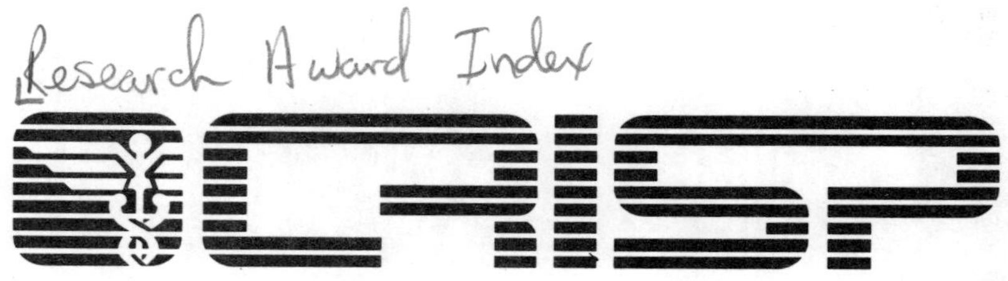

Biomedical Index to PHS-Supported Research

Fiscal Year 1991

Volume II

2. Project Number Listing
3. Investigator Listing

U.S. DEPARTMENT OF HEALTH
AND HUMAN SERVICES
Public Health Service
National Institutes of Health
Division of Research Grants
Bethesda, Maryland 20892

NIH Publication No. 92-200
May 1992

For sale by the U.S. Government Printing Office
Superintendent of Documents, Mail Stop: SSOP, Washington, DC 20402-9328
ISBN 0-16-041614-0

PROJECT NUMBER LISTING

PROJECT NO., ORGANIZATIONAL UNIT., INVESTIGATOR, ADDRESS, TITLE

N01AA-00013-00 (**) DEPARTMENT OF PSYCHIATRY LAPINLAHDENTIE 00180 HELSINKI 18 FINLAND Behavioral, biochemical, endocrine & genetic study of alcohol abuse

Z01AA-00024-13 (LMMB) VEECH, R L NIAAA Genetic and metabolic studies of human alcoholics

K05AA-00028-13 (ALCB) WEINER, HENRY PURDUE UNIVERSITY WEST LAFAYETTE, IN 47907 Aldehyde dehydrogenase and alcohol related problems

Z01AA-00036-05 (LMMB) SONG, B J NIAAA Regulation of ethanol-inducible cytochrome P450 gene

Z01AA-00037-05 (LMMB) SONG, B J NIAAA Structure & regulation of pyruvate dehydrogenase multienzyme complex (III) genes

Z01AA-00038-04 (LMMB) MCLAUGHLIN, A C NIAAA NMR studies of cerebral blood flow and energy metabolism

Z01AA-00039-04 (LMMB) MCLAUGHLIN, A C NIAAA Cerebral blood flow and energy metabolism in the rat

Z01AA-00040-04 (LMMB) MCLAUGHLIN, A C NIAAA Electrostatic properties of membrane

Z01AA-00042-03 (LMMB) MCLAUGHLIN, A C NIAAA Multiple quantum NMR studies of sodium and potassium in the rat brain

Z01AA-00044-02 (LMMB) CASAZZA, J P NIAAA Pig citrate synthase mechanism of action study using site directed mutagenesis

Z01AA-00045-02 (LMMB) DOBSON, G P NIAAA In vivo portal-hepatic venous gradients of glycogenic precursors in the rat

K05AA-00046-13 (ALCB) PIETRUSZKO, REGINA RUTGERS STATE UNIVERSITY OF NJ P.O. BOX 1089 PISCATAWAY, NJ 08855-1089 Aldehyde dehydrogenase and pathogenesis of alcoholism

Z01AA-00046-02 (LMMB) DOBSON, G P NIAAA Quantitation of 31P NMR

Z01AA-00047-02 (LMMB) JONES, J M NIAAA Effects of alcohol and acetate on leukocyte membrane receptor expression

K05AA-00048-12 (SRCA) WANDS, JACK R MOLECULAR HEPATOLOGY LABORATOR 149 13TH STREET CHARLESTOWN, MA 02129 Study of hepatitis B virus or variants in alcoholics

Z01AA-00048-02 (LMMB) MASUDA, T NIAAA Distribution in the perfused rat hearts--Effect of Pi and ethanol

Z01AA-00049-02 (LMMB) VEECH, R L NIAAA Enzymes and metabolites of the purine pathway in rat liver

Z01AA-00050-02 (LMMB) VEECH, R L NIAAA Relationship of cytokines to alcoholic liver disease

Z01AA-00051-02 (LMMB) MCLAUGHLIN, A C NIAAA Effect of ethanol on cerebral blood flow and energy metabolism in the rat

Z01AA-00052-01 (LMMB) MCLAUGHLIN, A C NIAAA In vivo measurement of intracellular calcium in the brain

Z01AA-00053-01 (LMMB) MCLAUGHLIN, A C NIAAA In vivo 17O NMR studies of cerebral oxygen consumption

Z01AA-00054-01 (LMMB) DOBSON, G P NIAAA The effects of ethanol on brain metabolism

Z01AA-00055-01 (LMMB) DOBSON, G P NIAAA Effects of ethanol on cardiac performance

Z01AA-00056-01 (LMMB) MCLAUGHLIN, A C NIAAA In vivo NMR exercise studies in panic disorder and alcoholic patients

Z01AA-00057-01 (LMMB) VEECH, R L NIAAA Effects of ethanol on natural killer (NK) cells

K02AA-00073-08 (ALCP) FILLMORE, KAYE M UNIV OF CALIF., SAN FRANCISCO BOX 0612, N631Y SAN FRANCISCO, CA 94143-0612 Situational and contextual factors in drinking practices

K02AA-00079-08 (ALCB) ERWIN, V GENE UNIVERSITY OF COLORADO CAMPUS BOX 297 BOULDER, CO 80309-0297 RSDA for pharmacogenetics of alcohol

K02AA-00081-08 (ALCB) CRABB, DAVID W INDIANA UNIV SCH OF MEDICINE 975 W. WALNUT STREET, IB424 INDIANAPOLIS, IN 46202-5121 Regulation of expression of alcohol dehydrogenase

K02AA-00087-05 (ALCB) THAYER, WILLIAM S HAHNEMANN UNIV SCH OF MEDICINE BROAD AND VINE PHILADELPHIA, PA 19102 Bioenergetic aspects of alcohol consumption

K02AA-00088-08 (ALCB) TARASCHI, THEODORE F THOMAS JEFFERSON UNIVERSITY PATHOLOGY AND CELL BIOLOGY PHILADELPHIA, PA 19107 Effects of ethanol and anesthetics on biologic membranes

K05AA-00093-06 (ALCB) DEITRICH, RICHARD A UNIVERSITY OF COLORADO DEPT. OF PHARMACOLOGY DENVER, CO 80262 Involvement of brain proteins in acute ethanol actions

K02AA-00098-05 (ALCB) EHLERS, CINDY L SCRIPPS RESEARCH INSTITUTE 10666 N TORREY PINES RD LA JOLLA, CA 92037 EEG & ERP markers of alcohol intoxication

K02AA-00101-05 (ALCB) FRYE, GERALD D TEXAS A & M UNIVERSITY 371 MEDICAL SCIENCES BUILDING COLLEGE STATION, TX 77843 GABAergic adaptation in ethanol

K02AA-00102-05 (ALCB) PALMER, MICHAEL R UNIV OF COLORADO HEALTH SCI CT 4200 EAST NINTH AVE BOX C236 DENVER, CO 80262 Ethanol effects on CNS tissue in vivo & in vitro

K02AA-00104-05 (ALCB) DEES, W LES TEXAS A&M RESEARCH FOUNDATION TEXAS A&M UNIVERSITY COLLEGE STATION, TX 77843 Alcohol and the onset of puberty

K02AA-00106-05 (ALCB) PETERSEN, DENNIS R UNIVERSITY OF COLORADO CAMPUS BOX 297 BOULDER, CO 80309-0297 Pharmacogenetics of ethanol neurotoxicity

K02AA-00107-05 (ALCB) RUDEEN, PAUL K SCHOOL OF MEDICINE UNIV OF MISSOURI-COLUMBIA COLUMBIA, MO 65212 Fetal alcohol neuroendocrinopathies

K05AA-00113-05 (ALCP) MARLATT, G ALAN UNIVERSITY OF WASHINGTON SEATTLE, WA 98195 Prevention of alcohol problems in the university setting

K02AA-00115-09 (ALCP) DAY, NANCY L WESTERN PSYCH INST & CLINIC 3811 O'HARA STREET PITTSBURGH, PA 15213 The effect of marihuana use on pregnancy outcome

K02AA-00118-04 (GER) MILES, MICHAEL FRANCIS ERNEST GALLO CLINIC & RES CTR SAN FRANCISCO, CA 94110 Ethanol responsive gene expression in neural cultures

PROJECT NO., ORGANIZATIONAL UNIT., INVESTIGATOR, ADDRESS, TITLE

FORT COLLINS, CO 80523 Factors controlling alcohol dehydrogenase transcription

K02AA-00121-03 (ALCB) HENDERSON, GEORGE I UNIV OF TX HEALTH SCI CTR DEPT. OF MEDICINE SAN ANTONIO, TX 78284-7878 Ethanol effects on vitamin transport/mitogenic signaling

K02AA-00123-02 (ALCB) RUBIN, RAPHAEL THOMAS JEFFERSON UNIVERSITY 11TH & WALNUT STREETS PHILADELPHIA, PA 19107 Effect of ethanol on signal transduction in platelets

K21AA-00125-03 (ALCB) HAYNE, HARLENE PRINCETON UNIVERSITY PRINCETON, NJ 08544-1010 The fetal alcohol syndrome--Research and training

K21AA-00126-02 (ALCB) MORING, JILL UNIV OF CONNECTICUT HEALTH CTR 263 FARMINGTON AVENUE FARMINGTON, CT 06030 Ethanol's effect on ion channel function and drug action

K21AA-00127-02 (ALCB) CHANDLER, LAWRENCE J UNIVERSITY OF FLORIDA BOX J-267 JHMHC GAINESVILLE, FL 32610 Alcohol and phospholipid derived second messengers

K02AA-00129-02 (ALCB) JERRELLS, THOMAS R LOUISIANA STATE UNIV MED CENTE PO BOX 33932 SHREVEPORT, LA 71130-3932 Effects of ethanol on the immune system

K05AA-00133-02 (ALCP) MILLER, WILLIAM R UNIVERSITY OF NEW MEXICO ALBUQUERQUE, NM 87131 Programmatic treatment innovation research

K21AA-00134-02 (ALCB) NIXON, SARA J UNIVERSITY OF OKLAHOMA 800 N E 15TH STREET OKLAHOMA CITY, OK 73104 Cognitive modeling-- Alcoholics and at-risk youth

K02AA-00135-02 (ALCB) PERIS, JOANNA COLLEGE OF PHARMACY BOX J-487, JHMHC GAINESVILLE, FL 32610 Nigrotectal GABA neurons in alcohol and kindled seizures

K02AA-00138-01 (ALCB) MEADOWS, GARY G WASHINGTON STATE UNIVERSITY PULLMAN, WA 99164-6510 Alcohol and natural killer cell activity

K05AA-00139-01 (ALCB) LANGE, LOUIS G JEWISH HOSPITAL OF ST LOUIS 216 S KINGSHIGHWAY ST LOUIS, MO 63110 Hepatic metabolism of alcohol by GSH transferase

K21AA-00140-01 (ALCB) HANNIGAN, JOHN H C.S. MOTT CTR HUMAN GROWTH DEV 275 EAST HANCOCK STREET DETROIT, MI 48201 Behavioral neuropharmacology of fetal alcohol exposure

K02AA-00141-01 (ALCB) WEHNER, JEANNE M UNIVERSITY OF COLORADO CAMPUS BOX 447 BOULDER, CO 80309-0447 ETOH/corticosterone/GABA interactions in LS/SS subjects

R01AA-00186-19 (ALCB) PIETRUSZKO, REGINA RUTGERS/STATE UNIVERSITY OF NJ P.O. BOX 1089 PISCATAWAY, NJ 08855-1089 Human aldehyde dehydrogenase isozymes and alcoholism

R01AA-00187-19 (ALCB) CERMAK, LAIRD S BOSTON VA MEDICAL CTR 116B 150 S HUNTINGTON AVE BOSTON, MA 02130 Cognitive deficits related to chronic alcoholism

R01AA-00200-19 (ALCB) WALKER, DON W Chronic alcohol consumption--Neurobiological correlates

Z01AA-00231-09 (LCS) ECKARDT, M NIAAA Central and peripheral nervous system function in abstinent alcoholics

Z01AA-00233-09 (LCS) BROWN, G NIAAA Family studies of alcoholism

Z01AA-00234-09 (LCS) NIELSEN, D NIAAA Molecular studies on tryptophan hydroxylase gene expression

Z01AA-00235-09 (LCS) SALEM, N NIAAA Nutritional effects on essential fatty acid composition

Z01AA-00237-09 (LCS) SHOAL, S NIAAA Individual variability in drug metabolism by carbon dioxide breath test

Z01AA-00238-09 (LCS) LINNOILA, M NIAAA CSF neuropeptides in alcohol withdrawal and brain disease

Z01AA-00239-08 (LCS) ECKARDT, M J NIAAA Alcoholism-associated cognitive impairment and organic brain syndrome

Z01AA-00240-12 (LCS) ECKARDT, M J NIAAA Cognitive function in male alcoholics

Z01AA-00249-08 (LCS) GEORGE, D NIAAA Pharmacologic reduction of alcohol consumption in alcoholic patients

Z01AA-00250-08 (LCS) ECKARDT, M NIAAA Electrophysiological studies of acute and chronic alcohol consumption

Z01AA-00257-07 (LCS) BROWN, G NIAAA Neuroendocrine studies in offspring of familial alcoholics

Z01AA-00258-07 (LCS) LINNOILA, M NIAAA Violent behavior, neurotransmitters, glucose metabolism, and alcohol abuse

R01AA-00259-20 (ALCP) WILSON, G TERENCE GRAD SCH APPLIED & PRO PSYCHGY BUSCH CAMPUS P O BOX 819 PISCATAWAY, N J 08854 Alcoholism/behavioral treatment---research & development

Z01AA-00262-09 (LCS) SALEM, N NIAAA Desaturation of essential fatty acids using stable isotope/mass spectrometry

Z01AA-00265-06 (LCS) GEORGE, D NIAAA Effects of alprazolam, diazepam, clonidine, and placebo upon ethanol withdrawal

Z01AA-00266-06 (LCS) GEORGE, D NIAAA Relationship of psychobiology to psychopathology in alcoholics

Z01AA-00267-06 (LCS) ECKARDT, M NIAAA Brain imaging

Z01AA-00268-06 (LCS) ECKARDT, M NIAAA The behavioral effects of alcohol and other psychotropic drugs

Z01AA-00272-04 (LCS) LINNOILA, M NIAAA CSF monoamine metabolites in alcoholic patients who attempt suicide

Z01AA-00273-03 (LCS) GEORGE, D NIAAA Effects of serotonergic activity on neuroendocrine and behavioral measures

Z01AA-00274-03 (LCS) GEORGE, D NIAAA Intravenous procaine in alcoholics and adult children of alcoholics

Z01AA-00275-03 (LCS) ECKARDT, M NIAAA Psychomotor and cognitive aspects of alcoholism

Z01AA-00276-03 (LCS) BROWN, G NIAAA Psychobiology and behavior of aggression and suicide in adults and children

Z01AA-00277-03 (LCS) HIGLEY, J NIAAA Non-human primate models of alcohol consumption and aggression

Z01AA-00278-02 (LCS) GEORGE, D NIAAA Behavioral and physiological effects of 2-deoxyglucose infusions

dehydrogenase

Z01AA-00279-02 (LCS) MOORE, V NIAAA Black and white offspring of parental alcoholics

Z01AA-00280-02 (LCS) GOLDMAN, D NIAAA Genetic studies of the electroencephalogram and event-related potentials

Z01AA-00281-02 (LCS) GOLDMAN,D NIAAA Molecular genetic studies on alcoholism in American Indians

Z01AA-00282-02 (LCS) GOLDMAN, D NIAAA Molecular genetic studies on the Dopamine D2 receptor

Z01AA-00283-02 (LCS) GOLDMAN, D NIAAA Molecular genetic studies on enzymes of alcohol metabolism

Z01AA-00284-02 (LCS) KIM, H Y NIAAA Alterations in lipid metabolism in the nervous system by ethanol

Z01AA-00285-02 (LCS) KARANIAN, J NIAAA Physiological functions of lipoxygenase products

Z01AA-00286-02 (LCS) GEORGE, D NIAAA Psychobiology of alcoholism in women

Z01AA-00287-01 (LCS) ESKAY, R NIAAA Stress axis, immune system-derived cytokines and ethanol

Z01AA-00288-01 (LCS) MORGAN, P NIAAA Central nervous system glutamate and c-fos mRNA in alcohol withdrawal

Z01AA-00289-01 (LCS) WOZNIAK, K NIAAA The effects of ethanol on central dopaminergic function

Z01AA-00290-01 (LCS) FILLING-KATZ, M NIAAA Studies on families with serotonin gene defects

Z01AA-00292-01 (LCS) SHOAF, S NIAAA Mechanisms responsible for altered drug metabolism follwing ethanol withdrawal

Z01AA-00400-06 (USP) GRANT, K A NIAAA Selective breeding for ethanol tolerance

Z01AA-00401-04 (LPPS) KUNOS, G NIAAA Interaction between the immune system and adrenergic receptors

Z01AA-00402-04 (LPPS) KUNOS, G NIAAA Brainstem neuro-mechanisms and blood pressure regulation

Z01AA-00403-04 (LPPS) KUNOS, G NIAAA Inverse regulation of hepatic alphal and beta-adrenergic receptors

Z01AA-00404-04 (LPPS) KINCAID, R L NIAAA Control of calcium and phosphorylation-regulated signalling pathways

Z01AA-00405-04 (LPPS) MARTENSEN, T M NIAAA Detection and regulation of specific cellular phosphoproteins

Z01AA-00479-08 (LPPS) WEIGHT, F F NIAAA Synaptic mechanisms and ethanol actions

Z01AA-00480-08 (LPPS) WEIGHT, F F NIAAA Nerve cell excitability and ethanol actions

Z01AA-00481-02 (LPPS) TAKACS, L NIAAA Regulation of IL-1 production

Z01AA-00482-02 (LPPS) TAKACS, L NIAAA Regulation of early steps in T-cell development

Z01AA-00483-02 (LPPS) FRASER, C M NIAAA Cloning, expression and site-directed mutagenesis of G protein-linked receptors

Z01AA-00484-02 (LPPS) FRASER, C M NIAAA Structure function analysis of the GABA-A receptor

Z01AA-00485-02 (LPPS) KIRKNESS, E F NIAAA Gene structure of GABA-A receptor subunits

Z01AA-00486-01 (LPPS) REINLIB, L NIAAA Mechanism of ethanol on GABA-channels in neurons

R01AA-00626-17 (ALCB) MEZEY, ESTEBAN JOHNS HOPKINS UNIV 600 N WOLFE ST., BLALOCK 903 BALTIMORE, MD 21205 Hormonal regulation of ethanol metabolism

Z01AA-00700-07 (LPPS) HOFFMAN, P NIAAA Ethanol effects on membrane-bound enzymes

Z01AA-00702-07 (LPPS) HOFFMAN, P NIAAA Ethanol modification of neurotransmitter receptor-effector coupling

Z01AA-00703-07 (LPPS) HOFFMAN, P NIAAA Neurohypophyseal peptides and ethanol tolerance

Z01AA-00705-05 (LPPS) HOFFMAN, P NIAAA In vitro models for ethanol effects on receptor-mediated processes

Z01AA-00706-03 (LPPS) RABE, C S NIAAA Effects of ethanol on NMDA-mediated neuronal function

Z01AA-00707-03 (LPPS) GRANT, K A NIAAA Behavioral pharmacology of ethanol

R01AA-01455-16 (SRCA) STREISSGUTH, ANN P UNIV OF WASHINGTON, GG-20 2707 NE BLAKELEY SEATTLE, WA 98195 Alcohol intake during pregnancy--Offspring development

R01AA-02054-12 (ALCB) SUN, ALBERT Y UNIV OF MISSOURI ONE HOSPITAL DRIVE COLUMBIA, MO 65212 Alcohol-membrane interaction on the brain--Aging effects

R37AA-02342-16 (ALCB) LI, TING-KAI INDIANA UNIVERSITY SCHOOL OF M 545 BARNHILL DRIVE INDIANAPOLIS, IN 46202-5124 Human alcohol and aldehyde dehydrogenases

R37AA-02666-15 (ALCB) WANDS, JACK R MGH EAST CANCER CENTER 149 13TH STREET, 7TH FLOOR CHARLESTOWN, MA 02129 Effects of alcohol on the liver

R37AA-02686-15 (SRCA) BEGLEITER, HENRI SUNY HLTH SCI CTR AT BROOKLYN 450 CLARKSON AVE., BOX 1203 BROOKLYN, N Y 11203 Brain dysfunction and alcoholism

R37AA-02863-12 (NSS) MOOS, RUDOLPH H STANFORD UNIVERSITY STANFORD, CA 94305 Evaluation of alcoholism-inducing community setting

R01AA-02887-15 (ALCB) CUNNINGHAM, CAROL C WAKE FOREST UNIVERSITY 300 SOUTH HAWTHORNE ROAD WINSTON-SALEM, NC 27103 Chronic alcoholism,liver,energy and lipid metabolism

R37AA-03037-14 (ALCP) JACOB, THEODORE WESTERN PSYCHIATRIC INSTITUTE 3811 O'HARA STREET PITTSBURGH, PA 15213 Alcoholism and family interaction

R37AA-03249-15 (ALCB) RILEY, EDWARD P SAN DIEGO STATE UNIVERSITY 5300 CAMPANILE DRIVE SAN DIEGO, CA 92182 Alcohol-induced behavioral teratogenesis

R01AA-03312-12 (ALCB) CEDERBAUM, ARTHUR I MOUNT SINAI SCHOOL OF MEDICINE ONE GUSTAVE L. LEVY PLACE NEW YORK, NY 10029 Effects of ethanol and acetaldehyde on liver function

R01AA-03490-12 (ALCB) DRUSE-MANTEUFFEL, MARY J LOYOLA UNIV MEDICAL SCHOOL 2160 SOUTH FIRST AVENUE MAYWOOD, IL 60153 Maternal alcoholism and CNS development in offspring

PROJECT NO., ORGANIZATIONAL UNIT., INVESTIGATOR, ADDRESS, TITLE

P50AA-03508-14 (SRCA) LIEBER, CHARLES S ALCOHOL RESEARCH CENTER 151/G 130 WEST KINGSBRIDGE RD BRONX, NY 10468 Metabolism of alcohol and associated pathologic effects

P50AA-03508-14 0001 (SRCA) ROSMAN, A Metabolism of alcohol and associated pathologic effects Markers of alcohol consumption

P50AA-03508-14 0004 (SRCA) CEDERBAUM, A Metabolism of alcohol and associated pathologic effects Interaction of pyrazole and glycerol with human microsomes and P-450IIEI

P50AA-03508-14 0005 (SRCA) BARAONA, E Metabolism of alcohol and associated pathologic effects Acetaldehyde metabolism and toxicity

P50AA-03508-14 0032 (SRCA) GARRO, ANTHONY J Metabolism of alcohol and associated pathologic effects Ethanol and cancer

P50AA-03508-14 0044 (SRCA) LASKER, J Metabolism of alcohol and associated pathologic effects Effects of ethanol on microsomal P-450 enzymes

P50AA-03508-14 0045 (SRCA) BARAONA, ENRIQUE Metabolism of alcohol and associated pathologic effects Effects of ethanol on hepatic lipids/serum lipoproteins

P50AA-03508-14 0046 (SRCA) ROJKIND, M Metabolism of alcohol and associated pathologic effects Pathogenesis of alcohol-induced fibrosis

P50AA-03508-14 0047 (SRCA) LIEBER, CHARLES S Metabolism of alcohol and associated pathologic effects Treatment and prevention of alcohol-induced liver injury

P50AA-03508-14 0048 (SRCA) LEO, M A Metabolism of alcohol and associated pathologic effects Ethanol-vitamin A interactions

P50AA-03508-14 0051 (SRCA) GENTRY, R T Metabolism of alcohol and associated pathologic effects Bioavailability and absorption kinetics of ethanol in alcoholics

P50AA-03508-14 0052 (SRCA) KORSTEN, M Metabolism of alcohol and associated pathologic effects Gastrointestinal consequences of alcohol abuse

P50AA-03508-14 9002 (SRCA) LIEBER, CHARLES S Metabolism of alcohol and associated pathologic effects Core--Biochemistry laboratory

P50AA-03508-14 9003 (SRCA) LIEBER, CHARLES S Metabolism of alcohol and associated pathologic effects Core--Pathology laboratory

P50AA-03508-14 9004 (SRCA) LIEBER, CHARLES S Metabolism of alcohol and associated pathologic effects Core--Animal facility

P50AA-03510-14 (SRCA) MEYER, ROGER E UNIV OF CONNECTICT HEALTH CTR FARMINGTON AVENUE FARMINGTON, CT 06032 Etiology and treatment of alcohol dependence

P50AA-03510-14 0003 (SRCA) KAPLAN, RICHARD Etiology and treatment of alcohol dependence Alcohol cue responsivity and CNS recovery after alcohol withdrawal

P50AA-03510-14 0011 (SRCA) KADDEN, RONALD M Etiology and treatment of alcohol dependence Alcoholism aftercare treatment matching--Longterm prognosis

P50AA-03510-14 0013 (SRCA) HESSELBROCK, VICTOR Etiology and treatment of alcohol dependence Prospective study

P50AA-03510-14 0014 (SRCA) BABOR, THOMAS Etiology and treatment of alcohol dependence Buspirone and fluvoxamine as adjuncts to a relapse prevention aftercare program

P50AA-03510-14 0015 (SRCA) ROUNSAVILLE, BRUCE J Etiology and treatment of alcohol dependence Comparison of coping skills training and fluvoxamine

P50AA-03510-14 0016 (SRCA) COONEY, NED L Etiology and treatment of alcohol dependence Alcohol and mood-related cue exposure for alcoholics

P50AA-03510-14 0017 (SRCA) DOLINSKY, ZELIG Etiology and treatment of alcohol dependence Neuroendocrine correlates of alcoholic's response to alcohol

P50AA-03510-14 0018 (SRCA) DOLINSKY, ZELIG Etiology and treatment of alcohol dependence Biobehavioral studies of alcohol consumption

P50AA-03510-14 0019 (SRCA) COONEY, NED L Etiology and treatment of alcohol dependence Reactivity to alcohol and mood-related stimuli in alcoholics

P50AA-03510-14 0020 (SRCA) HESSELBROCK, VICTOR Etiology and treatment of alcohol dependence Neuroelectric correlates of risk for alcohol dependence

P50AA-03510-14 0021 (SRCA) HESSELBROCK, VICTOR Etiology and treatment of alcohol dependence Drinking response in individuals at risk for alcoholism

P50AA-03510-14 0022 (SRCA) SHOEMAKER, WILLIAM Etiology and treatment of alcohol dependence Pre-clinical studies of membrane structure

P50AA-03527-14 (SRCA) ALBINO, JUDITH E N UNIVERSITY OF COLORADO 914 BROADWAY BOULDER, CO 80309 Genetic approaches to neuropharmacology of ethanol

P50AA-03527-14 0009 (SRCA) PETERSEN, DENNIS R Genetic approaches to neuropharmacology of ethanol Chronic ethanol and brain mitochondrial dysfunction

P50AA-03527-14 0016 (SRCA) FREEDMAN, ROBERT Genetic approaches to neuropharmacology of ethanol Detoxification and withdrawal

P50AA-03527-14 0017 (SRCA) WEHNER, JEANNE M Genetic approaches to neuropharmacology of ethanol Ethanol and the GABA-benzodiazepine complex

P50AA-03527-14 0018 (SRCA) HARRIS, R ADRON Genetic approaches to neuropharmacology of ethanol Ethanol effects--GABA, calcium and membrane physical properties

P50AA-03527-14 0019 (SRCA) DEITRICH, RICHARD A Genetic approaches to neuropharmacology of ethanol Protein kinase C and depressant effects of ethanol

P50AA-03527-14 0020 (SRCA) WEINER, NORMAN Genetic approaches to neuropharmacology of ethanol Ethanol sensitivity, thyroid function, neurotransmitters and development

P50AA-03527-14 0021 (SRCA) ERWIN, V GENE Genetic approaches to neuropharmacology of ethanol Neurotensin and calcium modulation of ethanol actions

P50AA-03527-14 9001 (SRCA) ERWIN, V GENE Genetic approaches to neuropharmacology of ethanol Core--Animal production

P50AA-03527-14 0001 (SRCA) WILSON, JAMES R Genetic approaches to neuropharmacology of ethanol Animal models

P50AA-03527-14 0003 (SRCA) MURPHY, ROBERT C Genetic approaches to neuropharmacology of ethanol Ethanol and inflammatory cells

P50AA-03527-14 0005 (SRCA) HOFFER, BARRY J Genetic approaches to neuropharmacology of ethanol Cellular basis for behavioral effects of ethanol

P50AA-03539-14 (SRCA) GUZE, SAMUEL B WASHINGTON UNIVERSITY 4940 AUDUBON AVENUE ST LOUIS, MO 63110 Neurobiology, genetics, epidemiology and alcoholism

P50AA-03539-14 9002 (SRCA) CICERO, THEODORE J Neurobiology, genetics, epidemiology and alcoholism Core--Animal breeding colony

P50AA-03539-14 9003 (SRCA) HEATH, ANDREW C Neurobiology, genetics, epidemiology and alcoholism Core--Alcoholism twin registry

P50AA-03539-14 9004 (SRCA) TODD, RICHARD D Neurobiology, genetics, epidemiology and alcoholism Core--Molecular neurobiology

P50AA-03539-14 9005 (SRCA) ROBINS, LEE N Neurobiology, genetics, epidemiology and alcoholism Core--Data analysis of existing data files

P50AA-03539-14 9006 (SRCA) ROBINS, LEE N Neurobiology, genetics, epidemiology and alcoholism Core--Biostatistical consultation

P50AA-03539-14 9007 (SRCA) ISENBERG, KEITH E Neurobiology, genetics, epidemiology and alcoholism Core--Cell and tissue culture

P50AA-03539-14 9008 (SRCA) BUCHOLZ, KATHLEEN K Neurobiology, genetics, epidemiology and alcoholism Core--Interview training

P50AA-03539-14 9009 (SRCA) GUZE, SAMUEL B Neurobiology, genetics, epidemiology and alcoholism Core--Follow up

R01AA-03624-13 (ALCB) THURMAN, RONALD G UNIV OF NORTH CAROLINA AT CH CB#7365, FACULTY LAB OFF BLDG CHAPEL HILL, N C 27599-7365 Control of drug and ethanol metabolism

R01AA-03972-12 (ALCB) ALKANA, RONALD L UNIV OF SOUTHERN CALIFORNIA 1985 ZONAL AVENUE LOS ANGELES, CA 90033 Low level hyperbaric ethanol antagonism

R01AA-04090-08 (ALCB) TICKU, MAHARAJ K UNIV OF TEXAS HLTH SCI CTR 7703 FLOYD CURL DRIVE SAN ANTONIO, TX 78284-7764 Ethanol GABA interactions in mammalian cultured neurons

R01AA-04368-12 (ALCB) MELLO, NANCY K MC LEAN HOSPITAL 115 MILL STREET BELMONT, MASS 02178 Alcohol and the menstrual cycle--Biobehavioral studies

R01AA-04425-11 (ALCB) VAN THIEL, DAVID H UNIVERSITY OF PITTSBURGH 3601 FIFTH AVENUE PITTSBURGH, PA 15261 Endocrine effects of alcohol abuse

R01AA-04570-09 (ALCP) AUSTIN, GREGORY A SOUTHWEST REGIONAL LABORATORY 4665 LAMPSON AVENUE LOS ALAMITOS, CA 90720 Historical review of alcohol abuse and control

R37AA-04610-10 (ALCP) WILSNACK, SHARON C UNIVERSITY OF NORTH DAKOTA 501 N. COLUMBIA ROAD GRAND FORKS, ND 58201 Problem drinking in women--A national survey followup

R37AA-04732-11 (NSS) MICHAELIS, ELIAS K UNIVERSITY OF KANSAS 2099 CONSTANT AVENUE CAMPUS WE LAWRENCE, KS 66047 Molecular actions of alcohol in brain-model membranes

R01AA-04961-11 (ALCB) TUMA, DEAN J VA MED CTR, MEDICAL RSCH SVCE 4101 WOOLWORTH AVENUE OMAHA, NE 68105 Alcoholic liver injury--Covalence of acetaldehyde

R01AA-05122-10 (ALCB) MICZEK, KLAUS A TUFTS UNIVERSITY MEDFORD, MASS 02155 Alcohol, benzodiazepines, and aggression

R37AA-05523-10 (ALCB) WEST, JAMES R UNIVERSITY OF IOWA COLLEGE OF MEDICINE IOWA CITY, IA 52242 Fetal alcohol syndrome--Third trimester model

R01AA-05524-09 (ALCB) BEGLEITER, HENRI SUNY HEALTH SCIENCES CENTER 450 CLARKSON AVENUE BROOKLYN, NY 11203 Neurophysiology in male children at high risk for alcoholism

R01AA-05526-09 (ALCP) SCHUCKIT, MARC A UNIV OF CALIFORNIA, SAN DIEGO 9500 GILMAN DRIVE LA JOLLA, CA 92093-0603 Reactions to brain depressants in sons of alcoholics

R01AA-05542-09 (ALCB) TREISTMAN, STEVEN N UNIVERSITY OF MASS MEDICAL SCH 55 LAKE AVENUE, NORTH WORCESTER, MA 01655 Ethanol action in individual neurons

R37AA-05591-09 (ALCP) MARLATT, G ALAN UNIVERSITY OF WASHINGTON SEATTLE, WA 98195 Prevention of alcohol problems in college students

R01AA-05592-08 (ALCB) PENTNEY, ROBERTA J STATE UNIVERSITY OF NEW YORK 317 FARBER HALL BUFFALO, NY 14214 Dendritic parameters--Age and ethanol effects

P50AA-05595-11 (SRCA) ROOM, ROBIN G MEDICAL RESEARCH INSTITUTE 2000 HEARST AVENUE BERKELEY, CA 94709-2176 Epidemiology of alcohol problems

P50AA-05595-11 0012 (SRCA) HILTON, MICHAEL Epidemiology of alcohol problems Trend & structure of alcohol dependence--General population 1990 survey data

P50AA-05595-11 0013 (SRCA) HILTON, MICHAEL Epidemiology of alcohol problems Epidemiology of alcohol problems and attitudes--National alcohol survey 1994/95

P50AA-05595-11 0014 (SRCA) CAETANO, RAUL Epidemiology of alcohol problems Longitudinal study of drinking among whites, blacks, and Hispanics

P50AA-05595-11 0015 (SRCA) HILTON, MICHAEL Epidemiology of alcohol problems Alcohol and mortality--National multiethnic sample

P50AA-05595-11 0016 (SRCA) TROCKI, KAREN Epidemiology of alcohol problems Drinking & risk-taking behavior--Longitudinal study in adolescents & young adults

P50AA-05595-11 0017 (SRCA) ROIZEN, RON Epidemiology of alcohol problems Alcohol and crime analysis

P50AA-05595-11 0018 (SRCA) CHERPITEL, CHERYL Epidemiology of alcohol problems Alcohol and casualty studies--Mississippi, California

P50AA-05595-11 0019 (SRCA) CAETANO, RAUL Epidemiology of alcohol problems Dimensions of alcohol dependence among white, black, and Mexican-American men

P50AA-05595-11 0020 (SRCA) SCHMIDT, LAURA Epidemiology of alcohol problems Alcohol dimensions in clients of homelessness services

P50AA-05595-11 0021 (SRCA) WEISNER, CONSTANCE Epidemiology of alcohol problems Study of those who provide services in alcoholism

P50AA-05595-11 0022 (SRCA) WEISNER, CONSTANCE Epidemiology of alcohol problems Alcohol treatment in the private sector--Health Maintenance Organization

P50AA-05595-11 0023 (SRCA) CHERPITEL, CHERYL Epidemiology of alcohol problems Alcohol and primary care studies

P50AA-05595-11 0024 (SRCA) WEISNER, CONSTANCE Epidemiology of alcohol problems Analysis across community epidemiology laboratory studies

P50AA-05595-11 9003 (SRCA) ROOM, ROBIN Epidemiology of alcohol problems Core

R01AA-05702-07 (ALCP) RUSSELL, MARCIA RESEARCH INST ON ALCOHOLISM 1021 MAIN STREET BUFFALO, NY 14203 Stress, race and alcohol use in a household population

R01AA-05763-09 (ALCB) YOSHIDA, AKIRA Y BECKMAN RES INST/CITY OF HOPE 1450 E DUARTE RD DUARTE, CA 91010 Human alcohol dehydrogenase and aldehyde dehydrogenase

R01AA-05809-10 (SRCA) LESLIE, STEVEN W Ethanol on calcium channels and NMDA receptors

R37AA-05812-08 (ALCB) WEINER, HENRY PURDUE UNIVERSITY WEST LAFAYETTE, IN 47907 Enzymology/molecular biology of aldehyde dehydrogenase

R01AA-05828-08 (SRCA) CRABBE, JOHN C OREGON HEALTH SCIENCES UNIV 3181 SW SAM JACKSON PARK ROAD PORTLAND, OR 97201 Selection of lines for ethanol thermal sensitivity

R01AA-05846-09 (ALCB) SHEFNER, SARAH A UNIV OF IL. COLL OF MED P.O. BOX 6998 CHICAGO, IL 60680 Intracellular study of ethanol effects on brain neurons

R01AA-05858-10 (ALCB) SLOMIANY, AMALIA UMDNJ-NEW JERSEY DENTAL SCHOOL 110 BERGEN STREET NEWARK, NJ 07103-2400 Effect of alcohol on gastric mucus glycoconjugates

R01AA-05868-09 (ALCB) DEITRICH, RICHARD A UNIV OF COLORADO HLTH SCIS CTR 4200 EAST 9TH AVENUE DENVER, CO 80262 Selective breeding for ethanol sensitivity

R01AA-05909-08 (ALCP) HILL, SHIRLEY Y WESTERN PSYCHIATRIC INST & CLI 3811 O'HARA STREET PITTSBURGH, PA 15213 Cognitive/personality factors in relatives of alcoholics

R01AA-05915-09 (ALCB) PALMER, MICHAEL R UNIV OF COLORADO HEALTH SCI CT 4200 E NINTH AVENUE DENVER, CO 80262 Ethanol effects on CNS tissue in vivo & in vitro

R01AA-05934-08 (ALCB) LIEBER, CHARLES S VETERANS ADMIN MED CTR 130 WEST KINGSBRIDGE ROAD BRONX, NY 10468 Interaction of ethanol with hepatic microsomes

R01AA-05950-08 (ALCB) KORNETSKY, CONAN BOSTON UNIVERSITY 80 EAST CONCORD STREET BOSTON, MA 02118 Effects of ethanol on brain-stimulation reward

R01AA-05965-09 (ALCB) PFEFFERBAUM, ADOLF VETERANS ADMINISTRATION 3801 MIRANDA PALO ALTO, CA 94304 CNS deficits -- interaction of age and alcoholism

R01AA-06014-08 (ALCB) KOZLOWSKI, GERALD P UNIV OF TX SW MED CTR /DALLAS 5323 HARRY HINES BLVD DALLAS, TX 75235-9040 Effect of alcohol on neuroendocrine cells

R01AA-06059-07 (ALCB) EHLERS, CINDY L SCRIPPS RESEARCH INSTITUTE 10666 N TORREY PINES RD LA JOLLA, CA 92037 EEG and ERP markers of alcohol intoxication

R01AA-06069-08 (ALCB) CREWS, FULTON T UNIVERSITY OF FLORIDA BOX J-267 ARB GAINESVILLE, FL 32610-0267 Ethanol effects on neurotransmission

R01AA-06092-08 (SRCA) ROLL, FREDRICK J UNIVERSITY OF CALIFORNIA 1001 POTRERO AVENUE SAN FRANCISCO, CA 94110 Pathogenesis of inflammation in alcoholic liver disease

R01AA-06135-08 (ALCB) PARSONS, OSCAR A OKLA UNIV HLTH SCIS CTR 800 N.E. 15TH STREET OKLAHOMA CITY, OK 73104 Alcoholism--Family, gender and CNS factors

R01AA-06201-07 (ALCP) HANSEN, WILLIAM B BOWMAN GRAY SCHOOL OF MEDICINE 300 SOUTH HAWTHORNE ROAD WINSTON-SALEM, NC 27103 Adolescent alcohol prevention trial

R01AA-06203-04A1 (ALCB) BAUER, RUSSELL M UNIVERSITY OF FLORIDA BOX J-165 JHMHC GAINESVILLE, FL 32610-0165 Psychophysiology of implicit memory in alcoholic amnesia

R01AA-06207-06 (ALCB) RABIN, RICHARD A STATE UNIVERSITY OF NEW YORK BUFFALO, NY 14214 Effects of ethanol on adenylate cyclase activity

R01AA-06221-08 (ALCB) COON, MINOR J UNIVERSITY OF MICHIGAN ANN ARBOR, MI 48109-0606 Alcohol metabolism role of P-450 oxygenases

R01AA-06223-08 (ALCB) PLAPP, BRYCE V UNIVERSITY OF IOWA 4-370 BOWEN SCIENCE BUILDING IOWA CITY, IA 52242 Structure-function studies of alcohol dehydrogenases

R01AA-06243-08 (ALCB) BELKNAP, JOHN K, JR OREGON HEALTH SCIENCES UNIV 3181 SW SAM JACKSON PARK RD PORTLAND, OR 97201 Alcohol predisposition--Comparative withdrawal syndromes

R01AA-06252-09 (SRCA) MENDELSON, JACK H MCLEAN HOSPITAL 115 MILL STREET BELMONT, MA 02178 Biobehavioral studies of alcohol problems in women

R01AA-06267-05 (SRCA) PELHAM, WILLIAM E WESTERN PSYCHIATRIC INST & CLI 3811 O'HARA STREET PITTSBURGH, PA 15213 Role of alcohol in adult-child interactions

P50AA-06282-09 (SRCA) HOLDER, HAROLD D PREVENTION RESEARCH CTR 2532 DURANT AVE BERKELEY, CA 94704 Environmental approaches to prevention

P50AA-06282-09 0001 (SRCA) SALTZ, ROBERT Environmental approaches to prevention Server intervention programs

P50AA-06282-09 0002 (SRCA) WAGENAAR, ALEX C Environmental approaches to prevention Alcohol related traffic crashes

P50AA-06282-09 0003 (SRCA) MOSKOWITZ, JOEL M Environmental approaches to prevention High school drinking policies and their implementation

P50AA-06282-09 0004 (SRCA) AMES, GENEVIEVE M Environmental approaches to prevention Family-level cultural model for prevention

P50AA-06282-09 0005 (SRCA) BREED, WARREN Environmental approaches to prevention Alcohol and the mass media

R01AA-06322-08 (ALCB) FRYE, GERALD D TEXAS A & M UNIVERSITY COLLEGE STATION, TX 77843 GABAergic adaptation in ethanol tolerance and dependence

R01AA-06324-08 (ALCP) DIELMAN, TEDDY E THE UNIV OF MICHIGAN G1210 TOWSLEY ANN ARBOR, MI 48109-0201 Countering pressures related to adolescent alcohol misuse

R01AA-06374-08 (BBCB) MAKINEN, MARVIN W UNIVERSITY OF CHICAGO 920 E 58TH STREET CHICAGO, IL 60637 The oxidation of alcohol by liver alcohol dehydrogenase

R01AA-06386-08 (ALCB) ZERN, MARK A ROGER WILLIAMS MED CTR 825 CHALKSTONE AVE PROVIDENCE, RI 02908 Bases of cirrhosis in alcoholic

PROJECT NO., ORGANIZATIONAL UNIT., INVESTIGATOR, ADDRESS, TITLE

liver disease

R01AA-06391-07 (ALCB) COLLINS, ALLAN C UNIVERSITY OF COLORADO CAMPUS BOX 447 BOULDER, CO 80309-0019 Ethanol/nicotine/cholinergic receptor interactions

R37AA-06399-09 (ALCB) HARRIS, ROBERT A UNIV OF CO HLTH SCI CTR 4200 EAST 9TH AVENUE DENVER, CO 80262 Brain membranes in alcohol and barbiturate dependence

P50AA-06420-08 (SRCA) BLOOM, FLOYD E RES INST OF SCRIPPS CLINIC 10666 NORTH TORREY PINES ROAD LA JOLLA, CA 92037 CNS effects of alcohol--Cellular neurobiology

P50AA-06420-08 9005 (SRCA) BLOOM, FLOYD E CNS effects of alcohol--Cellular neurobiology Core--Chronic alcohol administration model

P50AA-06420-08 9006 (SRCA) BLOOM, FLOYD E CNS effects of alcohol--Cellular neurobiology Core--Peptide biology laboratory

P50AA-06420-08 0001 (SRCA) SIGGINS, GEORGE R CNS effects of alcohol--Cellular neurobiology Neuronal and synaptic actions of alcohol

P50AA-06420-08 0002 (SRCA) KODA, LEONARD Y CNS effects of alcohol--Cellular neurobiology Autonomic neuropharmacology--Toxic effects of ethanol metabolites

P50AA-06420-08 0003 (SRCA) SHOEMAKER, WILLIAM J CNS effects of alcohol--Cellular neurobiology Developmental neurobiology--Fetal alcohol syndrome

P50AA-06420-08 0006 (SRCA) VALE, WYLIE W CNS effects of alcohol--Cellular neurobiology Neuroendocrine effects of ethanol

P50AA-06420-08 0007 (SRCA) FOOTE, STEPHEN L CNS effects of alcohol--Cellular neurobiology Systemic neuropharmacology

P50AA-06420-08 0008 (SRCA) KOOB, GEORGE F CNS effects of alcohol--Cellular neurobiology Behavioral pharmacology

P50AA-06420-08 0009 (SRCA) HENRIKSEN, STEVEN J CNS effects of alcohol--Cellular neurobiology Electroencephalographic indices of alcohol intoxication

P50AA-06420-08 0010 (SRCA) NEVILLE, HELEN J CNS effects of alcohol--Cellular neurobiology Human evoked potentials

P50AA-06420-08 9001 (SRCA) BLOOM, FLOYD E CNS effects of alcohol--Cellular neurobiology Core--Computer facility

R01AA-06434-07 (ALCB) CRABB, DAVID W INDIANA UNIV SCH OF MEDICINE 975 W WALNUT STREET INDIANAPOLIS, IN 46202-5121 Regulation of expression of liver alcohol dehydrogenase

R01AA-06451-07 (ALCB) DIAMOND, IVAN ERNEST GALLO CLINIC & RES CTR SAN FRANCISCO, CA 94110 Chronic effects of ethanol on neural cells in culture

R01AA-06460-08 (ALCB) EDENBERG, HOWARD J INDIANA UNIVERSITY 635 BARNHILL DRIVE INDIANAPOLIS, IN 46202-5122 Structure and expression of mammalian ADH genes

R01AA-06478-06 (ALCB) MC GIVERN, ROBERT F SAN DIEGO STATE UNIVERSITY 5300 CAMPANILE DRIVE SAN DIEGO, CA 92182 Prenatal alcohol--Endocrine and sexually dimorphic effects

R01AA-06483-04A1 (ALCB) LIGHT, KIM E UNIV OF ARKANSAS FOR MED SCI 4301 WEST MARKHAM STREET LITTLE ROCK, AR 72205 Postnatal ethanol exposure and neurochemical development

R01AA-06498-06 (ALCB) CRABBE, JOHN C JR OREGON HEALTH SCIENCES UNIV 3181 S W SAM JACKSON PARK ROAD PORTLAND, OR 97201 Selection of genetic lines for ethanol-induced activity

R01AA-06548-06 (ALCB) SAVAGE, DANIEL D, II UNIVERSITY OF NEW MEXICO ALBUQUERQUE, NM 87131-5316 Hippocampal neurotransmitter systems in fetal alcohol rats

R01AA-06555-04A2 (ALCB) YOST, GAROLD S UNIVERSITY OF UTAH 112 SKAGGS HALL SALT LAKE CITY, UT 84112 Ethanol induction of UDP-glucuronyltransferase

R01AA-06571-09 (ALCP) ERNHART, CLAIRE B METROHEALTH MEDICAL CENTER 3395 SCRANTON ROAD CLEVELAND, OH 44109 Alcohol--A behavioral teratogen in child development

R01AA-06601-06 (ALCB) VAN THIEL, DAVID H UNIVERSITY OF PITTSBURGH 3550 TERRACE STREET PITTSBURGH, PA 15261 Alcoholic liver pathology--Hepatic cerebral interaction

R01AA-06603-09 (ALCB) TSUKAMOTO, HIDEKAZU CASE WESTERN RESERVE UNIVERSIT 3395 SCRANTON RD CLEVELAND, OH 44109 Pathogenesis of progressive alcoholic liver injury

R01AA-06604-07 (ALCB) ANDERSON, ROBERT A, JR RUSH-PRESBY-ST LUKE'S MED CENT 1653 WEST CONGRESS PARKWAY CHICAGO, IL 60612 Ethanol's effects on male sexual development

R01AA-06608-07 (ALCB) FELDER, MICHAEL R DEPARTMENT OF BIOLOGICAL SCI COLUMBIA, SC 29208 Molecular genetics of genes of alcohol metabolism

R37AA-06610-07 (ALCB) CEDERBAUM, ARTHUR I MOUNT SINAI SCHOOL OF MEDICINE ONE GUSTAVE LEVY PLACE NEW YORK, NY 10029 Alcohol and pyrazole reaction and metabolism by microsomes

R01AA-06611-06 (ALCB) MIDDAUGH, LAWRENCE D 171 ASHLEY AVENUE ROOM 803 RESEARCH BUILDING CHARLESTON, SC 29425-0742 Mechanisms for long-term prenatal effects of alcohol

R01AA-06636-07 (ALCB) HOJNACKI, JEROME L UNIVERSITY OF LOWELL RIVERSIDE STREET LOWELL, MA 01854 Effect of ethanol on sex hormones and HDL metabolism

R01AA-06659-06 (ALCB) LANDAU, EMMANUEL M MT SINAI SCHOOL OF MEDICINE ONE GUSTAVE LEVY PLACE BOX 123 NEW YORK, NY 10029 Ethanol effects--Locus coeruleus and hippocampal neurons

R01AA-06661-07 (ALCB) SUN, GRACE Y UNIVERSITY OF MISSOURI COLUMBIA, MO 65212 Ethanol action on brain acidic phospholipids

R01AA-06662-07 (ALCB) CHARNESS, MICHAEL E W. ROXBURY VA MED CTR 1400 VFW PARKWAY WEST ROXBURY, MA 02132 Ethanol modulates opioid receptors in neural cell lines

R01AA-06665-06 (ALCB) GRUOL, DONNA L RES INST OF SCRIPPS CLINIC 10666 NORTH TORREY PINES RD LA JOLLA, CA 92037 Ethanol effects on CNS development and function

R01AA-06666-07 (ALCP) DAY, NANCY L WESTERN PSYCHIATRIC INST/CLIN 3811 O'HARA STREET PITTSBURGH, PA 15213 Alcohol use during pregnancy--A longitudinal study

R01AA-06699-06 (ALCP) MOOS, RUDOLPH H STANFORD UNIVERSITY STANFORD, CA 94305 Problem drinking and life stress among older adults

R01AA-06702-09 (ALCB) GEER, BILLY W KNOX COLLEGE GALESBURG, IL 61401 Genetic and dietary control of alcohol metabolism

R01AA-06721-06 (ALCB) HANNIGAN, JOHN H MOTT CTR/HUMAN GROWTH/DEVEL 275 EAST HANCOCK DETROIT, MI 48201 The psychopharmacology of ethanol-induced teratogenesis

R01AA-06728-05 (ALCB) KLETZIEN, ROLF F WESTERN MICHIGAN UNIVERSITY KALAMAZOO, MI 49008 Ethanol glucocorticoid regulation of G-6-P dehydrogenase

R01AA-06755-06 (ALCB) EMANUELE, MARY ANN VETERANS ADMIN HOSPITAL MEDICAL SERVICES (111) HINES, IL 60141 Effects of ethanol on male reproduction

R29AA-06758-05 (ALCB) WINSTON, GARY W LOUISIANA STATE UNIVERSITY 322 CHOPPIN HALL BATON ROUGE, LA 70893 Ethanol ingestion--Activation of industrial pollutants

R01AA-06772-07 (ALCB) GAVALER, JUDITH S UNIVERSITY OF PITTSBURGH 3515 FIFTH AVE PITTSBURGH, PA 15261 Alcohol effects in postmenopausal women

R01AA-06776-06 (ALCP) GEORGE, WILLIAM H STATE UNIV OF NY AT BUFFALO 235 PARK HALL-AMHERST CAMPUS AMHERST, NEW YORK 14260 Perceived alcohol effects on women II--Beliefs and sexuality

R01AA-06794-07 (ALCP) LEX, BARBARA W MCLEAN HOSPITAL 115 MILL STREET BELMONT, MA 02178 Alcoholism and family history in women

R01AA-06845-06 (ALCB) SAMSON, HERMAN H UNIVERSITY OF WASHINGTON 3937 15TH AVENUE NE SEATTLE, WA 98195 Models of drinking initiation--Behavioral study

R01AA-06860-06 (ALCB) POTTER, BARRY J MOUNT SINAI SCH OF MEDICINE 1 GUSTAVE L LEVY PLACE NEW YORK, NY 10029 Effects of alcohol on iron homeostasis

R01AA-06865-06 (ALCB) MEZEY, ESTEBAN JOHNS HOPKINS SCH OF MED 725 N. WOLFE ST. BALTIMORE, MD 21205 Effects of ethanol on glutathione metabolism

R01AA-06867-04A1 (ALCB) YORK, JAMES L RESEARCH INST ON ALCOHOLISM 1021 MAIN STREET BUFFALO, NY 14203 Aging and musculo-motor consequences of alcohol abuse

R01AA-06890-06 (ALCB) LAL, HARBANS TEXAS COLL OF OSTEOPATHIC MED 3500 CAMP BOWIE BLVD FORT WORTH, TX 76107-2690 Characterization of ethanol withdrawal

R01AA-06902-07 (ALCB) RILEY, EDWARD P SAN DIEGO STATE UNIVERSITY SAN DIEGO, CA 92182 Behavioral effects of neonatal alcohol exposure

R01AA-06916-08 (ALCB) MILLER, MICHAEL W UNIVERSITY OF IOWA 500 NEWTON RD/MEB IOWA CITY, IA 52242 Experimental fetal alcohol syndrome

R01AA-06925-03 (ALCP) BARNES, GRACE M RESEARCH INST ON ALCOHOLISM 1021 MAIN STREET BUFFALO, NY 14203 Family factors and adolescent alcohol use

R01AA-06926-06 (ALCP) PERRINE, MERVYN W VERMONT ALCOHOL RES CTR 2000 MOUNTAIN VIEW DRIVE COLCHESTER, VT 05446 Probabilities of drunken driving among convicted DUI's

R01AA-06927-06 (ALCB) SHOEMAKER, WILLIAM J UNIV OF CONNECTICUT HEALTH CTR 263 FARMINGTON AVENUE FARMINGTON, CT 06032 Opioid peptides, receptors and POMC mRNA in rat FAS

R01AA-06938-06 (ALCB) HALSTED, CHARLES H UNIV OF CALIFORNIA, DAVIS TB 156, SCHOOL OF MEDICINE DAVIS, CA 95616 Folate metabolism in alcoholism

R01AA-06965-06 (ALCB) CHAPIN, JOHN K HAHNEMANN UNIVERSITY BROAD & VINE PHILADELPHIA, PA 19102-1192 Ethanol effects on cortical circuits in sensory processing

R01AA-06971-04S1 (ALCB) EAGON, PATRICIA K UNIVERSITY OF PITTSBURGH 1000J SCAIFE HALL PITTSBURGH, PA 15261 Effect of alcohol on growth hormone - liver interaction

R01AA-06985-05 (ALCB) HEMPEL, JOHN D UNIVERSITY OF PITTSBURGH 3550 TERRACE STREET PITTSBURGH, PA 15261 Structural characterization of liver aldehyde dehydrogenase

R01AA-06989-06 (ALCB) LANGE, LOUIS G, III JEWISH HOSPITAL OF ST LOUIS 216 S KINGSHIGHWAY ST LOUIS, MO 63110 Specific myocardial metabolites of ethanol

R01AA-07010-06 (ALCB) EWALD, SANDRA J AUBURN UNIVERSITY COLLEGE OF VETERINARY MEDICINE AUBURN, AL 36849 Fetal alcohol syndrome and immune deficiency

R01AA-07032-07 (ALCB) GREENBERG, DAVID A UNIVERSITY OF CALIFORNIA SAN FRANCISCO GENERAL HOSPITAL SAN FRANCISCO, CA 94110 Ethanol and calcium channels in cultured neural cells

R01AA-07033-06 (ALCP) BROWN, SANDRA A UNIV OF CA, SAN DIEGO 9500 GILMAN DRIVE LA JOLLA, CA 92093-0603 Adolescent alcohol treatment outcome: recovery patterns

R01AA-07034-06 (ALCP) FILLMORE, KAYE UNIVERSITY OF CALIFORNIA BOX 0612 SAN FRANCISCO, CA 94143-0612 Collaborative alcohol-related longitudinal project

R01AA-07035-06 (ALCB) YESAVAGE, JEROME A STANFORD UNIVERSITY SCH OF MED STANFORD, CA 94305-5490 Pilot performance and alcohol

R01AA-07040-05 (ALCB) MILLER, KEITH W MASSACHUSETTS GENERAL HOSPITAL FRUIT STREET BOSTON, MA 02114 Action of ethanol on nicotinic membranes

R01AA-07042-06 (ALCB) PHILLIPS, DWIGHT E MONTANA STATE UNIVERSITY BOZEMAN, MT 59717 Gliogenesis, myelinogenesis and alcohol exposure

R01AA-07052-05 (ALCB) AMSEL, ABRAM UNIVERSITY OF TEXAS AT AUSTIN MEZES 330 AUSTIN, TX 78712 Fetal alcohol--Learning, memory, and neural development

R01AA-07065-05 (ALCP) ZUCKER, ROBERT A MICHIGAN STATE UNIVERSITY 129 PSYCHOLOGY RES BLDG EAST LANSING, MI 48824-1117 Risk and coping in children of alcoholics

R01AA-07070-04 (ALCP) MC CRADY, BARBARA S RUTGERS, THE STATE UNIV OF N J NEW BRUNSWICK, NJ 08903 Preventing relapses after couples' alcoholism treatment

R01AA-07101-03 (ALCB) DAR, M SAEED EAST CAROLINA UNIVERSITY SCHOOL OF MEDICINE GREENVILLE, NC 27858 Role of adenosine ethanol-induced motor disturbances

R01AA-07103-05 (ALCP) WALKER, R DALE UNIVERSITY OF WASHINGTON DEPT OF PSYCH ZB-20 (116 ATU) SEATTLE, WA 98195 Urban American Indian adolescent alcohol and drug abuse

R01AA-07112-05 (ALCB) BERMAN, MARLENE O BOSTON UNIV SCH OF MEDICINE 85 E CONCORD STREET BOSTON, MA 02118 Affective and cognitive changes in alcoholism

R01AA-07117-05 (ALCB) BOSRON, WILLIAM F INDIANA UNIVERSITY SCH

OF MED 635 BARNHILL DRIVE INDIANAPOLIS, IN 46202-5122 Structure and function of liver alcohol dehydrogenases

R01AA-07144-05 (ALCB) CICERO, THEODORE J WASHINGTON UNIVERSITY 4940 AUDUBON AVE ST LOUIS, MO 63110 Paternal and postnatal effects of alcohol on puberty

R29AA-07145-05 (ALCB) DAVIES, DAVID L UNIV OF ARKANSAS FOR MED SCIS 4301 WEST MARKHAM ST LITTLE ROCK, AR 72205-7199 Ethanol effects on glial responses to CNS tissue insult

R01AA-07147-04 (PCB) ROEHRS, TIMOTHY A HENRY FORD HOSPITAL 2921 W GRAND BLVD DETROIT, MI 48202 Ethanol, sleepiness/alertness, and impaired function

R01AA-07183-04 (ALCP) LEONARD, KENNETH E RES INST ON ALCOHOLISM 1021 MAIN STREET BUFFALO, NY 14203 Frequent heavy drinking and marital violence in newlyweds

P50AA-07186-06 (SRCA) RUBIN, EMANUEL THOMAS JEFFERSON UNIVERSITY 1020 LOCUST STREET PHILADELPHIA, PA 19107 Alcohol and the cell

P50AA-07186-06 0005 (SRCA) HOECK, JOANNES B Alcohol and the cell Effects of ethanol on Ca-mediated signal transduction systems

P50AA-07186-06 0007 (SRCA) CHANCE, BRITTON Alcohol and the cell NMR spectroscopy of liver

P50AA-07186-06 0011 (SRCA) TARASCHI, THEODORE Alcohol and the cell Molecular basis of membrane tolerance

P50AA-07186-06 0012 (SRCA) ELLINGSON, JOHN S Alcohol and the cell Role of phospholipids in membrane tolerance

P50AA-07186-06 0013 (SRCA) THOMAS, ANDREW P Alcohol and the cell Effects of ethanol on excitation-contraction coupling in cardiac muscle cells

P50AA-07186-06 0014 (SRCA) KALIA, MADHU Alcohol and the cell Ethanol effects on neurons and neuronal circuits

P50AA-07186-06 0015 (SRCA) DAMJANOV, IVAN Alcohol and the cell Cellular basis of fetal alcohol syndrome

P50AA-07186-06 0016 (SRCA) PROCKOP, DARWIN J Alcohol and the cell MRNA levels for collagens in cirrhosis

P50AA-07186-06 0017 (SRCA) FARBER, JOHN L Alcohol and the cell Sensitivity to oxidative stress after chronic ethanol treatment

R01AA-07192-05 (SRCD) BLUM, TERRY C COLLEGE OF MANAGEMENT GEORGIA INST OF TECHNOLOGY ATLANTA, GA 30332 Worksite integration of ADM prevention strategies

P01AA-07203-02 (SRCA) PERRINE, MERVYN W VERMONT ALCOHOL RES CTR 2000 MOUNTAIN VIEW DRIVE COLCHESTER, VT 05446 Psychobiological studies of alcohol tolerant drivers

P01AA-07203-02 0001 (SRCA) PERRINE, MERVYN W Psychobiological studies of alcohol tolerant drivers Behavioral and psychological aspects of alcohol tolerance

P01AA-07203-02 0002 (SRCA) BEIRNESS, DOUGLAS J Psychobiological studies of alcohol tolerant drivers Phenomenological aspects of alcohol tolerance

P01AA-07203-02 0003 (SRCA) LI, TING-KAI Psychobiological studies of alcohol tolerant drivers Biochemical aspects--Pharmacokinetics and genetics of alcohol metabolism

P01AA-07203-02 0004 (SRCA) HELZER, JOHN E Psychobiological studies of alcohol tolerant drivers Alcohol tolerance among alcoholics

P01AA-07203-02 9001 (SRCA) PERRINE, MERVYN W Psychobiological studies of alcohol tolerant drivers Core--Ad lib drinking & controlled doses with varying alcohol tolerance

R01AA-07212-06 (ALCB) SHAW, SPENCER V A MEDICAL CENTER 130 WEST KINGSBRIDGE RD BRONX, NY 10468 Iron mobilization and ethanol induced liver injury

P01AA-07215-06 (SRCA) RUBIN, EMANUEL THOMAS JEFFERSON UNIVERSITY 1020 LOCUST ST/RM 279 JAH PHILADELPHIA, PA 19107 Effects of alcohol on subcellular organelles of liver

P01AA-07215-06 0001 (SRCA) HOEK, JOANNES B Effects of alcohol on subcellular organelles of liver Ethanol and phospholipid-dependent signal transduction in liver

P01AA-07215-06 0002 (SRCA) THOMAS, ANDREW P Effects of alcohol on subcellular organelles of liver Effects of ethanol on phospholipid-dependent signal transduction

P01AA-07215-06 0003 (SRCA) STUBBS, CHRISTOPHER D Effects of alcohol on subcellular organelles of liver Ethanol effects on proteins interacting with the membrane surface

P01AA-07215-06 0004 (SRCA) TARASCHI, THEODORE F Effects of alcohol on subcellular organelles of liver The interaction of ethanol with liver cell membranes

P01AA-07215-06 9001 (SRCA) RUBIN, EMANUEL Effects of alcohol on subcellular organelles of liver Core--Lipid Laboratory

R01AA-07216-06 (ALCB) DEES, W LES TEXAS A&M UNIVERSITY COLL/VET MED: DEPT/VET ANATOMY COLLEGE STATION, TX 77843-4458 Neuroendocrine effects of alcohol on puberty

R01AA-07231-05 (ALCP) SHER, KENNETH J UNIVERSITY OF MISSOURI 210 MCALESTER HALL COLUMBIA, MO 65211 A prospective study of offspring of alcoholics

R01AA-07234-03 (ALCB) PETTY, FREDERICK DEPT OF VET AFFAIRS MED CTR 4500 SOUTH LANCASTER ROAD DALLAS, TX 75216 Plasma GABA--Biological marker for alcoholism?

R01AA-07250-04 (ALCP) BLUM, TERRY C COLLEGE OF MANAGEMENT GEORGIA INST OF TECHNOLOGY ATLANTA, GA 30332 Structure and content of employee alcoholism programs

R01AA-07261-06 (ALCB) DUESTER, GREGG L COLORADO STATE UNIVERSITY FORT COLLINS, CO 80523 Regulation of alcohol dehydrogenase gene expression

R01AA-07271-03 (ALCP) NORRIS, JEANETTE ALCOHOL & DRUG ABUSE INST 3937 15TH AVENUE, NE SEATTLE, WA 98105 Alcohol and social influence

R29AA-07276-02 (ALCP) BENNETT, ROBERT UNIV OF TEXAS MENTAL SCIS INST 1300 MOURSUND HOUSTON, TX 77030 Learned tolerance to alcohol in humans

R01AA-07284-06 (ALCB) FISHER, STANLEY E NORTH SHORE UNIVERSITY HOSPITA 300 COMMUNITY DRIVE MANHASSET, NY 11030 Ethanol and fetal growth--Role of the placenta

R01AA-07287-06 (SRCA) SPITZER, JOHN J LSU MEDICAL CENTER 1901 PERDIDO STREET NEW ORLEANS, LA 70112 Immune and metabolic modulation by alcohol and infection

R01AA-07292-06A1 (ALCB) WOOD, W GIBSON VA MEDICAL CENTER ONE VETERANS DRIVE MINNEAPOLIS, MN 55417 Transbilayer effects of alcohol on brain membranes

R01AA-07293-06 (ALCB) MEADOWS, GARY G WASHINGTON STATE UNIVERSITY PULLMAN, WA 99164-6510 Effect of alcohol on natural killer cell activity

R29AA-07302-04 (SRCD) KELLY, THOMAS H JOHNS HOPKINS UNIV SCH OF MED 600 N WOLFE ST HOUCK 2E BALTIMORE, MD 21205 Ethanol and aggressive behavior--Mechanisms of action

R01AA-07311-05 (ALCP) RICHMAN, JUDITH A UNIV OF ILLINOIS AT CHICAGO P.O. BOX 6998 CHICAGO, IL 60680 Problem drinking over time by future MDS

R01AA-07313-05 (ALCB) WEST, JAMES R UNIVERSITY OF IOWA COLLEGE OF MEDICINE IOWA CITY, IA 52242 Genetic influences on CNS fetal alcohol effects

R01AA-07317-03 (ALCB) NAGASAWA, HERBERT T 308 HARVARD STREET MINNEAPOLIS, MN 55455 Studies on the alcohol deterrent agent cyanamide

R01AA-07330-05 (ALCB) ERWIN, V GENE UNIVERSITY OF COLORADO CAMPUS BOX 297 BOULDER, CO 80309-0297 Neurotensinergic systems in ethanol actions

R01AA-07337-04 (ALCB) REINKE, LESTER A UNIV OF OKLAHOMA HEALTH SCIS C PO BOX 26901 OKLAHOMA CITY, OK 73190 Free radicals in alcoholic liver injury

R29AA-07351-06 (ALCB) SYAPIN, PETER J TEXAS TECH UNIV HEALTH SCI CTR LUBBOCK, TX 79430 Alcohol and peripheral-type benzodiazepine receptors

R29AA-07358-05 (ALCB) ADICKES, EDWARD D CREIGHTON UNIVERSITY CALIFORNIA AT 24TH STREET OMAHA, NE 68178 Teratogenic effects of ethanol on developing myocytes

R29AA-07360-04 (ALCP) COHEN, DEBORAH A UNIV OF SOUTHERN CALIFORNIA 1420 SAN PABLO STREET, PMB-B20 LOS ANGELES, CA 90033 Parenting skills, alcohol, and drug abuse prevention

R01AA-07361-03 (ALCP) ALTERMAN, ARTHUR VET ADMINISTRATION MEDICAL CTR UNIVERSITY & WOODLAND AVENUES PHILADELPHIA, PA 19104 Risk factors and the development of problematic drinking

R01AA-07365-03 (ALCB) HENRIKSEN, STEVEN J SCRIPPS RESEARCH INSTITUTE 10666 NORTH TORREY PINES RD LA JOLLA, CA 92037 CNS synaptic plasticity following acute ethanol exposure

P50AA-07378-04 (SRCA) GREDEN, JOHN F U OF MICHIGAN HOSP, BOX 0704 1500 E. MEDICAL CENTER DRIVE ANN ARBOR,MICHIGAN 48109-0704 Alcoholism and the aged--Central nervous system effects

P50AA-07378-04 0001 (SRCA) BERESFORD, T Alcoholism and the aged--Central nervous system effects Screening examinations for covert alcoholism in elderly individuals

P50AA-07378-04 0002 (SRCA) GOMBERG, E Alcoholism and the aged--Central nervous system effects Factors influencing treatment outcome in elderly alcoholics

P50AA-07378-04 0003 (SRCA) ADAMS, K Alcoholism and the aged--Central nervous system effects Neuropsychology and neurometabolism in aging and alcoholism

P50AA-07378-04 0004 (SRCA) GREDEN, J Alcoholism and the aged--Central nervous system effects Hippocampal degeneration and memory loss in elderly alcoholics

P50AA-07378-04 0005 (SRCA) KRONTOL, ZIAD Alcoholism and the aged--Central nervous system effects Alcohol, aging and immune function

P50AA-07378-04 0006 (SRCA) SHIPLEY, J Alcoholism and the aged--Central nervous system effects Sleep disregulation, sleep apnea and depression in elderly alcoholics

R01AA-07381-05 (SRCA) SEELIG, LEONARD L, JR LOUISIANA STATE UNIV MED CENTE P.O. BOX 33932 SHREVEPORT, LA 71130-3932 Maternal alcohol and lactational immune transfer

R29AA-07384-04 (ALCB) WAND, GARY S JOHNS HOPKINS UNIV SCH OF MED 720 RUTLAND AVENUE BALTIMORE, MD 21205 Ethanol and the hypothalamic-pituitary-adrenal axis

R01AA-07386-04 (ALCP) POWELL, BARBARA J VA MEDICAL CENTER 4801 LINWOOD BOULEVARD KANSAS CITY, MO 64128-2295 Pharmacological treatment of alcoholic subtypes

R01AA-07389-02 (SRCA) REDEI, EVA UNIVERSITY OF PENNSYLVANIA 422 CURIE BLVD. PHILADELPHIA, PA 19104-6141 Chronic & prenatal alcohol--Endocrine/immune interations

R01AA-07399-03 (ALCB) MCLANE, JERRY A HINES VA HOSPITAL BUILDING 1 ROOM D-203 HINES, IL 60141 Aging and ethanol as factors in axonal transport deficit

R01AA-07404-03 (ALCB) SAMSON, HERMAN H 3937 15TH AVENUE NE SEATTLE, WA 98105 Oral ethanol drinking and CNS dopamine-GABA systems

R01AA-07514-05 (ALCB) SCHENKER, STEVEN UNIVERSITY OF TEXAS 7703 FLOYD CURL DRIVE SAN ANTONIO, TX 78284-7878 Fetal alcohol syndrome--Role of placenta and of cocaine

R29AA-07517-03 (ALCP) VOLPICELLI, JOSEPH R VETERANS ADM MEDICAL CENTER BUILDING #15 (116) PHILADELPHIA, PA 19104 Naltrexone treatment of alcohol dependence

R01AA-07535-04 (ALCP) HEATH, ANDREW C WASHINGTON UNIVERSITY 4940 AUDUBON AVENUE ST LOUIS, MO 63110 Persistence and change in drinking habits--Twin study

R01AA-07536-04 (ALCP) HINGSON, RALPH W BOSTON UNIV SCHOOL OF MED 85 EAST NEWTON STREET BOSTON, MA 02118 Massachusetts 1987 Safe Roads Act/traffic safety program

R01AA-07537-04 (ALCB) URAY, NANDOR J KIRKSVILLE COLL OF OSTEOPA MED 800 WEST JEFFERSON KIRKSVILLE, MO 63501 Ethanol-hormonal interactions in cerebellar development

R01AA-07544-04 (SRCM) RODRIQUEZ, ORLANDO FORDHAM UNIVERSITY BRONX, N Y 10458 Spanish speaking mental health research and development center

R01AA-07548-03 (ALCB) DARUNA, JORGE H TULANE UNIVERSITY 1430 TULANE AVE NEW ORLEANS, LA 70112 Alcohol, P3 topography & family history of alcoholism

R29AA-07550-04 (ALCB) LUMPKIN, CHARLES K JR UNIV OF ARKANSAS FOR MED SCIS 4301 W MARKHAM LITTLE ROCK, AR 72205 Modulation of regeneration in alcoholic liver disease

R29AA-07551-04 (ALCP) REICH, GWENDOLYN G WASHINGTON UNIVERSITY 660 S. EUCLID AVENUE-BOX 8134 ST. LOUIS, MO 63110 Children's reactions to alcoholic parents' sobriety

R01AA-07554-04 (ALCP) MILLER, BRENDA A RESEARCH INST ON

ALCOHOLISM 1021 MAIN STREET BUFFALO, NY 14203 Impact of family violence on women's alcohol problems

R01AA-07559-03 (ALCB) BURT, DAVID R UNIV OF MD SCH OF MEDICINE 655 W. BALTIMORE STREET BALTIMORE, MD 21201 GABA receptor sequence and alcohol response

R01AA-07564-04 (ALCP) MILLER, WILLIAM R UNIVERSITY OF NEW MEXICO ALBUQUERQUE, NEW MEXICO 87131 Effectiveness of the community reinforcement approach

R01AA-07567-02 (ALCB) WEHNER, JEANNE M UNIVERSITY OF COLORADO CAMPUS BOX 447 BOULDER, CO 80309-0447 Ethanol-corticosterone-GABA interactions

R01AA-07569-03 (ALCB) MOORE, BLAKE W WASHINGTON UNIVERSITY 660 S EUCLID AVE/BOX 8134 ST LOUIS, MO 63110 Effects of ethanol on neural cells in culture

R29AA-07571-03 (ALCB) PONNAPPA, BIDDANDA C THOMAS JEFFERSON UNIVERSITY 1020 LOCUST STREET PHILADELPHIA, PA 19107 Alcohol & pancreatic digestive enzyme synthesis

R29AA-07573-03 (ALCB) FELLER, DANIEL J OREGON HEALTH SCIENCES UNIV PORTLAND, OR 97201 Ethanol selection--Compartive neurochemistry

R01AA-07582-03 (ALCP) LEWIS, COLLINS E WASHINGTON UNIVERSITY 600 S EUCLID AVE; BOX 8134 ST LOUIS, MO 63110 Diagnostic and cognitive vulnerabilities to relapse

R01AA-07585-03 (ALCB) SUN, ALBERT Y UNIVERSITY OF MISSOURI ONE HOSPITAL DRIVE COLUMBIA, MO 65212 The role of ethanol in free radical generation

R01AA-07595-03S1 (ALCP) COLLINS, R LORRAINE RESEARCH INSTITUTE ON ALCOHOLI 1021 MAIN STREET BUFFALO, NY 14203 Restraint and attributions--Risk factors in alcohol abuse

R01AA-07600-03 (ALCP) LIN, NAN DUKE UNIVERSITY 268 SOC-PSYCH BLDG. DURHAM, N C 27706 Life events, social support, and drinking

P50AA-07606-04 (SRCA) SOKOL, ROBERT J WAYNE STATE UNIVERSITY 540 EAST CANFIELD AVE DETROIT, MI 48201 Neurobehavioral aspects of fetal alcohol exposure

P50AA-07606-04 0001 (SRCA) ERNHART, CLAIRE B Neurobehavioral aspects of fetal alcohol exposure Analysis of the Cleveland prospective fetal alcohol data base

P50AA-07606-04 0002 (SRCA) JACOBSON, JOSEPH Neurobehavioral aspects of fetal alcohol exposure Research enhancement

P50AA-07606-04 0003 (SRCA) JACOBSON, SANDRA W Neurobehavioral aspects of fetal alcohol exposure Alcohol-related deficits in cognitive processing speed

P50AA-07606-04 0004 (SRCA) SMITH, MOYRA Neurobehavioral aspects of fetal alcohol exposure Molecular studies in alcohol-related birth defects

P50AA-07606-04 0005 (SRCA) SYNER, FRANK N Neurobehavioral aspects of fetal alcohol exposure Placental aldehyde dehydrogenase and adverse fetal outcome

P50AA-07606-04 0006 (SRCA) ABEL, ERNEST L Neurobehavioral aspects of fetal alcohol exposure Effects of paternal alcohol exposure

P50AA-07606-04 0007 (SRCA) SKOFF, ROBERT P Neurobehavioral aspects of fetal alcohol exposure Prenatal alcohol exposure and myelination

P50AA-07606-04 0008 (SRCA) BOTTOMS, SIDNEY Neurobehavioral aspects of fetal alcohol exposure Practical screening for risk drinking during pregnancy

P50AA-07606-04 9001 (SRCA) SOKOL, ROBERT J Neurobehavioral aspects of fetal alcohol exposure Clinical research core

P50AA-07606-04 9002 (SRCA) ABEL, ERNEST Neurobehavioral aspects of fetal alcohol exposure Laboratory research core

P50AA-07606-04 9003 (SRCA) AGER, JOEL Neurobehavioral aspects of fetal alcohol exposure Statistics and data base core

P50AA-07606-04 9004 (SRCA) VUCHINICH, RUDY E Neurobehavioral aspects of fetal alcohol exposure Education/training core

P50AA-07611-04 (SRCA) LI, TING-KAI INDIANA UNIV SCH OF MEDICINE 545 BARNHILL DRIVE INDIANAPOLIS, IN 46202-5124 Center on genetic determinants of alcohol ingestion

P50AA-07611-04 0003 (SRCA) LIN, RENEE C Center on genetic determinants of alcohol ingestion Pilot project--Heritability of plasma apolipoproteins

P50AA-07611-04 9001 (SRCA) LUMENG, LAWRENCE Center on genetic determinants of alcohol ingestion Core--Animal production

P50AA-07611-04 9002 (SRCA) CRABB, DAVID W Center on genetic determinants of alcohol ingestion Core--Molecular biology

P50AA-07611-04 9003 (SRCA) CHRISTIAN, JOE C Center on genetic determinants of alcohol ingestion Core--Human genetics and database

P50AA-07611-04 0001 (SRCA) WEINER, HENRY Center on genetic determinants of alcohol ingestion Pilot study--Liver mitochondrial aldehyde dehydrogenase

P50AA-07611-04 0002 (SRCA) LUMENG, LAWRENCE Center on genetic determinants of alcohol ingestion Pilot study--Aldehyde dehydrogenase isoenzymes in liver disease

R01AA-07624-02 (ALCP) GOOGINS, BRADLEY BOSTON UNIVERSITY 264 BAY STATE ROAD BOSTON, MA 02215 The role of work based social environments in alcoholism

R01AA-07641-04 (ALCB) CAMPBELL, BYRON A PRINCETON UNIVERSITY PRINCETON, N J 08544 Effect of fetal exposure to alcohol on aging

R01AA-07645-02 (ALCP) FAWCETT, JAN A RUSH-PRESBY-ST LUKE'S MED CENT 1720 WEST POLK STREET CHICAGO, IL 60612 Psychopharmacologic treatment of alcoholism

R01AA-07647-05 (SRCA) LUMENG, LAWRENCE INDIANA UNIVERSITY SCH OF MED 975 W. WALNUT STREET INDIANAPOLIS, IN 46202-5121 New diagnostic markers of alcohol abuse

R01AA-07653-04 (ALCB) NOBLE, ERNEST P NEUROPSYCHIATRIC INST 760 WESTWOOD PLAZA LOS ANGELES, CA 90024 Ethanol and phosphoinositide metabolism in astrocytes

R44AA-07657-03S1 (SRCA) SWETTE, LARRY L GINER, INC 14 SPRING STREET WALTHAM, MA 02254-9147 Alcohol measurements for treatment compliance

R44AA-07661-02A3 (SRCA) HIRSHBERG, LINDA CONSAD RESEARCH CORPORATION 121 NORTH HIGHLAND AVENUE PITTSBURGH, PA 15206 Development of a strategic issues Employee Assistance Program handbook

R29AA-07670-03 (ALCB) SUBRAMANIAN, MARAPPA G WAYNE STATE UNIVERSITY C S MOTT CENTER, 275 E HANCOCK DETROIT, MI 48201 Alcohol and lactation--Effects on prolactin release

PROJECT NO., ORGANIZATIONAL UNIT., INVESTIGATOR, ADDRESS, TITLE

R01AA-07683-03 (ALCP) BLAKE, RICHARD H UNIVERSITY OF NEBRASKA OMAHA KAYSER HALL 421 OMAHA, NE 68182-0167 Older persons problem drinking identification screen

R01AA-07694-03 (ALCP) GOODMAN, ALLEN C WAYNE STATE UNIVERSITY DETROIT, MI 48202 Economic analysis of alcohol treatment offset effects

R29AA-07700-04 (ALCP) SMITH, GORDON S JOHNS HOPKINS UNIVERSITY 615 N WOLFE ST BALTIMORE, MD 21205 Alcohol related drownings and fatal occupational injuries

R01AA-07702-04 (ALCB) CUNNINGHAM, CHRISTOPHER L OREGON HEALTH SCIENCES UNIV 3181 SW SAM JACKSON PARK ROAD PORTLAND, OR 97201 Modulation of alcohol reinforcement

R01AA-07707-03 (ALCB) CANNON, DALE S VETERANS ADM MEDICAL CENTER 4500 S LANCASTER ROAD DALLAS, TX 75216 Ethanol preference and taste aversion learning

R29AA-07710-04 (ALCB) NELSON, STEVE LSU MEDICAL CENTER 1542 TULANE AVENUE NEW ORLEANS, LA 70112 Effect of alcoholism on TNF and host defense

R01AA-07712-02 (ALCP) RYCHTARIK, ROBERT G RESEARCH INSTITUTE ON ALCOHOLI 1021 MAIN STREET BUFFALO, NY 14203 Coping skills in spouses of alcoholics

R01AA-07728-04 (ALCP) HEATH, ANDREW C WASHINGTON UNIVERSITY 4940 AUDUBON AVENUE ST LOUIS, MO 63110 Natural history of alcohol use and abuse--Genetic models

R01AA-07731-05 (SRCA) JERRELLS, THOMAS R LSU MEDICAL CENTER P O BOX 33932 SHREVEPORT, LA 71130 Mechanism of ethanol-induced impairments in immunity

R01AA-07732-03 (ALCB) LOOSEN, PETER T VA MEDICAL CENTER 1310 24TH AVENUE SOUTH NASHVILLE, TN 37203 Neuroendocrinology of alcoholism

R01AA-07733-03 (ALCB) LEUNG, BENJAMIN S UNIV OF MINNESOTA 420 DELAWARE ST SE, BOX 395 UM MINNEAPOLIS, MN 55455 Alcohol-induced intrauterine growth retardation

R01AA-07735-03 (ALCB) KNIGHT, LINDA C TEMPLE UNIVERSITY HOSPITAL 3401 N BROAD ST PHILADELPHIA, PA 19140 Effect of alcohol on gastric motor function

R01AA-07740-02 (ALCP) POWER, THOMAS G UNIVERSITY OF HOUSTON HOUSTON, TX 77204-5341 Attachment, autonomy, and patterns of adolescent drinking

R01AA-07747-03 (ALCB) MC DONOUGH, KATHLEEN H LOUISIANA STATE UNIV MED CTR 433 BOLIVAR, 8TH FLOOR NEW ORLEANS, LA 70112 Alcohol enhanced infection-induced cardiac depression

R29AA-07749-04 (ALCP) FORTINI, MARY-ELLEN OCCUPATIONAL HEALTH SERVICES I 125 E SIR FRANCIS DRAKE BLVD LARKSPUR, CA 94939 Adolescent drinking-and-driving attitudes and behaviors

R29AA-07750-03 (ALCB) MILES, MICHAEL F ERNEST GALLO CLINIC & RES CTR BUILDING 1, ROOM 101 SAN FRANCISCO, CA 94110 Ethanol effects on gene expression in neural cell cultures

R01AA-07751-03 (SRCA) TARNAWSKI, ANDRZEJ S LONG BEACH VA MEDICAL CENTER 5901 EAST 7TH STREET LONG BEACH, CA 90822 Cellular mechanisms of alcohol injury of gastric mucosa

R01AA-07754-04 (ALCB) GEORGE, FRANK R UNIVERSITY OF NEW MEXICO ALBUQUERQUE, NEW MEXICO 87131 Pharmacogenetics--Ethanol reinforecment and effects

R44AA-07772-03 (SRCA) LUBRANO, GLENN J UNIVERSAL SENSORS, INC 5258 VETERANS BLVD, SUITE D METAIRIE, LA 70006 A non-invasive alcohol probe

R01AA-07789-04 (ALCB) WEINBERG, JOANNE UNIVERSITY OF BRITISH COLUMBIA VANCOUVER, BC,V6T 1W5,CANADA Alcohol and stress --Interactive effects

R01AA-07791-03 (ALCB) BECKER, HOWARD C VA MEDICAL CENTER 109 BEE STREET CHARLESTON, SC 29403 Prenatal ethanol--Effect on later ethanol responsiveness

R01AA-07794-02 (ALCB) CHAN, ARTHUR W K RESEARCH INST ON ALCOHOLISM 1021 MAIN STREET BUFFALO, NY 14203 Detection of alcoholism and heavy alcohol intake

R01AA-07796-03 (ALCP) WELLS-PARKER, ELISABETH N MISSISSIPPI STATE UNIVERSITY P.O. BOX 6156 MISSISSIPPI STATE, MS 39762 DUI treatment meta-analysis and database/revision

R01AA-07799-02 (ALCB) MANOWITZ, PAUL UMDNJ-ROBERT W JOHNSON MED SCH 671 HOES LANE PISCATAWAY, NJ 08854-5633 An enzyme defect in alcoholic patients

R01AA-07802-04 (SRCA) LIEBER, CHARLES S VETERANS ADMIN MED CTR 130 WEST KINGSBRIDGE ROAD BRONX, NY 10468 Validation of biological markers of alcohol consumption

R01AA-07809-02 (ALCB) MASON, GEORGE A UNIV OF N CAROLINA/CHAPEL HILL 203 BIOLOGICAL SCI RES CTR CHAPEL HILL, NC 27599-7250 Interaction of alcohol and the HPT-axis

R01AA-07810-04 (ALCB) MAHER, JACQUELYN J 1001 POTRERO AVENUE BUILDING 40, RM 4102 SAN FRANCISCO, CA 94110 Mechanism of sinusoidal fibrosis in alcoholic hepatitis

R01AA-07812-04 (ALCP) LONGABAUGH, RICHARD H CTR FOR ALC/ADDICTION STUDIES BROWN UNIV, BOX G PROVIDENCE, RI 02912 Matching patients to treatment focus

R01AA-07817-03 (ALCB) TANG, BING-KOU UNIVERSITY OF TORONTO MEDICAL SCIENCES BUILDING TORONTO, ONTARIO CANADA M5S 1 Biological markers of chronic excess ethanol consumption

R01AA-07818-03 (ALCB) KLASSEN, LYNELL W UNIV OF NEBRASKA MEDICAL CENTE 600 SOUTH 42ND STREET OMAHA, NE 68198-3332 Immune response to acetaldehyde adducts on liver cells

R01AA-07825-03 (ALCP) LYDIARD, R BRUCE MEDICAL UNIV OF SOUTH CAROLINA 171 ASHLEY AVENUE CHARLESTON, SC 29425 Imipramine treatment of alcoholics with panic disorder

R01AA-07827-04 (ALCB) GORDON, ADRIENNE S ERNEST GALLO CLINIC & RES CTR BUILDING 1, ROOM 101 SAN FRANCISCO, CA 94110 CAMP signal transduction in lymphocytes from alcoholics

R01AA-07831-04 (ALCP) PETTINATI, HELEN M CARRIER FOUNDATION PO BOX 147 ROUTE 601 BELLE MEADE, NJ 08502 Cocaine and alcohol--Inpatient versus outpatient treatments

R29AA-07832-05 (ALCB) RECTOR, WILLIAM G, JR GASTROENTEROLOGY DIVISION 2045 FRANKLIN ST DENVER, CO 80205 Determinants of renal sodium retention in cirrhosis

R01AA-07836-04 (ALCB) NARAHASHI, TOSHIO NORTHWESTERN UNIVERSITY

PROJECT NO., ORGANIZATIONAL UNIT., INVESTIGATOR, ADDRESS, TITLE

MED 303 E. CHICAGO AVENUE CHICAGO, IL 60611 Cellular mechanism of action of alcohol

R01AA-07838-03 (ALCB) BELCHER, JOHN D UNIV OF MINNESOTA 1300 SOUTH SECOND STREET MINEAPOLIS, MN 55454-1015 Biological markers of alcohol consumption

R29AA-07839-04 (ALCP) ABDEL-RAHMAN, ABDEL A EAST CAROLINA UNIVERSITY GREENVILLE, NC 27858 Negative impact of alcohol on antihypertensive therapy

R29AA-07846-04 (ALCB) CASEY, CAROL A VETS ADMINISTRATION MED CENTER 4101 WOOLWORTH AVENUE OMAHA, NE 68105 Effect of ethanol on receptor-mediated endocytosis in liver

R01AA-07848-02 (ALCB) RHOADS, DENNIS E UNIVERSITY OF RHODE ISLAND 117 MORRILL LIFE SCIENCE BLDG KINGSTON, RI 02881 Synaptic amino acid transport--Alcohol and alcoholism

R01AA-07849-03 (ALCB) MUELLER, GERALD C UNIVERSITY OF WISCONSIN 1400 UNIVERSITY AVE. MADISON, WI 53706 Role of phosphatidylethanol synthesis in alcoholism

R01AA-07850-04 (ALCP) MONTI, PETER M PROVIDENCE VA MEDICAL CENTER DAVIS PARK PROVIDENCE, RI 02908 Cue exposure and social skills treatment for alcoholics

R01AA-07852-02 (ALCP) HAYS, RONALD D RAND CORPORATION 1700 MAIN STREET, PO BOX 2138 SANTA MONICA, CA 90407-2138 Microcomputer assessment of alcohol use

R01AA-07854-03 (ALCB) ACARA, MARGARET A STATE UNIVERSITY OF NEW YORK 102 FARBER HALL, SCHOOL OF MED BUFFALO, NY 14214 Magnetic resonance detection of alcohol effects

R01AA-07861-04 (ALCP) WINDLE, MICHAEL T RESEARCH INST ON ALCOHOLISM 1021 MAIN STREET BUFFALO, NY 14203 Vulnerability factors and adolescent drinking

R01AA-07862-02 (ALCB) YOUNG, STUART W STANFORD UNIVERSITY SCH OF MED STANFORD, CA 94305-5105 Alcohol toxicity measured by MRI contrast agents

R01AA-07863-02 (ALCB) CAVANAGH, PETER R PENNSYLVANIA STATE UNIVERSITY UNIVERSITY PARK, PA 16802 Gait, posture, and falls in elderly-- Role of alcohol

R01AA-07876-04 (ALCP) PERRINE, MERVYN W VERMONT ALCOHOL RES CTR 2000 MOUNTAIN VIEW DRIVE COLCHESTER, VT 05446 Alcohol tolerance and adaptation among drinking drivers

R01AA-07982-04 (ALCP) CLONINGER, CLAUDE R WASHINGTON UNIVERSITY 660 S. EUCLID - BOX 8134 ST LOUIS, MO 63110 Prediction of alcohol abuse in Swedish adoptees

R01AA-08003-04 (ALCB) TREISTMAN, STEVEN N UNIVERSITY OF MASSACHUSETTS 55 LAKE AVENUE NORTH WORCESTER, MA 01655 Alcohol action on nerve terminals in selected strains of rats

R01AA-08007-03 (ALCP) DONOVAN, JOHN E UNIVERSITY OF COLORADO CAMPUS BOX 483 BOULDER, CO 80309-0483 Drink-driving and risky driving in adolescents and youth

R01AA-08008-03 (ALCP) JOHNSON, PATRICK B FORDHAM UNIVERSITY HISPANIC RESEARCH CENTER BRONX, NY 10458 A comparison of Puerto Rican and Irish American drinking

R29AA-08009-03 (ALCB) LANCASTER, FRANCINE E TEXAS WOMAN'S UNIVERSITY 1130 M.D. ANDERSON BOULEVARD HOUSTON, TX 77030 Neuroamines of beer drinking rats and their offspring

R01AA-08020-03 (ALCB) NOBLE, ERNEST P UNIV OF CA, LOS ANGELES 760 WESTWOOD PLAZA LOS ANGELES, CA 90024-1759 CNS predictors of problem drinking by boys

R29AA-08022-03 (ALCB) STUBBS, CHRISTOPHER D THOMAS JEFFERSON UNIVERSITY 1020 LOCUST STREET PHILADELPHIA, PA 19107 Ethanol effect--protein-lipid interactions in membranes

R01AA-08024-03 (ALCB) BREESE, GEORGE R UNIV OF N CAROLINA AT CH HILL CHAPEL HILL, N C 27599 Neuropharmacology of the anti-conflict action of ethanol

R01AA-08025-03 (ALCB) MCARDLE, JOSEPH J UMDNJ-NEW JERSEY MEDICAL SCHOO 185 SOUTH ORANGE AVE NEWARK, NJ 07103-2714 Ethanol and gene modulation of CNS function and development

R01AA-08026-03 (ALCB) VERNADAKIS, ANTONIA O UNIVERSITY OF COLORADO 4200 EAST NINTH AVE DENVER, CO 80262 Alcohol effect in neuroembryogenesis--In ovo and culture

R01AA-08028-03 (SRCA) CLONINGER, CLAUDE R WASHINGTON UNIVERSITY 660 S EUCLID AVE, BOX 8134 ST LOUIS, MO 63110 Molecular genetic studies of alcoholic subtypes

R01AA-08029-03 (ALCB) SNYDER, ANN K UNIVERSITY OF HEALTH SCIS/ 3333 GREEN BAY ROAD NORTH CHICAGO, IL 60064 Role of embryonic fuels in fetal alcohol syndrome

R01AA-08030-03 (ALCP) QUITKIN, FREDERIC M NY STATE PSYCHIATRIC INSTITUTE 722 WEST 168TH STREET NEW YORK, NY 10032 Imipramine treatment of alcoholism with depression

R01AA-08031-02 (ALCP) POLLOCK, VICKI E UNIV OF SOUTHERN CALIFORNIA 1934 HOSPITAL PLACE LOS ANGELES, CA 90033 Alcoholism risk--Psychobiological alcohol effects in men

R01AA-08033-03 (ALCP) O'MALLEY, STEPHANIE S 285 ORCHARD STREET NEW HAVEN, CT 06511 Anxiety and vulnerability to alcoholism in young adults

P50AA-08037-04 (SRCA) WATSON, RONALD R UNIVERSITY OF ARIZONA 1501 N. CAMBELL AVENUE TUCSON, AZ 85724 Alcohol--Immunomodulation and disease pathogenesis

P50AA-08037-04 0001 (SRCA) MCCUSKEY, R Alcohol--Immunomodulation and disease pathogenesis Alcohol and hepatic microvascular dysfunction

P50AA-08037-04 0002 (SRCA) WATSON, RONALD Alcohol--Immunomodulation and disease pathogenesis Ethanol and murine retrovirus infection--Disease resistance

P50AA-08037-04 0003 (SRCA) EARNEST, DAVID L Alcohol--Immunomodulation and disease pathogenesis Ethanol and immuostimulants on kupffer cells function

P50AA-08037-04 0004 (SRCA) WITTE, MARLYS Alcohol--Immunomodulation and disease pathogenesis Alcohol, sinusoidal capillarization and immunodeficiency

R01AA-08051-01A4 (ALCP) WINDLE, MICHAEL T RESEARCH INST ON ALCOHOLISM 1021 MAIN STREET BUFFALO, NY 14203 Behavioral risk for AIDS among alcoholics

R01AA-08072-01A2 (ALCB) REYES, EDWARD UNIVERSITY OF NEW MEXICO 915 STANFORD, NE ALBUQUERQUE, NM 87131 Relationship between alcohol toxicity and glutatione

PROJECT NO., ORGANIZATIONAL UNIT., INVESTIGATOR, ADDRESS, TITLE

R01AA-08076-02 (ALCP) CONNORS, GERARD J RESEARCH INST ON ALCOHOLISM 1021 MAIN STREET BUFFALO, NY 14203 Secondary prevention of alcohol problems in women

R29AA-08080-03 (ALCB) KELLY, SANDRA J UNIV OF SOUTH CAROLINA COLUMBIA, SC 29208 Alcohol exposure during the brain growth spurt

R01AA-08082-02 (ALCP) HILL, SHIRLEY Y WESTERN PSYCHIATRIC INST & CLI 3811 O'HARA STREET PITTSBURGH, PA 15213 Biological risk factors in relatives of alcoholic women

R29AA-08089-04 (ALCB) WOODWARD, JOHN J MEDICAL COLL OF VA/VCU MCGUIRE HALL,RM 301, BOX 524 RICHMOND, VA 23298-0524 Modulation of calcium channels by ethanol

R01AA-08097-02 (ALCP) GRUBE, JOEL W PREVENTION RESEARCH CENTER 2532 DURANT AVENUE BERKELEY, CA 94704 Adolescent drinking in the United States and Ireland

R01AA-08098-02 (ALCP) JACOB, THEODORE UNIVERSITY OF ARIZONA FCR 210 TUCSON, AZ 85721 Family assessment in alcohol research

R01AA-08104-03 (ALCB) LESLIE, STEVEN W THE UNIV OF TEXAS AT AUSTIN COLLEGE OF PHARMACY AUSTIN, TX 78712-1074 Effect of aging and alcohol on neuronal calcium metabolism

R01AA-08105-03 (ALCP) COLES, CLAIRE D GEORGIA MENTAL HEALTH INST 1256 BRIARCLIFF ROAD, NE ATLANTA, GA 30306 Maternal alcohol use--Development outcome at school age

R01AA-08111-02 (ALCB) MASON, BARBARA J NEW YORK HOSP-CORNELL MED CENT 525 E 68TH ST NEW YORK, NY 10021 Desipramine metabolism in recovering alcoholics

R01AA-08116-03 (SRCA) FRENCH, SAMUEL W L.A. CO. HARBOR-UCLA MED CTR 1000 WEST CARSON STREET TORRANCE, CA 90509 Pathogenesis of experimental alcoholic liver disease

R01AA-08117-02 (ALCB) MESSING, ROBERT O ERNEST GALLO CLINIC & RES CTR BLDG 1, ROOM 101 SAN FRANCISCO, CA 94110 Ethanol, calcium channels & protein kinase C

R01AA-08118-03 (ALCP) WILSON, JAMES R UNIVERSITY OF COLORADO CAMPUS BOX 447 BOULDER, CO 80309-0447 Behavioral genetic analyses of alcohol consumption

R01AA-08125-03 (ALCB) MCCLEARN, GERALD E THE PENNSYLVANIA STATE UNIV S-211 HENDERSON BLDG UNIVERSITY PARK, PA 16802 Genetic markers and alcohol-related behavior in mice

R01AA-08128-02 (ALCP) LEONARD, KENNETH E RESEARCH INSTITUTE ON ALCOHOLI 1021 MAIN STREET BUFFALO, NY 14203 Experimental study of alcohol and marital aggression

R29AA-08139-04 (ALCB) RAUCY, JUDY L UNIVERSITY OF NEW MEXICO COLLEGE OF PHARMACY ALBUQUERQUE, NM 87131 Characterization of human liver cytochromes P450

R01AA-08149-04 (ALCB) LAKSHMAN, RAJ VA MEDICAL CENTER 50 IRVING ST, NW WASHINGTON, DC 20422 Mechanisms of omega-3 fatty acid on alcoholic hyperlipidemia

R01AA-08150-02 (ALCB) MANKES, RUSSELL F ALBANY MEDICAL COLLEGE 47 NEW SCOTLAND AVENUE ALBANY, NY 12208 Alcoholic embryopathy & maternal hypertension

R01AA-08153-02 (ALCP) KUNITZ, STEPHEN J UNIVERSITY OF ROCHESTER MED CT 601 ELMWOOD AVENUE; BOX 644 ROCHESTER, NY 14642 A follow-up study of alcohol abuse

R01AA-08154-01A2 (ALCB) COSTA, LUCIO G UNIVERSITY OF WASHINGTON SEATTLE, WA 98195 Ethanol and phosphoinositides during brain development

R01AA-08157-01A2 (ALCP) WELTE, JOHN W RESEARCH INST ON ALCOHOLISM 1021 MAIN STREET BUFFALO, NY 14203 Drinking and delinquency in young men

R01AA-08159-02 (ALCP) HASIN, DEBORAH S RESEARCH FDN FOR MENTAL HYGIEN 722 WEST 168TH STREET NEW YORK, NY 10032 Alcohol dependence--General population validity

R29AA-08161-03 (ALCB) COWLEY, DEBORAH S UNIVERSITY OF WASHINGTON RP-10 SEATTLE, WA 98195 Benzodiazepine sensitivity in sons of alcoholics

R01AA-08162-03 (ALCB) CHEDID, ANTONIO UNIV OF HLTH SCI/CHICAGO MED S 3333 NORTH GREEN BAY ROAD NORTH CHICAGO, IL 60064 The immunology of alcoholic liver disease

R29AA-08164-03 (ALCB) WEISS, FRIEDBERT RES INST OF SCRIPPS CLINIC 10666 N TORREY PINES RD, BCR 1 LA JOLLA, CA 92037 Brain dialysis and ethanol self-administration

R01AA-08166-03 (ALCB) DANIELL, LAURA C MEDICAL COLLEGE OF GA AUGUSTA, GA 30912-2300 Ethanol and releasable stores of intracellular calcium

R01AA-08169-03 (ALCB) WANDS, JACK R MASSACHUSETTS GENERAL HOSPITAL 149 13TH ST 7TH FL CHARLESTOWN, MA 02129 Study of HBV and/or variants in alcoholics

R29AA-08172-02 (ALCB) TWOMBLY, DENNIS A NORTHWESTERN UNIVERSITY 303 EAST CHICAGO AVENUE CHICAGO, IL 60611 Ethanol & anticonvulsant modulation of ion channels

R01AA-08176-03 (ALCP) GOODWIN, DONALD W UNIV OF KANSAS MED CENTER 39TH & RAINBOW KANSAS CITY, KS 66103 Thirty-year follow-up of men at high-risk for alcoholism

R29AA-08182-02 (ALCB) HAWTHORN, MARK H STATE UNIVERSITY OF NEW YORK 311 HOCHSTETTER HALL BUFFALO, NY 14260 Effects of alcohol on calcium channel subtypes

R01AA-08189-03 (ALCP) SPEIGLMAN, RICHARD C THE MARIN INSTITUTE 24 BELVEDERE STREET SAN RAFAEL, CA 94901 Justice system referrals and alcoholism treatment impact

R01AA-08195-02 (SRCA) SCHLEIFER, STEVEN J UMDNJ-NEW JERSEY MEDICAL SCHOO 185 SOUTH ORANGE AVENUE NEWARK, NJ 07103-2714 Alcohol dependence--Psychoimmunology and AIDS risk

R01AA-08203-03 (ALCP) ELLIOTT, DELBERT S UNIVERSITY OF COLORADO CAMPUS BOX 483 BOULDER, CO 80309 In-vehicle BAC test devices as a deterrent to DUI

R01AA-08204-03 (ALCB) SULIK, KATHLEEN K UNIV OF NC, CHAPEL HILL 108 TAYLOR HALL CB 7090 CHAPEL HILL, NC 27599-7090 Alcohol--Pathogenesis of early malformation

R01AA-08212-03 (ALCB) KALANT, HAROLD UNIVERSITY OF TORONTO TORONTO, ONTARIO CANADA M5S 1A8 Vasopressin and membrane mechanisms of ethanol tolerance

R01AA-08213-02 (ALCB) BADGER, THOMAS M UNIVERSITY OF ARKANSAS MED SCI 4301 W MARKHAM STREET LITTLE ROCK, AR 72205-7199 Alcohol, pulsatile hormones and molecular mechanisms

PROJECT NO., ORGANIZATIONAL UNIT., INVESTIGATOR, ADDRESS, TITLE

R01AA-08214-02 (ALCP) SCHIAVI, RAUL C MT SINAI SCHOOL OF MEDICINE ONE GUSTAVE L LEVY PLACE NEW YORK, NY 10029 Chronic alcoholism and male sexual dysfunction
R01AA-08219-03 (ALCB) ALLAN, ANDREA M 4940 AUDUBON AVE ST LOUIS, MO 63110 Alcohol actions--A behavioral pharmacogenetics approach
R01AA-08233-02 (ALCP) STALL, RONALD D UNIV OF CALIFORNIA 74 NEW MONTGOMERY STREET SAN FRANCISCO, CA 94105 AIDS risk reduction through substance abuse counseling
R03AA-08235-02 (ALCB) MITLER, MERRILL M SCRIPPS RESEARCH INSTITUTE 10666 NORTH TORREY PINES ROAD LA JOLLA, CA 92037 Ethanol and respiratory drive during sleep
R01AA-08237-03 (SRCA) COHEN, DONALD A UNIVERSITY OF KENTUCKY 800 ROSE STREET LEXINGTON, KY 40536-0084 Alcohol and AIDS - a murine model
R01AA-08238-02 (SRCA) HULLEY, STEPHEN B UNIVERSITY OF CALIFORNIA 74 NEW MONTGOMERY STREET SAN FRANCISCO, CA 94105 HIV risk and infection among alcoholics seeking therapy
R01AA-08241-03 (ALCB) YOKOYAMA, SHOZO SYRACUSE UNIVERSITY 130 COLLEGE PLACE SYRACUSE, NY 13244-1220 Genetics of alcohol sensitivity
R01AA-08246-02 (ALCB) SHEU, KWAN-FU R BURKE MEDICAL RESEARCH INSTITU 785 MAMARONECK AVE WHITE PLAINS, NY 10605 Predispositions to complications of alcoholism
R01AA-08247-02 (ALCB) LANGE, LOUIS G, III JEWISH HOSPITAL OF ST. LOUIS 216 S. KINGSHIGHWAY ST LOUIS, MO 63110 Hepatic metabolism of alcohol by GSH transferases
R01AA-08254-01A1 (ALCB) LE, DZUNG A ADDICTION RESEARCH FOUNDATION 33 RUSSELL STREET TORONTO,ONTARIO, CANADA M5S 2S Behavioral/biological determinants of ethanol preference
R29AA-08258-03 (ALCB) WHITMIRE, DAVID R UNIV OF GEORGIA DRIFTMIER ENG CENTER ATHENS, GA 30602 Rapid ethanol lowering--A bioengineering approach
R29AA-08260-03 (ALCB) DIEHL, ANNA M E JOHNS HOPKINS UNIVERSITY 725 N WOLFE STREET BALTIMORE, MD 21205 Effect of ethanol on regulation of liver regeneration
R01AA-08262-03 (ALCB) PERIS, JOANNA UNIVERSITY OF FLORIDA BOX J-487 JHMHC GAINESVILLE, FL 32610-0487 Nigrotectal GABA neurons in alcohol and kindled seizures
R01AA-08263-02 (ALCP) SENCHAK, MARILYN RESEARCH INST ON ALCOHOLISM 1021 MAIN STREET BUFFALO, NY 14203 Interpersonal skills of adult children of alcoholics
R01AA-08266-02 (ALCP) CUELLAR, JOSE B PREVENTION RESEARCH CENTER 2532 DURANT AVENUE BERKELEY, CA 94704 U.S. Mexicans and alcohol study
R01AA-08268-02 (ALCP) SHORE, ELSIE R WICHITA STATE UNIVERSITY BOX 34, 1845 FAIRMOUNT WICHITA, KS 67208 Business women's abuse prevention project followup study
R01AA-08269-02 (ALCP) KANTOR, GLENDA K UNIVERSITY OF NEW HAMPSHIRE HORTON SOCIAL SCIENCE CENTER DURHAM, NH 03824 Alcohol and marital conflict--A longitudinal analysis
R01AA-08275-01A1 (ALCB) WALTENBAUGH, CARL R NORTHWESTERN UNIV MEDICAL SCH 303 EAST CHICAGO AVENUE CHICAGO, IL 60611 Modification of specific immune responses by alcohol
R01AA-08277-02 (ALCP) WATERS, WILLIAM J RHODE ISLAND DEPT OF HEALTH THREE CAPITOL HILL PROVIDENCE, RI 02908-5097 Community alcohol abuse/injury prevention project
R01AA-08278-02 (ALCP) BUCHSBAUM, DAVID G MEDICAL COLLEGE OF VIRGINIA BOX 102 - MCV STATION RICHMOND, VA 23298 Improving physician management of alcohol disorders
R01AA-08281-01A2 (ALCB) BONDY, STEPHEN C UNIVERSITY OF CALIFORNIA IRVINE, CA 92717 Mitigation of the adverse effects of ethanol in the CNS
R29AA-08284-03 (ALCP) CORNELIUS, MARIE D WESTERN PSYCHIATRIC INST & CLI 3811 O'HARA STREET PITTSBURGH, PA 15213 Alcohol use among teenagers and infant outcome
R01AA-08285-03 (ALCB) ANTONY, VEENA B VAMC 1481 W 10TH ST 111P INDIANAPOLIS, IN 46202-2884 Alcohol induced adveolar macrophage dysfunction in AIDS
R01AA-08302-03 (ALCP) BEAUVAIS, FREDERICK COLORADO STATE UNIVERSITY C78 CLARK BLDG FT COLLINS, CO 80523 Alcohol use, dropouts, and Indian youth
R01AA-08307-03 (ALCB) ANTONY, ASOK C INDIANA UNIVERSITY SCH OF MED 975 W WALNUT ST INDIANAPOLIS, IN 46202-5121 How alcohol perturbs placental/hepatic folate transport
R01AA-08311-03 (ALCP) SMITH, ELIZABETH M WASHINGTON UNIV-SCH OF MED 660 S EUCLID AVE, BOX 8134 ST LOUIS, MO 63110 A prospective long term follow-up of alcoholics
R29AA-08312-03 (ALCB) FROEHLICH, JANICE C INDIANA UNIV SCH OF MED 545 BARNHILL DRIVE INDIANAPOLIS, IN 46202-5124 Enkephalinergic involvement in voluntary alcohol drinking
R01AA-08315-02 (ALCP) ROSE, RICHARD J INDIANA UNIVERSITY BLOOMINGTON, IN 47405 Longitudinal twin-family studies: use and abuse of alcohol
R01AA-08320-01A2 (ALCP) HOWLAND, JONATHAN BOSTON UNIV SCH OF PUBLIC HEAL 85 EAST NEWTON STREET BOSTON, MA 02118 National survey of drinking in aquatic settings
R01AA-08328-02 (ALCB) WIMALASENA, JAYANTHA UNIVERSITY OF NEBRASKA 600 SOUTH 42ND STREET OMAHA, NE 68198-6810 Effects of alcohol on human ovarian cell function
R29AA-08329-03 (ALCP) BRANNON, BONNIE R UNIVERSITY OF WASHINGTON 3937 15TH AVENUE NE SEATTLE, WA 98195 Institutional efficacy influences on school norms
R01AA-08331-01A1 (ALCP) SMITH, JANE E UNIVERSITY OF NEW MEXICO ALBUQUERQUE, NM 87131 Community reinforcement approach with the homeless
R01AA-08333-01A1 (ALCP) GOLDMAN, MARK S UNIVERSITY OF SOUTH FLORIDA 4202 E FOWLER TAMPA, FL 33620 Alcohol expectancies--Mediators of biopsychosocial risk?
R01AA-08335-02 (ALCP) SMITH, ELIZABETH M WASHINGTON UNIVERSITY 660 SOUTH EUCLID AVE, BOX 8134 ST LOUIS, MO 63110 Characteristics of homeless women & their children
R01AA-08338-02 (ALCB) HOLLOWAY, FRANK A UNIVERSITY OF OKLAHOMA P.O. BOX 26901 OKLAHOMA CITY, OK 73190-3000 Biobehavioral correlates of acute ethanol withdrawal

PROJECT NO., ORGANIZATIONAL UNIT., INVESTIGATOR, ADDRESS, TITLE

R01AA-08341-03 (ALCP) DRAKE, ROBERT E DARTMOUTH MEDICAL SCHOOL 9 MAYNARD STREET HANOVER, NH 03756 Treatment of dual diagnosis and homelessness
R01AA-08345-02 (SRCA) PAULY, MARK V UNIVERSITY OF PENNSYLVANIA 133 SOUTH 36TH STREET PHILADELPHIA, PA 19104-3246 Economic causes and effects of state alcoholism spending
R01AA-08349-02 (SRCA) SAFFER, HENRY NATL BUREAU OF ECONOMIC RES, I 269 MERCER STREET NEW YORK, NY 10003 Alcohol advertising and highway fatality rates
P01AA-08353-03 (SRCA) DIAMOND, IVAN ERNEST GALLO CLINIC & RES CTR BLDG 1, ROOM 101 SAN FRANCISCO, CA 94110 Cell biology and genetics of alcoholism
P01AA-08353-03 9001 (SRCA) MILES, MICHAEL Cell biology and genetics of alcoholism Core--Cell culture
P01AA-08353-03 9002 (SRCA) MESSING, ROBERT O Cell biology and genetics of alcoholism Core--Scientific
P01AA-08353-03 0001 (SRCA) GORDON, ADRIENNE S Cell biology and genetics of alcoholism Adenosine and adaptation to ethanol in human lymphocytes
P01AA-08353-03 0002 (SRCA) DIAMOND, IVAN Cell biology and genetics of alcoholism Identification of a genetic marker for alcoholism in cultures lymphocytes
P01AA-08353-03 0003 (SRCA) MILES, MICHAEL F Cell biology and genetics of alcoholism Ethanol-responsive gene expression in lymphocytes from alcoholism
P01AA-08353-03 0004 (SRCA) MESSING, ROBERT Cell biology and genetics of alcoholism Ethanol modulation of neuronal differentiation in cultured cells
P01AA-08353-03 0005 (SRCA) MOCHLY-ROSEN, DARIA Cell biology and genetics of alcoholism Ethanol modulation of cardiac myocyte function
R01AA-08354-02 (SRCA) SLOAN, FRANK A VANDERBILT UNIVERSITY BOX 1503 - STATION B NASHVILLE, TN 37235 Heavy drinking and drunk driving--Which deterrents work?
R01AA-08359-03 (SRCA) GROSSMAN, MICHAEL NATL BUREAU/ECONOMIC RES INC. 269 MERCER STREET NEW YORK, NY 10003 Alcohol use, addiction, and price
R03AA-08361-01A1 (ALCP) SCRIBNER, RICHARD INST FOR HEALTH PROMOTION AND 35 NORTH LAKE AVENUE PASADENA, CA 91101 City-level alcohol related problems and database
R01AA-08364-02 (SRCA) SALKEVER, DAVID S JOHNS HOPKINS UNIVERSITY 624 NORTH BROADWAY BALTIMORE, MD 21205-1901 Role of nonprofit providers--Policy impacts
R01AA-08366-02 (SRCA) COATE, DOUGLAS C NATIONAL BUREAU OF ECONOMIC RE 269 MERCER STREET, 8TH FLOOR NEW YORK, NY 10003 Moderate drinking and coronary heart disease mortality
R01AA-08370-02 (SRCA) MCKNIGHT, A JAMES NATL PUBLIC SERVICES RES INST 8201 CORPORATE DRIVE LANDOVER, MD 20785 Cost benefit analysis of alcohol service laws enforcement
R01AA-08371-02 (SRCA) SALKEVER, DAVID S JOHNS HOPKINS UNIVERSITY 624 NORTH BROADWAY BALTIMORE, MD 21205 Child health impacts of parental alcohol use
R01AA-08379-02 (SRCA) DOOLEY, DAVID C UNIV OF CA, IRVINE 310 SOCIAL ECOLOGY BUILDING IRVINE, CA 92717 Relationship of economic conditions and alcohol use
R01AA-08381-02 (SRCA) FISCHHOFF, BARUCH CARNEGIE MELLON UNIVERSITY PITTSBURGH, PA 15213 Adolescents' risk judgements--Elicitation & evaluation
R01AA-08382-02 (SRCA) LEHTO, MARK R PURDUE UNIVERSITY WEST LAFAYETTE, IN 47907 Decision-making model of alcohol related behavior
R01AA-08383-03 (SRCA) MAZIS, MICHAEL B THE AMERICAN UNIVERSITY 4400 MASSACHUSETTS AVENUE, NW WASHINGTON, DC 20016 Evaluating health warning labels for alcoholic beverages
R01AA-08393-02 (SRCA) PHELPS, CHARLES E UNIVERSITY OF ROCHESTER ROCHESTER, NY 14627 Reducing drunk driving with taxes, laws, and information
R01AA-08394-02 (SRCA) SINDELAR, JODY L LEPH PO BOX 3333/60 COLLEGE STREET NEW HAVEN, CT 06405 The economics of alcoholism and alcohol consumption
R01AA-08395-03 (SRCA) GRUENEWALD, PAUL J PREVENTION RESEARCH CENTER 2532 DURANT AVENUE BERKELEY, CA 94704 A socioeconomic model of alcohol problem prevention
U10AA-08401-03 (SRCA) BEGLEITER, HENRI SUNY HEALTH SCIENCE CENTER 450 CLARKSON AVE, BOX 1203 BROOKLYN, NY 11203 Coordinating center--Collaborative studies on the genetics of alcoholism
U10AA-08402-03 (SRCA) CROWE, RAYMOND R UNIV OF IOWA COLL OF MEDICINE 500 NEWTON ROAD IOWA CITY, IA 52242 Genetic linkage study of alcoholism
U10AA-08403-03 (SRCA) BEGLEITER, HENRI SUNY HEALTH SCIENCE CENTER 450 CLARKSON AVE, BOX 1203 BROOKLYN, NY 11203 A collaborative study on the genetics of alcoholism
R01AA-08404-03 (SRCA) MOLOF, MARTIN J INTEGRATED RESEARCH SERVS, INC 66 CLUB ROAD EUGENE, OR 97401 Server training models to prevent driving under influence of alcohol--Economics
U10AA-08428-03 (SRCA) RANDALL, CARRIE L VA MEDICAL CENTER 109 BEE STREET CHARLESTON, SC 29403 Alcoholics with social phobia--Treatment matching
U10AA-08430-03 (SRCA) BABOR, THOMAS F UNIV OF CONNECTICUT HEALTH CTR 263 FARMINGTON AVENUE FARMINGTON, CT 06032 Alcoholism treatment clinical trial--Coordinating center
U10AA-08431-03 (SRCA) CONNORS, GERARD J RESEARCH INST ON ALCOHOLISM 1021 MAIN STREET BUFFALO, NY 14203 Multistage patient matching to treatment and aftercare
U10AA-08432-03 (SRCA) DICLEMENTE, CARLO C UNIVERSITY OF HOUSTON 4800 CALHOUN HOUSTON, TX 77204-5341 Univ Houston-VA alcoholism treatment matching clinical research unit
U10AA-08435-03 (SRCA) MILLER, WILLIAM R UNIVERSITY OF NEW MEXICO ALBUQUERQUE, NM 87131 Strategies for matching clients to treatments
U10AA-08436-03 (SRCA) WALKER, R DALE UNIVERSITY OF WASHINGTON SEATTLE, WA 98195 Relapse prevention--Broad spectrum multistage matching
U10AA-08438-03 (SRCA) KADDEN, RONALD M UNIV OF CONNECTICUT HLTH CTR 263 FARMINGTON AVENUE FARMINGTON, CT 06032 Matching patients to alcoholism treatments

PROJECT NO., ORGANIZATIONAL UNIT., INVESTIGATOR, ADDRESS, TITLE

U10AA-08442-03 (SRCA) ZWEBEN, ALLEN UNIV OF WI-MILWAUKEE SCHOOL OF SOCIAL WELFARE MILWAUKEE, WI 53201 The efficacy of brief intervention with problem drinkers

U10AA-08443-03 (SRCA) LONGABAUGH, RICHARD H CTR FOR ALC/ADDICTION STUDIES 345 BLACKSTONE BOULEVARD PROVIDENCE, RI 02906 A multisite matching of treatment focus to dysfunction

R01AA-08447-01A2 (ALCP) DIELMAN, TEDDY E UNIVERSITY OF MICHIGAN ANN ARBOR, MI 48109-0201 Altering family norms regarding adolescent alcohol misuse

R01AA-08454-03 (ALCB) JONES, BYRON C PENNSYLVANIA STATE UNIVERSITY UNIVERSITY PARK, PA 16802 Pharmacogenetic analysis of low-dose ethanol effects

R01AA-08455-01A1 (ALCP) FILSTEAD, WILLIAM J PARKSIDE LUTHERAN HOSPITAL 1700 LUTHER LANE PARK RIDGE, IL 60068 Alcoholism treatment--Expectations, motivation and effort

R01AA-08459-02 (ALCB) KOOB, GEORGE F RSCH INST OF THE SCRIPPS CLINI 10666 N TORREY PINES RD, BCR 1 LA JOLLA, CA 92037 Neuropharmacology of ethanol reinforcement

R01AA-08461-01A1 (ALCP) LEIGH, BARBARA C UNIVERSITY OF WASHINGTON 3937 15TH AVENUE NE SEATTLE, WA 98195 Alcohol expectancies, memory accessibility & alcohol use

R01AA-08465-01A1 (ALCB) JANOWSKY, AARON J VETERANS ADM MEDICAL CENTER 3710 SW US VETERANS HOSPITAL R PORTLAND, OR 97201 Glutamate linked ion channels during alcohol withdrawal

R01AA-08473-01A1 (ALCB) BALSTER, ROBERT L MEDICAL COLLEGE OF VIRGINIA VIRGINIA COMMONWEALTH UNIVERSI RICHMOND, VA 23298-0613 Neural basis of the behavioral effects of alcohol

R01AA-08474-01A1 (ALCP) MANSON, SPERO M UNIV OF COLORADO HLTH SCIS CTR 4200 EAST NINTH AVE, BOX C249 DENVER, CO 80262 Alcohol use/abuse among Indian boarding school students

R29AA-08475-03 (ALCP) JOHNSTONE, BRYAN M UNIVERSITY OF KENTUCKY COLLEGE OF MEDICINE LEXINGTON, KY 40536 Alcohol and diet--General population relationships

R01AA-08477-01A1 (SRCA) BRYANT, RICHARD R UNIVERSITY OF MISSOURI 106 HUMANITIES-SOCIAL SCIENCES ROLLA, MO 65401 Impact of substance abuse on labor supply and wages

R03AA-08479-02 (ALCB) RICHIE, JOHN P, JR AMERICAN HEALTH FOUNDATION ONE DANA ROAD VALHALLA, NY 10595 Altered alcohol toxicity and glutathione status in aging

R01AA-08480-02 (ALCP) ALTERMAN, ARTHUR I UNIVERSITY OF PENNSYLVANIA 3910 CHESTNUT STREET PHILADELPHIA, PA 19104-6178 Sociopathy and treatment outcome in alcoholic patients

R01AA-08484-01A1 (ALCB) GONZALES, RUEBEN A UNIVERSITY OF TEXAS AUSTIN, TX 78712-1074 Ethanol and NMDA receptor function

R01AA-08492-02 (SRCA) MARTIN, PETER R VANDERBILT UNIVERSITY NASHVILLE, TN 37232 Genetic mechanisms of alcoholic organic brain disease

R01AA-08497-02 (ALCP) FARQUHAR, JOHN W STANFORD UNIVERSITY 1000 WELCH ROAD PALO ALTO, CA 94304-1885 A middle school curriculum in alcohol abuse prevention

R01AA-08499-01A1 (ALCB) POHORECKY, LARISSA A RUTGERS STATE UNIV OF NEW JERS PO BOX 1089 PISCATAWAY, NJ 08855-0969 Social status and preference for ethanol

R01AA-08512-01A1 (ALCP) FLEMING, MICHAEL F UNIVERSITY OF WISCONSIN 777 S MILLS STREET MADISON, WI 53715 A trial of physician treatment of problem drinkers

R03AA-08520-02 (ALCB) ROTTER, ANDREJ OHIO STATE UNIVERSITY 1645 NEIL AVENUE COLUMBUS, OH 43210 Alcohol & expression of GABA/BZ receptor RNA

R03AA-08530-02 (ALCB) LANTZ, ROBERT C UNIV OF ARIZONA HEALTH SCIS CT 1501 N CAMPBELL AVENUE TUCSON, AZ 85724 Alcohol & alveolar macrophage dysfunction

R03AA-08531-02 (ALCP) REYNOLDS, KIM D UNIVERSITY OF ALABAMA SUITE 502, CBB BIRMINGHAM, AL 35294 An alcohol prevention program for pregnant women

R03AA-08532-02 (ALCB) WEINER, HENRY PURDUE UNIVERSITY SOUTH UNIVERSITY DRIVE WEST LAFAYETTE, IN 47907 NMR determination of structure of ALDH signal peptide

R01AA-08536-02 (ALCB) SONNTAG, WILLIAM E WAKE FOREST UNIV/BOWMAN GRAY 300 SOUTH HAWTHORNE ROAD WINSTON-SALEM, NC 27103 Chronic ethanol and insulin-like growth factors

R01AA-08537-01A1 (ALCP) BALCH, GEORGE I UNIVERSITY OF ILLINOIS BOX 4348 M/C 307 CHICAGO, IL 60680 Enhancing the effectiveness of alcohol warning labels

R01AA-08545-02 (SRCA) MARIN, GERARDO UNIVERSITY OF SAN FRANCISCO IGNATIAN HEIGHTS SAN FRANCISCO, CA 94117-1080 Effects of alcohol warning labels on Hispanics

R01AA-08547-03 (SRCA) MACKINNON, DAVID POTER ARIZONA STATE UNIVERSITY TEMPE, AZ 85287-1104 Effects of alcohol labeling legislation on adolescents

P01AA-08553-02 (SRCA) LI, TING-KAI INDIANA UNIVERSITY SCHOOL OF M 545 BARNHILL DRIVE INDIANAPOLIS, IN 46202-5124 Neurobiology and genetics of alcohol-seeking behavior

P01AA-08553-02 0001 (SRCA) LI, TING-KAI Neurobiology and genetics of alcohol-seeking behavior Animal and molecular genetics

P01AA-08553-02 0002 (SRCA) MURPHY, JAMES M Neurobiology and genetics of alcohol-seeking behavior Behavioral pharmacology

P01AA-08553-02 0003 (SRCA) MCBRIDE, WILLIAM J Neurobiology and genetics of alcohol-seeking behavior Neurochemistry

P01AA-08553-02 0004 (SRCA) ZHOU, FENG Neurobiology and genetics of alcohol-seeking behavior Neuroanatomy

P01AA-08553-02 0005 (SRCA) FROEHLICH, JANICE C Neurobiology and genetics of alcohol-seeking behavior Nueroendocrine studies

R03AA-08554-02 (ALCB) WERBER, ANDREW H ALBANY MEDICAL COLLEGE 47 NEW SCOTLAND AVE-A136 ALBANY, NY 12208 Effect of alcohol on cerebral microcirculation

R01AA-08557-02 (SRCA) GREENFIELD, THOMAS K MED RES INST OF SAN FRANCISCO 2000 HEARST AVENUE BERKELEY, CA 94709 Impact of alcoholic beverage warning labels

R01AA-08559-02 (HUD) HENDRICKS, JON OREGON STATE UNIVERSITY CORVALLIS, OR 97331-3703 Social factors in medication and alcohol use by the aged

R01AA-08561-02 (SRCA) HANKIN, JANET R WAYNE STATE UNIVERSITY 656 W. KIRBY AVENUE DETROIT, MI 48202 Impact of labeling & education on antenatal drinking

PROJECT NO., ORGANIZATIONAL UNIT., INVESTIGATOR, ADDRESS, TITLE

R01AA-08564-04 (SRCA) TEMPLE, MARK ALCOHOL RES GROUP/MED RES INST 2000 HEARST AVENUE BERKELEY, CA 94709 Epidemiology of alcohol problems--Risk of AIDS

R01AA-08565-01 (ALCB) CHAWLA, RAJENDER K EMORY UNIVERSITY BOX 23410 ATLANTA, GA 30322 Abnormal metabolism in alcoholic cirrhosis

R29AA-08577-02 (SRCA) SZABO, GYONGYI UNIV OF MASSACHUSETTS MED CENT 55 LAKE AVENUE NORTH WORCESTER, MA 01655 Ethanols role in mediation of monocyte immunosuppression

R01AA-08578-02 (SRCA) ROLF, JON E 624 NORTH BROADWAY BALTIMORE, MD 21205 AIDS and alcohol and other drugs prevention project for Navajo youth

R03AA-08582-01A1 (ALCB) CALHOON, LINDA L NEW MEXICO HIGHLANDS UNIVERSIT LAS VEGAS, NM 87701 Biological markers of alcohol consumption among women

R29AA-08584-01A1 (ALCB) SINGLETARY, KEITH W COLLEGE OF AGRICULTURE 905 SOUTH GOODWIN AVENUE URBANA, IL 61801 Dietary ethanol and initiation of DMBA tumorigenesis

R01AA-08593-01A1 (ALCP) SOBELL, LINDA C ADDICTION RESEARCH FOUNDATION 33 RUSSELL STREET TORONTO, ONTARIO M5S 2S1 CANA Stability of natural recoveries from alcohol problems

R01AA-08596-02 (ALCP) PERRY, CHERYL L UNIVERSITY OF MINNESOTA 515 DELAWARD STREET SE MINNEAPOLIS, MN 55455 Community-wide prog to prevent adolescent alcohol abuse

R03AA-08598-02 (ALCB) SCHECHTER, MARTIN D NORTHEASTERN OHIO UNIVERSITIES 4209 S. ROUTE 44 ROOTSTOWN, OH 44272 Preference for alcohol--Effect of training and heredity

R01AA-08599-02 (ALCB) GLICK, STANLEY D ALBANY MEDICAL COLLEGE 47 NEW SCOTLAND AVENUE ALBANY, NY 12208 Neurohumoral and prenatal determinants of alcohol intake

R01AA-08604-02 (ALCP) BURGE, SANDRA K UNIV OF TEXAS HLTH SCIENCE CTR 7703 FLOYD CURL DRIVE SAN ANTONIO, TX 78284-7795 Primary care intervention for alcohol abuse

R01AA-08605-01A1 (ALCB) ZIMMERBERG, BETTY WILLIAMS COLLEGE BRONFMAN SCIENCE CTR WILLIAMSTOWN, MA 01267 Prenatal exposure to alcohol and thermoregulation

R01AA-08608-03 (ALCB) KOOP, DENNIS R OREGON HEALTH SCIENCES UNIV 3181 S.W. SAM JACKSON PARK ROA PORTLAND, OR 97201-3098 Alcohol toxicity--Role of ethanol-inducible P-450

P01AA-08621-02 (SRCA) CRABBE, JOHN C OREGON HEALTH SCIENCES UNIV 3181 SW SAM JACKSON PARK ROAD PORTLAND, OR 97201 Genetic analyses of neuroadaptation to ethanol

P01AA-08621-02 0001 (SRCA) CUNNINGHAM, CHRISTOPHER L Genetic analyses of neuroadaptation to ethanol Genetic basis of ethanol's hedonic effects /mice/

P01AA-08621-02 0002 (SRCA) PHILLIPS, TAMARA J Genetic analyses of neuroadaptation to ethanol Genetic co-determination of alcohol stimulant-reinforcement potency

P01AA-08621-02 0003 (SRCA) GALLAHER, EDWARD J Genetic analyses of neuroadaptation to ethanol Genetic basis of ethanol tolerance

P01AA-08621-02 0004 (SRCA) KEITH, L DONALD Genetic analyses of neuroadaptation to ethanol Genetic determinants of acute and chronic withdrawal seizures

P01AA-08621-02 0005 (SRCA) BELKNAP, JOHN K Genetic analyses of neuroadaptation to ethanol Neurochemistry and molecular biology

R03AA-08630-02 (ALCP) CARMAN, WENDY J UNIVERSITY OF MICHIGAN 109 OBSERVATORY STREET ANN ARBOR, MI 48109-2029 Alcohol use in Tecumseh, Michigan--1959-1978

R01AA-08631-01A1 (ALCP) SCHWARTZ, JOSEPH E SUNY/STONY BROOK PUTNAM HALL-SOUTH CAMPUS STONY BROOK, NY 11794-8790 Job characteristics and alcoholism in white collar workers

R01AA-08632-01A1 (ALCP) BAER, JOHN S UNIVERSITY OF WASHINGTON SEATTLE, WA 98195 Prediction of stability of high risk drinking

R03AA-08634-01A1 (ALCB) PERRY, HORACE M, III ST LOUIS UNIVERSITY 1402 SOUTH GRAND BOULEVARD ST LOUIS, MO 63104 In Vivo studies of ethanol aging and osteopenia

R01AA-08636-02 (ALCB) YORK, JAMES L RESEARCH INST ON ALCOHOLISM 1021 MAIN STREET BUFFALO, NY 14203 Age-dependent acquisition and loss of ethanol tolerance

R01AA-08637-01A1 (ALCP) O'FARRELL, TIMOTHY J ALCOHOL & FAMILY STUDIES LAB 940 BELMONT ST BROCKTON, MA 02401 Behavioral marital therapy in alcoholism treatment

R03AA-08641-02 (ALCB) SIGNS, STEVEN A NORTHEASTERN OHIO UNIVERSITIES 4206 STATE ROUTE 44 ROOTSTOWN, OH 44272 Molecular cloning of brain mRNA in ethanol dependence

R01AA-08645-02 (ALCB) BADGER, THOMAS M UNIVERSITY OF ARKANSAS 4301 W MARKHAM STREET LITTLE ROCK, AR 72205-7199 Alcohol--Direct and indirect effects on drug metabolism

R01AA-08650-02 (ALCB) PARSONS, OSCAR A UNIVERSITY OF OKLAHOMA HSC 800 NORTHEAST 15TH STREET OKLAHOMA CITY, OK 73104 Cognitive model of memory deficits in alcoholics

R01AA-08651-02 (ALCP) MUTHEN, BENGT O UCLA 405 HILGARD AVENUE LOS ANGELES, CA 90024-1521 Psychometric advances for alcohol & depression studies

R01AA-08661-02 (ALCB) EMANUELE, MARY A LOYOLA UNIVERSITY OF CHICAGO 2160 SOUTH FIRST AVENUE MAYWOOD, IL 60153 The effect of ETOH on GHRF - GH axis, puberty to adult

R01AA-08663-02 (ALCP) GRUENEWALD, PAUL J PREVENTION RESEARCH CENTER 2532 DURANT AVENUE BERKELEY, CA 94704 Advertising and youthful experimentation with alcohol

R01AA-08666-02 (ALCB) RODIER, PATRICIA M UNIVERSITY OF ROCHESTER 601 ELMWOOD AVENUE ROCHESTER, NY 14642 Neuroendocrine effects of prenatal exposure to alcohol

R01AA-08669-01A1 (ALCP) GREENBERG, EDWARD S UNIVERSITY OF COLORADO CAMPUS BOX 487 BOULDER, CO 80309-0487 Workplace risk factors for alcohol abuse

R24AA-08671-02 (SRCM) WENTOWSKI, GLORIA J BENNETT COLLEGE 900 EAST WASHINGTON STREET GREENSBORO, NC 27401-3239 Faculty research development and support program

R24AA-08671-02 0001 (SRCM) MOORE, CAROLYN A Faculty research development and support program Self-concepts/socio-cultural realities and alcohol addiction of African-Americans

PROJECT NO., ORGANIZATIONAL UNIT., INVESTIGATOR, ADDRESS, TITLE

R24AA-08671-02 0002 (SRCM) LINSTER, MICHELLE L Faculty research development and support program Factor of race/ethnicity in treatment for female alcoholics

R01AA-08672-02 (EPS) HEWITT, JOHN K VIRGINIA COMMONWEALTH UNIV MCV BOX 33 RICHMOND, VA 23298-0033 Personality and clinical psychobiology genetics

R01AA-08674-02 (ALCB) ALTURA, BURTON M SUNY HEALTH SCIENCE CENTER 450 CLARKSON AVENUE, BOX 31 BROOKLYN, NY 11203 Basis for alcohol and cocaine strokes--Role of mg2+

R03AA-08683-02 (MSM) BREAKEFIELD, XANDRA O MASS GENERAL HOSPITAL 13TH STREET CHARLESTOWN, MA 02129 Allelic variations in human monoamine oxidase genes

R01AA-08689-02 (ALCP) FINNEY, JOHN W JR VA MEDICAL CENTER (152MPD) 3801 MIRANDA AVE PALO ALTO, CA 94304 Meta-analysis of alcoholism treatment outcome research

R01AA-08706-02 (SRCA) CUNNINGHAM, CAROL C WAKE FOREST UNIVERSITY DEPT OF BIOCHEMISTRY WINSTON-SALEM, NC 27157 Alcohol-oxygen tension interactions in liver

R01AA-08709-02 (ALCB) MELCHIOR, CHRISTINE L VAMC, WEST LOS ANGELES WILSHIRE & SAWTELLE BLVDS LOS ANGELES, CA 90073 Alcohol and GABA-active neurosteroids

R01AA-08714-01A1 (ALCB) HOEK, JOANNES B THOMAS JEFFERSON UNIVERSITY 1020 LOCUST STREET PHILADELPHIA, PA 19107 Alcohol and the control of liver regeneration

R29AA-08716-02 (ALCB) KENNEDY, JOHN M UNIV OF ILLINOIS AT CHICAGO 835 SOUTH WOLCOTT AVENUE CHICAGO, IL 60612 Ethanol-induced cardiomyopathy during development

R03AA-08727-02 (ALCB) MARTIN, DAVID DUKE UNIVERSITY MEDICAL CENTER P.O. BOX 3813 DURHAM, NC 27710 NMDA receptors after prenatal ethanol exposure

R03AA-08731-01A1 (ALCB) HEYMAN, GENE M HARVARD UNIVERSITY 980 WILLIAM JAMES HALL CAMBRIDGE, MA 02138 Maintenance and development of need for alcohol

R01AA-08732-02 (SRCA) BOOTH, BRENDA M VA MEDICAL CENTER HSR&D FIELD PROGRAM (152) IOWA CITY, IA 52246 Alcoholism treatment and health care utilization

R01AA-08734-01A1 (ALCP) MONTI, PETER M BROWN UNIVERSITY DIVISION OF BIOLOGY & MEDICINE PROVIDENCE, RI 02912 Smoking, alcoholics' reactivity and treatment motivation

R03AA-08738-01A1 (ALCB) GOODRIDGE, ALAN G UNIVERSITY OF IOWA BOWEN SCIENCE BUILDING IOWA CITY, IA 52242 Targeted mutations to study alcohol-induced liver injury

R01AA-08742-02 (ALCB) POTTER, BARRY J MOUNT SINAI SCHOOL OF MEDICINE 1 GUSTAVE L LEVY PLACE NEW YORK, NY 10029 Effects of ethanol on hepatic organic anion uptake

P50AA-08746-02 (SRCA) GERSHON, SAMUEL WESTERN PSYCHIATRIC INST & CLI 3811 O'HARA STREET PITTSBURGH, PA 15213 Adolescent alcohol abuse--Biobehavioral manifestations

P50AA-08746-02 0001 (SRCA) ANTELMAN, SEYMOUR Adolescent alcohol abuse--Biobehavioral manifestations Stress-induced time dependent sensitization and ethanol consumption

P50AA-08746-02 0002 (SRCA) FERNSTROM, JOHN Adolescent alcohol abuse--Biobehavioral manifestations Effects of ethanol on growth hormone regulation

P50AA-08746-02 0003 (SRCA) BLOCK, GEOFFREY Adolescent alcohol abuse--Biobehavioral manifestations Nutrition and sex--Does it matter to the alcoholic teen?

P50AA-08746-02 0004 (SRCA) VAN THIEL, DAVID Adolescent alcohol abuse--Biobehavioral manifestations Immunogenetic factors in the development of alcoholic liver disease

P50AA-08746-02 0005 (SRCA) CLARK, DUNCAN Adolescent alcohol abuse--Biobehavioral manifestations Anxiety and alcoholism in adolescence

P50AA-08746-02 0006 (SRCA) MEZZICH, ADA Adolescent alcohol abuse--Biobehavioral manifestations Depression and alcohol abuse in female adolescents

P50AA-08746-02 9001 (SRCA) VAN THIEL, DAVID H Adolescent alcohol abuse--Biobehavioral manifestations Core--Biochemical laboratory

P50AA-08746-02 9002 (SRCA) MEZZICH, JUAN Adolescent alcohol abuse--Biobehavioral manifestations Core--Clinical research and database

P50AA-08746-02 9003 (SRCA) TARTAR, RALPH Adolescent alcohol abuse--Biobehavioral manifestations Core--Education and training

P50AA-08747-02 (SRCA) MC CRADY, BARBARA S RUTGERS THE STATE UNIV OF NJ P.O. BOX 1089 PISCATAWAY, NJ 08855-1089 Alcohol treatment: integrating basic & applied research

P50AA-08747-02 0004 (SRCA) LEVENTHAL, ELAINE A Alcohol treatment: integrating basic & applied research Elder-specific treatment matching

P50AA-08747-02 0005 (SRCA) MORGENSTERN, JONATHAN Alcohol treatment: integrating basic & applied research A causal model of treatment outcome

P50AA-08747-02 0006 (SRCA) BATES, MARSHA E Alcohol treatment: integrating basic & applied research Neuropsychological functioning and pattern of recovery over time

P50AA-08747-02 9001 (SRCA) MC CRADY, BARBARA S Alcohol treatment: integrating basic & applied research Core--Measurement battery

P50AA-08747-02 0001 (SRCA) WILSON, G TERENCE Alcohol treatment: integrating basic & applied research Cue exposure treatment of alcoholism

P50AA-08747-02 0002 (SRCA) PETTINATI, HELEN M Alcohol treatment: integrating basic & applied research Fluoxetine and cue exposure to reduce alcohol craving

P50AA-08747-02 0003 (SRCA) MC CRADY, BARBARA S Alcohol treatment: integrating basic & applied research Medical patients--Matching consultation to stage of change

R01AA-08753-01A1 (ALCB) WOOTEN, MARIE W AUBURN UNIVERSITY 331 FUNCHESS HALL AUBURN UNIVERSITY, AL 36849-54 Alcohol and transmembrane signalling

R01AA-08757-01A1 (ALCB) SARKAR, DIPAK K WASHINGTON STATE UNIVERSITY PULLMAN, WA 99164-6520 Role of opiates in alcohol-induced neurotoxicity

R01AA-08759-01A1 (ALCB) LAMB, ROBERT G VIRGINIA COMMONWEALTH UNIVERSI BOX 524, MCV STATION RICHMOND, VA 23298-0127 An in vitro model of ethanol-dependent liver cell injury

PROJECT NO., ORGANIZATIONAL UNIT., INVESTIGATOR, ADDRESS, TITLE

R01AA-08763-01A1 (ALCP) GAINES, LAWRENCE S VANDERBILT UNIVERSITY 1601 23RD AVENUE, SOUTH NASHVILLE, TN 37212 Beliefs about drinking and risk for alcoholism

R21AA-08764-01 (ALCP) WINTERS, KEN C UNIVERSITY OF MINNESOTA HARVARD ST AT EAST RIVER ROAD MINNEAPOLIS, MN 55455 Alcoholism assessment and treatment for adolescents

R01AA-08765-02 (SRCA) HOLDER, HAROLD D PREVENTION RESEARCH CENTER 2532 DURANT AVENUE BERKELEY, CA 94704 Community prevention study for alcohol problems

R29AA-08769-01 (ALCB) SISSON, JOSEPH H UNIV OF NEBRASKA MED CENTER 600 SOUTH 42ND STREET OMAHA, NE 68198 Acetaldehyde-mediated bronchial cilia dysfunction

R01AA-08770-02 (GMA) SIMON, FRANCIS R UNIVERSITY OF COLORADO 4200 EAST 9TH AVENUE DENVER, CO 80262 Effect of alcohol on hepatic function

R01AA-08771-02 (ALCB) CHAN, ALBERT UNIVERSITY OF MISSISSIPPI 2500 NORTH STATE STREET JACKSON, MS 39216-4505 Ethanol and hypothalamic unit activity

U01AA-08773-02 (SRCA) SOSIN, MICHAEL R UNIVERSITY OF CHICAGO 969 EAST 60TH STREET CHICAGO, IL 60637 Demonstration of case management and supported housing

U01AA-08774-02 (SRCA) JEKEL, JAMES CENTER FOR HEALTH POLICY & RES 350 CONGRESS AVENUE NEW HAVEN, CT 06519 Research on services for homeless substance abusers

U01AA-08775-02 (SRCA) WRIGHT, JAMES D TULANE UNIVERSITY 220 NEWCOMB HALL NEW ORLEANS, LA 70118 New Orleans homeless substance abuse project

U01AA-08778-02 (SRCA) BRAUCHT, GEORGE NICHOLAS UNIVERSITY OF DENVER UNIVERSITY PARK DENVER, CO 80208 Intensive case management for homeless substance abusers

U01AA-08783-01S1 (SRCA) FRANKLIN, JOHN E UMDNJ - NEW JERSEY MED SCHL 30 BERGEN STREET NEWARK, NJ 07107-3000 Homelessness, substance abuse--Investigating two interventions

U01AA-08788-02 (SRCA) STEVENS, SALLY J AMITY INC 316 S 6TH AVE TUCSON, AZ 85701 Southern Arizona alcohol/drug program for the homeless

U01AA-08798-02 (SRCA) COX, GARY B UNIVERSITY OF WASHINGTON 1959 NORTH EAST PACIFIC RP-10 SEATTLE, WA 98195 Intensive case management for chronic public inebriates

U01AA-08802-02 (SRCA) SHIPLEY, THOMAS E TEMPLE UNIVERSITY PHILADELPHIA, PA 19122 Assessing treatments for homeless poly-addicted men

U01AA-08804-02 (SRCA) SMITH, ELIZABETH M WASHINGTON UNIVERSITY 660 S EUCLID AVE - BOX 8134 ST LOUIS, MO 63110 Substance-abusing homeless families--Breaking the cycle

U01AA-08815-02 (SRCA) LAPHAM, SANDRA C LOVELACE MEDICAL FOUNDATION 1650 UNIVERSITY BLVD. N.E. ALBUQUERQUE, NM 87102 Substance abuse treatment programs for homeless persons

U01AA-08818-02 (SRCA) CONRAD, KENDON J CTR FOR HEALTH SVCS & POLICY R 629 NOYES STREET EVANSTON, IL 60208 Case managed residential care for homeless addicts

U01AA-08819-02 (SRCA) MILBY, JESSE B THE UNIV OF AL AT BIRMINGHAM UAB STATION - 101 MTB BIRMINGHAM, ALABAMA 35294 Comparative substance abuse treatments for the homeless

U01AA-08821-02 (SRCA) BURNAM, M AUDREY RAND CORPORATION 1700 MAIN STREET SANTA MONICA, CA 90407-2138 Evaluation of treatment options for the dually diagnosed

U01AA-08840-02 (SRCA) DRAKE, ROBERT E DARTMOUTH MEDICAL SCHOOL 2 WHIPPLE PLACE LEBANON, NH 03766 Washington DC homeless dual diagnosis project

R01AA-08845-01 (ALCB) SHELLITO, JUDD E LSU MEDICAL CENTER 1542 TULANE AVENUE NEW ORLEANS, LA 70112 Alcohol, immunosuppression, and Pneumocystis carinii

R29AA-08846-01A1 (ALCB) BAUTISTA, ABRAHAM P LOUISIANA STATE UNIV MED CTR 1901 PERDIDO STREET NEW ORLEANS, LA 70112 Role of liver in the immunodeficiency of alcoholics

R01AA-08848-01 (ALCB) MESSNER, RONALD P UNIV OF MINNESOTA HOSPITALS 420 DELAWARE STREET, SE MINNEAPOLIS, MN 55455 Selective reduction of immune clearance by ethanol

R01AA-08854-02 (CPA) FRAENKEL-CONRAT, HEINZ UNIVERSITY OF CALIFORNIA 229 WENDELL M. STANLEY HALL BERKELEY, CA 94720 Biochemical studies of a new type of nucleoside adduct

R01AA-08857-01 (ALCB) AGUAYO, LUIS G CATHOLIC UNIV AT VALPARAISO AVENIDA BRASIL 4059 CASILLA 4059, VAPARAAISO, CHIL Interaction of ethanol with GABA-A receptors

R01AA-08867-01 (ALCB) WONDERGEM, ROBERT EAST TENNESSEE STATE UNIVERSIT PO BOX 19,780A JOHNSON CITY, TN 37614-0002 Hepatocyte volume control and alcoholic injury

R01AA-08887-01 (ALCB) ZOELLER, ROBERT T UNIVERSITY OF MISSOURI COLUMBIA, MO 65212 Molecular basis for ethanol-induced hypothyroidism

R01AA-08914-01 (ALCB) EAGON, PATRICIA K UNIVERSITY OF PITTSBURGH 1000-J SCAIFE HALL PITTSBURGH, PA 15261 Effect of alcohol on hormone responsive liver function

R29AA-08920-01 (ALCP) WIECZOREK, WILLIAM F RESEARCH INST OF ALCOHOLISM 1021 MAIN STREET BUFFALO, NY 14203 Treatment-oriented typology of DWI offenders

R01AA-08924-01 (ALCB) RIVIER, CATHERINE SALK INST FOR BIOLOGICAL STUDI PO BOX 85800 SAN DIEGO, CA 92138 Alcohol-interleukin interactions on the rat hpa axis

R01AA-08925-01 (ALCP) CARMELLI, DORIT SRI INTERNATIONAL 333 RAVENSWOOD AVENUE MENLO PARK, CA 94025 Alcohol consumption and mortality in veteran twins

R43AA-08958-01 (SRCA) WALDORF, RONALD A OCULOKINETICS, INC 2291 W 205TH STREET TORRANCE, CA 90501 Analysis of EM/2 alcohol and drug impairment screener data

R43AA-08961-01 (SRCA) SMITH, KELLY L BEND RESEARCH, INC 64550 RESEARCH ROAD BEND, OR 97701-8599 Controlled-release implants of disulfiram metabolites

R01AA-08967-02 (ALCB) ARMSTRONG, ROBERT D UNIV OF MARYLAND SCH OF PHARMA 20 NORTH PINE STREET BALTIMORE, MD 21201 Rat model of mental deficits induced by prenatal alcohol

R01AA-08968-01 (ALCB) FEIN, GEORGE SAN FRANCISCO VA MEDICAL

PROJECT NO., ORGANIZATIONAL UNIT., INVESTIGATOR, ADDRESS, TITLE

CENTE 4150 CLEMENT STREET SAN FRANCISCO, CA 94121 Effects of chronic alcohol abuse on HIV CNS morbidity

R01AA-08970-02 (ALCP) BEUTLER, LARRY E UNIVERSITY OF CALIFORNIA SANTA BARBARA, CA 93106 Family vs behavioral treatment of alcoholism

R43AA-08971-01 (SRCA) RAWSON, RICHARD MATRIX CENTER, INC 8447 WILSHIRE BLVD BEVERLY HILLS, CA 90211 Outpatient alcoholism treatment neurobehavioral model

R01AA-08983-01 (ALCP) KAYE, WALTER H WESTERN PSYCHIATRIC INST & CLI 3811 O'HARA STREET PITTSBURGH, PA 15213 Genetic epidemiology--Alcohol abuse in eating disorders

R01AA-08986-01 (ALCB) LOVINGER, DAVID M VANDERBILT UNIVERSITY SCH OF M 702 LIGHT HALL NASHVILLE, TN 37232-0615 Ethanol inhibition of NMDA receptor-mediated responses

R01AA-08989-01 (ALCP) AMES, GENEVIEVE M PREVENTION RESEARCH CENTER 2532 DURANT AVENUE BERKELEY, CA 94704 Social control and alcohol in the workplace

R01AA-08992-01 (ALCP) STOUT, ROBERT L BUTLER HOSPITAL 345 BLACKSTONE BLVD PROVIDENCE, RI 02906 Time dynamics of alcohol treatment outcome

R01AA-09000-01 (ALCB) WAND, GARY S JOHNS HOPKINS UNIV SCH OF MED 725 N WOLFE ST HUNTERIAN 817 BALTIMORE, MD 21205 Molec/biochem analysis of adenylyl cyclase in alcoholism

R29AA-09002-01 (ALCP) HERD, DENISE A UNIVERSITY OF CALIFORNIA 518 WARREN HALL BERKELEY, CA 94720 Cultural predictors of black and white drinking behavior

R01AA-09004-01 (ALCP) ARANGO, VICTORIA WESTERN PSY INSTITUTE & CLINIC 3811 O'HARA STREET PITTSBURGH, PA 15213 Monoamine systems in alcoholism and suicide

R01AA-09005-01 (ALCB) HOFFMAN, PAULA L UNIVERSITY OF COLORADO 4200 EAST 9TH STREET DENVER, CO 80262 NMDA receptor function in ethanol withdrawal

R03AA-09008-01 (ALCP) PANETH, NIGEL S MICHIGAN STATE UNIVERSITY EAST LANSING, MI 48824-1316 Prenatal alcohol, neonatal brain injury and development

R03AA-09012-01 (ALCB) AGRE, PETER C JOHNS HOPKINS UNIVERSITY 725 N WOLFE STREET BALTIMORE, MD 21205 Red cell membrane protein defects in alcoholism

R01AA-09013-01 (ALCB) MORROW, A LESLIE UNIVERSITY OF NORTH CAROLINA CB #7175, MEDICAL RES BLDG A CHAPEL HILL, NC 27599 Ethanol regulation of GABAa receptor expression in brain

R01AA-09014-01 (ALCB) TABAKOFF, BORIS UNIV OF COLORADO HEALTH SCI CT 4200 EAST 9TH AVENUE DENVER, CO 80262 Alcohol and neuronal signal transduction

R13AA-09017-01 (SRCA) BABOR, THOMAS F UNIV OF CONNECTICUT HEALTH CTR 263 FARMINGTON AVENUE FARMINGTON, CT 06030 Alcoholic subtypes-- A conference proposal

R01AA-09026-01 (ALCP) WALLER, PATRICIA F UNIVERSITY OF MICHIGAN 2901 BAXTER ROAD ANN ARBOR, MI 48109-2150 Psychosocial correlates of adolescent driving behaviors

R01AA-09038-01 (ALCB) DUDEK, BRUCE C UNIVERSITY AT ALBANY - SUNY 1400 WASHINGTON AVE ALBANY, NY 12222 Genetic aspects of alcohol's behavioral activation

R01AA-09042-01 (ALCB) JAGUST, WILLIAM J LAWRENCE BERKELEY LABORATORY 1 CYCLOTRON RD BERKELEY, CA 94720 Alcohol and memory--A PET study

R13AA-09051-01 (ALCP) MILLER, WILLIAM R UNIVERSITY OF NEW MEXICO ALBUQUERQUE, NEW MEXICO 87131 Research on Alcoholics Anonymous--Opportunities and approaches

R43AA-09059-01 (SRCA) GROSS DE NUNEZ, GAYLE SAVANTES 2409 PERKINS RD DURHAM, NC 27706 Alcohol education--Computer animated video

R03AA-09067-01 (ALCB) WOLCOTT, ROBERT M LSU MED CTR SCH OF MED PO BOX 33932 SHREVEPORT, LA 71130-3932 Alcohol and the development of natural killer cells

R01AA-09142-01 (SRCA) WAGENAAR, ALEXANDER C UNIVERSITY OF MINNESOTA 1300 S. SECOND ST. SUITE 300 MINNEAPOLIS, MN 55454-1015 Reducing youth access to alcohol--A randomized community trial

R03AA-09143-01 (ALCP) SCHULENBERG, JOHN E UNIVERSITY OF MICHIGAN SURVEY RESEARCH CENTER ANN ARBOR, MI 48106-1248 Stability and change in alcohol use among youth

R01AA-09146-01 (SRCA) HOLDER, HAROLD D PREVENTION RESEARCH CENTER 2532 DURANT AVE BERKELEY, CA 94704 Preventing alcohol trauma--A community trial

R29AA-09173-01 (ALCB) MELLENCAMP, MARTHA A VETERANS AFFAIRS MEDICAL CTR 4801 LINWOOD BLVD KANSAS CITY, MO 64128-2295 Effects of chronic ethanol feeding on neutrophils

S15AA-09241-01 (SRCA) MC CUSKEY, ROBERT S UNIVERSITY OF ARIZONA 1501 N CAMPBELL AVE TUCSON, AZ 85724 Small instrumentation grant

S15AA-09242-01 (SRCA) SHERIDAN, JUDSON D UNIVERSITY OF MISSOURI 202 JESSE HALL COLUMBIA, MO 65211 Small instrumentation grant

S15AA-09243-01 (SRCA) HAWTHORN, MARK H STATE UNIVERSITY OF NEW YORK 463 HOCHSTETTER HALL BUFFALO, NY 14260 Small instrumentation grant

S15AA-09244-01 (SRCA) BLANE, HOWARD T RESEARCH INST ON ALCOHOLISM 1021 MAIN STREET BUFFALO, NY 14203 Small instrumentation grant

S15AA-09246-01 (SRCA) MANKES, RUSSELL F ALBANY MEDICAL COLLEGE 47 NEW SCOTLAND AVENUE ALBANY, NY 12208 Small instrumentation grant

S15AA-09250-01 (SRCA) ROBINSON, JOHN A LOYOLA UNIV. MEDICAL CENTER 2160 S FIRST AVE MAYWOOD, IL 60153 ASIP - Loyola University of Chicago

S15AA-09251-01 (SRCA) NEEL, JAMES W SAN DIEGO STATE UNIVERSITY SAN DIEGO, CA 92182-0413 Small instrumentation grant

S15AA-09252-01 (SRCA) BLOOM, FLOYD E SCRIPPS RESEARCH INSTITUTE 10666 NORTH TORREY PINES RD LA JOLLA, CA 92037 Small instrumentation grant

S15AA-09253-01 (SRCA) WELT, CAROL UNIV OF MED & DENT OF NEW JERS 185 SOUTH ORANGE AVE NEWARK, NJ 07103-2714 Small instrumentation grant

S15AA-09254-01 (SRCA) MC CLEARN, GERALD E PENNSYLVANIA STATE UNIV UNIVERSITY PARK, PA 16802 Small instrumentation grant

S15AA-09255-01 (SRCA) AMSEL, ABRAM UNIVERSITY OF TEXAS AT AUSTIN AUSTIN, TX 78712 Small instrumentation grant

PROJECT NO., ORGANIZATIONAL UNIT., INVESTIGATOR, ADDRESS, TITLE

S15AA-09256-01 (SRCA) HOFFMAN, DOUGLAS W DARTMOUTH MEDICAL SCHOOL HANOVER, NH 03756 Small instrumentation grant

S15AA-09258-01 (SRCA) WOODWARD, JOHN J VIRGINIA COMMONWEALTH UNIVERSI BOX 524, MCV STATION RICHMOND, VA 23298-0524 Small instrumentation grant

S15AA-09259-01 (SRCA) DE FRIES, JOHN C UNIVERSITY OF COLORADO CAMPUS BOX 19 BOULDER, CO 80309-0019 Small instrumentation grant

S15AA-09260-01 (SRCA) COLBERN, DEBORAH L UNIVERSITY OF ILLINOIS PO BOX 6998, M/C 901 CHICAGO, IL 60680 Small instrumentation grant

S15AA-09261-01 (SRCA) DEITRICH, RICHARD A UNIV OF COLORADO HLTH SCI CTR 4200 EAST 9TH AVENUE DENVER, CO 80262 Small instrumentation grant

S15AA-09262-01 (SRCA) GRUENEWALD, PAUL J PREVENTION RESEARCH CENTER 2532 DURANT AVENUE BERKELEY, CA 94704 Small instrumentation grant

S15AA-09263-01 (SRCA) KLING, O RAY UNIV OF OKLAHOMA HLTH SCI CTR 1000 STANTON L YOUNG BLVD OKLAHOMA CITY, OK 73190 Small instrumentation grant

S15AA-09264-01 (SRCA) BOWDEN, CHARLES L UNIV OF TEXAS HLTH SCI CTR 7703 FLOYD CURL DRIVE SAN ANTONIO, TX 78284-7792 Small instrumentation grant

S15AA-09265-01 (SRCA) EISENMAN, JOSEPH S MOUNT SINAI SCHOOL OF MEDICINE ONE GUSTAVE L LEVY PLACE NEW YORK, NY 10029-6574 Small instrumentation grant

S15AA-09266-01 (SRCA) MIDDAUGH, LAWRENCE D MEDICAL UNIV OF SOUTH CAROLINA 171 ASHLEY AVENUE CHARLESTON, SC 29425-0742 Small instrumentation grant

R24AA-09294-02 (SRCM) JOHNSON, MELVIN A, JR CENTRAL STATE UNIVERSITY 115 WESLEY HALL WILBERFORCE, OH 45384 Institutional research development plan

R24AA-09294-02 0001 (SRCM) RODNEY, H ELAINE Institutional research development plan Impact of parental alcoholism on minority adult children of alcoholics

R24AA-09294-02 0002 (SRCM) MARTIN-STANLEY, CHARLES Institutional research development plan Psychosocial factors as predictors of drug abuse among Black males

S15AA-09303-01 (SRCA) SWANN, ALAN C 6431 FANNIN HOUSTON, TX 77225 Small instrumentation grant

S15AA-09304-01 (SRCA) GALLETTI, PIERRE M BROWN UNIVERSITY BOX G A117 PROVIDENCE, R I 02912 Small instrumentation grant

R29AA-09312-01 (ALCP) SEARLES, JOHN S VERMONT ALCOHOL RESEARCH CENTE 2000 MOUNTAIN VIEW DR COLCHESTER, VT 05446-1910 Differences in alcoholic and non-alcoholic siblings

R01AA-09325-01 (ALCB) ONTKO, JOSEPH A LSU MEDICAL CENTER 1100 FLORIDA AVE NEW ORLEANS, LA 70119 Alcohol and fatty acid ethyl ester metabolism/transport

N01AA-10006-00 ( ) UNIV OF NEW MEXICO** SCHOLES HALL, ROOM 102 ALBUQUERQUE, NEW MEXICO 87112 Treatment research validation and extension program

N01AA-10007-00 ( ) RES FDN FOR MENTAL HYGIENE, IN** 1021 MAIN STREET BUFFALO, NEW YORK 14203 Treatment research validation and extension program

N01AA-10008-00 ( ) INTERSYSTEMS, INC** 820 WEST END AVENUE, 15E NEW YORK, NEW YORK 10025 Video alcohol education for Native American families

N01AA-10009-00 ( ) DEVELOPMENT ASSOC. INC** 1730 NORTH LYNN STREET ARLINGTON, VA 22209-2009 MITS Substance abuse prevention package for Black families

N01AA-10010-00 ( ) ANALYSIS & SIMULATION, INC** 172 HOLTZ ROAD BUFFALO, NEW YORK 14225 Integrated facility for analysis of complex surveys

N01AA-10011-00 ( ) BROWN UNIVERSITY CTR FOR ALCOHOL &** ADDICTION ST BOX G PROVIDENCE, RHODE ISLAND 02912 Treatment research validation and extension program

N01AA-60003-00 ( ) MACRO SYSTEM, INC** MACRO SYSTEMS 8630 FENTON ST SILVER SPRING, MD 20910 Alcohol policy analysis system

N01AA-80003-00 ( ) ROW SCIENCE, INC** 5515 SECURITY LANE SUITE 510 ROCKVILLE, MD 20852 Community demonstration projects for alcohol and drug abuse treatment

R25AD-00004-01 (SRCD) MILLER, LESLIE M BAYLOR COLLEGE OF MEDICINE ONE BAYLOR PLAZA/RM 633E HOUSTON, TX 77030 Houston science education partnership--Brain-link

R25AD-00006-01 (SRCD) HELLER, H CRAIG STANFORD UNIVERSITY STANFORD, CA 94305-2160 Interactive multimedia for middle grades life sciences

R25AD-00027-01 (SSS) HAYWARD, PATRICIA C FLORIDA STATE UNIV 227 CONRADI BUILDING B-142 TALLAHASSEE, FL 32306 Animal models in basic research-- A workshop for teacher

R25AD-00033-01 (SRCD) WHITLOW, JESSE W, JR RUTGERS UNIVERSITY 311 N 5TH CAMDEN, NJ 08102 Rutgers-Camden partners in life sciences

R25AD-00035-01 (SRCD) MALCOM, SHIRLEY M AMERICAN ASSOC/ADV OF SCIENCE 1333 H STREET NORTHWEST WASHINGTON, DC 20005 The AAAS Black Church health connection project

R25AD-00052-01 (SRCM) CUNNINGHAM, SUSANNA L UNIVERSITY OF WASHINGTON SCHOOL OF NURSING SEATTLE, WA 98195 Making connections, making choices--A partnership

R25AD-00056-01 (SSS) VOLTMER, RITA K MIAMI UNIVERSITY 255 MCGUFFEY HALL OXFORD, OH 45056 Health science partnerships for the middle/junior high school

R25AD-00059-01 (SSS) CHASE, CHRISTOPHER H HAMPSHIRE COLLEGE WEST STREET AMHERST, MA 01002 New program for science education--Brain and cognition

R25AD-00064-01 (SSS) KESSEL, RAYMOND UNIVERSITY OF WISCONSIN 445 HENRY MALL MADISON, WI 53706 Summer institute for biology education

R25AD-00066-01 (SRCD) BELLAMY, MARY L NATL ASSOC OF BIOLOGY TEACHERS 11250 ROGER BACON DRIVE RESTON, VA 22090 NABT and SN partnership in neurobiology education

R25AD-00076-01 (SRCM) NICKENS, HERBERT W ASSOCIATION OF AMERICAN MED CO ONE DUPONT CIRCLE, SUITE 200 WASHINGTON, DC 20036 Partnerships for future minority health scientists

R25AD-00077-01 (SSS) DAVIS, CINDA-SUE G 330 E LIBERTY ANN ARBOR, MI 48104-2289 Science for life--Summer program for high school women

P01AG-00001-17A2 (AGE) **PETERS, ALAN** BOSTON UNIVERSITY 80 EAST CONCORD STREET BOSTON, MA 02118 **Neural substrates of cognitive decline in aging monkeys**

P01AG-00001-17A2 0015 (AGE) **KEMPER, THOMAS** Neural substrates of cognitive decline in aging monkeys Age-related neuropathological changes in monkey brain

P01AG-00001-17A2 0016 (AGE) **PETERS, ALAN** Neural substrates of cognitive decline in aging monkeys Age changes in neurones and neuroglia of prefrontal cortex

P01AG-00001-17A2 0017 (AGE) **ROSENE, DOUGLAS L** Neural substrates of cognitive decline in aging monkeys Aged-related changes in the limbic system of the primate brain

P01AG-00001-17A2 0020 (AGE) **MOSS, MARK B** Neural substrates of cognitive decline in aging monkeys Age-related cognitive dysfunction in the monkey

P01AG-00001-17A2 0021 (AGE) **VOLICER, LADISLAV** Neural substrates of cognitive decline in aging monkeys Free radicals & aged-induced neurochemical changes in the monkey

P01AG-00001-17A2 0022 (AGE) **ABRAHAM, CARMELA** Neural substrates of cognitive decline in aging monkeys Mechanisms of amyloid deposition in the aging monkey brain

P01AG-00001-17A2 9002 (AGE) **ROSENE, DOUGLAS** Neural substrates of cognitive decline in aging monkeys Scientific core

P01AG-00001-17A2 9003 (AGE) **MOSS, MARK B** Neural substrates of cognitive decline in aging monkeys Core--Animal

Z01AG-00013-16 (LCP) **HARMAN, S M** NIA, NIH Hormones, hormone receptors and aging.III--Aging and human endocrine regulation

Z01AG-00015-33 (LSB) **FOZARD, J L** NIA, NIH The Baltimore longitudinal study of aging

Z01AG-00021-28 (LCP) **PLATO, C C** NIA, NIH Study of normal human variability and cross cultural aging

Z01AG-00022-15 (LCP) **PLATO, C C** NIA, NIH Bone loss with age--Epidemiology, familial and cross-cultural considerations

Z01AG-00023-15 (LCP) **HARMAN, S M** NIA, NIH Hormones and aging--Pituitary-hypothalamic function in experimental animals

Z01AG-00028-15 (LCP) **PLATO, C C** NIA, NIH Epidemiological and genetic studies of ALS/PD complex of Guam

R01AG-00029-17 (MGN) **PATTERSON, DAVID** ELEANOR ROOSEVELT INST FOR CNC 1899 GAYLORD STREET DENVER, CO 80206 **Gene expression in somatic cells in the aging process**

Z01AG-00044-18 (LCMB) **EICHHORN, G** NIA, NIH Metal ions and information transfer--Mechanism of RNA synthesis

Z01AG-00046-21 (LCMB) **PITHA, J** NIA, NIH Molecular recognition of lipids and lipophiles by cyclodextrin derivatives

Z01AG-00047-21 (LCMB) **RIFKIND, J M** NIA, NIH Structure-function relationships in hemoglobin and erythrocytes

Z01AG-00063-23 (LBS) **ENGEL, B T** NIA, NIH Learned modification of visceral function in animals

Z01AG-00072-06 (LBS) **ENGEL, B T** NIA, NIH Behavioral assessment and treatment of incontinence in nursing home residents

Z01AG-00073-03 (LBS) **TALAN, M I** NIA, NIH Physiology of thermoregulation and aging in rodents

Z01AG-00093-19 (LCP) **NORDIN, A A** NIA, NIH Cellular basis of regulation of the humoral immune response

Z01AG-00095-18 (LCP) **ADLER, W H** NIA, NIH The role of cell membrane structure in cellular recognition

Z01AG-00096-18 (LCP) **BROCK, M A** NIA, NIH Lymphocyte activation and function in aging individuals

Z01AG-00104-15 (LCP) **ADLER, W H** NIA, NIH Clinical immune survey of the longitudinal project participants

Z01AG-00120-14 (LNS) **GREIG, N H** NIA, NIH Blood-brain barrier and central nervous system function

Z01AG-00121-14 (LNS) **WADHWANI, K C** NIA, NIH Function and structure of peripheral nerve

Z01AG-00123-11 (LNS) **AULT, B** NIA, NIH Neuronal development in tissue culture

Z01AG-00125-13 (LNS) **SONCRANT, T** NIA, NIH Cerebral metabolism, relation to brain function and aging

Z01AG-00126-11 (LNS) **Schapiro, M** NIA, NIH Brain function in aging and dementia

Z01AG-00128-11 (LNS) **SONCRANT, T** NIA, NIH Analytical drug methods

Z01AG-00129-11 (LNS) **SMITH, Q R** NIA, NIH Distribution of nutrients, metals and toxins within central nervous system

Z01AG-00130-01 (LNS) **HAXBY, J V** NIA, NIH Neuropsychological function in aging and dementia

Z01AG-00131-08 (LNS) **GRADY, C** NIA, NIH Neurological function in aging and dementia

Z01AG-00132-09 (LNS) **DECARLI, C** NIA, NIH Brain anatomy in aging and dementia

Z01AG-00133-09 (LNS) **SONCRANT, T** NIA, NIH Clinical pharmacokinetics, pharmacodynamics and therapeutics

Z01AG-00134-08 (LNS) **PURDON, D** NIA, NIH Brain lipid metabolism, relation to function and aging

Z01AG-00135-08 (LNS) **CHANDRASEKARAN, K** NIA, NIH Molecular biology of brain aging and disease

Z01AG-00140-08 (LNS) **SCHAPIRO, M B** NIA, NIH Cerebrospinal fluid chemistry in aging and dementia

Z01AG-00180-05 (LPC) **MCCRAE, R R** NIA, NIH Stress, coping and personality in aging men and women

Z01AG-00183-03 (LPC) **COSTA, P T** NIA, NIH Basic research in personality

Z01AG-00184-03 (LPC) **COSTA, P T** NIA, NIH Psychosocial predictors of mental and physical health

Z01AG-00185-03 (LPC) **ZONDERMAN, A B** NIA, NIH Early markers of Alzheimer's disease in longitudinal participants

Z01AG-00188-01 (LPC) **WEINGARTNER, H** NIA, NIH Determinants of cognitive change in normal and impaired elderly

Z01AG-00189-01 (LPC) **GIAMBRA, L M** NIA, NIH Attentional processes in normal and impaired elderly

Z01AG-00204-06 (LCP) **TOBIN, J** NIA, NIH Nutritional studies in the Baltimore Longitudinal study of aging

PROJECT NO., ORGANIZATIONAL UNIT., INVESTIGATOR, ADDRESS, TITLE

Z01AG-00213-01 (LCP) **BERNIER, M** NIA, NIH Tyrosine phosphatases and insulin resistance in the aged

Z01AG-00214-01 (LCP) **EGAN, J** NIA, NIH Insulin secretion from beta cells of pancreas in diabetes and aging

Z01AG-00215-01 (LCP) **SORKIN, J** NIA, NIH Cholesterol as a risk factor for coronary heart disease in elderly men

Z01AG-00216-01 (LCP) **SORKIN, J** NIA, NIH Alterations in carbohydrate metabolism in normal aging

Z01AG-00217-01 (LCP) **MULLER, DC** NIA, NIH Plasma insulin levels--Relationships with blood pressure,age,obesity and sex

Z01AG-00218-01 (LCP) **ANDRES, R** NIA, NIH Respiratory quotient and metabolic rate as predictors of major weight gain

Z01AG-00226-09 (LCS) **JANCZEWSKI, A** NIA, NIH Excitation-contraction in isolated cardiac cells

Z01AG-00228-08 (LCS) **FLEG, J L** NIA, NIH Age-associated changes in cardiac rhythm and conduction

Z01AG-00231-07 (LCS) **HANSFORD, R** NIA, NIH Regulation of energy metabolism in aging and disease

Z01AG-00243-05 (LCS) **LAKATTA, E G** NIA, NIH Augmented Ca2+ release and arrhythmogenesis in Ca2+ stress in aging heart

Z01AG-00249-05 (LCS) **HANSFORD, R G** NIA, NIH Cellular and subcellar calcium ion homeostasis

Z01AG-00257-03 (LCS) **SILVERMAN, H** NIA,NIH Oxidant-induced intracellular calcium loading in cardiac myocytes

Z01AG-00258-03 (LCS) **DUBELL, W** NIA,NIH Cytosolic calcium modulation of the action potential

Z01AG-00259-03 (LCS) **VENTURA, C** NIA,NIH Mechanism for signal transduction of opioid peptides

Z01AG-00260-03 (LCS) **VENTURE, C** NIA,NIH Novel positive cardiac inotropic agents

Z01AG-00261-04 (LCS) **SOLLOTT, S** NIA, NIH A novel technique to assess cytosolic free Ca2+ in single cardiac myocytes

Z01AG-00262-03 (LCS) **BLANK, P S** NIA,NIH PH regulation in cardiac myocytes

Z01AG-00263-02 (LCS) **SILVERMAN, H S** NIA,NIH Intracellular Na+] and [Ca+] regulation in hypoxic cardiac myocyte

Z01AG-00264-02 (LCS) **LAKATTA, E** NIA, NIH Regulation of left ventricular volumes at rest and during stress

Z01AG-00265-02 (LCS) **FLEG, J** NIA, NIH Effects of age and gender on exercise cardiac performance

Z01AG-00266-02 (LCS) **FROEHLICH, J P** NIA,NIH Ion transport mechanisms and aging

Z01AG-00267-02 (LCS) **CHENG, L** NIA,NIH Vascular cell function and aging

Z01AG-00268-02 (LCS) **LAKATTA, E G** NIA,NIH Cardiac gene expression with adult aging

Z01AG-00269-02 (LCS) **GAMBASSI, G** NIA, NIH Signal transduction of alpha-adrenergic stimulation in cardiac myocytes

Z01AG-00270-02 (LCS) **LAKATTA, E** NIA, NIH Age associated changes in vascular properties

Z01AG-00271-01 (LCS) **BOLUYT, M** NIA, NIH Involvement of cardiac opioids in response of the heart to stress

Z01AG-00272-01 (LCS) **ZIEGELSTEIN, R** NIA, NIH Mechanism for signal transduction of shear stress forces in endothelial cells

Z01AG-00273-01 (LCS) **CROW, M** NIA, NIH MyoD1 and developmental gene expression in skeletal muscle

Z01AG-00274-01 (LCS) **CROWN, M** NIA, NIH Vascular smooth muscle gene expression and cellular differentiation

Z01AG-00275-01 (LCS) **GAMBASSI, G** NIA, NIH Modulation of myofilament Ca2+ sensitivity as a positive inotropic intervention

Z01AG-00276-01 (LCS) **MIYATA, H** NIA, NIH Mitochondrial Ca2+ measurement in single cardiac myocytes

Z01AG-00277-01 (LCS) **KINSELLA, J** NIA, NIH Angiogenesis endothelial cell function and aging

Z01AG-00278-01 (LCS) **PAULY, R** NIA, NIH Vascular smooth muscle cells in development and progression of vascular disease

Z01AG-00279-01 (LCS) **XIAO, R P** NIA, NIH Contrasting cellular effects of beta1 and beta2 adrenergic receptor stimulation

Z01AG-00280-01 (LCS) **XIAO, R P** NIA, NIH Interaction of sigma opioid and beta adrenergic receptors in cardiac myocytes

Z01AG-00281-01 (LCP) **HARMAN, S M** NIA, NIH Hormones, hormone receptors and aging IV hormone replacement in menopausal women

Z01AG-00290-06 (LCP) **TOBIN, J D** NIA, NIH Osteoarthritis and aging

Z01AG-00293-03 (LCP) **TOBIN, J D** NIA, NIH Biochemical parameters of bone metabolism--Age and sex contrasts

K12AG-00294-07 (AGE) **WEI, JEANNE Y** HARVARD MEDICAL SCHOOL 643 HUNTINGTON AVENUE BOSTON, MA 02115 **Physician scientist program award**

Z01AG-00301-08 (LCMB) **ROTH, G S** NIA, NIH Regulation of physiological functions during aging--I. hormone action

K07AG-00302-06 (AGE) **COE, RODNEY M** ST. LOUIS UNIV SCH OF MED 1402 SO. GRAND BLVD. ST. LOUIS, MO 63104 **Geriatric leadership academic award**

Z01AG-00302-08 (LCMB) **INGRAM, D K** NIA, NIH Regulation of physiological functions during aging--III. behavioral biology

Z01AG-00303-07 (LCMB) **CUTLER, R G** NIA, NIH Regulation of physiological functions during aging--IV. genes and longevity

Z01AG-00304-05 (LCMB) **ROTH, G S** NIA, NIH Regulation of physiological functions during aging--V. assessment of primate

Z01AG-00306-03 (LCMB) **JOSEPH, J A** NIA, NIH Regulation of physiological functions during aging-II.neurotransmitter response

R37AG-00322-17 (PBC) **NEMETHY, GEORGE** DEPT. OF BIOMATHMATICAL SCIENC P. O. BOX 1023 NEW YORK, NY 10029 **Aging--Conformational changes of collagen**

K11AG-00325-06 (AGE) **SOLSKY, MARILYN A** ORTHOPAEDIC HOSPITAL 2400 SOUTH FLOWER STREET LOS ANGELES, CA 90007 **Cartilage metabolism in aging and osteoarthritis**

K08AG-00341-05 (AGE) **SLOANE, PHILIP D** UNIV. OF NC AT CHAPEL HILL DEPT OF FAMILY MED, CB#7595 CHAPEL HILL, N C 27599 **NIA academic awards--Dizziness in the elderly**

K08AG-00342-05 (GER) **SIU, ALBERT L** UNIVERSITY OF CALIFORNIA 10833 LE CONTE AVENUE LOS ANGELES, CALIF 90024 **Health policy and functional status**

PROJECT NO., ORGANIZATIONAL UNIT., INVESTIGATOR, ADDRESS, TITLE

K12AG-00353-05 (GER) SEEGMILLER, JARVIS E UNIVERSITY OF CALIFORNIA DEPT OF MEDICINE (M-0131) LA JOLLA, CA 92093 Physician scientist program award

K08AG-00358-05 (GER) MEIER, DIANE E MOUNT SINAI MEDICAL CENTER ONE GUSTAVE L LEVY PLACE NEW YORK, N Y 10029 Influence of age and race on bone health

K07AG-00359-05 (AGE) HAMERMAN, DAVID MONTEFIORE MEDICAL CENTER 111 EAST 210TH STREET BRONX, NY 10467 Geriatric leadership academic award

K08AG-00363-05 (GER) LAVIZZO-MOUREY, RISA UNIVERSITY OF PENNSYLVANIA 3615 CHESTNUT STREET PHILADELPHIA, PA 19104-2683 Risk factors for dehydration among the elderly

K08AG-00367-05 (GER) LYLES, KENNETH W DUKE UNIVERSITY MEDICAL CENTER BOX 3881 DURHAM, NC 27710 Estrogen effects on mineral homeostasis in aging rats

K07AG-00368-05 (AGE) LUCHI, ROBERT J BAYLOR COLLEGE OF MEDICINE ONE BAYLOR PLAZA HOUSTON, TX 77030 Geriatric leadership academic award

K04AG-00369-05 (MGN) JOHNSON, THOMAS E INST. FOR BEHAVIORAL GENETICS UNIVERSITY OF COLORADO BOULDER, CO 80309-0447 Molecular genetic analysis of the specification of aging

K11AG-00371-05 (AGE) DOVE, S BRENT UNIVERSITY OF TEXAS 7703 FLOYD CURL DRIVE SAN ANTONIO, TX 78284 Effect of aging on immunogenetics of secretory IgA

P30AG-00371-18 (AGE) COHEN, HARVEY J DUKE UNIVERSITY MEDICAL CTR BOX 3003 DURHAM, N C 27710 Research support services for gerontology center

K04AG-00374-05 (IMS) THOMAN, MARILYN L SCRIPPS CLINIC & RES FNDN 10666 N TORREY PINES ROAD LA JOLLA, CA 92037 Interleukin 2 synthesis and activity in aged mice

P01AG-00378-20 (AGE) CRISTOFALO, VINCENT J MEDICAL COLL OF PENNSYLVANIA 3300 HENRY AVENUE PHILADELPHIA, PA 19129 Cellular senescence and control of cell proliferation

P01AG-00378-20 0009 (AGE) DUKER, NAHUM J Cellular senescence and control of cell proliferation Modulation of DNA excision repair at cellular senescence

P01AG-00378-20 0010 (AGE) BRADLEY, MATTHEWS O Cellular senescence and control of cell proliferation Cell structure and function in aging

P01AG-00378-20 9001 (AGE) CRISTOFALO, VINCENT J Cellular senescence and control of cell proliferation Core--Cell culture

P01AG-00378-20 9002 (AGE) BASERGA, RENATO L Cellular senescence and control of cell proliferation Core--Molecular biology of aging

P01AG-00378-20 0003 (AGE) CRISTOFALO, VINCENT J Cellular senescence and control of cell proliferation Regulation of cellular proliferation and senescence

P01AG-00378-20 0008 (AGE) BASERGA, RENATO L Cellular senescence and control of cell proliferation Molecular biology of aging

Z01AG-00381-01 (LCMB) SPENCER, R G NIA, NIH NMR studies of aging in cells, organs, and animals

K11AG-00382-05 (AGE) LYTTON, WILLIAM SALK INSTITUTE P O BOX 85800 SAN DIEGO, CA 92186-5800 Connectionist modeling in the neurology of aging

Z01AG-00382-01 (LCMB) SPENCER, R G NIA, NIH Molecular studies by solid-state NMR

K08AG-00383-05 (GER) BUSBY, MARY J FRANCIS SCOTT KEY MED CTR 4940 EASTERN AVE BALTIMORE, MD 21224 Physical activity and metabolic function in older men

K08AG-00387-05 (AGE) MADER, SCOTT L UNIVERSITY HOSP OF CLEVELAND HANNA HOUSE #110 CLEVELAND, OHIO 44106 Postural hypotension, autonomic function and aging

K01AG-00390-04 (AGE) CHEUNG, HOU T ILLINOIS STATE UNIVERSITY NORMAL, ILL 61761 Nutrition, aging, and immunity

K01AG-00394-05 (AGE) VERBRUGGE, LOIS M UNIVERSITY OF MICHIGAN 300 NORTH INGALLS ANN ARBOR, MI 48109-2007 Arthritis and daily life

K11AG-00396-05 (AGE) GROLLMAN, EDWIN M UNIV OF ROCHESTER MED CTR 601 ELMWOOD AVENUE ROCHESTER, NY 14642 Cytoskeletal proteins & trophic factors in aging and Alzheimer's disease

Z01AG-00403-06 (LNS) SCHAPIRO, M NIA, NIH Genetics and nongenetic factors in Alzheimer's disease

Z01AG-00404-05 (LNS) HORWITZ, B NIA, NIH Functional interactions among brain regions in aging and dementia

Z01AG-00405-05 (LNS) SHAPIRO, M NIA, NIH New investigations in aging and dementia

K11AG-00406-04 (AGE) KANG, UN J UNIV. OF CALIF, SAN DIEGO 9500 GILMAN DRIVE LA JOLLA, CA 92093-0624 Neurotransmitter gene expression in aging brain

Z01AG-00406-01 (LNS) RAPOPORT, S NIA, NIH Mechanisms for Alzheimer's disease

K08AG-00407-04 (AGE) BRASHEAR, HARRY R UNIVERSITY OF VIRGINIA BOX 394 - NEUROLOGY DEPT CHARLOTTESVILLE, VA 22908 The diagonal band--Organization and changes in dementia

K08AG-00408-04 (MHK) BIERER, LINDA M VA MEDICAL CENTER 130 WEST KINGSBRIDGE ROAD BRONX, NEW YORK 10468 Cholinergic and noradrenergic treatment of Alzheimer's disease

K08AG-00411-05 (AGE) TENOVER, JOYCE S WESLEY WOODS HOSPITAL 1821 CLIFTON RD, N.E. ATLANTA, GA 30329 NIA academic award--Androgen action in the elderly male

K01AG-00412-04 (AGE) KELLEHER, JOANNE K GEORGE WASHINGTON UNIVERSITY 2300 EYE ST. NW. WASHINGTON, DC. 20037 Mathematical models of intermediary metabolism in aging

K01AG-00414-02 (AGE) VERDERY, ROY B BOWMAN GRAY SCHOOL OF MEDICINE 300 S HAWTHORNE RD WINSTON-SALEM, NC 27103 Nutrition, acute phase mediators and decubitus ulcers

K04AG-00415-04 (NLS) PERRY, GEORGE CASE WESTERN RESERVE UNIV 2040 ADELBERT ROAD CLEVELAND, OH 44106 Amyloid precursor in Alzheimer's disease

K04AG-00417-04 (BNP) HOPKINS, PAUL B UNIVERSITY OF WASHINGTON DEPT. OF CHEMISTRY, BG-10 SEATTLE, WA 98195 Organic and bio-organic chemistry

K01AG-00420-04 (AGE) BALES, CONNIE W DUKE UNIVERSITY BOX 3003 DURHAM, NC 27710 Vitamin D metabolism--A function of kidney donor/recipient age

K07AG-00421-04 (BCA) ETTINGER, WALTER H WAKE FOREST UNIVERSITY 300 SOUTH HAWTHORNE ROAD WINSTON-SALEM, NC 27103 Geriatric leadership academic award

PROJECT NO., ORGANIZATIONAL UNIT., INVESTIGATOR, ADDRESS, TITLE

K04AG-00422-04 (IMB) BONDADA, SUBBARAO UNIVERSITY OF KENTUCKY 205 SANDERS-BROWN BLDG LEXINGTON, KY 40536-0230 B lymphocyte activation in young and aged animals

K04AG-00423-04 (RAP) SEALS, DOUGLAS R UNIVERSITY OF ARIZONA 228B MCKALE CENTER TUCSON, AZ 85721 Hypertension in the elderly--Effects of exercise

R01AG-00424-29 (MEP) WALFORD, ROY 405 HILGARD AVE UCLA SCHOOL OF MEDICINE LOS ANGELES, CA 90024 The role of immune phenomena in the aging process

K11AG-00425-04 (AGE) DE LA MONTE, SUZANNE M MASSACHUSETTS GENERAL HOSPITAL FRUIT STREET BOSTON, MA 02114 CNS plasticity & Alzheimer's disease--Molecular studies

R37AG-00425-27 (RAP) HOLLOSZY, JOHN O WASHINGTON UNIVERSITY 4566 SCOTT AVENUE ST LOUIS, MO 63110 Exercise-induced biochemical and anatomic adaptations

K08AG-00426-04 (AGE) ADES, PHILIP A MEDICAL CENTER HOSP OF VERMONT DIVISION OF CARDIOLOGY BURLINGTON, VT 05401 Exercise conditioning in older coronary patients

K04AG-00427-04 (IMB) EFFROS, RITA B UCLA MEDICAL SCHOOL 405 HILGARD AVE LOS ANGELES, CA 90024 Studies on senescence in human T lymphocyte cultures

K08AG-00428-03 (AGE) TAFFET, GEORGE E BAYLOR COLLEGE OF MEDICINE ONE BAYLOR PLAZA, DEPT OF MED HOUSTON, TX 77030 Modulation of relaxation in the senescent heart

K01AG-00429-03 (AGE) MC DONALD, ROGER B UNIVERSITY OF CALIFORNIA 275 MRAK HALL DAVIS, CA 95616 Aging, high sucrose diets and pracreatic function

K08AG-00430-03 (AGE) TROY, CAROL M COLUMBIA UNIVERSITY 630 W 168TH ST NEW YORK, NY 10032 Calcium and the cytoskeleton in Alzheimer's and related diseases

K04AG-00431-03 (NURS) BURGIO, KATHRYN L UNIV OF PITTSBURGH MEDICAL SCH B45 LOTHROP HAL, 190 LOTHROP S PITTSBURGH, PA 15213 Behavioral vs drug intervention for urinary incontinence

K11AG-00432-03 (AGE) SCHULZ, PAUL E BAYLOR COLLEGE OF MEDICINE ONE BAYLOR PLAZA HOUSTON,TX 77030 Cholinergic modulation of hippocampal mossy fiber LTP

K08AG-00433-03 (AGE) SUPIANO, MARK A UNIVERSITY OF MICHIGAN 972SE/2007 300 NIB ANN ARBOR, MI 48109-2007 NIA academic award--Sympathetic function in elderly human hypertension

K01AG-00434-03 (AGE) GARRARD, JUDITH UNIVERSITY OF MINNESOTA 420 DELAWARE STREET BOX 729 MINNEAPOLIS, MN 55455-0392 Discharge of nursing home elderly to the community

K04AG-00436-04 (ECS) WEI, JEANNE Y BETH ISRAEL HOSPITAL 330 BROOKLINE AVENUE BOSTON, MASS 02215 Effect of age on cardiovascular reflex function

K08AG-00437-02 (AGE) COLVIN, PERRY L, JR BOWMAN GRAY SCHOOL OF MEDICINE WAKE FOREST UNIVERSITY WINSTON-SALEM, NC 27157-1051 Nia academic award: Dietary acclimation

K01AG-00440-03 (AGE) KING, ABBY C STANFORD UNIVERSITY SCH OF MED 730 WELCH ROAD, SUITE B PALO ALTO, CA 94304-1885 Exercise and stress-related response in older adults

K04AG-00441-03 (NLS) GERHARDT, GREG A UNIV OF COLORADO HLTH SCI CTR 4200 E. 9TH AVENUE DENVER, CO 80262 Age-induced changes in monoamine presynaptic function

Z01AG-00441-04 (LCP) ADLER, W H NIA, NIH Host factors relating to HIV infections

K04AG-00443-02 (HUD) KEMPER, SUSAN UNIVERSITY OF KANSAS 426 FRASER HALL LAWRENCE, KS 66045 Language across the life-span

R37AG-00443-17 (CMS) SCHIFFMAN, SUSAN S DUKE UNIVERSITY DURHAM, NC 27706 Gustatory and olfactory quality changes with age

K01AG-00444-03 (AGE) YARASHESKI, KEVIN E WASHINGTON UNIVERSITY SCH OF M 660 S EUCLID AVE, BOX 8127 ST LOUIS, MO 63110 Anabolic effects of weight training and growth hormone in aging males

K11AG-00445-03 (AGE) HOLTZMAN, DAVID M DEPT. OF NEUROLOGY, M-794 UNIV. OF CALIFORNIA SAN FRANCISCO, CA 94143 Mouse trisomy 16 and NGF--Effects on CNS gene expression

K08AG-00446-03 (AGE) HULETTE, CHRISTINE M DUKE UNIVERSITY MEDICAL CTR PO BOX 3712 DURHAM, NC 27710 Brain reactive autoantibodies in Alzheimer's disease

K04AG-00450-03 (BCE) LAKOSKI, JOAN M UNIV OF TEXAS MEDICAL BRANCH 10TH AND MARKET STREET GALVESTON, TX 77550 Aging and estrogen on biogenic amine physiology

K11AG-00452-02 (AGE) DONALDSON, DEIRDRE H UNIV OF COLORADO HEALTH SCI CT 4200 E 9TH AVENUE DENVER, CO 80262 Molecular biology of neurodegenerative diseases

K08AG-00453-02 (AGE) BOULT, CHARLES E UNIVERSITY OF MINNESOTA 516 DELAWARE ST, SE-UMHC BOX 3 MINNEAPOLIS, MN 55455 NIA academic award--Predictors of functional ability

K11AG-00454-02 (AGE) NORTON, PEGGY A UNIVERSITY OF UTAH SCH OF MED 50 NORTH MEDICAL DRIVE SALT LAKE CITY, UT 84132 Connective tissue and etiology of genitourinary prolapse

K08AG-00455-02 (AGE) DAVIS, KENNETH M HARVARD MEDICAL SCHOOL 643 HUNTINGTON AVENUE BOSTON, MA 02215 NIA academic award--Physiology of volume regulation in the elderly

K07AG-00461-02 (AGE) CASSEL, CHRISTINE K UNIV OF CHICAGO MEDICAL CENTER 5841 S MARYLAND AVE BOX 12 CHICAGO, ILL 60637 Geriatric leadership academic award

K01AG-00463-01 (AGE) REDFERN, MARK S EYE & EAR INST OF PITTSBURGH 203 LOTHROP STREET PITTSBURGH, PA 15213 Postural control in the elderly

K04AG-00465-01 (REB) JOHNSON, LARRY TEXAS A & M UNIVERSITY COLLEGE OF VET MEDICINE COLLEGE STATION, TX 77843-445 Biology of the aging human testis

K07AG-00466-01 (AGE) WARSHAW, GREGG A UNIVERSITY OF CINCINNATI 231 BETHESDA AVENUE CINCINNATI, OH 45267-0582 Geriatric leadership academic award

K07AG-00469-02 (AGE) MASORO, EDWARD J UNIVERSITY OF TEXAS 7703 FLOYD CURL DRIVE SAN ANTONIO, TEX 78284 Geriatric leadership academic award

K11AG-00470-01A1 (AGE) LOURY, MARK C JOHNS HOPKINS HOSPITAL 600 NORTH WOLFE STREET BALTIMORE MD 21205 Odorant binding protein in the

aged olfactory system
K08AG-00471-03 (AGE) MANDELBLATT, JEANNE S MEMORIAL HOSP FOR CANCER 1275 YORK AVENUE NEW YORK, NY 10021 Breast and cervix cancer control in the elderly
K07AG-00474-02 (AGE) POTTER, JANE F UNIV OF NEBRASKA MEDICAL CTR 42ND AND DEWEY AVENUE OMAHA, NE 68105 Geriatric leadership academic award
K07AG-00485-02 (AGE) ERSHLER, WILLIAM B INST ON AGING & ADULT LIFE 425 HENRY MALL MADISON, WI 53706 Geriatric leadership academic award
K11AG-00486-02 (AGE) JONAS, ELIZABETH A YALE UNIVERSITY 333 CEDAR ST/PO BOX 3333 NEW HAVEN, CT 06510 Modulation of Ca current in Aplysia bag cell neurons
K08AG-00487-02 (AGE) STINEMAN, MARGARET G 3615 CHESTNUT STREET PHILADELPHIA, PA 19104 Geriatric--Rehabilitation prognostic staging system
K12AG-00488-01 (AGE) CASSEL, CHRISTINE K UNIV OF CHICAGO 5841 S MARYLAND AVE CHICAGO, ILL 60637 Geriatric academic program award
K12AG-00489-02 (AGE) SOLOMON, DAVID H UNIVERSITY OF CALIFORNIA 10833 LE CONTE AVE, (CHS) LOS ANGELES, CA 90024-1687 Geriatric academic program award
K01AG-00491-02 (AGE) BURGIO, LOUIS D UNIVERSITY OF PITTSBURGH 190 LOTHROP ST PITTSBURGH, PA 15213 Urinary incontinence in the nursing home
K04AG-00492-02 (CTY) SCHWARTZ, LAWRENCE M UNIVERSITY OF MASSACHUSETTS AMHERST, MA 01003 Molecular analysis of cell death genes
K08AG-00494-03 (AGE) PRATLEY, RICHARD E VETERANS ADMINISTRATION MED CT 3900 LOCH RAVEN BLVD BALTIMORE, MD 21218 Metabolic function in elderly hypertensives
K08AG-00495-02 (AGE) WEISS, JOHN H STANFORD UNIV MED CENTER 300 PASTEUR DRIVE STANFORD, CA 94305-5235 The chronic neurotoxicity of BMAA and non-NMDA agonists
K08AG-00497-03 (AGE) KATZEL, LESLIE I VETERANS ADMINISTRATION MED CT 3900 LOCH RAVEN BLVD BALTIMORE, MD 21218 Dyslipoproteinemia in older men with silent ischemia
K08AG-00499-01 (AGE) BRANDEIS, GABRIEL H HARVARD MEDICAL SCHOOL 643 HUNTINGTON AVENUE BOSTON, MA 02115 Urinary incontinence in frail elderly women
K12AG-00503-01 (AGE) ABRASS, ITAMAR B HARBORVIEW MED CTR, ZA-87 325 - 9TH AVENUE SEATTLE, WA 98104 Geriatric academic program award
K12AG-00503-01 0001 (AGE) DOBIE, DORCAS Geriatric academic program award REGULATION OF VASOPRESSIN GENE EXPRESSION IN AGING
K12AG-00503-01 0002 (AGE) GRUENEWALD, DAVID Geriatric academic program award Aging and brain regulation of male reproduction
K08AG-00504-01 (AGE) BLACK, RONALD S W.M. BURKE MEDICAL RES. INST. 785 MAMARONECK AVE WHITE PLAINS, NY 10605 Studies of ubiquitin in Alzheimer's disease
K01AG-00508-01 (NBSA) LEVKOFF, SUE E HARVARD MEDICAL SCHOOL 643 HUNTINGTON AVENUE BOSTON, MA 02115 Excess disability in cognitively impaired aged
K11AG-00509-01 (BCA) JURIVICH, DONALD A NORTHWESTERN UNIVERSITY 303 EAST COLLEGE AVENUE CHICAGO, IL 60611 Regulation of heat shock gene expression in senescence
K08AG-00510-01 (BCA) GURWITZ, JERRY H HARVARD MEDICAL SCHOOL 643 HUNTINGTON AVE BOSTON, MA 02115 Drug induced illness in the elderly--NSAIDs as a model
K11AG-00516-01 (BCA) CHOI, AUGUSTINE M JOHNS HOPKINS HOSPITAL 600 NORTH WOLFE STREET BALTIMORE, MD 21205 Genetic responses of the aging lung to oxidative stress
K01AG-00519-01 (BCA) ALEXANDER, NEIL B UNIVERSITY OF MICHIGAN NI3A00/0405 300 NORTH INGALLS ANN ARBOR, MI 48109-0405 Aging, chair mobility, and musculoskeletal impairment
K12AG-00521-01 (BCA) WEINER, LESLIE P UNIV OF SOUTHERN CALIFORNIA 2025 ZONAL AVENUE LOS ANGELES, CA 90033 Physican scientist program award – Neurogerontology
K11AG-00523-01 (BCA) GERHARD, GLENN S UNIVERSITY OF PENNSYLVANIA 422 CURIE BLVD - CRB PHILADELPHIA, PA 19104-6145 Targeting serum binding proteins in development
K08AG-00524-01 (BCA) INOUYE, SHARON K YALE SCHOOL OF MEDICINE 20 YORK STREET NEW HAVEN, CT 06504 Clinical predictors of delirium in the elderly
K08AG-00525-01 (BCA) MONTAMAT, STEPHEN C VA MEDICAL CENTER RES SERVICE 500 WEST FORT STREET (151) BOISE, ID 83702-4598 NIA academic award--Aging and cardiac regulation
K08AG-00526-01 (BCA) SCHMADER, KENNETH E DUKE UNIVERSITY MEDICAL CENTER PO BOX 3469 DURHAM, NC 27710 Epidemiology of herpes zoster and postherpetic neuralgia
K07AG-00532-01 (BCA) CRISTOFALO, VINCENT J MEDICAL COLL OF PENNSYLVANIA 3300 HENRY AVENUE PHILADELPHIA, PA 19129 Geriatric leadership academic award
K11AG-00533-01 (NBSA) VOCI, JAMES M 2074 ABINGTON RD CLEVELAND, OH 44106 Neurotrophin 4-- Characterization of a novel neurotrophic factor
K08AG-00537-01 (BCA) RUBINSTEIN, DANIEL B NEW ENGLAND MEDICAL CENTER 750 WASHINGTON STREET/BOX 245 BOSTON, MA 02111 Immune senescence, autoimmunity, and aging
P01AG-00538-15 (AGE) COTMAN, CARL W UNIVERSITY OF CALIFORNIA 249 STEINHAUS HALLL IRVINE, CA 92717 Behavioral and neural plasticity in the aged
P01AG-00538-15 0017 (AGE) COTMAN, CARL Behavioral and neural plasticity in the aged Molecular cascades following brain injury
P01AG-00538-15 9001 (AGE) GEDDES, JIM W Behavioral and neural plasticity in the aged Core--Tissue repository
P01AG-00538-15 0009 (AGE) LYNCH, GARY S Behavioral and neural plasticity in the aged Role of calcium ion activated proteases in aging and pathology
P01AG-00538-15 0014 (AGE) CUNNINGHAM, DENNIS Behavioral and neural plasticity in the aged Protease nexin 1--Alterations in Alzheimer's Disease
P01AG-00538-15 0015 (AGE) GALL, CHRISTINE Behavioral and neural plasticity in the aged NGF regulation and the aged brain
P01AG-00538-15 0016 (AGE) ISACKSON, PAUL Behavioral and neural plasticity in the aged NGF expression in aged brain
K11AG-00566-01 (BCA) SEIFER, DAVID B WOMEN & INFANTS HOSPITAL OF RI 101 DUDLEY STREET PROVIDENCE, RI 02905 Endocrinologic basis of reproductive aging
K01AG-00567-01 (BCA) GUCCIONE, ANDREW A MASSACHUSETTS GENERAL HOSPITAL FRUIT STREET BOSTON, MA 02114 Development of a comorbidity index for arthritis research
Z01AG-00600-03 (LBS) ANDERSON, D E NIA, NIH Respiratory factors in blood pressure regulation
Z01AG-00601-03 (LBS) MCCORMICK, K A NIA,NIH Exercise influences in aging man
Z01AG-00602-03 (LBS) MCCORMICK, K A NIA, NIH Diaphragmatic breathing challenge in man
Z01AG-00603-02 (LBS) ENGEL, B T NIA, NIH Clinical implications of nocturnal hemodynamic events
Z01AG-00604-03 (LBS) ANDERSON, D E NIA, NIH Behavior factors in blood pressure regulation
Z01AG-00605-03 (LBS) ANDERSON, D E NIA, NIH Cardiovascular interactions of stress and salt in the micropig
Z01AG-00606-01 (LBS) ENGEL, B T NIA, NIH Behavioral intervention for Alzheimer's patients and their caregivers
Z01AG-00622-04 (LSB) METTER, E J NIA,NIH Health and disease status in the BLSA--Clinical health evaluation
Z01AG-00623-03 (LSB) BRANT, L J NIA,NIH Development of statistical methodology for the analysis of studies of aging
Z01AG-00624-02 (LSB) FOZARD, J L NIA, NIH BLSA population dynamics
Z01AG-00625-02 (LSB) SHEFRIN, E A NIA, NIH Baltimore longitudinal study of aging data management
Z01AG-00626-02 (LSB) FOZARD, J L NIA, NIH Age changes in visual functioning
Z01AG-00627-02 (LSB) WEST, S NIA, NIH Risk factors for age related ocular changes
Z01AG-00628-02 (LSB) GORDON-SALANT, S NIA, NIH Aging and auditory characteristics
Z01AG-00629-02 (LSB) METTER, E J NIA, NIH Health and disease status in the BLSA men--Distribution of diseases
Z01AG-00630-02 (LSB) METTER, E J NIA, NIH Health and disease status in the BLSA women--Distribution of diseases
Z01AG-00631-02 (LSB) METTER, E J NIA, NIH Health and disease status in the BLSA men--Bias issues
Z01AG-00632-02 (LSB) METTER, E J NIA, NIH Health and disease status in the BLSA men--Perceived health status
Z01AG-00633-02 (LSB) METTER, E J NIA, NIH Health and disease status in the BLSA--The prostate gland
Z01AG-00634-02 (LSB) TOCKMAN, M S NIA, NIH Age changes in pulmonary function
Z01AG-00635-02 (LSB) FOZARD, J L NIA, NIH Age changes in response speed and nerve conduction
Z01AG-00636-02 (LSB) FRIED, L P NIA, NIH Study of physical activities in the BLSA
Z01AG-00637-02 (LSB) BRANT, L J NIA, NIH Individual variability in human aging
Z01AG-00638-02 (LSB) BRANT, L J NIA, NIH Health promotion, modifiable risk factors and aging
R01AG-00677-14 (CBY) RUTHERFORD, CHARLES L VA POLYTECHNIC INST & ST UNIV 2119 DERRING HALL BLACKSBURG, VA 24061 Alternate pathways in cellular aging
Z01AG-00706-06 (LMG) DANNER, D B NIA, NIH Cloning of a gene involved in shutting off cell growth
Z01AG-00713-04 (LMG) HOLBROOK, N J NIA, NIH gadd153, a gene expressed in response to DNA damage and growth arrest
Z01AG-00719-03 (LMG) HOLBROOK, N J NIA,NIH Heat shock protein gene expression in response to stress and aging
Z01AG-00720-02 (LMG) MARTIN, G R NIA, NIH Gene expression in chronic wounds and aged cells
Z01AG-00721-01 (LMG) HOLBROOK, N J NIA, NIH Genotoxic response to oxidative damage
R01AG-00783-12 (IMB) WEIGLE, WILLIAM O RES INST OF CRIPPS CLINIC 10666 NORTH TORREY PINES ROAD LA JOLLA, CA 92037 Effect of aging on immune states
R01AG-00947-14 (CTY) STEIN, GRETCHEN H UNIVERSITY OF COLORADO CAMPUS BOX 347 BOULDER, CO 80309-0347 Growth regulation: senescent vs nonsenescent cells
R01AG-01121-12 (NEUA) COLEMAN, PAUL D UNIVERSITY OF ROCHESTER NEUROBIOLOGY & ANATOMY-BOX 603 ROCHESTER, NY 14642 Computer aided study of dendrites in aging human brain
R37AG-01136-14 (NEUC) YEN, SHU-HUI C ALBERT EINSTEIN COLLEGE 1300 MORRIS PARK AVENUE BRONX, N Y 10461 The aging brain--Immunohistology and biochemistry
R01AG-01159-15 (BEM) MANTON, KENNETH G DUKE UNIVERSITY 2117 CAMPUS DRIVE DURHAM, N C 27706 A demographic study of multiple causes of death
P01AG-01188-13 (AGE) MCCARTER, ROGER UNIVERSITY OF TEXAS 7703 FLOYD CURL DRIVE SAN ANTONIO, TEX 78284 Nutritional probe of the aging process
P01AG-01188-13 0006 (AGE) MC CARTER, ROGER J Nutritional probe of the aging process Food restrictions,aging,energy metabolism and physical activity
P01AG-01188-13 0007 (AGE) KALU, DIKE N Nutritional probe of the aging process Food restriction and the c-cell endocrine system
P01AG-01188-13 0009 (AGE) FERNANDES, GABRIEL Nutritional probe of the aging process Effect of food restriction on immunity and aging
P01AG-01188-13 0010 (AGE) DEPAOLO, LOUIE V. Nutritional probe of the aging process Couplers of food restrictions to aging--Corticosterone, glucose, insulin
P01AG-01188-13 0011 (AGE) HERLIHY, JEREMIAH T. Nutritional probe of the aging process Couplers of food restriction to aging-Sympath. nervous sys., thyroid hormone
P01AG-01188-13 0012 (AGE) WARD, WALTER F. Nutritional probe of the aging process Food restriction on the turnover of metabolic enzymes in the aging rat
P01AG-01188-13 0013 (AGE) YU, BYUNG P Nutritional probe of the

PROJECT NO., ORGANIZATIONAL UNIT., INVESTIGATOR, ADDRESS, TITLE

aging process Dietary modulation of age-related lipid peroxidation
P01AG-01188-13 0014 (AGE) MASORO, EDWARD J. Nutritional probe of the aging process Dietry program--Animal models, longevity and pathology
P01AG-01188-13 9001 (AGE) MASORO, EDWARD J Nutritional probe of the aging process Statistical core
R37AG-01228-13 (CTY) WRIGHT, WOODRING E U OF TEXAS SW MED CENTER 5323 HARRY HINES BOULEVARD DALLAS, TX 75235 Gene expression in aging and development
R37AG-01274-13 (PBC) GRACY, ROBERT W TEXAS COLLEGE OSTEOPATHIC MED 3500 CAMP BOWIE BLVD FORT WORTH, TX 76107-2690 Effects of aging on lymphocyte activation
R37AG-01437-11 (REB) DAVIDSON, JULIAN M STANFORD UNIVERSITY STANFORD, CA 94305-4125 Pharmacologic factors & sexuality in aging hypertension
R01AG-01548-08A1 (NTN) RICHARDSON, ARLAN G UNIVERSITY OT TEXAS UNIVERSITY OF TEXAS SAN ANTONIO, TX 78284 Effect of dietary restriction on gene expression
R01AG-01739-11 (GEN) MAHAFFEY, JAMES W NORTH CAROLINA STATE UNIV P O BOX 7614 RALEIGH, NC 27695-7614 Genetic control of catalase expression in drosophila
P01AG-01743-12 (AGE) KLINMAN, NORMAN R SCRIPPS CLINIC/RESEARCH FDN 10666 NORTH TORREY PINES ROAD LA JOLLA, CA 92037 Immunobiology and immunopathology of aging
P01AG-01743-12 0002 (AGE) KLINMAN, NORMAN R Immunobiology and immunopathology of aging The B-cell repertoire of aged mice
P01AG-01743-12 0005 (AGE) WEIGLE, WILLIAM O Immunobiology and immunopathology of aging Effect of aging on inducible autoimmune diseases
P01AG-01743-12 0006 (AGE) DIXON, FRANK J Immunobiology and immunopathology of aging Molecular mechanisms underlying longevity in murine SLE
P01AG-01743-12 9001 (AGE) KLINMAN, NORMAN R Immunobiology and immunopathology of aging Core facilities
P01AG-01751-13 (BCA) MARTIN, GEORGE M UNIVERSITY OF WASHINGTON SEATTLE, WA 98195 Gene action in the pathobiology of aging
P01AG-01751-13 0007 (BCA) LOEB, LAURENCE A Gene action in the pathobiology of aging Oxygen free radicals and aging
P01AG-01751-13 0008 (BCA) MONNAT, RAYMOND J Gene action in the pathobiology of aging Molecular analysis of the Werner Syndrome mutator phenotype
P01AG-01751-13 0009 (BCA) KAVANAGH, TERRANCE J Gene action in the pathobiology of aging Alertations in glutathione metabolism -- implications for aging
P01AG-01751-13 9001 (BCA) MARTIN, GEORGE M Gene action in the pathobiology of aging Core--Cell and tissue culture facility
P01AG-01751-13 9002 (BCA) WOLF, NORMAN Gene action in the pathobiology of aging Core--Animal facility
P01AG-01751-13 9003 (BCA) RABINOVITCH, PETER S Gene action in the pathobiology of aging Core--Cytogenetics and flow cytometry
P01AG-01751-13 0001 (BCA) NORWOOD, THOMAS H Gene action in the pathobiology of aging Gene action and in vitro replicative life span
P01AG-01751-13 0003 (BCA) RABINOVITCH, PETER S Gene action in the pathobiology of aging Cellular aging and signal transduction
P01AG-01751-13 0005 (BCA) WOLF, NORMAN S Gene action in the pathobiology of aging In vivo analysis of replicative lifespan in a somatic cell system
P01AG-01751-13 0006 (BCA) MARTIN, GEORGE M Gene action in the pathobiology of aging Chromosomal mutations in aging somatic cells
R01AG-01760-11 (EDC) KLAG, MICHAEL J JOHNS HOPKINS UNIV 550 N BROADWAY BALTIMORE, MARYLAND 21205 Precursors of premature disease and death
R01AG-01822-12 (GEN) SHEARN, ALLEN D JOHNS HOPKINS UNIVERSITY 3400 N CHARLES ST BALTIMORE, MD 21218 Role of specific genes in imaginal disc determination
R01AG-02038-09A1 (SSP) HERZOG, ANNA R UNIVERSITY OF MICHIGAN 426 THOMPSON STREET ANN ARBOR, MI 48106-1248 Non-sampling errors in panel surveys of older adults
R37AG-02049-12 (NTN) GARRY, PHILIP J UNIVERSITY NEW MEXICO SURGE BLDG ROOM 215 ALBUQUERQUE, NM 87131 A prospective study of nutrition in the elderly
N01AG-02105-23 (**) OSTFELD, ADRIAN Establish populations for epidemiological studies
N01AG-02106-18 (**) WALLACE, ROBERT Establish populations for epidemiological studies
N01AG-02107-26 (**) TAYLOR, JAMES O Establish populations for epidemiological studies
N01AG-02109-01 (**) ALLEN, ANTON Pathology monitoring, F344 rat colony
P01AG-02126-11 (AGE) MAROTTA, CHARLES A MC LEAN HOSPITAL 115 MILL STREET BELMONT, MASS 02178 Molecular biology of neuronal aging
P01AG-02126-11 0006 (AGE) NIXON, RALPH A Molecular biology of neuronal aging Phosphorylation and turnover of neuronal cytoskeleton-associated proteins
P01AG-02126-11 0008 (AGE) ZAIN, SAYEDA B Molecular biology of neuronal aging Amyloid cDNA transfected cells and transgenic mice
P01AG-02126-11 0009 (AGE) MAROTTA, CHARLES A Molecular biology of neuronal aging Amyloid accumulation in aged brain, Alzheimeris and transgenic mice
P01AG-02126-11 0010 (AGE) JUNGALWALA, FIROZE B Molecular biology of neuronal aging Role of neuronal marker, A2B5 antigen in Alzheimer's disease
P01AG-02126-11 0011 (AGE) MAROTTA, CHARLES A Molecular biology of neuronal aging Transcription, translation and RNA metabolism in Alzheimer's disease brain
P01AG-02126-11 0012 (AGE) ST GEORGE-HYSLOP, PETER H Molecular biology of neuronal aging Identification of the gene causing Alzheimer's disease
P01AG-02126-11 0013 (AGE) NIXON, RALPH A Molecular biology of neuronal aging Neuronal cell death in a late-onset genetic disorder in mice
P01AG-02126-11 0014 (AGE) FINKELSTEIN, SETH P Molecular biology of neuronal aging Fibroblast growth factors in the aging brain

PROJECT NO., ORGANIZATIONAL UNIT., INVESTIGATOR, ADDRESS, TITLE

P01AG-02126-11 9001 (AGE) MAJOCHA, RONALD E Molecular biology of neuronal aging Core--Molecular neurocytology and neuroanatomy
R01AG-02128-11 (PBC) FESSLER, JOHN H UNIVERSITY OF CALIFORNIA 405 HILGARD AVENUE LOS ANGELES, CALIF 90024 Basement membrane biosynthesis
P01AG-02132-11 (AGE) PRUSINER, STANLEY B UNIVERSITY OF CALIFORNIA SCHOOL OF MEDICINE SAN FRANCISCO, CA 94143-0518 Viral degenerative and dementing diseases of aging
P01AG-02132-11 0001 (AGE) PRUSINER, STANLEY B Viral degenerative and dementing diseases of aging Purification and molecular structure of the scrapie agent
P01AG-02132-11 0004 (AGE) DE ARMOND, STEPHEN J. Viral degenerative and dementing diseases of aging Pathogenic mechanisms in scrapie
P01AG-02132-11 0005 (AGE) LINGAPPA, VISHWANATH R Viral degenerative and dementing diseases of aging Biogenesis and processing of prior proteins in scrapie
P01AG-02132-11 0006 (AGE) MCKINLEY, MICHAEL P Viral degenerative and dementing diseases of aging Cell biology of prion proteins
P01AG-02132-11 9001 (AGE) PRUSINER, STANLEY B Viral degenerative and dementing diseases of aging Core--scientific
R01AG-02152-10 (IMB) STUTMAN, OSIAS SLOAN-KETTERING INSTITUTE 1275 YORK AVENUE NEW YORK, NY 10021 T-cell development and aging
R01AG-02163-10 (LCR) MADDEN, DAVID J DUKE UNIVERSITY BOX 2980 DURHAM, NC 27710 Age and selective attention in visual search
P01AG-02219-11 (AGE) MOHS, RICHARD C VA MEDICAL CENTER DEPT OF PSYCHIATRY BRONX, NEW YORK 10468 Cholinergic treatment of memory deficits in the aged
R37AG-02224-12 (NSS) WISE, PHYLLIS M UNIV OF MARYLAND AT BALTIMORE 655 WEST BALTIMORE STREET BALTIMORE, MD 21201 Neuroendocrine and neurochemical function during aging
R01AG-02246-12 (GEN) TEMPLETON, ALAN R WASHINGTON UNIVERSITY DEPT OF BIOLOGY ST LOUIS, MO 63130 The aging effects associated with a polygenic complex
R01AG-02287-11 (EDC) BOSSE, RAYMOND NORMATIVE AGING STUDY (151) 200 SPRINGS RD BLDG 70 BEDFORD, MA 01730 The effect of retirement on physical health
R01AG-02325-10 (RNM) LEES, SIDNEY FORSYTH DENTAL CENTER 140 FENWAY BOSTON, MASS 02115 Mechano-ultrasonic properties of bone in aging
R01AG-02329-15 (IMB) YUNIS, EDMOND J DANA-FARBER CANCER INSTITUTE 44 BINNEY STREET BOSTON, MA 02115 Immunological aspects of aging
R01AG-02331-11 (END) CLEMMONS, DAVID R U N C AT CHAPEL HILL 3041 OLD CLIN BLDG. CB #7005 CHAPEL HILL, N C 27599 Control of fibroblast replication by IGF-I and its binding protein
R01AG-02338-09 (IMS) O'LEARY, JAMES J UNIVERSITY OF MINNESOTA 420 DELAWARE AVENUE MINNEAPOLIS, MN 55455 Mechanisms of depressed immune function in aging man
R37AG-02452-12 (HUD) LIGHT, LEAH L PITZER COLLEGE 1050 NORTH MILLS AVENUE CLAREMONT, CA 91711 direct and indirect measures of memory in old age
R01AG-02467-10 (MEDB) KUSHNER, IRVING METROHEALTH MEDICAL CENTER 3395 SCRANTON ROAD CLEVELAND, OHIO 44109 Induction of acute phase protein biosynthesis
R37AG-02577-09 (ORTH) NIMNI, MARCEL E USC ORTHOPAEDIC HOSPITAL 2400 S FLOWER ST LOS ANGELES, CA 90007 Osteogenesis--Development, modulation, and aging
R01AG-02711-13 (HUD) ANCOLI-ISRAEL, SONIA UNIVERSITY OF CALIFORNIA LA JOLLA, CA 92093-0603 Prevalence of sleep apnea in an aged population
R37AG-02751-10 (HUD) HOWARD, DARLENE V GEORGETOWN UNIVERSITY DEPARTMENT OF PSYCHOLOGY WASHINGTON, D C 20057 Studies of aging, semantic processing, and memory
R01AG-02822-11 (CTY) STOCKDALE, FRANK E STANFORD UNIVERSITY MEDICAL CT STANFORD, CA 94305-5306 Developmental age and changes in myosin isozymes
P01AG-02908-11 (BCA) BERG, PAUL STANFORD UNIVERSITY STANFORD, CA 94305-5307 DNA transactions and genome integrity in aging
P01AG-02908-11 0001 (BCA) KORNBERG, ARTHUR DNA transactions and genome integrity in aging Fidelity of genome replication
P01AG-02908-11 0006 (BCA) LEHMAN, I ROBERT DNA transactions and genome integrity in aging Mutagenesis and genomic rearrangements in eukaryotes
P01AG-02908-11 0007 (BCA) BERG, PAUL DNA transactions and genome integrity in aging Recombination repair of double-strand gaps & deletions in DNA
P01AG-02908-11 0011 (BCA) DAVIS, RONALD W DNA transactions and genome integrity in aging Regulation of chromosomal replication
P01AG-02908-11 0012 (BCA) HANAWALT, PHILIP C DNA transactions and genome integrity in aging DNA transactions and genome integrity
P01AG-02908-11 0013 (BCA) LIEBER, MICHAEL DNA transactions and genome integrity in aging Lymphoid DNA recombinases in aging and development
R01AG-03051-08 (LCR) REISBERG, BARRY NEW YORK UNIVERSITY MEDICAL CT 550 FIRST AVE NEW YORK, NY 10016 Aging and dementia--Longitudinal course of subgroups
R37AG-03055-10 (HUD) ELIAS, MERRILL F UNIVERSITY OF MAINE LITTLE HALL ORONO, ME 04469 Age hypertension and intellective performance
P01AG-03104-10 (GER) EGER, EDMOND I UNIV OF CALIF, SAN FRANCISCO S-455 SAN FRANCISCO, CA 94143 Aging and anesthesia
P01AG-03104-10 0005 (GER) STANSKI, DONALD R Aging and anesthesia Intravenous anesthetics and the aged
P01AG-03104-10 0007 (GER) CAHALAN, MICHAEL K Aging and anesthesia Pharmacology of nitroglycerin in the elderly
P01AG-03104-10 0008 (GER) KOBLIN, DONALD D Aging and anesthesia Nitrous oxide and folate metabolism in the aged
P01AG-03104-10 0009 (GER) MILLER, RONALD D Aging and anesthesia Pharmacokinetics of the antagonists of neuromuscular blockage
P01AG-03104-10 9001 (GER) SCHEINER, LEWIS B Aging and anesthesia Modelling and data analysis core
P01AG-03106-09 (AGE) MANUELIDIS, LAURA YALE UNIV. SCHOOL OF MEDICINE 333 CEDAR STREET NEW HAVEN, CT 06510 Animal models for the

study of dementias and aging
P01AG-03106-09 0002 (AGE) KIM, JUNG H Animal models for the study of dementias and aging Inbred rodent strains and independent CJD isoltes--Manifestation of disease
P01AG-03106-09 0003 (AGE) MANUELIDIS, ELIAS E Animal models for the study of dementias and aging Creutzfeldt-Jakob variants of disputed, questionable or genetic origin
P01AG-03106-09 0004 (AGE) MANUELIDIS, LAURA Animal models for the study of dementias and aging Therapeutic approaches to experimental dementias
P01AG-03106-09 0006 (AGE) MANUELIDIS, LAURA Animal models for the study of dementias and aging RNA studies and the Creutzfeldt-Jacob disease agent
P01AG-03106-09 0007 (AGE) MANUELIDES, LAURA Animal models for the study of dementias and aging Chromosome 21 sequences in brain--Alzheimer's and CJD
P01AG-03106-09 9001 (AGE) MANUELIDIS , LAURA Animal models for the study of dementias and aging Core
P01AG-03106-09 0001 (AGE) MANUELIDIS, ELIAS E Animal models for the study of dementias and aging Transmissions and morphological studies of humn dementias
R37AG-03188-10 (BEM) WOODBURY, MAX A DUKE UNIVERSITY 2117 CAMPUS DRIVE DURHAM, NC 27706 Longitudinal models of correlates of aging and longevity
R01AG-03376-11 (BPO) BARNES, CAROL A UNIVERSITY OF ARIZONA LIFE SCIENCES NORTH BUILDING TUCSON, AZ 85724 Neurobehavioral relations in senescent hippocampus
R01AG-03417-11 (SSS) FERNANDES, GABRIEL UNIVERSITY OF TEXAS HLTH SCI C 7703 FLOYD CURL DR SAN ANTONIO, TX 78284 Influence of diet on regulation, autoimmunity, and aging
R37AG-03501-10 (SSP) LEVENTHAL, HOWARD INST. ON HEALTH & AGING POLICY 30 COLLEGE AVENUE NEW BRUNSWICK, NJ 08903 Symptom and emotion stimuli to health action in the elderly
R01AG-03527-09A1 (PC) CHATTERJEE, BANDANA UNIV OF TEXAS HEALTH SCI CNTR 7703 FLOYD CURL DRIVE SAN ANTONIO, TX 78284 Age and hormone-dependent regulation of a hepatic protein
P01AG-03644-07 (AGE) HAMILL, ROBERT W UNIV-ROCHESTER SCH OF MED-DENT 601 ELMWOOD AVENUE ROCHESTER, N Y 14642 Neuroplasticity in aging and dementia
P01AG-03644-07 0005 (AGE) MC NEILL, THOMAS H Neuroplasticity in aging and dementia Alzheimer's disease--Histochemical-immunocytochemical study
P01AG-03644-07 0006 (AGE) FLOOD, DOROTHY G Neuroplasticity in aging and dementia Quantitative study of dendrites in aging and dementia
P01AG-03644-07 0007 (AGE) COLEMAN, PAUL D Neuroplasticity in aging and dementia Neurons, glia and growth-associated protein in aging and AD
P01AG-03644-07 0008 (AGE) HAMILL, ROBERT W Neuroplasticity in aging and dementia Neurochemical correlates of neuroplasticity in aging and AD
P01AG-03644-07 0009 (AGE) FAHNESTOCK, MARGARET Neuroplasticity in aging and dementia Nerve growth factor and Alzheimer's disease
P01AG-03644-07 9002 (AGE) TARIOT, PIERRE Neuroplasticity in aging and dementia Clinical core
P01AG-03644-07 9003 (AGE) LAPHAM, LOWELL W Neuroplasticity in aging and dementia Neuropathology, core
R44AG-03796-02 (HUD) VERTREES, JAMES C SOLON CONSULTING GROUP 12501 PROSPERITY DRIVE SILVER SPRING, MD 20904 Making aging data available to researchers
P01AG-03853-09 (AGE) BLASS, JOHN P WM BURKE MEDICAL RESEARCH INST 785 MAMARONECK AVENUE WHITE PLAINS, NY 10605 Geriatric dementia research clinic
P01AG-03853-09 0011 (AGE) BLASS, JOHN P Geriatric dementia research clinic Neural and Alzheimer antigens in cultured fibroblasts
P01AG-03853-09 0012 (AGE) GIBSON, GARY E Geriatric dementia research clinic Signal transduction in Alzheimer and control fibroblasts
P01AG-03853-09 0013 (AGE) COOPER, ARTHUR J L Geriatric dementia research clinic Metabolism of Alzheimer and control fibroblasts
P01AG-03853-09 0014 (AGE) SZABO, PAUL Geriatric dementia research clinic Chromosomal fragility in Alzheimer and control fibroblasts
P01AG-03853-09 0015 (AGE) ADLER, JOSHUA E Geriatric dementia research clinic Mechanism of reduction in neuronal plasticity with aging
P01AG-03853-09 9001 (AGE) BLASS, JOHN P Geriatric dementia research clinic Core--Clinical/neuropathology
P01AG-03853-09 9002 (AGE) KO, LI-WEN Geriatric dementia research clinic Core--Tissue culture
P01AG-03853-09 9003 (AGE) SHEU, KWAN-FU REX Geriatric dementia research clinic Core--Immunobiots/immunochemical assays
P01AG-03853-09 9004 (AGE) THALER, HOWARD Geriatric dementia research clinic Core--Statistics
R01AG-03884-10 (PC) WRIGHT, BARBARA E UNIVERSITY OF MONTANA MISSOULA, MT 59812 Computer analysis of aging in dictyostelium
P01AG-03934-10 (AGE) KAYE, DONALD MEDICAL COLL OF PENNSYLVANIA 3300 HENRY AVENUE PHILADELPHIA, PA 19129 Teaching nursing home
P01AG-03934-10 0000 (AGE) KAYE, D Teaching nursing home
P01AG-03934-10 0001 (AGE) KAYE, DONALD Teaching nursing home Urinary tract infections in a geriatric population
P01AG-03934-10 0003 (AGE) ALAVI, ABASS Teaching nursing home Cerebral structure and function in aging and dementia
P01AG-03934-10 0004 (AGE) POSNER, JOEL D Teaching nursing home Effects of exercise in older adults with chronic disease
P01AG-03934-10 0005 (AGE) PACK, ALLAN I Teaching nursing home Sleep apnea in the elderly
P01AG-03934-10 0006 (AGE) KATZ, IRA R. Teaching nursing home Metabolic brain disease in the aged--Prospective study
P01AG-03934-10 0007 (AGE) SCHUMACHER, RALPH H. Teaching nursing home Aging crystals and inflammation in osteoarthritis
P01AG-03934-10 9001 (AGE) KAYE, DONALD Teaching nursing home Core
P01AG-03949-10 (AGE) CRYSTAL, HOWARD ALBERT EINSTEIN COLLEGE OF MED 1300 MORRIS PARK AVENUE BRONX, NY 10461 Teaching nursing home
P01AG-03949-10 0001 (AGE) CRYSTAL, HOWARD A Teaching nursing home Alzheimer's disease--Markers and course
P01AG-03949-10 0002 (AGE) HAMERMAN, DAVID Teaching nursing home Osteoarthritis
P01AG-03949-10 0005 (AGE) GROBER, ELLEN Teaching nursing home Age-associated memory impairment
P01AG-03949-10 0006 (AGE) MARANTZ, PAUL R Teaching nursing home Clinical congestive heart failure in the elderly
P01AG-03949-10 9001 (AGE) KATZMAN, ROBERT Teaching nursing home Core
R01AG-03978-10 (IMS) MILLER, RICHARD A INSTITUTE OF GERONTOLOGY 300 NORTH INGALLS BUILDING ANN ARBOR, MI 48109-2007 Effect of aging on helper T cell function
P01AG-03991-08 (AGE) BERG, LEONARD WASH UNIV SCHOOL OF MEDICINE 660 S. EUCLID AVE ST LOUIS, MO 63110 Healthy aging and senile dementia
P01AG-03991-08 0003 (AGE) RAICHLE, MARCUS E Healthy aging and senile dementia PET-- Microvascular function in aging and SDAT
P01AG-03991-08 0005 (AGE) BERG, LEONARD Healthy aging and senile dementia Intellectual function and Alzheimer changes in the very old
P01AG-03991-08 0006 (AGE) MORRIS, JOHN C. Healthy aging and senile dementia Parkinsonism in SDAT vs. Parkinson's disease
P01AG-03991-08 0007 (AGE) BARTOLA, DAVID A. Healthy aging and senile dementia Memory processing in healthy aging and SDAT
P01AG-03991-08 0008 (AGE) ROBBINS, LEE N. Healthy aging and senile dementia Validity of lay interviewer assessment of dementia
P01AG-03991-08 0009 (AGE) PRICE, JOSEPH L. Healthy aging and senile dementia Anatomical mapping of neuropathological markers in dementia and aging
P01AG-03991-08 9001 (AGE) BERG, LEONARD Healthy aging and senile dementia Core--clinical
P01AG-03991-08 9002 (AGE) STORANDT, MARTHA Healthy aging and senile dementia Core--psychometrics
P01AG-03991-08 9003 (AGE) MCKEEL, DANIEL W. Healthy aging and senile dementia Core-- Neuropathology
P01AG-03991-08 9004 (AGE) STORANDT, MARTHA Healthy aging and senile dementia
R01AG-04058-07 (VISB) WERNER, JOHN S UNIVERSITY OF COLORADO CAMPUS BOX 345 BOULDER, CO 80309-0345 Optical & neural changes in the aging visual system
R37AG-04085-08 (HAR) MURPHY, CLAIRE L SAN DIEGO STATE UNIVERSITY 5300 CAMPANILE DRIVE SAN DIEGO, CA 92182-0350 Chemosensory perception and psychophysics in the aged
R55AG-04100-08A1 (IMS) KIPPS, THOMAS J UNIV OF CA 9500 GILMAN DR LA JOLLA, CA 92093-0945 Immunologic aging and autoimmunity
R01AG-04139-04 (SSP) STEWMAN, SHELBY CARNEGIE MELLON UNIVERSITY 5000 FORBES AVENUE PITTSBURGH, PA 15213 Aging and labor demand
R01AG-04145-09 (NEUA) YEN, SHU-HUI C ALBERT EINSTEIN COLLEGE 1300 MORRIS PARK AVENUE BRONX, NY 10461 Aging and Alzheimer dementia--Role of fibrous protein
R01AG-04146-07A1 (HUD) BOOTH, ALAN PENNSLYVANIA STATE UNIVERSITY N253 BURROWES BUILDING UNIVERSITY PARK, PA 16801 Marital instability over the life course
R01AG-04180-09 (ALY) KOHLER, HEINZ SAN DIEGO REGIONAL CANCER CENT 3099 SCIENCE PARK ROAD SAN DIEGO, CA 92121 Idiotype recognizing t-helper cells
R01AG-04212-09 (VISB) OWSLEY, CYNTHIA UNIVERSITY OF ALABAMA UAB STATION BIRMINGHAM, ALA 35294 Spatial vision and aging--Underlying mechanisms
P01AG-04220-07A1 (AGE) WISNIEWSKI, HENRYK M NYS INST FOR BASIC RESEARCH 1050 FOREST HILL ROAD STATEN ISLAND, NY 10314 Aging and senile dementia of the alzheimer type
P01AG-04220-07A1 0005 (AGE) MILLER, DAVID Aging and senile dementia of the alzheimer type Regulation of expression of the Alzheimer amyloid precursor gene
P01AG-04220-07A1 0007 (AGE) GRUNDKE-IGBAL, INGE Aging and senile dementia of the alzheimer type Biochemistry of readily soluble paired helical filaments
P01AG-04220-07A1 0008 (AGE) BOLTON, DAVID Aging and senile dementia of the alzheimer type Structural studies of PHF proteins
P01AG-04220-07A1 0009 (AGE) WISNIEWSKI, HENRY K Aging and senile dementia of the alzheimer type Production and processing of APP by cultured canine microglia
P01AG-04220-07A1 9002 (AGE) KOZLOWSKI, P B Aging and senile dementia of the alzheimer type Core--Frozen tissue bank and neuropathology
R37AG-04287-09 (NSS) STEVENS, JOSEPH C JOHN PIERCE LABORATORY INC 290 CONGRESS AVE NEW HAVEN, CT 06519 Chemical senses and aging
R01AG-04306-06 (HUD) HASHER, LYNN A DUKE UNIVERSITY DURHAM, NC 27706 Aging, inhibition, & the contents of working memory
R37AG-04307-09 (SSS) CHASE, MICHAEL H UNIV OF CALIF - L A 405 HILGARD AVE LOS ANGELES, CA 90024 State-dependent somatomotor processes
R01AG-04337-07A3 (HUD) CUNNINGHAM, WALTER R UNIVERSITY OF FLORIDA GAINESVILLE, FL 32611 -2065 Age changes in intellectual abilities in the elderly
P01AG-04342-09 (AGE) OLDSTONE, MICHAEL B SCRIPPS CLINIC AND RES FNDN 10666 N TORREY PINES ROAD LA JOLLA, CA 92037 Virologic and immunologic studies--Molecular basic of aging
P01AG-04342-09 0001 (AGE) OLDSTONE, MICHAEL B Virologic and immunologic studies--Molecular basic of aging Persistent viral infection with LCM virus
P01AG-04342-09 0002 (AGE) SOUTHERN, PETER J Virologic and immunologic studies--Molecular basic of aging LCM virus induced endocrine dysfunction
P01AG-04342-09 0005 (AGE) WILSON, CURTIS B Virologic and immunologic studies--Molecular basic of aging Immunopathological mechanisms of glomerulosclerosis and aging
P01AG-04342-09 0006 (AGE) NELSON, JAY A Virologic and immunologic studies--Molecular basic of aging Viral latency and reactivation in relation to aging
P01AG-04342-09 0007 (AGE) WHITTON, J LINDSAY Virologic and immunologic studies--Molecular basic of aging LCM viral persistence and host humoral immunity

PROJECT NO., ORGANIZATIONAL UNIT., INVESTIGATOR, ADDRESS, TITLE

P01AG-04342-09 9001 (AGE) OLDSTONE, MICHAEL B Virologic and immunologic studies--Molecular basic of aging Core--Tissue culture

R37AG-04344-08 (REB) PORTER, JOHN C THE UNIV OF TX SOUTHWESTERN 5323 HARRY HINES BOULEVARD DALLAS, TX 75235-9032 Aging and molecular neuroendocrine impairment

R01AG-04360-09 (ALY) FARR, ANDREW G UNIVERSITY OF WASHINGTON SM-20 SEATTLE, WA 98195 Age dependent modulation of T cell function

P01AG-04390-08 (AGE) LIPSITZ, LEWIS A HEBREW REHAB CENTER FOR AGED 1200 CENTRE ST BOSTON (ROSLINDALE), MA 02131 HRCA/Harvard research nursing home

P01AG-04390-08 0001 (AGE) ROWE, JOHN W HRCA/Harvard research nursing home Postprandial hypotension in the elderly

P01AG-04390-08 0002 (AGE) RESNICK, NEIL M HRCA/Harvard research nursing home pathophysiology of urinary incontinence in the frail elderly

P01AG-04390-08 0003 (AGE) HOLICK, MICHAEL F HRCA/Harvard research nursing home Vitamin D nutrition in the institutionalized elderly

P01AG-04390-08 0004 (AGE) MORRIS, JOHN N HRCA/Harvard research nursing home Identification of persons at risk of institutional placement

P01AG-04390-08 0005 (AGE) ALBERT, MARILYN HRCA/Harvard research nursing home Clinical and neuroendocrine measures of depression in SDAT

P01AG-04390-08 0006 (AGE) MINAKER, KENNETH HRCA/Harvard research nursing home Vasopressin release in dementia

P01AG-04390-08 0007 (AGE) MINAKER, KENNETH L. HRCA/Harvard research nursing home Atrial naturetic factor--Index of volume status in elderly

P01AG-04390-08 0008 (AGE) KAMINSKAS, EDVARDAS HRCA/Harvard research nursing home DNA repair in lymphocytes of Alzheimer's disease patients

P01AG-04391-09 (AGE) FORD, AMASA B CASE WESTERN RESERVE UNIV SCHOOL OF MEDICINE CLEVELAND, OH 44106 Academic teaching nursing home award

P01AG-04391-09 0005 (AGE) ELLNER, JERROLD J Academic teaching nursing home award Immunosenescence and tuberculosis in the elderly

P01AG-04391-09 0006 (AGE) GILMORE, GROVER C Academic teaching nursing home award Visual perception and Alzheimer's disease

P01AG-04391-09 0007 (AGE) HUDGEL, DAVID W Academic teaching nursing home award Physiology of obstructive sleep apnea in the elderly

P01AG-04391-09 9001 (AGE) FOOD, AMASA B Academic teaching nursing home award CORE

P01AG-04391-09 0004 (AGE) FORD, AMASA B Academic teaching nursing home award Selected respiratory and GI infections of the elderly

P01AG-04393-07 (AGE) WARREN, JOHN W UNIV OF MARYLAND SCHOOL OF MED 10 SOUTH PINE STREET BALTIMORE, MD 21201 Complications of long-term urinary catheters in the aged

P01AG-04393-07 0004 (AGE) MOBLEY, HARRY L T Complications of long-term urinary catheters in the aged Proteus mirabilis pathogenesis in urinary tract infection

P01AG-04393-07 0005 (AGE) WARREN, JOHN W Complications of long-term urinary catheters in the aged E. coli hemolysin kills human renal epithelial cells

P01AG-04393-07 0008 (AGE) DONNENBERG, MICHAEL Complications of long-term urinary catheters in the aged Mechanism of E. coli invasion of the renal parenchyma

P01AG-04393-07 0009 (AGE) FLETCHER, MADILYN Complications of long-term urinary catheters in the aged Polymicrobial colonization of catheter surfaces

P01AG-04393-07 9004 (AGE) WARREN, JOHN W Complications of long-term urinary catheters in the aged Core

P01AG-04402-09 (AGE) SHAPIRO, JAY FRANCIS SCOTT KEY MED CENTER 4940 EASTERN AVENUE BALTIMORE, MD 21224 Academic teaching nursing home award

P01AG-04402-09 0002 (AGE) GOLDBERG, ANDREW P Academic teaching nursing home award Physical activity, glucose and fat metabolism in seniors

P01AG-04402-09 0003 (AGE) SMITH, PHILIP L Academic teaching nursing home award Prevention of sleep apnea in a aging population

P01AG-04402-09 0005 (AGE) GOTTLIEB, SIDNEY O Academic teaching nursing home award Physical activity and cardiac function in elderly men

P01AG-04402-09 0006 (AGE) VERDERY, ROY B Academic teaching nursing home award Mechanism of age changes in lipoprotein metabolism

P01AG-04402-09 0007 (AGE) BLEECKER, MARGIT L Academic teaching nursing home award Neurobehavioral aging--Risk factors for cerebrovascolar, cardivascular disease

P01AG-04402-09 0008 (AGE) WHITEHEAD, WILLIAM E Academic teaching nursing home award Constipation in the elderly

P01AG-04402-09 9001 (AGE) BLEECKER, EUGENE R Academic teaching nursing home award Core--Scientific and data management

P01AG-04418-08 (NBSA) HOFFER, BARRY J UNIV OF COLORADO HLTH SCI CTR 4200 E NINTH AVENUE DENVER, CO 80262 Aminergic function in aging and Alzheimer's disease

P01AG-04418-08 0002 (NBSA) ZAHNISER, NANCY R Aminergic function in aging and Alzheimer's disease Adrenergic receptors during aging

P01AG-04418-08 0004 (NBSA) HOFFER, BARRY J Aminergic function in aging and Alzheimer's disease Physiological and chemical CNS transplants

P01AG-04418-08 0006 (NBSA) BICKFORD-WIMER, PAULA C Aminergic function in aging and Alzheimer's disease Aminergic neurotransmission in situ in aged rat brain

P01AG-04418-08 0009 (NBSA) BROWNING, MICHAEL Aminergic function in aging and Alzheimer's disease Protein phosphorylation and LTP in aged animals

P01AG-04418-08 0011 (NBSA) OLSON, LARS Aminergic function in aging and Alzheimer's disease Neuronotrophic factors in aging and Alzheimer's disease

P01AG-04418-08 9001 (NBSA) HOFFER, BARRY J Aminergic function in aging and Alzheimer's disease Core--Aging animals

P01AG-04418-08 9002 (NBSA) ZERBE, GARY O Aminergic function in aging and Alzheimer's disease Core--Statistics

R37AG-04517-08 (HUD) WINGFIELD, ARTHUR BRANDEIS UNIVERSITY WALTHAM, MA 02254 Age and decision strategies in running memory for speech

R01AG-04518-08 (EDC) HUI, SIU LUI INDIANA UNIVERSITY 702 BARNHILL DR INDIANAPOLIS, IN 46202-5200 Longitudinal studies of bone loss in aging

R01AG-04542-07 (NEUB) LANDFIELD, PHILIP W UNIVERSITY OF KENTUCKY CHANDLER MEDICAL CENTER LEXINGTON, KY 40536 Hippocampal synaptic structure-physiology during aging

P30AG-04590-07 (AGE) CLUBB, JEROME M INST FOR SOCIAL RESEARCH P O BOX 1248 ANN ARBOR, MI 48109-1248 Factors in aging-- continued development research resource

R01AG-04594-08 (SAT) STANSKI, DONALD R V A MEDICAL CENTER 3801 MIRANDA AVENUE PALO ALTO, CA 94304 IV anesthetic disposition in the aged hemodynamic state

R01AG-04736-08 (PBC) THONAR, EUGENE J RUSH PRESBY-ST LUKE'S MED CTR 1653 WEST CONGRESS PARKWAY CHICAGO, IL 60612 Age-related differences in cartilage proteoglycans

R55AG-04743-05A2 (HUD) ALWIN, DUANE F UNIVERSITY OF MICHIGAN 426 THOMPSON STREET ANN ARBOR, MI 48106-1248 Aging, personality, and social change

R37AG-04791-08 (HUD) NEBES, ROBERT D WESTERN PSYCHIATRIC INST 3811 O'HARA STREET PITTSBURGH, PA 15213 Semantic memory in Alzheimer disease

R37AG-04810-08 (BCE) LU, JOHN K UNIVERSITY OF CALIFORNIA DEPT OF OBSTETRIC & GYNECOLOGY LOS ANGELES, CA 90024-1740 Hormone secretion and pregnancy during aging

R01AG-04821-09 (VR) OZER, HARVEY L UMDNJ-NEW JERSEY MEDICAL SCHOO 185 SOUTH ORANGE AVE NEWARK, NJ 07103-2714 Immortalization of SV40-transformed human cells

P01AG-04860-08 (AGE) THORBECKE, GEERTRUIDA J NEW YORK UNIVERSITY MED CENTER 550 FIRST AVENUE NEW YORK, N Y 10016 The effect of aging on the immune response

P01AG-04860-08 0001 (AGE) THORBECKE, G JEANETTE The effect of aging on the immune response Effect of aging on germinal center formation in lymphoid tissue

P01AG-04860-08 0002 (AGE) BELSITO, DONALD V The effect of aging on the immune response Langerhans cells in the aged

P01AG-04860-08 0003 (AGE) GOTTESMAN, SUSAN R The effect of aging on the immune response T-cell functions and aging

P01AG-04860-08 0004 (AGE) BASCH, ROSS S The effect of aging on the immune response T cell precursors and aging

P01AG-04860-08 0005 (AGE) CRONSTEIN, BRUCE The effect of aging on the immune response Neutrophil function in the elderly

P01AG-04860-08 9001 (AGE) THORBECKE, GEERTRUIDA J The effect of aging on the immune response Core - Animal facility

P01AG-04875-08 (AGE) RIGGS, BYRON L MAYO FOUNDATION 200 FIRST STREET SOUTHWEST ROCHESTER, MINN 55905 Physiology of bone metabolism in an aging population

P01AG-04875-08 0001 (AGE) RIGGS, LAWRENCE B. Physiology of bone metabolism in an aging population Pathophysiology of involutional osteoporosis

P01AG-04875-08 0002 (AGE) MELTON, JOSEPH L. Physiology of bone metabolism in an aging population Risk factors for hip fractures among the elderly

P01AG-04875-08 0004 (AGE) MANN, KENNETH G Physiology of bone metabolism in an aging population Biochemical quantitation of bone-specific proteins

P01AG-04875-08 0005 (AGE) SPELSBERG, THOMAS C. Physiology of bone metabolism in an aging population Sex steroids, growth factors and bone cell function

P01AG-04875-08 0006 (AGE) RIGGS, B. LAWRENCE Physiology of bone metabolism in an aging population Prevention of age-related bone loss by calcium therapy

P01AG-04875-08 9001 (AGE) O'FALLON, WILLIAM M Physiology of bone metabolism in an aging population Biostatistics core

R01AG-04895-06 (HUD) ECKERT, J KEVIN UNIVERSITY OF MARYLAND SOCIOLOGY/ANTHROPOLOGY DEPT BALTIMORE, MD 21228 Caregivers to at-risk elderly board/care home residents

R01AG-04932-07 (CMS) SMITH, JAMES C FLORIDA STATE UNIVERSITY DEPARTMENT OF PSYCHOLOGY TALLAHASSEE, FLA 32306 The age related effect of the sweet taste in the rat

P01AG-04953-08 (AGE) ALBERT, MARILYN S MASSACHUSETTS GENERAL HOSPITAL CNY-9 BOSTON, MA 02114 Age-related changes of cognition in health and disease

P01AG-04953-08 0001 (AGE) ALBERT, MARILYN S Age-related changes of cognition in health and disease Neuropsychological assessments

P01AG-04953-08 0002 (AGE) DUFFY, FRANK H Age-related changes of cognition in health and disease BEAM EEG and EP analysis

P01AG-04953-08 0003 (AGE) SANDOR, TAMAS Age-related changes of cognition in health and disease Computerized tomography

P01AG-04953-08 0004 (AGE) JOLESZ, FERENC Age-related changes of cognition in health and disease Magnetic resonance imaging

P01AG-04953-08 0005 (AGE) HOLMAN, LEONARD B Age-related changes of cognition in health and disease Single photon emission computed tomography

P01AG-04953-08 9001 (AGE) ALBERT, MARILYN Age-related changes of cognition in health and disease Statistical core

P01AG-04953-08 9002 (AGE) SANDOR, TAMAS Age-related changes of cognition in health and disease Image analysis core

R01AG-04954-08 (EDC) EAVES, LINDON J MEDICAL COLLEGE OF VIRGINIA DEPARTMENT OF HUMAN GENETICS RICHMOND, VA 23298-0001 Genetic models of development and ageing

R01AG-04980-28S3 (ALY) THORBECKE, GEERTRUIDA J NEW YORK UNIVERSITY MED CENTER 550 FIRST AVENUE NEW YORK, N Y 10016 Lymphoid cells--Production of antibodies and complement

R01AG-04984-06 (TOX) RIKANS, LORA E U OF OKLAHOMA HEALTH SCI CTR PO BOX 26901 OKLAHOMA CITY, OK 73190 Influence of aging on hepatotoxicity

R01AG-05107-08 (SSP) CRIMMINS, EILEEN M ANDRUS GERONTOLOGY CENTER UNIV OF SOUTHERN CA LOS ANGELES, CA 90089-0191 Does improvement in mortality mean better health?

R01AG-05110-06 (HUD) MADDEN, DAVID J DUKE UNIVERSITY MEDICAL CENTER BOX 2980 DURHAM, NC 27710 Adult age differences in component processes of reading

P01AG-05119-07 (AGE) MARKESBERY, WILLIAM R UNIVERSITY OF KENTUCKY 101 SANDERS-BROWN BLDG LEXINGTON, KY 40536-0230 Biochemical, morphological, and trace element studies--Alzheimer's disease
P01AG-05119-07 0003 (AGE) MARKESBERY, WILLIAM R Biochemical, morphological, and trace element studies--Alzheimer's disease Trace elements studies in Alzheimer's disease
P01AG-05119-07 0005 (AGE) SPARKS, LARRY D. Biochemical, morphological, and trace element studies--Alzheimer's disease Serotonergic dysfunction in Alzheimer's disease
P01AG-05119-07 0006 (AGE) SLEVIN, JOHN T. Biochemical, morphological, and trace element studies--Alzheimer's disease Alzheimer's disease
P01AG-05119-07 9001 (AGE) MARKESBERG, WILLIAM R Biochemical, morphological, and trace element studies--Alzheimer's disease Core
P50AG-05128-08 (AGE) ROSES, ALLEN D ALZHEIMER'S DISEASE RES CTR 725 BROAD ST DURHAM, NC 27705 Alzheimer disease research center
P50AG-05128-08 0008 (AGE) SCHIFFMAN, SUSAN Alzheimer disease research center Taste and smell measurements of patients at risk for Alzheimer's disease
P50AG-05128-08 0009 (AGE) DAWSON, DEBORAH Alzheimer disease research center Age of onset in familial Alzheimer's disease
P50AG-05128-08 0010 (AGE) BREITNER, JOHN Alzheimer disease research center Clinical, genetic and neuropathic heterogeneity in Alzheimer's disease
P50AG-05128-08 0011 (AGE) CRAIN, BARBARA Alzheimer disease research center Pathology of fascia dentata in Alzheimer's disease
P50AG-05128-08 0012 (AGE) SCHMECHEL, DONALD E Alzheimer disease research center Aging in prosimian primate--Model for Alzheimer's disease pathology
P50AG-05128-08 0013 (AGE) ANHOLT, ROBERT Alzheimer disease research center Pilot project--Steroids in Alzheimer's disease
P50AG-05128-08 0014 (AGE) PADILLA, GEORGE Alzheimer disease research center Pilot project--Regulation of neuronal cell differentiation and viability
P50AG-05128-08 0015 (AGE) LASTRA, ANSELMO Alzheimer disease research center Pilot projects--Computer solutions to multipoint linkage analysis
P50AG-05128-08 0016 (AGE) ROBERTSON, DAVID Alzheimer disease research center Pilot project--Electron microscopic studies of Alzheimer's disease
P50AG-05128-08 9001 (AGE) ROSES, ALLEN Alzheimer disease research center Core--Clinical research development
P50AG-05128-08 9003 (AGE) CRAIN, BARBARA Alzheimer disease research center Core--Neuropathology
P50AG-05128-08 9005 (AGE) GWYTHER, LISA Alzheimer disease research center Core--Education and information transfer
P50AG-05128-08 9006 (AGE) CONNEALLY, MICHAEL Alzheimer disease research center Core--National cell bank
P50AG-05131-08 (AGE) KATZMAN, ROBERT UNIVERSITY OF CALIFORNIA 3350 LA JOLLA VILLAGE DRIVE SAN DIEGO, CA 92161 Alzheimer's disease research center
P50AG-05131-08 0020 (AGE) YOUNG, STEPHEN J Alzheimer's disease research center Pilot project--Cytoskeletal and endomembrane system
P50AG-05131-08 9001 (AGE) TERRY, ROBERT D Alzheimer's disease research center Core--Neuropathology
P50AG-05131-08 9002 (AGE) KATZMAN, ROBERT Alzheimer's disease research center Core--Clinical
P50AG-05131-08 9003 (AGE) JACKSON, J EDWARD Alzheimer's disease research center Core--Research training and information transfer
P50AG-05131-08 0001 (AGE) GILLIN, J CHRISTIAN Alzheimer's disease research center Chronobiology of demented, depressed and normal patients
P50AG-05131-08 0003 (AGE) MORRISON, JOHN H Alzheimer's disease research center Neuropathological indices of aging and dementia
P50AG-05131-08 0006 (AGE) SEEGMILLER, J EDWIN Alzheimer's disease research center Genetic markers
P50AG-05131-08 0012 (AGE) SAITOH, TSUNAO Alzheimer's disease research center Identification of function of amyloid beta-protein precursor
P50AG-05131-08 0013 (AGE) SALMON, DAVID P Alzheimer's disease research center Neuropsychological studies of dementia
P50AG-05131-08 0014 (AGE) TERRY, ROBERT D Alzheimer's disease research center Neuronal populations in dementia
P50AG-05131-08 0015 (AGE) THAL, LEON J Alzheimer's disease research center Cognitive effects of nerve growth factor
P50AG-05131-08 0016 (AGE) KATZ, BARRETT Alzheimer's disease research center Pilot project--Pattern electroretinogram in Alzheimer's disease
P50AG-05131-08 0017 (AGE) LANGLAIS, PHILIP J Alzheimer's disease research center Pilot project--Locus coeruleus and physostigmine response
P50AG-05131-08 0018 (AGE) OSTERGAARD, ARNE L Alzheimer's disease research center Pilot project--Implicit memory in dementia
P50AG-05131-08 0019 (AGE) JESTE, DILIP V Alzheimer's disease research center Pilot project--Alzheimer's disease psychosis and neuropsychological deficits
P50AG-05133-08 (AGE) PETTEGREW, JAY W WESTERN PSYCHIATRIC INST & CLN 3811 O'HARA STREET PITTSBURGH, PA 15213 Alzheimer disease research center
P50AG-05133-08 0001 (AGE) PETTEGREW, JAY W Alzheimer disease research center Membrane studies in Alzheimer's disease
P50AG-05133-08 0006 (AGE) NEBES, ROBERT D Alzheimer disease research center Cognitive slowing in Alzheimer's disease and depression
P50AG-05133-08 0007 (AGE) PALMER, ALAN M Alzheimer disease research center Excitatory amino acid neurons and receptors in Alzheimer's disease
P50AG-05133-08 0008 (AGE) LEWIS, DAVID Alzheimer disease research center Catecholaminergic neurons in human cerebral cortex
P50AG-05133-08 0009 (AGE) KLUNK, WILLIAM E Alzheimer disease research center Pilot--Alzheimer's beta amyloid and EFG-like growth factors
P50AG-05133-08 0010 (AGE) HOCH, CAROLINE C Alzheimer disease research center Pilot--Sleep apnea, mental status and behavior in Alzheimer's disease
P50AG-05133-08 0011 (AGE) PEREL, JAMES M Alzheimer disease research center Pilot--Binding to basic drugs and alpha-1-acidic glycoprotein in Alzheimer's
P50AG-05133-08 0012 (AGE) BAKER, JAMES T Alzheimer disease research center Pilot--Functional dissociation of the memory deficit in Alzheimer's disease
P50AG-05133-08 0013 (AGE) SILVERMAN, MYRNA Alzheimer disease research center Pilot--Alzheimer's caregiver support group--Feasibility study
P50AG-05133-08 0014 (AGE) WEBSTER, CHARLES W Alzheimer disease research center Pilot--A computer model of depression and dementia
P50AG-05133-08 9001 (AGE) REZEK, DONALD L Alzheimer disease research center Core--Clinical core
P50AG-05133-08 9002 (AGE) MOOSSY, JOHN Alzheimer disease research center Core--Neuropathology core
P50AG-05133-08 9004 (AGE) DETRE, KATHERINE Alzheimer disease research center Core--Data management core
P50AG-05133-08 9005 (AGE) SILVERMAN, MYRNA Alzheimer disease research center Core--Training and information core
P50AG-05134-08 (AGE) GROWDON, JOHN H MASSACHUSETTS GENERAL HOSPITAL FRUIT STREET BOSTON, MA 02114 Alzheimer's disease research center
P50AG-05134-08 0005 (AGE) MESULAM, MAREK-MARSEL Alzheimer's disease research center Cholinesterases in Alzheimer's disease
P50AG-05134-08 0006 (AGE) NIXON, RAPLH A Alzheimer's disease research center Pathobiology of altered neuronal protease expression
P50AG-05134-08 0012 (AGE) CORKIN, SUZANNE Alzheimer's disease research center Priming and language competence in Alzheimer's disease
P50AG-05134-08 0013 (AGE) HAMOS, JAMES E Alzheimer's disease research center Pathogenesis of dementia--A multi-factorial approach
P50AG-05134-08 0014 (AGE) KOWALL, NEIL W Alzheimer's disease research center Histochemistry of the cytoskeleton in Alzheimer's disease
P50AG-05134-08 0015 (AGE) DE GENNARO, LOUIS J Alzheimer's disease research center Pilot project--synapsin gene expression as a biomarker in dementia
P50AG-05134-08 0016 (AGE) GROWDON, JOHN H Alzheimer's disease research center Pilot project--Phospholipid abnormalities in Alzheimer's disease
P50AG-05134-08 9001 (AGE) GROWDON, JOHN H Alzheimer's disease research center Clinical core
P50AG-05134-08 9002 (AGE) HEDLEY-WHYTE, E TESSA Alzheimer's disease research center Neuropathology core
P50AG-05134-08 9004 (AGE) LIPSITZ, LEWIS A Alzheimer's disease research center Core--Research training and information transfer
P50AG-05136-08 (AGE) MARTIN, GEORGE M UNIVERSITY OF WASHINGTON SEATTLE, WA 98195 Alzheimer disease research center
P50AG-05136-08 0006 (AGE) RASKIND, MURRAY Alzheimer disease research center Noradrenergic function in Alzheimer's disease
P50AG-05136-08 0007 (AGE) SNOW, ALAN Alzheimer disease research center Proteoglycans in Alzheimer's disease and Down's syndrome
P50AG-05136-08 0008 (AGE) BOTHWELL, MARK Alzheimer disease research center Nerve growth factor in Alzheimer's spinal fluid
P50AG-05136-08 0009 (AGE) WONG, TIMOTHY Alzheimer disease research center Biased hypermutation and degenerative disease
P50AG-05136-08 0010 (AGE) ARNETT, CAROL Alzheimer disease research center Pilot project--PET imaging approach to early diagnosis of Alzheimer's disease
P50AG-05136-08 0011 (AGE) MARTIN, GEORGE Alzheimer disease research center Pilot project--Bioassay of human DNA via YAC clones
P50AG-05136-08 0012 (AGE) MONNAT, RAYMOND Alzheimer disease research center Pilot project--Mitochondrial DNA mutation in Alzheimer's disease
P50AG-05136-08 0013 (AGE) STORM, DANIEL Alzheimer disease research center Pilot project--Neuromodulin in Alzheimer brain
P50AG-05136-08 0014 (AGE) WESTRUM, LESNICK E Alzheimer disease research center Pilot project--Olfactory transplants--An Alzheimer's model
P50AG-05136-08 0015 (AGE) TEMPLE, BRUCE Alzheimer disease research center Pilot project--K+ channel gene expression in Alzheimer's disease
P50AG-05136-08 9001 (AGE) TERI, LINDA Alzheimer disease research center Training and information transfer core
P50AG-05136-08 9002 (AGE) RASKIND, MURRY Alzheimer disease research center Core--Clinical/data management
P50AG-05136-08 9003 (AGE) SUMI, SHUZO M Alzheimer disease research center General autopsy and neuropathology core
P50AG-05136-08 9004 (AGE) NORWOOD, THOMAS H Alzheimer disease research center Cell, tissue and fluids bank, cell culture and cytogenetics core
P50AG-05136-08 0003 (AGE) BIRD, THOMAS D Alzheimer disease research center Linkage analysis in familial Alzheimer's disease
P50AG-05138-08 (AGE) DAVIS, KENNETH L MOUNT SINAI SCHOOL OF MEDICINE ONE GUSTAVE LEVY PLACE NEW YORK, NY 10029 Alzheimer's disease research center
P50AG-05138-08 0001 (AGE) HAROUTUNIAN, VAHRAM Alzheimer's disease research center Animal models of Alzheimer's disease -- Neurotransmitter interactions
P50AG-05138-08 0006 (AGE) LAZZARINI, ROBERT A. Alzheimer's disease research center Neuron specific gene regulation
P50AG-05138-08 0007 (AGE) MORRISON, JOHN H. Alzheimer's disease research center Cellular pathology of cerebral cortex
P50AG-05138-08 0008 (AGE) ROBAKIS, NIKOLAOS K. Alzheimer's disease research center Expressing and processing of the amyloid precursor
P50AG-05138-08 0009 (AGE) PERL, DANIEL P. Alzheimer's disease research center Aluminum and Alzheimer's disease -- Microprobe study
P50AG-05138-08 0010 (AGE) DAVIS, KENNETH L. Alzheimer's disease research center Noradrenergic markers in Alzheimer's disease
P50AG-05138-08 0011 (AGE) MOHS, RICHARD C. Alzheimer's disease research center HPA axis in Alzheimer's disease
P50AG-05138-08 0012 (AGE) FILLIT, HOWARD M. Alzheimer's disease

research center Pilot study -- Heparan sulfate proteoglycans in Alzheimer's disease

P50AG-05138-08 0013 (AGE) GABRIEL, STEVEN M Alzheimer's disease research center Pilot study -- Galanin neurons and Alzheimer's disease neuropathology

P50AG-05138-08 0014 (AGE) WALLACE, WILLIAM C. Alzheimer's disease research center Pilot study -- Altered phosphoproteins regulating AD protein synthesis

P50AG-05138-08 9002 (AGE) PERL, DANIEL P. Alzheimer's disease research center Autopsy core

P50AG-05138-08 9003 (AGE) GREENWALD, BLAINE S. Alzheimer's disease research center Core -- Clinical research support

P50AG-05138-08 9004 (AGE) BUTLER, ROBERT N. Alzheimer's disease research center Core -- Information transfer

P50AG-05142-08 (AGE) FINCH, CALEB E UNIV OF SOUTHERN CALIFORNIA 3715 MCCLINTOCK AVE LOS ANGELES, CA 90089-0191 ADRC consortium of Los Angeles and Orange Counties

P50AG-05142-08 0007 (AGE) BUCHSBAUM, MONTE S. ADRC consortium of Los Angeles and Orange Counties Pilot study--Brain metabolism of preserved motor learning

P50AG-05142-08 0008 (AGE) TOKES, ZOLTON A. ADRC consortium of Los Angeles and Orange Counties Pilot study--Serine proteases in Alzheimer brain specimens

P50AG-05142-08 9001 (AGE) MILLER, CAROL A ADRC consortium of Los Angeles and Orange Counties Core--Neuropathology

P50AG-05142-08 9004 (AGE) CHUI, HELENA ADRC consortium of Los Angeles and Orange Counties Core-- Quantimet

P50AG-05142-08 9007 (AGE) HENDERSON, VICTOR W. ADRC consortium of Los Angeles and Orange Counties Core--Clinical

P50AG-05142-08 9008 (AGE) SOBEL, EUGENE L. ADRC consortium of Los Angeles and Orange Counties Core--Biostatistics and epidemiology

P50AG-05142-08 9009 (AGE) KNIGHT, ROBERT ADRC consortium of Los Angeles and Orange Counties Core--outreach and information transfer

P50AG-05142-08 0004 (AGE) BLANKS, JANET C. ADRC consortium of Los Angeles and Orange Counties Neuronal degeneration in the visual system of AD patients

P50AG-05142-08 0005 (AGE) NALCIOGLU, ORHAN ADRC consortium of Los Angeles and Orange Counties MRI analysis of Alzheimer's disease

P50AG-05142-08 0006 (AGE) THOMPSON, RICHARD F. ADRC consortium of Los Angeles and Orange Counties Aging, stress and the hippocampus

P50AG-05144-08 (AGE) MARKESBERY, WILLIAM R UNIVERSITY OF KENTUCKY 101 SANDERS-BROWN BUILDING LEXINGTON, KY 40536-0230 Alzheimer disease research center

P50AG-05144-08 0003 (AGE) SCHEFF, STEPHEN W Alzheimer disease research center Synaptic density and gene expression of NCAM in Alzheimer's disease

P50AG-05144-08 0005 (AGE) MATTSON, MARK P Alzheimer disease research center Cellular signaling and Alzheimer-like neurodegeneration

P50AG-05144-08 0006 (AGE) SISKEN, J E Alzheimer disease research center Alteration in calcium metabolism in familial Alzheimer's disease

P50AG-05144-08 0007 (AGE) SPARKS, DAVID L Alzheimer disease research center Senile plaques in Alzheimer's and heart diseases

P50AG-05144-08 0008 (AGE) WATT, DAVID S Alzheimer disease research center GTP photoaffinity probes from Alzheimer's disease brain

P50AG-05144-08 0009 (AGE) ZIMMER, STEPHEN G Alzheimer disease research center Search for transmissible agents in Alzheimer's disease hippocampus

P50AG-05144-08 9001 (AGE) KNOX, CRAIG Alzheimer disease research center Clinical research core

P50AG-05144-08 9002 (AGE) MARKESBERY, WILLIAM R Alzheimer disease research center Core--Neuropathology/neurochemistry

P50AG-05144-08 9003 (AGE) WEKSTEIN, DAVID R Alzheimer disease research center Training and information transfer core

P50AG-05146-09 (AGE) PRICE, DONALD L JOHNS HOPKINS HOSPITAL 600 NORTH WOLFE STREET BALTIMORE, MD 21205 Aging and Alzheimer disease, and Down's syndrome

P50AG-05146-09 0008 (AGE) PRICE, DONALD L Aging and Alzheimer disease, and Down's syndrome Studies of amyloid and chromosome 21

P50AG-05146-09 0009 (AGE) TRONCOSO, JUAN C Aging and Alzheimer disease, and Down's syndrome Biology of age-associated cognitive abnormalities

P50AG-05146-09 0010 (AGE) CORK, LINDA C Aging and Alzheimer disease, and Down's syndrome Neurobiology of Down's syndrome

P50AG-05146-09 0011 (AGE) ROSS, CHRISTOPHER A Aging and Alzheimer disease, and Down's syndrome Depression and psychosis in Alzheimer's disease

P50AG-05146-09 0012 (AGE) PRICE, DONALD L Aging and Alzheimer disease, and Down's syndrome Therapies for central cholinergic systems

P50AG-05146-09 0013 (AGE) RUTKOWSKI, J LYNN Aging and Alzheimer disease, and Down's syndrome Pilot study--NGF effects on primate neurons in vitro

P50AG-05146-09 0014 (AGE) RANCE, NAOMI E Aging and Alzheimer disease, and Down's syndrome Pilot study--Reproductive aging and the human hypothalamus

P50AG-05146-09 0015 (AGE) MARTIN, LEE J Aging and Alzheimer disease, and Down's syndrome Pilot study--Innervation of basal forebrain cholinergic neurons

P50AG-05146-09 0016 (AGE) ATURKKAN, JAYLAN S Aging and Alzheimer disease, and Down's syndrome Pilot study--Memory and associative learning in Alzheimer's disease

P50AG-05146-09 0017 (AGE) QUAID, KIMBERLY A Aging and Alzheimer disease, and Down's syndrome Pilot study--Proxy consent for autopsy

P50AG-05146-09 9001 (AGE) FOLSTEIN, MARSHAL F Aging and Alzheimer disease, and Down's syndrome Core--Clinical studies

P50AG-05146-09 9003 (AGE) TRONCOSO, JUAN C Aging and Alzheimer disease, and Down's syndrome Core--Neuropathology

P50AG-05146-09 9004 (AGE) FOLSTEIN, MARSHAL F Aging and Alzheimer disease, and Down's syndrome core--Training and information transfer

P50AG-05146-09 9005 (AGE) MUMA, NANCY A Aging and Alzheimer disease, and Down's syndrome Core--Molecular biology

U01AG-05170-07 (AGE) FANTL, JOHN A MEDICAL COLLEGE OF VIRGINIA BOX 34 RICHMOND, VA 23298 Urinary incontinence in community-dwelling women

U01AG-05170-07 0001 (AGE) WYMAN, JEAN F Urinary incontinence in community-dwelling women Behavioral intervention

U01AG-05170-07 0002 (AGE) FANTL, J ANDREW Urinary incontinence in community-dwelling women Estrogen supplementation

U01AG-05170-07 0003 (AGE) BUMP, RICHARD C Urinary incontinence in community-dwelling women Urogynecologic surgery in older women

U01AG-05170-07 9001 (AGE) MCCLISH, DONNA K Urinary incontinence in community-dwelling women Core--Biostatistics

R01AG-05198-02S1 (EDC) BARKER, WILLIAM H KAISER FOUNDATION HOSPITALS 4610 S E BELMONT STREET PORTLAND, OR 97215 Mortality decline among the aged: explanatory factors

R01AG-05213-06 (SRCM) FRIEDMAN, DAVID RES FDN FOR MENTAL HYGIENE INC 722 WEST 168 ST NEW YORK, NY 10032 Effects of aging on cognitive ERPS/cardiac waveform

R01AG-05214-07 (NLS) ELLIS, JOHN UNIVERSITY OF VERMONT BURLINGTON, VT 05405 Responses of subpopulations of muscarinic receptors

R01AG-05223-06 (VISB) WARREN, WILLIAM H, JR BROWN UNIVERSITY BOX 1853 PROVIDENCE, RI 02912 Visual control of locomotion

R01AG-05233-04 (BEM) FREEDMAN, ROBERT R LAFAYETTE CLINIC 951 E LAFAYETTE DETROIT, MI 48207 Behavioral treatment of menopausal hot flashes

R37AG-05284-06 (EDC) DAVIS, MARADEE A UNIV OF SO CALIF, HSW-1699 DEPT. OF EPIDEMOLOGY SAN FRANCISCO, CALIF 94143 Living arrangements diet and survival of older

R01AG-05309-05 (IMB) EFFROS, RITA B UCLA MEDICAL SCHOOL 405 HILGARD AVE LOS ANGELES, CA 90024 Senescence in human T lymphocyte cultures

R01AG-05317-04A3 (ORTH) WOOLLACOTT, MARJORIE H UNIVERSITY OF OREGON EUGENE, OR 97403 Age-related changes in posture and movement

R01AG-05324-07 (PBC) REISER, KAREN M CALIFORNIA PRIMATE RES CENTER UNIVERSITY OF CALIFORNIA DAVIS, CA 95616 Age-associated changes in collagen

R01AG-05333-07 (CTY) PEREIRA-SMITH, OLIVIA M BAYLOR COLLEGE OF MEDICINE ONE BAYLOR PLAZA HOUSTON, TEX 77030 A genetic analysis of indefinite division in human cells

R01AG-05366-05 (NEUB) WITKIN, JOAN W COLUMBIA UNIV COLL. P & S 630 WEST 168TH STREET NEW YORK, N Y 10032 Aging LHRH system/EM immunocytochemical studies

R01AG-05374-04A2 (IMB) SZAKAL, ANDRAS K VIRGINIA COMMONWEALTH UNIV BOX 709 MVC STATION RICHMOND, VA 23298-0709 Role of antigen transport by dendritic cells in aging

R01AG-05394-06 (EDC) GRIMM, RICHARD H UNIVERSITY OF MINNESOTA 515 DELAWARE ST SE MINNEAPOLIS, MN 55455 Risk factors for hip and colles' fractures

R01AG-05407-06 (EDC) CUMMINGS, STEVEN R 74 NEW MONTGOMERY STREET SAN FRANCISCO, CA 94105 Risk factors for hip and colles' fractures

R01AG-05433-06 (NEUA) PROHOVNIK, ISAK A N Y S PSYCHIATRIC INSTITUTE 722 WEST 168TH STREET NEW YORK, N Y 10032 Regional cerebral blood flow in Alzheimer's disease

R01AG-05552-05A1 (HUD) HESS, THOMAS M NORTH CAROLINA STATE UNIV RALEIGH, N C 27695-7801 Schematic knowledge influences on memory in adulthood

P01AG-05561-06A1 (NBSA) HOUSE, JAMES S INSTITUTE FOR SOCIAL RESEARCH PO BOX 1248 ANN ARBOR, MI 48106-1248 Productivity, stress and health in middle and late life

P01AG-05561-06A1 0001 (NBSA) HERZOG, A REGULA Productivity, stress and health in middle and late life Productive activities in middle and later life

P01AG-05561-06A1 0002 (NBSA) JACKSON, JAMES S Productivity, stress and health in middle and late life Sociocultural factors in productive aging

P01AG-05561-06A1 0003 (NBSA) HOUSE, JAMES S Productivity, stress and health in middle and late life Stratification, adaptation, aging, and health

P01AG-05561-06A1 0004 (NBSA) WORTMAN, CAMILLE B Productivity, stress and health in middle and late life Widowhood, bereavement and coping

P01AG-05561-06A1 9001 (NBSA) LEPKOWSKI, JAMES Productivity, stress and health in middle and late life Core--Administrative and data base core

P01AG-05562-07 (AGE) HOLLOSZY, JOHN O WASH UNIV SCHOOL OF MEDICINE 4566 SCOTT AVENUE ST LOUIS, MO 63110 Physiological adaptations to exercise in the elderly

P01AG-05562-07 0008 (AGE) HOLLOSZY, JOHN O Physiological adaptations to exercise in the elderly Follow-up study of master athletes

P01AG-05562-07 9001 (AGE) HOLLOSZY, JOHN O Physiological adaptations to exercise in the elderly Core

P01AG-05562-07 0002 (AGE) EHSANI, ALI A Physiological adaptations to exercise in the elderly Cardiovascular adaptation to training in the elderly

P01AG-05562-07 0005 (AGE) SCHONFELD, GUSTAV Physiological adaptations to exercise in the elderly Exercise, weight loss and lipoproteins

P01AG-05562-07 0006 (AGE) BIRGE, STANLEY J Physiological adaptations to exercise in the elderly Interaction of estrogen and exercise on bone mass

P01AG-05562-07 0007 (AGE) BIER, DENNIS M Physiological adaptations to exercise in the elderly Protein anabolic effects of weight training in the elderly

R01AG-05601-07 (PC) MONNIER, VINCENT M CASE WESTERN RESERVE UNIV 2085 ADELBERT ROAD CLEVELAND, OH 44106 Browning of human collagen in diabetes mellitus and aging

R37AG-05604-06 (NLS) NIXON, RALPH MC LEAN HOSPITAL 115 MILL STREET BELMONT, MA 02178 Dynamics of the neuronal cytoskeleton in aging brain

R01AG-05627-07 (PHRA) BLASCHKE, TERRENCE F STANFORD UNIV MEDICAL CENTER STANFORD, CA 94305-5113 Aging and in vivo vascular responsiveness in man

R37AG-05628-07 (IMB) GOOD, ROBERT A ALL CHILDREN'S HOSPITAL 801

PROJECT NO., ORGANIZATIONAL UNIT., INVESTIGATOR, ADDRESS, TITLE

6TH STREET SOUTH ST PETERSBURG, FL 33701 Cellular engineering to treat and prevent diseases of aging

R01AG-05633-07A1 (NTN) GOOD, ROBERT A ALL CHILDREN'S HOSPITAL 801 6TH STREET SOUTH ST PETERSBURG, FL 33701 Reduced calories, proliferation, immunity, cancer, aging

P50AG-05681-08 (AGE) BERG, LEONARD WASH UNIV SCHOOL OF MEDICINE 660 S EUCLID AVE. ST LOUIS, MO 63110 Washington University Alzheimer's disease research center

P50AG-05681-08 0004 (AGE) OLNEY, JOHN W Washington University Alzheimer's disease research center Excitatory transmitters and Alzheimer's disease

P50AG-05681-08 0006 (AGE) JOHNSON, EUGENE M Washington University Alzheimer's disease research center Molecular mechanisms of natural occurring neuronal death

P50AG-05681-08 0012 (AGE) WOZNIAK, DAVID F Washington University Alzheimer's disease research center Glutamate receptors and memory

P50AG-05681-08 0013 (AGE) ZORUMSKI, CHARLES F Washington University Alzheimer's disease research center Long term potentiation and excitatory amino acids

P50AG-05681-08 0014 (AGE) PARKINSON, DAVID Washington University Alzheimer's disease research center Biochemistry of dopamine in Alzheimer's disease

P50AG-05681-08 0015 (AGE) TRICK, GARY Washington University Alzheimer's disease research center Visual function in SDAT

P50AG-05681-08 0016 (AGE) PRICE, JOSEPH L Washington University Alzheimer's disease research center Pilot--Protein synthesis and neuronal death

P50AG-05681-08 0017 (AGE) GOTTLIEB, DAVID I Washington University Alzheimer's disease research center Pilot--Neuronal precursor proliferation

P50AG-05681-08 0018 (AGE) BALICE-GORDON, RITA Washington University Alzheimer's disease research center Pilot--Aging synapses visualized over time in aging mice

P50AG-05681-08 0019 (AGE) NOETZEL, MICHAEL Washington University Alzheimer's disease research center Pilot--Neurofilament protein phosphorylation in trisomy 16

P50AG-05681-08 0020 (AGE) CRAFT, SUZANNE Washington University Alzheimer's disease research center Pilot--Glucose and memory in mild SDAT

P50AG-05681-08 9001 (AGE) MILLER, J PHILIP Washington University Alzheimer's disease research center Biostatistics core

P50AG-05681-08 9002 (AGE) MORRIS, JOHN C Washington University Alzheimer's disease research center Clinical core

P50AG-05681-08 9003 (AGE) STORANDT, MARTHA Washington University Alzheimer's disease research center Psychometrics core

P50AG-05681-08 9004 (AGE) MCKEEL, DANIEL W JR Washington University Alzheimer's disease research center Morphology/neuropathology core

P50AG-05681-08 9005 (AGE) HIBBARD, LYNDON S Washington University Alzheimer's disease research center Morphology/image analysis core

P50AG-05681-08 9006 (AGE) BERG, LEONARD Washington University Alzheimer's disease research center Training and information transfer core

R37AG-05683-07 (NLS) GLENNER, GEORGE G UNIV OF CALIFORNIA, SAN DIEGO BASIC SCIENCE BLDG LA JOLLA, CA 92093 Cerebrovascular amyloid protein in Alzheimer's disease

R01AG-05717-07 (EI) KRISHNARAJ, RAJABATHER UNIVERSITY OF ILLINOIS 840 SOUTH WOOD (787) CHICAGO, IL 60612 Age-associated alterations in human NK cell system

R01AG-05731-04A3 (IMB) BONDADA, SUBBARAO UNIVERSITY OF KENTUCKY 205 SANDERS-BROWN BLDG LEXINGTON, KY 40536-0230 Age associated changes in B lymphocyte function

R01AG-05739-06 (VISB) BALL, KARLENE K WESTERN KENTUCKY UNIVERSITY BOWLING GREEN, KY 42101 Improvement of visual processing in older adults

P01AG-05793-06 (AGE) JOHNSTON, C CONRAD, JR INDIANA UNIV SCHOOL OF MED 545 BARNHILL DRIVE INDIANAPOLIS, IN 46202-5124 Some determinants of bone mass in the elderly

P01AG-05793-06 0004 (AGE) MILLER, JUDY Z Some determinants of bone mass in the elderly Effects of calcium on bone mass--A co-twin control study

P01AG-05793-06 0005 (AGE) PEACOCK, MUNRO Some determinants of bone mass in the elderly Prevention of bone loss at the hip with calcium or vitamin D

P01AG-05793-06 9001 (AGE) HUI, SIU L Some determinants of bone mass in the elderly Core--Biostatistics and epidemiology core

P01AG-05793-06 9002 (AGE) LONGCOPE, CHRISTOPHER Some determinants of bone mass in the elderly Core--Steroid dynamics core

P01AG-05793-06 9003 (AGE) PEACOCK, MUNRO Some determinants of bone mass in the elderly Core--Calcium absorption and biochemistry core

P01AG-05793-06 0001 (AGE) JOHNSTON, C CONRAD Some determinants of bone mass in the elderly Role of sex steroids in age-related bone loss

P01AG-05793-06 0002 (AGE) CHRISTIAN, JOE C Some determinants of bone mass in the elderly Twin and family studies of bone mass

P01AG-05842-06 (AGE) WISE, DAVID A NATL BUREAU OF ECONOMIC RES 1050 MASSACHUSETTS AVENUE CAMBRIDGE, MA 02138 The economics of aging

P01AG-05842-06 0001 (AGE) WISE, DAVID A The economics of aging Labor market behavior

P01AG-05842-06 0002 (AGE) BERNHEIM, B DOUGLAS The economics of aging Financial status--Retirement saving programs

P01AG-05842-06 0003 (AGE) MC FADDEN, DANIEL L The economics of aging Housing and living arrangements

P01AG-05842-06 0004 (AGE) KOTLIKOFF, LAURENCE J The economics of aging Family support

P01AG-05842-06 0005 (AGE) GARBER, ALAN M The economics of aging Health care

P01AG-05842-06 9001 (AGE) MC FADDEN, DANIEL L The economics of aging Core--New data acquisition

R01AG-05885-03S1 (EDC) MODAN, BARUCH CHAIM SHEBA MEDICAL CENTER TEL HASHOMER 52621 ISRAEL A national epidemiological study of the oldest old

R37AG-05890-07 (RNM) BUDINGER, THOMAS F UNIV OF CALIFORNIA, LIFE SCIS 1 CYCLOTRON ROAD BERKELEY, CA 94720 Cerebral blood flow patterns in Alzheimer's disease

PROJECT NO., ORGANIZATIONAL UNIT., INVESTIGATOR, ADDRESS, TITLE

R01AG-05891-07 (NEUA) FRANGIONE, BLAS N.Y.U. MEDICAL CENTER 550 FIRST AVENUE NEW YORK, NY 10016 Amyloidosis and Alzheimer's disease

R01AG-05892-10 (NLS) IQBAL, KHALID NY/ST/INS/BASIC/RES DEV DISABI 1050 FOREST HILL ROAD STATEN ISLAND, N Y 10314 Alzheimer neurofibrillary tangles--biochemical studies

R01AG-05893-12 (NLS) HERSH, LOUIS B THE UNIV OF TEXAS SOUTHWESTERN 5323 HARRY HINES BOULEVARD DALLAS, TEX 75235 Choline acetyltransferse

R01AG-05894-19 (NEUB) FINE, RICHARD E BOSTON UNIVERSITY SCH OF MED 80 EAST CONCORD ST RM# K-402 BOSTON, MA 02118 Coated vesicles -- membrane transport in muscle & brain

R01AG-05917-07 (NLS) ROTUNDO, RICHARD L UNIVERSITY OF MIAMI 1600 N W 10TH AVENUE MIAMI, FL 33101 Regulation of acetylcholinesterase synthesis and assembly

R01AG-05940-06 (PHRA) SCHWARTZ, JANICE B UNIVERSITY OF CALIFORNIA SAN FRANCISCO, CA 94143-0446 Effect of aging on calcium blocker kinetics/dynamics

R01AG-05944-05 (NEUA) CHANG, HOWARD T UNIVERSITY OF TENNESSEE 875 MONROE AVE MEMPHIS, TN 38163 Limbic-basal ganglia-cortex interactions

R01AG-05963-05 (HUD) RICE, GRACE E ARIZONA ST UNIV OLDER ADULTS MEMORY PROJECT TEMPE, AZ 85287-1308 Older adults' memory for written medical information

R01AG-05972-06 (HUD) BOWLES, NANCY L VA OUTPATIENT CLINIC 251 CAUSEWAY ST BOSTON, MA 02108 An analysis of word retrieval deficits in the aged

R01AG-06036-06 (BPO) ARNSTEN, AMY F YALE UNIVERSITY SCH OF MED PO BOX 3333 NEW HAVEN, CT 06510 Cognitive loss with age--Role of cortical catecholamines

R01AG-06041-04A3 (HUD) HOYER, WILLIAM J SYRACUSE UNIVERSITY 430 HUNTINGTON HALL SYRACUSE, NY 13244-2340 Aging, skill, and knowledge use

R37AG-06060-06 (NSS) FELTEN, DAVID L UNIV OF ROCHESTER SCH OF MED 601 ELMWOOD AVENUE ROCHESTER, N Y 14642 MPTP--Degeneration of monoamine systems, and aging

R01AG-06066-05 (SSS) DEMENT, WILLIAM C STANFORD UNIV, SCHL OF MED SCIENCES BUILDING T D, ROOM 11 STANFORD, CA 94305 Follow-up of elderly patients with sleep apnea

R01AG-06072-07 (HUD) CZEISLER, CHARLES A BRIGHAM AND WOMEN'S HOSPITAL 221 LONGWOOD AVE BOSTON, MA 02115 Disrupted sleep in the elderly--Response to phototherapy

R37AG-06079-08 (NSS) HOLICK, MICHAEL F BOSTON UNIV SCHOOL OF MEDICINE 80 EAST CONCORD ST M-1013 BOSTON, MA 02118 Influence of age on 7-dehydrocholesterol in the skin

R01AG-06088-05A1 (NEUB) GAGE, FRED H UNIV OF CALIFORNIA, SAN DIEGO LA JOLLA, CA 92093 Embryonic nerve cell transplantation in aged brain

R01AG-06093-19 (NEUB) NAKAJIMA, YASUKO UNIV OF ILLINOIS COLL OF MED 808 SOUTH WOOD ST CHICAGO, IL 60612 Ultrastructure and function of nerve and muscle

R37AG-06108-07 (CTY) HORNSBY, PETER J MEDICAL COLLEGE OF GEORGIA 1120 15TH ST AUGUSTA, GA 30612-2100 Aging of endocrine cells in culture

R37AG-06116-07 (PBC) DICE, JAMES F, JR TUFTS UNIVERSITY 136 HARRISON AVENUE BOSTON, MA 02111 Protein degradation in aging human fibroblasts

R01AG-06127-05 (PTHA) GILDEN, DONALD H UNIV OF COLORADO HLTH SCI CTR 4200 EAST NINTH AVENUE DENVER, CO 80262 Neurobiology of Varicella-Zoster virus

R01AG-06157-05 (RAP) FAULKNER, JOHN A UNIV OF MICHIGAN MED SCHOOL 7775 MEDICAL SCIENCE II BLDG. ANN ARBOR, MI 48109-0622 Exercise injury and repair of muscle fibers in aged mice

R01AG-06159-04A1 (NEUB) VIJAYAN, VIJAYA K UNIVERSITY OF CALIFORNIA DAVIS, CA 95616-8643 Reactive properties of brain neuroglia in aging rats

R01AG-06168-06 (MBC) JAZWINSKI, S MICHAL LOUISIANA STATE UNIVERSITY 1901 PERDIDO STREET NEW ORLEANS, LA 70112 Cellular aging in a yeast model system

R01AG-06170-06 (NLS) POTTER, LINCOLN T UNIV OF MIAMI SCHOOL OF MED PO BOX 016189, RM 189 MIAMI, FL 33101 Cholinergic mechanisms in aging and Alzheimer's disease

R37AG-06173-06 (NEUA) SELKOE, DENNIS J BRIGHAM AND WOMEN'S HOSPITAL 75 FRANCIS STREET BOSTON, MA 02115 Aging in the brain--Role of the fibrous proteins

R01AG-06217-05 (NEUB) FELDMAN, MARTIN L BOSTON UNIVERSITY 80 EAST CONCORD STREET BOSTON, MASS 02118 Auditory anatomy in aging rats with extended lifespans

R01AG-06221-06 (ECS) TATE, CHARLOTTE A UNIVERSITY OF HOUSTON 4800 CALHOUN HOUSTON, TX 77204 Myocardial response to exercise during senescence

R01AG-06226-05 (NLS) MEYER, EDWIN M UNIVERSITY OF FLORIDA P O BOX J-267 GAINESVILLE, FL 32610 Aging and brain acetylcholine release

R01AG-06232-05 (NTN) HARRISON, DAVID E THE JACKSON LABORATORY 600 MAIN STREET BAR HARBOR, ME 04609-0800 Nutritional effects on aging

R01AG-06246-06 (IMB) KELLEY, KEITH W UNIVERSITY OF ILLINOIS 1207 WEST GREGORY DRIVE URBANA, IL 61801 Hormonal restoration of a funtional thymus during aging

R44AG-06259-03 (NTN) DENNISON, KATHRYN F DINE SYSTEMS, INC 586 NORTH FRENCH ROAD, SUITE 2 AMHERST, NY 14228 Computerized nutrition program for senior citizens

R01AG-06265-06A1 (HUD) PARK, DENISE C UNIVERSITY OF GEORGIA HERTY DRIVE ATHENS, GA 30602 Effects of context on the aging memory

R01AG-06278-06 (IMB) ALBRIGHT, JULIA W GEORGE WASHINGTON UNIVERSITY 2300 I STREET N W WASHINGTON, D C 20037 Aging of immunity to parasites

R01AG-06299-07 (HEM) GALILI, URI MEDICAL COLL OF PENNSYLVANIA 3300 HENRY AVENUE PHILADELPHIA, PA 19129 Anti-Gal IgG on human red cells--A model for cell aging

R01AG-06322-03 (EDC) MAGAZINER, JAY UNIVERSITY OF MARYLAND 660 WEST REDWOOD ST BALTIMORE, MD 21201 Epidemiologic study--Determinants of recovery from hip fracture

R01AG-06346-04S1 (GEN) ROSE, MICHAEL R UNIV OF CALIFORNIA, IRVINE 816C ENGINERRING BUILDING IRVINE, CA 92717 Genetically - postponed senescence in Drosophila

R01AG-06347-05 (MEP) BUSBEE, DAVID L TEXAS A&M UNIVERSITY BOX 3578 COLLEGE STATION, TX 77843 Age-related inhibition of DNA synthesis initiation

R01AG-06348-05A1 (NEUC) GASKIN, FELICIA UNIV OF VIRGINIA SCH OF MED 6 EAST BLUE RIDGE HOSPITAL CHARLOTTESVILLE, VA 22901 Autoantibodies in Alzheimer's disease and normal aging

R01AG-06380-03 (SSP) KOTLIKOFF, LAURENCE J BOSTON UNIVERSITY 270 BAY STATE ROAD BOSTON, MA 02215 The increased annuitization of the elderly--Estimates A

R01AG-06432-05 (NEUA) HALSEY, JAMES H, JR UNIVERSITY OF ALABAMA AT BIRM DEPT. OF NEUROLOGY BIRMINGHAM, ALA 35294 Regional cerebral blood flow in progressive dementia

R01AG-06457-06 (HAR) HORAK, FAY B GOOD SAMARITAN HOSP & MED CENT 1120 N W 20TH AVENUE PORTLAND, OR 97209 Peripheral and central postural disorders in the elderly

R37AG-06490-06 (NSS) DEMENT, WILLIAM C STANFORD UNIVERSITY SCIENCES BLDG TD STANFORD, CA 94305 Sleep, exercise, aging and the circadian system

R01AG-06528-05A1 (PBC) DAVIDSON, JEFFREY M VANDERBILT UNIVERSITY 21ST AND GARLAND ST NASHVILLE, TN 37232-2561 Elastin and collagen in the aging process

R01AG-06533-06 (CBY) WILSON, PATRICIA D UMDNJ-R W JOHNSON MED/SCH 675 HOES LA/PHYSIO & BIOPHYS PISCATAWAY, NJ 08854-5635 Effect of aging on renal epithelial cells

R01AG-06537-06 (RAP) SEALS, DOUGLAS R UNIVERSITY OF ARIZONA MCKALE CENTER, RM 228-B TUCSON, AZ 85721 Sympathetic nervous system activity and human aging

R01AG-06557-06 (NEUB) ROPER, STEPHEN D COLORADO STATE UNIVERSITY DEPARTMENT OF ANATOMY FORT COLLINS, CO 80523 Neural influence on aging of receptor cells

R37AG-06559-04 (HUD) JOHNSON, COLLEEN L UNIVERSITY OF CALIFORNIA 1350 7TH AVE, CSBS-317 SAN FRANCISCO, CA 94143 The social world of the oldest old

P01AG-06569-05 (AGE) HARRELL, LINDY E UNIV OF ALA. AT BIRMINGHAM UAB STATION BIRMINGHAM, ALA 35294 Alzheimer's disease--A multidisciplinary approach

P01AG-06569-05 0005 (AGE) HALEY, WILLIAM E Alzheimer's disease--A multidisciplinary approach Caregiver coping--Racial and longitudinal effects

P01AG-06569-05 0006 (AGE) FOLKS, DAVID G Alzheimer's disease--A multidisciplinary approach Depression, life quality, and cognition in Alzheimer's dementia

P01AG-06569-05 0007 (AGE) POWERS, RICHARD Alzheimer's disease--A multidisciplinary approach Immunocytochemistry of tau epitopes--Aging and Alzheimer's autopsy

P01AG-06569-05 0008 (AGE) CASEY, MICHAEL Alzheimer's disease--A multidisciplinary approach Hippocampus morphology in aging

P01AG-06569-05 0009 (AGE) JOHNSON, GAIL Alzheimer's disease--A multidisciplinary approach Proteolysis and phosphorylation of MAPS in aging brain

P01AG-06569-05 0010 (AGE) HARRELL, LINDY E Alzheimer's disease--A multidisciplinary approach Hippocampal neuronal reorganization and phosphoinositol metabolism

P01AG-06569-05 9001 (AGE) HARRELL, LINDY E Alzheimer's disease--A multidisciplinary approach Clinical core

P01AG-06569-05 9002 (AGE) POWERS, RICHARD Alzheimer's disease--A multidisciplinary approach Tissue procurement and immunocytochemistry core

P01AG-06569-05 0001 (AGE) JOPE, RICHARD S Alzheimer's disease--A multidisciplinary approach Modulation of the release of membrane-bound choline

P01AG-06569-05 0004 (AGE) BINDER, LESTER I Alzheimer's disease--A multidisciplinary approach Microtubule proteins in Alzheimer's disease

R01AG-06584-06 (HUD) GIVEN, CHARLES W MICHIGAN STATE UNIVERSITY DEPARTMENT OF FAMILY PRACTICE EAST LANSING, MI 48824 Caregiver responses to managing elderly patients at home

R01AG-06601-05 (NEUC) KOSIK, KENNETH S BRIGHAM & WOMEN'S HOSPITAL 75 FRANCIS STREET, THORN 1226 BOSTON, MASS 02115 The pathobiology of tau protein

R37AG-06605-05 (HUD) CORKIN, SUZANNE H MASSACHUSETTS INST TECHNOLOGY E10-003A CAMBRIDGE, MA 02139 Theoretical analysis of learning in age-related disease

R01AG-06633-05 (NLS) SAPOLSKY, ROBERT M STANFORD UNIVERSITY STANFORD, CA 94305 Aging and hippocampal neuron loss -- Role of glucocorticoid

R01AG-06641-05 (NEUB) ROBBINS, NORMAN CASE WESTERN RESERVE UNIV 2119 ABINGTON ROAD CLEVELAND, OH 44106 Plasticity of motor nerve terminals in young & old mice

R37AG-06643-05 (HUD) LIANG, JERSEY UNIVERSITY OF MICHIGAN 300 NORTH INGALLS BLDG ANN ARBOR, MI 48109-2007 Well-being among the American and Japanese elderly

R01AG-06647-04A1 (NEUB) MORRISON, JOHN H MT SINAI SCHOOL OF MEDICINE ONE GUSTAVE L LEVY PLACE NEW YORK, N Y 10029 Cortico-cortical loss in Alzheimers disease in the aged

R01AG-06656-05 (NEUB) YOUNKIN, STEVEN G CASE WESTERN RESERVE UNIV SCHOOL OF MEDICINE CLEVELAND, OHIO 44106 AChE, ChaT & cholinergic neurons in aging & Alzheimer's disease

R01AG-06665-04 (RAP) HORWITZ, BARBARA A UNIVERSITY OF CALIFORNIA DAVIS, CA 95616-8519 Exercise effects on responses to cold in aging rats

U01AG-06781-05 (AGE) LARSON, ERIC B UNIVERSITY OF WASHINGTON DEPT OF MEDICINE, RG-20 SEATTLE, WA 98195 Alzheimer's disease patient registry

U01AG-06786-06 (AGE) KURLAND, LEONARD T MAYO FOUNDATION 200 FIRST STREET SOUTHWEST ROCHESTER, MN 55905 alzheimer's disease patient registry

U01AG-06790-06 (AGE) HEYMAN, ALBERT DUKE UNIVERSITY MEDICAL CENTER BOX 3203 DURHAM, NC 27710 Consortium to establish a registry for Alzheimer's disease

U01AG-06790-06 0001 (AGE) MORRIS, JOHN C. Consortium to establish a registry for Alzheimer's disease Clinical component

U01AG-06790-06 0002 (AGE) MOHS, RICHARD C. Consortium to establish a registry for Alzheimer's disease Neuropsychology component

U01AG-06790-06 0003 (AGE) GADO, MOKHTAR H. Consortium to establish a registry for Alzheimer's disease Neuroimaging (MRI) component

U01AG-06790-06 0004 (AGE) MIRRA, SUZANNE S. Consortium to establish a registry for Alzheimer's disease Neuropathology component

U01AG-06790-06 0005 (AGE) VAN BELLE, GERALD Consortium to establish a registry for Alzheimer's disease Methodology and data management

P01AG-06803-05 (AGE) DAVIES, PETER ALBERT EINSTEIN COLL OF MED 1300 MORRIS PARK AVE BRONX, NY 10461 Fundamental studies on Alzheimer's disease

P01AG-06803-05 0001 (AGE) DAVIES, PETER Fundamental studies on Alzheimer's disease Studies of a new protein in the Alzheimer's brain

P01AG-06803-05 0002 (AGE) SHAFIT-ZAGARDO, BRIDGET Fundamental studies on Alzheimer's disease Molecular probes for Alzheimer neurofibrillary tangles

P01AG-06803-05 0003 (AGE) DICKSON, DENNIS Fundamental studies on Alzheimer's disease Pathobiology of senile plaques and cerebral amyloid

P01AG-06803-05 0005 (AGE) KSIEZAK-REDING, HANNA Fundamental studies on Alzheimer's disease Tau proteins in Alzheimer's disease

P01AG-06803-05 9001 (AGE) DAVIES, PETER Fundamental studies on Alzheimer's disease Core

R01AG-06806-04 (HUD) KIRASIC, KATHLEEN C UNIVERSITY OF S CAROLINA DEPT. OF PSYCHOLOGY COLUMBIA, SC 29208 Aging, cognitive processing, and learning abilities

R29AG-06810-05 (EDC) GOING, SCOTT B UNIVERSITY OF ARIZONA INA E. GITTINGS BUILDING TUCSON, ARIZONA 85721 Fat and fat free body composition in older men and women

P01AG-06815-05 (GER) PECK, WILLIAM A JEWISH HOSPITAL OF ST LOUIS 216 SOUTH KINGS HIGHWAY ST LOUIS, MO 63110 Falls and hip fractures-- Causes, risks and outcomes

R37AG-06826-06 (HUD) SALTHOUSE, TIMOTHY A GEORGIA INST OF TECHNOLOGY SCHOOL OF PSYCHOLOGY ATLANTA, GA 30332 Adult age difference in reasoning and spatial abilities

P01AG-06836-04 (GER) MONK, TIMOTHY H WESTERN PSYCH INST & CLINIC 3811 O'HARA STREET PITTSBURGH, PA 15213 Aging, temperature and sleep--Cyclic regulatory mechanisms

P01AG-06836-04 0001 (GER) REYNOLDS, CHARLES F. Aging, temperature and sleep--Cyclic regulatory mechanisms Sleep intensity and propensity in later life

P01AG-06836-04 0002 (GER) MONK, TIMOTHY H. Aging, temperature and sleep--Cyclic regulatory mechanisms Circadian rhythms in the old old

P01AG-06836-04 0003 (GER) MONK, TIMOTHY H. Aging, temperature and sleep--Cyclic regulatory mechanisms Phase shift tolerance in the old old

P01AG-06836-04 0004 (GER) KITTRELL, E. MELANIE Aging, temperature and sleep--Cyclic regulatory mechanisms Circadian rhythms and thermoregulation in elderly rats

P01AG-06836-04 9001 (GER) MONK, TIMOTHY H Aging, temperature and sleep--Cyclic regulatory mechanisms Core--Sleep and time isolation laboratories

P01AG-06836-04 9002 (GER) MONK, TIMOTHY H. Aging, temperature and sleep--Cyclic regulatory mechanisms Core--Biostatistics and subject recruitment

R01AG-06841-05 (CMS) BEIDLER, LLOYD M FLORIDA STATE UNIVERSITY DEPT OF BIOLOGICAL SCIENCE TALLAHASSEE, FLA 32306 The effect of age on taste

R29AG-06849-04 (HUD) OSTERGAARD, ARNE L UNIV OF CALIF., SAN DIEGO 9500 GILMAN DRIVE LA JOLLA, CALIF 92093-0603 Priming & memory in amnesia & Alzheimers disease

R29AG-06854-04 (IMS) SCHWAB, RISE CORNELL UNIV MEDICAL COLLEGE 1300 YORK AVENUE NEW YORK, NY 10021 Impaired proliferation of T lymphocytes from aged humans

R01AG-06860-05 (GMA) CATHCART, EDGAR S BEDFORD VA HOSPITAL 200 SPRINGS ROAD BEDFORD, MA 01730 Amyloid, aging and diet

P01AG-06872-05 (BCA) BOWMAN, BARBARA H UNIVERSITY OF TEXAS 7703 FLOYD CURL DR SAN ANTONIO, TX 78284-7762 Molecular genetic mechanisms of aging

P01AG-06872-05 0001 (BCA) BOWMAN, BARBARA H Molecular genetic mechanisms of aging Transferrin and haptoglobin gene expression during aging

P01AG-06872-05 0002 (BCA) YANG, FUNMEI Molecular genetic mechanisms of aging Regulation of acute phase reactant genes during aging

P01AG-06872-05 0003 (BCA) JAGADEESWARAN, PURDUR Molecular genetic mechanisms of aging Factor IX gene transcriptional regulation during aging

P01AG-06872-05 0004 (BCA) CHATTERJEE, BANDANA Molecular genetic mechanisms of aging Hepatic androgen sensitivity during aging

P01AG-06872-05 9001 (BCA) JAGADEESWARAN, PUDUR Molecular genetic mechanisms of aging Core--Transgenic mouse

R01AG-06886-05 (MGN) MC GUE, MATTHEW K UNIVERSITY OF MINNESOTA 75 EAST RIVER ROAD MINNEAPOLIS, MN 55455 A twin study of normal aging

R01AG-06912-05 (SRC) DUCKLES, SUE P UNIVERSITY OF CALIFORNIA DEPT. OF PHARMACOLOGY IRVINE, CALIF 92717 Vascular adrenergic responsiveness during aging

R01AG-06929-05 (SRC) PREUSS, HARRY G GEORGETOWN UNIV SCH OF MED 4000 RESERVOIR ROAD,. N W WASHINGTON, DC 20007 Macronutrients on age-related hypertension

R01AG-06942-05 (SRC) VIRMANI, RENU ARMED FORCES INST OF PATHOLGOY 14TH STREET & ALASKA AVENUE NW WASHINGTON, DC 20306 Mechanisms responsible for age-related hypertension

R01AG-06943-05 (SRC) VLASSARA, HELEN ROCKEFELLER UNIVERSITY 1230 YORK AVE NEW YORK, NY 10021 Glycosylated proteins in age and hypertension

R01AG-06945-05 (EDC) BLAIR, STEVEN N INSTITUTE FOR AEROBICS RES 12330 PRESTON ROAD DALLAS, TX 75230 Impact of physical fitness and exercise on health

R01AG-06946-05A2 (BM) ORME, IAN M COLORADO STATE UNIVERSITY FORT COLLINS, CO 80523 Aging and immunity to tuberculosis

R44AG-06957-03 (HUD) LEIRER, VON O DECISION SYSTEMS 1473 MIRAMONTE BLDG #2 LOS ALTOS, CA 94022 Computerized medication reminder system for the elderly

R01AG-06969-04A1 (NEUB) BINDER, LESTER I UNIVERSITY OF ALABAMA UAB

PROJECT NO., ORGANIZATIONAL UNIT., INVESTIGATOR, ADDRESS, TITLE

STATION BIRMINGHAM, AL 35294 MAPs--Segregation and function
R37AG-07001-05 (HUD) LAWTON, M POWELL PHILADELPHIA GERIATRIC CENTER 5301 OLD YORK ROAD PHILADELPHIA, PA 19141 Affect, normal aging, and personal competence
R29AG-07004-05 (RAP) KENNEY, WILLIAM L PENNSYLVANIA STATE UNIV 102 NOLL LABORATORY UNIVERSITY PARK, PA 16802 Heat stress and thermoregulation: age and gender effects
R37AG-07025-05 (AGE) MANTON, KENNETH G DUKE UNIVERSITY 2117 CAMPUS DRIVE DURHAM, N C 27706 Forecasting life expectancy and active life
Z01AG-07030-03 (EDBP) BROCK, D B NIA, NIH NHANES III -- Health of older persons
Z01AG-07040-02 (EDBP) WHITE, L R NIA, NIH Honolulu aging study
R01AG-07046-25 (PB) HULTQUIST, DONALD E UNIVERSITY OF MICHIGAN 1301 CATHERINE ROAD ANN ARBOR, MI 48109-0606 Redox systems of erythrocytes
R01AG-07057-02 (MET) JACKSON, RODWIN A MIDDLESEX HOSP/COBBOLD LABS MORTIMER STREET LONDON W1, UK Normal aging and diabetes--Their metabolic distinction
R29AG-07069-05 (BPO) NORMILE, HOWARD J LAFAYETTE CLINIC 951 E LAFAYETTE DETROIT, MI 48207 Animal models of dementia--Neurotransmitter interactions
P01AG-07094-05 (AGE) WALLACE, ROBERT B UNIVERSITY OF IOWA 2800 STEINDLER IOWA CITY, IA 52242 Teaching nursing home
P01AG-07094-05 0001 (AGE) WALLACE, ROBERT B Teaching nursing home Case control study--Environmental risk factors in Parkinson's disease
P01AG-07094-05 0002 (AGE) SOWERS, MARYFRAN Teaching nursing home Bone density study
P01AG-07094-05 0003 (AGE) RUSSELL, DANIEL W Teaching nursing home Longitudinal study of caretakers of Alzheimer's patients
P01AG-07094-05 9001 (AGE) WALLACE, ROBERT B Teaching nursing home Core
R01AG-07113-05 (EDC) MEIER, DIANE E MOUNT SINAI MEDICAL CENTER BOX 1070 NEW YORK, NY 10029 Influence of race and age on bone homeostasis
R01AG-07114-05 (AGE) GILCHREST, BARBARA A BOSTON UNIVERSITY SCH OF MED 80 EAST CONCORD STREET BOSTON, MA 02118 Aging--Cell growth and differentiation
R01AG-07114-05 0002 (AGE) CAMPISI, JUDITH Aging--Cell growth and differentiation Cellular senescence and control of oncogene expression
R01AG-07114-05 0003 (AGE) MILLER, RICHARD A Aging--Cell growth and differentiation Activation defects in aging T cells
R01AG-07114-05 0004 (AGE) DOBSON, DEBORAH Aging--Cell growth and differentiation Adipocyte gene expression--Effects of aging in vitro and in vivo
R01AG-07114-05 9001 (AGE) GILCHREST, BARBARA A Aging--Cell growth and differentiation Core
R01AG-07114-05 0001 (AGE) GILCHREST, BARBARA A Aging--Cell growth and differentiation In vivo aging of skin derived cells
P01AG-07123-04 (AGE) SMITH, JAMES R BAYLOR COLLEGE OF MEDICINE ONE BAYLOR PLAZA HOUSTON, TX 77030 Molecular approaches to the study of cellular aging
P01AG-07123-04 0001 (AGE) SMITH, JAMES R Molecular approaches to the study of cellular aging Senescent cell proliferation and gene expression
P01AG-07123-04 0002 (AGE) PEREIRA-SMITH, OLIVIA M Molecular approaches to the study of cellular aging Mechanisms of reversal of senescence in human cells
P01AG-07123-04 0003 (AGE) DARLINGTON, GRETCHEN J Molecular approaches to the study of cellular aging Molecular analysis of fibronectin expression
P01AG-07123-04 0004 (AGE) MOSES, ROBB E Molecular approaches to the study of cellular aging Genetic defects in human aging
P01AG-07123-04 9001 (AGE) SMITH, JAMES R Molecular approaches to the study of cellular aging Core--Microinjection
P01AG-07123-04 9003 (AGE) DARLINGTON, GRETCHEN J Molecular approaches to the study of cellular aging Core--Molecular biology
R29AG-07127-06 (NEUA) PERLMUTTER, LYNN S UNIV OF SOUTHERN CALIFORNIA 2025 ZONAL AVENUE LOS ANGELES, CA 90033 Calpain and substrates in aged and Alzheimer brains
R29AG-07135-05 (PHRA) GALINSKY, RAYMOND E UNIVERSITY OF UTAH 301 SKAGGS HALL SALT LAKE CITY, UTAH 84112 Ethanol, the aging liver, and drug sulfation
R01AG-07137-05 (HUD) MC ARDLE, J JACK UNIVERSITY OF VIRGINIA GILMER HALL CHARLOTTESVILLE, VA 22903-2477 Growth curves of adult intelligence modeled with the human
R01AG-07139-04 (OBM) JETTE, ALAN M NEW ENGLAND RESEARCH INSTITUTE 9 GALEN STREET WATERTOWN, MA 02172 Oral health of older adults
R29AG-07141-05 (NEUB) CLAIBORNE, BRENDA J UNIVERSITY OF TEXAS DIVISION OF LIFE SCIENCES SAN ANTONIO, TEXAS 78285 Age-related structural changes in mammalian neurons
R01AG-07146-03 (EDC) BARON, JOHN A DARTMOUTH MEDICAL SCHOOL HANOVER, NH 03756 Fracture epidemiology and outcomes in the elderly
R01AG-07178-04 (EDC) ALLMAN, RICHARD M UNIVERSITY OF ALABAMA UNIVERSITY STATION BIRMINGHAM, ALABAMA 35294 Pressure sores among bedridden hospitalized elderly
R29AG-07179-05 (HUD) CHATTERS, LINDA M UNIVERSITY OF MICHIGAN SCHOOL OF PUBLIC HEALTH ANN ARBOR, MI 48109-2029 Subjective well-being of older blacks
R29AG-07180-05 (RAP) MAZZEO, ROBERT S UNIVERSITY OF COLORADO BOX 354 BOULDER, CO 80309-0354 Catecholamine response with age and training
R37AG-07181-05 (EDC) BARRETT-CONNOR, ELIZABETH L UNIV OF CALIF, SAN DIEGO LA JOLLA, CA 92093 Study of risk factors for osteoporosis in the elderly
R37AG-07182-05 (EDC) MC KINLAY, JOHN B NEW ENGLAND RESEARCH INST INC. 9 GALEN STREEN WATERTOWN, MA 02172 Pathways to provision of care for frail older persons
R01AG-07195-03S1 (AGE) FORD, AMASA B CASE WESTERN RESERVE UNIV SCHOOL OF MEDICINE CLEVELAND, OH 44106 Cleveland GAO study of the elderly
R37AG-07198-05 (SDI) MANTON, KENNETH G DUKE UNIVERSITY 2117 CAMPUS DRIVE DURHAM, NC 27706 Functional and health changes of the elderly, 1982-1988
R01AG-07218-05 (MEP) HERMAN, BRIAN A UNC AT CHAPEL HILL 232 SWING BLDG CB # 7090 CHAPEL HILL, N C 27599 Mechanisms of cell death in hepatocytes
R01AG-07225-03 (CVB) WEI, JEANNE Y BETH ISRAEL HOSPITAL 330 BROOKLINE AVENUE BOSTON, MA 02215 Orthostatic hypotension in older persons
P01AG-07232-03 (AGE) MAYEUX, RICHARD P NEUROLOGICAL INSTITUTE 710 WEST 168TH STREET NEW YORK, N Y 10032 The epidemiology of dementia in an urban community
P01AG-07232-03 0001 (AGE) GURLAND, BARRY J The epidemiology of dementia in an urban community The North Manhattan Aging project
P01AG-07232-03 0002 (AGE) MOHR, J P The epidemiology of dementia in an urban community Incidence of dementia in stroke
P01AG-07232-03 0003 (AGE) MAYEUX, RICHARD P The epidemiology of dementia in an urban community Epidemiology of dementia in idiopathic Parkinson's disease
P01AG-07232-03 9001 (AGE) STERN, YAAKOV The epidemiology of dementia in an urban community Core--Clinical, diagnostic, epidemiology
P01AG-07232-03 9002 (AGE) GOLDMAN, JAMES E The epidemiology of dementia in an urban community Core-Neuropathology
P01AG-07347-04 (AGE) GILDEN, DONALD H UNIV OF COLORADO HLTH SCI CTR 4200 EAST 9TH AVE, BOX B182 DENVER, CO 80262 Chronic neurologic disease produced by neurotropic virus
P01AG-07347-04 0001 (AGE) GLIDEN, DONALD H Chronic neurologic disease produced by neurotropic virus Morbidity in the aging--Persistence of varicella-zoster virus
P01AG-07347-04 0002 (AGE) VAFGI, ABBAS Chronic neurologic disease produced by neurotropic virus Varicella-zoster virus gene library and subunit vaccine
P01AG-07347-04 0003 (AGE) LEVIN, MYRON J Chronic neurologic disease produced by neurotropic virus Immunization to prevent herpes zoster in the elderly
P01AG-07347-04 0004 (AGE) PIZER, LEWIS I Chronic neurologic disease produced by neurotropic virus Analysis of HSV interactions with the nervous system
P01AG-07347-04 0005 (AGE) SARNOW, PETER Chronic neurologic disease produced by neurotropic virus Analysis of an untranslated region of poliovirus RNA
P01AG-07347-04 0006 (AGE) MURRAY, RONALD S Chronic neurologic disease produced by neurotropic virus Aging and the pathogenesis of Theiler's virus infection in mice
R29AG-07352-04 (ORTH) LARISH, DOUGLAS D ARIZONA STATE UNIVERSITY RM 210 TEMPE, AZ 85287 Economical walking in the aged
R29AG-07359-04 (CTY) BURMER, GLENNA C UNIVERSITY OF WASHINGTON DEPT OF PATHOLOGY SM-30 SEATTLE, WA 98195 Cloning of the Werner's syndrome defect
R01AG-07363-04 (HUD) WEISS, ROBERT S UNIVERSITY OF MASSACHUSETTS DOWNTOWN CAMPUS, ROOM 1107 BOSTON, MASS 02125 Transition to retirement from managerial roles
R01AG-07367-04 (NEUA) ROGERS, JOSEPH P.O. BOX 1278 13220 N. 105TH AVE. SUN CITY, AZ 85372 Complement activation in Alzheimer's disease pathogenesis
R01AG-07370-03 (EDC) STERN, YAAKOV NEUROLOGICAL INSTITUTE 710 WEST 168TH STREET NEW YORK, NEW YORK 10032 Predictors of severity in Alzheimers disease
R37AG-07388-04 (NTN) YOUNG, VERNON R MASSACHUSETTS INST OF TECH 77 MASSACHUSETTS AVENUE CAMBRIDGE, MA 02139 Regulation of energy metabolism in aging man
R01AG-07410-01A3 (HUD) REITZES, DONALD C GEORGIA STATE UNIVERSITY UNIVERSITY PLAZA ATLANTA, GA 30303 Roles and self--Factors in development and retirement
R29AG-07424-04 (NEUB) ECKENSTEIN, FELIX P OREGON HEALTH SCIENCES UNIV 3181 SW SAM JACKSON PARK RD PORTLAND, OREGON 97201 Neurotrophic support in aging & Alzheimer's disease
R01AG-07425-04 (EDC) RICE, DOROTHY P KAISER PERMANENTE 3451 PIEDMONT AVENUE OAKLAND, CA 94611 Epidemiology of chronic disease in the oldest old
R01AG-07429-03 (CBY) HEPPEL, LEON A CORNELL UNIVERSITY ITHACA, NY 14853 biochemical changes in senescent human fibroblasts
R01AG-07433-03 (EDC) REID, L DOUGLAS KAISER FOUNDATION HOSPITALS CTR/HLTH RES: 4610 SE BELMONT PORTLAND, OR 97215 Antihypertensive drug use and functioning in the elderly
R01AG-07444-04 (CBY) WANG, YU-HWA E LADY DAVIS INST FOR MED RES 3755 CHEMIN COTE STE CATHERINE MONTREAL, QUEBEC H3T1E2 CANADA Growth control in aging fibroblasts
R01AG-07449-03 (EDC) TINETTI, MARY E YALE UNIVERSITY PO BOX 3333 NEW HAVEN, CT 06510 Injury and functional decline in elderly fallers
R01AG-07450-03 (CBY) MACIAG, THOMAS AMERICAN RED CROSS 15601 CRABBS BRANCH WAY ROCKVILLE, MD 20855 Human endothelial cell senescence genes
R29AG-07452-04 (REB) MATT, DENNIS W MEDICAL COLLEGE OF VIRGINIA BOX 34 MCV STATION RICHMOND, VA 23298 Reproductive aging and the hypothalamic-pituitary axis
R29AG-07465-04 (BEM) ALDWIN, CAROLYN M UNIVERSITY OF CALIFORNIA DAVIS, CA 95616 Psychosocial factors affecting health among older men
R01AG-07466-02 (HUD) PERLMUTTER, MARION UNIVERSITY OF MICHIGAN 300 NORTH INGALLS ANN ARBOR, MI 48109-0406 Age and activity effects on adult congnition
R01AG-07467-05 (TOX) OOKHTENS, MURAD UNIV OF SOUTHERN CALIFORNIA 1975 ZONAL AVE LOS ANGELES, CA 90033 Aging effects on efflux and turnover of hepatic glutathione
R01AG-07469-04 (HUD) MANTON, KENNETH G DUKE UNIVERSITY 2117 CAMPUS DRIVE DURHAM, N C 27706 Active life expectancy in old and oldest-old populations
R01AG-07472-04 (PBC) DICE, JAMES F, JR TUFTS UNIVERSITY 136 HARRISON AVENUE BOSTON, MA 02111 Degradation of abnormal proteins in senescent fibroblasts
R01AG-07476-04 (HUD) LEVENSON, ROBERT W UNIVERSITY OF CALIFORNIA 3210 TOLMAN HALL BERKELEY, CA 94720 Aging and effective

PROJECT NO., ORGANIZATIONAL UNIT., INVESTIGATOR, ADDRESS, TITLE

marital functioning

R29AG-07480-04 (EDC) IDLER, ELLEN L INST FOR HEALTH CARE POLICY 30 COLLEGE AVENUE NEW BRUNSWICK, NJ 08903 Epidemiology of chronic pain & self-assessed health

R44AG-07522-02 (BPO) MC GOWAN, EDWARD J EJ MCGOWAN & ASSOCIATES, INC 310 WEST LAKE ST, SUITE 110 ELMHURST, IL 60126-1530 Biofeedback system for urinary and fecal incontinence

P01AG-07542-05 (AMS) PARFITT, A MICHAEL HENRY FORD HOSPITAL 2799 W GRAND BOULEVARD DETROIT, MI 48202 Bone remodeling --Amount/quality of bone and fractures

R01AG-07547-03 (NEUB) PERETZ, BERTRAM UNIVERSITY OF KENTUCKY DPT OF PHYSIOLOGY/BIOPHYSICS LEXINGTON, KY 40536-0084 Neuron viability in the adult nervous system

R01AG-07552-04 (NEUA) PERRY, GEORGE CASE WESTERN RESERVE UNIV 2085 ADELBERT ROAD CLEVELAND, OH 44106 Amyloid precursor in Alzheimer disease

R37AG-07554-04 (HAR) WILLOTT, JAMES F NORTHERN ILLINOIS UNIVERSITY DEPT OF PSYCHOLOGY DEKALB, ILL 60115 Aging and central auditory system morphology

R01AG-07562-03 (EDC) GANGULI, MARY UNIVERSITY OF PITTSBURGH 130 DESOTO STREET PITTSBURGH, PA 15261 Epidemiology of dementia--A prospective community study

R01AG-07569-03 (HUD) PARASURAMAN, RAJA CATHOLIC UNIVERSITY OF AMERICA WASHINGTON, DC 20064 Attention in aging and early Alzheimer's dementia

R01AG-07572-04 (ORTH) KALU, DIKE N UNIV OF TEXAS HLTH SCI CTR 7703 FLOYD CURL DR SAN ANTONIO, TX 78284-7756 Modulation of aging bone loss by anabolic hormones

R01AG-07584-04 (EDC) KUKULL, WALTER A UNIVERSITY OF WASHINGTON SEATTLE, WA 98195 Genetic differences in Alzheimers cases and controls

R01AG-07591-03S1 (BNP) KOZIKOWSKI, ALAN P UNIVERSITY OF PITTSBURGH 1101 CHEVRON SCIENCE CENTER PITTSBURGH, PA 15260 Agents for the treatment of memory & learning disorders

R01AG-07592-03 (MET) BARNARD, ROY J UNIVERSITY OF CALFORNIA 405 HILGARD AVENUE LOS ANGELES, CALIF 90024 Mechanisms of aging induced insulin resistance

R29AG-07597-04 (HUD) STULL, DONALD E UNIVERSITY OF AKRON DEPT. OF SOCIOLOGY AKRON, OH 44325 Caring for elders--Impact of social support and burden

R01AG-07603-04 (GMA) KAWANISHI, HIDERNORI ROBERT WOOD JOHNSON MEDICAL SC 1 ROBERT WOOD JOHNSON PL NEW BRUNSWICK, NJ 08903 Immune interventions of aged gut mucosal T cell defects

R01AG-07607-02 (HUD) BLANCHARD-FIELDS, FREDDA H LOUISIANA STATE UNIVERSITY 236 AUDOBON HALL BATON ROUGE, LA 70803-5501 Attributional processes in adulthood and aging

R01AG-07618-03 (EDC) BEYENE, YEWOUBDAR UNIVERSITY OF CALIFORNIA 1350 SEVENTH AVE SAN FRANCISCO, CA 94143 Menopause, aging & osteoporosis--Cross-cultural inquiry

R01AG-07624-03 (PTHA) CHUI, HELENA C DEPT. OF NEUROLOGY 12838 ERICKSON STREET DOWNEY, CA 90242 Alzheimer's disease and cerebral amyloid angiopathy

R01AG-07631-04 (PHRA) BRATER, DONALD C WISHARD MEMORIAL HOSPITAL 1001 W. 10TH ST. INDIANAPOLIS, IN 46202-2879 Clinical pharmacology of NSAIDS in the elderly

R37AG-07637-03 (SSP) HERMALIN, ALBERT I POPULATION STUDIES CENTER 1225 SOUTH UNIVERSITY AVE ANN ARBOR, MI 48104-2590 Comparative study of the elderly in four Asian countries

R01AG-07648-02 (PYB) GOLD, PAUL E UNIVERSITY OF VIRGINIA CHARLOTTESVILLE, VA 22903-247 Aging and memory

R29AG-07651-04 (SSP) GARBER, ALAN M STANFORD UNIVERSITY MED SCH OFFICE BLDG, X-214 STANFORD, CA 94305-5475 Health economics of aging

R01AG-07654-04A1 (HUD) FISK, ARTHUR D GA INST OF TECHNOLOGY ATLANTA, GA 30332-0170 Automatic and controlled processing and aging

R01AG-07660-05 (NTN) GOLDBERG, ANDREW P VETERANS ADMINISTRATION MED CT 3900 LOCH RAVEN BLVD BALTIMORE, MD 21218 Aerobic capacity and metabolic function in seniors

P01AG-07669-03 (AGE) RAINWATER, LEE P HARVARD UNIVERSITY 33 KIRKLAND STREET CAMBRIDGE, MA 02138 Comparative life course research on economic well-being

P01AG-07669-03 0001 (AGE) RAINWATER, LEE P. Comparative life course research on economic well-being Economic well-being of the elderly

P01AG-07669-03 0002 (AGE) SORENSON, ANNAMETTE Comparative life course research on economic well-being Life course variations in women's economic well-being

P01AG-07669-03 0003 (AGE) RAINWATER, LEE P. Comparative life course research on economic well-being Economic well-being over the life course

P01AG-07669-03 9001 (AGE) RAINWATER, LEE P. Comparative life course research on economic well-being Core--Construction of a multi-national cohort database

P01AG-07669-03 9002 (AGE) SMEEDLING, TIMOTHY M. Comparative life course research on economic well-being Core--Institutional data on cash and in-kind income sources

R01AG-07671-04 (NEUB) SCHMECHEL, DONALD E DUKE UNIV MEDICAL CENTER BOX 3145 DURHAM, NC 27710 An animal model of cholinergic deficiency

R29AG-07676-02 (HUD) MITTMAN, BRIAN S RAND CORPORATION 1700 MAIN STREET SANTA MONICA, CA 90406 Reactions-older workers promotion & employment prospects

R01AG-07677-03 (NEUB) SHAFIT-ZAGARDO, BRIDGET ALBERT EINSTEIN COLLEGE OF MED 1300 MORRIS PARK AVENUE BRONX, NY 10461 Second messengers in astrocytes and precursor cells

P01AG-07687-04 (AGE) SIMON, MELVIN I CALIFORNIA INST OF TECHNOLOGY DIVISION OF BIOLOGY PASADENA, CALIFORNIA 91125 Aging in the nervous system of transgenic mice

R01AG-07695-04 (AGE) LAL, HARBANS TEXAS COLLEGE OF OSTEO MED 3500 CAMP BOWIE BLVD. FORT WORTH, TX 76107 Neurobehavioral & immunological markers of aging

R01AG-07700-04 (AGE) FREDMAN, EITAN MED COLL OF PENNSYLVANIA 3200 HENRY AVENUE PHILADELPHIA, PA 19129 Aging, protein kinase C and serotonin release

R01AG-07711-04 (AGE) REISER, KAREN M CALIFORNIA PRIMATE RES CENTER UNIVERSITY OF CALIFORNIA-DAVIS DAVIS, CA 95616 Collagen crosslinks--Biomarkers of aging

PROJECT NO., ORGANIZATIONAL UNIT., INVESTIGATOR, ADDRESS, TITLE

R01AG-07719-04 (AGE) MURASKO, DONNA M MEDICAL COLLEGE OF PA 3300 HENRY AVENUE PHILADELPHIA, PA 19129 Immune and neurologic parameters as biomarkers of aging

R01AG-07723-04 (AGE) GALLOP, PAUL M HARVARD SCHOOL OF DENTAL MED 188 LONGWOOD AVENUE BOSTON, MASS 02115 Biomarkers of aging--Circulating and deposited osteocalcin

R01AG-07724-04 (AGE) WOLF, NORMAN S UNIVERSITY OF WASHINGTON DEPT OF PATHOLOGY SM-30 SEATTLE, WA 98195 Cell renewal, size & cloning as biomarkers of aging

R01AG-07732-04 (AGE) DIAMOND, JACK MC MASTER UNIVERSITY 1200 MAIN STREET HAMILTON, ONTARIO L8N 3Z5 Peripheral NGF-related sensory markers of aging in skin

R01AG-07735-04 (AGE) OLTON, DAVID S JOHNS HOPKINS UNIVERSITY 34TH AND CHARLES STREETS BALTIMORE, MD 21218 Behavioral and physiological biomarkers of aging

R01AG-07736-05 (AGE) DAVIS, PAUL J ALBANY MEDICAL COLLEGE 47 NEW SCOTLAND AVENUE ALBANY, N Y 12208 Cellular biomarkers of aging

R01AG-07739-04 (AGE) BUSBEE, DAVID L TEXAS A&M UNIVERSITY COLLEGE STATION, TX 77843 DNA polymerase alpha expression--A biomarker of aging

R01AG-07747-04 (AGE) BRONSON, RODERICK T TUFTS VETERINARY DIAGNOSTIC LA 305 SOUTH STREET JAMAICA PLAIN, MA 02130 Age related lesions as biomarkers of aging

R01AG-07750-04 (AGE) RANDERATH, KURT BAYLOR COLLEGE OF MEDICINE ONE BAYLOR PLAZA HOUSTON, TX 77030 DNA modifications (I-compounds) as biomarkers of aging

R01AG-07752-04 (AGE) SONNTAG, WILLIAM E BOWMAN GRAY SCHOOL OF MEDICINE 300 S HAWTHORNE RD WINSTON-SALEM, N C 27103 Growth hormone (GH) & GH-dependent biomarkers of aging

R01AG-07767-04 (AGE) LANDFIELD, PHILIP W UNIVERSITY OF KENTUCKY CHANDLER MEDICAL CENTER LEXINGTON, KY 40536 Biomarkers of brain aging

R01AG-07771-05 (NEUB) NORTH, WILLIAM G DARTMOUTH MEDICAL SCHOOL DEPT. OF PHYSIOLOGY HANOVER, NH 03756 Neuropeptides in central disorders-- Alzheimer's disease

R01AG-07772-04 (RAP) GUILLEMINAULT, CHRISTIAN STANFORD UNIVERSITY SCIENCES-BLDG TD STANFORD, CA 94305 Sleep, circadian rhythms, activity, and the heart

R01AG-07778-02 (HUD) NYDEGGER, CORINNE N UNIVERSITY OF CALIFORNIA 1350-7TH AVENUE/BOX 0850 SAN FRANCISCO, CA 94143 Intergenerational relations in the business family

R01AG-07793-04 (NEUA) JAGUST, WILLIAM J UNIVERSITY OF CALIFORNIA BIOLOGY & MEDICINE DIVISION BERKELEY, CA 94720 Longitudinal SPECT and PET studies of dementia

R01AG-07794-03 (HUD) STOLLER, ELEANOR P S U N Y DEPARTMENT OF SOCIOLOGY PLATTSBURGH, NY 12901 Self care-lay response to illness

R01AG-07795-02 (BCE) MILLER, MARILYN M ROYAL VICTORIA HOSPITAL 687 PINE AVENUE WEST MONTREAL, QUEBEC CANADA H3A 1A Neuroendocrine regulation in the aging hypothalamus

R01AG-07801-04 (TOX) MONTGOMERY, MARK R JAMES A HALEY VETERANS HOSP 13000 N BRUCE B. DOWNS BLVD TAMPA, FLA 33612 Toxicology of pulmonary oxidant injury in aging

R01AG-07805-03 (NLS) GRIFFITH, WILLIAM H, III TEXAS A&M UNIVERSITY COLLEGE OF MEDICINE COLLEGE STATION, TX 77843 Physiology of cholinergic basal forebrain neurons

R01AG-07806-02 (CMS) LABOV, WILLIAM LINGUISTICS LABORATORY 418 SERVICE DRIVE PHILADELPHIA, PA 19104-6021 Longitudinal study of language in normal aging

R01AG-07812-02 (HUD) GILINSKY, ALBERTA S UNIVERSITY OF BRIDGEPORT 185 MINE HILL ROAD FAIRFIELD, CT 06430 Judgment and reasoning across the life span

R01AG-07820-02 (HUD) MORRIS, JOHN N HEBREW REHAB CTR AGED 1200 CENTRE STREET BOSTON, MA 02131 High risk elders and community residence

R37AG-07823-03 (HUD) KAHANA, EVA F CASE WESTERN RESERVE UNIVERSIT MATHER MEMORIAL BLDG., #226 CLEVELAND, OH 44106 Adaptation to frailty among dispersed elderly

R01AG-07831-03 (NTN) ERSHLER, WILLIAM B UNIVERISTY OF WISCONSIN 425 HENRY MALL MADISON, WI 53706 Calorie restriction and aging in non-human primates

R01AG-07849-03 (HUD) HENRETTA, JOHN C UNIVERSITY OF FLORIDA 3357 TURLINGTON HALL GAINESVILLE, FL 32611 Joint retirement in two-worker couples

R29AG-07854-04 (HUD) MITCHELL, DAVID B SOUTHERN METHODIST UNIVERSITY DEPT. OF PSYCHOLOGY DALLAS, TX 75275 Normal aging--Evidence for multiple memory systems

R29AG-07855-04 (NEUA) PETERSON, CHRISTINE UNIV. OF SOUTHERN CALIFORNIA 3715 MCCLINTOCK AVE LOS ANGELES, CALIF 90089-0191 Altered calcium homeostasis to diagnose Alzheimer disease

R29AG-07857-04 (NTN) POEHLMAN, ERIC T UNIVERSITY OF VERMONT METABOLIC UNIT BURLINGTON, VT 05405 Physical activity & energy metabolism in aging man

R01AG-07861-04 (EDC) FELSON, DAVID T BOSTON UNIV SCHOOL OF MEDICINE 80 E CONCORD-ARTHRITIS CTR A20 BOSTON, MA 02118 Osteoarthritis and physical disability in the elderly

R01AG-07886-04 (HUD) HOLLAND, AUDREY L UNIVERSITY OF ARIZONA TUCSON, AZ 85721 Discourse and everyday remembering in Alzheimer diseases

R01AG-07891-03 (VISA) BLANKS, JANET M DOHENY EYE FOUNDATION 1355 SAN PABLO ST LOS ANGELES, CA 90033 Mechanisms 0f retinal defects in alzheimers disease

R01AG-07892-03 (NEUB) MORGAN, DAVID G UNIVERSITY OF S CALIFORNIA 3715 MCCLINTOCK AVE MC 0191 LOS ANGELES, CA 90089-0191 Changes in brain astrocytes with aging

R29AG-07904-02 (SSP) WILLIAMS, DAVID R YALE UNIVERSITY 140 PROSPECT ST/PO BOX 1965 NEW HAVEN, CT 06520 SES differences in morbidity/mortality in mid/late life

R01AG-07906-03 (NEUA) GROWDON, JOHN H MASSACHUSETTS GENERAL HOSPITAL BOSTON, MA 02114 Phospholipid abnormalities in Alzheimer's disease

R29AG-07907-05 (HUD) MC AULEY, EDWARD UNIVERSITY OF ILLINOIS S GOODWIN AVENUE URBANA, IL 61801 Self-efficacy cognitions, exercise, and aging

R35AG-07909-03 (AGE) FINCH, CALEB E UNIV. OF SOUTHERN CALIFORNIA UNIVERSITY PARK, MC 0191 LOS ANGELES, CA 90089-0191 Leadership and excellence in Alzheimer's disease

R35AG-07909-03 0001 (AGE) FINCH, CALEB E Leadership and excellence in Alzheimer's disease Gene regulation in hippocampus in Alzheimer's disease

R35AG-07909-03 0002 (AGE) MORGAN, DAVID G Leadership and excellence in Alzheimer's disease Mechanisms of glial hyperactivity

R35AG-07909-03 0003 (AGE) MAY, PATRICK C Leadership and excellence in Alzheimer's disease Pilot project--Corticoids, glutamine synthetase and neurodegeneration

R35AG-07909-03 0004 (AGE) NICHOLS, NANCY R Leadership and excellence in Alzheimer's disease Pilot project--Stress-related changes in brain RNA

R35AG-07909-03 0005 (AGE) JOHNSON, STEVEN A Leadership and excellence in Alzheimer's disease Pilot project--Messenger RNA and interventions into neuronal atrophy

R35AG-07911-04 (AGE) SELKOE, DENNIS J BRIGHAM AND WOMEN'S HOSPITAL 75 FRANCIS STREET BOSTON, MA 02115 Leadership and excellence in Alzheimer's disease

R35AG-07911-04 0001 (AGE) SELKOE, DENNIS J Leadership and excellence in Alzheimer's disease Regional processing of beta-amyloid precursor protein

R35AG-07911-04 0002 (AGE) LEE, GLORIA Leadership and excellence in Alzheimer's disease Studies on human tau protein

R35AG-07911-04 0003 (AGE) KOSIK, KENNETH S Leadership and excellence in Alzheimer's disease Phosphorylation of tau proteins

R35AG-07911-04 0004 (AGE) JOACHIM, CATHERINE L Leadership and excellence in Alzheimer's disease Processing of amyloid protein

R35AG-07911-04 0005 (AGE) SELKOE, DENNIS J Leadership and excellence in Alzheimer's disease Pilot study--Tropic or toxic effects of microinjected beta-amyloid protein

R35AG-07911-04 0006 (AGE) KOSIK, KENNETH S Leadership and excellence in Alzheimer's disease Pilot study--Effects of synthetic beta-amyloid peptides on neurons in culture

R35AG-07911-04 0007 (AGE) LEE, GLORIA Leadership and excellence in Alzheimer's disease Pilot study--Naturally-occuring analogs of Alzheimer's amyloid

R35AG-07911-04 0008 (AGE) KOSIK, KENNETH S Leadership and excellence in Alzheimer's disease Pilot study--Correlates of microtubule-associated proteins with neuronal form

R35AG-07914-03 (AGE) PRICE, DONALD L JOHNS HOPKINS HOSPITAL 600 N WOLFE STREET BALTIMORE, MD 21205 Molecular neuropathology of aging and dementia

R35AG-07914-03 0001 (AGE) PRICE, DONALD L Molecular neuropathology of aging and dementia Molecular approaches to aging and degenerative diseases of brain

R35AG-07914-03 0002 (AGE) MUMA, NANCY A Molecular neuropathology of aging and dementia Neuronal mRNA following injury

R35AG-07914-03 0003 (AGE) KOO, EDWARD H Molecular neuropathology of aging and dementia Gene expression after injury

R35AG-07914-03 0004 (AGE) APPLEGATE, MICHAEL E Molecular neuropathology of aging and dementia Expression of neurofilament proteins and neuronal cell size

R35AG-07914-03 0005 (AGE) PRICE, DONALD L Molecular neuropathology of aging and dementia Pilot study--In vitro polymerization of the beta amyloid protein

R35AG-07914-03 0006 (AGE) PRICE, DONALD L Molecular neuropathology of aging and dementia Pilot study--Expression of constructs containing chimeric B-protein precursor

R35AG-07918-03 (AGE) COTMAN, CARL W UNIVERSITY OF CALIFORNIA STEINHAUS HALL, ROOM 249 IRVINE, CA 92717 Neuronal plasticity versus pathology in Alzheimer's

R35AG-07918-03 0007 (AGE) NALCIOGLU, ORHAN Neuronal plasticity versus pathology in Alzheimer's Pilot study--MR imaging of limbic hippocampal circuitry in Alzheimer's disease

R35AG-07918-03 0008 (AGE) KEAN, MARY-LOUISE Neuronal plasticity versus pathology in Alzheimer's Pilot study--Motor memory compared to verbal memory in AD

R35AG-07918-03 0001 (AGE) COTMAN, CARL W Neuronal plasticity versus pathology in Alzheimer's Neuronal plasticity versus pathology in Alzheimer's disease

R35AG-07918-03 0002 (AGE) GEDDES, JAMES Neuronal plasticity versus pathology in Alzheimer's Cellular and molecular basis of neuritic plaque formation

R35AG-07918-03 0003 (AGE) BRIDGES, RICHARD Neuronal plasticity versus pathology in Alzheimer's Regulation of glial transport processes in aging and Alzheimer's disease

R35AG-07918-03 0004 (AGE) PETERSON, CHRISTINE Neuronal plasticity versus pathology in Alzheimer's Calcium homeostasis in peripheral cells from aged and Alzheimer's patients

R35AG-07918-03 0005 (AGE) ISACKSON, PAUL Neuronal plasticity versus pathology in Alzheimer's Pilot study--Regulation of nerve growth factor mRNA in neurons and glid

R35AG-07918-03 0006 (AGE) LEON, MICHAEL Neuronal plasticity versus pathology in Alzheimer's Pilot study--Detoxification mechanisms in aged and Alzheimer's disease

R35AG-07922-04 (AGE) ROSES, ALLEN D DIVISION OF NEUROLOGY 725 BROAD STREET DURHAM, N C 27705 Genetics of late and early onset alzheimer's disease

R35AG-07922-04 0001 (AGE) ROSES, ALLEN D Genetics of late and early onset alzheimer's disease Molecular genetics

R35AG-07922-04 0002 (AGE) CLARK, CHRISTOPHER Genetics of late and early onset alzheimer's disease Development of Alzheimer's disease family pedigrees

R35AG-07922-04 0003 (AGE) BREITNER, JOHN C S Genetics of late and early onset alzheimer's disease Environmental and genetic causes in twins ith Alzheimer's disease

R35AG-07922-04 0004 (AGE) DAWSON, DEBORAH V Genetics of late and early onset alzheimer's disease Applications of sib-pair linkage tests to Alzheimer's disease

R35AG-07922-04 0005 (AGE) BARTLETT, RICHARD J Genetics of late and early onset alzheimer's disease Molecular genetic analysis of early onset Alzheimers disease

R29AG-07933-03 (HUD) ERICKSON, KENNETH R GOOD SAMARITAN HOSPITAL 1040 N.W. 22ND AVENUE PORTLAND, OR 97210 Evoked potentials early Alzheimers disease detection

R01AG-07972-03 (CTY) DENHARDT, DAVID T RUTGERS, THE STATE UNIVERSITY DEPARTMENT OF BIOLOGICAL SCIS PISCATAWAY, N.J. 08855 Altered gene expression in immortal/senescent cells

R01AG-07973-03 (SSP) PARNES, HERBERT S 921 CHATHAM LANE, SUITE 200 COLUMBUS, OH 43221-2418 NLS resurvey--Older male survivors & decedents' widows

R37AG-07977-09 (LCR) BENGTSON, VERN L UNIV OF SOUTHERN CALIFORNIA UNIVERSITY PARK, MC 0191 LOS ANGELES, CA 90089-0191 Longitudinal study of generations and mental health

R01AG-07980-01A3 (PHRA) HURWITZ, ARYEH UNIVERSITY OF KANSAS MEDICAL C 3901 RAINBOW BOULEVARD KANSAS CITY, KS 66160-7320 Age-related gastric changes and drug absorption

R01AG-07988-02 (NTN) BODEN, GUENTHER TEMPLE UNIVERSITY HOSPITAL 3401 NORTH BROAD ST PHILADELPHIA, PA 19140 Nutritional effects of ethanol in the elderly

R29AG-07991-02 (HUD) MCDOWD, JOAN M UNIV OF SOUTHERN CALIFORNIA LABORATORY FOR ATTENTION LOS ANGELES, CA 90089-0191 Inhibitory process in selective attention and aging

R01AG-07992-03 (CBY) WRIGHT, WOODRING E UNIV. OF TEXAS SOUTHWESTERN ME 5323 HARRY HINES BOULEVARD DALLAS, TX 75235 Mechanisms of cellular immortalization

P01AG-07996-03 (AGE) SEEGMILLER, J EDWIN UNIVERSITY OF CALIFORNIA INSTITUTE FOR AGING, M013I LA JOLLA, CA 92093 Studies of joint aging and osteoarthritis

P01AG-07996-03 0001 (AGE) SEEGMILLER, EDWIN J. Studies of joint aging and osteoarthritis Purine metabolism in aging and osteoarthritis cartilage

P01AG-07996-03 0002 (AGE) SARTORIS, DAVID J. Studies of joint aging and osteoarthritis Magnetic resonance imaging in osteoarthritis and aging

P01AG-07996-03 0003 (AGE) LOTZ, MARTIN Studies of joint aging and osteoarthritis Role of neuropeptides and intrerleukin 6 in aging of cartilage

P01AG-07996-03 9001 (AGE) JONES, KENNETH L. Studies of joint aging and osteoarthritis Core--Tissue culture

P01AG-07996-03 9002 (AGE) AMIEL, DANIEL Studies of joint aging and osteoarthritis Core--Animal care

P01AG-07996-03 9003 (AGE) SCHAFFLER, MITCHELL B. Studies of joint aging and osteoarthritis Core--Morphology

R01AG-07998-03 (HAR) DIVENYI, PIERRE L VET ADMIN MED CTR 150 MUIR ROAD MARTINEZ, CA 94553 Speech perception under non-optimal conditions in aging

R01AG-07999-03 (HUD) QUANDT, SARA A UNIVERSITY OF KENTUCKY 211 LAFFERTY HALL LEXINGTON, KY 40506-0024 Nutritional strategies & dietary status of rural elderly

R01AG-08010-03 (NURS) BURGIO, KATHRYN L UNIVERSITY OF PITTSBURGH 190 LOTHROP ST/B-45 LOTHROP HA PITTSBURGH, PA 15213 Behavioral vs drug intervention for urinary incontinence

P50AG-08012-04 (AGE) WHITEHOUSE, PETER J UNIV HOSPITALS OF CLEVELAND 2074 ABINGTON ROAD CLEVELAND, OH 44106 UHC/CWRU Alzheimers disease research center

P50AG-08012-04 0006 (AGE) SMYTH, KATHLEEN UHC/CWRU Alzheimers disease research center Pilot study--Socially desirable response tendency and caregiver burden

P50AG-08012-04 9001 (AGE) WHITEHOUSE, PETER J UHC/CWRU Alzheimers disease research center Core--Clinical

P50AG-08012-04 9002 (AGE) CIVIL, RICHARD UHC/CWRU Alzheimers disease research center Core--Research training and information transfer

P50AG-08012-04 9003 (AGE) UNNERSTALL, JAMES R UHC/CWRU Alzheimers disease research center Core--Image analysis

P50AG-08012-04 9004 (AGE) GAMBETTI, PIERLUIGI UHC/CWRU Alzheimers disease research center Core--Neuropathology

P50AG-08012-04 0001 (AGE) HARIK, SAMI I UHC/CWRU Alzheimers disease research center Vessels of the brain in aging and Alzheimer's disease

P50AG-08012-04 0002 (AGE) YOUNKIN, STEVEN G UHC/CWRU Alzheimers disease research center Characterization of amyloid in Alzherimer's disease

P50AG-08012-04 0003 (AGE) RIPICH, DANIELLE UHC/CWRU Alzheimers disease research center Functional communication decline in Alzeheimer's disease

P50AG-08012-04 0004 (AGE) CAPLAN, ARNOLD UHC/CWRU Alzheimers disease research center Pilot study--Immunostain fingerprints of extracellular matrix of neural tissue

P50AG-08012-04 0005 (AGE) PERRY, GEORGE UHC/CWRU Alzheimers disease research center Pilot study--Paired helical filament binding proteins

P50AG-08013-04 (AGE) ROSENBERG, ROGER N UNIV OF TEXAS S W MED CTR DALL 5323 HARRY HINES BOULEVARD DALLAS, TEX 75235 Neurobiology of Alzheimers disease and aging

P50AG-08013-04 0001 (AGE) HERSH, LOUIS B Neurobiology of Alzheimers disease and aging Regulation of choline acetyltransferase

P50AG-08013-04 0002 (AGE) SPARKMAN, DENNIS R Neurobiology of Alzheimers disease and aging Cloning the gene for Alzheimer paired helical filament

P50AG-08013-04 0003 (AGE) RAESE, JOACHIM Neurobiology of Alzheimers disease and aging Heat shock genes in Alzheimer's disease

P50AG-08013-04 0004 (AGE) MORRISON, MARCELLS Neurobiology of Alzheimers disease and aging Regulation of expression of amyloid and paired helical filament proteins

P50AG-08013-04 0005 (AGE) GERMAN, DWIGHT C Neurobiology of Alzheimers disease and aging Loss of cortical afferents in Alzheimer's disease

P50AG-08013-04 0006 (AGE) TINTNER, RON Neurobiology of Alzheimers disease and aging Pilot study--R-CBF, behavior and CSF after pharmacologic challange in AD

P50AG-08013-04 0007 (AGE) CHAFETZ, PAUL Neurobiology of Alzheimers disease and aging Pilot study--Behavioral and cognitive outcomes of special AD care units

PROJECT NO., ORGANIZATIONAL UNIT., INVESTIGATOR, ADDRESS, TITLE

P50AG-08013-04 9001 (AGE) WEINER, MYRON F Neurobiology of Alzheimers disease and aging Core--Clinical

P50AG-08013-04 9002 (AGE) WHITE, CHARLES L Neurobiology of Alzheimers disease and aging Core--Neuropathology

P50AG-08013-04 9003 (AGE) JENNINGS, LINDA W Neurobiology of Alzheimers disease and aging Core--Data management

P50AG-08013-04 9004 (AGE) WEST, HELEN L Neurobiology of Alzheimers disease and aging Core--Education and information transfer

P30AG-08014-02 (AGE) BECKER, ROBERT E SOUTHERN ILLINOIS U SCH OF MED PO BOX 19230 SPRINGFIELD, IL 62794-9230 Alzheimers disease center core grant

P30AG-08014-02 9001 (AGE) CLARKE, BRENT Alzheimers disease center core grant Core--Neuropathology

P30AG-08014-02 9002 (AGE) COLLIVER, JERRY Alzheimers disease center core grant Core--Research support

P30AG-08014-02 9003 (AGE) BARROWS, HOWARD Alzheimers disease center core grant Information transfer core

P30AG-08017-02 (AGE) ZIMMERMAN, EARL A OREGON HEALTH SCIENCES UNIV 3181 SW SAM JACKSON PARK ROAD PORTLAND, OR 97201 Alzheimer's disease research center

P30AG-08017-02 9001 (AGE) HERNDON, ROBERT Alzheimer's disease research center Core--Training and information transfer

P30AG-08017-02 9002 (AGE) KAYE, JEFFREY Alzheimer's disease research center Core--Clinical

P30AG-08017-02 9003 (AGE) SEXTON, GARY Alzheimer's disease research center Core--Data management

P30AG-08017-02 9004 (AGE) BALL, MELVYN Alzheimer's disease research center Core--Neuropathology

P30AG-08031-02 (AGE) KURLAND, LEONARD T MAYO FOUNDATION 200 FIRST STREET SOUTHWEST ROCHESTER, MN 55905 Alzheimer's disease center core grant

P30AG-08031-02 9001 (AGE) PETERSON, RONALD C Alzheimer's disease center core grant Core--Clinical and research support

P30AG-08031-02 9002 (AGE) OKAZAKI, HAROU Alzheimer's disease center core grant Core--Neuropathology

P30AG-08031-02 9003 (AGE) TANGALOS, ERIC G Alzheimer's disease center core grant Core--Research training/information transfer

R29AG-08047-02 (EDC) NEWMAN, ANNE B UNIVERSITY OF PITTSBURGH 130 DESOTO STREET PITTSBURGH, PA 15261 Epidemiology of arterial disease in the elderly

P30AG-08051-02 (AGE) FERRIS, STEVEN H NEW YORK MEDICAL CENTER 550 FIRST AVENUE NEW YORK, N Y 10016 Alzheimers disease center core grant

P30AG-08051-02 9001 (AGE) REISBERG, BARRY Alzheimers disease center core grant Core--Clinical assessment and tracking

P30AG-08051-02 9002 (AGE) MILLER, DOUGLAS Alzheimers disease center core grant Core--Neuropathology

P30AG-08051-02 9003 (AGE) MITTLEMAN, MARY Alzheimers disease center core grant Core--Database management and statistical analysis

P30AG-08051-02 9004 (AGE) SELBY, MICHAEL Alzheimers disease center core grant Core--Training and information transfer

R37AG-08055-03 (AGE) SCHAIE, K WARNER PENNSYLVANIA STATE UNIVERSITY S-110 HENDERSON BUILDING UNIVERSITY PARK, PA 16802 Longitudinal studies of adult cognitive development

R37AG-08055-03 0001 (AGE) PLOMIN, ROBERT Longitudinal studies of adult cognitive development Family resemblances in cognitive performance in adults

R37AG-08055-03 0002 (AGE) SCHAIE, K. WARNER Longitudinal studies of adult cognitive development Health history and age changes in cognitive behavior

R37AG-08055-03 0003 (AGE) WILLIS, SHERRY L. Longitudinal studies of adult cognitive development Long-term effects of cognitive training

R37AG-08055-03 0004 (AGE) SCHAIE, K. WARNER Longitudinal studies of adult cognitive development Longitudinal-sequential studies of adult cognition

R37AG-08055-03 9001 (AGE) SHAIE, K. WARNER Longitudinal studies of adult cognitive development Core-- Seattle longitudinal study

R01AG-08060-03 (HUD) PLUDE, DANA JEFFREY UNIVERSITY OF MARYLAND DEPT OF PSYCHOLOGY COLLEGE PARK, MD 20742-4411 Aging, feature integration, & visual selective attention

R01AG-08076-01A3 (NEUA) IQBAL, KHALID NY/ST/INS/BASIC/RES DEV DISABI 1050 FOREST HILL ROAD STATEN ISLAND, N Y 10314 Neuronal cytoskeletal alterations in Alzheimer's disease

R01AG-08084-03 (NEUC) POTTER, HUNTINGTON HARVARD MEDICAL SCHOOL DEPT OF NEUROBIOLOGY BOSTON, MASS 02115 Amyloid deposition--Aging and Alzheimers disease

R01AG-08092-02 (IMB) SCHWAB, RISE CORNELL UNIV MEDICAL COLLEGE 1300 YORK AVENUE NEW YORK, NY 10021 Subcellular basis for human T cell senescence

R01AG-08094-03 (HUD) LIANG, JERSEY 300 N. INGALLS ANN ARBOR, MI 48109-2007 Well-being among the aged--a three-nation study

R01AG-08099-03 (NEUB) TORAN-ALLERAND, C DOMINIQUE COLUMBIA UNIVERSITY 630 WEST 168TH STREET NEW YORK, N Y 10032 Interactions of NGF/estrogen in CNS development & aging

R01AG-08102-03 (NLS) GROSSMANN, ANGELIKA UNIVERSITY OF WASHINGTON SEATTLE, WA 98195 Intracellular calcium regulation in Alzheimer's disease

R01AG-08106-03 (HUD) WALSH, DAVID A UNIV OF SOUTHERN CALIFORNIA UNIVERSITY PARK LOS ANGELES, CA 90089-1061 Individual decision making and successful aging

R01AG-08109-07 (PC) O'CONNOR, CLARE M WORCESTER FDN FOR EXP BIOL INC 222 MAPLE AVE SHREWSBURY, MA 01545 Methylation of atypical protein aspartyl residues

R01AG-08117-03 (CMS) CORKIN, SUZANNE H MASSACHUSETTS INST TECHNOLOGY E10-003A CAMBRIDGE, MA 02139 Effects of AD on basic and high-order sensory capacities

R01AG-08122-03 (EDC) WOLF, PHILIP A BOSTON UNIV SCH OF MED 80 E CONCORD ST, BOSTON, MA 02118 Epidemiology of dementia in the Framingham cohort

R01AG-08131-02 (SSP) SUTCH, RICHARD C UNIVERSITY OF CALIFORNIA 156 BARROWS HALL BERKELEY, CA 94720 Work and retirement in the United States--1900-1940

R29AG-08133-03 (BPO) COLLIER, TIMOTHY J UNIVERSITY OF ROCHESTER 601 ELMWOOD AVENUE, BOX 603 ROCHESTER, N Y 14642 Norepinephrine supplementation in aging

R29AG-08134-04 (HUD) ANDERSON, TRUDY B UNIVERSITY OF NORTH CAROLINA 211 STONE GREENSBORO, NC 27417-5001 Aging couples: last stage of family life/human

R01AG-08145-03S1 (HSR) RICE, DOROTHY P UNIV. OF CALIF., BOX 0612 3RD & PARNASSUS AVENUES SAN FRANCISCO, CA 94143 Costs of formal and informal care Alzheimer's patients

R37AG-08146-03 (SSP) WISE, DAVID A NATL BUREAU OF ECONOMIC RES 1050 MASSACHUSETTS AVENUE CAMBRIDGE, MA 02138 Pension plan provisions and early retirement

R01AG-08148-03 (CMS) DOTY, RICHARD L HOSPITAL OF UNIV OF PA 3400 SPRUCE STREET PHILADELPHIA, PA 19104 Early diagnosis of Alzheimer's disease & Parkinsonism

R44AG-08151-02 (HUD) LERNER, NEIL D COMSIS CORPORATION 8737 COLESVILLE RD SILVER SPRING, MD 20910 Smoke detector/emergency egress product for older users

R37AG-08155-03 (NEUC) GAMBETTI, PIERLUIGI CASE WESTERN RESERVE UNIV 2085 ADELBERT ROAD CLEVELAND, OHIO 44106 Molecular pathology of alzheimer disease

R01AG-08172-04 (SRC) MOORE, ROBERT Y WESTERN PSYCHIATRIC INST 3811 O'HARA STREET PITTSBURGH, PA 15213 Circadian rhythms and thermoregulation in elderly rats

R01AG-08173-04 (SRC) PORTER, JOHN C U.T. SOUTHWESTERN MED CENTER 5323 HARRY HINES BOULEVARD DALLAS, TX 75235-9032 Impaired secretion by aging neurons--Molecular and cellular studies

R01AG-08174-04 (SRC) SIMPSON, EVAN R U.T. SOUTHWESTERN MED CENTER 5323 HARRY HINES BOULEVARD DALLAS, TEXAS 75235-9051 Aging and the regulation of aromatase in adipose tissue

R01AG-08175-04 (SRC) MASON, JAMES I U.T. SOUTHWESTERN MED CENTER 5323 HARRY HINES BOULEVARD DALLAS, TX 75235-9051 Regulation of adrenal C19 steroid biosynthesis

R01AG-08177-04 (AGE) ABRAHAM, GEORGE N UNIV OF ROCHESTER MEDICAL CTR 601 ELMWOOD AVENUE ROCHESTER, N Y 14642 Clonal B-cell analysis in human monoclonal gammapathies

R01AG-08178-04 (AGE) LEDDY, JOHN P UNIVERSITY OF ROCHESTER 601 ELMWOOD AVENUE ROCHESTER, N Y 14642 Pathogenesis of erythrocyte autoantibody formation

R01AG-08179-04 (AGE) ZAUDERER, MAURICE UNIVERSITY OF ROCHESTER 601 ELMWOOD AVE ROCHESTER, N Y 14642 Variable gene utilization in specific t-cell responses

R01AG-08189-03S1 (SSP) DAVANZO, JULIE S RAND CORPORATION 1700 MAIN STREET SANTA MONICA, CA 90406 Demographic change and family decision making (Malaysia)

R55AG-08192-04 (IMS) KELSOE, GARNETT H UNIVERSITY OF MARYLAND 655 WEST BALTIMORE STREET BALTIMORE, MD 21201 Age's immunological consequences - Analysis of clones

R43AG-08195-01A1 (SSS) OGNIBENE, PETER J APPLIED SYSTEMS INST, INC 1420 K STREET NW WASHINGTON, DC 20005 Smart pharmacy cards to reduce adverse drug reactions

R01AG-08196-04 (MGN) RIGGS, ARTHUR D BECKMAN RES INSTCITY OF HOPE 1450 E DUARTE ROAD DUARTE, CA 91010 X-chromosome inactivation, DNA methylation, & gene regul

R29AG-08199-04 (MGN) TURKER, MITCHELL S MARKEY CANCER CENTER 800 ROSE ST/ROOM 306 LEXINGTON, KY 40536 Somatic mutation and aging: a model system

R01AG-08200-04 (NEUC) ROBAKIS, NILOLAOS K MOUNT SINAI SCHOOL MEDICINE ONE GUSTAVE LEVY PLACE BOX 12 NEW YORK, NY 10029 Cytoskeletal association of full length and truncated APP

R01AG-08201-04 (AGE) TERRY, ROBERT D UNIV OF CALIFORNIA, SAN DIEGO DEPT. OF NEUROSCIENCES, 0624 LA JOLLA, CALIF 92093 Structure and function in Alzheimer's disease

R01AG-08203-04 (AGE) MURPHY, CLAIRE L SAN DIEGO STATE UNIVERSITY DEPARTMENT OF PSYCHOLOGY SAN DIEGO, CA 92182-0350 Olfactory dysfunction in alzheimer' disease

R01AG-08204-04 (AGE) BUTTERS, NELSON M SAN DIEGO VA MEDICAL CENTER 3350 LA JOLLA VILLAGE DRIVE LA JOLLA, CA 92161 Neuropathological-memory correlates in DAT

R01AG-08205-04 (NLS) SAITOH, TSUNAO UNIV OF CALIFORNIA LA JOLLA, CA 92093 Altered protein kinases in Alzheimers disease

R01AG-08206-05 (AGE) ARMSTRONG, DAVID M GEORGETOWN UNIVERSITY MED CNTR 3900 RESERVOIR ROAD, N W WASHINGTON, D C 20007 Transmitter neuroanatomy in Alzheimer's disease

R01AG-08207-04 (NEUB) FINKLESTEIN, SETH P MASSACHUSETTS GENERAL HOSP-EAS BOSTON, MA 02114 Fibroblast growth factors in the aging brain

R01AG-08211-01A1 (EDC) MAGAZINER, JAY UNIVERSITY OF MARYLAND 660 WEST REDWOOD ST BALTIMORE, MD 21201 Epidemiology of dementia in aged nursing home admissions

R01AG-08214-03 (HUD) KAUSLER, DONALD H MC ALESTER HALL UNIVERSITY OF MISSSOURI COLUMBIA, MO 65211 Aging and retrieval processes in activity/action memory

R01AG-08226-03 (PHRA) ABERNETHY, DARRELL R ROGER WILLIAMS MEDICAL CENTER PROVIDENCE, RI 02908 Calcium antagonists, aging, and hypertension

R01AG-08240-03 (LCR) SULLIVAN, MARK D UNIV OF WASHINGTON MED SCHOOL DPT OF PSYCHIATRY & BEHAVIORAL SEATTLE, WA 98195 Disabling tinnitus and depression in the elderly

R01AG-08245-03 (PBC) VLASSARA, HELEN ROCKEFELLER UNIVERSITY 1230 YORK AVENUE NEW YORK, NY 10021 Regulation of tissue remodeling in aging and diabetes

R01AG-08249-01A2 (BCE) COLLINS, THOMAS J 200 UNIVERSITY BLVD GALVESTON, TX 77550 LH function in aging female mice

R29AG-08256-01A2 (HUD) CUSHMAN, LAURA A SCHOOL OF MEDICINE 601 ELMWOOD AVENUE ROCHESTER, NEW YORK 14642 Cognitive factors in the safety of older drivers

R01AG-08269-02 (HUD) BROWN, JUDITH K OAKLAND UNIVERSITY ROCHESTER, MI 48309-4401 Being in charge--A cross-cultural view of middle aged women

R01AG-08270-03 (SSP) JUSTER, F T 3240 INSTITUTE FOR SOCIAL RES P.O. BOX 1248 ANN ARBOR, MI 48106 Saving, wealth, and health among older americans

R01AG-08273-01A1 (HUD) MORGAN, DAVID L PORTLAND STATE UNIVERSITY

PO BOX 751-IOA PORTLAND, OR 97202-0751 Change over time in the social networks of recent widows
R01AG-08276-02 (HCT) SILVERMAN, MYRNA UNIVERSITY OF PITTSBURGH 130 DESOTO STREET PITTSBURGH, PA 15261 Geriatric assessment--A multicenter controlled evaluation
R01AG-08278-10 (NLS) NIXON, RALPH A MC LEAN HOSPITAL 115 MILL STREET BELMONT, MASS 02178 Human brain proteolysis in aging and Alzheimer's disease
R01AG-08279-01A2 (HUD) MARKUS, HAZEL UNIVERSITY OF MICHIGAN 426 THOMPSON STREET ANN ARBOR, MI 48106-1248 Self-concept in later adulthood--Past, current, possible
R01AG-08288-02 (BEM) WYKLE, MAY CASE WESTERN RESERVE UNIVERSIT CLEVELAND, OH 44106 MD style, self-care & compliance of chronically ill aged
R01AG-08289-02 (ORTH) JOHNSON, MARK MASSACHUSETTS INST OF TECHNOLO 77 MASSACHUSETTS AVENUE/RM 3-1 CAMBRIDGE, MA 02139 Age-related changes in connective tissue permeability
P01AG-08291-03 (AGE) LILLARD, LEE A RAND CORPORATION 1700 MAIN ST PO BOX 2138 SANTA MONICA, CA 90407 Social and economic functioning in older populations
P01AG-08291-03 0001 (AGE) LILLARD, LEE A Social and economic functioning in older populations Economic consequences of poor health in old age
P01AG-08291-03 0002 (AGE) WAITE, LINDA J Social and economic functioning in older populations Kin networks of older adults--Implications for health
P01AG-08291-03 0003 (AGE) WAITE, LINDA J Social and economic functioning in older populations Marriage, divorce, widowhood and financial well-being
P01AG-08291-03 0004 (AGE) GERTLER, PAUL J Social and economic functioning in older populations Payment mechanisms and nursing home outcomes
P01AG-08291-03 0005 (AGE) WARE, JOHN E Social and economic functioning in older populations Social and psychologic factors in health and functioning
P01AG-08291-03 9001 (AGE) LILLARD, LEE A Social and economic functioning in older populations Core--Data acquisition
R01AG-08293-02 (CMS) HUMES, LARRY E INDIANA UNIVERSITY BLOOMINGTON, IN 47405 Speech recognition by the hearing-impaired elderly
R37AG-08303-03 (MGN) MARTIN, GEORGE M UNIVERSITY OF WASHINGTON PATH DEPT/HLTH SCI BLDG D-509 SEATTLE, WA 98195 Homozygosity mapping of the werner syndrome locus
R01AG-08313-02 (NEUA) KUTAS, MARTA UNIV OF CALIF., SAN DIEGO 9500 GILMAN DRIVE LA JOLLA, CA 92093-0515 Brain potentials (erps), language, memory, and aging
R01AG-08319-02 (SSP) ZARKIN, GARY A DUKE UNIVERSITY DURHAM, NC 27706 Labor market transitions of older workers
P01AG-08321-03 (AGE) ZIRKIN, BARRY R JOHNS HOPKINS UNIVERSITY 615 N WOLFE STREET BALTIMORE, MD 21205 Aging and male reproductive tract structure and function
P01AG-08321-03 0001 (AGE) EWING, LARRY L Aging and male reproductive tract structure and function Effect of aging on the rat leydig cell
P01AG-08321-03 0002 (AGE) ZIRKIN, BARRY R Aging and male reproductive tract structure and function Age and spermatogenic cell response to intratesticular testosterone
P01AG-08321-03 0003 (AGE) WRIGHT, WILLIAM W Aging and male reproductive tract structure and function Age effects on number and function of sertoli cells and spermatogonia
P01AG-08321-03 0004 (AGE) MC CARREY, JOHN R Aging and male reproductive tract structure and function Does the male germ line age?
P01AG-08321-03 9001 (AGE) STRANDBERG, JOHN D Aging and male reproductive tract structure and function Core--Animal
R55AG-08322-04 (CTY) JOHNSON, THOMAS E UNIVERSITY OF COLORADO CAMPUS BOX 447 BOULDER, CO 80309-0447 Molecular genetic specification of aging processes
R01AG-08324-02 (NURS) EVANS, LOIS K UNIVERSITY OF PENNSYLVANIA 420 SERVICE DRIVE PHILADELPHIA, PA 19104-6096 Reducing restraints in nursing homes--A clinical trial
R01AG-08325-02 (EDC) KAWAS, CLAUDIA H JOHNS HOPKINS MEDICAL INSTS 4940 EASTERN AVENUE BALTIMORE, MD 21224 Risk factors and early signs in Alzheimer's disease/BLSA
R01AG-08327-03 (HUD) KEYL, PENELOPE M JOHNS HOPKINS UNIVERSITY 615 NORTH WOLFE STREET BALTIMORE, MD 21205 Effects of Alzheimer's disease and aging on driving
R01AG-08332-01A1 (END) KOWAL, JEROME CASE WESTERN RESERVE UNIVERSIT 12200 FAIRHILL RD CLEVELAND, OH 44120 Metabolism and function in the aging adrenal gland
R37AG-08346-02 (SSP) LILLARD, LEE A RAND CORPORATION 1700 MAIN STREET SANTA MONICA, CA 90406 Intergenerational transfers in Malaysia
R01AG-08353-03 (CMS) FOX, ROBERT A 1070 CARMACK ROAD COLUMBUS, OH 43210-1002 Age related changes in the perception of speech
R01AG-08371-03 (NEUA) PETTEGREW, JAY W WESTERN PSYCHIATRIC INST & CLN 3811 O'HARA STREET PITTSBURGH, PA 15213 In vivo metabolism in Alzheimer's disease
R01AG-08374-01A2 (NEUA) ROGERS, JOSEPH INST FOR BIOGERONTOLOGY RES PO BOX 1278 SUN CITY, AZ 85372 Amygdala in Alzheimer's disease and normal aging
R01AG-08375-03 (ALCP) AHERN, FRANK M PENNSYLVANIA STATE UNIVERSITY UNIVERSITY PARK, PA 16802 Alcohol & prescription drug interaction in the elderly
R01AG-08377-03 (NEUA) RAICHLE, MARCUS E WASHINGTON UNIV SCH OF MED 510 SOUTH KINGSHIGHWAY ST LOUIS, MO 63110 The brain microvasculature in aging and dementia
R01AG-08380-02 (BEM) HANLON, JOSEPH T DUKE UNIV MEDICAL CENTER BOX 3003 DURHAM, NC 27710 Pharmacy interventions for polypharmacy in the elderly
R29AG-08382-05 (HUD) STINE, ELIZABETH A L UNIVERSITY OF HAMPSHIRE DURHAM, NH 03824 Adult age differences in online processing of discourse
R29AG-08387-03 (EDC) COHN, BARBARA A CALIFORNIA DEPT OF HEALTH SERV 2151 BERKELEY WAY, ANNEX 2 BERKELEY, CA 94704-9980 Age, sex & survival-stability of associations over time
R44AG-08406-03 (SSS) SCHENK, DALE B ATHENA NEUROSCIENCES, INC. 800F GATEWAY BOULEVARD SOUTH SAN FRANCISCO, CA 94080 Characterization of b-amyloid precursor fragments in AD
R44AG-08407-02A1 (SSS) CHURCHILL, RUSSELL J AMERICAN RES CORP OF VIRGINIA PO BOX 3406 RADFORD, VA 24143-3406 Memory assist device to improve prescription compliance
R01AG-08415-03 (EDC) ANCOLI-ISRAEL, SONIA UNIV. OF CALIF., SAN DIEGO LA JOLLA, CA 92093-0603 Sleep consolidation in a nursing home population
R01AG-08419-03 (PCB) RASKIND, MURRAY A UNIVERSITY OF WASHINGTON 1959 NE PACIFIC ST RP-10 SEATTLE, WA 98195 Psychopathology of alzheimer's-psychoneuroendocrinology
R01AG-08435-01A2 (HUD) KRAMER, ARTHUR F UNIVERSITY OF ILLINOIS 603 EAST DANIEL STREET CHAMPAIGN, IL 61820 Development of skilled performance in the elderly
R01AG-08438-01A2 (GMA) MAJUMDAR, ADHIP N VA MEDICAL CENTER ALLEN PARK, MI 48101 Gastric mucosal injury and aging
R01AG-08441-03 (HUD) SCHACTER, DANIEL L HARVARD UNIVERSITY 33 KIRKLAND STREET CAMBRIDGE, MA 02138 Studies of aging memory
R01AG-08444-04 (NLS) KAY, MARGUERITE M B UNIVERSITY OF ARIZONA 1501 N CAMPBELL AVE TUCSON, AZ 85724 Membrane changes in neurologic and aging diseases
R01AG-08459-03 (CTY) SOHAL, RAJINDAR S SOUTHERN METHODIST UNIVERSITY DEPARTMENT OF BIOLOGY DALLAS, TX 75275 Antioxidant enzymes and aging in transgenic Drosophila
R01AG-08470-03 (BNP) LANSBURY, PETER T JR MASSACHUSETTS INST OF TECH 77 MASSACHUSETTS AVE CAMBRIDGE, MA 02139 Amyloid deposition in Alzheimer's disease
R01AG-08475-01A2 (HUD) ROWLES, GRAHAM D UNIVERSITY OF KENTUCKY 101 SANDERS-BROWN BUILDING LEXINGTON, KY 40536-0230 Family involvement in nursing home decision-making
R01AG-08476-02 (BEM) MARTIN, JOHN E SAN DIEGO STATE UNIVERSITY 6363 ALVARADO COURT SAN DIEGO, CA 92182 Health effects of exercise in elderly hypertensives
R01AG-08479-03 (NLS) SONSALLA, PATRICIA K UMDNJ-ROBERT W JOHNSON MED SCH DEPARTMENT OF NEUROLOGY PISCATAWAY, NJ 08854-5635 Dopaminergic neurotoxins and aging
R01AG-08481-03 (HUD) RUBINSTEIN, ROBERT L PHILADELPHIA GERIATRIC CENTER 5301 OLD YORK ROAD PHILADELPHIA, PA 19141 The middle aged child's experience of parental death
R29AG-08487-03 (NEUA) HYMAN, BRADLEY T MASSACHUSETTS GENERAL HOSPITAL FRUIT STREET BOSTON, MA 02114 Pathological alterations in alzheimer's disease
R01AG-08491-02 (HUD) KRAUSE, NEAL M UNIVERSITY OF MICHIGAN 1420 WASHINGTON HEIGHTS ANN ARBOR, MI 48109-2029 Social support among aged
R01AG-08494-03 (HUD) MEYD, CONSTANCE JOHNS HOPKINS UNIV SCHOOL OF M 4940 EASTERN AVENUE BALTIMORE, MD 21224 Biological factors responsible for neurobehavioral aging
R01AG-08504-02 (MBC) JAZWINSKI, S MICHAL LOUISIANA STATE UNIV MED CTR 1901 PERDIDO STREET NEW ORLEANS, LA 70112 Control of proliferation in senescent yeast cells
R01AG-08510-03 (EDC) BAUMGARTNER, RICHARD N UNIVERSITY OF NEW MEXICO ALBUQUERQUE, NM 87131 Body composition methods for the elderly
R37AG-08511-03 (EDC) DIOKNO, ANANIAS C UNIVERSITY OF MICHIGAN 1150 WEST MEDICAL CENTER DRIVE ANN ARBOR, MI 48109-0666 Geriatric urinary incontinence: Long-term follow-up
R01AG-08513-03 (NTN) BOILEAU, RICHARD A UNIVERSITY OF ILLINOIS 906 S GOODWIN AVE;125 FREER HA URBANA, IL 61801 Fat and fat-free body composition development in aging
R01AG-08514-03 (NEUB) GAGE, FRED H UNIVERSITY OF CALIFORNIA 9500 GILMAN DRIVE LA JOLLA, CA 92093-0624 Grafting genetically modified cells to the brain
R01AG-08521-03 (HUD) MORROW, DANIEL G DECISION SYSTEMS 1473 MIRAMONTE BLDG 2 LOS ALTOS, CA 94022 Aging, expertise, text organization, and comprehension
R01AG-08522-03 (HUD) POWELL, DONALD A UNIVERSITY OF SOUTH CAROLINA NEUROSCIENCE LAB., 151A COLUMBIA, SC 29201 Associative learning and aging
R01AG-08523-01A2 (EDC) MYERS, GEORGE C DUKE UNIVERSITY 2117 CAMPUS DRIVE DURHAM, NC 27706 A collaborative study of aging in the U.S and Australia
R01AG-08545-04 (HEM) DALE, GEORGE KL UNIVERSITY OF OKLAHOMA P O BOX 26901 OKLAHOMA CITY, OK 73190 Studies on erythrocyte senescence
R01AG-08549-03 (EDC) BREITNER, JOHN C DUKE UNIVERSITY MEDICAL CENTER BOX 3925 DURHAM, NC 27710 Genetic epidemiology Alzheimer disease in twins
R01AG-08552-03 (IMS) DANIELS, CHRISTOPHER K VA MEDICAL CENTER 500 WEST FORT ST BOISE, ID 83702 Regulation of mucosal immunocompetence in the aging rat
R29AG-08554-02 (HUD) UMBERSON, DEBRA UNIVERSITY OF TEXAS AUSTIN, TX 78712 Death of a parent--Impact on adult children and families
R37AG-08557-01A2 (NURS) HAUG, MARIE R CASE WESTERN RESERVE UNIV 2009 ADELBERT ROAD CLEVELAND, OH 44106 Stresses, strains and elderly physical health
R01AG-08562-03 (HUD) WILLIAMS, PAMELA HOSPITAL FOR SPECIAL SURGERY 535 EAST 70TH ST NEW YORK, NY 10021 A trial of epidural versus general anesthesia
R01AG-08567-01A2 (EDC) DAVANIPOUR, ZOREH LOMA LINDA UNIVERSITY SCH OF M SCHOOL OF MEDICINE LOMA LINDA, CA 92350 Alzheimer's disease among Seventh-Day Adventists
R29AG-08568-04 (EDC) FRANCIS, JOSEPH UNIVERSITY OF TENNESSEE, MEMPH 66 N. PAULINE, SUITE 232 MEMPHIS, TN 38163 Outcomes of delirium in hospitalized elderly
R01AG-08572-03 (NLS) KIRSCHNER, DANIEL A CHILDREN'S HOSPITAL 300 LONGWOOD AVENUE BOSTON, MA 02115 Abnormal fibrous assemblies of Alzheimer's disease
R01AG-08573-09 (CTY) BANDMAN, EVERETT UNIVERVSITY OF CALIFORNIA DEPT. OF FOOD SCIENCE & TECH. DAVIS, CA 95616 Immunobiochemical study of muscle myosin isoforms
R01AG-08574-04 (HEM) KAY, M M B UNIV OF ARIZONA 1501 N. CAMPBELL AVE. TUCSON AZ 85724 Cellular & molecular biology of altered

band 3

R01AG-08575-01A2 (NEUA) ARIEFF, ALLEN I VETERANS AFFAIRS MED CTRTER 4150 CLEMENT ST (111G) SAN FRANCISCO, CA 94121 Dementia, hyponatremia and aging--Peptide hormone role

R29AG-08589-02 (HUD) TSANG, PAMELA WRIGHT STATE UNIVERSITY DAYTON, OH 45435 Aging & pilot time-sharing performance

R44AG-08605-02 (HUD) STERNS, RONNI S EVENING STAR PRODUCTIONS 11818 CLIFTON BOULEVARD LAKEWOOD, OH 44107 Video programming and formats to enhance older adult fun

R01AG-08617-03 (HCT) BRENNAN, PATRICIA F CASE WESTERN RESERVE UNIV 2121 ABINGTON RD CLEVELAND, OHIO 44106 Supporting home care via a community computer network

R01AG-08633-01A2 (HUD) MARKIDES, KYRIAKOS S UNIV OF TEXAS MEDICAL BRANCH GALVESTON, TX 77550-2777 Intergenerational relationships in Mexican Americans

R01AG-08644-03 (SRC) SPITZE, GLENNA D STATE UNIVERSITY OF NEW YORK ALBANY, NY 12222 Family structure and intergenerational relations

R01AG-08651-03 (SRC) WOLF, DOUGLAS A THE URBAN INSTITUTE 2100 M STREET, NW WASHINGTON, DC 20037 Intergenerational families--Structure, dynamics exchanges

R01AG-08659-02 (ARR) MURASKO, DONNA M MEDICAL COLLEGE OF PENNSYLVANI 3300 HENRY AVE PHILADELPHIA, PA 19129 Effect of age on retrovirus disease and immunosuppression

P50AG-08664-03 (AGE) APPEL, STANLEY H BAYLOR COLLEGE OF MEDICINE ONE BAYLOR PLAZA HOUSTON, TX 77030 Alzheimer's disease research center

P50AG-08664-03 0001 (AGE) JOHNSTON, DANIEL Alzheimer's disease research center Pharmacology of mossy fiber synapatic plasticity

P50AG-08664-03 0002 (AGE) BOSTWICK, JAMES R Alzheimer's disease research center Phosphoethanolamine enhances brain cholinergic functions

P50AG-08664-03 0003 (AGE) PAPASOZOMENOS, SOZOS CH Alzheimer's disease research center Tau protein in dementia of the Alzheimer type

P50AG-08664-03 0004 (AGE) STRITTMATTER, WARREN J Alzheimer's disease research center Pilot study--Brain metalloendoprotease in amyloid A4 production

P50AG-08664-03 0005 (AGE) CASKEY, C THOMAS Alzheimer's disease research center Pilot study--Analysis of familial Alzheimer disease by DNA linkage

P50AG-08664-03 0006 (AGE) DOODY, RACHELLE S Alzheimer's disease research center Pilot study--Semantics of sentence accent in Alzheimer's disease

P50AG-08664-03 0007 (AGE) SMITH, LOUIS C Alzheimer's disease research center Pilot study--Eigenanalysis of high resolution chromosomes

P50AG-08664-03 9001 (AGE) STRITTMATTER, WARREN J Alzheimer's disease research center Core--clinical

P50AG-08664-03 9002 (AGE) INBODY, STEVEN B Alzheimer's disease research center Core--Information transfer and research training

P50AG-08664-03 9003 (AGE) KIRKPATRICK, JOEL B Alzheimer's disease research center Core--Neuropathology

P30AG-08665-02 (AGE) COLEMAN, PAUL D UNIV OF ROCHESTER SCH OF MED 601 ELMWOOD AVENUE, BOX 603 ROCHESTER, NY 14642 Alzheimers disease center core grant

P30AG-08665-02 9001 (AGE) HAMIL, ROBERT Alzheimers disease center core grant Core--Clinical

P30AG-08665-02 9002 (AGE) LAPHAM, LOWELL Alzheimers disease center core grant Core--Neuropathology

P30AG-08665-02 9003 (AGE) COLEMAN, PAUL Alzheimers disease center core grant Core--Training and information transfer

P50AG-08671-03 (AGE) GILMAN, SID UNIVERSITY OF MICHIGAN 1500 E MEDICAL CENTER DR ANN ARBOR, MI 48109-0316 Michigan Alzheimer's disease research center

P50AG-08671-03 0007 (AGE) WOLF, FREDRIC M Michigan Alzheimer's disease research center Pilot study--Improving communication with patients with early dementia

P50AG-08671-03 0008 (AGE) ALGASE, DONNA L Michigan Alzheimer's disease research center Pilot study--Impact of nurse-resident interaction on wandering

P50AG-08671-03 9001 (AGE) FOSTER, NORMAN L Michigan Alzheimer's disease research center Core--clinical

P50AG-08671-03 9002 (AGE) PENNEY, JOHN B Michigan Alzheimer's disease research center Core--Neuropathology

P50AG-08671-03 9003 (AGE) SHOPE, JEAN T Michigan Alzheimer's disease research center Core--Research training and information transfer

P50AG-08671-03 0001 (AGE) GILMAN, SID Michigan Alzheimer's disease research center Motor correlates of dementia

P50AG-08671-03 0002 (AGE) PENNEY, JOHN B Michigan Alzheimer's disease research center Dopaminergic and cholinergic markers in dementia

P50AG-08671-03 0003 (AGE) YOUNG, ANNE B Michigan Alzheimer's disease research center Glutamate receptors in the dementias

P50AG-08671-03 0004 (AGE) ALBIN, ROGER L Michigan Alzheimer's disease research center Pilot study--GABAergic cortical neurons in Alzheimer's disease

P50AG-08671-03 0005 (AGE) ALDRICH, MICHAELS Michigan Alzheimer's disease research center Pilot study--Sleep disturbance and motor abnormalities in Alzheimer's disease

P50AG-08671-03 0006 (AGE) MATA, MARINA Michigan Alzheimer's disease research center Pilot study--Calcium homeostasis in aging and Alzheimer's disease

R01AG-08673-01A2 (MET) SCHWARTZ, ROBERT S HARBORVIEW MEDICAL CENTER 325 NINTH AVENUE, ZA-67 SEATTLE, WA 98104 Adipose distribution and adrenergic mechanisms in aging

R29AG-08674-03 (LCR) ROHRER, JAMES E UNIVERSITY OF IOWA 2700 STEINDLER BUILDING IOWA CITY, IA 52242 Mental illness and outcomes of nursing home care

R01AG-08675-06 (LCR) COHEN-MANSFIELD, JISKA HEBREW HOME/GREATER WASHINGTON 6105 MONTROSE ROAD, RES INST ROCKVILLE, MD 20852 Mental health agitation in nursing home elderly

R37AG-08678-02 (NURS) OUSLANDER, JOSEPH G JEWISH HOMES FOR AGING 18855 VICTORY BLVD RESEDA, CA 91335 Assessment and treatment of incontinence in nursing homes

P50AG-08702-03 (AGE) SHELANSKI, MICHAEL L COLUMBIA UNIVERSITY 630 W 168TH ST NEW YORK, NY 10032 Alzheimer's disease research center

P50AG-08702-03 0001 (AGE) KANDEL, ERIC R Alzheimer's disease research center Molecular biological approaches to LTP in hippocampus

P50AG-08702-03 0002 (AGE) SCHON, ERIC A Alzheimer's disease research center Biosynthesis of the amyloid-beta protein precursor

P50AG-08702-03 0003 (AGE) JOH, TONG H Alzheimer's disease research center Neurotransmitter gene expression in CNS degeneration

P50AG-08702-03 0004 (AGE) TROY, CAROL M Alzheimer's disease research center Pilot-study--Expression of cytoskeletal mRNAs and proteins

P50AG-08702-03 0005 (AGE) ALETTA, JOHN M Alzheimer's disease research center Pilot study--High molecular mass map1 in alzheimer brain

P50AG-08702-03 0006 (AGE) GURLAND, BARRY J Alzheimer's disease research center Pilot-study--Comprehensive assessment of elderly with dementia

P50AG-08702-03 0007 (AGE) COTE, LUCIEN Alzheimer's disease research center Pilot study--Novel cholinesterase inhibitors

P50AG-08702-03 0008 (AGE) PROHOVNIK, ISAK Alzheimer's disease research center Pilot study--Cerebral blood flow as marker for Alzheimer's disease

P50AG-08702-03 9001 (AGE) MAYEUX, RICHARD Alzheimer's disease research center Core--Clinical

P50AG-08702-03 9002 (AGE) GOLDMAN, JAMES M Alzheimer's disease research center Core--Neuropathology

P50AG-08702-03 9003 (AGE) GURLAND, BARRY J Alzheimer's disease research center Core--Research training and information transfer

R37AG-08707-02 (IMB) WEKSLER, MARC E CORNELL UNIV MEDICAL COLLEGE 1300 YORK AVENUE NEW YORK, NY 10021 Autoimmune reactions in aging

R01AG-08708-02 (CTY) GOLDSTEIN, SAMUEL UNIVERSITY OF ARKANSAS 4300 WEST 7TH ST LITTLE ROCK, AR 72205 Molecular genetics of Werner syndrome and biological aging

R29AG-08710-02 (NEUA) ROBERTS, EUGENE L, JR UNIV OF MIAMI SCH OF MED PO BOX 016960 MIAMI, FL 33101 Age-related changes in brain metabolic neurophysiology

R29AG-08713-02 (RNM) BECK, THOMAS J JOHNS HOPKINS UNIV SCH OF MED 600 N WOLFE STREET BALTIMORE, MD 21205 Structural analysis of hip bone mineral image data

R01AG-08714-01A2 (HUD) OKEN, BARRY S OREGON HEALTH SCIS UNIVERSITY 3181 SW SAM JACKSON PARK ROAD PORTLAND, OR 97201-3098 Age-related changes in alertness and visual processing

R29AG-08718-02 (HUD) SWARTZ, KENNETH P UNIV OF ROCHESTER MEDICAL CTR 601 ELMWOOD AVE, BOX 629 ROCHESTER, NY 14642 Neuropsychology of music in aging & Alzheimers dementia

R01AG-08721-02 (PTHA) FRANGIONE, BLAS NEW YORK UNIVERSITY MEDICAL CT 550 FIRST AVENUE NEW YORK, NY 10016 Amyloid angiopathy, early plaques, and aging

R01AG-08724-02 (EDC) GATZ, MARGARET J UNIV OF SOUTHERN CALIFORNIA LOS ANGELES, CA 90089-1061 Dementia in Swedish twins

R29AG-08729-02 (SSP) LEIBSON, CYNTHIA MAYO FOUNDATION 200 FIRST STREET SOUTHWEST ROCHESTER, MN 55905 Trends in elderly mortality morbidity and hospital use

R01AG-08740-02 (RNM) FROST, J JAMES JOHNS HOPKINS HOSPITAL 600 NORTH WOLFE STREET BALTIMORE, MD 21205 Opiate receptor quantification in Alzheimer's disease

R01AG-08751-02 (BEM) KLAIBER, EDWARD L WORCESTER FOUNDATION 222 MAPLE AVENUE SHREWSBURY, MASS 01545 Estrogen treatment of mood disturbances in the menopause

P01AG-08761-02 (AGE) VAUPEL, JAMES W HUMPHREY INST OF PUBLIC AFFAIR 301 19TH AVE SOUTH MINNEAPOLIS, MN 55455 Oldest-old mortality--Demographic models and analyses

P01AG-08761-02 0001 (AGE) VAUPEL, JAMES W Oldest-old mortality--Demographic models and analyses Oldest-old mortality in Sweden and the U.S. /human/

P01AG-08761-02 0002 (AGE) VAUPEL, JAMES W Oldest-old mortality--Demographic models and analyses Oldest-old mortality among Danish twins /human/

P01AG-08761-02 0003 (AGE) CAREY, JAMES R Oldest-old mortality--Demographic models and analyses Oldest-old mortality for Mediterranean fruit flies

P01AG-08761-02 0004 (AGE) CURTSINGER, JAMES W Oldest-old mortality--Demographic models and analyses Oldest-old mortality for inbred lines of Drosophila

P01AG-08761-02 9001 (AGE) LOUIS, THOMAS A Oldest-old mortality--Demographic models and analyses Core--Statistical development

P01AG-08761-02 9002 (AGE) LANE, DAVID A Oldest-old mortality--Demographic models and analyses Core--Paradigm adjudication

R01AG-08762-01A1 (EDC) NISSINEN, MIRJA A UNIVERISTY OF KUOPIO PO BOX 6 KUOPIO, FINLAND SF-70211 Determinants of disability in elderly men

R01AG-08768-02 (HUD) SELTZER, MARSHA M UNIVERSITY OF WISCONSIN 1500 HIGHLAND AVE MADISON, WI 53705 Aging mothers of retarded adults; impacts of caregiving

R29AG-08776-02 (ORTH) CODY, DIANNA D HENRY FORD HOSPITAL 2799 W GRAND BLVD DETROIT, MI 48202 Strength density & microstructure in the proximal femur

P01AG-08777-01 (AGE) MANN, KENNETH G UNIVERSITY OF VERMONT GIVEN BLDG BURLINGTON, VT 05405 The regulation of bone formation

P01AG-08777-01 0001 (AGE) MANN, KENNETH G The regulation of bone formation Characterization of bone-related proteins

P01AG-08777-01 0002 (AGE) TRACY, RUSSELL P The regulation of bone formation Characterization of the extracellular matrix of bone

P01AG-08777-01 0003 (AGE) LONG, GEORGE L The regulation of bone formation Genetic expression of noncollagenous bone proteins

P01AG-08777-01 0004 (AGE) LONG, MICHAEL W The regulation of bone formation Bone protein expression in hematopoietic tissue

P01AG-08777-01 0005 (AGE) TRACY, RUSSELL P The regulation of bone formation New bone protein

P01AG-08777-01 0006 (AGE) MANN, KENNETH G The regulation of bone formation Immunochemical quantitation of bone-specific proteins

P01AG-08777-01 9001 (AGE) GENDREAU, MARK The regulation of bone formation Materials core

R01AG-08794-03 (BPN) DETOLEDO-MORRELL, LEYLA RUSH-PRESBYTERIAN-ST LUKES 1653 W. CONGRESS PARKWAY CHICAGO, IL 60612 Synaptic substrates of age-related memory dysfunction

R01AG-08796-02 (BPO) DISTERHOFT, JOHN F NORTHWESTERN UNIV MED SCHOOL 303 EAST CHICAGO AVENUE CHICAGO, IL 60611 Mechanisms of nimodipine learning enhancement in aging

P01AG-08802-02 (AGE) KURLAND, LEONARD T MAYO FOUNDATION 200 FIRST STREET SOUTHWEST ROCHESTER, MN 55905 Epidemiology of dementia and Micronesia

P01AG-08802-02 0001 (AGE) KURLAND, LEONARD T Epidemiology of dementia and Micronesia Epidimiology of dementia in Micronesia

P01AG-08802-02 0002 (AGE) PERL, DANIEL P Epidemiology of dementia and Micronesia Clinicopathologic correlation

P01AG-08802-02 0003 (AGE) PERL, DANIEL P Epidemiology of dementia and Micronesia Manifestations of olfactory system damage

P01AG-08802-02 9001 (AGE) KURLAND, LEONARD T Epidemiology of dementia and Micronesia Island core

P01AG-08802-02 9002 (AGE) O'BRIEN, PETER C Epidemiology of dementia and Micronesia Biostatistics core

P30AG-08808-03 (AGE) HALTER, JEFFREY B UNIVERSITY OF MICHIGAN 300 N. INGALLS STREET ANN ARBOR, MI 48109-0405 Michigan geriatrics research and training center

P30AG-08808-03 0005 (AGE) ORWOLL, LUCINDA J Michigan geriatrics research and training center Pilot study--Wisdom in later adulthood--Psychological correlates

P30AG-08808-03 9001 (AGE) SCHULTZ, ALBERT B Michigan geriatrics research and training center Core--Biomechanics

P30AG-08808-03 9002 (AGE) COHEN, BENNETT J Michigan geriatrics research and training center Core--Facility for aging rodents

P30AG-08808-03 9003 (AGE) FRIES, BRANT E Michigan geriatrics research and training center Core--Data management and analysis

P30AG-08808-03 9004 (AGE) PERLMUTTER, MARION Michigan geriatrics research and training center Core--Human subjects

P30AG-08808-03 9005 (AGE) ADELMAN, RICHARD C Michigan geriatrics research and training center Core--Research development

P30AG-08808-03 0001 (AGE) BRADLEY, SUZANNE F Michigan geriatrics research and training center Pilot study--Aging and the acute phase response /human/

P30AG-08808-03 0002 (AGE) ALEXANDER, NEIL B Michigan geriatrics research and training center Pilot study--Biomechanics of rising from a chair /elderly/

P30AG-08808-03 0003 (AGE) ALBIN, ROGER L Michigan geriatrics research and training center Pilot study--GABAergic cortical neurons in Alzheimer's disease /human/

P30AG-08808-03 0004 (AGE) ROSENBLATT, DORRIE E Michigan geriatrics research and training center Pilot study--Protease nexin I, a glial-derived trophic factor

P30AG-08808-03 0005 (AGE) SUPIANO, MARK A Michigan geriatrics research and training center Pilot study--Sympathetic function in elderly hypertensives /human/

P30AG-08812-02 (AGE) WEI, JEANNE Y 643 HUNTINGTON AVENUE BOSTON, MA 02115 Center of excellence in geriatric research and training

P30AG-08812-02 0001 (AGE) GREENSPAN, SUSAN L Center of excellence in geriatric research and training Pilot study--The coenzyme PQQ in age-related dopamine regulation

P30AG-08812-02 0002 (AGE) DAVIS, KENNETH M Center of excellence in geriatric research and training Pilot study--Predicting volume status using ANP in elderly

P30AG-08812-02 0003 (AGE) MANNING, WARREN J Center of excellence in geriatric research and training Pilot study--Myocardial response to hemodynamic stress in aging

P30AG-08812-02 0004 (AGE) BAUMANN, MARGARET M Center of excellence in geriatric research and training Pilot study--Intracellular mechanisms of contractility in bladder

P30AG-08812-02 0005 (AGE) GURWITZ, JERRY H Center of excellence in geriatric research and training Pilot study--Do thiazides precipitate diabetes in the old?

P30AG-08812-02 0006 (AGE) CLARK, BARBARA A Center of excellence in geriatric research and training Pilot study--Hormonal regulation of extracellular fluid volume in the old

P30AG-08812-02 9001 (AGE) LIPSITZ, LEWIS A Center of excellence in geriatric research and training Core--Subject recruitment

P30AG-08812-02 9002 (AGE) RESNICK, NEIL M Center of excellence in geriatric research and training Core--Diagnostic evaluation

P30AG-08812-02 9003 (AGE) AVORN, JEROME L Center of excellence in geriatric research and training Core--Data management

P30AG-08812-02 9004 (AGE) ELAHI, DARIVSH Center of excellence in geriatric research and training Core--Clinical physiology

P30AG-08812-02 9005 (AGE) WEI, JEANNE Y Center of excellence in geriatric research and training Core--Biomedical engineering and physics

P30AG-08812-02 9006 (AGE) MINAKER, KENNETH L Center of excellence in geriatric research and training Core--Research development

R01AG-08816-02 (HUD) CARSTENSEN, LAURA L STANFORD UNIVERSITY STANFORD, CA 94305-2130 Social interaction in old age

R29AG-08820-02 (CMS) SMITH, STANLEY D GOOD SAMARITAN HOSP & MED CENT 1120 N.W. 20TH AVE PORTLAND, OR 97209 Alzheimer's disease: lexicalsemantic and event knowledge

R01AG-08825-02 (BEM) FRIEDMAN, HOWARD S UNIVERSITY OF CALIFORNIA RIVERSIDE, CA 92521 Social and emotional predictors of health and longevity

R01AG-08835-02 (HUD) BURKE, DEBORAH M POMONA COLLEGE DEPT OF PSYCHOLOGY CLAREMONT, CA 91711 Memory and language in old age

R01AG-08836-01A2 (HUD) RUBINSTEIN, ROBERT L PHILADELPHIA GERIATRIC CENTER 5301 OLD YORK ROAD PHILADELPHIA, PA 19141 Lifestyles and generativity of childless older men

R01AG-08837-02 (BEM) HAMPSON, SARAH E OREGON RESEARCH INSTITUTE 1899 WILLAMETTE EUGENE, OR 97401 Older patients personal models of chronic disease

R29AG-08843-01A1 (NLS) ANDERSON, KEVIN J UNIVERSITY OF FLORIDA BOX J-144, JHMHC GAINESVILLE, FL 32610-0144 Excitatory amino acid systems in the aged brain

R01AG-08849-01A1 (HUD) DALTON, ARTHUR J NYS INSTITUTE FOR BASIC RESEAR 1050 FOREST HILL ROAD STATEN ISLAND, NY 10314 Dementia in Down syndrome--Longitudinal evaluation

R01AG-08861-02 (MGN) MCCLEARN, GERALD E PENNSYLVANIA STATE UNIVERSITY S-211 HENDERSON BUILDING UNIVERSITY PARK, PA 16802 Origins of variance in the old-old--Octogenarian twins

R01AG-08870-01A1 (NEUA) COSLETT, HARRY B TEMPLE UNIVERSITY HOSPITAL 3401 NORTH BROAD STREET PHILADELPHIA, PA 19140 The neuropsychology of perceptual disorders in dementia

R01AG-08882-02 (HUD) EKERDT, DAVID J UNIVERSITY OF KANSAS MEDICAL C 39TH & RAINBOW BLVD. KANSAS CITY, KS 66103 The retirement process in men

R01AG-08885-02 (CMS) ALTSCHULER, RICHARD A KRESGE HEARING RESEARCH INST 1301 EAST ANN STREET ANN ARBOR, MI 48109-0506 Mechanisms of age-related auditory sensory deficits

R01AG-08886-03 (SRC) ROBBINS, NORMAN CASE WESTERN RESERVE UNIV 2119 ABINGTON ROAD CLEVELAND, OH 44106 Mechanisms of aging at the neuromuscular junction

R01AG-08887-03 (SRC) LASEK, RAYMOND J CASE WESTERN RESERVE UNIV 2119 ABINGTON ROAD CLEVELAND, OH 44106 Aging changes in neuronal function and structure

R44AG-08895-02 (HUD) CARD, JOSEFINA J SOCIOMETRICS CORPORATION 170 STATE STREET LOS ATLOS, CA 94022-2812 Microcomputer data archive of social research on aging

R01AG-08909-03 (GMA) YAAR, MINA BOSTON UNIVERSITY SCHOOL OF ME 80 EAST CONCORD ST BOSTON, MA 02118-2394 Growth regulation of normal and malignant keratinocytes

R43AG-08910-01 (HUD) PARKER, MARY H SENIOR HOUSING RESEARCH GROUP 920 SOUTH ALFRED STREET ALEXANDRIA, VA 22314 Development of in-home care quality assurance process

R01AG-08918-03 (NEUC) CHRISTIAN, JOE C INDIANA UNIVERSITY SCHOOL OF M 975 WEST WALNUT STREET, IB-130 INDIANAPOLIS, IN 46202-5251 Huntington disease: A neurological marker of aging

R01AG-08920-06 (CTY) ROSENTHAL, NADIA A BOSTON UNIV SCHOOL OF MEDICINE 80 EAST CONCORD STREET BOSTON, MA 02118 Myosin light chain transcriptional regulatory elements

R29AG-08921-03 (EDC) BORENSTEIN GRAVES, AMY BATTELLE HUMAN RESEARCH CENTER 4000 NORTHEAST 41ST STREET SEATTLE, WA 98105 Aluminum in the epidemiology of alzheimer's disease

R01AG-08932-11 (PBC) CAPLAN, ARNOLD I CASE WESTERN RESERVE UNIV BIOLOGY DEPARTMENT CLEVELAND, OH 44106 Proteoglycan synthesis during development and aging

R01AG-08936-02 (IMB) WALFORD, ROY L UNIV OF CALIFORNIA SCHOOL OF M 10833 LE CONTE AVENUE LOS ANGELES, CA 90024 Major histocompatibility complex, aging and transgenic mice

R37AG-08937-01 (EDC) HEYMAN, ALBERT DUKE UNIVERSITY MEDICAL CENTER BOX 3203 DURHAM, NC 27710 Race differences in prevalence and incidence of dementia

P01AG-08938-07 (HDMR) EPSTEIN, CHARLES J UNIVERSITY OF CALIFORNIA 3RD AVENUE & PARNASSUS SAN FRANCISCO, CALIF 94143 Biology of Down syndrome

R01AG-08945-03 (DABR) HILLER, JACOB M NEW YORK UNIV MEDICAL CENTER 550 FIRST AVENUE NEW YORK, NY 10016 The endogenous opioid system in aging human & rat CNS

R01AG-08948-02 (HUD) TERESI, JEANNE A COMMUNITY RESEARCH APP. INC. 5901 PALISADES AVENUE RIVERDALE, NEW YORK 10471 Impact of special care units in nursing homes

R01AG-08951-01A1 (HUD) SCHUMAN, HOWARD UNIVERSITY OF MICHIGAN 426 THOMPSON STREET ANN ARBOR, MI 48106 Generational effects--Past present and future

R01AG-08957-01A1 (NURS) SCHMITT, MADELINE H UNIVERSITY OF ROCHESTER 601 ELMWOOD AVE ROCHESTER, NY 14642 The quality of geriatric team functioning

R01AG-08958-01A1 (HAR) JERGER, JAMES F BAYLOR COLLEGE OF MEDICINE 6501 FANNIN HOUSTON, TX 77030 Auditory rehabilitation of the elderly

R29AG-08959-01A1 (HAR) BELL, THEODORE S UCLA SCHOOL OF MEDICINE REHABILITATION CENTER LOS ANGELES, CA 90024-1624 Receptive communication problems of the elderly

R01AG-08961-01A2 (EDC) FRASER, GARY E LOMA LINDA UNIVERSITY NICHOL HALL, ROOM 2008 LOMA LINDA, CA 92350 Effect of health habits on survival in Adventists

R35AG-08967-02 (AGE) PRUSINER, STANLEY B UNIV/CAL SAN FRANCISCO SAN FRANCISCO, CA 94143 Leadership and excellence in Alzheimer's disease

R35AG-08967-02 0001 (AGE) PRUSINER, STANLEY B Leadership and excellence in Alzheimer's disease New approaches to prion diseases

R35AG-08967-02 0002 (AGE) HSIAO, KAREN Leadership and excellence in Alzheimer's disease Characterization of PrP mutations in inherited prion diseases

R35AG-08967-02 0003 (AGE) WESTAWAY, DAVID A Leadership and excellence in Alzheimer's disease Molecular biology of natural scrapie

R35AG-08967-02 0004 (AGE) SCOTT, MICHEAL R Leadership and excellence in Alzheimer's disease Random mutation analysis of the PrP gene

R35AG-08967-02 0005 (AGE) PRUSINER, STANLEY B Leadership and excellence in Alzheimer's disease Pilot project--Study of scrapie isolates in cell culture

R35AG-08967-02 0006 (AGE) PRUSINER, STANLEY B Leadership and excellence in Alzheimer's disease Pilot project--Identification of cellular proteins binding scrapie

R29AG-08969-03 (NEUB) SPRINGER, JOE E HAHNEMANN UNIVERSITY SCH OF ME BROAD AND VINE PHILADELPHIA, PA 19102-1192 CNS regeneration: effects of NGF-rich transplants

R01AG-08973-01A1 (HUD) BECKER, GAYLENE UNIVERSITY OF CALIFORNIA SAN FRANCISCO, CA 94143-0612 Gender and the disruption of life course structure

R35AG-08974-01 (AGE) PETTEGREW, JAY W WESTERN PSYCHIATRIC INST & CLN 3811 O'HARA STREET PITTSBURGH, PA 15213 Molecular studies in Alzheimer's disease

PROJECT NO., ORGANIZATIONAL UNIT., INVESTIGATOR, ADDRESS, TITLE

R35AG-08974-01 0005 (AGE) KLUNK, W E Molecular studies in Alzheimer's disease Chemical and physical studies of beta amyloid protein

R35AG-08974-01 0006 (AGE) MINSHEW, NANCY J Molecular studies in Alzheimer's disease In vivo brain chemistry in Down's syndrome

R35AG-08974-01 0007 (AGE) PALMER, ALAN M Molecular studies in Alzheimer's disease Relationship between PME and EAA neurons and receptors

R35AG-08974-01 0008 (AGE) GEDDES, J W Molecular studies in Alzheimer's disease Pilot study--Correlation of neuritic sprouting with the levels of PME and PDE

R35AG-08974-01 0001 (AGE) PETTEGREW, JAY Molecular studies in Alzheimer's disease Analysis of membrane metabolism in Alzheimer's disease

R35AG-08974-01 0002 (AGE) PETTEGREW, JAY Molecular studies in Alzheimer's disease Analysis of membrane phospholipid enzymes in Alzheimer's disease

R35AG-08974-01 0003 (AGE) PETTEGREW, JAY Molecular studies in Alzheimer's disease The effect of brain develop & aging on response to graded hypoxia/ischemia

R35AG-08974-01 0004 (AGE) PETTEGREW, JAY Molecular studies in Alzheimer's disease Modeling of phosphomonoester--Relationship to L-glutamate and GABA

R01AG-08991-02 (CTY) VARSHAVSKY, ALEXANDER J MASSACHUSETTS INST OF TECH 77 MASSACHUSETTS AVENUE CAMBRIDGE, MA 02139 Studies on stress, repair, and aging

R35AG-08992-01 (AGE) GAMBETTI, PIERLUIGI CASE WESTERN RESERVE UNIV 2085 ADELBERT ROAD CLEVELAND, OH 44106 Cellular and molecular pathology of Alzheimer's disease

R35AG-08992-01 0001 (AGE) GAMBETTI, PIERLUIGI Cellular and molecular pathology of Alzheimer's disease Heat shock proteins

R35AG-08992-01 0002 (AGE) LEBLANC, ANDREA Cellular and molecular pathology of Alzheimer's disease Gene expression of ubiquitin

R35AG-08992-01 0003 (AGE) COHEN, MARK Cellular and molecular pathology of Alzheimer's disease Amyloid deposition

R35AG-08992-01 0004 (AGE) PERRY, GEORGE Cellular and molecular pathology of Alzheimer's disease Studies of neurofibril.patho. in Alzheimer's disease

R35AG-08992-01 0005 (AGE) GAMBETTI, PIERLUIGI Cellular and molecular pathology of Alzheimer's disease Pilot 1---Identification of polypeptide components of PHF

R35AG-08992-01 0006 (AGE) COHEN, MARK Cellular and molecular pathology of Alzheimer's disease Pilot 2---Protease and beta amyloid peptide

R35AG-08992-01 0007 (AGE) YOUNKIN, STEVEN Cellular and molecular pathology of Alzheimer's disease Pilot 3---Putative AD genes

R35AG-08992-01 0008 (AGE) PERRY, GEORGE Cellular and molecular pathology of Alzheimer's disease pilot 4—Aged or alcohalic rats as an model of neuro.degeneration

R01AG-09000-02 (RAP) ENOKA, ROGER M UNIVERSITY OF ARIZONA TUCSON, AZ 85721 Aging and training effects on motor units in exercise

R01AG-09006-02 (BIO) SIPE, JEAN D BOSTON UNIV SCH OF MED 80 EAST CONCORD STREET BOSTON, MA 02118 Cellular metabolism of amyloid proteins in aging

R01AG-09009-02 (NLS) COLE, GREGORY M UNIV OF CALIF., SAN DIEGO LA JOLLA, CA 92093 Metabolism of Alzheimer amyloid b-protein precursor

R35AG-09014-01 (AGE) BLASS, JOHN P W M BURKE MED RESEARCH INST, I 785 MAMARONECK AVENUE WHITE PLAINS, NY 10605 Clinical-cell biological studies in Alzheimer's disease

R35AG-09014-01 0001 (AGE) BLASS, JOHN Clinical-cell biological studies in Alzheimer's disease Clin.sign. of abnor. in cells cult. from pat. with Alzheimer disease

R35AG-09014-01 0002 (AGE) BLACK, RONALD Clinical-cell biological studies in Alzheimer's disease Immun.quant. of paired hel.fil. and related prot. in ALZ.brain and fib.

R35AG-09016-02 (AGE) COLEMAN, PAUL D UNIVERSITY OF ROCHESTER 601 ELMWOOD AVENUE, BOX 603 ROCHESTER, NY 14642 Leadership & excellence in Alzheimer's disease award

R35AG-09016-02 0001 (AGE) COLEMAN, PAUL D Leadership & excellence in Alzheimer's disease award Alzheimer's disease, plastic neurites and neuron-gliainteraction

R35AG-09016-02 0002 (AGE) HIGGINS, GERALD A Leadership & excellence in Alzheimer's disease award NGF-Responsiveness and amyloid gene expression in Alzheimer's disease

R35AG-09016-02 0003 (AGE) RICHFIELD, ERIK K Leadership & excellence in Alzheimer's disease award Vulnerability and compensation of dopamaine systems in Alzheimer's and Aging

R35AG-09016-02 0004 (AGE) SLEMMON, J RANDALL Leadership & excellence in Alzheimer's disease award Differential peptide expression in Alzheimer's disease

R35AG-09016-02 0005 (AGE) ROGERS, KATHRYN E Leadership & excellence in Alzheimer's disease award Pilot project–MAP 2 mRNA in aging and Alzheimer's disease brain

R35AG-09016-02 0006 (AGE) SLADEK, CELIA D Leadership & excellence in Alzheimer's disease award Pilot project–Gene regulation in vasopressin neurons during aging

R35AG-09016-02 0007 (AGE) HAMILL, ROBERT W Leadership & excellence in Alzheimer's disease award Pilot project–Hippocampal glucocorticoid receptors in Alzheimer's disease

P01AG-09017-02 (AGE) CARP, RICHARD I NYS INST FOR BASIC RESEARCH 1050 FOREST HILL ROAD STATEN ISLAND, NY 10314 Search for a transmissible agent in Alzheimer's disease

P01AG-09017-02 0004 (AGE) PETTEGREW, JAY W Search for a transmissible agent in Alzheimer's disease Membrane metabolism in scrapie and Alzheimer's disease

P01AG-09017-02 9001 (AGE) SERSEN, EUGENE A Search for a transmissible agent in Alzheimer's disease Core--Data management

P01AG-09017-02 0001 (AGE) CARP, RICHARD I Search for a transmissible agent in Alzheimer's disease Transmission

P01AG-09017-02 0002 (AGE) RUBENSTEIN, RICHARD Search for a transmissible agent in Alzheimer's disease Detection of PrP in hamsters

P01AG-09017-02 0003 (AGE) KASCSAK, RICHARD J Search for a transmissible agent in Alzheimer's disease Differential gene expression in buffy coat cells

R15AG-09020-01 (BCE) CALLAHAN, PHYLLIS A MIAMI UNIVERSITY OXFORD, OH 45056 Age related changes in pituitary lactotrophs

R01AG-09029-01A1 (EDC) FARRER, LINDSAY A BOSTON UNIVERSITY 80 EAST CONCORD STREET BOSTON, MA 02118 Genetic epidemiological studies of Alzheimers disease

R01AG-09031-02 (NEUA) BINDER, LESTER I UNIVERSITY OF ALABAMA UAB STATION BIRMINGHAM, AL 35294 Microtubule proteins in Alzheimer's disease

R01AG-09033-01A1 (NTN) SEYBERT, DAVID W DUQUESNE UNIVERSITY 600 FORBES AVENUE PITTSBURGH, PA 15282 Lipid peroxidation in disease and aging

R15AG-09034-01A1 (CTY) HOOPES, LAURA L OCCIDENTAL COLLEGE 1600 CAMPUS ROAD LOS ANGELES, CA 90041 DNA repair and age-related methylation changes

R29AG-09055-02 (HUD) SHIMAMURA, ARTHUR P UNIVERSITY OF CALIFORNIA ASSESSMENT AND RESEARCH BERKELEY, CA 94720 Aging and memory--A neuropsychological analysis

R01AG-09063-02 (NLS) CONNOR, JAMES R PENNSYLVANIA STATE UNIVERSITY HERSHEY, PA 17033 Ferritin and transferrin in CNS aging and disease

R01AG-09065-01A1 (HUD) LUBORSKY, MARK R PHILADELPHIA GERIATRIC CENTER 5301 OLD YORK ROAD PHILADELPHIA, PA 19141 Continuity of personal meaning and well being in old age

U01AG-09078-02 (AGE) FIATARONE, MARIA A HEBREW REHABILITATION CTR AGED 1200 CENTRE STREET BOSTON, MA 02131 Muscle strengthening intervention in the frail elderly

U01AG-09087-02 (AGE) TINETTI, MARY E YALE UNIVERSITY SCHOOL OF MED 333 CEDAR ST, PO BOX 3333 NEW HAVEN, CT 06510 Community-based multiple fall risk factor intervention trial

U01AG-09089-02 (AGE) HORNBROOK, MARK C KAISER FDN HOSPTIAL 4610 S E BELMONT STREET PORTLAND, OR 97215-1795 Behavorial approach to falls prevention in the elderly

U01AG-09095-02 (AGE) BUCHNER, DAVID M UNIVERSITY OF WASHINGTON SEATTLE, WA 98195 Health status effects of endurance and strength training

U01AG-09098-02 (AGE) MILLER, J PHILIP 660 S EUCLID AVENUE, BX 8067 ST LOUIS, MO 63110 Reducing frailty & injuries in older persons

U01AG-09117-02 (AGE) MULROW, CYNTHIA D AUDIE L MURPHY VETERANS HOSPIT 7400 MERTON MINTER BLVD SAN ANTONIO, TX 78284 Effects of physical therapy in nursing home residents

R01AG-09121-02 (NEUA) LANGSTON, J WILLIAM CALIFORNIA PARKINSON'S FDN 2444 MOORPARK AVE SAN JOSE, CA 95128 Aging and environmental toxins

U01AG-09124-02 (AGE) WOLF, STEVEN L 1441 CLIFTON RD NE ATLANTA, GA 30322 Reducing frailty in elders--Two exercise interventions

R01AG-09127-02 (HUD) REISBERG, BARRY NEW YORK UNIVERSITY MEDICAL CT 550 FIRST AVE NEW YORK, NY 10016 Behavioral and psychotic symptoms in Alzheimer's disease

R01AG-09140-02 (IMB) MEYDANI, SIMIN N TUFTS UNIVERSITY 711 WASHINGTON STREET BOSTON, MA 02111 Vitamin E and the aging immune response

R01AG-09145-02 (HSR) FEDSON, DAVID S UNIV OF VIRGINIA HEALTH SCI CT BOX 494 CHARLOTTESVILLE, VA 22908 The Manitoba influenza study

R44AG-09167-02 (HUD) TRAPNELL, GORDON R ACTUARIAL RESEARCH CORPORATION 6928 LITTLE RIVER TURNPIKE ANNANDALE, VA 22003 Long term care insurance--A manual for regulators

R01AG-09176-01A1 (HUD) BECKER, GAY UNIVERSITY OF CALIFORNIA BOX 0612 SAN FRANCISCO, CA 94143-0612 From independence to dependence among the oldest old

R01AG-09179-02 (HUD) JAGACINSKI, RICHARD J OHIO STATE UNIVERSITY 1885 NEIL AVE COLUMBUS, OH 43210-1222 Auditory aiding for perceptual motor decline in aging

R01AG-09186-01A1 (CMS) MALMGREN, LESLIE T SUNY HEALTH SCIENCES CTR 750 EAST ADAMS STREET SYRACUSE, NY 13210 Aging human laryngeal protective mechanism

R01AG-09188-01A1 (NLS) BURKE, WILLIAM J 3635 VISTA AT GRAND PO BOX 152 ST LOUIS, MO 63110-0250 Degeneration of epinephrine neurons in Alzheimer's disease

R01AG-09191-01 (HAR) GORDON-SALANT, SANDRA M UNIVERSITY OF MARYLAND LEFRAK HALL COLLEGE PARK, MD 20742 Auditory temporal processes, speech perception and aging

R01AG-09195-01A1 (HUD) GLISKY, ELIZABETH L UNIVERSITY OF ARIZONA TUCSON, AZ 85721 Computer training for older adults

R01AG-09198-02 (HUD) TOBIN, SHELDON S RINGEL INST OF GERONTOLOGY 135 WESTERN AVENUE ALBANY, NY 12222 Permanent residential planning by parents of MR adults

R01AG-09199-01 (ORTH) HAYASHI, MASANDO UMDNJ-ROBERT W JOHNSON MED SCH PISCATAWAY, NJ 08854-5635 Vertebral endochondral ossification

R01AG-09200-01A1 (NEUA) TALAMO, BARBARA R TUFTS UNIVERSITY 136 HARRISON AVENUE BOSTON, MA 02111 Human olfactory tissue-- Aging and Alzheimer's disease

R01AG-09202-01A1 (EDC) GANGULI, MARY UNIVERSITY OF PITTSBURGH 130 DESOTO STREET PITTSBURGH, PA 15261 An Indo-US cross national dementia epidemiology study

R01AG-09203-01A1 (HUD) LABOUVIE-VIEF, GISELA WAYNE STATE UNIVERSITY 71 WEST WARREN DETROIT, MI 48202 Cognitive emotional maturity in adulthood and aging

R29AG-09208-01A1 (HUD) ZABRUCKY, KAREN M GEORGIA STATE UNIVERSITY UNIVERSITY PLAZA ATLANTA, GA 30303 Aging and evaluation and regulation of understanding

R29AG-09214-01A1 (BCE) RANCE, NAOMI E UNIVERSITY OF ARIZONA 1501 N CAMPBELL AVENUE TUSCON, AZ 85724 Reproductive aging and the human hypothalamus

P01AG-09215-02 (AGE) TROJANOWSKI, JOHN Q UNIV OF PENNSYLVANIA SCH OF ME MALONEY BASEMENT PHILADELPHIA, PA 19104-4283 Molecular substrates of aging and neuron death

P01AG-09215-02 0001 (AGE) JOYCE, JEFFREY N Molecular substrates of aging and neuron death Dopamine receptors

PROJECT NO., ORGANIZATIONAL UNIT., INVESTIGATOR, ADDRESS, TITLE

P01AG-09215-02 0002 (AGE) TROJANOWSKI, JOHN Q Molecular substrates of aging and neuron death Amyloid protein deposition

P01AG-09215-02 0003 (AGE) LEE, VIRGINIA M-Y Molecular substrates of aging and neuron death Kinases and cytoskeletal proteins

P01AG-09215-02 9001 (AGE) HURTIG, HOWARD I Molecular substrates of aging and neuron death Core--Clinbical assessment

P01AG-09215-02 9002 (AGE) TROJANOWSKI, JOHN Q Molecular substrates of aging and neuron death Core--Neuropathology

P01AG-09215-02 9003 (AGE) LEE, VIRGINIA M-Y Molecular substrates of aging and neuron death Core--Hybridoma and peptides

R01AG-09216-01 (NEUA) CRAIN, BARBARA J DUKE UNIVERSITY MED CTR BOX 3712 DURHAM, NC 27710 Pathology of fascia dentata in Alzheimer's disease

R01AG-09219-01A1 (NEUB) BARNES, CAROL A UNIVERSITY OF ARIZONA TUCSON, ARIZONA 85721 Transcription factor genes, neuronal plasticity, and aging

R01AG-09220-01 (REN) NELSON, JAMES F UNIV OF TEXAS HEALTH SCIENCE C 7703 FLOYD CURL DRIVE SAN ANTONIO, TX 78284-7756 Aging and the regulation of estrogen action in the brain

R01AG-09221-01A1 (LCR) KRAUSE, NEAL M UNIVERSITY OF MICHIGAN 1420 WASHINGTON HEIGHTS ANN ARBOR, MI 48109-2029 Well-being among the aged/personal control and self-esteem

R29AG-09229-02 (NEUB) YANKNER, BRUCE A CHILDRENS HOSPITAL CORPORATION 300 LONGWOOD AVE BOSTON, MA 02115 Amyloid neurotoxicity and biological function

R01AG-09231-02 (NEUB) LOY, REBEKAH MONROE COMMUNITY HOSPITAL 435 EAST HENRIETTA ROAD ROCHESTER, NY 14620 NGF receptor, memory and aging

R01AG-09235-02 (CPA) NEBERT, DANIEL W UNIVERSITY OF CINCINNATI 3223 EDEN AVE CINCINNATI, OH 45267-0056 Oxidative stress cell death and the [AH] gene battery

R01AG-09241-01 (ORTH) WRONSKI, THOMAS J UNIVERSITY OF FLORIDA BOX J-144, JHMHC GAINESVILLE, FLA 32610 Restoration of lost bone mass after ovariectomy

R01AG-09246-01A1 (IMB) O'LEARY, JAMES J UNIVERSITY OF MINNESOTA 420 DELAWARE AVENUE MINNEAPOLIS, MN 55455 Effect of advanced age on human naive and memory T cells

R55AG-09250-01A1 (EDC) COHN, BARBARA A CALIFORNIA PUBLIC HEALTH FDN 2001 ADDISON STREET BERKELEY, CA 94704-1103 Epidemiology of sex differences in cancer survival

R01AG-09253-02 (HUD) HASHTROUDI, SHAHIN GEORGE WASHINGTON UNIVERSITY WASHINGTON, DC 20052 Effects of aging on memory for source of information

R01AG-09265-02 (HUD) CAVANAUGH, JOHN C BOWLING GREEN STATE UNIVERSITY DEPARTMENT OF PSYCHOLOGY BOWLING GREEN, OH 43403 Caregiv burden over time/a stress and coping approach

R01AG-09276-02 (BEM) BAREFOOT, JOHN C DUKE UNIVERSITY MEDICAL CENTER BOX 31217 DURHAM, NC 27710 Gender and age differences in hostility

R01AG-09278-02 (CBY) WANG, YU-HWA E LADY DAVIS INST FOR MED RESEAR 3755 CHEMIN COTE STE-CATHERINE MONTREAL, QUEBEC H3T 1E2 CANA Fibroblast aging and programmed cell death

R01AG-09279-01 (PBC) MILLIS, ALBERT J STATE UNIVERSITY OF NEW YORK 1400 WASHINGTON AVENUE ALBANY, NY 12222 Gene expression in senescent cells

R29AG-09282-01A1 (HUD) ALLEN, PHILIP A CLEVELAND STATE UNIVERSITY EUCLID AVENUE AT EAST 24TH ST CLEVELAND, OH 44115 Adult age differences in cognitive noise

R01AG-09287-02 (PTHA) PERRY, GEORGE CASE WESTERN UNIVERSITY 2085 ADELBERT ROAD CLEVELAND, OH 44106 Neurofibrillary pathology in Alzheimer disease

R01AG-09291-01A1 (HUD) BOURGEOIS, MICHELLE S UNIV OF PITTSBURGH-UCSUR 121 UNIVERSITY PLACE PITTSBURGH, PA 15260 Interventions to change caregiver & Alzheimer's disease patient outcomes

R01AG-09295-01A1 (SSP) MC LAUGHLIN, STEVEN D BATTELLE HUMAN AFFAIRS RES CTR 4000 NE 41ST STREET SEATTLE, WA 98105 Parents marital history and support from adult children

R01AG-09297-01A1 (BPO) TUREK, FRED W NORTHWESTERN UNIVERSITY 2153 SHERIDAN ROAD EVANSTON, IL 60208 Effects of age on mammalian circadian clock

R01AG-09300-01A1 (EDC) FELSON, DAVID T BOSTON UNIV SCHOOL OF MEDICINE 80 EAST CONCORD STREET BOSTON, MA 02118 Longitudinal osteoarthritis study in an elderly cohort

R01AG-09301-02 (HUD) SATLIN, ANDREW MCLEAN HOSPITAL 115 MILL STREET BELMONT, MA 02178 Senile changes in circadian rhythms and behavior

R01AG-09302-02 (VISA) READY, DONALD F PURDUE UNIVERSITY WEST LAFAYETTE, IN 47907 A cellular and genetic analysis of cell death

R01AG-09304-01A1 (NTN) WINCHURCH, RICHARD A ASTHMA AND ALLERGY CENTER 301 BAYVIEW BLVD BALTIMORE, MD 21224 Nutritional requirements for immunity in the aged

R01AG-09309-02 (NEUB) SENGELAUB, DALE R INDIANA UNIVERSITY BLOOMINGTON, IN 47405 Steroids as trophic factors in an aging neuromuscular system

R13AG-09316-02 (AGE) BROWN, W TED NORTH SHORE UNIV HOSP 300 COMMUNITY DRIVE MANHASSET, NY 11030 The genetic basis of aging and longevity

R01AG-09320-02 (NEUC) GOLDGABER, DMITRY Y SUNY AT STONY BROOK STONY BROOK , NY 11794-8101 Regulation of Alzheimer amyloid precursor gene

R01AG-09321-01A1 (BPO) FLOOD, JAMES F VA MEDICAL CENTER 915 NORTH GRAND BLVD ST LOUIS, MO 63106 Model of dementia -- Senescence accelerated

R37AG-09326-02 (MGN) EDELMAN, GERALD M THE ROCKEFELLER UNIVERSITY 1230 YORK AVENUE NEW YORK, NY 10021-6399 Control of CAM expression in transgenic mice

R01AG-09331-02 (SRC) ALTER, GEORGE C INDIANA UNIVERSITY FOR RESEARCH AND TRAINING BLOOMINGTON, IN 47405 Kin, saving, and households of the elderly

R01AG-09333-02 (MGN) MCCLEARN, GERALD E PENNSYLVANIA STATE UNIVERSITY S-211 HENDERSON BUILDING UNIVERSITY PARK, PA 16802 Dimensions of aging--Genetic and environmental influence

PROJECT NO., ORGANIZATIONAL UNIT., INVESTIGATOR, ADDRESS, TITLE

R01AG-09337-01A1 (NLS) KLEIN, WILLIAM L NORTHWESTERN UNIVERSITY 2153 SHERIDAN RD EVANSTON, IL 60208 Molecular cell biology of amyloid precursor protein

R01AG-09338-02 (HUD) HAYWARD, MARK D UNIV OF SOUTERN CALIFORNIA LOS ANGELES, CA 90089-0191 Retirement from a life-course perspective

R01AG-09341-06A1 (EDC) SWAN, GARY E SRI INTERNATIONAL 333 RAVENSWOOD AVENUE MENLO PARK, CA 94025 CVD and cognitive decline in the elderly

R29AG-09344-02 (HUD) LAWRENCE, RENEE H PHILADELPHIA GERIATRIC CENTER 5301 OLD YORK ROAD PHILADELPHIA, PA 19141 Physical and emotional health among the elderly

R43AG-09358-01A1 (HUD) KIRKPATRICK, MARK, III CARLOW ASSOC INC 8315 LEE HIGHWAY FAIRFAX, VA 22031-2269 Development of a memory aid interface for elderly users

R43AG-09368-01A1 (HUD) LUCERO, MARY E GERIATRIC RESOURCES, INC 5450 BARTON DRIVE ORLANDO, FL 32807 Products for Alzheimers patients with null behavior

R01AG-09375-02 (EDC) MC GARVEY, STEPHEN T THE MIRIAM HOSPITAL 164 SUMMIT AVENUE PROVIDENCE, RI 02906 Adiposity insulin electrolytes and Samoan blood pressure

R13AG-09382-01 (AGE) HAREVEN, TAMARA K UNIVERSITY OF DELEWARE COLLEGE OF HUMAN RESOURCES NEWARK, DE 19716 Aging and generational relations conference

R01AG-09383-01A1 (CTY) GREIDER, CAROL W COLD SPRING HARBOR LABORATORY P O BOX 100 COLD SPRING HARBOR, NY 11724 Structure and function of telomeres in mammalian aging

R13AG-09398-01 (AGE) STUEN, CYNTHIA NATL CENTER FOR VISION & AGING 111 EAST 59TH STREET NEW YORK, NY 10022 Aging and sensory change-- A challenge to research

R01AG-09399-01 (CMS) GROSSMAN, MURRAY HOSP OF THE UNIV OF PENNSYLVAN 3400 SPRUCE STREET PHILADELPHIA, PA 19104-4283 Cognitive profiles in Alzheimer's disease and aging

R01AG-09411-01 (MEDB) GLENNER, GEORGE G UNIVERSITY OF CALIFORNIA LA JOLLA, CA 92093 Paired helical filament and plaque amyloid proteins

R01AG-09412-02 (ORTH) RUFF, CHRISTOPHER B JOHNS HOPKINS UNIVERSITY 725 NORTH WOLFE STREET BALTIMORE, MD 21205 Effects of aging and exercise on bone mass in beagles

R01AG-09413-01A1 (CTY) SHMOOKLER-REIS, ROBERT J J MCCLELLAN MEMORIAL VA HOSPIT 4300 WEST 7TH STREET LITTLE ROCK, AR 72205 Polymorphic genes modulating lifespan in C elegans

R01AG-09416-01A1 (HUD) MILLER, BAILA H UNIVERSITY OF ILLINOIS 808 S WOOD ST MC 778 CHICAGO, IL 60612 Gender and race in care of the cognitively impaired

R01AG-09417-01 (AGE) SCHNECK, STUART A UNIV OF COLORADO HEALTH SCI CT 4200 E 9TH AVE, BOX B-183 DENVER, CO 80262 Metabolic studies in dementia, aging and demyelination

P01AG-09417-01 0001 (AGE) PARKER, W DAVIS Metabolic studies in dementia, aging and demyelination Alzheimer's disease in mitochondrial genes

P01AG-09417-01 0002 (AGE) FILLEY, CHRISTOPHER Metabolic studies in dementia, aging and demyelination Cytochrome oxidase deficiency in Alzheimer's disease

P01AG-09417-01 0003 (AGE) BOYSON, SALLY J Metabolic studies in dementia, aging and demyelination Complex I in Parkinson's disease

P01AG-09417-01 0004 (AGE) STABLER, SALLY P Metabolic studies in dementia, aging and demyelination Prevalence and spectrum of B12 deficiency in the aged

P01AG-09417-01 0005 (AGE) ENGLAND, JOHN D Metabolic studies in dementia, aging and demyelination Efects of demyelination and aging upon sodium channels

P01AG-09417-01 9001 (AGE) SCHNECK, STUART A Metabolic studies in dementia, aging and demyelination Clinical-scientific core

R01AG-09430-01 (IMS) THEOFILOPOULOS, ARGYRIOS N RES INST OF SCRIPPS CLINIC 10666 NORTH TORREY PINES ROAD LA JOLLA, CA 92037 T cell receptor gene repertoire in aging

R29AG-09433-01A1 (HUD) HUMMERT, MARY L UNIVERSITY OF KANSAS 3090 WESCOE HALL LAWRENCE, KS 66045 Stereotypes of the elderly and communication

R01AG-09439-01 (HUD) SILVERMAN, WAYNE P NYS INST FOR BASIC RESEARCH DD 1050 FOREST HILL ROAD STATEN ISLAND, NY 10314 Aging and mental retardation--Changes in processing rate

R55AG-09440-01A1 (EDC) TALLEY, NICHOLAS J MAYO FOUNDATION 200 FIRST STREET SOUTHWEST ROCHESTER, MN 55905 Impact of functional bowel disease in the elderly

R01AG-09453-01A1 (PTHA) VLASSARA, HELEN ROCKEFELLER UNIVERSITY 1230 YORK AVE NEW YORK, NY 10021 Aging and vascular disease role of glycation

R13AG-09454-01 (AGE) KUNA, SAMUEL T UNIV OF TEXAS MEDICAL BRANCH ROUTE E-61 GALVESTON, TX 77550 Symposium on sleep and respiration in aging adults

R01AG-09458-01A1 (HEM) LIPSCHITZ, DAVID A UNIV OF ARKANSAS FOR MED SCIS 4301 WEST MARKHAM STREET LITTLE ROCK, AR 72205 Neutrophil function and aging

R29AG-09462-01 (HUD) LEVIN, JEFFREY S EASTERN VIRGINIA MEDICAL SCHOO PO BOX 1980 NORFOLK, VA 23501 Religion, health, and psychological well-being in the aged

P30AG-09463-01 (AGE) COHEN, HARVEY J DUKE UNIVERSITY MEDICAL CENTER BOX 3003 DURHAM, NC 27710 Geriatric research and training centers

P30AG-09463-01 0001 (AGE) HACKEL, ANDREA Geriatric research and training centers Autonomic functioning in elderly with unexplained syncope

P30AG-09463-01 0002 (AGE) SCHMADER, KENNETH E Geriatric research and training centers Epidemiology of herpes zoster and postherpetic neuralgia

P30AG-09463-01 0003 (AGE) KITZMAN, DALANE Geriatric research and training centers Age and cardiovascular function with rest and exercise

P30AG-09463-01 0004 (AGE) LOPREST, LORRAINE Geriatric research and training centers Linkage studies in Alzheimer's disease

P30AG-09463-01 9001 (AGE) BLAZER, DAN G Geriatric research and training centers Core--Human population laboratory

PROJECT NO., ORGANIZATIONAL UNIT., INVESTIGATOR, ADDRESS, TITLE

P30AG-09463-01 9002 (AGE) WILLIAMS, REDFORD B Geriatric research and training centers Core--Cardiovascular and autonomic physiology
P30AG-09463-01 9003 (AGE) GEORGE, LINDA K Geriatric research and training centers Core--Epidemiology /health services research
P30AG-09463-01 9004 (AGE) ROSES, ALLEN D Geriatric research and training centers Core--Genetic analysis laboratory
P30AG-09463-01 9005 (AGE) MARSH, GAIL R Geriatric research and training centers Core--Research development
P01AG-09464-01 (AGE) GREENGARD, PAUL ROCKEFELLER UNIVERSITY 1230 YORK AVENUE NEW YORK, NY 10021 Signal transduction and Alzheimer's disease
P01AG-09464-01 0001 (AGE) GREENGARD, PAUL Signal transduction and Alzheimer's disease Signal transduction & Alzheimer's disease--Enzymological studies
P01AG-09464-01 0002 (AGE) GANDY, SAMUEL E Signal transduction and Alzheimer's disease Signal transduction & Alzheimer's disease--Cell biological studies
P01AG-09464-01 0003 (AGE) GUSTAFSON, ERIC L Signal transduction and Alzheimer's disease Signal transduction & Alzheimer's disease--Anatomical studies
P01AG-09464-01 0004 (AGE) SCHAEFFER, ERIC Signal transduction and Alzheimer's disease Signal transduction and Alzheimer's disease--Molecular biological studies
P01AG-09464-01 9001 (AGE) CZERNIK, ANDREW J Signal transduction and Alzheimer's disease Core--Immunochemistry/protein chemistry/molecular biology
P01AG-09466-01 (AGE) DETOLEDO-MORRELL, LEYLA RUSH-PRESBYTERIAN-ST. LUKE'S 1653 W CONGRESS PKWY CHICAGO, IL 60612 Anatomic, physiologic and cognitive pathology of AD
P01AG-09466-01 0001 (AGE) DETOLEDO-MORRELL, LEYLA Anatomic, physiologic and cognitive pathology of AD Electrophysiological markers of early AD
P01AG-09466-01 0002 (AGE) GABRIELI, JOHN D Anatomic, physiologic and cognitive pathology of AD Knowledge systems analysis of early AD
P01AG-09466-01 0003 (AGE) GEINISMAN, YURI Anatomic, physiologic and cognitive pathology of AD Hippocampal synaptic connectivity in Alzheimer's disease
P01AG-09466-01 0004 (AGE) KORDOWER, JEFFREY H Anatomic, physiologic and cognitive pathology of AD NGF tropism in Alzheimer's disease
P01AG-09466-01 0005 (AGE) SAPER, CLIFFORD B Anatomic, physiologic and cognitive pathology of AD Chemical neuroanatomy of Alzheimer's disease
P01AG-09466-01 9001 (AGE) FOX, JACOB Anatomic, physiologic and cognitive pathology of AD Core--Clinical
P01AG-09466-01 9002 (AGE) COCHRAN, ELIZABETH J Anatomic, physiologic and cognitive pathology of AD Core--Neuropathology
P01AG-09466-01 9003 (AGE) NORUSIS, MARIJA J Anatomic, physiologic and cognitive pathology of AD Core--Statistics
R01AG-09468-01 (SSP) SLOAN, FRANK A VANDERBILT UNIVERSITY BOX 1503 - STATION B NASHVILLE, TN 37235 Effects of public subsidies on use of long term care
R01AG-09470-01 (NEUC) GLORIOSO, JOSEPH C UNIVERSITY OF PITTSBURGH E1246 BIOMEDICAL SCIENCE TOWER PITTSBURGH, PA. 152611 Studies of Alzheimer's disease using HSV gene transfer
P01AG-09480-01 (AGE) LLINAS, RODOLFO R NEW YORK UNIV MEDICAL CENTER 550 FIRST AVENUE NEW YORK, NY 10016 Aging and neuronal death--The role of cytosolic calcium
P01AG-09480-01 0001 (AGE) LLINAS, RODOLFO R Aging and neuronal death--The role of cytosolic calcium Electrophysiological characterization of aged Purkinje cells and cell death
P01AG-09480-01 0002 (AGE) CHERKSEY, BRUCE D Aging and neuronal death--The role of cytosolic calcium Molecular physiology of aging--Aging and ion channels
P01AG-09480-01 0003 (AGE) HILLMAN, DEAN E Aging and neuronal death--The role of cytosolic calcium Neuromorphology and subcellular structure in aging
P01AG-09480-01 9001 (AGE) LLINAS, RODOLFO R Aging and neuronal death--The role of cytosolic calcium Core--Computer, histological, and shop facility
R29AG-09486-01A1 (HUD) CHAPMAN, SANDRA B UNIVERSITY OF TEXAS 1966 INWOOD ROAD DALLAS, TX 75235 Cognitive discourse processing in elderly populations
R01AG-09488-01 (NLS) MEANEY, MICHAEL J MCGILL-DOUGLAS HOSP RESEARCH C 6875, BOUL LASALLE MONTREAL, QUEBEC H4H 1R3 CANAD Glucocorticoids, stress, and hippocampal aging
R01AG-09519-01 (EDC) KEEFOVER, ROBERT CHESTNUT RIDGE HOSPITAL MORGANTOWN , WV 26506 Screening for Alzheimers disease in a rural population
R01AG-09521-06 (CTY) BLAU, HELEN M STANFORD UNIVERSITY 125 PANAMA ST STANFORD, CA 94305 Cytoplasmic activators of human muscle genes
P01AG-09525-01 (AGE) BLUSZTAJN, JAN K BOSTON UNIVERSITY 85 EAST NEWTON ST,RM M1009 BOSTON, MA 02118 Aging of brain -- Effects of perinatal choline exposure
P01AG-09525-01 0001 (AGE) BLUSZTAJN, JAN K Aging of brain -- Effects of perinatal choline exposure Brain aging-- Biochemical effects of perinatal choline
P01AG-09525-01 0002 (AGE) LOY, REBEKAH Aging of brain -- Effects of perinatal choline exposure Perinatal choline effects-- Basal forebrain growth and aging
P01AG-09525-01 0003 (AGE) MECK, WARREN H Aging of brain -- Effects of perinatal choline exposure Perinatal choline supplementation, memory, and aging
P01AG-09525-01 0004 (AGE) WILLIAMS, CHRISTINA L Aging of brain -- Effects of perinatal choline exposure Time frames of choline enhancement of memory
P01AG-09525-01 0005 (AGE) ZEISEL, STEVEN H Aging of brain -- Effects of perinatal choline exposure Biochemistry of supplemental choline in neonatal rats
R01AG-09550-01 (PHRA) SCHWARTZ, JANICE B UNIVERSITY OF CALIFORNIA SAN FRANCISCO, CA 94143-0446 Regulation of cardiac rhythm & conduction with aging
R01AG-09557-01 (END) STRONG, RANDY VA MEDICAL CENTER ST LOUIS, MO 63125 Modulation of TH gene expression by reserpine and age
R01AG-09559-01 (PHRA) VESTAL, ROBERT E VA MEDICAL CENTER 500 WEST FORT STREET BOISE, ID 83702-4598 Age-related cardiac response to theophylline in man
R01AG-09560-01 (PHRA) VOELKER, JAMES R WISHARD MEMORIAL HOSPITAL 1001 WEST 10TH STREET INDIANAPOLIS, IN 46202-2879 Captopril and angiotensin vascular effects in senescence
R55AG-09566-01 (PHRA) O'CONNELL, MARY E UNIVERSITY OF MINNESOTA 308 HARVARD STREET SOUTHEAST MINNEAPOLIS, MN 55455 Estrogens in older women--Bone density and lipid effect
R01AG-09568-01 (EDC) JINKS, MARTIN J WASHINGTON STATE UNIVERSITY WEST 601 FIRST AVENUE SPOKANE, WA 99204-0399 Reduction in adrs via computerized pharmacy intervention
R01AG-09574-01 (GMB) RUBIN, ROBERT L SCIPPS CLINIC & RESEARCH FDN 10666 N TORREY PINES ROAD LA JOLLA, CA 92037 Neutrophil mediated drug toxicity in the elderly
R01AG-09587-01A1 (NLS) UNNERSTALL, JAMES R UNIV OF ILLINOIS PO BOX 6998 (M/C 512) CHICAGO, IL 60680 Neurochemical plasticity of locus coeruleus in aging
R01AG-09594-01 (GMB) SMITH, PHILIP C UNIVERSITY OF TEXAS AUSTIN, TX 78712 Protein glycation by acyl glucuronides in the elderly
R01AG-09597-01 (BCE) HOFFMAN, BRIAN B VETERANS AFFRS MEDICAL CENTER 3801 MIRANDA AVENUE PALO ALTO, CA 94304 Molecular pharmacology of adrenergic receptors in aging
R01AG-09611-01 (EDC) LIPTON, HELENE L UNIVERSITY OF CALIFORNIA 1388 SUTTER STREET, 11TH FLOOR SAN FRANCISCO, CA 94109 Reducing geriatric drug therapy--Two approaches
R01AG-09632-01A1 (EDC) GRAVENSTEIN, STEFAN UNIVERSITY OF WISCONSIN MADISON, WI 53706 The use of amantadine in the nursing home
R01AG-09634-01 (EDC) AVORN, JEROME L BETH ISRAEL HOSPITAL 330 BROOKLINE AVE, 3RD FLOOR BOSTON, MA 02115 Drug-induced parkinsonian symptoms in the elderly
P20AG-09646-02 (AGE) HOGAN, DENNIS P PENNSYLVANIA STATE UNIVERSITY UNIVERSITY PARK, PA 16802 Exploratory center on aging and health in rural America
P20AG-09648-02 (AGE) DEFRIESE, GORDON H UNIVERSITY OF NORTH CAROLINA CB# 7490 CHASE HALL CHAPEL HILL, NC 27599-7490 Program on health research for older rural populations
P20AG-09649-01 (AGE) COWARD, RAYMOND T UNIVERSITY OF FLORIDA/BOX J-17 GAINESVILLE, FL 32610-0177 Florida exploratory center on the health of rural elders
R01AG-09657-01 (PHRA) LANDEFELD, C SETH UNIVERSITY HOSP OF CLEVELAND 2074 ABINGTON ROAD CLEVELAND, OH 44106 Anticoagulant therapy in older patients
R01AG-09662-01 (NEUA) KAMEN, GARY P BOSTON UNIVERSITY 1 UNIVERSITY ROAD BOSTON, MA 02215 Control properties of aged human motor units
R01AG-09663-01 (BEM) REVES, J G DUKE UNIVERSITY MEDICAL CTR BOX 31186 THE HEART CENTER DURHAM, NC 27710 Aging and cognition after cardiac surgery
R01AG-09665-05A1 (NEUC) POTTER, HUNTINGTON HARVARD MEDICAL SCHOOL 220 LONGWOOD AVE BOSTON, MA 02115 Expression studies on Alzheimer's disease related genes
U01AG-09675-02 (AGE) WOLFSON, LESLIE UNIV OF CONNECTICUT HEALTH CTR 263 FARMINGTON AVE FARMINGTON, CT 06032 Training balance and strength of elderly to improve function
R01AG-09681-01 (NLS) TOKES, ZOLTAN A UNIVERSITY SOUTHERN CALIFORNIA 1303 N MISSION RD CRL 102 LOS ANGELES, CA 90033 Study of metalloproteases MP-130,-100 in Alzheimer brain
P20AG-09682-01 (AGE) WALLACE, ROBERT B UNIVERSITY OF IOWA IOWA CITY, IA 52242 Center for research on older rural populations
P20AG-09682-01 0001 (AGE) KROSS, BURTON C Center for research on older rural populations The older agricultural worker
P20AG-09682-01 0002 (AGE) WALLACE, ROBERT B Center for research on older rural populations Special rural populations
P20AG-09682-01 0003 (AGE) COLSHER, PATRICIA L Center for research on older rural populations Longitudinal study of end-stage renal disease
P20AG-09682-01 0004 (AGE) HOYT, D Center for research on older rural populations Social demography of the rural elderly
P20AG-09682-01 0005 (AGE) CHRISCHILLES, ELIZABETH A Center for research on older rural populations Self-care and pharmaceutical access
P20AG-09682-01 9001 (AGE) WALLACE, ROBERT B Center for research on older rural populations Core--biostatistic Facilities
R01AG-09683-01 (NEUB) KIM, HELEN UNIVERSITY OF ALABAMA 1918 UNIVERSITY BLVD BHSB 656 BIRMINGHAM, AL 35294 Acetylated tubulin in developing and aging rat brain
R01AG-09686-01 (CMS) BAKER, HARRIET D CORNELL UNIVERSITY MED COLLEGE 785 MAMARONECK AVE WHITE PLAINS, NY 10605 Plasticity in the aging olfactory system
R01AG-09690-01 (NEUA) FLOYD, ROBERT A OKLAHOMA MEDICAL RESEARCH FDN 825 N.E. 13TH STREET OKLAHOMA CITY, OK 73104 Age influence on ischemia reperfusion in brain
R37AG-09692-02 (HUD) WOLINSKY, FREDRIC D REGENSTRIEF INSTITUTE 1001 WEST 10TH ST - 5TH FLOOR INDIANAPOLIS, IN 46202-2859 A panel analysis of the aged's use of health services
R01AG-09693-01 (NEUB) BALOH, ROBERT W UNIVERSITY OF CALIFORNIA LOS ANGELES, CA 90024-1769 Dizziness in older people
R01AG-09694-01A1 (NEUC) BENDHEIM, PAUL E NYS INSTITUTE/BASIC RESEARCH 1050 FOREST HILL ROAD STATEN ISLAND, NY 10314 Aging and brain amyloid precursors on lymphocytes
R55AG-09700-01 (SSS) AUSTAD, STEVEN N HARVARD UNIV/BIOL LABORATORIES 16 DIVINITY AVE CAMBRIDGE, MA 02138 Manipulation of aging rate in the Virginia opossum
R43AG-09705-01 (SSS) CORDELL, BARBARA CALIFORNIA BIOTECHNOLOGY INC 2450 BAYSHORE PARKWAY MOUNTAIN VIEW , CA 94043 Recombinant CNTF for treatment of neuropathies
R43AG-09715-01 (HUD) JETTE, ALAN M NEW ENGLAND RESEARCH INST, INC 9 GALEN STREET WATERTOWN, MA 02172 Exercise video to improve muscle strength/older women
R43AG-09716-01 (SSS) PINCUS, STEVEN M CHAOTIC DYNAMICAL SYSTEMS

990 MOOSE HILL ROAD GUILFORD, CT 06437 Nonlinear cardiovascular dynamics of aging
R43AG-09719-01 (HUD) DALL, OWEN B CHESAPEAKE COMPUTING, INC 8401 CORPORATE DRIVE LANDOVER, MD 20785 Computerized assistance for service credit banking
R43AG-09720-01 (HUD) AVIS, NANCY NEW ENGLAND RESEARCH INST, INC 9 GALEN STREET WATERTOWN, MA 02172 Videotape to train interviewers in surveys of old people
R43AG-09725-01 (HUD) VERTREES, JAMES C SOLON CONSULTING GROUP 12501 PROSPERITY DRIVE SILVER SPRING, MD 20904 Integrated database for aging research
R43AG-09727-01 (VISB) KEIRN, PHILIP A VISUAL RESOURCES INC 225 THIRD AVE PO BOX 51524 BOWLING GREEN, KY 42101 Perceptual assessment / improvement of the older driver
R01AG-09735-10 (BIO) BRADSHAW, RALPH A UNIVERSITY OF CALIFORNIA IRVINE, CA 92717 Structure and function of nerve growth factor
R13AG-09737-01 (NBSA) ROGERS, ANDREI UNIVERSITY OF COLORADO CAMPUS BOX 19 BOULDER, CO 80309-0019 Conference on elderly migration and settlement
U01AG-09740-02 (AGE) JUSTER, F THOMAS UNIVERSITY OF MICHIGAN 426 THOMPSON STREET ANN ARBOR, MI 48106-1248 Health and retirement study
P01AG-09743-01 (AGE) BURKHAUSER, RICHARD V SYRACUSE UNIVERSITY MAXWELL HALL SYRACUSE, NY 13244-1090 The wellbeing of the elderly in a comparative context
P01AG-09743-01 0001 (AGE) BURKHAUSER, RICHARD The wellbeing of the elderly in a comparative context Economic risks to women--USA-German aging policy comparisons
P01AG-09743-01 0002 (AGE) SMEEDING, TIMOTHY The wellbeing of the elderly in a comparative context Elderly east and west and budgetary cost of retirement
P01AG-09743-01 0003 (AGE) SMEEDING, TIMOTHY The wellbeing of the elderly in a comparative context Equivalence scales and cost of disability
P01AG-09743-01 9001 (AGE) BURKHAUSER, RICHARD The wellbeing of the elderly in a comparative context Core--National comparative database
R01AG-09744-01A1 (HUD) JOHNSON, MARCIA K PRINCETON UNIVERSITY PRINCETON, NJ 08544-1010 Semantic memory and Alzheimer's disease
R01AG-09752-01 (HUD) WOODRUFF-PAK, DIANA S PHILADELPHIA GERIATRIC CENTER 5301 OLD YORK ROAD PHILADELPHIA, PA 19141 Aging, classical conditioning, and memory systems
R01AG-09755-01 (HUD) MACKAY, DON G UNIVERSITY OF CALIFORNIA LOS ANGELES, CA 90024-1563 The organization of cognitive processes in old age
R01AG-09761-02 (BBCA) GAFNI, ARI UNIVERSITY OF MICHIGAN 300 N INGALLS ANN, ARBOR, MI 48109-2007 Laser spectroscopy of triplet states in proteins
R13AG-09763-01 (BCA) RICHARDSON, ARLAN G UNIVERSITY OF TEXAS 7703 FLOYD CURL DRIVE SAN ANTONIO, TX 78284 1991 Gordon Research Conference on the biology of aging
R01AG-09769-01 (EDC) LARSON, ERIC B UNIV OF WASHINGTON MED CTR 1959 NE PACIFIC STREET SEATTLE, WA 98195 Epidemiology of dementia in older Japanese Americans
R01AG-09773-01A1 (BCA) ESPELAND, MARK A WAKE FOREST UNIV/PUB HLTH SCIS 300 SOUTH HAWTHORNE ROAD WINSTON-SALEM, NC 27103 Dietary interventions in the Elderly Trial (DIET)
R01AG-09775-01 (SSP) HAUSER, ROBERT M 425 HENRY MALL MADISON, WI 53706 Longitudinal study-- Parents and children at age 50
R01AG-09778-02 (CTY) PHILLIPS, PAUL D MEDICAL COLL OF PENNSYLVANIA Cell aging--Growth factor control of early response gene
R01AG-09779-04 (CEP) LANG, PETER J UNIVERSITY OF FLORIDA BOX J-165, JHMHC GAINESVILLE, FL 32610 Emotion and aging in women--Psychophysiology of imagery
R13AG-09782-01 (BCA) COHEN, HARVEY J DUKE UNIVERITY MEDICAL CENTER BOX 3003 DURHAM, N C 27710 AGS summer workshop--Geriatrics clinical research method
R29AG-09785-01 (EDC) HAAN, MARY KAISER FDN RESEARCH INSTITUTE 3451 PIEDMONT AVENUE OAKLAND, CA 94611 Epidemiology of survival in older blacks and whites
R13AG-09787-01 (NBSA) SCHAIE, K WARNER PENNSYLVANIA STATE UNIVERSITY UNIVERSITY PARK, PA 16802 Conference program on social structure and aging
P01AG-09793-01 (NBSA) HEFTI, FRANZ F UNIV OF SOUTHERN CALIFORNIA LOS ANGELES, CA 90089-0191 Dopaminergic and basal plasticity in aging
P01AG-09793-01 0001 (NBSA) HEFTI, FRANZ Dopaminergic and basal plasticity in aging Trophic control of dopaminergic neurons
P01AG-09793-01 0002 (NBSA) MCNEILL, THOMAS H Dopaminergic and basal plasticity in aging Synaptic remodelling of the striatum after deafferentation
P01AG-09793-01 0003 (NBSA) WALSH, JOHN Dopaminergic and basal plasticity in aging Electrophysiology of aging in the nigrostriatal system
P01AG-09793-01 0004 (NBSA) FINCH, CALEB Dopaminergic and basal plasticity in aging Gene expression during acute & chronic responses to nigrostriatal lesions
P01AG-09793-01 0005 (NBSA) MORGAN, DAVID Dopaminergic and basal plasticity in aging Cellular and molecular bases of D2 declines with age
P01AG-09793-01 9001 (NBSA) FINCH, CALEB E Dopaminergic and basal plasticity in aging Core--Animal resources
R37AG-09801-02 (IMB) MILLER, RICHARD A INSTITUTE OF GERONTOLOGY 300 NORTH INGALLS STREET ANN ARBOR, MI 48109-2007 Activation defects in aging T cells
R01AG-09827-01 (ORTH) WEAVER, DAVID S BOWMAN GRAY SCH OF MED 300 S HAWTHORNE ROAD WINSTON-SALEM, NC 27103 Anabolic steroid effects on bone and arteries
R01AG-09833-01 (NTN) WELLE, STEPHEN L MONROE COMMUNITY HOSPITAL 435 EAST HENRIETTA ROAD ROCHESTER, NY 14620 Effect of age on muscle protein synthesis
R01AG-09834-01 (NTN) STABLER, SALLY P UNIVERSITY OF COLORADO 4200 EAST NINTH AVENUE DENVER, CO 80262 Prevalence and spectrum of B12 deficiency in the aged
R55AG-09837-01 (NTN) KINOSIAN, BRUCE UNIVERSITY OF PENNSYLVANIA 3615 CHESTNUT STREET PHILADELPHIA, PA 19104-2683 Assessment of malnutrition in the hospitalized elderly
R01AG-09839-01 (NTN) ROSS, ALTA C THE MED COLL OF PENNSYLVANIA 3300 HENRY AVENUE PHILADELPHIA, PA 19129 Nutrition and aging -- Vitamin A and immune functions
R15AG-09840-01 (BCE) TOMASI, THOMAS E SOUTHWEST MISSOURI STATE UNIV SPRINGFIELD, MO 65804 Patterns of thyroid hormone dynamics with aging
R01AG-09862-02 (HUD) SNOWDON, DAVID A SANDERS-BROWN CTR ON AGING 800 S LIMESTONE LEXINGTON, KY 40536-0230 Independent and dependent life in the elderly
R01AG-09869-01 (NEUB) VAUGHAN, DEBORAH W BOSTON UNIVERSITY 80 EAST CONCORD STREET BOSTON, MA 02118-2394 Age, axon injury and motor neuron synaptology
R01AG-09873-01 (NLS) LONGO, FRANK M UNIVERSITY OF CALIFORNIA 505 PARNASSUS/BOX 0114 SAN FRANCISCO, CA 94143 Aging and neuronal death--A first generation of NGF analogs
R15AG-09881-01 (MET) STILLWELL, WILLIAM H PURDUE UNIVERSITY 1125 EAST 38TH STREET INDIANAPOLIS, IN 46205 Prevention of mitochondrial aging by omega-3 fatty acids
R01AG-09884-01 (NLS) WOLFE, BARRY B GEORGETOWN UNIV SCH OF MED 3900 RESERVOIR RD N W WASHINGTON, DC 20007 Aging and central cholinergic systems
R01AG-09900-01 (NLS) EBERWINE, JAMES UNIVERSITY OF PENNSYLVANIA 36TH & HAMILTON WALK PHILADELPHIA, PA 19104-6084 Gene expression in single aging neurons and glia
R55AG-09901-01 (EDC) MAGAZINER, JAY UNIVERSITY OF MARYLAND 660 WEST REDWOOD ST BALTIMORE, MD 21201 Determinants of recovery from hip fx/sup
R01AG-09902-01 (EDC) MAGAZINER, JAY UNIVERSITY OF MARYLAND 655 WEST REDWOOD ST BALTIMORE, MD 21201 Determinants of recovery from hip fracture in elderly--Self/proxy reports
R01AG-09905-01 (NLS) ABRAHAM, CARMELA R BOSTON UNIVERSITY MEDICAL CAMP 80 E CONCORD ST K-5 BOSTON, MA 02118 Amyloidogenesis--The role of reactive astrocytes
R43AG-09907-01 (SSS) LERNER, NEIL D COMSIS CORPORATION 8737 COLESVILLE RD SILVER SPRING, MD 20910 An integrated climbing/reaching device for the elderly
R01AG-09909-02 (CBY) CAMPISI, JUDITH LAWRENCE BERKELEY LABORATORY 1 CYCLOTRON ROAD BERKELEY, CA 94720 Cellular senescence and control of gene expression
R43AG-09910-01 (SSS) CRAINE, BRIAN L WESTERN RESEARCH COMPANY, INC 2127 EAST SPEEDWAY TUCSON, AZ 85719 Antibody based assay for quinolicic acid
R43AG-09911-01 (MHSB) GLASKY, ALVIN J ADVANCED IMMUNOTHERAPEUTICS 2691 RICHTER AVENUE, SUITE 105 IRVINE, CA 92714-5124 AIT-082; a drug for treatment of Alzheimer's disease
R29AG-09927-02 (GMA) PEACOCKE, MONICA NEW ENGLAND MEDICAL CTR HOSPIT 750 WASHINGTON STREET BOSTON, MA 02111 Effect of aging on retinoic acid receptor gene expression
R01AG-09931-01 (HSDG) STEWART, ANITA UNIVERSITY OF CALIFORNIA BOX 0612, N631Y SAN FRANCISCO, CA 94143-0612 Increasing physical activity of elders in the community
R01AG-09936-01 (HUD) HORN, JOHN L UNIV OF SOUTHERN CALIFORNIA UNIVERSITY PARK, MC 1061 LOS ANGELES, CA 90089-1061 Causes in adult development of differences in abilities
R13AG-09942-01 (NBSA) OWSLEY, CYNTHIA UNIVERSITY OF ALABAMA UAB STATION BIRMINGHAM, AL 35294 Older driver capability--Predicting accident risk
R55AG-09948-01 (IMB) THOMAN, MARILYN L THE SCRIPPS CLINIC RES INST 10666 NORTH TORREY PINES RD LA JOLLA, CA 92037 Peripheral T cell maintenance and thymic activity in the aged
R01AG-09956-01 (EDC) HENDRIE, HUGH C INDIANA UNIVERSITY SCH OF MED 534 CLINICAL DRIVE INDIANAPOLIS, IN 46202 Dementias--Indianapolis-Ibadan comparative prevalence
R13AG-09961-01 (BCA) STEEL, R KNIGHT BOSTON UNIVERSITY MEDICAL CENT 720 HARRISON AVENUE BOSTON, MA 02118 1991 Summer Institute in Geriatric Medicine
R13AG-09962-01 (BCA) LEVINE, ELLIOT M WISTAR INSTITUTE 3601 SPRUCE STREET PHILADELPHIA, PA 19104-4268 Molecular basis for cellular aging
R01AG-09965-01 (HUD) BARTLETT, JAMES C UNIVERSITY OF TX AT DALLAS 2601 N FLOYD RD/BOX 830688 RICHARDSON, TX 75083-0688 Aging in perception and cognition of music
R01AG-09966-01 (EDC) EVANS, DENIS A RUSH-PRESBY-ST LUKE'S MED CENT 1653 WEST CONGRESS PARKWAY CHICAGO, IL 60612 Epidemiologic study of persons with Alzheimer's disease
R13AG-09968-01 (BCA) JOHNSON, THOMAS E UNIVERSITY OF COLORADO 1450 30TH STREET BOULDER, CO 80309-0447 The molecular basis of aging and longevity--Conference
P01AG-09973-01 (NBSA) GALLAGHER, MICHELA UNIV OF N C AT CHAPEL HILL CAMPUS BOX 3270, DAVIE HALL CHAPEL HILL, N C 27599-3270 Cognition and hippocampal/cortical systems in aging
P01AG-09973-01 0001 (NBSA) RAPP, PETER R Cognition and hippocampal/cortical systems in aging Neuroanatomical studies of the aged hippocampal formation
P01AG-09973-01 0002 (NBSA) GALLAGHER, MICHELA Cognition and hippocampal/cortical systems in aging Neurochemical changes in hippocampal /cortical systems
P01AG-09973-01 0003 (NBSA) WOLFE, BARRY Cognition and hippocampal/cortical systems in aging Subtypes of acetylcholine receptors in aged rat brain
P01AG-09973-01 0004 (NBSA) MCKINNEY, MICHAEL Cognition and hippocampal/cortical systems in aging The septo-hippocampal cholinergic phenotype in aging
P01AG-09973-01 0005 (NBSA) EICHENBAUM, HOWARD Cognition and hippocampal/cortical systems in aging Functional coding in hippocampal /cortical systems
P01AG-09973-01 9001 (NBSA) GALLAGHER, MICHELA Cognition and hippocampal/cortical systems in aging Core-- Animal resource
P01AG-09973-01 9002 (NBSA) BURCHINAL, MARGARET Cognition and hippocampal/cortical systems in aging Core-- Data management component
P01AG-09975-01 (NBSA) CZEISLER, CHARLES A BRIGHAM AND WOMEN'S

PROJECT NO., ORGANIZATIONAL UNIT., INVESTIGATOR, ADDRESS, TITLE

HOSPITAL 221 LONGWOOD AVE BOSTON, MASS 02115 Sleep, aging and circadian rhythm disorders

P01AG-09975-01 0001 (NBSA) CZEISLER, CHARLES A Sleep, aging and circadian rhythm disorders Advanced sleep phase in the elderly-- Circadian etiology

P01AG-09975-01 0002 (NBSA) DAVIS, FREDERICK Sleep, aging and circadian rhythm disorders Transplantation analysis of circadian rhythms and aging

P01AG-09975-01 0003 (NBSA) CZEISLER, CHARLES Sleep, aging and circadian rhythm disorders Circadian rhythms sleep disorders in the blind

P01AG-09975-01 9001 (NBSA) KRONAUER, RICHARD E Sleep, aging and circadian rhythm disorders Core-- Analytical

R29AG-09976-01 (HUD) JOHNSON, MITZI M UNIV OF KENTUCKY LEXINGTON, KY 40536-0086 Age differences in decision-making performance

R01AG-09984-01 (HUD) BRANNON, DIANE PENNSYLVANIA STATE UNIVERSITY UNIVERSITY PARK, PA 16802 A test of transfer of training effects in nursing homes

R13AG-09985-01 (BCA) CRISTOFALO, VINCENT J MEDICAL COLL OF PENNSYLVANIA 3300 HENRY AVENUE PHILADELPHIA, PA 19129 Aging and cellular defense mechanisms

R01AG-09988-01 (HUD) FRIEDMAN, DAVID RES FDN FOR MENTAL HYGIENE 722 WEST 168 STREET NEW YORK, N Y 10032 Age-related ERP measures in Alzheimer's disease

R01AG-09989-09 (CTY) COWAN, NICHOLAS J NEW YORK MEDICAL CENTER 550 FIRST AVENUE NEW YORK, NY 10016 Structure and expression of human tubulin genes

R55AG-09991-01 (EDC) HASKELL, WILLIAM L STANFORD UNIVERSITY 1000 WELCH ROAD PALO ALTO, CA 94304 Community exercise training in older women and men

R01AG-10002-01 (NLS) FASMAN, GERALD D BRANDEIS UNIVERSITY WALTHAM, MA 02254-9110 Studies on synthetic models of Alzheimer proteins

R01AG-10004-04 (CBY) CAMPISI, JUDITH LAWRENCE BERKELEY LABORATORY 1 CYCLOTRON ROAD BERKELEY, CA 94720 Growth regulation in normal and tumorigenic cells

R01AG-10009-01 (HAR) FURMAN, JOSEPH M THE EAR & EYE INST OF PITTSBUR 203 LOTHROP ST SUITE 500 PITTSBURGH, PA 15213 Vestibulo-ocular function in the elderly

R01AG-10010-01 (HSR) BOAZ, RACHEL F GRADUAZTE CTR CUNY 33 WEST 42ND STREET NEW YORK, NY 10036 Improved versus deteriorated physical functioning -- Long term disabled elders

R01AG-10015-01 (BPO) OLTON, DAVID S JOHNS HOPKINS UNIVERSITY 34TH AND CHARLES STREETS BALTIMORE, MD 21218 Aging, memory and septohippocampal function

R01AG-10034-01 (NLS) DUBINSKY, JANET M UNIV OF TEXAS HLTH SCI CTR 7703 FLOYD CURL DRIVE SAN ANTONIO, TX 78284-7756 Interaction of hypoxic and excitotoxic neuronal injury

R29AG-10047-01 (HUD) MUTTER, SHARON A WESTERN KENTUCKY UNIVERSITY BOWLING GREEN, KY 42101 Judgment and decision making across the life span

R55AG-10064-01 (NURS) SCHNELLE, JOHN F UCLA SCHOOL OF MEDICINE 10833 LECONTE AVENUE LOS ANGELES, CA 90024-1687 Statistical quality control and restraint use management

R55AG-10070-01 (PBC) BAKER, JOHN R UNIVERSITY OF ALABAMA 1808 7TH AVE SOUTH BIRMINGHAM, AL 35294 Cartilage matrix protein interactions--Changes with age

R43AG-10076-01 (SSS) LLOYD, CYNTHIA A ATHENS RESEARCH & TECH, INC PO BOX 5494 ATHENS, GA 30604 Use of antibodies to modified alpha 1 antichymotrypsin

R43AG-10082-01 (HUD) AVIS, NANCY E NEW ENGLAND RESEARCH INST, INC 9 GALEN ST WATERTOWN, MA 02172 Women in the middle--Middle aged women and menopause video

R43AG-10083-01 (NTN) HEASLEY, SUSAN G BASIC FORE INC 6101 PEMBRIDGE DR TOLEDO, OH 43615 Method and apparatus for planning geriatric nutrition

R43AG-10087-01 (HUD) HUNT, GAIL G GIBSON-HUNT ASSOCIATES, LTD 1629 K STREET, NW WASHINGTON, DC 20006 What drives corporate eldercare utilization?

R01AG-10101-01 (SRC) LOCKSHIN, RICHARD A ST JOHN'S UNIVERSITY GRAND CENTRAL & UTOPIA PKWYS JAMAICA, NY 11439 Cell death in a high connectivity invertebrate model

R01AG-10102-01 (EDC) GORELICK, PHILIP B RUSH-PRESBYT-ST LUKE'S MED CTR 1653 WEST CONGRESS PARKWAY CHICAGO, IL 60612 Studies of dementia in the black aged--Alzheimer's and multi-infarct

R01AG-10104-01 (CBY) HERMAN, BRIAN A UNIVERSITY OF NORTH CAROLINA CB #7090, 232 TAYLOR HALL CHAPEL HILL, NC 27599-7090 Calcium and cell growth

P30AG-10123-01 (NBSA) CUMMINGS, JEFFREY L UCLA 710 WESTWOOD PLAZA LOS ANGELES, CA 90024-1769 UCLA Alzheimer's disease center

P30AG-10123-01 9003 (NBSA) VINTERS, HARRY UCLA Alzheimer's disease center Core-- Neuropathology

P30AG-10123-01 9004 (NBSA) SMALL, GARY UCLA Alzheimer's disease center Core-- Education /information transfer

P30AG-10123-01 0001 (NBSA) BREDESEN, DALE UCLA Alzheimer's disease center An in vitro model of Alzheimer's disease

P30AG-10123-01 0002 (NBSA) EDWARDS, ROBERT UCLA Alzheimer's disease center Oxidative phosphorylation and cellular vulnerability in Alzheimer's disease

P30AG-10123-01 0003 (NBSA) MILLER, BRUCE UCLA Alzheimer's disease center Proton spectroscopy in dementing conditions

P30AG-10123-01 9001 (NBSA) LEUCHTER, ANDREW UCLA Alzheimer's disease center Core-- Clinical

P30AG-10123-01 9002 (NBSA) MAZZIOTTA, JOHN UCLA Alzheimer's disease center Core-- Neuroimaging

P30AG-10124-01 (NBSA) TROJANOWSKI, JOHN Q UNIV OF PENNSYLVANIA SCH OF ME 36TH & SPRUCE STREETS PHILADELPHIA, PA 19104-4283 Alzheimer's disease center core

P30AG-10124-01 0001 (NBSA) SPITALNIK, STEVEN L Alzheimer's disease center core Glycosylation of amyloid precursor proteins

P30AG-10124-01 0002 (NBSA) RESNICK, SUSAN M Alzheimer's disease center core Association between late onset depression and Alzheimer's disease

P30AG-10124-01 0003 (NBSA) EBERWINE, JIM Alzheimer's disease center core Molecular analyses of the hippocampus in Alzheimer's disease

P30AG-10124-01 0004 (NBSA) DOTY, RICHARD Alzheimer's disease center core Sensory changes in early Alzheimer's disease

P30AG-10124-01 9001 (NBSA) GOTTLIEB, GARY Alzheimer's disease center core Core-- Clinical

P30AG-10124-01 9002 (NBSA) TROJANOWSKI, JOHN Q Alzheimer's disease center core Core-- Neuropathology

P30AG-10124-01 9003 (NBSA) ELLIS, NANCY B Alzheimer's disease center core Core-- Education and information transfer

P30AG-10129-01 (NBSA) JAGUST, WILLIAM J UCD NORTHERN CA ALZHEIMERS DIS 2001 DWIGHT WAY BERKELEY, CA 94704 UC Davis Alzheimer's disease center core

P30AG-10129-01 0001 (NBSA) MATHIS, CHESTER UC Davis Alzheimer's disease center core 18F Benzovesamicol ligands for cholinergic studies

P30AG-10129-01 0002 (NBSA) MUNGAS, DAN UC Davis Alzheimer's disease center core Serotonin and behavior in Alzheimer's disease

P30AG-10129-01 0003 (NBSA) BIEGON, ANAT UC Davis Alzheimer's disease center core Beta adrenergic receptors in Alzheimer's disease

P30AG-10129-01 9001 (NBSA) WEILER, PHILIP UC Davis Alzheimer's disease center core Core-- Clinical

P30AG-10129-01 9002 (NBSA) ELLIS, WILLIAM UC Davis Alzheimer's disease center core Core-- Neuropathology

P30AG-10129-01 9003 (NBSA) LINDEMAN, DAVID UC Davis Alzheimer's disease center core Core-- Education and information transfer

P30AG-10130-01 (NBSA) MIRRA, SUZANNE S VAMC 1670 CLAIRMONT RD DECATUR, GA 30033 Alzheimer's disease center core

P30AG-10130-01 0001 (NBSA) WALLACE, DOUGLAS C Alzheimer's disease center core Mitochondrial genes and Alzheimer's disease

P30AG-10130-01 0002 (NBSA) WOOD, JOHN G Alzheimer's disease center core Role of cytokines in Alzhemier's disease pathology

P30AG-10130-01 0003 (NBSA) DOETCH, PAUL Alzheimer's disease center core Oxidative DNA damage and transcription-- A model for neural cell death

P30AG-10130-01 0004 (NBSA) WILKINSON, KEITH D Alzheimer's disease center core Ubiquitin-dependent proteolysis in Alzheimer's disease and aging

P30AG-10130-01 9001 (NBSA) GREEN, ROBERT Alzheimer's disease center core Core--Clinical

P30AG-10130-01 9002 (NBSA) MIRRA, SUZANNE S Alzheimer's disease center core Core-- Neuropathology

P30AG-10130-01 9003 (NBSA) KARP, HERBERT R Alzheimer's disease center core Core-- Education and information transfer

P30AG-10130-01 9004 (NBSA) WALLACE, DOUGLAS C Alzheimer's disease center core Core-- Molecular biology

P30AG-10133-01 (NBSA) GHETTI, BERNARDINO INDIANA UNIV SCH OF MED 635 BARNHILL DRIVE INDIANAPOLIS, IN 46202-5120 Indiana Alzheimer's disease core center

P30AG-10133-01 9002 (NBSA) GHETTI, BERNARDINO Indiana Alzheimer's disease core center Core-- Neuropathology

P30AG-10133-01 9003 (NBSA) AUSTROM, MARY Indiana Alzheimer's disease core center Core-- Education

P30AG-10133-01 0001 (NBSA) LAHIRI, DEBOMOY Indiana Alzheimer's disease core center Beta-amyloid gene promoter expression in various cell types

P30AG-10133-01 0002 (NBSA) ABEL, LARRY Indiana Alzheimer's disease core center Ocular motor function in Alzheimer's disease

P30AG-10133-01 0003 (NBSA) SANGAMESWAREN, LAKSHMI Indiana Alzheimer's disease core center Expression of APP and prion protein mRNAs in cerebellar neurons

P30AG-10133-01 0004 (NBSA) YU, LEI Indiana Alzheimer's disease core center Effect of Alzheimer's disease on serotonin receptors

P30AG-10133-01 9001 (NBSA) FARLOW, MARTIN Indiana Alzheimer's disease core center Core-- Clinical

R01AG-10143-09 (GMA) CLARK, RICHARD A SUNY AT STONY BROOK SCHOOL OF MEDICINE STONY BROOK, N Y 11794 Fibronectin and cell recruitment

R43AG-10150-01 (NURS) D'ERASMO, MARTHA J BIRCH & DAVIS ASSOC, INC 8905 FAIRVIEW ROAD SILVER SPRING, MD 20910 Improving nursing documentation with computer technology

R01AG-10154-04 (BPN) GREENOUGH, WILLIAM T BECKMAN INSTITUTE 405 NORTH MATHEWS AVENUE URBANA, IL 61801 Physical exercise, mental activity, and brain aging

P30AG-10161-01 (NBSA) EVANS, DENIS A RUSH-PRESBY-ST LUKE'S MED CENT 1653 WEST CONGRESS PARKWAY CHICAGO, IL 60612 Rush Alzheimer's disease center core

P30AG-10161-01 0001 (NBSA) EVANS, DENIS Rush Alzheimer's disease center core Pilot for a study of Alzheimer's disease in a biracial community

P30AG-10161-01 0002 (NBSA) GILLEY, DAVID Rush Alzheimer's disease center core Short-term stability of clinical tests

P30AG-10161-01 0003 (NBSA) MUFSON, ELLIOT Rush Alzheimer's disease center core Nerve growth factor receptor expression in Alzheimer's disease

P30AG-10161-01 0004 (NBSA) GABRIELI, JOHN Rush Alzheimer's disease center core Memory systems analysis of age-related change in learning capacities

P30AG-10161-01 9001 (NBSA) BENNETT, DAVID Rush Alzheimer's disease center core Core-- Clinical

P30AG-10161-01 9002 (NBSA) FARRAN, CAROL Rush Alzheimer's disease center core Core-- Education and information transfer

P30AG-10161-01 9003 (NBSA) COCHRAN, ELIZABETH Rush Alzheimer's disease center core Core-- Neuropathology

P30AG-10163-01 (NBSA) HARRELL, LINDY E UNIVERSITY OF ALABAMA UNIVERSITY STATION BIRMINGHAM, AL 35294 Alzheimer's disease center core

P30AG-10163-01 0001 (NBSA) BROWN, GEORGE Alzheimer's disease center core Human brain sodium channels in Alzheimer's disease

P30AG-10163-01 0002 (NBSA) DUKE, LINDA Alzheimer's disease center core Recognition of gated words in Alzheimer's and normal elderly listeners

P30AG-10163-01 0003 (NBSA) WYSS, MICHAEL Alzheimer's disease center

core Morphological changes in retrosplenial cortex in Alzheimer's patients
P30AG-10163-01 9001 (NBSA) FOLKS, DAVID Alzheimer's disease center core Core– Clinical
P30AG-10163-01 9002 (NBSA) HALEY, WILLIAM Alzheimer's disease center core Core– Education and information transfer
P30AG-10163-01 9003 (NBSA) POWERS, RICHARD Alzheimer's disease center core Core– Neuropathology
R01AG-10173-01 (BCE) SARTER, MARTIN F OHIO STATE UNIVERSITY 1885 NEIL AVENUE COLUMBUS, OH 43210-1222 Aging, attention, and benzodiazepine receptor ligands
P30AG-10182-01 (NBSA) KOLLER, WILLIAM C UNIV OF KANSAS MEDICAL CENTER 39TH & RAINBOW BLVD KANSAS CITY, KS 66103-8410 Alzheimer's disease center core grant
P30AG-10182-01 0001 (NBSA) GLATT, SANDER Alzheimer's disease center core grant Herbicide /pesticide exposure in Alzheimer's disease
P30AG-10182-01 0002 (NBSA) KEMPER, SUSAN Alzheimer's disease center core grant Language of dementia
P30AG-10182-01 0003 (NBSA) FESTOFF, BARRY Alzheimer's disease center core grant Serine proteases and their serpins in amyloidogenesis
P30AG-10182-01 0004 (NBSA) NELSON, STANLEY Alzheimer's disease center core grant Free radical enzyme damage– An Alzheimer's disease model
P30AG-10182-01 9001 (NBSA) GLATT, SANDER Alzheimer's disease center core grant Core– Clinical
P30AG-10182-01 9002 (NBSA) HANDLER, MICHAEL Alzheimer's disease center core grant Core– Neuropathology
P30AG-10182-01 9003 (NBSA) BEISECKER, ANALEE Alzheimer's disease center core grant Core– Education and information transfer
S15AG-10230-01 (NSS) ABRAHAM, GEORGE N UNIVERSITY OF ROCHESTER 601 ELMWOOD AVE, PO BOX 706 ROCHESTER, NY 14642 Small instrumentation grant
S15AG-10231-01 (NSS) WODARSKI, JOHN S UNIVERSITY OF AKRON AKRON, OH 44325-2102 Small instrumentation grant
S15AG-10232-01 (NSS) KABISCH, WILLIAM T SOUTHERN ILLINOIS UNIVERSITY P O BOX 19230 SPRINGFIELD, IL 62794-9230 Small instrumentation grant
S15AG-10233-01 (NSS) DAVIS, JOSEPH H MCLEAN HOSPITAL 115 MILL STREET BELMONT, MA 02178 Small instrumentation grant
S15AG-10234-01 (NSS) ROSS, LEONARD MEDICAL COLLEGE OF PENNSYLVANI 3300 HENRY AVE PHILADELPHIA, PA 19129 Small instrumentation grant
S15AG-10235-01 (NSS) GOLDSTEIN, SOLOMON GRAD SCH & UNIV CTR OF CUNY 33 WEST 42ND STREET NEW YORK, NY 10036 Small instrumentation grant
S15AG-10236-01 (NSS) BISHOP, VERNON S UNIV OF TEXAS HLTH SCI CTR 7703 FLOYD CURL DRIVE SAN ANTONIO, TX 78284-7764 Small instrumentation grant
S15AG-10237-01 (NSS) SIMPKINS, JAMES W UNIVERSITY OF FLORIDA BOX J-487 GAINESVILLE, FL 32610 Small instrumentation grant
S15AG-10238-01 (NSS) ANGELAKOS, E T HAHNEMANN UNIVERSITY BROAD & VINE PHILADELPHIA, PA 19102-1192 Small instrumentation grant
S15AG-10239-01 (NSS) PROENZA, LUIS M UNIVERSITY OF ALASKA 306 SINGNERS' HALL FAIRBANKS, AK 99775 Small instrumentation grant
S15AG-10240-01 (NSS) COOK, EDWIN W UNIVERSITY OF ALABAMA UAB STATION BIRMINGHAM, AL 35294 Small instrumentation grant
S15AG-10241-01 (NSS) KOZLOWSKI, PIOTR B NYS INSTITUTE FOR BASIC RES.. 1050 FOREST HILL ROAD STATEN ISLAND, NY 10314 Small instrumentation grant
S15AG-10242-01 (NSS) CRUZE, ALVIN M RESEARCH TRIANGLE INSTITUTE PO BOX 12194 RES TRIANGLE PARK, NC 27709 Small instrumentation grant
S15AG-10243-01 (NSS) KORN, DAVID STANFORD UNIVERSITY MEDICAL BLDG RM M-121 STANFORD, CA 94305 Small instrumentation grant
S15AG-10244-01 (NSS) LAWTON, M POWELL PHILADELPHIA GERIATRIC CENTER 5301 OLD YORK ROAD PHILADELPHIA, PA 19141 Small instrumentation grant
S15AG-10245-01 (NSS) WISE, DAVID A NATL BUREAU OF ECONOMIC RES 1050 MASSACHUSETTS AVENUE CAMBRIDGE, MA 02138 Small instrumentation grant
S15AG-10246-01 (NSS) MC DOWELL, FLETCHER H BURKE REHABILITATION CENTER 785 MAMARONECK AVE WHITE PLAINS, NY 10605 Small instrumentation grant
S15AG-10247-01 (NSS) WOLF, DOUGLAS A URBAN INSTITUTE 2100 M STREET, NW WASHINGTON, DC 20037 Small instrumentation grant
R01AG-10248-01 (SSS) JOHNSON, THOMAS E UNIVERSITY OF COLORADO CAMPUS BOX 447 BOULDER, CO 80309-0447 RFLP-mapping of QTLS for life span and life history
R55AG-10251-01 (EDC) KLINE, JENNIE K RES FOUND FOR MENT HYG 722 WEST 168TH ST / BOX 53 NEW YORK, NY 10032 The epidemiology of trisomy and aging
R01AG-10257-01 (ECS) BARBER, B J TOBACCO & HEALTH RESEARCH INST COOPER & UNIVERSITY DRIVES LEXINGTON, KY 40546-0235 Age related changes in protein and water distribution
U01AG-10304-01 (BCA) LAWTON, M POWELL 5301 OLD YORK ROAD PHILADELPHIA, PA 19141 A stimulation - retreat program for Alzheimers patients
U01AG-10305-01 (BCA) MORRIS, JOHN N HEBREW REHAB CTR AGED 1200 CENTRE STREET BOSTON, MA 02131 Evaluating a family partnership program in SCUs
U01AG-10306-01 (BCA) KUTNER, NANCY G EMORY UNIVERSITY 1331 CLIFTON RD NE ATLANTA, GA 30322 Budd Terrace–SCU care model–Multidimensional analysis
U01AG-10311-01 (BCA) LINDEMAN, DAVID A CALIFORNIA ALZHEIMER'S DIS CTR 2001 DWIGHT WAY BERKELEY, CA 94704 Alzheimers special care units-longitudinal outcome study
U01AG-10313-01 (BCA) SLOANE, PHILIP D UNIVERSITY OF NORTH CAROLINA CB #7595 CHAPEL HILL, NC 27599-7595 Outcomes of Alzheimer's special care units in five states
U01AG-10317-01 (BCA) LEON, JOEL GEORGE WASHINGTON UNIVERSITY 2150 PENNSYLVANIA AVE NW 5TH F WASHINTON, DC 20037 National evaluation of special care units
U01AG-10318-01 (BCA) MONTGOMERY, RHONDA J WAYNE STATE UNIVERSITY 71 C EAST FERRY DETROIT, MI 48202 Special care units–Impact on AD residents, family, staff
R01AG-10327-01 (EDC) YU, ELENA S H SAN DIEGO STATE UNIVERSITY DIVISION OF EPIDEMIOLOGY SAN DIEGO, CA 92182 Alzheimer's disease and dementia in China
U01AG-10328-01 (BCA) GRANT, LESLIE A DIV OF HEALTH SERVS ADMIN C309 MAYO BOX 97 MINNEAPOLIS, MN 55455 Special care units in Minnesota nursing homes
U01AG-10330-01 (BCA) HOLMES, DOUGLAS HEBREW HOME FOR THE AGED 5901 PALISADE AVE RIVERDALE, NY 10471 Differential costs and inputs for special care units
R44AG-10347-02 (HUD) WHITWORTH, DONALD P, JR ANNAPOLIS SCIENCE CENTER 120 ADMIRAL COCHRANE DRIVE ANNAPOLIS, MD 21401 Using telephone media to plan for retirement
U01AG-10353-01 (BCA) DAWSON-HUGHES, BESS USDA HUMAN NUTRITION RES CTR 711 WASHINGTON ST BOSTON, MA 02111 Effect of calcium and vitamin D on bone loss from the hip
R01AG-10358-01 (BCA) GALLAGHER, J CHRISTOPHER BONE METABOLISM UNIT 601 N 30TH ST STE 5730 OMAHA, NE 68131 Pathophysiology of senile (type 11) osteoporosis
R03AG-10361-01 (SRC) AGURS, TANYA D PENNSYLVANIA STATE UNIV S 126 HENDERSON BLDG UNIVERSITY PARK, PA 16802 Weight loss/exercise in aged blacks with chronic disease
R03AG-10362-01 (SRC) BROWN, VALERIE S CASE WESTERN RESERVE UNIV CLEVELAND, OH 44146 Effects of poverty environments on elderly well being
R03AG-10372-01 (SRC) JACKSON, JAMES D UNIV OF KANSAS 426 FRASER LAWRENCE, KS 66045 Text summarization by older adults
U01AG-10373-01 (BCA) GALLAGHER, J CHRISTOPHER BONE METABOLISM UNIT 601 N 30TH ST STE 5730 OMAHA, NE 68131 Treatment for osteoporosis of the hip
R01AG-10374-01 (BCA) CODY, DIANNA D HENRY FORD HOSPITAL 2799 W GRAND BLVD DETROIT, MICHIGAN 48202 Proximal femur architecture in older women
R03AG-10376-01 (SRC) HORTON, TONYA LYNETTE UNIV OF NORTH CAROLINA C B #7360 CHAPEL HILL, NC 27599-7360 Effects of aging on the pharmacodynamics of morphine
R01AG-10381-01 (BCA) PARFITT, A MICHAEL HENRY FORD HOSPITAL ER7092 2799 W GRAND BOULEVARD DETROIT, MI 48202 ERT and focal balance between resorption and formation
U01AG-10382-01 (BCA) DALSKY, GAIL P UNIV OF CONNECTICUT HLTH CTR 309 FARM HOLLOW- STE C 208 FARMINGTON, CT 06030 Effect of exercise on femoral bone mass in older adults
U01AG-10383-01 (BCA) RUDMAN, DANIEL MEDICAL COLLEGE OF WISCONSIN 5000 W NATIONAL AVE MILWAUKEE, WI 53295 Effect of testosterone on bone density in hypogonadal men
R03AG-10390-01 (SRC) MCGADNEY, BRENDA F UNIVERSITY OF CHICAGO 969 E 60TH CHICAGO, IL 60637 Stress, and social supports as predictors of burden for caregivers
R03AG-10396-01 (SRC) MARTI, GERARDO UNIV OF SOUTHERN CALIFORNIA LOS ANGELES, CA 90089-0191 Intergenerational continuity and family solidarity
R03AG-10398-01 (SRC) KEYNTON, ROBERT S UNIVERSITY OF AKRON 301 SIDNEY OLSON RESEARCH CENT AKRON, OH 44325-0302 Effect of arterial graft caliber upon patency
R03AG-10405-01 (SRC) MONTOYA, HELEN MARIE HELEN MONTOYA RFD 2, BOX 229 NORFOLK, NE 68701 Service providers construal of elderly patients
U01AG-10407-01 (BCA) KLEEREKOPER, MICHAEL HENRY FORD HOSPITAL 2799 WEST GRAND BOULEVARD DETROIT, MI 48202 Estrogen in the prevention of bone loss from the hip
R01AG-10410-01 (NBSA) LEIGH, J PAUL SAN JOSE STATE UNIVERSITY SAN JOSE, CA 95192-0114 Education, arthritis and disability among minority seniors
R01AG-10412-01 (NBSA) ROSS, PHILIP D 846 SOUTH HOTEL ST HONOLULU, HAWAII 96813 Falls and fractures among elderly Japanese-Americans
P60AG-10415-01 (BCA) BECK, JOHN C UNIVERSITY OF CALIFORNIA 10833 LE CONTE AVENUE (CHS) LOS ANGELES, CA 90024-1687 UCLA older Americans independence center
P60AG-10415-01 0001 (BCA) SIU, ALBERT UCLA older Americans independence center Randomized trial of post-discharge geriatric assessment
P60AG-10415-01 0002 (BCA) SCHNELLE, JOHN F UCLA older Americans independence center Reduce dependency in nursing home residents
P60AG-10415-01 0003 (BCA) REUBEN, DAVID UCLA older Americans independence center Improving the effectiveness of geriatric assessment
P60AG-10415-01 9001 (BCA) KEELER, EMMETT UCLA older Americans independence center Research resources core–Cost effectiveness
P60AG-10415-01 9002 (BCA) HAHN, THEODORE UCLA older Americans independence center Research development core
P60AG-10415-01 9003 (BCA) BECK, JOHN UCLA older Americans independence center Core–Demonstration and dissemination project–Training research into practice
R01AG-10430-01 (NBSA) MILES, TONI P UNIV OF ILLINOIS AT CHICAGO PO BOX 6998 (M/C 922) CHICAGO, IL 60680 Black elderly twin study
P01AG-10435-01 (NBSA) GAGE, FRED H UNIVERSITY OF CALIFORNIA 9500 GILMAN DRIVE LA JOLLA, CA 92093-0624 Gene therapy for Alzheimer's disease
P01AG-10435-01 0001 (NBSA) GAGE, FRED Gene therapy for Alzheimer's disease Intracerebral neurotrophic factor delivery
P01AG-10435-01 0002 (NBSA) FISHER, LISA J Gene therapy for Alzheimer's disease Neurotransmitter delivery for cognitively impaired rats
P01AG-10435-01 0003 (NBSA) TUSZYNSKI, MARK Gene therapy for Alzheimer's disease Genetically modified cells in primates
P01AG-10435-01 9001 (NBSA) RAY, JASODHARA Gene therapy for Alzheimer's disease Core– Cellular and molecular genetics
R01AG-10436-01 (NBSA) MILLER, DOUGLAS K ST LOUIS UNIVERSITY 1402 S GRAND BLVD ST LOUIS, MO 63104 Physical frailty in urban African-Americans
R01AG-10444-01 (NBSA) HAZUDA, HELEN P UNIV OF TEXAS HEALTH SCIENCE C 7703 FLOYD CURL DRIVE SAN ANTONIO, TX 78284-7873 San

Antonio longitudinal study of aging
P01AG-10446-01 (NBSA) PARKER, WILLIAM D, JR UNIV OF COLORADO/HLTH SCI CTR 4200 E 9TH AVE C233 DENVER, CO 80262 Drug mechanisms in Alzheimer's disease treatment
P01AG-10446-01 0002 (NBSA) EATON, SANDRA Drug mechanisms in Alzheimer's disease treatment Alzheimer's-- The role of radicals
P01AG-10446-01 0003 (NBSA) WILCOX, CHRISTINE Drug mechanisms in Alzheimer's disease treatment The role of nerve growth factor in Alzheimer's disease
P01AG-10446-01 0001 (NBSA) PARKER, WILLIAM DAVIS Drug mechanisms in Alzheimer's disease treatment Mitochondrial effects of Alzheimer's disease drugs
R01AG-10454-01 (NBSA) KELSEY, JENNIFER L STANFORD MEDICAL SCHOOL STANFORD, CA 94305-5092 Osteoporosis and falls in Mexican-American elders
R01AG-10462-01 (BBCA) ANDERSON, STEPHEN CTR FOR ADV BIOTECHNOLOGY & ME 679 HOES LANE PISCATAWAY, NJ 08854-5638 Biochemistry & biophysics of BPTI folding mutants
P60AG-10463-01 (BCA) HAMILL, ROBERT W UNIV-ROCHESTER SCH OF MED-DENT 601 ELMWOOD AVENUE ROCHESTER, N Y 14642 Rochester Area Pepper Center
P60AG-10463-01 0001 (BCA) WELLS, THELMA Rochester Area Pepper Center Urinary incontinence--Treatment algorithm
P60AG-10463-01 0002 (BCA) HALL, WILLIAM Rochester Area Pepper Center Acute respiratory tract infection in the elderly
P60AG-10463-01 0003 (BCA) WELLE, STEPHEN Rochester Area Pepper Center Muscle hypertrophy and protein synthesis--Effect of age
P60AG-10463-01 0004 (BCA) TARIOT, PIERRE Rochester Area Pepper Center Carbamazepine therapy of agitation in dementia
P60AG-10463-01 0005 (BCA) PODGORSKI, CAROL Rochester Area Pepper Center Demonstration and dissemination project
P60AG-10463-01 9001 (BCA) PANZER, ROBERT Rochester Area Pepper Center Core--Geriatric assessment
P60AG-10463-01 9002 (BCA) ZIMMER, JAMES Rochester Area Pepper Center Core--Health services research
P60AG-10463-01 9003 (BCA) TANNER, MARTIN Rochester Area Pepper Center Core--Biostatistics
P60AG-10463-01 9004 (BCA) GRIGGS, ROBERT Rochester Area Pepper Center Core--Research development
P01AG-10480-01 (NBSA) HEFTI, FRANZ F UNIV OF SOUTHERN CALIFORNIA UNIVERSITY PARK, MC-0191 LOS ANGELES, CA 90089-0191 Therapeutic potential of neurotrophins in Alzheimer's disease
P01AG-10480-01 0001 (NBSA) NIKOLICS, KAROLY Therapeutic potential of neurotrophins in Alzheimer's disease Modified neurotrophins and neurotrophic antibodies
P01AG-10480-01 0002 (NBSA) HEFTI, FRANZ F Therapeutic potential of neurotrophins in Alzheimer's disease Biological actions of neurotrophins on rat brain cells in vitro & in vivo
P01AG-10480-01 0003 (NBSA) PRICE, DONALD L Therapeutic potential of neurotrophins in Alzheimer's disease Neurotrophins in models of neuronal degeneration
P01AG-10481-01 (NBSA) KRAFFT, GRANT A ABBOTT LABORATORIES 9MN AP9A ABBOTT PARK, IL 60064-3500 Neural proteases-- New Alzheimer's disease drug targets
P01AG-10481-01 0001 (NBSA) KRAFFT, GRANT Neural proteases-- New Alzheimer's disease drug targets Probes, inhibitors and structure of neural proteases
P01AG-10481-01 0002 (NBSA) GHANBARI, HOSSEIN Neural proteases-- New Alzheimer's disease drug targets Neural proteases as markers in Alzheimer's disease
P01AG-10481-01 0003 (NBSA) HOLZMAN, THOMAS Neural proteases-- New Alzheimer's disease drug targets Biochemistry of neural proteases
P01AG-10481-01 0004 (NBSA) FRAIL, DONALD Neural proteases-- New Alzheimer's disease drug targets Molecular biology of amyloid precursor protein and proteases
P01AG-10481-01 0005 (NBSA) KLEIN, WILLIAM Neural proteases-- New Alzheimer's disease drug targets Cell biology of neurodegenerative proteases
P01AG-10481-01 9001 (NBSA) MILLER, BARNEY Neural proteases-- New Alzheimer's disease drug targets Core-- Tissue bank
P01AG-10481-01 9002 (NBSA) KLASS, MICHAEL Neural proteases-- New Alzheimer's disease drug targets Core-- Biotechnology resources
P01AG-10481-01 9003 (NBSA) IANNACONE, PHILIP Neural proteases-- New Alzheimer's disease drug targets Core-- Northwestern University transgenic facility
P01AG-10481-01 9004 (NBSA) DECKER, MICHAEL Neural proteases-- New Alzheimer's disease drug targets Core-- Psychopharmacology and cognitive behavior
P01AG-10481-01 9005 (NBSA) GREER, JONATHAN Neural proteases-- New Alzheimer's disease drug targets Core-- Molecular structure and biophysical studies
U01AG-10483-01 (NBSA) THAL, LEON J VA MEDICAL CENTER 3350 LA JOLLA VILLAGE DRIVE SAN DIEGO, CA 92161 Alzheimer disease cooperative study unit
U01AG-10483-01 0003 (NBSA) GROWDON, JOHN Alzheimer disease cooperative study unit Deprenyl treatment for Alzheimer's disease
U01AG-10483-01 9001 (NBSA) HILL, ROBERT Alzheimer disease cooperative study unit Core-- Data management
U01AG-10483-01 0001 (NBSA) THAL, LEON J Alzheimer disease cooperative study unit Alzheimer's disease study units
U01AG-10483-01 0002 (NBSA) FERRIS, STEVEN H Alzheimer disease cooperative study unit Development of improved efficacy assessment measures
P60AG-10484-01 (BCA) HAZZARD, WILLIAM R BOWMAN GRAY SCHOOL OF MEDICINE MEDICAL CENTER BLVD WINSTON-SALEM, N C 27157-1052 Claude D Pepper Older Americans Independence Center
P60AG-10484-01 0001 (BCA) ETTINGER, WALTER H Claude D Pepper Older Americans Independence Center Therapeutic exercise for knee osteoarthritis
P60AG-10484-01 0002 (BCA) APPLEGATE, WILLIAM Claude D Pepper Older Americans Independence Center Non-pharmacologic treatment of systolic hypertension
P60AG-10484-01 0003 (BCA) APPLEGATE, WILLIAM Claude D Pepper Older Americans Independence Center Pharmacologic/non-pharmacologic treatment of osteoporosis
P60AG-10484-01 9001 (BCA) TELL, GRETHE Claude D Pepper Older Americans Independence Center Core--Recruitment
P60AG-10484-01 9002 (BCA) MORGAN, TIMOTHY Claude D Pepper Older Americans Independence Center Core--Biostatistics
P60AG-10484-01 9003 (BCA) SCHUMAKER, SALLY A Claude D Pepper Older Americans Independence Center Core--Quality of life/cost-effectiveness
P60AG-10484-01 9004 (BCA) ETTINGER, WALTER Claude D Pepper Older Americans Independence Center Core--Research development
P60AG-10484-01 9005 (BCA) SUGGS, PATRICIA Claude D Pepper Older Americans Independence Center Core--Demonstration and dissemination
P01AG-10485-01 (NBSA) SIMPKINS, JAMES W UNIVERSITY OF FLORIDA BOX J-487 GAINESVILLE, FL 32610 Discovery of novel drugs for Alzheimer's disease
P01AG-10485-01 0001 (NBSA) CREWS, FULTON J Discovery of novel drugs for Alzheimer's disease Phosphoinositide modulation, calcium and Alzheimer's disease
P01AG-10485-01 0002 (NBSA) MEYER, EDWIN M Discovery of novel drugs for Alzheimer's disease Anabaseine and DMAB-anabaseine as enhancers of neuron viability
P01AG-10485-01 0003 (NBSA) BODOR, NICHOLAS S Discovery of novel drugs for Alzheimer's disease Brain targeted delivery of thyrotropin releasing factor
P01AG-10485-01 0004 (NBSA) SIMPKINS, JAMES W Discovery of novel drugs for Alzheimer's disease Brain enhanced delivery of neurotrophomodulators
P01AG-10485-01 9001 (NBSA) CREWS, FULTON T Discovery of novel drugs for Alzheimer's disease Core-- Tissue culture
P01AG-10485-01 9002 (NBSA) MILLARD, WILLIAM J Discovery of novel drugs for Alzheimer's disease Core-- Neurochemistry
R01AG-10489-01 (NBSA) LANTIGUA, RAFAEL COLUMBIA UNIVERSITY 100 HAVEN AVE/TOWER 3-30F NEW YORK, NY 10032 Active life expectancy among urban minority elderly
P01AG-10491-01 (NBSA) GREENGARD, PAUL ROCKEFELLER UNIVERSITY 1230 YORK AVENUE NEW YORK, NY 10021 Interdisciplinary approach to Alzheimer drug discovery
P01AG-10491-01 0001 (NBSA) FRANGIONE, BLAS Interdisciplinary approach to Alzheimer drug discovery Processing of amyloid precursor protein by cerebral vessel walls
P01AG-10491-01 0002 (NBSA) GANDY, SAMUEL E Interdisciplinary approach to Alzheimer drug discovery Cell biology of amyloid precursor protein processing in vitro, in vivo
P01AG-10491-01 0003 (NBSA) PRICE, DONALD L Interdisciplinary approach to Alzheimer drug discovery Studies of cholinergic systems and amyloidogenesis
P01AG-10491-01 0004 (NBSA) BARTFAI, TAMAS Interdisciplinary approach to Alzheimer drug discovery Galanin-Acetylcholine interactions in basal forebrain
P01AG-10491-01 9001 (NBSA) RAMABHADRAN, T Interdisciplinary approach to Alzheimer drug discovery Core-- Scientific
R01AG-10499-02 (ARRF) NORR, KATHLEEN F UNIVERSITY OF ILLINOIS PO BOX 6998 CHICAGO, IL 60680 Peer education for AIDS prevention among Botswanan women
R01AG-10559-01 (BCE) JI, TAE H UNIVERSITY OF WYOMING BOX 3944, UNIVERSITY STATION LARAMIE, WY 82071-3944 Identification of LH-receptor gene regulatory sequences
R01AG-10560-01 (NEUC) LEVITT, PAT R MED COLLEGE OF PENNSYLVANIA 3200 HENRY AVENUE PHILADELPHIA, PA 19129 Role of non-neuronal cells in CNS formation and injury
S15AG-10561-01 (NSS) NEELON, VIRGINIA J UNIVERSITY OF NORTH CAROLINA CB# 7460, CARRINGTON HALL CHAPEL HILL, NC 27599 Small instrumentation grant
S15AG-10562-01 (NSS) KNAFL, KATHLEEN A UNIVERSITY OF ILLINOIS 845 SOUTH DAMEN AVENUE, M/C 80 CHICAGO, IL 60612 Small instrumentation grant
S15AG-10563-01 (NSS) ANDERSON, CAROLE A OHIO STATE UNIVERSITY 1585 NEIL AVENUE COLUMBUS, OH 43210 Small instrumentation grant
R01AG-10596-09 (PBC) CUNNINGHAM, DENNIS D UNIVERSITY OF CALIFORNIA IRVINE, CA 92717 Regulation of protease nexin 1 activity and secretion
R01AG-10599-01 (PBC) COOPERMAN, BARRY S UNIVERSITY OF PENNSYLVANIA 133 SOUTH 36TH STREET PHILADELPHIA, PA 19104 Antichymotrypsin interaction with serine proteases
R01AG-10604-01 (NEUA) POLICH, JOHN M SCRIPPS CLINIC & RESEARCH FDN 10666 NORTH TORREY PINES ROAD LA JOLLA, CA 92037 Assessment of Alzheimer's disease with P300
R01AG-10612-06 (CLIN) HANSEN, BARBARA C OBESITY & METABOLISM LABORATOR 10 SOUTH PINE STREET BALTIMORE, MD 21201 Obesity and the regulation of appetite
R01AG-10634-01 (NEUA) SANES, JEROME N BROWN UNIVERSITY BOX 1953 PROVIDENCE, RI 02912 Neural control of voluntary movements
R01AG-10638-01 (LCR) PROHOVNIK, ISAK NY ST PSYCHIATRIC INST 722 WEST 168TH STREET NEW YORK, N Y 10032 Alzheimer's diseased-like pathology in elderly schizophrenia
R01AG-10641-01 (NRRC) JACKSON, MARY E SYSTEMETRICS/MCGRAW-HILL HARTWELL AVENUE LEXINGTON, MA 02173 Estimates, predictors and outcomes of behavior problems
R01AG-10642-01 (NRRC) COHEN-MANSFIELD, JISKA HEBREW HOME/GREATER WASHINGTON 6121 MONTROSE RD ROCKVILLE, MD 20852 Management of screaming in nursing home residents
R01AG-10643-01 (NRRC) DEMENT, WILLIAM C STANFORD UNIVERSITY STANFORD, CA 94305 Sundown syndrome in a skilled nursing facility
R01AG-10644-01 (NRRC) KENNEDY, ROBERT D MONTEFIORE MEDICAL CENTER 111 EAST 210TH ST BRONX, NY 10467 Management of resistance to bathing activities
R01AG-10645-01 (NRRC) KOREN, MARY J NYS DEPT OF HEALTH EMPIRE STATE PLAZA ALBANY, NY 12237 Behavior management for persons with dementia
R01AG-10646-01 (NRRC) BONDER, BETTE R CLEVELAND STATE UNIVERSITY 24TH & EUCLID AVENUE CLEVELAND, OH 44115 Assessment and intervention--ADL in Alzheimer's disease
R01AG-10647-01 (NRRC) GILLEY, DAVID W RUSH-PRESBY-ST LUKE'S MED

CENT 1653 WEST CONGRESS PARKWAY CHICAGO, IL 60612 Aggressive behavior in persons with Alzheimer's disease
R01AG-10648-01 (NRRC) HORNER, JENNIFER DUKE UNIVERSITY MEDICAL CENTER BOX 3867 DURHAM, NC 27710 Dysphagia in Alzheimer's disease
R01AG-10664-01 (SRC) MARKESBERY, WILLIAM R UNIVERSITY OF KENTUCKY SANDERS-BROWN BLDG RM 101 LEXINGTON, KY 40536-0230 Alzheimer's disease, dental amalgams and mercury
R01AG-10665-01 (SRC) CORDELL, BARBARA L CALIFORNIA BIOTECHNOLOGY INC 2450 BAYSHORE PARKWAY MOUNTAIN VIEW, CA 94043 Transgenic mouse model of Alzheimer's disease amyloidosis
R01AG-10667-01 (SRC) MOISES, HYLAN C UNIVERSITY OF MICHIGAN 7806 MEDICAL SCIENCE II BLDG ANN ARBOR, MI 48109-0622 Nerve growth factor and cholinergic function in adult and
R01AG-10668-01 (SRC) MUFSON, ELLIOTT J RUSH-PRESBYTERIAN-ST LUKE MED 1725 WEST HARRISON, SUITE 1140 CHICAGO, IL 60612 Galanin in Alzheimer's disease
R01AG-10669-01 (SRC) MARSH, RICHARD F 1655 LINDEN DRIVE MADISON, WI 53706 Study of the protein in mink encephalopathy
R01AG-10670-01 (SRC) OTVOS, LASZLO WISTAR INSTITUTE 36TH & SPRUCE STREETS PHILADELPHIA, PA 19104 Conformation of phosphorylated brain peptides
R01AG-10671-01 (SRC) BREDESEN, DALE E UNIVERSITY OF CALIFORNIA 710 WESTWOOD PLAZA LOS ANGELES, CA 90024-1769 A genetically tractable in vitro model of ALZ.D
R01AG-10672-01 (SRC) MOBLEY, WILLIAM C UNIVERSITY OF CALIFORNIA BOX 0114 SAN FRANCISCO, CA 94143-0114 Neurotrophic factor therapy for Alzheimer's disease
R01AG-10673-01 (SRC) JOHNSON, STEVEN A UNIVERSITY OF SOUTHERN CALIF 3715 MCCLINTOCK AVE LOS ANGELES, CA 90089-0191 Complement expression in Alzheimer's disease brain
R01AG-10675-01 (SRC) MALTER, JAMES S TULANE UNIVERSITY MEDICAL CENT 1430 TULANE AVENUE NEW ORLEANS, LA 70112 APP mRNA dysregulation and Alzheimer's disease
R01AG-10676-01 (SRC) SALTON, STEPHEN R MT SINAI SCHOOL OF MEDICINE 1 GUSTAVE LEVY PLACE, BOX 1065 NEW YORK, NY 10029 Regulation of VGF by neurotrophic growth factors
R01AG-10677-01 (SRC) BROWN, GREGORY G HENRY FORD HOSPITAL (K-11) 2799 W GRAND BLVD DETROIT, MI 48202 Spectroscopy of Alzheimer's disease & vascular dementia
R01AG-10678-01 (SRC) GEDDES, JAMES W UNIVERSITY OF KENTUCKY SANDERS-BROWN BLDG RM 209 LEXINGTON, KY 40536-0230 MAP5, sprouting, and Alzheimer's disease pathology
R01AG-10679-01 (SRC) GONZALEZ, R GILBERTO MGH NMR CENTER 13TH STREET CHARLESTOWN, MA 02129 Neuroimaging in the diagnosis of Alzheimer's disease
R01AG-10681-01 (SRC) CARLSON, GEORGE A MCLAUGHLIN RESEARCH INSTITUTE 1625 3RD AVE N GREAT FALLS, MT 59401 Transgenic mouse models for Alzheimer's disease
R01AG-10682-01 (SRC) STOPA, EDWARD G SUNY HLTH SCIENCE CTR 750 E ADAMS ST SYRACUSE, NY 13210 Heparin-binding growth factors in aging and Alzheimer's
R01AG-10683-01 (SRC) VIOLA, MICHAEL V STATE UNIVERSITY OF NEW YORK STONY BROOK, NY 11794-8174 A transomic mouse model for Alzheimer's disease
R01AG-10684-01 (SRC) SIMONS, ELIZABETH R BOSTON UNIV SCH OF MEDICINE 80 E CONCORD ST BOSTON, MA 02118 Platelet-endothelial cell interactions in Alzheimer's
R01AG-10685-01 (SRC) FRAUTSCHY, SALLY A THE WHITTIER INSTITUTE 9894 GENESEE AVENUE LA JOLLA, CA 92037 Mechanism of beta-amyloid neurotoxicity in the rat brain
R01AG-10686-01 (SRC) KRUEGER, BRUCE K UNIVERSITY OF MARYLAND 660 W REDWOOD ST BALTIMORE, MD 21201 Glial-neuronal interactions in neurodengeneration
R01AG-10687-01 (SRC) LEVINE, ROBERT A LAFAYETTE CLINIC 951 E LAFAYETTE DETROIT, MI 48207 Biopterin/catecholamine metabol.in Alzheimer's & aging
R01AG-10689-01 (SRC) MASLIAH, ELIEZER UNIV OF CALIFORNIA LA JOLLA, CA 92093-0624 Subcellular basis of synaptic pathology Alzheimer dis
R01AG-10747-01 (BPO) BOOZE, ROSEMARIE M UNIVERSITY OF KENTUCKY CHANDLER MEDICAL CTR/MS-301 LEXINGTON, KY 40536 Progressive cholinergic dysfunction in aging brain
R01AG-10755-01 (SRC) ROSE, GREGORY M UNIVERSITY OF CO HLTH SCI CTR 4200 E 9TH AVENUE DENVER, CO 80262 Cholinergic circuits and hippocampal function in aging
R29AG-10756-01 (EDC) WRIGLEY, J MICHAEL UNIVERSITY OF ALABAMA/BIRMINGH UAB STATION BIRMINGHAM, AL 35294-2016 A demographic study of dementia among the elderly
R01AG-10757-01 (HUD) WORTMAN, CAMILLE B STATE UNIVERSITY OF NEW YORK STONY BROOK, NY 11794-2500 Widowhood, bereavement and coping
R01AG-10760-01 (LCR) VITALIANO, PETER P UNIV OF WASHINGTON SEATTLE, WA 98195 Caregiver mental health and Alzheimer's disease outcomes
N01AG-12101-00 (**) MULIVOR, RICHARD A Selection, production, characterization of genetically marked cells
N01AG-12102-00 (**) BLAZER, DAN Renewal of the established populations for epidemologic studies of the elderly
N01AG-12112-00 (**) FRIED, LINDA Women's aging study
N01AG-12117-00 (**) RUSSELL, ROBERT J Development and maintenance of a long-term colony of aged hybrid rats
N01AG-12118-00 (**) YIN, FRANK C Vascular stiffness, arterial pressure and cardiac mass
N01AG-32103-21 (**) CAIL, STEPHEN P Maintain a colony of genetically defined aged mice
N01AG-42110-10 (**) BLAZER, DAN Establishment of a population for studies of the elderly
N01AG-52115-10 (**) CAIL, STEPHEN P Maintenance of a long-term colony of aged hybrid rats
N01AG-62109-08 (**) GREENE, ARTHUR E Production, characterization of genetically marked cell for aging study
N01AG-72102-05 (**) COHEN, BENNETT J Pathology monitoring of aged hybrid rat colony
N01AG-92116-01 (**) WEISFELDT, MYRON Noninvasive assessment of cardiac structure & function
N01AG-92118-02 (**) ALLEN, ANTON Pathology monitoring for multigenotypic mouse colony
Z01AI-00013-28 (LIP) LEWIS, A M NIAID, NIH Immunobiology and pathogenesis of DNA virus infections
Z01AI-00020-16 (ODIR) LEVY, H B NIAID, NIH Clinical studies with polyICLC
Z01AI-00027-24 (LMM) TULLY, J G NIAID, NIH Basic studies of mycoplasmas
Z01AI-00030-23 (LI) PAUL, W E NIAID, NIH Antigen recognition and activation of immunocompetent cells
Z01AI-00035-18 (LI) INMAN, J K NIAID, NIH Specificity in immune response
Z01AI-00036-26 (LI) MAGE, R G NIAID, NIH Ig genetics--Ontogeny and differentiation of cells of the rabbit immune system
Z01AI-00043-26 (LCI) BENNETT, J E NIAID,NIH Immunology and chemotherapy of systemic mycoses
Z01AI-00045-23 (LCI) FRANK, M M NIAID, NIH Studies on interaction of antibody and complement on production of immune damage
Z01AI-00048-21 (LCI) FRANK, M M NIAID, NIH The pathophysiology of autoimmune hemolytic anemia
Z01AI-00057-18 (LCI) KWON-CHUNG, K J NIAID, NIH Basic studies on pathogenic fungi
Z01AI-00058-18 (LCI) STRAUS, S E NIAID, NIH The pathogenesis and chemotherapy of herpes virus infections in man
Z01AI-00072-20 (LPVD) LODMELL, D L NIAID, NIH Role of host and viral factors in resistance to rabies virus infections in mice
Z01AI-00074-19 (LPVD) CHESEBRO, B NIAID, NIH Genetically controlled mechanisms of recovery from Friend virus-induced leukemia
Z01AI-00085-14 (LPVD) BLOOM, M E NIAID, NIH Pathogenesis of aleutian disease virus infection
Z01AI-00086-15 (LPVD) PORTIS, J L NIAID, NIH Pathogenesis of diseases induced by non-oncogenic retroviruses
Z01AI-00094-32 (LPD) DIAMOND, L S NIAID, NIH Entamoeba histolytica-- Molecular taxonomy and genetic mechanisms of virulence
Z01AI-00097-33 (LPD) MERCADO, T I NIAID, NIH Physiological and cytochemical pathology of parasitic diseases
Z01AI-00098-35 (LPD) WEINBACH, E C NIAID, NIH Biochemical mechanisms of energy metabolism in mammalian and parasitic organisms
Z01AI-00099-21 (LPD) DVORAK, J A NIAID, NIH Biophysical parasitology
Z01AI-00102-17 (LPD) NEVA, F A NIAID, NIH Pathogenesis of disease caused by infection with intracellular parasites
Z01AI-00108-20 (LPD) MILLER, L H NIAID, NIH Studies on the immunobiology of malaria
Z01AI-00123-25 (LVD) MERCHLINSKY, M NIAID, NIH Structure and replication of poxvirus DNA
Z01AI-00126-19 (LVD) DEFILIPPES, F NIAID, NIH Functional analyses of vaccinia virus DNA
Z01AI-00134-29 (LI) ASOFSKY, R NIAID, NIH Control of immunoglobulin synthesis in mice
Z01AI-00143-22 (LIG) BAKER, P J NIAID, NIH Genetic control of the antibody response to microbial antigens
Z01AI-00144-27 (LIG) BAKER, P J NIAID, NIH Regulation of the antibody response to microbial polysaccharide antigens
Z01AI-00145-24 (LIG) BAKER, P J NIAID, NIH Mode of action of thymus derived (T) suppressor and amplifier cells
Z01AI-00154-17 (LCI) KALINER, M A NIAID, NIH Events in immediate hypersensitivity
Z01AI-00155-16 (LHD) GALLIN, J I NIAID, NIH Clinical studies of abnormal host defense
Z01AI-00161-14 (LPD) NASH, T E NIAID, NIH Immunochemistry of parasitic diseases
Z01AI-00162-15 (LPD) DWYER, D M NIAID, NIH Biochemical cytology of host-parasite interactions in parasitic protozoa
Z01AI-00166-14 (LIG) KINDT, T J NIAID, NIH Characterization of rabbit MHC antigens
Z01AI-00168-14 (LIG) KINDT, T J NIAID, NIH Cell surface markers of rabbit lymphocytes
Z01AI-00169-15 (BRB) COLIGAN, J NIAID, NIH Analysis of murine and human transplantation antigens and genes
Z01AI-00170-14 (LIG) LONG, E NIAID, NIH Molecular and functional analysis of human class II histocompatibility antigens
Z01AI-00171-14 (LIG) KINDT, T J NIAID, NIH Infection of rabbits with human immunodeficiency virus I
Z01AI-00172-13 (BRB) COLIGAN, J E NIAID, NIH Synthesis of peptide antigens
Z01AI-00180-13 (LIG) KINDT, T J NIAID, NIH Properties of transformed rabbit cell lines
Z01AI-00190-13 (LMM) MARTIN, M A NIAID, NIH Molecular genetics of eukaryotic cells and their viruses
Z01AI-00193-12 (LMSF) SWANSON, J NIAID, NIH Gonococcal surface components--Structure and function
Z01AI-00197-12 (LPD) NUTMAN, T B NIAID, NIH Immunoregulation and immune recognition in filariasis and non-filarial diseases
Z01AI-00208-11 (LPD) MCCUTCHAN, T NIAID, NIH The isolation and characterization of plasmodial genes
Z01AI-00210-11 (LIR) KEHRL, J H NIAID, NIH Immunoregulation of human lymphocyte function
Z01AI-00213-11 (LIR) HOFFMAN, G S NIAID, NIH Vasculitides and other immune-mediated diseases
Z01AI-00216-11 (LICP) CALDWELL, H D NIAID, NIH Immunochemistry of Chlamydial surface antigens
Z01AI-00218-10 (LMM) REPASKE, R NIAID, NIH Biochemical and chemical studies on retroviral DNA
Z01AI-00224-10 (LI) SHEVACH, E M NIAID, NIH Receptors, co-receptors, and counter-receptors in T cell activation
Z01AI-00226-10 (LI) MAGE, R G NIAID, NIH Rabbit allotypes--Structure, organization and regulated expression of Ig genes
Z01AI-00240-10 (LPD) KASLOW, D NIAID, NIH MCCUTCHAN, TF Antigenic analysis of sexual stages of malaria parasites

PROJECT NO., ORGANIZATIONAL UNIT., INVESTIGATOR, ADDRESS, TITLE

Z01AI-00241-10 (LPD) MILLER, L H NIAID, NIH Identification of receptors for merozoite invasion of erythrocytes
Z01AI-00246-09 (LPD) SHER, A NIAID, NIH Molecular studies of the genome and surface of Schistosoma mansoni
Z01AI-00248-10 (LPD) GWADZ, R W NIAID, NIH Genetics and physiology of vector capacity in Anopheline mosquitos
Z01AI-00249-10 (LCI) METCALFE, D D NIAID, NIH The pathogenesis, diagnosis, and treatment of systemic mast cell disorders
Z01AI-00251-10 (LPD) SHER, A NIAID, NIH Immunologic studies on schistosomiasis
Z01AI-00253-10 (LPD) OTTESEN, E A NIAID, NIH Studies of the immunologic responses to filarial infections
Z01AI-00255-10 (LPD) OTTESEN, E A NIAID, NIH Studies of the immunologic responses to non-filarial parasitic infections
Z01AI-00256-10 (LPD) SACKS, D L NIAID, NIH Developmental biology of Leishmania promastigotes
Z01AI-00257-10 (LPD) NEVA, F A NIAID, NIH Immunology of strongyloidiasis
Z01AI-00262-10 (LPVD) COE, J E NIAID, NIH Role of pentraxins in acute and chronic pathology
Z01AI-00263-10 (LPVD) BLOOM, M E NIAID, NIH Structure and function of the ADV genome
Z01AI-00265-10 (LPVD) RACE, R E NIAID, NIH Immunobiology of scrapie virus infection
Z01AI-00266-10 (LPVD) EVANS, L H NIAID, NIH Genetic structure of murine retroviruses
Z01AI-00275-10 (LCI) GAITHER, T NIAID, NIH The complement receptor and C3 mediated opsonization
Z01AI-00279-10 (LCI) KALINER, M A NIAID, NIH Studies on mucous glycoproteins
Z01AI-00284-10 (LIP) HARTLEY, J W NIAID, NIH Characterization of pathogenic murine leukemia viruses
Z01AI-00286-10 (LIP) HARTLEY, J W NIAID, NIH Genetic control of murine leukemia viruses and virus-induced neoplasms
Z01AI-00294-10 (LVD) ROSE, J A NIAID, NIH Structure and function of adenovirus DNA
Z01AI-00295-10 (LVD) ROSE, J A NIAID, NIH Helper factors required for expression of the adeno-associated virus genome
Z01AI-00296-10 (LVD) ROSE, J A NIAID, NIH Characterization and production of parvovirus proteins
Z01AI-00297-10 (LVD) ROSE, J A NIAID, NIH Mechanism and regulation of adeno-associated virus DNA replication
Z01AI-00298-10 (LVD) MOSS, B NIAID, NIH Development of vaccinia virus as an expression vector
Z01AI-00300-10 (LMM) KOZAK, C A NIAID, NIH Genetic aspects of viral oncogenesis in wild mouse species and laboratory mice
Z01AI-00301-10 (LMM) KOZAK, C NIAID, NIH Genetic mapping of mouse chromosomal genes
Z01AI-00304-10 (LMM) SILVER, J NIAID, NIH Pathogenesis of retroviral diseases
Z01AI-00306-10 (LVD) BULLER, R M NIAID, NIH Pathogenesis of orthopoxvirus infections
Z01AI-00307-10 (LVD) MOSS, B NIAID, NIH Regulation of vaccinia virus gene expression
Z01AI-00311-11 (LID) PURCELL, R H NIAID, NIH Search for new hepatitis agents
Z01AI-00314-11 (LID) MILLER, R NIAID, NIH Woodchuck virus--Molecular biological studies
Z01AI-00323-11 (LID) COLLINS, P L NIAID, NIH Structure and expression of parainfluenza type 3 virus genes
Z01AI-00324-10 (LID) MURPHY, B R NIAID, NIH Laboratory studies of influenza viruses
Z01AI-00325-09 (LID) MURPHY, B R NIAID, NIH Respiratory viruses in primates
Z01AI-00326-10 (LID) MURPHY, B R NIAID, NIH Respiratory viruses in volunteers
Z01AI-00327-10 (LID) HALL, S L NIAID, NIH Laboratory studies of parainfluenza type 3 virus
Z01AI-00333-10 (LID) KAPIKIAN, A Z NIAID, NIH A longitudinal study of viral gastroenteritis in infants and young children
Z01AI-00339-10 (LID) HOSHINO, Y NIAID, NIH Isolation and serotypic characterization of human and animal rotaviruses
Z01AI-00340-10 (LID) HOSHINO, Y NIAID, NIH Genetic studies of rotavirus pathogenesis
Z01AI-00341-10 (LID) KAPIKIAN, A Z NIAID, NIH Evaluation of live attenuated rotavirus vaccines
Z01AI-00342-10 (LID) KAPIKIAN, A Z NIAID, NIH Studies of gastroenteritis viruses by electron microscopy
Z01AI-00343-10 (LID) GREEN, K NIAID, NIH The role of Norwalk virus & related Norwalk-like viruses in viral gastroenteritis
Z01AI-00345-10 (LID) MURPHY, B R NIAID, NIH Laboratory studies of respiratory syncytial virus
Z01AI-00346-09 (LID) FLORES, J NIAID, NIH Genetic characterization of rotavirus by hybridization techniques
Z01AI-00347-09 (LPD) CHEEVER, A W NIAID, NIH Schistosomal hepatic fibrosis
Z01AI-00349-09 (LI) GERMAIN, R N NIAID, NIH Structure and function of murine class II MHC genes and gene products
Z01AI-00350-09 (LPD) NASH, T E NIAID, NIH DNA analysis of parasites
Z01AI-00352-09 (BRB) COLIGAN, J NIAID, NIH Characterization of cell surface molecules important for immune function
Z01AI-00353-09 (LMM) KHAN, A S NIAID, NIH Structural and functional studies of mammalian endogenous retroviral sequences
Z01AI-00354-09 (LCI) JAMES, S P NIAID, NIH Immunoregulatory defects in inflammatory bowel disease
Z01AI-00356-09 (LCI) STROBER, W NIAID, NIH Studies of the regulation of IgA immunoglobulin synthesis
Z01AI-00358-10 (LIR) QUINN, T C NIAID, NIH Immunopathogenesis of Chlamydia trachomatis infections
Z01AI-00361-09 (LIR) QUINN, T C NIAID, NIH International studies on the acquired immunodeficiency syndrome
Z01AI-00368-08 (LID) COLLINS, P L NIAID, NIH Structural analysis of respiratory syncytial virus genome
Z01AI-00370-08 (LID) OLMSTED, R NIAID, NIH Studies of simian acquired immune deficiency syndrome
Z01AI-00372-09 (LID) COLLINS, P L NIAID, NIH RSV proteins--Roles in host immunity and immunoprophylaxis
Z01AI-00389-08 (LIG) ROBINSON, M A NIAID, NIH Molecular genotype analyses in HLA and TCR genes in human families
Z01AI-00390-08 (LIR) LANE, H C NIAID, NIH Clinical investigation of AIDS
Z01AI-00394-08 (LI) MARGULIES, D H NIAID, NIH Molecular genetic analysis of lymphocyte function
Z01AI-00403-08 (LI) GERMAIN, R N NIAID, NIH Molecular genetic analysis of T cell receptor structure and repertoire
Z01AI-00415-08 (LMM) MARTIN, M A NIAID,NIH Molecular biology of retroviruses associated with AIDS
Z01AI-00416-08 (LVD) MOSS, B NIAID, NIH Recombinant vaccines against retroviruses associated with leukemia and AIDS
Z01AI-00418-08 (LPVD) MAURY, W NIAID, NIH Immunobiology of equine infectious anemia virus, a retrovirus model for AIDS
Z01AI-00425-07 (LI) CHUSED, T M NIAID, NIH Lymphocyte physiology
Z01AI-00427-07 (LI) SITKOVSKY, M V NIAID, NIH Antigen-specific and antigen-nonspecific cellular cytotoxicity
Z01AI-00429-07 (LCI) KALINER, M A NIAID, NIH Studies on nasal responses
Z01AI-00430-07 (LCI) STRAUS, S E NIAID, NIH Molecular biology of Varicella-Zoster virus infections
Z01AI-00431-07 (LIR) SIEBENLIST, U NIAID, NIH A molecular biologic approach to immune activation
Z01AI-00432-06 (LCI) JAMES, S P NIAID, NIH Regulation of mucosal immune responses in non-human primates
Z01AI-00437-07 (LMM) HOGGAN, M D NIAID, NIH The biology and genetics of the AIDS retrovirus
Z01AI-00439-07 (LPD) OTTESEN, E A NIAID, NIH Clinical and therapeutic studies in human filariasis
Z01AI-00445-08 (LVD) CHALLBERG, M NIAID, NIH Mechanisms of viral DNA replication
Z01AI-00446-07 (LID) FLORES, J NIAID, NIH Testing of rotavirus vaccine candidates in Venezuela and Peru
Z01AI-00459-06 (LID) ZHANG, C NIAID, NIH Expression of Dengue and other flavivirus proteins using baculovirus vector
Z01AI-00465-06 (LIP) MORSE, H C NIAID, NIH Retrovirus-induced murine immunodeficiency syndrome
Z01AI-00467-06 (LMM) VENKATESAN, S NIAID, NIH HIV-1 particle formation, RNA packaging and virus morphogenesis
Z01AI-00468-06 (LPVD) CHESEBRO, B NIAID, NIH Biology of human AIDS retrovirus
Z01AI-00469-06 (LCI) MCKENZIE, R NIAID, NIH Complement--Studies in viral infection
Z01AI-00470-06 (LCI) STRAUS, S E NIAID, NIH Chronic Epstein Barr virus infection and chronic fatigue syndrome
Z01AI-00480-06 (LVP) SCHWAN, T G NIAID, NIH Pathogen-arthropod interactions of vector-borne diseases affecting public health
Z01AI-00481-06 (LHD) MALECH, H L NIAID, NIH Human phagocyte NADPH oxidase
Z01AI-00483-06 (LPD) WELLEMS, T E NIAID, NIH Molecular genetics of drug resistance and red cell invasion in malaria
Z01AI-00484-05 (LIP) HOLMES, K L NIAID, NIH Mechanisms in hematopoietic cell differentiation
Z01AI-00485-05 (LCMI) SCHWARTZ, R H NIAID, NIH T cell activation
Z01AI-00486-05 (LCMI) FOWLKES, B J NIAID, NIH T cell differentiation
Z01AI-00487-05 (LPD) CHEEVER, A W NIAID, NIH Studies on the quantitative parasitology of schistosome infections
Z01AI-00488-05 (LVP) GARON, C F NIAID, NIH Ultrastructural analysis of antigenic determinants in pathogens
Z01AI-00492-05 (LVP) SCHWAN, T G NIAID, NIH Molecular basis for infection by Borrelia burgdorferi
Z01AI-00493-06 (LI) PAUL, W E NIAID, NIH B cell stimulatory factor-1 (BSF-1)/interleukin-4
Z01AI-00494-05 (LPD) SACKS, D NIAID, NIH Analysis of T cell responses in human leishmaniasis
Z01AI-00495-06 (LCI) KALINER, M A NIAID, NIH Biochemical events in mast cell secretion
Z01AI-00496-05 (LCI) STRAUS, S E NIAID, NIH Interactions between the human immunodeficiency virus and herpesviruses
Z01AI-00498-05 (LID) COLLINS, P L NIAID, NIH Synthesis processing and function of human RSV proteins
Z01AI-00500-05 (LID) FALGOUT, B NIAID, NIH Processing and immunogenicity of Dengue type 4 virus nonstructural protein NS1
Z01AI-00501-05 (LID) MARKOFF, L NIAID, NIH Processing of dengue viral glycoproteins
Z01AI-00502-05 (LID) MARKOFF, L NIAID, NIH Antigenic analysis of the dengue envelope glycoprotein using synthetic peptides
Z01AI-00507-05 (LID) GREEN, K NIAID, NIH Molecular characterization of rotavirus serotypes
Z01AI-00512-04 (LPD) NUTMAN, T B NIAID, NIH Molecular definition of filarial antigens
Z01AI-00513-04 (LCI) METCALFE, D D NIAID, NIH Molecular biology of mast cell growth and differentiation
Z01AI-00514-04 (LCI) METCALFE, D D NIAID, NIH Diagnosis and treatment of adverse reactions to foods and additives
Z01AI-00516-04 (LMSF) PINCUS, S H NIAID, NIH Immunoglobulin biology
Z01AI-00519-04 (LICP) MORRISON, R P NIAID, NIH Immunopathogenesis of chlamydial infections
Z01AI-00520-04 (LI) GERMAIN, R N NIAID, NIH Analysis of T lymphocyte responses to HIV proteins
Z01AI-00521-04 (LHD) GALLIN, J I NIAID, NIH Effect of cytokines in host defense and inflammation
Z01AI-00522-04 (BRB) COLIGAN, J NIAID, NIH Protein sequence analyses

PROJECT NUMBER LISTING

PROJECT NO., ORGANIZATIONAL UNIT., INVESTIGATOR, ADDRESS, TITLE

Z01AI-00523-04 (BRB) HOLMES, K L NIAID, NIH Flow cytometry analysis
Z01AI-00524-04 (LPVD) PERRY, L L NIAID, NIH Immunologic factors in susceptibility and resistance to rabies virus in mice
Z01AI-00525-04 (LIG) LONG, E O NIAID, NIH Molecular analysis of human natural killer cells
Z01AI-00527-04 (LMM) THEODORE, T S NIAID, NIH Molecular cloning and characterization of retroviruses associated with AIDS
Z01AI-00528-03 (LMM) VENKATESAN, S NIAID,NIH Functional studies of HIV-1 regulatory proteins
Z01AI-00530-04 (LID) MILLER, R H NIAID, NIH Molecular and computer analysis of the hepatitis B virus genome
Z01AI-00531-04 (LID) FALGOUT, B NIAID, NIH Functional analysis of dengue nonstructural proteins, NS2B and NS3
Z01AI-00533-04 (LID) GREEN, K NIAID, NIH Analysis of rotavirus proteins with monoclonal antibodies
Z01AI-00534-04 (LID) QIAN, Y NIAID, NIH Molecular studies of non-group A rotaviruses
Z01AI-00537-04 (LIR) FAUCI, A S NIAID,NIH Immunopathogenic mechanisms of human immunodeficiency virus infection
Z01AI-00538-04 (LVD) BERGER, E NIAID, NIH Interaction of human immunodeficiency virus with the CD4 receptor
Z01AI-00539-04 (LVD) MOSS, B NIAID, NIH Virus-cell interactions, viral pathogenesis and host immunity
Z01AI-00540-04 (LVD) FRENKEL, N NIAID, NIH Molecular biology of human herpesviruses
Z01AI-00541-04 (LVD) YEWDELL, J NIAID, NIH Folding assembly, and transport of viral glycoproteins
Z01AI-00542-04 (LVD) YEWDELL, J W NIAID, NIH Processing of viral proteins for T cell recognition
Z01AI-00543-04 (BRB) COLIGAN, J E NIAID, NIH Recognition of peptidic antigens by virus-specific cytotoxic T lymphocytes
Z01AI-00544-03 (LIP) CHATTOPADHYAY, S K NIAID,NIH Molecular basis of pathogenesis of murine leukemia virus infections
Z01AI-00545-03 (LI) GERMAIN, R N NIAID,NIH Antigen processing and presentation
Z01AI-00547-03 (LMM) JEANG, K-T NIAID,NIH Molecular mechanism(s) of human retrovirus trans-regulatory proteins
Z01AI-00548-03 (LCI) STRAUS, S E NIAID, NIH Prevention of genital herpes simplex infection
Z01AI-00549-03 (LMSF) ROSA, P A NIAID,NIH Pathogenesis of infection with the Lyme disease spirochete, Borrelia burgdorferi
Z01AI-00550-03 (LPVD) PERRY, L L NIAID, NIH EAE--Immunoregulation of relapsing disease
Z01AI-00551-03 (LPVD) PERRY, L L NIAID, NIH Cellular interactions during HIV infection in vitro
Z01AI-00552-03 (LVP) CIEPLAK, W NIAID,NIH Immunopathobiology of bacterial toxins
Z01AI-00553-03 (LVP) CIEPLAK, W NIAID,NIH Molecular biology and immunology of pathogenic Campylobacter
Z01AI-00554-03 (LVP) GARON, C F NIAID,NIH Structural characterization of microbial genes and nucleic acid molecules
Z01AI-00557-03 (LID) MARKOFF, L J NIAID, NIH Cross-reactive antibodies to clotting factors in Dengue virus infections
Z01AI-00558-03 (LID) FLORES, J NIAID, NIH Prediction of rotavirus serotypes by hybridization specific to probes
Z01AI-00562-03 (LIR) VITKOVIC, L NIAID,NIH Neuroimmunology and neuropathogenesis of HIV infection
Z01AI-00564-03 (LVD) ROSE, J A NIAID, NIH Development of a parvoviral vector that regulates gene expression
Z01AI-00565-02 (LI) LENARDO, M NIAID, NIH The family of kappaB regulators for genes in the immune response
Z01AI-00566-02 (LI) LENARDO, M NIAID, NIH Gene regulatory events in T cell tolerance and thymic T cell maturation
Z01AI-00567-01 (LICP) HACKSTADT, T NIAID, NIH Rickettsial surface structure and function
Z01AI-00568-02 (LMSF) HEINEMANN, J NIAID,NIH Molecular basis and extent of microbial sex
Z01AI-00569-02 (LID) EMERSON, SUZANNE NIAID, NIH Determination of genetic markers of virulence and adaptation to CC of hepA virus
Z01AI-00570-02 (LID) MILLER, R NIAID, NIH Molecular biology of hepatitis C virus
Z01AI-00571-02 (LID) PETHEL, M NIAID, NIH Amino acid substitution at the NSI-NS2A cleavage junction of Dengue protein
Z01AI-00572-02 (LID) CAHOUR, A NIAID, NIH Processing of Dengue virus polyprotein NS3-NS4A-NS4B-NS5 domain
Z01AI-00573-02 (LID) GREEN, K NIAID, NIH Expression of rotavirus proteins in Salmonella bacteria
Z01AI-00574-02 (LID) LARRALDE, G NIAID, NIH Expression/distribution of conserved/serotype-specific epitopes on rotavirus VP8
Z01AI-00576-02 (LID) RASOOL, N NIAID, NIH Serotype analysis and characterization of rotaviruses from Malaysia
Z01AI-00578-02 (LIP) SHAPIRO, M NIAID, NIH Role of oncogenes in B cell neoplasia
Z01AI-00579-02 (LPD) SHER, A NIAID, NIH Studies on immune regulation in toxoplasmosis
Z01AI-00580-02 (LPVD) CAUGHEY, B NIAID, NIH Biochemistry of scrapie pathogenesis
Z01AI-00581-02 (LCMI) MATZINGER, P NIAID,NIH T cell memory and T cell tolerance
Z01AI-00582-02 (LID) GORZIGLIA, M NIAID, NIH Expression and recovery of recombinant rotavirus VP4 from insect cell cultures
Z01AI-00583-02 (LID) LI, BAOGUANG NIAID, NIH Expression of the outer capsid protein of VP4 of human and porcine rotaviruses
Z01AI-00585-02 (LIR) LANE, HC NIAID,NIH Pathogenic mechanism in HIV and other retroviral infections
Z01AI-00586-02 (LIR) KOENIG, S NIAID,NIH Immune reponse to HIV and related retroviruses
Z01AI-00587-02 (LIR) DAYTON, A NIAID,NIH Regulation of gene expression of the HIV
Z01AI-00588-02 (LMM) KHAN, A NIAID,NIH Molecular biology of simian immunodeficiency virus

PROJECT NO., ORGANIZATIONAL UNIT., INVESTIGATOR, ADDRESS, TITLE

Z01AI-00589-02 (LCI) RUSSO, T NIAID, NIH Identification of complement resistance determinants in Escherichia coli
Z01AI-00590-02 (LCI) SNELLER, M NIAID, NIH Studies of primary immunodeficiency diseases
Z01AI-00594-02 (ODIR) KINET, J NIAID, NIH Structure and function of Fc(gamma) and Fc(epsilon) receptors
Z01AI-00595-01 (LCI) HAMMER, C H NIAID, NIH Purification, characterization and function of proteins of the complement system
Z01AI-00601-01 (LID) GORZIGLIA, M NIAID, NIH Development of recombinant BCG-VP8 vaccines
Z01AI-00602-01 (LID) GORZIGLIA, M NIAID, NIH Expression of rotavirus outer capsid protein VP4 by recombinant adenovirus
Z01AI-00603-01 (LID) GORZIGLIA, M NIAID, NIH Monoclonal antibodies directed to VP8 subunit of VP4
Z01AI-00604-01 (LID) HOSHINO, Y NIAID, NIH Cold adaptation of human rotaviruses
Z01AI-00605-01 (LID) KAPIKIAN, A Z NIAID, NIH Experimental infection of chimpanzees by human rotavirus
Z01AI-00606-01 (LID) STEELE, A D NIAID, NIH Molecular biology of neonatal rotavirus strains detected in South Africa
Z01AI-00607-01 (LCI) PARRIS, B NIAID,NIH Regulation of cytokine gene expression in mast cells
Z01AI-00608-01 (LMSF) BELLAND, R J NIAID, NIH Expression and phase variation of gonococcal opa genes
Z01AI-00609-01 (LMSF) BHAT, K S NIAID, NIH Synthetic gene approach to study the action of antibacterial genes in mammals
Z01AI-00610-01 (LPVD) PERRY, L L NIAID, NIH Role of H-2 I-E in recovery from Friend virus induced leukemia
Z01AI-00611-01 (LPVD) SPANGRUDE, G J NIAID, NIH Enrichment of hematopoietic stem cells from mouse bone marrow
Z01AI-00612-01 (LICP) MANNING, D S NIAID, NIH Expression and analysis of recombinant chlamydial antigens
Z01AI-00613-01 (LCMI) SCHWARTZ, R H NIAID, NIH T cell subsets
Z01AI-00614-01 (LHD) LETO, T L NIAID, NIH Structure and function of phagocyte proteins
Z01AI-00615-01 (LHD) MURPHY, P NIAID, NIH Chemoattractant receptors of human phagocytes
Z01AI-00617-01 (LCI) RUSSO, T A NIAID,NIH Regulation of capsule synthesis in a pathogenic E. coli isolate
Z01AI-00618-01 (LCI) RUSSO, T A NIAID,NIH Acquisition of an increased resistance to host defenses in vivo
Z01AI-00619-01 (LVD) YEWDELL, J W NIAID, NIH Intracellular antibody-mediated virus neutralization
Z01AI-00620-01 (LVD) FRENKEL, N NIAID, NIH Molecular epidemiology of human herpesviruses 6 and 7
Z01AI-00621-01 (LCI) COHEN, J I NIAID,NIH Molecular biology of transformation by Epstein-Barr virus
K11AI-00683-05 (MID) GOLDFELD, ANNE E MASSACHUSETTS GENERAL HOSPITAL FRUIT STREET BOSTON, MA 02114 Training in infectious disease and molecular biology
K11AI-00739-05 (MID) MOSCONA, ANNE MOUNT SINAI SCHOOL OF MEDICINE ONE GUSTAVE L LEVY PLACE NEW YORK, N Y 10029 Molecular basis for variation of influenza viruses
K04AI-00742-05 (MBC) KHAN, SALEEM A UNIVERSITY OF PITTSBURGH PITTSBURGH, PA 15261 Plasmid pT181 DNA replication in Staphylococcus aureus
K11AI-00759-05 (MID) SNEDEKER, JEFFREY D DUKE UNIVERSITY MEDICAL CTR BOX 31085 DURHAM, N C 27710 Autoantibodies as probes of virus-host interactions
K04AI-00760-05 (MBC) MORAN, CHARLES P, JR EMORY UNIVERSITY 560 WOODRUFF MEMORIAL BLDG ATLANTA, GA 30322 Gene regulation in bacterial differentiation
K11AI-00768-05 (AITC) ADAMS, BARBARA S UNIV OF MICHIGAN MED SCH 4540 KRESGE I ANN ARBOR, MI 48109-0358 Biochemical regulation of gene activation in T cells
K11AI-00780-04 (MID) WIEST, PETER M MIRIAM HOSPITAL 164 SUMMIT AVENUE PROVIDENCE, RI 02906 Biogenesis of surface membrane of Schistosoma mansoni
K11AI-00793-05 (AITC) PERENTESIS, JOHN P UMHC, UNIV OF MINNESOTA HOSPIT HARVARD ST AT RIVER RD MINNEAPOLIS, MN 55455 Molecular study of ribosomal toxins and applications in oncology
K04AI-00799-05 (IMB) ECKELS, DAVID D BLOOD CTR OF SOUTHEASTERN WISC 1701 WEST WISCONSIN AVENUE MILWAUKEE, WI 53233 Immunoregulatory role of human class II MHC molecules
K04AI-00800-05 (MBC) LUCKEY, MARY SAN FRANCISCO STATE UNIVERSITY SAN FRANCISCO, CA 94132 Lamb protein transport channel in E. coli outer membran
K11AI-00803-05 (MID) GABRIEL, ABRAM JOHNS HOPKINS UNIV SCH OF MED 725 N WOLFE STREETT BALTIMORE, MD 21205 Transcription in trypanosomatid Crithidia fasciculata
K11AI-00804-05 (AITC) MACDONALD, SUSAN M JOHNS HOPKINS 301 BAYVIEW BLVD BALTIMORE, MD 21229 Studies of IgE dependent histamine releasing factors
K04AI-00813-05 (MCHA) CURRAN, DENNIS P UNIVERSITY OF PITTSBURGH DEPARTMENT OF CHEMISTRY PITTSBURGH, PA 15260 New strategies in total synthesis
K04AI-00815-05 (TMP) WOOD, DAVID O UNIVERSITY OF SOUTH ALABAMA MOBILE, AL 36688 Genetic analysis of rickettsial intracellular parasitism
K04AI-00834-04 (BM) JUDD, RALPH C UNIVERSITY OF MONTANA MISSOULA, MT 59812 Studies on outer membrane of neisseria gonorrhoeae
K04AI-00838-05 (MBC) REAM, LLOYD W OREGON STATE UNIVERSITY AGRICULTURAL CHEM DEPT CORVALLIS, OR 97331 T-DNA integration during crown gall tumorigenesis
K11AI-00840-05 (MID) GOLENBOCK, DOUGLAS T MAXWELL FINLAND LABORATORY 774 ALBANY STREET BOSTON, MA 02118 Lipid a metabolism and membrane protein interactions
K04AI-00843-05 (IMB) DORSHKIND, KENNETH A UNIVERSITY OF CALIFORNIA 1126 WEBBER HALL WEST RIVERSIDE, CA 92521 Immunobiology of B cell differentiation
K11AI-00846-05 (AITC) CROGHAN, THOMAS WOODWARD UNIVERSITY OF FLORIDA BOX J-221, JHMHC GAINESVILLE, FL 32610 Genetic control of the immune response

PROJECT NO., ORGANIZATIONAL UNIT., INVESTIGATOR, ADDRESS, TITLE

K04AI-00856-05 (BM) DEEPE, GEORGE S UNIV OF CINCINNATI 231 BETHESDA AVENUE CINCINNATI, OH 45267-0560 H. capsulatum-reactive murine T cell clones and hybrids

K11AI-00865-05 (MID) DERMODY, TERENCE S VANDERBILT UNIVERSITY MED CTR 1161 21ST AVENUE SO NASHVILLE, TN 37232 Molecular basis of persistent reovirus infection

K11AI-00866-05 (AITC) SILVERMAN, GREGG J UNIVERSITY OF CALIFORNIA LA JOLLA, CA 92093-0945 Variable region gene expression in human autoantibodies

K11AI-00870-04 (MID) ROSENTHAL, PHILIP J SAN FRANCISCO GENERAL HOSPITAL 1000 POTRERO STREET SAN FRANCISCO, CA 94110 Molecular approaches to a malarial cysteine

K11AI-00873-04 (MID) STEELE, MARILYN I OK CHILDREN'S MEMORIAL HOSP P O BOX 26307 OKLAHOMA CITY, OK 73126 Capsule synthesis by mucoid pseudomonas aeruginosa

K04AI-00874-04 (MBY) JAEHNING, JUDITH A INDIANA UNIVERSITY BLOOMINGTON, IN 47405 Molecular studies of pseudomonas aeruginosa exotoxin a

K04AI-00875-04 (EVR) HOLLAND, THOMAS C WAYNE STATE UNIVERSITY SCHOOL OF MEDICINE DETROIT, MI 48202 Properties of HSV-I glycoproteins and membrane proteins

K04AI-00876-04 (BM) GALLOWAY, DARRELL R OHIO STATE UNIVERSITY 484 WEST TWELFTH AVENUE COLUMBUS, OHIO 43210 Molecular studies of pseudomonas aeruginosa exotoxin A

K11AI-00877-04 (MID) PIROFSKI, LISE-ANNE ALBERT EINSTEIN COLLEGE OF MED 1300 MORRIS PARK AVENUE BRONX, NY 10461 Antibody structure in mouse adenovirus infection

K04AI-00878-04 (VR) SANDRI-GOLDIN, ROZANNE M THE REGENTS OF UNIV. OF CALIF. DEPT MICROBIO. & MOL. GENETICS IRVINE, CA 92717 Herpes simplex virus gene regulation

K04AI-00881-04 (BM) LOW, DAVID A UNIVERSITY OF UTAH SALT LAKE CITY, UT 84132 Analysis of escherichia coli virulence determinants

K04AI-00882-05 (MBC) BRUSILOW, WILLIAM S WAYNE STATE UNIVERSITY 540 E CANFIELD AVENUE DETROIT, MI 48201 Synthesis, assembly & function of bacterial H+ Atpases

K07AI-00884-04 (MID) PROBER, CHARLES G STANFORD UNIV MEDICAL CENTER STANFORD, CA 94305 Epidemiology & outcome of gestational HSV infections

K04AI-00889-04 (VR) OFFIT, PAUL A CHILDREN'S HOSP OF PHILA 34TH ST & CIVIC CENTER BLVD PHILADELPHIA, PA 19104 Protection against viral gastroenteritis by ctls

K11AI-00892-04 (MID) WILSON, CRAIG M UNIV OF ALABAMA AT BIRMINGHAM UNIVERSITY STATION BIRMINGHAM, AL 35294 Drug resistant malaria molecular and genetic studies

K11AI-00903-03 (AITC) PARKER, CHRISTINA M DANA-FARBER CANCER INST 44 BINNEY ST/MAYER 640 BOSTON, MA 02115 Functional T cell receptor gamma delta cells and genes

K11AI-00906-04 (MID) KLEIN, BRUCE S UNIVERSITY OF WISCONSIN 600 HIGHLAND AVE, H4/572 MADISON, WI 53792 Antifungal role & action of human cytolytic lymphocytes

K04AI-00908-04 (VR) PEEPLES, MARK E RUSH MEDICAL COLLEGE 1653 WEST CONGRESS PARKWAY CHICAGO, IL 60612 Identification of a cell receptor for hepatitis B virus

K04AI-00910-04 (IMB) RIGBY, WILLIAM F DEPARTMENT OF MICROBIOLOGY DARTMOUTH MEDICAL SCHOOL HANOVER, NH 03756 Regulation of the immune response by vitamin D

K11AI-00912-04 (AIDS) MULLIGAN, MARK J UNIVERSITY OF ALABAMA DEPT. MICROBIOLOGY BIRMINGHAM, AL 35294 HIV-2 envelope glycoproteins and cell fusion

K11AI-00917-03 (MID) MILLER, SAMUEL I MASSACHUSETTS GENERAL HOSPITAL INFECTIOUS DIS UNIT, GREY 4 BOSTON, MA 02114 Bacterial genetics molecular pathogenesis of Salmonella

K04AI-00919-03 (ALY) WETSEL, RICK A CHILDREN'S HOSPITAL 400 S KINGSHIGHWAY ST LOUIS, MO 63110 Complement C5 deficiency--Molecular analysis

K11AI-00922-03 (MID) MARKS, GILBERT L UNIVERSITY OF SOUTH ALABAMA CANCER CTR / CLINICAL BLDG MOBILE, AL 36688 Genetics of Rickettsia prowazekii surface antigens

K04AI-00923-03 (EVR) FREY, TERYL K GEORGIA STATE UNIVERSITY UNIVERSITY PLAZA ATLANTA, GA 30303 Replication of rubella virus

K11AI-00924-03 (MID) JENSEN, WAYNE A COLORADO STATE UNIVERSITY FORT COLLINS, CO 80523 Effect of bovine leukemia virus on lymphokine expression

K08AI-00926-03 (AITC) MCCARTHY, PHILIP L BRIGHAM AND WOMEN'S HOSPITAL 75 FRANCIS STREET BOSTON, MA 02115 Homologous recombination in embryonal stem cells

K11AI-00929-04 (AIDS) KURITZKES, DANIEL R UNIVERSITY OF COLORADO 4200 E NINTH AVE DENVER, CO 80262 HIV epitopes recognized by cytotoxic T lymphocytes

K11AI-00930-04 (AIDS) POMERANTZ, ROGER J JEFFERSON MEDICAL COLLEGE 1025 WALNUT STREET PHILADELPHIA, PA 19107 Cellular tropism of HIV

K04AI-00932-03 (TMP) KASPER, LLOYD H DARTMOUTH MEDICAL SCHOOL SECTION OF NEUROLOGY HANOVER, NH 03756 Toxoplasma gondii--Immunology and pathogenesis

K04AI-00934-03 (VR) PINTEL, DAVID J UNIV OF MISSOURI SCH OF MED COLUMBIA, MO 65212 Molecular and genetic analysis of MVM gene expression

K04AI-00935-04 (MBC) GOURSE, RICHARD L UNIV OF WISCONSIN-MADISON 1550 LINDEN DR MADISON, WI 53706 Activation and control of rrna transcription

K04AI-00936-03 (SAT) BARBER, WILLIAM H UNIVERSITY OF ALABAMA 756 LYONS HARRISON RESEARCH BL BIRMINGHAM, AL 35294 Donor marrow tolerance in human and canine allografts

K08AI-00937-03 (MID) PAMER, ERIC G UNIVERSITY OF WASHINGTON 1264 HEALTH SCIENCES BUILDING SEATTLE, WA 98195 Characterization of a Trypansoma brucei protease

K08AI-00938-03 (MID) RYAN, CAROLINE A VETERANS ADMINISTRATION MED CT 1660 SOUTH COLUMBIAN WAY SEATTLE, WA 98108 Characterization of erythromycin resistant campylobacter

K11AI-00944-02 (SRC) WADE, NANCY A NEW YORK STATE DEPT OF HEALTH PO BOX 509 ALBANY, NY 12201-0509 Genetic polymorphism of CD4 and CD8--Relationship to AIDS

PROJECT NO., ORGANIZATIONAL UNIT., INVESTIGATOR, ADDRESS, TITLE

K11AI-00945-03 (MID) HEROLD, BETSY C NORTHWESTERN UNIVERSITY 303 E CHICAGO AVE CHICAGO, IL 60611 Role of herpesvirus complement-binding glycoprotein in virus infection

K04AI-00948-03 (IMS) HUFF, THOMAS F BOX 678, MCV STATION RICHMOND, VA 23298-0678 Differentiation of mast cell progenitors

K11AI-00951-02 (MID) CHUCK, STEVEN L UNIVERSITY OF CALIFORNIA BOX 0414 SAN FRANCISCO, CA 94143 Assembly of subviral particles of hepatitis B virus

K11AI-00952-03 (AIDS) DOW, STEVEN W COLORADO STATE UNIVERSITY FORT COLLINS, CO 80523 Mechanisms of retrovirus-induced neural dysfunction

K04AI-00955-03 (BIO) SMITH, GEORGIA F ARIZONA STATE UNIVERSITY TEMPE, AZ 85287-1501 A (2'-5')a n -dependent endonuclease and interferon acti

K08AI-00958-02 (AITC) WIEDMEIER, SUSAN E UNIVERSITY OF WASHINGTON SEATTLE, WA 98195 Immunobiology of bone marrow transplantation

K07AI-00961-02 (AITC) MARQUARDT, DIANA L U OF CALIF, SAN DIEGO MED CTR 225 DICKINSON ST, H-811-G SAN DIEGO, CA 92103 Mast cell adenosine receptor signal transduction

K11AI-00963-02 (AIDS) CLABOUGH, DEBRA L NC STATE UNIVERSITY 4700 HILLSBOROUGH STREET RALEIGH, NC 27606 Molecular and cellular basis of equine infectious anemia virus disease

K04AI-00964-02 (BM) WHITTAM, THOMAS S PENNSYLVANIA STATE UNIVERSITY 208 MUELLER LABORATORY UNIVERSITY PARK, PA 16802 Clonal structure of pathogenic E. coli

K11AI-00965-02 (MID) LIU, LEO X BETH ISRAEL HOSPITAL 330 BROOKLINE AVE BOSTON, MA 02215 Filarial eicosanoids--Biosynthesis and cellular actions

K04AI-00968-02 (BM) KRAUSE, DUNCAN C UNIVERSITY OF GEORGIA 803 BIOLOGICAL SCIENCES BUILDI ATHENS, GA 30602 A genetic approach to Mycoplasma pneumoniae virulence

K11AI-00971-02 (MID) ROTHMAN, ALAN L UNIVERSITY OF MASS MED CTR 55 LAKE AVENUE NORTH WORCESTER, MA 01655 Murine T lymphocyte responses to dengue virus

K11AI-00972-02 (AIDS) MCNEARNEY, TERRY ANN 660 S EUCLID AVE/BOX 8125 ST LOUIS, MO 63110 The molecular basis of HIV-1 cell specific tropism

K08AI-00973-02 (MID) CHAMBERS, THOMAS J WASHINGTON UNIVERSITY BOX 8230 ST LOUIS, MO 63110 Proteolytic control of flavivirus polyprotein processing

K08AI-00974-02 (AITC) CHANG, TIEN-LAN MASSACHUSETTS GENERAL HOSPITAL FRUIT STREET BOSTON, MA 02114 Helper T cells in mucosal immune respone

K11AI-00979-02 (AIDS) WEISS, CAROL D UNIV OF CALIFORNIA SCHOOL OF M 513 PARNASSUS AVENUE SAN FRANCISCO, CA 94143 Fusion mechanism of the HIV envelope glycoprotein

K11AI-00981-02 (MID) MADOFF, LAWRENCE C CHANNING LABORATORY 180 LONGWOOD AVE BOSTON, MA 02115 C proteins in immunity to group B streptococcus

K08AI-00982-02 (AIDS) FLEXNER, CHARLES W JOHNS HOPKINS UNIVERSITY 600 N WOLFE STREET BALTIMORE, MD 21205 Inhibition of lentivirus envelope-mediated cell fusion

K11AI-00983-02 (MID) JANKELEVICH, SHIRLEY 74 MIDWOOD ROAD BRANFORD, CT 06405 Interaction of Epstein-Barr virus with nuclear matrix

K11AI-00984-02 (AITC) HAEGER, ELISABETH B UNIV OF CALIFORNIA, SAN DIEGO 9500 GILMAN DRIVE LA JOLLA, CA 92093-0063 Development of immune system in T cell receptor in transgenic mice

K11AI-00986-02 (MID) CHAPMAN, ALGER B, III UNIVERSITY OF CALIFORNIA 3333 CALIFORNIA ST SUITE 150 SAN FRANCISCO, CA 94118 Regulation of transcription in trypanosomes

K11AI-00988-02 (SRC) LUBAN, JEREMY COLUMBIA UNIVERSITY 630 WEST 168TH STREET NEW YORK, NY 10032 Mutagenesis of HIV-1 gag coding region

K04AI-00990-02 (VR) PATTON, JOHN T UNIVERSITY OF MIAMI SCH OF MED PO BOX 016960 (R-138) MIAMI, FL 33101 Replication of rotavirus RNA

K07AI-00995-02 (AITC) LEMANSKE, ROBERT F, JR 600 HIGHLAND AVE MADISON, WI 53792 Pathogenesis of pulmonary allergic responses

K11AI-00996-02 (MID) MANNICK, JOAN B HARVARD MEDICAL SCHOOL 75 FRANCIS STREET BOSTON, MA 02115 Epstein-Barr nuclear antigen leader protein in EBV-induced transformation

K08AI-00997-03 (AITC) SHAW, ANDREY SHIN-YEE WASHINGTON UNIV SCH OF MED ST LOUIS, MO 63110 Signalling through a T cell kinase p56lck

K11AI-00999-02 (AITC) BELL, GREGORY M SAN FRANCISCO VA MEDICAL CENTE 4150 CLEMENT STREET SAN FRANCISCO, CA 94143 Characterization of gp35 a T cell signalling molecule

K11AI-01001-01A1 (MID) HONDALUS, MARY K TEMPLE UNIV SCHOOL OF MEDICINE 3400 NORTH BROAD STREET PHILADELPHIA, PA 19140 Macrophage recongnition and phagocytosis of rhodococcus

K04AI-01006-01 (EVR) FRASER, MALCOLM J UNIVERSITY OF NOTRE DAME NOTRE DAME, IND 46556 Transposon mutagenesis of nuclear polyhedrosis viruses

K08AI-01012-01 (AIDS) WILLERFORD, DENNIS M FRED HUTCHINSON CANCER RES CTR 1124 COLUMBIA STREET SEATTLE, WA 98104 Role of memory T cells in the pathogenesis of AIDS

K08AI-01015-01 (AIDS) ALBRECHT, MARY A NEW ENGLAND DEACONESS HOSP 185 PILGRIM ROAD BOSTON, MA 02215 HIV-HSV interactions in vitro

K08AI-01017-01 (AIDS) GABUZDA, DANA H DANA-FARBER CANCER INSTITUTE 44 BINNEY STREET BOSTON, MA 02115 Function of the HIV-1 envelope glycoprotein c-terminus

K11AI-01019-01 (MID) KRON, MICHAEL A MICHIGAN STATE UNIVERSITY B309 CLINICAL CENTER EAST LANSING, MI 48824 Immune responses to Onchocerca volvulus in Ecuador

K04AI-01021-01 (BM) MINION, F CHRIS IOWA STATE UNIVERSITY ELWOOD DR AMES, IA 50011 Mechanisms of pathogenesis in Myoplasma pulmonis

K08AI-01022-02 (SRC) BEDROSIAN, CAMILLE L DUKE UNIVERSITY MEDICAL CENTER PO BOX 31078 DURHAM, NC 27710 Molecular analysis of BPV-1 replication

K04AI-01023-01 (TMP) VAN VOORHIS, WESLEY C UNIVERSITY OF WASHINGTON SEATTLE, WA 98195 The immune response in chronic

infections
K07AI-01026-01 (AITC) UMETSU, DALE T STANFORD UNIVERSITY MEDICAL CT STANFORD, CA 94305-5119 Heterogeneity among human CD4+ T cells
K11AI-01027-01 (AIDS) MARGOLIS, DAVID M UNIV OF MASSACHUSETTS MED CENT 373 PLANTATION STREET WORCESTER, MA 01605 A study of the molecular mechanism of HIV Tat function
K08AI-01028-01 (MID) UPDIKE, WANDA S UNIVERSITY OF UTAH 5C334 MEDICAL CENTER SALT LAKE CITY, UT 84132 The polymerase and RNA replication of hepatitis a virus
K08AI-01029-01 (MID) DIAZ, PAMELA S UNIVERSITY OF CHICAGO 5841 S MARYLAND AVENUE CHICAGO, IL 60637 Herpes simplex virus GE and GI protein specific T-cells
K11AI-01030-01 (AITC) WANG, STEWART C UNIVERSITY OF PITTSBURGH 3550 TERRACE STREET PITTSBURGH, PA 15261 Cytokine regulation of rejection in vivo
K11AI-01031-01 (MID) JONES, SIAN UNIVERSITY OF PENNSYLVANIA 209 JOHNSON PAVILION PHILADELPHIA, PA 19104-6076 Role of phospholipase C in listeria pathogenesis
K08AI-01032-01 (MID) HERWALDT, LOREEN A UNIVERSITY OF IOWA C-41 GH IOWA CITY, IA 52242 Iron acquisition by staphylococci
K08AI-01033-01 (AIDS) SILBERMAN, SANDRA L BRIGHAM & WOMEN'S HOSPITAL 75 FRANCIS ST BOSTON, MA 02115 CD4-- Structural and binding studies
K11AI-01035-01 (AITC) HENDRICKSON, BARBARA A CHILDREN'S HOSPITAL ENDERS 6, 300 LONGWOOD AVENUE BOSTON, MA 02115 Analysis of CD2 function by targeted mutagenesis
K04AI-01036-01 (BM) WASHBURN, RONALD G BOWMAN GRAY SCHOOL OF MEDICINE 300 SOUTH HAWTHORNE ROAD WINSTON-SALEM, NC 27103 Aspergillus fumigatus complement inhibitor
K11AI-01037-01 (MID) MIRDA, DANIEL P UNIVERSITY OF CALIFORNIA DEPARTMENT OF MEDICINE SAN FRANCISCO, CA 94143-0130 Interaction of HSV with fibroblast growth factor receptor
K08AI-01039-01 (AIDS) GOLDMAN, FREDERICK D NAT JEWISH CTR FOR IMM RES MED 1400 JACKSON ST DENVER, CO 80206 Gp120-mediated uncoupling of T cell receptor signals
K08AI-01043-01 (MID) HEFFERNAN, EDWIN J UNIVERSITY OF CALIFORNIA 225 DICKINSON STREET SAN DIEGO, CA 92103 Plasmid-mediated serum resistance in salmonella
K04AI-01044-01 (MGN) KWAN, SAU-PING RUSH-PRESBYT-ST LUKE'S MED CTR 1653 WEST CONGRESS PARKWAY CHICAGO, IL 60612 Molecular studies of Wiskott Aldrich syndrome
K08AI-01046-01 (AIDS) SKOLNIK, PAUL R NEW ENGLAND MEDICAL CTR HOSPIT 750 WASHINGTON STREET BOSTON, MA 02111 Vitamin D and CMV--Effects on HIV infected monocytes
K04AI-01051-01 (BBCA) PARDI, ARTHUR UNIVERSITY OF COLORADO CAMPUS BOX 215 BOULDER, CO 80309-0215 Heteronuclear multi-dimensional NMR studies of RNA
K11AI-01061-01 (MID) MCQUILLEN, DANIEL P MAXWELL FINLAND LABORATORY 774 ALBANY ST BOSTON, MA 02118 Immune interactions of gonorrhea and vaccine development
K08AI-01062-01 (AITC) BALLOU, STANLEY P METROHEALTH MEDICAL CENTER 3395 SCRANTON RD CLEVELAND, OH 44109 Interaction of C-reactive protein with human monocytes
K08AI-01067-01 (AITC) SYLVESTRE, DIANA SLOAN-KETTERING INSTITUTE 1275 YORK AVE NEW YORK, NY 10021 Regulation of the low affinity Fc receptor locus
K08AI-01085-01 (SRC) FLANIGAN, TIMOTHY P THE MIRIAM HOSPITAL 164 SUMMIT AVENUE PROVIDENCE, RI 02904 Modulation of in vitro Cryptosporidium parvum infection
K11AI-01086-01 (MID) GRAHAM, MARY B UNIVERSITY OF VIRGINIA HEALTH SCIENCES CENTER (MR-4) CHARLOTTESVILLE, VA 22908 T cell function in antiviral immunity
R01AI-01278-35 (BNP) RINEHART, KENNETH L 454 ROGER ADAMS LAB, BOX 45-5 1209 W CALIFORNIA STREET URBANA, IL 61801 Chemistry and biochemistry of certain antibiotics
R37AI-01462-36 (GEN) PERKINS, DAVID D STANFORD UNIVERSITY STANFORD, CA 94305-5020 Genetics of neurospora
R01AI-01466-35 (VR) KAESBERG, PAUL J UNIVERSITY OF WISCONSIN 1525 LINDEN DRIVE MADISON, WIS 53706 Structure & function of the genomes of small viruses
K06AI-01826-29 (NSS) LIU, CHIEN UNIV OF KANSAS MEDICAL CENTER 39TH AND RAINBOW BLVD. KANSAS CITY, KS 66103 Pathogenetic study & diagnosis of infectious diseases
K06AI-02372-29 (NSS) VAN VUNAKIS, HELEN BRANDEIS UNIVERSITY WALTHAM, MA 02254 Structure & activity of biologically important molecules
N01AI-02500-06 ( ) SILVERMAN, JOHN** Technical/logistical support servs as specified herein
R37AI-02753-32 (TMP) CRAIG, GEORGE B, JR UNIVERSITY OF NOTRE DAME DEPT OF BIOLOGICAL SCIENCES NOTRE DAME, IN 46556 Factors affecting vector competence in Aedes triseriatus
R01AI-02908-33 (TMP) EISNER, THOMAS CORNELL UNIVERSITY ITHACA, NY 14853-2702 Secretions of arthropods
R01AI-03075-30A3 (ALY) OVARY, ZOLTAN NYU SCHOOL OF MEDICINE 550 FIRST AVENUE NEW YORK, N Y 10016 Immunology mechanism of anaphylaxis
R01AI-03260-32 (BM) KARNOVSKY, MANFRED L HARVARD MEDICAL SCHOOL 25 SHATTUCK STREET BOSTON, MA 02115 Biochemical basis of phagocytosis
R01AI-03771-30 (VR) CROWELL, RICHARD L HAHNEMANN UNIVERSITY BROAD AND VINE STREET PHILADELPHIA, PA 19102 Viral interference in carrier cultures
R01AI-03958-30 (IMB) NOSSAL, GUSTAV J WALTER & ELIZA HALL INST SINGLE CELL LABORATORY VICTORIA 3050, AUSTRALIA Mechanisms of lymphocyte-antigen interactions
R01AI-04043-30 (MBC) SIX, ERICH W UNIVERSITY OF IOWA IOWA CITY, IA 52242 Genetic studies of phage-prophage interactions
R01AI-04156-30 (MBC) NEILANDS, JOHN B UNIV OF CALIFORNIA, BERKELEY BERKELEY, CA 94720 Microbial iron metabolism
R01AI-04615-30 (MBC) NEUHAUS, FRANCIS C NORTHWESTERN UNIVERSITY 2153 SHERIDAN RD, HOGAN BLDG EVANSTON, IL 60208 Biosynthesis of bacterial cell wall components
R37AI-04717-30 (TMP) REMINGTON, JACK S PALO ALTO MEDICAL FOUNDATION 860 BRYANT STREET PALO ALTO, CA 94301 Toxoplasmosis--Nature of infection and immune response
K06AI-04739-30 (NSS) GREEN, MAURICE ST LOUIS UNIVERSITY 3681 PARK AVENUE ST LOUIS, MO 63110 Biochemistry of viral replication
R01AI-04769-30 (BNP) RINEHART, KENNETH L UNIVERSITY OF ILLINOIS BOX 45-5/1209 W CALIFORNIA ST URBANA, IL 61801 Structures of antibiotics and related compounds
R37AI-04866-29 (IMS) NORMAN, PHILLIP S JOHNS HOPKINS AST & ALGY CTR 301 BAYVIEW BLVD BALTIMORE, MD 21224 A study of allergy to ragweed pollen
R01AI-05044-28 (MBC) SHOCKMAN, GERALD D TEMPLE U SCH OF MED 3400 NORTH BROAD ST. PHILADELPHIA, PA 19140 Biosynthesis of bacterial cell walls and membranes
N01AI-05045-05 ( ) BROWN, LAWRENCE** Community program for clinical research on AIDS--Stage 1
N01AI-05046-05 ( ) HOLLOWAY, WILLIAM** Community program for clinical research on AIDS--Stage 1
N01AI-05049-06 ( ) DOLIN, RAPHEAL** Control measures against human infectious diseases other than AIDS
N01AI-05050-04 ( ) WRIGHT, PETER F** Control measures against human infectious diseases other than AIDS
N01AI-05051-04 ( ) BELSHE, ROBERT** Control measures against human infectious diseases other than AIDS
N01AI-05053-01 ( ) MAASSAB, H F** Development of live attenuated cold adapted influenza vaccines
N01AI-05054-05 ( ) KAPLAN, CHARLES S** Community program for clinical research on AIDS--Stage 1
N01AI-05055-01 ( ) NOVOTNY, JOROSLAV** Resynthesis of therapeutic agents for infectious disease
N01AI-05056-03 ( ) MURRILL, EVELYN** Analytical chemistry of chemicals and pharmaceuticals
N01AI-05057-04 ( ) KESSLER, MATT J** Animal research and maintenance facility
N01AI-05058-07 ( ) SALZMAN, NORMAN** Molecular virology and immunology laboratory
N01AI-05059-01 ( ) ANDERSON, PORTER** Operation of a Haemophilus influenzae type B reference
N01AI-05060-02 ( ) SATTERFIELD, WILLIAM C** AIDS-infected chimpanzees
N01AI-05061-04 ( ) CLEMENTS, MARY LOU** AIDS vaccine evaluation unit
N01AI-05062-04 ( ) WRIGHT, PETER F** AIDS vaccine evaluation unit
N01AI-05063-05 ( ) DOLIN, RAPHAEL** AIDS vaccine evaluation unit
N01AI-05064-04 ( ) BELSHE, ROBERT** AIDS vaccine evaluation unit
N01AI-05065-04 ( ) COREY, LAWRENCE** AIDS vaccine evaluation units
N01AI-05066-04 ( ) BRADBURY, RICHARD** Facility for non-human primates utilized in infectious
N01AI-05067-03 ( ) BRADBURY, RICHARD** Care and housing of AIDS research animals
N01AI-05068-03 ( ) SCHWARTZ, RONALD** Mouse breeding facility
N01AI-05069-03 ( ) BRADBURY, RICHARD** Facility for animal models utilized for viral hepatitis
N01AI-05070-03 ( ) SCHUELER, RONALD L** Holding and maintenance of HIV AIDS infected rabbits
N01AI-05071-04 ( ) WRIGHT, CRAIG D** Community project for clinical research in AIDS (CPCRA) operations center
N01AI-05072-06 ( ) MCKINLAY, SONJA M** Data center for epidemiologic investigations of HIV
N01AI-05073-02 ( ) NEATON, JAMES D** Community programs for clinical research on AIDS
N01AI-05074-01 ( ) BRENNAN, PATRICK J** Isolation, purification and characterization of mycobacteria antigen
N01AI-05075-01 ( ) BRUCE, JOHN L** Maintenance and supply of schistosome infected snails and mammals
N01AI-05076-02 ( ) SCHUELER, RONALD L** Maintenance of a rabbit breeding and holding facility
N01AI-05077-03 ( ) HOLLAND, LOUIS E** In vitro test systems for combined chemotherapies against HIV
N01AI-05078-03 ( ) SHINAGI, RAYMOND F** In vitro test systems for combined chemotherapies against HIV
N01AI-05079-02 ( ) HOOVER, EDWARD A** In vivo test systems for combined chemotherapies against HIV
N01AI-05080-03 ( ) MC CUNE, MICHAEL J** In vivo test systems for combined chemotherapies against HIV
N01AI-05081-05 ( ) WHITTEN, KIM** Clinical site monitoring
N44AI-05083-04 ( ) MATSUOKA, YUMIKO** Cloning and expression of human parainfluenza virus cycloprotein genes
N01AI-05084-03 ( ) BROWN, RONALD L** Reagent resource support for AIDS vaccine development
N01AI-05086-02 ( ) HOLLINGSHEAD, M** In vivo test systems for combined chemotherapies against HIV
N01AI-05087-02 ( ) BUCKHEIT, ROBERT** Technical support for the basic research and development program-- Virology
N01AI-05088-01 ( ) CURTIS, TOMMIE G** Coordinating center for the basic research and development program
R37AI-05090-29 (MBC) PARK, JAMES T TUFTS UNIVERSITY 136 HARRISON AVENUE BOSTON, MA 02111 Chemistry and biosynthesis of microbial cell walls
R37AI-05371-29 (MBC) CLARK, ALVIN J UNIVERSITY OF CALIFORNIA 401 BARKER HALL BERKELEY, CA 94720 Physiology of bacterial conjugation and recombination
R37AI-05388-29 (MBC) FOX, MAURICE S MASSACHUSETTS INST OF TECHNOLO 77 MASSACHUSETTS AVE CAMBRIDGE, MA 02139 Genetic recombination and microbial DNA synthesis
R37AI-05629-29 (VR) MERIGAN, THOMAS C STANFORD UNIVERSITY 125 PANAMA ST/JORDAN QUAD BIRC STANFORD, CA 94305-4125 Interferon, immunity and latent viruses
R01AI-05664-28 (ALY) GOODMAN, JOEL W UNIVERSITY OF CALIFORNIA 3RD & PARNASSUS AVE, BOX 0414 SAN FRANCISCO, CA 94143 Structure of immunologic determinants of proteins

PROJECT NO., ORGANIZATIONAL UNIT., INVESTIGATOR, ADDRESS, TITLE

R01AI-05802-27 (TMP) LUCAS, JOHN J SUNY-HEALTH SCIENCES CTR SYRACUSE, NY 13210 Lipids of leishmanias and trypanosomes
R37AI-05875-27 (IMB) COHN, MELVIN THE SALK INSTITUTE P O BOX 85800 SAN DIEGO, CA 92186-5800 Antibody synthesis
R22AI-05920-29 (VR) STOLLAR, VICTOR UNIV OF MED/DENT OF NEW JERSEY 675 HOES LANE PISCATAWAY, NJ 08854-5635 Arbovirus replication in mosquito and vertebrate cells
R37AI-06045-28 (NSS) RICHARDSON, CHARLES C HARVARD UNIVERSITY 25 SHATTUCK STREET CAMBRIDGE, MA 02138 Structure and synthesis of DNA
R01AI-06246-27 (EVR) STEVENS, JACK G UNIVERSITY OF CALIFORNIA 405 HILGARD AVENUE LOS ANGELES, CA 90024-1747 Latency in herpesvirus infections of cells & tissues
R01AI-06264-27 (VR) YOUNGNER, JULIUS S UNIVERSITY OF PITTSBURGH DEPT OF MOL. GENETICS & BIOCHE PITTSBURGH, PA 15261 Live virus vaccines as dominant negative mutants
R37AI-07012-26 (NSS) COHN, ZANVIL A ROCKEFELLER UNIVERSITY 1230 YORK AVENUE NEW YORK, N Y 10021 The physiology of macrophages
R37AI-07079-26 (NSS) KOSHLAND, MARIAN E UNIVERSITY OF CALIFORNIA 439 LIFE SCIENCE ADDITION BERKELEY, CA 94720 Mechanisms of antibody biosynthesis
R01AI-07118-26 (TMP) BLOOM, BARRY R ALBERT EINSTEIN COLLEGE OF MED 1300 MORRIS PARK AVENUE BRONX, N Y 10461 Biochemical basis of delayed hypersensitivity
R01AI-07194-26 (MBC) HELINSKI, DONALD R UNIVERSITY OF CALIFORNIA 9500 GILMAM DRIVE LA JOLLA, CA 92093-0634 Structure and genetic control of colicines
R37AI-07289-26 (ALY) NATHENSON, STANLEY G ALBERT EINSTEIN COLLEGE OF MED 1300 MORRIS PARK AVENUE BRONX, NY 10461 Biochemical studies of histocompatability antigens
R01AI-07290-26 (IMS) LICHTENSTEIN, LAWRENCE M GOOD SAMARITAN HOSPITAL 5601 LOCH RAVEN BLVD BALTIMORE, MD 21218 In vitro studies of human anaphylaxis
R37AI-07757-25 (ALY) MC DEVITT, HUGH O STANFORD UNIV SCH OF MED FAIRCHILD BLDG, D-345 STANFORD, CA 94305-5402 Genetic control of the immune response
R37AI-07763-25 (BM) KLEBANOFF, SEYMOUR J UNIVERSITY OF WASHINGTON SEATTLE, WA 98195 Antimicrobial effect of peroxidase in leucocytes
R37AI-08054-25 (ALY) STEINER, LISA A MASSACHUSETTS INST OF TECH 77 MASSACHUSETTS AVENUE CAMBRIDGE, MA 02139 Structure and diversity in the immune system
R37AI-08270-24 (NSS) LICHTENSTEIN, LAWRENCE M JOHNS HOPKINS UNIVERSITY 301 BAYVIEW BLVD BALTIMORE, MD 21224 An in vitro approach to problems of clinical allergy
R01AI-08427-23 (BBCA) MAESTRE, MARCOS F LAWRENCE BERKELEY LABORATORY LIFE SCIENCES BERKELEY, CA 94720 Physical structure of viruses, chromosomes & cell nuclei
R37AI-08499-24 (NSS) NUSSENZWEIG, VICTOR NEW YORK UNIVERSITY MED CTR 550 FIRST AVENUE NEW YORK, N Y 10016 Surface membrane defenses against complement attack
R01AI-08573-24 (MBC) CAMPBELL, ALLAN M STANFORD UNIVERSITY STANFORD, CALIF 94305 Genetics of lambda prophage--Biotin operon
R37AI-08619-24 (NSS) COHEN, STANLEY N STANFORD UNIVERSITY SCHOOL OF MEDICINE STANFORD, CA 94305 Genetic mechanisms in bacterial antibiotic resistance
R37AI-08722-23 (MBC) CALENDAR, RICHARD L UNIVERSITY OF CALIFORNIA 401 BARKER HALL BERKELEY, CA 94720 DNA replication by satellite phage P4 and its helper, P2
R01AI-08746-23 (MBC) ADLER, JULIUS UNIV OF WISCONSIN-MADISON MADISON, WI 53706 Behavior of bacteria--Biochemistry and genetics
R37AI-08795-23 (ALY) DUTTON, RICHARD W UNIVERSITY OF CALIF., SAN DIEG 9500 GILMAN DRIVE LA JOLLA, CA 93092-0063 Cellular mechanisms in the immune response
R37AI-08831-23 (EVR) WEBSTER, ROBERT G ST JUDE CHILDREN'S RES HOSP 332 NORTH LAUDERDALE, BOX 318 MEMPHIS, TN 38101 Studies of pandemic influenza virus
R01AI-08909-23 (VR) JOKLIK, WOLFGANG K DUKE UNIVERSITY PO BOX 3020 DURHAM, NC 27710 Macromolecular synthesis in virus-infected cells
R37AI-08998-23 (MBC) HUTCHISON, CLYDE A, III UNIV OF N C AT CHAPEL HILL CB7290, 804 FLOB CHAPEL HILL, NC 27599 Genetics, DNA chemistry and phage Phi-X-174
R01AI-09100-22 (BM) MOEHRING, THOMAS J UNIVERSITY OF VERMONT BURLINGTON, VT 05405 Genetics of resistance to Pseudomonas Toxin and viruses
R37AI-09102-23 (TMP) SIMPSON, LARRY UNIVERSITY OF CALIFORNIA 405 HILGARD AVENUE LOS ANGELES, CA 90024 Function of the kinetoplast in the hemoflagellates
R37AI-09167-23 (NSS) MOORE, PETER B YALE UNIVERSITY 1504A YALE STATION NEW HAVEN, CT 06520 Ribosome structure and function
R01AI-09169-19 (BM) MC CALL, CHARLES E WAKE FOREST UNIVERSITY BOWMAN GRAY SCH OF MED WINSTON-SALEM, N C 27103 Functional and metabolic properties of toxic neutrophils
R01AI-09352-21 (MBC) TROY, FREDERIC A UNIVERSITY OF CALIFORNIA MEDICAL SCIENCES BLDG, IA DAVIS, CA 95616 Chemistry and biosynthesis of cell-surface polymers
R01AI-09483-22 (TMP) SAZ, HOWARD J UNIVERSITY OF NOTRE DAME NOTRE DAME, IN 46556 Intermediary metabolism of helminths
R37AI-09484-22 (EVR) OLDSTONE, MICHAEL B SCRIPPS CLINIC & RESEARCH FDN 10666 N TORREY PINES ROAD LA JOLLA, CA 92037 Pathogenesis of persistent viral infection
R37AI-09504-21 (NSS) MANDELL, GERALD L UNIVERSITY OF VIRGINIA CHARLOTTESVILLE, VA 22908 Mechanism of phagocyte microbicidal activity
R01AI-09556-21 (TMP) OLIVER, JAMES H, JR GEORGIA SOUTHERN UNIVERSITY BOX 8042 STATESBORO, GA 30460 Reproduction in ticks and mites
R01AI-09580-17 (BMT) EMERY, THOMAS F UTAH STATE UNIVERSITY LOGAN, UT 84322-0300 Mechanisms of microbial iron transport
R37AI-09644-22 (MBC) NIKAIDO, HIROSHI UNIVERSITY OF CALIFORNIA BERKELEY, CA 94720 Biochemistry of bacterial cell membranes
R01AI-09648-21 (ALY) BECKER, ELMER L UNIVERSITY OF CONNECTICUT 263 FARMINGTON AVE FARMINGTON, CT 06030 Immunologically activated enzyme systems of cells

PROJECT NO., ORGANIZATIONAL UNIT., INVESTIGATOR, ADDRESS, TITLE

R37AI-09706-21 (NSS) KOPROWSKI, HILARY WISTAR INSTITUTE 36TH & SPRUCE STREETS PHILADELPHIA, PA 19104 Study of rabies and rabies virus antigens
R37AI-09728-21 (ALY) GLEICH, GERALD J MAYO FOUNDATION 200 FIRST STREET SOUTHWEST ROCHESTER, MN 55905 The functions of eosinophils
R01AI-10060-21 (IMS) ISHIZAKA, TERUKO LA JOLLA INSTITUTE 1149 NORTH TORREY PINES ROAD LA JOLLA, CA 92037 Relation of gamma globulin structure to hypersensitivity
R55AI-10085-28 (BM) DALE, JAMES B VA MEDICAL CENTER 1030 JEFFERSON AVE MEMPHIS, TN 38104 Chemistry and immunology of streptococcal M proteins
R37AI-10142-21 (MBC) RICHARDSON, JOHN P INDIANA UNIVERSITY BLOOMINGTON, IN 47405 Factors that control RNA transcription
R01AI-10187-21 (SSS) NAKANISHI, KOJI COLUMBIA UNIVERSITY HAVEMEYER HALL NEW YORK, NY 10027 Studies bioactive compounds and receptors
R37AI-10242-30 (EI) ROWLEY, DONALD A UNIVERSITY OF CHICAGO DIVISION OF BIOLOGICAL SCIENCE CHICAGO, IL 60637 Pathologic studies of inflammation and immunity
R01AI-10311-21 (MBC) DUBNAU, DAVID A PUBLIC HLTH RES INST CUNY INC 455 FIRST AVENUE NEW YORK, NY 10016 Genetic recombination in Bacillus subtilis
R01AI-10318-20 (MBC) CLEWELL, DON B UNIVERSITY OF MICHIGAN ANN ARBOR, MI 48109-0402 Transferable streptococcal transposon, Tn916
R01AI-10333-21 (MBC) MILLER, CHARLES G UNIVERSITY OF ILLINOIS 407 S GOODWIN AVE URBANA, IL 61801 Genetics and biochemistry of intracellular proteolysis
R37AI-10343-20 (BIO) HIRSCHHORN, ROCHELLE NEW YORK UNIVERSITY MEDICAL CT 550 FIRST AVENUE NEW YORK, NY 10016 Activation of immunocompetent lymphocytes
P50AI-10404-21 (AITC) HONG, RICHARD UNIV OF WISCONSIN HOSPITAL 600 HIGHLAND AVE (K4-434) MADISON, WI 53792 Asthma and allergic disease center
P50AI-10404-21 0002 (AITC) BUCKNER, CARL K Asthma and allergic disease center Parainfluenza 3 virus on the control of the airways
P50AI-10404-21 0006 (AITC) BUSSE, WILLIAM W Asthma and allergic disease center Rhinovirus effects on pulmonary mast cell secretion
P50AI-10404-21 0007 (AITC) GRAZIANO, FRANK M Asthma and allergic disease center Parainfluenza 3 infection on pulmonary mast cell mediator release
P50AI-10404-21 0008 (AITC) LEMANSKE, ROBERT F Asthma and allergic disease center Effects of viral infection on asthamic reaction
P50AI-10404-21 0009 (AITC) HONG, RICHARD Asthma and allergic disease center Effector mechanisms of virus induced asthma
P50AI-10404-21 0010 (AITC) CASTLEMAN, WILLIAM L Asthma and allergic disease center Effects of viral bronchiolitis in infant rats
P50AI-10404-21 9001 (AITC) HONG, RICHARD Asthma and allergic disease center Core support
R01AI-10615-21 (BM) GOTSCHLICH, EMIL C ROCKEFELLER UNIVERSITY 1230 YORK AVENUE NEW YORK, NY 10021-6399 Immunochemical studies on gonococcal surface antigens
R01AI-10627-20S1 (TMP) DESPOMMIER, DICKSON D COLUMBIA UNIVERSITY 630 W 168TH ST NEW YORK, NY 10032 Functional antigens of Trichinella spiralis
R22AI-10645-20 (TMP) AIKAWA, MASAMICHI CASE WESTERN RESERVE UNIV 2085 ADELBERT ROAD CLEVELAND, OH 44106 Electron microscopy of plasmodium-host interactions
P01AI-10702-20 (SRC) NATHENSON, STANLEY G ALBERT EINSTEIN COLLEGE OF MED 1300 MORRIS PARK AVENUE BRONX, N Y 10461 Cell biology of lymphoid cells
P01AI-10702-20 0001 (SRC) RAJAN, THIRUCHANDURAI V Cell biology of lymphoid cells Somatic cell genetics
P01AI-10702-20 0002 (SRC) NATHENSON, STANLEY G Cell biology of lymphoid cells Cell replication, immunoglobulins, transplantation antigens
P01AI-10702-20 0004 (SRC) BLOOM, BARRY R Cell biology of lymphoid cells Cellular basis of resistance to microorganisms
P01AI-10702-20 0005 (SRC) DIAMOND, BETTY A Cell biology of lymphoid cells Macrophage biology
P01AI-10702-20 0006 (SRC) BIRSHSTEIN, BARBARA K Cell biology of lymphoid cells Control of gene expression
R01AI-10704-31 (PTHA) MICHAEL, ALFRED F 516 DELWARE ST SE MINNEAPOLIS, MN 55455 Study of renal diseases in childhood
R01AI-10732-20 (BM) BASS, DAVID A BOWMAN GRAY SCHOOL OF MEDICINE 300 S HAWTHORNE ROAD WINSTON-SALEM, N C 27103 Pathophysiology and metabolism of the leukocyte
R01AI-10734-18 (ALY) SPIEGELBERG, HANS L UNIV OF CALIFORNIA SAN DIEGO 9500 GILMAN DR LA JOLLA, CA 92093-0609 IgE and IgG subclass formation
R37AI-10793-18 (NSS) STRAUSS, JAMES H CALIFORNIA INST OF TECHNOLOGY 1201 E CALIFORNIA BLVD PASADENA, CA 91125 A genetic analysis of sindbis virus
R01AI-10811-24A1 (IMS) CHIORAZZI, NICHOLAS NORTH SHORE UNIV HOSPITAL 300 COMMUNITY DRIVE MANHASSET, NY 11030 Serologic,cellular and molecular studies of autoantibodies
R01AI-10964-18 (MCHA) WHITE, JAMES D OREGON STATE UNIVERSITY CORVALLIS, OR 97331-4003 Synthesis of macrolide antibiotics
R01AI-10971-20 (MBC) HIGGINS, MICHAEL L TEMPLE UNIV SCH OF MEDICINE 3400 NORTH BROAD STREET PHILADELPHIA, PA 19140 Cell division and surface growth
R37AI-10984-20 (VR) TESH, ROBERT B YALE UNIV SCHOOL OF MEDICINE 60 COLLEGE STREET; PO BOX 3333 NEW HAVEN, CT 06510-8034 Support for world reference center for arboviruses
R37AI-11112-25 (EVR) WAGNER, ROBERT R UNIVERSITY OF VIRGINIA SCHOOL OF MEDICINE - BOX 441 CHARLOTTESVILLE, VA 22908 Cellular resistance to viral infection
R01AI-11183-19 (IMB) SERCARZ, ELI E UNIVERSITY OF CALIFORNIA 405 HILGARD AVENUE LOS ANGELES, CA 90024 Regulatory circuitry using defined protein antigens
R01AI-11202-19 (IMS) ISHIZAKA, KIMISHIGE LA JOLLA INST FOR ALLERGY/IMMU 11149 NORTH TORREY PINES ROAD LA JOLLA, CA 92037 Regulation of reaginic antibody response

PROJECT NO., ORGANIZATIONAL UNIT., INVESTIGATOR, ADDRESS, TITLE

PROJECT NO., ORGANIZATIONAL UNIT., INVESTIGATOR, ADDRESS, TITLE

R37AI-11219-19 (NSS) ROSSMANN, MICHAEL G PURDUE UNIVERSITY WEST LAFAYETTE, IND 47907 Structure of a small spherical virus

R37AI-11234-20 (NSS) KNIGHT, KATHERINE L LOYOLA UNIVERSITY OF CHICAGO 2160 SOUTH FIRST AVENUE MAYWOOD, IL 60153 Structure and genetic control of IgA

R37AI-11240-19 (NSS) CAMPBELL, PRISCILLA A NATL JEWISH CTR/IMM RESP MED 1400 JACKSON STREET DENVER, CO 80206-1997 Cell biology of the immune response to bacteria

R37AI-11289-19 (TMP) COLLEY, DANIEL G VA MEDICAL CENTER 1310-24TH AVENUE, SOUTH NASHVILLE, TN 37212-2637 Immunologic responses to Schistosoma mansoni

R01AI-11361-16 (TMP) CASTRO, GILBERT A UNIV OF TEXAS MEDICAL SCHOOL PO BOX 20708 HOUSTON, TX 77225 Immunoregulation of gut epithelium to escape parasitism

R22AI-11373-17 (TMP) DAVIS, GEORGE MORGAN ACADEMY OF NATURAL SCIENCES 19TH & THE PARKWAY PHILADELPHIA, PA 19103 Analysis of molluscan faunas and Asian schistosomiasis

R37AI-11377-18 (VR) SCHLESINGER, SONDRA WASHINGTON UNIV SCH OF MED BOX 8230 ST LOUIS, MO 63110 Structure and replication of enveloped RNA viruses

P50AI-11403-19 (AITC) PATTERSON, ROY NORTHWESTERN UNIV MEDICAL SCH 303 E CHICAGO AVENUE EVANSTON, IL 60611 Immunologic airway disease clinical and basic studies

P50AI-11403-19 0009 (AITC) GREENBERGER, PAUL A Immunologic airway disease clinical and basic studies Allergic bronchopulmonary aspergillosis

P50AI-11403-19 0010 (AITC) ZEISS, C RAYMOND Immunologic airway disease clinical and basic studies Animal models of immunologic lung disease

P50AI-11403-19 0011 (AITC) LAWRENCE, IRA Immunologic airway disease clinical and basic studies Skin mast cells

P50AI-11403-19 0012 (AITC) SMITH, LEWIS J Immunologic airway disease clinical and basic studies Bioactive mediators

R01AI-11459-19 (MBC) FRIEDMAN, DAVID I UNIVERSITY OF MICHIGAN M6722 MEDICAL SCIENCE BLDG II ANN ARBOR, MI 48109-0620 Host and viral influences on phage lambda development

R01AI-11479-17 (MBC) KHORANA, HAR G MASSACHUSETTS INST OF TECH 77 MASSACHUSETTS AVENUE CAMBRIDGE, MA 02139 Studies of biological membranes

R01AI-11490-18 (MCHA) PAQUETTE, LEO ARMAND OHIO STATE UNIVERSITY 120 WEST 18TH AVENUE COLUMBUS, OH 43210-1173 Polycondensed alicyclics and their antiviral role

R01AI-11573-18 (BBCB) SCHUSTER, TODD M UNIVERSITY OF CONNECTICUT 75 NORTH EAGLEVILLE ROAD STORRS, CT 06269-3125 Biophysical studies of virus assembly

R37AI-11676-17 (MBC) BLACK, LINDSAY W UNIVERSITY OF MARYLAND 660 WEST REDWOOD STREET BALTIMORE, MD 21201 Phage T4 head assembly and initiation of infection

R01AI-11709-16 (BM) CLARK, VIRGINIA L UNIV OF ROCHESTER MEDICAL CTR ROCHESTER, NY 14642 Function of gonococcal anaerobically induced proteins

R01AI-11744-17 (BMT) RAYMOND, KENNETH N UNIVERSITY OF CALIFORNIA BERKELEY, CA 94720 Coordination chemistry of microbial iron transport

R37AI-11772-19 (EVR) KRUG, ROBERT M RUTGERS UNIVERSITY 679 HOES LANE PISCATAWAY, NJ 08855-1179 Replication of influenza virus

R37AI-11822-18 (BM) FISCHETTI, VINCENT A THE ROCKEFELLER UNIVERSITY 1230 YORK AVENUE NEW YORK, NEW YORK 10021-6399 Properties of streptococcal M protein

R01AI-11823-18 (EVR) PALESE, PETER M MOUNT SINAI SCHOOL OF MEDICINE ONE GUSTAVE L LEVY PLACE NEW YORK, NY 10029 Studies with synthetic neuraminidase substrates

P01AI-11851-18 (AITC) UHR, JONATHAN W UNIV OF TEXAS SW MEDICAL CENTE 5323 HARRY HINES BLVD DALLAS, TX 75235 Activation and differentiation of lymphocytes

P01AI-11851-18 0006 (AITC) UHR, JONATHAN W Activation and differentiation of lymphocytes Molecular interaction on the plasma membrane

P01AI-11851-18 0008 (AITC) VITETTA, ELLEN S Activation and differentiation of lymphocytes Structure and function of alloantigens

P01AI-11851-18 0010 (AITC) UHR, JONATHAN W Activation and differentiation of lymphocytes Biochemical basis of attachment of Ig to plasma membrane

P01AI-11851-18 0011 (AITC) KETTMAN, JOHN Activation and differentiation of lymphocytes Function of B-cell subsets

P01AI-11851-18 0012 (AITC) KETTMAN, JOHN Activation and differentiation of lymphocytes Abelson virus-induced transformation of B-lymphocyte

P01AI-11851-18 0013 (AITC) UHR, JONATHAN W Activation and differentiation of lymphocytes Binding of specific T cells to antigen-pulsed macrophages

P01AI-11851-18 0014 (AITC) UHR, JONATHAN W Activation and differentiation of lymphocytes Functional correlates of macrophage-antigen-T cell interaction

P01AI-11851-18 0015 (AITC) UHR, JONATHAN W Activation and differentiation of lymphocytes Generation of functional T cell hybrids

P01AI-11851-18 0016 (AITC) VITETTA, ELLEN S Activation and differentiation of lymphocytes Antigens on virus-infected cells which are recognized by cytotoxic T cells

P01AI-11851-18 0017 (AITC) VITETTA, ELLEN Activation and differentiation of lymphocytes Molecular basis of isotype switching in murine B cells

P01AI-11851-18 0018 (AITC) TUCKER, PHILIP Activation and differentiation of lymphocytes Lymphokine induction of protein DNA interactions during class switching

P01AI-11851-18 0019 (AITC) CAPRA, J. DONALD Activation and differentiation of lymphocytes Developmentr of the human HIV repertoire

P01AI-11851-18 0020 (AITC) FORMAN, JAMES Activation and differentiation of lymphocytes Role of L3T4 cell in the regulation of CTL responses

P01AI-11851-18 0021 (AITC) KETTMAN, JOHN Activation and differentiation of lymphocytes Extra-thymic T cell maturation in epithelial tumors

P01AI-11851-18 9001 (AITC) UHR, JONATHAN W Activation and differentiation of lymphocytes Core--Cell culture

P01AI-11851-18 9002 (AITC) FORMAN, JAMES Activation and differentiation of lymphocytes Core--Animal colony

P01AI-11851-18 9003 (AITC) KETTMAN, JOHN Activation and differentiation of lymphocytes Core flow cytometry

R01AI-11855-17 (BBCB) THOMAS, GEORGE J, JR UNIVERSITY OF MISSOURI SCHOOL OF BASIC LIFE SCIENCES KANSAS CITY, MO 64110-2499 Molecular structure and interactions of viruses

R01AI-11949-17 (VR) PORTNER, ALLEN ST JUDE CHILDREN'S RES HOSP 332 N LAUDERDALE, P O BOX 318 MEMPHIS, TN 38101 Biosynthesis of paramyxoviruses

R37AI-12001-15 (NSS) MARGOLIASH, EMANUEL UNIVERSITY OF ILLINOIS P O BOX 4348 CHICAGO, IL 60680 Antigenicity of globular proteins

R01AI-12020-19 (BNP) MEINWALD, JERROLD CORNELL UNIVERSITY BAKER LABORATORY ITHACA, NY 14853-1301 Chemistry of arthropod secretions

R01AI-12052-18 (VR) GINSBERG, HAROLD S COLUMBIA UNIVERSITY 650 WEST 168TH STREET NEW YORK, NY 10032 Biochemical changes in adeno-transformed and infected cells

R37AI-12069-17 (ARR) SCHLOSSMAN, STUART F DANA-FARBER CANCER INSTITUTE 44 BINNEY STREET BOSTON, MA 02115 Human T cell subsets--Isolation and characterization

R01AI-12103-14A1 (BM) COLE, BARRY C UNIV OF UTAH MED CENTER 50 NORTH MEDICAL DRIVE SALT LAKE CITY, UT 84132 Mycoplasma superantigen MAM in disease and autoimmunity

R37AI-12127-17 (ALY) CAPRA, J DONALD UNIV OF TEXAS SOUTHWESTERN 5323 HARRY HINES BLVD DALLAS, TX 75235 Immunoglobulin V region structures--Genetic implications

R01AI-12184-16 (IMB) CANTOR, HARVEY I DANA-FARBER CANCER INSTITUTE 44 BINNEY STREET BOSTON, MA 02115 T-cell subpopulations in transplantation immunity

R01AI-12202-18 (MBC) MACNAB, ROBERT M YALE UNIVERSITY, SCH OF MED P. O. BOX 3333 NEW HAVEN, CT 06510 Principles of sensory reception and motor function

R37AI-12211-18 (ALY) ASKENASE, PHILIP W YALE UNIV SCH OF MEDICINE 333 CEDAR STREET NEW HAVEN, CT 06510 Immunology of cutaneous basophil hypersensitivity

R01AI-12227-16S1 (MBC) HENDRIX, ROGER W UNIVERSITY OF PITTSBURGH PITTSBURGH, PA 15260 Assembly and structure of bacteriophage lambda

R01AI-12277-18 (MBC) WOLFE, RALPH S UNIVERSITY OF ILLINOIS 407 S GOODWIN/131 BURRILL HALL URBANA, IL 61801 New microbial vitamin-coenzyme relationships

R01AI-12316-15S1 (VR) SUMMERS, DONALD F UNIVERSITY OF UTAH SCHOOL OF M SALT LAKE CITY, UT 84132 Composition, assembly and replication of RNA viruses

R37AI-12320-17 (PBC) LENGYEL, PETER DEPT-MOLEC BIOPHYS & BIOCHEM 260 WHITNEY AVE, P O BOX 6666 NEW HAVEN, CT 06511 Interferon, animal viruses and protein synthesis

R01AI-12387-17 (EVR) EHRENFELD, ELVERA R UNIVERSITY OF UTAH DEPARTMENT OF BIOCHEMISTRY SALT LAKE CITY, UT 84132 Control of translation in poliovirus infected cells

R01AI-12459-16 (TMP) RIDDIFORD, LYNN M SEATTLE, WA 98195 NJ-15 Hormonal regulation of the insect epidermisa

R37AI-12464-16 (NSS) WERTZ, GAIL W UNIVERSITY OF ALABAMA BOX 70 BHSB BIRMINGHAM, AL 35294 Studies of viral ribonucleic acid replication

R01AI-12467-14 (VR) IORIO, RONALD M UNIV OF MASSACHUSETTS MED SCH 55 LAKE AVENUE, NORTH WORCESTER, MA 01655 Molecular biology of NDV membrane proteins

R37AI-12520-17 (VR) SAMUEL, CHARLES E UNIVERSITY OF CALIFORNIA SANTA BARBARA, CA 93106 Mechanism of interferon action

R01AI-12533-17 (ALY) CLAFLIN, J LATHAM UNIVERSITY OF MICHIGAN 6748/0620 MED SCI BLDG II ANN ARBOR, MI 48109-0620 Control of antibody diversity and expression

R01AI-12575-17 (MBC) ROTHMAN-DENES, LUCIA B BIOPHYSICS & THEORETICAL BIOL AND CELL BIOLOGY CHICAGO, IL 60637 Novel transcribing activities in N-4 infected E coli

R01AI-12601-15 (BM) MILLER, JAMES N UNIVERSITY OF CALIFORNIA 405 HILGARD AVENUE LOS ANGELES, CA 90024 Immune mechanisms in experimental syphilis

R37AI-12603-17 (NSS) FLAHERTY, LORRAINE A WADSWORTH CTR FOR LAB & RESEAR PO BOX 509 ALBANY, NY 12201-0509 Immunogenetics and differentiation

R37AI-12680-17 (VR) COMPANS, RICHARD W UAB UAB STATION BIRMINGHAM, AL 35294 Influenza virus structure, biosynthesis, and assembly

R01AI-12710-16 (BM) WEIDANZ, WILLIAM P UNIVERSITY OF WISCONSIN 1300 UNIVERSITY AVENUE MADISON, WI 53706 Mechanisms of nonsterilizing immunity in malaria

R37AI-12734-16 (NSS) SHREFFLER, DONALD C WASHINGTON UNIV SCH OF MEDICIN BOX 8031, 660 SO EUCLID ST LOUIS, MO 63110 Organization and functions of the H-2 gene complex

R01AI-12749-16 (VR) NAYAK, DEBI P UNIVERSITY OF CALIFORNIA 43-239 CHS LOS ANGELES, CA 90024-1747 Interference by defective influenza viruses--Mechanism

R01AI-12770-14 (BM) TANOWITZ, HERBERT B ALBERT EINSTEIN COLL OF MEDICI 1300 MORRIS PARK AVENUE BRONX, NY 10461 Trypanosoma cruzi: pathogenesis of infection

R01AI-12806-13A1 (BM) DOMER, JUDITH E TULANE UNIVERSITY SCH OF MED 1430 TULANE AVENUE NEW ORLEANS, LA 70112 Host respones in experimental candidiasis

R01AI-12851-16 (MBC) FEISS, MICHAEL G UNIVERSITY OF IOWA DEPARTMENT OF MICROBIOLOGY IOWA CITY, IA 52242 Virus chromosome structure--Role in development

R37AI-12913-16 (TMP) BOROS, DOV L WAYNE STATE UNIVERSITY 540 E CANFIELD AVE DETROIT, MI 48201 Immunoregulation of the schistosome egg granuloma

R01AI-12936-15 (SB) ALEXANDER, J WESLEY UNIVERSITY OF CINCINNATI 231 BETHESDA AVE CINCINNATI, OHIO 45267-0558 Host defense mechanisms--Control of surgical infection

R01AI-13002-16 (VR) LENARD, JOHN UMDNJ-ROBERT W JOHNSON MED SCH 675 HOES LANE PISCATAWAY, NJ 08854-5635 VSV structure, budding,

PROJECT NO., ORGANIZATIONAL UNIT., INVESTIGATOR, ADDRESS, TITLE

entry using membrane mutants
R37AI-13013-15 (NSS) STEINMAN, R M ROCKEFELLER UNIVERSITY 1230 YORK AVENUE NEW YORK, N Y 10021 Characterization of lymphoid dendritic cells
R37AI-13128-14 (TMP) KUHN, RAYMOND E WAKE FOREST UNIVERSITY WINSTON-SALEM, NC 27109 Immunobiology of Chagas' disease
R01AI-13150-14 (BM) HILL, HARRY R UNIVERSITY OF UTAH 50 NORTH MEDICAL DR SALT LAKE CITY, UT 84132 Mechanisms of host resistance to group B streptococci
R37AI-13178-16 (NSS) FIELDS, BERNARD N HARVARD MEDICAL SCHOOL 200 LONGWOOD AVE BOSTON, MA 02115 Genetics of reovirus
R01AI-13323-16 (ALY) BOSMA, MELVIN J INSTITUTE FOR CANCER RESEARCH 7701 BURHOLME AVENUE PHILADELPHIA, PA 19111 SCID mice and the control of lymphocyte differentiation
R37AI-13357-16 (NSS) GEFTER, MALCOLM L MASSACHUSETTS INST OF TECH 77 MASSACHUSETTS AVENUE CAMBRIDGE, MA 02139 Regulatory mechanisms in normal and neoplastic cells
R01AI-13446-12A1 (BM) WYRICK, PRISCILLA B UNIV OF NORTH CAROLINA CB# 7290, FLOB 804 CHAPEL HILL, NC 27599 Virulence factors of Chlamydiae
R37AI-13509-16 (ALY) BIRSHTEIN, BARBARA K ALBERT EINSTEIN COLL OF MED 1300 MORRIS PARK AVE BRONX, NY 10461 Cellular and structural studies of myeloma mutants
R37AI-13526-16 (NSS) ROBINSON, WILLIAM S STANFORD UNIVERSITY STANFORD, CA 94305 The viruses of hepatitis B
R55AI-13541-14A1 (IMS) WIRA, CHARLES R DARTMOUTH MEDICAL SCHOOL HANOVER, NH 03756 Sex hormone regulation of the mucosal immune system
R37AI-13544-15 (BM) LANDY, ARTHUR BROWN UNIVERSITY PROVIDENCE, RI 02912 Mechanisms of site-specific recombination
R01AI-13550-16 (BM) ABRAHAM, SOMAN N WASHINGTON UNIV MED CTR 216 S KINGSHIGHWAY ST LOUIS, MO 63110 Ligand receptor interaction in bacterial adherence
R01AI-13562-16 (VR) STINSKI, MARK F UNIVERSITY OF IOWA IOWA CITY, IA 52242 The genes that regulate human cytomegalovirus expression
R01AI-13574-14 (EVR) LESNAW, JUDITH A UNIVERSITY OF KENTUCKY 101 T H MORGAN BUILDING LEXINGTON, KY 40506 Replication of negative strand RNA viruses
R37AI-13587-16 (BBCB) MCCONNELL, HARDEN M STANFORD UNIVERSITY STANFORD, CA 94305 Immunology and biophysics of reconstituted membranes
R01AI-13600-15 (IMB) CANTOR, HARVEY I DANA-FARBER CANCER INSTITUTE 44 BINNEY STREET BOSTON, MA 02115 Immunobiology of Ly+ T-cell subclasses
R01AI-13654-15 (BBCB) WILEY, DON C HARVARD UNIVERSITY 7 DIVINITY AVENUE CAMBRIDGE, MA 02138 Viral membrane and glycoprotein structure.
R01AI-13718-15 (VR) GIBSON, D WADE JOHNS HOPKINS SCH OF MEDICINE 725 NORTH WOLFE STREET BALTIMORE, MD 21205 Herpesvirus proteins synthesis and virion assembly
R01AI-13725-13A2 (IMB) PRESS, JOAN L BRANDEIS UNIVERSITY DEPARTMENT OF BIOLOGY, ROOM 51 WALTHAM, MA 02254-9110 Immunogenetic analysis of B cell differentiation
R01AI-13915-16 (IMB) PIERCE, CARL W JEWISH HOSPITAL 216 SOUTH KINGHIGHWAY ST LOUIS, MO 63110 Cell interactions in immune responses in vitro
R01AI-13926-14 (BM) FERRIERI, PATRICIA UNIVERSITY OF MINNESOTA BOX 134 MAYO MINNEAPOLIS, MN 55455 Host responses to group B streptococci
R01AI-13967-14 (IMS) KAPP-PIERCE, JUDITH A JEWISH HOSPITAL OF ST LOUIS 1500 WALLACE BLVD ST LOUIS, MO 63110 Role of MHC genes in immunoregulation
R37AI-13989-15 (EI) GERHARD, WALTER WISTAR INSTITUTE 36TH AND SPRUCE STREETS PHILADELPHIA, PA 19104 Antigenicity and immunogenicity of influenza virus
R01AI-14032-13 (SAT) SIMMONS, RICHARD L UNIVERSITY OF PITTSBURGH PITTSBURGH, PA 15261 Pathogenesis and treatment of experimental peritonitis
R22AI-14065-15 (BM) COLLINS, FRANK M TRUDEAU INSTITUTE, INC P O BOX 59 SARANAC LAKE, N Y 12983 A mouse infection model of lepromatous leprosy
R01AI-14107-15 (BM) HOLMES, RANDALL K USUHS/F E HERBERT SCH OF MED 4301 JONES BRIDGE ROAD BETHESDA, MD 20814-4799 Control of bacterial toxins by viruses and plasmids
R37AI-14157-20 (ALY) ALPER, CHESTER A CENTER FOR BLOOD RESEARCH, INC 800 HUNTINGTON AVENUE BOSTON, MA 02115 Investigations of human complement
R01AI-14162-14 (VR) HACKETT, CHARLES J WISTAR INSTITUTE 36TH AND SPRUCE STREETS PHILADELPHIA, PA 19104 Cell mediated immunity in influenza
R01AI-14176-14 (MBC) SAIER, MILTON H JR UNIVERSITY OF CALIFORNIA LA JOLLA, CA 92093 Mechanism of carbohydrates transport in bacteria
R01AI-14209-13 (BM) KOZEL, THOMAS R UNIVERSITY OF NEVADA RENO, NV 89557 Cryptococcal polysaccharide--Inhibition of phagocytosis
R01AI-14332-15 (IMS) ZWEIMAN, BURTON UNIVERSITY OF PENNSYLVANIA 512 JOHNSON PAVILION PHILADELPHIA, PA 19104-6057 Inflammatory responses in allergic reactions and asthma
R01AI-14349-13 (ALY) MURPHY, DONAL B NYST DEPT OF HLTH/HLTH RES, IN PO BOX 509 ALBANY, NY 12201-0509 Expression and function of MHC class I and class II genes
R01AI-14367-12 (EVR) BRIAN, DAVID A UNIVERSITY OF TENNESSEE M-409 WALTERS LIFE SCIS BUILDI KNOXVILLE, TN 37996-0845 Coronavirus structure and replication
R01AI-14426-15 (MBC) IPPEN-IHLER, KARIN A TEXAS A&M UNIVERSITY COLLEGE STATION, TX 77843 The genetics and biochemistry of plasmid transfer
R01AI-14490-13 (TMP) APPLETON, JUDITH A J A BAKER INST ANIM HLTH, NYS COL OF VET MED, CORNELL UNIV ITHACA, NY 14853-6401 Immunity to parasitic infection
R01AI-14551-15 (SAT) MONACO, ANTHONY P NEW ENGLAND DEACONESS HOSPITAL 185 PILGRIM ROAD BOSTON, MA 02215 Experimental and clinical allograft unresponsiveness
R37AI-14579-13 (IMS) JANEWAY, CHARLES A, JR YALE UNIV SCHOOL OF MEDICINE 310 CEDAR STREET NEW HAVEN, CT 06510 Influence of H-2 antigens on mouse T cell responses

PROJECT NO., ORGANIZATIONAL UNIT., INVESTIGATOR, ADDRESS, TITLE

R37AI-14584-25 (ALY) EDIDIN, MICHAEL A JOHNS HOPKINS UNIVERSITY 3400 N CHARLES STREET BALTIMORE, MD 21218 Chemistry and development of transplantation antigens
R01AI-14594-15 (VR) MOYER, SUE A UNIVERSITY OF FLORIDA GAINESVILLE, FL 32610 Replication and interference of RNA viruses
R37AI-14627-24 (VR) HOLLAND, JOHN J UNIVERSITY OF CALIFORNIA 9500 GILMAN DRIVE LA JOLLA, CA 92093-0116 Synthesis in normal, virus infected and tumor cells
R22AI-14710-11 (EVR) BROWN, DENNIS T UNIVERSITY OF TEXAS BIO 220 AUSTIN, TX 78713 Development of a virus membrane
R01AI-14747-18 (EI) CLARK, WILLIAM R UNIVERSITY OF CALIFORNIA MOLECULAR BIOLOGY INSTITUTE LOS ANGELES, CA 90024 Degranulation functions of cytotoxic T lymphocytes
R37AI-14764-15 (IMB) DAVID, CHELLA S MAYO FOUNDATION 200 FIRST STREET SOUTHWEST ROCHESTER, MN 55905 Structure,expression,regulation of murine and human Ia genes
R01AI-14782-14 (IMB) KEARNEY, JOHN F UNIV OF ALABAMA @ BIRMINGHAM UAB STATION BIRMINGHAM, AL 35294 Regulation of B cell clonal diversity
R37AI-14784-15 (NSS) ISHIZAKA, KIMISHIGE LA JOLLA INST ALLERGY/IMMUNOLO 11149 NORTH TORREY PINES RD LA JOLLA, CA 92037 Ontogeny and differentiation of IgE-B lymphocytes
R01AI-14826-13 (BM) ROSENTHAL, RAOUL S INDIANA UNIVERSITY 635 BARNHILL DRIVE INDIANAPOLIS, IN 46202-5120 Role of peptidoglycan in health and disease
R37AI-14885-14 (MBC) LACKS, SANFORD A BROOKHAVEN NATIONAL LABORATORY ASSOCIATED UNIVERSITIES, INC UPTON, N Y 11973 DNA mismatch repair in transformation and mutagenesis
R01AI-14908-13 (ALY) KLAPPER, DAVID G UNIV OF NC AT CHAPEL HILL CB#7290 804 FLOB CHAPEL HILL, N C 27599 Structure/function of ragweed pollen allergen antigen E
R01AI-14910-12A1 (IMB) HUBER, BRIGITTE T TUFTS UNIV./SCHOOL OF MEDICINE 136 HARRISON AVENUE BOSTON, MA 02111 B lymphocytes--Differentiation and triggering
R01AI-14929-12 (HEM) BASS, DAVID A BOWMAN GRAY SCH OF MED OF WAKE MEDICAL CENTER BOULEVARD WINSTON-SALEM, NC 27157-1054 Priming & stimulation of granulocytes
R01AI-14937-13 (MCHA) TOWNSEND, CRAIG A JOHNS HOPKINS UNIVERSITY CHARLES & 34TH STREETS BALTIMORE, MD 21218 Biosynthesis of beta-lactam antibiotics
R01AI-14969-14 (ALY) CHESS, LEONARD COLUMBIA UNIVERSITY 630 WEST 168TH STREET NEW YORK, N Y 10032 Differentiation antigens on human T cell subclasses
R01AI-14981-14 (VR) ROUSE, BARRY T UNIVERSITY OF TENNESSEE DEPARTMENT OF MICROBIOLOGY KNOXVILLE, TN 37996-0845 Immunity mechanisms in herpesvirus infections
R37AI-15027-14 (MCHA) HEATHCOCK, CLAYTON H UNIVERSITY OF CALIFORNIA BERKELEY, CA 94720 Acyclic stereoselection in natural product synthesis
R01AI-15035-14 (TMP) WINKLER, HERBERT H UNIVERSITY OF SOUTH ALABAMA COLLEGE OF MEDICINE MOBILE, AL 36688 Permeability of the epidemic typhus rickettsia
R01AI-15066-14 (EI) TERHORST, CORNELIS P BETH ISRAEL HOSPITAL 330 BROOKLINE BOSTON, MA 02215 Cell surface receptors on cytotoxic T cells
N01AI-15082-00 (**) DISMUKES, WILLIAM E Clinical trial for antimicrobial therapy of systemic mycotic infections
N01AI-15093-00 (**) MURPHEY-CORB, MICHAEL Evaluation of vaccines for SAIDS in monkeys
N01AI-15094-00 (**) MORTON, WILLIAM R Evaluation of vaccines for SAIDS in monkeys
N01AI-15095-00 (**) CLEMENTS, MARY LOU Facility for the study of infectious agents,vaccines and antimicrobials
N01AI-15096-00 (**) LEVINE, MYRON M Enteric diseases vaccine evaluation and treatment unit
N01AI-15097-00 (**) SIDWELL, ROBERT W Animal models of human viral infections
N01AI-15098-00 (**) KERN, EARL R Animal models of human viral infections
N01AI-15099-00 (**) WYDE, PHILIP R Animal models of human viral infections
N01AI-15100-00 (**) DUNKEL, EDMUND C Animal models of human viral infections
N01AI-15101-00 (**) MYERS, MARTIN G Animal models of human viral infections
N01AI-15103-00 (**) COUCH, ROBERT Establishment of an acute viral respiratory disease unit
N01AI-15104-02 (**) JOHNSON, KARL Operations office
N01AI-15105-00 (**) WITTES, JANET Data coordinating center for the national cooperative study
N01AI-15106-00 (**) BOLOGNESI, DAN P Central immunology laboratory for AIDS vaccine clinical trials
N01AI-15107-00 (**) MCCALL, JOHN Filariae respository
N01AI-15108-00 (**) EXPOSITO, LORENZO Research and development support for CMRS of NIAID
N01AI-15110-00 (**) POPE, ANDREW Health effects indoor/allergens
N01AI-15111-00 (**) MACGREGOR, JAMES Investigation of new opportunistic infection drug toxicology
N01AI-15112-00 (**) LEWIS, FRED A Production and delivery of Schistosoma mansoni
N01AI-15113-00 (**) WHITLEY, RICHARD D Clinical trials of therapies for severe herpesvirus infections
N01AI-15114-00 (**) WYAND, MICHAEL S Evaluation in monkeys of candidate vaccines for simian AIDS
N01AI-15115-00 (**) DUQUESNOY, RENE J Alloantisera and molecular probes for public specificities of the MHC
N01AI-15116-00 (**) WARD, FRANCES E Alloantisera and molecular probes for public specificities of the MHC
N01AI-15117-00 (**) SHAW, JERRI Outreach, education and technology transfer

PROJECT NO., ORGANIZATIONAL UNIT., INVESTIGATOR, ADDRESS, TITLE

N01AI-15118-00 (**) UNADKAT, J D Evaluation of pharmacokinetics of AIDS therapies in nonhuman primates

N01AI-15119-00 (**) MARTIN, LOUIS Evaluation of AIDS therapies in animal models of retroviral disease

N01AI-15120-00 (**) TSAI, CHE'CHEUNG Evaluation of AIDS therapies in animal retroviral models

R37AI-15122-18 (EVR) WIMMER, ECKARD A SUNY - AT STONY BROOK STONY BROOK, N Y 11794 Poliovirus--Molecular biology and surface structure

N01AI-15123-00 (**) DURAKO, STEPHEN Clinical trials to evaluate therapies of HIV disease

R01AI-15123-14 (EVR) SAWICKI, DOROTHEA L MEDICAL COLLEGE OF OHIO 3000 ARLINGTON AVE TOLEDO, OHIO 43614 Regulation of alphavirus transcription

N01AI-15124-00 (**) WARD, JOEL I Evaluation of vaccine proph. against infect. diseases in children

N01AI-15125-00 (**) OLIN, PATRICK Pertussis clinical trial part 2)

N01AI-15126-00 (**) GLEZEN, PAUL Maternal immunization of infectious diseases in neonates

N01AI-15127-00 (**) FISHER, FRANKLIN G Laboratory support services

N01AI-15128-00 (**) MCGHEE, JERRY Mucosal immunization research group

N01AI-15129-01 (**) POTASH, LOUIS Vaccine production facility

N01AI-15130-00 (**) STOTO, MICHAEL A Study on the adverse reactions of childhood vaccines

N01AI-15131-00 (**) THOMAS, MARILYN Coordinated center for clinical & epidemiologic studies in infectious diseases

R01AI-15136-13 (PTHB) ULEVITCH, RICHARD J SCRIPPS CLINIC & RES FDN 10666 NORTH TORREY PINES ROAD LA JOLLA, CA 92037 The molecular pathology of LPS-induced injury

R22AI-15193-12 (TMP) PHILLIPS, S MICHAEL UNIV OF PENNA, SCH OF MEDICINE 36TH & HAMILTON WALK PHILADELPHIA, PA 19104 S. mansoni vitellogenesis and granuloma formation

R01AI-15230-12 (TMP) STAY, BARBARA A UNIVERSITY OF IOWA IOWA CITY, IA 52242 Control of juvenile hormone synthesis

R01AI-15231-14 (IMS) GLEICH, GERALD J MAYO FOUNDATION 200 FIRST STREET SOUTHWEST ROCHESTER, MN 55905 Eosinophils in human disease

R01AI-15235-13 (TMP) SHEAR, HANNAH L NEW YORK UNIVERSITY MED CTR 550 FIRST AVENUE NEW YORK, N Y 10016 Macrophage activation in experimental malaria

R01AI-15251-13 (ALY) SAXON, ANDREW UNIVERSITY OF CALIFORNIA 10833 LECONTE AVE LOS ANGELES, CA 90024-1680 Regulation of human IgE in health and disease

R01AI-15257-21 (VR) PLAGEMANN, PETER G UNIVERSITY OF MINNESOTA BOX 196 MAYO HOSPITAL MINNEAPOLIS, MN 55455 LDH virus--Growth in macrophages and persistent infection

R01AI-15284-13 (EI) GOODMAN, MICHAEL G RES INST OF SCRIPPS CLINIC 10666 NORTH TORREY PINES ROAD LA JOLLA, CA 92037 Mechanism of lymphocyte activation by thiol compounds

R01AI-15286-14 (MBC) LINDAHL, LASSE A UNIVERSITY OF ROCHESTER HUTCHINSON HALL 478 ROCHESTER, NY 14627 Coordination of E coli ribosomal protein synthesis

P50AI-15322-14 (AITC) UNANUE, EMIL R WASHINGTON UNIV. SCHOOL OF MED 660 SOUTH EUCLID AVENUE ST LOUIS, MO 63110 Centers for interdisciplinary research in immunologic diseases

P50AI-15322-14 0008 (AITC) WEDNER, H JAMES Centers for interdisciplinary research in immunologic diseases Psychosocial techniques to enhance asthma management

P50AI-15322-14 0009 (AITC) PARKER, CHARLES W Centers for interdisciplinary research in immunologic diseases Genetic factors in IgE with mediated allergy

P50AI-15322-14 0010 (AITC) SCHWARTZ, BENJAMIN D Centers for interdisciplinary research in immunologic diseases Class II restriction of influenza specific T-cell clones

P50AI-15322-14 0012 (AITC) UNANUE, EMIL R Centers for interdisciplinary research in immunologic diseases Macrophage activation and Ia expression in SCID

P50AI-15322-14 0013 (AITC) LOH, DENNIS Centers for interdisciplinary research in immunologic diseases MHC transgenic mouse model

P50AI-15322-14 0014 (AITC) CHAPLIN, DAVID D Centers for interdisciplinary research in immunologic diseases Immunogenetics of SLE and class III genes of MHC

P50AI-15322-14 0015 (AITC) LUBLIN, DOUGLAS Centers for interdisciplinary research in immunologic diseases Decay accelerating factor gene structure

P50AI-15332-14 (AITC) FAHEY, JOHN L UCLA SCHOOL OF MEDICINE 405 HILGARD AVENUE LOS ANGELES, CA 90024-1747 Center for interdisciplinary research in immunologic diseases

P50AI-15332-14 0006 (AITC) FAHEY, JOHN L Center for interdisciplinary research in immunologic diseases Immunologic effects of lymphokine therapy

P50AI-15332-14 0011 (AITC) TARGAN, STEPHEN R Center for interdisciplinary research in immunologic diseases Role of in vivo primed CTL in immune disorders

P50AI-15332-14 0012 (AITC) STIEHM, E RICHARD Center for interdisciplinary research in immunologic diseases Monocyte function in pediatric AIDS

P50AI-15332-14 0014 (AITC) SAXON, ANDREW Center for interdisciplinary research in immunologic diseases Retinoids/lymphokines to enhance defective human B cells

P50AI-15332-14 0015 (AITC) CLEMENT, LORAN T Center for interdisciplinary research in immunologic diseases Differentiation of CD8+ cytotoxic suppressor cells

P50AI-15332-14 0016 (AITC) FAHEY, JOHN L Center for interdisciplinary research in immunologic diseases Outreach, education and demonstration program in immunological diseases

P50AI-15332-14 9001 (AITC) GIORGI, J V Center for interdisciplinary research in immunologic diseases Core--Flow cytometry laboratory

P50AI-15332-14 9002 (AITC) CLEMENT, LORAN T Center for interdisciplinary research in immunologic diseases Core--Immune function laboratory

R01AI-15338-13A1 (BM) DIAMOND, RICHARD D UNIVERSITY HOSPITAL 88 EAST NEWTON STREET BOSTON, MA 02118 Pulmonary and systemic killing of opportunistic fungi

P01AI-15351-13 (SRC) KAZURA, JAMES W UNIVERSITY HOSPITALS 2074 ABINGTON ROAD CLEVELAND, OH 44106 Tropical disease research units

P01AI-15351-13 0001 (SRC) MAHMOUD, ADEL A Tropical disease research units Protective antigens of schistosoma mansoni

P01AI-15351-13 0005 (SRC) KUZURA, JAMES W Tropical disease research units Protective antigens of Brugia malayi

P01AI-15351-13 0007 (SRC) TARTAKOFF, ALAN M Tropical disease research units Biology of Schistosoma mansoni glycocalyx

P01AI-15351-13 9002 (SRC) SALATA, ROBERT A Tropical disease research units Lymphocyte cloning--Core

P01AI-15351-13 9003 (SRC) AIKAWA, MASAMICHI Tropical disease research units Ultrastructure--Core

P01AI-15351-13 9004 (SRC) BLANTON, RICHARD E Tropical disease research units Life cycles--Core

P01AI-15353-13 (SRC) PIERCE, CARL W JEWISH HOSPITAL OF ST LOUIS 216 SOUTH KINGSHIGHWAY ST LOUIS, MO 63110 Lymphocyte biology, the MHC and immune regulation

P01AI-15353-13 9004 (SRC) LITTLE, J RUSSELL Lymphocyte biology, the MHC and immune regulation Core--Special cell facility

P01AI-15353-13 9001 (SRC) LAKE, JEFFREY P Lymphocyte biology, the MHC and immune regulation Core--Animal production facility

P01AI-15353-13 9003 (SRC) DAVIE, JOSEPH M Lymphocyte biology, the MHC and immune regulation Core--Hybrid cell facility

R37AI-15394-13 (IMB) RICH, ROBERT R BAYLOR COLLEGE OF MEDICINE ONE BAYLOR PLAZA/DEBAKEY CTR HOUSTON, TX 77030-3498 Human immune responses to haptens in vitro

R01AI-15429-13 (TMP) STRETTON, ANTONY O UNIVERSITY OF WISCONSIN 1117 W JOHNSON STREET MADISON, WI 53706 Physiological studies on a parasitic nematode

R01AI-15446-09 (ALY) KIM, BYUNG S NORTHWESTERN UNIV MED SCH 303 E CHICAGO AVENUE CHICAGO, IL 60611 T cells responses to phosphorylcholine

R01AI-15486-13 (IMB) DE MARS, ROBERT I UNIVERSITY OF WISCONSIN-MADISO 445 HENRY MALL MADISON, WI 53706 T lymphocyte hybrids and lymphoblastoid variants

R01AI-15488-13 (EVR) ROIZMAN, BERNARD UNIVERSITY OF CHICAGO 910 EAST 58TH STREET CHICAGO, ILLINOIS 60637 Herpes simplex virus multiplication

R01AI-15495-10A1 (BM) MC MURRAY, DAVID N TEXAS A&M UNIVERSITY REYNOLDS MEDICAL BUILDING COLLEGE STATION, TX 77843 Dietary deficiencies and tuberculosis vaccine efficacy

R01AI-15503-14 (TMP) YOSHINO, TIMOTHY P UNIV OF WISCONSIN-MADISON 2015 LINDEN DRIVE WEST MADISON, WI 53706 Immunobiology of schistosome-mollusk interactions

R01AI-15539-13 (EVR) FLANEGAN, JAMES B UNIVERSITY OF FLORIDA GAINESVILLE, FLA 32610 Molecular biology of poliovirus RNA replication

R37AI-15607-13 (BM) VOLANAKIS, JOHN E UNIVERSITY OF ALABAMA UAB STATION BIRMINGHAM, AL 35294 C-reactive protein phospholipid interactions

R37AI-15608-12 (VR) BRACIALE, THOMAS J UNIVERSITY OF VIRGINIA HEALTH CHARLOTTESVILLE, VA 22908 Cytotoxic T lymphocyte response to influenza virus

R37AI-15614-13 (PTHA) DINARELLO, CHARLES A NEW ENGLAND MED CENTER HOSPITA 750 WASHINGTON STREET, BOX 041 BOSTON, MA 02111 Pathogeneneesis of fever in humans

R01AI-15619-12 (MBC) BURDETT, VICKERS DUKE UNIV MED CTR BOX 2030 DURHAM, N C 27710 Streptococcus plasmide--Molecular genetic analysis

R01AI-15650-14 (MBC) CRONAN, JOHN E, JR UNIVERSITY OF ILLINOIS 407 S GOODWIN/131 BURRILL HALL URBANA, ILLINOIS 61801 Genetic approaches to regulation of lipid metabolism

R01AI-15662-12 (TMP) HAPP, GEORGE M UNIVERSITY OF VERMONT MARSH LIFE SCIENCE BLDG. BURLINGTON, VT 05405 Control of reproductive maturation--An insect model

R01AI-15669-14 (EI) STROMINGER, JACK L DANA-FARBER CANCER INSTITUTE 44 BINNEY STREET BOSTON, MA 02115 Chemical & serological studies of lymphocyte surfaces

R01AI-15706-13 (PC) SAUER, ROBERT T MASSACHUSETTS INST OF TECHNOLO 77 MASSACHUSETTS AVE CAMBRIDGE, MA 02139 Sequence determinants of protein structure & stability

R01AI-15716-12 (BM) MURPHY, JUNEANN W UNIV OF OKLAHOMA HLTH SCIS CTR P O BOX 26901 OKLAHOMA CITY, OK 73190 Role of T cells in immunity to cryptococcosis

R01AI-15722-13 (VR) MOYER, RICHARD W UNIVERSITY OF FLORIDA BOX J-266 JHMHC GAINESVILLE, FL 32610 Gene regulation of mammalian DNA viruses

R01AI-15732-13 (ALY) JONES, PATRICIA P STANFORD UNIVERSITY STANFORD, CA 94305-5020 Genetics, structure, and expression of Ia antigens

R01AI-15749-13 (BM) WILKINS, TRACY D VIRGINIA POLYTECHNIC INST & STATE UNIV, ANAEROBE LAB BLACKSBURG, VA 24061 Isolation of toxins from C difficile and C sordellii

R37AI-15761-12 (NSS) WEIGLE, WILLIAM O SCRIPPS CLINIC & RESEARCH FDN 10666 NORTH TORREY PINES ROAD LA JOLLA, CA 92037 Regulation of lymphocyte activation

R01AI-15775-13 (IMB) CRESSWELL, PETER YALE MEDICAL SCHOOL 310 CEDAR STREET NEW HAVEN, CT 06510 Regulation of HLA antigen expression

R37AI-15797-14 (NSS) KLINMAN, NORMAN R SCRIPPS CLINIC/RESEARCH FDN 10666 NORTH TORREY PINES ROAD LA JOLLA, CA 92037 Clonal analysis of the immune mechanism

R37AI-15803-13 (IMS) WORTIS, HENRY H TUFTS UNIVERSITY 136 HARRISON AVENUE BOSTON, MA 02111 Lymphocyte development

R01AI-15834-11 (BM) HURST, JAMES K OREGON GRADUATE INSTITUTE 19600 N W VON NEUMANN DRIVE BEAVERTON, OR 97006-1999 Molecular basis for microbicidal action in leukocytes

R55AI-15892-13 (VR) LYLES, DOUGLAS S BOWMAN GRAY SCHOOL OF MEDICINE WINSTON-SALEM, NC 27157-1064 Assembly of enveloped viruses

R01AI-15939-12 (IMS) OGRA, PEARAY L UNIVERSITY OF TEXAS 301

UNIVERSITY OF TEXAS GALVESTON, TX 77550-2774 Mucosal immune response to respiratory syncytial virus

R01AI-15940-12 (BM) VASIL, MICHAEL L UNIVERSITY OF COLORADO 4200 E NINTH AVENUE DENVER, CO 80262 Genetics virulence in Pseudomonas species

R01AI-15955-10A2 (VR) PETERSON, DARRELL L VIRGINIA COMMONWEALTH UNIV BOX 614 MCV STATION RICHMOND, VA 23298-0614 Structure of hepatitis B antigens

R22AI-16006-12 (TMP) LEWIS, FRED A BIOMEDICAL RESEARCH INSTITUTE 12111 PARKLAWN DRIVE ROCKVILLE, MD 20852 Immunity in a Schistosoma mansoni abortive infection

R01AI-16052-16 (IMB) WETTSTEIN, PETER J MAYO FOUNDATION 200 FIRST STREET SW ROCHESTER, MN 55905 Non-H-2 histocompatibility genes & encoded antigens

R01AI-16099-12 (VR) KEENE, JACK D DUKE UNIV MED CENTER P O BOX 3020 DURHAM, N C 27710 Replicative mechanisms of the negative strand viruses

R22AI-16137-09 (TMP) BAYNE, CHRISTOPHER J OREGON STATE UNIVERSITY CORVALLIS, OR 97331 Schistosome-snail compatibility--Underlying mechanisms

R01AI-16165-13 (VR) PAULSON, JAMES C CYTEL CORPORATION 11099 N TORREY PINES RD LA JOLLA, CA 92037 Sialyloligosaccharide receptors of animal viruses

R01AI-16242-10 (BM) KEUSCH, GERALD T NEW ENGLAND MED CTR HOSPS,INC 750 WASHINGTON ST/NEMCH BOX 41 BOSTON, MA 02111 Shigella exotoxin--Cell receptors and mode of action

R01AI-16262-13 (PBC) SEHGAL, PRAVINKUMAR B NEW YORK MEDICAL COLLEGE VALHALLA, NY 10595 Regulation of interleukin-6 & interferon production

P01AI-16282-13 (SRC) JOHNSON, WARREN D, JR CORNELL UNIV MEDICAL COLLEGE 1300 YORK AVE, RM A-431 NEW YORK, NY 10021 Basic and applied research in protozoan diseases

P01AI-16282-13 0004 (SRC) BADARO, ROBERTO Basic and applied research in protozoan diseases Epidemiology and natural history of leishmaniasis

P01AI-16282-13 0005 (SRC) CARVALHO, EDGAR M Basic and applied research in protozoan diseases Cellular immunology of leishmaniasis

P01AI-16282-13 0006 (SRC) REED, STEVEN G Basic and applied research in protozoan diseases Molecular biology of leishmania and T. cruzi

P01AI-16282-13 0007 (SRC) MARSDEN, PHILIP D. Basic and applied research in protozoan diseases Immunotherapy and chemotherapy of leishmaniasis

P01AI-16305-13 (SRC) DAVID, JOHN R HARVARD SCH OF PUBLIC HEALTH 665 HUNTINGTON AVENUE BOSTON, MA 02115 Studies on four tropical diseases in Brazil

P01AI-16305-13 0007 (SRC) DOURADO, HEITOR V Studies on four tropical diseases in Brazil Amazonas--Leishmaniasis, malaria, and snake bites

P01AI-16305-13 0009 (SRC) ANDRADE, Z Studies on four tropical diseases in Brazil Bahia--Schistosomiasis and leishmaniasis

P01AI-16305-13 0012 (SRC) ALENCAR, JOAQUIN E Studies on four tropical diseases in Brazil Ceara--Leishmaniasis

P01AI-16305-13 9001 (SRC) DAVID, JOHN R Studies on four tropical diseases in Brazil Core

P01AI-16312-13 (SRC) JENSEN, JAMES B BRIGHAM YOUNG UNIVERSITY PROVO, UTAH 84602 Collaborative research on parasitic diseases in Sudan

P01AI-16312-13 0002 (SRC) JENSON, JAMES B Collaborative research on parasitic diseases in Sudan Immunology of falciparum malaria in sudan

P01AI-16312-13 0003 (SRC) WILLIAMS, JEFFREY F Collaborative research on parasitic diseases in Sudan Immunology of onchocerca volvulus infection and response to therapy

P01AI-16312-13 0006 (SRC) BENNETT, JAMES L Collaborative research on parasitic diseases in Sudan A biochemical-immunological study of symmer's fibrosis

P01AI-16312-13 9001 (SRC) WILLIAMS, JEFFREY F Collaborative research on parasitic diseases in Sudan Core--Khartoum laboratory

P50AI-16337-13 (AITC) KAPLAN, ALLEN P SUNY AT STONY BROOK STONY BROOK, NY 11794 Pathogenesis of allergic diseases of the skin & lungs

P50AI-16337-13 0001 (AITC) KAPLAN, ALLEN P Pathogenesis of allergic diseases of the skin & lungs Vasoactive mediators in inflammatory disorders

P50AI-16337-13 0002 (AITC) KAPLAN, ALLEN P Pathogenesis of allergic diseases of the skin & lungs Cytokines and histamine release

P50AI-16337-13 0004 (AITC) DATTWYLER, RAYMOND Pathogenesis of allergic diseases of the skin & lungs Humoral mediators of inflammation in human Lyme Borreliosis

P50AI-16337-13 0005 (AITC) GOREVIC, PETER Pathogenesis of allergic diseases of the skin & lungs Mediators of inflammation in cryoglobulinemia

P50AI-16337-13 0006 (AITC) SMALDONE, GERALD Pathogenesis of allergic diseases of the skin & lungs Lung mechanics--Reactivity and mucus clearance in asthma

R01AI-16348-12 (VR) NAYAK, DEBI P UCLA SCHOOL OF MEDICINE 405 HILGARD AVENUE LOS ANGELES, CA 90024-1747 Cloning and expression of influenza viral RNA segments

R01AI-16463-12 (MBC) GUINEY, DONALD G UCSD MEDICAL CENTER 225 DICKINSON STREET SAN DIEGO, CA 92103 Antibiotic resistance of bacteroides

R37AI-16478-12 (MBC) BERG, HOWARD C HARVARD UNIVERSITY 16 DIVINITY AVENUE CAMBRIDGE, MA 02138 Sensory transduction in bacterial chemotaxis

R01AI-16480-09 (SSS) CRAMER, EVA B SUNY HLTH SCIENCE CENTER 450 CLARKSON AVE (BOX #5) BROOKLYN, NY 11203 Transepithelial migration of human neutrophils

R01AI-16501-11 (TMP) MANSOUR, TAG E STANFORD UNIVERSITY STANFORD, CA 94305-5332 Regulatory enzymes in parasitic helminths

R01AI-16567-10 (MBC) MAGEE, PAUL T UNIVERSITY OF MINNESOTA COLLEGE OF BIOLOGICAL SCIENCES ST. PAUL, MN 55108 Establishment of a genetic system in Candida albicans

R01AI-16611-12 (ALY) KNIGHT, KATHERINE L UNIV OF ILLINOIS AT CHICAGO 2160 SOUTH FIRST AVENUE MAYWOOD, IL 60153 Genetic control of immunoglobulin variable regions

R01AI-16618-09 (BM) FRIEDMAN, HERMAN COLLEGE OF MEDICINE 12901 NO 30TH STREET TAMPA, FLA 33612 Legionnaire's disease--Cell mediated immunity

R01AI-16637-11 (GMA) WESTON, WILLIAM L U OF COLORADO HLTH SCIS CTR 4200 EAST NINTH AVE B153 DENVER, CO 80262 Erythema multiforme--A clinical pathogenetic study

R22AI-16687-12 (EVR) RAMIG, ROBERT F BAYLOR COLLEGE OF MEDICINE ONE BAYLOR PLAZA HOUSTON, TEX 77030 Genetics of the rotaviruses

R37AI-16689-12 (IMB) PIOUS, DONALD A UNIVERSITY OF WASHINGTON SEATTLE, WA 98195 Genetic regulation of lymphoid differentiation antigens

R01AI-16692-11 (BM) NORGARD, MICHAEL V UNIV OF TEX SW MEDICAL CTR 5323 HARRY HINES BOULEVARD DALLAS, TX 75235-9048 Molecular analysis of T. pallidum membrane immunogens

R01AI-16722-09 (BM) CLEARY, P PATRICK UNIVERSITY OF MINNESOTA MINNEAPOLIS, MN 55455 Genetic control of virulence in group A streptococci

R01AI-16732-11 (BM) KLEMPNER, MARK S NEW ENGLAND MEDICAL CENTER 750 WASHINGTON STREET BOSTON, MA 02111 Biology of the human neutrophil plasma membrane

R01AI-16756-09 (BM) LEVY, STUART B TUFTS UNIV MEDICAL SCHOOL 136 HARRISON AVENUE BOSTON, MA 02111 Multiple resistance to antibiotics

R22AI-16776-13 (BM) FINKELSTEIN, RICHARD A UNIVERSITY OF MISSOURI COLUMBIA, MO 65212 Escherichia coli LT-related enterotoxins

R37AI-16790-12 (NSS) CHAKRABARTY, ANANDA M UNIV OF ILLINOIS COLLEGE OF ME 835 SOUTH WOLCOTT AVE CHICAGO, IL 60612 Pseudomonas infection in cystic fibrosis

R37AI-16794-10 (BM) TOMASZ, ALEXANDER ROCKEFELLER UNIVERSITY 1230 YORK AVENUE NEW YORK, NY 10021 Beta lactam resistance and tolerance in pneumococci

R01AI-16795-11 (BM) THOMAS, EDWIN L UNIV OF TENNESSEE, MEMPHIS 894 UNION AVENUE MEMPHIS, TN 38163 Myeloperoxidase and leukocyte granule components

R37AI-16869-12 (SAT) SIMMONS, RICHARD L UNIVERSITY OF PITTSBURGH 497 SCAIFE HALL PITTSBURGH, PA 15261 Effectors in the allograft response

R01AI-16892-12 (MBC) SAUER, ROBERT T MASSACHUSETTS INST OF TECH 77 MASSACHUSETTS AVE CAMBRIDGE, MA 02139 Repressor and antirepressor proteins of bacteriophage

R01AI-16919-13 (IMB) MELVOLD, ROGER W NORTHWEST UNIV MEDICAL SCHOOL 303 EAST CHICAGO AVENUE CHICAGO, IL 60611 Maintenance of a histocompatibility mutant mouse colony

R01AI-16943-12 (MCHA) DANISHEFSKY, SAMUEL J YALE UNIVERSITY 1504A YALE STATION NEW HAVEN, CT 06520 The synthesis of potential antibodies

R01AI-16945-10 (TMP) MC LEOD, RIMA L MICHAEL REESE HOSPITAL LAKE SHORE DRIVE AT 31ST ST. CHICAGO, IL 60616 Immune response to ingested Toxoplasma

R01AI-16963-12 (TMP) MURRAY, HENRY W CORNELL UNIV MEDICAL COLL 1300 YORK AVENUE NEW YORK, NY 10021 Mononuclear phagocyte killing of leishmania parasites

R01AI-17021-12 (ALY) KING, TE PIAO ROCKEFELLER UNIVERSITY 1230 YORK AVENUE NEW YORK, N Y 10021 Immunochemical studies of insect venom allergens

R01AI-17069-12 (EDC) ADLER, STUART P MEDICAL COLLEGE OF VIRGINIA PO BOX 163, MCV STATION RICHMOND, VA 23298 Epidemiology of cytomegalovirus

R37AI-17134-12 (IMB) KAPPLER, JOHN W NATIONAL JEWISH CENTER 1400 JACKSON STREET DENVER, CO 80206 Regulatory mechanisms in the immune response

R01AI-17142-12 (IMB) TEW, JOHN G VIRGINIA COMMONWEALTH UNIV BOX 678 - MCV STATION RICHMOND, VA 23298-0678 Role of follicular antigen-binding dendritic cells

R01AI-17162-10 (EI) VOLKMAN, ALVIN EAST CAROLINA UNIVERSITY SCHOOL OF MEDICINE GREENVILLE, NC 27858-4353 Mechanisms of macrophage diversity

R01AI-17205-12 (VR) PAGANO, JOSEPH S UNIV OF NC AT CHAPEL HILL CB# 7295 CHAPEL HILL, NC 27599 Antiviral drugs and Epstein-Barr virus infection states

R01AI-17242-10 (BM) SANFORD, BARBARA A UNIV OF TEXAS HLTH SCI CTR 7703 FLOYD CURL DRIVE SAN ANTONIO, TX 78284-7758 Mechanism of bacterial superinfection

R01AI-17246-11 (EVR) WILCOX, KENT W MEDICAL COLLEGE OF WISCONSIN 8701 WATERTOWN PLANK RD MILWAUKEE, WI 53226 Regulation of gene expression in HSV infected cells

R01AI-17252-07A3 (TMP) ARLIAN, LARRY G WRIGHT STATE UNIVERSITY 235A BIOLOGICAL SCIENCES BLDG DAYTON, OH 45435 Scabies--biology, culture, host specificity and antigens

R01AI-17258-12 (SSS) BURAKOFF, STEVEN J DANA-FARBER CANCER INSTITUTE 44 BINNEY STREET BOSTON, MA 02115 CD4 and CD8 in induction and specificity of T lymphocytes

R01AI-17265-11 (EVR) FLINT, SARAH J PRINCETON UNIVERSITY LEWIS THOMAS LABORATORY PRINCETON, NJ 08544 Regulation of gene expression in ad2 infected cells

R01AI-17270-12 (BBCB) BURNETT, ROGER M WISTAR INSTITUTE 36TH & SPRUCE STREETS PHILADELPHIA, PA 19104 Molecular structure of the adenovirus capsid

R01AI-17287-10 (PC) WYKLE, ROBERT L WAKE FOREST UNIVERSITY 300 SOUTH HAWTHORNE ROAD WINSTON-SALEM, N C 27103 Stimulation of neutrophil arachidonate metabolism

R01AI-17292-12 (MBC) BASSFORD, PHILIP J, JR UNIV OF NORTH CAROLINA CB7290 804 FLOB CHAPEL HILL, NC 27599 Factors determining protein localization in E coli

R01AI-17297-12 (TMP) LEA, ARDEN O UNIVERSITY OF GEORGIA ATHENS, GA 30602 Endocrinology of mosquito reproduction

R01AI-17330-11 (ALY) PERRY, ROBERT P INSTITUTE FOR CANCER RESEARCH 7701 BURHOLME AVENUE PHILADELPHIA, PA 19111 Studies of immunoglobulin and ribosomal protein genes

R01AI-17331-11 (EVR) PALMENBERG, ANN C UNIV OF WISCONSIN 1655 LINDEN DRIVE MADISON, WI 53706 Cardioviral proteases and comparative genome structure

R01AI-17340-11 (BM) BACCHI, CYRUS J PACE UNIV/HASKINS LABS 41

PARK ROW NEW YORK, NY 10038 Polyamines in trypanosomes - function and metabolism
P01AI-17354-10S1 (SRC) PETERSON, PER A SCRIPPS CLINIC & RES FDN 10666 NORTH TORREY PINES RD LA JOLLA, CA 92037 Complement--Immunology and structure
P01AI-17354-10S1 0001 (SRC) MULLER-EBERHARD, HANS J Complement--Immunology and structure Biochemistry of human complement
P01AI-17354-10S1 0002 (SRC) COCHRANE, CHARLES G Complement--Immunology and structure Molecular mechanisms of leukocyte stimulation
P01AI-17354-10S1 0003 (SRC) COOPER, NEIL R Complement--Immunology and structure Complement--Immunology and strucutre
P01AI-17354-10S1 0004 (SRC) HUGLI, TONY E Complement--Immunology and structure Receptors to inflammatory mediators
P01AI-17354-10S1 0006 (SRC) FEY, GEORG H Complement--Immunology and structure Human leukocyte receptors for chemotactic peptides
P01AI-17354-10S1 0007 (SRC) TACK, BRIAN F Complement--Immunology and structure Structure of factor H and its homolog--The C3b receptor
P01AI-17354-10S1 9001 (SRC) MULLER-EBERHARD, HANS J Complement--Immunology and structure Core
R01AI-17375-10 (TMP) STUART, KENNETH D SEATTLE BIOMEDICAL RES INST 4 NICKERSON ST. #100 SEATTLE, WA 98109-1651 Trypanosome variant antigen genes
R01AI-17386-10 (VR) EHRENFELD, ELVERA R UNIVERSITY OF UTAH SCHOOL OF MEDICINE SALT LAKE CITY, UTAH 84132 Poliovirus RNA replication
R01AI-17416-06 (TMP) SILVERMAN, DAVID J UNIVERSITY OF MARYLAND 655 W BALTIMORE STREET BALTIMORE, MD 21201 Rickettsia rickettsii in human endothelial cells
R01AI-17418-11 (VR) WEISS, SUSAN R UNIVERSITY OF PENNSYLVANIA SCH OF MED/JOHNSON PAVILION PHILADELPHIA, PA 19104-6076 Coronaviruses--Molecular biology and persistence
R37AI-17474-11 (BM) IANDOLO, JOHN J KANSAS STATE UNIVERSITY VCS BUILDING MANHATTAN, KS 66506 Studies on staphylococcal toxins
R01AI-17484-10 (BM) BELL, ROBIN G CORNELL UNIVERSITY NYS COLLEGE OF VET MEDICINE ITHACA, NY 14853-6401 Immunobiology of rapid expulsion
R01AI-17508-11 (MBC) GUSSIN, GARY N UNIVERSITY OF IOWA IOWA CITY, IA 52242 Genetic and biochemical analysis of promoter function
R01AI-17565-11 (IMB) HOOD, LEROY E CALIFORNIA INST OF TECHNOLOGY PASADENA, CA 91125 Isolation and characterization of T-cell receptor genes
R01AI-17572-11 (BM) MUNSON, ROBERT S ST LOUIS CHILDREN'S HOSPITAL 400 SOUTH KINGSHIGHWAY ST LOUIS, MO 63110 Outer membrane proteins of Haemophilus influenzae
R01AI-17595-11 (MCHA) MC GARVEY, GLENN J UNIVERSITY OF VIRGINIA MCCORMICK ROAD CHARLOTTESVILLE, VA 22901 Synthetic studies on the polyene macrolide antibiotics
R22AI-17615-11 (TMP) WYLER, DAVID J NEW ENGLAND MED CTR HOSP NEMCH BOX 041 750 WASHINGTON S BOSTON, MA 02111 Fibroblast stimulation in Schistosomiasis
R01AI-17621-11 (BM) HANSEN, ERIC J U OF TX SOUTHWSTN MED CTR @ DA DALLAS, TX 75235 Surface antigens of Haemophilus influenzae type B
R37AI-17651-12 (ALY) TERHORST, CORNELIS P BETH ISRAEL HOSPITAL 330 BROOKLINE AVENUE BOSTON, MA 02215 Biochemical studies of human T cell surface markers
R01AI-17653-10 (MET) LIPSKY, PETER E UNIV OF TEXAS SW MED CTR 5323 HARRY HINES BLVD DALLAS, TX 75235 Sterol metabolism and human mononuclear cell function
R01AI-17654-08 (EVR) KITCHINGMAN, GEOFFREY R ST JUDE CHILDREN'S RES HOSP 322 N LAUDERDALE ST/BOX 318 MEMPHIS, TN 38101-0318 Genetic and biochemical analysis of Ad5 region 2
R01AI-17672-12 (EI) WELSH, RAYMOND M, JR UNIVERSITY OF MASS MED CTR WORCESTER, MA 01655 Immunity and virus disease
R37AI-17712-12 (ALY) MARCUS, DONALD M BAYLOR COLLEGE OF MEDICINE ONE BAYLOR PLAZA HOUSTON, TX 77030 Glycolipid cell membrane antigens
R01AI-17758-10 (IMS) KLEBANOFF, SEYMOUR J UNIVERSITY OF WASHINGTON SCHOOL OF MEDICINE SEATTLE, WA 98195 Mast cell-eosinophil interaction in allergic injury
R01AI-17808-11 (MBC) DAHLQUIST, FREDERICK W UNIVERSITY OF OREGON EUGENE, OR 97403 Mechanistic studies of bacterial chemotaxis
R01AI-17828-08A2 (TMP) AZAD, ABDU F UNIV OF MARYLAND SCH OF MED 655 WEST BALTIMORE STREET BALTIMORE, MD 21201 Murine typhus--Vector biology and transmission
R01AI-17876-11 (MBC) SALYERS, ABIGAIL A UNIVERSITY OF ILLINOIS MICROBIO DPT/131 BURRILL HALL URBANA, IL 61801 Catabolism of polysaccharides by colonic bacteroides
R37AI-17879-11 (NSS) TONEGAWA, SUSUMU MASSACHUSETTS INST OF TECH 77 MASSACHUSETTS AVENUE CAMBRIDGE, MA 02139 Developmental regulations
R37AI-17892-11 (ALY) PARHAM, PETER STANFORD UNIVERSITY SCH OF MED SHERMAN FAIRCHILD SCIENCE BLDG STANFORD, CA 94305-5400 Structural biology of HLA-A, B antigens
R01AI-17897-10 (ALY) COOK, RICHARD G BAYLOR COLLEGE OF MEDICINE MICHAEL E DEBAKEY CTR HOUSTON, TX 77030 Biochemistry of Qa-TLa region gene products
R01AI-17899-04A5 (TMP) CLARKSON, ALLEN B, JR NEW YORK UNIVERSITY 550 FIRST AVE NEW YORK, NY 10016 Mitochondrial electron transport in African trypanosomes
R01AI-17904-06 (BM) SCHELD, W MICHAEL UNIVERSITY OF VIRGINIA BOX 385 CHARLOTTESVILLE, VA 22908 Pathogenesis and pathophysiology of bacterial meningitis
R01AI-17938-11 (BM) ANDERSON, PORTER W UNIVERSITY OF ROCHESTER 601 ELMWOOD AVE; BOX 690 ROCHESTER, NY 14642 Carbohydrate vaccines for H influenzae B and S pneumoniae
R01AI-17962-10 (BM) GRANOFF, DAN M ST LOUIS CHILDREN'S HOSPITAL 400 S. KINGSHIGHWAY BLVD. ST. LOUIS, MO 63110 Genetic control of immune responses to polysaccharides
R01AI-17966-11 (ALY) WAKELAND, EDWARD K UNIVERSITY OF FLORIDA BOX J-275, JHMHC/COLL OF MED GAINESVILLE, FL 32610 Structural analysis of I region variance
R01AI-17979-09 (EI) WALKER, WILLIAM S ST JUDE CHILDREN'S RES HOSP 332 N LAUDERDALE, BOX 318 MEMPHIS, TN 38101 The ontogeny of mononuclear phagocytes
R01AI-17986-10 (PB) PRATT, REX F WESLEYAN UNIVERSITY MIDDLETOWN, CT 06457 Beta-lactamases--Active site chemistry
R01AI-17992-11 (BBCB) WRIGHT, CHRISTINE S VA COMMONWEALTH UNIV/MED COLL BOX 614 MCV STATION RICHMOND, VA 23298-0614 Structure and interaction of proteins with membranes
R01AI-17997-12 (ALY) CEBRA, JOHN J UNIVERSITY OF PENNSYLVANIA PHILADELPHIA, PA 19104 Cellular and humoral bases of mucosal immune response
R01AI-18000-10 (BM) HEWLETT, ERIK L UNIVERSITY OF VIRGINIA BOX 419, SCHOOL OF MEDICINE CHARLOTTESVILLE, VA 22908 Bordetella cyclase--Structure and biological activity
R01AI-18016-12 (ALY) TUCKER, PHILIP W UNIV OF TX SOUTHWESTERN MED CT 5323 HARRY HINES BLVD DALLAS, TX 75235 Chain gene organization in transformed B lymphocytes
R01AI-18029-09 (VR) THIMMAPPAYA, BAYAR NORTHWESTERN UNIV MED SCHOOL 303 E CHICAGO AVENUE CHICAGO, IL 60611 Structure and function of adenovirus genome
R37AI-18045-11 (BM) MEKALANOS, JOHN J MICRO & MOLECULAR GENETICS 200 LONGWOOD AVE BOSTON, MA 02115 Genetic analysis of toxinogenesis in vibrio cholerae
R01AI-18073-10A1 (ALY) KURLANDER, ROGER J DUKE MEDICAL CENTER DEPT OF MEDICINE DURHAM, N C 27710 T cell phagocyte interaction in antimicrobial immunity
R01AI-18083-11 (VR) REISS, CAROL S NEW YORK UNIVERSITY WASHINGTON SQUARE NEW YORK, NY 10003 Regulation & specificity of the immune response to VSV-g
R01AI-18094-11 (EVR) CONDIT, RICHARD C UNIVERSITY OF FLORIDA BOX J-266 GAINESVILLE, FL 31610 Vaccinia virus biochemical genetics
R01AI-18124-11 (ALY) ORR, HARRY T UNIVERSITY OF MINNESOTA BOX 198 UMHC MINNEAPOLIS, MN 55455 Molecular biological studies on the HLA system
R01AI-18125-10 (BM) SIBER, GEORGE R DANA-FARBER CANCER INSTITUTE 44 BINNEY STREET BOSTON, MA 02115 Preparation of bacterial polysaccharide immune globulin
R01AI-18149-09 (BM) ZABRISKIE, JOHN B ROCKEFELLER UNIVERSITY 1230 YORK AVENUE NEW YORK, NY 10021 Mechanisms of streptococcal-host interactions
R01AI-18188-11 (BM) MUNFORD, ROBERT S U TEXAS SW MED CTR AT DALLAS 5323 HARRY HINES BOULEVARD DALLAS, TX 75235 Interactions of endotoxin with human plasma & cells
R01AI-18203-09 (EVR) AIR, GILLIAN M UNIV OF ALABAMA AT BIRMINGHAM UNIVERSITY STATION BIRMINGHAM, AL 35294 Influenza B--Gene sequences
R01AI-18220-10 (IMS) THOMPSON, LINDA F OKLAHOMA MEDICAL RES FDN 825 N E 13TH STREET OKLAHOMA CITY, OK 73104 Purine metabolism and human lymphocyte maturation
R01AI-18228-10 (EVR) LEVINE, MYRON THE UNIVERSITY OF MICHIGAN MEDICAL SCHOOL ANN ARBOR, MI 48109-0618 Genetics of herpesvirus-host cell interactions
R01AI-18234-11 (MBC) POTEETE, ANTHONY R DEPT OF MOL GENETICS & MICROBI 55 LAKE AVENUE NORTH WORCESTER, MA 01655 Bacteriophage P22 essential recombination function
R37AI-18270-11 (VR) BALL, LAURENCE A UNIV OF ALABAMA @ BIRMINGHAM UAB STATION BIRMINGHAM, AL 35294 Vaccinia virus DNA recombination and recombinants
R01AI-18272-10 (EVR) DASGUPTA, ASIM UCLA SCHOOL OF MEDICINE 43-239 CHS LOS ANGELES, CA 90024-1747 In vitro replication of poliovirus
R01AI-18283-11 (MBC) WEISBLUM, BERNARD UNIV OF WISCONSIN SYSTEM 1300 UNIVERSITY AVENUE MADISON, WISC 53706 Inducible antibiotic resistance
R01AI-18289-11 (VR) COHEN, GARY H UNIV. OF PENNSYLVANIA DEPT OF MICROBIOLOGY PHILADELPHIA, PA 19104-6002 Studies of glycoprotein D of herpes simplex virus
R01AI-18306-11 (ALY) BAIRD, BARBARA A CORNELL UNIVERSITY ITHACA, NY 14853 Structure-function relationships of the IgE receptor
R01AI-18316-11 (EVR) BONA, CONSTANTIN A MOUNT SINAI SCHOOL OF MEDICINE ONE GUSTAVE LEVY PL/BOX 1124 NEW YORK, NY 10029 Idiotype vaccine producing anti-influenza virus immunity
R37AI-18357-11 (BM) BRENNAN, PATRICK J COLORADO STATE UNIVERSITY FORT COLLINS, CO 80523 Specific antigens of atypical mycobacteria
R01AI-18382-08 (EVR) BRINTON, MARGO A GEORGIA STATE UNIVERSITY UNIVERSITY PLAZA ATLANTA, GA 30303 Cellular gene product modulates flavivirus RNA synthesis
R01AI-18384-10 (BM) APICELLA, MICHAEL A S U N Y @ BUFFALO CLINICAL CTR ERIE CTY MED CTR/462 GRIDER ST BUFFALO, NY 14215 Lipopolysaccharide of N. gonorrhoeae
R01AI-18398-09 (BNP) RODRIGUEZ, ELOY UNIVERSITY OF CALIFORNIA PHYTOCHEMISTRY & TOXICOLOGY LA IRVINE, CA 92717 Dermatotoxicological studies of allergenic plants
R01AI-18401-10 (BM) PETERSON, JOHNNY W UNIV OF TEXAS MEDICAL BRANCH DEPT OF MICROBIOLOGY, J-19 GALVESTON, TX 77550 Virulence factors in the pathogenesis of salmonellosis
K06AI-18424-29 (NSS) MALEK, EMILE A TULANE MEDICAL CENTER 1501 CANAL STREET NEW ORLEANS, LA 70112 Epidemiology and control of schistosomiasis
R01AI-18427-10 (BM) KOMUNIECKI, RICHARD W UNIVERSITY OF TOLEDO TOLEDO, OH 43606 Volatile acid formation by parasitic helminths
R01AI-18449-10 (VR) RUYECHAN, WILLIAM T UNIFORMED SERV UNIV HEALTH SCI 4301 JONES BRIDGE ROAD BETHESDA, MD 20814-4799 Structure and function of varicella zoster DNA
R01AI-18462-09 (BM) HULL, RICHARD A BAYLOR COLL OF MED 1 BAYLOR PLAZA HOUSTON, TX 77030 Virulence factors in uropathogenic enterobacteriaceae
R01AI-18471-09 (BM) ELLNER, JERROLD J UNIV HOSPITALS OF CLEVELAND 2109 ADELBERT ROAD CLEVELAND, OH 44106 Immunosuppression in mycobacterial diseases
R01AI-18499-10 (IMB) CAPRA, J DONALD U OF TEXAS SW MED CTR AT DALLA 5323 HARRY HINES BLVD DALLAS, TX 75235 Nucleic acid studies of anti-arsonate hybridomas

PROJECT NO., ORGANIZATIONAL UNIT., INVESTIGATOR, ADDRESS, TITLE

R01AI-18571-10 (BM) WEISS, JERROLD P NEW YORK UNIV MEDICAL CENTER 550 FIRST AVENUE NEW YORK, NY 10016 Neutrophils and bacterial phospholipid degradation
R37AI-18599-10 (VR) HELENIUS, ARI H YALE UNIVERSITY 333 CEDAR STREET NEW HAVEN, CT 06510 Cell biology of virus entry
R37AI-18613-10 (IMS) BUCKLEY, REBECCA H DUKE UNIVERSITY MEDICAL CENTER BOX 2898 DURHAM, NC 27710 Haploidentical stem cell education in the human thymus
R01AI-18634-09 (IMB) GREY, HOWARD M CYTEL CORPORATION 11099 NORTH TORREY PINES ROAD LA JOLLA, CA 92037 Molecular events in antigen recognition
R01AI-18637-09 (BM) BLAKE, MILAN S THE ROCKEFELLER UNIVERSITY 1230 YORK AVENUE NEW YORK, NY 10021-6399 The functional role of the major outer membrane protein
R01AI-18641-10 (VR) MASON, WILLIAM S INSTITUTE FOR CANCER RESEARCH 7701 BURHOLME AVENUE PHILADELPHIA, PA 19111 Molecular basis for hepadnaviral infections
R01AI-18694-08 (TMP) RIBEIRO, JOSE M C UNIVERSITY OF ARIZONA 410 FORBES BLDG TUCSON, AZ 85721 Regulation and function of salivation in vectors
R01AI-18697-11 (ALY) CONRAD, DANIEL H VIRGINIA COMMONWEALTH UNIV BOX 678 MCV STATION RICHMOND, VA 23298-0678 Structure and function of the B lymphocyte Fc receptor
R37AI-18738-11 (MBC) HERSKOWITZ, IRA UNIVERSITY OF CALIFORNIA SAN FRANCISCO, CA 94143-0448 Genetic control of mating in yeast
P01AI-18745-10 (AITC) MESTECKY, JIRI F UNIV OF ALABAMA AT BIRMINGHAM UAB STATION BIRMINGHAM, AL 35294 Physiology and immunopathology of IgA immune system
P01AI-18745-10 0001 (AITC) MESTECKY, JIRI F Physiology and immunopathology of IgA immune system Common mucosal system in humans
P01AI-18745-10 0002 (AITC) GALLA, JOHN H Physiology and immunopathology of IgA immune system Immunopathogenesis of IgA nephropathy
P01AI-18745-10 0003 (AITC) SCHROHENLOHER, RALPH E Physiology and immunopathology of IgA immune system IgA rheumatoid factors and its complexes
P01AI-18745-10 0004 (AITC) COOPER, MAX D Physiology and immunopathology of IgA immune system Role of IgA B-cells in disease
P01AI-18745-10 9001 (AITC) MESTECKY, JIRI F Physiology and immunopathology of IgA immune system Core--Tissue processing and cell culture
R01AI-18757-11 (EVR) THORLEY-LAWSON, DAVID A TUFTS UNIVERSITY 136 HARRISON AVENUE BOSTON, MA 02111 Host immunity to EBV infection in vivo and in vitro
R01AI-18758-11 (BBCA) THOMAS, GEORGE J, JR UNIVERSITY OF MISSOURI 5100 ROCKHILL ROAD KANSAS CITY, MO 64110-2499 Structure interactions and exchanges of nucleic acids
R01AI-18764-10 (BBCA) JOHNSON, JOHN E PURDUE UNIVERSITY WEST LAFAYETTE, IN 47907 High resolution structure of multi component viruses
R01AI-18768-07A4 (TMP) ALDERETE, JOHN F UNIV OF TEXAS HEALTH SCI CTR 7703 FLOYD CURL DRIVE SAN ANTONIO, TX 78284-7758 Biology of Trichomonas vaginalis cytadherence
R01AI-18782-10 (EVR) GANEM, DONALD E UNIVERSITY OF CALIFORNIA 3RD & PARNASSUS AVENUES SAN FRANCISCO, CA 94143 Molecular biology of the hepatitis B-type viruses
R01AI-18785-10 (IMB) KAPPLER, JOHN W NATL JEWISH CTR/IMM & RESP MED 1400 JACKSON STREET DENVER, CO 80206 Characteristics of T cell receptors
R01AI-18790-10 (IMB) SAKANO, HITOSHI UNIV OF CALIF-3573 LIFE SCIE BERKELEY, CA 94720 Somatic DNA recombination in antibody genes
R01AI-18797-09 (BM) VOGEL, STEFANIE N UNIFORMED SERVICES UNIVERSITY 4301 JONES BRIDGE ROAD BETHESDA, MD 20814 Differentiative signals for macrophage activation
R01AI-18841-09 (TMP) RAVDIN, JONATHAN I V.A. MEDICAL CENTER 10701 EAST BOULEVARD CLEVELAND, OH 44106 Mechanisms of E histolytica adherence and cytolysis
R22AI-18867-09 (TMP) LOVERDE, PHILIP T STATE UNIVERSITY OF NEW YORK 203 SHERMAN HALL BUFFALO, NY 14214 A molecularly-defined vaccine for schistosomiasis
R01AI-18873-09 (BM) MANNING, JERRY E UNIV OF CALIFORNIA, IRVINE IRVINE, CA 92717 Trypanosoma cruzi--Isolation of surface antigen genes
R01AI-18882-09 (IMB) RICH, ROBERT R BAYLOR COLLEGE OF MEDICINE ONE BAYLOR PLAZA HOUSTON, TX 77030 T cell responses to non-H-2 antigens of chromosome 17
R37AI-18895-10 (BM) MURPHY, JUNEANN W UNIV OF OKLAHOMA HLTH SCIS CTR P O BOX 26901 OKLAHOMA CITY, OK 73190 Natural cell-mediated resistance in cryptococcosis
R37AI-18939-08 (ALY) PIERCE, SUSAN K NORTHWESTERN UNIVERSITY 2153 SHERIDAN ROAD EVANSTON, IL 60208 Specificity of individual helper T lymphocytes
R01AI-18958-10 (IMS) MC GHEE, JERRY R UNIV OF ALABAMA UAB STATION BIRMINGHAM, AL 35294 Cellular and molecular basis for the IgA response
R01AI-18985-10 (MBC) MATSUMURA, PHILIP UNIVERSITY OF ILLINOIS PO BOX 4348 CHICAGO, IL 60680 Molecular biology of MOT and the CHE gene products
R01AI-18987-11 (BIO) KOWALCZYKOWSKI, STEPHEN C UNIVERSITY OF CALIFORNIA DAVIS, CA 95616-8665 Mechanistic studies of genetic recombination
R01AI-18988-08 (BM) LUKEHART, SHEILA A HARBORVIEW MEDICAL CENTER 325 NINTH AVENUE SEATTLE, WA 98104 Immunogens of T. pallidum--Identification and function
R37AI-18998-10 (EVR) PALESE, PETER M MOUNT SINAI SCHOOL OF MEDICINE 1 GUSTAVE L LEVY PL, BOX 1124 NEW YORK, NY 10029 Genetic analysis of influenza A, B and C viruses
R01AI-19007-08 (EI) BACH, FRITZ H UNIVERSITY OF MINNESOTA 420 DELEWARE STREET S E MINNEAPOLIS, MN 55455 Molecular studies of NK cells and NK/LAK function
R01AI-19018-10 (MBC) CROSA, JORGE H OREGON HEALTH SCIENCES UNIV 3181 SW SAM JACKSON PARK RD PORTLAND, OR 97201 Iron uptake as a virulence factor in pathogenic vibrios

PROJECT NO., ORGANIZATIONAL UNIT., INVESTIGATOR, ADDRESS, TITLE

R37AI-19031-10 (BM) ANDERSON, DONALD C TEXAS CHILDREN'S CLIN CARE CTR 8080 N STADIUM DRIVE, STE 2100 HOUSTON, TX 77054 PMN leukocyte motility and adherence in neonates
R01AI-19032-10 (PC) SKLAR, LARRY A UNIVERSITY OF NEW MEXICO 915 STANFORD DR ALBUQUERQUE, NM 87131 Ligand-receptor-G protein dynamics and neutrophil response
R01AI-19036-09 (MBC) SUSKIND, MIRIAM UNIV OF SOUTHERN CALIFORNIA 825 WEST 37TH ST/SHS 172 MC 13 LOS ANGELES, CA 90089-1340 Molecular mechanisms of DNA transportation
R01AI-19042-07A2 (ALY) KABAT, ELVIN A COLUMBIA UNIVERSITY 701 W 168TH STREET NEW YORK, N Y 10032 Hybridoma and myeloma antibody combining sites
R01AI-19047-09 (IMB) BIKOFF, ELIZABETH K MOUNT SINAI SCHOOL OF MEDICINE ONE GUSTAVE L LEVY PLACE NEW YORK, NY 10029 Inherited control mechanism in Ig gene expression
R01AI-19053-11 (ALY) FANGER, MICHAEL W DARTMOUTH MEDICAL SCHOOL DEPARTMENT OF MICROBIOLOGY HANOVER, NH 03756 Human leukocyte subpopulations
R01AI-19071-18 (SAT) TILNEY, NICHOLAS L BRIGHAM AND WOMEN'S HOSPITAL 75 FRANCIS STREET BOSTON, MA 02115 Role of IL-2 receptor positive cells in transplantation
R37AI-19084-09 (EVR) AIR, GILLIAN M UNIV OF ALABAMA AT BIRMINGHAM UNIVERSITY STATION BIRMINGHAM, AL 35294 Structure of antigenic sites on influenza virus proteins
P50AI-19093-08 (AITC) RICHERSON, HAL B UNIVERSITY OF IOWA COLLEGE OF MEDICINE IOWA CITY, IA 52242 Immunologic mechanisms in atopic bronchial asthma
P50AI-19093-08 0002 (AITC) HUNNINGHAKE, GARY W Immunologic mechanisms in atopic bronchial asthma Pathogenic mechanisms in asthma at sites of disease
P50AI-19093-08 0005 (AITC) RICHERSON, HAL B Immunologic mechanisms in atopic bronchial asthma Immunopathology and pathophysiology of allergic bronchial asthma
P50AI-19093-08 0006 (AITC) CASALE, THOMAS B Immunologic mechanisms in atopic bronchial asthma Effects of mast cell mediators and drugs on lung receptors
P50AI-19093-08 0007 (AITC) MERCHANT, J A Immunologic mechanisms in atopic bronchial asthma Epidemiological assessment of laboratory animal allergy
R01AI-19146-08 (BM) OHMAN, DENNIS E UNIV OF TENNESSEE, MEMPHIS MEMPHIS, TN 38163 Activation of alginate genes in pseudomonas aeruginosa
R01AI-19148-10 (ALY) SEIDMAN, JONATHAN G HARVARD MEDICAL SCHOOL 25 SHATTUCK STREET BOSTON, MA 02115 T-cell antigen receptor--Function and development
R01AI-19149-06 (BM) COLE, GARRY T UNIVERSITY OF TEXAS AUSTIN, TX 78713-7640 Immunoreactive macromolecules in coccidioides cell types
R22AI-19199-08 (MBC) KLEI, THOMAS R LOUISIANA STATE UNIVERSITY SCHOOL OF VETERINARY MEDICINE BATON ROUGE, LA 70803 Lymphatic lesion pathogenesis in Brugia-infected jirds
R37AI-19217-10 (BM) STRAND, METTE JOHNS HOPKINS U SCH OF MED 725 N WOLFE ST BALTIMORE, MD 21205 Immuno-protective and pathogenic schistosome antigens
R01AI-19222-10 (IMS) TACK, BRIAN F RESEARCH INST OF SCRIPPS CLINI 10666 NORTH TORREY PINES RD LA JOLLA, CA 92037 Structural basis of C3 functions
R01AI-19244-10 (VR) LAI, MICHAEL M UNIV OF SOUTHERN CALIFORNIA 2011 ZONAL AVENUE LOS ANGELES, CA 90033 Murine coronavirus RNA synthesis
R01AI-19262-08 (HAR) FIREMAN, PHILIP CHILDREN'S HOSP OF PITTSBURGH 3705 FIFTH AVE AT DESOTO ST PITTSBURGH, PA 15213 Immune mechanisms of middle ear disease
R01AI-19276-10 (MBC) SHUMAN, HOWARD A COLUMBIA UNIVERSITY 701 WEST 168TH ST NEW YORK, NY 10032 Active transport of maltose in E. coli
R01AI-19278-08S1 (ALY) WINKELSTEIN, JERRY A JOHNS HOPKINS HOSPITAL 600 N WOLFE STREET BALTIMORE, MD 21205 Genetically determined deficiency of C3
R01AI-19296-10 (MBC) SIMON, MELVIN I CALIFORNIA INST OF TECHNOLOGY PASADENA, CA 91125 Mechanisms of motility/chemotaxis in bacteria
R22AI-19302-06 (BM) GORMUS, BOBBY J TULANE UNIVERSITY DELTA REGIONAL PRIMATE RES CTR COVINGTON, LA 70433 Experimental leprosy/vaccine studies in mangabeys
R01AI-19304-07S1 (BM) FERRETTI, JOSEPH J UNIV OF OKLAHOMA HEALTH SCI CT 940 STANTON L YOUNG BLVD OKLAHOMA CITY, OK 73104 Determinants of virulence in group A streptococci
R01AI-19310-09 (MBC) DUNNY, GARY M UNIVERSITY OF MINNESOTA 1479 GORTNER AVENUE ST PAUL, MN 55108 Genetic functions of conjugative Streptococcal R factor
R37AI-19335-11 (IMB) BEVAN, MICHAEL J UNIVERSITY OF WASHINGTON SEATTLE, WA 98195 Cytotoxic response to histocompatibility antigens
R01AI-19347-08 (TMP) HANDMAN, EMANUELA WALTER & ELIZA HALL INST/MED R P O ROYAL MELBOURNE HOSP VICTORIA 3050, AUSTRALIA Characterization and cloning of Leishmania antigens
R01AI-19350-07A1 (IMS) SHACKELFORD, PENELOPE G WASHINGTON UNIVERSITY 400 S. KINGSHIGHWAY ST LOUIS, MO 63110 Children's antibodies to polysaccharides-- V region genes
R01AI-19353-08 (BM) BRUBAKER, ROBERT R MICHIGAN STATE UNIVERSITY EAST LANSING, MI 48824-1101 Ca2+ & the VWA+ virulence factor of Yersiniae
R01AI-19358-10 (BIO) SANTI, DANIEL V UNIVERSITY OF CALIFORNIA SAN FRANCISCO, CA 94143-0446 Enzymes of folate metabolism in protozoa--Leishmania
R37AI-19411-10 (IMS) WINCHESTER, ROBERT J HOSPITAL FOR JOINT DISEASES 301 EAST 17TH STREET NEW YORK, NY 10003 B cell alloatigens, molecular basis and disease aspects
R37AI-19428-09 (NSS) CERAMI, ANTHONY ROCKEFELLER UNIVERSITY 1230 YORK AVENUE NEW YORK, N Y 10021 Biochemistry of trypanosomatids--Basis for drug design
R01AI-19469-08 (BM) BLAKE, MILAN S ROCKEFELLER UNIVERSITY 1230 YORK AVENUE NEW YORK, N Y 10021-6399 Surface proteins of Neisseria

gonorrhoeae

R01AI-19478-10 (ALY) ESSER, ALFRED F UNIVERSITY OF FLORIDA GAINESVILLE, FL 32610 Impairment of membrane function by complement

R01AI-19490-10 (EI) STEWART, CARLETON C N Y STATE DEPT OF HEALTH 666 ELM STREET BUFFALO, N Y 14263 Proliferation and function of mononuclear phagocytes

R01AI-19494-10 (EVR) SCHLESINGER, MILTON J WASHINGTON UNIVERSITY SCHOOL OF MEDICINE ST. LOUIS, MO 63110 RNA-envelope virus formation in animal cells

R01AI-19497-08 (BM) MALAMY, MICHAEL H TUFTS UNIVERSITY 136 HARRISON AVENUE BOSTON, MA 02111 Genetic systems to study virulence in bacteroides

P01AI-19499-08 (SRC) KLINMAN, NORMAN R THE SCRIPPS RESEARCH INSTITUTE 10666 NORTH TORREY PINES ROAD LA JOLLA, CA 92037 Basis of determinant recognition by the immune system

P01AI-19499-08 0002 (SRC) LERNER, RICHARD A Basis of determinant recognition by the immune system Catalytic antibodies

P01AI-19499-08 0003 (SRC) KLINMAN, NORMAN R Basis of determinant recognition by the immune system Molecular analysis of B cell clonal development

P01AI-19499-08 0006 (SRC) BEVAN, MICHAEL J Basis of determinant recognition by the immune system Repertoire selection of class I restricted T cells

P01AI-19499-08 0008 (SRC) GETZOFF, ELIZABETH D Basis of determinant recognition by the immune system Structured chemistry of antibody binding to cytochrome c

P01AI-19499-08 9001 (SRC) KLINMAN, NORMAN R Basis of determinant recognition by the immune system Core--Comuptation and computer graphics

P01AI-19512-09 (AITC) MC DEVITT, HUGH O STANFORD UNIVERSITY SCHOOL OF MEDICINE STANFORD, CA 94305-5402 Lymphocyte and macrophage genes proteins and receptors

P01AI-19512-09 0008 (AITC) DAVIS, MARK Lymphocyte and macrophage genes proteins and receptors T cell tolerance in transgenic models

P01AI-19512-09 0009 (AITC) GOODNOW, CHRISTOPHER Lymphocyte and macrophage genes proteins and receptors Transgenic mouse models for B lymphocyte tolerance and autoimmunity

P01AI-19512-09 0010 (AITC) HERZENBERG, LEONARD Lymphocyte and macrophage genes proteins and receptors Selected spontaneous hybridomas and site-specific antigen binding variants

P01AI-19512-09 0011 (AITC) PARNES, JANE Lymphocyte and macrophage genes proteins and receptors Regulation and function of CD8 in transgenic mouse

P01AI-19512-09 0012 (AITC) JONES, PATRICIA Lymphocyte and macrophage genes proteins and receptors MHC control of T cell receptor repertoire for an autoantigen

P01AI-19512-09 0013 (AITC) MCDEVITT, HUGH Lymphocyte and macrophage genes proteins and receptors Production and expression of Ii polypeptide chains

P01AI-19512-09 0014 (AITC) WIESSMAN, IRVING Lymphocyte and macrophage genes proteins and receptors Granzyme A

P01AI-19512-09 9001 (AITC) MCDEVITT, HUGH Lymphocyte and macrophage genes proteins and receptors Core-- Transgenic mouse facility

R37AI-19530-09 (NSS) CLEM, LESTER W UNIV OF MISSISSIPPI MED CTR 2500 NORTH STATE STREET JACKSON, MS 39216-4505 Immunologic studies in ectothermic vertebrates

R01AI-19545-05 (EVR) BROWN, DENNIS T THE UNIV OF TEXAS AT AUSTIN COLLEGE OF NATURAL SCIENCES AUSTIN, TX 78713 Arbovirus growth in cultured insect cells

P01AI-19554-08S1 (MID) NAHMIAS, ANDRE J EMORY UNIVERSITY SCHOOL OF MED 69 BUTLER STREET, S E ATLANTA, GA 30303 Epidemiology and natural history of genital herpes

P01AI-19554-08S1 0001 (MID) PEREIRA, LENORE Epidemiology and natural history of genital herpes HSV proteins and monoclonal antibody production

P01AI-19554-08S1 0002 (MID) DRAGALIN, DAN Epidemiology and natural history of genital herpes HSV antibodies and genital herpes in HMO population

P01AI-19554-08S1 0003 (MID) THOMPSON, SUMNER Epidemiology and natural history of genital herpes Epidemiology and history of genital herpes during pregnancy

P01AI-19554-08S1 0004 (MID) GIBSON, JAMES J Epidemiology and natural history of genital herpes HSV antibodies and genital herpes in college undergraduates

P01AI-19554-08S1 0005 (MID) THOMPSON, SUMNER Epidemiology and natural history of genital herpes HSV antibodies in a population of homosexual men

P01AI-19554-08S1 0006 (MID) JOHNSON, ROBERT E Epidemiology and natural history of genital herpes HSV antibodies in a sample of the U.S. population

P01AI-19554-08S1 0007 (MID) WHITTINGTON, WILLIAM L Epidemiology and natural history of genital herpes Sexual transmission patterns of HSV

P01AI-19554-08S1 0008 (MID) NAHMIAS, ANDRE J Epidemiology and natural history of genital herpes Immunology and genetics of genital HSV infection

P01AI-19554-08S1 0009 (MID) KEYSERLING, HARRY Epidemiology and natural history of genital herpes HSV type antibody testing in pregnant women

P01AI-19554-08S1 9002 (MID) KEYSERLING, HARRY Epidemiology and natural history of genital herpes Clinical-epidemiology coordination core

P01AI-19554-08S1 9003 (MID) NIGIDA, STEVE Epidemiology and natural history of genital herpes Laboratory core

P01AI-19554-08S1 9004 (MID) BROGAN, DONNA Epidemiology and natural history of genital herpes Biostatistics and computer core

R22AI-19585-09 (BM) PERKINS, MARGARET E ROCKEFELLER UNIVERSITY 1230 YORK AVE, BOX 282 NEW YORK, NY 10021 Biochemical studies on erythrocyte invasion by plasmodia

R01AI-19622-09 (EI) SHIN, MOON L UNIVERSITY OF MARYLAND 10 S PINE STREET BALTIMORE, MD 21201 Mechanism of complement attack on nucleated cells

R01AI-19624-09 (IMB) HOOD, LEROY E CALIFORNIA INST OF TECHNOLOGY PASADENA, CA 91125 Transplantation antigens--Expression and function

R01AI-19635-09 (MBC) GROSS, CAROL A UNIVERSITY OF WISCONSIN 1550 LINDEN DRIVE MADISON, WI 53706 Mutational analysis of E coli core RNA polymerase

R01AI-19641-09 (BM) MURPHY, TIMOTHY F SUNY AT BUFFALO/CLIN CTR 462 GRIDER STREET BUFFALO, N Y 14215 Outer membrane proteins of nontypeable H. influenzae

R01AI-19656-09 (HEM) COHEN, HARVEY J UNIV OF ROCHESTER MEDICAL CTR 601 ELMWOOD AVENUE ROCHESTER, NY 14642 White blood cell oxidase--Normal and abnormal

R37AI-19659-09 (NSS) WINKLER, HERBERT H UNIVERSITY OF SOUTH ALABAMA 307 UNIVERSITY BOULEVARD MOBILE, ALA 36688 Lymphokine and antibody--Host defense against rickettsiae

R01AI-19674-07 (IMS) KIYONO, HIROSHI UNIVERSITY OF ALABAMA UAB STATION BIRMINGHAM, AL 35294 Regulation of IgA response in LPS

R01AI-19687-10 (IMB) HANSEN, TED H WASHINGTON UNIV SCH OF MED 660 S EUCLID, BOX 8232 ST LOUIS, MO 63110 H-2D heterogeneity--Immunogenetic and molecular studies

R37AI-19693-09 (TMP) SPIELMAN, ANDREW HARVARD SCHOOL OF PUBLIC HEALT 665 HUNTINGTON AVENUE BOSTON, MA 02115 Host abundance and transmission of Ixodes-borne zoonoses

R22AI-19716-09 (MBC) KAPER, JAMES B UNIV OF MARYLAND SCH OF MED 10 SOUTH PINE STREET BALTIMORE, MD 21201 Development of a live oral cholera vaccine

R55AI-19727-09 (ALY) MARSH, DAVID G JOHNS HOPKINS ASTHMA/ALLERGY C 301 BAYVIEW BLVD BALTIMORE, MD 21224 Immunochemical studies of human response to allergens

R01AI-19737-09 (PTHB) PITHA-ROWE, PAULA M JOHNS HOPKINS UNIV 418 N BOND ST BALTIMORE, MD 21231 Regulation of IFN alpha gene expression

R37AI-19744-10 (NSS) RUTTER, WILLIAM J UNIVERSITY OF CALIFORNIA SAN FRANCISCO, CA 94143-0534 Molecular analysis of hepatitis B virus

R01AI-19747-10 (IMS) LIU, FU-TONG SCRIPPS CLINIC & RESEARCH FDN 10666 N TORREY PINES RD LA JOLLA, CA 92037 Molecular studies of Fc receptors for immunoglobulin E

R01AI-19752-09 (ALY) ROTHENBERG, ELLEN CALIFORNIA INST OF TECHNOLOGY 1201 E CALIFORNIA BLVD PASADENA, CA 91125 Molecular analysis of murine thymocyte differentiation

R37AI-19769-09 (TMP) CHRISTENSEN, BRUCE M UNIVERSITY OF WISCONSIN 1655 LINDEN DRIVE MADISON, WI 53706 Immune response of mosquitoes to filarial worms

R01AI-19775-10 (IMB) AUGUSTIN, ANDREI A NAT. JEWISH CTR/IMM & RESP MED 1400 JACKSON STREET DENVER, CO 80206 T cells--Function and antigen recognition

R01AI-19782-07 (BM) BYRNE, GERALD I UNIV OF WISCONSIN MEDICAL SCH MADISON, WI 53706 Immunity and latency in chlamydial infections

R01AI-19793-08 (PB) ROSEN, BARRY P WAYNE STATE UNIVERSITY 540 E CANFIELD AVE DETROIT, MI 48201 The ATP-coupled arsenical pump of Escherichia coli

R01AI-19800-09 (BM) EDWARDS, MORVEN S BAYLOR COLLEGE OF MEDICINE ONE BAYLOR PLAZA HOUSTON, TX 77030 Opsonins in neonatal immunity to group B streptococci

R01AI-19807-09 (IMB) REINHERZ, ELLIS L DANA-FARBER CANCER INSTITUTE 44 BINNEY STREET BOSTON, MA 02115 Human T cell antigen-recognition structures

R01AI-19838-09 (VR) COEN, DONALD M HARVARD MEDICAL SCHOOL 250 LONGWOOD AVENUE BOSTON, MA 02115 Molecular genetics of HSV DNA polymerase gene

R01AI-19844-09 (BM) MC CLANE, BRUCE A UNIV OF PITTSBURG SCH OF MED MICRO,BIOCHEM & MOLEC BIO DEPT PITTSBURGH, PA 15261 Mechanism of action of C perfringens enterotoxin

R01AI-19863-08 (TMP) GILLIN, FRANCES D UCSD MEDICAL CENTER 225 DICKINSON STREET SAN DIEGO, CA 92093-0934 Secretory defenses against giardia lamblia

R01AI-19881-09 (MBC) BASTIA, DEEPAK DUKE UNIVERSITY MEDICAL CTR BOX 3020 DURHAM, NC 27710 Mechanism of replication of drug resistance factors

R01AI-19883-09 (CBY) ZIGMOND, SALLY H BIOLOGY DEPARTMENT UNIVERSITY OF PENNSYLVANIA PHILADELPHIA, PA 19104-6018 Cell biology of locomotion & chemotaxis of leukocytes

R01AI-19884-10 (ALY) KINCADE, PAUL W OKLAHOMA MEDICAL RES FDN 825 N E 13TH STREET OKLAHOMA CITY, OK 73104 Developmental defects affecting humoral immunity

R01AI-19888-06 (SSS) EDELSON, PAUL J CORNELL UNIV MEDICAL COLLEGE 1300 YORK AVE NEW YORK, NY 10021 Leishmania and host defense

R01AI-19896-09 (IMS) TEALE, JUDY M UNIV OF TEXAS HEALTH SCI CTR 7703 FLOYD CURL DRIVE SAN ANTONIO, TX 78284 B cell and repertoire development in vitro

R01AI-19957-09 (IMB) BUTCHER, EUGENE C STANFORD UNIV SCH OF MEDICINE STANFORD, CA 94305 Leukocyte receptors for endothelium

R01AI-19964-07 (ALY) JONES, PATRICIA P Regulation of MHC antigen expression

R01AI-19968-08 (TMP) KAYES, STEPHEN G UNIV OF SOUTH ALABAMA 2042 MEDICAL SCIENCES BLDG MOBILE, ALA 36688 Nematode-induced pulmonary granuloma formation

R01AI-19973-09 (VR) WARD, DAVID C YALE UNIVERSITY 333 CEDAR STREET,P.O. BOX 3333 NEW HAVEN, CT 06510 Molecular and genetic analysis of parvovirus replication

R01AI-19990-07 (BM) EDWARDS, JOHN E, JR UNIV OF CALIF, INFEC DIS DIV 1000 WEST CARSON ST, E-5 TORRANCE, CA 90509 Candida adherence and penetration of vascular endothelium

R01AI-20001-08 (PTHA) CHISARI, FRANCIS V THE SCRIPPS RESEARCH INSTITUTE 10666 NORTH TORREY PINES ROAD LA JOLLA, CA 92037 Pathogenesis of liver disease in hepatitis

R01AI-20006-08 (BM) NORRIS, STEVEN J UNIV OF TEXAS MED SCHOOL P O BOX 20708 HOUSTON, TX 77225 Physiologic characteristics of Treponema pallidum

R37AI-20015-09 (PBC) STAHL, PHILIP D WASHINGTON U SCH OF MED 660 SOUTH EUCLID AVE/BOX 8228 ST LOUIS, MO 63110 Expression/function of macrophage mannose receptors

R01AI-20016-08 (BM) CLEARY, P PATRICK UNIVERSITY OF MINNESOTA BOX 196 MAYO BLDG MINNEAPOLIS, MN 55455 A streptococcal inactivator of human chemoattractants

R01AI-20017-09 (EVR) RACANIELLO, VINCENT R COLUMBIA UNIVERSITY

701 W 168TH ST NEW YORK, N Y 10032 Studies on poliovirus using infectious viral cDNA clones
R01AI-20038-08 (IMB) DE FRANCO, ANTHONY L UNIV OF CALIFORNIA, SAN FRANCIS DEPT OF MICROBIOLOGY/IMMUNOLOG SAN FRANCISCO, CA 94143-0552 Regulation of B lymphocyte proliferation by antigen
R37AI-20047-09 (ALY) ALT, FREDERICK W COLUMBIA UNIVERSITY 701 WEST 168TH STREET NEW YORK, NY 10032 Assembly and expression of Ig variable region genes
R22AI-20052-08 (TMP) VICKERY, ANN C UNIVERSITY OF SOUTH FLORIDA 13301 N 30TH STREET, MHH 104 TAMPA, FL 33612 Filarial immunology in nude mice
R01AI-20059-09 (IMS) MARSH, DAVID G JOHNS HOPKINS ASTHMA & ALRGY C 301 BAYVIEW BLVD BALTIMORE, MD 21224 Genetic studies of human immune response
R01AI-20060-09 (IMS) PATTERSON, ROY NORTHWESTERN UNIV MEDICAL SCH 303 E CHICAGO AVENUE CHICAGO, IL 60611 Animal models of asthma and occupational lung disease
R01AI-20065-10 (HEM) BOXER, LAURENCE A UNIVERSITY OF MICHIGAN F6515 MOTT CHILDREN'S HOSP ANN ARBOR, MI 48109-0238 Regulation of granulocyte secretion
R37AI-20067-08 (EI) GIGLI, IRMA UNIV OF CALIFORNIA MED CTR 225 DICKINSON STREET, H-811J SAN DIEGO, CA 92103 Activation of the complement system
R01AI-20068-09 (MBC) SMITH, JOHN M SEATTLE BIOMEDICAL RES INST 4 NICKERSON ST SEATTLE, WA 98109-1651 The regulation of purine biosynthesis in E. coli k12
R37AI-20069-09 (ALY) KINCADE, PAUL W OKLAHOMA MEDICAL RES FDN 825 N E 13TH STREET OKLAHOMA CITY, OK 73104 Role of regulatory peptides in pulmonary hypertension
R01AI-20080-09 (TMP) RAY, DAN S UNIVERSITY OF CALIFORNIA 405 HILGARD AVENUE LOS ANGELES, CA 90024 Regulation of trypanosome DNA replication
R22AI-20148-09 (BM) O'BRIEN, ALISON D F. EDWARD HERBERT SCH OF MED 4301 JONES BRIDGE ROAD, USUHS BETHESDA, MD 20814-4799 Shiga-like toxin of Escherichia coli
R01AI-20154-04 (BM) BJORNSON, ANN B JAMES N GAMBLE INST OF MED RES 2141 AUBURN AVENUE CINCINNATI, OH 45219 Humoral factors of host defense against Bacteroides
R01AI-20181-10 (VR) WERTZ, GAIL W UAB - MICRO DEPT UNIVERSITY STATION BIRMINGHAM, AL 35294 Analysis of respiratory syncytial virus gene products
R01AI-20182-07 (ALY) STROMINGER, JACK L DANA-FARBER CANCER INSTITUTE 44 BINNEY STREET BOSTON, MA 02115 Structure/function relationships in human MHC molecules
R01AI-20190-09 (TMP) MALLAVIA, LOUIS P WASHINGTON STATE UNIVERSITY PULLMAN, WA 99164-4233 Surface change and virulence in Coxiella burnetii
R37AI-20201-09 (VR) LAMB, ROBERT A NORTHWESTERN UNIVERSITY 2153 SHERIDAN ROAD EVANSTON, IL 60208-3500 Structure and function of the influenza virus genome
R01AI-20211-08 (VR) MOCARSKI, EDWARD S, JR STANFORD UNIVERSITY STANFORD, CA 94305 Cytomegalovirus DNA replication and inversion
R01AI-20232-08 (IMS) SIDMAN, CHARLES L THE JACKSON LABORATORY 600 MAIN STREET BAR HARBOR, ME 04609-0800 Mechanisms of autoimmunity
R01AI-20241-08 (ALY) WELLER, PETER F BETH ISRAEL HOSPITAL 330 BROOKLINE AVENUE BOSTON, MA 02215 Human eosinophile--Mechanisms of functioning
R01AI-20245-09 (TMP) ANDERSON, JOHN R UNIVERSITY OF CALIFORNIA 201 WELLMAN HALL BERKELEY, CA 94720 Biological control of mosquitoes with Lambornella clarki
R01AI-20248-09 (ALY) ROCK, KENNETH L DANA FARBER CANCER INSTITUTE 44 BINNEY STREET BOSTON, MA 02115 Immunobiology of MHC restriction of T cells
R01AI-20253-07 (ALY) MACGLASHAN, DONALD W, JR GOOD SAMARITAN HOSPITAL 5601 LOCH RAVEN BLVD BALTIMORE, MD 21239 Mechanisms of human basophil and mast cell desensitization
R01AI-20264-09 (BNP) FLOSS, HEINZ G UNIVERSITY OF WASHINGTON BG-10 SEATTLE, WA 98195 Biologically active microbial metabolites
R01AI-20279-09 (MBC) STAUFFER, GEORGE V UNIVERSITY OF IOWA IOWA CITY, IA 52242 Regulatory biology of pseudomonas tryptophan synthase
R37AI-20288-09 (IMB) FRELINGER, JEFFREY A UNIVERSITY OF NORTH CAROLINA CB7290, 804 FLOB CHAPEL HILL, NC 27599 Genetics and function of murine Ia antigens
R01AI-20313-08 (IMS) TEALE, JUDY M UTHSC AT SAN ANTONIO 7703 FLOYD CURL DRIVE SAN TONIO, TX 78284 Regulation of immunoglobulin class expression
R01AI-20319-09 (BM) MORAN, CHARLES P, JR EMORY UNIV SCHOOL OF MEDICINE ATLANTA, GA 30322 Role of RNA polymerase in bacterial differentiation
R01AI-20323-09 (BM) WELCH, RODNEY A UNIVERSITY OF WISCONSIN 1300 UNIVERSITY AVENUE MADISON, WI 53706 Analysis of the E. coli hemolysin and related toxins
R01AI-20325-08 (BM) DONOHUE-ROLFE, ARTHUR M NEW ENGLAND MED CTR HOSPITALS 750 WASHINGTON ST, BOX 041 BOSTON, MA 02111 Shigella toxin--Structure and function relationships
R01AI-20331-07A1 (IMS) LEHRER, SAMUEL B TULANE MEDICAL CENTER 1700 PERDIDO STREET NEW ORLEANS, LA 70112 Isolation and characterization of basidiospore allergens
R01AI-20336-09 (MBC) ORDAL, GEORGE W UNIVERSITY OF ILLINOIS 506 SOUTH MATHEWS AVE URBANA, IL 61801 Chemotactic sensory transduction in Bacillus subtilis
R55AI-20337-07 (BM) WRIGHT, ANDREW TUFTS UNIVERSITY 136 HARRISON AVENUE BOSTON, MA 02111 Studies of bacterial IgA proteases
R01AI-20355-09 (TMP) STRETTON, ANTONY O ZOOLOGY RESEARCH BUILDING 1117 W JOHNSON STREET MADISON, WI 53706 Cellular and molecular studies on ascaris neuropeptides
R01AI-20382-09 (EVR) FINBERG, ROBERT W DANA-FARBER CANCER INSTITUTE 44 BINNEY ST JF319 BOSTON, MA 02115 Cell mediated immune response to murine viruses
R01AI-20384-09 (TMP) WOOD, DAVID O UNIVERSITY OF SOUTH ALABAMA 307 UNIVERSITY BLVD MOBILE, AL 36688 Genetic analysis of Rickettsia prowazekii
R01AI-20385-09 (TMP) FALLON, ANN M UNIVERSITY OF MINNESOTA 1980 FOLWELL AVENUE ST PAUL, MN 55108 Synthesis and degradation of ribosomes in the mosquito
R01AI-20387-07 (BM) FRETER, ROLF G THE UNIVERSITY OF MICHIGAN ANN ARBOR, MI 48109-0620 Bacterial adhesion in the microecology of the large gut
R01AI-20408-08 (VR) ENGLER, JEFFREY A UNIVERSITY OF ALABAMA UAB STATION BIRMINGHAM, AL 35294-0005 Initiation of adenovirus-2 DNA replication
R01AI-20451-07 (ALY) KUMAR, VINAY THE UNIVERSITY OF TEXAS DEPARTMENT OF PATHOLOGY DALLAS, TX 75235 Origin and differentiation of natural killer cells
R01AI-20452-08 (TMP) MCKERROW, JAMES H UNIVERSITY OF CALIFORNIA SAN FRANCISCO, CA 94143-0506 Characterization of cercarial proteinase of S mansoni
R01AI-20459-09 (EVR) ARVIN, ANN M STANFORD UNIV SCHOOL OF MED S-332 MEDICAL CENTER STANFORD, CA 94305 Immunity and viral replication in children with varicella
R37AI-20460-09 (NSS) STILLMAN, BRUCE W COLD SPRING HARBOR LABORATORY P O BOX 100 COLD SPRING HARBOR, N Y 11724 Initiation of DNA replication at virus and cell origins
R01AI-20484-20 (VR) THACH, ROBERT E WASHINGTON UNIVERSITY SCHOOL OF ARTS AND SCIENCES ST LOUIS, MO 63130 Replication of virulent and oncogenic viruses
R01AI-20486-08 (BM) CHANG, KWANG-POO UNIVERSITY OF HEALTH SCIENCES THE CHICAGO MEDICAL SCHOOL NORTH CHICAGO, IL 60064 Leishmania-macrophage cellular interactions in vitro
R37AI-20487-09 (PBC) SCHWARTZ, LAWRENCE B VIRGINIA COMMONWEALTH UNIVERSI BOX 263, MCV STATION RICHMOND, VA 23298-0263 Biochemistry of mast cell secretory granule enzymes
R01AI-20506-08 (BM) ABRAMSON, JON S WAKE FOREST UNIVERSITY 300 SOUTH HAWTHORNE ROAD WINSTON-SALEM, NC 27103 Phagocytic cell dysfunction due to influenza virus
R01AI-20516-08 (EI) SILVERSTEIN, SAMUEL C COLUMBIA UNIVERSITY 630 WEST 168TH STREET NEW YORK, NY 10032 Role of mononuclear leukocytes in immunity
R01AI-20519-09 (ALY) CAMBIER, JOHN C NATIONAL JEWISH CENTER 1400 JACKSON STREET DENVER, CO 80206 Molecular biology of B cell tolerance and activation
R01AI-20530-08 (EVR) KNIPE, DAVID M HARVARD MEDICAL SCHOOL 25 SHATTUCK STREET BOSTON, MA 02115 Maturation of herpesviral nuclear proteins
R01AI-20551-08 (EVR) ROBINSON, WILLIAM S STANFORD UNIV SCH OF MEDICINE STANFORD, CALIF 94305 Animal models of HBV infection and disease
R01AI-20565-08 (IMS) PLATTS-MILLS, THOMAS A UNIVERSITY OF VIRGINIA HEALTH SCI CENTER, BOX 225 CHARLOTTESVILLE, VA 22908 Dust mite, cockroach and cat allergens in houses--Asthma
R01AI-20566-09 (BBCB) HOGLE, JAMES M HARVARD UNIVERSITY 240 LONGWOOD AVENUE BOSTON, MA 02115 High resolution crystallographic studies of poliovirus
R01AI-20591-08 (VR) WEBSTER, ROBERT G ST JUDE CHILDREN'S RES HOSP 332 NORTH LAUDERDALE, BOX 318 MEMPHIS, TN 38101 Host cell selection of influenza virus
R22AI-20597-07 (TMP) VEZZA, ANNE C UAB DEPT OF MEDICINE BIRMINGHAM, AL 35294 Transcriptional analyses of the P. falciparum RNA genes
R01AI-20603-07 (BM) COOPER, MORRIS D SOUTHERN ILLINOIS UNIVERSITY P O BOX 19230 SPRINGFIELD, IL 62794-9230 Immunobiology of gonococcal infection in human tissues
R01AI-20608-06 (VR) WALSH, EDWARD E ROCHESTER GENERAL HOSPITAL 1425 PORTLAND AVENUE ROCHESTER, NY 14621 Antibody in respiratory syncytial virus infection
R01AI-20611-08 (EVR) SAMUEL, CHARLES E UNIVERSITY OF CALIFORNIA SANTA BARBARA, CA 93106 Interferon action and protein phosphorylation
R22AI-20612-08 (VR) STRAUSS, JAMES H CALIFORNIA INST OF TECHNOLOGY BIOLOGY DIVISION PASADENA, CALIF 91125 Togavirus replication strategies and evolution
R01AI-20624-07 (PBC) HOOK, MAGNUS UAB/BHSB 508 1918 UNIVERSITY BLVD BIRMINGHAM, AL 35294 Binding of bacteria to fibronectin
R01AI-20634-08 (PTHA) SCHULMAN, EDWARD S 621 BOBST BUILDING BROAD & VINE PHILADELPHIA, PA 19102 Mechanisms of human lung hypersensitivity reactions
R37AI-20642-08 (MBY) MANIATIS, THOMAS P HARVARD UNIVERSITY 7 DIVINITY AVENUE CAMBRIDGE, MA 02138 Human beta-interferon gene regulation
R01AI-20644-07 (PB) BARRETT, ANTHONY G COLORADO STATE UNIVERSITY FORT COLLINS, CO 80523 Total synthesis of avermectin and calyculin
R01AI-20662-08 (EVR) HUTT-FLETCHER, LINDSEY M UNIVERSITY OF FLORIDA BOX J-145/JHMHC GAINESVILLE, FL 32610 Initiation of cell infection with Epstein-Barr virus
R01AI-20671-08 (SRC) RUBINSTEIN, ARYE ALBERT EINSTEIN COLLEGE OF MED 1300 MORRIS PARK AVENUE BRONX, NY 10461 Materno-fetal HIV transmission - Model for vaccines
R01AI-20671-08 0002 (SRC) RUBINSTEIN, ARYE Materno-fetal HIV transmission - Model for vaccines Development of an AIDS transmission blocking vaccine
R01AI-20671-08 9001 (SRC) RUBINSTEIN, ARYE Materno-fetal HIV transmission - Model for vaccines Virus production, purification, neutralization ---Core
R01AI-20671-08 9002 (SRC) RUBINSTEIN, ARYE Materno-fetal HIV transmission - Model for vaccines Vaccine core laboratory
R01AI-20671-08 0001 (SRC) RUBINSTEIN, ARYE Materno-fetal HIV transmission - Model for vaccines Maternal-fetal transmission of HIV
R01AI-20673-09 (ARR) HUGHES, WALTER T ST JUDE CHILDREN'S RES HOSP 332 NORTH LAUDERDALE MEMPHIS, TN 38105 Development therapeutics for P. carinii pneumonitis
R01AI-20686-08 (SAT) MAKI, TAKASHI NEW ENGLAND DEACONESS HOSPITAL 185 PILGRIM ROAD BOSTON, MA 02215 Suppressor lymphokine involved in allograft unresponsiveness
R01AI-20720-07A1 (IMB) MILICH, DAVID R SCRIPPS CLINIC & RESEARCH FDN 10666 N TORREY PINES ROAD LA JOLLA, CA 92037 MHC-control cell correlates of the hepatitis B surface antigen immune response

PROJECT NO., ORGANIZATIONAL UNIT., INVESTIGATOR, ADDRESS, TITLE

R01AI-20723-06 (BM) SCOTT, JUNE R EMORY UNIVERSITY 3001 ROLLINS RESEARCH CENTER ATLANTA, GA 30322 Genetic analysis of Streptococcal M protein

R01AI-20729-06 (ARR) LETVIN, NORMAN L NEW ENGLAND PRIMATE RES CTR ONE PINE HILL DRIVE SOUTHBOROUGH, MA 01772 Immunoregulation in AIDS

R01AI-20738-06 (BM) SANTOSHAM, MATHURAM JOHNS HOPKINS UNIVERSITY 615 N WOLFE STREET BALTIMORE, MD 21205 Propholaxis of H. influenzae and other infections

R01AI-20745-06 (ALY) BENJAMIN, DAVID C UNIVERSITY OF VIRGINIA BOX 441 CHARLOTTESVILLE, VA 22908 Molecular basis of antigenicity

R01AI-20770-07 (BBCB) OPELLA, STANLEY J UNIVERSITY OF PENNSYLVANIA 231 S 34TH STREET / CHEM DEPT PHILADELPHIA, PA 19104-6323 NMR of membrane bound phage coat proteins

R01AI-20778-06 (BBCB) LYLES, DOUGLAS S BOWMAN GRAY SCHOOL OF MEDICINE MEDICAL CENTER BLVD WINSTON-SALEM, NC 27157-1064 Analysis of viral and H-2 antigen interactions

R01AI-20792-09 (HEM) LOBUGLIO, ALBERT F UAB UAB STATION BIRMINGHAM, AL 35294 Human immune cytopenias--Studies with monoclonal antibody

R01AI-20845-09 (MBC) SO, MAGDALENE H OREGON HEALTH SCIENCE UNIV 3181 SW SAM JACKSON PARK RD PORTLAND, OR 97201 Genetic regulation of pilus expression of N gonorrhoeae

R01AI-20846-07 (ALY) KAMOUN, MALEK UNIVERSITY OF PENNSYLVANIA 286 J MORGAN BLDG, 37TH & HML PHILADELPHIA, PA 19104-6082 Biology of the CD2/E-receptor complex

R01AI-20850-07 (BM) NORROD, ERMINIA P VASSAR COLLEGE POUGHKEEPISE, N Y 12601 Reduction of molecular oxygen by neisseria gonorrhoeae

R37AI-20866-06 (BM) CLARK, ROBERT A UNIV OF IOWA COLLEGE OF MED SW 54-15/GH IOWA CITY, IA 52242 Neutrophil activation of the oxidative burst

R01AI-20880-06 (BM) DENSEN, PETER UNIVERSITY OF IOWA IOWA CITY, IA 52242 Interaction of gonococci with neutrophils and serum

R37AI-20896-10 (VR) HUANG, ALICE S NEW YORK UNIVERSITY 6 WASHINGTON SQUARE NORTH NEW YORK, NY 10003 Replication of vesicular stomatitis virus

R01AI-20897-07 (BM) REST, RICHARD F HAHNEMANN UNIV SCH OF MEDICINE BROAD AND VINE PHILADELPHIA, PA 19102-1192 Intracellular fate of neisseria gonorrhoeae

R01AI-20900-07A1 (BM) BEAMAN, BLAINE L UNIV OF CALIFORNIA SCH OF MED DAVIS, CA 95616 Determinants of infection in nocardiosis

R01AI-20922-07 (ALY) SOLOSKI, MARK J JOHNS HOPKINS UNIV MED SCH 725 N WOLFE STREET BALTIMORE, MD 21205 Functional analysis of tissue-specific class I molecules

R22AI-20938-07A1 (TMP) TRAGER, WILLIAM ROCKEFELLER UNIVERSITY 1230 YORK AVENUE NEW YORK, NY 10021-6399 Extracellular development in vitro of malaria parasites

R01AI-20940-07 (ARR) GRAVES, DONALD C UNIVERSITY OF OKLAHOMA P O BOX 26901 OKLAHOMA CITY, OK 73190 Assay for pneumocystosis in immunodeficient hosts

R01AI-20941-07 (PC) TURCO, SALVATORE J U OF KENTUCKY MED CTR MS627A 800 ROSE STREET LEXINGTON, KY 40536-0084 Glycoconjugates of leishmania

R01AI-20943-06 (PTHA) HUANG, CHI-KUANG UNIV OF CONNECTICUT HLTH CTR 263 FARMINGTON AVE FARMINGTON, CT 06030 Chemotactic neutrophil activation and phosphoproteins

R01AI-20953-07 (VR) FELDMAN, LAWRENCE T UCLA, SCHOOL OF MEDICINE 405 HILGARD AVE LOS ANGELES, CA 90024 Transactivation by the pseudorabies virus IEP protein

R01AI-20954-05 (VR) SPECTOR, DEBORAH H UNIV OF CALIFORNIA SAN DIEGO 9500 GILMAN DR LA JOLLA, CA 92093-0116 Murine cmv, molecular biology and in vivo pathogenesis

R01AI-20958-08 (IMS) LIU, FU-TONG SCRIPPS RESEARCH INSTITUTE 10666 NORTH TORREY PINES RD LA JOLLA, CA 92037 Gene expression, structure and function of IgE

R01AI-20963-08 (EI) ENGELHARD, VICTOR H UNIVERSITY OF VIRGINIA BOX 441 CHARLOTTESVILLE, VA 22908 Antigenic determinants on HLA-B7 and -A2

R01AI-20980-07 (MBC) STOCK, JEFFRY B PRINCETON UNIVERSITY PRINCETON, N J 08544 Mechanisms of sensory processing in chemotaxis

R01AI-21002-06 (SSS) DEMBO, MICAH LOS ALAMOS NATIONAL LABORATORY T-10, MAIL STOP K710 LOS ALAMOS, NM 87545 Biophysical models of cell motility

R01AI-21009-07A1 (BM) HULL, SHEILA I BAYLOR COLLEGE OF MEDICINE 1 BAYLOR PLAZA HOUSTON, TX 77030-3498 Genetic dissection and reconstruction of a uropathogen

R01AI-21017-08 (MBC) STRALEY, SUSAN C UNIVERSITY OF KENTUCKY LEXINGTON, KY 40536-0084 Plasmid pCD-encoded virulence determinants in plague

R01AI-21025-06 (TMP) BOOTHROYD, JOHN C STANFORD UNIVERSITY D-305 FAIRCHILD BUILDING STANFORD, CA 94305-5402 Molecular basis of pathogenicity of African trypanosomes

R01AI-21029-08 (MBC) GEORGOPOULOS, CONSTANTINE P UNIVERSITY OF UTAH SCHOOL OF MEDICINE SALT LAKE CITY, UT 84132 Analysis of the heat shock response in E. coli

R01AI-21049-08 (BM) TESH, ROBERT B YALE UNIVERSITY SCHOOL OF MED P O BOX 3333, 333 CEDAR STREET NEW HAVEN, CT 06510-8034 Biology of Leishmania in phlebotomine sandflies

R01AI-21067-08 (ALY) VOLANAKIS, JOHN E UNIV OF ALABAMA AT BIRMINGHAM UAB STATION BIRMINGHAM, AL 35294 Assembly and regulation of complement C3-convertases

R01AI-21069-09 (IMB) RAULET, DAVID H UNIV. OF CALIF. AT BERKELEY DIVISION OF IMMUNOLOGY BERKELEY, CA 94720 Requirements for T cell activation

R01AI-21073-08 (IMS) ADKINSON, N FRANKLIN, JR JOHNS HOPKINS ASTHMA & ALL CTR 301 BAYVIEW BLVD BALTIMORE, MD 21224 Immunotherapy of childhood asthma

R01AI-21075-05 (BM) HOUSTON, CLIFFORD W UNIVERSITY OF TEXAS MED BRANCH GALVESTON, TX 77550 The role of Aeromonas hydrophila virulence factors

R01AI-21083-09 (ALY) HOCH, SALLIE O AGOURON INSTITUTE 505 COAST BOULEVARD SOUTH LA JOLLA, CA 92037 Nuclear proteins and autoimmunity

R01AI-21089-06 (BM) LONG, CAROLE A HAHNEMANN UNIV SCH OF MED BROAD AND VINE PHILADELPIA, PA 19102-1192 Idiotype and immunity to malaria

R01AI-21144-06 (BBCB) KORNBERG, ROGER D STANFORD UNIVERSITY FAIRCHILD BLDG D123 STANFORD, CA 94305-5400 Structure of immunoglobulin isotypes, variants, complexes

R01AI-21150-07 (BM) SHAFER, WILLIAM M EMORY UNIVERSITY ATLANTA, GA 30322 Gonococci--Genetics of resistance to PMN proteins

R01AI-21159-06A3 (BM) HILL, GEORGE C MEHARRY MEDICAL COLLEGE DIV OF BIOMEDICAL SCIENCES NASHVILLE, TN 37208 Electron transport systems in trypanosomes

R01AI-21165-08 (IMB) SCHWABER, JERROLD HAHNEMANN UNIVERSITY BROAD AND VINE PHILADELPHIA, PA 19102 Regulation of Ig rearrangement in pre-B and B cells

R01AI-21171-06 (BM) GRIFFISS, J MCLEOD U OF CALIFORNIA, SAN FRANCISCO DEPT OF LAB MED, BOX 0134 SAN FRANCISCO, CA 94143 The role of IgA in bacterial disease

R22AI-21214-08 (TMP) VANDER JAGT, DAVID L UNIV OF NEW MEXICO 915 STANFORD DRIVE N E ALBUQUERQUE, N M 87131 Protein degradation in P falciparum

R01AI-21226-06 (ALY) REINHERZ, ELLIS L DANA-FARBER CANCER INSTITUTE 44 BINNEY STREET BOSTON, MA 02115 Genes encoding T cell receptors

R01AI-21229-07 (IMB) VITETTA, ELLEN S UNIV. OF TEXAS SW MED CTR/DALL 5323 HARRY HINES BOULEVARD DALLAS, TX 75235 The activation of antigen-specific memory B cells

R01AI-21236-06S2 (BM) JUDD, RALPH C UNIVERSITY OF MONTANA MISSOULA, MT 59812 Peptide analyses of protein 1 of Neisseria gonorrhoeae

R01AI-21242-06 (TMP) WALKER, DAVID H UNIV OF TEXAS MED BRANCH 301 UNIVERSITY BLVD GALVESTON, TX 77550-2774 Analysis of spotted fever rickettsial antigens

R01AI-21251-04A1 (TMP) SHERMAN, IRWIN W UNIVERSITY OF CALIFORNIA RIVERSIDE, CA 92521 Erythrocyte-endothelial interactions in malaria

R01AI-21255-08 (IMS) REED, CHARLES E MAYO FOUNDATION 200 FIRST STREET SW ROCHESTER, MN 55905 Immunological assay of aeroallergens

R01AI-21256-08 (IMB) DORSHKIND, KENNETH A UNIVERSITY OF CALIFORNIA RIVERSIDE, CA 92521-0121 Immunobiology of B cell differentiation

P01AI-21289-08 (AITC) RICH, ROBERT R BAYLOR COLLEGE OF MEDICINE ONE BAYLOR PLACE HOUSTON, TX 77030 Regulatory abnormalities in immunologic diseases

P01AI-21289-08 0001 (AITC) RICH, SUSAN S Regulatory abnormalities in immunologic diseases Growth factors for suppressor T cells in normal and autoimmune mice

P01AI-21289-08 0002 (AITC) RICH, ROBERT R Regulatory abnormalities in immunologic diseases Pathophysiology of human suppressor T cell activation and growth

P01AI-21289-08 0003 (AITC) THOMAS, JAMES W Regulatory abnormalities in immunologic diseases Regulation of human immune responses to insulin

P01AI-21289-08 0004 (AITC) POLLACK, MARILYN S Regulatory abnormalities in immunologic diseases Lymphocytotoxic antibodies in patients with AIDS

P01AI-21289-08 9001 (AITC) LEWIS, DOROTHY E Regulatory abnormalities in immunologic diseases Core--Flow cytometry facility

P01AI-21289-08 9002 (AITC) POLLACK, MARILYN S Regulatory abnormalities in immunologic diseases Core--Tissue typing laboratory

R01AI-21301-08 (HEM) WEISS, STEPHEN J UNIVERSITY OF MICHIGAN 11150 W MEDICAL CENTER DR ANN ARBOR, MI 48109-0668 Human phagocytes, oxygen metabolites and inflammation

R01AI-21302-07 (VR) PINTEL, DAVID J UNIV OF MISSOURI-COLUMBIA MEDICAL SCIENCE BUILDING COLUMBIA, MO 65212 Molecular and genetic analysis of mvm gene expression

R01AI-21309-08 (MBC) RICK, PAUL D USUHS-F EDWARD HEBERT SCH OF M 4301 JONES BRIDGE ROAD BETHESDA, MD 20814-4799 Biosynthesis of enterobacterial common antigen

R01AI-21324-06 (BBCB) WILEY, DON C HARVARD UNIVERSITY 7 DIVINITY AVENUE CAMBRIDGE, MA 02138 X-ray structure of African trypanosome surface antigen

R01AI-21328-07 (IMB) FINKELMAN, FRED D F E HEBERT SCHOOL OF MEDICINE 4301 JONES BRIDGE ROAD BETHESDA, MD 20814 In vivo and in vitro B lymphocyte activation

R01AI-21334-08 (PC) ENGLUND, PAUL T JOHNS HOPKINS UNIVERSITY 725 N. WOLFE STREET BALTIMORE, MD 21205 Trypanosome variant surface glycoprotein

R01AI-21335-08 (EVR) HRUBY, DENNIS E OREGON STATE UNIVERSITY COLLEGE OF SCIENCE CORVALLIS, OR 97331-3804 Expression and regulation of vaccinia virus late genes

R01AI-21343-07A1 (BM) CZUPRYNSKI, CHARLES J UNIVERSITY OF WISCONSIN 2015 LINDEN DRIVE WEST MADISON, WI 53706 Inflammation in resistance to bacterial infection

R01AI-21352-08 (BM) LOVETT, MICHAEL A UNIV OF CALIFORNIA, LOS ANGELE LOS ANGELES, CA 90024-1747 Genetics of Treponema pallidum pathogenicity

R01AI-21359-07 (TMP) CERAMI, ANTHONY ROCKEFELLER UNIVERSITY 1230 YORK AVENUE NEW YORK, NY 10021 Parasite induced catabolism in mammals

R22AI-21362-08 (VR) GREENBERG, HARRY B STANFORD UNIVERSITY MEDICAL CT STANFORD, CA 94305 Viral gastroenteritis--Basis of virulence and protection

R01AI-21365-05 (BM) WIRTH, DYANN F HARVARD SCHOOL OF PUBLIC HLTH 665 HUNTINGTON AVENUE BOSTON, MA 02115 Developmentally regulated genes in Leishmania sp

R01AI-21372-08 (ALY) HEDRICK, STEPHEN M UNIV OF CALIFORNIA, SAN DIEGO 9500 GILMAN DR 0063 LA JOLLA, CA 92093-0063 T cell receptor--Molecular structure & expression

R01AI-21389-07A1 (EVR) FREY, TERYL K GEORGIA STATE UNIVERSITY UNIVERSITY PLAZA ATLANTA, GA 30303 Molecular biology of rubella virus

R01AI-21393-08 (IMB) ENGELHARD, VICTOR H UNIVERSITY OF VIRGINIA BOX 441 CHARLOTTESVILLE, VA 22908 Xenogeneic cytotoxic T cell responses

R01AI-21401-06 (TMP) HAJDUK, STEPHEN L UNIVERSITY OF ALABAMA

PROJECT NO., ORGANIZATIONAL UNIT., INVESTIGATOR, ADDRESS, TITLE

UAB STATION BIRMINGHAM, AL 35294 Gene expression during trypanosome differentiation

R01AI-21414-06 (ARR) KOTLER, DONALD P ST LUKES/ROOSEVELT HOSP CTR AMSTERDAM AVENUE & 114TH STREE NEW YORK, NY 10025 Pathogenesis of intestinal dysfunction in AIDS

R01AI-21420-06 (EI) RICH, SUSAN S BAYLOR COLLEGE OF MEDICINE ONE BAYLOR PLAZA HOUSTON, TX 77030 Regulation of suppressor T cell growth and differentiation

R01AI-21423-06 (TMP) BOOTHROYD, JOHN C STANFORD UNIVERSITY D-305 FAIRCHILD BUILDING STANFORD, CA 94305-5402 Antigens of Toxoplasma gondii and their genes

R01AI-21431-06 (MBC) COX, REBECCA A PO BOX 23340, 2303 SE MILITARY SAN ANTONIO, TX 78223 Biologically active Coccidioides immitis antigens

R01AI-21443-06 (TMP) RAI, KARAMJIT S UNIVERSITY OF NOTRE DAME NOTRE DAME, IN 46556 Genetic differentiation in Aedes albopictus subgroup

R01AI-21451-06 (BM) LORY, STEPHEN UNIVERSITY OF WASHINGTON MICROBIOLOGY SC-42 SEATTLE, WA 98195 Studies of P. aeruginosa virulence determinants

R22AI-21478-06 (VR) PATTON, JOHN T UNIVERSITY OF MIAMI SCH OF MED P O BOX 01690 MIAMI, FL 33101 Viral proteins in rotavirus replication

R01AI-21487-06 (EI) SPRENT, JONATHAN SCRIPPS CLINIC AND RES FDN 10666 N. TORREY PINES ROAD LA JOLLA, CA 92037 H-2 control of T-helper cells function in vivo

R01AI-21490-06 (IMB) BONDADA, SUBBARAO ROOM 205 SANDERS BROWN BLDG LEXINGTON, KY 40536-0230 B-lymphocyte receptors for growth and maturation factors

R22AI-21494-06 (EVR) RAMIG, ROBERT F BAYLOR COLLEGE OF MEDICINE ONE BAYLOR PLAZA HOUSTON, TEX 77030 Genetics and pathogenesis of bluetongue virus

R22AI-21496-06 (BM) GODSON, G NIGEL NYU MED CTR, BIOCHEMISTRY DEPT 550 FIRST AVENUE NEW YORK, NY 10016 Molecular biology of the malaria organism P. knowlesi

R01AI-21501-06A1 (EVR) READ, GEORGE S, JR UNIVERSITY OF MISSOURI SCHOOL BASIC LIFE SCIENCES KANSAS CITY, MO 64110-2499 Control of mRNA stability in HSV infected cells

R01AI-21515-06 (VR) SANDRI-GOLDIN, ROZANNE M UNIVERSITY OF CALIFORNIA IRVINE, CA 92717-4025 Herpes simplex virus gene regulation

R01AI-21531-06 (TMP) CROSS, GEORGE A THE ROCKEFELLER UNIVERSITY 1230 YORK AVENUE NEW YORK, NY 10021-6399 Structure and processing of trypanosome variant antigens

R01AI-21533-06 (MBC) CRAIG, NANCY L 725 NORTH WOLFE STREET BALTIMORE, MD 21205 Transposition of Tn7

R01AI-21548-06 (BM) BRILES, DAVID E UNIVERSITY OF ALABAMA 801 SDB, UNIVERSITY STATION BIRMINGHAM, AL 35294 Protective immunity to pneumococcal surface proteins

P01AI-21568-07 (SRC) REICHLIN, MORRIS OKLAHOMA MEDICAL RESEARCH FDN 825 N E 13TH STREET OKLAHOMA CITY, OK 73104 Autoantibodies in SLE and polymyositis

P01AI-21568-07 0002 (SRC) HARLEY, JOHN B Autoantibodies in SLE and polymyositis Autoantigenicity of the 60 kD Ro/SSA protein

P01AI-21568-07 0005 (SRC) REICHLIN, MORRIS Autoantibodies in SLE and polymyositis Antibodies to the isomorphic forms of Ro/SSA and lupus nephritis

P01AI-21568-07 0006 (SRC) FRANK, MARK BARTON Autoantibodies in SLE and polymyositis T cell receptors and anti-Ro/SSA antibody production

P01AI-21568-07 0007 (SRC) TARGOFF, IRA N Autoantibodies in SLE and polymyositis Molecular analysis of polymyositis-associated antigens

P01AI-21568-07 9001 (SRC) TARGOFF, IRA N Autoantibodies in SLE and polymyositis Core--Patient accrual and HLA serological analysis

P01AI-21568-07 9002 (SRC) HARLEY, JOHN B Autoantibodies in SLE and polymyositis Core--Experimental design and statistical analysis

R01AI-21569-06 (ALY) GLIMCHER, LAURIE H HARVARD SCH OF PUBLIC HEALTH 665 HUNTINGTON AVENUE BOSTON, MA 02115 Structural basis of functional class II gene expression

R01AI-21572-06A3 (EVR) PERRAULT, JACQUES SAN DIEGO STATE UNIVERSITY COLLEGE OF SCIENCES SAN DIEGO, CA 92182 VSV polymerase regulation and DI replication

R01AI-21620-06 (BM) GRIFFISS, J MCLEOD U OF CALIFORNIA, SAN FRANCISCO 4150 CLEMENT SAN FRANCISCO, CA 94121 Immunochemistry of gonococcal lipopolysaccharide

R01AI-21628-07A1 (BM) MURPHY, JOHN R UNIVERSITY HOSPITAL 88 EAST NEWTON STREET BOSTON, MA 02118 Molecular mechanisms of diphtheria tox gene regulation

R01AI-21640-07 (VR) NELSON, JAY A THE SCRIPPS RESEARCH INSTITUTE 10666 N. TORREY PINES ROAD LA JOLLA, CA 92037 Molecular aspects of cytomegalovirus latency

R22AI-21657-06 (MBC) KAPER, JAMES B UNIV OF MARYLAND SCH OF MEDICI 10 SOUTH PINE STREET BALTIMORE, MD 21201 Molecular genetics of enteropathogenic E coli adhesion

R01AI-21674-07 (EVR) EDSON, CLARK MC WHORTER TUFTS UNIV SCH OF MEDICINE 136 HARRISON AVENUE BOSTON, MA 02111 Varicella-zoster virus membrane antigens

R01AI-21678-06 (MBC) GUNSALUS, ROBERT P UNIVERSITY OF CALIFORNIA 405 HILGARD AVENUE LOS ANGELES, CA 90024 Anaerobic expression of fumarate reductase in E. coli

R01AI-21702-07 (MBC) SAIER, MILTON H, JR UNIVERSITY OF CALIFORNIA 9500 GILMAN DRIVE LA JOLLA, CA 92093-0116 ATP-dependent protein kinases in Streptococci

R37AI-21729-07 (TMP) CROSS, GEORGE A THE ROCKEFELLER UNIVERSITY 1230 YORK AVENUE NEW YORK, NY 10021-6399 Molecular genetics of trypanosome antigenic variation

R01AI-21736-07 (IMB) MILLER, MARCIA MADSEN BECKMAN RES INST/CITY OF HOPE 1450 EAST DUARTE ROAD DUARTE, CA 91010-0269 Immunobiology of the major histocompatibility complex

R01AI-21747-07 (EVR) WELLER, SANDRA K UNIVERSITY OF CONNECTICUT MEDICAL/DENTAL BASIC HLTH SCI FARMINGTON, CT 06032 Genetics of HSV DNA replication

R01AI-21758-07 (VR) TRAKTMAN, PAULA CORNELL UNIV MEDICAL COLLEGE 1300 YORK AVENUE NEW YORK, N Y 10021 Vaccinia DNA replication--Genetics and molecular biology

PROJECT NO., ORGANIZATIONAL UNIT., INVESTIGATOR, ADDRESS, TITLE

R01AI-21761-06 (GMB) MANOLAGAS, STAVROS C VA MEDICAL CENTER 1481 W TENTH STREET INDIANAPOLIS, IN 46202-2884 1,25 dihydroxy vitamin d3 and cellular immunity

R01AI-21768-07A1 (ALY) CAMBIER, JOHN C NATIONAL JEWISH CENTER 1400 JACKSON STREET DENVER, CO 80206 Signal transduction in B cell activation

R01AI-21772-06 (MBC) ARCHER, GORDON L MEDICAL COLL OF VIRGINIA BOX 49, MCV STATION RICHMOND, VA 23298-0049 Antimicrobial resistance gene mobility in staphylococci

R01AI-21784-07 (TMP) VAN DER PLOEG, L H COLLEGE/PHYSICIANS & SURGEONS OF COLUMBIA UNIVERSITY NEW YORK, NY 10032 Mechanism of antigenic variation in Trypanosoma brucei

R01AI-21786-07 (BM) WANG, CHING C UNIVERSITY OF CALIFORNIA 926 MEDICAL SCIENCES BUILDING SAN FRANCISCO, CA 94143-0446 Cross-linked glycosome enzymes of trypanosoma brucei

R01AI-21818-06 (PTHA) PINCKARD, R NEAL UNIV OF TEXAS HLTH SCI CTR 7703 FLOYD CURL DR SAN ANTONIO, TX 78284 Platelet activating factor (PAF) synthesis and release

R01AI-21833-06 (BM) MONTE-WICHER, VICTORIA WADSWORTH CTR FOR LABS/RESEARC EMPIRE STATE PLAZA ALBANY, NY 12201 Experimental syphilis--Guniea pig model

R01AI-21842-05 (EDC) OSTERHOLM, MICHAEL T MINNESOTA DEPARTMENT OF HEALTH 717 DELAWARE STREET SOUTHEAST MINNEAPOLIS, MN 55440 Impact of vaccination on hemophilus disease incidence

R01AI-21862-07 (BM) PATTON, CURTIS L YALE UNIV, SCHOOL OF MEDICINE P O BOX 3333, 333 CEDAR STR NEW HAVEN, CT 06510 Calmodulin and regulation in trypanosomes

R01AI-21870-05 (ALY) BLOMBERG, BONNIE B UNIVERSITY OF MIAMI P O BOX 016960 (R-138) MIAMI, FL 33101 Studies on human lambda light chain immunoglobulin genes

R01AI-21884-07 (TMP) MERRITT, RICHARD W MICHIGAN STATE UNIVERSITY EAST LANSING, MI 48824 Feeding ecology of larval mosquitoes in natural habitats

R01AI-21885-07 (EDC) GRAYSTON, J THOMAS UNIVERSITY OF WASHINGTON SC -36 SEATTLE, WA 98195 Human infection with chlamydia

R01AI-21897-07 (SSS) GANGADHARAM, PATTISAPU R UNIVERSITY OF ILLINOIS 840 S WOOD STREET CHICAGO, IL 60680 Immunopathology of mycobacterium intracellulare in AIDS

R01AI-21903-07 (TMP) BEVERLEY, STEPHEN M HARVARD MEDICAL SCHOOL 250 LONGWOOD AVENUE BOSTON, MA 02115 Mechanism of gene amplification in leishmania

P01AI-21912-08 (MID) BROOKS, GEO F U OF CALIFORNIA, SAN FRANCISCO SAN FRANCISCO, CA 94143-0100 Bay area STD research program

P01AI-21912-08 0004 (MID) BOLAN, G Bay area STD research program Behavior in recurrent gonococcal infection

P01AI-21912-08 0005 (MID) PALEFSKY, J Bay area STD research program Manifestations and biology of HPV in sexual partners

P01AI-21912-08 0006 (MID) STEPHEN, R Bay area STD research program Serologic evaluation on chlamydia in SIDS

P01AI-21912-08 0007 (MID) BROOKS, G Bay area STD research program Gonococcal antigen-mediated damage to human fallopian tube

P01AI-21912-08 0008 (MID) GRIFFIS, M Bay area STD research program Gonococcal LOS interactions with cell surface lectins

P01AI-21912-08 9001 (MID) SCHACTER, J Bay area STD research program Clinical core

P01AI-21912-08 9004 (MID) BROOKS, G Bay area STD research program Core projects

R01AI-21946-07 (BM) BARROW, WILLIAM W TEXAS COLLEGE OF OSTEOPATHIC M 3500 CAMP BOWIE BLVD FORT WORTH, TX 76107 Processing of AIDS related mycobacterial antigens

R01AI-21951-07 (BM) LIPSCOMB, MARY F UNIV OF TEXAS SW MED CTR DALLAS, TX 75235-9072 Pulmonary defenses in opportunistic infections

R01AI-21961-07 (HEM) GABIG, THEODORE G INDIANA UNIVERSITY 975 WEST WALNUT STREET INDIANAPOLIS, IN 46202-5121 Oxidant generation by blood neutrophils and monocytes

R01AI-21964-06 (CBY) ARNAOUT, M AMIN MASSACHUSETTS GENERAL HOSPITAL FRUIT STREET BOSTON, MA 02114 Molecular basis of mo1/1fa1 deficiency in man--Disease modl

R01AI-21973-12 (EVR) ROHRMANN, GEORGE F OREGON STATE UNIVERSITY CORVALLIS, OR 97331 Nucleopolyhedrosis viruses of Orgyia pseudotsugata

R01AI-21975-07 (TMP) AGABIAN, NINA M UNIV OF CALIF, SAN FRANCISCO 926 MEDICAL SCIENCES BLDG. SAN FRANCISCO, CA 94143-0446 Molecular basis of antigenic variation

R01AI-22001-08 (EVR) O'CALLAGHAN, DENNIS J LOUISIANA STATE UNIV MED CTR 1501 KING'S HIGHWAY SHREVEPORT, LA 71130-3932 Study of nucleic acids of herpesvirus infected cells

R01AI-22003-08 (ALY) WRIGHT, SAMUEL D ROCKEFELLER UNIVERSITY 1230 YORK AVENUE NEW YORK, NY 10021 Structure and function of human C3 receptors

R01AI-22005-08 (ALY) SILVER, JACK NORTH SHORE UNIV HOSPITAL 300 COMMUNITY DRIVE MANHASSET, NY 11030 Functional analysis of human Ia

R01AI-22009-07 (ALY) ZAUDERER, MAURICE UNIVERSITY OF ROCHESTER 601 ELMWOOD AVE, BOX 704 ROCHESTER, NY 14642 Subsets of helper T cells in immune regulation

R37AI-22021-08 (MBC) COLLIER, ROBERT J HARVARD MEDICAL SCHOOL 25 SHATTUCK STREET BOSTON, MA 02115 Molecular mechanisms of bacterial pathogenesis

R01AI-22033-07 (ALY) UNANUE, EMIL R WASHINGTON UNIVERSITY SCH OF M 660 SOUTH EUCLID AVE, BOX 8118 ST LOUIS, MO 63110 Studies of antigen stimulation

R22AI-22038-07 (TMP) INSELBURG, JOSEPH W DARTMOUTH MEDICAL SCHOOL HANOVER, NH 03756 Plasmodium falciparum antigens for vaccine

R01AI-22039-07 (ALY) PARHAM, PETER R STANFORD UNIVERSITY SHERMAN FAIRCHILD BUILDING STANFORD, CA 94305 Interactions between HLA-A, B & antigen receptors of CTL

R01AI-22070-05 (TMP) TARLETON, RICK L DEPARTMENT OF ZOOLOGY UNIVERSITY OF GEORGIA ATHENS, GA 30602 Immunoregulation in experimental Chagas' disease

R01AI-22072-05 (GMA) STREILEIN, WAYNE J UNIVERSITY OF MIAMI PO BOX 016960 MIAMI, FL 33101 Langerhans cells in contact hypersensitivity

R01AI-22082-05 (BM) KUO, CHO-CHOU UNIVERSITY OF WASHINGTON

SEATTLE, WA 98195 Subcutaneous model of chlamydial salpingitis in monkeys

R01AI-22116-06 (EVR) PELUSO, RICHARD W MOUNT SINAI SCHOOL OF MEDICINE ONE GUSTAVE L LEVY PLACE NEW YORK, N Y 10029 Mechanism of RNA replication of negative-strand viruses

R01AI-22119-06 (TMP) SCOTT, THOMAS W UNIVERSITY OF MARYLAND DIV OF AGRIC. & LIFE SCIENCES COLLEGE PARK, MD 20742-5575 Multiple blood feeding by mosquitoes

R01AI-22125-07 (EI) SWAIN, SUSAN L UNIV OF CALIFORNIA, SAN DIEGO 9500 GILMAN DRIVE, 0063 LA JOLLA, CA 92093-0063 The role of helper T cells in the B cell response

R37AI-22144-07 (GEN) SELANDER, ROBERT K PENNSYLVANIA STATE UNIVERSITY MUELLER LAB UNIVERSITY PARK, PA 16802 Molecular population genetics of pathogenic bacteria

R01AI-22159-07 (BM) NOVICK, RICHARD P PUBLIC HEALTH RESEARCH INST 455 FIRST AVENUE NEW YORK, NY 10016 Biology and genetics of toxic shock syndrome toxin-1

R01AI-22160-06 (BM) TAINER, JOHN A THE SCRIPPS RESEARCH INSTITUTE 10666 NORTH TORREY PINES ROAD LA JOLLA, CA 92037 Assembly and structure of neisseria gonorrheae pili

R01AI-22166-06 (MBY) FEY, GEORG H SCRIPPS CLINIC & RESEARCH FDN DEPT OF IMMUNOLOGY, IMM14 LA JOLLA, CA 92037 Structure and regulation of liver acute phase genes

R01AI-22176-06 (BM) GOGUEN, JON D UNIV OF MASSACHUSETTS MED SCH 55 LAKE AVENUE NORTH WORCESTER, MA 01655 Plasmids and virulence in plague

R01AI-22181-07 (IMB) KRAIG, ELLEN B UNIV OF TEXAS HLTH SCI CTR 7703 FLOYD CURL DRIVE SAN ANTONIO, TX 78284-7762 Antigen receptor genes from T-helper and T-suppressor cells

R01AI-22183-07 (MBC) ROTHFIELD, LAWRENCE I UNIV OF CONNECTICUT HLTH CTR 263 FARMINGTON AVENUE FARMINGTON, CT 06032 Studies of bacterial cell division

R01AI-22186-06 (VR) JOHNSTON, ROBERT E UNIVERSITY OF N.C. @ CHAPEL HI DEPT OF MICROBIO/IMMUNOLOGY CHAPEL HILL, NC 27599 Molecular basis of alphavirus neurovirulence

R01AI-22192-07 (VR) AURELIAN, LAURE UNIVERSITY OF MARYLAND 10 SOUTH PINE STREET BALTIMORE, MD 21201 Vaccinia vectored HSV genes in protective immunity

R01AI-22193-07 (HEM) SCHREIBER, ALAN D 3400 SPRUCE STREET PHILADELPHIA, PA 19104 Human blood monocyte receptor expression and modulation

R01AI-22199-08 (BM) SCHELL, RONALD F UNIV OF WISCONSIN MED SCH 1300 UNIVERSITY AVENUE MADISON, WI 53706 Specific immune reactivity to treponemal infection

R01AI-22214-07 (IMS) TACK, BRIAN F RES INST OF SCRIPPS CLINIC 10666 NORTH TORREY PINES ROAD LA JOLLA, CA 92037 Molecular analysis of complement component C5

R01AI-22223-07 (MBC) ORNDORFF, PAUL E NORTH CAROLINA STATE UNIV COL OF VET MED, BOX 8401 RALEIGH, NC 27606 Control and expression of type 1 pili in E coli

R01AI-22229-06 (TMP) CROSS, GEORGE A M ROCKEFELLER UNIVERSITY 1230 YORK AVENUE NEW YORK, NY 10021-6399 Trypanosome gene expression and environmental adaptation

R01AI-22243-05 (BM) GOLDMAN, WILLIAM E WASHINGTON UNIV SCHOOL OF MED BOX 8093 ST LOUIS, MO 63110 Bordetella pertussis tracheal cytotoxin

R37AI-22251-08 (EVR) BERNS, KENNETH I CORNELL MEDICAL COLLEGE 1300 YORK AVE; BOX 62 NEW YORK, NY 10021 Molecular biology of adeno-associated virus

R01AI-22252-07 (PB) BARRETT, ANTHONY G COLORADO STATE UNIVERSITY FORT COLLINS, CO 80523 Total synthesis of antifungal agents

R01AI-22259-07 (IMB) PALMER, EDWARD NAT'L JEWISH CTR/IMM & RES MED 1400 JACKSON STREET DENVER, CO 80206 Genetics of T lymphocyte antigen receptors

R01AI-22277-07 (ALY) KENNERLY, DONALD A U OF TEX SW MED CTR/INT MED 5323 HARRY HINES BLVD DALLAS, TX 75235-9030 Role of diacylglycerol metabolism in mast cell secretion

R01AI-22280-07 (EVR) ARVIN, ANN M STANFORD UNIV SCHOOL OF MED STANFORD, CA 94305 Varicella-Zoster infection/immunity in guinea pigs

R01AI-22293-06 (SB) THOMAS, JUDITH M EAST CAROLINA UNIVERSITY BRODY BUILDING GREENVILLE, NC 27858-4354 A preclinical model of allograft tolerance

P01AI-22295-07 (SRC) MARRACK, PHILIPPA C NTN'L JEWISH CTR FOR I & R MED 1400 JACKSON STREET DENVER, CO 80206 Antigen recognition by T cells

P01AI-22295-07 0001 (SRC) MARRACK, PHILIPPA C Antigen recognition by T cells Generation of antibodies to T cell receptor

P01AI-22295-07 0002 (SRC) AUGUSTIN, ANDREI A Antigen recognition by T cells T cell receptos--Diversity and connectivity

P01AI-22295-07 0004 (SRC) CAMBIER, JOHN C Antigen recognition by T cells T cell receptor mediated transmembrane signaling

P01AI-22295-07 0005 (SRC) GREY, HOWARD M Antigen recognition by T cells Requirements for class I restricted E cell recognition of antigen

P01AI-22295-07 0006 (SRC) PALMER, EDWARD Antigen recognition by T cells The regulation of V alpha 7 expressing T cells

P01AI-22295-07 9001 (SRC) CAMBIER, JOHN C Antigen recognition by T cells Flow cytometry facility core

P01AI-22295-07 9002 (SRC) FREED, JOHN Antigen recognition by T cells Chemistry facility core

R01AI-22296-06 (ET) BAKER, DAVID C UNIVERSITY OF TENNESSEE KNOXVILLE, TN 37996-1600 Biosynthesis of Ara-2, 2'-deoxycoformycin analogues

R01AI-22307-06 (EVR) KENNEDY, RONALD C SOUTHWEST FDN FOR BIOMED RES P O BOX 28147 SAN ANTONIO, TX 78228-0147 Idiotypic analysis of the immune response to HBV

R37AI-22346-09 (NSS) BALTIMORE, DAVID ROCKEFELLER UNIVERSITY 1230 YORK AVENUE NEW YORK, N Y 10021 Molecular biology of picornaviruses

R01AI-22350-05 (HEM) WEILER, JOHN M UNIVERSITY OF IOWA HOSPITALS IOWA CITY, IA 52242 Protamine hypersensitivity and polyion biology

R01AI-22374-12A2 (SAT) NELSON, ROBERT D UNIVERSITY OF MINNESOTA BOX 124 UHMC MINNEAPOLIS, MN 55455 Mechanism of human leukocyte chemotaxis

P01AI-22380-07 (SRC) BASEMAN, JOEL B UNIV OF TEXAS HLTH SCIS CTR 7703 FLOYD CURL DRIVE SAN ANTONIO, TX 78284-7758 Program on sexually transmitted diseases

P01AI-22380-07 0001 (SRC) ALDERETE, JOHN F Program on sexually transmitted diseases Immunochemistry of Trichomonas vaginalis surfaces and immunogens

P01AI-22380-07 0002 (SRC) BASEMAN, JOEL B Program on sexually transmitted diseases Molecular analysis of Treponema pallidum adherence

P01AI-22380-07 0003 (SRC) MATTINGLY, STEPHEN J Program on sexually transmitted diseases Virulence of group B streptococci in neonatal disease

P01AI-22380-07 0004 (SRC) WILLIAMS, DWIGHT M Program on sexually transmitted diseases Cellular immunity in Chlamydia trachomatis infection

P01AI-22380-07 0005 (SRC) KENNEDY, RONALD C Program on sexually transmitted diseases Monoclonal anti-idiotype vaccine strategies for Hepatis B virus

P01AI-22380-07 9002 (SRC) MORRISON-PLUMMER, JANICE Program on sexually transmitted diseases Antibody core

P01AI-22380-07 9003 (SRC) GIBBS, RONALD S Program on sexually transmitted diseases Clinical core

R01AI-22383-06 (MBC) SALYERS, ABIGAIL A UNIVERSITY OF ILLINOIS 407 SOUTH GOODWIN AVENUE URBANA, IL 61801 Conjugal transfer of bacteroides antibiotic resistances

R01AI-22415-06 (ALY) DISCIPIO, RICHARD G SCRIPPS RESEARCH INSTITUTE 10666 NORTH TORREY PINES RD LA JOLLA, CA 92037 Lytic factors of the immune system

R01AI-22420-07 (IMB) PEASE, LARRY R MAYO FOUNDATION 200 FIRST ST-SW ROCHESTER, MN 55905 Diversity in H-2 haplotypes

R01AI-22421-06 (BM) HORWITZ, MARCUS A UCLA SCHOOL OF MEDICINE CTR FOR THE HLTH SCI, 37-121 LOS ANGELES, CA 90024-1406 Immune responses to an intracellular pulmonary pathogen

R01AI-22436-05 (IMS) METCALF, ELEANOR S UNIFORMED SERV UNIV/HLTH SCIS 4301 JONES BRIDGE ROAD BETHESDA, MD 20814 Host environment and B cell repertoire expression

R01AI-22441-07 (BM) MANSFIELD, JOHN M UNIVERSITY OF WISCONSIN 1655 LINDEN DRIVE MADISON, WI 53706 Immunobiology of African trypansomiasis

R01AI-22449-06 (ALY) HOLOWKA, DAVID A CORNELL UNIVERSITY ITHACA, N Y 14853 Antigen binding, crosslinking and transmembrane signaling

R01AI-22456-06 (BM) MARKHAM, RICHARD B JOHNS HOPKINS UNIVERSITY SCHOOL OF PUBLIC HEALTH BALTIMORE, MD 21205 T cell killing of extracellular bacteria

R01AI-22468-07 (EVR) RUYECHAN, WILLIAM T USUHS 4301 JONES BRIDGE ROAD BETHESDA, MD 20814 Proteins involved in replication and expression of HSV DNA

R01AI-22470-05 (EVR) WHITE, JUDITH M UNIVERSITY OF CALIFORNIA DEPARTMENT OF PHARMACOLOGY SAN FRANCISCO, CA 94143-0450 Mechanism of viral membrane fusion proteins

R22AI-22488-07 (TMP) WEIL, GARY J JEWISH HOSP/WASH U MED CTR 216 S KINGSHIGHWAY ST LOUIS, MO 63110 Circulating parasite antigens in human filariasis

R01AI-22498-07 (BM) RUBENS, CRAIG E CHILDREN'S HOSPITAL & MED CTR 4800 SAND POINT WAY N E SEATTLE, WA 98105 Genetics of virulence of type III group B streptococcus

R01AI-22501-07 (EDC) LANE, ROBERT S UNIVERSITY OF CALIFORNIA 201 WELLMAN HALL BERKELEY, CA 94720 Lyme disease in western USA--Ecology and epidemiology

R01AI-22503-07 (VR) GANEM, DONALD E U OF CALIF AT SAN FRANCISCO 3RD & PARNASSUS AVENUES SAN FRANCISCO, CA 94143-0414 Hepatitis B surface antigen secretion and assembly

R01AI-22510-07 (EVR) SEN, GANES C CLEVELAND CLINIC FOUNDATION 9500 EUCLID AVENUE CLEVELAND, OH 44195-5178 Antiviral actions of interferons

R01AI-22511-07 (IMB) DAVIS, MARK M STANFORD UNIVERSITY BECKMAN CENTER/SCHOOL OF MED STANFORD, CALIFORNIA 94305-542 Murine T-cell receptor structure and recognition

R37AI-22519-08 (IMB) WILSON, DARCY B LA JOLLA INST/EXPERIMENTAL MED 11099 N TORREY PINES RD, STE 1 LA JOLLA, CA 92037 Lymphocytes & histocompatibility antigens

R22AI-22520-06 (TMP) TRACY, JAMES W UNIVERSITY OF WISCONSIN 2015 LINDEN DRIVE WEST MADISON, WI 53706-1102 Biochemistry of schistosome glutathione s-transferases

R01AI-22528-06 (IMB) HEBER-KATZ, ELLEN WISTAR INST 36TH & SPRUCE ST PHILADELPHIA, PA 19104 Immunobiology of anti-viral T cell responses

R37AI-22531-07 (ALY) AUSTEN, K FRANK SEELEY G MUDD BUILDING 250 LONGWOOD AVENUE BOSTON, MA 02115 In vitro studies of the mechanism of anaphylaxis

R01AI-22532-07 (IMB) DAVID, JOHN R BRIGHAM AND WOMEN'S HOSP INC. SEELY G. MUDD BLDG/FIFTH FLOOR BOSTON, MA 02115 Studies on cellular immunity

R01AI-22535-07 (BM) PIER, GERALD B CHANNING LABORATORY 180 LONGWOOD AVENUE BOSTON, MA 02115-5899 Polysaccharide vaccine to pseudomonas aeruginosa

R22AI-22553-08 (BM) MODLIN, ROBERT L UNIV OF CALIFORNIA, LOS ANGELE 10833 LE CONTE AVENUE LOS ANGELES, CA 90024-1750 Immunoregulatory cells in leprosy lesions

R01AI-22557-07 (EVR) FOUNG, STEVEN K H STANFORD UNIVERSITY BLOOD CTR 800 WELCH ROAD PALO ALTO, CA 94304 Human monoclonal antibodies to cytomegalovirus

R01AI-22563-07 (TMP) SOBERMAN, ROY J SEELEY G MUDD BUILDING 250 LONGWOOD AVENUE BOSTON, MA 02115 Biosynthesis, biology and metabolism of the leukotrienes

R01AI-22564-07 (HEM) MCPHAIL, LINDA C BOWMAN GRAY SCH OF MED 300 SOUTH HAWTHORNE ROAD WINSTON-SALEM, N C 27103 Regulation of oxygen metabolism in blood neutrophils

R01AI-22571-06A1 (PTHA) WELLER, PETER F BETH ISRAEL HOSPITAL 330

PROJECT NO., ORGANIZATIONAL UNIT., INVESTIGATOR, ADDRESS, TITLE

BROOKLINE AVENUE BOSTON, MA 02215 Cytoplasmic lipid bodies of inflammatory cells

R01AI-22603-06A1 (PBC) HASTY, KAREN A UNIV OF TENNESSEE, MEMPHIS 875 MONROE AVENUE MEMPHIS, TN 38163 Characterization of human neutrophil collagenase

R01AI-22610-06 (EVR) FRASER, MALCOLM J, JR UNIVERSITY OF NOTRE DAME COLLEGE OF SCIENCE NOTRE DAME, IN 46556 Transposon mutagenesis of nuclear polyhedrosis viruses

R22AI-22616-06 (BM) KAPLAN, GILLA ROCKEFELLER UNIVERSITY 1230 YORK AVENUE BOX 280 NEW YORK, NY 10021 Pathobiology of human leprosy

R37AI-22624-07 (ARR) JOHNSON, WARREN D, JR CORNELL UNIV MEDICAL COLLEGE 1300 YORK AVE NEW YORK, NY 10021 Natural history of HIV infection in Haiti

R01AI-22627-07 (VR) CHOW, MARIE MASSACHUSETTS INST OF TECH 77 MASSACHUSETTS AVE, 56-217 CAMBRIDGE, MA 02139 Molecular analysis of poliovirus neutralizing epitopes

R01AI-22635-05 (TMP) PARSONS, MARILYN SEATTLE BIOMEDICAL RES INST 4 NICKERSON STREET SEATTLE, WA 98109-1651 Molecular analysis of the Trypanosome glycosome

R01AI-22646-07 (EVR) KATZE, MICHAEL G UNIVERSITY OF WASHINGTON SEATTLE, WA 98195 Translational control in influenza virus infected cells

R22AI-22653-06 (BM) MOHAGHEGHPOUR, NAHID MED RES INST OF SAN FRANCISCO 2200 WEBSTER STREET SAN FRANCISCO, CA 94115 Immunologic defects in lepromatous leprosy

R01AI-22662-05 (TMP) SCHAD, GERHARD A UNIVERSITY OF PENNSYLVANIA 3800 SPRUCE ST PHILADELPHIA, PA 19104 Human strongyloidiasis--development of a canine model

R01AI-22664-07 (SAT) KAHAN, BARRY D THE UNIV OF TEXAS MED SCHOOL 6431 FANNIN STREET HOUSTON, TX 77030 A clinical model of donor-specific unresponsiveness

R01AI-22667-06 (VR) STANBERRY, LAWRENCE R CHILDREN'S HOSPITAL RES FDN ELLAND AND BETHESDA AVENUE CINCINNATI, OHIO 45229 -2899 Viral persistence--studies with herpes simplex virus

N01AI-22668-26 (**) GALUN, RACHEL Epidemiology and control of arthropod-borne diseases

R01AI-22674-06 (ALY) GALLI, STEPHEN J BETH ISRAEL HOSPITAL 330 BROOKLINE AVENUE BOSTON, MA 02215 Role of mast cells in inflammation and immunity

R01AI-22687-05 (ALY) BERGER, MELVIN CASE WESTERN RESERVE UNIV 2101 ADELBERT ROAD CLEVELAND, OH 44106 Complement receptor expression on human neutrophils

R01AI-22693-07 (VR) SEMLER, BERT L UNIVERSITY OF CALIFORNIA CALIFORNIA COLLEGE OF MEDICINE IRVINE, CA 92717 Poliovirus gene function and regulation

R01AI-22697-07 (PBC) SHEPHERD, VIRGINIA L VANDERBILT UNIVERSITY B-1308, MEDICAL CENTER NORTH NASHVILLE, TN 37232 Mechanisms of mannose receptor modulation in macrophage

R01AI-22711-07 (VR) GIBSON, D WADE JOHNS HOPKINS SCHOOL OF MEDICI 725 NORTH WOLFE STREET BALTIMORE, MD 21205 Cytomegalovirus proteins--Immunochemical studies

R01AI-22726-06 (TMP) REED, STEVEN G SEATTLE BIOMED RES INST 4 NICKERSON STREET SEATTLE, WA 98109-1651 Immunosuppression in Trypanosoma cruzi infections

R01AI-22730-06 (IMB) DAILEY, MORRIS O UNIVERSITY OF IOWA COLLEGE COLLEGE OF MEDICINE IOWA CITY, IA 52242 Characterization of leukocyte endothelial cell receptors

R01AI-22735-06 (HEM) JESAITIS, ALGIRDAS J MONTANA STATE UNIVERSITY BOZEMAN, MT 59717 Regulation of chemoattractant activation of neutrophils

R01AI-22745-07 (SSS) GOLDSTEIN, ELLIOT UNIVERSITY OF KANSAS 39TH AND RAINBOW BOULEVARD KANSAS CITY, KANSAS 66103-841 Development of a computer-assisted assay of cell motion

R44AI-22760-03 (SSS) BOCHNER, BARRY R BIOLOG, INC 3447 INVESTMENT BLVD HAYWARD, CA 94545 Rapid accurate identification of yeasts

R01AI-22795-06A1 (EVR) GROSE, CHARLES F UNIVERSITY OF IOWA NEWTON ROAD IOWA CITY, IA 52242 Antigenic determinants of varicella virus

R01AI-22801-06 (EI) WEISER, WEISHUI Y BRIGHAM AND WOMEN'S HOSPITAL 250 LONGWOOD AVENUE BOSTON, MA 02115 Recombinant migration inhibitory factor

R01AI-22802-06 (ALY) ABBAS, ABUL K BRIGHAM & WOMEN'S HOSPITAL 75 FRANCIS STREET BOSTON, MA 02115 Regulatory mechanisms in antibody production

R01AI-22806-06 (BM) PIER, GERALD B CHANNING LABORATORY 180 LONGWOOD AVENUE BOSTON, MA 02115 Immunochemical study of P. aeruginosa mucoid antigens

R01AI-22809-06 (PB) LAMBETH, JOHN D EMORY UNIVERSITY SCH OF MED DEPT OF BIOCHEMISTRY ATLANTA, GA 30322 Neutrophil plasma membrane oxidative enzymes

R37AI-22813-25 (NSS) RUECKERT, ROLAND R UNIVERSITY OF WISCONSIN 1525 LINDEN DRIVE MADISON, WI 53706 Structure and synthesis of retro- and adenoviruses

R01AI-22832-06 (IMB) ECKELS, DAVID D BLOOD CTR SOUTHEASTERN WISCON 1701 WEST WISCONSIN AVENUE MILWAUKEE, WI 53233 Genetic regulation of human T-Lymphocyte clones

R01AI-22833-08 (ALY) FEARON, DOUGLAS T JOHNS HOPKINS UNIVERSITY 725 N WOLFE ST, 617 HUNTERIAN BALTIMORE, MD 21205 Biology and biochemistry of the human C3b receptor

R37AI-22835-07 (NSS) PREISS, JACK MICHIGAN STATE UNIVERSITY EAST LANSING, MI 48824-1319 Regulation of polysaccharide synthesis

R01AI-22839-06 (BM) LEHRER, ROBERT I UCLA SCHOOL OF MEDICINE CENTER FOR HEALTH SCIENCES LOS ANGELES, CA 90024 Defensins--Antimicrobial peptides of human neutrophils

R01AI-22848-06 (BM) COLLIER, ROBERT J HARVARD MEDICAL SCHOOL 200 LONGWOOD AVENUE BOSTON, MA 02115 Recombinant toxoids of bacterial exotoxins

R01AI-22871-06 (IMB) MOSIER, DONALD E MEDICAL BIOLOGY INSTITUTE 11077 NORTH TORREY PINES ROAD LA JOLLA, CA 92037 Induction and regulation of B lymphocyte activation

R01AI-22881-05 (VR) RAWLINS, DAN R EMORY UNIVERSITY 3119 ROLLINS RESEARCH CTR ATLANTA, GA 30322 Control of lytic Epstein-Barr virus DNA replication

PROJECT NO., ORGANIZATIONAL UNIT., INVESTIGATOR, ADDRESS, TITLE

R01AI-22882-05S1 (IMB) STROM, TERRY B BETH ISRAEL HOSPITAL 330 BROOKLINE AVE BOSTON, MA 02215 Interleukin 2 receptor target therapy in transplantation

R01AI-22894-06 (EVR) CAUGHMAN, GRETCHEN B MEDICAL COLLEGE OF GEORGIA 1120 15TH STREET AUGUSTA, GA 30912-1126 Regulation of herpes proteins in persistent infection

R01AI-22898-05 (BBCB) HERRON, JAMES N UNIVERSITY OF UTAH 421 WAKARA WAY SALT LAKE CITY, UT 84108 Molecular basis of antigenic specificity

R01AI-22900-06 (ALY) RAO, ANJANA DANA-FARBER CANCER INSTITUTE 44 BINNEY STREET BOSTON, MA 02115 Analysis of T cell receptor function by gene transfer

R01AI-22931-07 (BM) SELSTED, MICHAEL E UNIVERSITY OF CALIFORNIA COLLEGE OF MEDICINE IRVINE, CA 92717 Moleculoar aspects of leukocyte antimicrobial peptides

R01AI-22933-06 (BM) HEFFRON, FRED OREGON HEALTH SCIENCES UNIV 3181 SW SAM JACKSON PARK RD PORTLAND, OR 97201-3098 Salmonella genes required for survival in the macrophage

R01AI-22940-05 (IMS) GRANT, J ANDREW UNIV OF TEXAS MEDICAL BRANCH CLINICAL SCIENCES 409 GALVESTON, TX 77550 Mononuclear cell factors affecting basophils and mast cells

R01AI-22946-04A2 (TMP) BUCK, GREGORY A VIRGINIA COMMONWEALTH UNIVERSI BOX 678, MCV STATION RICHMOND, VA 23298-0678 Novel RNA capping activities in Trypanosoma cruzi

R37AI-22959-06 (NSS) MILLER, I GEORGE, JR YALE UNIVERSITY 333 CEDAR ST/ BOX 3333 NEW HAVEN, CT 06510 Pathogenesis of Epstein-Barr virus infections

R01AI-22963-06 (BM) HOWARD, DEXTER H UCLA SCH OF MED CTR/HLTH SCIS LOS ANGELES, CA 90024-1747 Molecular bases of interferon-induced fungistasis

R01AI-22983-06 (BM) SO, MAGADALENE Y H OREGON HEALTH SCIENCES UNIV 3181 SW JACKSON PARK RD PORTLAND, OR 97201-3098 Novel salmonella/vector system for antigen delivery

R01AI-22993-04A3 (TMP) KERWIN, JAMES L UNIVERSITY OF WASHINGTON SEATTLE, WA 98195 Morphogenesis of the mosquito pathogen Lagenidium

R01AI-22998-06 (BM) YAMASAKI, RYOHEI UNIVERSITY OF CALIFORNIA 4150 CLEMENT ST SAN FRANCISCO, CA 94121 Stereochemistry of the gonococcal LOS epitopes

R01AI-23004-07 (TMP) MCMAHON-PRATT, DIANE M YALE UNIVERSITY SCHOOL OF MED 60 COLLEGE ST, P.O. BOX 3333 NEW HAVEN, CT 06510 Leishmania antigens-biochemical and immunologic studies

R01AI-23007-05 (BBCB) CROSS, TIMOTHY A FLORIDA STATE UNIVERSITY TALLAHASSEE, FL 32306 Dynamic and structural elucidation of gramicidin A

R01AI-23010-05 (MBY) EISEN, HARVEY A FRED HUTCHINSON CANCER RES CTR 1124 COLUMBIA STREET SEATTLE, WA 98104 Molecular biology of gene expression in Trypanosomes

R01AI-23017-06 (BM) DEEPE, GEORGE S UNIVERSITY OF CINCINNATI 321 BETHESDA AVENUE CINCINNATI, OH 45267-0560 Studies of H capsulatum-reactive murine T cell clones (mice)

R01AI-23039-05 (MBC) VIMR, ERIC R UNIVERSITY OF ILLINOIS 2001 SOUTH LINCOLN AVENUE URBANA, IL 61801 Mechanisms of polysialic acid assembly in E coli

R01AI-23044-06 (BM) RANK, ROGER G UNIVERSITY OF ARKANSAS MED SCI 4301 WEST MARKHAM LITTLE ROCK, AR 72205 Immunity to chlamydial genital and eye infections

R01AI-23047-05S1 (IMS) GRIFFIN, DIANE E JOHNS HOPKINS UNIVERSITY 600 N. WOLFE ST., MEYER 6-181 BALTIMORE, MD 21205 Immune response during measles virus infection

R01AI-23052-06 (ALY) LOBB, CRAIG J U OF MISSISSIPPI MED CTR 2500 NORTH STATE STREET JACKSON, MS 39216-4505 Systemic and mucosal immunity in ectotherms

R01AI-23081-07 (IMS) CRESSWELL, PETER YALE MEDICAL SCHOOL 310 CEDAR STREET NEW HAVEN, CT 06510 Role of endocytosis in cell recognition

R22AI-23083-07 (TMP) CAULFIELD, JOHN P SYNTEX (U.S.A.) INC 3401 HILLVIEW AVE, S3-6 PALO ALTO, CA 94304 S. mansoni: immune induced surface changes

R01AI-23140-02A3 (BM) SCALARONE, GENE M IDAHO STATE UNIVERSITY BOX 8007 POCATELLO, ID 83209 Enzyme immunoassays for the diagnosis of blastomycosis

R01AI-23168-07 (MBC) FISHER, SUSAN H BOSTON UNIV SCHOOL OF MEDICINE 80 E CONCORD BOSTON, MA 02118 The regulation of glutamine synthetase in streptomyces

R01AI-23173-06 (VR) LAMB, ROBERT A NORTHWESTERN UNIVERSITY 2153 SHERIDAN ROAD EVANSTON, IL 60208-3500 Structure and expression of the paramyxovirus SV5 genome

R01AI-23181-06 (IMS) BUSSE, WILLIAM W UNIVERSITY OF WISCONSIN 600 HIGHLAND AVENUE MADISON, WI 53792 Function of the isolated eosinophil in asthma

R01AI-23244-06A2 (BM) LEE, JEAN C CHANNING LABORATORY 180 LONGWOOD AVENUE BOSTON, MA 02115-5899 Staphylococcus aureus--Capsular antigens and immunity

R01AI-23246-04 (ALY) CHIN, YEE HON UNIVERSITY OF MIAMI R-138 P O BOX 016960 MIAMI, FL 33101 Cell surface structures in lymphocyte migration

R37AI-23253-07 (NSS) HILDEBRAND, JOHN G UNIVERSITY OF ARIZONA 611 GOULD-SIMPSON SCI BLDG TUCSON, AZ 85721 Central mechanisms of antennal senses in insects

R01AI-23262-07 (HEM) SOUTHWICK, FREDERICK S UNIV OF FLORIDA COLL OF MED BOX J-277 JHMHC GAINESVILLE, FL 32610-0217 Regulation of actin filament formation in phagocytes

P01AI-23271-06 (AITC) CAPRA, J DONALD UNIV OF TEXAS SOUTHWESTERN 5323 HARRY HINES BLVD DALLAS, TX 75235 Major histocompatibility complex in human disease

P01AI-23271-06 0001 (AITC) CAPRA, J DONALD Major histocompatibility complex in human disease HLA-D and T cell receptor genes in human disease

P01AI-23271-06 0002 (AITC) STASTNY, PETER Major histocompatibility complex in human disease T cells in allergy to mountain cedar pollen allergen

P01AI-23271-06 0003 (AITC) SULLIVAN, TIMOTHY J Major histocompatibility complex in human disease Immunochemical and

immunogenetic studies of mountain cedar allergy
P01AI-23271-06 9001 (AITC) CAPRA, J DONALD Major histocompatibility complex in human disease Core--Tissue culture and molecular biology
P01AI-23271-06 9002 (AITC) STASTNY, PETER Major histocompatibility complex in human disease Core--HLA typing
R01AI-23283-07 (MGN) STAVNEZER, JANET M UNIV OF MASSACHUSETTS MED SCH 55 LAKE AVENUE NORTH WORCESTER, MA 01655 Molecular basis of immunoglobulin heavy chain switch
P01AI-23287-06 (AITC) DUTTON, RICHARD W UNIVERSITY OF CALIFORNIA CANCER CENTER Q-063 LA JOLLA, CA 92093 Lymphocyte receptors, ligands, and biological function
P01AI-23287-06 0001 (AITC) SWAIN, SUSAN L Lymphocyte receptors, ligands, and biological function Consequences of direct helper T cell-B cell interaction
P01AI-23287-06 0002 (AITC) DUTTON, RICHARD W Lymphocyte receptors, ligands, and biological function Molecular characterization of BCGFII lymphokine and BCGFII receptors
P01AI-23287-06 0003 (AITC) HEDRICK, STEPHEN M Lymphocyte receptors, ligands, and biological function Functional analysis of gamma/delta bearing T cells in transgenic mice
P01AI-23287-06 0004 (AITC) BRAIN, ADRIENNE Lymphocyte receptors, ligands, and biological function Membrane associated lymphocyte growth factors
P01AI-23287-06 0005 (AITC) SINGER, S JONATHAN Lymphocyte receptors, ligands, and biological function Intracellular events induced by receptor-ligand interactions in immune system
P01AI-23287-06 0006 (AITC) DUTTON, RICHARD Lymphocyte receptors, ligands, and biological function Dynamcis of cell interactions with other cells
P01AI-23287-06 0007 (AITC) VARKI, AJIT Lymphocyte receptors, ligands, and biological function Effects of gangliosides on T-B cell interaction
P01AI-23287-06 9003 (AITC) SWAIN, SUSAN Lymphocyte receptors, ligands, and biological function Core-cell culture, hybridoma and flow cytometry
R01AI-23302-06 (ARR) GIGLIOTTI, FRANCIS UNIVERSITY OF ROCHESTER 601 ELMWOOD AVENUE ROCHESTER, NY 14642 Monoclonal antibodies for the study of P carinii
R01AI-23328-06 (BM) MOBLEY, HARRY L UNIVERSITY OF MARYLAND 10 SOUTH PINE STREET BALTIMORE, MD 21201 Bacterial urease in urinary tract infection
R01AI-23335-05 (BM) PIER, GERALD B CHANNING LABORATORY 180 LONGWOOD AVENUE BOSTON, MA 02115 Adhesins of coagulase negative staphylococci
R01AI-23338-07 (IMB) LITMAN, GARY W UNIVERSITY OF SOUTH FLORIDA 801 SIXTH ST SOUTH, BOX 707 ST PETERSBURG, FL 33701 Early evolutionary origin of immunoglobulin genes
R01AI-23339-07 (BM) KASPER, DENNIS L CHANNING LABORATORY 180 LONGWOOD AVENUE BOSTON, MA 02115 group b streptococcal polysaccharides
R01AI-23348-04A2 (MBC) LOW, DAVID A UNIVERSITY OF UTAH 50 NORTH MEDICAL DRIVE SALT LAKE CITY, UT 84132 The role of DNA methylation in pili gene regulation
R01AI-23350-05 (IMS) RILEY, RICHARD L UNIVERSITY OF MIAMI PO BOX 016960 MIAMI, FL 33101 The B cell repertoire of normal and autoimmune mice
R01AI-23357-05A2 (BM) DYER, DAVID W STATE UNIVERSITY OF NEW YORK BUFFALO, NY 14214 Transferrin and pathogenesis of Neisseriae
P01AI-23360-07 (AITC) CARPENTER, CHARLES B BRIGHAM AND WOMEN'S HOSP, INC 75 FRANCIS STREET BOSTON, MA 02115 Program project in transplantation immunology
P01AI-23360-07 9001 (AITC) WEINBERG, DAVID Program project in transplantation immunology Pathology core
P01AI-23360-07 0002 (AITC) CARPENTER, CHARLES B Program project in transplantation immunology Immunogenetics of T cell regulation
P01AI-23360-07 0004 (AITC) SCHLOSSMAN, STUART F Program project in transplantation immunology Selective manipulation of the host's immune response
P01AI-23360-07 0005 (AITC) KIRKMAN, ROBERT L Program project in transplantation immunology Specific immunotherapy in primate renal transplantation
R01AI-23362-06 (BM) KRAUSE, DUNCAN C UNIV OF GEORGIA 523 BIOLOGICAL SCIENCES BLDG ATHENS, GA 30602 Genetic analysis of mycoplasma pneumoniae cell adherence
R01AI-23366-06 (BM) HANSEN, ERIC J U OF TEXAS SW MED CTR @ DALLAS DALLAS, TX 75235 Pulmonary immunity to nontypable Haemophilus influenzae
R01AI-23371-05 (IMB) JOHNSON, ARMEAD H GEORGETOWN UNIVERSITY MED SCHO 3900 RESERVOIR RD NW, PO BOX 6 WASHINGTON, DC 20007 Immunogenetics of the HLA-D region in American Blacks
R01AI-23398-06 (BNP) CIARDELLI, THOMAS L DARTMOUTH MEDICAL SCHOOL HANOVER, NH 03756 Structure-activity of interleukin 2 and related peptides
R01AI-23416-04A2 (BM) CHAFFIN, WELDA L TEXAS TECH UNIV HLTH SCIS CTR LUBBOCK, TX 79430 Cell surface dynamics of mannoproteins of C. albicans
R22AI-23417-04A2 (BM) RICHARDSON, KATHLEEN OREGON HLTH SCIENCES UNIVERSIT 3181 SW SAM JACKSON PARK ROAD PORTLAND, OR 97201-3098 Vibrio cholerae immunogenic components and pathogenesis
R01AI-23429-04 (BM) GALLOWAY, DARRELL R OHIO STATE UNIVERSITY 484 WEST TWELFTH AVENUE COLUMBUS, OH 43210-1292 Immunochemical analysis of exotoxin A from P. aeruginosa
R29AI-23430-06 (ALY) KATZ, HOWARD R BRIGHAM AND WOMENS HOSPITAL 250 LONGWOOD AVENUE BOSTON, MA 02115 Membrane glycolipid probes of mast cell heterogeneity
R01AI-23446-05 (EVR) GREGORIADES, ANASTASIA NEW YORK COLL OF PODIATRIC MED 53 EAST 124 STREET NEW YORK, NY 10035 Membrane assembly and influenza virus replication
R37AI-23447-06 (BM) MORRISON, DAVID C UNIVERSITY OF KANSAS MED CTR 39TH AND RAINBOW BLVD KANSAS CITY, KS 66103-8410 Immunochemistry of endotoxin unresponsive C3H/HeJ mice
R01AI-23450-05 (VR) ANKEL, HELMUT K MEDICAL COLLEGE OF WISCONSIN 8701 WATERTOWN PLANK ROAD MILWAUKEE, WI 53226 Antiviral activity of prostaglandins
R01AI-23454-05 (IMB) ROTHSTEIN, THOMAS L UNIVERSITY HOSPITAL 88 EAST NEWTON STREET BOSTON, MA 02118 Analysis of B cell stimulation induced by cytochalasin
R01AI-23455-05 (BM) HINRICHS, DAVID J CHILES RES INST/PROVIDENCE MED 4805 NE GLISAN PORTLAND, OR 97213 Immunoregulation of anti-listeria immunity
R01AI-23459-05A1 (BM) TUOMANEN, ELAINE I ROCKEFELLER UNIVERSITY 1230 YORK AVENUE NEW YORK, NY 10021 Adherence of Bordetella pertussis to human cells
R01AI-23463-06 (IMS) MELMON, KENNETH L STANFORD UNIVERSITY SCH OF MED STANFORD, CA 94305-5102 Autacoids as pharmacologic modifiers of human immunity
R01AI-23467-05 (SAT) DUQUESNOY, RENE J UNIVERSITY OF PITTSBURGH 3550 DESOTO & TERRANCE STREETS PITTSBURGH, PA 15261 Lymphocyte analysis in human heart transplants
R01AI-23470-05 (BM) CLARK-CURTISS, JOSEPHINE E WASHINGTON UNIVERSITY CAMPUS BOX 1137 ST. LOUIS, MO 63130 Mycobacterium leprae taxonomy and genetics
R01AI-23474-06 (MBC) O'BRIEN, THOMAS F BRIGHAM AND WOMEN'S HOSPITAL 75 FRANCIS STREET BOSTON, MASS 02115 Epidemiology of antibiotic resistance plasmids
R01AI-23482-05 (EVR) BERNSTEIN, DAVID I JAMES N GAMBLE INST OF MED RES 2141 AUBURN AVENUE CINCINNATI, OH 45219 Immunobiology of genital HSV-2 infection in guinea pigs
R01AI-23483-04A2 (PBC) STEVENS, RICHARD L BRIGHAM & WOMENS HOSPITAL, INC 250 LONGWOOD AVE BOSTON, MA 02115 Secretory granule proteoglycans and cellular immunity
R01AI-23484-06 (SAT) WELLS, CAROL L UNIVERSITY OF MINNESOTA 1919 UNIVERSITY AVE ST PAUL, MN 55104 Translocating bacteria -- Role in postsurgical sepsis
R01AI-23498-06 (BBCB) WILSON, IAN A RESEARCH INST/SCRIPPS CLINIC 10666 N TORREY PINES RD/MB-13 LA JOLLA, CA 92037 Crystallographic studies antibody-antigen recognition
R01AI-23499-06 (HEM) CHEN, BEN D M WAYNE STATE UNIV SCHOOL OF MED P O BOX 02188 - HEM/ONCOL DIV DETROIT, MI 48201 Macrophage growth--Role of colony stimulating factor
R01AI-23504-04A1 (IMS) MAYER, LLOYD F MOUNT SINAI HOSPITAL 1 GUSTAVE L LEVY PL/BOX 1089 NEW YORK, NY 10029 Functional role of Ia on GI tract epithelial cells
R01AI-23513-05 (ALY) LITTMAN, DAN R UNIVERSITY OF CALIFORNIA BOX 0414 SAN FRANCISCO, CA 94143 Function of CD4 & CD8 in T cell development
R01AI-23520-06 (EVR) SCHULZE, IRENE T ST LOUIS UNIVERSITY 1402 SOUTH GRAND BOULEVARD ST LOUIS, MO 63104 Molecular determinants of influenza virus host range
R01AI-23521-05 (PTHA) ANDERSON, DONALD C TEXAS CHILDREN'S CLIN CARE CTR 8080 N STADIUM DR, SUITE 2100 HOUSTON, TX 77054 Role of LFA-1/Mac-1/p150,95 in PMN leukocyte adherence
R01AI-23524-06A1 (ARRB) SCOTT, GWENDOLYN B UNIV OF MIAMI SCHOOL OF MED PO BOX 016960 MIAMI, FL 33101 Infants of HIV-1 seropositive mothers
R01AI-23534-04 (SSS) SCHAFFER, WILLIAM M UNIVERSITY OF ARIZONA TUCSON, AZ 85721 Dynamics of infectious diseases
R01AI-23538-05 (BM) ISBERG, RALPH R TUFTS UNIVERSITY SCHOOL OF MEDICINE BOSTON, MA 02111 Molecular basis of yersinia host cell interaction
R01AI-23542-05 (BM) CZOP, JOYCE K SEELEY G MUDD BUILDING 250 LONGWOOD AVENUE BOSTON, MA 02115 Study of phagocytosis via beta-glucan receptors
R01AI-23544-05 (BM) HAVELL, EDWARD A TRUDEAU INSTITUTE, INC PO BOX 59 SARANAC LAKE, NY 12983 Antimicrobial functions of cytokines
R37AI-23545-06 (NSS) BLOOM, BARRY R ALBERT EINSTEIN COLLEGE OF MED 1300 MORRIS PARK AVENUE BRONX, NY 10461 Mycobacterial genes, antigens and vaccines
R01AI-23547-06 (HEM) COATES, THOMAS D CHILDRENS HOSP OF LOS ANGELES 4650 SUNSET BOULEVARD LOS ANGELES, CA 90027 Role of granules and organelles in leukocyte activation
R01AI-23548-07 (ALY) RIBLET, ROY J MEDICAL BIOLOGY INSTITUTE 11077 NORTH TORREY PINES ROAD LA JOLLA, CA 92037 Genetic analysis of the immune response
R01AI-23549-06 (BM) SHUMAN, HOWARD A COLUMBIA UNIVERSITY 701 WEST 168TH ST NEW YORK, NY 10032 Genetic analysis of monocyte killing by bacteria
R01AI-23555-05 (BM) COX, REBECCA A SAN ANTONIO STATE CHEST HOSPIT 2303 S E MILITARY DRIVE SAN ANTONIO, TX 78223 Immunoregulation in coccidioidomycosis
R01AI-23568-05 (ALY) MONROE, JOHN G UNIV OF PENNA SCHOOL OF MEDICI 36TH & HAMILTON WALK PHILADELPHIA, PA 19104-6082 Studies of receptor immunoglobulin mediated signalling
R01AI-23591-07 (VR) KLESSIG, DANIEL F RUTGERS-THE STATE UNIV OF NJ PO BOX 759 PISCATAWAY, NJ 08855-0759 The multifunctional adenovirus DNA binding protein
R01AI-23594-07 (VR) GETHING, MARY-JANE H U T SOUTHWESTERN MEDICAL CTR 5323 HARRY HINES BLVD DALLAS, TX 75235-9038 Molecular genetics of influenza virus hemagglutinin
R01AI-23598-06 (ALY) MEDOF, M EDWARD CASE WESTERN RESERVE UNIV 2085 ADELBERT ROAD CLEVELAND, OH 44106 Role of DAF in the complement cascade and in PNH
R01AI-23653-06 (IMB) STEINMULLER, DAVID UNIVERSITY OF IOWA IOWA CITY, IA 52242 Skin-specific alloantigens
R01AI-23659-04A2 (EI) COWING, CAROL O MEDICAL BIOLOGY INSTITUTE 11077 NORTH TORREY PINES ROAD LA JOLLA, CA 92037 Role of accessory cells in immune responses
R01AI-23667-06 (IMB) KLEIN, JAN UNIVERSITY OF MIAMI PO BOX 016960 MIAMI, FL 33101 Polymorphism of the major histocompatibility complex
R01AI-23668-05 (IMB) BELLER, DAVID I UNIVERSITY HOSPITAL, INC 88 E NEWTON ST BOSTON, MA 02118 Control of macrophage antigen-presenting function
R01AI-23682-07 (TMP) ULLMAN, BUDDY OREGON HEALTH SCIENCES UNIV 3181 S W SAM JACKSON PARK ROAD PORTLAND, OR 97201 Genetic analysis of purine metabolism in L donovani

PROJECT NO., ORGANIZATIONAL UNIT., INVESTIGATOR, ADDRESS, TITLE

P50AI-23694-06 (AITC) **COOPER, MAX D** UNIVERSITY OF ALABAMA UAB STATION, WTI 263 BIRMINGHAM, AL 35294-3300 Center for interdisciplinary research on immunological diseases

P50AI-23694-06 0001 (AITC) **BONNER, JAMES R** Center for interdisciplinary research on immunological diseases Public and physician education in allergy and clinical immunology

P50AI-23694-06 0004 (AITC) **GRIFFIN, JOHANNA A** Center for interdisciplinary research on immunological diseases Molecular mechanisms controlling immunoglobulin isotype

P50AI-23694-06 0007 (AITC) **VOLANAKIS, JOHN** Center for interdisciplinary research on immunological diseases MHC class III genes and immunologic diseases

P50AI-23694-06 0008 (AITC) **KIDD, VINCENT** Center for interdisciplinary research on immunological diseases Altered galactosylation in autoimmune disease

P50AI-23694-06 0009 (AITC) **BUCY, PAT** Center for interdisciplinary research on immunological diseases Studies of chicken T cell sublineages

P50AI-23694-06 0010 (AITC) **MOUNTZ, JOHN** Center for interdisciplinary research on immunological diseases Role of CD4+ T cells in MRL-lpr mice

P50AI-23694-06 0011 (AITC) **SCHROEDER, HARRY** Center for interdisciplinary research on immunological diseases Analysis of the VH antibody repertoire in XLA

P50AI-23694-06 0012 (AITC) **VAKIL, MEENAL** Center for interdisciplinary research on immunological diseases Distortion of immune responses in newborn and adult mice

R01AI-23695-05 (BM) **WEISS, ALISON A** VIRGINIA COMMONWEALTH UNIV BOX 678, MCV STATION RICHMOND, VA 23298-0678 Analysis of virulence mutants of bordetella pertussis

R01AI-23700-04A1 (TMP) **GRANATH, WILLARD O, JR** UNIVERSITY OF MONTANA MISSOULA, MT 59812 Molecular biology of schistosome-snail interactions

R01AI-23705-03 (BM) **SOHNLE, PETER G** VA MEDICAL CENTER RESEARCH SERVICE/151 MILWAUKEE, WI 53295 Early host responses to cutaneous candidiasis

R37AI-23719-06 (NSS) **MILLER, LOIS K** UNIVERSITY OF GEORGIA CEDAR STREET ATHENS, GA 30602 The molecular biology of baculoviruses

R01AI-23721-04A2 (BM) **SCHENGRUND, CARA L** MILTON S HERSHEY MEDICAL CENTE P O BOX 850 HERSHEY, PA 17033 Blockage of toxin-cell interactions by oligosaccharides

R01AI-23730-05 (TMP) **FRENKEL, JACOB K** UNIVERSITY OF KANSAS MED CNTR 39TH & RAINBOW BLVD KANSAS CITY, KS 66103 Transmission of toxoplasma in Panama

R01AI-23731-04 (BM) **KLIMPEL, GARY** UNIVERSITY OF TEXAS GALVESTON, TX 77550 Natural cytotoxic activity to bacteria-infected cells

R01AI-23739-04A3 (ALY) **MANSER, TIMOTHY L** THOMAS JEFFERSON UNIVERSITY 1025 WALNUT STREET PHILADELPHIA, PA 19107 Expression of antibody diversity during immune responses

R37AI-23742-06 (NSS) **KAESBERG, PAUL J** UNIVERSITY OF WISCONSIN 1525 LINDEN DRIVE MADISON, WIS 53706 Molecular biology of multipartite genome viruses

R01AI-23762-04A1 (VR) **SPINDLER, KATHERINE R** UNIVERSITY OF GEORGIA ATHENS, GA 30602 Molecular biology and pathogenesis of mouse adenovirus

R01AI-23764-06 (IMB) **KUPFER, ABRAHAM** NAT OF JEWISH CTR FOR IMMUN 1400 JACKSON STREET DENVER, CO 80206 Cell biology of immune interactions

R01AI-23771-04A1 (BM) **MOSELEY, STEPHEN L** UNIVERSITY OF WASHINGTON SEATTLE, WA 98195 New adhesins of diarrhea-associated E. coli

R01AI-23774-05 (IMS) **ROBERTS, NORBERT J, JR** UNIVERSITY OF ROCHESTER 601 ELMWOOD AVENUE ROCHESTER, NY 14642 Viral infection and human immunoregulation

R01AI-23786-04A2 (EI) **EZEKOWITZ, R ALAN B** CHILDREN'S HOSPITAL 300 LONGWOOD AVE BOSTON, MA 02115 Regulation of human macrophage mannose receptor gene

R01AI-23788-04 (SSS) **STITES, DANIEL P** UNIVERSITY OF CALIFORNIA BOX 0100 - IMMUNOLOGY SAN FRANCISCO, CA 94143 T cell immunity to AIDS virus

R01AI-23796-06 (BM) **TOMPKINS, LUCY S** STANFORD UNIV SCH OF MEDICINE FAIRCHILD BUILDING STANFORD, CA 94305-5402 Genetic determinants of virulence in campylobacter

R01AI-23830-06 (BM) **CANNON, JANNE G** U N C AT CHAPEL HILL CB #7290 CHAPEL HILL, NC 27599 Genetics and function of meningococcal surface proteins

R01AI-23847-04 (SAT) **KUPIEC-WEGLINSKI, JERZY W** HARVARD MEDICAL SCHOOL 260 LONGWOOD AVE BOSTON, MA 02115 Cd4/cd25 targeted therapy in sensitized graft recipients

R01AI-23850-04A2 (BM) **SCHERER, STEWART** UNIV OF MINNESOTA MED SCHOOL BX 196 UMHC, 420 DELAWARE ST, MINNEAPOLIS, MN 55455 Mobile DNA in Candida albicans biology and epidemiology

R01AI-23859-07 (HEM) **GOYERT, SANNA M** NORTH SHORE UNIV HOSPITAL 300 COMMUNITY DRIVE MANHASSET, N Y 11030 Structure and function of monocyte/granulocyte antigens

R01AI-23869-05 (HEM) **QUESENBERRY, PETER J** UNIVERSITY OF VIRGINIA SCHOOL OF MEDICINE, BOX 502 CHARLOTTESVILLE, VA 22908 The effect of pertussis toxin on hemopoiesis

R01AI-23876-04A1 (HEM) **WEISS, STEPHEN J** UNIVERSITY OF MICHIGAN 102 OBSERVATORY STREET ANN ARBOR, MI 48109-0724 Activation of collagenolytic enzymes in neutrophils

R01AI-23884-06 (ARR) **PINTER, ABRAHAM** PUBLIC HEALTH RESEARCH INST 455 FIRST AVENUE NEW YORK, NY 10016 Characterization of AIDS virus env proteins

R01AI-23886-06 (EVR) **PICKUP, DAVID J** DUKE UNIVERSITY MEDICAL CTR P O BOX 3020 DURHAM, NC 27710 The structure and function of poxvirus genes

R01AI-23900-05 (IMS) **CERNY, JAN** UNIVERSITY OF MARYLAND 655 WEST BALTIMORE STREET BALTIMORE, MD 21201 Immunoregulation by anti-idiotopes

R01AI-23902-03 (IMS) **MOHANAKUMAR, THALACHALLOUR** WASHINGTON UNIVERSITY 4960 AUDUBON AVE BOX 8109 ST LOUIS, MO 63110 Function and biochemistry of human IgG Fc receptors

R01AI-23909-06 (ALY) **SHARON, JACQUELINE** BOSTON UNIVERSITY DEPT OF PATHOLOGY BOSTON, MA 02118 Structural requirements of antibody combining sites

R01AI-23923-04 (BBCA) **FOX, ROBERT O** YALE UNIVERSITY 260 WHITNEY AVENUE NEW HAVEN, CT 06511 Constraining beta-turn structure in model immunogens

R01AI-23927-06 (ALY) **WIDERA, GEORG** RESEARCH INST/SCRIPPS CLINIC 10666 N TORREY PINES RD LA JOLLA, CA 92037 Molecular approaches to Ia gene function and regulation

R01AI-23939-03 (BM) **COHEN, MYRON S** UNIV OF NORTH CAROLINA AT CH 547 BURNETT-WOMACK CB# 7030 CHAPEL HILL, NC 27599-7030 Phagocytes, free radicals and cellular consequences

R37AI-23945-06 (NSS) **FALKOW, STANLEY** STANFORD UNIVERSITY STANFORD, CA 94305-5402 Bordetella pertussis virulence determinants

R01AI-23950-06 (IMB) **LANDRETH, KENNETH S** WEST VIRGINIA UNIV MED CTR HEALTH SCIENCES CENTER/NORTH MORGANTOWN, WV 26506 Regulation of B lymphopoiesis

R01AI-23952-05 (ARR) **JACKSON, SUSAN** UNIVERSITY OF ALABAMA BIRMINGHAM, AL 35294 The mucosal and serum IgA systems in AIDS

R01AI-23963-04 (ALY) **TRUCCO, MASSIMO M** CHILDRENS'S HOSP OF PITTSUBURG 3705 FIFTH AVENUE PITTSBURGH, PA 15213 DNA level study of alloreactive T-cell clone targets

P01AI-23968-06 (MID) **FRASER, NIGEL W** WISTAR INSTITUTE 36TH AND SPRUCE STREETS PHILADELPHIA, PA 19104 Mechanism of latency of herpes simplex virus

P01AI-23968-06 0001 (MID) **FRASER, NIGEL W** Mechanism of latency of herpes simplex virus Gene expression during HSV-1 latency and reactivation

P01AI-23968-06 0002 (MID) **SPIVACK, JORDAN G** Mechanism of latency of herpes simplex virus HSV-1 latency-associated transcripts and gene products

P01AI-23968-06 0004 (MID) **WROBLEWSKA, ZOFIA** Mechanism of latency of herpes simplex virus Detection of latent herpes viruses in human tissue

P01AI-23968-06 0005 (MID) **BLOCK, TIMOTHY** Mechanism of latency of herpes simplex virus Viral genetics of herpes simplex virus latency

R01AI-23970-06 (EVR) **CEBRA, JOHN J** UNIVERSITY OF PENNSYLVANIA PHILADELPHIA, PA 19104-6018 Reoviruses as probes of gut mucosal T-cell response

R01AI-23975-05 (BM) **BURNS, JANE L** CHILDREN'S HOSP & MEDICAL CTR 4800 SAND POINT WAY NE SEATTLE, WA 98105 Outer membrane permeability of Pseudomonas cepacia

R01AI-23978-05 (IMB) **SHERR, DAVID H** HARVARD MEDICAL SCHOOL 25 SHATTUCK STREET BOSTON, MA 02115 The immunobiology of auto-(idiotype-) reactive B helper

R01AI-23980-04 (EDC) **ALLEN, SUSAN ANN** USCF PREVENTION SCIENCES GROUP 74 NEW MONTGOMERY STREET SAN FRANCISCO, CA 94105 African AIDS--Risk factors, virology and pathology

R01AI-23985-04A1 (BM) **NEWMAN, SIMON L** UNIVERSITY OF CINCINNATI 231 BETHESDA AVENUE CINCINNATI, OH 45267-0560 Receptor function on human monocytes and macrophages

R01AI-23988-06 (MBC) **HOOPER, DAVID C** MASSACHUSETTS GENERAL HOSPITAL 12 FRUIT STREET BOSTON, MA 02114-2696 Mechanisms of action and resistance to quinolone agents

R01AI-23990-06 (ALY) **GALLI, STEPHEN J** BETH ISRAEL HOSP 330 BROOKLINE AVENUE BOSTON, MA 02215 Regulation and significance of mast cell heterogeneity

R01AI-23996-03 (SSS) **VILLEMEZ, CLARENCE L, JR** UNIVERSITY OF WYOMING DEPT OF MOLECULAR BIOLOGY LARAMIE, WY 82071 Toward a protozoan immunotoxin

P01AI-24009-05 (SRC) **ROIZMAN, BERNARD** UNIVERSITY OF CHICAGO 910 EAST 58TH STREET CHICAGO, IL 60637 Molecular mechanisms of Herpes simplex virus latency

P01AI-24009-05 0001 (SRC) **WHITELY, RICHARD J** Molecular mechanisms of Herpes simplex virus latency Basic aspects of herpesvirus virulence and biology

P01AI-24009-05 0002 (SRC) **ROIZMAN, BERNARD** Molecular mechanisms of Herpes simplex virus latency Analysis of viral gene expression by HSV-1 mutants

P01AI-24009-05 0003 (SRC) **SEARS, AMY** Molecular mechanisms of Herpes simplex virus latency State of viral DNA in latently infected cells

P01AI-24009-05 0004 (SRC) **FRENKEL, NIZA** Molecular mechanisms of Herpes simplex virus latency Molecular basis of viral DNA replication during latency

P01AI-24010-05 (SRC) **SCHAFFER, PRISCILLA A** DANA-FARBER CANCER INSTITUTE 44 BINNEY ST BOSTON, MA 02115 Mechanism of latency of Herpes simplex virus

P01AI-24010-05 0001 (SRC) **TENSOR, RICHARD B** Mechanism of latency of Herpes simplex virus Viral and neural factors in HSV

P01AI-24010-05 0002 (SRC) **KNIPE, DAVID** Mechanism of latency of Herpes simplex virus Detection of HSV antigens

P01AI-24010-05 0003 (SRC) **COHEN, DONALD M** Mechanism of latency of Herpes simplex virus HSV replication

P01AI-24010-05 0004 (SRC) **SCHAFFER, PRISCILLA A.** Mechanism of latency of Herpes simplex virus HSV gene functions in latency

P01AI-24010-05 9001 (SRC) **SCHAFFER, PRISCILLA A** Mechanism of latency of Herpes simplex virus Core--Mouse facility

R22AI-24011-06 (TMP) **WANG, CHING C** UNIVERSITY OF CALIFORNIA BOX 0446 SAN FRANCISCO, CA 94143 Purine metabolism in Schistosoma mansoni

R01AI-24012-06 (HEM) **MITCHELL, BEVERLY S** UNIVERSITY OF MICHIGAN 1150 W MEDICAL CENTER DR ANN ARBOR, MI 48109 Overproduction of adenosine deaminase in erythrocytes

R01AI-24021-06A2 (EVR) **GERSHON, ANNE A** COLUMBIA UNIVERSITY 630 WEST 168TH STREET NEW YORK, NY 10032 Vz virus--Clinical implications of immunity

R01AI-24030-05 (ARR) **ROBINSON, JAMES E** LSU MEDICAL CENTER 1542 TULANE AVENUE NEW ORLEANS, LA 70112 Human monoclonal antibodies to HIV-1 gp120

R01AI-24083-04 (MBC) **POTEETE, ANTHONY R** UNIV OF MASSACHUSETTS MED SCH 55 LAKE AVENUE NORTH WORCESTER, MA 01655 Genetic analysis of bacteriophage lysozyme structure

R01AI-24134-05 (EVR) **RICE, CHARLES M** WASHINGTON UNIVERSITY BOX

PROJECT NO., ORGANIZATIONAL UNIT., INVESTIGATOR, ADDRESS, TITLE

8230/SCHOOL OF MEDICINE ST. LOUIS, MO 63110 Molecular genetics of Sindbis virus replication
R01AI-24136-05 (BM) ROBERTS, MARILYN C UNIVERSITY OF WASHINGTON SCH OF PUBLIC HLTH & COMM MED SEATTLE, WA 98195 Tetracycline resistance in urogenital bacteria
R01AI-24137-05 (IMB) FARR, ANDREW G UNIVERSITY OF WASHINGTON SCHOOL OF MEDICINE SEATTLE, WA 98195 Thymic environment and T cell differentiation
R01AI-24138-04 (ALY) KARR, ROBERT W UNIV OF IOWA COLLEGE OF MED IOWA CITY, IA 52242 Molecular cloning of the Dr7-associated Ia genes
R29AI-24139-05 (ALY) MOORE, FRANCIS D BRIGHAM AND WOMEN'S HOSPITAL 75 FRANCIS STREET BOSTON, MA 02115 Complement receptors on murine Kupffer cells
R01AI-24141-04A1 (BM) WING, EDWARD J MONTEFIORE UNIV HOSPITAL 3459 FIFTH AVENUE PITTSBURGH, PA 15213 Host defense mechanisms in Listeria infection
R01AI-24145-04 (BM) BLASER, MARTIN J VANDERBILT UNIVERSITY DEPARTMENT OF MEDICINE NASHVILLE, TN 37232 Cell-surface proteins in campylobacter fetus virulence
R01AI-24146-05 (TMP) PASCAL, ROBERT ANTHONY, JR PRINCETON UNIVERSITY PRINCETON, NJ 08544 Inhibitors of lipid biosynthesis in parasitic protozoa
R01AI-24155-06 (TMP) HARRIS, BEN G TEXAS COLL OF OSTEOPATHIC MED BIOCHEM DPT/3500 CAMP BOWIE BL FORT WORTH, TX 76107-2690 Regulation of metabolism in parasitic helminths
R01AI-24156-05 (EDC) OWNBY, DENNIS R HENRY FORD HOSPITAL 2799 WEST GRAND BLVD DETROIT, MI 48202-2689 Environmental factors as determinants of childhood atopy
R01AI-24157-05 (IMB) ALLEN, PAUL M WASHINGTON UNIVERSITY DEPARTMENT OF PATHOLOGY ST LOUIS, MO 63110 Processing and presentation of self-proteins
R01AI-24158-04A1 (ALY) WEIS, JOHN H UNIV OF UTAH SCH OF MEDICINE 50 NORTH MEDICAL DRIVE SALT LAKE CITY, UT 84132 Characterization of the murine complement receptors
R01AI-24162-05 (BM) HOSTETTER, MARGARET K UNIVERSITY OF MINNESOTA 420 DELAWARE ST, SE/BOX 296 UM MINNEAPOLIS, MN 55455 Interactions of C3 with bacterial pathogens
R01AI-24178-04 (SSS) NELSON, JAY A SCRIPPS RESEARCH INSTITUTE 10666 N TORREY PINES RD LA JOLLA, CA 92037 Pathogenesis of AIDS--Role of cytomegalovirus
R01AI-24194-05 (ARR) RICHARDS, FRANK F YALE UNIVERSITY SCH OF MEDICIN 333 CEDAR ST-P O BOX 3333 NEW HAVEN, CT 06510 The cyst wall of Pneumocystis carinii
R01AI-24199-03 (TMP) NAPPI, ANTHONY J LOYOLA UNIVERSITY OF CHICAGO DEPT OF BIOLOGY CHICAGO, IL 60626 Biochemical mechanisms in insect immunity
R01AI-24204-05 (MBC) BROOKER, ROBERT J UNIVERSITY OF MINNESOTA 1479 GORTNER AVENUE ST PAUL, MN 55108 Microbial physiology and structure of the lactose carrier
R37AI-24227-07 (BM) BABIOR, BERNARD M THE SCRIPPS RESEARCH INSTITUTE 10666 NORTH TORREY PINES ROAD LA JOLLA, CA 92037 Function of normal and malignant phagocytes
R01AI-24239-05 (EDC) STEVENS, CLADD E NEW YORK BLOOD CENTER 310 EAST 67 STREET NEW YORK, NY 10021 AIDS virus infection in a cohort of homosexual men
R29AI-24252-05 (IMB) PROVVEDINI, DIEGO M SCRIPPS CLINIC & RES FNDN 10666 NORTH TORREY PINES RD LA JOLLA, CA 92037 Role of 1,25(OH)2D3 & the thymus gland
R55AI-24258-06 (ALY) PARHAM, PETER R STANFORD UNIVERSITY STANFORD, CA 94305-5400 The nature of HLA-a, b, c polymorphism
R29AI-24261-05 (IMS) HEYMANN, PETER W UNIV OF VIRGINIA HLTH SCI CTR BOX 386 CHARLOTTESVILLE, VA 22908 IgE antibody & exposure to mite allergens in asthma
R37AI-24272-06 (NSS) NISONOFF, ALFRED BRANDEIS UNIVERSITY ROSENSTIEL RESEARCH CENTER WALTHAM, MA 02254 Idiotypic analysis of the antibody repertoire
R01AI-24283-05 (PTHA) GOLDMAN, DANIEL W GOOD SAMARITAN HOSPITAL 5601 LOCH RAVEN BLVD BALTIMORE, MD 21239 Regulation of the leukotriene B receptor system
R01AI-24285-04 (TMP) GILLIN, FRANCES D UCSD MED CTR/INF DIS DIV-H811F 225 DICKINSON STREET SAN DIEGO, CA 92117 Encystation & chitin synthetase of parasitic protozoa
P01AI-24286-05 (SRC) VOLBERDING, PAUL A SAN FRANCISCO GENERAL HOSPITAL 995 POTRERO AVENUE SAN FRANCISCO, CA 94110 Laboratory and clinical studies of AIDS
P01AI-24286-05 0001 (SRC) LEVY, JAY A Laboratory and clinical studies of AIDS Biological, serologic and molecular features of HIV infection
P01AI-24286-05 0002 (SRC) LEVY, JAY A Laboratory and clinical studies of AIDS HIV nucleotide sequence variation
P01AI-24286-05 0003 (SRC) LITTMAN, DON R Laboratory and clinical studies of AIDS Role of CD antigen on HIV infection of cells
P01AI-24286-05 0004 (SRC) MCGRATH, MICHAEL Laboratory and clinical studies of AIDS Monoclonal antibodies to HIV subcomponents
P01AI-24286-05 0005 (SRC) STISTES, DANIEL Laboratory and clinical studies of AIDS Autoimmunity in HIV infections
P01AI-24286-05 0006 (SRC) MCGRATH, MICHAEL Laboratory and clinical studies of AIDS HIV related lymphomogenesis
P01AI-24286-05 0007 (SRC) BECKSTEAD, JAY H Laboratory and clinical studies of AIDS Immunologic pathology in HIV
P01AI-24286-05 9001 (SRC) VOLBERDING, PAUL A Laboratory and clinical studies of AIDS Grant support--Core
P01AI-24286-05 9002 (SRC) FEIGEL, DAVID Laboratory and clinical studies of AIDS Laboratory data and communication services
P01AI-24286-05 9003 (SRC) GREENSPAN, JOHN Laboratory and clinical studies of AIDS Tissue and services processing facility
R01AI-24291-04A1 (ARRA) MC GUIRE, TRAVIS C WASHINGTON STATE UNIVERSITY COLLEGE OF VETERINARY MEDICINE PULLMAN, WA 99164-7040 Immune control of equine infectious anemia lentivirus
R22AI-24298-04 (BM) ELLNER, JERROLD J CASE WESTERN RESERVE UNIVERSIT 10900 EUCLID AVE CLEVELAND, OH 44106-4984 Protective/diagnostic recombinant mycobacterial antigens
R01AI-24303-05 (ALY) PARKER, DAVID C UNIV OF MASSACHUSETTS MED SCH 55 LAKE AVENUE NORTH WORCESTER, MA 01655 B lymphocyte activation
R22AI-24307-04A1 (TMP) MIKKELSEN, ROSS B MEDICAL COLLEGE OF VIRGINIA BOX 58 - MCV STATION RICHMOND, VA 23298-0058 Parasitophorous and plasma membranes of P falciparum
R29AI-24313-05 (TMP) MOSSER, DAVID M TEMPLE UNIVERSITY SCH OF MED 3400 NORTH BROAD ST PHILADELPHIA, PA 19140 The macrophage receptors for leishmania
R01AI-24319-05 (IMS) HESS, ALLAN D JOHNS HOPKINS ONCOLOGY CENTER 600 N WOLFE STREET BALTIMORE, MD 21205 Syngeneic graft-versus-host disease
R01AI-24320-05 (BM) KASLOW, HARVEY R UNIV OF SOUTHERN CALIFORNIA 1333 SAN PABLO STREET LOS ANGELES, CA 90033 Pertussis toxin and the pertussis vaccine
R01AI-24322-06 (ALY) UNKELESS, JAY C MOUNT SINAI SCHOOL OF MEDICINE 1 GUSTAVE L. LEVY PLACE NEW YORK, N Y 10029 Fc receptor structure and function
R01AI-24335-05 (IMB) KELSOE, GARNETT H UNIVERSITY OF MARYLAND 660 WEST REDWOOD ST BALTIMORE, MD 21201 Analysis of the murine antibody repertoire
R01AI-24340-05 (TMP) LOKER, ERIC S UNIVERSITY OF NEW MEXICO DEPARTMENT OF BIOLOGY ALBUQUERQUE, NM 87131 The role of lectins in snail-trematode associations
R37AI-24345-05 (VR) ROSE, JOHN K YALE UNIVERSITY 310 CEDAR ST, BML-342 NEW HAVEN, CT 06510 Ribosome recognition and animal virus gene expression
R01AI-24348-04A2 (IMB) RIGBY, WILLIAM F C TRUSTEES OF DARTMOUTH COLLEGE HANOVER, NH 03756 Modulation of the immune response by vitamin D
R01AI-24355-06 (TMP) WASSOM, DONALD L U OF WISC, SCH OF VET MED 2015 LINDEN DRIVE - WEST MADISON, WI 53706 Immunogenetics of Trichinella spiralis in the mouse
R01AI-24356-06 (VR) ETCHISON, DIANE UNIVERSITY OF KANSAS MED CTR DEPARTMENT OF MICROBIOLOGY KANSAS CITY, KS 66103 Poliovirus-induced alterations in protein synthesis
R01AI-24424-05 (TMP) BARBOUR, ALAN G UNIV OF TEXAS HLTH SCI CTR 7703 FLOYD CURL DRIVE SAN ANTONIO, TX 78284 Molecular basis of Borrelia pathogenesis
R01AI-24428-06 (MBC) MINION, F CHRIS IOWA STATE UNIVERSITY ELWOOD DRIVE AMES, IA 50011 Mechanism of pathogenesis in mycoplasma pulmonis
R01AI-24431-05 (BM) OBRIG, TOM G UNIV OF ROCHESTER MED CTR 601 ELMWOOD AVE, PO BOX 672 ROCHESTER, NY 14642 Shiga toxin mode of action in bacterial diseases
R29AI-24432-04 (TMP) YOUNG, KAREN M U OF WISCONSIN SCH OF VET MED 2015 LINDEN DRIVE WEST MADISON, WI 53706 Regulation of eosinophilopoiesis in parasitic infection
R29AI-24433-04 (TMP) BURGESS, ELIZABETH C UNIV OF WISCONSIN-MADISON 2015 LINDEN DR-WEST MADISON, WI 53706 Animal reservoirs of Borrelia burgdorferi
R01AI-24436-04 (BM) GANEM, DONALD E UNIVERSITY OF CALIFORNIA BOX 0502 SAN FRANCISCO, CA 94143 Molecular biology of chlamydial development
R01AI-24439-05 (IMS) SAMPSON, HUGH A JOHNS HOPKINS HOSPITAL 600 N WOLFE STREET BALTIMORE, MD 21205 Mechanisms of food hypersensitivity in atopic dermatitis
R29AI-24452-04 (BM) STEIN, DANIEL C UNIVERSITY OF MARYLAND MICROBIOLOGY BUILDING COLLEGE PARK, MD 20742 Lipooligosaccharide biosynthesis in neisseriaceae
R55AI-24454-04A1 (MBC) HANSEN, J NORMAN UNIVERSITY OF MARYLAND COLLEGE PARK, MD 20742 Molecular genetics and mechanism of protein antibiotics
P01AI-24460-04 (MID) PALESE, PETER M MOUNT SINAI SCHOOL OF MEDICINE 1 GUSTAVE L LEVY PL, BOX 1124 NEW YORK, NY 10029 Development of antiviral strategies--Molecular approaches
P01AI-24460-04 0001 (MID) BONA, CONSTANTIN A Development of antiviral strategies--Molecular approaches Immunoglobulin recombinant vaccine
P01AI-24460-04 0002 (MID) PALESE, PETER Development of antiviral strategies--Molecular approaches Inhibition of influenza virus replication via anti-sense RNA expression
P01AI-24460-04 0003 (MID) GORDON, JON W Development of antiviral strategies--Molecular approaches Antisense retroviral genes in transgenic mice
P01AI-24460-04 9001 (MID) PALESE, PETER Development of antiviral strategies--Molecular approaches Core
R01AI-24465-05 (IMB) SELSING, ERIK TUFTS UNIVERSITY SCHOOL OF MED 136 HARRISON AVE BOSTON, MA 02111 Immunity in transgenic mice
R01AI-24484-05 (SSS) WIGDAHL, BRIAN MILTON S HERSHEY MED CTR PENN STATE UNIV, P.O. BOX 850 HERSHEY, PA 17033 HTLV-III neurobiology--Molecular pathogenesis and control
R29AI-24489-05 (SSS) MOSCA, JOSEPH D 1500 EAST GUDE DRIVE ROCKVILLE, MD 20850 HTLV-III sequences at the transcriptional level
R29AI-24490-03 (TMP) CHAPPELL, CYNTHIA L BAYLOR COLLEGE OF MEDICINE ONE BAYLOR PLAZA HOUSTON, TX 77030 Diagnosis of schistosomiasis with a parasite proteinase
R29AI-24500-05 (TMP) SYPEK, JOSEPH P NEW ENGLAND MED CTR HOSP 750 WASHINGTON ST BOX 041 BOSTON, MA 02111 Cell mediated host defense in leishmaniasis
R29AI-24511-05 (TMP) TITUS, RICHARD G HARVARD SCH OF PUBLIC HEALTH 665 HUNTINGTON AVENUE BOSTON, MA 02115 Cutaneous leishmaniasis--Relative role of T cell
R29AI-24520-04 (TMP) HOWARD, RANDALL F SEATTLE BIOMEDICAL RES. INST. 4 NICKERSON STREET SEATTLE, WA 98109-1651 Rhoptry antigens of Plasmodium falciparum merozoites
P01AI-24526-05 (SRC) MOSIER, DONALD MEDICAL BIOLOGY INSTITUTE 11077 NORTH TORREY PINES ROAD LA JOLLA, CA 92037 Specialized molecules of the immune system
R22AI-24528-03 (TMP) VANDERBERG, JEROME P NYU MEDICAL CENTER 550 FIRST AVENUE NEW YORK, NY 10016 Plasmodium sporozoite-host cell interactions
R29AI-24531-04 (TMP) CORDINGLEY, JOHN S UNIVERSTIY OF WYOMING BOX 3944 UNIVERSITY STATION LARAMIE, WY 82071 The immune response to cloned schistosome antigens

PROJECT NO., ORGANIZATIONAL UNIT., INVESTIGATOR, ADDRESS, TITLE

R01AI-24533-05 (BM) CURTISS, ROY, III WASHINGTON UNIVERSITY ONE BROOKINGS DRIVE ST LOUIS, MO 63130 **Molecular genetic analysis of salmonella pathogenicity**

R01AI-24540-05 (ALY) STEINMAN, RALPH M ROCKEFELLER UNIVERSITY 1230 YORK AVENUE NEW YORK, NY 10021 **Human lymphocyte activation--Role of dendritic cells**

R01AI-24541-05 (ALY) CATON, ANDREW THE WISTAR INSTITUTE 36TH AND SPRUCE STREETS PHILADELPHIA, PA 19104 **Antibody diversity in recognition of influenza HA**

R29AI-24544-05 (IMB) ROOPENIAN, DERRY C JACKSON LABORATORY 600 MAIN STREET BAR HARBOR, ME 04609-0800 **T cell responses to weak transplantation antigens**

R01AI-24545-05 (VR) FLINT, SARAH J PRINCETON UNIVERSITY PRINCETON, N J 08544 **Adenovirus nucleoproteins**

R29AI-24565-05 (BM) VUKAJLOVICH, STANLEY W UNIV OF KANSAS MEDICAL CTR 39TH RAINBOW BOULEVARD KANSAS CITY, KS 66103 **Interaction of lipopolysaccharides with serum proteins**

R22AI-24566-05 (BM) WHITTAM, THOMAS S PENNSYLVANIA STATE UNIVERSITY 208 MUELLER LABORATORY UNIVERSITY PARK, PA 16802 **The clonal nature of cytotoxigenic E. coli**

R29AI-24570-02 (TMP) FURLONG, STEPHEN T SEELEY G MUDD BUILDING 250 LONGWOOD AVENUE BOSTON, MA 02115 **Lipid analyses of Schistosoma mansoni**

R01AI-24571-06 (IMB) DEKRUYFF, ROSMARIE H LSP CHILDREN'S HOSP AT STANFOR 725 WELCH ROAD STANFORD, CA 94304 **Activation and function of CD4+ T cell subsets**

R01AI-24576-05 (VR) HAYWARD, GARY S JOHNS HOPKINS UNIVERSITY 725 N WOLFE STREET BALTIMORE, MD 21205 **The immediate-early regulatory genes of cytomegalovirus**

R29AI-24582-05 (IMB) CHOI, EDMUND M U OF CINCINNATI MED CTR 231 BETHESDA AVENUE CINCINNATI, OH 45267-0524 **Structural-functional relationships of the Ia antigen**

R01AI-24585-05 (ALY) COWING, CAROL O MEDICAL BIOLOGY INSTITUTE 11077 NORTH TORREY PINES ROAD LA JOLLA, CA 92037 **Regulation and function of MHC class II transgenes**

R29AI-24598-05 (IMS) GEORGITIS, JOHN W BOWMAN GRAY SCH OF MED OF W F WINSTON-SALEM, N C 27103 **Pathophysiology of allergic rhinitis**

R29AI-24615-04 (TMP) STEWART, MICHAEL J NEW YORK UNIV MEDICAL CENTER DEPT/MEDICAL & MOLEC PARASIT NEW YORK, NY 10016 **Motility and invasiveness of Plasmodium sporozoites**

R01AI-24616-04 (BM) APICELLA, MICHAEL A SUNY AT BUFFALO SCH OF MED CLINICAL CENTER BUFFALO, N Y 14215 **Lipooligosaccharides of haemophilus influenzae**

R29AI-24624-05 (IMB) PISCHEL, KEN D UCSD MEDICAL CENTER 225 DICKINSON STREET SAN DIEGO, CA 92103 **Allotypic variation of LFA-1 antigens**

R01AI-24627-06 (TMP) RUBEN, LAWRENCE S SOUTHERN METHODIST UNIVERSITY 220 FONDREN SCIENCE BLDG DALLAS, TX 75275 **Molecular biology of calcium pathways in trypanosomes**

R01AI-24630-05 (BM) MENDELMAN, PAUL M CHILDREN'S HOSP & MED CTR 4800 SAND POINT WAY N E SEATTLE, WA 98105 **H. influenzae--Penicillin binding proteins and cell wall**

R29AI-24635-05 (ALY) KRANZ, DAVID M UNIVERSITY OF ILLINOIS 1209 W CALIFORNIA STREET URBANA, IL 61801 **Antigen-specific T cell receptors**

R01AI-24639-05 (IMB) THIELE, DWAIN L UT SOUTHWESTERN MEDICAL CENTER 5323 HARRY HINES BOULEVARD DALLAS, TX 75235-8887 **The role of cytotoxic cells in alloimmune responses**

R01AI-24643-06 (SSS) LAGAKOS, STEPHEN W DANA-FARBER CANCER INSTITUTE 44 BINNEY STREET BOSTON, MA 02115 **Statistical methods in AIDS research**

R29AI-24645-05 (BM) KING, CHARLES H CASE WESTERN RESERVE UNIVERSIT 2109 ADELBERT RD CLEVELAND, OH 44106 **The role of membrane protease in neutrophil activation**

R01AI-24650-04 (BNP) RICH, DANIEL H UNIV OF WISCONSIN/SCH OF PHARM 425 NORTH CHARTER STREET MADISON, WI 53706 **Synthesis of cyclosporin photoaffinity-labeling reagents**

R01AI-24656-03 (BM) MAURELLI, ANTHONY T U.S.U.H.S. 4301 JONES BRIDGE RD BETHESDA, MD 20814-4799 **Temperature regulation of shigella virulence genes**

R01AI-24669-03 (IMS) PLATSOUCAS, CHRIS D U OF TEXAS / ANDERSON CANCER C 1515 HOLCOMBE BLVD HOUSTON, TX 77030 **Hybridoma-derived human suppressor factors**

P01AI-24671-04 (SRC) BONA, CONSTANTIN A MOUNT SINAI SCHOOL OF MEDICINE ONE GUSTAVE L. LEVY PLACE NEW YORK, NY 10029-6574 **Cellular and molecular studies of autoimmune diseases**

P01AI-24671-04 9002 (SRC) MAYER, LLOYD Cellular and molecular studies of autoimmune diseases Core-- Flow cytometry facility

P01AI-24671-04 0001 (SRC) BONA, CONSTANTIN A Cellular and molecular studies of autoimmune diseases Origin and characteristics of self repertoire in scleroderma

P01AI-24671-04 0002 (SRC) UNKELESS, JAY C Cellular and molecular studies of autoimmune diseases Autoimmune Fc receptor in mononuclear cell activation

P01AI-24671-04 0003 (SRC) MAYER, LLOYD Cellular and molecular studies of autoimmune diseases Immunoregulatory defects in IBD--Mechanisms of T cell activation

P01AI-24671-04 0004 (SRC) FILLIT, HOWARD Cellular and molecular studies of autoimmune diseases Autoimmunity to proteoglycans in autoimmune disease

P01AI-24671-04 9001 (SRC) MORAN, THOMAS Cellular and molecular studies of autoimmune diseases Core--Central hybridoma laboratory

R01AI-24676-04 (SAT) FERGUSON, RONALD M OHIO STATE UNIVERSITY 1655 UPHAM DRIVE COLUMBUS, OH 43210 **Pre- and post-operative T cell function**

R29AI-24677-04 (BM) NIESEL, DAVID W UNIVERSITY OF TEXAS MED BRANCH DEPT OF MICROBIOLOGY, J19 GALVESTON, TX 77550 **Ca++-mediated enhancement of salmonella invasion**

R29AI-24681-06 (IMB) SCHULZE, DAN H UNIV OF MARYLAND 655 WEST BALTIMORE STREET BALTIMORE, MD 21201 **Characterization and expression of an Ig VH gene family**

R29AI-24682-04 (EI) ESA, AHMED H THE JOHNS HOPKINS ONCOLOGY CTR 600 NORTH WOLF STREET BALTIMORE, MD 21205 **Modulation of accessory cell functions by cyclosporine**

PROJECT NO., ORGANIZATIONAL UNIT., INVESTIGATOR, ADDRESS, TITLE

R29AI-24684-05 (BM) DREYFUS, LAWRENCE A UNIVERSITY OF MISSOURI 5100 ROCKHILL RD KANSAS CITY, MO 64110 **Virulence associated traits & Legionella pathogenesis**

R29AI-24687-04 (ALY) CHAPMAN, MARTIN D UNIVERSITY OF VIRGINIA MED CTR BOX 225 CHARLOTTESVILLE, VA 22908 **Antigenic structure of purified house dust mite allergen**

R29AI-24691-05 (IMB) MARTINEZ-MAZA, OTONIEL UCLA SCHOOL OF MEDICINE CENTER FOR HEALTH SCIENCES LOS ANGELES, CA 90024-1740 **Defective cellular control-activated B lymphocytes-AIDS**

R01AI-24695-05 (BNP) SCHULTZ, PETER G UNIVERSITY OF CALIFORNIA BERKELEY, CA 94720 **Synthesis of catalytic antibodies**

R01AI-24699-05 (BM) DJEU, JULIE Y UNIVERSITY OF SOUTH FLORIDA 12901 BRUCE B DOWNS BLVD TAMPA, FL 33612 **Cytokine regulation of PMN responses against C. albicans**

R29AI-24704-05 (TMP) KUMAR, NIRBHAY JOHNS HOPKINS UNIVERSITY 615 N WOLFE ST BALTIMORE, MD 21205 **Membrane antigens of P. falciparum anti-gamete immunity**

R01AI-24709-05 (HEM) ZUCALI, JAMES R UNIV OF FLORIDA COLLEGE OF MED BOX J-277, JHMHC GAINESVILLE, FL 32610 **Interleukin 1 and the regulation of hematopoiesis**

R22AI-24710-05 (TMP) BARNWELL, JOHN W NEW YORK UNIV MEDICAL SCHOOL 341 EAST 25TH STREET NEW YORK, NY 10010 **Molecular analysis of Plasmodium vivax surface antigens**

R29AI-24711-05 (TMP) KIRCHHOFF, LOUIS V DEPT. OF MEDICINE UNIVERSITY OF IOWA HOSPITALS IOWA CITY, IA 52242 **Recombinant Trypanosoma cruzi protein vaccines**

R01AI-24716-05A1 (TMP) RAIKHEL, ALEXANDER S MICHIGAN STATE UNIVERSITY EAST LANSING, MI 48824-1115 **Regulation of vitellogenin synthesis in the mosquito**

R01AI-24717-05 (GMA) HARLEY, JOHN B OKLAHOMA MEDICAL RESEARCH FDN 825 NE 13TH STREET OKLAHOMA CITY, OK 73104 **HLA-DQ gene complementation in lupus**

R01AI-24720-06 (ALY) MOLD, CAROLYN UNIV OF NEW MEXICO HOSPITAL 2211 LOMAS NE, 7TH FLOOR SOUTH ALBUQUERQUE, NM 87131 **Membrane activation of alternative complement pathway**

R01AI-24731-05 (BM) EISENSTEIN, BARRY I UNIVERSITY OF MICHIGAN 6643 MEDICAL SCIENCE BLDG II ANN ARBOR, MI 48109-0620 **Molecular immunopathogenesis of legionella proteins**

R01AI-24734-06 (BM) EISENSTEIN, BARRY I UNIVERSITY OF MICHIGAN 6703 MEDICAL SCIENCE BLDG II ANN ARBOR, MI 48109-0620 **E. coli fimbriae--Structure-function and regulation**

R37AI-24739-05 (ALY) COLTEN, HARVEY R WASHINGTON UNIVERSITY 400 SOUTH KINGSHIGHWAY BLVD ST LOUIS, MO 63110 **Molecular genetics of the MHC-linked complement genes**

R37AI-24742-05 (ALY) UNANUE, EMIL R WASHINGTON UNIV SCH OF MED 660 S EUCLID AVE, BOX 8118 ST LOUIS, MO 63110 **Antigen presentation--Role of Ia molecules**

R01AI-24745-05 (SSS) RATNER, LEE WASHINGTON UNIV 660 S EUCLID AVE ST LOUIS, MO 63110 **Pathogenesis of human immunodeficiency virus infection**

R37AI-24748-05 (EI) CHESS, LEONARD COLUMBIA-PRESBYTERIAN MED CTR 630 WEST 168TH STREET NEW YORK, N Y 10032 **Ontogeny of human T cell receptors**

R01AI-24755-05 (ARR) SODROSKI, JOSEPH G DANA-FARBER CANCER INSTITUTE 44 BINNEY STREET BOSTON, MA 02115 **Role of the HIV-1 envelope glycoprotein in virus and cytopathicity**

P01AI-24756-05 (SRC) HOLMES, KING K HARBORVIEW MEDICAL CENTER 325 NINTH AVENUE SEATTLE, WA 98104 **Chlamydial infections and pelvic inflammatory disease**

P01AI-24756-05 0001 (SRC) ESCHENBACH, DAVID A Chlamydial infections and pelvic inflammatory disease Acute pelvic inflammatory disease

P01AI-24756-05 0002 (SRC) PATTON, DOROTHY L Chlamydial infections and pelvic inflammatory disease Pathogenesis of chlamydia salpingitis

P01AI-24756-05 0003 (SRC) STERGACHIS, ANDREAS S Chlamydial infections and pelvic inflammatory disease Chlamydia trachomatis control program in a primary care setting

P01AI-24756-05 9001 (SRC) STAMM, WALTER E Chlamydial infections and pelvic inflammatory disease Core--Chlamydia laboratory

P01AI-24756-05 9002 (SRC) HOLMES, KING K Chlamydial infections and pelvic inflammatory disease Core--Neisseria reference laboratory

P01AI-24756-05 9003 (SRC) DEROVEN, TIMOTHY A Chlamydial infections and pelvic inflammatory disease Core--Statistics

P01AI-24760-05 (SRC) RICE, PETER A MAXWELL FINLAND LABORATORY 774 ALBANY STREET BOSTON, MASS 02118 **Clinical and laboratory studies of PID**

P01AI-24760-05 0001 (SRC) DALE, PETER A Clinical and laboratory studies of PID Male to female transmission of C. trachomatis or N. gonorhoeae and PID

P01AI-24760-05 0002 (SRC) RICE, PETER A Clinical and laboratory studies of PID Immune interactions of human hosts with Neisseria gonorrhoeae

P01AI-24760-05 0003 (SRC) MCDONALD, A BRUCE Clinical and laboratory studies of PID Role of Chlamydia in pelvic inflammatory disease

P01AI-24760-05 0004 (SRC) TAUBER, ALFRED I Clinical and laboratory studies of PID Biochemical interactions of the human neutrophil with Chlamydia

P01AI-24760-05 9001 (SRC) RICE, PETER A Clinical and laboratory studies of PID Core facilities

R01AI-24762-05 (VR) ROUSE, BARRY T UNIVERSITY OF TENNESSEE KNOXVILLE, TENN 37996-0845 **Liposome microencapsulation of vaccine antigens**

P01AI-24768-05 (SRC) SWEET, RICHARD L SAN FRANCISCO GENERAL HOSPITAL 1001 POTRERO AVENUE SAN FRANCISCO, CA 94110 **Reproductive infectious disease program**

P01AI-24768-05 0001 (SRC) SWEET, RICHARD L Reproductive infectious disease program Consequences of PID (pelvic inflammatory disease)

P01AI-24768-05 0002 (SRC) SCHACHTER, JULIUS Reproductive infectious disease program Is a specific chlamydial protein seen in PID sequelae?

P01AI-24768-05 0003 (SRC) SWEET, RICHARD L Reproductive infectious disease program Evaluation of therapeutic regimens for treatment of PID

P01AI-24768-05 9001 (SRC) SWEET, RICHARD L Reproductive infectious

PROJECT NO., ORGANIZATIONAL UNIT., INVESTIGATOR, ADDRESS, TITLE

disease program Core--Clinical facilities

R29AI-24770-05 (VR) IORIO, RONALD M UNIVERSITY OF MASSACHUSETTS 55 LAKE AVENUE NORTH WORCESTER, MA 01655 **Neutralization of NDV by monoclonal antibodies**

R01AI-24771-06 (TMP) STUART, KENNETH D SEATTLE BIOMEDICAL RES. INST. 4 NICKERSON STREET, #100 SEATTLE, WA 98109-1651 **Small nucleic acids in Leishmania and Endothrypainum**

P01AI-24775-05 (AITC) COHN, ZANVIL A ROCKEFELLER UNIVERSITY 1230 YORK AVENUE NEW YORK, NY 10021 **Cell mediated immunity--A clinical and laboratory program**

P01AI-24775-05 0001 (AITC) COHN, ZANVIL Cell mediated immunity--A clinical and laboratory program The interaction of monocytes, T cells and components of the vessel wall

P01AI-24775-05 0002 (AITC) STEINMAN, RALPH M Cell mediated immunity--A clinical and laboratory program Dendritic cells in rheumatoid arthritis and AIDS

P01AI-24775-05 0003 (AITC) GRANELLI-PIPERNO, ANGELA Cell mediated immunity--A clinical and laboratory program Generation of cytolytic T cells in man

P01AI-24775-05 0004 (AITC) WRIGHT, SAMUEL D Cell mediated immunity--A clinical and laboratory program Adhesion promoting receptors in immunity

P01AI-24775-05 0005 (AITC) NATHAN, CARL F Cell mediated immunity--A clinical and laboratory program Oxidative injury by human neutrophils

P01AI-24775-05 9001 (AITC) STEINMAN, RALPH M Cell mediated immunity--A clinical and laboratory program Core--Laboratory for monoclonal antibodies

R01AI-24779-01A3 (BNP) RODRIGUEZ, ELOY UNIVERSITY OF CALIFORNIA PHYTOCHEMISTRY/TOXICOLOGY/LAB IRVINE, CA 92717 **Chemical studies of novel sulfur containing antibiotics**

R01AI-24782-06 (BM) JOHNSTON, RICHARD B, JR CHILDREN'S HOSPITAL 34TH & CIVIC CENTER BOULEVARD PHILADELPHIA, PA 19104 Mechanisms of resistance to bacterial infection

R44AI-24832-03 (SSS) NICKOL, ALLEN D MERIDIAN DIAGNOSTICS, INC 3471 RIVER HILLS DRIVE CINCINNATI, OH 45244 **Diagnostics for mycoplasma hominis and pneumoniae**

R01AI-24835-06 (ALY) DOWTON, S BRUCE WASHINGTON UNIV SCH OF MED 400 SOUTH KINGSHIGHWAY ST LOUIS, MO 63110 **Regulation of C-reactive protein gene expression**

R01AI-24836-06 (ALY) COLTEN, HARVEY R WASHINGTON UNIV SCH OF MED 400 SOUTH KINGSHIGHWAY BLVD ST LOUIS, MO 63110 **Complement biosynthesis**

R01AI-24837-06 (BM) PEREIRA, MIERCIO E NEW ENGLAND MED CTR HOSPITALS BOX 41, 750 WASHINGTON ST BOSTON, MA 02111 **Surface receptors in Trypanosoma cruzi**

R01AI-24838-06 (HEM) CURNUTTE, JOHN T, III THE SCRIPPS RESEARCH INST 10666 NORTH TORREY PINES ROAD **Regulation of Superoxide production by human neutrophils**

R01AI-24840-05 (HEM) KORCHAK, HELEN M CHILDREN'S HOSP OF PHILADELPHI 34TH & CIVIC CENTER BLVD PHILADELPHIA, PA 19104 **Activation of the human neutrophil**

R01AI-24841-06 (SSS) MARKS, MELVIN I MEMORIAL MEDICAL CENTER 2801 ATLANTIC AVENUE LONG BEACH, CA 90801-1428 **Antibiotic prophylaxis in infants with cystic fibrosis**

U01AI-24845-06 (SRC) HASELTINE, WILLIAM A DANA-FARBER CANCER INSTITUTE 44 BINNEY STREET BOSTON, MA 02115 **Screening and drug design of HIV-1 therapeutics**

U01AI-24845-06 0009 (SRC) GOFF, STEPHEN P Screening and drug design of HIV-1 therapeutics Inhibitors of HTLV-III pol gene products expressed in E. coli

U01AI-24845-06 0010 (SRC) ROSENBERG, MARTIN Screening and drug design of HIV-1 therapeutics Screening and drug design using selective HIV-1 molecular targets

U01AI-24845-06 0011 (SRC) RUPRECHT, RUTH M Screening and drug design of HIV-1 therapeutics Chemoprophylaxis after SIV exposure

U01AI-24845-06 0007 (SRC) HASELTINE, WILLIAM A Screening and drug design of HIV-1 therapeutics Molecular approaches to development of anti-HIV-1 drugs

U01AI-24845-06 0008 (SRC) SODROSKI, JOSEPH Screening and drug design of HIV-1 therapeutics HIV-1 gp120 interactions with the CD4 viral receptor

U01AI-24846-06 (AIDS) ZAMECNIK, PAUL C WORCESTER FDN FOR EXP BIOLOGY 222 MAPLE AVENUE SHREWSBURY, MA 01545 **Oligonucleotide inhibition of HIV**

P50AI-24848-05 (AITC) ROSENWASSER, LANNY J NAT JWSH CTR/IMMUN & RESP MED 1400 JACKSON STREET DENVER, CO 80206 **Immunoregulation in allergic disease**

P50AI-24848-05 0001 (AITC) OHMAN, JOHN Immunoregulation in allergic disease Epidemiology and immunotherapy of human allergy to mice

P50AI-24848-05 0004 (AITC) PINCUS, STEPHANIE H Immunoregulation in allergic disease Eosinophil-lymphocyte interactions

P50AI-24848-05 0005 (AITC) KLEMPNER, MARK S Immunoregulation in allergic disease Acute phase protein synthesis and amyloidogenesis

P50AI-24848-05 0006 (AITC) BORISH, LARRY Immunoregulation in allergic disease Pathophysiology of late phase asthmatic reactions

P50AI-24848-05 0007 (AITC) ROSENWASSER, LARRY Immunoregulation in allergic disease Identification & experission of IL-1 receptors on human immune/inflammatory cells

P01AI-24854-05 (AITC) UNANUE, EMIL R WASHINGTON UNIV SCH OF MED 660 SOUTH EUCLID AVENUE ST LOUIS, MO 63110 **Program project in transplantation biology**

P01AI-24854-05 0001 (AITC) UNANUE, EMIL R Program project in transplantation biology Role in the regulation of IL-1

P01AI-24854-05 0002 (AITC) SCHREIBER, R{OBERT Program project in transplantation biology Role of IFN in initiating cellular immune responses

P01AI-24854-05 0003 (AITC) LACY, PAUL Program project in transplantation biology Effect of MABS to lymphokines on islet allograft rejection

P01AI-24854-05 0004 (AITC) FLYE, M WAYNE Program project in transplantation biology Antigen presentation by the Kupffer cell

P01AI-24854-05 9001 (AITC) UNANUE, EMIL R Program project in transplantation biology Core--Hybridoma and histology resources

R01AI-24855-04 (IMS) STETLER, DEAN A UNIVERSITY OF KANSAS LAWRENCE, KS 66045 **RNA polymerase I and autoantibodies in murine SLE**

R01AI-24870-04 (BM) SCOTT, JUNE R EMORY UNIVERSITY 1510 CLIFTON ROAD **Regulation of expression of adherence factors**

R01AI-24874-03 (BIO) KIERSZENBAUM, FELIPE MICHIGAN STATE UNIVERSITY 148 GILTNER HALL EAST LANSING, MI 48824 **Polyamines in Trypanosoma cruzi infection**

R01AI-24876-02 (IMS) FILLIT, HOWARD M MT SINAI SCHOOL OF MEDICINE ONE GUSTAVE L LEVY PLACE NEW YORK, NY 10029 **Specificity of human autoantibodies to proteoglycans**

R29AI-24888-05 (VR) GONZALEZ-SCARANO, FRANCISCO UNIVERSITY OF PENNSYLVANIA 209 JOHNSON PAVILION PHILADELPHIA, PA 19104-6076 **Fusion function of La Crosse bunyavirus**

R01AI-24899-05 (SSS) OLIVER, JAMES H, JR GEORGIA SOUTHERN UNIVERSITY PO BOX 8042 STATESBORO, GA 30460 **Ixodes ticks and borrelia burgdorferi in southeast U.S.**

R29AI-24902-04 (EVR) HINSHAW, VIRGINIA S UNIVERSITY OF WISCONSIN 2015 LINDEN DR. - WEST MADISON, WI 53706 **Cytotoxic T lymphocytes in influenza virus evolution**

R29AI-24905-03 (MBC) IKEDA, RICHARD A GEORGIA INST OF TECHNOLOGY SCHOOL OF CHEMISTRY ATLANTA, GA 30332 **The molecular basis of function of t7 RNA polymerase**

R29AI-24909-06 (IMB) BROOKS, KATHRYN H MICHIGAN STATE UNIVERSITY EAST LANSING, MI 48824-1101 **Activation of Lyl+b cells and their regulatory role**

R01AI-24912-04 (BM) CUTLER, JIMMY E MONTANA STATE UNIVERSITY BOZEMAN, MT 59717 **Candida albicans surface antigens**

R29AI-24915-04 (BIO) SMITH, GEORGIA F ARIZONA STATE UNIVERSITY TEMPE, AZ 85287 **A (2'-5')an-dependent endonuclease and interferon action**

R01AI-24916-03 (EDC) ADAMS, HARRY G ECU SCHOOL OF MEDICINE DEPT OF MEDICINE GREENVILLE, NC 27858-4354 **Sexual transmission of herpes simplex virus**

R29AI-24922-04 (VR) EIDEN, JOSEPH J JOHNS HOPKINS HOSPITAL 600 N WOLFE STREET BALTIMORE, MD 21205 **Group B rotaviruses--Structure and clinical significance**

R01AI-24935-05 (HEM) SHA'AFI, RAMADAN I UNIVERSITY OF CONNECTICUT 263 FARMINGTON AVE FARMINGTON, CT 06032 **Role of calcium in platelet activating factor action**

R01AI-24939-05 (VR) RUECKERT, ROLAND R UNIVERSITY OF WISCONSIN 1525 LINDEN DRIVE MADISON, WIS 53706 **Structure, synthesis and assembly of picornaviruses**

R01AI-24943-04 (VR) ANDREWS, PETER W WISTAR INSTITUTE 36TH AND SPRUCE STREETS PHILADELPHIA, PA 19104 **Replication of HCMV in human teratocarcinoma cells**

R29AI-24952-04 (ALY) KURT-JONES, EVELYN A BRIGHAM AND WOMEN'S HOSPITAL 75 FRANCIS STREET BOSTON, MA 02115 **Biology & biochemistry of membrane interleukin 1**

R29AI-24972-05 (EVR) SEEGER, CHRISTOPH INSTITUTE FOR CANCER RESEARCH 7701 BURHOLME AVENUE PHILADELPHIA, PA 19111 **Replication of hepadnaviruses**

R29AI-24976-05 (BM) STAMM, LOLA V UNIV. OF NC AT CHAPEL HILL ROSENAU HALL CHAPEL HILL, NC 27599 **Surface & extracellular antigens of T pallidum**

R29AI-24985-05 (BIO) CHILTON, FLOYD HAROLD BOWMAN GRAY SCHOOL OF MEDICINE MEDICAL CENTER BOULEVARD WINSTON-SALEM, NC 27157-1052 **Biochemical interactions between lipid mediator classes**

R01AI-24987-03 (SB) ADCOCK, GAYLE D EASTERN VIRGINIA MED SCHOOL P O BOX 1980 NORFOLK, VA 23501 **Monocyte and endothelial interactions in vein grafts**

R29AI-24989-05 (TMP) REPIK, PATRICIA M THE MEDICAL COLLEGE OF PA 3300 HENRY AVENUE PHILADELPHIA, PA 19129 **Molecular investigation of the ecology of EE virus**

R29AI-24992-04 (GMA) BARRETT, KIM E UNIV OF CALIFORNIA, SAN DIEGO 225 DICKINSON STREET SAN DIEGO, CA 92103 **Mucosal mast cells and intestinal diseases**

R01AI-24996-05 (BM) SIBER, GEORGE R DANA-FARBER CANCER INSTITUTE 44 BINNEY STREET BOSTON, MA 02115 **Diversity of human antibody to H. influenzae B capsule**

R01AI-24998-05 (VR) ESTES, MARY K BAYLOR COLLEGE OF MEDICINE ONE BAYLOR PLAZA HOUSTON, TX 77030 **Subunit rotavirus vaccines and mucosal immunity**

R01AI-25005-05 (EVR) MORROW, CASEY D UNIVERSITY OF ALABMA UNIVERSITY STATION BIRMINGHAM, AL 35294 **Expression of functional poliovirus replication genes**

R01AI-25008-06 (BM) LUCAS, ALEXANDER H CHILDREN'S HOSP OAKLAND RES IN 747 52ND STREET OAKLAND, CA 94609 **Human antibody repertoire to H. influenzae B**

R29AI-25009-06 (SSS) JABBAR, MOHAMED A THE CLEVELAND CLINIC FOUNDATIO 9500 EUCLID AVENUE CLEVELAND, OH 44195 **Topogenic repertoire of AIDS virus envelope glycoprotein**

R55AI-25011-04A1 (ALY) WETSEL, RICK A WASHINGTON UNIVERSITY 400 S KINGSHIGHWAY ST LOUIS, MO 63110 **Complement C5 and the C5a-receptor -- Molecular genetics**

R01AI-25016-05 (EVR) COOPER, NEIL R SCRIPPS RESEARCH INST 10666 NORTH TORREY PINES ROAD LA JOLLA, CA 92037 **Cytomegalovirus--Infection and immunoregulation**

R29AI-25019-05 (BM) GIVNER, LAURENCE B BOWMAN GRAY SCH/MED/WAKE FORES MEDICAL CENTER BOULEVARD WINSTON-SALEM, NC 27157 **Hyperimmune human IgG for type III group B streptococcus**

R01AI-25022-05 (IMB) ABBAS, ABUL K BRIGHAM AND WOMENS HOSPITAL 221 LONGWOOD AVE LMRC 521 BOSTON, MA 02115 **Function and activation of helper T lymphocytes**

R29AI-25024-04 (EDC) KREISS, JOAN K HARBORVIEW MEDICAL CENTER 325 - 9TH AVENUE SEATTLE, WA 98104 **Epidemiology of HIV transmission in Africa**

R29AI-25031-05 (TMP) LANGER, PAMELA J UNIV OF WYOMING/MOLEC BIO DEPT UNIVERSITY STATION, BOX 3944 LARAMIE, WY 82071 **Leishmania surface protein genes**

R01AI-25032-05 (BM) ADEREM, ALAN A ROCKEFELLER UNIVERSITY 1230 YORK AVENUE NEW YORK, NY 10021 **LPS regulation of macrophage function**

R29AI-25037-05 (BM) WASHBURN, RONALD G BOWMAN GRAY SCHOOL OF MEDICINE MEDICAL CENTER BLVD WINSTON-SALEM, NC 27157 **Aspergillus**

PROJECT NO., ORGANIZATIONAL UNIT., INVESTIGATOR, ADDRESS, TITLE

fumigatus complement inhibitor
R01AI-25038-04A1 (MBC) REED, STEVEN G SEATTLE BIOMEDICAL RES INST 4 NICKERSON STREET SEATTLE, WA 98109-1651 Leishmania antigens defined by human immune responses
R01AI-25055-03 (BM) PARKER, CHARLOTTE D UNIVERSITY OF MISSOURI M642 MEDICAL SCIENCE BLDG COLUMBIA, MO 65212 Delivery of pertussis vaccine antigens by other microbes
R29AI-25062-03 (IMS) JYONOUCHI, HARUMI UNIVERSITY OF MINNESOTA BOX 391 UMHC MINNEAPOLIS, MN 55455 Studies of soluble immunoregulators in murine lupus
R29AI-25071-02 (IMS) WEINBERG, KENNETH I CHILDREN'S HOSP OF LOS ANGELES 4650 SUNSET BOULEVARD LOS ANGELES, CA 90027 Genetic defects of the IL2/IL2 receptor axis
R29AI-25076-04 (BM) WALLIS, ROBERT S CASE WESTERN RESERVE UNIV 2109 ADELBERT ROAD CLEVELAND, OH 44106 Hybridoma selction of recombinant mycobacterial antigens
R29AI-25082-05 (GMA) KUPPER, THOMAS S WASHINGTON UNIV SCH OF MED 660 SOUTH EUCLID AVENUE ST LOUIS, MO 63110 Immunophysiology of keratinocyte cytokines
R29AI-25085-05 (TMP) NARDIN, ELIZABETH H NEW YORK UNIV SCHOOL OF MED 341 EAST 25TH ST NEW YORK, NY 10010 T cell epitopes of the malaria CS proteins
R29AI-25086-05 (IMB) GRITZMACHER, CHRISTINE A SCRIPPS CLINIC & RESEARCH FOUN 10666 N. TORREY PINES ROAD LA JOLLA, C92037 IgE heavy chain class switching a molecular analysis
R22AI-25096-05 (BM) TAYLOR, RONALD K UNIVERSITY OF TENNESSEE 858 MADISON AVENUE MEMPHIS, TN 38163 Genetic determinants of virulence in Vibrio cholerae
R29AI-25098-04 (BM) PERRY, ROBERT D LOUISIANA STATE UNIV MED CTR 1501 KINGS HIGHWAY, POB 33932 SHREVEORT, LA 71130-3932 Iron storage and uptake in Yersinia pestis
R01AI-25099-03 (ARR) SZOKA, FRANCIS C, JR UNIVERSITY OF CALIFORNIA 926 MEDICAL SCIECNES BLDG SAN FRANCISCO, CA 94143-0446 Targeted chemotherapy to hIV infected macrophages
R29AI-25105-05 (EVR) SARNOW, PETER UNIVERSITY OF COLORADO HSC 4200 EAST NINTH AVE DENVER, CO 80262 Structure and function of the poliovirus RNA genome
R29AI-25108-05 (SSS) LI, YEN HARVARD MEDICAL SCHOOL ONE PINE HILL DRIVE SOUTHBOROUGH, MA 01772 Molecular genetics of Simian immunodeficiency virus
R01AI-25111-03 (TMP) MARCIANO-CABRAL, FRANCINE VIRGINIA COMMONWEALTH UNIVERSI BOX 678 MCV STATION RICHMOND, VA 23298-0678 Resistance--Pathogenic naegleria to macrophage cytolytic factors
R01AI-25117-05 (IMS) KWAN, SAU-PING RUSH-PRESBYT-ST LUKE'S MED CTR 1653 WEST CONGRESS PARKWAY CHICAGO, IL 60612 Molecular approaches to XLA in B cell immunodeficiency
R29AI-25126-05 (SAT) SHAPIRO, MICHAEL E BETH ISREAL HOSPITAL 330 BROOKLINE AVENUE BOSTON, MA 02215 Transplant alloimmunity generated by viral infection
R01AI-25129-05 (IMB) CONLEY, MARY E ST JUDE CHILDREN'S RES HOSP 332 N LAUDERDALE MEMPHIS, TN 38101 Genetic aspects of immunodeficiency
R01AI-25132-04A1 (BM) ZIEGLER, HARRY K EMORY UNIV SCH OF MED 3001 ROLLINS RESEARCH CENTER ATLANTA, GA 30322 Regulation of macrophage function by lipopolysaccharide
R29AI-25134-05 (BM) WU-HSIEH, BETTY UCLA SCHOOL OF MEDICINE LOS ANGELES, CA 90024-1747 Role of IFN-gamma in experimental murine histoplasmosis
R22AI-25136-01A4 (TMP) KROGSTAD, DONALD J WASHINGTON UNIV SCH OF MED 660 S EUCLID AVE/BOX 8118 ST LOUIS, MO 63110 Antimalarial action and resistance
R01AI-25144-05 (ALY) MOSTOV, KEITH E UNIV OF CALIFORNIA SAN FRANCISCO, CA 94143-0452 Transport of immunoglobulins across epithelial cells
R29AI-25151-05 (SSS) KANDA, PATRICK S W FDN/BIOMEDICAL RESEARCH POST OFFICE BOX 28147 SAN ANTONIO, TX 78228-0147 Immune response to HIV synthetic peptides
R29AI-25166-05 (EVR) KIRKEGAARD, KARLA A UNIVERSITY OF COLORADO CAMPUS BOX 347 BOULDER, CO 80309-0347 Nucleic acid-protein interactions & poliovirus
R29AI-25183-05 (EVR) MCLACHLAN, ALAN SCRIPPS CLINIC 10666 NORTH TORREY PINES RD LA JOLLA, CALIF 92037 Hepatitis B virus gene expression
R29AI-25184-05 (EI) MARGOLICK, JOSEPH B JOHNS HOPKINS UNIVERSITY 615 NORTH WOLFE STREET BALTIMORE, MD 21205 Biologic role of phagocytosis-inducing factor
R01AI-25185-05 (IMB) PURE, ELLEN ROCKEFELLER UNIVERSITY 1230 YORK AVENUE NEW YORK, NY 10021 Structure and function of B lymphoblast receptors
R01AI-25187-05 (EDC) YUNGINGER, JOHN W MAYO FOUNDATION 200 FIRST STREET SOUTHWEST ROCHESTER, MINN 55905 Epidemiology of asthma
R01AI-25210-05 (SAT) SUCIU-FOCA, NICOLE COLL OF PHYS/SURG OF COLUM UNI 630 WEST 168TH STREET NEW YORK, NY 10032 Idiotypic network regulation of immune response
R01AI-25214-04 (HEM) HOWARD, THOMAS H UNIVERSITY OF ALABAMA 1600 7TH AVE SOUTH BIRMINGHAM, AL 35233 Neutrophil movement--Cellular and molecular control
R29AI-25222-05 (IMS) PERRY, GREG A UNIV OF NEBRASKA MED CTR 600 SOUTH 42ND STREET OMAHA, NE 68198 Role of proximal colonic lymphoid tissue in immunity
R01AI-25224-05 (EVR) SOUTHERN, PETER J UNIV OF MINNESOTA MED SCH 420 DELAWARE ST, S E BX 196 MINNEAPOLIS, MN 55455-0312 Molecular basis of persistent virus infection
R01AI-25230-05 (HEM) ACKERMAN, STEVEN J BETH ISRAEL HOSPITAL 330 BROOKLINE AVE BOSTON, MA 02215 Molecular biology and functions of eosinophil proteins
R01AI-25231-04 (EVR) HOLMES, KATHRYN V UNIFORMED SERVS UNIV/HLTH SCIS 4301 JONES BRIDGE ROAD BETHESDA, MD 20814-4799 Molecular genetics of the receptor for MHV
R01AI-25255-05 (MGN) KELLEMS, RODNEY E BAYLOR COLLEGE OF MEDICINE ONE BAYLOR PLAZA HOUSTON, TX 77030 Regulation of adenosine deaminase gene expression
R01AI-25273-05 (SRC) MULLINS, JAMES I STANFORD UNIVERSITY D-333

PROJECT NO., ORGANIZATIONAL UNIT., INVESTIGATOR, ADDRESS, TITLE

SHERMAN FAIRCHILD BLDG STANFORD, CA 94305-5402 Viral genetic basis of AIDS immunopathogenesis in cats
R01AI-25280-06 (SRC) CHESNUT, ROBERT W CYTEL CORPORATION 3525 JOHN HOPKINS COURT SAN DIEGO, CA 92121 HIV envelope protein epitopes recognized by T cells
R01AI-25284-05 (ARR) MAYER, CECILIA C UNIVERSITY OF CALIFORNIA 3RD & PARNASSUS AVE SAN FRANCISCO, CA 94143 Function of the nef gene in HIV replication and pathogenesis
R01AI-25287-05 (SRC) WILEY, DON C CHILDREN'S HOSPITAL 320 LONGWOOD AVENUE BOSTON, MA 02115 Structural studies of HIV envelope glycoprotein
R01AI-25288-05 (ARR) GAYNOR, RICHARD B UNIVERSITY OF TEXAS SW MED CTR 5323 HARRY HINES BLVD DALLAS, TX 75235-9030 Regulation of HIV gene expression
R01AI-25291-05 (SRC) HAHN, BEATRICE H UNIVERSITY OF ALABAMA UAB STATION BIRMINGHAM, AL 35294 Molecular structure-function studies of HTLV-4 and HIV
R01AI-25304-05 (SRC) HAMMARSKJOLD, MARIE-LOUISE SUNY AT BUFFALO 3435 MAIN ST BUFFALO, NY 14214 Molecular interactions between EBV & HIV
R01AI-25308-04A1 (ARRC) RICE, ANDREW P BAYLOR COLLEGE OF MEDICINE ONE BAYLOR PLAZA HOUSTON, TX 77030 Molecular mechanism of Tat transactivation
R01AI-25316-04A1 (ARRA) KORNBLUTH, RICHARD S VA MEDICAL CENTER 3350 LA JOLLA VILLAGE DRIVE SAN DIEGO, CA 92161 HIV effects on T cell activation of macrophage functions
R01AI-25319-05 (SRC) EISERLING, FREDERICK A UNIVERSITY OF CALIFORNIA 405 HILGARD AVENUE LOS ANGELES, CA 90024 Structural studies of HIV envelope glycoprotein
R01AI-25321-05 (ARR) SWANSTROM, RONALD I U OF N CAROLINA AT CHAPEL HILL COMPREHENSIVE LINEBERGER CANCE CHAPEL HILL, NC 27599 Molecular analysis of HIV pol gene products
R01AI-25328-04 (ARRC) DESROSIERS, RONALD C N E REGIONAL PRIMATE RES CTR ONE PINE HILL DRIVE SOUTHBOROUGH, MA 01772 Molecular basis for SIV pathogenicity
R29AI-25361-02 (TMP) YARLETT, NIGEL R PACE UNIVERSITY 41 PARK ROW NEW YORK, NY 10038 Polyamine biosynthesis & metabolism in Trichomonas
R01AI-25372-04 (IMB) ANSARI, AFTAB A JOHNS HOPKINS ASTHMA/ALLERGY C 301 BAYVIEW BLVD BALTIMORE, MD 21229 Immunobiology of Ia-determinant & HLA-D interaction
R01AI-25376-03 (EVR) HAY, JOHN UNIFORMED SVCS UNIV/HLTH SCIS 4301 JONES BRIDGE RD BETHESDA, MD 20814-4799 Functional analysis of Hantaan virus proteins
P01AI-25380-05 (SRC) REDDY, PREMKUMAR E THE WISTAR INSTITUTE 36TH AND SPRUCE STREETS PHILADELPHIA, PA 19104 Role of HIV in AIDS and AIDS-associated neoplasms
P01AI-25380-05 0001 (SRC) REDDY, PREMKUMAR E Role of HIV in AIDS and AIDS-associated neoplasms Mutational analysis of the HIV envelope gene
P01AI-25380-05 0002 (SRC) HOXIE, JAMES A Role of HIV in AIDS and AIDS-associated neoplasms Biology of HIV envelope interactions with human cells
P01AI-25380-05 0003 (SRC) KOPROWSKI, HILARY Role of HIV in AIDS and AIDS-associated neoplasms Anti-idiotype antibodies in AIDS
P01AI-25380-05 0004 (SRC) CROCE, CARLO Role of HIV in AIDS and AIDS-associated neoplasms Lymphoadenopathy syndrome (LAS) & non-Hodgkin's lymphomas in AIDS
P01AI-25380-05 9001 (SRC) KHAN, SHABBIR A Role of HIV in AIDS and AIDS-associated neoplasms Peptide synthesis core
P01AI-25380-05 9002 (SRC) PLOTKIN, STANLEY Role of HIV in AIDS and AIDS-associated neoplasms Clinical core
R01AI-25505-04 (ALY) RUDD, CHRISTOPHER E DANA-FARBER CANCER INSTITUTE 44 BINNEY STREET BOSTON, MA 02115 Analysis of a new human T cell-activation antigen 2H1
R55AI-25507-04 (ALY) MARQUARDT, DIANA L THE REGENTS OF THE UNIV OF CAL 225 DICKINSON STREET SAN DIEGO, CA 92103 Characterization of the mast cell adenosine receptor
R29AI-25513-04 (TMP) FEAGIN, JEAN E SEATTLE BIOMED RESEARCH INST 4 NICKERSON ST, #100 SEATTLE, WA 98109-1651 Mitochondrial genes of Plasmodium falciparum
R29AI-25522-05 (EVR) SALVATO, MARIA S UNIVERSITY OF WISCONSIN 1300 UNIVERSITY AVENUE MADISON, WI 53706 Molecular determinants of the cytotoxic T cell response
R29AI-25523-04 (IMS) STEIN, LEONARD D U OF N CAROLINA AT CHAPEL HILL BURNETT WOMACK BUILDING CB# 72 CHAPEL HILL, NC 27599 Ontogeny of the autoimmune B cell repertoire in man
R01AI-25526-04 (IMS) RICHARDSON, BRUCE C UNIVERSITY OF MICHIGAN R4550 KRESGE I, BOX 018 ANN ARBOR, MI 48109 DNA methylation, gene expression and autoimmunity
R29AI-25529-04 (SSS) ZEGER, SCOTT L THE JOHNS HOPKINS UNIVERSITY 615 NORTH WOLFE STREET BALTIMORE, MD 21205-3179 Regression for time-dependent data
R29AI-25530-04 (EVR) SAMULSKI, R JUDE UNIVERSITY OF PITTSBURGH 269 CRAWFORD HALL PITTSBURGH, PA 15260 AAV-specific integration & rescue in human cells
R55AI-25531-04A1 (ARRC) KUMAR, AJIT GEORGE WASHINGTON UNIV 2300 EYE ST NW WASHINGTON, DC 20037 Mechanism of action of HIV regulatory protein
R01AI-25534-05 (EVR) DUZGUNES, NEJAT A UNIVERSITY OF PACIFIC 2155 WEBSTER STREET SAN FRANCISCO, CA 94115 Kinetics and mechanisms of virus-cell membrane fusion
R01AI-25535-03 (IMB) GAULTON, GLEN N UNIVERSITY OF PENNSYLVANIA 36TH & HAMILTON WALK PHILADELPHIA, PA 19104-6082 Immunotherapy with anti-IL2 receptor monoclonal antibody
R01AI-25537-04 (IMS) HUFF, THOMAS F VIRGINIA COMMONWEALTH UNIV BOX 678 MCV STATION RICHMOND, VA 23298-0678 Studies of mast cell differentiation in vitro
R01AI-25542-04 (IMS) SULLIVAN, JOHN L UNIV OF MASSACHUSETTS MED SCH 55 LAKE AVENUE, NORTH WORCESTER, MA 01655 Immunoregulation during infectious mononucleosis
R29AI-25550-03 (SAT) KITTUR, DILIP S HARVEY 805 600 NORTH WOLF STREET BALTIMORE, MD 21205 MHC class II induction in allograft

rejection
R01AI-25552-02 (VR) RHODE, SOLON L, III UNIV OF NEBRASKA MEDICAL CENTE 600 SOUTH 42ND STREET OMAHA, NE 68198-6810 Parvovirus DNA replication, NS1 and DNA polymerase delta
R01AI-25555-04 (TOX) BUSS, WILLIAM C UNIVERSITY OF NEW MEXICO SCHOOL OF MEDICINE ALBUQUERQUE, NM 87131 Studies on the toxicity of cyclosporine
R29AI-25557-04 (VR) FRIESEN, PAUL D UNIV OF WISCONSIN-MADISON 1525 LINDEN DRIVE MADISON, WI 53706 A characterization of baculovirus early gene expression
R29AI-25563-04 (BM) TOBIAS, PETER S RES INSTITUTE OF SCRIPPS CLIN 10666 NORTH TORREY PINES RD LA JOLLA, CA 92037 Molecular pathology of LPS host-protein complexes
R01AI-25567-03 (BM) MOBLEY, HARRY L UNIVERSITY OF MARYLAND 10 SOUTH PINE STREET BALTIMORE, MD 21201 Urease and gene expression in Campylobacter pylori
R01AI-25568-04 (TMP) TAYLOR, TERRIE E MICHIGAN STATE UNIVERSITY B-527 WEST FEE HALL EAST LANSING, MI 48824-1316 Immunotherapy in pediatric cerebral malaria
R29AI-25570-04 (RNM) RUSCKOWSKI, MARY UNIV OF MASSACHUSETTS MED CTR 55 LAKE AVENUE NORTH WORCESTER, MA 01655 Monoclonal antibodies for in vivo labeled blood products
R01AI-25574-04A1 (BM) BETLEY, MARSHA J UNIVERSITY OF WISCONSIN 1550 LINDEN DR MADISON, WI 53706 Staphylococcal enterotoxins--Structure and function
R29AI-25582-03 (ARR) STEVENSON, MARIO UNIVERSITY OF NEBRASKA MED CTR SWANSON CTR 2020, 42ND & DEWEY OMAHA, NE 68105 Studies on HIV cytopathicity, antisense RNA approach
R01AI-25586-04 (VR) PEEPLES, MARK E RUSH MEDICAL CENTER 1653 WEST CONGRESS PARKWAY CHICAGO, ILL 60612 Identification of a cell receptor for hepatitis B virus
R22AI-25587-03 (TMP) WEIL, GARY J JEWISH HOSPITAL/WASH UNIV 216 S KINGWHIGHWAY ST LOUIS, MO 63110 Surface antigens of infective larvae and immunity in filariasis
R01AI-25606-04 (BM) ROSEN, HENRY SWEDISH HOSPITAL MEDICAL CTR 747 SUMMIT AVE SEATTLE, WA 98104 Oxidative neutrophil microbicidal mechanisms
R29AI-25608-04 (BM) PARSONNET, JEFFREY DARTMOUTH-HITCHCOCK MED CENTER 2 MAYNARD STREET HANOVER, NH 03756 Role of monokines in pathogenesis of S aureus infections
R01AI-25616-04 (SSS) KABAT, ELVIN A COLUMBIA UNIVERSITY 701 W 168TH STREET NEW YORK, N Y 10032 Sequences of proteins of immunological interest
R01AI-25629-04 (TMP) BEATY, BARRY J COLORADO STATE UNIVERSITY FORT COLLINS, CO 80523 Molecular genetic control of mosquito vector potential
R01AI-25630-01A3 (BM) GILSDORF, JANET R UNIV OF MICHIGAN MEDICAL CTR 1500 EAST MEDICAL CENTER DRIVE ANN ARBOR, MI 48109-0244 Molecular and functional studies of H. influenzae B pili
R01AI-25634-03 (BM) MORRIS, JOHN GLENN JR UNIV OF MARYLAND AT BALTIMORE 10 SOUTH PINE STREET BALTIMORE, MD 21201 Studies of the Yesinia enterocolitica virulence plasmid
R29AI-25635-04 (GMA) GILBERT, RICHARD J ST ELIZABETH'S HOSP OF BOSTON 736 CAMBRIDGE STREET BRIGHTON, MA 02135 Intestinal muscle effects of Clostridium difficile toxin
R29AI-25637-04 (TMP) VILLALTA, FERNANDO MEHARRY MEDICAL COLLEGE 1005 D. B. TODD BLVD NASHVILLE, TN 37208 Host cell invasion by Trypanosoma cruzi
R29AI-25640-03 (MBC) DYBVIG, KEVIN F UAB VOLKER HALL-503 BIRMINGHAM, AL 35294 Development of TN916 into a mycoplasma genetic tool
R29AI-25641-04 (HEM) BALAZOVICH, KENNETH J UNIVERSITY OF MICHIGAN PED HEMATOLOGY/ONCOLOGY DEPT ANN ARBOR, MI 48109 Protein kinase in human neutrophils
R29AI-25644-04 (SSS) RINGLER, DOUGLAS J ONE PINE HILL DR SOUTTBORO, MA 01772 Immunomorphologic basis for SIV pathogenecity
R01AI-25650-04 (EVR) GRAVES, MICHAEL C REED NEUROLOGICAL RESEARCH CEN 710 WESTWOOD PLAZA LOS ANGELES, CALIFORNIA 90024 Viral infection of glial cells and induction of immunity
R01AI-25651-04 (TOX) BOWERS, LARRY D UNIVERSITY OF MINNESOTA 420 DELAWARE ST, SE MINNEAPOLIS, MN 55455 Characterization of cyclosporine metabolites
R55AI-25656-05A1 (HEM) ENGLISH, DENIS METHODIST HOSPITAL OF INDIANA 1701 NORTH SENATE BLVD INDIANAPOLIS, IN 46202 Neutrophil Ca++ influx and phosphoinositide hydrolysis
R01AI-25669-04 (BM) IGLEWSKI, BARBARA H SCHOOL OF MEDICINE & DENTISTRY 601 ELMWOOD AVE ROCHESTER, N Y 14642 Role of exoenzyme S in Pseudomonas aeruginosa infections
R01AI-25693-05 (SRC) LEHRER, ROBERT I UCLA SCHOOL OF MEDICINE CENTER FOR THE HEALTH SCIENCES LOS ANGELES, CA 90024 Antifungal properties of human mononuclear cells
U01AI-25696-05 (SRC) GANJU-KRISHAN, AWTAR UNIVERSITY OF MIAMI P O BOX 016960 (R-71) CORAL GABLES, FL 33101 Miami--National cooperative drug discovery group--AIDS
U01AI-25696-05 9005 (SRC) DUNCAN, ROBERT Miami--National cooperative drug discovery group--AIDS Core--Biostatistics
U01AI-25696-05 0001 (SRC) MIAN, ABDUL MOHSIN Miami--National cooperative drug discovery group--AIDS Synthesis of nucleoside analogs as potential anti-AIDS drugs
U01AI-25696-05 0002 (SRC) PETTIT, GEORGE R Miami--National cooperative drug discovery group--AIDS Natural products
U01AI-25696-05 0003 (SRC) RESNICK, LIONEL Miami--National cooperative drug discovery group--AIDS Antiviral screening program
U01AI-25696-05 0004 (SRC) DOWNEY, KATHLEEN Miami--National cooperative drug discovery group--AIDS Viral polymerase screening--Reverse transcriptase study
U01AI-25696-05 0005 (SRC) WIERENGA, WENDEL Miami--National cooperative drug discovery group--AIDS Molecular modeling
U01AI-25696-05 0006 (SRC) GANJU-KRISHAN, AWTAR Miami--National cooperative drug discovery group--AIDS Cellular pharmacology program
U01AI-25696-05 9001 (SRC) LAZARUS, HERBERT Miami--National cooperative drug discovery group--AIDS Core--Tissue culture
U01AI-25696-05 9002 (SRC) GANJU-KRISHAN, AWTAR Miami--National cooperative drug discovery group--AIDS Core--Flow cytometry resource
U01AI-25696-05 9003 (SRC) MASOUD, ASAAD Miami--National cooperative drug discovery group--AIDS Analytical pharmacology resource--Core
U01AI-25696-05 9004 (SRC) LAVOIE, LAWRENCE Miami--National cooperative drug discovery group--AIDS Core--Data management
U01AI-25697-05 (SRC) LOO, TI L GEORGE WASHINGTON UNIV MED SCH 2300 EYE STREET, NW. WASHINGTON, D C 20037 Pharmacologic disposition of potential anti-AIDS agents
U01AI-25697-05 0001 (SRC) MCKENNA, CHARLES E Pharmacologic disposition of potential anti-AIDS agents Development of anti-HIV agents
U01AI-25697-05 0002 (SRC) BODNER, ANNE J Pharmacologic disposition of potential anti-AIDS agents Development of anti-HIV compounds
U01AI-25697-05 0003 (SRC) CHENG, YUNG-CHI Pharmacologic disposition of potential anti-AIDS agents Development of anti-AIDS agents
U01AI-25697-05 0006 (SRC) LOO, TI LI Pharmacologic disposition of potential anti-AIDS agents Development of anti-HIV agents
R01AI-25715-04 (ARRA) ROSOWSKY, ANDRE DANA-FARBER CANCER INSTITUTE 44 BINNEY STREET BOSTON, MA 02115 Multifunctional phosphonoformate prodrugs against HIV-1
U01AI-25721-05 (SRC) REKOSH, DAVID M S U N Y AT BUFFALO 3435 MAIN STREET BUFFALO, N Y 14214 In vitro and in vivo models to study HIV-cell interaction
U01AI-25721-05 0001 (SRC) HAMMARSKJOLD, MARIE L In vitro and in vivo models to study HIV-cell interaction Studies on the mechanism underlying rev function
U01AI-25721-05 0003 (SRC) REKOSH, DAVID In vitro and in vivo models to study HIV-cell interaction Studies on virus assembly
U01AI-25721-05 9001 (SRC) SYNDER, GRAYSON H In vitro and in vivo models to study HIV-cell interaction Core--Oligonucleotide and peptide synthesis
U01AI-25721-05 9002 (SRC) CICCARELLI, RICHARD In vitro and in vivo models to study HIV-cell interaction Core--Drug screening
U01AI-25722-05 (SRC) CLOYD, MILES W UNIVERSITY OF TEXAS MEDICAL BR GALVESTON, TX 77550 Mechanisms of HIV cytotoxicity and ways to counteract
U01AI-25722-05 0001 (SRC) ROJKO, JENNIFER L Mechanisms of HIV cytotoxicity and ways to counteract Mechanisms of FeLV-C cytopathology
U01AI-25722-05 0002 (SRC) ROJKO, JENNIFER L Mechanisms of HIV cytotoxicity and ways to counteract Mechanisms of FIV cytopathology
U01AI-25722-05 0003 (SRC) CLOYD, MILES W Mechanisms of HIV cytotoxicity and ways to counteract Mechanisms of T4 cell resistance to HIV
R01AI-25731-05 (TMP) PERRYMAN, LANCE E WASHINGTON STATE UNIVERSITY PULLMAN, WA 99164-7040 Control of cryptosporidiosis by neutralization antibodies
R01AI-25738-05 (BM) CALDERONE, RICHARD A GEORGETOWN UNIVERSITY SCHOOL OF MEDICINE WASHINGTON, DC 20007 The C3d complement receptor of Candida albicans
U01AI-25739-04 (SRC) DRACH, JOHN C UNIVERSITY OF MICHIGAN 1011 N UNIVERSITY ANN ARBOR, MI 48109-1078 Nucleosides & thiosemicarbazones as selective inhibitors
U01AI-25739-04 0001 (SRC) TOWNSEND, LEROY B. Nucleosides & thiosemicarbazones as selective inhibitors Nucleosides as potential inhibitors of HIV
U01AI-25739-04 0002 (SRC) SHIPMAN, CHARLES Nucleosides & thiosemicarbazones as selective inhibitors Evaluation of compounds as selective inhibitors of HIV
U01AI-25739-04 0003 (SRC) HILL, DONALD L. Nucleosides & thiosemicarbazones as selective inhibitors Pharmacologic and toxicologic evaluation of antivirals
R01AI-25751-05 (SRC) MORAHAN, PAGE S MED COLLEGE OF PENNSLYVANIA 3300 HENRY AVENUE PHILADELPHIA, PA 19129 Macrophage and NK cell resistance vs herpesviruses
R01AI-25765-05 (ARR) SIDMAN, CHARLES L THE JACKSON LABORATORY 600 MAIN STREET BAR HARBOR, ME 04609-0800 Murine models of Pneumocystis carinii infection
R01AI-25769-05 (ARR) YOUNG, LOWELL S MED RES INST OF SAN FRANCISCO 2200 WEBSTER STREET SAN FRANCISCO, CA 94115 Pathogenesis and host defense against M. avium
R01AI-25773-05 (SRC) FISCHL, MARGARET A UNIVERSITY OF MIAMI SCH OF MED P O BOX 016960 MIAMI, FL 33101 Heterosexual transmission of HIV
R01AI-25780-05 (BM) LEVITZ, STUART M UNIVERSITY HOSPITAL 88 EAST NEWTON STREET BOSTON, MA 02118 Role of macrophages in cryptococcal infections
R01AI-25783-05 (ARR) MITCHELL, THOMAS G DUKE UNIVERSITY MEDICAL CENTER BOX 3803 DURHAM, NC 27710 Studies of Cryptococcus neoformans associated with AIDS
U01AI-25784-05 (SRC) WHITLEY, RICHARD J UNIVERSITY OF ALABAMA 1600 7TH AVENUE SOUTH BIRMINGHAM, AL 35294 Birmingham national cooperative drug development group
U01AI-25784-05 9001 (SRC) SOMMADOSSI, JEAN-PIERRE Birmingham national cooperative drug development group Core laboratories
U01AI-25784-05 0001 (SRC) HUNTER, ERIC Birmingham national cooperative drug development group Structure of the HIV env gene product
U01AI-25784-05 0002 (SRC) SECRIST, JOHN A Birmingham national cooperative drug development group Design of inhibitors in the processing of linked oligosaccharides
U01AI-25784-05 0003 (SRC) COMPANS, RICHARD W Birmingham national cooperative drug development group Identification of novel inhibitions which affect HIV glycoproteins
R29AI-25790-05 (IMB) KAUMAYA, PRAVIN T P OHIO STATE UNIVERSITY 1654 UPHAM DRIVE COLUMBUS, OH 43210 Conformational peptides to probe immune responses
R01AI-25799-05 (SRC) ELLNER, JERROLD J CASE WESTERN RESERVE UNIVERSIT 10900 EUCLID AVE CLEVELAND, OH 44106-4984 Mycobacterial diseases in AIDS
R01AI-25802-05 (ARR) PEDERSEN, NIELS C UNIV OF CALIFORNIA SCHOOL OF VETERINARY MEDICINE DAVIS, CA 95616 FIV infection of cats as a model for HIV infection
R01AI-25816-04 (BM) NELSON, ROBERT D UNIVERSITY OF MINNESOTA

PROJECT NO., ORGANIZATIONAL UNIT., INVESTIGATOR, ADDRESS, TITLE

BOX 124 UMHC MINNEAPOLIS, MN 55455 Candidiasis--Immuno-inhibition by mannan catabolites

R01AI-25817-04 (SRC) PFEFFERKORN, ELMER R DARTMOUTH MEDICAL SCHOOL HANOVER, NH 03756 Anticoccidial drugs and drug resistance in toxoplasmosis

R29AI-25818-04 (BM) CZINN, STEVEN J CASE WESTERN RESERVE UNIV 2040 ADELBERT ROAD CLEVELAND, OHIO 44106 Immunology of Campylobacter pylori in gastric disease

R01AI-25820-03 (IMS) SHARP, JOHN G UNIV OF NEBRASKA MEDICAL CTR 600 SOUTH 42ND STREET OMAHA, NE 68198-6395 Microenvironment influence GALT location and ontogeny

R01AI-25825-05 (SRC) ELDER, JOHN H SCRIPPS RESEARCH INSTITUTE 10666 NORTH TORREY PINES RD LA JOLLA, CA 92037 Feline T-lymphotropic virus as a model for HIV vaccine

R01AI-25827-04 (BM) HOSTETTER, MARGARET K UNIVERSITY OF MINNESOTA 420 DELAWARE ST, SE MINNEAPOLIS, MN 55455 A molecular marker for invasive Candida albicans

R01AI-25828-05 (SRC) MAYER, KENNETH H MEMORIAL HOSPITAL PROSPECT STREET PAWTUCKET, RI 02860 Heterosexual HIV transmission in greater Providence

U01AI-25831-05 (SRC) CHEESEMAN, SARAH H UNIVERSITY OF MASSACHUSETTS 55 LAKE AVENUE NORTH WORCESTER, MA 01655 AIDS in central Mass.--Therapy, immunity and education

U01AI-25831-05 0001 (SRC) CHEESEMAN, SARAH H AIDS in central Mass.--Therapy, immunity and education Antiviral HIV therapy in hemophiliacs, IV drug abusers in central Mass.

U01AI-25831-05 0002 (SRC) ENNIS, FRANCIS A AIDS in central Mass.--Therapy, immunity and education Role of MHC restricted cytoxic lymphocytes in AIDS

U01AI-25831-05 0003 (SRC) BLACKLOW, NEIL R AIDS in central Mass.--Therapy, immunity and education HIV educational outreach

R01AI-25836-04 (ALY) MIZEL, STEVEN B BOWMAN GRAY SCH OF MED D MICR & IMM 300 S HAWTHORNE R WINSTON-SALEM, N C 27103 Interleukin 1 synthesis and secretion

R01AI-25850-05 (SRC) MONTELARO, RONALD C UNIVERSITY OF PITTSBURGH SCHOOL OF MEDICINE PITTSBURGH, PA 15261 Immunologic management of lentivirus infections--EIAV

U01AI-25859-05 (SRC) JONES, ROBERT B INDIANA UNIV/DEPT OF MEDICINE 545 BARNHILL DRIVE INDIANAPOLIS, IN 46202-5124 Indiana AIDS clinical research group

U01AI-25859-05 0001 (SRC) FIFE, KENNETH H Indiana AIDS clinical research group Clinical evaluation of anti-AIDS compounds

U01AI-25859-05 0002 (SRC) WALKER, EDWIN B Indiana AIDS clinical research group Multiple parameter flow cytology analysis in AIDS

U01AI-25859-05 0003 (SRC) WHEAT, LAWRENCE J Indiana AIDS clinical research group Histoplasmosis in AIDS

U01AI-25859-05 0004 (SRC) BLACK, JOHN R Indiana AIDS clinical research group Alternative therapy for Pneumocystis pneumonia in AIDS

U01AI-25859-05 0005 (SRC) SMITH, JAMES W Indiana AIDS clinical research group Genetic immunologic & susceptibility study of pneumocystis

U01AI-25859-05 9001 (SRC) JONES, ROBERT B Indiana AIDS clinical research group Clinical core

U01AI-25859-05 9002 (SRC) BRATER, D CRAIG Indiana AIDS clinical research group Clinical pharmacology core

U01AI-25859-05 9003 (SRC) KATZ, B P Indiana AIDS clinical research group Biostatistics-computer core

U01AI-25867-05 (SRC) SCHULOF, RICHARD S GEORGE WASHINGTON UNIV 2150 PENNSYLVANIA AVE, NW WASHINGTON, D.C. 20052 Combination therapy of HIV infection

U01AI-25867-05 0001 (SRC) SCHULOF, RICHARD S Combination therapy of HIV infection Ribavirin and isoprinosine--Lymphadenopathy patients

U01AI-25867-05 0002 (SRC) SCHULOF, RICHARD S Combination therapy of HIV infection AZT and alpha interferon--AIDS related Kaposi sarcoma patients

U01AI-25867-05 0003 (SRC) SCHULOF, RICHARD S Combination therapy of HIV infection AZT and ampligen in patients with AIDS or ARC

U01AI-25867-05 9001 (SRC) SCHLESSELMAN, SARAH E Combination therapy of HIV infection Core--Biostatistics

U01AI-25868-05 (SRC) VAN DER HORST, CHARLES M UNIV. OF N.C. AT CHAPEL HILL CB#7030, 516 BURNETT-WOMACK CHAPEL HILL, NC 27599-7030 University of North Carolina AIDS clinical study group

U01AI-25868-05 0001 (SRC) LEMON, STANLEY University of North Carolina AIDS clinical study group Clinical studies of antiretroviral therapies

U01AI-25868-05 0002 (SRC) PAGANO, JOSEPH University of North Carolina AIDS clinical study group Treatment failures--Testing of virus drug resistance

U01AI-25868-05 0003 (SRC) KENNEY, SHANNON University of North Carolina AIDS clinical study group Biological interactions between the Herpesvirus and HIV

U01AI-25868-05 0004 (SRC) HUANG, ENG-SHANG University of North Carolina AIDS clinical study group The role of cytomegalovirus infection in AIDS

U01AI-25868-05 0005 (SRC) SWANSTROM, RONALD University of North Carolina AIDS clinical study group HIV transmission and evolution

U01AI-25868-05 0006 (SRC) LANDIS, SUZANNE University of North Carolina AIDS clinical study group Contact tracing strategies for HIV infection

U01AI-25868-05 9001 (SRC) FOLDS, JAMES University of North Carolina AIDS clinical study group Core--Clinical retrovirology laboratory

R29AI-25869-05 (SRC) ROYER, ROBERT E UNIV OF NEW MEXICO SCH OF MED 915 STANFORD DRIVE N E ALBUQUERQUE, NM 87131 Gossypol derivatives as covalent carriers of antivirals

U01AI-25879-04S2 (SRC) LEDERMAN, MICHAEL M CASE WESTERN RESERVE UNIVERSIT 10900 EUCLID AVENUE CLEVELAND, OH 44106-4984 Establishment of an AIDS clinical studies group

U01AI-25879-04S2 0001 (SRC) LEDERMAN, MICHAEL Establishment of an AIDS clinical studies group Clinical trials study group

U01AI-25879-04S2 0003 (SRC) CALABRESE, LEONARD Establishment of an AIDS clinical studies group Outreach programs

U01AI-25883-05 (SRC) CONNOR, EDWARD M UMDNJ-NEW JERSEY MEDICAL SCH 185 SOUTH ORANGE AVENUE NEWARK, NJ 07107-3007 Network of AIDS

PROJECT NO., ORGANIZATIONAL UNIT., INVESTIGATOR, ADDRESS, TITLE

clinical studies groups

U01AI-25893-05 (SRC) STEIGBIGEL, ROY T SUNY AT STONY BROOK SCHOOL OF MEDICINE STONY BROOK, NY 11794-8153 SUNY Stony Brook AIDS clinical studies group

U01AI-25893-05 0001 (SRC) STEIGBIGEL, ROY T SUNY Stony Brook AIDS clinical studies group Effect of HIV on macrophage function

U01AI-25893-05 0002 (SRC) BURGER, HAROLD SUNY Stony Brook AIDS clinical studies group Viral and cellular determinants of HIV pathogenesis

U01AI-25893-05 0003 (SRC) WEISER, BARBARA SUNY Stony Brook AIDS clinical studies group Viral cofactors in HIV infection

U01AI-25893-05 0004 (SRC) LUFT, BENJAMIN J SUNY Stony Brook AIDS clinical studies group Effect of Toxoplasma gondii on pathogenesis of HIV

U01AI-25893-05 0005 (SRC) SAMPSON, MICHAEL G SUNY Stony Brook AIDS clinical studies group Early detection of Pneumocystis carinii in AIDS

U01AI-25893-05 0006 (SRC) SMALDONE, GERALD C SUNY Stony Brook AIDS clinical studies group Aerosol therapy for Pneumocystis pneumonia

U01AI-25893-05 0007 (SRC) MORRISON, SIDONIE A SUNY Stony Brook AIDS clinical studies group Mechanisms of hemostatic compromise in AIDS

U01AI-25893-05 0008 (SRC) SCHUBACH, WILLIAM H SUNY Stony Brook AIDS clinical studies group Role of EBV in AIDS lymphomas

U01AI-25893-05 0009 (SRC) WALTON, ROSE A SUNY Stony Brook AIDS clinical studies group AIDS outreach and education

U01AI-25897-05 (SRC) FRAME, PETER T UNIV OF CINCINNATI COLL OF MED EDEN AND BETHESDA AVENUES CINCINNATI, OH 45267-0405 Therapy/basic studies/outreach programs in HIV infection

U01AI-25897-05 0001 (SRC) WALZER, PETER D Therapy/basic studies/outreach programs in HIV infection Pneumonia in HIV infection

U01AI-25897-05 9001 (SRC) FRAME, PETER Therapy/basic studies/outreach programs in HIV infection Core patient management unit

R01AI-25899-05 (ARR) CHU, CHUNG K UNIVERSITY OF GEORGIA ATHENS, GA 30602 Synthesis and biotransformation of anti-HIV prodrugs

U01AI-25902-05 (SRC) GRIECO, MICHAEL H ST LUKE'S-ROOSEVELT HOSP CTR 428 WEST 59TH STREET NEW YORK, NY 10019 AIDS clinical studies group

U01AI-25902-05 0001 (SRC) P15606271 AIDS clinical studies group AIDS research treatment program

U01AI-25902-05 0002 (SRC) VOLSKY, , DAVID J AIDS clinical studies group Anti-HIV therapy and host-cell gene expression

U01AI-25902-05 0003 (SRC) CLEVELAND, WILLIAM L AIDS clinical studies group Specificity, and regulation of anti-HIV antibodies

U01AI-25902-05 0004 (SRC) INADA, YORITARO AIDS clinical studies group Circulating immune complexes in AIDS

U01AI-25903-05 (SRC) RATNER, LEE WASHINGTON UNIV SCH OF MED 660 S EUCLID AVE ST LOUIS, MO 63110 AIDS clinical study group

U01AI-25903-05 0001 (SRC) CLIFFORD, DAVID B AIDS clinical study group Psychometric, neurologic and CSF analysis of HIV-infected patients

U01AI-25903-05 0002 (SRC) POSNER, MICHAEL I AIDS clinical study group Neuropsychologic studies of AIDS dementia

U01AI-25903-05 0003 (SRC) HONG, BARRY A AIDS clinical study group Psychologic study--Patient response to HIV antibody testing

U01AI-25903-05 0004 (SRC) GELB, LAWRENCE D AIDS clinical study group Dideoxycytidine vs. AZT therapy in patients with HIV infection

U01AI-25903-05 0005 (SRC) MEDOFF, GERALD AIDS clinical study group Developing more effective therapy for cryptococcal infections in AIDS patients

U01AI-25903-05 0006 (SRC) RATNER, LEE AIDS clinical study group Biological markers of HIV infection

U01AI-25903-05 0007 (SRC) BROWN, ERIC J AIDS clinical study group Receptor expression and function--HIV infected leukocytes

U01AI-25903-05 0008 (SRC) KROGSTAD, DONALD J AIDS clinical study group Endocytosis, phagosome acidification in mononuclear phagocytes--AIDS patients

U01AI-25903-05 0009 (SRC) MEDOFF, GERALD AIDS clinical study group Model systems--Developing therapy for cryptococcal meningitis in AIDS

U01AI-25903-05 0010 (SRC) HONG, BARRY A AIDS clinical study group Community outreach program

U01AI-25903-05 9001 (SRC) STORCH, GREGORY A AIDS clinical study group Core--Virology laboratory

U01AI-25903-05 9002 (SRC) POLMAR, STEPHEN H AIDS clinical study group Core--Immunology Laboratory

U01AI-25903-05 9003 (SRC) KROGSTAD, DONALD J AIDS clinical study group Core--Drug assay and pharmacokinetics laboratory

U01AI-25903-05 9004 (SRC) RATNER, LEE AIDS clinical study group Core--Computer facility

U01AI-25903-05 9005 (SRC) MILLER, J PHILIP AIDS clinical study group Core--Biostatistics

R01AI-25904-04 (EI) JOHNSON, HOWARD M UNIVERSITY OF FLORIDA 1053 MCCARTY HALL GAINESVILLE, FL 32611 Staphylococcal enterotoxins--Potent inducers of brms

R01AI-25909-05 (ARR) AGRAWAL, KRISHNA C TULANE UNIV SCHOOL OF MEDICINE 1430 TULANE AVENUE NEW ORLEANS, LA 70112 Novel approaches to antiviral chemotherapy

U01AI-25914-04S2 (SRC) GOCKE, DAVID J UMDNJ/ROBERT WOOD JOHNSON MED ONE ROBERT WOOD JOHNSON PLACE NEW BRUNSWICK, NJ 08903-0019 The Central Jersey AIDS clinical studies group

U01AI-25914-04S2 0001 (SRC) GOCKE, DAVID J The Central Jersey AIDS clinical studies group Evaluation of 2'3'dideoxycytidine (DDC) therapy in HIV-infected patients

U01AI-25914-04S2 0002 (SRC) WEINSTEIN, MELVIN P The Central Jersey AIDS clinical studies group Corticosteroid treatment of Pneumocystis carinii pneumonia (PCP)

U01AI-25914-04S2 0003 (SRC) PESTKA, SIDNEY The Central Jersey AIDS clinical studies group Sequence analysis & detection of HIV nucleic acid; antisense RNA therapy

U01AI-25914-04S2 0004 (SRC) PESTKA, SIDNEY The Central Jersey AIDS clinical studies group Antiviral and antiproliferative effects of human interferons on HIV in vitro

U01AI-25914-04S2 9001 (SRC) SCHWARTZER, THOMAS A The Central Jersey AIDS clinical studies group Core--HIV culture laboratory

PROJECT NUMBER LISTING

PROJECT NO., ORGANIZATIONAL UNIT., INVESTIGATOR, ADDRESS, TITLE

U01AI-25914-04S2 9002 (SRC) RASKA, KAREL The Central Jersey AIDS clinical studies group Core--Clinical immunology laboratory
U01AI-25915-05 (SRC) PHAIR, JOHN P NORTHWESTERN UNIVERSITY 680 N LAKE SHORE DRIVE CHICAGO, IL 60611 Clinical treatment and laboratory studies of AIDS
U01AI-25917-04 (SRC) MURRAY, HENRY W CORNELL UNIVERSITY MED COLLEGE 1300 YORK AVENUE NEW YORK, NY 10021 New treatments for AIDS and AIDS-related infections
U01AI-25917-04 0001 (SRC) MURRAY, HENRY W New treatments for AIDS and AIDS-related infections Interaction of AZT and gamma interferon in patients treated with both
U01AI-25917-04 0002 (SRC) SOAVE, ROSEMARY New treatments for AIDS and AIDS-related infections Spiramycin for cryptosporidiosis
U01AI-25917-04 0003 (SRC) ROBERTS, RICHARD B New treatments for AIDS and AIDS-related infections Fansidar prophylaxis against reactivated toxoplasmosis
U01AI-25917-04 0004 (SRC) HARTMAN, BARRY J New treatments for AIDS and AIDS-related infections Fluconazole therapy for crytococcosis
U01AI-25917-04 9001 (SRC) MURRAY, HENRY W New treatments for AIDS and AIDS-related infections Core--Biostatistics
R01AI-25920-04 (TMP) LANDFEAR, SCOTT M OREGON HLTH SCIS UNIVERSITY 3181 S W SAM JACKSON PK RD PORTLAND, OR 97201-3098 Stage specific genes in Leishmania enriettii
U01AI-25922-05 (SRC) ENGLEMAN, EDGAR G STANFORD UNIVERSITY BLOOD BANK 800 WELCH ROAD PALO ALTO, CA 94304 National cooperative drug discovery group for AIDS
U01AI-25922-05 0001 (SRC) ENGLEMAN, EDGAR G National cooperative drug discovery group for AIDS HIV spacific cytolytic clones
U01AI-25922-05 0002 (SRC) LIFSON, JEFFREY National cooperative drug discovery group for AIDS Interaction between HIV envelope glycoprotein and CD4
U01AI-25922-05 0003 (SRC) FRY, KIRK National cooperative drug discovery group for AIDS HIV specific human and chimeric monoclonal antibodies
U01AI-25922-05 9001 (SRC) ENGLEMAN, EDGAR G National cooperative drug discovery group for AIDS Immune functin bioassay--Core
U01AI-25922-05 9002 (SRC) LIFSON, JEFFREY National cooperative drug discovery group for AIDS HIV bioassay--Core
U01AI-25922-05 9003 (SRC) HWANG, KOU National cooperative drug discovery group for AIDS Core--Protein chemistry and immunoconjugation
U01AI-25924-05 (SRC) FASS, ROBERT J OHIO STATE UNIV. MEDICAL CENTE 410 W 10TH AVE COLUMBUS, OH 43210-1228 AIDS clinical study group
U01AI-25924-05 0001 (SRC) PARA, MICHAEL F AIDS clinical study group Establishment of a cohort and clinical management
U01AI-25924-05 0002 (SRC) TRIOZZI, PIERRE L AIDS clinical study group Combination therapy of HIV infection with interferon and AZT
U01AI-25924-05 0003 (SRC) GAGINELLA, TIMOTHY S AIDS clinical study group Role of VIP and other intestinal peptides in HIV associated diarrhea
U01AI-25924-05 0004 (SRC) ZWILLING, BRUCE S AIDS clinical study group Effects of HIV infection on Ia expression by monocytes
U01AI-25924-05 9001 (SRC) WHITACRE, CAROLINE C AIDS clinical study group Core--Laboratory
U01AI-25924-05 9002 (SRC) RICE, ROBET R AIDS clinical study group Database and analysis core
U01AI-25928-05 (SRC) EYSTER, M ELAINE MILTON S. HERSEY MED CENTER P O BOX 850 HERSHEY, PA 17033 Therapy of early HIV infections in hemophiliacs
U01AI-25934-05 (SRC) MC INTOSH, KENNETH CHILDREN'S HOSPITAL 300 LONGWOOD AVE, ENDERS 6 BOSTON, MA 02115 Prevention, treatment and study of childhood AIDS
U01AI-25934-05 0001 (SRC) MC INTOSH, KENNETH Prevention, treatment and study of childhood AIDS Natural history and therapy in childhood AIDS
U01AI-25934-05 0002 (SRC) WINTER, HARLAND Prevention, treatment and study of childhood AIDS Gastrointestinal and nutritional studies of HIV infection
U01AI-25934-05 9001 (SRC) MCINTOSH, KENNETH Prevention, treatment and study of childhood AIDS Clinical core
U01AI-25934-05 9002 (SRC) HUANG, ALICE S Prevention, treatment and study of childhood AIDS Laboratory core
R01AI-25938-04 (BM) CATES, KATHRYN LYNN RAINBOW BABIES & CHILDRENS HOS 2074 ABINGTON ROAD CLEVELAND, OH 44106 Interaction of complement and Haemophilus influenzae
R01AI-25944-03 (MBC) KOLTER, ROBERTO G HARVARD MEDICAL SCHOOL 200 LONGWOOD AVENUE BOSTON, MA 02115 Molecular genetics of peptide export in E coli
U01AI-25959-05 (SRC) ZAIA, JOHN A CITY OF HOPE NATIONAL MED CTR 1500 EAST DUARTE ROAD DUARTE, CA 91010 Development and delivery of antiviral RNA for AIDS
U01AI-25959-05 0001 (SRC) ROSSI, JOHN J Development and delivery of antiviral RNA for AIDS Development of antisense therapy for AIDS
U01AI-25959-05 0004 (SRC) ZAIA, JOHN A Development and delivery of antiviral RNA for AIDS Development and delivery of antiviral RNA for AIDS
U01AI-25959-05 0005 (SRC) CHASE, JOHN W Development and delivery of antiviral RNA for AIDS Synthetic approach to ribozyme development
U01AI-25959-05 0006 (SRC) KOHN, DONALD B Development and delivery of antiviral RNA for AIDS Anti-HIV ribozyme transduction by retroviral vectors
R44AI-25983-03 (SSS) KORBA, BRENT E MOLEC DIAGNOSTIC SYSTEMS, INC 4 RESEARCH COURT ROCKVILLE, MD 20850 In vitro testing for agents that inhibit HBV replication
U01AI-25993-05 (SRC) STEIGBIGEL, ROY T SUNY AT STONY BROOK STONY BROOK, NY 11794-8153 NCDDG for the treatment of AIDS
U01AI-25993-05 0004 (SRC) WEISER, BARBARA NCDDG for the treatment of AIDS Viral cofactors in HIV infection as targets for therapy
U01AI-25993-05 9001 (SRC) STEIGBIGEL, ROY NCDDG for the treatment of AIDS Immunology and virology core
U01AI-25993-05 0001 (SRC) WIMMER, ECKARD NCDDG for the treatment of AIDS Inhibitors of HIV-specific proteinase--Treatment of AIDS
U01AI-25993-05 0002 (SRC) JOHNSON, FRANCIS NCDDG for the treatment of AIDS Synthesis of potential inhibitors of HIV reverse transcriptase
U01AI-25993-05 0003 (SRC) STEIGBIGEL, ROY NCDDG for the treatment of AIDS Role of macrophage of HIV infection
R44AI-26019-03 (SSS) BRESLER, HERBERT S BIOTRONIC SYSTEMS CORPORATION 9620 MEDICAL CENTER DRIVE ROCKVILLE, MD 20850 Rapid biosensor assay of AIDS virus antibodies
R44AI-26028-03 (SSS) PANICALI, DENNIS L APPLIED BIOTECHNOLOGY, INC 80 ROGERS STREET CAMBRIDGE, MA 02142 Attenuation of the NYCBH vaccine strain of vaccinia
U01AI-26029-05 (SRC) BERGSTROM, DONALD E PURDUE UNIVERSITY WEST LAFAYETTE, IN 47907 Design and synthesis of oligonucleotide analogue antivirals
U01AI-26031-03S1 (SRC) FOUNG, STEVEN K H STANFORD UNIVERSITY BLOOD CTR 800 WELCH ROAD PALO ALTO, CA 94304 Innovative targeted approaches to CMV infections
U01AI-26035-03S1 (SRC) GOODING, LINDA R EMORY UNIVERSITY 507 WOODRUFF MEMORIAL BLDG ATLANTA, GA 30322 Molecular mechanisms of TNF-adenovirus interactions
U01AI-26049-05 (SRC) MANGEL, WALTER F BROOKHAVEN NATIONAL LABORATORY UPTON, NY 11973 The adenovirus 2 proteinase--Target for antiviral therapy
U01AI-26056-05S1 (SRC) ARMSTRONG, DONALD SLOAN-KETTERING INST/CA RES 1275 YORK AVENUE NEW YORK, N Y 10021 Drug discovery for treatment of AIDS
R29AI-26064-04 (EVR) HUANG, DIANA D RUSH PRESBY-ST LUKE MEDICAL CT 1653 WEST CONGRESS PARKWAY CHICAGO, IL 60612 Persistence of avian arthritis agent (reovirus) in vivo
R29AI-26070-04 (EVR) GRAY, WAYNE L UNIV OF ARKANSAS FOR MED SCI 4301 WEST MARKHAM LITTLE ROCK, AR 72205-7199 Simian varicella--A model for human VZV infections
U01AI-26075-05 (SRC) HOLMES, KATHRYN V UNIFORMED SERVS U OF HLTH SCIS 4301 JONES BRIDGE ROAD BETHESDA, MD 20814-4799 Coronavirus-receptor interactions
U01AI-26077-05 (SRC) COEN, DONALD M HARVARD MEDICAL SCHOOL 250 LONGWOOD AVENUE BOSTON, MA 02115 Combined approach to targeted anti-herpesvirus drugs
R55AI-26081-04 (ARRA) TILLEY, SHERMAINE A PUBLIC HEALTH RESEARCH INSTITU 455 FIRST AVENUE NEW YORK, NY 10016 Human monoclonal antibodies against HIV-1
R29AI-26098-04 (SSS) PLAEGER-MARSHALL, SUSAN F U C L A SCHOOL OF MEDICINE 405 HILGARD AVENUE LOS ANGELES, CA 90024 Defective CD8 T cell-mediated control in AIDS
R01AI-26103-02 (IMS) FELSBURG, PETER J PURDUE UNIVERSITY WEST LAFAYETTE, IN 47907 Model of X-linked severe combined immunodeficiency
R01AI-26109-04 (VR) TATTERSALL, PETER J YALE UNIVERSITY SCHOOL OF MED 333 CEDAR STREET NEW HAVEN, CT 06510 Molecular genetics of parvoviral DNA replication
R29AI-26113-03 (IMB) CHEN, YUNG-WU TEMPLE UNIV. SCHOOL OF MEDICIN 3400 NORTH BROAD STREET PHILADELPHIA, PA 19140 IL-4 induced IGM/IGG expression in normal murine B cells
R01AI-26121-03 (IMS) CATHCART, MARTHA K CLEVELAND CLINIC FOUNDATION 9500 EUCLID AVENUE CLEVELAND, OH 44106 Immunosuppression by an inhibitor of interleukin 2
R01AI-26122-04 (EVR) BERNS, KENNETH I CORNELL UNIVERSITY MED COLL 1300 YORK AVENUE NEW YORK, N Y 10021 Negative regulation of AAV DNA replication
R37AI-26123-04 (ARRA) PITHA-ROWE, PAULA M JOHNS HOPKINS UNIV 418 N BOND ST BALTIMORE, MD 21231 The role of cytokines in the pathogenesis of AIDS
R01AI-26128-04 (SSS) DEBS, ROBERT J UNIV CALIFORNIA, SAN FRANCISCO 3RD AND PARNASSUS SAN FRANCISCO, CA 94143-0128 Targeted therapy for AIDS-related pneumonias
R01AI-26144-02 (TMP) SUYAMA, YOSHITAKA UNIVERSITY OF PENNSYLVANIA 207 LEIDY LAB PHILADELPHIA, PA 19104 Imported tRNAs in mitochondria of Leishmania tarentolae
R29AI-26148-04 (BM) HOISETH, SUSAN K GEORGETOWN UNIVERSITY 3900 RESERVOIR RD., N.W. WASHINGTON, D.C. 20007 Genetic analysis of H. influenzae capsule expression
R29AI-26150-03 (IMS) KATONA, ILDY M UNIFORMED SERV U OF HLTH SCIS 4301 JONES BRIDGE ROAD BETHESDA, MD 20814-4799 Regulation of in vivo IgE responses
R01AI-26152-03 (BM) GARIEPY, JEAN THE ONTARIO CANCER INSTITUTE TORONTO, ONTARIO M4X 1K9, CANADA Characterization of the E coli enterotoxin st I receptor
R22AI-26153-03 (TMP) TAYLOR, DIANE WALLACE GEORGETOWN UNIVERSITY 37TH & O STS., N.W. WASHINGTON, D C 20057 Rodent malarial antigen--Py117
R01AI-26154-04 (TMP) ELDRIDGE, BRUCE F UNIVERSITY OF CALIFORNIA DAVIS, CA 95616 Ecology of California & Bunyamwera serogroup viruses
R29AI-26157-04 (TMP) JASMER, DOUGLAS P WASHINGTON STATE UNIVERSITY DEPT OF VETERINAY MICRO/PATH PULLMAN, WA 99164 Regulation of muscle gene expression in trichinosis
R01AI-26158-04 (TMP) SAUER, JOHN R OKLAHOMA STATE UNIVERSITY 501 LIFE SCIENCES WEST STILLWATER, OK 74078 Salivary secretion in a blood-sucking arthropod
R22AI-26170-03 (BM) JACOBS, WILLIAM R, JR ALBERT EINSTEIN COLL OF MED 1300 MORRIS PARK AVENUE BRONX, NY 10461 Molecular genetic analysis of Mycobacterium tuberculosis
R29AI-26173-04 (ALY) FINNEGAN, ALISON RUSH-PRESB-ST LUKE'S MED CTR 1653 WEST CONGRESS PARKWAY CHICAGO, IL 60612 T cell recognition of antigen
R01AI-26178-03 (TMP) DENLINGER, DAVID L OHIO ST UNIV ENTOMOLOGY DEPT. 1735 NEIL AVENUE COLUMBUS, OH 43210 Regulation of metamorphosis behavior in the Tsetse fly
R01AI-26195-04 (BM) FALKOW, STANLEY STANFORD UNIVERSITY STANFORD, CA 94305 The genetic and molecular basis of bacterial invasion
R01AI-26197-02 (TMP) CROSS, GEORGE A THE ROCKEFELLER UNIVERSITY 1230 YORK AVENUE NEW YORK, NY 10021 Structure and function of T. cruzi surface glycoproteins
R01AI-26232-02 (BM) ENGLEBERG, N CARY UNIVERSITY OF MICHIGAN ANN ARBOR, MI 48109-0620 Mutation of L pneumophila virulence genes

PROJECT NO., ORGANIZATIONAL UNIT., INVESTIGATOR, ADDRESS, TITLE

R01AI-26239-01A2 (EVR) KETNER, GARY W JOHNS HOPKINS UNIVERSITY 615 N WOLFE STREET BALTIMORE, MD 21205 Adenovirus gene expression--Genetics of early region 4

R01AI-26244-04 (EVR) OU, JING-HSIUNG J UNIV OF SOUTHERN CA SCH OF MED 2011 ZONAL AVE HMR 401 LOS ANGELES, CA 90033 Gene expression and molecular pathogenesis of HBV

R01AI-26249-05 (NEUB) YAKSH, TONY L UNIV OF CALIF, SAN DIEGO LA JOLLA, CA 92093 Peptide release from peripheral terminals of afferents

R01AI-26251-02 (VR) OFFIT, PAUL A JOSEPH STOKES JR., RSCH INST. DEPARTMENT OF PEDIATRICS PHILADELPHIA, PA 19104 Protection from viral gastroenteritis by intestinal CTLS

R01AI-26256-05 (EVR) GALINSKI, MARK S CLEVELAND CLINIC FOUNDATION 9500 EUCLID AVE CLEVELAND, OH 44195 Analysis of Parainfluenza 3 virus mediated fusion

R01AI-26259-01A2 (MCHA) BUNNELLE, WILLIAM H UNIVERSITY OF MISSOURI 123 CHEMISTRY BUILDING COLUMBIA, MO 65211 Electron rich peroxides as analogs of artemisinin

R01AI-26261-04 (PB) DAVES, G DOYLE, JR RENSSELAER POLYTECHNIC INST TROY, N Y 12180-3590 C-nucleosides as anti-AIDS agents

R29AI-26265-04 (BM) FRANZBLAU, SCOTT G GILLIS W LONG HANSEN'S DIS CTR PHARMACOLOGY RES DEPT GARVILLE, LA 70721 Metabolic maintenance & growth of Mycobacterium leprae

R29AI-26279-03 (BM) WESTERINK, MARIA ANNA JULIA SUNY CLINICAL CENTER ERIE COUNTY MEDICAL CENTER BUFFALO, NY 14215 Meningococcal anti-idiotype vaccines

R01AI-26280-04 (BM) BAVOIL, PATRIK M UNIVERSITY OF ROCHESTER 601 ELMWOOD AVE ROCHESTER, NY 14642 Molecular basis of chlamydial development/pathogenesis

R29AI-26284-04 (IMS) SANTORO, THOMAS J UNIV OF COLORADO HLTH SCI CTR 4200 E 9TH AVE (BOX B 115) DENVER, CO 80262 Membrane lipids and their potential role in lupus

R01AI-26289-04 (BM) MEKALANOS, JOHN J HARVARD MEDICAL SCHOOL 25 SHATTUCK STREET BOSTON, MA 02115 Coordinate regulation of bacterial virulence factors

R01AI-26292-03 (ALY) JACK, RICHARD M BRIGHAM AND WOMEN'S HOSPITAL 250 LONGWOOD AVENUE BOSTON, MA 02115 CR1 of human neutrophils--Biosynthesis and biology

R01AI-26296-02 (IMB) NOELLE, RANDOLPH J DARTMOUTH MEDICAL SCHOOL HANOVER, NH 03756 Cognate activation of B lymphocytes

R22AI-26305-03 (BM) GILLIS, THOMAS P GILLIS W LONG HANSEN'S DIS CTR CARVILLE, LA 70721 Characterization of T-cell clones to Mycobacterium leprae

R01AI-26322-03 (IMS) UMETSU, DALE T STANFORD UNIVERSITY SCH OF MED STANFORD, CA 94305-5119 Heterogeneity among human CD4+T cell clones

R29AI-26323-04 (EVR) SRIVASTAVA, ARUN INDIANA UNIV SCHOOL OF MEDICIN 635 BARNHILL DRIVE INDIANAPOLIS, IN 46202-5120 Studies on the human parvovirus B19

R29AI-26334-03 (IMB) SRIVASTAVA, RAKESH THE SCRIPPS RESEARCH INSTITUTE 10666 NORTH TORREY PINES ROAD LA JOLLA, CA 92037 Structure and expression of non HLA-A, B, C class I genes

R01AI-26339-03 (PHRA) SCHREIER, HANS UNIVERSITY OF FLORIDA COLLEGE OF PHARMACY/BOX J494 GAINESVILLE, FL 32610 Micobacterium avium disease--Inhaled liposome anti-TB drug therapy

R01AI-26350-04 (VR) SUMMERS, DONALD F UNIVERSITY OF UTAH SCH OF MED SALT LAKE CITY, UTAH 84132 Replication & capsid antigenes of Hepatitis A virus

R01AI-26363-04 (ALY) THOMAS, MATTHEW L WASHINGTON UNIV SCH OF MED 660 S. EUCLID AVENUE ST LOUIS, MO 63110 Leukocyte surface glycoproteins--Function and regulation

R01AI-26371-04 (VR) STOLLAR, VICTOR UNIV OF MED/DENT OF NEW JERSEY 675 HOES LANE PISCATAWAY, NJ 08854-5635 The genome of the cell fusing agent from mosquito cells

R01AI-26386-03 (BIO) PAINTER, RICHARD G UNIVERSITY OF TEXAS HLTH CTR P O BOX 2003 TYLER, TX 75710 Regulation of neutrophil chemotaxis in inflammation

R44AI-26387-03 (HUD) PARMS, CLIFFORD A INTERSYSTEMS INCORPORATED 820 W END AVE NEW YORK, NY 10025 Preventing HIV infection among minority group youth

R44AI-26430-03 (SSS) MCCULLOUGH, DOUGLAS IMMUNODIAGNOSTICS INC 562 1ST AVE SOUTH SEATTLE, WA 98104-2866 Immunological aspects of AIDS-related synthetic peptides

R44AI-26434-02 (SSS) BORAKER, DAVID K CHROMOGEN, INC PO BOX 128 MILTON, VT 05468 Enhanced ELISA performance using acoustic microstreaming

R44AI-26438-03 (SSS) SMITH, RICHARD H BIOQUANT, INC 1919 GREEN ROAD ANN ARBOR, MI 48105 Solid state enzyme-based immunosensors

R01AI-26449-11 (IMS) LAMM, MICHAEL E CASE WESTERN RESERVE UNIV 2085 ADELBERT ROAD CLEVELAND, OH 44106 Studies on secretory immunoglobulin

R01AI-26450-05 (EI) SCHWARTZ, ROBERT S NEW ENGLAND MED CTR HOSP 750 WASHINGTON STREET BOSTON, MA 02111 Monoclonal human lupus autoantibodies

U01AI-26462-04 (AIDS) KENNEDY, RONALD C SOUTHWEST FDN FOR BIOMED RES P O BOX 28147 SAN ANTONIO, TX 78228-0147 Strategy to develop idiotype based vaccines against HIV

U01AI-26462-04 0001 (AIDS) BUCK DAVID Strategy to develop idiotype based vaccines against HIV Mouse monoclonal antibodies against human CD4 molecule

U01AI-26462-04 0002 (AIDS) ESTESS PILA Strategy to develop idiotype based vaccines against HIV Generate chimeric CD4 molecules and chimeric anti CD4 molecules

U01AI-26462-04 0003 (AIDS) CHANH TRAN C Strategy to develop idiotype based vaccines against HIV Produce anti-id reagents against anti CD4

U01AI-26462-04 0004 (AIDS) KANDA PATRICK Strategy to develop idiotype based vaccines against HIV Synthetic peptides analogous to anti-cd4 monoclonal antibodies

U01AI-26462-04 0005 (AIDS) KENNEDY RONALD Strategy to develop idiotype based vaccines against HIV Anti-idiotypic antibodies to anti-HIV reagents

U01AI-26462-04 0006 (AIDS) ALLAN JONATHAN S Strategy to develop idiotype based vaccines against HIV Evaluation of idiotype-based vaccines in rhesus macaque/SIV model

PROJECT NO., ORGANIZATIONAL UNIT., INVESTIGATOR, ADDRESS, TITLE

U01AI-26462-04 0007 (AIDS) EICHBERG JORG W Strategy to develop idiotype based vaccines against HIV Evaluate idiotype-based vaccine in chimpanzees

U01AI-26463-04 (AIDS) YOUNG, RICHARD A WHITEHEAD INST FOR BIOMED RES NINE CAMBRIDGE CENTER CAMBRIDGE, MA 02142 Immune & biological strategies for AIDS vaccines

U01AI-26463-04 0001 (AIDS) YOUNG, RICHARD A Immune & biological strategies for AIDS vaccines Immune assessment and vaccine vehicles for AIDS

U01AI-26463-04 0002 (AIDS) BALTIMORE, DAVID Immune & biological strategies for AIDS vaccines Intracellular immunization

U01AI-26463-04 0003 (AIDS) DEROSIERS, RONALD C Immune & biological strategies for AIDS vaccines SIV neutralizing epitopes and vaccine development

U01AI-26463-04 0004 (AIDS) SCHOOLEY, ROBERT T Immune & biological strategies for AIDS vaccines Characterization of cytotoxic responses to HIV antigens

U01AI-26471-04 (AIDS) GARDNER, MURRAY B UNIVERSITY OF CALIFORNIA SCHOOL OF MEDICINE DAVIS, CA 95616 Vaccination for HIV and AIDS

U01AI-26471-04 0001 (AIDS) GARDNER, MURRY B Vaccination for HIV and AIDS Development of AIDS vaccines with different strains of HIV

U01AI-26471-04 0002 (AIDS) LEVY, JAY A Vaccination for HIV and AIDS Identify and classify HIV for AIDS vaccines

U01AI-26471-04 0003 (AIDS) STEIMER, KATHELYN S Vaccination for HIV and AIDS Genetically engineered polypeptides as vaccine against HIV

U01AI-26471-04 0004 (AIDS) EICHBERG, JORG W Vaccination for HIV and AIDS Efficacy of candidate HIV vaccines in chimpanzees

P01AI-26482-03S1 (SRC) ROBBINS, FREDERICK C CASE WESTERN RESERVE UNIV 10900 EUCLID AVENUE CLEVELAND, OH 44106-4984 HIV infection and AIDS in Uganda

P01AI-26482-03S1 0001 (SRC) GOLDFARB, JOHANNA HIV infection and AIDS in Uganda Transmission and course of HIV infection in infants

P01AI-26482-03S1 0002 (SRC) DANIEL, THOMAS M HIV infection and AIDS in Uganda Preventing, serodiagnosis, course of tuberculosis in HIV-infected patients

P01AI-26482-03S1 0003 (SRC) KAZURA, JAMES HIV infection and AIDS in Uganda Lymphotropic viruses in Kaposi's sarcoma & non-Hodgkins lymphoma

P01AI-26482-03S1 0004 (SRC) SCHUMANN, DEBRA HIV infection and AIDS in Uganda Family structure and social organization of risk behaviors

P01AI-26482-03S1 9001 (SRC) ROBBINS, FREDERICK C HIV infection and AIDS in Uganda Core--Data management

P01AI-26482-03S1 9002 (SRC) DOWNING, ROBERT HIV infection and AIDS in Uganda Core--Virology and molecular biology

R01AI-26483-04 (SRC) REEM, GABRIELLE H NEW YORK UNIVERSITY MED CENTER 550 FIRST AVENUE NEW YORK, NY 10016 Cyclosporine and gene expression by human thymocytes

P01AI-26487-03S1 (SRC) MUELLER, NANCY E HARVARD SCHOOL OF PUBLIC HEALT 677 HUNTINGTON AVENUE BOSTON, MA 02115 The AIDS epidemic in Mexico

P01AI-26487-03S1 9002 (SRC) MEULLER, NANCY E The AIDS epidemic in Mexico Core--Epidemiology

P01AI-26487-03S1 9003 (SRC) KANKI, PHYLLIS J The AIDS epidemic in Mexico Core--Virology of HIV infection in Mexico

P01AI-26487-03S1 0001 (SRC) MUELLER, NANCY E The AIDS epidemic in Mexico Surveillance of HIV infection in Mexico

P01AI-26487-03S1 0002 (SRC) GORTMAKER, STEVEN L The AIDS epidemic in Mexico Homosexual transmission of HIV infection--Preventive intervention

P01AI-26487-03S1 0003 (SRC) MEULLER, NANCY E The AIDS epidemic in Mexico Heterosexual transmission of HIV infection

P01AI-26487-03S1 9001 (SRC) KANKI, PHYLLIS J The AIDS epidemic in Mexico Core--Laboratory

R01AI-26490-03 (IMB) GELFAND, ERWIN W NATIONAL JEWISH CENTER 1400 JACKSON ST DENVER, CO 80206-1997 Ionic,biochemical,genetic basis for cyclosporin activity

P01AI-26491-03 (SRC) BLOOM, BARRY R ALBERT EINSTEIN COLLEGE OF MED 1300 MORRIS PARK AVENUE BRONX, NY 10461 Immunology and vaccines for leprosy and leishmaniasis

P01AI-26491-03 0001 (SRC) BLOOM, BARRY R. Immunology and vaccines for leprosy and leishmaniasis Molecular biology and immunology of M. leprae

P01AI-26491-03 0002 (SRC) BLOOM, BARRY R. Immunology and vaccines for leprosy and leishmaniasis Molecular biology and immunology of american cutaneous leishmaniasis

P01AI-26491-03 0003 (SRC) CONVIT, JACINTO Immunology and vaccines for leprosy and leishmaniasis Immunoregulation in leishmaniasis and leprosy

P01AI-26491-03 0004 (SRC) BLOOM, BARRY R. Immunology and vaccines for leprosy and leishmaniasis Epidem. and vaccine field studies of Amer. cutaneous leishmaniasis

P01AI-26491-03 0005 (SRC) BLOOM, BARRY R. Immunology and vaccines for leprosy and leishmaniasis Genetics of resistance to leprosy and leishmaniasis

P01AI-26491-03 9001 (SRC) CONVIT, JACINTO Immunology and vaccines for leprosy and leishmaniasis Core-- Molecular biology

P01AI-26497-03 (SRC) DECKELBAUM, RICHARD J COLUMBIA UNIVERSITY 630 WEST 168TH STREET NEW YORK, NY 10032 Giardiasis and cryptosporidiosis in children

P01AI-26497-03 0001 (SRC) NAGGAN, LECHAIM Giardiasis and cryptosporidiosis in children Cryptosporidium and giardiasis among Bedouin children

P01AI-26497-03 0002 (SRC) GRANOT, ESTHER Giardiasis and cryptosporidiosis in children Giardia lamblia & cryptosporidium associated diarrhea in hospital & community

P01AI-26497-03 0003 (SRC) SPIRA, DAN T Giardiasis and cryptosporidiosis in children Characterization of giardia and Cryptosporidium strains

P01AI-26497-03 0004 (SRC) VAN DER PLOEG, LEX Giardiasis and cryptosporidiosis in children Genetic and antigenic variability in Giardia lamblia

P01AI-26497-03 9001 (SRC) SCHLESINGER, MICHAEL Giardiasis and cryptosporidiosis in children Immunology core

P01AI-26497-03 9002 (SRC) NEUMANN, LILY Giardiasis and cryptosporidiosis in children Biostatistics core

P01AI-26499-03S1 (SRC) SAAH, ALFRED J THE JOHNS HOPKINS UNIVERSITY 550 NORTH BROADWAY, SUITE 763 BALTIMORE, MD 21205 HIV infection in Malawian mothers and their children

P01AI-26499-03S1 0001 (SRC) POLK, B FRANK HIV infection in Malawian mothers and their children Epidemiology of HIV infection in pregnant Malawian women

P01AI-26499-03S1 0002 (SRC) SAAH, ALFRED J HIV infection in Malawian mothers and their children Probability of infant HIV infection at birth with maternal HIV infection

P01AI-26499-03S1 0003 (SRC) SAAH, ALFRED J HIV infection in Malawian mothers and their children Longitudinal study--Seroconversion of HIV-negative mothers, fathers and infants

P01AI-26499-03S1 0004 (SRC) NELSON, KENRAD HIV infection in Malawian mothers and their children Risk of severe morbidity or mortality--Mothers and babies

P01AI-26499-03S1 9001 (SRC) FARZADEGAN, HOMAYOON HIV infection in Malawian mothers and their children Core--Serology, virology and immunology of HIV infection

P01AI-26499-03S1 9002 (SRC) HOOK, EDWARD HIV infection in Malawian mothers and their children Core--Clinical microbiology of sexually transmitted diseases

P01AI-26499-03S1 9003 (SRC) MUNOZ, ALVARO HIV infection in Malawian mothers and their children Core--Epidemiologic and statistical resource

U01AI-26503-04 (AIDS) COREY, LAWRENCE PACIFIC MEDICAL CENTER 1200 12TH AVENUE SOUTH SEATTLE, WA 98144 Subunit immunodeficiency virus vaccines

U01AI-26503-04 0001 (AIDS) HU SHU-LOK Subunit immunodeficiency virus vaccines Construction of subunit immunodeficiency virus vaccines

U01AI-26503-04 0002 (AIDS) MORTON WILLIAM Subunit immunodeficiency virus vaccines Immune response to subunit immunodeficiency virus vaccines in primates

U01AI-26503-04 0003 (AIDS) GREENBERG PHIL Subunit immunodeficiency virus vaccines Cellular immune responses to subunit immunodeficiency virus vaccines

U01AI-26503-04 0004 (AIDS) BUCHANAN THOMAS Subunit immunodeficiency virus vaccines Synthetic peptides for the purification and testing of SIV and HIV-2 vaccines

U01AI-26503-04 0005 (AIDS) COREY LAWRENCE Subunit immunodeficiency virus vaccines Evaluation of the reactogenicity and immunogenicity of HIV vaccines

U01AI-26503-04 9001 (AIDS) THOULESS MARGARET Subunit immunodeficiency virus vaccines Core--Virology/serology laboratory

P01AI-26505-03 (SRC) COLLEY, DANIEL G VA MEDICAL CENTER 1310-24TH AVENUE, SOUTH NASHVILLE, TN 37212 Studies on schistosomiasis & Chagas' disease in Brazil

P01AI-26505-03 0001 (SRC) GAZZINELLI, GIOVANNI Studies on schistosomiasis & Chagas' disease in Brazil Immunology of schistomiasis

P01AI-26505-03 0002 (SRC) COLLEY, DANIEL G. Studies on schistosomiasis & Chagas' disease in Brazil Immunolgy of Chagas' disease

P01AI-26505-03 0003 (SRC) KEMP, W. MICHAEL Studies on schistosomiasis & Chagas' disease in Brazil Molecular biology of Schistosoma mansoni

P01AI-26505-03 0004 (SRC) ROMANHA, ALVARO J. Studies on schistosomiasis & Chagas' disease in Brazil Molecular biological aspects of Trypanosoma cruzi

P01AI-26505-03 9001 (SRC) GAZZINELLI, GIOVANNI Studies on schistosomiasis & Chagas' disease in Brazil Core -- Laboratory

P01AI-26506-04 (SRC) JOHNSON, WARREN D, JR CORNELL UNIV MEDICAL COLLEGE 1300 YORK AVE, RM A-431 NEW YORK, NY 10021 Collaborative AIDS research in Brazil

P01AI-26506-04 0001 (SRC) GALVAO, PAULO AYROZA Collaborative AIDS research in Brazil Seroprevalence of HIV infection and characterization of HIV isolates

P01AI-26506-04 0002 (SRC) BADARO, ROBERTO Collaborative AIDS research in Brazil HIV infection in sexual partners and children of HIV infected adults

P01AI-26506-04 0003 (SRC) CARVALHO, EDGAR Collaborative AIDS research in Brazil Clinical AIDS in Brazil--Coinfection with endemic pathogens

U01AI-26507-03 (AIDS) PANICALI, DENNIS L APPLIED BIOTECHNOLOGY, INC 80 ROGERS STREET CAMBRIDGE, MA 02142 Development of vaccinia-based vaccines for HIV and SIV

U01AI-26507-03 0001 (AIDS) ROBERTS, BRYAN E Development of vaccinia-based vaccines for HIV and SIV Genetic engineering and expression analysis

U01AI-26507-03 0002 (AIDS) SULLIVAN, JOHN L Development of vaccinia-based vaccines for HIV and SIV HIV vaccinia recombinant vaccine--HIV specific immunity

U01AI-26507-03 0003 (AIDS) DESROSIERS, RONALD C Development of vaccinia-based vaccines for HIV and SIV Vaccine trials in macaques with vaccinia-SIV recombinants

P01AI-26512-03 (SRC) GUERRANT, RICHARD L UNIV OF VIRGINIA SCHOOL OF MED BOX 485 CHARLOTTESVILLE, VA 22908 Recognition and expression of tropical infectious diseases

P01AI-26512-03 0001 (SRC) GUERRANT, RICHARD L Recognition and expression of tropical infectious diseases Epidemiology, predisposing factors, etiologies of prolonged diarrhea

P01AI-26512-03 0002 (SRC) WEIKEL, CYNTHIA S Recognition and expression of tropical infectious diseases Cryptosporidiosis--Disease expression, epidemiology and humoral immunity

P01AI-26512-03 0003 (SRC) NATIONS, MARILYN K Recognition and expression of tropical infectious diseases "Illness of the child"--Recognition of a childhood syndrome

P01AI-26512-03 0004 (SRC) LIMA, NOELIA Recognition and expression of tropical infectious diseases Nosocomial diarrhea in northeastern brazil

P01AI-26512-03 0005 (SRC) PEARSON, RICHARD D Recognition and expression of tropical infectious diseases Disease expression and immunity in American visceral leishmaniasis

P01AI-26512-03 9001 (SRC) LIMA, ALDO Recognition and expression of tropical infectious diseases Core--UVA/UFC collaborative care research laboratory

R01AI-26521-04 (EDC) HALSEY, NEAL A JOHNS HOPKINS UNIVERSITY 615 NORTH WOLFE STREET BALTIMORE, MD 21205 HIV and HTLV-I cohort studies of Haitian women and infants

R01AI-26522-14 (EVR) TAYLOR, JOHN M INSTITUTE FOR CANCER RESEARCH 7701 BURHOLME AVENUE PHILADELPHIA, PA 19111 Reverse transcription

R01AI-26532-04 (BM) JOHNSON, WILLIAM UNIVERSITY OF IOWA IOWA CITY, IA 52242 Virulent to avirulent conversion of Leginella pneumophila

R01AI-26534-03 (TMP) BLUM, JACOB J DUKE UNIVERSITY MEDICAL CENTER PO BOX 3709-S DURHAM, NC 27710 Intermediary metabolism of leishmania

R01AI-26538-04 (BIO) LEHMAN, I R STANFORD UNIVERSITY SCHOOL OF MEDICINE STANFORD, CA 94305 Enzymatic mechanism of herpesvirus DNA replication

R01AI-26539-04 (EVR) MC KNIGHT, JENNIFER L UNIVERSITY OF PITTSBURGH GRADUATE SCHOOL OF PUBLIC HEAL PITTSBURGH, PA 15261 Characterization of two novel HSV-1 regulatory proteins

R01AI-26542-03 (TMP) KIERSZENBAUM, FELIPE MICHIGAN STATE UNIVERSITY MICROBIOLOGY & PUBLIC HEALTH EAST LANSING, MI 48824 Lymphocyte modulation by Trypanosoma cruzi

R37AI-26558-04 (BM) GOTSCHLICH, EMIL C ROCKEFELLER UNIVERSITY 1230 YORK AVENUE NEW YORK, NY 10021-6399 Molecular biology of meningococcal surface proteins

R01AI-26560-04 (BM) BLANCHARD, D KAY UNIVERSITY OF SOUTH FLORIDA 12901 N BRUCE B DOWNS BLVD TAMPA, FL 33612 Resistance of opportunistic infection by Mycobacteria

R29AI-26561-03 (ALY) GREENSPAN, NEIL S CASE WESTERN RESERVE UNIV 2085 ADELBERT ROAD CLEVELAND, OH 44106 Constant domain modulation of antibody activity

R01AI-26579-02 (MBC) PERLIN, MICHAEL H UNIVERSITY OF LOUISVILLE LOUISVILLE, KY 40292 Active-site characterization for aminoglycoside 3'-phosphotransferase

R29AI-26580-04 (GMA) KALISH, RICHARD S SUNY AT STONY BROOK STONY BROOK, N Y 11794 T-cell mechanisms of pathology in DTH & drug eruptions

R01AI-26585-04 (VR) BANERJEE, AMIYA K CLEVELAND CLINIC FOUNDATION 9500 EUCLID AVENUE CLEVELAND, OH 44106 Gene expression of negative strand RNA viruses

R01AI-26589-03 (BM) SPITZNAGEL, JOHN K EMORY UNIVERSITY ATLANTA, GA 30322 Salmonella resistance to cationic proteins in PMN

R01AI-26598-04 (ALY) SAITO, HARUO DANA-FARBER CANCER INSTITUTE 44 BINNEY STREET BOSTON, MA 02115 Structure and function of human leukocyte common antigen

R01AI-26600-03 (ARR) MCHENRY, CHARLES S UNIVERSITY OF COLORADO CB B121/4200 E 9TH AVENUE DENVER, CO 80262 Biochemistry of human immunodeficiency virus replication

R29AI-26603-04 (EVR) DENISON, MARK R VANDERBILT UNIVERSITY MED CTR 1161 S. 21ST AVE S. D-7226 MCN NASHVILLE, TN 37232-2581 Coronavirus--Analysis of polymerase gene products

R01AI-26604-03 (ALY) SHASTRI, NILABH UNIVERSITY OF CALIFORNIA BERKELEY, CA 94720 Molecular model for T cell receptor-ligand interactions

R01AI-26609-04 (IMS) BUSSE, WILLIAM W UNIV OF WISCONSIN HOSPITAL 600 HIGHLAND AVE (H6/367) MADISON, WI 53792 Airway biology of rhinovirus 16 infection and asthma

R01AI-26610-04 (MGN) PETERSON, PER A RESEARCH INST OF SCRIPPS CLIN 10666 NORTH TORREY PINES ROAD LA JOLLA, CA 92037 Expression of human class II antigensa

R29AI-26629-03 (IMS) BURKS, ARVIL W JR ARKANSAS CHILDREN'S HOSPITAL 800 MARSHALL STREET LITTLE ROCK, AR 72202 Allergenicity of major component proteins of soybean

R01AI-26641-04 (SRC) SCHLEGEL, ROBERT A PENNSYLVANIA STATE UNIVERSITY 101 SOUTH FREAR LABORATORY UNIVERSITY PARK, PA 16802 Membrane lipid order and lymhocyte function

R01AI-26644-04 (SRC) IMBODEN, JOHN B VETERANS ADMIN MED CTR-111R 4150 CLEMENT STREET SAN FRANCISCO, CA 94121 Regulation of inositol lipids by the T cell molecule CD5

R01AI-26646-04 (IMS) SULLIVAN, TIMOTHY J UNIV OF TEXAS SW MEDICAL CTR 5323 HARRY HINES BLVD DALLAS, TX 75235-9030 Studies of beta-lactam antibiotic allergy

R01AI-26649-03 (TMP) PETRI, WILLIAM A, JR UNIV. OF VA, MR4 RM 2115, DEPT. OF INT. MED. CHARLOTTESVILLE, VA 22908 Structure & function of E histolytica adherence lectin

R29AI-26651-04 (TMP) BZIK, DAVID J DARTMOUTH MEDICAL SCHOOL HANOVER, NH 03756 Gene expression & regulation in P. falciparum

R01AI-26652-03 (ARR) MODAK, MUKUND J UNIV OF MED & DENT OF NEW JERS 185 SOUTH ORANGE AVENUE NEWARK, NJ 07103-2757 Structure-function relation in HIV reverse transcription

R01AI-26653-04 (IMS) KORNGOLD, ROBERT JEFFERSON MEDICAL COLLEGE 1020 LOCUST STREET PHILADELPHIA, PA 19107 EAE susceptibility analysis with radiation chimeras

R01AI-26655-03 (MBC) SILVER, RICHARD P 601 ELMWOOD AVE/BOX 672 ROCHESTER, NY 14642 Translocation of the E coli KI capsular polysaccharide

R29AI-26663-04 (EVR) KRYSTAL, MARK R MT. SINAI SCHOOL OF MEDICINE ONE GUSTAVE LEVY PLACE NEW YORK, NY 10029 Molecular studies on influenza virus replication

R29AI-26665-04 (SSS) MONESTIER, MARC CENTER FOR MOLECULAR MEDICINE 1 BRUCE STREET NEWARK, NJ 07103 Induction of anti-DNA autoantibodies in normal mice

R29AI-26672-04 (VR) GEBALLE, ADAM P FRED HUTCHINSON CANCER RES. CT 1124 COLUMBIA ST SEATTLE, WA 98104 Translational control of cytomegalovirus gene expression

R01AI-26675-04 (NEUC) RICHERT, JOHN R GEORGETOWN UNIVERSITY MED CTR 3800 RESERVOIR ROAD, N W WASHINGTON, D C 20007 Human T cell recognition sites on myelin basic protein

R01AI-26689-03 (IMS) ASKENASE, PHILIP W YALE UNIV SCH OF

PROJECT NO., ORGANIZATIONAL UNIT., INVESTIGATOR, ADDRESS, TITLE

MEDICINE 333 CEDAR STREET NEW HAVEN, CT 06510 Initiator T cells in delayed-type hypersensitivity

P01AI-26698-03S1 (SRC) KEUSCH, GERALD T NEW ENGLAND MEDICAL CTR HOSP 750 WASHINGTON STREET, BOX 041 BOSTON, MA 02111 AIDS-associated diarrhea and wasting syndrome in Africa

P01AI-26698-03S1 0001 (SRC) COLEBUNDERS, ROBERT AIDS-associated diarrhea and wasting syndrome in Africa The incidence and history of AIDS associated diarrhea and wasting

P01AI-26698-03S1 0002 (SRC) RUSSELL, ROBERT M AIDS-associated diarrhea and wasting syndrome in Africa Mechanism of diarrhea and malabsorption in African AIDS

P01AI-26698-03S1 0003 (SRC) DDONOHUE-ROLFE, ARTHUR AIDS-associated diarrhea and wasting syndrome in Africa Microbial etiology of AIDS associated diarrhea

P01AI-26698-03S1 0004 (SRC) CANNON,JOSEPH G AIDS-associated diarrhea and wasting syndrome in Africa Host factor in AIDS associated diarrhea and wasting syndrome

P01AI-26698-03S1 9001 (SRC) ONDERDONK, ANDREW AIDS-associated diarrhea and wasting syndrome in Africa Core--Microbiology

P01AI-26698-03S1 9002 (SRC) LENCER, WAYNE AIDS-associated diarrhea and wasting syndrome in Africa Clinical study--Core

P01AI-26698-03S1 9003 (SRC) LENCER, WAYNE AIDS-associated diarrhea and wasting syndrome in Africa Gastrointestinal function/metabolism--Core

P01AI-26698-03S1 9004 (SRC) RAND, WILLIAM AIDS-associated diarrhea and wasting syndrome in Africa Biostatistic--Core

R29AI-26710-04 (IMS) GAVALCHIN, JERRIE SUNY HEALTH SCIENCE CENTER 750 EAST ADAMS ST SYRACUSE, NY 13210 Nephritogenic idiotypes in normal and autoimmune mice

R01AI-26711-05 (HEM) JESAITIS, ALGIRADAS JOSEPH MONTANA STATE UNIVERSITY DEPARTMENT OF CHEMISTRY BOZEMAN, MT 59717 Role of cytochrome B in neutrophil superoxide production

R01AI-26718-04 (VR) AIR, GILLIAN M UAB (BASIC HLTH SC BLDG--360) UAB STATION BIRMINGHAM, ALA 35294 Structure and activity of influenza B neuraminidases

R29AI-26733-02 (PBC) BOHNSACK, JOHN F UNIVERSITY OF UTAH MED CENTER 50 NORTH MEDICAL DRIVE SALT LAKE CITY, UT 84132 Structure and function of a neutrophil lamanin receptor

R01AI-26734-04 (GEN) POSTLETHWAIT, JOHN H UNIVERSITY OF OREGON EUGENE, OR 97403 Molecular genetics of immunity in Drosophila

R29AI-26735-04 (GMA) MAGILAVY, DANIEL B UNIVERSITY OF CHICAGO E 65TH ST AT LAKE MICHIGAN CHICAGO, IL 60649 Liver natural killer & accessory cells in murine lupus

R01AI-26741-04 (EVR) LAI, MICHAEL M UNIV OF SOUTHERN CALIFORNIA 2011 ZONAL AVENUE LOS ANGELES, CA 90033 Molecular biology of Hepatitis delta virus

R29AI-26756-04 (BM) RADOLF, JUSTIN D UNIV OF TEXAS SOUTHWESTERN MEDICAL CENTER AT DALLAS DALLAS, TX 75235-9030 Membrane proteins of Treponema pallidum

R01AI-26761-01A2 (GMA) CHIN, YEE HON UNIVERSITY OF MIAMI R-138 P O BOX 016960 MIAMI, FL 33101 Lymphocyte migration and skin diseases

R01AI-26762-04 (SSS) TANG, JORDAN J OKLAHOMA MEDICAL RESEARCH FDN 825 N E 13TH STREET OKLAHOMA CITY, OK 73104 Studies on the protease of human immunodeficiency virus

R01AI-26763-04 (VR) HUANG, HENRY WASHINGTON UNIVERSITY BOX 8230 ST LOUIS, MO 63110-1093 Mechanism of alphavirus subgenomic mRNA synthesis

R01AI-26765-03S1 (VR) SEMLER, BERT L UNIVERSITY OF CALIFORNIA COLLEGE OF MEDICINE IRVINE, CA 92717 Genetics of 5'-noncoding regions of picornavirus RNAs

R01AI-26769-02 (VR) BUJARSKI, JOZEF NORTHERN ILLINOIS UNIVESITY DEKALB, IL 60115 Studies on recombination in the multipartite RNA viruses

R01AI-26771-04 (SRC) CHILTON, FLOYD HAROLD BOWMAN GRAY SCHOOL OF MEDICINE MEDICAL CENTER BLVD WINSTON, N C 27157-1052 Relationship between platelet activating factor and eicosanoids

R01AI-26774-03 (EI) HASKILL, STEPHEN UNIVERSITY OF NORTH CAROLINA CB# 7295 CHAPEL HILL, NC 27599-7295 Adherence regulated monocyte genes

R01AI-26782-02 (IMB) HARDY, RICHARD R INSTITUTE FOR CANCER RESEARCH 7701 BURHOLME AVENUE PHILADELPHIA, PA 19111 Ly-1 B cells--Lineage determination and antibody repertoire

R01AI-26787-04 (TMP) SCOTT, THOMAS W UNIVERSITY OF MARYLAND DIV. OF AGRIC. AND LIFE SCIENC COLLEGE PARK, MD 20742 Togavirus-vector interactions /birds,hamsters/

R01AI-26788-03 (EDC) KOMAROFF, ANTHONY L BRIGHAM AND WOMENS HOSPITAL 75 FRANCIS STREET BOSTON, MA 02115 Prevalence of chronic fatigue syndrome

R01AI-26791-04 (IMB) BOTTOMLY, KIM YALE UNIV SCH OF MEDICINE PO BOX 3333 NEW HAVEN, CT 06510 Differential activation of CD4+ T cell subsets

R01AI-26800-04 (EVR) FLANAGAN, THOMAS D RESEARCH FDN OF SUNY 218 SHERMAN HALL BUFFALO, NY 14214 The role of viral glycoproteins in membrane fusion

R29AI-26804-04 (BM) THOMAS, DEBORA DENEE UNIVERSITY OF TEXAS HLTH SCI C 7703 FLOYD CURL DR SAN ANTONIO, TX 78284 Interactions of pathogenic spirochetes with host cells

R01AI-26806-01A3 (ARRA) FITZGERALD-BOCARSLY, PATRICIA UMDNJ-NEW JERSEY MEDICAL SCHOO 185 SO ORANGE AVE NEWARK, NJ 07103-2714 Role of interferon-alpha in AIDS pathogenesis

R01AI-26807-03 (BM) DE LA MAZA, LUIS M UNIVERSITY OF CALIFORNIA MEDICAL SCIENCES I D440 IRVINE, CA 92717 Recombinant polytypic chlamydia vaccine

R01AI-26810-03 (IMB) JANEWAY, CHARLES A, JR YALE UNIVERSITY, SCHOOL OF MED 310 CEDAR STREET NEW HAVEN, CONN 06510 Ligands and accessory factors in CD4+ T cell priming

R29AI-26813-03 (BM) MULDROW, LYCURGUS L ATLANTA UNIVERSITY CTR, INC 440 WESTVIEW DRIVE, SW ATLANTA, GA 30310 Molecular analysis of Clostridium difficile toxin genes

R29AI-26814-04 (IMB) LACEY, DAVID L JEWISH HOSP AT WASHINGTON UNIV 216 SOUTH KINGSHIGHWAY ST LOUIS, MO 63110 Bone-seeking hormones and the immune system

R01AI-26815-04 (TMP) BARTHOLD, STEPHEN W YALE UNIVERSITY 333 CEDAR STREET NEW HAVEN, CT 06510 A rat model of Lyme disease

R01AI-26818-03 (ARR) CEASE, KEMP B UNIVERSITY OF MICHIGAN 102 OBSERVATORY ROAD ANN ARBOR, MI 48109-0724 Rational peptide component vaccines for AIDS

P50AI-26821-04 (AITC) BELLANTI, JOSEPH A GEORGETOWN UNIV SCH OF MED 3800 RESERVOIR ROAD, N W WASHINGTON, D C 20007 Centers for interdisciplinary research on immunolgic diseases

P50AI-26821-04 0004 (AITC) RICHERT, JOHN Centers for interdisciplinary research on immunolgic diseases Development of T cell immunity to viral and autoantigens

P50AI-26821-04 0005 (AITC) ZUCKERMAN, ALAN Centers for interdisciplinary research on immunolgic diseases Asthma patient education project

P50AI-26821-04 0001 (AITC) BELLANTI, JOSEPH Centers for interdisciplinary research on immunolgic diseases Phagocytic cell function in newborn and developing infant

P50AI-26821-04 0002 (AITC) VOGEL, CARL WILHEIM Centers for interdisciplinary research on immunolgic diseases Structure-function analysis of complement protein C3

P50AI-26821-04 0003 (AITC) COLE, MICHAEL Centers for interdisciplinary research on immunolgic diseases Development of mucosal immunity to commensal oral bacteria

R01AI-26827-04 (IMB) RITTENBERG, MARVIN B OREGON HLTH SCIS UNIVERSITY 3181 SW SAM JACKSON PK RD PORTLAND, OR 97201 Evolution of molecular diversity & epitope recognition

R01AI-26833-04 (IMS) MARION, TONY N UNIV OF TENNESSEE, MEMPHIS 858 MADISON AVE, SUITE 801 MEMPHIS, TN 38163 Structure and ontogeny of autoimmune anti-DNA antibodies

R29AI-26835-04 (ALY) FINGEROTH, JOYCE D DANA-FARBER CANCER INSTITUTE 44 BINNEY STREET BOSTON, MA 02115 The putative murine complement receptor type 2

R37AI-26837-04 (BM) SPARLING, PHILIP F UNIV. OF NC AT CHAPEL HILL CB# 7290, 804 FLOB CHAPEL HILL, N C 27599 Genetics and biology of gonococcal protein I

R29AI-26844-04 (ALY) CLARKE, STEPHEN H UNIV OF NC, AT CHAPEL HILL CB#7290, 804 FLOB CHAPEL HILL, NC 27599 Structure/function of anti-hemagglutinin antibodies

R01AI-26847-04 (EI) BLUESTONE, JEFFREY A UNIV OF CHICAGO, BOX 424 5841 S MARYLAND AVENUE CHICAGO, IL 60637 Immunobiology of TcR gamma delta T cells

R22AI-26848-02 (TMP) MESHNICK, STEVEN R CUNY MEDICAL SCHOOL CONVENT AVENUE AT 138TH STREET NEW YORK, NY 10031 Oxidant effects in malaria-infected erythrocytes

R29AI-26853-04 (GMA) CRAFT, JOSEPH E YALE UNIVERSITY SCHOOL OF MED 333 CEDAR ST., P. O. BOX 3333 NEW HAVEN, CT 06510 Structure and autoimmunogenic potential of the Thsn RNP/human

R29AI-26863-04 (HEM) SUCHARD, SUZANNE J UNIVERSITY OF MICHIGAN F6515 MOTT HOSPITAL, BOX 0238 ANN ARBOR, MI 48109 Membrane cytoskeleton interactions in neutrophils

R29AI-26865-03 (ARR) NABEL, GARY J UNIVERSITY OF MICHIGAN 1150 W MEDICAL CENTER DRIVE ANN ARBOR, MI 48109-0650 Control of HIV and inducible T cell gene products

R01AI-26872-04 (EI) TEDDER, THOMAS F DANA-FARBER CANCER INSTITUTE 44 BINNEY STREET BOSTON, MA 02115 Molecular analysis of B lymphocyte-restricted proteins

R29AI-26875-02 (IMB) YOUNG, JAMES W ROCKEFELLER UNIVERSITY 1230 YORK AVENUE NEW YORK, NY 10021-6399 Generation of primary human cytolytic T lymphocytes

R01AI-26879-04 (EVR) ROY, POLLY UNIV OF ALABAMA AT BIRMINGHAM UNIVERSITY STATION BIRMINGHAM, AL 35294 Bluetongue virus morphogenesis

R01AI-26880-02 (IMB) FREED, JOHN H NATL JEW CTR-IMMUN & RESP MED 1400 JACKSON STREET DENVER, CO 80206 Mixed isotype class II molecules--Function and occurrence

R01AI-26884-04 (ALY) OHARA, JUN-ICHI UNIV OF COLORADO HLTH SC CTR 4200 E 9TH AVE DENVER, CO 80262 Molecular studies of interleukin-4 receptor

P01AI-26886-04 (SRC) CHESS, LEONARD COLUMBIA UNIVERSITY 630 WEST 168TH STREET NEW YORK, N Y 10032 Pathogenesis of AIDS--Molecular and cellular mechanisms

P01AI-26886-04 0001 (SRC) CHESS, LEONARD Pathogenesis of AIDS--Molecular and cellular mechanisms Biologic and functional consequences of CD4-gp120 interactions

P01AI-26886-04 0002 (SRC) SILVERSTEIN, SAMUEL C Pathogenesis of AIDS--Molecular and cellular mechanisms Humoral and cellular immunity to HIV infection in vitro

P01AI-26886-04 0003 (SRC) GINSBERG, HAROLD S Pathogenesis of AIDS--Molecular and cellular mechanisms Virologic and pathogenic investigation of AIDS incubation period

P01AI-26886-04 0004 (SRC) GOFF, STEPHEN Pathogenesis of AIDS--Molecular and cellular mechanisms Construction of hybrid viral genomes and their use in the study of HIV latency

P01AI-26886-04 0005 (SRC) WEINBERGER, JUDAH Pathogenesis of AIDS--Molecular and cellular mechanisms HIV gene expression in primary human monocytes

P01AI-26886-04 9001 (SRC) GINSBERG, HAROLD S Pathogenesis of AIDS--Molecular and cellular mechanisms Core--HIV isolation culture and containment facility

P01AI-26886-04 9002 (SRC) KNOWLES, DANIEL Pathogenesis of AIDS--Molecular and cellular mechanisms Core--AIDS specimen procurement

R01AI-26887-04 (EI) SWAIN, SUSAN L UNIV OF CALIFORNIA, SAN DIEGO SCHOOL OF MEDICINE LA JOLLA, CA 92093-0063 Characterization of helper T cell subsets

R01AI-26889-02 (TMP) RUSSELL, DAVID G WASHINGTON UNIVERSITY BOX 8230 ST LOUIS, MO 63110-1093 Leishmania antigens important to host cell infection

R01AI-26896-03 (VR) TYRING, STEPHEN K UNIV OF TEXAS MEDICAL SCHOOL GALVESTON, TX 77550 Mechanisms of interferon action against papillomaviruses

R01AI-26899-03 (IMB) HURLEY, CAROLYN K GEORGETOWN UNIVERSITY 3900 RESERVOIR RD, N.W. WASHINGTON, DC 20007 Allogeneic response--Role of T cell receptor diversity

PROJECT NO., ORGANIZATIONAL UNIT., INVESTIGATOR, ADDRESS, TITLE

R22AI-26904-03 (TMP) **WASSOM, DONALD L** UNIV OF WISCONSIN-MADISON 2015 LINDEN DRIVE - WEST MADISON, WI 53706 Immunoregulation in murine malaria

R01AI-26905-03 (TMP) **ZIEGLER, ROLF** UNIVERSITY OF ARIZONA BIOSCIENCES WEST 351 TUCSON, AZ 85721 Control of peptide hormone levels in insects

R29AI-26912-03 (TMP) **RATHOD, PRADIPSINH K** CATHOLIC UNIVERSITY OF AMERICA 103 MCCORT-WARD BIOLOGY BLDG WASHINGTON, DC 20064 Antimalarial activity of orotic acid analogs

R01AI-26918-04 (TMP) **LOCKSLEY, RICHARD M** UNIVERSITY OF CALIFORNIA BOX 0654, RM C-443 SAN FRANCISCO, CA 94143-0654 Helper T cell subsets in leishmanisis

R01AI-26923-04 (PTHB) **OWNBY, CHARLOTTE L** OKLAHOMA STATE UNIVERSITY STILLWATER, OKLA 74078 Development of a new polyvalent antivenom for snakebite

R01AI-26928-04 (EI) **SUNG, SUN-SANG J** MEDICAL COLLEGE OF VIRGINIA BOX 58 MCV STATION RICHMOND, VA 23298 Human lymphocyte production of tumor necrosis factor

R01AI-26932-01A3 (IMS) **SUTHANTHIRAN, MANIKKAM** CORNELL UNIV MEDICAL COLLEGE 1300 YORK AVENUE NEW YORK, NY 10021 Cyclosporine--Mechanisms of immunosuppressive action

R01AI-26937-04 (EVR) **GLORIOSO, JOSEPH C** UNIVERSITY OF PITTSBURGH 3550 TERRACE STREET PITTSBURGH, PA 15261 Genetics and function of HSV gb and gd in virus entry

R29AI-26940-04 (IMS) **LEWIS, DAVID B** UNIVERSITY OF WASHINGTON DEPARTMENT OF PEDIATRICS SEATTLE, WA 98105 Ontogeny of interferon-gamma & interleukin-4 production

R01AI-26941-03 (SAT) **BURLINGHAM, WILLIAM J** UNIVERSITY OF WISCONSIN F4/315 CSC MADISON, WI 53792 Desensitization by antiidiotypic Ab-2 to MHC class I

R01AI-26942-04 (ALY) **ALLISON, JAMES P** UNIVERSITY OF CALIFORNIA BERKELEY, CA 94720 The murine gamma/delta antigen receptor

R01AI-26943-03 (EVR) **WOLINSKY, JERRY S** UNIV OF TEXAS HEALTH SCI CTR PO BOX 20708 HOUSTON, TX 77225 Molecular immune response determinants of rubella virus

R01AI-26950-03 (EI) **MESCHER, MATTHEW F** MEDICAL BIOLOGY INSTITUTE 11077 N TORREY PINES RD LA JOLLA, CA 92037 Transmembrane signalling in cytotoxic T lymphocytes

R44AI-26965-03 (SSS) **LIN, TSUE-MING** DIAMEDIX CORPORATION 2140 N MIAMI AVENUE MIAMI, FL 33127 Rapid safe & inexpensive immunoassay for Lyme disease

R44AI-26971-03 (SSS) **FUNG, SEK-CHUNG** TANOX BIOSYSTEMS, INC 10301 STELLA LINK HOUSTON, TX 77025 Anti-idiotypic vaccines for AIDS

R44AI-26983-03 (SSS) **PAPSIDERO, LAWRENCE D** CELLULAR PRODUCTS, INC 688 MAIN STREET BUFFALO, NY 14202 Neutralization of HIV

R44AI-27006-02A2 (SSS) **DE CASTRO, AURORA F** GDS TECHNOLOGY, INC PO BOX 473 ELKHART, IN 46515 A new enzymatic strip-test for theophylline

R01AI-27007-03 (SSS) **DEICH, ROBERT A** PRAXIS BIOLOGICS, INC 300 EAST RIVER ROAD ROCHESTER, NY 14623 Mutant nontoxic forms of pertussis toxin for vaccine

R01AI-27026-04 (BBCB) **PARDI, ARTHUR** UNIVERSITY OF COLORADO CAMPUS BOX 215 BOULDER, CO 80309-0215 Solution structures of antimicrobial peptides

R01AI-27028-03 (VR) **WHITTON, J LINDSAY** SCRIPPS CLINIC & RES FDN 10666 N TORREY PINES ROAD LA JOLLA, CA 92037 Analyses of cytotoxic T cell response to virus infection

R01AI-27035-03 (ARR) **HIZI, AMNON** SACKLER SCHOOL OF MEDICINE TEL AVIV, ISRAEL 69978 Studies of human immunodeficiency virus enzymes

R01AI-27039-03 (MBC) **NICHOLAS, ROBERT A** UNC AT CHAPEL HILL CB#7365 FACULTY LAB OFF BLDG CHAPEL HILL, NC 27599-7365 Relating structure/function in E. coli penicillin-PBPS

R01AI-27044-03 (TMP) **BENACH, JORGE L** S.U.N.Y. AT STONY BROOK HEALTH SCIENCES CENTER STONY BROOK, NY 11794 Antigen specific interactions of borrelia with tick

R29AI-27050-04 (SSS) **WONG, JOHNSON T** MASSACHUSETTS GENERAL HOSPITAL FRUIT STREET BOSTON, MA 02114 T cell subsets strategies in AIDS and transplantation

R29AI-27053-04 (SSS) **SIEKEVITZ, MIRIAM L** MOUNT SINAI SCHOOL OF MEDICINE ONE GUSTAVE LEVY PLACE NEW YORK, N.Y. 10029 Control of HIV-I & interleukin-2 in activated T cells

R01AI-27054-03 (ARR) **FAY, PHILIP J** UNIVERSITY OF ROCHESTER 601 ELMWOOD AVE, PO BX 610 ROCHESTER, NY 14642 DNA synthesis and recombination by hiv DNA polymerase

R01AI-27057-04 (SSS) **ANSARI, AFTAB A** EMORY UNIV SCHOOL OF MED 783 WOODRUFF MEMORIAL BLDG ATLANTA, GA 30322 Role of virus specific T cell immunity in primate AIDS

R01AI-27076-04 (SSS) **DAVIS, RONALD W** STANFORD UNIVERSITY STANFORD, CA 94305 Regulatory sites and factors for the AIDS virus HIV1

R01AI-27090-03 (TMP) **BAUMANN, PAUL** UNIVERSITY OF CALIFORNIA DAVIS, CA 95616 Genetics and physiology of bacterial mosquito toxins

R01AI-27091-03 (EDC) **ADLER, STUART P** MEDICAL COLLEGE OF VIRGINIA P O BOX 163, MCV STATION RICHMOND, VA 23298 Epidemiology of human parvovirus B19

R01AI-27094-03 (ARR) **CLARK, ALICE M** UNIVERSITY OF MISSISSIPPI UNIVERSITY, MS 38677 New drugs for opportunistic infectious diseases

R01AI-27107-04 **BELAS, MICHAEL R, JR** UNIVERSITY OF MARYLAND SYSTEM 600 EAST LOMBARD STREET BALTIMORE, MD 21202 Regulation of Proteus differentiation

R01AI-27111-04 (SSS) **MAIO, JOSEPH J** ALBERT EINSTEIN COL OF MED 1300 MORRIS PARK AVENUE BRONX, N Y 10461 Cellular regulation of HIV-1 expression

R01AI-27123-03 (IMB) **HANSEN, TED H** WASHINGTON UNIV SCH OF MED 660 SOUTH EUCLID ST LOUIS, MO 63110 Role of b2m in MHC class I expression and conformation

R01AI-27128-03 (TMP) **EDMAN, JEFFREY C** UNIVERSITY OF CALIFORNIA SAN FRANCISCO, CA 94143-0534 Molecular biology of pneumocystis carinii

R29AI-27130-03 (TMP) **CHANG, SANDRA P** UNIVERSITY OF HAWAII 3675 KILAUEA AVENUE HONOLULU, HI 96816 B cell and T cell recognition sites of P falciparum gp195

P01AI-27135-04 (AIDS) **ALBERSHEIM, PETER** COMPLEX CARBOHYDRATES RES CTR 220 RIVERBEND ROAD ATHENS, GA 30602 Structure of HIV and CD4 glycoproteins

P01AI-27135-04 0001 (AIDS) **HASELTINE, WILLIAM** Structure of HIV and CD4 glycoproteins Molecular studies of HIV carbohydrates

P01AI-27135-04 0002 (AIDS) **SEALS, JONATHAN** Structure of HIV and CD4 glycoproteins Large scale purification of CD4 and HIV-1 GP120 and GP41

P01AI-27135-04 0003 (AIDS) **CUMMINGS, RICHARD** Structure of HIV and CD4 glycoproteins Analysis of the carbohydrates of HIV and its receptor

P01AI-27135-04 0004 (AIDS) **VAN HLBEEK, HERMAN** Structure of HIV and CD4 glycoproteins Determining the structure of HIV and CD4 carbohydrates

U01AI-27136-03 (AIDS) **BURNY, ARSENE L** UNIVERSITY OF BRUSSELS 67, RUE DES CHEVAUX 1640 RHODE-ST-GENESE - BELGIUM SIV vaccination as a model for AIDS vaccines

U01AI-27136-03 0001 (AIDS) **BURRY, ARSENE** SIV vaccination as a model for AIDS vaccines SIV recombinant antigens--Production and presentation

U01AI-27136-03 0002 (AIDS) **MULLINS, JAMES I** SIV vaccination as a model for AIDS vaccines Identification and analysis of a SIV pathogen

U01AI-27136-03 0003 (AIDS) **FULTZ, PATRICIA N** SIV vaccination as a model for AIDS vaccines Immunization and challenge of Macaques with SIV

R01AI-27156-03 (SRC) **COLLINS, FRANK M** TRUDEAU INSTITUTE, INC P O BOX 59 SARANAC LAKE, N Y 12983 Protective epitopes of BCG protective sensitins

R01AI-27161-03 (VR) **BEACHY, ROGER N** WASHINGTON UNIVERSITY ONE BROOKINGS DRIVE ST LOUIS, MO 63130 Tmv-coat protein in engineered cross-protection

R01AI-27163-03 (ALY) **MIZEL, STEVEN B** WAKE FOREST UNIVERSITY 300 SO HAWTHORNE ROAD WINSTON-SALEM, N C 27103 The mechanism of interleukin 1 action

R01AI-27168-03 (EI) **TENNER, ANDREA J** AMERICAN RED CROSS 15601 CRABBS BRANCH WAY ROCKVILLE, MD 20855 Interactions of C1q with phagocytic cells

R29AI-27171-03 (TMP) **NICKELL, STEVEN P** JOHNS HOPKINS UNIVERSITY 615 NORTH WOLFE STREET BALTIMORE, MD 21205 Immune T cell recognition Trypanosoma cruzi antigens

R01AI-27175-03 (BBCB) **HERZBERG, OSNAT** CTR FOR ADV RES IN BIOTECH 9600 GUDELSKY DRIVE ROCKVILLE, MD 20850 Crystallographic studies of beta-lactamase

U01AI-27179-04 (SRC) **GORDON, JEFFREY I** WASHINGTON U SCH OF MED 660 S EUCLID AVE, BOX 8231 ST LOUIS, MO 63110 Analogs of myristic acid to modulate HIV-1 assembly

R01AI-27180-03 (TMP) **MALLAVIA, LOUIS P** WASHINGTON STATE UNIVERSITY PULLMAN, WA 99164-4233 Cell mediated immune response to C. burnetti isolates

R29AI-27181-03 (GMA) **TARGOFF, IRA N** OKLAHOMA MEDICAL RESEARCH FDN 825 NORTHEAST 13TH STREET OKLAHOMA CITY, OK 73104 Autoantibodies in dermatomyositis

R01AI-27187-02 (VR) **GERSHON, ANNE A** COLUMBIA UNIVERSITY 630 WEST 168TH STREET NEW YORK, NY 10032 Varicella-zoster--Receptors and infective mechanisms

R22AI-27189-03 (BM) **NAVALKAR, RAMCHANDRA G** MOREHOUSE SCHOOL OF MEDICINE 720 WESTVIEW DR, SW ATLANTA, GA 30310 Reactivity of moleculariy defined mycobacterial antigens

R29AI-27195-03 (BM) **SEIFERT, H STEVEN** NORTHWESTERN UNIVERSITY 303 EAST CHICAGO AVENUE CHICAGO, IL 60611 Regulation of pilin expression

U01AI-27196-04 (SRC) **BOYKIN, DAVID W** GEORGIA STATE UNIV RESEARCH FN UNIVERSITY PLAZA ATLANTA, GA 30303-3083 National cooperative drug discovery group/AIDS

U01AI-27196-04 0001 (SRC) **DIXON, DABNEY W** National cooperative drug discovery group/AIDS Phthalocyanines and porphyrins as anti HIV agents

U01AI-27196-04 0002 (SRC) **STREKOWSKI, LUCJAN** National cooperative drug discovery group/AIDS Novel heterocyclic anti HIV agents

U01AI-27196-04 0003 (SRC) **BOYKIN, DAVID W** National cooperative drug discovery group/AIDS Modified aryldiamidines to increase RNA binding as anti HIV agents

U01AI-27196-04 0004 (SRC) **WILSON, DAVID W** National cooperative drug discovery group/AIDS Molecular modelling--Anti-HIV drug stepwise design

U01AI-27196-04 9001 (SRC) **SCHINAZI, RAYMOND** National cooperative drug discovery group/AIDS Biological core

R01AI-27199-03 (VR) **HORWITZ, MARSHALL S** ALBERT EINSTEIN COLL OF MED 1300 MORRIS PARK AVENUE BRONX, N Y 10461 Adenovirus pathogenesis and the class I MHC

R01AI-27201-03 (BM) **MCDANIEL, LARRY S** UNIVERSITY OF ALABAMA 802 DSB BIRMINGHAM, AL 35294 Pneumococcal cell surface protection eliciting molecules

R01AI-27203-03 (AR) **MONTALI, RICHARD J** NATIONAL ZOOLOGICAL PARK 3000 CONNECTICUT AVENUE, N.W. WASHINGTON, D.C. 20008 Characterization of new primate hepatitis virus

R01AI-27204-02 (BM) **MC MURRAY, DAVID N** TEXAS A&M UNIVERSITY REYNOLDS MEDICAL BUILDING COLLEGE STATION, TX 77843 Immunoregulatory T cells in pulmonary tuberculosis

U01AI-27205-04 (SRC) **VARMUS, HAROLD E** UNIVERSITY OF CALIFORNIA 3RD AND PARNASSUS AVES SAN FRANCISCO, CA 94143-0414 Development of new approaches to inhibit growth of HIV

U01AI-27205-04 0001 (SRC) **VARMUS, HAROLD E.** Development of new approaches to inhibit growth of HIV Development of new approaches to inhibit HIV

U01AI-27205-04 0002 (SRC) **GESTELAND, RAYMOND F.** Development of new approaches to inhibit growth of HIV Screening for drugs that alter frameshifting

U01AI-27205-04 0003 (SRC) **BROWN, PATRICK O.** Development of new approaches to inhibit growth of HIV HIV integration mechanisms and inhibitors

R01AI-27214-03 (ALY) **KARR, ROBERT W** UNIVERSITY OF IOWA EMRB IOWA CITY, IA 52242 HLA class II structure-function relationships

R29AI-27218-02 (TMP) **WARD, HONORINE D** NEW ENGLAND MEDICAL CTR HOSPIT 750 WASHINGTON ST, BOX 041 BOSTON, MA 02111 Biology of giardia--Role of carbohydrate residues

R22AI-27219-03 (TMP) **LOVERDE, PHILIP T** STATE UNIVERSITY OF NEW

PROJECT NO., ORGANIZATIONAL UNIT., INVESTIGATOR, ADDRESS, TITLE

YORK 203 SHERMAN HALL BUFFALO, NY 14214 Molecular basis for schistosome reproductive development
U01AI-27220-04 (SRC) PLATTNER, JACOB ABBOTT LABORATORIES D-47E/AP9A-LL ABBOTT PARK, IL 60064 Discovery and design of inhibitors of HIV protease
U01AI-27220-04 0001 (SRC) SIMMER, ROBERT L Discovery and design of inhibitors of HIV protease Protein engineering in HIV protease
U01AI-27220-04 0002 (SRC) HOMANDBERG, GENE A Discovery and design of inhibitors of HIV protease Biochemistry of HIV protease
U01AI-27220-04 0003 (SRC) PLATTNER, JACOB J Discovery and design of inhibitors of HIV protease Chemical sysntesis of HIV protease inhibitors
U01AI-27220-04 0004 (SRC) ERICKSON, JOHN W Discovery and design of inhibitors of HIV protease X-ray crystallography of HIV protease
U01AI-27220-04 0005 (SRC) FESIK, STEPHEN W Discovery and design of inhibitors of HIV protease NMR of HIV protease
U01AI-27221-03 (SRC) MAK, TAK W ONTARIO CANCER INSTITUTE 500 SHERBOURNE STREET TORONTO, ONT, CANADA M4X 1K9 Discovery and rational development of novel AIDS drugs
U01AI-27221-03 0001 (SRC) MAK, TAK W Discovery and rational development of novel AIDS drugs Functional interactions with the HIV receptor CD4
U01AI-27221-03 0002 (SRC) STROMINGER, JACK L Discovery and rational development of novel AIDS drugs Inhibition of the CD4 and class II MHC interaction
U01AI-27221-03 0003 (SRC) CHEN, IRWIN S Discovery and rational development of novel AIDS drugs Analysis of non-structural HIV functions
U01AI-27221-03 0004 (SRC) DAVIES, R WYNE Discovery and rational development of novel AIDS drugs Functional domain definition and structural studies
U01AI-27221-03 0005 (SRC) KAPLITE, PAUL V Discovery and rational development of novel AIDS drugs High volume in vitro screening for novel AIDS drugs
R01AI-27235-03 (SRC) JACOBS, WILLIAM R ALBERT EINSTEIN COLL OF MED 1300 MORRIS PARK AVENUE BRONX, NY 10461 Diagnosis of tuberculosis by recombinant shuttle phasmid
R01AI-27236-03 (SRC) COATES, ANTHONY M LONDON HOSPITAL MEDICAL COLLEG TURNER STREET, LONDON E1 2AD, UNITED KINGDOM Improved vaccinia recombinants for tuberculosis vaccine
R01AI-27243-03 (SRC) BOOM, WILLEM H CASE WESTERN RESERVE UNIVERSIT 2109 ADELBERT ROAD CLEVELAND, OH 44106 Heterogeneity of CD4+ T-cells--M. tuberculosis infection
R22AI-27247-03 (TMP) TARASCHI, THEODORE F THOMAS JEFFERSON UNIVERSITY 1020 LOCUST ST PHILADELPHIA, PA 19107-6799 Membrane trafficking in malaria infected erythrocytes
R01AI-27249-02 (BM) MURRAY, BARBARA E DIV OF INFECTIOUS DISEASES 6431 FANNIN STREET HOUSTON, TX 77030 Studies of enterococcal beta-lactamase
R01AI-27251-03 (ARR) KALMAN, THOMAS I S U N Y AT BUFFALO 457 COOKE HALL BUFFALO, N Y 14260 Molecular approaches to anti-AIDS drug development
R29AI-27260-04 (TMP) ANDREWS, NORMA W YALE UNIVERSITY SCHOOL OF MED. 800 LCI, 333 CEDAR STREET NEW HAVEN, CT 06510 Trypanosoma cruzi hemolysin
R01AI-27272-03 (SRC) WISE, DONALD L NORTHEASTERN UNIVERSITY 342 SNELL ENGINEERING CENTER BOSTON, MA 02115 Tuberculosis chemotherapy with biodegradable polymers
U01AI-27280-03 (SRC) NONOYAMA, MEIHAN TAMPA BAY RESEARCH INSTITUTE 10900 ROOSEVELT BOULEVARD ST PETERSBURG, FL 33716 Development of the pine cone extract as a novel drug for AIDS treatment
U01AI-27280-03 0001 (SRC) NONOYAMA, MEIHAN Development of the pine cone extract as a novel drug for AIDS treatment Pine cone extract mechanism of inhibition of HIV replication
U01AI-27280-03 0002 (SRC) KONNO, KUNIO Development of the pine cone extract as a novel drug for AIDS treatment Pine cone extract purification, structure and toxicology
R01AI-27284-03 (SRC) EISENACH, KATHLEEN MCCLELLAN MEMORIAL VETS HOSP 4300 W 7H / MED RES SERV - 151 LITTLE ROCK, AR 72205 Mycobacterium genome structure and repeated sequences
R01AI-27285-03 (SRC) BARNES, PETER F UNIV OF SOUTHERN CALIFORNIA 2025 ZONAL AVENUE LOS ANGELES, CA 90033 Immunologic significance of cell walls in tuberculosis
R01AI-27288-03 (SRC) BRENNAN, PATRICK J COLORADO STATE UNIVERSITY DEPT OF MICROBIOLOGY FORT COLLINS, CO 80523 Defined native antigens and immunity to tuberculosis
P01AI-27290-04 (SRC) HAHN, BEATRICE H UNIV OF ALABAMA AT BIRMINGHAM UNIVERSITY STATION, BHS 284 BIRMINGHAM, AL 35294 HIV replication and pathogenesis
P01AI-27290-04 0001 (SRC) HAHN, BEATRICE H. HIV replication and pathogenesis Determinants of HIV 2 pathogenicity
P01AI-27290-04 0002 (SRC) HUNTER, ERIC HIV replication and pathogenesis Retroviral glycoprotein precursor cleavage
P01AI-27290-04 0003 (SRC) COMPANS, RICHARD W. HIV replication and pathogenesis HIV-2 envelope glycoproteins and cell fusion
P01AI-27290-04 0004 (SRC) MORROW, CASEY D. HIV replication and pathogenesis Molrcular analysis of HIV-1 reverse transcription
P01AI-27290-04 0005 (SRC) BENVENISTE, ETTY N. HIV replication and pathogenesis Functional analysis of HIV-1 infected human astrocytes
P01AI-27290-04 0006 (SRC) COOPER, MAX D. HIV replication and pathogenesis Relationship of CD4 and T-cell activations to AIDS
P01AI-27290-04 0007 (SRC) SHAW, GEORGE M. HIV replication and pathogenesis Replication and virulence determinants of HIV-1 in vivo
P01AI-27290-04 9001 (SRC) SAAG, MICHAEL S. HIV replication and pathogenesis Clinical core
P01AI-27290-04 9002 (SRC) SHAW, GEORGE M. HIV replication and pathogenesis Central virus core
P01AI-27291-04 (SRC) LINIAL, MAXINE L FRED HUTCHINSON CANCER RES CTR 1124 COLUMBIA STREET SEATTLE, WA 98104 Molecular analysis of HIV replication
P01AI-27291-04 0001 (SRC) LINIAL, MAXINE L. Molecular analysis of HIV replication Identification of HIV packaging sequences; generation of packaging cell lines
P01AI-27291-04 0002 (SRC) ERSENMAN, ROBERT N. Molecular analysis of HIV replication Regulation of HIV assembly
P01AI-27291-04 0003 (SRC) GROUDINE, MARK T. Molecular analysis of HIV replication Analysis of transcripyional termination and anti-termination sequences in HIV
P01AI-27291-04 0004 (SRC) MILLER, A. DUSTY Molecular analysis of HIV replication Anti-sense RNA inhibition of viral replication
P01AI-27291-04 0005 (SRC) GEBALLE, ADAM P. Molecular analysis of HIV replication Reciprocal effects of HIV and CMV on gene expression
P01AI-27291-04 0006 (SRC) GALLATIN, W MICHAEL Molecular analysis of HIV replication
P01AI-27291-04 9001 (SRC) LINIAL, MAXINE L. Molecular analysis of HIV replication Core
P01AI-27297-04 (SRC) NARAYAN, OPENDRA JOHNS HOPKINS UNIV SCH OF MED 720 RUTLAND AVENUE BALTIMORE, MD 21205 Pathogenesis of AIDS--The simian immunodefiency virus-Macaque model
P01AI-27297-04 0001 (SRC) NARAYAN, O. Pathogenesis of AIDS--The simian immunodefiency virus-Macaque model Pathogenesis of SIV infection in Rhesus monkeys
P01AI-27297-04 0002 (SRC) CLEMENTS, JANICE F. Pathogenesis of AIDS--The simian immunodefiency virus-Macaque model Molecular basis of cellular tropism of SIV in Rhesus monkeys
P01AI-27297-04 0003 (SRC) DONNENBERG, ALBERT D. Pathogenesis of AIDS--The simian immunodefiency virus-Macaque model Effect of HIV infection on hematopoiesis in Rhesus monkeys
P01AI-27297-04 0004 (SRC) PITHA-ROWE, PAULA M. Pathogenesis of AIDS--The simian immunodefiency virus-Macaque model The role of cytokines in SIV infection
P01AI-27297-04 9001 (SRC) ADAMS, R J Pathogenesis of AIDS--The simian immunodefiency virus-Macaque model Rhesus monkey facility core
P01AI-27297-04 9002 (SRC) NARAYAN, O. Pathogenesis of AIDS--The simian immunodefiency virus-Macaque model Biohazard/sterilization facility core
U01AI-27302-04 (SRC) MARSHALL, GARLAND R WASHINGTON UNIVERSITY 660 S EUCLID AVE ST LOUIS, MO 63110 Inhibitors of retroviral protease
U01AI-27302-04 0001 (SRC) MARSHALL, GARLAND R Inhibitors of retroviral protease Synthesis and structure of HIV protease and inhibitors
U01AI-27302-04 0002 (SRC) RICH, DANIEL H Inhibitors of retroviral protease Synthesis of transition state analog inhibitors
U01AI-27302-04 0003 (SRC) RATNER, LEE Inhibitors of retroviral protease The HIV protease and its role in virus replication
U01AI-27310-04 (SRC) ROSSMANN, MICHAEL G PURDUE UNIVERSITY WEST LAFAYETTE, IN 47907 The structure of HIV components for the design of antiviral agents
U01AI-27310-04 0002 (SRC) DIXON, JACK E. The structure of HIV components for the design of antiviral agents Structure and characterization of the CD4 receptor
U01AI-27310-04 0003 (SRC) JOHNSON, JOHN E. The structure of HIV components for the design of antiviral agents Learning drug design--Inhib. of uncoating in insect and plant RNA viruses
U01AI-27310-04 9001 (SRC) POIESZ, BERNARD The structure of HIV components for the design of antiviral agents Core A -- SUNY Syracuse
U01AI-27310-04 0001 (SRC) ROSSMAN, MICHAEL G. The structure of HIV components for the design of antiviral agents Structure of p24--Design of antiviral agents targeted at p24
R01AI-27314-02 (NEUA) KOMAROFF, ANTHONY L BRIGHAM AND WOMENS HOSPITAL 75 FRANCIS STREET BOSTON, MA 02115 Neuroimmunologic studies of chronic fatigue syndrome
R01AI-27316-03 (TMP) HAJDUK, STEPHEN L UNIV OF ALABAMA AT BIRMINGHAM UAB STATION BIRMINGHAM, AL 35294 Lysis of Trypanosoma brucei by human HDL lipoprotein
R29AI-27317-03 (TMP) BLANTON, RONALD E UNIVERSITY HOSPITALS 2074 ABINGTON ROAD CLEVELAND, OH 44106 Gene regulation during transformation in Schistosoma
R01AI-27318-03 (ALY) BLATTNER, FREDERICK R UNIVERSITY OF WISCONSIN 445 HENRY MALL MADISON, WI 53706 Engineered mutation of the antibody genes
R01AI-27320-03 (EVR) PLAGEMANN, PETER G UNIV OF MINNESOTA MEDICAL SCHO 420 DELAWARD ST, S.E. MINNEAPOLIS, MN 55455 Ldh virus/akr MuLV interaction in poliomyelitis of mice
R01AI-27323-03 (VR) TRIEZENBERG, STEVEN J MICHIGAN STATE UNIVERSITY COLLEGE OF HUMAN MEDICINE EAST LANSING, MI 48824 Trans-activated expression of HSV immediate early genes
R01AI-27324-02 (IMB) SCHIFFENBAUER, JOEL UNIVERSITY OF FLORIDA BOX J-221 JHMHC GAINESVILLE, FL 32610 The study of class II genes in autoimmune mice
R29AI-27329-03 (BM) CALDERWOOD, STEPHEN B MASSACHUSETTS GENERAL HOSPITAL FRUIT ST./INFECTIOUS DIS UNIT BOSTON, MA 02114 Genetic and biochemical analyses of shiga-like toxins
R01AI-27331-02 (SAT) CLICK, ROBERT E UNIV OF WISCONSIN-RIVER FALLS 410 SOUTH THIRD STREET RIVER FALLS, WI 54022 Xenograft transplantation
U01AI-27336-04 (SRC) REINHERZ, ELLIS L DANA-FARBER CANCER INSTITUTE 44 BINNEY STREET BOSTON, MA 02115 Comprehensive national coop drug discovery group-AIDS
U01AI-27336-04 0001 (SRC) REINHERZ, ELLIS L Comprehensive national coop drug discovery group-AIDS The HIV gp120 binding site of CD4
U01AI-27336-04 0002 (SRC) VITETTA, ELLEN S Comprehensive national coop drug discovery group-AIDS Specific killing of HIV-infected T-cell by CD4 ricin a chain conjugates
U01AI-27336-04 0003 (SRC) SILICIFANO, ROBERT F Comprehensive national coop drug discovery group-AIDS Human T-cell recognition of HIV envelope glycoproteins
U01AI-27336-04 0004 (SRC) KOLODNER, RICHARD Comprehensive national coop drug discovery group-AIDS Purification of HIV reverse transcriptase and integrase
U01AI-27336-04 9001 (SRC) REINHERZ, ELLIS L Comprehensive national coop drug discovery group-AIDS Core--Baculoviral core
R01AI-27342-03 (BM) MILLER, VIRGINIA L UNIV OF CALIFORNIA, LOS ANGELE 405 HILGARD AVE. LOS ANGELES, CA 90024-1489 Molecular basis of epithelial cell invasion by Yersinia

PROJECT NO., ORGANIZATIONAL UNIT., INVESTIGATOR, ADDRESS, TITLE

R01AI-27382-03 (TMP) RAINEY, PETRIE M YALE SCHOOL OF MEDICINE P O BOX 3333 NEW HAVEN, CT 06510 Mechanisms of antileishmanial drugs

U01AI-27397-04 (SRC) HSU, MING-CHU HOFFMANN-LA ROCHE INC. BUILDING 58 NUTLEY, NJ 07110 Discovery of drugs inhibiting HIV regulatory genes

U01AI-27397-04 0001 (SRC) HSU, MING-CHU Discovery of drugs inhibiting HIV regulatory genes Inhibitors of tat III and art as anti-HIV agents

U01AI-27397-04 0002 (SRC) ROSEN, CRAIG A Discovery of drugs inhibiting HIV regulatory genes Mechanism of action of the HIV art protein

U01AI-27397-04 0003 (SRC) ROEDER, ROBERT G Discovery of drugs inhibiting HIV regulatory genes Mechanism of HIV promoter activation

U01AI-27397-04 0004 (SRC) VOLSKY, DAVID J Discovery of drugs inhibiting HIV regulatory genes Cooperative drug discovery group project for AIDS treatment

R01AI-27401-03 (OBM) REDDY, MOLAKALA S 3435 MAIN STREET BUFFALO, NY 14214 Salivary and tracheobronchial mucins in disease

R29AI-27403-03 (TMP) WHEELER, DIANA ESTHER UNIVERSITY OF ARIZONA DEPARTMENT OF ENTOMOLOGY TUCSON, AZ 85721 Oogenesis & mechanisms of sterility in social insects

R01AI-27404-04 (GMA) TIGELAAR, ROBERT E YALE UNIV., SCHOOL OF MEDICINE 333 CEDAR ST NEW HAVEN, CT 06510 Heterogeneity of thy-1+ cells in epidermis

R29AI-27406-03 (BM) CHAMBERS, HENRY F, III SAN FRANCISCO GENERAL HOSPITAL 1001 POTRERO STREET SAN FRANCISCO, CA 94143 Methicillin resistance of Staphylococcus aureus

R01AI-27409-03 (EI) PETTY, HOWARD R WAYNE STATE UNIVERSITY DETROIT, MI 48202 Watching target cell oxidation and cytolysis

R01AI-27411-02 (EI) GEHA, RAIF S CHILDREN'S HOSPITAL 300 LONGWOOD AVENUE BOSTON, MA 02115 Interaction between staph toxin and MHC class II molecules

R01AI-27416-03 (MGN) MCIVOR, R S UNIVERSITY OF MINNESOTA HARVARD ST AT EAST RIVER ROAD MINNEAPOLIS, MN 55455 Nucleoside phosphorylase gene insertion and expression

R29AI-27417-04 (IMB) FINK, PAMELA J UNIVERSITY OF WASHINGTON I-164 HEALTH SCIENCES CENTER SEATTLE, WA 98195 Developmental influences on T cell receptor expression

R01AI-27422-03 (ARR) KHAN, SHABBIR A WISTAR INSTITUTE 36TH & SPRUCE STREETS PHILADELPHIA, PA 19104 Tat and art proteins of HIV--Structure-function studies

R29AI-27429-03 (ALY) BOCHNER, BRUCE S JOHNS HOPKINS ASTHMA & ALL CTR 301 BAYVIEW BLVD BALTIMORE, MD 21224 Basophil activation and recruitment in allergic disease

R01AI-27431-03 (EVR) DE LUCA, NEAL A DANA-FARBER CANCER INSTITUTE 44 BINNEY STREET BOSTON, MA 02115 Structure and mechanism of action of HSV-1 ICP4

R01AI-27435-03 (EVR) ERTL, HILDEGUND THE WISTAR INSTITUTE 36TH & SPRUCE STREETS PHILADELPHIA, PA 19104 Anti-idiotypic antibodies to T cells as vaccines

R01AI-27436-02 (BNP) GLOER, JAMES B UNIVERSITY OF IOWA IOWA CITY, IA 52242 Coprophilous fungi--New sources of bioactive metabolites

R29AI-27440-03 (EVR) GOODMAN, JESSE L UNIV OF MINNESOTA HOSPITAL 516 DELAWARD ST, SE - BOX 250 MINNEAPOLIS, MN 55455 Biological characterization of HSV invasiveness genes

R22AI-27448-01A3 (TMP) HARN, DONALD A HARVARD SCHOOL PUBLIC HEALTH 665 HUNTINGTON AVE BOSTON, MA 02115 Immune responses in vivo to egg antigens of S mansoni

R01AI-27449-04 (EVR) LAZAROWITZ, SONDRA G UNIVERSITY OF ILLINOIS 407 S GOODWIN AVENUE URBANA, IL 61801 Molecular genetics of geminiviruses SqLCV and MSV

R29AI-27450-03 (EVR) GUARINO, LINDA A TEXAS A&M UNIVERSITY COLLEGE STATION, TEX 77843 Enhancer-independent and dependent ACNPV gene activation

R01AI-27451-03 (EVR) DASGUPTA, ASIM UNIVERSITY OF CALIFORNIA SCHOOL OF MEDICINE LOS ANGELES, CALIF 90024 Inhibition of host-cell transcription by poliovirus

R01AI-27457-03 (SAT) LEFKOWITH, JAMES B WASHINGTON UNIV MEDICAL SCH 660 SOUTH EUCLID AVE, BOX 8045 ST LOUIS, MO 63110 Role of lipids in organ immunogenicity

R29AI-27458-03 (TMP) ZAVALA, FIDEL NEW YORK UNIV SCHL OF MED 341 EAST 25TH STREET NEW YORK, NY 10010 Role of T cells in of antisporozoite immunity

R29AI-27461-03 (TMP) HEINZEL, FREDERICK P UCSF MEDICAL CENTER BOX 0654 SAN FRANCISCO, CA 94143-0654 Cytokine function during murine leishmaniasis

R01AI-27465-03 (CBY) MOND, JAMES J UNIFORM SERVICES UNIV HLTH SCI 4301 JONES BRIDGE ROAD BETHESDA, MD 20814-4799 Analysis of intracellular events in B cell activation

R01AI-27466-03 (BM) LITTLE, J RUSSELL JEWISH HOSP/WASH UNIV MED CTR 216 S. KINGSHIGHWAY ST. LOUIS, MO 63110 H. capsulatum interactions with murine macrophages

R01AI-27471-03 (SSS) DELISI, CHARLES BOSTON UNIVERSITY 44 CUMMINGTON STREET BOSTON, MA 02212 Computer assisted approaches to vaccine and drug design

R29AI-27497-02 (VR) NAEVE, CLAYTON W ST JUDE CHILDREN'S RESEARCH HO 332 N LAUDERDALE, P O BOX 318 MEMPHIS, TN 38101 Influenza hemagglutinin as a model acylprotein

R29AI-27506-03 (PTHA) SCHRAUFSTATTER, INGRID U THE SCRIPPS RESEARCH INSTITUTE 10666 NORTH TORREY PINES ROAD LA JOLLA, CA 92037 Role of oxidants in acute inflammatory injury

R01AI-27508-03 (ALY) KABAT, ELVIN A COLUMBIA UNIVERSITY 701 WEST 168TH STREET NEW YORK, NY 10032 Human myeloma proteins with anti-carbohydrate activity

R01AI-27511-03 (TMP) TITUS, RICHARD G HARVARD SCHOOL OF PUBLIC HEALT 665 HUNTINGTON AVENUE BOSTON, MA 02115 Role of sandfly saliva in leishmaniasis

R01AI-27517-03 (ALY) SCHWARTZ, LAWRENCE B MEDICAL COLLEGE OF VIRGINIA VCU, BOX 263, MCV STATION RICHMOND, VA 23298-0263 Characterization of different types of human mast cells

R29AI-27518-03 (BBCB) LUO, MING UNIV OF ALABAMA AT BIRMINGHAM UAB STATION BIRMINGHAM, AL 35294 Structure of an influenza B neuraminidase-Fab complex

R01AI-27530-03 (TMP) MC LEOD, RIMA L MICHAEL REESE HOSPITAL LAKE SHORE DR AT 31ST ST CHICAGO, IL 60616 Treatment of congenital toxoplasmosis

U01AI-27533-03 (AIDS) RUBINSTEIN, ARYE ALBERT EINSTEIN COLLEGE OF MED 1300 MORRIS PARK AVENUE BRONX, NY 10461 Expansion of the pediatric AIDS clinical trial group

U01AI-27535-03 (AIDS) WILFERT, CATHERINE M DUKE UNIVERSITY MEDICAL CTR ERWIN ROAD, BOX 2951 DURHAM, NC 27710 Pediatric AIDS treatment group

U01AI-27535-03 0001 (AIDS) WILFERT, CATHERINE M Pediatric AIDS treatment group Clinical trials in HIV infected children

U01AI-27535-03 0002 (AIDS) MCKINNEY, ROSS E Pediatric AIDS treatment group Immunology and early diagnosis of HIV-1 infection in the neonate

U01AI-27541-04 (AIDS) WARA, DIANE W UNIVERSITY OF CALIFORNIA THIRD & PARNASSUS AVE SAN FRANCISCO, CA 94143 Northern California Pediatric AIDS treatment center

U01AI-27550-04 (AIDS) BRYSON, YVONNE J UNIVERSITY OF CALIFORNIA 10833 LECONTE AVENUE LOS ANGELES, CA 90024-1752 Expansion of the pediatric AIDS clinical trials group

U01AI-27551-04 (AIDS) SHEARER, WILLIAM T BAYLOR COLLEGE OF MEDICINE ONE BAYLOR PLAZA HOUSTON, TX 77030 Pediatric AIDS clinical trials group

U01AI-27553-04 (AIDS) BORKOWSKY, WILLIAM NEW YORK UNIVERSITY MEDICAL CT 550 FIRST AVENUE NEW YORK, NY 10016 Pediatric AIDS clinical trials group

U01AI-27554-04 (AIDS) SACKS, HENRY S MOUNT SINAI MEDICAL CENTER 1 GUSTAVE L LEVY PLACE NEW YORK, NY 10029-6574 Pediatric AIDS clinical trials group

R01AI-27556-01A3 (NEUC) KLUGER, MATTHEW J UNIVERSITY OF MICHIGAN 7620 MEDICAL SCI BLDG II ANN ARBOR, MI 48109-0622 The physiologic role of cytokines in lipopolysaccharide

U01AI-27557-04 (AIDS) PELTON, STEPHEN I BOSTON CITY HOSP 818 HARRISON AVE BOSTON, MA 02118 Pediatric AIDS clinical trials group

U01AI-27559-04 (AIDS) YOGEV, RAM CHILDREN'S MEMORIAL HOSPITAL 2300 CHILDREN'S PLAZA, BOX 20 CHICAGO, IL 60614 Pediatric AIDS clinical trials group

U01AI-27560-04 (AIDS) SCOTT, GWENDOLYN B UNIVERSITY OF MIAMI PO BOX 016960 MIAMI, FL 33101 Pediatric AIDS clinical trials group

U01AI-27562-05 (AIDS) GERSHON, ANNE A COLUMBIA UNIVERSITY 630 WEST 168TH STREET NEW YORK, NY 10032 Expansion of pediatric AIDS clinical trials group

U01AI-27563-04 (AIDS) SPECTOR, STEPHEN A UCSD MEDICAL CENTER 225 DICKINSON STREET, H-814-H SAN DIEGO, CA 92103 Pediatric AIDS clinical trials group

U01AI-27565-04 (AIDS) YOLKEN, ROBERT H JOHNS HOPKINS HOSPITAL 600 N WOLFE ST/CMSC 1104 BALTIMORE, MD 21205 Baltimore pediatric AIDS clinical trials group

R01AI-27568-03 (IMB) CONNOLLY, JANET M WASHINGTON UNIVERSITY 660 S EUCLID BOX 8232 ST LOUIS, MO 63110 CD8 (Lyt-2) recognition of the class I alpha 3 domain

R01AI-27573-01A3 (GMA) CAULFIELD, MICHAEL J CLEVELAND CLINIC FOUNDATION 9500 EUCLID AVE/1 CLINIC CTR CLEVELAND, OH 44195 Characterzation of a pathogenic autoimmune response

R44AI-27605-03 (SSS) ANDERSEN, PHILIP R IDEXX CORP 100 FORE STREET PORTLAND, ME 04101 FIV as a small laboratory animal model of HIV

R44AI-27614-02 (SSS) SWANSON, MELVIN BIO-METRIC SYSTEMS, INC 9924 WEST 74TH STREET EDEN PRAIRIE, MN 55344 Novel supports for carbohydrate immobilization

R01AI-27652-09 (ARR) FRIDLAND, ARNOLD ST JUDE CHILDREN'S RES HOSP 332 N LAUDERDALE MEMPHIS, TN 38101 Arabinonucleoside activation in leukemia cells

R29AI-27655-04 (BM) PORTNOY, DANIEL A UNIV OF PENNSYLVANIA MED SCH 209 JOHNSON PAVILION/MICROBIO PHILADELPHIA, PA 19104-6076 Listeria hemolysin and intracellular growth

U01AI-27658-05S1 (NSS) REICHMAN, RICHARD C UNIVERSITY OF ROCHESTER 601 ELMWOOD AVE ROCHESTER, NY 14642 Establishment of an AIDS clinical trials group

U01AI-27659-05S2 (NSS) HIRSCH, MARTIN S MASSACHUSETTS GENERAL HOSPITAL FRUIT STREET BOSTON, MA 02114 AIDS clinical trials group

U01AI-27660-05S2 (NSS) MITSUYASU, RONALD T UCLA SCHOOL OF MEDICINE DEPT OF MEDICINE LOS ANGELES, CA 90024-1793 AIDS clinical trials group conversion from ATEU

U01AI-27661-06 (NSS) BALFOUR, HENRY H, JR UNIV OF MINNESOTA MEDICAL SCH 420 DELAWARE ST, S E, BOX 437 MINNEAPOLIS, MN 55455 The establishment of AIDS clinical trials units

U01AI-27662-06 (NSS) BARTLETT, JOHN A DUKE UNIVERSITY MEDICAL CENTER PO BOX 3284 DURHAM, NC 27710 The establishment of AIDS treatment evaluation unit

U01AI-27663-05S2 (NSS) MILLS, JOHN SAN FRANCISCO GENERAL HOSP 995 POTRERO ST., BLDG. 80 SAN FRANCISCO, CA 94110 AIDS clinical trials group

U01AI-27664-05S3 (NSS) COREY, LAWRENCE PACIFIC MEDICAL CENTER 1200 12TH AVE S SEATTLE, WA 98144 AIDS clinical trials unit

U01AI-27665-05S2 (NSS) VALENTINE, FRED T NEW YORK UNIVERSITY MED CENTER 550 FIRST AVENUE NEW YORK, NY 10016 AIDS clinical trials unit

U01AI-27666-05S1 (NSS) MERIGAN, THOMAS C STANFORD UNIVERSITY 125 PANAMA ST JORDAN QUAD/BIRC STANFORD, CA 94305-4125 AIDS clinical trials unit

U01AI-27667-06 (NSS) SACKS, HENRY S MOUNT SINAI MEDICAL CENTER 1 GUSTAVE L LEVY PLACE NEW YORK, NY 10029 The establishment of AIDS treatment evaluation unit

U01AI-27668-05S2 (NSS) BARTLETT, JOHN G JOHNS HOPKINS HOSPITAL 600 N WOLFE STREET BALTIMORE, MD 21205 Conversion of JHH ATEU to ACTU

U01AI-27669-05S2 (NSS) ARMSTRONG, DONALD MEM SLOAN-KETTERING CANCER CTR 1275 YORK AVENUE NEW YORK, NY 10021 AIDS clinical trial group

U01AI-27670-05S1 (NSS) SPECTOR, STEPHEN A UCSD MEDICAL CENTER 225 DICKINSON STREET SAN DIEGO, CA 92103 AIDS clinical trials group

U01AI-27671-06 (NSS) SOEIRO, RUY ALBERT EINSTEIN COLLEGE OF MED 1300 MORRIS PARK AVE BRONX, NY 10461 The establishment of AIDS clinical trials units

PROJECT NO., ORGANIZATIONAL UNIT., INVESTIGATOR, ADDRESS, TITLE

PROJECT NO., ORGANIZATIONAL UNIT., INVESTIGATOR, ADDRESS, TITLE

U01AI-27672-05S1 (NSS) HO, MONTO UNIVERSITY OF PITTSBURGH A427 CRABTREE HALL PITTSBURGH, PA 15261 An AIDS treatment evaluation unit

U01AI-27673-05S2 (NSS) LEEDOM, JOHN M LAC/USC MEDICAL CENTER 1200 NORTH STATE STREET LOS ANGELES, CA 90033 The establishment of AIDS treatment evaluation units

U01AI-27674-06 (NSS) HYSLOP, NEWTON E, JR TULANE UNIV/SCHOOL OF MEDICINE 1430 TULANE AVENUE NEW ORLEANS, LA 70112 Establishment of an AIDS clinical trials unit

U01AI-27675-05S2 (NSS) FISCHL, MARGARET A UNIVERSITY OF MIAMI PO BOX 016960 MIAMI, FL 33101 Establishment of AIDS treatment evaluation units

R01AI-27681-02 (ARR) DEBS, ROBERT J UNIVERSITY OF CALIFORNIA SAN FRANCISCO, CA 94143-0128 Anti-retroviral therapy and immunomodulation of HIV

R01AI-27685-03 (ARR) CLARKSON, ALLEN B, JR NEW YORK UNIVERSITY MED CENTER 550 FIRST AVENUE NEW YORK, NY 10016 Polyamine metabolism and AIDS associated pneumonia

R01AI-27689-02 (ARR) HERSH, EVAN M ARIZONA CANCER CENTER 1501 NORTH CAMPBELL AVENUE TUCSON, AZ 85724 Human monoclonal antibodies to HIV

R01AI-27690-03 (ARR) ARNOLD, EDWARD CABM 675 HOES LANE PISCATAWAY, NJ 08854 Structure determination of HIV reverse transcriptase

R01AI-27692-03 (ARR) BROOM, ARTHUR D UNIVERSITY OF UTAH 308 SKAGGS HALL SALT LAKE CITY, UT 84112 Polynucleotides as anti-aids agents

R01AI-27697-01A1 (ARRD) HONG, CHUNG I ROSWELL PARK MEMORIAL INST ELM & CARLTON STREETS BUFFALO, N Y 14263 Anti-AIDS nucleoside conjugates of ether phospholipids

R01AI-27698-02 (ARR) MARX, PRESTON A NEW MEXICO STATE UNIVERSITY DEPT OF VIROLOGY & IMMUNOLOGY HOLLOMAN AFB, NM 88330-1027 Evolution of SIV in West Africa

R01AI-27702-03 (ARR) SODROSKI, JOSEPH G DANA-FARBER CANCER INSTITUTE 44 BINNEY STREET BOSTON, MA 02115 Development of HIV as a vector system

R01AI-27703-03 (ARR) MOSIER, DONALD E MEDICAL BIOLOGY INSTITUTE 11077 NORTH TORREY PINES ROAD LA JOLLA, CA 92037 T cell-macrophage interactions in murine models of AIDS

R01AI-27711-02 (ARR) REED, STEVEN G SEATTLE BIOMEDICAL RESEARCH IN 4 NICKERSON STREET SEATTLE, WA 98109-1651 Infection of macrophages with HIV and protozoan parasite

P30AI-27713-04 (SRC) BYRN, STEPHEN R PURDUE UNIVERSITY SCHOOL OF PHARM & PHARM SCIENC WEST LAFAYETTE, IN 47907 AIDS research center support

P30AI-27713-04 9001 (SRC) GILHAM, PETER T AIDS research center support Core--Biotechnology facility

P30AI-27713-04 9002 (SRC) WEITH, H LEE AIDS research center support Core--Computational biochemistry facility

P30AI-27713-04 9003 (SRC) GORENSTEIN, DAVID G AIDS research center support Core--Solution structural biology facility

P30AI-27713-04 9004 (SRC) ROSSMAN, MICHAEL G AIDS research center support Core--X-ray structure facility

R01AI-27722-03 (ARRA) STOCKER, BRUCE A STANFORD UNIVERSITY SCHOOL OF MEDICINE STANFORD, CA 94305-5402 Salmonella-HIV chimera as vaccine

R01AI-27727-03 (ARR) HOOK, EDWARD W, III JOHNS HOPKINS HOSPITAL 600 N WOLFE STREET BALTIMORE, MD 21205 Genital ulceration as a risk factor for HIV infection

R01AI-27729-03 (ARR) ARDMAN, BLAIR NEW ENGLAND MED CTR HOSPS, INC 750 WASHINGTON STREET BOSTON, MA 02111 Anti-CD4 autoantibodies in HIV infection

P30AI-27732-04 (SRC) GARDNER, MURRAY B UNIVERSITY OF CALIFORNIA SCHOOL OF MEDICINE DAVIS, CA 95616 Immunodeficiency retroviruses in man and animals

P30AI-27732-04 9001 (SRC) CARLSON, JAMES R Immunodeficiency retroviruses in man and animals Core--Clinical virology

P30AI-27732-04 9002 (SRC) HENDRICKS, ANDREW G Immunodeficiency retroviruses in man and animals Core--Primate center

P30AI-27732-04 9003 (SRC) LUCIW, PAUL Immunodeficiency retroviruses in man and animals Core--Molecular virology

P30AI-27732-04 9004 (SRC) HINRICHS, STEVEN H Immunodeficiency retroviruses in man and animals Core--Transgenic facility

R01AI-27740-03 (ARR) SY, MAN-SUN MASSACHUSETTS GENERAL HOSPITAL 149 13TH STREET CHARLESTOWN, MA 02129 Immune response to HIV-1 encoded antigens in mice

P30AI-27741-04 (SRC) RUBINSTEIN, ARYE ALBERT EINSTEIN COLLEGE OF MED 1300 MORRIS PARK AVENUE BRONX, NY 10461 Molecular and immune interdiction of AIDS

P30AI-27741-04 9001 (SRC) RUBINSTEIN, ARYE Molecular and immune interdiction of AIDS Core--Flow cytometry

P30AI-27741-04 9002 (SRC) SCHARFF, MATTHEW D Molecular and immune interdiction of AIDS Core--Hybridoma facility

P30AI-27741-04 9003 (SRC) NATHENSON, STANLEY G Molecular and immune interdiction of AIDS Core--Nucleic acid and peptide synthesis

P30AI-27742-03 (SRC) LAWRENCE, H SHERWOOD NEW YORK UNIVERSITY MED CTR 550 FIRST AVENUE NEW YORK, NY 10016 Center for AIDS research

P30AI-27742-03 9004 (SRC) MARMOR, MICHAEL Center for AIDS research Core--HIV registry and education center

P30AI-27742-03 9005 (SRC) JAVITT, NORMAN B. Center for AIDS research Core--Pharmacology laboratory

P30AI-27742-03 9006 (SRC) CHACHOUA, ABRAHAM Center for AIDS research Core--Clinical trials management

P30AI-27742-03 9007 (SRC) VALENTINE, FRED T. Center for AIDS research Core--Flow cytometry

P30AI-27742-03 9008 (SRC) PASTERNACK, BERNARD S. Center for AIDS research Core--Biostatistics

P30AI-27742-03 9001 (SRC) PINTER, ABRAHAM Center for AIDS research Core--Viral culture

P30AI-27742-03 9002 (SRC) FRIEDMAN, KIEN, ALVIN E. Center for AIDS research Core--Immunovirology

P30AI-27742-03 9003 (SRC) KRASINSKI, KEITH Center for AIDS research Core--Specimen management

R01AI-27744-03 (ARR) GORENSTEIN, DAVID G PURDUE UNIVERSITY WEST LAFAYETTE, IN 47907-1393 NMR, structure and design of HIV regulatory agents

R01AI-27747-03 (ARR) LETVIN, NORMAN L NEW ENGLAND REG PRIM/RES CTR ONE PINE HILL DRIVE SOUTHBOROUGH, MA 01772 Experimental models for GI disease in HIV infection

P30AI-27757-04 (SRC) HOLMES, KING K CENTER FOR AIDS & STD SUITE 215 SEATTLE, WA 98122 Center for AIDS research

P30AI-27757-04 9001 (SRC) GREENBERG, PHILIP Center for AIDS research Core--Immunology

P30AI-27757-04 9002 (SRC) COREY, LAWRENCE Center for AIDS research Core--Retrovirology of AIDS

P30AI-27757-04 9003 (SRC) HANMOSFIELD, H HUNTER Center for AIDS research Core--AIDS research

P30AI-27757-04 9004 (SRC) FISHER, LLOYD D Center for AIDS research Core--AIDS research

P30AI-27762-03 (SRC) MERIGAN, THOMAS C STANFORD UNIV SCH OF MEDICINE DIV OF INFECTIOUS DISEASES STANFORD, CA 94305 AIDS research center core support grant

P30AI-27762-03 9001 (SRC) MERIGAN, THOMAS C AIDS research center core support grant Core--Clinical trials/viral immunology

P30AI-27762-03 9002 (SRC) ENGELMAN, EDGER AIDS research center core support grant Core--Pathogenesis

P30AI-27762-03 9003 (SRC) BLASCHKE, TERRENCE F AIDS research center core support grant Core--Clinical pharmacology

P30AI-27762-03 9004 (SRC) ROBINSON, WILLIAM S AIDS research center core support grant Core--Virology

P30AI-27763-04 (SRC) VOLBERDING, PAUL A SAN FRANCISCO GENERAL HOSPITAL 995 POTRERO AVENUE SAN FRANCISCO, CA 94110 San Francisco center for AIDS research

P30AI-27763-04 9001 (SRC) FEIGAL, DAVID W San Francisco center for AIDS research Core--Data management and biostatistics support

P30AI-27763-04 9002 (SRC) GREENSPAN, JOHN S San Francisco center for AIDS research Core--Centralized AIDS specimen processing and storage

P30AI-27763-04 9003 (SRC) BENOWITZ, NEAL L San Francisco center for AIDS research Core--Clinical pharmacology laboratory

P30AI-27763-04 9004 (SRC) WINKELSTEIN, WARREN San Francisco center for AIDS research Core--Epidemilogy consortium

P30AI-27763-04 9005 (SRC) HEYWORTH, MARTIN F San Francisco center for AIDS research Core--Monoclonal antibody facility

P30AI-27763-04 9006 (SRC) VYAS, GIRISH N San Francisco center for AIDS research Core--Polymerase chain reacion facility

R01AI-27766-04 (ARR) BLANK, KENNETH J HAHNEMANN UNIVERSITY BROAD AND VINE PHILADELPHIA, PA 19102 Murine retrovirus infection and resistance to Candida

P30AI-27767-04 (SRC) HUNTER, ERIC UNIV OF ALABAMA AT BIRMINGHAM UAB STATION BIRMINGHAM, AL 35294 Birmingham center for AIDS research

P30AI-27767-04 9001 (SRC) SHAW, GEORGE M Birmingham center for AIDS research Central virus core

P30AI-27767-04 9002 (SRC) WHITLEY, RICHARD J Birmingham center for AIDS research Core--Clinical

P30AI-27767-04 9003 (SRC) MORROW, CASEY Birmingham center for AIDS research Core--Molecular biology

P30AI-27767-04 9004 (SRC) ENGLER, JEFFREY A Birmingham center for AIDS research Core--DNA sequencing

P30AI-27767-04 9005 (SRC) JACKSON, SUSAN Birmingham center for AIDS research Core--Flow cytometry

R01AI-27771-12 (EI) ROSS, GORDON D UNIVERSITY OF LOUISVILLE SCHOOL OF MEDICINE LOUISVILLE, KY 40292 Membrane components of the leukocyte complement system

R01AI-27774-01A2 (TMP) NAYAR, J K UNIVERSITY OF FLORIDA 200 9TH STREET, SE VERO BEACH, FL 32962 Intracellular melanization of filarids in mosquitoes

R22AI-27777-02 (TMP) LEWIS, FRED A BIOMEDICAL RESEARCH INSTITUTE 12111 PARKLAWN DRIVE ROCKVILLE, MD 20852 Snail/schistosome genetic influences on cercariogenesis

R29AI-27779-03 (EVR) RICO-HESSE, REBECA YALE UNIVERSITY 60 COLLEGE STREET NEW HAVEN, CT 06510 Molecular determinants of VEE virus epidemiology

R01AI-27783-03 (SSS) SMITH, HAMILTON O JOHNS HOPKINS U SCH OF MED 725 N WOLFE STREET BALTIMORE, MD 21205 Mapping the Haemophilus influenzae Rd genome

R01AI-27790-03 (EI) HAYES, COLLEEN E UNIVERSITY OF WISCONSIN 420 HENRY MALL MADISON, WI 53706 Helper T lymphocyte function in vitamin A deficiency

R01AI-27791-03 (IMS) JOHNSON, LAWRENCE L TRUDEAU INSTITUTE, INC PO BOX 59 SARANAC LAKE, NY 12983 Basis of naturally acquired immunological tolerance

R01AI-27795-01A3 (EDC) ADLER, STUART P MEDICAL COLLEGE OF VIRGINIA PO BOX 163 MCV STATION RICHMOND, VA 23298 Epidemiology of cytomegalovirus

R01AI-27796-01A3 (TOX) HOENER, BETTY A UNIVERSITY OF CALIFORNIA 926 MEDICAL SCIENCES BUILDING SAN FRANCISCO, CA 94143-0446 Comparative toxicities of 5-nitrofurans

R01AI-27803-02 (TMP) EISEN, HARVEY A FRED HUTCHINSON CANCER RES CTR 1124 COLUMBIA STREET SEATTLE, WA 98104 Cross-reactive antigens in Chagas' Disease

R29AI-27809-04 (PTHA) CAVENDER, DRUIE E UNIV OF MIAMI SCH OF MEDICINE PO BOX 016960/MICRO & IMMUNOLO MIAMI, FL 33101 Cytokine effects on endothelium in chronic inflammation

R01AI-27811-03 (BM) MCMAHON-PRATT, DIANE M YALE UNIVERSITY SCHOOL OF MED PO BOX 3333/60 COLLEGE ST NEW HAVEN, CT 06510 Studies of differentially expressed leishmania antigens

R01AI-27828-01A3 (TMP) FARRELL, JAY P UNIVERSITY OF PENNSYLVANIA 3800 SPRUCE STREET PHILADELPHIA, PA 19104 T cell subsets in cutaneous leishmaniasis

R29AI-27832-03 (VR) CARRINGTON, JAMES C TEXAS A&M UNIVERSITY COLLEGE STATION, TX 77843 Activity and transport of tobacco etch virus proteinase

R29AI-27835-03 (ALY) PILLAI, SHIV S MASSACHUSETTS GENERAL HOSPITAL FRUIT STREET BOSTON, MA 02114 Studies on the pre-b to B lymphocyte transition

R29AI-27837-03 (BM) KOOMEY, J MICHAEL UNIVERSITY OF MICHIGAN

6711 MED SCI BLDG II ANN ARBOR, MI 48109-0620 Gonococcal pili--Studies of structure and function

R01AI-27849-03 (ALY) SEED, BRIAN MASSACHUSETTS GENERAL HOSPITAL BOSTON, MA 02114 Genetic analysis of human Fc receptors

R01AI-27850-03 (EI) AURON, PHILIP E THE CENTER FOR BLOOD RESEARCH 800 HUNTINGTON AVENUE BOSTON, MA 02115 Accessory cell activation in the immune response

R01AI-27853-03 (ALY) GOODENOW, ROBERT A BAXTER HEALTHCARE CORP 3015 S DAIMLER STREET SANTA ANA, CA 92705 Molecular dissection of allogeneic T cell recognition

R01AI-27855-03 (IMB) JANEWAY, CHARLES A, JR YALE UNIVERSITY SCHOOL OF MED 310 CEDAR STREET NEW HAVEN, CT 06510 Specificty, distrubution, function of gamma--Delta i cells

R29AI-27857-03 (TMP) JOHNSON, PATRICIA JEAN MICROBIOLOGY & IMMUNOLOGY UCLA SCH OF MED 43-239 CHS LOS ANGELES, CA 90024-1747 Biogenesis of hydrogenosomes of a trichomonad parasite

R01AI-27858-04 (TMP) JERRELLS, THOMAS R LSU MEDICAL CENTER P O BOX 33932 SHREVEPORT, LA 71130-3932 T-cell mediated immunity to Rickettsia tustusgamushi

R29AI-27862-04 (BM) SCHREIBER, JOHN R RAINBOW BABIES/CHILDRENS HOSP 2101 ADELBERT RD CLEVELAND, OH 44106 Anti-idiotype induced immunity against P. aeruginosa

R29AI-27863-02 (BM) SPINOLA, STANLEY M SUNY CLINICAL CENTER 462 GRIDER STREET BUFFALO, NY 14215 Pathogenesis of Haemophilus ducreyi infections

R29AI-27864-02 (IMS) ALAM, RAFEUL UNIVERSITY OF TEXAS MED BRANCH CLINICAL SCIENCE BLDG 409, G-6 GALVESTON, TX 77550 Characterization of histamine release inhibitory factor

R22AI-27872-02 (BM) WIRTH, DYANN F HARVARD SCHOOL OF PUBLIC HLTH 665 HUNTINGTON AVENUE BOSTON, MA 02115 Genetic basis of drug resistance in P falciparum

R01AI-27873-03 (BM) BASEMAN, JOEL B UNIVERSITY OF TEXAS 7703 FLOYD CURL DRIVE SAN ANTONIO, TX 78284 Molecular analysis of adhesin P1

R29AI-27877-03 (IMB) FLAJNIK, MARTIN F UNIVERSITY OF MIAMI MIAMI, FL 33101 Ontogeny and phylogeny of the MHC

R29AI-27879-02 (IMB) LUTZ, CHARLES T UNIVERSITY OF IOWA IOWA CITY, IA 52242 HLA-B7 transplantation antigen epitopes

R01AI-27880-03 (HEM) GREEN, TERRENCE R VA MEDICAL CENTER PO BOX 1034 PORTLAND, OR 97207 Enzymology of the neutrophil NADPH:O2 oxidoreductase

R29AI-27881-03 (HEM) BRESSLER, ROBERT B METHODIST HOSPITAL 6565 FANNIN STREET HOUSTON, TX 77030 Growth and differentiation of human mast cells

R01AI-27885-02 (IMS) HANDWERGER, BARRY S UNIV OF MARYLAND AT BALTIMORE 10 SOUTH PINE STREET BALTIMORE, MD 21201 Is murine SLE associated with Th1/Th2 cell dysfunction

R29AI-27886-02 (VR) KOUSOULAS, KONSTANTIN G LOUISIANA STATE UNIVERSITY SCHOOL OF VETERINARY MEDICINE BATON ROUGE, LA 70803-1806 Fusion domains of hsv-1 proteins

R01AI-27903-03 (IMB) BORN, WILLI K NATIONAL JEWISH CENTER FOR 1400 JACKSON STREET DENVER, CO 80206 Specificity & function of gamma/delta TCR T lymphocytes

R01AI-27906-02 (IMS) MACGLASHAN, DONALD W JOHNS HOPKINS ASTHMA/ALLERGY C 301 BAYVIEW BLVD BALTIMORE, MD 21224 Production of cytokines by activated mast cells

R29AI-27907-02 (BM) COLLINS, CARLEEN U OF MIAMI/SCH OF MED PO BOX 016960 MIAMI, FL 33101 Urease--Molecular studies and role in pathogenesis

R29AI-27908-02 (BM) PICKETT, CAROL L UNIVERSITY OF KENTUCY 800 ROSE ST LEXINGTON, KY 40536 Campylobacter jejuni cytotoxins

R01AI-27909-03 (IMB) PALLAVICINI, MARIA G UNIVERSITY OF CALIFORNIA 1855 FOLSOM STREET SAN FRANCISCO, CA 94143-0808 In-vivo repopulation kinetics of purified stem cells

R01AI-27913-03 (BM) TUOMANEN, ELAINE I ROCKEFELLER UNIVERSITY 1230 YORK AVENUE NEW YORK, NY 10021 Pneumococcal cell wall in meningitis

R01AI-27914-03 (EVR) LLOYD, RICHARD E UNIV OF OKLAHOMA HTLTH CTR PO BOX 26901 OKLAHOMA CITY, OK 73190 Control of translation by poliovirus proteinase

R01AI-27915-04 (PTHA) MADAIO, MICHAEL P UNIVERSITY OF PENNSYLVANIA 422 CURIE BLVD PHILADELPHIA, PA 19104-6144 Autoreactive T cells in murine lupus nephritis

R01AI-27917-03 (IMB) SHEIL, JAMES M WEST VIRGINIA UNIVERSITY MORGANTOWN, WV 26506 Peptide recognition by cytotoxic T lymphocytes

R01AI-27951-02 (IMB) MARTIN, PAUL J FRED HUTCHINSON CANCER RES CTR 1124 COLUMBIA STREET SEATTLE, WA 98104 Role of lymphoid cells in allogeneic marrow engraftment

R01AI-27957-02 (EI) PIERCE, SUSAN K NORTHWESTERN UNIVERSITY 2153 SHERIDAN ROAD EVANSTON, IL 60208 Targeting of native protein and peptide antigens

R29AI-27960-02 (VR) BRAUN, DANIEL K UNIV OF MICHIGAN MEDICAL CENTE 1500 E MEDICAL CTR DR, BOX 037 ANN ARBOR, MI 48109-0378 Mapping and analysis of human herpes virus 6 antigen

R15AI-27975-01A2 (GMA) KOVACS, SHIRLEY A CALIFORNIA STATE UNIVERSITY CEDAR & SHAW AVENUES FRESNO, CA 93740-0073 Characterization of rheumatoid antigens in cyanobacteria

R01AI-27976-02 (IMB) THANAVALA, YASMIN ROSWELL PARK MEMORIAL INST 666 ELM STREET BUFFALO, NY 14263 Murine human T cell response to HBS-AG versus anti-id

R15AI-27978-01A2 (VR) CAFRUNY, WILLIAM A UNIVERSITY OF SOUTH DAKOTA SCHOOL OF MEDICINE VERMILLION, SD 57069 Regulation of viral infectivity

R29AI-27983-03 (IMB) TAN, KUT-NIE DANA-FARBER CANCER INSTITUTE 44 BINNEY STREET BOSTON, MA 02115 T cell receptor recognition mechanism

R01AI-27985-02 (SAT) BARBER, WILLIAM H UNIVERSITY OF ALABAMA 756 LYONS HARRISON RES BLDG BIRMINGHAM, AL 35294 Donor marrow tolerance in human & canine allografts

R01AI-27989-03 (EI) FATHMAN, C GARRISON STANFORD UNIVERSITY DIV OF IMMUNOLOGY/S-021 STANFORD, CA 94305-5111 Study of a ternary complex that drives T cell activation

R01AI-27992-02 (EI) PARDOLL, DREW M JOHNS HOPKINS UNIVERSITY DEPARTMENT OF MEDICINE BALTIMORE, MD 21205 Role of TCR gamma/delta T cells in the immune response

R01AI-27994-03 (IMS) TEALE, JUDY M UNIVERSITY OF TEXAS 7703 FLOYD CURL DRIVE SAN ANTONIO, TX 78284 B cell immune repertoire in autoimmune mice

R01AI-27998-03 (IMB) JENKINS, MARC K UNIV OF MINNESOTA MEDICAL SCH 420 DELAWARE STREET/SE/BOX 196 MINNEAPOLIS, MN 55455 Costimulatory signals in CD4+ T cell activation

R29AI-28003-04 (TMP) WALTERS, LAUREL L UNIV OF ALASKA FAIRBANKS INSTITUTE OF ARCTIC BIOLOGY FAIRBANKS, AK 99775-0180 Ultrastructural studies of leishmania-sandfly interaction

R01AI-28018-02 (BM) PEREIRA, H ANNE EMORY UNIVERSITY ATLANTA, GA 30322 A monocyte-specific chemoattractant from human PMN

R01AI-28034-03 (HEM) BAXTER-LOWE, LEE A BLOOD CTR OF SE WISCONSIN 1701 W WISCONSIN AVENUE MILWAUKEE, WI 53233 Definition and relevance of HLA-DQ micropolymorphism

R01AI-28035-02 (TMP) REED, SHARON L UCSD MEDICAL CENTER 225 DICKENSON STREET SAN DIEGO, CA 92103 Cysteine proteinases and virulence of E. histolytica

R01AI-28040-02 (BM) WESSELS, MICHAEL R CHANNING LABORATORY 180 LONGWOOD AVENUE BOSOTN, MA 02115 Group B streptococcal capsule and virulence

P01AI-28046-03 (AITC) TERHORST, CORNELIS P BETH ISRAEL HOSPITAL 330 BROOKLINE AVENUE BOSTON, MA 02215 The T cell receptor/CD3 complex in immunologic diseases

P01AI-28046-03 0001 (AITC) GEHA, RAIF The T cell receptor/CD3 complex in immunologic diseases Childhood T cell immunodeficiency diseases

P01AI-28046-03 0002 (AITC) GEHA, RAIF The T cell receptor/CD3 complex in immunologic diseases Eczema--A dermatological disease modulated by immune mechanisms

P01AI-28046-03 0003 (AITC) TERHORST, CORNELIS The T cell receptor/CD3 complex in immunologic diseases Design of T cell immunodeficiences in transgenic mice

P01AI-28046-03 0004 (AITC) TERHORST, CORNELIS The T cell receptor/CD3 complex in immunologic diseases Design of novel anti-CD3 and monoclonals for preclinical trials

R01AI-28048-03 (ARR) GARRY, ROBERT F, JR TULANE SCHOOL OF MEDICINE MICROBIOLOGY & IMMUNOLOGY DEPT NEW ORLEANS, LA 70112 Alterations of transport systems in HIV-infected cells

R01AI-28065-03 (ARR) ZARLING, JOYCE M ONCOGEN 3005 FIRST AVENUE SEATTLE, WA 98121 Immunity in HIV immunized and infected primates and humans

R01AI-28071-03 (ARR) ROSSEN, ROGER D BAYLOR COLLEGE OF MEDICINE 1 BAYLOR PLAZA HOUSTON, TX 77030 Monocyte HIV-1 infection and neurological function

R01AI-28076-03 (ARR) PAGANO, MARCELLO HARVARD SCH OF PUBLIC HEALTH 677 HUNTINGTON AVENUE BOSTON, MA 02115 Statistical model of the AIDS epidemic

R01AI-28086-03 (ARR) POLLACK, MARILYN S METHODIST HOSPITAL 6565 FANNIN STREET, F-501 HOUSTON, TX 77030 Immunogenetic factors in the prognosis of HIV infections

R29AI-28104-04 (VR) MUNOZ, JOSE L NEW YORK UNIVERSITY MED CTR 550 FIRST AVENUE NEW YORK, N Y 10016 T cells to specific respiratory syncytial virus proteins

R01AI-28108-04 (SSS) SILICIANO, ROBERT F JOHNS HOPKINS UNIV SCH OF MED 725 NORTH WOLFE STREET BALTIMORE, MD 21205 Analysis of human T cell recognition of the GP 120 of HIV

R01AI-28110-01A2 (TMP) ONGERTH, JERRY E UNIVERSITY OF WASHINGTON SC-34 SEATTLE, WA 98195 Identification and control of G. lamblia in drinking water

R01AI-28115-04 (IMB) POTTER, TERRY A NAT'L JEWISH CTR FOR IMMUNOLOG 1400 JACKSON ST DENVER, CO 80206-1997 Role of CD8 in T cell activation and thymic selection

R44AI-28124-03 (PSF) HAHN, ELLIOT F BAKER CUMMINS PHARMACEUTICALS 8800 NW 36TH STREET MIAMI, FL 33178-2404 Nucleotide dimers as anti-HIV agents

R44AI-28125-02 (SSS) DURAN, LISE W BIO-METRIC SYSTEMS, INC 9924 W. SEVENTY FOURTH ST EDEN PRAIRIE, MN 55344 Immobilization of antimicrobial peptides

R44AI-28126-03 (PSF) STEARNS, JAY F SERES LABORATORIES, INC PO BOX 470 SANTA ROSA, CA 95402 Antifusogenic antivirals--Design and testing

R44AI-28127-02 (SSS) LARRICK, JAMES W GENELABS, INCORPORATED 505 PENOBSCOT DRIVE REDWOOD CITY, CA 94063 Inhibitors of interleukin 1

U01AI-28147-03 (SRC) COMPANS, RICHARD W UNIV OF ALABAMA AT BIRMINGHAM DEPARTMENT OF MICROBIOLOGY BIRMINGHAM, AL 35294 Mucosal and systematic immunity to SIV and HIV vaccines

U01AI-28147-03 0001 (SRC) COMPANS, RICHARD W. Mucosal and systematic immunity to SIV and HIV vaccines Expression of the HIV envelope protein

U01AI-28147-03 0002 (SRC) ELDRIDGE, JOHN H. Mucosal and systematic immunity to SIV and HIV vaccines Microcapsules as delivery systems for hiv and siv antigens

R44AI-28148-03 (SSS) LAWRENCE, PAUL J LITMUS CONCEPTS, INC 3485-A KIFER ROAD SANTA CLARA, CA 95051 A metabolic screening test for infectious vaginitis

R44AI-28151-02 (SSS) KIM, YOUNG W TANOX BIOSYSTEMS, INC 10301 STELLA LINK HOUSTON, TX 77025 Neutralizing immunotoxin therapy for AIDS

U01AI-28167-02 (AIDS) NEWMAN, MARK J CAMBRIDGE BIOSCIENCE CORP 365 PLANTATION ST WORCESTER, MA 01605 SIVAGM pathogenesis and vaccine development in Macaca nemestrina

U01AI-28167-02 0001 (AIDS) MARCIANI, DANTE SIVAGM pathogenesis and vaccine development in Macaca nemestrina Formulation of an effective HIV-2 subunit vaccine

U01AI-28167-02 0002 (AIDS) HERRMANN, JOHN SIVAGM pathogenesis and vaccine development in Macaca nemestrina Immunological assessment of adjuvant effectiveness

U01AI-28167-02 0003 (AIDS) NEWMAN, MARK SIVAGM pathogenesis and vaccine development in Macaca nemestrina Lentivirus (HIV-2) vaccine testing in Rhesus macaques

PROJECT NO., ORGANIZATIONAL UNIT., INVESTIGATOR, ADDRESS, TITLE

U01AI-28167-02 9001 (AIDS) WYAND, MIKE SIVAGM pathogenesis and vaccine development in Macaca nemestrina Core-- HIV-2 gp160 vaccine study in Rhesus macaques
U01AI-28171-03 (AIDS) YOUNG, JAMES F MEDIMMUNE, INC GAITHERSBURG, MD 20878 Vaccine development for immunodeficiency viruses
U01AI-28171-03 0001 (AIDS) HOCKMEYER, WAYNE T Vaccine development for immunodeficiency viruses HIV T and B cell epitopes and development of subunit vaccines constructs
U01AI-28171-03 0002 (AIDS) MANNINO, RAPHAEL J Vaccine development for immunodeficiency viruses Liposome immunopotentiation of HIV vaccines
U01AI-28171-03 0003 (AIDS) FUERST, THOMAS R Vaccine development for immunodeficiency viruses Vaccina virus vectored HIV vaccines
U01AI-28171-03 0004 (AIDS) BLOOM, BARRY R Vaccine development for immunodeficiency viruses Mycobacterial vectors for AIDS vaccines
U01AI-28171-03 9001 (AIDS) DE LA CRUZ, VIDAL F Vaccine development for immunodeficiency viruses Core--Immunology
R29AI-28186-04 (IMB) QUILL, HELEN R UNIV OF PENNA, M-163 36TH & HAMILTON WALK PHILADELPHIA, PA 19104-6082 The in vitro induction of helper T cell tolerance
R29AI-28188-05 (TMP) TORIAN, BRUCE E IDAHO STATE UNIVERSITY CAMPUS BOX 8334 POCATELLO, ID 83209-8334 Surface antigens and pathogenesis of amebiasis
R55AI-28189-04 (ARRC) NORTH, THOMAS W UNIVERSITY OF MONTANA MISSOULA, MT 59812 Feline lentivirus model for drug resistance
R01AI-28191-04 (AITC) FEARON, DOUGLAS T JOHNS HOPKINS UNIVERSITY 725 N WOLFE STREET BALTIMORE, MD 21205 Role of complement receptor in the immune response
R01AI-28193-03 (ARR) TERWILLIGER, ERNEST F DANA-FARBER CANCER INSTITUTE 44 BINNEY STREET BOSTON, MA 02115 Molecular biology of the vpu gene of HIV-1
R01AI-28194-02 (ARR) CELADA, FRANCO INST OF MOLECULAR BIOLOGY 301 EAST 17TH STREET NEW YORK, NY 10003 Neutralizing responses to HIV gp120 complexed with CD4 A
R01AI-28196-03 (ARR) BERMAN, MONIQUE A UNIV CALIFORNIA/CA COLL OF MED IRVINE, CA 92717 Pathogenesis of AIDS--Role of monokines
R01AI-28197-04 (ARR) ALTMAN, AMNON LA JOLLA INST-ALLERGY & IMMUNO 11149 NORTH TORREY PINES RD LA JOLLA, CA 92037 T cell immunity and synthetic peptide AIDS vaccines
R01AI-28201-03 (ARR) GREEN, MAURICE ST LOUIS UNIVERSITY 3681 PARK AVENUE ST LOUIS, MO 63110 Regulation of HIV gene expression by tat mutant peptide
R55AI-28202-01A2 (ARRD) RIDEOUT, DARRYL C SCRIPPS CLINIC & RES FDN 10666 N TORREY PINES RD LA JOLLA, CA 92037 Self-assembling antiretroviral agents
R01AI-28204-03 (ARR) BURGESS, KEVIN RICE UNIVERSITY PO BOX 1892 HOUSTON, TX 77251 Synthetic analogues of castanospermine
R01AI-28206-03 (ARR) STRAND, METTE JOHNS HOPKINS UNIV SCH OF MED 725 N WOLFE STREET BALTIMORE, MD 21205 Mechanism of HIV GP41 - mediated immunosuppression
R01AI-28208-03 (ARR) HOXIE, JAMES A HOSP OF THE U OF PENNSYLVANIA 3400 SPRUCE STREET PHILADELPHIA, PA 19104 Pathogenesis of HIV in CD4 cells
R01AI-28210-02 (ARR) GOODENOW, MAUREEN M UNIVERSITY OF FLORIDA BOX J-275 JHMHC GAINESVILLE, FL 32610 Biological effects of HIV-1 genetic variability
R01AI-28213-03 (ARR) FARQUHAR, DAVID U OF TEX/M D ANDERSON CANCER C 1515 HOLCOMBE BLVD HOUSTON, TX 77030 Cell-permeable anti-HIV nucleotide analogues
R01AI-28214-03 (ARR) SANDBORG, CHRISTY IRENE UNIVERSITY OF CALIFORNIA IRVINE, CA 92717 Role of monokines in B cell abnormalities in AIDS
R01AI-28215-03 (ARR) REINHOLD, VERNON N 665 HUNTINGTON AVENUE BOSTON, MA 02115 Structure-function relationships in gp120
R01AI-28220-02 (ARR) REGEN, STEVEN L LEHIGH UNIVERSITY BETHLEHEM, PA 18105 Supramolecular surfactants as anti-HIV agents
R29AI-28233-03 (ARR) CULLEN, BRYAN R DUKE UNIVERSITY MEDICAL CENTER BOX 3025 DURHAM, NC 27710 Mechanism of action of the HIV-1 rev gene product
R01AI-28236-03 (ARR) REMMEL, RORY P UNIVERSITY OF MINNESOTA 308 HARVARD STREET S.E. MINNEAPOLIS, MN 55455 Carbovir prodrugs--Synthesis, metabolism, and kinetics
R01AI-28240-03 (ARR) GREENE, WARNER C DUKE UNIVERSITY MEDICAL CENTER PO BOX 3037 DURHAM, NC 27710 The nef gene of HIV-1
R01AI-28241-03 (ARR) HSIUNG, GUEH-DJEN VA MEDICAL CENTER WEST SPRING STREET WEST HAVEN, CT 06516 Chemotherapy of HIV infection--Ultrastructural approaches
U01AI-28243-03 (SRC) MURPHEY-CORB, MICHAEL A DELTA REGIONAL PRIMATE RES CTR THREE RIVERS ROAD COVINGTON, LA 70433 Development of an AIDS prototype vaccine using SIV
U01AI-28243-03 0001 (SRC) MURPHEY-CORB, MICHAEL A. Development of an AIDS prototype vaccine using SIV Immunization of macaques with whole killed SIV vaccines
U01AI-28243-03 0002 (SRC) NEWMAN, MARK J. Development of an AIDS prototype vaccine using SIV Cell-mediated immunity to Simian immunodeficiency virus
U01AI-28243-03 0003 (SRC) MONTELARO, RONALD C. Development of an AIDS prototype vaccine using SIV Elucidation of SIV immunogenicity by synthetic peptides
U01AI-28243-03 0004 (SRC) PUTNEY, SCOTT D. Development of an AIDS prototype vaccine using SIV Development of pubunit vaccine for SIV
U01AI-28243-03 9001 (SRC) MURPHEY-CORB, MICHAEL A. Development of an AIDS prototype vaccine using SIV SIV vaccine testing in rhesus monkey--Core
R37AI-28246-03 (ARR) HAASE, ASHLEY T UNIV OF MINNESOTA MEDICAL SCH BOX 196 UMHC/420 DELAWARE ST, MINNEAPOLIS, MN 55455 The pathogenesis of hiv induced immunodeficiency
R01AI-28253-03 SILVERMAN, ROBERT H CLEVELAND CLINIC FOUNDATION ONE CLINIC CENTER CLEVELAND, OH 44195 Activation of antiviral proteins by HIV-1 leader RNA
R01AI-28256-03 (ARR) DANCIS, JOSEPH NYU MEDICAL CENTER 550 FIRST AVENUE NEW YORK, NY 10016 Placental transfer & metabolism of drugs for AIDS

PROJECT NO., ORGANIZATIONAL UNIT., INVESTIGATOR, ADDRESS, TITLE

R01AI-28264-03 (ARR) FARZADEGAN, HOMAYOON JHU SCH OF HYGIENE & PUBLIC HL 615 NORTH WOLFE STREET BALTIMORE, MD 21205 Detection of HIV-1 by PCR in seronegative drug users
R01AI-28270-03 (ARR) SPECTOR, STEPHEN A UNIV OF CALIFORNIA, SAN DIEGO 225 DICKINSON STREET SAN DIEGO, CA 92103 Molecular interaction of HIV HCMV
R01AI-28272-02 (ARR) KHALILI, KAMEL THOMAS JEFFERSON UNIVERSITY 1020 LOCUST STREET PHILADELPHIA, PA 19107 Transactivation of JCV expression by HIV-1 tat protein
R01AI-28273-03 (ARR) ALLAN, JONATHAN S SOUTHWEST FDN/BIOMED RESEARCH PO BOX 28147 SAN ANTONIO, TX 78228-0147 Pathobiology of african green monkey retroviruses
R01AI-28279-03 (MID) CASSELL, GAIL H UNIVERSITY OF ALABAMA UAB STATION BIRMINGHAM, AL 35294 Identification and characterization of urealyticum antigen
R01AI-28281-03 (SRCD) PAHWA, SAVITA NORTH SHORE UNIVERSITY HOSP 300 COMMUNITY DRIVE MANHASSET, NY 11030 HIV envelope glycoproteins and immunity
R29AI-28282-03 (ARR) NEUDORF, STEVEN CHILDREN'S HOSPITAL OF PGH 3705 FIFTH AVE PITTSBURGH, PA 15213 Signal transduction via the Cd4 molecule
R01AI-28283-03 (SSS) WONG, PAUL K Y UNIV OF TEX SYSTEM CANCER CTR P O BOX 389 SMITHVILLE, TX 78957 Retrovirus-induced immune & neural disorders-AIDS model
R01AI-28284-04 (SAT) ASCHER, NANCY L U OF CALIFORNIA, SAN FRANCISCO 533 PARNASSUS AVENUE SAN FRANCISCO, CA 94143-0780 Modification of local and systemic allograft rejection
R01AI-28290-03 (HEM) PEREZ, HECTOR D UNIVERSITY OF CALIFORNIA 3RD & PARNASSUS AVES/BOX 0868 SAN FRANCISCO, CA 94143-0868 Formyl peptide receptor of human neutrophils
R01AI-28304-03 (BM) MURPHY, TIMOTHY F STATE UNIVERSITY OF NEW YORK 3495 BAILEY AVENUE BUFFALO, NY 14215 Pathogenesis of branhamella catarrhalis infections
R01AI-28308-03 (EDC) SHAPIRO, EUGENE D YALE UNIV SCHOOL OF MED 333 CEDAR ST/BOX 3333 NEW HAVEN, CT 06510 The efficacy of conjugate vaccines against H influenzae
R01AI-28309-02 (EVR) MCCLURE, MARCELLA A UNIVERSITY OF CALIFORNIA 716 ENGINEERING BUILDING IRVINE, CA 92717 Computer-based analysis and RNA virus evolution
R37AI-28317-03 (EVR) BRACIALE, THOMAS J UNIVERSITY OF VIRGINIA HEALTH CHARLOTTESVILLE, VA 22908 Human T lymphocyte response to viral antigens
R01AI-28320-02 (ALY) PEASE, LARRY R MAYO FOUNDATION 200 FIRST ST-SW ROCHESTER, MN 55905 Structural basis of immune function in the MHC
R01AI-28332-03 (IMB) FORMAN, JAMES M UNIV OF TEXAS SW MEDICAL CTR 5323 HARRY HINES BOULEVARD DALLAS, TX 75235 Immune reactivity against organ specific MHC molecules
R01AI-28338-03 (EVR) FELDMAN, LAWRENCE T UNIV. OF CALIF. SCH OF MEDICIN 10833 LE CONTE AVENUE LOS ANGELES, CA 90024-1747 Hsv-1 gene expression in latently infected neurons
R01AI-28341-01A2 (VR) MOCARSKI, EDWARD S, JR STANFORD UNIVERSITY SHERMAN FAIRCHILD SCI BLDG STANFORD, CA 94305-5402 Cytomegalovirus--Gene functions and virus localization
R01AI-28342-02 (HEM) BADWEY, JOHN A BOSTON BIOMEDICAL RESEARCH INS 20 STANIFORD STREET BOSTON, MA 02114 Synergistic stimulation and priming of neutrophils
R01AI-28354-02 (ARR) HARMSEN, ALLEN G TRUDEAU INSTITUTE, INC PO BOX 59 ALGONQUIN AVE SARANAC LAKE, NY 12983 Reconstitution of immunity to pneumocystis in SCID mice
R01AI-28356-03 (SAT) MOHANAKUMAR, THALACHALLOUR WASHINGTON UNIV SCHOOL OF MED 4939 AUDUBON AVE, BOX 8109 ST LOUIS, MO 63110 Immunoregulatory role of antiidiotypic antibodies to HLA
R29AI-28358-02 (GMA) DU CLOS, TERRY W UNIVERSITY OF NEW MEXICO SCHOOL OF MEDICINE ALBUQUERQUE, NM 87131 Reactions of C-reactive protein with nuclear antigens
R01AI-28362-03 (VR) MULLER, MARK T OHIO STATE UNIVERSITY 484 W 12TH AVENUE COLUMBUS, OH 43210 Immediate early gene regulation in herpes simplex virus
R01AI-28364-03 (EI) TSOUKAS, CONSTANTINE SAN DIEGO STATE UNIV SAN DIEGO, CA 92182 Signal transduction in T cells
R01AI-28365-03 (IMS) JENKINS, MARC K UNIVERSITY OF MINNESOTA MED SC BOX 196 UMHC 402 DELAWARE ST S MINNEAPOLIS, MN 55455 Effects of cyclosporine A on T cell development
R01AI-28367-02 (IMS) CROW, MARY K HOSPITAL FOR SPECIAL SURGERY 535 E 70TH ST NEW YORK, NY 10021 The role of activated B lymphocytes in immune responses
R01AI-28368-03 (TMP) BRADFIELD, JAMES Y TEXAS A&M UNIVERSITY COLLEGE STATION, TX 77843 Insect adipokinetic hormone gene expression
R01AI-28372-02 (BM) ROGERS, THOMAS J TEMPLE UNIVERSITY SCHOOL OF ME 3400 NORTH BROAD STREET PHILADELPHIA, PA 19140 Candida dimorphism--Virulence and immunomodulatory action
R29AI-28378-02 (EVR) FULLER, A OVETA UNIVERSITY OF MICHIGAN ANN ARBOR, MI 48109-0620 Functions of glycoprotein D in herpesvirus infection
R01AI-28385-02 (EVR) PARRISH, COLIN R CORNELL UNIVERSITY N Y S COLLEGE OF VET MEDICINE ITHACA, NY 14853 Parvovirus structure, function and host range
R01AI-28386-03 (HEM) PIKE, MARILYN C MASS GENERAL HOSP (BULFINCH 1) FRUIT ST (ARTHRITIS UNIT) BOSTON, MA 02114 Leukocyte activation--Cytoskeleton / membrane protein interactions
R01AI-28388-01A2 (BM) PERFECT, JOHN R DUKE UNIVERSITY MEDICAL CENTER BOX 3353 DURHAM, NC 27710 Genetic and molecular biology of virulence in C. neoformans
P01AI-28392-02 (SRC) BULLOCK, WARD E UNIVERSITY OF CINCINNATI 231 BETHESDA AVENUE CINCINNATI, OH 45267-0560 Molecular and cell biology of fungal pathogens
P01AI-28392-02 0005 (SRC) STRINGER, JAMES R Molecular and cell biology of fungal pathogens Molecular genetic analysis of pneumocystis
P01AI-28392-02 0001 (SRC) DEAN, GARY Molecular and cell biology of fungal pathogens Histoplasma proton pumps genes and proteins
P01AI-28392-02 0002 (SRC) NEWMAN, SIMON Molecular and cell biology

of fungal pathogens Interaction of histoplasma capsulatum with human macrophages

P01AI-28392-02 0003 (SRC) RHODES, JUDITH Molecular and cell biology of fungal pathogens Molecular biology of Aspergillus elastase

P01AI-28392-02 0004 (SRC) WONG, BRIAN Molecular and cell biology of fungal pathogens Polyol metabolites of pathogenic fungi as markers for infection

R29AI-28395-03 (TMP) SAMUELSON, JOHN C HARVARD SCHOOL OF PUBLIC HEALT 665 HUNTINGTON AVENUE BOSTON, MA 02115 Molecular genetics of drug resistance in E histolyica

R22AI-28396-03 (BM) VAIDYA, AKHIL B HAHNEMAN UNIVERSITY BROAD AND VINE PHILADELPHIA, PA 19102-1192 Organelle genomes of malarial parasites

R01AI-28399-03 (TMP) SPRING, JEFFREY H UNIVERSITY OF S W LOUISIANA DEPT OF BIOLOGY LAFAYETTE, LA 70504-2451 Neuroendocrine regulation of water balance in insects

R29AI-28401-03 (BM) BOHACH, GREGORY A UNIVERSITY OF IDAHO BACTERIOLOGY & BIOCHEM DEPT MOSCOW, ID 83843 Molecular analysis of staphylococcal type C enterotoxins

P01AI-28408-02 (SRC) DIAMOND, RICHARD D UNIVERSITY HOSPITAL 88 EAST NEWTON STREET BOSTON, MA 02118 Regulatory mechanisms determining fungicidal responses

P01AI-28408-02 0001 (SRC) DIAMOND, RICHARD D Regulatory mechanisms determining fungicidal responses Bases of divergent cytokine effects on hyphal killing

P01AI-28408-02 0002 (SRC) SMAIL, EDWIN H Regulatory mechanisms determining fungicidal responses Characterization of leukocyte inhibitor from C. albicans

P01AI-28408-02 0003 (SRC) LEVITZ, STUART M Regulatory mechanisms determining fungicidal responses Receptor-ligand interactions in Cryptococcosis

P01AI-28408-02 0004 (SRC) SUGAR, ALAN M Regulatory mechanisms determining fungicidal responses Human macrophage effector mechanisms in Blastomycosis

P01AI-28408-02 0005 (SRC) HAUSER, WILLIAM E Regulatory mechanisms determining fungicidal responses Natural killer cell responses to opportunistic mycosis

P01AI-28408-02 9001 (SRC) SIMONS, ELIZABETH R Regulatory mechanisms determining fungicidal responses Core--Cell analysis resource/single cell functional responses

P01AI-28408-02 9002 (SRC) MESHULAM, TOVA Regulatory mechanisms determining fungicidal responses Core--Cell analysis resource: Lipid biochemistry and receptors

P01AI-28412-03 (SRC) CLARK, ROBERT A UNIV OF IOWA COLLEGE OF MED SW 54-15/GH IOWA CITY, IA 52242 Basis of oxygen-dependent neutrophil host defenses

P01AI-28412-03 0001 (SRC) CLARK, ROBERT A Basis of oxygen-dependent neutrophil host defenses Cytosolic components of the neutrophil oxidase system

P01AI-28412-03 0002 (SRC) BRITIGAN, BRADLEY E Basis of oxygen-dependent neutrophil host defenses Modulation of neutrophil hydoxyl radical formation

P01AI-28412-03 0003 (SRC) NAUSEEF, WILLIAM M Basis of oxygen-dependent neutrophil host defenses Molecular determinants of myeloperoxidase targetting

P01AI-28412-03 9001 (SRC) BRITIGAN, BRADLEY E Basis of oxygen-dependent neutrophil host defenses Core--cell preparation and culture

R01AI-28414-03 (IMS) BUCKLEY, REBECCA H DUKE UNIVERSITY MEDICAL CENTER BOX 2898 DURHAM, NC 27710 The regulation of human IgE synthesis by cytokines

R01AI-28419-03 (IMS) SERCARZ, ELI E UNIV OF CALIFORNIA 405 HILGARD AVENUE LOS ANGELES, CA 90024 T cell response to mbp: repertoire/dominance/suppression

R29AI-28421-02 (BM) GULIG, PAUL A UNIVERSITY OF FLORIDA BOX J-266 GAINESVILLE, FL 32610-0266 Analysis of the Salmonella typhimurium virulence plasmid

R29AI-28422-03 (IMB) MC COY, KATHLEEN L VIRGINIA COMMONWEALTH UNIV BOX 678, MCV STATION RICHMOND, VA 23298-0678 Intracellular transport pathways for processing antigens

R01AI-28425-01A2 (ET) OKUNEWICK, JAMES P ALLEGHENY-SINGER RESEARCH INST 320 EAST NORTH AVENUE PITTSBURGH, PA 15212 Effect of prior donor pregnancy on graft-vs-host disease

R55AI-28427-01A3 (TMP) BALBER, ANDREW E DUKE UNIV MEDICAL CENTER PO BOX 3010 DURHAM, NC 27710 Glycoproteins of a trypanosome membrane domain

R01AI-28432-03 (EVR) BROYLES, STEVEN S PURDUE RESEARCH FOUNDATION SCHOOL OF AGRICULTURE WEST LAFAYETTE, IN 47907 Vaccinia virus transcription

R01AI-28433-02 (SSS) PERELSON, ALAN S UNIVERSITY OF CALIFORNIA PO BOX 1663, MAIL STOP K710 LOS ALAMOS, NM 87545 Immune system modeling

R01AI-28449-03 (IMB) FLOMENBERG, NEAL MILWAUKEE COUNTY MEDICAL COMPL 8700 W WISCONSIN AVENUE MILWAUKEE, WI 53226 Structure and function of human CD8 alpha and CD8 beta

R01AI-28457-03 (BM) YOTHER, JANET L UAB, 236 LHR BIRMINGHAM, AL 35294 Genetics and virulence of pneumococcal capsular types

P01AI-28465-03 (SRC) ARNAOUT, AMIN MASSACHUSETTS GENERAL HOSPITAL 13TH STREET BOSTON, MA 02129 The neutrophil membrane

P01AI-28465-03 0004 (SRC) STOSSEL, THOMAS P The neutrophil membrane The actin system and the PMN membrane

P01AI-28465-03 0001 (SRC) ARNAOUT, AMIN The neutrophil membrane Gene regulation of human leukocyte receptor CD11/CD18

P01AI-28465-03 0002 (SRC) PIKE, MARILYN The neutrophil membrane Polyphosphoinositide metabolism and neutrophil membrane signaling

P01AI-28465-03 0003 (SRC) ROBINSON, DWIGHT The neutrophil membrane PMN lipid modification

R01AI-28468-03 (EI) NOELLE, RANDOLPH J DARTMOUTH MEDICAL SCHOOL HANOVER, NH 03756 Reconstitution of the humoral immune response

R01AI-28471-03 (TMP) STRINGER, JAMES R UNIVERSITY OF CINCINNATI 231 BETHESDA AVENUE CINCINNATI, OH 45267-0524 Molecular genetic analysis of Pneumocystic

R29AI-28478-03 (SAT) HENRY, MITCHELL L OHIO STATE UNIVERSITY 1654 UPHAM DR COLUMBUS, OH 43210 Ex vivo xenoantibody adsorption

R01AI-28479-03 (HEM) BABIOR, BERNARD M SCRIPPS CLINIC & RESEARCH FDN 10666 NORTH TORREY PINES ROAD LA JOLLA, CA 92037 Oxidase-related 48K phosphoprotein of human neutrophils

R01AI-28480-02 (SAT) FLYE, M WAYNE ONE BARNES HOSPITAL PLAZA SUITE 5108 QUEENY TOWER ST LOUIS, MO 63110 Modification of the immune response by the liver

R01AI-28481-03 (BM) SCHACHTER, JULIUS SAN FRANCISCO GENERAL HOSPITAL 1001 POTRERO AVE/BLDG 30 RM 41 SAN FRANCISCO, CA 94110 Noninvasive screening for STDS in asymptomatic males

R01AI-28487-02 (BM) CURTIS, ROY WASHINGTON UNIVERSITY LINDELL & SKINKER BOULEVARDS ST LOUIS, MO 63130 Genetic analysis of bordetella avium virulence

R01AI-28495-03 (IMB) KOTZIN, BRIAN L NATL JEWISH CTR FOR IMMUNOLOGY 1400 JACKSON STREET DENVER, CO 80206-1997 Autoimmunity in murine graft-versus-host disease

R22AI-28499-01A1 (TMP) SHOEMAKER, CHARLES HARVARD SCHOOL OF PUBLIC HEALT 665 HUNTINGTON AVENUE BOSTON, MA 02115 S. mansoni homologues of EGF receptor and P-glycoprotein

R29AI-28500-02 (BM) MICHEL, JAMES L CHANNING LABORATORY 180 LONGWOOD AVE BOSTON, MA 02115 Genetic analysis of C proteins in group B streptococcus

R29AI-28502-03 (BM) PETERSON, KENNETH M LSU MEDICAL CENTER P O BOX 33932 SHREVEPORT, LA 71130-3932 Analysis of V. cholerae genes involved in colonization

R29AI-28503-03 (IMB) WILLIAMS, WILLIAM V UNIV OF PENNSYLVANIA 3600 SPRUCE STREET PHILADELPHIA, PA 19104 Molecular analysis of an internal image autoantibody

R01AI-28506-02 (EVR) SAWICKI, STANLEY G MEDICAL COLLEGE OF OHIO PO BOX 10008 TOLEDO, OH 43699 Coronavirus RNA synthesis--Lytic & persistent infections

R29AI-28508-03 (ALY) BAND, HAMID DANA-FARBER CANCER INSTITUTE 44 BINNEY STREET/MAYER 640 BOSTON, MA 02115 Antigen recognition by gamma-delta T cell receptor

R01AI-28520-03 (EVR) RYAN, JAMES P UNIV OF TENNESSEE, MEMPHIS 858 MADISON AVENUE MEMPHIS, TN 38163 Genetic analysis of herpesvirus glycoproteins

R29AI-28523-03 (IMB) SYMINGTON, FRANK W SEATTLE BIOMEDICAL RES INST 4 NIKCERSON STREET SEATTLE, WA 98109-1651 Cytokines in human graft-versus-host disease

R29AI-28525-03 (TMP) SIBERSTEIN, DAVID S BRIGHAM & WOMEN'S HOSPITAL, IN 250 LONGWOOD AVENUE BOSTON, MA 02115 Structure and biological function of the monokine ecef

R01AI-28526-03 (BM) SULTZER, BARNET M STATE UNIV OF NEW YORK 450 CLARKSON AVE BROOKLYN, NY 11203 Suppression of activated lymphocytes by endotoxin

R01AI-28528-03 (BM) TESH, ROBERT B YALE UNIV SCHOOL OF MEDICINE 60 COLLEGE STREET; PO BOX 3333 NEW HAVEN, CT 06510-8034 Epidemiology and control of visceral leishmaniasis

P50AI-28532-03 (AITC) RUDDY, SHAUN MEDICAL COLLEGE OF VIRGINIA BOX 263 MCV STATION RICHMOND, VA 23298-0263 Cellular mechanisms of inflammation and allergy

P50AI-28532-03 0001 (AITC) FREER, RICHARD Cellular mechanisms of inflammation and allergy Regulation and chemotactic peptide receptors

P50AI-28532-03 0002 (AITC) FREER, RICHARD Cellular mechanisms of inflammation and allergy Regulation and chemotactic peptide receptors

P50AI-28532-03 0003 (AITC) TEW, JOHN Cellular mechanisms of inflammation and allergy Regulation of IgE--Role of dendritic cells

P50AI-28532-03 0004 (AITC) HUFF, THOMAS Cellular mechanisms of inflammation and allergy Differentiation of mast cell progenitors

R01AI-28535-03 (BBCB) WESTBROOK, EDWIN M ARGONNE NATIONAL LABORATORY 9700 SOUTH CASS AVENUE ARGONNE, IL 60439-4833 Structure and function of cholera toxin

R01AI-28537-03 (EVR) SCHAFFER, PRISCILLA A DANA-FARBER CANCER INSTITUTE 44 BINNEY STREET BOSTON, MA 02115 Genetics of HSV DNA replication and recombination

R55AI-28539-01A2 (EI) CORLEY, RONALD B DUKE UNIVERSITY MEDICAL CENTER BOX 3010 DURHAM, NC 27710 Functional analysis of an autoreactive B cell repertoire

R01AI-28540-03 (IMB) MULLEN, HELEN B UNIVERSITY OF MISSOURI COLUMBIA, MO 65212 Mechanism of T cell activation by type 2 antigens

R29AI-28542-03 (EVR) HOROHOV, DAVID W LOUISIANA STATE UNIVERSITY SCH OF VETERINARY MEDICINE BATON ROUGE, LA 70803 Signal requirement for memory cytotoxic T lymphocytes

R29AI-28544-03 (EVR) MATSON, DAVID O BAYLOR COLLEGE COLL OF MEDICIN ONE BAYLOR PLAZA HOUSTON, TX 77030 Moleculair biology of human calciviruses

R01AI-28545-03 (BM) TAYLOR, JOHN W UNIVERSITY OF CALIFORNIA BERKELEY, CA 94720 Medical mycology--PCR rDNA phylogeny and identification

R29AI-28551-02 (TMP) ADAM, RODNEY D UNIVERSITY OF ARIZONA 1501 N. CAMPBELL AVENUE TUCSON, AZ 85724 Antigenic variaton in Giardia lamblia

R29AI-28552-03 (ALY) DIMENT, STEPHANIE NEW YORK UNIVERSITY MEDICAL SC 550 FIRST AVENUE NEW YORK, NY 10016 Endosomal proteolysis in antigen presentation

R29AI-28554-03 (ALY) BIERER, BARBARA E DANA-FARBER CANCER INSTITUTE 44 BINNEY STREET BOSTON, MA 02115 Interaction of CD-2 with LFA-3 in T cell activation

R29AI-28559-03 (BNP) MEIER, GUY P MEDICAL UNIV OF SOUTH CAROLINA 171 ASHLEY AVENUE CHARLESTON, SC 29425 Olefinic analogs of CaA--new agents

R29AI-28566-03 (ARR) PEREZ, LAUTARO G UNIVERSITY OF MINNESOTA 420 DELAWARE STREET SE MINNEAPOLIS, MN 55455 Oligomerization of the HIV glycoproteins

R01AI-28568-03 (ARR) WALKER, BRUCE D MASSACHUSETTS GENERAL HOSPITAL 32 FRUIT STREET BOSTON, MA 02114 HIV-1-specific T cell clones

R01AI-28570-02 (ARR) MALLEY, ARTHUR OREGON REGIONAL PRIM RES CTR 505 NW 185TH AVENUE BEAVERTON, OR 97006 Synthetic peptides to develop simian retroviral vaccine

R01AI-28571-03 (ARR) DUNN, BEN M UNIVERSITY OF FLORIDA 223 GRINTER HALL GAINESVILLE, FL 32611 Human immunodeficiency virus

proteinase
R01AI-28572-03 (ARR) KABAT, DAVID OREGON HEALTH SCIENCES UNIV 3181 SW SAM JACKSON PARK RD PORTLAND, OR 97201 Novel vertebrate protein production -- HIV
R01AI-28580-03 (ARR) LUCIW, PAUL A UNIVERSITY OF CALIFORNIA DAVIS, CA 95616 Feline immunodeficiency virus gene expression
R01AI-28586-03 (IMS) OHMAN, JOHN L JR NEW ENGLAND MEDICAL CENTER 750 WASHINGTON STREET BOSTON, MA 02111 Immunology of occupational allergy to mice
R44AI-28600-02 (SSS) HORAN, PAUL K ZYNAXIS CELL SCIENCE, INC 371 PHOENIXVILLE PIKE MALVERN, PA 19355 A new method of tracking lymphocytes to metastatic tumor
R44AI-28605-02 (SSS) THIEME, THOMAS R EPITOPE, INC 15425 SW KOLL PARKWAY BEAVERTON, OR 97006 Rapid assay for HIV-1 antibodies in saliva
R44AI-28628-02A1 (SSS) SMITH, DAVID F SEALITE SCIENCES, INC 3453 HOLCOMB BRIDGE RD ATLANA, GA 30092 Luminescence detection reagents for food pathogens
R44AI-28650-02 (SSS) MACKIE, HUGH GLEN RESEARCH CORPORATION 44901 FALCON PLACE STERLING, VA 22170 Production of therapeutic antisense oligonucleotides
R44AI-28654-02A1 (SSS) HIRSCHEL, MARK D ENDOTRONICS, INC 8500 EVERGREEN BLVD COON RAPIDS, MN 55433 Compact cell culture device for cellular immunotherapy
P30AI-28662-03 (SRC) BOLOGNESI, DANI P DUKE UNIVERSITY MEDICAL CENTER PO BOX 2926 DURHAM, NC 27710 Duke University Medical Center for AIDS research
P30AI-28662-03 9001 (SRC) CULLEN, BAGAN R Duke University Medical Center for AIDS research Core--Gene expression
P30AI-28662-03 9002 (SRC) PALKER, THOMAS J Duke University Medical Center for AIDS research Core--Peptide synthesis
P30AI-28662-03 9003 (SRC) WEINHOLD, KENT J Duke University Medical Center for AIDS research Core--Retroviral biology
P30AI-28662-03 9004 (SRC) DENNING, STEPHEN M Duke University Medical Center for AIDS research Core--Flow cytology
P30AI-28662-03 9005 (SRC) RICHTER, CONRAD Duke University Medical Center for AIDS research Core--scid-Hu/transgenic mouse facility
P30AI-28662-03 9006 (SRC) AUSTIN, ARTHUR A Duke University Medical Center for AIDS research Core--Data management
U01AI-28666-03 (SRC) BONA, CONSTANTIN A MOUNT SINAI SCHOOL OF MEDICINE ONE GUSTAVE L LEVY PLACE NEW YORK, NY 10029 Adjuvanticity of stearyl-tyrosine for subunit and HIV synthetic antigens
U01AI-28676-03 (SRC) HUNTER, ROBERT L, JR EMORY UNIVERSITY 1364 CLIFTON RD ATLANTA, GA 30322 Development of BCG as an adjuvant and vaccine vector
U01AI-28679-03 (SRC) THURIN, JAN WISTAR INSTITUTE 36TH AND SPRUCE STREETS PHILADELPHIA, PA 19104 ISCOM glycoside adjuvant and HIV-1 vaccine
U01AI-28681-03 (SRC) CEASE, KEMP B UNIVERSITY OF MICHIGAN 102 OBSERVATORY ROAD ANN ARBOR, MI 48109-0724 Adjuvant strategies using T cell help enhancer peptides
U01AI-28685-03 (SRC) MERIGAN, THOMAS C STANFORD UNIVERSITY SCH OF MED STANFORD, CA 94305 Antigen presenting vehicles in HSV and HIV infections
P30AI-28691-03 (SRC) JANICKI, BERNARD W DANA-FARBER CANCER INSTITUTE 44 BINNEY STREET BOSTON, MA 02115 AIDS center support grant
P30AI-28691-03 9004 (SRC) ROSOWSKY, ANDRE AIDS center support grant Core -- Pharmacology
P30AI-28691-03 9005 (SRC) BREITMEYER, JAMES B. AIDS center support grant Core --Mammalian cell culture core
P30AI-28691-03 9001 (SRC) SODROSKI, JOSEPH G. AIDS center support grant Core --Biohazard containment
P30AI-28691-03 9002 (SRC) RUPRECHT, RUTH M. AIDS center support grant Core --Animal biohazard
P30AI-28691-03 9003 (SRC) KOLODNER, RICHARD D. AIDS center support grant Core --Molecular biology
P30AI-28696-01 (SRC) KENNEDY, RONALD C SOUTHWEST FDN FOR BIOMED RES PO BOX 28147 SAN ANTONIO, TX 78228-0147 Multidisciplinary center for AIDS related research
P30AI-28696-01 9001 (SRC) CHANH, C Multidisciplinary center for AIDS related research Monoclonal antibody facility core
P30AI-28696-01 9002 (SRC) EICHBERG, JORG Multidisciplinary center for AIDS related research Veterinary resources core
P30AI-28696-01 9003 (SRC) KANDA, P Multidisciplinary center for AIDS related research Peptide chemistry facility
P30AI-28696-01 9004 (SRC) ALLAN, JONATHAN Multidisciplinary center for AIDS related research Virus production and reagent facility
P30AI-28696-01 9005 (SRC) BOSWELL, R Multidisciplinary center for AIDS related research Human clinical resources core
P30AI-28696-01 9006 (SRC) KENNEDY, R Multidisciplinary center for AIDS related research Developmental program core
P30AI-28697-01 (SRC) CHEN, IRVIN S UCLA - SCHOOL OF MEDICINE 11-262 FACTOR BUILDING LOS ANGELES, CA 90024-1678 Center for AIDS research
P30AI-28697-01 9001 (SRC) MILES, STEVEN Center for AIDS research Specimen bank core
P30AI-28697-01 9002 (SRC) SAXON, ANDREW Center for AIDS research SCID mouse colony core
P30AI-28697-01 9003 (SRC) GIORGI, JANIS Center for AIDS research Flow cytometry/cell separation core
P30AI-28697-01 9004 (SRC) CHEN, IRVIN Center for AIDS research Virology core support
P30AI-28697-01 9005 (SRC) CHEN, IRVIN Center for AIDS research Pediatric/Perinatal HIV program core
P30AI-28697-01 9006 (SRC) ELASHOFF, ROBERT Center for AIDS research Biostatistics core
P30AI-28697-01 9007 (SRC) TOUTELLOTE, W Center for AIDS research Neurological core
P30AI-28697-01 9008 (SRC) DETELES, ROGER Center for AIDS research Epidemiology consultative service core
P30AI-28697-01 9009 (SRC) CHEN, IRVIN Center for AIDS research Development/seed grants
U01AI-28701-03 (SRC) TAM, JAMES P ROCKEFELLER UNIVERSITY 1230 YORK AVENUE NEW YORK, NY 10021-6399 Vaccine adjuvants for AIDS
U01AI-28702-03 (SRC) MANNINO, RAPHAEL J UNIV OF MED & DENT OF NEW JERS 185 SOUTH ORANGE AVENUE NEWARK, NJ 07103-2714 Immune response to peptide-phospholipid conjugates
R01AI-28711-03 (ARR) KOTLOFF, KAREN L CENTER FOR VACCINE DEVELOPMENT 10 SOUTH PINE STREET BALTIMORE, MD 21201 Prevalence of HIV-1 infection in college students
R01AI-28715-03 (ARR) BLANK, KENNETH J HAHNEMANN UNIVERSITY BROAD AND VINE PHILADELPHIA, PA 19102 Genetic basis for persistent MULV infection
R01AI-28716-03 (ARR) ALLEN, PAUL M WASHINGTON UNIV SCH OF MEDICIN ST LOUIS, MO 63110 Identification and enhancement of HIV-1 T cell epitopes
U01AI-28718-03 (SRC) FOX, BARBARA S UNIVERSITY OF MARYLAND 10 SOUTH PINE STREET BALTIMORE, MD 21201 Effect of adjuvants on murine helper T cells
R01AI-28721-01A2 (ARRA) RINALDO, CHARLES R, JR UNIVERSITY OF PITTSBURGH GRADUATE SCH OF PUBLIC HLTH PITTSBURGH, PA 15261 Natural killer cell response to HIV
R01AI-28724-03 (ARR) ROOS, DAVID S UNIVERSITY OF PENNSYLVANIA LEIDY LABORATORY OF BIOLOGY PHILADELPHIA, PA 19104-6017 Folate metabolism and drug resistance in toxoplasma
R01AI-28731-03 (ARR) LIOTTA, DENNIS C EMORY UNIVERSITY ATLANTA, GA 30322 Non-carbohydrate approaches to anti-AIDS nucleosides
R29AI-28732-02 (ARR) STRAUBINGER, ROBERT M STATE UNIVERSITY OF NEW YORK BUFFALO, NY 14260 Cell biology/ therapy of mycobacterial infection in AIDS
R01AI-28733-02 (ARR) MERIGAN, THOMAS C STANFORD UNIVERSITY DEPT OF MEDICINE STANFORD, CA 94305-5107 Murine retroviral model for HIV drug evaluation
R01AI-28734-01A3 (ARRC) LANGHOFF, ERIK DANA-FARBER CANCER INSTITUTE 44 BINNEY STREET BOSTON, MA 02115 Function and expression of HIV 1 genes in pure leukocytes
R29AI-28735-02 (ARR) TONG, SANDRA E UNIVERSITY OF CALIFORNIA 3RD & PARNASSUS AVES SAN FRANCISCO, CA 94143-0724 Regulation of HIV gene expression in activated T cells
R01AI-28736-03 (ARR) CENTER, DAVID M BOSTON UNIV SCH OF MEDICINE 80 EAST CONCORD STREET, K-6 BOSTON, MA 02118 Effects of HIV gp120 and infection on T cell responses
R01AI-28741-02 (ARR) DONEHOWER, LAWRENCE A BAYLOR COLLEGE OF MEDICINE ONE BAYLOR PLAZA HOUSTON, TX 77030 Role of viral genes in HIV-1 replication
R01AI-28747-04 (ARR) HO, DAVID D NEW YORK CITY AIDS RESEARCH CT 455 FIRST AVENUE 7TH FLOOR NEW YORK, N Y 10016 HIV-1 infection of CD4-negative neuronal cells
P30AI-28748-03 (SRC) ADA, GORDON JOHNS HOPKINS UNIVERSITY 615 NORTH WOLFE STREET BALTIMORE, MD 21205 The center for AIDS research - The Johns Hopkins Medical Institutions
P30AI-28748-03 9001 (SRC) MARKHAM, RICHARD B The center for AIDS research - The Johns Hopkins Medical Institutions Core--SCID-Hu mouse
P30AI-28748-03 9002 (SRC) MARGOLICK, JOSEPH B The center for AIDS research - The Johns Hopkins Medical Institutions Core--Flow cytometry
P30AI-28748-03 9003 (SRC) AUGUST, J THOMAS The center for AIDS research - The Johns Hopkins Medical Institutions Core--Protein sequencing and peptide synthesis
P30AI-28748-03 9004 (SRC) FARZADEGAN, HAMAYOON The center for AIDS research - The Johns Hopkins Medical Institutions Core--HIV virology
P30AI-28748-03 9005 (SRC) CLEMENTS, JANICE E The center for AIDS research - The Johns Hopkins Medical Institutions Core--Molecular resources
P30AI-28748-03 9006 (SRC) SAAH, ALFRED J The center for AIDS research - The Johns Hopkins Medical Institutions Core--Biostatistic and epidemiology
P30AI-28748-03 9007 (SRC) JOHNSON, RICHARD The center for AIDS research - The Johns Hopkins Medical Institutions Core--New investigators award program
R01AI-28757-03 (ARR) WIENTJES, M GUILL OHIO STATE UNIVERSITY 456 W 10TH AVE COLUMBUS, OH 43210 Delivery of anti-AIDS drug 2',3'-dideoxyinosine
R01AI-28758-02 (ARR) FARAS, ANTHONY J UNIVERSITY OF MINNESOTA BX 206 UMHC/HARVARD ST AT E RI MINNEAPOLIS, MN 55455 Nature of HIV-related genetic sequences in human DNA
R01AI-28760-03 (ARR) PARDRIDGE, WILLIAM M UCLA SCHOOL OF MEDICINE LOS ANGELES, CA 90024-1682 Aids delivery through the blood-brain barrier
R01AI-28761-03 (ARR) HENDERSON, EARL E TEMPLE UNIV SCH OF MEDICINE 3400 NORTH BROAD STREET PHILADELPHIA, PA 19140 Inhibition of hiv replication by dhea and its analogs
R29AI-28767-03 (ARR) WEINER, DAVID B THE WISTAR INSTITUTE 36TH & SPRUCE STREETS PHILADELPHIA, PA 19104 Cell entry of HIV-1
R01AI-28771-03 (ARR) GILBOA, ELI SLOAN-KETTERING INST CANCER RE 1275 YORK AVENUE NEW YORK, NY 10021 Antisense RNA inhibition of HIV via retroviral vectors
P01AI-28778-02 (SRC) RICHARDS, FRANK F YALE UNIVERSITY SCH OF MEDICIN 60 COLLEGE STREET NEW HAVEN, CT 06510 The biology of the kinetoplastida and their vectors
P01AI-28778-02 0001 (SRC) ULLU, ELISABETTA The biology of the kinetoplastida and their vectors Transcription and RNA processing in trypanosomes
P01AI-28778-02 0002 (SRC) RICHARDS, FRANK F The biology of the kinetoplastida and their vectors Parasites, retrotransposons and vector symbionts
P01AI-28778-02 0003 (SRC) TESH, ROBERT B The biology of the kinetoplastida and their vectors Insect symbiosis and vector competence
P01AI-28778-02 0004 (SRC) CROTHERS, DONALD M The biology of the kinetoplastida and their vectors Spliced leader RNA structure and interactions
P01AI-28778-02 9001 (SRC) TESH, ROBERT B The biology of the kinetoplastida and their vectors Core--Insectary
P01AI-28780-01A1 (MID) GREENE, BRUCE M UNIVERSITY OF ALABAMA 1025 18TH ST SOUTH, UAB STATIO BIRMINGHAM, AL 35294 Molecular parasitology and parasitic disease

PROJECT NO., ORGANIZATIONAL UNIT., INVESTIGATOR, ADDRESS, TITLE

P01AI-28780-01A1 0001 (MID) GREENE, BRUCE Molecular parasitology and parasitic disease Onchocercal disease--Relation to defined antigens
P01AI-28780-01A1 0002 (MID) UNNASCH, THOMAS Molecular parasitology and parasitic disease Molecular cloning of disease associated antigens
P01AI-28780-01A1 0003 (MID) FREEDMAN, DAVID Molecular parasitology and parasitic disease Cell determinants of Onchocercal disease
P01AI-28780-01A1 0004 (MID) CHAKRAVARTI, BULBUL Molecular parasitology and parasitic disease Ocular disease associated Onchocercal antigens
P01AI-28780-01A1 9001 (MID) CHAKRABARTI, DEB Molecular parasitology and parasitic disease Protein chemistry core unit
P01AI-28781-02 (SRC) CHRISTENSEN, BRUCE M UNIVERSITY OF WISCONSIN 1655 LINDEN DRIVE MADISON, WI 53706 Parasite function in response to the host environment
P01AI-28781-02 0003 (SRC) TRACY, JAMES W Parasite function in response to the host environment Enzymatic basis of drug activation by schistosomes
P01AI-28781-02 0004 (SRC) YOSHINO, TIMOTHY P Parasite function in response to the host environment Parasitic castration in snail vectors of schistosomiasis
P01AI-28781-02 0005 (SRC) CHRISTENSEN, BRUCE M Parasite function in response to the host environment Genetic control of filariae development in mosquitoes
P01AI-28781-02 0001 (SRC) MANSFIELD, JOHN M Parasite function in response to the host environment Biological variation within trypanosome population
P01AI-28781-02 0002 (SRC) WASSUM, DONALD L Parasite function in response to the host environment Host-parasite genetic interactions in murine malaria
R01AI-28785-06 (ARR) HASELTINE, WILLIAM A DANA-FARBER CANCER INSTITUTE 44 BINNEY STREET BOSTON, MA 02115 Molecular biology of the AIDS virus HTLV-III
R01AI-28798-02 (TMP) ULLU, ELISABETTA YALE UNIV SCHOOL OF MEDICINE DEPT OF INTERNAL MEDICINE NEW HAVEN, CT 06510 Transcription and RNA processing in trypanosomes
R01AI-28799-02 (TMP) NILSEN, TIMOTHY W CASE WESTERN RESERVE UNIV SCHOOL OF MEDICINE CLEVELAND, OHIO 44106 Gene expression in human parasitic nematodes
R01AI-28802-02 (IMB) ROOPENIAN, DERRY C JACKSON LABORATORY 600 MAIN STREET BAR HARBOR, ME 04609-0800 Non H-2 histocompatibility genes and antigens
R01AI-28807-02 (SSS) CANNON, JANNE G UNIVERSITY OF NC AT CHAPEL HIL CB #7290 DEPT OF MICROBIOLOGY CHAPEL HILL, NC 27599 Physical and genetic map of the gonococcal genome
R29AI-28809-02 (ALY) MELLINS, ELIZABETH D UNIVERSITY OF WASHINGTON SEATTLE, WA 98195 Processing of antigens for HLA restricted presentation
R01AI-28824-02 (EVR) NILES, EDWARD G STATE UNIVERSITY OF NEW YORK 3435 MAIN ST BUFFALO, NY 14214 Investigation of the vaccinia virus capping enzyme
R01AI-28825-02 (BM) HORWITZ, MARCUS A UCLA SCHOOL OF MEDICINE 405 HILGARD AVENUE LOS ANGELES, CA 90024 Iron and monocyte activation against a lung pathogen
R55AI-28827-01A2 (ALY) STAVNEZER, JANET M UNIV OF MASSACHUSETTS MED SCH 55 LAKE AVENUE NORTH WORCESTER, MA 01655 Regulation of antibody class switching to igg1 & igg2a
R29AI-28833-01A2 (BM) LIPUMA, JOHN J MEDICAL COLLEGE OF PENNSYLVANI 3300 HENRY AVENUE PHILADELPHIA, PA 19129 Haemophilus influenzae B virulence--Role of haemocin
R01AI-28835-02 (BM) CLEMENTS, JOHN D TULANE UNIVERSITY 1430 TULANE AVENUE NEW ORLEANS, LA 70112 Attenuated mutants of Salmonella as vaccine vectors
R01AI-28836-01A2 (BM) MITCHELL, THOMAS G DUKE UNIVERSITY MEDICAL CENTER BOX 3803 DURHAM, NC 27710 Molecular identification of pathogenic fungi
R01AI-28845-02 (BMT) SESSLER, JONATHAN L UNIVERSITY OF TEXAS AUSTIN, TX 78712 Biomedical applications of "expanded porphyrins"
R29AI-28847-02 (ALY) BISHOP, GAIL A UNIVERSITY OF IOWA IOWA CITY, IA 52242 Regulation of class II mediated B cell differentiation
R01AI-28851-02 (BMT) SHAPLEY, PATRICIA A UNIVERSITY OF ILLINOIS 1209 W CALIFORNIA ST BOX 60-5 URBANA, IL 61801 Reactivity models for isopenicillin-N-synthetase
R01AI-28852-02 (TMP) TELFER, WILLIAM UNIVERSITY OF PENNSYLVANIA PHILADELPHIA, PA 19104-6018 Polarized intercellular bridges in insect oogenesis
R01AI-28855-02 (TMP) SHAPIRO, THERESA A JOHNS HOPKINS UNIVERSITY 725 NORTH WOLFE ST BALTIMORE, MD 21205 Topoisomerase II--Target for anti-trypanosomal therapy
R22AI-28856-02 (BM) MORRIS, J GLENN UNIVERSITY OF MARYLAND 10 S PINE STREET BALTIMORE, MD 21201 Pathogenesis of non-O1 vibrio cholerae
R01AI-28858-01A2 (PBC) MENON, ANANT K ROCKEFELLER UNIVERSITY 1230 YORK AVE NEW YORK, NY 10021 Biosynthesis of membrane protein glycolipid anchors
R29AI-28867-02 (BM) ROOP, ROY M, II UNIV OF ARKANSAS FOR MED SCIS 4301 WEST MARKHAM SLOT 511 LITTLE ROCK, AR 72205-7199 Immunogenicity of recombinant Brucella abortus proteins
R29AI-28871-02 (BM) KIM, JANICE J VETERANS ADMIN MEDICAL CTR, 11 4150 CLEMENT STREET SAN FRANCISCO, CA 94121 Meningococcal lipooligosaccharide epitope expression
R01AI-28873-02 (ARR) WANG, TERESA S STANFORD UNIVERSITY SCHOOL OF MEDICINE STANFORD, CA 94305-5324 Mutational studies of AIDS therapeutic agents
R01AI-28884-01A1 (BM) SMITH, CHARLES J EAST CAROLINA UNIVERSITY SCHOOL OF MEDICINE GREENVILLE, NC 27858 -4354 B. fragilis multiple drug resistance--origin and control
R29AI-28892-02 (IMS) BUDD, RALPH C UNIVERSITY OF VERMONT GIVEN BUILDING BURLINGTON, VT 05405 Applications of the lpr mouse to T cell development
R01AI-28894-01A2 (EVR) BASAK, SUKLA UNIV. OF ALABAMA @ BIRMINGHAM BIRMINGHAM, AL 35294 Receptors and entry process of canine parvovirus
R01AI-28896-02 (IMS) MC DEVITT, HUGH O STANFORD UNIVERSITY D345 FAIRCHILD BUILDING STANFORD, CA 94305 The use of anti-Ia antisera in murine systemic lupus
R01AI-28899-02 (IMS) SCHWARTZ, ROBERT S NEW ENGLAND MED CTR 750 WASHINGTON STREET, BOX 245 BOSTON, MA 02111 Induction of autoimmunity with idiotypes
R01AI-28900-02 (VR) LEVY, DAVID E NEW YORK UNIVERSITY MEDICAL CT 550 FIRST AVENUE NEW YORK, NY 10016 Signal transduction pathway in IFN induced transcription
R01AI-28903-01A2 (ARRD) PATONAY, GABOR GEORGIA STATE UNIVERSITY UNIVERSITY PLAZA ATLANTA, GA 30303 NIR dyes as labels for immunoassays in AIDS and other infectious diseases
R29AI-28905-02 (ARR) DE GRUTTOLA, VICTOR HARVARD SCH OF PUBLIC HLTH 677 HUNTINGTON AVE BOSTON, MA 02115 Statistical modeling of progression of HIV infection
R01AI-28907-02 (IMS) GLIMCHER, LAURIE H HARVARD SCH OF PUBLIC HEALTH 665 HUNTINGTON AVENUE BOSTON, MA 02115 Interferon-gamma control of MHC genes in autoimmunity
R01AI-28923-02 (IMB) KAPLAN, DAVID R CASE WESTERN RESERVE UNIVERSIT 2085 ADELBERT ROAD CLEVELAND, OH 44106 Transfection of human T cell clones
R29AI-28927-02 (BM) HATFULL, GRAHAM F UNIVERSITY OF PITTSBURGH PITTSBURGH, PA 15260 Molecular biology of mycobacteria and their phages
R01AI-28928-02 (ARR) SEGREST, JERE P UNIV OF ALABAMA 1808 7TH AVENUE, SOUTH BIRMINGHAM, AL 35294 Amphipathic helixes, HDL, and HIV infectivity
R01AI-28931-02 (ALY) BJORKMAN, PAMELA J CALIFORNIA INST OF TECHNOLOGY 1201 E CALIFORNIA BLVD PASADENA, CA 91125 Characterization of peptide binding properties of HLA
R29AI-28943-02 (BM) WARREN, H SHAW MASSACHUSETTS GENERAL HOSPITAL INFECTIOUS DISEASES UNIT BOSTON, MA 02114 Mechanisms of endotoxin neutralization by antisera
R01AI-28944-02 (BM) BESSEN, DEBRA E ROCKEFELLER UNIVERSITY 1230 YORK AVE, BOX 276 NEW YORK, NY 10021-6399 Molecular properties of class I and II streptococci
R29AI-28950-02 (BM) KEATH, ELIZABETH J ST. LOUIS UNIVERSITY 221 NORTH GRAND BLVD ST. LOUIS, MO 63103 Virulence determinants in histoplasma capsulatum
R29AI-28954-02 (SB) PRUETT, TIMOTHY L UNVI OF VA HLTH SCI CTR BOX 181 CHARLOTTESVILLE, VA 22908 E coli virulence traits in intraabdominal infection
R01AI-28962-01A1 (TMP) BACIC, ANTONY UNIVERSITY OF MELBOURNE PARKVILLE, VIC, AUSTRALIA 305 Leishmania glycolipids--Structure and funtion
R01AI-28971-02 (VR) MARATOS-FLIER, ELEFTHERIA JOSLIN DIABETES CENTER ONE JOSLIN PLACE BOSTON, MA 02215 Molecular characterization of the reovirus receptor
R01AI-28973-02 (ALY) BRENNER, MICHAEL B DANA-FARBER CANCER INSTITUTE 44 BINNEY STREET, MAYER 640 BOSTON, MA 02115 T lympohocyte recognition
R01AI-28975-01A2 (TMP) NAIR, RAMACHANDRAN M S HERBERT H LEHMAN COLLEGE OF CU BRONX, NY 10468-1589 Production of artemesinin by cell cultures
R01AI-28993-02 (EI) LE, JUNMING NEW YORK UNIVERSITY MEDICAL CT 550 FIRST AVE NEW YORK, NY 10016 Synthesis and roles of TNF and IL-6 in T cell activation
R29AI-28995-02 (SSS) NEUHAUS, JOHN M UNIVERSITY OF CALIFORNIA 1699-HSW SAN FRANCISCO, CA 94143 Methods for longitudinal and clustered binary data
R22AI-29000-02 (TMP) BEIER, JOHN C JOHNS HOPKINS UNIVERSITY DEPT. OF IMMUN. & INFECT. DIS. BALTIMORE, MD 21205 Anopheles vector potential for malaria transmission
R01AI-29001-02 (TMP) REED, NORMAN D MONTANA STATE UNIVERSITY BOZEMAN, MONTANA 59717 Different imbalances of cytokines in nematode infections
R29AI-29002-02 (SAT) SEDMAK, DANIEL D OHIO STATE UNIVERSITY 4170 GRAVES HALL, 333 W 10TH A COLUMBUS, OH 43210 Virus-endothelial interactions in organ transplantation
R29AI-29003-02 (ALY) SANZ, IGNACIO UNIV OF TEXAS HEALTH SCI CTR 7703 FLOYD CURL DRIVE SAN ANTONIO, TX 78284 Genetics and mechanisms of diversity of human DH gene segments
R29AI-29004-02 (SSS) TSAI, WEI-YANN COLUMBIA UNIV SCH OF PUBLIC HL 600 WEST 168TH ST, 5TH FLOOR NEW YORK, NY 10032-3799 Statistical inference for incomplete survival data
R01AI-29008-02 (BM) VOLKMAN, DAVID J SUNY AT STONY BROOK STONY BROOK, NY 11794-8161 Human lyme borreliosis--Coordinate T and B cell responses
R29AI-29009-03 (VR) DORSKY, DAVID I UNIV OF CONNECTICUT HEALTH CTR FARMINGTON, CT 06032 Structure and function of the HSV DNA polymerase
R01AI-29026-02 (EVR) COURTNEY, RICHARD J PENNSYLVANIA STATE UNIVERSITY P.O. BOX 850 HERSHEY, PA 17033 Virion-associated immediate early proteins of HSV-1
R01AI-29027-01A1 (VR) MOREL, PENELOPE A PITTSBURGH CANCER INSTITUTE 3343 FORBES AVENUE PITTSBURGH, PA 15213 Genetics of human T cell response to cytomegalovirus
R01AI-29040-02 (BM) LEE, JEAN C CHANNING LABORATORY 180 LONGWOOD AVENUE BOSTON, MA 02115 Genetic analysis of S. aureus capsule production
R01AI-29042-02 (IMB) ERLICH, HENRY A CETUS CORPORATION 1400 FIFTY-THIRD STREET EMERYVILLE, CA 94608 HLA-DP sequence polymorphism and autoimmunity
R29AI-29064-02 (BM) BROWN, MARY B UNIVERSITY OF FLORIDA BOX J-137 JHMHC GAINESVILLE, FL 32610 IgA Fc receptors on mycoplasmas and impact on disease
R01AI-29088-02 (EI) FENTON, MATTHEW J UNIVERSITY HOSPITAL 88 EAST NEWTON ST BOSTON, MA 02118 Early events in accessory cell activation
R01AI-29092-03 (TMP) DEAN, DONALD H THE OHIO STATE UNIVERSITY 484 WEST TWELFTH AVENUE COLUMBUS, OH 43210-1292 Functional domains of bacillus thuringiensis endotoxin
R01AI-29102-02 (TMP) KRESINA, THOMAS F MIRIAM HOSPITAL 164 SUMMIT AVENUE PROVINDENCE, RI 02906 Molecular modulation of murine

schistosomiasis
R01AI-29103-02 (PTHA) MARTIN, THOMAS R SEATTLE VA MEDICAL CENTER 1660 S COLUMBIAN WAY SEATTLE, WA 98108 Alveolar macrophage-derived neutrophil chemoattractant
R01AI-29107-03 (ARR) CHEN, IRVIN S UNIVERSITY OF CALIFORNIA 10833 LE CONTE AVENUE LOS ANGELES, CA 90024-1678 Primary cell systems for the study of HIV-l latency
R01AI-29110-02 (PTHA) SHERRY, BARBARA A THE ROCKEFELLER UNIVERSITY 1230 YORK AVE NEW YORK, NY 10021-6399 Biochemistry and function of four novel monokines
R29AI-29113-02 (ARR) GREGERSEN, PETER K NORTH SHORE UNIVERSITY HOSPITA 300 COMMUNITY DRIVE MANHASSET, NY 10030 Regulation of immunity to HIV by HLA class II genes
R01AI-29117-03 (ARR) GREENE, WARNER C DUKE UNIVERSITY MEDICAL CENTER PO BOX 3037 DURHAM, NC 27710 Inhibition of HIV-1 growth by transcriptional silencer proteins
R01AI-29119-02 (ARR) LAURENCE, JEFFREY C CORNELL UNIV MEDICAL COLLEGE 1300 YORK AVENUE NEW YORK, NY 10021 Block of HIV induction by hormone-enhancer interactions
R01AI-29121-01A2 (ARRC) BINA, MINOU PURDUE UNIVERSITY BROWN BUILDING WEST LAFAYETTE, IN 47907 Regulation of HIV-1 gene expression
R01AI-29125-03 (ARR) KOHN, DONALD B CHILDRENS HOSPITAL LOS ANGELES 4650 SUNSET BLVD LOS ANGELES, CA 90027 Retroviral vector-mediated transfer of nef gene to inhib
R01AI-29131-03 (ARR) WEI, LEE-JEN HARVARD SCHOOL OF PUBLIC HEALT BOSTON, MA 02115 Statistical problems in AIDS studies
R01AI-29133-03 (ARR) AU, JESSIE L OHIO STATE UNIVERSITY 500 WEST 12TH AVENUE COLUMBUS, OH 43210 Pharmacology of dideoxynucleosides in small intestinal Epithelium
R01AI-29135-03 (ARR) FRANKEL, ALAN D WHITEHEAD INST/BIOMED RESEARCH NINE CAMBRIDGE CENTER CAMBRIDGE, MA 02142 Activity and inhibition of the tat protein from HIV
R01AI-29151-03 (ARR) CARSON, DENNIS A UNIV OF CALIFORNIA, SAN DIEGO 9500 GILMAN DRIVE LA JOLLA, CA 92093-0945 Nucleotide metabolism in lymphocytes and macrophages
R01AI-29153-03 (ARR) CHAN, THOMAS C PURDUE UNIVERSITY WEST LAFAYETTE, IN 47907 Potentiation of anti-viral nucleoside by pharmacologic entrapment
R01AI-29155-03 (ARR) AGARWAL, RAM P UNIVERSITY OF MIAMI SCH OF MED 1550 NW 10TH AVE (R-71) MIAMI, FL 33136 Mechanisms of selective actions of antiviral agents
R01AI-29157-03 (ARR) PARKER, WILLIAM B SOUTHERN RESEARCH INSTITUTE PO BOX 55305 BIRMINGHAM, AL 35255-5305 Molecular interactions of carbovir, AZT, and interferon
R01AI-29158-03 (ARR) LEE, MARIETTA Y UNIVERSITY OF MIAMI PO BOX 016960 MIAMI, FL 33101 Inhibition of human DNA polymerases by antiviral drugs
R01AI-29162-03 (ARR) JEWELL, NICHOLAS P UNIVERSITY OF CALIFORNIA 367 EVANS HALL BERKELEY, CA 94720 Statistical methodology in the natural history of AIDS
R01AI-29163-03 (ARR) MARKHAM, RICHARD B JOHNS HOPKINS UNIVERSITY 615 NORTH WOLFE STREET BALTIMORE, MD 21205 Use of SCID-human mice as a model for AIDS therapy
R01AI-29164-03 (ARR) RICHMAN, DOUGLAS D VA MEDICAL CENTER 3550 LA JOLLA VILLAGE DRIVE SAN DIEGO, CA 92161 Mechanisms of resistance in clinical isolates of HIV
R01AI-29167-03 (ARR) GAYNOR, RICHARD B UNIVERSITY OF TEXAS 5323 HARRY HINES BLVD DALLAS, TX 75235-9030 Cellular and viral proteins involved in HIV mRNA regulation
R01AI-29168-03 (ARR) FLEMING, THOMAS R UNIVERSITY OF WASHINGTON SEATTLE, WA 98195 Statisical issues in AIDS research
R01AI-29173-03 (ARR) CRUMPACKER, CLYDE S, II BETH ISRAEL HOSPITAL 330 BROOKLINE AVENUE BOSTON, MA 02215 Resistance of HIV to drugs in patients and in cloned RT genes
R01AI-29179-03 (ARR) NABEL, GARY J UNIV OF MICHIGAN MEDICAL CENTE 1150 WEST MEDICAL CENTER DRIVE ANN ARBOR, MI 48109-0650 Definition and regulation of cellular genes which control HIV transcription
R01AI-29182-03 (ARR) MOSIER, DONALD E MEDICAL BIOLOGY INSTITUTE 11077 NORTH TORREY PINES ROAD LA JOLLA, CA 92037 HIV-infected hu-SCID mice as models for AIDS therapy
R01AI-29184-03 (ARR) DUBIN, NEIL I NEW YORK UNIVERSITY MEDICAL CT 341 EAST 25TH STREET NEW YORK, NY 10010-2598 Modelling HIV latency using immunologic measures
R01AI-29193-02 (ARR) D'AQUILA, RICHARD T MASSACHUSETTS GENERAL HOSP 149 13TH STREET CHARLESTOWN, MA 02129 Nucleoside resistance of the HIV-1 reverse transcriptase
R01AI-29196-02 (ARR) TAYLOR, JEREMY M UNIV OF CALIF SCH OF PUBLIC HL 405 HILGARD AVENUE LOS ANGELES, CA 90024-1772 Statistical methods in AIDS research
R01AI-29197-03 (ARR) WANG, MEI-CHENG JOHNS HOPKINS UNIVERSITY 615 NORTH WOLFE STREET BALTIMORE, MD 21205 Statistical methods for AIDS prevalent cohort data
R01AI-29200-01A1 (ARRC) CHINNADURAI, GOVINDASWAMY ST LOUIS UNIVERSITY MED CTR 3681 PARK AVENUE ST LOUIS, MO 63110 Genetic manipulation of the regulatory circuits of HIV
U01AI-29207-03 (AIDS) YILMA, TILAHUN UNIVERSITY OF CALIFORNIA SCHOOL OF VETERINARY MEDICINE DAVIS, CA 95616 SIV in macaques is a model for AIDS vaccine development
R01AI-29213-02 (BM) MOSER, STEPHEN A JEWISH HOSP/WASH UNIV MED CTR 216 SOUTH KINGSHIGHWAY BLVD ST LOUIS, MO 63110 Blastomyces dermatitidis conidial-macrophage interactions
R44AI-29285-02 (SSS) ANDERSON, NORMAN G LARGE SCALE BIOLOGY CORPORATIO 9620 MEDICAL CENTER DRIVE ROCKVILLE, MD 20850 Automatic parallel peptides synthesizer for AIDS vaccine
R01AI-29306-02 (ARR) SRINIVASAN, ALAGARSAMY WISTAR INSTITUTE 36TH & SPRUCE STREETS PHILADELPHIA, PA 19104 Functional studies with hybrid HIVs
R01AI-29308-02 (ARR) ARLINGHAUS, RALPH B THE UNIVERSITY OF TEXAS DEPT OF MOLECULAR PATHOLOGY HOUSTON, TEX 77030 Selective induction of CTL-mediated immunity against HIV
R29AI-29311-02 (ARR) MOEN, LAURA K OLD DOMINION UNIV RES FOUNDATI NORFOLK, VA 23508-0869 Structure-function aspects of HIV reverse transcriptase
R01AI-29312-02 (ARR) EDMAN, JEFFREY C UNIVERSITY OF CALIFORNIA HORMONE RESEARCH INST SAN FRANCISCO, CA 94143-0534 Molecular biology of Cryptococcus neoformans
R01AI-29313-02 (ARR) PARSLOW, TRISTRAM G UNIVERSITY OF CALIFORNIA, SF4 PARNASSUS CAMPUS SAN FRANCISCO, CA 94143-0506 Function and inhibition of the rev gene product of HIV
R01AI-29314-02 (ARR) WAWER, MARIA J COLUMBIA UNIVERSITY 60 HAVEN AVENUE NEW YORK, NY 10032 HIV dynamics and prevention, Rakai district Uganda
R01AI-29316-02 (ARR) KANESHIRO, EDNA S DEPT-BIOLOGICAL SCIENCES UNIVERSITY OF CINCINNATI CINCINNATI, OH 45221-0006 Characterization of pneumocystis carinii lipids
R44AI-29317-02 (SSS) KALTER, SEYMOUR S VIRUS REFERENCE LAB, INC 7540 LOUIS PASTEUR SAN ANTONIO, TX 78229 Development of viral diagnostic kits
R01AI-29323-03 (ARR) MCCUNE, JOSEPH M SYSTEMIX, INC 3400 WEST BAYSHORE ROAD PALO ALTO, CA 94303 HIV infection in the SCID-hu mouse
R01AI-29324-02 (ARR) FRELINGER, JEFFREY A U N C AT CHAPEL HILL CB# 7290 804 FLOB CHAPEL HILL, NC 27599 Role of HLA class I molecules in the CTL response to HIV
R01AI-29326-01A3 (ARRA) MATTA, KHUSHI L ROSWELL PARK MEMORIAL INSTITUT ELM & CARLTON STREETS BUFFALO, NY 14263 Studies related to the carbohydrate moieties of gp120
R01AI-29327-03 (ARR) GIAM, CHOU-ZEN CASE WESTERN RESERVE UNIV 10900 EUCLID AVENUE CLEVELAND, OH 44106-4984 Mechanism of autocatalysis of HIV protease
R01AI-29328-02 (ARR) GASCON, PEDRO UMDNJ-NEW JERSEY MEDICAL SCHOO 185 SOUTH ORANGE AVENUE NEWARK, NJ 07103-2757 Defective erythropoiesis in AIDS with M. avium complex
R01AI-29329-02 (ARR) ROSSI, JOHN J BECKMAN RESEARCH INSTITUTE 1450 EAST DUARTE ROAD DUARTE, CA 91010 A yeast system for developing anti-HIV-1 ribozymes
R01AI-29331-02 (ARR) JUNE, CARL H NAVAL MEDICAL RESEARCH INST 8901 WISCONSIN AVENUE BETHESDA, MD 20814-5055 Effects of HIV-1 infection on T cell signal transduction
R01AI-29333-02 (ARR) HASELTINE, WILLIAM A DANA-FARBER CANCER INSTITUTE 44 BINNEY STREET BOSTON, MA 02115 Pathogenic provirus of SIVmac
R01AI-29335-02 (ARR) BENDER, STEVEN L UNIVERSITY OF CALIFORNIA IRVINE, CA 92717 Novel DNA analogs for antisense DNA therapy of AIDS
R01AI-29349-02 (ARR) DANCIS, JOSEPH NYU MEDICAL CENTER 550 FIRST AVENUE NEW YORK, NY 10016 Toxicity of AIDS drugs on human placenta
R29AI-29354-02 (ARR) PRATT, KAREN R UNIVERSITY OF VERMONT BURLINGTON, VT 05405 Repression of HIV-1 transcription by DNA methylation
P20AI-29360-02 (SRC) JACKSON, RUDOLPH E MOREHOUSE SCHOOL OF MEDICINE 720 WESTVIEW DR SW ATLANTA, GA 30310 Planning grant for AIDS consortium center
R01AI-29362-02 (ARR) RICCIARDI, ROBERT P WISTAR INSTITUTE 36TH AND SPRUCE STREETS PHILADELPHIA, PA 19104 Inhibiting transactivation of HIV-1
P01AI-29363-02 (SRC) GALLOWAY, DENISE A FRED HUTCHINSON CANCER CENTER 1124 COLUMBIA STREET SEATTLE, WA 98104 Natural history of human papillomavirus (HPV) infections
P01AI-29363-02 0001 (SRC) HOLMES, KING K Natural history of human papillomavirus (HPV) infections Perinatal and childhood transmission of human papillomavirus
P01AI-29363-02 0002 (SRC) KOUTSKY, LAURA ANN Natural history of human papillomavirus (HPV) infections Acquisition and natural history of human papillomavirus (HPV) genital infection
P01AI-29363-02 0003 (SRC) GALLOWAY, DENISE A Natural history of human papillomavirus (HPV) infections Humoral immune response to HPV 6 & 16 infection
P01AI-29363-02 0004 (SRC) MCDOUGALL, JAMES K Natural history of human papillomavirus (HPV) infections Human papillomavirus (HPV) expression in organotype cultures
P01AI-29363-02 9001 (SRC) BECKMANN, ANNA MARIE Natural history of human papillomavirus (HPV) infections Core--Molecular biology
P01AI-29363-02 9002 (SRC) KIVIAT, NANCY Natural history of human papillomavirus (HPV) infections Core--Cytology, histology, and dot blots
P01AI-29363-02 9003 (SRC) FISHER, LLOYD D Natural history of human papillomavirus (HPV) infections Core--Biostatistics
R01AI-29367-02 (VR) HRUBY, DENNIS E OREGON STATE UNIVERSITY CORVALLIS, OR 97331-3804 Proteolytic maturation of vaccinia core polypeptides
R01AI-29372-03 (ARR) SALZMAN, NORMAN P GEORGETOWN UNIVERSITY 3900 RESERVOIR ROAD, NW WASHINGTON, DC 20007 Glycosylation of SIV GP120--Role in the immune response
R01AI-29373-03 (ARR) NEURATH, ALEXANDER R NEW YORK BLOOD CENTER 310 EAST 67TH STREET NEW YORK, NY 10021 Epitope mapping of HIV-1 enhancing antibodies
R01AI-29375-03 (ARR) ENNIS, FRANCIS A UNIVERSITY OF MASSACHUSETTS 55 LAKE AVENUE NORTH WORCESTER, MA 01655 Antibody dependent enhancement of hiv infections
R01AI-29377-01A1 (ARRA) MONTEFIORI, DAVID C VANDERBILT UNIVERSITY RM C-3321 MED CTR NORTH NASHVILLE, TN 37232-2561 Immune responses to glycosylation-modified SIV vaccines
R55AI-29378-01A1 (ARR) NEUTRA, MARIAN R CHILDRENS HOSPITAL 300 LONGWOOD AVENUE BOSTON, MA 02115 Mucosal immune response to HIV envelope glycoproteins
R01AI-29382-03 (ARR) NARAYAN, OPENDRA THE JHU SCHOOL OF MEDICINE 720 RUTLAND AVENUE BALTIMORE, MD 21205 Enhancement of infection in mo with lentiviruses siv hiv
R01AI-29385-01A1 (IMB) MILLER, JACQUES F WALTER & ELIZA HALL INST/MED/R VICTORIA, 3050 AUSTRALIA Tolerance to extra-thymic antigens
R01AI-29390-01A1 (TMP) WIDMER, GIOVANNI CHILDREN'S HOSPITAL 300 LONGWOOD AVE/ENDERS 6 BOSTON, MA 02115 Molecular study of an RNA virus in Leishmania
R01AI-29394-03 (ARR) LEVY, JAY A UNIVERSITY OF CALIFORNIA BOX

0128 SAN FRANCISCO, CA 94143 Enhancing antibodies in HIV infection

R01AI-29395-03 (ARR) SODROSKI, JOSEPH G DANA-FARBER CANCER INSTITUTE 44 BINNEY STREET BOSTON, MA 02115 Role of glycosylation in HIV envelope immunogenicity

R01AI-29398-03 (ARR) MITCHELL, WILLIAM M VANDERBILT UNIVERSITY DEPT OF PATHOLOGY NASHVILLE, TN 37232 Analysis of C'-ADE and FCR-ADE in HIV & SIV infection

R01AI-29407-06 (IMB) DE LUCA, DOMINICK UNIVERSITY OF ARIZONA 1501 N. CAMBELL TUCSON, AZ 85724 Cell interactions in fetal development--Role of interleukin 1

R29AI-29417-03 (GMA) ROMAIN, PAUL L UNIV OF MASSACHUSETTS MED SCH 55 LAKE AVENUE NORTH WORCESTER, MA 01655 Normal and rheumatic disease T cell regulation via CD6

R29AI-29418-03 (EDC) JOHN, A MEREDITH PRINCETON UNIVERSITY PRINCETON, NJ 08544-2091 Infection, immunization and host population dynamics

R01AI-29426-02 (SSS) GANI, JOSEPH M UNIVERSITY OF CALIFORNIA SANTA BARBARA, CA 93106 The spatial spread of epidemics and their control

R01AI-29427-02 (VR) HEARING, PATRICK STATE UNIVERSITY OF NEW YORK STONY BROOK, N Y 11794-8621 Analysis of the hepatitis B virus enhancer region

R29AI-29428-01A1 (IMS) SLATER, JAY E CHILDREN'S NATIONAL MED CENTER 111 MICHIGAN AVENUE, NW WASHINGTON, DC 20010 Studies in rubber allergy and anaphylaxis

R01AI-29430-02 (ARR) LIN, TAI-SHUN YALE UNIVERSITY SCHOOL OF MED P O BOX 3333, 333 CEDAR STREET NEW HAVEN, CT 06510 3'-Deoxynucleoside analogs as potential antiviral agents

R01AI-29432-01A1 (BM) STEPHENS, RICHARD S UNIV OF CALIFORNIA, SAN FRANIS 3RD AVENUE & PARNASSUS STREET SAN FRANCISCO, CA 94143-0412 Microbiology of Chlamydia trachomatis development

R01AI-29433-01A1 (BM) SHERMAN, FRED UNIV OF ROCHESTER SCH-MED&DENY 601 ELMWOOD AVENUE ROCHESTER, NY 14642 Instabilities of the pathogenic yeast Candida albicans

R01AI-29434-02 (TMP) WELLS, MICHAEL A UNIVERSITY OF ARIZONA BIO SCIENCES WEST TUCSON, AZ 85721 Insect storage proteins

R29AI-29455-01A1 (MEDB) PFEFFERKORN, LORRAINE C DARTMOUTH MEDICAL SCHOOL HANOVER, NH 03756 Molecular basis of Fc gamma receptor I signaling

R29AI-29457-01A1 (TMP) SAKANARI, JUDY A UNIVERSITY OF CALIFORNIA SAN FRANCISCO, CA 94143-0506 Characterization of the serine protease from Anisakids

R01AI-29466-01A1 (IMB) SCHUBACH, WILLIAM H STATE UNIVERSITY OF NEW YORK DEPT OF MEDICINE STONY BROOK, NY 11794-8174 Control of expression of the lymphocyte Fc epsilon receptor CD23

R01AI-29470-01A1 (ALY) MORRISON, SHERIE L UNIVERSITY OF CALIFORNIA 405 HILGARD AVE LOS ANGELES, CA 90024-1489 Glycosylation and antibody function

R01AI-29471-02 (BM) LEVINE, MYRON M UNIVERSITY OF MARYLAND 10 S PINE STREET BALTIMORE, MD 21201 Recombinant and live oral Salmonella typhi hybrid vaccines

R01AI-29478-01A1 (TMP) BELLOFATTO, VIVIAN M ROCKEFELLER UNIVERSITY 1230 YORK AVENUE NEW YORK, NY 10021-6399 Analysis of trypanosome mRNA synthesis by gene transfer

R29AI-29485-02 (VR) YEE, JIING-KUAN UNIV OF CALIF, SAN DIEGO LA JOLLA, CA 92093 Properties of an enhancer and the X protein of HBV

R29AI-29487-02 (EVR) AIKEN, JUDD M UNIVERSITY OF WISCONSIN 1655 LINDEN DR MADISON, WI 53706 Mitochondrial involvement in scrapie infection

R01AI-29492-02 (EVR) WOLD, WILLIAM S ST. LOUIS UNIVERSITY 3681 PARK AVE ST LOUIS, MO 63110 RNA processing in adenovirus region E3

R01AI-29507-03 (SRC) MORRISON, DIANE M UNIVERSITY OF WASHINGTON 4101 15TH AVE NE SEATTLE, WA 98195 Understanding the decision to use condoms

R01AI-29508-03 (SRC) HOOK, EDWARD W, III DEPT OF MEDICINE 600 N WOLFE STREET BALTIMORE, MD 21205 Condom use to prevent STDS including AIDS in Baltimore

P01AI-29512-02 (SRC) COWAN, MORTON J UNIVERSITY OF CALIFORNIA THIRD & PARNASSUS AVENUES SAN FRANCISCO, CA 94143-0105 Induction of tolerance in marrow transplantion

P01AI-29512-02 0003 (SRC) HARRISON, MICHAEL R Induction of tolerance in marrow transplantion Marrow transplantation in fetal monkeys

P01AI-29512-02 0004 (SRC) PUROHIT, SARLA Induction of tolerance in marrow transplantion Downregulation of HLA class II antigens by antisense DNA

P01AI-29512-02 9001 (SRC) COWAN, MORTON J Induction of tolerance in marrow transplantion Core--Bone marrow transplant laboratory

P01AI-29512-02 9002 (SRC) COLOMBE, BETH W Induction of tolerance in marrow transplantion Core--Immunogenetics lab

P01AI-29512-02 0001 (SRC) COWEN, MORTON J Induction of tolerance in marrow transplantion Reconstitution and tolerance after haplocompatible BMT

P01AI-29512-02 0002 (SRC) GOLBUS, MITCHELL Induction of tolerance in marrow transplantion Hematopoietic stem cell transplantation in fetal mice

P01AI-29518-02 (SRC) HANSEN, JOHN A FRED HUTCHINSON CANCER RES CTR 1124 COLUMBIA STREET SEATTLE, WA 98104 Immunogenetics of marrow allografting

P01AI-29518-02 0001 (SRC) GERAGHTY, DANIEL Immunogenetics of marrow allografting Polymorphism and transplantation biology of novel HLA class I genes

P01AI-29518-02 0002 (SRC) CHOO, S YOON Immunogenetics of marrow allografting Polymorphism and transplantation biology of HLA-A, B, C antigens

P01AI-29518-02 0003 (SRC) BEATTY, PATRICK G Immunogenetics of marrow allografting Polymorphism and transplantation biology of HLA class II antigens

P01AI-29518-02 0004 (SRC) MARTIN, PAUL Immunogenetics of marrow allografting Induction of nonresponsiveness to alloantigens

P01AI-29518-02 0005 (SRC) ANASETTI, CLAUDIO Immunogenetics of marrow allografting Cellular regulation of alloimmune responses

P01AI-29518-02 9001 (SRC) MARTIN, PAUL Immunogenetics of marrow allografting Core--Cell bank and clinical data base

P01AI-29522-02 (AITC) LEDDY, JOHN P UNIVERSITY OF ROCHESTER 601 ELMWOOD AVENUE, BOX 695 ROCHESTER, NY 14642 Immunologic diseases--Cellular and molecular mechanisms

P01AI-29522-02 0001 (AITC) INSEL, RICHARD A Immunologic diseases--Cellular and molecular mechanisms Primary X-linked immunodeficiency diseases--Molecular analysis of genetic defects

P01AI-29522-02 0002 (AITC) ZWILLICH, SAMUEL H Immunologic diseases--Cellular and molecular mechanisms Seronegative arthritis--Analysis of T lymphocyte specificity

P01AI-29522-02 0003 (AITC) ABRAHAM, GEORGE N Immunologic diseases--Cellular and molecular mechanisms Lymphoproliferative disorders--Human endogenous retrovirus-like sequences

P01AI-29522-02 0004 (AITC) LEDDY, JOHN P Immunologic diseases--Cellular and molecular mechanisms Immune mediated vascular disorders--Properties of platelets and endothelial cells

R01AI-29524-02 (AITC) LANSDORP, PETER M TERRY FOX LABORATORY FOR DIVISION OF HEMATOLOGY VANCOUVER, BC CANADA V5Z 1L3 Activation and proliferation of hematopoietic stem cells

P01AI-29530-02 (SRC) RITZ, JEROME DANA-FARBER CANCER INSTITUTE 44 BINNEY STREET BOSTON, MA 02115 Allogeneic bone marrow transplantation

P01AI-29530-02 0001 (SRC) RITZ, JEROME Allogeneic bone marrow transplantation Allogenic transplantation with CD6 depleted bone marrow

P01AI-29530-02 0002 (SRC) MORIMOTO, CHIKAO Allogeneic bone marrow transplantation Characterization of immunoregulator T cells after allogenic BMT

P01AI-29530-02 0003 (SRC) RITZ, JEROME Allogeneic bone marrow transplantation Mixed chimerism following allogenic bone marrow transplantation

P01AI-29530-02 9001 (SRC) RITZ, JEROME Allogeneic bone marrow transplantation Core--Biostatistics/data management

P01AI-29531-02 (SRC) BLUESTONE, JEFFREY A BEN MAY INSTITUTE 5841 S MARYLAND AVE BOX 424 CHICAGO, IL 60637 Immunomodulation of transplant rejection

P01AI-29531-02 0001 (SRC) BLUESTONE, JEFFREY A Immunomodulation of transplant rejection Immunosuppressive effects of anti-T cell mAbs

P01AI-29531-02 0002 (SRC) FITCH, FRANK W Immunomodulation of transplant rejection Murine T lymphocyte subsets and allograft rejection

P01AI-29531-02 0003 (SRC) STUART, FRANK P Immunomodulation of transplant rejection Immunosuppressive regimens based on anti-human T cell mAbs

P01AI-29531-02 0004 (SRC) THISTLETHWAITE, JAMES R Immunomodulation of transplant rejection The hu-SCID mouse--A model for human allografting

P01AI-29531-02 9001 (SRC) THISTLETHWAITE, JAMES R Immunomodulation of transplant rejection Core--Animal facility

P01AI-29531-02 9002 (SRC) FITCH, FRANK W Immunomodulation of transplant rejection Core--Analytical

R01AI-29533-02 (TMP) NATHANSON, JAMES A MASSACHUSTTS GENERAL HOSPITAL 32 FRUIT STREET BOSTON, MA 02114 Structure of insect neurotransmitter receptors

R01AI-29541-02 (ARR) CHINNDAURAI, GOVINDASWAMY ST LOUIS UNIVERSITY MEDICAL CT 3681 PARK AVE ST LOUIS, MO 63110 Inhibition of HIV gene expression by adenovirus mutants

R01AI-29544-01A1 (IMB) PARKER, DAVID C UNIV OF MASSACHUSETTS MED SCH 55 LAKE AVENUE NORTH WORCESTER, MA 01655 Antigen presentation in acquired tolerance

R01AI-29549-01A1 (BM) HULTGREN, SCOTT J WASHINGTON UNIVERSITY BOX 8093 ST LOUIS, MO 63110 Chaperone-assisted pili assembly in pathogenic E. coli

R29AI-29550-02 (HEM) HARTSHORN, KEVAN L BOSTON UNIV SCH OF MED 80 EAST CONCORD STREET BOSTON, MA 02118 A novel viral probe of neutrophil activation

R01AI-29553-02 (IMB) DUKE, RICHARD C UNIV OF COLORADO HLTH SCI CTR BOX B-175/4200 EAST NINTH AVE DENVER, CO 80262 Self-recognition by T cells

R01AI-29564-01A1 (IMB) TING, JENNY P UNC-LINEBERGER CANCER RES CTR CB# 7295 CHAPEL HILL, NC 27599-7295 Coordinate control of human Ia antigens and Ii chain

R01AI-29566-02 (BM) BUCHMEIER, NANCY A UNIVERSITY OF CALIFORNIA 9500 GILMAN DR LA JOLLA, CA 92093-9125-F Salmonella proteins needed for survival in macrophages

R29AI-29574-02 (ALY) HOGAN, KEVIN T MEDICAL COLLEGE OF WISCONSIN 8701 WATERTOWN PLANK RD MILWAUKEE, WI 53226 Molecular analysis of B and T cell epitopes on HLA-A2

R01AI-29575-01A1 (IMB) SCHNECK, JONATHAN P JOHNS HOPKINS ASTHMA/ALLERGY C 5501 HOPKINS BAYVIEW CIRCLE BALTIMORE, MD 21224 Immunoregulatory functions of class I molecules

R01AI-29576-02 (ALY) CLARKE, STEPHEN H UNIV OF N.C. AT CHAPEL HILL CB# 7290 CHAPEL HILL, NC 27599 Variable region gene repertoire of Ly-1 B cells

R01AI-29579-02 (EVR) DOHERTY, PETER C ST JUDE CHILDREN'S RESERCH HOS 332 N LAUDERDALE/PO BOX 318 MEMPHIS, TN 38101 Cell-mediated immunity in influenza

R15AI-29591-01A1 (TMP) JARROLL, EDWARD L CLEVELAND STATE UNIVERSITY 1983 E 24TH ST CLEVELAND, OH 44115 Synthesis of N-acetylgalactosamine in encysting Giardia

R01AI-29595-02 (BM) LEHRER, ROBERT I UCLA SCHOOL OF MEDICINE CENTER FOR HEALTH SCIENCES LOS ANGELES, CA 90024-1406 Gastrointestinal and myeloid defensins

R01AI-29599-02 (EVR) KAWAOKA, YOSHIHIRO ST JUDE CHILDREN'S RES HOSPITA 332 NORTH LAUDERDALE, PO BOX 3 MEMPHIS, TN 38101 Molecular pathogenesis of influenza

R01AI-29606-02 (EVR) PEEPLES, MARK E RUSH-PRES-ST LUKE'S MEDICAL CT 1653 WEST CONGRESS PARKWAY CHICAGO, IL 60612 NDV M protein: virion assembly and nuclear location

R01AI-29609-02 (BM) KOBAYASHI, GEORGE S WASHINGTON UNIV SCHOOL OF MED 660 SOUTH EUCLILD AVE/BX 8051 ST LOUIS, MO 63110 Dimorphism and virulence in histoplasma capsulatum

R01AI-29611-01A1 (BM) STULL, TERRENCE L MED COLL OF PENNSYLVANIA

3300 HENRY AVENUE PHILADELPHIA, PA 19129 H. influenzae-- Mutagenesis and hydroxamate production
R01AI-29619-02 (BM) PORTNOY, DANIEL A UNIV OF PENNSYLVANIA MED SCH PHILADELPHIA, PA 19104-6076 Molecular biology of listeria-host cell interaction
R01AI-29623-01A1 (BM) AMBROSINO, DONNA M DANA-FARBER CANCER INSTITUTE 44 BINNEY STREET BOSTON, MA 02115 B cell and T cell responses to polysaccharides
R15AI-29627-01A1 (BM) VANDENBOSCH, JAMES L EASTERN MICHIGAN UNIVERSITY 316 MARK JEFFERSON YPSILANTI, MI 48197 Thermoregulation of serum-resistance in Salmonella typhimurium
R01AI-29646-02 (TMP) BEVERLEY, STEPHEN M HARVARD MEDICAL SCHOOL 240 LONGWOOD AVENUE BOSTON, MA 02115 Molecular genetics of Leishmania using DNA transfection
R29AI-29648-03 (EDC) REED, BARBARA D UNIVERSITY OF MICHIGAN 1018 FULLER, BOX 0708 ANN ARBOR, MI 48109-0708 Epidemiology of recurrent candida vulvovaginitis
R01AI-29650-02 (SAT) GOZZO, JAMES J NORTHEASTERN UNIVERSITY 360 HUNTINGTON AVENUE BOSTON, MA 02115 Tolerance to allografts induced with neonatal tissue
R01AI-29654-01A1 (PTHA) KIER, ANN B UNIVERSITY OF CINCINNATI MED C 231 BETHESDA AVENUE CINCINNATI, OH 45267-0529 Inflammatory response of the local Shwartzman reaction
R01AI-29657-01A1 (EI) HEAGY, WYRTA DANA-FARBER CANCER INSTITUTE 44 BINNEY STREET BOSTON, MA 02115 Opioids and opiates-- T cell motility
R01AI-29672-01A2 (IMB) FEENEY, ANN J MEDICAL BIOLOGY INSTITUTE 11077 NORTH TORREY PINES RD LA JOLLA, CA 92037 Analysis of junctional diversity in B and T cells
R01AI-29673-02 (ALY) LEIDEN, JEFFREY M MEDICAL SCIENCE RES BLDG I 1150 W MEDICAL CENTER DRIVE ANN ARBOR, MI 48109-0650 Transcriptional control of human T cell receptor genes
R29AI-29676-02 (BM) STEELE, PAUL E UNIVERSITY OF CINCINNATI 231 BETHESDA AVENUE CINCINNATI, OH 45267-0529 Histoplasma capsulatum genome structure and manipulation
R01AI-29680-02 (EDC) WEBSTER, ROBERT G ST JUDE CHILDREN'S RES HOSP 332 NORTH LAUDERDALE/BOX 318 MEMPHIS, TN 38101 Molecular epidemiology of pandemic influenza
R01AI-29681-01A1 (VR) BURKE, RAE L CHIRON CORPORATION 4560 HORTON STREET EMERYVILLE, CA 94608 Cellular immune response to genital herpes infection
R15AI-29683-01A1 (VR) BOYD, KENNETH R DUQUESNE UNIVERSITY PITTSBURGH, PA 15282 Molecular and genetic studies of Flanders virus
R01AI-29687-02 (EVR) STANBERRY, LAWRENCE R CHILDREN'S HOSPITAL RES FDN ELLAND AND BETHESDA AVENUE CINCINNATI, OHIO 45229 -2899 Molecular analysis of neuronal HSV latency/reactivation
R01AI-29689-02 (IMS) LO, DAVID SCRIPPS CLINIC & RESEARCH FNDN 10666 N TORREY PINES ROAD LA JOLLA, CA 92037 Immunological tolerance in transgenic mice
R01AI-29690-02 (IMS) ROTHSTEIN, THOMAS L UNIVERSITY HOSPITAL 88 E. NEWTON ROAD BOSTON, MA 02118 Phorbol ester responsive B lymphocytes
R01AI-29691-02 (ARR) SCOTT, DAVID W U OF ROCHESTER SCH OF MED & DE BOX 704/601 ELMWOOD AVENUE ROCHESTER, NY 14642 Regulation of specific B cell responses
R29AI-29693-03 (TMP) UNNASCH, THOMAS R UAB, DEPT OF MED, MLB, 2ND FL DIV OF GEOGRAPHIC MEDICINE BIRMINGHAM, AL 35294 Identification of O volvulus protective epitopes
R01AI-29704-02 (EI) GELFAND, ERWIN W NATIONAL JEWISH CENTER 1400 JACKSON STREET DENVER, CO 80206 Activation and transformation of human B cells by EB virus
R01AI-29719-02 (SRC) ISBERG, RALPH R TUFTS UNIVERSITY 136 HARRISON AVENUE BOSTON, MA 02111 Cellular entry and adhesion of Borrelia burgdorferi
R01AI-29724-02 (SRC) SPIELMAN, ANDREW HARVARD SCHOOL OF PUBLIC HLTH 665 HUNTINGTON AVENUE BOSTON, MA 02115 Mechanism of transmission of the agent of Lyme disease
R01AI-29731-02 (SRC) BARBOUR, ALAN G UNIV OF TEXAS HLTH SCI CTR 7703 FLOYD CURL DRIVE SAN ANTONIO, TX 78284 Genetic diversity and pathogenicity of Borrelia burgdorferi
R01AI-29733-02 (SRC) LOVETT, MICHAEL A UNIV OF CALIFORNIA, LOS ANGELE LOS ANGELES, CA 90024-1747 Pathogenic mechanisms in lyme borreliosis
R01AI-29735-02 (SRC) NORGARD, MICHAEL V UNIV OF TEXAS SW MED CENTER 5323 HARRY HINES BOULEVARD DALLAS, TX 75235 Membrane proteins of Borrelia burgdorferi
R01AI-29739-02 (SRC) JOHNSON, RUSSELL C UNIVERSITY OF MINNESOTA 420 DELAWARE STREET, S.E. MINNEAPOLIS, MN 55455 Antigenic and immunogenic components of Borrelia burgdorferi
R01AI-29740-03 (IMS) RAVECHE', ELIZABETH S UMDNJ-NEW JERSEY MED SCHOOL 185 SOUTH ORANGE AVENUE NEWARK, NJ 07103-2714 Immunoregulation by unique autoimmune Ly1+B cells
R29AI-29742-02 (ALY) VIK, DENNIS P SCRIPPS CLN & RESEARCH FDN 10666 NORTH TORREY PINES ROAD LA JOLLA, CA 92037 Structure and regulation of murine complement factor H
R01AI-29743-02 (SRC) CHARON, NYLES W WEST VIRGINIA UNIVERSITY 2095 HEALTH SCIENCES NORTH MORGANTOWN, WV 26506 An analysis of Borrelia burgdorferi motility
R01AI-29746-03 (TMP) JAMES, ANTHONY A UNIVERSITY OF CALIFORNIA IRVINE, CA 92717 Expression of exogenous genes in vector mosquitoes
R01AI-29747-01A1 (TMP) WITTNER, MURRAY ALBERT EINSTEIN COLL OF MED 1300 MORRIS PARK AVENUE BRONX, NY 10461 Pathogenesis of Trypanosoma cruzi induced cardiomyopathy
R01AI-29751-01A1 (PBC) VAN HALBEEK, HERMAN UNIVERSITY OF GEORGIA 220 RIVERBEND ROAD ATHENS, GA 30602 Trypanosome variant surface glycoprotein carbohydrates
R43AI-29772-01A1 (SSS) USINGER, WILLIAM R IMMUSINE, INC 1933 DAVIS ST SAN LEANDRO, CA 94577 Development of bacterial polysaccharide as an adjuvant
R43AI-29778-01A1 (SSS) LOEFFLER, HERBERT H LOEFFLER-MACONKEY, INC 26 DUDLEY STREET ARLINGTON, MA 02174 An automated slide stainer for molecular probes
P01AI-29796-06 (DDK) STROBER, SAMUEL STANFORD UNIV MED CTR MEDICINE/IMMUNOLOGY STANFORD, CA 94305-5111 Use of hybridomas and T cell clones in transplantation
P01AI-29796-06 0001 (DDK) STROBER, SAMUEL Use of hybridomas and T cell clones in transplantation Clinical trial--Renal transplantation
P01AI-29796-06 0002 (DDK) FATHMAN, C GARRISON Use of hybridomas and T cell clones in transplantation Anti-CD4 tolerance in rodents
P01AI-29796-06 0003 (DDK) HALL, BRUCE Use of hybridomas and T cell clones in transplantation Mechanisms of tolerance in rodents
P01AI-29796-06 0004 (DDK) GRUMET, CARL Use of hybridomas and T cell clones in transplantation Tolerance to soluble antigens
P01AI-29796-06 0005 (DDK) FATHMAN, C GARRISON Use of hybridomas and T cell clones in transplantation Anti-CD4 primate tolerance
P01AI-29796-06 0006 (DDK) ENGLEMAN, EDGAR Use of hybridomas and T cell clones in transplantation Antibodies to suppressor T cells
P01AI-29796-06 9001 (DDK) STROBER, SAMUEL Use of hybridomas and T cell clones in transplantation Core--Flow cytometry
P01AI-29796-06 9002 (DDK) STROBER, SAMUEL Use of hybridomas and T cell clones in transplantation Core--Immune monitoring
P01AI-29796-06 9003 (DDK) HALL, BRUCE Use of hybridomas and T cell clones in transplantation Core--Immunopathology
R01AI-29797-02 (ARR) RUPRECHT, RUTH M DANA-FARBER CANCER INSTITUTE 44 BINNEY STREET BOSTON, MA 02115 Isolation and characterization of rodent lentiviruses
R01AI-29799-02 (ARR) CARDIFF, ROBERT D UNIVERSITY OF CALIFORNIA DAVIS, CA 95616 Murine immunodeficiency lentivirus model for AIDS
R01AI-29800-02 (ARR) SAGE, RICHARD D UNIVERSITY OF MISSOURI 102 TUCKER HALL COLUMBIA, MO 65211 A search for murine immunodeficiency lentiviruses
R01AI-29802-03 (AITC) BEVAN, MICHAEL J UNIVERSITY OF WASHINGTON SEATTLE, WASHINGTON 98195 Repertoire of class I restricted T cells
R01AI-29810-02 (ARR) CROWLE, ALFRED J UNIV OF COLORADO HLTH SCI CTR 4200 EAST NINTH AVENUE DENVER, CO 80262 Defects in native anti-m avium immunity in AIDS
R01AI-29816-02 (ARR) KING, JAMES C UNIVERSITY OF MARYLAND 700 WEST LOMBARD ST, 2ND FLOOR BALTIMORE, MD 21201 Respiratory viral infection in HIV infected children
R01AI-29819-02 (ARR) GOODCHILD, JOHN WORCESTER FDN/EXPERIMENTAL BIO 222 MAPLE AVENUE SHREWSBURY, MA 01545 Ribozymes as inhibitors of HIV replication
R01AI-29821-02 (ARR) CULLEN, BRYAN R DUKE UNIVERSITY MEDICAL CENTER BOX 3025 DURHAM, NC 27710 Trans-dominant mutant repressors of HIV-1 replication
R01AI-29825-02 (ARR) PUTNEY, SCOTT D REPLIGEN CORPORATION ONE KENDALL SQUARE CAMBRIDGE, MA 02139 Neutralization resistant variants of HIV
R43AI-29829-01A1 (SSS) CASTOR, TREVOR P BIO-ENG, INC 216 SYLVIA STREET ARLINGTON, MA 02174 Biphasic aqueous polymer fractionation of lymphokines
R01AI-29833-02 (ARR) HARPER, JEFFREY W BAYLOR COLLEGE OF MEDICINE ONE BAYLOR PLAZA HOUSTON, TX 77030 Inhibition of TAR-mediated HIV trans-activation
R01AI-29834-02 (ARR) BONHOMME, FRANCOIS S UNIVERSITE MONTPELLIER II 34095 MONTPELLIER CEDEX 05 FRANCE Survey of immunodeficiency lentiviruses in wild mice
R01AI-29839-01A1 (ARRC) CUSHION, MELANIE T UC COLLEGE OF MEDICINE 231 BETHESDA AVENUE CINCINNATI, OH 45267-0560 Transmission of pneumocystis infection
R01AI-29842-02 (ARR) NAIR, VASU UNIVERSITY OF IOWA IOWA CITY, IA 52242 Potential synergistic inhibitors of HIV infectivity
R01AI-29847-02 (ARR) TENEN, DANIEL G BETH ISRAEL HOSPITAL 330 BROOKLINE AVE BOSTON, MA 02215 Development of anti-HIV vectors in monocytes/macrophages
R01AI-29848-03 (ARR) EL KOUNI, MAHMOUD HAMDI UNIVERSITY OF ALABAMA UAB STATION BOX 402 BIRMINGHAM, AL 35394 Purine analogue metabolism in toxoplasma gondii
R01AI-29850-02 (ARR) ORGEL, LESLIE E SALK INST/BIOLOGICAL STUDIES PO BOX 85800 SAN DIEGO, CA 92138 HIV inhibition by cross linking antisense RNA via platinum
R01AI-29852-02 (ARR) WEINHOLD, KENT J DUKE UNIVERSITY MEDICAL CENTER PO BOX 2926 DURHAM, NC 27710 Characterization of anti HIV-1 cellular cytotoxicities
R01AI-29855-02 (ARR) RINGLER, DOUGLAS J ONE PINE HILL DR SOUTHBOROUGH, MA 01772 Consequences of SIV infection of macrophages
R01AI-29856-01A1 (ARRC) EDWARDS, CYNTHIA A GENELABS, INC 505 PENOBSCOT DRIVE REDWOOD CITY, CA 94063 Characterization of a putative HIV-1 regulatory protein
R01AI-29857-02 (ARR) MAYER, CECILIA C UNIVERSITY OF CALIFORNIA BOX 0128 SN FRANCISCO, CA 94143 Structure/function relationships of HIV-1
R01AI-29869-02 (ARR) HOFFMANN, MICHAEL K NEW YORK MEDICAL COLLEGE VALHALLA, NY 10595 CD4-mediated immune suppression in AIDS
R01AI-29870-02 (ARR) HAMPEL, ARNOLD E NORTHERN ILLINOIS UNIVERSITY DEKALB, IL 60115 The "hairpin" catalytic RNA--characterization and application
R01AI-29871-01A2 (ARRE) ROSENSTREICH, DAVID L ALBERT EINSTEIN COLLEGE OF MED 1300 MORRIS PARK AVENUE BRONX, NY 10461 Sinusitis in human immunodeficiency virus disease
R01AI-29873-02 (ARR) HASELTINE, WILLIAM A DANA-FARBER CANCER INSTITUTE 44 BINNEY STREET BOSTON, MA 02115 Molecular biology of HIV-1 capsid proteins
R01AI-29876-02 (ARR) KOOPMAN, JAMES S UNIVERSITY OF MICHIGAN 109 OBSERVATORY STREET ANN ARBOR, MI 48109-2029 Assessment of HIV transmission risks and patterns
R01AI-29880-02 (ARR) REMOLD-O'DONNELL, EILEEN CENTER FOR BLOOD RESEARCH 800 HUNTINGTON AVENUE BOSTON, MA 02115 Role of macrophage sialophorin (CD43) in HIV defense
R01AI-29882-01A2 (ARRE) LEECH, JAMES H SAN FRANCISCO GENERAL HOSPITAL 1001 POTRERO STREET SAN FRANCISCO, CA 94110 Molecular biology of cryptosporidium
R01AI-29886-02 (ARR) NELSON, RICHARD G SAN FRANCISCO GENERAL HOSPITAL 1001 POTRERO AVE SAN FRANCISCO, CA 94110 Cryptosporidium dihydrofolate reductase as a chemotherapeutic target
R01AI-29889-02 (ARR) WONG-STAAL, FLOSSIE UNIV OF CALIFORNIA,

SAN DIEGO LA JOLLA, CA 92093-0613 In vivo and in vitro parameters of HIV-2 pathogenicity
R01AI-29892-02 (ARR) BURKE, JOHN M UNIVERSITY OF VERMONT BURLINGTON, VT 05405 Construction and optimization of anti-HIV ribozymes
R01AI-29893-03 (ARR) HUANG, LEAF UNIVERSITY OF PITTSBURGH W1351 BIOMEDICAL SCIENCE TOWER PITTSBURGH, PA 15261 Targeted gene therapies for AIDS
R29AI-29894-02 (ARR) O' BRIEN, WILLIAM A UCLA SCHOOL OF MEDICINE LOS ANGELES, CA 90024 Cellular tropism of a brain-derived HIV-1 isolate
R01AI-29895-02 (ARR) BURTON, JAMES A LABORATORY OF RATIONAL DRUG 88 EAST NEWTON STREET BOSTON, MA 02118 Design and synthesis of inhibitors of HIV-1 protease
R01AI-29900-01A2 (ARRD) PARKER, KATHLYN A BROWN UNIVERSITY PROVIDENCE, RI 02912 Synthesis of compounds with anti-HIV activity
R01AI-29902-02 (ARR) FLAVELL, RICHARD A YALE UNIVERSITY PO BOX 3333 NEW HAVEN, CT 06510-8023 Novel autoimmunity in AIDS related immunodeficiency
P01AI-29903-02 (SRC) CAMBIER, JOHN C NATL JEWISH CTR/IMMUN & RESP M 1400 JACKSON ST DENVER, CO 80206 Molecular basis of HIV induced immune suppression
P01AI-29903-02 0001 (SRC) CAMBIER, JOHN C Molecular basis of HIV induced immune suppression GP120 induced CD4 modulation of antigen receptor function
P01AI-29903-02 0002 (SRC) POTTER, TERRY A Molecular basis of HIV induced immune suppression CDF function in physiologic activation of T cells
P01AI-29903-02 0003 (SRC) MARRACK, PHILIPPA C Molecular basis of HIV induced immune suppression Effects of HIV gp120 on thymocyte maturation
P01AI-29903-02 0004 (SRC) CAMPBELL, PRISCILL A Molecular basis of HIV induced immune suppression Effects of GP120 and GP41 on macrophage function
P01AI-29903-02 9001 (SRC) CAMBIER, JOHN C Molecular basis of HIV induced immune suppression Core--Cytometry and reagents
R01AI-29904-02 (ARR) ROSOWSKY, ANDRE DANA-FARBER CANCER INSTITUTE 44 BINNEY STREET BOSTON, MASS 02115 Lipophilic antifolates and AIDS opportunistic infections
R01AI-29905-01A1 (ARRD) SIMPSON, MELVIN V SUNY AT STONY BROOK STONY BROOK, N Y 11794-5215 AZT toxicity and mitochondrial DNA replication in AIDS
R01AI-29906-02 (ARR) GEHA, RAIF S CHILDRENS HOSPITAL 300 LONGWOOD AVE BOSTON, MA 02115 T cell signalling in maternally acquired HIV infection
R29AI-29908-01A1 (ARRA) NOKTA, MOSTAFA A UNIV OF TEXAS MEDICAL BRANCH RT H82 GALVESTON, TX 77550 Transmembrane signaling in HIV infection
R01AI-29952-01A1 (BM) WESSELS, MICHAEL R CHANNING LABORATORY 180 LONGWOOD AVENUE BOSTON, MA 02115-5899 Immune response to the group A streptococcal capsule
R55AI-29953-01A1 (ALY) BERG, LESLIE J HARVARD UNIVERSITY 16 DIVINITY AVE CAMBRIDGE, MA 02138 Function of MHC class II mutants in transgenic mice
R01AI-29954-02 (IMB) PETERLIN, BORIS M UNIVERSITY OF CALIFORNIA 3RD AND PARNASSUS AVENUES SAN FRANCISCO, CA 94143 Bare lymphocyte syndrome II-- Defective proteins and genes
R01AI-29961-02 (VR) WEBER, PETER C PENNSYLVANIA STATE UNIVERSITY PO BOX 850 HERSHEY, PA 17033 Mechanism of recombination in the HSV-1 genome
R01AI-29963-02 (VR) BOROWIEC, JAMES A NEW YORK UNIVERSITY MEDICAL CT 550 FIRST AVENUE NEW YORK, NY 10016 Mechanisms of SV 40 DNA replication
R01AI-29971-01A1 (TMP) CUPP, EDDIE W UNIVERSITY OF ARIZONA 410 D FORBES BUILDING TUCSON, AZ 85721 Black fly (simulium spp) immunity to onchocerca spp
R29AI-29974-01A1 (IMS) BROIDE, DAVID H UNIVERSITY OF CALIFORNIA 225 DICKINSON ST SAN DIEGO, CA 92103-1990 Asthma--Cytokines and airway inflammation
R01AI-29976-02 (IMS) ISAKSON, PETER C SEARLE R&D DIV. OF MOLECULAR & CELL BIOLO ST LOUIS, MO 63198 Cell cycle progression in B lymphoblasts
R29AI-29981-02 (EI) YOKOYAMA, WAYNE M UNIVERSITY OF CALIFORNIA BOX 0868 SAN FRANCISCO, CA 94143-0868 Molecular characterization of the A1 multigene family
R01AI-29984-02 (EVR) MAKINO, SHINJI UNIVERSITY OF TEXAS AUSTIN, TEXAS 78712-1095 Molecular studies of coronavirus replication
R01AI-29988-02 (VR) SUGDEN, BILL MCARDLE LAB FOR CANCER RESEARC 1400 UNIVERSITY AVENUE MADISON, WI 53706 Genetic analysis of immortalizing functions of EBV
R01AI-29990-01A1 (IMS) HEDRICK, STEPHEN M UNIV OF CALIFORNIA, SAN DIEGO WARREN CAMPUS CENTER LA JOLLA, CA 92093 Regulation of CD4 gene expression
R01AI-30000-02 (ARR) KASPER, LLOYD H DARTMOUTH MEDICAL SCHOOL HANOVER, NH 03756 Toxoplasma gondii--Diagnosis and prevention in AIDS
R01AI-30006-01A1 (BM) CAMPAGNARI, ANTHONY A SUNY CLINICAL CENTER 462 GRIDER STREET BUFFALO, NY 14215 Structure analysis of Haemophilus ducreyi LOS
R01AI-30010-02 (TMP) RIKIHISA, YASUKO OHIO STATE UNIVERSITY 1925 COFFEY ROAD COLUMBUS, OH 43210-1005 Ehrlichiacidal mechanism by macrophage ca++ mobilization
R29AI-30020-02 (ALY) POLLOCK, ROBERTA R OCCIDENTAL COLLEGE 1600 CAMPUS ROAD LOS ANGELES, CA 90041 A novel assay for somatic mutation in Ig V genes in vivo
R01AI-30025-01A1 (ARRC) CARPENTER, SUSAN L IOWA STATE UNIVERSITY AND PREVENTIVE MEDICINE AMES, IA 50011 Biological variation of equine infectious anemia virus
R01AI-30026-02 (SSS) OLIVER, JAMES H, JR GEORGIA SOUTHERN UNIVERSITY STATESBORO, GA 30460 Tick systematics on a global basis
R01AI-30033-02 (ARR) PERNIS, BENVENUTO G COLUMBIA UNIVERSITY 701 W 168 STREET NEW YORK, NY 10032 Binding of HIV peptides to class II MHC on human cells
R01AI-30036-01A1 (IMB) RICH, ROBERT R BAYLOR COLLEGE OF MEDICINE ONE BAYLOR PLAZA HOUSTON, TX 77030-3498 Superantigens and the MHC--Structure and function
R55AI-30042-01A1 (TMP) GURRI GLASS, GREGORY E JOHNS HOPKINS UNIVERSITY 615 N WOLFE ST BALTIMORE, MD 21205 Transmission and risk factors of Borrelia in small mammals
R22AI-30046-02 (BM) RAJAN, THIRUCHANDURAI V UNIV OF CONNECTICUT HLTH CNTR 263 FARMINGTON AVE FARMINGTON, CT 06032 Immunodeficient SCID mouse model of lymphatic filariasis
R01AI-30048-02 (EVR) AHMED, RAFI UCLA SCHOOL SCHOOL OF MEDICINE LOS ANGELES, CA 90024-1747 T cell memory in viral infection
R29AI-30050-01A1 (BM) GOLDBERG, JOANNA B CHANNING LABORATORY 180 LONGWOOD AVENUE BOSTON, MA 02115-5899 Genetics and role of alginate in P. aeruginosa infection
R01AI-30060-02 (TMP) JOINER, KEITH A YALE UNIVERSITY 333 CEDAR STREET, LCI 8 NEW HAVEN, CT 06510 Cell attachment and invasion by Toxoplasma gondii
R29AI-30063-02 (BM) NOEL, GARY J CORNELL UNIVERSITY 1300 YORK AVE NEW YORK, NY 10021 Macrophage defenses against Haemophilus influenzae
R29AI-30064-02 (BM) CIANCIOTTO, NICHOLAS P WARD MEMORIAL BLDG 303 EAST CHICAGO AVE CHICAGO, IL 60611 Genetic analysis of the Legionella mip virulence factor
R01AI-30066-01A1 (TMP) LEVITT, ALEXANDRA M NEW YORK UNIV MEDICAL CENTER 550 FIRST AVENUE NEW YORK, NY 10016 Stage specific transcripts in human malaria parasites
R01AI-30068-02 (BM) RUBENS, CRAIG E CHILDREN'S HOSP & MEDICAL CTR 4800 SAND POINT WAY NE SEATTLE, WA 98105 Cellular invasion by group B streptococci
R01AI-30070-01A1 (EVR) MCLACHLAN, ALAN SCRIPPS CLINIC 10666 NORTH TORREY PINES RD LA JOLLA, CALIF 92037 Regulation of hepatitis B virus transcription
R01AI-30073-02 (TMP) SCOTT, PHILLIP A UNIV OF PENN SCHOOL OF MEDICIN 3800 SPRUCE STREET PHILADELPHIA, PA 19104 T cell responses in L major infected and immunized mice
R15AI-30074-01A1 (MBC) SHINNERS, ELIZABETH N MARQUETTE UNIVERSITY 604 N 16TH STREET MILWAUKEE, WI 53233 Genetic linkage relations of Neisseria gonorrhoeae
R29AI-30083-02 (MBC) BARCAK, GERARD J UNIVERSITY OF MARYLAND 660 W REDWOOD STREET BALTIMORE, MD 21201 Molecular genetics of haemophilus influenzae transformation genes
R29AI-30104-02 (EI) BISHOP, D KEITH UNIVERSITY OF UTAH MEDICAL CTR 50 NORTH MEDICAL DRIVE SALT LAKE CITY, UT 84132 Inflammatory endothelia-lymphocyte interactions in vivo
R01AI-30105-01A1 (VR) BRITT, WILLIAM J UNIV. OF ALABAMA AT BIRMINGHAM UAB STATION Antibody recognition of cytomegalovirus glycoproteins
R29AI-30126-01A1 (TMP) WILSON, MARY E UNIVERSITY OF IOWA IOWA CITY, IA 52242 Antigens eliciting a T cell response in leishmaniasis
R29AI-30127-02 (TMP) MC DONALD, GREGORY A UNIVERSITY OF MISSOURI COLUMBIA, MO 65212 Immunogenicity and regulation of rickettsial proteins
R01AI-30131-02 (IMB) REPASKY, ELIZABETH A ROSWELL PARK MEMORIAL INST 666 ELM STREET BUFFALO, N Y 14263 Lymphocyte spectrin association with immune function
R29AI-30136-02 (TMP) BARRY, WENDY C TEXAS A & M RESEARCH FOUNDATIO TEXAS A&M UNIVERSITY COLLEGE STATION, TX 77843 Immunology of babesiosis
R01AI-30138-01A1 (BM) NOVICK, RICHARD P PUBLIC HEALTH RESEARCH INST 455 FIRST AVENUE NEW YORK, N Y 10016 Molecular genetics of exotoxin regulation in S. aureus
R29AI-30142-01A1 (MEDB) BAULDRY, SUE A WAKE FOREST UNIVERSITY 300 S HAWTHORNE RD WINSTON-SALEM, NC 27103 Physiologic phospholipase A2 activation in neutrophils
R18AI-30151-01A1 (AIDS) LEWIS, MARYANN UNIV OF CALIFORNIA - LOS ANGEL 10833 LE CONTE AVENUE LOS ANGELES, CA 90024-6917 Community-based asthma education for Latino children
R01AI-30155-02 (ALY) PARNES, JANE R STANFORD UNIV SCHOOL OF MED 300 PASTEUR DR STANFORD, CA 94305 -5111 Function and expression of Lyb-2
R01AI-30162-02 (BM) BARBIERI, JOSEPH T MEDICAL COLLEGE OF WISCONSIN 8701 WATERTOWN PLANK ROAD MILWAUKEE, WI 53226 Acellular vaccines against bacterial pathogens
R29AI-30165-02 (BM) DING, AIHAO CORNELL UNIV MEDICAL COLLEGE 1300 YORK AVENUE NEW YORK, NY 10021 Role of microtubule in macrophage response to LPS
R29AI-30169-01A1 (ALY) REISER, HANS DANA FARBER CANCER INSTITUTE 44 BINNEY STREET BOSTON, MA 02115 Characterization of T cell activation antigen
R01AI-30171-03 (IMS) RAULET, DAVID H UNIVERSITY OF CALIFORNIA 415 LIFE SCIENCES ADDITION BERKELEY, CA 94720 Role of H-2 genes in T cell selection
R01AI-30177-02 (IMB) WABL, MATTHIAS R UNIVERSITY OF CALIFORNIA BOX 0414 SAN FRANCISCO, CA 94143-0414 Immunoglobulin gene targeting into the mouse germ line
R01AI-30178-02 (IMB) ARGON, YAIR DUKE MEDICAL CENTER PO BOX 3010 DURHAM, NC 27710 Traffic of immunoglobulins and MHC proteins in B cells
U01AI-30183-02 (SRC) LARTEY, PAUL A ABBOTT LABORATORIES DEPARTMENT 47M, BUILDING AP9A Discovery of novel fungicidal agents
U01AI-30183-02 9002 (SRC) FESIK, STEPHEN W Discovery of novel fungicidal agents Core--NMR spectroscopy
U01AI-30183-02 0001 (SRC) KLEIN, LARRY L Discovery of novel fungicidal agents Design and synthesis of novel fungicidal agents
U01AI-30183-02 0002 (SRC) SHEN, LINUS Discovery of novel fungicidal agents Fungal topoisomerases as targets for antifungal drug discovery
U01AI-30183-02 0003 (SRC) SELITRENNIKOFF, CLAUDE P Discovery of novel fungicidal agents Fungal cell wall enzymology--(1-3)-B-glucan synthase
U01AI-30183-02 0004 (SRC) MITSHER, LESTER A Discovery of novel fungicidal agents Novel antifungal agents form higher plants
U01AI-30183-02 9001 (SRC) MCALPINE, JAMES B Discovery of novel fungicidal agents Core--Microbial screening and fermentation
U01AI-30188-02 (SRC) GORDON, JEFFREY I WASHINGTON UNIVERSITY

PROJECT NO., ORGANIZATIONAL UNIT., INVESTIGATOR, ADDRESS, TITLE

660 SOUTH EUCLID AVE, BOX 8231 ST LOUIS, MO 63110 Modulation of protein n-myristoylation in myco pathogens
U01AI-30189-02 (SRC) BRENNAN, PATRICK J COLORADO STATE UNIVERSITY FORT COLLINS, CO 80523 Molecular biology and treatment of Mycobacterium avium
U01AI-30189-02 0001 (SRC) BRENNAN, PATRICK J Molecular biology and treatment of Mycobacterium avium Chemical basis of drug resistance in Mycobacterium avium
U01AI-30189-02 0002 (SRC) JACOBS, WILLIAM R Molecular biology and treatment of Mycobacterium avium Molecular genetic analysis of Mycobacterium avium drug targets
U01AI-30189-02 0003 (SRC) ORME, I M Molecular biology and treatment of Mycobacterium avium Innovative animal models of Mycobacterium avium infection
U01AI-30189-02 0004 (SRC) ELLNER, JERROLD J Molecular biology and treatment of Mycobacterium avium Discovery of new drugs active against Mycobacterium avium
R03AI-30219-02 (AIDS) MITCHELL, CHARLES D UNIV. OF MIAMI, SCHOOL OF MED PO BOX 016960 MIAMI, FL 33101 Congenital toxoplasmosis and maternal HIV-1 infection
U01AI-30223-02 (SRC) STERLING, CHARLES R UNIVERSITY OF ARIZONA BUILDING 90, ROOM 202 TUCSON, AZ 85721 Immunotherapy of cryptosporidiosis using monoclonals
U01AI-30223-02 0001 (SRC) STERLING, CHARLES R Immunotherapy of cryptosporidiosis using monoclonals Monoclonal antibody immunotherapy of cryptosporidiosis
U01AI-30223-02 0002 (SRC) RIGGS, MICHAEL W Immunotherapy of cryptosporidiosis using monoclonals Passive antibody mediated control of cryptosporidiosis
U01AI-30223-02 9001 (SRC) CAMA, VITIALIANO A Immunotherapy of cryptosporidiosis using monoclonals Core--cryptosporidium production and purification
U01AI-30223-02 9002 (SRC) RIGGS, MICHAEL W Immunotherapy of cryptosporidiosis using monoclonals Core--Evaluation of monoclonal antibodies in immunocompetent mice
U01AI-30230-02 (SRC) REMINGTON, JACK S PALO ALTO MEDICAL FOUNDATION 860 BRYANT STREET PALO ALTO, CA 94301 Drug discovery for treatment of toxoplasmosis in AIDS
U01AI-30230-02 0001 (SRC) REMINGTON, JACK S Drug discovery for treatment of toxoplasmosis in AIDS Drug discovery for treatment of toxoplasmosis in AIDS
U01AI-30230-02 0002 (SRC) MANSOUR, TAG E Drug discovery for treatment of toxoplasmosis in AIDS PPi-dependent glycolytic enzymes in T. gondii
U01AI-30230-02 0003 (SRC) BOOTHROYD, JOHN C Drug discovery for treatment of toxoplasmosis in AIDS Identification of drug targets through genetics
U01AI-30230-02 9001 (SRC) ARAUJO, FAUSTO Drug discovery for treatment of toxoplasmosis in AIDS Core--Preparation, supply of toxoplasma and immunologicals
U01AI-30230-02 9002 (SRC) CONLEY, FRANCES K Drug discovery for treatment of toxoplasmosis in AIDS Core--Neuropathology
U01AI-30238-02 (AIDS) WONG-STAAL, FLOSSIE UNIV. OF CALIF., SAN DIEGO LA JOLLA, CA 92093 Strategies for HIV vaccine development
U01AI-30238-02 0001 (AIDS) WONG-STAAL, F Strategies for HIV vaccine development Molecular approach to HIV vaccines
U01AI-30238-02 0002 (AIDS) WANG, CHANG Strategies for HIV vaccine development Epitope based synthetic HIV antigens as subunit vaccines
U01AI-30238-02 0003 (AIDS) ARNOLD, EDWARD Strategies for HIV vaccine development Human rhinovirus 14 (HRV14) as a vector for AIDS vaccines
U01AI-30238-02 0004 (AIDS) MORTON, WILLIAM R Strategies for HIV vaccine development HIV-2 vaccines--Testing in Macaques
U01AI-30238-02 0005 (AIDS) GREENBERG, PHILIP Strategies for HIV vaccine development Evaluation of the cellular immune responses to HIV and HIV vaccines
U01AI-30238-02 0006 (AIDS) MOSIER, DONALD E Strategies for HIV vaccine development HIV-infected hu-SCID mice as models for AIDS therapy
U01AI-30238-02 9001 (AIDS) LOONEY, DAVID Strategies for HIV vaccine development Virology core
R01AI-30242-02 (ARR) UHLENBECK, OLKE C UNIVERSITY OF COLORADO CAMPUS BOX 215 BOULDER, CO 80309-0215 Design of optimal ribozymes for cleavage of HIV RNA
U01AI-30243-02 (SRC) BUTEL, JANET S BAYLOR COLLEGE OF MEDICINE ONE BAYLOR PLAZA HOUSTON, TX 77030 Toward gene therapy for AIDS
U01AI-30243-02 9001 (SRC) LEWIS, DOROTHY E Toward gene therapy for AIDS Core--Specimen handling, flow cytometry, immune function
U01AI-30243-02 9002 (SRC) GIBBS, RICHARD A Toward gene therapy for AIDS Core--Nucleic acid service facility
U01AI-30243-02 9003 (SRC) BELMONT, JOHN W Toward gene therapy for AIDS Core--Gene therapy mouse facility
U01AI-30243-02 0001 (SRC) BELMONT, JOHN W Toward gene therapy for AIDS Induction fo resistance to HIV by receptor blockade
U01AI-30243-02 0002 (SRC) DONEHOWER, LAWRENCE A Toward gene therapy for AIDS Role of nef in inhibition of HIV-1 infection
U01AI-30243-02 0003 (SRC) HARPER, JEFFREY W Toward gene therapy for AIDS HIV TAR element as a target for gene therapy
R01AI-30248-02 (IMS) DE CAMILLI, PIETRO YALE UNIVERSITY 333 CEDAR ST PO BOX 3333 NEW HAVEN, CT 06510 Autoimmunity to GABA-ergic neurons in stiff-man syndrome
U01AI-30261-02 (SRC) SANTI, DANIEL V UNIVERSITY OF CALIFORNIA 513 PARNASSUS AVE SAN FRANCISCO, CA 94143-0962 Drug targets of opportunistic pathogens in AIDS
U01AI-30261-02 0001 (SRC) EDMAN, JEFFREY C Drug targets of opportunistic pathogens in AIDS Cloning and molecular biological characterization of antibiotic targets
U01AI-30261-02 0002 (SRC) SANTI, DANIEL V Drug targets of opportunistic pathogens in AIDS Heterologous expression, purification of enzymes--Screening effort
U01AI-30261-02 0003 (SRC) KUNTZ, IRWIN D Drug targets of opportunistic pathogens in AIDS Molecular modeling and computer assisted drug design
U01AI-30279-02 (SRC) PIPER, JAMES R SOUTHERN RESEARCH INSTITUTE 2000 9TH AVE, SOUTH/BOX 55305 BIRMINGHAM, AL 35255-5305 Agents against Pneumocystis and Toxoplasma
U01AI-30279-02 0001 (SRC) PIPER, JAMES R Agents against Pneumocystis and Toxoplasma Agents against Pneumocystis and Toxoplasma
U01AI-30279-02 0002 (SRC) VASANTHAKUMAR, GEETHA Agents against Pneumocystis and Toxoplasma Genetic and biochemical analysis of HGPRT from Toxoplasma gondii
U01AI-30279-02 0003 (SRC) PFEFFERKORN, ELMER R Agents against Pneumocystis and Toxoplasma Evaluation against toxoplasma in vivo and in vitro
U01AI-30279-02 0004 (SRC) SHANNON, WILLIAM M Agents against Pneumocystis and Toxoplasma Development of novel anti-HCMV drugs
R01AI-30283-02 (VR) ROOP, DENNIS R BAYLOR COLLEGE OF MEDICINE ONE BAYLOR PLAZA HOUSTON, TX 77030 Targeting human papilloma virus gene expression in mice
R01AI-30286-02 (BM) SCHWEINLE, JO ELLEN YALE UNIVERSITY PO BOX 3333 NEW HAVEN, CT 06510 Complement activation by mannose-binding protein
R43AI-30289-01A1 (SSS) HUANG, MANLEY T GENPHARM INTERNATIONAL 2375 GARCIA AVENUE MOUNTAIN VIEW, CA 94043 Transgenic approach to superior immunodeficient mice
R43AI-30290-01A1 (SSS) KENSIL, CHARLOTTE A CAMBRIDGE BIOSCIENCE CORPORATI 365 PLANTATION STREET WORCESTER, MA 01605 Recombinant subunit vaccine for human cytomegalovirus
R43AI-30301-01A1 (SSS) RABIN, LINDA SYSTEMIX, INC 3400 W BAYSHORE RD PALO ALTO, CA 94303 Testing of HIV vaccines in SCID-hu mice
R03AI-30344-02 (MID) KAPER, JAMES B UNIV OF MARYLAND-MEDICAL SCHOO 10 SOUTH PINE STREET BALTIMORE, MD 21201 INDO-US vaccine action programme
R03AI-30345-02 (MID) LEVIN, MYRON UNIV OF COLORADO HLTH SCI CTR 4200 E 9TH AVE, BOX C-227 DENVER, CO 80262 INDO-US vaccine action programme
R03AI-30346-02 (MID) GREENBERG, HARRY B STANFORD UNIVERSITY SCHOOL OF MEDICINE STANFORD, CA 94305 INDO-US vaccine action programme
R01AI-30349-01A1 (ARRA) JACOBS, BERTRAM L ARIZONA STATE UNIVBERSITY TEMPE, AZ 85287-2701 Mechanism of action of interferon against HIV
R01AI-30350-02 (ARR) LEVY, JAY A UNIVERSITY OF CALIFORNIA BOX 0128 SAN FRANCISCO, CA 94143 Suppression of HIV replication by CD8+ cells
R01AI-30356-01A1 (ARRC) WOOD, CHARLES UNIVERSITY OF KANSAS HAWORTH HALL LAWRENCE, KS 66045 Biology of HIV AND HHV-6 interactions
R01AI-30358-02 (ARRC) KOUP, RICHARD ALAN THE AARON DIAMOND AIDS RES CTR 455 FIRST VENUE NEW YORK, N Y 10016 Cellular immunity to HIV-- Studies in the Hu-SCID mouse
R01AI-30361-02 (ARR) HARRISON, STEPHEN C HARVARD UNIVERSITY 7 DIVINITY AVENUE CAMBRIDGE, MA 02138 Structure and interactions of human CD4
R01AI-30363-01A1 (ARRC) MOCARSKI, EDWARD S STANFORD UNIVERSITY SCHOOL OF MEDICINE STANFORD, CA 94305-5402 Cytomegalovirus pathogenesis in immunodeficiency
R01AI-30366-02 (ARR) KIYONO, HIROSHI UNIVERSITY OF ALABAMA BIRMINGHAM, AL 35294 Induction of SIV-specific CTLs by mucosal immunization
R01AI-30373-01A1 (ARRB) VON REYN, CHARLES F DARTMOUTH-HITCHCOCK MEDICAL CT 2 MAYNARD STREET HANOVER, NH 03756 Disseminated MAC in AIDS--International collaboration
R01AI-30374-01A1 (ARRA) ROSE, JOHN K YALE UNIVERSITY 310 CEDAR ST NEW HAVEN, CT 06510 HIV glycoprotein transport and signaling
R01AI-30376-01A1 (ARRA) FURMANSKI, PHILIP NEW YORK UNIVERSITY 1009 MAIN BUILDING NEW YORK, NY 10003 Mechanisms of eradication of virus infected macrophages
R01AI-30377-02 (ARR) DANDEKAR, SATYA UNIVERSITY OF CALIFORNIA DEPARTMENT OF INTERNAL MEDICIN DAVIS, CA 95616 Immune activation in vivo and FIV gene expression in cats
R01AI-30386-02 (ARR) STEVENSON, MARIO UNIVERSITY OF NEBRASKA MED CTR SWANSON CTR 2020, 42ND & DEWEY OMAHA, NE 68105 Molecular basis of HIV-1 persistence
R01AI-30389-02 (ARR) SHULTZ, LEONARD D JACKSON LABORATORY 600 MAIN STREET BAR HARBOR, ME 04609-0800 Development of new SCID mouse models for AIDS research
R29AI-30392-02 (ARR) TAYLOR, ETHAN W UNIVERSITY OF GEORGIA COLLEGE OF PHARMACY ATHENS, GA 30602 Molecular modeling studies and SAR of anti-HIV agents
R01AI-30395-02 (ARR) JAMESON, BRADFORD A THOMAS JEFFERSON UNIVERSITY 1020 LOCUST ST PHILADELPHIA, PA 19107 A study of the physical interaction between HIV and the CD4 protein
R01AI-30399-02 (ARR) REKOSH, DAVID M S U N Y AT BUFFALO 3435 MAIN STREET BUFFALO, NY 14214 Studies on HIV assembly
R01AI-30411-02 (ARRC) MATTHEWS, THOMAS J DUKE UNIVERSITY MED CENTER PO BOX 2926 DURHAM, NC 27710 Studies on the 3rd variable domain of the HIV-1 envelope
U01AI-30420-02 (SRC) YOLKEN, ROBERT H JOHNS HOPKINS UNIV SCH OF MED 600 NORTH WOLFE STREET BALTIMORE, MD 21205 Amplified nucleic acid-EIA for microbial diagnosis
U01AI-30448-02 (SRC) ESTES, MARY K BAYLOR COLLEGE OF MEDICINE ONE BAYLOR PLAZA HOUSTON, TX 77030 Development of diagnostic tests for Norwalk viruses
U01AI-30451-02 (SRC) LAKEMAN, FRED D UNIVERSITY OF ALABAMA 918 UNIVERSITY BLVD/UNIV STATI BIRMINGHAM, AL 35294 Diagnostic approaches to herpes simplex virus infections
U01AI-30456-02 (SRC) JORDAN, M COLIN UNIVERSITY OF MINNESOTA 420 DELAWARE ST S E MINNESPOLIS, MN 55455 Molecular diagnosis of cytomegalovirus disease
U01AI-30457-02 (SRC) RICHMAN, DOUGLAS D THE REGENTS OF THE UNIV OF CAL UNIV OF CALIFORNIA, SAN DIEGO LA JOLLA, CA 92093-0934 Rapid microbial diagnosis by nucleic acid amplification
R01AI-30462-02 (EVR) COHRS, RANDALL J UNIV OF COLORADO HLTH SCIS CTR 4200 E NINTH AVE/BOX B-182 DENVER, CO 80262 Control of 2-5a pathway by ts mutant of vaccinia
R01AI-30464-01 (TMP) HARVEY, WILLIAM R TEMPLE UNIVERSITY PHILADELPHIA, PA 19122 Physiology of insect amino acid transport

R01AI-30465-01A1 (TMP) PAX, RALPH A MICHIGAN STATE UNIVERSITY EAST LANSING, MI 48824 Analysis of ion channels in S. mansoni muscle fibers
R01AI-30475-01 (TMP) WANG, CHING C UNIVERSITY OF CALIFORNIA SAN FRANCISCO, CA 94143-0446 The double-stranded RNA viruses in Trichomonas and Giardia
R01AI-30479-01 (BM) MILLER, SAMUEL I MASSACHUSETTS GENERAL HOSPITAL FRUIT STREET BOSTON, MA 02114 Role of the phoP regulon in salmonella virulence
R13AI-30488-01 (MID) ESTES, MARY K BAYLOR COLLEGE OF MEDICINE ONE BAYLOR PLAZA HOUSTON, TX 77030 Third international symposium on double-stranded RNA viruses
R29AI-30492-01 (BM) GALAN, JORGE E SUNY AT STONY BROOK STONY BROOK, NY 11794-8621 Molecular genetic analysis of salmonella cell invasion
R29AI-30497-01A1 (TMP) PHILLIPS, NELSON B CASE WESTERN UNIVERSITY 2109 ADELBERT ROAD CLEVELAND, OH 44106 Analysis of Giardia pyrophosphate dependent kinases
R01AI-30499-01A1 (BM) PETERSON, ELLENA M UNIVERSITY OF CALIFORNIA MEDICINE SCIENCES IRVINE, CA 92717 Neutralizing epitopes of Chlamydia trachomatis
R01AI-30500-01 (BM) SILVERSTEIN, RICHARD UNIVERSITY OF KANSAS MED CTR 39TH & RAINBOW BOULEVARD KANSAS CITY, KS 66103-8410 Hydrazine and endotoxin, TNF in acute infectious disease
R29AI-30501-02 (IMS) BAKER, JAMES R, JR UNIVERSITY OF MICHIGAN ANN ARBOR, MI 48109-0380 Characterization of thyroid autoantibodies and autoantigens
R01AI-30502-01 (ALY) LACY, ELIZABETH H SLOAN-KETTERING CANCER CTR 1275 YORK AVENUE NEW YORK, NY 10021 Developmental regulation of T cell specific genes
R01AI-30517-01 (EVR) GUPTA, KAILASH C RUSH-PRESBYTERIAN-ST LUKE'S ME 1653 WEST CONGRESS PARKWAY CHICAGO, IL 60612 Structure & function of P and C proteins of Sendai virus
R01AI-30527-01 (EI) PIOUS, DONALD A UNIVERSITY OF WASHINGTON DIVISION OF DEV. BIOLOGY SEATTLE, WA 98195 Antigen processing genes and cell biology
R01AI-30534-01 (BIO) BURKE, JOHN M UNIVERSITY OF VERMONT BURLINGTON, VT 05405 Antiviral hairpin ribozymes
R01AI-30535-01 (SSS) DELISI, CHARLES BOSTON UNIVERSITY 44 CUMMINGTON STREET BOSTON, MA 02215 The molecular basis of antigen presentation
R01AI-30537-01A1 (TMP) JOHNSON, PATRICIA J UCLA SCHOOL OF MEDICINE LOS ANGELES, CA 90024-1747 Drug resistance in the parasite Trichomonas vaginalis
R01AI-30544-01 (VR) SEEGER, CHRISTOPH INST FOR CANCER RESEARCH 7701 BURHOLME AVE PHILADELPHIA, PA 19111 Functional analysis of the hepadna virus genome
R01AI-30546-02 (IMS) ZIER, KAREN S MOUNT SINAI SCHOOL OF MEDICINE ONE GUSTAVE L LEVY PLACE NEW YORK, NY 10029 Decreased IL-2 synthesis in type I diabetes
P01AI-30548-01A1 (MID) BARTHOLD, STEPHEN W YALE UNIVERSITY 333 CEDAR STREET NEW HAVEN, CT 06510 Lyme disease--Pathogenesis and protection
P01AI-30548-01A1 0002 (MID) MALAWISTA, STEPHEN Lyme disease--Pathogenesis and protection Probes for Borrelia Burgdorferi DNA in ticks, mice and men
P01AI-30548-01A1 0003 (MID) BARTHOLD, STEPHEN Lyme disease--Pathogenesis and protection Mouse model of lyme Borreliosis
P01AI-30548-01A1 0004 (MID) FLAVELL, RICHARD Lyme disease--Pathogenesis and protection A recombinant vaccine for Lyme Borreliosis
P01AI-30548-01A1 9001 (MID) BARTHOLD, STEPHEN Lyme disease--Pathogenesis and protection Animal laboratory core
P01AI-30548-01A1 9004 (MID) ANDERSON, JOHN Lyme disease--Pathogenesis and protection Entomologic and bacteriologic core
P01AI-30548-01A1 0001 (MID) KANTOR, FRED Lyme disease--Pathogenesis and protection Protective epitopes important in Lyme Borreliosis
R29AI-30550-01 (EI) CHATILA, TALAL A CHILDRENS HOSPITAL BOSTON, MA 02115 Molecular analysis of IL-2 deficiency states in SCIDS patients
R01AI-30554-01A1 (EI) JENSEN, PETER E EMORY UNIV SCHOOL OF MEDICINE 1639 PIERCE DRIVE ATLANTA, GA 30322 Regulation of antigen processing
R01AI-30556-01A1 (BM) WRIGHT, SAMUEL D ROCKEFELLER UNIVERSITY 1230 YORK AVENUE NEW YORK, NY 10021-6399 Recognition and respones to endotoxin
R01AI-30557-01A1 (BBCB) TAMM, LUKAS K UNIVERSITY OF VIRGINIA MED SCH HLTH SCIS CENTER BOX 449 CHARLOTTESVILLE, VA 22908 Mechanisms of viral spike glycoprotein-mediated membrane
R29AI-30559-01 (ALY) GOLDFIEN, ROBERT D SAN FRANCISCO VA MEDICAL CENTE 4150 CLEMENT STREET SAN FRANCISCO, CA 94121 The role of phospholipase C in T cell activation
R01AI-30561-01 (IMS) CRISPE, IAN N YALE UNIV., SCHOOL OF MEDICINE 310 CEDAR STREET NEW HAVEN, CT 06510 Function and specificity of CD4-/CD8- T cells with alpha,beta receptors
R01AI-30566-01 (VR) PALMENBERG, ANN C UNIVERSITY OF WISCONSIN 1655 LINDEN DRIVE MADISON, WI 53706 Cardioviral poly(c) tracts and virus pathogenicity
R01AI-30572-01 (EVR) MORRISON, TRUDY G UNIVERSITY OF MASSACHUSETTS 55 LAKE AVENEU NORTH WORCESTER, MA 01655 Mutational analysis of the NDV fusion glycoprotein
R01AI-30575-01 (IMB) FINKEL, TERRI H NATIONAL JEWISH CTR FOR DEPARTMENT OF PEDIATRICS DENVER, CO 80206 Signal transduction events of selection and tolerance
R01AI-30580-01 (BBCB) HOGLE, JAMES M SCRIPPS CLINIC & RES FDN 10666 N TORREY PINES ROAD LA JOLLA, CA 92037 Structure of poliovirus/antiviral drug complexes
R01AI-30581-01A1 (ALY) SPIES, THOMAS DANA FARBER CANCER INST 44 BINNEY STREET BOSTON, MA 02115 Novel immune response genes within the human MHC
P50AI-30601-01 (SRC) SANIEL, MEDIADORA C RESEARCH INST/TROPICAL MEDICIN ALABANG, MUNTINLUPA, METRO MANILA, PHILIPPINES 1702 Tropical medicine research center
P50AI-30601-01 0001 (SRC) OLVEDA, REMIGIO Tropical medicine research center Morbidity and resistance to reinfection in S. Japonica
P50AI-30601-01 0002 (SRC) RAMIREZ, BERNADETTE Tropical medicine research center Vaccine development against S. Japonicum
P50AI-30601-01 0003 (SRC) SALAZAR, NELIA Tropical medicine research center Factors affecting endemicity of Malaria--Implication for control
P50AI-30601-01 0004 (SRC) CHAN, GERTRUDE Tropical medicine research center Chemotherapy studies of multibacillary leprosy in the Philippines
P50AI-30601-01 9001 (SRC) MEDIADORA, SANIEL Tropical medicine research center Core--Portable field laboratory
P50AI-30601-01 9002 (SRC) MEDIADORA, SANIEL Tropical medicine research center Core--Data collection and biostatistics
P50AI-30603-01 (SRC) SARAVIA, NANCY G FUNDACION CIDEIM CALI, COLOMBIA Interdisciplinary studies of leishmania
P50AI-30603-01 0001 (SRC) TRAVI, BRUNO L Interdisciplinary studies of leishmania Vector biology, ecology and control (hamsters, mice)
P50AI-30603-01 0002 (SRC) WEIGLE, KRISTIN A Interdisciplinary studies of leishmania Detection of Leishmania genome & antigens in vivo--Diagnosis
P50AI-30603-01 0003 (SRC) SARAVIA, NANCY G Interdisciplinary studies of leishmania Pathogenesis, susceptibility and resistance
P50AI-30603-01 0004 (SRC) SARAVIA, NANCY G Interdisciplinary studies of leishmania Molecular determinants of parasite virulence (human, hamsters, mice)
P50AI-30603-01 9001 (SRC) WEIGLE, KRISTEN A Interdisciplinary studies of leishmania Biometry core
P50AI-30603-01 9002 (SRC) PALMA, GLORIA I Interdisciplinary studies of leishmania Clinical core
P50AI-30603-01 9003 (SRC) TRAVI, BRUNO L Interdisciplinary studies of leishmania Laboratory core
R01AI-30605-17 (IMS) FRITZ, ROBERT B MEDICAL COLLEGE OF WISCONSIN 8701 WATERTOWN PLANK RD MILWAUKEE, WI 53226 Immune function in allergic encephalomyelitis
R01AI-30606-02 (ARR) MC KAY, DAVID B STANFORD UNIVERSITY STANFORD, CA 94305 Crystallographic studies of catalytic hammerhead RNA
R01AI-30615-01A1 (SAT) ILDSTAD, SUZANNE T UNIVERSITY OF PITTSBURGH 497 SCAIFE HALL 5TH AVE PITTSBURGH, PA 15261 Organ transplantation -- Mixed chimerism induced tolerance
R01AI-30618-01 (BM) TOMPKINS, LUCY S STANFORD UNIVERSITY STANFORD, CA 94305-5402 Genetic determinant of pathogenicity in Legionella
R01AI-30624-01 (VR) KURANE, ICHIRO UNIV OF MASSACHUSETTS MED CTR 55 LAKE AVE NORTH WORCESTER, MA 01655 Human immune responses to dengue viruses
R01AI-30628-01A1 (BM) KASPER, DENNIS L CHANNING LABORATORY 180 LONGWOOD AVENUE BOSTON, MA 02115 Prevention of perinatal group B streptococcal infections
P50AI-30639-01 (SRC) CARVALHO, EDGAR M HOSP UNIV PROFESSOR E SANTOS RUA JOAO DAS BOTAS S/N CANELA 40140 SALVADOR, BAHIA, BRASIL Pathogenesis and therapy of tropical diseases
P50AI-30639-01 0001 (SRC) CARVALHO, EDGAR M Pathogenesis and therapy of tropical diseases Host immune response in schistosomiasis
P50AI-30639-01 0002 (SRC) BARRAL-NETTO, MANOEL Pathogenesis and therapy of tropical diseases T cell responses in leishmaniasis
P50AI-30639-01 0003 (SRC) BADERO, ROBERTO Pathogenesis and therapy of tropical diseases Immunotherapy of leishmaniasis and leprosy
R29AI-30643-01 (BM) CAPARON, MICHAEL WASHINGTON UNIVERSITY MED SCH BOX 8093 ST LOUIS, MO 63110-1093 Regulation of M protein expression in S. pyogenes
R01AI-30646-01 (BM) LEVY, STUART B TUFTS UNIV MEDICAL SCHOOL 136 HARRISON AVENUE BOSTON, MA 02111 Efflux mediated resistance to tetracyclines
R29AI-30648-01 (VR) CONE, RICHARD W CHILDREN'S HOSPITAL & MED CENT 4800 SAND POINT WAY, NE SEATTLE, WA 98105 The pathogenesis of HHV-6 in the immunocopromised host
R01AI-30653-02 (ALY) ECKHARDT, LAUREL A COLUMBIA UNIVERSITY 753A FAIRCHILD CTR NEW YORK, NY 10027 Control of gene expression in myeloma cells
R01AI-30656-01 (EI) MAKI, RICHARD A LA JOLLA CANCER RESEARCH FDN 10901 NORTH TORREY PINES ROAD LA JOLLA, CA 92037 Characterization of an ets related transcription factor
R22AI-30660-01 (TMP) CERAMI, ANTHONY THE ROCKEFELLER UNIVERSITY 1230 YORK AVENUE NEW YORK, NY 10021 Hemoglobin catabolism by Plasmodium falciparum
R01AI-30663-01 (BM) LOCKSLEY, RICHARD M UNIVERSITY OF CALIFORNIA BOX 0654, RM C-443 SAN FRANCISCO, CA 94143-0654 CD4+ T cell receptors in leishmaniasis
R01AI-30725-01 (BBCB) KIM, SUNG-HOU UNIVERSITY OF CALIFORNIA BERKELEY, CA 94720 Crystallographic studies of bacterial chemoreceptors
R01AI-30726-01 (BBCA) PARDI, ARTHUR UNIV OF COLORADO CAMPUS BOX 215 BOULDER, CO 80309-0215 Structures of ribozymes that can cleave targeted RNAs
P01AI-30731-01A1 (SRC) COREY, LAWRENCE CHILDREN'S HOSPITAL & MED CENT 4800 SAND POINT WAY NE SEATTLE, WA 98105 Epidemiology/pathogenesis of asymptomatic genital herpes
P01AI-30731-01A1 0001 (SRC) COREY, LAWRENCE Epidemiology/pathogenesis of asymptomatic genital herpes Clinical epidemiology and natural history of asymptomatic genital herpes
P01AI-30731-01A1 0002 (SRC) BROWN, ZANE A Epidemiology/pathogenesis of asymptomatic genital herpes The perinatal complications of asymptomatic genital herpes simplex virus
P01AI-30731-01A1 0003 (SRC) ASHLEY, RHODA L Epidemiology/pathogenesis of asymptomatic genital herpes Local immune responses to herpes simplex virus specific proteins
P01AI-30731-01A1 9001 (SRC) ASHLEY, RHODA L Epidemiology/pathogenesis of asymptomatic genital herpes Core--Virology
P01AI-30731-01A1 9002 (SRC) BENEDETTI, JACQUELINE

PROJECT NO., ORGANIZATIONAL UNIT., INVESTIGATOR, ADDRESS, TITLE

Epidemiology/pathogenesis of asymptomatic genital herpes
Core--Statistics

R01AI-30732-01A1 (SAT) LOWRY, ROBIN P EMORY UNIVERSITY 1364 CLIFTON ROAD, NORTHEAST ATLANTA, GA 30322 Conditioned unresponsiveness in organ transplantation

R29AI-30733-01 (TMP) MATHER, THOMAS N CENTER FOR BLOOD RESEARCH 800 HUNTINGTON AVE BOSTON, MA 02115 Dynamics of Lyme disease spirochete transmission

R29AI-30735-01 (PTHA) ELSTAD, MARK R UNIVERSITY OF UTAH SALT LAKE CITY, UTAH 84112 Regulation of platelet-activating factor acetylhydrolase

R01AI-30742-01 (HEM) BABIOR, BERNARD M SCRIPPS CLINIC AND RES FDN 10666 NORTH TORREY PINES ROAD LA JOLLA, CA 92037 NADPH-Binding protein of the respiratory burst oxidase

R01AI-30743-01 (BBCB) SCHUTT, CLARENCE E PRINCETON UNIVERSITY HOYT LABORATORY PRINCETON, NJ 08544 Structure determination of pertussis toxin

R01AI-30744-01A1 (IMS) MOUNTZ, JOHN D THE UNIVERITY OF ALABAMA UAB STATION BIRMINGHAM, AL 35294 Expression of transgenic TcR genes in autoimmune lpr/lpr mice

U01AI-30751-01 (SRC) KERCSMAR, CAROLYN M CASE WESTERN RESERVE UNIVERSIT 2101 ADELBERT ROAD CLEVELAND, OH 44106 Predictors of asthma morbidity in urban black children

U01AI-30752-01 (SRC) WEDNER, H JAMES WASHINGTON UNIVERSITY ONE BROOKINGS DRIVE ST LOUIS, MO 63110 St Louis asthma study unit

U01AI-30756-01 (SRC) EVANS, RICHARD, III CHILDREN'S MEMORIAL HOSPITAL 2300 CHILDREN'S PLAZA, BOX 60 CHICAGO, IL 60614 The Chicago inner-city asthma study

R29AI-30759-01A1 (ARRC) KATZMAN, MICHAEL MILTON S HERSHEY MEDICAL CENTE P O BOX 850 HERSHEY, PA 17033 Studies on HIV 1 integration

U01AI-30772-01 (SRC) KATTAN, MEYER MT SINAI SCHOOL OF MEDICINE 1 GUSTAVE L LEVY PL, BOX 1202 NEW YORK, NY 10029 National cooperative inner city asthma study

U01AI-30773-01 (SRC) EGGLESTON, PEYTON A JOHNS HOPKINS UNIVERSITY 600 N WOLFE STREET BALTIMORE, MD 21205 The role of the home environment in inner-city asthma

U01AI-30777-01 (SRC) CRAIN, ELLEN ALBERT EINSTEIN COLL OF MEDICI 1300 MORRIS PARK AVENUE BRONX, NY 10461 Reduction of inner-city asthma

U01AI-30779-01 (SRC) LEICKLY, FREDERICK E HENRY FORD HOSPITAL 2799 WEST GRAND BOULEVARD DETROIT, MI 48202 National cooperative inner-city asthma study

U01AI-30780-01 (SRC) MALVEAUX, FLOYD J HOWARD UNIVERSITY COLLEGE OF M 520 W STREET NW WASHINGTON, DC 20059 Inner city asthma--Washington D.C.

P01AI-30795-02 (AIDS) KANKI, PHYLLIS J HARVARD SCHOOL OF PUBLIC HEALT 665 HUNTINGTON AVENUE BOSTON, MA 02115 Natural history of HIV infections in Senegal

P01AI-30795-02 0001 (AIDS) LALLEMANT, MARC Natural history of HIV infections in Senegal Natural history of perinatally acquired HIV infection

P01AI-30795-02 0002 (AIDS) MARLINK, RICHARD Natural history of HIV infections in Senegal Comparitive studies of HIV disease in adults

P01AI-30795-02 0003 (AIDS) KANKI, PHYLLIS Natural history of HIV infections in Senegal HIV-2 infection and natural history in children

P01AI-30795-02 9001 (AIDS) KANKI, PHYLLIS Natural history of HIV infections in Senegal Virology and clinical laboratory core

P01AI-30795-02 9002 (AIDS) HSIEH, CHUNG Natural history of HIV infections in Senegal Data management and analysis core

R01AI-30797-01A1 (BM) GENCO, CAROLINE A EMORY UNIVERSITY 1462 CLIFTON ROAD, NE ATLANTA, GA 30322 Iron assimilation by pathogenic Neisseria species

R01AI-30798-02 (EVR) MCCANCE, DENNIS J UNIVERSITY OF ROCHESTER MED CT 601 ELMWOOD AVE, PO BOX 672 ROCHESTER, NY 14642 Effects of HPV6 & 16 on epithelial cell differentiation

R01AI-30803-02 (IMB) KANAGAWA, OSAMI WASH UNIV SCHO OF MEDICINE 660 SOUTH EUCLID AVENUE ST. LOUIS, MO 63110 Role of CD4/CD8 molecule in T cell specificity

R43AI-30814-01A1 (SSS) SIOUFI, HABIB A VIRAFREE CORPORATION 107 BROWNE STREET BROOKLINE, MA 02146 Investigation of safer test tubes for laboratory use

R43AI-30818-01A1 (HEM) LIN, LILY HRI RESEARCH, INC 2341 STANWELL DRIVE CONCORD, CA 94520 Methods for PCR sample preparation--Heme neutralization

R43AI-30821-01 (SSS) CROOKE, ROSANNE M ISIS PHARMACEUTICALS 2280 FARADAY AVE CARLSBAD, CA 92008 Polyamine oligonucleotides to enhance cellular uptake

R29AI-30822-01A1 (CBY) HORNBECK, PETER V UNIVERSITY OF MARYLAND 10 SOUTH PINE STREET BALTIMORE, MD 21201 Functional cell biology of phosphomyristin C

R43AI-30834-01 (SSS) XIONG, CHENG PARAVAX, INC 2301 RESEARCH BLVD FT. COLLINS, CO 80526 Vaccine potential of Toxoplasma gondii recombinant P30

R43AI-30837-01 (SSS) COUGHLIN, RICHARD T CAMBRIDGE BIOTECH CORP 365 PLANTATION STREET WORCESTER, MA 01605 Rapid diagnostic for Clostridium difficile toxin B

R43AI-30838-01 (SSS) BORAKER, DAVID K CHROMOGEN, INC PO BOX 128 MILTON, VT 05468 Enhanced electro-acoustic fusion for cell hybridization

R43AI-30839-01 (SSS) FULTON, ROBERT J INLAND LABORATORIES, INC 2600 STEMMONS FREEWAY DALLAS, TX 75207 Development of immunotoxins using a mutant of exotoxin A

R01AI-30840-01 (EI) PLATTS-MILLS, THOMAS A UNIVERSITY OF VIRGINIA HEALTH SCI CENTER, BOX 225 CHARLOTTESVILLE, VA 22908 Trichophyton and aspergillus-- Immunology and lung disease

R43AI-30843-01A1 (SSS) MARCELLETTI, JOHN F LIDAK PHARMACEUTICALS 11077 NORTH TORREY PINES RD LA JOLLA, CA 92037 The anti- retroviral effects of behenyl alcohol

R43AI-30847-01 (SSS) DISCIULLO, STEVEN O APPLIED BIOTECHNOLOGY, INC 80 ROGERS STREET CAMBRIDGE, MA 02142 Preparation of non-infectious HIV-like particles

R43AI-30851-01 (SSS) CAROME, EDWARD F EDJEWISE SENSOR PRODUCTS, INC. 3450 GREEN ROAD CLEVELAND, OH 44122 Fiberoptic sensor for HIV antibodies

R43AI-30854-01A1 (SSS) GARAY, GABRIEL L TRANSPHARM GROUP, INC 1642 FELL STREET SAN FRANCISCO, CA 94117 Drug delivery system to treat oro-esophageal candidiasis

R43AI-30858-01 (SSS) CIMINO, GEORGE D HRI RESEARCH, INC 2315 FIFTH STREET BERKELEY, CA 94710 Methods for PCR sample preparation--Target capture

R01AI-30861-01A1 (ARRC) PRASAD, VINAYAKA R ALBERT EINSTEIN COLLEGE OF MED 1300 MORRIS PARK AVE BRONX, NY 10461 Drug resistant HIV reverse transcriptases

R43AI-30863-01 (SSP) ROBINSON, J DANIEL SIMKIN, INC 406 WEST UNIVERSITY AVENUE GAINESVILLE, FL 32601 Drug usage evaluation and intervention in the AIDS population

R43AI-30864-01 (SSP) MILLSTEIN, JEFFREY A APPLIED BIOMATHEMATICS 100 NORTH COUNTRY ROAD SETAUKET, NY 11733 Detecting sites at risk of becoming foci of lyme disease

R43AI-30865-01 (SSP) WILLIAMS, BEN T UNIV PARK PATHOLOGY ASSOC 1408 WEST UNIVERSITY AVENUE URBANA, IL 61801 HIV screening aid for medical practice

R01AI-30873-05 (EVR) PEREIRA, LENORE UNIVERSITY OF CALIFORNIA DIV. ORAL BIOLOGY, HSW 604 SAN FRANCISCO, CA 94143-0512 Studies on the glycoprotein gb of hsv--An oral pathogen

R43AI-30876-01 (SSS) CHANDRASEKHARAN, RAMACHANDRAN TSRL, INC. PO BOX 7062 ANN ARBOR, MI 48107 Topical delivery of liposomally encapsulated interferon

P01AI-30879-17 (SRC) COOPER, MAX D UNIV. OF ALABAMA @ BIRMINGHAM UAB STATION, UNIVERSITY STATIO BIRMINGHAM, AL 35294 Cell differentiation studies in cancer immunobiology

P01AI-30879-17 0002 (SRC) KEARNEY, JOHN F Cell differentiation studies in cancer immunobiology Hybridomas

P01AI-30879-17 0003 (SRC) BALCH, CHARLES M Cell differentiation studies in cancer immunobiology Normal and abnormal lymphoid differentiation in humans

P01AI-30879-17 0005 (SRC) COOPER, MAX D Cell differentiation studies in cancer immunobiology Lymphoid differentiation in non-human vertebrates

P01AI-30879-17 9001 (SRC) COOPER, MAX D Cell differentiation studies in cancer immunobiology Biomedical facilities

R01AI-30880-01A2 (ARRC) CHIN, DANIEL J THE AGOURON INST 505 COAST BLVD SOUTH LA JOLLA, CA 92037 Optimal nuclear targets of anti-HIV oligodeoxynucleotides

R01AI-30882-01 (ARRC) JOYCE, GERALD F RESEARCH INST OF SCRIPPS CLINI 10666 NORTH TORREY PINES RD LA JOLLA, CA 92037 Evolutionary engineering of anti-HIV-1 ribozymes

R01AI-30885-01 (ARRB) FINKELSTEIN, DIANNE M MASSACHUSETTS GENERAL HOSPITAL BULFINCH 4 BOSTON, MA 02114 Statistical methods for failure time data in AIDS

R43AI-30887-01 (SSS) SPIELVOGEL, BERNARD F BORON BIOLOGICALS, INC 2811 O'BERRY STREET RALEIGH, NC 27607 Nucleoside phosphate analogues with boronated phosphates

R01AI-30890-08 (ALY) WOODLAND, ROBERT T UNIVERSITY OF MASSACHUSETTS 55 LAKE AVENUE NORTH WORCESTER, MA 01655 Regulation of B cell function

R29AI-30897-01 (ARRC) KIM, SUNYOUNG NEW ENGLAND DEACONESS HOSPITAL 185 PILGRIM ROAD BOSTON, MA 02215 Molecular virologic analysis of the nef gene of HIV

R55AI-30900-01 (ARRD) GANGJEE, ALEEM DUQUESNE UNIVERSITY 443 MELLON HALL OF SCIENCE PITTSBURGH, PA 15282 Tricyclic analogues of trimetrexate and piritrexim

R01AI-30901-01 (ARRC) RABSON, ARNOLD B CTR FOR ADVANCED BIOTECH & MED 679 HOES LANE PISCATAWAY, NJ 08854-5638 Role of DNA regulatory sequences in HIV infection

R01AI-30904-01A2 (ARRA) YAMAMOTO, JANET K UNIVERSITY OF CALIFORNIA DAVIS, CA 95616 Vaccines for feline immunodeficiency virus

R01AI-30914-01 (ARRA) WALKER, BRUCE D MASSACHUSETTS GENERAL HOSPITAL 55 FRUIT ST BOSTON, MA 02114 Inhibition of HIV-1 replication by cytotoxic lymphocytes

R01AI-30916-01 (ARRA) VISCIDI, RAPHAEL P JOHNS HOPKINS UNIV SCH OF MED 600 NORTH WOLFE STREET BALTIMORE, MD 21205 Studies of immunosuppressive activity of TAT from HIV-1

R01AI-30917-01A1 (ARRD) SUMMERS, MICHAEL F UNIV OF MARYLAND BALTIMORE CO BALTIMORE, MD 21228 NMR studies of HIV-1 proteins

R29AI-30924-01A1 (ARRC) MARKOVITZ, DAVID M UNIV OF MICHIGAN MEDICAL CENTE 1150 WEST MEDICAL CENTER DRIVE ANN ARBOR, MI 48109-0680 Activation of the HIV-2 enhancer

R01AI-30926-01A1 (ARRA) LIEBERMAN, JUDY NEW ENGLAND MEDICAL CENTER 750 WASHINGTON ST, BOX 245 BOSTON, MA 02111 The cytolytic T cell response to HIV-1

R01AI-30927-01A1 (ARRC) EMERMAN, MICHAEL FRED HUTCHINSON CANCER RES CTR 1124 COLUMBIA STREET SEATTLE, WA 98104 HIV host-cell interactions

R55AI-30937-01A1 (ARRC) GUPTA, PHALGUNI UNIVERSITY OF PITTSBURGH 426 PARRAN HALL PITTSBURGH, PA 15261 Role of various HIV-1 genes in pathogenesis

R01AI-30939-01A1 (ARRA) MOHAGHEGHPOUR, NAHID SRI INTERNATIONAL 333 RAVENSWOOD AVENUE MENLO PARK, CA 94025 Adjuvant activities of an algal glucan

R03AI-30945-02 (ARRD) BELL, THOMAS W S U N Y AT STONY BROOK COLLEGE OF ARTS AND SCIENCES STONY BROOK, NY 11794-3400 New methods for determination of pentamidine

R03AI-30973-02 (ARRD) CAMERON, MIRIAM L DUKE UNIV MEDICAL CTR BOX 3524 DURHAM, NC 27710 HIV-1 affects mononuclear phagocyte antifungal activity

R03AI-30985-02 (ARRD) FRITSCHE, THOMAS R UNIVERSITY OF WASHINGTON SEATTLE, WA 98195 Pathogenesis of toxoplasma in SIV-infected macaques

R01AI-30987-02 (PTHA) RABINOWE, STEVEN L JOSLIN DIABETES CENTER ONE JOSLIN PLACE BOSTON, MA 02215 Pathogenesis of autonomic neuropathy in type I diabetes

R01AI-30988-01 (ARRD) MILLER, MARVIN J UNIVERSITY OF NOTRE DAME NOTRE DAME, IN 46556 Drugs and delivery systems for opportunistic infections

R03AI-30993-01 (MID) SACK, BRADLEY JOHNS HOPKINS UNIVERSITY 615

NORTH WOLFE STREET BALTIMORE, MD 21218 Improved laboratory diagnosis of diarrhoeagenic E.coli A

R03AI-30994-02 (MID) BUTLER, THOMAS C TEXAS TECH UNIV HEALTH SCI CTR LUBBOCK, TX 79430 INDO-US vaccine action programme

R01AI-30997-09 (IMS) HAMILTON, BRIAN L UNIVERSITY OF MIAMI PO BOX 016960 MIAMI, FL 33101 Mechanisms of minor H antigen GVHD

R43AI-31003-01 (SSS) LONBERG, NILS GENPHARM INTERNATIONAL 2375 GARCIA AVENUE MOUNTAIN VIEW, CA 94043 A human antibody repertoire in a transgenic mouse

R01AI-31006-01A2 (ARRA) REMOLD, HEINZ G HARVARD MEDICAL SCHOOL 250 LONGWOOD AVE BOSTON, MA 02115 Mycobacterium avium-intracellulare infections and AIDS

R43AI-31007-01A1 (SSS) GAMPER, HOWARD B MICROPROBE CORPORATION 1725 220TH STREET SE, #104 BOTHELL, WA 98021 Anti- sense inhibition of HBsAg expression in hep g2 cell

R43AI-31008-01 (SSS) MOLDOVEANUA, ZINA SECRETECH, INC 1025 18TH STREET SOUTH BIRMINGHAM, AL 35205 New strategies for immunization against influenza virus

R13AI-31012-01 (AITC) PARKER, DAVID C UNIVERSITY OF MASSACHUSETTS 55 LAKE AVE NORTH WORCESTER, MA 01655 FASEB summer conference--Lymphocytes and antibody

R13AI-31013-01 (MID) DAVID, JOHN R HARVARD SCH OF PUBLIC HEALTH 665 HUNTINGTON AVENUE BOSTON, MA 02115 American society for Trop. Med. Hyg. bloc travel request

R22AI-31034-01 (TMP) LOUNIBOS, LEON P UNIVERSITY OF FLORIDA 200 9TH STREET S E VERO BEACH, FL 32962 Genetic and ecologic differentiation of malaria vectors

R13AI-31040-01 (MID) WHITLEY, RICHARD J UNIVERSITY OF ALABAMA 1600 7TH AVENUE SOUTH BIRMINGHAM, AL 35294 Fourth international conference on antiviral research

R01AI-31046-01 (SAT) SACHS, DAVID H MASSACHUSETTS GENERAL HOSPITAL FRUIT STREET BOSTON, MA 02114 Tolerance to vascular allografts in miniature swine

R29AI-31048-02 (BM) HAZEN, KEVIN C UNIV OF VIRGINIA HLTH SCI CTR BOX 168 CHARLOTTESVILLE, VA 22908 Molecular characterization of C. albicans hydrophobicity

R29AI-31057-01 (EDC) HALLORAN, MARY E EMORY UNIVERSITY 1599 CLIFTON RD NE ATLANTA, GA 30329 Study designs for malaria and other vector-borne disease

R22AI-31066-01 (BM) BARNES, PETER F UNIV OF SOUTHERN CALIFORNIA 2025 ZONAL AVENUE LOS ANGELES, CA 90033 Immunoregulatory role of gamma delta T cells in tuberculosis

R29AI-31072-01 (VR) SUREAU, CAMILLE SOUTHWEST FDN FOR BIOMED RES P O BOX 28147 SAN ANTONIO, TX 78228-0147 Genetic analysis of HDV/HBV interaction

R01AI-31075-01 (TMP) CUPP, EDDIE W UNIVERSITY OF ARIZONA TUCSON, AZ 85721 The role of black fly saliva in parasite transmission

R01AI-31079-01 (TMP) PAPPAS, CAROL D PERU STATE COLLEGE PERU, NE 68421 Relatedness of world wide Aedes albopictus populations

R29AI-31088-01 (BM) ARMSTRONG, SANDRA K EAST CAROLINA UNIVERSITY GREENVILLE, NC 27858-4354 Iron acquisition in Bordetella pertussis

U01AI-31089-02 (SRC) HEATH-CHIOZZI, MARGO E UNIVERSITY OF HAWAII 1960 EAST-WEST ROAD HONOLULU, HI 96822 Development of a Hawaii AIDS clinical trials unit

R01AI-31101-02 (VR) MESSNER, RONALD P UNIVERSITY OF MINNESOTA BOX 108 UMHC/420 DELAWARE ST, MINNEAPOLIS, MN 55455 Mechanisms of coxsackievirus induced polymyositis

U01AI-31107-02 (SRC) GREAVES, WAYNE L HOWARD UNIVERSITY HOSPITAL 2041 GEORGIA AVENUE, NW WASHINGTON, DC 20060 AIDS minority infrastucture

R13AI-31108-01 (MID) APICELLA, MICHAEL A SUNY CLINICAL CENTER 462 GRIDER STREET BUFFALO, NY 14215 Microbial virulence factors and the human response

R01AI-31119-01 (BM) HEWLETT, ERIK L UNIVERSITY OF VIRGINIA BOX 419, SCHOOL OF MEDICINE CHARLOTTESVILLE, VA 22908 Biological effects of pertussis toxin B-oligomer

U01AI-31122-02 (SRC) VAZQUEZ, GUILLERMO J UNIV OF PUERTO RICO GPO BOX 5067 SAN JUAN, PR 00936 ACTU infrastructure development in Puerto Rico

R29AI-31126-01 (PBC) SHIMIZU, YOJI UNIVERSITY OF MICHIGAN 6620 MEDICAL SCIENCE BLDG II ANN ARBOR, MI 48109-0620 Regulation of VLA integrin function on human T cells

R01AI-31129-01A1 (ALY) LEE, DAVID R UNIV OF MISSOURI-COLUMBIA SCHOOL OF MEDICINE COLUMBIA, MO 65212 Peptide binding and expression of MHC class I molecules

R29AI-31130-01 (TMP) BLISSARD, GARY W BOYCE THOMPSON INSTITUTE TOWER ROAD ITHACA, NY 14853-1801 Regulation of viral gene expression in insect cells

R29AI-31133-01 (IMB) BILL, JEROME R NAT'L JEWISH CENTER/IMMUN 1400 JACKSON STREET DENVER, CO 80206-1997 Requirement for non-MHC encoded genes in alloreactivity

R01AI-31137-01 (MEDB) RAY, ANURADHA ROCKEFELLER UNIVERSITY 1230 YORK AVENUE NEW YORK, NY 10021 Hormonal regulation of interleukin-6 gene expression

R01AI-31140-01 (BM) POSNETT, DAVID N CORNELL UNIVERSITY MED COLLEGE 1300 YORK AVENUE NEW YORK, NY 10021 Molecular sites reactive with Mycoplasma arthritidis mitogen

R01AI-31144-01 (MBC) DYBVIG, KEVIN F UNIV OF ALABAMA AT BIRMINGHAM UAB STATION BIRMINGHAM, AL 35294 Genetic recombination in mycoplasmas

R01AI-31145-04 (ARRD) FRIDLAND, ARNOLD ST JUDE CHILDREN'S RES HOSP 332 N LAUDERDALE MEMPHIS, TN 38101 Metabolism and cytotoxicity of C-nucleoside analogs

R01AI-31147-01 (ARRC) LE GRICE, STUART F J CASE WESTERN RESERVE UNIVERSIT 2109 ADELBERT ROAD CLEVELAND, OH 44106 Reverse transcriptase/primer tRNA interactions in HIV

R01AI-31155-01 (GMA) GLEICH, GERALD J MAYO FOUNDATION 200 FIRST STREET SOUTHWEST ROCHESTER, MN 55905 The pathogenesis of the eosinophilia-myalgia syndrome

R01AI-31158-01 (IMB) SYKES, MEGAN MASSACHUSETTS GENERAL HOSPITAL FRUIT STREET BOSTON, MA 02114 A new approach to preventing GVHD

R29AI-31160-01 (IMB) WADE, WILLIAM F UNIVERSITY OF NEBRASKA 13 MANTER HALL LINCOLN, NE 68588-0118 The B chain of I-A --Structure and function

R01AI-31168-01 (ALY) PARHAM, PETER R STANFORD UNIVERSITY STANFORD, CA 94305 Evolution, selection and origins of class I MHC molecule

R15AI-31180-01 (TMP) WRIGHT, JAMES C AUBURN UNIVERSITY AUBURN UNIV, AL 36849-5519 Transmission and diagnosis of canine Lyme disease

R15AI-31187-01 (TMP) HOOK, REUEL R, JR 1600 EAST ROLLINS RD COLUMBIA, MO 65211 Role of RF-like IgM in resistance to malaria

R15AI-31191-01 (VR) MCQUEEN, NANCY L CALIFORNIA STATE UNIVERSITY 5151 STATE UNIVERSITY DRIVE LOS ANGELES, CA 90032 Cloning expression and transport studies of Sendai virus

R15AI-31194-01 (BM) BRODKIN, MARC A WIDENER UNIVERSITY 437 KIRKBRIDE HALL CHESTER, PA 19013 Role of T cells in immunity to Salmonella typhimurium

R15AI-31197-01 (BM) CASTRIC, PETER A DUQUESNE UNIVERSITY PITTSBURGH, PA 15282 Pilin regulatory genes of pseudomonas aeruginosa

R15AI-31205-01 (BM) SINGH, SHIVA P ALABAMA STATE UNIVERSITY 915 SOUTH JACKSON STREET MONTGOMERY, AL 36101 Immunoprotective potential of porins and anti-porin monoclonal antibodies

R01AI-31209-01 (ALY) CORLEY, RONALD B DUKE UNIVERSITY MEDICAL CENTER BOX 3010 DURHAM, N C 27710 IgM polymerization and J chain expression

R15AI-31211-01 (BM) PRICE, STUART B AUBURN UNIVERSITY 264 GREENE HALL AUBURN, AL 36849 Analysis of the pH 6 antigen of Yersinia pestis

R29AI-31213-02 (IMS) PORTNOY, JAY M THE CHILDREN'S MERCY HOSPITAL 24TH AT GILLHAM ROAD KANSAS CITY, MO 64108 Analysis of alternaria antigens

R15AI-31214-01 (PHRA) WHITE, CATHERINE A UNIVERSITY OF HOUSTON 1441 MOURSUND ST HOUSTON, TX 77030 Improved antibiotic therapy with liposomal targeting

R01AI-31220-01 (EVR) WRIGHT, CYNTHIA F ARMED FORCES INST OF PATHOLOGY WASHINGTON, DC 20306-6000 Vaccinia virus late transcription

R13AI-31222-01 (AITC) FOX, C FRED KEYSTONE CENTER PO BOX 606 KEYSTONE, CO 80435 Conference on cytokines and their receptors

R22AI-31224-01 (TMP) KNOPF, PAUL M BROWN UNIVERSITY PROVIDENCE, RI 02912-9707 Expression of a gene for an S mansoni vaccine antigen

P01AI-31229-01 (SRC) LIPSKY, PETER E U OF TEXAS HLTH SCI CTR/DALLAS 5323 HARRY HINES BLVD DALLAS, TX 75235 Molecular analysis of autoantibody formation

P01AI-31229-01 0001 (SRC) LIPSKY, PETER E Molecular analysis of autoantibody formation The frequency of human autoantibody producing B cells

P01AI-31229-01 0002 (SRC) CAPRA, DONALD J Molecular analysis of autoantibody formation Molecular analysis of the human B cells repertoire

P01AI-31229-01 0003 (SRC) MEEK, KATHERYN D Molecular analysis of autoantibody formation Recombination in the generation of autoantibodies

P01AI-31229-01 0004 (SRC) TUCKER, PHILLIP W Molecular analysis of autoantibody formation Recapitulation of autoimmunity in transgenic mice

P01AI-31229-01 9001 (SRC) LIPSKY, PETER E Molecular analysis of autoantibody formation Core--Cell culture

R55AI-31230-01A1 (PTHA) EMANCIPATOR, STEVEN N CASE WESTERN RESERVE UNIVERSIT 2085 ADELBERT RD CLEVELAND, OH 44106 Enzymolysis of immune complexes in vivo

R29AI-31231-02 (EI) KAYE, JONATHAN G SCRIPPS CLINIC & RES FOUNDATIO 10666 NORTH TORREY PINES RD LA JOLLA, CA 92037 Analysis of T cell development in transgenic mice

R15AI-31232-01 (MET) GRUND, VERNON R UNIVERSITY OF CINCINNATI MED C 3223 EDEN AVENUE CINCINNATI, OH 45267-0004 Immunochemical modulation of metabolic homeostasis

R15AI-31234-01 (BM) DEZFULIAN, MANOUCHER FLORIDA INTERNATIONAL UNIVERSI COLLEGE OF HEALTH MIAMI, FL 33199 Monoclonal antibody based ELISA for botulinum neurotoxin

P01AI-31238-01 (SRC) UNANUE, EMIL R WASHINGTON UNIV SCH OF MED 660 S EUCLID AVE, BOX 8118 ST LOUIS, MO 63110 T cell autoimmunity

P01AI-31238-01 0004 (SRC) MURPHY, KENNETH M T cell autoimmunity Cellular basis of T cell activation

P01AI-31238-01 0001 (SRC) UNANUE, EMIL R T cell autoimmunity Antigen presentation in insulin dependent diabetes mellitus

P01AI-31238-01 0002 (SRC) ALLEN, PAUL T cell autoimmunity The role of T cells in autoimmune myocarditis

P01AI-31238-01 0003 (SRC) BRACIALE, THOMAS J T cell autoimmunity A transgenic model for insulin dependent diabetes mellitus

P01AI-31241-01 (SRC) NEPOM, GERALD T VIRGINIA MASON RESEARCH CENTER 1000 SENECA STREET SEATTLE, WA 98101 Molecular and genetic mechanisms of autoimmunity

P01AI-31241-01 0001 (SRC) CONCANNON, PATRICK J Molecular and genetic mechanisms of autoimmunity Structural features of T cell receptor recognition in autoimmunity

P01AI-31241-01 0002 (SRC) NEPOM, GERALD T Molecular and genetic mechanisms of autoimmunity HLA class II interactions in antigen presentation

P01AI-31241-01 0003 (SRC) NAPOM, BARBARA S Molecular and genetic mechanisms of autoimmunity Allelic polymorphism in HLA-DRB regulatory region genes

P01AI-31241-01 0004 (SRC) MILNER, ERIC C B Molecular and genetic mechanisms of autoimmunity Antibody repertoires and autoimmunity

P01AI-31241-01 9001 (SRC) NEPOM, GERALD T Molecular and genetic mechanisms of autoimmunity Core--DNA and cell bank

R29AI-31249-01 (EVR) ANDERS, DAVID G WADSWORTH CTR FOR LAB & RES EMPIRE STATE PLAZA ALBANY, NY 12201-0509 Structure and function of a CMV origin of DNA replication

R15AI-31256-01 (BNP) BAKER, BILL J FLORIDA INSTITUTE TECHNOLOGY MELBOURNE, FL 32901 Biosynthetic studies of eudistomins C E K and L

R01AI-31262-02 (ARR) BENJAMIN, DAVID OHIO STATE UNIVERSITY 410 W 10TH AVE COLUMBUS, OH 43210 HIV-1 and B cell lymphokines-- Role and effects

PROJECT NO., ORGANIZATIONAL UNIT., INVESTIGATOR, ADDRESS, TITLE

R29AI-31265-01 (IMS) WALDSCHMIDT, THOMAS J UNIVERSITY OF IOWA COLL OF MED IOWA CITY, IA 52242 Functional characterization of FceR- and FceR+ B cells

R01AI-31269-01 (ALY) CLAYTON, LINDA K DANA FARBER CANCER INST 44 BINNEY STREET BOSTON, MA 02115 Molecular and functional analysis of CD3 zeta and eta isoforms

R13AI-31270-01 (AITC) FOX, C FRED KEYSTONE CENTER PO BOX 606 KEYSTONE, CO 80435 Conference on the molecular basis of oxidative damage by leukocytes

R01AI-31272-02 (ARR) GREEN, MICHAEL R UNIV OF MASS MEDICAL SCHOOL 373 PLANTATION STREET WORCESTER, MA 01605 Transcription activation by the HIV tat and HTLV tax protein

R13AI-31277-01 (AITC) FOX, C FRED KEYSTONE CENTER PO BOX 606 KEYSTONE, CO 80435 Conference on self reactivity and its regulation

R43AI-31284-01 (SSS) MORROW, WILLIAM J IDEC 11099 N. TORREYPINES RD, #160 LA JOLLA, CA 92037 Identification of pathogenic autoantibodies

R43AI-31285-01 (SSS) DENIS, KATHLEEN A SPECIALTY LABORATORIES INC 2211 MICHIGAN AVENUE SANTA MONICA, CA 90404-3900 Generation of antigen-specific MABs using SCID-hu mice

R43AI-31287-01 (SSS) KONIGSBERG, PAULA J VESTAR, INC. 650 CLIFFSIDE DR. SAN DIMAS, CA 91773 IL-2 liposomes as delivery agents for immunotherapeutics

R43AI-31295-01 (SSS) JOLLY, DOUGLAS J VIAGENE INC 11075 ROSELLE STREET SAN DIEGO, CA 92121 Improved quantitative commercial HIV assay

R43AI-31300-01 (SSS) LIN, LILY HRI RESEARCH, INC 2315 FIFTH STREET BERKELEY, CA 94710 Validation test for pathogen inactivation using the PCR

R43AI-31310-01 (SSS) KANG, CHANG-YUIL IDEC PHARMACEUTICALS CORPORATI 11099 NORTH TORREY PINES ROAD LA JOLLA, CA 92037 The anti-idiotype antibody approach for an HIV vaccine

R43AI-31313-01 (SSS) GARDNER, FRED A BIOMEDICAL DEVELOPMENT CORP 737 ISOM ROAD SAN ANTONIO, TX 78216 Salmonella control on poultry using a disinfectant dip

R43AI-31315-01 (SSS) GAMPER, HOWARD B MICROPROBE CORPORATION 1725 220TH STREET SE, #104 BOTHELL, WA 98021 HIV reporter cell line for screening anti-sense agents

R01AI-31326-01 (ARRD) ROBINSON, WILLIAM E, JR VANDERBILT UNIVERSITY NASHVILLE, TN 37232-2561 Testing of anti-HIV compounds from medicinal plants

R29AI-31331-01 (ARRB) BACCHETTI, PETER SAN FRANCISCO GENERAL HOSPITAL 995 POTRERO AVE SAN FRANCISCO, CA 94110 Smoothed incomplete-data methods for studying epidemics

R01AI-31334-01 (ARRC) GRANDGENETT, DUANE P ST LOUIS UNIV MEDICAL CENTER 3681 PARK AVENUE ST LOUIS, MO 63110 HIV-1 integration protein

R01AI-31335-07 (IMS) NACLERIO, ROBERT M JOHNS HOPKINS ASTHMA/ALLERGY C 5501 HOPKINS BAYVIEW CIRCLE BALTIMORE, MD 21224 Evaluation of the nasal late phase response to antigen

R01AI-31337-01 (ARRA) ROCK, KENNETH L DANA FARBER CANCER INSTITUTE 44 BINNEY STREET BOSTON, MA 02115 Vaccine for CTL immunity to human immunodeficiency virus

R01AI-31338-01 (ARRE) HORWITZ, MARCUS A UCLA SCHOOL OF MEDICINE LOS ANGELES, CA 90024-1688 Immunoprotective determinants of M. tuberculosis in AIDS

R55AI-31340-01A1 (ARRA) HUSO, DAVID L JOHNS HOPKINS UNIV/SCH OF MED 301 BAYVIEW BLVD BALTIMORE, MD 21224 Envelope carbohydrates of CAEV -- Insight into HIV biology

R01AI-31342-01A1 (ARRC) DEWHURST, STEPHEN UNIVERSITY OF ROCHESTER MED CT 601 ELMWOOD AVENUE, BOX 672 ROCHESTER, NY 14642 Characterization of SIV long terminal repeat

R55AI-31343-01A1 (ARRD) LEE-HUANG, SYLVIA NEW YORK UNIVERSITY MED CTR 550 FIRST AVENUE NEW YORK, N Y 10016 Rational development of novel anti-AIDS drugs

R01AI-31344-01 (ARRE) HILL, JOSEPH O TRUDEAU INSTITUTE, INC BOX 59 ALGONQUIN AVE SARANAC LAKE, NY 12983 Immunity against opportunistic Cryptococcus neoformans

R43AI-31349-01 (BIOL) KRAUS, LEWIS E INFOUSE 1995 UNIVERSITY AVENUE BERKELEY, CA 94704 Interactive video to teach children about HIV prevention

R01AI-31354-01A1 (ARRC) TERWILLIGER, ERNEST F DANA-FARBER CANCER INSTITUTE 44 BINNEY STREET BOSTON, MA 02115 Structure, function and mechanism of the HIV-1 vpr gene

R55AI-31355-01 (ARRC) VIGLIANTI, GREGORY A UNIVERSITY OF MASSACHUSETTS 55 LAKE AVENUE NORTH WORCESTER, MA 01655 Tar RNA splicing in siv mac

R55AI-31356-01A1 (ARRB) DUPONT, HERBERT L UT HEALTH SCIENCES CENTER PO BOX 20186 HOUSTON, TX 77225 HIV-associated diarrhea and wasting in Zambia

R29AI-31360-01 (ARRE) KUHLS, THOMAS L CHILDRENS HOSPITAL OF OKLAHOMA 940 NORTH EAST 13TH OKLAHOMA CITY, OK 73104 Cryptosporidium parvum - enterocyte interactions

R29AI-31373-01 (ARRE) JANOFF, EDWARD N VA MEDICAL CENTER 1 VETERANS DRIVE MINNEAPOLIS, MN 55417 Immunity to pneumococcus in persons with HIV

R55AI-31375-01 (ARRC) SCOTT, WALTER A UNIVERSITY OF MIAMI PO BOX 016129 MIAMI, FL 33101 Drug resistant HIV in children treated with AZT or ddi

R01AI-31378-01A1 (ARRC) WONG-STAAL, FLOSSIE UNIVERSITY OF CALIFORNIA LA JOLLA, CA 92093 The rev/rex transactivation pathway of HIV/HTLV

R01AI-31383-01A1 (ARRA) MARTHAS, MARTA L UNIVERSITY OF CALIFORNIA VIROLOGY & IMMUNOLOGY UNIT DAVIS, CA 95616-8542 Vaccination against infection with cell-associated SIV

R01AI-31386-01A1 (ARRA) SOPORI, MOHAN L LOVELACE MEDICAL FOUNDATION 2425 RIDGECREST DR, SE ALBUQUERQUE, NM 87108-5127 Role of autoreactive T cells in murine acquired immunodeficiency syndrome

R01AI-31414-01 (TMP) VAN VOORHIS, WESLEY C UNIVERSITY OF WASHINGTON SEATTLE, WA 98195 Immune response in acute and chronic Chagas's disease

R13AI-31415-01 (AIDS) SHULTZ, LEONARD D JACKSON LABORATORY 600 MAIN STREET BAR HARBOR, ME 04609-0800 Seventh international workshop on immune deficient animals

R13AI-31416-01 (MID) MOCARSKI, EDWARD S, JR STANFORD UNIVERSITY FAIRCHILD SCIENCE CENTER STANFORD, CA 94305-5402 Sixteenth international herpesvirus workshop

PROJECT NO., ORGANIZATIONAL UNIT., INVESTIGATOR, ADDRESS, TITLE

R13AI-31424-01 (MID) HILL, GEORGE C MEHARRY MEDICAL COLLEGE DIV OF BIOMEDICAL SCIENCES NASHVILLE, TN 37208 Eighth annual tropical diseases symposium

R01AI-31427-01 (SSS) MOREL, PENELOPE A PITTSBURGH CANCER INSTITUTE LOTHROP STREET PITTSBURGH, PA 15213 Mathematical modeling of immunological reactions

R01AI-31431-01 (TMP) WALKER, DAVID H UNIVERSITY OF TEXAS MED BRANCH 301 UNIVERSITY BLVD GALVESTON, TX 77550 Antigenic composition of medically related Ehrlichiae

R29AI-31436-01 (PTHA) CROCKETT-TORABI, ELAHE UNIVERSITY OF MICHIGAN 1301 CATHERINE RD ANNARBOR, MI 48109-0602 Fc receptor dependent neutrophil activation

U01AI-31440-01 (SRC) DELMONICO, FRANCIS L MASSACHUSETTS GENERAL HOSPITAL FRUIT STREET BOSTON, MA 02114 Comparison of OKT4A to conventional immunosuppression

U01AI-31442-01 (SRC) LIGHT, JIMMY A MEDLANTIC RES FOUNDATION 108 IRVING STREET NW WASHINGTON, DC 20010 Improving the safety and efficacy of immunosuppression

U01AI-31445-01 (SRC) STUART, FRANK P UNIVERSITY OF CHICAGO 5801 SOUTH MARYLAND AVENUE CHICAGO, IL 60637 Therapeutic monoclonal antibodies in renal trasplantation

R13AI-31447-01 (MID) RICHARDS, FRANK F YALE UNIVERSITY DEPT. OF INTERNAL MEDICINE NEW HAVEN CT 06510 2nd international workshop on AIDS related parasites

U01AI-31448-01 (SRC) HOLMES, KING K HARBORVIEW MEDICAL CENTER 325 NINTH AVENUE SEATTLE, WA 98104 University of Washington STD cooperative research center

U01AI-31448-01 9001 (SRC) DEROUEN, TIMOTHY University of Washington STD cooperative research center Biostatistics /epidemiology core

U01AI-31448-01 9002 (SRC) STAMM, WALTER E University of Washington STD cooperative research center Laboratory core

U01AI-31448-01 9003 (SRC) HANDSFIELD, H HUNTER University of Washington STD cooperative research center Behavioral and clinical core

U01AI-31448-01 9004 (SRC) STAMM, WALTER E University of Washington STD cooperative research center Developmental awards core

U01AI-31448-01 0001 (SRC) PLUMMER, FRANK University of Washington STD cooperative research center Immunology of gonorrhea in Nairobi prostitute cohort

U01AI-31448-01 0002 (SRC) BRUNHAM, ROBERT University of Washington STD cooperative research center PID in developing countries--Relation to HIV and the pill

U01AI-31448-01 0003 (SRC) LUKEHART, SHEILA A University of Washington STD cooperative research center Pathogenesis and therapy of experimental neurosyphilis

U01AI-31448-01 0004 (SRC) HILLIER, SHARON L University of Washington STD cooperative research center H(2)O(2) producing Lactobacilli and STD resistance in women

U01AI-31448-01 0005 (SRC) GALLOWAY, DENISE A University of Washington STD cooperative research center HPV-6 and 16 infections--Molecular epidemiology

U01AI-31448-01 0006 (SRC) COREY, LAWRENCE University of Washington STD cooperative research center HSV 2 serologic testing--Strategy for STD control

U01AI-31448-01 0007 (SRC) MORRISON, DIANE M University of Washington STD cooperative research center STD behavioral intervention--Risk assessment and triage

U01AI-31448-01 0008 (SRC) HOLMES, KING K University of Washington STD cooperative research center Sex partner networks, recruitment and STD epidemiology

U01AI-31448-01 0009 (SRC) GILLMORE, MARY L R University of Washington STD cooperative research center STD outcomes after condom education in adolescents

U01AI-31449-01 (SRC) ALEXANDER, J WESLEY UNIVERSITY OF CINCINNATI 231 BETHESDA AVE CINCINNATI, OHIO 45267-0558 Tolerance induction using DST-donor specific transfusion and cyclosporine

U01AI-31457-01 (SRC) BARBER, WILLIAM H UNIVERSITY OF ALABAMA UAB STATION BIRMINGHAM, AL 35294 Donor bone marrow as a biologic immunosuppressive agent

R01AI-31460-01 (TMP) SAUER, JOHN R OKLAHOMA STATE UNIVERSITY 501 LIFE SCIENCES WEST STILLWATER, OK 74078 Arachidonate metabolism in tick salivary glands

R01AI-31473-01 (BM) NAHM, MOON H WASHINGTON UNIV SCH OF MED 660 SOUTH EUCLID AVENUE ST. LOUIS, MO 63110 Human antibody response to Haemophilus influenzae B

R01AI-31474-01 (BM) SOLL, DAVID R UNIVERSITY OF IOWA IOWA CITY, IA 52242 Vaginotropic and vaginopathic strains of Candida albicans

R01AI-31478-01 (TMP) JACOBS-LORENA, MARCELO CASE WESTERN RESERVE UNIV 2109 ADELBERT ROAD CLEVELAND, OH 44106 Gut-specific genes of Simulium

R29AI-31479-01 (BM) KLEIN, BRUCE S UNIVERSITY OF WISCONSIN 600 HIGHLAND AVE MADISON, WI 53792 Antifungal role and action of human T-cell subsets

R29AI-31489-01 (IMS) BLACKMAN, MARCIA A ST JUDE CHILDRENS RES HOSPITAL 332 N LAUDERDALE MEMPHIS, TN 38105 T cell tolerance by clonal anergy in transgenic mice

U01AI-31490-01 (SRC) HUNSICKER, LAWRENCE G UNIV OF IOWA HOSPITAL IOWA CITY, IA 52242 Clinical trials of immunosuppression in renal transplant

U01AI-31492-01 (SRC) ROSENTHAL, J THOMAS UCLA SCHOOL OF MEDICINE 10833 LE CONTE AVE LOS ANGELES, CA 90024 Cooperative clinical trials in renal transplantation

U01AI-31494-01 (SRC) JONES, ROBERT B UNIVERSITY OF INDIANA 545 BARNHILL DRIVE INDIANAPOLIS, IN 46202-5124 Midwest sexually transmitted diseases research center

U01AI-31494-01 0001 (SRC) SPEAR, PATRICIA G Midwest sexually transmitted diseases research center Variability in herpes simplex virus glycoproteins and infectivity

U01AI-31494-01 0002 (SRC) SEIFERT, H STEVEN Midwest sexually transmitted diseases research center Gonococcal pilin serology and gene usage in vivo

U01AI-31494-01 0003 (SRC) BYRNE, GERALD I Midwest sexually transmitted diseases research center T cell responses in chlamydial disease

U01AI-31494-01 0004 (SRC) FIFE, KENNETH H Midwest sexually transmitted diseases research center Papillomavirus infections in pregnancy

U01AI-31494-01 0005 (SRC) ROMAN, ANN Midwest sexually transmitted diseases research center Human papillomavirus type 6 gene expression regulation

U01AI-31494-01 0006 (SRC) WILDE, CHARLES E Midwest sexually transmitted diseases research center Molecular biology of gonococcal OMP-MC

U01AI-31494-01 0007 (SRC) ORR, DONALD P Midwest sexually transmitted diseases research center Computer assisted STD interventions for adolescents

U01AI-31494-01 9001 (SRC) BLYTHE, MARGARET J Midwest sexually transmitted diseases research center Clinical core

U01AI-31494-01 9002 (SRC) KATZ, BARRY P Midwest sexually transmitted diseases research center Biostatistics core

U01AI-31494-01 9003 (SRC) JONES, ROBERT B Midwest sexually transmitted diseases research center Chlamydia culture core

U01AI-31496-01 (SRC) SPARLING, PHILIP F UNIVERSITY OF NORTH CAROLINA 3033 OLD CLINIC CHAPEL HILL, NC 27599-7005 North Carolina STD cooperative research center

U01AI-31496-01 9001 (SRC) COHEN, MYRON S North Carolina STD cooperative research center Core--Microbiology

U01AI-31496-01 0001 (SRC) SPARLING, PHILIP F North Carolina STD cooperative research center Structure and function of gonococcal iron regulated proteins

U01AI-31496-01 0002 (SRC) CANNON, JANNE G North Carolina STD cooperative research center Properties of Neisseria gonorrhoeae opa outer membrane proteins

U01AI-31496-01 0003 (SRC) COHEN, MYRON S North Carolina STD cooperative research center Inoculation of mutants into urethra

U01AI-31496-01 0004 (SRC) STAMM, LOLA V North Carolina STD cooperative research center Pathogenesis and immunity of Treponema pallidum proteins

U01AI-31496-01 0005 (SRC) WYRICK, PRISCILLA B North Carolina STD cooperative research center Immunopathogenesis of genital Chlamydia trachomatis

U01AI-31496-01 0006 (SRC) THOMAS, JAMES C North Carolina STD cooperative research center The epidemiology of STDs in rural North Carolina

U01AI-31498-01 (SRC) BASEMAN, JOEL B UNIV OF TEXAS HLTH SCIS CTR 7703 FLOYD CURL DRIVE SAN ANTONIO, TX 78284-7758 Sexually transmitted diseases cooperative research center

U01AI-31498-01 0001 (SRC) ALDERETE, JOHN F Sexually transmitted diseases cooperative research center Antigenic diversity genes of Trichomonas vaginalis

U01AI-31498-01 0002 (SRC) TRYON, VICTOR V Sexually transmitted diseases cooperative research center Treponema pallidum and the human host

U01AI-31498-01 0003 (SRC) DEB, SWATI P Sexually transmitted diseases cooperative research center Herpes simplex virus replication from STD patients

U01AI-31498-01 0004 (SRC) SHAIN, ROCHELLE N Sexually transmitted diseases cooperative research center Modifying STD risk behavior among Mexican American women

U01AI-31498-01 0005 (SRC) SUMAYA, CIRO V Sexually transmitted diseases cooperative research center STD education and training center for South Texas

U01AI-31498-01 9001 (SRC) TRYON, VICTOR V Sexually transmitted diseases cooperative research center Biotechnology core

U01AI-31498-01 9002 (SRC) NEWTON, EDWARD R Sexually transmitted diseases cooperative research center Clinical core

U01AI-31498-01 9003 (SRC) PERDUE, SONDRA T Sexually transmitted diseases cooperative research center Statistical core

U01AI-31498-01 9004 (SRC) BASEMAN, JOEL B Sexually transmitted diseases cooperative research center Developmental core

U01AI-31499-01 (SRC) SCHACHTER, JULIUS SAN FRANCISCO GENERAL HOSPITAL 1001 POTRERO AVENUE SAN FRANCISCO, CA 94110 San Francisco STD cooperative research center

U01AI-31499-01 0001 (SRC) PALEFSKY, JOEL M San Francisco STD cooperative research center Cell-mediated immune response to HPV infection

U01AI-31499-01 0002 (SRC) STEPHENS, RICHARD S San Francisco STD cooperative research center Host immune response to chlamydia trachmotasis infections

U01AI-31499-01 0003 (SRC) PADIAN, NANCY S San Francisco STD cooperative research center Sexual partners and risk of pelvic inflammatory disease

U01AI-31499-01 0004 (SRC) SWEET, RICHARD L San Francisco STD cooperative research center Inapparent PID in female contacts of men with urethritis

U01AI-31499-01 0005 (SRC) SHAFER, MARY ANN B San Francisco STD cooperative research center Military-based intervention to prevent urethritis/STDs

U01AI-31499-01 9001 (SRC) SCHACHTER, JULIUS San Francisco STD cooperative research center Core--Laboratory

U01AI-31499-01 9002 (SRC) BOLAN, GAIL San Francisco STD cooperative research center Core--Clinical

U01AI-31499-01 9003 (SRC) MOSS, ANDREW R San Francisco STD cooperative research center Core--Epidemiology and biostatistics

R01AI-31500-01 (EVR) KNIPE, DAVID M HARVARD MEDICAL SCHOOL 200 LONGWOOD AVE BOSTON, MA 02115 HSV DNA replication protein and late gene expression

R01AI-31501-01 (VR) RICE, CHARLES M WASHINGTON UNIVERSITY 660 S EUCLID AVE, BOX 8093 ST. LOUIS, MO 63110 Proteolytic control of flavivirus replication

R13AI-31511-01 (MID) SVANBORG, CATHARINA LUND UNIVERSITY SOLVEGATAN 23 S-223 62 LUND, SWEDEN Gordon conference on microbial adhesion mechanisms

PROJECT NO., ORGANIZATIONAL UNIT., INVESTIGATOR, ADDRESS, TITLE

R01AI-31519-01 (BM) KLIMPEL, GARY UNIVERSITY OF TEXAS GALVESTON, TX 77550 Bacteria induced cytokine production in the gut

R01AI-31524-01 (ALY) MESCHER, MATTHEW F MEDICAL BIOLOGY INSTITUTE 11077 N TORREY PINES RD LA JOLLA, CA 92037 Molecular mechanisms of MHC class I antigen recognition

R29AI-31527-01 (IMS) PERKINS, DAVID L BRIGHAM AND WOMEN'S HOSPITAL, 75 FRANCIS STREET BOSTON, MA 02115 Peripheral T cell tolerance induced by superantigens

R13AI-31531-01 (MID) STEWART, GEORGE C UNIVERSITY OF KANSAS 7042 HAWORTH HALL LAWRENCE, KS 66045-2103 Gordon conference on staphylococcal disease

R01AI-31537-01 (BM) GOLDFINE, HOWARD UNIVERSITY OF PENNSYLVANIA 209 JOHNSON PAVILION PHILADELPHIA, PA 19104-6076 Phospholipases and the pathogenesis of Listeria

U01AI-31541-01 (SRC) GEHA, RAIF S CHILDREN'S HOSPITAL CORPORATIO 300 LONGWOOD AVE BOSTON, MA 02115 Molecular basis of immune function in health and disease

U01AI-31541-01 0004 (SRC) CHATILA, TALAL A Molecular basis of immune function in health and disease Signal transduction by MHC class II molecules

U01AI-31541-01 0005 (SRC) GLIMCHER, LAURIE A Molecular basis of immune function in health and disease Models of class II deficiency

U01AI-31541-01 0006 (SRC) ROSEN, FRED S Molecular basis of immune function in health and disease The Wiskott-Aldrich syndrome--A calpain/calpastatin defect

U01AI-31541-01 0007 (SRC) HOMER, CHARLES J Molecular basis of immune function in health and disease Urban patient and provider management training for asthma

U01AI-31541-01 0001 (SRC) ALT, FREDERICK W Molecular basis of immune function in health and disease Control of IgE isotype switching

U01AI-31541-01 0002 (SRC) GEHA, RAIF S Molecular basis of immune function in health and disease Role of CD40 in the induction of IgE synthesis

U01AI-31541-01 0003 (SRC) TERHORST, CORNELIUS P Molecular basis of immune function in health and disease Signal transduction by membrane immunoglobulins

R29AI-31545-01 (GMA) PICKER, LOUIS J UNIVERSITY OF TEXAS SW MED CTR 5323 HARRY HINES BLVD DALLAS, TX 75235-9072 Molecular basis of human T-cell homing to inflamed skin

R29AI-31548-01 (BM) MILLER, JEFFERY F UCLA SCHOOL OF MEDICINE 10833 LE CONTE AVE LOS ANGELES, CA 90024-1747 Sensory transduction and the bordetella/ host interaction

R01AI-31558-01 (ALY) WINOTO, ASTAR UNIV OF CALIFORNIA, BERKELEY 472 LIFE SCIENCE ADDITION BERKELEY, CA 94720 Molecular mechanisms of alpha beta cell development

U01AI-31559-01 (SRC) MATAS, ARTHUR J UNIVERSITY OF MINNESOTA 420 DELAWARE STREET SOUTH EAST MINNEAPOLIS, MN 55455 Transplant study unit application

R01AI-31563-01 (EVR) WALKER, BRUCE D MASSACHUSETTS GENERAL HOSPITAL 55 FRUIT ST/GRAY 5 BOSTON, MA 02114 Cell-mediated immunity in hepatitis C virus infection

R13AI-31565-01 (MID) ROSE, JOHN K UNIV OF RHODE ISLAND 310 CEDAR ST NEW HAVEN, CT 06510 Gordon conference on animal cells and viruses

R01AI-31580-01 (EDC) WARD, JOEL I HARBOR-UCLA MEDICAL CENTER 1124 W CARSON ST TORRANCE, CA 90502 Haemophilus influenzae B conjugate vaccine efficacy

R13AI-31581-01 (MID) CAMPBELL, ALLAN STANFORD UNIVERSITY STANFORD, CA 94305 Population biology and evolution of microorganisms

R01AI-31584-01 (GMA) HARLEY, JOHN B OKLAHOMA MEDICAL RESEARCH FDN 825 NE 13TH STREET OKLAHOMA CITY, OK 73104 Y RNA sequences and Ro RNP function

R01AI-31588-01 (BM) O'BRIEN, REBECCA L NATIONAL JEWISH CENTER FOR 1400 JACKSON STREET DENVER, CO 80206 Heat shock protein recognition by gamma,delta T cell subset

R01AI-31591-01 (IMS) GREEN, DOUGLAS R LA JOLLA INST/ALLERGY/IMMUNOLO 11149 N TORREY PINES RD LA JOLLA, CA 92037 Activation-induced apoptosis in T cell development

R29AI-31592-01 (ALY) WARD, ELIZABETH S UNIVERSITY OF TEXAS 5323 HARRY HINES BLVD DALLAS, TX 75235-8576 Soluble T cell receptor expressions in Escherichia coli

U01AI-31595-01 (SRC) SPIEGELBERG, HANS L UNIV OF CALIFORNIA 9500 GILMAN DR LA JOLLA, CA 92093-0609 Role of cytokines in allergic disorders

U01AI-31595-01 0001 (SRC) WASSERMAN, STEPHEN Role of cytokines in allergic disorders Asthma in the Indo-Chinese

U01AI-31595-01 0002 (SRC) SPIEGELBERG, HANS L Role of cytokines in allergic disorders Il-4, IgE and IgG4 formation in atopy

U01AI-31595-01 0003 (SRC) BROIDE, DAVID H Role of cytokines in allergic disorders Mast cells and endothelium

U01AI-31595-01 0004 (SRC) BARRETT, KIM E Role of cytokines in allergic disorders Interaction of mast cells with the airway epithelium

U01AI-31595-01 0005 (SRC) GIGLI, IRMA Role of cytokines in allergic disorders Phototoxin and UV light modulation of cellular function

U01AI-31595-01 9001 (SRC) FIRESTEIN, GARY Role of cytokines in allergic disorders Molecular biology core

P01AI-31596-01 (MID) DOHERTY, PETER C ST JUDE CHILDREN'S RESERCH HOS 332 N LAUDERDALE MEMPHIS, TN 38105 Cellular immune response in respiratory virus infections

P01AI-31596-01 0001 (MID) PORTNER, ALAN Cellular immune response in respiratory virus infections Parainfluenza virus proteins and their role in immunity

P01AI-31596-01 0002 (MID) ALLEN, JANE Cellular immune response in respiratory virus infections Specificity of human T cells for human parainfluenza 1 virus

P01AI-31596-01 0003 (MID) KATZ, JACQUELINE Cellular immune response in respiratory virus infections Sendai virus pathogenesis and cell mediated immunity

P01AI-31596-01 0004 (MID) DOHERTY, PETER Cellular immune response in respiratory virus infections T cell memory to sendai viruses

P01AI-31596-01 0005 (MID) COLECLOUGH, CHRISTOPHER Cellular immune response in respiratory virus infections Antibody genes in sendai

PROJECT NO., ORGANIZATIONAL UNIT., INVESTIGATOR, ADDRESS, TITLE

virus-specific memory B cells
P01AI-31596-01 9001 (MID) PORTNER, ALLEN Cellular immune response in respiratory virus infections Virus molecular reagents and monoclonal antibodies
P01AI-31596-01 9002 (MID) DOHERTY, PETER Cellular immune response in respiratory virus infections Monoclonal antibodies, flow cytometry, and histopathology
U01AI-31599-01 (SRC) AUSTEN, K FRANK BRIGHAM & WOMEN'S HOSPITAL 250 LONGWOOD AVE BOSTON, MA 02115 Cellular basis of hypersensitivity diseases in humans
U01AI-31599-01 0001 (SRC) DRAZEN, JEFFREY M Cellular basis of hypersensitivity diseases in humans Urinary and excretion of LTR as an index of airway responses
U01AI-31599-01 0002 (SRC) FANTA, CHRISTOPHER H Cellular basis of hypersensitivity diseases in humans Asthma morbidity among city minorities -- Educational intervention
U01AI-31599-01 0003 (SRC) OWEN, WILLIAM F Cellular basis of hypersensitivity diseases in humans Eosinophil phenotypes in chronic eosinophilic pneumonia
U01AI-31599-01 0004 (SRC) STEVENS, RICHARD L Cellular basis of hypersensitivity diseases in humans Anti-peptide antibodies and oligonucleotide probes recognizing mast cell protease
U01AI-31599-01 0005 (SRC) WEIDNER, NOEL Cellular basis of hypersensitivity diseases in humans Mast cell phenotype, activation profile in various physical allergies
U01AI-31599-01 0006 (SRC) WEIDNER, NOEL Cellular basis of hypersensitivity diseases in humans Mast cells distribution and phenotype in systemic mastocytosis
U01AI-31599-01 0007 (SRC) WEIDNER, NOEL Cellular basis of hypersensitivity diseases in humans Bullous pemphigoid
R29AI-31608-01 (EDC) SCHWARTZ, BRIAN JHU SCH OF HYGIENE & PUBLIC HL 615 NORTH WOLFE STREET BALTIMORE, MD 21205 Anti - tick antibody in Lyme disease research
R55AI-31612-01 (BM) HANDWERGER, SANDRA BETH ISRAEL MEDICAL CENTER FIRST AVENUE AT 16TH STREET NEW YORK, NY 10003 Glycopeptide resistance in enterococcus
R29AI-31615-01 (TMP) GOLDBERG, DANIEL E JEWISH HOSP AT WASH UNIV MED C BOX 8230 660 S EUCLID ST LOUIS, MO 63110 Function and inhibition of P falciparum digestive vacuoles
R13AI-31620-01 (AITC) KAPLAN, ALAN M UNIVERSITY OF KENTUCKY 800 ROSE ST LEXINGTON, KY 40536-0084 Autumn immunology conference
R29AI-31622-01 (VR) MASTERS, PAUL S NEW YORK STATE DEPT OF HEALTH LABORATORY OF VIROLOGY ALBANY, NY 12201-0509 Coronavirus protein - RNA interactions
R55AI-31641-01 (SAT) FOX, IRA J COLUMBIA UNIVERSITY 630 WEST 168TH STREET NEW YORK, NY 10032 Gene therapy in induction of transplant tolerance
R55AI-31644-01 (SAT) MC CARTHY, SUSAN A MONTEFIORE HOSPITAL 3459 FIFTH AVENUE PITTSBURGH, PA 15213 Organ transplantation -- Role of CD8 in cytotoxic T cells
R29AI-31645-01 (BM) DIRITA, VICTOR J UNIVERSITY OF MICHIGAN 018 ANIMAL RESEARCH FACILITY ANN ARBOR, MI 48109 Role of ToxT in regulation of Vibrio cholerae virulence
R01AI-31646-01 (BM) OSBORN, MARY J UNIVERSITY OF CONNECTICUT 263 FARMINGTON AVE FARMINGTON, CT 06030 Regulation of O-antigen synthesis in Salmonella
R29AI-31649-01 (GMA) CRUZ, PONCIANO D JR 5323 HARRY HINES BOULEVARD DALLAS, TX 75235 In vitro models of contact hypersensitivity
R01AI-31650-01 (IMS) RAULET, DAVID H UNIVERSITY OF CALIFORNIA 415 LIFE SCIENCES ADDITION BERKELEY, CA 94720 Regulation and MHC-dependence of gamma delta T cells
R01AI-31656-01 (BM) WISE, KIM S UNIV OF MISSOURI-COLUMBIA M642 SCHOOL OF MEDICINE COLUMBIA, MO 65212 Molecular genetic basis of mycoplasma antigen variation
R01AI-31657-01 (VR) VIRSHUP, DAVID M PRIMARY CHILDREN'S MEDICAL CTR 100 N MEDICAL DRIVE SALT LAKE CITY, UT 84113 Regulation of initiation of SV40 DNA replication
R29AI-31660-01 (ARRD) MOLINSKI, TADEUSZ F UNIVERSITY OF CALIFORNIA DAVIS, CA 95616 Mechanism selective antifungals-- Potential AIDS adjuvant
R29AI-31662-01 (ALY) MATHUR, AMBIKA UNIV OF MINNESOTA 515 DELAWARE STREET, SE MINNEAPOLIS, MN 55455 Host regulation of IgE synthesis in murine hybridomas
R29AI-31665-01 (BM) FRANK, DARA W MEDICAL COLLEGE OF WISCONSIN 8701 WATERTOWN PLANK RD MILWAUKEE, WI 53226 Regulation of exoenzyme S in Pseudomonas
R29AI-31669-01 (IMB) MUELLER, DANIEL L UNIV OF TX SOUTHWESTERN MED CN 5323 HARRY HINES BLVD DALLAS, TX 75235-8884 Protein phosphorylation in T-cell clonal anergy
U01AI-31686-01 (SRC) GROOPMAN, JEROME E NEW ENGLAND DEACONESS HOSPITAL 185 PILGRAM RD BOSTON, MA 02215 Cellular immunotherapy for HIV
U01AI-31686-01 0001 (SRC) CAPON, DANIEL J Cellular immunotherapy for HIV Universal donor, non-MHC-restricted CTL's for HIV therapy
U01AI-31686-01 0002 (SRC) GROOPMAN, JEROME E Cellular immunotherapy for HIV Cellular cytotoxic immune response to HIV, CMV in HIV infected patients
U01AI-31686-01 0003 (SRC) MOSIER, DONALD E Cellular immunotherapy for HIV Testing of cellular immunotherapy in hu-PBL-SCID mice
U01AI-31696-01 (SRC) SELSTED, MICHAEL E UNIVERSITY OF CALIFORNIA IRVINE, CA 92717 Drug discovery for treatment of cryptoccal disease
U01AI-31696-01 0001 (SRC) SELSTED, MICHAEL E Drug discovery for treatment of cryptoccal disease Antifungal peptides for treatment of cryptococcosis
U01AI-31696-01 0002 (SRC) EDWARDS, JOHN E Drug discovery for treatment of cryptoccal disease Cryptococcosis--Enhancement of host clearance mechanisms
U01AI-31696-01 0003 (SRC) COURCHESNE, WILLIAM E Drug discovery for treatment of cryptoccal disease Pheromone control of Cryptococcus neoformans growth
U01AI-31696-01 0004 (SRC) KOZEL, THOMAS R Drug discovery for treatment of cryptoccal disease Cryptococcosis--Passive immunization with monoclonal antibody
U01AI-31696-01 9001 (SRC) LUPAN, DAVID M Drug discovery for treatment of cryptoccal disease Animal studies core
U01AI-31696-01 9002 (SRC) SELSTED, MICHAEL E Drug discovery for treatment of cryptoccal disease Peptide synthesis and characterization core
U01AI-31696-01 9003 (SRC) JANOFF, ANDREW S Drug discovery for treatment of cryptoccal disease Lipid/liposomology core
U01AI-31702-01 (SRC) WALZER, PETER D UNIV OF CINCINNATI COLL OF MED 231 BETHESDA AVE CINCINNATI, OH 45267-0560 Metabolic studies of opportunistic fungi and protozoa
U01AI-31702-01 0001 (SRC) CUSHION, MELANIE T Metabolic studies of opportunistic fungi and protozoa Development of an axenic culture for Pneumocystis
U01AI-31702-01 0002 (SRC) KANESHIRO, EDNA S Metabolic studies of opportunistic fungi and protozoa Lipid uptake and metabolism in Pneumocystis carinii
U01AI-31702-01 0003 (SRC) ILTZSCH, MAX H Metabolic studies of opportunistic fungi and protozoa Purine metabolism in Toxoplasma gondii and Pneumocystis carinii
U01AI-31702-01 0004 (SRC) WONG, BRIAN Metabolic studies of opportunistic fungi and protozoa D-mannitol metabolism in Cryptococcus neoformans
U01AI-31702-01 0005 (SRC) KALB, VERNON F Metabolic studies of opportunistic fungi and protozoa Lanosterol demethylation mutants and antifungal agents
R43AI-31707-01 (SSS) CULLMAN, LOUIS C FOCUS/MRL INCORPORATED 10703 PROGRESS WAY CYPRESS, CA 90603-4738 Preparation of envelope glycoprotein rich HIV-1
R43AI-31708-01 (SSS) BABU, Y S BIOCRYST INC 1075 13TH STREET SOUTH BIRMINGHAM, AL 35205 Structure based design of inhibitors for flu neuraminidase
R43AI-31712-01 (SSS) HIGGINS, PAUL J REPLIGEN CORPORATION ONE KENDALL SQUARE CAMBRIDGE, MA 02139 Antibody heteroconjugates for treatment of SIV infection
R43AI-31713-01 (SSS) PROFY, ALBERT T REPLIGEN CORPORATION ONE KENDALL SQUARE CAMBRIDGE, MA 02139 Effect of gp120 proteolysis on HIV-1 infection
R43AI-31714-01 (HEM) LIN, LILY HRI RESEARCH, INC 2315 FIFTH STREET BERKELEY, CA 94710 Decontamination of platelet concentrates
U01AI-31718-01 (SRC) TOWNSEND, LEROY B 428 CHURCH STREET ANN ARBOR, MI 48109-1065 Heterocyclic compounds as selective inhibitors of HCMV
U01AI-31718-01 0001 (SRC) TOWNSEND, LEROY B Heterocyclic compounds as selective inhibitors of HCMV Heterocyclic compounds as selective inhibitors of human cytomegalovirus
U01AI-31718-01 0002 (SRC) DRACH, JOHN C Heterocyclic compounds as selective inhibitors of HCMV In vitro evaluation and biochemistry
U01AI-31718-01 9001 (SRC) KERN, EARL R Heterocyclic compounds as selective inhibitors of HCMV Core--In vivo antiviral evaluation
R43AI-31722-01 (SSS) HOPP, THOMAS P PROTEIN RESEARCH LABORATORIES 562 1ST AVE S SEATTLE, WA 98104 Crystallization of IL-3--An antibody mediated approach
R43AI-31724-01 (SSS) KOHLER, HEINZ IDEC PHARMACEUTICAL CORP 11099 N TORREY PINES ROAD LA JOLLA, CA 92037 Cloning human anti-gp120 B cells for AIDS therapy
R43AI-31729-01 (SSS) BARONAS-LOWELL, DIANE M ONCOGENE SCIENCE INC 350 COMMUNITY DRIVE MANHASST, NY 11030 Detecting protein interactions by a yeast genetic system
R43AI-31730-01 (SSS) NEWMAN, ROLAND A IDEC PHARMACEUTICALS CORP 11099 N TORREY PINES RD LA JOLLA, CA 92037 Molecular cloning and expression of human anti-gp120
R43AI-31738-01 (SSS) LAWRENCE, PAUL J LITMUS CONCEPTS, INC 3485 KIFER ROAD SANTA CLARA, CA 95051 A screening test for chlamydia trachomatis in women
R43AI-31739-01 (SSS) GIBSON, ROGER M GIBSON ENTERPRISES OF N AMERIC 3446 NE KINCAID TOPEKA, KS 66617 Development and bacteriological studies of the SNAP CAP
R43AI-31740-01 (SSS) VERCELLOTTI, SHARON V V-LABS INC 423 N THEARD ST COVINGTON, LA 70433 Sulfated chitosan derivatives as anti HIV 1 agents
R43AI-31743-01 (SSS) MADDON, PAUL J PROGENICS PHARMACEUTICALS, INC OLD SAW MILL RIVER ROAD TARRYTOWN, NY 10591 High-level expression of HIV gp120 in mammalian cells
R43AI-31748-01 (HUD) BEERY, MADELINE P AIDS IMPACT INC 200 SECOND AVE W, PO BOX 9443 SEATTLE, WA 98109 the HIV AIDS adolescent risk reduction project (HAARP)
R43AI-31750-01 (HUD) TANKE, ELIZABETH D DECISION SYSTEMS 1473 MIRAMONTE, BLDG #2 LOS ALTO, CA 94022 Intervention for increasing compliance in tuberculosis
R43AI-31753-01 (SSS) FISCHER, RANDY S METAGENE CORPORATION ONE PROCESS BLVD BOX 26 ALACHUA, FL 32615 Cost-efficient preparation of L-arogenate
R43AI-31757-01 (HUD) WRIGHT, MICHAEL P SCIENTIFIC SOCIAL RESEARCH 811 W BOYD NORMAN, OK 73069 Microcomputer software for Chlamydia risk assessment
R43AI-31761-01 (SSS) GREENER, ALAN L STRATEGENE, INC 11099 NORTH TORREY PINES ROAD LA JOLLA, CA 92037 New bacterial hosts for expressing foreign genes
R43AI-31763-01 (SSS) VIOLANTE, MICHAEL R STERILIZATION TECH SERV, INC 7500 WEST HENRIETTA ROAD RUSH, N Y 14543 Improved inhalation therapy of AIDS-related infections
R01AI-31769-01 (ARRE) CHERNIAK, ROBERT GEORGIA STATE UNIVERSITY UNIVERSITY PLAZA ATLANTA, GA 30303-3083 Cryptococcus neoformans--Epitope specific antibodies/and structure
R01AI-31774-01 (ARRE) UPTON, STEVE J KANSAS STATE UNIVERSITY MANHATTAN, KS 66506 In vitro studies on cryptosporidium, an opportunistic infection of AIDS
R43AI-31782-01 (SSS) KURACINA, THOMAS C INJECTIMED INC 216 EAST EUCALYPTUS STREET OJAI, CA 93023-2707 Safety syringe cap minimizing needlestick probability
R01AI-31783-01 (ARRA) SODROSKI, JOSEPH G DANA-FARBER CANCER

PROJECT NO., ORGANIZATIONAL UNIT., INVESTIGATOR, ADDRESS, TITLE

INSTITUTE 44 BINNEY STREET BOSTON, MA 02115 Molecular characterization of neutralizing monoclonal antibodies
R01AI-31789-01 (ARRB) TSIATIS, ANASTASIOS A HARVARD SCHOOL OF PUBLIC HEALT 677 HUNTINGTON AVE BOSTON, MA 02115 Statistical methods for AIDS clinical trials
R29AI-31804-01 (ARRD) ANDERSON, MARY E CORNELL UNIV MEDICAL COLLEGE 1300 YORK AVE NEW YORK, NY 10021 Novel AIDS therapies based on glutathione metabolism
R01AI-31806-01 (ARRC) HILDRETH, JAMES E JOHNS HOPKINS UNIV 725 N WOLFE ST BALTIMORE, ME 21205 Role of leukocyte adhesion receptors in the pathobiology
U01AI-31808-01 (SRC) JOINER, KEITH A YALE UNIVERSITY PO BOX 3333 NEW HAVEN, CT 06510 Mechanism based drug selection and design for T. gondii
U01AI-31808-01 0001 (SRC) LUFT, BENJAMIN J Mechanism based drug selection and design for T. gondii Effect of antibiotics on protein synthesis of T. gondii
U01AI-31808-01 0002 (SRC) ROOS, DAVID S Mechanism based drug selection and design for T. gondii Mechanism-based drug selection and design for T. gondii
U01AI-31808-01 0003 (SRC) JOINER, KEITH A Mechanism based drug selection and design for T. gondii Transport of antibiotics into Toxoplasma gondii
U01AI-31808-01 0004 (SRC) JOINER, KEITH A Mechanism based drug selection and design for T. gondii Transport of nucleosides into Toxoplasma gondii
U01AI-31808-01 9001 (SRC) LARTEY, PAUL A Mechanism based drug selection and design for T. gondii Core--Macrolide drug discovery
U01AI-31808-01 9002 (SRC) JOINER, KEITH A Mechanism based drug selection and design for T. gondii Core--Facilities and reagents
R29AI-31812-01 (ARRA) SPEAR, GREGORY T RUSH-PRES ST LUKES MEDICAL CTR 1653 W CONGRESS PARKWAY CHICAGO, IL 60612 Interaction of HIV-1 with complement
R55AI-31815-01 (ARRC) SHANK, PETER R BROWN UNIVERSITY BOX G-B629 PROVIDENCE, RI 02912 Characterization of HIV TAT-mediated transactivation
R29AI-31816-01 (ARRC) KAPPES, JOHN C UNIV OF ALABAMA UAB STATION BIRMINGHAM, AL 35294 Functional analysis of the HIV-2 vpx and vpr genes
R29AI-31823-01 (ARRC) RAPPAPORT, JAY F UNIVERSITY OF CALIFORNIA 9500 GILMAN DRIVE LA JOLLA, CA 92093 HIV-TAT specificity domain and TAR-binding host factors
R01AI-31826-01 (ARRC) HERNANDEZ, NOURIA T COLD SPRING HARBOR LABORTORY PO BOX 100 COLD SPRING HARBOR, NY 11724 Formation of short transcripts in the HIV 1 long terminal repeat
R01AI-31827-01 (ARRD) LIOTTA, DENNIS C EMORY UNIVERSITY DIVISION OF ARTS AND SCIENCES ATLANTA, GA 30322 Novel heterocyclic anti-AIDS agents
R01AI-31828-01 (ARRD) LEUNG, WAI-CHOI UNIVERSITY OF ARKANSAS 4301 W MARKHAM LITTLE ROCK, AR 72205 Molecular studies of tumor necrosis factor
R01AI-31830-01 (ARRE) LO, SHYH-CHING AMERICAN REGISTRY OF PATHOLOGY BUILDING 54 WASHINGTON DC, 20306-6000 Study of AIDS associated mycoplasma
R01AI-31852-01 (ARRC) BOTO, WILLIAM THE CITY COLLEGE OF CUNY CONVENT AVE AND 138TH ST NEW YORK, NY 10031 Nucleotide sequence of Ugandan HIV isolates
R29AI-31854-01 (ARRA) HO, RODNEY J UNIVERSITY OF WASHINGTON MAIL STOP BG-20 SEATTLE, WA 98195 Pharmacologic and biologic studies of antigen carriers
R01AI-31866-01 (ARRA) BACHOVCHIN, WILLIAM W TUFTS UNIVERSITY 136 HARRISON AVENUE BOSTON, MA 02111 Dipeptidyl peptidase IV and immune system regulation
U01AI-31867-01 (SRC) NORMAN, PHILLIP S JOHNS HOPKINS UNIV 301 BAYVIEW BLVD BALTIMORE, MD 21224 Immunologic disease cooperative research center
U01AI-31867-01 0014 (SRC) MALVEAUX, FLOYD J Immunologic disease cooperative research center Asthma management in inner city patients
U01AI-31867-01 0015 (SRC) GOLDEN, DAVID B Immunologic disease cooperative research center Natural history of food allergy in adults
U01AI-31867-01 9001 (SRC) LICHTENSTEIN, LAWRENCE M Immunologic disease cooperative research center Science core
U01AI-31867-01 0002 (SRC) SCHLEIMER, ROBERT P Immunologic disease cooperative research center Mechanism of action of steroids on inflammation
U01AI-31867-01 0004 (SRC) NORMAN, PHILIP S Immunologic disease cooperative research center Pathophysiology and treatment of allergic rhinitis
U01AI-31867-01 0010 (SRC) LIU, MARK C Immunologic disease cooperative research center Inflammation in airway disease
U01AI-31867-01 0012 (SRC) LAUBE, BETH Immunologic disease cooperative research center Airway deposition of inhaled drugs for asthma
U01AI-31867-01 0013 (SRC) ADKINSON, FRANKLIN Immunologic disease cooperative research center Studies of allergic drug reactions
R01AI-31868-09 (EI) BURAKOFF, STEVEN J DANA-FARBER CANCER INSTITUTE 44 BINNEY STREET BOSTON, MA 02115 Regulation of human cytolytic T lymphocytes
R29AI-31870-01 (ARRA) VOLAND, JOSEPH R UNIVERSITY OF CALIFORNIA 9500 GILMAN DR 0063 LA JOLLA, CA 92093-0063 T cell subsets in HIV infected patients
R01AI-31871-04 (BM) ESCHENBACH, DAVID A UNIVERSITY OF WASHINGTON SEATTLE, WA 98195 Infection and histopathology in preterm labor
R01AI-31872-10 (EVR) PROBER, CHARLES G STANFORD UNIV MEDICAL CENTER STANFORD, CA 94305 Herpes simplex, pregnancy neonatal risk, host defense
R01AI-31873-01 (EI) GERAGHTY, DANIEL E FRED HUTCHINSON CANCER RES CTR 1124 COLUMBIA STREET, M718 SEATTLE, WA 98104 Expression and function of three new HLA class I antigens
U01AI-31876-01 (SRC) ROBERTSON, HUGH D CORNELL UNIV MED COLLEGE 1300 YORK AVE/RM E-004 NEW YORK, NY 10021 RNA-level therapeutics for hepatitis B and delta viruses

PROJECT NO., ORGANIZATIONAL UNIT., INVESTIGATOR, ADDRESS, TITLE

U01AI-31883-01 (SRC) NEMEROW, GLEN R SCRIPPS CLINIC & RESEARCH FDN 10666 NORTH TORREY PINES ROAD LA JOLLA, CA 92037 Inhibition of Epstein-Barr virus receptor interaction
U01AI-31888-01 (SRC) LUO, MING UNIV OF ALABAMA BOX 79 THT/BHSB RM 274 BIRMINGTON, AL 35294 Design inhibitors of influenza virus, HAV and RSV
U01AI-31889-01 (SRC) SCHLESINGER, MILTON J WASHINGTON UNIV SCHOOL OF MED BOX 8230 ST LOUIS, MO 63110-1093 Peptide-based inhibitors of enveloped virus assembly
R01AI-31918-01 (ARRD) TUNG, FRANK Y UNIVERSITY OF FLORIDA PO BOX J-275; JHMHC GAINESVILLE, FL 32610-0275 An animal model of gene therapies for AIDS
U01AI-31921-01 (SRC) SPRINGER, TIMOTHY A THE CENTER FOR BLOOD RESEARCH 800 HUNTINGTON AVENUE BOSTON, MA 02115 ICAM-1 receptor analogues as anti-rhinovirus agents
U01AI-31927-01 (SRC) TAYLOR, JOHN M INSTITUTE FOR CANCER RESEARCH 7701 BURHOLME AVENUE PHILADELPHIA, PA 19111 Delta virus as a vector for the delivery of biologically active RNAs
R43AI-31933-01 (SSS) MULLIS, KARY B SPECIALTY LABORATORIES INC 2211 MICHIGAN AVE SANTA MONICA, CA 90404-3900 Rapid DNA extraction for DNA diagnostics
U01AI-31934-01 (SRC) DUNN, BEN M UNIVERSITY OF FLORDIA GAINESVILLE, FL 32610-0245 Picornaviral processing proteinases
R13AI-31935-01 (AIDS) MARTIN, JOHN C GILEAD SCIENCES 344 LAKESIDE DRIVE FOSTER CITY, CA 94404 Gordon research conference on the chemotherapy of AIDS
R01AI-31938-01 (ARRC) GREEN, MICHAEL R UNIV OF MASS MEDICAL CENTER 373 PLANTATION STREET WORCESTER, MA 01605 The HIV-1 Rev protein-- Biochemical mechanisms
R03AI-31994-01 (MID) SIDDIQUI, ALEEM UNIV OF COLORADO HEALTH SCIS C 4200 E NINTH AVE, BOX B175 DENVER, CO 80262 Indo-U.S. vaccine action program
R01AI-32028-01A1 (ARRC) FRANZA, B ROBERT, JR COLD SPRING HARBOR LABORATORY PO BOX 100 COLD SPRING HARBOR, NY 11724 Cellular control of HIV expression
R01AI-32031-16 (ALY) SMITH, KENDALL A DARTMOUTH MEDICAL SCHOOL HANOVER, NH 03756 The regulation of T-cell proliferation
R01AI-32154-05 (TMP) RAIKHEL, ALEXANDER S MICHIGAN STATE UNIVERSITY EAST LANSING, MI 48824-1115 Mosquito oocytes--Mechanism of protein accumulation
S15AI-32162-01 (NSS) STURMAN, LAWRENCE WADSWORTH CTR FOR LABS/RESEARC ALBANY, NY 12201 Small instrumentation grant
S15AI-32163-01 (NSS) HENSON, PETER M NATIONAL JEWISH CTR/IMMUN/RESP 1400 JACKSON STREET DENVER, CO 80206 Small instrumentation grant
S15AI-32164-01 (NSS) MORIARTY, C MICHAEL UNIVERSITY OF GEORGIA ATHENS, GA 30602 Small instrumentation grant
S15AI-32165-01 (NSS) ROLFE, RIAL D TEXAS TECH UNIV. HLTH. SCI. CT LUBBOCK, TX 79430 Small instrumentation grant
S15AI-32166-01 (NSS) RATTAZZI, MARIO C NORTH SHORE UNIVERSITY HOSP 300 COMMUNITY DRIVE MANHASSET, NY 11030 Small instrumentation grant
S15AI-32167-01 (NSS) RODGERS, FRANK G UNIVERSITY OF NEW HAMPSHIRE DURHAM, NH 03824-3544 Small instrumentation grant
S15AI-32169-01 (NSS) MOSIER, DONALD E MEDICAL BIOLOGY INSTITUTE 11077 NORTH TORREY PINES ROAD LA JOLLA, CA 92037 Small instrumentation grant
S15AI-32170-01 (NSS) SMITH, ARNOLD L CHILDREN'S HOSP & MED CTR 4800 SAND POINT WAY N E SEATTLE, WA 98105 Small instrumentation grant
S15AI-32171-01 (NSS) GIOLAS, THOMAS G UNIVERSITY OF CONNECTICUT BOX U-133, 438 WHITNEY RD EXT STORRS, CT 06269-1133 Small instrumentation grant
S15AI-32172-01 (NSS) SAFWAT, FUAD M UNIVERSITY OF MASSACHUSETTS HARBOR CAMPUS BOSTON, MA 02125 Small instrumentation grant
S15AI-32173-01 (NSS) IBRAHIM, MICHEL A UNIVERSITY OF NORTH CAROLINA CB #7400 ROSENAU HALL CHAPEL HILL, NC 27599 Small instrumentation grant
S15AI-32174-01 (NSS) WILCZYNSKI, WALTER UNIVERSITY OF TEXAS 330 MEZES HALL AUSTIN, TX 78712 Small instrumentation grant
S15AI-32175-01 (NSS) YOUNG, ROBERT C INSTITUTE FOR CANCER RESEARCH 7701 BURHOLME AVENUE PHILADELPHIA, PA 19111 Small instrumentation grant
S15AI-32176-01 (NSS) COMINGS, DAVID E CITY OF HOPE NAT MED CTR 1500 EAST DUARTE ROAD DUARTE, CA 91010 Small instrumentation grant
R01AI-32177-01 (MGN) BEAUDET, ARTHUR L BAYLOR COLLEGE OF MEDICINE ONE BAYLOR PLAZA HOUSTON, TEX 77030 Mouse mutants for cell adhesion molecules
S15AI-32182-01 (NSS) GOODWIN, WILLIAM J SW FDN FOR BIOMEDICAL RESEARCH PO BOX 28147 SAN ANTONIO, TX 78228-0147 Small instrumentation grant
S15AI-32183-01 (NSS) RAYMOND, KATHLEEN C UNIVERSITY OF MONTANA MISSOULA, MT 59812-1002 Small instrumentation grant
S15AI-32184-01 (NSS) STUART, KENNETH D SEATTLE BIOMEDICAL RES INST 4 NICKERSON STREET SEATTLE, WA 98109-1651 Small instrumentation grant
S15AI-32185-01 (NSS) DEWILLE, JAMES W OHIO STATE UNIVERSITY 1925 COFFEY RD COLUMBUS, OH 43210 Small instrumentation grant
S15AI-32186-01 (NSS) COOPER, ALLEN D PALO ALTO MEDICAL RESEARCH FDN 860 BRYANT STREET PALO ALTO, CA 94301 Small instrumentation grant
S15AI-32187-01 (NSS) LEVIN, ROBERT M BOSTON CITY HOSPITAL 818 HARRISON AVENUE BOSTON, MA 02118 Small instrumentation grant
S15AI-32188-01 (NSS) LIEBERMAN, SEYMOUR 428 W 59TH ST AJA 118 NEW YORK, NY 10019 Small instrumentation grant
S15AI-32189-01 (NSS) AVADHANI, NARAYAN G UNIVERSITY OF PENNSYLVANIA 3800 SPRUCE STREET PHILADELPHIA, PA 19104-6048 Small instrumentation grant
S15AI-32190-01 (NSS) OKUNEWICK, JAMES P ALLEGHENY SINGER RES INST 320 E NORTH AVE PITTSBURGH, PA 15212-9986 Small instrumentation grant
S15AI-32191-01 (NSS) BERNSTEIN, DAVID I JAMES N GAMBLE INST OF MED RES 2141 AUBURN AVENUE CINCINNATI, OH 45219 Small instrumentation grant
S15AI-32192-01 (NSS) FOGEL, BERNARD J UNV OF MIAMI, SCH OF MED

PROJECT NO., ORGANIZATIONAL UNIT., INVESTIGATOR, ADDRESS, TITLE

R-699 P O BOX 016960 MIAMI, FLA 33101 Small instrumentation grant
S15AI-32193-01 (NSS) ROBINSON, JOHN A LOYOLA UNIVERSITY MEDICAL CENT 2160 S FIRST AVE MAYWOOD, IL 60153 Small instrumentation grant
S15AI-32194-01 (NSS) NORTH, ROBERT J TRUDEAU INSTITUE, INC PO BOX 59 SARANAC LAKE, NY 12983 Small instrumentation grant
S15AI-32195-01 (NSS) LOEHR, THOMAS M OREGON GRADUATE INSTITUTE 19600 N W VON NEUMANN DR BEAVERTON, OR 97006-1999 Small instrumentation grant
S15AI-32196-01 (NSS) FRANKS, RONALD D UNIVERSITY OF MINNESOTA DULUTH DULUTH, MN 55812 Small instrumentation grant
S15AI-32197-01 (NSS) JANICKI, BERNARD W DANA-FARBER CANCER INSTITUTE 44 BINNEY STREET BOSTON, MA 02115 Small instrumentation grant
S15AI-32198-01 (NSS) BROWN, DAVID M UNIVERSITY OF MINNESOTA BOX 293 MINNEAPOLIS, MN 55455 Small instrumentation grant
S15AI-32199-01 (NSS) SPENCE, JOSEPH T SUNY AT BUFFALO DEPT. OF BIOMEDICAL SCIENCES BUFFALO, NY 14214 Small instrumentation grant
S15AI-32200-01 (NSS) TAYLOR, BENJAMIN A THE JACKSON LABORATORY 600 MAIN STREET BAR HARBOR, ME 04609-0800 Small instrumentation grant
S15AI-32201-01 (NSS) NORROD, E PININA VASSAR COLLEGE BOX 141 POUGHKEEPISE, N Y 12601 Small instrumentation grant
S15AI-32202-01 (NSS) LAMARTINIERE, CORAL A UNIVERSITY OF ALABAMA UAB STATION BIRMINGHAM, AL 35294 Small instrumentation grant
S15AI-32203-01 (NSS) RABKIN, MITCHELL T BETH ISRAEL HOSPITAL 330 BROOKLINE AVE BOSTON, MA 02215 Small instrumentation grant
S15AI-32204-01 (NSS) OMENN, GILBERT S UNIVERSITY OF WASHINGTON SCHOOL OF PUBLIC HEALTH, SC-30 SEATTLE, WASH 98195 Small instrumentation grant
S15AI-32205-01 (NSS) WOLLMAN, HARRY HAHNEMANN UNIVERSITY BROAD AND VINE PHILADELPHIA, PA 19102-1192 Small instrumentation grant
S15AI-32206-01 (NSS) MORRIS, N RONALD ROBERT WOOD JOHNSON MED SCH 675 HOES LANE, R109 PISCATAWAY, NJ 08854 Small instrumentation grant
S15AI-32207-01 (NSS) PALADE, GEORGE E UNIVERSITY OF CALIFORNIA 9500 GILMAN DRIVE LA JOLLA, CA 92093-0602 Small instrumentation grant
S15AI-32208-01 (NSS) ROSS, GORDON D UNIVERSITY OF LOUISVILLE SCHOOL OF MEDICINE LOUISVILLE, KY 40292 Small instrumentation grant
S15AI-32209-01 (NSS) HOCK, JANET M TUFTS UNIVERSITY 1 KNEELAND STREET BOSTON, MA 02111 Small instrumentation grant
S15AI-32210-01 (NSS) WORLAND, STEPHEN T AGOURON INSTITUTE 505 COAST BLVD SOUTH LA JOLLA, CA 92037 Small instrumentation grant
S15AI-32211-01 (NSS) SMITH, RICHARD T UNIV OF FLORIDA COL OF MED BOX J-215 JHMHC GAINESVILLE, FL 32610 Small instrumentation grant
S15AI-32212-01 (NSS) BECK, RAYMOND W UNIVERSITY OF TENNESSEE KNOXVILLE, TN 37996-0830 Small instrumentation grant
S15AI-32213-01 (NSS) IDE, CHARLES F TULANE UNIVERSITY 6823 ST CHARLES AVE NEW ORLEANS, LA 70118 Small instrumentation grant
S15AI-32214-01 (NSS) BREDECK, HENRY E MICHIGAN STATE UNIVERSITY 238 ADMINISTRATION BUILDING EAST LANSING, MI 48824-1046 Small instrumentation grant
S15AI-32215-01 (NSS) DRATZ, EDWARD A MONTANA STATE UNIVERSITY 108 GAINES HALL BOZEMAN, MT 59717 Small instrumentation grant
S15AI-32216-01 (NSS) BAYNE, CHRISTOPHER J OREGON STATE UNIVERSITY CORVALLIS, OR 97331-2914 Small instrumentation grant
S15AI-32217-01 (NSS) SAWYER, RICHARD T MERCER UNIV SCHOOL OF MEDICINE 1550 COLLEGE STREET MACON, GA 31207 Small instrumentation grant
S15AI-32218-01 (NSS) BONDURANT, STUART UNIVERSITY OF NORTH CAROLINA 125 MACNIDER BLDG CB# 7000 CHAPEL HILL, NC 27599 Small instrumentation grant
S15AI-32222-01 (NSS) RUSSELL, JAMES D MEHARRY MEDICAL COLLEGE 1005 DB TODD JR BLVD NASHVILLE, TN 37208 Small instrumentation grant
R43AI-32227-01 (SSS) WALFIELD, ALAN M UNITED BIOMEDICAL, INC 2 NEVADA DRIVE LAKE SUCCESS, NY 11042 Synthetic hepatitis C antigens for subunit vaccine
R01AI-32243-05 (IMS) CHEN, POJEN P UNIV OF CALIFORNIA, SAN DIEGO LA JOLLA, CA 92093 Molecular genetics of autoantibodies in humans
U01AI-32246-01 (SRC) KOMAROFF, ANTHONY L BRIGHAM AND WOMENS HOSPITAL 75 FRANCIS STREET BOSTON, MA 02115 Chronic fatigue syndrome cooperative research center
U01AI-32246-01 0001 (SRC) KOMAROFF, ANTHONY L Chronic fatigue syndrome cooperative research center Chronic fatigue syndrome, fibromyalgia and depression
U01AI-32246-01 0002 (SRC) WANG, FREDERICK C S Chronic fatigue syndrome cooperative research center Cytokines and chronic fatigue syndrome
U01AI-32246-01 9001 (SRC) KOMAROFF, ANTHONY L Chronic fatigue syndrome cooperative research center Core--Clinical core
U01AI-32246-01 9002 (SRC) BUCHWALD, DEDRA S Chronic fatigue syndrome cooperative research center Core--Clinical core
U01AI-32247-01 (SRC) NATELSON, BENJAMIN H UMDNJ-NEW JERSEY MEDICAL SCHOO 88 ROSS STREET NEWARK, NJ 07108 A syndromic approach to the chronic fatigue syndrome
U01AI-32247-01 0001 (SRC) NATELSON, BENJAMIN H A syndromic approach to the chronic fatigue syndrome Classification of chronic fatigue syndrome patients
U01AI-32247-01 0002 (SRC) HAY, JOHN A syndromic approach to the chronic fatigue syndrome Virology assessment of chronic fatigue syndrome patients
U01AI-32247-01 0003 (SRC) GAUSE, WILLIAM C A syndromic approach to the chronic fatigue syndrome Immunological assessment of chronic fatigue syndrome patients
U01AI-32247-01 9001 (SRC) NATELSON, BENJAMIN H A syndromic approach to the chronic fatigue syndrome Core--Data analysis
R03AI-32253-01 (MID) DEBROY, CHITRITA PENNSYLVANIA STATE UNIVERSITY COLLEGE OF AGRICULTURE UNIVERSITY PARK, PA 16801 Characterization of aggregative E. Coli
R01AI-32298-01 (ARRD) DANCIS, JOSEPH NEW YORK UNIVERSITY MED CTR 550 FIRST AVENUE NEW YORK, NY 10016 In vitro model of polarized trophoblast
R01AI-32299-01 (ARRD) TARANTAL, ALICE F CA REGIONAL PRIMATE RESEARCH C DAVIS, CA 95616-8542 Toxicity of anti-HIV drugs in pre and

PROJECT NO., ORGANIZATIONAL UNIT., INVESTIGATOR, ADDRESS, TITLE

postnatal macaques
R01AI-32301-01 (ARRB) HUANG, RU C JOHNS HOPKINS UNIVERSITY 34TH NORTH CHARLES STREET BALTIMORE, MD 21218 Effects of HIV and DU5H proteins on embryos in culture
R01AI-32302-01 (ARRB) MURPHEY-CORB, MICHAEL A TULANE REGIONAL PRIMATE RES CT 18703 THREE RIVERS RD COVINGTON, LA 70433 SIV and macaque model for fetal infection and disease
R01AI-32305-01 (ARRB) EPSTEIN, LEON G UNIVERSITY OF ROCHESTER MED CT 601 ELMWOOD AVE, BOX 631 ROCHESTER, NY 14642 HIV infection of human fetal neural xenografts
R01AI-32306-01 (ARRB) CALVELLI, THERESA A ALBERT EINSTEIN COLL OF MEDICI 1300 MORRIS PARK AVENUE BRONX, NY 10461 Transplacental passage of HIV and immunoglobulin
R01AI-32307-01 (ARRB) DOUGLAS, GORDON C UNIV OF CALIFORNIA SCH OF MED DAVIS, CA 95616-8643 Interaction of HIV with isolated placental cells
R01AI-32309-01 (ARRB) RINGLER, DOUGLAS J NEW ENGLAND REG PRIMATE RES CT ONE PINE HILL DRIVE SOUTHBOROUGH, MA 01772-9102 Determinants of SIV and HIV-1 transplacental infection
R01AI-32310-01 (ARRB) TOMPKINS, WAYNE A NORTH CAROLINA STATE UNIV 4700 HILLSBOROUGH STREET RALEIGH, NC 27606 Feline/FIV model for pediatric AIDS
R01AI-32314-01 (ARRD) STARK, RAYMOND I COLUMBIA UNIVERSITY DEPT OF PEDIATRICS NEW YORK, NY 10032 Evaluation of anti-HIV drugs in pregnant and fetal baboons
R01AI-32316-01 (ARRD) CAPCO, DAVID G ARIZONA STATE UNIVERSITY TEMPE, AZ 85287-1501 Interaction of anti-HIV drugs with placental models
R01AI-32317-01 (ARRB) OCHS, HANS D UNIVERSITY OF WASHINGTON SEATTLE, WA 98195 Maternal-fetal transmission of SIV in macaques
R01AI-32319-01 (ARRD) MILLER, RICHARD K UNIVERSITY OF ROCHESTER 601 ELMWOOD AVENUE ROCHESTER, NY 14642 Placenta-- Anti-HIV therapy
R01AI-32330-01 (ARRB) RUPRECHT, RUTH M DANA-FARBER CANCER INSTITUTE 44 BINNEY STREET BOSTON, MA 02115 SIV pathogenesis during ontogeny
R01AI-32332-01 (ARRD) HO, RODNEY J UNIVERSITY OF WASHINGTON MAIL STOP BG-20 SEATTLE, WA 98195 Anti-HIV drugs and the placenta-- Intracellular metabolism
R01AI-32339-01 (ARRB) GOLOS, THADDEUS G UNIVERSITY OF WISCONSIN 1223 CAPITOL CT MADISON, WI 53715-1299 SIV infection of rhesus syncytiotrophoblasts in vitro
R01AI-32341-01 (ARRB) NAHMIAS, ANDRE J EMORY UNIVERSITY 69 BUTLER ST SE ATLANTA, GA 30303 HIV placental infection in vitro experimental models
R01AI-32384-01 (ARRA) KOHL, STEVE SAN FRANCISCO GEN'L HOSPITAL 1001 POTRERO AVENUE SAN FRANCISCO, CA 94110 Maternal and infant immune determinants of HIV infection
R01AI-32388-01 (ARRA) SCHWARTZ, DAVID H JOHNS HOPKINS UNIVERSITY 624 NORTH BROADWAY BALTIMORE, MD 21205 Vertical transmission of human immunodeficiency virus
R01AI-32391-01 (ARRA) SULLIVAN, JOHN L UNIV OF MASSACHUSETTS 55 LAKE AVENUE, NORTH WORCHESTER, MA 01655 Killer cells and viral load in vertical HIV infection
R01AI-32393-01 (ARRA) GREENBERG, MICHAEL L DUKE UNIVERSITY MEDICAL CENTER PO BOX 2926 DURHAM, NC 27710 Immunity and perinatal HIV-1 transmission in Tanzania
R01AI-32395-01 (ARRA) JACKSON, JAY B CASE WESTERN RESERVE MEDICAL S 2085 ADELBERT ROAD CLEVELAND, OH 44106 HIV in Ugandan mothers and infants--Immunity and detection
R01AI-32397-01 (ARRA) ANDIMAN, WARREN A YALE UNIV SCHOOL OF MEDICINE 333 CEDAR STREET NEW HAVEN, CT 06510 Syncytium inhibition antibodies and maternal-infant AIDS
R01AI-32403-01 (SRC) PERSING, DAVID H MAYO FOUNDATION 200 FIRST ST SOUTHWEST ROCHESTER, MN 55902 Multi-locus molecular detection of Borrelia burgdorferi
R01AI-32412-06 (IMB) GLIMCHER, LAURIE H HARVARD SCH OF PUBLIC HEALTH 665 HUNTINGTON AVENUE BOSTON, MA 02115 Regulation of class II gene expression
R01AI-32424-01 (ARRA) ZOLLA-PAZNER, SUSAN VETERANS AFFAIRS MEDICAL CENTE 423 EAST 23RD ST NEW YORK, NY 10010 Human monoclonal antibodies to prevent fetal HIV disease
R01AI-32427-01 (ARRA) BORKOWSKY, WILLIAM NEW YORK UNIVERSITY MEDICAL CT 550 FIRST AVENUE NEW YORK, NY 10016 Viral and immune correlates of perinatal HIV transmission
R01AI-32429-01 (ARRA) VALENTINE, FRED T NEW YORK UNIVERSITY MED CENTER 550 FIRST AVENUE NEW YORK, N Y 10016 Pathogenicity of HIV isolates-- Role in fetal transmission
R01AI-32439-01 (ARRA) SKOWRON, GAIL ROGER WILLIAMS MEDICAL CENTER 825 CHALKSTONE AVE PROVIDENCE, RI 02908 HIV immunity-- Correlation with vertical transmission
R01AI-32440-01 (ARRA) PLAEGER-MARSHALL, SUSAN F UNIVERSITY OF CALIFORNIA 10833 LE CONTE AVENUE LOS ANGELES, CA 90024-1752 Cellular immunity to HIV in mothers and infants
R01AI-32444-01 (ARRA) CLOYD, MILES W UNIVERSITY OF TEXAS MEDICAL BR SCHOOL OF MEDICINE GALVESTON, TX 77550 HIV in infants-- Early immunity and genetic susceptibility
R01AI-32446-01 (ARRA) KLIKS, SRISAKUL C UNIV OF CALIFORNIA BOX 0128 SAN FRANCISCO, CA 94143 Maternal antibodies in vertical transmission of HIV
R01AI-32454-01 (SRC) LUFT, BENJAMIN J SUNY AT STONY BROOK HSC T-15 080 STONY BROOK, NY 11794-8153 Development of diagnostics for Lyme borreliosis
R01AI-32456-01 (ARRA) LEE, FRANCIS K PEDIATRIC INFECTIOUS DISEASES 69 BUTLER ST, SE ATLANTA, GA 30303 Perinatal HIV immune factors in mothers and infants
R01AI-32457-01 (ARRA) SACKS, HENRY S MOUNT SINAI MEDICAL CENTER 1 GUSTAVE L LEVY PLACE NEW YORK, NY 10029-6574 Early diagnosis of pediatric HIV infection
R01AI-32466-01 (ARRA) SHEARER, WILLIAM T BAYLOR COLLEGE OF MEDICINE ONE BAYLOR PLAZA HOUSTON, TX 77030 Role of the placenta in transmission of HIV
R01AI-32468-01 (ARRA) HALSEY, NEAL A JOHNS HOPKINS UNIVERSITY 615 NORTH WOLFE STREET BALTIMORE, MD 21205 HIV in mothers and

infants– Immunity and early diagnosis

R01AI-32469-01 (ARRA) WALKER, BRUCE D MASS GENERAL HOSPITAL 55 FRUIT ST BOSTON, MA 02114 HIV-1 specific immunity and maternal-fetal transmission

R13AI-32476-01 (AITC) IBER, RICHARD I INTL ASSOC ALLERGO AND CLN IMM 611 EAST WELLS STREET MILWAUKEE, WI 53202 XIV international congress of allergology– Travel grant

R01AI-32478-01 (ARRA) LANDAY, ALAN L RUSH-PRESBYTERIAN-ST. LUKES ME 1653 WEST CONGRESS PARKWAY CHICAGO, IL 60612 Cellular markers of HIV immunity in mothers and infants

U01AI-32480-01 (SRC) HOGLE, JAMES M HARVARD MEDICAL SCHOOL 240 LONGWOOD AVE BOSTON, MA 02115 Poliovirus as a model for the design of antiviral drugs

R01AI-32489-01 (MBY) DARNELL, JAMES E ROCKEFELLER UNIVERSITY 1230 YORK AVENUE NEW YORK, NY 10021 Gene control and cell growth regulation by interferon

N01AI-32535-38 (**) PHAU, JOHN P The natural history of AIDS in homosexual men

R01AI-32687-01 (ARRA) BROUILLETTE, CHRISTIE G SOUTHERN RESEARCH INSTITUTE 2000 NINTH AVENUE SOUTH BIRMINGHAM, AL 35255-5305 Domain stability and interactions in CD4

R01AI-32736-01 (BM) DREYFUS, LAWRENCE A UNIVERSITY OF MISSOURI 5100 ROCKHILL ROAD, BSB 109 KANSAS CITY, MO 64110 Analysis of the E. coli STb heat stable enterotoxin

R01AI-32744-01 (ARRA) SEDMAK, DANIEL D OHIO STATE UNIVERSITY 1645 NEIL AVENUE COLUMBUS, OH 43210 Syncytiotrophoblast IgG Fc receptors and HIV infection

R01AI-32764-01 (ALY) SCHWARTZ, BENJAMIN D WASHINGTON UNIV SCH OF MED 660 S EUCLID AVE/BOX 8045 ST LOUIS, MO 63110 Antibody detection of class II - peptide complexes

R01AI-32784-01 (ARRD) SANTI, DANIEL V UNIVERSITY OF CALIFORNIA RBOX 0448 SAN FRANCISCO, CA 94143 Enzyme targets of opportunistic pathogens in AIDS

R01AI-32788-01 (ARRA) WEINER, DAVID B THE WISTAR INSTITUTE 36TH & SPRUCE STREETS PHILADELPHIA, PA 19104 Humoral immunity in maternal and fetal HIV infection

R29AI-32794-01 (ARRD) JOHNSON, VICTORIA A UNIVERSITY OF ALABAMA BIRMINGHAM, AL 35294 Breakthrough of HIV-1 replication during drug therapy

U01AI-32834-01 (SRC) TAN, ENG M THE SCRIPPS RESEARCH INSTITUTE 10666 NORTH TORREY PINES ROAD LA JOLLA, CA 92037 Asthama, allergy and autoimmunity

U01AI-32834-01 0001 (SRC) TAN, ENG M Asthama, allergy and autoimmunity Autoimmunity and B cell epitopes

U01AI-32834-01 0002 (SRC) ZURAW, BRUCE L Asthama, allergy and autoimmunity Kallikrein-kinin system in allergic disease

U01AI-32834-01 0003 (SRC) HUGLI, TONY E Asthama, allergy and autoimmunity Aspirin-sensitive asthma and arachidonate metabolites

U01AI-32834-01 0004 (SRC) ISHIZAKA, KIMISHIGE Asthama, allergy and autoimmunity Allergen-specific human Ts hybridoma construction

U01AI-32834-01 0005 (SRC) LIU, FU-TONG Asthama, allergy and autoimmunity Endogenous lectins an allergic inflammation

U01AI-32834-01 0006 (SRC) CHRISTIANSEN, SANDRA Asthama, allergy and autoimmunity Inner city asthma

U01AI-32834-01 9001 (SRC) TAN, ENG M Asthama, allergy and autoimmunity Clinical core

R01AI-32912-01 (SRC) TIDWELL, RICHARD R UNIVERSITY OF NORTH CAROLINA CAMPUS BOX 7525 CHAPEL HILL, NC 27599-7525 Dicationic drugs–Metabolism and toxicity

R01AI-32917-01 (EDC) WHEELER, COSETTE M UNIVERSITY OF NEW MEXICO 900 CAMINO DE SALUD, NE ALBUQUERQUE, NM 87131-5306 A PCR-based natural history study of HPV infections

P01AI-32918-09 (SRC) O'REILLY, RICHARD J SLOANE-KETTERING INST CANCER R 1275 YORK AVENUE NEW YORK, NY 10021 Marrow transp./SCID & other lethal congenital immunodeficiencies

P01AI-32918-09 9002 (SRC) FLOMENBERG, NEAL Marrow transp./SCID & other lethal congenital immunodeficiencies Immunologic monitoring of T-cell and B-cell lines–Core

P01AI-32918-09 9003 (SRC) GROSHEN, SUSAN Marrow transp./SCID & other lethal congenital immunodeficiencies Biostatistics and data management

P01AI-32918-09 0001 (SRC) BORDIGNON, CLAUDIA Marrow transp./SCID & other lethal congenital immunodeficiencies Transplantation in patients with SCID

P01AI-32918-09 0002 (SRC) DUPONT, BO Marrow transp./SCID & other lethal congenital immunodeficiencies T-cell defects in lethal combined immunodeficiencies

P01AI-32918-09 0006 (SRC) INCFEY, GENEVIEVE S Marrow transp./SCID & other lethal congenital immunodeficiencies Interaction between thymus and hemapoietic cells in SCID

P01AI-32918-09 0008 (SRC) O'REILLY, RICHARD J Marrow transp./SCID & other lethal congenital immunodeficiencies Transplantation of lethal congenital immunodeficiencies

P01AI-32918-09 0009 (SRC) HOFFMAN, MICHAEL Marrow transp./SCID & other lethal congenital immunodeficiencies Production of interleukin-1 by monocytes from SCID patients

P01AI-32918-09 0010 (SRC) FLOMENBERG, NEAL Marrow transp./SCID & other lethal congenital immunodeficiencies Tolerance to host HLA-determinants–Allogenic bone marrow chimeric SCID patients

P01AI-32918-09 0011 (SRC) LUM, LAWRENCE Marrow transp./SCID & other lethal congenital immunodeficiencies B cell function and immune response

P01AI-32918-09 0012 (SRC) KEIVER, CAROLYN A Marrow transp./SCID & other lethal congenital immunodeficiencies Humoral immune deficiencies

P01AI-32918-09 0013 (SRC) GILBOA, ELI Marrow transp./SCID & other lethal congenital immunodeficiencies Capacity of retroviral vectors to transfer ADA gene

P01AI-32918-09 9001 (SRC) CHAGANTI, RAJU S Marrow transp./SCID & other lethal congenital immunodeficiencies Cytogenetics core

N01AI-42532-14 (**) RAO, A VIJAYA Prevention of prematurity by treatment of genitourinary infections

N01AI-62515-12 (**) CLEMENTS, MARY LOU Facility for study of infectious agents and vaccines

PROJECT NO., ORGANIZATIONAL UNIT., INVESTIGATOR, ADDRESS, TITLE

N01AI-62521-08 (**) SOIKE, KENNETH F Models for antiviral evaluation

N01AI-62528-18 (**) LEVINE, MYRON M Facility for study of infectious disease and vaccines

N01AI-62553-14 (**) LEVINE, MYRON M Study of malaria vaccines in human volunteers

N01AI-72620-06 (**) HAMMERLING, ULRICH Development of method for bulk preparation of alloantibodies

N01AI-72621-10 (**) YUNGINGER, JOHN W Allergen resource reference laboratory

N01AI-72622-08 (**) PETERS, ROBERT Mouse leukemia virus project

N01AI-72623-38 (**) GERIN, JOHN L Operate a molecular virology and immunology laboratory

N01AI-72629-11 (**) COUCH, ROBT B Evaluation control measures against infectious diseases

N01AI-72631-16 (**) DETELS, ROGERS Natural history of acquired immunodeficiency syndrome

N01AI-72632-15 (**) RINALDO, CHARLES History of acquired immune deficiency in homosexual men

N01AI-72634-14 (**) SAAL, ALFRED The natural history of acquired immunodeficiency syndrome

N01AI-72636-06 (**) ISEMAN, MICHAEL D Drugs to treat M. avium intracellular infections

N01AI-72637-07 (**) YOUNG, LOWELL S Drugs to treat M. avium intracellular infections

N01AI-72638-07 (**) CLARK, ALICE M Develop drugs for treatment of candidiasis

N01AI-72640-10 (**) KOBAYASHI, GEORGE S Development of additional drugs for treatment of candidiasis

N01AI-72641-09 (**) DRACH, JOHN Development of antiviral drugs for treatment of human

N01AI-72642-10 (**) SHANNON, WILLIAM Drugs to treat human cytomegalovirus (HCMV) infections

N01AI-72643-09 (**) REIST, ELMER Development of antiviral drugs

N01AI-72644-09 (**) WRIGHT, GEORGE Development of antiviral drugs

N01AI-72645-10 (**) SCHNELLER, STEWART W Development of antiviral drugs

N01AI-72646-07 (**) WALZER, PETER Development of additional drugs for pneumocystis carinii

N01AI-72647-11 (**) SMITH, JAMES W Drugs for treatment of pneumocystis carinii

N01AI-72648-06 (**) TIDWELL, RICHARD R Development of additional drugs for treatment of pneumocystis carinii

N01AI-72649-04 (**) ST JOHN, RONALD K HIV infection in the Caribbean and Latin America

N01AI-72650-07 (**) CHELLA, DAVID Production of reagents against H-2 cell membrane antigens

N01AI-72651-10 (**) FRELINGER, JEFFREY A Reagents against H-2 cell membrane antigens

N01AI-72656-09 (**) GIORGI, JANIA V Correlates-markers of immunity in the acquired immodeficiency syndrome

N01AI-72658-08 (**) PAZNER, ZOLLASUSAN Correlates-markers of immunity in the acquired immunodeficiency syndrome

N01AI-72659-08 (**) VALENTINE, FRED T Correlates-markers of immunity in the acquired immunodeficiency syndrome

N01AI-72662-12 (**) MCGOWAN, JOHN J Evaluating biological response modifiers as therapies

N01AI-72663-09 (**) HOOVER, EDWARD A Evaluating biological response modifiers as therapies

N01AI-72665-08 (**) TOMPKINS, WAYNE A Evaluating biological response modifiers as therapies

N01AI-72676-11 (**) MUNOZ, ALVARD Data coordinating center /natural history of AIDS

N01AI-82500-09 (**) KOVAK, JOEL AIDS vaccine trial data coordinating and analysis center

N01AI-82505-11 (**) RICH, KENNETH Perinatal transmission of HIV and retroviral infections

N01AI-82506-09 (**) PITT, JANE Perinatal transmission of HIV and related retroviruses

N01AI-82507-17 (**) TOUMALA, RUTH Perinatal transmission of HIV and related retroviruses

N01AI-82509-04 (**) REICHMAN, RICHARD C Combination therapy for patients with condyloma acumina

N01AI-82511-07 (**) THOMPSON, JOHN S Clinical trial for the use of monoclonal antibodies

N01AI-82512-08 (**) KIRKMAN, ROBERT Clinical trial for the use of monoclonal antibodies

N01AI-82513-08 (**) BARGER, BRUCE O Screening, characterization, and acquisition of regents

N01AI-82514-07 (**) JOHNSON, ARMEAD Screening, characterization and acquisition of regents

N01AI-82517-08 (**) HOLLINGER, BLAINE Research and development contract–virology quality control

N01AI-82518-03 (**) KERN, EARL R Antiviral screen for herpesvirus

N01AI-82519-03 (**) WYDE, PHILIP R Antiviral screen for respiratory viruses

N01AI-82520-04 (**) LAUER, BRIAN A Immunoglobulin prophylaxis for children at risk to severe RSV infections

N01AI-82678-09 (**) LUSHER, JEANNE Recruiting and following HIV infected hemophilic patients

N01AI-82680-07 (**) BAKER, DAVID C To target drugs to the central nervous system for AIDS therapy

N01AI-82681-06 (**) POTASH, LOUIS Operation of an experimental virus vaccine production laboratory

N01AI-82683-09 (**) JOHNSON, DAVID Resource support services for the acquired immunodeficiency syndrome

N01AI-82684-24 (**) STERN, SUSAN A Acquisition, analysis, storage and distribution of cells

N01AI-82685-09 (**) OSTROUR, JEFFREY M Production of

PROJECT NO., ORGANIZATIONAL UNIT., INVESTIGATOR, ADDRESS, TITLE

retrovirus stocks for AIDS research
N01AI-82687-03 ( ) KERGDER, JOHN W** A papillomavirus animal model for evaluation
N01AI-82688-04 ( ) FARAS, ANTHONY J** A papillomavirus animal model for evaluation
N01AI-82689-07 ( ) EBY, RONALD J** Development of protein-polysaccharide pneumococcal conjugate vaccine
N01AI-82696-05 ( ) GORECKI, MARIAN** Production of antisera and recombinant proteins for research in AIDS
N01AI-82698-07 ( ) TENNANT, BUD C** Breeding and experimental facility for woodchucks
N01AI-82699-03 ( ) SCHIFFMAN, GERALD** Operation of a pneumococcal polysaccharide serological laboratory
N01AI-85001-06 ( ) STROBER, SAMUEL** Combined syngeneic and allogenic bone marrow transplantation & supressor cells
N01AI-85002-04 ( ) BLAZAR, BRUCE R** Transplantation/immune cell depleted/marrow grafts
N01AI-85003-03 ( ) ANDREWS, ROBERT G** Hematopoietic reconstitution using isolated progenitor
N01AI-85005-10 ( ) DIAZ, CLEMENTE** Collaborative prospective cohort studies of perinatal AIDS
N01AI-85006-07 ( ) ILEANA, QUINTAS** Logistical support contract
N01AI-87240-09 ( ) QUEENER, SHERRY** Antifolate screen for drugs/opportunistic infect/AIDS
N01AI-87248-19 ( ) FERINDE, JOHN** Storage and distribution of clinical drugs for AIDS
N01AI-95010-04 ( ) WAXDAL, MYRON** Flow cytometry quality control
N01AI-95012-07 ( ) PAN, PERCY S** Repository and distribution center for reagents
N01AI-95014-05 ( ) LANDESMAN, SHELDON H** Heterosexual transmissions of HIV and related retroviruses
N01AI-95015-09 ( ) CORNELL, RICHARD G** Data coordinating center for HIV studies
N01AI-95016-08 ( ) LEEF, JAMES** Repository for human immunodeficiency (HIV) specimens
N01AI-95024-03 ( ) MOBRAATEN, LARRY E** Cryopreserved mouse embryo repository
N01AI-95025-05 ( ) WILLIAMS, EDNA** Support for the epidemiology branch, DAIDS
N01AI-95027-07 ( ) THOMPSON, MELANIE** Community programs for clinical research on AIDS -- Stage I
N01AI-95028-06 ( ) CRANE, LAWRENCE** Community programs for clinical research on AIDS -- Stage I
N01AI-95029-06 ( ) EL-SADR, WAFAA** Community programs for clinical research on AIDS -- Stage I
N01AI-95030-06 ( ) LAGAKOS, STEPHEN** Statistical and data analysis center
N01AI-95031-06 ( ) LAM, SI-HOI** Community programs for clinical research on AIDS -- Stage I
N01AI-95032-06 ( ) BESCH, LYNN** Community programs for clinical research on AIDS -- Stage I
N01AI-95033-06 ( ) COHN, DAVID** Community program for clinical research on AIDS -- Stage II
N01AI-95034-04 ( ) KERKERING, THOMAS** Community programs for clinical research on AIDS -- Stage II
N01AI-95035-06 ( ) ABRAMS, DONALD I** Community programs for clinical research on AIDS
N01AI-95036-04 ( ) SARAVOLATZ, LOUIS** Community programs for clinical research on AIDS -- Stage II
N01AI-95037-06 ( ) SAMPSON, JAMES H** Community programs for clinical research on AIDS -- Stage I
N01AI-95038-05 ( ) ERNST, JEROME** Community programs for clinical research on AIDS
N01AI-95039-06 ( ) PEREZ, GEORGE** Community programs for clinical research on AIDS
N01AI-95040-02 ( ) CHIN, TING-FONG** Development and manufacture of dosage forms of compounds
N01AI-95041-03 ( ) HOWSON, CHRISTOPHER** Review of the adverse consequences of pertussis and rubella vaccines
K08AR-01482-05 (AMS) AWBREY, BRIAN J MASSACHUSETTS GENERAL HOSPITAL 1014 JACKSON TOWER BOSTON, MA 02114 Collagenase activator protein & interleukin-1
K11AR-01537-05 (ADDK) RIENHOFF, HUGH Y, JR JOHN HOPKINS UNIVERSITY 720 RUTLAND AVENUE BALTIMORE, MD 21205 Transcriptional control of murine serum amyloid A genes
K04AR-01684-05 (IMS) MARSHAK-ROTHSTEIN, ANN BOSTON U. SCHOOL OF MEDICINE 80 EAST CONCORD STREET BOSTON, MA 02118 Analysis of immunoregulatory defect
K04AR-01686-05 (GMA) ANHALT, GRANT J THE JOHNS HOPKINS UNIVERSITY 600 NORTH WOLFE STREET BALTIMORE, MD 21205 Pathogenicity of pemphigus and pemphigold antibodies
K04AR-01694-05 (OBM) VIGNERY, AGNES M YALE UNIVERSITY MEDICAL SCHOOL 333 CEDAR STREET NEW HAVEN, CT 06510 Osteoclasts and giant cells--Implications of cell fusion
K08AR-01714-05 (ADDK) MA, SHAU P UNIVERSITY OF CHICAGO 5841 S MARYLAND AVE, BOX 409 CHICAGO, IL 60637 Membrane proteins or epidermal keratinocytes
K04AR-01737-05 (ORTH) WRIGHT, TIMOTHY M HOSPITAL FOR SPECIAL SURGERY 535 EAST 70TH STREET NEW YORK, NY 10021 Fracture mechanics in design of total joint replacement
K08AR-01749-05 (ADDK) CARPENTER, THOMAS O YALE UNIVERSITY MEDICAL SCHOOL 333 CEDAR ST., P. O. BOX 3333 NEW HAVEN, CT 06510 Mitochondrial vitamin D metabolism in hypophosphatemia
K04AR-01765-05 (GMA) ELMETS, CRAIG A UNIV. HOSPITALS OF CLEVELAND 2074 ADELBERT ROAD CLEVELAND, OH 44106 UVB radiation--Immunodermatologic effects in humans
K08AR-01770-05 (ADDK) COOPER, KEVIN D R5538 KRESGE I BOX 530 ANN ARBOR MI 48109 UV light-induced epidermal antigen presenting cells
K04AR-01782-05 (GMA) MORHENN, VERA B SRI INTERNATIONAL 333 RAVENSWOOD AVE MENLO PARK, CA 94025 Characterization and culture of human langerhans cells

PROJECT NO., ORGANIZATIONAL UNIT., INVESTIGATOR, ADDRESS, TITLE

K04AR-01784-05 (GMA) SONTHEIMER, RICHARD D UNIV. OF TX H.S.C. AT DALLAS 5323 HARRY HINES BOULEVARD DALLAS, TX 75235 Mechanisms of cutaneous injury in lupus erythematosus
K08AR-01787-05 (AMS) PETERSEN, MARTA J UNIVERSITY OF UTAH 50 NORTH MEDICAL DRIVE SALT LAKE CITY, UTAH 84132 Purification and study of human keratinocyte collagenase
K04AR-01788-04 (BBCA) SHRIVER, JOHN W SOUTHERN ILLINOIS UNIVERSITY DEPT OF CHEMISTRY & BIOCHEM CARBONDALE, ILL 62901 Biophysical studies of the myosin ATPase
K04AR-01789-05 (GMB) GUNDBERG, CAREN M YALE UNIV. SCHOOL OF MEDICINE 333 CEDAR ST., P. O. BOX 3333 NEW HAVEN, CT 06510 Regulation of osteocalcin concentrations in blood
K04AR-01792-05 (GMA) ELKON, KEITH B HOSPITAL FOR SPECIAL SURGERY 535 EAST 70TH STREET NEW YORK, NY 10021 Molecular analysis and clinical associations of p/anti-p
K11AR-01793-05 (AMS) DEDRICK, DALE K TC2912 TAUBMAN HEALTH CENTER ORTHOPAEDIC SURGERY ANN ARBOR, MI 48109-0328 Trabecular bone physiologic response to applied stress
K04AR-01799-04 (ORTH) WEBBER, RICHARD J UNIVERSITY OF ARKANSAS 4301 W. MARKHAM, SLOT 517 LITTLE ROCK, AR 72205 Fibrocartilaginous knee joint Menisci--Biology and repair
K04AR-01803-04 (GMA) ISSEROFF, ROSLYN-RIVKAH UNIV CA, DAVIS SCHOOL OF MED, TB 192 DAVIS, CALIF 95616 Control of keratinocyte differentiation by fatty acids
K08AR-01804-04 (AMS) KVEDAR, JOSEPH C MASSACHUSETTS GENERAL HOSPITAL 32 FRUIT STREET BOSTON, MA 02114 Composition of the cornified envelope of mouse epidermis
K08AR-01805-05 (AMS) BLEICHER, PAUL A MASSACHUSETTS GENERAL HOSPITAL FRUIT STREET BOSTON, MA 02114 Structure and regulation of the Cd1 multigene family
K08AR-01806-04 (AMS) DAVIDSON, ANNE ALBERT EINSTEIN COLLEGE OF MED 1300 MORRIS PARK AVENUE BRONX, NY 10461 Antibodies bearing an SLE associated idiotype
K08AR-01808-02 (AMS) RICO, M JOYCE DUKE UNIVERSITY MEDICAL CTR BOX 3135 DUHAM, NC 27710 Characterization of B and T cell epitopes on BP antigen
K04AR-01810-04 (PHRA) NAVARRO, JAVIER V BOSTON UNIVERSITY 80 E CONCORD ST BOSTON, MA 02118 Modulation of calcium channels in muscle cells
K08AR-01811-02 (AMS) PALLER, AMY S CHILDREN'S MEMORIAL HOSPITAL CHICAGO, IL 60614 Gangliosides and epidermal growth and differentiation
K11AR-01812-03 (AMS) WINAND, NENA NYS COLLEGE OF VETERINARY MED 123 DAY HALL ITHACA, NY 14853 Molecular genetics of canine x-linked muscular dystrophy
K11AR-01813-03 (AMS) WILSON, RAYMOND W BAYLOR COLLEGE OF MEDICINE ONE BAYLOR PLAZA HOUSTON, TX 77030 Molecular genetics of leukocyte adhesion molecules
K11AR-01816-04 (AMS) HINKES, MICHAEL T THE CHILDREN'S HOSPITAL 300 LONGWOOD AVENUE BOSTON, MA 02115 Cell surface proteoglycan in epidermal development
K08AR-01817-03 (AMS) VARGA, JOHN THOMAS JEFFERSON UNIVERSITY RM M-46, JEFFERSON ALUMNI HALL PHILADELPHIA, PA 19107 Mechanisms of collagen synthesis regulation by TGF-B
K08AR-01819-03 (AMS) ORY, PETER A SEATTLE VA MEDICAL CENTER 1660 S. COLUMBIAN WAY SEATTLE, WASHINGTON 98108 Characterization of CD16 on neutrophils
K04AR-01823-03 (GMA) NICKOLOFF, BRIAN J UNIVERSITY OF MICHIGAN 1301 GATHERINE RDAD ANN ARBOR, MI 48109-0602 Role of adhesive molecules in skin diseases
K08AR-01824-03 (AMS) GRAVALLESE, ELLEN M HARVARD SCHOOL OF PUBLIC HEALT 665 HUNTINGTON AVENUE BOSTON, MA 02115 Role of lipopolysaccharide in connective tissue disease
K11AR-01825-03 (AMS) SAITTA, MICHAEL R DUKE UNIVERSITY MEDICAL CENTER BOX 3020 DURHAM, NC 27710 Molecular biology of the RO-RNP autoantigen
K08AR-01828-02 (AMS) MORELLI, JOSEPH G UNIVERSITY OF COLORADO 4200 E NINTH AVE, BOX B153 DENVER, CO 80262 UV light induced eicosanoid formation & metabolism
K11AR-01829-02 (AMS) LEE, RANDALL J STANFORD UNIVERSITY STANFORD, CA 94305 Structure and function of the myosin tail
K04AR-01831-02 (CTY) PUTKEY, JOHN A U. OF TEXAS MED. CNTR./HOUSTON PO BOX 20708 HOUSTON, TX 77225 Mutation of functional domains in cardiac troponin C
K04AR-01833-02 (ORTH) CORDO, PAUL J GOOD SAMARITAN HOSP./MED. CTR. 1120 N W 20TH AVE PORTLAND, OR 97210 Kinesthetic control of targeted limb movements
K04AR-01837-02 (CTY) MOON, RANDALL T UNIVERSITY OF WASHINGTON SCHOOL OF MEDICINE SEATTLE, WA 98195 Inhibition of nonerythroid spectrin by antisense RNA
K08AR-01838-01A1 (AMS) PRYSTOWSKY, JANET H COLUMBIA UNIVERSITY 630 WEST 168TH STREET NEW YORK, NY 10032 Regulation of ornithine decarboxylase in human skin
K04AR-01841-01A1 (PHY) KIRLEY, TERENCE L UNIVERSITY OF CINCINNATI 231 BETHESDA AVENUE CINCINNATI, OH 45267-0575 Characterization of transverse tubule Mg--ATPase
K11AR-01846-02 (AMS) SLACK, JAMES L UNIVERSITY OF WASHINGTON SJ-70 SEATTLE, WA 98195 Transformation-induced changes in matrix gene expression
K08AR-01847-02 (AMS) GILKESON, GARY S DUKE UNIVERSITY MEDICAL CTR PO BOX 2918 DURHAM, NC 27710 Immunopathogenesis of induced anti-DNA responses
K04AR-01849-02 (GMA) PENTLAND, ALICE P WASHINGTON UNIV SCH OF MED 660 S EUCLID AVE/BOX 8123 ST LOUIS, MO 63110 Mechanisms of enhanced eicosanoid synthesis in UV injury
K11AR-01850-01A1 (AMS) KIM, YOUN H STANFORD UNIV MED CTR 300 PASTEUR DR STANFORD, CA 94305 1h-MRS study of tumorigenesis and malignant transformation
K08AR-01852-01 (AMS) IVASHKIV, LIONEL B HARVARD SCH OF PUBLIC HEALTH 665 HUNTINGTON AVENUE BOSTON, MA 02115 The role of MXBP, a transcription factor, in autoimmune
K08AR-01853-01 (AMS) MAURO, THEODORA M UNIVERSITY OF CALIFORNIA 1605 ALHAMBRA BLVD SACRAMENTO, CA 95816 Membrane current control of

keratinocyte differentiation
K08AR-01854-01 (AMS) PORCELLI, STEVEN A DANA FARBER CANCER INST 44 BINNEY ST MAYER BLDG BOSTON, MA 02115 Immune recognition by CD4-8-T lymphocytes
K08AR-01856-01 (AMS) BATHON, JOAN M JOHNS HOPKINS UNIVERSITY 301 BAYVIEW BOULEVARD BALTIMORE, MD 21224 Regulation of synovial cell responsiveness to bradykinin
K08AR-01860-01 (AMS) BRICE, SYLVIA L UNIVERSITY OF COLORADO HSC 4200 E NINTH AVENUE/B153 DENVER, CO 80262 Immunopathogenesis of recurrent aphthous stomatitis
K08AR-01862-01 (AMS) GEORGE, ALFRED L DEPARTMENT OF MEDICINE 518 GLEN ARBOR DRIVE WYNNEWOOD, P A 19096 Human muscle sodium channels in period paralysis
K08AR-01863-01 (AMS) HIGGINS, GLORIA C UNIVERSITY OF TENNESSEE 956 COURT AVE G326 MEMPHIS, TENNESSEE Specific synovial fluid inhibitor of interleukin-1a
K08AR-01864-02 (AMS) CLARK, MARCUS R NATIONAL JEWISH CENTER 1400 JACKSON STREET DENVER, CO 80206 Molecular characterization of FC receptors
K08AR-01866-01 (AMS) BLOCH, DONALD B MASSACHUSETTS GENERAL HOSPITAL 15 FRUIT STREET BOSTON, MA 02114 Characterization of atypical speckled autoantigens
K11AR-01867-01 (AMS) BRIDGES, STANLEY LOUIS JR UNIVERSITY OF ALABAMA UAB STATION BIRMINGHAM, AL 35294 Immunoglobulin gene repertoire in rheumatoid synovium
K08AR-01868-01 (AMS) YOHN, JOSEPH J UNIV OF COLORADO HLTH SCI CENT 4200 E NINTH AVE/B153 DENVER, CO 80262 Regulation of human melanocyte antioxidant defenses
K11AR-01870-01 (AMS) FELDMAN, JONATHAN D 333 CEDAR ST NEW HAVEN, CT 06510-8026 Molecular mechanism of acetylcholine receptor clustering
K11AR-01871-01 (AMS) LESH, RYAN E UNIVERSITY OF VIRGINIA PO BOX 449 JORDAN HALL CHARLOTTESVILLE, VA 22908 Signal transduction adrenergic receptor and Na/K-ATPase
K11AR-01872-01 (AMS) KATZENSTEIN, PAUL L UNIV OF TX HLTH SCI CTR PO BOX 20708 HOUSTON, TX 77225 Molecular biology of osteoarthritis and chondrodysplasias
K08AR-01881-01 (AMS) FRYBURG, DAVID A UNIV OF VIRGINIA HLTH SCI CTR PO BOX 511-66 CHARLOTTESVILLE, VA 22908 Hormonal regulation of skeletal muscle metabolism in man
N01AR-22201-02 ( ) BASSIN, GAIL D** National arthritis and musculoskeletal and skin diseases
R01AR-02255-31 (BM) COLE, BARRY C UNIVERSITY OF UTAH 50 NORTH MEDICAL DRIVE SALT LAKE CITY, UTAH 84132 Mycoplasma arthritidis T cell mitogen
R37AR-02594-33 (ALY) FRANGIONE, BLAS N.Y.U. MEDICAL CENTER 550 FIRST AVENUE NEW YORK, NY 10016 Structure of immunoglobulins and related proteins
P01AR-03555-32A1 (AMS) VOLANAKIS, JOHN E UNIV OF ALABAMA UAB STATION - 437 THT BIRMINGHAM, AL 35294 Coordinated studies in rheumatic diseases
P01AR-03555-32A1 0003 (AMS) KOOPMAN, WILLIAM J Coordinated studies in rheumatic diseases Pathological immunoglobulins
P01AR-03555-32A1 0006 (AMS) SCHROEDER, HARRY W Coordinated studies in rheumatic diseases Tissue-specific antigen receptor repertoires in RA
P01AR-03555-32A1 0007 (AMS) MOUNTZ, JOHN D Coordinated studies in rheumatic diseases Expression of transgenic TcR genes in autoimmune lpr/lpr mice
P01AR-03555-32A1 0008 (AMS) BUCY, R PAT Coordinated studies in rheumatic diseases Effect of cycloesporin A on TCR ontogeny and autoimmune disease
P01AR-03555-32A1 0009 (AMS) VOLANAKIS, JOHN E Coordinated studies in rheumatic diseases Regulation of C2 gene expression in SLE
P01AR-03564-32 (AMS) KRANE, STEPHEN M MASSACHUSETTS GENERAL HOSPITAL 32 FRUIT STREET BOSTON, MA 02114 Study of mesenchymal tissues and their diseases
P01AR-03564-32 0001 (AMS) KRANE, STEPHEN Study of mesenchymal tissues and their diseases Collagen degradation in inflammation
P01AR-03564-32 0002 (AMS) GOLDRING, MARY Study of mesenchymal tissues and their diseases Collagen synthesis in inflammation
P01AR-03564-32 0019 (AMS) KRANE, STEVEN Study of mesenchymal tissues and their diseases Monocyte differentiation and function
P01AR-03564-32 0021 (AMS) YEH, EDWARD Study of mesenchymal tissues and their diseases Genetic approach to T cell activation
P01AR-03564-32 0022 (AMS) GOLDRING, STEVEN Study of mesenchymal tissues and their diseases Skeletal cell differentiation and response
P01AR-03564-32 0023 (AMS) SIMON, LEE Study of mesenchymal tissues and their diseases Collagen metabolism in human disease
P01AR-03564-32 0024 (AMS) ROBINSON, DWIGHT Study of mesenchymal tissues and their diseases Control of eicosanoid metabolism inflammation
P01AR-03564-32 9004 (AMS) KRANE, STEPHEN Study of mesenchymal tissues and their diseases Tissue cultureand ultrastructure--Core
R37AR-04349-32 (BBCB) HARRINGTON, WILLIAM F THE JOHNS HOPKINS UNIVERSITY CHARLES AND 34TH STREETS BALTIMORE, MD 21218 Biophysical chemical studies of muscle proteins
R01AR-07912-26 (EDC) HEANEY, ROBERT P CREIGHTON UNIVERSITY CALIFORNIA AT 24TH STREET OMAHA, NE 68178 Longitudinal study of a pre-osteoporosis population
R01AR-08662-26 (ORTH) HOWELL, DAVID S UNIV OF MIAMI SCH OF MEDICINE PO BOX 016960 MIAMI, FL 33101 Role of phospholipids in mineralization of osteoid
R13AR-09431-26 (AMS) WUEPPER, KIRK D OREGON HEALTH SCI UNIV 3181 S W SAM JACKSON PARK ROAD PORTLAND, OREG 97201 Annual symposia on the biology of skin
P01AR-09989-27 (AMS) LIPSKY, PETER E UNIV OF TEXAS SOUTHWESTERN MED 5323 HARRY HINES BLVD DALLAS, TX 75235-8884 Immunologic and other aspects of rheumatic disease
P01AR-09989-27 0001 (AMS) LIPSKY, PETER E Immunologic and other aspects of rheumatic disease Immunoregulatory abnormalities in systemic lupus
P01AR-09989-27 0003 (AMS) SONTHEIMER, RICHARD D Immunologic and other aspects of rheumatic disease Immunobiology of the human dermal microvascular unit
P01AR-09989-27 0004 (AMS) OPPENHEIMER, NANCY Immunologic and other aspects of rheumatic disease Lymphocyte endothelial cell interaction in chronic inflammation
P01AR-09989-27 0006 (AMS) TAUROG, JOEL Immunologic and other aspects of rheumatic disease Experimental arthritis in transgenic rats and mice
P01AR-09989-27 0025 (AMS) LIPSKY, P. Immunologic and other aspects of rheumatic disease Abnormalities of T cell function in SLE
P01AR-09989-27 0026 (AMS) LIPSKY, P. Immunologic and other aspects of rheumatic disease Regulation of B cell function in SLE
P01AR-09989-27 9003 (AMS) LIPSKY, PETER Immunologic and other aspects of rheumatic disease Core--Tissue culture
P01AR-09989-27 9004 (AMS) LIPSKY, PETER Immunologic and other aspects of rheumatic disease Core--Electron microscopy
R01AR-10493-25 (BM) MALAWISTA, STEPHEN E YALE UNIVERSITY 333 CEDAR STREET NEW HAVEN, CT 06510 Biophysical mechanisms in leukocytes and melanocytes
R01AR-10531-26 (PBC) JOURDIAN, GEORGE W UNIVERSITY OF MICHIGAN 4633 KRESGE MED RES BLDG I ANN ARBOR, MICH 48109-0531 Biochemistry of mucopolysaccharides
R37AR-10546-26 (GMA) BRIGGAMAN, ROBERT A UNIVERSITY OF NORTH CAROLINA CB #7600 CHAPEL HILL, NC 27514 Utilization of epidermal cell model from human skin
R01AR-10551-26 (PHY) FUCHS, FRANKLIN UNIVERSITY OF PITTSBURGH 3550 TERRACE STREET PITTSBURGH, PA 15261 Analysis of cellular calcium compartments in muscle
R01AR-10728-25 (GMA) CASTOR, C WILLIAM UNIV OF MICHIGAN MEDICAL CTR WASHTENAW PLACE, RM 4570 KRESG ANN ARBOR, MICH 48109 Connective tissue activation in rheumatic diseases
R37AR-11248-25 (PBC) BORNSTEIN, PAUL UNIVERSITY OF WASHINGTON 201 ADMINISTRATION SEATTLE, WA 98195 Biogenesis and function of connective tissue proteins
R01AR-11262-25 (GMB) STERN, PAULA H NORTHWESTERN UNIVERSITY 303 EAST CHICAGO AVENUE CHICAGO, ILL 60611 Effects of hormones on bone resorption in vitro
R01AR-11476-24 (PTHA) MANNIK, MART UNIVERSITY OF WASHINGTON DEPT OF MEDICINE RG 28 SEATTLE, WA 98195 Studies on the renal disease of systemic lupus
R37AR-11949-24 (BIO) WEISSMANN, GERALD NEW YORK UNIV MEDICAL CENTER 550 FIRST AVENUE NEW YORK, NY 10016 Mechanisms of arthritis
R37AR-12129-24 (GMA) EISEN, ARTHUR Z DIVISION OF DERMATOLOGY BOX 8123 4950 AUDUBON AVENUE ST. LOUIS, MO 63110 Extracellular matrix degradation in normal/abnormal skin
N01AR-12202-01 ( ) TILLEY, BARBARA C** Assessment of the efficacy of minocycline in rheumatoid arthritis
N01AR-12203-01 ( ) KAPLAN, DAVID** Minocycline clinical trial for rheumatoid arthritis
N01AR-12204-20 ( ) WARD, JOHN R** Cooperative systematic studies of rheumatic diseases
N01AR-12205-01 ( ) TRENTHAM, DAVID** Minocycline clinical trial for rheumatoid arthritis
N01AR-12206-01 ( ) CLEGG, DANIEL O** Minocycline clinical trial for rheumatoid arthritis
N01AR-12207-01 ( ) ALARCON, GRACEILA** Minocycline clinical trial for rheumatoid arthritis
R37AR-12433-24 (NSS) FUKUYAMA, KIMIE UNIVERSITY OF CALIFORNIA 3RD & PARNASSUS AVENUES SAN FRANCISCO, CA 94143-0536 Cytochemical studies on the keratinization process
R37AR-12683-23 (PBC) TANZER, MARVIN L UNIV OF CONNECTICUT 263 FARMINGTON AVE FARMINGTON, CT 06030 Structure, function and properties of collagen
R01AR-12803-32 (CPA) CARLSON, FRANCIS D THE JOHNS HOPKINS UNIVERSITY 3400 N CHARLES STREET BALTIMORE, MD 21218 The structural basis of cellular function
R37AR-12849-23 (NSS) MANNIK, MART UNIVERSITY OF WASHINGTON SEATTLE, WA 98195 Immunologic studies in rheumatoid arthritis
R01AR-13812-20A2 (ORTH) BRIGHTON, CARL T UNIVERSITY OF PENNSYLVANIA 36TH AND HAMILTON WALK PHILADELPHIA, PA 19104-6081 Stimulation of extremity growth by electrical fields
R55AR-13824-21A2 (GMA) WILLIAMS, RALPH C, JR UNIVERSITY OF FLORIDA BOX J-221, JHMHC GAINESVILLE, FL 32610 Interactions of cellular and humoral immunity
R37AR-13921-31 (PBC) VEIS, ARTHUR NORTHWESTERN UNIV-DENTAL SCH 303 E CHICAGO AVENUE CHICAGO, IL 60611 Structure and assembly of collagen molecules and fibrils
R01AR-14317-20 (CTY) REEDY, MICHAEL K DUKE UNIVERSITY MEDICAL CENTER BOX 3011 DURHAM, NC 27710 Myofibrillar, structure in striated muscle
R37AR-15781-20 (GMB) HAUSSLER, MARK R UNIVERSITY OF ARIZONA DEPARTMENT OF BIOCHEMISTRY TUCSON, AZ 85724 Function of vitamin D metabolites and bone disease
R01AR-15888-18 (GMB) DEFTOS, LEONARD J UNIVERSITY OF CALIFORNIA LA JOLLA, CA 92093 Calcitropic hormones
R37AR-15963-26 (BBCB) SZENT-GYORGYI, ANDREW G BRANDEIS UNIVERSITY WALTHAM, MA 02254 Regulation in striated, smooth and cardiac muscle
R01AR-16061-20A1 (AMS) PAK, CHARLES Y UNIVERSITY OF TEXAS 5323 HARRY HINES BLVD DALLAS, TEX 75235 Theoretical and therapeutic aspects of calcification
R01AR-16209-18 (GMA) JASIN, HUGO E UNIV OF ARKASAS FOR MED SCIS 4301 WEST MARKHAM LITTLE ROCK, ARK 72205 Role of immune complexes in chronic inflammation
R01AR-16265-17A3 (ORTH) MANKIN, HENRY J MASSACHUSETTS GENERAL HOSPITAL 32 FRUIT STREET BOSTON, MA 02114 Metabolism in normal and osteoarthritic cartilage
R01AR-16404-17 (PBC) BENYA, PAUL D USC ORTHOPAEDIC HOSPITAL 2400 S FLOWER ST LOS ANGELES, CA 90007-2697 Collagen in osteoarthritic cartilage
R37AR-16940-19 (GMA) WOESSNER, J FREDERICK, JR UNIV OF MIAMI SCHOOL OF MED PO BOX 016960 MIAMI, FL 33101 Human cartilage proteases in arthritis

PROJECT NO., ORGANIZATIONAL UNIT., INVESTIGATOR, ADDRESS, TITLE

R37AR-17128-19 (GMA) PINNELL, SHELDON R DUKE UNIV. MEDICAL CENTER BOX 3135 DURHAM, NC 27710 Collagen biosynthesis in connective tissue disease
R01AR-17172-16 (ORTH) COONEY, WILLIAM P MAYO FOUNDATION 200 FIRST STREET SOUTHWEST ROCHESTER, MN 55905 Functional forces in normal and abnormal fingers
R01AR-17220-19 (PBC) TANZER, MARVIN L UNIV OF CONNECTICUT 263 FARMINGTON AVE FARMINGTON, CT 06030 Biological role of laminin carbohydrates
R37AR-17323-19 (NSS) KENYON, GEORGE L UNIVERSITY OF CALIFORNIA SAN FRANCISCO, CA 94143-0446 Active sites of creatine kinase from heart and muscle
R37AR-17346-18 (BBCB) COHEN, CAROLYN BRANDEIS UNIVERSITY P O BOX 9110 WALTHAM, MA 02254-9110 Muscle structure and the contractile mechanism
R37AR-17350-19 (NSS) LOWEY, SUSAN BRANDEIS UNIVERSITY PO BOX 9110 WALTHAM, MA 02254 Chemistry of muscle proteins
R37AR-17803-18 (NSS) ALMERS, WOLFHARD UNIVERSITY OF WASHINGTON SJ-40 SEATTLE, WA 98195 Electric studies of excitation, secretion and contraction
R37AR-18033-18 (ORTH) BRIGHTON, CARL T UNIVERSITY OF PENNSYLVANIA STEMMLER HALL PHILADELPHIA, PA 19104 Acceleration of fracture healing by electrical fields
R01AR-18063-17A2 (ORTH) RAISZ, LAWRENCE G UNIVERSITY OF CONNECTICUT 263 FARMINGTON AVENUE FARMINGTON, CT 06032 Factors influencing bone metabolism
R01AR-18140-15 (ORTH) TAYLOR, C RICHARD HARVARD UNIVERSITY MUSEUM OF COMPARATIVE ZOOLOGY CAMBRIDGE, MASS 02138 Locomotion--idling metabolism and gait dynamics
R01AR-18549-16A1 (GMA) POH-FITZPATRICK, MAUREEN B NEW YORK MEDICAL COLLEGE VALHALLA, NY 10595 Erythropoietic protoporphyria--Mechanisms of disease
R37AR-18687-16 (PHY) MEISSNER, GERHARD W UNIV OF NC AT CHAPEL HILL DEPT OF BIOCHEMISTRY, CB#7260 CHAPEL HILL, NC 27599-7260 Sarcoplasmic reticulum function and reassembly
R01AR-18860-15 (CTY) HAUSCHKA, STEPHEN D UNIVERSITY OF WASHINGTON DEPT. OF BIOCHEMISTRY, SJ-70 SEATTLE, WA 98195 Mitogenic regulation of skeletal muscle differentiation
R37AR-18880-15 (PBC) KAGAN, HERBERT M BOSTON U. SCHOOL OF MEDICINE 80 EAST CONCORD STREET BOSTON, MA 02118 Properties of aortic lysyl oxidase
R01AR-18983-15 (OBM) WUTHIER, ROY E UNIVERSITY OF SOUTH CAROLINA 424 PHYSICAL SCIENCES BLDG COLUMBIA, SC 29208 Role of matrix vesicles in calcification
R01AR-19098-16 (GMA) ELIAS, PETER M VETERANS ADMIN MEDICAL CTR 4150 CLEMENT STREET SAN FRANCISCO, CA 94121 Nature of mammalian cutaneous permeability barrier
R01AR-19101-15 (GMA) SONTHEIMER, RICHARD D UNIVERSITY OF TEXAS 5323 HARRY HINES BLVD DALLAS, TX 75235 Mechanisms of cutaneous injury in lupus erythematosus
R37AR-19393-15 (RAP) BOOTH, FRANK W UNIV OF TEXAS MEDICAL SCHOOL PO BOX 20708 HOUSTON, TX 77225 Exercise-induced growth of adult rat skeletal muscle
R37AR-19537-16 (GMA) BAUER, EUGENE A STANFORD UNIVERSITY EDWARDS BLDG STANFORD, CA 94305 Control of collagenase in human fibroblast cultures
R01AR-19616-15 (GMA) JIMENEZ, SERGIO A THOMAS JEFFERSON UNIVERSITY 1020 LOCUST STREET PHILADELPHIA, PA 19107 Biochemical and vascular alterations in scleroderma
R37AR-19622-15 (PC) SCHWARTZ, NANCY B UNIVERSITY OF CHICAGO 5801 S ELLIS AVENUE CHICAGO, IL 60637 Regulation of biosynthesis of proteoglycan
R01AR-19626-13A1 (PBC) BRODSKY, BARBARA M UNIV OF MED & DENT OF NJ 675 HOES LANE PISCATAWAY, NJ 08854-5635 Structural studies of connective tissues
R01AR-19969-12 (ORTH) YAMAUCHI, MITSUO UNIVERSITY OF NORTH CAROLINA DENTAL RESEARCH CENTER CHAPEL HILL, N C 27514 Chemistry and physiology of bone -Vitamin D nutrition
R01AR-19980-11 (EVR) MILLS, BARBARA G UNIV OF SOUTHERN CALIFORNIA UNIVERSITY PARK MC 0641 LOS ANGELES, CALIF 90089-0641 Study of possible causes of Paget's disease of bone
R01AR-20358-16 (GMA) STEERE, ALLEN C NEW ENGLAND MED CTR 750 WASHINGTON ST BOSTON, MA 02111 Lyme arthritis--A new epidemic disease
P01AR-20553-15 (AMS) KEFALIDES, NICHOLAS A CONNECTIVE TISSUE RES INST 3624 MARKET STREET PHILADELPHIA, PA 19104 Chemistry and metabolism of connective tissues
P01AR-20553-15 0001 (AMS) ROSENBLOOM, JOEL Chemistry and metabolism of connective tissues Molecular genetics of human elastin
P01AR-20553-15 0003 (AMS) KEFALIDES, NICHOLAS A Chemistry and metabolism of connective tissues Chemistry, metabolism of basement membranes
P01AR-20553-15 0008 (AMS) NEILSON, ERIC G Chemistry and metabolism of connective tissues Nephritogenic tubular antigens in interstitial nephritis
P01AR-20553-15 0010 (AMS) MYERS, J C Chemistry and metabolism of connective tissues Structure-expression of collagen and fibronectin in transcripts
P01AR-20553-15 9001 (AMS) ALPER, ROBERT Chemistry and metabolism of connective tissues Core analytical facility
P60AR-20557-13 (AMS) PALELLA, THOMAS D UNIV. OF MICHIGAN MED. CENTER TAUBMAN H.C.C., ROOM 3105 ANN ARBOR, MI 48109-0368 The University of Michigan multipurpose arthritis center
P60AR-20557-13 9001 (AMS) TODD, ROBERT F The University of Michigan multipurpose arthritis center Flow cytometry core facility
P60AR-20557-13 9002 (AMS) FOX, DAVID The University of Michigan multipurpose arthritis center Hybridoma core facility
P60AR-20557-13 9003 (AMS) OXENDER, DALE The University of Michigan multipurpose arthritis center Molecular biology core
P60AR-20557-13 9004 (AMS) PERINI, FULVIO The University of Michigan multipurpose arthritis center Protein structure and design
P60AR-20557-13 9005 (AMS) GOLDSTEIN, STEVEN The University of Michigan multipurpose arthritis center The biomechanics core facility
P60AR-20557-13 0057 (AMS) FOX, DAVID The University of Michigan multipurpose arthritis center Molecular characteriztion of a novel synovial T cell antigen
P60AR-20557-13 0059 (AMS) FOX, IRVING The University of Michigan multipurpose arthritis center Adenosine a2 receptor effect on coupling
P60AR-20557-13 0060 (AMS) RICHARDSON, BRUCE The University of Michigan multipurpose arthritis center 5-Azacytidine induced autoreactive t cells in autoimmune disease
P60AR-20557-13 0061 (AMS) STOOLMAN, L M The University of Michigan multipurpose arthritis center The role of lymphocyte migration in chronic inflammatory arthritis
P60AR-20557-13 0062 (AMS) CARTER-SU The University of Michigan multipurpose arthritis center Connective tissue activating protein an glucose transport
P60AR-20557-13 0063 (AMS) BOLE, G G The University of Michigan multipurpose arthritis center Bone cartilage interface in experimental osteoarthritis
P60AR-20557-13 0064 (AMS) DAVIS, W K The University of Michigan multipurpose arthritis center Ambulatory care training for primary care house officers
P60AR-20557-13 0065 (AMS) MCMAHON, L F The University of Michigan multipurpose arthritis center Hospital admission variation in musculoskeletal disease
P60AR-20557-13 0066 (AMS) THOMPSON, CRAIG B The University of Michigan multipurpose arthritis center Regulation of CD28 activation pathway in autoimmune disease
P60AR-20557-13 0067 (AMS) WILSON, JAMES N The University of Michigan multipurpose arthritis center Gene therapy of leukocyte adhesion deficiency
P60AR-20557-13 0068 (AMS) CAMPER, SALLY ANN The University of Michigan multipurpose arthritis center Autoantibodies in transgenic mice
P60AR-20582-14 (ADDK) BRANDT, KENNETH D INDIANA U. SCHOOL OF MEDICINE 541 CLINICAL DRIVE INDIANAPOLIS, IN 46202-5103 Multipurpose arthritis center
P60AR-20582-14 0001 (ADDK) SRIVASTAVA, ARUN Multipurpose arthritis center Human parvovirum B19 and rheumatoid arthritis
P60AR-20582-14 0002 (ADDK) KLUVE-BECKMAN, BARBARA Multipurpose arthritis center Interaction of SAA with Ia molecules--T-cell recognition of self-antigens
P60AR-20582-14 0003 (ADDK) LIEPNIEKS, JURIS J Multipurpose arthritis center Biochemical mechanisms of prealbumin amyloid formation
P60AR-20582-14 0004 (ADDK) HUGENBERG, STEVEN T Multipurpose arthritis center Sensitivity to IGF-1 of osteoarthritic and atrophic cartilage
P60AR-20582-14 9004 (ADDK) BENSON, MERRILL Multipurpose arthritis center Core--Protein structure
P60AR-20582-14 9005 (ADDK) KLUVE-BECKERMAN, BARBARA Multipurpose arthritis center Core--Molecular biology
P60AR-20582-14 9006 (ADDK) KATZ, BARRY P Multipurpose arthritis center Core--Statistics
P60AR-20582-14 9007 (ADDK) MAZZUCA, STEVEN Multipurpose arthritis center Core--Interviews
P60AR-20610-14 (ADDK) HOLMAN, HALSTED R STANFORD UNIVERSITY 1000 WELCH RD, SUITE 203 PALO ALTO, CA 94304 Multipurpose arthritis center
P60AR-20610-14 0004 (ADDK) FRIES, JAMES F Multipurpose arthritis center Community component--Outcome in rheumatoid arthritis
P60AR-20610-14 0006 (ADDK) MOOS, RUDOLF Multipurpose arthritis center Community component--Social outcome of juvenile arthritis
P60AR-20610-14 0013 (ADDK) HOLMAN, HALSTED R Multipurpose arthritis center Education component--Arthritis self management
P60AR-20610-14 0016 (ADDK) FRIES, JAMES F Multipurpose arthritis center Community component--Osteoarthritis, osteoporosis and running
P60AR-20610-14 9001 (ADDK) FRIES, JAMES F Multipurpose arthritis center Core--Biostatistics, computer, outcome assessment and experimental design
P60AR-20610-14 9002 (ADDK) FATHMAN, C GARRISON Multipurpose arthritis center Core--T-cell cloning
P60AR-20613-14 (ADDK) MEENAN, ROBERT F BOSTON UNIVERSITY SCH OF MED 71 E. CONCORD STREET, K-5 BOSTON, MA 02118 Multipurpose arthritis center
P60AR-20613-14 0011 (ADDK) MEENAN, ROBERT F Multipurpose arthritis center Arthritis impact measurement scales
P60AR-20613-14 0019 (ADDK) JU, SHYR-TE Multipurpose arthritis center Feasibility study--Murine amyloid enhancing factor--Immunologic approach
P60AR-20613-14 0023 (ADDK) FELSON, DAVID T Multipurpose arthritis center Rheumatologic applications of metaanalysis
P60AR-20613-14 0024 (ADDK) FELSON, DAVID T Multipurpose arthritis center Epidemiology of osteoporosis
P60AR-20613-14 0025 (ADDK) ABRAHAM, CARMELA R Multipurpose arthritis center Serine proteases in human aging and Alzheimer's disease
P60AR-20613-14 0026 (ADDK) SIMMS, ROBERT Multipurpose arthritis center Muscle metabolism and muscle fatigue in fibromyalgia syndrome
P60AR-20613-14 9001 (ADDK) COHEN, ALAN S Multipurpose arthritis center Core--Amyloid studies unit
P60AR-20613-14 9002 (ADDK) FELSON, DAVID Multipurpose arthritis center Core--Research and evaluation support unit
P60AR-20614-14 (ADDK) KOOPMAN, WILLIAM J UNIV OF ALABAMA UAB STATION/THT 429A BIRMINGHAM, AL 35294 Multipurpose arthritis center
P60AR-20614-14 0006 (ADDK) STRAATON, KARIN Multipurpose arthritis center Vocational evaluation of patients with rheumatoid arthritis
P60AR-20614-14 0007 (ADDK) MAISIAK, RICHARD Multipurpose arthritis center Dissemination of arthritis information by telephone
P60AR-20614-14 0008 (ADDK) BRILES, DAVID E Multipurpose arthritis center Rheumatoid factor--Origin and relation to fatal pneumonia
P60AR-20614-14 0009 (ADDK) COUCHMAN, JOHN R Multipurpose arthritis center Cell matrix interactions in systemic sclerosis
P60AR-20614-14 0010 (ADDK) HARDY, KENNETH J Multipurpose arthritis center Cell and molecular analysis of human cytokine regulation in RA
P60AR-20614-14 0011 (ADDK) BARNUM, SCOTT Multipurpose arthritis center Biosynthesis and regulation of human C4-binding protein
P60AR-20614-14 9001 (ADDK) ACCAVITTI, MARY ANN Multipurpose arthritis center Core--Hybridoma facility

PROJECT NO., ORGANIZATIONAL UNIT., INVESTIGATOR, ADDRESS, TITLE

P60AR-20614-14 9002 (ADDK) ELDRIDGE, JOHN Multipurpose arthritis center Flow cytometry--Core
P60AR-20614-14 9003 (ADDK) BARGER, BRUCE Multipurpose arthritis center Immunomolecular genetics--Core
P60AR-20614-14 0005 (ADDK) LORISH, CHRISTOPHER Multipurpose arthritis center Coping and health status variability in rheumatoid arthritis
P60AR-20618-13 (AMS) MOSKOWITZ, ROLAND W CASE WESTERN RESERVE UNIV. 2073 ABINGTON ROAD CLEVELAND, OH 44106 Northeast Ohio multipurpose arthritis center
P60AR-20618-13 0015 (AMS) KING, CHARLES Northeast Ohio multipurpose arthritis center Protease enhancement of neutrophil inflammatory response
P60AR-20618-13 0016 (AMS) BLOSSEY, BETTY Northeast Ohio multipurpose arthritis center Inducible expression in insulin-like growth factor-1
P60AR-20618-13 0017 (AMS) MAGNUSON, TERRY Northeast Ohio multipurpose arthritis center Expression of C-reactive protein in transgenic mice
P60AR-20618-13 0018 (AMS) JENTOFT, JOYCE E Northeast Ohio multipurpose arthritis center Investigation of the Clq binding site on IgG
P60AR-20618-13 0019 (AMS) COULTON, CLAUDIA Northeast Ohio multipurpose arthritis center The impact of total hip arthroplasty
P60AR-20618-13 0020 (AMS) LEVINE, STEPHEN Northeast Ohio multipurpose arthritis center Sexual adjustment in women with SLE
P60AR-20618-13 0021 (AMS) MILLIGAN, SHARON Northeast Ohio multipurpose arthritis center Coping, social support and sense of control by women in SLE
P60AR-20618-13 0022 (AMS) HAQQI, TARIQ Northeast Ohio multipurpose arthritis center T cell receptor Vb gene expression
P60AR-20618-13 9001 (AMS) HULL, ALAN Northeast Ohio multipurpose arthritis center Core--Evaluation/education
P60AR-20618-13 9004 (AMS) MEHRABAN, FUAD Northeast Ohio multipurpose arthritis center Hybridoma core laboratory
P60AR-20618-13 9005 (AMS) STEVENSON, SHARON Northeast Ohio multipurpose arthritis center Immunohistochemistry core
P60AR-20621-13 (AMS) ROTHFIELD, NAOMI F UNIVERSITY OF CONNECTICUT H.C. 263 FARMINGTON AVENUE FARMINGTON, CT 06032 Multipurpose arthritis center
P60AR-20621-13 0020 (AMS) AFFLECK, GLENN G Multipurpose arthritis center Community component--Coping responses to rheumatoid arthritis
P60AR-20621-13 0022 (AMS) REISINE, SUSAN T Multipurpose arthritis center Community component--Role performance limitations in rheumatoid arthritis patient
P60AR-20621-13 0023 (AMS) REISINE, SUSAN T Multipurpose arthritis center Education component--Outcomes in total point arthroplasty
P60AR-20621-13 0026 (AMS) GRONOWICZ, GLORIA Multipurpose arthritis center Effect of glucocorticoids on bone organ culture
P60AR-20621-13 0027 (AMS) PADULA, STEVEN Multipurpose arthritis center Regulation of collagen production by scleroderma fibroblasts
P60AR-20621-13 0029 (AMS) TANZER, JASON Multipurpose arthritis center Sjogren's syndrome--Oral flora and disease
P60AR-20621-13 0030 (AMS) ZERNIK, JOSEPH Multipurpose arthritis center Molecular studies of rat bone alkaline phosphatase
P60AR-20621-13 9001 (AMS) SHEEHAN, JOSEPH Multipurpose arthritis center Core--Statistics and evaluation
P60AR-20684-14 (AMS) GOLDSTEIN, IRA M UNIV OF CAL, SAN FRANCISCO P.O. BOX 0868 SAN FRANCISCO, CA 94143-0868 U C S F Multipurpose arthritis center
P60AR-20684-14 0022 (AMS) CURTIS, JEFFREY U C S F Multipurpose arthritis center Lymphocyte homing in autoimmune lung diseases
P60AR-20684-14 0023 (AMS) ERNST, JOEL D. U C S F Multipurpose arthritis center CDNA cloning of Ca2+ dependent phospholipid binding protein
P60AR-20684-14 0024 (AMS) CLARKSON, SARAH B. U C S F Multipurpose arthritis center Structure-function relationships of human Fc receptor
P60AR-20684-14 0025 (AMS) BRODSKY, FRAN U C S F Multipurpose arthritis center Cell biology of antigen presentation
P60AR-20684-14 0028 (AMS) NEVIT, MICHAEL U C S F Multipurpose arthritis center Falls and injury among persons with rheumatoid arthritis
P60AR-20684-14 0029 (AMS) DAVIS, MARADEE U C S F Multipurpose arthritis center Outcomes associate with knee osteoarthritis
P60AR-20684-14 0030 (AMS) HENKE, CURTIS U C S F Multipurpose arthritis center Utilization and cost of rheumatoid arthritis patients
P60AR-20684-14 0031 (AMS) YELIN, E. U C S F Multipurpose arthritis center Musculoskeletal disability and the elderly
P60AR-20684-14 0032 (AMS) HENKE, CURTIS U C S F Multipurpose arthritis center Arthritis treatment in changing Medicaid system
P60AR-20684-14 9002 (AMS) YELIN, EDWARD U C S F Multipurpose arthritis center Core-rheumatoid arthritis
P60AR-20684-14 0020 (AMS) ROSEN, STEVEN U C S F Multipurpose arthritis center Lymphocyte migration into arthritic joints
R01AR-20702-13 (ORTH) ANDRIACCHI, THOMAS P RUSH-PRES-ST LUKE'S MED CTR 1653 WEST CONGRESS PARKWAY CHICAGO, IL 60612 Biomechanical study of total knee replacement
R01AR-20793-11 (PBC) MINOR, RONALD R CORNELL U./DEPT. OF PATHOL. 323 VETERINARY RSRCH. TOWER ITHACA, NY 14853 Heritable diseases of connective tissue
R01AR-21172-13 (ORTH) GROOD, EDWARD S UNIVERSITY OF CINCINNATI ML 627 CINCINNATI, OH 45221-0627 A/p translation in the knee--changes after acl surgery
R01AR-21175-15 (GMA) VAUGHAN, JOHN H UNIVERSITY OF CALIFORNIA LA JOLLA, CA 92093 Epstein-Barr virus and autoimmune disease
R18AR-21393-17 (AMS) FRIES, JAMES F 701 WELCH RD PALO ALTO, CA 94304 A national arthritis data resource
R18AR-21393-17 0019 (AMS) STEEN, VIRGINIA A national arthritis data resource Outcome studies in systemic sclerosis
R18AR-21393-17 0020 (AMS) ODDIS, CHESTER A national arthritis data resource Natural history of polymyositis-dermatomyositis
R18AR-21393-17 0021 (AMS) HUNDER, GENE A national arthritis data resource Outcome of vasculitis
R18AR-21393-17 0022 (AMS) FRIES, JAMES A national arthritis data resource Applications of a toxicity index
R18AR-21393-17 0023 (AMS) LUGGEN, MICHAEL A national arthritis data resource Nonsteroidal anti-inflammatory drugs in rheumatoid and osteoarthritis
R18AR-21393-17 0024 (AMS) LUGGEN, MICHAEL A national arthritis data resource Development of optimal monitoring strategies for anti-rheumatic therapy
R18AR-21393-17 0025 (AMS) ESDAILE, JOHN A national arthritis data resource Evaluation of diffuse idiopathic skeletal hyperostosis
R18AR-21393-17 0026 (AMS) WOLFE, FREDERICK A national arthritis data resource Outcome of fibromyalgia
R18AR-21393-17 0027 (AMS) ALTMAN, ROY A national arthritis data resource Paget's disease of bone
R18AR-21393-17 0028 (AMS) MEDSGER, THOMAS A national arthritis data resource Rheumatic disease registry and outcome assessment
R18AR-21393-17 0001 (AMS) HUBERT, HELEN A national arthritis data resource Risk factors for osteoarthritis and musculoskeletal aging
R18AR-21393-17 0002 (AMS) HUBERT, HELEN A national arthritis data resource Precursors of arthritis and musculoskeletal aging
R18AR-21393-17 0003 (AMS) LEIGH, J A national arthritis data resource Occupational hazards and arthritis
R18AR-21393-17 0004 (AMS) FRIES, JAMES A national arthritis data resource Schooling, gender gap, selection bias, and arthritis
R18AR-21393-17 0005 (AMS) ALTMAN, ROY A national arthritis data resource Progression in osteoarthritis on the knee
R18AR-21393-17 0006 (AMS) FRIES, JAMES A national arthritis data resource Is rheumatoid arthritis changing
R18AR-21393-17 0008 (AMS) SCHURMAN, DAVID A national arthritis data resource Joint replacement
R18AR-21393-17 0009 (AMS) CALLAHAN, LEIGH A national arthritis data resource Socioeconomic and comorbidity effects in rheumatoid arthritis
R18AR-21393-17 0010 (AMS) PINCUS, THEODORE A national arthritis data resource Monitoring of rheumatoid arthritis in private practice
R18AR-21393-17 0011 (AMS) PINCUS, THEODORE A national arthritis data resource Staging of rheumatoid arthritis
R18AR-21393-17 0012 (AMS) WOLFE, FREDERICK A national arthritis data resource The course of rheumatoid arthritis in the elderly
R18AR-21393-17 0013 (AMS) LOVELL, DANIEL A national arthritis data resource Predictors of outcome in juvenile rheumatoid arthritis
R18AR-21393-17 0014 (AMS) RUSSELL, I A national arthritis data resource Rheumatoid arthritis in Hispanics
R18AR-21393-17 0015 (AMS) EDWORTHY, STEVEN A national arthritis data resource Multi-center for systemic lupus erythematosus (SLE)
R18AR-21393-17 0016 (AMS) HOCHBERG, MARC A national arthritis data resource Longitudinal studies in systemic lupus erythematosus
R18AR-21393-17 0017 (AMS) SIBLEY, JOHN A national arthritis data resource Clinical predictors of outcome in SLE
R18AR-21393-17 0018 (AMS) EDWORTHY, STEVEN A national arthritis data resource Lupus state model
R37AR-21496-14 (NSS) ROSENBERG, LAWRENCE C MONTEFIORE MEDICAL CENTER 111 EAST 210TH STREET BRONX, N Y 10467 Structure of epiphyseal and growth plate cartilage
P01AR-21557-13 (ADDK) HALBROOK, KAREN A UNIVERSITY OF WASHINGTON 1959 PACIFIC NORTHEAST SEATTLE, WA 98195 Interdisciplinary basic research in dermatology
P01AR-21557-13 0001 (ADDK) DALE, BEVERLY A Interdisciplinary basic research in dermatology structural proteins in disorders of keratinization
P01AR-21557-13 0002 (ADDK) BYERS, PETER H Interdisciplinary basic research in dermatology EM and biochemistry on inherited collagen disorders
P01AR-21557-13 0003 (ADDK) OLERUD, JOHN E Interdisciplinary basic research in dermatology Ultrasonic characterization of wounds by acoustic microscopy
P01AR-21557-13 0004 (ADDK) FLECKMAN, PHILIP Interdisciplinary basic research in dermatology In vitro epidermal differentiation
P01AR-21557-13 0005 (ADDK) WIGHT, THOMAS N Interdisciplinary basic research in dermatology a
P01AR-21557-13 9001 (ADDK) HOLBROOK, KAREN Interdisciplinary basic research in dermatology Core laboratory
R37AR-21617-14 (RAP) TERJUNG, RONALD L S U N Y HEALTH SCIENCE CTR DEPARTMENT OF PHYSIOLOGY SYRACUSE, NY 13210 Adenine nucleotide metabolism in skeletal muscle
R37AR-21673-14 (BBCB) TAO, TERENCE C BOSTON BIOMEDICAL RESEARCH 20 STANIFORD STREET BOSTON, MA 02114 Proximity relationships among muscle proteins
R01AR-21707-11 (GMB) CANALIS, ERNESTO M ST FRANCIS HOSPITAL & MED CTR 114 WOODLAND STREET HARTFORD, CT 06105 Effect of growth factors on aspects of bone formation
R01AR-21896-13 (ORTH) TOMFORD, WILLIAM W MASSACHUSETTS GENERAL HOSPITAL FRUIT STREET BOSTON, MA 02114 Bone and cartilage allografts in bone tumor treatment
R01AR-22031-14 (BBCB) REISLER, EMIL UNIVERSITY OF CALIFORNIA 405 HILGARD AVENUE LOS ANGELES, CA 90024-1569 Dynamic events in myosin during contraction of muscle
R01AR-22083-12S1 (GMA) DOWNING, DONALD UNIV. OF IOWA COLLEGE OF MED. 270 MEDICAL LABORATORIES IOWA CITY, IA 52242 Evaluation of pathogenic factors in acne vulgaris
R01AR-24015-14 (IMS) EMLEN, JAMES W UNIVERSITY OF COLORADO H.S.C. RHEUMATOLOGY/BOX B-115 DENVER, CO 80262 Studies on the role of DNA in systemic lupus
R01AR-25193-13 (BBCB) CHEUNG, HERBERT C UNIVERSITY OF ALABAMA UAB STATION / 520 CH19 BIRMINGHAM, AL 35294 Studies on muscle regulatory proteins
R01AR-25201-12 (PHY) VERGARA, JULIO L U.C.L.A. SCHOOL OF MEDICINE 405 HILGARD AVENUE LOS ANGELES, CA 90024 Excitation-contraction coupling in skeletal muscle
R01AR-25271-13 (GMB) DZIAK, ROSEMARY S U N Y- AT BUFFALO 3435 MAIN ST/320 FOSTER HALL BUFFALO, NY 14214 Bone cell calcium regulation
R01AR-25339-14 (GMA) SATO, KENZO UNIVERSITY OF IOWA 270 MED LABS IOWA CITY, IOWA 52242 Mechanism of eccrine sweat gland function
R01AR-25395-11 (GMA) PARRISH, JOHN A MASSACHUSETTS GENERAL

PROJECT NO., ORGANIZATIONAL UNIT., INVESTIGATOR, ADDRESS, TITLE

HOSPITAL 32 FRUIT ST BOSTON, MA 02114 Optics and phototoxicity in human skin

R37AR-25443-13 (IMS) CARSON, DENNIS A UNIV. OF CALIFORNIA, SAN DIEGO 9500 GILMAN DRIVE Rheumatoid factor--Genetics, pathogenesis, and modulation

R01AR-25527-10 (PBC) ORKIN, ROSLYN W MASSACHUSETTS GENERAL HOSPITAL 32 FRUIT STREET BOSTON, MA 02114 Hyaluronidase in morphogenesis and tissue remodeling

R01AR-25871-13 (GMA) O'KEEFE, EDWARD J UNIVERSITY OF NORTH CAROLINA 137 NC MEMORIAL HOSPITAL CHAPEL HILL, NC 27514 Desmosome--Structure and function

R01AR-25921-12A1 (GMB) PRICE, PAUL A UNIVERSITY OF CALIFORNIA 9500 GILMAN DRIVE LA JOLLA, CA 92093-0322 Regulation of vitamin K-dependent bone proteins

R01AR-26009-11 (GMA) MARCELO, CYNTHIA L UNIVERSITY OF MICHIGAN KRESGE I, R6558, BOX 0528 ANN ARBOR, MI 48109-0528 Modulation of keratinocyte growth and specialization

R01AR-26034-11 (PBC) POSTLETHWAITE, ARNOLD E UNIVERSITY OF TENNESSEE 956 COURT AVENUE, G326 MEMPHIS, TENN 38163 Fibroblast activation

R01AR-26287-12 (ORTH) AN, KAI-NAN MAYO FOUNDATION 200 FIRST STREET SOUTHWEST ROCHESTER, MN 55905 Force and stability analysis of human elbow

R01AR-26446-09 (ORTH) MOTE, CLAYTON D, JR UNIVERSITY OF CALIFORNIA BERKELEY, CA 94720 Human response and lower extremity injury

R01AR-26574-11 (GMA) EISENBERG, ROBERT A UNIV OF N C AT CHAPEL HILL 932 FLOB CB# 7280 CHAPEL HILL, N C 27599-7280 Mechanisms of autoreactivity in SLE

R01AR-26599-12 (GMA) BRINCKERHOFF, CONSTANCE E DARTMOUTH MEDICAL SCHOOL DEPT OF MEDICINE HANOVER, NH 03756 Regulation of metalloproteinase gene expression

R37AR-26710-11 (ORTH) BIZZI, EMILIO MASSACHUSETTS INST. OF TECH. 77 MASSACHUSETTS AVENUE CAMBRIDGE, MA 02139 Processes underlying arm trajectory formation

R01AR-26833-10 (ORTH) SCHURMAN, DAVID J STANFORD UNIVERSITY SCHOOL OF MEDICINE STANFORD, CA 94305-5326 Infectious arthritis and cartilage destruction

R01AR-26846-12 (PHY) GOLDMAN, YALE E UNIVERSITY OF PENNSYLVANIA 37TH & HAMILTON WALK PHILADELPHIA, PA 19104-6085 Kinetics of the muscle contractile apparatus

R01AR-26928-11 (GMB) FITZGERALD, ROBERT H, JR DEPT. OF ORTHO SURGERY 4707 ST. ANTOINE 1 SOUTH DETROIT, MI 48201 Orthopedic sepsis--pathogenesis, diagnosis and treatment

R01AR-26957-06 (SB) GRISTINA, ANTHONY G 2190 FOX MILL ROAD HERNDON, VA 22071 Bacterial colonization of surgical biomaterials

Z01AR-27000-29 (LPB) PODOLSKY, R J NIAMS, NIH The mechanism of muscular contraction

Z01AR-27001-17 (LPB) SCHOENBERG, M NIAMS, NIH Contractility of skeletal and smooth muscle

Z01AR-27002-13 (LSBR) STEVEN, A C NIAMS, NIH Structural biology of macromolecular structure

Z01AR-27003-32 (LPB) KEMPNER, E S NIAMS, NIH Biophysical studies of metabolic activity and control

Z01AR-27004-22 (LPB) GERSHFELD, N L NIAMS, NIH The dynamic properties of cell membranes and related systems

Z01AR-27006-09 (LPB) MURAYAMA, M NIAMS, NIH Aggregation of human platelets induced by decommpression

Z01AR-27012-07 (LPB) YU, L C NIAMS, NIH Structural and mechanical properties of muscle fibers

R37AR-27029-12 (NSS) PRICE, PAUL A UNIVERSITY OF CALIFORNIA LA JOLLA, CA 92093 Function of the vitamin K-dependent bone protein

R01AR-27032-12 (PHY) DREZNER, MARC K DUKE UNIVERSITY MEDICAL CENTER BOX 3285 DURHAM, NC 27710 Pathogenesis of vitamin D refractory diseases

R01AR-27065-12 (EDC) MELTON, LEE JOSEPH MAYO FOUNDATION 200 FIRST STREET SOUTHWEST ROCHESTER, MN 55905 Epidemiology of age related bone loss & fracture

R01AR-27110-11 (GMA) WEINSTEIN, GERALD D UNIVERSITY OF CALIFORNIA IRVINE, CA 92717 Pathophysiology & chemotherapy in psoriasis and cancer

R01AR-27130-11 (CBY) RICE, ROBERT H UNIVERSITY OF CALIFORNIA DAVIS, CA 95616-8588 Keratinocyte transglutaminase--Anchorage and cloning

R37AR-27214-11 (GMA) GINSBERG, MARK H SCRIPPS CLINIC & RES FDN 10666 N TORREY PINES ROAD LA JOLLA, CA 92037 Platelets in rheumatic disease

R01AR-27663-11 (GMA) BYSTRYN, JEAN-CLAUDE NEW YORK UNIV MED CTR 560 FIRST AVENUE NEW YORK, NY 10016 Humoral immunity to pigmented cells in vitiligo

R01AR-27680-11 (VR) CHEEVERS, WILLIAM P WASHINGTON STATE UNIVERSITY PULLMAN, WA 99164-7040 Pathogenesis of lentivirus-induced arthritis of goats

R01AR-27807-12 (CBY) HOOK, MAGNUS UAB UNIVERSITY STATION BIRMINGHAM, ALABAMA 35294 Structure and function of the extracellular matrix

R01AR-27883-11 (PC) FUCHS, ELAINE V UNIVERSITY OF CHICAGO 920 E 58TH ST, BIOCHEM DEPT CHICAGO, ILL 60637 Gene expression & differentiation in human epidermis

R01AR-27926-10 (ORTH) GENANT, HARRY K UNIV OF CALIFORNIA DEPT OF RADIOLOGY, BOX 0628 SAN FRANCISCO, CA 94143-0628 Quantitative tomography for bone mineral assessment

R01AR-27940-09A1 (GMA) DONALDSON, DONALD J UNIVERSITY OF TENNESSEE 875 MONROE AVENUE MEMPHIS, TN 38163 Cell-substrate interactions in epidermal cell migration

R01AR-28069-11 (GMA) EPSTEIN, ERVIN H, JR SAN FRANCISCO GENERAL HOSPITAL 1001 POTRERO STREET SAN FRANCISCO, CA 94110 Steroid sulfatase and stratum corneum cell cohesion

R37AR-28149-12 (NSS) MUNDY, GREGORY R UNIV OF TEXAS HEALTH SCI CTR 7703 FLOYD CURL DRIVE SAN ANTONIO, TX 78284-7877 Monocyte-macrophage system and bone resorption

R01AR-28292-11 (GMB) HADDAD, JOHN G, JR UNIVERSITY OF PENNSYLVANIA 531 JOHNSON PAVILION PHILADELPHIA, PA 19104-6067 Functions of the plasma vitamin D binding protein

PROJECT NO., ORGANIZATIONAL UNIT., INVESTIGATOR, ADDRESS, TITLE

R01AR-28304-09 (GMA) PINNELL, SHELDON R DUKE UNIV MEDICAL CENTER BOX 3135 DURHAM, NC 27710 Collagen biosynthesis in human skin fibroblasts

R01AR-28401-09A1 (BBCB) LU, RENNE C BOSTON BIOMEDICAL RESEARCH INS 20 STANIFORD STREET BOSTON, MA 02114 Structure function relations in myosin

R01AR-28450-09 (GMA) UITTO, JOUNI J THOMAS JEFFERSON UNIVERSITY 1020 LOCUST STREET PHILADELPHIA, PA 19107 Biochemistry and morphology of connective tissue

R01AR-28467-10 (ORTH) COUTTS, RICHARD D UNIV. OF CALIFORNIA, SAN DIEGO 3032 & 3028 BASIC SCIENCES BLV LA JOLLA, CA 92093 Evaluation of cartilage grown from rib perichondrium

R01AR-28566-12 (GMA) PEREZ, HECTOR D UNIVERSITY OF CALIFORNIA THIRD & PARNASSUS AVENUES SAN FRANCISCO, CA 94143-0868 Host defenses in systemic lupus erythematosus

R01AR-29846-10 (IMS) HORWITZ, DAVID A USC SCHOOL OF MEDICINE 2011 ZONAL AVENUE LOS ANGELES, CA 90033 Immunoregulatory mechanisms in the rheumatic diseases

R01AR-29850-11 (ORTH) KREAM, BARBARA E UNIV. OF CT HLTH. CNTR. FARMINGTON, CT 06030-1850 Hormonal regulation of bone collagen metabolism

R01AR-29908-09 (GMA) WILLIAMS, MARY L VETERANS ADMIN MED CTR 4150 CLEMENT STREET SAN FRANCISCO, CA 94121 Normal skin lipid metabolism and cornification disorders

R01AR-29983-08A3 (GMB) LICHTLER, ALEXANDER UNIV OF CONNECTICUT HLTH CTR 263 FARMINGTON AVENUE FARMINGTON, CT 06030 Hormone regulation of bone collagen synthesis

R01AR-30036-10 (IMS) BLUESTEIN, HARRY G UCSD MEDICAL CENTER 225 W DICKINSON ST/H-811-G SAN DIEGO, CA 92103 SLE antibodies to neurons and lymphocytes--Pathobiology

R01AR-30102-11 (GMB) BROADUS, ARTHUR E YALE UNIVERSITY 333 CEDAR ST BOX 3333 NEW HAVEN, CT 06510 Malignancy-associated hypercalcemia

R01AR-30134-13 (GMA) MOSKOWITZ, ROLAND W UNIVERSITY HOSPITALS 2074 ABINGTON RD CLEVELAND, OH 44106 Pathogneis and therapy of experimental osteoarthritis

R01AR-30346-10 (CVA) BALDWIN, KENNETH M UNIVERSITY OF CALIFORNIA, IRVN MED SCI I D340 IRVINE, CA 92717 Activity regulation of skeletal isomyosin expression

R01AR-30426-10 (GMB) ROWE, DAVID W UNIVERSITY OF CONNECTICUT 263 FARMINGTON AVE FARMINGTON, CT 06032 Type I collagen biosynthesis in osteogenesis imperfecta

R01AR-30431-10 (GMA) LEROY, E CARWILE MEDICAL UNIV OF SOUTH CAROLINA 171 ASHLEY AVENUE CHARLESTON, S C 29425 Scleroderma

R01AR-30442-11 (BBCB) KENSLER, ROBERT W UNIVERSITY OF MISSOURI 5100 ROCKHILL ROAD KANSAS CITY, MO 64110-2499 Thick filament myosin and C-protein arrangement

R01AR-30475-09 (GMA) GAMMON, WALTER R UNIVERSITY OF NORTH CAROLINA CB# 700, 137 NCMH/DEP OF DERM CHAPEL HILL, N C 27514 An in vitro model of bullous pemphigoid

R01AR-30481-10 (PBC) MAYNE, RICHARD UNIV OF ALABAMA AT BIRMINGHAM UNIVERSITY STATION BIRMINGHAM, AL 35294 Collagens of hyaline cartilage

R01AR-30556-10 (PBC) FURTHMAYR, HEINZ STANFORD UNIVERSITY STANFORD, CA 94305-5324 Structural composition-organization of basement membrane

R01AR-30582-26 (EDC) MELTON, L JOSEPH MAYO FOUNDATION 200 FIRST STREET, SW ROCHESTER, MN 55905 Rochester epidemiology project

R01AR-30587-08 (PBC) YAMAUCHI, MITSO UNIVERSITY OF NORTH CAROLINA DENTAL RESEARCH CENTER CHAPEL HILL, N C 27514 Biochemistry and structure of collagen tissue matrices

R01AR-30682-10 (GMA) FREEDBERG, IRWIN M NEW YORK UNIV MEDICAL CENTER 550 FIRST AVENUE NEW YORK, NY 10016 Epidermal macromolecular metabolism

P60AR-30692-08 (ADDK) POPE, RICHARD M NORTHWESTERN UNIVERSITY 303 E CHICAGO AVE CHICAGO, IL 60611 Multipurpose arthritis center

P60AR-30692-08 0018 (ADDK) MANHEIM, LARRY Multipurpose arthritis center National survey of rheumatologists and their practices

P60AR-30692-08 9001 (ADDK) DYER, ALAN R Multipurpose arthritis center Core--Biostatistics and data management

P60AR-30692-08 0003 (ADDK) CONNELL, KAREN Multipurpose arthritis center Education--Enhancing educational status arthritis patients

P60AR-30692-08 0006 (ADDK) HUGHES, SUSAN L Multipurpose arthritis center Community component--musculoskeletal disease in the elderly

P60AR-30692-08 0011 (ADDK) KOCH, ALISA E. Multipurpose arthritis center Feasibility study--Monocyte/macrophage heterogeneity in rheumatoid arthris

P60AR-30692-08 0015 (ADDK) CONNELL, KAREN Multipurpose arthritis center Education--Ambulatory arthritis elective for medical students

P60AR-30692-08 0016 (ADDK) MYONES, BARRY L Multipurpose arthritis center Characterization of binding sites on the EBV/C3dg receptor

P60AR-30692-08 0017 (ADDK) KIM, BYUNG S Multipurpose arthritis center Analysis of pathogenic epitopes in rheumatoid arthritis

P60AR-30701-10 (AMS) WINFIELD, JOHN B DIVISION OF RHEUMATOLOGY 932 FLOB, UNC-CH SCHOOL OF MED CHAPEL HILL, NC 27514 Multipurpose arthritis center

P60AR-30701-10 0010 (AMS) HUNT, STEPHEN Multipurpose arthritis center Anti-lymphocyte antibody target antigen genes in SLE

P60AR-30701-10 0011 (AMS) COHEN, PHILIP Multipurpose arthritis center Characterization of B-cell specific gene

P60AR-30701-10 0014 (AMS) EISENBERG, ROBERT A Multipurpose arthritis center Genetic control of the anti-chromatin response in autoimmune mice

P60AR-30701-10 0015 (AMS) REED, WILLIAM Multipurpose arthritis center Construction of expression vectors encoding complement receptor

P60AR-30701-10 0016 (AMS) MCGAGHIE, WILLIAM C Multipurpose arthritis center Education and evaluating medical students

P60AR-30701-10 0017 (AMS) BLALOCK, SUSAN J Multipurpose arthritis center Adjustment to rheumatoid arthritis

P60AR-30701-10 0018 (AMS) DEVELLIS, ROBERT Multipurpose arthritis center Selective remembering of information by arthritis patients

P60AR-30701-10 0021 (AMS) BLALOCK, SUSAN J Multipurpose arthritis

center
P60AR-30701-10 9003 (AMS) ROSS, GORDON Multipurpose arthritis center Immunology core
P60AR-30701-10 9004 (AMS) FRYER, JOHN Multipurpose arthritis center Numerical sciences core
R01AR-30752-06 (IMB) DAVID, CHELLA S MAYO FOUNDATION 200 FIRST STREET SOUTHWEST ROCHESTER, MN 55905 Immunogenetics of collagen induced arthritis in mice
R01AR-30833-10 (ORTH) GOLDBERG, VICTOR M CASE WESTERN RESERVE UNIV. 2074 ABINGTON ROAD CLEVELAND, OH 44106 Structure and metabolism of vascularized allografts
R01AR-30863-10 (IMS) WINFIELD, JOHN B UNIVERSITY OF NORTH CAROLINA 932 FLOB; CB# 7280 CHAPEL HILL, NC 27599-7280 Autoantibodies to activated lymphocytes in SLE
R01AR-30868-10 (BBCB) COOKE, ROGER A UNIVERSITY OF CALIFORNIA 841 HEALTH SCIENCES WEST SAN FRANCISCO, CA 94143-0524 Studies of muscle proteins using paramagnetic probes
R01AR-30917-08 (BBCB) GRACEFFA, PHILIP J BOSTON BIOMED RES INST 20 STANIFORD STREET BOSTON, MA 02114 Tropomyosin in muscle regulation
R01AR-30965-11 (GMA) GOLDSMITH, LOWELL A UNIVERSITY OF ROCHESTER 601 ELMWOOD AVE PO BOX 697 ROCHESTER, NY 14642 Monoclonal antibodies to human epidermis
R01AR-30988-10 (GMB) HOMSHER, EARL E UNIVERSITY OF CALIFORNIA 10833 LE CONTE AVE LOS ANGELES, CA 90024-1751 Muscle energetics and chemomechanical transduction
R01AR-31017-08 (ORTH) CORDO, PAUL J 1120 NW 20TH AVE PORTLAND, OR 97209 Spatial and temporal control of targeted limb movement
R01AR-31062-09 (GMB) BAYLINK, DAVID J PETTIS V. A. HOSPITAL 11201 BENTON STREET LOMA LINDA, CA 92357 Endosteal bone volume regulation and osteoporosis
R01AR-31068-09 (ORTH) TRIPPEL, STEPHEN B MASSACHUSETTS GENERAL HOSPITAL ORTHOPAEDIC RESEARCH LAB BOSTON, MASSACHUSETTS 02114 Role of peptide growth factors in skeletal development
R01AR-31133-09A1 (GMA) REICHLIN, MORRIS OKLAHOMA MEDICAL RESEARCH FDN 825 N E 13TH STREET OKLAHOMA CITY, OK 73104 Immune response to non-DNA containing antigens in SLE
R01AR-31203-09 (GMA) THEOFILOPOULOS, ARGYRIOS N SCRIPPS CLINIC & RES FOUND. 10666 NORTH TORREY PINES RD LA JOLLA, CA 92037 Murine models of generalized autoimmunity
R01AR-31239-06A2 (BBCB) CHEUNG, HERBERT C UNIVERSITY OF ALABAMA UAB STATION BIRMINGHAM, AL 35294 Interaction of myosin with actin
R01AR-31263-10 (ORTH) LORENZO, JOSEPH A UNIVERSITY OF CT HEALTH CENTER DEPARTMENT OF MEDICINE AM047 FARMINGTON, CT 06032 Cytokines in bone
R01AR-31283-09 (EDC) MARICQ, HILDEGARD R MED. UNIV. OF SOUTH CAROLINA 171 ASHLEY AVENUE CHARLESTON, SC 29425 Epidemiology of Raynaud phenomenon
R01AR-31330-08 (ORTH) GLOWACKI, JULIEANNE BRIGHAM AND WOMEN'S HOSP, INC 75 FRANCIS STREET BOSTON, MASS 02115 A model for studying regulation of bone resorption
R01AR-31636-09 (GMB) GODT, ROBERT E MEDICAL COLLEGE OF GEORGIA DEPT OF PHYSIO & ENDOCRINOLOGY AUGUSTA, GA 30912-3000 Calcium and contractile activation in striated muscle
R01AR-31737-09 (CTY) FUCHS, ELAINE V UNIVERSITY OF CHICAGO 5841 SOUTH MARYLAND CHICAGO, IL 60637 Vitamin a and keratinization in human epithelial cells
R01AR-31793-06A3 (ORTH) GOLDSTEIN, STEVEN A UNIVERSITY OF MICHIGAN G-0161 400 N INGALLS/0486 ANN ARBOR, MI 48109-0486 Trabecular bone remodeling--Response to applied stress
R01AR-31806-09A1 (PHY) MOSS, RICHARD L UNIVERSITY OF WISCONSIN 1300 UNIVERSITY AVE MADISON, WI 53706 Myosin isozymes and contraction in developing muscles
R01AR-31814-09 (PHY) HOROWICZ, PAUL UNIVERSITY OF ROCHESTER 601 ELMWOOD AVENUE ROCHESTER, NY 14642 Ionic properties of skeletal muscle membranes
R01AR-31839-06A1 (PBC) BERG, RICHARD A UMDNJ-R W JOHNSON MEDICAL SCHO 675 HOES LANE PISCATAWAY, NJ 08854-5635 Regulation of prolyl hydroxylase
R01AR-31891-09 (IMS) SCHLEIMER, ROBERT P JOHNS HOPKINS UNIVERSITY 301 BAYVIEW BLVD BALTIMORE, MD 21224 Glucocorticosteroid action in inflammatory disease
R01AR-31901-09 (GMA) WINTROUB, BRUCE U UCSF, DEPT OF DERMATOLOGY 5333 PARNASSUS AVE, RM U126 SAN FRANCISCO, CA 94143-0318 Human skin mast cell granule enzymes: skin diseases
R01AR-32007-09 (BNP) RICH, DANIEL H UNIVERSITY OF WISCONSIN 425 N CHARTER STREET MADISON, WI 53706 Synthesis and activity of cyclosporin analogues
R37AR-32063-10 (IMS) TAN, ENG M RESEARCH INST OF SCRIPPS CLINI 10666 NORTH TORREY PINES ROAD LA JOLLA, CA 92037 Autoimmunity to nuclear antigens
R37AR-32081-10 (GMA) DIAZ, LUIS A MEDICAL COLLEGE OF WISCONSIN 8701 WATERTOWN PLANK ROAD MILWAUKEE, WISCONSIN 53226 Pemphigus and pemphigoid
P01AR-32087-09 (AMS) AVIOLI, LOUIS V JEWISH HOSPITAL OF ST LOUIS 216 SOUTH KINGSHIGHWAY BLVD ST LOUIS, MO 63110 Calcium transport, bone cell function, aging
P01AR-32087-09 0010 (AMS) FEDDE, KENTON N. Calcium transport, bone cell function, aging Biogenesis of physiologic function & alkaline phosphatase in osteoblasts
P01AR-32087-09 0011 (AMS) AVIOLI, LOUIS V Calcium transport, bone cell function, aging Hormonal control of osteoblastic growth, differentiation, function
P01AR-32087-09 0012 (AMS) HRUSKA, KEITH A Calcium transport, bone cell function, aging Regulation of cell calcium and differentiation
P01AR-32087-09 0013 (AMS) GLUCK, STEPHEN Calcium transport, bone cell function, aging Expression and targeting of proton pumps during osteoclast differentiation
P01AR-32087-09 0014 (AMS) Y Calcium transport, bone cell function, aging Osteoclast mediated bone remodeling
P01AR-32087-09 9001 (AMS) PECK, WILLIAM A Calcium transport, bone cell function, aging Core--Tissue and cell culture laboratory
R01AR-32145-08A2 (ORTH) OEGEMA, THEODORE R, JR UNIVERSITY OF MINNESOTA 420 DELAWARE ST SE BOX 310 MINNEAPOLIS, MI 55455 Recovery of intervertebral disc after enzyme treatment
R01AR-32147-10 (CTY) FISCHMAN, DONALD A CORNELL UNIV MEDICAL COLLEGE DEPT OF CELL BIOLOGY & ANATOMY NEW YORK, NY 10021 Myofibril assembly in striated muscle
R01AR-32192-09 (GMA) COHEN, IRUN R WEIZMANN INSTITUTE OF SCIENCE PO BOX 26 REHOVOT, ISRAEL 76100 Autoimmune arthritis--Disease/protection by T cell lines
R01AR-32196-07A1 (GMB) CATHERWOOD, BAYARD D V A MEDICAL CENTER 1670 CLAIRMONT RD, NE DECATUR, GA 30033 1,25-Dihydroxyvitamin D regulation of parathyroid hormone action
R01AR-32214-07 (IMS) REICHLIN, MORRIS OKLAHOMA MEDICAL RESEARCH FDN 825 NORTHEAST 13TH STREET OKLAHOMA CITY, OKLA 73104 Definition of autoimmune responses in polymyositis
R01AR-32343-08 (GMA) KORN, JOSEPH H UNIVERSITY OF CONNECTIUT 263 FARMINGTON AVENUE FARMINGTON, CT 06032 Immune mediated alterations in connective tissue
R01AR-32371-09 (IMS) DIAMOND, BETTY A ALBERT EINSTEIN COLL OF MEDICI 1300 MORRIS PARK AVENUE BRONX, NY 10461 Anti-DNA antibodies in systemic lupus erythematosus
R01AR-32374-08 (GMA) DOWNING, DONALD T UNIVERSITY OF IOWA 270 MEDICAL LABORATORIES IOWA CITY, IA 52242 Structure and function of polar lipids in human skin
R37AR-32461-10 (CTY) TAYLOR, D LANSING CARNEGIE-MELLON UNIVERSITY 4400 FIFTH AVENUE PITTSBURGH, PA 15213 Structural and chemical dynamics of cell movement
R01AR-32490-09 (GMA) ANHALT, GRANT J THE JOHNS HOPKINS UNIVERSITY 600 NORTH WOLFE ST, BLALOCK 90 BALTIMORE, MD 21205 Pathophysiology of experimentally induced pemphigus
R01AR-32549-08 (GMA) HARDIN, JOHN A YALE UNIVERSITY 333 CEDAR STREET NEW HAVEN, CONN 06510 Immune response to nuclear constituents in SLE
R01AR-32564-07 (GMA) JIMENEZ, SERGIO A THOMAS JEFFERSON UNIVERSITY 1020 LOCUST STREET PHILADELPHIA, PA 19107 Collagen metabolism in a model for scleroderma
R01AR-32593-07A1 (GMA) ELMETS, CRAIG A UNIV. HOSPITALS OF CLEVELAND 2074 ADELBERT ROAD CLEVELAND, OH 44106 UVB radiation--Immunodermatologic effects in humans
R01AR-32599-09 (GMA) DIAZ, LUIS A MEDICAL COLLEGE OF WISCONSIN 8701 WATERTOWN PLANK ROAD MILWAUKEE, WISCONSIN 53226 Etiology and pathogenesis of pemphigus
R01AR-32634-09 (GMA) LEVINE, JON D UNIVERSITY OF CALIFORNIA 533 PARNASSUS AVE-BOX 0724 SAN FRANCISCO, CA 94143-0724 Synovial nociceptors in experimental arthritis
R01AR-32764-08 (BBCB) PHILLIPS, GEORGE N, JR RICE UNIV/DEPT OF BIOCHEM P O BOX 1892 HOUSTON, TX 77251 Crystallography of tropomyosin and troponin
R01AR-32788-08 (GMB) TEITELBAUM, STEVEN L JEWISH HOSP AT WASHINGTON UNIV 216 SOUTH KINGSHIGHWAY ST. LOUIS, MO 63110 Mechanisms of orthopedic implant loosening
R37AR-32805-09 (PHY) MAGLEBY, KARL L UNIVERSITY OF MIAMI POST OFFICE BOX 016430 MIAMI, FL 33101 Mechanisms of ionic channel activity
R01AR-32808-09 (GMB) RIOS, EDUARDO ST LUKE'S MEDICAL CENTER 1653 WEST CONGRESS PARKWAY CHICAGO, IL 60612 Calcium movements in excitation-contraction coupling
R01AR-32811-08S1 (GMA) SIMKIN, PETER A UNIVERSITY OF WASHINGTON SEATTLE, WA 98195 Patterns of pathophysiology in articular diseases
R01AR-32858-06 (BBCB) CHANTLER, PETER D MEDICAL COLLEGE OF PENN EPPI DIVISION, 3200 HENRY AVE PHILADELPHIA, PA 19129 Myosin linked regulation in muscle and non-muscle cells
R01AR-32927-08 (GMB) OSDOBY, PHILIP A WASHINGTON UNIV 660 S EUCLID AVE BOX 8100 ST LOUIS, MO 63110 The cell surface & osteoclast development
R01AR-32961-08 (BBCA) THOMAS, DAVID D UNIVERSITY OF MINNESOTA 435 DELAWARE STREET SE MINNEAPOLIS, MN 55455 Molecular dynamics of muscle contraction
R01AR-33062-08 (GMA) KIMBERLY, ROBERT P HOSPITAL FOR SPECIAL SURGERY 535 EAST 70TH STREET NEW YORK, NY 10021 Mononuclear phagocyte function in immunologic diseases
R01AR-33066-09 (ORTH) EDWARDS, W THOMAS S U N Y - HLTH SCI CENTER 750 EAST ADAMS STREET SYRACUSE, N Y 13210 Biomechanics of vertebral fracture in osteoporosis
R01AR-33097-13 (ORTH) GELBERMAN, RICHARD H MASS GENERAL HOSPITAL BOSTON, MA 02114 Flexor tendon--Restoration of the gliding surface
R01AR-33098-09 (ORTH) WONG, GLENDA L UNIVERSITY OF COLORADO AUSTIN BLUFFS PARKWAY COLORADO SPRINGS, CO 80933-71 Hormone responses in isolated bone cells
R01AR-33141-06 (BBCB) DEATHERAGE, JAMES F UNIV OF ARIZONA BIOSCIS W BLDG TUSCSON, AZ 85721 Structure of the Z disk of striated muscle
R01AR-33189-08 (ORTH) GOTTLIEB, GERALD L RUSH-PRESBYTERIAN-ST. LUKE'S M 1653 WEST CONGRESS PARKWAY CHICAGO, IL 60612 Elastic/plastic joint compliance
R01AR-33236-08 (ORTH) GRODZINSKY, ALAN J MASSACHUSETTS INST. OF TECH. 50 VASSAR STREET, ROOM 38-377 CAMBRIDGE, MA 02139 Electromechanics of cartilage--Synthesis and degradation
R01AR-33278-09 (GMA) STEINMAN, CHARLES R STONY BROOK, N Y 11794-8161 Etiology of rheumatoid arthritis and SLE
R01AR-33625-09 (GMA) WOODLEY, DAVID T STANFORD UNIV MEDICAL CTR 300 PASTEUR DRIVE STANFORD, CA 94305-5334 Purification of epidermolysis bullosa acquisita antigen
R01AR-33663-07A1 (GMA) DE LEO, VINCENT A COLUMBIA UNIVERSITY 630 WEST 168TH STREET NEW YORK, N Y 10032 UV radiation and epidermal membrane messenger systems
R01AR-33713-07 (IMS) MORIMOTO, CHIKAO DANA-FARBER CANCER INSTITUTE 44 BINNEY STREET BOSTON, MASS 02115 Immunoregulatory circuits in man
R01AR-33887-07 (GMA) COHEN, PHILIP L UNIVERSITY OF NORTH CAROLINA 932 F.L.O.B., 231H CHAPEL HILL, NC 27514 T cell control of autoreactivity in murine SLE
R01AR-33920-08 (ORTH) LIAN, JANE B UNIV OF MASSACHUSETTS MED SCH 55 LAKE AVENUE NORTH WORCESTER, MA 01655 Synthesis of osteocalcin in bone

PROJECT NO., ORGANIZATIONAL UNIT., INVESTIGATOR, ADDRESS, TITLE

R01AR-33948-09 (MEP) SCHULTZ, ALBERT B UNIVERSITY OF MICHIGAN DEPT. OF MECHANICAL ENGR. ANN ARBOR, MI 48109-2125 Biomechanical studies of idiopathic scoliosis

R01AR-33962-07 (IMS) HAHN, BEVRA H UNIVERSITY OF CALIFORNIA 10833 LE CONTE AVENUE LOS ANGELES, CA 90024-1736 Pathogenesis and therapy of systemic lupus erythematosus

R01AR-33983-11 (GMA) FOX, ROBERT I SCRIPPS CLINIC & RES FND 10666 NORTH TORREY PINES ROAD LA JOLLA, CALIF 92037 Immune response in human autoimmune diseases

R37AR-34081-07 (ORTH) GLIMCHER, MELVIN J CHILDREN'S HOSPITAL CORP 300 LONGWOOD AVENUE BOSTON, MA 02115 Nature of bone mineral--Inception, maturation and aging

R01AR-34156-07 (IMS) EISENBERG, ROBERT A UNIV OF N C AT CHAPEL HILL 932 FLOB CB# 7280 CHAPEL HILL, N C 27599-7280 Experimental induction of systemic lupus erythematosus by altered Ia

R37AR-34264-08 (ORTH) AKESON, WAYNE H UCSD MEDICAL CTR 225 DICKINSON ST SAN DIEGO, CA 92103 Anterior cruciate ligament healing

R01AR-34295-07 (GMA) BENNETT, ROBERT M OREGON HEALTH SCIENCES UNIV. 3181 S.W. SAM JACKSON PARK RD. PORTLAND, OR 97201 DNA receptor autoimmunity and idiotypic mimicry in SLE

R01AR-34313-07 (CBY) MACINTYRE, STEPHEN S CLEVELAND METRO GENERAL HOSP 3395 SCRANTON RD CLEVELAND, OH 44109 Regulation of C-reactive protein secretion

R01AR-34358-08 (IMS) RUBIN, ROBERT L SCRIPPS CLINIC & RSRCH. FNDTN. 10666 NORTH TORREY PINES ROAD LA JOLLA, CA 92037 Mechanisms underlying procainamide-induced autoimmunity

R01AR-34377-06 (PHY) PALADE, PHILIP T UNIV OF TEXAS MEDICAL BRANCH PHYSIOLOGY & BIOPHYSICS DEPT GALVESTON, TX 77550 Ca release from sarcoplasmic reticulum: The frog package

R01AR-34399-06 (ORTH) GOLDSTEIN, STEVEN A UNIVERSITY OF MICHIGAN G-0161 400 N INGALLS/0486 ANN ARBOR, MI 48109-0486 Trabecular architectural effects on material properties

R01AR-34411-07 (GMB) SHAPIRO, IRVING M UNIV OF PENN SCH OF DENTAL MED 4001 SPRUCE STREET PHILADELPHIA, PA 19104-6003 Role of metabolic factors in bone formation

R01AR-34511-08 (GMA) SUN, TUNG-TIEN NEW YORK UNIVERSITY MED SCHOOL 550 FIRST AVENUE NEW YORK, NY 10016 Markers of epidermal differention

R01AR-34602-17 (PHY) BARANY, MICHAEL UNIVERSITY ILLINOIS 1853 W POLK STREET CHICAGO, IL 60612 Protein phosphorylation in smooth muscle

R01AR-34614-07 (SB) ROSENBERG, LAWRENCE C MONTEFIORE MEDICAL CENTER 111 EAST 210TH STREET BRONX, N Y 10467 Pathobiology of articular cartilage degeneration

R01AR-34711-07 (CTY) CRAIG, ROGER W UNIVERSITY OF MASSACHUSETTS 55 LAKE AVENUE NORTH WORCESTER, MA 01605 Structure of contractile filaments of muscle

R01AR-34718-07 (GMA) HALL, RUSSELL P, III DUKE UNIVERSITY BOX 3135 DURHAM, NC 27710 Dermatitis herpetiformis & the mucosal immune response

R01AR-34744-07 (TMP) JOHNSON, RUSSELL C 1460 MAYO BLDG., BOX 196 420 DELAWARE STREET, S.E. MINNEAPOLIS, MN 55455 Lyme disease--Study of the etiological agent

R01AR-34808-07 (GMA) PHONG, LE T DUKE UNIVERSITY MEDICAL CENTER SCHOOL OF MEDICINE DURHAM, NC 27710 Epithelial differentiation--Comparison of skin and thymus

R01AR-34861-04A3 (GMA) FINE, JO-DAVID UNIV OF NC AT CHAPEL HILL 137 UNC HOSPITALS CHAPEL HILL, NC 27514 Skin basement membrane zone and epidermolysis bullosa

R01AR-34872-07 (PHY) WARSHAW, DAVID M UNIVERSITY OF VERMONT GIVEN MEDICAL BUILDING BURLINGTON, VT 05405 Crossbridge cycle kinetics in single smooth muscle cells

R01AR-35004-06 (OBM) VIGNERY, AGNES M YALE UNIV SCH OF MED 333 CEDAR ST PO BOX 3333 NEW HAVEN, CT 06510 Osteoclasts & giant cells-mechanisms & functional implications of cell fusion

R01AR-35056-07 (ORTH) NISHIMOTO, SATORU K UNIVERSITY OF TENNESSEE 800 MADISON AVENUE MEMPHIS, TN 38163 Metabolism of noncollagenous bone proteins

R01AR-35068-07 (GMA) BERGSTRESSER, PAUL R UNIV OF TEXAS MED SCH 5323 HARRY HINES BOULEVARD DALLAS, TX 75235 Biology of the thy-1 antigen-bearing epidermal cells

R01AR-35132-06 (GMB) DONALDSON, SUE K UNIVERSITY OF MINNESOTA 308 HARVARD ST SE MINNEAPOLIS, MN 55455 Skeletal muscle excitation-contraction coupling

R01AR-35155-07 (ORTH) WILSMAN, NORMAN J UNIVERSITY OF WISCONSIN 2015 LINDEN DRIVE WEST MADISON, WI 53706 The hypertrophic chondrocyte and its pericellular matrix

R01AR-35166-06 (ORTH) LIAN, JANE B UNIV OF MASSACHUSETTS MED SCH 55 LAKE AVENUE NORTH WORCESTER, MA 01655 Osteocalcin function in resorption

R01AR-35186-07 (BBCB) RAYMENT, IVAN UNIVERSITY OF WISCONSIN 1710 UNIVERSITY AVENUE MADISON, WIS 53705 X-ray diffraction studies on myosin subfragment-1

R01AR-35188-05 (ORTH) ROODMAN, GARSON D UNIV OF TEXAS HLTH SCI CTR 7703 FLOYD CURL DR SAN ANONIO, TX 78284 Developmental aspects of osteoclast formation in-vitro

R01AR-35192-06 (ORTH) LIEBER, RICHARD L VETERANS ADMINISTRATION MED CT 3350 LA JOLLA VILLAGE DRIVE SAN DIEGO, CA 92161 Torque generation following surgical tendon transfers

R01AR-35216-07 (ECS) CHALOVICH, JOSEPH M EAST CAROLINA UNIVERSITY GREENVILLE, NC 27858 Actin based regulation of smooth muscle contraction

R01AR-35230-06 (IMS) MARSHAK-ROTHSTEIN, ANN BOSTON UNIVERSITY 80 EAST CONCORD STREET BOSTON, MA 02118 B cell hyperactivity in autoimmune

R01AR-35270-06A1 (BEM) KEEFE, FRANCIS J DUKE UNIVERSITY MEDICAL CENTER BOX 3159 DURHAM, NC 27710 Coping with osteoarthritic knee pain

R01AR-35322-06 (PBC) NEAME, PETER J UNIV OF SOUTH FLORIDA 12901 BRUCE B DOWNS BLVD, BOX6 TAMPA, FL 33612 Structure and function in cartilage link protein

R01AR-35409-05 (EDC) GRISSO, JEANE A UNIVERSITY OF PENNSYLVANIA 420 SERVICE DRIVE PHILADELPHIA, PA 19140 Causes of hip fractures among black & white women

PROJECT NO., ORGANIZATIONAL UNIT., INVESTIGATOR, ADDRESS, TITLE

R01AR-35487-07 (GMA) AGNELLO, VINCENT LAHEY CLINIC MEDICAL CENTER 41 MALL ROAD BURLINGTON, MA 01805 Human immune complex diseases

R01AR-35506-06 (IMB) WELSH, RAYMOND M, JR UNIVERSITY OF MASS MEDICAL SCH 55 LAKE AVE NORTH WORCESTER, MA 01655 Virus-induced immunopathology

R01AR-35532-08 (GMA) BURGESON, ROBERT E MASSACHUSETTS GENERAL HOSPITAL BLDG 149 13TH STREET CHARLESTOWN, MA 02129 Characterization of a new human collagen

R01AR-35582-06 (EDC) CAULEY, JANE A UNIVERSITY PITTSBURGH 130 DESOTO STREET PITTSBURGH, PA 15261 Risk factors for hip and Colles' fractures

R01AR-35583-06 (EDC) VOGT, THOMAS M KAISER FOUNDATION HOSPITAL 4610 SE BELMONT ST PORTLAND, OR 97215 Risk factors for hip and Colles' fractures

R01AR-35584-06 (EDC) SHERWIN, ROGER W UNIV OF MD AT BALTIMORE 660 WEST REDWOOD ST BALTIMORE, MD 21201 Risk factors for hip and Colles' fracture

R01AR-35587-06 (BM) WISE, KIM S UNIVERSITY OF MISSOURI M642 SCHOOL OF MEDICINE COLUMBIA, MO 65212 Organization and expression of mycoplasma genes

R01AR-35590-07 (ORTH) BROWN, STANLEY A CASE WESTERN RESERVE UNIV 2040 ADELBERT ROAD CLEVELAND, OH 44106 In vitro and in vivo corrosion of orthopaedic implants

R01AR-35651-05 (ORTH) TURNER, RUSSELL T MAYO FOUNDATION 200 FIRST STREET SOUTHWEST ROCHESTER, MN 55905 Bone and mineral homeostatis in immobilization

R01AR-35661-04A1 (PHY) SWEENEY, H LEE THE UNIVERSITY OF PENNSYLVANIA 37TH AND HAMILTON WALK PHILADELPHIA, PA 19104-6085 Physiology and myosin isozymes of skeletal muscle fibers

R01AR-35664-06 (GMA) LUST, GEORGE CORNELL UNIVERSITY NYS COLLE OF VETERINARY MED ITHACA, NY 14853 Fibronectin and cartilage destruction in osteoarthritis

R01AR-35689-07 (GMA) BURGESON, ROBERT E MASSACHUSETTS GENERAL HOSPITAL BLDG 149 13TH STREET CHARLESTOWN, MA 02129 Characterization of sub-epithelial antigens

R01AR-35788-04 (SB) BROWN, THOMAS D UNIVERSITY OF IOWA 4 JESSUP HALL IOWA CITY, IA 52242 Pathomechanics of femoral head aseptic necrosis

R01AR-35805-08 (GMA) WELGUS, HOWARD G JEWISH HOSPITAL 216 S KINGSHIGHWAY ST LOUIS, MO 63110 Biological role of human TIMP in matrix turnover

R01AR-35837-04A2 (ORTH) MALLUCHE, HARTMUT H UNIVERSITY OF KENTUCKY 800 ROSE STREET LEXINGTON, KY 40536-0084 Bone loss after ovariectomy

R01AR-35858-06 (EDC) KULLER, LEWIS H UNIVERSITY OF PITTSBURGH 130 DE SOTO STREET PITTSBURGH, PA 15261 Epidemiology of hormones and osteoporosis

R01AR-35906-07 (ORTH) SLEDGE, CLEMENT B BRIGHAM AND WOMEN' HOSP, INC 75 FRANCIS STREET BOSTON, MASS 02115 The development of radiation synovectomy in arthritis

P30AR-35907-07 (AMS) SCHUR, PETER H BRIGHAM AND WOMEN'S HOSP, INC 75 FRANCES STREET BOSTON, MASS 02115 Rheumatic disease--Core center

P30AR-35907-07 0001 (AMS) SCHUR, PETER H Rheumatic disease--Core center Clinical research unit in rheumatic diseases

P30AR-35907-07 9001 (AMS) SCHUR, PETER H Rheumatic disease--Core center Inpatient and outpatient core

P30AR-35907-07 9002 (AMS) KATZ, HOWARD R Rheumatic disease--Core center Flow cytometry core

P30AR-35907-07 9003 (AMS) WEIS, JOHN H Rheumatic disease--Core center Molecular biology core

P30AR-35907-07 9004 (AMS) CAULFIELD, JOHN Rheumatic disease--Core center Morphology core

P30AR-35907-07 9005 (AMS) SCHUR, PETER H Rheumatic disease--Core center Support laboratory

R01AR-35973-07 (CBY) IP, WALLACE S UNIV OF CINCINNATI COLL OF MED 231 BETHESDA AVE, ML 521 CINCINNATI, OH 45267-0521 Structure and assembly of intermediate filaments

R01AR-36008-06 (GMA) LEIFERMAN, KRISTIN M MAYO FOUNDATION 200 FIRST STREET SOUTHWEST ROCHESTER, MN 55905 Eosinophil leukocytes and atopic dermatitis

R01AR-36028-06 (GMA) HABICHT, GAIL S STATE UNIVERSITY OF NEW YORK STONY BROOK, NY 11794-8691 Interleukin 1, inflammation and aging

R01AR-36066-06A2 (ORTH) BELL, NORMAN H VA MEDICAL CENTER 109 BEE STREET CHARLESTON, SC 29403 Bone and mineral metabolism in blacks and whites

R01AR-36110-07 (PBC) VOGEL, KATHRYN G THE UNIVERSITY OF NEW MEXICO DEPARTMENT OF BIOLOGY ALBUQUERQUE, NM 87131 Proteoglycan structure, metabolism and role in tendon

R01AR-36239-08 (OBM) MARSH, MARY E UNIV OF TEXAS HLTH SCI CTR PO BOX 20068 HOUSTON, TX 77225 Tissue calcification--structure and chemistry

R01AR-36281-07A1 (PHY) KUSHMERICK, MARTIN J UNIVERSITY OF WASHINGTON MED C 1959 NE PACIFIC ST SEATTLE, WA 98195 Skeletal muscle energy metabolism

R01AR-36294-15 (NEUB) ONTELL, MARCIA B UNIVERSITY OF PITTSBURGH 3550 TERRACE STREET PITTSBURGH, PA 15261 Muscle satellite cell--Reaction to disease and trauma

P60AR-36308-07 (ADDK) LIANG, MATTHEW H BRIGHAM & WOMEN'S HOSPITAL 75 FRANCIS STREET BOSTON, MA 02115 Robert B. Brigham multipurpose arthritis center

P60AR-36308-07 0013 (ADDK) LIANG, MATTHEW H Robert B. Brigham multipurpose arthritis center Education--Primary prevention program for low back injury at the worksite

P60AR-36308-07 0014 (ADDK) BRENNER, MICHAEL Robert B. Brigham multipurpose arthritis center Antigen specific responses in RA

P60AR-36308-07 0015 (ADDK) LIPSON, STEVEN Robert B. Brigham multipurpose arthritis center Prospective study of predictors of successful spinal stenosis surgery

P60AR-36308-07 9001 (ADDK) LARSON, MARTIN Robert B. Brigham multipurpose arthritis center Core--Biometry

P60AR-36308-07 9003 (ADDK) KATZ, HOWARD Robert B. Brigham multipurpose arthritis center Core--Flow cytometry

PROJECT NO., ORGANIZATIONAL UNIT., INVESTIGATOR, ADDRESS, TITLE

P60AR-36308-07 9004 (ADDK) SCHUR, PETER Robert B. Brigham multipurpose arthritis center Core--Immunogenetics

P60AR-36308-07 9005 (ADDK) JACK, RICHARD Robert B. Brigham multipurpose arthritis center Core--Hybridoma facility

P60AR-36308-07 9006 (ADDK) CAULFIELD, JOHN F Robert B. Brigham multipurpose arthritis center Core--Morphology

R29AR-36416-06 (ORTH) BARANOWSKI, THOMAS J, JR EMORY UNIVERSITY 69 BUTLER STREET ATLANTA, GA 30303 Electromagnetic effects on bone tissue and its chemistry

R01AR-36457-06A1 (GMA) COUCHMAN, JOHN R UNIVERSITY OF ALABAMA UNIVERSITY BOULEVARD BIRMINGHAM, AL 35294 Basement membrane proteoglycans

R01AR-36460-06 (RNM) SCHAUWECKER, DONALD S WISHARD MEM HOSP 1001 W 10TH ST INDIANAPOLIS, IN 46202 Osteomyelitis detection with In-111 C13 and In-111 wbc's

R01AR-36794-06 (PBC) EYRE, DAVID R UNIVERSITY OF WASHINGTON DEPT OF ORTHOPAEDICS, RK-10 SEATTLE, WA 98195 Biochemistry of the intervertebral disc

R01AR-36819-07 (PBC) OLSEN, BJORN R HARVARD MEDICAL SCHOOL 25 SHATTUCK STREET BOSTON, MA 02115 Biogenesis of extracellular matrix

R01AR-36820-07 (PBC) OLSEN, BJORN R HARVARD MEDICAL SCHOOL 25 SHATTUCK STREET BOSTON, MA 02115 Collagen gene structure and expression

P60AR-36834-05 (AMS) HAHN, BEVRA H UNIVERSITY OF CALIFORNIA 10833 LE CONTE AVE LOS ANGELES, CA 90024-1736 Multipurpose arthritis center

P60AR-36834-05 0001 (AMS) BRAHN, ERNEST Multipurpose arthritis center Pathogenic T cell clones in collagen arthritis

P60AR-36834-05 0004 (AMS) HAHN, BEVRA Multipurpose arthritis center Development of transgenic mice with rearranged gamma globulin

P60AR-36834-05 0005 (AMS) HARBER, PHILIP Multipurpose arthritis center Occupational rheumatology

P60AR-36834-05 0006 (AMS) KAPLAN, SHERRIE Multipurpose arthritis center Education of rheumatoid arthritis patients

P60AR-36834-05 0007 (AMS) TSAO, BETTY Multipurpose arthritis center Peptides that promote production of pathogenic autoantibodies in lupus nephritis

P60AR-36834-05 0008 (AMS) BERKANOVIC, EMIL Multipurpose arthritis center Analysis of role of depression in functional outcomes in patients with RA

P60AR-36834-05 9001 (AMS) EBLING, FANNY Multipurpose arthritis center Core--Monoclonal antibody laboratory

R01AR-36865-06 (MBY) NADAL-GINARD, BERNARDO CHILDRENS HOSPITAL 300 LONGWOOD AVE BOSTON, MA 02115 Alternative splicing of contractile protein genes

R01AR-36867-05 (GMA) GERSHWIN, MERRILL E UNIVERSITY OF CALIFORNIA DAVIS, CA 95616 Immunoregulation in avian scleroderma

R01AR-36963-06 (PHY) HOLICK, MICHAEL F BOSTON UNIVERSITY 80 EAST CONCORD ST, M-1013 BOSTON, MA 02118 Photobiology of vitamin D3

R01AR-36994-05 (PBC) SANDELL, LINDA J UNIVERSITY OF WASHINGTON DEPT. OF ORTHOPAEDICS, RK-10 SEATTLE, WA 98195 Regulation of gene expression in cartilage

R01AR-37003-04A2 (PBC) BIRK, DAVID E ROBERT WOOD JOHNSON MEDICAL SC 675 HOES LANE PISCATAWAY, NJ 08854-5635 Extracellular compartments--Matrix development and repair

R01AR-37070-06 (IMB) PALMER, EDWARD NAT'L JEWISH CTR/IMM & RES MED 1400 JACKSON ST DENVER, CO 80206 Genetics of autoimmunity

R01AR-37095-05 (MEP) THRALL, MARY A COLORADO STATE UNIVERSITY FORT COLLINS, CO 80523 Marrow transplant therapy for mucopolysaccharidosis

R01AR-37145-04 (CTY) ETLINGER, JOSEPH D NEW YORK MEDICAL COLLEGE BASIC SCIENCE BUILDING VALHALLA, NY 10595 Mechanism of disuse atrophy in skeletal muscle

R01AR-37277-03 (PHY) GILBERT, SUSAN H UNIV,. OF MASS,. MED. CTR. 373 PLANTATION STREET WORCESTER, MA 01605 Kinetics of energy liberation in active skeletal muscle

R01AR-37296-06 (GMA) NEPOM, GERALD T VIRGINIA MASON RESEARCH CENTER 1000 SENECA STREET SEATTLE, WA 98101 HLA susceptibility genes in rheumatoid arthritis

R01AR-37308-04A2 (ORTH) QUARLES, DARRYL L DUKE UNIVERSITY MEDICAL CENTER PO BOX 3285 DURHAM, NC 27710 Pharmacologically induced neo-osteogenesis

R01AR-37318-06 (PBC) EYRE, DAVID R UNIVERSITY OF WASHINGTON SCHOOL OF MEDICINE SEATTLE, WA 98195 Pathobiology of inborn skeletal diseases

R01AR-37344-09 (CTY) SCHACHAT, FREDERICK H DUKE UNIVERSITY MEDICAL CENTER ANATOMY DEPT BOX 3011 DURHAM, NC 27710 Patterns of gene expression in mammalian muscle fibers

R01AR-37399-05 (ORTH) ADAMS, JOHN S CEDARS-SINAI MEDICAL CENTER 8700 BEVERLY BLVD LOS ANGELES, CA 90048 Rickets and osteomalacia

R01AR-37499-04 (BBCB) HIGHSMITH, STEFAN UNIVERSITY OF THE PACIFIC 2155 WEBSTER STREET SAN FRANCISCO, CA 94115 Dynamics and elasticity of myosins

R01AR-37507-05 (ORTH) BIGOS, STANLEY J UNIVERSITY WASHINGTON MAIL STOP RK-10 SEATTLE, WA 98195 Premorbid risk factors for back disorders vs absenteeism

R01AR-37520-05 (ORTH) ALOIA, JOHN F WINTHROP-UNIVERSITY HOSPITAL 259 FIRST STREET MINEOLA, N Y 11501 Prevention of postmenopausal bone loss

R01AR-37560-03 (ORTH) CLARK, CHARLES C UNIVERSITY OF PENNSYLVANIA 36TH & HAMILTON WALK/424 STEMM PHILADELPHIA, PA 19104-6081 Structure and metabolism of cartilage collagens

R01AR-37562-04 (ORTH) GENANT, HARRY K UNIVERSITY OF CALIFORNIA DEPARTMENT OF RADIOLOGY SAN FRANCISCO, CALIF 94143 Enhancement of peak bone mass in young women

R01AR-37594-06 (GMA) MILSTONE, LEONARD M YALE UNIVERSITY PO BOX 3333 NEW HAVEN, CT 06510 Parathyroid hormone-like peptide from keratinocytes

R01AR-37606-05 (PHY) PATLAK, JOSEPH B UNIVERSITY OF VERMONT GIVEN BUILDING BURLINGTON, VT 05405 Modes of single Na channel gating during late currents

R01AR-37643-24 (PHY) CHANDLER, WILLIAM K YALE MEDICAL SCHOOL 333 CEDAR STREET NEW HAVEN, CT 06510 Electrical and contractile properties of muscle

R01AR-37661-05 (ORTH) BOSKEY, ADELE L HOSPITAL FOR SPECIAL SURGERY 535 EAST 70TH STREET NEW YORK, NY 10021 In vitro initiation of biological calcification

R01AR-37716-05 (ORTH) KAHN, ARNOLD J UNIVERSITY OF CALIFORNIA BOX 0640 C-734 SAN FRANCISCO, CA 94143-0640 Biochemical characterization of osteoclasts

R01AR-37726-06 (ORTH) GOLDBERG, VICTOR M CASE WESTERN RESERVE UNIV 2074 ABINGTON ROAD CLEVELAND, OHIO 44106 Controlled cartilage repair

R01AR-37909-04 (TMP) KURTTI, TIMOTHY J UNIVERSITY OF MINNESOTA 219 HUDSON HL/1980 FOLWELL AVE SAINT PAUL, MN 55108 Lyme disease spirochetes in tick organ and cell culture

R01AR-37945-05 (CBY) KNUDSEN, KAREN A LANKENAU MEDICAL RES CENTER 100 LANCASTER AVE W OF CITY LI WYNNEWOOD, PA 19096 Glycoproteins mediating myoblast recognition/fusion

R01AR-37986-05 (GMA) ROTHFIELD, NAOMI F UNIV OF CONNECTICUT HLTH CTR 263 FARMINGTON AVENUE FARMINGTON, CT 06032 Autoantibodies in scleroderma and Raynaud's phenomenon

R29AR-38007-05 (ORTH) RIMNAC, CLARE M HOSPITAL FOR SPECIAL SURGERY 535 EAST 70TH STREET NEW YORK, NY 10021 Permanent deformation of compact bone

R01AR-38018-05A1 (ALY) SY, MAN-SUN MASSACHUSETTS GENERAL HOSPITAL 149 13TH ST CHARLESTOWN, MA 02129 T cell abnormalities in autoimmune 1pr/1pr mice

R01AR-38121-05 (ORTH) BANES, ALBERT J UNIVERSITY NORTH CAROLINA 253 CLINICAL SCIENCES BLDG CHAPEL HILL, NC 27599 Tendon cells - Interactions and responses to stress

R01AR-38159-03 (ORTH) AMIEL, DAVID UNIVERSITY OF CALIFORNIA LA JOLLA, CA 92093-0630 Effect of proteases during immobilization

R01AR-38174-05 (PBC) GOLDBERG, BURTON D UNIVERSITY OF WISCONSIN 470 NORTH CHARTER STREET MADISON, WI 53706 Procollagen--Secretion, assembly and cell receptors

P01AR-38188-07 (AMS) PROCKOP, DARWIN J JEFFERSON MEDICAL COLLEGE 1020 LOCUST STREET PHILADELPHIA, PA 19107 Biochemistry of normal and diseased connective tissue

P01AR-38188-07 0001 (AMS) HOJIMA, YOSHIO Biochemistry of normal and diseased connective tissue Type I procollagen N-proteinase & type I procollagen C-proteinase

P01AR-38188-07 0002 (AMS) PROCKOP, DARWIN J Biochemistry of normal and diseased connective tissue Conversion of procollagen to collagen fibrils

P01AR-38188-07 0003 (AMS) PROCKOP, DARWIN J Biochemistry of normal and diseased connective tissue Mutations causing brittle bones and related disorders

P01AR-38188-07 0004 (AMS) LICHU, MON Biochemistry of normal and diseased connective tissue Analysis of procollagen genes in osteogenesis imperfecta

P01AR-38188-07 9001 (AMS) PROCKOP, DARWIN J Biochemistry of normal and diseased connective tissue Core--Tissue culture

P01AR-38188-07 9003 (AMS) PROCKOP, DARWIN J Biochemistry of normal and diseased connective tissue Molecular biology--Core

R29AR-38193-05 (PBC) KINGSTON, WILLIAM J UNIVERSITY OF ROCHESTER 601 ELMWOOD AVENUE, BOX 673 ROCHESTER, NY 14642 Anabolic actions of insulin in neuromuscular disease

R01AR-38319-05 (GMA) TAUROG, JOEL D UNIV OF TEXAS HLTH SCI CTR DEPT OF INTERNAL MEDICINE DALLAS, TX 75235 Antigenic structure of HLA-B27

R01AR-38346-05 (ORTH) JEE, WEBSTER SHEW S UNIV OF UTAH, SCH OF MEDICINE DIV OF RADIOBIOLOGY, BLDG 351 SALT LAKE CITY, UTAH 84112 Making new bone trabeculae in osteopenic aged skeleton

R01AR-38349-05 (ORTH) HAUSCHKA, PETER V CHILDREN'S HOSPITAL CORP 300 LONGWOOD AVENUE BOSTON, MA 02115 Osteoinduction and the biology of bone growth factors

R01AR-38386-05 (GMA) BIKLE, DANIEL D VETERANS ADMIN MEDICAL CENTER 4150 CLEMENT STREET SAN FRANCISCO, CA 94121 Vitamin D and the differentiation of keratinocytes

R01AR-38398-05 (ORTH) LEWIS, JACK L UNIVERSITY OF MINNESOTA 420 DELAWARE ST SE/BOX 289 UMH MINNEAPOLIS, MINNESOTA 55455 Biomechanics of anterior cruciate repair

R29AR-38404-06 (PHY) ROME, LAWRENCE C UNIVERSITY OF PENNSYLVANIA 415 S. UNIVERSITY AVE PHILADELPHIA, PA 19104-6018 Muscle function during locomotion

R01AR-38421-04 (PBC) CHEUNG, HERMAN S MILWAUKEE COUNTY MED. COMPLEX 8700 WEST WISCONSIN AVE BOX 11 MILWAUKEE, WI 53226 Biological effects of basic calcium phosphate crystals

R29AR-38454-05 (BBCB) WINKELMANN, DONALD A U. OF MED & DENT OF N.J. 675 HOES LANE PISCATAWAY, NJ 08854 Molecular probes of myosin structure and interactions

R01AR-38460-06 (ORTH) GUNDBERG, CAREN M YALE UNIV SCHOOL OF MEDICINE 333 CEDAR ST, P O BOX 3333 NEW HAVEN, CT 06510 Osteocalcin synthesis and catabolism in vivo and in vitro

R01AR-38477-06 (GMA) FOX, DAVID A UNIVERSITY OF MICHIGAN 4570 KRESGE I/0531 ANN ARBOR, MI 48109 Unique surface structures on synovial cells

R29AR-38489-05 (ORTH) MC AFEE, PAUL C 1217 SAINT PAUL STREET BALTIMORE, MD 21202 A histomorphometric analysis of spinal stabilization

R01AR-38501-06 (GMA) ZURIER, ROBERT R UNIVERSITY OF MASSACHUSETTS 55 LAKE AVENUE NORTH WORCESTER, MA 01655 Regulation of cell activation by fatty acids

P60AR-38520-04 (AMS) CHRISTIAN, CHARLES L HOSPITAL FOR SPECIAL SURGERY 535 EAST 70TH STREET NEW YORK, N Y 10021 Multipurpose arthritis center

P60AR-38520-04 0001 (AMS) BHARDWAJ, NINA Multipurpose arthritis center Monoclonal antibodies to human dendritic cells

P60AR-38520-04 0003 (AMS) KIMBERLY, ROBERT Multipurpose arthritis center Marine lipids and receptor signal transduction

P60AR-38520-04 0004 (AMS) SALMON, JANE Multipurpose arthritis center Modulation of monocyte effector functions by adenosine

P60AR-38520-04 0005 (AMS) TORZILLI, PETER Multipurpose arthritis center Mechanical stress and chondrocyte metabolism

P60AR-38520-04 0006 (AMS) JOHANSON, NORMAN Multipurpose arthritis

center Bone mass in total hip replacement--Prosthetic loosening
P60AR-38520-04 0007 (AMS) HEALY, JOHN Multipurpose arthritis center Calcitonin in prevention of bone loss in temporal arteritis
P60AR-38520-04 0008 (AMS) KOBASA, SUZANNE Multipurpose arthritis center Stress and stress resistance in lupus pregnancy
P60AR-38520-04 0009 (AMS) REVENSON, TRACEY Multipurpose arthritis center Patient and marital adaptation to rheumatic disease
P60AR-38520-04 0010 (AMS) ELKON, KEITH B Multipurpose arthritis center Model of directly pathogenic autoantibodies
P60AR-38520-04 9001 (AMS) KINBERLY, ROBERT Multipurpose arthritis center Flow cytometry and cell sorting core facility
P60AR-38520-04 9002 (AMS) FRIEDMAN, STEVEN Multipurpose arthritis center Cell culture core
P60AR-38520-04 9003 (AMS) CHARLSON, MARY Multipurpose arthritis center Research methodology core
R01AR-38540-04 (PTHA) BHATTACHARYA, SYAMAL K UNIVERSITY OF TENNESSEE 956 COURT AVE, SUITE E225 MEMPHIS, TN 38163 Regulation of membrane mediated muscle degeneration
R29AR-38551-05 (PC) MANTZOURANIS, EVANGELIA C BOSTON CITY HOSPITAL 818 HARRISON AENUE BOSTON, MA 02118 Serum amyloid P component--Regulation of gene expression
R01AR-38576-03 (PHY) KIRLEY, TERENCE L UNIVERSITY OF CINCINNATI 231 BETHESDA AVENUE CINCINNATI, OHIO 45267-0575 Characterization of transverse tubule Mg2+-ATPase
R01AR-38580-06 (PBC) SANDY, JOHN D SHRINERS HOSP/CRIPPLED CHILD 12502 NORTH PINE DRIVE TAMPA, FL 33612-4799 Extracellular processing of cartilage proteoglycans
R01AR-38630-04 (ORTH) KRAG, MARTIN H UNIV OF VERMONT BURLINGTON, VT 05405 Internal and external deformations of the lumbar disc
R29AR-38636-04 (GMB) GRONOWICZ, GLORIA A UNIV OF CONNECTICUT HLTH CTR 263 FARMINGTON AVENUE FARMINGTON, CT 06032 Extracellular matrix proteins in cell and organ culture of bone
R29AR-38640-05 (ORTH) VIEGAS, STEVEN F UNIVERSITY OF TEXAS 6 136 MCCULLOUGH G-92 GALVESTON, TX 77550 Contact pressure in the radiocarpal joint
R01AR-38648-06 (PBC) RAMIREZ, FRANCESCO MOUNT SINAI SCHOOL OF MEDICINE ONE GUSTAVA L LEVY PLACE NEW YORK, NY 10029 Pathophysiology of human fibrillar collagen types
R01AR-38650-04 (ORTH) KIMURA, JAMES H HENRY FORD HOSPITAL 2799 WEST GRAND BLVD DETROIT, MI 48202 Tissue culture models of cartilage metabolism
R01AR-38656-05 (GMA) RYAN, LAWRENCE M MEDICAL COLLEGE OF WISCONSIN BOX 118-8700 WEST WISCONSIN AV MILWAUKEE, WI 53226 Inorganic pyrophosphate metabolism in arthritis
R01AR-38658-05 (GMA) MORHENN, VERA B SRI INTERNATIONAL 333 RAVENSWOOD AVE MENLO PARK, CA 94025 Characterization & culture of human langerhans cells
R01AR-38671-05 (ORTH) WOOD, MICHAEL B MAYO FOUNDATION 200 FIRST STREET SOUTHWEST ROCHESTER, MN 55905 Prolonged anoxia and responsiveness of bone vascular bed
R01AR-38698-05 (BEM) RUDY, THOMAS E PAIN EVAL & TREATMENT INST BAUM BOULEVARD AT CRAIG STREET PITTSBURG, PA 15213 CBP: A biobehavioral model of function capacity
R01AR-38719-03 (ORTH) BUTLER, DAVID L UNIVERSITY OF CINCINNATI CINCINNATI, OH 45221-0048 Biomechanics of ACL allografts--Sterilization effects
R01AR-38728-04 (ORTH) MOW, VAN C COLUMBIA-PRESBYERIAN MED CTR 630 WEST 168TH ST RM 1412 NEW YORK, NY 10032 Biomechanics of normal human and bovine meniscus
R01AR-38782-06 (RAP) KUSHMERICK, MARTIN J DEPT. OF RADIOLOGY, SB-05 UNIVERSITY OF WASHINGTON SEATTLE, WA 98195 Circulatory and metabolic adaptations in ischemic limbs
R01AR-38796-06 (PHY) MOCZYDLOWSKI, EDWARD G YALE UNIVERSITY PO BOX 3333 NEW HAVEN, CT 06510 Enzymology of single Na-channels in artificial bilayers
R01AR-38821-06 (ALY) BARRETT, KATHLEEN J NEW ENGLAND MED CTR HOSP, INC 750 WASHINGTON STREET BOSTON, MA 02111 Organization of autoantibody VH genes
R29AR-38844-04 (IMS) BRAHN, ERNEST UCLA SCHOOL OF MEDICINE 1000 VETERAN AVENUE LOS ANGELES, CA 90024-1670 Collagen induced arthritis--Specificity of T cells
R01AR-38847-03 (GMA) STUART, MARIE J ST CHRISTOPHERS HOSPITAL 5TH AND LEHIGH AVENUE PHILADELPHIA, PA 19133 Role of eicosanoids in hemophilic arthropathy
R29AR-38850-05 (GMA) NOONAN, FRANCES P GEORGE WASHINGTON UNIVERSITY 2300 I ST., ROSS HALL, 101B WASHINGTON, D.C. 20037 Immunosuppression by ultraviolet B radiation
R29AR-38858-05 (PBC) LIAO, WARREN S-L M. D. ANDERSON HOSPITAL 1515 HOLCOMBE BLVD HOUSTON, TX 77030 Molecular aspects of amyloidosis
R29AR-38867-04 (PC) FAGAN, JULIE M RUTGERS UNIVERSITY BARTLETT HALL, P O BOX 231 NEW BRUNSWICK, N J 08903 Role of ATP-dependent proteolysis in mammalian cells
R29AR-38869-04 (ORTH) CHEAL, EDWARD J BRIGHAM & WOMEN'S HOSPITAL 75 FRANCIS STREET BOSTON, MA 02115 Interfragmentary strain hypothesis and fracture healing
R29AR-38872-05 (CTY) FREGIEN, NEVIS L UNIVERSITY OF MIAMI 1600 NORTHWEST 10TH AVENUE MIAMI, FL 33101 Effects of mitogens on muscle growth and gene expression
R29AR-38881-04 (PHY) PUTNAM, ROBERT W WRIGHT STATE UNIV SCH OF MED BOX 927 DAYTON, OH 45401 PH regulation in skeletal muscle--Design & plasticity /frogs,mice
R29AR-38883-05 (IMB) NEPOM, BARBARA S VIRGINIA MASON RSRCH. CNTR. IMMUNOLOGY/1000 SENECA SEATTLE, WA 98101 HLA genes and hybrid molecules in pauciarticular Jra
R29AR-38884-04 (GMA) STRICKLAND, PAUL T JOHNS HOPKINS UNIVERSITY 615 NORTH WOLFE STREET BALTIMORE, MD 21205 Susceptibility determinants for photocarcinogenesis
R01AR-38888-05 (CTY) IKEBE, MITSUO CASE WESTERN RESERVE UNIV. 2119 ABINGTON ROAD CLEVELAND, OH 44106 Molecular mechanism of the regulation in smooth muscle
R01AR-38889-03 (IMS) SALMON, JANE EVA HOSPITAL FOR SPECIAL SURGERY 535 EAST 70TH STREET NEW YORK, N Y 10021 HLA-associated Fc receptor function in normals and SLE
R01AR-38894-03 (MET) MOXLEY, RICHARD T, III UNIV OF ROCHESTER MED CTR 601 ELMWOOD AVE BX 673/DPT NEU ROCHESTER, NY 14642 Anabolic actions of insulin in neuromuscular disease
R01AR-38899-05 (BBCB) HUXLEY, HUGH E ROSENSTIEL CENTER 415 SOUTH STREET WALTHAM, MA 02254 Structural studies of muscle contraction mechanism
R01AR-38905-05 (ORTH) WRIGHT, TIMOTHY M HOSPITAL FOR SPECIAL SURGERY 535 EAST 70TH STREET NEW YORK, NY 10021 Surface failure in UHMWPE joint components
R01AR-38910-04A1 (CBY) JANMEY, PAUL A BRIGHAM AND WOMEN'S HOSPITAL 75 FRANCIS STREET BOSTON, MA 02115 Reversible formation and structure of actin networks
R01AR-38912-05 (PBC) CHU, MON-LI H THOMAS JEFFERSON UNIVERSITY 1020 LOCUST STREET PHILADELPHIA, PA 19107-6799 Structure of type VI collagen and its role in disease
R01AR-38915-04 (GMA) ELKON, KEITH B HOSPITAL FOR SPECIAL SURGERY 535 EAST 70TH STREET NEW YORK, NY 10021 Molecular analysis of p/anti-p
R01AR-38917-04 (BIO) HILLE, CHARLES R OHIO STATE UNIVERSITY 5170 GRAVES HALL COLUMBUS, OH 43210-1239 Mechanistic studies of xanthine oxidase
R29AR-38918-01A3 (GMA) HASAN, TAYYABA MASSACHUSETTS GENERAL HOSPITAL FRUIT STREET BOSTON, MA 02114 Tetracycline phototoxicity photobiology & photophysics
P01AR-38923-05 (AMS) UITTO, JOUNI J JEFFERSON MEDICAL COLLEGE 233 S 10TH STREET PHILADELPHIA, PA 19107-5541 Molecular genetics of skin basement membrane zone
P01AR-38933-05 (AMS) RAISZ, LAWRENCE G UNIVERSITY OF CONNECTICUT 263 FARMINGTON AVENUE FARMINGTON, CT 06030 Pathogenesis and prevention of osteoporosis
P01AR-38933-05 0001 (AMS) RAISZ, LAWRENCE G Pathogenesis and prevention of osteoporosis Role of prostaglandins in the pathogenesis of osteoporosis
P01AR-38933-05 0002 (AMS) KREAM, BARBARA E Pathogenesis and prevention of osteoporosis Glucocorticoids & collagen on bone collagen synthesis and gene expression
P01AR-38933-05 0003 (AMS) ROWE, DAVID W Pathogenesis and prevention of osteoporosis Genetic factors in osteoporosis
P01AR-38933-05 0004 (AMS) SMITH, JO-ANNE A Pathogenesis and prevention of osteoporosis Exercise and estrogen in prevention of osteoporosis
P01AR-38933-05 0005 (AMS) LORENZO, JOSEPH A Pathogenesis and prevention of osteoporosis Cytokines and growth factors on bone resorption
P01AR-38933-05 0006 (AMS) GUNNESS-HEY, MICHELE Pathogenesis and prevention of osteoporosis Racial and ethnic determinants of bone mass and structure
P01AR-38933-05 0007 (AMS) LICHTLER, ALEX Pathogenesis and prevention of osteoporosis Immortalization of rat bone cells
P01AR-38933-05 0008 (AMS) RUBIN, KAREN Pathogenesis and prevention of osteoporosis Adolescent idiopathic scoliosis as a marker for adult osteoporosis
P01AR-38933-05 9001 (AMS) RAISZ, LAWRENCE G Pathogenesis and prevention of osteoporosis Core--Bone histomorphometry laboratory
R29AR-38945-05 (ORTH) ROSIER, RANDY N DEPT. OF ORTHOPAEDICS, BOX 665 STRONG MEMORIAL/601 ELMWOOD ROCHESTER, NY 14642 Growth factors and epiphyseal chondrocyte maturation
R01AR-38970-05 (PHY) STEFANI, ENRICO BAYLOR COLLEGE OF MEDICINE ONE BAYLOR PLAZA HOUSTON, TX 77030 Ca channels in skeletal muscle fibers
R01AR-38972-04A1 (PHY) MEYER, RONALD A MICHIGAN STATE UNIVERSITY EAST LANSING, MI 48824 NMR studies of mammalian skeletal muscle metabolism
R29AR-38976-05 (BBCB) SAFER, DANIEL UNIVERSITY OF PENNSYLVANIA DEPT. OF BIOCHEM. & BIOPHYS. PHILADELPHIA, PA 19104-6089 Crossbridge structure & geometry
R01AR-38980-06 (PHY) MAUGHAN, DAVID W UNIVERSITY OF VERMONT BURLINGTON, VT 05405 Microanalysis of intracellular fluid from muscle
R44AR-38987-03 (SSS) HSIA, JAMES C CANDELA LASER CORPORATION 530 BOSTON POST ROAD WAYLAND, MA 01778 Pulsed laser treatment of pigmented lesions
R29AR-39021-03 (PHRA) PERSHING, LYNN K UNIV OF UTAH DPT OF INTERNAL MEDICINE SALT LAKE CITY, UT 84132 Percutaneous absorption and metabolism in human skin
R01AR-39148-03 (GMA) MAHOWALD, MAREN L MINNEAPOLIS VA MED CTR ONE VETERANS DRIVE MINNEAPOLIS, MN 55417 Microvascular mechanisms of articular damage in antigen
R01AR-39153-04 (IMS) HANSEN, JOHN A F. HUTCHINSON CANCER CENTER 1124 COLUMBIA STREET, ROOM 718 SEATTLE, WA 98104 HLA-D polymorphism and disease susceptibility
R01AR-39155-04 (BBCB) MILLIGAN, RONALD A SCRIPPS CLINIC & RSRCH. FNDTN. 10666 NORTH TORREY PINES ROAD LA JOLLA, CA 92037 Cryo-electron microscopy of muscle filaments
R01AR-39157-03 (IMS) DATTA, SYAMAL K NEW ENGLAND MEDICAL CNTR HOSPI 750 WASHINGTON STREET, BOX 52 BOSTON, MA 02111 Pathogenic anti-dNA antibodies:regulation in human lupus
R01AR-39158-03 (CTY) SPEICHER, DAVID W THE WISTAR INSTITUTE 36TH AND SPRUCE STREET PHILADELPHIA, PA 19104 Domain structure of human smooth muscle filamin
P60AR-39162-05 (AMS) HAYNES, BARTON F DUKE MEDICAL CENTER BOX 3258 DURHAM, NC 27710 Specialized center of research in rheumatoid arthritis
P60AR-39162-05 0001 (AMS) HAYNES, BARTON F. Specialized center of research in rheumatoid arthritis Cytokine and T cell activation in rheumatoid synovial microenvironment
P60AR-39162-05 0002 (AMS) WEINBERG, J. BRICE Specialized center of research in rheumatoid arthritis Effector cell function by inflammatory mediators in rheumatoid arthritis
P60AR-39162-05 0003 (AMS) MCCACHREN, S SPENCE Specialized center of research in rheumatoid arthritis Inflammation and synovial cell proliferation in rheumatoid arthritis
P60AR-39162-05 0004 (AMS) ST. CLAIR, E. WILLIAM Specialized center

of research in rheumatoid arthritis Autoantibody response in Sjogren's syndrome and rheumatoid arthritis
P50AR-39162-05 0005 (AMS) PISETSKY, DAVID S. Specialized center of research in rheumatoid arthritis Immunopathogenesis of arthritis in MRL mice
P50AR-39162-05 0006 (AMS) KEEFE, FRANCIS J Specialized center of research in rheumatoid arthritis Pain coping strategies in rheumatoid arthritis
P50AR-39162-05 9001 (AMS) SINGER, KAY H Specialized center of research in rheumatoid arthritis Tissue laboratory core
P50AR-39162-05 9002 (AMS) KAUFMAN, RUSSEL E. Specialized center of research in rheumatoid arthritis Molecular biology core
P50AR-39166-05 (AMS) KANG, ANDREW H UNIV. OF TENNESSEE, MEMPHIS 956 COURT AVENUE, G326 MEMPHIS, TN 38163 SCOR on the pathogenesis of rheumatoid arthritis
P50AR-39166-05 0001 (AMS) STUART, J M SCOR on the pathogenesis of rheumatoid arthritis Structural basis of collagen arthritis
P50AR-39166-05 0002 (AMS) MYERS, L K SCOR on the pathogenesis of rheumatoid arthritis Antigen specific suppression of collagen arthritis
P50AR-39166-05 0003 (AMS) ENDRES, R SCOR on the pathogenesis of rheumatoid arthritis Synovial T lymphocytes in rheumatoid arthritis
P50AR-39166-05 0004 (AMS) POSTLETHWAITE, A E SCOR on the pathogenesis of rheumatoid arthritis Structure function relationships of IL-1 alpha and beta
P50AR-39166-05 0005 (AMS) MAINARDI, CARLO SCOR on the pathogenesis of rheumatoid arthritis Synovial cell metalloproteinases in rheumatoid arthritis
P50AR-39166-05 0006 (AMS) MAINARDI, CARLO SCOR on the pathogenesis of rheumatoid arthritis Neutrophil collagenases in rheumatoid arthritis
P50AR-39166-05 0007 (AMS) STUART, J M SCOR on the pathogenesis of rheumatoid arthritis Mechanisms of joint destruction in collagen arthritis
P50AR-39166-05 0008 (AMS) RAGHOW, R SCOR on the pathogenesis of rheumatoid arthritis Regulation of collagen gene expression in fibroblasts
P50AR-39166-05 9001 (AMS) ENDRES, ROBERT SCOR on the pathogenesis of rheumatoid arthritis Hybridoma core
P50AR-39166-05 9002 (AMS) SEYER, J H SCOR on the pathogenesis of rheumatoid arthritis Protein chemistry - Core
P50AR-39169-05 (AMS) LIPSKY, PETER E UNIV OF TEXAS SW MED CTR 5323 HARRY HINES BLVD DALLAS, TX 75235 Specialized center of research in rheumatoid arthritis
P50AR-39169-05 0001 (AMS) STASTNY, P Specialized center of research in rheumatoid arthritis Genetic basis for rheumatoid factor production in rheumatoid arthritis
P50AR-39169-05 0002 (AMS) CAPRA, J D Specialized center of research in rheumatoid arthritis Immunoglobulin variable region gene polymorphism in rheumatoid arthritis patients
P50AR-39169-05 0003 (AMS) TAUROG, J Specialized center of research in rheumatoid arthritis Role of humoral and cellular immunity ininflammatory arthritis
P50AR-39169-05 0004 (AMS) LIPSKY, P Specialized center of research in rheumatoid arthritis Cellular basis of rheumatoid arthritis
P50AR-39169-05 0006 (AMS) LIPSKY, P E Specialized center of research in rheumatoid arthritis Therapeutic modulation of immune reactivity in patient with rheumatoid arthritis
R01AR-39189-04 (PBC) NAGASE, HIDEAKI UNIV. OF KANSAS MEDICAL CENTER 39TH AND RAINBOW BOULEVARD KANSAS CITY, KS 66103 Metalloproteases in connective tissue matrix breakdown
R01AR-39190-03S1 (GMA) DOTTO, GIAN-PAOLO YALE UNIVERSITY 310 CEDAR STREET NEW HAVEN, CT 06510 Growth differentiation control in primary keratinocytes
P50AR-39191-05 (AMS) LINDSAY, ROBERT HELEN HAYES HOSPITAL HAYES HOSPITAL, ROUTE 9W WEST HAVERSTRAW, NY 10993 Specialized centers of research in osteoporosis
P50AR-39191-05 0001 (AMS) DEMPSTER, DAVID W Specialized centers of research in osteoporosis Mode of action and regulation of the osteoclast
P50AR-39191-05 0002 (AMS) SHEN, VICTOR Specialized centers of research in osteoporosis Ovarian function, skeletal remodeling and the calcium-vitamin D endocrine system
P50AR-39191-05 0003 (AMS) BILEZIKAIN, JOHN P Specialized centers of research in osteoporosis Phosphate as an activator of the osteoporotic skeleton
P50AR-39191-05 0004 (AMS) KELSEY, JENNIFER L Specialized centers of research in osteoporosis Epidemiology of bone mass in young adults
P50AR-39191-05 9001 (AMS) SHEN, VICTOR Specialized centers of research in osteoporosis Biochemistry - Core
P50AR-39191-05 9002 (AMS) DEMPSTER, DAVID W Specialized centers of research in osteoporosis Bone histomorphometry -Core
P50AR-39191-05 9003 (AMS) LINDSAY, ROBERT Specialized centers of research in osteoporosis Non-invasive measurement of bone mineral
R29AR-39201-04 (PBC) CENTRELLA, MICHAEL SAINT FRANCIS HOSP & MED CNTR LL4 WOODLAND STREET HARTFORD, CT 06105 Bone collagen production by bone-derived TGFbeta
R01AR-39209-02 (ORTH) PANJABI, MANOHAR M YALE UNIVERSITY MEDICAL SCHOOL PO BOX 3333 NEW HAVEN, CT 06510 Spinal injuries of thoracolumbar spine
R01AR-39213-04 (ORTH) POPE, MALCOLM H UNIVERSITY OF VERMONT COLLEGE OF MEDICINE/GIVEN BLDG BURLINGTON, VT 05405 In vivo measuring of anterior cruciate ligament strain
R01AR-39218-04 (CTY) PUTKEY, JOHN A U. OF TEXAS MED. CNTR./HOUSTON PSOT OFFICE BOX 20708 HOUSTON, TX 77225 Mutation of functional domains in cardiac troponin c
P50AR-39221-05 (AMS) RECKER, ROBERT R CREIGHTON UNIVERSITY 601 NORTH 30TH STREET OMAHA, NE 68131 Specialized center of research in osteoporosis
P50AR-39221-05 9005 (AMS) KIMMEL, DANIEL B Specialized center of research in osteoporosis Histomorphometry core
P50AR-39221-05 0001 (AMS) GALLAGHER, J C Specialized center of research in osteoporosis Family studies in osteoporosis
P50AR-39221-05 0002 (AMS) RECKER, ROBERT R Specialized center of research in osteoporosis Bone histomorphometry before and after menopause
P50AR-39221-05 0003 (AMS) KIMMEL, DONALD B Specialized center of research in osteoporosis Nutrition and bone loss after ovariectomy
P50AR-39221-05 0004 (AMS) HEANEY, ROBERT P Specialized center of research in osteoporosis Identification and treatment of calcium deficiency
P50AR-39221-05 0005 (AMS) HEANEY, ROBERT P Specialized center of research in osteoporosis Calcium bioavailability from certain plant sources
P50AR-39221-05 0006 (AMS) RECKER, ROBERT R Specialized center of research in osteoporosis Restoration of bone mass by coherence treatment
P50AR-39221-05 0007 (AMS) GALLAGHER, J C Specialized center of research in osteoporosis Effect of strength training on bone density
P50AR-39221-05 9001 (AMS) HEANEY, ROBERT P Specialized center of research in osteoporosis Biochemistry - Core
P50AR-39221-05 9002 (AMS) DAVIES, K MICHAEL Specialized center of research in osteoporosis Data management - Core
P50AR-39221-05 9003 (AMS) GALLAGHER, J C Specialized center of research in osteoporosis Densitometry core
P50AR-39221-05 9004 (AMS) GALLAGHER, J C Specialized center of research in osteoporosis Immunoassay - Core
P50AR-39226-05 (AMS) BRIGHTON, CARL T 425 MEDICAL EDUCATION BUILDING 36TH & HAMILTON WALK PHILADELPHIA, PA 19104-6081 Interaction of hormones and physical stress on bone mass
P50AR-39226-05 0001 (AMS) BRIGHTON, CARL T Interaction of hormones and physical stress on bone mass Effects of an applied electric field on bone loss
P50AR-39226-05 0002 (AMS) HADDAD, JOHN G Interaction of hormones and physical stress on bone mass Skeletal effects of calcitonin and estrogen
P50AR-39226-05 0003 (AMS) POLLACK, SOLOMON Interaction of hormones and physical stress on bone mass Zeta potential of bone in relation to osteoporosis
P50AR-39226-05 0004 (AMS) WILLIAMS, JOHN L Interaction of hormones and physical stress on bone mass Osteon biomechanics--Effects of disuse, age and hormones
P50AR-39226-05 0005 (AMS) DUCHEYNE, PAUL Interaction of hormones and physical stress on bone mass Hormones, stress and electricity, and porus ingrowth
P50AR-39226-05 0006 (AMS) ATTIE, MAURICE F Interaction of hormones and physical stress on bone mass Genetic study of bone mineral density
P50AR-39226-05 9001 (AMS) WILLIAMS, JOHN L Interaction of hormones and physical stress on bone mass Mechanical testing core
P50AR-39226-05 9002 (AMS) IANNOTTI, JOSEPH P Interaction of hormones and physical stress on bone mass Histomorphometry core
P50AR-39226-05 9003 (AMS) WILLIAMS, JOHN L Interaction of hormones and physical stress on bone mass Computation core
R01AR-39234-03 (ORTH) SANDLER, RIVKA B UNIVERSITY OF PITTSBURGH 121 MEYRAN AVENUE PITTSBURGH, PA 15260 Muscle strength and postmenopausal bone loss
P50AR-39239-05 (AMS) KUETTNER, KLAUS E RUSH PRESBYTERIAN--ST. LUKE'S 1653 WEST CONGRESS PARKWAY CHICAGO, IL 60612-3864 Specialized center of research in osteoarthritis
P50AR-39239-05 0001 (AMS) AYDELOTTE, MARGARET B Specialized center of research in osteoarthritis Metabolism of sub-populations of articular chondrocytes
P50AR-39239-05 0003 (AMS) KUETTNER, KLAUS Specialized center of research in osteoarthritis Protease inhibitors in normal and disease cartilage
P50AR-39239-05 0004 (AMS) THONAR, EUGENE Specialized center of research in osteoarthritis Keratan sulfate--Marker for cartilage catabolism in osteoarthritis
P50AR-39239-05 0005 (AMS) ANDRIACCHI, THOMAS Specialized center of research in osteoarthritis Factors influencing function following hip replacement
P50AR-39239-05 9001 (AMS) KIMURA, JAMES H Specialized center of research in osteoarthritis Cell and tissue culture
P50AR-39239-05 9002 (AMS) KUSZAK, JEROME Specialized center of research in osteoarthritis Morphology and ultrastructure
R01AR-39241-03 (GMB) LUBEN, RICHARD A UNIVERSITY OF CALIFORNIA DIVISION OF BIOMEDICAL SCIENCE RIVERSIDE, CALIF 92521 Bone cell antigens related to PTH receptors
R01AR-39244-04 (PC) BAKER, JOHN R U. A. B. UNIVERSITY STATION BIRMINGHAM, AL 35294 Structure and interactions of proteoglycans
P50AR-39250-05 (AMS) BRANDT, KENNETH D INDIANA UNIVERSITY 541 CLINICAL DRIVE INDIANAPOLIS, IN. 46202-5103 Specialized center of research in osteoarthritis
P50AR-39250-05 0001 (AMS) SMITH, G N Specialized center of research in osteoarthritis Changes in pericellular matrix chondrocytes in osteoarthritis
P50AR-39250-05 0002 (AMS) FIFE, F R Specialized center of research in osteoarthritis Cartilage matrix glycoprotein as a serum marker of osteoarthritis
P50AR-39250-05 0003 (AMS) O'CONNOR, BRIAN Specialized center of research in osteoarthritis Neurogenic acceleration of experimental osteoarthritis
P50AR-39250-05 0004 (AMS) MYERS, STEPHEN Specialized center of research in osteoarthritis Synovitis and cartilage repair in osteoarthritis
P50AR-39250-05 9001 (AMS) O'CONNER, BRIAN Specialized center of research in osteoarthritis Histology/photomicrography--Core
P50AR-39250-05 9002 (AMS) HECK, D A Specialized center of research in osteoarthritis Orthopedic procedures--Core
P50AR-39250-05 9003 (AMS) SMITH, G N Specialized center of research in osteoarthritis Biochemistry--Core
P50AR-39250-05 9004 (AMS) KATZ, B Specialized center of research in osteoarthritis Biostatistics--Core
R01AR-39254-05 (GMA) FU, SHU MAN UNIV OF VIR HEALTH SCI CTR SCH OF MED/DEPT OF MED CHARLOTTESVILLE, VA 22908 Autoantibodies in rheumatoid arthritis and other states

PROJECT NO., ORGANIZATIONAL UNIT., INVESTIGATOR, ADDRESS, TITLE

P50AR-39255-05 (AMS) THOMPSON, ROBY C, JR DEPT. OF ORTHOPAEDIC SURGERY 420 DELAWARE ST. S.E., BOX 189 MINNEAPOLIS, MN 55455 Specialized center of research in osteoarthritis

P50AR-39255-05 0001 (AMS) THOMPSON, R Specialized center of research in osteoarthritis Biologic responses in osteoarthritis

P50AR-39255-05 0002 (AMS) BRADFORD, DAVID Specialized center of research in osteoarthritis Spine

P50AR-39255-05 0003 (AMS) LEWIS, JACK Specialized center of research in osteoarthritis Clinical knee motion

P50AR-39255-05 9001 (AMS) LEWIS, JACK Specialized center of research in osteoarthritis Biomechanics--Core

P50AR-39255-05 9002 (AMS) OEGEMA, T. R. Specialized center of research in osteoarthritis Biology--Core

R01AR-39273-05 (GMB) BUTLER, WILLIAM T UNIVERSITY TEXAS HEALTH SCI CT 6516 JOHN FREEMAN AVE HOUSTON, TX 77030 Bone proteins--chemistry, synthesis, tissue localization

R01AR-39278-04A1 (ORTH) RUBIN, CLINTON T STATE UNIV OF NEW YORK HEALTH SCIENCE CENTER STONY BROOK, NY 11794-8181 Attenuation of wolff's law by systemic disorders

R01AR-39280-04 (CBY) MACLENNAN, DAVID H UNIVERSITY OF TORONTO 112 COLLEGE STREET TORONTO, ONTARIO CANADA M5G1L6 Site-specific mutagenesis of the Ca2+-ATPase

R29AR-39282-04 (IMS) NELSON, JUDITH L FRED HUTCHINSON CANCER RESEARC 1124 COLUMBIA STREET, RM 718 SEATTLE, WASH 98104 HLA-d alloantigens--rheumatoid arthritis & reproductivity

R01AR-39286-04 (BBCA) MORRISON, HARRY A PURDUE UNIVERSITY WEST LAFAYETTE, IND 47907 Studies related to tetracycline cutaneous phototoxicity

R01AR-39288-02 (BBCB) BURGHARDT, THOMAS P MAYO FOUNDATION 200 FIRST ST, SOUTHWEST ROCHESTER, MN 55905 Molecular angle transitions in muscle

R01AR-39297-04 (SAT) HULL, BARBARA E WRIGHT STATE UNIVERSITY 235 BIOLOGICAL SCIENCES DEPT DAYTON, OH 45435 Transplantation of allogeneic skin equivalents

R01AR-39299-03 (RAP) KASPEREK, GEORGE J EAST CAROLINA UNIVERSITY GREENVILLE, NC 27858 Effect of exercise on protein degradation

R01AR-39310-03 (ORTH) GALANTE, JORGE O RUSH-PRESB-ST LUKE'S MED CTR 1653 WEST CONGRESS PARKWAY CHICAGO, ILL 60612 Systemic implications of total joint replacement

R29AR-39318-04 (ORTH) MARSH, RICHARD L NORTHEASTERN UNIVERSITY 360 HUNTINGTON AVE. BOSTON, MA. 02115 Functional & structural properties of skeletal muscle

R01AR-39320-04 (CTY) STOCKDALE, FRANK E STANFORD UNIVERSITY MED CTR DIV OF ONCOLOGY ROOM M-211 STANFORD, CALF 94305-5306 Avian myogenic cell commitment

R29AR-39325-04 (GMA) REVEILLE, JOHN D UNIV OF TEXAS MED SCHOOL PO BOX 20708 HOUSTON, TX 77225 Molecular genetic analysis of ankylosing spondylitis

R29AR-39361-04 (IMS) PADULA, STEVEN J UNIVERSITY OF CONNECTICUT 263 FARMINGTON AVENUE FARMINGTON, CT 06032 Rheumatoid arthritis & Lyme disease--T cell receptor

R29AR-39366-03 (EDC) KWOH, C KENT UNIV OF PITTSBURGH 985 SACIFE HALL/DEPT MED PITTSBURGH, PA 15261 Epidemiology of rhematoid arthitis--Genetic determinants

R01AR-39378-04 (RAP) STAINSBY, WENDELL N UNIVERSITY OF FLORIDA BOX J-274, JHMCH GAINESVILLE, FL 32610 Role of 02 transport in determining V02 max of muscle

R29AR-39380-03 (ORTH) ZALESKE, DAVID J MASSACHUSETTS GENERAL HOSPITAL FRUIT STREET BOSTON, MA 02114 Epiphyseal reconstruction

R55AR-39382-04 (GMA) BOMALASKI, JOHN S VA MEDICAL CENTER 39TH & WOODLAND PHILADELPHIA, PA 19104 Rheumatoid arthritis phospholipases and inflammation

R29AR-39396-03 (ORTH) MILLER, RAYMOND R CLEVELAND CLINIC FOUNDATION 9500 EUCLID AVENUE CLEVELAND, OHIO 44106 Growth plate vascularization/endochondral ossification

R01AR-39405-04 (PBC) GERSTENFELD, LOUIS C CHILDREN'S HOSPITAL CORPORATIO 300 LONGWOOD AVE BOSTON, MA 02115 Cartilage expression and regulation

R01AR-39420-06 (BNP) CHEDEKEL, MILES ROBERT UNIVERSITY OF CALIFORNIA 9 HUTCHINSON HALL DAVIS, CA 95616 Biosynthetic and structural studies on melanins

R01AR-39421-04 (MEP) ANDRIACCHI, THOMAS P RUSH-PRES-ST LUKE'S MED CTR 1653 WEST CONGRESS PARKWAY CHICAGO, IL 60612 Anterior cruciate ligament-functional biomechanics

R29AR-39423-04 (MBY) WIECZOREK, DAVID F UNIV OF CINCINNATI 231 BETHESDA AVE CINCINNATI, OH 45267-0524 Regulation of alternative RNA splicing in a-tropomyosin

R44AR-39427-02A2 (SSS) PARISH, HARLIE A MOLECULAR DESIGN INT'L, INC PO BOX 41777 MEMPHIS, TN 38174 Topical drugs for the treatment of psoriasis

P01AR-39448-04 (AMS) ELIAS, PETER M VETERANS ADMIN MEDICAL CTR 4150 CLEMENT STREET SAN FRANCISCO, CALIF 94121 Relationship of keratinocyte function to differentiation

P01AR-39448-04 0004 (AMS) GOLDYNE, MARK E. Relationship of keratinocyte function to differentiation Eicosanoids and fibroblast-keratinocyte interactions

P01AR-39448-04 0005 (AMS) GRAYSON, STEPHEN Relationship of keratinocyte function to differentiation Proteolipids and keratinocyte function

P01AR-39448-04 9001 (AMS) WILLIAMS, MARY Relationship of keratinocyte function to differentiation Core--Cell culture

P01AR-39448-04 9002 (AMS) GRAYSON, STEPHEN Relationship of keratinocyte function to differentiation Core--Morphology

P01AR-39448-04 0001 (AMS) BIKLE, DANIEL D. Relationship of keratinocyte function to differentiation Differentiation of transformed keratinocytes

P01AR-39448-04 0002 (AMS) BOYER, THOMAS E. Relationship of keratinocyte function to differentiation Keratinocyte differentiation and detoxification

P01AR-39448-04 0003 (AMS) ELIAS, PETER Relationship of keratinocyte function to differentiation Sphingolipid metabolism and keratinocyte differentiation

PROJECT NO., ORGANIZATIONAL UNIT., INVESTIGATOR, ADDRESS, TITLE

R01AR-39460-04 (GMA) GERATZ, JOACHIM D UNIV OF NORTH CAROLINA CHAPEL HILL, N C 27599 Suppression of erosive arthritis by protease inhibitors

R29AR-39467-04 (CTY) OLWIN, BRADLEY B UNIVERSITY OF WISCONSIN 420 HENRY HALL MADISON, WI 53706 Analysis of myogenic growth and differentiation

R01AR-39472-03 (PBC) GOLDBERG, GREGORY I WASHINGTON UNIV SCH OF MED 660 SOUTH EUCLID AVE BOX 8123 ST LOUIS, MO 63110 ECM proteases in inflammation, fibrosis & tumorigenesis

R01AR-39480-03 (GMA) SCHWAB, JOHN H UNIV OF NC/CB#7290 804 FLOB DEPT MICROBIO & IMMUN CHAPEL HILL, NC 27599 Regulation of inflammation in experimental arthritis

R29AR-39481-04 (BEM) BUCKELEW, SUSAN P UMC SCHOOL OF MEDICINE 5RO1 RUSK REHABILITATION CENTE COLUMBIA, MO 65212 Biofeedback and physical therapy treatment of PFS

R29AR-39489-03 (IMS) ROSTAMI, ABDOLMOHAMMAD HOSP OF UNIV OF PENNSYLVANIA 3400 SPRUCE STREET PHILADELPHIA, PA 19104 Immunopathogenesis of experimental allergic myositis

R01AR-39496-03 (RAP) HICKSON, ROBERT C UNIVERSITY OF ILLINOIS/CHICAGO BOX 4348 CHICAGO, IL 60680 Exercise and muscle atrophy prevention

R01AR-39499-01A3 (MGN) HERMAN, GAIL E BAYLOR COLLEGE OF MEDICINE ONE BAYLOR PLAZA S911 HOUSTON, TX 77030 Molecular studies of X-linked chondrodysplasia punctata

R29AR-39507-01A3 (ORTH) KNUDSON, CHERYL B RUSH-PRESBYTERIAN-ST LUKES MED 1653 W CONGRESS PKWY CHICAGO, IL 60612 Hyaluronate-cell interactions during limb morphogenesis

R01AR-39514-03 (EDC) PERTSCHUK, MICHAEL J THE GRADUATE HOSPITAL 1800 LOMBARD ST PHILADELPHIA, PA 19146 Longitudinal study of bone density in anorexia nervosa

R01AR-39515-04 (ORTH) GOLDRING, STEVEN R ARTHRITIS UNIT MASSACHUSETTS GENERAL HOPITAL BOSTON, MA 02114 Biochemical & cellular responses to biomaterials

R29AR-39522-05 (PHY) RASGADO-FLORES, HECTOR F UNIVERSITY OF HEALTH SCIENCES/ 3333 GREEN BAY ROAD NOTHE CHICAGO, ILLINOIS 60064 Volume regulation in muscle cells

P01AR-39529-02 (AMS) MUNDY, GREGORY R UNIV OF TEXAS HEALTH SCI CTR 7703 FLOYD CURL DRIVE SAN ANTONIO, TX 78284-7877 The osteoclast and its regulation

P01AR-39529-02 0001 (AMS) MUNDY, GREGORY The osteoclast and its regulation Molecular mechanisms of osteoclast activation

P01AR-39529-02 0002 (AMS) CHIRGWIN, JOHN M The osteoclast and its regulation Gene expression during osteoclast differentiation

P01AR-39529-02 0003 (AMS) BONEWALD, LYNDA The osteoclast and its regulation Role of TGF beta and binding proteins in bone remodelings

P01AR-39529-02 0004 (AMS) ROODMAN, G DAVID The osteoclast and its regulation Bone remodeling in Paget's disease

P01AR-39529-02 9001 (AMS) MUNDY, GREGORY The osteoclast and its regulation Laboratory core

R01AR-39541-03 (EDC) LA PORTE, RONALD E UNIVERSITY OF PITTSBURGH 130 DESOTO STREET PITTSBURGH, PA 15261 Epidemiology of sports injuries

R01AR-39547-01A3 (GMA) PITTELKOW, MARK R MAYO FOUNDATION 200 FIRST ST SOUTHWEST ROCHESTER, MN 55905 Transforming growth factor-alpha regulation in keratinocytes

R29AR-39552-03 (IMS) BHARDWAJ, NINA ROCKEFELLER UNIVERSITY 1230 YORK AVENUE NEW YORK, NY 10021 The production of cytokines by antigen presenting cells

R01AR-39555-04 (GMA) THEOFILOPOULOS, ARGYRIOS N RES INST OF SCRIPPS CLINIC 10666 NORTH TORREY PINES ROAD LA JOLLA, CA 92037 T cell antigen receptor genes in autoimmunity

R01AR-39559-03 (EDC) LOHMAN, TIMOTHY G UNIVERSITY OF ARIZONA INA E GITTINGS BLDG/DPT EXERCI TUSCON, AZ 85721 Effects of exercise on bone mineral content in women

R01AR-39560-01A1 (ORTH) WEAVER, CONNIE M PURDUE UNIVERSITY WEST LAFAYETTE, IN 47907 Exercise and bone mass in young women

R01AR-39561-04 (OBM) HRUSKA, KEITH A JEWISH HOSPITAL 216 S KINGSHIGHWAY ST LOUIS, MO 63110 Hormonal regulation of osteoblast function

R01AR-39571-03 (GMB) INSOGNA, KARL L YALE UNIVERSITY 333 CEDAR ST, PO BOX 3333 NEW HAVEN, CT 06510 A malignancy-associated PTH-like peptide--effect on bone

R01AR-39574-04 (ORTH) COCHRAN, GEORGE V ROUTE 9W WEST HAVERSTRAW, N Y 10993 Factors affecting streaming potentials in living bone

R29AR-39576-04 (IMS) FIRESTEIN, GARY S UCSD MEDICAL CENTER 225 DICKINSON STREET SAN DIEGO, CA 92103 Lymphokines in rheumatoid arthritis

R01AR-39577-03 (IMS) HARLEY, JOHN B OKLAHOMA MEDICAL RESEARCH FDN 825 NE 13TH STREET OKLAHOMA CITY, OK 73104 Antiidiotypes in congenital heart block & neonatal lupus

R01AR-39582-04 (IMS) BRENNER, MICHAEL B DANA-FARBER CANCER INSTITUTE 44 BINNEY STREET BOSTON, MA 02115 T cells and disease

R01AR-39583-03 (RAP) CAMPBELL, KENNETH B WASHINGTON STATE UNIVERSITY PULLMAN, WA 99164-6520 Bioenergetic and Ca2+ regulation of muscle in fatigue

R01AR-39588-02 (PBC) STEIN, GARY S UNIV OF MASSACHUSETTS MED CNTR 55 LAKE AVENUE NORTH WORCESTER, MA 01655 Control of osteoblast proliferation and differentiation

R01AR-39590-01A3 (CBY) PEPE, FRANK A UNIVERSITY OF PENNSYLVANIA SCHOOL OF MEDICINE PHILADELPHIA, PA 19104-6058 Myosin rod sequences and their role in filament assembly

R01AR-39595-03 (RAP) CANNON, JOSEPH G TUFTS UNIVERSITY 711 WASHINGTON ST BOSTON, MA 02111 Muscle damage in aging--inflammatory mechanisms

R01AR-39602-04 (PHRA) NAVARRO, JAVIER V BOSTON UNIVERSITY 80 E CONCORD ST BOSTON, MA 02118 Modulation of calcium channels in muscle cells

R01AR-39603-03 (PHY) SCHACHAT, FREDERICK H DUKE UNIVERSITY MEDICAL CENTER BOX 3011 DURHAM, NC 27710 Physiological adaptation and muscle protein transitions

R01AR-39617-04 (CBY) CAPETANAKI, YASSEMI BAYLOR COLLEGE OF MEDICINE ONE BAYLOR PLAZA HOUSTON, TX 77030 Desmin and vimentin

during myogenesis
R01AR-39623-03 (ORTH) CHAMBERS, TIMOTHY J ST GEORGE'S HOSPITAL MEDICAL S CRANMER TERRACE, TOOTING LONDON SW17 ORE, UK Regulation of bone resorption
R01AR-39626-04 (GMA) WINCHESTER, ROBERT J COLUMBIA UNIVERSITY 630 W. 168TH STREET NEW YORK, NY 10032 Cutaneous & articular manifestations in HIV diseases
R29AR-39627-04 (PHY) SIMON, BRUCE J THE UNIV OF TEXAS MED BRANCH 301 UNIVERSITY BOULEVARD GALVESTON, TX 77550 Calcium-dependent inactivation of sarcoplasmic reticulum calcium release
R01AR-39632-03 (GMA) LAWLEY, THOMAS J EMORY UNIVERSITY DERMATOLOGY DPT CLIFTON ROAD ATLANTA, GA 30322 Human dermal endothelial cells in skin disease
R01AR-39639-01A3 (GMA) FEINGOLD, KENNETH R VA MEDICAL CENTER 4150 CLEMENT STREET SAN FRANCISCO, CA 94121 Regulation of epidermal lipid synthesis
R01AR-39643-03 (PHY) PATE, EDWARD F WASHINGTON STATE UNIVERSITY PULLMAN, WA 99164 Analysis of cross-bridge mechanics
R29AR-39651-03 (EDC) SOWERS, MARY F UNIVERSITY OF MICHIGAN 109 OBSERVATORY RM 3037 ANN ARBOR, MI 48109 Effect of lactation on bone
R29AR-39652-03 (PHY) REISER, PETER J UNIVERSITY OF ILLINOIS P.O. BOX 6998 CHICAGO, IL 60680 Factors regulating properties of skeletal muscle
R01AR-39657-03 (EDC) KLEEREKOPER, MICHAEL HENRY FORD HOSPITAL 2799 WEST GRAND BOULEVARD DETROIT, MI 48202 Biochemical markers and bone loss in older women
R29AR-39658-02 (GMA) FALANGA, VINCENT UNIVERSITY OF MIAMI PO BOX 016250 MIAMI, FL 33101 Transforming growth factor-beta & scleroderma
P01AR-39674-03 (AMS) LAZARUS, GERALD S 422 CURIE BLVD PHILADELPHIA, PA 19104-6142 Proteinases and mediators in cutaneous biology
P01AR-39674-03 0001 (AMS) SCHECHTER, NORMAN M Proteinases and mediators in cutaneous biology Role of serine proteinases from mast cells and skin
P01AR-39674-03 0002 (AMS) LAVKER, ROBERT M Proteinases and mediators in cutaneous biology Modulation of skin mast cells and their microenvironment
P01AR-39674-03 0003 (AMS) JENSEN, PAMELA J Proteinases and mediators in cutaneous biology Keratinocyte plasminogen activator system
P01AR-39674-03 0004 (AMS) LAZARUS, GERALD S Proteinases and mediators in cutaneous biology The role of proteinases in cutaneous disease
P01AR-39674-03 9001 (AMS) MURPHY, GEORGE F Proteinases and mediators in cutaneous biology Morphology--Core
P01AR-39674-03 9002 (AMS) JENSEN, PAMELA J Proteinases and mediators in cutaneous biology Tissue culture--Core
P01AR-39674-03 9003 (AMS) SCHECHTER, NORMAN M Proteinases and mediators in cutaneous biology Instrument--Core
R29AR-39677-03 (CTY) YABLONKA-REUVENI, ZIPORA UNIVERSITY OF WASHINGTON DPT OF BIOLOGICAL STRUCTURE SM SEATTLE, WA 98195 Skeletal muscle satellite cell
R29AR-39678-03 (CTY) KARGACIN, GARY J UNIV OF MASSACHUSETTS MED SCH 55 LAKE AVENUE NORTH WORCESTER, MA 01655 Structural organization of contracting smooth muscle
R01AR-39682-03 (GMA) STRICKLIN, GEORGE P VA MEDICAL CENTER 1310 24TH AVENUE SOUTH NASHVILLE, TN 37212 Extracellular matrix degradation in skin
R01AR-39683-03 (ORTH) WOO, SAVIO L-Y UNIVERSITY OF PITTSBURGH 986 SCAIFE HALL PITTSBURGH,PA 15261 Structure and function of anterior cruciate ligament
R29AR-39684-03 (ORTH) LITSKY, ALAN S DAVIS MEDICAL RESEARCH CENTER WEST NINTH AVENUE COLUMBUS, OH 43210 Bone-cement interface biomechanics
R01AR-39688-02 (NTN) LIPKIN, EDWARD W UNIVERSITY OF WASHINGTON MAIL STOP RG-26 SEATTLE, WA 98195 Mechanisms of parenteral nutrition associated bone loss
R29AR-39691-03 (GMA) FISHER, GARY J UNIVERSITY OF MICHIGAN KRESG I, R6558/0528 ANN ARBOR, MI 48109 Phospholipase C /protein kinase C in psoriatic epidermis
R29AR-39700-04 (PHY) HUDSON, RANDALL L UNIVERSITY OF ILLINOIS BOX 6998 CHICAGO, IL 60680 Mechanism of calcium mineralization
R01AR-39703-03 (ORTH) GROOD, EDWARD S UNIVERSITY OF CINCINNATI CINCINNATI, OH 45221-0627 In-vivo knee ligament forces
R01AR-39705-03 (PBC) PACIFICI, MAURIZIO UNIVERSITY OF PENNSYLVANIA 4001 SPRUCE ST PHILADELPHIA, PA 19104 Control of type X collagen gene expression
R29AR-39706-02 (ORTH) PACIFICI, ROBERTO THE JEWISH HOSP OF ST LOUIS 216 SOUTH KINGSHIGHWAY BLVD ST LOUIS, MO 63110 The role of interleukin-1 in human osteoporosis
R01AR-39708-04 (ORTH) BURR, DAVID B INDIANA UNIVERSITY SCH OF MED 635 BARNHILL DRIVE INDIANAPOLIS, IN 46202-5120 Prevention of stress fractures in bone
R01AR-39710-03 (BBCB) MENDELSON, ROBERT A, JR UNIVERSITY OF CALIFORNIA 3RD & PARNASSUS AVE SAN FRANCISCO, CA 94143-0524 Neutron diffraction studies of muscle contraction
R29AR-39715-03 (EDC) GORDON, NEIL F INSTITUTE FOR AEROBICS RESEARC 12330 PRESTON ROAD DALLAS, TX 75230 Musculoskeletal fitness and health
R29AR-39722-03 (CTY) PRIESS, JAMES R, JR 1124 COLUMBIA STREET SEATTLE, WA 98104 Muscle cell determination in C. elegans embryos
R29AR-39724-03 (GMA) POLAKOWSKA, RENATA R UNIVERSITY OF ROCHESTER DEPARTMENT OF DERMATOLOY ROCHESTER, NY 14642 Epidermal trans-acting factors in skin development
R01AR-39726-03 (BM) RANK, ROGER G UNIVERSITY OF ARKANSAS DEPT OF MICROBIOLOGY/IMMUNOLOG LITTLE ROCK, ARK 72205 Immunopathology of chlamydia--induced reactive arthritis
R01AR-39728-03 (PHY) YATES, LAWRENCE D OKLAHOMA STATE UNIVERSITY 104 ANIMAL SCIENCE BLDG STILLWATER, OK 74078 Pathways in calcium regulation of muscle contraction
R29AR-39730-03 (GMA) RESING, KATHERYN A UNIVERSITY OF WASHINGTON SEATTLE, WA 98195 Protein processing in epidermal differentiation
R01AR-39737-01A1 (ORTH) MARKS, SANDY C, JR UNIV OF MASSACHUSETTS MED CTR 55 LAKE AVE NORTH WORCESTER, MA 01655 Vitamin D and bone modeling
P01AR-39740-03 (AMS) JIMENEZ, SERGIO A RHEUMATOLOGY RESEARCH LABS 1020 LOCUST STREET, RM M-46 PHILADELPHIA, PA 19107 Molecular biology of heritable osteoarthritis
P01AR-39740-03 0001 (AMS) KNOWLTON, ROBERT G Molecular biology of heritable osteoarthritis Genetic linkage analysis of heritable osteoarthritis
P01AR-39740-03 0002 (AMS) JIMENEZ, SERGIO A Molecular biology of heritable osteoarthritis Genetic defects in biosynthesis of cartilage collagens in OA
P01AR-39740-03 0003 (AMS) PROCKOP, DARWIN J Molecular biology of heritable osteoarthritis Analysis of mutated genes causing heritable OA
P01AR-39740-03 0004 (AMS) PROCKOP, DARWIN J Molecular biology of heritable osteoarthritis Expression of mutated procollagen genes in transgenic mice
P01AR-39740-03 9001 (AMS) UITTO, JOUNI Molecular biology of heritable osteoarthritis Core-cartilage collagen gene clones, constructs and sequences
P01AR-39740-03 9002 (AMS) BASHEY, REZA I Molecular biology of heritable osteoarthritis Core--Tissue culture
P01AR-39740-03 9003 (AMS) BALDWIN, CLINTON T Molecular biology of heritable osteoarthritis Molecular biology and DNA repository--Core
R01AR-39741-03 (GMA) COUCHMAN, JOHN R UNIVERSITY OF ALABAMA ROOM 762 DIABETES HOSPITAL BIRMINGHAM, AL 35294 Fibronectin and skin development
R01AR-39742-02 (BIO) BAKER, RODNEY C UNIV OF COLORADO HLTH SCI CENT 4200 E 9TH AVENUE DENVER, CO 80262 Biotransformation of platelet activating factor
R01AR-39743-03 (GMB) PARTRIDGE, NICOLA C PEDIATRIC RESEARCH INSTITUTE 3662 PARK AVENUE ST LOUIS, MO 63110 Parathyroid hormone regulation of osteoblastic mRNA
P30AR-39749-04 (AMS) FREEDBERG, IRWIN M NEW YORK UNIV MEDICAL CENTER 550 FIRST AVENUE NEW YORK, NY 10016 Skin diseases research center
P30AR-39749-04 9001 (AMS) LIM, HENRY Skin diseases research center Biological response modifier--Core
P30AR-39749-04 9002 (AMS) SUN, TUNG-TIEN Skin diseases research center Cell and tissue culture-Core
P30AR-39749-04 9003 (AMS) BYSTRYN, JEAN-CLAUDE Skin diseases research center Immunofluorescence-Core
P30AR-39749-04 9004 (AMS) BLUMENBERG, MIROSLAV Skin diseases research center Molecular biology-Core
P30AR-39750-04 (AMS) BICKERS, DAVID R CASE WESTERN RESERVE UNIV DEPARTMENT OF DERMATOLOGY CLEVELAND, OHIO 44106 Skin diseases research center of Northeast Ohio
R01AR-39754-03 (BBCA) THOMAS, DAVID D UNIVERSITY OF MINNESOTA 435 DELAWARE STREET SE MINNEAPOLIS, MN 55455 Time resolved EPR spectroscopy of muscle
R01AR-39760-03 (MEP) HAYES, WILSON C BETH ISRAEL HOSPITAL 330 BROOKLINE AVENUE BOSTON, MA 02215 Multiscan photon absorptiometry and osteoporotic fracture
R29AR-39761-03 (SSS) MORRISON, LYNNE H OREGON HEALTH SCIENCE UNIV 3181 S W SAM JACKSON PARK ROAD PORTLAND, OR 97201 Herpes gestationis antigen/autoantibody system
R01AR-39787-01A2 (RAP) MANOHAR, MURLI UNIVERSITY OF ILLINOIS 212 LARGE ANIMAL CLINIC URBANA, IL 61801 Respiratory muscle energetics during exercise
R01AR-39794-03 (EDC) BAUER, RICHARD L UNIV OF TEXAS HLTH SCI CTR 7703 FLOYD CURL DRIVE SAN ANTONIO, TX 78284 Osteoporosis in Mexican Americans and nonhispanic whites
R29AR-39795-01A1 (GMA) BIGBY, MICHAEL E MASSACHUSETTS GENERAL HOSPITAL 149 13TH ST CHARLESTOWN, MA 02129 Use of T-cell hybridomas to study cutaneous immunology
R01AR-39799-01A2 (GMA) LOTZ, MARTIN K UNIV OF CALIFORNIA, SAN DIEGO LA JOLLA, CA 92039 Pathogenetic mediators in arthritis
R29AR-39801-03 (BBCB) LERNER, LAURA E UNIVERSITY OF WISCONSIN 1101 UNIVERSITY AVE MADISON, WI 53706 An nmr study of proteoglycan aggregate components
R01AR-39807-02 (EDC) GRISSO, JEANE A UNIVERSITY OF PENNSYLVANIA 317R NURSING EDUCATION BLDG PHILADELPHIA, PA 19104-6095 A case-control study of risk factors for hip fracture
R01AR-39818-03 (RNM) OLERUD, JOHN E UNIVERSITY OF WASHINGTON DIVISION OF DERMATOLOGY, RM-14 SEATTLE, WA 98195 Ultrasonic assessment of surgical wounds
R29AR-39827-03 (ORTH) SUMNER, DALE R RUSH-PRESBYTERIAN-ST LUKE'S 1653 WEST CONGRESS PARKWAY CHICAGO, IL 60612 Bone ingrowth/remodeling in cementless knee arthroplasty
R01AR-39828-01A1 (ORTH) BIEWENER, ANDREW A UNIVERSITY OF CHICAGO 1025 E 57TH ST RM 400 CHICAGO, IL 60637 Effect of exercise on bone modeling during growth
R01AR-39831-01A1 (GMA) ROBBINS, DICK L UNIVERSITY OF CALIFORNIA DAVIS, CA 95616 The molecular genetic basis of RF in RA
R29AR-39836-02 (GEN) BENIAN, GUY M EMORY UNIVERSITY SCHOOL OF MED PATH, RM 717 WOODRUFF MEM BLDG ATLANTA, GA 30322 Studies of unc-22 protein of C. elegans muscle
R29AR-39837-04 (PBC) COHN, DANIEL H CEDARS-SINAI MEDICAL CENTER BOX 48750-MEDICAL GENETICS LOS ANGELES, CA 90048 Genetic and molecular basis of osteogenesis imperfecta
R01AR-39848-02 (GMA) HALABAN, RUTH YALE UNIVERSITY SCH OF MEDICIN 333 CEDAR ST, PO BOX 3333 NEW HAVEN, CT 06510 Genes involved in albinism and partial albinism
R01AR-39849-03 (CTY) OLSON, ERIC N UNIVERSITY OF TEXAS 1515 HOLCOMBE BLVD HOUSTON, TX 77030 Regulation of myoblast differentiation
R29AR-39854-03 (ORTH) PELKER, RICHARD R YALE UNIVERSITY DEPT OF ORTHOPAEDICS NEW HAVEN, CT 06510 Fracture healing - effects of radiation
R01AR-39860-03 (CTY) HAM, RICHARD G UNIVERSITY OF COLORADO DEPT OF MOLECULAR/CELL/DEV BIO BOULDER, CO 80309-0347 Control of human

muscle cell growth and differentiation

R01AR-39869-03 (GMA) LERNER, AARON B YALE UNIVERSITY SCHOOL OF MED 333 CEDAR STREET NEW HAVEN, CT 06510 Studies on vitiligo, melanomas and albinism

R01AR-39870-04 (ORTH) SHAPIRO, JAY R JOHNS HOPKINS UNIVERSITY 4940 EASTERN AVE BALTIMORE, MD 21224 Collagen metabolism in osteogenesis imperfecta osteoblasts

R29AR-39872-03 (RAP) ESSIG, DAVID A UNIVERSITY OF ILLINOIS AT CHIC PO BOX 4348/PHYSICAL EDUC DEPT CHICAGO, IL 60680 Induction of aminolevulinic acid synthase by exercise

R01AR-39875-03 (GMA) DAVID, CHELLA S MAYO FOUNDATION 200 FIRST STREET SOUTHWEST ROCHESTER, MN 55905 Enterobacteria in HLA-B27 linked spondyloarthropathies

R29AR-39876-01A3 (OBM) POPOFF, STEVEN N TEMPLE UNIVERSITY SCHOOL OF ME 3400 NORTH BROAD STREET PHILADELPHIA, PA 19140 Bone resorption-- Immune and endocrine relationships

R15AR-39887-01A2 (HED) DIBENNARDO, ROBERT LEHMAN COLLEGE 250 BEDFORD PARK BLVD, WEST BRONX, NY 10468 Age related closure of the lumbosacral vertebral laminae

R01AR-39892-03 (MGN) SPRITZ, RICHARD A UNIVERSITY OF WISCONSIN 445 HENRY MALL 317 LAB OF GENE MADISON, WI 53706 Genetic studies of oculocutaneous albinism

R15AR-39893-01A2 (RAP) HOYT, DONALD F CALIFORNIA STATE POLYTECH UNIV 3801 WEST TEMPLE AVENUE POMONA, CA 91768 Detraining in hibernators

R01AR-39894-02 (RAP) FITTS, ROBERT H MARQUETTE UNIVERSITY 530 NORTH FIFTEENTH STREET MILWAUKEE, WI 53233 Exercise-induced changes in single muscle fiber function

R15AR-39905-01A2 (GMA) BOWERS, ROGER R CALIFORNIA STATE UNIVERSITY 5151 STATE UNIVERSITY DR LOS ANGELES, CA 90032 Dominant white (I) gene of chickens -- Model for vitiligo

R01AR-39910-02 (ALY) HASHIMOTO, YASUHIRO UNIVERSITY OF PENNSYLVANIA PHILADELPHIA, PA 19104-6082 Gene regulation of normal and autoimmune T cell receptor

R01AR-39915-03 (ARR) DUVIC, MADELEINE UNIVERSITY OF TEXAS MEDICAL SC 6431 FANNIN HOUSTON, TX 77030 Pathogenesis of AIDS/HIV associated psoriasis

R29AR-39918-03 (GMA) MILNER, ERIC C VIRGINIA MASON RESEARCH CENTER 1000 SENECA STREET SEATTLE, WA 98101 Antibody vh gene selection in rheumatoid arthritis

R01AR-39921-01A1 (EDC) LIANG, MATTHEW H BRIGHAM & WOMEN'S HOSPITAL 75 FRANCIS STREET BOSTON, MA 02115 Modifiable risk factors in Blacks with systemic lupus erythematosus

R01AR-39922-03 (RAP) TROTTER, JOHN A UNIVERSITY OF NEW MEXICO DEPT OF ANATOMY/ SCH OF MED ALBURQUERQUE, NM 87131 Long muscles with series fibers -- Ultrastructural analysis

R01AR-39939-03 (BM) STEINMAN, CHARLES R SUNY AT STONY BROOK SCHOOL OF MEDICINE STONY BROOK, N Y 11794-8161 Eubacterial infection in idiopathic human disease

R15AR-39940-01A2 (ORTH) NELSON, DAVID A MICHIGAN TECH UNIVERSITY 1400 TOWNSEND AVE HOUGHTON, MI 49931 Analysis of hyperthermia of giant cell tumors of bone

R01AR-39950-02 (IMS) AREND, WILLIAM P UNIV OF COLORADO HLTH SCI CTR 4200 E 9TH AVENUE, BOX B 115 DENVER, CO 80262 Regulation of IL-1 beta and IL-1 inhibitor gene expression

R01AR-39959-03 (GMA) EPSTEIN, ERVIN H, JR SAN FRANCISCO GENERAL HOSPITAL 1001 POTRERO STREET SAN FRANCISCO, CA 94110 Basal cell carcinoma--Cloning of a tumor suppressor gene

R01AR-39965-03 (ORTH) SHAPIRO, FREDERIC D CHILDREN'S HOSPITAL 300 LONGWOOD AVENUE BOSTON, MA 02115 Cell-cell communication in cortical bone repair

R29AR-39974-02 (RAP) BALON, THOMAS W UNIVERSITY OF IOWA FIELD HOUSE 506B IOWA CITY, IA 52242 Exercise and hormonal regulation of muscle metabolism

R01AR-39979-03 (GMA) GLASS, DAVID N CHILDREN'S HOSPITAL MED CENTER ELLAND AND BETHESDA AVENUES CINCINNATI, OH 45229-2899 Pauci juvenile rheumatoid arthritis--HLA gene DNA

R01AR-39993-03 (IMS) KURNICK, JAMES T PATHOLOGY RESEARCH LABORATORY 149 13TH ST 7TH FL CHARLESTOWN, MA 02129 Clonal dominance of T-Lymphocytes in arthritis

R01AR-39998-03 (RAP) VANDENBURGH, HERMAN H MIRIAM HOSPITAL 164 SUMMIT AVE PROVIDENCE, RI 02906 Prostaglandins and skeletal muscle hypertrophy

R29AR-40001-03 (GMA) OETTING, WILLIAM S UNIVERSITY OF MINNESOTA HOSP 420 DELAWARE ST/BOX 485 MINNEAPOLIS, MN 55455 Molecular biology of dopachrome oxidoreductase

R01AR-40004-03 (ORTH) DAVY, DWIGHT T CASE WESTERN RESERVE UNIVERSIT 2040 ADELBERT ROAD CLEVELAND, OH 44106 Patellar geometry and knee extensor mechanics

R29AR-40015-03 (CTY) BURGHES, ARTHUR M OHIO STATE UNIVERSITY HOSPITAL 1654 UPHAM DRIVE COLUMBIA, OH 43210 Determination of proteins associated with dystrophin

R29AR-40016-03 (GMA) ELDER, JAMES T UNIVERSITY OF MICHIGAN MED SCH C560A MSRBII, BOX 0672 ANN ARBOR, MI 48109-0672 TGF-alpha and tyrosine kinase activation in psoriasis

R01AR-40018-01A2 (GMA) ANHALT, GRANT J JOHNS HOPKINS UNIVERSITY 600 N WOLFE ST BALTIMORE, MD 21205 Characterization of the pemphigus foliaceus antigen

R29AR-40022-02 (GMA) HICKOK, NOREEN J THOMAS JEFFERSON UNIVERSITY 1020 LOCUST STREET PHILADELPHIA, PA 19107 Keratinocytes--Modulation by retinoic acid

R01AR-40029-03 (ORTH) HOGAN, NEVILLE MASSACHUSETTS INST OF TECHNOLO 77 MASSACHUSETTS AVENUE CAMBRIDGE, MA 02139 Study of tool use by amputees and able persons

R01AR-40032-03 (ORTH) RATCLIFFE, ANTHONY COLUMBIA UNIVERSITY 630 WEST 168TH ST NEW YORK, NY 10032 Cartilage turnover in disease models of disuse and osteoarthritis

R01AR-40036-01A1 (ORTH) MANN, ROBERT W MASS INSTITUTE OF TECHNOLOGY 77 MASSACHUSETTS AVENUE CAMBRIDGE, MA 02139 In vivo measure versus dynamic estimate of hip force

R01AR-40042-02 (GMA) BERGSTRESSER, PAUL R UNIV OF TEXAS SW MEDICAL CENTE 5323 HARRY HINES BLVD DALLAS, TX 75235-9069 Modulation of langerhans cell function by UVB radiation

R01AR-40046-01A1 (PBC) RAO, VELIDI UNIVERSITY OF NEBRASKA MED CTR 42ND AND DEWEY AVE OMAHA, NE 68105 The pathogenesis of osteogenesis imperfecta

R01AR-40050-03 (ORTH) LIEBER, RICHARD L VETERANS ADMINISTRATION MED CT 3350 LAJOLLA VILLAGE DRIVE SAN DIEGO, CA 92161 Muscle injury--mechanism, prevention and treatment

R01AR-40056-03 (RAP) GONYEA, WILLIAM J UNIV OF TX SOUTHWESTERN MED CT 5323 HARRY HINES BLVD DALLAS, TEX 75235 Cellular mechanisms for muscle fiber proliferation

R01AR-40057-03 (EDC) WARD, R H UNIVERSITY OF UTAH MED SCHOOL 501 WINTROBE BLDG/50 N MEDICAL SALT LAKE CITY, UT 84132 Genetic epidemiology of rheumatoid arthritis in Utah

R01AR-40064-03 (ORTH) STRATES, BASIL S UNIVERSITY OF FLORIDA 1600 SW ARCHER RD GAINESVILLE, FL 32610 Bone induction and repair enhancement--Modes and modulations

R01AR-40065-03 (GMA) NICKOLOFF, BRIAN J UNIVERSITY OF MICHIGAN 1301 CATHERINE ROAD ANN ARBOR, MI 48109-0602 Role of adhesion molecules in psoriasis

R01AR-40072-02 (GMA) CRAFT, JOSEPH E YALE UNIVERSITY 333 CEDAR STREET NEW HAVEN, CT 06510 Molecular characterization of the Sm snRNP polypeptides

R01AR-40073-03 (OBM) HOROWITZ, MARK C YALE UNIVERSITY, SCH OF MED 333 CEDAR ST NEW HAVEN, CT 06510 Mechanisms of osteoblast activation and regulation

R01AR-40075-02 (OBM) LEBOY, PHOEBE S UNIVERSITY OF PENNSYLVANIA 4001 SPRUCE STREET PHILADELPHIA, PA 19104 Regulation of mineralization in chondrocyte cultures

R01AR-40080-03 (CTY) MOON, RANDALL T UNIVERSITY OF WASHINGTON SEATTLE, WA 98195 Inhibition of nonerythroid spectrin by antisense RNA

R01AR-40093-02 (GMA) STOKES, IAN A UNIVERSITY OF VERMONT GIVEN MEDICAL BLDG BURLINGTON, VT 05405 Analysis and simulation of surgical spinal fusion

R01AR-40095-03 (BBCB) BOREJDO, JULIAN BAYLOR RESEARCH FOUNDATION 3500 GASTON AVENUE DALLAS, TX 75246 Rotation of myosin cross-bridges in skeletal muscles

R44AR-40113-02 (SSS) PEARSON, GLENN F CIVILIZED SOFTWARE, INC 7735 OLD GEORGETOWN ROAD BETHESDA, MD 20814 Improved foot controllers for personal computers

R01AR-40124-03 (GMA) KUPPER, THOMAS S WASHINGTON UNIV SCHOOL OF MED 660 SOUTH EUCLID AVENUE ST LOUIS, MO 63110 Role of Il-1 receptors in cutaneous disease

R01AR-40135-02 (GMA) AREND, WILLIAM P UNIVERSITY OF COLORADO HSC 4200 EAST NINTH AVENUE, B 115 DENVER, CO 80262 Role of interleukin-1 inhibitor--Inflammatory synovitis

R01AR-40138-01A2 (GMA) COOPER, SHELDON M UNIVERSITY OF VERMONT BURLINGTON, VT 05405 Clonality and TCR genes of RA and Lyme synovial T cells

R29AR-40152-02 (PBC) BALDWIN, CLINTON T BOSTON UNIVERSITY SCH MED 801 COMMONWEALTH AVENUE BOSTON, MA 02215 Defective proteoglycans in osteoarthritis

R29AR-40155-01A1 (RAP) HOGAN, MICHAEL C UNIV OF CALIFORNIA, SAN DIEGO DIVISION OF PHYSIOLOGY, M-023A LA JOLLA, CA 92093-0623 Determinants of muscle maximal 02 uptake and performance

R29AR-40159-02 (IMS) ROKEACH, LUIS A AGOURON INSTITUTE 505 CAST BOULEVARD SOUTH LA JOLLA, CALIFORNIA 92037 Autoantigens and rheumatic disease

R01AR-40166-01A2 (ORTH) GOEL, VIJAY K UNIVERSITY OF IOWA IOWA CITY, IA 52242 Mechanics of spine surgery--A finite element analysis

R01AR-40169-01A2 (EDC) SPECKER, BONNY L UNIV OF CINCINNATI/COLL OF MED 231 BETHESDA AVE CINCINNATI, OH 45267-0541 Effect of race and activity on infant calcium status

R01AR-40174-02 (ORTH) JOHNSON, ROBERT J UNIVERSITY OF VERMONT GIVEN BLDG BURLINGTON, VT 05405 In vivo strain measurement of reconstructed ac ligament

R01AR-40176-02 (ORTH) MINKIN, CEDRIC UNIV OF SOUTHERN CALIFORNIA UNIVERSITY PARK MC-0641 LOS ANGELES, CA 90089-0641 Systemic and local regulation of osteoclast ontogeny

R29AR-40184-03 (PBC) BENNETT, VICKIE DEE THOMAS JEFFERSON UNIVERSITY 1015 WALNUT STREET PHILADELPHIA, PA 19107 Functions of alternatively spliced cartilage fibronectin

R01AR-40185-02 (GMB) BARON, ROLAND E YALE UNIV SCHOOL OF MEDICINE 333 CEDAR STREET NEW HAVEN, CT 06510 Bone formation and anion exchange in osteoblasts

R01AR-40190-02 (BBCA) SHRIVER, JOHN W SOUTHERN ILLINOIS UNIVERSITY CHEMISTRY & BIOCHEMSITRY DEPT. CARBONDALE, IL 62901 DSC of immobilized proteins

R01AR-40191-03 (ORTH) RIMNAC, CLARE M HOSPITAL FOR SPECIAL SURGERY 535 EAST 70TH STREET NEW YORK, NY 10021 Degradation in polyethylene joint components

R01AR-40194-01A1 (ORTH) DUCHEYNE, PAUL UNIVERSITY OF PENNSYLVANIA 220 S 33RD STREET PHILADELPHIA, PA 19104 Mechanisms of ion release from titanium and its alloys

R01AR-40197-01A1 (CTY) WALSH, KENNETH CASE WESTERN RESERVE UNIVERSIT 2119 ABINGTON ROAD CLEVELAND, OH 44106 Molecular control during myogenesis

R01AR-40199-02 (ORTH) COLE, KELLY J UNIVERSITY OF IOWA S501 FIELD HOUSE IOWA CITY, IA 52242 Properties of knee ligament mechanoreceptive afferents

R01AR-40217-02 (ORTH) DARLING, WARREN G UNIVERSITY OF IOWA 506A FIELD HOUSE IOWA CITY, IA 52242 Control of index finger movements

R29AR-40225-02 (PC) KESTER, MARK CASE WESTERN RESERVE UNIV 2040 ADELBERT RD CLEVELAND, OH 44106 Endogenous diradylglycerols in smooth muscle cell types

R01AR-40227-02 (GMA) STROBER, SAMUEL STANFORD UNIVERSITY DIVISION OF IMMUNOLOGY STANFORD, CA 94305 In vitro model of rheumatoid arthritis

R01AR-40231-01A2 (ORTH) HANGARTNER, THOMAS N WRIGHT STATE UNIVERSITY ONE WYOMING STREET DAYTON, OH 45409 Bone density changes in spinal-cord injured patients

R01AR-40234-02 (PHY) MAUGHAN, DAVID W UNIVERSITY OF VERMONT BURLINGTON, VT 05405 Contractile properties of mutant drosophila muscle

R29AR-40239-02 (GMA) HILLSON, JAN L UNIVERSITY OF WASHINGTON SEATTLE, WA 98195 Origin of rheumatoid factors and molecular cloning
R01AR-40240-02 (GMA) ROOP, DENNIS R BAYLOR COLLEGE OF MEDICINE ONE BAYLOR PLAZA HOUSTON, TX 77030 Regulation and function of a major cell envelope protein
R01AR-40242-01A2 (ORTH) LINSCHEID, RONALD L MAYO FOUNDATION 200 FIRST STREET SOUTHWEST ROCHESTER, MN 55905 Biomechanics of the normal and pathological wrist
R01AR-40243-02 (PHY) HEINY, JUDITH A UNIVERSITY OF CINCINNATI CINCINNATI, OH 45267-0576 Optical studies of T-system function in E-C coupling
R29AR-40246-02 (PHY) BLOCK, BARBARA A UNIVERSITY OF CHICAGO 1025 E 57TH STREET CHICAGO, IL 60637 Excitation-thermogenic coupling/heat producing muscles
R01AR-40248-02 (MGN) KWON, BYOUNG S INDIANA UNIVERSITY SCH OF MED 635 BARNHILL DRIVE, MS 255 INDIANAPOLIS, IN 46202 - 5120 Melanin biosynthesis and oculocutaneous albinism
R01AR-40252-02 (BBCA) PHILLIPS, GEORGE N, JR RICE UNIVERSITY P O BOX 1892 HOUSTON, TX 77251 Structural determinates of ligand binding to myoglobin
R29AR-40253-02 (ORTH) RAPUANO, BRUCE EDWARD HOSPITAL FOR SPECIAL SURGERY 535 EAST 70TH STREET NEW YORK, NY 10021 Control of prostaglandins and cancer-mediated osteolysis
R01AR-40259-02 (PHY) HAEBERLE, JOE R UNIVERSITY OF VERMONT GIVEN BUILDING BURLINGTON, VT 05405 Caldesmon and regulation of smooth muscle contraction
R44AR-40278-02 (SSS) LESIECKI, MICHAEL CANDELA LASER CORPORATION 530 BOSTON POST ROAD WAYLAND, MA 01778 Percutaneous laser diskectomy
R29AR-40284-02 (GMA) ALLEN-HOFFMANN, B LYNN 5638 MEDICAL SCIENCES CENTER MADISON, WI 53706 Regulation of differentiation in human epithelial cells
R01AR-40300-01 (CTY) BRANDT, PHILIP W COLUMBIA UNIVERSITY 630 WEST 168TH STREET NEW YORK, N Y 10032 Cooperativity between thin filament regulatory proteins
R55AR-40301-01A1 (GMA) BERTOLINO, ARTHUR P NEW YORK UNIVERSITY MED CTR 550 FIRST AVE NEW YORK, NY 10016 Hair keratin expression and gene regulation
R01AR-40310-02 (ORTH) GLANT, TIBOR T RUSH-PRESBYTERIAN-ST LUKES 1653 WEST CONGRESS PARKWAY CHICAGO, IL 60612-3864 Study of autoimmune progressive polyarthritis
R01AR-40312-02 (GMA) MODLIN, ROBERT L UNIVERSITY OF CALIFORNIA 10833 LE CONTE AVENUE LOS ANGELES, CA 90024-1750 T-lymphocyte receptor gamma/delta lymphocytes in human skin lesions
R01AR-40321-01A1 (ORTH) HAYES, WILSON C BETH ISRAEL HOSPITAL 330 BROOKLINE AVENUE BOSTON, MA 02215 Fall biomechanics and hip fracture risk
R01AR-40324-02 (GMA) SUNDBERG, JOHN P THE JACKSON LABORATORY 600 MAIN STREET BAR HARBOR, ME 04609 Flaky skin mouse--a papulosquamous disease
R55AR-40325-01A1 (ORTH) ROSIER, RANDY N UNIV OF ROCHESTER 601 ELMWOOD AVE ROCHESTER, NY 14642 Autocrine and ionic regulation of chondrocyte phenotype
R01AR-40330-01A2 (RAP) MARKOLF, KEITH L UNIVERSITY OF CALIFORNIA 405 HILGARD AVENUE LOS ANGELES, CA 90024 In vitro measurements of cruciate ligament forces
R01AR-40335-02 (PBC) DE CROMBRUGGHE, BENOIT U OF TEXAS SYSTEM CANCER CTR 1515 HOLCOMBE HOUSTON, TEXAS 77030 Functional analysis of collagens in transgenic mice
R01AR-40339-02 (CTY) OLSON, ERIC N UNIVERSITY OF TEXAS 1515 HOLCOMBE BLVD HOUSTON, TX 77030 Genes that regulate myogenesis
R01AR-40342-03 (RAP) GLADDEN, L BRUCE AUBURN UNIVERSITY 2050 JOEL H EAVES-MEM COLISEUM AUBURN UNIVERSITY, AL 36849 Factors determining lactate uptake by skeletal muscle
R01AR-40343-03 (ORTH) TIDBALL, JAMES G UNIVERSITY OF CALIFORNIA 405 HILGARD AVENUE LOS ANGELES, CA 90024-1568 Myotendinous junctions--adaptations to exercise and disuse
R01AR-40364-02 (ORTH) CATERSON, BRUCE UNIVERSITY OF NORTH CAROLINA CB #7055 CHAPEL HILL, NC 27599-7055 Proteoglycan metabolism in osteoarthritis
R01AR-40391-02 (IMS) REEVES, WESTLEY H UNIVERSITY OF NORTH CAROLINA 932 FLOB CB# 7280 CHAPEL HILL, NC 27599-7280 Mechanisms of autoantibody production in systemic lupus erythematosus
R01AR-40393-01A1 (ORTH) NUNAMAKER, DAVID M UNIVERSITY OF PENNSYLVANIA 382 WEST STREET ROAD KENNETT SQUARE, PA 19348 Fatigue of bone relationships to exercise
R01AR-40404-01A1 (GMA) BIGLER, ROBERT D HAHNEMANN UNIVERSITY BROAD & VINE PHILADELPHIA, PA 19102-1192 Anti-idiotype antibodies in cutaneous T cell lymphoma
R29AR-40408-02 (ORTH) BUCHANAN, THOMAS S REHAB INSTITUTE OF CHICAGO 345 EAST SUPERIOR STREET CHICAGO, IL 60611 Biomechanics of muscle control during static postures
R29AR-40409-01A1 (GMA) TUAN, TAI-LAN ORTHOPAEDIC HOSPITAL 2400 SOUTH FLOWER STREET LOS ANGELES, CA 90007 Fibrin gel contraction & matrix synthesis by fibroblasts
R29AR-40410-02 (GMA) GIUDICE, GEORGE J MEDICAL COLLEGE OF WISCONSIN 8701 WATERTOWN PLANK RD BOX265 MILWAUKEE, WI 53226 Hemidesmosomes in bullous pemphigoid
R01AR-40411-01A1 (ECS) BRAND, RICHARD A UNIV OF IOWA HOSPITALS COLLEGE OF MEDICINE IOWA CITY, IA 52242 Mechanical factors initiating bone remodeling
R01AR-40414-01A1 (GMA) SKINNER, MARTHA BOSTON UNIV SCHOOL OF MEDICINE 71 EAST CONCORD STREET BOSTON, MA 02118 Transthyretin in familial amyloidotic polyneuropathy
R01AR-40416-02 (ORTH) RUDDLE, NANCY H YALE UNIVERSITY 225 WHITNEY AVENUE NEW HAVEN, CT. 06520 High bone turnover in HTLV-1 tax transgenic animals
R29AR-40423-01A1 (BEM) CRONAN, THEREASA A SAN DIEGO STATE UNIVERSITY 5300 CAMPNILE DRIVE SAN DIEGO, CA 92182 Social support and health care use in osteoarthritis
R01AR-40425-01A1 (ORTH) RYMER, WILLIAM Z REHABILITATION INST OF CHICAGO 345 EAST SUPERIOR CHICAGO, IL 60611 Mechanism for compensation of neuromuscular fatigue
R01AR-40427-01A1 (ORTH) SPECTOR, MYRON BRIGHAM AND WOMEN'S HOSPITAL 75 FRANCIS STREET BOSTON, MA 02115 Calcium phosphate coating for orthopedic prostheses
R29AR-40428-01A2 (OBM) SILVERTON, SUSAN F UNIVERSITY OF PENNSYLVANIA 4010 LOCUST STREET PHILADELPHIA, PA 19101-6002 Osteoclast activation and carbonic anhydrase
R01AR-40431-02 (EDC) NEVITT, MICHAEL C UNIVERSITY OF CALIFORNIA BOX 0886 SAN FRANCISCO, CA 94143 Osteoarthritis and osteoporosis in elderly women
R01AR-40438-01A1 (IMS) WILLIAMS, RALPH C, JR UNIV OF FLORIDA COLLEGE OF MED BOX J 221 JHMHC GAINESVILLE, FL 32610 Studies of rheumatoid factor specificity
R01AR-40445-02 (AMS) BENACH, JORGE L SUNY AT STONY BROOK STONY BROOK, NY 11794 Borrelia burgdorferi--invasion and chronicity
R01AR-40448-02 (AMS) GOODMAN, JESSE L UNIVERSITY OF MINNESOTA MED SC 516 DELAWARD ST, SE/BOX 250 MINNEAPOLIS, MN 55455 Molecular pathogenesis and diagnosis of Lyme disease
R01AR-40451-02 (EDC) SHAPIRO, EUGENE D YALE UNIV SCHOOL OF MED PO BOX 3333 NEW HAVEN, CT 06510-8064 Prevention of Lyme disease--A randomized clinical trial
R01AR-40452-02 (AMS) MALAWISTA, STEPHEN E YALE UNIVERSITY 333 CEDAR ST, PO BX 3333 NEW HAVEN, CT 06510 Pathogenesis of Lyme disease: Molecular probes
R01AR-40470-02 (AMS) COYLE, PATRICIA K SUNY HEALTH SCIENCES CENTER STONY BROOK, NY 11794 Immune complex analysis in lyme neuroborreliosis
R01AR-40476-02 (AMS) PACHNER, ANDREW R GEORGETOWN UNIVERSITY 37TH AND O STREETS, NW WASHINGTON, DC 20057 Murine lyme borreliosis
R01AR-40488-01A1 (ARRE) NICKOLOFF, BRIAN J UNIVERSITY OF MICHIGAN 1301 CATHERINE RD ANN ARBOR, MI 48109-0602 Dermal dendrocytes and AIDS-related psoriasis
R01AR-40494-02 (RAP) STIREWALT, WILLIAM S UNIVERSITY OF VERMONT GIVEN MEDICAL BLDG D-212 BURLINGTON, VT 05405 Activity induced growth of skeletal muscle
R01AR-40495-02 (AMS) WINCHESTER, ROBERT J HOSPITAL FOR JOINT DISEASES 301 EAST 17TH STREET NEW YORK, NY 10003 Immunogenetic basis of Lyme disease susceptibility
R01AR-40507-01A1 (ORTH) HOROWITZ, MARK C YALE UNIVERSITY, SCH OF MED 333 CEDAR ST NEW HAVEN, CT 06510 Analysis of bone allograft induced alloreactivity
R44AR-40512-02A2 (SSS) MAINIGI, KUSUM K INTERSCIENCES DEVELOPMENT ASSO 3508 MARKET STREET, SUITE 212 PHILADELPHIA, PA 19104 Improved long bone measuring device
R29AR-40514-01A1 (GMA) LONGLEY, BRUCE J YALE UNIVERSITY 333 CEDAR STREET NEW HAVEN, CT 06510 Antigen presenting cells of the skin
R01AR-40520-02 (GMA) DUVIC, MADELEINE UNIVERSITY OF TEXAS MEDICAL SC 6431 FANNIN HOUSTON, TX 77030 Selective manipulation of gene expression in skin
R01AR-40525-02 (IMS) FIRESTEIN, GARY S UNIV OF CALIFORNIA SAN DIEGO 225 DICKINSON STREET SAN DIEGO, CA 92103 Cytokine interactions in inflammatory arthritis
R01AR-40540-01A1 (PHY) CHALOVICH, JOSEPH M EAST CAROLINA UNIVERSITY GREENVILLE, NC 27858 Weakly bound crossbridges in muscle contraction
R01AR-40544-02 (GMA) HOLOSHITZ, JOSEPH UNIVERSITY OF MICHIGAN R4570 KRESGE I ANN ARBOR, MI 48109-0531 T cell clones from rheumatoid arthritic synovial fluid
R01AR-40553-02 (ORTH) WEAVER, CONNIE M PURDUE UNIVERSITY DEPT OF FOODS & NUTRITION WEST LAFAYETTE, IN 47907 Calcium metabolism in adolescent girls and young women
R01AR-40554-01A1 (ORTH) BONE, HENRY G HENRY FORD HOSPITAL 2799 W GRAND BLVD DETROIT, MI 48202 Bone remodeling in Paget's disease
R29AR-40556-02 (PBC) STOLLE, CATHERINE A UMDNJ-ROBERT WOOD JOHNSON MED DIV OF PULMONARY/CRITICAL CARE NEW BRUNSWICK, NJ 08903-0019 Pathobiochemistry of Ehlers-Danlos syndrome Type 1
R01AR-40558-01A1 (ORTH) KOENEMAN, JAMES B HARRINGTON ARTHRITIS RES CTR 1800 EAST VAN BUREN PHOENIX, AZ 85006 Testing of adaptive bone change hypotheses
R29AR-40561-01A1 (IMS) SASSO, ERIC H UNIVERSITY OF WASHINGTON 3935 UNIVERSITY WAY NE, JM-24 SEATTLE, WA 98195 V gene polymorphism in systemic lupus erythematosus and rheumatoid arthritis
R01AR-40574-02 (GMA) PENTLAND, ALICE P WASHINGTON UNIV SCH OF MED 660 SOUTH EUCLID AVENUE ST LOUIS, MO 63110 Mechanisms of enhanced eicosanoid synthesis in UV injury
R01AR-40576-02 (AMS) STEERE, ALLEN C NEW ENGLAND MED CTR HOSP, INC 750 WASHINGTON ST/BOX 406 BOSTON, MA 02111 T and B cell epitopes of B Burgdorferi in Lyme disease
R29AR-40580-01A1 (CVA) WEIR, LAWRENCE ST ELIZABETH'S HOSPITAL 736 CAMBRIDGE STREET BOSTON, MA 02135 Restenosis and the expression of nonmuscle myosin
R01AR-40586-01A1 (GMA) WENSTRUP, RICHARD J DUKE UNIVERSITY MEDICAL CENTER P. O. BOX 3351 DURHAM, NC 27710 Mutational analysis of type I collagen function
R01AR-40593-02 (PHY) HOWARD, JONATHON UNIVERSITY OF WASHINGTON SJ-40 SEATTLE, WA 98195 Mechanics of kinesin--A microtubule-based motor protein
R29AR-40595-01A1 (GMA) MYERS, LINDA K UNIVERSITY OF TENNESSEE 956 COURT AVE MEMPHIS, TN 38163 Immunogenic epitopes of collagen critical in arthritis
R55AR-40598-01A1 (RAP) NOSEK, THOMAS M MEDICAL COLLEGE OF GEORGIA AUGUSTA, GA 30912-3000 Failure of the contractile process in fatigue
R01AR-40601-01A1 (GMA) HOCH, SALLIE O AGOURON INSTITUTE 505 COAST BOULEVARD SOUTH LA JOLLA, CA 92037 Autoimmune antigens and systemic sclerosis
R01AR-40614-01A1 (ORTH) LAU, KIN-HING W JERRY L PETTIS V A HOSPITAL 11201 BENTON STREET LOMA LINDA, CA 92357 Serum osteoclastic acid phosphatase immunoassay
R01AR-40615-01A1 (PHY) WAGENKNECHT, TERENCE C NEW YORK STATE DEPT OF HEALTH EMPIRE STATE PLAZA-PO BOX 509 ALBANY, NY 12201-0509 Structure of channels in excitation-contraction coupling
R01AR-40620-02 (IMS) EISENBERG, ROBERT A UNIV. OF NC AT CHAPEL HILL 932 FLOB CB#7280 CHAPEL HILL, NC 27599 B cells in murine SLE
R43AR-40645-01A1 (SSS) WINGET, RODNER R BIOMARINE TECHNOLOGIES

PROJECT NO., ORGANIZATIONAL UNIT., INVESTIGATOR, ADDRESS, TITLE

INC BOX 20159 SEATTLE, WA 98102 Eicosapentaenoic acid for topical skin disease treatment
R55AR-40655-01A1 (ORTH) BURR, DAVID B INDIANA UNIVERSITY 635 BARNHILL DRIVE INDIANAPOLIS, IN 46202-5120 Bone adaptation--Experimental and theoretical studies
R01AR-40661-01 (ORTH) PARTRIDGE, NICOLA C PEDIATRIC RESEARCH INSTITUTE 3662 PARK AVENUE ST LOUIS, MO 63110 Osteoblast mediated turnover of collagenase in bone
R01AR-40671-01A1 (RNM) WEHRLI, FELIX W UNIVERSITY OF PENNSYLVANIA 308 MEDICAL EDUCATION BUILDING PHILADELPHIA, PA 19104-6086 Evaluation of trabecular bone marrow by MR
R29AR-40672-01 (GMA) HAQQI, TARIQ M CASE WESTERN RESERVE UNIVERSIT 2074 ABINGTON ROAD CLEVELAND, OH 44106 T cell receptor V genes in collagen induced arthritis
R43AR-40673-01A1 (SSS) MAGEE, FRANK P IATROMED, INC 2850 S 36TH STREET PHOENIX, AZ 85040 Electromagnetic stimulation of cartilage tissue
R01AR-40678-01 (GMA) ANSEL, JOHN C VA MEDICAL CENTER 3710 SW US VETERANS HOSPITAL R PORTLAND, OR 97201 Neurokinin activation of normal human keratinocytes
R01AR-40679-01A1 (ORTH) BONADIO, JEFFREY F HOWARD HUGHES MED INST 1150 WEST MEDICAL CENTER DRIVE ANN ARBOR, MI 48109-0650 Transgenic model of osteogenesis imperfecta type I
R29AR-40682-01A1 (CTY) LIM, ROBERT W UNIVERSITY OF MISSOURI ONE HOSPITAL DRIVE COLUMBIA, MO 65212 Growth factor regulation of muscle differentiation
R29AR-40688-02 (ECS) TURNER, CHARLES HALL INDIANA UNIVERSITY 541 CLINICAL DRIVE INSIANAPOLIS, IN 46202-5111 Mechanically induced stimulation of bone formation
R29AR-40689-01A1 (PC) LEACH, ROBIN J UNIV OF TEXAS HLTH SCI CENTER 7703 FLOYD CURL DRIVE SAN ANTONIO, TX 78284 -7762 Regulation of osteoblast specific gene expression
R55AR-40701-01A1 (ORTH) EINHORN, THOMAS A MOUNT SINAI SCHOOL OF MEDICINE ONE GUSTAVE L LEVY PL BOX 1188 NEW YORK, NY 10029-6574 Cytokines in fracture healing
R29AR-40705-01 (ORTH) KOHRT, WENDY M WASHINGTON UNIVERSITY 4566 SCOTT AVE ST LOUIS, MO 63110 Non weight bearing exercise and bone mass in older women
R01AR-40727-01A1 (PHY) POTTER, JAMES D UNIVERSITY OF MIAMI PO BOX 016189 MIAMI, FL 33101 Mutation of skeletal troponin C functional domains
R01AR-40736-01A1 (ORTH) MATKOVICH, VELIMIR OHIO STATE UNIVERSITY 480 W 9TH AVE DAVIS RES CTR COLUMBUS, OH 43212 Calcium on bone mass formation during puberty
R01AR-40740-01 (GMA) CARTER-SU, CHRISTIN UNIVERSITY OF MICHIGAN 1301 CATHERINE STREET ANN ARBOR, MI 48109-0622 Regulation of glucose transport by CTAP-III isoforms
R01AR-40741-01A1 (GMA) ZONANA, JONATHAN OREGON HEALTH SCIENCES UNIV 3181 SW SAM JACKSON PARK ROAD PORTLAND, OR 97201-3098 The ectodermal dysplasias-- Molecular genetic analysis
R01AR-40765-01A1 (MEDB) SAMOLS, DAVID R CASE WESTERN RESERVE UNIV 2119 ABINGTON ROAD CLEVELAND, OH 44106 Studies of the in vivo role of C-reactive protein in transgenic mice
R01AR-40766-01A1 (MEDB) SABINA, RICHARD L 8701 WATERTOWN PLANK ROAD MILWAUKEE, WI 53226 Unique amino domains and AMP deaminase isoform diversity
P60AR-40770-01A1 (AMS) CARSON, DENNIS A UNIV OF CALIFORNIA SAN DIEGO LA JOLLA, CA 92093 Multipurpose arthritis and musculoskeletal diseases center
P60AR-40770-01A1 0001 (AMS) CARRERA, CARLOS J Multipurpose arthritis and musculoskeletal diseases center Effects of CdA on monocyte function and phenotype in RA
P60AR-40770-01A1 0002 (AMS) POLLARD, KENNETH Multipurpose arthritis and musculoskeletal diseases center Evaluation of new animal model of systemic autoimmunity induced by mercuric Cl
P60AR-40770-01A1 0003 (AMS) SILVERMAN, GREGG J Multipurpose arthritis and musculoskeletal diseases center Human humoral response to carbohydrate determinants
P60AR-40770-01A1 0004 (AMS) TIGHE, HELEN P Multipurpose arthritis and musculoskeletal diseases center Transgenic mouse model--RF function and regulation in health and disease
P60AR-40770-01A1 0005 (AMS) BARRETT-CONNOR, ELIZABETH Multipurpose arthritis and musculoskeletal diseases center Predictors of musculoskeletal problems in a retirement community
P60AR-40770-01A1 0006 (AMS) KAPLAN, ROBERT M Multipurpose arthritis and musculoskeletal diseases center Quality of life for arthritis patients in National Health Interview Survey
P60AR-40770-01A1 9001 (AMS) RICE, JOHN A Multipurpose arthritis and musculoskeletal diseases center Biostatistics and evaluation core
P60AR-40770-01A1 9002 (AMS) CHEN, POJEN Multipurpose arthritis and musculoskeletal diseases center Molecular biology core
R01AR-40771-01A1 (RAP) MOSELEY, POPE L UNIVERSITY OF IOWA C33K GENERAL HOSPITAL IOWA CITY, IOWA 52242 Exercise heat and thermotolerance -- Molecular mechanisms
R29AR-40776-01A1 (ORTH) FYHRIE, DAVID P HENRY FORD HOSPITAL 2799 W GRAND BLVD DETROIT, MI 48202 Strength and micro-strain in vertebral trabecular bone
R01AR-40780-01 (CTY) WOLD, BARBARA J CALIFORNIA INST OF TECHNOLOGY 1201 EAST CALIFORNIA BOULEVARD PASADENA, CA 91125 Positive acting regulators of myogenesis
R43AR-40787-01 (SSS) RAMAN, RAMAS V CERACON INCORPORATED 1101 N MARKET BLVD #9 SACRAMENTO, CA 95834 Fabricating high performance prostheses
R43AR-40796-01 (SSS) CARIGNAN, FOREST J ADVANCED MECHANICAL TECH, INC 151 CALIFORNIA ST NEWTON, MA 02158 Foot pressure measurement with hall effect sensors
R43AR-40797-01 (SSS) KLAUSNER, MITCHELL MATTEK CORPORATION 200 HOMER AVENUE ASHLAND, MA 01721 Cell culture surfaces for bone research
R43AR-40799-01 (SSS) CRAINE, ERIC R WESTERN RESEARCH COMPANY, INC 2127 E SPEEDWAY, SUITE 209 TUCSON, AZ 85719 Video comparator for isolation of dermatological lesions
R01AR-40801-02 (PHY) MILTON, RICHARD L BALL STATE UNIVERSITY

PROJECT NO., ORGANIZATIONAL UNIT., INVESTIGATOR, ADDRESS, TITLE

2000 UNIVERSITY AVENUE MUNCIE, IN 47306 Endplate Na channels in skeletal muscle fibers
R43AR-40807-01 (SSS) MOORE, LARRY J EASTERN ANALYTICAL, INC 335 PAINT BRANCH DRIVE COLLEGE PARK, MD 20742 Calcium isotopic analysis using laser autoionization
R13AR-40812-01 (AMS) BARON, ROLAND YALE UNIV SCHOOL OF MEDICINE 333 CEDAR STREET NEW HAVEN, CT 06510 Gordon Research Conference on Cellular and Molecular Biology of Bones
R13AR-40817-01 (AMS) LIPSKY, PETER E U OF TEXAS HLTH SCI CTR/DALLAS 5323 HARRY HINES BLVD DALLAS, TX 75235 Conference on HLA-B27 related disorders
R01AR-40820-01 (GMB) LEE, MINAKO Y UNIVERSITY OF WASHINGTON SM-20 SEATTLE, WA 98195 Tumor cell-derived osteoclast growth factor
R01AR-40824-01 (GMA) ULLRICH, STEPHEN E U T MD ANDERSON CANCER CENTER 1515 HOLCOMBE BOULEVARD, BOX 1 HOUSTON, TX 77030 Keratinocyte-derived immunosuppressive cytokines
R29AR-40829-01 (PBC) HERING, THOMAS M CASE WESTERN RESERVE UNIVERSIT 2074 ABINGTON ROAD CLEVELAND, OH 44106 Cartilage proteoglycan aggregate functional interactions
R13AR-40831-01 (AMS) KEFALIDES, NICHOLAS A CONNECTIVE TISSUE RES INST 3624 MARKET STREET PHILADELPHIA, PA 19104 International Symposium on Basement Membranes
R01AR-40832-01 (ORTH) RECKER, ROBERT R CREIGHTON UNIVERSITY 601 NORTH 30TH ST SUITE 5740 OMAHA, NE 68132 An efficacy trial of calcium in fracture prevention
R01AR-40835-01 (ORTH) KOSHLAND, GAIL F UNIVERSITY OF ARIZONA HEALTH SCIENCES CTR TUCSON, AZ 85724 Muscle activity at onset of human three-joint movement
R55AR-40836-01 (CTY) SALAMA, GUY UNIVERSITY OF PITTSBURGH 3500 TERRACE ST PITTSBURGH, PA 15261 106-kDa Ca2+ release channels in SR
R29AR-40839-01 (CBY) PENG, ISSAC ROBERT WOOD JOHNSON MED SCHOOL 675 HOES LANE PISCATAWAY, NJ 08854 Actin incorporation into myofibrils and nonmuscle filaments
R01AR-40840-01 (CTY) NACHMIAS, VIVIANNE T UNIVERSITY OF PENNSYLVANIA SCHOOL OF MEDICINE PHILADELPHIA, PA 19104-6058 A 5 kDa peptide and its interaction with actin
R29AR-40844-01 (GMA) WOOD, GARY S VETERANS ADMINISTRATION 10701 EAST BOULEVARD CLEVELAND, OH 44106 Analysis of dendritic cell leukocyte common antigen
R01AR-40849-01 (CTY) WILLIAMS, ROBERT S UNIVERSITY OF TEXAS SW MED CTR 5323 HARRY HINES BLVD DALLAS, TX 75235-9013 Molecular genetics of muscle specialization
R29AR-40854-01 (GMA) NAIDES, STANLEY J UNIVERSITY OF IOWA HOSP DIVISION OF RHEUMATOLOGY IOWA CITY, IA 52242 Persistant infection in chronic B19 arthropathy
R01AR-40857-01 (ORTH) BATTIE, MICHELLE C UNIVERSITY OF WASHINGTON SEATTLE, WA 98195 Spine pathology and low back pain determinants in identical twins
R01AR-40864-01 (MGN) CHAMBERLAIN, JEFFREY S UNIVERSITY OF MICHIGAN ANN ARBOR, MI 48109-0618 Dystrophin replacement in mdx mice
R29AR-40873-01 (GMA) ALBERS, KATHRYN M UNIVERSITY OF KENTUCKY 800 ROSE STREET LEXINGTON, KY 40536-0093 Keratin function in epidermal growth and differentiation
R13AR-40887-01 (AMS) RAMIREZ, FRANCESCO B MOUNT SINAI SCHOOL OF MEDICINE ONE GUSTAVE L LEVY PLACE,BOX 1 NEW YORK, NY 10029 Gordon Conference - Structural Macromolecules--Collagen
R15AR-40894-01 (IMS) TYMOCZKO, JOHN L CARLETON COLLEGE ONE NORTH COLLEGE STREET NORTHFIELD, MN 55057 Structure/function study of human autoimmune antigens
R29AR-40901-01 (RAP) THOMASON, DONALD B UNIVERSITY OF TENNESSEE 894 UNION AVE MEMPHIS, TN 38163 Activity-dependent polypeptide elongation in muscle
R13AR-40910-01 (AMS) FOX, C FRED KEYSTONE CENTER PO BOX 606 KEYSTONE, CO 80435 Joint conference on muscle and cardiovascular in biology
R13AR-40911-01 (AMS) FOX, C FRED KEYSTONE CENTER PO BOX 606 KEYSTONE, CO 80435 Conference on immunopathogenesis of rheumatoid arthritis
R15AR-40913-01 (ORTH) KINCAID, STEVEN A COLLEGE OF VETERINARY MEDICINE 109 GREEN HALL AUBURN UNIV, AL 36849-5518 Hyaluronic acid/TGF-B composite to treat osteoarthritis
R15AR-40914-01 (CTY) POWELL, JEANNE A SMITH COLLEGE CLARK SCIENCE CTR NORTHAMPTON, MA 01063 Fusion and nuclear rescue domains in dysgenic mice
R29AR-40917-02 (BBCB) CREMO, CHRISTINE R WASHINGTON STATE UNIVERSITY PULLMAN, WA 99164-4660 Topographical studies of smooth muscle myosin
P01AR-40919-01 (SRC) HAHN, BEVRA H UNIVERSITY OF CALIFORNIA 10833 LE CONTE LOS ANGELES, CA 90024-1736 Molecular interactions mediating autoimmune mechanisms
P01AR-40919-01 0003 (SRC) KLOTZ, JOAN L Molecular interactions mediating autoimmune mechanisms Self reactive T cells in murine lupus
P01AR-40919-01 0004 (SRC) BRAHN, ERNEST Molecular interactions mediating autoimmune mechanisms Collagen arthritis--Arthritogenic and suppressor epitopes
P01AR-40919-01 0005 (SRC) YU, DAVID T Y Molecular interactions mediating autoimmune mechanisms Relationship between HLA-B27 and arthritis
P01AR-40919-01 0006 (SRC) SERCARZ, ELI E Molecular interactions mediating autoimmune mechanisms Molecular mimicry in the MBP/EAE system
P01AR-40919-01 9001 (SRC) MILLER, ALEXANDER Molecular interactions mediating autoimmune mechanisms Core--Peptide synthesis
P01AR-40919-01 9002 (SRC) BOHMAN, ROGER Molecular interactions mediating autoimmune mechanisms Flow cytometry and cell sorting core
P01AR-40919-01 0001 (SRC) TSAO, BETTY P Molecular interactions mediating autoimmune mechanisms Immunoregulation of antibodies to DNA
P01AR-40919-01 0002 (SRC) HAHN, BEVRA H Molecular interactions mediating autoimmune mechanisms Peptides in immunoglobulin regulate anti-DNA in SLE
R15AR-40923-01 (GMB) GORSKI, JEFFREY P UNIVERSITY OF MISSOURI 5100 ROCKHILL ROAD KANSAS CITY, MO 64110-2499 In vivo/in vitro studies of bone acidic glycoprotein-75

PROJECT NO., ORGANIZATIONAL UNIT., INVESTIGATOR, ADDRESS, TITLE

R01AR-40926-02 (ORTH) CHIPMAN, STEWART D JOHNS HOPKINS SCHOOL OF MEDICI 4940 EASTERN AVENUE BALTIMORE, MD 21224 Fluoride effects on osteoblast extracellular matrix
R13AR-40927-01 (AMS) FOX, C FRED KEYSTONE CENTER PO BOX 606 KEYSTONE, CO 80435 Conference on Wound Repair and Fibroblasts
R29AR-40933-01 (GMA) GASPARI, ANTHONY A UNVIERSITY OF ROCHESTER 601 ELMWOOD AVE, BOX 697 ROCHESTER, NY 14642 In vitro studies of human T-cell unresponsiveness
R43AR-40948-01 (SSS) ELFORD, HOWARD L MOLECULES FOR HEALTH, INC 3313 GLOUCESTER ROAD RICHMOND, VA 23227 Potential new topical anti-psoriasis agents
R43AR-40954-01 (SSS) MILDER, FREDRIC L APPLIED PHYSICS CORP 204 CLINTON ROAD BROOKLINE, MA 02146-5814 Pediatric XRF bone lead with an X-ray generator
R43AR-40958-01 (SSS) GOODALL, ELEANOR TOPICAL TESTING,INC. 421 WAKARA WAY, RESEARCH PARK SALT LAKE CITY, UT 84108 Monitoring of limb position
R29AR-40959-02 (ORTH) GRANDE, DANIEL NORTH SHORE UNIVERSITY HOSPITA 300 COMMUNITY DRIVE MANHASSET, NY 11030 Chondrogenic repair in cartilage defects
R13AR-40962-01 (AMS) FINERMAN, GERALD A UCLA SCHOOL OF MEDICINE 10833 LE CONTE AVE LOS ANGELES, CA 90024 Workshop on biology & biomechanics of the synovial joint
R29AR-40981-01 (IMS) FOX, HOWARD S SCRIPPS CLINIC & RESEARCH FOUN 10666 NORTH TORREY PINES RD LA JOLLA, CA 92037 The effect of estrogen on the immune system
R13AR-40984-01 (AMS) UITTO, JOUNI J THOMAS JEFFERSON UNIVERSITY 1020 LOCUST ST PHILADELPHIA, PA 19107 Symposium--BMZ Biology and Pathology in EB
R01AR-40994-01 (GMA) NAGASE, HIDEAKI UNIV OF KANSAS MEDICAL CENTER 39TH AND RAINBOW BOULEVARD KANSAS CITY, KS 66103-8410 Structure and function of collagenase inhibitors
R01AR-40997-01 (BBCB) STOKES, DAVID L UNIVERSITY OF VIRGINIA BOX 449 JORDAN HALL CHARLOTTESVILLE, VA 22908 Frozen-hydrated electron microscopy of caATPase
R13AR-40999-01 (AMS) POTTS, RUSSELL O PFIZER, INC EASTERN POINT ROAD GROTON, CT 06340 Gordon Research Conference on Barrier Function of Mammalian Skin
R01AR-41003-01 (GMA) PLATSOUCAS, CHRIS D UNIVERSITY OF TEXAS 1515 HOLCOMBE BLVD HOUSTON, TX 77030 T-cell receptors in rheumatoid arthritis
R55AR-41008-01 (GMA) KORMAN, NEIL J CASE WESTERN RESERVE UNIVERSIT 2074 ABINGTON ROAD CLEVELAND, OH 44106 Characterization of epidermal bullous pemphigoid antigen
R01AR-41018-01 (ORTH) PERRY, JACQUELIN RANCHO LOS AMIGOS MED CTR 12808 ERICKSON AVENUE DOWNEY, CA 90242 SCI shoulder function with wheelchairs and transfers
Z01AR-41020-24 (ARB) STEINBERG, A D NIAMS, NIH Pathogenesis of autoimmunity in mice with SLE-like illness
Z01AR-41023-17 (ARB) STEINBERG, A D NIAMS, NIH Studies of patients with immune-mediated diseases
R01AR-41025-01 (PHY) HOFFMAN, ERIC PAUL UNIV OF PITTSBURGH SCH OF MED PITTSBURGH, PA 15261 Molecular basis for periodic paralysis
Z01AR-41025-20 (ARB) METZGER, H NIAMS, NIH Cell surface receptors for IgE
R13AR-41034-01 (AMS) WONG, PATRICK Y NEW YORK MEDICAL COLLEGE VALHALLA, NY 10595 Conference--Cytokines And Lipid Mediators As Regulators Of Cell Function
R13AR-41036-01 (AMS) DALE, BEVERLY A UNIVERSITY OF WASHINGTON SEATTLE, WA 98195 Epithelial differentiation and keratinization--Gordon Conference
R55AR-41040-01 (ORTH) RUBIN, CLINTON T STATE UNIV OF NEW YORK MUSCULO-SKELETAL RESEARCH LAB STONY BROOK, NY 11794-8181 Prevention of osteopenia by low energy electric fields
Z01AR-41040-19 (ARB) STEINBERG, A D NIAMS, NIH Various cytotoxic drug programs in diffuse lupus nephritis
R01AR-41042-01 (PBC) ADAMS, SHERRILL L UNIV OF PA SCH OF DENTAL MED 4001 SPRUCE STREET PHILADELPHIA, PA 19104-6003 Molecular mechanisms regulating alfa2(I) collagen gene E
R29AR-41046-01 (ORTH) SAAVEDRA, RAUL A CHILDREN'S HOSPITAL 300 LONGWOOD AVE BOSTON, MA 02115 Function of osteopontin--A molecular genetics approach
Z01AR-41048-12 (ARB) WILDER, R L NIAMS, NIH Bacterial cell wall induced arthritis and hepatic granuloma formation
R29AR-41051-01 (IMB) HOFFMAN, ROBERT W UNIVERSITY OF MISSOURI MA 427 HEALTH SCIENCE CENTER COLUMBIA, MO 65212 Human immune response to the U1-70kD snRNP autoantigen
Z01AR-41066-09 (ARB) WILDER, R L NIAMS, NIH Characterization of synovial tissue from patients w/RA & related conditions
R55AR-41072-01 (BBCB) TAYLOR, RONALD P UNIVERSITY OF VIRGINIA BOX 440 SCH OF MEDICINE CHARLOTTESVILLE, VA 22908 Cr1-proteoliposomes for immune complex binding in SLE
R13AR-41073-01 (AMS) PICOU, DAVID CCMRC/OFFICE OF THE DIRECTOR 20 SCHNEIDER GARDENS TRINIDAD, WEST INDIES CCMRC Meeting - collaborative research planning effort
R01AR-41074-01 (OBM) WU, CHOU BING UNIVERSITY OF BRITISH COLUMBIA 2199 WESTBROOK MALL VANCOUVER, BC V6T 1Z77 Molecular mechanism of matrix protein phosphorylation
Z01AR-41074-04 (ARB) PLOTZ, P H NIAMS, NIH Etiology and pathogenesis of idiopathic inflammatory myopathy in humans
R43AR-41076-01A1 (HUD) CONNELL, KAREN J INST FOR INQUIRY IN EDUCATION 35 EAST WACKER DRIVE CHICAGO, IL 60601 Multi media dissemination of EDUCIZE for arthritis
Z01AR-41076-04 (ARB) PLOTZ, P H NIAMS, NIH Therapeutic trials in idiopathic inflammatory myopathies
Z01AR-41080-03 (ARB) PLOTZ, P H NIAMS, NIH Use of MRI to detect inflammation in muscle of myositis
Z01AR-41083-02 (ARB) KASTNER, D L NIAMS, NIH Genetics of familial Mediterranean fever
Z01AR-41084-02 (LSB) STEINERT, P NIAMS, NIH Structural features of keratin and related intermediate filaments
Z01AR-41085-02 (LSB) STEINERT, P NIAMS, NIH Expression, structure and function of filaggrin

PROJECT NO., ORGANIZATIONAL UNIT., INVESTIGATOR, ADDRESS, TITLE

Z01AR-41086-02 (LSB) STEINERT, P NIAMS, NIH Expression, structure and function of loricrin, a major cell envelope protein
Z01AR-41087-02 (LSB) STEINERT, P NIAMS, NIH Epidermal transglutaminases
Z01AR-41088-01 (ARB) WILDER, R L NIAMS, NIH Neuroendocrine factors in the autoimmune diseases
R43AR-41093-01 (SSS) SILBERGLITT, RICHARD S TECHNOLOGY ASSESSMENT & TRANSF 133 DEFENSE HWY ANNAPOLIS, MD 21401 Phase change heat storage devices for arthritis therapy
R43AR-41094-01 (SSS) KONIGSBERG, PAULA J VESTAR, INC. 650 CLIFFSIDE DR. SAN DIMAS, CA 91773 Liposomal gold compounds--improved antiarthritic therapy
R43AR-41109-01 (GMA) TIPTON, ARTHUR J ATRIX LABORATORIES INC 1625 SHARP POINT DRIVE FT COLLINS, CO 80522-2501 A biodegradable wound treatment
R43AR-41110-01 (GMA) BARTEL, RONNDA L MARROW TECH INCORPORATED 10933 N TORREY PINES RD LA JOLLA, CA 92037 A physiological skin replacement
R43AR-41123-01 (SSS) CRAINE, BRIAN L WESTERN RESEARCH COMPANY, INC 2127 EAST SPEEDWAY TUCSON, AZ 85719 Computer nail bed capillaroscopy
R43AR-41124-01 (SSS) COONS, TERESA A RHOMED INCORPORATED 4261 BALLOON PARK RD., NE ALBUQUERQUE, NM 87109 99m Tc-PHA-L4 labeled lymphocytes
R01AR-41129-01 (PHY) STEINHARDT, RICHARD A UNIVERSITY OF CALIFORNIA 391 LIFE SCIENCE ADDITION BERKELEY, CA 94720 Calcium channels in normal and diseased tissue
R01AR-41221-01 (EDC) FELSON, DAVID T BOSTON UNIV SCHOOL OF MEDICINE 80 EAST CONCORD STREET BOSTON, MA 02118 Rheumatoid arthritis drug therapy in the elderly
S15AR-41227-01 (NSS) ARNOLD, ROLAND R UNIVERSITY OF NORTH CAROLINA CHAPEL HILL, NC 27599-7455 Small instrumentation grant
S15AR-41228-01 (NSS) NEPOM, GERALD T VIRGINIA MASON RESEARCH CENTER 1000 SENECA STREET SEATTLE, WA 98101 Small instrumentation grant
S15AR-41229-01 (NSS) WRIGHT, TIMOTHY M HOSPITAL FOR SPECIAL SURGERY 535 EAST 70TH STREET NEW YORK, NY 10021 Small instrumentation grant
S15AR-41230-01 (NSS) MELCHIOR, DONALD L UNIV OF MASSACHUSETTS/MED SCH 55 LAKE AVENUE NORTH WORCESTER, MA 01655 Small instrumentation grant
S15AR-41231-01 (NSS) STERN, PAULA H NORTHWESTERN UNIVERSITY 303 EAST CHICAGO AVENUE CHICAGO, IL 60611 Small instrumentation grant
S15AR-41232-01 (NSS) BRUCE, ALICE E UNIVERSITY OF MAINE ORONO, ME 04469 Small instrumentation grant
S15AR-41233-01 (NSS) GLADDEN, L BRUCE AUBURN UNIVERSITY 2050 MEMORIAL COLISEUM AUBURN UNIVERSITY, AL 36849 Small instrumentation grant
S15AR-41234-01 (NSS) PERRY, JACQUELIN RANCHO LOS AMIGOS MED CTR 12808 ERICKSON AVENUE DOWNEY, CA 90242 Small instrumentation grant
S15AR-41235-01 (NSS) KAHN, ARNOLD J UNIVERSITY OF CALIFORNIA BOX 0640 C-734 SAN FRANCISCO, CA 94143-0640 Small instrumentation grant
S15AR-41236-01 (NSS) LOKER, ERIC S UNIVERSITY OF NEW MEXICO ALBUQUERQUE, NM 87131-6003 Small instrumentation grant
S15AR-41237-01 (NSS) FRIED, WALTER RUSH-PRESBYTERIAN-ST LUKE'S 1653 WEST CONGRESS PARKWAY CHICAGO, IL 60612 Small instrumentation grant
S15AR-41238-01 (NSS) PUTNAM, ROBERT W 3640 COLONEL GLENN HIGHWAY DAYTON, OH 45435 Small instrumentation grant
S15AR-41239-01 (NSS) LOW, ROBERT UNIVERSITY OF VERMONT GIVEN BLDG BURLINGTON, VT 05405 Small instrumentation grant
S15AR-41240-01 (NSS) FORDTRAN, JOHN S BAYLOR UNIV MED CTR 3812 ELM ST DALLAS, TX 75246 Small instrumentation grant
S15AR-41241-01 (NSS) CANALIS, ERNESTO ST FRANCIS HOSPITAL & MED CTR 114 WOODLAND STREET HARTFORD, CT 06105-1299 Small instrumentation grant
S15AR-41242-01 (NSS) NORMAN, ANTHONY W UNIVERSITY OF CALIFORNIA RIVERSIDE, CA 92521-0121 Small instrumentation grant
S15AR-41243-01 (NSS) GOLDSTEIN, BERNARD SAN FRANCISCO STATE UNIVERSITY 1600 HOLLOWAY AVE SAN FRANCISCO, CA 94132 Small instrumentation grant
S15AR-41244-01 (NSS) MATTOON, JAMES R UNIVERSITY OF COLORADO SCIENCE BLDG 250 COLORADO SPRINGS, CO 80933-71 Small instrumentation grant
S15AR-41245-01 (NSS) SINGER, BURTON H YALE UNIVERSITY P O BOX 3333, 60 COLLEGE ST NEW HAVEN, CT 06510 Small instrumentation grant
S15AR-41246-01 (NSS) THURMAN, WILLIAM G OKLAHOMA MED RESEARCH FDN 825 NE 13TH STREET OKLAHOMA CITY, OK 73104 Small instrumentation grant
S15AR-41247-01 (NSS) ABRAMS, DAVID B MIRIAM HOSPITAL 164 SUMMIT AVENUE PROVIDENCE, R I 02906 Small instrumentation grant
S15AR-41248-01 (NSS) MACKENZIE, IAN C U OF TEXAS HLTH SCI CTR PO BOX 20068 HOUSTON, TX 77225 Small instrumentation grant
S15AR-41249-01 (NSS) ROSENBLOOM, JOEL UNIVERSITY OF PENNSYLVANIA 4001 SPRUCE STREET PHILADELPHIA, PA 19104-6003 Small instrumentation grant
S15AR-41250-01 (NSS) LABERGE, MARTINE CLEMSON UNIVERSITY 301 RHODES RESEARCH CENTER CLEMSON, SC 29634-0905 Small instrumentation grant
S15AR-41251-01 (NSS) OSDOBY, PHILIP A WASHINGTON UNIVERSITY 4559 SCOTT AVENUE ST LOUIS, MO 63110 Small instrumentation grant
S15AR-41252-01 (NSS) WINCHESTER, ROBERT J HOSPITAL FOR JOINT DISEASES 301 EAST 17TH STREET NEW YORK, N Y 10003 Small instrumentation grant
S15AR-41253-01 (NSS) PAPLAUSKAS, LEONARD P UNIV OF CONNECTICUT HLTH CTR 263 FARMINGTON AVE FARMINGTON, CT 06030-9984 Small instrumentation grant
S15AR-41254-01 (NSS) RYMER, WILLIAM Z REHABILITATION INST RESEARCH C 345 EAST SUPERIOR CHICAGO, IL 60611 Small instrumentation grant
R01AR-41309-01 (CBY) DEDMAN, JOHN R UNIVERSITY OF CINCINNATI 231 BETHESDA AVE CINCINNATI, OH 45267-0576 Regulation of Ca2+

PROJECT NO., ORGANIZATIONAL UNIT., INVESTIGATOR, ADDRESS, TITLE

homeostasis in skeletal muscle
R01AR-41313-01 (AMS) MANOLAGAS, STAVROS C VA MEDICAL CENTER 1481 W TENTH STREET INDIANAPOLIS, IN 46202-2884 Hormonal control of cytokines in bone and stromal cells
R01AR-41319-01 (AMS) NELSON, DOROTHY A HENRY FORD HOSPITAL 2799 W GRAND BLVD DETROIT, MI 48202 Accumulation of skeletal mass in prepubertal school children
R01AR-41336-01 (AMS) ROODMAN, GARSON D UNIV OF TEXAS HLTH SCI CTR 7703 FLOYD CURL DR SAN ANTONIO, TX 78284-7880 Effects of estrogen on osteoclasts from transgenic mice
R01AR-41339-01 (AMS) BARON, ROLAND E YALE UNIV SCHOOL OF MEDICINE 333 CEDAR STREET/SHM IE55 NEW HAVEN, CT 06510 Characterization of an osteoclast specific proton pump
R01AR-41342-01 (AMS) CHRISTAKOS, SYLVIA S UNIV OF MED/DENT OF NEW JERSEY 185 SOUTH ORANGE AVE NEWARK, NJ 07103-2714 Osteoporosis/dihydroxyvitamin regulated gene expression
R01AR-41344-01 (AMS) TELL, GRETHE S WAKE FOREST UNIVERSITY MEDICAL CENTER BOULEVARD WINSTON-SALEM, NC 27157-1063 Incidence and risk factors for falls in older adults
R01AR-41347-01 (AMS) HOLETS, VICKY R UNIVERSITY OF MIAMI 1600 NW 10TH AVE MIAMI, FL 33136 Spinal cord injury induced osteoporosis
R01AR-41349-01 (AMS) GOLDSTEIN, STEVEN A UNIVERSITY OF MICHIGAN G-0161, 400 N INGALLS/0486 ANN ARBOR, MI 48109-0486 Tissue morphology and architecture effects on bone
R01AR-41366-01 (AMS) SPECKER, BONNY L UNIVERSITY OF CINCINNATI MED C 231 BETHESDA AVE CINCINNATI, OH 45267-0541 Effect of lactation and weaning on calcium status
R01AR-41376-01 (AMS) DIBIANCA, FRANK A BAPTIST MEMORIAL HOSPITAL 899 MADISON AVE/BIOMED ENGR MEMPHIS, TN 38163 Novel densitometric techniques for osteoporosis research
R01AR-41383-01 (AMS) COLDITZ, GRAHAM A CHANNING LABORATORY 180 LONGWOOD AVE BOSTON, MA 02115 Prospective study of fractures in men and women
R01AR-41386-01 (AMS) PARISIEN, MAY HELEN HAYES HOSPTITAL ROUTE 9W WEST HAVERSTRAW, NY 10993 Skeletal homeostasis in blacks and whites
R01AR-41392-01 (AMS) HAUSCHKA, PETER V CHILDREN'S HOSPITAL CORP 300 LONGWOOD AVENUE BOSTON, MASS 02115 Osteocalcin receptor function in bone resorption
R01AR-41398-01 (AMS) KIEL, DOUGLAS P RHODE ISLAND HOSPITAL PROVIDENCE, RI 02903 Risk factors for vertebral fracture and bone loss
R01AR-41409-01 (AMS) EISMAN, JOHN A GARVAN INSTITUTE OF MEDICAL RE 384 VICTORIA ST DALINGHURST, AUSTRALIA NSW 201 Molecular mechanisms of genetic regulation of bone mass
R01AR-41412-01 (AMS) PACIFICI, ROBERTO WASHINGTON UNIV MED CTR 216 SOUTH KINGSHIGHWAY BLVD ST LOUIS, MO 63110 Rat IL-1 receptor antagonist in ovariectomy induced bone loss
R01AR-41418-01 (AMS) TURNER, RUSSELL T MAYO FOUNDATION 200 FIRST STREET SOUTHWEST ROCHESTER, MN 55905 Regulation of bone balance by estrogen and tamoxifen
R01AR-41425-01 (AMS) SNYDER, PETER J UNIVERSITY OF PENNSYLVANIA 422 CURIE BLVD PHILADELPHIA, PA 19104-6149 Will testosterone increse bone mineral density in elderly men?
R01AR-41439-13 (GMA) UITTO, JOUNI J THOMAS JEFFERSON UNIVERSITY 1025 LOCUST ST PHILADELPHIA, PA 19107 Collagen biosynthesis by cultured fibroblasts
R01AR-41463-01 (ORTH) KEY, L LYNDON, JR MEDICAL UNIV OF SOUTH CAROLINA 171 ASHLEY AVENUE CHARLESTON, SC 29425 Superoxide and bone resorption
R01AR-41497-01 (AMS) PERSING, DAVID H MAYO FOUNDATION 200 FIRST STREET SW ROCHESTER, MN 55905 Molecular diagnosis and monitoring of Lyme disease
R01AR-41500-01 (AMS) KLEMPNER, MARK S NEW ENGLAND MED CTR HOSP, INC 750 WASHINGTON ST, BOX 041 BOSOTN, MA 02111 Diagnosis of early Lyme disease
R01AR-41507-01 (AMS) NORRIS, STEVEN J UNIVERSITY OF TEXAS PO BOX 20708 HOUSTON, TX 77225 Virulence-associated proteins in Lyme disease diagnosis
R01AR-41508-01 (AMS) NADELMAN, ROBERT B WESTCHESTER MEDICAL CENTER MACY PAVILION RM 209SE VALHALLA, NY 10595 Controlled treatment trial of patients with Lyme disease
R01AR-41511-01 (AMS) SCHWARTZ, IRA S NEW YORK MEDICAL COLLEGE VALHALLA, NY 10595 Nucleic acid-based diagnostic probes for Lyme disease
R01AR-41517-01 (AMS) PICKEN, ROGER N BAXTER HEALTHCARE CORP 909 ORCHARD ST MUNDELEIN, IL 60060 Lyme disease diagnosis by PCR/DNA probe system
R01AR-41518-01 (AMS) SCHUTZER, STEVEN E UMDNJ-NEW JERSEY MEDICAL SCHOO 185 SOUTH ORANGE AVENUE NEWARK, NJ 07103-2714 Complexed antibody in early diagnosis and course of Lyme disease
R01AR-41522-01 (AMS) JOHNSON, RUSSELL C UNIVERSITY OF MINNESOTA 420 DELAWARE ST, SE/BOX 196 UM MINNEAPOLIS, MN 55455 In vitro and in vivo antimicrobial studies of B. burgdorferi
R01AR-41547-01 (AMS) WILLIAMS, WILLIAM V UNIV OF PENNSYLVANIA 3600 SPRUCE STREET PHILADELPHIA, PA 19104 Molecular diagnosis and therapy of Lyme borreliosis
R01AR-41551-01 (AMS) BAUER, EUGENE A STANFORD UNIVERSITY 300 PASTEUR DRIVE STANFORD, CA 94305-5334 Candidate protein clones in EB
R01AR-41551-01 0001 (AMS) BAUER, EUGENE A Candidate protein clones in EB DNA protein clones in recessive dystrophic, junctional and acquired EB
R01AR-41551-01 0002 (AMS) WOODLEY, DAVID T Candidate protein clones in EB Keratinocyte locomotion and protease expression
R01AR-41551-01 0003 (AMS) KARASEK, MARVIN A Candidate protein clones in EB Metabolism of dermal microvascular BM in epidermolysis bullosa
R01AR-41551-01 0004 (AMS) MCGUIRE, JOSEPH S Candidate protein clones in EB Chronic injury enhanced proteolysis and carcinogenesis in RDEB
R01AR-41551-01 0005 (AMS) LANE, ALFRED T Candidate protein clones in EB Fetal wound response
R01AR-41551-01 0006 (AMS) FURTHMAYR, HEINZ Candidate protein clones in EB Keratinocyte interaction with basement membrane
R01AR-41551-01 9001 (AMS) KARASEC, MARVIN A Candidate protein clones in EB Cell culture and tissue facility
R43AR-41573-01 (GMA) COHEN, LAWRENCE K SOMATIX THERAPY CORPORATION 850 MARINA VILLAGE PARKWAY ALAMEDA, CA 94501-1034 Cell-based delivery of wound healing growth factors
R29AR-41606-01 (NLS) IGWE, ORISA J UNIV OF MISSOURI-KANSAS CITY M3-104 MED SCH BLDG /2411 HOLM KANSAS CITY, MO 64108-2792 Regulation of substance P in prolonged nociception
R29AR-41607-01 (EDC) RAMSEY-GOLDMAN, ROSALIND NORTHWESTERN UNIV MEDICAL SCHO 303 E CHICAGO AVE, WARD 3-315 CHICAGO, IL 60611 Epidemiology of lupus pregnancy--Maternal/fetal outcome
N01AR-62271-08 (**) SAMS, W MITCHELL, JR Establish a clinical site for the National Epidermolysis Bullosa Registry
N01AR-82200-04 (**) FITZGERALD, GWEN H Holding facility for autoimmune mice
N01AR-92200-03 (**) SHEA, JOHN M Support services/national arthritis advisory board
Z01BA-01001-10 (LAP) ANDERSON, M C FDA Potency levels in standardized allergenic extracts
Z01BA-01002-15 (LAP) ANDERSON, M C FDA Standardization of allergenic extracts of pollens
Z01BA-01003-06 (LAP) ANDERSON, M C FDA Studies and standardization of house dust mite extracts
Z01BA-01004-04 (LAP) ANDERSON, M C FDA Continuing studies of cat allergy
Z01BA-01005-02 (LAP) ANDERSON, M C FDA Isoelectric focusing procedures for allergenic extracts
Z01BA-01006-04 (LAP) ANDERSON, M C FDA Development of the fluorescent relatice potency test
Z01BA-01007-02 (LAP) MATTHEWS, J FDA Clinical application of allergy units
Z01BA-01008-02 (LAP) TURKELTAUB, P C FDA Prevalence of allergic and non allergic respiratory disease in U. S. population
Z01BA-01009-02 (LAP) TURKELTAUB, P C FDA Safety and efficacy of ragweed extracts differing in potency and composition
Z01BA-01010-02 (LAP) MATTHEWS, J FDA Accuracy and precision of parallel-line skin test estimates of relative potency
Z01BA-01011-02 (LAP) TURKELTAUB, P C FDA The effect of early versus late onset of childhood asthma
Z01BA-01012-02 (LAP) TURKELTAUB, P C FDA Allergen skin test reactivity and respiratory disease in the U.S. population
Z01BA-01014-06 (LAP) TURKELTAUB, P C FDA Fatalities from immunotherapy and skin testing with allergenic extracts
Z01BA-01016-02 (LAP) TURKELTAUB, P C FDA The Hymenoptera venom study III--Safety of venom immunotherapy
Z01BA-01017-01 (LAP) MATTHEWS, J FDA In vivo determination of compositional differences in standardized cat extracts
Z01BA-01018-01 (LAP) MATTHEWS, J FDA In vivo determination of stability of standardized grass extracts
Z01BA-01019-01 (LAP) ANDERSON, M C FDA Study of the allergenicity of latex
Z01BA-01020-01 (LAP) ANDERSON, M C FDA Study of cockroach allergens
Z01BA-01021-01 (LAP) ANDERSON, M C FDA Alternate test method for assay of hyaluronidase in Hymenoptera venoms
Z01BA-02002-03 (LBP) RUBINSTEIN, Y R FDA Genetic and structural analysis of Neisseria meningitidis outer membrane proteins
Z01BA-02003-03 (LBP) ARAKERE, G FDA Role of the lipid tail of the group C polysaccharide
Z01BA-02005-06 (LBP) RUBINSTEIN, L FDA Immunity to group C Neisseria meningitidis in mice
Z01BA-02006-09 (LBP) STEIN, K E FDA Regulation of the immune response to polysaccharide antigens
Z01BA-02007-09 (LBP) VANN, W F FDA Biosynthesis of capsular polysaccharides of pathogenic bacteria
Z01BA-02008-04 (LBP) STEIN, K E FDA Ontogeny of immunoglobulin variable region expression
Z01BA-02009-02 (LBP) STEIN, K E FDA Mitogenic capacity of various components from gram negative bacteria
Z01BA-02010-08 (LBP) TSAI, C M FDA Immunochemical studies of meningococcal lipooligosaccharide antigens
Z01BA-02011-03 (LBP) TSAI, C M FDA Chemical quantitation of polysaccharide content in Hib-conjugate vaccines
Z01BA-02012-02 (LBP) GU, X X FDA Preparation of N. meningitidis lipooligosaccharide with high yield
Z01BA-02013-02 (LBP) GU, X X FDA Preparation of monoclonal antibody against meningococcal lipooligosaccharide
Z01BA-02015-02 (LBP) BANKS, S FDA Molecular cloning of pneumolysin gene from S. pneumoniae type 19F
Z01BA-02017-02 (LBP) LI, J FDA Expression and distribution of pneumolysin in S. pneumoniae
Z01BA-02018-02 (LBP) LU, C S FDA Immunogenicity of pneumococcal group 9 polysaccharide-protein complex
Z01BA-02020-02 (LBP) LEE, C J FDA Enhancement of 19F antibody response by 19F PS-inactivated pneumolysin conjugate
Z01BA-02021-01 (LBP) ARAKERE, G FDA astress induced proteins of group B Neisseria meningitidis
Z01BA-02022-01 (LBP) BANKS, S D FDA Characteristics and expression of group 19 pneumolysin genes
Z01BA-02023-01 (LBP) LEE, C J FDA Ultrastructural location of pneumolysin in S. pneumoniae
Z01BA-02024-01 (LBP) LEE, C J FDA Maternal immunity and antibody responses of offspring to pneumococcal type 19FPS
Z01BA-02025-01 (LBP) VANN, W F FDA Structure and immunochemistry of capsular polysaccharides
Z01BA-03001-02 (LBT) HALPERN, J L FDA Identification of the ganglioside binding domain of tetanus toxin
Z01BA-03003-02 (LBT) STIBITZ, E S FDA Global regulation of virulence factor in Bordetella pertussis
Z01BA-03004-02 (LBT) ANSHER, S FDA Models for evaluating the toxicity of cytokines
Z01BA-03005-02 (LBT) ANSHER, S FDA The effects of DPT vaccine

on hepatic drug metabolism
Z01BA-03006-01 (LBT) JOHNSON, V G FDA Structure-function relationships of diphtheria toxin
Z01BA-04001-06 (LCP) KENIMER, J G FDA Identification of neutralizing epitopes on pertussis toxin
Z01BA-04003-06 (LCP) KARPAS, A B FDA Production and characterization of monoclonal antibodies
Z01BA-04004-03 (LCP) LEININGER, E FDA Characterization of bacterial adhesins
Z01BA-04005-02 (LCP) LEININGER, E FDA Characterization of bacterial mutants in cell adhesins
Z01BA-04006-02 (LCP) LEININGER, E FDA Monoclonal antibodies directed against filamentous hemaglutinins
Z01BA-04007-02 (LCP) LEININGER, E FDA Characterization of bacterial receptors on mammalian cells
Z01BA-04008-01 (LCP) PROBST, P G FDA Synthesis of oligonucleotides
Z01BA-04009-01 (LCP) ELLISON, J S FDA Fusion phage epitope library
Z01BA-05001-04 (LI) MORRIS, S L FDA Characterization of Mycobacterium intracellulare lambda-gt11 recombinant clones
Z01BA-05002-03 (LI) ROUSE, D A FDA Characterization of Mycobacterium avium lambda-gt11 library
Z01BA-05003-03 (LI) MORRIS, S L FDA Characterization of Mycobacterium kansasii antigens in a lambda-gt11 gene library
Z01BA-05004-03 (LI) MORRIS, S L FDA AIDS-related mycobacterial disease--Antibodies to M. avium in AIDS sera
Z01BA-05005-02 (LI) MACKALL, J FDA Analysis of natural and synthetic antigens and epitopes of mycobacteria
Z01BA-06001-08 (LM) BARILE, M F FDA Mycoplasma pneumoniae-induced pneumonia in chimpanzees
Z01BA-06003-02 (LM) BARILE, M F FDA Evaluation of Mycoplasma pneumoniae vaccines in chimpanzees
Z01BA-06004-04 (LM) BARILE, M F FDA Mycoplasma studies on rheumatoid arthritis and schizophrenia
Z01BA-06005-04 (LM) OLSON, L D FDA Molecular analysis of Mycoplasma hominis
Z01BA-06006-04 (LM) BARILE, M F FDA Mycoplasma infection of cell cultures
Z01BA-06007-02 (LM) OLSON, L D FDA Characterization of non-P1 proteins involved in Mycoplasma pneumoniae attachment
Z01BA-06008-01 (LM) OLSON, L D FDA Sera immunoblots of chimpanzee infected with Mycoplasma pneumoniae
Z01BA-06009-01 (LM) BARILE, M F FDA Mycoplasma-induced septic arthritis in chimpanzees
Z01BA-06010-01 (LM) OLSON, L D FDA DNA methylation by different strains of M. hominis
Z01BA-06011-01 (LM) OLSON, L D FDA Attachment specificity of Mycoplasma hominis
Z01BA-06012-01 (LM) OLSON, L D FDA Analysis of the pathogenicity of strains of Mycoplasma fermentans
Z01BA-06013-01 (LM) BARILE, M F FDA Wegener's granulomatosis
Z01BA-07001-23 (LP) MEADE, B D FDA Serologic methods for pertussis research--Development and standardization
Z01BA-07002-02 (LP) BURNS, D L FDA Serological response to Bordetella pertussis antigens
Z01BA-07003-03 (LP) MEADE, B D FDA Evaluation of serodiagnostic methods for pertussis
Z01BA-07004-03 (LP) MINK, C M FDA Epidemiology and diagnosis of Bordetella pertussis infection in Washington DC
Z01BA-07005-08 (LP) MEADE, B D FDA Immune response to three versus four doses of DTP vaccine
Z01BA-07006-02 (LP) MEADE, B D FDA Evaluation of the human antibody response to acellular pertussis vaccines
Z01BA-07007-12 (LP) SHAHIN, R D FDA Aerosol infection of mice as a model for pertussis infection
Z01BA-07008-04 (LP) SHAHIN, R D FDA Evaluation of antigens protective in the mouse aerosol model
Z01BA-07009-02 (LP) SHAHIN, R D FDA Mucosal immunity to pertussis antigens in mice
Z01BA-07010-04 (LP) MINK, C M FDA Mucosal immunity to pertussis in humans
Z01BA-07011-07 (LP) BURNS, D L FDA Studies on the structure and function of pertussis toxin
Z01BA-07012-03 (LP) BURNS, D L FDA Studies on the structure and function of heat-labile toxin from Bordetella
Z01BA-07015-03 (LP) BRENNAN, M J FDA Adhesins of Bordetella pertussis
Z01BA-07016-02 (LP) BRENNAN, M J FDA Pertactin and FHA as adhesive proteins of Bordetella pertussis
Z01BA-07017-04 (LP) BRENNAN, M J FDA Characterization of the porin protein of Bordetella pertussis
Z01BA-07018-02 (LP) BRENNAN, M J FDA Mammalian cell receptors for Bordetella pertussis
Z01BA-07019-02 (LP) BURNS, D L FDA Development of tests for acellular pertussis vaccines
Z01BA-07020-39 (LP) JANSEN, D L FDA Control testing
Z01BA-07021-24 (LP) MANCLARK, C R FDA Selective breeding to establish a "standard" mouse
Z01BA-07022-02 (LP) SHAHIN, R D FDA Microencapsulation of pertussis antigens
Z01BA-07023-01 (LP) BURNS, D L FDA Molecular chaperones
Z01BA-07024-01 (LP) FINN, T FDA Characterization of a new vir-regulated B. pertussis surface antigen
Z01BA-07025-01 (LP) BRENNAN, M J FDA Diagnosis of pertussis by molecular and immunological techniques
Z01BA-07026-01 (LP) BRENNAN, M J FDA Immunologically important epitopes on pertactin
Z01BB-01001-14 (LAC) MAY, J C FDA Analysis and characterization of mercurial preservatives in injectables
Z01BB-01002-17 (LAC) MAY, J C FDA Analysis and characterization of aluminum adjuvant in injectables
Z01BB-01003-16 (LAC) MAY, J C FDA Determination of residual moisture in freeze-dried biological products
Z01BB-01004-11 (LAC) MAY, J C FDA Trace metals in injectable biological products
Z01BB-01005-07 (LAC) MAY, J C FDA Determination of aluminum in human antihemophilic factor
Z01BB-01006-05 (LAC) DEL GROSSO, A V FDA Determination of chlorpheniramine in human blood serum
Z01BB-01007-06 (LAC) DEL GROSSO, A V FDA Determination of urushiol in allergenic extracts--Urushiol stability studies
Z01BB-01008-04 (LAC) DEL GROSSO, A V FDA High performance metal chelate interaction chromatography
Z01BB-01009-13 (LAC) MAY, J C FDA Quantitative determination of phenol, glycerin, formaldehyde, etc. in injectables
Z01BB-01010-01 (LAC) MAY, J C FDA Determination of nitrogen content (protein) of biological products
Z01BB-02001-02 (LBC) XI-QUING, C FDA Role of cis-acting elements in rubella virus replication
Z01BB-02002-02 (LBC) NAKHASI, H L FDA Host-cell protein interaction with stem-loop (-) strand RNA of rubella virus
Z01BB-02003-02 (LBC) XI-QUING, C FDA 3'-cis-acting element of rubella virus RNA with a DNA promoter activity
Z01BB-02004-02 (LBC) SINGH, N K FDA Purification of cellular rubella virus RNA-binding proteins
Z01BB-02006-09 (LBC) GOLDMAN, N FDA Molecular mechanism for the regulation of C-reactive protein
Z01BB-02007-04 (LBC) GOLDMAN, N FDA Eukaryotic gene expression of circumsporozoite protein for vaccine development
Z01BB-02008-02 (LBC) DEVRIES, Y L FDA Identification and characterization of cellular receptor(s) for HBV
Z01BB-02009-02 (LBC) GOLDMAN, N FDA Development of a recombinant viral vaccine expressing malaria antigen
Z01BB-02010-02 (LBC) GOLDMAN, N FDA Induction of CRP in liver cells
Z01BB-02011-02 (LBC) DEVRIES, Y FDA Endotoxin binding protein of Limulus amebocyte
Z01BB-02012-03 (LBC) SYIN, C FDA Development and differentiation of malaria parasite
Z01BB-02013-03 (LBC) BOYKINS, R FDA Protein chemistry
Z01BB-02014-01 (LBC) LIN, L FDA Biological significance of C-reactive protein
Z01BB-02015-01 (LBC) LIU, T FDA Limunectin--A PC-binding protein from Limulus with adhesion promoting properties
Z01BB-03002-02 (LBP) BULL, T E FDA Theoretical NMR development I
Z01BB-03003-02 (LBP) BULL, T E FDA Theoretical NMR development II
Z01BB-03004-02 (LBP) BULL, T E FDA Theoretical NMR development III
Z01BB-03005-07 (LBP) PASTOR, R W FDA Computer modeling and other theoretical studies of biopolymers
Z01BB-03006-03 (LBP) BYRD, R A FDA Structural studies of biomacromolecules via NMR spectroscopy
Z01BB-03009-02 (LBP) VENABLE, R M FDA Theoretical studies of macromolecules from HIV
Z01BB-04001-02 (LCMB) BERTIN, P FDA Molecular biology of chronic lymphocytic leukemia
Z01BB-04002-02 (LCMB) BRAHAM, P FDA Flow cytometry computer support program
Z01BB-04005-03 (LCMB) MARTI, G E FDA Cell analysis facility--Flow cytometry
Z01BB-04006-02 (LCMB) KASSIS, J A FDA Altering the insertion specificity of a transposable element
Z01BB-04007-02 (LCMB) KASSIS, J A FDA A fragment of engrailed DNA can mediate transvection
Z01BB-04009-03 (LCMB) KASSIS, J A FDA Control of gene expression during development
Z01BB-05001-10 (LCB) FRASER, B A FDA Structural analysis by mass spectrometry
Z01BB-06001-04 (LMI) EPSTEIN, S L FDA Antibody responses to Ia antigens--Idiotypes and antibody diversity
Z01BB-06002-03 (LMI) EPSTEIN, S L FDA Contract support, studies of antibody idiotypes
Z01BB-06003-06 (LMI) EPSTEIN, S L FDA Studies of immunity to CD4 and gp120
Z01BB-06005-02 (LMI) BERKOWER, I FDA gp120 conjugate vaccine
Z01BB-06006-02 (LMI) BERKOWER, I FDA Human T cell response to HBsAg--Cloning and expression of antigenic fragments
Z01BB-06007-01 (LMI) MILLER, F W FDA Human leukocyte antigen (HLA) gene associations with autoimmune myositis
Z01BB-07001-03 (LMP) JAMRICH, M A FDA Expression of Homeo-box containing genes during early Xenopus development
Z01BB-07002-02 (LMP) MCHUGH, E FDA Forskolin affinity labelling of adenylyl cyclase and glucose transporter
Z01BB-07003-03 (LMP) ROBBINS, J FDA Synthesis and characterization of forskolin derivatives
Z01BB-07004-02 (LMP) MOOS, M FDA Purification of adenylyl cyclase
Z01BB-07005-02 (LMP) BEAUCAGE, S L FDA An improved synthesis of oligodeoxyribonucleoside phosphorothioates
Z01BB-07006-01 (LMP) APPEL, N FDA Localization of adenylyl cyclase and the glucose transporter in rat brain
Z01BB-07007-01 (LMP) MORRIS, D FDA Forskolin photoaffinity labels as probes of diverse membrane proteins
Z01BB-07008-01 (LMP) BEAUCAGE, S L FDA Advances in the synthesis of oligonucleotides via the phosphoramidite approach
Z01BB-07009-01 (LMP) BEAUCAGE, S L FDA Oligothymidylates with alternating (3'-3') and (5'-5') phosphodiester linkages
Z01BB-07010-01 (LMP) BEAUCAGE, S L FDA Cellular uptake of oligonucleotide analogues
Z01BB-07011-01 (LMP) MOOS, M FDA Primary structure determination of signal transduction proteins
Z01BD-01001-03 (LCB) SHINAGAWA, SUSUMU FDA Activity of growth factors--Effects on cellular adhesion and cellular activity

PROJECT NO., ORGANIZATIONAL UNIT., INVESTIGATOR, ADDRESS, TITLE

Z01BD-01002-03 (LCB) SHINAGAWA, SUSUMU FDA Synthesis of peptide tertiary structural templates for AIDS vaccine development
Z01BD-01003-03 (LCB) LIU, SONG YUAN FDA Mechanisms of growth factor signal transduction-- EGF receptor
Z01BD-01004-03 (LCB) PACKARD, B FDA Tumor-derived soluble immunoregulatory factor
Z01BD-01005-03 (LCB) STROMBERG, K J FDA Autocrine role of ligands /receptors of the EGF family in ovarian carcinogenesis
Z01BD-01006-03 (LCB) PLUZNIK, D H FDA Differentiation of hematopoietic cells
Z01BD-01007-03 (LCB) PLUZNIK, D H FDA Biosynthesis of hematopoietic growth factors
Z01BD-01010-01 (LCB) JOHNSON, GIBBES R FDA The role and mechanism of action of amphiregulin in biological processes
Z01BD-01011-01 (LCB) KOMORIYA, AKIRA FDA Animal models for the long-term safety assessment of colony stimulating factors
Z01BD-02001-06 (LCI) SIEGEL, J P FDA Cytokine regulation of cytotoxic lymphocyte responses
Z01BD-02002-03 (LCI) PURI, R FDA Immunoregulation in vivo and in vitro by cytokines
Z01BD-02003-03 (LCI) PURI, R FDA IL-4 receptors on murine solid tumors and tumor infiltrating lymphocytes
Z01BD-02004-03 (LCI) PURI, R FDA Characterization of tumors and TIL from tumors induced by HHV-6
Z01BD-02007-03 (LCI) ROSENBERG, A FDA Cellular interactions and mechanisms of allograft rejection & tolerance induction
Z01BD-02012-01 (LCI) PURI, R FDA Expression of IL-4 receptors on human tumors
Z01BD-02016-01 (LCI) KOZAK, R W FDA Cytokines and the cascade of receptors--Lymphocyte activation
Z01BD-02017-01 (LCI) BLOOM, E T FDA Molecular and cellular regulation of natural killer cells
Z01BD-02018-01 (LCI) BLOOM, E T FDA Molecular and cellular regulation of cytolytic T cells and effects of age
Z01BD-03002-02 (LCR) HU, R Q FDA Evidence for multiple binding sites for several species of Hu IFN-alpha
Z01BD-03004-02 (LCR) BEKISZ, J FDA Antibodies to human IFN in J.L.P. patients treated with human IFN
Z01BD-03005-03 (LCR) MILLER, D M FDA Purification and characterization of natural human interferon alpha
Z01BD-03008-03 (LCR) HAYES, M FDA Regulation of interferon production by human monocytes
Z01BD-03009-02 (LCR) NGUYEN, N Y FDA Isolation of biologically active cytokines by non-denaturing PAGE
Z01BD-03010-03 (LCR) GERRARD, T L FDA Regulation and function of histocompatibility on human cells
Z01BD-03012-02 (LCR) GRUBER, M FDA Regulation of M-CSF message expression and M-CSF secretion by human monocytes
Z01BD-03013-02 (LCR) WEBB, D S FDA LFA-3, CD44, and CD45--Physiologic triggers of monocyte TNF and IL-1 release
Z01BD-03015-02 (LCR) WEBB, D S FDA Enhancement of ICAM-1 sensitizes tumor cells to monocyte-mediated lysis
Z01BD-03017-02 (LCR) CLOUSE-STREBEL, K FDA Identification of HIV proteins that stimulate monokine secretion
Z01BD-03018-02 (LCR) CLOUSE-STREBEL, K FDA Identification of EBV proteins that stimulate monokine secretion
Z01BD-03019-03 (LCR) FINBLOOM, D S FDA The role of cytokines and phagocytic cells in inflammation
Z01BD-03020-04 (LCR) LARNER, A FDA Mechanisms of IFN-regulated gene expression
Z01BD-03021-01 (LCR) HAYES, MARK P FDA Expression and characterization of recombinant human interferon alpha receptor
Z01BD-03022-03 (LCR) LIANG, SHU MEI FDA The effect of glutathione on interleukin-2 activity
Z01BD-03023-01 (LCR) LIANG, SHU-MEI FDA Production of anti-p24 monoclonal antibody against HIV-1 proteins
Z01BD-03024-01 (LCR) RONG, YANG FDA Structure /function studies of human interleukin-2
Z01BD-03025-01 (LCR) LIANG, SHU-MEI FDA Protein engineering of the interleukin-2 fusion protein
Z01BD-03026-01 (LCR) LIANG, SHU-MEI FDA Effect of glutathione on differentiation of primary activated lymphocytes
Z01BD-03027-01 (LCR) LIANG, SM FDA The effect of glutathione on interleukin-4 activity
Z01BD-03028-01 (LCR) FELDMAN, G FDA The role of cytokines in regulating inflammatory cell function
Z01BD-03029-01 (LCR) FELDMAN, G FDA Structural studies of the interleukin-4 receptor
Z01BD-03030-01 (LCR) HU, R Q FDA cDNA cloning and expression of human IFN-alpha species O
Z01BD-03031-01 (LCR) HU, R Q FDA Relation of structure and function of Hu IFN-gamma by site-directed mutagenesis
Z01BD-03032-01 (LCR) DONNELLY, R P FDA Regulation of interleukin-1 beta gene expression in human monocytes by IL-4
Z01BD-03033-01 (LCR) WEBB, D S FDA Self regulation of ICAM-1 expression in melanoma cells
Z01BD-03034-01 (LCR) WEBB, D S FDA Production of monocyte colony stimulating factor by human melanoma cells
Z01BD-03035-01 (LCR) CLOUSE-STREBEL, K A FDA Identification of the receptor(s) on human MO that binds to HIV-1 gp120
Z01BD-03036-01 (LCR) CLOUSE-STREBEL, K A FDA Identification of an NK cell derived factor that suppresses HIV infection of MO
Z01BD-04001-03 (LI) TOSATO, G FDA A role for interleukin 6 in the pathogenesis of HIV infection in humans
Z01BD-04002-03 (LI) TOSATO, G FDA Study of B cell growth by Epstein Barr virus
Z01BD-04003-03 (LI) FRUGONI, P FDA Immunoregulation of EBV-infected B lymphocytes
Z01BD-04008-03 (LI) MAX, E E FDA Gene regulation in B lymphocytes
Z01BD-04011-03 (LI) NORCROSS, M A FDA Involvement of proteoglycans and polyanionic polysaccharides in HIV infection
Z01BD-04012-03 (LI) NORCROSS, M A FDA Analysis of RAF-oncogene related novel protein kinase gene
Z01BD-04013-03 (LI) CALLAHAN, L FDA Characterization of human antibodies to HIV which block gp120-CD4 interactions
Z01BD-04014-01 (LI) TOSATO, G FDA Interleukin-6: A transcription activating cytokine
Z01BD-04015-01 (LI) TANNER, J FDA Biochemical and biological analysis of human recombinant IL-6
Z01BD-04016-01 (LI) TOSATO, G FDA IL-6 is tumorigenic for EBV immortalized B cells
Z01BD-04017-01 (LI) TOSATO, G FDA Interleukin-10 inhibits T cell proliferation and interferon gamma production
Z01BD-04018-01 (LI) NORCROSS, M A FDA Analysis of HIV-induced auto-antibodies to cryptic epitopes of human CD4
Z01BD-04019-01 (LI) MAX, E E FDA Lymphokine regulation of immunoglobulin isotype switching
Z01BE-01001-09 (LBT) HOCHSTEIN, H D FDA Comparison of limulus amebocyte lysate (LAL) test with the rabbit pyrogen test
Z01BE-01002-06 (LBT) LUKAS, J M FDA Development of in vitro potency assay for diphtheria antitoxin
Z01BE-01003-03 (LBT) RAMOS, R FDA Development of in vitro potency assay for tetanus antitoxin
Z01BE-01004-03 (LBT) HEINTZELMAN, M D FDA Diphtheria antitoxin master standard replacement
Z01BE-01005-01 (LBT) KEARNS, D FDA Fungistasis testing of some biological products
Z01BE-03001-09 (OD) FITZGERALD, E A FDA Comparison of in vivo and in vitro potency tests for rabies vaccine
Z01BE-03002-10 (OD) FITZGERALD, E A FDA Rabies immunization antibody detection in at-risk personnel
Z01BE-03003-07 (OD) ROSCIOLI, N E FDA Development of an SRID potency test for rabies vaccine
Z01BE-03004-03 (OD) ROSCIOLI, N A FDA Development of an ELISA for rabies vaccine potency
Z01BE-03005-02 (OD) CHUMAKOV, K FDA Molecular diagnostics of reversion to neurovirulence in poliovirus vaccines
Z01BE-03007-02 (OD) LEVENBOOK, I S FDA An improved ATG treated newborn rat model for metastasis study
Z01BE-03008-02 (OD) RIDGE, J FDA Development of an in vitro assay for neurovirulence of live poliovirus vaccines
Z01BF-01001-07 (LDVR) MARCUS-SEKURA, C J FDA Epitope mapping of the EBV membrane antigen
Z01BF-01002-02 (LDVR) MARCUS-SEKURA, C J FDA Expression of HIV antigens in E coli
Z01BF-01003-02 (LDVR) MARCUS-SEKURA, C J FDA Inhibition of gene expression by normal & modified antisense oligonucleotides
Z01BF-01004-02 (LDVR) MANISCHEWITZ, J F FDA Detection of human cytomegalovirus infections
Z01BF-01005-02 (LDVR) MANISCHEWITZ, J F FDA Virological studies of recipients of HIV-1 vaccines
Z01BF-01006-04 (LDVR) GOLDING, H FDA Analysis of chemical induced T cell mutants with resistance to HIV-1 infection
Z01BF-01007-02 (LDVR) GOLDING, H FDA Molecular mimicry and generation of immunosuppressive autoantibodies in AIDS
Z01BF-01008-02 (LDVR) GOLDING, H FDA Production of peptide-based, T cell independent HIV-1 vaccine
Z01BF-01009-02 (LDVR) MARCUS-SEKURA, C J FDA Detection of viruses in cell substrates
Z01BF-01010-02 (LDVR) RAZZAQUE, A FDA Mechanistic approaches to HCMV mtrIII-induced transformation
Z01BF-01011-02 (LDVR) RAZZAQUE, A FDA Oncogenic potential of human herpesvirus-6
Z01BF-01012-02 (LDVR) RAZZAQUE, A FDA HHV-6 DNA induced tumors and tumor infiltraion lymphocytes
Z01BF-01013-01 (LDVR) GOLDING, H FDA Studies of HIV-1 env-mediated membrane fusion and syncytia formation
Z01BF-01014-01 (LDVR) MANISCHEWITZ, J F FDA CMV induction of tumor necrosis factor (TNF alpha) in infected tissue
Z01BF-01015-06 (LDVR) ARMSTRONG, G R FDA Studies of Epstein-Barr virus, HTLV II and related diseases
Z01BF-02001-15 (LRVD) WILLIAMS, M S FDA Standardized reagents for potency testing of influenza virus vaccines
Z01BF-02002-06 (LRVD) LEVANDOWSKI, R A FDA Cellular and humoral immune responses to rhinoviruses
Z01BF-02003-03 (LRVD) LEVANDOWSKI, R A FDA Influenza vaccine development and use
Z01BF-02004-03 (LRVD) BEELER, J A FDA Antigenic and molecular characterization of the fusion glycoprotein of RSV
Z01BF-02005-01 (LRVD) BEELER, J FDA Sequencing of PCR amplified cDNA of the gene for the RSV fusion glycoprotein
Z01BF-02006-01 (LRVD) BEELER, J FDA Immune response to formalin treated respiratory syncytial virus
Z01BF-02007-01 (LVRD) LEVANDOWSKI, R A FDA Influenza reassortant virus--Biology and genetics
Z01BF-03002-06 (LPD) LUNDQUIST, R E FDA Analysis of the initial events in the in vivo replication of poliovirus RNA
Z01BF-03003-08 (LPD) LUNDQUIST, R E FDA Quantitation of poliovirus D-antigen in inactivated poliovirus vaccines
Z01BF-03005-02 (LPD) MULLER, J FDA Electron microscopy studies
Z01BF-03006-02 (LPD) SAWYER, L A FDA International collaborative study of polio reagents
Z01BF-03008-02 (LPD) SAWYER, L A FDA Varying reactivities of monoclonal antibodies with the same polio vaccine
Z01BF-03010-01 (LPD) ALBRECHT, P FDA Immunization of six and nine month old infants against measles
Z01BF-03011-01 (LPD) AALBRECHT, P FDA Measles outbreak in a fully vaccinated school population
Z01BF-03012-01 (LPD) LUNDQUIST, R E FDA Sequential propagation of poliovirus RNA genomes using improved transfection
Z01BF-03013-01 (LPD) SAWYER, L A FDA Reactions following immunization with Japanese encephalitis virus vaccine
Z01BF-03014-01 (LPD) SAWYER, L A FDA Nonresponders to human diploid cell rabies vaccine, intradermal
Z01BF-03015-01 (LPD) SAWYER, L A FDA Potency test for Japanese

encephalitis virus vaccine, inactivated, lyophilized
Z01BF-04001-06 (LRR) WELLS, M FDA HIV in patients and animals--Cell mediated immunity and viral isolation
Z01BF-04003-03 (LRR) KLINMAN, D M FDA B cell activation in pathologic states
Z01BF-04011-01 (LRR) SAWYER, L A FDA Further development of the rhesus monkey as a model of HIV infection
Z01BF-04012-01 (LRR) CARROW, E W FDA Neutralizing and PND-specific BA to HIV-1 strains in Japanese hemophiliac sera
Z01BF-04013-01 (LRR) CARROW, E W FDA Development of a method for measuring HIV-1 specific NA by inhibition of p24 Ag
Z01BF-04014-01 (LRR) VOJCIC, L K FDA Sera tested for neutralizating antibodies against autologous HIV-1 isolates
Z01BF-04015-01 (LRR) VUJCIC, L K FDA Preparation of HIV-1 reference reagents for the World Health Organization
Z01BF-04016-01 (LRR) VUJCIC, L K FDA V3 loop region synthetic peptides are used to block HIV-1 neutralization
Z01BF-05001-03 (LHR) FEINSTONE, S M FDA Antigenic structure of hepatitis A virus
Z01BF-05002-04 (LHR) FEINSTONE, S M FDA Molecular characterization of HAV
Z01BF-05003-03 (LHR) FEINSTONE, S M FDA Non-A non-B hepatitis
Z01BG-04001-02 (LH) BISWAS, R FDA Serum HBV-DNA and HBeAg in acute hepatitis predicts progression to chronicity
Z01BG-04002-02 (LH) BISWAS, R FDA Hepatitis C and therapeutic immunoglobulin product saftey--A chimpanzee study
Z01BG-04004-02 (LH) NEDJAR, S FDA Simultaneous detection of HIV-1 and HCV genomic sequences by PCR
Z01BG-04008-01 (LH) NEDJAR, S FDA Simultaneous detection of HBV and HCV genomic sequences by PCR
Z01BG-04009-01 (LH) WILSON, L FDA Analytical sensitivity of test kits to detect antibodies to hepatitis B antigens
Z01BG-06015-02 (LR) HEWLETT, I FDA Mechanism of antiviral activity of novel and established anti-HIV agents
Z01BG-06016-02 (LR) HEWLETT, I K FDA Assessment of HIV infection in Spanish seronegative IVDA's and their partners
Z01BG-06017-03 (LR) HEWLETT, I K FDA Detection of multiple viruses by PCR co-amplification
Z01BG-06018-03 (LR) HEWLETT, I K FDA Quantitative detection by PCR of HIV-1 DNA and RNA in serum and cultures
Z01BG-06021-02 (LR) HEWLETT, I K FDA Infection of non-hematopoietic cells with HIV-1 and HIV-2
Z01BG-06022-02 (LR) HEWLETT, I K FDA Induction of HIV-1 from latently infected cell lines by chemical carcinogens
Z01BG-06024-03 (LR) RUTA, M FDA Role of FGF receptor in tumors
Z01BG-06026-04 (LR) GEYER, S J FDA Optimization and quantification of markers of HIV infection and replication
Z01BG-06030-02 (LR) GEYER, S J FDA Characterization of messengers controlling HIV replication
Z01BG-06031-02 (LR) GEYER, S J FDA Characterization and mapping of HIV neutralizing antibodies
Z01BG-06033-02 (LR) GEYER, S J FDA HIV messengers and regulatory factors by FACS, IFA and hybridization
Z01BG-06035-01 (LR) EPSTEIN, J S FDA Inhibition of HIV-1 expression by deferoxamine, an iron chelating agent
Z01BG-06036-01 (LR) EPSTEIN, J S FDA Prevalence of Yersinia enterocolitica in stored red blood cells
Z01BG-06037-01 (LR) EPSTEIN, J S FDA Blood storage patterns and red cell contamination by Yersinia enterocolitica
Z01BG-06038-01 (LR) HEWLETT, I K FDA Cellular factors that control viral expression and regulation
Z01BG-06039-01 (LR) HEWLETT, I K FDA Efficacy of passive immunotherapy in AIDS assessed by PCR
Z01BG-06040-01 (LR) HEWLETT, I K FDA Immunization with HIV immune globulin in the prevention of HIV infection in Pan
Z01BG-06041-01 (LR) HEWLETT, I K FDA Inhibition and regulation of HIV gene expression with antisense oligonucleotides
Z01BG-06042-01 (LR) HEWLETT, I K FDA Viral determinants of HIV-1 pathogenesis by construction of recombinant viruses
Z01BG-06043-01 (LR) POFFENBERGER, K FDA Modulation of HIV-1 expression by antisense RNA
Z01BG-06044-01 (LR) POFFENBERGER, K FDA Modulation of HIV-1 expression with triple-helix-forming oligonucleotides
Z01BG-06045-01 (LR) POFFENBERGER, K FDA HIV infection of hematopoetic cells at differing stages of differentiation
Z01BG-06046-01 (LR) SELVAM, M P FDA Colon cancer cell growth inhibition using antisense oligos against CRYPTO
Z01BG-06047-01 (LR) SELVAM, M P FDA Comparative inhibition of HIV replication by nystatin A
Z01BG-06048-01 (LR) SELVAM, M P FDA HIV-1 protease inhibitor cerulenin as an antiviral agent
Z01BG-06049-01 (LR) SELVAM, M P FDA Specific delivery of antiviral agents using immunoliposomes
Z01BG-06050-01 (LR) SELVAM, M P FDA Development and characterization of a new RIPA for detection of HIV-2 antibodies
Z01BG-06051-01 (LR) MAYNER, R FDA Development and characterization of a new RIPA for detection of HIV-2 antibodies
Z01BG-06052-01 (LR) RUTA, M FDA Characterization of HTLV standards
Z01BG-06053-01 (LR) RUTA, M FDA HTLV-I reference reagents
Z01BG-06054-01 (LR) RUTA, M FDA T-cell line from an aplastic anemia patient that produces high levels of HTLV-II
Z01BG-06055-01 (LR) RUTA, M FDA Role of fibroblast growth factor receptor in stomach tumors
Z01BG-06056-01 (LR) GEYER, S J FDA HIV survival in packed red cells
Z01BH-01001-02 (LCH) HARVATH, L FDA Leukocyte common antigen (CD45) is involved in neutrophil chemotaxis
Z01BH-01003-06 (LCH) HARVATH, L FDA Biphasic filamentous-actin polymerization in activated neutrophils
Z01BH-01006-07 (LCH) HARVATH, L FDA Flow cytometry facility
Z01BH-01007-03 (LCH) HARVATH, L FDA Laser scanning confocal microscopy facility
Z01BH-01008-08 (LCH) PRODOUZ, K N FDA Effect of the photosensitizer merocyanine 540 on platelet membranes
Z01BH-01009-03 (LCH) PRODOUZ, K N FDA Inactivation of surrogate viruses with merocyanine 540
Z01BH-01010-05 (LCH) PRODOUZ, K N FDA Inactivation of viruses in blood products by inhibition of viral nucleic acid
Z01BH-01011-04 (LCH) PRODOUZ, K N FDA Photochemical inactivation of virus in blood products
Z01BH-01012-02 (LCH) PRODOUZ, K N FDA The effect of beta-lactam antibiotics on platelet proteins
Z01BH-01013-02 (LCH) PRODOUZ, K N FDA Development of new assays to evaluate function of stored platelets
Z01BH-01016-02 (LCH) ALAYASH, A I FDA Modified hemoglobins as a source of activated oxygen species
Z01BH-01017-02 (LCH) ALAYASH, A I FDA Modified hemoglobins and their reactions with ligands
Z01BH-01024-01 (LCH) FRATANTONI, J C FDA Investigation of the platelet response to hypotonic stress
Z01BH-01025-01 (LCH) PRODOUZ, K N FDA Induction of calpain activity during storage of platelet concentrates
Z01BH-01026-01 (LCH) ALAYASH, A I FDA Hypothermic conditions affect O2-carrying capacity of crosslinked hemoglobins
Z01BH-01027-01 (LCH) ALAYASH, A I FDA Autooxidation and stability of crosslinked hemoglobins
Z01BH-01028-01 (LCH) ALAYASH, A I FDA Interactions of modified hemoglobins with iron chelators
Z01BH-01029-01 (LCH) HARVATH, L FDA Lamin peptides stimulate human neutrophil chemokinesis
Z01BH-02001-02 (LCB) HOFFMAN, T FDA Regulation of arachidonate metabolism by lipid mediators and calcium
Z01BH-02002-02 (LCB) HOFFMAN, T FDA Regulation of lymphokine production and release by lipid mediators and calcium
Z01BH-02003-03 (LCB) JESSOP, J J FDA Mechanism for interleukin 1-beta release from human monocytes
Z01BH-02004-02 (LCB) TRIPATHI, A K FDA Mechanism of the monocyte-mediated antibody dependent cellular cytotoxicity
Z01BH-02005-02 (LCB) PURI, J FDA Monocyte differentiation: Role of tyrosine phosphorylation via CSF-1 receptor
Z01BH-02006-03 (LCB) MONOHAR, V FDA Development of a hemopoietic stem cell model: Further studies
Z01BH-02007-02 (LCB) PURI, J FDA Cross linking of class II molecules as a signal in regulation of monocytes
Z01BH-02008-02 (LCB) GOLDING, B FDA Immunoconjugates that will be effective in eliciting anti-HIV response
Z01BH-02009-02 (LCB) GOLDING, B FDA Effects of Brucella abortus and LPS-BA on lymphokine secretion
Z01BH-02010-03 (LCB) BONVINI, E FDA Signal transduction via the T cell receptor /CD3 complex
Z01BH-02012-03 (LCB) ALAVA, M A FDA Modulation of TCR /CD3 signal transduction by c-AMP /protein kinase A
Z01BH-02013-02 (LCB) CONTI, A FDA Analysis of inositol phosphate metabolism in lymphocytes by HPLC
Z01BH-02014-03 (LCB) DEBELL, K FDA Role of cytoskeleton in T cell receptor signal transduction
Z01BH-02017-01 (LCB) HOFFMAN, T FDA Regulation of arachidonate metabolism at the level of protein synthesis
Z01BH-02018-01 (LCB) BRUNSWICK, M FDA Analysis of signal transduction in normal murine B lymphocyte
Z01BH-02019-01 (LCB) HOFFMAN, T FDA Role of monocytes in adverse reactions to monoclonal antibody therapy
Z01BH-05012-02 (LPD) KAUFMAN, B FDA Antiidiotype vaccines against flaviviruses
Z01BH-05014-05 (LPD) SHRAKE, A F FDA Origins of ligand-induced multiphasic thermal protein denaturation
Z01BH-05015-09 (LPD) SHRAKE, A F FDA Physical characterization of colloidal plasma volume expanders
Z01BH-05016-02 (LPD) SHRAKE, A F FDA Ligand-induced biphasic protein unfolding by strong denaturants
Z01BH-05018-02 (LPD) TANKERSLEY, D L FDA Mechanism of formation of immunoglobulin G dimer
Z01BH-05021-03 (LPD) YEI, SS FDA Expression and characterization of preS peptides of HBsAg in E. coli
Z01BH-05022-02 (LPD) YU, M W FDA The protectivity of an anti-subtype d against HBV infection
Z01BH-05024-01 (LPD) SHRAKE, A F FDA Investigations of protein structure
Z01BH-05025-01 (LPD) TANKERSLEY, D L FDA Standardization of a reference immune globulin preparation
Z01BH-05026-01 (LPD) YU, M W FDA Preparation and characterization of polyclonal anti-rpreSes of HBsAg
Z01BH-07001-02 (LHT) LAMB, M A FDA Coagulation factor IX standardization study
Z01BH-07002-01 (LHT) LAMB, M A FDA Von Willebrand factor standardization study
Z01BH-07003-01 (LHT) LAMB, M A FDA Molecular integrity of FVIII in commercial FVIII concentrates
Z01BH-07004-02 (LHT) LEWIS, R M FDA Interaction of tissue factor pathway inhibitor with VIIa and Xa
Z01BH-07005-01 (LHT) LEWIS, R M FDA Development of antisera to tissue factor pathway inhibitor
Z01BH-07006-01 (LHT) BEEBE, D FDA Effect of various lipoprotein fractions on endothelial cells
Z01BH-07007-02 (LHT) BEEBE, D FDA Clearance studies in rabbits
Z01BH-07008-06 (LHT) BEEBE, D FDA Further characterization of the t-PA receptor on various cell lines
Z01BH-07009-06 (LHT) FRICKE, W FDA Seroconversion surveillance project
Z01BH-07010-01 (LHT) FRICKE, W FDA Comparison of the chromogenic and one-stage assays for factor IX
Z01BH-07011-01 (LHT) FRICKE, W FDA Activation of fVIII by fXa and inhibition by tissue factor pathway inhibitor
K06CA-00685-31 (NCR) MUELLER, GERALD C UNIV OF

PROJECT NO., ORGANIZATIONAL UNIT., INVESTIGATOR, ADDRESS, TITLE

PROJECT NO., ORGANIZATIONAL UNIT., INVESTIGATOR, ADDRESS, TITLE

WISCONSIN-MADISON 1400 UNIVERSITY AVENUE MADISON, WI 53706 Growth regulating mechanisms

K08CA-00961-05 (CT) YOUNG, JAMES W THE ROCKEFELLER UNIVERSITY 1230 YORK AVE NEW YORK, NY 10021-6399 Generation of primary human cytolytic T lymphocytes

K08CA-01102-06 (CT) MEEKER, TIMOTHY C VETERANS ADMIN MEDICAL CENTER 4150 CLEMENT ST., SECT. 111H SAN FRANCISCO, CA 94121 Molecular genetics of human leukemia and lymphoma

K04CA-01110-05 (GMA) WU, GEORGE Y UNIVERSITY OF CONNECTICUT 263 FARMINGTON AVE RM AM044 FARMINGTON, CT 06032 Drug targeting to hepatocytes

K04CA-01112-05 (EI) GREEN, WILLIAM R DARTMOUTH MEDICAL SCHOOL HANOVER, NH 03756 Cellular immunity to endogenous AKR/Gross leukemia virus

K08CA-01124-05 (CT) SULLIVAN, DANIEL MARK J.G. BROWN CANCER CENTER 529 SOUTH JACKSON STREET LOUISVILLE, KY 40292 DNA topoisomerase activity and cancer therapy

K04CA-01125-05 (HAR) LEONARD, REBECCA J UNIVERSITY OF CALIFORNIA, DAVI 2500 STOCKTON BLVD. SACRAMENTO, CALIFORNIA 95817 Articulatory dynamics in orofacial cancer patients

K04CA-01139-06 (EVR) SHALLOWAY, DAVID I CORNELL UNIVERSITY 120 DAY HALL ITHACA, NY 14853-2801 Regulation/activation of C-SRC transforming activity

K04CA-01152-05 (EDC) BUCKLEY, JONATHAN D UNIVERSITY OF SOUTHERN CALIF 2025 ZONAL AVENUE LOS ANGELES, CA 90033 Epidemiology of cancer in children

K04CA-01175-05 (CTY) BLOOM, KERRY S UNIVERSITY OF NORTH CAROLINA WILSON HALL, CB #3280 CHAPEL HILL, N C 27599-3280 Structural analysis of a eukaryotic centromere

K04CA-01179-05 (BNP) IRELAND, CHRIS M UNIVERSITY OF UTAH SALT LAKE CITY, UTAH 84112 Antineoplastic agents from marine organisms

K07CA-01181-06 (SRC) LYNCH, CHARLES F UNIVERSITY OF IOWA 2800 STEINDLER BUILDING IOWA CITY, IA 52242 Preventive oncology academic award

K04CA-01189-06 (MGN) SKLAR, JEFFREY LEWIS BRIGHAM AND WOMEN'S HOSPITAL 75 FRANCIS STREET BOSTON, MA 02115 Genetic analysis of human lymphoid neoplasia

K08CA-01199-05 (SRC) PELLEY, ROBERT J CASE WESTERN RESERVE UNIVERSIT 2074 ABINGTON ROAD CLEVELAND, OH 44106 Erb-B activation: from EGF-receptor to leukemia oncogene

K04CA-01205-05 (ET) HACKER, MILES P UNIVERSITY OF VERMONT BURLINGTON, VT 05405 Modulation of organ specific anticancer drug

K04CA-01208-06 (BMT) TULLIUS, THOMAS D JOHN HOPKINS UNIVERSITY CHARLES AND 34TH STREETS BALTIMORE, MARYLAND 21218 Using metals to study DNA and DNA-protein complexes

K04CA-01226-05 (CBY) BARNES, DAVID W OREGON STATE UNIVERSITY CORVALLIS, OREGON 97331 Cell-substratum interactions

K08CA-01227-06 (SRC) CROOP, JAMES M DANA-FARBER CANCER INSTITUTE 44 BINNEY STREET BOSTON, MA 02115 Multidrug resistance genes - analysis and applications

K08CA-01229-05 (SRC) KENNEY, SHANNON C UNIV OF N C AT CHAPEL HILL 210 LINEBERGER CCRC, CB#7295 CHAPEL HILL, N C 27599 NCI clinical investigator award

K04CA-01230-05 (CPA) KENSLER, THOMAS W THE JOHNS HOPKINS UNIVERSITY 615 NORTH WOLFE STREET BALTIMORE, MD 21205 Molecular mechanisms of anticarcinogenesis

K08CA-01240-05 (SRC) NEGLIA, JOSEPH P UNIVERSITY OF MINNESOTA 420 DELAWARE ST SE-BOX 484 MINNEAPOLIS, MN 55455 Second malignant neoplasms following childhood leukemia

K04CA-01241-05 (ET) SAVARESE, TODD M BROWN UNIVERSITY BOX G PROVIDENCE, RI 02912 Chemotherapeutic consequences of glutathione depletion

K08CA-01254-03 (CT) GREENBERG, JAMES M CHILDREN'S HOSPITAL MED CTR ELLAND AND BETHESDA AVENUE CINCINNATI, OH 45229-2899 Human T-cell gamma & delta rearranging genes in leukemia

K11CA-01272-05 (SRC) LICHT, JONATHAN D DANA-FARBER CANCER INSTITUTE 44 BINNEY STREET BOSTON, MA 02115 Molecular cloning of a eukaryotic transcription factor

K11CA-01279-07 (SRC) GAUWERKY, CHARLOTTE THOMAS JEFFERSON UNIVERSITY 1025 WALNUT STREET PHILADELPHIA, PA 19107 Molecular studies on the evolution of b-cell lymphomas

K11CA-01283-05 (SRC) ROSMARIN, ALAN G MIRIAM HOSPITAL 164 SUMMIT AVENUE PROVIDENCE, RI 02906 In situ hybridization study of myeloid gene expression

K07CA-01286-05 (SRC) GOTTLIEB, NELL H U T HEALTH SCI CTR AT HOUSTON POST OFFICE BOX 20186 HOUSTON, TX 77225 Preventive oncology academic award

K04CA-01287-05 (TOX) GUENTHNER, THOMAS M UNIV OF ILLINOIS AT CHICAGO 835 SO. WOLCOTT AVE CHICAGO, IL 60680 Multiplicity of human xenobiotic-metabolizing enzymes

K07CA-01291-06 (SRC) GARABRANT, DAVID H UNIVERSITY OF MICHIGAN 1522 SPH I ANN ARBOR, MI 48109-2029 Preventive oncology academic award

K08CA-01299-05 (SRC) PEACE, DAVID J UNIVERSITY OF WASHINGTON BB1321 HEALTH SCIENCES BLDG SEATTLE, WA 98195 NCI clinical investigator award

K04CA-01304-04 (CBY) MATSUMURA, FUMIO RUTGERS UNIVERSITY P O BOX 1059 PISCATAWAY, NJ 08854 Tropomyosins in normal and transformed cells

K11CA-01309-06 (SRC) BEAUCHAMP, ROBERT DANIEL UNIV OF TEXAS MEDICAL BRANCH GALVESTON, TX 77550 Growth factors and pancreatic cancer (hamsters, rats, mice)

K11CA-01314-05 (SRC) ROSENBLATT, JOSEPH D UNIVERSITY OF CALIFORNIA 405 HILGARD AVE LOS ANGELES, CA 90024 The role of novel X-region proteins in HTLV-1 and HTLV-11

K04CA-01319-04 (RNM) MATTREY, ROBERT F UNIV OF CALIFORNIA MED CTR 225 DICKINSON STREET SAN DIEGO, CA 92103-9981 Perfluorocarbon applications in diagnostic imaging

K04CA-01324-05 (HEM) GEWIRTZ, ALAN M UNIVERSITY OF PENNSYLVANIA 133 SOUTH 36TH STREET PHILADELPHIA, PA 19104-3246 Regulation of human megakaryocytopoiesis

K11CA-01326-04 (SRC) FRIEDMAN, ALAN D JOHNS HOPKINS HOSPITAL 600 NORTH WOLFE STREET BALTIMORE, MD 21205 Mechanisms of trans-activation of herpesvirus genes

K04CA-01330-04 (MCHA) WILLIARD, PAUL G DEPT OF CHEMISTRY BOX H BROWN UNIVERSITY PROVIDENCE, RI 02912 Structural studies of enolates for organic synthesis

K04CA-01335-04 (CPA) PENNING, TREVOR M UNIVERSITY OF PENNSYLVANIA PHILADELPHIA, PA 19104 Dihydrodiol dehydrogenase and PAH detoxification

K04CA-01337-05 (MCHA) WINKLER, JEFFREY DAVID UNIVERSITY OF PENNSYLVANIA 133 SOUTH 36TH STREET PHILADELPHIA, PA 19104-3246 New methodology for the synthesis of anti tumor agents

K08CA-01339-01A2 (CT) WARREN, STEPHEN L YALE UNIVERSITY SCHOOL OF MED P.O. BOX 3333 NEW HAVEN, CT 06510 Regulation of epithelial morphogenesis by pp60 c-src

K11CA-01341-05 (SRC) BIRKENBACH, MARK P HARVARD MEDICAL SCHOOL 25 SHATTUCK STREET BOSTON, MA 02115 Growth transformation of lymphocytes by Epstein-Barr virus infection

K11CA-01342-04 (CT) SKILLING, STEPHEN R UNIVERSITY OF MINNESOTA 1988 FITCH AV, VET MED BLDG ST PAUL, MN 55108 Modulation primary afferent activity: eaas & substance P

K04CA-01343-04 (PTHB) HOLMES, ERIC H PACIFIC NORTHWEST RES FDN 720 BROADWAY SEATTLE, WA 98122 Glycosyltransferase activation in colonic adenocarcinoma

K04CA-01349-04 (BNP) SKIBO, EDWARD B ARIZONA STATE UNIVERSITY TEMPE, AZ 85287 The design of antitumor reductive alkylators

K04CA-01350-04 (ET) MOKYR, MARGALIT B UNIVERSITY OF ILLINOIS 835 SOUTH WOLCOTT, M/C 790 CHICAGO, IL 60612 Mechanism of melphalan-mediated tumor eradication

K04CA-01351-03 (PTHB) BARSKY, SANFORD H UCLA SCHOOL OF MEDICINE 13-188 CHS 173216 LOS ANGELES, CA 90024-1732 Tumor cell-desmoplastic response interactions

K08CA-01352-02 (CT) STONE, RICHARD M DANA-FARBER CANCER INSTITUTE 44 BINNEY STREET BOSTON, MA 02115 Differentiation signal transduction in myeloid leukemia

K07CA-01353-05 (SRC) HO, E E NORTHERN CALIF CANCER CENTER 1301 SHOREWAY ROAD, SUITE 425 BELMONT, CA 94002 Preventive oncology academic award

K11CA-01358-04 (CT) KRAUS, VIRGINIA B DUKE UNIVERSITY MEDICAL CENTER P O BOX 3054 DURHAM, NC 27710 Cellular genes mediating ela-like transcription control

K08CA-01363-04 (CT) BROWN, MYLES A DANA-FARBER CANCER INSTITUTE 44 BINNEY STREET BOSTON, MA 02115 Regulation of estrogen receptor expression

K07CA-01364-04 (SRC) STANFORD, JANET L FRED HUTCHINSON CANCER RESEARC 1124 COLUMBIA STREET SEATTLE, WA 98104 Preventive oncology academic award

K04CA-01369-02 (HEM) CHIU, ING-MING OHIO ST UNIV/ DAVIS MED RES CT 480 WEST 9TH AVENUE COLUMBUS, OH 43210 Heparin-binding growth factor-1--Structure and function

K08CA-01371-04 (CT) WILEY, JOSEPH M JOHNS HOPKINS ONCOLOGY CENTER 600 NORTH WOLFE STREET BALTIMORE, MD 21205 Novel marrow purging regimens in rat leukemia

K04CA-01374-04 (EDC) DAVIS, SCOTT FRED HUTCHINSON CANCER RES CTR 1124 COLUMBIA STREET SEATTLE, WASH 98004 Etiologic studies of hematopoietic cancer and radiation

K07CA-01380-04 (SRC) KOH, HOWARD K BOSTON SCHOOL OF PUBLIC HEALTH 80 EAST CONCORD ST M-948 BOSTON, MA 02118 Preventive oncology academic award

K04CA-01382-04 (CPA) PELLING, JILL C UNIV OF NEBRASKA MED CNTR 600 SOUTH 42ND STREET OMAHA, NE 68198 Two-stage skin carcinogenesis and Ha-ras gene expression

K11CA-01385-04 (CT) DECAPRIO, JAMES DANA-FARBER CANCER INSTITUTE 44 BINNEY STREET BOSTON, MA 02115 Controlled regulation of SV40 T antigen synthesis

K11CA-01391-03 (CT) JENISON, STEVE A UNIVERSITY OF NEW MEXICO SCHOOL OF MEDICINE ALBUQUERQUE, NM 87131 Immune responses to HPVS involved in genital neoplasia

K11CA-01392-04 (CT) SWAMINATHAN, SANKAR HARVARD MEDICAL SCHOOL 25 SHATTUCK STREET BOSTON, MA 02115 Epstein-Barr encoded RNAs and latent gene expression

K07CA-01397-04 (SRC) BEGG, LISA UNIVERSITY OF PITTSBURGH 130 DESOTO STREET PITTSBURGH, PA 15261 Preventive oncology academic award

K04CA-01401-03 (ALY) YARMUSH, MARTIN L RUTGERS, STATE UNIV OF NJ P O BOX 909 PISCATAWAY, NJ 08855-0909 Dynamics of antigen-antibody interactions

K11CA-01408-02 (SRC) KELLY, KAREN L UNIV OF COLO HLTH SCIENCE CTR 4200 E. 9TH AVE. DENVER, CO 80262 Expression of mucin genes in lung cancer

K08CA-01412-03 (CT) EDER, JOSEPH P BETH ISRAEL HOSPITAL 330 BROOKLINE AVENUE BOSTON, MA 02115 The role of DNA repair in cisplatin resistance

K08CA-01418-03 (CT) TALCOTT, JAMES A DANA-FARBER CANCER INSTITUTE 44 BINNEY ST, MAYER 3A 28 BOSTON, MA 02115 Clinical and classical epidemiology in oncology

K11CA-01419-03 (CT) MACGREGOR, DOUGLAS N NEW YORK UNIVERSITY MEDICAL CT 550 FIRST AVENUE NEW YORK, NY 10016 A study of the genetic origins of medulloblastoma

K08CA-01422-02 (CT) DRUKER, BRIAN J DANA-FARBER CANCER INSTITUTE 44 BINNEY STREET BOSTON, MA 02115 Genetic analysis of the activation of a tyrosine kinase

K11CA-01423-01A3 (CT) ROH, MARK S U.T.M.D. ANDERSON CANCER CENTE 1515 HOLCOMBE BLVD HOUSTON, TX 77030 Immunology and liver metastases

K04CA-01424-03 (CPA) ASHENDEL, CURTIS L PURDUE UNIVERSITY R. HEINE PHARMACY BUILDING WEST LAFAYETTE, IN 47907 Molecular mechanisms of multi-stage carcinogenesis

K08CA-01429-03 (CT) DOWNING, JAMES R ST JUDE CHILDREN'S RES HOSP 332 N LAUDERDALE MEMPHIS, TN 38105 Csf-1 receptor tyrosine kinase

K04CA-01441-03 (RAD) DOETSCH, PAUL W EMORY UNIVERSITY ATLANTA, GA 30322 Radiation-induced DNA damage and repair in eukaryotes

K11CA-01443-03 (CT) ADAMS, ROBERTA H UNIVERSITY OF UTAH MEDICAL CTR 50 NORTH MEDICAL DRIVE SALT LAKE CITY, UT 84132 Molecular biology of translocation associated leukemias

K08CA-01449-02 (SRC) LIEBERMAN, JUDY NEW ENGLAND MEDICAL CENTER

750 WASHINGTON ST, BOX 245 BOSTON, MA 02111 The cytolytic mechanism of human T lymphocytes

K08CA-01451-03 (CT) **GEYER, J RUSSELL** UNIVERSITY OF WASHINGTON SEATTLE, WA 98195 Antineoplastic therapy toxicity in the developing CNS

K04CA-01457-04 (VR) **LIPSICK, JOSEPH STEVEN** SUNY AT STONY BROOK SCHOOL OF MEDICINE STONY BROOK, N Y 11794 Transformation by the myb oncogene

K11CA-01458-03 (CT) **KAUFMAN, PETER A** DUKE UNIVERSITY MEDICAL CTR BOX 3273 DURHAM, NC 27710 The tax protein of HTLV-I: mechanism of action and role

K07CA-01463-03 (SRC) **DUBROW, ROBERT D** YALE UNIVERSITY SCH OF MEDICIN 60 COLLEGE ST, PO BOX 3333 NEW HAVEN, CT 06510 Preventive oncology academic award

K11CA-01467-01A2 (CT) **FINE, HOWARD A** DANA-FARBER CANCER INSTITUTE 44 BINNEY ST BOSTON, MA 02115 Role of HTLV-1 X-region in cellular transformation

K07CA-01468-03 (SRC) **BAKER, MARY S** FRED HUTCHINSON CANCER RES CTR 1124 COLUMBIA STREET SEATTLE, WA 98104 Preventive oncology academic award

K11CA-01469-03 (CT) **UMBRICHT, CHRISTOPHER B** JOHNS HOPKINS UNIVERSITY 725 NORTH WOLFE ST, PCTB 602 BALTIMORE, MD 21205 Role of mammalian helicases in DNA replication

K08CA-01479-02 (CT) **MARKOVITZ, DAVID M** DIVISION OF INFECTIOUS DISEASE 3116 TAUBMAN HEALTH CENTER ANN ARBOR, MI 48109-0378 Cellular factors involved in HIV gene regulation

K04CA-01480-03 (EDC) **SILBER, JEFFREY H** CHILDREN'S HOSP OF PHILADELPHI 34TH & CIVIC CENTER BLVD PHILADELPHIA, PA 19104 Prediction and outcome measurement in childhood cancer

K08CA-01483-02 (CT) **SANDMAIER, BRENDA M** FRED HUTCHINSON CANCER RES CTR 1124 COLUMBIA STREET SEATTLE, WA 98104 Mechanism of antibody facilitated marrow engraftment

K08CA-01486-02 (CT) **HALL, CRAIG G** BETH ISRAEL HOSPITAL 330 BROOKLINE AVENUE BOSTON, MA 02215 Recognition of HLA-A2 molecule by human cytotoxic T cell

K08CA-01487-02 (SRC) **FETTEN, JAMES V** NORTH SHORE UNIV HOSPITAL 300 COMMUNITY DRIVE MANHASSET, NEW YORK 11030 Immunization via gene transfer

K08CA-01490-02 (CT) **BAHNSON, ROBERT R** UNIVERSITY OF PITTSBURGH 4414 PRESBYTERIAN UNIV. HOSPIT PITTSBURGH, PA 15213 Metallothionein and cytotoxic drug resistance

K11CA-01492-02 (CT) **WEN, PATRICK Y** BRIGHAM AND WOMEN'S HOSPITAL 75 FRANCIS STREET BOSTON, MA 02115 Immunotherapy for malignant gliomas

K11CA-01495-02 (CT) **SIMONS, JONATHAN W** THE JOHNS HOPKINS ONCOLOGY CTR 424 N. BOND STREET BALTIMORE, MD 21231 Characterization of human tumor suppressor genes

K04CA-01497-02 (ET) **AU, JESSIE L** OHIO STATE UNIVERSITY 500 WEST 12TH AVENUE COLUMBUS, OH 43210 Pharmacodynamics of agents for bladder cancer intravesical therapy

K11CA-01498-02 (CT) **FLETCHER, JONATHAN A** BRIGHAM AND WOMEN'S HOSPITAL 75 FRANCIS STREET BOSTON, MA 02115 Training in molecular cytogenetics of solid tumors

K08CA-01499-02 (SRC) **GRIBBIN, THOMAS E** 1150 W MED CTR DR/5510 MSRBI ANN ARBOR, MI 48109-0680 Cloning of t(3;4) a leukemia-associated translocation

K08CA-01501-03 (CT) **RATECH, HOWARD** DUKE UNIVERSITY MED CTR P O BOX 3250 DURHAM, N C 27710 Oncogenes and human B cell transformation

K11CA-01503-02 (CT) **ZUCKIER, LIONEL S** ALBERT EINSTEIN COLL OF MED 1300 MORRIS PARK AVE BRONX, NY 10461 Monoclonal antibody imaging in nuclear medicine

K11CA-01505-02 (CT) **LO, KWOK M** DANA FARBER CANCER INSTITUTE 44 BINNEY STREET BOSTON, MA 02115 Molecular mechanism of HTLV-I leukemogenesis

K08CA-01507-03 (CT) **MARASCO, WAYNE A** DANA-FARBER CANCER INSTITUTE 44 BINNEY STREET BOSTON, MA 02115 Cd23 - an autocrine growth factor and receptor

K08CA-01511-02 (CT) **WEBER, BARBARA L** UNIVERSITY OF MICHIGAN 1150 WEST MEDICAL CENTER DRIVE ANN ARBOR, MI 48109-0680 Molecular cloning and regulation of mammastatin

K11CA-01514-02 (CT) **ANDREWS, DAVID W** TEMPLE UNIVERSITY 3401 NORTH BROAD STREET PHILADELPHIA, PA 19140 Molecular pathogenesis of human primary brain tumors

K04CA-01517-03 (MEP) **GROOPMAN, JOHN D** JOHNS HOPKINS UNIV SCH/PUB HLT 615 NORTH WOLFE STREET BALTIMORE, MD 21205 Monitoring human exposure to aflatoxin

K07CA-01522-02 (SRC) **HELZLSOUER, KATHY J** JOHNS HOPKINS UNIVERSITY 615 N WOLFE ST BALTIMORE, MD 21205 Preventive oncology academic award

K11CA-01524-02 (SRC) **TSANG, SO-FAI** HARVARD MEDICAL SCHOOL BOSTON, MA 02115 The transactivation of CD23 by EBNA-2 and LMP

K11CA-01528-02 (SRC) **KAELIN, WILLIAM G, JR** DANA-FARBER CANCER INSTITUTE 44 BINNEY STREET BOSTON, MA 02115 Retinoblastoma susceptibility gene--Functional analysis

K08CA-01534-01A1 (CT) **DROBYSKI, WILLIAM** MEDICAL COLLEGE OF WISCONSIN 8701 WATERTOWN PLANK RD MILWAUKEE, WI 53226 Molecular detection of leukemia after allogeneic BMT

K07CA-01541-02 (SRC) **FIORE, MICHAEL C** CLINICAL SCIENCES CENTER 600 HIGHLAND AVE MADISON, WI 53792 Preventive oncology academic award

K08CA-01546-02 (SRC) **ROBERTS, WILLIAM M** ST JUDE CHILDREN'S RES HOSPITA 332 N LAUDERDALE MEMPHIS, TN 38105 Transcriptional regulation of the CSF-1 receptor gene

K08CA-01548-02 (SRC) **PILZ, RENATE B** UCSD MEDICAL CENTER 225 DICKINSON STREET SAN DIEGO, CA 92103 Role of G-kinase in differentiation--Use of HL-60 mutant

K08CA-01549-02 (SRC) **ROTH, MICHAEL D** UCLA MEDICAL CENTER 10833 LE CONTE AVENUE LOS ANGELES, CA 90024 Cytotoxic cell regulation by the pulmonary macrophage

K11CA-01551-02 (SRC) **SAWYERS, CHARLES L** UNIV OF CALIFORNIA, LOS ANGELE 405 HILGARD AVENUE LOS ANGELES, CA 90024-1570 P53 in chronic myelogenous leukemia

K08CA-01554-02 (SRC) **SCHENKEIN, DAVID P** NEW ENGLAND MED. CTR. HOSPITAL 750 WASHINGTON STREET, BOX 245 BOSTON, MA. 02111 Early events in retroviral replication

PROJECT NO., ORGANIZATIONAL UNIT., INVESTIGATOR, ADDRESS, TITLE

K11CA-01556-01 (CT) **MASHAL, ROBERT D** DANA-FARBER CANCER INSTITUTE 44 BINNEY STREET BOSTON, MA 02115 Detection of minimal residual disease in human cancer

K04CA-01557-01 (CPA) **FAGAN, JOHN B** MAHARISHI INTERNATIONAL UNIV FAIRFIELD, IA 52556 Carcinogen metabolizing p-450s-gene regulation

K11CA-01561-01 (CT) **KITCHELL, BARBARA E** RAF-1, QUAD 7, BUILDING 330 STANFORD, CALIFORNIA 94305 Molecular studies of retroviral oncogenesis

K08CA-01562-01 (CT) **POTTER, DAVID A** MASSACHUSETTS INST OF TECHNOLO 77 MASSACHUSETTS AVE CAMBRIDGE, MA 02139 Functional analysis of transcription factors in HIV-1

K11CA-01566-01 (CT) **BLACK, ALEXANDER C** UCLA MEDICAL CENTER 405 HILGARD AVE LOS ANGELES, CA 90024-1570 Regulation of HTLV II gene expression by Rex

K04CA-01571-02 (BNP) **GLOER, JAMES B** UNIVERSITY OF IOWA IOWA CITY, IA 52242 New antitumor and antifungal natural products from fungi

K11CA-01572-02 (CT) **CALIGIURI, MICHAEL A** ROSWELL PARK CANCER INSTITUTE CARLTON & ELM STREET BUFFALO, NY 14263 Characterization of thymic derived NK cells

K11CA-01573-01 (CT) **ROBERTS, DRUCILLA J** BRIGHAM & WOMEN'S HOSPITAL 75 FRANCIS STREET BOSTON, MA 02115 Pathobiology of parthenogenesis--Molecular controls

K11CA-01581-01 (CT) **BLUME, SCOTT** UNIV OF ALABAMA AT BIRMINGHAM UAB STATION BIRMINGHAM, AL 35294 Specific inhibition of DHFR and MDR1 transcription

K08CA-01586-01 (CT) **RUSTGI, ANIL K** MASSACHUSETTS GENERAL HOSPITAL 149 13TH STREET CHARLESTON, MA 02129 Myc-oncogenes in neuroblastoma and colon cancer

K04CA-01588-01 (ARRA) **MARTINEZ-MAZA, OTONIEL** UCLA SCHOOL OF MEDICINE SCHOOL OF MEDICINE LOS ANGELES, CA 90024-1740 Immune dysfunction and AIDS-related tumors

K08CA-01590-01 (CT) **RADANY, ERIC H** UNIVERSITY OF CALIFORNIA BOX 0552 SAN FRANCISCO, CA 94143 Molecular models for neoplasia in the gliomas

K07CA-01591-01 (CEC) **MC GLYNN, KATHERINE A** FOX CHASE CANCER CENTER 7701 BURHOLME AVE PHILADELPHIA, PA 19111 Preventive oncology academic award

K08CA-01595-01 (CT) **LEVITSKY, HYAM I** JOHNS HOPKINS UNIVERSITY 725 NORTH WOLFE STREET BALTIMORE, MD 21205 Analysis of a novel T cell subset-- The NK1+ alpha beta

K08CA-01599-01 (CT) **CASTLE, VALERIE P** UNIVERSITY OF MICHIGAN F6515 BOX 0238 ANN ARBOR, MI 48109 The role of thrombospondin in tumor cell biology

K08CA-01600-01 (CT) **CHERNY, RICHARD C** UNIVERSITY OF WASHINGTON SEATTLE, WA 98195 Role of vitronectin in tumor cell metastasis

K11CA-01602-01 (CT) **MASTRIANNI, DAVID M** BETH ISRAEL HOSPITAL 330 BROOKLINE AVENUE Molecular characterization of myelomonocytic leukemia

K07CA-01604-01 (CEC) **LERMAN, CARYN E** FOX CHASE CANCER CENTER 7701 BURHOLME AVENUE PHILADELPHIA, PA 19111 Impact of genetic counseling for breast cancer

K04CA-01605-01 (CTY) **SUDOL, MARIUS** THE ROCKEFELLER UNIVERSITY 1230 YORK AVENUE NEW YORK, NY 10021-6399 Functional analysis of proto-oncogenes

K11CA-01607-01 (CT) **BROWN, RUSSELL A** UNIV OF UTAH MEDICAL CENTER 50 N MEDICAL DRIVE SALT LAKE CITY, UT 84132 Structure and stability of the GCN4 leucine zipper

K04CA-01608-01 (END) **DE FRANCO, DONALD B** UNIVERSITY OF PITTSBURGH 552 CRAWFORD HALL PITTSBURGH, PA 15260 Intracellular mechanisms of glucocorticoid action

K11CA-01609-01 (CT) **HARPER, SEAN E** MASSACHUSETTS GENERAL HOSPITAL FRUIT STREET BOSTON, MA 02114 Tissue-specific transcription in the B lymphocyte

K08CA-01612-01 (CT) **RADICH, JERALD P** FRED HUTCHINSON CANCER RESEARC MOLECULAR MEDICINE AB133 SEATTLE, WA 98104-2092 Detection of minimal residual disease in acute leukemia

K08CA-01613-01 (CT) **SLAPAK, CHRISTOPHER A** NEW ENGLAND MEDICAL CENTER 750 WASHINGTON ST, BOX #245 BOSTON, MA 02111 Anthracycline efflux in multiresistant leukemia cells

K11CA-01614-01 (CT) **SKACH, WILLIAM R** UNIVERSITY OF CALIFORNIA, SF BOX 0128 SAN FRANCISCO, CA 94143 Biogenesis and functional reconstitution of human MDR1

K08CA-01615-01 (CT) **GULLEY, MARGARET L** UNIV OF NC AT CHAPEL HILL CB#7525, BRINKHOUS-BULLITT BLD CHAPEL HILL, NC 27599-7525 State of B cell differentiation and EBV gene expression

K08CA-01616-01 (CT) **ANDERSON, RUSSELL D** CASE WESTERN RESERVE UNIVERSIT HEMATOLOGY/ONCOLOGY DIVISION CLEVELAND, OH 44106 Specificity of intercalator directed genotoxicity

K08CA-01641-01 (CEC) **SANCHEZ, LORRAINE** UNM CANCER CENTER 900 CAMINO DE SALUD ALBUQUERQUE, NM 87131 Use of support systems by hispanic cancer patients of NM

K07CA-01642-01 (CEC) **ISSELL, BRIAN F** UNIVERSITY OF HAWAII 2540 MAILE WAY HONOLULU, HI 96822 Reducing cancer mortality in Hawaii's high risk minorities

K08CA-01643-01 (CEC) **FORD, JEAN** HARLEM HOSPITAL CENTER 506 LENOX AVE NEW YORK, NY 10037 Relation of serum oncoproteins to lung cancer

K08CA-01646-01 (CEC) **YANCEY, ANTRONETTE K** UNIV OF CALIF, L A 1100 GLENDON AVENUE, STE 711 LOS ANGELES, CA 90024-3511 Enhancing health behavior adherence in the underserved

K11CA-01660-01 (CT) **ROSS, HELEN J** UNIVERSITY OF CALIFORNIA, IRVI DIV HEMATOLOGY/ONCOLOGY IRVINE, CA 92717 Regulation of cytokine mRNA stability in tumor cells

R01CA-02071-38 (REN) **LEVITZ, MORTIMER** NEW YORK UNIV MED CTR 550 FIRST AVENUE NEW YORK, N Y 10016 Steroid metabolism and action in cancer

U10CA-02649-35 (CCI) **ORTEGA, JORGE A** CHILDREN'S HOSP OF LOS ANGELES 4650 SUNSET BOULEVARD LOS ANGELES, CA 90027 Children's cancer study group

R37CA-02758-35 (MET) **KANDUTSCH, ANDREW A** JACKSON LABORATORY 600 MAIN STREET BAR HARBOR, ME 04609-0800 Regulation of sterol biosynthesis

R13CA-02809-36 (SRC) GRODZICKER, TERRI I COLD SPRING HARBOR LABORATORY P O BOX 100 COLD SPRING HARBOR, NY 11724 Cold spring harbor symposia on quantitative biology

R01CA-02817-35 (ET) SARTORELLI, ALAN C YALE UNIVERSITY 333 CEDAR STREET NEW HAVEN, CT 06510 Biochemical pharmacology of antineoplastic agents

R01CA-02897-35 (BCE) GREENE, GEOFFREY L THE UNIV OF CHICAGO 5841 SOUTH MARYLAND AVE/B424 CHICAGO, ILL 60637 Steroids and growth

U10CA-02971-35 (CCI) HUTCHINSON, RAYMOND J UNIVERSITY OF MICHIGAN F6515 MOOT HOSP., BOX 0238 ANN ARBOR, MI 48109 Children's cancer study group

U10CA-03161-34 (CCI) FERNBACH, DONALD J TEXAS CHILDREN'S HOSPITAL 6621 FANNIN STREET HOUSTON, TX 77030 Pediatric oncology group

U10CA-03161-34 0041 (CCI) FERNBACH, DONALD J Pediatric oncology group POG8633--Postoperative chemotherapy and delayed irradiation for brain tumors

U10CA-03161-34 0042 (CCI) FERNBACH, DONALD J Pediatric oncology group POG8617--Therapy for B-cell acute lymphoblastic leukemia and lymphoma

U10CA-03161-34 0043 (CCI) FERNBACH, DONALD J Pediatric oncology group POG9139--Phase I study of cisplatin and irradiation in brain stem gliomas

U10CA-03161-34 0044 (CCI) FERNBACH, DONALD J Pediatric oncology group POG9079--Phase I study of L-PAM/CTX with ABM rescue for brain tumors in children

U10CA-03161-34 0045 (CCI) FERNBACH, DONALD J Pediatric oncology group POG9075--Phase I study of acivicin in children with solid tumors

U10CA-03161-34 0046 (CCI) FERNBACH, DONALD J Pediatric oncology group POG9074--Phase I study of xomazyme-H65 in children with T-cell ALL/lymphoma

U10CA-03161-34 0047 (CCI) FERNBACH, DONALD J Pediatric oncology group POG9072--Phase I chemotherapy for recurrent/resistant malignant solid tumors

U10CA-03161-34 0048 (CCI) FERNBACH, DONALD J Pediatric oncology group POG9061-Phase II systemic therapy and irradiation for ALL & CNS leukemia

U10CA-03161-34 0049 (CCI) FERNBACH, DONALD J Pediatric oncology group POG 9086--Phase I pilot study of therapy for T-cell ALL or NHL

U10CA-03161-34 0050 (CCI) FERNBACH, DONALD J Pediatric oncology group POG9071--Phase I trial of fazarabine in children with acute leukemia

U10CA-03161-34 0051 (CCI) FERNBACH, DONALD J Pediatric oncology group POG8970--Phase I trial of fazarabine in children with refractory solid tumors

U10CA-03161-34 0052 (CCI) FERNBACH, DONALD J Pediatric oncology group POG8973--Etoposide (VP-16) and carboplatin in children with acute leukemia

U10CA-03161-34 0053 (CCI) FERNBACH, DONALD J Pediatric oncology group POG8870--Phase I trial of ifosfamide/VP16/MESNA in children with acute leukemia

U10CA-03161-34 0054 (CCI) FERNBACH, DONALD J Pediatric oncology group POG8871--Phase I study of rTNF in children with refractory solid tumors

U10CA-03161-34 0055 (CCI) FERNBACH, DONALD J Pediatric oncology group POG8671--Phase I immunotherapy with rIL-2 in children with solid tumors

U10CA-03161-34 0056 (CCI) FERNBACH, DONALD J Pediatric oncology group POG8494--Phase I study of fludarabine phosphate in pediatric patients

U10CA-03161-34 0057 (CCI) FERNBACH, DONALD J Pediatric oncology group POG8930--A comprehensive genetic analysis of brain tumors

U10CA-03161-34 0058 (CCI) FERNBACH, DONALD J Pediatric oncology group POG8828--Late effects of Hodgkin's disease

U10CA-03161-34 0059 (CCI) FERNBACH, DONALD J Pediatric oncology group POG9046--Molecular genetic analysis of Wilm's tumors

U10CA-03161-34 0060 (CCI) FERNBACH, DONALD J Pediatric oncology group POG9153--Rhabdomyosarcoma study/laboratory evaluation of tumor

U10CA-03161-34 0001 (CCI) FERNBACH, DONALD J Pediatric oncology group POG9006--6-MP/methotrexate vs. alternating chemotherapy for ALL in childhood

U10CA-03161-34 0009 (CCI) FERNBACH, DONALD J Pediatric oncology group POG8725--Phase III chemotherapy +/- radiation therapy in pediatric Hodgkins

U10CA-03161-34 0010 (CCI) FERNBACH, DONALD J Pediatric oncology group POG8704--Phase III chemotherapy of childhood T cell ALL & lymphoblastic lymphoma

U10CA-03161-34 0011 (CCI) FERNBACH, DONALD J Pediatric oncology group POG8719--Phase III chemotherapy for non-Hodgkin's lymphoma in children

U10CA-03161-34 0012 (CCI) FERNBACH, DONALD J Pediatric oncology group POG8650--National Wilm's tumor and clear cell sarcoma study

U10CA-03161-34 0013 (CCI) FERNBACH, DONALD J Pediatric oncology group POG8616--Phase III chemotherapy for childhood Burkitt and non-Burkitts lymphoma

U10CA-03161-34 0014 (CCI) FERNBACH, DONALD J Pediatric oncology group POG8615--Phase III study of large cell lymphomas in children and adolescents

U10CA-03161-34 0015 (CCI) FERNBACH, DONALD J Pediatric oncology group POG8651--Phase III study of childhood nonmetastatic osteosarcoma

U10CA-03161-34 0016 (CCI) FERNBACH, DONALD J Pediatric oncology group POG8653--Phase III study of childhood soft tissue sarcomas

U10CA-03161-34 0017 (CCI) FERNBACH, DONALD J Pediatric oncology group POG8625--Phase III combined therapy in childhood Hodgkin's disease

U10CA-03161-34 0018 (CCI) FERNBACH, DONALD J Pediatric oncology group POG8451--Intergroup rhabdomyosarcoma study

U10CA-03161-34 0019 (CCI) FERNBACH, DONALD J Pediatric oncology group POG9110--Rotational drug therapy after first marrow relapse of non-T, non B ALL

U10CA-03161-34 0020 (CCI) FERNBACH, DONALD J Pediatric oncology group POG9107--Phase II pilot study of infant leukemia

U10CA-03161-34 0021 (CCI) FERNBACH, DONALD J Pediatric oncology group POG9140--Phase II therapy for recurrent or refractory neuroblastoma

U10CA-03161-34 0022 (CCI) FERNBACH, DONALD J Pediatric oncology group POG9048--Phase II study of malignant germ cell tumors in children

U10CA-03161-34 0023 (CCI) FERNBACH, DONALD J Pediatric oncology group POG9060--Intensive QOD ifosfamide treatment for CNS tumors in children

U10CA-03161-34 0024 (CCI) FERNBACH, DONALD J Pediatric oncology group POG8936--Phase II study of carboplatin treatment for optic pathway tumors

U10CA-03161-34 0025 (CCI) FERNBACH, DONALD J Pediatric oncology group POG8935--Phase II study of surgery and/or radiotherapy for optic pathway tumors

U10CA-03161-34 0026 (CCI) FERNBACH, DONALD J Pediatric oncology group POG8820--Phase II/III study of VP-16, AMSA +/- 5-azacytidine in childhood ANLL

U10CA-03161-34 0027 (CCI) FERNBACH, DONALD J Pediatric oncology group POG8889--Intergroup rhabdomyosarcoma study for clinical group IV disease

U10CA-03161-34 0028 (CCI) FERNBACH, DONALD J Pediatric oncology group POG8866--Phase II asparaginase therapy for acute lymphoblastic leukemia

U10CA-03161-34 0029 (CCI) FERNBACH, DONALD J Pediatric oncology group POG8862--Combination chemotherapy of acute T-lymphoblastic leukemia

U10CA-03161-34 0030 (CCI) FERNBACH, DONALD J Pediatric oncology group POG8863--Phase II study of high dose cytosine arabinoside in childhood tumors

U10CA-03161-34 0031 (CCI) FERNBACH, DONALD J Pediatric oncology group POG8827--Phase II treatment of children with Hodgkin's disease in relapse

U10CA-03161-34 0032 (CCI) FERNBACH, DONALD J Pediatric oncology group POG8865--Phase II recombinant alpha-interferon in relapsed T-cell disease

U10CA-03161-34 0033 (CCI) FERNBACH, DONALD J Pediatric oncology group--Phase II recombinant A-interferon in chronic myelogenous leukemia

U10CA-03161-34 0034 (CCI) FERNBACH, DONALD J Pediatric oncology group POG8832--Combination chemotherapy followed by radiotherapy for brain tumors

U10CA-03161-34 0035 (CCI) FERNBACH, DONALD J Pediatric oncology group POG8731--Phase II trial of methotrexate in treatment of brain tumors in children

U10CA-03161-34 0036 (CCI) FERNBACH, DONALD J Pediatric oncology group POG8788--Intergroup rhabdomyosarcoma study/pilot study for clinical group III

U10CA-03161-34 0037 (CCI) FERNBACH, DONALD J Pediatric oncology group POG8761--Phase II study of homoharringtonine therapy for nonlymphoblastic leukemi

U10CA-03161-34 0038 (CCI) FERNBACH, DONALD J Pediatric oncology group POG8739--Phase II immunotherapy with alpha-2 interferon for brain tumors

U10CA-03161-34 0039 (CCI) FERNBACH, DONALD J Pediatric oncology group POG8741--Treatment of patients with stage C and stage D neuroblastoma

U10CA-03161-34 0040 (CCI) FERNBACH, DONALD J Pediatric oncology group POG8751--Phase II methotrexate chemotherapy for rhabdomyosarcoma in children

U10CA-03161-34 0002 (CCI) FERNBACH, DONALD J Pediatric oncology group POG9005--Dose intensification of methotrexate & 6-mercaptourine in childhood ALL

U10CA-03161-34 0003 (CCI) FERNBACH, DONALD J Pediatric oncology group POG9031--Cisplatin/VP-16 therapy of medulloblastoma/pre vs. post irradiation

U10CA-03161-34 0004 (CCI) FERNBACH, DONALD J Pediatric oncology group POG8945--Phase III chemotherapy for hepatoblastoma & hepatocellular carcinoma

U10CA-03161-34 0005 (CCI) FERNBACH, DONALD J Pediatric oncology group POG9049--Phase III study of high-risk malignant germ cell tumors in children

U10CA-03161-34 0006 (CCI) FERNBACH, DONALD J Pediatric oncology group POG8844--Bone marrow transplant in children with stage D neuroblastoma

U10CA-03161-34 0007 (CCI) FERNBACH, DONALD J Pediatric oncology group POG8850--Phase III treatment of Ewing's sarcoma and neuroectodermal bone tumors

U10CA-03161-34 0008 (CCI) FERNBACH, DONALD J Pediatric oncology group POG8821--Phase III chemotherapy +/- autologous BMT in children with AML

R01CA-03352-35 (PTHB) BROWN, J MARTIN CANCER BIOLOGY RESEARCH LAB STANFORD UNIV SCHOOL/MEDICINE STANFORD, CA 94305-5468 Biological aspects of carcinogenesis by radiation

R01CA-03353-34 (RAD) KALLMAN, ROBERT F STANFORD UNIVERSITY RADIATION ONCOLOGY, RM AO-38 STANFORD, CA 94305-6060 Experimental radiotherapy-- Cellular responses in vivo

U10CA-03526-34 (CCI) PIOMELLI, SERGIO COLUMBIA UNIVERSITY 630 WEST 168TH STREET NEW YORK, N Y 10032 Children's cancer study group

U10CA-03713-33S1 (CCI) PINKEL, DONALD UNIV OF TEXAS SYSTEM CANC CTR 1515 HOLCOMBE BLVD HOUSTON, TX 77030 Pediatric oncology group

U10CA-03750-34 (CCI) RUYMANN, FREDERICK B CHILDREN'S HOSPITAL 700 CHILDREN'S DRIVE COLUMBUS, OHIO 43205 Children's cancer study group

U10CA-03888-34 (CCI) REAMAN, GREGORY CHILDREN'S HOSPITAL NAT MED CT 111 MICHIGAN AVENUE N W WASHINGTON, DC 20010 children's cancer study group

U10CA-03927-34 (CCI) COOPER, M ROBERT WAKE FOREST UNIVERSITY 300 SOUTH HAWTHORNE ROAD WINSTON-SALEM, N C 27103 Cancer and leukemia group B (CALGB)

R37CA-04186-33 (BBCA) RICH, ALEXANDER MASSACHUSETTS INST OF TECH 77 MASSACHUSETTS AVENUE CAMBRIDGE, MA 02139 The molecular structure of nucleic acids

PROJECT NO., ORGANIZATIONAL UNIT., INVESTIGATOR, ADDRESS, TITLE

U10CA-04326-33 (CCI) CORNWELL, GIBBONS G, III NORRIS COTTON CANCER CENTER DARTMOUTH HITCHCOCK MED CTR HANOVER, NH 03756 Cancer and leukemia group B
U10CA-04457-32 (CCI) HOLLAND, JAMES F MOUNT SINAI SCHOOL OF MEDICINE ONE GUSTAVE L LEVY PLACE NEW YORK, N Y 10029 Cancer and leukemia group B - Mount Sinai
R01CA-04484-33 (RAD) HUMPHREY, RONALD M UNIV OF TEX M D ANDEROSN CA CT PO BOX 389 SMITHVILLE, TX 78957 DNA repair and recovery in the mammalian cell cycle
U10CA-04919-32 (CCI) WEICK, JAMES K CLEVELAND CLINIC FOUNDATION 9500 EUCLID AVENUE CLEVELAND, OHIO 44106 Southwest oncology group
U10CA-04920-32 (CCI) BALCERZAK, STANLEY P OHIO STATE UNIV HOSPITALS 410 W 10TH AVE., ROOM N-1021 COLUMBUS, OHIO 43210 Southwest oncology group
R37CA-04946-30 (IMB) BOSMA, MELVIN J INSTITUTE FOR CANCER RESEARCH 7701 BURHOLME AVENUE PHILADELPHIA, PA 19111 Severe combined immunodeficiency
R01CA-05003-33 (GMA) PATHAK, MADHUKAR A MASSACHUSETTS GENERAL HOSPITAL WARREN 5, ROOM 562 BOSTON, MASS 02114 Skin reactions to light--Photosensitivity and cancer
R01CA-05262-31 (ARR) PRUSOFF, WILLIAM H YALE UNIVERSITY 333 CEDAR STREET NEW HAVEN, CT 06510 Iododeoxyuridine, Iodo-DNA and biological activity
P01CA-05388-31A1 (SRC) NANDI, SATYABRATA UNIVERSITY OF CALIFORNIA 447 LIFE SCIENCES ADDITION BERKELEY, CA 94720 Mammary tumorigenesis in rodents
P01CA-05388-31A1 0036 (SRC) CUNHA, GERALD R Mammary tumorigenesis in rodents: Stromal-epithelial interactions in growth/differentiation mammary epithelia
P01CA-05388-31A1 0035 (SRC) FIRESTONE, GARY L Mammary tumorigenesis in rodents Hormonal regulation of mammary tumor cell growth
P01CA-05388-31A1 0036 (SRC) CUNHA, GERALD R Mammary tumorigenesis in rodents Stromal-epithelial interactions in growth/differentiation mammary epithelia(mice
P01CA-05388-31A1 0037 (SRC) TALAMANTES, FRANK Mammary tumorigenesis in rodents Hormones/growth factors & receptors--Mammary chemical carcinogenesis
P01CA-05388-31A1 9001 (SRC) NANDI, SATYABRATA Mammary tumorigenesis in rodents Core-Mouse colony
P01CA-05388-31A1 9002 (SRC) NANDI, STAYABRATA Mammary tumorigenesis in rodents Core--Histology and immunocytochemistry
U10CA-05436-25 (CCI) GAYNON, PAUL S CLINICAL SCIENCE CENTER 600 HIGHLAND AVENUE, H4/436 MADISON, WI 53792 Children's cancer study group
U10CA-05587-31 (CCI) LAND, VITA J WASHINGTON UNIVERSITY 400 S KINGSHIGHWAY ST LOUIS, MO 63110 Pediatric oncology group
U10CA-05587-31 0020 (CCI) LAND, VITA J Pediatric oncology group POG9107--Phase II pilot study of infant leukemia
U10CA-05587-31 0021 (CCI) LAND, VITA J Pediatric oncology group POG9140--Phase II therapy for recurrent or refractory neuroblastoma
U10CA-05587-31 0022 (CCI) LAND, VITA J Pediatric oncology group POG9048--Phase II study of malignant germ cell tumors in children
U10CA-05587-31 0023 (CCI) LAND, VITA J Pediatric oncology group POG9060--Intensive COD ifosfamide treatment for CNS tumors in children
U10CA-05587-31 0024 (CCI) LAND, VITA J Pediatric oncology group POG8936--Phase II study of carboplatin treatment for optic pathway tumors
U10CA-05587-31 0025 (CCI) LAND, VITA J Pediatric oncology group POG8935--Phase II study of surgery and/or radiotherapy for optic pathway tumors
U10CA-05587-31 0026 (CCI) LAND, VITA J Pediatric oncology group POG8820--Phase II/III study of VP-16, AMSA +/- 5-azacytidine in childhood ANLL
U10CA-05587-31 0027 (CCI) LAND, VITA J Pediatric oncology group POG8889--Intergroup rhabdomyosarcoma study for clinical group IV disease
U10CA-05587-31 0028 (CCI) LAND, VITA J Pediatric oncology group POG8866--Phase II asparaginase therapy for acute lymphoblastic leukemia
U10CA-05587-31 0029 (CCI) LAND, VITA J Pediatric oncology group POG8862--Combination chemotherapy of acute T-lymphoblastic leukemia
U10CA-05587-31 0030 (CCI) LAND, VITA J Pediatric oncology group POG8863--Phase II study of high dose cytosine arabinoside in childhood tumors
U10CA-05587-31 0031 (CCI) LAND, VITA J Pediatric oncology group POG8827--Phase II treatment of children with Hodgkin's disease in relapse
U10CA-05587-31 0032 (CCI) LAND, VITA J Pediatric oncology group POG8865--Phase II recombinant alpha-interferon in relapsed T-cell disease
U10CA-05587-31 0033 (CCI) LAND, VITA J Pediatric oncology group --Phase II recombinant A-interferon in chronic myelogenous leukemia
U10CA-05587-31 0034 (CCI) LAND, VITA J Pediatric oncology group POG8832--Combination chemotherapy followed by radiotherapy for brain tumors
U10CA-05587-31 0035 (CCI) LAND, VITA J Pediatric oncology group POG8731--Phase II trial of methotrexate in treatment of brain tumors in children
U10CA-05587-31 0036 (CCI) LAND, VITA J Pediatric oncology group POG8788--Intergroup rhabdomyosarcoma study/pilot study for clinical group III
U10CA-05587-31 0037 (CCI) LAND, VITA J Pediatric oncology group POG8761--Phase II study of homoharringtonine therapy for nonlymphoblastic leukemi
U10CA-05587-31 0038 (CCI) LAND, VITA J Pediatric oncology group POG8739--Phase II immunotherapy with alpha-2 interferon for brain tumors
U10CA-05587-31 0039 (CCI) LAND, VITA J Pediatric oncology group POG8741--Treatment of patients with stage C and stage D neuroblastoma
U10CA-05587-31 0040 (CCI) LAND, VITA J Pediatric oncology group POG8751--Phase II methotrexate chemotherapy for rhabdomyosarcoma in children
U10CA-05587-31 0041 (CCI) LAND, VITA J Pediatric oncology group POG8633--Postoperative chemotherapy and delayed irradiation for brain tumors
U10CA-05587-31 0042 (CCI) LAND, VITA J Pediatric oncology group POG8617--Therapy for B-cell acute lymphoblastic leukemia and lymphoma
U10CA-05587-31 0043 (CCI) LAND, VITA J Pediatric oncology group POG9139--Phase I study of cisplatin and irradiation in brain stem gliomas
U10CA-05587-31 0044 (CCI) LAND, VITA J Pediatric oncology group POG9079--Phase I study of L-PAM/CTX with ABM rescue for brain tumors in children
U10CA-05587-31 0045 (CCI) LAND, VITA J Pediatric oncology group POG9075--Phase I study of acivicin in children with solid tumors
U10CA-05587-31 0046 (CCI) LAND, VITA J Pediatric oncology group POG9074--Phase I study of xomazyme-H65 in children with T-cell ALL/lymphoma
U10CA-05587-31 0047 (CCI) LAND, VITA J Pediatric oncology group POG9072--Phase I chemotherapy for recurrent/resistant malignant solid tumors
U10CA-05587-31 0048 (CCI) LAND, VITA J Pediatric oncology group POG9061-Phase II systemic therapy and irradiation for ALL & CNS leukemia
U10CA-05587-31 0049 (CCI) LAND, VITA J Pediatric oncology group POG 9086--Phase I pilot study of therapy for T-cell ALL or NHL
U10CA-05587-31 0050 (CCI) LAND, VITA J Pediatric oncology group POG9071--Phase I trial of fazarabine in children with acute leukemia
U10CA-05587-31 0051 (CCI) LAND, VITA J Pediatric oncology group POG8970--Phase I trial of fazarabine in children with refractory solid tumors
U10CA-05587-31 0001 (CCI) LAND, VITA J Pediatric oncology group POG9006--6-MP/methotrexate vs. alternating chemotherapy for ALL in childhood
U10CA-05587-31 0052 (CCI) LAND, VITA J Pediatric oncology group POG8973--Etoposide (VP-16) and carboplatin in children with acute leukemia
U10CA-05587-31 0053 (CCI) LAND, VITA J Pediatric oncology group POG8870--Phase I trial of ifosfamide/VP16/MESNA in children with acute leukemia
U10CA-05587-31 0054 (CCI) LAND, VITA J Pediatric oncology group POG8871--Phase I study of rTNF in children with refractory solid tumors
U10CA-05587-31 0055 (CCI) LAND, VITA J Pediatric oncology group POG8671--Phase I immunotherapy with rIL-2 in children with solid tumors
U10CA-05587-31 0056 (CCI) LAND, VITA J Pediatric oncology group POG8494--Phase I study of fludarabine phosphate in pediatric patients
U10CA-05587-31 0057 (CCI) LAND, VITA J Pediatric oncology group POG8930--A comprehensive genetic analysis of brain tumors
U10CA-05587-31 0058 (CCI) LAND, VITA J Pediatric oncology group POG8828--Late effects of Hodgkin's disease
U10CA-05587-31 0059 (CCI) LAND, VITA J Pediatric oncology group POG9046--Molecular genetic analysis of Wilm's tumors
U10CA-05587-31 0060 (CCI) LAND, VITA J Pediatric oncology group POG9153--Rhabdomyosarcoma study/laboratory evaluation of tumor
U10CA-05587-31 0002 (CCI) LAND, VITA J Pediatric oncology group POG9005--Dose intensification of methotrexate & 6-mercaptourine in childhood ALL
U10CA-05587-31 0003 (CCI) LAND, VITA J Pediatric oncology group POG9031--Cisplatin/VP-16 therapy of medulloblastoma/pre vs. post irradiation
U10CA-05587-31 0004 (CCI) LAND, VITA J Pediatric oncology group POG8945--Phase III chemotherapy for hepatoblastoma & hepatocellular carcinoma
U10CA-05587-31 0005 (CCI) LAND, VITA J Pediatric oncology group POG9049--Phase III study of high-risk malignant germ cell tumors in children
U10CA-05587-31 0006 (CCI) LAND, VITA J Pediatric oncology group POG8844--Bone marrow transplant in children with stage D neuroblastoma
U10CA-05587-31 0007 (CCI) LAND, VITA J Pediatric oncology group POG8850--Phase III treatment of Ewing's sarcoma and neuroectodermal bone tumors
U10CA-05587-31 0008 (CCI) LAND, VITA J Pediatric oncology group POG8821--Phase III chemotherapy +/- autologous BMT in children with AML
U10CA-05587-31 0009 (CCI) LAND, VITA J Pediatric oncology group POG8725--Phase III chemotherapy +/- radiation therapy in pediatric Hodgkins
U10CA-05587-31 0010 (CCI) LAND, VITA J Pediatric oncology group POG8704--Phase III chemotherapy of childhood T cell ALL & lymphoblastic lymphoma
U10CA-05587-31 0011 (CCI) LAND, VITA J Pediatric oncology group POG8719--Phase III chemotherapy for non-Hodgkin's lymphoma in children
U10CA-05587-31 0012 (CCI) LAND, VITA J Pediatric oncology group POG8650--National Wilm's tumor and clear cell sarcoma study
U10CA-05587-31 0013 (CCI) LAND, VITA J Pediatric oncology group POG8616--Phase III chemotherapy for childhood Burkitt and non-Burkitts lymphoma
U10CA-05587-31 0014 (CCI) LAND, VITA J Pediatric oncology group POG8615--Phase III study of large cell lymphomes in children and adolescents
U10CA-05587-31 0015 (CCI) LAND, VITA J Pediatric oncology group POG8651--Phase III study of childhood nonmetastatic osteosarcoma
U10CA-05587-31 0016 (CCI) LAND, VITA J Pediatric oncology group POG8653--Phase III study of childhood soft tissue sarcomas
U10CA-05587-31 0017 (CCI) LAND, VITA J Pediatric oncology group POG8625--Phase III combined therapy in childhood Hodgkin's disease
U10CA-05587-31 0018 (CCI) LAND, VITA J Pediatric oncology group POG8451--Intergroup rhabdomyosarcoma study
U10CA-05587-31 0019 (CCI) LAND, VITA J Pediatric oncology group POG9110--Rotational drug therapy after first marrow relapse of non-T, non B ALL
P01CA-05826-29 (SRC) BERTINO, JOSEPH R MEMORIAL HOSP, CNCR & ALLIED D 1275 YORK AVENUE NEW YORK, NY 10021 Cancer chemotherapy program project

PROJECT NO., ORGANIZATIONAL UNIT., INVESTIGATOR, ADDRESS, TITLE

P01CA-05826-29 0143 (SRC) YOUNG, CHARLES W Cancer chemotherapy program project Developmental therapy
P01CA-05826-29 0150 (SRC) CLARKSON, BAYARD D Cancer chemotherapy program project Chemotherapeutic studies of hematopoietic neoplasms
P01CA-05826-29 0154 (SRC) YAGODA, ALAN Cancer chemotherapy program project Chemotherapeutic studies in solid tumors
P01CA-05826-29 9002 (SRC) GELLER, NANCY Cancer chemotherapy program project Core--Biostatistics and data management
P01CA-05826-29 9003 (SRC) BERTINO, JOSEPH R Cancer chemotherapy program project Core--Pharmacology core
P01CA-05826-29 9004 (SRC) CHAGANTI, RAJU Cancer chemotherapy program project Core--Genetics
R01CA-05945-27 (MEP) SOROF, SAM INSTITUTE FOR CANCER RESEARCH 7701 BURHOLME AVENUE PHILADELPHIA, PA 19111 Ligand-protein complexes, growth and carcinogenesis
P01CA-06294-30 (SRC) PETERS, LESTER J U.T. M.D. ANDERSON CANCER CENT 1515 HOLCOMBE BOULEVARD HOUSTON, TEXAS 77030 Extension of radiotherapy research
P01CA-06294-30 0033 (SRC) MEYN, RAYMOND E Extension of radiotherapy research Programmed cell death--Normal & tumor tissue radiation response
P01CA-06294-30 0067 (SRC) TRAVIS, ELIZABETH L Extension of radiotherapy research Normal tissue pathobiology after radiation/cytotoxic chemotherapy
P01CA-06294-30 0068 (SRC) HITTELMAN, WALTER N Extension of radiotherapy research Induction & repair of chromosomal damage following irradiation
P01CA-06294-30 0072 (SRC) TOFILON, PHILIP J Extension of radiotherapy research In vitro investigation of radiation-induced CNS injury
P01CA-06294-30 0073 (SRC) BROCK, WILLIAM A Extension of radiotherapy research Lymphocytes, fibroblasts, keratinocytes radiosensitivity--In vitro assay
P01CA-06294-30 0078 (SRC) TRAVIS, ELIZABETH L Extension of radiotherapy research Irradiated volume effect on normal tissue response
P01CA-06294-30 0079 (SRC) PETERS, LESTER J Extension of radiotherapy research Accelerated fractionation in postoperative treatment of head/neck cancer
P01CA-06294-30 0080 (SRC) RICH, TYVIN A Extension of radiotherapy research Rectal cancer chemo/radiotherapy response--Tumor cell proliferation
P01CA-06294-30 9003 (SRC) MILAS, LUKA Extension of radiotherapy research Core--Specific pathogen free (SPF) mouse colony
P01CA-06294-30 9005 (SRC) HORTON, JOHN L Extension of radiotherapy research Core--Radiotherapy physics
P01CA-06294-30 9006 (SRC) TERRY, NICHOLAS H Extension of radiotherapy research Core--Flow cytometry
P01CA-06294-30 9007 (SRC) BROWN, BARRY W Extension of radiotherapy research Core--Biostatistics and data management
P30CA-06516-28 (CCS) BENACERRAF, BARUJ DANA-FARBER CANCER INSTITUTE 44 BINNEY STREET BOSTON, MA 02115 Cancer center support grant
P30CA-06516-28 0020 (CCS) CANELLOS, GEORGE P Cancer center support grant Clinical oncology
P30CA-06516-28 0022 (CCS) FREI, EMIL Cancer center support grant Medicine
P30CA-06516-28 0023 (CCS) LIVINGSTON, DAVID M Cancer center support grant Neoplastic disease mechanisms
P30CA-06516-28 0024 (CCS) BURAKOFF, STEVEN J Cancer center support grant Pediatric oncology
P30CA-06516-28 0025 (CCS) SCLOSSMAN, STUART Cancer center support grant Tumor immunology
P30CA-06516-28 9002 (CCS) REISS, CAROL S Cancer center support grant Core--Animal facility
P30CA-06516-28 9003 (CCS) SCHAFFER, PRISCILLA A Cancer center support grant Core--Library
P30CA-06516-28 9004 (CCS) ZELEN, MARVIN Cancer center support grant Biostatistics and epidemiology
P30CA-06516-28 9005 (CCS) SLAYTER, HENREY S Cancer center support grant Electron microscope laboratory
P30CA-06516-28 9007 (CCS) LIVINGSTON, DAVID M Cancer center support grant Biosafety
P30CA-06516-28 9009 (CCS) FREI, EMIL Cancer center support grant Research pharmacy
P30CA-06516-28 9011 (CCS) LIVINGSTON, DAVID M Cancer center support grant Media laboratory
P30CA-06516-28 9012 (CCS) SCHLOSSMAN, STUART F Cancer center support grant Cell surface phenotyping core lab
P30CA-06516-28 9013 (CCS) BERNAL, SAMMUEL D Cancer center support grant Flow cytometry core
P30CA-06516-28 9014 (CCS) RITZ, JEROME Cancer center support grant Bone marrow purging
P30CA-06516-28 0016 (CCS) FREI, EMIL Cancer center support grant Cancer pharmacology
R01CA-06576-28 (MEP) NOVIKOFF, PHYLLIS M ALBERT EINSTEIN COLLEGE OF MED 1300 MORRIS PARK AVENUE BRONX, N Y 10461 Biochemical cytology of normal and malignant tissues
U10CA-06594-27A1 (CCI) RUCKDESCHEL, JOHN C ALBANY MEDICAL COLLEGE 47 NEW SCOTLAND AVE ALBANY, NY 12208 Eastern cooperative oncology group
P30CA-06927-29 (CCS) YOUNG, ROBERT C FOX CHASE CANCER CENTER 7701 BURHOLME AVENUE PHILADELPHIA, PA 19111 Comprehensive cancer center program at Fox Chase
P30CA-06927-29 9022 (CCS) YOUNG, R Comprehensive cancer center program at Fox Chase Protein analysis--core
P30CA-06927-29 9023 (CCS) YOUNG, R Comprehensive cancer center program at Fox Chase Spectroscopy support--core
P30CA-06927-29 9024 (CCS) YOUNG, R Comprehensive cancer center program at Fox Chase Developmental funds
P30CA-06927-29 9025 (CCS) DUNCAN, JAMES Comprehensive cancer center program at Fox Chase Instrument shop--core
P30CA-06927-29 9026 (CCS) CATALANO, ROBERT Comprehensive cancer center program at Fox Chase Protocol management--core
P30CA-06927-29 9005 (CCS) LITWIN, SAMUEL Comprehensive cancer center program at Fox Chase Core--Biomathematics
P30CA-06927-29 9006 (CCS) SCHEIFER, MARTIN Comprehensive cancer center program at Fox Chase Core--Computer facility
P30CA-06927-29 9007 (CCS) EATON, GORDON J Comprehensive cancer center program at Fox Chase Core--Animal facilities
P30CA-06927-29 9008 (CCS) CUSTER, PHILIP Comprehensive cancer center program at Fox Chase Core--Pathology
P30CA-06927-29 9009 (CCS) BAYER, MANFRED E Comprehensive cancer center program at Fox Chase Core--Electron microscopy facility
P30CA-06927-29 9010 (CCS) GLUSKER, ROBERT Comprehensive cancer center program at Fox Chase Core--Organic synthesis laboratory
P30CA-06927-29 9014 (CCS) ALBERT, K Comprehensive cancer center program at Fox Chase Core--Research library
P30CA-06927-29 9015 (CCS) DURAY, PAUL Comprehensive cancer center program at Fox Chase Core--Tumor bank
P30CA-06927-29 9016 (CCS) YOUNG, ROBERT Comprehensive cancer center program at Fox Chase Word processing center--core
P30CA-06927-29 9017 (CCS) YOUNG, R Comprehensive cancer center program at Fox Chase Cell culture facility--core
P30CA-06927-29 9018 (CCS) YOUNG, R Comprehensive cancer center program at Fox Chase DNA and RNA sequencing--core
P30CA-06927-29 9019 (CCS) YOUNG, ANTHONY Comprehensive cancer center program at Fox Chase DNA synthesis--core
P30CA-06927-29 9020 (CCS) YOUNG, R Comprehensive cancer center program at Fox Chase Experimental histopathology--core
P30CA-06927-29 9021 (CCS) YOUNG, R Comprehensive cancer center program at Fox Chase Peptide synthesis--core
P30CA-06973-29 (CCS) OWENS, ALBERT H, JR JOHNS HOPKINS UNIVERSITY 600 NORTH WOLFE STREET BALTIMORE, MD 21205 Regional oncology research center
P30CA-06973-29 9001 (CCS) ISAACS, JOHN Regional oncology research center Animal resources..core
P30CA-06973-29 9002 (CCS) HARWOOD, PATRICIA M Regional oncology research center Core--Research pharmacy
P30CA-06973-29 9006 (CCS) SHARKIS, SAUL J Regional oncology research center Core--Cell sorting/flow microfluorimetry laboratory
P30CA-06973-29 9008 (CCS) ENTERLINE, JOHN P Regional oncology research center Core--Clinical information system/biostatistics unit
P30CA-06973-29 9010 (CCS) TUCKER, ROBERT W Regional oncology research center Core--Electron microscopy laboratory
P30CA-06973-29 9012 (CCS) GRIFFIN, C Regional oncology research center Clinical genetics...core
P30CA-06973-29 9013 (CCS) NOE, DENNIS Regional oncology research center Clinical pharmacology...core
P30CA-06973-29 9014 (CCS) LEVENTHAL, BRIGID Regional oncology research center Clinical research office...core
P30CA-06973-29 9015 (CCS) ENTERLINE, JOHN Regional oncology research center Information systems
P30CA-06973-29 9016 (CCS) MCGUIRE, DEBORAH Regional oncology research center Research nursing...core
P30CA-06973-29 9017 (CCS) WILLIAMS, JERRY Regional oncology research center Experimental irradiators...core
P30CA-06973-29 9018 (CCS) BAYLIN, STEPHEN Regional oncology research center Central laboratory support...core
P30CA-06973-29 9019 (CCS) BRAINE, HAYDEN Regional oncology research center Hemapheresis...core
P30CA-06973-29 9021 (CCS) HAMILTON, STANLEY Regional oncology research center Tissue depository...core
P30CA-06973-29 9022 (CCS) SANFORD, GORDON Regional oncology reseach center Nucleotide synthesizer...core
P30CA-06973-29 9023 (CCS) PITHA-ROWE, P Regional oncology research center Biosafety level 3 facility...core
P30CA-06973-29 9024 (CCS) OWENS, ALBERT Regional oncology research center Development....core
R01CA-07139-28 (VR) CONSIGLI, RICHARD A KANSAS STATE UNIVERSITY MANHATTAN, KANSAS 66506 Studies in polyoma transformed cells--Virion proteins
P30CA-07175-28 (CCS) PITOT, HENRY C UNIVERSITY OF WISCONSIN 1400 UNIVERSITY AVENUE MADISON, WI 53706 Cancer center support at the McArdle laboratory
P30CA-07175-28 9006 (CCS) PITOT, HENRY C Cancer center support at the McArdle laboratory Histotechnology laboratory
P30CA-07175-28 9008 (CCS) RIEGEL, ILSE L Cancer center support at the McArdle laboratory Library and scientific writing instruction--Core facility
P30CA-07175-28 9010 (CCS) MILLER, ELIZABETH C Cancer center support at the McArdle laboratory Biohazards and safety core
P30CA-07175-28 9011 (CCS) RISSER, REX G Cancer center support at the McArdle laboratory Irradiation facility--Core
P30CA-07175-28 9012 (CCS) PIFOT, HENRY C Cancer center support at the McArdle laboratory Development funds--Core
P30CA-07175-28 0001 (CCS) MILLER, ELIZABETH C Cancer center support at the McArdle laboratory Biochemical studies in chemical carcinogenesis
P30CA-07175-28 0002 (CCS) TEMIN, HOWARD M Cancer center support at the McArdle laboratory Molecular biology and genetics of tumor viruses
P30CA-07175-28 0003 (CCS) MUELLER, GERALD C Cancer center support at the McArdle laboratory Regulatory mechanisms in tumor biology
P30CA-07175-28 9002 (CCS) SUGDEN, BILL M Cancer center support at the McArdle laboratory Cell culture media preparation facility
P30CA-07175-28 9003 (CCS) ROSS, JEFFREY Cancer center support at the McArdle laboratory Radioactive isotope counting facility
P30CA-07175-28 9004 (CCS) PITOT, HENRY C Cancer center support at the McArdle laboratory Electron microscope facility
P30CA-07175-28 9005 (CCS) MILLER, ELIZABETH C Cancer center support at the McArdle laboratory Animal care facility
U10CA-07190-28 (CCI) KARP, DANIELS D NEW ENGLAND MEDICAL CENTER 750 WASH ST/BOX 452 ECOG OFC BOSTON, MA 02111 Eastern cooperative oncology group
U10CA-07306-28 (CCI) WOODS, WILLIAM G UNIVERSITY OF MINNESOTA BOX 454 MAYO MINNEAPOLIS, MN 55455 Children's cancer study group

R01CA-07340-28 (ET) PARKS, ROBERT E, JR BROWN UNIVERSITY BOX G-B429 PROVIDENCE, RI 02912 Adenosine analogs as cancer chemotherapeutic agents
U10CA-07431-28 (CCI) MURPHY, SHARON B CHILDRENS MEMORIAL HOSPITAL 2300 CHILDREN'S PLAZA CHICAGO, IL 60614 Pediatric oncology group
U10CA-07431-28 0056 (CCI) MURPHY, SHARON B Pediatric oncology group POG8494--Phase I study of fludarabine phosphate in pediatric patients
U10CA-07431-28 0057 (CCI) MURPHY, SHARON B Pediatric oncology group POG8930--A comprehensive genetic analysis of brain tumors
U10CA-07431-28 0058 (CCI) MURPHY, SHARON B Pediatric oncology group POG8828--Late effects of Hodgkin's disease
U10CA-07431-28 0059 (CCI) MURPHY, SHARON B Pediatric oncology group POG9046--Molecular genetic analysis of Wilm's tumors
U10CA-07431-28 0060 (CCI) MURPHY, SHARON B Pediatric oncology group POG9153--Rhabdomyosarcoma study/laboratory evaluation of tumor
U10CA-07431-28 0001 (CCI) MURPHY, SHARON B Pediatric oncology group POG9006--6-MP/methotrexate vs. alternating chemotherapy for ALL in childhood
U10CA-07431-28 0024 (CCI) MURPHY, SHARON B Pediatric oncology group POG8936--Phase II study of carboplatin treatment for optic pathway tumors
U10CA-07431-28 0025 (CCI) MURPHY, SHARON B Pediatric oncology group POG8935--Phase II study of surgery and/or radiotherapy for optic pathway tumors
U10CA-07431-28 0026 (CCI) MURPHY, SHARON B Pediatric oncology group POG8820--Phase II/III study of VP-16, AMSA +/- 5-azacytidine in childhood ANLL
U10CA-07431-28 0027 (CCI) MURPHY, SHARON B Pediatric oncology group POG8889--Intergroup rhabdomyosarcoma study for clinical group IV disease
U10CA-07431-28 0028 (CCI) MURPHY, SHARON B Pediatric oncology group POG8866--Phase II asparaginase therapy for acute lymphoblastic leukemia
U10CA-07431-28 0029 (CCI) MURPHY, SHARON B Pediatric oncology group POG8862--Combination chemotherapy of acute T-lymphoblastic leukemia
U10CA-07431-28 0030 (CCI) MURPHY, SHARON B Pediatric oncology group POG8863--Phase II study of high dose cytosine arabinoside in childhood tumors
U10CA-07431-28 0031 (CCI) MURPHY, SHARON B Pediatric oncology group POG8827--Phase II treatment of children with Hodgkin's disease in relapse
U10CA-07431-28 0032 (CCI) MURPHY, SHARON B Pediatric oncology group POG8865--Phase II recombinant alpha-interferon in relapsed T-cell disease
U10CA-07431-28 0033 (CCI) MURPHY, SHARON B Pediatric oncology group--Phase II recombinant A-interferon in chronic myelogenous leukemia
U10CA-07431-28 0034 (CCI) MURPHY, SHARON B Pediatric oncology group POG8832--Combination chemotherapy followed by radiotherapy for brain tumors
U10CA-07431-28 0035 (CCI) MURPHY, SHARON B Pediatric oncology group POG8731--Phase II trial of methotrexate in treatment of brain tumors in children
U10CA-07431-28 0036 (CCI) MURPHY, SHARON B Pediatric oncology group POG8788--Intergroup rhabdomyosarcoma study/pilot study for clinical group III
U10CA-07431-28 0037 (CCI) MURPHY, SHARON B Pediatric oncology group POG8761--Phase II study of homoharringtonine therapy for nonlymphoblastic leukemi
U10CA-07431-28 0038 (CCI) MURPHY, SHARON B Pediatric oncology group POG8739--Phase II immunotherapy with alpha-2 interferon for brain tumors (human)e
U10CA-07431-28 0039 (CCI) MURPHY, SHARON B Pediatric oncology group POG8741--Treatment of patients with stage C and stage D neuroblastoma
U10CA-07431-28 0040 (CCI) MURPHY, SHARON B Pediatric oncology group POG8751--Phase II methotrexate chemotherapy for rhabdomyosarcoma in children
U10CA-07431-28 0041 (CCI) MURPHY, SHARON B Pediatric oncology group POG8633--Postoperative chemotherapy and delayed irradiation for brain tumors
U10CA-07431-28 0042 (CCI) MURPHY, SHARON B Pediatric oncology group POG8617--Therapy for B-cell acute lymphoblastic leukemia and lymphoma
U10CA-07431-28 0043 (CCI) MURPHY, SHARON B Pediatric oncology group POG9139--Phase I study of cisplatin and irradiation in brain stem gliomas
U10CA-07431-28 0044 (CCI) MURPHY, SHARON B Pediatric oncology group POG9079--Phase I study of L-PAM/CTX with ABM rescue for brain tumors in children
U10CA-07431-28 0045 (CCI) MURPHY, SHARON B Pediatric oncology group POG9075--Phase I study of acivicin in children with solid tumors
U10CA-07431-28 0046 (CCI) MURPHY, SHARON B Pediatric oncology group POG9074--Phase I study of xomazyme-H65 in children with T-cell ALL/lymphoma
U10CA-07431-28 0047 (CCI) MURPHY, SHARON B Pediatric oncology group POG9072--Phase I chemotherapy for recurrent/resistant malignant solid tumors
U10CA-07431-28 0048 (CCI) MURPHY, SHARON B Pediatric oncology group POG9061-Phase II systemic therapy and irradiation for ALL & CNS leukemia
U10CA-07431-28 0049 (CCI) MURPHY, SHARON B Pediatric oncology group POG 9066--Phase I pilot study of therapy for T-cell ALL or NHL
U10CA-07431-28 0050 (CCI) MURPHY, SHARON B Pediatric oncology group POG9071--Phase I trial of fazarabine in children with acute leukemia
U10CA-07431-28 0051 (CCI) MURPHY, SHARON B Pediatric oncology group POG8970--Phase I trial of fazarabine in children with refractory solid tumors
U10CA-07431-28 0052 (CCI) MURPHY, SHARON B Pediatric oncology group POG8973--Etoposide (VP-16) and carboplatin in children with acute leukemia
U10CA-07431-28 0053 (CCI) MURPHY, SHARON B Pediatric oncology group POG8870--Phase I trial of ifosfamide/VP16/MESNA in children with acute leukemia
U10CA-07431-28 0054 (CCI) MURPHY, SHARON B Pediatric oncology group POG8871--Phase I study of rTNF in children with refractory solid tumors
U10CA-07431-28 0055 (CCI) MURPHY, SHARON B Pediatric oncology group POG8671--Phase I immunotherapy with rIL-2 in children with solid tumors
U10CA-07431-28 0002 (CCI) MURPHY, SHARON B Pediatric oncology group POG9005--Dose intensification of methotrexate & 6-mercaptourine in childhood ALL
U10CA-07431-28 0003 (CCI) MURPHY, SHARON B Pediatric oncology group POG9031--Cisplatin/VP-16 therapy of medulloblastoma/pre vs. post irradiation
U10CA-07431-28 0004 (CCI) MURPHY, SHARON B Pediatric oncology group POG8945--Phase III chemotherapy for hepatoblastoma & hepatocellular carcinoma
U10CA-07431-28 0005 (CCI) MURPHY, SHARON B Pediatric oncology group POG9049--Phase III study of high-risk malignant germ cell tumors in children
U10CA-07431-28 0006 (CCI) MURPHY, SHARON B Pediatric oncology group POG8844--Bone marrow transplant in children with stage D neuroblastoma
U10CA-07431-28 0007 (CCI) MURPHY, SHARON B Pediatric oncology group POG8850--Phase III treatment of Ewing's sarcoma and neuroectodermal bone tumors
U10CA-07431-28 0008 (CCI) MURPHY, SHARON B Pediatric oncology group POG8821--Phase III chemotherapy +/- autologous BMT in children with AML
U10CA-07431-28 0009 (CCI) MURPHY, SHARON B Pediatric oncology group POG8725--Phase III chemotherapy +/- radiation therapy in pediatric Hodgkins
U10CA-07431-28 0010 (CCI) MURPHY, SHARON B Pediatric oncology group POG8704--Phase III chemotherapy of childhood T cell ALL & lymphoblastic lymphoma
U10CA-07431-28 0011 (CCI) MURPHY, SHARON B Pediatric oncology group POG8719--Phase III chemotherapy for non-Hodgkin's lymphoma in children
U10CA-07431-28 0012 (CCI) MURPHY, SHARON B Pediatric oncology group POG8650--National Wilm's tumor and clear cell sarcoma study
U10CA-07431-28 0013 (CCI) MURPHY, SHARON B Pediatric oncology group POG8616--Phase III chemotherapy for childhood Burkitt and non-Burkitts lymphoma
U10CA-07431-28 0014 (CCI) MURPHY, SHARON B Pediatric oncology group POG8615--Phase III study of large cell lymphomas in children and adolescents
U10CA-07431-28 0015 (CCI) MURPHY, SHARON B Pediatric oncology group POG8651--Phase III study of childhood nonmetastatic osteosarcoma
U10CA-07431-28 0016 (CCI) MURPHY, SHARON B Pediatric oncology group POG8653--Phase III study of childhood soft tissue sarcomas
U10CA-07431-28 0017 (CCI) MURPHY, SHARON B Pediatric oncology group POG8625--Phase III combined therapy in childhood Hodgkin's disease
U10CA-07431-28 0018 (CCI) MURPHY, SHARON B Pediatric oncology group POG8451--Intergroup rhabdomyosarcoma study
U10CA-07431-28 0019 (CCI) MURPHY, SHARON B Pediatric oncology group POG9110--Rotational drug therapy after first marrow relapse of non-T, non B ALL
U10CA-07431-28 0020 (CCI) MURPHY, SHARON B Pediatric oncology group POG9107--Phase II pilot study of infant leukemia
U10CA-07431-28 0021 (CCI) MURPHY, SHARON B Pediatric oncology group POG9140--Phase II therapy for recurrent or refractory neuroblastoma
U10CA-07431-28 0022 (CCI) MURPHY, SHARON B Pediatric oncology group POG9048--Phase II study of malignant germ cell tumors in children
U10CA-07431-28 0023 (CCI) MURPHY, SHARON B Pediatric oncology group POG9060--Intensive QOD ifosfamide treatment for CNS tumors in children
R01CA-07535-28 (END) MACLEOD, ROBERT M UNIVERSITY OF VIRGINIA BOX 135 CHARLOTTESVILLE, VA 22903 Control of pituitary gland and pituitary tumor hormones
U10CA-07968-27 (CCI) SILVER, RICHARD T CORNELL UNIVERSITY 1300 YORK AVENUE NEW YORK, N Y 10021 Cancer and leukemia group B
R37CA-08010-27 (ET) BERTINO, JOSEPH R SLOAN-KETTERING INSTITUTE 1275 YORK AVE NEW YORK, NY 10021 Mechanism of action of folate antagonists
R01CA-08315-27 (PTHB) MELNYKOVYCH, GEORGE VETERANS AFFAIRS MEDICAL CENTE 4801 LINWOOD BLVD RM 151 KANSAS CITY, MO 64128 Steroid induced changes in cultured malignant cells
P01CA-08341-26 (SRC) HAIT, WILLIAM N YALE UNIVERSITY 333 CEDAR ST-PO BOX 3333 NEW HAVEN, CT 06510 Clinical pharmacology and cancer chemotherapy
P01CA-08341-26 0071 (SRC) HANDSCHUMACHER, ROBERT E Clinical pharmacology and cancer chemotherapy Physiological & biochemical modification of human colon cancer therapy
P01CA-08341-26 0072 (SRC) SARTORELLI, ALAN C Clinical pharmacology and cancer chemotherapy Squamous cell carcinoma differentiation
P01CA-08341-26 0075 (SRC) HAIT, WILLIAM N Clinical pharmacology and cancer chemotherapy Pharmacological studies of drugs altering multidrug resistance
P01CA-08341-26 0076 (SRC) TOOD, MARY B Clinical pharmacology and cancer chemotherapy Differentiation of leukemic cells with 6-thioguanine
P01CA-08341-26 0077 (SRC) COOPER, DENNIS L Clinical pharmacology and cancer chemotherapy Synthesis, chemistry and synergistic cytotoxicity with thymidine
P01CA-08341-26 9001 (SRC) BERTINO, JOSEPH R Clinical pharmacology and cancer chemotherapy Core--Clinical pharmacology
P01CA-08341-26 9002 (SRC) ERNSTOFF, MARC S Clinical pharmacology and cancer chemotherapy Core--Biostatistics
P01CA-08341-26 9003 (SRC) HAIT, WILLIAM N Clinical pharmacology and cancer chemotherapy Core--Clinical trials
P01CA-08341-26 9004 (SRC) HAIT, WILLIAM N Clinical pharmacology and cancer chemotherapy Core--Clinical diagnostic laboratory
R01CA-08349-24A2 (RNM) COUNSELL, RAYMOND E UNIV OF MICHIGAN MED SCH M6322 MEDICAL SCIENCE BLDG I ANN ARBOR, MI 48109-0626 Potential tumor or organ imaging agents
R37CA-08416-26 (NSS) PENMAN, SHELDON MASSACHUSETTS INST OF TECHNOLO 77 MASSACHUSETTS AVENUE CAMBRIDGE, MA 02139 Cytoskeletal architecture and gene expression

PROJECT NO., ORGANIZATIONAL UNIT., INVESTIGATOR, ADDRESS, TITLE

P30CA-08748-26 (SRC) MARKS, PAUL A MEM SLOAN-KETTERING CANCER CTR 1275 YORK AVENUE NEW YORK, N Y 10021 Cancer center support grant
P30CA-08748-26 9030 (SRC) WALTERS, MARY J Cancer center support grant Core--Glassware washing facility
P30CA-08748-26 9031 (SRC) LAUGHLIN, JOHN S Cancer center support grant Core--Cyclotron facility
P30CA-08748-26 9032 (SRC) HURWITZ, JERARD Cancer center support grant Core--Oligonucleotide synthesis facility
P30CA-08748-26 9033 (SRC) ROSEN, ORA M Cancer center support grant Core--Peptide synthesizer facility
P30CA-08748-26 9034 (SRC) MARIANS, KENNETH J Cancer center support grant Core--Fermenter facility
P30CA-08748-26 9035 (SRC) CHAGANTI, RAJU S K Cancer center support grant Core--Cytogenetics facility
P30CA-08748-26 9036 (SRC) CASPAR, EPHRIAM S Cancer center support grant Core--Clinical research support program
P30CA-08748-26 9037 (SRC) KLEINBERG, MICHAEL L Cancer center support grant Core--Pharmacy support program
P30CA-08748-26 9038 (SRC) BOYSE, EDWARD A Cancer center support grant Core--Congenic mouse facility
P30CA-08748-26 9010 (SRC) GODBOLD, JAMES Cancer center support grant Core--Biostatistics laboratory
P30CA-08748-26 9011 (SRC) STERNBERG, STEVEN S Cancer center support grant Core--Human tumor procurement center
P30CA-08748-26 9012 (SRC) OTTER, BRIAN A Cancer center support grant Core--Nuclear magnetic resonance facility
P30CA-08748-26 9013 (SRC) WATANABE, KYOICHI A Cancer center support grant Core--Preparative synthesis facility
P30CA-08748-26 9016 (SRC) MASTROIANNI, FRANK Cancer center support grant Core--Biosafety service
P30CA-08748-26 9017 (SRC) MYERS, DAVID D Cancer center support grant Core--General animal facility
P30CA-08748-26 9019 (SRC) WALTERS, MARY J Cancer center support grant Core--Central media preparation facility
P30CA-08748-26 9022 (SRC) MELAMED, MYRON R Cancer center support grant Core--Flow cytometry facility
P30CA-08748-26 9023 (SRC) MARKS, PAUL A Cancer center support grant Core--Planning and evaluation
P30CA-08748-26 9029 (SRC) MYERS, DAVID D Cancer center support grant Core--Animal health services
R37CA-08759-25 (PC) KORNFELD, STUART A WASH UNIV SCHOOL OF MED 660 S EUCLID AVENUE ST LOUIS, MO 63110 Structure, biosynthesis and biologic function of glycoprotein
R01CA-08964-24A1 (PC) RACKER, EFRAIM CORNELL UNIVERSITY 239 BIOTECHNOLOGY BUILDING ITHACA, NY 14853 In vitro reconstitutions of signal transduction pathways
R25CA-09353-13 (SRC) FOX, C FRED UNIVERSITY OF CALIFORNIA LOS ANGELES, CA 90024-1570 A workshop on the histopathology of neoplasia
R25CA-09481-10 (SRC) GRODZICKER, TERRI I COLD SPRING HARBOR LABORATORY P O BOX 100 COLD SPRING HARBOR, NY 11724 Support for cancer research center workshops
R25CA-09486-08 (SRC) GRANT, MARCIA M CITY OF HOPE NATIONAL 1500 E. DUARTE ROAD DUARTE, CA 91010 Cancer nursing research course
R25CA-09496-07 (SRC) JONES, CAROL E ROOSEVELT INST/CANCER RES IN 1899 GAYLORD STREET DENVER, CO 80206 Somatic cell and molecular genetics workshop
R01CA-10056-25 (IMS) SOLOMON, ALAN UNIV OF TENNESSEE MED CTR 1924 ALCOA HIGHWAY KNOXVILLE, TN 37920 Proteins in multiple myeloma & related blood diseases
R01CA-10197-24 (EVR) BALUDA, MARCEL A UCLA SCHOOL OF MEDICINE 405 HILGARD AVE LOS ANGELES, CA 90024-1732 Tumor induction by avian myeloblastosis virus
U10CA-10198-21 (CCI) O'BRIEN, RICHARD T UNIVERSITY OF UTAH 50 NORTH MEDICAL DRIVE SALT LAKE CITY, UT 84132 Children's cancer study group
U10CA-10382-25 (CCI) CHARD, RONALD L, JR CHILDREN'S ORTHOPEDIC HOSPITAL 4800 SAND PT WAY NE, BOX C5371 SEATTLE, WA 98105 Children's cancer study group
P30CA-10815-24 (CCS) KOPROWSKI, HILARY WISTAR INSTITUTE 36TH & SPRUCE STREETS PHILADELPHIA, PA 19104 Consolidated basic cancer research program
P30CA-10815-24 9003 (CCS) MAUL, GERD G Consolidated basic cancer research program Electron microscopy
P30CA-10815-24 9005 (CCS) KOPROWSKI, HILARY Consolidated basic cancer research program Animal breeding
P30CA-10815-24 9008 (CCS) KOPROWSKI, HILARY Consolidated basic cancer research program Shared resources
P30CA-10815-24 9010 (CCS) KOPROWSKI, HILARY Consolidated basic cancer research program Mycoplasma contamination service
P30CA-10815-24 9011 (CCS) KOPROWSKI, HILARY Consolidated basic cancer research program Cell sorter facility
P30CA-10815-24 9012 (CCS) KOPROWSKI, HILARY Consolidated basic cancer research program Computer facility
P01CA-10893-23 (SRC) BUSCH, HARRIS BAYLOR COLLEGE OF MEDICINE ONE BAYLOR PLAZA HOUSTON, TX 77030 Cancer research program
P01CA-10893-23 0047 (SRC) BUSCH, HARRIS Cancer research program Nuclear proteins of cancer cells
P01CA-10893-23 0048 (SRC) ROTHBLUM, LAWRENCE Cancer research program Gene control mechanisms for ribosomal DNA
P01CA-10893-23 0049 (SRC) REDDY, RAMACHANDRA Cancer research program Small RNPS of the nucleolus
P01CA-10893-23 9001 (SRC) BUSCH, HARRIS Cancer research program Core--Electron microscopy
R01CA-10925-42 (BMT) GLUSKER, JENNY P INSTITUTE FOR CANCER RESEARCH 7701 BURHOLME AVENUE PHILADELPHIA, PA 19111 Application of crystallographic techniques
R37CA-10951-24 (PB) PEDERSEN, PETER L THE JOHNS HOPKINS UNIVERITY DEPT OF BIOLOGICAL CHEMISTRY BALTIMORE, MD 21205 Control of enzymatic phosphate transfer in mitochondria
U10CA-10953-24 (CCI) HANSON, WILLIAM F UT MD ANDERSON CANCER CENTER 1515 HOLCOMBE BLVD HOUSTON, TX 77030 Radiological physics center
U10CA-11028-24 (CCI) RAI, KANTI R L I JEWISH MEDICAL CENTER NEW HYDE PARK, NY 11042 Multidisciplinary therapy for malignant disease - CALGB
R01CA-11034-23 (GEN) CARBON, JOHN A UNIVERSITY OF CALIFORNIA SANTA BARBARA, CA 93106 Studies on centromere structure and function
R01CA-11045-23 (BNP) BENTRUDE, WESLEY G UNIVERSITY OF UTAH SALT LAKE CITY, UT 84112 Cyclic nucleotides, cyclophosphamides, and antivirals
U10CA-11083-24 (CCI) BENNETT, JOHN M UNIV OF ROCHESTER SCH OF MED 601 ELMWOOD AVE/PO BOX 704 ROCHESTER, N Y 14642 Eastern cooperative oncology group
R01CA-11185-20 (MCHA) SHECHTER, HAROLD OHIO STATE UNIVERSITY 120 WEST 18TH AVE COLUMBUS, OH 43210 Novel uracils, pyrimidines, azoles and purines
R01CA-11196-22 (BNP) MARKHAM, GEORGE INSTITUTE FOR CANCER RESEARCH 7701 BURHOLME AVENUE PHILADELPHIA, PA 19111 Chemistry and enzymology of anticancer purine analogs
P30CA-11198-23 (CCS) COOPER, ROBERT A, JR UNIV OF ROCHESTER CANCER CTR 601 ELMWOOD AVENUE/BOX 704 ROCHESTER, NY 14642 Core cancer center support grant
P30CA-11198-23 9011 (CCS) PENNY, DAVID P Core cancer center support grant Experimental pathology--Core
P30CA-11198-23 9015 (CCS) HENSHAW, EDGAR C Core cancer center support grant Basic research services--Core
P30CA-11198-23 9016 (CCS) SIEMANN, DIETMAR W Core cancer center support grant Animal tumor research facility--Core
P30CA-11198-23 9017 (CCS) ODOROFF, CHARLES L Core cancer center support grant Biostatistics--Core
P30CA-11198-23 9018 (CCS) KING, PETER C Core cancer center support grant Cell separation/Flow cytometry facility
P30CA-11198-23 9019 (CCS) KING, PETER C Core cancer center support grant Flow cytometry facility--Core
P30CA-11198-23 9020 (CCS) PENNY, DAVID P Core cancer center support grant Experimental resources--Core
P30CA-11198-23 9021 (CCS) ZAIN, SAYEEDA Core cancer center support grant Tissue culture-gene characterization--Core
P30CA-11198-23 9022 (CCS) COOPER, ROBERT A Core cancer center support grant Developmental core--Analytical biochemistry lab
P30CA-11198-23 9023 (CCS) BARTH, RICHARD Core cancer center support grant Transgenic mouse facility
P30CA-11198-23 9024 (CCS) BRYANT, ROBERT Core cancer center support grant NMR facility
U10CA-11233-23 (CCI) NITSCHKE, RUPRECHT UNIVERSITY OF OKLAHOMA POST OFFICE BOX 26901 OKLAHOMA CITY, OK 73190 Pediatric oncology group
U10CA-11233-23 0012 (CCI) NITSCHKE, RUPRECHT Pediatric oncology group POG8650--National Wilm's tumor and clear cell sarcoma study
U10CA-11233-23 0013 (CCI) NITSCHKE, RUPRECHT Pediatric oncology group POG8616--Phase III chemotherapy for childhood Burkitt and non-Burkitts lymphoma
U10CA-11233-23 0014 (CCI) NITSCHKE, RUPRECHT Pediatric oncology group POG8615--Phase III study of large cell lymphomas in children and adolescents
U10CA-11233-23 0015 (CCI) NITSCHKE, RUPRECHT Pediatric oncology group POG8651--Phase III study of childhood nonmetastatic osteosarcoma
U10CA-11233-23 0016 (CCI) NITSCHKE, RUPRECHT Pediatric oncology group POG8653--Phase III study of childhood soft tissue sarcomas
U10CA-11233-23 0017 (CCI) NITSCHKE, RUPRECHT Pediatric oncology group POG8625--Phase III combined therapy in childhood Hodgkin's disease
U10CA-11233-23 0018 (CCI) NITSCHKE, RUPRECHT Pediatric oncology group POG8451--Intergroup rhabdomyosarcoma study
U10CA-11233-23 0019 (CCI) NITSCHKE, RUPRECHT Pediatric oncology group POG9110--Rotational drug therapy after first marrow relapse of non-T, non B ALL
U10CA-11233-23 0020 (CCI) NITSCHKE, RUPRECHT Pediatric oncology group POG9107--Phase II pilot study of infant leukemia
U10CA-11233-23 0021 (CCI) NITSCHKE, RUPRECHT Pediatric oncology group POG9140--Phase II therapy for recurrent or refractory neuroblastoma
U10CA-11233-23 0022 (CCI) NITSCHKE, RUPRECHT Pediatric oncology group POG9048--Phase II study of malignant germ cell tumors in children
U10CA-11233-23 0023 (CCI) NITSCHKE, RUPRECHT Pediatric oncology group POG9060--Intensive QOD ifosfamide treatment for CNS tumors in children
U10CA-11233-23 0024 (CCI) NITSCHKE, RUPRECHT Pediatric oncology group POG8936--Phase II study of carboplatin treatment for optic pathway tumors
U10CA-11233-23 0025 (CCI) NITSCHKE, RUPRECHT Pediatric oncology group POG8935--Phase II study of surgery and/or radiotherapy for optic pathway tumors
U10CA-11233-23 0026 (CCI) NITSCHKE, RUPRECHT Pediatric oncology group POG8820--Phase II/III study of VP-16, AMSA +/- 5-azacytidine in childhood ANLL
U10CA-11233-23 0027 (CCI) NITSCHKE, RUPRECHT Pediatric oncology group POG8889--Intergroup rhabdomyosarcoma study for clinical group IV disease
U10CA-11233-23 0028 (CCI) NITSCHKE, RUPRECHT Pediatric oncology group POG8866--Phase II asparaginase therapy for acute lymphoblastic leukemia
U10CA-11233-23 0029 (CCI) NITSCHKE, RUPRECHT Pediatric oncology group POG8862--Combination chemotherapy of acute T-lymphoblastic leukemia
U10CA-11233-23 0030 (CCI) NITSCHKE, RUPRECHT Pediatric oncology group POG8863--Phase II study of high dose cytosine arabinoside in childhood tumors
U10CA-11233-23 0031 (CCI) NITSCHKE, RUPRECHT Pediatric oncology group POG8827--Phase II treatment of children with Hodgkin's disease in relapse
U10CA-11233-23 0032 (CCI) NITSCHKE, RUPRECHT Pediatric oncology group POG8865--Phase II recombinant alpha-interferon in relapsed T-cell disease
U10CA-11233-23 0033 (CCI) NITSCHKE, RUPRECHT Pediatric oncology

group--Phase II recombinant A-interferon in chronic myelogenous leukemia
U10CA-11233-23 0034 (CCI) NITSCHKE, RUPRECHT Pediatric oncology group POG8832--Combination chemotherapy followed by radiotherapy for brain tumors
U10CA-11233-23 0035 (CCI) NITSCHKE, RUPRECHT Pediatric oncology group POG8731--Phase II trial of methotrexate in treatment of brain tumors in children
U10CA-11233-23 0036 (CCI) NITSCHKE, RUPRECHT Pediatric oncology group POG8788--Intergroup rhabdomyosarcoma study/pilot study for clinical group III
U10CA-11233-23 0037 (CCI) NITSCHKE, RUPRECHT Pediatric oncology group POG8761--Phase II study of homoharringtonine therapy for nonlymphoblastic leukemi
U10CA-11233-23 0038 (CCI) NITSCHKE, RUPRECHT Pediatric oncology group POG8739--Phase II immunotherapy with alpha-2 interferon for brain tumors
U10CA-11233-23 0039 (CCI) NITSCHKE, RUPRECHT Pediatric oncology group POG8741--Treatment of patients with stage C and stage D neuroblastoma
U10CA-11233-23 0040 (CCI) NITSCHKE, RUPRECHT Pediatric oncology group POG8751--Phase II methotrexate chemotherapy for rhabdomyosarcoma in children
U10CA-11233-23 0041 (CCI) NITSCHKE, RUPRECHT Pediatric oncology group POG8633--Postoperative chemotherapy and delayed irradiation for brain tumors
U10CA-11233-23 0042 (CCI) NITSCHKE, RUPRECHT Pediatric oncology group POG8617--Therapy for B-cell acute lymphoblastic leukemia and lymphoma
U10CA-11233-23 0043 (CCI) NITSCHKE, RUPRECHT Pediatric oncology group POG9139--Phase I study of cisplatin and irradiation in brain stem gliomas
U10CA-11233-23 0001 (CCI) NITSCHKE, RUPRECHT Pediatric oncology group POG9006--6-MP/methotrexate vs. alternating chemotherapy for ALL in childhood
U10CA-11233-23 0044 (CCI) NITSCHKE, RUPRECHT Pediatric oncology group POG9079--Phase I study of L-PAM/CTX with ABM rescue for brain tumors in children
U10CA-11233-23 0045 (CCI) NITSCHKE, RUPRECHT Pediatric oncology group POG9075--Phase I study of acivicin in children with solid tumors
U10CA-11233-23 0046 (CCI) NITSCHKE, RUPRECHT Pediatric oncology group POG9074--Phase I study of xomazyme-H65 in children with T-cell ALL/lymphoma
U10CA-11233-23 0047 (CCI) NITSCHKE, RUPRECHT Pediatric oncology group POG9072--Phase I chemotherapy for recurrent/resistant malignant solid tumors
U10CA-11233-23 0048 (CCI) NITSCHKE, RUPRECHT Pediatric oncology group POG9061-Phase II systemic therapy and irradiation for ALL & CNS leukemia
U10CA-11233-23 0049 (CCI) NITSCHKE, RUPRECHT Pediatric oncology group POG 9086--Phase I pilot study of therapy for T-cell ALL or NHL
U10CA-11233-23 0050 (CCI) NITSCHKE, RUPRECHT Pediatric oncology group POG9071--Phase I trial of fazarabine in children with acute leukemia
U10CA-11233-23 0051 (CCI) NITSCHKE, RUPRECHT Pediatric oncology group POG8970--Phase I trial of fazarabine in children with refractory solid tumors
U10CA-11233-23 0052 (CCI) NITSCHKE, RUPRECHT Pediatric oncology group POG8973--Etoposide (VP-16) and carboplatin in children with acute leukemia
U10CA-11233-23 0053 (CCI) NITSCHKE, RUPRECHT Pediatric oncology group POG8870--Phase I trial of ifosfamide/VP16/MESNA in children with acute leukemia
U10CA-11233-23 0054 (CCI) NITSCHKE, RUPRECHT Pediatric oncology group POG8871--Phase I study of rTNF in children with refractory solid tumors
U10CA-11233-23 0055 (CCI) NITSCHKE, RUPRECHT Pediatric oncology group POG8671--Phase I immunotherapy with rIL-2 in children with solid tumors
U10CA-11233-23 0056 (CCI) NITSCHKE, RUPRECHT Pediatric oncology group POG8494--Phase I study of fludarabine phosphate in pediatric patients
U10CA-11233-23 0057 (CCI) NITSCHKE, RUPRECHT Pediatric oncology group POG8930--A comprehensive genetic analysis of brain tumors
U10CA-11233-23 0058 (CCI) NITSCHKE, RUPRECHT Pediatric oncology group POG8826--Late effects of Hodgkin's disease
U10CA-11233-23 0059 (CCI) NITSCHKE, RUPRECHT Pediatric oncology group POG9046--Molecular genetic analysis of Wilm's tumors
U10CA-11233-23 0060 (CCI) NITSCHKE, RUPRECHT Pediatric oncology group POG9153--Rhabdomyosarcoma study/laboratory evaluation of tumor
U10CA-11233-23 0002 (CCI) NITSCHKE, RUPRECHT Pediatric oncology group POG9005--Dose intensification of methotrexate & 6-mercaptourine in childhood ALL
U10CA-11233-23 0003 (CCI) NITSCHKE, RUPRECHT Pediatric oncology group POG9031--Cisplatin/VP-16 therapy of medulloblastoma/pre vs. post irradiation
U10CA-11233-23 0004 (CCI) NITSCHKE, RUPRECHT Pediatric oncology group POG8945--Phase III chemotherapy for hepatoblastoma & hepatocellular carcinoma
U10CA-11233-23 0005 (CCI) NITSCHKE, RUPRECHT Pediatric oncology group POG9049--Phase III study of high-risk malignant germ cell tumors in children
U10CA-11233-23 0006 (CCI) NITSCHKE, RUPRECHT Pediatric oncology group POG8844--Bone marrow transplant in children with stage D neuroblastoma
U10CA-11233-23 0007 (CCI) NITSCHKE, RUPRECHT Pediatric oncology group POG8850--Phase III treatment of Ewing's sarcoma and neuroectodermal bone tumors
U10CA-11233-23 0008 (CCI) NITSCHKE, RUPRECHT Pediatric oncology group POG8821--Phase III chemotherapy +/- autologous BMT in children with AML
U10CA-11233-23 0009 (CCI) NITSCHKE, RUPRECHT Pediatric oncology group POG8725--Phase III chemotherapy +/- radiation therapy in pediatric Hodgkins
U10CA-11233-23 0010 (CCI) NITSCHKE, RUPRECHT Pediatric oncology group POG8704--Phase III chemotherapy of childhood T cell ALL & lymphoblastic lymphoma
U10CA-11233-23 0011 (CCI) NITSCHKE, RUPRECHT Pediatric oncology group POG8719--Phase III chemotherapy for non-Hodgkin's lymphoma in children
R37CA-11378-22 (PTHB) MC GUIRE, WILLIAM L UNIVERSITY OF TEXAS HLTH SCI C 7703 FLOYD CURL DRIVE SAN ANTONIO, TX 78284-7884 Mechanism of hormonal control of mammary carcinoma
R01CA-11430-25 (NEUB) ZIMMERMAN, STUART O UT M D ANDERSON CANCER CENTER 1515 HOLCOMBE BLVD HOUSTON, TX 77030 Biomathematics and computing in a cancer institute
R01CA-11430-25 0058 (NEUB) JOHNSTON, DENNIS A Biomathematics and computing in a cancer institute Cytometric measurement and estimation of cell kinetics
R01CA-11430-25 0066 (NEUB) THOMES, HOWARD D Biomathematics and computing in a cancer institute Radiobiological studies
R01CA-11430-25 0067 (NEUB) ZIMMERMAN, STUART O Biomathematics and computing in a cancer institute Analysis of structural models of interacting populations
R01CA-11430-25 0068 (NEUB) WHITE, R ALLEN Biomathematics and computing in a cancer institute In vivo cellular studies
R01CA-11430-25 0069 (NEUB) BROWN, BARRY W Biomathematics and computing in a cancer institute Aspects of cancer progression
R01CA-11430-25 0070 (NEUB) ATKINSON, E NEELY Biomathematics and computing in a cancer institute Minization of noisy functions
R01CA-11430-25 0071 (NEUB) ATKINSON, E NEELY Biomathematics and computing in a cancer institute Monte Carlo study of ill conditioning effects in nonlinear regression analysis
R01CA-11430-25 0072 (NEUB) BROWN, BARRY W Biomathematics and computing in a cancer institute Effects in designs for dose-response estimation in radiobiology
R01CA-11430-25 0073 (NEUB) DIXON, DENNIS O Biomathematics and computing in a cancer institute Statistical methods for mixture model with log-logistic failure times
U10CA-11488-21 (CCI) MEUNIER, FRANCOISE EORTC DATA CENTER AVENUE E. MOUNIER 83 BTE 11 1200 BRUSSELS, BELGIUM EORTC coordinating and data center
R01CA-11512-22 (VR) HORWITZ, MARSHALL S ALBERT EINSTEIN COLL OF MED DPT OF MICROBIOLOGY-IMMUNOLOGY BRONX, NY 10461 Adenovirus DNA synthesis and polypeptide assembly
R01CA-11685-21 (END) ORTH, DAVID N VANDERBILT UNIVERSITY SCHOOL OF MEDICINE NASHVILLE, TN 37232 Tumor cell synthesis & secretion of peptide hormones
R01CA-11695-22 (BBCB) GRIFFITH, O HAYES UNIVERSITY OF OREGON INSTITUTE OF MOLECULAR BIOLOGY EUGENE, OR 97403 Photoelectron imaging and properties of macromolecules
R01CA-11705-21A1 (BIO) GOULIAN, MEHRAN UNIV OF CALIFORNIA, SAN DIEGO LA JOLLA, CA 92093 DNA synthesis studies
R01CA-11778-22 (ET) WHITELEY, JOHN M SCRIPPS CLINIC & RES FDN 10666 N TORREY PINES ROAD LA JOLLA, CALIF 92037 Chemistry of folate and pteridine coenzymes
U10CA-11789-21 (CCI) GREEN, MARK R UNIV OF CALIFORNIA, SAN DIEGO 225 DICKINSON ST., H-811 K SAN DIEGO, CA 92103 Cancer and leukemia group B
U10CA-11796-22 (CCI) MEADOWS, ANNA T CHILDREN'S HOSPITAL 3400 CIVIC CENTER BLVD PHILADELPHIA, PA 19104 Children's cancer study group
R37CA-11861-22 (EVR) WAGNER, EDWARD K UNIVERSITY OF CALIFORNIA SCHOOL OF BIOLOGICAL SCIENCES IRVINE, CA 92717 Control of viral RNA synthesis in herpes virus infection
R37CA-11898-21 (PTHA) BIGNER, DARRELL D DUKE UNIV MEDICAL CENTER P O BOX 3156 DURHAM, N C 27710 Brain tumors--immunological and biological studies
R01CA-11944-19 (MEP) MEDINA, DANIEL BAYLOR COLLEGE OF MEDICINE ONE BAYLOR PLAZA HOUSTON, TEXAS 77030 Biology of mammary preneoplasias
R01CA-12010-29 (MCHA) KUEHNE, MARTIN E UNIVERSITY OF VERMONT BURLINGTON, VT 05405 Total syntheses of indole alkaloids
U10CA-12027-20 (SRC) FISHER, BERNARD UNIVERSITY OF PITTSBURGH 3550 TERRACE STREET PITTSBURGH, PA 15261 Primary cancer therapy group--(NSABP) headquarters
U10CA-12028-20 (SRC) FISHER, BERNARD UNIVERSITY OF PITTSBURGH 3550 TERRACE ST PITTSBURGH, PA 15261 Primary breast cancer therapy group (NSABP)
U10CA-12036-19 (SRC) JOCHIMSEN, PETER R UNIVERSITY OF IOWA HOSPITALS IOWA CITY, IOWA 52242 Primary breast cancer group (NSABP)
U10CA-12046-19 (CCI) PERRY, MICHAEL C UNIVERSITY OF MISSOURI ONE HOSPITAL DRIVE COLUMBIA, MO 65212 Cancer and leukemia group B
R37CA-12055-20 (EVR) MILLER, I GEORGE, JR YALE UNIVERSITY PO BOX 3333 333 CEDAR STREET NEW HAVEN, CT 06510 Studies of Epstein-Barr virus
R01CA-12115-21 (MCHA) PAQUETTE, LEO A OHIO STATE UNIVERSITY 120 WEST 18TH AVENUE COLUMBUS, OH 43210-1173 Cytotoxic, cocarcinogenic, and antileukemic agents
P30CA-12197-19 (CCS) CAPIZZI, ROBERT L BOWMAN GRAY SCHOOL OF MEDICINE 300 SOUTH HAWTHORNE ROAD WINSTON-SALEM, NC 27103 Cancer city of Wake Forest University
P30CA-12197-19 9003 (CCS) WAITE, B MOSELEY Cancer city of Wake Forest University Membrane biology core laboratory
P30CA-12197-19 9004 (CCS) KUCERA, LOUIS S Cancer city of Wake Forest University Tissue culture laboratory
P30CA-12197-19 9005 (CCS) SETHI, V SAGAR Cancer city of Wake Forest University Pharmacology core laboratory
P30CA-12197-19 9006 (CCS) SPURR, CHARLES L Cancer city of Wake Forest University Epi-stat program
P30CA-12197-19 9007 (CCS) CAPIZZI, ROBERT L. Cancer city of Wake Forest University Clinical research program
P30CA-12197-19 9008 (CCS) DOELLGAST, GEORGE J Cancer city of Wake Forest University Hybridoma--core laboratory
P30CA-12197-19 9009 (CCS) THOMAS, MICHAEL J Cancer city of Wake Forest University Gc/ms--core laboratory
P30CA-12197-19 9010 (CCS) LEWIS, JON C Cancer city of Wake Forest

PROJECT NO., ORGANIZATIONAL UNIT., INVESTIGATOR, ADDRESS, TITLE

University Electron microscopy--core laboratory

P30CA-12197-19 9011 (CCS) LIVELY, MARK O Cancer city of Wake Forest University Protein analysis core lab

P30CA-12197-19 9012 (CCS) BASS, DAVID A Cancer city of Wake Forest University Flow cytometry--core laboratory

P30CA-12197-19 9013 (CCS) THOMAS, MICHAEL J Cancer city of Wake Forest University Nuclear magnetic resonance core laboratory

P30CA-12197-19 9014 (CCS) POLLACK, BRIAN Cancer city of Wake Forest University DNA synthesis core lab

P30CA-12197-19 9015 (CCS) POWELL, BAYARD L. Cancer city of Wake Forest University Leukemia cell distribution—core

P30CA-12197-19 9016 (CCS) CAPIZZI, ROBERT L. Cancer city of Wake Forest University Developmental core

U10CA-12213-20 (CCI) NEIDHART, JAMES A UNM CANCER CENTER 900 CAMINO DE SALUD, N E ALBUQUERQUE, N M 87131 Cooperative study of cancer chemotherapy

P30CA-12227-20 (CCS) MYERS, ALLEN R TEMPLE UNIV SCH OF MEDICINE 3400 NORTH BROAD STREET PHILADELPHIA, PA 19140 Core program on carcinogenesis

P30CA-12227-20 9002 (CCS) CROCE, CARLO Core program on carcinogenesis Cell culture media preparation core

P30CA-12227-20 9003 (CCS) CROCE, CARLO Core program on carcinogenesis Computer facility

P30CA-12227-20 9004 (CCS) CROCE, CARLO Core program on carcinogenesis Electron microscopy facility

P30CA-12227-20 9005 (CCS) CROCE, CARLO Core program on carcinogenesis Equipment maintenance and repair core

P30CA-12227-20 9006 (CCS) CROCE, CARLO Core program on carcinogenesis Flow cytometry facility

P30CA-12227-20 9007 (CCS) CROCE, CARLO Core program on carcinogenesis Laboratory animal facility

P30CA-12227-20 9008 (CCS) CROCE, CARLO Core program on carcinogenesis Nucleic acid facility core

P30CA-12227-20 9009 (CCS) CROCE, CARLO Core program on carcinogenesis Protein chemistry laboratory core

P30CA-12227-20 9010 (CCS) CROCE, CARLO Core program on carcinogenesis Transgenic mouse laboratory

P30CA-12227-20 9011 (CCS) CROCE, CARLO Core program on carcinogenesis Developmental funds

P30CA-12227-20 9001 (CCS) CROCE, CARLO Core program on carcinogenesis Biohazard control and safety

R01CA-12421-20 (HEM) ADAMS, JERRY M W & E HALL INST OF MED RES PO ROYAL MELBOURNE HOSP PARKVILLE VIC 3050 AUSTRALIA Oncogenes in hematopoietic differentiation and neoplasia

R37CA-12428-22 (PC) FRIEDBERG, ERROL C UNIV OF TEX SW MED CTR AT DALL 5323 HARRY HINES BLVD DALLAS, TX 75235 DNA repair and its relationship to carcinogenesis

U10CA-12449-21 (CCI) CAREY, ROBERT W MASSACHUSETTS GENERAL HOSPITAL 100 BLOSSOM STREET BOSTON, MA 02114 Cancer and leukemia group B

R01CA-12464-21 (ARR) HIRSCH, MARTIN S MASSACHUSETTS GENERAL HOSPITAL FRUIT ST INFECTIOUS DIS UNIT BOSTON, MA 02114 Immune reactivity and oncogenic virus infections

P01CA-12536-20 (SRC) HALL, ERIC J COLUMBIA UNIVERSITY 630 W 168TH STREET NEW YORK, N Y 10032 The effects of small doses of radiation

P01CA-12536-20 0003 (SRC) HALL, ERIC J The effects of small doses of radiation Transformation, mutagenesis and repair

P01CA-12536-20 0009 (SRC) BOREK, CARMIA The effects of small doses of radiation Induction and modulation of radiogenic transformation

P01CA-12536-20 0011 (SRC) GEARD, CHARLES R The effects of small doses of radiation Radiation cytogenetics

P01CA-12536-20 0016 (SRC) KLIAUGA, PAUL The effects of small doses of radiation Experimental nanodosimetry of pulsed beams

P01CA-12536-20 0017 (SRC) ZAIDER, MARCO The effects of small doses of radiation Physico-chemical events in radiation action

P01CA-12536-20 0018 (SRC) BRENNER, DAVID J The effects of small doses of radiation Towards the new Q

P01CA-12536-20 9001 (SRC) HALL, ERIC J The effects of small doses of radiation Core program

P01CA-12582-19 (SRC) MORTON, DONALD L UNIVERSITY OF CALIFORNIA 405 HILGARD AVE LOS ANGELES, CA 90024-1406 Surgery immunology and immunotherapy of human cancer

P01CA-12582-19 0003 (SRC) GUPTA, RISHAB K Surgery immunology and immunotherapy of human cancer Circulating immune complexes and urinary antigens of cancer patients

P01CA-12582-19 0004 (SRC) MORTON, DONALD L Surgery immunology and immunotherapy of human cancer Clinical investigation of immunotherapy of malignant melanoma

P01CA-12582-19 0016 (SRC) GOLUB, SIDNEY H Surgery immunology and immunotherapy of human cancer In vivo regulation of nk cytotoxicity

P01CA-12582-19 0017 (SRC) IRIE, REIKO F Surgery immunology and immunotherapy of human cancer Tumor antigens that elicit humoral immune responses in cancer patients

P01CA-12582-19 9001 (SRC) MORTON, DONALD L. Surgery immunology and immunotherapy of human cancer Core support

R01CA-12623-18 (BNP) MOORE, RICHARD E UNIVERSITY OF HAWAII 2545 THE MALL HONOLULU, HI 96822 Anticancer agents from cyanophytes and marine organisms

U10CA-12644-20 (CCI) STEPHENS, RONALD L UNIV OF KANSAS MEDICAL CENTER 39TH AND RAINBOW BLVD KANSAS CITY, KS 66103 Southwest oncology group studies

P30CA-12708-21 (CCS) PEDERSON, THORU WORCESTER FDN FOR EXP BIOLOGY 222 MAPLE AVE SHREWSBURY, MA 01545 Cancer center support

P30CA-12708-21 9002 (CCS) PEDERSON, THORU Cancer center support Central service--Core

P30CA-12708-21 9003 (CCS) WITMAN, GEORGE Cancer center support Electron microscopy facility--Core

P30CA-12708-21 9004 (CCS) MILLER, F Cancer center support Marine animal facility--Core

P30CA-12708-21 9005 (CCS) GOODCHILD, JOHN Cancer center support Oligodeoxynucleotide synthesis--Core

P30CA-12708-21 9006 (CCS) HILDEBRANDT, JOHN Cancer center support Protein chemistry--Core

P30CA-12708-21 9007 (CCS) HILDEBRANDT, JOHN Cancer center support Developmental program--Core

P30CA-12708-21 9001 (CCS) HOAGLAND, MAHLON B Cancer center support Cell culture facility

P01CA-12800-18A1 (SRC) WALL, RANDOLPH UCLA SCHOOL OF MEDICINE CENTER FOR HEALTH SCIENCES Immune functions and cancer

P01CA-12800-18A1 0048 (SRC) WALL, RANDOLF Immune functions and cancer B cell genes--Expression, regulation, and function

P01CA-12800-18A1 0055 (SRC) DENNY, CHRISTOPHER Immune functions and cancer Analysis of lymphoid malignancy translocation oncogenes by DNA fragment transfer

P01CA-12800-18A1 0056 (SRC) BRAUN, JONATHAN Immune functions and cancer Ig variable region hypermutation in human B lymphocytes

P01CA-12800-18A1 0057 (SRC) SAXON, ANDREW Immune functions and cancer B cell responses in Common Variable Immunodeficiency

P01CA-13038-19 (SRC) MIHICH, ENRICO ROSWELL PARK CANCER INSTITUTE ELM AND CARLTON STREETS BUFFALO, NY 14263 Experimental therapeutics and cancer drug program

P01CA-13038-19 0097 (SRC) BERNACKI, RALPH J Experimental therapeutics and cancer drug program Drug development--In vitro & in vivo therapy evaluation

P01CA-13038-19 0101 (SRC) KANTER, PETER M Experimental therapeutics and cancer drug program Drug development--Toxicology, pathology, preclinical pharmacology

P01CA-13038-19 0104 (SRC) BOBEK, MIROSLAV Experimental therapeutics and cancer drug program Protein kinase C as potential target for tumor cell growth inhibition

P01CA-13038-19 0111 (SRC) RUSTUM, YOUCEF M Experimental therapeutics and cancer drug program Modification of drug resistance

P01CA-13038-19 0112 (SRC) MCGUIRE, JOHN J Experimental therapeutics and cancer drug program Folyl- & antifolylpolyglutamates in combination chemotherapy

P01CA-13038-19 0113 (SRC) DOLNICK, BRUCE J Experimental therapeutics and cancer drug program Antisense suppression of mdrl gene expression

P01CA-13038-19 0114 (SRC) KULESZ-MARTIN, MOLLY Experimental therapeutics and cancer drug program Cell regulation & therapeutics--Selectivity in tumors

P01CA-13038-19 0115 (SRC) EHRKE, M JANE Experimental therapeutics and cancer drug program Chemotherapy and biological response modifiers

P01CA-13038-19 9001 (SRC) MIHICH, ENRICO Experimental therapeutics and cancer drug program Core

P01CA-13106-20 (CAK) MATHEWS, MICHAEL B COLD SPRING HARBOR LABORATORY PO BOX 100 COLD SPRING HARBOR, NY 11724 Cold Spring Harbor Cancer research center

P01CA-13106-20 9002 (CAK) MATHEWS, MICHAEL B Cold Spring Harbor Cancer research center Scientific core

P01CA-13106-20 0001 (CAK) MATHEWS, MICHAEL B Cold Spring Harbor Cancer research center Protein synthesis section

P01CA-13106-20 0006 (CAK) GRODZICKER, TERRI I Cold Spring Harbor Cancer research center Adenovirus genetics section

P01CA-13106-20 0007 (CAK) ROBERTS, RICHARD J Cold Spring Harbor Cancer research center Nucleic acid chemistry section

P01CA-13106-20 0011 (CAK) HARLOW, EDWARD Cold Spring Harbor Cancer research center Protein immunochemistry

P01CA-13106-20 0012 (CAK) MARSHALS, DANIEL R Cold Spring Harbor Cancer research center Protein chemistry section

P01CA-13106-20 0013 (CAK) GLUZMAN, YAKUV Cold Spring Harbor Cancer research center Molecular biology of SV 40

P01CA-13106-20 0014 (CAK) HERR, WINSHIP Cold Spring Harbor Cancer research center Transcription control

P01CA-13106-20 0015 (CAK) MATHEWS, MICHAEL B Cold Spring Harbor Cancer research center Protein synthesis--Regulation of adenovirus RNA production

P01CA-13106-20 0016 (CAK) STILLMAN, BRUCE S Cold Spring Harbor Cancer research center DNA synthesis--SV 40 DNA replication

P01CA-13106-20 0017 (CAK) STILLMAN, BRUCE S Cold Spring Harbor Cancer research center Function of adenovirus EIB gene products

P30CA-13148-20 (SRC) LOBUGLIO, ALBERT F UNIV OF ALABAMA AT BIRMINGHAM UAB STATION BIRMINGHAM, AL 35294 Cancer center core support grant

P30CA-13148-20 9001 (SRC) BUGG, CHARLES E Cancer center core support grant Core facility--X-ray crystallography

P30CA-13148-20 9002 (SRC) KRISHNA, N RAMA Cancer center core support grant Core facility--NMR

P30CA-13148-20 9004 (SRC) COMPANS, RICHARD W Cancer center core support grant Core facility--Electron microscopy

P30CA-13148-20 9005 (SRC) COOPER, MAX D Cancer center core support grant Core facility--Media preparation, glassware washing and tissue culture

P30CA-13148-20 9009 (SRC) SOONG, SENG JAW Cancer center core support grant Core facility--Biostatistics

P30CA-13148-20 9011 (SRC) GRIZZLE, WILLIAM E Cancer center core support grant Core facility--Tissue procurement

P30CA-13148-20 9012 (SRC) RODU, BRAD Cancer center core support grant Core facility--Dental oncology

P30CA-13148-20 9015 (SRC) TAYLOR, KENNETH B Cancer center core support grant Core facility--Fermentation

P30CA-13148-20 9016 (SRC) ENGLER, JEFFREY A Cancer center core support grant Core facility--Oligonucleotide synthesis

P30CA-13148-20 9017 (SRC) AIR, GILLIAN M Cancer center core support grant Core--Protein analysis and peptide synthesis

P30CA-13148-20 9018 (SRC) GROSSI, CARLOS E Cancer center core support grant Core facility--Hematopoietic cell laboratory

P30CA-13148-20 9021 (SRC) WHEELER, RICHARD H Cancer center core support grant Core--Clinical studies unit

P30CA-13148-20 9022 (SRC) VINTER, D Cancer center core support grant Core facility--Digital imaging microscopy

R01CA-13195-17 (PC) SMULSON, MARK E GEORGETOWN UNIVERSITY 3900 RESERVOIR RD, N W WASHINGTON, D C 20007 Histone ADP-ribosylation and HeLa cell replication

R01CA-13202-20 (BBCB) HARRISON, STEPHEN C HARVARD UNIVERSITY 7

PROJECT NO., ORGANIZATIONAL UNIT., INVESTIGATOR, ADDRESS, TITLE

DIVINITY AVENUE CAMBRIDGE, MA 02138 Structure and assembly of viruses and of coated vesicles

R37CA-13267-20 (IMB) HYMAN, ROBERT A SALK INSTITUTE PO BOX 85800 SAN DIEGO, CA 92186-5800 Genetic basis of antigenic variation

R37CA-13311-20 (RAD) SUIT, HERMAN D MASSACHUSETTS GENERAL HOSPITAL FRUIT STREET BOSTON, MA 02114 Modification of tumor response to local irradiation

P30CA-13330-20 (CCS) SCHARFF, MATTHEW D ALBERT EINSTEIN COLLEGE OF MED 1300 MORRIS PARK AVENUE BRONX, NEW YORK 10461 Core support for cancer research center

P30CA-13330-20 9001 (CCS) FANT, JANE Core support for cancer research center The analytical ultrastructure center

P30CA-13330-20 9002 (CCS) SERRANO, LOUIS J Core support for cancer research center Animal institute barrier facility

P30CA-13330-20 9003 (CCS) WEST, MICHAEL Core support for cancer research center Biohazard facility

P30CA-13330-20 9004 (CCS) BLOOM, BARRY Core support for cancer research center Cell culture and media preparation

P30CA-13330-20 9005 (CCS) WIERNIK, PETER H Core support for cancer research center Clinical research unit

P30CA-13330-20 9008 (CCS) DIAMOND, BETTY A Core support for cancer research center Fluorescent activated cell sorter

P30CA-13330-20 9009 (CCS) SCHARFF, MATTHEW D Core support for cancer research center Hybridoma facility

P30CA-13330-20 9011 (CCS) GUPTA, RAJ K Core support for cancer research center NMR facility

P30CA-13330-20 9012 (CCS) WARNER, JONATHAN R Core support for cancer research center Oligonucleotide synthesis facility

P30CA-13330-20 9015 (CCS) SCHARFF, MATTHEW D Core support for cancer research center Shared equipment

P30CA-13330-20 9016 (CCS) SCHARFF, MATTHEW D Core support for cancer research center Developmental support

P30CA-13330-20 9017 (CCS) DEPINHO, RONALD Core support for cancer research center Transgenic mouse and stem cell facility

P30CA-13343-18 (CCS) UPTON, ARTHUR C NEW YORK UNIVERSITY MED CENTER 550 FIRST AVENUE NEW YORK, NEW YORK 10016 Research in environmental cancer

P30CA-13343-18 9001 (CCS) UPTON, ARTHUR C Research in environmental cancer Shared resources and services--Library

P30CA-13343-18 9002 (CCS) UPTON, ARTHUR C Research in environmental cancer Shared resources--Mass spectrometry

P30CA-13343-18 9003 (CCS) UPTON, ARTHUR C Research in environmental cancer Shared resources--Histopathology

P30CA-13343-18 9004 (CCS) ALTSHULER, BERNARD Research in environmental cancer Biostatistics and biomathematics--Core

P30CA-13343-18 9007 (CCS) UPTON, ARTHUR C Research in environmental cancer Computer facility

P30CA-13343-18 9008 (CCS) UPTON, ARTHUR C Research in environmental cancer Animal facility--Core

P30CA-13343-18 9010 (CCS) UPTON, ARTHUR C Research in environmental cancer Machine and electrical shop--Core

P30CA-13343-18 9011 (CCS) UPTON, ARTHUR C Research in environmental cancer Inhalation facility--Core

P30CA-13343-18 9012 (CCS) UPTON, ARTHUR C Research in environmental cancer Nucleotide synthesis facility--Core

P30CA-13343-18 9013 (CCS) UPTON, ARTHUR C Research in environmental cancer Developmental funds--Core

R37CA-13353-18 (RAD) SONG, CHANG W UNIV OF MINNESOTA MEDICAL SCH HARVARD ST AT E RIVER RD/494UM MINNEAPOLIS, MN 55455 Vascularity & reoxygenation in x-irradiated tumors

R01CA-13402-19 (PC) ATKINSON, PAUL H ALBERT EINSTEIN COLL OF MED 1300 MORRIS PARK AVENUE BRONX, N Y 10461 Surface membranes in normal and cancer cells

R01CA-13410-17A2 (REN) SONNENSCHEIN, CARLOS TUFTS UNIVERSITY 136 HARRISON AVENUE BOSTON, MA 02111-1800 Mechanism of hormone action on target cells in culture

P01CA-13525-19 (SRC) WILSON, CHARLES B DEPT OF NEUROLOGICAL SURGERY UNIVERSITY OF CALIFORNIA SAN FRANCISCO, CA 94143-0112 Program for treatment of malignant brain tumors

P01CA-13525-19 0015 (SRC) PRADOS, MICHAEL Program for treatment of malignant brain tumors Clinical therapy for malignant brain tumors

P01CA-13525-19 0020 (SRC) MARTON, LAWRENCE J Program for treatment of malignant brain tumors Polyamine-DNA interactions

P01CA-13525-19 0022 (SRC) FIKE, JOHN R Program for treatment of malignant brain tumors Modification of radiation and heat damage in normal brain

P01CA-13525-19 0023 (SRC) BODELL, WILLIAM J Program for treatment of malignant brain tumors Molecular mechanism for BCNU potential

P01CA-13525-19 0025 (SRC) DEEN, DENNIS Program for treatment of malignant brain tumors Modification of radiation recovery in human brain tumor cells

P01CA-13525-19 0026 (SRC) GUTIN, PHILIP Program for treatment of malignant brain tumors Vasogenic edema in the genesis of delayed radiation injury of spinal cord

P01CA-13525-19 9001 (SRC) DEEN, DENIS Program for treatment of malignant brain tumors Core project

R01CA-13533-20 (PTHB) SUSSMAN, HOWARD H STANFORD UNIVERSITY 300 PASTEUR DRIVE STANFORD, CALIF 94305 Ectopic placental proteins in cancer

U10CA-13539-19 (CCI) HAMMOND, DENMAN ORION MEDICAL SCIENCES INST 440 EAST HUNTINGTON DR. ARCADIA, CA 91006-6012 Children's cancer study group chairman's grant

R01CA-13605-18 (CBY) STEINBERG, MALCOLM S PRINCETON UNIVERSITY PRINCETON, NJ 08544-1014 Molecular basis of embryonic cell guidance

R01CA-13608-19 (VR) VOGT, MARGUERITE M SALK INST/BIOLOGICAL STUDIES P O BOX 85800 SAN DIEGO, CA 92138 Viral gene functions involved in transformation

U10CA-13612-18 (CCI) MILLER, THOMAS P UNIV OF ARIZ/HLTH SCIENCES CTR 1501 N CAMPBELL AVENUE TUCSON, AZ 85724 Southwest oncology group

U10CA-13650-19 (CCI) HAHN, RICHARD G MAYO FOUNDATION 200 FIRST STREET SOUTHWEST ROCHESTER, MN 55905 Eastern cooperative oncology group

PROJECT NO., ORGANIZATIONAL UNIT., INVESTIGATOR, ADDRESS, TITLE

P30CA-13696-19 (SRC) WEINSTEIN, I BERNARD HAMMER HLTH SCI CTR 701 WEST 168TH STREET NEW YORK, NY 10032 Cancer center core support grant

P30CA-13696-19 9007 (SRC) MOORE, BETTY Cancer center core support grant Information/communication services

P30CA-13696-19 9008 (SRC) ELLISON, ROSE R Cancer center core support grant Inpatient research facility

P30CA-13696-19 9009 (SRC) ELLISON, ROSE R Cancer center core support grant Clinical cancer outpatient facility

P30CA-13696-19 9013 (SRC) MESA-TEJADA, RICHARD Cancer center core support grant Central tumor tissue laboratory

P30CA-13696-19 9014 (SRC) CANTOR, CHARLES Cancer center core support grant Cell sorter facility

P30CA-13696-19 9015 (SRC) MORRISON, SHERIS Cancer center core support grant Core--Glassware facility

P30CA-13696-19 9016 (SRC) VAN DER PLOEG, LEX Cancer center core support grant Core--Biological contain ment facility

P30CA-13696-19 9017 (SRC) JEFFREY, ALAN Cancer center core support grant Core--Chemical biohazards

P30CA-13696-19 9018 (SRC) SMITH, CASSANDRA Cancer center core support grant Core--Peparative biochemistry facility

P30CA-13696-19 9019 (SRC) CANFIELD, ROBERT E, Cancer center core support grant Y

P30CA-13696-19 9020 (SRC) EFSTRATIADIS, ARGIRIS Cancer center core support grant Core--Oligonucleotide synthesis laboratory

P30CA-13696-19 9021 (SRC) SMITH, CASSANDRA Cancer center core support grant P04190946

P30CA-13696-19 9022 (SRC) CONSTANTINI, FRANKLIN D. Cancer center core support grant Core--Transgenic mice

P30CA-13696-19 9023 (SRC) ALT, FRED Cancer center core support grant Core--Oncogene diagnostic unit

P30CA-13696-19 9024 (SRC) WARBURTON, DOROTHY Cancer center core support grant Core--Cytogenetics facility

P30CA-13696-19 9025 (SRC) COX, JAMES D. Cancer center core support grant Radiation oncology facilities

P30CA-13696-19 9026 (SRC) TAUBK, ROBERT N. Cancer center core support grant Cancer control and regional activities facilities

P30CA-13696-19 9002 (SRC) NEIMANN, WENDELL Cancer center core support grant Core facility--Animal facility

P30CA-13696-19 9005 (SRC) SHAPIRO, LUCILLE Cancer center core support grant Core facility--Media preparation

P30CA-13696-19 9006 (SRC) HONIG, BARRY H. Cancer center core support grant Core--computer facility

U10CA-13809-19 (CCI) BREITFELD, PHILIP P INDIANA UNIV SCHOOL OF MED 702 BARNHILL DR/RM 2720 INDIANAPOLIS, IN 46202-5225 Children's cancer study group

R37CA-13881-19 (RAD) CLIFTON, KELLY H UNIVERSITY OF WISCONSIN 600 N HIGHLAND AVE MADISON, WI 53792 Radiation in vitro--Mammary neoplasia

R37CA-13884-19 (NSS) ECKHART, WALTER SALK INST FOR BIOLOGICAL STUDY POST OFFICE BOX 85800 SAN DIEGO, CA 92186-5800 Viral gene functions and regulation of cell growth

P30CA-13943-19 (CCS) MAIZEL, ABBY L ROGER WILLIAMS GENERAL HOSPITA 825 CHALKSTONE AVENUE PROVIDENCE, RI 02908 Clinical cancer research center (CCSG) core

P30CA-13943-19 0016 (CCS) CALABRESI, PAUL Clinical cancer research center (CCSG) core Developmental funds

P30CA-13943-19 0010 (CCS) CALABRESI, PAUL Clinical cancer research center (CCSG) core Cloning of genes for enzymes of pyrimidine and purine metabolism

P30CA-13943-19 0011 (CCS) CLARK, JEFFREY Clinical cancer research center (CCSG) core Inhibition of autocrine BFGF stimulated growth of melanoma cells

P30CA-13943-19 0012 (CCS) TAKEDA, AKIKA Clinical cancer research center (CCSG) core Variation of LFA-1 sialylation--Mechanism and effect

P30CA-13943-19 0013 (CCS) KING, THOMAS Clinical cancer research center (CCSG) core Molecular mechanisms of leukemogenesis

P30CA-13943-19 0014 (CCS) KASAIAN, MARION Clinical cancer research center (CCSG) core Effect of cyclosporine A on NK cells

P30CA-13943-19 9007 (CCS) CALABRESI, PAUL Clinical cancer research center (CCSG) core Animal care facility

P30CA-13943-19 9008 (CCS) CRABTREE, GERALD W Clinical cancer research center (CCSG) core High pressure liquid chromatography

P30CA-13943-19 9009 (CCS) CHU, SHIH HSI Clinical cancer research center (CCSG) core Medicinal chemistry facility

P30CA-13943-19 9011 (CCS) CALABRESI, PAUL Clinical cancer research center (CCSG) core Clinical trial management

P30CA-13943-19 9014 (CCS) CALABRESI, PAUL Clinical cancer research center (CCSG) core Tissue culture facility

P30CA-13943-19 9015 (CCS) CALABRESI, PAUL Clinical cancer research center (CCSG) core Biostatistics service

U10CA-14028-18 (CCI) BAKER, LAURENCE H WAYNE STATE UNIVERSITY PO BOX 02188 DETROIT, MI 48202 Southwest oncology group

P30CA-14051-20 (CCS) HYNES, RICHARD O MASSACHUSETTS INST OF TECHNOLO 77 MASS AVE/ BLDG E17-113 CAMBRIDGE, MA 02139 Cancer center support (core) grant

P30CA-14051-20 9001 (CCS) LURIA, SALVADOR E Cancer center support (core) grant Animal facility--Core

P30CA-14051-20 9002 (CCS) LURIA, SALVADOR E Cancer center support (core) grant Electron microscope facility--Core

P30CA-14051-20 9003 (CCS) LURIA, SALVADOR E Cancer center support (core) grant Media preparation facility--Core

P30CA-14051-20 9005 (CCS) SHARP, P Cancer center support (core) grant Biopolymer laboratory

P30CA-14051-20 9006 (CCS) SHARP, P Cancer center support (core) grant Cell analyzer and sorting facility

P30CA-14051-20 9007 (CCS) SHARP, P Cancer center support (core) grant Transgenic animal facility

P30CA-14051-20 9010 (CCS) SHARP, P Cancer center support (core) grant Development facility--Core

R01CA-14054-18 (MGN) KLEIN, GEORGE KAROLINSKA INSTITUTE PO BOX 60400 TOCKHOLM, SWEDEN S-104 01 Malignant behavior and cellular

antigen expression
P30CA-14089-16 (SRC) HENDERSON, BRIAN E USC CANCER CENTER PO BOX 33800 LOS ANGELES, CA 90033-0800 USC comprehensive cancer center (core) support
P30CA-14089-16 9001 (SRC) MCMILLAN, MINNIE USC comprehensive cancer center (core) support Microchemical core lab
P30CA-14089-16 9002 (SRC) HORWITZ, DAVID A USC comprehensive cancer center (core) support Cell sorter core lab
P30CA-14089-16 9003 (SRC) TOKES, ZOLTAN A USC comprehensive cancer center (core) support Cell culture core facility
P30CA-14089-16 9004 (SRC) CHAN, KENNETH K USC comprehensive cancer center (core) support Pharmacoanalytic lab--Core
P30CA-14089-16 9007 (SRC) CASGRANDE, JOHN T USC comprehensive cancer center (core) support Computer services--Core
P30CA-14089-16 9008 (SRC) THOMAS, DUNEAN C USC comprehensive cancer center (core) support Biostatistic core facility
P30CA-14089-16 9009 (SRC) SPICER, DARCY USC comprehensive cancer center (core) support Clinical investigations support facility
P30CA-14089-16 9010 (SRC) SIEGEL, STUART E USC comprehensive cancer center (core) support Clinical research support--CHLA
P30CA-14089-16 9011 (SRC) TAYLOR, BILL USC comprehensive cancer center (core) support Basic research core facility
P30CA-14089-16 9012 (SRC) HENDERSON, BRIAN E USC comprehensive cancer center (core) support Development funds--core
P30CA-14089-16 9013 (SRC) TRICHE, TIMOTHY J USC comprehensive cancer center (core) support Tumor bank core
R01CA-14113-19 (IMB) SHIN, HYUN S JOHNS HOPKINS UNIVERSITY 725 N WOLFE STREET BALTIMORE, MD 21205 Platelet-mediated cytotoxicity--Mechanisms & applications
R01CA-14134-20 (SSS) MELAMED, MYRON R NEW YORK MEDICAL COLLEGE VALHALLA, N.Y. 10595 Automated urinary cytology for cancer detection
P30CA-14195-18 (CCS) ECKHART, WALTER THE SALK INSTITUTE POST OFFICE BOX 85800 SAN DIEGO, CA 92186-5800 Cancer center support core grant
P30CA-14195-18 0038 (CCS) EVANS, RONALD M Cancer center support core grant Gene regulation in the neuroendocrine system
P30CA-14195-18 0039 (CCS) HUNTER, TONY Cancer center support core grant Transforming gene products of RNA or DNA tumor viruses
P30CA-14195-18 0040 (CCS) HYMAN, ROBERT A Cancer center support core grant Cell surface of hematopoietic cells
P30CA-14195-18 0041 (CCS) ROSE, JOHN K Cancer center support core grant Structure and expression of viral membrane proteins
P30CA-14195-18 0044 (CCS) VERMA, INDER M Cancer center support core grant Genome organization of retroviruses
P30CA-14195-18 0045 (CCS) SEFTON, BARTHOLOMEW M Cancer center support core grant Viral transformation and viral replication
P30CA-14195-18 0046 (CCS) VOGT, MARGUERITE M Cancer center support core grant Transformation of murine hematopoietic cell
P30CA-14195-18 0047 (CCS) GLENNEY, JOHN Cancer center support core grant Plasma membrane structure and function
P30CA-14195-18 0049 (CCS) EVANS, GLEN A Cancer center support core grant Developmental genetics of the thymus-leukemia antigens
P30CA-14195-18 0051 (CCS) HOLLEY, ROBERT W Cancer center support core grant Control of growth of mammalian cells
P30CA-14195-18 9001 (CCS) ECKHART, WALTER Cancer center support core grant Shared resources--Equipment
P30CA-14195-18 9002 (CCS) ECKHART, WALTER Cancer center support core grant Media preparation and shared services
P30CA-14195-18 9003 (CCS) ECKHART, WALTER Cancer center support core grant Shared resources--Flow cytometry
P30CA-14195-18 9004 (CCS) ECKHART, WALTER Cancer center support core grant Shared resources--Developmental program
P30CA-14195-18 9005 (CCS) ECKHART, WALTER Cancer center support core grant Shared resources--Transgenic animals
P30CA-14195-18 9006 (CCS) ECKHART, WALTER Cancer center support core grant Shared resources--DNA synthesis
P30CA-14195-18 0005 (CCS) ECKHART, WALTER Cancer center support core grant Cell transformation by polyoma virus
P30CA-14195-18 0009 (CCS) HUNTER, ANTHONY R Cancer center support core grant Mechanisms of viral transformation
P30CA-14195-18 0010 (CCS) HYMAN, ROBERT A Cancer center support core grant Regulation and function of cell surface antigens
P30CA-14195-18 0026 (CCS) VERMA, INDER M Cancer center support core grant Viral and cellular oncogenes
P30CA-14195-18 0033 (CCS) TROWBRIDGE, IAN S Cancer center support core grant Cell surface glycoproteins of hematopoietic cells
P30CA-14195-18 0035 (CCS) DULBECCO, RENATO Cancer center support core grant Normal and neoplastic development of the mammary gland
K06CA-14219-30 (NSS) TRENTIN, JOHN J BAYLOR COLLEGE OF MEDICINE ONE BAYLOR PLAZA HOUSTON, TX 77030 Tissue transplantation, radiobiology, and cancer biology
R01CA-14235-18 (EDC) SWIFT, MICHAEL R UNIV OF N C AT CHAPEL HILL CHAPEL HILL, NC 27599 Neoplasia predisposing genes of man
P30CA-14236-18 (SRC) BAST, ROBERT C, JR DUKE UNIVERSITY MEDICAL CENTER BOX 3814 DURHAM, N C 27710 Comprehensive cancer center support grant
P30CA-14236-18 9025 (SRC) ERICKSON, HAROLD P Comprehensive cancer center support grant Core--Microscopy
P30CA-14236-18 9026 (SRC) LINNEY, ELWOOD A Comprehensive cancer center support grant Core--Transgenic and genetically specified murine facility
P30CA-14236-18 9027 (SRC) SPICER, LEONARD D Comprehensive cancer center support grant Core--High resolution nmr spectroscopy center
P30CA-14236-18 9032 (SRC) SEIGLER, H F Comprehensive cancer center support grant Core--Multidisciplinary clinics
P30CA-14236-18 0928 (SRC) JIRTLE, RANDY L Comprehensive cancer center support grant Core--Animal and cell radiation facility
P30CA-14236-18 0929 (SRC) HAYNES, BARTON F Comprehensive cancer center support grant Core--Flow cytometry facility
P30CA-14236-18 0930 (SRC) PETER, WILLIAM Comprehensive cancer center support grant Core--Bone marrow transplant support
P30CA-14236-18 0931 (SRC) KUNTZBERG, JOANNE Comprehensive cancer center support grant Core--Hematopoietic progenitor assay unit
P30CA-14236-18 9002 (SRC) JOKLIK, WOLFGANG K Comprehensive cancer center support grant Core--Cell culture facility
P30CA-14236-18 9010 (SRC) BIGNER, DARRELL D Comprehensive cancer center support grant Core--animal and laboratory isolation facility
P30CA-14236-18 9012 (SRC) GEORGE, STEPHEN L Comprehensive cancer center support grant Core--Data management unit
P30CA-14236-18 9014 (SRC) BAST, ROBERT C Comprehensive cancer center support grant Core--Inpatient research unit
P30CA-14236-18 9018 (SRC) BIGNER, SANDRA H Comprehensive cancer center support grant Human tissue bank and cytogenetics
P30CA-14236-18 9021 (SRC) SEIGLER, HILLIARD F Comprehensive cancer center support grant Core--Support services for research in solid tumors
P30CA-14236-18 9022 (SRC) ZALUTSKY, MICHAEL R Comprehensive cancer center support grant Radiolabeling facility
P30CA-14236-18 9023 (SRC) PIZZO, SALVATORE Comprehensive cancer center support grant Core--Macromolecular facility
P30CA-14236-18 9024 (SRC) MODRICH, PAUL L Comprehensive cancer center support grant Core--Fermentation facility
R37CA-14394-19 (PC) SANTI, DANIEL V UNIVERSITY OF CALIFORNIA 513 PARNASSAS AVE SAN FRANCISCO, CA 94143-0446 Thymidylate synthetase and related enzymes
P30CA-14395-18A1 (CCS) ALTMAN, NORMAN H UNIVERSITY OF MIAMI P O BOX 016960 (D72) MIAMI, FL 33101 Cancer center core support grant
P30CA-14395-18A1 9009 (CCS) EAST, DAWN Cancer center core support grant Clinical research services...core
P30CA-14395-18A1 9010 (CCS) TRAPIDO, EDWARD Cancer center core support grant Biostatistics and computing...core
P30CA-14395-18A1 9011 (CCS) SAMY, T Cancer center core support grant Analytical pharmacology...core
P30CA-14395-18A1 9012 (CCS) OTRAKJI, CHRISTIAN Cancer center core support grant Tissue procurement...core
P30CA-14395-18A1 9013 (CCS) LICHTER, WOLF Cancer center core support grant Cell culture media and supplies...core
P30CA-14395-18A1 9014 (CCS) ALTMAN, NORMAN Cancer center core support grant Office support system...core
P30CA-14395-18A1 9015 (CCS) KRISHAN, AWTAR Cancer center core support grant Core equipment maintenance...core
P30CA-14395-18A1 9016 (CCS) BREW, KEITH Cancer center core support grant Protein analysis...core
P30CA-14395-18A1 9017 (CCS) KRISHAN, AWTAR Cancer center core support grant Analytical cytology...core
P30CA-14395-18A1 9018 (CCS) WERNER, RUDOLF Cancer center core support grant Oligonucleotide synthesis...core
P30CA-14395-18A1 9019 (CCS) KRISHAN, AWTAR Cancer center core support grant Histopathology...core
P30CA-14395-18A1 9020 (CCS) KRISHAN, AWTAR Cancer center core support grant Seminar series...core
P30CA-14395-18A1 9021 (CCS) ALTMAN, NORMAN Cancer center core support grant Developmental funds...core
R01CA-14462-19 (IMB) THORBECKE, GEERTRUIDA J NEW YORK UNIVERSITY MED CENTER 550 FIRST AVENUE NEW YORK, N Y 10016 Properties of lymphoid tumor cells in vivo and in vitro
R01CA-14464-18 (CTY) LOEWENSTEIN, WERNER R UNIV OF MIAMI PO BOX 016430 MIAMI, FL 33101 Intercellular communication and cancer
P30CA-14520-19 (CCS) CARBONE, PAUL P UNIV OF WI CLINICAL CA CTR 600 HIGHLAND AVENUE MADISON, WI 53792 Cancer center support
P30CA-14520-19 9003 (CCS) DEMETS, DAVID L Cancer center support Core--biostatistics resource
P30CA-14520-19 9005 (CCS) SONDEL, PAUL M Cancer center support Core--Scintillation counting services
P30CA-14520-19 9006 (CCS) MULCAHY, R TIMOTHY Cancer center support Core--Radiation sources
P30CA-14520-19 9007 (CCS) JORDAN, V CRAIG Cancer center support Core--analytical instrumentation
P30CA-14520-19 9009 (CCS) DOLNICK, BRUCE J Cancer center support Core--safety service
P30CA-14520-19 9010 (CCS) DEMETS, DAVID Cancer center support Core--Clinical trials data units
P30CA-14520-19 9013 (CCS) TORMEY, DOUGLASS C Cancer center support Core--biological sample and tissue acquisition
P30CA-14520-19 9014 (CCS) CARBONE, PAUL P. Cancer center support Cancer control resources--Core
P30CA-14520-19 9015 (CCS) CARBONE, PAUL P. Cancer center support Developmental funds--Core
U10CA-14548-17 (CCI) MANSOUR, EDWARD G METROHEALTH MEDICAL CENTER 3395 SCRANTON ROAD CLEVELAND, OH 44135 Eastern cooperative oncology group
R01CA-14551-16A4 (ET) RYSER, HUGUES J BOSTON UNIVERSITY 80 EAST CONCORD STREET BOSTON, MA 02118 Penetration of macromolecules into mammalian cells
U10CA-14560-18 (CCI) FINKLESTEIN, JERRY Z HARBOR-UCLA MEDICAL CENTER 1124 WEST CARSON STREET TORRANCE, CA 90509 Children's cancer study group A
P30CA-14599-18 (CCS) SCHILSKY, RICHARD L UNIVERSITY OF CHICAGO 5841 SOUTH MARYLAND AVENUE CHICAGO, IL 60637 Univ of Chgo Ca res ctr: Cancer center support grant
P30CA-14599-18 9002 (CCS) ROIZMAN, BERNARD Univ of Chgo Ca res ctr: Cancer center support grant Viral oncology core facility
P30CA-14599-18 9003 (CCS) SWIFT, HEWSON Univ of Chgo Ca res ctr: Cancer center support grant Cancer biology core facility
P30CA-14599-18 9004 (CCS) FRIED, JOSEF Univ of Chgo Ca res ctr: Cancer center support grant NMR spectroscopy cancer research facility
P30CA-14599-18 9005 (CCS) OLESKE, DENISE Univ of Chgo Ca res ctr: Cancer center support grant Biostatistical and data management core facility
P30CA-14599-18 9007 (CCS) ROIZMAN, BERNARD Univ of Chgo Ca res ctr: Cancer center support grant Oligopeptide synthesis--Core
P30CA-14599-18 9008 (CCS) SCHREILER, HANS Univ of Chgo Ca res ctr: Cancer center support grant Animal barrier core facility
P30CA-14599-18 9009 (CCS) ULTMANN, JOHN E. Univ of Chgo Ca res ctr: Cancer center support grant Developmental funds--Investigators only
R01CA-14609-18 (CBY) GRINNELL, FREDERICK L UNIV OF TX SW MED

CTR DALLAS 5323 HARRY HINES BOULEVARD DALLAS, TX 75235 Molecular basis of cellular adhesiveness
R01CA-14649-18 (MEP) OYASU, RYOICHI NORTHWESTERN UNIV MEDICAL SCH 303 EAST CHICAGO AVENUE CHICAGO, IL 60611 In vivo bladder carcinogenesis of nitrosamines
R01CA-14799-16A1 (CPA) BRENT, THOMAS P ST JUDE CHILDREN'S RES HOSP 332 N LAUDERDALE MEMPHIS, TN 38101-0318 Enzymes and reactions for repair of DNA in human cells
R01CA-14835-18 (BIO) WANG, TERESA S STANFORD UNIV-SCHOOL OF MEDICI STANFORD, CA 94305 DNA polymerases in normal and neoplastic human cells
R01CA-14906-17 (CPA) ALLFREY, VINCENT G THE ROCKEFELLER UNIVERSITY 1230 YORK AVENUE NEW YORK, NY 10021-6399 Nuclear proteins in carcinogenesis of the colon
U10CA-14958-17 (CCI) WIERNIK, PETER H ALBERT EINSTEIN COLLEGE OF MED 1300 MORRIS PARK AVENUE BRONX, NY 10461 Eastern cooperative oncology group
R01CA-15044-18 (PTHA) MANUELIDIS, LAURA M YALE UNIVERSITY SCH OF MED 333 CEDAR ST, P O BOX 3333 NEW HAVEN, CT 06510 Pathogenetic determinants of human CNS tumors
R37CA-15062-18 (NSS) AHMED, KHALIL US DEPT OF VA AFFRS/RES SVC15 MEDICAL CENTER, ONE VETERANS D MINNEAPOLIS, MN 55417-2319 Studies of normal and neoplastic prostate
P30CA-15083-18 (CCS) KOVACH, JOHN S MAYO FOUNDATION 200 FIRST STREET SOUTHWEST ROCHESTER, MN 55905 Cancer center support grant
P30CA-15083-18 9013 (CCS) WIEBEU, ERIC D Cancer center support grant Molecular probe--core
P30CA-15083-18 9014 (CCS) LIEBSON, PAUL Cancer center support grant Development funds--core
P30CA-15083-18 0001 (CCS) AMES, MATTHEW M Cancer center support grant Cancer pharmacology
P30CA-15083-18 0002 (CCS) MCKEAN, DAVID J Cancer center support grant Immunology
P30CA-15083-18 0003 (CCS) PRENDERGAST, FRAUKLYN G Cancer center support grant Biochemistry and molecular biology
P30CA-15083-18 0004 (CCS) O'CONNELL, MICHAEL J Cancer center support grant Clinical trials
P30CA-15083-18 9001 (CCS) AMES, MATTHEW Cancer center support grant Cancer pharmacology
P30CA-15083-18 9003 (CCS) O'FALLON, JUDITH R Cancer center support grant Statistical core
P30CA-15083-18 9004 (CCS) AMES, MATTHEW M Cancer center support grant Pharmacology core
P30CA-15083-18 9005 (CCS) BANKS, P M Cancer center support grant Surgical pathology--core
P30CA-15083-18 9006 (CCS) BURNHAM, NORA R Cancer center support grant Oncology pharmacy core
P30CA-15083-18 9007 (CCS) KATZMANN, JOHN A Cancer center support grant Monoclonal antibody core
P30CA-15083-18 9010 (CCS) MCKEAN, DAVID J Cancer center support grant Immunology core
P30CA-15083-18 9011 (CCS) KOVACH, JOHN S Cancer center support grant Cellular immunology laboratory--core
P30CA-15083-18 9012 (CCS) DEWALD, GORDON W Cancer center support grant Cytogenetics--core
R01CA-15142-18 (ET) MIHICH, ENRICO ROSWELL PARK CANCER INSTITUTE THERAPEUTICS BUFFALO, NY 14263 Cancer chemotherapy and immunologic effects
R01CA-15187-15 (BIO) BARIL, EARL F WORCESTER FOUNDATION 222 MAPLE AVENUE SHREWSBURY, MA 01545 DNA synthesis--Regulation in normal and cancer cells
R37CA-15201-18 (RAD) BROWN, JOHN M STANFORD MEDICAL CENTER STANFORD MEDICAL CENTER STANFORD, CA 94305-6060 Experimental radiotherapy--Basis and modification
R01CA-15237-17 (HEM) SHADDUCK, RICHARD K WEST PENN HOSPITAL FOUNDATION 4818 LIBERTY AVE PITTSBURGH, PA 15224 Regulation of granulopoiesis
R01CA-15325-17A2 (PC) GRAY, GARY R UNIVERSITY OF MINNESOTA 207 PLEASANT ST SE MINNEAPOLIS, MN 55455 Antitumor active components of BCG cell walls
R37CA-15378-18 (RAD) OLEINICK, NANCY L DIV OF BIOCHEMICAL ONCOLOGY 2058 ABINGTON ROAD CLEVELAND, OH 44106 Radiation induced modifications in protein synthesis
P01CA-15396-18 (SRC) SANTOS, GEORGE W JOHNS HOPKINS UNIV ONCOL CTR 600 NORTH WOLFE STREET BALTIMORE, MD 21205 Bone marrow transplantation in human disease
P01CA-15396-18 0001 (SRC) SANTOS, GEORGE W Bone marrow transplantation in human disease preparative regimens and therapeutic anti-tumor
P01CA-15396-18 0003 (SRC) HESS, ALLAN D Bone marrow transplantation in human disease Graft-versus-host reaction and disease
P01CA-15396-18 0007 (SRC) BURNS, WILLIAM H Bone marrow transplantation in human disease Biology of viral and other infections in bone marrow transplants
P01CA-15396-18 0008 (SRC) COLVIN, O MICHAEL Bone marrow transplantation in human disease Pharmacology in bone marrow transplantation
P01CA-15396-18 9001 (SRC) ZEHNBAUER, BARBARA Bone marrow transplantation in human disease Supportive services--cytogenetics core
P01CA-15396-18 9002 (SRC) BESCHORNER, WILLIAM E Bone marrow transplantation in human disease core--Pathology
P01CA-15396-18 9003 (SRC) ROWLEY, SCOTT D Bone marrow transplantation in human disease Core--Stem cell laboratory
P01CA-15396-18 9004 (SRC) MELLITS, E DAVID Bone marrow transplantation in human disease Core--Statistics and data
P01CA-15396-18 9005 (SRC) WINGARD, JOHN R Bone marrow transplantation in human disease Core--Outpatient facility
R37CA-15416-18 (PTHB) COFFEY, DONALD S JOHNS HOPKINS HOSPITAL MARBURG 121, 600 N WOLFE ST BALTIMORE, MD 21205 models of prostate cancer--Cell structure and function
U10CA-15488-19 (CCI) GLICK, JOHN H UNIV OF PA CANCER CENTER 3400 SPRUCE STREET PHILADELPHIA, PA 19104 Eastern cooperative oncology group
R01CA-15523-18 (RNM) ADELSTEIN, STANLEY J SHIELDS WARREN RADIATION LAB 50 BINNEY STREET BOSTON, MA 02115 Therapeutic/toxic action of electron-emitting nuclides
U10CA-15525-18 (CCI) FALLETTA, JOHN M DUKE UNIVERSITY MEDICAL CENTER PO BOX 2916 DURHAM, NC 27710 Pediatric Oncology Group studies
U10CA-15525-18 0011 (CCI) FALLETTA, JOHN M Pediatric Oncology Group studies POG8719--Phase III chemotherapy for non-Hodgkin's lymphoma in children
U10CA-15525-18 0012 (CCI) FALLETTA, JOHN M Pediatric Oncology Group studies POG8650--National Wilm's tumor and clear cell sarcoma study
U10CA-15525-18 0013 (CCI) FALLETTA, JOHN M Pediatric Oncology Group studies POG8616--Phase III chemotherapy for childhood Burkitt and non-Burkitts lymphoma
U10CA-15525-18 0014 (CCI) FALLETTA, JOHN M Pediatric Oncology Group studies POG8615--Phase III study of large cell lymphomas in children and adolescents
U10CA-15525-18 0015 (CCI) FALLETTA, JOHN M Pediatric Oncology Group studies POG8651--Phase III study of childhood nonmetastatic osteosarcoma
U10CA-15525-18 0016 (CCI) FALLETTA, JOHN M Pediatric Oncology Group studies POG8653--Phase III study of childhood soft tissue sarcomas
U10CA-15525-18 0017 (CCI) FALLETTA, JOHN M Pediatric Oncology Group studies POG8625--Phase III combined therapy in childhood Hodgkin's disease
U10CA-15525-18 0018 (CCI) FALLETTA, JOHN M Pediatric Oncology Group studies POG8451--Intergroup rhabdomyosarcoma study
U10CA-15525-18 0019 (CCI) FALLETTA, JOHN M Pediatric Oncology Group studies POG9110--Rotational drug therapy after first marrow relapse of non-T, non B ALL
U10CA-15525-18 0020 (CCI) FALLETTA, JOHN M Pediatric Oncology Group studies POG9107--Phase II pilot study of infant leukemia
U10CA-15525-18 0021 (CCI) FALLETTA, JOHN M Pediatric Oncology Group studies POG9140--Phase II therapy for recurrent or refractory neuroblastoma
U10CA-15525-18 0022 (CCI) FALLETTA, JOHN M Pediatric Oncology Group studies POG9048--Phase II study of malignant germ cell tumors in children
U10CA-15525-18 0023 (CCI) FALLETTA, JOHN M Pediatric Oncology Group studies POG9060--Intensive QOD ifosfamide treatment for CNS tumors in children
U10CA-15525-18 0024 (CCI) FALLETTA, JOHN M Pediatric Oncology Group studies POG8936--Phase II study of carboplatin treatment for optic pathway tumors
U10CA-15525-18 0025 (CCI) FALLETTA, JOHN M Pediatric Oncology Group studies POG8935--Phase II study of surgery and/or radiotherapy for optic pathway tumors
U10CA-15525-18 0026 (CCI) FALLETTA, JOHN M Pediatric Oncology Group studies POG8820--Phase II/III study of VP-16, AMSA +/- 5-azacytidine in childhood ANLL
U10CA-15525-18 0027 (CCI) FALLETTA, JOHN M Pediatric Oncology Group studies POG8889--Intergroup rhabdomyosarcoma study for clinical group IV disease
U10CA-15525-18 0028 (CCI) FALLETTA, JOHN M Pediatric Oncology Group studies POG8866--Phase II asparaginase therapy for acute lymphoblastic leukemia
U10CA-15525-18 0029 (CCI) FALLETTA, JOHN M Pediatric Oncology Group studies POG8862--Combination chemotherapy of acute T-lymphoblastic leukemia
U10CA-15525-18 0030 (CCI) FALLETTA, JOHN M Pediatric Oncology Group studies POG8863--Phase II study of high dose cytosine arabinoside in childhood tumors
U10CA-15525-18 0031 (CCI) FALLETTA, JOHN M Pediatric Oncology Group studies POG8827--Phase II treatment of children with Hodgkin's disease in relapse
U10CA-15525-18 0032 (CCI) FALLETTA, JOHN M Pediatric Oncology Group studies POG8865--Phase II recombinant alpha-interferon in relapsed T-cell disease
U10CA-15525-18 0033 (CCI) FALLETTA, JOHN M Pediatric Oncology Group--Phase II recombinant A-interferon in chronic myelogenous leukemia
U10CA-15525-18 0034 (CCI) FALLETTA, JOHN M Pediatric Oncology Group studies POG8832--Combination chemotherapy followed by radiotherapy for brain tumors
U10CA-15525-18 0035 (CCI) FALLETTA, JOHN M Pediatric Oncology Group studies POG8731--Phase II trial of methotrexate in treatment of brain tumors in children
U10CA-15525-18 0036 (CCI) FALLETTA, JOHN M Pediatric Oncology Group studies POG8788--Intergroup rhabdomyosarcoma study/pilot study for clinical group III
U10CA-15525-18 0037 (CCI) FALLETTA, JOHN M Pediatric Oncology Group studies POG8761--Phase II study of homoharringtonine therapy for nonlymphoblastic leukemi
U10CA-15525-18 0038 (CCI) FALLETTA, JOHN M Pediatric Oncology Group studies POG8739--Phase II immunotherapy with alpha-2 interferon for brain tumors
U10CA-15525-18 0039 (CCI) FALLETTA, JOHN M Pediatric Oncology Group studies POG8741--Treatment of patients with stage C and stage D neuroblastoma
U10CA-15525-18 0040 (CCI) FALLETTA, JOHN M Pediatric Oncology Group studies POG8751--Phase II methotrexate chemotherapy for rhabdomyosarcoma in children
U10CA-15525-18 0041 (CCI) FALLETTA, JOHN M Pediatric Oncology Group studies POG8633--Postoperative chemotherapy and delayed irradiation for brain tumors
U10CA-15525-18 0042 (CCI) FALLETTA, JOHN M Pediatric Oncology Group studies POG8617--Therapy for B-cell acute lymphoblastic leukemia and lymphoma
U10CA-15525-18 0001 (CCI) FALLETTA, JOHN M Pediatric Oncology Group studies POG9006--6-MP/methotrexate vs. alternating chemotherapy for ALL in childhood
U10CA-15525-18 0043 (CCI) FALLETTA, JOHN M Pediatric Oncology Group studies POG9139--Phase I study of cisplatin and irradiation in brain

stem gliomas
U10CA-15525-18 0044 (CCI) FALLETTA, JOHN M Pediatric Oncology Group studies POG9079--Phase I study of L-PAM/CTX with ABM rescue for brain tumors in children
U10CA-15525-18 0045 (CCI) FALLETTA, JOHN M Pediatric Oncology Group studies POG9075--Phase I study of acivicin in children with solid tumors
U10CA-15525-18 0046 (CCI) FALLETTA, JOHN M Pediatric Oncology Group studies POG9074--Phase I study of xomazyme-H65 in children with T-cell ALL/lymphoma
U10CA-15525-18 0047 (CCI) FALLETTA, JOHN M Pediatric Oncology Group studies POG9072--Phase I chemotherapy for recurrent/resistant malignant solid tumors
U10CA-15525-18 0048 (CCI) FALLETTA, JOHN M Pediatric Oncology Group studies POG9061-Phase II systemic therapy and irradiation for ALL & CNS leukemia
U10CA-15525-18 0049 (CCI) FALLETTA, JOHN M Pediatric Oncology Group studies POG 9086--Phase I pilot study of therapy for T-cell ALL or NHL
U10CA-15525-18 0050 (CCI) FALLETTA, JOHN M Pediatric Oncology Group studies POG9071--Phase I trial of fazarabine in children with acute leukemia
U10CA-15525-18 0051 (CCI) FALLETTA, JOHN M Pediatric Oncology Group studies POG8970--Phase I trial of fazarabine in children with refractory solid tumors
U10CA-15525-18 0052 (CCI) FALLETTA, JOHN M Pediatric Oncology Group studies POG8973--Etoposide (VP-16) and carboplatin in children with acute leukemia
U10CA-15525-18 0053 (CCI) FALLETTA, JOHN M Pediatric Oncology Group studies POG8870--Phase I trial of ifosfamide/VP16/MESNA in children with acute leukemia
U10CA-15525-18 0054 (CCI) FALLETTA, JOHN M Pediatric Oncology Group studies POG8871--Phase I study of rTNF in children with refractory solid tumors
U10CA-15525-18 0055 (CCI) FALLETTA, JOHN M Pediatric Oncology Group studies POG8671--Phase I immunotherapy with rIL-2 in children with solid tumors
U10CA-15525-18 0056 (CCI) FALLETTA, JOHN M Pediatric Oncology Group studies POG8494--Phase I study of fludarabine phosphate in pediatric patients
U10CA-15525-18 0057 (CCI) FALLETTA, JOHN M Pediatric Oncology Group studies POG8930--A comprehensive genetic analysis of brain tumors
U10CA-15525-18 0058 (CCI) FALLETTA, JOHN M Pediatric Oncology Group studies POG8828--Late effects of Hodgkin's disease
U10CA-15525-18 0059 (CCI) FALLETTA, JOHN M Pediatric Oncology Group studies POG9046--Molecular genetic analysis of Wilm's tumors
U10CA-15525-18 0060 (CCI) FALLETTA, JOHN M Pediatric Oncology Group studies POG9153--Rhabdomyosarcoma study/laboratory evaluation of tumor
U10CA-15525-18 0002 (CCI) FALLETTA, JOHN M Pediatric Oncology Group studies POG9005--Dose intensification of methotrexate & 6-mercaptourine in childhood ALL
U10CA-15525-18 0003 (CCI) FALLETTA, JOHN M Pediatric Oncology Group studies POG9031--Cisplatin/VP-16 therapy of medulloblastoma/pre vs. post irradiation
U10CA-15525-18 0004 (CCI) FALLETTA, JOHN M Pediatric Oncology Group studies POG8945--Phase III chemotherapy for hepatoblastoma & hepatocellular carcinoma
U10CA-15525-18 0005 (CCI) FALLETTA, JOHN M Pediatric Oncology Group studies POG9049--Phase III study of high-risk malignant germ cell tumors in children
U10CA-15525-18 0006 (CCI) FALLETTA, JOHN M Pediatric Oncology Group studies POG8844--Bone marrow transplant in children with stage D neuroblastoma
U10CA-15525-18 0007 (CCI) FALLETTA, JOHN M Pediatric Oncology Group studies POG8850--Phase III treatment of Ewing's sarcoma and neuroectodermal bone tumors
U10CA-15525-18 0008 (CCI) FALLETTA, JOHN M Pediatric Oncology Group studies POG8821--Phase III chemotherapy +/- autologous BMT in children with AML
U10CA-15525-18 0009 (CCI) FALLETTA, JOHN M Pediatric Oncology Group studies POG8725--Phase III chemotherapy +/- radiation therapy in pediatric Hodgkins
U10CA-15525-18 0010 (CCI) FALLETTA, JOHN M Pediatric Oncology Group studies POG8704--Phase III chemotherapy of childhood T cell ALL & lymphoblastic lymphoma
R01CA-15605-15 (CPA) EPSTEIN, JOHN H UNIVERSITY OF CALIFORNIA 3RD & PARNASSUS SAN FRANCISCO, CA 94143-0536 Chemotherapeutic agents and ultraviolet carcinogenesis
R01CA-15645-16 (BBCB) DUNLAP, R BRUCE UNIVERSITY OF SOUTH CAROLINA COLUMBIA, SC 29208 DTMP synthetase--NMR and mechanistic studies
P30CA-15704-18 (CCS) DAY, ROBERT W FRED HUTCHINSON CANCER RES CTR 1124 COLUMBIA STREET SEATTLE, WA 98104 Cancer center support grant
P30CA-15704-18 9020 (CCS) WEINTRAUB, HAROLD Cancer center support grant Seminar series--Core
P30CA-15704-18 9001 (CCS) SALE, GEORGE E Cancer center support grant Core--Electron microscopy service
P30CA-15704-18 9002 (CCS) SEEF, STEVEN Cancer center support grant Core--Biostatistics-epidemiology
P30CA-15704-18 9004 (CCS) JOHNSON, BARBARA Cancer center support grant Animal health resources--Core
P30CA-15704-18 9006 (CCS) WILSON, JOAN W Cancer center support grant Library--Core
P30CA-15704-18 9007 (CCS) BERNSTEIN, IRWIN D Cancer center support grant Flow cytometry--Core
P30CA-15704-18 9012 (CCS) SALE, GEORGE E Cancer center support grant Histology services--Core
P30CA-15704-18 9013 (CCS) KELLEHER, JOLEEN Cancer center support grant Nursing support--Shared resources
P30CA-15704-18 9014 (CCS) DAY, ROBERT W Cancer center support grant New program in clinical and experimental pathology--Developmental program
P30CA-15704-18 9017 (CCS) BLUMENSTEIN, BRENT A Cancer center support grant Compuer shared resources--Core
P30CA-15704-18 9018 (CCS) HILL, ROGER Cancer center support grant Cryobiology--Core
P30CA-15704-18 9019 (CCS) TOLENTINO, ERNEST Cancer center support grant Microchemistsry unit--Core
R01CA-15744-16 (PTHB) RUBIN, HARRY UNIVERSITY OF CALIFORNIA 229 WENDELL M STANLEY HALL BERKELEY, CA 94720 Cellular adaptation and progression to malignancy
R37CA-15751-18 (VR) LIVINGSTON, DAVID M DANA-FARBER CANCER INSTITUTE 44 BINNEY STREET BOSTON, MA 02115 Structure and function of SV40 non-virion proteins
R01CA-15776-14 (CPA) LEAV, IRWIN 136 HARRISON AVENUE BOSTON, MA 02111 Prostatic differentiation & sex hormone metabolism
P01CA-15822-17 (CAK) GREENE, MARK I UNIVERSITY OF PENNSYLVANIA 36TH & HAMILTON WALK PHILADELPHIA, PA 19104 Immunobiology of normal and neoplastic lymphocytes
P01CA-15822-17 0001 (CAK) WILSON, DARCY B Immunobiology of normal and neoplastic lymphocytes Immunobiology of T lymphocytes
P01CA-15822-17 0007 (CAK) NOWELL, PETER C Immunobiology of normal and neoplastic lymphocytes Lymphocyte population in chronic lymphocytic leukemia
P01CA-15822-17 0009 (CAK) SPRENT, JONATHON Immunobiology of normal and neoplastic lymphocytes Lymphocyte function in bone marrow chimeras
P01CA-15822-17 0010 (CAK) BLANK, KENNETH J Immunobiology of normal and neoplastic lymphocytes Effect of H-2 expression on MuLV-induced leukemogenesis
P01CA-15822-17 9001 (CAK) WILSON, DARCY B Immunobiology of normal and neoplastic lymphocytes Core program
R37CA-15901-17 (NSS) EVANS, HELEN H CASE WESTERN RESERVE UNIVERSIT 2058 ABINGTON ROAD CLEVELAND, OHIO 44106 Mutants and altered radioresponse of cells and tumors
R01CA-15979-18 (MET) SIPERSTEIN, MARVIN D VETERANS ADMIN MEDICAL CNTR 4150 CLEMENT STREET SAN FRANCISCO, CA 94121 Cholesterol metabolism in normal and malignant liver
U10CA-15989-17 (CCI) PULLEN, D JEANETTE UNIV OF MISSISSIPPI MEDICAL CT 2500 NORTH STATE STREET JACKSON, MS 39216 Pediatric oncology group
U10CA-15989-17 0020 (CCI) PULLEN, D JEANETTE Pediatric oncology group POG9107--Phase II pilot study of infant leukemia
U10CA-15989-17 0021 (CCI) PULLEN, D JEANETTE Pediatric oncology group POG9140--Phase II therapy for recurrent or refractory neuroblastoma
U10CA-15989-17 0022 (CCI) PULLEN, D JEANETTE Pediatric oncology group POG9048--Phase II study of malignant germ cell tumors in children
U10CA-15989-17 0023 (CCI) PULLEN, D JEANETTE Pediatric oncology group POG9060--Intensive QOD ifosfamide treatment for CNS tumors in children
U10CA-15989-17 0024 (CCI) PULLEN, D JEANETTE Pediatric oncology group POG8936--Phase II study of carboplatin treatment for optic pathway tumors
U10CA-15989-17 0025 (CCI) PULLEN, D JEANETTE Pediatric oncology group POG8935--Phase II study of surgery and/or radiotherapy for optic pathway tumors
U10CA-15989-17 0026 (CCI) PULLEN, D JEANETTE Pediatric oncology group POG8820--Phase II/III study of VP-16, AMSA +/- 5-azacytidine in childhood ANLL
U10CA-15989-17 0027 (CCI) PULLEN, D JEANETTE Pediatric oncology group POG8889--Intergroup rhabdomyosarcoma study for clinical group IV disease
U10CA-15989-17 0028 (CCI) PULLEN, D JEANETTE Pediatric oncology group POG8866--Phase II asparaginase therapy for acute lymphoblastic leukemia
U10CA-15989-17 0029 (CCI) PULLEN, D JEANETTE Pediatric oncology group POG8862--Combination chemotherapy of acute T-lymphoblastic leukemia
U10CA-15989-17 0030 (CCI) PULLEN, D JEANETTE Pediatric oncology group POG8863--Phase II study of high dose cytosine arabinoside in childhood tumors
U10CA-15989-17 0031 (CCI) PULLEN, D JEANETTE Pediatric oncology group POG8827--Phase II treatment of children with Hodgkin's disease in relapse
U10CA-15989-17 0032 (CCI) PULLEN, D JEANETTE Pediatric oncology group POG8865--Phase II recombinant alpha-interferon in relapsed T-cell disease
U10CA-15989-17 0033 (CCI) PULLEN, D JEANETTE Pediatric oncology group--Phase II recombinant A-interferon in chronic myelogenous leukemia
U10CA-15989-17 0034 (CCI) PULLEN, D JEANETTE Pediatric oncology group POG8832--Combination chemotherapy followed by radiotherapy for brain tumors
U10CA-15989-17 0035 (CCI) PULLEN, D JEANETTE Pediatric oncology group POG8731--Phase II trial of methotrexate in treatment of brain tumors in children
U10CA-15989-17 0036 (CCI) PULLEN, D JEANETTE Pediatric oncology group POG8788--Intergroup rhabdomyosarcoma study/pilot study for clinical group III
U10CA-15989-17 0037 (CCI) PULLEN, D JEANETTE Pediatric oncology group POG8761--Phase II study of homoharringtonine therapy for nonlymphoblastic leukemi
U10CA-15989-17 0038 (CCI) PULLEN, D JEANETTE Pediatric oncology group POG8739--Phase II immunotherapy with alpha-2 interferon for brain tumors
U10CA-15989-17 0039 (CCI) PULLEN, D JEANETTE Pediatric oncology group POG8741--Treatment of patients with stage C and stage D neuroblastoma
U10CA-15989-17 0040 (CCI) PULLEN, D JEANETTE Pediatric oncology group POG8751--Phase II methotrexate chemotherapy for rhabdomyosarcoma in children
U10CA-15989-17 0041 (CCI) PULLEN, D JEANETTE Pediatric oncology group POG8633--Postoperative chemotherapy and delayed irradiation for brain tumors
U10CA-15989-17 0042 (CCI) PULLEN, D JEANETTE Pediatric oncology

group POG8617--Therapy for B-cell acute lymphoblastic leukemia and lymphoma
U10CA-15989-17 0043 (CCI) PULLEN, D JEANETTE Pediatric oncology group POG9139--Phase I study of cisplatin and irradiation in brain stem gliomas
U10CA-15989-17 0044 (CCI) PULLEN, D JEANETTE Pediatric oncology group POG9079--Phase I study of L-PAM/CTX with ABM rescue for brain tumors in children
U10CA-15989-17 0045 (CCI) PULLEN, D JEANETTE Pediatric oncology group POG9075--Phase I study of acivicin in children with solid tumors
U10CA-15989-17 0046 (CCI) PULLEN, D JEANETTE Pediatric oncology group POG9074--Phase I study of xomazyme-H65 in children with T-cell ALL/lymphoma
U10CA-15989-17 0047 (CCI) PULLEN, D JEANETTE Pediatric oncology group POG9072--Phase I chemotherapy for recurrent/resistant malignant solid tumors
U10CA-15989-17 0048 (CCI) PULLEN, D JEANETTE Pediatric oncology group POG9061-Phase II systemic therapy and irradiation for ALL & CNS leukemia
U10CA-15989-17 0049 (CCI) PULLEN, D JEANETTE Pediatric oncology group POG 9086--Phase I pilot study of therapy for T-cell ALL or NHL
U10CA-15989-17 0050 (CCI) PULLEN, D JEANETTE Pediatric oncology group POG9071--Phase I trial of fazarabine in children with acute leukemia
U10CA-15989-17 0051 (CCI) PULLEN, D JEANETTE Pediatric oncology group POG8970--Phase I trial of fazarabine in children with refractory solid tumors
U10CA-15989-17 0001 (CCI) PULLEN, D JEANETTE Pediatric oncology group POG9006--6-MP/methotrexate vs. alternating chemotherapy for ALL in childhood
U10CA-15989-17 0052 (CCI) PULLEN, D JEANETTE Pediatric oncology group POG8973--Etoposide (VP-16) and carboplatin in children with acute leukemia
U10CA-15989-17 0053 (CCI) PULLEN, D JEANETTE Pediatric oncology group POG8870--Phase I trial of ifosfamide/VP16/MESNA in children with acute leukemia
U10CA-15989-17 0054 (CCI) PULLEN, D JEANETTE Pediatric oncology group POG8871--Phase I study of rTNF in children with refractory solid tumors
U10CA-15989-17 0055 (CCI) PULLEN, D JEANETTE Pediatric oncology group POG8671--Phase I immunotherapy with rIL-2 in children with solid tumors
U10CA-15989-17 0056 (CCI) PULLEN, D JEANETTE Pediatric oncology group POG8494--Phase I study of fludarabine phosphate in pediatric patients
U10CA-15989-17 0057 (CCI) PULLEN, D JEANETTE Pediatric oncology group POG8930--A comprehensive genetic analysis of brain tumors
U10CA-15989-17 0058 (CCI) PULLEN, D JEANETTE Pediatric oncology group POG8828--Late effects of Hodgkin's disease
U10CA-15989-17 0059 (CCI) PULLEN, D JEANETTE Pediatric oncology group POG9046--Molecular genetic analysis of Wilm's tumors
U10CA-15989-17 0060 (CCI) PULLEN, D JEANETTE Pediatric oncology group POG9153--Rhabdomyosarcoma study/laboratory evaluation of tumor
U10CA-15989-17 0002 (CCI) PULLEN, D JEANETTE Pediatric oncology group POG9005--Dose intensification of methotrexate & 6-mercaptourine in childhood ALL
U10CA-15989-17 0003 (CCI) PULLEN, D JEANETTE Pediatric oncology group POG9031--Cisplatin/VP-16 therapy of medulloblastoma/pre vs. post irradiation
U10CA-15989-17 0004 (CCI) PULLEN, D JEANETTE Pediatric oncology group POG8945--Phase III chemotherapy for hepatoblastoma & hepatocellular carcinoma
U10CA-15989-17 0005 (CCI) PULLEN, D JEANETTE Pediatric oncology group POG9049--Phase III study of high-risk malignant germ cell tumors in children
U10CA-15989-17 0006 (CCI) PULLEN, D JEANETTE Pediatric oncology group POG8844--Bone marrow transplant in children with stage D neuroblastoma
U10CA-15989-17 0007 (CCI) PULLEN, D JEANETTE Pediatric oncology group POG8850--Phase III treatment of Ewing's sarcoma and neuroectodermal bone tumors
U10CA-15989-17 0008 (CCI) PULLEN, D JEANETTE Pediatric oncology group POG8821--Phase III chemotherapy +/- autologous BMT in children with AML
U10CA-15989-17 0009 (CCI) PULLEN, D JEANETTE Pediatric oncology group POG8725--Phase III chemotherapy +/- radiation therapy in pediatric Hodgkins
U10CA-15989-17 0010 (CCI) PULLEN, D JEANETTE Pediatric oncology group POG8704--Phase III chemotherapy of childhood T cell ALL & lymphoblastic lymphoma
U10CA-15989-17 0011 (CCI) PULLEN, D JEANETTE Pediatric oncology group POG8719--Phase III chemotherapy for non-Hodgkin's lymphoma in children
U10CA-15989-17 0012 (CCI) PULLEN, D JEANETTE Pediatric oncology group POG8650--National Wilm's tumor and clear cell sarcoma study
U10CA-15989-17 0013 (CCI) PULLEN, D JEANETTE Pediatric oncology group POG8616--Phase III chemotherapy for childhood Burkitt and non-Burkitts lymphoma
U10CA-15989-17 0014 (CCI) PULLEN, D JEANETTE Pediatric oncology group POG8615--Phase III study of large cell lymphomas in children and adolescents
U10CA-15989-17 0015 (CCI) PULLEN, D JEANETTE Pediatric oncology group POG8651--Phase III study of childhood nonmetastatic osteosarcoma
U10CA-15989-17 0016 (CCI) PULLEN, D JEANETTE Pediatric oncology group POG8653--Phase III study of childhood soft tissue sarcomas
U10CA-15989-17 0017 (CCI) PULLEN, D JEANETTE Pediatric oncology group POG8625--Phase III combined therapy in childhood Hodgkin's disease
U10CA-15989-17 0018 (CCI) PULLEN, D JEANETTE Pediatric oncology group POG8451--Intergroup rhabdomyosarcoma study
U10CA-15989-17 0019 (CCI) PULLEN, D JEANETTE Pediatric oncology group POG9110--Rotational drug therapy after first marrow relapse of non-T, non B ALL

PROJECT NO., ORGANIZATIONAL UNIT., INVESTIGATOR, ADDRESS, TITLE

R01CA-16006-18 (MBY) DARNELL, JAMES E ROCKEFELLER UNIVERSITY 1230 YORK AVENUE NEW YORK, NY 10021 Liver differentiation and mrna regulation
P01CA-16038-18 (SRC) WEISSMAN, SHERMAN M YALE UNIVERSITY P O BOX 3333 NEW HAVEN, CT 06510 Program on the molecular basis of viral transformation
P01CA-16038-18 0006 (SRC) MILLER, I GEORGE Program on the molecular basis of viral transformation E B viral nuclear proteins in B-lympocyte immortalization
P01CA-16038-18 0010 (SRC) STEITZ, JOAN A Program on the molecular basis of viral transformation Viral small RNPs--Roles in cell transformation
P01CA-16038-18 0017 (SRC) TATTERSALL, PETER Program on the molecular basis of viral transformation In vitro analysis of oncosuppression by parvoviruses
P01CA-16038-18 0018 (SRC) LENGYEL, PETER Program on the molecular basis of viral transformation The genetics and biochemistry of oncogene action
P01CA-16038-18 0020 (SRC) DETTO, GIAN-PAOLO Program on the molecular basis of viral transformation Genetic control of keratinocyte and melanocyte transformation
P30CA-16042-17 (CCS) STECKEL, RICHARD J UCLA LOUIS FACTOR HLTH SCI BLD 10833 LE CONTE AVENUE LOS ANGELES, CA 90024-1781 Cancer center core support grant
P30CA-16042-17 9001 (CCS) ELASHOFF, ROBERT M Cancer center core support grant Biostatistics, analytic support and epidemiology (BASE) unit core
P30CA-16042-17 9002 (CCS) EISERLING, FREDERICK A Cancer center core support grant Biological structure core services
P30CA-16042-17 9003 (CCS) BUNTING, ALISON Cancer center core support grant Cancer information core service
P30CA-16042-17 9004 (CCS) WELLS, JOHN R Cancer center core support grant Cell separation core service
P30CA-16042-17 9005 (CCS) RAY, DAN S Cancer center core support grant Fermentor-preparation core facility
P30CA-16042-17 9006 (CCS) CLARK, WILLIAM R Cancer center core support grant Media preparation and cell freezing core service
P30CA-16042-17 9007 (CCS) FAHEY, JOHN L Cancer center core support grant Monoclonal antibody testing core service
P30CA-16042-17 9008 (CCS) HAYS, ESTHER F Cancer center core support grant Nude mouse core facility
P30CA-16042-17 9009 (CCS) SARNA, GREGORY P Cancer center core support grant Out-patient clinical research unit
P30CA-16042-17 9010 (CCS) BRESLOW, LESTER Cancer center core support grant Cancer control core
R01CA-16054-15 (PBC) BREWER, CURTIS F ALBERT EINSTEIN COLL OF MED 1300 MORRIS PARK AVENUE BRONX, N Y 10461 Carbohydrate and glycopeptide interactions with lectins
P30CA-16056-16 (CCS) TOMASI, THOMAS B, JR ROSWELL PARK MEMORIAL INST 666 ELM STREET BUFFALO, NY 14263 Roswell park memorial institute center core grant
P30CA-16056-16 9017 (CCS) PAUL, B Roswell park memorial institute center core grant Chemistry resource laboratory
P30CA-16056-16 9018 (CCS) REPASKY, ELIZABETH Roswell park memorial institute center core grant Electron microscopy facility
P30CA-16056-16 9019 (CCS) TOMASI, THOMAS Roswell park memorial institute center core grant Shared instrumentation
P30CA-16056-16 9020 (CCS) SLOCUM, H Roswell park memorial institute center core grant Tissue procurement
P30CA-16056-16 9021 (CCS) TOMASI, THOMAS Roswell park memorial institute center core grant GCDC central resources
P30CA-16056-16 9022 (CCS) STEWART, CARLTON Roswell park memorial institute center core grant Flow cytometry unit
P30CA-16056-16 9014 (CCS) MURPHY, GERALD P Roswell park memorial institute center core grant Shared resources--Developmental core support
P30CA-16056-16 9015 (CCS) TOMASI, THOMAS Roswell park memorial institute center core grant Biomathematics resource unit
P30CA-16056-16 9016 (CCS) SWANK, R Roswell park memorial institute center core grant Biopolymer facility
P30CA-16058-17 (CCS) SCHULLER, DAVID E ARTHUR G. JAMES CANC HOSP 300 W 10TH AVE RM 520 COLUMBUS, OH 43210 OSU comprehensive cancer center support (core) grant
P30CA-16058-17 9001 (CCS) BRUEGGEMEIER, ROBERT W OSU comprehensive cancer center support (core) grant Core--Analytical equipment laboratory
P30CA-16058-17 9002 (CCS) MILO, GEORGE E OSU comprehensive cancer center support (core) grant Core--Biosafety
P30CA-16058-17 9004 (CCS) GREVER, MICHAEL R OSU comprehensive cancer center support (core) grant Core--Interdisciplinary oncology unit
P30CA-16058-17 9005 (CCS) BALCERZAK, STANLEY P OSU comprehensive cancer center support (core) grant Core--Ambulatory oncology unit
P30CA-16058-17 9009 (CCS) TREWYN, RONALD W OSU comprehensive cancer center support (core) grant Core--Tumor procurement
P30CA-16058-17 9010 (CCS) STAUBUS, ALFRED E OSU comprehensive cancer center support (core) grant Core--Clinical pharmacology
P30CA-16058-17 9011 (CCS) ZWILLING, BRUCE OSU comprehensive cancer center support (core) grant Core--Flow cytometry laboratory
P30CA-16058-17 9012 (CCS) YOUNG, DONN OSU comprehensive cancer center support (core) grant Core--Epidemiology and biostatistics
P30CA-16058-17 9013 (CCS) STEPHENS, RALPH E OSU comprehensive cancer center support (core) grant Core--Cell culture service
P30CA-16058-17 9014 (CCS) TOMIE, DAVID L OSU comprehensive cancer center support (core) grant Core--clonogenic tumor cell assay
P30CA-16058-17 9015 (CCS) CSCHULLER, DAVID OSU comprehensive cancer center support (core) grant Peptide synthesis
P30CA-16058-17 9016 (CCS) SCHULLER, DAVID OSU comprehensive cancer center support (core) grant Monoclonal laboratory
P30CA-16058-17 9017 (CCS) SCHULLER, DAVID OSU comprehensive cancer center support (core) grant Development funds--Core
P30CA-16059-15 (CCS) GOLDMAN, I DAVID VIRGINIA COMMONWEALTH UNIVERSI BOX 230 MCV STATION RICHMOND, VA 23298 Massey cancer center

PROJECT NO., ORGANIZATIONAL UNIT., INVESTIGATOR, ADDRESS, TITLE

core support
P30CA-16059-15 9021 (CCS) GOLDMAN, DAVID Massey cancer center core support Developmental core
P30CA-16059-15 9009 (CCS) SCHOOK, LAWRENCE B Massey cancer center core support Hybridoma monoclonal antibody
P30CA-16059-15 9011 (CCS) GOLDMAN, DAVID Massey cancer center core support Flow cytometry
P30CA-16059-15 9012 (CCS) BUCK, GREGORY Massey cancer center core support Nucleic acid synthesis and analysis
P30CA-16059-15 9013 (CCS) WESTIN, ERIC Massey cancer center core support Molecular biology
P30CA-16059-15 9014 (CCS) ABRAHAM, DONALD Massey cancer center core support Structural molecular biology
P30CA-16059-15 9015 (CCS) GOLDMAN, DAVID Massey cancer center core support Bone marrow transplantation
P30CA-16059-15 9016 (CCS) WARE, JOY Massey cancer center core support Athymic nude mouse
P30CA-16059-15 9017 (CCS) STROM, STEPHEN Massey cancer center core support Human tissue acquisition and histopathology
P30CA-16059-15 9018 (CCS) CARTER, W Massey cancer center core support Biostatistical core
P30CA-16059-15 9019 (CCS) RETCHIN, SHELDON Massey cancer center core support Cancer surveillance
P30CA-16059-15 9020 (CCS) GOLDMAN, DAVID Massey cancer center core support Clinical research...core
P30CA-16086-17 (CCS) PAGANO, JOSEPH S UNIV OF NC AT CHAPEL HILL 102 LINEBERGER, CB# 7295 CHAPEL HILL, NC 27599 Cancer center support grant
P30CA-16086-17 9002 (CCS) GRIFFITH, JACK Cancer center support grant Electron microscope--Core facility
P30CA-16086-17 9003 (CCS) PAGANO, JOSEPH S Cancer center support grant Tissue culture facility
P30CA-16086-17 9006 (CCS) KAUFMAN, DAVID G Cancer center support grant Biohazards facility
P30CA-16086-17 9007 (CCS) HULKA, BARBARA S Cancer center support grant Epi-stat unit and developmental epidemiology
P30CA-16086-17 9008 (CCS) PAGANS, J S Cancer center support grant Clinical core
P30CA-16086-17 9009 (CCS) PAGANO, JOSEPH S Cancer center support grant Flow cytometry--Core
P30CA-16086-17 9011 (CCS) PAGANO, JOSEPH S Cancer center support grant Developmental projects--Core
P30CA-16086-17 9012 (CCS) LEE, DAVID Cancer center support grant Nucleic acid core
P30CA-16086-17 9013 (CCS) EDISON, LIU Cancer center support grant Tumor procurement and analysis core
P30CA-16086-17 9014 (CCS) BHASKER, JOHN Cancer center support grant Transgenic mouse/microinjection core
P30CA-16086-17 9015 (CCS) HERMAN, BRIAN Cancer center support grant Analytical microscopy core
P30CA-16086-17 9016 (CCS) JULIANO, RUDOLPH Cancer center support grant Drug screening core
P30CA-16087-14 (CCS) DEFENDI, VITTORIO DIRECTOR 550 FIRST AVENUE NEW YORK, NY 10016 Cancer center support (core) grant
P30CA-16087-14 9004 (CCS) BLUM, RONALD Cancer center support (core) grant Patient research unit
P30CA-16087-14 9005 (CCS) PASTERNACK, BERNARD Cancer center support (core) grant Epidemiology biostatistics unit
P30CA-16087-14 9006 (CCS) DEMOPOULOS, RITA Cancer center support (core) grant Clinical oncology patient registry
P30CA-16087-14 9007 (CCS) SCHLESINGER, DAVID H Cancer center support (core) grant Macromolecular sequencing--Core
P30CA-16087-14 9008 (CCS) DEFENDI, VITTORIO Cancer center support (core) grant Developmental program--Core
P30CA-16087-14 9009 (CCS) BASCH, R Cancer center support (core) grant Cell sorting unit
P30CA-16087-14 9010 (CCS) NEWCOMB, ELIZABETH Cancer center support (core) grant Transgenic mouse facility
P30CA-16087-14 9011 (CCS) SHRIVER, MARK Cancer center support (core) grant Core BRM laboratory.
P30CA-16087-14 9012 (CCS) COHEN, DEBRA Cancer center support (core) grant Coordinated resource for tumor data and samples.
U10CA-16116-18 (CCI) ETTINGER, DAVID S JOHNS HOPKINS HOSPITAL 130 ONCOLOGY CENTER BALTIMORE, MD 21205 Eastern cooperative oncology group
R01CA-16265-16A1 (CPA) JEFCOATE, COLIN R UNIV OF WISCONSIN MED SC 1300 UNIVERSITY AVENUE MADISON, WI 53706 Metabolism of polycyclic hydrocarbons and carcinogenesis
R37CA-16303-16 (END) ROSEN, JEFFREY M BAYLOR COLLEGE OF MEDICINE ONE BAYLOR PLAZA HOUSTON, TX 77030 Hormonal regulation of breast cancer
R01CA-16312-18 (VR) GRANDGENETT, DUANE P ST LOUIS UNIVERSITY 3681 PARK AVE ST LOUIS, MO 63110 Avian retrovirus DNA synthesis and its regulations
R01CA-16318-17 (ET) SCHIMKE, ROBERT T STANFORD UNIVERSITY 125 PANAMA STREET STANFORD, CA 94305-4125 Molecular mechanism in resistance to folate analogues
P30CA-16359-17 (CCS) SARTORELLI, ALAN C YALE UNIVERSITY 333 CEDAR STREET NEW HAVEN, CONN 06510 Comprehensive cancer center
P30CA-16359-17 9005 (CCS) SARTORELLI, ALAN C Comprehensive cancer center Core facility--cell sorter
P30CA-16359-17 9015 (CCS) JANERICH, DWIGHT Comprehensive cancer center Clinical research/ biostatistics core
P30CA-16359-17 9019 (CCS) WEISSMAN, SAMUEL M Comprehensive cancer center Central electron microscope facility--core
P30CA-16359-17 9020 (CCS) MURPHY, DONAL B Comprehensive cancer center Mouse tumor bank
P30CA-16359-17 9021 (CCS) CARTER, DARRYL Comprehensive cancer center Tissue retrieval system--core
P30CA-16359-17 9022 (CCS) SARTORELLI, ALLAN C. Comprehensive cancer center Mass spectrometry facility -- Core
P30CA-16359-17 9023 (CCS) DENNIS, COOPER L. Comprehensive cancer center Developmental funds- Medical oncology

PROJECT NO., ORGANIZATIONAL UNIT., INVESTIGATOR, ADDRESS, TITLE

P30CA-16359-17 9024 (CCS) SARTORELLI, ALLAN C. Comprehensive cancer center Transgenic mouse facility
P30CA-16359-17 0001 (CCS) COOPER, DENNIS L Comprehensive cancer center Developmental funds--Medical oncology
P30CA-16359-17 9004 (CCS) WEISSMAN, SHERMAN M Comprehensive cancer center Tissue culture facility--core
R37CA-16368-18 (MGN) SKOULTCHI, ARTHUR I ALBERT EINSTEIN COLLEGE OF MED 1300 MORRIS PARK AVENUE BRONX, NY 10461 Control of differentiation of erythroleukemic cells
U10CA-16385-17 (CCI) THIGPEN, JAMES T UNIV OF MISSISSIPPI MED CTR 2500 NORTH STATE STREET JACKSON, MS 39216 Southwest oncology group
U10CA-16395-17 (CCI) BLUM, RONALD H NEW YORK UNIVERSITY MED CTR 550 FIRST AVENUE NEW YORK, NY 10016 Eastern cooperative oncology group
R37CA-16448-17 (HEM) FIALKOW, PHILIP J UNIVERSITY OF WASHINGTON SEATTLE, WA 98195 Human cancer - Origin and genetic markers
U10CA-16450-17 (CCI) PETERSON, BRUCE A UNIVERSITY OF MINNESOTA BOX 348 UMHC MINNEAPOLIS, MN 55455 Cancer and leukemia group B - Minnesota oncology group
R01CA-16463-17 (END) SURKS, MARTIN I MONTEFIORE HOSP & MEDICAL CTR 111 EAST 210TH STREET BRONX, N Y 10467 L-triiodothyronine effects on cell regulation
R01CA-16502-17 (EVR) BOETTIGER, DAVID E UNIVERSITY OF PENNSYLVANIA 209 JOHNSON PAVILION G2 PHILADELPHIA, PA 19104 Genetic analysis of RNA tumor viruses
P01CA-16519-17 (SRC) KELLY, THOMAS J, JR THE JOHNS HOPKINS UNIVERSITY 725 N WOLFE ST/RM 602 PCTB BALTIMORE, MD 21205 Program on molecular biology of viral tumorigenesis
P01CA-16519-17 0001 (SRC) KELLY, THOMAS J JR Program on molecular biology of viral tumorigenesis Mechanisms of viral carcinogenesis
P01CA-16519-17 0006 (SRC) HIETER, PHILIP A Program on molecular biology of viral tumorigenesis Functional determinants of chromosome segregation
P01CA-16519-17 0007 (SRC) NATHANS, DANIEL Program on molecular biology of viral tumorigenesis Regulation of cell growth--Role of jun proteins
P01CA-16519-17 0008 (SRC) DESIDERIO, STEPHEN V Program on molecular biology of viral tumorigenesis DNA-protein interactions in lymphocyte differentiation
P01CA-16519-17 0009 (SRC) CORDEN, JEFFRY L Program on molecular biology of viral tumorigenesis RNA polymerase II largest subunit structure and function
P01CA-16519-17 0010 (SRC) BOEKE, JEF D Program on molecular biology of viral tumorigenesis Transposable elements as endogenous retroviruses
P01CA-16519-17 9001 (SRC) KELLY, THOMAS J JR Program on molecular biology of viral tumorigenesis Laboratory core
P30CA-16520-16 (SRC) GLICK, JOHN H UNIVERSITY OF PENNSYLVANIA 3400 SPRUCE STREET PHILADELPHIA, PA 19104 University of Pennsylvania cancer center support grant
P30CA-16520-16 9019 (SRC) KANT, JEFFREY A University of Pennsylvania cancer center support grant Core--Molecular diagnosis laboratory
P30CA-16520-16 9020 (SRC) GREENE, MARK I University of Pennsylvania cancer center support grant Core--Transgenic animal facility
P30CA-16520-16 9021 (SRC) LIVOLSI, VIRGINIA A University of Pennsylvania cancer center support grant Core--Tumor tissue facility
P30CA-16520-16 0001 (SRC) LU, PONZY University of Pennsylvania cancer center support grant Core--Nucleic acid facility
P30CA-16520-16 9002 (SRC) CASSILETH, PETER A University of Pennsylvania cancer center support grant Core--Clinical research unit
P30CA-16520-16 9011 (SRC) LUSK, EDWARD J University of Pennsylvania cancer center support grant Core--Biostatistics resource
P30CA-16520-16 9012 (SRC) PRYSTOWSKY, MICHAEL B University of Pennsylvania cancer center support grant Core--Flow cytometry and cell sorter facility
P30CA-16520-16 9014 (SRC) KENNETT, ROGER H University of Pennsylvania cancer center support grant Core--Cell center
P30CA-16520-16 9015 (SRC) GUERRY, DUPONT University of Pennsylvania cancer center support grant Core--Melanoma program
P30CA-16520-16 9017 (SRC) LU, PONZY University of Pennsylvania cancer center support grant Core--Nucleic acid facility
P30CA-16520-16 9018 (SRC) LAMBRIS, JOHN University of Pennsylvania cancer center support grant Core--Protein chemistry
P01CA-16599-17 (SRC) HAYWARD, WILLIAM S SLOAN-KETTERING INST/CANCER RE 1275 YORK AVE NEW YORK, NY 10021 Hematopoietic cell transformation by retroviruses
P01CA-16599-17 0017 (SRC) HAYWARD, WILLIAM Hematopoietic cell transformation by retroviruses Mechanisms of virus induced neoplasia
P01CA-16599-17 0018 (SRC) FLEISSNER, ERWIN J Hematopoietic cell transformation by retroviruses A comparative study of radiation and virus leukemogenesis
P01CA-16599-17 0019 (SRC) O'DONNELL, PAUL Hematopoietic cell transformation by retroviruses Influence of MuLV infection
P01CA-16599-17 0020 (SRC) OLIFF, ALLEN Hematopoietic cell transformation by retroviruses Molecular virology of mulv induced leukemia
P01CA-16599-17 0021 (SRC) RACEVSKIS, JANIS Hematopoietic cell transformation by retroviruses MuMTV antigens and transformation related genes
P01CA-16599-17 9001 (SRC) FLEISSNER, ERWIN J Hematopoietic cell transformation by retroviruses Core unit
R01CA-16642-17 (EI) NORTH, ROBERT J TRUDEAU INSTITUE, INC PO BOX 59 SARANAC LAKE, NY 12983 Immunological basis of tumor regression
R01CA-16660-14 (PTHB) HILF, RUSSELL UNIVERSITY OF ROCHESTER ROCHESTER, N Y 14642 Insulin and steroid interactions in breast cancer
R37CA-16669-16 (MEP) TEEBOR, GEORGE W NEW YORK UNIVERSITY MED CTR 550 FIRST AVENUE NEW YORK, N Y 10016 Repairability of oxidative damage to DNA
P30CA-16672-17 (SRC) BECKER, FREDERICK F THE UNIVERSITY OF TEXAS 1515 HOLCOMBE BLVD HOUSTON, TX 77030 Cancer center support

PROJECT NO., ORGANIZATIONAL UNIT., INVESTIGATOR, ADDRESS, TITLE

PROJECT NO., ORGANIZATIONAL UNIT., INVESTIGATOR, ADDRESS, TITLE

P30CA-16672-17 9007 (SRC) BROWN, BARRY W Cancer center support Core--Information systems support
P30CA-16672-17 9008 (SRC) JARDINE, JOHN H Cancer center support Core--experimental animals research MD anderson hospital
P30CA-16672-17 9010 (SRC) BECKER, FREDERICK F Cancer center support Core--Biosafety office
P30CA-16672-17 9012 (SRC) KEELING, MICHAEL E Cancer center support Core--experimental animal research support
P30CA-16672-17 9014 (SRC) BECKER, FREDERICK F Cancer center support Core--Centralized histopathology research laboratory
P30CA-16672-17 9015 (SRC) BARLOGIE, BARTHEL Cancer center support Core--Cell sorter facility
P30CA-16672-17 9016 (SRC) NICHOLSON, GARTH L Cancer center support Core--Scanning electron microscopy facility
P30CA-16672-17 9017 (SRC) WRIGHT, DAVID A Cancer center support Core--Recombinant DNA facility
P30CA-16672-17 9018 (SRC) FORD, RICHARD J Cancer center support Core--tissue procurement laboratory
R01CA-16707-17 (BBCA) TIMASHEFF, SERGE N BRANDEIS UNIVERSITY 415 SOUTH STREET WALTHAM, MA 02254-9110 Tubulin associations and effects of anticancer drugs
R01CA-16717-17 (RAD) DOUGHERTY, THOMAS J ROSWELL PARK MEMORIAL INST 666 ELM STREET BUFFALO, NY 14263 Activated dyes as anti-tumor agents
R01CA-16740-16 (PBC) QUIGLEY, JAMES P STATE UNIV OF NY AT STONY BROO BHS TOWER 9 RM 168 STONY BROOK, NY 11794 Proteases in growth control & malignant transformation
R01CA-16858-18 (ALY) MORRISON, SHERIE L UNIVERSITY OF CALIFORNIA 405 HILGARD AVE LOS ANGELES, CA 90024 Genetics and biochemistry of myeloma Ig production
R37CA-16861-17 (BMT) MEARES, CLAUDE F UNIV OF CALIFORNIA, DAVIS DAVIS, CA 95616 Bifunctional chelating agents in tumor localization
R01CA-16885-16 (ALY) RUDDLE, NANCY H YALE UNIVERSITY SCHOOL OF MED PO BOX 3333-60 COLLEGE ST NEW HAVEN, CT 06510 Propagation of thymus-derived lymphocyte lines
R01CA-16903-15 (MCHA) STANG, PETER J UNIVERSITY OF UTAH SALT LAKE CITY, UTAH 84112 Alkynl ester and alkynliodonium chemistry
R01CA-16924-16A1 (BCE) BARRACK, EVELYN JOHNS HOPKINS HOSPITAL 600 NORTH WOLFE STREET BALTIMORE, MD 21205 Role of growth factors in prostate cancer
R37CA-16954-16 (CPA) HOLLENBERG, PAUL F WAYNE STATE UNIVERSITY 540 E CANFIELD DETROIT, MI 48201 Hemoprotein-catalyzed oxygenations of carcinogens
R01CA-17007-16 (CBY) HYNES, RICHARD O MASSACHUSETTS INST OF TECHNOLO 77 MASSACHUSETTS AVENUE CAMBRIDGE, MA 02139-4307 Cell surface structure and transformations
P01CA-17054-16 (SRC) ROSS, RONALD K UNIV OF SOUTHERN CALIFORNIA 1974 ZONAL AVE - KAM B 34 LOS ANGELES, CA 90033 Epidemiology and biostatistics unit--Iatrogenic diseases
P01CA-17054-16 0001 (SRC) BERNSTEIN, LESLIE Epidemiology and biostatistics unit--Iatrogenic diseases Oral contraceptives and breast cancer in young women
P01CA-17054-16 0002 (SRC) ROSS, RONALD K Epidemiology and biostatistics unit--Iatrogenic diseases Hormone replacement therapy and breast cancer
P01CA-17054-16 0003 (SRC) PETERS, RUTH K Epidemiology and biostatistics unit--Iatrogenic diseases Oral contraceptives and adenocarcinoma of cervix in young women
P01CA-17054-16 0004 (SRC) YU, MIMI C Epidemiology and biostatistics unit--Iatrogenic diseases Analgesics, diuretics and cancers of the bladder and kidney
P01CA-17054-16 0005 (SRC) PRESTON-MARTIN, SUSAN Epidemiology and biostatistics unit--Iatrogenic diseases x-ray and drugs in the etiology of acute myelogenous leukemia
P01CA-17054-16 0006 (SRC) PRESTON-MARTIN, SUSAN Epidemiology and biostatistics unit--Iatrogenic diseases Estrogen replacement therapy and spinal meningiomas
P01CA-17054-16 9001 (SRC) PHILLIPS, ROLAND Epidemiology and biostatistics unit--Iatrogenic diseases Core--Cancer surveillance program
P01CA-17094-16 (CTR) SALMON, SYDNEY E UNIV OF ARIZONA COLLEGE OF MED 1501 N CAMPBELL AVENUE TUCSON, AZ 85724 Medical oncology program project
P01CA-17094-16 0017 (CTR) ALBERTS, DAVID S Medical oncology program project Pharmacokinetics in cancer chemotherapy
P01CA-17094-16 0019 (CTR) SALMON, SYDNEY E Medical oncology program project Medical oncology clinical research protocol development
P01CA-17094-16 0026 (CTR) HERSH, EVANS M Medical oncology program project In vitro models of biologicl therapy
P01CA-17094-16 0027 (CTR) THOMAS, GROGAN Medical oncology program project Immunobiology of non-Hodgkins's lymphoma
P01CA-17094-16 0028 (CTR) DALTON, WILLIAM S Medical oncology program project Drug resistance in breast cancer
P01CA-17094-16 0029 (CTR) SALMON, SYDNEY E Medical oncology program project HTCA and prediction of drug therapy effects
P01CA-17094-16 9002 (CTR) MCGEE, DANIELLE Medical oncology program project Core biostatistics and information processing
U10CA-17145-16 (CCI) BENSON, AL B NORTHWESTERN UNIV MED SCHOOL 303 E CHICAGO AVE, OLSON 8524 CHICAGO, IL 60611 Clinical trials--Eastern cooperative oncology group
R01CA-17229-14S2 (GMA) RUSSELL, JAMES D MEHARRY MEDICAL COLLEGE 1005 D. B. TODD BLVD. NASHVILLE, TN 37208 Keloids--An in vitro model of tumor growth regulation
R01CA-17289-16 (VR) SEFTON, BARTHOLOMEW M SALK INST FOR BIOLOGICAL STUDI PO BOX 85800 SAN DIEGO, CA 92138 Membranes and viral transformation
R01CA-17364-14 (ET) MEISTRICH, MARVIN L U.T. M.D. ANDERSON CANCER CENT 1515 HOLCOMBE BLVD HOUSTON, TX 77030 Mutagenic action of cancer therapy on testis cells
R01CA-17374-17 (BBCB) KRAUT, JOSEPH UNIV OF CALIFORNIA, SAN DIEGO 9500 GILMAN DRIVE LA JOLLA, CA 92093-0317 Crystallographic studies of dihydrofolate reductase
R01CA-17393-17 (ET) DONAHOE, PATRICIA K MASSACHUSETTS GENERAL HOSPITAL BOSTON, MA 02113 Mullerian inhibiting substance
R01CA-17395-17 (CPA) GROLLMAN, ARTHUR P SUNY STONY BROOK STONY BROOK, 11794-4466 Molecular pharmacology of tumor and virus inhibitors
R37CA-17542-16 (EVR) MARTIN, G STEVEN UNIVERSITY OF CALIFORNIA 401 BAKER HALL BERKELEY, CA 94720 Genetics of RNA tumor viruses
R01CA-17562-16 (BBCA) VAN DER HELM, DICK UNIVERSITY OF OKLAHOMA DEPARTMENT OF CHEMISTRY NORMAN, OK 73019 Structure of anticancer agents by x-ray diffraction
R37CA-17575-17 (HEM) HOUSMAN, DAVID E MASSACHUSETTS INST TECHNOLOGY 77 MASSACHUSETTS AVE/E-17-543 CAMBRIDGE, MA 02139-4307 Erythroid differentiation in Friend leukemia cell
P30CA-17613-17 (CCS) WYNDER, ERNST L AMERICAN HEALTH FOUNDATION 320 EAST 43RD STREET NEW YORK, NY 10017 Cancer center support grant
P30CA-17613-17 9006 (CCS) WYNDER, ERNST L Cancer center support grant Scientific information facility
P30CA-17613-17 9007 (CCS) WYNDER, ERNST L Cancer center support grant Biohazard facility
P30CA-17613-17 9008 (CCS) WYNDER, ERNST L Cancer center support grant Central laboratory service
P30CA-17613-17 9009 (CCS) WYNDER, ERNST L Cancer center support grant In vitro facility
P30CA-17613-17 9010 (CCS) WYNDER, ERNEST L. Cancer center support grant Developmental funds--Core
P30CA-17613-17 9011 (CCS) HALEY, NANCY J. Cancer center support grant Clinical biochemistry facility--Core
P30CA-17613-17 9002 (CCS) WYNDER, ERNST L Cancer center support grant Animal facility
P30CA-17613-17 9003 (CCS) WYNDER, ERNST L Cancer center support grant Histopathology laboratory
P30CA-17613-17 9004 (CCS) WYNDER, ERNST L Cancer center support grant Instrumentation facility
P30CA-17613-17 9005 (CCS) WYNDER, ERNST L Cancer center support grant Biostatistics and computer service
R01CA-17625-15 (BNP) LEE, KUO-HSIUNG UNIVERSITY OF NORTH CAROLINA CB#7360 BEARD HALL CHAPEL HILL, N C 27599-7360 Plant antitumor agents
R37CA-17733-17 (ALY) TROWBRIDGE, IAN S SALK INSTITUTE PO BOX 85800 SAN DIEGO, CA 92138 Lymphocyte antigens--Structure, function and synthesis
U10CA-17829-15 (CCI) ABLIN, ARTHUR R UNIVERSITY OF CALIFORNIA 505 PARNASSUS, M-643 SAN FRANCISCO, CA 94143 Childrens cancer study group
R01CA-17918-17 (BNP) VEDEJS, EDWIN UNIVERSITY OF WISCONSIN 1101 UNIVERSITY AVENUE MADISON, WI 53706 Cytotoxic nitrogen heterocycles
R25CA-17971-15 (SRC) HORTON, JOHN ALBANY MEDICAL COLLEGE 47 NEW SCOTLAND AVENUE ALBANY, NY 12208 Cancer education program
R25CA-17973-17 (SRC) HUTH, JAMES F UNIV OF NC AT CHAPEL HILL 3010 OLD CLINIC BLDG, CB #7210 CHAPEL HILL, NC 27599-7210 Professional oncology education program
R25CA-17998-16 (CEC) GREENBERG, RAYMOND S 1599 CLIFTON RD NE ATLANTA, GA 30329 Cancer education program grant
R01CA-18001-25 (RAD) MEINHOLD, CHARLES B NCRP 7910 WOODMONT AVE BETHESDA, MD 20814 Radiation protection and measurements
R25CA-18002-13 (SRC) BLUM, RONALD H NEW YORK UNIV MEDICAL CENTER 550 FIRST AVENUE NEW YORK, N Y 10016 Professional oncology education program
R25CA-18016-13 (SRC) FARRAR, WILLIAM B OHIO STATE UNIVERSITY 410 W 10TH AVE/N-907 DOAN HALL COLUMBUS, OH 43210 Cancer education program
R37CA-18023-17 (RAD) BEDFORD, JOEL S RADIOLOGICAL HEALTH SCIENCES COLORADO STATE UNIVERSITY FORT COLLINS, CO 80523 Dose and time factors in cellular radiosensitivity
P01CA-18029-16 (CCP) THOMAS, E DONNALL FRED HUTCHINSON CANCER RES CTR 1124 COLUMBIA STREET SEATTLE, WA 98104 Adult leukemia research center
P01CA-18029-16 0036 (CCP) MEYERS, JOEL Adult leukemia research center Viral infections
P01CA-18029-16 0037 (CCP) MARTIN, PAUL J Adult leukemia research center Prevention of graft vs-host disease
P01CA-18029-16 0038 (CCP) BENSINGER, WILLIAM I Adult leukemia research center Platelet alloimmunity in marrow transplantation
P01CA-18029-16 9003 (CCP) FLUORNOY, N Adult leukemia research center Biostatistics and information systems
P01CA-18029-16 9004 (CCP) BENSINGER, WILLIAM I Adult leukemia research center Transfusion support--Core
P01CA-18029-16 9005 (CCP) SALE, GEORGE E Adult leukemia research center Pathology parogram
P01CA-18029-16 9006 (CCP) THOMAS, E DONNALL Adult leukemia research center Nutritional services research
P01CA-18029-16 9007 (CCP) THOMAS, E DONNALL Adult leukemia research center Infectious diseases and microbiology
P01CA-18029-16 9008 (CCP) CLARK, JOAN G Adult leukemia research center Respiratory and critical care--Core
P01CA-18029-16 9009 (CCP) SCHUBERT, MARK Adult leukemia research center Oral medicine
P01CA-18029-16 9010 (CCP) MCDONALD, GEORGE B Adult leukemia research center Gastrointestinal and hepatic studies
P01CA-18029-16 9011 (CCP) SULLIVAN, KEITH Adult leukemia research center Outpatient care and long-term pediatric care
P01CA-18029-16 9012 (CCP) CLARK, KIM Adult leukemia research center Social service
P01CA-18029-16 0001 (CCP) THOMAS, E DONNALL Adult leukemia research center Allogeneic marrow grafting for treatment of acute leukemia
P01CA-18029-16 0002 (CCP) STORB, RAINER F Adult leukemia research center Allogeneic marrow transplant in aplastic anemia
P01CA-18029-16 0013 (CCP) BUCKNER, C DEAN Adult leukemia research center Adult leukemia research center
P01CA-18029-16 0019 (CCP) STORB, RAINER F Adult leukemia research center Adult leukemia research center
P01CA-18029-16 0020 (CCP) SINGER, JACK W Adult leukemia research center Adult leukemia research center
P01CA-18029-16 0021 (CCP) HANSEN, JOHN A Adult leukemia research center Adult leukemia research center

PROJECT NO., ORGANIZATIONAL UNIT., INVESTIGATOR, ADDRESS, TITLE

P01CA-18029-16 0025 (CCP) DURNAM, DIANE Adult leukemia research center Adult leukemia research center
P01CA-18029-16 0026 (CCP) THOMAS, E DONNALL Adult leukemia research center Nutritional services research
P01CA-18029-16 0030 (CCP) BUCKNER, DEAN C Adult leukemia research center Adult leukemia research center
P01CA-18029-16 0031 (CCP) DEEG,JOACHIM, H Adult leukemia research center Adult leukemia research center
P01CA-18029-16 0032 (CCP) CLIFT, ROBERT Adult leukemia research center Adult leukemia research center
P01CA-18029-16 0033 (CCP) DONEY, KRISTINE Adult leukemia research center Adult leukemia research center
P01CA-18029-16 0034 (CCP) CLIFT, ROBERT Adult leukemia research center Marrow transplantation for patients with cml
P01CA-18029-16 0035 (CCP) APPLEBAUM, FREDERICK Adult leukemia research center Marrow transplantation for patients with lymphoma
R01CA-18105-16 (EI) APPELBAUM, FREDERICK R FRED HUTCHINSON CANCER RES CTR 1124 COLUMBIA STREET SEATTLE, WA 98104 Immunotherapy studies in dogs with spontaneous malignancies
R01CA-18110-17 (BCE) GORSKI, JACK UNIV OF WISCONSIN-MADISON 420 HENRY MALL MADISON, WI 53706 Prolactin synthesis in normal and neoplastic tissue
R37CA-18119-15 (END) KATZENELLENBOGEN, BENITA S UNIVERSITY OF ILLINOIS 407 S GOODWIN, 524 BURRILL HAL URBANA, IL 61801 Antiestrogens-- Mechanism of antagonist action
R37CA-18137-16 (CPA) PEGG, ANTHONY E PENNSYLVANIA STATE UNIVERSITY POST OFFICE BOX 850 HERSHEY, PA 17033 Persistence of alkylated DNA in carcinogenesis
R37CA-18138-16 (BIO) PEGG, ANTHONY E PENNSYLVANIA STATE UNIVERSITY MILTON HERSEY MED CTR, PO BX 8 HERSHEY, PA 17033 Mammalian polyamine metabolism
R01CA-18141-16 (MCHA) HAUSER, FRANK M SUNY AT ALBANY ALBANY, NY 12203 Polynuclear anticancer antibiotics--selected syntheses
R37CA-18151-16 (EVR) WETTSTEIN, FELIX O UNIVERSITY OF CALIFORNIA 405 HILGARD AVENUE LOS ANGELES, CA 90024-1747 Analysis of the shope-papilloma carcinoma system
R25CA-18201-16 (SRC) MIRAND, EDWIN A ROSWELL PARK MEMORIAL INSTITUT 666 ELM STREET BUFFALO, NY 14263 Cancer education program
P01CA-18221-16 (CCP) STORB, RAINER F FRED HUTCHINSON CANCER RES CTR 1124 COLUMBIA STREET SEATTLE, WA 98104 Marrow grafting for treatment of hematologic maligancies
P01CA-18221-16 0001 (CCP) NOTTENBURG, CAROL Marrow grafting for treatment of hematologic maligancies B cell function and antigen-specific immune response
P01CA-18221-16 0002 (CCP) WITHERSPOON, ROBERT P Marrow grafting for treatment of hematologic maligancies: Long term follow up chronic graft-versus-host disease
P01CA-18221-16 0004 (CCP) TOROK-STORB, BEVERLY J Marrow grafting for treatment of hematologic maligancies Lymphocyte-marrow cell interactions
P01CA-18221-16 0009 (CCP) SYMINTON, FRAUK W Marrow grafting for treatment of hematologic maligancies Immune mechanisms of graft vs. host diseases
P01CA-18221-16 0010 (CCP) LOUGHRAN, THOMAS P Marrow grafting for treatment of hematologic maligancies Studies on marrow graft resistance
P01CA-18221-16 9001 (CCP) STORB, RAINER F Marrow grafting for treatment of hematologic maligancies Core support
R01CA-18234-14 (EI) ROSZMAN, THOMAS L UNIVERSITY OF KENTUCKY LEXINGTON, KY 40536-0084 Immunobiology of primary intracranial tumors
R01CA-18282-16 (VR) LINIAL, MAXINE L FRED HUTCHINSON CANCER RES CTR 1124 COLUMBIA ST SEATTLE, WA 98104 Viral coded functions in rous sarcoma virus
R01CA-18303-16 (EVR) FARAS, ANTHONY J UNIVERSITY OF MINNESOTA HARVARD ST. AT EAST RIVER RD. MINNEAPOLIS, MN 55455 RNA-directed DNA polymerase and 70s RNA of oncornaviruses
R01CA-18332-17 (SSS) DEMETS, DAVID L BIOSTATISTICS CENTER 420 NORTH CHARTER STREET MADISON, WI 53706 Statistical problems in cancer research
R01CA-18470-15 (IMB) KNOWLES, BARBARA B WISTAR INSTITUTE 36TH AND SPRUCE STREET PHILADELPHIA, PA 19104 Antigenicity and tumorigenicity of somatic cell hybrids
R01CA-18601-16 (BNP) WATANABE, KYOICHI A SLOAN-KETTERING INST/CNCR RES 1275 YORK AVENUE NEW YORK, NY 10021 Synthetic masked nucleosides for anticancer studies
R01CA-18611-16A1 (VR) COMPANS, RICHARD W UNIV OF ALABAMA AT BIRMINGHAM BIRMINGHAM, AL 35294 Directional transport of MuLV glycoproteins
R01CA-18614-15 (RAD) EPP, EDWARD R MASSACHUSETTS GENERAL HOSPITAL FRUIT STREET BOSTON, MA 02114 Radiation sensitization applied to cancer radiobiology
R37CA-18640-21 (IMB) SILVERS, WILLYS K UNIVERSITY OF PENNSYLVANIA 195 MEDICAL LABORATORIES/G3 PHILADELPHIA, PA 19104 Behavior of weak transplantation antigens
R01CA-18659-19 (IMB) GILL, THOMAS J, III UNIVERSITY OF PITTSBURGH 716 SCAIFE HALL PITTSBURGH, PA 15261 Chemical, genetic and cellular aspects of immunogenicity
R01CA-18689-16 (CBY) COOPER, GEOFFREY M DANA FARBER CANCER INSTITUTE 44 BINNEY STREET BOSTON, MA 02115 Infectious DNA for endogenous RNA tumor virus genes
R01CA-18734-15A1 (PTHB) JONES, CAROL A ELEANOR ROOSEVELT INSTITUTE 1899 GAYLORD STREET DENVER, CO 80206 Immunologic studies related to malignancy
R37CA-18808-17 (VR) TEGTMEYER, PETER J STATE UNIVERSITY OF NEW YORK STONY BROOK, NY 11794-0001 Tumor virus SV40--Protein function and DNA replication
R01CA-18846-16 (MCHA) KENDE, ANDREW S UNIVERSITY OF ROCHESTER RIVER CAMPUS , HUTCHISON HALL ROCHESTER, NY 14627 Synthesis of bridged & polycyclic antitumor agents
P01CA-18856-16 (SRC) SIROTNAK, FRANCIS M SLOAN-KETTERING INSTITUTE 1275 YORK AVE NEW YORK, NY 10021 A program on experimental therapeutics in cancer
P01CA-18856-16 0008 (SRC) SIROTNAK, FRANCIS M A program on experimental therapeutics in cancer Developmental antifolate therapy of cancer
P01CA-18856-16 0009 (SRC) WATANABE, KYOTCHI A A program on experimental therapeutics in cancer Design and synthesis of anticancer agents
P01CA-18856-16 0016 (SRC) CHOU, TING-CHAO A program on experimental therapeutics in cancer Toxicology and pharmacology of antitumor agents
P01CA-18856-16 0020 (SRC) BIEDLER, JUNE A program on experimental therapeutics in cancer Multidrug-resistance, P-glycoprotein and differentiation
P01CA-18856-16 0021 (SRC) SCOTTO, K A program on experimental therapeutics in cancer Multidrug-resitance-molecular biology
P01CA-18856-16 0022 (SRC) O'BRIEN, JAMES A program on experimental therapeutics in cancer Clinical studies of multidrug resistance
P01CA-18856-16 9001 (SRC) SIROTNAK, FRANCIS M A program on experimental therapeutics in cancer Core laboratory A --Cytotoxicity and antitumor testing
P01CA-18856-16 9002 (SRC) CHOU, T A program on experimental therapeutics in cancer Toxicology and pharmacology
P01CA-19014-14 (SRC) PAGANO, JOSEPH S CB# 7295 LINBERGER COMP CAN CT UNIV OF NC AT CHAPEL HILL CHAPEL HILL, NC 27599-7295 Viral oncogenesis and latency
P01CA-19014-14 0007 (SRC) PAGANO, JOSEPH S Viral oncogenesis and latency EBV DNA polynerase expression
P01CA-19014-14 0016 (SRC) BACHENHEIMOR, STEVEN L Viral oncogenesis and latency DNA- Protein interaction in HSV and EBV regulation
P01CA-19014-14 0017 (SRC) HUANG, ENG SHANG Viral oncogenesis and latency Cytomegalovirus- specific DNA polymevase
P01CA-19014-14 0018 (SRC) SWANSTON, ROBERT Viral oncogenesis and latency HIV-2 and SIV pol genes
P01CA-19014-14 0019 (SRC) LIN JUNG-CHUNG Viral oncogenesis and latency Epstein-Barr virus DNA-binding protein
P01CA-19014-14 0020 (SRC) SHANNON, KENNEY Viral oncogenesis and latency Negative regulation of EBV gene expression
P01CA-19014-14 0021 (SRC) RAAB- TRAUB, NANCY Viral oncogenesis and latency Oncogenic potential of EBV latency
P01CA-19014-14 9002 (SRC) GRIFFITH, JACK Viral oncogenesis and latency Electron microscopy core
P01CA-19014-14 9003 (SRC) HUANG, ENG SHANG Viral oncogenesis and latency Tissue culture core
P01CA-19014-14 9004 (SRC) SWANSTORM, RONALD Viral oncogenesis and latency Virus cantainment facility--core
R01CA-19033-16 (MCHA) SMITH, AMOS B, III UNIVERSITY OF PENNSYLVANIA 133 SOUTH 36TH ST PHILADELPHIA, PA 19104-3246 Synthesis of cyclopentenoid antitumor agents
P01CA-19138-15 (SRC) CASTRO, JOSEPH R UNIVERSITY OF CALIFORNIA 1 CYCLOTRON ROAD BERKELEY, CA 94720 Treatment of cancer with heavy charged particles
P01CA-19138-15 0001 (SRC) LYMAN, JOHN T Treatment of cancer with heavy charged particles Biophysics of charged particle radiotherapy
P01CA-19138-15 0002 (SRC) GRUNDER, HERMANN A Treatment of cancer with heavy charged particles Accerlerator operations
P01CA-19138-15 0003 (SRC) TOBIAS, CORNELIUS A Treatment of cancer with heavy charged particles Autoradioactive beams for target localization
P01CA-19138-15 0004 (SRC) CASTRO, JOSEPH R Treatment of cancer with heavy charged particles Pilot studies with helium particles
P01CA-19138-15 0005 (SRC) CHEN, GEORGE T Treatment of cancer with heavy charged particles Treatment planning with charged particles
P01CA-19138-15 0006 (SRC) CASTRO, JOSEPH R Treatment of cancer with heavy charged particles Phase III clinical trials
P01CA-19138-15 0007 (SRC) CASTRO, JOSEPH R Treatment of cancer with heavy charged particles Cooperative trial
P01CA-19138-15 0008 (SRC) PHILLIPS, THEODORE L Treatment of cancer with heavy charged particles Phase I-II clinical studies with heavy charged particles
P01CA-19138-15 9001 (SRC) ALONSO, JOSE R Treatment of cancer with heavy charged particles Radiotherapy facilities and beam delivery
R37CA-19144-17 (CBY) BUCK, CLAYTON A WISTAR INSTITUTE 36TH AND SPRUCE STREETS PHILADELPHIA, PA 19104 Membrane changes caused by tumor virus transformation
P01CA-19266-14A1 (SRC) SCHREIBER, HANS UNIVERSITY OF CHICAGO 5841 SOUTH MARYLAND AVENUE CHICAGO, ILLINOIS 60637 Immunity and cancer
P01CA-19266-14A1 0020 (SRC) FITCH, FRANK W Immunity and cancer Cell surface structures in T lymphocyte activation
P01CA-19266-14A1 0021 (SRC) SANT, ANDREA Immunity and cancer Dynamics of MHC class II restricted T cell activation
P01CA-19266-14A1 0022 (SRC) QUINTANS, JOSE Immunity and cancer T-T interactions and immune regulation
P01CA-19266-14A1 0023 (SRC) BLUESTONE, JEFFREY Immunity and cancer In vivo potentiation of immune responses
P01CA-19266-14A1 0024 (SRC) SINGH, HARINDER Immunity and cancer Function and control of Oct-2 expression in T lineage cells
P01CA-19266-14A1 0025 (SRC) SCHREIBER, HANS Immunity and cancer Immunity and tumor progression system
P01CA-19266-14A1 9002 (SRC) BLUESTONE, JEFFREY Immunity and cancer Flow cytometry core
P01CA-19266-14A1 9003 (SRC) FITCH, FRANK W Immunity and cancer Shared laboratory core
R01CA-19308-15 (VR) HOPKINS, NANCY H MASSACHUSETTS INST OF TECH 77 MASSACHUSETTS AVENUE CAMBRIDGE, MA 02139-4307 Studies on endogenous and other C-type viruses of mice
R25CA-19376-15 (SRC) NEWTON, SHEILA A HOWARD UNIVERSITY 2041 GEORGIA AVENUE, NORTHWEST WASHINGTON, D C 20060 Cancer education grant program
R25CA-19379-15 (CEC) BRESNICK, EDWARD DARTMOUTH MEDICAL SCHOOL HANOVER, NH 03756 Cancer education program
R01CA-19386-15 (RAD) HAHN, GEORGE M STANFORD UNIVERSITY 125 PANAMA STREET STANFORD, CA 94305-4125 Tumor radiochemotherapy--Effects of ultrasound and heat
R37CA-19401-16 (PTHB) STANBRIDGE, ERIC J UNIVERSITY OF CALIFORNIA COLLEGE OF MEDICINE IRVINE, CA 92717 Genetic Analysis of Human malignancy

PROJECT NUMBER LISTING

PROJECT NO., ORGANIZATIONAL UNIT., INVESTIGATOR, ADDRESS, TITLE

R01CA-19492-16A2 (BIO) COLEMAN, MARY S UNIV OF NC AT CHAPEL HILL CB#7260, 405 FLOB CHAPEL HILL, NC 27599-7260 Terminal transferase in mammalian hemopoietic tissue

R25CA-19536-13 (SRC) ALGER, ELIZABETH UMDNJ-NEW JERSEY MEDICAL SCH 185 SOUTH ORANGE AVENUE NEWARK, N J 07103-2757 Cancer education program

P01CA-19589-14A1 (SRC) FREI, EMIL, III DANA-FARBER CANCER INSTITUTE 44 BINNEY STREET BOSTON, MA 02115 Clinical/experimental pharmacology of respiratory cancer

P01CA-19589-14A1 0032 (SRC) ROLLINS, BARRETT J Clinical/experimental pharmacology of respiratory cancer Molecular phenotyping of carcinomas of the head and neck

P01CA-19589-14A1 0033 (SRC) CHEN, LAN BO Clinical/experimental pharmacology of respiratory cancer Mitochondria as a reservoir for agents against lung carcinoma

P01CA-19589-14A1 9002 (SRC) ROSOWSKY, ANDRE Clinical/experimental pharmacology of respiratory cancer Core--Clinical pharmacology

P01CA-19589-14A1 9003 (SRC) KALISH, LESLIE Clinical/experimental pharmacology of respiratory cancer Core--Biostatistics and data management

P01CA-19589-14A1 0005 (SRC) ROSOWSKY, ANDRE Clinical/experimental pharmacology of respiratory cancer Folate metabolism as a target for chemotherapy

P01CA-19589-14A1 0015 (SRC) FREI, EMIL Clinical/experimental pharmacology of respiratory cancer Clinical science

P01CA-19589-14A1 0029 (SRC) TEICHER, BEVERLY A Clinical/experimental pharmacology of respiratory cancer Perfluorochemical emulsions in cancer therapy

P01CA-19589-14A1 0030 (SRC) WAXMAN, DAVID J Clinical/experimental pharmacology of respiratory cancer Role of glutathione S-transferase in alkylating agent resistance

P01CA-19589-14A1 0031 (SRC) KUFE, DONALD W Clinical/experimental pharmacology of respiratory cancer Ethanol and gene expression in head and neck cancer

R01CA-19613-14 (ET) NORTH, WILLIAM G DARTMOUTH MEDICAL SCHOOL HANOVER, NH 03756 Neuropeptides and small cell carcinoma

R37CA-19616-17 (NSS) EDMUNDSON, ALLEN B DON/SYBIL HARRINGTON 1500 WALLACE BOULEVARD AMARILLO, TX 79106 Immunoglobulins in multiple myeloma and amyloidosis

R01CA-19816-16 (EVR) IMPERIALE, MICHAEL J UNIVERSITY OF MICHIGAN 6714 MEDICAL SCIENCE BLDG II ANN ARBOR, MI 48109-0620 Role of SV40 gene A in cellular transformation

R01CA-19931-13A3 (ARRA) LILLY, FRANK ALBERT EINSTEIN COLLEGE OF MED 1300 MORRIS PARK AVENUE BRONX, NY 10461 Mechanism of the H-2 effect of viral leukemogenesis

R01CA-20068-16 (VR) NEIMAN, PAUL E FRED HUTCHINSON CANCER RES CTR 1124 COLUMBIA ST SEATTLE, WA 98104 Molecular mechanisms in neoplasia

R37CA-20081-15 (VR) VOGT, VOLKER M CORNELL UNIV/BIOTECH BLDG DEPT OF BIOCHEM/MOL & CELL BIO ITHACA, N Y 14853 Avian retrovirus structure & assembly

U10CA-20148-15 (SRC) GLASS, ANDREW G CENTER FOR HEALTH RESEARCH 4610 S E BELMONT PORTLAND, OR 97215 Primary breast cancer therapy group (NSABP)

U10CA-20156-15 (SRC) MARGOLESE, RICHARD G JEWISH GENERAL HOSPITAL 3755 COTE ST CATHERINE RD MONTREAL, QUEBEC H3T 1E2 Primary breast cancer therapy group

R01CA-20164-15 (BNP) CORDELL, GEOFFREY A UNIV OF IL AT CHICAGO 833 S WOOD ST/COLL OF PHARMACY CHICAGO, IL 60612 Naturally-occurring anticancer principles

P01CA-20180-14 (SRC) LOOK, ALFRED T, JR ST JUDE CHILDREN'S RES HOSPITA 332 N LAUDERDALE, P.O. BOX 318 MEMPHIS, TN 38105 Leukemia program project grant

P01CA-20180-14 0001 (SRC) LOOK, A THOMAS Leukemia program project grant Therapy and cell biology of childhood acute lymphoblastic leukemia

P01CA-20180-14 0009 (SRC) MIRRO, JOSEPH Leukemia program project grant Therapy of acute myeloid leukemia

P01CA-20180-14 0010 (SRC) EVANS, WILLIAM E Leukemia program project grant Pharmacokinetics and pharmacodynamics of anticancer drugs in children

P01CA-20180-14 0011 (SRC) SHERR, CHARLES J Leukemia program project grant The CSF-1 and CSF-1 receptor genes in myeloid leukemia

P01CA-20180-14 0012 (SRC) IHLE, JAMES N Leukemia program project grant Cell biology of acute myelogenous leukemia

P01CA-20180-14 9001 (SRC) ROBERTSON, PAUL K Leukemia program project grant Biostatistics--Core

P01CA-20180-14 9002 (SRC) BEHM, FREDERICK G Leukemia program project grant Core--Central laboratory

U10CA-20187-15 (SRC) LERNER, HARVEY J PENNSYLVANIA HOSPITAL EIGHTH AND SPRUCE STREETS PHILADELPHIA, PA 19107 Primary cancer therapy group

P01CA-20194-14 (CCP) CLARKSON, BAYARD D SLOAN-KETTERING INST/CNC RES 1275 YORK AVENUE NEW YORK, N Y 10021 Human hematopoietic tumors program project

P01CA-20194-14 9005 (CCP) FRIED, JERROLD Human hematopoietic tumors program project Multi-user fluorescence activated cell sorter

P01CA-20194-14 0021 (CCP) ANDREEFF, MICHAEL Human hematopoietic tumors program project Flow cytometry of hematopoietic tumors

P01CA-20194-14 0023 (CCP) MOORE, MALCOLM A Human hematopoietic tumors program project Developmental hematopoiesis

P01CA-20194-14 0024 (CCP) CLARKSON, BAYARD D Human hematopoietic tumors program project Chronic myelogenous leukemia

P01CA-20194-14 0025 (CCP) KOZINER, BENJAMIN Human hematopoietic tumors program project Phenotypic characterization of B lymphocytes

P01CA-20194-14 0026 (CCP) MERTELSMANN, ROLAND H Human hematopoietic tumors program project Interleukin 2 in leukemia and immunodeficiency

P01CA-20194-14 9001 (CCP) CLARKSON, BAYARD D Human hematopoietic tumors program project Core component on human hematopoietic tumors

P01CA-20194-14 9002 (CCP) HIRSHAUT, YASHAR Human hematopoietic tumors program project Tumor procurement

P01CA-20194-14 9003 (CCP) CLARKSON, BAYARD D Human hematopoietic tumors program project Computerized data base - Core

PROJECT NO., ORGANIZATIONAL UNIT., INVESTIGATOR, ADDRESS, TITLE

P01CA-20194-14 9004 (CCP) MIKE, VALERIE Human hematopoietic tumors program project Biostatistics program - Core

U10CA-20203-15 (SRC) FOSTER, ROGER S, JR UNIVERSITY OF VERMONT ONE SOUTH PROSPECT ST BURLINGTON, VT 05401 Primary breast cancer therapy group (NSABP)

R37CA-20260-15 (EVR) SCHAFFER, PRISCILLA A DANA-FARBER CANCER INSTITUTE 44 BINNEY STREET BOSTON, MA 02115 Immediate-early genes of HSV

U10CA-20319-15 (CCI) RIVKIN, SAUL E SWEDISH HOSPITAL TUMOR INST 1221 MADISON STREET SEATTLE, WA 98104 Southwest oncology group

U10CA-20321-15 (SRC) SHIBATA, HENRY R ROYAL VICTORIAL HOSPITAL 687 PINE AVENUE WEST MONTREAL, H3A 1A1, CANADA Primary breast cancer therapy group

R37CA-20329-17 (ET) SUTHERLAND, ROBERT M SRI INTERNATIONAL 333 RAVENSWOOD AVENUE MENLO PARK, CA 94025 Combined radiotherapy-chemotherapy studies

U10CA-20371-15 (SRC) WOLTER, JANET M 1725 W HARRISON ST, SUITE 830 Primary cancer therapy group

R01CA-20408-15 (IMB) SHULTZ, LEONARD D JACKSON LABORATORY 600 MAIN STREET BAR HARBOR, ME 04609-0800 Immunodeficiency and tumorigenesis

R01CA-20421-15 (PC) KRAG, SHARON S THE JOHNS HOPKINS UNIVERSITY 615 NORTH WOLFE STREET BALTIMORE, MD 21205 Mutants altered in glycosylation of soluble and membrane proteins

R01CA-20424-15 (PBC) GOLDSTEIN, IRWIN J UNIVERSITY OF MICHIGAN 4320 MEDICAL SCIENCE I ANN ARBOR, MI 48109-0606 Murine ascites tumor cell glycoproteins

P01CA-20432-14 (SRC) CARBONE, PAUL P WISCON CLINICAL CANCER CENTER 600 HIGHLAND AVENUE MADISON, WI 53792 Concept to clinics--From models to multimodality trials

P01CA-20432-14 0019 (SRC) TORMEY, DOUGLASS C Concept to clinics--From models to multimodality trials Intensive treatment approaches in metastatic breast cancer

P01CA-20432-14 0031 (SRC) SONDEL, PAUL M Concept to clinics--From models to multimodality trials: Combining IL-2 with tumor-reactive human-mouse chimeric monoclonal antibody

P01CA-20432-14 0032 (SRC) SCHILLER, JOAN H Concept to clinics--From models to multimodality trials Biological response modifiers and 5-fluorouracil--Metastatic colorectal patients

P01CA-20432-14 0033 (SRC) ROBINS, H IAN Concept to clinics--From models to multimodality trials Carboplatin, systemic hyperthermia, and thymidine

P01CA-20432-14 0034 (SRC) BORDEN, ERNEST C Concept to clinics--From models to multimodality trials Studies of interferons with radiotherapy

P01CA-20432-14 0035 (SRC) STORER, BARRY E Concept to clinics--From models to multimodality trials Statistical methods in multimodal cancer therapy

P01CA-20432-14 9001 (SRC) TORMEY, DOUGLASS C Concept to clinics--From models to multimodality trials Core--Clinical support

P01CA-20432-14 9002 (SRC) DEMETS, DAVID L Concept to clinics--From models to multimodality trials Core--Biostatistics and biodata management

R25CA-20449-15 (SRC) FAHEY, THOMAS J MEMORIAL HOSPITAL FOR CANCER 1275 YORK AVENUE NEW YORK, NY 10021 Cancer education program

R37CA-20525-15 (EVR) EISENMAN, ROBERT N FRED HUTCHINSON CANCER RES CTR 1124 COLUMBIA STREET SEATTLE, WA 98104 Mechanisms in avian oncornavirus replication

R01CA-20531-15 (IMB) YUNIS, EDMOND J DANA-FARBER CANCER INSTITUTE 44 BINNEY STREET BOSTON, MA 02115 Genetic analysis of normal & malignant lymphocytes

R37CA-20535-15 (CTY) YAMAMOTO, KEITH R UNIV OF CALIF, SAN FRANCISCO SAN FRANCISCO, CA 94143 Gene regulation by steroid receptor proteins

U10CA-20549-15 (CCI) RAGAB, ABDELSALAM H EMORY UNIVERSITY CLINIC 2040 RIDGEWOOD DRIVE, N.E. ATLANTA, GA 30322 Pediatric Oncology Group

R01CA-20551-15 (EVR) ROHRSCHNEIDER, LARRY R FRED HUTCHINSON CANCER RES CTR 1124 COLUMBIA STREET SEATTLE, WA 98104 Mechanisms of oncornavirus-induced transformation

R01CA-20802-15 (VR) CARROLL, ROBERT B NEW YORK UNIVERSITY MED CENTER 550 FIRST AVENUE NEW YORK, NY 10016 Biochemical and functional properties of the SV40 T antigens

R01CA-20807-12 (CPA) KAUFFMAN, FREDERICK C RUTGERS STATE UNIVERSITY 41 GORDON RD PISCATAWAY, NJ 08855 Pharmacology of carcinogen activation in intact cells

R01CA-20816-16 (IMS) GERSHWIN, MERRILL E UNIVERSITY OF CALIFORNIA IMMUNOLOGY DAVIS, CA 95616 Pathogenesis of autoimmunity in New Zealand mice

R37CA-20822-14 (PBC) COLVIN, ROBERT B MASSACHUSETTS GENERAL HOSPITAL BLOSSOM STREET UNIT COX 5 BOSTON, MA 02114 Cell interaction and the clotting system

R37CA-20833-15 (EI) TRINCHIERI, GIORGIO THE WISTAR INSTITUTE 36TH AND SPRUCE STREETS PHILADELPHIA, PA 19104 Cell-mediated cytotoxicity in humans

R01CA-20851-14 (CPA) GEACINTOV, NICHOLAS E NEW YORK UNIVERSITY 4 WASHINGTON PLACE NEW YORK, NY 10003 Characterization of carcinogen nucleic acid complexes

U10CA-21060-15 (CCI) DUGGAN, DAVID B STATE UNIVERSITY OF NEW YORK 750 EAST ADAMS STREET SYRACUSE, N Y 13210 Participation in cancer and leukemia group B

P01CA-21071-14 (CTR) CREAVEN, PATRICK J ROSWELL PARK MEMORIAL INST. ELM AND CARLTON STREETS BUFFALO, NY 14263 Clinical biochemical pharmacology in cancer therapeutics

P01CA-21071-14 0001 (CTR) RUSTUM, YOUCEF M Clinical biochemical pharmacology in cancer therapeutics Response to antimetabolites in patients with ANLL

P01CA-21071-14 0006 (CTR) PREISLER, HARVEY D Clinical biochemical pharmacology in cancer therapeutics Determinants of anthracyclines in AML

P01CA-21071-14 0015 (CTR) RUSTUM, YOUCEF M Clinical biochemical pharmacology in cancer therapeutics metabolic modulation in cancer chemotherapy

PROJECT NO., ORGANIZATIONAL UNIT., INVESTIGATOR, ADDRESS, TITLE

P01CA-21071-14 0016 (CTR) BAKER, RAYMOND D. Clinical biochemical pharmacology in cancer therapeutics Multidrug- resistance in human tumors

P01CA-21071-14 0017 (CTR) BRENNER, DEAN E. Clinical biochemical pharmacology in cancer therapeutics Antineoplastic drug hepatic interaction

P01CA-21071-14 9002 (CTR) CREAVEN, PATRICK J Clinical biochemical pharmacology in cancer therapeutics Clinical Core

P01CA-21071-14 9005 (CTR) GRECO, WILLIAM R Clinical biochemical pharmacology in cancer therapeutics Core--biomathematics

P01CA-21071-14 9006 (CTR) SLOCUM, HARRY K Clinical biochemical pharmacology in cancer therapeutics Scientific Core

U10CA-21076-16 (CCI) TORMEY, DOUGLASS C UNIV OF WISC/CLNCL CANCER CTR 600 HIGHLAND AVE K4/632 MADISON, WI 53792 Eastern cooperative oncology--Wisconsin studies

R01CA-21103-10A3 (MEDB) LINDAHL, RONALD G UNIV OF SOUTH DAKOTA SCH OF ME VERMILLION, SD 57069 Gene-enzyme relationships of mammalian aldehyde dehydrogenases

P01CA-21111-15 (SRC) WEINSTEIN, I BERNARD HEALTH SCIENCES/COLUMBIA UNIV 701 WEST 168TH STREET NEW YORK, NY 10032 Molecular events in chemical carcinogenesis

P01CA-21111-15 0001 (SRC) JEFFREY, ALAN M Molecular events in chemical carcinogenesis Adduct formation between DNA and various activated carcinogens

P01CA-21111-15 0002 (SRC) GRUNBERGER, DEZIDER Molecular events in chemical carcinogenesis Changes in nucleic acids modified by chemical carcinogens

P01CA-21111-15 0004 (SRC) WEINSTEIN, I BERNARD Molecular events in chemical carcinogenesis Genetic analysis of the action of chemical carcinogens

P01CA-21111-15 0007 (SRC) SANTELLA, REGINA Molecular events in chemical carcinogenesis Antibodies and immunoassays for carcinogen-adducts

P01CA-21111-15 0008 (SRC) PATEL, DINSHAW Molecular events in chemical carcinogenesis NMR studies--Carcinogen modified DNA oligonucleotides

P01CA-21111-15 0009 (SRC) ROTHSTEIN, RODNEY J Molecular events in chemical carcinogenesis Studies on the genetic consequences of carcinogens in yeast

P01CA-21111-15 0010 (SRC) GOFF, STEVE Molecular events in chemical carcinogenesis Tumor suppressor genes in chemically transformed cells

U10CA-21115-16 (CCI) TORMEY, DOUGLASS C CLINICAL SCIENCE CENTER 600 HIGHLAND AVE, K4/614 MADISON, WI 53792 Ecog operations office

P01CA-21124-14 (CAK) KOPROWSKI, HILARY THE WISTAR INSTITUTE 36TH AND SPRUCE STREETS PHILADELPHIA, PA 19104 Virology and genetic of cancer

P01CA-21124-14 0006 (CAK) HUEBNER, KAY F Virology and genetic of cancer Molecular genetics of cervical carcinoma

P01CA-21124-14 0010 (CAK) KNOWLES, BARBARA B Virology and genetic of cancer Immune respone to potentially oncogenic viruses

P01CA-21124-14 0011 (CAK) ROVERA, GIOVANNI Virology and genetic of cancer Differentiation on myelomonocyatic cells

P01CA-21124-14 0012 (CAK) STEPLEWSKI, XENON Virology and genetic of cancer Colorectal cancer progression in polyposis coli

P01CA-21124-14 0013 (CAK) KOPROWSKI, HILARY Virology and genetic of cancer Immunotherapeutic agents for GI cancer

P01CA-21124-14 0014 (CAK) REDDY, PREMAKUR Virology and genetic of cancer Role of viral and oncogenes in leukemogenesis

P01CA-21124-14 9001 (CAK) KOPROWSKI, HILARY Virology and genetic of cancer Core component

P01CA-21239-15 (SRC) SUIT, HERMAN D MASSACHUSETTS GENERAL HOSPITAL FRUIT STREET BOSTON, MA 02114 Proton radiation therapy research

P01CA-21239-15 9001 (SRC) GOITEIN, M Proton radiation therapy research Physics--core

P01CA-21239-15 0001 (SRC) SUIT, HERMAN Proton radiation therapy research Clinical trials

P01CA-21239-15 0002 (SRC) SUIT, HERMAN Proton radiation therapy research Clinical investigations

P01CA-21239-15 0003 (SRC) GOITEIN, M Proton radiation therapy research To develop techniques for better proton treatment

R01CA-21246-13 (CBY) CHUNG, ALBERT E UNIVERSITY OF PITTSBURGH A519 THACKERAY HALL PITTSBURGH, PA 15260 Roles of laminin and entactin in cell adhesion

R01CA-21253-15 (CPA) MAHER, VERONICA M MICHIGAN STATE UNIVERSITY EAST LANSING, MI 48824-1316 Interaction of carcinogens with DNA--Spectra of mutation

R01CA-21327-14 (EVR) RUNDELL, MARY K NORTHWESTERN U SCHOOL OF MED 303 E CHICAGO AVENUE CHICAGO, ILLINOIS 60611 Functions of SV40 small-t antigen and cellular proteins

R01CA-21375-14 (VR) WILLIAMS, JAMES F CARNEGIE-MELLON UNIVERSITY 4400 FIFTH AVENUE PITTSBURGH, PA 15213 Genetic analysis of adenoviruses

R01CA-21445-15 (EI) LLOYD, KENNETH O SLOAN-KETTERING INST CAN RES 1275 YORK AVENUE NEW YORK, N Y 10021 Antigens of human malignant melanoma

R37CA-21463-14 (PTHB) FURCHT, LEO T UNIVERSITY OF MINNESOTA 420 DELAWARE ST. S.E. MINNEAPOLIS, MN 55455 Molecular mechanisms in metastasis -- Role of fibronectin

R37CA-21518-15 (END) SCHNEIDER, ARTHUR B MICHAEL REESE HOSPITAL & MED C 29TH STREET AND ELLIS AVENUE CHICAGO, IL 60616 Radiation induced thyroid cancer

R01CA-21615-14A1 (MBC) WALKER, GRAHAM C MASSACHUSETTS INST OF TECHNOLO 77 MASSACHUSETTS AVENUE CAMBRIDGE, MA 02139 Mutagenesis and repair of DNA

R01CA-21651-15 (MGN) ARTZT, KAREN UNIV OF TEXAS AT AUSTIN AUSTIN, TEXAS 78712-1064 Teratocarcinoma and embryonal tumors--surface antigens

U10CA-21661-16 (CCI) COX, JAMES D AMERICAN COLLEGE OF RADIOLOGY 1101 MARKET STREET, 14TH FLOOR PHILADELPHIA, PA 19107 Radiation therapy oncology group

R01CA-21663-15 (PC) HENSHAW, EDGAR C UNIVERSITY OF ROCHESTER 601 ELMWOOD AVE ROCHESTER, N Y 14642 Intermediary metabolism

PROJECT NO., ORGANIZATIONAL UNIT., INVESTIGATOR, ADDRESS, TITLE

R01CA-21673-11 (RAD) HOFER, KURT G FLORIDA STATE UNIVERSITY TALLAHASSEE, FL 32306-3015 Tumor cell hypoxia as a factor in cancer therapy

P01CA-21737-14 (CCP) KERSEY, JOHN H UNIV OF MINNESOTA BOX 803 HARVARD ST @ EAST RIVER RD MINNEAPOLIS, MN 55455 Pediatric oncology program project

P01CA-21737-14 0001 (CCP) LEBIEN, TUCKER Pediatric oncology program project Studies of ALL with monoclonal antibodies

P01CA-21737-14 0002 (CCP) UCKRUN, FATIH Pediatric oncology program project Immunotoxin against leukemic progenitor cells

P01CA-21737-14 0003 (CCP) RAMSAY, NORMA K. C. Pediatric oncology program project Acute lymphocytic leukemia

P01CA-21737-14 0004 (CCP) HURD, DAVID Pediatric oncology program project Lymphoma/ peripheral blood stem cells

P01CA-21737-14 0005 (CCP) MCGLAVE, PHILIP Pediatric oncology program project Bone marrow transplantation for CML

P01CA-21737-14 0006 (CCP) FILIPOVICH, ALEXANDRA Pediatric oncology program project Preventuion and treatment of graft versus host disease

P01CA-21737-14 0007 (CCP) BLAZAR, BRUCE Pediatric oncology program project Recombinant growth factors in B.M. transplantation

P01CA-21737-14 0008 (CCP) SLADIK, NORMAN Pediatric oncology program project Pharmacodynamics of cyclophosphamide therapy

P01CA-21737-14 0009 (CCP) KRIVIT, WILLIAM Pediatric oncology program project BM transplantation for inborn error of metabolism

P01CA-21737-14 0010 (CCP) JORDAN, COLIN Pediatric oncology program project Cytomegalovirus infection in B.M. transplantation

P01CA-21737-14 0011 (CCP) ROBISON, LESLIE Pediatric oncology program project Endocrine function

P01CA-21737-14 9001 (CCP) GOLDMAN, ANNE Pediatric oncology program project Biometric support facility--core

P01CA-21737-14 9002 (CCP) KERSEY, JOHN H. Pediatric oncology program project Patient support core

P30CA-21742-13 (SRC) LANSKY, SHIRLEY B ILLINOIS CANCER COUNCIL CENTER 36 SOUTH WABASH AVE, SUITE 700 CHICAGO, IL 60603 Cancer center support grant

P30CA-21765-14 (SRC) SIMONE, JOSEPH V ST JUDE CHILDS RESEARCH HOSP 332 NORTH LAUDERDALE MEMPHIS, TN 38101 Cancer center support (core) grant

P30CA-21765-14 9004 (SRC) MURTI, KURUGANTI G. Cancer center support (core) grant Core--Electron microscopy facility

P30CA-21765-14 9005 (SRC) METZGER, DENNIS W Cancer center support (core) grant Core--Monoclonal antibody facility

P30CA-21765-14 9006 (SRC) EVANS, WILLIAM E. Cancer center support (core) grant Core--Pharmacokinetics laboratory

P30CA-21765-14 9007 (SRC) WALKER, MARY EDITH Cancer center support (core) grant Core--Research reference center

P30CA-21765-14 9008 (SRC) WILLIAMS, BOBBY G. Cancer center support (core) grant Core--Biohazards control program

P30CA-21765-14 9009 (SRC) LOOK, THOMAS A. Cancer center support (core) grant Core--Flow cytometry and cell sorting laboratory

P30CA-21765-14 9010 (SRC) DOUGLAS, EDWIN C. Cancer center support (core) grant Core--Cytogenetics laboratory

P30CA-21765-14 9011 (SRC) JENKINS, JESSE J. Cancer center support (core) grant Core--Tumor bank

P30CA-21765-14 9012 (SRC) NAEVE, CLAYTON W Cancer center support (core) grant Core--Oligonucleotide and peptide synthesis and sequencing

P30CA-21765-14 9013 (SRC) FRIED, VICTOR A. Cancer center support (core) grant Core--Protein structure facility

P30CA-21765-14 9014 (SRC) WATTS, FRANK Cancer center support (core) grant Core--Biomedical engineering

P30CA-21765-14 9001 (SRC) REHG, JEROLD E Cancer center support (core) grant Core--Animal resources center

P30CA-21765-14 9002 (SRC) LUTHER, JERRY Cancer center support (core) grant Core--Biomedical communications

P30CA-21765-14 9003 (SRC) GEORGE, STEPHEN L. Cancer center support (core) grant Core--Biostatistics

R01CA-21773-12 (VR) HUANG, ENG-SHANG UNIV OF N C AT CHAPEL HILL CANCER CENTER CHAPEL HILL, N C 27599 Cytomegaloviruses and human malignancy

R37CA-21776-15 (EVR) SPEAR, PATRICIA G NORTHWESTERN UNIVERSITY 303 EAST CHICAGO AVENUE CHICAGO, IL 60611 Herpesvirus gene expression in transformed cells

R37CA-21923-14 (NSS) BAENZIGER, JACQUES U WASHINGTON UNIV SCH OF MED 660 S. EUCLID AVE-BOX 8118 ST LOUIS, MO 63110 Oligosaccharide structure and function in recognition

R01CA-21959-15 (CPA) PHILLIPS, DAVID H INSTITUTE OF CANCER RESEARCH 17A ONSLOW GARDENS LONDON SW7 3AL, ENGLAND Mechanisms of activation of polycylic hydrocarbons

R01CA-22008-14 (CPA) LI, JONATHAN J COLLEGE OF PHARMACY/WEGNER HAL WASHINGTON STATE UNIVERSITY PULLMAN, WA 99164-6510 Estrogen carcinogenicity and hormone dependent tumors

R25CA-22032-15 (SRC) BANKS, WILLIAM L, JR VIRGINIA COMMONWEALTH UNIVERSI BOX 614 MCV STATION RICHMOND, VA 23298-0614 Cancer education program

R01CA-22042-14 (CBY) STILES, CHARLES D DANA-FARBER CANCER INSTITUTE 44 BINNEY STREET BOSTON, MA 02115 Regulation of gene expression by PDGF

R37CA-22130-14 (VR) HAYWARD, GARY S JOHNS HOPKINS UNIVERSITY 725 N WOLFE STREET BALTIMORE, MD 21205 Structure and regulation of human herpesvirus genomes

R01CA-22153-15 (ET) PORTER, CARL W ROSWELL PARK MEMORIAL INST 666 ELM STREET BUFFALO, NY 14263 Polyamines as a potential chemotherapeutic target

R01CA-22186-12 (RAD) DETHLEFSEN, LYLE A UNIV OF UTAH HLT SCI CTR 50 NORTH MEDICAL DRIVE SALT LAKE CITY, UT 84132 Cell heterogeneity and tumor therapy

R37CA-22215-14 (NSS) KISHI, YOSHITO HARVARD UNIVERSITY 12 OXFORD STREET CAMBRIDGE, MA 02138 Synthesis of antitumor natural products

R01CA-22237-12 (MCHA) MARINO, JOSEPH P UNIVERSITY OF MICHIGAN 930 N UNIVERSITY ANN ARBOR, MI 48109-1055 Synthetic methods-site specific/latent antitumor agents

R37CA-22247-14 (ALY) MERUELO, DANIEL NY UNIVERSITY MED CENTER 550 FIRST AVENUE NEW YORK, NY 10016 Genetics of resistence to leukemia

R01CA-22294-14 (HEM) KINKADE, JOSEPH M, JR EMORY UNIVERSITY ATLANTA, GA 30322 Quantitative studies on granulocyte differentiation

P01CA-22427-14 (SRC) PARDEE, ARTHUR B DANA-FARBER CANCER INSTITUTE 44 BINNEY STREET BOSTON, MA 02115 Molecular analysis of malignant transformation

P01CA-22427-14 0010 (SRC) SPIEGELMAN, BRUCE M Molecular analysis of malignant transformation Process by which cells become committed pre-adipocytes

P01CA-22427-14 0011 (SRC) WAGNER, JOHN A Molecular analysis of malignant transformation Genes induced by nerve growth factor

P01CA-22427-14 0012 (SRC) KAPLAN, PAUL Molecular analysis of malignant transformation Differences in growth control between two embryo cell lines

P01CA-22427-14 9001 (SRC) PARDEE, ARTHUR B Molecular analysis of malignant transformation Core--scientific

P01CA-22427-14 0003 (SRC) PARDEE, ARTHUR B Molecular analysis of malignant transformation Molecular regulation of thymidine kinase production

P01CA-22427-14 0004 (SRC) CHEN, LAN B Molecular analysis of malignant transformation Lineage analysis of human cancer cells

P01CA-22427-14 0005 (SRC) STILES, CHARLES D Molecular analysis of malignant transformation The role of platelet wound hormone in transformation

P01CA-22427-14 0007 (SRC) GUDAS, LORRAINE J Molecular analysis of malignant transformation Retinoic acid effects on differentiation of teratocarcinoma cells

P01CA-22427-14 0008 (SRC) RHEINWALD, JAMES G Molecular analysis of malignant transformation Culture of normal, transformed, partially transformed keratinocytes

P01CA-22427-14 0009 (SRC) SAGER, RUTH Molecular analysis of malignant transformation Genomic changes associated with tumorigenesis

U10CA-22433-14 (CCI) WEISS, GEOFFREY R UNIV OF TEX HLTH SCIS CENTER 7703 FLOYD CURL DRIVE SAN ANTONIO, TX 78284 Southwest oncology group

P30CA-22435-11 (CCS) FOSTER, ROGER S, JR UNIVERSITY OF VERMONT 1 SOUTH PROSPECT STREET BURLINGTON, VT 05401 Cancer center support grant

P30CA-22435-11 9002 (CCS) STEWART, JAMES A Cancer center support grant Core--Clinical research management

P30CA-22435-11 9003 (CCS) HACKER, MILES P Cancer center support grant Core--Biochemical pharmacology laboratory

P30CA-22435-11 9009 (CCS) BRANDA, RICHARD Cancer center support grant Immunobiology core lab

P30CA-22435-11 9011 (CCS) SCHAEFFER, WARREN I Cancer center support grant Core--Flow cytometry facility

P30CA-22435-11 9012 (CCS) COSTANZA, MICHAEL C Cancer center support grant Core--Biostatistical resource

P30CA-22435-11 9014 (CCS) FOSTER, ROGER Cancer center support grant Research publications--core

P30CA-22435-11 9015 (CCS) FOSTER, ROGER Cancer center support grant Developmental core

P01CA-22443-14 (CAK) TEMIN, HOWARD M MCARDLE LAB FOR CANCER RESEARC 1400 UNIVERSITY AVENUE MADISON, WI 53706 Molecular biology and genetics of tumor viruses

P01CA-22443-14 0001 (CAK) TEMIN, HOWARD M Molecular biology and genetics of tumor viruses Retroviruses (mice, rats, birds)

P01CA-22443-14 0002 (CAK) MERTZ, JANET E Molecular biology and genetics of tumor viruses Regulation of SV40 late gene expression

P01CA-22443-14 0003 (CAK) RISSER, REX Molecular biology and genetics of tumor viruses Determinants of retrovirus envelope function

P01CA-22443-14 0004 (CAK) SUGDEN, BILL M Molecular biology and genetics of tumor viruses Epstein-barr virus and cellular transformation (human tissue)

P01CA-22443-14 0005 (CAK) PANGANIBAN, ANTONITO Molecular biology and genetics of tumor viruses Retroviral DNA integration, gene expression

R37CA-22451-18 (CBY) TRINKAUS, JOHN P YALE UNIVERSITY POST OFFICE BOX 6666 NEW HAVEN, CT 06511-8112 Contact behavior of developing and transformed cells

P30CA-22453-14 (SRC) BAKER, LAWRENCE H WAYNE STATE UNIVERSITY P O BOX 02188 DETROIT, MI 48202 Cancer center support grant

P30CA-22453-14 9007 (SRC) PAINE, PHILLIP L Cancer center support grant Protein separation facility--Core

P30CA-22453-14 9008 (SRC) NEGENDANK, WILLIAM G Cancer center support grant Center participation and evaluation--Core

P30CA-22453-14 9009 (SRC) NAKEFF, ALEXANDER Cancer center support grant Flow cytometry facility--Core

P30CA-22453-14 9010 (SRC) NEGENDANK, WILLIAM G Cancer center support grant NMR facility--Core

P30CA-22453-14 9011 (SRC) VALDIEVIESE, MANUEL Cancer center support grant Clinical trials office--Core

P30CA-22453-14 9012 (SRC) BRENNAN, MICHAEL J Cancer center support grant Developmental funds--Core

P30CA-22453-14 0001 (SRC) KING, CHARLES Cancer center support grant Chemical carcinogenesis

P30CA-22453-14 0002 (SRC) HONN, KENNETH V Cancer center support grant Tumor metastasis

P30CA-22453-14 0003 (SRC) HEPPNER, GLORIA Cancer center support grant Breast cancer program

P30CA-22453-14 0004 (SRC) VALERIOTE, FRED Cancer center support grant Developmental therapeutics program

P30CA-22453-14 0005 (SRC) SWANSON, MARIE G Cancer center support grant Epidemiology

P30CA-22453-14 9001 (SRC) KEMPFF, MAYA Cancer center support grant Mass spectrometry--Core

P30CA-22453-14 9002 (SRC) MOLS, OLE Cancer center support grant NMR spectroscopy--Core

P30CA-22453-14 9003 (SRC) HEEG, MARY Cancer center support grant X-ray crystallography--Core

P30CA-22453-14 9004 (SRC) HEINZ-BROSS, KARL Cancer center support grant Instrumentation--Core

P30CA-22453-14 9005 (SRC) OWNBY, HELEN Cancer center support grant Biological and human tissue resources

P30CA-22453-14 9006 (SRC) SWANSON, MARIE G Cancer center support grant Biostatistical support--Core

P01CA-22484-14 (CAK) PITOT, HENRY C UNIVERSITY OF WISCONSIN-MADISO 1400 UNIVERSITY AVE MADISON, WI 53706-1599 Biochemical studies in chemical carcinogenesis

P01CA-22484-14 0001 (CAK) MILLER, JAMES A Biochemical studies in chemical carcinogenesis Roles of electrophilic metabolites in carcinogenesis

P01CA-22484-14 0004 (CAK) PITOT, HENRY C Biochemical studies in chemical carcinogenesis Cell and molecular biology of hepatocarcinogenesis

P01CA-22484-14 0005 (CAK) KASPER, CHARLES B Biochemical studies in chemical carcinogenesis Regulation of membrane-bound enzymes

P01CA-22484-14 0006 (CAK) DRINKWATER, NORMAN R Biochemical studies in chemical carcinogenesis Genetic control of hepatocarcinogenesis

P01CA-22484-14 0007 (CAK) FAHL, WILLIAM E Biochemical studies in chemical carcinogenesis Glutathione S-transferase and its regultion

P01CA-22484-14 0008 (CAK) POLAND, ALAN Biochemical studies in chemical carcinogenesis The Ah receptors

P01CA-22484-14 9001 (CAK) MILLER, ELIZABETH C Biochemical studies in chemical carcinogenesis Histotechnology laboratory--Core

U10CA-22489-14 (SRC) KAVANAH, MAUREEN T THE UNIVERSITY HOSPITAL 88 EAST NEWTON ST BOSTON, MA 02118 Primary breast cancer therapy group

R01CA-22540-27 (PBC) SPRINGER, GEORG F UHS/THE CHICAGO MEDICAL SCH 3333 GREEN BAY ROAD NORTH CHICAGO, IL 60064 Characterization of human carcinoma T and Tn autoantigens

R01CA-22555-14 (VR) BUTEL, JANET S BAYLOR COLLEGE OF MEDICINE ONE BAYLOR PLAZA HOUSTON, TX 77030 Biological properties of SV40 early proteins

R01CA-22556-14 (HEM) METCALF, DONALD WALTER & ELIZA HALL INSTITUTE P O BOX 3050 VICTORIA, AUSTRALIA Differentiation of granulocytes and macrophages

R37CA-22677-14 (NSS) SCHREIBER, HANS UNIVERSITY OF CHICAGO 5841 SOUTH MARYLAND AVE CHICAGO, IL 60637 Manipulation of tumor-specific immunity

R01CA-22682-12S1 (CPA) MICHL, JOSEF STATE UNIVERSITY OF NEW YORK 450 CLARKSON AVE BROOKLYN, N Y 11203 An in vitro model of pancreas carcinogenesis

R37CA-22704-15 (RAD) KENNEDY, ANN R HOSP OF THE UNIV OF PENN 3400 SPRUCE ST PHILADELPHIA, PA 19104-4283 Radiation and chemical in vitro malignant transformation

R37CA-22729-14 (CBY) GELEHRTER, THOMAS D UNIV OF MICHIGAN MED SCH 1500 E MEDICAL CENTER DR ANN ARBOR, MI 48109-0618 Hormonal regulation of membrane phenotype

R01CA-22754-14 (ET) PRIEST, DAVID G MEDICAL UNIV OF SOUTH CAROLINA 171 ASHLEY AVENUE CHARLESTON, SC 29425 5-Fluorouracil target in eucaryotic cells

R01CA-22762-14 (MEP) AVADHANI, NARAYAN G UNIVERSITY OF PENNSYLVANIA 3800 SPRUCE ST PHILADELPHIA, PA 19104 Mitochondrial genetic lesions during carcinogenesis

R01CA-22764-14 (ET) SIROTNAK, FRANCIS M SLOAN-KETTERING INSTITUTE 1275 YORK AVENUE NEW YORK, NY 10021 Pharmacology of selective antitumor action/antifols

R01CA-22786-14 (ALY) BANKERT, RICHARD B ROSWELL PARK MEMORIAL INST 666 ELM STREET BUFFALO, N Y 14263 Receptor dynamics and normal/tumor cell function

R01CA-22794-15 (EI) SEEGER, ROBERT C CHILDRENS HOSP OF LOS ANGELES 4650 SUNSET BOULEVARD LOS ANGELES, CA 90027 Human neuroblastoma antigens

R01CA-22807-14 (BNP) SMITH, AMOS B, III OFFICE OF RESEARCH ADMIN 133 SOUTH 36TH ST PHILADELPHIA, PA 19104-3246 Synthesis of novel antitumor agents

R37CA-22860-14 (RAD) GERWECK, LEO E MASSACHUSETTS GENERAL HOSPITAL FRUIT ST BOSTON, MA 02114 Metabolic factors in heat & radiation lethality

P30CA-23074-14 (CCS) SALMON, SYDNEY E UNIV OF ARIZONA HLTH SCIS CTR 1501 N CAMPBELL AVENUE TUCSON, AZ 85724 Cancer center core support grant

P30CA-23074-14 9006 (CCS) DORR, ROBERT T Cancer center core support grant Cancer research pharmacy service

P30CA-23074-14 9007 (CCS) TRENT, JEFFREY M Cancer center core support grant Cytogenetic core service

P30CA-23074-14 9010 (CCS) GERNER, EUGENE Cancer center core support grant Experimental radiation--core

P30CA-23074-14 9011 (CCS) LEIBOVITZ, ALBERT Cancer center core support grant Tissue culture--Core

P30CA-23074-14 9012 (CCS) SALMON, SYDNEY E Cancer center core support grant Development core

P30CA-23074-14 9013 (CCS) NEWKIRK, DEBORAH Cancer center core support grant Computer services--core

P30CA-23074-14 9014 (CCS) HERSH, EVAN Cancer center core support grant Flow cytometry services--core

P30CA-23074-14 9015 (CCS) DUFFY, JOHN Cancer center core support grant Molecular biology services--core

P30CA-23074-14 9001 (CCS) JONES, STEVEN E Cancer center core support grant Clinical cancer research program--Core

P30CA-23074-14 9002 (CCS) MOON, THOMAS E Cancer center core support grant Biometry, epidemiology and processing of information service unit

P01CA-23076-14 (CAK) DOVE, WILLIAM F UNIV OF WI; MCARDLE LAB 1400 UNIVERSITY AVENUE MADISON, WI 53706 The cell cycle and differentiation in tumor biology

P01CA-23076-14 0001 (CAK) BURGESS, RICHARD R The cell cycle and differentiation in tumor biology RNA polymerase and control of transcription

P01CA-23076-14 0002 (CAK) DOVE, WILLIAM F The cell cycle and differentiation in tumor biology Developmental genes in three types of P polycephalum

P01CA-23076-14 0004 (CAK) MUELLER, GERALD C The cell cycle and

PROJECT NO., ORGANIZATIONAL UNIT., INVESTIGATOR, ADDRESS, TITLE

differentiation in tumor biology Molecular mechanisms controlling cancer cell growth
P01CA-23076-14 0005 (CAK) ROSS, JEFFREY The cell cycle and differentiation in tumor biology Regulation of mRNA degradation
P01CA-23076-14 0007 (CAK) FARNHAM, PEGGY J The cell cycle and differentiation in tumor biology Transcription factors responsive to alterations
P01CA-23076-14 9001 (CAK) DOVE, WILLIAM F The cell cycle and differentiation in tumor biology Core
R01CA-23086-14 (EVR) ROBINSON, HARRIET L UNIVERSITY OF MASSACHUSETTS 55 LAKE AVE, NORTH WORCESTER, MA 01655 Retrovirus-host interactions
P01CA-23099-13 (CTR) CRIST, WILLIAM M ST JUDE CHILDREN'S RES HOSPITA 332 N LAUDERDALE, P O BOX 318 MEMPHIS, TN 38101 Studies of childhood solid tumors
P01CA-23099-13 0001 (CTR) PRATT, CHARLES Studies of childhood solid tumors Phase I and 2 studies in childhood colon cancer
P01CA-23099-13 0008 (CTR) HANGHTON, PETER J Studies of childhood solid tumors Rhabdosarcoma
P01CA-23099-13 0010 (CTR) PRATT, CHARLES B Studies of childhood solid tumors Phase I-II pharmacological studies in children with solid tumor
P01CA-23099-13 0011 (CTR) HOUGHTON, JANET A Studies of childhood solid tumors Interaction of 5-FU and leucovorin in solid tumor
P01CA-23099-13 0012 (CTR) EVANS, WILLIAM Studies of childhood solid tumors Pharmacokinetics
P01CA-23099-13 0013 (CTR) BELT, JUDITH A Studies of childhood solid tumors Selective therapy for rhabdomyosarcoma
P01CA-23099-13 0014 (CTR) DYALOWICH, JACK C Studies of childhood solid tumors Modulation of etoposide activity
P01CA-23099-13 0015 (CTR) HANGHTON, JANET A Studies of childhood solid tumors Cross-resistance between melphalan and vincristine
P01CA-23099-13 0016 (CTR) BRENT, THOMAS P Studies of childhood solid tumors Relation of DNA repair processes
P01CA-23099-13 0017 (CTR) LOOK, THOMAS A Studies of childhood solid tumors Clinical staging by genetic studies
P01CA-23099-13 9002 (CTR) GEORGE, STEPHEN L Studies of childhood solid tumors Biostatistics--Core
P01CA-23099-13 9003 (CTR) LOOK, THOMAS A Studies of childhood solid tumors Cell distribution laboratory--Core
P01CA-23099-13 9004 (CTR) HANGHTON, PETER J Studies of childhood solid tumors Xenograft core facility
P30CA-23100-11 (CCS) BURROW, GERARD N UNIV OF CALIFORNIA, SAN DIEGO CANCER CENTER, T-010 LA JOLLA, CA 92093 Specialized cancer center core support grant
P30CA-23100-11 9001 (CCS) MENDELSOHN, JOHN Specialized cancer center core support grant Biostatistics core
P30CA-23100-11 9002 (CCS) YEN, SAMUEL S Specialized cancer center core support grant Endocrine and radioiodination core
P30CA-23100-11 9003 (CCS) HOWELL, STEPHEN B Specialized cancer center core support grant Pharmacology and cytokinetics core
P30CA-23100-11 9004 (CCS) MENDELSOHN, JOHN Specialized cancer center core support grant Radiobiology laboratory--Core
P30CA-23100-11 9005 (CCS) VARKI, AJIT P Specialized cancer center core support grant Developmental program--Core
P30CA-23100-11 0003 (CCS) ROYSTON, IVOR Specialized cancer center core support grant Cell sorting and surface marker laboratory--Core
P30CA-23108-14 (CCS) MC INTYRE, O ROSS DARTMOUTH-HITCHCOCK MED CTR TWO MAYNARD ST, HB 7920 HANOVER, NH 03756 Cancer center support core
P30CA-23108-14 9001 (CCS) FREEMAN, DANIEL H Cancer center support core Core--Biostatistics
P30CA-23108-14 9004 (CCS) MEMOLI, VINCENT A Cancer center support core Core--Histology
P30CA-23108-14 9007 (CCS) GUYRE, PAUL M Cancer center support core Core--Flow cytometry facility
P30CA-23108-14 9008 (CCS) DOUPLE, EVAN B Cancer center support core Core--Irradiation service
P30CA-23108-14 9011 (CCS) FANGER, MICHAEL W Cancer center support core Core--Hybridoma library and monoclonal production
P30CA-23108-14 9012 (CCS) MC INTYRE, O ROSS Cancer center support core Core---DNA synthesis service
P30CA-23108-14 9013 (CCS) MC INTYRE, O ROSS Cancer center support core Developmental core
P01CA-23113-13 (SRC) DAVIS, LAWRENCE W ALBERT EINSTEIN MED COLLEGE & 1825 EAST CHESTER RD BRONX, NY 10461 Particle clinical trials - headquarters and statistics
R25CA-23146-13 (SRC) HAYS, DANIEL M CHILDRENS HOSP OF LOS ANGELES 4650 SUNSET BLVD LOS ANGELES, CA 90027 Professional oncology education program
P30CA-23168-14 (CCS) BAIRD, WILLIAM M PURDUE CANCER CENTER PURDUE UNIVERSITY WEST LAFAYETTE, IN 47907 Cancer center support
P30CA-23168-14 9001 (CCS) JACOBSON, LINDA B Cancer center support Cell culture lab--Core
P30CA-23168-14 9002 (CCS) BAIRD, WILLIAM M. Cancer center support Spectroscopy core
P30CA-23168-14 9003 (CCS) BAIRD, WILLIAM M. Cancer center support Electron microscopy core
P30CA-23168-14 9004 (CCS) BAIRD, WILLIAM M. Cancer center support Peptide core
P30CA-23168-14 9005 (CCS) BAIRD, WILLIAM M. Cancer center support Flow cytometer--core
P30CA-23168-14 9006 (CCS) BAIRD, WILLIAM M. Cancer center support Developmental core
R01CA-23226-20 (PTHA) FAUSTO, NELSON BROWN UNIVERSITY BOX G PROVIDENCE, RI 02912 Gene expression in regenerating and neoplastic livers
R37CA-23296-15 (ET) DARZYNKIEWICZ, ZBIGNIEW NEW YORK MEDICAL COLLEGE 100 GRASSLANDS RD ELMSFORD, NY 10532 Effects of new anticancer drugs on the cell cycle
U10CA-23306-12 (SRC) SUTHERLAND, CARL M TULANE UNIVERSITY 1430 TULANE AVENUE NEW ORLEANS, LA 70112 Primary breast cancer therapy group

PROJECT NO., ORGANIZATIONAL UNIT., INVESTIGATOR, ADDRESS, TITLE

U10CA-23318-15 (CCI) HARRINGTON, DAVID DANA-FARBER CANCER INSTITUTE 44 BINNEY STREET BOSTON, MA 02115 ECOG Statistical Coordinating Center
R01CA-23365-13 (BIO) CHANG, LUCY M UNIFORMED SER/UNIV HLTH SCI 4301 JONES BRIDGE ROAD BETHESDA, MD 20889-4799 DNA polymerases in normal and cancer cells
R01CA-23378-12 (ET) KESSEL, DAVID H WAYNE STATE UNIV SCH OF MED 540 E. CANFIELD STREET DETROIT , MI 48201 Porphyrin photosensitization and phototherapy
R37CA-23386-14 (CPA) KING, CHARLES M MICHIGAN CANCER FOUNDATION 110 EAST WARREN AVENUE DETROIT, MI 48201 Mechanistic approaches to carcinogenesis
R01CA-23449-13 (CPA) LOMBARDI, BENITO UNIV OF PITTSBURGH SCH OF MED 3550 TERRACE AT DESOTO STREETS PITTSBURGH, PA 15261 Choline deficiency and hepatocarcinogenesis
R37CA-23751-13 (ORTH) CHAO, EDMUND Y MAYO FOUNDATION 200 FIRST STREET S W ROCHESTER, MN 55905 Segmental bone and joint replacement after tumor resection
R01CA-23753-14 (PTHB) RIFKIN, DANIEL B NEW YORK UNIVERSITY MED CTR 550 FIRST AVENUE NEW YORK, N Y 10016 Proteases and the malignant phenotype
P01CA-23766-14 (SRC) O'REILLY, RICHARD J SLOANE-KETTERING INST CANCER R 1275 YORK AVENUE NEW YORK, N Y 10021 Marrow transplantation in leukemia and other diseases
P01CA-23766-14 0003 (SRC) MOORE, MALCOLM A Marrow transplantation in leukemia and other diseases Hematopoietic growth factors for allogenic bone marrow transplant
P01CA-23766-14 0022 (SRC) FLOMENBERG, NEAL Marrow transplantation in leukemia and other diseases: Immunoregulation in graft-vs-host reactions & graft-host tolerance
P01CA-23766-14 0023 (SRC) O'REILLY, RICHARD J Marrow transplantation in leukemia and other diseases Marrow transplantation for experimental therapy evaluation
P01CA-23766-14 0024 (SRC) O'REILLY, RICHARD J Marrow transplantation in leukemia and other diseases Marrow transplantation in acute and chronic leukemia treatment
P01CA-23766-14 0030 (SRC) DUPONT, BO Marrow transplantation in leukemia and other diseases Immunogenetics of HLA and bone marow transplantation
P01CA-23766-14 0031 (SRC) KERNAN, NANCY A Marrow transplantation in leukemia and other diseases Marrow graft failure with T-cell depleted transplants--Host resistance
P01CA-23766-14 0032 (SRC) CASTRO-MALASPINA, HUGO Marrow transplantation in leukemia and other diseases Marrow graft failure following T-cell depletion-Stroma mech
P01CA-23766-14 0033 (SRC) KEEVER, CAROLYN A Marrow transplantation in leukemia and other diseases Cellular systems contributing to leukemia resistance
P01CA-23766-14 0034 (SRC) EMANUEL, DAVID Marrow transplantation in leukemia and other diseases CMV infections--improved diagnosis & host resistance potentiation
P01CA-23766-14 9002 (SRC) GROSHEN, SUSAN Marrow transplantation in leukemia and other diseases Biostatistics core
P01CA-23766-14 9007 (SRC) CHAGANTI, RAJU S Marrow transplantation in leukemia and other diseases Cytogenetic studies in bone marrow--Core
P01CA-23766-14 9008 (SRC) COLLINS, NANCY H Marrow transplantation in leukemia and other diseases Monitoring of bone marrow depletions--Core
P01CA-23766-14 9009 (SRC) FLOMENBERG, NEAL Marrow transplantation in leukemia and other diseases Immunologic monitoring in therapeutic marrow transplantation
P01CA-23767-13 (CAK) AXEL, RICHARD COLUMBIA UNIVERSITY 722 W. 168TH ST. NEW YORK, NY 10032 Molecular virology
P01CA-23767-13 0001 (CAK) AXEL, RICHARD Molecular virology T4--Cell surface receptor for AIDS virus
P01CA-23767-13 0006 (CAK) ALT, FREDERICK W Molecular virology Selective gene amplification in normal and neoplastic cells
P01CA-23767-13 0007 (CAK) SILVERSTEIN, SAUL J Molecular virology Papilloma viruses in cervical cancer
P01CA-23767-13 0008 (CAK) GOFF, STEPHEN P Molecular virology Targeting of retrovirus genome into selected genes
P01CA-23767-13 0009 (CAK) GOTTESMAN, MAXWELL E Molecular virology Genetic rearrangement in prokaryotes
P01CA-23767-13 9001 (CAK) AXEL, RICHARD Molecular virology Cell growth facility--Core
R01CA-23800-13 (CPA) WANG, CHING Y MICHIGAN CANCER FOUNDATION 110 EAST WARREN AVENUE DETROIT, MICH 48201 Mechanisms of bladder tumorigenesis
R01CA-23857-14 (MEP) WILKINS, TRACY D VA POLYTECHNIC INST & ST UNIV 301 BURRUSS HALL BLACKSBURG, VA 24061 Relationships of fecal mutagens to colon cancer
R01CA-23931-14 (EVR) ISOM, HARRIET C PENNSYLVANIA STATE UNIVERSITY P O BOX 850 HERSHEY, PA 17033 Regulation of differentiation in hepatocytes in vitro
R25CA-23944-11 (SRC) WILIMAS, JUDITH A ST JUDE CHILDREN'S RES HOSP PO BOX 318 MEMPHIS, TN 38101-0318 Professional oncology education
R01CA-24071-13 (END) CARPENTER, GRAHAM F VANDERBILT UNIVERSITY 21ST AVE S AT GARLAND ST NASHVILLE, TN 37232-0146 Studies of the receptor for epidermal growth factor
R01CA-24101-12A1 (BMT) KALLENBACH, NEVILLE R NEW YORK UNIVERSITY 4 WASHINGTON PLACE, 514 NEW YORK, NY 10003 Ligand interactions of DNA junctions
R01CA-24144-13 (CPA) GRISHAM, JOE W UNIV OF N C AT CHAPEL HILL CB# 7525 BRINKHOUS-BULLITT CHAPEL HILL, N C 27599-7525 Mechanisms of DNA-dependent cytotoxicity by chemicals
R01CA-24158-13 (PC) COLLINS, JAMES M MCV STATION P O BOX 614 RICHMOND, VA 23298-0614 Replicative enzymes and rates of DNA synthesis
R01CA-24220-13 (EVR) ROSENBERG, NAOMI E TUFTS UNIVERSITY 136 HARRISON AVENUE BOSTON, MA 02111 Abelson leukemia virus transformation
R01CA-24321-13 (PTHB) KIM, YOUNG S VA MEDICAL CENTER 4150

CLEMENT STREET SAN FRANCISCO, CA 94121 Glycoconjugates in pancreatic cancer

R37CA-24347-13 (END) THOMPSON, E AUBREY, JR UNIV OF TEXAS MED BR GALVESTON, TX 77550 Hormonal control of proliferation malignant thymocytes

R01CA-24385-12 (CBY) MASTRO, ANDREA M PENNSYLVANIA STATE UNIVERSITY 431 SOUTH FREAR BLDG UNIVERSITY PARK, PA 16802 Effects of phorbol esters on lymphocyte stimulation

R01CA-24429-16 (IMS) WINKELSTEIN, ALAN MONTEFIORE HOSPITAL 3459 FIFTH AVENUE PITTSBURGH, PA 15213 T cell colony formation in normals and AIDS

R01CA-24432-20 (ALY) MARGOLIES, MICHAEL N MASSACHUSETTS GENERAL HOSPITAL JACKSON 14 BOSTON, MA 02114 Sequence, shape and specificity of antibodies

R37CA-24442-23 (ALY) SERCARZ, ELI E UNIVERSITY OF CALIFORNIA 405 HILGARD AVENUE LOS ANGELES, CA 90024-1489 Chemical basis for receptor recognition of lysozymes

R01CA-24473-14 (IMB) DAVID, CHELLA S MAYO FOUNDATION 200 FIRST STREET SOUTHWEST ROCHESTER, MN 55905 Genetics and function of (H-2 linked) I region

R01CA-24487-13 (BNP) CLARDY, JON C CORNELL UNIVERSITY ITHACA, NY 14853-1301 Structural studies on bioactive natural products

U10CA-24507-13 (SRC) MAURER, HAROLD M MEDICAL COLLEGE OF VIRGINIA MCV STATION, BOX 646 RICHMOND, VA 23298 Intergroup rhabdomyosarcoma study

P01CA-24530-12 (CAK) COFFIN, JOHN M TUFTS UNIVERSITY 136 HARRISON AVENUE BOSTON, MASSACHUSETTS 02111 Molecular genetics of cancer

P01CA-24530-12 0001 (CAK) SCHWARTZ, ROBERT S Molecular genetics of cancer Immunology of murine leukemia virus GP70

P01CA-24530-12 0004 (CAK) COFFIN, JOHN M Molecular genetics of cancer Molecular biology of murine retrovirus

P01CA-24530-12 0007 (CAK) ROSENBERG, NAOMI E Molecular genetics of cancer Immortalization of B-cells by retrovirus

P01CA-24530-12 0010 (CAK) ANDROPHY, ELLIOT E Molecular genetics of cancer Control of papilloma virus expression

P01CA-24530-12 0011 (CAK) SCHAFFHAUSEN, BRIAN S Molecular genetics of cancer Tumor virus gene products

P01CA-24530-12 9001 (CAK) SWHWARTZ, ROBERT S Molecular genetics of cancer Core-program

R01CA-24553-12 (ET) HUANG, LEAF UNIVERSITY OF TENNESSEE DEPT OF BIOCHEMISTRY KNOXVILLE, TENN 37996-0840 Targeting of liposome to tumor cells

R37CA-24607-13 (IMB) ENGLEMAN, EDGAR G STANFORD UNIVERSITY BLOOD CENT 800 WELCH ROAD PALO ALTO, CA 94304 Suppressor T cells of mixed leukocyte reaction in man

R01CA-24628-08 (BM) NOWOTNY, ALOIS H UNIVERSITY OF PENNSYLVANIA 4010 LOCUST STREET PHILADELPHIA, PA 19104 Relation of structure to function in endotoxin

R01CA-24634-12 (BNP) KLEIN, ROBERT S MONTEFIORE MEDICAL CENTER 111 EAST 210 STREET BRONX, N Y 10467 Synthesis of C-nucleosides for anticancer studies

R01CA-24652-13 (RAD) MOULDER, JOHN E MEDICAL COLLEGE OF WISCONSIN 8700 W WISCONSIN AVENUE MILWAUKEE, WI 53226 Kidney response to radiation and chemotherapy

R01CA-24665-13 (MCHA) KOCH, TAD H UNIVERSITY OF COLORADO CAMPUS BOX 215 BOULDER, CO 80309-0215 New drugs to alleviate adriamycin cardiotoxicity

R55CA-24694-14 (EVR) TEVETHIA, MARY J PENNSYLVANIA STATE UNIVERSITY P O BOX 850 HERSHEY, PA 17033 Mutagenesis of specific regions of the SV40 genome

R01CA-24710-13 (VR) WOLD, WILLIAM S ST LOUIS UNIVERSITY 3681 PARK AVE ST LOUIS, MO 63110 Adenovirus 2 coded early glycoprotein

R01CA-24715-13 (VR) LIVINGSTON, DAVID M DANA-FARBER CANCER INSTITUTE 44 BINNEY STREET BOSTON, MA 02115 Isolation and function of small SV40 T antigen

R01CA-24806-12 (RNM) DOI, KUNIO UNIVERSITY OF CHICAGO SCH MED 5841 S MARYLAND AVE CHICAGO, ILLINOIS Radiographic imaging for cancer diagnosis

R37CA-24844-13 (CPA) STAMPFER, MARTHA R LAWRENCE BERKELEY LABORATORY 1 CYCLOTRON ROAD BERKELEY, CA 94720 Characterization of human mammary cells

R01CA-24873-13 (EI) BANKHURST, ARTHUR D UNIVERSITY OF NEW MEXICO SCHOOL OF MEDICINE ALBUQUERQUE, NM 87131 Immunosuppression in cancer patients

R37CA-25000-14 (VR) TEVETHIA, SATVIR S THE MILTON S HERSHEY MED CTR PENN STATE UNIV P O BOX 850 HERSHEY, PA 17033 Biology of SV40 specific transplantation antigen

R01CA-25012-13 (CPA) SINCLAIR, PETER R VA MEDICAL & REGIONAL OFFICE C WHITE RIVER JUNCTION, VT 0500 Liver cell cultures for study of carcinogen activation

R37CA-25027-24 (RAD) BOX, HAROLD C ROSWELL PARK CANCER INST ELM & CARLTON STREETS BUFFALO, NY 14263 Transfer mechanisms in irradiated biological systems

R01CA-25078-13 (PBC) JACOB, SAMSON T UNIV-HLTH SCIEN/CHICAGO MED SC 3333 GREEN BAY ROAD NORTH CHICAGO, IL 60064 Poly(a) polymerase and mRNA processing

R01CA-25098-14 (PTHB) CHIU, JEN-FU UNIV OF VERMONT COL OF MED B405 GIVEN BUILDING BURLINGTON, VT 05405 Regulation of alpha-fetoprotein in fetal and cancer liver

R01CA-25142-10A3 (BNP) PARRY, RONALD J RICE UNIVERSITY P O BOX 1892 HOUSTON, TX 77251 Biosynthesis of some microbial metabolites

R01CA-25185-13 (BNP) KOREEDA, MASATO UNIVERSITY OF MICHIGAN ANN ARBOR, MI 48109 Synthesis and reactions of polycyclic aromatic hydrocarbon metabolites

R01CA-25215-13 (VR) BUTEL, JANET S BAYLOR COLLEGE OF MEDICINE ONE BAYLOR PLAZA HOUSTON, TX 77030 Tumor virus effects on mammary epithelial cells

U10CA-25224-12 (CCI) MOERTEL, CHARLES G MAYO FOUNDATION 200 FIRST STREET SOUTHWEST ROCHESTER, MN 55905 The north central cancer treatment group

R37CA-25235-13 (EVR) BERK, ARNOLD J UNIVERSITY OF CALIFORNIA 405 HILGARD AVE LOS ANGELES, CA 90024 Biosynthesis of adenovirus early RNAs

PROJECT NO., ORGANIZATIONAL UNIT., INVESTIGATOR, ADDRESS, TITLE

R01CA-25236-12 (ET) PIPER, JAMES R SOUTHERN RESEARCH INSTITUTE 2000 9TH AVE, SOUTH/BOX 55305 BIRMINGHAM, AL 35255-5305 Developmental antifolate therapy of cancer

R01CA-25250-12 (IMB) KLEIN, EVA KAROLINSKA INSTITUTE BOX 60400 STOCKHOLM, SWEDEN S-104 01 Target sites and genetic control in NK and LAK cells

R01CA-25253-13 (ALY) BANKERT, RICHARD B ROSWELL PARK MEMORIAL INST 666 ELM STREET BUFFALO, N Y 14263 Immunoregulatory network probed by cell hybridization

R01CA-25298-13 (PTHB) HALPERN, ALLAN C UNIV OF PA SCH OF MED 422 CURIE BLVD PHILADELPHIA, PA 19104 Biology of human cutaneous malignant melanoma

R01CA-25344-13 (CPA) SMULSON, MARK E GEORGETOWN UNIVERSITY 3900 RESERVOIR RD, N W WASHINGTON, D C 20007 Carcinogens and chromatin structure and function

R01CA-25362-11 (CPA) GURTOO, HIRA L ROSWELL PARK MEMORIAL INSTITUT 666 ELM STREET BUFFALO, N Y 14263 Genetics of aflatoxin metabolism role in carcinogenesis

R01CA-25394-11 (ET) ROSOWSKY, ANDRE DANA-FARBER CANCER INSTITUTE 44 BINNEY STREET BOSTON, MA 02115 New approaches to antifolate chemotherapy

U10CA-25408-13 (CCI) CASTLEBERRY, ROBERT P CHILDREN'S HOSPITAL, 651 1600 7TH AVENUE SOUTH BIRMINGHAM, AL 35233 Pediatric Oncology Group

U10CA-25408-13 0001 (CCI) CASTLEBERRY, ROBERT P Pediatric Oncology Group POG9006--6-MP/methotrexate vs. alternating chemotherapy for ALL in childhood

U10CA-25408-13 0002 (CCI) CASTLEBERRY, ROBERT P Pediatric Oncology Group POG9005--Dose intensification of methotrexate & 6-mercaptourine in childhood ALL

U10CA-25408-13 0003 (CCI) CASTLEBERRY, ROBERT P Pediatric Oncology Group POG9031--Cisplatin/VP-16 therapy of medulloblastoma/pre vs. post irradiation

U10CA-25408-13 0004 (CCI) CASTLEBERRY, ROBERT P Pediatric Oncology Group POG8945--Phase III chemotherapy for hepatoblastoma & hepatocellular carcinoma

U10CA-25408-13 0005 (CCI) CASTLEBERRY, ROBERT P Pediatric Oncology Group POG9049--Phase III study of high-risk malignant germ cell tumors in children

U10CA-25408-13 0006 (CCI) CASTLEBERRY, ROBERT P Pediatric Oncology Group POG8844--Bone marrow transplant in children with stage D neuroblastoma

U10CA-25408-13 0007 (CCI) CASTLEBERRY, ROBERT P Pediatric Oncology Group POG8850--Phase III treatment of Ewing's sarcoma and neuroectodermal bone tumors

U10CA-25408-13 0008 (CCI) CASTLEBERRY, ROBERT P Pediatric Oncology Group POG8821--Phase III chemotherapy +/- autologous BMT in children with AML

U10CA-25408-13 0009 (CCI) CASTLEBERRY, ROBERT P Pediatric Oncology Group POG8725--Phase III chemotherapy +/- radiation therapy in pediatric Hodgkins

U10CA-25408-13 0010 (CCI) CASTLEBERRY, ROBERT P Pediatric Oncology Group POG8704--Phase III chemotherapy of childhood T cell ALL & lymphoblastic lymphoma

U10CA-25408-13 0011 (CCI) CASTLEBERRY, ROBERT P Pediatric Oncology Group POG8719--Phase III chemotherapy for non-Hodgkin's lymphoma in children

U10CA-25408-13 0012 (CCI) CASTLEBERRY, ROBERT P Pediatric Oncology Group POG8650--National Wilm's tumor and clear cell sarcoma study

U10CA-25408-13 0013 (CCI) CASTLEBERRY, ROBERT P Pediatric Oncology Group POG8616--Phase III chemotherapy for childhood Burkitt and non-Burkitts lymphoma

U10CA-25408-13 0021 (CCI) CASTLEBERRY, ROBERT P Pediatric Oncology Group POG9140--Phase II therapy for recurrent or refractory neuroblastoma

U10CA-25408-13 0022 (CCI) CASTLEBERRY, ROBERT P Pediatric Oncology Group POG9048--Phase II study of malignant germ cell tumors in children

U10CA-25408-13 0023 (CCI) CASTLEBERRY, ROBERT P Pediatric Oncology Group POG9060--Intensive QOD ifosfamide treatment for CNS tumors in children

U10CA-25408-13 0024 (CCI) CASTLEBERRY, ROBERT P Pediatric Oncology Group POG8936--Phase II study of carboplatin treatment for optic pathway tumors

U10CA-25408-13 0025 (CCI) CASTLEBERRY, ROBERT P Pediatric Oncology Group POG8935--Phase II study of surgery and/or radiotherapy for optic pathway tumors

U10CA-25408-13 0026 (CCI) CASTLEBERRY, ROBERT P Pediatric Oncology Group POG8820--Phase II/III study of VP-16, AMSA +/- 5-azacytidine in childhood ANLL

U10CA-25408-13 0027 (CCI) CASTLEBERRY, ROBERT P Pediatric Oncology Group POG8889--Intergroup rhabdomyosarcoma study for clinical group IV disease

U10CA-25408-13 0028 (CCI) CASTLEBERRY, ROBERT P Pediatric Oncology Group POG8866--Phase II asparaginase therapy for acute lymphoblastic leukemia

U10CA-25408-13 0029 (CCI) CASTLEBERRY, ROBERT P Pediatric Oncology Group POG8862--Combination chemotherapy of acute T-lymphoblastic leukemia

U10CA-25408-13 0030 (CCI) CASTLEBERRY, ROBERT P Pediatric Oncology Group POG8863--Phase II study of high dose cytosine arabinoside in childhood tumors

U10CA-25408-13 0031 (CCI) CASTLEBERRY, ROBERT P Pediatric Oncology Group POG8827--Phase II treatment of children with Hodgkin's disease in relapse

U10CA-25408-13 0032 (CCI) CASTLEBERRY, ROBERT P Pediatric Oncology Group POG8865--Phase II recombinant alpha-interferon in relapsed T-cell disease

U10CA-25408-13 0033 (CCI) CASTLEBERRY, ROBERT P Pediatric Oncology Group--Phase II recombinant A-interferon in chronic myelogenous leukemia

U10CA-25408-13 0034 (CCI) CASTLEBERRY, ROBERT P Pediatric Oncology

PROJECT NO., ORGANIZATIONAL UNIT., INVESTIGATOR, ADDRESS, TITLE

Group POG8832--Combination chemotherapy followed by radiotherapy for brain tumors

U10CA-25408-13 0035 (CCI) CASTLEBERRY, ROBERT P Pediatric Oncology Group POG8731--Phase II trial of methotrexate in treatment of brain tumors in children

U10CA-25408-13 0036 (CCI) CASTLEBERRY, ROBERT P Pediatric Oncology Group POG8788--Intergroup rhabdomyosarcoma study/pilot study for clinical group III

U10CA-25408-13 0037 (CCI) CASTLEBERRY, ROBERT P Pediatric Oncology Group POG8761--Phase II study of homoharringtonine therapy for nonlymphoblastic leukemi

U10CA-25408-13 0038 (CCI) CASTLEBERRY, ROBERT P Pediatric Oncology Group POG8739--Phase II immunotherapy with alpha-2 interferon for brain tumors

U10CA-25408-13 0039 (CCI) CASTLEBERRY, ROBERT P Pediatric Oncology Group POG8741--Treatment of patients with stage C and stage D neuroblastoma

U10CA-25408-13 0040 (CCI) CASTLEBERRY, ROBERT P Pediatric Oncology Group POG8751--Phase II methotrexate chemotherapy for rhabdomyosarcoma in children

U10CA-25408-13 0041 (CCI) CASTLEBERRY, ROBERT P Pediatric Oncology Group POG8633--Postoperative chemotherapy and delayed irradiation for brain tumors

U10CA-25408-13 0042 (CCI) CASTLEBERRY, ROBERT P Pediatric Oncology Group POG8617--Therapy for B-cell acute lymphoblastic leukemia and lymphoma

U10CA-25408-13 0043 (CCI) CASTLEBERRY, ROBERT P Pediatric Oncology Group POG9139--Phase I study of cisplatin and irradiation in brain stem gliomas

U10CA-25408-13 0044 (CCI) CASTLEBERRY, ROBERT P Pediatric Oncology Group POG9079--Phase I study of L-PAM/CTX with ABM rescue for brain tumors in children

U10CA-25408-13 0045 (CCI) CASTLEBERRY, ROBERT P Pediatric Oncology Group POG9075--Phase I study of acivicin in children with solid tumors

U10CA-25408-13 0046 (CCI) CASTLEBERRY, ROBERT P Pediatric Oncology Group POG9074--Phase I study of xomazyme-H65 in children with T-cell ALL/lymphoma

U10CA-25408-13 0047 (CCI) CASTLEBERRY, ROBERT P Pediatric Oncology Group POG9072--Phase I chemotherapy for recurrent/resistant malignant solid tumors

U10CA-25408-13 0048 (CCI) CASTLEBERRY, ROBERT P Pediatric Oncology Group POG9061-Phase II systemic therapy and irradiation for ALL & CNS leukemia

U10CA-25408-13 0049 (CCI) CASTLEBERRY, ROBERT P Pediatric Oncology Group POG 9086--Phase I pilot study of therapy for T-cell ALL or NHL

U10CA-25408-13 0014 (CCI) CASTLEBERRY, ROBERT P Pediatric Oncology Group POG8615--Phase III study of large cell lymphomas in children and adolescents

U10CA-25408-13 0015 (CCI) CASTLEBERRY, ROBERT P Pediatric Oncology Group POG8651--Phase III study of childhood nonmetastatic osteosarcoma

U10CA-25408-13 0016 (CCI) CASTLEBERRY, ROBERT P Pediatric Oncology Group POG8653--Phase III study of childhood soft tissue sarcomas

U10CA-25408-13 0017 (CCI) CASTLEBERRY, ROBERT P Pediatric Oncology Group POG8625--Phase III combined therapy in childhood Hodgkin's disease

U10CA-25408-13 0018 (CCI) CASTLEBERRY, ROBERT P Pediatric Oncology Group POG8451--Intergroup rhabdomyosarcoma study

U10CA-25408-13 0019 (CCI) CASTLEBERRY, ROBERT P Pediatric Oncology Group POG9110--Rotational drug therapy after first marrow relapse of non-T, non B ALL

U10CA-25408-13 0020 (CCI) CASTLEBERRY, ROBERT P Pediatric Oncology Group POG9107--Phase II pilot study of infant leukemia

U10CA-25408-13 0050 (CCI) CASTLEBERRY, ROBERT P Pediatric Oncology Group POG9071--Phase I trial of fazarabine in children with acute leukemia

U10CA-25408-13 0053 (CCI) CASTLEBERRY, ROBERT P Pediatric Oncology Group POG8870--Phase I trial of ifosfamide/VP16/MESNA in children with acute leukemia

U10CA-25408-13 0054 (CCI) CASTLEBERRY, ROBERT P Pediatric Oncology Group POG8871--Phase I study of rTNF in children with refractory solid tumors

U10CA-25408-13 0055 (CCI) CASTLEBERRY, ROBERT P Pediatric Oncology Group POG8671--Phase I immunotherapy with rIL-2 in children with solid tumors

U10CA-25408-13 0056 (CCI) CASTLEBERRY, ROBERT P Pediatric Oncology Group POG8494--Phase I study of fludarabine phosphate in pediatric patients

U10CA-25408-13 0057 (CCI) CASTLEBERRY, ROBERT P Pediatric Oncology Group POG8930--A comprehensive genetic analysis of brain tumors

U10CA-25408-13 0058 (CCI) CASTLEBERRY, ROBERT P Pediatric Oncology Group POG8828--Late effects of Hodgkin's disease

U10CA-25408-13 0059 (CCI) CASTLEBERRY, ROBERT P Pediatric Oncology Group POG9046--Molecular genetic analysis of Wilm's tumors

U10CA-25408-13 0060 (CCI) CASTLEBERRY, ROBERT P Pediatric Oncology Group POG9153--Rhabdomyosarcoma study/laboratory evaluation of tumor

U10CA-25408-13 0051 (CCI) CASTLEBERRY, ROBERT P Pediatric Oncology Group POG8970--Phase I trial of fazarabine in children with refractory solid tumors

U10CA-25408-13 0052 (CCI) CASTLEBERRY, ROBERT P Pediatric Oncology Group POG8973--Etoposide (VP-16) and carboplatin in children with acute leukemia

R37CA-25417-13 (EVR) TJIAN, ROBERT T UNIV OF CALIFORNIA 401 BARKER HALL BERKELEY, CA 94720 The SV40 tumor antigen

R01CA-25462-12 (EVR) FARAS, ANTHONY J UNIVERSITY OF MINNESOTA BOX 206 UMHC/HARVARD ST MINNEAPOLIS, MN 55455 Human papillomaviruses and malignant disease

R01CA-25526-09 (ET) PAPAHADJOPOULOS, P DEMETRIOS UNIVERSITY OF CALIFORNIA CANCER RESEARCH INST BOX 0128 SAN FRANCISCO, CA 94143 Liposome targeting to tumor cells in vivo

R37CA-25583-13 (NSS) LOPEZ, DIANA M P O BOX 016960 MIAMI, FL 33101 Cell mediated immunity in mammary tumor models

R01CA-25636-10 (RAD) FOX, MICHAEL H COLORADO STATE UNIVERSITY FORT COLLINS, CO 80523 Mechanisms of cell killing by hyperthermia

U10CA-25769-12 (SRC) GUEVIN, RAYMOND M SAINT-LUC'S HOSPITAL 1058, ST-DENIS STREET MONTREAL, QUEBEC, CANADA Primary breast cancer therapy group - NSABP

P01CA-25803-13 (SRC) SPRENT, JONATHAN RES INST OF SCRIPPS CLINIC 10666 NORTH TORREY PINES ROAD LA JOLLA, CA 92037 Control of normal and abnormal cell development

P01CA-25803-13 0001 (SRC) BEVAN, MICHAEL J Control of normal and abnormal cell development Cell lineages of the thymus

P01CA-25803-13 0004 (SRC) SHERMAN, LINDA A Control of normal and abnormal cell development Utilization and recognition by mouse T lymphocytes of human MHC molecules

P01CA-25803-13 0007 (SRC) SPRENT, JONATHAN Control of normal and abnormal cell development Role of CD4+ cells in graft-versus-host disease

P01CA-25803-13 9001 (SRC) BEVAN, MICHAEL J Control of normal and abnormal cell development Core

R01CA-25810-13 (VR) KABAT, DAVID OREGON HEALTH SCIENCES UNIV 3181 SW SAM JACKSON PARK RD PORTLAND, OR 97201-3098 Leukemogenic membrane glycoproteins: gp55s of SFFVs

R01CA-25836-12 (BCE) KATZENELLENBOGEN, JOHN A UNIVERSITY OF ILLINOIS URBANA, IL 61801 Rational design of breast tumor imaging agents

P01CA-25842-11 (SRC) MARTIN, DANIEL S 89-15 WOODHAVEN BLVD WOODHAVEN, N Y 11421 Cancer therapy with biochemical modulators BRMS and CSFCCA

P01CA-25842-11 0001 (SRC) MARTIN, DANIEL S Cancer therapy with biochemical modulators BRMS and CSFCCA Experimental chemotherapy

P01CA-25842-11 0002 (SRC) SAWYER, ROBERT S Cancer therapy with biochemical modulators BRMS and CSFCCA Biochemical studies

P01CA-25842-11 0003 (SRC) BERTINO, JOSEPH Cancer therapy with biochemical modulators BRMS and CSFCCA Clinical studies

P01CA-25842-11 9001 (SRC) STOLFI, ROBERT L Cancer therapy with biochemical modulators BRMS and CSFCCA Core--Animal facilities

P01CA-25874-12 (SRC) HERLYN, MEENHARD WISTAR INSTITUTE 36TH & SPRUCE STREETS PHILADELPHIA, PA 19104 Human melanoma--Etiology and progression

P01CA-25874-12 0013 (SRC) RODECK, ULRICH Human melanoma--Etiology and progression Tumor progression and growth control

P01CA-25874-12 0014 (SRC) WESTERMARK, BENGT Human melanoma--Etiology and progression Mechanisms of PDGF and PDGF receptor regulation

P01CA-25874-12 0015 (SRC) CLARK, WALLACE H Human melanoma--Etiology and progression Metastasis--Blood vascular intravasation and the lymphatic vascular cascade

P01CA-25874-12 9001 (SRC) MEENHARD, HERLYN Human melanoma--Etiology and progression Core

P01CA-25874-12 0004 (SRC) HERLYN, MEENHARD Human melanoma--Etiology and progression Maturation, tumor progression and differentiation

P01CA-25874-12 0007 (SRC) HERLYN, DOROTHEE Human melanoma--Etiology and progression Immunogenicity of various preparations of melanoma-associated antigens

P01CA-25874-12 0009 (SRC) LINNEBACH, ALBAN J Human melanoma--Etiology and progression Melanoma oncogenes and antioncogenes

P01CA-25874-12 0011 (SRC) DUPONT, GERRY Human melanoma--Etiology and progression Treatment of patients with disseminated melanoma with monoclonal antibodies

P01CA-25874-12 0012 (SRC) SPEICHER, DAVID Human melanoma--Etiology and progression Biochemistry and differential expression of melanoma-associated antigens

R37CA-25917-12 (EI) DAYNES, RAYMOND A UNIV OF UTAH, MED SCHOOL 50 NORTH MEDICAL DRIVE SALT LAKE CITY, UTAH 84132 Efferent control of cellular immune responses

R01CA-25933-12 (ET) GALIVAN, JOHN H NEW YORK STATE DEPT OF HLTH EMPIRE STATE PLAZA ALBANY, NY 12201-0509 Methotrexate and metabolism in hepatic cells

R01CA-25951-11 (CPA) JIRTLE, RANDY L DUKE UNIVERSITY MEDICAL CENTER BOX 3433 DURHAM, N C 27710 Survival and carcinogenesis in transplanted hepatocytes

R01CA-25956-13 (ET) SHAPIRO, JOAN RANKIN ST JOSEPH'S HOSP AND MED CTR 350 WEST THOMAS ROAD PHOENIX, AZ 85013 Human glioma heterogeneity and chemosensitivity

R01CA-25957-12 (RAD) WARTERS, RAYMOND L UNIVERSITY OF UTAH 1400 EAST 2ND SOUTH SALT LAKE CITY, UTAH 84132 Chromatin replication and heat-induced cell death

R01CA-25972-11 (HEM) METCALF, DONALD WALTER & ELIZA HALL INSTITUTE PO BOX 3050 ROYAL MELBOURNE HO VICTORIA, AUSTRALIA Self renewal in normal and leukemic hemopoietic stem cells

U10CA-25988-13 (CCI) HARRIS, JULES E RUSH-PRESBY-ST LUKES MED CTR 1653 W CONGRESS PKWY CHICAGO, IL 60612 Collaborative clinical trials with the ecog

R01CA-25990-13 (ET) BROWN, J MARTIN STANFORD UNIV SCHOOL OF MED STANFORD, CA 94305 Combined modalities--Cell, tumor and tissue effects

R01CA-26001-13 (VR) GALLOWAY, DENISE A FRED HUTCHINSON CANCER RES CTR 1124 COLUMBIA STREET SEATTLE, WA 98104 Herpesvirus expression in transformation & latency

R01CA-26038-12 (HEM) KOEFFLER, H PHILLIP UNIVERSITY OF CALIFORNIA 405 HILGARD AVENUE LOS ANGELES, CA 90024-1678 Differentiation and proliferation of myeloid cells

U10CA-26044-13 (CCI) NEERHOUT, ROBERT C OREGON HEALTH SCIENCES UNIV 3181 S W SAM JACKSON PARK ROAD PORTLAND, OR 97201 Children's cancer study group

R37CA-26056-12 (CPA) WEINSTEIN, I BERNARD CANCER CTR/INST OF CANCER RES 701 WEST 168TH STREET NEW YORK, NY 10032 Cellular and biochemical effects of tumor promoters

R01CA-26122-13 (CBY) BAUMANN, HEINZ ROSWELL PARK MEMORIAL INST 666 ELM STREET BUFFALO, NY 14263 Effects of hormones on cell membrane properties

U10CA-26126-13 (CCI) WELLS, ROBERT J CHILDREN'S HOSPITAL RES FDN ELLAND & BETHESDA AVENUES CINCINNATI, OHIO 45229-2899 Children's cancer study group

R01CA-26169-13 (EI) BOSE, HENRY R, JR UNIVERSITY OF TEXAS

AUSTIN, TX 78712 Immunosuppression by avian acute leukemia viruses
U10CA-26270-11 (CCI) LUKENS, JOHN N VANDERBILT UNIVERSITY NASHVILLE, TN 37232 Children's cancer study group
R37CA-26279-12 (NSS) WARD, JOHN F UNIV OF CALIFORNIA, SAN DIEGO 9500 GILMAM DR LA JOLLA, CA 92093-0610 Mechanisms in shouldered survival curves
R01CA-26297-12 (ALY) MC KEAN, DAVID J MAYO FOUNDATION 200 FIRST STREET S W ROCHESTER, MN 55905 structure-function analysis of Ia antigens
R01CA-26312-10A1 (RAD) MEYN, RAYMOND E U.T. M.D. ANDERSON CANCER CENT 1515 HOLCOMBE BLVD HOUSTON, TX 77030 Repair of radiation damage in vitro and in vivo
R37CA-26345-12 (VR) KNIPE, DAVID M HARVARD MEDICAL SCHOOL 25 SHATTUCK STREET BOSTON, MA 02115 Genetics of herpesvirus transformation
R01CA-26350-12 (RAD) URANO, MUNEYASU UNIVERSITY OF KENTUCKY MED CTR 800 ROSE STREET LEXINGTON, KY 40536-0084 Tumor response to hyperthermia and irradiation
R01CA-26376-12 (ET) LUDUENA, RICHARD F UNIV OF TEXAS HLTH SCI CTR 7703 FLOYD CURL DRIVE SAN ANTONIO, TX 78284-7760 Mechanism of action of anti-tumor drugs
R37CA-26386-12 (EI) BERNSTEIN, IRWIN D FRED HUTCHINSON CANCER RES CTR 1124 COLUMBIA STREET SEATTLE, WA 98104 Monoclonal antibody therapy of cancer
R01CA-26391-12 (BIO) COLEMAN, MARY S UNIV OF NC AT CHAPEL HILL 405 FACULTY LAB OFC BLDG CB 72 CHAPEL HILL, NC 27599-7260 Molecular pathology of leukemia and lymphoma
R37CA-26504-13 (HEM) STANLEY, EVAN R ALBERT EINSTEIN COLLEGE OF MED 1300 MORRIS PARK AVENUE BRONX, NY 10461 Regulation of granulocyte and macrophage production
R01CA-26556-12 (MEP) SHINOZUKA, HISASHI UNIVERSITY OF PITTSBURGH 776 SCAIFE HALL PITTSBURGH, PA 15261 Dietary modification & promotion of liver carcinogenesis
R01CA-26582-11 (SRC) CLEELAND, CHARLES S UNIV OF WI HOSP & CLINICS 600 HIGHLAND AVENUE MADISON, WI 53792 A pilot study of cancer pain
R01CA-26656-14 (PTHB) RHEINWALD, JAMES G BIOSURFACE TECHNOLOGY, INC 64 SIDNEY STREET CAMBRIDGE, MA 02139 An autocrine basis of epithelial growth and neoplasia
R01CA-26659-11S1 (EI) WRIGHT, GEORGE L, JR EASTERN VIRGINIA MED SCH P O BOX 1980 NORFOLK, VA 23501 Monoclonal antibodies to prostate tumor antigens
P01CA-26712-11S1 (SRC) HYNES, RICHARD O M I T CENTER FOR CANCER RES BLDG E17, RM 227 CAMBRIDGE, MA 02139 Molecular analyses of cellular proteins and their genes
P01CA-26712-11S1 0002 (SRC) HYNES, RICHARD O Molecular analyses of cellular proteins and their genes Structure-function relationships of fibronectin
P01CA-26712-11S1 0003 (SRC) ROBBINS, PHILLIPS W Molecular analyses of cellular proteins and their genes Biological consequences of altered protein glycosylation
P01CA-26712-11S1 0004 (SRC) SOLOMON, FRANK Molecular analyses of cellular proteins and their genes Cytoplasmic microtubules associated proteins
P01CA-26712-11S1 0007 (SRC) HOUSMAN, DAVID E Molecular analyses of cellular proteins and their genes Molecular analysis of NA+ K+ ATPase
P01CA-26712-11S1 9001 (SRC) HYNES, RICHARD O Molecular analyses of cellular proteins and their genes Core support
U10CA-26730-12 (SRC) BORNSTEIN, RICHARD S MT SINAI MEDICAL CENTER ONE MT SINAI DRIVE CLEVELAND, OHIO 44106 Primary breast cancer therapy group - NSABP
P01CA-26731-12 (SRC) TANNENBAUM, STEVEN R MASSACHUSETTS INST OF TECH 77 MASSACHUSETTS AVENUE CAMBRIDGE, MA 02139 Endogenous nitrite carcinogenesis in man
P01CA-26731-12 0005 (SRC) TANNENBAUM, STEVEN R Endogenous nitrite carcinogenesis in man Chemistry of carcinogens
P01CA-26731-12 0006 (SRC) DEEN, WILLIAM M Endogenous nitrite carcinogenesis in man Pharmacokinetics of nitrite and nitrosamines
P01CA-26731-12 0007 (SRC) MARLETTA, MICHAEL A Endogenous nitrite carcinogenesis in man Formation of nitrite and nitrate
P01CA-26731-12 0008 (SRC) FOX, JAMES G Endogenous nitrite carcinogenesis in man Endogenous nitrosation--Animal models
P01CA-26731-12 0009 (SRC) WOGAN, GERALD N Endogenous nitrite carcinogenesis in man Genetic alterations during gastric carcinogenesis
P01CA-26731-12 9001 (SRC) WISHNOK, JOHN S Endogenous nitrite carcinogenesis in man Core--Analytic chemical services
P01CA-26731-12 9002 (SRC) FOX, JAMES R Endogenous nitrite carcinogenesis in man Core--Animal resource and experimental surgery model
R01CA-26750-13 (MCHA) PADWA, ALBERT EMORY UNIVERSITY ATLANTA, GA 30322 Synthesis of fused heterocyclic compounds
R01CA-26751-12 (MCHA) PADWA, ALBERT EMORY UNIVERSITY DEPARTMENT OF CHEMISTRY ATLANTA, GA 30322 Heterocyclic ring compounds for alkaloid synthesis
P01CA-26803-11 (SRC) HANASH, SAMIR M UNIVERSITY OF MICHIGAN F6515 MOTT CHILDREN'S HOSPITAL ANN ARBOR, MI 48109 Program project--Study of human mutation
P01CA-26803-11 0002 (SRC) SKOLNICK, MICHAEL Program project--Study of human mutation Automated analysis of two-dimensional gels
P01CA-26803-11 0003 (SRC) CHU, ERNEST H Program project--Study of human mutation Mutagenesis in somatic cells
P01CA-26803-11 0004 (SRC) HANASH, SAMIR M Program project--Study of human mutation Germinal & somatic mutations in cancer patients with radiotherapy & chemotherapy
P01CA-26803-11 9001 (SRC) HANASH, SAMIR M Program project--Study of human mutation 2-d gel core
U10CA-26806-12 (CCI) WEISS, RAYMOND B WALTER REED ARMY MEDICAL CTR HEMATOLOGY-ONCOLOGY MED CTR WASHINGTON, D C 20307-5001 Support of studies in the cancer and leukemia group B
R01CA-26852-10S1 (EDC) WINAWER, SIDNEY J MEMORIAL HOSPITAL FOR CANCER 1275 YORK AVENUE NEW YORK, NY 10021 Control of large bowel cancer following polypectomy
R01CA-26869-12 (REN) HORWITZ, KATHRYN B UNIV OF COLORADO HLTH SCI CTR 4200 EAST NINTH AVENUE DENVER, CO 80262 Nuclear steroid hormone receptors in breast cancer
R01CA-26905-12 (VR) PRIVES, CAROL L COLUMBIA UNIVERSITY 818A FAIRCHILD CENTER NEW YORK, NY 10027 Polyoma and SV40 T antigen roles in viral DNA synthesis
R37CA-26914-11 (PTHB) LOEPPKY, RICHARD N UNIVERSITY OF MISSOURI 123 CHEMISTRY BUILDING COLUMBIA, MO 65211 Carcinogenesis--Nitrosamine formation and inhibition
U10CA-27057-12 (CCI) NATALE, RONALD B UNIVERSITY OF MICHIGAN 102 OBSERVATORY ANN ARBOR, MI 48109 Southwest oncology group
R01CA-27101-11 (ET) NAIR, MADHAVAN G UNIVERSITY OF SOUTH ALABAMA 307 UNIVERSITY BOULEVARD MOBILE, AL 36688 Cancer chemotherapy--New folate analogues
R01CA-27223-12 (VR) ROBINSON, HARRIET L UNIV OF MASSACHUSETTS MED SCH 55 LAKE AVE. NORTH WORCESTER, MA 01655 Avian leukosis viruses and cancer
R01CA-27306-13 (CPA) BOUCK, NOEL P NORTHWESTERN UNIVERSITY 303 E CHICAGO AVENUE CHICAGO, IL 60611 Genetic analysis of malignant transformation
R01CA-27343-12 (SSS) SHAFER, RICHARD H UNIVERSITY OF CALIFORNIA 926 MEDICAL SCIENCES BUILDING SAN FRANCISCO, CA 94143-0446 Experimental studies of drug-nucleic acid interactions
R01CA-27419-13 (ET) HEPPNER, GLORIA H MICHIGAN CANCER FOUNDATION 110 EAST WARREN AVENUE DETROIT, MICH 48201 Chemotherapeutic consequence of tumor heterogeneity
R01CA-27440-13 (BCE) BRODIE, ANGELA M UNIVERSITY OF MARYLAND 660 W REDWOOD STREET BALTIMORE, MD 21201 Aromatase inhibitors, breast cancer, and other diseases
R01CA-27466-13 (HEM) QUESENBERRY, PETER J UNIVERSITY OF VIRGINIA MR4, BOX 1131 CHARLOTTESVILLE, VA 22908 Endothelial colony-stimulating activity
U10CA-27469-11 (CCI) PARK, ROBERT C GYNECOLOGIC ONCOLOGY GROUP 1234 MARKET STREET SUITE 1945 PHILADELPHIA, PA 19107 Gynecologic oncology group headquarters
P01CA-27489-12 (SRC) LERNER, RICHARD A RESEARCH INST OF SCRIPPS CLINI 10666 NORTH TORREY PINES ROAD LA JOLLA, CA 92037 Consequences of endogenous retroviral expression
P01CA-27489-12 0004 (SRC) DIXON, FRANK J Consequences of endogenous retroviral expression T cell receptor studies
P01CA-27489-12 0005 (SRC) PETERSON, PER Consequences of endogenous retroviral expression Analysis of the CD8-Class I MHC interaction
P01CA-27489-12 0006 (SRC) LERNER, RICHARD A Consequences of endogenous retroviral expression Genetics and structure of the Fv fragments of antibodies
P01CA-27489-12 0007 (SRC) BALCH, WILLIAM Consequences of endogenous retroviral expression Regulation of membrane recycling by ras-related proteins
P01CA-27489-12 9001 (SRC) HOUGHTEN, RICHARD Consequences of endogenous retroviral expression Core--Research support
P01CA-27502-11 (SRC) ALBERTS, DAVID S UNIVERSITY OF ARIZONA 1515 NORTH CAMPBELL AVE TUCSON, AZ 85724 Chemoprevention and vitamin A program project
P01CA-27502-11 0009 (SRC) PLEZIA, PATRICIA M Chemoprevention and vitamin A program project Clinical pharmacology of Beta-carotene in normal subjects
P01CA-27502-11 0012 (SRC) GENSLER, HELEN L Chemoprevention and vitamin A program project Prevention of photocarcinogenesis
P01CA-27502-11 0015 (SRC) MOON, THOMAS E Chemoprevention and vitamin A program project Epidemiology of cutaneous cancers--Predicting skin cancer risks
P01CA-27502-11 0016 (SRC) MOON, THOMAS E Chemoprevention and vitamin A program project Chemoprevention of skin cancer by retinoids
P01CA-27502-11 0017 (SRC) GAREWAL, HARINDER Chemoprevention and vitamin A program project Chemoprevention trials in skin and oral cancers
P01CA-27502-11 9002 (SRC) MOON, THOMAS E Chemoprevention and vitamin A program project Core--Biometry and information processing
P01CA-27502-11 9003 (SRC) PENG, YEI-MEI Chemoprevention and vitamin A program project Core--Analytical chemistry
P01CA-27502-11 9004 (SRC) RITENBAUGH, CHERYL Chemoprevention and vitamin A program project Core--Dietary evaluation
P01CA-27502-11 9005 (SRC) ATWOOD, JAN Chemoprevention and vitamin A program project Core--Behavioral science
P01CA-27503-12 (CAK) TEVETHIA, SATVIR PENNSYLVANIA STATE UNIVERSITY P O BOX 850 HERSHEY, PA 17033 DNA viruses and neoplasia
P01CA-27503-12 0001 (CAK) RAPP, FRED DNA viruses and neoplasia Herpes virus latency
P01CA-27503-12 0002 (CAK) ISOM, HARRIET C DNA viruses and neoplasia Oncogenicity of cytomegaloviruses
P01CA-27503-12 0004 (CAK) TEVETHIA, SATVIR S DNA viruses and neoplasia Herpes simplex virus proteins
P01CA-27503-12 0005 (CAK) TEVETHIA, MARY J DNA viruses and neoplasia Genetic anlysis of cytomegalovirus
P01CA-27503-12 0006 (CAK) HOWETT, MARY K DNA viruses and neoplasia Human papillomavirus infection
P01CA-27503-12 0009 (CAK) KREIDER, JOHN DNA viruses and neoplasia Transformation of cells by papilomarirus
P01CA-27503-12 9001 (CAK) RAPP, FRED DNA viruses and neoplasia Core support
R01CA-27523-11 (IMS) EVANS, ROBERT THE JACKSON LABORATORY 600 MAIN STREET BAR HARBOR, ME 04609-0800 Macrophages and tumor growth
U10CA-27525-13 (CCI) COMIS, ROBERT L FOX CHASE CANCER CENTER 7701 BURHOLME AVENUE PHILADELPHIA, PA 19111 Eastern cooperative oncology group
R01CA-27564-10 (PTHB) HOFFMAN, ROBERT M UNIV OF CALIF, SAN DIEGO LA JOLLA, CA 92093-0609 Methionine dependence, a metabolic marker in cancer
R01CA-27578-11 (EVR) PARSONS, J THOMAS UNIVERSITY OF VIRGINIA BOX 441 CHARLOTTESVILLE, VA 22908 Expression of avian retrovirus transforming genes
R01CA-27603-13 (MCHA) HECHT, SIDNEY M UNIVERSITY OF VIRGINIA CHARLOTTESVILLE, VA 22901 Synthesis of bleomycin group antibiotics

PROJECT NO., ORGANIZATIONAL UNIT., INVESTIGATOR, ADDRESS, TITLE

R01CA-27605-11 (ET) MORAN, RICHARD G UNIV OF SOUTHERN CALIFORNIA 1303 Z MISSION ROAD LOS ANGELES, CA 90033 Evaluation of a new approach to antifolate chemotherapy
R37CA-27607-12 (MGN) LEE, AMY S USC SCHOOL OF MEDICINE 1441 EASTLAKE AVE LOS ANGELES, CA 90033 Co-ordinated gene expression in mammalian cells
R01CA-27632-12 (MGN) KING, MARY C UNIVERSITY OF CALIFORNIA BERKELEY, CA 94720 Genetic analysis of breast cancer in families
U10CA-27678-12 (CCI) FEIG, STEPHEN A U.C.L.A. SCHOOL OF MEDICINE 10833 LE CONTE AVENUE LOS ANGELES, CA 90024 Children's cancer study group
R01CA-27706-11 (MEP) IP, CLEMENT C Y ROSWELL PARK CANCER INST ELM AND CARLTON STREETS BUFFALO, NY 14263 Selenium metabolism & chemoprevention
R01CA-27755-11 (PBC) CULP, LLOYD A CASE WESTERN RESERVE UNIVERSIT SCHOOL OF MEDICINE CLEVELAND, OH 44106 Fibronectin--proteoglycan binding in adhesion
R01CA-27791-10A1 (RAD) RUBIN, PHILIP UNIV OF ROCHESTER CANCER CTR 601 ELMWOOD AVE, BOX 647 ROCHESTER, NY 14642 Pulmonary surfactant system and radiation pneumonitis
R01CA-27808-09 (NEUC) TISCHLER, ARTHUR S NEW ENGLAND MED CTR HOSP, INC. 750 WASHINGTON STREET BOSTON, MA 02111 Pathobiology of adrenal medullary tumors
R01CA-27809-11 (MEP) SAUER, LEONARD A MARY IMOGENE BASSETT HOSP ONE ATWELL ROAD COOPERSTOWN, N Y 13326 Pathways of energy metabolism in malignancy in vivo
R01CA-27821-11 (BEM) PROCHASKA, JAMES O UNIVERSITY OF RHODE ISLAND FLAGG ROAD KINGSTON, RI 02881 Self-help models & interventions for smoking cessation
R37CA-27834-11 (EVR) HUNTER, ERIC UNIV OF ALABAMA AT BIRMINGHAM UAB STATION BIRMINGHAM, AL 35294 Genetics of primate 'D' type retroviruses
R37CA-27903-16 (EI) EPSTEIN, LOIS B UNIVERSITY OF CALIFORNIA 3RD AVE AND PARNASSUS SAN FRANCISCO, CA 94143 The biology of the antitumor actions of interferons
R01CA-27931-11 (ET) HITTELMAN, WALTER N UNIV OF TX MD ANDERSON CANCER 1515 HOLCOMBE BLVD HOUSTON, TX 77030 Chromosome aberrations with therapeutic agents
R37CA-27951-12 (VR) BRUGGE, JOAN S UNIVERSITY OF PENNSYLVANIA 422 CURIE BLVD PHILADELPHIA, PA 19104-6148 Pp60 src & the polyma mt protein interaction
R01CA-27967-12 (MEP) AWASTHI, YOGESH C UNIV OF TEXAS MEDICAL BRANCH 301 KEILLER BLDG ROUTE F20 GALVESTON, TX 77550 Mechanism of anti-carcinogenic effect of antioxidants
R37CA-28000-12 (MEP) MALEJKA-GIGANTI, DANUTA VETERANS MEDICAL CENER ONE VETERANS DRIVE MINNEAPOLIS, MN 55417 Mammary carcinogenesis by N-substituted aryl compounds
R01CA-28010-12 (BCE) PRATT, WILLIAM B M6322 MEDICAL SCIENCE BLDG I UNIV OF MICHIGAN MED SCHOOL ANN ARBOR, MI 48109-0626 Steroid receptor transformation
R01CA-28038-11 (CPA) BROYDE, SUSE B NEW YORK UNIVERSITY 100 WASHINGTON SQUARE EAST NEW YORK, NY 10003 Carcinogen-DNA adducts--Linkage site and conformation
R01CA-28051-12 (VR) STOLTZFUS, CONRAD M UNIVERSITY OF IOWA IOWA CITY, IA 52242 Avian retrovirus RNA metabolism
P01CA-28103-13 (SRC) KRUMDIECK, CARLOS L UNIVERSITY OF ALABAMA UAB STATION BOX 188 BIRMINGHAM, AL 35294 Core clinical nutrition research center
P01CA-28103-13 9002 (SRC) HOWERDE, E SAUBERLICH Core clinical nutrition research center Core--nutrition research support laboratory
P01CA-28103-13 9003 (SRC) HEIMBURGER, DOUGLAS C Core clinical nutrition research center Core--Clinical nutrition
P01CA-28103-13 9005 (SRC) CRAIG, CAROL Core clinical nutrition research center Core--nutrition information service special component
P01CA-28103-13 9007 (SRC) GRUBBS, CLINTON J Core clinical nutrition research center Core--experimental carcinogenesis
P01CA-28103-13 9008 (SRC) CORNWELL, ANNIE Core clinical nutrition research center Core--Computerized nutrient data bank
P01CA-28103-13 9009 (SRC) GRUBBS, CLINTON J Core clinical nutrition research center Core--histopathology
P01CA-28103-13 9010 (SRC) BARTOLUCCI, ALFRED H Core clinical nutrition research center Core--Statistics
P01CA-28103-13 9011 (SRC) KRUMDIECK, CARLOS L Core clinical nutrition research center Core--Image analysis laboratory
P01CA-28103-13 9012 (SRC) WEINSIER, ROLAND L Core clinical nutrition research center Core--Nutrition education
R01CA-28119-11 (MCHA) FUKUYAMA, TOHRU RICE UNIVERSITY PO BOX 1892 HOUSTON, TX 77251 Synthesis of antitumor antibiotics
R01CA-28139-11 (EI) FELDMAN, MICHAEL WEIZMANN INSTITUTE OF SCIENCE PO BOX 26 REHOVOT, 76100 ISRAEL Immunobiology of tumor metastases
P01CA-28146-11 (SRC) TEGTMEYER, PETER J STATE UNIVVERSITY OF NEW YORK STONY BROOK, NY 11794-8621 Tumor virus host interactions
P01CA-28146-11 0004 (SRC) HEARING, PATRICK Tumor virus host interactions Cis and trans regulation of adenovirus transcription
P01CA-28146-11 0005 (SRC) TEGTMEYER, PETER J Tumor virus host interactions Transformation by SV40 T antigen and the p53 oncogene
P01CA-28146-11 0006 (SRC) WIMMER, ECKARD Tumor virus host interactions Characterization of the cellular receptor for poliovirus
P01CA-28146-11 0007 (SRC) ENRIETTO, PAULA Tumor virus host interactions The role of c-rel and c-myc in oncogenesis
P01CA-28146-11 0008 (SRC) HAYMAN, MICHAEL Tumor virus host interactions Mechanisms of action of the erbB oncogene
P01CA-28146-11 0009 (SRC) MUZYCZKA, NICHOLAS Tumor virus host interactions Role of AAV proteins in transcriptional regulation
P01CA-28146-11 0010 (SRC) LIPSICK, JOSEPH S Tumor virus host interactions myb-Related genes in animals and lower eukaryotes
P01CA-28146-11 9001 (SRC) BYNUM, DAVID Tumor virus host interactions Core--Laboratory support services
R37CA-28149-11 (NSS) VITETTA, ELLEN S U OF TX SOUTHWESTERN MED CTR. 5323 HARRY HINES BLVD DALLAS, TX 75235 New stradegies for immunotoxin therapy
R01CA-28231-10S1 (IMB) CARLSON, GEORGE A MCLAUGHLIN RESEARCH INSTITUTE 1625 3RD AVENUE NORTH GREAT FALLS, MT 59401 H-2 associated natural resistance
R01CA-28240-12 (PTHB) SCOTT, ROBERT E UNIV OF TENNESSEE, MEMPHIS 800 MADISON AVENUE MEMPHIS, TN 38163 Pathology in the control of differentiation in cancer
R25CA-28297-12 (SRC) LALLY, EDWARD T UNIVERSITY OF PENNSYLVANIA 4001 SPRUCE STREET PHILADELPHIA, PA 19104 Cancer education program
R01CA-28332-11 (RAD) LORD, EDITH M UNIVERSITY OF ROCHESTER 601 ELMWOOD AVENUE, BOX 704 ROCHESTER, N Y 14642 In situ antitumor immunity and effects of radiation
R01CA-28343-12 (RNM) GOODWIN, DAVID A V A MEDICAL CENTER 3801 MIRANDA AVENUE PALO ALTO, CA 94304 Bifunctional chelates in cancer imaging and therapy
R01CA-28366-12 (PTHB) MILLER, FRED R MICHIGAN CANCER FOUNDATION 110 EAST WARREN AVENUE DETROIT, MI 48201 Natural site preference in mammary cancer biology
R01CA-28379-11 (VR) ALWINE, JAMES C UNIV OF PENNSYLVANIA 422 CURIE BLVD PHIADELPHIA, PA 19104-6142 Regulation of DNA tumor virus gene expression
U10CA-28383-12 (CCI) BRECHER, MARTIN L ROSWELL PARK CANCER INSTITUTE ELM & CARLTON STREETS BUFFALO, NY 14263 Treatment of childhood cancer
U10CA-28383-12 0046 (CCI) BRECHER, MARTIN L Treatment of childhood cancer POG9074--Phase I study of xomazyme-H65 in children with T-cell ALL/lymphoma
U10CA-28383-12 0047 (CCI) BRECHER, MARTIN L Treatment of childhood cancer POG9072--Phase I chemotherapy for recurrent/resistant malignant solid tumors
U10CA-28383-12 0048 (CCI) BRECHER, MARTIN L Treatment of childhood cancer POG9061-Phase II systemic therapy and irradiation for ALL & CNS leukemia
U10CA-28383-12 0049 (CCI) BRECHER, MARTIN L Treatment of childhood cancer POG 9066--Phase I pilot study of therapy for T-cell ALL or NHL
U10CA-28383-12 0050 (CCI) BRECHER, MARTIN L Treatment of childhood cancer POG9071--Phase I trial of fazarabine in children with acute leukemia
U10CA-28383-12 0051 (CCI) BRECHER, MARTIN L Treatment of childhood cancer POG8970--Phase I trial of fazarabine in children with refractory solid tumors
U10CA-28383-12 0052 (CCI) BRECHER, MARTIN L Treatment of childhood cancer POG8973--Etoposide (VP-16) and carboplatin in children with acute leukemia
U10CA-28383-12 0053 (CCI) BRECHER, MARTIN L Treatment of childhood cancer POG8870--Phase I trial of ifosfamide/VP16/MESNA in children with acute leukemia
U10CA-28383-12 0054 (CCI) BRECHER, MARTIN L Treatment of childhood cancer POG8871--Phase I study of rTNF in children with refractory solid tumors
U10CA-28383-12 0055 (CCI) BRECHER, MARTIN L Treatment of childhood cancer POG8671--Phase I immunotherapy with rIL-2 in children with solid tumors
U10CA-28383-12 0056 (CCI) BRECHER, MARTIN L Treatment of childhood cancer POG8494--Phase I study of fludarabine phosphate in pediatric patients
U10CA-28383-12 0057 (CCI) BRECHER, MARTIN L Treatment of childhood cancer POG8930--A comprehensive genetic analysis of brain tumors
U10CA-28383-12 0058 (CCI) BRECHER, MARTIN L Treatment of childhood cancer POG8828--Late effects of Hodgkin's disease
U10CA-28383-12 0059 (CCI) BRECHER, MARTIN L Treatment of childhood cancer POG9046--Molecular genetic analysis of Wilm's tumors
U10CA-28383-12 0060 (CCI) BRECHER, MARTIN L Treatment of childhood cancer POG9153--Rhabdomyosarcoma study/laboratory evaluation of tumor
U10CA-28383-12 0001 (CCI) BRECHER, MARTIN L Treatment of childhood cancer POG9006--6-MP/methotrexate vs. alternating chemotherapy for ALL in childhood
U10CA-28383-12 0014 (CCI) BRECHER, MARTIN L Treatment of childhood cancer POG8615--Phase III study of large cell lymphomas in children and adolescents
U10CA-28383-12 0015 (CCI) BRECHER, MARTIN L Treatment of childhood cancer POG8651--Phase III study of childhood nonmetastatic osteosarcoma
U10CA-28383-12 0016 (CCI) BRECHER, MARTIN L Treatment of childhood cancer POG8653--Phase III study of childhood soft tissue sarcomas
U10CA-28383-12 0017 (CCI) BRECHER, MARTIN L Treatment of childhood cancer POG8625--Phase III combined therapy in childhood Hodgkin's disease
U10CA-28383-12 0018 (CCI) BRECHER, MARTIN L Treatment of childhood cancer POG8451--Intergroup rhabdomyosarcoma study
U10CA-28383-12 0019 (CCI) BRECHER, MARTIN L Treatment of childhood cancer POG9110--Rotational drug therapy after first marrow relapse of non-T, non B ALL
U10CA-28383-12 0020 (CCI) BRECHER, MARTIN L Treatment of childhood cancer POG9107--Phase II pilot study of infant leukemia
U10CA-28383-12 0021 (CCI) BRECHER, MARTIN L Treatment of childhood cancer POG9140--Phase II therapy for recurrent or refractory neuroblastoma
U10CA-28383-12 0022 (CCI) BRECHER, MARTIN L Treatment of childhood cancer POG9048--Phase II study of malignant germ cell tumors in children
U10CA-28383-12 0023 (CCI) BRECHER, MARTIN L Treatment of childhood cancer POG9060--Intensive QOD ifosfamide treatment for CNS tumors in children
U10CA-28383-12 0024 (CCI) BRECHER, MARTIN L Treatment of childhood cancer POG8936--Phase II study of carboplatin treatment for optic pathway tumors
U10CA-28383-12 0025 (CCI) BRECHER, MARTIN L Treatment of childhood cancer POG8935--Phase II study of surgery and/or radiotherapy for optic pathway tumors
U10CA-28383-12 0026 (CCI) BRECHER, MARTIN L Treatment of childhood cancer POG8820--Phase II/III study of VP-16, AMSA +/- 5-azacytidine in childhood ANLL
U10CA-28383-12 0027 (CCI) BRECHER, MARTIN L Treatment of childhood cancer POG8889--Intergroup rhabdomyosarcoma study for clinical group

IV disease
U10CA-28383-12 0028 (CCI) BRECHER, MARTIN L Treatment of childhood cancer POG8866--Phase II asparaginase therapy for acute lymphoblastic leukemia
U10CA-28383-12 0029 (CCI) BRECHER, MARTIN L Treatment of childhood cancer POG8862--Combination chemotherapy of acute T-lymphoblastic leukemia
U10CA-28383-12 0030 (CCI) BRECHER, MARTIN L Treatment of childhood cancer POG8863--Phase II study of high dose cytosine arabinoside in childhood tumors
U10CA-28383-12 0031 (CCI) BRECHER, MARTIN L Treatment of childhood cancer POG8827--Phase II treatment of children with Hodgkin's disease in relapse
U10CA-28383-12 0032 (CCI) BRECHER, MARTIN L Treatment of childhood cancer POG8865--Phase II recombinant alpha-interferon in relapsed T-cell disease
U10CA-28383-12 0033 (CCI) BRECHER, MARTIN L Treatment of childhood cancer--Phase II recombinant A-interferon in chronic myelogenous leukemia
U10CA-28383-12 0034 (CCI) BRECHER, MARTIN L Treatment of childhood cancer POG8832--Combination chemotherapy followed by radiotherapy for brain tumors
U10CA-28383-12 0035 (CCI) BRECHER, MARTIN L Treatment of childhood cancer POG8731--Phase II trial of methotrexate in treatment of brain tumors in children
U10CA-28383-12 0036 (CCI) BRECHER, MARTIN L Treatment of childhood cancer POG8788--Intergroup rhabdomyosarcoma study/pilot study for clinical group III
U10CA-28383-12 0037 (CCI) BRECHER, MARTIN L Treatment of childhood cancer POG8761--Phase II study of homoharringtonine therapy for nonlymphoblastic leukemi
U10CA-28383-12 0038 (CCI) BRECHER, MARTIN L Treatment of childhood cancer POG8739--Phase II immunotherapy with alpha-2 interferon for brain tumors
U10CA-28383-12 0039 (CCI) BRECHER, MARTIN L Treatment of childhood cancer POG8741--Treatment of patients with stage C and stage D neuroblastoma
U10CA-28383-12 0040 (CCI) BRECHER, MARTIN L Treatment of childhood cancer POG8751--Phase II methotrexate chemotherapy for rhabdomyosarcoma in children
U10CA-28383-12 0041 (CCI) BRECHER, MARTIN L Treatment of childhood cancer POG8633--Postoperative chemotherapy and delayed irradiation for brain tumors
U10CA-28383-12 0002 (CCI) BRECHER, MARTIN L Treatment of childhood cancer POG9005--Dose intensification of methotrexate & 6-mercaptourine in childhood ALL
U10CA-28383-12 0003 (CCI) BRECHER, MARTIN L Treatment of childhood cancer POG9031--Cisplatin/VP-16 therapy of medulloblastoma/pre vs. post irradiation
U10CA-28383-12 0004 (CCI) BRECHER, MARTIN L Treatment of childhood cancer POG8945--Phase III chemotherapy for hepatoblastoma & hepatocellular carcinoma
U10CA-28383-12 0005 (CCI) BRECHER, MARTIN L Treatment of childhood cancer POG9049--Phase III study of high-risk malignant germ cell tumors in children
U10CA-28383-12 0006 (CCI) BRECHER, MARTIN L Treatment of childhood cancer POG8844--Bone marrow transplant in children with stage D neuroblastoma
U10CA-28383-12 0007 (CCI) BRECHER, MARTIN L Treatment of childhood cancer POG8850--Phase III treatment of Ewing's sarcoma and neuroectodermal bone tumors
U10CA-28383-12 0008 (CCI) BRECHER, MARTIN L Treatment of childhood cancer POG8821--Phase III chemotherapy +/- autologous BMT in children with AML
U10CA-28383-12 0042 (CCI) BRECHER, MARTIN L Treatment of childhood cancer POG8617--Therapy for B-cell acute lymphoblastic leukemia and lymphoma
U10CA-28383-12 0043 (CCI) BRECHER, MARTIN L Treatment of childhood cancer POG9139--Phase I study of cisplatin and irradiation in brain stem gliomas
U10CA-28383-12 0044 (CCI) BRECHER, MARTIN L Treatment of childhood cancer POG9079--Phase I study of L-PAM/CTX with ABM rescue for brain tumors in children
U10CA-28383-12 0045 (CCI) BRECHER, MARTIN L Treatment of childhood cancer POG9075--Phase I study of acivicin in children with solid tumors
U10CA-28383-12 0009 (CCI) BRECHER, MARTIN L Treatment of childhood cancer POG8725--Phase III chemotherapy +/- radiation therapy in pediatric Hodgkins
U10CA-28383-12 0010 (CCI) BRECHER, MARTIN L Treatment of childhood cancer POG8704--Phase III chemotherapy of childhood T cell ALL & lymphoblastic lymphoma
U10CA-28383-12 0011 (CCI) BRECHER, MARTIN L Treatment of childhood cancer POG8719--Phase III chemotherapy for non-Hodgkin's lymphoma in children
U10CA-28383-12 0012 (CCI) BRECHER, MARTIN L Treatment of childhood cancer POG8650--National Wilm's tumor and clear cell sarcoma study
U10CA-28383-12 0013 (CCI) BRECHER, MARTIN L Treatment of childhood cancer POG8616--Phase III chemotherapy for childhood Burkitt and non-Burkitts lymphoma
U10CA-28439-12 0017 (CCI) KUNG, FAITH H Pediatric oncology group POG8625--Phase III combined therapy in childhood Hodgkin's disease
U10CA-28439-12 0018 (CCI) KUNG, FAITH H Pediatric oncology group POG8451--Intergroup rhabdomyosarcoma study
U10CA-28439-12 0019 (CCI) KUNG, FAITH H Pediatric oncology group POG9110--Rotational drug therapy after first marrow relapse of non-T, non B ALL
U10CA-28439-12 0020 (CCI) KUNG, FAITH H Pediatric oncology group POG9107--Phase II pilot study of infant leukemia
U10CA-28439-12 0021 (CCI) KUNG, FAITH H Pediatric oncology group POG9140--Phase II therapy for recurrent or refractory neuroblastoma
U10CA-28439-12 0022 (CCI) KUNG, FAITH H Pediatric oncology group POG9048--Phase II study of malignant germ cell tumors in children
U10CA-28439-12 0023 (CCI) KUNG, FAITH H Pediatric oncology group POG9060--Intensive COD ifosfamide treatment for CNS tumors in children
U10CA-28439-12 0024 (CCI) KUNG, FAITH H Pediatric oncology group POG8936--Phase II study of carboplatin treatment for optic pathway tumors
U10CA-28439-12 0025 (CCI) KUNG, FAITH H Pediatric oncology group POG8935--Phase II study of surgery and/or radiotherapy for optic pathway tumors
U10CA-28439-12 0026 (CCI) KUNG, FAITH H Pediatric oncology group POG8820--Phase II/III study of VP-16, AMSA +/- 5-azacytidine in childhood ANLL
U10CA-28439-12 0027 (CCI) KUNG, FAITH H Pediatric oncology group POG8889--Intergroup rhabdomyosarcoma study for clinical group IV disease
U10CA-28439-12 0028 (CCI) KUNG, FAITH H Pediatric oncology group POG8866--Phase II asparaginase therapy for acute lymphoblastic leukemia
U10CA-28439-12 0029 (CCI) KUNG, FAITH H Pediatric oncology group POG8862--Combination chemotherapy of acute T-lymphoblastic leukemia
U10CA-28439-12 0030 (CCI) KUNG, FAITH H Pediatric oncology group POG8863--Phase II study of high dose cytosine arabinoside in childhood tumors
U10CA-28439-12 0031 (CCI) KUNG, FAITH H Pediatric oncology group POG8827--Phase II treatment of children with Hodgkin's disease in relapse
U10CA-28439-12 0032 (CCI) KUNG, FAITH H Pediatric oncology group POG8865--Phase II recombinant alpha-interferon in relapsed T-cell disease
U10CA-28439-12 0033 (CCI) KUNG, FAITH H Pediatric oncology group--Phase II recombinant A-interferon in chronic myelogenous leukemia
U10CA-28439-12 0034 (CCI) KUNG, FAITH H Pediatric oncology group POG8832--Combination chemotherapy followed by radiotherapy for brain tumors
U10CA-28439-12 0035 (CCI) KUNG, FAITH H Pediatric oncology group POG8731--Phase II trial of methotrexate in treatment of brain tumors in children
U10CA-28439-12 0036 (CCI) KUNG, FAITH H Pediatric oncology group POG8788--Intergroup rhabdomyosarcoma study/pilot study for clinical group III
U10CA-28439-12 0037 (CCI) KUNG, FAITH H Pediatric oncology group POG8761--Phase II study of homoharringtonine therapy for nonlymphoblastic leukemi
U10CA-28439-12 0038 (CCI) KUNG, FAITH H Pediatric oncology group POG8739--Phase II immunotherapy with alpha-2 interferon for brain tumors (human)e
U10CA-28439-12 0039 (CCI) KUNG, FAITH H Pediatric oncology group POG8741--Treatment of patients with stage C and stage D neuroblastoma
U10CA-28439-12 0040 (CCI) KUNG, FAITH H Pediatric oncology group POG8751--Phase II methotrexate chemotherapy for rhabdomyosarcoma in children
U10CA-28439-12 0041 (CCI) KUNG, FAITH H Pediatric oncology group POG8633--Postoperative chemotherapy and delayed irradiation for brain tumors
U10CA-28439-12 0042 (CCI) KUNG, FAITH H Pediatric oncology group POG8617--Therapy for B-cell acute lymphoblastic leukemia and lymphoma
U10CA-28439-12 0043 (CCI) KUNG, FAITH H Pediatric oncology group POG9139--Phase I study of cisplatin and irradiation in brain stem gliomas
U10CA-28439-12 0044 (CCI) KUNG, FAITH H Pediatric oncology group POG9079--Phase I study of L-PAM/CTX with ABM rescue for brain tumors in children
U10CA-28439-12 0045 (CCI) KUNG, FAITH H Pediatric oncology group POG9075--Phase I study of acivicin in children with solid tumors
U10CA-28439-12 0046 (CCI) KUNG, FAITH H Pediatric oncology group POG9074--Phase I study of xomazyme-H65 in children with T-cell ALL/lymphoma
U10CA-28439-12 0047 (CCI) KUNG, FAITH H Pediatric oncology group POG9072--Phase I chemotherapy for recurrent/resistant malignant solid tumors
U10CA-28439-12 0048 (CCI) KUNG, FAITH H Pediatric oncology group POG9061-Phase II systemic therapy and irradiation for ALL & CNS leukemia
U10CA-28439-12 (CCI) KUNG, FAITH H UNIV OF CALIFORNIA, SAN DIEGO LA JOLLA, CA 92093 Pediatric oncology group
U10CA-28439-12 0049 (CCI) KUNG, FAITH H Pediatric oncology group POG 9086--Phase I pilot study of therapy for T-cell ALL or NHL
U10CA-28439-12 0050 (CCI) KUNG, FAITH H Pediatric oncology group POG9071--Phase I trial of fazarabine in children with acute leukemia
U10CA-28439-12 0051 (CCI) KUNG, FAITH H Pediatric oncology group POG8970--Phase I trial of fazarabine in children with refractory solid tumors
U10CA-28439-12 0052 (CCI) KUNG, FAITH H Pediatric oncology group POG8973--Etoposide (VP-16) and carboplatin in children with acute leukemia
U10CA-28439-12 0053 (CCI) KUNG, FAITH H Pediatric oncology group POG8870--Phase I trial of ifosfamide/VP16/MESNA in children with acute leukemia
U10CA-28439-12 0054 (CCI) KUNG, FAITH H Pediatric oncology group POG8871--Phase I study of rTNF in children with refractory solid tumors
U10CA-28439-12 0055 (CCI) KUNG, FAITH H Pediatric oncology group POG8671--Phase I immunotherapy with rIL-2 in children with solid tumors
U10CA-28439-12 0056 (CCI) KUNG, FAITH H Pediatric oncology group POG8494--Phase I study of fludarabine phosphate in pediatric patients
U10CA-28439-12 0057 (CCI) KUNG, FAITH H Pediatric oncology group POG8930--A comprehensive genetic analysis of brain tumors
U10CA-28439-12 0058 (CCI) KUNG, FAITH H Pediatric oncology group POG8828--Late effects of Hodgkin's disease
U10CA-28439-12 0059 (CCI) KUNG, FAITH H Pediatric oncology group POG9046--Molecular genetic analysis of Wilm's tumors
U10CA-28439-12 0060 (CCI) KUNG, FAITH H Pediatric oncology group

PROJECT NO., ORGANIZATIONAL UNIT., INVESTIGATOR, ADDRESS, TITLE

POG9153--Rhabdomyosarcoma study/laboratory evaluation of tumor
U10CA-28439-12 0001 (CCI) KUNG, FAITH H Pediatric oncology group POG9006--6-MP/methotrexate vs. alternating chemotheray for ALL in childhood
U10CA-28439-12 0002 (CCI) KUNG, FAITH H Pediatric oncology group POG9005--Dose intensification of methotrexate & 6-mercaptourine in childhood ALL
U10CA-28439-12 0003 (CCI) KUNG, FAITH H Pediatric oncology group POG9031--Cisplatin/VP-16 therapy of medulloblastoma/pre vs. post irradiation
U10CA-28439-12 0004 (CCI) KUNG, FAITH H Pediatric oncology group POG8945--Phase III chemotherapy for hepatoblastoma & hepatocellular carcinoma
U10CA-28439-12 0005 (CCI) KUNG, FAITH H Pediatric oncology group POG9049--Phase III study of high-risk malignant germ cell tumors in children
U10CA-28439-12 0006 (CCI) KUNG, FAITH H Pediatric oncology group POG8844--Bone marrow transplant in children with stage D neuroblastoma
U10CA-28439-12 0007 (CCI) KUNG, FAITH H Pediatric oncology group POG8850--Phase III treatment of Ewing's sarcoma and neuroectodermal bone tumors
U10CA-28439-12 0008 (CCI) KUNG, FAITH H Pediatric oncology group POG8821--Phase III chemotherapy +/- autologous BMT in children with AML
U10CA-28439-12 0009 (CCI) KUNG, FAITH H Pediatric oncology group POG8725--Phase III chemotherapy +/- radiation therapy in pediatric Hodgkins
U10CA-28439-12 0010 (CCI) KUNG, FAITH H Pediatric oncology group POG8704--Phase III chemotherapy of childhood T cell ALL & lymphoblastic lymphoma
U10CA-28439-12 0011 (CCI) KUNG, FAITH H Pediatric oncology group POG8719--Phase III chemotherapy for non-Hodgkin's lymphoma in children
U10CA-28439-12 0012 (CCI) KUNG, FAITH H Pediatric oncology group POG8650--National Wilm's tumor and clear cell sarcoma study
U10CA-28439-12 0013 (CCI) KUNG, FAITH H Pediatric oncology group POG8616--Phase III chemotherapy for childhood Burkitt and non-Burkitts lymphoma
U10CA-28439-12 0014 (CCI) KUNG, FAITH H Pediatric oncology group POG8615--Phase III study of large cell lymphomas in children and adolescents
U10CA-28439-12 0015 (CCI) KUNG, FAITH H Pediatric oncology group POG8651--Phase III study of childhood nonmetastatic osteosarcoma
U10CA-28439-12 0016 (CCI) KUNG, FAITH H Pediatric oncology group POG8653--Phase III study of childhood soft tissue sarcomas
R01CA-28471-12 (MEP) DVORAK, HAROLD F BETH ISRAEL HOSPITAL 330 BROOKLINE AVENUE BOSTON, MA 02215 Biology of solid & ascites tumor growth
R01CA-28473-11 (VR) HAYWARD, GARY S 725 N. WOLFE STREET BALTIMORE, MD 21205 Cellular transformation by DNA of human herpesvirus
U10CA-28476-12 (CCI) LEVENTHAL, BRIGID G JOHNS HOPKINS UNIVERSITY 550 N. BROADWAY, SUITE 1121 BALTIMORE, MD 21205 Pediatric oncology group membership
U10CA-28476-12 0018 (CCI) LEVENTHAL, BRIGID G Pediatric oncology group membership POG8451--Intergroup rhabdomyosarcoma study
U10CA-28476-12 0019 (CCI) LEVENTHAL, BRIGID G Pediatric oncology group membership POG9110--Rotational drug therapy after first marrow relapse of non-T, non B ALL
U10CA-28476-12 0020 (CCI) LEVENTHAL, BRIGID G Pediatric oncology group membership POG9107--Phase II pilot study of infant leukemia
U10CA-28476-12 0021 (CCI) LEVENTHAL, BRIGID G Pediatric oncology group membership POG9140--Phase II therapy for recurrent or refractory neuroblastoma
U10CA-28476-12 0022 (CCI) LEVENTHAL, BRIGID G Pediatric oncology group membership POG9048--Phase II study of malignant germ cell tumors in children
U10CA-28476-12 0023 (CCI) LEVENTHAL, BRIGID G Pediatric oncology group membership POG9060--Intensive QOD ifosfamide treatment for CNS tumors in children
U10CA-28476-12 0024 (CCI) LEVENTHAL, BRIGID G Pediatric oncology group membership POG8936--Phase II study of carboplatin treatment for optic pathway tumors
U10CA-28476-12 0025 (CCI) LEVENTHAL, BRIGID G Pediatric oncology group membership POG8935--Phase II study of surgery and/or radiotherapy for optic pathway tumors
U10CA-28476-12 0026 (CCI) LEVENTHAL, BRIGID G Pediatric oncology group membership POG8820--Phase II/III study of VP-16, AMSA +/- 5-azacytidine in childhood ANLL
U10CA-28476-12 0027 (CCI) LEVENTHAL, BRIGID G Pediatric oncology group membership POG8889--Intergroup rhabdomyosarcoma study for clinical group IV disease
U10CA-28476-12 0028 (CCI) LEVENTHAL, BRIGID G Pediatric oncology group membership POG8866--Phase II asparaginase therapy for acute lymphoblastic leukemia
U10CA-28476-12 0029 (CCI) LEVENTHAL, BRIGID G Pediatric oncology group membership POG8862--Combination chemotherapy of acute T-lymphoblastic leukemia
U10CA-28476-12 0030 (CCI) LEVENTHAL, BRIGID G Pediatric oncology group membership POG8863--Phase II study of high dose cytosine arabinoside in childhood tumors
U10CA-28476-12 0031 (CCI) LEVENTHAL, BRIGID G Pediatric oncology group membership POG8827--Phase II treatment of children with Hodgkin's disease in relapse
U10CA-28476-12 0032 (CCI) LEVENTHAL, BRIGID G Pediatric oncology group membership POG8865--Phase II recombinant alpha-interferon in relapsed T-cell disease
U10CA-28476-12 0033 (CCI) LEVENTHAL, BRIGID G Pediatric oncology group--Phase II recombinant A-interferon in chronic myelogenous leukemia
U10CA-28476-12 0034 (CCI) LEVENTHAL, BRIGID G Pediatric oncology group membership POG8832--Combination chemotherapy followed by radiotherapy for brain tumors
U10CA-28476-12 0035 (CCI) LEVENTHAL, BRIGID G Pediatric oncology group membership POG8731--Phase II trial of methotrexate in treatment of brain tumors in children
U10CA-28476-12 0036 (CCI) LEVENTHAL, BRIGID G Pediatric oncology group membership POG8788--Intergroup rhabdomyosarcoma study/pilot study for clinical group III
U10CA-28476-12 0037 (CCI) LEVENTHAL, BRIGID G Pediatric oncology group membership POG8761--Phase II study of homoharringtonine therapy for nonlymphoblastic leukemi
U10CA-28476-12 0038 (CCI) LEVENTHAL, BRIGID G Pediatric oncology group membership POG8739--Phase II immunotherapy with alpha-2 interferon for brain tumors
U10CA-28476-12 0039 (CCI) LEVENTHAL, BRIGID G Pediatric oncology group membership POG8741--Treatment of patients with stage C and stage D neuroblastoma
U10CA-28476-12 0040 (CCI) LEVENTHAL, BRIGID G Pediatric oncology group membership POG8751--Phase II methotrexate chemotherapy for rhabdomyosarcoma in children
U10CA-28476-12 0041 (CCI) LEVENTHAL, BRIGID G Pediatric oncology group membership POG8633--Postoperative chemotherapy and delayed irradiation for brain tumors
U10CA-28476-12 0042 (CCI) LEVENTHAL, BRIGID G Pediatric oncology group membership POG8617--Therapy for B-cell acute lymphoblastic leukemia and lymphoma
U10CA-28476-12 0043 (CCI) LEVENTHAL, BRIGID G Pediatric oncology group membership POG9139--Phase I study of cisplatin and irradiation in brain stem gliomas
U10CA-28476-12 0044 (CCI) LEVENTHAL, BRIGID G Pediatric oncology group membership POG9079--Phase I study of L-PAM/CTX with ABM rescue for brain tumors in children
U10CA-28476-12 0045 (CCI) LEVENTHAL, BRIGID G Pediatric oncology group membership POG9075--Phase I study of acivicin in children with solid tumors
U10CA-28476-12 0046 (CCI) LEVENTHAL, BRIGID G Pediatric oncology group membership POG9074--Phase I study of xomazyme-H65 in children with T-cell ALL/lymphoma
U10CA-28476-12 0047 (CCI) LEVENTHAL, BRIGID G Pediatric oncology group membership POG9072--Phase I chemotherapy for recurrent/resistant malignant solid tumors
U10CA-28476-12 0048 (CCI) LEVENTHAL, BRIGID G Pediatric oncology group membership POG9061-Phase II systemic therapy and irradiation for ALL & CNS leukemia
U10CA-28476-12 0049 (CCI) LEVENTHAL, BRIGID G Pediatric oncology group membership POG 9086--Phase I pilot study of therapy for T-cell ALL or NHL
U10CA-28476-12 0001 (CCI) LEVENTHAL, BRIGID G Pediatric oncology group membership POG9006--6-MP/methotrexate vs. alternating chemotherapy for ALL in childhood
U10CA-28476-12 0050 (CCI) LEVENTHAL, BRIGID G Pediatric oncology group membership POG9071--Phase I trial of fazarabine in children with acute leukemia
U10CA-28476-12 0051 (CCI) LEVENTHAL, BRIGID G Pediatric oncology group membership POG8970--Phase I trial of fazarabine in children with refractory solid tumors
U10CA-28476-12 0052 (CCI) LEVENTHAL, BRIGID G Pediatric oncology group membership POG8973--Etoposide (VP-16) and carboplatin in children with acute leukemia
U10CA-28476-12 0053 (CCI) LEVENTHAL, BRIGID G Pediatric oncology group membership POG8870--Phase I trial of ifosfamide/VP16/MESNA in children with acute leukemia
U10CA-28476-12 0054 (CCI) LEVENTHAL, BRIGID G Pediatric oncology group membership POG8871--Phase I study of rTNF in children with refractory solid tumors
U10CA-28476-12 0055 (CCI) LEVENTHAL, BRIGID G Pediatric oncology group membership POG8671--Phase I immunotherapy with rIL-2 in children with solid tumors
U10CA-28476-12 0056 (CCI) LEVENTHAL, BRIGID G Pediatric oncology group membership POG8494--Phase I study of fludarabine phosphate in pediatric patients
U10CA-28476-12 0057 (CCI) LEVENTHAL, BRIGID G Pediatric oncology group membership POG8930--A comprehensive genetic analysis of brain tumors
U10CA-28476-12 0058 (CCI) LEVENTHAL, BRIGID G Pediatric oncology group membership POG8828--Late effects of Hodgkin's disease
U10CA-28476-12 0059 (CCI) LEVENTHAL, BRIGID G Pediatric oncology group membership POG9046--Molecular genetic analysis of Wilm's tumors
U10CA-28476-12 0060 (CCI) LEVENTHAL, BRIGID G Pediatric oncology group membership POG9153--Rhabdomyosarcoma study/laboratory evaluation of tumor
U10CA-28476-12 0002 (CCI) LEVENTHAL, BRIGID G Pediatric oncology group membership POG9005--Dose intensification of methotrexate & 6-mercaptopurine in childhood ALL
U10CA-28476-12 0003 (CCI) LEVENTHAL, BRIGID G Pediatric oncology group membership POG9031--Cisplatin/VP-16 therapy of medulloblastoma/pre vs. post irradiation
U10CA-28476-12 0004 (CCI) LEVENTHAL, BRIGID G Pediatric oncology group membership POG8945--Phase III chemotherapy for hepatoblastoma & hepatocellular carcinoma
U10CA-28476-12 0005 (CCI) LEVENTHAL, BRIGID G Pediatric oncology group membership POG9049--Phase III study of high-risk malignant germ cell tumors in children
U10CA-28476-12 0006 (CCI) LEVENTHAL, BRIGID G Pediatric oncology group membership POG8844--Bone marrow transplant in children with stage D neuroblastoma
U10CA-28476-12 0007 (CCI) LEVENTHAL, BRIGID G Pediatric oncology group membership POG8850--Phase III treatment of Ewing's sarcoma and neuroectodermal bone tumors
U10CA-28476-12 0008 (CCI) LEVENTHAL, BRIGID G Pediatric oncology group membership POG8821--Phase III chemotherapy +/- autologous BMT in children with AML
U10CA-28476-12 0009 (CCI) LEVENTHAL, BRIGID G Pediatric oncology group membership POG8725--Phase III chemotherapy +/- radiation therapy in pediatric Hodgkins
U10CA-28476-12 0010 (CCI) LEVENTHAL, BRIGID G Pediatric oncology

group membership POG8704–Phase III chemotherapy of childhood T cell ALL & lymphoblastic lymphoma
U10CA-28476-12 0011 (CCI) LEVENTHAL, BRIGID G Pediatric oncology group membership POG8719–Phase III chemotherapy for non-Hodgkin's lymphoma in children
U10CA-28476-12 0012 (CCI) LEVENTHAL, BRIGID G Pediatric oncology group membership POG8650–National Wilm's tumor and clear cell sarcoma study
U10CA-28476-12 0013 (CCI) LEVENTHAL, BRIGID G Pediatric oncology group membership POG8616–Phase III chemotherapy for childhood Burkitt and non-Burkitts lymphoma
U10CA-28476-12 0014 (CCI) LEVENTHAL, BRIGID G Pediatric oncology group membership POG8615–Phase III study of large cell lymphomas in children and adolescents
U10CA-28476-12 0015 (CCI) LEVENTHAL, BRIGID G Pediatric oncology group membership POG8651–Phase III study of childhood nonmetastatic osteosarcoma
U10CA-28476-12 0016 (CCI) LEVENTHAL, BRIGID G Pediatric oncology group membership POG8653–Phase III study of childhood soft tissue sarcomas
U10CA-28476-12 0017 (CCI) LEVENTHAL, BRIGID G Pediatric oncology group membership POG8625–Phase III combined therapy in childhood Hodgkin's disease
R01CA-28495-10 (ET) BEERMAN, TERRY A ROSWELL PARK CANCER INSTITUTE ELM & CARLTON ST BUFFALO, NY 14263 Mechanism of action of DNA-reactive antitumor drugs
U10CA-28530-12 (CCI) MAURER, HAROLD M MEDICAL COLLEGE OF VIRGINIA MCV STATION BOX 646 RICHMOND, VA 23298 Pediatric Oncology Group
R01CA-28533-12 (IMB) RUSSELL, JOHN H WASHINGTON UNIVERSITY MED SCH 660 SOUTH EUCLID ST. LOUIS, MO 63110 Mechanisms of tumor destruction by immune effectors
R01CA-28548-11 (CBY) JOHNSON, ROSS G UNIVERSITY OF MINNESOTA 1445 GORTNER AVENUE ST PAUL, MN 55108-1095 Developing immunological probes for gap junctions
U10CA-28572-10S1 (CCI) MAYBEE, DAVID A WALTER REED ARMY MEDICAL CTR WASHINGTON, DC 20307-5001 Support of Southwest oncology group studies, WRAMS
R01CA-28595-10 (ET) BIEDLER, JUNE L SLOAN-KETTERING INST/CNCR RES 1275 YORK AVENUE NEW YORK, N Y 10021 Cellular concomitants of vincristine resistance
R01CA-28596-11 (ET) PLUNKETT, WILLIAM K UT MD ANDERSON CANCER CTR 1515 HOLCOMBE BLVD HOUSTON, TX 77030 Biochemical basis for therapeutic activity
R37CA-28681-12 (BIO) TOMASZ, MARIA HUNTER COLLEGE OF CUNY 695 PARK AVE NEW YORK, NY 10021 Adducts of mitomycin C with nucleotides
R01CA-28704-12 (PTHA) DARZYNKIEWICZ, ZBIGNIEW NEW YORK MED COLL AT VALHALLA 100 GRASSLANDS RD ELMSFORD, NY 10523 Probes for flow cytometry
R01CA-28711-10 (MGN) ADAIR, GERALD M SCIENCE PARK-RESEARCH DIVISION PO BOX 389 SMITHVILLE, TX 78957 Expression of genetic variation in cultured cells
R01CA-28725-11 (BIO) SCHUSTER, SHELDON M UNIVERSITY OF FLORIDA J HILLIS MILLER HLTH CTR GAINESVILLE, FL 32610 Asparagine biosynthesis in normal and tumor cells
R01CA-28771-12 (SSS) BARLOGIE, BART UNIVERSITY OF ARKANSAS MED SCI 4301 WEST MARKHAM LITTLE ROCK, AR 72205 Heterogencity of malignant lymphoma/human
R01CA-28783-12 (ET) DE GRAW, JOSEPH I SRI INTERNATIONAL 333 RAVENSWOOD AVENUE MENLO PARK, CA 94025 Deaza analogs of folic acid and methotrexate
R01CA-28824-12 (MCHA) DANISHEFSKY, SAMUEL J YALE UNIVERSITY 225 PROSPECT STREET NEW HAVEN, CT 06511-8118 The synthesis of antitumor natural products
R37CA-28825-12 (NSS) BAIRD, WILLIAM M PURDUE UNIVERSITY ROBERT HEINE PHARMACY BUILDING WEST LAFAYETTE, IN 47907 Modifiers of chemical carcinogenesis in cell culture
R01CA-28834-12 (CPA) DVORAK, ANN M BETH ISRAEL HOSPITAL 330 BROOKLINE AVENUE BOSTON, MA 02215 Basophil/mast cell function
U10CA-28837-11 (SRC) DIMITROV, NIKOLAY V MICHIGAN STATE UNIVERSITY B220 LIFE SCIENCES BLDG EAST LANSING, MI 48824-1317 Primary cancer therapy (NSABP)
U10CA-28841-11 (CCI) VATS, TRIBHAWAN S UNIV OF KANSAS MED CTR 39TH & RAINBOW BLVD. RM 3032 D KANSAS CITY, KS 66103-8410 Pediatric Oncology Group studies
U10CA-28841-11 0004 (CCI) VATS, TRIBHAWAN S Pediatric Oncology Group studies POG8945–Phase III chemotherapy for hepatoblastoma & hepatocellular carcinoma
U10CA-28841-11 0005 (CCI) VATS, TRIBHAWAN S Pediatric Oncology Group studies POG9049–Phase III study of high-risk malignant germ cell tumors in children
U10CA-28841-11 0006 (CCI) VATS, TRIBHAWAN S Pediatric Oncology Group studies POG8844–Bone marrow transplant in children with stage D neuroblastoma
U10CA-28841-11 0007 (CCI) VATS, TRIBHAWAN S Pediatric Oncology Group studies POG8850–Phase III treatment of Ewing's sarcoma and neuroectodermal bone tumors
U10CA-28841-11 0008 (CCI) VATS, TRIBHAWAN S Pediatric Oncology Group studies POG8821–Phase III chemotherapy +/- autologous BMT in children with AML
U10CA-28841-11 0009 (CCI) VATS, TRIBHAWAN S Pediatric Oncology Group studies POG8725–Phase III chemotherapy +/- radiation therapy in pediatric Hodgkins
U10CA-28841-11 0010 (CCI) VATS, TRIBHAWAN S Pediatric Oncology Group studies POG8704–Phase III chemotherapy of childhood T cell ALL & lymphoblastic lymphoma
U10CA-28841-11 0011 (CCI) VATS, TRIBHAWAN S Pediatric Oncology Group studies POG8719–Phase III chemotherapy for non-Hodgkin's lymphoma in children
U10CA-28841-11 0012 (CCI) VATS, TRIBHAWAN S Pediatric Oncology Group studies POG8650–National Wilm's tumor and clear cell sarcoma study
U10CA-28841-11 0013 (CCI) VATS, TRIBHAWAN S Pediatric Oncology

PROJECT NO., ORGANIZATIONAL UNIT., INVESTIGATOR, ADDRESS, TITLE

Group studies POG8616–Phase III chemotherapy for childhood Burkitt and non-Burkitts lymphoma
U10CA-28841-11 0014 (CCI) VATS, TRIBHAWAN S Pediatric Oncology Group studies POG8615–Phase III study of large cell lymphomas in children and adolescents
U10CA-28841-11 0015 (CCI) VATS, TRIBHAWAN S Pediatric Oncology Group studies POG8651–Phase III study of childhood nonmetastatic osteosarcoma
U10CA-28841-11 0016 (CCI) VATS, TRIBHAWAN S Pediatric Oncology Group studies POG8653–Phase III study of childhood soft tissue sarcomas
U10CA-28841-11 0017 (CCI) VATS, TRIBHAWAN S Pediatric Oncology Group studies POG8625–Phase III combined therapy in childhood Hodgkin's disease
U10CA-28841-11 0018 (CCI) VATS, TRIBHAWAN S Pediatric Oncology Group studies POG8451–Intergroup rhabdomyosarcoma study
U10CA-28841-11 0019 (CCI) VATS, TRIBHAWAN S Pediatric Oncology Group studies POG9110–Rotational drug therapy after first marrow relapse of non-T, non B ALL
U10CA-28841-11 0020 (CCI) VATS, TRIBHAWAN S Pediatric Oncology Group studies POG9107–Phase II pilot study of infant leukemia
U10CA-28841-11 0021 (CCI) VATS, TRIBHAWAN S Pediatric Oncology Group studies POG9140–Phase II therapy for recurrent or refractory neuroblastoma
U10CA-28841-11 0022 (CCI) VATS, TRIBHAWAN S Pediatric Oncology Group studies POG9048–Phase II study of malignant germ cell tumors in children
U10CA-28841-11 0023 (CCI) VATS, TRIBHAWAN S Pediatric Oncology Group studies POG9060–Intensive QOD ifosfamide treatment for CNS tumors in children
U10CA-28841-11 0024 (CCI) VATS, TRIBHAWAN S Pediatric Oncology Group studies POG8936–Phase II study of carboplatin treatment for optic pathway tumors
U10CA-28841-11 0025 (CCI) VATS, TRIBHAWAN S Pediatric Oncology Group studies POG8935–Phase II study of surgery and/or radiotherapy for optic pathway tumors
U10CA-28841-11 0026 (CCI) VATS, TRIBHAWAN S Pediatric Oncology Group studies POG8820–Phase II/III study of VP-16, AMSA +/- 5-azacytidine in childhood ANLL
U10CA-28841-11 0027 (CCI) VATS, TRIBHAWAN S Pediatric Oncology Group studies POG8889–Intergroup rhabdomyosarcoma study for clinical group IV disease
U10CA-28841-11 0028 (CCI) VATS, TRIBHAWAN S Pediatric Oncology Group studies POG8866–Phase II asparaginase therapy for acute lymphoblastic leukemia
U10CA-28841-11 0029 (CCI) VATS, TRIBHAWAN S Pediatric Oncology Group studies POG8862–Combination chemotherapy of acute T-lymphoblastic leukemia
U10CA-28841-11 0030 (CCI) VATS, TRIBHAWAN S Pediatric Oncology Group studies POG8863–Phase II study of high dose cytosine arabinoside in childhood tumors
U10CA-28841-11 0031 (CCI) VATS, TRIBHAWAN S Pediatric Oncology Group studies POG8827–Phase II treatment of children with Hodgkin's disease in relapse
U10CA-28841-11 0032 (CCI) VATS, TRIBHAWAN S Pediatric Oncology Group studies POG8865–Phase II recombinant alpha-interferon in relapsed T-cell disease
U10CA-28841-11 0033 (CCI) VATS, TRIBHAWAN S Pediatric Oncology Group–Phase II recombinant A-interferon in chronic myelogenous leukemia
U10CA-28841-11 0034 (CCI) VATS, TRIBHAWAN S Pediatric Oncology Group studies POG8832–Combination chemotherapy followed by radiotherapy for brain tumors
U10CA-28841-11 0035 (CCI) VATS, TRIBHAWAN S Pediatric Oncology Group studies POG8731–Phase II trial of methotrexate in treatment of brain tumors in children
U10CA-28841-11 0001 (CCI) VATS, TRIBHAWAN S Pediatric Oncology Group studies POG9006–6-MP/methotrexate vs. alternating chemotherapy for ALL in childhood
U10CA-28841-11 0036 (CCI) VATS, TRIBHAWAN S Pediatric Oncology Group studies POG8788–Intergroup rhabdomyosarcoma study/pilot study for clinical group III
U10CA-28841-11 0037 (CCI) VATS, TRIBHAWAN S Pediatric Oncology Group studies POG8761–Phase II study of homoharringtonine therapy for nonlymphoblastic leukemi
U10CA-28841-11 0038 (CCI) VATS, TRIBHAWAN S Pediatric Oncology Group studies POG8739–Phase II immunotherapy with alpha-2 interferon for brain tumors
U10CA-28841-11 0039 (CCI) VATS, TRIBHAWAN S Pediatric Oncology Group studies POG8741–Treatment of patients with stage C and stage D neuroblastoma
U10CA-28841-11 0040 (CCI) VATS, TRIBHAWAN S Pediatric Oncology Group studies POG8751–Phase II methotrexate chemotherapy for rhabdomyosarcoma in children
U10CA-28841-11 0041 (CCI) VATS, TRIBHAWAN S Pediatric Oncology Group studies POG8633–Postoperative chemotherapy and delayed irradiation for brain tumors
U10CA-28841-11 0042 (CCI) VATS, TRIBHAWAN S Pediatric Oncology Group studies POG8617–Therapy for B-cell acute lymphoblastic leukemia and lymphoma
U10CA-28841-11 0043 (CCI) VATS, TRIBHAWAN S Pediatric Oncology Group studies POG9139–Phase I study of cisplatin and irradiation in brain stem gliomas
U10CA-28841-11 0044 (CCI) VATS, TRIBHAWAN S Pediatric Oncology Group studies POG9079–Phase I study of L-PAM/CTX with ABM rescue for brain tumors in children
U10CA-28841-11 0045 (CCI) VATS, TRIBHAWAN S Pediatric Oncology Group studies POG9075–Phase I study of acivicin in children with solid tumors
U10CA-28841-11 0046 (CCI) VATS, TRIBHAWAN S Pediatric Oncology Group studies POG9074–Phase I study of xomazyme-H65 in children with T-cell ALL/lymphoma
U10CA-28841-11 0047 (CCI) VATS, TRIBHAWAN S Pediatric Oncology

PROJECT NO., ORGANIZATIONAL UNIT., INVESTIGATOR, ADDRESS, TITLE

Group studies POG9072--Phase I chemotherapy for recurrent/resistant malignant solid tumors

U10CA-28841-11 0048 (CCI) VATS, TRIBHAWAN S Pediatric Oncology Group studies POG9061-Phase II systemic therapy and irradiation for ALL & CNS leukemia

U10CA-28841-11 0049 (CCI) VATS, TRIBHAWAN S Pediatric Oncology Group studies POG 9086--Phase I pilot study of therapy for T-cell ALL or NHL

U10CA-28841-11 0050 (CCI) VATS, TRIBHAWAN S Pediatric Oncology Group studies POG9071--Phase I trial of fazarabine in children with acute leukemia

U10CA-28841-11 0051 (CCI) VATS, TRIBHAWAN S Pediatric Oncology Group studies POG8970--Phase I trial of fazarabine in children with refractory solid tumors

U10CA-28841-11 0052 (CCI) VATS, TRIBHAWAN S Pediatric Oncology Group studies POG8973--Etoposide (VP-16) and carboplatin in children with acute leukemia

U10CA-28841-11 0053 (CCI) VATS, TRIBHAWAN S Pediatric Oncology Group studies POG8870--Phase I trial of ifosfamide/VP16/MESNA in children with acute leukemia

U10CA-28841-11 0054 (CCI) VATS, TRIBHAWAN S Pediatric Oncology Group studies POG8871--Phase I study of rTNF in children with refractory solid tumors

U10CA-28841-11 0055 (CCI) VATS, TRIBHAWAN S Pediatric Oncology Group studies POG8671--Phase I immunotherapy with rIL-2 in children with solid tumors

U10CA-28841-11 0056 (CCI) VATS, TRIBHAWAN S Pediatric Oncology Group studies POG8494--Phase I study of fludarabine phosphate in pediatric patients

U10CA-28841-11 0057 (CCI) VATS, TRIBHAWAN S Pediatric Oncology Group studies POG8930--A comprehensive genetic analysis of brain tumors

U10CA-28841-11 0058 (CCI) VATS, TRIBHAWAN S Pediatric Oncology Group studies POG8828--Late effects of Hodgkin's disease

U10CA-28841-11 0059 (CCI) VATS, TRIBHAWAN S Pediatric Oncology Group studies POG9046--Molecular genetic analysis of Wilm's tumors

U10CA-28841-11 0060 (CCI) VATS, TRIBHAWAN S Pediatric Oncology Group studies POG9153--Rhabdomyosarcoma study/laboratory evaluation of tumor

U10CA-28841-11 0002 (CCI) VATS, TRIBHAWAN S Pediatric Oncology Group studies POG9005--Dose intensification of methotrexate& 6-mercaptopurine for childhood ALL

U10CA-28841-11 0003 (CCI) VATS, TRIBHAWAN S Pediatric Oncology Group studies POG9031--Cisplatin/VP-16 therapy of medulloblastoma/pre vs. post irradiation

P01CA-28842-09 (SRC) CORREA, PELAYO LSU MEDICAL CENTER 1901 PERDIDO ST NEW ORLEANS, LA 70112 Etiologic studies of gastric carcinoma

P01CA-28842-09 0001 (SRC) CORREA, PELAYO Etiologic studies of gastric carcinoma Histopathology

P01CA-28842-09 0008 (SRC) TANNENBAUM, STEVEN R Etiologic studies of gastric carcinoma N-Nitroso compounds and gastric cancer

P01CA-28842-09 0009 (SRC) CORREA, PELAYO Etiologic studies of gastric carcinoma Helicobacter pylori and gastric cancer

P01CA-28842-09 0011 (SRC) CORREA, PELAYO Etiologic studies of gastric carcinoma Chemoprevention of gastric dysplasia

P01CA-28842-09 0012 (SRC) WOGAN, GERALD N Etiologic studies of gastric carcinoma Genetic alterations during gastric tumor development

U10CA-28851-11 (CCI) TUBERGEN, DAVID G CHILDREN'S HOSPITAL 1056 EAST NINETEENTH AVENUE DENVER, CO 80218 Children's cancer study group

U10CA-28862-11 (CCI) BONNET, JOHN D SCOTT AND WHITE CLINIC 2401 SOUTH 31ST STREET TEMPLE, TX 76508 Southwest oncology group

R37CA-28865-13 (MCHA) GRIECO, PAUL A INDIANA UNIVERSITY BLOOMINGTON, IN 47405 Tumor inhibitors and related substances

P01CA-28881-07A1 (SRC) HILAL, SADEK K NEUROLOGICAL INSTITUTE 710 WEST 168TH STREET NEW YORK, NY 10032 Evaluation of high field medical NMR imaging

P01CA-28881-07A1 0001 (SRC) HILAL, SADEK K Evaluation of high field medical NMR imaging Grading & sizing of brain tumors by MR sodium imaging

P01CA-28881-07A1 0002 (SRC) JOHNSON, GLYN Evaluation of high field medical NMR imaging Proton chemical shift imaging

P01CA-28881-07A1 0003 (SRC) JOHNSON, GLYN Evaluation of high field medical NMR imaging Data processing for chemical shift imaging

P01CA-28881-07A1 0004 (SRC) OH, CHANG-HYUH Evaluation of high field medical NMR imaging MR spectroscopy/imaging--High order magnetic field gradients

P01CA-28881-07A1 0005 (SRC) HALL, ERIC J Evaluation of high field medical NMR imaging Study of safety of NMR up to 5.0 T

P01CA-28881-07A1 9001 (SRC) HILAL, SADEK K Evaluation of high field medical NMR imaging Core

U10CA-28882-11 (CCI) GILCHRIST, GERALD S MAYO FOUNDATION 200 FIRST STREET SOUTHWEST ROCHESTER, MN 55905 Children's cancer study group

P01CA-28896-11 (SRC) RUOSLAHTI, ERKKI I LA JOLLA CANCER RESEARCH FDN 10901 NORTH TORREY PINES ROAD LA JOLLA, CA 92037 Cell-matrix interactions in neoplasia and development

P01CA-28896-11 0001 (SRC) RUOSLAHTI, ERKKI I Cell-matrix interactions in neoplasia and development Cell adhesion proteins and receptors

P01CA-28896-11 0003 (SRC) ENGVALL, EVA S Cell-matrix interactions in neoplasia and development Merosin, a tissue-restricted basement membrane component

P01CA-28896-11 0005 (SRC) ROUSLAHTI, ERKKI I Cell-matrix interactions in neoplasia and development Proteoglycans in normal and malignant cells

P01CA-28896-11 0006 (SRC) PIERSCHBACHER, MICHAEL D Cell-matrix interactions in neoplasia and development Cell attachment mechanisms

P01CA-28896-11 9001 (SRC) RUOSLAHTI, ERKKI I Cell-matrix interactions in neoplasia and development Core program

R01CA-28936-11 (EI) HAYNES, BARTON F DUKE MEDICAL CENTER BOX 3258 DURHAM, NC 27710 Mechanisms of human T lymphocyte development

R37CA-28950-10 (CPA) STONER, GARY D MEDICAL COLLEGE OF OHIO HLTH ED BLDG/202/C.S.#10008 TOLEDO, OH 43699 Carcinogenesis studies in the esophagus

PROJECT NO., ORGANIZATIONAL UNIT., INVESTIGATOR, ADDRESS, TITLE

R01CA-28954-10 (CPA) GOULD, MICHAEL N UNIVERSITY OF WISCONSIN 600 HIGHLAND AVENUE MADISON, WIS 53792 factors controlling susceptibility to mammary cancer

U10CA-29013-11 (CCI) ROGERS, PAUL CHILDRENS HOSPITAL 4480 OAK STREET VANCOUVER, BC, V6H 3V4 CANADA Participate children's cancer study group

R01CA-29026-11 (RAD) THAMES, HOWARD D, JR UNIV OF TX M.D. ANDERSON CAN/C 1515 HOLCOMBE BLVD HOUSTON, TX 77030 Low-dose limit of effective fractionation

R01CA-29048-10 (PTHB) COFFINO, PHILIP UNIVERSITY OF CALIFORNIA THIRD & PARNASSUS AVENUES SAN FRANCISCO, CA 94143 Mechanisms of ornithine decarboxylase regulation

R01CA-29078-11 (PTHB) IANNACCONE, PHILIP M NORTHWESTERN UNIVERSITY 303 EAST CHICAGO AVENUE CHICAGO, IL 60611 Cellular origins of rat hepatic preneoplasias

R01CA-29088-08 (CPA) GOLD, BARRY I UNIVERSITY OF NEBRASKA 600 SOUTH 42ND STREET OMAHA, NE 68198 Activation and transportation of nitrosamines

R01CA-29101-09S1 (PTHB) LA BRECQUE, DOUGLAS R UNIV OF IOWA HOSP & CLINICS C109 GH IOWA CITY, IA 52242 Characterization of a liver specific growth promotor

R01CA-29108-10 (MCHA) BOECKMAN, ROBERT K, JR UNIVERSITY OF ROCHESTER ROCHESTER, NY 14627 Synthesis of antitumor substances

R01CA-29117-10 (SB) GILLETTE, EDWARD L COLORADO STATE UNIVERSITY COMPARATIVE ONCOLOGY UNIT FORT COLLINS, CO 80523 Experimental intraoperative radiotherapy

U10CA-29139-11 (CCI) KRISCHER, JEFFREY P PEDIATRIC ONCOLOGY GROUP 4110 SW 34 STREET, SUITE 22 GAINESVILLE, FL 32608-2516 Pediatric oncology group statistical office

R01CA-29200-10 (EI) GUERRY, DUPONT UNIVERSITY OF PENNSYLVANIA 3400 SPRUCE STREET PHILADELPHIA, PA 19104 Autologous immunity to human cultured melanoma

R01CA-29243-11 (EVR) PARSONS, J THOMAS UNIVERSITY OF VIRGINIA BOX 441 HEALTH SCIENCES CTR CHARLOTTESVILLE, VA 22908 Sarcoma virus specific tumor antigens

R01CA-29258-10 (CPA) ROSSMAN, TOBY G NEW YORK UNIVERSITY MED CTR 550 FIRST AVENUE NEW YORK, N Y 10016 Mutagenesis by metals of environmental significance

R01CA-29270-10 (VR) FLUCK, MICHELE M MICHIGAM STATE UNIVERSITY EAST LANSING, MI 48824-1101 Genome integration and control of viral gene expression

U10CA-29281-11 (CCI) GROSS, SAMUEL UNIVERSITY OF FLORIDA BOX J-296, JHM HEALTH CENTER GAINESVILLE, FL 32610 Pediatric oncology group - University of Florida

U10CA-29281-11 0032 (CCI) GROSS, SAMUEL Pediatric oncology group - University of Florida POG8865--Phase II recombinant alpha-interferon in relapsed T-cell disease

U10CA-29281-11 0033 (CCI) GROSS, SAMUEL Pediatric oncology group - University of Florida--Phase II recombinant A-interferon in chronic myelogenous leukemia

U10CA-29281-11 0034 (CCI) GROSS, SAMUEL Pediatric oncology group - University of Florida POG8832--Combination chemotherapy followed by radiotherapy for brain tumors

U10CA-29281-11 0035 (CCI) GROSS, SAMUEL Pediatric oncology group - University of Florida POG8731--Phase II trial of methotrexate in treatment of brain tumors in children

U10CA-29281-11 0036 (CCI) GROSS, SAMUEL Pediatric oncology group - University of Florida POG8788--Intergroup rhabdomyosarcoma study/pilot study for clinical group III

U10CA-29281-11 0037 (CCI) GROSS, SAMUEL Pediatric oncology group - University of Florida POG8761--Phase II study of homoharringtonine therapy for nonlymphoblastic leukemi

U10CA-29281-11 0038 (CCI) GROSS, SAMUEL Pediatric oncology group - University of Florida POG8739--Phase II immunotherapy with alpha-2 interferon for brain tumors

U10CA-29281-11 0039 (CCI) GROSS, SAMUEL Pediatric oncology group - University of Florida POG8741--Treatment of patients with stage C and stage D neuroblastoma

U10CA-29281-11 0040 (CCI) GROSS, SAMUEL Pediatric oncology group - University of Florida POG8751--Phase II methotrexate chemotherapy for rhabdomyosarcoma in children

U10CA-29281-11 0041 (CCI) GROSS, SAMUEL Pediatric oncology group - University of Florida POG8633--Postoperative chemotherapy and delayed irradiation for brain tumors

U10CA-29281-11 0042 (CCI) GROSS, SAMUEL Pediatric oncology group - University of Florida POG8617--Therapy for B-cell acute lymphoblastic leukemia and lymphoma

U10CA-29281-11 0043 (CCI) GROSS, SAMUEL Pediatric oncology group - University of Florida POG9139--Phase I study of cisplatin and irradiation in brain stem gliomas

U10CA-29281-11 0044 (CCI) GROSS, SAMUEL Pediatric oncology group - University of Florida POG9079--Phase I study of L-PAM/CTX with ABM rescue for brain tumors in children

U10CA-29281-11 0045 (CCI) GROSS, SAMUEL Pediatric oncology group - University of Florida POG9075--Phase I study of acivicin in children with solid tumors

U10CA-29281-11 0046 (CCI) GROSS, SAMUEL Pediatric oncology group - University of Florida POG9074--Phase I study of xomazyme-H65 in children with T-cell ALL/lymphoma

U10CA-29281-11 0047 (CCI) GROSS, SAMUEL Pediatric oncology group - University of Florida POG9072--Phase I chemotherapy for recurrent/resistant malignant solid tumors

U10CA-29281-11 0048 (CCI) GROSS, SAMUEL Pediatric oncology group - University of Florida POG9061-Phase II systemic therapy and irradiation for ALL & CNS leukemia

U10CA-29281-11 0049 (CCI) GROSS, SAMUEL Pediatric oncology group - University of Florida POG 9086--Phase I pilot study of therapy for T-cell ALL or NHL

U10CA-29281-11 0050 (CCI) GROSS, SAMUEL Pediatric oncology group - University of Florida POG9071--Phase I trial of fazarabine in children with acute leukemia

U10CA-29281-11 0051 (CCI) GROSS, SAMUEL Pediatric oncology group - University of Florida POG8970--Phase I trial of fazarabine in children with refractory solid tumors
U10CA-29281-11 0052 (CCI) GROSS, SAMUEL Pediatric oncology group - University of Florida POG8973--Etoposide (VP-16) and carboplatin in children with acute leukemia
U10CA-29281-11 0053 (CCI) GROSS, SAMUEL Pediatric oncology group - University of Florida POG8870--Phase I trial of ifosfamide/VP16/MESNA in children with acute leukemia
U10CA-29281-11 0054 (CCI) GROSS, SAMUEL Pediatric oncology group - University of Florida POG8871--Phase I study of rTNF in children with refractory solid tumors
U10CA-29281-11 0055 (CCI) GROSS, SAMUEL Pediatric oncology group - University of Florida POG8671--Phase I immunotherapy with rIL-2 in children with solid tumors
U10CA-29281-11 0056 (CCI) GROSS, SAMUEL Pediatric oncology group - University of Florida POG8494--Phase I study of fludarabine phosphate in pediatric patients
U10CA-29281-11 0057 (CCI) GROSS, SAMUEL Pediatric oncology group - University of Florida POG8930--A comprehensive genetic analysis of brain tumors
U10CA-29281-11 0058 (CCI) GROSS, SAMUEL Pediatric oncology group - University of Florida POG8828--Late effects of Hodgkin's disease
U10CA-29281-11 0059 (CCI) GROSS, SAMUEL Pediatric oncology group - University of Florida POG9046--Molecular genetic analysis of Wilm's tumors
U10CA-29281-11 0060 (CCI) GROSS, SAMUEL Pediatric oncology group - University of Florida POG9153--Rhabdomyosarcoma study/laboratory evaluation of tumor
U10CA-29281-11 0001 (CCI) GROSS, SAMUEL Pediatric oncology group - University of Florida POG9006--6-MP/methotrexate vs. alternating chemotherapy for ALL in childhood
U10CA-29281-11 0002 (CCI) GROSS, SAMUEL Pediatric oncology group - University of Florida POG9005--Dose intensification of methotrexate & 6-mercaptourine in childhood ALL
U10CA-29281-11 0003 (CCI) GROSS, SAMUEL Pediatric oncology group - University of Florida POG9031--Cisplatin/VP-16 therapy of medulloblastoma/pre vs. post irradiation
U10CA-29281-11 0004 (CCI) GROSS, SAMUEL Pediatric oncology group - University of Florida POG8945--Phase III chemotherapy for hepatoblastoma & hepatocellular carcinoma
U10CA-29281-11 0005 (CCI) GROSS, SAMUEL Pediatric oncology group - University of Florida POG9049--Phase III study of high-risk malignant germ cell tumors in children
U10CA-29281-11 0006 (CCI) GROSS, SAMUEL Pediatric oncology group - University of Florida POG8844--Bone marrow transplant in children with stage D neuroblastoma
U10CA-29281-11 0007 (CCI) GROSS, SAMUEL Pediatric oncology group - University of Florida POG8850--Phase III treatment of Ewing's sarcoma and neuroectodermal bone tumors
U10CA-29281-11 0008 (CCI) GROSS, SAMUEL Pediatric oncology group - University of Florida POG8821--Phase III chemotherapy +/- autologous BMT in children with AML
U10CA-29281-11 0009 (CCI) GROSS, SAMUEL Pediatric oncology group - University of Florida POG8725--Phase III chemotherapy +/- radiation therapy in pediatric Hodgkins
U10CA-29281-11 0010 (CCI) GROSS, SAMUEL Pediatric oncology group - University of Florida POG8704--Phase III chemotherapy of childhood T cell ALL & lymphoblastic lymphoma
U10CA-29281-11 0011 (CCI) GROSS, SAMUEL Pediatric oncology group - University of Florida POG8719--Phase III chemotherapy for non-Hodgkin's lymphoma in children
U10CA-29281-11 0012 (CCI) GROSS, SAMUEL Pediatric oncology group - University of Florida POG8650--National Wilm's tumor and clear cell sarcoma study
U10CA-29281-11 0013 (CCI) GROSS, SAMUEL Pediatric oncology group - University of Florida POG8616--Phase III chemotherapy for childhood Burkitt and non-Burkitts lymphoma
U10CA-29281-11 0014 (CCI) GROSS, SAMUEL Pediatric oncology group - University of Florida POG8615--Phase III study of large cell lymphomas in children and adolescents
U10CA-29281-11 0015 (CCI) GROSS, SAMUEL Pediatric oncology group - University of Florida POG8651--Phase III study of childhood nonmetastatic osteosarcoma
U10CA-29281-11 0016 (CCI) GROSS, SAMUEL Pediatric oncology group - University of Florida POG8653--Phase III study of childhood soft tissue sarcomas
U10CA-29281-11 0017 (CCI) GROSS, SAMUEL Pediatric oncology group - University of Florida POG8625--Phase III combined therapy in childhood Hodgkin's disease
U10CA-29281-11 0018 (CCI) GROSS, SAMUEL Pediatric oncology group - University of Florida POG8451--Intergroup rhabdomyosarcoma study
U10CA-29281-11 0019 (CCI) GROSS, SAMUEL Pediatric oncology group - University of Florida POG9110--Rotational drug therapy after first marrow relapse of non-T, non B ALL
U10CA-29281-11 0020 (CCI) GROSS, SAMUEL Pediatric oncology group - University of Florida POG9107--Phase II pilot study of infant leukemia
U10CA-29281-11 0021 (CCI) GROSS, SAMUEL Pediatric oncology group - University of Florida POG9140--Phase II therapy for recurrent or refractory neuroblastoma
U10CA-29281-11 0022 (CCI) GROSS, SAMUEL Pediatric oncology group - University of Florida POG9048--Phase II study of malignant germ cell tumors in children
U10CA-29281-11 0023 (CCI) GROSS, SAMUEL Pediatric oncology group - University of Florida POG9060--Intensive QOD ifosfamide treatment for CNS tumors in children
U10CA-29281-11 0024 (CCI) GROSS, SAMUEL Pediatric oncology group - University of Florida POG8936--Phase II study of carboplatin treatment for optic pathway tumors
U10CA-29281-11 0025 (CCI) GROSS, SAMUEL Pediatric oncology group - University of Florida POG8935--Phase II study of surgery and/or radiotherapy for optic pathway tumors
U10CA-29281-11 0026 (CCI) GROSS, SAMUEL Pediatric oncology group - University of Florida POG8820--Phase II/III study of VP-16, AMSA +/- 5-azacytidine in childhood ANLL
U10CA-29281-11 0027 (CCI) GROSS, SAMUEL Pediatric oncology group - University of Florida POG8889--Intergroup rhabdomyosarcoma study for clinical group IV disease
U10CA-29281-11 0028 (CCI) GROSS, SAMUEL Pediatric oncology group - University of Florida POG8866--Phase II asparaginase therapy for acute lymphoblastic leukemia
U10CA-29281-11 0029 (CCI) GROSS, SAMUEL Pediatric oncology group - University of Florida POG8862--Combination chemotherapy of acute T-lymphoblastic leukemia
U10CA-29281-11 0030 (CCI) GROSS, SAMUEL Pediatric oncology group - University of Florida POG8863--Phase II study of high dose cytosine arabinoside in childhood tumors
U10CA-29281-11 0031 (CCI) GROSS, SAMUEL Pediatric oncology group - University of Florida POG8827--Phase II treatment of children with Hodgkin's disease in relapse
U10CA-29293-11 (CCI) FORMAN, EDWIN N RHODE ISLAND HOSPITAL 593 EDDY STREET PROVIDENCE, RI 02902 Pediatric oncology group
U10CA-29293-11 0035 (CCI) FORMAN, EDWIN N Pediatric oncology group POG8731--Phase II trial of methotrexate in treatment of brain tumors in children
U10CA-29293-11 0036 (CCI) FORMAN, EDWIN N Pediatric oncology group POG8788--Intergroup rhabdomyosarcoma study/pilot study for clinical group III
U10CA-29293-11 0037 (CCI) FORMAN, EDWIN N Pediatric oncology group POG8761--Phase II study of homoharringtonine therapy for nonlymphoblastic leukemi
U10CA-29293-11 0038 (CCI) FORMAN, EDWIN N Pediatric oncology group POG8739--Phase II immunotherapy with alpha-2 interferon for brain tumors
U10CA-29293-11 0039 (CCI) FORMAN, EDWIN N Pediatric oncology group POG8741--Treatment of patients with stage C and stage D neuroblastoma
U10CA-29293-11 0040 (CCI) FORMAN, EDWIN N Pediatric oncology group POG8751--Phase II methotrexate chemotherapy for rhabdomyosarcoma in children
U10CA-29293-11 0041 (CCI) FORMAN, EDWIN N Pediatric oncology group POG8633--Postoperative chemotherapy and delayed irradiation for brain tumors
U10CA-29293-11 0042 (CCI) FORMAN, EDWIN N Pediatric oncology group POG8617--Therapy for B-cell acute lymphoblastic leukemia and lymphoma
U10CA-29293-11 0043 (CCI) FORMAN, EDWIN N Pediatric oncology group POG9139--Phase I study of cisplatin and irradiation in brain stem gliomas
U10CA-29293-11 0044 (CCI) FORMAN, EDWIN N Pediatric oncology group POG9079--Phase I study of L-PAM/CTX with ABM rescue for brain tumors in children
U10CA-29293-11 0045 (CCI) FORMAN, EDWIN N Pediatric oncology group POG9075--Phase I study of acivicin in children with solid tumors
U10CA-29293-11 0046 (CCI) FORMAN, EDWIN N Pediatric oncology group POG9074--Phase I study of xomazyme-H65 in children with T-cell ALL/lymphoma
U10CA-29293-11 0047 (CCI) FORMAN, EDWIN N Pediatric oncology group POG9072--Phase I chemotherapy for recurrent/resistant malignant solid tumors
U10CA-29293-11 0048 (CCI) FORMAN, EDWIN N Pediatric oncology group POG9061--Phase II systemic therapy and irradiation for ALL & CNS leukemia
U10CA-29293-11 0049 (CCI) FORMAN, EDWIN N Pediatric oncology group POG 9086--Phase I pilot study of therapy for T-cell ALL or NHL
U10CA-29293-11 0050 (CCI) FORMAN, EDWIN N Pediatric oncology group POG9071--Phase I trial of fazarabine in children with acute leukemia
U10CA-29293-11 0051 (CCI) FORMAN, EDWIN N Pediatric oncology group POG8970--Phase I trial of fazarabine in children with refractory solid tumors
U10CA-29293-11 0052 (CCI) FORMAN, EDWIN N Pediatric oncology group POG8973--Etoposide (VP-16) and carboplatin in children with acute leukemia
U10CA-29293-11 0053 (CCI) FORMAN, EDWIN N Pediatric oncology group POG8870--Phase I trial of ifosfamide/VP16/MESNA in children with acute leukemia
U10CA-29293-11 0054 (CCI) FORMAN, EDWIN N Pediatric oncology group POG8871--Phase I study of rTNF in children with refractory solid tumors
U10CA-29293-11 0055 (CCI) FORMAN, EDWIN N Pediatric oncology group POG8671--Phase I immunotherapy with rIL-2 in children with solid tumors
U10CA-29293-11 0056 (CCI) FORMAN, EDWIN N Pediatric oncology group POG8494--Phase I study of fludarabine phosphate in pediatric patients
U10CA-29293-11 0057 (CCI) FORMAN, EDWIN N Pediatric oncology group POG8930--A comprehensive genetic analysis of brain tumors
U10CA-29293-11 0058 (CCI) FORMAN, EDWIN N Pediatric oncology group POG8828--Late effects of Hodgkin's disease
U10CA-29293-11 0059 (CCI) FORMAN, EDWIN N Pediatric oncology group POG9046--Molecular genetic analysis of Wilm's tumors
U10CA-29293-11 0060 (CCI) FORMAN, EDWIN N Pediatric oncology group POG9153--Rhabdomyosarcoma study/laboratory evaluation of tumor
U10CA-29293-11 0001 (CCI) FORMAN, EDWIN N Pediatric oncology group POG9006--6-MP/methotrexate vs. alternating chemotherapy for ALL in childhood
U10CA-29293-11 0003 (CCI) FORMAN, EDWIN N Pediatric oncology group POG9031--Cisplatin/VP-16 therapy of medulloblastoma/pre vs. post irradiation
U10CA-29293-11 0004 (CCI) FORMAN, EDWIN N Pediatric oncology group POG8945--Phase III chemotherapy for hepatoblastoma & hepatocellular carcinoma
U10CA-29293-11 0005 (CCI) FORMAN, EDWIN N Pediatric oncology group POG9049--Phase III study of high-risk malignant germ cell tumors in children
U10CA-29293-11 0006 (CCI) FORMAN, EDWIN N Pediatric oncology group POG8844--Bone marrow transplant in children with stage D neuroblastoma
U10CA-29293-11 0007 (CCI) FORMAN, EDWIN N Pediatric oncology group POG8850--Phase III treatment of Ewing's sarcoma and neuroectodermal

bone tumors
U10CA-29293-11 0008 (CCI) FORMAN, EDWIN N Pediatric oncology group POG8821--Phase III chemotherapy +/- autologous BMT in children with AML
U10CA-29293-11 0009 (CCI) FORMAN, EDWIN N Pediatric oncology group POG8725--Phase III chemotherapy +/- radiation therapy in pediatric Hodgkins
U10CA-29293-11 0010 (CCI) FORMAN, EDWIN N Pediatric oncology group POG8704--Phase III chemotherapy of childhood T cell ALL & lymphoblastic lymphoma
U10CA-29293-11 0011 (CCI) FORMAN, EDWIN N Pediatric oncology group POG8719--Phase III chemotherapy for non-Hodgkin's lymphoma in children
U10CA-29293-11 0012 (CCI) FORMAN, EDWIN N Pediatric oncology group POG8650--National Wilm's tumor and clear cell sarcoma study
U10CA-29293-11 0013 (CCI) FORMAN, EDWIN N Pediatric oncology group POG8616--Phase III chemotherapy for childhood Burkitt and non-Burkitts lymphoma
U10CA-29293-11 0014 (CCI) FORMAN, EDWIN N Pediatric oncology group POG8615--Phase III study of large cell lymphomas in children and adolescents
U10CA-29293-11 0015 (CCI) FORMAN, EDWIN N Pediatric oncology group POG8651--Phase III study of childhood nonmetastatic osteosarcoma
U10CA-29293-11 0016 (CCI) FORMAN, EDWIN N Pediatric oncology group POG8653--Phase III study of childhood soft tissue sarcomas
U10CA-29293-11 0017 (CCI) FORMAN, EDWIN N Pediatric oncology group POG8625--Phase III combined therapy in childhood Hodgkin's disease
U10CA-29293-11 0018 (CCI) FORMAN, EDWIN N Pediatric oncology group POG8451--Intergroup rhabdomyosarcoma study
U10CA-29293-11 0019 (CCI) FORMAN, EDWIN N Pediatric oncology group POG9110--Rotational drug therapy after first marrow relapse of non-T, non B ALL
U10CA-29293-11 0020 (CCI) FORMAN, EDWIN N Pediatric oncology group POG9107--Phase II pilot study of infant leukemia
U10CA-29293-11 0021 (CCI) FORMAN, EDWIN N Pediatric oncology group POG9140--Phase II therapy for recurrent or refractory neuroblastoma
U10CA-29293-11 0022 (CCI) FORMAN, EDWIN N Pediatric oncology group POG9048--Phase II study of malignant germ cell tumors in children
U10CA-29293-11 0023 (CCI) FORMAN, EDWIN N Pediatric oncology group POG9060--Intensive OOD ifosfamide treatment for CNS tumors in children
U10CA-29293-11 0024 (CCI) FORMAN, EDWIN N Pediatric oncology group POG8936--Phase II study of carboplatin treatment for optic pathway tumors
U10CA-29293-11 0025 (CCI) FORMAN, EDWIN N Pediatric oncology group POG8935--Phase II study of surgery and/or radiotherapy for optic pathway tumors
U10CA-29293-11 0026 (CCI) FORMAN, EDWIN N Pediatric oncology group POG8820--Phase II/III study of VP-16, AMSA +/- 5-azacytidine in childhood ANLL
U10CA-29293-11 0027 (CCI) FORMAN, EDWIN N Pediatric oncology group POG8889--Intergroup rhabdomyosarcoma study for clinical group IV disease
U10CA-29293-11 0028 (CCI) FORMAN, EDWIN N Pediatric oncology group POG8866--Phase II asparaginase therapy for acute lymphoblastic leukemia
U10CA-29293-11 0029 (CCI) FORMAN, EDWIN N Pediatric oncology group POG8862--Combination chemotherapy of acute T-lymphoblastic leukemia
U10CA-29293-11 0030 (CCI) FORMAN, EDWIN N Pediatric oncology group POG8863--Phase II study of high dose cytosine arabinoside in childhood tumors
U10CA-29293-11 0031 (CCI) FORMAN, EDWIN N Pediatric oncology group POG8827--Phase II treatment of children with Hodgkin's disease in relapse
U10CA-29293-11 0032 (CCI) FORMAN, EDWIN N Pediatric oncology group POG8865--Phase II recombinant alpha-interferon in relapsed T-cell disease
U10CA-29293-11 0033 (CCI) FORMAN, EDWIN N Pediatric oncology group--Phase II recombinant A-interferon in chronic myelogenous leukemia
U10CA-29293-11 0034 (CCI) FORMAN, EDWIN N Pediatric oncology group POG8832--Combination chemotherapy followed by radiotherapy for brain tumors
U10CA-29293-11 0002 (CCI) FORMAN, EDWIN N Pediatric oncology group POG9005--Dose intensification of methotrexate & 6-mercaptourine in childhood ALL
R01CA-29303-11 (EVR) TATTERSALL, PETER J YALE UNIVERSITY SCHOOL OF MED 333 CEDAR STREET NEW HAVEN, CT 06510 Molecular basis of parvovirus target cell specificity
U10CA-29314-11 (CCI) TANNOUS, RAYMOND UNIVERSITY OF IOWA 2520 JCP - GENERAL HOSPITAL IOWA CITY, IOWA 52242 Childrens cancer study group
R37CA-29323-11 (PTHB) GRISHAM, J W U OF N CAROLINA AT CHAPEL HILL CB# 7525, BRINKHOUS-BULLITT BL Clonal analysis of carcinogenesis in vitro
R01CA-29339-12 (VR) WANG, LU-HAI MOUNT SINAI SCH OF MED/MICROBI 5TH AVENUE AND 100TH STREET NEW YORK, NY 10029 Transforming genes of avian sarcoma viruses
R01CA-29360-09 (ET) GANJU-KRISHAN, AWTAR UNIVERSITY OF MIAMI MED SCH PO BOX 016960 (R-71) MIAMI, FL 33101 Adriamycin effects on tumor cell proliferation
R01CA-29414-10 (CPA) SIROVER, MICHAEL A TEMPLE UNIVERSITY SCH OF MED 3420 NORTH BROAD STREET PHILADELPHIA, PA 19140 Regulation of DNA repair in human carcinogenesis
R01CA-29431-11 (ET) KUFE, DONALD W DANA-FARBER CANCER INSTITUTE 44 BINNEY STREET BOSTON, MA 02115 Molecular modulations of Ara-C therapy in man
R37CA-29476-12 (CPA) TRENT, JEFFREY M UNIVERSITY OF MICHIGAN RM. C560 BOX 0668 ANN ARBOR, MICHIGAN 48109 Clonal karyotypic evolution in human solid tumors
P01CA-29502-11A1 (SRC) RIVLIN, RICHARD S MEM HOSP FOR CANCER & ALLIED D 1275 YORK AVENUE NEW YORK, NY 10021 Cooperative core lab and clinical nutrition research
P01CA-29502-11A1 9004 (SRC) CUNNINGHAM-RUNDLES, SUSANNA Cooperative core lab and clinical nutrition research Core--Immunology laboratory
P01CA-29502-11A1 9006 (SRC) BRESLOW, JAN L Cooperative core lab and clinical nutrition research Core--Lipids laboratory
P01CA-29502-11A1 9007 (SRC) TELANG, NITIN T Cooperative core lab and clinical nutrition research Core--Carcinogenesis and nutrition laboratory
P01CA-29502-11A1 9008 (SRC) LANE, JOSEPH M Cooperative core lab and clinical nutrition research Core--Metabolic bone disease laboratory
P01CA-29502-11A1 0034 (SRC) LEVINE, BARBARA Cooperative core lab and clinical nutrition research Nutrition information center
P01CA-29502-11A1 0035 (SRC) TIWARI, RAJ K Cooperative core lab and clinical nutrition research Modulation of gene expression by fatty acids
P01CA-29502-11A1 0036 (SRC) CUNNINGHAM-RUNDLES, SUSANNA Cooperative core lab and clinical nutrition research Immune deficiency, malabsorption and risk of malignancy in children
P01CA-29502-11A1 0037 (SRC) MURRAY, HENRY W Cooperative core lab and clinical nutrition research Killing of visceral leishmanial parasites
P01CA-29502-11A1 0038 (SRC) YEH, JAMES K Cooperative core lab and clinical nutrition research Effects of ovariectomy, estrogen replacement, and exercise on glutathione
P01CA-29502-11A1 0039 (SRC) KIM, JAE HO Cooperative core lab and clinical nutrition research Preferential killing of glucose depleted HeLa cells by vitamin K3 and hyperthermi
P01CA-29502-11A1 0040 (SRC) DENNISON, BARBARA Cooperative core lab and clinical nutrition research Clinical trial of psyllium to lower cholesterol in children
P01CA-29502-11A1 0041 (SRC) BIGLER, RODNEY E Cooperative core lab and clinical nutrition research Radiation-induced vascular and metabolic changes in brain
P01CA-29502-11A1 0043 (SRC) GERTNER, JOSEPH M Cooperative core lab and clinical nutrition research Energy intake and energy expenditure during growth hormone therapy
P01CA-29502-11A1 0044 (SRC) BOECK, M Cooperative core lab and clinical nutrition research Pilot--Energy expenditure and body composition in patients with anorexia nervosa
P01CA-29502-11A1 0045 (SRC) CUNNINGHAM-RUNDLES, SUSANNA Cooperative core lab and clinical nutrition research Evaluation of zinc level and immune response in the elderly
P01CA-29502-11A1 0046 (SRC) GIARDINA, P V Cooperative core lab and clinical nutrition research Role of iron and the effect of in vitro chelation on immune response
P01CA-29502-11A1 0047 (SRC) SALVATORE, R Cooperative core lab and clinical nutrition research Immune modulation by 1,25 dihydroxyvitamin D3
P01CA-29502-11A1 0048 (SRC) CARTER, D M Cooperative core lab and clinical nutrition research Malnutrition and immune response in Epidermolysis Bullosa
P01CA-29502-11A1 0049 (SRC) VEBER, M Cooperative core lab and clinical nutrition research Malnutrition in HIV infected pediatric patients
P01CA-29502-11A1 0050 (SRC) BERNER, Y Cooperative core lab and clinical nutrition research Modulation of immune response in vitro
P01CA-29502-11A1 0051 (SRC) BOCKMAN, R Cooperative core lab and clinical nutrition research Pilot--Gallium nitrate for the treatment of bone disorder
P01CA-29502-11A1 0052 (SRC) BAJORUNAS, D R Cooperative core lab and clinical nutrition research Pilot--Bone metabolism in premature menopausal women with breast cancer
P01CA-29502-11A1 0053 (SRC) WEINERMAN, S Cooperative core lab and clinical nutrition research Pilot--Calcium citrate supplementation in women with a history of renal stones
P01CA-29502-11A1 0054 (SRC) WARRELL, R Cooperative core lab and clinical nutrition research Pilot--Gallium nitrate for treatment of advanced Paget's disease of bone
P01CA-29502-11A1 0055 (SRC) BRINTON, ELIOT A Cooperative core lab and clinical nutrition research Pilot--Molecular genetic basis of dietary control of apo A-1 metabolism
P01CA-29502-11A1 0056 (SRC) DONNER, DAVID B Cooperative core lab and clinical nutrition research Pilot--TNF receptor regulation in cancer-associated cachexia
P01CA-29502-11A1 0057 (SRC) GALBRAITH, RICHARD A Cooperative core lab and clinical nutrition research Pilot--Nutrition, trace metals and drugs on P450 homeostasis
P01CA-29502-11A1 0058 (SRC) GERTNER, JOSEPH M Cooperative core lab and clinical nutrition research Pilot--Pregnancy and the control of calcium absorption
P01CA-29502-11A1 0059 (SRC) KINNEY, JOHN M Cooperative core lab and clinical nutrition research Pilot--Relation of blood flow to metabolism in human adipose tissue
P01CA-29502-11A1 0060 (SRC) SGOUROS, GEORGE Cooperative core lab and clinical nutrition research Pilot--Mechanisms of radiation induced activation of the PPP in rat brain
P01CA-29502-11A1 0061 (SRC) TRAKTMAN, PAULA Cooperative core lab and clinical nutrition research Pilot--Expression of the osteoblastic phenotype in vitro
P01CA-29502-11A1 9002 (SRC) HESTON, WARREN D W Cooperative core lab and clinical nutrition research Core--Metabolism and oncology laboratory
P01CA-29502-11A1 9003 (SRC) BIGLER, RODNEY E Cooperative core lab and clinical nutrition research Core--Biophysics laboratory
U10CA-29511-12 (CCI) GLICKSMAN, ARVIN S ROGER WILLIAMS GENERAL HOSPITA 825 CHALKSTONE AVENUE PROVIDENCE, RI 02908 Quality assurance review center
R01CA-29525-11 (CPA) REZNIKOFF, CATHERINE A WISCONSIN CLINICAL SCIENCE CTR 600 HIGHLAND AVENUE MADISON, WI 53792 Transformation in vitro of human uroepithelial cells
R01CA-29561-33A1 (VR) GREEN, MAURICE ST LOUIS UNIVERSITY 3681 PARK AVE ST LOUIS, MO 63110 Biochemical functions of adenovirus oncogenes
P01CA-29580-11 (SRC) HOFFMANN, DIETRICH AMERICAN HEALTH FOUNDATION ONE DANA RD VALHALLA, NY 10595 Experimental tobacco carcinogenesis

PROJECT NO., ORGANIZATIONAL UNIT., INVESTIGATOR, ADDRESS, TITLE

P01CA-29580-11 0001 (SRC) HECHT, STEPHEN S Experimental tobacco carcinogenesis Carcinogenesis of tobacco-specific N-nitrosamines
P01CA-29580-11 0004 (SRC) LAVOIE, EDMOND J Experimental tobacco carcinogenesis Tobacco flavor compounds
P01CA-29580-11 0006 (SRC) BRUNNEMANN, KLAUS D Experimental tobacco carcinogenesis Analytical studies in tobacco carcinogenesis
P01CA-29580-11 0007 (SRC) PROKOPCZYK, BOGDAN Experimental tobacco carcinogenesis Formation of carcinogens during chewing of tobacco mixtures
P01CA-29580-11 0009 (SRC) HALEY, NANCY J Experimental tobacco carcinogenesis Sidestream smoke carcinogenicity
P01CA-29580-11 9001 (SRC) RIVENSON,ABRAHAM S. Experimental tobacco carcinogenesis Core--research animal facility
P01CA-29580-11 9002 (SRC) RIVENSON, ABRAHAM Experimental tobacco carcinogenesis Core--Histology facility
P01CA-29582-10A1 (SRC) GILLETTE, EDWARD L VETERINARY TEACHING HOSPITAL COLORADO STATE UNIVERSITY FORT COLLINS, CO 80523 Comparative oncology research program
P01CA-29582-10A1 0002 (SRC) PAGE, RODNEY L Comparative oncology research program Whole body hyperthermia and chemotherapy of lymphosarcomas
P01CA-29582-10A1 0005 (SRC) WITHROW, STEPHEN J Comparative oncology research program Limb sparing and local release of cisplatin for osteosarcoma
P01CA-29582-10A1 0006 (SRC) GILLETTE, EDWARD Comparative oncology research program Whole body hyperthermia and radiation for brain and tumor response
P01CA-29582-10A1 9001 (SRC) GILLETTE, EDWARD L Comparative oncology research program Core--Animal tumor center
P01CA-29582-10A1 9002 (SRC) GEORGE, STEPHEN Comparative oncology research program Core--Biostatistics
P01CA-29589-10 (SRC) ADAMS, DOLPH O DUKE UNIVERSITY MEDICAL CTR PO BOX 3712 DURHAM, NC 27710 Macrophage activation--Development and regulation
P01CA-29589-10 0001 (SRC) ADAMS, DOLPH O Macrophage activation--Development and regulation Regulation and genomic/functional role of Na+/H+ antiport activation
P01CA-29589-10 0003 (SRC) SNYDERMAN, RALPH Macrophage activation--Development and regulation GTP-binding proteins in mononuclear phagocyte activation
P01CA-29589-10 0006 (SRC) PIZZO, SALVATORE Macrophage activation--Development and regulation The alpha 2-macroglobulin receptor recognition site
P01CA-29589-10 0007 (SRC) TING, JENNY P Y Macrophage activation--Development and regulation IFN-gamma induced genomic regulation of class II MHC-genes in macrophages
P01CA-29589-10 9003 (SRC) UHING, RONALD J Macrophage activation--Development and regulation Cell biology and biochemistry core
P01CA-29589-10 9005 (SRC) LEWIS, JAMES G Macrophage activation--Development and regulation Animal core
R01CA-29591-12 (REN) HOCHBERG, RICHARD B YALE UNIVERSITY SCH OF MED 333 CEDAR ST PO BOX 3333 NEW HAVEN, CT 06510-8063 Steroid hormones in breast cancer
R37CA-29592-11 (EI) KAHAN, BARRY D UNIVERSITY OF TEXAS MED SCHOOL 6431 FANNIN, SUITE 6240 HOUSTON, TX 77030 Active specific immunotherapy in man--A murine model
P01CA-29605-10 (SRC) MORTON, DONALD L UNIVERSITY OF CALIFORNIA 405 HILGARD AVENUE LOS ANGELES, CA 90024-1406 New approaches to surgical oncology
P01CA-29605-10 0002 (SRC) EILBER, FREDERICK R New approaches to surgical oncology New approaches to skeletal and soft tissue sarcomas
P01CA-29605-10 0003 (SRC) IRIE, REIKO F New approaches to surgical oncology Hybridomas for monoclonal antibodies to melanoma
P01CA-29605-10 0004 (SRC) STORM, F KRISTIAN New approaches to surgical oncology Surgical oncology with combination thermo-chemotherapy
P01CA-29605-10 9001 (SRC) MORTON, DONALD L New approaches to surgical oncology Core support
P01CA-29605-10 0001 (SRC) MORTON, DONALD L New approaches to surgical oncology Malignant melanoma
R01CA-29614-09 (EDC) ANDERSON, DAVID E UNIV OF TEXAS MD ANDERSON CA C 1515 HOLCOMBE BLVD/HBM BOX 209 HOUSTON, TX 77030 Genetics of breast cancer
R01CA-29639-10 (RNM) NELP, WIL B UNIVERSITY OF WASHINGTON UNIV HOSPITAL RC-70 SEATTLE, WA 98195 Tumor imaging with radiolabelled monoclonal antibody
R37CA-29653-11 (RNM) CETAS, THOMAS C UNIVERSITY OF ARIZONA ARIZONA HLTH SCI CTR TUCSON, AZ 85724 Thermal dosimetry in hyperthermia
R01CA-29660-10 (EI) VAAGE, JAN ROSWELL PARK MEMORIAL INST 666 ELM STREET BUFFALO, NY 14263-0001 Immune control of mammary tumor growth
U10CA-29691-11 (CCI) RAVINDRANATH, YADDANAPUDI CHILDREN'S HOSPITAL OF MICHIGA 3901 BEAUBIEN DETROIT, MI 48201 Pediatric oncology group
U10CA-29691-11 0056 (CCI) RAVINDRANATH, YADDANAPUDI Pediatric oncology group POG8494--Phase I study of fludarabine phosphate in pediatric patients
U10CA-29691-11 0057 (CCI) RAVINDRANATH, YADDANAPUDI Pediatric oncology group POG8930--A comprehensive genetic analysis of brain tumors
U10CA-29691-11 0058 (CCI) RAVINDRANATH, YADDANAPUDI Pediatric oncology group POG8828--Late effects of Hodgkin's disease
U10CA-29691-11 0059 (CCI) RAVINDRANATH, YADDANAPUDI Pediatric oncology group POG9046--Molecular genetic analysis of Wilm's tumors
U10CA-29691-11 0060 (CCI) RAVINDRANATH, YADDANAPUDI Pediatric oncology group POG9153--Rhabdomyosarcoma study/laboratory evaluation of tumor
U10CA-29691-11 0001 (CCI) RAVINDRANATH, YADDANAPUDI Pediatric oncology group POG9006--6-MP/methotrexate vs. alternating chemotherapy for ALL in childhood
U10CA-29691-11 0024 (CCI) RAVINDRANATH, YADDANAPUDI Pediatric oncology group POG8936--Phase II study of carboplatin treatment for optic pathway tumors
U10CA-29691-11 0025 (CCI) RAVINDRANATH, YADDANAPUDI Pediatric oncology group POG8935--Phase II study of surgery and/or radiotherapy for optic pathway tumors
U10CA-29691-11 0026 (CCI) RAVINDRANATH, YADDANAPUDI Pediatric oncology group POG8820--Phase II/III study of VP-16, AMSA +/- 5-azacytidine in childhood ANLL
U10CA-29691-11 0027 (CCI) RAVINDRANATH, YADDANAPUDI Pediatric oncology group POG8889--Intergroup rhabdomyosarcoma study for clinical group IV disease
U10CA-29691-11 0028 (CCI) RAVINDRANATH, YADDANAPUDI Pediatric oncology group POG8866--Phase II asparaginase therapy for acute lymphoblastic leukemia
U10CA-29691-11 0029 (CCI) RAVINDRANATH, YADDANAPUDI Pediatric oncology group POG8862--Combination chemotherapy of acute T-lymphoblastic leukemia
U10CA-29691-11 0030 (CCI) RAVINDRANATH, YADDANAPUDI Pediatric oncology group POG8863--Phase II study of high dose cytosine arabinoside in childhood tumors
U10CA-29691-11 0031 (CCI) RAVINDRANATH, YADDANAPUDI Pediatric oncology group POG8827--Phase II treatment of children with Hodgkin's disease in relapse
U10CA-29691-11 0032 (CCI) RAVINDRANATH, YADDANAPUDI Pediatric oncology group POG8865--Phase II recombinant alpha-interferon in relapsed T-cell disease
U10CA-29691-11 0033 (CCI) RAVINDRANATH, YADDANAPUDI Pediatric oncology group--Phase II recombinant A-interferon in chronic myelogenous leukemia
U10CA-29691-11 0034 (CCI) RAVINDRANATH, YADDANAPUDI Pediatric oncology group POG8832--Combination chemotherapy followed by radiotherapy for brain tumors
U10CA-29691-11 0035 (CCI) RAVINDRANATH, YADDANAPUDI Pediatric oncology group POG8731--Phase II trial of methotrexate in treatment of brain tumors in children
U10CA-29691-11 0036 (CCI) RAVINDRANATH, YADDANAPUDI Pediatric oncology group POG8788--Intergroup rhabdomyosarcoma study/pilot study for clinical group III
U10CA-29691-11 0037 (CCI) RAVINDRANATH, YADDANAPUDI Pediatric oncology group POG8761--Phase II study of homoharringtonine therapy for nonlymphoblastic leukemi
U10CA-29691-11 0038 (CCI) RAVINDRANATH, YADDANAPUDI Pediatric oncology group POG8739--Phase II immunotherapy with alpha-2 interferon for brain tumors
U10CA-29691-11 0039 (CCI) RAVINDRANATH, YADDANAPUDI Pediatric oncology group POG8741--Treatment of patients with stage C and stage D neuroblastoma
U10CA-29691-11 0040 (CCI) RAVINDRANATH, YADDANAPUDI Pediatric oncology group POG8751--Phase II methotrexate chemotherapy for rhabdomyosarcoma in children
U10CA-29691-11 0041 (CCI) RAVINDRANATH, YADDANAPUDI Pediatric oncology group POG8633--Postoperative chemotherapy and delayed irradiation for brain tumors
U10CA-29691-11 0042 (CCI) RAVINDRANATH, YADDANAPUDI Pediatric oncology group POG8617--Therapy for B-cell acute lymphoblastic leukemia and lymphoma
U10CA-29691-11 0043 (CCI) RAVINDRANATH, YADDANAPUDI Pediatric oncology group POG9139--Phase I study of cisplatin and irradiation in brain stem gliomas
U10CA-29691-11 0044 (CCI) RAVINDRANATH, YADDANAPUDI Pediatric oncology group POG9079--Phase I study of L-PAM/CTX with ABM rescue for brain tumors in children
U10CA-29691-11 0045 (CCI) RAVINDRANATH, YADDANAPUDI Pediatric oncology group POG9075--Phase I study of acivicin in children with solid tumors
U10CA-29691-11 0046 (CCI) RAVINDRANATH, YADDANAPUDI Pediatric oncology group POG9074--Phase I study of xomazyme-H65 in children with T-cell ALL/lymphoma
U10CA-29691-11 0047 (CCI) RAVINDRANATH, YADDANAPUDI Pediatric oncology group POG9072--Phase I chemotherapy for recurrent/resistant malignant solid tumors
U10CA-29691-11 0048 (CCI) RAVINDRANATH, YADDANAPUDI Pediatric oncology group POG9061-Phase II systemic therapy and irradiation for ALL & CNS leukemia
U10CA-29691-11 0049 (CCI) RAVINDRANATH, YADDANAPUDI Pediatric oncology group POG 9086--Phase I pilot study of therapy for T-cell ALL or NHL
U10CA-29691-11 0050 (CCI) RAVINDRANATH, YADDANAPUDI Pediatric oncology group POG9071--Phase I trial of fazarabine in children with acute leukemia
U10CA-29691-11 0051 (CCI) RAVINDRANATH, YADDANAPUDI Pediatric oncology group POG8970--Phase I trial of fazarabine in children with refractory solid tumors
U10CA-29691-11 0052 (CCI) RAVINDRANATH, YADDANAPUDI Pediatric oncology group POG8973--Etoposide (VP-16) and carboplatin in children with acute leukemia
U10CA-29691-11 0053 (CCI) RAVINDRANATH, YADDANAPUDI Pediatric oncology group POG8870--Phase I trial of ifosfamide/VP16/MESNA in children with acute leukemia
U10CA-29691-11 0054 (CCI) RAVINDRANATH, YADDANAPUDI Pediatric oncology group POG8871--Phase I study of rTNF in children with refractory solid tumors
U10CA-29691-11 0055 (CCI) RAVINDRANATH, YADDANAPUDI Pediatric oncology group POG8671--Phase I immunotherapy with rIL-2 in children with solid tumors
U10CA-29691-11 0002 (CCI) RAVINDRANATH, YADDANAPUDI Pediatric oncology group POG9005--Dose intensification of methotrexate & 6-mercaptourine in childhood ALL
U10CA-29691-11 0003 (CCI) RAVINDRANATH, YADDANAPUDI Pediatric oncology group POG9031--Cisplatin/VP-16 therapy of medulloblastoma/pre vs. post irradiation
U10CA-29691-11 0004 (CCI) RAVINDRANATH, YADDANAPUDI Pediatric oncology group POG8945--Phase III chemotherapy for hepatoblastoma &

PROJECT NO., ORGANIZATIONAL UNIT., INVESTIGATOR, ADDRESS, TITLE

hepatocellular carcinoma

U10CA-29691-11 0005 (CCI) RAVINDRANATH, YADDANAPUDI Pediatric oncology group POG9049--Phase III study of high-risk malignant germ cell tumors in children

U10CA-29691-11 0006 (CCI) RAVINDRANATH, YADDANAPUDI Pediatric oncology group POG8844--Bone marrow transplant in children with stage D neuroblastoma

U10CA-29691-11 0007 (CCI) RAVINDRANATH, YADDANAPUDI Pediatric oncology group POG8850--Phase III treatment of Ewing's sarcoma and neuroectodermal bone tumors

U10CA-29691-11 0008 (CCI) RAVINDRANATH, YADDANAPUDI Pediatric oncology group POG8821--Phase III chemotherapy +/- autologous BMT in children with AML

U10CA-29691-11 0009 (CCI) RAVINDRANATH, YADDANAPUDI Pediatric oncology group POG8725--Phase III chemotherapy +/- radiation therapy in pediatric Hodgkins

U10CA-29691-11 0010 (CCI) RAVINDRANATH, YADDANAPUDI Pediatric oncology group POG8704--Phase III chemotherapy of childhood T cell ALL & lymphoblastic lymphoma

U10CA-29691-11 0011 (CCI) RAVINDRANATH, YADDANAPUDI Pediatric oncology group POG8719--Phase III chemotherapy for non-Hodgkin's lymphoma in children

U10CA-29691-11 0012 (CCI) RAVINDRANATH, YADDANAPUDI Pediatric oncology group POG8650--National Wilm's tumor and clear cell sarcoma study

U10CA-29691-11 0013 (CCI) RAVINDRANATH, YADDANAPUDI Pediatric oncology group POG8616--Phase III chemotherapy for childhood Burkitt and non-Burkitts lymphoma

U10CA-29691-11 0014 (CCI) RAVINDRANATH, YADDANAPUDI Pediatric oncology group POG8615--Phase III study of large cell lymphomas in children and adolescents

U10CA-29691-11 0015 (CCI) RAVINDRANATH, YADDANAPUDI Pediatric oncology group POG8651--Phase III study of childhood nonmetastatic osteosarcoma

U10CA-29691-11 0016 (CCI) RAVINDRANATH, YADDANAPUDI Pediatric oncology group POG8653--Phase III study of childhood soft tissue sarcomas

U10CA-29691-11 0017 (CCI) RAVINDRANATH, YADDANAPUDI Pediatric oncology group POG8625--Phase III combined therapy in childhood Hodgkin's disease

U10CA-29691-11 0018 (CCI) RAVINDRANATH, YADDANAPUDI Pediatric oncology group POG8451--Intergroup rhabdomyosarcoma study

U10CA-29691-11 0019 (CCI) RAVINDRANATH, YADDANAPUDI Pediatric oncology group POG9110--Rotational drug therapy after first marrow relapse of non-T, non B ALL

U10CA-29691-11 0020 (CCI) RAVINDRANATH, YADDANAPUDI Pediatric oncology group POG9107--Phase II pilot study of infant leukemia

U10CA-29691-11 0021 (CCI) RAVINDRANATH, YADDANAPUDI Pediatric oncology group POG9140--Phase II therapy for recurrent or refractory neuroblastoma

U10CA-29691-11 0022 (CCI) RAVINDRANATH, YADDANAPUDI Pediatric oncology group POG9048--Phase II study of malignant germ cell tumors in children

U10CA-29691-11 0023 (CCI) RAVINDRANATH, YADDANAPUDI Pediatric oncology group POG9060--Intensive QOD ifosfamide treatment for CNS tumors in children

R01CA-29797-10 (EVR) RICCIARDI, ROBERT P THE WISTAR INSTITUTE 36TH AND SPRUCE STREETS PHILADELPHIA, PA 19104 Organization and expression of adenovirus genes

R01CA-29850-07A2 (ET) VOGLER, WILLIAM R EMORY UNIVERSITY PO BOX AE ATLANTA, GA 30322 Effects of alkyl-lysophospholipids in leukemia

R37CA-29884-11 (EVR) HUNTER, ERIC UNIVERSITY OF ALABAMA UAB STATION BIRMINGHAM, AL 35294 Site specific mutagenesis in the env gene of RSV

R01CA-29894-10 (CBY) ANDREWS, PETER W WISTAR INSTITUTE 36TH AND SPRUCE STREETS PHILADELPHIA, PA 19104 Human teratocarcinoma derived cell lines

R01CA-29995-11 (PTHB) FURCHT, LEO T UNIVERSITY OF MINNESOTA 420 DELAWARE ST SE/BOX 609 MINNEAPOLIS, MN 55455 Laminin peptides/receptors in metastatic cell function

R01CA-29997-09 (PTHB) HONN, KENNETH V WAYNE STATE UNIVERSITY 431 CHEMISTRY DETROIT, MI 48202 Role of eicosanoids in tumor cell metastasis

R01CA-30002-10 (EVR) ROBERTS, THOMAS M DANA-FARBER CANCER INSTITUTE 44 BINNEY STREET BOSTON, MA 02115 Molecular mechanisms of polyoma induced transformation

R01CA-30015-11 (IMB) MORTENSEN, RICHARD F OHIO STATE UNIVERSITY 484 W 12TH AVENUE COLUMBUS, OHIO 43210 Acute phase reactants--Induction and host resistance

R01CA-30088-11 (ET) DRAY, SHELDON UNIV OF ILLINOIS AT CHICAGO DEPT MICROB/IMM, P O BOX 6998 CHICAGO, IL 60680 Synergy of tumor chemotherapy and host immunity

R01CA-30101-09A1 (PTHB) ANTONIADES, HARRY N CENTER FOR BLOOD RESEARCH 800 HUNTINGTON AVE BOSTON, MA 02115 PDGF and neoplastic transformation

R01CA-30103-11 (ET) BECK, WILLIAM T ST JUDE CHILDREN'S RES HOSP 332 NORTH LAUDERDALE MEMPHIS, TN 38101 Microdetection assay for drug-resistant tumors

U10CA-30138-11 (SRC) GEHAN, EDMUND A PEDIATRIC INTERGROUP STAT CTR 1515 HOLCOMBE HOUSTON, TX 77030 Statistical center--Pediatric intergroup studies

R01CA-30147-12 (ALY) GOTTLIEB, PAUL D UNIVERSITY OF TEXAS AT AUSTIN AUSTIN, TX 78712 Genetic markers, leukemogenesis and thymic function

P01CA-30195-11 (CTR) MC GUIRE, WILLIAM L UNIVERSITY OF TEXAS HLTH SCI C 7703 FLOYD CURL DRIVE SAN ANTONIO, TX 78284 Medical oncology program project--Therapeutic research

P01CA-30195-11 0007 (CTR) MC GUIRE, WILLIAM L Medical oncology program project--Therapeutic research Mechanism of antiestrogen action in breast cancer

P01CA-30195-11 0008 (CTR) EDWARDS, DEAN P Medical oncology program project--Therapeutic research Antibodies to progesterone receptors

P01CA-30195-11 0009 (CTR) CLARK, GARY M Medical oncology program project--Therapeutic research Breast cancer cell kinetics

P01CA-30195-11 0010 (CTR) JOCOBS, JOHN W Medical oncology program project--Therapeutic research Hormonal control of gene expression in breast cancer

P01CA-30195-11 0011 (CTR) CHAMNESS, GARY C Medical oncology program project--Therapeutic research Cytochemical methods for steroid receptors in breast cancer

P01CA-30195-11 0012 (CTR) EDWARDS, DEAN P Medical oncology program project--Therapeutic research Monoclonal antibodies to breast tumor cell antigens

P01CA-30195-11 9001 (CTR) EDWARDS, DEAN P Medical oncology program project--Therapeutic research Antibody core laboratory

P01CA-30195-11 9002 (CTR) MC GUIRE, WILLIAM L Medical oncology program project--Therapeutic research Core facility

P30CA-30199-11 (CCS) RUOSLAHTI, ERKKI LA JOLLA CANCER RES FOUNDATION 10901 NORTH TORREY PINES ROAD LA JOLLA, CA 92037 Cancer center support grant

P30CA-30199-11 9006 (CCS) PIERSCHBACHER, MICHAEL D Cancer center support grant Protein chemistry facility

P30CA-30199-11 9007 (CCS) RICHARD, M Cancer center support grant DNA chemistry

P30CA-30199-11 9008 (CCS) ERKI, RUOSLAHTI Cancer center support grant Development of program support

P30CA-30199-11 9001 (CCS) ENGVALL, EVA S Cancer center support grant Animal facility

P30CA-30199-11 9002 (CCS) BIRDWELL, CHARLES R Cancer center support grant Electron microscopy

P30CA-30199-11 9004 (CCS) SANFORD, GERRY Cancer center support grant Photography service

P30CA-30199-11 9005 (CCS) FUKUDA, MINORU Cancer center support grant Shared carbohydrate chemistry

P01CA-30206-10 (SRC) FORMAN, STEPHEN J CITY OF HOPE NATIONAL MED CTR 1500 E. DUARTE ROAD DUARTE, CA 91010-0269 Bone marrow transplantation for hematologic malignancies

P01CA-30206-10 0001 (SRC) FORMAN, STEPHEN J Bone marrow transplantation for hematologic malignancies Allogeneic bone marrow transplantation for hematological malignancy

P01CA-30206-10 0005 (SRC) ZAIA, JOHN A Bone marrow transplantation for hematologic malignancies Biology of cytomegalovirus infection

P01CA-30206-10 0009 (SRC) WALLACE, BRUCE R Bone marrow transplantation for hematologic malignancies Molecular genetic aspects of BMT

P01CA-30206-10 0010 (SRC) MCLAUGHLIN-TAYLOR, ELIZABETH Bone marrow transplantation for hematologic malignancies Antigen specific immune response to HCMV--Antigen and vaccine

P01CA-30206-10 0011 (SRC) SHANLEY, JOHN D Bone marrow transplantation for hematologic malignancies The role of cytokines in CMV-associated interstitial pneumonitis

P01CA-30206-10 9001 (SRC) NILAND, JOYCE C Bone marrow transplantation for hematologic malignancies Core--Biostatistics

R01CA-30241-12 (CPA) MICHALOPOULOS, GEORGE K UNIVERSITY OF PITTSBURGH 3550 TERRACE AT DESOTO PITTSBURGH, PA 15261 Cell culture and transplantation of human hepatocytes

P01CA-30246-11 (CAK) JOKLIK, WOLFGANG K DUKE UNIVERSITY POST OFFICE BOX 3020 DURHAM, N C 27710 Regulatory functions of protein nucleic acid interaction

P01CA-30246-11 0002 (CAK) BASTIA, DEEPAK Regulatory functions of protein nucleic acid interaction DNA-protein and protein-protein interactions

P01CA-30246-11 0003 (CAK) JOKLIK, WOLFGANG K Regulatory functions of protein nucleic acid interaction RNA-protein interaction in reovirus formation

P01CA-30246-11 0004 (CAK) KEENE, JACK D Regulatory functions of protein nucleic acid interaction Cellular ribonucleoproteins

P01CA-30246-11 0005 (CAK) OSTRONSKI, M C Regulatory functions of protein nucleic acid interaction Gene expression in transformed cells

P01CA-30246-11 0006 (CAK) PICKUP, D J Regulatory functions of protein nucleic acid interaction

P01CA-30246-11 9001 (CAK) JOKLIK, WOLFGANG K Regulatory functions of protein nucleic acid interaction Core component

R01CA-30264-10 (EI) KLEIN , GEORGE KAROLINSKA INSTITUTE BOX 60400 STOCKHOLM, SWEDEN S-104 01 Immune effector mechanisms in EBV carrying patients

R01CA-30276-11 (VISA) NIEDERKORN, JERRY Y UNIV OF TEXAS SW MED CTR 5323 HARRY HINES BLVD DALLAS, TX 75235 Immunological modulation of ocular tumor metastasis

R01CA-30280-10 (EI) WEISBART, RICHARD H VA MEDICAL CENTER 16111 PLUMMER STREET SEPULVEDA, CA 91343 Molecular events in neutrophil phagocytosis by IgA

R01CA-30289-09 (PBC) VLODAVSKY, ISRAEL HADASSAH UNIVERSITY HOSPITAL KIRYAT HADASSAH, POB 12000 JERUSALEM 91120, ISRAEL Role of heparanase in tumor invasion and angiogenesis

R01CA-30295-11 (CPA) GOULD, MICHAEL N UNIVERSITY OF WISCONSIN 600 HIGHLAND AVENUE MADISON, WI 53792 Mammary carcinogenesis-interspecies comparisons

R37CA-30356-10 (VR) HAYWARD, S DIANE JOHNS HOPKINS UNIVERSITY 600 N WOLFE STREET BALTIMORE, MD 21205 EBV genome expression--Localization of specific functions

R37CA-30388-11 (NSS) GOLDE, DAVID W DIV OF HEMATOLOGY-ONCOLOGY 37-068 CHS LOS ANGELES, CA 90024-1678 Humoral regulation of normal and malignant hemopoiesis

R37CA-30488-11 (VR) GOFF, STEPHEN P COLUMBIA UNIV/HEALTH SCIENCES 701 WEST 168 STREET NEW YORK, NY 10032 Construction and analysis of retrovirus mutants

R37CA-30490-11 (EVR) BOTCHAN, MICHAEL R UNIVERSITY OF CALIFORNIA 171 GPB BUILDING BERKELEY, CA 94720 Regulatory interactions between tumor viruses and cells

R01CA-30515-09 (EI) SIDELL, NEIL UNIVERSITY OF CALIFORNIA 741 CIRCLE DR S LOS ANGELES, CA 90024-1732 Immunological aspects of retinoids in human cancer

R01CA-30545-07 (CBY) KANO-SUEOKA, TAMIKO UNIVERSITY OF COLORADO CAMPUS BOX 347 BOULDER, CO 80309-0347 Phosphatidylethanolamine and cell proliferation

PROJECT NO., ORGANIZATIONAL UNIT., INVESTIGATOR, ADDRESS, TITLE

R37CA-30558-11 (EI) CHEEVER, MARTIN A UNIVERSITY OF WASHINGTON SEATTLE, WA 98195 Specific immunotherapy of murine tumors
R37CA-30645-11 (PC) STANLEY, PAMELA M ALBERT EINSTEIN COLL OF MED 1300 MORRIS PARK AVENUE BRONX, NY 10461 Glycosylation mutants of animal cells
R01CA-30674-10 (EVR) STEFFEN, DAVID L COLLEGE OF MEDICINE ONE BAYLOR PLAZA HOUSTON, TX 77030 Analysis of cellular oncogenes in virus-induced tumors
R01CA-30688-09 (MGN) ALBERTINI, RICHARD J UNIVERSITY OF VERMONT 32 NORTH PROSPECT STREET BURLINGTON, VT 05401 Direct mutagenicity testing in man
R01CA-30909-08 (MCHA) MC LAUGHLIN, JERRY L PURDUE UNIVERSITY WEST LAFAYETTE, IN 47907 Antitumor fractionation of plants using simple bioassays
R01CA-30931-10 (EDC) HOLFORD, THEODORE R YALE UNIVERSITY SCH OF MEDICIN PO BOX 3333 NEW HAVEN, CT 06510 Systematic analysis: cancer incidence and mortality trends
U10CA-30969-11 (CCI) VIETTI, TERESA J WASHINGTON UNIVERSITY 4949 WEST PINE BLVD, SUITE 2A ST LOUIS, MO 63108 Pediatric Oncology Group - Operations office
R01CA-30981-11 (EVR) GAYNOR, RICHARD B UNIVERSITY OF TEXAS SW MED CTR 5323 HARRY HINES BOULEVARD DALLAS, TX 75235-9030 Transcriptional regulation by the adenovirus E1A protein
R01CA-31101-10 (MEP) KULESZ-MARTIN, MOLLY F ROSWELL PARK MEMORIAL INST 666 ELM ST BUFFALO, NY 14263 Quantitative carcinogenesis in cultured epithelial cells
R01CA-31102-10A2 (EVR) BEDIGIAN, HENDRICK G JACKSON LABORATORY 600 MAIN STREET BAR HARBOR, ME 04609-0800 A new murine model for the study of myeloid leukemia
R01CA-31199-11 (IMB) RUSSELL, STEPHEN W UNIV OF KANSAS MEDICAL CENTER 39TH AND RAINBOW BLVD KANSAS CITY, KANSAS 66103 Macrophage-mediated injury causing tumor regression
P01CA-31224-06S1 (CTR) MOERTEL, CHARLES G MAYO FOUNDATION 200 FIRST STREET SOUTHWEST ROCHESTER, MN 55905 New approaches to treatment by gastrointestinal cancer
P01CA-31224-06S1 0001 (CTR) O'CONNELL, MICHAEL J New approaches to treatment by gastrointestinal cancer Colorectal carcinoma
P01CA-31224-06S1 0003 (CTR) MOERTEL, CHARLES G New approaches to treatment by gastrointestinal cancer Less common gastrointestinal carcinomas
P01CA-31224-06S1 0004 (CTR) KOVACH, JOHN S New approaches to treatment by gastrointestinal cancer In vivo cellular pharmacokinetics of 5-Fu
P01CA-31224-06S1 0005 (CTR) MCKEAN, D J New approaches to treatment by gastrointestinal cancer Clonal expression and targeting cytotoxic lymphocytes
P01CA-31224-06S1 9001 (CTR) O'FALLON, JUDITH R New approaches to treatment by gastrointestinal cancer Core--Statistics
P01CA-31224-06S1 9002 (CTR) MOERTEL, CHARLES G New approaches to treatment by gastrointestinal cancer Pathology-Core
R37CA-31230-09 (RAD) GOMER, CHARLES J CHILDRENS HOSPITAL 4650 SUNSET BLVD LOS ANGELES, CA 90027 Hematoporphyrin distribution and photosensitization
R01CA-31346-09 (IMB) MERUELO, DANIEL NEW YORK UNIV MEDICAL CTR 550 FIRST AVENUE NEW YORK, NY 10016 Study of MuLV sequences in the MHC and cloning minor H genes
R01CA-31363-10 (EVR) DESROSIERS, RONALD C HARVARD MEDICAL SCHOOL ONE PINE HILL DRIVE SOUTHBORO, MASS 01772 Molecular basis for herpesvirus saimiri oncogenicity
R37CA-31397-10 (RAD) LI, GLORIA C SLOAN KETTERING INST FOR CAN R 1275 YORK AVENUE NEW YORK, NY 10021 Fractionated hyperthermia and heat shock proteins
R01CA-31472-07 (MGN) PAPACONSTANTINOU, JOHN UNIVERSITY OF TEXAS MED BR 613 BASIC SCIENCE BUILDING GALVESTON, TX 77550 Mechanism of gene regulation in somatic cell hybrids
R01CA-31526-10 (ET) BURNS, CHARLES P UNIVERSITY OF IOWA HOSPITALS DEPARTMENT OF MEDICINE IOWA CITY, IOWA 52242 Tumor lipids and hyperthermia/chemotherapy
R01CA-31534-10 (EI) TUCKER, PHILIP W UNIV OF TX SOUTHWESTERN MED CT 5323 HARRY HINES BLVD DALLAS, TX 75235 Isotype switching in a neoplastic B cell model, BCL1
U10CA-31566-10 (CCI) PUI, CHING-HON ST JUDE CHILDRENS RES HOSP 332 N LAUDERDALE MEMPHIS, TN 38101 Pediatric oncology group participation
U10CA-31566-10 0010 (CCI) PUI, CHING-HON Pediatric oncology group participation POG8704--Phase III chemotherapy of childhood T cell ALL & lymphoblastic lymphoma
U10CA-31566-10 0011 (CCI) PUI, CHING-HON Pediatric oncology group participation POG8719--Phase III chemotherapy for non-Hodgkin's lymphoma in children
U10CA-31566-10 0012 (CCI) PUI, CHING-HON Pediatric oncology group participation POG8650--National Wilm's tumor and clear cell sarcoma study
U10CA-31566-10 0013 (CCI) PUI, CHING-HON Pediatric oncology group participation POG8616--Phase III chemotherapy for childhood Burkitt and non-Burkitts lymphoma
U10CA-31566-10 0014 (CCI) PUI, CHING-HON Pediatric oncology group participation POG8615--Phase III study of large cell lymphomas in children and adolescents
U10CA-31566-10 0015 (CCI) PUI, CHING-HON Pediatric oncology group participation POG8651--Phase III study of childhood nonmetastatic osteosarcoma
U10CA-31566-10 0016 (CCI) PUI, CHING-HON Pediatric oncology group participation POG8653--Phase III study of childhood soft tissue sarcomas
U10CA-31566-10 0017 (CCI) PUI, CHING-HON Pediatric oncology group participation POG8625--Phase III combined therapy in childhood Hodgkin's disease
U10CA-31566-10 0018 (CCI) PUI, CHING-HON Pediatric oncology group participation POG8451--Intergroup rhabdomyosarcoma study
U10CA-31566-10 0019 (CCI) PUI, CHING-HON Pediatric oncology group participation POG9110--Rotational drug therapy after first marrow relapse of non-T, non B ALL

PROJECT NO., ORGANIZATIONAL UNIT., INVESTIGATOR, ADDRESS, TITLE

U10CA-31566-10 0020 (CCI) PUI, CHING-HON Pediatric oncology group participation POG9107--Phase II pilot study of infant leukemia
U10CA-31566-10 0021 (CCI) PUI, CHING-HON Pediatric oncology group participation POG9140--Phase II therapy for recurrent or refractory neuroblastoma
U10CA-31566-10 0022 (CCI) PUI, CHING-HON Pediatric oncology group participation POG9048--Phase II study of malignant germ cell tumors in children
U10CA-31566-10 0023 (CCI) PUI, CHING-HON Pediatric oncology group participation POG9060--Intensive QOD ifosfamide treatment for CNS tumors in children
U10CA-31566-10 0024 (CCI) PUI, CHING-HON Pediatric oncology group participation POG8936--Phase II study of carboplatin treatment for optic pathway tumors
U10CA-31566-10 0025 (CCI) PUI, CHING-HON Pediatric oncology group participation POG8935--Phase II study of surgery and/or radiotherapy for optic pathway tumors
U10CA-31566-10 0026 (CCI) PUI, CHING-HON Pediatric oncology group participation POG8820--Phase II/III study of VP-16, AMSA +/- 5-azacytidine in childhood ANLL
U10CA-31566-10 0027 (CCI) PUI, CHING-HON Pediatric oncology group participation POG8889--Intergroup rhabdomyosarcoma study for clinical group IV disease
U10CA-31566-10 0028 (CCI) PUI, CHING-HON Pediatric oncology group participation POG8866--Phase II asparaginase therapy for acute lymphoblastic leukemia
U10CA-31566-10 0029 (CCI) PUI, CHING-HON Pediatric oncology group participation POG8862--Combination chemotherapy of acute T-lymphoblastic leukemia
U10CA-31566-10 0030 (CCI) PUI, CHING-HON Pediatric oncology group participation POG8863--Phase II study of high dose cytosine arabinoside in childhood tumors
U10CA-31566-10 0031 (CCI) PUI, CHING-HON Pediatric oncology group participation POG8827--Phase II treatment of children with Hodgkin's disease in relapse
U10CA-31566-10 0032 (CCI) PUI, CHING-HON Pediatric oncology group participation POG8865--Phase II recombinant alpha-interferon in relapsed T-cell disease
U10CA-31566-10 0033 (CCI) PUI, CHING-HON Pediatric oncology group--Phase II recombinant A-interferon in chronic myelogenous leukemia
U10CA-31566-10 0034 (CCI) PUI, CHING-HON Pediatric oncology group participation POG8832--Combination chemotherapy followed by radiotherapy for brain tumors
U10CA-31566-10 0035 (CCI) PUI, CHING-HON Pediatric oncology group participation POG8731--Phase II trial of methotrexate in treatment of brain tumors in children
U10CA-31566-10 0036 (CCI) PUI, CHING-HON Pediatric oncology group participation POG8788--Intergroup rhabdomyosarcoma study/pilot study for clinical group III
U10CA-31566-10 0037 (CCI) PUI, CHING-HON Pediatric oncology group participation POG8761--Phase II study of homoharringtonine therapy for nonlymphoblastic leukemi
U10CA-31566-10 0038 (CCI) PUI, CHING-HON Pediatric oncology group participation POG8739--Phase II immunotherapy with alpha-2 interferon for brain tumors
U10CA-31566-10 0039 (CCI) PUI, CHING-HON Pediatric oncology group participation POG8741--Treatment of patients with stage C and stage D neuroblastoma
U10CA-31566-10 0040 (CCI) PUI, CHING-HON Pediatric oncology group participation POG8751--Phase II methotrexate chemotherapy for rhabdomyosarcoma in children
U10CA-31566-10 0041 (CCI) PUI, CHING-HON Pediatric oncology group participation POG8633--Postoperative chemotherapy and delayed irradiation for brain tumors
U10CA-31566-10 0001 (CCI) PUI, CHING-HON Pediatric oncology group participation POG9006--6-MP/methotrexate vs. alternating chemotherapy for ALL in childhood
U10CA-31566-10 0042 (CCI) PUI, CHING-HON Pediatric oncology group participation POG8617--Therapy for B-cell acute lymphoblastic leukemia and lymphoma
U10CA-31566-10 0043 (CCI) PUI, CHING-HON Pediatric oncology group participation POG9139--Phase I study of cisplatin and irradiation in brain stem gliomas
U10CA-31566-10 0044 (CCI) PUI, CHING-HON Pediatric oncology group participation POG9079--Phase I study of L-PAM/CTX with ABM rescue for brain tumors in children
U10CA-31566-10 0045 (CCI) PUI, CHING-HON Pediatric oncology group participation POG9075--Phase I study of acivicin in children with solid tumors
U10CA-31566-10 0046 (CCI) PUI, CHING-HON Pediatric oncology group participation POG9074--Phase I study of xomazyme-H65 in children with T-cell ALL/lymphoma
U10CA-31566-10 0047 (CCI) PUI, CHING-HON Pediatric oncology group participation POG9072--Phase I chemotherapy for recurrent/resistant malignant solid tumors
U10CA-31566-10 0048 (CCI) PUI, CHING-HON Pediatric oncology group participation POG9061-Phase II systemic therapy and irradiation for ALL & CNS leukemia
U10CA-31566-10 0049 (CCI) PUI, CHING-HON Pediatric oncology group participation POG 9086--Phase I pilot study of therapy for T-cell ALL or NHL
U10CA-31566-10 0050 (CCI) PUI, CHING-HON Pediatric oncology group participation POG9071--Phase I trial of fazarabine in children with acute leukemia
U10CA-31566-10 0051 (CCI) PUI, CHING-HON Pediatric oncology group participation POG8970--Phase I trial of fazarabine in children with refractory solid tumors
U10CA-31566-10 0052 (CCI) PUI, CHING-HON Pediatric oncology group participation POG8973--Etoposide (VP-16) and carboplatin in children with acute leukemia
U10CA-31566-10 0053 (CCI) PUI, CHING-HON Pediatric oncology group participation POG8870--Phase I trial of ifosfamide/VP16/MESNA in

PROJECT NO., ORGANIZATIONAL UNIT., INVESTIGATOR, ADDRESS, TITLE

children with acute leukemia
U10CA-31566-10 0054 (CCI) PUI, CHING-HON Pediatric oncology group participation POG8871--Phase I study of rTNF in children with refractory solid tumors
U10CA-31566-10 0055 (CCI) PUI, CHING-HON Pediatric oncology group participation POG8671--Phase I immunotherapy with rIL-2 in children with solid tumors
U10CA-31566-10 0056 (CCI) PUI, CHING-HON Pediatric oncology group participation POG8494--Phase I study of fludarabine phosphate in pediatric patients
U10CA-31566-10 0057 (CCI) PUI, CHING-HON Pediatric oncology group participation POG8930--A comprehensive genetic analysis of brain tumors
U10CA-31566-10 0058 (CCI) PUI, CHING-HON Pediatric oncology group participation POG8828--Late effects of Hodgkin's disease
U10CA-31566-10 0059 (CCI) PUI, CHING-HON Pediatric oncology group participation POG9046--Molecular genetic analysis of Wilm's tumors
U10CA-31566-10 0060 (CCI) PUI, CHING-HON Pediatric oncology group participation POG9153--Rhabdomyosarcoma study/laboratory evaluation of tumor
U10CA-31566-10 0002 (CCI) PUI, CHING-HON Pediatric oncology group participation POG9005--Dose intensification of methotrexate & 6-mercaptourine in childhood ALL
U10CA-31566-10 0003 (CCI) PUI, CHING-HON Pediatric oncology group participation POG9031--Cisplatin/VP-16 therapy of medulloblastoma/pre vs. post irradiation
U10CA-31566-10 0004 (CCI) PUI, CHING-HON Pediatric oncology group participation POG8945--Phase III chemotherapy for hepatoblastoma & hepatocellular carcinoma
U10CA-31566-10 0005 (CCI) PUI, CHING-HON Pediatric oncology group participation POG9049--Phase III study of high-risk malignant germ cell tumors in children
U10CA-31566-10 0006 (CCI) PUI, CHING-HON Pediatric oncology group participation POG8844--Bone marrow transplant in children with stage D neuroblastoma
U10CA-31566-10 0007 (CCI) PUI, CHING-HON Pediatric oncology group participation POG8850--Phase III treatment of Ewing's sarcoma and neuroectodermal bone tumors
U10CA-31566-10 0008 (CCI) PUI, CHING-HON Pediatric oncology group participation POG8821--Phase III chemotherapy +/- autologous BMT in children with AML
U10CA-31566-10 0009 (CCI) PUI, CHING-HON Pediatric oncology group participation POG8725--Phase III chemotherapy +/- radiation therapy in pediatric Hodgkins
R37CA-31612-10 (RAD) WITHERS, H RODNEY UCLA CENTER FOR HEALTH SCI 10833 LECONTE AVE LOS ANGELES, CA 90024-1714 Late effects of radiotherapy: biology and quantitation
R01CA-31615-10 (HEM) KAUSHANSKY, KENNETH UNIVERSITY OF WASHINGTON SEATTLE, WA 98195 Growth factors in normal & neoplastic hematopoiesis
R01CA-31618-10 (RAD) VALLERA, DANIEL A UNIV OF MINNESOTA MEDICAL SCHO HARVARD ST AT EAST RIVER ROAD MINNEAPOLIS, MN 55455 Irradiation and the immune system
R01CA-31635-07A3 (ET) HRUSHESKY, WILLIAM J M ALBANY V A MED. CENTER (111C) 113 HOLLAND AVE ALBANY, NY 12208 Clinical application of chronobiology to cancer medicine
R01CA-31641-07A2 (MEP) LOTLIKAR, PRABHAKAR D FELS INST FOR CANCER RESEARCH 3420 NORTH BROAD STREET PHILADELPHIA, PA 19140 Modulation of mycotoxin carcinogenesis by glutathione
R01CA-31680-10 (CPA) DERUBERTIS, FREDERICK R VA MEDICAL CENTER UNIVERSITY DR C PITTSBURGH, PA 15240 Phospholipid derived signals in colon epithelial growth
R01CA-31685-10 (IMB) LEBIEN, TUCKER W UNIVERSITY OF MINNESOTA PO BOX 609 UMHC MINNEAPOLIS, MN 55455 Differentiative programs of lymphoid progenitor cells
R01CA-31719-10 (EVR) CHINNADURAI, GOVINDASWAMY ST LOUIS UNIVERSITY 3681 PARK AVENUE ST LOUIS, MO 63110 Genetic analysis of adenovirus 2 early genes
R01CA-31721-10 (CPA) MITRA, SANKAR OAK RIDGE NATIONAL LAB PO BOX 2009 OAK RIDGE, TN 37831-8077 DNA repair and nitrosamine-induced carcinogenesis
R01CA-31733-10 (CPA) KAUFMAN, DAVID G UNIV OF N C AT CHAPEL HILL CB 7525 CHAPEL HILL, NC 27599-7525 Promotion of chemical carcinogenesis in uterine tissue
R01CA-31753-09 (ET) HAWTHORNE, M FREDERICK UNIV OF CALIF AT LA 405 HILGARD AVENUE LOS ANGELES, CA 90024 Boron-10-labeled antibodies in cancer therapy
R01CA-31760-10 (CBY) GOLDMAN, ROBERT D NORTHWESTERN UNIV MED SCH 303 EAST CHICAGO AVENUE CHICAGO, IL 60611 Interactions between intermediate filaments and nucleus
R01CA-31770-09 (NEUA) NEUWELT, EDWARD A OREGON HEALTH SCIENCES UNIV 3181 S W SAM JACKSON PARK ROAD PORTLAND, OR 97201 Osmotic opening of the blood-brain-barrier
R01CA-31781-11 (MGN) DAVIDSON, RICHARD L UNIVERSITY OF ILLINOIS 808 S WOOD ST, COLLEGE OF MED CHICAGO, ILL 60612 Mechanisms of chemical mutagenesis in mammalian cells
R01CA-31787-11 (HEM) STORB, RAINER F FRED HUTCHINSON CANCER RES CTR 1124 COLUMBIA STREET SEATTLE, WA 98104 Irradiation and marrow transplantation
R01CA-31789-13 (IMB) DATTA, SYAMAL K NEW ENGLAND MEDICAL CENTER HOS 750 WASHINGTON STREET; BOX 52 BOSTON, MA 02111 Genetic-viral-immunologic studies
R01CA-31798-11 (IMB) SPRINGER, TIMOTHY A CENTER FOR BLOOD RESEARCH 800 HUNTINGTON AVENUE BOSTON, MA 02115 Lymphocyte function-associated (LFA) antigens
R37CA-31799-11 (IMB) SPRINGER, TIMOTHY A CENTER FOR BLOOD RESEARCH 800 HUNTINGTON AVENUE BOSTON, MA 02115 The leukocyte adhesion receptors mac-1 and p150,95
R01CA-31808-11 (RAD) DEWEY, WILLIAM C UNIVERSITY OF CALIFORNIA MCB 200, BOX 0806 SAN FRANCISCO, CA 94143 Molecular basis of radiosensitization by hyperthermia
U10CA-31809-09 (CCI) COOPER, BERNARD A MCGILL CANCER CENTER 3655 DRUMMOND STREET, MONTREAL QUEBEC, CANADA H3G 1Y6 cancer and leukemia group b
R01CA-31810-11 (BIO) ROTTMAN, FRITZ M CASE WESTERN RESERVE UNIVERSIT 2109 ADELBERT ROAD CLEVELAND, OH 44106 N6 methyladenosine formation and function in eukaryotic mRNA
R37CA-31813-11 (NSS) DEWEY, WILLIAM C UNIV OF CA, SAN FRANCISCO CED 200, BOX 0806 SAN FRANCISCO, CA 94143-0806 Cellular responses to irradiation
R01CA-31841-11 (BNP) WENDER, PAUL A STANFORD UNIVERSITY STANFORD, CA 94305 Synthetic studies on tumor promoters and inhibitors
R01CA-31845-11 (MCHA) WENDER, PAUL A STANFORD UNIVERSITY STANFORD, CA 94305-5080 Synthetic studies related to cancer research/treatment
R01CA-31888-09 (ET) BALL, EDWARD D MONTEFIORE UNIVERSITY HOSPITAL 2 NORTH PITTSBURGH, PA 15213 Monoclonal antibodies for the treatment of leukemia
R37CA-31893-10 (VR) THORLEY-LAWSON, DAVID A TUFTS UNIVERSITY SCHOOL OF MED 136 HARRISON AVENUE BOSTON, MA 02111 Epstein-Barr virus membrane antigens
R01CA-31894-10 (PC) JACOB, SAMSON T THE CHICAGO MEDICAL SCHOOL 3333 GREEN BAY ROAD NORTH CHICAGO, IL 60064 Control of rRNA synthesis by carcinogens and hormones
U10CA-31946-10 (CCI) MCINTYRE, ROSS O DARTMOUTH-HITCHCOCK MED CTR NORRIS COTTON CANCER CTR HANOVER, NH 03756 Cancer and Leukemia Group B-Chairman's grant
R01CA-31949-08A3 (EVR) NONOYAMA, MEIHAN TAMPA BAY RESEARCH INSTITUTE 10900 ROOSEVELT BOULEVARD ST PETERSBURG, FL 33716 Marek's disease virus--transformation & oncogenesis
U10CA-31983-10 (CCI) AISNER, JOSEPH UNIV OF MARYLAND HOSPITAL 22 SOUTH GREENE STREET BALTIMORE, MD 21201 Participation in CALGB
U10CA-32053-09 (CCI) CAMITTA, BRUCE M MEDICAL COLLEGE OF WISCONSIN 8701 WATERTOWN PLANK ROAD MILWAUKEE, WI 53226 Pediatric oncology group participation
U10CA-32053-09 0047 (CCI) CAMITTA, BRUCE M Pediatric oncology group participation POG9072--Phase I chemotherapy for recurrent/resistant malignant solid tumors
U10CA-32053-09 0048 (CCI) CAMITTA, BRUCE M Pediatric oncology group participation POG9061-Phase II systemic therapy and irradiation for ALL & CNS leukemia
U10CA-32053-09 0049 (CCI) CAMITTA, BRUCE M Pediatric oncology group participation POG 9086--Phase I pilot study of therapy for T-cell ALL or NHL
U10CA-32053-09 0050 (CCI) CAMITTA, BRUCE M Pediatric oncology group participation POG9071--Phase I trial of fazarabine in children with acute leukemia
U10CA-32053-09 0051 (CCI) CAMITTA, BRUCE M Pediatric oncology group participation POG8970--Phase I trial of fazarabine in children with refractory solid tumors
U10CA-32053-09 0052 (CCI) CAMITTA, BRUCE M Pediatric oncology group participation POG8973--Etoposide (VP-16) and carboplatin in children with acute leukemia
U10CA-32053-09 0053 (CCI) CAMITTA, BRUCE M Pediatric oncology group participation POG8870--Phase I trial of ifosfamide/VP16/MESNA in children with acute leukemia
U10CA-32053-09 0054 (CCI) CAMITTA, BRUCE M Pediatric oncology group participation POG8871--Phase I study of rTNF in children with refractory solid tumors
U10CA-32053-09 0055 (CCI) CAMITTA, BRUCE M Pediatric oncology group participation POG8671--Phase I immunotherapy with rIL-2 in children with solid tumors
U10CA-32053-09 0056 (CCI) CAMITTA, BRUCE M Pediatric oncology group participation POG8494--Phase I study of fludarabine phosphate in pediatric patients
U10CA-32053-09 0057 (CCI) CAMITTA, BRUCE M Pediatric oncology group participation POG8930--A comprehensive genetic analysis of brain tumors
U10CA-32053-09 0058 (CCI) CAMITTA, BRUCE M Pediatric oncology group participation POG8828--Late effects of Hodgkin's disease
U10CA-32053-09 0059 (CCI) CAMITTA, BRUCE M Pediatric oncology group participation POG9046--Molecular genetic analysis of Wilm's tumors
U10CA-32053-09 0060 (CCI) CAMITTA, BRUCE M Pediatric oncology group participation POG9153--Rhabdomyosarcoma study/laboratory evaluation of tumor
U10CA-32053-09 0001 (CCI) CAMITTA, BRUCE M Pediatric oncology group participation POG9006--6-MP/methotrexate vs. alternating chemotherapy for ALL in childhood
U10CA-32053-09 0015 (CCI) CAMITTA, BRUCE M Pediatric oncology group participation POG8651--Phase III study of childhood nonmetastatic osteosarcoma
U10CA-32053-09 0016 (CCI) CAMITTA, BRUCE M Pediatric oncology group participation POG8653--Phase III study of childhood soft tissue sarcomas
U10CA-32053-09 0017 (CCI) CAMITTA, BRUCE M Pediatric oncology group participation POG8625--Phase III combined therapy in childhood Hodgkin's disease
U10CA-32053-09 0018 (CCI) CAMITTA, BRUCE M Pediatric oncology group participation POG8451--Intergroup rhabdomyosarcoma study
U10CA-32053-09 0019 (CCI) CAMITTA, BRUCE M Pediatric oncology group participation POG9110--Rotational drug therapy after first marrow relapse of non-T, non B ALL
U10CA-32053-09 0020 (CCI) CAMITTA, BRUCE M Pediatric oncology group participation POG9107--Phase II pilot study of infant leukemia
U10CA-32053-09 0021 (CCI) CAMITTA, BRUCE M Pediatric oncology group participation POG9140--Phase II therapy for recurrent or refractory neuroblastoma
U10CA-32053-09 0022 (CCI) CAMITTA, BRUCE M Pediatric oncology group participation POG9048--Phase II study of malignant germ cell tumors in children
U10CA-32053-09 0023 (CCI) CAMITTA, BRUCE M Pediatric oncology group participation POG9060--Intensive QOD ifosfamide treatment for CNS tumors in children
U10CA-32053-09 0024 (CCI) CAMITTA, BRUCE M Pediatric oncology group participation POG8936--Phase II study of carboplatin treatment for

PROJECT NO., ORGANIZATIONAL UNIT., INVESTIGATOR, ADDRESS, TITLE

optic pathway tumors
U10CA-32053-09 0025 (CCI) CAMITTA, BRUCE M Pediatric oncology group participation POG8935–Phase II study of surgery and/or radiotherapy for optic pathway tumors
U10CA-32053-09 0026 (CCI) CAMITTA, BRUCE M Pediatric oncology group participation POG8620–Phase II/III study of VP-16, AMSA +/- 5-azacytidine in childhood ANLL
U10CA-32053-09 0027 (CCI) CAMITTA, BRUCE M Pediatric oncology group participation POG8889–Intergroup rhabdomyosarcoma study for clinical group IV disease
U10CA-32053-09 0028 (CCI) CAMITTA, BRUCE M Pediatric oncology group participation POG8866–Phase II asparaginase therapy for acute lymphoblastic leukemia
U10CA-32053-09 0029 (CCI) CAMITTA, BRUCE M Pediatric oncology group participation POG8862–Combination chemotherapy of acute T-lymphoblastic leukemia
U10CA-32053-09 0030 (CCI) CAMITTA, BRUCE M Pediatric oncology group participation POG8863–Phase II study of high dose cytosine arabinoside in childhood tumors
U10CA-32053-09 0031 (CCI) CAMITTA, BRUCE M Pediatric oncology group participation POG8827–Phase II treatment of children with Hodgkin's disease in relapse
U10CA-32053-09 0032 (CCI) CAMITTA, BRUCE M Pediatric oncology group participation POG8865–Phase II recombinant alpha-interferon in relapsed T-cell disease
U10CA-32053-09 0033 (CCI) CAMITTA, BRUCE M Pediatric oncology group–Phase II recombinant A-interferon in chronic myelogenous leukemia
U10CA-32053-09 0034 (CCI) CAMITTA, BRUCE M Pediatric oncology group participation POG8832–Combination chemotherapy followed by radiotherapy for brain tumors
U10CA-32053-09 0035 (CCI) CAMITTA, BRUCE M Pediatric oncology group participation POG8731–Phase II trial of methotrexate in treatment of brain tumors in children
U10CA-32053-09 0036 (CCI) CAMITTA, BRUCE M Pediatric oncology group participation POG8788–Intergroup rhabdomyosarcoma study/pilot study for clinical group III
U10CA-32053-09 0037 (CCI) CAMITTA, BRUCE M Pediatric oncology group participation POG8761–Phase II study of homoharringtonine therapy for nonlymphoblastic leukemi
U10CA-32053-09 0038 (CCI) CAMITTA, BRUCE M Pediatric oncology group participation POG8739–Phase II immunotherapy with alpha-2 interferon for brain tumors
U10CA-32053-09 0039 (CCI) CAMITTA, BRUCE M Pediatric oncology group participation POG8741–Treatment of patients with stage C and stage D neuroblastoma
U10CA-32053-09 0040 (CCI) CAMITTA, BRUCE M Pediatric oncology group participation POG8751–Phase II methotrexate chemotherapy for rhabdomyosarcoma in children
U10CA-32053-09 0041 (CCI) CAMITTA, BRUCE M Pediatric oncology group participation POG8633–Postoperative chemotherapy and delayed irradiation for brain tumors
U10CA-32053-09 0042 (CCI) CAMITTA, BRUCE M Pediatric oncology group participation POG8617–Therapy for B-cell acute lymphoblastic leukemia and lymphoma
U10CA-32053-09 0043 (CCI) CAMITTA, BRUCE M Pediatric oncology group participation POG9139–Phase I study of cisplatin and irradiation in brain stem gliomas
U10CA-32053-09 0044 (CCI) CAMITTA, BRUCE M Pediatric oncology group participation POG9079–Phase I study of L-PAM/CTX with ABM rescue for brain tumors in children
U10CA-32053-09 0045 (CCI) CAMITTA, BRUCE M Pediatric oncology group participation POG9075–Phase I study of acivicin in children with solid tumors
U10CA-32053-09 0046 (CCI) CAMITTA, BRUCE M Pediatric oncology group participation POG9074–Phase I study of xomazyme-H65 in children with T-cell ALL/lymphoma
U10CA-32053-09 0002 (CCI) CAMITTA, BRUCE M Pediatric oncology group participation POG9005–Dose intensification of methotrexate & 6-mercaptopurine in childhood ALL
U10CA-32053-09 0003 (CCI) CAMITTA, BRUCE M Pediatric oncology group participation POG9031–Cisplatin/VP-16 therapy of medulloblastoma/pre vs. post irradiation
U10CA-32053-09 0004 (CCI) CAMITTA, BRUCE M Pediatric oncology group participation POG8945–Phase III chemotherapy for hepatoblastoma & hepatocellular carcinoma
U10CA-32053-09 0005 (CCI) CAMITTA, BRUCE M Pediatric oncology group participation POG9049–Phase III study of high-risk malignant germ cell tumors in children
U10CA-32053-09 0006 (CCI) CAMITTA, BRUCE M Pediatric oncology group participation POG8844–Bone marrow transplant in children with stage D neuroblastoma
U10CA-32053-09 0007 (CCI) CAMITTA, BRUCE M Pediatric oncology group participation POG8850–Phase III treatment of Ewing's sarcoma and neuroectodermal bone tumors
U10CA-32053-09 0008 (CCI) CAMITTA, BRUCE M Pediatric oncology group participation POG8821–Phase III chemotherapy +/- autologous BMT in children with AML
U10CA-32053-09 0009 (CCI) CAMITTA, BRUCE M Pediatric oncology group participation POG8725–Phase III chemotherapy +/- radiation therapy in pediatric Hodgkins
U10CA-32053-09 0010 (CCI) CAMITTA, BRUCE M Pediatric oncology group participation POG8704–Phase III chemotherapy of childhood T cell ALL & lymphoblastic lymphoma
U10CA-32053-09 0011 (CCI) CAMITTA, BRUCE M Pediatric oncology group participation POG8719–Phase III chemotherapy for non-Hodgkin's lymphoma in children
U10CA-32053-09 0012 (CCI) CAMITTA, BRUCE M Pediatric oncology group participation POG8650–National Wilm's tumor and clear cell sarcoma study
U10CA-32053-09 0013 (CCI) CAMITTA, BRUCE M Pediatric oncology group participation POG8616–Phase III chemotherapy for childhood Burkitt and non-Burkitts lymphoma

PROJECT NO., ORGANIZATIONAL UNIT., INVESTIGATOR, ADDRESS, TITLE

U10CA-32053-09 0014 (CCI) CAMITTA, BRUCE M Pediatric oncology group participation POG8615–Phase III study of large cell lymphomas in children and adolescents
R01CA-32066-08 (MGN) KIDD, KENNETH K YALE UNIVERSITY SCH OF MED 333 CEDAR STREET NEW HAVEN, CT 06510 Genetic linkage in multiple endocrine neoplasia, type II
U10CA-32102-11 (CCI) COLTMAN, CHARLES A, JR CANCER THERAPY & RESEARCH CTR 4450 MEDICAL DRIVE SAN ANTONIO, TX 78229 Southwest oncology group–Operations office
U10CA-32115-10 (CCI) PAJAK, THOMAS F AMERICAN COLLEGE OF RADIOLOGY 1101 MARKET ST. 14TH FLOOR PHILADELPHIA, PA 19107 Radiation therapy oncology group-statistical unit
R01CA-32126-06 (MEP) MC COY, GEORGE D CASE WESTERN RESERVE UNIV 2109 ADELBERT ROAD CLEVELAND, OH 44106 Role of ethanol in the etiology of head & neck cancer
R37CA-32157-10 (CPA) RANDERATH, KURT BAYLOR COLLEGE OF MEDICINE ONE BAYLOR PLAZA HOUSTON, TX 77030 32p-labeling test for nucleic acid damage by carcinogens
R01CA-32186-17 (HEM) SALSER, WINSTON A DEPARTMENT OF BIOLOGY LOS ANGELES, CA 90024 Rec-DNA analysis of human hematopoietic differentiation
R01CA-32197-10 (EDC) PAGANINI- HILL, ANNLIA UNIV OF SOUTHERN CALIFORNIA 1441 EASTLAKE AVENUE #802 LOS ANGELES, CA 90033 Estrogens and life-style practices in disease prevention
R01CA-32226-10 (ET) HARMON, JEFFREY M UNIFORMED SERVICES UNIVERSITY 4301 JONES BRIDGE ROAD BETHESDA, MD 20814 Steroid resistance in human leukemic cells
R01CA-32241-09 (SRC) DEEN, DARWIN D JR RGNL NTRTN CTR/NY ACDMY MED 2 EAST 103RD STREET NEW YORK, NY 10029 The regional center for clinical nutrition education
R01CA-32248-09 (RNM) BERNS, MICHAEL W UNIVERSITY OF CALIFORNIA BECKMAN LASER INST & MED CLINI IRVINE, CA 92717 Laser photoradiation therapy of malignant tumors
R01CA-32259-09 (RAD) LIN, CHI-WEI MASSACHUSETTS GENERAL HOSPITAL FRUIT STREET BOSTON, MA 02114 Photo therapy of bladder cancer : new photosensitizers
U10CA-32291-10 (CCI) CANELLOS, GEORGE P 44 BINNEY STREET BOSTON, MA 02115 Cancer and leukemia group B
R01CA-32317-11 (EVR) SHALLOWAY, DAVID I CORNELL UNIV OFC OF SPON PROG 120 DAY HALL ITHACA, NY 14853-2801 Role of pp60c-src homolog of the RSV oncogenic protein
R01CA-32369-09 (HEM) ROTHENBERG, SHELDON P SUNY HLTH SCI CTR AT BROOKLYN 450 CLARKSON AVENUE BROOKLYN, N Y 11203 Folate binders in hematopoiesis and cell replication
R01CA-32387-09 (BCE) TINDALL, DONALD J MAYO FOUNDATION 200 FIRST STREET SOUTHWEST ROCHESTER, MN 55905 Androgen receptors in cancerous prostatic tissue
R37CA-32436-10 (CPA) STRAUSS, BERNARD S UNIVERSITY OF CHICAGO 920 E 58TH STREET CHICAGO, IL 60637 Error prone DNA synthesis and oncogene mutagenesis
R01CA-32455-11 (VR) FAN, HUNG Y UNIVERSITY OF CALIFORNIA IRVINE, CA 92717 Expression and pathogenesis of murine leukemia virus
R01CA-32513-08S2 (PTHB) COHEN, SAMUEL MONROE UNIV OF NEBRASKA MED CTR 600 SOUTH 42ND STREET OMAHA, NE 68198-3135 Studies on experimental bladder tumors
R37CA-32546-16 (RAD) BERNHARD, WILLIAM A UNIVERSITY OF ROCHESTER ROCHESTER, N Y 14642 Solid state radiation chemistry of nucleic acid bases
R01CA-32551-10 (HEM) STANLEY, EVAN R ALBERT EINSTEIN COLLEGE OF MED 1300 MORRIS PARK AVENUE BRONX, NY 10461 Hemopoietic stem cell differentiation to macrophages
R01CA-32553-10 (EI) POLLACK, SYLVIA B SCHOOL OF MEDICINE UNIVERSITY OF WASHINGTON SEATTLE, WA 98195 Production of natural killer cells
R01CA-32579-10 (RAD) GRIFFITHS, T DANIEL NORTHERN ILLINOIS UNIVERSITY DEKALB, IL 60115 DNA replication after insult wth UV
R01CA-32605-10 (VR) SHAFRITZ, DAVID A ALBERT EINSTEIN COLL OF MED 1300 MORRIS PARK AVE BRONX, N Y 10461 Hepatitis B virus - chronic hepatitis - liver cancer
R01CA-32613-09 (ET) HOUGHTON, JANET A ST JUDE CHILDREN'S RES HOSPITA 332 NORTH LAUDERDALE MEMPHIS, TN 38101 Selective therapy for colon carcinoma
P01CA-32617-09A1 (SRC) WYNDER, ERNST L AMERICAN HEALTH FOUNDATION 320 EAST 43RD STREET NEW YORK, NY 10017 Interdisciplinary studies in cancer epidemiology
P01CA-32617-09A1 0001 (SRC) KABAT, GEOFFREY C Interdisciplinary studies in cancer epidemiology General epidemiology of tobacco-related cancers
P01CA-32617-09A1 0007 (SRC) MURPHY, SHARON E Interdisciplinary studies in cancer epidemiology Tobacco-specific nitrosamine hemoglobin adducts in tobacco users
P01CA-32617-09A1 0008 (SRC) HARRIS, RANDALL E Interdisciplinary studies in cancer epidemiology Comparison of tobacco-related cancers in blacks and whites
P01CA-32617-09A1 0009 (SRC) RICHIE, JOHN P Interdisciplinary studies in cancer epidemiology Metabolic epidemiology of tobacco-related cancers in blacks and whites
P01CA-32617-09A1 9001 (SRC) ZANG, EDITH A Interdisciplinary studies in cancer epidemiology Core–Biostatistics and computer facility
R01CA-32638-11 (EVR) LANCASTER, WAYNE D WAYNE STATE UNIVERSITY 540 E CANFIELD/3216 SCOTT HALL DETROIT, MI 48201 Papillomavirus DNA and antigens in cervical neoplasia
R01CA-32685-10 (IMB) SONDEL, PAUL M UW CLINICAL CANCER CENTER 600 HIGHLAND AVENUE MADISON, WI 53792 The immunobiology of human antileukemic lymphocytes
R01CA-32695-08 (EVR) PETERSON, DAVID O TEXAS A & M UNIVERSITY COLLEGE STATION, TX 77843 Genetic and molecular analysis of steroid responsiveness
R01CA-32713-10 (ET) JORDAN, VIRGIL C UNIVERSITY OF WISCONSIN 600 HIGHLAND AVE, K4/646 CSC MADISON, WI 53792 Structure function relationship of antiestrogen
U10CA-32734-10 (CCI) BERENBERG, JEFFREY L CANCER CENTER OF HAWAII 2540 MAILE WAY HONOLULU, HI 96822 Southwest oncology group

PROJECT NO., ORGANIZATIONAL UNIT., INVESTIGATOR, ADDRESS, TITLE

studies
R01CA-32742-09 (PB) PEDERSEN, PETER L JOHNS HOPKINS UNIVERSITY 725 NORTH WOLFE STREET BALTIMORE, MD 21205-2185 Glucose metabolism in neoplastic tissues
R01CA-32745-09 (RAD) TOMASOVIC, STEPHEN P U.T. M.D. ANDERSON CANCER CENT 1515 HOLCOMBE BLVD HOUSTON, TX 77030 Hyperthermic stress proteins and thermotolerance
R01CA-32779-07 (ARRD) ZEMLICKA, JIRI MICHIGAN CANCER FOUNDATION 110 EAST WARREN AVENUE DETROIT, MI 48201 Antitumor and antiviral nucleoside analogues
R01CA-32826-10 (PC) MACHER, BRUCE A SAN FRANCISCO STATE UNIVERSITY 1600 HOLLOWAY AVE SAN FRANCISCO, CA 94132 Glycosphingolipids in oncogenesis and differentiation
R01CA-32827-09 (RAD) HAHN, GEORGE M STANFORD U. SCHOOL OF MEDICINE STANFORD, CA 94305 Hyperthermia membrane structure and function
R01CA-32839-09 (ET) PLUNKETT, WILLIAM K U.T. M.D. ANDERSON CANCER CENT 1515 HOLCOMBE BLVD HOUSTON, TX 77030 Cellular pharmacology in cancer chemotherapy
P01CA-32845-29 (CCP) WAGNER, HENRY N, JR JOHNS HOPKINS UNIVERSITY 615 N WOLFE ST BALTIMORE, MD 21205 Nuclear instrumentation and chemistry in medicine
P01CA-32845-29 0020 (CCP) BURNS, H DONALD Nuclear instrumentation and chemistry in medicine Relationship of structure to biodistribution of technetium complex
P01CA-32845-29 0022 (CCP) BURNS, H DONALD Nuclear instrumentation and chemistry in medicine Lipophilic cations for myocardial imaging
P01CA-32845-29 0025 (CCP) KRAMER, ALFRED V Nuclear instrumentation and chemistry in medicine Technetium-99m labeling of monoclonal antibodies
P01CA-32845-29 9001 (CCP) WAGNER, HENRY N Nuclear instrumentation and chemistry in medicine Core support
R01CA-32846-21 (RNM) ROGERS, W LESLIE UNIVERSITY OF MICHIGAN 3480 KRESGE III BUILDING ANN ARBOR, MI 48109-0552 Radionuclides--radiation detection and quantification
R01CA-32853-15 (RNM) MCAFEE, JOHN G THE GEORGE WASHINGTON UNIVERSI 901 23RD STREET N W WASHINGTON, D C 20037 Radioactive labeling of blood cells and their products
R01CA-32857-12 (RNM) LONG, DAVID M UNIV OF CALIF, S D MED CTR 225 DICKINSON STREET SAN DIEGO, CA 92103 Radiopaque fluorocarbon in diagnostic radiology
R01CA-32863-12 (RNM) MAXON, HARRY R UNIV OF CINCINNATI MEDICAL CTR MAIL LOCATION 577 CINCINNATI, OHIO 45267-0577 Efficacious skeletal imaging radiopharmaceuticals
R01CA-32870-11 (RNM) KUNDEL, HAROLD L UNIV OF PENNSYLVANIA 36TH ST & HAMILTON WALK PHILADELPHIA, PA 19104 Visual search and film reader error in radiology
R01CA-32873-11 (RNM) BROWNELL, GORDON L MASSACHUSETTS GENERAL HOSPITAL FRUIT STREET BOSTON, MA 02114 Analog coded systems for positron tomography
R01CA-32897-09 (SSS) FOLEY, KATHLEEN M MEMORIAL HOSP/CA & ALLIED DIS 1275 YORK AVENUE NEW YORK, N Y 10021 Cancer pain: pharmacokinetic correlates of analgesia
R01CA-32898-10 (HEM) TRINCHIERI, GIORGIO THE WISTAR INSTITUTE 36TH AND SPRUCE STREETS PHILADELPHIA, PA 19104 Differentiation and function of human monocytes
P30CA-32911-08 (CCS) HOOD, LEROY E CALIFORNIA INST OF TECHNOLOGY 1201 E CALIFORNIA BLVD PASADENA, CA 91125 Cancer center support grant
P30CA-32911-08 9001 (CCS) HOOD, LEROY E Cancer center support grant Microchemical facility--Core
P30CA-32911-08 9002 (CCS) HOOD, LEROY E Cancer center support grant Computer facility--Core
P30CA-32911-08 9003 (CCS) HOOD, LEROY E Cancer center support grant Cell sorting facility--Core
P30CA-32911-08 9004 (CCS) SIMON, MELVIN Cancer center support grant Animal facility—core
R37CA-32926-07 (VR) BESMER, PETER SLOAN-KETTERING INST/CANCER RE 1275 YORK AVENUE NEW YORK, N Y 10021 C-kit & v-kit--Normal function & oncogenic activation
R01CA-32927-08 (PHY) LEVINSON, CHARLES UNIV OF TEXAS HLTH SCIENCE CTR 7703 FLOYD CURL DRIVE SAN ANTONIO, TX 78284-7756 Anion transport in Ehrlich carcinoma cells
U01CA-32934-10 (SRC) GREENBERG, E ROBERT DARTMOUTH HITCHCOCK MED CTR 2 MAYNARD ST/HB 7925 HANOVER, NH 03756 Chemopreventive trial of beta carotene in skin cancer
R55CA-32937-07A2 (CPA) ASCH, BONNIE B ROSWELL PARK CANCER INST ELM & CARLTON STS BUFFALO, NY 14263 Markers of mammary cell differentiation and neoplasia
R01CA-32940-10 (VR) WILLIAMS, JAMES F CARNEGIE-MELLON UNIVERSITY 4400 FIFTH AVENUE PITTSBURGH, PA 15213 Type 12 adenovirus transformation - defective mutants
R01CA-32949-09 (BCE) RUDDON, RAYMOND W EPPLEY INSTITUTE FOR RESEARCH 600 SOUTH 42ND STREET OMAHA, NE 68198-6805 Biosynthesis and secretion of HCG by human trophoblasts
R01CA-32974-09 (MCHA) WULFF, WILLIAM D UNIVERSITY OF CHICAGO 5735 SOUTH ELLIS AVENUE CHICAGO, IL 60637 Synthesis of anthracyclinones
R01CA-32979-07 (EVR) RAAB-TRAUB, NANCY UNIV OF NC AT CHAPEL HILL CHAPEL HILL, NC 27599-7295 EBV expression in nasopharyngeal carcinoma
R01CA-33000-11 (PBC) FUKUDA, MINORU LA JOLLA CANCER RESEARCH FDN 10901 NORTH TORREY PINES ROAD LA JOLLA, CA 92037 Glycoproteins in differentiation and oncogenesis
R01CA-33019-09 (EDC) MEHTA, CYRUS R DANA-FARBER CANCER INSTITUTE 44 BINNEY STREET BOSTON, MA 02115 New statistical methods for cancer treatment
R01CA-33021-10 (MBY) PERUCHO, MANUEL CALIFORNIA INST OF BIOL RES 11099 N TORREY PINES ROAD LA JOLLA, CA 92037 Expression of the human c-K-ras gene
R01CA-33047-06 (MCHA) FARNSWORTH, NORMAN R UNIV OF ILLINOIS AT CHICAGO 833 S WOOD STREET CHICAGO, IL 60680 Plant antitumor agents--isolation and identification

PROJECT NO., ORGANIZATIONAL UNIT., INVESTIGATOR, ADDRESS, TITLE

P01CA-33049-09 (SRC) OETTGEN, HERBERT F MEMORIAL HOSP FOR C&A DISEASES 1275 YORK AVENUE NEW YORK, N Y 10021 Biological approaches to the treatment of cancer
P01CA-33049-09 0004 (SRC) LIVINGSTON, PHILIP O Biological approaches to the treatment of cancer Development of cancer vaccines
P01CA-33049-09 0005 (SRC) HOUGHTON, ALAN N Biological approaches to the treatment of cancer Diagnostic and therapeutic trials with monoclonal antibodies
P01CA-33049-09 0006 (SRC) LLOYD, KENNETH G Biological approaches to the treatment of cancer Monoclonal antibodies for treatment of carcinomas
P01CA-33049-09 0007 (SRC) CHEUNG, NAI-KUNG V Biological approaches to the treatment of cancer Monoclonal antibodies for treatment of neuroblastoma
P01CA-33049-09 0008 (SRC) NATHAN, CARL F Biological approaches to the treatment of cancer PMN antitumor effects augmented by monoclonal antibodies in cancer
P01CA-33049-09 9001 (SRC) OETTGEN, HERBERT F Biological approaches to the treatment of cancer Core--Biostatistics--Monoclonal antibody facility
R01CA-33056-09 (CPA) CALOS, MICHELE P STANFORD UNIVERSITY SCHOOL OF MEDICINE STANFORD, CA 94305 Mutation in cells at the DNA sequence level
R01CA-33065-10 (EI) DAYNES, RAYMOND A UNIVERSITY OF UTAH 50 NORTH MEDICAL DRIVE SALT LAKE CITY, UTAH 84132 Immunobiology of UVL-induced tumors
R37CA-33084-09 (EI) GREENBERG, PHILIP D UNIVERSITY OF WASHINGTON BB1321 HEALTH SCIENCES BLDG SEATTLE, WA 98195 Mechanisms of murine tumor eradication by immunotherapy
R01CA-33093-10 (MGN) TAYLOR, BENJAMIN A THE JACKSON LABORATORY 600 MAIN STREET BAR HARBOR, ME 05609-0800 Recombinant inbred strains and cancer
R01CA-33097-09 (BEM) COPELAND, DONNA R UNIV TEXAS/M D ANDERSON CA CTR 1515 HOLCOMBE BOULEVARD HOUSTON, TX 77030 Neuropsychological assessment of children with cancer
R01CA-33099-07 (EVR) PADMANABHAN, RADHA K UNIV OF KANSAS MEDICAL CENTER 39TH AND RAINBOW BLVD KANSAS CITY, KS 66103 Structure and functional analysis of adenovirus genomes
R01CA-33119-07A1 (EI) WARNKE, ROGER A STANFORD UNIVERSITY MEDICAL CT STANFORD, CA 94305 Tumor host relationships in human lymphomas in vivo
R01CA-33135-07A2 (PTHB) SIDDIQUI, ALEEM UNIV OF COLORADO HEALTH SCIS C 4200 EAST NINTH AVE DENVER, CO 80262 Expression of HBV genes and hepatoma
R01CA-33148-10 (ET) WHEELESS, LEON L UNIV OF ROCHESTER MED CENTER 601 ELMWOOD AVENUE ROCHESTER, NY 14642 Multidimensional slit-scan detection of bladder cancer
R01CA-33192-07A2 (EVR) BOSE, HENRY R, JR UNIVERSITY OF TEXAS AT AUSTIN 24TH & SPEEDWAY AUSTIN, TX 78712 Transformation by avian reticuloendotheliosis virus
U01CA-33193-10 (SRC) VAINIO, HARRI INTL AGCY/RESEARCH ON CANCER 150 COURS ALBERT THOMAS FRANCE Evaluation of carcinogenic risk of chemicals to humans
R01CA-33225-10 (HEM) PELUS, LOUIS M 709 SWEDELAND ROAD KING OF PRUSSIA, PA 19406 Regulation of myeloid progenitor cell differentiation
R01CA-33240-09 (MEP) IP, MARGOT M ROSWELL PARK MEMORIAL INST ELM AND CARLTON STREETS BUFFALO, NY 14263 Lipid modulation of mammary proliferation & differentiation
R01CA-33314-10 (PTHB) YUNIS, JORGE J HAHNEMANN UNIVERSITY BROAD & VINE STS, MAIL STOP 41 PHILADELPHIA, PA 19102-1192 Molecular pathogenesis of follicular lymphoma
R01CA-33326-09 (MCHA) CASSADY, JOHN M OHIO STATE UNIVERSITY 500 WEST TWELFTH AVENUE COLUMBUS, OH 43210 Novel antineoplastic agents from higher plants
R01CA-33369-09 (CPA) BUTEL, JANET S BAYLOR COLLEGE OF MEDICINE ONE BAYLOR PLAZA HOUSTON, TX 77030 Carcinogen-viral oncogene interactions in mammary cancer
R37CA-33399-10 (ET) LEVY, RONALD STANFORD UNIVERSITY STANFORD, CA 94305-6060 Anti-idiotype therapy of human B cell malignancy
R01CA-33405-11 (RAD) HENLE, KURT J UNIVERSITY OF ARKANSAS 4301 W MARKHAM LITTLE ROCK, AR 72205 Modulators of cellular heat sensitivity
R01CA-33497-08 (CPA) MALKINSON, ALVIN M UNIVERSITY OF COLORADO SCHOOL OF PHARMACY BOULDER, CO 80309-0297 Lung tumor promotion by BHT
R01CA-33505-10 (ET) YEN, ANDREW CORNELL UNIVERSITY NYS COLLEGE OF VETERINARY MED ITHACA, NY 14853 Cell cycle specific control of cellular differentiation
R01CA-33511-07A1 (MEP) OYASU, RYOICHI NORTHWESTERN UNIVERSITY MED SC 303 EAST CHICAGO AVENUE CHICAGO, IL 60611 Experimental urinary bladder carcinogenesis
R01CA-33537-08 (RNM) PENG, CHIN-TZU SCH OF PHAR UNIV OF CA, SAN FR 926 MEDICAL SCIENCES BUILDING SAN FRANCISCO, CA 94143-0446 Tritium labeling-mechanisms and methods
R01CA-33541-09 (RNM) JASZCZAK, RONALD J DUKE UNIVERSITY MEDICAL CENTER PO BOX 3949 DURHAM, NC 27710 In vivo radionuclide quantitation using emission CT
P30CA-33572-11 (SRC) CHERVENICK, PAUL A BECKMAN RESEARCH INSTITUTE 1450 EAST DUARTE ROAD DUARTE, CA 91010 Cancer center support (core) grant
P30CA-33572-11 9003 (SRC) FORREST, GERALD Cancer center support (core) grant Core--DNA cloning
P30CA-33572-11 9004 (SRC) KLEVECZ, ROBERT Cancer center support (core) grant Core--Analytical cytometry
P30CA-33572-11 9005 (SRC) PAXTON, RAYMOND Cancer center support (core) grant Core--Protein microsequencing
P30CA-33572-11 9006 (SRC) NILAND, JOYCE C Cancer center support (core) grant Core--Biostatistics
P30CA-33572-11 9008 (SRC) KAPLAN, BRUCE E Cancer center support (core) grant Core--DNA and peptide synthesis
P30CA-33572-11 9009 (SRC) FORREST, GERALD Cancer center support (core) grant Core--DNA sequencing
P30CA-33572-11 9010 (SRC) WU, ANNA M Cancer center support (core)

grant Core--Nucleic acid extraction facility
P30CA-33572-11 9011 (SRC) WALLACE, R BRUCE Cancer center support (core) grant Core--DNASTAR
P30CA-33572-11 9012 (SRC) LEE, TERRY D Cancer center support (core) grant Core--Mass spectrometry
P30CA-33572-11 9013 (SRC) CHEN, SHIUAN Cancer center support (core) grant Core--Circular dichroism and fourier transform infrared spectrophotometry
P30CA-33572-11 9014 (SRC) MAS, MARIA Cancer center support (core) grant Core--Molecular graphics
P30CA-33572-11 9015 (SRC) BATTIFORA, HECTOR Cancer center support (core) grant Core--Frozen tumor bank, tissue procurement, and immunohistochemistry
U10CA-33587-09 (CCI) WHITEHEAD, VICTOR M MONTREAL CHILDRENS HOSPITAL 2300 TUPPER STREET CANADA H3H 1P3 Pediatric oncology group
U10CA-33587-09 0032 (CCI) WHITEHEAD, VICTOR M Pediatric oncology group POG8865--Phase II recombinant alpha-interferon in relapsed T-cell disease
U10CA-33587-09 0033 (CCI) WHITEHEAD, VICTOR M Pediatric oncology group--Phase II recombinant A-interferon in chronic myelogenous leukemia
U10CA-33587-09 0034 (CCI) WHITEHEAD, VICTOR M Pediatric oncology group POG8832--Combination chemotherapy followed by radiotherapy for brain tumors
U10CA-33587-09 0035 (CCI) WHITEHEAD, VICTOR M Pediatric oncology group POG8731--Phase II trial of methotrexate in treatment of brain tumors in children
U10CA-33587-09 0036 (CCI) WHITEHEAD, VICTOR M Pediatric oncology group POG8788--Intergroup rhabdomyosarcoma study/pilot study for clinical group III
U10CA-33587-09 0037 (CCI) WHITEHEAD, VICTOR M Pediatric oncology group POG8761--Phase II study of homoharringtonine therapy for nonlymphoblastic leukemi
U10CA-33587-09 0038 (CCI) WHITEHEAD, VICTOR M Pediatric oncology group POG8739--Phase II immunotherapy with alpha-2 interferon for brain tumors
U10CA-33587-09 0039 (CCI) WHITEHEAD, VICTOR M Pediatric oncology group POG8741--Treatment of patients with stage C and stage D neuroblastoma
U10CA-33587-09 0040 (CCI) WHITEHEAD, VICTOR M Pediatric oncology group POG8751--Phase II methotrexate chemotherapy for rhabdomyosarcoma in children
U10CA-33587-09 0041 (CCI) WHITEHEAD, VICTOR M Pediatric oncology group POG8633--Postoperative chemotherapy and delayed irradiation for brain tumors
U10CA-33587-09 0042 (CCI) WHITEHEAD, VICTOR M Pediatric oncology group POG8617--Therapy for B-cell acute lymphoblastic leukemia and lymphoma
U10CA-33587-09 0043 (CCI) WHITEHEAD, VICTOR M Pediatric oncology group POG9139--Phase I study of cisplatin and irradiation in brain stem gliomas
U10CA-33587-09 0044 (CCI) WHITEHEAD, VICTOR M Pediatric oncology group POG9079--Phase I study of L-PAM/CTX with ABM rescue for brain tumors in children
U10CA-33587-09 0045 (CCI) WHITEHEAD, VICTOR M Pediatric oncology group POG9075--Phase I study of acivicin in children with solid tumors
U10CA-33587-09 0046 (CCI) WHITEHEAD, VICTOR M Pediatric oncology group POG9074--Phase I study of xomazyme-H65 in children with T-cell ALL/lymphoma
U10CA-33587-09 0047 (CCI) WHITEHEAD, VICTOR M Pediatric oncology group POG9072--Phase I chemotherapy for recurrent/resistant malignant solid tumors
U10CA-33587-09 0048 (CCI) WHITEHEAD, VICTOR M Pediatric oncology group POG9061-Phase II systemic therapy and irradiation for ALL & CNS leukemia
U10CA-33587-09 0049 (CCI) WHITEHEAD, VICTOR M Pediatric oncology group POG 9086--Phase I pilot study of therapy for T-cell ALL or NHL
U10CA-33587-09 0050 (CCI) WHITEHEAD, VICTOR M Pediatric oncology group POG9071--Phase I trial of fazarabine in children with acute leukemia
U10CA-33587-09 0051 (CCI) WHITEHEAD, VICTOR M Pediatric oncology group POG8970--Phase I trial of fazarabine in children with refractory solid tumors
U10CA-33587-09 0052 (CCI) WHITEHEAD, VICTOR M Pediatric oncology group POG8973--Etoposide (VP-16) and carboplatin in children with acute leukemia
U10CA-33587-09 0053 (CCI) WHITEHEAD, VICTOR M Pediatric oncology group POG8870--Phase I trial of ifosfamide/VP16/MESNA in children with acute leukemia
U10CA-33587-09 0054 (CCI) WHITEHEAD, VICTOR M Pediatric oncology group POG8871--Phase I study of rTNF in children with refractory solid tumors
U10CA-33587-09 0055 (CCI) WHITEHEAD, VICTOR M Pediatric oncology group POG8671--Phase I immunotherapy with rIL-2 in children with solid tumors
U10CA-33587-09 0056 (CCI) WHITEHEAD, VICTOR M Pediatric oncology group POG8494--Phase I study of fludarabine phosphate in pediatric patients
U10CA-33587-09 0057 (CCI) WHITEHEAD, VICTOR M Pediatric oncology group POG8930--A comprehensive genetic analysis of brain tumors
U10CA-33587-09 0058 (CCI) WHITEHEAD, VICTOR M Pediatric oncology group POG8828--Late effects of Hodgkin's disease
U10CA-33587-09 0059 (CCI) WHITEHEAD, VICTOR M Pediatric oncology group POG9046--Molecular genetic analysis of Wilm's tumors
U10CA-33587-09 0060 (CCI) WHITEHEAD, VICTOR M Pediatric oncology group POG9153--Rhabdomyosarcoma study/laboratory evaluation of tumor
U10CA-33587-09 0001 (CCI) WHITEHEAD, VICTOR M Pediatric oncology group POG9006--6-MP/methotrexate vs. alternating chemotherapy for ALL in childhood
U10CA-33587-09 0002 (CCI) WHITEHEAD, VICTOR M Pediatric oncology group POG9005--Dose intensification of methotrexate & 6-mercaptourine in childhood ALL
U10CA-33587-09 0003 (CCI) WHITEHEAD, VICTOR M Pediatric oncology group POG9031--Cisplatin/VP-16 therapy of medulloblastoma/pre vs. post irradiation
U10CA-33587-09 0004 (CCI) WHITEHEAD, VICTOR M Pediatric oncology group POG8945--Phase III chemotherapy for hepatoblastoma & hepatocellular carcinoma
U10CA-33587-09 0005 (CCI) WHITEHEAD, VICTOR M Pediatric oncology group POG9049--Phase III study of high-risk malignant germ cell tumors in children
U10CA-33587-09 0006 (CCI) WHITEHEAD, VICTOR M Pediatric oncology group POG8844--Bone marrow transplant in children with stage D neuroblastoma
U10CA-33587-09 0007 (CCI) WHITEHEAD, VICTOR M Pediatric oncology group POG8850--Phase III treatment of Ewing's sarcoma and neuroectodermal bone tumors
U10CA-33587-09 0008 (CCI) WHITEHEAD, VICTOR M Pediatric oncology group POG8821--Phase III chemotherapy +/- autologous BMT in children with AML
U10CA-33587-09 0009 (CCI) WHITEHEAD, VICTOR M Pediatric oncology group POG8725--Phase III chemotherapy +/- radiation therapy in pediatric Hodgkins
U10CA-33587-09 0010 (CCI) WHITEHEAD, VICTOR M Pediatric oncology group POG8704--Phase III chemotherapy of childhood T cell ALL & lymphoblastic lymphoma
U10CA-33587-09 0011 (CCI) WHITEHEAD, VICTOR M Pediatric oncology group POG8719--Phase III chemotherapy for non-Hodgkin's lymphoma in children
U10CA-33587-09 0012 (CCI) WHITEHEAD, VICTOR M Pediatric oncology group POG8650--National Wilm's tumor and clear cell sarcoma study
U10CA-33587-09 0013 (CCI) WHITEHEAD, VICTOR M Pediatric oncology group POG8616--Phase III chemotherapy for childhood Burkitt and non-Burkitts lymphoma
U10CA-33587-09 0014 (CCI) WHITEHEAD, VICTOR M Pediatric oncology group POG8615--Phase III study of large cell lymphomas in children and adolescents
U10CA-33587-09 0015 (CCI) WHITEHEAD, VICTOR M Pediatric oncology group POG8651--Phase III study of childhood nonmetastatic osteosarcoma
U10CA-33587-09 0016 (CCI) WHITEHEAD, VICTOR M Pediatric oncology group POG8653--Phase III study of childhood soft tissue sarcomas
U10CA-33587-09 0017 (CCI) WHITEHEAD, VICTOR M Pediatric oncology group POG8625--Phase III combined therapy in childhood Hodgkin's disease
U10CA-33587-09 0018 (CCI) WHITEHEAD, VICTOR M Pediatric oncology group POG8451--Intergroup rhabdomyosarcoma study
U10CA-33587-09 0019 (CCI) WHITEHEAD, VICTOR M Pediatric oncology group POG9110--Rotational drug therapy after first marrow relapse of non-T, non B ALL
U10CA-33587-09 0020 (CCI) WHITEHEAD, VICTOR M Pediatric oncology group POG9107--Phase II pilot study of infant leukemia
U10CA-33587-09 0021 (CCI) WHITEHEAD, VICTOR M Pediatric oncology group POG9140--Phase II therapy for recurrent or refractory neuroblastoma
U10CA-33587-09 0022 (CCI) WHITEHEAD, VICTOR M Pediatric oncology group POG9048--Phase II study of malignant germ cell tumors in children
U10CA-33587-09 0023 (CCI) WHITEHEAD, VICTOR M Pediatric oncology group POG9060--Intensive QOD ifosfamide treatment for CNS tumors in children
U10CA-33587-09 0024 (CCI) WHITEHEAD, VICTOR M Pediatric oncology group POG8936--Phase II study of carboplatin treatment for optic pathway tumors
U10CA-33587-09 0025 (CCI) WHITEHEAD, VICTOR M Pediatric oncology group POG8935--Phase II study of surgery and/or radiotherapy for optic pathway tumors
U10CA-33587-09 0026 (CCI) WHITEHEAD, VICTOR M Pediatric oncology group POG8820--Phase II/III study of VP-16, AMSA +/- 5-azacytidine in childhood ANLL
U10CA-33587-09 0027 (CCI) WHITEHEAD, VICTOR M Pediatric oncology group POG8889--Intergroup rhabdomyosarcoma study for clinical group IV disease
U10CA-33587-09 0028 (CCI) WHITEHEAD, VICTOR M Pediatric oncology group POG8866--Phase II asparaginase therapy for acute lymphoblastic leukemia
U10CA-33587-09 0029 (CCI) WHITEHEAD, VICTOR M Pediatric oncology group POG8862--Combination chemotherapy of acute T-lymphoblastic leukemia
U10CA-33587-09 0030 (CCI) WHITEHEAD, VICTOR M Pediatric oncology group POG8863--Phase II study of high dose cytosine arabinoside in childhood tumors
U10CA-33587-09 0031 (CCI) WHITEHEAD, VICTOR M Pediatric oncology group POG8827--Phase II treatment of children with Hodgkin's disease in relapse
U10CA-33601-12 (CCI) GEORGE, STEPHEN L DUKE UNIV MEDICAL CTR BOX 3958 DURHAM, NC 27710 Cancer and leukemia group B statistical center
U10CA-33603-09 (CCI) LINK, MICHAEL P CHILDREN'S HOSPITAL AT STANFOR 520 SAND HILL ROAD PALO ALTO, CA 94304 Pediatric oncology group
U10CA-33603-09 0001 (CCI) LINK, MICHAEL P Pediatric oncology group POG9006--6-MP/methotrexate vs. alternating chemotherapy for ALL in childhood
U10CA-33603-09 0034 (CCI) LINK, MICHAEL P Pediatric oncology group POG8832--Combination chemotherapy followed by radiotherapy for brain tumors
U10CA-33603-09 0002 (CCI) LINK, MICHAEL P Pediatric oncology group POG9005--Dose intensification of methotrexate & 6-mercaptourine in childhood ALL
U10CA-33603-09 0003 (CCI) LINK, MICHAEL P Pediatric oncology group POG9031--Cisplatin/VP-16 therapy of medulloblastoma/pre vs. post irradiation
U10CA-33603-09 0004 (CCI) LINK, MICHAEL P Pediatric oncology group POG8945--Phase III chemotherapy for hepatoblastoma & hepatocellular carcinoma
U10CA-33603-09 0005 (CCI) LINK, MICHAEL P Pediatric oncology group

POG9049–Phase III study of high-risk malignant germ cell tumors in children
U10CA-33603-09 0006 (CCI) LINK, MICHAEL P Pediatric oncology group POG8844–Bone marrow transplant in children with stage D neuroblastoma
U10CA-33603-09 0007 (CCI) LINK, MICHAEL P Pediatric oncology group POG8850–Phase III treatment of Ewing's sarcoma and neuroectodermal bone tumors
U10CA-33603-09 0008 (CCI) LINK, MICHAEL P Pediatric oncology group POG8821–Phase III chemotherapy +/- autologous BMT in children with AML
U10CA-33603-09 0009 (CCI) LINK, MICHAEL P Pediatric oncology group POG8725–Phase III chemotherapy +/- radiation therapy in pediatric Hodgkins
U10CA-33603-09 0010 (CCI) LINK, MICHAEL P Pediatric oncology group POG8704–Phase III chemotherapy of childhood T cell ALL & lymphoblastic lymphoma
U10CA-33603-09 0011 (CCI) LINK, MICHAEL P Pediatric oncology group POG8719–Phase III chemotherapy for non-Hodgkin's lymphoma in children
U10CA-33603-09 0012 (CCI) LINK, MICHAEL P Pediatric oncology group POG8650–National Wilm's tumor and clear cell sarcoma study
U10CA-33603-09 0013 (CCI) LINK, MICHAEL P Pediatric oncology group POG8616–Phase III chemotherapy for childhood Burkitt and non-Burkitts lymphoma
U10CA-33603-09 0014 (CCI) LINK, MICHAEL P Pediatric oncology group POG8615–Phase III study of large cell lymphomas in children and adolescents
U10CA-33603-09 0015 (CCI) LINK, MICHAEL P Pediatric oncology group POG8651–Phase III study of childhood nonmetastatic osteosarcoma
U10CA-33603-09 0035 (CCI) LINK, MICHAEL P Pediatric oncology group POG8731–Phase II trial of methotrexate in treatment of brain tumors in children
U10CA-33603-09 0036 (CCI) LINK, MICHAEL P Pediatric oncology group POG8788–Intergroup rhabdomyosarcoma study/pilot study for clinical group III
U10CA-33603-09 0037 (CCI) LINK, MICHAEL P Pediatric oncology group POG8761–Phase II study of homoharringtonine therapy for nonlymphoblastic leukemi
U10CA-33603-09 0038 (CCI) LINK, MICHAEL P Pediatric oncology group POG8739–Phase II immunotherapy with alpha-2 interferon for brain tumors (human)e
U10CA-33603-09 0039 (CCI) LINK, MICHAEL P Pediatric oncology group POG8741–Treatment of patients with stage C and stage D neuroblastoma
U10CA-33603-09 0040 (CCI) LINK, MICHAEL P Pediatric oncology group POG8751–Phase II methotrexate chemotherapy for rhabdomyosarcoma in children
U10CA-33603-09 0041 (CCI) LINK, MICHAEL P Pediatric oncology group POG8633–Postoperative chemotherapy and delayed irradiation for brain tumors
U10CA-33603-09 0042 (CCI) LINK, MICHAEL P Pediatric oncology group POG8617–Therapy for B-cell acute lymphoblastic leukemia and lymphoma
U10CA-33603-09 0043 (CCI) LINK, MICHAEL P Pediatric oncology group POG9139–Phase I study of cisplatin and irradiation in brain stem gliomas
U10CA-33603-09 0044 (CCI) LINK, MICHAEL P Pediatric oncology group POG9079–Phase I study of L-PAM/CTX with ABM rescue for brain tumors in children
U10CA-33603-09 0045 (CCI) LINK, MICHAEL P Pediatric oncology group POG9075–Phase I study of acivicin in children with solid tumors
U10CA-33603-09 0046 (CCI) LINK, MICHAEL P Pediatric oncology group POG9074–Phase I study of xomazyme-H65 in children with T-cell ALL/lymphoma
U10CA-33603-09 0047 (CCI) LINK, MICHAEL P Pediatric oncology group POG9072–Phase I chemotherapy for recurrent/resistant malignant solid tumors
U10CA-33603-09 0048 (CCI) LINK, MICHAEL P Pediatric oncology group POG9061-Phase II systemic therapy and irradiation for ALL & CNS leukemia
U10CA-33603-09 0049 (CCI) LINK, MICHAEL P Pediatric oncology group POG 9086–Phase I pilot study of therapy for T-cell ALL or NHL
U10CA-33603-09 0050 (CCI) LINK, MICHAEL P Pediatric oncology group POG9071–Phase I trial of fazarabine in children with acute leukemia
U10CA-33603-09 0051 (CCI) LINK, MICHAEL P Pediatric oncology group POG8970–Phase I trial of fazarabine in children with refractory solid tumors
U10CA-33603-09 0052 (CCI) LINK, MICHAEL P Pediatric oncology group POG8973–Etoposide (VP-16) and carboplatin in children with acute leukemia
U10CA-33603-09 0053 (CCI) LINK, MICHAEL P Pediatric oncology group POG8870–Phase I trial of ifosfamide/VP16/MESNA in children with acute leukemia
U10CA-33603-09 0054 (CCI) LINK, MICHAEL P Pediatric oncology group POG8871–Phase I study of rTNF in children with refractory solid tumors
U10CA-33603-09 0055 (CCI) LINK, MICHAEL P Pediatric oncology group POG8671–Phase I immunotherapy with rIL-2 in children with solid tumors
U10CA-33603-09 0056 (CCI) LINK, MICHAEL P Pediatric oncology group POG8494–Phase I study of fludarabine phosphate in pediatric patients
U10CA-33603-09 0057 (CCI) LINK, MICHAEL P Pediatric oncology group POG8930–A comprehensive genetic analysis of brain tumors
U10CA-33603-09 0058 (CCI) LINK, MICHAEL P Pediatric oncology group POG8828–Late effects of Hodgkin's disease
U10CA-33603-09 0059 (CCI) LINK, MICHAEL P Pediatric oncology group POG9046–Molecular genetic analysis of Wilm's tumors
U10CA-33603-09 0060 (CCI) LINK, MICHAEL P Pediatric oncology group POG9153–Rhabdomyosarcoma study/laboratory evaluation of tumor
U10CA-33603-09 0016 (CCI) LINK, MICHAEL P Pediatric oncology group POG8653–Phase III study of childhood soft tissue sarcomas
U10CA-33603-09 0017 (CCI) LINK, MICHAEL P Pediatric oncology group POG8625–Phase III combined therapy in childhood Hodgkin's disease
U10CA-33603-09 0018 (CCI) LINK, MICHAEL P Pediatric oncology group POG8451–Intergroup rhabdomyosarcoma study
U10CA-33603-09 0019 (CCI) LINK, MICHAEL P Pediatric oncology group POG9110–Rotational drug therapy after first marrow relapse of non-T, non B ALL
U10CA-33603-09 0020 (CCI) LINK, MICHAEL P Pediatric oncology group POG9107–Phase II pilot study of infant leukemia
U10CA-33603-09 0021 (CCI) LINK, MICHAEL P Pediatric oncology group POG9140–Phase II therapy for recurrent or refractory neuroblastoma
U10CA-33603-09 0022 (CCI) LINK, MICHAEL P Pediatric oncology group POG9048–Phase II study of malignant germ cell tumors in children
U10CA-33603-09 0023 (CCI) LINK, MICHAEL P Pediatric oncology group POG9060–Intensive QOD ifosfamide treatment for CNS tumors in children
U10CA-33603-09 0024 (CCI) LINK, MICHAEL P Pediatric oncology group POG8936–Phase II study of carboplatin treatment for optic pathway tumors
U10CA-33603-09 0025 (CCI) LINK, MICHAEL P Pediatric oncology group POG8935–Phase II study of surgery and/or radiotherapy for optic pathway tumors
U10CA-33603-09 0026 (CCI) LINK, MICHAEL P Pediatric oncology group POG8820–Phase II/III study of VP-16, AMSA +/- 5-azacytidine in childhood ANLL
U10CA-33603-09 0027 (CCI) LINK, MICHAEL P Pediatric oncology group POG8889–Intergroup rhabdomyosarcoma study for clinical group IV disease
U10CA-33603-09 0028 (CCI) LINK, MICHAEL P Pediatric oncology group POG8866–Phase II asparaginase therapy for acute lymphoblastic leukemia
U10CA-33603-09 0029 (CCI) LINK, MICHAEL P Pediatric oncology group POG8862–Combination chemotherapy of acute T-lymphoblastic leukemia
U10CA-33603-09 0030 (CCI) LINK, MICHAEL P Pediatric oncology group POG8863–Phase II study of high dose cytosine arabinoside in childhood tumors
U10CA-33603-09 0031 (CCI) LINK, MICHAEL P Pediatric oncology group POG8827–Phase II treatment of children with Hodgkin's disease in relapse
U10CA-33603-09 0032 (CCI) LINK, MICHAEL P Pediatric oncology group POG8865–Phase II recombinant alpha-interferon in relapsed T-cell disease
U10CA-33603-09 0033 (CCI) LINK, MICHAEL P Pediatric oncology group–Phase II recombinant A-interferon in chronic myelogenous leukemia
R01CA-33616-12 (EVR) CHINNADURAI, GOVINDASWAMY ST LOUIS UNIVERSITY 3681 PARK AVENUE ST LOUIS, MO 63110 Adenovirus lp locus–Role in oncogenic transformation
P01CA-33619-09 (SRC) KOLONEL, LAURENCE N UNIVERSITY OF HAWAII 1236 LAUHALA STREET, SUITE 407 HONOLULU, HI 96813 Epidemiologic studies of diet and cancer in Hawaii
P01CA-33619-09 0008 (SRC) GOODMAN MARC T Epidemiologic studies of diet and cancer in Hawaii Case-control study of diet and endometrial cancer risk
P01CA-33619-09 0009 (SRC) LE MARCHAND, LOIC Epidemiologic studies of diet and cancer in Hawaii Case-control study of diet and malignant melanoma
P01CA-33619-09 0010 (SRC) YOSHIZAWA, CARL Epidemiologic studies of diet and cancer in Hawaii Ecologic study of diet and cancer among migrants in Hawaii
P01CA-33619-09 9001 (SRC) KOLONEL, LAURENCE N Epidemiologic studies of diet and cancer in Hawaii Core–Biostatistics
P01CA-33619-09 0001 (SRC) KOLONEL, LAURENCE N Epidemiologic studies of diet and cancer in Hawaii Prospective cohort study of diet and cancer
P01CA-33619-09 0006 (SRC) HANKIN, JEAN Epidemiologic studies of diet and cancer in Hawaii Telephone interview for quantitative diet history assessment
P01CA-33619-09 0007 (SRC) LE MARCHAND, LOIC Epidemiologic studies of diet and cancer in Hawaii Case-control study of diet and colorectal cancer
P01CA-33620-08 (CAK) PRIVES, CAROL L COLUMBIA UNIVERSITY 818A FAIRCHILD CENTER NEW YORK, NY 10027 Directed SV40 mutation–Cell molecular consequences
P01CA-33620-08 0001 (CAK) PRIVES, CAROL Directed SV40 mutation–Cell molecular consequences Protein interactions in SV40 oncogenesis
P01CA-33620-08 0002 (CAK) MANLEY, JAMES L Directed SV40 mutation–Cell molecular consequences Controlling splicing of SV40 early mRNA
P01CA-33620-08 0003 (CAK) POLLACK, ROBERT E Directed SV40 mutation–Cell molecular consequences Control of viral and cellular gene expression in SV40-cells
P01CA-33620-08 0004 (CAK) BARTON, JACQUELINE Directed SV40 mutation–Cell molecular consequences Mapping local DNA structures on SV40 genome
P01CA-33620-08 9001 (CAK) POLLACK, ROBERT E Directed SV40 mutation–Cell molecular consequences Core
U10CA-33622-09 (SRC) HAMM, JOHN T UNIVERSITY OF LOUISVILLE LOUISVILLE, KY 40292 Primary breast cancer therapy group–NSABP
U10CA-33625-09 (CCI) BUCHANAN, GEORGE R UNIV OF TX SW MED CTR AT DALLA 5323 HARRY HINES BLVD DALLAS, TX 75235 Pediatric oncology group activities
U10CA-33625-09 0053 (CCI) BUCHANAN, GEORGE R Pediatric oncology group activities POG8870–Phase I trial of ifosfamide/VP16/MESNA in children with acute leukemia
U10CA-33625-09 0054 (CCI) BUCHANAN, GEORGE R Pediatric oncology group activities POG8871–Phase I study of rTNF in children with refractory solid tumors
U10CA-33625-09 0055 (CCI) BUCHANAN, GEORGE R Pediatric oncology group activities POG8671–Phase I immunotherapy with rIL-2 in children with solid tumors
U10CA-33625-09 0056 (CCI) BUCHANAN, GEORGE R Pediatric oncology group activities POG8494–Phase I study of fludarabine phosphate in pediatric patients
U10CA-33625-09 0057 (CCI) BUCHANAN, GEORGE R Pediatric oncology group activities POG8930–A comprehensive genetic analysis of brain tumors
U10CA-33625-09 0058 (CCI) BUCHANAN, GEORGE R Pediatric oncology

group activities POG8828–Late effects of Hodgkin's disease
U10CA-33625-09 0059 (CCI) BUCHANAN, GEORGE R Pediatric oncology group activities POG9046–Molecular genetic analysis of Wilm's tumors
U10CA-33625-09 0060 (CCI) BUCHANAN, GEORGE R Pediatric oncology group activities POG9153–Rhabdomyosarcoma study/laboratory evaluation of tumor
U10CA-33625-09 0001 (CCI) BUCHANAN, GEORGE R Pediatric oncology group activities POG9006–6-MP/methotrexate vs. alternating chemotherapy for ALL in childhood
U10CA-33625-09 0021 (CCI) BUCHANAN, GEORGE R Pediatric oncology group activities POG9140–Phase II therapy for recurrent or refractory neuroblastoma
U10CA-33625-09 0022 (CCI) BUCHANAN, GEORGE R Pediatric oncology group activities POG9048–Phase II study of malignant germ cell tumors in children
U10CA-33625-09 0023 (CCI) BUCHANAN, GEORGE R Pediatric oncology group activities POG9060–Intensive QOD ifosfamide treatment for CNS tumors in children
U10CA-33625-09 0024 (CCI) BUCHANAN, GEORGE R Pediatric oncology group activities POG8936–Phase II study of carboplatin treatment for optic pathway tumors
U10CA-33625-09 0025 (CCI) BUCHANAN, GEORGE R Pediatric oncology group activities POG8935–Phase II study of surgery and/or radiotherapy for optic pathway tumors
U10CA-33625-09 0026 (CCI) BUCHANAN, GEORGE R Pediatric oncology group activities POG8820–Phase II/III study of VP-16, AMSA +/- 5-azacytidine in childhood ANLL
U10CA-33625-09 0027 (CCI) BUCHANAN, GEORGE R Pediatric oncology group activities POG8889–Intergroup rhabdomyosarcoma study for clinical group IV disease
U10CA-33625-09 0028 (CCI) BUCHANAN, GEORGE R Pediatric oncology group activities POG8866–Phase II asparaginase therapy for acute lymphoblastic leukemia
U10CA-33625-09 0029 (CCI) BUCHANAN, GEORGE R Pediatric oncology group activities POG8862–Combination chemotherapy of acute T-lymphoblastic leukemia
U10CA-33625-09 0030 (CCI) BUCHANAN, GEORGE R Pediatric oncology group activities POG8863–Phase II study of high dose cytosine arabinoside in childhood tumors
U10CA-33625-09 0031 (CCI) BUCHANAN, GEORGE R Pediatric oncology group activities POG8827–Phase II treatment of children with Hodgkin's disease in relapse
U10CA-33625-09 0032 (CCI) BUCHANAN, GEORGE R Pediatric oncology group activities POG8865–Phase II recombinant alpha-interferon in relapsed T-cell disease
U10CA-33625-09 0033 (CCI) BUCHANAN, GEORGE R Pediatric oncology group activities–Phase II recombinant A-interferon in chronic myelogenous leukemia
U10CA-33625-09 0034 (CCI) BUCHANAN, GEORGE R Pediatric oncology group activities POG8832–Combination chemotherapy followed by radiotherapy for brain tumors
U10CA-33625-09 0035 (CCI) BUCHANAN, GEORGE R Pediatric oncology group activities POG8731–Phase II trial of methotrexate in treatment of brain tumors in children
U10CA-33625-09 0036 (CCI) BUCHANAN, GEORGE R Pediatric oncology group activities POG8788–Intergroup rhabdomyosarcoma study/pilot study for clinical group III
U10CA-33625-09 0037 (CCI) BUCHANAN, GEORGE R Pediatric oncology group activities POG8761–Phase II study of homoharringtonine therapy for nonlymphoblastic leukemi
U10CA-33625-09 0038 (CCI) BUCHANAN, GEORGE R Pediatric oncology group activities POG8739–Phase II immunotherapy with alpha-2 interferon for brain tumors
U10CA-33625-09 0039 (CCI) BUCHANAN, GEORGE R Pediatric oncology group activities POG8741–Treatment of patients with stage C and stage D neuroblastoma
U10CA-33625-09 0040 (CCI) BUCHANAN, GEORGE R Pediatric oncology group activities POG8751–Phase II methotrexate chemotherapy for rhabdomyosarcoma in children
U10CA-33625-09 0041 (CCI) BUCHANAN, GEORGE R Pediatric oncology group activities POG8633–Postoperative chemotherapy and delayed irradiation for brain tumors
U10CA-33625-09 0042 (CCI) BUCHANAN, GEORGE R Pediatric oncology group activities POG8617–Therapy for B-cell acute lymphoblastic leukemia and lymphoma
U10CA-33625-09 0043 (CCI) BUCHANAN, GEORGE R Pediatric oncology group activities POG9139–Phase I study of cisplatin and irradiation in brain stem gliomas
U10CA-33625-09 0044 (CCI) BUCHANAN, GEORGE R Pediatric oncology group activities POG9079–Phase I study of L-PAM/CTX with ABM rescue for brain tumors in children
U10CA-33625-09 0045 (CCI) BUCHANAN, GEORGE R Pediatric oncology group activities POG9075–Phase I study of acivicin in children with solid tumors
U10CA-33625-09 0046 (CCI) BUCHANAN, GEORGE R Pediatric oncology group activities POG9074–Phase I study of xomazyme-H65 in children with T-cell ALL/lymphoma
U10CA-33625-09 0047 (CCI) BUCHANAN, GEORGE R Pediatric oncology group activities POG9072–Phase I chemotherapy for recurrent/resistant malignant solid tumors
U10CA-33625-09 0048 (CCI) BUCHANAN, GEORGE R Pediatric oncology group activities POG9061–Phase II systemic therapy and irradiation for ALL & CNS leukemia
U10CA-33625-09 0049 (CCI) BUCHANAN, GEORGE R Pediatric oncology group activities POG 9086–Phase I pilot study of therapy for T-cell ALL or NHL
U10CA-33625-09 0050 (CCI) BUCHANAN, GEORGE R Pediatric oncology group activities POG9071–Phase I trial of fazarabine in children with acute leukemia
U10CA-33625-09 0051 (CCI) BUCHANAN, GEORGE R Pediatric oncology group activities POG8970–Phase I trial of fazarabine in children with refractory solid tumors
U10CA-33625-09 0052 (CCI) BUCHANAN, GEORGE R Pediatric oncology group activities POG8973–Etoposide (VP-16) and carboplatin in children with acute leukemia
U10CA-33625-09 0002 (CCI) BUCHANAN, GEORGE R Pediatric oncology group activities POG9005–Dose intensification of methotrexate& 6-mercaptopurine for childhood ALL
U10CA-33625-09 0003 (CCI) BUCHANAN, GEORGE R Pediatric oncology group activities POG9031–Cisplatin/VP-16 therapy of medulloblastoma/pre vs. post irradiation
U10CA-33625-09 0004 (CCI) BUCHANAN, GEORGE R Pediatric oncology group activities POG8945–Phase III chemotherapy for hepatoblastoma & hepatocellular carcinoma
U10CA-33625-09 0005 (CCI) BUCHANAN, GEORGE R Pediatric oncology group activities POG9049–Phase III study of high-risk malignant germ cell tumors in children
U10CA-33625-09 0006 (CCI) BUCHANAN, GEORGE R Pediatric oncology group activities POG8844–Bone marrow transplant in children with stage D neuroblastoma
U10CA-33625-09 0007 (CCI) BUCHANAN, GEORGE R Pediatric oncology group activities POG8850–Phase III treatment of Ewing's sarcoma and neuroectodermal bone tumors
U10CA-33625-09 0008 (CCI) BUCHANAN, GEORGE R Pediatric oncology group activities POG8821–Phase III chemotherapy +/- autologous BMT in children with AML
U10CA-33625-09 0009 (CCI) BUCHANAN, GEORGE R Pediatric oncology group activities POG8725–Phase III chemotherapy +/- radiation therapy in pediatric Hodgkins
U10CA-33625-09 0010 (CCI) BUCHANAN, GEORGE R Pediatric oncology group activities POG8704–Phase III chemotherapy of childhood T cell ALL & lymphoblastic lymphoma
U10CA-33625-09 0011 (CCI) BUCHANAN, GEORGE R Pediatric oncology group activities POG8719–Phase III chemotherapy for non-Hodgkin's lymphoma in children
U10CA-33625-09 0012 (CCI) BUCHANAN, GEORGE R Pediatric oncology group activities POG8650–National Wilm's tumor and clear cell sarcoma study
U10CA-33625-09 0013 (CCI) BUCHANAN, GEORGE R Pediatric oncology group activities POG8616–Phase III chemotherapy for childhood Burkitt and non-Burkitts lymphoma
U10CA-33625-09 0014 (CCI) BUCHANAN, GEORGE R Pediatric oncology group activities POG8615–Phase III study of large cell lymphomas in children and adolescents
U10CA-33625-09 0015 (CCI) BUCHANAN, GEORGE R Pediatric oncology group activities POG8651–Phase III study of childhood nonmetastatic osteosarcoma
U10CA-33625-09 0016 (CCI) BUCHANAN, GEORGE R Pediatric oncology group activities POG8653–Phase III study of childhood soft tissue sarcomas
U10CA-33625-09 0017 (CCI) BUCHANAN, GEORGE R Pediatric oncology group activities POG8625–Phase III combined therapy in childhood Hodgkin's disease
U10CA-33625-09 0018 (CCI) BUCHANAN, GEORGE R Pediatric oncology group activities POG8451–Intergroup rhabdomyosarcoma study
U10CA-33625-09 0019 (CCI) BUCHANAN, GEORGE R Pediatric oncology group activities POG9110–Rotational drug therapy after first marrow relapse of non-T, non B ALL
U10CA-33625-09 0020 (CCI) BUCHANAN, GEORGE R Pediatric oncology group activities POG9107–Phase II pilot study of infant leukemia
R01CA-33643-09 (CTY) GETZ, MICHAEL J MAYO FOUNDATION 200 FIRST STREET SOUTHWEST ROCHESTER, MINN 55905 Mechanisms of regulation of cell proliferation
R01CA-33644-09 (EDC) NOMURA, ABRAHAM M KUAKINI MEDICAL CENTER 347 NORTH KUAKINI STREET HONOLULU, HAWAII 96817 Cancer epidemiology of the migrant Japanese in Hawaii
R37CA-33657-11 (RAD) WALLACE, SUSAN S UNIVERSITY OF VERMONT GIVEN MEDICAL BUILDING BURLINGTON, VT 05405 Repair of DNA damage induced by ionizing radiation
R01CA-33771-09 (EVR) ROSENBERG, NAOMI E TUFTS UNIVERSITY SCHOOL OF MED 136 HARRISON AVENUE BOSTON, MA 02111 RNA tumor virus–Hematopoietic cell interaction
R01CA-33825-08 (ET) ENSMINGER, WILLIAM D 1310 EAST CATHERINE ROAD 3709 UPJOHN CENTER ANN ARBOR, MI 48109-0504 Hepatic tumor microcirculation and microsphere therapy
R01CA-33834-09 (PTHB) KRAMER, RANDALL H UNIVERSITY OF CALIFORNIA DIV OF ORAL BIOLOGY/HSW 604 SAN FRANCISCO, CA 94143 Tumor cell invasion of microvessel subendothelial matrix
R01CA-33895-09 (PTHB) FUKUDA, MINORU LA JOLLA CANCER RESEARCH FDN 10901 NORTH TORREY PINES ROAD LA JOLLA, CA 92037 Glycoproteins in normal and leukemic cell differentiation
R01CA-33907-08A1 (BNP) WATANABE, KYOICHI A SLOAN-KETTERING INST/CNCR RES 1275 YORK AVENUE NEW YORK, NY 10021 Synthesis of antitumor/viral pyrimidine C-nucleosides
R01CA-33922-08 (RNM) ROEMER, ROBERT B UNIVERSITY OF ARIZONA 1501 NORTH CAMPBELL TUCSON, AZ 85724 Ultrasound hyperthermia system for cancer therapy
R01CA-33936-09 (HEM) KOEFFLER, PHILLIP H UNIVERSITY OF CALIFORNIA LOS ANGELES, CA 90024-1678 Action of retinoids on myeloid leukemia
R01CA-34025-08 (PBC) SENGER, DONALD R BETH ISRAEL HOSPITAL 330 BROOKLINE AVENUE BOSTON, MA 02215 Secreted phosphoproteins associated with tumorigenicity
R01CA-34061-09 (CPA) SCARPELLI, DANTE G NORTHWESTERN UNIV MEDICAL SCH 303 EAST CHICAGO AVENUE CHICAGO, IL 60611 Pancreatic duct carcinogens–Species differences
R01CA-34062-08 (IMB) KAPLAN, ALAN M UNIVERSITY OF KENTUCKY LEXINGTON, KY 40536-0084 T-cell interactions with cloned Ia+ accessory cells
R01CA-34085-09 (ET) MITCHELL, BEVERLY S UNIV OF NC AT CHAPEL HILL CB# 7365, FLOB CHAPEL HILL, NC 27599-7365 Inhibitors of purine nucleoside phosphorylase
R01CA-34126-09 (EVR) TIBBETTS, CLARK J VANDERBILT UNIVERSITY NASHVILLE, TN 37232 Adenovirus genome expression–Physical mapping studies
R01CA-34141-10 (IMS) GODFREY, HENRY P NEW YORK MEDICAL COLLEGE

PROJECT NO., ORGANIZATIONAL UNIT., INVESTIGATOR, ADDRESS, TITLE

BASIC SCIENCE BUILDING VALHALLA, NY 10595 Macrophage agglutination factor

R01CA-34151-09S1 (PTHB) HAAS, MARTIN UNIV OF CALIFORNIA, SAN DIEGO 9500 GILMAN DR, 0063 LA JOLLA, CA 92093 Viral malignant lymphomagenesis in X-irradiated mice

R01CA-34158-11 (RAD) KOVAL, THOMAS M MAYO FOUNDATION 200 FIRST STREET SOUTHWEST ROCHESTER, MN 55905 Insect cells--A basis for radioresistance

P01CA-34183-08 (SRC) SCHLOSSMAN, STUART F DANA-FARBER CANCER INSTITUTE 44 BINNEY STREET BOSTON, MA 02115 Biology and treatment of leukemia and lymphoma

P01CA-34183-08 0016 (SRC) TENEN, DANIEL G Biology and treatment of leukemia and lymphoma Regulation of gene for human stem cell antigen CD34 in leukemic cells

P01CA-34183-08 0017 (SRC) SCHLOSSMAN, STUART F Biology and treatment of leukemia and lymphoma Novel immunotherapeutic strategies

P01CA-34183-08 9001 (SRC) GELBER, RICHARD Biology and treatment of leukemia and lymphoma Biostatistics and computer resources

P01CA-34183-08 9002 (SRC) RITZ, JEROME Biology and treatment of leukemia and lymphoma Clinical research support core

P01CA-34183-08 0003 (SRC) GRIFFIN, JAMES D Biology and treatment of leukemia and lymphoma Biology of acute myeloblastic leukemia

P01CA-34183-08 0005 (SRC) KUFE, DONALD W Biology and treatment of leukemia and lymphoma C-FMS and CSF-1 expression in myeloid differentiation and leukemia

P01CA-34183-08 0010 (SRC) NADLER, LEE M Biology and treatment of leukemia and lymphoma B cell non-Hodgkin's lymphoma--New therapeutic strategies

P01CA-34183-08 0013 (SRC) RITZ, JEROME Biology and treatment of leukemia and lymphoma Multi-disciplinary strategies for the treatment of acute myeloid leukemia

P01CA-34183-08 0014 (SRC) TEDDER, THOMAS F Biology and treatment of leukemia and lymphoma CD20--B lymphocyte-specific ion channel

P30CA-34196-09 (CCS) PAIGEN, KENNETH JACKSON LABORATORY 600 MAIN STREET BAR HARBOR, ME 04609-0800 Cancer center support (core) grant

P30CA-34196-09 9006 (CCS) SIDMAN, CHARLES Cancer center support (core) grant Flow cytometry--Core

P30CA-34196-09 9007 (CCS) MOBRAATEN, LARRY E Cancer center support (core) grant Genetic information resources

P30CA-34196-09 9008 (CCS) KAZAK, LESLIE P Cancer center support (core) grant Transgenic mouse resources

P30CA-34196-09 9010 (CCS) JONES, ALBERT M Cancer center support (core) grant Laboratory animal medicine

P30CA-34196-09 9011 (CCS) JONES, ALBERT M Cancer center support (core) grant Pathology--core

P30CA-34196-09 9013 (CCS) EPPIG, JOHN J Cancer center support (core) grant Electron microscopy services

P30CA-34196-09 9014 (CCS) TAYLOR, FREDRICK Cancer center support (core) grant Microchemistry service--Core

P30CA-34196-09 9015 (CCS) PAIGEN, KENNETH Cancer center support (core) grant Conference and seminars--Core

P30CA-34196-09 9016 (CCS) PAIGEN, KENNETH Cancer center support (core) grant Developmental funds--Core

P01CA-34200-09 (SRC) STRUCK, ROBERT F SOUTHERN RESEARCH INSTITUTE PO BOX 55305 BIRMINGHAM, AL 35255-5305 Development of new antitumor agents

P01CA-34200-09 0002 (SRC) SECRIST, JOHN A Development of new antitumor agents Nucleosides with altered metabolism

P01CA-34200-09 0004 (SRC) SECRIST, JOHN A Development of new antitumor agents Carbocyclic analogues of nucleosides for anticancer and antiviral chemotherapy

P01CA-34200-09 0005 (SRC) STRUCK, ROBERT F Development of new antitumor agents Chemically reactive compounds for cancer chemotherapy

P01CA-34200-09 0011 (SRC) PARKER, WILLIAM B Development of new antitumor agents DNA primase as a target for cancer chemotherapy

P01CA-34200-09 0012 (SRC) SIROTNAK, FRANK Development of new antitumor agents Developmental antifolate therapy of cancer

P01CA-34200-09 0013 (SRC) STRUCK, ROBERT F Development of new antitumor agents Phosphoramide mustards--Cytoxicity and effects on DNA

P01CA-34200-09 0014 (SRC) SIMPSON-HERREN, LINDA Development of new antitumor agents Intratumor distribution of anticancer drugs

P01CA-34200-09 9001 (SRC) ELLIOTT, ROBERT D Development of new antitumor agents Core--Organic preparations and analytical laboratory

P01CA-34200-09 9003 (SRC) BENNETT, LEE L Development of new antitumor agents Core--Biochemical support

P01CA-34200-09 9007 (SRC) HILL, DONALD L Development of new antitumor agents Core--Pharmacology of potential anticancer agents

P01CA-34200-09 9008 (SRC) SHANNON, WILLIAM M Development of new antitumor agents Core--Antiviral evaluations

P01CA-34200-09 9009 (SRC) HARRISON, STEADMAN Development of new antitumor agents Core--Chemotherapy

P01CA-34233-09 (SRC) LEVY, RONALD STANFORD UNIVERSITY STANFORD MEDICAL CENTER STANFORD, CA 94305-5306 Clinical and laboratory studies of malignant lymphomas

P01CA-34233-09 0010 (SRC) LEVY, RONALD Clinical and laboratory studies of malignant lymphomas Monoclonal antibody therapy of Mycosis Fungoides

P01CA-34233-09 0017 (SRC) LEVY, RONALD Clinical and laboratory studies of malignant lymphomas Biologic studies of follicular lymphoma and diffuse large cell lymphoma

P01CA-34233-09 0018 (SRC) KRENSKY, ALAN M Clinical and laboratory studies of malignant lymphomas CTL recognition of non-Hodgkin's lymphoma

P01CA-34233-09 0019 (SRC) CLEARY, MICHAEL L Clinical and laboratory studies of malignant lymphomas Isolation of novel oncogenes from malignant lymphomas

P01CA-34233-09 0021 (SRC) HORNING, SANDRA J Clinical and laboratory studies of malignant lymphomas HLA and Hodgkin's disease

P01CA-34233-09 0022 (SRC) LIEBER, MICHAEL R Clinical and laboratory studies of malignant lymphomas Lymphoid-specific DNA enzymes in human lymphoma

P01CA-34233-09 0023 (SRC) CHU, GILBERT Clinical and laboratory studies of malignant lymphomas Translocation and activation of c-myc in human lymphomas

PROJECT NO., ORGANIZATIONAL UNIT., INVESTIGATOR, ADDRESS, TITLE

P01CA-34233-09 9002 (SRC) WARNKE, ROGER Clinical and laboratory studies of malignant lymphomas Core--Pathology

P01CA-34233-09 9003 (SRC) BROWN, BYRON W Clinical and laboratory studies of malignant lymphomas Core--Information and data management

P01CA-34233-09 9007 (SRC) HOPPE, RICHARD T Clinical and laboratory studies of malignant lymphomas Core--Patient resource

P01CA-34233-09 0001 (SRC) ROSENBERG, SAUL A Clinical and laboratory studies of malignant lymphomas Clinical investigations of the management of adults with Hodgkin's disease

P01CA-34233-09 0002 (SRC) HORNING, SANDRA Clinical and laboratory studies of malignant lymphomas Clinical and pathologic studies in non-Hodgkin's lymphoma

P01CA-34233-09 0004 (SRC) DONALDSON, SARAH S Clinical and laboratory studies of malignant lymphomas Clinical investigations in pediatric Hodgkin's disease

P01CA-34233-09 0005 (SRC) BROWN, BYRON W Clinical and laboratory studies of malignant lymphomas Statistical aspects of lymphoma studies

R01CA-34247-09 (MCHA) MARSHALL, JAMES A UNIVERSITY OF SOUTH CAROLINA COLUMBIA, SC 29208 Synthesis of macrocyclic antitumor antibiotics

U01CA-34256-08 (SRC) MOON, THOMAS E UNIVERSITY OF ARIZONA 1515 NORTH CAMPBELL AVENUE TUCSON, AZ 85724 Chemoprevention of skin cancer by vitamin A

R01CA-34269-08 (RAD) BELLI, JAMES A UNIV OF TEXAS MED BRANCH GALVESTON, TX 77550 Radiation and drug effects in mammalian cells

R01CA-34282-08 (CBY) RIFKIN, DANIEL B NEW YORK UNIVERSITY MED CTR 550 FIRST AVENUE NEW YORK, N Y 10016 Biochemical mechanisms of cellular invasion

U01CA-34290-08 (SRC) MCLARTY, JERRY W UNIV OF TEXAS HLTH CTR PO BOX 2003 TYLER, TX 75710 Beta-carotene and lung cancer chemoprevention

R01CA-34301-08 (ET) DOLNICK, BRUCE J ROSWELL PARK CANCER INSTITUTE THERAPEUTICS BUFFALO, N Y 14263 Effects of antimetabolites on RNA metabolism

R01CA-34303-09 (MCHA) WEINREB, STEVEN M PENNSYLVANIA STATE UNIVERSITY 152 DAVEY LABORATORY UNIVERSITY PARK, PA 16802 Natural product synthesis via electron deficient imines

R01CA-34398-07 (RNM) EDMONDS, PETER D SRI INTERNATIONAL 333 RAVENSWOOD AVENUE MENLO PARK, CA 94025 Ultrasonic properties of normal and pathological tissues

R01CA-34442-08 (EI) GOLUB, SIDNEY H UNIVERSITY OF CALIFORNIA 405 HILGARD AVENUE LOS ANGELES, CA 90024 In vitro induction of NK cytotoxicity

R01CA-34443-08 (CPA) FISCHER, SUSAN M UT MD ANDERSON CANCER CTR SCIENCE PARK - RESEARCH DIVISI SMITHVILLE, TX 78957 Role of arachidonate metabolites in tumor promotion

R01CA-34456-08 (EVR) DONOGHUE, DANIEL J UNIV OF CALIFORNIA SAN DIEGO LA JOLLA, CA 92093-0322 Expression of retroviral envelope gene fusion proteins

R01CA-34461-09 (EI) WELSH, RAYMOND M UNIV OF MASSACHUSETTS MED CTR 55 LAKE AVENUE NORTH WORCESTER, MA 01655 Regulation of natural killer cells

R01CA-34472-08 (CTY) TUCKER, ROBERT W JOHNS HOPKINS UNIVERSITY 600 NORTH WOLFE STREET BALTIMORE, MD 21205 Calcium-growth in neoplastic-nonneoplastic fibroblasts

R01CA-34493-08 (EDC) HOLMES, KING K HARBORVIEW MEDICAL CENTER 325 NINTH AVENUE SEATTLE, WA 98104 Etiology and natural history of cervical neoplasia

R01CA-34544-08 (ET) KALLMAN, ROBERT F STANFORD UNIVERSITY DIV OF RADIATION ONCOL, RM AO- STANFORD, CALIF 94305 Combined modalities--Radiotherapy and chemotherapy

R01CA-34546-11 (IMS) FU, SHU MAN DIV OF RHEUMATOLOGY BOX 412 UNIVERSITY OF VIRGINIA CHARLOTTESVILLE, VA 22908 Studies on human lymphocyte activation

R01CA-34569-09 (PBC) MALTESE, WILLIAM A GEISINGER CLINIC/WEIS CENTER NORTH ACADEMY AVENUE DANVILLE, PA 17822 Isoprenoid synthesis and tumor cell growth

R37CA-34570-09 (RNM) RASEY, JANET S UNIVERSITY OF WASHINGTON 1959 NE PACIFIC STREET SEATTLE, WA 98195 Nuclear imaging of tumors--biological and chemical basis

R01CA-34588-07 (EDC) PASTERNACK, BERNARD S NEW YORK UNIVERSITY MED CENTER 550 FIRST AVENUE NEW YORK, NY 10016 Endocrine and environmental factors in breast cancer

R01CA-34590-10 (PTHB) RICHMOND, ANN VANDERBILT UNIV SCH OF MED C-2310 M C N NASHVILLE, TN 37232 Melanoma growth stimulatory activity

R01CA-34610-09 (CBY) MASSAGUE, JOAN SLOAN-KETTERING INSTITUTE 1275 YORK AVENUE NEW YORK, NY 10021 Receptors for transforming growth factor-beta

R01CA-34619-10 (ET) BORCH, RICHARD F UNIV OF ROCHESTER MEDICAL CTR 601 ELMWOOD AVENUE ROCHESTER, NY 14642-8411 Mechanisms of cyclophosphamide activation

R01CA-34620-09 (ET) BORCH, RICHARD F UNIVERSITY OF ROCHESTER 601 ELMWOOD AVENUE ROCHESTER, NY 14642 Reduction of toxicity in cancer chemotherapy

R01CA-34627-08A1 (CPA) HEIN, DAVID W UNIVERSITY OF NORTH DAKOTA 501 NORTH COLUMBIA ROAD GRAND FORKS, ND 58203 Pharmacogenetics of drug and carcinogen metabolism

R01CA-34691-08 (HEM) SEGEL, GEORGE B UNIV OF ROCHESTER SCH OF MED 601 ELMWOOD AVENUE ROCHESTER, NY 14642 A specific abnormality in chronic leukemic lymphocytes

R01CA-34695-09 (CPA) TERZAGHI-HOWE, MARGARET OAK RIDGE NATIONAL LABORATORY PO BOX 2009 OAK RIDGE, TN 37831-8077 Cell interactions--Expression of preneoplastic markers

R01CA-34714-08 (BBCA) CODY, VIVIAN MEDICAL FDN OF BUFFALO INC 73 HIGH STREET BUFFALO, N Y 14203 Molecular & electronic structures of antifolate drugs

R37CA-34722-09 (EVR) SCHAFFHAUSEN, BRIAN S TUFTS UNIVERSITY 136 HARRISON AVENUE BOSTON, MA 02111 Products of the transforming genes of polyoma virus

R01CA-34732-08A1 (MEP) BAILEY, GEORGE S OREGON STATE UNIVERSITY CORVALLIS, OR 97331 Mechanisms of inhibition of chemical carcinogenesis

R01CA-34734-06 (EVR) MURPHY, EDWIN C, JR UNIV OF TEXAS/M D A CANCER CTR 1515 HOLCOMBE BLVD HOUSTON, TX 77030 MuSVts110--Thermosensitive RNA splicing in intact cells

R01CA-34738-06 (GMB) STREWLER, GORDON J VA MEDICAL CENTER 4150 CLEMENT STREET (111N) SAN FRANCISCO, CA 94121 Malignancy associated hypercalcemia

R01CA-34763-06 (CBY) LEAVITT, JOHN C PALO ALTO MEDICAL FDN 860 BRYANT ST PALO ALTO, CA 94301 Roles of microfilament proteins in neoplasia/metastasis

R01CA-34775-06 (MGN) CHAGANTI, RAJU S SLOAN-KETTERING INSTITUTE 1275 YORK AVE NEW YORK, NY 10021 Mapping chromosomes and genes in relation to leukemia

R01CA-34780-07 (VR) DUDLEY, JAQUELIN P UNIVERSITY OF TEXAS AT AUSTIN AUSTIN, TX 78712-1095 Regulation of MMTV in T-cell tumors

R01CA-34787-09 (ALY) TROWBRIDGE, IAN S SALK INSTITUTE PO BOX 85800 SAN DIEGO, CA 92138 Human cell surface antigens--Transferrin receptors

R01CA-34841-10 (HEM) HOFFMAN, RONALD INDIANA UNIVERSITY SCH OF MED 975 WEST WALNUT ST, IB442 INDIANAPOLIS, IN 46202-5121 Regulation of hematopoiesis in cancer

P01CA-34847-09 (SRC) HENDERSON, MAUREEN M FRED HUTCHINSON CANCER RES CTR 1124 COLUMBIA STREET SEATTLE, WA 98104 Cancer prevention research unit renewal application

P01CA-34847-09 0001 (SRC) OMENN, GILBERT S Cancer prevention research unit renewal application Efficacy of beta-carotene and retinal in high risk for lung cancer

P01CA-34847-09 0002 (SRC) GOODMAN, GARY E Cancer prevention research unit renewal application Side effects in chemoprevention with beta-carotene and retinal

P01CA-34847-09 0003 (SRC) CHU, JOSEPH Cancer prevention research unit renewal application Chemoprevention (or prevention) of cervical cancer with folic acid

P01CA-34847-09 0012 (SRC) WHITE, EMILY Cancer prevention research unit renewal application Health of husbands of participants in the womens' health trial

P01CA-34847-09 0015 (SRC) SARASON, IRWIN G Cancer prevention research unit renewal application The role of local churches in eating behavior changes

P01CA-34847-09 0016 (SRC) URBAN, NICOLE Cancer prevention research unit renewal application Promotion of breast cancer screening in a community

P01CA-34847-09 0017 (SRC) TAPLIN, STEPHEN Cancer prevention research unit renewal application Mammography recruitment strategies

P01CA-34847-09 0018 (SRC) PETERSON, ARTHUR Cancer prevention research unit renewal application Prevention of smokeless tobacco use in children

P01CA-34847-09 0019 (SRC) THOMPSON, BETI Cancer prevention research unit renewal application A stepped approach to smoking reduction

P01CA-34847-09 0020 (SRC) KOEPSELL, THOMAS Cancer prevention research unit renewal application Methodology of community-based intervention studies

P01CA-34847-09 9002 (SRC) WAGNER, EDWARD H Cancer prevention research unit renewal application Core--Mini population laboratory

P01CA-34847-09 9003 (SRC) WHITE, EMILY Cancer prevention research unit renewal application Core--Surveillance and investigation section

P01CA-34847-09 9004 (SRC) THOMPSON, BETI Cancer prevention research unit renewal application Core--Social research support section shared resource

P01CA-34847-09 9005 (SRC) KRISTAL, ALAN Cancer prevention research unit renewal application Core--Nutrition epidemiology section

P01CA-34847-09 9006 (SRC) URBAN, NICOLE Cancer prevention research unit renewal application Core--Cost analysis section

P01CA-34847-09 9007 (SRC) SARASON, IRWIN Cancer prevention research unit renewal application Core--Behavioral science measurement shared resource

P01CA-34847-09 9009 (SRC) KINNE, SUSAN Cancer prevention research unit renewal application Core--Study of worksite smoking policies

P01CA-34856-09 (SRC) ENGSTROM, PAUL F FOX CHASE CANCER CENTER 7701 BURHOLME AVENUE PHILADELPHIA, PA 19111 Enhancing adherence to cancer control regimens

P01CA-34856-09 0002 (SRC) RIMER, BARBARA Enhancing adherence to cancer control regimens Mobile mammography

P01CA-34856-09 0005 (SRC) ORLEANS, TRACY Enhancing adherence to cancer control regimens Clear horizons--Adherence to smoking cessation

P01CA-34856-09 0006 (SRC) BALSHEM, MARTHA Enhancing adherence to cancer control regimens Check-up on health

P01CA-34856-09 0007 (SRC) MYERS, RONALD E Enhancing adherence to cancer control regimens Colo-record study

P01CA-34856-09 9001 (SRC) DAYAL, HARI Enhancing adherence to cancer control regimens Epidemiology/statistics core

P01CA-34856-09 9002 (SRC) RIMER, BARBARA Enhancing adherence to cancer control regimens Behavioral research

R01CA-34869-09 (CPA) WETTERHAHN, KAREN E DARTMOUTH COLLEGE STEELE HALL HANOVER, NH 03755 Mechanism of chromium carcinogenicity

R01CA-34871-09 (BEM) JAY, SUSAN M CHILDRENS HOSP OF LOS ANGELES 4650 SUNSET BOULEVARD LOS ANGELES, CA 90027 Bone marrow aspirations in children; treatment outcome

P01CA-34936-08 (SRC) STRONG, LOUISE C UNIV OF TEX MD ANDERSON CA CTR 1515 HOLCOMBE BLVD BOX 209 HOUSTON, TX 77030 A mutational model for childhood cancer

P01CA-34936-08 0001 (SRC) STRONG, LOUISE C A mutational model for childhood cancer Etiology of childhood sarcoma

P01CA-34936-08 0002 (SRC) FERRELL, ROBERT C A mutational model for childhood cancer Genetic analysis of childhood sarcoma families

P01CA-34936-08 0003 (SRC) SAUNDERS, GRADY F A mutational model for childhood cancer Gene probes for Wilm's tumor

P01CA-34936-08 0004 (SRC) SICILIANO, MICHAEL J A mutational model for childhood cancer DNA repair genes in childhood cancer

P01CA-34936-08 0005 (SRC) WILLIAMS, WICK R A mutational model for childhood cancer Genetic epidemiology of childhood sarcoma

P01CA-34936-08 0006 (SRC) TYINSKY, MICHAEL A mutational model for childhood cancer Molecular basis of the familial predisposition to cancer

P01CA-34936-08 9001 (SRC) PATHAK, SEN A mutational model for childhood cancer Cytogenetics

P01CA-34936-08 9002 (SRC) GIOVANELLA, BEPPINO A mutational model for childhood cancer Establishment of cell lines and tumorigenicity

R01CA-34970-13 (RNM) JONES, ALUN G HARVARD MEDICAL SCHOOL 50 BINNEY STREET BOSTON, MASS 02115 The chemistry of technetium related to nuclear medicine

R01CA-34979-08 (SSS) FINBERG, ROBERT W DANA-FARBER CANCER INSTITUTE 44 BINNEY ST BOSTON, MA 02115 Animal models of AIDS

R37CA-34988-09 (NSS) FISCHL, MARGARET A UNIVERSITY OF MIAMI PO BOX 016960 MIAMI, FL 33101 Heterosexual and household tranmission of HTLV-III

R37CA-34992-09 (BMT) LIPPARD, STEPHEN J MASSACHUSETTS INST OF TECHNOLO CAMBRIDGE, MA 02139 Chemistry and biology of platinum anticancer drugs

R01CA-35020-09 (ARRA) HIRSCH, MARTIN S MASSACHUSETTS GENERAL HOSPITAL FRUIT ST BOSTON, MA 02114 Viruses, acquired immunodeficiency, and Kaposi's sarcoma

R01CA-35035-09 (RAD) PRAKASH, SATYA UNIVERSITY OF ROCHESTER ROCHESTER, N Y 14627 Excision repair of UV irradiated DNA in yeast

U10CA-35090-08 (SRC) GROSS, HOWARD M COX HEART INSTITUTE 3525 SOUTHERN BLVD DAYTON, OH 45429 Dayton community clinical oncology program

U10CA-35091-08 (SRC) WALLACE, HAROLD J, JR RUTLAND REGIONAL MEDICAL CENTE 160 ALLEN STREET RUTLAND, VT 05701 Green Mountain community clinical oncology group

U10CA-35096-08 (SRC) ROSENBLUTH, RICHARD J BERGEN-PASSAIC COMMUNITY CLINI HACKENSACK MEDICAL CENTER HACKENSACK, NJ 07601 Bergen-Passaic community clinical oncology program

U10CA-35101-08 (SRC) MORTON, ROSCOE F IOWA ONCOLOGY RESEARCH ASSN 1044 SEVENTH STREET DES MOINES, IA 50314 Iowa oncology research association CCOP

U10CA-35103-08 (SRC) TSCHETTER, LOREN K SIOUX COMMUNITY CANCER CTM 1000 EAST 21ST STREET SIOUX FALLS, SD 57105 Sioux community cancer consortium

U10CA-35113-08 (SRC) GERSTNER, JAMES B ILLINOIS ONCOLOGY RSRCH ASSN 900 MAIN STREET SUITE 780 PEORIA, IL 61602 Illinois oncology research association CCOP

U10CA-35117-08 (SRC) PUGH, REGINALD P ALLEGHENY-SINGER RESEARCH INST 320 EAST NORTH AVENUE PITTSBURGH, PA 15212-9986 Allegheny community clinical oncology program

U10CA-35119-08 (SRC) MC CULLOCH, JOHN H 1776 SKYLYN DRIVE PO BOX 2768 SPARTANBURG, SC 29304 Spartanburg community clinical oncology program

U10CA-35128-08 (SRC) HENRY, PATRICK H MERCY DRS. BLDG, TOWER B 621 SOUTH NEW BALLAS ROAD ST LOUIS, MO 63141 St Louis-Cape Girardeau CCOP

U10CA-35157-08 (SRC) TALBERT, JAMES L FLA ASSOC OF PED TUMOR PGRMS PO BOX 13372 GAINESVILLE, FL 32604-1372 Community clinical oncology program

U10CA-35176-08 (SRC) BELT, ROBERT J BAPTIST MEDICAL CENTER 6601 ROCKHILL ROAD KANSAS CITY, MO 64131 Kansas City community clinical oncology program

U10CA-35178-08 (SRC) BORST, JAMES R BUTTERWORTH HOSPITAL 100 MICHIGAN, NE GRAND RAPIDS, MI 49503 Grand Rapids community clinical oncology program

U10CA-35184-08 (SRC) STOTT, PHILLIP B KALAMAZOO CCOP 1521 GULL ROAD KALAMAZOO, MI 49001 Kalamazoo community clinical oncology program

U10CA-35192-08 (SRC) EINSTEIN, ALBERT B, JR VIRGINIA MASON CLINIC 1100 9TH AVE, PO BOX 900 SEATTLE, WA 98111 Community clinical oncology program

U10CA-35195-08 (SRC) HATFIELD, ALAN K 602 W. UNIVERSITY AVE. URBANA, IL 61801 Carle cancer center community clinical oncology program

U10CA-35199-08 (SRC) KHANDEKAR, JANARDAN D EVANSTON HOSPITAL 2650 RIDGE AVE EVANSTON, IL 60201 Community clinical oncology program

U10CA-35200-08 (SRC) PRESANT, CARY A LOS ANGELES ONCOLOGIC INST 2131 WEST THIRD STREET LOS ANGELES, CA 90057 Central Los Angeles community clinical oncology program

R01CA-35212-07 (BNP) KALMAN, THOMAS I S U N Y AT BUFFALO 457 COOKE HALL BUFFALO, N Y 14260 Mechanism-based enzyme inhibitors--Novel antifolates

R01CA-35215-08 (RAD) ROCKWELL, SARA C YALE UNIV SCH OF MEDICINE P. O. BOX 3333 NEW HAVEN, CT 06510 Fluorochemical emulsions as adjuncts to radiotherapy

R01CA-35249-07 (CPA) FAUSTO, NELSON BROWN UNIVERSITY DIV OF BIOLOGY AND MEDICINE PROVIDENCE, R I 02912 Protooncogenes and cell lineages in liver carcinogenesis

R01CA-35251-08 (BBCA) KRUGH, THOMAS R UNIVERSITY OF ROCHESTER ROCHESTER, NY 14627 Structure of carcinogen-nucleic acid complexes

U10CA-35261-08 (SRC) LAUFMAN, LESLIE R COLUMBUS CCOP 1151 South High Street COLUMBUS, OH 43206 Columbus community clinical oncology program

U10CA-35262-08 (SRC) KING, DAVID K GREATER PHOENIX COMMUNITY 925 EAST MCDOWELL ROAD PHOENIX, AZ 85006-2726 Greater Phoenix community clinical oncology program

U10CA-35267-08 (SRC) FLYNN, PATRICK J COMM CLINICAL ONCOLOGY PRGM 5000 WEST 39TH STREET ST LOUIS PARK, MN 55416 W Metro-Minneapolis community clinical oncology program

U10CA-35269-08 (SRC) KROOK, JAMES E DULUTH CLINIC, LTD 400 EAST THIRD STREET DULUTH, MN 55805 Duluth community clinical oncology program

U10CA-35272-08 (SRC) KARDINAL, CARL G OCHSNER CANCER INST 1516 JEFFERSON HIGHWAY NEW ORLEANS, LA 70121 Ochsner community clinical oncology program

U10CA-35279-08 (SRC) VINCIGUERRA, VINCENT P NORTH SHORE UNIVERSITY HOSPITA 300 COMMUNITY DRIVE MANHASSET, NY 11030 North shore univ community clinical oncology program

U10CA-35281-08 (SRC) PIERCE, IRVING 314 S K STREET TACOMA, WA 98405 Northwest community clinical oncology program

U10CA-35283-07A1 (SRC) FLAM, MARSHALL S 3636 N. FIRST FRESNO, CA

PROJECT NO., ORGANIZATIONAL UNIT., INVESTIGATOR, ADDRESS, TITLE

93726 San Joaquin Valley community clinical oncology program

R01CA-35329-06 (BIO) MATTA, KHUSHI L ROSWELL PARK MEMORIAL INST. BUFFALO, NY 14263 Systematic study of three types of glycosyltransferases

R01CA-35362-06 (PTHB) SUDILOVSKY, OSCAR CASE WESTERN RESERVE UNIV 2085 ADELBERT RD CLEVELAND, OH 44106 DNA content of dysplastic lesions in human and rat liver

R01CA-35368-06 (CPA) VERMA, AJIT K UNIV OF WI, CLIN CANC CTR 600 HIGHLAND AVENUE MADISON, WI 53792 Ca2+-dependent processes involved in phorbol ester tumor

R01CA-35373-09 (CPA) MICHALOPOULOS, GEORGE K UNIVERSITY OF PITTSBURGH SCHOOL OF MEDICINE PITTSBURGH, PA 15261 Hepatopoietins, liver regeneration and carcinogenesis

U10CA-35412-08 (SRC) BANERJEE, TARIT K MARSHFIELD CLINIC 1000 NORTH OAK AVENUE MARSHFIELD, WI 54449 Marshfield community clinical oncology program

U10CA-35415-08 (SRC) SCHAEFER, PAUL TOLEDO COMMUNITY HSP ONCOL PRG 3314 COLLINGWOOD BOULEVARD TOLEDO, OH 43610 Toledo community clinical oncology program

U10CA-35421-08 (SRC) ELLERTON, JOHN A SOUTHERN NEVADA CANCER RES FDN 501 S RANCHO DR - SUITE C-14 LAS VEGAS, NV 89106 Southern Nevada Cancer Research Foundation--CCOP

U10CA-35431-08 (SRC) HYNES, HENRY E ST FRANCIS REGIONAL MEDICAL CT 929 N ST FRANCIS WICHITA, KS 67214 Community clinical oncology program

U10CA-35435-08 (SRC) BOSELLI, BRUCE ROBERT PACKER HOSPITAL GUTHRIE SQUARE SAYRE, PA 18840 Twin Tiers community clinical oncology program

U10CA-35448-08 (SRC) BERNATH, ALBERT M GEISINGER MEDICAL CENTER NORTH ACADEMY AVENUE DANVILLE, PA 17822 Geisinger community clinical oncology program

R01CA-35464-08 (SSS) TANNER, MARTIN A UNIV OF ROCHESTER MED CENTER 601 ELMWOOD AVE PO BOX 630 ROCHESTER, NY 14642 Nonparametric analysis of censored data

R01CA-35480-07 (REN) MARKAVERICH, BARRY M BAYLOR COLLEGE OF MEDICINE 4000 RESEARCH FOREST DRIVE THE WOODLANDS, TX 77381 Cell growth inhibition and estrogen action

R01CA-35482-07 (ALY) MERUELO, DANIEL NEW YORK UNIVERSITY MED CTR 550 FIRST AVENUE NEW YORK, N Y 10016 Cloning and study of a major gene involved on oncogenesis

R37CA-35494-08 (CPA) VOGELSTEIN, BERT JOHNS HOPKINS UNIVERSITY 424 N. BOND STREET/ROOM 109 BALTIMORE, MARYLAND 21231 Clonal analysis of human neoplasia

R01CA-35519-08 (CPA) EL-BAYOUMY, KARAM E AMERICAN HEALTH FOUNDATION ONE DANA ROAD VALHALLA, NY 10595 Nitroaromatics--Carcinogenicity and metabolism

R01CA-35531-07 (ET) GANAPATHI, RAM N CLEVELAND CLINIC FOUNDATION 9500 EUCLID AVENUE CLEVELAND, OH 44195 Effect of calmodulin inhibitors on adriamycin resistance

R01CA-35541-08 (CPA) ROSNER, MARSHA R UNIVERSITY OF CHICAGO 5841 SOUTH MD AVE BOX 424 CHICAGO, IL 60637 Modulation of cellular phosphorylation by tumor promoter

R01CA-35568-08 (VR) GALLOWAY, DENISE A FRED HUTCHINSON CANCER RES CTR 1124 COLUMBIA STREET SEATTLE, WA 98104 Molecular studies on herpesvirus proteins

R01CA-35580-07S1 (RAD) MARGULIES, LOLA NEW YORK MEDICAL COLLEGE VALHALLA, NY 10595 Ionizing radiation and transposon mobility

R01CA-35581-08 (CPA) MACLEOD, MICHAEL C U OF TEX/MD ANDERSON CANCER CT PO BOX 389 SMITHVILLE, TX 78957 Specificity of diol epoxide--Chromatin interactions

R01CA-35675-08 (CPA) FISHER, PAUL B COLUMBIA UNIVERSITY 630 WEST 168TH ST NEW YORK, NY 10032 Analysis of progression of the transformed phenotype (rats)

R01CA-35711-08 (PTHB) WANDS, JACK R MOLECULAR HEPATOLOGY LABORATOR 149 13TH ST. 7TH FLOOR CHARLESTOWN, MA 02129 Pathogenensis, immunodiagnosis, and therapy of HCC

R01CA-35767-08 (RAD) HENNER, WILLIAM D OREGON HEALTH SCIENCES UNIV 3181 S W SAM JACKSON PARK ROAD PORTLAND, OR 97201 Ionizing radiation induced DNA damage and repair

R01CA-35961-07 (EI) MORAHAN, PAGE S MED COLLEGE OF PENNSLYVANIA 3300 HENRY AVENUE PHILADELPHIA, PA 19129 Macrophage resistance vs viruses and tumors

R01CA-35977-08 (EI) SUZUKI, TSUNEO UNIV OF KANSAS MEDICAL CENTER 39TH AND RAINBOW BLVD KANSAS CITY, KS 66103-8410 Receptor-mediated regulation of macrophage functions

U10CA-36015-08 (CCI) ALBO, VINCENT C CHILDREN'S HOSP OF PITTSBURGH ONE CHILDREN'S PLACE PITTSBURGH, PA 15213-2583 Children's cancer study group

U10CA-36047-07 (CCI) SHAPIRO, WILLIAM R ST. JOSEPH'S HOS. & MED. CENTE 350 WEST THOMAS ROAD PHOENIX, AZ 85013 Brain tumor cooperative group--cns tumor biology therapy

R01CA-36054-09 (ET) MORAN, RICHARD G UNIV OF SOUTHERN CALIFORNIA 1303 N MISSION ROAD LOS ANGELES, CA 90033 Metabolic limitations to the efficacy of 5FU

R01CA-36097-08 (BNP) HARVEY, RONALD G UNIVERSITY OF CHICAGO 5841 SOUTH MARYLAND AVE CHICAGO, IL 60637 Mechanism of carcinogenesis of polycyclic hydrocarbons

R01CA-36106-09 (CPA) BRESNICK, EDWARD DARTMOUTH MEDICAL SCHOOL H.B. 7650 HANOVER, NH 03756 Polycyclic hydrocarbon metabolism and carcinogenesis

R01CA-36111-07 (VR) WALTER, GERNOT F UNIV OF CALIF, SAN DIEGO LA JOLLA, CA 92093-0612 SV40 and polyoma virus transforming proteins

R01CA-36118-07 (VR) SIMMONS, DANIEL T SCHOOL OF LIFE/HLT SCIENCES UNIVERSITY OF DELAWARE NEWARK, DE 19716 The structure and function of the SV40 tumor antigen

R37CA-36146-18 (END) BOURGEOIS-COHN, SUZANNE SALK INST FOR BIOL STUDIES P O BOX 85800 SAN DIEGO, CA 92186-5800 Regulation in E. coli extended to lymphomas

R01CA-36167-08 (HEM) GRIFFIN, JAMES D DANA-FARBER CANCER INSTITUYE 44 BINNEY STREET BOSTON, MA 02115 Surface antigens of human myeloid progenitor cells

R01CA-36200-08 (EVR) CHOW, LOUISE T UNIV OF ROCHESTER SCH OF MED 601 ELMWOOD AVENUE - BOX 607 ROCHESTER, NY 14642 Human papilloma virus gene expression

R01CA-36204-07 (EVR) NEMEROW, GLEN R RESEARCH INST OF SCRIPPS CLIN 10666 NORTH TORREY PINES ROAD LA JOLLA, CA 92037 Infection of B lymphocytes by Epstein-Barr virus

R01CA-36233-08 (EI) MITCHELL, MALCOLM S USC CANCER CENTER 2025 ZONAL AVE, GH 10-442 LOS ANGELES, CA 90033 Specific active immunotherapy of human melanoma

R01CA-36241-08 (ET) BLOCH, ALEXANDER NEW YORK STATE DEPT OF HEALTH ELM & CARLTON STREETS BUFFALO, NY 14263 Chemodifferentiation as an approach to cancer therapy

R37CA-36245-08 (PTHA) TROJANOWSKI, JOHN Q UNIVERSITY OF PENNSYLVANIA 3400 SPRUCE ST PHILADELPHIA, PA 19104 Neurofilament expression and tumor progression

R01CA-36246-08 (MBY) MARCU, KENNETH B SUNY AT STONY BROOK STONY BROOK, N Y 11794-5215 Chromosome translocated oncogenes and neoplasia

R01CA-36250-08 (PTHB) GOWN, ALLEN M UNIVERSITY OF WASHINGTON SEATTLE, WA 98195 Cytoskeletal hybridoma monoclonal antibodies as diagnostic reagents

R01CA-36306-08 (HEM) BAGBY, GROVER C OREGON HLTH SCIS UNIVERSITY 3181 S W SAM JACKSON PARK ROAD PORTLAND, OR 97201-3098 Monokines in hematopoiesis

R01CA-36327-08 (MGN) PELLICER, ANGEL G NEW YORK UNIV MEDICAL CENTER 550 FIRST AVENUE NEW YORK, NY 10016 Ras gene mutation time and structure in mouse lymphomas

R01CA-36342-08 (CPA) GARTE, SEYMOUR J NEW YORK UNIVERSITY MED CENTER LONG MEADOW ROAD TUXEDO, NY 10987 Transforming genes in inhalation carcinogenesis

R37CA-36353-09 (CPA) O'BRIEN, THOMAS G THE LANKENAU MEDICAL RES CTR 100 LANCASTER AVE. WYNNEWOOD, PA 19096 Ionic regulation and tumor promotion

R01CA-36355-08 (MGN) SONENSHEIN, GAIL E BOSTON UNIVERSITY SCH OF MED 80 EAST CONCORD ST BOSTON, MA 02118 Expression of oncogenes and IgA genes in transformed cells

R01CA-36361-08 (RAD) NAIRN, RODNEY S UT MD ANDERSON CANC CTR P O BOX 389 SMITHVILLE, TX 78957 Repair and recombination in radiation-sensitive cells

R01CA-36362-08 (MGN) SKOLNICK, MARK GENETIC EPIDEMIOLOGY SUITE 102, 410 CHIPETA WAY SALT LAKE CITY, UT 84108 Linkage analysis and multiple loci

R01CA-36387-08 (EDC) HAILE, ROBERT W UNIVERSITY OF CALIFORNIA LOS ANGELES, CA 90024-1772 Genetic - epidemiologic study of bilateral breast cancer

R55CA-36390-07 (EDC) HELZLSOUER, KATHY J JOHNS HOPKINS UNIVERSITY 615 N WOLFE ST BALTIMORE, MD 21205 Serologic precursors of cancer

R37CA-36401-08 (PHRA) EVANS, WILLIAM E ST JUDE CHILDREN'S RESEARCH HO 332 N LAUDERDALE MEMPHIS, TN 38105 Hepatic drug clearance in children

R01CA-36428-07 (RAD) ROEMER, ROBERT B UNIVERSITY OF ARIZONA AEROSPACE BUILDING, ROOM 309D TUCSON, AZ 85724 Hyperthermia--estimation of complete temperature fields

R01CA-36434-08 (CBY) STANLEY, PAMELA M ALBERT EINSTEIN COLL OF MED 1300 MORRIS PARK AVENUE BRONX, NY 10461 Glycosylation defects of lectin-resistant tumor cells

R01CA-36447-06 (RAD) WALDREN, CHARLES A COLORADO STATE UNIVERSITY FORT COLLINS, CO 80523 Cell genetic damage at low dose and low dose rate

R01CA-36448-09 (EVR) SORGE, JOSEPH A STRATAGENE CLONING SYSTEMS 11099 NORTH TORREY PINES ROAD LA JOLLA, CA 92037 Gene transfer and expression using retroviruses

R37CA-36464-08 (HEM) BROXMEYER, HAL E INDIANA UNIV SCHOOL OF MED 975 W. WALNUT STREET INDIANAPOLIS, IN 46202-5121 Colony stimulating factors, lactoferrin and myelopoiesis

R01CA-36481-08 (PBC) SLOANE, BONNIE F WAYNE STATE UNIVERSITY 540 E CANFIELD DETROIT, MI 48201 Cathepsin b-like cysteine proteinases and tumor invasion

R01CA-36485-08 (RAD) RASEY, JANET S UNIVERSITY OF WASHINGTON 1959 N E PACIFIC ST SEATTLE, WASH 98195 Radioprotective drugs--mechanistic and biological studies

R01CA-36517-07A1 (BNP) OTTER, BRIAN A MONTEFIORE MEDICAL CENTER 111 EAST 210TH STREET BRONX, NY 10467 Analogs of 6-vinyluracil as antitumor agents

R01CA-36543-05 (MCHA) RIGBY, JAMES H WAYNE STATE UNIVERSITY DETROIT, MI 48202 Synthesis of cocarcinogenic diterpenes

R01CA-36544-06 (BNP) TAM, JAMES P ROCKEFELLER UNIVERSITY 1230 YORK AVENUE NEW YORK, NY 10021-6399 Synthetic transforming growth factors

R01CA-36606-09 (MBY) MILCAREK, CHRISTINE A UNIVERSITY OF PITTSBURGH PITTSBURGH, PA 15261 Immunoglobulin gene expression in myeloma mutants

R01CA-36622-09 (BNP) IRELAND, CHRIS M UNIVERSITY OF UTAH 306 SKAGGS HALL SALT LAKE CITY, UT 84112 Antineoplastic agents from marine organisms

R01CA-36642-11 (IMS) CORLEY, RONALD B DUKE UNIVERSITY MEDICAL CENTER BOX 3010 DURHAM, NC 27710 Cellular and molecular events in B lymphocyte activation

R01CA-36679-09 (CPA) BRESNICK, EDWARD DARTMOUTH MEDICAL SCHOOL H B 7650 HANOVER, NH 03756 DNA repair after polycyclic hydrocarbon administration

R01CA-36700-09 (ALY) FREED, JOHN H NAT JEWISH CTR FOR IMMUNOLOGY 1400 JACKSON STREET DENVER, CO 80206 Structural-functional analysis of MHC class II molecules

R01CA-36701-08 (PTHB) YAGER, JAMES D JOHNS HOPKINS UNIVERSITY 615 NORTH WOLFE STREET BALTIMORE, MD 21205 Role of gonadal steroids in hepatocarcinogenesis

R01CA-36725-06 (ET) VALLERA, DANIEL A BOX 367 MAYO MEMORIAL BUILDING 420 DELAWARE STREET S E MINNEAPOLIS, MN 55455 Immunotoxins in human bone marrow transplantation

P30CA-36727-08 (CCS) RUDDON, RAYMOND W UNIV OF NEBRASKA MED CTR 600 S. 42ND STREET OMAHA, NE 68198-6805 Laboratory cancer research center support (core) grant

P30CA-36727-08 9007 (CCS) EASTMAN, ALAN Laboratory cancer research center support (core) grant Cell culture facility--Core

PROJECT NO., ORGANIZATIONAL UNIT., INVESTIGATOR, ADDRESS, TITLE

P30CA-36727-08 9008 (CCS) RHODE, SOLON Laboratory cancer research center support (core) grant Molecular biology core laboratory

P30CA-36727-08 9009 (CCS) ARMITAGE, JAMES Laboratory cancer research center support (core) grant Lymphoma/leukemia study group

P30CA-36727-08 9010 (CCS) BRESNICK, EDWARD Laboratory cancer research center support (core) grant Computer network--Core

P30CA-36727-08 9001 (CCS) CONRAD, ROBERT D Laboratory cancer research center support (core) grant Animal facility core

P30CA-36727-08 9002 (CCS) ROGAN, ELEANOR G Laboratory cancer research center support (core) grant Microbial mutagenesis core

P30CA-36727-08 9003 (CCS) ISSENBERG, PHILLIP Laboratory cancer research center support (core) grant Mass spectrometry core

P30CA-36727-08 9004 (CCS) POUR, PARVIZ M Laboratory cancer research center support (core) grant Histology-pathology facility core

P30CA-36727-08 9005 (CCS) NAGEL, DONALD L Laboratory cancer research center support (core) grant NMR facility core

P30CA-36727-08 9006 (CCS) VOLSKY, DAVID J Laboratory cancer research center support (core) grant Fluorescence activated cell sorter core

R37CA-36745-09 (NSS) BRASITUS, THOMAS A THE UNIVERSITY OF CHICAGO 5841 S. MARYLAND AVENUE CHICAGO, IL 60637 Colonic epithelial cell plasma membranes

R25CA-36762-07 (SRC) COSTANZA, MARY E UNIV OF MASSACHUSETTS MED CTR 55 LAKE AVE NORTH WORCESTER, MA 01655 Student assistantships in cancer research

R01CA-36773-08 (ET) BENZ, CHRISTOPHER C UNIVERSITY OF CALIFORNIA M-1282 BOX 0128 SAN FRANCISCO, CA 94143 Therapeutic modulation of breast cancer oncogenes and estrogen receptors

R01CA-36777-08 (ET) KUO, JYH-FA EMORY UNIVERSITY ATLANTA, GA 30322 Protein kinase C in cell growth and differentiation

R01CA-36798-08 (CCG) GRADY, KATHLEEN E MASS INST OF BEHAVIORAL MED 1145 MAIN STREET SPRINGFIELD, MA 01103 Women's acceptance of breast self-examination

R01CA-36799-07 (RNM) MATTREY, ROBERT F UNIV OF CALIFORNIA MED CTR 225 DICKINSON STREET SAN DIEGO, CA 92103 PFCs as CT/ultrasound contrast agents

R01CA-36810-06 (RAD) NELSON, WILLIAM H DEPT OF PHYSICS & ASTRONOMY GEORGIA STATE UNIVERSITY ATLANTA, GA 30303 Direct ionization effects in DNA

R01CA-36827-08 (PTHB) SLAMON, DENNIS J UNIV OF CALIFORNIA 10833 LE CONTE AVE LOS ANGELES, CA 90024-1678 Oncogenes in physiologic & pathological states

R01CA-36856-08 (RAD) HILF, RUSSELL UNIVERSITY OF ROCHESTER 601 ELMWOOD AVE BOX 607 ROCHESTER, NY 14642 Actions of HpD and photoradiation of mammary tumors

R01CA-36858-08 (RAD) SIEMANN, DIETMAR W UNIVERSITY OF ROCHESTER 601 ELMWOOD AVENUE ROCHESTER, NY 14642 Radiation and drug effects on tumor cell subpopulations

R01CA-36860-09 (EI) GREEN, WILLIAM R DARTMOUTH MEDICAL SCHOOL P O BOX 7 HANOVER, NH 03756 Cellular immunity to endogenous AKR leukemia viruses

R01CA-36888-07 (SSS) BRENT, THOMAS P ST JUDE CHILDREN'S RES HOSP 332 NORTH LAUDERDALE/PO BX 318 MEMPHIS, TN 38101 DNA crosslink repair enzymes in human cells

R01CA-36896-08A1 (HEM) GEWIRTZ, ALAN M UNIVERSITY OF PENNSYLVANIA 36TH & HAMILTON WALK PHILADELPHIA, PA 19104-6082 Regulation of human megakaryocytopoiesis

R01CA-36902-08 (CVB) JAIN, RAKESH K MASSACHUSETTS GENERAL HOSPITAL STEEL LAB FOR TUMOR BIOLOGY BOSTON, MA 02114 Macromolecular transport in neoplastic capillary beds

R01CA-36920-06 (ET) ANDERSON, JAMES H JOHNS HOPKINS HOSPITAL 720 RUTLAND AVENUE BALTIMORE, MD 21205 Diagnostic radiology-imaging, chemotherapy-brain tumor

R01CA-36921-08 (IMS) BENNETT, MICHAEL UT SOUTHWESTERN MED CTR 5323 HARRY HINES BOULEVARD DALLAS, TX 75235-9051 Immunogenetics of hybrid resistance

R01CA-36922-08 (IMS) BENNETT, MICHAEL UNIV OF TX SW MED CTR AT DALLA 5323 HARRY HINES BLVD DALLAS, TX 75248 Immunobiology of hybrid resistance

R01CA-36946-07A1 (ET) KENNEDY, KATHERINE A GEORGE WASHINGTON UNIV MED CTR 2300 EYE ST, NW WASHINGTON, DC 20037 Biochemical responses of hypoxic cells to chemotherapy

R01CA-36974-08 (EVR) HASELTINE, WILLIAM A DANA-FARBER CANCER INSTITUTE 44 BINNEY STREET BOSTON, MA 02115 Study of the px region of HTLV I and II

R01CA-36979-08 (CPA) DIGIOVANNI, JOHN UNIV OF TEX M D ANDERSON CAN C P O BOX 389 SMITHVILLE, TEX 78957 The role of DNA binding in mouse skin tumor initiation

R01CA-36993-07 (PTHB) CRAIGHEAD, JOHN E UNIVERSITY OF VERMONT SOULE MEDICAL ALUMNI BUILDING BURLINGTON, VT 05405 Experimental asbestos-induced mesothelioma

U10CA-37027-09 (CCI) BLOOMFIELD, CLARA D ROSWELL PARK CANCER INSTITUTE ELM AND CARLTON STREETS BUFFALO, N Y 14263 Cancer and leukemia group B immunology and cytogenetics

R37CA-37037-08 (CPA) YANG, CHUNG S RUTGERS STATE UNIV OF NEW JERS LAB/CANCER RES BLDG/PO BOX 078 PISCATAWAY, NJ 08855-0789 Metabolic activation of n-nitrosamines

U10CA-37055-08 (CCI) BARCOS, MAURICE ROSWELL PARK MEMORIAL INST ELM & CARLTON STREETS BUFFALO, N Y 14263 Cancer & leukemia group B pathology committee

R01CA-37062-08 (ET) ISRAEL, MERVYN UNIV OF TENNESSEE-MEMPHIS 874 UNION AVENUE MEMPHIS, TN 38163 Preparation of adriamycin analogs and derivatives

R01CA-37099-08 (IMB) GOODENOW, ROBERT A BAXTER HEALTHCARE CORPORATION FENWAL DIVISION SANTA ANA, CA 92705 Molecular immunogenetics of novel MHC tumor antigens

R01CA-37111-09 (CPA) DIGIOVANNI, JOHN UT M D ANDERSON CANCER CENTER P O BOX 389 SMITHVILLE, TX 78957 Mechanism of skin tumor promotion by chrysarobin

R01CA-37126-07 (OBM) GOLTZMAN, DAVID ROYAL VICTORIA HOSP RM. H4.67 687 PINE AVENUE WEST MONTREAL, QC, CANADA H3A 1A1 Effects of prostate cancer on skeletal tissue

R01CA-37130-08 (ET) LING, VICTOR ONTARIO CANCER INSTITUTE 500 SHERBOURNE STREET TORONTO, ONTARIO CANADA M4X 1 Multidrug resistance and P-glycoprotein in human cancer

PROJECT NO., ORGANIZATIONAL UNIT., INVESTIGATOR, ADDRESS, TITLE

R01CA-37139-08 (PB) TUKEY, ROBERT H UNIVERSITY OF CALIFORNIA 9500 GILMAN DR LA JOLLA, CA 92093-0812 Cytochrome P-450 genes and chemical carcinogenesis

R01CA-37155-07 (EI) PERUSSIA, BICE THOMAS JEFFERSON UNIVERSITY 1025 WALNUT ST PHILADELPHIA, PA 19107 Receptors for immunoglobulin G on leukocytes

R01CA-37156-07 (IMB) SCHREIBER, HANS THE UNIVERSITY OF CHICAGO 5841 MARYLAND AVNEUE CHICAGO, IL 60637 Immunology of unique tumor-specific antigens

R01CA-37157-08 (VR) DIMAIO, DANIEL C YALE UNIVERSITY 333 CEDAR STREET NEW HAVEN, CT 06510 Analysis of cell transformation by bovine papillomavirus

R01CA-37165-08 (MGN) DALLA-FAVERA, RICCARDO COLUMBIA UNIV HLTH SCI 630 WEST 168TH ST NEW YORK, NY 10032 C-myc rearrangements in human hematopoietic neoplasias

R01CA-37166-07 (CPA) DRINKWATER, NORMAN R UNIVERSITY OF WISCONSIN 1400 UNIVERSITY AVENUE MADISON, WI 53706 Molecular analysis of carcinogen-induced mutations

R01CA-37194-08 (CPA) BATTIFORA, HECTOR A CITY OF HOPE NATIONAL MED CTR 1500 E DUARTE ROAD DUARTE, CA 91010 Monoclonal antibodies in the immunohistochemical class

R01CA-37209-06 (ET) ISRAEL, MERVYN UNIVERSITY OF TENNESSEE 874 UNION AVENUE MEMPHIS, TN 38163 Pharmacologic evaluation of new adriamycin analogs

R01CA-37225-07 (VR) KNOWLES, BARBARA B WISTAR INSTITUTE 36TH & SPRUCE STREETS PHILADELPHIA, PA 19104 Hepatitis B virus and primary hepatocellular carcinoma

R01CA-37232-08 (EVR) ROGLER, CHARLES E ALBERT EINSTEIN COLLEGE OF MED 1300 MORRIS PARK AVENUE BRONX, NY 10461 WHV and HBV associated hepatocellular carcinoma

R01CA-37239-06 (RAD) JAIN, RAKESH K MASSACHUSETTS GENERAL HOSPITAL STEELE LAB OF TUMOR BIOLOGY BOSTON, MA 02114 Normal & tumor tissues in hyperthermia & hyperglycemia

R01CA-37245-08 (RAD) LYNCH, DANIEL R DARTMOUTH COLLEGE THAYER SCHOOL OF ENGINEERING HANOVER, N H 03755 Computerized thermal dosimetry for hyperthermia

R01CA-37259-06 (PTHB) ROSENTHAL, LEONARD J GEORGETOWN MEDICAL CENTER 3900 RESERVOIR ROAD NW WASHINGTON, DC 20007 Transformation by HCMV strain Towne mtrII AND mtrIII

U01CA-37287-08 (SRC) GREENBERG, E ROBERT NORRIS COTTON CANCER CENTER 2 MAYNARD ST/HB 7925 HANOVER, NH 03756 Nutritional prevention of polyps in the large bowel

R37CA-37295-08 (ARR) DALLA-FAVERA, RICCARDO COLUMBIA UNIVERSITY 630 WEST 168TH STREET NEW YORK, NY 10032 AIDS-associated lymphoproliferative disorders

R01CA-37298-07 (BEM) MATTES, RICHARD D MONELL CHEMICAL SENSES CENTER 3500 MARKET STREET PHILADELPHIA, PA 19104 Effects of cancer chemotherapy on dietary habits

R01CA-37351-07 (PTHB) FRIEDMAN, ROBERT M UNIFORMED SERV UNIV HLTH SCI 4301 JONES BRIDGE ROAD BETHESDA, MD 20814 Inhibition of human oncogene expression by interferon

R01CA-37352-08 (SSS) BIBBO, MARLUCE UNIVERSITY OF CHICAGO 5841 S MARYLAND AVE, HM-449 CHICAGO, IL 60637 Objective grading of prostate carcinoma

R01CA-37370-09 (END) GOODMAN, RICHARD H OREGON HELATH SCIS UNIVERSITY 3181 SW SAM JACKSON PARK ROAD PORTLAND, OR 97201-3098 Ectopic hormone synthesis in pheochromocytoma cells

R01CA-37372-08 (PC) GEAHLEN, ROBERT L PURDUE UNIVERSITY SCH OF PHARM WEST LAFAYETTE, IN 47907-1333 Tyrosine protein kinases and lymphocyte activation

R01CA-37374-10 (ALY) MICHAELSON, JAMES S MGH CANCER CENTER BLDG 149, 13TH STREET, FLOOR 7 CHARLESTOWN, MA 02129 Immunochemical genetics of murine alloantigens

U10CA-37377-07 (SRC) FISHER, BERNARD UNIVERSITY OF PITTSBURGH 3550 TERRACE ST. 914 SCAIFE HA PITTSBURGH, PA 15261 Community clinical oncology program-NSABP research base

U10CA-37379-07 (SRC) KRISCHER, JEFFREY P 4110 SW 34 ST.-SUITE 22 GAINESVILLE, FL 32608 Pediatric oncology group as a CCOP research base

U10CA-37379-07 0041 (SRC) KRISCHER, JEFFREY P Pediatric oncology group as a CCOP research base POG8633--Postoperative chemotherapy and delayed irradiation for brain tumors

U10CA-37379-07 0042 (SRC) KRISCHER, JEFFREY P Pediatric oncology group as a CCOP research base POG8617--Therapy for B-cell acute lymphoblastic leukemia and lymphoma

U10CA-37379-07 0043 (SRC) KRISCHER, JEFFREY P Pediatric oncology group as a CCOP research base POG9139--Phase I study of cisplatin and irradiation in brain stem gliomas

U10CA-37379-07 0044 (SRC) KRISCHER, JEFFREY P Pediatric oncology group as a CCOP research base POG9079--Phase I study of L-PAM/CTX with ABM rescue for brain tumors in children

U10CA-37379-07 0045 (SRC) KRISCHER, JEFFREY P Pediatric oncology group as a CCOP research base POG9075--Phase I study of acivicin in children with solid tumors

U10CA-37379-07 0046 (SRC) KRISCHER, JEFFREY P Pediatric oncology group as a CCOP research base POG9074--Phase I study of xomazyme-H65 in children with T-cell ALL/lymphoma

U10CA-37379-07 0047 (SRC) KRISCHER, JEFFREY P Pediatric oncology group as a CCOP research base POG9072--Phase I chemotherapy for recurrent/resistant malignant solid tumors

U10CA-37379-07 0048 (SRC) KRISCHER, JEFFREY P Pediatric oncology group as a CCOP research base POG9061-Phase II systemic therapy and irradiation for ALL & CNS leukemia

U10CA-37379-07 0049 (SRC) KRISCHER, JEFFREY P Pediatric oncology group as a CCOP research base POG 9086--Phase I pilot study of therapy for T-cell ALL or NHL

U10CA-37379-07 0050 (SRC) KRISCHER, JEFFREY P Pediatric oncology group as a CCOP research base POG9071--Phase I trial of fazarabine in children with acute leukemia

U10CA-37379-07 0051 (SRC) KRISCHER, JEFFREY P Pediatric oncology group as a CCOP research base POG8970--Phase I trial of fazarabine in

PROJECT NO., ORGANIZATIONAL UNIT., INVESTIGATOR, ADDRESS, TITLE

children with refractory solid tumors
U10CA-37379-07 0052 (SRC) KRISCHER, JEFFREY P Pediatric oncology group as a CCOP research base POG8973--Etoposide (VP-16) and carboplatin in children with acute leukemia
U10CA-37379-07 0053 (SRC) KRISCHER, JEFFREY P Pediatric oncology group as a CCOP research base POG8870--Phase I trial of ifosfamide/VP16/MESNA in children with acute leukemia
U10CA-37379-07 0054 (SRC) KRISCHER, JEFFREY P Pediatric oncology group as a CCOP research base POG8871--Phase I study of rTNF in children with refractory solid tumors
U10CA-37379-07 0055 (SRC) KRISCHER, JEFFREY P Pediatric oncology group as a CCOP research base POG8671--Phase I immunotherapy with rIL-2 in children with solid tumors
U10CA-37379-07 0056 (SRC) KRISCHER, JEFFREY P Pediatric oncology group as a CCOP research base POG8494--Phase I study of fludarabine phosphate in pediatric patients
U10CA-37379-07 0057 (SRC) KRISCHER, JEFFREY P Pediatric oncology group as a CCOP research base POG8930--A comprehensive genetic analysis of brain tumors
U10CA-37379-07 0058 (SRC) KRISCHER, JEFFREY P Pediatric oncology group as a CCOP research base POG8828--Late effects of Hodgkin's disease
U10CA-37379-07 0059 (SRC) KRISCHER, JEFFREY P Pediatric oncology group as a CCOP research base POG9046--Molecular genetic analysis of Wilm's tumors
U10CA-37379-07 0060 (SRC) KRISCHER, JEFFREY P Pediatric oncology group as a CCOP research base POG9153--Rhabdomyosarcoma study/laboratory evaluation of tumor
U10CA-37379-07 0001 (SRC) KRISCHER, JEFFREY P Pediatric oncology group as a CCOP research base POG9006--6-MP/methotrexate vs. alternating chemotherapy for ALL in childhood
U10CA-37379-07 0002 (SRC) KRISCHER, JEFFREY P Pediatric oncology group as a CCOP research base POG9005--Dose intensification of methotrexate & 6-mercaptourine in childhood ALL
U10CA-37379-07 0003 (SRC) KRISCHER, JEFFREY P Pediatric oncology group as a CCOP research base POG9031--Cisplatin/VP-16 therapy of medulloblastoma/pre vs. post irradiation
U10CA-37379-07 0004 (SRC) KRISCHER, JEFFREY P Pediatric oncology group as a CCOP research base POG8945--Phase III chemotherapy for hepatoblastoma & hepatocellular carcinoma
U10CA-37379-07 0005 (SRC) KRISCHER, JEFFREY P Pediatric oncology group as a CCOP research base POG9049--Phase III study of high-risk malignant germ cell tumors in children
U10CA-37379-07 0006 (SRC) KRISCHER, JEFFREY P Pediatric oncology group as a CCOP research base POG8844--Bone marrow transplant in children with stage D neuroblastoma
U10CA-37379-07 0007 (SRC) KRISCHER, JEFFREY P Pediatric oncology group as a CCOP research base POG8850--Phase III treatment of Ewing's sarcoma and neuroectodermal bone tumors
U10CA-37379-07 0008 (SRC) KRISCHER, JEFFREY P Pediatric oncology group as a CCOP research base POG8821--Phase III chemotherapy +/- autologous BMT in children with AML
U10CA-37379-07 0009 (SRC) KRISCHER, JEFFREY P Pediatric oncology group as a CCOP research base POG8725--Phase III chemotherapy +/- radiation therapy in pediatric Hodgkins
U10CA-37379-07 0010 (SRC) KRISCHER, JEFFREY P Pediatric oncology group as a CCOP research base POG8704--Phase III chemotherapy of childhood T cell ALL & lymphoblastic lymphoma
U10CA-37379-07 0011 (SRC) KRISCHER, JEFFREY P Pediatric oncology group as a CCOP research base POG8719--Phase III chemotherapy for non-Hodgkin's lymphoma in children
U10CA-37379-07 0012 (SRC) KRISCHER, JEFFREY P Pediatric oncology group as a CCOP research base POG8650--National Wilm's tumor and clear cell sarcoma study
U10CA-37379-07 0013 (SRC) KRISCHER, JEFFREY P Pediatric oncology group as a CCOP research base POG8616--Phase III chemotherapy for childhood Burkitt and non-Burkitts lymphoma
U10CA-37379-07 0014 (SRC) KRISCHER, JEFFREY P Pediatric oncology group as a CCOP research base POG8615--Phase III study of large cell lymphomas in children and adolescents
U10CA-37379-07 0015 (SRC) KRISCHER, JEFFREY P Pediatric oncology group as a CCOP research base POG8651--Phase III study of childhood nonmetastatic osteosarcoma
U10CA-37379-07 0016 (SRC) KRISCHER, JEFFREY P Pediatric oncology group as a CCOP research base POG8653--Phase III study of childhood soft tissue sarcomas
U10CA-37379-07 0017 (SRC) KRISCHER, JEFFREY P Pediatric oncology group as a CCOP research base POG8625--Phase III combined therapy in childhood Hodgkin's disease
U10CA-37379-07 0018 (SRC) KRISCHER, JEFFREY P Pediatric oncology group as a CCOP research base POG8451--Intergroup rhabdomyosarcoma study
U10CA-37379-07 0019 (SRC) KRISCHER, JEFFREY P Pediatric oncology group as a CCOP research base POG9110--Rotational drug therapy after first marrow relapse of non-T, non B ALL
U10CA-37379-07 0020 (SRC) KRISCHER, JEFFREY P Pediatric oncology group as a CCOP research base POG9107--Phase II pilot study of infant leukemia
U10CA-37379-07 0021 (SRC) KRISCHER, JEFFREY P Pediatric oncology group as a CCOP research base POG9140--Phase II therapy for recurrent or refractory neuroblastoma
U10CA-37379-07 0022 (SRC) KRISCHER, JEFFREY P Pediatric oncology group as a CCOP research base POG9048--Phase II study of malignant germ cell tumors in children
U10CA-37379-07 0023 (SRC) KRISCHER, JEFFREY P Pediatric oncology group as a CCOP research base POG9060--Intensive QOD ifosfamide treatment for CNS tumors in children
U10CA-37379-07 0024 (SRC) KRISCHER, JEFFREY P Pediatric oncology group as a CCOP research base POG8936--Phase II study of carboplatin treatment for optic pathway tumors
U10CA-37379-07 0025 (SRC) KRISCHER, JEFFREY P Pediatric oncology group as a CCOP research base POG8935--Phase II study of surgery and/or radiotherapy for optic pathway tumors

PROJECT NO., ORGANIZATIONAL UNIT., INVESTIGATOR, ADDRESS, TITLE

U10CA-37379-07 0026 (SRC) KRISCHER, JEFFREY P Pediatric oncology group as a CCOP research base POG8820--Phase II/III study of VP-16, AMSA +/- 5-azacytidine in childhood ANLL
U10CA-37379-07 0027 (SRC) KRISCHER, JEFFREY P Pediatric oncology group as a CCOP research base POG8889--Intergroup rhabdomyosarcoma study for clinical group IV disease
U10CA-37379-07 0028 (SRC) KRISCHER, JEFFREY P Pediatric oncology group as a CCOP research base POG8866--Phase II asparaginase therapy for acute lymphoblastic leukemia
U10CA-37379-07 0029 (SRC) KRISCHER, JEFFREY P Pediatric oncology group as a CCOP research base POG8862--Combination chemotherapy of acute T-lymphoblastic leukemia
U10CA-37379-07 0030 (SRC) KRISCHER, JEFFREY P Pediatric oncology group as a CCOP research base POG8863--Phase II study of high dose cytosine arabinoside in childhood tumors
U10CA-37379-07 0031 (SRC) KRISCHER, JEFFREY P Pediatric oncology group as a CCOP research base POG8827--Phase II treatment of children with Hodgkin's disease in relapse
U10CA-37379-07 0032 (SRC) KRISCHER, JEFFREY P Pediatric oncology group as a CCOP research base POG8865--Phase II recombinant alpha-interferon in relapsed T-cell disease
U10CA-37379-07 0033 (SRC) KRISCHER, JEFFREY P Pediatric oncology group as a CCOP research base--Phase II recombinant A-interferon in chronic myelogenous leukemia
U10CA-37379-07 0034 (SRC) KRISCHER, JEFFREY P Pediatric oncology group as a CCOP research base POG8832--Combination chemotherapy followed by radiotherapy for brain tumors
U10CA-37379-07 0035 (SRC) KRISCHER, JEFFREY P Pediatric oncology group as a CCOP research base POG8731--Phase II trial of methotrexate in treatment of brain tumors in children
U10CA-37379-07 0036 (SRC) KRISCHER, JEFFREY P Pediatric oncology group as a CCOP research base POG8788--Intergroup rhabdomyosarcoma study/pilot study for clinical group III
U10CA-37379-07 0037 (SRC) KRISCHER, JEFFREY P Pediatric oncology group as a CCOP research base POG8761--Phase II study of homoharringtonine therapy for nonlymphoblastic leukemi
U10CA-37379-07 0038 (SRC) KRISCHER, JEFFREY P Pediatric oncology group as a CCOP research base POG8739--Phase II immunotherapy with alpha-2 interferon for brain tumors
U10CA-37379-07 0039 (SRC) KRISCHER, JEFFREY P Pediatric oncology group as a CCOP research base POG8741--Treatment of patients with stage C and stage D neuroblastoma
U10CA-37379-07 0040 (SRC) KRISCHER, JEFFREY P Pediatric oncology group as a CCOP research base POG8751--Phase II methotrexate chemotherapy for rhabdomyosarcoma in children
R37CA-37392-10 (CBY) KLAGSBRUN, MICHAEL CHILDREN'S HOSPITAL CORP 300 LONGWOOD AVENUE BOSTON, MA 02115 **Angiogenic endothelial cell growth factors**
R37CA-37393-10 (PTHB) ZETTER, BRUCE R CHILDREN'S HOSPITAL CORPORATIO 300 LONGWOOD AVENUE BOSTON, MA 02115 **Tumor cell interactions with the vasculature**
R37CA-37395-10 (PTHA) FOLKMAN, M JUDAH CHILDREN'S HOSPITAL 300 LONGWOOD AVENUE BOSTON, MA 02115 **Mechanisms of angiogenesis in transgenic tumorigenesis**
U10CA-37400-08 (SRC) HAMMOND, DENMAN 440 E HUNTINGTON DRIVE ARCADIA, CA 91066-6012 **CCSG research base for CCOP**
U10CA-37403-07 (SRC) TORMEY, DOUGLAS CLINICAL SCIENCE CTR 600 HIGHLAND AVENUE MADISON, WI 53792 **ECOG CCOP research base**
U10CA-37404-07 (SRC) MOERTEL, CHARLES G MAYO FOUNDATION 200 FIRST STREET SOUTHWEST ROCHESTER, MN 55905 **Community clinical oncology program**
U10CA-37417-08 (SRC) LEVITT, RALPH ROGER MARIS CANCER CENTER 820 NORTH 4TH STREET FARGO, NORTH DAKOTA 58122 **St Lukes Hospital CCOP**
U10CA-37420-07 (SRC) MORROW, GARY R 601 ELMWOOD AVE/BOX 704 ROCHESTER, NY 14642 **University of Rochester cancer center-CCOP research base**
U10CA-37423-07 (SRC) LIST, MARCY A ILLINOIS CANCER COUNCIL 36 S WABASH AVE/SUITE 700 CHICAGO, IL 60603 **ICC community clinical oncology program research base**
U10CA-37429-07 (SRC) COLTMAN, CHARLES A, JR SOUTHWEST ONCOLOGY GROUP SUITE 618 SAN ANTONIO, TX 78229-6197 **Southwest oncology group-CCOP research base**
R01CA-37435-09 (RAD) GRDINA, DAVID J ARGONNE NATIONAL LABORATORY 9700 SOUTH CASS AVENUE ARGONNE, IL 60439 **Experimental radiotherapy, carcinogenesis, and protector**
U10CA-37447-08 (SRC) MCINTYRE, O ROSS DARTMOUTH-HITCHCOCK MEDICAL CT NORRIS COTTON CANCER CTR HANOVER, NH 03756 **CALGB research base community clinical oncology program**
R01CA-37461-08 (ARR) SCHOOLEY, ROBERT T UNIV OF CO HLTH SCIENCE CTR 4200 E 9TH AVENUE DENVER, CO 80262 **Cell mediated immune response to human retroviruses**
R01CA-37465-07 (ARR) VOLSKY, DAVID J ST LUKE'S-ROOSEVELT HOSP CTR 428 WEST 59TH ST/ANTENUCCI BLD NEW YORK, NY 10019 **Viral etiology of AIDS--Role of HIV-induced membrane injury**
R01CA-37483-06 (RNM) SOMMER, FRANK G STANFORD UNIVERSITY RADIO/NUCLEAR MED RM P-1009 STANFORD, CA 94305 **Ultrasonic characterization of abdominal tissues**
P01CA-37497-07 (SRC) ROYSTON, IVOR SAN DIEGO REGIONAL CANCER CENT 3099 SCIENCE PARK ROAD SAN DIEGO, CA 92121 **Monoclonal antibodies in cancer detection and treatment**
P01CA-37497-07 0001 (SRC) ROYSTON, IVOR Monoclonal antibodies in cancer detection and treatment B cell neoplasm cross reactive idiotypes--monoclonal antibodies
P01CA-37497-07 0002 (SRC) TAETLE, RAYMOND Monoclonal antibodies in cancer detection and treatment Therapy with anti-transferrin receptor antibody
P01CA-37497-07 0003 (SRC) BOERNER, PAULA Monoclonal antibodies in cancer detection and treatment In vitro immun. & human MOAB production to tumor-assoc. antigens
P01CA-37497-07 0006 (SRC) ROYSTON, IVOR Monoclonal antibodies in cancer detection and treatment Anti-idiotype therapy of B cell lymphoma
P01CA-37497-07 0007 (SRC) KIPPS, THOMAS J. Monoclonal antibodies in

cancer detection and treatment Molecular analysis of idiotype diversity in B cell lymphoma
P01CA-37497-07 0006 (SRC) ROYSTON, IVOR Monoclonal antibodies in cancer detection and treatment Active immunotherapy of T cell lymphoma
P01CA-37497-07 9001 (SRC) PARKER, BARBARA A. Monoclonal antibodies in cancer detection and treatment Core--Patient support
P01CA-37497-07 9002 (SRC) ROYSTON, IVOR Monoclonal antibodies in cancer detection and treatment Immunologic monitoring core
P01CA-37497-07 9003 (SRC) OLSHEN, RICHARD A. Monoclonal antibodies in cancer detection and treatment Biostatistics core
U10CA-37517-07 (CCI) BLESSING, JOHN A ROSWELL PARK MEMORIAL INST 666 ELM STREET BUFFALO, NY 14263 Gynecologic oncology group statistical office
R01CA-37553-06 (RAD) BLOOMER, WILLIAM D JOINT RADIATION ONCOLOGY CENTE 230 LOTHROP STREET PITTSBURGH, PA 15213 Receptor mediated radiation oncology
R01CA-37570-05 (NEUC) HIRAMOTO, RAYMOND N UNIV OF ALABAMA AT BIRMINGHAM MICROBIOLOGY BIRMINGHAM, AL 35294 CNS effects on interferon production and NK cell activity
R01CA-37585-06 (ET) CENTER, MELVIN S KANSAS STATE UNIVERSITY ACKERT HALL MANHATTAN, KANSAS 66506 Mechanisms regulating cell resistance to adriamycin
R01CA-37586-11 (RNM) VON RAMM, OLAF T DUKE UNIVERSITY DURHAM, NC 27706 High-speed ultrasound imaging
P01CA-37589-08 (SRC) MC KEEHAN, WALLACE L W A JONES CELL SCI CTR, INC 10 OLD BARN ROAD LAKE PLACID, N Y 12946 Cell culture factors and their relation to cancer biology
P01CA-37589-08 0002 (SRC) SERRERO, GINETTE Cell culture factors and their relation to cancer biology Factors produced by teratoma variants and in vivo tumorigenicity
P01CA-37589-08 0003 (SRC) SATO, GORDON H Cell culture factors and their relation to cancer biology Monoclonal antibodies to human factor receptors
P01CA-37589-08 0005 (SRC) MC KEEHAN, WALLACE L Cell culture factors and their relation to cancer biology Prostate cells biology
P01CA-37589-08 0006 (SRC) HAYASHI, JUN Cell culture factors and their relation to cancer biology Molecular biology of thymulin
P01CA-37589-08 0007 (SRC) STEVENS, JAMES L Cell culture factors and their relation to cancer biology Growth factor and renal cancer
P01CA-37589-08 0008 (SRC) JAKEN, SUSAN Cell culture factors and their relation to cancer biology Regulation of protein kinase C in transformed cells
P01CA-37589-08 9001 (SRC) CRABB, JOHN W Cell culture factors and their relation to cancer biology Core--Protein chemistry
P01CA-37589-08 9002 (SRC) MANSSON, PER-ERIK Cell culture factors and their relation to cancer biology Core--Molecular biology
R01CA-37601-07 (BNP) BROOM, ARTHUR D UNIVERSITY OF UTAH 306 SKAGGS HALL SALT LAKE CITY, UT 84112 Multisubstrate enzyme inhibitors
U01CA-37606-08 (SRC) PORTER, CARL W ROSWELL PARK MEMORIAL INST ELM & CARLTON STREETS BUFFALO, N Y 14263 Inhibitors of polyamine biosynthesis and/or function
U01CA-37606-08 0004 (SRC) PEGG, ANTHONY E Inhibitors of polyamine biosynthesis and/or function Biochemistry underlying polyamine metabolism
U01CA-37606-08 0005 (SRC) PORTER, CARL W Inhibitors of polyamine biosynthesis and/or function Antitumor activity of polyamine inhibitors
U01CA-37606-08 0006 (SRC) MORTON, LAURENCE L Inhibitors of polyamine biosynthesis and/or function Modification of intracellular polyamine content and cancer therapy
U01CA-37606-08 0007 (SRC) CASERO, ROBERT Inhibitors of polyamine biosynthesis and/or function Polyamine antimetabolite effects on human cancer cells
U01CA-37606-08 0001 (SRC) BERGERON, RAYMOND J Inhibitors of polyamine biosynthesis and/or function Design and synthesis of polyamine antiproliferatives
U01CA-37606-08 0002 (SRC) COWARD, JAMES K Inhibitors of polyamine biosynthesis and/or function Inhibitors of spermine and spermidine synthesis
U01CA-37606-08 0003 (SRC) SUFRIN, JANICE R Inhibitors of polyamine biosynthesis and/or function Modifiers and markers of polyamine biosynthesis
R01CA-37613-07 (CPA) WELSCH, CLIFFORD W MICHIGAN STATE UNIVERSITY EAST LANSING, MI 48824 Caffeine and experimental mammary gland tumorigenesis
R01CA-37618-08 (RAD) SUTHERLAND, ROBERT M SRI INTERNATIONAL 333 RAVENSWOOD AVENUE MENLO PARK, CA 94025 Basic studies of experimental tumor models
R01CA-37626-07 (MEDB) CUMMINGS, RICHARD D UNIVERSITY OF GEORGIA BOYD GRADUATE STUDIES RESEARCH ATHENS, GA 30602 Surface oligosaccharides in embryonal carcinoma cells
U01CA-37641-07 (SRC) MENDELSOHN, JOHN SLOAN-KETTERING INSTITUTE FOR 1275 YORK AVENUE NEW YORK, NY 10021 Anti-receptor monoclonal antibodies in cancer treatment
U01CA-37641-07 0001 (SRC) TROWBRIDGE, IAN S Anti-receptor monoclonal antibodies in cancer treatment Therapy with antitransferrin receptor monoclonal antibodies
U01CA-37641-07 0002 (SRC) TAETLE, RAYMOND Anti-receptor monoclonal antibodies in cancer treatment Anti-receptor monoclonal antibodies--Preclinical studies
U01CA-37641-07 0003 (SRC) MENDELSOHN, JOHN Anti-receptor monoclonal antibodies in cancer treatment Anti-EGF receptor monoclonal antibodies
U01CA-37641-07 9001 (SRC) TROWBRIDGE, IAN S Anti-receptor monoclonal antibodies in cancer treatment Core--Recombinant receptor and monoclonal antibody production
U01CA-37641-07 9002 (SRC) TAETLE, RAYMOND Anti-receptor monoclonal antibodies in cancer treatment Core--Nude mice
R01CA-37667-08 (VR) GARCEA, ROBERT L DANA-FARBER CANCER INSTITUTE 44 BINNEY STREET BOSTON, MA 02115 Mechanisms in polyoma virus assembly
R01CA-37702-08 (GEN) TATCHELL, KELLY G NORTH CAROLINA STATE UNIV 4543 GARDNER HALL BOX 7615 RALEIGH, NC 27695-7615 The function of the RAS oncogene homolog in yeast
R01CA-37706-07 (IMB) DENNERT, GUNTHER UNIV OF SOUTHERN CALIFORNIA 2011 ZONAL AVENUE LOS ANGELES, CA 90033 Nk cells and bone marrow rejection
R01CA-37778-07 (PTHB) MACLEOD, CAROL L UNIV OF CALIF, SAN DIEGO CANCER CENTER, 0812 LA JOLLA, CA 92093-0812 SI12 t-lymphoma: a new model for gene control in tumors
R01CA-37785-07S1 (CBY) MC KEOWN-LONGO, PAULA J ALBANY MEDICAL COLLEGE 47 NEW SCOTLAND AVENUE ALBANY, NY 12208 Regulation of fibronectin matrix assembly
R01CA-37794-06 (ET) SCHTEINGART, DAVID E UNIV OF MICHIGAN MED CTR 1500 EAST MEDICAL CTR DRIVE ANN ARBOR, MI 48109-0678 Development of mitotane analogs for adrenal cancer
R01CA-37806-07 (BNP) JOHNSON, CARL R WAYNE STATE UNIVERSITY DETROIT, MI 48202 Biomolecules and analogues as antiviral/antitumor agents
R01CA-37831-07 (CPA) DEMPLE, BRUCE LABORATORY OF TOXICOLOGY 665 HUNTINGTON AVE BOSTON, MA 02115 Oxidative DNA damage--Repair and cellular responses
R01CA-37853-07 (PC) GLICK, MARY C JOSEPH STOKES JR, RES INSTITUT 34TH & CIVIC CENTER BLVD PHILADELPHIA, PA 19104 Structures of neurectoderm tumor glycoproteins
R01CA-37858-06S1 (MEP) FRENKEL, KRYSTYNA NEW YORK UNIV MEDICAL CENTER 550 FIRST AVENUE NEW YORK, NY 10016 Tumor promoters effecting base modification in DNA
R01CA-37868-08 (EI) BALL, EDWARD D MONTEFIORE UNIVERSITY HOSPITAL 2 NORTH ROOM 14 PITTSBURGH, PA 15213 Monoclonal antibodies/small cell carcinoma of the lung
R01CA-37870-06 (RNM) ANDERSON, JAMES H JOHNS HOPKINS UNIVERSITY 720 RUTLAND AV/330 TRAYLOR BL BALTIMORE, MD 21205 Diagnostic radiology-imaging-metabolism of tumors
R01CA-37879-08 (ET) OLIVE, PEGGY L BRITISH COL CANCER RES CTR VANCOUVER, B C CANADA V5Z 1L3 Quantitation of hypoxic tumor cells
R01CA-37880-07 (CPA) FOSTER, PATRICIA L BOSTON UNIVERSITY 80 EAST CONCORD STREET BOSTON, MASS 02118 Mechanisms of mutagenesis by chemical carcinogens
R01CA-37881-06 (ET) FITCHEN, JOHN H EPITOPE, INC 15425 S.W. KOLL PARKWAY BEAVERTON, OR 97006 Use of MTAase deficiency in cancer treatment
R01CA-37887-07A1 (PTHB) GARVIN, ABBOTT J MEDICAL UNIV OF SOUTH CAROLINA 171 ASHLEY AVENUE CHARLESTON, SC 29425 Malignant potential of the components of Wilms tumors
R01CA-37895-06 (EI) SHARKEY, ROBERT M CENTER FOR MOLECULAR MED & IMM 1 BRUCE STREET NEWARK, NJ 07103 Improved radioimmunotherapy of cancer
R01CA-37907-07 (PTHB) ALBINO, ANTHONY P SLOAN-KETTERING INSTITUTE 1275 YORK AVENUE NEW YORK, NY 10021 Role of oncogenes in the pathogenesis of melanoma
R01CA-37912-06 (CPA) RICHIE, ELLEN R U TEXAS/M D ANDERSON CANCER CR 1515 HOLCOMBE BLVD HOUSTON, TX 77030 Mechanisms of MNU induced lymphoma
R01CA-37926-08 (SAT) RATLIFF, TIMOTHY L JEWISH HOSPITAL 216 SOUTH KINGSHIGHWAY ST LOUIS, MO 63110 Mechanisms of surgical adjuvant intravesical BCG therapy
R01CA-37944-06 (EI) RAAM, SHANTHI TUFTS UNIV MEDICAL CANCER UNIT 170 MORTON STREET JAMAICA PLAIN, MA 02130 Immunohistochemical classification of human breast tumors
R01CA-37959-08 (EI) FERRONE, SOLDANO NEW YORK MEDICAL COLLEGE VALHALLA, NY 10595 Human melanoma, immunotherapy, antiidiotype antibodies
R01CA-37961-06S1 (MCHA) KAHL, STEPHEN B UNIVERSITY OF CALIFORNIA 926 MEDICAL SCIENCES BUILDING SAN FRANCISCO, CA 94143 Porphyrins and phthalocyanine for cancer radiotherapy
U10CA-37981-08 (CCI) BARLOGIE, BARTHEL UNIV OF ARKANSAS FOR MED SCIS 4301 WEST MARKHAM STREET LITTLE ROCK, AR 72205 Southwest oncology group
R01CA-37993-08 (RAD) RIEDERER, STEPHEN J MAYO FOUNDATION 200 FIRST STREET, SW ROCHESTER, MN 55905 Magnetic resonance fluoroscopy
R01CA-38006-05 (EI) LAMON, EDDIE W UNIV OF ALABAMA AT BIRMINGHAM UAB STATION BIRMINGHAM, AL 35294 Idiotype-anti-idiotype modulation of immunity to M-MuLV
R01CA-38024-07 (CTY) SIRBASKU, DAVID A UNIV/TEXAS HLTH SCIENCE CTR POST OFFICE BOX 20708 HOUSTON, TEX 77225 Monoclonal antibodies to mammary tumor growth factors
R01CA-38038-05 (MBY) HANSEN, ULLA M DANA-FARBER CANCER INSTITUTE 44 BINNEY STREET BOSTON, MA 02115 Role for transcription factor LSF in mammalian cells
R01CA-38043-08 (ALY) LACHMAN, LAWRENCE B U.T. M.D. ANDERSON CANCER CENT 1515 HOLCOMBE BLVD BOX 173 HOUSTON, TX 77030 Biological studies of human interleukin I
R01CA-38046-08 (PC) LEIS, JONATHAN P CASE WESTERN RESERVE UNIV 2119 ABINGTON ROAD CLEVELAND, OH 44106 Retroviral proteins involved in DNA integration/virion assembly
R01CA-38047-07 (EVR) TSICHLIS, PHILIP N FOX CHASE CANCER CTR 7701 BURHOLME AVENUE PHILADELPHIA, PA 19111 DNA rearrangements in MoMuLV induced thymomas
R01CA-38055-07 (HEM) FLEIT, HOWARD B S U N Y AT STONY BROOK DEPARTMENT OF PATHOLOGY STONY BROOK, N Y 11794 Fc receptor expression during myeloid differentiation
R55CA-38079-08 (RAD) FREEMAN, MICHAEL L VANDERBILT UNIVERSITY HOSPITAL E-1200 MEDICAL UNIV HOSPITAL NASHVILLE, TN 37232 Biochemistry of hyperthermic cellular inactivation
R01CA-38106-07 (ET) TRAVIS, ELIZABETH L U.T. M.D. ANDERSON CANCER CENT 1515 HOLCOMBE BLVD, BOX 66 HOUSTON, TEXAS 77030 Residual radiation damage in normal tissues
R01CA-38128-06 (CPA) GOULD, MICHAEL N UNIV OF WI CLINICAL CANC CTR 600 HIGHLAND AVENUE MADISON, WI 53792 Modulation of carcinogenesis by monoterpenoids
R01CA-38151-07 (SSS) CASSADY, JOHN M OHIO STATE UNIVERSITY 500 WEST TWELFTH AVENUE COLUMBUS, OH 43210 Novel natural inhibitors of carcinogenesis
R01CA-38173-04 (ET) BRATTAIN, MICHAEL G BAYLOR COLLEGE OF MEDICINE ONE BAYLOR PLAZA HOUSTON, TX 77030 Mechanism of action of differentiation agents

PROJECT NO., ORGANIZATIONAL UNIT., INVESTIGATOR, ADDRESS, TITLE

R01CA-38177-06 (MEP) BROITMAN, SELWYN A BOSTON UNIVERSITY SCH OF MED 80 E CONCORD STREET BOSTON, MA 02118 Lipid diet effects on colon tumor growth and metastases

R01CA-38189-07 (HEM) LEE, MINAKO Y UNIVERSITY OF WASHINGTON SM-20 SEATTLE, WA 98195 Bone-bone marrow mice interaction

R01CA-38193-07 (PTHB) VERONESI, UMBERTO INTERNTNL UNION AGAINST CANCER 3 RUE DU CONSEIL-GENERAL 1205 GENEVA SWITZERLAND Project on the tnm classification of malignant tumors

R01CA-38269-08 (BEM) PETERSON, ARTHUR V FRED HUTCHINSON CANCER RES CTR 1124 COLUMBIA STREET SEATTLE, WA 98104 Hutchinson smoking prevention project

R01CA-38273-07 (BEM) BIGLAN, ANTHONY OREGON RESEARCH INSTITUTE 1899 WILLAMETTE EUGENE, OREGON 97401 Community intervention to reduce adolescent tobacco use

R01CA-38325-08 (HEM) NEWBURGER, PETER E UNIV OF MASSACHUSETTS MED SCH 55 LAKE AVENUE NORTH WORCESTER, MA 01655 White blood cell oxidase in leukemia and normal cells

R01CA-38350-11 (EI) BOTTOMLY, KIM YALE UNIV SCH OF MEDICINE PO BOX 3333 NEW HAVEN, CT 06510 Activation of humoral and cell responses by T cells

R01CA-38351-14 (IMB) HAMMERLING, ULRICH G SLOAN-KETTERING INST CA RES 1275 YORK AVENUE NEW YORK, NY 10021 Ontogenetic development of lymphocytes

R37CA-38355-08 (EI) SPRENT, JONATHAN RES INST OF SCRIPPS CLINIC 10666 NORTH TORREY PINES ROAD LA JOLLA, CA 92037 Lymphocyte function in normal and chimeric mice

R01CA-38395-06 (SSP) SECKER-WALKER, ROGER H UNIVERSITY OF VERMONT 235 ROWELL BUILDING BURLINGTON, VT 05405 Smoking prevention through mass media and school program

R01CA-38400-11 (RNM) LIZZI, FREDERIC L RIVERSIDE RESEARCH INST 330 WEST 42ND STREET NEW YORK, NY 10036 Advanced clinical ultrasonic tissue characterization

R37CA-38450-06 (EDC) MUELLER, NANCY E HARVARD SCHOOL OF PUBLIC HLTH 677 HUNTINGTON AVENUE BOSTON, MA 02115 Risk factors for human T-cell leukemia virus infection

P01CA-38493-06S1 (SRC) FREI, EMIL, III DANA-FARBER CANCER INSTITUTE 44 BINNEY STREET BOSTON, MA 02115 Solid tumor autologous marrow program

P01CA-38493-06S1 0002 (SRC) TEICHER, BEVERLY A Solid tumor autologous marrow program Preclinical studies of combined alkylating agents

P01CA-38493-06S1 0003 (SRC) FREI, EMIL Solid tumor autologous marrow program Pharmacokinetics of STAMP alkylating agents

P01CA-38493-06S1 0004 (SRC) SCHNIPPER, LOWELL Solid tumor autologous marrow program Modulation of alkylation of dna with inhibitors of topoisomerase II

P01CA-38493-06S1 0006 (SRC) ANTMAN, KAREN H Solid tumor autologous marrow program Bone marrow growth factor studies

P01CA-38493-06S1 0007 (SRC) BERNAL, SAMUEL D Solid tumor autologous marrow program STAMP marrow tumor detection and purging

P01CA-38493-06S1 9001 (SRC) BEGG, COLIN Solid tumor autologous marrow program Core--Biostatistical support of STAMP

P01CA-38493-06S1 9005 (SRC) FREI, EMIL Solid tumor autologous marrow program Core--Clinical

P01CA-38493-06S1 0001 (SRC) ANTMAN, KAREN Solid tumor autologous marrow program Solid tumor autologous marrow program--STAMP clinical studies

R01CA-38515-06 (RNM) OPHIR, JONATHAN UNIV OF TEXAS HEALTH SCIENCE C 6431 FANNIN ST/MSB 2130 HOUSTON, TX 77030 Quantitative ultrasonic differentiation of liver disease

R01CA-38538-08 (VR) FOLK, WILLIAM R UNIVERSITY OF MISSOURI M121 MEDICAL SCIENCES BLDG COLUMBIA, MO 65212 Mammalian cell transformation by oncogenic viruses

R37CA-38544-07 (BMT) HECHT, SIDNEY M UNIV OF VIRGINIA MCCORMICK ROAD CHARLOTTESVILLE, VA 22901 Chemistry of activated bleomycin

P01CA-38548-07 (SRC) BARTELS, PETER H UNIVERSITY OF ARIZONA TUCSON, ARIZONA 85721 Fast digital microscope designs for tumor diagnosis

P01CA-38548-07 0001 (SRC) PAPLANUS, P Fast digital microscope designs for tumor diagnosis Ultrafast laser scanner microscope in diagnostic laboratory

P01CA-38548-07 0002 (SRC) SHACK, ROLAND Fast digital microscope designs for tumor diagnosis High speed fluorescence scanner

P01CA-38548-07 0003 (SRC) SHOEMAKER, R Fast digital microscope designs for tumor diagnosis Multiprocessor computer system for medical imaging

P01CA-38552-05A1 (SRC) CHAPMAN, C RICHARD FRED HUTCHINSON CAN RES CTR 1124 COLUMBIA STREET SEATTLE, WA 98104 Improving management of chemoradiotherapy toxicity

P01CA-38552-05A1 0001 (SRC) SYRJALA, K L Improving management of chemoradiotherapy toxicity Cognitive behavioral pain management with a family coach during BMT

P01CA-38552-05A1 0002 (SRC) MACKIE, A Improving management of chemoradiotherapy toxicity Improvements in patient-controlled analgesia for bone marrow transplant patients

P01CA-38552-05A1 0005 (SRC) HILL, HARLAN Improving management of chemoradiotherapy toxicity Tailored infusions of opiods--Agonists, partial agonists and agonist antagonists

P01CA-38552-05A1 0009 (SRC) SCHUBERT, M Improving management of chemoradiotherapy toxicity Oral toxicity/ Complications following bone marrow transplants

P01CA-38552-05A1 0010 (SRC) CODA, BARBARA Improving management of chemoradiotherapy toxicity Laboratory investigation of epidural opioid analgesia in humans

P01CA-38552-05A1 9002 (SRC) DONALDSON, G Improving management of chemoradiotherapy toxicity Core--Information management

P01CA-38552-05A1 9003 (SRC) HILL, HARLAN Improving management of chemoradiotherapy toxicity Core--Pharmacology

U01CA-38567-06 (SRC) VERONESI, UMBERTO ISTITUTO NAZIONALE TUMORI VIA G VENEZIAN, 1 20133 MILANO, ITALY Breast cancer prevention with synthetic retinoid (HPR)

R01CA-38571-07 (MBY) CALAME, KATHRYN L COLUMBIA UNIVERSITY 701 WEST 168TH ST NEW YORK, N Y 10032 C-myc oncogene regulation in normal and malignant cells

PROJECT NO., ORGANIZATIONAL UNIT., INVESTIGATOR, ADDRESS, TITLE

R01CA-38579-08 (PTHB) PERUCHO, MANUEL CALIF. INST. OF BIO. RESEARCH LA JOLLA, CA92037 Mutant ras oncogenes in human tumors

R01CA-38587-07 (EI) JOHNSON, HOWARD M UNIVERSITY OF FLORIDA DEPT. MICROBIOL. & CELL SCIENC Regulatory and antitumor effects of gamma interferon

R37CA-38597-07 (VR) CHEN, IRVIN S UNIVERSITY OF CALIFORNIA 405 HILGARD AVE LOS ANGELES CALIF 90024 A molecular genetic study of human T-cell leukemia virus

R01CA-38621-08 (MGN) SKLAR, JEFFREY LEWIS BRIGHAM AND WOMEN'S HOSPITAL 75 FRANCIS STREET BOSTON, MA 02115 Genetic studies of human B cell cancer

R01CA-38635-07 (PTHB) BRINSTER, RALPH L UNIVERSITY OF PENNSYLVANIA DEPT OF ANIMAL BIOLOGY PHILADELPHIA, PA 19104 Onc gene introduction and expression in transgenic mice

R01CA-38637-07 (RAD) SIEMANN, DIETMAR W UNIVERSITY OF ROCHESTER 601 ELMWOOD AVENUE, BOX 704 ROCHESTER, N Y 14642 Sensitizers plus combined modalities in lung tumors

R01CA-38645-07 (ORTH) BOCKMAN, RICHARD S THE HOSP FOR SPECIAL SURGERY 535 EAST 70 STREET NEW YORK, N Y 10021 The effect of gallium on bone

R01CA-38651-05 (GMA) SINGH, POMILA UNIV OF TEXAS MEDICAL BRANCH 6.202 OLD JOHN SEALY, E32 GALVESTON, TX 77550 Gastrointestinal hormones in gastrointestinal cancer

R01CA-38655-06 (CPA) FAGAN, JOHN B MAHARISHI INTERNATIONAL UNIV FAIRFIELD, IA 52556 Cytochrome P-450 gene structure and regulation

R01CA-38656-07 (RAD) COSS, RONALD A 1020 SANSOM ST PHILADELPHIA, PA 19107-5004 Cellular mechanisms of hyperthermia damage

R01CA-38661-09 (VR) RUBIN, BERISH Y FORDHAM UNIVERSITY LARKIN HALL 160 BRONX, NY 10458 Interferons--Properties, action and patient prescreening

R01CA-38683-08 (PHRA) DUFFEL, MICHAEL W UNIVERSITY OF IOWA IOWA CITY, IOWA 52242 Aryl sulfotransferase in drug & xenobiotic metabolism

R01CA-38701-06 (CBY) VARKI, AJIT P UNIV OF CALIF, SAN DIEGO 9500 GILMAN DRIVE LA JOLLA, CALIF 92093 N-linked oligosaccharides of normal and malignant cells

R55CA-38725-04A1 (MGN) DIAZ, MANUEL O UNIVERSITY OF CHICAGO 5841 S MARYLAND AVENUE BOX 420 CHICAGO, IL 60637 Molecular genetics of lymphoid neoplasia

R37CA-38757-07 (VR) LEVINE, ARNOLD J PRINCETON UNIVERSITY PRINCETON, NJ 08544-1014 Viral induced tumorigenesis

R01CA-38773-07S1 (PBC) DOYLE, DARRELL J SUNY AT BUFFALO 109 COOKE HALL BUFFALO, NY 14260 Proteins of the hepatoma cell plasma membrane

R01CA-38779-06 (EI) RUSSELL, STEPHEN W WILKINSON LABORATORY UNIV OF KANSAS MEDICAL CENTER KANSAS CITY, KS 66103-8410 Gamma interferon receptor on tumorilytic macrophages

R01CA-38789-07 (VR) FRISQUE, RICHARD J PENNSYLVANIA STATE UNIVERSITY 433 S FREAR BUILDING UNIVERSITY PARK, PA 16802 A molecular approach to the unique biology of IC virus

R01CA-38790-07 (RNM) KORAL, KENNETH F UNIV OF MICHIGAN MEDICAL CENTE 1500 EAST MEDICAL CENTER DRIVE ANN ARBOR, MI 48109-0028 Developing dosimetry of radionuclides given for therapy

R01CA-38797-05 (PBC) BHAVANANDAN, VEER P MILTON S HERSHEY MEDICAL CTR P O BOX 850 HERSHEY, PA 17033 Studies on Ca antigen epipectin and related glycoproteins

R01CA-38808-07 (CBY) HUANG, JUNG S ST LOUIS UNIV SCH OF MED 1402 S GRAND BOULEVARD ST LOUIS, MO 63104 Role of platelet derived growth factor in cell growth

R01CA-38817-05 (PBC) BISWAS, CHITRA TUFTS UNIV SCH OF MEDICINE 136 HARRISON AVE BOSTON, MA 02111 Fibroblast tumor cell interactions in tumor invasion

R01CA-38821-07 (PC) CASNELLIE, JOHN E UNIVERSITY OF ROCHESTER DPT OF PHARMACOLOGY ROCHESTER, N Y 14642-8411 Properties of a lymphoma cell tyrosine protein kinase

R01CA-38823-07 (VR) PRIVALSKY, MARTIN L UNIVERSITY OF CALIFORNIA DAVIS, CA 95616 Characterization of the v-erb B oncogene protein of AEV

U10CA-38859-05S1 (CCI) LIPTON, JEFFREY M MOUNT SIANI HOSPITAL ONE GUSTAVE LEVY PLACE NEW YORK, N Y 10029 Multidisciplinary studies in childhood cancer-POG

R01CA-38877-07A1 (EVR) SIXBEY, JOHN W ST JUDE CHILDREN'S RES HOSP 332 N LAUDERDALE MEMPHIS, TN 38101 Epstein-Barr virus expression in normal human epithelium

R01CA-38888-08 (CBY) MACARA, IAN GREGORY UNIVERSITY OF VERMONT MEDICAL ALUMNI BUILDING BURLINGTON, CT 05405 Oncogene phosphoinositide kinase activity and cancer/kinase C

R01CA-38921-07 (CPA) RUSSO, JOSE FOX CHASE CANCER CENTER 7701 BURHOLME AVENUE PHILADELPHIA, PA 19111 Human breast susceptibility to transformation

U10CA-38926-06 (CCI) CROWLEY, JOHN J FRED HUTCHINSON CANCER RES CTR 1124 COLUMBIA STREET SEATTLE, WA 98104-2092 Southwest oncology group statistical center

R01CA-38929-07 (EDC) STRONG, LOUISE C UNIV OF TEX MD ANDERSON CA CTR 1515 HOLCOMBE BLVD HOUSTON, TX 77030 Genetic epidemiology of childhood sarcoma

R01CA-38942-07 (EI) HUDIG, DOROTHY UNIVERSITY OF NEVADA HOWARD BUILDING RENO, NV 89557-0046 Protease that function in nk-lymphocyte killing

R01CA-38951-08 (IMB) KORNGOLD, ROBERT THOMAS JEFFERSON UNIVERSITY 1020 LOCUST STREET PHILADELPHIA, PA 19107 Etiology and pathogenesis of murine graft vs host disease

R37CA-38965-08 (VR) SHENK, THOMAS E PRINCETON UNIVERSITY PRINCETON, N J 08544 -1014 Structure and function of DNA tumor virus genomes

R01CA-38976-07 (CPA) GOLD, BARRY I UNIVERSITY OF NEBRASKA MED CTR 600 SOUTH 42ND STREET OMAHA, NE 68198-4370 Metabolism and genetoxicity of nitrosamines

R01CA-38981-08 (END) FURLANETTO, RICHARD W UNIVERSITY OF ROCHESTER 601 ELMWOOD AVENUE BOX 777 ROCHESTER, NY 14642 Somatomedin actions in normal and transformed cells

R01CA-38992-07 (PB) LEVENSON, ROBERT YALE UNIVERSITY 333 CEDAR STREET NEW HAVEN, CT 06510 Molecular analysis of Na+/K+-ATPase

PROJECT NO., ORGANIZATIONAL UNIT., INVESTIGATOR, ADDRESS, TITLE

R01CA-38994-07 (VR) MAJORS, JOHN E WASH UNIV SCH OF MED 660 S. EUCLID AVENUE/BOX 8094 ST LOUIS, MO 63110 Analysis of retroviral transcriptional regulation
R01CA-39016-06 (ARR) YAMAMOTO, JANET K SCHOOL OF VETERINARY MEDICINE UNIVERSITY OF CALIFORNIA DAVIS, CA 95616 Functional & phenotypic analysis of T-cells in FIV-FAIDS
R01CA-39018-06A2 (CPA) WEBER, WENDELL W UNIVERSITY OF MICHIGAN ANN ARBOR, MI 48109-0626 Acetylation pharmacogenetics--Arylamines and DNA damage
R01CA-39027-07 (BBCA) ALDERFER, JAMES L ROSWELL PARK MEMORIAL INST ELM & CARLTON STREETS BUFFALO, N Y 14263 Effects of light on nucleic acids
R01CA-39036-08 (CTY) GUDAS, LORRAINE J CORNELL UNIVERSITY MED COLLEGE 1300 YORK AVENUE NEW YORK, NY 10021 Retinoic acid--Role in differentiation and carcinogenesis
R01CA-39045-05 (CPA) LANGE, CHRISTOPHER S SUNY-HEALTH SCIENCE CTR PO BOX 1212-450 CLARKSON AVE BROOKLYN, NY 11203 Determination of cell survival from DNA parameters
R01CA-39053-08 (BIO) MORRIS, DAVID R UNIVERSITY OF WASHINGTON SEATTLE, WA 98195 Growth regulation of polyamine synthesis
R01CA-39063-07 (SSS) KANGARLOO, HOOSHANG UNIVERSITY OF CALIFORNIA 405 HILGARD AVENUE LOS ANGELES, CA 90024-1046 Digital viewing stations for diagnostic images
R01CA-39064-08 (PTHA) TODD, ROBERT F, III UNIVERSITY OF MICHIGAN 102 OBSERVATORY DR ANN ARBOR, MI 48109-1248 Cell surface antigens of human macrophages
R01CA-39066-08 (MGN) LINNEY, ELWOOD A DUKE UNIV MEDICAL CENTER PO BOX 3020 DURHAM, NC 27710 Embryonal carcinoma growth and differentiation
R01CA-39068-11 (MGN) DUNNICK, WESLEY A UNIVERSITY OF MICHIGAN 6743 MED SCIENCE BLDG II ANN ARBOR, MI 48109-0620 DNA sequences involved in the heavy chain switch
R01CA-39070-06 (IMB) WOODWARD, JEROLD G UNIVERSITY OF KENTUCKY MS 401 MEDICAL CENTER LEXINGTON, KY 40536-0084 Cellular and molecular control of Ia antigen expression
R37CA-39076-08 (CBY) WEBER, MICHAEL J UNIVERSITY OF VIRGINIA BOX 441 MEDICAL CTR CHARLOTTESVILLE, VA 22908 Signal transmission by the SRC oncogens
R01CA-39077-08 (CBY) CHEN, WEN-TIEN GEORGETOWN UNIV SCH OF MED 3900 RESERVOIR ROAD, N W WASHINGTON, D C 20007 Molecular ultrastructure and cell adhesion
R01CA-39078-08 (EI) STREILEIN, J WAYNE UNIVERSITY OF MIAMI SCH OF MED POST OFFICE BOX 016960 R-138 MIAMI, FL 33101 Analysis of neonatal H-2 tolerance
U10CA-39086-07 (SRC) FISHER, BERNARD UNIV OF PITTSBURGH 3550 TERRACE STREET PITTSBURGH, PA 15261 Cooperative group outreach program
U10CA-39088-07 (CCI) TORMEY, DOUGLASS C FRONTIER SCI & TECH RES FOUND 303 BOYLSTON STREET BROOKLINE, MA 02146 Eastern cooperative oncology group outreach program
U10CA-39091-07 (SRC) COLTMAN, CHARLES A, JR CANCER THERAPY & RES CTR 4450 MEDICAL DRIVE SAN ANTONIO, TX 78229 Cooperative group outreach program
U10CA-39097-07 (SRC) MC INTYRE, O ROSS CALGB 444 MOUNT SUPPORT RD LEBANON, NH 03766 Cooperative group outreach program
R01CA-39099-08 (MEP) BUCHER, NANCY L R BOSTON UNIVERSITY SCH OF MED 80 E CONCORD STREET BOSTON, MA 02118 Cytoplasmic factors in cellular growth
R01CA-39192-08 (MBY) COLE, MICHAEL D PRINCETON UNIVERSITY PRINCETON, NJ 08544-1014 DNA rearrangements and the c-myc oncogene
R01CA-39201-08 (EI) PODACK, ECKHARD R UNIVERSITY OF MIAMI PO BOX 016960 (R-138) MIAMI, FL 33101 Molecular mechanism of lymphocyte mediated tumor lysis
R37CA-39207-07 (VR) KUNG, HSING-JIEN MOLECULAR BIOLOGY & MICROBIOLO CASE WESTERN RESERVE UNIV CLEVELAND, OH 44106 Avian erythroleukemia and c-erbB activation
R01CA-39224-10 (RNM) ZAGZEBSKI, JAMES A UNIVERSITY OF WISCONSIN 1300 UNIVERSITY AVENUE MADISON, WIS 53706 Accurate in vivo ultrasonic scattering assessments
R01CA-39225-07 (PTHB) SIRICA, ALPHONSE E BOX 662 MCV STATION RICHMOND, VA 23298-0662 Hepatic oval cells in culture and in vivo
U10CA-39227-07 (CCI) SKEEL, ROLAND T MEDICAL COLLEGE OF OHIO P. O. BOX 10008 TOLEDO, OH 43699 Eastern cooperative oncology group studies - Toledo, Ohio
U10CA-39229-07 (CCI) KIRKWOOD, JOHN M UNIVERSITY OF PITTSBURGH MONTEFIORE UNIVERSITY HOSPITAL PITTSBURGH, PA 15213 Eastern cooperative oncology group
R01CA-39230-17 (RNM) MILLER, MORTON W UNIVERSITY OF ROCHESTER SCHOOL OF MEDICINE & DENTISTRY ROCHESTER, NY 14642 Biophysical bases of pulsed ultrasound bioeffects
R01CA-39233-07 (GMA) BOLAND, C RICHARD UNIVERSITY OF MICHIGAN 3014 ADMINISTRATIVE BUILDING ANN ARBOR, MI 48109 Cancer-associated colonic mucins
R01CA-39237-07 (BIO) SPINDEL, ELIOT R OREGON REGIONAL PRIMATE RES CT 505 N W 185TH AVENUE BEAVERTON, OR 97006 Bombesin-like peptides: structure & physiology
P01CA-39240-07 (SRC) CZECH, MICHAEL P UNIV OF MASSACHUSETTS MED SCH DEPARTMENT OF BIOCHEMISTRY WORCESTER, MA 01655 Growth factor receptor signal transduction
P01CA-39240-07 0006 (SRC) STEIN, JANET L Growth factor receptor signal transduction Genes regulating adipocyte differentiation
P01CA-39240-07 9002 (SRC) DAVIS, ROGER J Growth factor receptor signal transduction Core--Tissue culture and media preparation
P01CA-39240-07 9003 (SRC) STEIN, JANET L Growth factor receptor signal transduction Recombinant DNA/nucleic acids--Core
P01CA-39240-07 9005 (SRC) MASSAGUE, JOAN Growth factor receptor signal transduction Peptide synthesis--Core
P01CA-39240-07 0001 (SRC) CZECH, MICHAEL P Growth factor receptor signal transduction Role of casein kinase II in signalling T kinases
P01CA-39240-07 0002 (SRC) MASSAGUE, JOAN Growth factor receptor signal transduction Cell surface receptor regulation
P01CA-39240-07 0003 (SRC) JOHNSON, GARY L Growth factor receptor signal transduction Genetic analysis of phorbol ester growth arrest of S49 cells
P01CA-39240-07 0004 (SRC) DAVIS, ROGER J Growth factor receptor signal transduction Regulation of EGF receptors
P01CA-39240-07 0005 (SRC) ROBINSON, HARRIET L Growth factor receptor signal transduction Phosphorylation of erb B and cell transformation
R01CA-39248-07 (ET) BERD, DAVID THOMAS JEFFERSON UNIVERSITY 1015 WALNUT ST PHILADELPHIA, PA 19107 Augmentation of human immunity by cyclophosphamide
R01CA-39259-07 (VR) COLE, CHARLES N DARTMOUTH MEDICAL SCHOOL DEPARTMENT OF BIOCHEMISTRY HANOVER, N H 03756 The molecular biology of SV40 large T antigen
R18CA-39260-07 (SRC) PEREZ-STABLE, ELISEO J UNIV OF CA, SAN FRANCISCO 400 PARNASSUS AVE, A-405 SAN FRANCISCO, CA 94143-0320 Smoking cessation interventions in Hispanics
R18CA-39304-05S1 (SRC) MCGRAW, SARAH A NEW ENGLAND RESEARCH INST, INC 9 GALEN STREET WATERTOWN, MA 02172 Smoking prevention in hispanic (Puerto Rican) adolescents
R01CA-39312-06 (SSS) REDPATH, JOHN L UNIVERSITY OF CALIFORNIA IRVINE, CA 92717 Radiobiological studies of human hybrid cell lines
R01CA-39319-06 (PTHB) IRIMURA, TATSURO UNIVERSITY OF TEXAS 1515 HOLCOMBE BLVD HOUSTON, TX 77030 Colorectal cancer metastasis
R01CA-39351-05 (MCHA) FRANCK, RICHARD W HUNTER COLLEGE OF CUNY 695 PARK AVENUE NEW YORK, NY 10021 Anthracyclines from isoquinolines
R01CA-39360-08 (CPA) MAGUN, BRUCE E OREGON HEALTH SCIENCES UNIV 3181 S W SAM JACKSON PARK ROAD PORTLAND, OR 97201-3098 Mechanisms of tumor promotion in vivo
R01CA-39365-07 (MGN) RONINSON, IGOR B UNIVERSITY OF ILLINOIS 808 SOUTH WOOD STREET CHICAGO, IL 60612 Isolation of amplified genes from human tumors
R01CA-39374-06 (RNM) APFEL, ROBERT E YALE UNIVERSITY 2159 YALE STATION NEW HAVEN, CT 06520-2159 Assessment of cavitation from diagnostic ultrasound
R01CA-39390-08 (VR) LANFORD, ROBERT E SW FOUNDATION FOR BIOMED RES P O BOX 28147 SAN ANTONIO, TX 78228-0147 SV40 T antigen--Model for nuclear transport of proteins
R37CA-39392-08 (PTHB) LIEBERMAN, MICHAEL W BAYLOR COLLEGE OF MEDICINE ONE BAYLOR PLAZA HOUSTON, TX 77030 Carcinogen activation of unexpressed mammalian genes
R01CA-39416-06 (PTHB) KENSLER, THOMAS W JOHNS HOPKINS UNIVERSITY 615 NORTH WOLFE ST BALTIMORE, MD 21205 Mechanisms of anticarcinogenesis by dithiolthiones
R01CA-39417-06 (MEP) ONEILL, IAN K INTERN AGENCY FOR RES ON CANCE 150 COURS ALBERT THOMAS 69372 LYON CEDEX 08, FRANCE In vivo microcapsule monitoring of carcinogens
R01CA-39427-05 (ET) CHU, SHIH-HSI BROWN UNIVERSITY BOX G,B-B6 PROVIDENCE, RI 02912 Pyrimidine nucleoside phosphorylases in chemotherapy
R01CA-39438-07 (EVR) PARSONS, SARAH J UNIVERSITY OF VIRGINIA CHARLOTTESVILLE, VA 22908 Role of C-src in retroviral transformation
R01CA-39441-05 (ALY) JONES, C MICHAEL UNIVERSITY OF TEXAS MED SCHOOL 6431 FANNIN STREET HOUSTON, TX 77030 Studies of a human monocyte cytotoxicity-inducing factor
R01CA-39448-06 (ET) MATTHAY, KATHERINE K UNIV OF CALIFORNIA MED CTR M-650 BOX 0106 SAN FRANCISCO, CA 94143 Treatment of leukemia by antibody-directed liposomes
R01CA-39456-03 (MEP) WALKER, BRUCE E MICHIGAN STATE UNIVERSITY EAST LANSING, MI 48824-1316 Transplacental carcinogenesis and diet
R01CA-39463-06 (SSS) TSUI, BENJAMIN M UNIV OF NC AT CHAPEL HILL CB #7575, 152 MACNIDER HALL CHAPEL HILL, NC 27599 Corrective image reconstruction methods for SPECT
R01CA-39481-07 (PBC) IOZZO, RENATO V THOMAS JEFFERSON UNIVERSITY 1020 LOCUST STREET PHILADELPHIA, PA 19107 Neoplastic modulation of proteoglycan metabolism
R01CA-39492-07 (EI) BERNSTEIN, IRWIN D FRED HUTCHINSON CANCER RES CTR 1124 COLUMBIA STREET SEATTLE, WA 98104 Monoclonal antibodies against leukemia
R01CA-39504-06 (CPA) PENNING, TREVOR M UNIVERSITY OF PENNSYLVANIA 37TH & HAMILTON WALK PHILADELPHIA, PA 19104-6084 Dihydrodiol dehydrogenase and the aspirin-like drugs
R01CA-39527-07 (CPA) HOGAN, MICHAEL E BAYLOR COLLEGE OF MEDICINE 4000 RESEARCH FOREST DR. THE WOODLANDS, TX 77381 Mapping carcinogen binding sites on genes
P01CA-39542-07 (SRC) BURAKOFF, STEVEN J CHILDREN'S HOSPITAL 300 LONGWOOD AVE BOSTON, MA 02115 Cellular studies of bone marrow transplantation
P01CA-39542-07 0004 (SRC) GEHA, RAIF S Cellular studies of bone marrow transplantation Th2 T cells and lymphokines post-transplantation and in GVH disease
P01CA-39542-07 0005 (SRC) ABBAS, ABUL Cellular studies of bone marrow transplantation Immunodeficiency associated with graft versus host disease
P01CA-39542-07 9001 (SRC) ANTIN, JOSEPH Cellular studies of bone marrow transplantation Core--Clinical marrow transplantation
P01CA-39542-07 9002 (SRC) SMITH, BRIAN R Cellular studies of bone marrow transplantation Core--Flow cytometry
P01CA-39542-07 0001 (SRC) NATHAN, DAVID G Cellular studies of bone marrow transplantation Hematopoiesis following bone marrow transplantation
P01CA-39542-07 0002 (SRC) ORKIN, STUART H Cellular studies of bone marrow transplantation Molecular studies of bone marrow transplantation
P01CA-39542-07 0003 (SRC) BURAKOFF, STEVEN J Cellular studies of bone marrow transplantation T cell function after bone marrow transplantation
R01CA-39545-06 (TOX) WILLIAMS, GARY M AMERICAN HEALTH FOUNDATION ONE DANA ROAD VALHALLA, NY 10595 Biochemical toxicity of agents increasing reactive 02
R01CA-39547-07 (CPA) GRUNBERGER, DEZIDER 701 W 168 STREET NEW YORK, NY 10032 Mechanism of mutation induced in mammalian gene
R01CA-39553-07 (CPA) KRAUTER, KENNETH S ALBERT EINSTEIN COLLEGE OF MED 1300 MORRIS PARK AVE BRONX, NY 10461 Induction of gene expression by chemical carcinogens

PROJECT NO., ORGANIZATIONAL UNIT., INVESTIGATOR, ADDRESS, TITLE

R01CA-39566-06 (RNM) SHIELDS, ANTHONY F SEATTLE VA MEDICAL CENTER 1660 S COLUMBIAN WAY SEATTLE, WA 98108 Labeled thymidine--Development as a PET imaging agent
R01CA-39582-07 (RAD) FAHEY, ROBERT C UNIV OF CALIFORNIA, SAN DIEGO DEPARTMENT OF CHEMISTRY, 0506 LA JOLLA, CA 92093 Mechanism of radioprotection by aminothiols
R01CA-39605-07 (ALY) ROTHENBERG, ELLEN CALIFORNIA INSTITUTE OF TECH 1201 E. CALIFORNIA BLVD. PASADENA, CA 91125 Expression of growth control genes in functional T cells
R01CA-39612-07 (IMB) CRABTREE, GERALD R STANFORD UNIVERSITY STANFORD, CA 94305 Pathways of T lymphocyte activation
R01CA-39617-08 (VR) PEARSON, GARY R GEORGETOWN UNIVERSITY 3900 RESERVOIR RD, N W WASHINGTON, D C 20007 EBV spefic antigens
R01CA-39621-08 (EI) HAMILTON, THOMAS A CLEVELAND CLINIC FOUNDATION 9500 EUCLID AVENUE CLEVELAND, OH 44106 Induced macrophage tumoricidal activation
R01CA-39623-06 (IMB) DENNERT, GUNTHER UNIV OF SOUTHERN CALIFORNIA 2011 ZONAL AVE. LOS ANGELES, CA 90033 Target cell lysis by cytolytic effector cells
R01CA-39629-06S1 (ET) SPEARS, COLIN P USC COMPREHENSIVE CANCER CTR 1303 N MISSION ROAD LOS ANGELES, CA 90033 Biochemistry of 5-fluorouracil effects
R01CA-39633-07 (RNM) KWOCK, LESTER UNIV NO CAROLINA/CHAPEL HILL CHAPEL HILL, NC 27599 Analysis of metastatic potential of tumors
R01CA-39640-07 (SSS) LAGAKOS, STEPHEN W DANA-FARBER CANCER INSTITUTE 44 BINNEY STREET BOSTON, MA 02115 Biostatistical problems in cancer research
R01CA-39662-07 (ET) LIU, LEROY F JOHNS HOPKINS UNIVERSITY 725 N WOLFE STREET BALTIMORE, MD 21205 Mechanism of action of antitumor drugs
R01CA-39681-07 (CPA) KOHWI-SHIGEMATSU, TERUMI LA JOLLA CANCER RESEARCH FDN 10901 N TORREY PINES RD LA JOLLA, CA 92037 Studies on non-B DNA structure with chemical carcinogens
R01CA-39687-07 (ET) MORAN, RICHARD G U S C CANCER CENTER 1303 NORTH MISSION ROAD LOS ANGELES, CA 90033 Antifolates inhibitory to folylpolyglutamate synthetase
R01CA-39691-04A1 (VR) AURELIAN, LAURE UNIVERSITY OF MARYLAND 10 SOUTH PINE STREET BALTIMORE, MD 21201 Protein kinase activity and HSV-2 transforming potential
R01CA-39698-06 (RAD) COGGIN, JOSEPH H, JR UNIVERSITY OF SOUTH ALABAMA COLLEGE OF MEDICINE MOBILE, AL 36688 Role of oncofetal antigens in radiation carcinogenesis
R01CA-39712-07 (BIO) MANNING, DAVID R UNIVERSITY OF PENNSYLVANIA 36TH AND HAMILTON WALK PHILADELPHIA, PA 19104-6084 Signal transduction in cell proliferation
R35CA-39723-06 (SRC) COHEN, STANLEY HAHNEMANN UNIV SCH OF MED BROAD AND VINE PHILADELPHIA, PA 19102 Activation and regulation of normal and neoplastic cell
R01CA-39742-07 (EDC) FOLSOM, AARON R 611 BEACON STREET SE MINNEAPOLIS, MN 55455 Distribution of body fat and cancer risk in women
R01CA-39745-07 (MEP) BOYNTON, ALTON L PACIFIC NORTHWEST RESEARCH FDN 720 BROADWAY SEATTLE, WA 98122 Assays for and mechanisms of action of tumor promoters
R01CA-39755-08 (CBY) BULINSKI, JEANNETTE C COLUMBIA UNIVERSITY 630 WEST 168TH STREET NEW YORK, NY 10032 Mechanism of segregation of modified tubulin in vivo
R01CA-39771-07 (MGN) BRODEUR, GARRETT M WASHINGTON UNIVERSITY 400 SOUTH KINGSHIGHWAY BLVD ST LOUIS, MO 63110 Molecular genetic analysis of human neuroblastoma
R35CA-39779-07 (SRC) WEISS, NOEL S UNIVERSITY OF WASHINGTON SEATTLE, WA 98195 Research in cancer epidemiology
R35CA-39780-07 (SRC) HUNTER, ANTHONY R SALK INST FOR BIO STUDIES P O BOX 85800 SAN DIEGO, CA 92138 Role of protein phosphorylation in growth control
R35CA-39782-08 (SRC) CANTOR, CHARLES R, LAWRENCE BERKELEY LABORATORY ONE CYCLOTRON ROAD Gene structure, arrangement, dynamics and expression
R35CA-39790-07 (SRC) DORF, MARTIN E HARVARD MEDICAL SCHOOL 25 SHATTUCK STREET BOSTON, MA 02115 Cellular pathways involved in immunoregulation
R35CA-39805-07 (SRC) ESSEX, MYRON E HARVARD SCH OF PUBLIC HEALTH 665 HUNTINGTON AVENUE BOSTON, MA 02115 NCI outstanding investigator grant
R35CA-39807-07 (SRC) GOLDMAN, ISRAEL D MEDICAL COLLEGE OF VIRGINIA BOX 230, MCV STATION RICHMOND, VA 23298-0001 Cellular pharmacology of anticancer agents
R35CA-39809-07 (SRC) FREIREICH, EMIL J U.T. M.D. ANDERSON CANCER CENT 1515 HOLCOMBE BOULEVARD HOUSTON, TX 77030 Therapy and the biology of human leukemia
R01CA-39811-07 (MBY) FERAMISCO, JAMES R SAN DIEGO CANCER CENTER/T-011 SAN DIEGO signal transduction by cellular rotooncogenes
R35CA-39814-07 (SRC) SAGER, RUTH DANA-FABER CANCER INSTITUTE 44 BINNEY STREET BOSTON, MA 02115 Genomic changes in cancer--Mechanisms and consequences
R35CA-39821-07 (SRC) HORWITZ, SUSAN B ALBERT EINSTEIN COLL OF MEDICI 1300 MORRIS PARK AVENUE BRONX, NY 10461 Antitumor drugs--Mechanisms of action and resistance
R35CA-39825-07 (SRC) SIITERI, PENTTI K UNIVERSITY OF CALIFORNIA HSW 1656 SAN FRANCISCO, CA 94143 Sex hormones and cancer
R35CA-39826-07 (SRC) WEINBERG, ROBERT A WHITEHEAD INST FOR BIOMED RES NINE CAMBRIDGE CENTER CAMBRIDGE, MA 02142 Molecular basis of carcinogenesis
R35CA-39827-08 (SRC) BOYSE, EDWARD A UNIV OF ARIZONA COLL OF MEDICI 1501 N CAMPBELL AVENUE TUCSON, AZ 85724 Normal and abnormal cell surface genetics
R35CA-39829-07 (SRC) WIGLER, MICHAEL H COLD SPRING HARBOR LABORATORY PO BOX 100 COLD SPRING HARBOR, NY 11724 Genetics of cell proliferation
R35CA-39832-07 (SRC) VARMUS, HAROLD E UNIVERSITY OF CALIFORNIA 3RD AND PARNASSUS AVES SAN FRANCISCO, CA 94143-0414 Molecular analysis of retroviruses and oncogenes

PROJECT NO., ORGANIZATIONAL UNIT., INVESTIGATOR, ADDRESS, TITLE

R35CA-39836-07 (SRC) HUENNEKENS, FRANK M RES INST OF SCRIPPS CLINIC 10666 NORTH TORREY PINES ROAD LA JOLLA, CA 92037 Folate and B12 coenzymes
R35CA-39838-07 (SRC) SCHARFF, MATTHEW D ALBERT EINSTEIN COLLEGE OF MED 1300 MORRIS PARK AVE BRONX, NY 10461 Somatic cell genetics of Ig genes
R35CA-39841-07 (SRC) GOLDENBERG, DAVID M CTR FOR MOLECULAR MED/IMMUNOLO ONE BRUCE STREET NEWARK, NJ 07103 Radioimmunodetection of cancer
R35CA-39844-07 (SRC) EINHORN, LAWRENCE H INDIANA UNIVERSITY SCH OF MED 926 WEST MICHIGAN ST. INDIANAPOLIS, IN 46202-5265 NCI outstanding investigator grant
R37CA-39851-08 (HEM) GREENBERGER, JOEL S UNIV OF MASSACHUSETTS MED CTR 55 LAKE AVENUE NORTH WORCESTER, MA 01655 Stem cell age and X-ray chemotherapy leukemogenesis
R37CA-39853-08 (PTHB) FROST, PHILIP UNIV OF TX M D ANDERSON CA CTR 1515 HOLCOMBE BLVD HOUSTON, TX 77030 Genomic instability and clonality in tumor progression
R35CA-39860-07 (SRC) CROCE, CARLO M THOMAS JEFFERSON UNIVERSITY 1025 WALNUT STREET PHILADELPHIA, PA 19107 Genetics of human hematopoietic neoplasias
R35CA-39903-07 (SRC) LOEB, LAWRENCE A UNIVERSITY OF WASHINGTON SEATTLE, WA 98195 The fidelity of DNA replication
R35CA-39910-07 (SRC) AMES, BRUCE N UNIVERSITY OF CALIFORNIA 401 BARKER HALL BERKELEY, CA 94720 Mutagenesis and carcinogenesis
R35CA-39915-07 (SRC) DUESBERG, PETER H UNIVERSITY OF CALIFORNIA 229 STANLEY HALL BERKELEY, CA 94720 Retroviral onc genes and cellular proto onc genes
R01CA-39926-07 (SSS) EMANUEL, BEVERLY S CHILDRENS HOSP OF PHILADELPHIA 34TH & CIVIC CENTER BLVD PHILADELPHIA, PA 19104 Cytogenetic and molecular studies of human chromosome 22
R01CA-39929-07 (SSS) HARRINGTON, DAVID P DANA-FARBER CANCER INSTITUTE 44 BINNEY STREET, MAYER 415 BOSTON, MA 02115 Nonparametric statistical tests for censored data
R01CA-39930-08 (ET) BAST, ROBERT DEPT. OF MEDICINE DUKE UNIVERSITY MEDICAL CENTER Specific immunotherapy with monoclonal antibodies
R01CA-39932-08 (PTHB) CERIANI, ROBERTO L JOHN MUIR CNCR/AGING RES INST 2055 NORTH BROADWAY WALNUT CREEK, CA 94596 Circulating tumor components
R01CA-39936-07 (CPA) CERIANI, ROBERTO L JOHN MUIR CNCR/AGING RES INST 2055 NORTH BROADWAY WALNUT CREEK, CA 94596 Breast cancer prognosis with cellular markers
R01CA-39947-06A2 (CPA) BERTRAM, JOHN S CANCER RESEARCH CENTER OF HAWA 1236 LAUHALA STREET HONOLULU, HI 96813 Inhibition of in vitro transformation by retinoids
R01CA-40003-06 (SSS) SCHALLY, ANDREW V TULANE UNIVERSITY 1430 TULANE AVENUE NEW ORLEANS, LA 70112 Use of LH-RH agonists and antagonists in prostate cancer
R01CA-40004-06 (SSS) SCHALLY, ANDREW V TULANE UNIVERSITY SCH OF MED 1430 TULANE AVE NEW ORLEANS, LA 70112 Use of LH-RH analogs in breast and ovarian cancer
P01CA-40007-06A1 (SRC) LOGEMANN, JERILYN A NORTHWESTERN UNIVERSITY 2299 SHERIDAN RD EVANSTON, IL 60208-3540 CCSP in head and neck cancer rehabilitation
P01CA-40007-06A1 0003 (SRC) LOGEMANN, JERILYN A CCSP in head and neck cancer rehabilitation Biomechanics of swallow after head and neck cancer
P01CA-40007-06A1 0004 (SRC) MCCONNEL, FRED CCSP in head and neck cancer rehabilitation Effects of surgical reconstitution on speech and swallowing
P01CA-40007-06A1 0005 (SRC) LIST, MARCY A CCSP in head and neck cancer rehabilitation Performance outcome assessment in laryngeal cancer
P01CA-40007-06A1 9001 (SRC) HANSON, DAVID CCSP in head and neck cancer rehabilitation Core--Data reduction, analysis, and storage
P01CA-40007-06A1 0001 (SRC) MCCONNEL, FRED CCSP in head and neck cancer rehabilitation Comparison of three methods of swallowing
P01CA-40007-06A1 0002 (SRC) LOGEMANN, JERILYN A CCSP in head and neck cancer rehabilitation Biomechanical effects of tracheostomy tubes
R25CA-40008-07 (SRC) CASSILETH, PETER A UNIVERSITY OF PENNSYLVANIA 3400 SPRUCE ST PHILADELPHIA, PA 19104 Cancer education program
P01CA-40011-07 (SRC) SANTEN, RICHARD J MILTON S. HERSHEY MEDICAL CTR. P.O. BOX 850 HERSHEY, PA 17033 Mitotic modifiers of hormone-dependent cancers
P01CA-40011-07 0001 (SRC) MANNI, ANDREA Mitotic modifiers of hormone-dependent cancers Hormone stimulation plus chemotherapy in breast and prostate cancer
P01CA-40011-07 0002 (SRC) MANNI, ANDREA Mitotic modifiers of hormone-dependent cancers Polyamines and the autocrine control of breast cancer growth
P01CA-40011-07 0003 (SRC) SATYASWAROOP, P G Mitotic modifiers of hormone-dependent cancers Treatment strategies for endometrial carcinoma
P01CA-40011-07 0004 (SRC) ENGLISH, HUGH R Mitotic modifiers of hormone-dependent cancers Androgen priming plus chemotherapy for prostate cancer
P01CA-40011-07 0005 (SRC) SANTEN, R Mitotic modifiers of hormone-dependent cancers Determinants of tissue estradiol concentration
P01CA-40011-07 0007 (SRC) OHLSON-WILHELM, BETSY Mitotic modifiers of hormone-dependent cancers: Prognostic significance of intratumor heterogeneity in endometrial cancer
P01CA-40011-07 0008 (SRC) SATYASWAROOP, P G Mitotic modifiers of hormone-dependent cancers Progesterone receptor regulation
P01CA-40011-07 0009 (SRC) MANNI, ANDREA Mitotic modifiers of hormone-dependent cancers: Evaluation of polyamines effects on breast tumor growth in vivo
P01CA-40011-07 9001 (SRC) OHLSSON-WILHELM, BETSY Mitotic modifiers of hormone-dependent cancers Core A--Cell identification and cell kinetics laboratories
P01CA-40011-07 9002 (SRC) DEMERS, LAWRENCE Mitotic modifiers of

hormone-dependent cancers Core B--Endocrine laboratory
P01CA-40011-07 9003 (SRC) LANDIS, RICHARD Mitotic modifiers of hormone-dependent cancers Core C--Biostatistical unit
R25CA-40021-07 (SRC) CONRAD, MARCEL E USA CANCER CENTER UNIVERSITY OF SOUTH ALABAMA MOBILE, AL 36688 Cancer education program
R35CA-40029-07 (SRC) GREEN, HOWARD HARVARD MEDICAL SCHOOL 25 SHATTUCK STREET BOSTON, MA 02115 Terminal differentiation of epidermal and adipose cells
P01CA-40035-06 (SRC) MUNDY, GREGORY R UNIV OF TEXAS HEALTH SCI CTR 7703 FLOYD CURL DRIVE SAN ANTONIO, TX 78284 Solid tumors--Humoral hypercalcemia of malignancy
P01CA-40035-06 0001 (SRC) RBONEWALD, LINDA F Solid tumors--Humoral hypercalcemia of malignancy Solid tumors--Humoral hypercalcemia of malignancy
P01CA-40035-06 0004 (SRC) ROODMAN, G DAVID Solid tumors--Humoral hypercalcemia of malignancy Bone resorbing lymphokines in hematologic malignancies
P01CA-40035-06 0005 (SRC) MUNDY, GREGORY R Solid tumors--Humoral hypercalcemia of malignancy Effects of tumor-associated factors on the skeleton
P01CA-40035-06 0007 (SRC) CHIRGWIN, JOHN M Solid tumors--Humoral hypercalcemia of malignancy Stimulation of bone resorption by breast cancer cells
P01CA-40035-06 9001 (SRC) JACOBS, JOHN W Solid tumors--Humoral hypercalcemia of malignancy Core--Laboratory
R37CA-40041-08 (NSS) ALLISON, JAMES P MOLECULAR & CELL BIOLOGY 415 LIFE SCIENCES ADDITION BERKELEY, CA 94720 Surface antigens of murine T lymphomas
P01CA-40042-07 (CAK) PARSONS, J THOMAS UNIVERSITY OF VIRGINIA SCHOOL OF MEDICINE BOX 441 CHARLOTTESVILLE, VA 22908 Oncogenes and mitogens--Intracellular mechanisms
P01CA-40042-07 0006 (CAK) BENDER, TIMOTHY P Oncogenes and mitogens--Intracellular mechanisms Regulation of c-myb expression by attenuation
P01CA-40042-07 0001 (CAK) WEBER, MICHAEL J Oncogenes and mitogens--Intracellular mechanisms Effects of pp60 SRC on mitogen receptors
P01CA-40042-07 0002 (CAK) PARSONS, THOMAS J Oncogenes and mitogens--Intracellular mechanisms Structure and function of a cellular tyrosine protein kinase
P01CA-40042-07 0003 (CAK) CREUTZ, CARL E Oncogenes and mitogens--Intracellular mechanisms Role of c-SRC in adrenal chromaffin cell secretion
P01CA-40042-07 0004 (CAK) GARRISON, JAMES C Oncogenes and mitogens--Intracellular mechanisms Possible role for the c-RAS gene product
P01CA-40042-07 0005 (CAK) SANDO, JULIANNE J Oncogenes and mitogens--Intracellular mechanisms Control of lymphocytes growth and differentiation
P01CA-40042-07 9001 (CAK) WEBER, MICHAEL J Oncogenes and mitogens--Intracellular mechanisms Core component
P01CA-40046-05S2 (CAK) STRAUSS, BERNARD S UNIVERSITY OF CHICAGO 5841 SOUTH MARYLAND AVENUE CHICAGO, IL 60637 Etiology of treatment-induced secondary leukemia
P01CA-40046-05S2 0001 (CAK) WEICHSELBAUM, RALPH Etiology of treatment-induced secondary leukemia mutagen sensitivity and cancer susceptibility
P01CA-40046-05S2 0002 (CAK) STRAUSS, BERNARD Etiology of treatment-induced secondary leukemia Methyltransferase in secondary tumor formation
P01CA-40046-05S2 0003 (CAK) LEBEAU, MICHELLE Etiology of treatment-induced secondary leukemia Molecular-cytogenetic analysis of chromosome in myeloid disorders.
P01CA-40046-05S2 9001 (CAK) LARSON, RICHARD Etiology of treatment-induced secondary leukemia Patient access and data management.
P01CA-40053-06 (SRC) BORTIN, MORTIMER M INT'L BONE MARROW TRANSPLANT R 8701 WATERTOWN PLANK ROAD MILWAUKEE, WI 53226 A collaborative bone marrow transplant program
P01CA-40053-06 0001 (SRC) BORTIN, MORTIMER M A collaborative bone marrow transplant program Critical and unresolved issues in allogenic bone marrow transplantation
P01CA-40053-06 0002 (SRC) BORTIN, MORTIMER M A collaborative bone marrow transplant program Immunogenetic problems and transplant-related events in allogenic BMT
P01CA-40053-06 0003 (SRC) BORTIN, MORTIMER M A collaborative bone marrow transplant program Critical and unresolved issues in autologous bone marrow transplantation
P01CA-40053-06 9001 (SRC) RIMM, ALFRED A A collaborative bone marrow transplant program Core
R01CA-40064-06 (CPA) ETHIER, STEPHEN P UNIVERSITY OF MICHIGAN DEPT OF RADIATION ONCOLOGY ANN ARBOR, MI 48109 Growth factor independence in mammary neoplasia
R01CA-40065-05 (CPA) SHAY, JERRY W U T SOUTHWESTERN MED CTR DALLA 5323 HARRY HINES BLVD DALLAS, TX 75235 A cytoplasmic role in carcinogen-induced tumorigenicity
R01CA-40077-06 (SSS) SCHALLY, ANDREW V TULANE UNIVERSITY 1430 TULANE AVENUE NEW ORLEANS, LA 70112 Use of hypothalamic hormones in pancreatic cancer
R01CA-40080-05 (MEP) NEWBERNE, PAUL M MALLORY INST OF PATHOLOGY FDN 784 MASSACHUSETTS AVENUE BOSTON, MA 02118 Zinc deficiency and related factors in esophageal cancer
R01CA-40081-05A2 (BNP) JOULLIE, MADELEINE M UNIVERSITY OF PENNSYLVANIA 34TH AND SPRUCE STREETS PHILADELPHIA, PA 19104-6323 Synthesis of biologically active cyclodepsipeptides
R01CA-40090-05A2 (ET) ZWELLING, LEONARD A U.T. M.D. ANDERSON CANCER CENT 1515 HOLCOMBE BLVD HOUSTON, TX 77030 Biochemical pharmacology of DNA intercalating agents
R01CA-40095-06 (EDC) CORREA, PELAYO LSU MEDICAL CTR/PATHOLOGY 1901 PERDIDO STREET NEW ORLEANS, LA 70112 Lung cancer in non-smoking women
R01CA-40099-07 (PTHB) OREN, MOSHE WEIZMANN INSTITUTE OF SCIENCE POB 26 REHOVOT 76100, ISRAEL Functional analysis of the P53 cellular tumor antigen
R01CA-40104-07 (REN) HASLAM, SANDRA Z MICHIGAN STATE UNIVERSITY EAST LANSING, MI 48824 Role of stroma in mammary gland cell proliferation
R01CA-40145-04A3 (CPA) CLAWSON, GARY A PENN STATE U/M S HERSHEY MED C 500 UNIVERSITY DR, P O BOX 85 HERSHEY, PA 17033 Mechanisms of RNA transport
R01CA-40157-06 (BMT) LIEBESKIND, LANNY S EMORY UNIVERSITY ATLANTA, GA 30322 An organotransition metal entry to antitumor quinones
R01CA-40160-07 (MEP) NANDI, SATYABRATA UNIV CALIFORNIA CAN RES LAB 447 LIFE SCIENCES ADDITION BERKELEY, CA 94720 Lipid turnover & growth of normal & tumor mammary cells
R01CA-40162-07 (PTHB) KORC, MURRAY UNIVERSITY OF CALIFORNIA IRVINE, CA 92717 Pancreatic cancer and epidermal growth factor receptor
R01CA-40163-07 (HEM) GASSON, JUDITH C DIV HEMATOLOGY/ONCOLOGY - UCLA LOS ANGELES, CA 90024-1678 Mechanism of action of a human granulopoietin
R01CA-40172-05 (RAD) JIRTLE, RANDY L DUKE UNIVERSITY MEDICAL CENTER BOX 3433 DURHAM, NC 27710 Radiobiology of hepatocytes
R01CA-40189-07 (CTY) RICHTER, JOEL D WORCESTER FDN FOR EXP BIO 222 MAPLE AVENUE SHREWSBURY, MASS 01545 Nuclear targeting of protein
R01CA-40211-06 (MEP) HAYES, WILSON C BETH ISRAEL HOSPITAL 330 BROOKLINE AVENUE BOSTON, MA 02215 Biomechanics of metastatic defects in bone
R01CA-40216-07 (EI) NADLER, LEE M DANA-FARBER CANCER INSTITUTE 44 BINNEY ST BOSTON, MA 02115 Function of the B7 antigen on normal/neoplastic B cells
R01CA-40225-07 (PTHB) BARSKY, SANFORD H UCLA SCH OF MED/PATH 173216 405 HILGARD AVENUE LOS ANGELES, CA 90024-1732 The desmoplastic response to tumor invasion
R01CA-40228-07 (MEP) BAIRD, WILLIAM M PURDUE UNIVERSITY ROBERT HEINE PHARMACY BUILDING WEST LAFAYETTE, IN 47907 Molecular mechanisms of hydrocarbon DNA interactions
R01CA-40251-06 (RAD) LEPOCK, JAMES R UNIVERSITY OF WATERLOO WATERLOO, ONT CANADA N2L 3G1 Cellular thermostability and thermotolerance
R01CA-40256-06 (HEM) TRINCHIERI, GIORGIO WISTAR INSTITUTE 36TH AND SPRUCE STREETS PHILADELPHIA, PA 19104 Regulation of hematopoiesis by NK cells
R01CA-40263-07 (CPA) LIEBERMAN, MICHAEL W BAYLOR COLLEGE OF MEDICINE ONE BAYLOR PLAZA HOUSTON, TX 77030 Molecular pathology of transgenic liver and kidney cancer
R01CA-40272-06 (SSS) GALLATIN, WILLIAM M ICOS CORPORATION 22021 - 20TH AVENUE SE BOTHELL, WA 98021 Lymphocyte homing in simian AIDS affected primates
R01CA-40282-04A1 (ET) YEAGER, ANDREW M JOHNS HOPKINS ONCOLOGY CTR 600 NORTH WOLFE STREET BALTIMORE, MD 21205 Studies of ex- vivo pharmacologic purging in rat leukemia
R01CA-40303-06 (SSS) ROSEN, BRUCE R MASSACHUSETTS GENERAL HOSPITAL FRUIT STREET BOSTON, MA 02114 NMR proton chemical shift imaging
R01CA-40330-07 (ET) SUBJECK, JOHN R ROSWELL PARK MEMORIAL INST 666 ELM STREET BUFFALO, NY 14263 Stress proteins, drug tolerance and cellular deprivation
R01CA-40333-07 (ET) RONINSON, IGOR B UNIVERSITY OF ILLINOIS 808 SOUTH WOOD ST CHICAGO, IL 60612 Human multidrug resistance p-glycoprotein genes
R01CA-40355-07 (RNM) DEWHIRST, MARK W DUKE UNIV MEDICAL CTR BOX 3455 DUMC DURHAM, NC 27710 Heat and radiation effects in tumor microcirculation
R37CA-40356-07 (EDC) SPEIZER, FRANK E CHANNING LABORATORY 180 LONGWOOD AVENUE BOSTON, MA 02115 Prospective study of diet and cancer in women
R01CA-40360-07 (NSS) HENNEKENS, CHARLES H BRIGHAM & WOMEN'S HOSPITAL 55 POND AVENUE BROOKLINE, MA 02146 A randomized trial of aspirin and mortality in US MDS
R01CA-40402-06 (PTHB) SAWICKI, JANET A LANKENAU MEDICAL RESEARCH CENT LINE The transforming potential of cellular oncogenes
R01CA-40406-06 (PTHB) O'BRIEN, TIMOTHY J UNIVERSITY OF ARKANSAS 4301 WEST MARKHAM-SLOT 518 LITTLE ROCK, AR 72205 Tumor antigen CA125 in ovarian cancer patients
R01CA-40411-06 (RAD) ACKERMAN, JOSEPH J WASH UNIV/CHEM DEPT BOX 1134 ONE BROOKINGS DRIVE ST LOUIS, MO 63130 Physiologic determinants of tumor response
R01CA-40414-07 (EVR) KELLY, THOMAS J JOHNS HOPKINS UNIV MEDICAL SCH 725 NORTH WOLFE STREET BALTIMORE, MD 21205 Replication of the SV40 genome
R01CA-40423-06 (REN) TAPPER, DAVID CHILDREN'S HOSPITAL & MED CTR 4800 SAND POINT WAY, NORTHEAST SEATTLE, WA 98105 Determination of a new growth factor in breast milk
R01CA-40440-07 (EVR) SRINIVAS, RANGA V UNIV OF ALABAMA, BIRMINGHAM UNIVERSITY STATION BIRMINGHAM, ALA 35294 Site-specific modification of SFFV glycoproteins
R01CA-40453-06 (CPA) LEADON, STEVEN ANTHONY UNIV OF NC -CHAPEL HILL CB7512 NC CLINICAL CANCER CENT CHAPEL HILL, NC 27599 DNA repair in specific sequences of mammalian cells
R01CA-40456-06 (RNM) HUANG, H K UNIVERSITY OF CALIFORNIA 405 HILGARD AVENUE LOS ANGELES, CALIF 90024-1406 Radiological image compression
R01CA-40458-05 (REN) MAGARIAN, ROBERT A UNIV OF OKLAHOMA/HLTH SCI CTR 1110 NORTH STONE WALL OKLAHOMA CITY, OK 73190 Resolution and antitumor testing of chiral antiestrogens
R01CA-40463-07 (BNP) TAYLOR, JOHN-STEPHEN A WASHINGTON UNIVERSITY ONE BROOKINGS DRIVE ST LOUIS, MO 63130 DNA photolesion structure-activity relationships
R01CA-40468-06 (EDC) YU, MIMI C UNIVERSITY OF S CALIFORNIA 1441 EASTLAKE AVENUE LOS ANGELES, CA 90033-0800 Salted fish and nasopharyngeal carcinoma
R01CA-40475-08 (CBY) BARNES, DAVID W OREGON STATE UNIVERSITY CORVALLIS, OREG 97330 Cell-substratum interactions
R37CA-40489-07 (PTHA) CHISARI, FRANCIS V RESEARCH INST OF

PROJECT NO., ORGANIZATIONAL UNIT., INVESTIGATOR, ADDRESS, TITLE

SCRIPPS CLINC 10666 NORTH TORREY PINES ROAD LA JOLLA, CA 92037 Pathogenesis of hepatitis B

R01CA-40500-05 (RAD) DOUPLE, EVAN B DARTMOUTH HITCHCOCK MED CTR 2 MAYNARD STREET HANOVER, NH 03756 Potentiation of radiation therapy by carboplatin

R01CA-40512-05 (CTY) FRANZA, B ROBERT, JR COLD SPRING HARBOR LABORATORY PO BOX 100 COLD SPRING HARBOR, NY 11724 Identification of cell cycle specific proteins affected by oncogenes

R01CA-40516-07 (RAD) VARNES, MARIE E UNIVERSITY HOSPITALS 2058 ABINGTON ROAD CLEVELAND, OH 44106 Metabolic modification of repair of radiation damage

R37CA-40530-08 (ET) DIASIO, ROBERT B UNIVERSITY OF ALABAMA UAB STATION BOX 600 BIRMINGHAM, AL 35294 Mechanism of toxicity of fluorocytosine and fluorouracil

R01CA-40532-04A2 (ET) LIVINGSTON, PHILIP O MEMORIAL HOSPITAL FOR 1275 YORK AVENUE NEW YORK, N Y 10021 Immunization of melanoma patients with gangliosides

R01CA-40533-07 (CPA) NEWCOMB, ELIZABETH W NEW YORK UNIV MEDICAL CENTER 550 FIRST AVENUE NEW YORK, N Y 10016 Mechanism of oncogene activation in mouse lymphomas

R01CA-40534-07 (CPA) YAMASAKI, HIROSHI INTL AGENCY FOR RES ON CANCER 150 COURS ALBERT THOMAS 69372 LYON CEDEX, 08 FRANCE Role of intercellular communication in carcinogenesis

R01CA-40540-07 (MBY) CORCES, VICTOR G JOHNS HOPKINS UNIVERSITY 34TH AND CHARLES STREET BALTIMORE, MD 21218 Molecular basis of neoplastic transformation by ras oncogenes

R29CA-40545-06 (HEM) BENDER, JAMES G BAXTER TECHNOLOGY PARK WG2-2S ROUND LAKE, IL 60073-0490 Characterization of bone marrow derived granulocytes

R01CA-40570-07 (ET) BECK, WILLIAM T ST JUDE CHILDREN'S RESEARCH HO 332 NORTH LAUDERDALE MEMPHIS, TN 38101 Multiple drug resistance in human tumors

R01CA-40573-07 (CBY) DONOGHUE, DANIEL J UNIV OF CALIFORNIA, SAN DIEGO DEPT OF CHEMISTRY, B-022 LA JOLLA, CA 92093 Molecular studies of transforming growth factors

R01CA-40575-07 (HEM) VAN ZANT, GARY E TEXAS TECH UNIV HEALTH SCI CTR HEALTH SCI CTR, 3601 4TH ST LUBBOCK TX 79430 Hematopoietic stem cell proliferation and function

R13CA-40577-06 (SRC) KING, THOMAS J GEORGETOWN UNIVERSITY 3800 RESERVOIR RD NW WASHINGTON, DC 20007 Young minority scientists in the field of cancer

R01CA-40583-05A1 (ORTH) CHAO, EDMUND Y MAYO FOUNDATION 200 FIRST STREET S W ROCHESTER, MN 55905 Fixation of massive bone transplants in tumor surgery

R01CA-40584-07 (MEP) BOWDEN, GEORGE T UNIVERSITY OF ARIZONA ARIZONA HEALTH SCIENCES CTR TUCSON, AZ 85724 Oncogene activation during skin tumor progression

R37CA-40586-07 (EVR) PIPAS, JAMES M UNIVIVERSITY OF PITTSBURGH PITTSBURGH, PA 15260 Genetic analysis of the SV40 large tumor antigen

R01CA-40598-08 (CPA) MEEHAN, THOMAS D UNIVERSITY OF CALIFORNIA 926 MEDICAL SCIENCE BLDG SAN FRANCISCO, CA 99143-0446 Physical and chemical interactions of BPDE and DNA

R01CA-40602-07 (CBY) RULEY, HENRY E MASSACHUSETTS INST OF TECHNOLO 77 MASSACHUSETTS AVENUE CAMBRIDGE, MA 02139 Oncogene collaborations in cell transformation

R01CA-40605-06 (CPA) ROMANO, LOUIS J WAYNE STATE UNIVERSITY 4002 FACULATY ADMIN BLDG, 656 DETROIT, MI 48202 Biological consequences of site-specific damage to DNA

R01CA-40615-07 (CPA) POVIRK, LAWRENCE F VIRGINIA COMMONWEALTH UNIV BOX 613, MCV STATION RICHMOND, VA 23298 Genotoxicity of DNA-directed antineoplastic agents

R01CA-40629-08 (BCE) ASCOLI, MARIO UNIVERSITY OF IOWA COLLEGE OF MEDICINE IOWA CITY, IA 52242-1109 Gonadotropin actions in Leydig tumor cells

R01CA-40636-06 (MGN) ASTRIN, SUSAN M INSTITUTE FOR CANCER RESEARCH 7701 BURHOLME AVENUE PHILADELPHIA, PA 19111 Deregulation of oncogene expression in human tumors

R01CA-40640-04A2 (MEP) IGLEHART, J DIRK DUKE UNIVERSITY MEDICAL CENTER BOX 3873 DURHAM, NC 27710 Expression of oncogenes in human tumors

R01CA-40644-07 (SSS) BRESLOW, NORMAN E UNIVERSITY OF WASHINGTON SEATTLE, WA 98195 Statistical methods in cancer epidemiology

R01CA-40660-06 (EVR) PALKER, THOMAS J DUKE UNIVERSITY MEDICAL CTR BOX 3307 DURHAM, N C 27710 HTLV-I--Study of host-virus interactions

R01CA-40675-05 (BBCB) GORE, JOHN C YALE UNIVERSITY 155 WHITNEY AVE NEW HAVEN, CT 06511 Proton relaxation mechanisms in tissues for NMR imaging

R01CA-40696-06 (SSS) BRAIN, JOSEPH D HARVARD UNIVERSITY 665 HUNTINGTON AVE BOSTON, MA 02115 Magnetic field effects on macrophages

R01CA-40714-06 (EVR) MATHES, LAWRENCE E OHIO STATE UNIVERSITY 1925 COFFEY ROAD COLUMBUS, OH 43210-1005 Immunoprevention of HTLV infection

R01CA-40725-07 (EI) RUDDERS, RICHARD A VETERANS ADMINISTRATION MED CT 150 S HUNTINGTON AVE BOSTON, MA 02130 Clonal evolution of human malignant lymphomas

P01CA-40737-06 (SRC) LONDON, W THOMAS FOX CHASE CANCER CENTER PHILADELPHIA, PA 19111 Cancer clinical research at the fox chase center - HBV A

P01CA-40737-06 0043 (SRC) LONDON, W THOMAS Cancer clinical research at the fox chase center - HBV A Prevention of primary hepatocellular carcinoma--Woodchuck hepatitis virus

P01CA-40737-06 0044 (SRC) LONDON, W THOMAS Cancer clinical research at the fox chase center - HBV A Replication of hepatitis B virus and the risk of liver cancer

P01CA-40737-06 0050 (SRC) LUSTBADER, EDWARD D Cancer clinical research at the fox chase center - HBV A Statistical methodology--Case control studies of primary hepatocellular cancer

P01CA-40737-06 0052 (SRC) LONDON, W Cancer clinical research at the fox chase center - HBV A A trial of phyllanthus amarus in pekin ducklings

P01CA-40737-06 0053 (SRC) BUETOW, K Cancer clinical research at the fox chase center - HBV A Molecular genetic change in human carcinoma

PROJECT NO., ORGANIZATIONAL UNIT., INVESTIGATOR, ADDRESS, TITLE

P01CA-40737-06 9001 (SRC) LUSTBADER, EDWARD D Cancer clinical research at the fox chase center - HBV A Core--Computational facilities and statistics

P01CA-40737-06 9003 (SRC) O'CONNELL, ANNA P Cancer clinical research at the fox chase center - HBV A Core--Blood collection

P01CA-40737-06 9004 (SRC) MILLMAN, IRVING Cancer clinical research at the fox chase center - HBV A Central laboratory services

P01CA-40737-06 9005 (SRC) HALBHERR, THERESA Cancer clinical research at the fox chase center - HBV A Core--Staff safety

R01CA-40758-05 (PTHB) OSSOWSKI, LILIANA MOUNT SINAI MEDICAL CENTER 1 GUSTAVE L LEVY PL, BX 1178 NEW YORK, NY 10029 Factors involved in malignant behavior of human tumors

R01CA-40811-05 (MEP) FELTON, JAMES S UNIVERSITY OF CALIFORNIA P O BOX 5507, L-452 LIVERMORE, CA 94550 Quantification of cooked-food mutagens by immunoassay

R01CA-40823-07 (CPA) REINERS, JOHN J, JR U T M D ANDERSON CANCER CENTER P O BOX 389 SMITHVILLE, TX 78957 Epidermal polycyclic aromatic hydrocarbon metabolism

R01CA-40847-07 (CPA) PELLING, JILL C EPPLEY INST FOR RESEARCH 42ND & DEWEY AVE OMAHA, NEBRASKA 68105 Two-stage skin carcinogenesis and altered gene expression

R01CA-40874-06 (MEP) MC CORMICK, DAVID L IIT RESEARCH INSTITUTE 10 WEST 35TH STREET CHICAGO, IL 60616 Arachidonic acid metabolism and cancer chemoprevention

R01CA-40889-06 (SRC) SURWIT, EARL A UNIVERSITY OF ARIZONA TUCSON, AZ 85724 Phase III intervention trial for cervical dysplasia

R01CA-40895-06 (MEP) DAVIES, DONALD S ROYAL POSTGRADUATE MED SCHOOL LONDON, W12 ONN - UK The metabolic fate of mutagenic amines in animals and man

R01CA-40929-07 (NLS) WAGNER, JOHN A CORNELL UNIVERSITY MED COLL 1300 YORK AVENUE NEW YORK, NY 10021 Regulation of neural development by protein kinases

R01CA-40931-07 (EI) DAY, NOORBIBI K ALL CHILDREN'S HOSPITAL 801 6TH ST SOUTH BOX 31020 ST PETERSBURG, FL 33731-8920 Analysis of acquired immunodeficiency syndrome in cats

R01CA-40987-07 (HEM) ROHRSCHNEIDER, LARRY R FRED HUTCHINSON CANCER RES CTR 1124 COLUMBIA STREET, M421 SEATTLE, WA 98104 Tumor cell biology of the fms oncogene proteins

R01CA-41068-05 (RAD) WEICHSELBAUM, RALPH R UNIVERSITY OF CHICAGO 5841 S MARYLAND AVE, BOX 442 CHICAGO, IL 60637 X-ray & molecular probes of retinoblastoma

R01CA-41072-06 (CBY) COOPER, JONATHAN A FRED HUTCHINSON CANCER RES CTR 1124 COLUMBIA STREET SEATTLE, WA 98104 Protein phosphorylation & cell growth regulation

P01CA-41078-05 (SRC) BROWN, TRUMAN R FOX CHASE CANCER CENTER 7701 BURHOLME AVENUE PHILADELPHIA, PA 19111 NMR studies of metabolism in cancer and diabetes

P01CA-41078-05 0002 (SRC) BROWN, TRUMAN R NMR studies of metabolism in cancer and diabetes NMR studies of arterial perfused hepatomas

P01CA-41078-05 0005 (SRC) SZWERGOLD, BENJAMIN S NMR studies of metabolism in cancer and diabetes Phospholipid metabolism in transformed cells

P01CA-41078-05 0006 (SRC) BROWN, TRUMAN R NMR studies of metabolism in cancer and diabetes Development of chemical shift imaging techniques

P01CA-41078-05 0007 (SRC) OTTERY, FAITH NMR studies of metabolism in cancer and diabetes NMR evaluation of nutritional intervention in cancer cachexia

P01CA-41078-05 9001 (SRC) MURPHY-BOESCH, JOSEPH NMR studies of metabolism in cancer and diabetes Instrumentation and computer core

P01CA-41078-05 9002 (SRC) KAPPLER, FRANCIS NMR studies of metabolism in cancer and diabetes Chemistry core

P01CA-41081-06A1 (SRC) UHR, JONATHAN W UNIV TEXAS SOUTHWESTERN MED CT 5323 HARRY HINES BOULEVARD DALLAS, TX 75235 Immunotoxin therapy for patients with B cell tumors

P01CA-41081-06A1 0003 (SRC) STONE, MARVIN J Immunotoxin therapy for patients with B cell tumors B cell lymphoma phase I trial with IGG-anti-CD19-dgA

P01CA-41081-06A1 0004 (SRC) FAY, JOSEPH Immunotoxin therapy for patients with B cell tumors B cell lymphoma phase II clinical trial with IgG-CD22-dgA

P01CA-41081-06A1 0005 (SRC) STONE, MARVIN Immunotoxin therapy for patients with B cell tumors B cell lymphoma Phase II clinical trial with IgG-anti-CD19-SMPT-dgA

P01CA-41081-06A1 9001 (SRC) VITETTA, ELLEN S Immunotoxin therapy for patients with B cell tumors Core--Immunotoxin preparation, quality control, and toxicology

U10CA-41082-06 (CCI) TOLEDANO, STUART R UNIVERSITY OF MIAMI P O BOX 016960 MIAMI, FL 33101 Pediatric oncology group

U10CA-41082-06 0001 (CCI) TOLEDANO, STUART R Pediatric oncology group POG9006--6-MP/methotrexate vs. alternating chemotherapy for ALL in childhood

U10CA-41082-06 0002 (CCI) TOLEDANO, STUART R Pediatric oncology group POG9005--Dose intensification of methotrexate & 6-mercaptourine in childhood ALL

U10CA-41082-06 0003 (CCI) TOLEDANO, STUART R Pediatric oncology group POG9031--Cisplatin/VP-16 therapy of medulloblastoma/pre vs. post irradiation

U10CA-41082-06 0004 (CCI) TOLEDANO, STUART R Pediatric oncology group POG8945--Phase III chemotherapy for hepatoblastoma & hepatocellular carcinoma

U10CA-41082-06 0005 (CCI) TOLEDANO, STUART R Pediatric oncology group POG9049--Phase III study of high-risk malignant germ cell tumors in children

U10CA-41082-06 0006 (CCI) TOLEDANO, STUART R Pediatric oncology group POG8844--Bone marrow transplant in children with stage D neuroblastoma

U10CA-41082-06 0007 (CCI) TOLEDANO, STUART R Pediatric oncology group POG8850--Phase III treatment of Ewing's sarcoma and neuroectodermal bone tumors

U10CA-41082-06 0008 (CCI) TOLEDANO, STUART R Pediatric oncology group POG8821--Phase III chemotherapy +/- autologous BMT in children with AML

PROJECT NO., ORGANIZATIONAL UNIT., INVESTIGATOR, ADDRESS, TITLE

U10CA-41082-06 0041 (CCI) TOLEDANO, STUART R Pediatric oncology group POG8633--Postoperative chemotherapy and delayed irradiation for brain tumors

U10CA-41082-06 0009 (CCI) TOLEDANO, STUART R Pediatric oncology group POG8725--Phase III chemotherapy +/- radiation therapy in pediatric Hodgkins

U10CA-41082-06 0010 (CCI) TOLEDANO, STUART R Pediatric oncology group POG8704--Phase III chemotherapy of childhood T cell ALL & lymphoblastic lymphoma

U10CA-41082-06 0011 (CCI) TOLEDANO, STUART R Pediatric oncology group POG8719--Phase III chemotherapy for non-Hodgkin's lymphoma in children

U10CA-41082-06 0012 (CCI) TOLEDANO, STUART R Pediatric oncology group POG8650--National Wilm's tumor and clear cell sarcoma study

U10CA-41082-06 0013 (CCI) TOLEDANO, STUART R Pediatric oncology group POG8616--Phase III chemotherapy for childhood Burkitt and non-Burkitts lymphoma

U10CA-41082-06 0014 (CCI) TOLEDANO, STUART R Pediatric oncology group POG8615--Phase III study of large cell lymphomas in children and adolescents

U10CA-41082-06 0015 (CCI) TOLEDANO, STUART R Pediatric oncology group POG8651--Phase III study of childhood nonmetastatic osteosarcoma

U10CA-41082-06 0016 (CCI) TOLEDANO, STUART R Pediatric oncology group POG8653--Phase III study of childhood soft tissue sarcomas

U10CA-41082-06 0017 (CCI) TOLEDANO, STUART R Pediatric oncology group POG8625--Phase III combined therapy in childhood Hodgkin's disease

U10CA-41082-06 0018 (CCI) TOLEDANO, STUART R Pediatric oncology group POG8451--Intergroup rhabdomyosarcoma study

U10CA-41082-06 0019 (CCI) TOLEDANO, STUART R Pediatric oncology group POG9110--Rotational drug therapy after first marrow relapse of non-T, non B ALL

U10CA-41082-06 0042 (CCI) TOLEDANO, STUART R Pediatric oncology group POG8617--Therapy for B-cell acute lymphoblastic leukemia and lymphoma

U10CA-41082-06 0043 (CCI) TOLEDANO, STUART R Pediatric oncology group POG9139--Phase I study of cisplatin and irradiation in brain stem gliomas

U10CA-41082-06 0044 (CCI) TOLEDANO, STUART R Pediatric oncology group POG9079--Phase I study of L-PAM/CTX with ABM rescue for brain tumors in children

U10CA-41082-06 0045 (CCI) TOLEDANO, STUART R Pediatric oncology group POG9075--Phase I study of acivicin in children with solid tumors

U10CA-41082-06 0046 (CCI) TOLEDANO, STUART R Pediatric oncology group POG9074--Phase I study of xomazyme-H65 in children with T-cell ALL/lymphoma

U10CA-41082-06 0047 (CCI) TOLEDANO, STUART R Pediatric oncology group POG9072--Phase I chemotherapy for recurrent/resistant malignant solid tumors

U10CA-41082-06 0048 (CCI) TOLEDANO, STUART R Pediatric oncology group POG9061-Phase II systemic therapy and irradiation for ALL & CNS leukemia

U10CA-41082-06 0049 (CCI) TOLEDANO, STUART R Pediatric oncology group POG 9086--Phase I pilot study of therapy for T-cell ALL or NHL

U10CA-41082-06 0050 (CCI) TOLEDANO, STUART R Pediatric oncology group POG9071--Phase I trial of fazarabine in children with acute leukemia

U10CA-41082-06 0051 (CCI) TOLEDANO, STUART R Pediatric oncology group POG8970--Phase I trial of fazarabine in children with refractory solid tumors

U10CA-41082-06 0052 (CCI) TOLEDANO, STUART R Pediatric oncology group POG8973--Etoposide (VP-16) and carboplatin in children with acute leukemia

U10CA-41082-06 0053 (CCI) TOLEDANO, STUART R Pediatric oncology group POG8870--Phase I trial of ifosfamide/VP16/MESNA in children with acute leukemia

U10CA-41082-06 0054 (CCI) TOLEDANO, STUART R Pediatric oncology group POG8871--Phase I study of rTNF in children with refractory solid tumors

U10CA-41082-06 0055 (CCI) TOLEDANO, STUART R Pediatric oncology group POG8671--Phase I immunotherapy with rIL-2 in children with solid tumors

U10CA-41082-06 0056 (CCI) TOLEDANO, STUART R Pediatric oncology group POG8494--Phase I study of fludarabine phosphate in pediatric patients

U10CA-41082-06 0057 (CCI) TOLEDANO, STUART R Pediatric oncology group POG8930--A comprehensive genetic analysis of brain tumors

U10CA-41082-06 0058 (CCI) TOLEDANO, STUART R Pediatric oncology group POG8828--Late effects of Hodgkin's disease

U10CA-41082-06 0059 (CCI) TOLEDANO, STUART R Pediatric oncology group POG9046--Molecular genetic analysis of Wilm's tumors

U10CA-41082-06 0060 (CCI) TOLEDANO, STUART R Pediatric oncology group POG9153--Rhabdomyosarcoma study/laboratory evaluation of tumor

U10CA-41082-06 0020 (CCI) TOLEDANO, STUART R Pediatric oncology group POG9107--Phase II pilot study of infant leukemia

U10CA-41082-06 0021 (CCI) TOLEDANO, STUART R Pediatric oncology group POG9140--Phase II therapy for recurrent or refractory neuroblastoma

U10CA-41082-06 0022 (CCI) TOLEDANO, STUART R Pediatric oncology group POG9048--Phase II study of malignant germ cell tumors in children

U10CA-41082-06 0023 (CCI) TOLEDANO, STUART R Pediatric oncology group POG9060--Intensive QOD ifosfamide treatment for CNS tumors in children

U10CA-41082-06 0024 (CCI) TOLEDANO, STUART R Pediatric oncology group POG8936--Phase II study of carboplatin treatment for optic pathway tumors

U10CA-41082-06 0025 (CCI) TOLEDANO, STUART R Pediatric oncology group POG8935--Phase II study of surgery and/or radiotherapy for optic pathway tumors

U10CA-41082-06 0026 (CCI) TOLEDANO, STUART R Pediatric oncology group POG8820--Phase II/III study of VP-16, AMSA +/- 5-azacytidine in childhood ANLL

PROJECT NO., ORGANIZATIONAL UNIT., INVESTIGATOR, ADDRESS, TITLE

U10CA-41082-06 0027 (CCI) TOLEDANO, STUART R Pediatric oncology group POG8889--Intergroup rhabdomyosarcoma study for clinical group IV disease

U10CA-41082-06 0028 (CCI) TOLEDANO, STUART R Pediatric oncology group POG8866--Phase II asparaginase therapy for acute lymphoblastic leukemia

U10CA-41082-06 0029 (CCI) TOLEDANO, STUART R Pediatric oncology group POG8862--Combination chemotherapy of acute T-lymphoblastic leukemia

U10CA-41082-06 0030 (CCI) TOLEDANO, STUART R Pediatric oncology group POG8863--Phase II study of high dose cytosine arabinoside in childhood tumors

U10CA-41082-06 0031 (CCI) TOLEDANO, STUART R Pediatric oncology group POG8827--Phase II treatment of children with Hodgkin's disease in relapse

U10CA-41082-06 0032 (CCI) TOLEDANO, STUART R Pediatric oncology group POG8865--Phase II recombinant alpha-interferon in relapsed T-cell disease

U10CA-41082-06 0033 (CCI) TOLEDANO, STUART R Pediatric oncology group--Phase II recombinant A-interferon in chronic myelogenous leukemia

U10CA-41082-06 0034 (CCI) TOLEDANO, STUART R Pediatric oncology group POG8832--Combination chemotherapy followed by radiotherapy for brain tumors

U10CA-41082-06 0035 (CCI) TOLEDANO, STUART R Pediatric oncology group POG8731--Phase II trial of methotrexate in treatment of brain tumors in children

U10CA-41082-06 0036 (CCI) TOLEDANO, STUART R Pediatric oncology group POG8788--Intergroup rhabdomyosarcoma study/pilot study for clinical group III

U10CA-41082-06 0037 (CCI) TOLEDANO, STUART R Pediatric oncology group POG8761--Phase II study of homoharringtonine therapy for nonlymphoblastic leukemi

U10CA-41082-06 0038 (CCI) TOLEDANO, STUART R Pediatric oncology group POG8739--Phase II immunotherapy with alpha-2 interferon for brain tumors

U10CA-41082-06 0039 (CCI) TOLEDANO, STUART R Pediatric oncology group POG8741--Treatment of patients with stage C and stage D neuroblastoma

U10CA-41082-06 0040 (CCI) TOLEDANO, STUART R Pediatric oncology group POG8751--Phase II methotrexate chemotherapy for rhabdomyosarcoma in children

P01CA-41086-06 (SRC) SHENK, THOMAS E PRINCETON UNIVERSITY PRINCETON, N J 08544 Viral and cellular oncogenes - mechanism of action

P01CA-41086-06 0001 (SRC) SHENK, THOMAS E Viral and cellular oncogenes - mechanism of action Ad5 E1B transforming gene and estrogen-dependent breast tumor induction by Ad9

P01CA-41086-06 0003 (SRC) COLE, MICHAEL D Viral and cellular oncogenes - mechanism of action Function of the c-myc oncogene

P01CA-41086-06 0004 (SRC) BROACH, JAMES R Viral and cellular oncogenes - mechanism of action Function of yeast RAS oncogene homologs

P01CA-41086-06 0005 (SRC) LEVINE, ARNOLD J Viral and cellular oncogenes - mechanism of action P53, A cellular tumor suppressor

P01CA-41086-06 9001 (SRC) SHENK, THOMAS E Viral and cellular oncogenes - mechanism of action Core component

R01CA-41101-07 (BNP) BOGER, DALE L SCRIPPS RESEARCH INST 10666 NORTH TORREY PINES RD LA JOLLA, CA 92037 Deoxybouvardin and vouvardin--Antitumor agents

P01CA-41108-05 (SRC) ALBERTS, DAVID S UNIVERSITY OF ARIZONA 1515 NORTH CAMPBELL AVE TUCSON, AZ 85724 Colon cancer prevention program project

P01CA-41108-05 9002 (SRC) RITENBAUGH, CHERYL Colon cancer prevention program project Nutrition core

P01CA-41108-05 9003 (SRC) ATWOOD, JAN R Colon cancer prevention program project Adherence core

P01CA-41108-05 9004 (SRC) ALBERTS, DAVID S Colon cancer prevention program project Analytical core

P01CA-41108-05 0001 (SRC) ALBERTS, DAVID S Colon cancer prevention program project Wheat bran fiber effect on colonic adenomatous polyp recurrence

P01CA-41108-05 0002 (SRC) EARNEST, DAVID L Colon cancer prevention program project Cancer prevention--Piroxicam effects on colon mucosa

P01CA-41108-05 0004 (SRC) MEYSKENS, FRANK L Colon cancer prevention program project Polyamine synthesis inhibitor difluoromethylornithine colon mucosa effect

P01CA-41108-05 9001 (SRC) MCGEE, DANIEL Colon cancer prevention program project Biometry core

R01CA-41165-07 (EI) HOOVER, RICHARD G DEPARTMENT OF PATHOLOGY COLLEGE OF MEDICINE LITTLE ROCK, AK 72205 Tumor suppressive T cells with Fc receptors in myeloma

P01CA-41167-06 (CCP) HOLLENBERG, NORMAN K BRIGHAM & WOMEN'S HOSPITAL 75 FRANCIS STREET BOSTON, MA 02115 Diagnostic radiology research center

P01CA-41167-06 0001 (CCP) KIJEWSKI, MARIE Diagnostic radiology research center Maximum likelyhood estimation of physical quantities from CT.

P01CA-41167-06 0002 (CCP) MOORE, STEPHEN Diagnostic radiology research center Physical improvements for SPECT imaging.

P01CA-41167-06 0003 (CCP) PHILLIP, JUDI Diagnostic radiology research center Observer efficiency in detection and discrimination tasks.

P01CA-41167-06 0004 (CCP) KASSIS, AMIN Diagnostic radiology research center New approaches to labeling antibodies for radiodiag.of cancer.

P01CA-41167-06 0005 (CCP) SELTZER, STEPHEN Diagnostic radiology research center Improved imaging of tumors.

P01CA-41167-06 0006 (CCP) JOLESSZ, FERENC Diagnostic radiology research center Proton magnetic resonance of myelin and demyelination.

P01CA-41167-06 0007 (CCP) HOLLENBERG, NORMAN Diagnostic radiology research center Collateral blood vessel tone, reactivity and growth.

P01CA-41167-06 0008 (CCP) SOHN, MIRIAM Diagnostic radiology

PROJECT NO., ORGANIZATIONAL UNIT., INVESTIGATOR, ADDRESS, TITLE

research center Atherosclerotic vascular disease imaging using MRI.

P01CA-41167-06 9001 (CCP) SANDOR, TAMAS Diagnostic radiology research center Digital image processing.

P01CA-41167-06 9002 (CCP) HURLBERT, ANDREA Diagnostic radiology research center Radiology animal research core

P01CA-41167-06 9003 (CCP) MCNEILL, BARBARA Diagnostic radiology research center Radiological analytic core

P01CA-41183-05 (SRC) SALMON, SYDNEY UNIVERSITY OF ARIZONA ARIZONA HEALTH SCIENCES CTR TUCSON, AZ 85724 Cytogenetic oncology program project

P01CA-41183-05 0001 (SRC) MELTZER, PAUL S Cytogenetic oncology program project Molecular analysis of multiple drug resistance

P01CA-41183-05 0002 (SRC) TRENT, JEFFREY M Cytogenetic oncology program project Comparative cytogenetics of drug resistant and sensitive human tumor cells

P01CA-41183-05 0003 (SRC) VOGELSTEIN, BERT Cytogenetic oncology program project Karyology and prognosis of human malignant melanoma

P01CA-41183-05 0004 (SRC) ALBERTS, DAVID S Cytogenetic oncology program project Clinical correlation of chromosome change in ovary cancer

P01CA-41183-05 0005 (SRC) DALTON, WILLIAM S Cytogenetic oncology program project Chromosomal change in breast cancer

P01CA-41183-05 0006 (SRC) SANDBERG, AVERY A Cytogenetic oncology program project Cytogenetics of soft tissue and urologic tumors

P01CA-41183-05 9001 (SRC) MCGEE, DANIEL Cytogenetic oncology program project Biostatistics core

P01CA-41183-05 9002 (SRC) LEIBOVITZ, ALBERT Cytogenetic oncology program project Cell culture core

P01CA-41183-05 9003 (SRC) DAVIS, JOHN R Cytogenetic oncology program project Pathologic review core

U10CA-41188-06 (CCI) BERRY, DAISILEE H ARKANSAS CHILDREN'S HOSPITAL 800 MARSHALL STREET LITTLE ROCK, AR 72202 Pediatric oncology group

U10CA-41188-06 0038 (CCI) BERRY, DAISILEE H Pediatric oncology group POG8739--Phase II immunotherapy with alpha-2 interferon for brain tumors

U10CA-41188-06 0039 (CCI) BERRY, DAISILEE H Pediatric oncology group POG8741--Treatment of patients with stage C and stage D neuroblastoma

U10CA-41188-06 0040 (CCI) BERRY, DAISILEE H Pediatric oncology group POG8751--Phase II methotrexate chemotherapy for rhabdomyosarcoma in children

U10CA-41188-06 0041 (CCI) BERRY, DAISILEE H Pediatric oncology group POG8633--Postoperative chemotherapy and delayed irradiation for brain tumors

U10CA-41188-06 0042 (CCI) BERRY, DAISILEE H Pediatric oncology group POG8617--Therapy for B-cell acute lymphoblastic leukemia and lymphoma

U10CA-41188-06 0043 (CCI) BERRY, DAISILEE H Pediatric oncology group POG9139--Phase I study of cisplatin and irradiation in brain stem gliomas

U10CA-41188-06 0044 (CCI) BERRY, DAISILEE H Pediatric oncology group POG9079--Phase I study of L-PAM/CTX with ABM rescue for brain tumors in children

U10CA-41188-06 0045 (CCI) BERRY, DAISILEE H Pediatric oncology group POG9075--Phase I study of acivicin in children with solid tumors

U10CA-41188-06 0046 (CCI) BERRY, DAISILEE H Pediatric oncology group POG9074--Phase I study of xomazyme-H65 in children with T-cell ALL/lymphoma

U10CA-41188-06 0047 (CCI) BERRY, DAISILEE H Pediatric oncology group POG9072--Phase I chemotherapy for recurrent/resistant malignant solid tumors

U10CA-41188-06 0048 (CCI) BERRY, DAISILEE H Pediatric oncology group POG9061-Phase II systemic therapy and irradiation for ALL & CNS leukemia

U10CA-41188-06 0049 (CCI) BERRY, DAISILEE H Pediatric oncology group POG 9086--Phase I pilot study of therapy for T-cell ALL or NHL

U10CA-41188-06 0050 (CCI) BERRY, DAISILEE H Pediatric oncology group POG9071--Phase I trial of fazarabine in children with acute leukemia

U10CA-41188-06 0051 (CCI) BERRY, DAISILEE H Pediatric oncology group POG8970--Phase I trial of fazarabine in children with refractory solid tumors

U10CA-41188-06 0052 (CCI) BERRY, DAISILEE H Pediatric oncology group POG8973--Etoposide (VP-16) and carboplatin in children with acute leukemia

U10CA-41188-06 0053 (CCI) BERRY, DAISILEE H Pediatric oncology group POG8870--Phase I trial of ifosfamide/VP16/MESNA in children with acute leukemia

U10CA-41188-06 0054 (CCI) BERRY, DAISILEE H Pediatric oncology group POG8871--Phase I study of rTNF in children with refractory solid tumors

U10CA-41188-06 0055 (CCI) BERRY, DAISILEE H Pediatric oncology group POG8671--Phase I immunotherapy with rIL-2 in children with solid tumors

U10CA-41188-06 0056 (CCI) BERRY, DAISILEE H Pediatric oncology group POG8494--Phase I study of fludarabine phosphate in pediatric patients

U10CA-41188-06 0057 (CCI) BERRY, DAISILEE H Pediatric oncology group POG8930--A comprehensive genetic analysis of brain tumors

U10CA-41188-06 0058 (CCI) BERRY, DAISILEE H Pediatric oncology group POG8828--Late effects of Hodgkin's disease

U10CA-41188-06 0059 (CCI) BERRY, DAISILEE H Pediatric oncology group POG9046--Molecular genetic analysis of Wilm's tumors

U10CA-41188-06 0060 (CCI) BERRY, DAISILEE H Pediatric oncology group POG9153--Rhabdomyosarcoma study/laboratory evaluation of tumor

U10CA-41188-06 0001 (CCI) BERRY, DAISILEE H Pediatric oncology group POG9006--6-MP/methotrexate vs. alternating chemotherapy for ALL in childhood

U10CA-41188-06 0006 (CCI) BERRY, DAISILEE H Pediatric oncology group POG8844--Bone marrow transplant in children with stage D neuroblastoma

U10CA-41188-06 0002 (CCI) BERRY, DAISILEE H Pediatric oncology

PROJECT NO., ORGANIZATIONAL UNIT., INVESTIGATOR, ADDRESS, TITLE

group POG9005--Dose intensification of methotrexate & 6-mercaptourine in childhood ALL

U10CA-41188-06 0003 (CCI) BERRY, DAISILEE H Pediatric oncology group POG9031--Cisplatin/VP-16 therapy of medulloblastoma/pre vs. post irradiation

U10CA-41188-06 0004 (CCI) BERRY, DAISILEE H Pediatric oncology group POG8945--Phase III chemotherapy for hepatoblastoma & hepatocellular carcinoma

U10CA-41188-06 0005 (CCI) BERRY, DAISILEE H Pediatric oncology group POG9049--Phase III study of high-risk malignant germ cell tumors in children

U10CA-41188-06 0007 (CCI) BERRY, DAISILEE H Pediatric oncology group POG8850--Phase III treatment of Ewing's sarcoma and neuroectodermal bone tumors

U10CA-41188-06 0008 (CCI) BERRY, DAISILEE H Pediatric oncology group POG8821--Phase III chemotherapy +/- autologous BMT in children with AML

U10CA-41188-06 0009 (CCI) BERRY, DAISILEE H Pediatric oncology group POG8725--Phase III chemotherapy +/- radiation therapy in pediatric Hodgkins

U10CA-41188-06 0010 (CCI) BERRY, DAISILEE H Pediatric oncology group POG8704--Phase III chemotherapy of childhood T cell ALL & lymphoblastic lymphoma

U10CA-41188-06 0011 (CCI) BERRY, DAISILEE H Pediatric oncology group POG8719--Phase III chemotherapy for non-Hodgkin's lymphoma in children

U10CA-41188-06 0012 (CCI) BERRY, DAISILEE H Pediatric oncology group POG8650--National Wilm's tumor and clear cell sarcoma study

U10CA-41188-06 0013 (CCI) BERRY, DAISILEE H Pediatric oncology group POG8616--Phase III chemotherapy for childhood Burkitt and non-Burkitts lymphoma

U10CA-41188-06 0014 (CCI) BERRY, DAISILEE H Pediatric oncology group POG8615--Phase III study of large cell lymphomas in children and adolescents

U10CA-41188-06 0015 (CCI) BERRY, DAISILEE H Pediatric oncology group POG8651--Phase III study of childhood nonmetastatic osteosarcoma

U10CA-41188-06 0016 (CCI) BERRY, DAISILEE H Pediatric oncology group POG8653--Phase III study of childhood soft tissue sarcomas

U10CA-41188-06 0017 (CCI) BERRY, DAISILEE H Pediatric oncology group POG8625--Phase III combined therapy in childhood Hodgkin's disease

U10CA-41188-06 0018 (CCI) BERRY, DAISILEE H Pediatric oncology group POG8451--Intergroup rhabdomyosarcoma study

U10CA-41188-06 0019 (CCI) BERRY, DAISILEE H Pediatric oncology group POG9110--Rotational drug therapy after first marrow relapse of non-T, non B ALL

U10CA-41188-06 0020 (CCI) BERRY, DAISILEE H Pediatric oncology group POG9107--Phase II pilot study of infant leukemia

U10CA-41188-06 0021 (CCI) BERRY, DAISILEE H Pediatric oncology group POG9140--Phase II therapy for recurrent or refractory neuroblastoma

U10CA-41188-06 0022 (CCI) BERRY, DAISILEE H Pediatric oncology group POG9048--Phase II study of malignant germ cell tumors in children

U10CA-41188-06 0023 (CCI) BERRY, DAISILEE H Pediatric oncology group POG9060--Intensive QOD ifosfamide treatment for CNS tumors in children

U10CA-41188-06 0024 (CCI) BERRY, DAISILEE H Pediatric oncology group POG8936--Phase II study of carboplatin treatment for optic pathway tumors

U10CA-41188-06 0025 (CCI) BERRY, DAISILEE H Pediatric oncology group POG8935--Phase II study of surgery and/or radiotherapy for optic pathway tumors

U10CA-41188-06 0026 (CCI) BERRY, DAISILEE H Pediatric oncology group POG8820--Phase II/III study of VP-16, AMSA +/- 5-azacytidine in childhood ANLL

U10CA-41188-06 0027 (CCI) BERRY, DAISILEE H Pediatric oncology group POG8889--Intergroup rhabdomyosarcoma study for clinical group IV disease

U10CA-41188-06 0028 (CCI) BERRY, DAISILEE H Pediatric oncology group POG8866--Phase II asparaginase therapy for acute lymphoblastic leukemia

U10CA-41188-06 0029 (CCI) BERRY, DAISILEE H Pediatric oncology group POG8862--Combination chemotherapy of acute T-lymphoblastic leukemia

U10CA-41188-06 0030 (CCI) BERRY, DAISILEE H Pediatric oncology group POG8863--Phase II study of high dose cytosine arabinoside in childhood tumors

U10CA-41188-06 0031 (CCI) BERRY, DAISILEE H Pediatric oncology group POG8827--Phase II treatment of children with Hodgkin's disease in relapse

U10CA-41188-06 0032 (CCI) BERRY, DAISILEE H Pediatric oncology group POG8865--Phase II recombinant alpha-interferon in relapsed T-cell disease

U10CA-41188-06 0033 (CCI) BERRY, DAISILEE H Pediatric oncology group--Phase II recombinant A-interferon in chronic myelogenous leukemia

U10CA-41188-06 0034 (CCI) BERRY, DAISILEE H Pediatric oncology group POG8832--Combination chemotherapy followed by radiotherapy for brain tumors

U10CA-41188-06 0035 (CCI) BERRY, DAISILEE H Pediatric oncology group POG8731--Phase II trial of methotrexate in treatment of brain tumors in children

U10CA-41188-06 0036 (CCI) BERRY, DAISILEE H Pediatric oncology group POG8788--Intergroup rhabdomyosarcoma study/pilot study for clinical group III

U10CA-41188-06 0037 (CCI) BERRY, DAISILEE H Pediatric oncology group POG8761--Phase II study of homoharringtonine therapy for nonlymphoblastic leukemi

R01CA-41233-06 (PTHB) KERBEL, ROBERT S SUNNYBROOK HEALTH SCIENE CENTR 2075 BAYVIEW AVENUE TORONTO, ONTARIO M4N 3M5 **New approach to study human melanoma metastasis**

R01CA-41248-06 (MEP) THOMPSON, JOHN A UNIV OF CO/SCH OF

PHARMACY CAMPUS BOX 297 BOULDER, CO 80309 Bioactivation of dietary phenols by hemoproteins

R01CA-41261-06 (RAD) **PRAKASH, SATYA** UNIVERSITY OF ROCHESTER ROCHESTER, NY 14627 Repair of UV irradiated DNA--Excision genes of yeast

R01CA-41267-04A3 (CPA) **OBERLEY, LARRY W** UNIVERSITY OF IOWA 14 MEDICAL LABORATORIES IOWA CITY, IA 52242 Superoxide dismutase levels in tumor cells

R01CA-41268-06 (IMB) **BIRON, CHRISTINE A** BROWN UNIVERSITY DIVISION OF BIO/MED, BOX G PROVIDENCE, RI 02912 Natural killer cell growth and development

R01CA-41270-07 (RAD) **SCHNEIDERMAN, MARTIN H** UNIVERSITY OF NEBRASKA MED CTR 600 SOUTH 42ND ST OOMAHA, NE 68198 Radiation-induced division delay & cell survival

P01CA-41285-07 (SRC) **PREISLER, HARVEY D** UNIVERSITY OF CINCINNATI BARRET CANCER CENTER CINCINNATI, OHIO 45267 Clinical and biological studies of the myeloid leukemias

P01CA-41285-07 0004 (SRC) **PREISLER, HARVEY D** Clinical and biological studies of the myeloid leukemias Leukemic cell differentiation & development of acute myelogenous leukemia

P01CA-41285-07 0005 (SRC) **KINNIBURGH, ALAN J** Clinical and biological studies of the myeloid leukemias Oncogene expression in myeloid leukemia

P01CA-41285-07 9001 (SRC) **SANDBERG, AVERY A** Clinical and biological studies of the myeloid leukemias Core--Cytogenetics

P01CA-41285-07 9002 (SRC) **PRIORE, ROGER L** Clinical and biological studies of the myeloid leukemias Core--Statistics

P01CA-41285-07 9003 (SRC) **MAYERS, GEORGE** Clinical and biological studies of the myeloid leukemias Core--Monoclonal antibody development for chemotherapy

P01CA-41285-07 9004 (SRC) **BARCOS, MAURICE** Clinical and biological studies of the myeloid leukemias Core--Cell lineage and level of maturation in myeloid disorders

P01CA-41285-07 0001 (SRC) **PREISLER, HARVEY D** Clinical and biological studies of the myeloid leukemias Biology of myeloid differentiation and proliferation in vitro

P01CA-41285-07 0002 (SRC) **RAZA, AZRA** Clinical and biological studies of the myeloid leukemias Cellular proliferation and differentiation in myeloid diseases

U10CA-41287-06 (CCI) **VOGELZANG, NICHOLAS J** UNIV OF CHICAGO MEDICAL CENTER 5841 S MARYLAND AVENUE BOX 420 CHICAGO, IL 60637 Cancer and leukemia group B

R01CA-41295-04A1 (RNM) **HAYES, WILSON C** BETH ISRAEL HOSPITAL 330 BROOKLINE AVENUE BOSTON, MA 02215 Hip fracture risk prediction by QDR

R01CA-41302-06 (EVR) **SUGDEN, BILL** UNIVERSITY OF WISCONSIN 1400 UNIVERSITY AVENUE MADISON, WI 53706 Biological and molecular studies of A-MULV tumorigenesi

R01CA-41314-06 (ET) **MODEST, EDWARD J** BOSTON UNIV SCHOOL OF MEDICINE 80 EAST CONCORD STREET BOSTON, MA 02118 Pharmacological effects of ether lipid analogs

R01CA-41316-07 (RAD) **SKIBBA, JOSEPH L** ELLIS FISCHEL HOSPITAL 115 BUSINESS LOOP 70 WEST COLUMBIA, MD 65203 Hyperthermic liver injury and lipid peroxidation

R01CA-41323-06 (BBCB) **FINER-MOORE, JANET S** UNIVERSITY OF CALIFORNIA DEPT OF BIOCHEM AND BIOPHYSICS SAN FRANCISCO, 94143-0448 Crystallographic studies of thymidylate synthase

R01CA-41324-07 (RNM) **SEHGAL, CHANDRA M** UNIVERSITY OF PENNSYLVANIA 36TH ST & HAMILTON WALK PHILADELPHIA, PA 19104 Acoustic nonlinearity for tissue characterization

R01CA-41325-06 (MCHA) **DOERING, WILLIAM V** HARVARD UNIVERSITY 12 OXFORD ST CAMBRIDGE, MA 02138-2902 Semi-rigid conjugated polyenes as model anticarcinogens

R01CA-41349-06 (MCHA) **SWINDELL, CHARLES S** BRYN MAWR COLLEGE BRYN MAWR, PA 19010 Synthesis of taxinine and taxol

U10CA-41357-06 (SRC) **COUTURE, JEAN** ST SACREMENT HOSPITAL 1050 CHEMIN STE-FOY QUEBEC, G1S 4L8, CANADA Primary breast cancer therapy group--NSABP

R01CA-41359-05 (PTHA) **PETERS, BARRY P** NORTH CAROLINA STATE UNIV 4700 HILLSBOROUGH STREET RALEIGH, NC 27606 Biosynthesis of basal lamina by human malignant cells

R01CA-41372-06 (PTHB) **AUGENLICHT, LEONARD H** MONTEFIORE MEDICAL CENTER 111 EAST 210TH STREET BRONX, NY 10467 Gene expression in human colon cancer

R29CA-41375-05 (ET) **MEYERS, MARIAN B** SLOAN-KETTERING INSTITUTE 1275 YORK AVENUE NEW YORK, N Y 10021 Egf receptor in normalized multidrug-resistant cells

R01CA-41386-06 (REN) **EDWARDS, DEAN P** UNIV OF COLORADO HLTH SCIS CTR 4200 EAST NINTH AVENUE DENVER, CO 80262 Immunologic probes for study of progesterone receptor

R55CA-41387-04A2 (MEP) **LI, JONATHAN J** WASHINGTON STATE UNIVERSITY PULLMAN, WA 99164-6510 Sex hormones and hepatocellular carcinomas

R01CA-41407-06 (ET) **THOMPSON, E BRAD** UNIV OF TEXAS MEDICAL BRANCH 603 BASIC SCIENCE BLDG. F-45 GALVESTON, TX 77550 The human glucocorticoid receptor, its gene and actions

R37CA-41424-08 (CBY) **BRINKLEY, BILL R** BAYLOR COLLEGE OF MEDICINE ONE BAYLOR PLAZA HOUSTON, TX 77030 Studies of mitosis in normal and neoplastic cells/mice,human,deer,hamsters/

R01CA-41450-06 (VR) **HUMPHRIES, ERIC H** MARY BABB RANDOLPH CANCER CTR SCHOOL OF MEDICINE MORGANTOWN, WEST VIRGINIA 265 Expression and function of v-rel in lymphoid tissue

R01CA-41456-06 (HEM) **TENEN, DANIEL G** BETH ISRAEL HOSPITAL 330 BROOKLINE AVENUE BOSTON, MA 02215 Molecular biology of human myeloid differentiation

R01CA-41461-07 (ET) **FREISHEIM, JAMES H** MEDICAL COLLEGE OF OHIO C S 10008 TOLEDO, OH 43699 Structure-function studies of dihydrofolate reductase

R01CA-41464-06 (RNM) **HYDE, JAMES S** MEDICAL COLLEGE OF WISCONSIN 8701 WATERTOWN PLANK ROAD MILWAUKEE, WI 53226 Loop-gap resonator coils for MRI P31 spectroscopy

R01CA-41490-08 (RAD) **JETTE, DAVID** INST OF APPLIED PHYSIOLOGY/MED 701 16TH AVENUE SEATTLE, WA 98122 Multiple scattering theory applied to electron dosimetry

R01CA-41510-05 (EVR) **HOLLAND, CHRISTIE A** UNIV OF MASS MEDICAL SCHOOL 55 LAKE AVE, NORTH WORCESTER, MA 01655 Oncogenicity of mink cell focus-inducing retroviruses

R01CA-41520-06 (PTHA) **BIEDLER, JUNE L** SLOAN-KETTERING INST/CANCER RE 1275 YORK AVENUE NEW YORK, NY 10021 Human neuroblastoma cell transdifferentiation

R01CA-41521-06 (PTHB) **HOLMES, ERIC H** PACIFIC NORTHWEST RES FDN 720 BROADWAY SEATTLE, WA 98122 Regulation of synthesis of glycolipid tumor antigens

R01CA-41524-06 (PBC) **NAKAJIMA, MOTOWO** UNIVERSITY OF TEXAS 1515 HOLCOMBE BLVD HOUSTON, TX 77030 Tumor basement membrane degrading enzymes

R01CA-41525-06 (PTHB) **FROST, PHILIP** U.T.M.D.ANDERSON CANCER CENTER 1515 HOLCOMBE BLVD BOX 173 HOUSTON, TX 77030 Alien gene transfection in the therapy of metastases

R37CA-41530-06 (NSS) **THOMAS, DAVID B** FRED HUTCHINSON CANCER RES CTR 1124 COLUMBIA STREET SEATTLE, WA 98104 Trace elements and cancers of larynx, esophagus and mouth

R01CA-41556-05 (PTHB) **REISS, MICHAEL** YALE UNIVERSITY 333 CEDAR STREET P.O. BOX 333 NEW HAVEN, CT 06510 Growth control of malignant and normal keratinocytes

U10CA-41573-06 (CCI) **SALLAN, STEPHEN E** DANA-FARBER CANCER INSTITUTE 44 BINNEY STREET, ROOM 1842 BOSTON, MA 02115 Pediatric oncology group

U10CA-41573-06 0001 (CCI) **SALLAN, STEPHEN E** Pediatric oncology group POG9006--6-MP/methotrexate vs. alternating chemotherapy for ALL in childhood

U10CA-41573-06 0002 (CCI) **SALLAN, STEPHEN E** Pediatric oncology group POG9005--Dose intensification of methotrexate & 6-mercaptourine in childhood ALL

U10CA-41573-06 0003 (CCI) **SALLAN, STEPHEN E** Pediatric oncology group POG9031--Cisplatin/VP-16 therapy of medulloblastoma/pre vs. post irradiation

U10CA-41573-06 0004 (CCI) **SALLAN, STEPHEN E** Pediatric oncology group POG8945--Phase III chemotherapy for hepatoblastoma & hepatocellular carcinoma

U10CA-41573-06 0005 (CCI) **SALLAN, STEPHEN E** Pediatric oncology group POG9049--Phase III study of high-risk malignant germ cell tumors in children

U10CA-41573-06 0006 (CCI) **SALLAN, STEPHEN E** Pediatric oncology group POG8844--Bone marrow transplant in children with stage D neuroblastoma

U10CA-41573-06 0007 (CCI) **SALLAN, STEPHEN E** Pediatric oncology group POG8850--Phase III treatment of Ewing's sarcoma and neuroectodermal bone tumors

U10CA-41573-06 0008 (CCI) **SALLAN, STEPHEN E** Pediatric oncology group POG8821--Phase III chemotherapy +/- autologous BMT in children with AML

U10CA-41573-06 0009 (CCI) **SALLAN, STEPHEN E** Pediatric oncology group POG8725--Phase III chemotherapy +/- radiation therapy in pediatric Hodgkins

U10CA-41573-06 0010 (CCI) **SALLAN, STEPHEN E** Pediatric oncology group POG8704--Phase III chemotherapy of childhood T cell ALL & lymphoblastic lymphoma

U10CA-41573-06 0011 (CCI) **SALLAN, STEPHEN E** Pediatric oncology group POG8719--Phase III chemotherapy for non-Hodgkin's lymphoma in children

U10CA-41573-06 0012 (CCI) **SALLAN, STEPHEN E** Pediatric oncology group POG8650--National Wilm's tumor and clear cell sarcoma study

U10CA-41573-06 0013 (CCI) **SALLAN, STEPHEN E** Pediatric oncology group POG8616--Phase III chemotherapy for childhood Burkitt and non-Burkitts lymphoma

U10CA-41573-06 0014 (CCI) **SALLAN, STEPHEN E** Pediatric oncology group POG8615--Phase III study of large cell lymphomas in children and adolescents

U10CA-41573-06 0015 (CCI) **SALLAN, STEPHEN E** Pediatric oncology group POG8651--Phase III study of childhood nonmetastatic osteosarcoma

U10CA-41573-06 0016 (CCI) **SALLAN, STEPHEN E** Pediatric oncology group POG8653--Phase III study of childhood soft tissue sarcomas

U10CA-41573-06 0017 (CCI) **SALLAN, STEPHEN E** Pediatric oncology group POG8625--Phase III combined therapy in childhood Hodgkin's disease

U10CA-41573-06 0018 (CCI) **SALLAN, STEPHEN E** Pediatric oncology group POG8451--Intergroup rhabdomyosarcoma study

U10CA-41573-06 0019 (CCI) **SALLAN, STEPHEN E** Pediatric oncology group POG9110--Rotational drug therapy after first marrow relapse of non-T, non B ALL

U10CA-41573-06 0020 (CCI) **SALLAN, STEPHEN E** Pediatric oncology group POG9107--Phase II pilot study of infant leukemia

U10CA-41573-06 0021 (CCI) **SALLAN, STEPHEN E** Pediatric oncology group POG9140--Phase II therapy for recurrent or refractory neuroblastoma

U10CA-41573-06 0022 (CCI) **SALLAN, STEPHEN E** Pediatric oncology group POG9048--Phase II study of malignant germ cell tumors in children

U10CA-41573-06 0023 (CCI) **SALLAN, STEPHEN E** Pediatric oncology group POG9060--Intensive QOD ifosfamide treatment for CNS tumors in children

U10CA-41573-06 0024 (CCI) **SALLAN, STEPHEN E** Pediatric oncology group POG8936--Phase II study of carboplatin treatment for optic pathway tumors

U10CA-41573-06 0029 (CCI) **SALLAN, STEPHEN E** Pediatric oncology group POG8862--Combination chemotherapy of acute T-lymphoblastic leukemia

U10CA-41573-06 0030 (CCI) **SALLAN, STEPHEN E** Pediatric oncology group POG8863--Phase II study of high dose cytosine arabinoside in childhood tumors

U10CA-41573-06 0031 (CCI) **SALLAN, STEPHEN E** Pediatric oncology group POG8827--Phase II treatment of children with Hodgkin's disease in relapse

U10CA-41573-06 0032 (CCI) **SALLAN, STEPHEN E** Pediatric oncology group POG8865--Phase II recombinant alpha-interferon in relapsed T-cell disease

U10CA-41573-06 0033 (CCI) **SALLAN, STEPHEN E** Pediatric oncology

PROJECT NO., ORGANIZATIONAL UNIT., INVESTIGATOR, ADDRESS, TITLE

group–Phase II recombinant A-interferon in chronic myelogenous leukemia

U10CA-41573-06 0034 (CCI) SALLAN, STEPHEN E Pediatric oncology group POG8832–Combination chemotherapy followed by radiotherapy for brain tumors

U10CA-41573-06 0035 (CCI) SALLAN, STEPHEN E Pediatric oncology group POG8731–Phase II trial of methotrexate in treatment of brain tumors in children

U10CA-41573-06 0036 (CCI) SALLAN, STEPHEN E Pediatric oncology group POG8788–Intergroup rhabdomyosarcoma study/pilot study for clinical group III

U10CA-41573-06 0037 (CCI) SALLAN, STEPHEN E Pediatric oncology group POG8761–Phase II study of homoharringtonine therapy for nonlymphoblastic leukemi

U10CA-41573-06 0038 (CCI) SALLAN, STEPHEN E Pediatric oncology group POG8739–Phase II immunotherapy with alpha-2 interferon for brain tumors

U10CA-41573-06 0039 (CCI) SALLAN, STEPHEN E Pediatric oncology group POG8741–Treatment of patients with stage C and stage D neuroblastoma

U10CA-41573-06 0040 (CCI) SALLAN, STEPHEN E Pediatric oncology group POG8751–Phase II methotrexate chemotherapy for rhabdomyosarcoma in children

U10CA-41573-06 0041 (CCI) SALLAN, STEPHEN E Pediatric oncology group POG8633–Postoperative chemotherapy and delayed irradiation for brain tumors

U10CA-41573-06 0042 (CCI) SALLAN, STEPHEN E Pediatric oncology group POG8617–Therapy for B-cell acute lymphoblastic leukemia and lymphoma

U10CA-41573-06 0043 (CCI) SALLAN, STEPHEN E Pediatric oncology group POG9139–Phase I study of cisplatin and irradiation in brain stem gliomas

U10CA-41573-06 0044 (CCI) SALLAN, STEPHEN E Pediatric oncology group POG9079–Phase I study of L-PAM/CTX with ABM rescue for brain tumors in children

U10CA-41573-06 0045 (CCI) SALLAN, STEPHEN E Pediatric oncology group POG9075–Phase I study of acivicin in children with solid tumors

U10CA-41573-06 0046 (CCI) SALLAN, STEPHEN E Pediatric oncology group POG9074–Phase I study of xomazyme-H65 in children with T-cell ALL/lymphoma

U10CA-41573-06 0047 (CCI) SALLAN, STEPHEN E Pediatric oncology group POG9072–Phase I chemotherapy for recurrent/resistant malignant solid tumors

U10CA-41573-06 0048 (CCI) SALLAN, STEPHEN E Pediatric oncology group POG9061–Phase II systemic therapy and irradiation for ALL & CNS leukemia

U10CA-41573-06 0049 (CCI) SALLAN, STEPHEN E Pediatric oncology group POG 9086–Phase I pilot study of therapy for T-cell ALL or NHL

U10CA-41573-06 0050 (CCI) SALLAN, STEPHEN E Pediatric oncology group POG9071–Phase I trial of fazarabine in children with acute leukemia

U10CA-41573-06 0051 (CCI) SALLAN, STEPHEN E Pediatric oncology group POG8970–Phase I trial of fazarabine in children with refractory solid tumors

U10CA-41573-06 0052 (CCI) SALLAN, STEPHEN E Pediatric oncology group POG8973–Etoposide (VP-16) and carboplatin in children with acute leukemia

U10CA-41573-06 0053 (CCI) SALLAN, STEPHEN E Pediatric oncology group POG8870–Phase I trial of ifosfamide/VP16/MESNA in children with acute leukemia

U10CA-41573-06 0054 (CCI) SALLAN, STEPHEN E Pediatric oncology group POG8871–Phase I study of rTNF in children with refractory solid tumors

U10CA-41573-06 0055 (CCI) SALLAN, STEPHEN E Pediatric oncology group POG8671–Phase I immunotherapy with rIL-2 in children with solid tumors

U10CA-41573-06 0056 (CCI) SALLAN, STEPHEN E Pediatric oncology group POG8494–Phase I study of fludarabine phosphate in pediatric patients

U10CA-41573-06 0057 (CCI) SALLAN, STEPHEN E Pediatric oncology group POG8930–A comprehensive genetic analysis of brain tumors

U10CA-41573-06 0058 (CCI) SALLAN, STEPHEN E Pediatric oncology group POG8828–Late effects of Hodgkin's disease

U10CA-41573-06 0059 (CCI) SALLAN, STEPHEN E Pediatric oncology group POG9046–Molecular genetic analysis of Wilm's tumors

U10CA-41573-06 0060 (CCI) SALLAN, STEPHEN E Pediatric oncology group POG9153–Rhabdomyosarcoma study/laboratory evaluation of tumor

U10CA-41573-06 0025 (CCI) SALLAN, STEPHEN E Pediatric oncology group POG8935–Phase II study of surgery and/or radiotherapy for optic pathway tumors

U10CA-41573-06 0026 (CCI) SALLAN, STEPHEN E Pediatric oncology group POG8820–Phase II/III study of VP-16, AMSA +/- 5-azacytidine in childhood ANLL

U10CA-41573-06 0027 (CCI) SALLAN, STEPHEN E Pediatric oncology group POG8889–Intergroup rhabdomyosarcoma study for clinical group IV disease

U10CA-41573-06 0028 (CCI) SALLAN, STEPHEN E Pediatric oncology group POG8866–Phase II asparaginase therapy for acute lymphoblastic leukemia

R01CA-41579-06 (RNM) GREEN, PHILIP S SRI INTERNATIONAL MENLO PARK, CALIF 94025 Ultrasonic reflex transmission imaging

R01CA-41581-06 (ET) KHOKHAR, ABDUL R M D ANDERSON CANCER CTR 1515 HOLCOMBE BLVD/BOX 052 HOUSTON, TX 77030 Therapeutic index of oncolytic isomeric platinum drugs

R01CA-41582-06 (SSS) KOZIOL, JAMES A SCRIPPS CLINIC & RESEARCH FDN 10666 NORTH TORREY PINES ROAD LA JOLLA, CA 92037 Topics in biostatistics

R01CA-41583-06 (EI) MAYER, LLOYD F MOUNT SINAI HOSPITAL ONE GUSTAVE L LEVY PL NEW YORK, NY 10029 Lymphokine regulation of human B cell maturation

R01CA-41619-04 (EI) RITZ, JEROME DANA-FARBER CANCER INSTITUTE 44 BINNEY STREET BOSTON, MA 02115 Characterization of functional structures on NK cells

PROJECT NO., ORGANIZATIONAL UNIT., INVESTIGATOR, ADDRESS, TITLE

R01CA-41635-04 (RAD) NUSSBAUM, GILBERT H WASHINGTON UNIVERSITY 510 S KINGSHIGHWAY ST LOUIS, MO 63110 Vasodilator-assisted hyperthermia of deep seated tumors

R01CA-41644-06 (PTHB) LE BEAU, MICHELLE M UNIVERSITY OF CHICAGO 5841 S MARYLAND AVE, BOX 420 CHICAGO, IL 60637 Molecular analysis of chromosomal fragile sites

R01CA-41655-07 (BIO) ECHOLS, HARRISON UNIVERSITY OF CALIFORNIA 401 BARKER HALL BERKELEY, CA 94720 Mutagenesis and its control in E coli

U10CA-41721-06 (CCI) DUBOWY, RONALD L SUNY HLTH SCI CTR AT SYRACUSE 750 EAST ADAMS STREET SYRACUSE, NY 13210 Participation in the Pediatric Oncology Group

U10CA-41721-06 0056 (CCI) DUBOWY, RONALD L Participation in the Pediatric Oncology Group POG8494–Phase I study of fludarabine phosphate in pediatric patients

U10CA-41721-06 0057 (CCI) DUBOWY, RONALD L Participation in the Pediatric Oncology Group POG8930–A comprehensive genetic analysis of brain tumors

U10CA-41721-06 0058 (CCI) DUBOWY, RONALD L Participation in the Pediatric Oncology Group POG8828–Late effects of Hodgkin's disease

U10CA-41721-06 0059 (CCI) DUBOWY, RONALD L Participation in the Pediatric Oncology Group POG9046–Molecular genetic analysis of Wilm's tumors

U10CA-41721-06 0060 (CCI) DUBOWY, RONALD L Participation in the Pediatric Oncology Group POG9153–Rhabdomyosarcoma study/laboratory evaluation of tumor

U10CA-41721-06 0001 (CCI) DUBOWY, RONALD L Participation in the Pediatric Oncology Group POG9006–6-MP/methotrexate vs. alternating chemotherapy for ALL in childhood

U10CA-41721-06 0024 (CCI) DUBOWY, RONALD L Participation in the Pediatric Oncology Group POG8936–Phase II study of carboplatin treatment for optic pathway tumors

U10CA-41721-06 0025 (CCI) DUBOWY, RONALD L Participation in the Pediatric Oncology Group POG8935–Phase II study of surgery and/or radiotherapy for optic pathway tumors

U10CA-41721-06 0026 (CCI) DUBOWY, RONALD L Participation in the Pediatric Oncology Group POG8820–Phase II/III study of VP-16, AMSA +/- 5-azacytidine in childhood ANLL

U10CA-41721-06 0002 (CCI) DUBOWY, RONALD L Participation in the Pediatric Oncology Group POG9005–Dose intensification of methotrexate & 6-mercaptourine in childhood ALL

U10CA-41721-06 0003 (CCI) DUBOWY, RONALD L Participation in the Pediatric Oncology Group POG9031–Cisplatin/VP-16 therapy of medulloblastoma/pre vs. post irradiation

U10CA-41721-06 0004 (CCI) DUBOWY, RONALD L Participation in the Pediatric Oncology Group POG8945–Phase III chemotherapy for hepatoblastoma & hepatocellular carcinoma

U10CA-41721-06 0005 (CCI) DUBOWY, RONALD L Participation in the Pediatric Oncology Group POG9049–Phase III study of high-risk malignant germ cell tumors in children

U10CA-41721-06 0006 (CCI) DUBOWY, RONALD L Participation in the Pediatric Oncology Group POG8844–Bone marrow transplant in children with stage D neuroblastoma

U10CA-41721-06 0007 (CCI) DUBOWY, RONALD L Participation in the Pediatric Oncology Group POG8850–Phase III treatment of Ewing's sarcoma and neuroectodermal bone tumors

U10CA-41721-06 0027 (CCI) DUBOWY, RONALD L Participation in the Pediatric Oncology Group POG8889–Intergroup rhabdomyosarcoma study for clinical group IV disease

U10CA-41721-06 0028 (CCI) DUBOWY, RONALD L Participation in the Pediatric Oncology Group POG8866–Phase II asparaginase therapy for acute lymphoblastic leukemia

U10CA-41721-06 0029 (CCI) DUBOWY, RONALD L Participation in the Pediatric Oncology Group POG8862–Combination chemotherapy of acute T-lymphoblastic leukemia

U10CA-41721-06 0030 (CCI) DUBOWY, RONALD L Participation in the Pediatric Oncology Group POG8863–Phase II study of high dose cytosine arabinoside in childhood tumors

U10CA-41721-06 0031 (CCI) DUBOWY, RONALD L Participation in the Pediatric Oncology Group POG8827–Phase II treatment of children with Hodgkin's disease in relapse

U10CA-41721-06 0032 (CCI) DUBOWY, RONALD L Participation in the Pediatric Oncology Group POG8865–Phase II recombinant alpha-interferon in relapsed T-cell disease

U10CA-41721-06 0033 (CCI) DUBOWY, RONALD L Pediatric Oncology Group–Phase II recombinant A-interferon in chronic myelogenous leukemia

U10CA-41721-06 0034 (CCI) DUBOWY, RONALD L Participation in the Pediatric Oncology Group POG8832–Combination chemotherapy followed by radiotherapy for brain tumors

U10CA-41721-06 0035 (CCI) DUBOWY, RONALD L Participation in the Pediatric Oncology Group POG8731–Phase II trial of methotrexate in treatment of brain tumors in children

U10CA-41721-06 0036 (CCI) DUBOWY, RONALD L Participation in the Pediatric Oncology Group POG8788–Intergroup rhabdomyosarcoma study/pilot study for clinical group III

U10CA-41721-06 0037 (CCI) DUBOWY, RONALD L Participation in the Pediatric Oncology Group POG8761–Phase II study of homoharringtonine therapy for nonlymphoblastic leukemi

U10CA-41721-06 0038 (CCI) DUBOWY, RONALD L Participation in the Pediatric Oncology Group POG8739–Phase II immunotherapy with alpha-2 interferon for brain tumors

U10CA-41721-06 0039 (CCI) DUBOWY, RONALD L Participation in the Pediatric Oncology Group POG8741–Treatment of patients with stage C and stage D neuroblastoma

U10CA-41721-06 0040 (CCI) DUBOWY, RONALD L Participation in the Pediatric Oncology Group POG8751–Phase II methotrexate chemotherapy for rhabdomyosarcoma in children

U10CA-41721-06 0041 (CCI) DUBOWY, RONALD L Participation in the Pediatric Oncology Group POG8633–Postoperative chemotherapy and delayed irradiation for brain tumors

U10CA-41721-06 0042 (CCI) DUBOWY, RONALD L Participation in the Pediatric Oncology Group POG8617–Therapy for B-cell acute

lymphoblastic leukemia and lymphoma
U10CA-41721-06 0043 (CCI) DUBOWY, RONALD L Participation in the Pediatric Oncology Group POG9139--Phase I study of cisplatin and irradiation in brain stem gliomas
U10CA-41721-06 0044 (CCI) DUBOWY, RONALD L Participation in the Pediatric Oncology Group POG9079--Phase I study of L-PAM/CTX with ABM rescue for brain tumors in children
U10CA-41721-06 0045 (CCI) DUBOWY, RONALD L Participation in the Pediatric Oncology Group POG9075--Phase I study of acivicin in children with solid tumors
U10CA-41721-06 0046 (CCI) DUBOWY, RONALD L Participation in the Pediatric Oncology Group POG9074--Phase I study of xomazyme-H65 in children with T-cell ALL/lymphoma
U10CA-41721-06 0047 (CCI) DUBOWY, RONALD L Participation in the Pediatric Oncology Group POG9072--Phase I chemotherapy for recurrent/resistant malignant solid tumors
U10CA-41721-06 0048 (CCI) DUBOWY, RONALD L Participation in the Pediatric Oncology Group POG9061-Phase II systemic therapy and irradiation for ALL & CNS leukemia
U10CA-41721-06 0049 (CCI) DUBOWY, RONALD L Participation in the Pediatric Oncology Group POG 9086--Phase I pilot study of therapy for T-cell ALL or NHL
U10CA-41721-06 0050 (CCI) DUBOWY, RONALD L Participation in the Pediatric Oncology Group POG9071--Phase I trial of fazarabine in children with acute leukemia
U10CA-41721-06 0051 (CCI) DUBOWY, RONALD L Participation in the Pediatric Oncology Group POG8970--Phase I trial of fazarabine in children with refractory solid tumors
U10CA-41721-06 0052 (CCI) DUBOWY, RONALD L Participation in the Pediatric Oncology Group POG8973--Etoposide (VP-16) and carboplatin in children with acute leukemia
U10CA-41721-06 0053 (CCI) DUBOWY, RONALD L Participation in the Pediatric Oncology Group POG8870--Phase I trial of ifosfamide/VP16/MESNA in children with acute leukemia
U10CA-41721-06 0054 (CCI) DUBOWY, RONALD L Participation in the Pediatric Oncology Group POG8871--Phase I study of rTNF in children with refractory solid tumors
U10CA-41721-06 0055 (CCI) DUBOWY, RONALD L Participation in the Pediatric Oncology Group POG8671--Phase I immunotherapy with rIL-2 in children with solid tumors
U10CA-41721-06 0008 (CCI) DUBOWY, RONALD L Participation in the Pediatric Oncology Group POG8821--Phase III chemotherapy +/- autologous BMT in children with AML
U10CA-41721-06 0009 (CCI) DUBOWY, RONALD L Participation in the Pediatric Oncology Group POG8725--Phase III chemotherapy +/- radiation therapy in pediatric Hodgkins
U10CA-41721-06 0010 (CCI) DUBOWY, RONALD L Participation in the Pediatric Oncology Group POG8704--Phase III chemotherapy of childhood T cell ALL & lymphoblastic lymphoma
U10CA-41721-06 0011 (CCI) DUBOWY, RONALD L Participation in the Pediatric Oncology Group POG8719--Phase III chemotherapy for non-Hodgkin's lymphoma in children
U10CA-41721-06 0012 (CCI) DUBOWY, RONALD L Participation in the Pediatric Oncology Group POG8650--National Wilm's tumor and clear cell sarcoma study
U10CA-41721-06 0013 (CCI) DUBOWY, RONALD L Participation in the Pediatric Oncology Group POG8616--Phase III chemotherapy for childhood Burkitt and non-Burkitts lymphoma
U10CA-41721-06 0014 (CCI) DUBOWY, RONALD L Participation in the Pediatric Oncology Group POG8615--Phase III study of large cell lymphomas in children and adolescents
U10CA-41721-06 0015 (CCI) DUBOWY, RONALD L Participation in the Pediatric Oncology Group POG8651--Phase III study of childhood nonmetastatic osteosarcoma
U10CA-41721-06 0016 (CCI) DUBOWY, RONALD L Participation in the Pediatric Oncology Group POG8653--Phase III study of childhood soft tissue sarcomas
U10CA-41721-06 0017 (CCI) DUBOWY, RONALD L Participation in the Pediatric Oncology Group POG8625--Phase III combined therapy in childhood Hodgkin's disease
U10CA-41721-06 0018 (CCI) DUBOWY, RONALD L Participation in the Pediatric Oncology Group POG8451--Intergroup rhabdomyosarcoma study
U10CA-41721-06 0019 (CCI) DUBOWY, RONALD L Participation in the Pediatric Oncology Group POG9110--Rotational drug therapy after first marrow relapse of non-T, non B ALL
U10CA-41721-06 0020 (CCI) DUBOWY, RONALD L Participation in the Pediatric Oncology Group POG9107--Phase II pilot study of infant leukemia
U10CA-41721-06 0021 (CCI) DUBOWY, RONALD L Participation in the Pediatric Oncology Group POG9140--Phase II therapy for recurrent or refractory neuroblastoma
U10CA-41721-06 0022 (CCI) DUBOWY, RONALD L Participation in the Pediatric Oncology Group POG9048--Phase II study of malignant germ cell tumors in children
U10CA-41721-06 0023 (CCI) DUBOWY, RONALD L Participation in the Pediatric Oncology Group POG9060--Intensive QOD ifosfamide treatment for CNS tumors in children
R01CA-41722-05 (HUD) EVANS, RICHARD I UNIVERSITY OF HOUSTON HOUSTON, TX 77204-5341 Teenage smokeless tobacco use--Process/prevention
R01CA-41733-05S1 (SSS) D'ONOFRIO, CAROL N UNIV OF CALIFORNIA, BERKELEY 519 WARREN HALL BERKELEY, CALIF 94720 Curtailing the use of smokeless tobacco through 4-H
R01CA-41740-07 (HEM) CHITAMBAR, CHRISTOPHER R MILWAUKEE COUNTY MED COMPLEX 8700 W WISCONSIN AVENUE MILWAUKEE, WI 53226 Cellular uptake and interaction of gallium and iron
R01CA-41746-06 (ET) MURPHY, JOHN R UNIVERSITY HOSPITAL 88 EAST NEWTON STREET BOSTON, MA 02118 Diphtheria toxin-related peptide hormone gene fusions
R29CA-41757-05 (BIO) FEUERSTEIN, BURT G UNIVERSITY OF CALIFORNIA SAN FRANCISCO, CA 94143-0134 Rational development of polyamine analogues
R01CA-41829-07 (END) STEIN, JOSEPH P SUNY HLTH SCI CTR AT SYRACUSE 766 IRVING AVENUE SYRACUSE, NY 13210 Retinoid regulation of gene expression
R01CA-41843-04A2 (ET) BRANDA, RICHARD F GENETICS LABORATORY 32 NORTH PROSPECT ST BURLINGTON, VT 05401 Effect of folate on chromosomes in breast cancer
R44CA-41846-03 (SSS) MILLER, RICHARD A IDEC PHARMACEUTICALS CORPORATI 291 N BERNARDO AVENUE MOUNTAIN VIEW, CA 94043 Shared tumor idiotopes of B cell neoplasms
R01CA-41982-06 (IMB) KUNG, JOHN T UNIVERSITY OF TEXAS 7703 FLOYD CURL DRIVE SAN ANTONIO, TEX 78284 Immune functions of Il-2 on cytotoxic T cell precursors
R01CA-41986-08 (BNP) BOGER, DALE L RESEARCH INST OF SCRIPPS CLINI 10666 NORTH TORREY PINES ROAD LA JOLLA, CA 92037 Antitumor antibiotics: cc-1065 and bleomycins
R01CA-41991-07 (BIO) SHANE, BARRY UNIVERSITY OF CALIFORNIA 119 MORGAN HALL BERKELEY, CA 94720 Regulation of folylpolyglutamate synthesis
R01CA-41993-05 (IMB) WEBB, SUSAN R RESEARCH INST OF SCRIPPS CLINI 10666 NORTH TORREY PINES ROAD LA JOLLA, CA 92037 Immunobiology of Mls responses
R01CA-41996-07 (BIO) TAMANOI, FUYUHIKO UNIVERSITY OF CHICAGO 920 EAST 58TH STREET CHICAGO, IL 60637 Structural and functional analyses of yeast ras proteins
R01CA-41997-07 (EI) O'DORISIO, MARY S CHILDREN'S HOSPITAL RES FDN 700 CHILDREN'S DRIVE COLUMBUS, OH 43205 Immune effector vasoactive intestinal peptide receptors
R01CA-42003-08 (AR) ALTMAN, NORMAN H UNIV OF MIAMI SCH OF MEDICINE PO BOX 016960 MIAMI, FL 33101 Production of rats with isologously transplanted r3327
R01CA-42006-06 (IMS) CHOI, YONG S ALTON OCHSNER MEDICAL FOUNDATI 1516 JEFFERSON HIGHWAY NEW ORLEANS, LA 70121 Human B-cell growth factors
R01CA-42009-05 (REN) BOLANDER, FRANKLYN F, JR UNIVERSITY OF SOUTH CAROLINA COLUMBIA, SC 29208 MMTV regulation in normal mouse mammary epithelium
P30CA-42014-06 (CCS) STEWART, J ROBERT UNIVERSITY OF UTAH 2C110 MEDICAL CENTER SALT LAKE CITY, UT 84132 Utah regional cancer center
P30CA-42014-06 9001 (CCS) DETHLEFSEN, LYLE A Utah regional cancer center Cell analysis center
P30CA-42014-06 9002 (CCS) WHITE, RAYMOND L Utah regional cancer center DNA / peptide facility
P30CA-42014-06 9003 (CCS) WHITE, RAYMOND L Utah regional cancer center UTAH population data base--Core
P30CA-42014-06 9005 (CCS) DEWITT, CHARLES W Utah regional cancer center Inbred rodent facility--Core
P30CA-42014-06 9007 (CCS) EGGER, MARLENE J Utah regional cancer center Biostatistical core resources
P30CA-42014-06 9008 (CCS) EYRE, HARMON T Utah regional cancer center Clinical research support service--core
P30CA-42014-06 9009 (CCS) STEWART, J ROBERT Utah regional cancer center Development funds--Core
P30CA-42014-06 9010 (CCS) MCWHORTER, WILLIAM P. Utah regional cancer center Utah cancer registry--Core
P30CA-42014-06 9011 (CCS) MCCLOSKEY, JAMES A. Utah regional cancer center Mass and NMR spectroscopy
R37CA-42024-07 (CPA) FAHL, WILLIAM E UNIVERSITY OF WISCONSIN-MADISO 1400 UNIVERSITY AVENUE MADISON, WI 53706 Carcinogen-transformed human cells--Genetic traits
R01CA-42026-07 (RAD) ILIAKIS, GEORGE THOMAS JEFFERSON UNIV HOSPITAL 11TH AND WALNUT STREET PHILADELPHIA, PA 19107 Has cellular repair a common molecular base?
R01CA-42031-07 (MCHA) HOLTON, ROBERT A FLORIDA STATE UNIVERSITY TALLAHASSEE, FL 32306 Total synthesis of antitumor taxanes
R01CA-42032-07 (PBC) DAMSKY, CAROLINE H UNIVERSITY OF CALIFORNIA SAN FRANCISCO, CA 94143-0515 Cytoskeleton-membrane interactions--Antiserum induced changes
P01CA-42045-06 (SRC) KROHN, KENNETH A UNIVERSITY OF WASHINGTON SCHOOL OF MEDICINE, RC-05 SEATTLE, WA 98195 Metabolic imaging of cancer and its response to therapy
P01CA-42045-06 0001 (SRC) SPENCE, ALEXANDER M Metabolic imaging of cancer and its response to therapy Metabolic imaging of malignant glioma
P01CA-42045-06 0003 (SRC) SHIELDS, ANTHONY F Metabolic imaging of cancer and its response to therapy Metabolic measurement in lymphoma treated with chemotherapy
P01CA-42045-06 0004 (SRC) GRAHAM, MICHAEL M Metabolic imaging of cancer and its response to therapy Vascular permeability in tumor and normal tissue
P01CA-42045-06 0006 (SRC) RASEY, JANET S Metabolic imaging of cancer and its response to therapy Imaging hypoxia in tumors and normal tissue
P01CA-42045-06 0007 (SRC) KROHN, KENNETH A Metabolic imaging of cancer and its response to therapy Mapping oxidation-reduction status of tumors--Response to therapy
P01CA-42045-06 0008 (SRC) HAYNOR, DAVID R Metabolic imaging of cancer and its response to therapy Chemical shift imaging in human tumors
P01CA-42045-06 9001 (SRC) KROHN, KENNETH A Metabolic imaging of cancer and its response to therapy Core--Radiochemistry
P01CA-42045-06 9002 (SRC) LEWELLEN, THOMAS K Metabolic imaging of cancer and its response to therapy Core--Physics support for the PET
P01CA-42045-06 9003 (SRC) BASSINGTHWAIGHTE, JAMES B Metabolic imaging of cancer and its response to therapy Core--Modeling in experiment design and analysis
P01CA-42045-06 9004 (SRC) GRAHAM, MICHAEL M Metabolic imaging of cancer and its response to therapy Core--Tomography facility
P01CA-42045-06 9005 (SRC) SHUMAN, WILLIAM P Metabolic imaging of cancer and its response to therapy Core--NMR
P01CA-42045-06 9007 (SRC) MODELL, HAROLD I Metabolic imaging of cancer and its response to therapy Core--animal support
R01CA-42046-06 (EI) POSNETT, DAVID N CORNELL UNIVERSITY MED COLLEGE 515 EAST 71 STREET NEW YORK, NY 10021 T cell leukemia and the human T cell antigen receptor

R01CA-42049-08 (IMB) **MARCHALONIS, JOHN J** UNIVERSITY OF ARIZONA 1501 N CAMPBELL AVENUE TUCSON, AZ 85724 Immunoglobulin-related T lymphocyte surface receptors

R01CA-42056-08 (MCHA) **BOGER, DALE L** RES INST OF SCRIPPS CLINIC 10666 NORTH TORREY PINES RD LA JOLLA, CA 92037 Antitumor-antibiotics

R37CA-42060-07 (EI) **MENDELSOHN, JOHN** SLOAN KETTERING INSTITUTE 1275 YORK AVENUE NEW YORK, NY 10021 Antitumor activities of antireceptor antibodies

P01CA-42063-06 (SRC) **SHARP, PHILLIP A** MASSACHUSETTS INST OF TECHNOLO 77 MASSACHUSETTS AVENUE CAMBRIDGE, MA 02139 Expression by oncogenes and anti-oncogenes

P01CA-42063-06 0002 (SRC) **HOUSMAN, DAVID** Expression by oncogenes and anti-oncogenes Molecular genetics of Wilms' Tumor

P01CA-42063-06 0004 (SRC) **COCHRAN, BRENT H** Expression by oncogenes and anti-oncogenes Molecular analysis of the sis/PDGF inducible factor

P01CA-42063-06 0005 (SRC) **RULEY, HENRY E** Expression by oncogenes and anti-oncogenes Use of retrovirus promoter trap vectors to identify oncogenes and anti-oncogenes

P01CA-42063-06 0006 (SRC) **SHARP, PHILLIP A** Expression by oncogenes and anti-oncogenes Transcription regulation by oncogenes

P01CA-42063-06 9001 (SRC) **SHARP, PHILLIP A** Expression by oncogenes and anti-oncogenes Core

R01CA-42091-04A2 (END) **HARRISON, ROBERT W** UNIV OF ARKANSAS FOR MED SCIS 4301 WEST MARKHAM STREET LITTLE ROCK, AR 72205 Physiology of pituitary cell glucocorticoid binding

P01CA-42101-06 (SRC) **SARTORELLI, ALAN C** YALE UNIV SCHOOL OF MEDICINE 333 CEDAR STREET NEW HAVEN, CT 06510 Cancer control research unit

P01CA-42101-06 0001 (SRC) **JANERICH, DWIGHT T** Cancer control research unit Improving early detection of cervical cancer

P01CA-42101-06 0003 (SRC) **KASL, STANISLAV V** Cancer control research unit Effects of race and social factors on stage at diagnosis

P01CA-42101-06 0004 (SRC) **THOMPSON,W DOUGLAS** Cancer control research unit Interventions to improve use of breast cancer screening

P01CA-42101-06 0005 (SRC) **THOMPSON, W DOUGLAS** Cancer control research unit Case-control study of lethal melanoma and skin examination

P01CA-42101-06 0007 (SRC) **POLEDNAK, ANTHONY P** Cancer control research unit Cancer in Hispanics in Connecticut and Long Island

P01CA-42101-06 0008 (SRC) **DUBROW, ROBERT** Cancer control research unit Risk profile for colorectal adenomatous polyps

P01CA-42101-06 0009 (SRC) **THOMPSON, W DOUGLAS** Cancer control research unit Frequency of mammography and death due to breast cancer

P01CA-42101-06 0010 (SRC) **GOODWIN, W JARRAD** Cancer control research unit Beta-carotene chemoprevention in early head and neck cancer

P01CA-42101-06 0011 (SRC) **SALOVEY, PETER** Cancer control research unit Cognitive & affective influences on perceptions of cancer risk & vulnerability

P01CA-42101-06 0012 (SRC) **BERKMAN, LISA** Cancer control research unit Premorbid predictors of cancer, stage at diagnosis, therapy, mortality in elderly

P01CA-42101-06 9001 (SRC) **MORRA, MARION** Cancer control research unit Core--Field applications

P01CA-42101-06 9003 (SRC) **FLANNERY, JOHN T** Cancer control research unit Core--Cancer control surveillance in Connecticut tumor registry

R01CA-42103-04A1 (ET) **GORDON, JON W** MT SINAI SCHOOL OF MEDICINE 1 GUSTAVE L LEVY PLACE NEW YORK, NY 10029 Cancer chemotherapy in transgenic rats and mice

R35CA-42107-05 (SRC) **FIDLER, ISAIAH J** THE UNIV OF TEXAS M D A C CTR 1515 HOLCOMBE BLVD HOUSTON, TX 77030 Human cancer metastasis--Biology and treatment

R01CA-42129-06 (EVR) **PINTER, ABRAHAM** PUBLIC HEALTH RESEARCH INST 455 FIRST AVENUE NEW YORK, N Y 10016 Biochemical and genetic studies of MuLV env proteins

R01CA-42157-06 (CPA) **CONTI, CLAUDIO J** UNIV OF TX M D ANDERSON CA CTR SCIENCE PARK RESEARCH DIV HOUSTON, TX 77030 Chromosome alteration during chemical carcinogenesis

R01CA-42165-04A1 (RNM) **KING, MICHAEL A** UNIV OF MASS MED SCHOOL 55 LAKE AVENUE NORTH WORCESTER, MA 01655 Digital restoration and quantitation of SPECT images

R01CA-42167-07 (RAD) **HELD, KATHRYN D** MASSACHUSETTS GENERAL HOSPITAL FRUIT STREET BOSTON, MA 02114 Mechanisms of radioprotection and toxicity of SH compounds

R01CA-42179-06 (RNM) **HEINEMAN, WILLIAM R** UNIVERSITY OF CINCINNATI BIOMEDICAL CHEMISTRY RES CTR CINCINNATI, OH 45221-0172 99m-Tc brain imaging agents for use with SPECT

R01CA-42211-05 (CPA) **FISCHER, SUSAN M** UNIVERSITY OF TEXAS P O BOX 389 SMITHVILLE, TX 78957 Tumor promoter-induced oxidants from epidermal cells

R01CA-42229-04 (CBY) **MOSCATELLI, DAVID A** NEW YORK UNIVERSITY MED CTR 550 FIRST AVENUE NEW YORK, NY 10016 Fibroblast growth factor-FGF receptor interactions

R35CA-42232-06 (SRC) **NOWELL, PETER C** UNIVERSITY OF PENNSYLVANIA SCHOOL OF MEDICINE PHILADELPHIA, PA19101-3246 Studies of neoplastic and normal leukocytes

R01CA-42239-06 (CPA) **BOWDEN, GEORGE T** UNIVERSITY OF ARIZONA MED SCHO 1501 N CAMPBELL AVE TUCSON, AZ 85724 Radiation induced skin tumors and oncogene activation

R01CA-42245-06 (EVR) **HAYWARD, S DIANE** JOHNS HOPKINS UNIVERSITY 600 N WOLFE STREET BALTIMORE, MD 21205 Regulation of replication and latency by EBV EBNA-1

R01CA-42246-06 (EI) **TODD, ROBERT F, III** UNIV OF MICHIGAN/SIMPSON INST 102 OBSERVATORY DR/INT MED ANN ARBOR, MI 48109 Human macrophage activation antigens

R01CA-42275-05 (CBY) **MCNEIL, PAUL L** HARVARD MEDICAL SCHOOL 220 LONGWOOD AVENUE BOSTON, MA 02115 Activation of quiescent cells in vitro and in vivo

R01CA-42276-06 (EI) **MERCURIO, ARTHUR M** NEW ENGLAND DEACONESS HOSPITAL 185 PILGRIM ROAD BOSTON, MA 02215 Glycoconjugates and macrophage-tumor cell interactions

R01CA-42278-06 (RAD) **HENDERSON, BARBARA W** ROSWELL PARK MEMORIAL INSTITUT 666 ELM STREET Oxygen and light dependency of photodynamic therapy

PROJECT NO., ORGANIZATIONAL UNIT., INVESTIGATOR, ADDRESS, TITLE

R01CA-42286-04A2 (ET) **POWIS, GARTH** MAYO FOUNDATION 200 FIRST STREET SOUTHWEST Intracellular free Ca2+ and anticancer drug action

R01CA-42300-06 (ET) **BEARDSLEY, GEORGE P** YALE UNIVERSITY SCH OF MEDICIN 333 CEDAR STREET NEW HAVEN, CT 06510 Molecular studies DNA structural lesions

R01CA-42302-06 (PTHB) **OSHIMA, ROBERT G** LA JOLLA CANCER RESEARCH FDN 10901 NORTH TORREY PINES ROAD LA JOLLA, CA 92037 Early development control of human and mouse cytokeratin

R01CA-42324-06 (RNM) **ZALUTSKY, MICHAEL R** DUKE UNIVERSITY P O BOX 3808 DURHAM, NC 27710 Astatine and iodine radiolabeled monoclonal antibodies

R01CA-42325-07 (ET) **MULCAHY, R TIMOTHY** UNIVERSITY OF WISCONSIN 600 HIGHLAND AVENUE MADISON, WI 53792 Radiation sensitizers--interactions with other modalities

U10CA-42326-07 (CCI) **GREEN, DANIEL M** ROSWELL PARK CANCER INSTITUTE ELM AND CARLTON STREETS BUFFALO, N Y 14263 National Wilms' tumor study-4

R01CA-42329-05 (RNM) **WONG, JEFFERY Y C** CITY OF HOPE NATIONAL MED CTR 1500 E DUARTE RD DUARTE, CA 91010 Innovative immunoimaging for presurgical cancer staging

R01CA-42350-06 (VR) **SEFTON, BARTHOLOMEW M** SALK INST FOR BIOLOGICAL STUDI PO BOX 85800 SAN DIEGO, CA 92138 Thymoma tyrosine protein kinase

R01CA-42352-05S1 (MEP) **AUSMAN, LYNNE M** TUFTS UNIVERSITY MEDFORD, MA 02155 Nutritional influences on colon cancer

R01CA-42354-05 (ET) **MAXWELL, IAN H** 4200 EAST 9TH AVENUE DENVER, CO 80262 Tumor cell killing by expression of a toxin gene

R01CA-42357-05 (EVR) **SCHNEIDER, ROBERT J** NEW YORK UNIV MEDICAL CENTER 550 FIRST AVENUE NEW YORK, NY 10016 Translational regulation of adenovirus gene expression

R01CA-42361-06 (EI) **LADISCH, STEPHAN K** CHILDREN'S RESEARCH INSTITUTE 111 MICHIGAN AVE, N.W. WASHINGTON, DC 20010 Immunosuppressive neuroblastoma tumor gangliosides

R01CA-42367-06 (ET) **TAYLOR, EDWARD C** PRINCETON UNIVERSITY DEPARTMENT OF CHEMISTRY PRINCETON, NJ 08544 Design and synthesis of antitumor dideaza tetrahydrofolic acid analogs

R01CA-42368-06 (PBC) **HEMLER, MARTIN E** DANA-FARBER CANCER INSTITUTE 44 BINNEY STREET, MAYER 613 BOSTON, MA 02115 novel adhesion proteins in the VLA family

R01CA-42381-05 (MEP) **WEISBURGER, JOHN H** AMERICAN HEALTH FOUNDATION ONE DANA RD VALHALLA, NY 10595 Metabolism of the carcinogen aminomethylimidazoquinoline

R01CA-42385-06 (BIO) **KOLESNICK, RICHARD N** SLOAN-KETTERING INST/CNCR RES 1275 YORK AVENUE NEW YORK, NY 10021 Mechanism of phorbol ester-induced lipid metabolism

R01CA-42391-06A1 (ET) **COLEMAN, C NORMAN** JOINT CENTER FOR RADIATION 50 BINNEY STREET Chemical modifiers of radiation and chemotherapy

R01CA-42409-07 (CBY) **SHIPLEY, GARY D** OREGON HEALTH SCIENCES UNIV 3181 SW SAM JACKSON PARK ROAD PORTLAND, OR 97201 Fibroblast growth factor and neoplastic transformation

R01CA-42414-06 (EVR) **BOTCHAN, MICHAEL R** UNIVERSITY OF CALIFORNIA MOLECULAR AND CELL BIOLOGY BERKELEY, CA 94720 Bovine papilloma virus--model systems

R01CA-42426-05 (BIO) **SADLER, SUSAN E** UNIVERSITY OF DENVER UNIVERSITY PARK DENVER, CO 80208 Regulation of cAMP levels in xenopus oocytes

R01CA-42439-06 (ET) **THOMAS, THRESIA** U OF MED/DENT OF NJ-RW JOHNSON 675 HOES LANE PISCATAWAY, NJ 08854-5635 Role of polyamines in estrogen function in breast cancer

R01CA-42448-05 (CPA) **LISTOWSKY, IRVING** ALBERT EINSTEIN COLLEGE OF MED 1300 MORRIS PARK AVENUE BRONX, N Y 10461 High affinity high capacity steroid and carcinogen binder

R01CA-42453-05 (RNM) **BERBAUM, KEVIN S** UNIVERSITY OF IOWA IOWA CITY, IA 52242 Satisfaction of search in diagnostic radiology

R01CA-42460-08 (VR) **COURTNEY, RICHARD J** PA ST UNIV COLL OF MD P.O. BOX 850 HERSHEY, PA 17033 Studies of purified herpes simplex virus glycoproteins

R01CA-42465-04A2 (MEP) **MEADOWS, GARY G** WASHINGTON STATE UNIVERSITY COLLEGE OF PHARMACY PULLMAN, WA 99164-6510 Mechanism of dietary modulation of metastasis

R01CA-42471-06 (IMB) **RAO, ANJANA** DANA-FARBER CANCER INSTITUTE 44 BINNEY STREET BOSTON, MA 02115 Role of myc and fos oncogenes in lymphocyte growth

R01CA-42476-06 (ET) **CHAN, PUI-KWONG** BAYLOR COLLEGE OF MEDICINE ONE BAYLOR PLAZA HOUSTON, TEX 77030 Drug effects on functions of phosphoprotein B23

R01CA-42486-06 (PBC) **HART, GERALD W** JOHNS HOPKINS UNIV SCH OF MED BIOCHEM DEP 725 N WOLFE ST BALTIMORE, MD 21205 Role of cell-surface glycosylation in tumor metastasis

R01CA-42500-05A2 (CPA) **PINCUS, MATTHEW R** SUNY/HEALTH SCIENCE CENTER 750 EAST ADAMS STREET SYRACUSE, NY 13210 Protein structure and oncogenesis

R35CA-42504-06 (SRC) **EISEN, HERMAN N** M I T DEPARTMENT OF BIOLOGY 77 MASSACHUSETTS AVENUE CAMBRIDGE, MA 02139 Reactions of cytotoxic T lymphocytes with target cells

R35CA-42505-07 **HAKOMORI, SEN-ITIROH** BIOMEMBRANE INSTITUTE 201 ELLIOTT AVE W, SUITE 305 SEATTLE, WA 98119 Glycolipids in differentation and oncogenesis

R35CA-42506-06 (SRC) **WEINTRAUB, HAROLD M** FRED HUTCHINSON CANCER RES CTR 1124 COLUMBIA STREET SEATTLE, WA 98104 Generation of development mutants with cloned DNA vector

R35CA-42507-06 (SRC) **RUOSLAHTI, ERKKI I** LA JOLLA CANCER RES FOUNDATION 10901 NORTH TORREY PINES ROAD LA JOLLA, CA 92037 Molecular mechanisms of cell adhesion

R35CA-42508-06 (SRC) **REISFELD, RALPH A** SCRIPPS CLINIC & RESEARCH FDN 10666 N TORREY PINES RD LA JOLLA, CALIF 92037 Molecular profile of melanoma and neuroblastoma antigen

R35CA-42509-06 (SRC) **HERZENBERG, LEONARD A** STANFORD UNIVERSITY DEPARTMENT OF GENETICS STANFORD, CA 94305 Genetics of immunoglobulins and lymphocyte molecules

R35CA-42510-06 (SRC) **WEBER, GEORGE** INDIANA UNIVERSITY SCH OF MED 702 BARNHILL DRIVE INDIANAPOLIS, IN 46202-5200 Enzyme pattern-targeted chemotherapy

R35CA-42517-06 (SRC) **WIED, GEORGE L** UNIVERSITY OF CHICAGO 5841 SOUTH MARYLAND AVENUE CHICAGO, ILL 60637 Computer-based expert system for cervical cytology

R01CA-42520-05 (HEM) **ELIAS, LAURENCE** UNIVERSITY OF NEW MEXICO 900 CAMINO DE SALUD NE ALBUQUERQUE, NM 87131 Mn+2-phospholipid stimulated protein kinase and leukemic differentiation

R01CA-42522-04A1 (ET) **WEI, WEI-ZEN** MICHIGAN CANCER FOUNDATION 110 EAST WARREN AVENUE DETROIT, MI 48201-1379 Immunomodulation of mouse mammary neoplastic progression

R01CA-42533-06 (HEM) **KRAFT, ANDREW S** UNIV OF ALABAMA DIV OF HEMATOLOGY/ONCOLOGY BIRMINGHAM, AL 35294 Control of differentiation of human promyelocytes

R35CA-42542-06 (SRC) **SUMMERS, JESSE W** UNIVERSITY OF NEW MEXICO ALBUQUERQUE, N MEX 87131 Persistent infections by hepadnaviruses

R35CA-42551-06 (SRC) **WEISSMAN, IRVING L** STANFORD UNIVERSITY STANFORD, CA 94305 Normal and neoplastic lymphocyte maturation

R35CA-42556-06 (SRC) **WEISSMAN, SHERMAN M** YALE UNIVERSITY SCH OF MED 333 CEDAR ST-PO BOX 3333 NEW HAVEN, CT 06510 Molecular genetics of cancer and the immune system

R35CA-42557-06 (SRC) **ROWLEY, JANET D** UNIVERSITY OF CHICAGO BOX 420 Chromosome abnormalities and human leukemia and lymphoma

R35CA-42560-06 (SRC) **MINTZ, BEATRICE** INSTITUTE FOR CANCER RESEARCH 7701 BURHOLME AVENUE PHILADELPHIA, PA 19111 Development vs neoplastic proliferation of stem cells

R35CA-42564-06 (SRC) **VOGT, PETER K** UNIV OF SOUTHERN CALIFORNIA 2011 ZONAL AVENUE, HMR 401 LOS ANGELES, CA 90033-1054 Onc genes in virus and cell

R35CA-42567-06 (SRC) **ROEDER, ROBERT G** ROCKEFELLER UNIVERSITY 1230 YORK AVENUE NEW YORK, NY 10021-6399 Molecular basis of cell growth and transformation

R35CA-42568-06 (SRC) **BASILICO, CLAUDIO** NEW YORK UNIV MEDICAL CENTER 550 FIRST AVENUE NEW YORK, N Y 10016 Viral and cellular gene expression and growth regulation

R01CA-42571-07 (EI) **ST JOHN, THOS P** ICOS CORPORATION 22021 - 20TH AVENUE SE BOTHELL, WA 98021 Homing receptor gene expression in lymphoid tumors

R35CA-42572-06 (SRC) **MOSES, HAROLD L** VANDERBILT UNIVERSITY SCHOOL O DEPARTMENT OF CELL BIOLOGY NASHVILLE, TN 37232 Transforming growth factors in neoplastic transformation

R01CA-42573-06 (EVR) **HAYMAN, MICHAEL J** STATE UNIVERSITY OF NEW YORK SCHOOL OF MEDICINE STONY BROOK, NY 11794-8621 Interaction of oncogenes with avian erythroid cells

R35CA-42580-06 (SRC) **ERIKSON, RAYMOND L** HARVARD UNIVERSITY 16 DIVINITY AVENUE CAMBRIDGE, MA 02138 Biochemistry of the cancer cell

R35CA-42581-06 (SRC) **MACK, THOMAS M** UNIV OF SOUTHERN CALIFORNIA 2025 ZONAL AVENUE LOS ANGELES, CA 90033 Epidemiologic research in cancer etiology

R01CA-42585-05 (MEP) **VERMA, AJIT K** U OF WISCONSIN-CLINICAL SCI CT 600 HIGHLAND AVE-RM K4/532 MADISON, WI 53792 Inhibition of ornithine decarboxylase by retinoic acid

R01CA-42593-05 (RNM) **LEWELLEN, THOMAS K** UNIVERSITY OF WASHINGTON SEATTLE, WA 98195 Simulation system for emission tomography

R01CA-42595-06 (BIO) **MILLAN, JOSE L** LA JOLLA CANCER RES FOUNDATION 10901 N. TORREY PINES ROAD LA JOLLA, CA 92037 Cancer-related placental-type alkaline phosphatases

R01CA-42596-05 (RAD) **WEICHSELBAUM, RALPH R** UNIVERSITY OF CHICAGO 5841 S MARYLAND AVE, BOX 442 CHICAGO, IL 60637 Assays of tumor response to radiotherapy

R01CA-42605-06A1 (BIO) **CARADONNA, SALVATORE J** UNIV OF MED & DENT OF NJ 401 S CENTRAL PLAZA STRATFORD, NEW JERSEY 08084 Genetics and enzymology of human DNA repair

R01CA-42607-06 (RAD) **DOETSCH, PAUL W** EMORY UNIVERSITY WOODRUFF MEMORIAL BLDG ATLANTA, GA 30322 Repair of oxidative and radiation-induced DNA damage

R44CA-42615-03 (SSS) **SIMS, COLIN** DYNAMIC DIGITAL DISPLAYS, INC 130 RADNOR-CHESTER RD #100 ST. DAVIDS, PA 19087 Real-time 3D visualization for radiotherapy planning

R01CA-42633-06 (RAD) **UCKUN, FATIH M** UNIV OF MINNESOTA HEALTH CTR HARVARD ST @ E RIVER RD/BX 356 MINNEAPOLIS, MN 55455 Biological and physical factors in TBI

R01CA-42664-07 (HEM) **MILLER, DONALD M** 1918 UNIVERSITY BLVD BHSB 288 BIRMINGHAM, AL 35294 In vivo and in vitro differentiation of leukemic cells

R44CA-42670-03 (SSS) **GUIRE, PATRICK E** 9924 WEST 74TH STREET Immobilization of biomolecules

P01CA-42710-06A1 (SRC) **HEBER, DAVID** UCLA-DIV OF CLINICAL NUTRITION 1000 VETERAN AVE-REHAB CTR A1- LOS ANGELES, CA 90024-1742 The UCLA clinical nutrition research unit

P01CA-42710-06A1 0001 (SRC) **MILLER, CARL W** The UCLA clinical nutrition research unit Vitamin D effect on leukemic cells--Molecular analysis

P01CA-42710-06A1 9002 (SRC) **HEBER, DAVID** The UCLA clinical nutrition research unit Lipid/hormone core

P01CA-42710-06A1 9003 (SRC) **SWENDSEID, MARIAN E** The UCLA clinical nutrition research unit Vitamin/trace element core

P01CA-42710-06A1 9004 (SRC) **BRASEL, JO ANNE** The UCLA clinical nutrition research unit Stable isotope core

P01CA-42710-06A1 9006 (SRC) **KOEFFLER, H PHILIP** The UCLA clinical nutrition research unit Cellular and molecular biology core

P01CA-42710-06A1 9007 (SRC) **ECKHERT, CURTIS** The UCLA clinical nutrition research unit Nutrition education core

P01CA-42710-06A1 9008 (SRC) **ELASHOFF, ROBERT** The UCLA clinical nutrition research unit Statistical coordinating core

R01CA-42713-07 (CBY) **PLEDGER, WARREN J** VANDERBILT UNIVERSITY SCHOOL OF MEDICINE NASHVILLE, TN 37232 Regulation of the mammalian cell cycle

R01CA-42714-06 (PTHB) **HIXSON, DOUGLAS C** RHODE ISLAND HOSPITAL 593 EDDY STREET PROVIDENCE, RI 02903 Molecular determinants of multicellular organization

R01CA-42715-06 (PTHB) **HIXSON, DOUGLAS C** RHODE ISLAND HOSPITAL 593 EDDY STREET PROVIDENCE, RI 02902 Cellular origins of liver cancer

PROJECT NO., ORGANIZATIONAL UNIT., INVESTIGATOR, ADDRESS, TITLE

R01CA-42730-07 (BEM) **POMERLEAU, OVIDE F** UNIVERSITY OF MICHIGAN 900 WALL STREET ANN ARBOR, MI 48105 Smoking and the effects of nicotine in women

R01CA-42735-06 (IMB) **CLEMENT, LORAN T** UNIVERSITY OF CALIFORNIA LOS ANGELES, CA 90024-1752 Ontogeny and functions of human helper T cell subsets

R01CA-42736-07 (CPA) **SINGER, BEA A** LAWRENCE BERKELEY LABORATORY UNIVERSITY OF CALIFORNIA BERKELEY, CALIF 94720 Alkylation of polynucleotides in vitro in vivo

R01CA-42739-06 (IMB) **PHIPPS, RICHARD P** UNIV OF ROCHESTER SCH OF MED 601 ELMWOOD AVE BX 704 CAN CTR ROCHESTER, NY 14642 accessory cell modulation of B cell tolerance

R37CA-42742-07 (CBY) **MATSUMURA, FUMIO** NELSON LABS/BUSCH CAMPUS P.O. BOX 1059 PISCATAWAY, NJ 08855-1059 Microfilament organization

P01CA-42745-05 (SRC) **DEWHIRST, MARK W** DUKE UNIVERSITY MEDICAL CTR PO BOX 3455 DURHAM, NC 27710 Hyperthermia and perfusion effects in cancer therapy

P01CA-42745-05 0001 (SRC) **THRALL, DONALD W** Hyperthermia and perfusion effects in cancer therapy Whole body and local hyperthermia in malignancies

P01CA-42745-05 0002 (SRC) **PAGE, RODNEYES E** Hyperthermia and perfusion effects in cancer therapy Hyperthermia and platinum compounds in dogs

P01CA-42745-05 0003 (SRC) **OLSEN, JAMES R** Hyperthermia and perfusion effects in cancer therapy Regional/local/interstitial heat plus XRT

P01CA-42745-05 0004 (SRC) **CLEGG, SCOTT** Hyperthermia and perfusion effects in cancer therapy Full thermal modeling

P01CA-42745-05 0005 (SRC) **SOSTMAN, DIRK** Hyperthermia and perfusion effects in cancer therapy MRI and MRS in clinical hyperthermia--Radiation therapy of sarcoma

P01CA-42745-05 9002 (SRC) **THRALL, DONALD E** Hyperthermia and perfusion effects in cancer therapy Animal core

P01CA-42745-05 9003 (SRC) **COX, EDWIN B** Hyperthermia and perfusion effects in cancer therapy Biostatistics and data management -- core

P01CA-42745-05 9004 (SRC) **JOINES, WILLIAM T** Hyperthermia and perfusion effects in cancer therapy Engineering core

R01CA-42755-07 (HEM) **DISTELHORST, CLARK W** UNIVERSITY HOSPS OF CLEVELAND 2074 ABINGTON ROAD CLEVELAND, OH 44106 Mechanism of glucocorticoid in lymphoid malignancy

P01CA-42760-06 (SRC) **WARNECKE, RICHARD B** UNIVERSITY OF ILLINOIS CHICAGO, IL 60680 Community interventions for cancer prevention

P01CA-42760-06 0001 (SRC) **WARNECKE, RICHARD B** Community interventions for cancer prevention Televised self-help program for smoking cessation

P01CA-42760-06 0002 (SRC) **KVIZ, FREDERICK J.** Community interventions for cancer prevention Psychosocial response to televised smoking cessation intervention

P01CA-42760-06 0003 (SRC) **GRUDER, CHARLES L** Community interventions for cancer prevention Social support in smoking cessation

P01CA-42760-06 0004 (SRC) **MANFREDI, CLARA** Community interventions for cancer prevention Cancer prevention strategies among low-SES black women

P01CA-42760-06 0005 (SRC) **BURTON, DEE** Community interventions for cancer prevention Motivation and mobilizing the confirmed smoker

P01CA-42760-06 9002 (SRC) **WARNECKE, RICHARD B** Community interventions for cancer prevention Survey methodology--Core

P01CA-42760-06 9003 (SRC) **DANGENBERG, PATRICIA** Community interventions for cancer prevention Core--Statistics and methods

P01CA-42762-05 (SRC) **TS'O, PAUL O** JOHN HOPKINS UNIVERSITY 615 NORTH WOLFE STREET BALTIMORE, MD 21205 Oligonucleotide analogs as gene regulation agents

P01CA-42762-05 0001 (SRC) **MILLER, PAUL S** Oligonucleotide analogs as gene regulation agents Chemistry of oligonucleotide methylphosphonates

P01CA-42762-05 0002 (SRC) **TS'O, PAUL O** Oligonucleotide analogs as gene regulation agents Physiochemistry and molecular cytology

P01CA-42762-05 0003 (SRC) **CHANG, ESTHER H** Oligonucleotide analogs as gene regulation agents Modulation of tumor growth in vitro and in vivo

P01CA-42762-05 0004 (SRC) **AURELIAN, LAURE** Oligonucleotide analogs as gene regulation agents Oligonucleotide analogs as antiviral/anticancer agents

P01CA-42762-05 9001 (SRC) **MILLER, PAUL S** Oligonucleotide analogs as gene regulation agents Core--Scientific

U10CA-42764-06 (CCI) **STEINHERZ, PETER G** MEM HOSP FOR CA & ALLIED DIS 1275 YORK AVENUE NEW YORK, N Y 10021 Childrens cancer study group

P01CA-42765-04 (SRC) **KAUFMAN, DAVID G** UNIV OF N C AT CHAPEL HILL 515 BRINKHOUS-BULLITT CB# 7525 CHAPEL HILL, N C 27599 Cycle-dependent mechanisms of chemical carcinogenesis

P01CA-42765-04 0001 (SRC) **GRISHAM, J W** Cycle-dependent mechanisms of chemical carcinogenesis Cell cycle and cell transformation in vitro

P01CA-42765-04 0002 (SRC) **KAUFMAN, DAVID G** Cycle-dependent mechanisms of chemical carcinogenesis Cell cycle dependent hepatocarcinogenesis

P01CA-42765-04 0003 (SRC) **KAUFMAN, DAVID G** Cycle-dependent mechanisms of chemical carcinogenesis DNA replication and susceptibility to transformation

P01CA-42765-04 0004 (SRC) **KAUFMAN, WILLIAM K** Cycle-dependent mechanisms of chemical carcinogenesis Influence of cell cycle on DNA repair processes

P01CA-42765-04 0005 (SRC) **CORDEIRO-STONE, MARILA** Cycle-dependent mechanisms of chemical carcinogenesis Timing of oncogene replication and carcinogenesis

P01CA-42765-04 0006 (SRC) **SMITH, GARY J** Cycle-dependent mechanisms of chemical carcinogenesis Mechanisms of mutation as function of cell cycle

P01CA-42765-04 9001 (SRC) **KAUFMAN, DAVID G** Cycle-dependent mechanisms of chemical carcinogenesis Scientific core

U10CA-42777-04 (CCI) **BRAUN, THOMAS J** UNIVERSITY OF COLORADO 4200 EAST 9TH AVE DENVER, CO 80262 University of colorado - southwest oncology group

U10CA-42782-04 (CCI) **COOPER, HERBERT A** UNIV OF NC AT CHAPEL HILL BURNETT-WOMACK BLDG, CB#7220 CHAPEL HILL, NC 27599 Collaborative

PROJECT NO., ORGANIZATIONAL UNIT., INVESTIGATOR, ADDRESS, TITLE

studies with the children's cancer study g

P01CA-42792-05 (SRC) MC DOUGALL, JAMES K FRED HUTCHINSON CANCER RES CTR 1124 COLUMBIA STREET SEATTLE, WA 98104 Hpv: biology, clinical significance and epidemiology

P01CA-42792-05 0001 (SRC) GALLOWAY, DENISE A Hpv: biology, clinical significance and epidemiology HPV expression and antigenicity

P01CA-42792-05 0002 (SRC) MCDOUGALL, JAMES E Hpv: biology, clinical significance and epidemiology Oncogenic potential of HPV

P01CA-42792-05 0003 (SRC) DALING, JANET R Hpv: biology, clinical significance and epidemiology Epidemiology of condylomata acuminatum

P01CA-42792-05 0004 (SRC) DALING, JANET R Hpv: biology, clinical significance and epidemiology Anogenital cancer--Epidemiology, biochemistry and immunology

P01CA-42792-05 0005 (SRC) CHU, JOSEPH Hpv: biology, clinical significance and epidemiology Relationship of cervical intraepithelial neoplasia III and HPV

P01CA-42792-05 9001 (SRC) BECKMAN, ANNA M Hpv: biology, clinical significance and epidemiology Core a--Molecular biology laboratory

P01CA-42792-05 9002 (SRC) KIVIAT, NANCY Hpv: biology, clinical significance and epidemiology Core B--Histology--Cytology laboratory

P01CA-42792-05 9003 (SRC) MCDOUGALL, JAMES K Hpv: biology, clinical significance and epidemiology

R01CA-42802-05 (ET) KUFE, DONALD W DANA-FARBER CANCER INSTITUTE 44 BINNEY STREET BOSTON, MA 02115 Differentiating agents in hematologic malignancies

R01CA-42804-06 (HEM) LOOK, ALFRED T, JR ST JUDE CHILDRENS RES HOSPITAL 332 N LAUDERDALE, BOX 318 MEMPHIS, TN 38101 Mechanisms of gene regulation in myelopoiesis

R01CA-42808-07 (RAD) HILL, COLIN K UNIV OF SOUTHERN CALFORNIA 1414 SOUTH HOPE STREET LOS ANGELES,CA 90015 Neutron dose protraction effect on transformation

R01CA-42810-04A3 (PTHB) TAINSKY, MICHAEL A UNIVERSITY OF TEXAS 1515 HOLCOMBE BLVD HOUSTON, TX 77030 Regulatory mechanisms for tumor suppressors

R01CA-42829-05 (CPA) SCHULLER, HILDEGARD M UNIVERSITY OF TENNESSEE P O BOX 1071 KNOXVILLE, TN 37901-1071 Transplacental carcinogenicity of NNK

R01CA-42835-06 (CTY) TAPAROWSKY, ELIZABETH J PURDUE UNIVERSITY DEPARTMENT OF BIOLOGICAL SCIS WEST LAFAYETTE, IN 47907 Cooperative effects of viral and cellular oncogenes

R01CA-42836-06 (CBY) LEOF, EDWARD B VANDERBILT UNIVERSITY SCHOOL OF MEDICINE NASHVILLE, TN 37232 Proto-oncogenes and cellular proliferation

R01CA-42854-05 (CPA) FLOYD, ROBERT A OKLAHOMA MEDICAL RESEARCH FDN 825 N.E. 13TH STREET OKLAHOMA CITY, OK 73104 Oxygen free radicals in carcinogenesis

R01CA-42876-04A2 (CPA) WELSCH, CLIFFORD W MICHIGAN STATE UNIVERSITY EAST LANSING, MI 48824 Dietary fat and human breast carcinoma growth

R01CA-42890-06 (EI) DAWSON, JEFFREY R DUKE UNIVERSITY MED CTR BOX 3010 DURHAM, NC 27710 Natural killer cell--Target cell recognition

R01CA-42898-05 (ET) BERNACKI, RALPH J ROSWELL PARK MEMORIAL INSTITUT ELM & CARLTON STREETS BUFFALO, NY 14263 Development of antimetastatic therapy and models

R01CA-42908-05A1 (ET) LATTIME, EDMUND C JEFFERSON MEDICAL COLLEGE 1015 WALNUT ST, RM 1005 PHILADELPHIA, PA 19107 In-vivo and in-vitro tumor lysis by TNF producing cells

R01CA-42919-04A2 (PTHB) DE CLERCK, YVES A CHILDREN'S HOSPITAL OF L. A. 4650 SUNSET BOULEVARD LOS ANGELES, CA 90027 Inhibition of tumor invasion by metalloproteinase inhibitors

R01CA-42922-04A1 (EI) VLOCK, DANIEL R VETERANS ADMINISTRATION MED CT ROOM E7-146 PITTSBURGH, PA 15240 Immunobiology of melanoma

R01CA-42944-05 (PTHB) SUMMERHAYES, IAN C NEW ENGLAND DEACONESS HOSPITAL 185 PILGRIM ROAD BOSTON, MA 02215 Oncogenesis of bladder epithelial cells

R01CA-42947-07 (RNM) MILLER, DOUGLAS L BATTELLE MEMORIAL INSTITUTE PO BOX 999 RICHLAND, WA 99352 Bioeffects of gas body activation in medical ultrasound

R01CA-42949-05 (SSS) THOMAS, DUNCAN C USC SCHOOL OF MEDICINE 2025 ZONAL AVENUE, PMB B201 LOS ANGELES, CA 90033 Time related factors in cancer epidemiology

R01CA-42951-06 (PTHA) LLOYD, RICARDO V 1500 E MEDICAL CTR DR ANN ARBOR, MI 48109-0054 Studies of normal and neoplastic human pituitary tissue

R01CA-42954-05 (PTHB) ISAACS, JOHN T JOHNS HOPKINS HOSPITAL 422 NORTH BOND STREET BALTIMORE, MD 21231 Genetic factors and the suppression of mammary cancer

R01CA-42971-06 (MEP) CLEARY, MICHAEL L STANFORD UNIVERSITY MEDICAL CT 300 PASTEUR DRIVE STANFORD, CA 94305-5324 Molecular pathology of human lymphoid malignancies

R01CA-42978-05 (PTHB) DER, CHANNING J LA JOLLA CANCER RESEARCH FDN 10901 NORTH TORREY PINES ROAD LA JOLLA, CA 92037 Biological activity of human h/ras oncogenes

R01CA-42981-06 (PTHB) ITZKOWITZ, STEVEN H MOUNT SINAI MEDICAL CENTER BOX 1069/ONE GUSTAVE L LEVY PL NEW YORK, NY 10029 Incompatible blood group antigens in colon cancer

R01CA-42986-06 (CPA) BIRT, DIANE F UNIVERSITY OF NEBRASKA MED CTR 600 SOUTH 42ND STREET OMAHA, NE 68198 Dietary fat, calories and two-stage tumorigenesis

R01CA-42992-06 (ET) KLEINERMAN, EUGENIE S UNIVERSITY OF TEXAS 1515 HOLCOMBE BLVD/HMB BOX 173 HOUSTON, TX 77030 Liposome therapy--a potential adjuvant for osteosarcoma

R01CA-43037-04A1 (END) DE FRANCO, DONALD B UNIVERSITY OF PITTSBURGH 552 CRAWFORD HALL PITTSBURGH, PA 15260 Intracellular mechanisms of glucocorticoid action

R01CA-43054-05 (MBY) WANG, JEAN Y UNIV OF CALIFORNIA, SAN DIEGO 9500 GILMAN DRIVE LA JOLLA, CA 92093-0166 Structure and function of C-abl proto-oncogene

R01CA-43058-06 (CLN) EDELSON, RICHARD L YALE UNIVERSITY P.O. BOX 3333 NEW HAVEN, CT 06510 Immunobiology of cutaneous T cell lymphoma

R01CA-43059-05 (ALY) SCHREIBER, ROBERT D WASHINGTON UNIV SCH OF MEDICIN 660 S. EUCLID AVE-BOX 8118 ST LOUIS, MO 63110 Molecular regulation of macrophage cytocidal activity

PROJECT NO., ORGANIZATIONAL UNIT., INVESTIGATOR, ADDRESS, TITLE

R01CA-43068-05 (BMT) SCHRAM, KARL H UNIVERSITY OF ARIZONA COLLEGE OF PHARMACY TUCSON, AZ 85721 Mass spectrometry of urinary nucleosides

R01CA-43090-06 (RAD) BULL, JOAN M UNIV OF TEXAS MEDICAL SCHOOL 6431 FANNIN ST RM 5016 MS HOUSTON, TX 77030 Hyperthermal and chemotherapy--On tumor and normal tissue

R01CA-43092-05 (EDC) ROSS, RONALD K UNIV OF SOUTHERN CALIFORNIA 2025 ZONAL AVENUE LOS ANGELES, CA 90033 Dietary factors in the etiology of cancer

R01CA-43121-04 (EI) BONAVIDA, BENJAMIN UNIV OF CALIFORNIA LOS ANGELES, CA 90024 The programming for lysis stage in NK cytotoxicity

R01CA-43122-05 (EVR) YATES, JOHN L ROSWELL PARK MEMORIAL INST 666 ELM STREET BUFFALO, NY 14263 The functions of epstein-barr virus nuclear antigen 1

R01CA-43143-06 (EVR) SPECK, SAMUEL H 44 BINNEY STREET BOSTON, MA 02115 Viral transcription in EBV transformed human B cells

R01CA-43151-06 (CPA) BOSLAND, MAARTEN C NEW YORK UNIVERSITY MED CENTER 550 FIRST AVENUE NEW YORK, NY 10016 Chemical induction of prostatic adenocarcinomas

R01CA-43159-06 (CPA) CHUNG, FUNG-LUNG AMERICAN HEALTH FOUNDATION ONE DANA ROAD VALHALLA, NY 10595 Enals in tumorigenesis

R37CA-43175-06 (NSS) SHORE, ROY E NEW YORK UNIVERSITY MEDICAL CT 341 EAST 25TH STREET NEW YORK, NY 10010-2598 Follow-up of patients X-irradiated for scalp ringworm

R01CA-43187-04 (EI) COOK, JAMES L NAT'L JEWISH CTR-IMMUNOLOGY 1400 JACKSON STREET DENVER, CO 80206-1997 Oncogenes and tumor cell/immune response interactions

U10CA-43189-03 (CCI) STEWART, JAMES A UNIV OF VT/REGIONAL CNCR CTR 1 SOUTH PROSPECT ST BURLINGTON, VT 05401 Eastern cooperative oncology group

R01CA-43194-06 (RAD) HALL, ERIC J COLUMBIA UNIV HLTH SCIS 630 WEST 168TH STREET NEW YORK, NY 10032 Hyperthermia, chemotherapy and oncogenic transformation

R01CA-43198-05 (ET) ROTI ROTI, JOSEPH L WASH UNIV SCHOOL OF MEDICINE 4511 FOREST PARK BLVD ST LOUIS, MO 63108 Nuclear protein content and heat-induced cell killing

R01CA-43199-05 (RAD) GARTE, SEYMOUR J NEW YORK UNIV MEDICAL CENTER 550 FIRST AVENUE NEW YORK, NY 10016 Oncogene activation in radiation carcinogenesis

R01CA-43201-07 (ET) OZER, HOWARD UNIV OF N C AT CHAPEL HILL CB#7305 3009 OLD CLINIC BLDG CHAPEL HILL, NC 27599-7305 Immunoregulatory effects of the interferons (human) /mice,rabbits

R01CA-43208-05 (CPA) FISHER, PAUL B COLUMBIA UNIVERSITY 630 WEST 168TH STREET NEW YORK, NY 10032 Multifactor interactions in carcinogenesis

R01CA-43211-06 (CPA) KNUDSON, ALFRED G INSTITUTE FOR CANCER RESEARCH 7701 BURHOLME AVENUE PHILADELPHIA, PA 19111 Hereditary and induced cancer in an animal model

R01CA-43216-06 (ARR) HOOVER, EDWARD A COLORADO STATE UNIVERSITY FORT COLLINS, CO 80523 Pathogenesis of feline leukemia virus induced AIDS

R01CA-43217-05 (CCG) LONDON, W THOMAS FOX CHASE CANCER CENTER 7701 BURHOLME AVENUE PHILADELPHIA, PA 19111 Prevention of liver cancer in east Asian populations in Philadelphia

R01CA-43218-05 (EI) GOLD, DAVID V CTR FOR MOLECULAR MED/IMMUNOLO 1 BRUCE ST NEWARK, NJ 07103 Monoclonal antibodies for management of GI cancer

R01CA-43222-05 (MGN) GLOVER, THOMAS W UNIVERSITY OF MICHIGAN D1109 MED. PROF. BLDG. BX 0718 ANN ARBOR, MI 48109 Role of fragile sites in chromosome breakage and cancer

R01CA-43225-05A2 (HEM) CAYRE, YVON E COLUMBIA UNIVERSITY 630 WEST 168TH STREET NEW YORK, NY 10032 Transcriptional regulation of myeloblastin expression

R01CA-43232-06 (MEP) LIEHR, JOACHIM G UNIV OF TEXAS MEDICAL BRANCH 301 UNIVERSITY BLVD. GALVESTON, TX 77550-2774 Prevention of estrogen-induced tumors by chemical means

R37CA-43233-07 (NSS) LIEHR, JOACHIM G UNIV. TEXAS MEDICAL BRANCH GALVESTON, TEXAS 77550 Mechanism of estrogen-induced renal carcinogenesis

R01CA-43237-04 (HEM) GOORHA, RAKESH M ST JUDE CHILDREN'S RES HOSP 332 N LAUDERDALE, P O BOX 318 MEMPHIS, TENNESSEE 38101-0318 Gene rearrangement and expression in T-cell leukemia

R01CA-43264-06 (EI) MEDVECZKY, PETER UNIVERSITY OF SOUTH FLORIDA 12901 BRUCE B DOWNS BLVD TAMPA, FL 33612 Growth factors and herpesvirus saimiri induced lymphomas

R01CA-43297-05 (ET) DANIEL, LARRY W BOWMAN GRAY SCHOOL OF MEDICINE 300 SOUTH HAWTHORNE ROAD WINSTON-SALEM, NC 27103 Leukemic cell inhibition and maturation by ether lipids

R01CA-43315-05 (ARR) NEURATH, A ROBERT NEW YORK BLOOD CENTER 310 EAST 67TH STREET NEW YORK, NY 10021 Synthetic HIV-1 envelope protein analogs for future vaccines

R01CA-43318-06 (PTHB) BAYLIN, STEPHEN B ONCOLOGY CENTER RESEARCH LABS 424 NORTH BOND STREET BALTIMORE, MD 21231 Methylation of the calcitonin gene in human tumors

R01CA-43322-07 (RAD) ULLRICH, ROBERT L UNIV OF TX MED BR/DIV OF RES 3310 GAIL BORDEN BLDG/RAD GALVESTON, TX 77550-2774 Carcinogenic interactions of radiation and chemicals

R01CA-43324-07 (RAD) CLAYCAMP, H GREGG UNIVERSITY OF PITTSBURGH A512 CRABTREE HALL PITTSBURGH, PA 15261 Radiation biochemistry of DNA base damage

R01CA-43334-05 (RNM) TRAHEY, GREGG E DUKE UNIVERSITY 136 ENGINEERING BLDG DURHAM, NC 27706 Adaptive ultrasonic imaging

R37CA-43342-05 (CPA) MAGEE, PETER N TEMPLE UNIVERSITY 3400 NORTH BROAD STREET PHILADELPHIA, PA 19140 Formation and metabolism of nitrosamines in pigs

R44CA-43444-03 (ET) LISHKO, VALERYI K ANTICANCER, INC 5325 METRO STREET SAN DIEGO, CA 92110 Methioninase for methionine dependent chemotherapy

P01CA-43447-06 (SRC) BOLOGNESI, DANI P DUKE UNIVERSITY MEDICAL CENTER PO BOX 2926 DURHAM, NC 27710 Pre-clinical studies on prevention and intervention in AIDS

P01CA-43447-06 0007 (SRC) HAYNES, BARTON F Pre-clinical studies on prevention and intervention in AIDS Immune responses to HIV induced by synthetic peptide constructs

P01CA-43447-06 0008 (SRC) MATTHEWS, THOMAS J Pre-clinical studies on prevention and intervention in AIDS Challenge of chronically infected chimps with a divergent HIV isolate

P01CA-43447-06 0009 (SRC) WEINHOLD, KENT J Pre-clinical studies on prevention and intervention in AIDS Cellular anti-HIV-1 cytotoxicities in infected and immunized nonhuman primates

P01CA-43447-06 0010 (SRC) PALKER, THOMAS J Pre-clinical studies on prevention and intervention in AIDS Protective immune response to SIVmac251 with synthetic peptide vaccine

P01CA-43447-06 9002 (SRC) LANGLOIS, ALPHONSE J Pre-clinical studies on prevention and intervention in AIDS Core--Virology and immunology

P01CA-43447-06 9003 (SRC) GREENBERG, MICHAEL Pre-clinical studies on prevention and intervention in AIDS Core--Molecular Biology

R01CA-43455-06 (EI) FAND, IRWIN CTR FOR MOL MEDICINE & IMM 1 BRUCE STREET NEWARK, NJ 07103 Whole-body autoradiography in tumor RAID

R01CA-43460-09 (PTHB) VOGELSTEIN, BERT JOHNS HOPKINS ONCOLOGY CENTER 424 NORTH BOND ST, RM 109 BALTIMORE, MD 21231 The P53 gene in human neoplasia

P01CA-43461-05 (SRC) GRITZ, ELLEN R UNIVERSITY OF CALIFORNIA 1100 GLENDON AVESTE 711 LOS ANGELES, CA 90024-3511 UCLA cancer control science program

P01CA-43461-05 9001 (SRC) ELASHOFF, ROBERT UCLA cancer control science program Statistical coordinating unit

P01CA-43461-05 9002 (SRC) GRITZ, ELLEN R UCLA cancer control science program Organization and administration - Core

P01CA-43461-05 9003 (SRC) GRITZ, ELLEN R UCLA cancer control science program Administration - Core

P01CA-43461-05 0001 (SRC) GANZ, PATRICIA A UCLA cancer control science program Improving adherence to cancer rehabilitation regimens

P01CA-43461-05 0002 (SRC) MARCUS, ALBERT C UCLA cancer control science program Adherence among low-income women with abnormal pap smear

P01CA-43461-05 0003 (SRC) GRITZ, ELLEN R UCLA cancer control science program Smoking cessation in head and neck cancer patients

P01CA-43461-05 0004 (SRC) HEBER, DAVID UCLA cancer control science program Adherence to low-fat diet to prevent breast cancer

R01CA-43475-06 (ARR) GREEN, WILLIAM R DARTMOUTH MEDICAL SCHOOL DEPARTMENT OF MICROBIOLOGY HANOVER, NH 03756 The development and assessment of retroviral vaccines

R01CA-43500-06 (ET) MC GUIRE, JOHN J ROSWELL PARK MEMORIAL INST ELM & CARLTON STREETS BUFFALO, NY 14263 Human leukemia folypolyglutamate synthetase inhibitors

R18CA-43521-06 (CCG) LEARY, MARY DEPT OF PUBLIC HEALTH 150 TREMONT STREET BOSTON, MA 02111 A model statewide cancer control program

R01CA-43532-06 (EVR) HARDWICK, J MARIE JOHNS HOPKINS UNIV SCHOOL OF M 600 NORTH WOLFE STREET BALTIMORE, MD 21205 Epstein-Barr virus regulation of gene function

R01CA-43540-04A1 (PTHB) CORY, SUZANNE WALTER/ELIZA HALL INSTITUTE POST OFFICE VICTORIA, AUSTRALIA 3050 Oncogene-induced leukemogenesis in transgenic mice

R01CA-43544-03 (EI) MURRAY, JAMES L UNIV OF TEXAS 1515 HOLCOMBE BLVD HOUSTON, TX 77030 Optimization of monoclonal antibody localization

R01CA-43551-06 (CBY) MACARA, IAN G UNIV OF ROCHESTER MEDICAL CTR BOX BPHYS ROCHESTER, N Y 14642 Regulation of cellular differentiation

R01CA-43585-06 (ET) LIANG, JAN C U.T. M.D. ANDERSON CANCER CENT 1515 HOLCOMBE BLVD HOUSTON, TX 77030 Assessment of germ cell damage induced by chemotherapy

R01CA-43592-05 (VR) LIPSICK, JOSEPH S SUNY AT STONY BROOK SCHOOL OF MEDICINE STONY BROOK, N Y 11794 Mechanism of transformation by the v-myb oncogene

U10CA-43595-05 (SRC) WAGMAN, LAWRENCE D CITY OF HOPE NATIONAL MED CTR 1500 E DUARTE ROAD DUARTE, CA 91010 Primary breast cancer therapy group--NSABP

R01CA-43600-06 (EVR) STAVNEZER, EDWARD UNIVERSITY OF CINCINNATI 231 BETHESDA AVENUE CINCINNATI, OH 45267-0522 The origin, structure and biological activity of skvs

R01CA-43610-06A1 (IMB) NATHAN, CARL F CORNELL UNIVERSITY MED COLLEGE 1300 YORK AVE NEW YORK, NY 10021 Macrophage deactivation

R01CA-43618-02 (HEM) LIEBERMANN, DAN A UNIV OF PENN SCHOOL OF MEDICIN ANATOMY-CHEMISTRY BLDG PHILADELPHIA, PA 19104-6059 Myelopoiesis, leukemia and its suppression

R01CA-43629-06 (PTHB) STOLER, MARK H CLEVELAND CLINIC FOUNDATION 9500 EUCLID AVENUE CLEVELAND, OH 44195-5138 Human papillomavirus -- Host gene expression in neoplasia

R01CA-43632-06 (PTHB) MICHALOPOULOS, GEORGE K UNIVERSITY OF PITTSBURGH 3550 TERRACE AT DESOTA PITTSBURGH, PA 15261 A1 adrenoreceptor, liver carcinogenesis and regeneration

R29CA-43651-05 (EVR) LICHTMAN, ANDREW H BRIGHAM & WOMEN'S HOSPITAL 75 FRANCIS STREET BOSTON, MA 02115 In-vitro models of viral leukemogenesis

U10CA-43652-05 (SRC) DEFUSCO, PATRICIA A HARTFORD HOSPITAL 80 SEYMOUR STREET HARTFORD, CT 06115 Primary breast cancer therapy group--NSABP

R01CA-43659-05 (ET) SARTORELLI, ALAN C YALE COMPREHENSIVE CANCER CTR 333 CEDAR STREET, PO BOX 3333 NEW HAVEN, CT 06510 Hypoxic cell selective chemotherapeutic agents

R29CA-43660-04 (ET) PRITSOS, CHRIS A UNIVERSITY OF NEVADA AT RENO DEPT OF NUTRITION RENO, NV 89557-0014 Enhanced preferential cytotoxicity by radical scavengers

R01CA-43676-05 (EI) TOMPKINS, MARY B NC STATE UNVERSITY 4700 HILLSBOROUGH STREET RALEIGH, NC 27606 FELV-induced alterations of feline hematopoietic cells

P30CA-43703-04A1 (CCS) BERGER, NATHAN A CASE WESTERN RESERVE UNIV 2040 ADELBERT RD CLEVELAND, OH 44106 CWRU cancer research center

P30CA-43703-04A1 9012 (CCS) GERSON, STANTON CWRU cancer research center Hematopoietic stem cell--Core

P30CA-43703-04A1 9001 (CCS) EVANS, HELEN CWRU cancer research center Tissue culture support facility--Core

P30CA-43703-04A1 9002 (CCS) DEHASETH, PETER CWRU cancer research center Molecular biology facility--Core

P30CA-43703-04A1 9003 (CCS) JACOBBERGER, JAMES CWRU cancer research center Flow cytometry--Core

P30CA-43703-04A1 9004 (CCS) BERGER, NATHAN A CWRU cancer research center Core--Biostatistics/ clinical trials facility

P30CA-43703-04A1 9007 (CCS) OLEINICK, NANCY CWRU cancer research center Radiation resource facility--Core

P30CA-43703-04A1 9008 (CCS) VOIGHT, ROBERT A CWRU cancer research center Athymic animal facility--Core

P30CA-43703-04A1 9010 (CCS) BERGER, NATHAN CWRU cancer research center Developmental funds--Core

P30CA-43703-04A1 9011 (CCS) PRETLOW, THOMAS CWRU cancer research center Histology--Core

R01CA-43713-03 (BNP) MITSCHER, LESTER A UNIVERSITY OF KANSAS CARRUTH-O'LEARY HALL LAWRENCE, KS 66045-2506 Novel antimutagenic compounds

R01CA-43719-04A1 (MEP) GLAUERT, HOWARD P UNIVERSITY OF KENTUCKY 212 FUNKHOUSER BLDG LEXINGTON, KY 40506-0054 Diet and carcinogenesis by peroxisome proliferators

P01CA-43720-05 (CAK) COHEN, STANLEY VANDERBILT UNIVERSITY SCH OF M 21ST AVENUE SOUTH NASHVILLE, TN 37232 Mechanism of action of epidermal growth factor

P01CA-43720-05 0001 (CAK) MROEKOWSKI, BARBARA Mechanism of action of epidermal growth factor Molecular biology approaches to the action of EGF

P01CA-43720-05 0002 (CAK) CARPENTER, GRAHAM Mechanism of action of epidermal growth factor Stimulation of the inositol triphosphate pathway by EGF

P01CA-43720-05 0003 (CAK) CARPENTER, GRAHAM Mechanism of action of epidermal growth factor Biology of an EGF-dependent cell line

P01CA-43720-05 0004 (CAK) PLEDGER, JACK W Mechanism of action of epidermal growth factor Modulation of the EGF receptors

P01CA-43720-05 0005 (CAK) OSHEROFF, NEIL Mechanism of action of epidermal growth factor Effect of EGF on topoisomerase activity

P01CA-43720-05 0006 (CAK) MCKANNA, JAMES Mechanism of action of epidermal growth factor Morphological analysis of EGF

P01CA-43720-05 0007 (CAK) STAROS, JAMES V Mechanism of action of epidermal growth factor Studies of EGF-receptors dynamics

P01CA-43720-05 9001 (CAK) COHEN, STANLEY Mechanism of action of epidermal growth factor Program Core

P01CA-43720-05 9002 (CAK) MROCZKOWSKI, BARBARA Mechanism of action of epidermal growth factor Preparation and instrument support--Core

R37CA-43722-05 (PTHA) BIGNER, SANDRA H DUKE UNIV MEDICAL CENTER BOX 3712 DURHAM, NC 27710 Growth control and cytogenetics of malignant gliomas

R01CA-43728-03 (EVR) COCKERELL, GARY L COLORADO STATE UNIVERSITY FORT COLLINS, CO 80523 Latency and leukomogenicity of bovine leukemia virus

R01CA-43769-05 (RAD) RINALDY, AUGUSTINUS UNIV OF TENNESSEE, MEMPHIS 956 COURT AVENUE, ROOM H300 MEMPHIS, TN 38163 Molecular cloning of human DNA repair gene

R01CA-43783-06 (ET) TEW, KENNETH D FOX CHASE CANCER CENTER 7701 BURHOLME AVENUE PHILADELPHIA, PA 19111 Estramustine as an antimicrotubule agent in the prostate

P01CA-43791-04A1 (SRC) WILLIAMS, JERRY R JOHNS HOPKINS ONCOLOGY CENTER 600 NORTH WOLFE STREET BALTIMORE, MD 21205 Radiolabeled immunoglobulin therapy of human cancer

P01CA-43791-04A1 0001 (SRC) DILLEHAY, LARRY Radiolabeled immunoglobulin therapy of human cancer Radiobiology of RIT

P01CA-43791-04A1 0002 (SRC) KLEIN, JERRY Radiolabeled immunoglobulin therapy of human cancer Factors in immunoglobulin tumor binding in RIT

P01CA-43791-04A1 0003 (SRC) LEICHNER, PETER K Radiolabeled immunoglobulin therapy of human cancer Normal tissue dosimetry in RIT

P01CA-43791-04A1 0004 (SRC) WILLIAMS, JERRY Radiolabeled immunoglobulin therapy of human cancer Integration of RIT with external beam and chemotherapy

P01CA-43791-04A1 9001 (SRC) Quadri, Syed Radiolabeled immunoglobulin therapy of human cancer Linker immunoconjugate synthesis--Core

P01CA-43791-04A1 9002 (SRC) WILLIAMS, JERRY Radiolabeled immunoglobulin therapy of human cancer Biological support--Core

R01CA-43793-05 (CBY) LEE, DAVID C UNIV OF NC AT CHAPEL HILL CANCER CENTER, CB# 7295 CHAPEL HILL, NC 27599 Regulation of transforming growth factors

R01CA-43803-05 (CBY) ROBERTS, THOMAS M DANA-FARBER CANCER INSTITUTE 44 BINNEY STREET BOSTON, MA 02115 Pp60 c-src in growth transformation and differentiation

R29CA-43823-05 (ET) WAYS, DOUGLAS K EAST CAROLINA UNIVERSITY BRODY MEDICAL SCIENCES BLDG GREENVILLE, NC 27858 Phorbol ester induced differentiation of leukemic cells

R01CA-43830-06 (ET) TEW, KENNETH D FOX CHASE CANCER CENTER 7701 BURHOLME AVE PHILADELPHIA, PA 19111 Intranuclear reactions and drug resistance

R01CA-43840-07 (RAD) BOYER, ARTHUR L U OF TX/M D ANDERSON CANCER CT 1515 HOLCOMBE BLVD HOUSTON, TX 77030 Fast fourier dose computation for conformal therapy

R01CA-43855-05 (MBY) GREENBERG, MICHAEL E HARVARD MEDICAL SCHOOL BOSTON, MA 02115 Nerve growth factor regulation of gene expression

R01CA-43856-03 (MEP) KRITCHEVSKY, DAVID WISTAR INSTITUTE 36TH & SPRUCE ST PHILADELPHIA, PA 19104 Caloric restriction in tumor promotion--Mechanisms

R01CA-43860-05 (PBC) OLIVER, NOELYNN A TUFTS UNIVERSITY 136 HARRISON AVENUE BOSTON, MA 02111 Cis and trans acting factors in neoplastic transformation

R01CA-43882-05 (MGN) SURTI, URVASHI MAGEE WOMENS HOSPITAL 300 HALKET ST PITTSBURGH, PA 15213 Genetics and biology of human ovarian teratomas

R01CA-43888-04A1 (ET) HAIT, WILLIAM N YALE UNIVERSITY P O BOX 3333 NEW HAVEN, CT 06510 Drug-sensitivity of calcium-modulators from

PROJECT NO., ORGANIZATIONAL UNIT., INVESTIGATOR, ADDRESS, TITLE

brain tumors
R01CA-43894-06 (CPA) JACOBSON, MYRON K TEXAS COL OF OSTEOPATHIC MED 3500 CAMP BOWIE BLVD FORT WORTH, TX 76107-2690 Alteration of NAD metabolism by chemical carcinogens
R01CA-43909-04A1 (PTHB) LOCKER, JOSEPH D UNIVERSITY OF PITTSBURGH 3550 TERRACE AT DESOTA STREET PITTSBURGH, PA 15261 Developmental & neoplastic gene expression in the liver
R29CA-43914-05 (PTHB) AGINS, ALAN P BROWN UNIVERSITY BOX G-B416 PROVIDENCE, R I 02912 Prostaglandin metabolism and receptors in leukemia
R01CA-43917-06 (ET) LAZO, JOHN S UNIV OF PITTSBURGH SCH OF MED E1340 BIOMEDICAL SCIENCE TOWER PITTSBURGH, PA 15261 Biochemical regulators of bleomycin - induced pulmonary toxicity
R01CA-43920-04A1 (RNM) GREENLEAF, JAMES F MAYO FOUNDATION 200 FIRST STREET SOUTHWEST Composite transducers for medical ultrasonics
R01CA-43924-04 (PTHA) MC CARTHY, JAMES B UNIVERSITY OF MINNESOTA 420 DELAWARE ST SE ST PAUL, MN 55455 Metastasis inhibition by fibronectin-tumor interactions
R01CA-43926-03 (ET) EVELHOCH, JEFFREY L WAYNE STATE UNIVERSITY SCHL ME DETROIT, MICH 48201 P-31 mrs--Chemotherapy response predictor
R01CA-43950-06 (ET) MIER, JAMES W NEW ENGLAND MEDICAL CTR HOSP-I 750 WASHINGTON ST BOSTON, MA 02111 Immunobiology of LAK cells
R01CA-43967-05 (PBC) SENGER, DONALD R BETH ISRAEL HOSPITAL 330 BROOKLINE AVENUE BOSTON, MA 02215 Tumor-secreted vascular permeability factor
R01CA-43969-05 (MCHA) WILLIAMS, ROBERT M COLORADO STATE UNIVERSITY FORT COLLINS, CO 80523 Quinocarcin mechanism of action
R01CA-44013-05 (ET) BERGER, FRANKLIN G UNIVERSITY OF SOUTH CAROLINA COLUMBIA, SC 29208 Thymidylate synthase and fluorodeoxyuridine resistance
R01CA-44014-04 (RNM) SHELLOCK, FRANK G CEDARS-SINAI MEDICAL CENTER 8700 BEVERLY BLVD LOS ANGELES, CA 90048 Thermophysiologic effects of magnetic resonance imaging
R01CA-44029-05 (PTHA) DALLA-FAVERA, RICCARDO HEALTH SCIENCES, COLUMBIA UNIV 630 WEST 168TH STREET NEW YORK, N Y 10032 Molecular pathology of human lymphoid malignancies
R01CA-44042-05 (MBY) ZIFF, EDWARD B NEW YORK UNIVERSITY MEDICAL CT 550 FIRST AVE NEW YORK, NY 10016 Dynamics of c-fos protein interactions
R01CA-44060-04A1 (BLR) BEARD, DAVID V UNIVERSITY OF NORTH CAROLINA CHAPEL HILL, NC 27599 New visualizations for medical image workstation
U10CA-44064-05 (SRC) LEES, ALAN W CROSS CANCER INSTITUTE 11560 UNIVERSITY AVENUE EDMONTON, AB CANADA T6G 1Z2 Primary breast cancer therapy group--NSABP
U10CA-44066-05 (SRC) ROBIDOUX, ANDRE HOTEL DIEU OF MONTREAL 3840 ST-URBAIN MONTREAL, QUEBEC, CANADA H2W 1 primary breast cancer therapy group--NSABP
U10CA-44067-05 (SRC) KARP, DANIEL D NEW ENGLAND MEDICAL CENTER 171 HARRISON AVE/BOX 452 BOSTON, MA 02111 Primary breast cancer therapy group--NSABP
R01CA-44069-06 (MEP) LIEHR, JOACHIM G UNIVERSITY OF TEXAS MEDICAL BR GALVESTON, TX 77550-2774 Prevention of estradiol-induced tumors by vitamin C
R44CA-44076-03 (SSS) KNOTT, GARY CIVILIZED SOFTWARE, INC 7735 OLD GEORGETOWN ROAD BETHESDA, MD 20814 Clinsys: software for clinical trials
R01CA-44114-04A2 (RAD) SONG, CHANG W HARVARD ST AT EAST RIVER RD MINNEAPOLIS, MN 55455 Physiological factors in hyperthermia
R01CA-44124-05 (RAD) CAIN, CHARLES A THE UNIV OF MICHIGAN 3302 GGB DOW CONNECTOR ANN ARBOR, MI 48109-2125 New ultrasound phased applicator for hyperthermia
R01CA-44131-06 (PTHB) COLE, LAURENCE A YALE UNIVERSITY SCHOOL OF MED 333 CEDAR ST NEW HAVEN, CT 06510 O-glycosylation of HCG and cancer
R01CA-44133-05 (SRC) HAYS, DANIEL M CHILDRENS HOSP OF LOS ANGELES 4650 SUNSET BLVD LOS ANGELES, CA 90027 Aiding childhood cancer patients confront adult issues
R01CA-44140-05 (SRC) LANSKY, SHIRLEY B ILLINOIS CANCER COUNCIL 36 S WABASH, SUITE 700 CHICAGO, IL 60603-2965 Behavioral management protocol for school attendance
R01CA-44166-06 (EVR) YOSHIMURA, FAYTH K UNIVERSITY OF WASHINGTON SEATTLE, WA 98195 DNA forms of murine leukemia viruses
R01CA-44173-06 (ET) BUCHSBAUM, DONALD J UNIV OF ALABAMA AT BIRMINGHAM 619 SOUTH 19TH ST BIRMINGHAM, AL 35233 Treatment of colon cancer with radiolabeled CEA antibody
R01CA-44174-05 (VR) ANDROPHY, ELLIOT J NEW ENGLAND MED CTR HOSP 750 WASHINGTON ST/BOX 114 BOSTON, MA 02111 Characterization of papillomavirus e6 proteins
R01CA-44247-06 (CPA) FRIEDBERG, ERROL C UNIVERSITY OF TEXAS SW MED CTR 5323 HARRY HINES BLVD DALLAS, TX 75235 DNA repair and cancer-prone hereditary human disease
R44CA-44249-03 (SSS) GRABOWY, RICHARD S MICROWAVE MEDICAL SYSTEMS, INC PO BOX 188/9 GOLDSMITH STREET LITTLETON, MA 10460-0188 Optimizing microwave scanning to detect breast cancer
R35CA-44257-04 (SRC) GOLDBERG, IRVING H HARVARD MEDICAL SCHOOL 250 LONGWOOD AVENUE BOSTON, MA 02115 Molecular pharmacology of anticancer drugs
R35CA-44338-06 (SRC) BISHOP, J M UNIVERSITY OF CALIFORNIA SAN FRANCISCO, CA 94143 Retroviruses and cancer genes
R35CA-44339-05 (SRC) JAENISCH, RUDOLF WHITEHEAD INST FOR BIOMED RES NINE CAMBRIDGE CENTER CAMBRIDGE, MA 02142 Retroviruses, oncogenes & mammalian development
R35CA-44343-05 (SRC) BENJAMIN, THOMAS L HARVARD MEDICAL SCHOOL 25 SHATTUCK STREET BOSTON, MA 02115 Natural and unnatural roles of the polyoma Hr-t gene
R35CA-44344-03 (SRC) PETTIT, GEORGE R ARIZONA STATE UNIVERSITY CANCER RESEARCH INSTITUTE TEMPE, AZ 85287-2404 NCI outstanding investigator grant
R35CA-44349-05 (SRC) HANAWALT, PHILIP C STANFORD UNIVERSITY HERRIN BIOLOGICAL LABS STANFORD, CA 94305-5020 Cellular processing of damaged DNA--Role in oncogenesis
R35CA-44352-05 (SRC) NICOLSON, GARTH L UNIVERSITY OF TEXAS 1515 HOLCOMBE HOUSTON, TX 77030 Tumor metastasis

PROJECT NO., ORGANIZATIONAL UNIT., INVESTIGATOR, ADDRESS, TITLE

R35CA-44353-05 (SRC) GUENGERICH, F PETER VANDERBILT UNIVERSITY 21ST AVE SOUTH AND GARLAND NASHVILLE, TN 37232 Enzymic activation of chemical carcinogens
R35CA-44355-05 (SRC) MALEY, FRANK NY STATE DPT HLTH/HLTH RSRCH EMPIRE STATE PLAZA ALBANY, NY 12201 NCI outstanding investigators grant
R35CA-44356-05 (SRC) HANAFUSA, HIDESABURO ROCKEFELLER UNIVERSITY 1230 YORK AVENUE NEW YORK, N Y 10021 Cell transformation by retrovirus
R35CA-44358-05 (SRC) CHENG, YUNG-CHI YALE UNIV SCHOOL OF MEDICINE SHM B313 333 CEDAR STREET NEW HAVEN, CT 510 Development of anti-cancer and anti-viral compounds
R35CA-44360-04 (SRC) VERMA, INDER M SALK INST/BIOLOGICAL STUDIES P O BOX 85800 SAN DIEGO, CA 92138 Oncogenes, proto-oncogenes and retroviral vectors
R01CA-44365-05 (PTHB) SEHGAL, PRAVINKUMAR B ROCKEFELLER UNIVERSITY 1230 YORK AVENUE NEW YORK, NY 10021-6399 Tumor necrosis factor induces a new regulatory cytokine
R35CA-44372-05 (SRC) FITCH, FRANK W UNIV OF CHICAGO 5841 SOUTH MARYLAND AVENUE CHICAGO, IL 60637 Regulation of T lymphocyte immune responses
R35CA-44377-05 (SRC) HECHT, STEPHEN S AMERICAN HEALTH FOUNDATION 320 EAST 43RD STREET NEW YORK, NY 10017 Metabolic activation of carcinogens
R01CA-44383-03 (MEP) BLACK, HOMER S BAYLOR COLLEGE ONE BAYLOR PLAZA HOUSTON, TX 77030 Skin cancer prophylaxis by low-fat dietary intervention
R01CA-44384-05 (RAD) MC BRIDE, WILLIAM H UNIVERSITY OF CALIFORNIA 10833 LECONTE AVENUE LOS ANGELES, CA 90024-1714 Response of brain to radiation
R35CA-44385-05 (SRC) COFFIN, JOHN M TUFTS UNIVERSITY BOSTON, MA 02111 The molecular biology of retroviruses
R01CA-44387-05 (CPA) GOULD, MICHAEL N UNIVERSITY OF WISCONSIN 600 HIGHLAND AVE MADISON, WI 53792 Characterizing early events in mammary carcinogenesis
R01CA-44395-05 (BNP) SCOTT, A IAN TEXAS A&M UNIVERSITY COLLEGE STATION, TX 77843 Biosynthesis of the antitumor alkaloids of catharanthus
R01CA-44401-05 (EDC) PETERS, RUTH K UNIV OF SOUTHERN CALIFORNIA 1420 SAN PABLO STREET LOS ANGELES, CA 90033 Case-control study of adenocarcinoma of the cervix
R01CA-44404-05 (BMT) LIEBESKIND, LANNY S EMORY UNIVERSITY ATLANTA, GA 30322 Alkylidene cyclopentenones--organometallic entries
R01CA-44416-02 (CPA) CHANG, CHING-JER PURDUE UNIV SCH OF PHARMACY WEST LAFAYETTE, IN 47907 DNA modifications by pyruvaldehyde
R55CA-44426-04 (ET) RATLIFF, TIMOTHY L JEWISH HOSPITAL 216 SOUTH KINGSHIGHWAY ST LOUIS, MO 63110 Intravesical BCG for bladder cancer -- Role of fibronectin
R29CA-44441-06 (CTY) BISHAYEE, SUBAL CORIELL INST FOR MEDICAL RES 401 HADDON AVENUE CAMDEN, N J 08103 Analysis of the receptor for c-sis protein
R01CA-44446-05 (EI) EPSTEIN, LOIS B 1282 MOFFITT HOSPITAL UNIV CALIFORNIA SAN FRANCISCO SAN FRANCISCO, CA 94143 Comparative biology of human TNF and IL-1
R01CA-44460-05 (SSS) HASELTINE, WILLIAM A DANA-FARBER CANCER INSTITUTE 44 BINNEY STREET BOSTON, MA 02115 Molecular biology of the art gene of HTLV-III
R29CA-44464-06 (CBY) WHEELOCK, MARGARET J UNIVERSITY OF TOLEDO 2801 WEST BANCROFT TOLEDO, OH 43606 Adhesion related proteins of human epithelial cells
R01CA-44470-03S1 (PTHB) WEISSMAN, BERNARD E UNIV OF N C AT CHAPEL HILL CB# 7295 CHAPEL HILL, N C 27599 Characterization of pediatric recessive cancer genes
R01CA-44499-06 (ET) LUDLUM, DAVID B UNIV OF MASSACHUSETTS MED SCH 55 LAKE AVENUE NORTH WORCESTER, MA 01655 Sensitivity and resistance to nitrosourea-like agents
R29CA-44504-05 (RAD) GENSLER, HELEN L UNIVERSITY OF ARIZONA HEALTH SCIENCES CENTER TUCSON, AZ 85724 UV modulation of chemical carcinogenesis
R29CA-44505-04 (ET) RIDEOUT, DARRYL C SCRIPPS CLINIC AND RES FDN 10666 N TORREY PINES RD LA JOLLA, CA 92037 Antitumor specificity amplification
R29CA-44507-05 (PBC) UMBREIT, J N UNIVERSITY OF SOUTH ALABAMA USA CANCER CENTER MOBILE, AL 36688 Mammary gland glycosaminoglycan structure and turnover
R01CA-44522-04 (RAD) YOUNG, ALFRED B UNIV OF KENTUCKY MED CTR LEXINGTON, KY 40536 Interstitial neutron therapy for glioblastoma
P01CA-44530-05 (SRC) TALALAY, PAUL JOHNS HOPKINS UNIVERSITY 725 NORTH WOLFE STREET BALTIMORE, MD 21205 Novel strategies for chemoprotection against cancer
P01CA-44530-05 0001 (SRC) TALALAY, PAUL Novel strategies for chemoprotection against cancer Mechanisms of induction of chemoprotective enzymes
P01CA-44530-05 0002 (SRC) KENSLER, THOMAS Novel strategies for chemoprotection against cancer Interference with tumor promotion and progression by antioxidants
P01CA-44530-05 0003 (SRC) GORDON, GARY Novel strategies for chemoprotection against cancer Development of dehydroepiandrosterone as a chemoprotective agent
P01CA-44530-05 0004 (SRC) POSNER, GARY H Novel strategies for chemoprotection against cancer Relation of chemical structure to chemoprotective activity
R01CA-44537-05 (RAD) NATH, RAVINDER YALE UNIVERSITY, SCH OF MED P O BOX 3333 333 CEDAR ST., NEW HAVEN, CT 06510 Enhancement of IUdR sensitization by low energy photons
R29CA-44542-04 (PTHB) HALABAN, RUTH YALE UNIVERSITY 333 CEDAR STREET NEW HAVEN, CT 06510 Proliferation & malignant transformation of melanocytes
R01CA-44546-05 (EDC) BERNSTEIN, LESLIE USC SCHOOL OF MEDICINE 2025 ZONAL AVENUE LOS ANGELES, CA 90033 A case-control study of breast cancer in young women
R37CA-44550-05 (RAD) CORRY, PETER M WILLIAM BEAUMONT HOSPITAL 3601 WEST THIRTEEN MILE ROAD ROYAL OAK, MI 48072 Preferential killing

of melanized tissues
R01CA-44578-04 (EDC) MUELLER, NANCY E HARVARD SCHOOL OF PUB SCHOOL 677 HUNTINGTON AVENUE BOSTON, MA 02115 The epidemiology of "classic" Kaposi's sarcoma
P30CA-44579-04A1 (CCS) WAGNER, ROBERT R UNIVERSITY OF VIRGINIA SCH OF MED, BOX 441 CHARLOTTESVILLE, VA 22908 Cancer research center
P30CA-44579-04A1 9002 (CCS) FLICKENGER, CHARLES Cancer research center Central electron microscope facility--Core
P30CA-44579-04A1 9003 (CCS) FOX, JAY W Cancer research center Central protein and nucleic acid research center
P30CA-44579-04A1 9005 (CCS) HERR, JOHN C Cancer research center Lymphocyte culture/hybridoma center
P30CA-44579-04A1 9006 (CCS) WAGNER, ROBERT R Cancer research center Development funds - Core
P30CA-44579-04A1 9009 (CCS) SJOKA, NICHOLAS Cancer research center Vivarium facility--Core
P30CA-44579-04A1 9012 (CCS) OWENS, G Cancer research center Cell sorter facility--Core
R01CA-44580-05 (RNM) JOSEPH, PETER M UNIVERSITY OF PENNSYLVANIA 3400 SPRUCE STREET PHILADELPHIA, PA 19104 Multinuclear MRI of tumors in animals
R29CA-44597-05 (ET) FERNANDES, DANIEL J WAKE FOREST UNIVERSITY MEDICAL CENTER BOULVARD WINSTON-SALEM, NC 27157 Antimetabolites and nuclear matrix-bound DNA
R29CA-44602-05 (PTHB) CARR, BRIAN I 5C FALK CLINIC 3601 FIFTH AVENUE PITTSBURGH, PA 15213 TGFD beta receptors in hepatocarcinogenesis
R29CA-44611-05 (PC) DEGEN, JAY L CHILDREN'S HOSPITAL MED CTR ELLAND AND BETHESDA AVES CINCINNATI, OH 45229 Protein phosphorylation and plasminogen activator
R01CA-44627-05 (PBC) SCHWARZBAUER, JEAN E PRINCETON UNIVERSITY PRINCETON, NJ 08544-1014 Functional role of fibronectin subunit heterogeneity
R01CA-44633-06 (EVR) FLYER, DAVID C THE MILTON S HERSHEY MED CTR P O BOX 850 HERSHEY, PA 17033 Specificity of the ctl response to murine leukemia virus
R01CA-44649-04A1 (HEM) MAY, WILLIAM S JR JOHNS HOPKINS UNIVERSITY 720 RUTLAND AVE BALTIMORE, MD 21205 Characterization of the IL-3 growth factor receptor (rabbits, rats,guinea pigs),
R29CA-44659-05 (PTHB) BAJKOWSKI, ANDREW S LOYOLA UNIVERSITY 2160 SOUTH FIRST AVENUE MAYWOOD, IL 60153 Processing and secretion of cathepsin B in metastasis
P01CA-44665-04 (CCP) HAHN, GEORGE M STANFORD UNIVERSITY SCH OF MED DEPT. OF RADIATION ONCOLOGY STANFORD, CA 94305 Hyperthermia--Heterogeneity of tissue responses
P01CA-44665-04 0005 (CCP) SOMMER, GRAHAM F Hyperthermia--Heterogeneity of tissue responses Magnetic resonance imaging and spectroscopy
P01CA-44665-04 0006 (CCP) KAPP, DANIEL S Hyperthermia--Heterogeneity of tissue responses Prediction of tumor response
P01CA-44665-04 0001 (CCP) KAPP, DANIEL S Hyperthermia--Heterogeneity of tissue responses Radiation therapy and hyperthermia
P01CA-44665-04 0002 (CCP) CARLSON, ROBERT W Hyperthermia--Heterogeneity of tissue responses Chemotherapy and hyperthermia
P01CA-44665-04 0003 (CCP) FASSENDEN, PETER Hyperthermia--Heterogeneity of tissue responses Microwave equipment development
P01CA-44665-04 0004 (CCP) FESSENDEN, PETER Hyperthermia--Heterogeneity of tissue responses Interstitial RF equipment development
P01CA-44665-04 0007 (CCP) HAHN, GEORGE M Hyperthermia--Heterogeneity of tissue responses Modification of response
P01CA-44665-04 9001 (CCP) HAHN, GEORGE M Hyperthermia--Heterogeneity of tissue responses Core
R01CA-44673-05 (EVR) HEARING, PATRICK RESEARCH FOUNDATION OF SUNY DEPT OF MICROBIOLOGY STONY BROOK, N Y 11794 Analysis of a polyomavirus enhancer & binding protein
R01CA-44676-06 (ET) MELERA, PETER W UNIV OF MARYLAND 660 W REDWOOD ST BALTIMORE, MD 21201 Multidrug resistance in mammalian cells
R01CA-44683-03 (EDC) HSIEH, CHUNG-CHENG HARVARD SCHOOL OF PUBLIC HLTH 677 HUNTINGTON AVENUE BOSTON, MA 02115 Case-control study of cancer of extrahepatic bile duct
R01CA-44684-04 (EDC) SANDLER, ROBERT S UNIV OF NORTH CAROLINA AT CH 423 BURNETT-WOMACK BLDG CB# 70 CHAPEL HILL, NC 27599-7080 Risk factors for colon adenomas
R01CA-44686-04 (CPA) CAVALIERI, ERCOLE UNIV OF NEBRASKA MED CENTER 600 SOUTH 42ND STREET OMAHA, NE 68198-6805 Mechanisms of tumor initiation by benzopyrene and derivatives
U10CA-44691-07 (CCI) SCHILSKY, RICHARD L UNIVERSITY OF CHICAGO 5841 S MARYLAND BOX 420 CHICAGO, IL 60637 Chemotherapy committee: CALGB
R29CA-44700-05 (MGN) WESTBROOK, CAROL A UNIVERSITY OF CHICAGO 5841 SOUTH MARYLAND AVENUE Molecular genetic study of chromosome 9 translocations
P01CA-44704-04A1 (SRC) STEELE, GLENN D, JR NEW ENGLAND DEACONESS HOSPITAL 185 PILGRIM ROAD BOSTON, MA 02215 The pathobiology of colorectal cancer
P01CA-44704-04A1 0002 (SRC) MERCURIO, ARTHUR The pathobiology of colorectal cancer Differentiation and basement membrane interactions
P01CA-44704-04A1 0003 (SRC) MATSUDAIRA, PAUL The pathobiology of colorectal cancer Cytoskeleton and colon carcinoma differentiation
P01CA-44704-04A1 0004 (SRC) SUMMERHAYES, IAN The pathobiology of colorectal cancer Oncogenes and colon epithelial transformation
P01CA-44704-04A1 0005 (SRC) CHAN, LAN BO The pathobiology of colorectal cancer Molecular markers for human colorectal cancer
P01CA-44704-04A1 0007 (SRC) THOMAS, PETER The pathobiology of colorectal cancer Role of cell surface and secreted CEA family members in metastases
P01CA-44704-04A1 0008 (SRC) JESSUP, J MILBURN The pathobiology of colorectal cancer Evaluation of markers and prognosis in colorectal cancer
P01CA-44704-04A1 9004 (SRC) GOLDMAN, HARVEY The pathobiology of colorectal cancer Core--Pathology component
P01CA-44704-04A1 9005 (SRC) MATSUDAIRA, PAUL The pathobiology of colorectal cancer Core--Electron microscopy and protein sequencing
R01CA-44709-05 (CPA) SHAW, BARBARA R DUKE UNIVERSITY 101 GROSS CHEMISTRY DURHAM, NC 27706 Ionized base pairs and cross-strand mutagenesis
R01CA-44723-05 (RAD) KENG, PETER C UNIVERSITY OF ROCHESTER MED CT 601 ELMWOOD AVENUE ROCHESTER, NY 14642 Radiation sensitivity of quiescent tumor cells
R01CA-44728-04 (RAD) PHILPOTT, GORDON W JEWISH HOSPITAL OF ST LOUIS 216 S KINGSHIGHWAY ST LOUIS, MO 63110 Tumor localization and imaging using -colon cancer ma
R01CA-44729-05 (ET) TRITTON, THOMAS R UNIVERSITY OF VERMONT COLLEGE OF MEDICINE, GIVEN BLD BURLINGTON, VT 05405 Membrane targets in cancer chemotherapy
R29CA-44734-05 (CPA) LEWIS, JAMES G DUKE UNIVERSITY MEDICAL CTR BOX 3712 DURHAM, NC 27710 Xenobiotics, inflammation and carcinogenesis
R01CA-44737-05 (ET) GANJU-KRISHAN, AWTAR UNIVERSITY OF MIAMI P O BOX 016960 MIAMI, FLA 33101 Multiple drug resistance in human solid tumors
R29CA-44741-04 (CPA) TELANG, NITIN T SLOAN-KETTERING INST FOR CANCE 1275 YORK AVENUE NEW YORK, NY 10021 In vitro induction and modulation of mammary preneoplasia
R01CA-44747-04 (CBY) DONNER, DAVID B SLOAN-KETTERING INSTITUTE 1275 YORK AVENUE NEW YORK, NY 10021 Tumor necrosis factor receptor--Structure and function
R29CA-44754-05 (PTHB) FUNG, YUEN K CHILDREN'S HOSPITAL 4650 SUNSET BLVD LOS ANGELES, CA 90054-0700 Cloning and characterization of the retinoblastoma gene
R29CA-44761-03 (CBY) CHERINGTON, VAN TUFTS UNIVERSITY SCHOOL OF MED 136 HARRISON AVE BOSTON, MA 02111 An oncogene sensitive regulation of differentiation
R29CA-44764-05 (MGN) NAYLOR, SUSAN L UNIV OF TEXAS HLTH SCIENCE CTR 7703 FLOYD CURL DRIVE SAN ANTONIO, TX 78284 Molecular analysis of chromosome aberrations in cancer
P01CA-44768-05 (SRC) SMITH, HELENE S MEDICAL RESEARCH INSTITUTE 2200 WEBSTER STREET SAN FRANCISCO, CA 94115 Molecular and cellular predictors of breast cancer prognosis
P01CA-44768-05 0001 (SRC) BENZ, CHRISTOPHER C Molecular and cellular predictors of breast cancer prognosis Activation of oncogenes and receptors in breast cancer
P01CA-44768-05 0002 (SRC) SMITH, HELENE S Molecular and cellular predictors of breast cancer prognosis Genetic markers for predicting prognosis of breast cancers
P01CA-44768-05 0003 (SRC) STERN, ROBERT Molecular and cellular predictors of breast cancer prognosis Stromal-epithelial interactions in breast cancer
P01CA-44768-05 0004 (SRC) WALDMAN, FRED Molecular and cellular predictors of breast cancer prognosis Breast tumor interphase cytogenetics
P01CA-44768-05 9001 (SRC) LJUNG, BRITT-MARIE Molecular and cellular predictors of breast cancer prognosis Clinical core project
P01CA-44768-05 9003 (SRC) MAYALL, BRIAN H Molecular and cellular predictors of breast cancer prognosis Cytometry and biostatistics--Core
P01CA-44768-05 9004 (SRC) THOR, ANN Molecular and cellular predictors of breast cancer prognosis Immunopathology core
P01CA-44768-05 9005 (SRC) SMITH, HELENE S Molecular and cellular predictors of breast cancer prognosis Cell culture core
R01CA-44771-04 (REN) BROOKS, SAM C WAYNE STATE UNIVERSITY 540 CANFIELD DETROIT, MI 48201 Estrogen structure-receptor function relationships
R01CA-44783-05 (ET) VOGELSANG, GEORGIA JOHNS HOPKINS ONCOLOGY CENTER 600 N WOLFE STREET BALTIMORE, MD 21205 Immunopharmacology of thalidomide
R29CA-44786-06 (EI) SRIVASTAVA, PRAMOD K MT SINAI SCHOOL OF MEDICINE BOX 1215 NEW YORK, NY 10029 Genetic determinants of polymorphic sarcoma antigens
R25CA-44789-02A2 (CEC) BURZYNSKI, NORBERT J UNIVERSITY OF LOUISVILLE LOUISVILLE, KY 40292 Cancer education grant program
R29CA-44790-05 (EDC) WHITE, EMILY FRED HUTCHINSON CANCER RES CTR 1124 COLUMBIA STREET SEATTLE, WA 98104 Epidemiology of physical activity and colon cancer
R01CA-44794-05 (EI) FANGER, MICHAEL W DEPT OF MICROBIOLOGY DARTMOUTH MEDICAL SCHOOL HANOVER, NH 03756 Heteroantibody mediated killing of lymphoma cells
R01CA-44799-02 (SB) ADRIAN, THOMAS E CREIGHTON UNIVERSITY 2500 CALIFORNIA ST OMAHA, NE 68178 Cholecystokinin effect on pancreatic growth and tumors
R01CA-44806-04 (CPA) BOX, HAROLD C ROSWELL PARK MEMORIAL INST 666 ELM STREET BUFFALO, NY 14263 DNA damage, promotion and the prooxidant state
R01CA-44822-05 (EVR) LENZ, JOHN R ALBERT EINSTEIN COLL OF MED 1300 MORRIS PARK AVENUE BRONX, NY 10461 Leukemogenesis by murine retroviruses
R29CA-44838-05 (PTHB) MILLER, ALAN M UNIVERSITY OF FLORIDA PO BOX 100277 COLL OF MED GAINESVILL, FL 32610-0277 Metabolic and molecular control of myelopoiesis
R01CA-44848-05 (MCHA) FENICAL, WILLIAM H UNIV OF CALIFORNIA, SAN DIEGO LA JOLLA, CALIFORNIA 92093-02 Antitumor-antibiotics from marine microorganisms
R01CA-44877-05 (PTHB) HERLYN, MEENHARD WISTAR INSTITUTE 36TH & SPRUCE STREETS PHILADELPHIA, PA 19104 Growth regulation in normal and malignant cells
R01CA-44881-05 (RAD) WITHERS, H RODNEY UNIVERSITY OF CALIFORNIA DEPT OF RADIATION ONCOLOGY LOS ANGELES, CA 90024 Response of spinal cord to low radiation poses
R55CA-44887-04 (ET) DONNENBERG, ALBERT D MONTEFIORE UNIVERSITY HOSPITAL 3459 FIFTH AVE PITTSBURGH, PA 15213 Depletion of bone marrow

lymphocytes

R29CA-44890-04 (ET) SWEATMAN, TREVOR W UNIV OF TENNESSEE-MEMPHIS 874 UNION AVENUE MEMPHIS, TN 38163 The pharmacology of new intravesical therapeutics

R01CA-44903-04 (HUD) SCHINKE, STEVEN P COLUMBIA UNIVERSITY 622 WEST 113TH STREET NEW YORK, NY 10025 Preventing tobacco use among native American adolescents

R01CA-44907-06 (HUD) SUSSMAN, STEVEN Y DEPT OF HLTH BEHAVIOR RES INST 35 N LAKE AVE , SUITE 200 PASADENA, CA 91101 Smokeless tobacco--Onset, prevention, and cessation

R01CA-44921-05 (HUD) ELDER, JOHN SAN DIEGO STATE UNIVERSITY SAN DIEGO, CA 92182 Smokeless tobacco prevention in public schools

R29CA-44940-05 (RAD) CALDERWOOD, STUART K DANA FARBER CANCER INSTITUTE 44 BINNEY STREET BOSTON, MA 02115 Role of calcium in cellular responses to hyperthermia

R01CA-44949-05 (CPA) CHU, GILBERT STANFORD UNIVERSITY MED CTR DIV OF ONCOLOGY, RM M211 STANFORD, CA 94305 Finding the molecular defect in xeroderma pigmentosum

R55CA-44958-04A1 (EVR) DYNAN, WILLIAM S UNIVERSITY OF COLORADO BOULDER, COLO 80309 Functional organization of bk virus promoter/enhancer

R01CA-44960-05 (SRC) RICCIARDI, ROBERT P WISTAR INSTITUTE 36TH AND SPRUCE STREETS PHILADELPHIA, PA 19104 Role of BKV enhancers in virus regulation and cancer

U01CA-44968-04 (SRC) GRIZZLE, WILLIAM E UNIV OF AL AT BIRMINGHAM UAB STATION BIRMINGHAM, AL 35294 Cooperative human tissue network

R01CA-44970-05 (SRC) FRISQUE, RICHARD J PENNSYLVANIA STATE UNIVERSITY 433 S FREAR BUILDING UNIVERSITY PARK, PA 16802 Human polyomaviruses- oncogenic potential and mechanisms

U01CA-44971-04 (SRC) CLAUSEN, KATHRYN P OHIO STATE UNIVERSITY 2078 GRAVES HALL COLUMBUS, OH 43210 Cooperative human tissue network

U01CA-44974-04 (SRC) LIVOLSI, VIRGINIA A HOSPITAL OF UNIV OF PENNSYLVAN 3400 SPRUCE STREET PHILADELPHIA, PA 19104 Comprehensive human tissue network

R37CA-44976-06 (NSS) TILGHMAN, SHIRLEY M PRINCETON UNIVERSITY PRINCETON, NJ 08544 Regulation of alpha-fetoprotein gene expression

R01CA-44977-06 (EI) TRUCCO, MASSIMO CHILDREN'S HOSP OF PITTSBURGH 3705 FIFTH AVE PITTSBURGH, PA 15213 Lymphokines involved in immunosurveillance

R01CA-44980-06 (CPA) KLEIN-SZANTO, ANDRES J FOX CHASE CANCER CENTER 7701 BURHOLME AVENUE PHILADELPHIA, PA 19111 Markers of skin tumor progression

R01CA-44981-05 (MEP) KLEIN-SZANTO, ANDRES J FOX CHASE CANCER CENTER 7701 BURHOLME AVENUE PHILADELPHIA, PA 19111 Carcinogenesis of xenotransplanted human epithelia

R37CA-44982-05 (RAD) BIAGLOW, JOHN E UNIVERSITY OF PENNSYLVANIA 3508 MARKET STREET/B30 PHILADELPHIA, PA 19104-3357 Modification of x-ray response of anoxic-hypoxic cells

R01CA-44983-06 (ALY) ANDERSON, CLARK L 480 W. NINTH AVENUE COLUMBUS, OH 43210-1228 Fc receptor structure and function

P01CA-44991-04 (SRC) BERNSTEIN, IRWIN D FRED HUTCHINSON CANCER RES CTR 1124 COLUMBIA STREET SEATTLE, WA 98104 Therapy of leukemia/lymphoma with monoclonal antibodies

P01CA-44991-04 0001 (SRC) PRESS, OLIVER W Therapy of leukemia/lymphoma with monoclonal antibodies Radiolabelled antibody therapy of B-cell lymphoma

P01CA-44991-04 0003 (SRC) APPELBAUM, FREDERICK Therapy of leukemia/lymphoma with monoclonal antibodies Radiolabelled antibody therapy of acute leukemia

P01CA-44991-04 0004 (SRC) NELP, WILL B Therapy of leukemia/lymphoma with monoclonal antibodies Radiolabelled antibody biodistribution, internal dosimetry/radiotherapy

P01CA-44991-04 9001 (SRC) BERNSTEIN, IRWIN D Therapy of leukemia/lymphoma with monoclonal antibodies Statistics--Core

P01CA-44991-04 9003 (SRC) EARY, JANET F Therapy of leukemia/lymphoma with monoclonal antibodies Radiochemistry--Core

R01CA-44998-05 (PHRA) IYENGAR, SRINIVAS R MOUNT SINAI SCHOOL OF MEDICINE ONE GUSTAVE LEVY PLACE, BOX 12 NEW YORK, NY 10029 Molecular mechanism of desensitization

R01CA-45003-06 (SSS) FOX, SARAH A UNIVERSITY OF CALIFORNIA 10833 LE CONTE AVENUE LOS ANGELES, CA 90024-1683 Increasing screening mammography for women over 65

R29CA-45011-06 (RAD) YASUI , LINDA S NORTHERN ILLINOIS UNIVERSITY DEPT OF BIOLOGICAL SCIENCES DEKALB, IL 60115 Cytotoxicity of 125I decay produced lesions in chromatin

R01CA-45028-04 (MEP) CHRISTMAN, JUDITH K MICHIGAN CANCER FOUNDATION 110 EAST WARREN AVE DETROIT, MI 48201 Mechanism of 5-azacr-mediated alteration in gene activity

R01CA-45033-04 (SRC) FOLK, WILLIAM R UNIVERSITY OF MISSOURI M121 MEDICAL SCIS BUILDING COLUMBIA, MO 65212 Mechanism of transformation by BK virus

R29CA-45049-05 (EI) WHITE, HILLARY D DARTMOUTH MEDICAL SCHOOL HANOVER, NH 03756 Recognition of leukemia antigen by anti-viral CTL's

R01CA-45052-05 (MGN) KRONTIRIS, THEODORE G NEW ENGLAND MEDICAL CENTER 750 WASHINGTON STREET BOSTON, MA 02111 Analysis of human oncogene polymorphisms

R01CA-45055-09 (REB) KOOS, ROBERT D 655 WEST BALTIMORE STREET BALTIMORE, MD 21201 Ovarian angiogenesis

R01CA-45078-06 (RAD) ROSENSTEIN, BARRY S MOUNT SINAI SCHOOL OF MEDICINE ONE GUSTAVE LEVY PLACE NEW YORK, NY 10029 Repair of solar UV induced DNA damage

R01CA-45124-06 (VR) WONG, PAUL K UNIV OF TEX/MD ANDERSON CAN CT PO BOX 389 SMITHVILLE, TX 78957 Paralytogenesis induced by MuLV mutants

R01CA-45125-05 (EVR) ARLINGHAUS, RALPH B UT MD ANDERSON CANCER CTR 1515 HOLCOMB BLVD HOUSTON, TX 77030 Studies on viral & cellular mos proteins

R01CA-45127-06 (EVR) SARKAR, NURUL H MEDICAL COLLEGE OF GEORGIA CB-2607 AUGUSTA, GA 30912-2400 Effect of diet on murine mammary tumorigenesis

R37CA-45128-06 (NSS) GORBACH, SHERWOOD L TUFTS UNIVERSITY 136 HARRISON AVENUE BOSTON, MA 02111 Diet, estrogens, and breast cancer

R01CA-45131-05 (SSS) HINTON, DAVID E UNIVERSITY OF CALIFORNIA SCHOOL OF VETINARY MEDICINE DAVIS, CA 95616 Mechanistic hepatocarcinogenesis in fish

R29CA-45141-05 (RAD) CORNFORTH, MICHAEL N UNIV OF TEXAS MED BRANCH 3.310 GAIL BORDEN BLDG GALVESTON, TX 77550 Cytogenetic effects pertaining to low doses of radiation

R29CA-45145-04 (BBCA) GOLDSTEIN, BARRY M UNIVERSITY OF ROCHESTER 601 ELMWOOD AVENUE ROCHESTER, NY 14642 Conformational studies of new antitumor agents

R37CA-45148-06 (NSS) MAIZEL, ABBY L ROGER WILLIAMS GENERAL HOSP 825 CHALKSTONE AVENUE PROVIDENCE, RI 02908 Biomolecular nature of human B cell growth factor

R55CA-45153-04 (BNP) COY, DAVID H TULANE UNIVERSITY MED CTR 1430 TULANE AVENUE NEW ORLEANS, LA 70112 Anti-mitogenic bombesin antagonists

R01CA-45154-05 (RAD) WARTERS, RAYMOND L UNIVERSITY OF UTAH MEDICAL CTR SALT LAKE CITY, UT 84132 Heat-induced radiosensitization

R01CA-45156-05 (RAD) WHEELER, KENNETH T, JR BOWMAN GRAY SCH OF MED MEDICAL CENTER BLVD WINSTON-SALEM, NC 27157 DNA damage and repair in irradiated normal and tumor cells

R01CA-45158-05 (EVR) CHANG, ESTHER H UNIFORMED SERVS UNIV/HEALTH SC 4301 JONES BRIDGE ROAD BETHESDA, MD 20814-4799 Oncogenes in human cancer induction

P01CA-45164-04A1 (SRC) IP, CLEMENT C Y ROSWELL PARK MEMORIAL INST 666 ELM STREET BUFFALO, NY 14263 Mechanism of selenium chemoprevention of carcinogenesis

P01CA-45164-04A1 0001 (SRC) IP, CLEMENT Mechanism of selenium chemoprevention of carcinogenesis Mammary cancer prevention by novel selenium compounds

P01CA-45164-04A1 0002 (SRC) GANTHER, HOWARD Mechanism of selenium chemoprevention of carcinogenesis Selenium metabolism and anticarcinogenic action

P01CA-45164-04A1 0003 (SRC) MEDINA, DANIEL Mechanism of selenium chemoprevention of carcinogenesis Selenoproteins in rat mammary tumorigenesis

P01CA-45164-04A1 0004 (SRC) SUNDE, ROGER A Mechanism of selenium chemoprevention of carcinogenesis Selenium metabolism and selenoproteins with high selenium

P01CA-45164-04A1 0005 (SRC) THOMPSON, HENRY Mechanism of selenium chemoprevention of carcinogenesis Mechanisms of selenium anticancer and toxic activities

R37CA-45187-05 (ET) ROTH, JACK A UNIVERSITY OF TEXAS 1515 HOLCOMBE BLVD HOUSTON, TX 77030 Tumor antigens expressed by oncogene-transformed cells

U01CA-45202-04S1 (SRC) ZERHOUNI, ELIAS A JOHNS HOPKINS MED INST 600 N WOLFE ST, MRI RM 143 BALTIMORE, MD 21205 National collaborative diagnostic imaging trial

U01CA-45205-04S1 (SRC) QUINT, LESLIE E UNIVERSITY OF MICHIGAN HOSP 1500 EAST MEDICAL CTR DRIVE ANN ARBOR, MI 48109-0030 National collaborative diagnostic imaging trial project

R29CA-45208-05 (EVR) SNAPKA, ROBERT M OHIO STATE UNIVERSITY 103 WISEMAN HALL COLUMBUS, OH 43210 Aberrant papovavirus replication after genotoxic damage

R29CA-45213-05 (CPA) ELLIOTT, MARK S OLD DOMINION UNIVERSITY NORFOLK, VA 23529 Modulation of queuine levels with tumor promoters

R29CA-45216-04 (RAD) TAYLOR, JEREMY M UNIV OF CALIFORNIA LOS ANGELES 10833 LE CONTE LOS ANGELES, CA 90024-1714 Radiation research quantitative methods and models

R01CA-45217-05 (EVR) ARLINGHAUS, RALPH B U OF TEXAS/M D ANDERSON CA CTR 1515 HOLCOMBE BLVD/BOX 89 HOUSTON, TX 77030 A temperature-sensitive retrovirus spicing mutant

R01CA-45218-05 (HEM) NATHAN, CARL F CORNELL UNIVERSITY 1300 YORK AVENUE NEW YORK, N Y 10021 Oxidative injury by human neutrophils

U01CA-45226-03S1 (SRC) PAUSHTER, DAVID M CLEVELAND CLINIC FOUNDATION 9500 EUCLID AVENUE CLEVELAND, OH 44195 Imaging techniches in prostate cancer

R01CA-45229-04A1 (RNM) NALCIOGLU, ORHAN UNIVERSITY OF CALIFORNIA DIV OF PHYSICS & ENGINEERING IRVINE, CA 92717 Incoherent flow imaging by NMR

R01CA-45233-04 (CBY) BRACKENBURY, ROBERT W UNIVERSITY OF CINCINNATI 231 BETHESDA AVENUE, ML #521 CINCINNATI, OH 45267-0521 Cell-cell interactions in malignancy

R01CA-45234-06 (MGN) HANAHAN, DOUGLAS UNIVERSITY OF CALIFORNIA SAN FRANCISCO, CA 94143-0534 Targeted oncogenesis and diabetes in transgenic mice

R29CA-45236-05 (IMB) YAGI, MAYUMI SEATTLE BIOMEDICAL RES INST 4 NICKERSON STREET SEATTLE, WA 98109-1651 Analysis of a novel proliferation-associated antigen

R29CA-45240-05 (CTY) FARNHAM, PEGGY J UNIV OF WISCONSIN 1400 UNIVERSITY AVENUE MADISON, WI 53706-1599 Transcriptional regulation of growth-related genes

R29CA-45241-05 (HEM) ANDERSON, STEVEN M SUNY AT STONY BROOK ROOM 153, BHS-9 STONY BROOK, NY 11794 Modulation of hematopoietic stem cell proliferation

U01CA-45254-04S1 (SRC) RIFKIN, MATTHEW D MAIN BUILDING 11TH AND SANSOM STREETS PHILADELPHIA, PA 19107 National collaborative diagnostic imaging project

U01CA-45256-04S2 (SRC) MC NEIL, BARBARA J HARVARD MEDICAL SCHOOL 25 SHATTUCK ST/PARCEL B-1ST FL BOSTON, MA 02115 Radiological diagnostic oncology group

R29CA-45272-05 (ALY) YARMUSH, MARTIN L RUTGERS UNIVERSITY P O BOX 909 PISCATAWAY, NJ 08854 Structure and dynamics of immune complexes

R01CA-45277-06 (RAD) STAMATO, THOMAS LANKENAU MEDICAL RESEARCH CENT LANCASTER AVE WEST OF CITY LIN PHILADELPHIA, PA 19151 Isolation of radiation sensitive mammalian cell

R01CA-45279-03 (HEM) HOFFMAN, RONALD INDIANA UNIVERSITY SCH OF MED 975 WEST WALNUT STREET INDIANAPOLIS, IN 46202-5121 Purification of primitive hematopoietic progenitor cells

R01CA-45284-04 (EI) PERUSSIA, BICE THOMAS JEFFERSON UNIV MED COLL 1020 LOCUST ST PHILADELPHIA, PA 19107 Activation of non MHC-restricted cytotoxic lymphocytes

R29CA-45285-05 (VR) PALLAS, DAVID C DANA-FARBER CANCER

INSTITUTE 44 BINNEY STREET BOSTON, MA 02115 The role of cellular proteins in polyoma transformation

R01CA-45290-04A1 (PTHB) NEWTON, SHEILA HOWARD UNIVERSITY CANCER CENTE 2041 GEORGIA AVENUE, NW WASHINGTON, DC 20060 Mechanism of fibronectin mediated adhesion

R29CA-45293-05 (GMA) MORRIS, REBECCA J U T M D ANDERSON CANCER CENTER P O BOX 389 SMITHVILLE, TX 78957 Epidermal stem cells in two-stage carcinogenesis

R01CA-45303-05 (ET) HANDSCHUMACHER, ROBERT E YALE UNIV SCHOOL OF MED 333 CEDAR STREET/BOX 3333 NEW HAVEN, CONN 06510 Transport metabolic control of pyrimidine nucleoside

R29CA-45306-05 (RNM) BLACKBAND, STEPHEN J THE HOPKINS UNIV SCHOOL OF MED 720 RUTLAND AVENUE BALTIMORE, MD 21205 NMR microscopy and localized spectroscopy at 360 and 200 MHZ

R29CA-45310-04 (CBY) BOCKUS, BEVERLY J TUFTS UNIVERSITY 136 HARRISON AVENUE C-myc phosphorylation and growth related kinases

R29CA-45312-05 (PTHB) VUK-PAVLOVIC, STANIMIR MAYO FOUNDATION 200 FIRST STREET S W ROCHESTER, MN 55905 Autocrine mechanisms in micrometastasis models

R29CA-45313-05 (SSS) STORER, BARRY E MEDICAL SCIENCES CENTER 420 NORTH CHARTER STREET MADISON, WI 53706 Biostatistical methods for cancer research

R29CA-45316-05 (PTHB) DIAKUN, KATE R ROSWELL PARK MEMORIAL INST 666 ELM STREET BUFFALO, NY 14263 Sialylated carbohydrate antigens related to Ca 125

R29CA-45327-04 (MEP) SOUBA, WILEY W DEPARTMENT OF SURGERY BOX J-28 COLLEGE OF MEDICINE GAINESVILLE, FL 32610 Glutamine metabolism in the tumor bearing rat

R01CA-45339-05 (HEM) LEMISCHKA, IHOR R PRINCETON UNVIERSITY P O BOX 5292 PRINCETON, NJ 08544-1014 In vivo behavior of hematopoietic stem cell clones

R29CA-45354-04 (PTHB) SAMLOWSKI, WOLFRAM E UNIVERSITY OF UTAH 50 NORTH MEDICAL DRIVE SALT LAKE CITY, UT 84132 Endothelial cell toxicity of marrow ablative agents

R29CA-45357-06 (RAD) PAULSEN, KEITH D THAYER SCHOOL OF ENGINEERING DARTMOUTH COLLEGE HANOVER, NH 03755 Numerical analysis of electromagnetic hyperthermia

R01CA-45358-03 (ET) WALLACK, MARC KENNETH ST VINCENT'S HOSPITAL 153 WEST 11TH ST NEW YORK, NY 10011 Phase III randomized trial of vaccinia melanoma oncolysate

R29CA-45360-05 (EVR) SCHWARTZ, RICHARD C MICHIGAN STATE UNIVERSITY GILTNER HALL EAST LANSING, MI 48824-1101 Synergy of viral ras & myc in lymphoid transformation

R01CA-45361-05 (MEP) RAJALAKSHMI, S UNIVERSITY OF TORONTO 1 KINGS COLLEGE CIRCLE TORONTO, ONTARIO M5S 1A8 CANAD Glycosylation in experimental carcinogenesis

R01CA-45363-04 (PBC) BLASZCZYK-THURIN, MAGDALENA THE WISTAR INSTITUTE 36TH & SPRUCE STREETS PHILADELPHIA, PA 19104 Tumor-associated fucosyltransferase

U10CA-45374-03 (SRC) BROWNING, SCOTT M KAISER PERMANENTE 4647 ZION AVENUE SAN DIEGO, CA 92120 Community clinical oncology program

U10CA-45377-05 (SRC) DOTY, GORDON L PROVIDENCE MEDICAL CENTER 4805 N E GLISAN PORTLAND, OR 97213 Columbia River community clinical oncology program

R01CA-45382-05 (EVR) CARMICHAEL, GORDON G UNIV OF CONNECTICUT HLTH CENTE 263 FARMINGTON AVE FARMINGTON, CT 06030 Processing and function of polyoma RNA

U10CA-45389-05 (SRC) DIFINO, SANTO M HEMATOLOGY-ONCOLOGY ASSOC OF C 5789 WIDEWATERS PARKWAY DEWITT, NY 13214 Syracuse hematology-oncology CCOP

U10CA-45400-03 (SRC) HART, RONALD D 2901 W KINNICKINNIC RIVER PKWY MILWAUKEE, WI 53215-3690 Community clinical oncology program--Milwaukee

R01CA-45408-05 (RAD) DRITSCHILO, ANATOLY GEORGETOWN UNIV MEDICAL CTR 3800 RESERVOIR ROAD, NW WASHINGTON, DC 20007 Molecular studies of radiation resistant tumor cells

U10CA-45418-05 (SRC) BERKOWITZ, IRVING M THE MEDICAL CENTER OF DELAWARE P O BOX 6001 NEWARK, DE 19718 Community clinical oncology program

R29CA-45422-04 (MEP) KLINE, KIMBERLY THE UNIV OF TEXAS AT AUSTIN AUSTIN, TX 78712 Micronutrients in immunomodulations & cancer

R01CA-45423-03 (ET) PEREZ-SOLER, ROMAN U T MD ANDERSON CANCER CTR PO BOX 80-1515 HOLCOMBE BLVD HOUSTON, TX 77030 Development of new lipophilic cisplatin analogues

R01CA-45424-04A1 (RAD) SEVILLA, MICHAEL D OAKLAND UNIVERSITY ROCHESTER, MI 48063 Radiation induced sulfhydryl autoxidation and the OER

R29CA-45425-05 (ET) STEARNS, MARK E MEDICAL COLLEGE OF PENNSYLVANI 3300 HENRY AVE PHILADELPHIA, PA 19129 Estramustine's therapeutic effects--Tumor cell kinesin

U10CA-45450-05 (SRC) FRANKLIN, ERNEST W ST JOSEPH'S HOSPITAL/SUITE 100 5665 PEACHTREE DUNWOODY ROAD ATLANTA, GA 30342-1701 Atlanta regional community clinical oncology program

U10CA-45459-05 (SRC) KELLER, ALAN M ST FRANCIS HOSPITAL/NWBCC 6161 SOUTH YALE TULSA, OK 74136 Saint Francis Hospital/Natalie Warren Bryant CCOP

U10CA-45461-03 (SRC) CASSIDY, MICHAEL J BAY AREA TUMOR INSTITUTE 2844 SUMMIT STREET SUITE 204 OAKLAND, CA 94609 Community clinical oncology program

U10CA-45466-05 (SRC) CAGGIANO, VINCENT SUTTER COMMUNITY HOSPITALS 5275 F STREET SACRAMENTO, CA 95819 Sacramento community clinical oncology program

R29CA-45468-04 (MEP) MC GARRITY, THOMAS J MILTON S HERSHEY MEDICAL CTR P O BOX 850 HERSHEY, PA 17033 Experimental and clinical studies in colorectal cancer

R01CA-45480-05 (SSS) PENMAN, SHELDON S MASSACHUSETTS INST OF TECHNOLO 77 MASSACHUSETTS AVENUE CAMBRIDGE, MA 02139 Nuclear proteins specific to cell type and malignancy

R01CA-45484-03 (EI) EBERLEIN, TIMOTHY J BRIGHAM & WOMEN'S HOSPITAL 75 FRANCIS STREET BOSTON, MA 02115 An alternative method of adoptive immunotherapy

R01CA-45504-04 (SRC) WYNDER, ERNST L AMERICAN HEALTH FOUNDATION 320 EAST 43RD STREET NEW YORK, NY 10017 Low-fat diet in stage II breast cancer--Randomized study

P30CA-45508-05 (CCS) ROBERTS, RICHARD J COLD SPRING HARBOR LABORATORY POST OFFICE BOX 100 COLD SPRING HARBOR, NY 11724 CSHL cancer center support grant

P30CA-45508-05 9001 (CCS) HANAHAN, DOUGLAS CSHL cancer center support grant Core--Animals facilities

P30CA-45508-05 9002 (CCS) ROBERTS, RICHARD J CSHL cancer center support grant Core--Electromechanical workshop

P30CA-45508-05 9003 (CCS) HARLOW, EDWARD E CSHL cancer center support grant Core--Monoclonal antibody facility

P30CA-45508-05 9004 (CCS) ROBERTS, RICHARD J CSHL cancer center support grant Core--Computer services

P30CA-45508-05 9006 (CCS) WIGLER, MICHAEL H CSHL cancer center support grant Core--Flow cytometry facility

P30CA-45508-05 9007 (CCS) MARSHAK, DANIEL R CSHL cancer center support grant Core--Protein chemistry

P30CA-45508-05 9008 (CCS) SPECTOR, DAVID L CSHL cancer center support grant Core--Electron microscope facility

P30CA-45508-05 9009 (CCS) ZOLLER, MARK J CSHL cancer center support grant Core--Oligonucleotide synthesis facility

R29CA-45513-05 (EDC) STOCKWELL, HEATHER G UNIVERSITY OF SOUTH FLORIDA 13301 N 30TH STREET TAMPA, FL 33612 Epidemiology of lung cancer in non-smoking women

R01CA-45528-05A1 (ET) BERNAL, SAMUEL D UNIVERSITY OF HOSPITAL 88 E NEWTON STREET BOSTON, MA 02118 Chemotherapy resistance of human respiratory carcinomas

R29CA-45541-05 (RAD) FIELD, ELIZABETH H VETERANS AFFAIRS MED CENTER HIGHWAY 6 WEST IOWA CITY, IA 52246 Mechanism of TLI-induced immunosuppression in nzb/nzw

P01CA-45548-05 (CAK) FOLKMAN, MOSES J CHILDREN'S HOSPITAL 300 LONGWOOD AVENUE BOSTON, MA 02115 Regulation of angiogenesis

P01CA-45548-05 0001 (CAK) INGBER, DONALD Regulation of angiogenesis Regulation of angiogenesis by growth factors

P01CA-45548-05 0002 (CAK) INGBER, DONALD Regulation of angiogenesis Extracellular matrix as a solid state regulator

P01CA-45548-05 0003 (CAK) D'AMORE, PATRICIA A Regulation of angiogenesis Role of pericytes in the regulation of angiogenesis

P01CA-45548-05 0004 (CAK) ZETTER, BRUCE R Regulation of angiogenesis Role of mast cells in angiogenesis

P01CA-45548-05 0005 (CAK) GLOWACKI, JULIANNE Regulation of angiogenesis The regulation of vascularization in vivo

P01CA-45548-05 0006 (CAK) FOLKMAN, JUDAH Regulation of angiogenesis Regulation of angiogenesis by its inhibitors

P01CA-45548-05 9001 (CAK) Regulation of angiogenesis

P01CA-45548-05 9002 (CAK) FOLKMAN, JUDAH Regulation of angiogenesis Laboratory service core

P01CA-45548-05 9003 (CAK) D'AMORE, PATRICIA A Regulation of angiogenesis Photography core

P01CA-45548-05 9004 (CAK) SHING, YUEN Regulation of angiogenesis Tissue culture--Growth factor unit

U10CA-45553-03 (SRC) EBBERT, LARRY P RAPID CITY MEDICAL CENTER 728 COLUMBUS STREET RAPID CITY, SD 57701 Rapid City regional group community clinical oncology program

R01CA-45557-05 (RAD) ILIAKIS, GEORGE THOMAS JEFFERSON UNIVERSITY 10TH & WALNUT STS PHILADELPHIA, PA 19107 Radiosensitization by BrdUrd/IdUrd--Cellular molecular effects

U10CA-45558-04A1 (SRC) HEIM, WILLIAM J MERCY HOSPITAL 746 JEFFERSON AVE, SUITE 205 SCRANTON, PA 18501 Mercy hospital CCOP (MCCOP)

R01CA-45559-04A1 (HEM) SIEFF, COLIN A DANA-FARBER CANCER INSTITUTE 44 BINNEY ST BOSTON, MA 02115 The sources and actions of human GM-CSF and multi-CSF

U10CA-45560-05 (SRC) GOODWIN, WENDALL J 1000 E. PRIMROSE/ SUITE 450 SPRINGFIELD, MO 65807 Ozarks regional community clinical oncology program

U10CA-45564-05 (SRC) DAVILA, ENRIQUE MOUNT SINAI MEDICAL CENTER 4300 ALTON ROAD MIAMI BEACH, FL 33140 Community clinical oncology program

R01CA-45571-05 (HEM) BOSWELL, H SCOTT INDIANA UNIVERSITY 975 W. WALNUT ST IB442 INDIANAPOLIS, IN 46202-5121 Mechanisms of hemopoietic immortalization

R29CA-45587-05 (PTHB) BYERS, HUGH R DEPARTMENT OF PATHOLOGY BOSTON, MA 02114 Pathology and mechanism of melanoma cell migration

R01CA-45590-04 (RAD) BROOKS, ANTONE L BATTELLE MEMORIAL INSTITUTE P O BOX 999 RICHLAND, WA 99352 Radiation induced chromosome damage in vivo

R01CA-45593-06 (BBCA) KIM, SUNG-HOU UNIVERSITY OF CALIFORNIA 336 SPROUL HALL BERKELEY, CA 94720 X-ray crystallographic studies of ras oncogene products

R01CA-45611-05 (HEM) CHIU, ING-MING OHIO STATE UNIVERSITY 480 W 9TH AVE RM S2052 COLUMBUS, OH 43210 Molecular and functional analysis of human class 1 HBGF

R01CA-45614-04 (EDC) HOLLY, ELIZABETH A NORTHERN CALIFORNIA CANCER CTR 1301 SHOREWAY ROAD SUITE 425 BELMONT, CA 94002 Epidemiology of non-Hodgkin's lymphoma & retroviral test

R29CA-45620-05 (ET) DANHAUSER, LYNN L UNIV TEXAS M D ANDERSON CAN CT 1515 HOLCOMBE BLVD HOUSTON, TX 77030 Enhanced cancer therapeutic activity by host protection

R29CA-45626-05 (EI) HARPER, JOHN R TELIOS PHARMACEUTICALS INC 2909 SCIENCE PARK ROAD SAN DIEGO, CA 92121 Molecular profiles of small cell lung carcinoma antigens

R01CA-45628-05 (ET) ERICKSON, LEONARD C LOYOLA UNIV MEDICAL CTR 2160 SOUTH FIRST AVE MAYWOOD, IL 60153 Biochemical modulation of drug resistance in tumor cells

R01CA-45634-06 (PTHB) GINDER, GORDON D UNIVERSITY OF MINNESOTA BOX 236 UMHC/411 MASONIC CTR MINNEAPOLIS, MN 55455 Regulation of HLA-class I gene expression in human tumor

R29CA-45640-03 (ET) FRONDOZA, CARMELITA G JOHNS HOPKINS UNIV SCH OF PUB 615 N. WOLFE STREET BALTIMORE, MD 21205 Plasmacytoma resistance to alkylating agents

R01CA-45642-05 (MBY) GILMAN, MICHAEL Z COLD SPRING HARBOR LAB PO BOX 100-1 BUNGTOWN RD COLD SPRING HARBOR, NY 11724 Induction of c-fos expression by extracellular signals

PROJECT NO., ORGANIZATIONAL UNIT., INVESTIGATOR, ADDRESS, TITLE

R01CA-45643-03 (BBCA) DROBNY, GARY P UNIVERSITY OF WASHINGTON DEPT OF CHEMISTRY, BG-10 SEATTLE, WA 98195 NMR studies of the anticancer drug neocarzinostatin

R29CA-45658-05 (EI) PASTERNACK, MARK S MASSACHUSETTS GENERAL HOSPITAL INFECTIOUS DISEASE UNIT BOSTON, MA 02114 Analysis of cytotoxic T lymphocyte serine esterase

R29CA-45664-05 (CPA) SNOW, ELIZABETH T NY UNIVERSITY MED CTR 550 FIRST AVE NEW YORK NY 10016 Mechanisms of metal mutagenesis--Cr, Ni, and Be

R55CA-45667-04 (ET) GEAHLEN, ROBERT L PURDUE UNIVERSITY SCHOOL OF PHARMACY WEST LAFAYETTE, IN 47907 Inhibitors of protein myristoylation as anticancer drugs

R29CA-45671-05 (ET) BHALLA, KAPIL MEDICAL UNIV OF SOUTH CAROLINA 171 ASHLEY AVENUE CHARLESTON, S C 29425 Deoxycytidine mediated protection of myeloid progenitor cells

R01CA-45674-05 (ET) JOHNSON, CANDACE SUE EYE & EAR INST OF PITTSBURGH 203 LOTHROP STREET PITTSBURGH, PA 15213 Mechanisms of the anti-leukemic effects of TNF

R01CA-45677-06 (HEM) GABIG, THEODORE G INDIANA UNIV SCH OF MED 975 W. WALNUT STREET INDIANAPOLIS, IN 46202-5121 IL-3 response--Control by G proteins and PIP 2 hydrolyssis

R01CA-45682-05 (ALY) PERLMUTTER, ROGER M UNIVERSITY OF WASHINGTON SL-15 SEATTLE, WA 98195 Lymphocyte-specific protein tyrosine kinase genes

R01CA-45689-04 (RNM) DUNN, FLOYD UNIVERSITY OF ILLINOIS 1406 WEST GREEN STREET URBANA, IL 61801 Ultrasonic absorption by biological media

R29CA-45690-05 (PBC) SPITALNIK, STEVEN L UNIVERSITY OF PENNSYLVANIA 217 MED LABS PHILADELPHIA, PA 19104 Shedding, secretion, and transfer of glycosphingolipids

R01CA-45700-05 (CPA) PITOT, HENRY C UNIVERSITY OF WISCONSIN-MADISO 1400 UNIVERSITY AVE MADISON, WI 53706-1599 Instability of tumor promotion in hepatocarcinogenesis

R01CA-45708-04A1 (PTHB) STERN, DAVID F YALE UNIV SCHOOL OF MEDICINE 310 CEDAR ST/ BOX 3333 NEW HAVEN, CT 06510 Transformation by the neu oncogene product and EGF

R01CA-45726-04 (EI) CHERESH, DAVID A SCRIPPS CLINIC & RES FDN 10666 NORTH TORREY PINES ROAD LA JOLLA, CALIF 92037 Regulation of tumor cell attachment by surface antigens

R29CA-45727-06 (MEP) SIEGAL, GENE P UNIVERSITY OF ALABAMA UAB STATION BIRMINGHAM, AL 35223 Chemical progression and inhibition of neoplasia

R01CA-45734-05 (CPA) BILLINGS, PAUL C HOSP OF UNIV OF PENNSYLVANIA 3400 SPRUCE ST / 2 DONNER BLDG PHILADELPHIA, PA 19104-4283 Target proteases of anticarcinogenic protease inhibitors

R01CA-45735-04A1 (MEP) WETTERHAHN, KAREN E DARTMOUTH COLLEGE HANOVER, NH 03755 Effect of chromium on gene expression

R01CA-45743-04 (RNM) JOLESZ, FERENC A BRIGHAM AND WOMEN'S HOSPITAL 75 FRANCIS STREET BOSTON, MA 02115 NMR imaging of laser-tissue interactions

R01CA-45745-04 (PTHB) TESTA, JOSEPH R FOX CHASE CANCER CENTER 7701 BURHOLME AVENUE PHILADELPHIA, PA 19111 Cytogenetics of human lung cancer and mesothelioma

R29CA-45757-05 (CTY) SUDOL, MARIUS ROCKEFELLER UNIVERSITY 1230 YORK AVENUE NEW YORK, NY 10021 Structural and functional analysis of the yes proto-oncogene

R37CA-45762-04 (EDC) ROSENBERG, LYNN BOSTON UNIV SCH OF MEDICINE 1371 BEACON STREET BROOKLINE, MA 02146 Case control surveillance of serious illnesses and drugs

R01CA-45767-06 (SSS) OSEROFF, ALLAN R ROSWELL PARK CANCER INSTITUTE ELM & CARLTON STREETS BUFFALO, NY 14263 Selective photochemotherapy--development and application

R01CA-45799-05 (MGN) SHAPER, JOEL H JOHNS HOPKINS UNIV SCH OF MED 600 NORTH WOLFE STREET BALTIMORE, MD 21205 Mouse galtransferase--Structure/expression in development

U10CA-45807-06 (SRC) WADE, JAMES L MEMORIAL MEDICAL CENTER 800 NORTH RUTLEDGE STREET SPRINGFIELD, IL 62781-0001 Central Illinois community clinical oncology program

U10CA-45808-05 (SRC) SPURR, CHARLES L SOUTHEAST CANCER CONTROL 2062 BEACH ST WINSTON-SALEM, NC 27103-2614 Southeast cancer control consortium--CCOP

U10CA-45809-04 (SRC) WINN, RODGER J UT M.D. ANDERSON CANCER CTR 1515 HOLCOMBE BLVD HOUSTON, TX 77030 Community clinical oncology program

R01CA-45814-04 (HEM) MC GLAVE, PHILIP B UNIV OF MINNESOTA - BOX 480 UM 420 DELAWARE ST SE MINNEAPOLIS, MN 55455 Regulation of hematopoiesis in chronic myelogenous leukemia

R01CA-45822-05 (ET) VADAS, MATHEW A INST OF MEDICAL & VETERINARY S BOX 14 RUNDLE MALL POST OFFICE ADELAIDE, SOUTH AUSTRALIA, 500 Role of human IL-3 in normal and leukemic myeloid cells

R01CA-45834-05 (SRC) ENGSTROM, PAUL F FOX CHASE CANCER CENTER 7701 BURHOLME AVENUE PHILADELPHIA, PA 19111 Reducing avoidable mortality from breast cancer

R01CA-45847-05 (SRC) SAVAGE, EDWARD W CHARLES R. DREW MED SCH/OB/GYN 1621 E 120TH STREET LOS ANGELES, CA 90059 Reduction in cervical cancer mortality in Los Angeles

R29CA-45860-05 (ET) CULLUM, MALFORD E 801 SOUTH PAULINA - M/C 860 CHICAGO, IL 60612 Function of 13-cis-retinoic acid in HL-60 cells

R44CA-45869-03 (SSS) GIBSON, WILLIAM A PELLISSIPPI INTERNATIONAL, INC 110 RIDGEWAY CENTER OAK RIDGE, TN 37830 A new device for microdosimetry

R44CA-45903-03 (SSS) MITCHELL, ANN D GENESYS RESEARCH, INC 2300 ENGLERT DRIVE DURHAM, NC 27733 L5178y mouse lymphoma TK locus host-mediated assay

R44CA-45913-03 (SSS) BLOSSER, GABE F MEDCYC CORP 609 BEECH ST EAST LANSING, MI 48823 Multi-rod variable collimator for radiation therapy

R44CA-45915-02A1 (SSS) DINES, KRIS A XDATA CORPORATION 611 N CAPITOL AVE, RM 108 INDIANAPOLIS, IN 46220 Expert radiology assistant--Phase II

R01CA-45919-04 (PTHB) PINKEL, DANIEL LABORATORY FOR CELL ANALYSIS 1855 FOLSOM ST RM 230 SAN FRANCISCO, CA 94143-0808 Tumor cytogenetics by floresence in situ hybridization

R01CA-45954-08 (MGN) ROSS, SUSAN R UNIVERSITY OF ILLINOIS 1853 W POLK STREET CHICAGO, IL 60612 The developmental control of introduced genes in mice

R01CA-45957-05 (EI) MALEK, THOMAS R UNIVERSITY OF MIAMI SCH OF MED 1600 NW 10TH AVENUE MIAMI, FL 33101 The interleukin 2 receptor and T lymphocyte growth

U01CA-45957-05 (SRC) BRATTAIN, MICHAEL G BAYLOR COLLEGE OF MEDICINE ONE BAYLOR PLAZA HOUSTON, TX 77030 Growth regulation of human colonic neoplasms

U01CA-46088-05 (SRC) JOHNSTON, MICHAEL R UNIV OF COLORADO HLTH SCI CTR 4200 E 9TH AVENUE #C310 DENVER, CO 80262 Targeted therapy for lung cancer

U01CA-46088-05 0001 (SRC) JOHNSTON, MICHAEL R Targeted therapy for lung cancer Targeting therapy for lung cancer by isolated perfusion

U01CA-46088-05 0002 (SRC) BUNN, PAUL A Targeted therapy for lung cancer Monoclonal antibodies in the treatment of lung cancer

U01CA-46088-05 0003 (SRC) DAWSON, CHRISTOPHER A Targeted therapy for lung cancer Lung function and lung cancer therapy

U01CA-46088-05 0004 (SRC) GILLETTE, EDWARD L Targeted therapy for lung cancer Irradiation and hyperthermia for lung cancer therapy

R01CA-46096-05 (EI) MALEK, THOMAS R UNIVERSITY OF MIAMI SCH OF MED 1600 NW 10TH AVENUE MIAMI, FL 33101 Biological function Ly-6 alloantigens

U10CA-46113-04 (CCI) FLETCHER, WILLIAM S OREGON HLTH SCIENCES UNIV 3181 S W SAM JACKSON PARK RD PORTLAND, OR 97201 Southwest oncology group

R01CA-46121-05 (VR) MANLEY, JAMES L COLUMBIA UNIVERSITY 753A FAIRCHILD NEW YORK, NY 10027 Mechanism of alternative splicing of SV40 pre mrna

P01CA-46128-04 (CAK) JAMIESON, JAMES D YALE UNIVERSITY 333 CEDAR STREET NEW HAVEN, CT 06510 Membrane protein traffic in normal and transformed cells

P01CA-46128-04 0007 (CAK) ROSE, JOHN K Membrane protein traffic in normal and transformed cells Protein signals and intracellular membrane traffic

P01CA-46128-04 9001 (CAK) FARQUHAR, MARILYN G Membrane protein traffic in normal and transformed cells Immunoelectron microscopy core

P01CA-46128-04 9002 (CAK) MELLAMN, IRA Membrane protein traffic in normal and transformed cells Monoclonal antibody-cell production--Core

P01CA-46128-04 9003 (CAK) NOVICK, PETER Membrane protein traffic in normal and transformed cells Media preparation--Core

P01CA-46128-04 0001 (CAK) FARQUHAR, MARILYN G Membrane protein traffic in normal and transformed cells Membrane traffic through Golgi subcompartments

P01CA-46128-04 0002 (CAK) NOVICK, SUSAN F Membrane protein traffic in normal and transformed cells Application of in-vitro mutagenesis

P01CA-46128-04 0003 (CAK) HELENIUS, ARI H Membrane protein traffic in normal and transformed cells Role of protein conformation

P01CA-46128-04 0004 (CAK) JAMIESON, JAMES D Membrane protein traffic in normal and transformed cells Role of BIP in post-translation process

P01CA-46128-04 0005 (CAK) MELLMAN, IRA Membrane protein traffic in normal and transformed cells Protein signals and membrane traffic during endocytosis

P01CA-46128-04 0006 (CAK) PALADE, GEORGE E Membrane protein traffic in normal and transformed cells Control of vesticular traffic in transformed cells

R29CA-46134-05 (EI) PRESS, OLIVER W UNIVERSITY OF WASHINGTON SEATTLE, WA 98195 Receptor mediated endocytosis of lymphocyte antigens

U10CA-46136-04 (CCI) NEEFE, JOHN R UNIV OF KENTUCKY 800 ROSE ST LEXINGTON, KY 40536 SWOG cooperative group clinical studies

R29CA-46251-04 (EI) SCHANTZ, STIMSON P MEMORIAL HOSPITAL FOR CANCER 1275 YORK AVENUE NEW YORK, N Y 10021 Head & neck cancer: clinical impact of natural immunity

R01CA-46256-04 (ET) STETSON, PHILIP L UNIV OF MICHIGAN/UPJOHN CENTER 1310 CATHERINE ROAD ANN ARBOR, MI 48109 Host/tumor response to BUDR/IUDR administration

R01CA-46269-03S1 (SRC) BROTHMAN, ARTHUR R EASTERN VIRGINIA MEDICAL SCH 700 OLNEY ROAD/BOX 1980 NORFOLK, VA 23501 Cytogenetic analysis of cells derived from prostatic car

R01CA-46274-03 (NEUC) EMANUEL, BEVERLY S CHILDRENS HOSP OF PHILADELPHIA 34TH & CIVIC CENTER BLVD PHILADELPHIA, PA 19104 Molecular cytogenetics--Pediatric CNS tumors

U10CA-46282-04 (CCI) FISHER, RICHARD I LOYOLA UNIVERSITY MEDICAL CTR 2160 SOUTH FIRST AVENUE MAYWOOD, IL 60153 SWOG grant application for Loyola University

R01CA-46283-04 (EVR) VAN DYKE, TERRY A UNIVERSITY OF PITTSBURGH 274 CRAWFORD HALL PITTSBURGH, PA 15260 SV40 T antigen mediated oncogenesis in transgenic mice

R01CA-46288-03 (MEP) NEWBERNE, PAUL M MALLORY INST OF PATHOLOGY FDN 784 MASSACHUSETTS AVE RM 213 BOSTON, MA 02118 Lipotrope deficiency and liver cancer in rats

R29CA-46292-04 (BMT) SOLORZANO, CARMEN P BRIGHAM AND WOMEN'S HOSPITAL 75 FRANCIS STREET BOSTON, MA 02115 Development of new Gd contrast agents for NMR imaging

R01CA-46295-03 (RAD) WARD, JOHN F UNIV OF CALIFORNIA SAN DIEGO LA JOLLA, CA 92093 Biologically significant damage in DNA

R01CA-46296-04 (RAD) RAABE, OTTO G UNIVERSITY CALIFORNIA DAVIS, CALIFORNIA 95616 Cancer, & injury risk assessment for radionuclides

R01CA-46330-03 (HSR) WEINERT, CLARANN MONTANA STATE UNIVERSITY BOZEMAN, MT 59717 Home care of rural cancer patients in Montana

U01CA-46339-04 (SRC) MARLETT, JUDITH A UNIVERSITY OF WISCONSIN 1415 LINDEN DRIVE MADISON, WI 53706 Physiochemical effects of dietary fiber in humans

R01CA-46349-03 (REN) SATYASWAROOP, P G PENNSYLVANIA STATE UNIVERSITY HERSHEY, PA 17033 Progesterone receptor regulation in endometrial cancer

R01CA-46350-03 (ET) STROBL, JEANNINE S PHARMACOLOGY/TOXICOLOGY DEPT WEST VIRGINIA UNIVERSITY MORGANTOWN, WV 26506 Calcium and estrogen action in human breast cancer

R01CA-46361-04 (MBY) SEIDMAN, JONATHAN G HARVARD MEDICAL SCHOOL 25 SHATTUCK STREET BOSTON, MA 02115 Regulation of murine 21-hydroxylase gene expression

U10CA-46368-04 (CCI) DOROSHOW, JAMES H CITY OF HOPE NATIONAL MED CTR 1500 E DUARTE ROAD DUARTE, CA 91010 COH southwest oncology group clinical trials
P01CA-46370-04 (CAK) WIGLER, MICHAEL H COLD SPRING HARBOR LABORATORY PO BOX 100 COLD SPRING HARBOR, NY 11724 Molecular biology of cellular transformation
P01CA-46370-04 0001 (CAK) WIGLER, MICHAEL Molecular biology of cellular transformation Human oncogenes
P01CA-46370-04 0002 (CAK) HANAHAN, DOUGLASS Molecular biology of cellular transformation Oncogenesis in transgenic mice
P01CA-46370-04 0003 (CAK) GILMAN, MICHAEL Molecular biology of cellular transformation Fos transcriptional activation
P01CA-46370-04 0004 (CAK) HELFMAN, DAVID Molecular biology of cellular transformation Tropomyosins and transformation
P01CA-46370-04 0005 (CAK) FERAMISCO, JAMES Molecular biology of cellular transformation Membrane signal transduction
P01CA-46370-04 9001 (CAK) WIGLER, MICHAEL Molecular biology of cellular transformation Scientific core
R29CA-46371-04 (SSS) GASPER, PETER W COLORADO STATE UNIVERSITY FORT COLLINS, COLO 80523 Marrow transplant therapy for retrovirus infections
R55CA-46374-04 (VR) RADKE, KATHRYN UNIVERSITY OF CALIFORNIA, DAVI DAVIS, CA 95616 Cellular regulation of bovine leukemia virus replication
R01CA-46406-04 (MEP) OLSON, JAMES A IOWA STATE UNIVERSITY BIOCHEMISTRY & BIOPHYSICS AMES, IA 50011 Human metabolism of deuterated caroteoids
R29CA-46410-04 (ET) ALI-OSMAN, FRANCIS UNIVERSITY OF TEXAS BOX 88, 1515 HOLCOMBE BLVD HOUSTON, TX 77030 Glutathione in brain tumor resistance to nitrosoureas
R01CA-46413-04 (MEP) COFFEY, ROBERT J VANDERBILT UNIVERSITY C 2104, MEDICAL CENTER NORTH NASHVILLE, TN 37232 Role of transforming growth factor alpha in neoplasia
R29CA-46418-04 (PTHB) PENNO, MARGARET B JOHNS HOPKINS HOSPITAL 600 N WOLFE ST, BLALOCK 1017 BALTIMORE, MD 21205 Antisense RNA and DNA inhibition of Ki-ras translation
R29CA-46423-04 (REN) MEHTA, RAJESHWARI R UNIVERSITY OF ILLINOIS 840 SOUTH WOOD STREET CHICAGO, IL 60612 Metabolic transformation of steroids in breast cells
R01CA-46433-03 (CPA) BEER, DAVID G UNIVERSITY OF MICHIGAN B560 MSRB II, BOX 0686 ANN ARBOR, MI 48109 Altered gene expression during lung carcinogenesis
R29CA-46436-04 (MBY) MORAN, ELIZABETH COLD SPRING HARBOR LABORATORY POST OFFICE BOX 100 COLD SPRING HARBOR, N Y 11724 The cell growth control functions of E1A oncogene
U10CA-46441-04 (CCI) MEYERS, FREDERICK J UNIVERSITY OF CALIFORNIA SCHOOL OF MEDICINE DAVIS, CA 95616 Southwest oncology group--University of California
R01CA-46446-05 (BNP) NICOLAOU, KYRIACOS C RESEARCH INST OF SCRIPPS CLINI 10666 NORTH TORREY PINES ROAD LA JOLLA, CA 92037 Total synthesis of anticancer agents
R29CA-46452-04 (ET) SHEWACH, DONNA S 5514 MSRB I 1150 W MEDICAL CENTER DRIVE ANN ARBOR, MI 48109 Activation of chemotherapeutic agents in leukemic cells
R29CA-46455-05 (PTHB) SRIVASTAVA, SHIVA KUMAR UNIFORMED SERVICES UNIV HLTH S 4301 JONES BRIDGE ROAD BETHESDA, MD 20814-4799 Studies on the human dbl oncogene product
P01CA-46456-02 (SRC) WORDEN, JOHN K UNIVERSITY OF VERMONT 235 ROWELL BUILDING BURLINGTON, VT 05405 Breast screening program project
P01CA-46456-02 0001 (SRC) WORDEN, JOHN K Breast screening program project Coordinating community resources to promote participation in breast screening
P01CA-46456-02 0002 (SRC) SOLOMON, LAURA J Breast screening program project Enhancing BSE maintenance through self-reward strategies
P01CA-46456-02 0003 (SRC) SECKER-WALKER, ROGER H Breast screening program project Cost-effectiveness of breast cancer screening promotion programs
P01CA-46456-02 9001 (SRC) COSTANZA, MICHAEL C Breast screening program project Core--Biometry
P01CA-46456-02 9002 (SRC) FLYNN, BRIAN S Breast screening program project Core--Community service
R01CA-46462-02 (PC) ESKO, JEFFREY D UNIVERSITY OF ALABAMA UNIV OF ALABAMA AT BIRMINGHAM BIRMINGHAM, AL 35294 Tumor formation dependent on proteoglycans
R01CA-46465-04 (PBC) PESTKA, SIDNEY UMDNJ-ROBERT W JOHNSON MED SCH 675 HOES LANE PISCATAWAY, NJ 08854-5635 Interferon gamma receptors-- Regulation and function
R01CA-46507-05 (ALY) PARNES, JANE R STANFORD UNIV MEDICAL CENTER STANFORD, CA 94305 Regulation and function of the L3T4
R01CA-46508-05 (BIO) LAMBETH, J DAVID EMORY UNIVERSITY SCHOOL OF MED ATLANTA, GA 30322 Regulation of neutrophil function
R01CA-46527-13 (CPA) TOPAL, MICHAEL D UNIV OF NORTH CAROLINA CB# 7295 CHAPEL HILL, NC 27599-7295 Molecular basis of environmentally induced mutations
R01CA-46533-04 (BBCB) PATEL, DINSHAW J COLUMBIA UNIV, HEALTH SCI DEPT BIOCHEM/630 WEST 168 ST NEW YORK, N Y 10032 DNA damage sites--Mutagenic and carcinogenic lesions
U01CA-46535-05 (SRC) HECHT, STEPHEN S AMERICAN HEALTH FOUNDATION 320 EAST 43RD STREET NEW YORK, N Y 10017 Isothiocyanates and nitrosamine carcinogenesis
R29CA-46550-06 (ET) ARMSTRONG, R DOUGLAS UNIVERSITY OF MICHIGAN 3074 H. H. DOW BLDG ANN ARBOR, MI 48109-2136 Therapeutic relevance of queuine to human cancer
R01CA-46551-04 (RNM) NORTH, WILLIAM G DARTMOUTH MEDICAL SCHOOL HANOVER, N H 03756 Radiodiagnosis of SCCL with antibodies to neurophysins
R29CA-46552-04 (EDC) VAUGHAN, THOMAS L FRED HUTCHINSON CANCER RES CTR 1124 COLUMBIA ST SEATTLE, WA 98104 An epidemiological study of nasopharyngeal cancer
P01CA-46560-03 (SRC) BAKER, LAURENCE H WAYNE STATE UNIVERSITY P O BOX 02188 DETROIT, MI 48201 Developmental therapeutics of new solid tumor anticancer
P01CA-46560-03 0001 (SRC) CORBETT, THOMAS H. Developmental therapeutics of new solid tumor anticancer Drug discovery--Primary assays in vitro and in vivo
P01CA-46560-03 0002 (SRC) CORBETT, THOMAS H. Developmental therapeutics of new solid tumor anticancer Experimental therapeutics of new anticancer agents
P01CA-46560-03 0003 (SRC) VALERIOTE, FREDERICK Developmental therapeutics of new solid tumor anticancer Biochemical pharmacology and mechanism of action
P01CA-46560-03 0004 (SRC) VALDIVIESO, MANUEL Developmental therapeutics of new solid tumor anticancer Clinical trials of new anticancer agents
P01CA-46560-03 9001 (SRC) HEILBRUN, LANCE K. Developmental therapeutics of new solid tumor anticancer Core--Biostatistics
P01CA-46560-03 9002 (SRC) NEGENDANK, WILLIAM G. Developmental therapeutics of new solid tumor anticancer Core--NMR facility
R01CA-46562-04 (RAD) LEAVITT, DENNIS D UNIVERSITY OF UTAH MEDICAL 50 NORTH MEDICAL DRIVE Optimization of electron arc by dynamic therapy
R01CA-46565-05 (CTY) LAU, LESTER F UNIV OF ILLINOIS COLL OF MED 808 S WOOD ST MAIL CODE 669 CHICAGO, IL 60612 Growth-related genes regulated with c-fos
R01CA-46567-02 (EDC) ARMSTRONG, R WARWICK UNIV OF IL AT URBANA-CHAMPAIGN 1206 S FOURTH ST CHAMPAIGN, IL 61820 Nasopharyngeal carcinoma and dust and smoke in Malaysia
R01CA-46574-05 (SRC) WARD, KATHY NEBRASKA DEPT OF HEALTH 301 CENTENNIAL MALL SOUTH LINCOLN, NB 68509-5007 Developing data-based interventions in cancer control
R01CA-46582-04 (SRC) STOODT, GEORJEAN DIVISION OF ADULT HEALTH P O BOX 27687 RALEIGH, NC 27611-7687 Data-based interventions for cancer control in North Carolina
R01CA-46586-05 (SRC) NASCA, PHILIP C NEW YORK STATE DEPT OF HEALTH EMPIRE STATE PLAZA-TOWER BLDG ALBANY, NY 12237 Data-based interventions in cancer control--New York State
R01CA-46587-05 (SRC) LARAMEY, CHARLENE TEXAS DEPARTMENT OF HEALTH 1100 W 49TH STREET AUSTIN, TX 78756 Development of data-based interventions for cancer control
U01CA-46589-05 (SRC) REDDY, BANDARU S AMERICAN HEALTH FOUNDATION 320 EAST 43RD STREET NEW YORK, NY 10017 Chemoprevention of colon cancer by organoselenium
U01CA-46589-05 0001 (SRC) EL-BAYOUMY, KARAM Chemoprevention of colon cancer by organoselenium Synthesis and metabolism of organoselenium compounds
U01CA-46589-05 0002 (SRC) CONAWAY, C CLIFFORD Chemoprevention of colon cancer by organoselenium Toxicology of organoselenium compounds
U01CA-46589-05 0003 (SRC) REDDY, BANDARU S Chemoprevention of colon cancer by organoselenium In vivo efficacy of organoselenium compounds
U01CA-46589-05 0004 (SRC) SOHN, OCK SOON Chemoprevention of colon cancer by organoselenium Pharmacology of organoselenium compounds
U01CA-46589-05 0005 (SRC) FIALA, EMERICH S Chemoprevention of colon cancer by organoselenium Organoselenium compounds as inhibitors of carcinogen activation
R01CA-46591-02 (BEM) MILLER, SUZANNE M TEMPLE UNIVERSITY WEISS HALL PHILADELPHIA, PA 19122 Cancer control and coping in cervical dysplasia
P30CA-46592-04 (CCS) WICHA, MAX S UNIV OF MICHIGAN CANCER CENTER 101 SIMPSON DRIVE ANN ARBOR, MI 48109-0752 University of michigan cancer center
P30CA-46592-04 9001 (CCS) NATALE, RONALD B University of michigan cancer center Clinical trials core
P30CA-46592-04 9002 (CCS) CORNELL, RICHARD G University of michigan cancer center Biostatistics core
P30CA-46592-04 9003 (CCS) STETSON, PHILLIP L University of michigan cancer center Drug analysis core
P30CA-46592-04 9005 (CCS) ABRAMS, GERALD University of michigan cancer center Tissue procurement core
P30CA-46592-04 9006 (CCS) GLAZER, GARY M University of michigan cancer center Tumor imaging core
P30CA-46592-04 9007 (CCS) OXENDER, DALE L University of michigan cancer center Molecular biology and protein chemistry
P30CA-46592-04 9009 (CCS) WELSH, MICHAEL J University of michigan cancer center Morphology core
P30CA-46592-04 9010 (CCS) HUDSON, JERRY L University of michigan cancer center Cytometry core
P30CA-46592-04 9011 (CCS) WICHA, MAX S University of michigan cancer center Developmental core
P30CA-46592-04 9012 (CCS) WOTRING, LINDA University of michigan cancer center In vitro drug evaluation...core
P30CA-46592-04 9013 (CCS) LAWRENCE, THEODORE University of michigan cancer center Experimental irradiation...core
R01CA-46593-04 (PTHB) BAER, RICHARD J UNIV OF TEXAS SOUTHWESTERN 5323 HARRY HINES BLVD DALLAS, TX 75235-9048 The role of the TAL gene in human T cell leukemia
R01CA-46595-05 (CBY) BLENIS, JOHN HARVARD MEDICAL SCHOOL 25 SHATTUCK STREET BOSTON, MA 02115 Oncogenic regulation of s6 protein kinase & cell growth
R29CA-46612-04 (BNP) GLOER, JAMES B UNIVERSITY OF IOWA DEPARTMENT OF CHEMISTRY IOWA CITY, IO 52242 Antibiotics and antitumor agents from marine fungi
R01CA-46613-04 (EVR) KUNG, HSING-JIEN CASE WESTERN RESERVE UNIV SCHOOL OF MEDICINE CLEVELAND, OHIO 44106 Oncogene activation in avian B & T lymphoma
R29CA-46617-04 (VR) BRAUN, LUNDY A BROWN UNIVERSITY BOX G PROVIDENCE, RI 02912 Oncogenes & growth factors in human gynecologic cancers
R29CA-46627-04 (RAD) HYNYNEN, KULLERVO H UNIVERSITY OF ARIZONA RADIATION ONCOLOGY DEPARTMENT TUCSON, AZ 85724 High temperature ultrasound hyperthermia
R29CA-46637-02 (CPA) SMART, ROBERT C NORTH CAROLINA STATE UNIV CAMPUS BOX 7633 RALEIGH, NC 27695-7633 Diacylglycerols as tumor promoters
R01CA-46640-04 (RAD) WILLIAMSON, JEFFREY F WASHINGTON UNIVERSITY 510 SOUTH KINGSHIGHWAY BLVD ST LOUIS, MO 63110 Heterogeneity corrections in brachytherapy dosimetry

PROJECT NO., ORGANIZATIONAL UNIT., INVESTIGATOR, ADDRESS, TITLE

R29CA-46641-04 (RAD) KASID, USHA N GEORGETOWN UNIVERSITY 3800 RESERVOIR ROAD, NW WASHINGTON, DC 20007 RAF oncogene analysis and radiation resistant tumor cell
R29CA-46645-04 (EI) EVANS, SHARON S ROSWELL PARK CANCER INST ELM & CARLTON STREETS BUFFALO, N Y 14263 Role of alpha-interferon receptor in human immunoregulation
R01CA-46657-04 (HEM) CLARKE, MICHAEL F UNIVERSITY OF MICHIGAN 1150 W MEDICAL CENTER DRIVE ANN ARBOR, MI 48109 Hematopoietic growth factors, oncogenes, & leukemia
R29CA-46667-05 (IMB) JENSEN, PETER E EMORY UNIV SCHOOL OF MEDICINE WOODRUFF MEMORIAL BUILDING ATLANTA, GA 30322 Insulin-specific regulatory T cells in nonresponders
R01CA-46668-04 (SRC) STERNBERG, EDITH ILLINOIS DEPT OF PUBLIC HLTH 525 W JEFFERSON SPRINGFIELD, IL 62761 Data-based interventions for cancer control in Illinois
R01CA-46673-04 (ET) SIROTNAK, FRANCIS M SLOAN KETTERING INST/CNCR RES 1275 YORK AVENUE NEW YORK, N Y 10021 New therapeutics related to tumor cell folate transport
R01CA-46675-04 (RNM) LASSER, ELLIOTT C UNIVERSITY OF CALIFORNIA 9500 GILMAN DR LA JOLLA, CA 92093-0632 Study of nonionic reactions: can steroids modify?
R01CA-46676-04A1 (CBY) NISHIKURA, KAZUKO WISTAR INSTITUTE 36TH AND SPRUCE STREETS PHILDELPHIA, PA 19104 Roles of c-oncogenes in cell growth and differentiation
R29CA-46677-03 (VR) FOSTER, DAVID A HUNTER COLLEGE OF CUNY 695 PARK AVENUE NEW YORK, NY 10021 The basis for transformation by fujinami sarcoma virus
R29CA-46683-05 (CBY) SPARKS, RODNEY L TULANE UNIVERSITY Differentiation control in normal and transformed cells
R01CA-46686-03 (HEM) CROUSE, DAVID A UNIVERSITY OF NEBRASKA 600 SOUTH 42nd STREET OMAHA, NE 68198-6395 Characterization of circulating hematopoietic stem cells
R01CA-46720-04 (PTHB) SAUNDERS, GRADY F UNIVERSITY OF TEXAS 1515 HOLCOMBE BOULEVARD HOUSTON, TEXAS 77030 DNA sequence organization in the Wilm's tumor locus
R29CA-46723-04 (MGN) WILLIAMS, MICHAEL E UNIVERSITY OF VIRGINIA BOX 502 CHARLOTTESVILLE, VA 22908 Molecular genetics of human multiple myeloma
R01CA-46732-03 (ET) GRECO, WILLIAM R ROSWELL PARK MEMORIAL INST ELM AND CARLTON STREETS BUFFALO, N Y 14263 Determination of synergism, additivity and antagonism
U01CA-46738-05 (SRC) BELL, ROBERT M DUKE UNIVERSITY MEDICAL CENTER 212 MSIA RESEARCH DRIVE DURHAM, NC 27710 Protein kinase C inhibitors as chemopreventive agents
U01CA-46738-05 0001 (SRC) CARROLL, F IVY Protein kinase C inhibitors as chemopreventive agents Development of chemopreventive agents
U01CA-46738-05 0002 (SRC) BELL, ROBERT M Protein kinase C inhibitors as chemopreventive agents Enzyme activity assessments/mechanisms
U01CA-46738-05 0003 (SRC) HANNUN, YUSEL Protein kinase C inhibitors as chemopreventive agents Cellular activity assessments
U01CA-46738-05 0004 (SRC) COOK, C EDGAR Protein kinase C inhibitors as chemopreventive agents in vivo antipromoter activity and disposition
R01CA-46764-04 (OBM) JACOBS, JOHN R WAYNE STATE UNIVERSITY 540 EAST CANFIELD, UHC-5E DETROIT, MI 48201 Cricopharyngeal myotomy
R01CA-46778-04 (BNP) PATEL, DINSHAW J COLUMBIA UNIV, HEALTH SCI 630 WEST 168 ST NEW YORK, N Y 10032 DNA complexes--Antitumor drugs and chemotherapy
R01CA-46782-05 (PTHB) CALABRETTA, BRUNO THOMAS JEFFERSON UNIVERSITY 233 LOCUST STREET PHILADELPHIA, PA 19107 Altered growth regulation in human leukemia
R01CA-46785-03 (CPA) SCHAFFNER, CARL P P O BOX 759 PISCATAWAY, NJ 08855-0759 Prostatic glutathione s-epoxide transferases
R01CA-46788-03S1 (ET) KOSLOW, MAXIM NYU MEDICAL CENTER 550 FIRST AVENUE NEW YORK, NY 10016 Intracavitary LAK/Il-2 in brain tumors
R01CA-46798-03 (ET) TOFILON, PHILIP J U T M D ANDERSON CANCER CENTER 1515 HOLCOMBE BLVD HOUSTON, TX 77030 Drug-induced SCEs in human primary tumor cell culture
R01CA-46806-04A1 (PTHB) NOLL, WALTER W DARTMOUTH-HITCHCOCK MED CTR HANOVER, NH 03756 Genetic mapping of familial medullary thyroid carcinoma
R29CA-46809-05 (EI) AKPORIAYE, EMMANUEL T UNIVERSITY OF ARIZONA 1501 N. CAMPBELL AVENUE TUSCON, ARIZONA 85724 Immunological characterization of cells
R01CA-46812-04 (EI) SEAMAN, WILLIAM E SAN FRANCISCO VA MED CTR 4150 CLEMENT ST. (111R) SAN FRANCISCO, CA 94121 Transmembrane signaling in the activation of NK cells
R29CA-46818-04 (CPA) BIGGART, NEAL W SAN DIEGO STATE UNIVERSITY 5300 CAMPANILE DRIVE SAN DIEGO, CALIF 92182-0057 Reactive oxygen-mediated mutagenesis by CdC1-2 and TPA
R01CA-46820-04 (IMB) DJEU, JULIE Y UNIVERSITY OF SOUTH FLORIDA 12901 BRUCE B DOWNS BLVD TAMPA, FL 33612 Mechanism of activity of LAK cells against macrophages
R01CA-46823-04 (EDC) THOMAS, DAVID B FRED HUTCHINSON CANCER RES CTR 1124 COLUMBIA STREET SEATTLE, WASH 98104 Randomized trial of breast self examination in Shanghai
R01CA-46828-04A1 (PTHB) COLE, LAURENCE A YALE UNIVERSITY SCHOOL OF MED 333 CEDAR ST NEW HAVEN, CT 06510 Urinary hCG beta subunit/core fragment in gynecologic cancer
R01CA-46830-04 (PTHB) MUSCHEL, RUTH J UNIVERSITY OF PENNSYLVANIA 422 CURIE BLVD PHILADELPHIA, PA 19104 Molecular mechanisms in metastasis
R01CA-46843-04 (CPA) MATRISIAN, LYNN M VANDERBILT UNIVERSITY SCHOOL OF MEDICINE NASHVILLE, TN 37232 Role of transin in tumor promotion and progression
R29CA-46866-04 (REN) TABIBZADEH, SIAMAK S UNIVERSITY OF SOUTH FLORIDA 12901 BRUCE B DOWNS BLVD. TAMPA, FL 33612 Role of cytokines and HLA-DR in endometrial epithelium
R29CA-46878-04 (ET) MCIVOR, R S UNIVERSITY OF MINNESOTA HARVARD ST AT EAST RIVER ROAD MINNEAPOLIS, MN 55455 Methotrexate-resistance gene insertion in tumor therapy

PROJECT NO., ORGANIZATIONAL UNIT., INVESTIGATOR, ADDRESS, TITLE

R29CA-46880-04 (RAD) HAHN, PETER J SUNY HEALTH SCIENCE CENTER 750 EAST ADAMS STREET SYRACUSE, NY 13210 X-irradiation, drug resistance and gene amplification
R01CA-46882-04 (MEP) KIM, KI-HAN PURDUE UNIVERSITY SCHOOL OF AGRICULTURE WEST LAFAYETTE, IND 47907 Tumor necrosis factor & fatty acid synthesis
R01CA-46883-04 (SRC) ANDERSON, HENRY A WISCONSIN DIVISION OF HEALTH P O BOX 309 MADISON, WI 53701-0309 Wisconsin cancer control project
R01CA-46885-03 (CPA) HOSICK, HOWARD L WASHINGTON STATE UNIVERSITY PULLMAN, WA 99164-4220 Role of mesenchyme in mammary tumor progression
R55CA-46886-04 (MEP) FISCHER, SUSAN M UT MD ANDERSON CANCER CTR P.O. BOX 389 SMITHVILLE, TX 78957 Role of PUFA in cancer prevention
R01CA-46896-03 (CPA) SHARMA, MINOTI ROSWELL PARK MEMORIAL INST ELM & CARLTON ST BUFFALO, N Y 14263 Fluorescence postlabeling assay for DNA damage
R01CA-46903-02 (PTHB) LOUGHRAN, THOMAS P, JR FRED HUTCHINSON CANCER RES CTR 1124 COLUMBIA STREET SEATTLE, WA 98104 Studies of large granular lymphocyte leukemia
R01CA-46907-03 (SSS) WOODS, WILLIAM G UNIV OF MINNESOTA BOX 454 UMHC MINNEAPOLIS, MN 55455 Screening for neuroblastoma in infants
R01CA-46909-06 (RNM) GREEN, MARK A PURDUE UNIVERSITY WEST LAFAYETTE, IN 47907 Radiopharmaceuticals labeled with metal radionuclides
U01CA-46927-04 (SRC) BARON, JOHN A DARTMOUTH-HITCHCOCK MEDICAL CT 2 MAYNARD ST HANOVER, NH 03756 Calcium in the prevention of neoplastic polyps
P30CA-46934-04 (CCS) BUNN, PAUL A, JR UNIVERSITY OF COLORADO 4200 E 9TH AVE, BOX B 171 DENVER, CO 80262 Cancer center core grant
P30CA-46934-04 9001 (CCS) ARCHER, PHILIP G Cancer center core grant Biostatistics--core
P30CA-46934-04 9002 (CCS) BUNN, PAUL Cancer center core grant Clinical investigations--Core
P30CA-46934-04 9003 (CCS) GEMMILL, ROBERT Cancer center core grant Cytogenetics--Core
P30CA-46934-04 9004 (CCS) BUNN, PAUL Cancer center core grant Flow cytometry--Core
P30CA-46934-04 9005 (CCS) STEVENS, JAMES Cancer center core grant Laboratory animals--Core
P30CA-46934-04 9006 (CCS) MILLER, GARY J Cancer center core grant Histopathology/Tissue procurement core
P30CA-46934-04 9007 (CCS) HIRS, WERNER C M Cancer center core grant Macromolecular resources core--Core
P30CA-46934-04 9008 (CCS) HENDRICK, E Cancer center core grant Radiological sciences--core
P30CA-46934-04 9009 (CCS) EDWARDS, DEAN P Cancer center core grant Tissue culture and monoclonal antibody--core
P30CA-46934-04 9010 (CCS) BUNN, PAUL A Cancer center core grant Developmental funds--core
R01CA-46938-04 (BCE) EDWARDS, DEAN P UNIV OF COLORADO HLTH SCIS CTR 4200 EAST NINTH AVENUE DENVER, CO 80262 Progesterone receptor binding to specific DNA sequences
R29CA-46956-04 (EI) AHRENS, PATRICIA B MEDICAL COLLEGE OF WISCONSIN 8701 WATERTOWN PLANK ROAD MILWAUKEE, WI 53226 The role of carbohydrate in natural killer cytotoxicity
R29CA-46964-06 (BIO) ATLURU, DURGAPRASADARAO 701 PARK AVE MINNEAPOLIS, MN 55415 Role of endogenous leukotriene production in lymphocyte
R35CA-46967-05 (SRC) BENACERRAF, BARUJ DANA-FARBER CANCER INST 44 BINNEY ST BOSTON, MA 02115 Studies on antigen-processing and T cell repertoire
R44CA-46973-03 (SSS) MEHTA, CYRUS R CYTEL SOFTWARE CORPORATION 137 ERIE ST CAMBRIDGE, MA 02139 Statistical software for group sequential clinical trials
R35CA-47006-05 (SRC) KIEFF, ELLIOTT D BRIGHAM & WOMEN'S HOSPITAL 75 FRANCIS ST BOSTON, MA 02115 Molecular biology of Epstein-Barr virus infection
R01CA-47043-05 (RNM) DOI, KUNIO UNIVERSITY OF CHICAGO 5841 SOUTH MARYLAND AVENUE CHICAGO, IL 60637 Computerized angiographic analysis of stenotic lesions
R01CA-47050-04 (MEP) ERICKSON, KENT L UNIVERSITY OF CALIFORNIA SCHOOL OF MEDICINE DAVIS, CA 95616 Dietary fatty acids, eicosanoids and macrophage function
R29CA-47053-05 (EDC) BERKOWITZ, GERTRUD S MOUNT SINAI SCHOOL OF MEDICINE ONE GUSTAVE L LEVY PLACE NEW YORK, NY 10029 The prevalence and epidemiology of cryptorchidism
R01CA-47056-12 (CBY) ERICKSON, HAROLD P DUKE UNIVERSITY MEDICAL CENTER DURHAM, N C 27710 Electron microscopy of plasma and cell surface proteins
R35CA-47064-04 (SRC) SHERR, CHARLES J ST. JUDE CHILDREN'S RES HOSP 332 NORTH LAUDERDALE MEMPHIS, TN 38105 The fms oncogene (CSF-1 receptor)
R29CA-47075-04 (VR) CUNNINGHAM, JAMES M BRIGHAM AND WOMEN'S HOSPITAL 75 FRANCIS STREET BOSTON, MA 02115 Isolation and analysis of murine leukemia virus receptor
R01CA-47082-04 (MEP) PRESTON-MARTIN, SUSAN UNIV OF SOUTHERN CALIFORNIA 2025 ZONAL AVENUE LOS ANGELES, CA 90033 Childhood brain tumors and N-nitroso exposures
R01CA-47088-04A1 (ARRC) BARKLIS, ERIC OREGON HEALTH SCIENCES UNIV 3181 S W SAM JACKSON PARK ROAD PORTLAND, OR 97201-3098 Core assembly of the human immunodeficiency virus
R29CA-47098-03 (EVR) BURR, JOHN G UNIVERSITY OF TEXAS P O BOX 830688 RICHARDSON, TX 75083-0688 Purification of tyrosine phosphoproteins
R01CA-47106-02 (CPA) CONTI, CLAUDIO J U OF TEXAS/ANDERSON CANCER CTR 1515 HOLCOMBE BLVD SMITHVILLE, TEXAS 78957 Multistage carcinogenesis of the cervix and vagina
R01CA-47112-04 (CPA) MEDINA, DANIEL BAYLOR COLLEGE OF MEDICINE 1200 MOURSUND AVENUE HOUSTON, TX 77030 Early events in chemical carcinogen induced mammary tumorigenesis
R29CA-47127-04 (VR) SMOTKIN, DAVID UNIVERSITY OF UTAH 50 NORTH MEDICAL DRIVE SALT LAKE CITY, UTAH 84132 Human papillomavirus gene

expression in cervical cancer
R01CA-47132-04 (MEP) LAWRENCE, K SILBART UNIVERISTY OF CONNECTICUT U-39 3636 HORSEBARN RD EXT STORRS, CT 06269-4039 The mucosal immune response to aflatoxin B1
R01CA-47135-03 (BNP) CREWS, PHILLIP UNIV OF CALIFORNIA ROOM 313 THIMANN LAB SANTA CRUZ, CA 95064 Novel cytotoxic natural products from marine sponges
R29CA-47142-05 (PTHB) GOPALAKRISHNA, RAYUDU UNIV OF SOUTHERN CALIFORNIA 2025 ZONAL AVENUE MMR-512 LOS ANGELES, CA 90033 Tumor promoters & protein kinase C in cancer metastasis
R01CA-47147-04 (EDC) NEWCOMB, POLLY A UNIVERSITY OF WISCONSIN 1300 UNIVERSITY AVE, RM 6795 MADISON, WI 53706 Alcohol consumption, lactation, and breast cancer risk
R29CA-47148-04 (MCHA) MYERS, ANDREW G CALIFORNIA INST OF TECHNOLOGY 1201 EAST CALIFORNIA BOULEVARD PASADENA, CA 91125 Mechanistic and synthetic studies of neocarzinostatin
R01CA-47150-03 (END) PERDUE, JAMES F AMERICAN NATIONAL RED CROSS 15601 CRABBS BRANCH WAY ROCKVILLE, MD 20855 The role of IGFS in Wilms tumor development
R01CA-47159-03 (PTHB) HERLYN, MEENHARD THE WISTAR INSTITUTE 36TH AND SPRUCE STREETS PHILADELPHIA, PA 19104 Metastatic--Biological phenotype and models for therapy
R29CA-47161-03 (ET) SCHOR, NINA F CHILDRENS HOSPITAL 3705 FIFTH AVENUE AT DESOTO ST PITTSBURGH, PA 15213 Oxygen radicals, neurotransmitters and neural tumors
P01CA-47179-03 (CTR) BRENNAN, MURRAY R MEMORIAL HOSPITAL 1275 YORK AVENUE NEW YORK, NY 10021 Soft tissue sarcoma program project
P01CA-47179-03 0001 (CTR) BRENNAN, MURRAY Soft tissue sarcoma program project Localized-resectable soft tissue sarcoma
P01CA-47179-03 0002 (CTR) MURRAY, BRENNAN Soft tissue sarcoma program project Immunopathology of soft tissue sarcoma
P01CA-47179-03 0003 (CTR) BERTINO, JOSEPH Soft tissue sarcoma program project Natural and acquired drug resistance in soft tissue sarcoma.
P01CA-47179-03 9001 (CTR) BRENNAN, MURRAY Soft tissue sarcoma program project Clinical core
P01CA-47179-03 9002 (CTR) HAJDU, STEVEN Soft tissue sarcoma program project Pathology core
P01CA-47179-03 9004 (CTR) GAYNOR, JEFFREY Soft tissue sarcoma program project Biostatistical core
R29CA-47206-03 (MGN) SRIVATSAN, ERI S CHILDRENS HOSP OF LOS ANGELES 4650 SUNSET BOULEVARD LOS ANGELES, CA 90027 Precise localization of a human tumor suppressor gene
R29CA-47207-04 (EVR) BROWN, ANTHONY M C CORNELL UNIVERSITY MED COL 1300 YORK AVENUE NEW YORK, NY 10021 Action of the oncogene int-1 in mouse mammary tumors
R29CA-47217-04 (ET) NYCE, JONATHAN W EAST CAROLINA UNIVERSITY GREENVILLE, NC 27858 Drug-induced hypermethylation of DNA & drug resistance
R01CA-47227-04 (RNM) NG, THIAN C CLEVELAND CLINIC FOUNDATION 9500 EUCLID AVENUE CLEVELAND, OH 44106 Nmr studies of heterogeneity & radioresistance of tumors
R29CA-47228-04 (ET) DOLAN, MARY E 5841 SOUTH MARYLAND AVE CHICAGO, IL 60637 Modulation of alkyltransferases to enhance chemotherapy
R01CA-47234-04 (CPA) HUMAYUN, M ZAFRI NEW JERSEY MEDICAL SCHOOL 185 SOUTH ORANGE AVENUE NEWARK, NJ 07103-2714 Mechanisms of mutagenesis by cyclic DNA adducts
R44CA-47241-03 (SSS) MC DANIEL, JOE R FEIN-MARQUART ASSOCIATES, INC 7215 YORK RD BALTIMORE, MD 21212 Optical scanner input of graphical chemical structure
R01CA-47248-03 (PTHB) SORENSON, GEORGE D DARTMOUTH MEDICAL SCHOOL HANOVER, NH 03756 Molecular genetic studies of metastasis in lung cancer
R29CA-47249-04 (MCHA) PANEK, JAMES S BOSTON UNIVERSITY 590 COMMONWEALTH AVENUE BOSTON, MA 02215 Enantioselective approach to antitumor agents
R01CA-47282-02 (PTHA) IOZZO, RENATO V THOMAS JEFFERSON UNIVERSITY 1020 LOCUST STREET PHILADELPHIA, PA 19107 Heparan sulfate and transformation
R29CA-47292-04 (PTHB) KACINSKI, BARRY M YALE UNIVERSITY SCHOOL OF MED 333 CEDAR STREET NEW HAVEN, CT 06510 FMS-related genes in ovarian and endometrial neoplasia
R29CA-47296-04 (PTHB) LOZANO, GUILLERMINA U OF TX M.D. ANDERSON CAN CTR 1515 HOLCOMBE BOULEVARD HOUSTON, TX 77030 Relation of P53 and other factors in transgenic mice
R01CA-47305-04 (EDC) MACMAHON, BRIAN HARVARD SCHOOL/PUBLIC HEALTH 677 HUNTINGTON AVENUE BOSTON, MA 02115 Alcohol consumption, lactation, and breast cancer risk
R01CA-47307-04 (EI) YOUNG, JOHN D THE ROCKEFELLER UNIVERSITY 1230 YORK AVENUE NEW YORK, NY 10021 Molecular mechanisms of lymphocyte mediated killing
R01CA-47327-04 (CPA) LONGNECKER, DANIEL S DARTMOUTH MEDICAL SCHOOL HANOVER, NH 03756 Transgenic mouse models of pancreatic carcinogenesis
R01CA-47333-05 (CPA) SHALLOWAY, DAVID I CORNELL UNIVERSITY 120 DAY HALL ITHACA, N Y 14853-2801 Interaction of src and other proteins in transformation
R01CA-47342-03 (MEP) WALASZEK, ZBIGNIEW UNIV TX M.D. ANDERSON CAN CTR P.O. BOX 389 SMITHVILLE, TX 78957 Mechanism of glucarate inhibition of mammary cancer
R29CA-47346-04 (PTHB) JUNEJA, HARINDER S UNIV OF TX HLTH SCI CTR, HOUST P O BOX 20036, RM 5.016 MSB HOUSTON, TX 77225 Leukemia cell adherence protein in marrow metastasis
R01CA-47354-03 (RNM) KRESSEL, HERBERT Y HOSPITAL OF THE UNIV OF PENN PHILADELPHIA, PA 19104 MR of colorectal hepatic metastases--Response to therapy
R01CA-47369-04 (PTHB) PIERCE, G BARRY UNIVERSITY OF COLORADO 4200 EAST NINTH AVENUE DENVER, CO 80262 Embryonic induction in differentiation therapy
R01CA-47373-04 (PTHB) DEFTOS, LEONARD J UNIV OF CALIFORNIA, SAN DIEGO DEPT. OF MEDICINE, V-111 C LA JOLLA, CA 92093 Endocrine cancer
R01CA-47377-03 (ET) WIEMAN, THOMAS J UNIVERSITY OF LOUISVILLE LOUISVILLE, KY 40292 Effect of photodynamic therapy on blood flow
R01CA-47379-04 (RAD) TEICHER, BEVERLY A DANA-FARBER CANCER INSTITUTE 44 BINNEY STREET BOSTON, MA 02115 Pt complexes--Heat, pH and hypoxia effects on mechanism
R29CA-47384-03 (BCE) MIKSICEK, RICHARD J STATE UNIVERSITY OF NEW YORK BST T8, ROOM 140 STONY BROOK, N Y 11794-8651 Ligand/protein interactions in estrogen receptors
R29CA-47391-04 (CBY) FEIG, LARRY A 136 HARRISON AVENUE BOSTON, MASSACHUSETTS 02111 Genetic analysis of ras and G protein function
R01CA-47396-04 (BIO) GERNER, EUGENE W UNIVERSITY OF ARIZONA RADIATION ONCOLOGY TUCSON, AZ 85724 Polyamines in cell growth and responses to stress
R01CA-47399-04 (CBY) HANN, STEPHEN R VANDERBILT UNIVERSITY C-2310 MCN NASHVILLE, TN 37232 Two c-myc protein--Role in cell growth and oncogenesis
R29CA-47401-04 (ALY) GRAY, LLOYD S UNIVERSITY OF VIRGINIA BOX 286 CHARLOTTESVILLE, VA 22908 Tumor cell destruction by CTL--Path from binding to lysis
R01CA-47404-04 (CBY) MAGUN, BRUCE E OREGON HEALTH SCIENCES UNIV 3181 SW SAM JACKSON PARK ROAD PORTLAND, OR 97201-3098 EGF/TGF-beta control of second messenger and transcription
R01CA-47407-04 (RAD) CALDERWOOD, STUART K DANA FARBER CANCER INSTITUTE 50 BINNEY ST BOSTON, MA 02115 Transmembrane signal modulation by hyperthermia
R01CA-47409-03 (CPA) MORITA, MICHIO COLORADO STATE UNIVERSITY FT COLLINS, CO 80523 Transformation and tumor regression-- A stem cell model
R01CA-47411-04 (BCE) RIDGWAY, CHESTER E UNIV OF COLORADO HLTH SCIS CTR 4200 EAST NINTH AVENUE - B151 DENVER, CO 80262 Alteration of T3 receptors in a pituitary tumor
R01CA-47424-02 (HEM) CHEN, BEN D WAYNE STATE UNIVERSITY PO BOX 02188 DETROIT, MI 48201 Growth regulation in normal and transformed phagocytes
R29CA-47428-05 (REN) MADDOX, ANNE-MARIE UNIV OF AR FOR MED SCIENCES 4301 WEST MARKHAM SLOT 508 LITTLE ROCK, AR 72205 Autocrine factors in breast cancer
R29CA-47430-03 (RNM) EARY, JANET F UNIV OF WASHINGTON HOSPITAL 1959 NE PACIFIC STREET SEATTLE, WA 98195 Quantitation of radiolabeled antibody distribution
R35CA-47439-04 (SRC) CASPAR, DONALD L BRANDEIS UNIVERSITY 415 SOUTH STREET WALTHAM, MA 02254 Switching in virus and membrane assemblies
P01CA-47445-03 (SRC) HERBERMAN, RONALD B PITTSBURGH CANCER INSTITUTE 200 MEYRAN AVE PITTSBURGH, PA 15213 Cancer in organ transplant recipients
P01CA-47445-03 0001 (SRC) HO, MONTO Cancer in organ transplant recipients EBV in post-transplantation lymphoproliferative disease (PTLD)
P01CA-47445-03 0002 (SRC) WHITESIDE, THERESA L Cancer in organ transplant recipients Immunologic effector cells in de novo post-transplant malignancies
P01CA-47445-03 0003 (SRC) WHITESIDE, THERESA L Cancer in organ transplant recipients Recurrent liver tumor effector cells in immunosuppressed allograft patients
P01CA-47445-03 0004 (SRC) LEVY, SANDRA Cancer in organ transplant recipients Stress & coping behavior--Predictors of infection & tumors in transplant patients
P01CA-47445-03 9001 (SRC) HERBERMAN, RONALD B Cancer in organ transplant recipients Core--Clinical
R35CA-47448-03 (SRC) WHITTEMORE, ALICE S STANFORD UNIVERSITY DEPT OF HEALTH RESEARCH/POLICY STANFORD, CA 94305-5092 Research in cancer epidemiology and biostatistics
R35CA-47451-04 (SRC) ROIZMAN, BERNARD UNIVERSITY OF CHICAGO 910 EAST 58TH STREET CHICAGO, ILL 60637 Molecular biology of herpes simplex viruses
R55CA-47456-04 (PTHB) GROFFEN, JOHN H CHILDREN'S HOSP OF LOS ANGELES 4650 SUNSET BLVD LOS ANGELES, CA 90027 Characterization of bcr and abl related genes
R29CA-47457-05 (CPA) GALLAGHER, PATRICIA E WEST VIRGINIA UNIVERSITY P O BOX 6057 MORGANTOWN, W VA 26506-6057 Enzymatic repair of carcinogenic damage to DNA
R35CA-47479-04 (SRC) MARNETT, LAWRENCE J VANDERBILT UNIVERSITY SCHOOL OF MEDICINE NASHVILLE, TN 37232 Polyunsaturated fatty acid metabolism and carcinogenesis
R01CA-47480-04 (PTHB) NELKIN, BARRY D JOHNS HOPKINS ONCOLOGY CTR LAB 424 N BOND STREET BALTIMORE, MD 21231 Differentiation of medullary thyroid carcinoma cells
R01CA-47482-05 (VR) WILLS, JOHN W HERSHEY MED CTR/PENN STATE UNI P.O. BOX 850 HERSHEY, PA 17033 Analysis of Gag domains required for retrovirus assembly
R35CA-47486-02 (SRC) SKALKA, ANNA M INSTITUTE FOR CANCER RESEARCH 7701 BURHOLME AVENUE PHILADELPHIA, PA 19111 RNA tumor viruses--Control of DNA integration & gene expression
R29CA-47492-04 (ET) CASERO, ROBERT A, JR THE JOHNS HOPKINS ONCOLOGY CTR 424 N. BOND STREET BALTIMORE, MD 21231 Mechanisms human tumor response to polyamine inhibitors
R35CA-47497-04 (SRC) ELKIND, MORTIMER M COLORADO STATE UNIVERSITY RADIOLOGICAL HEALTH SCIENCES FORT COLLINS, COLO 80523 Radiobiology of lethality, mutation, & transformation
R01CA-47503-04 (EDC) COMSTOCK, GEORGE W TRAINING CENTER FOR PHR BOX 2067 HAGERSTOWN, MD 21742 Blood & data bank for cancer risk factor studies
R01CA-47512-03 (PTHB) HERZ, FRITZ MONTEFIORE MEDICAL CENTER 111 EAST 210TH STREET BRONX, N Y 10467 Selected markers in noninvasive bladder tumors
R01CA-47526-03S1 (SRC) FRADET, YVES LAVAL UNIVERSITY 11 COTE DU PALAIS QUEBEC, QUE G1R 2J6 CANADA New markers for detection and evaluation of bladder tumors
R01CA-47537-03 (PTHB) MAYALL, BRIAN H UNIV CALIFORNIA/SAN FRANCISCO 505 PARNASSUS AVENUE SAN FRANCISCO, CA 94143-0134 Cytometric and other markers of human bladder cancer
R01CA-47538-03S1 (SRC) CORDON-CARDO, CARLOS MEMORIAL HOSP/CNCR/ALLD DISE 1275 YORK AVENUE NEW YORK, N Y 10021 Markers of

exfoliated benign and malignant bladder cells

R35CA-47542-04 (SRC) LITTLE, JOHN B HARVARD UNIVERSITY 665 HUNTINGTON AVENUE BOSTON, MA 02115 Effects of radiation on mammalian cells

U10CA-47545-04 (CCI) OMURA, GEORGE A UNIVERSITY OF ALABAMA UNIVERSITY STATION BIRMINGHAM, AL 35294 Cancer and leukemia group B

U10CA-47546-04 (CCI) LYSS, ALAN P JEWIS HOSPITAL OF ST. LOUIS ST LOUIS, MO 63110 Cancer and leukemia group B

R29CA-47547-03 (ET) HILL, ANNA B ARIZONA STATE UNIVERSITY TEMPE, AZ 85287-1501 Transformation associated enhancement of drug resistance

R01CA-47548-03 (EI) NORIN, ALLEN J SUNY HEALTH SCIENCE CTR 450 CLARKSON AVE BROOKLYN, NY 11203 Cell surface target of Il-2 activated killer cells

R01CA-47549-03 (CPA) WEITZMAN, SIGMUND A NORTHWESTERN UNIV MED SCHOOL 303 E CHICAGO AVE, 8524 OLSON CHICAGO, IL 60611 Oxygen radical-induced malignant transformation

R35CA-47554-04 (SRC) STROMINGER, JACK L HAVARD UNIVERSITY 7 DIVINITY AVENUE Chemistry and biology of human lymphocytes

U10CA-47555-04 (CCI) MAUER, ALVIN M UNIV OF TENNESSEE, MEMPHIS 3 N DUNLAP ST/VAN FLEET BLDG MEMPHIS, TN 38163 Cancer and leukemia group B

R29CA-47558-04 (PTHA) MCKEEVER, PAUL E UNIVERSITY OF MICHIGAN 1500 E MEDICAL CENTER DRIVE ANN ARBOR, MI 48109 Antigenic heterogeneity and instability in human gliomas

U10CA-47559-01A1 (CCI) OZER, HOWARD UNIV OF NC AT CHAPEL HILL CB#7305 3009 OLD CLINIC BLDG CHAPEL HILL, NC 27599 Cancer and leukemia group B

R29CA-47566-04 (HEM) TYKOCINSKI, MARK L CASE WESTERN RESERVE UNIVERSIT 2085 ADELBERT ROAD CLEVELAND, OH 44106 Human leukemic differentiation--Anti-sense RNA studies

R01CA-47571-04 (PTHB) ZARBL, HELMUT MASSACHUSETTS INST OF TECH 77 MASSACHUSETTS AVENUE CAMBRIDGE, MA 02139 Cloning of transformation effector and suppressor genes

R01CA-47572-04 (CBY) BRUGGE, JOAN S UNIVERSITY OF PENNSYLVANIA PHILADELPHIA, PA 19104-6076 Studies on the c-src proto-oncogene product in neurons

U10CA-47577-04 (CCI) TRUMP, DONALD L DUKE UNIVERSITY MEDICAL CENTER BOX 3398 DURHAM, N C 27710 Cancer and leukemia group B (calgb)

R01CA-47589-04 (HEM) SANTOLI, DANIELA THE WISTAR INSTITUTE 36TH AND SPRUCE STREETS PHILADELPHIA, PA 19104 Growth factor-dependent normal and leukemic cell growth

R01CA-47591-03 (CPA) BARTSCH, HELMUT INTRNTNL AGENCY FOR RES/CANCER 150 COURS ALBERT THOMAS 69372 LYON CEDEX 08, FRANCE Bacteria, DNA damage in stomach and bladder cancers

R01CA-47609-04 (ALY) KRENSKY, ALAN M STANFORD UNIVERSITY SCH MEDICI STANFORD, CA 94305 Cellular and molecular studies of HLA recognition

R29CA-47610-06 (RAD) CHENG, KWAN HON TEXAS TECH UNIVERSITY LUBBOCK, TX 79409 Inactivation of Ca-transport proteins by hyperthermia

R29CA-47611-05 (EVR) DAS, GOKUL C UNIVERSITY OF TEXAS HLTH CTR PO BOX 2003 TYLER, TEXAS 75710 Regulation of transcription in polyoma virus

R01CA-47622-04 (SRC) KREIDER, JOHN W PENNSYLVANIA STATE UNIVERSITY P O BOX 850 HERSHEY, PA 17033 Studies on papillomavirus host interaction

R55CA-47629-04 (PTHB) IZANT, JONATHAN G YALE UNIVERSITY 333 CEDAR ST, PO BOX 3333 NEW HAVEN, CT 06510 Enhancement and modulation of anti-sense RNA activity

R01CA-47631-04 (SRC) HOLMES, EDWARD W, JR UNIVERSITY OF PENNSYLVANIA 3400 SPRUCE STREET PHILADELPHIA, PA 19104-4283 Retroviral anti-sense RNA--Cellular and viral responses

R01CA-47632-05 (SRC) HANAHAN, DOUGLAS HORMONE RESEARCH INSTITUTE UNIVERSITY OF CALIFORNIA SAN FRANCISCO, CA 94143-0534 Oncogenesis by papillomavirus DNAs in transgenic mice

U10CA-47642-04 (CCI) CLAMON, GERALD H UNIVERSITY HOSPITALS IOWA CITY, IA 52242 University of Iowa institutional CALGB grant

R44CA-47644-03 (SSS) BRAUNLICH, PETER F INTL SENSOR TECHNOLOGY NE 1425 TERRE VIEW DRIVE PULLMAN, WA 99163 Feasibility study of fiber-optic fast neutron dosimetry

R29CA-47652-05 (ET) SAFA, AHMAD R THE UNIVERSITY OF CHICAGO 5841 SOUTH MARYLAND AVENUE CHICAGO, IL 60637 Functional role of gp150-180 in multidrug resistance

R01CA-47657-26 (IMB) CLAMAN, HENRY N UNIV OF COLORADO HLTH SCIS CTR 4200 EAST NINTH AVENUE DENVER, CO 80262 Immunocompetence of thymus cells

R01CA-47658-04 (SSS) MOOLGAVKAR, SURESH H FRED HUTCHINSON CNCR RES CTR 1124 COLUMBIA STREET SEATTLE, WA 98104 Biomathematical approaches to cancer

R01CA-47659-04 (SOH) MILLER, SCOTT C UNIVERSITY OF UTAH SALT LAKE CITY, UT 84112 Occupational risk reduction by radiotoxin chelation

R01CA-47669-05 (ET) WRIGHT, SUSAN C PALO ALTO INST FOR MOLEC MED 2462 WYANDOTTE STREET MOUNTAIN VIEW, CA 94043 Variant cells resistant to diverse cytotoxic agents

R01CA-47676-04 (PTHB) CRUM, CHRISTOPHER P BRIGHAM AND WOMEN'S HOSPITAL 75 FRANCIS STREET BOSTON, MA 02115 Pathobiology of cervical intraepithelial neoplasia

R01CA-47718-05 (ARRA) HERRMANN, STEVEN H GENETICS INSTITUTE 87 CAMBRIDGE PARK DR CAMBRIDGE, MA 02140 Biochemistry of CTL-target interactions

R44CA-47720-03 (MEP) LAM, LUKE K T LKT LABORATORIES, INC. MINNEAPOLIS, MN 55413 Natural chemopreventive agents

R01CA-47722-04 (PTHA) SPRIGGS, DAVID R CLINICAL SCIENCES CENTER 600 HIGHLAND AVE MADISON, WI 57392 Molecular mechanisms of tumor necrosis factor

R01CA-47723-04 (CPA) SINGER, BEA A LAWRENCE BERKELEY LABORATORY UNIVERSITY OF CALIFORNIA BERKELEY, CALIF 94720 Biochemical mechanisms of vinyl chloride carcinogenesis

R01CA-47724-04 (ALY) BRENNER, MICHAEL B DANA-FARBER CANCER INSTITUTE 44 BINNEY STREET BOSTON, MA 02115 T cell receptor gamma, delta

R29CA-47735-05 (MGN) STATES, J CHRISTOPHER METROPOLITAN CTR FOR HIGH TECH 2727 SECOND AVENUE, 4TH FLOOR DETROIT, MI 48201 Genetics of human DNA repair

P01CA-47741-02 (SRC) PETERS, WILLIAM P DUKE UNIV MEDICAL CENTER PO BOX 3961 DURHAM, NC 27710 Autologous bone marrow transplants in breast/ovarian cancer

P01CA-47741-02 0005 (SRC) HANNUN, YUSUF Autologous bone marrow transplants in breast/ovarian cancer Platelet dysfunction with high dose chemotherapy & bone marrow support

P01CA-47741-02 9001 (SRC) PETERS, WILLIAM P Autologous bone marrow transplants in breast/ovarian cancer Core--Cryopreservation laboratory

P01CA-47741-02 9002 (SRC) ROSNER, GARY Autologous bone marrow transplants in breast/ovarian cancer Core--Statistical support and data management

P01CA-47741-02 0001 (SRC) PETERS, WILLIAM P Autologous bone marrow transplants in breast/ovarian cancer High dose combination breast/ovary cancer chemotherapy with ABMS--Clinical trials

P01CA-47741-02 0002 (SRC) CLARK-PEARSON, DANIEL Autologous bone marrow transplants in breast/ovarian cancer Therapeutic approaches to ovary/breast cancer--High dose chemotherapy & ABMS

P01CA-47741-02 0003 (SRC) BAST, ROBERT C JR Autologous bone marrow transplants in breast/ovarian cancer Immunodetection/immunopharmacological elimination of breast/ovary cancer cells

P01CA-47741-02 0004 (SRC) PETERS, WILLIAM P Autologous bone marrow transplants in breast/ovarian cancer Clinical and experimental approaches to hematopoietic reconstitution

P01CA-47748-03 (SRC) BUCKNER, C DEAN FRED HUTCHINSON CANCER RES CTR 1124 COLUMBIA ST E100 SEATTLE, WA 98104 Autologous marrow transplantation

P01CA-47748-03 0001 (SRC) DONEY, KRISTINE Autologous marrow transplantation Autologous marrow transplantation for patients with acute lymphoblastic leukemia

P01CA-47748-03 0002 (SRC) APPLEBAUM, FREDERICK Autologous marrow transplantation Autologous marrow transplantation for patients with acute nonlymphoblatic leukemi

P01CA-47748-03 0003 (SRC) APPLEBAUM, FREDERICK Autologous marrow transplantation Autologous marrow transplantation for patients with malignant lymphoma

P01CA-47748-03 0004 (SRC) BENSINGER, WILLIAM Autologous marrow transplantation Autologous marrow transplantation for multiple myelemal

P01CA-47748-03 0005 (SRC) ANDREWS, ROBERT Autologous marrow transplantation Hematopoietic reconstitution using isolated progenitor cell

P01CA-47748-03 0006 (SRC) BEVENSON, RONALD Autologous marrow transplantation Selected and transplantation of human hematopoietic progenitor cells

P01CA-47748-03 0007 (SRC) TOROK-STORH, BEVERLY Autologous marrow transplantation Hematopoietic reconstitution--The role of stromal cells

P01CA-47748-03 0008 (SRC) SINGER, JACK W Autologous marrow transplantation Recombinant hematopoietic growth factors in AHT--Effect of hematopoietic progena

P01CA-47748-03 0009 (SRC) FEFER, ALEXANDER Autologous marrow transplantation Lymphokines and immunotherapy following bone marrow transplantation

P01CA-47748-03 0010 (SRC) BENSINGER, WILLIAM Autologous marrow transplantation In vitro detection of residual leukemia

P01CA-47748-03 9001 (SRC) FISHER, LLOYD Autologous marrow transplantation Core--Biostatistics

P01CA-47748-03 9002 (SRC) MARTIN, PAUL Autologous marrow transplantation Marrow processing and evaluation core

P01CA-47748-03 9003 (SRC) SULLIVAN, KEITH Autologous marrow transplantation Core--Outpatientcare and long term follow up

P01CA-47748-03 9004 (SRC) SALE, GEORGE Autologous marrow transplantation Core--Pathology

R01CA-47749-03 (EDC) BERESFORD, SHIRLEY A A UNIVERSITY OF WASHINGTON DEPT OF EPIDEMIOLOGY, SC-36 SEATTLE, WA 98195 Endometrial cancer risk and post-menopausal hormone use

R01CA-47752-02 (EI) LEIBSON, PAUL J MAYO FOUNDATION 200 FIRST STREET SOUTHWEST ROCHESTER, MN 55905 Mechanisms of human natural killer cell activation

R01CA-47756-04 (RAD) PECK, JEFFREY W UNIV OF UTAH HLTH SCI CTR SALT LAKE CITY, UT 84132 X-ray & heat interactions & murine jejunal fibrosis

R29CA-47763-04 (PTHB) GILMORE, THOMAS D BOSTON UNIVERSITY 2 CUMMINGTON STREET BOSTON, MA 02215 Transformation of cells by the v-rel oncogene

R01CA-47767-04 (CTY) ROTHMAN, JAMES E SLOAN-KETTERING INSTITUTE 1275 YORK AVENUE NEW YORK, N.Y. 10021 Ras oncogene-related proteins and secretion

R29CA-47775-05 (ET) CHAKRABARTY, SUBHAS UNIVERSITY OF TEXAS 1515 HOLCOMBE BLVD HOUSTON, TX 77030 Transforming growth factors action in colon cancer

R25CA-47779-04 (SRC) SKOULTCHI, ARTHUR I ALBERT EINSTEIN COLLEGE OF MED 1300 MORRIS PARK AVE BRONX, NY 10461 Summer cancer research program

R25CA-47785-04 (SRC) LOVE, RICHARD C UNIVERSITY OF WISCONSIN 1300 UNIV AVE, SUITE 7C MADISON, WI 53706 Oncology education--Summer research and prevention

R01CA-47786-02 (RAD) TOMASOVIC, STEPHEN P UNIV TEXAS ANDERSON CANCER CTR 1515 HOLCOMBE ROAD HOUSTON, TX 77030 Optimization of hyperthermic and macrophage cytotoxicity

R29CA-47809-04 (VR) JOVE, RICHARD UNIVERSITY OF MICHIGAN 6606 MEDICAL SCIENCE BLDG II ANN ARBOR, MI 48109-0620 Mechanisms of cell transformation by the viral src gene

R01CA-47812-02 (EDC) JENSEN, OLE M ROSENVANGETS HOVEDVEJ 35 P O BOX 839 2100 COPENHAGEN, DENMARK Human papillomavirus and cervical cancer in Copenhagen

R01CA-47815-03 (CBY) WEBER, MICHAEL J UNIV OF VIRGINIA BOX 441 MED CTR CHARLOTTESVILLE, VA 22908 Regulation of glucose transporters by the src oncogene

PROJECT NO., ORGANIZATIONAL UNIT., INVESTIGATOR, ADDRESS, TITLE

R29CA-47816-04 (MGN) BUETOW, KENNETH H FOX CHASE CANCER CENTER 7701 BURHOLME AVENUE PHILADELPHIA, PA 19111 Genetic changes in primary hepatocellular carcinoma

R01CA-47828-03 (BIO) IVES, DAVID H OHIO STATE UNIVERSITY 484 WEST 12TH AVENUE COLUMBUS, OH 43212 Deoxycytidine kinase--Regulation and molecular biology

P01CA-47829-04 (SRC) DENARDO, GERALD L UNIVERSITY OF CALIFORNIA 1508 ALHAMBRA BLVD SACRAMENTO, CA 95816 Studies to improve cancer therapy with antibodies

P01CA-47829-04 0001 (SRC) DENARDO, GERALD L Studies to improve cancer therapy with antibodies B-cell malignancy treated with radiolabeled monoclonal antibody

P01CA-47829-04 0002 (SRC) DE NARDO, SALLY J Studies to improve cancer therapy with antibodies Development of immunoconjugate therapy for breast cancer

P01CA-47829-04 0004 (SRC) MEARES, CLAUDE F Studies to improve cancer therapy with antibodies Antibody-chelate conjugates

P01CA-47829-04 9001 (SRC) DENARDO, GERALD L Studies to improve cancer therapy with antibodies Core--Biostatistics and data management

P01CA-47829-04 9002 (SRC) DENARDO, GERALD L Studies to improve cancer therapy with antibodies Core--Quantitative imaging and dosimetry

P01CA-47829-04 9003 (SRC) DENARDO, SALLY J Studies to improve cancer therapy with antibodies Core--Antibody pharmacy

P01CA-47829-04 9004 (SRC) DENARDO, SALLY J Studies to improve cancer therapy with antibodies Core--Immunopathology

P01CA-47829-04 9005 (SRC) DENARDO, SALLY J Studies to improve cancer therapy with antibodies Core--Cellular and molecular immunobiology

R29CA-47844-04 (ET) GIBSON, NEIL W UNIV OF SOUTHERN CA SCH OF PHA 1303 N MISSION ROAD LOS ANGELES, CA 90033 Mechanism of action of sulfonate ester anticancer drugs

R01CA-47845-03 (PBC) SCHROIT, ALAN J UNIV OF TX MD ANDERSON CANCER 1515 HOLCOMBE BLVD (HMB 173) HOUSTON, TX 77030 Phosphatidylserine in pathology and macrophage recognition

R29CA-47855-04 (RAD) TAYLOR, YVONNE C WASHINGTON UNIV SCH MEDICINE 4511 FOREST PARK BLVD, # 404 ST LOUIS, MO 63108 Chromatin conformation and PLD repair

R01CA-47858-04 (EI) QUARANTA, VITO THE SCRIPPS RESEARCH INSTITUTE 10666 NORTH TORREY PINES ROAD LA JOLLA, CA 92037 A new class of tumor-associated antigens

R01CA-47860-03 (ET) BHATTACHARYA-CHATTERJEE, MALAY ROSWELL PARK MEMORIAL INST 666 ELM STREET BUFFALO, NY 14263 Idiotype approach to therapy of human T cell leukemia

R01CA-47866-03 (HEM) LAWRENCE, HUGH J VETERANS AFFAIRS MED CTR 150 MUIR RD MARTINEZ, CA 94553 Homeotic gene expression in human hematopoietic cells

R01CA-47869-03 (EI) ZALMAN, LEORA S INSTITUTE OF SCRIPPS CLINIC 10666 NORTH TORREY PINES RD. LA JOLLA, CA 92037 Mechanism of lymphocyte cytotoxicity and self protection

R29CA-47872-05 (VR) JONES, CLINTON J UNIV OF NEBRASKA, LINCOLN EAST CAMPUS LINCOLN, NE 68583-0905 Mechanistic approaches to HSV-2 induced transformation

R25CA-47877-04 (SRC) LOPEZ-S, ALFREDO LSU MEDICAL CENTER 1542 TULANE AVENUE NEW ORLEANS, LA 70112 Nutrition-cancer education program LSUMC

R01CA-47878-04 (EI) RUDDLE, NANCY H YALE UNIV/816 LEPH P. O. BOX 3333 NEW HAVEN, CONN 06510 Lymphotoxin mechanisms

R01CA-47881-04 (CBY) BERTICS, PAUL J UNIVERSITY OF WISCONSIN-MADISO 1300 UNIV AVE/571 MED SCI BLDG MADISON, WI 53706 EGF receptor function and control by phosphorylation

R25CA-47883-04 (SRC) HANDSCHUMACHER, ROBERT E YALE UNIV SCHOOL OF MED 333 CEDAR STREET/BOX 3333 NEW HAVEN, CT 06510 Cancer education program

R25CA-47888-04 (SRC) HEIMBURGER, DOUGLAS UAB STATION WEBB BLDG. ROOM 22 BIRMINGHAM, AL 35294 Cancer prevention and control training program

R01CA-47891-03 (ET) ITOH, KYOGO UNIV OF TX MD ANDERSON CANCER 1515 HOLCOMBE BLVD HOUSTON, TX 77030 Biology of human tumor infiltrating lymphocytes

P30CA-47904-04 (CCS) HERBERMAN, RONALD B PITTSBURGH CANCER INST LOTHROP STREET PITTSBURGH, PA 15261 Cancer center support grant

P30CA-47904-04 9014 (CCS) HEMPLE, JOHN Cancer center support grant Protein synthesis facility

P30CA-47904-04 9015 (CCS) HERBERMAN, RONALD Cancer center support grant Developmental funds --core

P30CA-47904-04 9016 (CCS) WATKINS, SIMON Cancer center support grant Electron microscopy--Core

P30CA-47904-04 9017 (CCS) YASKO, J Cancer center support grant Clinical research support services--Core

P30CA-47904-04 9018 (CCS) KHAN, SALEEM Cancer center support grant DNA sequencing facility--Core

P30CA-47904-04 9019 (CCS) HERBERMAN, RONALD Cancer center support grant Cytogenetics laboratory

P30CA-47904-04 9001 (CCS) DAY, ROGER S. Cancer center support grant Biostatics Unit - Core

P30CA-47904-04 9004 (CCS) CHUNG, ALBERT Cancer center support grant Hybridoma facility

P30CA-47904-04 9005 (CCS) HERBERMAN, RONALD Cancer center support grant Immunologic monitoring and diagnostic lab--Core

P30CA-47904-04 9006 (CCS) WHITESIDE, THERESA L. Cancer center support grant Serum and tissue bank - - core

P30CA-47904-04 9008 (CCS) MCCOY, PHILIP J. Cancer center support grant Flow cytometry facility

P30CA-47904-04 9009 (CCS) HOFMANN, KLAUS Cancer center support grant Protein sequencing facility

P30CA-47904-04 9010 (CCS) ROSENBERG, JOHN M. Cancer center support grant DNA synthesis facility

P30CA-47904-04 9013 (CCS) BRAMSON, PAUL Cancer center support grant Animal facility --Core

R25CA-47905-04 (SRC) BAKEMEIER, RICHARD F UNIVERSITY OF COLORADO 4200 E 9TH AVE, BOX B190 DENVER, CO 80262 Cancer education program

PROJECT NO., ORGANIZATIONAL UNIT., INVESTIGATOR, ADDRESS, TITLE

R01CA-47929-03 (ET) ERICKSON, LEONARD C LOYOLA UNIV MED CTR 2160 SOUTH FIRST AVENUE MAYWOOD, IL 60153 Interaction of antitumor agents with activated oncogenes

R01CA-47937-04 (CTY) REDDY, PREMKUMAR E THE WISTAR INSTITUTE 36TH AND SPRUCE STREETS PHILADELPHIA, PA 19104 Transformation & differentiation by v and c-abl genes

R01CA-47941-03 (ET) BECK, WILLIAM T ST JUDE CHILDREN'S RES HOSP 332 NORTH LAUDERDALE MEMPHIS, TN 38101 Altered topoisomerase in atypical multidrug resistance

R29CA-47943-04 (MEP) LIEBLER, DANIEL C UNIVERSITY OF ARIZONA COLLEGE OF PHARMACY TUCSON, ARIZONA 85721 Vitamin E turnover and chemical toxicity

R29CA-47944-04 (HEM) GEIB, ROY W TERRE HAUTE CTR/MEDICAL EDUC 135 HOLMSTEDT HALL AT ISU TERRE HAUTE, IN 47809 Analysis of a Friend virus-like disease in Fv-2rr mice

R01CA-47953-03 (PTHB) BOSS, JEREMY M EMORY UNIVERSITY 1510 CLIFTON RD ATLANTA, GA 30322 Cloning of tumor necrosis factor induced genes

R01CA-47956-04 (PTHB) REED, JOHN C UNIVERSITY OF PENNSYLVANIA 207 JOHN MORGAN BUILDING PHILADELPHIA, PA 19104 Investigation of bcl-2 function through gene transfer

R01CA-47958-04 (ET) WANG, JAMES C HARVARD UNIVERSITY 7 DIVINITY AVENUE CAMBRIDGE, MA 02138 Cell-killing by topoisomerase-active anticancer drugs

R29CA-47963-03 (MEP) STARNES, H F, JR STANFORD UNIVERSITY MED CENTER DIV OF GEN SURGERY, RM S-067 STANFORD, CA 94305-5101 Metabolic effects on the tumor necrosis factor

R01CA-47969-02 (REN) JACOBSON, HERBERT I ALBANY MEDICAL COLLEGE 47 NEW SCOTLAND AVENUE ALBANY, NY 12208 Regulation of breast cancer growth by alpha-fetoprotein

R01CA-47975-04 (MGN) BAER, RICHARD J UNIV OF TX SOUTHWESTERN MED CT 5323 HARRY HINES BLVD DALLAS, TX 75235-9048 Chromosome 14 inversion in human T cell oncogenesis

R29CA-47980-04 (CBY) CHANEY, WILLIAM G UNIVERSITY OF NEBRASKA MED CTR 600 SOUTH 42ND STREET OMAHA, NE 68198-4525 Glycosylation changes in oncogenesis

P01CA-47982-04 (SRC) PIZER, STEPHEN M UNIVERSITY OF NORTH CAROLINA CB# 3174, SITTERSON HALL CHAPEL HILL, NC 27599-3175 Medical image presentation

P01CA-47982-04 0001 (SRC) FUCHS, HENRY Medical image presentation 3D display approaches

P01CA-47982-04 0002 (SRC) PIZER, STEPHEN M Medical image presentation 2D and 3D object definition

P01CA-47982-04 0004 (SRC) ROSENMAN, JULIAN G Medical image presentation Clinical applications of 3D display

P01CA-47982-04 0007 (SRC) BURBECK, CHRISTINA A Medical image presentation Human vision project

P01CA-47982-04 0008 (SRC) PISANO, ETTA D Medical image presentation Clinical 2D image quality project

P01CA-47982-04 0009 (SRC) BEARD, DAVID V Medical image presentation Integrated radiology workstation

P01CA-47982-04 9002 (SRC) MULLER, KEITH E Medical image presentation Statistics core

P01CA-47982-04 9003 (SRC) GASH, A GRAHAM Medical image presentation Facilities Core

P01CA-47983-04 (SRC) ROVERA, GIOVANNI J-S-JR.-R-I/CHILDREN'S HOSP 34TH STREET & CIVIC CTR BLVD PHILADELPHIA, PA 19104 Molecular analysis of pediatric cancers

P01CA-47983-04 0005 (SRC) RAUSCHER, FRANK J Molecular analysis of pediatric cancers Analysis of the structure and function of the Wilms tumor gene

P01CA-47983-04 0006 (SRC) SCHER, CHARLES D Molecular analysis of pediatric cancers Mitogenic signals in osteogenic sarcomas

P01CA-47983-04 9001 (SRC) WOMER, R Molecular analysis of pediatric cancers Tumor procurement

P01CA-47983-04 9002 (SRC) BIEGEL, JACLYN Molecular analysis of pediatric cancers Cytogenetics core

P01CA-47983-04 0001 (SRC) ROVERA, GIOVANNI Molecular analysis of pediatric cancers Molecular diagnosis of relapse B lineage acute lymphoblastic leukemia

P01CA-47983-04 0003 (SRC) EMANUEL, BEVERLY Molecular analysis of pediatric cancers Investigation of the t(2;13) translocation in alveolar rhabdomyosarcoma

P01CA-47983-04 0004 (SRC) PLEASURE, DAVID Molecular analysis of pediatric cancers NGF signal-transcription coupling in human neuroectodermal tumors

R01CA-47988-01A1 (EDC) BURING, JULIE E 55 POND AVE BROOKLINE, MA 02146 Trial of beta-carotene & lung cancer in high risk women

R01CA-47989-04 (SRC) BALMES, JOHN R 1001 POTRERO AVENUE BUILDING 9, ROOM 109 SAN FRANCISCO, CA 94110 Chemoprevention trial beta carotene and retinol

R29CA-47992-04 (HEM) BROWN, MELISSA A OREGON HLTH SCI UNIV 3181 SW SAM JACKSON PARK ROAD PORTLAND, OR 97201 Regulation of hematopoietic growth factor interleukin 4

R01CA-47993-04 (HEM) SHARKIS, SAUL J THE JOHNS HOPKINS UNVI SCH/MED 600 NORTH WOLFE STREET BALTIMORE, MD 21205 Mechanism of action of bryostatins on hematopoiesis

R01CA-47994-03 (MEP) GARRETT, CARLETON T GEORGE WASHINGTON UNIVERSITY 2300 Eye Street, NW WASHINGTON, DC 20037 Ras gene mutations in human neoplasia

P01CA-47995-02 (SRC) GROLLMAN, ARTHUR P SUNY AT STONY BROOK SCH OF MED, HLTH SCI CENTER STONY BROOK, NY 11794-8651 Chemistry and biology of exocyclic DNA adducts

P01CA-47995-02 0001 (SRC) JOHNSON, FRANCIS Chemistry and biology of exocyclic DNA adducts Exocyclic adducts--Synthetic and analytic studies

P01CA-47995-02 0002 (SRC) GROLLMAN, ARTHUR P Chemistry and biology of exocyclic DNA adducts Exocyclic adducts and site-specific mutagenesis

P01CA-47995-02 0003 (SRC) EISENBERG, MOISES Chemistry and biology of exocyclic DNA adducts Structure and thermodynamic properties of exocyclic DNA adducts

P01CA-47995-02 0004 (SRC) PATEL, DINSHAW Chemistry and biology of

exocyclic DNA adducts NMR studies on exocyclic DNA adducts
P01CA-47995-02 9001 (SRC) IDEN, CHARLES R Chemistry and biology of exocyclic DNA adducts Core
R29CA-47996-04 (EVR) KHALILI, KAMEL JEFFERSON MEDICAL COLLEGE 1020 LOCUST STREET PHILADELPHIA, PA 19107 Tissue specific transcription of JCV in glial cells
P01CA-47997-03 (SRC) BERTINO, JOSEPH R MEMORIAL HOSPITAL FOR CANCER 1275 YORK AVENUE NEW YORK, N Y 10021 Regional chemotherapy of liver metastasis from colon cancer
P01CA-47997-03 0001 (SRC) KEMENY, NANCY Regional chemotherapy of liver metastasis from colon cancer Clinical trials--Fluorodeoxyuridine
P01CA-47997-03 0002 (SRC) COHEN, ALFRED M Regional chemotherapy of liver metastasis from colon cancer Clinical trials--Imaging
P01CA-47997-03 0003 (SRC) BERTINO, JOSEPH R Regional chemotherapy of liver metastasis from colon cancer Resistance to FUDR and dichloromethotrexate in colorectal carcinoma
P01CA-47997-03 0004 (SRC) SIGURDSON, ELIN R Regional chemotherapy of liver metastasis from colon cancer Design and evaluation of reginal chemotherapy strategies in a rat model
P01CA-47997-03 0005 (SRC) KOUTCHER, JASON A Regional chemotherapy of liver metastasis from colon cancer NMR evaluation of liver metastasis from colon cancer
P01CA-47997-03 9001 (SRC) NIEDZWEICKI, DONNA Regional chemotherapy of liver metastasis from colon cancer Core--Biostatistics
P01CA-47997-03 9002 (SRC) TONG, WILLIAM Regional chemotherapy of liver metastasis from colon cancer Core--Pharmacokinetics
R01CA-48002-02 (RNM) DERENZO, STEVE E LAWRENCE BERKELEY LABORATORY 1 CYCLOTRON ROAD BERKELEY, CA 94720 Search for ultra-fast, heavy atom scintillators
R29CA-48003-03 (EDC) BECKER, THOMAS M UNIV OF NEW MEXICO SCHOOL OF MEDICINE ALBUQUERQUE, N M 87131 Epidemiology of cervical dysplasia in minority women
R01CA-48004-03 (SSS) JACKSON, VALERIE P INDIANA UNIVERSITY MED CENTER 1001 W 10TH ST, DEPT RADIOLOGY INDIANAPOLIS, IN 46202-2879 Stereotactic mammographic fine needle breast biopsy
R25CA-48010-03 (SRC) HAGHBIN, MAHROO THOMAS JEFFERSON UNIV HOSPTIAL 11TH & SANSOM STREETS PHILADELPHIA, PA 19107 Short research experience for student assistants
R29CA-48022-04 (MEP) MONNAT, RAYMOND J, JR UNIVERSITY OF WASHINGTON DEPT OF PATHOLOGY SM-30 SEATTLE, WA 98195 Oxygen mutagenesis in human somatic cells
R01CA-48023-03 (MGN) THOMPSON, CRAIG B MEDICAL SCIENCE RES BLDG I 1150 W MED CTR DRIVE, RM 4510 ANN ARBOR, MI 48109 Gene conversion in myc-induced bursal lymphomas
R01CA-48031-04 (GNM) SMITH, DAVID I WAYNE STATE UNIV SCH OF MED 3136 SCOTT HALL DETROIT, MI 48201 Chromosome breakpoints and renal and small cell lung cancer
R01CA-48032-04 (MEP) PRETLOW, THERESA P CASE WESTERN RESERVE UNIV 2085 ADELBERT ROAD CLEVELAND, OH 44106 Colonic putative preneoplastic foci
R01CA-48041-04 (MBY) PETERSON, DAVID O TEXAS A & M UNIVERSITY COLLEGE STATION, TX 77843 Mechanisms of steroid hormone-regulated transcription
R01CA-48049-03 (CBY) NICHOLSON, BRUCE J STATE UNIVERSITY OF NEW YORK 619 COOKE HALL BUFFALO, NY 14260 Mechanisms for control of cell growth by gap junctions
R01CA-48051-04 (EDC) ROBISON, LESLIE L UNIVERSITY OF MINNESOTA BOX 422 MAYO BLDG MINNEAPOLIS, MN 55455 Epidemiology of childhood acute lymphoblastic leukemia
R01CA-48054-04 (MBY) GOLDFARB, MITCHELL P 630 WEST 168 ST NEW YORK, N Y 10032 The c-fgf3 and SAOS2 oncogenes
R29CA-48061-04 (SSS) RYAN, LOUISE DANA FARBER CANCER INSTITUTE 44 BINNEY STREET BOSTON, MA 02115 Biostatistical topics in carcinogenicity and teratology
R25CA-48062-03 (SRC) ST JEOR, SACHIKO T UNIVERSITY OF NEVADA SCH OF MED/BRIGHAM BLDG. RENO, NEVADA 89557 Curricular integration of nutrition in cancer and health
R01CA-48066-03 (CPA) MAHER, VERONICA M MICHIGAN STATE UNIVERSITY EAST LANSING, MI 48824 Mechanisms of homologous recombination in human cells
R01CA-48068-04 (ET) RAMAKRISHNAN, SUNDARAM UNIVERSITY OF MINNESOTA 435 DELAWARE ST, SE MINNEAPOLIS, MN 55455 Inhibition of tumor cell growth by immunotoxins
R01CA-48069-02 (ET) ELLIS, THOMAS M LOYOLA UNIV SCHOOL OF MEDICINE 2160 SOUTH FIRST AVENUE MAYWOOD, IL 60153 Differentiation and heterogeneity of human LAK cells
R01CA-48071-03 (PTHB) MOODY, TERRY W GEORGE WASHINGTON UNIVERSITY 2300 EYE STREET/NORTHWEST WASHINGTON, DC 20037 VIP and EGF receptors in non-small cell lung cancer
R01CA-48075-04 (ET) BEAR, HARRY D VIRGINIA COMMONWEALTH UNIV PO BOX 11, MCV STATION RICHMOND, VA 23298-0011 Expansion of anti-tumor T cells from tumor-bearing hosts
R01CA-48080-02 (ET) YOUNG, M RITA HINES VA HOSPITAL HINES, IL 60141 Myeloid differentiation therapy reduces suppressor cells
R01CA-48081-04 (CPA) BAYLIN, STEPHEN B THE ONCOLOGY CENTER LABS 424 N BOND STREET BALTIMORE, MARYLAND 21231 Regulation of tumor progression in small cell lung cancer
R01CA-48084-02 (MEP) BOSLAND, MAARTEN C NEW YORK UNIV MEDICAL CENTER 550 FIRST AVENUE NEW YORK, NY 10016 Hormonal vs chemical carcinogenesis in the rat prostate
R01CA-48085-06 (EI) HARRIS, DAVID T UNIVERSITY OF ARIZONA PHARM/MICRO BLDG. 90 TUCSON, AZ 85721 Analysis of a natural killer cell target cell antigen
R01CA-48088-02 (RAD) COLACCHIO, THOMAS ANTHONY DARTMOUTH-HITCHCOCK MED CTR 2 MAYNARD STREET HANOVER, N H 03756 Intraoperative radiation therapy & hyperthermia
R29CA-48091-04 (CBY) GENTRY, LARRY E MEDICAL COLLEGE OF OHIO 3000 ARLINGTON AVE/BOX 10008 TOLEDO, OHIO 43699-0008 Transforming growth factor beta1--Structural and functional analysis
R25CA-48094-02 (SRC) MAMTANI, RAVINDER NEW YORK MEDICIAL COLLEGE AND PREVENTIVE MEDICINE VALHALLA, NY 10595 Cancer and nutrition curriculum program
R29CA-48096-04 (RAD) OKUNIEFF, PAUL MASSACHUSETTS GENERAL HOSPITAL BOSTON, MA 02114 Predicting the response of tumor to radiation
P01CA-48112-01A3 (SRC) PEZZUTO, JOHN M UNIV OF ILLINOIS AT CHICAGO 833 S WOOD STREET (M/C 781) CHICAGO, IL 60612 Natural inhibitors of carcinogenesis
P01CA-48112-01A3 0001 (SRC) FONG, HARRY H S Natural inhibitors of carcinogenesis Chemopreventive agents--Provision of source materials
P01CA-48112-01A3 0002 (SRC) KINGHORN, A DOUGLAS Natural inhibitors of carcinogenesis Chemopreventive agents--Isolation and identification
P01CA-48112-01A3 0003 (SRC) PEZZUTO, JOHN M Natural inhibitors of carcinogenesis Chemopreventive agents--In vitro evaluation
P01CA-48112-01A3 0004 (SRC) WALL, MONROE E Natural inhibitors of carcinogenesis Chemopreventive agents--Antimutagenesis
P01CA-48112-01A3 0005 (SRC) MOON, RICHARD C Natural inhibitors of carcinogenesis Chemopreventive agents--Carcinogenesis inhibition
P01CA-48112-01A3 0006 (SRC) MORIARTY, ROBERT M Natural inhibitors of carcinogenesis Chemopreventive agents--Synthesis and modification
P01CA-48112-01A3 9001 (SRC) HAN, MOON-CHULL Natural inhibitors of carcinogenesis Core--Biostatistics
P01CA-48112-01A3 9002 (SRC) BEECHER, CHRIS W W Natural inhibitors of carcinogenesis Core--Information management
R01CA-48121-04 (CPA) MULLIN, JAMES M LANKENAU MED RES CENTER LANCASTER AVE. W CITY LINE WYNNEWOOD, PA 19096 Epithelial cell division--Polarity and phorbol esters
R01CA-48129-05 (RNM) CHAN, HEANG-PING UNIVERSITY OF MICHIGAN ANN ARBOR, MI 48109 Development of computer-based techniques in mammography
R01CA-48146-03 (EI) HOCHMAN, JACOB D THE HEBREW UNIV OF JERUSALEM JERUSALEM 91904 ISRAEL Monoclonal antibodies to human multi drug resistance
R01CA-48162-04 (SRC) CROOP, JAMES M DANA-FARBER CANCER INSTITUTE 44 BINNEY STREET BOSTON, MA 02115 Immunologic analysis of the multidrug resisant gene family
R01CA-48172-02 (ET) KOVACS, CHARLES J EAST CAROLINA UNIVERSITY SCHOOL OF MEDICINE GREENVILLE, NC 27858 Cytokine sequencing and toxicity-- Marrow and GI studies
R29CA-48174-04 (CPA) PRESTON, BRADLEY D RUTGERS UNIVERSITY P. O. BOX 789 PISCATAWAY, NJ 08855-0789 Mutagenesis by chemical carcinogens in transgenic mice
R01CA-48175-04 (MCHA) MASAMUNE, SATORU MASSACHUSETTS INST OF TECH DEPARTMENT OF CHEMISTRY CAMBRIDGE, MA 02139 Syntheses of antitumor agents calyculin and scytophycin
R01CA-48184-03 (PTHB) DE FREITAS, ELAINE C WISTAR INSTITUTE 36TH AND SPRUCE STREETS PHILADELPHIA, PA 19104 Activation and growth regulation of Sezary T cells
R01CA-48196-04 (SRC) KEOGH, JAMES P UNIV OF MARYLAND AT BALTIMORE 405 W REDWOOD ST, 2ND FLOOR BALTIMORE, MD 21201 Phase IV chemoprevention trial beta-carotene/retinol
R01CA-48198-03 (EVR) SHIH, CHIAHO UNIVERSITY OF PENNSYLVANIA PHILADELPHIA, PA 19104-6059 Dissection of the life cycle of human hepatitis B virus
R01CA-48200-04 (SRC) CULLEN, MARK R YALE UNIV SCH OF MED BOX 3333 NEW HAVEN, CT 06510 Beta-carotene/retinol chemoprevention trial in asbestos exposed group
R01CA-48203-04 (SRC) VALANIS, BARBARA G KAISER FOUNDATION HOSPITALS 4610 S.E. BELMONT STREET PORTLAND, OR 97215 Chemoprevention of lung cancer--Retinoids/beta-carotene
R01CA-48210-04 (PBC) SLOANE, BONNIE F WAYNE STATE UNIVERSITY SCHOOL OF MEDICINE DETROIT, MI 48201 Characterization of tumor cysteine proteinase inhibitors
R01CA-48219-04 (VR) GOODING, LINDA R EMORY UNIVERSITY 507 WOODRUFF MEMORIAL BLDG ATLANTA, GA 30322 Mechanism of adenovirus-induced tnf resistance
R01CA-48236-04 (SSS) KNOWLES, DANIEL M COLUMBIA UNIVERSITY 630 WEST 168TH STREET NEW YORK, NY 10032 Immunopathology of lymphoid neoplasia in AIDS
R55CA-48255-01A3 (SSS) WOLF, WALTER UNIV OF SOUTHERN CALIFORNIA 1985 ZONAL AVENUE LOS ANGELES, CA 90033 Metabolic imaging of drugs using 18f PET and 19f NMR
R01CA-48263-07 (PBC) HUANG, RU-CHIH C JOHNS HOPKINS UNIVERSITY 34TH AND CHARLES STREETS BALTIMORE, MD 21218 Activation of a type viral gene expression during aging
R01CA-48269-02 (RNM) MACOVSKI, ALBERT STANFORD UNIVERSITY DURAND BUILDING, ROOM 109 STANFORD, CA 94305 Magnetic resonance spectroscopic neoplasm imaging
R01CA-48280-02 (NURS) SMITH, ROBERTA A UNIV OF ILLINOIS AT CHICAGO ONE ILLINI DRIVE, BOX 1649 PEORIA, IL 61656-1649 Self-care & control--A multifaceted approach
R01CA-48286-03 (SRC) WELCH, MICHAEL J WASHINGTON UNIV, SCH OF MED 510 SOUTH KINGSHIGHWAY ST LOUIS, MO 63110 In vivo assessment of tumor receptor levels using PET
U01CA-48369-04 (SRC) HONG, WAUN K U OF TX M.D. ANDERSON CAN CTR 1515 HOLCOMBE BLVD HOUSTON, TEXAS 77030 Chemoprevention in human bronchial metaplasia/dysplasia
U01CA-48405-04 (SRC) WAHL, GEOFFREY M SALK INSTITUTE P O BOX 85800 SAN DIEGO, CA 92186-5800 Detection and curing of amplified genes in human cancer
U01CA-48409-05 (SRC) GROOPMAN, JOHN D THE JOHNS HOPKINS UNIVERSITY 615 NORTH WOLFE STREET BALTIMORE, MD 21205 Monitoring human exposure to aflatoxins in the Gambia
R01CA-48432-02 (NURS) HINDS, PAMELA S ST JUDE CHILDREN'S RESEARCH HO 332 N. LAUDERDALE MEMPHIS, TN 38105 Self-care outcomes in adolescents with cancer
R01CA-48450-03 (NURS) BRADEN, CARRIE JO UNIVERSITY OF ARIZONA COLLEGE OF NURSING TUCSON, AZ 85721 Nurse interventions promoting self help response to cancer
U01CA-48460-04 (SRC) BLUMBERG, BARUCH S INST CANCER RESEARCH/FOX CHASE 7701 BURHOLME AVENUE PHILADELPHIA, PA 19111 Chemoprevention of primary liver cancer
R01CA-48492-03 (PTHB) BABU, V RAMESH UNIV OF SOUTHERN CALIFORNIA 1441 EASTLAKE AVENUE LOS ANGELES, CA 90031 Cytogenetic and molecular genetic study of bladder cancer
R44CA-48530-03 (SSS) TOURVILLE, DONALD R ZEUS SCIENTIFIC, INC

200 EVANS WAY/ PO BOX 8108 SOMERVILLE, NJ 08876 Fluorescent steroid binding in endometrical carcinoma
R44CA-48534-03 (SSS) HUANG, CHUN-MING PHARMINGEN 11555 SORRENTO VALLEY ROAD SAN DIEGO, CA 92121 Monoclonal antibody against retinoblastoma gene product
R44CA-48541-03 (SSS) DOIRON, DANIEL R LASERGUIDE, INC PO BOX 1965 94 COMMERCE DR BUELLTON, CA 93427-1965 Red nd:yag laser for photodynamic therapy
R44CA-48544-03 (SSS) STOLLER, MILTON LORAD MEDICAL SYSTEMS INC 262 PRESTIGE PARK RD EAST HARTFORD, CT 06108 Lorad Medical Systems, Inc
R44CA-48570-03 (SSS) SCHWARTZ, ABRAHAM CARIBBEAN MICROPARTICLES CORP PO BOX 4344 HATO REY, PUERTO RICO 00919 Development of a quantitative antibody binding kit
R01CA-48594-04 (EVR) HOOVER, EDWARD A COLORADO STATE UNIVERSITY DEPARTMENT OF PATHOLOGY FORT COLLINS, COLO 80523 Mechanisms of retrovirus induced aplastic anemia
U01CA-48626-04 (SRC) MURPHY, JOHN R THE UNIVERSITY HOSPITAL 88 EAST NEWTON STREET BOSTON, MA 02118 Growth factor receptor targeted toxins for leukemia/lymphoma
U01CA-48626-04 0003 (SRC) STROM, TERRY B Growth factor receptor targeted toxins for leukemia/lymphoma Immunology program
U01CA-48626-04 0001 (SRC) MURPHY, JOHN R Growth factor receptor targeted toxins for leukemia/lymphoma Molecular biology program
U01CA-48626-04 0002 (SRC) MCCAFFREY, RONALD P Growth factor receptor targeted toxins for leukemia/lymphoma Cell biologic program
R01CA-48635-03 (HSDG) SCHULZ, RICHARD UNIV OF PITTSBURGH FIFTH AVE & BIGELOW BLVD PITTSBURGH, PA 15260 Living with homecare--Cancer patients and caregivers
R01CA-48636-05 (RAD) STAMATO, THOMAS D LANKENAU MEDICAL RESEARCH CTR LANCASTER AVE. WEST OF CITY LI PHILADELPHIA, PA 19151 Poly (adp-ribose) and repair of radiation induced damage
R01CA-48641-03 (CBY) GREENE, JAMES J CATHOLIC UNIVERSITY OF AMERICA WASHINGTON, DC 20064 Antiproliferative genes in the regulation of cell growth
R01CA-48642-04 (CPA) PAULI, BENDICHT U NYS COLLEGE VET MED/CORNELL ITHACA, NY 14853 Carcinogenesis testing of sintered porous cocrmo implant
R01CA-48648-07 (HEM) PRYSTOWSKY, MICHAEL B U OF PENNSYLVANIA MED SCH PATHOLOGY & LAB MED DEPT PHILADELPHIA, PA 19104-6082 The role of T lymphocyte factors in hemopoiesis
R29CA-48654-04 (BIO) JACOBS, BERTRAM L ARIZONA STATE UNIVERSITY TEMPE, AZ 85287 Control of the interferon-induced protein kinase
R29CA-48656-05 (VR) FEITELSON, MARK A JEFFERSON MEDICAL COLLEGE OF 1020 LOCUST STREET PHILADELPHIA, PA 19107 Products of the x and polymerase genes of hepadnaviruses
R01CA-48662-03 (CBY) STACEY, DENNIS W CLEVELAND CLINIC FOUNDATION 9500 EUCLID AVENUE CLEVELAND, OH 44106 The role of proto-oncogenes in cellular proliferation
R29CA-48664-04 (IMB) FOX, BARBARA S UNIVERSITY OF MD 10 SOUTH PINE STREET BALTIMORE, MD. 21201 Influence of immunization regimen on helper T cells
R29CA-48667-04 (CBY) FEUERSTEIN, NILI H UNIV OF PENN SCHOOL OF MED 36TH & HAMILTON WALK PHILADELPHIA, PA 19104-6015 Nuclear proteins and regulation of lymphocyte growth
R29CA-48672-03 (RAD) TUCKER, SUSAN L UNIV OF TX M.D. ANDERSON CAN C 1515 HOLCOMBE BOULEVARD HOUSTON, TX 77030 Evaluation of predictors of tumor response to radiation
R29CA-48707-03 (EVR) BABISS, LEE E THE ROCKEFELLER UNIVERSITY 1230 YORK AVE. NEW YORK, NY 10021-6399 Transformation progression and ad5 gene regulation
R01CA-48709-04 (EVR) GIAM, CHOU-ZEN CASE WESTERN RESERVE UNIVERSIT 10900 EUCLID AVENUE CLEVELAND, OH 44106-4984 Biochemical mechanism of trans-activation in HTLV-I
P01CA-48711-02 (SRC) SKOLNICK, MARK H UNIVERSITY OF UTAH 410 CHIPETA WAY #105 SALT LAKE CITY, UT 84108 Genetic epidemiology of cancer and predisposing lesions
P01CA-48711-02 0001 (SRC) MEYER, LAURENCE J Genetic epidemiology of cancer and predisposing lesions Genetic epidemiology of nevi and melanoma
P01CA-48711-02 0002 (SRC) BURT, RANDALL W Genetic epidemiology of cancer and predisposing lesions Genetic epidemiology of adenomatous polyps and colon cancer
P01CA-48711-02 0003 (SRC) WARD, JOHN H Genetic epidemiology of cancer and predisposing lesions Genetic epidemiology of proliferative breast disease and breast cancer
P01CA-48711-02 0004 (SRC) SKOLNICK, MARK H Genetic epidemiology of cancer and predisposing lesions Linkage analysis of common cancers
P01CA-48711-02 9001 (SRC) CANNON-ALBRIGHT, LISA A Genetic epidemiology of cancer and predisposing lesions Core--Genetics lab
P01CA-48711-02 9002 (SRC) GOLDGAR, DAVID Genetic epidemiology of cancer and predisposing lesions Core--Data analysis
R29CA-48713-03 (ET) SAMOSZUK, MICHAEL K UNIVERSITY OF CALIFORNIA PATHOLOGY DEPT, CCM D-440 IRVINE, CA 92717 Enzyme immunoaugmentation of Hodgkin's disease
R29CA-48716-03 (RAD) JORGENSEN, TIMOTHY J GEORGETOWN UNIV MED CTR 3800 RESERVOIR ROAD, N. W. WASHINGTON, D.C. 20007 Biochemistry of radiation-induced DNA strand breaks
R01CA-48717-03 (SRC) DESAI, PRAFUL UICC RUE DU CONSEIL-GENERAL 3 1205 GENEVA, SWITZERLAND NGO participation in national cancer plans
R29CA-48718-03 (VR) ROBERTS, JAMES M FRED HUTCHINSON CANCER RES CTR 1124 COLUMBIA STREET SEATTLE, WA 98104 Control of viral replication
R01CA-48723-04A1 (ARRB) BROOKMEYER, RONALD S JOHNS HOPKINS UNIVERSITY 615 NORTH WOLFE STREET BALTIMORE, MD 21205-3179 Statistical methods in AIDS research
R01CA-48725-02 (ET) POWIS, GARTH MAYO FOUNDATION 200 FIRST STREET SOUTHWEST ROCHESTER, MN 55905 Metabolism and the activity of quinone anticancer drugs
P01CA-48729-03 (SRC) BRADY, THOMAS J MASS GENERAL HOSP-NMR CENTER BLDG 149, 13TH STREET CHARLESTON, MA 02129 Biomedical implications of magnetic susceptibility in MR imaging
P01CA-48729-03 0005 (SRC) BRADY, THOMAS J Biomedical implications of magnetic susceptibility in MR imaging MR imging of liver metastases
P01CA-48729-03 9001 (SRC) ACKERMAN, JEROME L Biomedical implications of magnetic susceptibility in MR imaging Core--NMR facilities
P01CA-48729-03 9002 (SRC) PEARLMAN, JUSTIN D Biomedical implications of magnetic susceptibility in MR imaging Core--NMR computer and technologies
P01CA-48729-03 9003 (SRC) LAUFFER, RANDALL A Biomedical implications of magnetic susceptibility in MR imaging Core--NMR contrast agents
P01CA-48729-03 0001 (SRC) ROSEN, BRUCE R Biomedical implications of magnetic susceptibility in MR imaging MR imaging of brain perfusion
P01CA-48729-03 0002 (SRC) KANTOR, HOWARD L Biomedical implications of magnetic susceptibility in MR imaging MR studies of myocardial perfusion
P01CA-48729-03 0003 (SRC) THULBORN, KEITH R Biomedical implications of magnetic susceptibility in MR imaging Biochemical and multinuclear MR studies of hemorrhage
P01CA-48729-03 0004 (SRC) WEDEEN, VAN J Biomedical implications of magnetic susceptibility in MR imaging MR imaging of deep venous thrombosis
P01CA-48733-02 (SRC) MORGAN, ALAN R UNIVERSITY OF TOLEDO 2801 WEST BANCROFT STREET TOLEDO, OHIO 43606 PDT-- Sensitizers, delivery systems and biologic response
P01CA-48733-02 0001 (SRC) MORGAN, ALAN R PDT-- Sensitizers, delivery systems and biologic response Structure-activity relationships for sensitizers in PDT
P01CA-48733-02 0002 (SRC) GARBO, GRETA PDT-- Sensitizers, delivery systems and biologic response Effect of drug delivery systems on PDT
P01CA-48733-02 0003 (SRC) KESSEL, DAVID PDT-- Sensitizers, delivery systems and biologic response Determinants of tumor localization
P01CA-48733-02 0004 (SRC) SELMAN, STEVEN H PDT-- Sensitizers, delivery systems and biologic response Biologic response to PDT
P01CA-48733-02 9001 (SRC) SELMAN, STEVEN H PDT-- Sensitizers, delivery systems and biologic response In vivo core
P01CA-48735-02 (SRC) OLEINICK, NANCY L CASE WESTERN RESERVE UNIVERSIT 2058 ABINGTON ROAD CLEVELAND, OH 44106 Phthalocyanine photodynamic therapy--Mechanistic studies
P01CA-48735-02 0001 (SRC) KENNEY, MALCOLM E Phthalocyanine photodynamic therapy--Mechanistic studies Synthesis of phthalocyanines for tumor phototherapy
P01CA-48735-02 0002 (SRC) OLEINICK, NANCY L Phthalocyanine photodynamic therapy--Mechanistic studies Cytotoxic responses in phthalocyanine photodynamic phototherapy
P01CA-48735-02 0003 (SRC) BERGER, NATHAN A Phthalocyanine photodynamic therapy--Mechanistic studies Metabolic alterations in photodynamic purging of bone marrow
P01CA-48735-02 0004 (SRC) MUKHTAR, HASAN Phthalocyanine photodynamic therapy--Mechanistic studies Phthalocyanine photodynamic therapy--In vivo responses and mechanisms
P01CA-48735-02 9001 (SRC) DUNBAR, ROBERT C Phthalocyanine photodynamic therapy--Mechanistic studies Core--Light source facility
R01CA-48737-03 (PBC) FUKUDA, MINORU LA JOLLA CANCER RESEARCH FDN 10901 NORTH TORREY PINES ROAD LA JOLLA, CA 92037 Lysosomal membrane glycoproteins--Structure and biosynthesis
R01CA-48741-03 (MEP) COHEN, LEONARD A ONE DANA ROAD VALHALLA, N Y 10595 Voluntary exercise as means of mammary cancer prevention
U10CA-48743-03 (CCI) DONALDSON, MILTON H THREE COOPER PLAZA CAMDEN, N.J. 08103 Childrens cancer study group
R01CA-48746-03 (EVR) BEEMON, KAREN L JOHNS HOPKINS UNIVERSITY 3400 NORTH CHARLES STREET BALTIMORE, MD 21218 Retroviral regulatory sequences within coding sequences
R01CA-48763-03 (GMA) ELMETS, CRAIG A UNIV HOSPITALS OF CLEVELAND 2074 ABINGTON ROAD CLEVELAND, OH 44106 Skin cancer: Immunotoxic mechanisms
R01CA-48774-03 (EDC) PIKE, MALCOLM C USC MEDICAL SCHOOL PMB A-201 2025 ZONAL AVENUE LOS ANGELES, CA 90033 Case-control study of post-menopausal endometrial cancer
R01CA-48780-04 (PTHB) PRESS, MICHAEL F UNIV OF SOUTHERN CALIFORNIA 2011 ZONAL AVENUE, HMR 204 LOS ANGELES, CA 90033 Pathobiology of breast cancer and hormone receptors
P01CA-48799-03 (SRC) PLEDGER, WARREN J VANDERBILT UNIV SCHOOL OF MED C-2310 MCN NASHVILLE, TN 37232-2175 Growth inhibitors, differentiation and cancer
P01CA-48799-03 0001 (SRC) PLEDGER, WARREN J Growth inhibitors, differentiation and cancer Gene expression regulating calcium-induced differentiation
P01CA-48799-03 0002 (SRC) MATRISIAN, LYNN M Growth inhibitors, differentiation and cancer Cellular RNAs modulated by growth inhibitory effects of TGF-beta
P01CA-48799-03 0003 (SRC) HNN, STEPHEN R Growth inhibitors, differentiation and cancer C-MYC proteins in differenilation and growth inhibition
P01CA-48799-03 0004 (SRC) HOGAN, BRIGID L.M. Growth inhibitors, differentiation and cancer Role of TGF-beta regulated genes in embryonic development
P01CA-48799-03 9001 (SRC) WATTERSON, D. MARTIN Growth inhibitors, differentiation and cancer Core--microchemical resource
P01CA-48799-03 9002 (SRC) HOLT, JEFFRY T. Growth inhibitors, differentiation and cancer Core-Molecular and cellular biology
P01CA-48799-03 9003 (SRC) HOGAN, BRIGID L.M. Growth inhibitors, differentiation and cancer Core-Transgenic mouse facility
R01CA-48801-02 (EVR) LEVY, LAURA S TULANE UNIV SCH OF MEDICINE 1430 TULANE AVENUE NEW ORLEANS, LA 70112 Molecular genetics of feline retroviruses
R01CA-48802-03 (MGN) LYNCH, HENRY T CREIGHTON UNIVERSITY CALIFORNIA AT 24TH STREET OMAHA, NE 68178 Linkage studies in hereditary breast cancer
R01CA-48815-03 (BBCB) MAUDSLEY, ANDREW A VA MEDICAL CENTER 4150 CLEMENT STREET SAN FRANCISCO, CA 94121 Spectroscopic NMR imaging of proton metabolites in vivo
R01CA-48828-02 (PTHB) ANDERSON, GARTH R ROSEWELL PARK MEMORIAL INST 666 ELM STREET BUFFALO, NY 14263 Anoxia responsive VL30 elements

PROJECT NO., ORGANIZATIONAL UNIT., INVESTIGATOR, ADDRESS, TITLE

R01CA-48900-03 (RAD) PETTI, PAULA L LAWRENCE BERKELEY LABORATORY 1 CYCLOTRON RD BERKELEY, CA 94720 Multiple scattering in 3d charged particles tmt planning
R29CA-48902-03 (RAD) MACKIE, THOMAS R 1530 MEDICAL SCIENCES CENTER 1300 UNIVERSITY AVENUE MADISON, WI 53706 Radiation dose calculation using convolution
R01CA-48905-02 (ET) SEBTI, SAID M UNIV OF PITTS SCHOOL OF MED W1354 BIOMEDICAL SCIENCE TOWER PITTSBURGH, PA 15261 Bleomycin hydrolase and tumor resistance to bleomycin
R29CA-48906-03 (ET) DONATO, NICHOLAS J UNIVERSITY OF TEXAS 1515 HOLCOMBE BOULEVARD HOUSTON, TX 77030 Early biochemical events in tumor necrosis factor action
P01CA-48919-01A2 (SRC) BUKOWSKI, RONALD M CLEVELAND CLINIC FOUNDATION 9500 EUCLID AVE/ONE CLINIC CTR CLEVELAND, OH 44195 Biology of renal cell carcinoma
P01CA-48919-01A2 0001 (SRC) BUDD, G THOMAS Biology of renal cell carcinoma Combined cytokine therapy
P01CA-48919-01A2 0002 (SRC) FINKE, JAMES H Biology of renal cell carcinoma IL-2 /IL-4 Synergy in T-cell response-- Mechanism of action
P01CA-48919-01A2 0003 (SRC) HAMILTON, THOMAS ALAN Biology of renal cell carcinoma Mechanisms of interferon/interleukin-2 induced macrophage gene expression
P01CA-48919-01A2 9001 (SRC) TUBBS, RAYMOND Biology of renal cell carcinoma Core-- Immunotyping
P01CA-48919-01A2 9002 (SRC) KLEIN, ERIC A Biology of renal cell carcinoma Core-- Tissue culture
R29CA-48922-03 (PTHB) ALDAZ, CLAUDIO M U OF TEXAS M D ANDERSON CA CTR P.O. BOX 389 SMITHVILLE, TX 78957 Chromosomal abnormalities in rat mammary carcinogenesis
R25CA-48924-03 (SRC) WRIGHT, JOHN R S U N Y - AT BUFFALO 204 FARBER HALL BUFFALO, NY 14214 Summer student oncology fellowship program
R01CA-48927-02 (REN) RUSSO, JOSE FOX CHASE CANCER CENTER 7701 BURHOLME AVENUE PHILADELPHIA, PA 19111 Influence of puberty on breast topography and neoplasia
R01CA-48930-03 (ET) BOUCEK, ROBERT J, JR VANDERBILT UNIVERSITY MED CTR D-2217 MCN NASHVILLE, TN 37232-2572 Sarcoplasmic reticulum: membrane target of anthracycline
R01CA-48932-03 (CPA) FEINBERG, ANDREW P UNIV OF MICHIGAN MEDICAL CTR 1150 W MEDICAL CAMPUS DRIVE ANN ARBOR, MI 48109 Identification of the earliest steps in transformation
R01CA-48939-01A2 (ET) HYNYNEN, KULLERVO H UNIVERSITY OF ARIZONA ARIZONA HEALTH SCIENCES CENTER TUCSON, AZ 85724 Intracavitary ultrasound hyperthermia system
R01CA-48943-03 (CPA) SUKUMAR, SARASWATI SALK INST/BIOLOGICAL STUDIES P O BOX 85800 SAN DIEGO, CA 92138 Role of ras oncogenes in chemical carcinogenesis
R01CA-48945-01A2 (ET) SAUNDERS, PRISCILLA P U.T. M.D. ANDERSON CANCER CENT 1515 HOLCOMBE BOULEVARD HOUSTON, TX 77030 Nucleoside analogs--interactions with NAD synthesis
R01CA-48956-02 (NEUA) BERNSTEIN, JERALD J GEORGE WASHINGTON UNIVERSITY 2150 PENNSYLVANIA AVE WASHINGTON, DC 20037 Therapy & migration of human malignant astrocytomas
R01CA-48961-03 (BMT) WHITTEN, DAVID G UNIV OF ROCHESTER- RIVER CAMPU HUTCHISON HALL 404 ROCHESTER, NY 14627 Picket fence porphyrins for photodynamic therapy
R01CA-48964-03 (RNM) ORVIG, CHRISTOPHER E UNIVERSITY OF BRITISH COLUMBIA 2036 MAIN MALL VANCOUVER, BC CANADA V6T 1Z1 Hydroxyketone ligands in nuclear medicine
R01CA-48974-02 (BNP) KINGSTON, DAVID G VA POLYT.INST & ST UNIV. BLACKSBURG, VA 24061-0212 Photoaffinity labeling of tubulin by taxol
R01CA-48985-02 (RNM) GIGER, MARYELLEN L UNIVERSITY OF CHICAGO 5841 SOUTH MARYLAND AVE CHICAGO, IL 60637 Digital image analysis for cancer detection
R29CA-48990-03 (VR) PIRISI, LUCIA A UNIVERSITY OF SOUTH CAROLINA DEPT. OF PATHOLOGY SMC 661 COLUMBIA, SC 29208 Papillomavirus transformation of human keratinocytes
R01CA-48995-03 (BIO) DANIEL, LARRY W BOWMAN GRAY SCH/WAKE FOREST UN 300 SOUTH HAWTHORNE ROAD WINSTON-SALEM, NC 27103 Phosphatidylcholine, a source of diglyceride mediators
R01CA-48996-01A2 (EDC) SHERMAN, KAREN J FRED HUTCHINSON CANCER RES CTR 1124 COLUMBIA STREET SEATTLE, WA 98104 Oral cancer--Epidemiology, biochemistry, and immunology
R01CA-48998-01A2 (EDC) SLATTERY, MARTHA L UNIV OF UTAH SCH OF MED 50 N MEDICAL DR, ROOM 1C26 SALT LAKE CITY, UT 84132 Diet, activity & reproduction as risks for colon cancer
R29CA-49002-03 (CPA) HAMILTON, JOSHUA W DARTMOUTH COLLEGE HANOVER, NH 03755 Effect of carcinogens on gene expression in vivo
R01CA-49004-03 (RAD) BRYANT, ROBERT G UNIV OF ROCHESTER MEDICAL CTR 601 ELMWOOD AVE/BOX BPHYS ROCHESTER, NY 14642 Tumor response to therapy characterized by NMR
R29CA-49017-03 (RAD) MACKLIS, ROGER M 50 BINNEY STREET BOSTON, MA 02115 Animal models in immunochelate radiotherapy
R01CA-49018-03 (RAD) LASZLO, ANDREI WASHINGTON UNIV SCHL OF MED 4511 FOREST PARK BLVD ST LOUIS, MO 63130 Mechanisms of thermotolerance--Protection or repair
R29CA-49024-04 (ET) MAIER, TOM J OREGON HEALTH SCIENCES UNIV 611 S.W. CAMPUS DRIVE PORTLAND, OR 97201 Natural suppressor cells--cancer therapy and tolerance induction
R01CA-49039-03 (PTHB) FARBER, ROSANN A CB#7525 BRINKHOUS-BULLITT BLDG UNIV OF N C AT CHAPEL HILL CHAPEL HILL, NC 27599-7525 Molecular genetics of treatment-induced leukemia
R01CA-49044-02 (EDC) THOMAS, DAVID B FRED HUTCHINSON CANCER RES CTR 1124 COLUMBIA STREET SEATTLE, WA 98104 Papilloma viruses and cervical cancer in Bangkok
R29CA-49047-04 (VR) STRAIR, ROGER K YALE UNIVERSITY P O BOX 3333 NEW HAVEN, CT 06510 Isolation of a human E1A-like factor
R01CA-49052-03 (CBY) HOLT, JEFFREY T VANDERBILT UNIVERSITY SCHOOL OF MEDICINE NASHVILLE, TN 37232 Functions of c-fos protein in cellular physiology
R01CA-49056-03 (MGN) WALDMAN, FREDERIC M UNIV OF CALIFORNIA 1855 FOLSOM STREET SAN FRANCISCO, CA 94143-0808 Nuclear organization by fluorescence in situ hybridization

PROJECT NO., ORGANIZATIONAL UNIT., INVESTIGATOR, ADDRESS, TITLE

P01CA-49062-02 (SRC) HALL, ERIC J COLUMBIA UNIV HLTH SCIS 630 WEST 168TH STREET NEW YORK, NY 10032 Radiation biology of simulated radon-daughter alphas
P01CA-49062-02 0001 (SRC) HALL, ERIC J Radiation biology of simulated radon-daughter alphas Alpha particles, asbestosis fibers, chemical carcinogens--SHE cell transformation
P01CA-49062-02 0002 (SRC) HEI, TOM K Radiation biology of simulated radon-daughter alphas Human-hamster hybrid cell mutations induced by radon simulated alpha particles
P01CA-49062-02 0003 (SRC) GRUNBERGER, DEZIDER Radiation biology of simulated radon-daughter alphas Mechanism of mutation induced in mammalian gene by alpha particles
P01CA-49062-02 0004 (SRC) WEINSTEIN, BERNARD I Radiation biology of simulated radon-daughter alphas: Asynchronous DNA replication--inducible responses to alpha particle radiation
P01CA-49062-02 0005 (SRC) GEARD, CHARLES R Radiation biology of simulated radon-daughter alphas Cytogenetics--Alpha particle-induced chromosomal changes
P01CA-49062-02 9001 (SRC) HALL, ERIC J Radiation biology of simulated radon-daughter alphas Core--Development of radon simulation facility and bioinstrument shop
U01CA-49076-03 (SRC) ZERHOUNI, ELIAS A JOHNS HOPKINS HOSPITAL BALTIMORE, MD 21205 National collaborative diagnostic imaging trial projects
U01CA-49077-03 (SRC) FRANCIS, ISAAC R UNIV OF MICHIGAN HOSPITAL DEPT OF RADIOLOGY - 0030 ANN ARBOR, MI 48109-0030 National collaborative diagnostic imaging trial project
U01CA-49078-03 (SRC) MOSS, ALBERT A UNIVERSITY OF WASHINGTON DEPT OF RADIOLOGY, SB-05 SEATTLE, WA 98195 National collaborative diagnostic imaging trial projects
U01CA-49079-03 (SRC) MEGIBOW, ALEC J NEW YORK UNIV MEDICAL CENTER 560 FIRST AVENUE HW205 NEW YORK, NY 10016 Imaging trials in pancreatic and colo-rectal carcinoma
R01CA-49081-01A3 (REB) ATAYA, KHALID M CASE WESTERN UNIVERSITY 3395 SCRANTON RD CLEVELAND, OH 44109 Chemotherapy-induced ovarian failure--Prevention
R01CA-49084-18 (BNP) FAULKNER, D JOHN SCRIPPS INST. OF OCEANOGRAPHY LA JOLLA, CA 92093-0212 Antibiotics from marine organisms
U01CA-49088-03 (SRC) BALFE, DENNIS M MALLINCKRODT INST OF RADIOLOGY 510 S KINGSHIGHWAY BLVD ST LOUIS, MO 63110 National collaborative diagnostic imaging trial projects
P01CA-49089-03 (SRC) GIROTTI, ALBERT W MEDICAL COLLEGE OF WISCONSIN 8701 WATERTOWN PLANK RD MILWAUKEE, WI 53226 Mechanisms of merocyanine-mediated phototherapy
P01CA-49089-03 0001 (SRC) KALYANARAMAN, BALARAMAN Mechanisms of merocyanine-mediated phototherapy Photochemical-photophysical studies on merocyanine 540
P01CA-49089-03 0002 (SRC) GIROTTI, ALBERT W Mechanisms of merocyanine-mediated phototherapy Photodynamic action of merocyanine on cell membranes
P01CA-49089-03 0003 (SRC) SIEBER, FRITZ Mechanisms of merocyanine-mediated phototherapy Cellular targets of dye-mediated photosensitization
P01CA-49089-03 9001 (SRC) GIROTTI, ALBERT W Mechanisms of merocyanine-mediated phototherapy Core
P30CA-49095-04 (SRC) BERNARD, LOUIS J MEHARRY MEDICAL COLLEGE 1005 D.B. TODD BOULEVARD NASHVILLE, TENNESSEE 37208 Drew Meharry Morehouse Consortium Cancer Center
P30CA-49095-04 9001 (SRC) BROWN, C PERRY Drew Meharry Morehouse Consortium Cancer Center Core--Epidemiology/Biostatistics
P30CA-49095-04 9002 (SRC) HUNTER, ROY Drew Meharry Morehouse Consortium Cancer Center Core--Editorial office
P30CA-49095-04 9003 (SRC) CLAYTON, LINDA Drew Meharry Morehouse Consortium Cancer Center Core--Clinical trials
R01CA-49096-03 (EI) DUPONT, BO SLOAN-KETTERING INST/CANCER RE 1275 YORK AVENUE NEW YORK, NY 10021 Serine esterases in human cytolytic lymphocytes
R01CA-49114-03 (IMB) GOLDFARB, RONALD H PITTSBURGH CANCER INSTITUTE 3343 FORBES AVENUE PITTSBURGH, PA 15213 Natural killer cell proteolytic enzymes--functional role
R01CA-49127-04 (MEP) LEVINE, ALAN E UT HEALTH SCI CTR AT HOUSTON P O BOX 20069 HOUSTON, TEXAS 77225 Autocrine role of transforming growth factor
R01CA-49133-03 (PTHB) DIAZ, MANUEL O 5841 SOUTH MARYLAND CHICAGO, IL 60637 Interferon gene deletions in human leukemia cell lines
R01CA-49135-03 (CPA) IVERSEN, PATRICK L UNIVERSITY OF NEBRASKA MED CTR 600 SOUTH 42ND ST OMAHA, NE 68198-6260 Gene specific inhibition of cytochrome P-450 isoforms
R01CA-49143-03 (ET) BRAUNSCHWEIGER, PAUL G UNIVERSITY OF MIAMI SCH OF MED 1600 NW 10TH AVE MIAMI, FL 33136 Antitumor activity of recombinant interleukin I
R01CA-49150-04 (ET) SCHILSKY, RICHARD LEWIS UNIVERSITY OF CHICAGO 5841 SOUTH MARYLAND, BOX 420 CHICAGO, IL 60637 Cellular pharmacology of the stereoisomers of leucovorin
R01CA-49152-03 (PTHB) NEEL, BENJAMIN BETH ISRAEL HOSPITAL 330 BROOKLINE AVE, RW663 BOSTON, MA 02215 Molecular analysis of suppression of transformation
R44CA-49164-03 (SSS) POWER, ROBERT L INNOVATIVE IMAGINING SCIENCES 1095 EAST 2100 SOUTH #295 SALT LAKE CITY, UT 84106 Light equalization radiographic screen/film cassette
R44CA-49166-03 (SSS) DEJARNETTE, WAYNE T DEJARNETTE RESEARCH SYS INC 10 WONDERVIEW COURT TIMONIUM, MD 21093 Development of a low cost ACR-NEMA PACS interface
R01CA-49181-04 (RAD) SHADLEY, JEFFREY D MEDICAL COLLEGE OF WISCONSIN 8700 W WISCONSIN AVE MILWAUKEE, WI 53226 Study of inducible repair response in human lymphocytes
R01CA-49186-03 (ET) HANDE, KENNETH R VANDERBILT UNIVERSITY 1956 THE VANDERBILT CLINIC NASHVILLE, TN 37232 Pharmacogentic aspects of antineoplastic drug metabolism
R01CA-49195-01A3 (MEP) RUSSELL, ROBERT M 711 WASHINGTON STREET BOSTON, MA 02111 Intestinal metabolism of b-carotene

R01CA-49203-08 (PTHB) KLEVECZ, ROBERT R BECKMAN RESEARCH INSTITUTE 1450 EAST DUARTE ROAD DUARTE, CA 91010 Timing of mammalian cell cycle events
R29CA-49207-03 (HEM) MCKEITHAN, TIMOTHY WAYNE UNIVERSITY OF CHICAGO MED CTR BOX 414 Molecular analysis of the 14;19 translocation
P01CA-49210-03 (SRC) CAVALIERI, ERCOLE L UNIV OF NEBRASKA MED CENTER 600 SOUTH 42ND STREET OMAHA, NE 68198-6805 Mechanisms of 7,12-dimethylbenzanthracene carcinogenesis
P01CA-49210-03 0001 (SRC) CAVALIERI, ERCOLE L Mechanisms of 7,12-dimethylbenzanthracene carcinogenesis Chemical and biological formation of DMBA-DNA adducts
P01CA-49210-03 0002 (SRC) GROSS, MICHAEL L Mechanisms of 7,12-dimethylbenzanthracene carcinogenesis Mass spectrometry for DNA adducts structures
P01CA-49210-03 0003 (SRC) SMALL, GERALD J. Mechanisms of 7,12-dimethylbenzanthracene carcinogenesis DNA damage analysis by fluorescence line narrowing
R01CA-49218-03 (BEM) BAKER, FRANK JOHNS HOPKINS UNIVERSITY 615 NORTH WOLFE STREET BALTIMORE, MD 21205 Psychosocial factors in adjustment of BMT survivors
R01CA-49227-03 (MEP) BROITMAN, SELWYN A MALLORY INST OF PATHOLOGY FDN 784 MASSACHUSETTS AVENUE BOSTON, MA 02118 Detection of LDL-receptors in colon and colon tumors
R01CA-49228-03 (PTHB) LYNCH, RICHARD G UNIV OF IOWA COLL OF MED 144ML IOWA CITY, IOWA 52242 Tumor immunology of T cell IgE fc receptors
R01CA-49231-04 (ET) SHU, SUYU UNIVERSITY OF MICHIGAN 2926 TAUBMAN CTR/SURGERY DEPT ANN ARBOR, MI 48109-0331 Adoptive T cell immunotherapy of nonimmunogenic tumors
R01CA-49232-04 (EI) REINHERZ, ELLIS L DANA-FARBER CANCER INSTITUTE 44 BINNEY STREET BOSTON, MA 02115 Structure-function analysis of common acute lymphoblastic leukemia antigen
R01CA-49238-03 (PTHB) LEBOWITZ, PAUL YALE MEDICAL SCHOOL 333 CEDAR ST., P.O. BOX 3333 NEW HAVEN, CONN 06510 Bcr-abl and ras in CML evolution, phenotype, prognosis
R01CA-49240-03 (HEM) LIU, EDISON T UNIV OF N C AT CHAPEL HILL LINEBERGER COMPREHENSIVE CA CT CHAPEL HILL, N C 27599 Molecular determinants in human leukemic progression
R01CA-49243-03 (PTHB) SPIRO, ROBERT C RES INST OF SCRIPPS CLINIC 10666 N TORREY PINES ROAD LA JOLLA, CA 92037 Structure & function of a cell-associated proteoglycan
R01CA-49248-01A2 (ET) WAXMAN, DAVID J DANA FARBER CANCER INST 44 BINNEY ST BOSTON, MA 02115 Hepatic metabolism of anti cancer drugs
R01CA-49254-03 (ET) RASO, VICTOR A BOSTON BIOMEDICAL RES INST 20 STANIFORD STREET BOSTON, MA 02114 Model to test the therapeutic value of toxin conjugates
R01CA-49256-03 (PTHB) STOOLMAN, LLOYD M 1301 CATHERINE ROAD ANN ARBOR, MI 48109-0602 Endothelial-binding lectins of lymphoid malignancies
R29CA-49258-04 (PTHB) BENADE, LEONARD E AMERICAN RED CROSS/HOLLAND LAB 15601 CRABBS BRANCH WAY ROCKVILLE, MD 20855 Derivation of revertants of ras-transformed human cells
R01CA-49259-03 (PBC) CARTER, WILLIAM G FRED HUTCHINSON CANCER RES CTR 1124 COLUMBIA ST SEATTLE, WA 98104 Extracellular matrix receptors in tissue morphogenesis
R01CA-49260-04 (ET) BLUESTONE, JEFFREY A BEN MAY INSTITUTE 5841 S MARYLAND AVE, BOX 424 CHICAGO, IL 60637 In vivo potentiation of immune responses
R01CA-49261-03 (SSS) DALLAS, WILLIAM J UNIVERSITY OF ARIZONA TUCSON, AZ 85724 Viewing console for Picture Archiving and Communications System
R01CA-49271-03 (VR) LEVINE, ARNOLD J PRINCETON UNIVERSITY PRINCETON, NJ 08544-1014 Proteins and gene functions of Epstein-Barr virus
R29CA-49275-03 (RNM) MORTON, KATHRYN A UNIVERSITY OF UTAH MEDICAL DEPARTMENT OF RADIOLOGY Tumor imaging with nuclides that bind to metallothionein
R01CA-49283-08 (IMS) FRIEDMAN, STEVEN M HOSPITAL FOR SPECIAL SURGERY 535 EAST 70TH STREET NEW YORK, N Y 10021 Hapten specific human T cell lines
R01CA-49296-04 (EVR) MONTELARO, RONALD C UNIVERSITY OF PITTSBURGH PITTSBURGH, PA 15261 Gene expression during lentivirus infections--EIAV
R29CA-49297-04 (ET) GAMETCHU, BAHIRU MEDICAL COLLEGE OF WISCONSIN 8701 WATERTOWN PLANK ROAD MILWAUKEE, WI 53226 Membrane glucocorticoid receptor in lymphocytolysis
R01CA-49298-03 (CBY) GLENNEY, JOHN R UNIV OF KENTUCKY MEDICAL CENTE 800 ROSE STREET LEXINGTON, KY 40536-0084 Cytoskeletal substrates of the tyrosine kinase pp60 VSRC
R01CA-49308-03 (PTHB) BRAUN, JONATHAN UCLA, CENTER FOR HLTH SCIENCES 405 HILGARD AVENUE LOS ANGELES, CA 90024-1732 Immunoglobulin gene expression in B-lyl cells
R44CA-49310-02 (ET) MORGAN, LEE ROY DEKK-TEC, INC 3839 ULLOA ST NEW ORLEANS, LA 70119 Phenylhydrazones with anticancer activities
R44CA-49328-02 (SSS) HAUGLAND, RICHARD P MOLECULAR PROBES, INC 4849 PITCHFORD AVENUE EUGENE, OR 97402 Photochemotherapy-synthesis of cationic photosensitizers
R44CA-49337-02A1 (SSS) HALEY, JOHN D ONCOGENE SCIENCE INC 350 COMMUNITY DRIVE MANHASSET, NY 11030 TGF-beta 3 production in eucaryotes and procaryotes
R44CA-49338-02 (SSS) REYNOLDS, FRED H ONCOGENE SCIENCE, INC 106 CHARLES LINDBERGH BLVD UNIONDALE, NY 11553 Immunologic assays to activated ras oncogene proteins
R44CA-49347-03 (SSS) PATEL, GORDHAN N JP LABORATORIES, INC 26 HOWARD STREET PISCATAWAY, NJ 08854 Film dosimeter for neutron therapy
R01CA-49359-03 (PBC) FONG, DUNNE RUTGERS THE STATE UNIV OF N J NELSON BIOLOGICAL LABS PISCATAWAY, NJ 08855-1059 Proteinase function and cancer metastasis
R01CA-49374-03 (SRC) NANDI, SATYABRATA UNIVERSITY OF CALIFORNIA 447 LIFE SCIENCES ADDITION BERKELEY, CA 94720 Transformation of human breast epithelial cells in vitro
R01CA-49384-03 (SRC) MC COY, GEORGE D CASE WESTERN RESERVE UNIV 2119 ABINGTON ROAD CLEVELAND, OH 44106 Oral cancer--Etiological role of tobacco and alcohol
R01CA-49394-04 (IMB) CHESNUT, ROBERT W CYTEL CORPORATION 11099 NORTH TORREY PINES ROAD LA JOLLA, CA 92037 Recognition of EBV latent membrane protein
R01CA-49401-04 (SRC) MARSHALL, MILTON VIRGIL PARK ONE RESEARCH LABS, INC 12852 PARK ONE DRIVE SUGAR LAND, TX 77478 Tobacco products and oral cavity cancer
R44CA-49405-02A1 (SSS) BINKLEY, DAVID M COMPUTER TECHNOLOGY & IMAGING 810 INNOVATION DRIVE KNOXVILLE, TN 37932 A timing system for positron emission tomography
R29CA-49409-02 (ET) BASU, HIRAK S UNIVERSITY OF CALIFORNIA BOX 0520 SAN FRANCISCO, CA 94143 Development of polyamine analogs as anticancer agents
R01CA-49411-03 (RAD) KANTOR, GEORGE J WRIGHT STATE UNIVERSITY 3640 COLONEL GLENN HWY DAYTON, OH 45435 Domain-specific DNA excision repair in human cells
R01CA-49414-12 (GMA) BRAVERMAN, IRWIN M YALE UNIVERSITY P O BOX 3333, 333 CEDAR STREET NEW HAVEN, CT 06510 Pathogenesis of mycosis fungoides
R01CA-49416-02 (RAD) YATVIN, MILTON B OREGON HEALTH SCIENCES UNIV 3181 S W SAM JACKSON PARK RD PORTLAND, OR 97201 Role of membrane lipids in heat injury
R01CA-49417-02 (PTHB) THIERY, JEAN P CNRS-ECOLE NORMALE SUPERIEURE 46 RUE D'ULM-8EME ETAGE PARIS, FRANCE 75230 CEDEX 05 Epithelio-mesenchymal conversion in tumor metastasis
R01CA-49419-03 (HEM) WILSON, E LYNETTE NEW YORK UNIVERSITY MED CTR 550 FIRST AVENUE NEW YORK, NY 10016 The role of plasminogen activators in myelopoiesis
R01CA-49422-03 (MEP) HALL, ALAN K UMDNJ-NEW JERSEY MED SCHOOL 185 SOUTH ORANGE AVE., (G-536) NEWARK, NJ 07103-2757 Molecular actions of retinoids in neoplastic cell growth
R01CA-49423-03 (CPA) LIN, CHING-SHWUN PALO ALTO MEDICAL FOUNDATION 860 BRYANT STREET PALO ALTO, CA 94301 Role of metaschematin proteins in neoplasia
R25CA-49425-03 (SRC) BERRY, DAISILEE H UNIVERSITY OF ARKANSAS 4301 WEST MARKHAM LITTLE ROCK, AR 72205 Partners in research
R01CA-49429-02 (RAD) STEEVES, RICHARD A UNIVERSITY OF WISCONSIN MADISON, WI 53792 Ferromagnetic hyperthermia & iodine-125 brachytherapy
R01CA-49431-02 (BEM) ANDRYKOWSKI, MICHAEL A UNIVERSITY OF KENTUCKY LEXINGTON, KY 40536-0086 Quality of life following bone marrow transplantation
R29CA-49435-02 (PBC) MATSUURA, HIDEMITSU 8420 SOUTHEAST 39TH STREET MERCER ISLAND, WA 98040 Alpha-GalNAc transferase regulating oncofetal epitope
R01CA-49437-03 (IMB) OKUNEWICK, JAMES P ALLEGHENY GENERAL HOSPITAL 320 E NORTH AVE PITTSBURGH, PA 15212 Influence of T-cell subtypes on graft-vs-leukemia
R01CA-49438-02 (PBC) DEAN, DOUGLAS C WASHINGTON UNIV SCHOOL OF MED 660 S EUCLID, BX 8052 ST LOUIS, MO 63110 Regulation of fibronectin expression
R01CA-49443-03 (PTHB) LEE, MING-SHENG THE UNIVERSITY OF TEXAS MD ANDERSON CANCER CTR, BOX 73 HOUSTON, TX 77030 Minimal residual disease in lymphomas with the t(14;18)
R01CA-49446-03 (EDC) PAFFENBARGER, RALPH S, JR STANFORD UNIV SCH OF MEDICINE HRP BUILDING, ROOM 113 STANFORD, CA 94305-5092 Prostate cancer in high, medium and low risk populations
R01CA-49449-03 (EDC) SPEIZER, FRANK E CHANNING LABORATORY 180 LONGWOOD AVENUE BOSTON, MA 02115 Biochemical markers in the nurses' health study cohort
R01CA-49450-03 (EDC) ROBISON, LESLIE L BOX 422 UMCH UNIVERSITY OF MINNESOTA MINNEAPOLIS, MN 55455 Acute nonlymphoblastic leukemia in children
R01CA-49455-03 (MGN) SEIZINGER, BERND R MASSACHUSETTS GENERAL HOSPITAL 32 FRUIT STREET BOSTON, MA 02114 Isolation of gene defect in von Hippel-Lindau disease
R01CA-49466-02 (PTHB) MC CORMICK, PAULETTE J SUNY ALBANY 1400 WASHINGTON AVENUE ALBANY, N Y 12222 Analysis of a non-tumorigenic teratocarcinoma cell line
R01CA-49469-03 (RAD) NATH, RAVINDER YALE UNIVRSITY SCHOOL OF MED PO BOX 3333, 333 CEDAR STREET NEW HAVEN, CT 06510 Dosimetry of pd-103 for interstitial brachytherapy
R29CA-49472-03 (CTY) DAILEY, LISA A THE ROCKEFELLER UNIVERSITY 1230 YORK AVENUE NEW YORK, NY 10021-6399 Regulatory mechanisms in the G1 phase of the cell cycle
R01CA-49474-02 (PTHB) DEFTOS, LEONARD J UNIVERSITY OF CALIFORNIA DEPARTMENT OF MEDICINE LA JOLLA, CA 92093 Cancer & hypercalcemia
R29CA-49477-02 (RAD) MURRAY, DAVID U OF TEXAS M D ANDERSON CA CTR 1515 HOLCOMBE, BOX 66 HOUSTON, TX 77030 Mechanism of action of radiomodifying agents
P01CA-49488-01A2 (SRC) AMOSS, MAX S TEXAS A&M UNIVERSITY COLLEGE STATION, TX 77843 A developmental model of melanoma
P01CA-49488-01A2 0001 (SRC) TISSOT, ROBERT G A developmental model of melanoma Genetic factors in Sinclair swine melanoma
P01CA-49488-01A2 0002 (SRC) BEATTIE, CRAIG W A developmental model of melanoma Gene expression during swine melanoma histogenesis
P01CA-49488-01A2 0003 (SRC) AMOSS, MAX S A developmental model of melanoma Growth factors in Sinclair swine cutaneous melanoma
P01CA-49488-01A2 9001 (SRC) AMOSS, MAX S A developmental model of melanoma Core--Sinclair swine herd
R01CA-49498-03 (RAD) KOCH, CAMERON J 3400 SPRUCE STREET DONNER II PHILADELPHIA, PA 19104 Mechanisms of cellular and molecular radiosensitivity
R29CA-49499-02 (OBM) HORN-ROSS, PAMELA L NORTHERN CALIFORNIA CANCER CTR 1420 HARBOR BAY PKWY ALAMEDA, CA 94501 Epidemiology of salivary gland cancer
R01CA-49501-03 (RAD) BEDFORD, JOEL S COLORADO STATE UNIVERSITY FORT COLLINS, COLORADO 80523 Radiation cytogenetics
R01CA-49506-03 (REN) LEHRER, STEVEN P MOUNT SINAI MEDICAL CTR NEW YORK, NY 10029 Polymorphic estrogen receptor m-RNA in breast cancer
R01CA-49507-03 (CBY) GOLD, LESLIE I NEW YORK UNIVERSITY MED CENTER 400 EAST 34TH STREET, RR806 NEW YORK, NY 10016 Distribution

PROJECT NO., ORGANIZATIONAL UNIT., INVESTIGATOR, ADDRESS, TITLE

and functional aspects of TGF-beta-3

R01CA-49515-03 (PBC) DE CROMBRUGGHE, BENOIT U OF TX/M D ANDERSON CAN CTR 1515 HOLCOMBE BLVD HOUSTON, TX 77030 Control mechanism in synthesis of extracellular matrix by fibroblast

R01CA-49516-04 (RNM) TAYLOR, JUNE S ST JUDE CHILDREN'S RES HOSPITA 332 N LAUDERDALE MEMPHIS, TN 38101 Localized NMR spectroscopy of human brain tumors

R01CA-49522-03 (SRC) WELTY, THOMAS K PHS INDIAN HOSPITAL 3200 CANYON LAKE DR RAPID CITY, SD 57702 Cancer and cancer risk factor among Sioux Indians

R01CA-49529-03 (ET) GOREN, MARSHALL P ST. JUDE CHILDREN'S RES. HOSP. 332 N LAUDERDALE PO BX318 MEMPHIS, TN 38101 Chloroacetaldehyde and ifosfamide toxicity

R01CA-49530-03 (EVR) LIVINGSTON, DAVID M DANA-FARBER CANCER INSTITUTE 44 BINNEY STREET BOSTON, MA 02115 Repressor control of SV40 transformation

R29CA-49531-02 (EDC) WEINSTOCK, MARTIN A ROGER WILLIAM GENERAL HOSPITAL 825 CHALKSTONE AVENUE PROVIDENCE, RI 02908 A case control study of dysplastic nevi

R01CA-49532-03 (EDC) GILLES, FLOYD H CHILDRENS HOSP OF LOS ANGELES 4650 SUNSET BLVD LOS ANGELES, CA 90027 Childhood brain tumors: prognoses and homogeneity

R01CA-49536-02 (ET) MELERA, PETER W UNIVERSITY OF MARYLAND 665 W BALTIMORE STREET BALTIMORE, MD 21201 Dihydrofolate reductase mediated antifolate resistance in mammalian cells

R01CA-49540-04 (EVR) CARLIN, CATHLEEN R CASE WESTERN RESERVE UNIVERSIT 2109 ADELBERT ROAD CLEVELAND, OH 44106 Egf receptor down-regulation by adenovirus

R01CA-49553-03 (SRC) FARMER, GAIL C CALIFORNIA ST UNIV/LONG BEACH HLTH SCI, 1250 BELLFLOWER BLVD LONG BEACH, CA 90840 Cervical cancer among American Indian women

R01CA-49562-03 (SSS) CHU, WILLIAM T LAWRENCE BERKELEY LAB 1 CYCLOTRON RD BERKELEY, CA 94720 Raster-scanner development for 3D conformational therapy

R01CA-49564-02 (BBCB) VICTOR, THOMAS A EVANSTON HOSPITAL 2650 RIDGE AVE EVANSTON, IL 60201 Breast cancer metabolism studies by P-31 and C-13 NMR

R25CA-49565-03 (SRC) LI, VIRGINIA C UCLA SCHOOL OF PUBLIC HEALTH 10833 LECONTE AVE, RM 21-261 C LOS ANGELES, CA 90024-1772 Cancer education program for chronic disease prevention

R01CA-49569-03 (SRC) YU, ELENA S H SAN DIEGO STATE UNIVERSITY 5300 CAMPANILE DRIVE SAN DIEGO, CA 92182 Developmental research in cancer control among Asian Americans

R01CA-49578-03 (SRC) FRATE, DENNIS A UNIVERSITY OF MISSISSIPPI RURAL HLTH RES PROG/PO BOX 283 GOODMAN, MS 39079 Institutionalizing dietary changes for cancer prevention

R01CA-49582-03 (GEN) HOFFMANN, F MICHAEL MCARDLE LAB FOR CANCER RES UNIVERSITY OF WISCONSIN MADISON, WI 53706 Genetic analysis of Drosophila Abelson tyrosine kinase

R01CA-49588-04 (STC) SIMON, KENNETH J MARY BABB RANDOLPH CANCER CTR MORGANTOWN, WV 26506 Reducing cervical cancer mortality in West Virginia

P01CA-49605-03 (SRC) BLUME, KARL G STANFORD UNIVERSITY HOSPITAL 300 PASTEUR DRIVE STANFORD, CA 94305-5112 Bone marrow grafting for leukemia and lymphoma

P01CA-49605-03 0001 (SRC) BLUME, KARL G Bone marrow grafting for leukemia and lymphoma Allogenic marrow grafting for leukemia /human/

P01CA-49605-03 0002 (SRC) HORNING, SANDRA J Bone marrow grafting for leukemia and lymphoma Autologous marrow grafting for lymphoma /human/

P01CA-49605-03 0003 (SRC) SKLAR, JEFFREY L Bone marrow grafting for leukemia and lymphoma Detection of minimal malignant disease in bone marrow transplantation

P01CA-49605-03 0004 (SRC) WEISSMAN, IRVING L Bone marrow grafting for leukemia and lymphoma Identify & isolate human bone marrow hematopoietic stem cells

P01CA-49605-03 0005 (SRC) SIKIC, BRANIMIR I Bone marrow grafting for leukemia and lymphoma Multidrug resistance as a prognostic factor in bone marrow transplant /human/

P01CA-49605-03 0006 (SRC) KRENSKY, ALAN M Bone marrow grafting for leukemia and lymphoma Tumor specific cytotoxic T-lymphocytes in bone marrow transplant /human/

P01CA-49605-03 0007 (SRC) LEVY, RONALD Bone marrow grafting for leukemia and lymphoma Peritransplant idiotype vaccination for patients with B-cell lymphoma /also mice/

P01CA-49605-03 0008 (SRC) ARVIN, ANN M Bone marrow grafting for leukemia and lymphoma Varicella-zoster virus infections after bone marrow transplant /human/

P01CA-49605-03 9001 (SRC) BROWN, BYRON W, JR Bone marrow grafting for leukemia and lymphoma Core--Biostatistics

R01CA-49608-02 (CPA) HENDERSON, EARL E TEMPLE UNIV SCH OF MEDICINE 3400 NORTH BROAD STREET PHILADELPHIA, PA 19140 Endonuclease V expression in human cells

R01CA-49609-02 (RAD) LAMON, EDDIE W UNIV OF ALABAMA AT BIRMINGHAM UNIVERSITY STATION BIRMINGHAM, AL 35294 Effects of hyperthermia on immune functions in vitro

R25CA-49612-02 (SRC) GORBACH, SHERWOOD L TUFTS UNIV SCH OF MEDICINE 136 HARRISON AVENUE BOSTON, MA 02111 Tufts medical-dental nutrition/cancer education program

R01CA-49619-02 (SRC) GIEBEL, GREGORY LABORERS NATL HLTH/SAFETY FUND 905 16TH STREET, NW WASHINGTON, DC 20006 Cancer control for laborers'

R29CA-49624-03 (VR) HINRICHS, STEVEN H UNIV OF NEBRASKA MED CTR 600 SOUTH 42ND ST OMAHA, NE 68198-6495 Effect of HTLV-I TAT expression in transgenic mice

R01CA-49629-03 (MGN) SKARE, JAMES C BOSTON UNIVERSITY 80 E CONCORD ST, L402 BOSTON, MA 02118 Genetics of the x-linked lymphoproliferative syndrome

R29CA-49633-02 (PTHB) FREEMAN, JAMES W UNIV OF KENTUCKY MEDICAL CTR 800 ROSE ST, 313 COMBS BLDG LEXINGTON, KY 40536-0093 Role of antigen P120 in cell proliferation

R29CA-49634-03 (PTHB) DAVIDSON, NANCY E JOHNS HOPKINS UNIVERSITY 720 RUTLAND AVE/SCH OF MED BALTIMORE, MD 21205 Epidermal growth

PROJECT NO., ORGANIZATIONAL UNIT., INVESTIGATOR, ADDRESS, TITLE

factor receptor in human breast cancer

P01CA-49639-02 (SRC) DEISSEROTH, ALBERT B UNIVERSITY OF TEXAS 1515 HOLCOMBE BLVD HOUSTON, TX 77030 Therapy of CML

P01CA-49639-02 0001 (SRC) DEISSEROTH, ALBERT B Therapy of CML Therapy of CML Ph1-positive--Diploid hematopoiesis restoration

P01CA-49639-02 0002 (SRC) LEE, MING-SHENG Therapy of CML Polymerase chain reaction for abl-bcr mRNA and ras mutation

P01CA-49639-02 0003 (SRC) ARLINGHAUS, RALPH B Therapy of CML Serum & cellular P210 quantitation in chronic CML before & after therapy

P01CA-49639-02 0004 (SRC) DEISSEROTH, ALBERT Therapy of CML Molecular changes--Sensitivity & resistance to CML biological therapy

P01CA-49639-02 0005 (SRC) EMERSON, STEPHEN G Therapy of CML Cellular regulation of clonal proliferation in CML

P01CA-49639-02 9001 (SRC) DEISSEROTH, ALBERT B Therapy of CML Core--Cell and serum collection, bone marrow transplantation

P01CA-49639-02 9002 (SRC) LIANG, JAN C Therapy of CML Core--Markers and cytogenetics

R01CA-49641-02 (HCT) SIMINOFF, LAURA A WESTERN PSYCHIATRIC INST & CLI 3811 O'HARA STREET PITTSBURGH, PA 15213 Referral to cancer trials--A population-based model

R01CA-49643-03 (BEM) BERESFORD, SHIRLEY A UNIVERSITY OF WASHINGTON SEATTLE, WA 98195 Dietary intervention trial in primary care practices

R01CA-49644-03 (EI) SHIN, HYUN S JOHNS HOPKINS UNIVERSITY 725 N WOLFE STREET BALTIMORE, MD 21205 Eradication of residual leukemia by antibody therapy

R29CA-49649-04 (MGN) LEE, EVA Y H P UNIVERSITY OF TEXAS HLTH SCI C 7703 FLOYD CURL DRIVE SAN ANTONIO, TX 78284 Cancer suppressing & developmental functions of RB gene

R01CA-49667-03 (PTHB) FRAZIER, MARSHA L UT MD ANDERSON CANCER CTR 1515 HOLCOMBE BLVD HOUSTON, TX 77030 Transgenic animal model/pancreatic duct cell adenocarcinoma

R01CA-49670-03 (VR) LAIMINS, LAIMONIS UNIVERSITY OF CHICAGO 920 EAST 58TH STREET CHICAGO, IL 60637 Hpv-18 effects on epithelial cell differentiation

R01CA-49672-03 (RAD) GEARD, CHARLES R COLUMBIA UNIVERSITY 630 WEST 168TH ST. NEW YORK, NY 10032 Short-range radiations--lesions and chromosomal changes

R29CA-49675-03 (ET) RAVDIN, PETER M UNIV OF TEXAS HLTH SCI CTR 7703 FLOYD CURL DR SAN ANTONIO, TX 78284-7884 Autocrine growth factors--Effects of immunoneutralization

R01CA-49695-02 (BIO) CHEN, KUANG Y RUTGERS, STATE UNIV OF N J P O BOX 939 PISCATAWAY, NJ 08855-0939 Hypusine formation: Biochemistry and function

R01CA-49696-03 (RAD) LIBER, HOWARD L HARVARD SCHOOL OF PUB HEALTH 665 HUNTINGTON AVENUE BOSTON, MA 02115 Ionizing radiation mutagenesis in human cells

R01CA-49697-02 (BLR) GRAY, ROBERT M 133 DURAND BUILDING STANFORD, CA 94305 Medical image compression by vector quantization

R01CA-49708-03 (EI) VLOCK, DANIEL R VETERANS ADMINISTRATION HOSP UNIVERSITY DRIVE C RM E7146 PITTSBURGH, PA 15240 Serologic studies of squamous cell carcinoma

P01CA-49712-03 (SRC) DEUEL, THOMAS F JEWISH HOSPITAL 216 S KINGSHIGHWAY ST LOUIS, MO 63110 Gene regulation in normal and transformed cells

P01CA-49712-03 0001 (SRC) BRODEUR, GARRETT M Gene regulation in normal and transformed cells Analysis of NGF receptor in neuroblastomas/human

P01CA-49712-03 0002 (SRC) DEUEL, THOMAS F Gene regulation in normal and transformed cells Roles of growth factors in neoplastic transformation

P01CA-49712-03 0003 (SRC) KORSMEYER, STANLEY J Gene regulation in normal and transformed cells Transcriptional regulation, role of Bcl-2 in development and neoplasia

P01CA-49712-03 0004 (SRC) LEY, TIMOTHY J Gene regulation in normal and transformed cells Regulation of cathepsin G gene--Normal, leukemic cells

P01CA-49712-03 0005 (SRC) MILBRANDT, JEFFREY D Gene regulation in normal and transformed cells Role of NGF I-A and NGF I-B in differentiation and development

P01CA-49712-03 9001 (SRC) CROUCH, EDMOND C Gene regulation in normal and transformed cells Core--Morphology

P01CA-49712-03 9002 (SRC) KORSMEYER, STANLEY J Gene regulation in normal and transformed cells Core-Transgenic mouse facil

P01CA-49712-03 9003 (SRC) MILBRANDT, JEFFREY D Gene regulation in normal and transformed cells Core-Oligonucleotides

R29CA-49715-04 (RAD) BORRELLI, MICHAEL J WM BEAUMONT HOSP/DEPT RAD ONC 3601 W THIRTEEN MILE ROAD ROYAL OAK, MI 48073-6769 Determination of hyperthermic cell killing mechanisms

R35CA-49721-03 (SRC) KERSEY, JOHN H UNIV OF MINNESOTA BOX 86, UMHC MINNEAPOLIS, MN 55455 Outstanding investigator award

R01CA-49729-02 (RAD) ROSE, SETH D ARIZONA STATE UNIVERSITY COLLEGE OF LIB. ARTS & SCI. TEMPE, AZ 85287-1604 Photosensitized pyrimidine dimer splitting

R35CA-49731-01A2 (SRC) VILCEK, JAN T NEW YORK UNIVERSITY MED CTR 550 FIRST AVE NEW YORK, NY 10016 Mechanisms of TNF/cytokine actions

R35CA-49734-03 (SRC) MC DEVITT, HUGH O STANFORD UNIVERSITY D-345 FAIRCHILD BUILDING STANFORD, CA 94305-5402 Structure/function of class II MHC molecules in the immune response

R01CA-49741-02 (EVR) PANGANIBAN, ANTONITO T UNIVERSITY OF WISCONSIN 1400 UNIVERSITY AVENUE MADISON, WI 53706-1599 Template switching during reverse transcription

R01CA-49743-02 (EI) GRIMES, WILLIAM J UNIVERSITY OF ARIZONA BIOSCIENCES WEST TUCSON, AZ 85721 Tumor cell recognition by activated lymphocytes

R01CA-49749-02 (CBY) SCHLEGEL, ROBERT HARVARD SCH OF PUBLIC HLTH 665 HUNTINGTON AVENUE BOSTON, MA 02115 Regulation of mitosis in normal and transformed cells

R35CA-49751-03 (SRC) HURLEY, LAURENCE H COL PHARMACY/DRUG DYNAMICS INS AUSTIN, TX 78712 Novel approaches to antitumor drug development

R35CA-49756-02 (SRC) CONNEY, ALLAN H RUTGERS STATE UNIVERSITY OF NJ PO BOX 789 PISCATAWAY, NJ 08855-0789 Cancer cause & prevention

PROJECT NO., ORGANIZATIONAL UNIT., INVESTIGATOR, ADDRESS, TITLE

research

R35CA-49758-03 (SRC) JONES, PETER A USC SCHOOL OF MEDICINE 1441 EASTLAKE AVENUE LOS ANGELES, CA 90033 DNA methylation in development and cancer

R35CA-49761-03 (SRC) FRIEDMAN, GARY D DIV RSRCH/KAISER PERMANENTE 3451 PIEDMONT AVENUE OAKLAND, CA 94611 Cancer epidemiology in a large health care plan

U10CA-49762-01A2 (CCI) VOGLER, WILLIAM R EMORY UNIVERSITY 718 WOODRUFF MEMORIAL BLDG ATLANTA, GA 30322 Eastern cooperative oncology group

R01CA-49764-04 (MEP) CLARK, LARRY C UNIV OF ARIZONA/CANCER CENTER 1515 N CAMPBELL/EPIDEMIOLOGY TUCSON, AZ 85724 The prevention of non-melanoma skin cancer with a nutr S

R29CA-49765-04 (MGN) NAGARAJAN, LALITHA M D ANDERSON CANCER CENTER 1515 HOLCOMBE/HEMATOLOGY/BOX24 HOUSTON, TX 77030 Studies on the human pim-1 gene

R01CA-49776-03 (SRC) LILLEMOE, KEITH D JOHNS HOPKINS HOSPITAL 600 N WOLFE STREET BALTIMORE, MD 21205 Pain control in patients with pancreatic cancer

R01CA-49783-03 (SRC) WANG, CHING Y MICHIGAN CANCER FOUNDATION 110 EAST WARREN AVENUE DETROIT, MICH 48201 Genetic alterations involved in bladder carcinogenesis

R01CA-49784-03 (SRC) KELSEN, DAVID P MEMORIAL HOSPITAL FOR 1275 YORK AVENUE NEW YORK, NY 10021 Pain assessment in patients with pancreas cancer

R01CA-49785-03 (SRC) WOLF, GERALD L NMR-CENTER, MGH-EAST BUILDING 149, 13TH STREET CHARLESTOWN, MA 02129 Validation of in vivo MR tissue perfusion methods

R01CA-49786-03 (SRC) BRASCH, ROBERT C UNIVERSITY OF CALIFORNIA, S F BOX 0628 SAN FRANCISCO, CA 94143-0628 Enhanced MRI for tumor vascular integrity and perfusion

R01CA-49792-02 (RAD) JAIN, RAKESH K MASSACHUSETTS GENERAL HOSPITAL DEPT OF RADIATION ONCOLOGY BOSTON, MA 02114 Heterogeneous distribution of antibodies in tumors

R29CA-49797-02 (CPA) ST CLAIR, DARET K BOWMAN GRAY SCHOOL OF MEDICINE 300 S HAWTHORNE RD WINSTON-SALEM, NC 27103 Mechanism of MnSOD expression in normal and tumor cells

R01CA-49798-02 (CPA) FRENKEL, KRYSTYNA NEW YORK UNIV MEDICAL CENTER 550 FIRST AVENUE NEW YORK, N Y 10016 Metals and nucleoside hydroperoxide mediated genetic damage

R01CA-49816-03 (SRC) AU, JESSIE L OHIO STATE UNIVERSITY 500 W 12TH AVE, COLL OF PHARMA COLUMBUS, OH 43210 Pharmacodynamics of agents for bladder cancer intravesical therapy

R01CA-49820-02 (ET) O'DWYER, PETER FOX CHASE CANCER CTR 7701 BURHOLME AVE PHILADELPHIA, PA 19111 Chemosensitizers and drug resistance

R29CA-49826-03 (CPA) WEYAND, ERIC H RUTGERS STATE UNIVERSITY BUSCH CAMPUS, PO BOX 789 PISCATAWAY, NJ 08855-0789 Initiation of mammary carcinogenesis in the rat

R29CA-49832-03 (PTHB) OZTURK, MEHMET MGH CANCER CTR/MGH EAST 149 13TH STREET 7TH FLOOR CHARLESTOWN, MA 02129 Studies on human hepatoma cell surface protein P50

R01CA-49835-02 (PTHB) STACKPOLE, CHRISTOPHER W NEW YORK MEDICAL COLLEGE DEPARTMENT OF PATHOLOGY VALHALLA, N Y 10595 Organ patterning of B 16 melanoma secondary metastasis

R01CA-49837-01A2 (MEP) CURLEY, ROBERT W, JR OHIO STATE UNIVERSITY 500 WEST 12TH AVENUE COLUMBUS, OH 43210 Analog studies of retinoid glucuronide activity

R01CA-49843-03 (ET) AVRAMIS, VASSILIOS I CHILDRENS HOSP OF LOS ANGELES 4650 SUNSET BLVD/HEM-ONCOLOGY LOS ANGELES, CA 90027 Deoxycytidine kinase control and Ara-C resistance

R29CA-49845-03 (CPA) LEBOVITZ, RUSSELL M BAYLOR COLLEGE OF MEDICINE ONE BAYLOR PLAZA HOUSTON, TX 77030 Hepatocarcinogenesis in vitro using activated fos genes

R01CA-49850-02 (ET) CHEEVER, MARTIN A UNIVERSITY OF WASHINGTON BB1321 HEALTH SCIENCES BLDG. SEATTLE, WA 98195 Specific T cell immunity to autologous melanoma

R01CA-49856-02 (ET) RASO, VICTOR A BOSTON BIOMEDICAL RES INST 20 STANIFORD STREET BOSTON, MA 02114 Targeting toxins with acid-triggered hybrid antibodies

R29CA-49858-03 (CPA) NOTARIO-RUIZ, VICENTE GEORGETOWN UNIV MEDICAL CTR 3800 RESERVOIR RD, NW WASHINGTON, DC 20007 Oncogenes in carcinogen-initiated hamster tumor cells

R29CA-49859-03 (PTHB) MUTTER, GEORGE L BRIGHAM AND WOMEN'S HOSPITAL 75 FRANCIS STREET BOSTON, MA 02115 Cellular oncogenes in germ cell tumors

R01CA-49866-03 (VR) BOETTIGER, DAVID E DEPARTMENT OF MICROBIOLOGY UNIVERSITY OF PENNSYLVANIA PHILADELPHIA, PA 19104-6076 Role of integrin in viral transformation

R01CA-49869-03 (MEP) TEEBOR, GEORGE W NEW YORK UNIVERSITY MED CTR 550 FIRST AVENUE NEW YORK, N Y 10016 Genomic distribution and phylogeny of DNA repair

R01CA-49870-04 (EI) KIPPS, THOMAS J UNIV OF CA, SAN DIEG0 LA JOLLA, CA 92093-0945 Antibody V gene expression in human B cell malignancies

R01CA-49875-02 (BNP) REMERS, WILLIAM A UNIVERSITY OF ARIZONA COLLEGE OF PHARMACY TUCSON, AZ 85721 Design of DNA binding agents for resistant tumors

R01CA-49879-03 (SRC) UNGER, EVAN C UNIVERSITY OF ARIZONA 1501 N. CAMPBELL AVE TUCSON, AZ 85724 Liposomal contrast agents for magnetic resonance imaging

U10CA-49883-03 (CCI) EINHORN, LAWRENCE H INDIANA UNIVERSITY SCH OF MED 926 WEST MICHIGAN ST INDIANAPOLIS, IN 46202-5265 Eastern cooperative oncology group

R01CA-49906-02 (BCE) DE SOMBRE, EUGENE R UNIVERSITY OF CHICAGO 5841 SOUTH MARYLAND AVE, BOX 4 CHICAGO, IL 60637 Estrogen receptor-directed therapy with Auger electrons

R01CA-49912-03 (EVR) TUREK, LUBOMIR P UNIVERSITY OF IOWA COLLEGE OF MEDICINE IOWA CITY, IA 52242 Human papillomavirus-16 regulation in cervical cancer

R29CA-49916-03 (CPA) JOHNSON, MARK D NORTHWESTERN UNIV MED SCHOOL 303 EAST CHICAGO AVE CHICAGO, IL 60611 Mechanism of growth factor-induced transformation

PROJECT NO., ORGANIZATIONAL UNIT., INVESTIGATOR, ADDRESS, TITLE

R01CA-49917-01A2 (CPA) CAVALIERI, ERCOLE UNIV OF NEBRASKA MED CENTER 600 SOUTH 42ND STREET OMAHA, NE 68198-6805 Mechanisms of carcinogenesis of dibenzo(a,l)pyrene

R01CA-49926-02 (PTHB) FREGIEN, NEVIS L UNIV OF MIAMI SCH OF MED 1600 NORTHWEST 10TH AVE, R124 MIAMI, FL 33101 Glycosyltransferase gene expression in transformed cells

R01CA-49932-02 (EVR) ROTH, MONICA J UMDNJ-R W JOHNSON MEDICAL SCHO 675 HOES LANE PISCATAWAY, NJ 08854 The envelope gene products of murine leukemia virus

R01CA-49933-03 (IMB) HAMMERLING, ULRICH G SLOAN-KETTERING INST CA RES 1275 YORK AVENUE NEW YORK, NY 10021 Lipid growth factor for normal and malignant B cells

R01CA-49935-03 (CPA) REINERS, JOHN J, JR UNIV OF TX M D ANDERSON CA CTR P O BOX 389 SMITHVILLE, TX 78957 Immunomodulation and chemically induced carcinogenesis

R01CA-49936-03 (CPA) DAY, RUFUS S III CROSS CANCER INSTITUTE 11560 UNIVERSITY AVE EDMONTON, ALBERTA CNDA T6G 1Z2 Cellular DNA repair response to methylating agents

R01CA-49938-03 (PTHB) DE BUSTROS, ANDREE C JOHNS HOPKINS UNIVERSITY 424 N BOND ST BALTIMORE, MD 21231 Ectopic production of calcitonin by tumors

R01CA-49950-03 (ET) BARNA, BARBARA P 9500 EUCLID AVENUE CLEVELAND, OH 44195-5131 Synthetic CRP peptide: therapy for cancer metastases

U10CA-49952-01A2 (CCI) OBLON, DAVID J UNIVERSITY FLORIDA BOX J-277 JHMHC GAINESVILLE, FL 32610 Eastern cooperative oncology group

U10CA-49957-03 (CCI) JOHNSON, DAVID H MEDICAL ONCOLOGY 1956 THE VANDERBILT CLINIC NASHVILLE, TN 37232 Eastern cooperative oncology group

R01CA-49963-03 (PTHB) MERCOLA, DANIEL A UNIVERSITY OF CALIFORNIA DEPT OF PATHOLOGY, V-151 LA JOLLA, CA 92093-0023 Application of antisense fos and sis RNA to human tumors

R29CA-49975-03 (PTHB) CHELLADURAI, MOHANATHASAN WAYNE STATE UNIVERSITY 431 CHEM BLDG/RAD ONCOL DEPT DETROIT, MI 48202 Tumor procoagulant--Role in metastasis

R29CA-49976-04 (SSS) DHAWAN, ATAM P UNIVERSITY OF CINCINNATI 826 RHODES HALL CINCINNATI, OH 45221-0030 Early detection of cutaneous malignant melanoma

R25CA-49981-03 (SRC) BAKEMEIER, RICHARD F UNIV OF COLORADO CANCER CTR 4200 E 9TH AVE BOX B190 DENVER, CO 80262 University of colorado cancer education program

R01CA-49982-02 (BBCA) PATEL, DINSHAW J COLUMBIA UNIVERSITY 630 WEST 168TH STREET NEW YORK, NY 10032 Molecular toxicology--exocyclic DNA adducts/cross-links

R29CA-49986-02 (ALY) CARROLL, WILLIAM L WASHINGTON UNIV/SCH OF MED 400 S. KINGSHIGHWAY ST LOUIS, MO 63110 The molecular basis of immunoglobulin gene hypermutation

R01CA-49987-01A2 (ET) EPSTEIN, ALAN L UNIV OF SOUTHERN CALIFORNIA 2011 ZONAL AVENUE LOS ANGELES, CA 90033 Tumor necrosis treatment of cancer

R01CA-49992-03 (MCHA) SHIMIZU, YUZURU UNIVERSITY OF RHODE ISLAND DEPT OF PHARMACOGNOSY KINGSTON, R I 02881 Antitumor, antiviral agents in microalgae

R55CA-49995-01A2 (EI) BLUMENTHAL, ROSALYN D CTR/MOLECULAR MED & IMMUNOLOGY 1 BRUCE STREET NEWARK, NJ 07103 Reduction of radioantibody-induced nontumor toxicity

R01CA-49996-03 (BCE) CUNHA, GERALD R UNIVERSITY OF CALIFORNIA 513 PARNASSUS AVE SAN FRANCISCO, CA 94143-0452 Prostatic regression--A developmental approach

R01CA-50030-03 (SRC) PEREZ-STABLE, ELISEO J UNIVERSITY OF CALIFORNIA 400 PARNASSUS AVE RM A-405 SAN FRANCISCO, CA 94143-0320 Development of cancer control interventions for hispanics

R44CA-50031-02 (SSS) SHEFER, RUTH E SCIENCE RESEARCH LABORATORY, I 15 WARD STREET SOMERVILLE, MA 02143 Accelerator production of epithermal neutrons for boron neutron capture therapy

R44CA-50045-02 (NTN) PETERSEN, BARBARA J TECHNICAL ASSESSMENT SYS, INC 1000 POTOMAC STREET, NW WASHINGTON, DC 20007 Dietary constituent cancer modulation analysis system

R01CA-50054-03 (ET) POSNER, MARSHALL R NEW ENGLAND DEACONESS HOSPITAL 185 PILGRIM RD BOSTON, MA 02215 Human monoclonal antibodies to study and treat leukemias

R44CA-50077-03 (SSS) KING, CHARLES R MOLECULAR ONCOLOGY, INC 19 FIRSTFIELD ROAD GAITHERSBURG, MD 20878 Applications of anti-erbb-2 monoclonal antibodies

P01CA-50084-03 (SRC) BASTANI, ROSHAN UNIVERSITY OF CALIFORNIA 1100 GLENDON AVENUE SUITE 711 LOS ANGELES, CA 90024-3511 Los Angeles County cancer prevention research unit

P01CA-50084-03 0006 (SRC) CRANE, LORI Los Angeles County cancer prevention research unit Barriers to screening mammography

P01CA-50084-03 9001 (SRC) BASTANI, ROSHAN Los Angeles County cancer prevention research unit Core--Centralized evaluation and data acquisition

P01CA-50084-03 9002 (SRC) ELASHOFF, ROBERT Los Angeles County cancer prevention research unit Core--Stastical coordinations

P01CA-50084-03 0001 (SRC) HENNEMAN, CAROL Los Angeles County cancer prevention research unit Extending cervical cancer screening in L.A. County Dept Health Services

P01CA-50084-03 0002 (SRC) MARCUS, ALFRED C Los Angeles County cancer prevention research unit Improving adherence behavior among women with abnormal Pap smears

P01CA-50084-03 0003 (SRC) PEARCE, JOHN Los Angeles County cancer prevention research unit Extending breast cancer screening in L.A. County Dept Health Services

P01CA-50084-03 0004 (SRC) ABBOTT, MARY I Los Angeles County cancer prevention research unit Quality assurance of cytology laboratories

P01CA-50084-03 0005 (SRC) BASSETT, LAWRENCE Los Angeles County cancer prevention research unit Professional education program for screening mammography

P01CA-50087-03 (SRC) PROCHASKA, JAMES O UNIVERSITY OF RHODE ISLAND 420 CHAFEE BUILDING KINGSTON, RI 02881 Accelerating the process of change for cancer prevention

P01CA-50087-03 0001 (SRC) PROCHASKA, JAMES O Accelerating the process of change for cancer prevention Self-help programs for

PROJECT NO., ORGANIZATIONAL UNIT., INVESTIGATOR, ADDRESS, TITLE

accelerating smoking cessation
P01CA-50087-03 0002 (SRC) ABRAMS, DAVID Accelerating the process of change for cancer prevention Accelerating worksite smoking control programs
P01CA-50087-03 0003 (SRC) GOLDSTEIN, MICHAEL G Accelerating the process of change for cancer prevention Accelerating physicians adoption of smoking protocols
P01CA-50087-03 0004 (SRC) RAKOWSKI, WILLIAM Accelerating the process of change for cancer prevention Accelerating screening mammography rates in Rhode Island
P01CA-50087-03 9001 (SRC) VELICER, WAYNE F Accelerating the process of change for cancer prevention Evaluation core
R01CA-50107-03 (EI) RICHES, DAVID W NAT'L JEWISH CTR/IMMUNO/RESP M 1400 JACKSON STREET DENVER, CO 80206-1997 Regulation of the tumoricidal macrophage phenotype
U01CA-50109-03 (SRC) SPENGLER, ROBERT F VERMONT DEPARTMENT OF HEALTH 60 MAIN STREET - PO BOX 70 BURLINGTON, VT 05402 Vermont cancer prevention and control project
U01CA-50112-03 (SRC) SOUTHARD, JOHN W DEPT/HEALTH & MENTAL HYGIENE 201 WEST PRESTON ST, RM 306 BALTIMORE, MD 21201 Data-based interventions in cancer control in Maryland
U01CA-50116-02 (SRC) EPSTEIN, SUSAN D NH DIV OF PUBLIC HEALTH SERVIC 6 HAZEN DRIVE CONCORD, NH 03301-6527 New Hampshire inter-agency cancer control initiative
U01CA-50117-03 (SRC) STEINER, CAROL B DEPARTMENT OF HUMAN RESOURCES 878 PEACHTREE STREET, NE ATLANTA, GA 30309 Data-based cancer control in Georgia
U01CA-50118-02 (SRC) WEINBERG, GENE B PENNSYLVANIA DEPT OF HEALTH PO BOX 90 HARRISBURG, PA 17120 Pennsylvania cancer control data-based demonstration project
U01CA-50121-03 (SRC) KIRKCONNELL, SHIRLEY OFFICE OF PUBLIC HEALTH PO BOX 60630 NEW ORLEANS, LA 70160 Data-based intervention research for Louisiana
R01CA-50131-03 (ARR) AMBINDER, RICHARD F JOHNS HOPKINS UNIVERSITY 600 N WOLFE ST/173 ONCOLOGY CT BALTIMORE, MD 21205 Bone marrow transplantation for HIV patients with cancer
U01CA-50133-03 (SRC) MCDONOUGH, STEPHEN L STATE DEPT HEALTH/CONSOL LABS CAPITOL BUILDING JUDICIAL WING BISMARCK, ND 58505 Data-based intervention research for public health agencies
U01CA-50135-03 (SRC) WADSWORTH, B JO OFC OF HEART DISEASE/CAN PREV MAIL STOP: LK-13 OLYMPIA, WASHINGTON 98504 Data-based intervention research for public health agencies
U01CA-50137-03 (SRC) KOFIE, VINCENT Y DEPT OF HUMAN SERVICES 1660 L STREET, NW WASHINGTON, DC 20036 Data-based intervention research for public health agencies
R01CA-50139-03 (SRC) LETVIN, NORMAN L NEW ENGLAND PRIMATE RES CTR ONE PINE HILL DRIVE SOUTHBOROUGH, MA 01772 Immune regulations in SIV infections
R01CA-50141-03 (SRC) DAVIS, WILLIAM C WASHINGTON STATE UNIVERSITY DEPT OF VET MICROBIO AND PATH PULLMAN, WA 99164 Animal models for research on AIDS-related lentiviruses
R01CA-50146-03 (SRC) LI, YEN HARVARD MEDICAL SCHOOL ONE PINE HILL DRIVE SOUTHBOROUGH, MA 01772 Diversity and pathogenesis of SIVagm
R01CA-50151-03 (SRC) NELSON, JAY A SCRIPPS CLINIC & RESEARCH FDN 10666 NORTH TORREY PINES ROAD LA JOLLA, CA 92037 A transgenic model for HIV/opportunistic interactions
R01CA-50157-02 (ARR) GREEN, WILLIAM R DARTMOUTH MEDICAL SCHOOL HANOVER, NH 03756 The pathogenesis of MAIDS and specific T cell responses
R01CA-50158-03 (SRC) PITHA-ROWE, PAULA M JOHNS HOPKINS SCH OF MED 418 N. BOND STREET BALTIMORE, MD 21231 Retrovirus-induced immunodeficiency--Role of cytokines
R01CA-50159-03 (SRC) ROTH, JAMES A IOWA STATE UNIVERSITY AMES, IA 50011 Bovine lentivirus as a model for HIV infection
R01CA-50168-02 (ARR) PAYNE, SUSAN L CASE WESTERN RESERVE UNIVERSIT SCHOOL OF MEDICINE CLEVELAND, OH 44106 Lentiviral diseases--EIAV genome structure
R01CA-50174-01A2 (RAD) HERMAN, TERENCE S DANA-FARBER CANCER INSTITUTE 44 BINNEY STREET Trimodality (x-rays/heat/drugs) therapeutic studies
R01CA-50175-04 (BNP) KOZIKOWSKI, ALAN P MAYO FOUNDATION 200 FIRST STREET SOUTHWEST ROCHESTER, MN 55905 Synthesis of inactivators of protein kinase C
R01CA-50179-03 (SRC) PEDERSEN, NIELS C UNIV OF CALIFORNIA, DAVIS SCHOOL OF VETERINARY MEDICINE DAVIS, CA 95616 Incidental infectious diseases as cofactors in the transmission of HIV
R01CA-50182-03 (SRC) JENSON, A BENNETT GEORGETOWN UNIV MED SCHOOL 4000 RESERVOIR ROAD WASHINGTON, DC 20007 Antigenic determinants of the papillomavirus L1 capsid protein
R01CA-50183-02 (SRC) DENHARDT, DAVID T RUTGERS, STATE UNIVERSITY PO BOX 1059 PISCATAWAY, NJ 08855-1059 Mechanism of anticarcinogenic action of TIMP
R01CA-50189-03 (MEP) BECKER, DOROTHEA MONTEFIORE UNIV HOSPITAL 3459 FIFTH AVENUE PITTSBURGH, PA 15213 Importance of BFGF in the progression of human melanoma
R01CA-50192-03 (RAD) BROCK, WILLIAM A U.T. M.D. ANDERSON CANCER CENT 1515 HOLCOMBE BOULEVARD HOUSTON, TX 77030 Human tumor cell radiosensitivity versus radiocurability
R01CA-50193-03 (EDC) SCHLESSELMAN, JAMES J H M JACKSON FDN/ADV MILITARY M 4301 JONES BRIDGE ROAD BETHESDA, MD 20814-4799 Oral contraceptives and cancer
R01CA-50195-03 (SRC) SHAY, JERRY W UNIV TEXAS SOUTHWESTERN MED CT 5323 HARRY HINES BOULEVARD DALLAS, TX 75235 In vitro transformation of human mammary epithelial cell
R01CA-50207-02 (RAD) TOFILON, PHILIP J UNIV OF TEXAS MD ANDERSON CA C 1515 HOLCOMBE BLVD HOUSTON, TX 77030 Cell differentiation and repair of radiation damage
R01CA-50210-03 (PTHA) DAVIS, RICHARD L UNIVERSITY OF CALIFORNIA BRAIN TUMOR RES CENTER/BOX 052 SAN FRANCISCO, CA 94143 Rapid estimation of human brain tumor growth kinetics
R01CA-50211-02 (PC) DESCHENES, ROBERT J UNIVERSITY OF IOWA COLLEGE OF MEDICINE IOWA CITY, IA 52242 Structural changes and the function of RAS oncogenes
R55CA-50220-01A2 (RAD) SMITH, KENDRIC C STANFORD UNIV SCHOOL OF MED 125 PANAMA ST JORDAN/QUAD/BIRC STANFORD, CA 94305-5105 Mechanisms of ionizing radiation mutagenesis
R55CA-50224-01A2 (ET) EASTMAN, ALAN DARTMOUTH MED SCHOOL HANOVER, NH 03756 Cell death induced by anticancer agents
R01CA-50229-03 (REN) DJAKIEW, DANIEL GEORGETOWN UNIVERSITY 3900 RESERVOIR RD, N W WASHINGTON, DC 20007 Polarized secretion by prostatic cells
R01CA-50231-03 (PTHB) IRIMURA, TATSURO UNIVERSITY OF TEXAS 1515 HOLCOMBE BOULEVARD HOUSTON, TX 77030 Metastasis specific carbohydrate antigens
R01CA-50234-02 (EVR) NERENBERG, MICHAEL I RES INST. OF SCRIPPS CLINIC 10666 N TORREY PINES ROAD LA JOLLA, CA 92037 Mouse models for HTLV-1 induced pathogenesis
R01CA-50239-03 (SSS) KORSMEYER, STANLEY J WASHINGTON UNIVERSITY 660 S EUCLID/BOX 8045 ST LOUIS, MO 63110 Molecular analysis of human chromosome segment 18q21.3
R01CA-50244-03 (HEM) PHARR, PAMELA P VA MEDICAL CENTER 109 BEE ST CHARLESTON, SC 29403 Retroviral infection of hemopoietic stem cells
R29CA-50246-03 (PBC) ROTHBERG, PAUL G UNIVERSITY OF MISSOURI SCHOOL OF MEDICINE KANSAS CITY, MO 64110 Synthesis and stability of myc RNA on colon cancer cells
R01CA-50248-01A1 (PTHB) HEISTERKAMP, NORA C CHILDREN'S HOSP OF LOS ANGELES 4650 SUNSET BOULEVARD LOS ANGELES, CA 90027 Mouse model for Ph' positive CML and ALL
R01CA-50261-03 (CBY) BROEK, DANIEL L NORRIS CANCER CENTER 1441 EASTLAKE AVENUE LOS ANGELES, CA 90033-0800 Isolation and analysis of proteins which regulate RAS function
R01CA-50264-02 (MEP) HAWRYLEWICZ, ERVIN J MERCY HOSPITAL & MEDICAL CTR STEVENSON EXP AT KING DRIVE CHICAGO, IL 60616 Diet methionine--S-ado, polyamines and mammary tumors
R01CA-50267-01A2 (MEP) KELLEHER, PHILIP C UNIVERSITY OF VERMONT BURLINGTON, VT 05405 Premalignant and malignant hepatocyte AFP glycosylation
R01CA-50270-01A2 (ET) PEREZ-SOLER, ROMAN U.T. M.D. ANDERSON CANCER CTR 1515 HOLCOMBE BLVD HOUSTON, TX 77030 Anthracyclines with high affinity for lipid membranes
R01CA-50275-03 (HEM) CLINE, MARTIN J DEPARMENT OF MEDICINE/ UNIV OF CALIFORNIA,LOS ANGELES LOS ANGELES, CA 90024 Molecular events in blast crisis of CML
R01CA-50285-02 (EVR) MAXWELL, IAN H UNIV OF COLORADO HLTH SCIS CTR 4200 EAST 9TH AVENUE DENVER, CO 80262 Autonomous parvovirus vectors for cancer therapy
R01CA-50286-03 (PBC) CHERESH, DAVID A RESEARCH INST OF SCRIPPS CLNC 10666 NORTH TORREY PINES ROAD LA JOLLA, CA 92037 Integrin-dependent cell adhesion --Structure-function
U01CA-50298-03 (SRC) MEYER, LAURENCE J UNIV OF UTAH SCHOOL OF MED 50 NORTH MEDICAL DRIVE SALT LAKE CITY, UT 84132 Biology and chemoprevention of melanoma in nevus grafts
R29CA-50303-03 (PTHB) SMITH, JILL P PENNSYLVANIA STATE UNIVERSITY PO BOX 850 HERSHEY, PA 17033 Effects of cholecystokinin on human pancreatic cancer
P01CA-50305-02 (SRC) POTTER, JOHN D UNIV OF MINNESOTA 515 DELAWARE STREET SE MINNEAPOLIS, MN 55455 A colon cancer prevention research unit
P01CA-50305-02 9002 (SRC) BELCHER, JOHN A colon cancer prevention research unit Laboratory core
P01CA-50305-02 9003 (SRC) SELLERS, TOM A colon cancer prevention research unit Clinical core
P01CA-50305-02 0001 (SRC) POTTER, JOHN D A colon cancer prevention research unit Adenomatous polyps case study--Family history, diet, alcohol, exercise
P01CA-50305-02 0002 (SRC) GRAVES, KAREN A colon cancer prevention research unit Dietary intervention on recurrence of adenomatous polyps--Vegetables & fruit
P01CA-50305-02 0003 (SRC) ELMER, PATRICIA J A colon cancer prevention research unit Evaluation and development of dietary methods
P01CA-50305-02 0004 (SRC) SLAVIN, JOANNE L A colon cancer prevention research unit Feeding studies to test biomarkers of vegetable & fruit consumption
P01CA-50305-02 9001 (SRC) ELMER, PATRICIA A colon cancer prevention research unit Dietary core
R01CA-50329-03 (MBY) PRYWES, RON M COLUMBIA UNIVERSITY 813B FAIRCHILD NEW YORK, NY 10027 Transcriptional regulation of c-fos
R29CA-50330-02 (MEP) KLEIN, SAMUEL UNIVERSITY OF TEXAS MED BRANCH 4.106 MCCULLOUGH BLVD, G-64 GALVESTON, TX 77550 Effect of enteral feeding on metabol in cancer patient
R01CA-50331-02 (PTHB) HANSEN, MARC F UNIV OF TX/M D ANDERSON CAN CT 1515 HOLCOMBE BLVD HOUSTON, TX 77030 Molecular genetics of familial mixed cancer
R01CA-50339-03 (SRC) WETTSTEIN, FELIX O UCLA SCHOOL OF MEDICINE 10833 LE CONTE AVENUE LOS ANGELES, CA 90024-1747 Immunology of virus induced rabbit papillomas/carcinomas
R29CA-50341-01A2 (PTHB) WEISS, LAWRENCE M CITY OF HOPE NATIONAL MED CTR 1500 E DUARTE ROAD DUARTE CA 91010 In situ hybridization in Hodgkin's disease
R01CA-50342-02 (PTHB) LOBO, PETER ISSAC UNIVERSITY OF VIRGINIA HEALTH SCIENCES CENTER CHARLOTTESVILLE, VA 22908 MHC gene products in protecting cells against NK lysis
R01CA-50350-03 (RAD) LEITH, JOHN T BROWN UNIVERSITY BOX G RM B-003 PROVIDENCE, RI 02912 Tumor bed effect -- Influence on growth factor expression
R01CA-50353-02 (RNM) STARK, DAVID D MASSACHUSETTS GENERAL HOSPITAL 32 FRUIT STREET BOSTON, MA 02114 Particulate contrast agents for MRI
R29CA-50354-02 (REN) WELSHONS, WADE V UNIV OF MISSOURI-COLUMBIA W116 VETERINARY MEDICINE COLUMBIA, MO 65211 Regulation of steroid receptor turnover in cancer cells
R01CA-50355-02 (PTHB) GELMANN, EDWARD P LOMBARDI CANCER RESEARCH CENTE 3800 RESERVOIR ROAD NW WASHINGTON, DC 20007 Molecular mechanisms for prostate cancer cell growth
R01CA-50364-01A2 (ET) BERMAN, MICHAEL L CLINICAL CANCER CTR,

UCIMC 101 THE CITY DRIVE SOUTH ORANGE, CA 92668 Chemoprevention of cervical cancer with beta-carotene
R01CA-50376-03 (PTHB) KERN, FRANCIS G V T LOMBARDI CANCER RES CENTER 3800 RESERVOIR ROAD, NW WASHINGTON, DC 20007 Genetic mechanisms of breast tumor progression
R01CA-50377-03 (CPA) ROSEN, NEAL SLOAN-KETTERING INSTITUTE 1275 YORK AVENUE NEW YORK, N.Y. 10021 Role of the lck protein tyrosine kinase in colon cancer
R01CA-50378-02 (PTHB) ZARBL, HELMUT MASSACHUSETTS INST OF TECHNOLO CAMBRIDGE, MA 02139 Aberrant gene regulation induced by v-fos transformation
R01CA-50380-01A3 (ET) SIDDIK, ZAHID H U.T. M.D. ANDERSON CANCER CENT 1515 HOLCOMBE BLVD. HOUSTON, TX 77030 Improving the theraupeutic index of platinum complexes
R29CA-50381-03 (EDC) GLASER, SALLY L NORTHERN CALIFORNIA CANCER CTR 1301 SHOREWAY ROAD, SUITE 425 BELMONT, CA 94002 Reproductive factors in Hodgkin's disease in women
R01CA-50382-03 (RNM) MISTRETTA, CHARLES A UNIVERSITY OF WISCONSIN 600 HIGHLAND AVENUE MADISON, WI 53792 Single-exposure dual-energy radiography
R29CA-50383-03 (EDC) SCHWARTZ, ANN G UNIVERSITY OF PITTSBURGH SCHOOL OF MEDICINE PITTSBURGH, PA 15261 Familial risk of lung cancer
R01CA-50385-03 (EDC) WILLETT, WALTER C HARVARD SCHOOL PUBLIC HEALTH 677 HUNTINGTON AVENUE BOSTON, MA 02115 Risk factors for breast cancer among younger nurses
R01CA-50387-03 (RAD) ELICEIRI, GEORGE L ST LOUIS UNIV SCHOOL OF MED 1402 S GRAND BLVD ST LOUIS, MO 63104 Uv-induced inhibition of small nuclear RNA synthesis
R01CA-50391-02 (MEP) YEOMAN, LYNN C BAYLOR COLLEGE OF MEDICINE ONE BAYLOR PLAZA HOUSTON, TX 77030 EGF-R modulation and responses in colon carcinoma
U01CA-50399-03 (SRC) LUK, GORDON D WAYNE STATE UNIV SCHOOL OF MED 540 EAST CANFIELD DETROIT, MI 48201 Phase I chemoprevention using DFMO to modulate ODC
R01CA-50412-02 (ET) MUGGIA, FRANCO M UNIV OF SOUTHERN CALIFORNIA 1441 EASTLAKE AVENUE LOS ANGELES, CA 90033 Intraperitoneal floxuridine plus leucovorin
R01CA-50414-03 (BIO) MARLETTA, MICHAEL A UNIVERSITY OF MICHIGAN 428 CHURCH ST ANN ARBOR, MI 48109-1065 A novel pathway of arginine metabolism in macrophages
R01CA-50430-03 (SRC) CHANG, CHIA-CHENG MICHIGAN STATE UNIVERSITY B236 LIFE SCIENCES BUILDING EAST LANSING, MI 48824 Transformation of human breast epithelial cells in vitro
R01CA-50432-02 (CPA) LOECHLER, EDWARD L BOSTON UNIVERSITY 2 CUMMINGTON STREET BOSTON, MA 02215 Molecular modeling in chemical carcinogenesis
R01CA-50434-03 (CPA) PELLICER, ANGEL G NEW YORK UNIV MEDICAL CENTER 550 FIRST AVENUE NEW YORK, NY 10016 DMBA-induced self-regressing tumors--Role of H-ras in-evolution
R01CA-50435-03 (ET) KAUFMANN, SCOTT H JOHNS HOPKINS HOSPITAL 600 N. WOLFE STREET BALTIMORE, MD 21205 Topoisomerase II and drug resistance in acute leukemia
R01CA-50443-03 (PTHB) DENNY, CHRISTOPHER T DEPT PEDIATRICS/RM A2-422 MDCC UCLA MEDICAL CENTER LOS ANGELES, CA 90024-1752 Molecular study of Ewing sarcoma t(11/22) translocation
R01CA-50445-03 (MEP) MARTIN, MARY B GEORGETOWN UNIV MEDICAL CENTER 3800 RESERVOIR RD NW WASHINGTON, DC 20007 Regulation of estrogen receptor in human breast cancer
R01CA-50453-03 (PTHB) DVORAK, HAROLD F BETH ISRAEL HOSPITAL 330 BROOKLINE AVENUE BOSTON, MA 02215 Prospective study of ovarian carcinoma
R01CA-50457-02 (MEP) BRATTAIN, MICHAEL G BAYLOR COLLEGE OF MEDICINE ONE BAYLOR PLAZA HOUSTON, TX 77030 Control of differentiation in colonic carcinoma
R01CA-50458-02 (MEP) TAYLOR, DOUGLAS D FOX CHASE CANCER CTR 7701 BURHOLME AVENUE PHILADELPHIA, PA 19111 Induction of altered lipid metabolism in cancer
R01CA-50459-03 (CBY) FALLER, DOUGLAS V BOSTON UNIVERSITY SCHOOL OF ME 80 EAST CONCORD STREET BOSTON, MA 02118 Control of cell growth by oncogenes
R01CA-50465-02 (RAD) ONODA, JAMES M WAYNE STATE UNIVERSITY 431 CHEMISTRY DETROIT, MI 48202 Radiation effects on plasma membrane receptors
R01CA-50468-02 (EDC) DUPONT, WILLIAM D 21ST & GARLAND AVENUES NASHVILLE, TN 37232-2637 Epidemiology of molecular risk factors for breast cancer
R29CA-50473-03 (ET) KRAMER, ROBERT A LEDERLE LABORATORIES BLDG 60B PEARL RIVER, NY 10965 Role of glutathione in multidrug resistance
R01CA-50486-03 (PTHA) YATES, ALLAN J OHIO STATE UNIVERSITY 473 W 12TH AVE COLUMBUS, OH 43210 Role of gangliosides in the pathogenesis of gliomas
R01CA-50489-02 (EDC) SWIFT, MICHAEL R UNIV OF NC AT CHAPEL HILL CB #7250, BDRC CHAPEL HILL, NC 27599-7250 Cancer risk of ataxia-telangiectasia heterozygotes
R01CA-50497-03 (MGN) BALE, ALLEN E YALE UNIVERSITY 333 CEDAR ST, PO BOX 3333 NEW HAVEN, CT 06510 Isolation of the gene for multiple endocrine neoplasia 1
R29CA-50503-03 (RAD) HUNT, CLAYTON R WASHINGTON UNIVERSITY 4511 FOREST PARK BLVD ST LOUIS, MO 63108 Hsp70 regulation in cells recovering from hyperthermia
R01CA-50505-02 (RNM) KHAW, BAN-AN MASSACHUSETTS GENERAL HOSPITAL FRUIT STREET BOSTON, MA 02114 Negative charge-modified monoclonal antibodies
R01CA-50512-02 (MCHA) MAGNUS, PHILIP D UNIVERSITY OF TEXAS AT AUSTIN AUSTIN, TX 78712 Esperamicin and neocarzinostatin--syntheses and mechanisms
R01CA-50516-03 (CBY) ROSEN, ELIOT M YALE UNIV SCH OF MEDICINE 333 CEDAR STREET NEW HAVEN, CT 06510 Scatter factor regulates endothelial/epithelial mobility
R01CA-50519-03 (RAD) CHEN, DAVID J LOS ALAMOS NATIONAL LABORATORY GENETICS GROUP LOS ALAMOS, NM 87545 Molecular cloning of a human radiation repair gene
R01CA-50520-03 (SRC) FREEMAN, HAROLD P HARLEM HOSPITAL CENTER 506 LENOX AVENUE NEW YORK, NY 10037 Emergency room cancer screening program
R01CA-50523-03 (EVR) TANAKA, AKIKO TAMPA BAY RESEARCH INSTITUTE 10900 ROOSEVELT BLVD ST PETERSBURG, FL 33716 Marek's disease virus-analysis of latent genes
P01CA-50528-03 (SRC) FERAMISCO, JAMES R UNIVERSITY OF CALIFORNIA The function of nuclear oncogenes in cancer cells
P01CA-50528-03 0001 (SRC) FERAMISCO, JAMES R The function of nuclear oncogenes in cancer cells Protein phosphorylation in oncogene action
P01CA-50528-03 0002 (SRC) KARIN, MICHAEL The function of nuclear oncogenes in cancer cells Function and regulation of the C-jun protooncogene
P01CA-50528-03 0003 (SRC) LIPSICK, JOSEPH The function of nuclear oncogenes in cancer cells Regulation of c-myb expression in normal and malignant cells
P01CA-50528-03 0004 (SRC) WACHSMAN, WILLIAM The function of nuclear oncogenes in cancer cells Regulation of gene expression by HTLV and Rex
P01CA-50528-03 0005 (SRC) TSENG, BEN Y The function of nuclear oncogenes in cancer cells Regulation of expression of DNA synthetic enzymes
P01CA-50528-03 9001 (SRC) FERAMISCO, JAMES R The function of nuclear oncogenes in cancer cells Core--Microinjection
P01CA-50528-03 9002 (SRC) LIPSICK, JOSEPH The function of nuclear oncogenes in cancer cells Core--Antibody/peptide synthesis and nucleotide synthesis/sequencing
P01CA-50529-01A2 (SRC) POTMESIL, MILAN NEW YORK UNIV MEDICAL CENTER 550 FIRST AVENUE NEW YORK, NY 10016 DNA topoisomerase I-targeted therapy of colonic cancer
P01CA-50529-01A2 0001 (SRC) WALL, MONROE DNA topoisomerase I-targeted therapy of colonic cancer Drug development--Camptothecin analogs
P01CA-50529-01A2 0002 (SRC) LIU, LEROY F DNA topoisomerase I-targeted therapy of colonic cancer Molecular biology
P01CA-50529-01A2 0003 (SRC) POTMESIL, MILAN DNA topoisomerase I-targeted therapy of colonic cancer Cell biology
P01CA-50529-01A2 0004 (SRC) GIOVANELLA, BEPPINO C DNA topoisomerase I-targeted therapy of colonic cancer Tumor biology
P01CA-50529-01A2 9001 (SRC) HOCHSTER, HOWARD DNA topoisomerase I-targeted therapy of colonic cancer Core--Colon oncology
R01CA-50532-03 (VR) NORKIN, LEONARD C UNIVERSITY OF MASSACHUSETTS AMHERST, MA 01003 Interaction of SV40 with MHC class 1 proteins
R01CA-50539-03 (RNM) HASEGAWA, BRUCE H UNIVERSITY OF CALIFORNIA SAN FRANCISCO, CA 94143 Development of an emission-transmission CT system
R01CA-50540-02 (CBY) QUINLAN, MARGARET P 858 MADISON AVENUE MEMPHIS, TN 38163 Immortalization of primary epithelial cells by AD5 12S
R01CA-50542-03 (BIO) HINDSGAUL, OLE UNIVERSITY OF ALBERTA EDMONTON, ALBERTA Inhibitors of glycosyltransferases
R01CA-50551-03 (HEM) TSUJIMOTO, Y WISTAR INSTITUTE 36TH AND SPRUCE STREETS PHILADELPHIA, PA 19104 Function of the bcl-2 protein
R01CA-50558-03 (PTHB) CLARK, JEFFREY ROGER WILLIAMS MEDICAL CENTER 825 CHALKSTONE AVE PROVIDENCE, RI 02908 Mechanism of 1, 25-D3 anti-proliferative action in CML
R01CA-50559-03 (PTHB) LAUG, WALTER E CHILDRENS HOSPITAL/LOS ANGELES 4650 SUNSET BOULEVARD LOS ANGELES, CA 90027 Modulation of tumor invasion & metastasis
R01CA-50574-02 (VR) KASAMATSU, HARUMI UNIVERSITY OF CALIFORNIA 405 HILGARD AVE LOS ANGELES, CA 90024-1606 Assembly and morphogenesis of DNA tumor viruses
R01CA-50585-03 (MEP) DOVE, WILLIAM F UNIVERSITY OF WISCONSIN 1400 UNIVERSITY AVENUE MADISON, WI 53706 Spontaneous intestinal carcinogenesis in mouse mutant
R01CA-50588-03 (CPA) THOMPSON, TIMOTHY C BAYLOR COLLEGE OF MEDICINE 6535 FANNIN F427A HOUSTON, TX 77030 Mechanisms of progression in oncogene-induced prostate Cancer
R01CA-50589-01A1 (PTHB) PRESS, MICHAEL F UNIV OF SOUTHERN CALIFORNIA 2011 ZONAL AVE-HMR 910 LOS ANGELES, CA 90033 HER-2 neu proto-oncogene in ovarian & endometrial cancer
R29CA-50590-03 (CPA) WILDING, GEORGE UNIVERSITY OF WISCONSIN 600 HIGHLAND AVENUE MADISON, WI 53792 Peptide growth factors in human prostate carcinogenesis
R01CA-50595-02 (RAD) KINSELLA, TIMOTHY J UNIV WISCONSIN CLIN CANCER CTR 600 HIGHLAND AVENUE, K4/312 MADISON, WI 53792 Radiation and chemosensitization with iododeoxyuridine
R01CA-50597-03 (EDC) ROSNER, BERNARD A CHANNING LABORATORY 180 LONGWOOD AVENUE BOSTON, MA 02115 Measurement errors in cancer/respiratory epidemiology
R01CA-50601-02 (PTHB) ISAACS, JOHN T 422 NORTH BOND STREET BALTIMORE, MD 21231 Programmed death of normal and malignant prostatic cells
R01CA-50604-03 (MGN) RICHIE, ELLEN R U TEXAS/M D ANDERSON CANCER CR P.O. BOX 389 SMITHVILLE, TX 78957 Characterization of a murine tumor suppressor gene model
R01CA-50608-01A1 (CPA) PARDEE, ARTHUR B DANA-FARBER CANCER INSTITUTE 44 BINNEY STREET BOSTON, MA 02115 Role of topoisomerase I in DNA repair and chemotherapy
R01CA-50609-02 (MEP) WARE, JOY L VIRGINIA COMMONWEALTH UNIVERSI BOX 662/MED COLL OF VIRGINIA/V RICHMOND, VA 23298 Role of growth factors in human prostate carcinoma
R01CA-50616-01A2 (REN) TERRANOVA, PAUL F UNIVERSITY OF KANSAS MED CTR 39TH & RAINBOW BOULEVARD KANSAS CITY, KS 66103 Ovarian tumor necrosis factor
R01CA-50618-01A2 (ET) SCANLON, KEVIN J CITY OF HOPE NATIONAL MED CTR 1500 EAST DUARTE ROAD DUARTE, CA 91010 Development of a fos ribozyme
R01CA-50628-03 (RAD) GOITEIN, MICHAEL MASSACHUSETTS GENERAL HOSPITAL BOSTON, MA 02114 Assessment & optimization of radiation therapy
R01CA-50629-03 (RAD) BALCER-KUBICZEK, ELIZABETH K UMBC/SCH OF

PROJECT NO., ORGANIZATIONAL UNIT., INVESTIGATOR, ADDRESS, TITLE

MED/6-015 BRESSLER 655 WEST BALTIMORE STREET BALTIMORE, MD 21201 Neoplastic transformation by neutrons and gamma rays
R01CA-50633-03 (ET) WEINER, LOUIS M FOX CHASE CANCER CENTER 7701 BURHOLME AVE PHILADELPHIA, PA 19111 Bispecific anti-tumor/FCYR III monoclonal antibodies
R29CA-50638-02 (ET) SINGH, SHIVENDRA V UNIVERSITY OF MIAMI P O BOX 016960 (R-71) MIAMI, FL 33101 Glutathione and related enzymes in cellular drug resistance
R01CA-50641-02 (RNM) KING, MICHAEL A UNIV OF MASSACHUSETTS MED SCH 55 LAKE AVENUE NORTH WORCESTER, MA 01655 Three dimensional edge detection for SPECT images
R01CA-50645-02 (MEP) FRIEDMAN, EILEEN A MEMORIAL HOSPITAL 1275 YORK AVENUE NEW YORK, NY 10021 Tumor promoter induced protein phosphorylation
R01CA-50658-01A2 (EDC) WESTHOFF, CAROLYN L 630 WEST 168 STREET NEW YORK, NY 10032 Case control study of benign ovarian neoplasms
P01CA-50661-03 (SRC) LIVINGSTON, DAVID M DANA-FARBER CANCER INSTITUTE 44 BINNEY STREET BOSTON, MA 02115 Papovavirus transforming mechanisms
P01CA-50661-03 9001 (SRC) LIVINGSTON, DAVID M PAPOVAVIRUS TRANSFORMING MECHANISMS Hybridoma resources
P01CA-50661-03 9002 (SRC) LIVINGSTON, DAVID M PAPOVAVIRUS TRANSFORMING MECHANISMS Animal pathology study unit
P01CA-50661-03 0001 (SRC) ROBERTS, THOMAS M PAPOVAVIRUS TRANSFORMING MECHANISMS Molecular analysis of c-Raf activation
P01CA-50661-03 0002 (SRC) SMITH, ALAN E PAPOVAVIRUS TRANSFORMING MECHANISMS Tyrosine kinase binding and Polyomavirus antigen activation
P01CA-50661-03 0003 (SRC) GARCEA, ROBERT L PAPOVAVIRUS TRANSFORMING MECHANISMS Cell recognition by polyomavirus
P01CA-50661-03 0004 (SRC) LIVINGSTON, DAVID M PAPOVAVIRUS TRANSFORMING MECHANISMS SV40 T-Rb interactions
P01CA-50661-03 0005 (SRC) SCHAFFHAUSEN, BRIAN S PAPOVAVIRUS TRANSFORMING MECHANISMS N-terminal domain of polyoma virus large T antigen
R01CA-50675-02 (MGN) HELD, WILLIAM A ROSWELL PARK MEMORIAL INST 666 ELM STREET BUFFALO, NY 14263 Androgen conditional carcinogenesis in transgenic mice
R01CA-50676-02 (PTHB) PFAHL, MAGNUS LA JOLLA CANCER RESEARCH FDN 10901 NORTH TORREY PINES ROAD LA JOLLA, CA 92037 The retinoic acid receptor in development and disease
R01CA-50677-03 (ET) FRANKFURT, OSKAR S CEDARS MEDICAL CENTER 1400 NW 12TH AVENUE MIAMI, FL 33136 Flow cytometric study of anticancer drug effects on DNA
R29CA-50679-03 (RAD) HALPERN, HOWARD J UNIVERSITY OF CHICAGO 5841 S MARYLAND AVE/BOX 442 CHICAGO, ILL 60637 Imaging oxygen w/low frequency electron spin resonance
R29CA-50681-03 (ET) VAN HOUTEN, BENNETT UNIVERSITY OF VERMONT BURLINGTON, VT 05405 Repair of platinum-DNA adducts in mammalian cells
R01CA-50684-03 (CPA) LIEBERMAN, MICHAEL W BAYLOR COLLEGE OF MEDICINE ONE BAYLOR PLAZA HOUSTON, TX 77020 Metallothionein activation--a model of carcinogen action
R01CA-50694-01A2 (PTHB) SIEGFRIED, JILL M UNIVERSITY OF PITTSBURGH 3550 TERRACE STREET PITTSBURGH, PA 15261 IGF-I related peptides in the pathology of lung cancer
R29CA-50703-03 (RNM) GARWOOD, MICHAEL G UNIV OF MINNESOTA MED SCHOOL 385 EAST RIVER ROAD MINNEAPOLIS, MN 55455 In vivo MRS and MRI methods: application to brain tumors
R29CA-50706-03 (PTHB) FAGIN, JAMES A CEDARS-SINAI MEDICAL CENTER 8700 BEVERLY BOULEVARD LOS ANGELES, CA 90048 Molecular pathophysiology of thyroid cell growth
R29CA-50710-04 (MEP) LIU, KATHERINE JUNG-MEI COOK COUNTY HOSPITAL 1835 W HARRISON STREET CHICAGO, ILLINOIS 60612 Gluconeogenic substrate metabolism in cancer
R29CA-50715-02 (ET) AL-KATIB, AYAD M WAYNE STATE UNIVERSITY ONCOLOGY DETROIT, MI 48201-0188 Differentiation-related proteins in malignant cells
R01CA-50720-01A2 (MCHA) PARKER, KATHLYN A BROWN UNIVERSITY PROVIDENCE, RI 02912 Synthesis of c-aryl glycosides
R01CA-50721-03 (ET) BEARDSLEY, G PETER YALE UNIV SCHOOL OF MEDICINE BOX 3333 NEW HAVEN, CT 06510 Biochemical and cellular pharmacology of deazatetrahydrofolates
R01CA-50726-01A1 (SOH) CROUCH, EDMUND A TUFTS UNIVERSITY SCHOOL OF MED 136 HARRISON AVENUE BOSTON, MA 02111 Analysis of the Carcinogenisis Bioassay Data System database
R29CA-50733-03 (SSS) KRIEG-KOWALD, MARIANNE MEDICAL COLLEGE OF WISCONSIN 8701 WATERTOWN PLANK ROAD MILWAUKEE, WI 53226 Mechanism of photodynamic action of cyanine dyes
R01CA-50735-03 (CBY) NIYOGI, SALIL K OAK RIDGE NATIONAL LABORATORY P.O. BOX 2009 OAK RIDGE, TN 37831-8077 Human epidermal growth factor--Site-directed mutagenesis
R01CA-50738-03 (ARR) KIVIAT, NANCY HARBORVIEW MEDICAL CENTER 325 NINTH AVENUE SEATTLE, WA 98104 Anal dysplasia in HIV positive and negative men
R01CA-50739-02 (PTHB) NEWCOM, SAMUEL R EMORY UNIVERSITY 46 ARMSTRONG STREET ATLANTA, GA 30303 High molecular wt transforming growth factor beta in Hodgkin's disease
U01CA-50743-03 (SRC) CHANG, CHING-JER SCHOOL OF PHARMACY PURDUE UNIVERSITY WEST LAFAYETTE, IN 47907 Mechanism-based discovery of antitumor agents
R01CA-50749-02 (SRC) HRUSHESKY, WILLIAM J 47 NEW SCOTLAND AVE (A52) 113 HOLLAND AVE (111C) ALBANY, NY 12208 Chronobiological investigation of TNF and IL-2
U01CA-50750-03 (SRC) CLARDY, JON C CORNELL UNIVERSITY BAKER LABORATORY ITHACA, NY 14853-1301 New anticancer drugs from cultured and collected marine organisms
U01CA-50750-03 0001 (SRC) CLARDY, JON C New anticancer drugs from cultured and collected marine organisms Structure studies on anticancer drugs from marine organisms
U01CA-50750-03 0002 (SRC) CASAZZA, ANN M New anticancer drugs from cultured and collected marine organisms Pharmacologaical studies on anticancer and drugs from marine organisms
U01CA-50750-03 0003 (SRC) FAULKNER, D JOHN New anticancer drugs from cultured and collected marine organisms
U01CA-50750-03 0004 (SRC) FENICAL, WILLIAM New anticancer drugs from cultured and collected marine organisms Anticancer and anti-HIV agents from marine microorganisms and coelenterates
U01CA-50750-03 0005 (SRC) IRELAND, CHRIS M New anticancer drugs from cultured and collected marine organisms Anticancer drugs from marine organisms and blue-green algae
U01CA-50750-03 0006 (SRC) SHIMIZU, YUZUVU New anticancer drugs from cultured and collected marine organisms Anticancer drugs from marine organisms and microalgae
R01CA-50752-02 (SRC) FLEISCHMANN, WILLIAM R, JR UNIVERSITY OF TEXAS MED BRANCH GALVESTON, TX 77550 Chronobiology of interferon therapy
R29CA-50767-03 (EVR) PIWNICA-WORMS, HELEN M TUFTS UNIVERSITY 136 HARRISON AVENUE BOSTON, MA 02111 Role of tyrosine kinases in middle T ag transformation
U01CA-50771-03 (SRC) HECHT, SIDNEY M UNIVERSITY OF VIRGINIA CHARLOTTESVILLE, VA 22901 Mechanism-based discovery of novel antitumor agents
U01CA-50771-03 0001 (SRC) JOHNSON, RANDALL Mechanism-based discovery of novel antitumor agents Smith Klein & French Laboratories
U01CA-50771-03 0002 (SRC) KINGSTON, DAVID G Mechanism-based discovery of novel antitumor agents Dept Chemistry, Virginia Polytechnic
U01CA-50771-03 0003 (SRC) HECHT, SIDNEY Mechanism-based discovery of novel antitumor agents Dept Chemistry, University of Virginia
U01CA-50771-03 0004 (SRC) VON HOFF, DANIEL D Mechanism-based discovery of novel antitumor agents Dept Medicine, Univ Texas, San Antonio
R29CA-50773-02 (VR) REICH, NANCY C STATE UNIVERSITY OF NEW YORK STONY BROOK, NY 11794-8691 Cellular & oncogenic control of interferon induced genes
R29CA-50774-02 (CBY) JOSEPH, LOREN J UNIVERSITY OF CHICAGO 5841 SOUTH MARYLAND AVENUE CHICAGO, IL 60637 Zinc finger proteins implicated in mitogenesis
R29CA-50777-03 (ARR) DOUGHERTY, JOSEPH P UMDNJ-ROBERT WOOD JOHNSON M S 675 HOES LANE PISCATAWAY, NJ 08854-5635 Determination of retrovirus mutation rates
R29CA-50780-03 (ET) ECONOMOU, JAMES S UNIVERSITY OF CALIFORNIA 405 HILGARD AVENUE LOS ANGELES, CA 90024-1406 Therapeutic regulation of TNF in IL-2 immunotherapy
R44CA-50788-02 (SSS) RHODES, BUCK A RHOMED INCORPORATED 1020 TIJERAS NE ALBUQUERQUE, NM 87106 Improved technetium-99m labeling for cancer imaging
R01CA-50795-02 (EDC) CHU, JOSEPH FRED HUTCHINSON CANCER RES CTR 1124 COLUMBIA ST SEATTLE, WA 98104 The relationship of CIN III and human papilloma virus
R44CA-50800-02 (SSS) JACQUEZ, GEOFFREY M APPLIED BIOMATHEMATICS 100 NORTH COUNTRY ROAD SETAUKET, NY 11733 Statistical detection of cancer clusters
R44CA-50811-02 (SSS) KING, CHARLES R MOLECULAR ONCOLOGY, INC 19 FIRSTFIELD ROAD GAITHERSBURG, MD 20878 New molecular markers on malignancy of breast cancer
R44CA-50826-02 (SSS) O'FOGHLUDHA, FEARGHUS QUANTUM RESEARCH SERVICES, INC 100 CAPITOLA DR DURHAM, NC 27713-4411 Development of a 3-D electron treatment planning system
R44CA-50842-02A1 (SSS) SCHIPMA, PETER B I S GRUPE INC 948 SPRINGER DR LOMBARD, IL 60148 Epidemiology information resource on optical disc
R44CA-50843-02A1 (ET) BACUS, JAMES W CELL ANALYSIS SYSTEMS, INC. 909 SOUTH ROUTE 83 ELMHURST, IL 60126-4944 Quantitation of oncogene products in cells and tissue
R01CA-50847-03 (SRC) ALLEN, SUSAN A UNIVERSITY OF CALIFORNIA BOX 0886 SAN FRANCISCO, CA 94143 HIV, HPV-cancer in Rwanda
R01CA-50849-03 (SRC) RAGNI, MARGARET V HEMOPHILIA CTR OF WESTERN PA 812 FIFTH AVENUE PITTSBURGH, PA 15219 Study of HIV-associated malignancy in hemophiliacs
R01CA-50850-03 (SRC) LEVINE, ALEXANDRA M UNIV OF SOUTHERN CALIFORNIA 1975 ZONAL AVENUE KAM #500 LOS ANGELES, CA 90033 Epidemiology of HIV-related lymphoma
R01CA-50851-03 (BLR) UDUPA, JAYARAM K UNIVERSITY OF PENNSYLVANIA 418 SERVICE DRIVE 4TH FLOOR PHILADELPHIA, PA 19104-6021 Unix-based software for 3D display and analysis
R01CA-50856-02 (ARR) KIVIAT, NANCY HARBORVIEW MEDICAL CENTER 325 NINTH AVENUE SEATTLE, WA 98104 Cervical neoplasia and HIV infection in Senegal
R29CA-50858-01A1 (BEM) BOWEN, DEBORAH J FRED HUTCHINSON CANCER RES CTR 1124 COLUMBIA STREET SEATTLE, WA 98104 Tryptophan as an adjunct to smoking cessation therapy
R01CA-50872-03 (SRC) KWOK, CHEUK SANG HAMILTON REGIONAL CANCER CENTR 711 CONCESSION STREET HAMILTON, ONTARIO/CANADA L8V 1 Electron dosimetry in radioimmunotherapy
R01CA-50886-03 (SRC) CHIN, LEE M NEW ENGLAND DEACONESS HOSPITAL 185 PILGRIM ROAD BOSTON, MA 02215 Novel approaches to radio-immunoconjugate dosimetry in-vitro
R01CA-50891-02 (SRC) DYE, EARL S TRUDEAU INSTITUTE, INC PO BOX 59 SARANAC LAKE, NY 12983 Influence of bioperiodicity on tumor immunotherapy
R01CA-50897-03 (MGN) GERMAN, JAMES L, III NEW YORK BLOOD CENTER 310 EAST 67TH STREET NEW YORK, N Y 10021 Molecular analysis of somatic recombination
R29CA-50898-03 (HEM) GIMBLE, JEFFREY M OKLAHOMA MEDICAL RESEARCH FDN 825 N E 13TH ST OKLAHOMA CITY, OK 73104 Gene regulation in lymphohemopoietic stromal cells
U01CA-50905-03 (SRC) JENKINS, ROBERT B MAYO FOUNDATION 200 FIRST ST SOUTHWEST ROCHESTER, MN 55905 An investigation of the molecular pathology of gliomas
R01CA-50906-03 (GMB) CLEMENS, THOMAS L CEDARS-SINAI MEDICAL CENTER 8700 BEVERLY BLVD, RM B131 LOS ANGELES, CA 90048 Actions of parathyroid hormone-like human tumor factor
R01CA-50909-03 (MEP) CHRISTMAN, JUDITH K MICHIGAN CANCER FOUNDATION 110 EAST WARREN AVE DETROIT, MI 48201 "Cloning the gene for a novel tpa-induced protein"

PROJECT NO., ORGANIZATIONAL UNIT., INVESTIGATOR, ADDRESS, TITLE

U01CA-50910-03 (SRC) YATES, ALLAN J OHIO STATE UNIVERSITY 473 WEST 12TH AVENUE COLUMBUS, OH 43210 The value of glycolipids for classifying astrocytomas

R44CA-50916-02 (SSS) LINDMAYER, JOSEPH QUANTEX CORPORATION 2 RESEARCH COURT ROCKVILLE, MD 20850 High sensitivity phosphor for X-ray imaging--Phase II

U01CA-50931-03 (SRC) JOHNSON, PETER C ST JOSEPH'S HOSPITAL & MED CTR 350 WEST THOMAS ROAD PHOENIX, AZ 85013 Improved classification of human astrocytes

R01CA-50937-02 (RAD) FOWLER, JOHN F UNIV OF WI CLINICAL CANCER CTR 600 HIGHLAND AVE MADISON, WI 53792 Proliferation in human tumors during radiotherapy

R01CA-50947-01A1 (ET) ANDERSON, KENNETH C DANA-FARBER CANCER INST 44 BINNEY ST BOSTON, MA 02115 Characterization of growth factor responsive B cells

R01CA-50948-02 (RNM) MACOVSKI, ALBERT STANFORD UNIVERSITY DURAN BUILDING STANFORD, CA 94305 High-speed MRI tumor imaging

P01CA-50956-02 (SRC) WYNDER, ERNST L AMERICAN HEALTH FOUNDATION 320 EAST 43RD STREET NEW YORK, NY 10017 Minority cancer prevention research unit

P01CA-50956-02 0001 (SRC) ROYCE, JACQUELINE M Minority cancer prevention research unit Urban health clinic nurses and smoking control

P01CA-50956-02 0002 (SRC) SCHILLING, ROBERT F Minority cancer prevention research unit Nicotine fading and relapse prevention among african-american smokers

P01CA-50956-02 0003 (SRC) ORLANDI, MARIO A Minority cancer prevention research unit Housing project interventions to prevent cancer among african-american smokers

P01CA-50956-02 0004 (SRC) SCHINKE, STEVEN P Minority cancer prevention research unit Computer-based interventions to prevent cancer among african-american youth

P01CA-50956-02 0005 (SRC) BOTVIN, GILBERT J Minority cancer prevention research unit School-based approaches to prevention of tobacco use with african-american youth

P01CA-50956-02 9001 (SRC) SCHINKE, STEVEN P Minority cancer prevention research unit Core--Intervention development

P01CA-50956-02 9002 (SRC) ZANG, EDITH A Minority cancer prevention research unit Core--Information management, statistics and program evaluation

P01CA-50956-02 9003 (SRC) FREEMAN, HAROLD P Minority cancer prevention research unit Core--Community liaison

R01CA-50980-02 (MEP) WATTENBERG, LEE W UNIVERSITY OF MINNESOTA 6-133 JACKSON HALL MINNEAPOLIS, MN 55455 Studies of carcinogenicity of fecapentaenes

R01CA-50985-01A1 (RNM) KRESSEL, HERBERT Y UNIVERSITY OF PENNSYLVANIA DEVON CENTER-3400 SPRUCE ST PHILADELPHIA, PA 19104 MRI/MRS in the evaluation of prostatic carcinoma

R01CA-50991-02 (MCHA) MARTIN, STEPHEN F UNIVERSITY OF TEXAS AUSTIN, TX 78712 Strategies for the synthesis of anticancer agents

R01CA-50995-02 (RAD) RALEIGH, JAMES A UNIV OF NC-CHAPEL HILL CB 7512 CHAPEL HILL, NC 27599 Histochemical markers of tumor hypoxia

R29CA-51001-02 (PHRA) RELLING, MARY V ST. JUDE CHILDREN'S RES HOSP 332 NORTH LAUDERDALE MEMPHIS, TN 38105 Polymorphic metabolism of antineoplastics in children

R01CA-51007-02 (SSS) PIERCE, DONALD A OREGON STATE UNIVERSITY CORVALLIS, OR 97331-4606 Statistical analysis of cancer in atomic bomb survivors

P30CA-51008-02 (CCS) LIPPMAN, MARC E GEORGETOWN UNIV MEDICAL CENTER 3800 RESERVOIR ROAD, NW WASHINGTON, DC 20007 CCSG for the Vincent T Lombardi cancer research center

P30CA-51008-02 9001 (CCS) CLARKE, ROBERT CCSG for the Vincent T Lombardi cancer research center Animal core facility

P30CA-51008-02 9002 (CCS) PICKLE, LINDA CCSG for the Vincent T Lombardi cancer research center Biostatistics unit

P30CA-51008-02 9003 (CCS) CHEN, WEN TIEN CCSG for the Vincent T Lombardi cancer research center Cytochemistry and morphology core laboratory

P30CA-51008-02 9004 (CCS) BLAIR, OWEN CCSG for the Vincent T Lombardi cancer research center Flow cytometry/cell sorting core facility

P30CA-51008-02 9005 (CCS) HURLEY, CAROLYN CCSG for the Vincent T Lombardi cancer research center Macromolecules core facility

P30CA-51008-02 9006 (CCS) STEAKLEY, CARYN CCSG for the Vincent T Lombardi cancer research center Clinical reseach management office

P30CA-51008-02 9007 (CCS) BHATIA, KISHORE CCSG for the Vincent T Lombardi cancer research center Development core support

R01CA-51012-02 (ARR) HALL, WILLIAM W NORTH SHORE UNIVERSITY HOSPITA 300 COMMUNITY DRIVE MANHASSET, NY 11030 Concomitant infections with HIV and HTLV-I/HTLV-II

R01CA-51015-02 (GMA) ANANTHASWAMY, HONNAVARA N UNIV OF TEXAS MD ANDERSON CA C 1515 HOLCOMBE BOULEVARD HOUSTON, TX 77030 Cellular and molecular basis for basal cell nevus syndrome

R01CA-51020-02 (PTHB) IHLE, JAMES N DEPARTMENT OF BIOCHEMISTRY 332 NORTH LAUDERDALE MEMPHIS, TN 38101-0318 Molecular mechanisms in myeloid transformation

R01CA-51033-02 (PTHB) TANNOCK, IAN F ONTARIO CANCER INSTITUTE 500 SHERBOURNE ST ONTARIO, CANADA M4X 1K9 PH regulation and cancer

R29CA-51053-02 (PTHB) PRICE, JANET E THE UNIV. OF TEXAS 1515 HOLCOMBE BLVD., HMB 173 HOUSTON TEXAS, 77030 The biology of metastatic human breast carcinoma

R01CA-51054-02 (BBCB) MOUNTFORD, CAROLYN E UNIVERSITY OF SYDNEY NSW, 2006, AUSTRALIA Plasma membrane involvement in malignancy and metastasis

R29CA-51060-02 (MEP) BOORSTEIN, ROBERT NEW YORK UNIVERSITY MED CTR 550 FIRST AVE NEW YORK, NY 10016 HmUra mutagenicity and base excision repair

R29CA-51061-02 (PTHB) COHN, SUSAN L CHILDREN'S MEMORIAL HOSPITAL 2300 CHILDREN'S PLAZA CHICAGO, IL 60614 Molecular mechanisms of differentiation in neuroblastoma

R01CA-51064-02 (RAD) CHOU, WEN-GANG UNIV OF ROCHESTER MEDICAL CTR 601 ELMWOOD AVENUE ROCHESTER, NY 14642 Radiation associated gene products

PROJECT NO., ORGANIZATIONAL UNIT., INVESTIGATOR, ADDRESS, TITLE

R29CA-51065-02 (EVR) SPECK, NANCY A DARTMOUTH MEDICAL SCHOOL HANOVER, NH 03756 Genetics and biochemistry of viral leukemogenesis

R29CA-51068-02 (MEP) CELANO, PAUL ONCOLOGY CTR RESEARCH LABS 424 N BOND ST BALTIMORE, MD 21231 Regulation of growth gene expression by the polyamines

R01CA-51071-02 (RNM) O'BRIEN-PENNEY, BILL C UNIV OF MASSACHUSETTS MED CTR 55 LAKE AVE NORTH WORCESTER, MA 01655 Reconstruction methods for radiolabeled antibody imaging

R01CA-51076-02 (RAD) PHILLIPS, MARK H LAWRENCE BERKELEY LABORATORY 1 CYCLOTRON ROAD BERKELEY, CA 94720 Dose comparison of stereotactic radiosurgical modalities

R01CA-51077-01A1 (RNM) SMITH, BRUCE D UNIVERSITY OF CINCINNATI ML 30 CINCINNATI, OH 45221-0030 Evaluation of novel cone-beam reconstruction for spect

R01CA-51080-02 (ARR) OVERBAUGH, JULIE M UNIVERSITY OF WASHINGTON SEATTLE, WA 98195 Regulation of FeLV expression and pathogenisis

R01CA-51085-02 (ET) CASERO, ROBERT A, JR JOHNS HOPKINS RESEARCH LABS 424 NORTH BOND STREET BALTIMORE, MD 21231 Spermidine N1-acetylase induction in lung cancers

R01CA-51086-01A2 (EDC) VINEIS, PAOLO UNIVERSITY OF TORINO VIA SANTENA 7 TORINO, ITALY 10126 Hematolymphopoietic malignancies in Italy

R01CA-51088-02 (CPA) MUFTI, SIRAJ I UNIVERSITY OF ARIZONA DEPT PHARMACOLOGY/TOXICOLOGY TUCSON, AZ 85721 Tobacco-alcohol related carcinogenesis models--Aerodigestive tract

R01CA-51093-02 (PTHA) WONG, ALBERT J FOX CHASE CANCER CENTER 7701 BURHOLME AVENUE PHILADELPHIA, PA 19111 Altered EGF receptors in human gliomas

R01CA-51096-01A2 (CPA) VOS, JEAN-MICHEL H UNIV OF NC AT CHAPEL HILL CHAPEL HILL, NC 27599 Replicon misfunctions in human carcinogenesis

R55CA-51103-01A1 (CPA) VONHOFE, ERIC H UNIV OF MASSACHUSETTS MED SCH 55 LAKE AVE NORTH WORCESTER, MA 01655 Specific DNA damage and neoplastic transformation

R01CA-51105-02 (PTHB) LIEBER, MICHAEL R STANFORD UNIV, SCH OF MEDICINE 300 PASTEUR DRIVE STANFORD, CA 94305 Human VDJ recombinase in neoplastic and primary cells

R01CA-51106-02 (CPA) CURPHEY, THOMAS J DARTMOUTH MEDICAL SCHOOL HANOVER, NH 03756 Solid-phase electrophile trapping agents

P01CA-51116-02 (SRC) ROTI ROTI, JOSEPH L WASHINGTON UNIVERSITY 4511 FOREST PARK BLVD, #404 ST LOUIS, MO 63108 Nuclear determinants of therapeutic response

P01CA-51116-02 0001 (SRC) ROTI, JOSEPH Nuclear determinants of therapeutic response Changes in nuclear polypeptide composition and radiosensitivity development

P01CA-51116-02 0002 (SRC) TAYLOR, YVONNE Nuclear determinants of therapeutic response Cell shape as mediator of radiation sensitivity

P01CA-51116-02 0003 (SRC) LASZIO, ANDREI Nuclear determinants of therapeutic response Predictors of tumor cell response to hyperthermia

P01CA-51116-02 0004 (SRC) LIN, HSIU-SAN Nuclear determinants of therapeutic response Effects of hyperthermia on the mononuclear phagocyte system

P01CA-51116-02 0005 (SRC) TOLMACH, L Nuclear determinants of therapeutic response Mechanisms of control of cell-cycle progression

P01CA-51116-02 9001 (SRC) HIGASHIKUBO, RYUJI Nuclear determinants of therapeutic response Core--Cytometry

R01CA-51117-02 (EDC) MODAN, BARUCH CHAIM SHEBA MEDICAL CENTER TEL HASHOMER 52621 ISRAEL Brain tumors and n-nitroso exposures

R01CA-51119-02 (REN) SIMPSON, EVAN R U.T. SOUTHWESTERN MED CENTER 5323 HARRY HINES BOULEVARD DALLAS, TEX 75235-9051 Aromatase structure function relationships and cancer

R01CA-51124-01A2 (RAD) EHMAN, RICHARD L MAYO FOUNDATION 200 FIRST STREET SW ROCHESTER, MN 55905 Adaptive techniques for MR imaging of moving structures

R01CA-51127-02 (EVR) LUSKY, MONIKA D CORNELL UNIV MEDICAL COLLEGE 1300 YORK AVENUE NEW YORK, NY 10021 Regulation of bovine papillomavirus replication

R01CA-51130-02 (EI) EDWARDS, BRUCE S LOVELACE MEDICAL FOUNDATION 2425 RIDGECREST DIRVE, S E ALBUQUERQUE, NM 87108 NK and target cell biodynamic mechanisms

R01CA-51132-02 (PC) SAITO, HARUO DANA-FARBER CANCER INSTITUTE 44 BINNEY STREET BOSTON, MA 02115 Receptor-linked protein tyrosine phosphatases

R29CA-51142-02 (BEM) BASTANI, ROSHAN UNIV OF CALIFORNIA LOS ANGELES 1100 GLENDON, SUITE 711 LOS ANGELES, CA 90024 Promoting screening mammography among high-risk women

R01CA-51148-02 (PTHA) YUNG, WAI-KWAN A U.T. M.D.ANDERSON CANCER CTR 1515 HOLCOMBE BLVD HOUSTON, TX 77030 Autocrine growth regulation in human gliomas

R01CA-51149-02 (RAD) MCKENNA, WILLIAM G HOSP OF THE UNIV OF PENN 3400 SPRUCE STREET PHILADELPHIA, PA 19104 Genetics of radiation resistance

R01CA-51150-01A2 (RAD) FREYER, JAMES P LOS ALAMOS NATIONAL LABORATORY PO BOX 1663 LOS ALAMOS, NM 87545 Nmr spectroscopy and imaging of tumor models

R55CA-51160-01A2 (ET) RINEHART, JOHN J SCOTT & WHITE MEMORIAL HOSPITA 2401 S 31ST ST TEMPLE, TX 76508 Chemotherapy and biologics in a murine tumor model

R01CA-51161-01A2 (RNM) QUADRI, SYED M UNIV OF NEBRASKA MED CTR 600 S 42ND ST OMAHA, NE 68198-1210 Linker-modulated distribution of radioimmunoconjugates

R01CA-51165-02 (ET) HEBER, DAVID UCLA SCHOOL OF MEDICINE 1000 VETERAN AVENUE LOS ANGELES, CA 90024 Megestrol acetate for treatment of cancer cachexia

R29CA-51167-02 (PTHB) DUBEAU, LOUIS K NORRIS JR COMP CANCER CENTER 1441 EASTLAKE AVENUE LOS ANGELES, CA 90033 Sequential genetic changes during tumor development

R29CA-51170-02 (MBY) HALL, DAVID J THOMAS JEFFERSON UNIVERSITY 208 BLSB; 233 SOUTH 10TH ST PHILADELPHIA, PA 19107 Analysis of the murine c-myc promoter

R01CA-51175-02 (ET) OZOLS, ROBERT F FOX CHASE CANCER CENTER 7701 BURHOLME AVENUE PHILADELPHIA, PA 19111 Reversal of drug resistance in ovarian cancer

P01CA-51183-01A1 (SRC) BERGER, NATHAN A CASE WESTERN RESERVE UNIV 2040 ADELBERT RD CLEVELAND, OH 44106 Modulation of alkylating agent chemotherapy in colon cancer

P01CA-51183-01A1 0001 (SRC) WILLSON, JAMES K Modulation of alkylating agent chemotherapy in colon cancer Models of alkylating agent resistance in colon cancer

P01CA-51183-01A1 0002 (SRC) VARNES, MARIE E Modulation of alkylating agent chemotherapy in colon cancer Thiol metabolism in alkylation agent resistant human colon cancer

P01CA-51183-01A1 0003 (SRC) BERGER, NATHAN A Modulation of alkylating agent chemotherapy in colon cancer Modulation of poly(ADP-ribose) and DNA repair in colon cancer chemotherapy

P01CA-51183-01A1 0004 (SRC) GERSON, STANTON L Modulation of alkylating agent chemotherapy in colon cancer Modulation of O-6 alkylguanine alkyltransferase in colon cancer chemotherapy

P01CA-51183-01A1 0005 (SRC) MARKOWITZ, SANFORD Modulation of alkylating agent chemotherapy in colon cancer Altered gene expression in alkylating agent resistant human colon cancer

P01CA-51183-01A1 0006 (SRC) LAZARUS, HILLARD Modulation of alkylating agent chemotherapy in colon cancer Clinical trials for the treatment of colon cancer

P01CA-51183-01A1 9001 (SRC) WILLSON, JAMES K Modulation of alkylating agent chemotherapy in colon cancer Core--Cell culture

P01CA-51183-01A1 9002 (SRC) HOPPEL, CHARLES L Modulation of alkylating agent chemotherapy in colon cancer Core--Pharmacology

R01CA-51189-03 (RAD) SAPARETO, STEPHEN A CITY OF HOPE NATIONAL MED CTR 1500 E DUARTE RD DUARTE, CA 91010 Quantitative evaluation of clinical hyperthermia

R01CA-51196-02 (EDC) PERERA, FREDERICA P COLUMBIA UNIV SCH OF PUBLIC HL 60 HAVEN AVENUE, B-109 NEW YORK, NY 10032 Biomarkers of environmental tobacco smoke exposure

R01CA-51197-02 (CBY) MAIHLE, NITA J MAYO FOUNDATION 200 FIRST STREET SOUTHWEST ROCHESTER, MN 55905 Tissue specific oncogenesis mediated by c-erb B

P01CA-51198-02 (SRC) HUANG, H K UNIV OF CALIFORNIA, LOS ANGELE BL-CHS CENTER FOR HEALTH SCIEN LOS ANGELES, CA 90024 PACS in radiology

P01CA-51198-02 0001 (SRC) KANGARLOO, HOOSHANG PACS in radiology PACS for intensive care units

P01CA-51198-02 0002 (SRC) LUFKIN, ROBERT B PACS in radiology PACS in neuroradiology

P01CA-51198-02 0003 (SRC) ABERLE, DENISE R PACS in radiology PACS for thoracic imaging

P01CA-51198-02 0004 (SRC) CHAN, KELBY PACS in radiology Radiological image compression

P01CA-51198-02 9001 (SRC) HUANG, H K PACS in radiology Core--Research and development of PACS-related technology

R01CA-51206-02 (ET) LUK, GORDON D WAYNE STATE UNIV SCH OF MEDICI 540 E CANFIELD/SCOTT HALL 2125 DETROIT, MI 48201 ODC as a therapeutic target--Gene function analysis

R01CA-51207-02 (ET) BERAN, MILOSALV U.T. M.D. ANDERSON CANCER CENT 1515 HOLCOMBE BLVD. HOUSTON, TEXAS 77030 MAMSA resistance and expression of p76 protein

R01CA-51210-02 (ET) ROSS, DAVID UNIVERSITY OF COLORADO CAMPUS BOX 297 BOULDER, COLORADO 80309-0297 Activation of the antitumor quinone AZQ by DT-diaphorase

R55CA-51211-01A1 (CPA) SCHULLER, HILDEGARD M UNIVERSITY OF TENNESSEE P O BOX 1071/COLL OF VET MED KNOXVILLE, TN 37901-1071 Mechanisms of neuroendocrine lung carcinogenesis by nitrate

R01CA-51218-02 (ET) GUENTHNER, THOMAS M UNIV OF ILLINOIS 835 S WOLCOTT CHICAGO, IL 60612 Mechanisms of enhancement of melphalan cytotoxicity

R01CA-51220-02 (ET) CHANG, ALFRED E UNIVERSITY OF MICHIGAN MED CTR 1500 EAST MEDICAL CENTER DRIVE ANN ARBOR, MI 48109-0331 Adoptive therapy of human cancer with sensitized T cells

R01CA-51228-02 (ET) HAMILTON, THOMAS FOX CHASE CANCER CENTER 7701 BURHOLME AVE PHILADELPHIA, PA 19111 DNA repair and resistance to cisplatin in ovarian cancer

R29CA-51229-01A1 (ET) GAMCSIK, MICHAEL P JOHNS HOPKINS UNIVERSITY 310 TRAYLOR, 720 RUTLAND AVE BALTIMORE, MD 21205 Drug resistance mechanisms in cancer cells

R01CA-51245-01A1 (RNM) LEVIN, DAVID N UNIVERSITY OF CHICAGO 5841 S MARYLAND AVE, BOX 429 CHICAGO, IL 60637 Integrated 3D display of MR, CT, and PET images

R01CA-51248-02 (RNM) GUR, DAVID UNIVERSITY OF PITTSBURGH 3550 TERRACE STREET PITTSBURGH, PA 15261 Digital acquisition and display of chest images

R01CA-51323-02 (EDC) MOSCICKI, BARBARA UNIV OF CALIFORNIA, SF 400 PARNASSUS AVENUE SAN FRANCISCO, CA 94143 Natural history of HPV in teens--infection to neoplasia

R01CA-51324-02 (RNM) LEE, SOO-YOUNG CORNELL UNIVERSITY ENGINEERING & THEORY CTR 336 ITHACA, NY 14853 Parallel image reconstruction for 3-D positron CT

R01CA-51325-03 (PTHB) PARCHMENT, RALPH E HIPPLE CANCER RESEARCH CENTER 4100 SOUTH KETTERING BLVD DAYTON, OH 45439-2092 Cell death, chalones, and cytotoxic metabolites

R01CA-51326-03 (PTHB) FULTON, AMY M UNIV OF MD SCHOOL OF MED 10 S PINE STREET BALTIMORE, MD 21201 Macrophage-induced tumor progression

R01CA-51329-02 (RNM) CHANG, WEI RUSH-PRESBYTERIAN 1653 WEST CONGRESS PARKWAY CHICAGO, IL 60612 Development of a multi-crystal brain spect system

R01CA-51345-01A1 (ET) KRADIN, RICHARD L MASSACHUSETTS GENERAL HOSPITAL 100 BLOSSOM STREET BOSTON, MA 02114 Adoptive immunotherapy of renal cell cancer

R01CA-51377-01A1 (CPA) KOHWI, YOSHINORI LA JOLLA CANCER RESEARCH FDN 10901 NORTH TORREY PINES RD LA JOLLA, CA 92037 Reaction of carcinogens with DNA and biological effects

R01CA-51388-02 (RAD) LITTLEFIELD, L GAYLE OAK RIDGE ASSOCIATED UNIV P. O. BOX 117 OAK RIDGE, TN 37831 Cytogenetic indices--Direct vs indirect radiation action

R01CA-51395-02 (PTHB) KLINGER, HAROLD P ALBERT EINSTEIN COLL OF MED 1300 MORRIS PARK AVENUE BRONX, NY 10461 Genomic alterations in cervical carcinoma

R01CA-51397-02 (RAD) ANTONUK, LARRY E UNIVERSITY OF MICHIGAN MED CTR 1500 E MEDICAL CTR DR ANN ARBOR, MI 48109-0010 MASDA, an amorphous silicon imager for radiotherapy

R01CA-51406-02 (ARR) LOTZ, MARTIN K UNIV OF CALIFORNIA, SAN DIEGO LA JOLLA, CA 92093 TGF beta and the pathogenesis of HIV

R01CA-51410-01A2 (PTHA) JACOBY, LEE B MASSACHUSETTS GENERAL HOSP-EAS 149 13TH STREET CHARLESTOWN, MA 02129 Clonal analysis of nervous system tumors

R01CA-51425-02 (IMB) UCKUN, FATIH M UNIV OF MINNESOTA HEALTH CTR HARVARD ST @ E RIVER RD/BX 356 MINNEAPOLIS, MN 55455 Immunobiology of normal and leukemic B-cell precursors

R01CA-51426-01A3 (EI) YUAN, DOROTHY C UT SOUTHWESTERN MED CTR 5323 HARRY HINES BLVD DALLAS, TX 75235-9072 Interactions between B lymhocytes and NK cells

R01CA-51434-02 (EI) KOHLER, HEINZ SAN DIEGO REGIONAL CANCER CENT 3099 SCIENCE PARK ROAD SAN DIEGO, CA 92121 Preclinical anti-idiotype therapy of cancer

R29CA-51438-01A2 (CPA) BUBLEY, GLENN J BETH ISRAEL HOSPITAL 330 BROOKLINE AVENUE BOSTON, MA 02215 Mechanisms of platinum-induced mutagenesis

R01CA-51443-02 (CPA) ROBERTSON, FREDIKA M UNIV OF MED & DENT OF NEW JERS ONE ROBERT W JOHNSON PLACE NEW BRUNSWICK, NJ 08903-0019 Role of keratinocyte sub-populations in tumor promotion

R29CA-51449-02 (VR) LACY, JILL YALE UNIVERSITY 333 CEDAR STREET/P O BOX 3333 NEW HAVEN, CT 06510 EBV transformation--Study of EBV-induced genes

R29CA-51452-03 (ET) MULDER, KATHLEEN M PENN STATE/ HERSHEY MEDICAL CT P O BOX 850 HERSHEY, PA 17033 Mechanisms of TGF-beta resistance in colon carcinoma cells

R01CA-51462-03 (SSS) BALTIMORE, DAVID THE ROCKEFELLER UNIVERSITY 1230 YORK AVENUE NEW YORK, N Y 10021 Malignancy & normal dev in pre-B lymphocytes

R01CA-51477-02 (SRC) PENG, YEI-MEI UNIVERSITY OF ARIZONA 1515 NORTH CAMPBELL AVENUE TUCSON, AZ 85724 The relationship between blood and tissue micronutrient

R01CA-51479-02 (SRC) NIERENBERG, DAVID W DARTMOUTH MEDICAL SCHOOL HINMAN BOX 7650 HANOVER, NH 03756 Human blood and tissue levels of vitamins A, E, and Carotenoids

R01CA-51482-05 (BCE) KATZENELLENBOGEN, BENITA S UNIVERSITY OF ILLINOIS 407 SOUTH GOODWIN AVENUE URBANA, IL 61801 Progesterone receptor regulation

R01CA-51485-02 (PTHB) ROY-BURMAN, PRADIP UNIV OF SOUTHERN CALIFORNIA 2011 ZONAL AVENUE - HMR 212 LOS ANGELES, CA 90033 Pathogenetic mechanisms in feline leukemia

R01CA-51487-02 (ET) KIANG, DAVID T UNIVERSITY OF MINNESOTA HARVARD ST EAST RIVER RD MINNEAPOLIS, MN 55455 Modulation of cell-cell communication in breast cancer

P01CA-51495-02 (SRC) LEE, WEN-HWA UNIV OF CALIFORNIA, SAN DIEGO LA JOLLA, CA 92093 Mechanisms of cancer suppression by the human retinoblastoma

P01CA-51495-02 0003 (SRC) FRIEDMANN, THEODORE Mechanisms of cancer suppression by the human retinoblastoma Gene delivery system

P01CA-51495-02 0004 (SRC) LEE, WEN-HWA Mechanisms of cancer suppression by the human retinoblastoma Cellular function of the retinoblastoma gene product

P01CA-51495-02 0001 (SRC) LEE, WEN-HWA Mechanisms of cancer suppression by the human retinoblastoma Mechanisms of cancer suppression by the retinoblastoma gene

P01CA-51495-02 0002 (SRC) LEE, WEN-HWA Mechanisms of cancer suppression by the human retinoblastoma Retinoblastoma gene -- Second transcription

P01CA-51495-02 0005 (SRC) HEDRICH, STEPHEN Mechanisms of cancer suppression by the human retinoblastoma Transgenic RB gene expression

P01CA-51495-02 9001 (SRC) SCULLY, PETER Mechanisms of cancer suppression by the human retinoblastoma Pathology and nude mice

P01CA-51495-02 9002 (SRC) LEE, WEN-HWA Mechanisms of cancer suppression by the human retinoblastoma DNA synthesizer and antibody production

R01CA-51496-03 (CBY) BLAIR, LESLIE A C YALE UNIV, SCHOOL OF MED 333 CEDAR ST, PO BX 3333 NEW HAVEN, CT 06510 The function of the mas oncogene

R29CA-51497-02 (PTHB) DANG, CHI V JOHNS HOPKINS UNIV MEDICAL SCH 720 RUTLAND AVENUE BALTIMORE, MD 21205 Functional domains of c-myc protein

R01CA-51498-02 (MEP) MORDAN, LAWRENCE J UNIV HAWAII/CNCR RES CTR HAWAI 1236 LAUHALA STREET HONOLULU, HI 96813 Retinoids effects on Ca2+ and mitogenesis in carcinogenesis

R29CA-51504-02 (PTHB) MARKOWITZ, SANFORD D CASE WESTERN RESERVE UNIVERSIT 11001 CEDAR AVE CLEVELAND, OH 44106 Novel oncogene related product detected in human colon

R01CA-51506-02 (SRC) KRINSKY, NORMAN I TUFTS UNIVERSITY SCHOOL OF MED 136 HARRISON AVENUE BOSTON, MA 02111 Fat soluble micronutrients in human plasma and tissues

R29CA-51512-02 (ET) POLLOCK, RAPHAEL E UNIV TEXAS M.D. ANDERSON CAN C 1515 HOLCOMBE BLVD HOUSTON, TX 77030 Surgical stress impairment of human NK cell cytotoxicity

R01CA-51515-02 (ET) NGO, FRANK Q CLEVELAND CLINIC FOUNDATION 9500 EUCLID AVENUE CLEVELAND, OH 44106 Tumor blood flow after neutron irradiation

R01CA-51524-02 (BIO) PORTER, CARL W ROSWELL PARK MEMORIAL INST ELM & CARLTON STREETS BUFFALO, NY 14263 Implications of inducible polyamine catabolism

R29CA-51539-03 (MEP) BOYD, DOUGLAS DAVID UNIV OF TX MD ANDERSON CAN CTR 1515 HOLCOMBE BLVD. HOUSTON, TX 77030 Regulation of urokinase and its receptor in colon cancer

R01CA-51540-01A1 (PTHB) TURLEY, EVA ANN MANITOBA INSTITUTE/ CELL BIOLO WINNIPEG, MANITOBA R3E 0V9 CANADA Role of hyaluronan in tumor cell locomotion

R01CA-51549-06 (MEP) GOLDFARB, STANLEY UNIV OF WISCONSIN MED SCH 1300 UNIVERSITY AVENUE MADISON, WI 53706 Biology of the mouse hepatocarcinogenesis

PROJECT NO., ORGANIZATIONAL UNIT., INVESTIGATOR, ADDRESS, TITLE

PROJECT NO., ORGANIZATIONAL UNIT., INVESTIGATOR, ADDRESS, TITLE

R43CA-51553-01A1 (HUD) CLARK, D JOSEPH VIDEODISCOVERY, INC 1700 WESTLAKE AVENUE NORTH SEATTLE, WA 98109-3012 Interactive videodisc and cancer prevention

R43CA-51568-01A1 (ET) RAYCHAUDHURI, SYAMAL IDEC PHARMACEUTICALS CORPORATI 11099 N TORREY PINES ROAD LA JOLLA, CA 92037 Anti-I cell receptor antibodies for cancer immunotherapy

R44CA-51576-02 (SSS) HENDRICKS, JOHN B PO BOX 2470 HUNTSVILLE, AL 35804 A cryocooler for superconducting imaging systems

R44CA-51595-02 (SSS) MCGRATH, CHARLES M GRACE BIO-ONCOLOGY LABORATORY 900 AUBURN ROAD PONTIAC, MI 48057 Freeze-transfer method for in situ detection of RNA

R01CA-51605-03 (ARR) CHAMPOUX, JAMES J UNIVERSITY OF WASHINGTON SCHOOL OF MEDICINE SEATTLE, WA 98195 Plus-strand priming & integration by MULV & HIV

U01CA-51610-03 (SRC) MEYSKENS, FRANK JR CANCER CENTER, UCIMC 101 THE CITY DRIVE ORANGE, CA 92688 Chemoprevention of human melanoma

R01CA-51621-03 (ARR) GILL, PARKASH S UNIV OF S CALIF/KENNETH NORRIS 1441 EASTLAKE AVE LOS ANGELES, CA 90033 Pathogenisis of Kaposi's sarcoma

R01CA-51657-03 (ET) YALOWICH, JACK C UNIVERSITY OF PITTSBURGH W1355 BIOMEDICAL SCIENCE TOWER PITTSBURGH, PA 15261 Mechanisms and modulation of etoposide (VP-16) resistance

R01CA-51664-02 (PTHB) YUNIS, JORGE J HAHNEMANN UNIVERSITY-M.S. 412 BROAD & VINE PHILADELPHIA, PA 19102-1192 Gene defects of band 11q23 in hematologic malignancies

U01CA-51671-03 (SRC) ERIKSEN, MICHAEL P U OF TEXAS, MD ANDERSON CA CTR 1515 HOLCOMBE BOULEVARD HOUSTON, TX 77030 Cancer prevention for rural energy workers

U01CA-51686-03 (SRC) SORENSEN, GLORIAN C UNIV OF MASSACHUSETTS MED SCH 55 LAKE AVENUE, NORTH WORCESTER, MA 01605 Worksite cancer prevention project

U01CA-51687-03 (SRC) VARNES, JILL W COLL OF HLTH & HUMAN PERFORMAN 232 FLG, UNIVERSITY OF FLORIDA GAINESVILLE, FL 32611-2834 GTE--Good for me--Cancer prevention campaign A

U01CA-51688-03 (SRC) GRIZZLE, JAMES E FRED HUTCHINSON CANCER RES CTR 1124 COLUMBIA STREET SEATTLE, WA 98104 Coordinating worksite health promotion interventions

R01CA-51712-02 (PTHB) YARDEN, YOSEF WEIZMANN INSTITUTE OF SCIENCE PO BOX 26 REHOVOT, ISRAEL 76100 Reverse genetics of the neu and kit protooncogenes

R01CA-51714-01A2 (PTHB) RAZ, AVRAHAM MICHIGAN CANCER FDN 110 E WARREN AVENUE DETROIT, MI 48201-1379 Characterization of motility factor receptor

R01CA-51716-01A1 (CPA) SCOTT, ROBERT E THE UNIV OF TENNESSEE 800 MADISON AVENUE MEMPHIS, TN 38163 Pathology in anticancer/cancer suppressor regulation

R29CA-51728-02 (ET) CORNWELL, MARILYN M UW CLINICAL CANCER CENTER 600 N HIGHLAND AVENUE MADISON, WI 53792 Multidrug resistance--Transcription of the mdrl gene

R01CA-51729-01A1 (BLR) NATHWANI, BHARAT N UNIV OF SOUTHERN CALIFORNIA 2011 ZONAL AVE LOS ANGELES, CA 90033 Clinical trials of expert system on lymph node pathology

R01CA-51735-02 (CPA) HOLT, JEFFREY T VANDERBILT UNIVERSITY SCHOOL OF MEDICINE NASHVILLE, TN 37232 Transcriptional mechanisms of carcinogenesis

R01CA-51748-03 (PBC) FREYTAG, SVEND O HENRY FORD HOSPITAL 2799 WEST GRAND BLVD DETRIOT, MI 48202 Mechanisms of c-myc oncogene action

R01CA-51756-01A1 (ET) WEBB, THOMAS E OHIO STATE UNIV RES FDN 371 HAMILTON HALL COLUMBUS, OH 43210 Anti-tumor activity of glucarate and HPR

R01CA-51770-01A1 (ET) JAYARAM, HIREMAGALUR N INDIANA UNIV SCHOOL OF MED 702 BARNHILL DRIVE INDIANAPOLIS, IN 46202-5200 Metabolism of tiazofurin in human leukemia cells

R01CA-51771-02 (RAD) FINGAR, VICTOR H UNIVERSITY OF LOUISVILLE LOUISVILLE, KENTUCKY 40292 Mechanistic studies of PDT-induced vascular damage

R01CA-51779-02 (EVR) JAY, GILBERT AMERICAN RED CROSS 15601 CRABBS BRANCH WAY ROCKVILLE, MD 20855 Neoplasia disorders induced by HTLV-1 in transgenic mice

R55CA-51782-01A1 (MEP) CLARKE, ROBERT GEORGETOWN UNIVERSITY 3800 RESERVOIR ROAD, NW WASHINGTON, DC 20007 Hormonal autonomy in hormone dependent tumors

R01CA-51792-02 (VR) ENRIETTO, PAULA STATE UNIVERSITY OF NEW YORK STONY BROOK, NY 11794-8621 Characterization of proteins that interact with rel

R01CA-51794-02 (MCHA) HUA, DUY H KANSAS STATE UNIVERSITY WILLARD HALL MANHATTAN, KS 66506 Sulfinyl ketimines

R01CA-51802-02 (OMA) MUKHTAR, HASAN UNIV HOSPITALS OF CLEVELAND 2074 ABINGTON ROAD CLEVELAND, OH 44106 Phthalocyanine photodynamic therapy of skin tumors

R01CA-51814-01A2 (ET) FERRONE, SOLDANO NEW YORK MEDICAL COLLEGE BASIC SCIENCES BUILDING VALHALLA, NEW YORK 10595 Immunotherapy of melanoma with antidiotypic antibodies

R55CA-51823-01A1 (ET) SKLAREW, ROBERT J NEW YORK MEDICAL COLLEGE 100 GRASSLANDS ROAD ELMSFORD, NY 10523 Breast cancer receptor paterns, ploidy and kinetics

R01CA-51825-02 (CPA) SNOW, ELIZABETH T NEW YORK UNIVERSITY MED CTR 550 FIRST AVENUE NEW YORK, NY 10016 Carcinogen-induced deletion mutagenesis in V79 cells

R01CA-51826-02 (ET) SKLAR, MARSHALL D RADIATION ONCOLOGY (D-31) P O BOX 016960 MIAMI, FL 33101 Characterization of cisplatinum resistances genes

R01CA-51830-02 (MEP) CHUNG, FUNG-LUNG AMERICAN HEALTH FOUNDATION 0NE DANA ROAD VALHALLA, NY 10595 Endogenous enals in nitrosamine carcinogenesis

R01CA-51831-01A1 (EDC) KOEHLER, KENNETH J IOWA STATE UNIVERSITY AMES, IA 50011 Statistical methods for correlated survival data

R29CA-51841-01A1 (MEP) BARCELLOS-HOFF, MARY H LAWRENCE BERKELEY LABORATORY 1 CYCLOTRON RD, MAILSTOP 74-15 BERKELEY, CA 94720 Stromal influence on expression of preneoplasia

R01CA-51852-01A1 (PTHB) GETZ, MICHAEL J MAYO FOUNDATION 200 FIRST STREET SOUTHWEST ROCHESTER, MN 55905 Genetics and cell physiology of murine tissue factor

R01CA-51857-02 (ET) SHAW, DENISE R UNIV OF AL AT BIRMINGHAM UAB STATION BIRMINGHAM, AL 35294 Human tumor-specific antibodies produced in SCID mice

R29CA-51860-01A2 (CPA) SCICCHITANO, DAVID A NEW YORK UNIVERSITY 100 WASHINGTON SQUARE EAST NEW YORK, NY 10003 Sequence-specific repair of alkylated cellular DNA

R01CA-51864-02 (PTHB) TSUJIMOTO, Y WISTAR INSTITUTE 36TH AND SPRUCE STREETS PHILADELPHIA, PA 19104 Study on the bc1-2 rearrangements in CLL

R01CA-51870-01A1 (RAD) MURRAY, DAVID U OF TEXAS/ANDERSON CANCER CTR 1515 HOLCOMBE BLVD HOUSTON, TX 77030 DNA damage in the radiation response of tissues & tumors

U01CA-51880-02 (SRC) HOUSTON, L L CETUS CORPORATION 1400 53RD STREET EMERYVILLE, CA 94608 Engineered antibreast cancer single-chain fv immunotoxin

U01CA-51880-02 0001 (SRC) HUSTON, JAMES S Engineered antibreast cancer single-chain fv immunotoxin Genetic engineering and protein production

U01CA-51880-02 0002 (SRC) HOUSTON, LOU L Engineered antibreast cancer single-chain fv immunotoxin Chemical crosslinking and immunology

U01CA-51880-02 0003 (SRC) WEINER, LOUIS M Engineered antibreast cancer single-chain fv immunotoxin In vivo and in vitro pharmacology studies

U01CA-51880-02 0004 (SRC) STAFFORD, WALTER F Engineered antibreast cancer single-chain fv immunotoxin Biophysical analysis

R01CA-51884-02 (PTHB) KRAMER, RANDALL H UNIV OF CALIF, SAN FRANCISCO HSW 604 SAN FRANCISCO, CA 94143-0512 Integrin receptor for laminin in malignant melanoma

R01CA-51886-02 (CPA) JAY, GILBERT AMERICAN RED CROSS 15601 CRABBS BRANCH WAY ROCKVILLE, MD 20855 Role of the hepatitis B virus in inducing malignancies in transgenic mice

R01CA-51887-02 (ALY) RUDD, CHRISTOPHER E DANA-FARBER CANCER INSTITUTE 44 BINNEY STREET BOSTON, MA 02115 Molecular analysis of the CD4/CD8:p56 lck complex

R01CA-51888-01A1 (PBC) DIXIT, VISHVA M 1301 CATHERINE STREET ANN ARBOR, MI 48109-0602 Novel thrombospondin receptors on squamous carcinoma cells

R01CA-51890-02 (PC) BUSS, JANICE E LA JOLLA CANCER RESEARCH FDN 10901 NORTH TORREY PINES ROAD LA JOLLA, CA 92037 Control of membrane binding and oncogenes by p21ras

R01CA-51893-01A1 (PTHB) TSICHLIS, PHILIP N FOX CHASE CANCER CTR 7701 BURHOLME AVENUE PHILADELPHIA, PA 19111 Role of MLVI-1 and MLVI-4 genes in human oncogenesis

U01CA-51908-02 (SRC) LIPPMAN, MARC E LOMBARDI CANCER RESEARCH CTR 3800 RESERVOIR RD, NW WASHINGTON, DC 20007 Growth regulation as targets in breast cancer treatment

U01CA-51908-02 0001 (SRC) MARTIN, MARY BETH Growth regulation as targets in breast cancer treatment Hormonal regulation of gene expression

U01CA-51908-02 0002 (SRC) SAUSVILLE, EDWARD A Growth regulation as targets in breast cancer treatment Signal transduction

U01CA-51908-02 0003 (SRC) CLARK, ROBERT Growth regulation as targets in breast cancer treatment Control of malignant progression

U01CA-51908-02 0004 (SRC) WELLSTEIN, ANTON Growth regulation as targets in breast cancer treatment Heparin binding growth factors

U01CA-51908-02 0005 (SRC) DICKSON, ROBERT B Growth regulation as targets in breast cancer treatment Regulation of invasion

R01CA-51912-01A1 (PTHB) TLSTY, THEA D UNIV OF NC AT CHAPEL HILL CHAPEL HILL, NC 27599-7295 Gene amplification-- A tool to study neoplasia

R01CA-51918-01A1 (PTHB) SHOWE, LOUISE C WISTAR INSTITUTE 36TH AND SPRUCE STREETS PHILADELPHIA, PA 19104 Interactions of V-ERBA/V-ERBB/band 3 in erythroleukemia

R01CA-51921-01A2 (EDC) TONIOLO, PAOLO G NEW YORK UNIVERSITY MED CTR 341 EAST 25TH STREET NEW YORK, NY 10010 Mammographic parenchymal patterns and breast cancer risk

R01CA-51923-01A1 (EDC) HAILE, ROBERT W UNIVERSITY OF CALIFORNIA LOS ANGELES, CA 90024-1772 Sigmoidoscopy based case control study of polyps

R29CA-51926-01A1 (BEM) CELLA, DAVID F RUSH CANCER CENTER 1725 W HARRISON STREET CHICAGO, IL 60612 Improving quality of life in advanced cancer

R01CA-51932-02 (EDC) POTTER, JOHN D UNIV OF MINNESOTA SCHOOL OF PH 611 BEACON STREET, SE MINNEAPOLIS, MN 55455 Calcium and colorectal epitelial cell proliferation

R01CA-51935-01A2 (RNM) GLICKSON, JERRY D JOHNS HOPKINS UNIV SCH OF MED 600 NORTH WOLFE ST, MRI-110 BALTIMORE, MD 21205 NMR prediction and monitoring of radiation response

R01CA-51945-02 (REN) FEY, EDWARD G UNIV OF MASSACHUSETTS MED SCH 55 LAKE AVENUE NORTH WORCESTER, MA 01655 Antibodies to nuclear proteins in cervical cancer

U01CA-51946-02 (SRC) REISFELD, RALPH A SCRIPPS RESEARCH INSTITUTE 10666 N TORREY PINES RD LA JOLLA, CA 92037 New tumor models for the development of immunotherapy

U01CA-51946-02 0001 (SRC) GILLIES, STEPHEN D New tumor models for the development of immunotherapy Production of chimeric antibodies

U01CA-51946-02 0002 (SRC) REISFELD, RALPH A New tumor models for the development of immunotherapy Tumor model system

U01CA-51946-02 9001 (SRC) MULLER, BARBARA M New tumor models for the development of immunotherapy Nude and SCID mouse core

R01CA-51949-02 (ET) HOUGHTON, PETER J ST JUDE CHILDREN'S RESEARCH HO 332 NORTH LAUDERDALE/PO BOX 31 MEMPHIS, TN 38101-0318 Therapy of colon cancer with diarylsulfonylureas

R01CA-51950-01A1 (RNM) GLICKSON, JERRY D JOHNS HOPKINS UNIV SCH OF MED 600 NORTH WOLFE STREET BALTIMORE, MD 21205 In Vivo NMR of tumors and their response to chemotherapy

U01CA-51958-02 (SRC) STEPLEWSKI, ZENON S THE WISTAR INSTITUTE 36TH AND SPRUCE STREETS PHILADELPHIA, PA 19104 Radioisotope-antibody conjugates for cancer therapy

U01CA-51958-02 0001 (SRC) CURTIS, PETER Radioisotope-antibody conjugates for cancer therapy Modified antibodies for radioisotope coupling

PROJECT NO., ORGANIZATIONAL UNIT., INVESTIGATOR, ADDRESS, TITLE

U01CA-51958-02 0002 (SRC) MAUSNER, LEONARD Radioisotope-antibody conjugates for cancer therapy Evaluation of immunoconjugates of Cu-67 and Sm-153

U01CA-51958-02 0003 (SRC) HAINFIELD, JAMES F Radioisotope-antibody conjugates for cancer therapy Radioactive gold cluster immunoconjugates

U01CA-51958-02 9001 (SRC) STEPLEWSKI, ZENON S Radioisotope-antibody conjugates for cancer therapy Core--Radioisotope-antibody conjugates for cancer therapy

R01CA-51960-02 (RNM) THAKUR, MADHUKAR L THOMAS JEFFERSON UNIVERSITY 11TH AND WALNUT STREET PHILADELPHIA, PA 19107 Simplified labeling of antibodies with Tc-99m and Re-186

R01CA-51962-02 (SSS) TSIATIS, ANASTASIOS A DANA-FARBER CANCER INSTITUTE 44 BINNEY STREET BOSTON, MA 02115 Statistical analysis of time to event data in cancer

R01CA-51968-01A1 (PBC) LIU, BRIAN C S MT SINAI SCHOOL OF MEDICINE ONE GUSTAVE L LEVY PL, BOX 127 NEW YORK, NY 10029 Protease inhibitors in human bladder cancer invasion

R29CA-51971-02 (PTHB) POWELL, MARIANNE B UNIV OF AZ, AZ CANCER CENTER 1515 N CAMPBELL AVE TUCSON, AZ 85724 Immortalization and transformation of human melanocytes

R01CA-51972-02 (ET) WELLS, WILLIAM W MICHIGAN STATE UNIVERSITY EAST LANSING, MI 48824 Thioltransferase in normal and transformed cells

R29CA-51982-03 (VR) BOS, TIMOTHY J EASTERN VA MEDICAL SCHOOL 700 WEST OLNEY RD, PO BOX 1980 NORFOLK, VA 23501 Analysis of target genes activated by the jun oncoprotei

R01CA-51985-01A1 (MGN) KRONTIRIS, THEODORE G NEW ENGLAND MEDICAL CENTER 750 WASHINGTON S, BOX 245 BOSTON, MA 02111 Determinants of bc12 oncogene translocations

P01CA-51987-02 (SRC) MESSING, EDWARD M CLINICAL SCIENCE CENTER 600 HIGHLAND AVENUE MADISON, WI 53792 Selected mechanisms of human bladder carcinogenesis

P01CA-51987-02 0001 (SRC) REZNIKOFF, CATHERINE A Selected mechanisms of human bladder carcinogenesis: Chromosomal losses in multistep transformation of human uroepithelial cells

P01CA-51987-02 0002 (SRC) SWAMINATHAN, SANTHANAM Selected mechanisms of human bladder carcinogenesis Susceptibility factors in bladder carcinogenesis

P01CA-51987-02 0003 (SRC) MESSING, EDWARD M Selected mechanisms of human bladder carcinogenesis Mechanisms of urothelial responsiveness to epidermal growth factor

P01CA-51987-02 9001 (SRC) REZNIKOFF, CATHERINE A Selected mechanisms of human bladder carcinogenesis Core--Tissue culture facility

U01CA-51992-02 (SRC) MCCORMICK, FRANK P CETUS CORPORATION 1400 53RD ST EMERYVILLE, CA 94608 Discovery of drugs inhibiting oncogenic ras proteins

U01CA-51992-02 0001 (SRC) MCCORMICK, FRANK Discovery of drugs inhibiting oncogenic ras proteins Interaction of ras, p21, and GAP

U01CA-51992-02 0002 (SRC) WITTINGHOFER, ALFRED Discovery of drugs inhibiting oncogenic ras proteins X-ray crystallographic analysis of ras, p21, and GAP

U01CA-51992-02 0003 (SRC) WOOD, ALEX Discovery of drugs inhibiting oncogenic ras proteins Ident. and analysis of chemical inhibitors of ras function

U01CA-51992-02 0004 (SRC) REDFIELD, ALFRED Discovery of drugs inhibiting oncogenic ras proteins NMR analysis of P-21 and GAP

U01CA-51992-02 9001 (SRC) SHERMAN, MICHAEL Discovery of drugs inhibiting oncogenic ras proteins Core facility

P01CA-51993-01A1 (SRC) DAWSON, MARCIA I SRI INTERNATIONAL 333 RAVENSWOOD AVENUE MENLO PARK, CA 94025 Receptor selective cancer chemopreventive retinoids

P01CA-51993-01A1 0001 (SRC) DAWSON, MARCIA I Receptor selective cancer chemopreventive retinoids Retinoid design and synthesis

P01CA-51993-01A1 0002 (SRC) CRAMER, RICHAARD D Receptor selective cancer chemopreventive retinoids Retinal theoretical studies

P01CA-51993-01A1 0003 (SRC) PFAHL, MAGNUS Receptor selective cancer chemopreventive retinoids Nuclear receptors as mediators of retinal response

P01CA-51993-01A1 0004 (SRC) ELY, KATHRYN R Receptor selective cancer chemopreventive retinoids Molecular structure of retinoic acid receptors

P01CA-51993-01A1 9001 (SRC) RUDD, COLETTE J Receptor selective cancer chemopreventive retinoids Bioassay core

R29CA-51995-01A1 (CPA) RONAI, ZEEV A AMERICAN HEALTH FOUNDATION ONE DANA ROAD VALHALLA, NY 10595 Mechanisms of UV-radiation inducible protein expression

R29CA-51998-02 (GMA) KAETZEL, CHARLOTTE S CASE WESTERN RESERVE UNIVERSIT 2085 ADELBERT ROAD CLEVELAND, OH 44106 Regulation of the polymeric immunoglobulin receptor

R01CA-52001-01A1 (EI) FARBER, JOSHUA M JOHNS HOPKINS UNIV SCH OF MED 725 N WOLFE STREET BALTIMORE, MD 21205 Novel macrophage derived interferon induced cytokines

R01CA-52003-01A1 (TOX) LINZ, JOHN E MICHIGAN STATE UNIVERSITY 234B FOOD SCIENCE BLDG. EAST LANSING, MI 48824-1224 Aflatoxin B-1 biosynthesis in Aspergillus parasiticus

R01CA-52004-02 (VR) SPECK, SAMUEL H DANA-FARBER CANCER INSTITUTE 44 BINNEY STREET BOSTON, MA 02115 Control of EBV lytic gene expression during latency

R01CA-52006-01A1 (MEP) WARGOVICH, MICHAEL J UNIV OF TEX M D ANDERSON CAN C 1515 HOLCOMBE BOULEVARD HOUSTON, TX 77030 Calcium inhibition of colon cancer progression

R29CA-52008-01A1 (ET) KARCZMAR, GREGORY S UNIVERSITY OF CHICAGO MED CENT BOX 429/5841 SOUTH MARYLAND AV CHICAGO, IL 60637 Response of tumors to TNF studied by magnetic resonance

P01CA-52009-01A1 (SRC) REDDY, PREMKUMAR E THE WISTAR INSTITUTE 36TH AND SPRUCE STREETS PHILADELPHIA, PA 19104 Viruses and oncogenes in hematopoietic malignancies

P01CA-52009-01A1 0001 (SRC) REDDY, PREMKUMAR E Viruses and oncogenes in hematopoietic malignancies Role of myb gene in cell growth and differentiation

P01CA-52009-01A1 0002 (SRC) ROVERA, GIOVANNI Viruses and oncogenes in hematopoietic malignancies Genetic analysis of growth factor dependent myelomonocytic differentiation

P01CA-52009-01A1 0003 (SRC) RAUSCHER, FRANK J Viruses and oncogenes in hematopoietic malignancies Transcription factor fos-jun family--Hematopoietic cell growth & differentiation

P01CA-52009-01A1 0004 (SRC) RICCIARDI, ROBERT P Viruses and oncogenes in hematopoietic malignancies HHV-6 new protein in HTLV-1 activation & cellular transformation

U01CA-52020-02 (SRC) MCCAFFREY, RONALD P UNIVERSITY HOSPITAL 88 E NEWTON STREET BOSTON, MA 02118 Specific therapy for TdT-positive leukemia/lymphoma

U01CA-52020-02 0001 (SRC) MCCAFFREY, RONALD P Specific therapy for TdT-positive leukemia/lymphoma Cell biology program

U01CA-52020-02 0002 (SRC) BEARDSLEY, G PETER Specific therapy for TdT-positive leukemia/lymphoma Biochemical pharmacology program

U01CA-52020-02 0003 (SRC) CHU, CHUNG K Specific therapy for TdT-positive leukemia/lymphoma Medicinal chemistry program

R29CA-52025-02 (RAD) FRANKLIN, WILLIAM A MONTEFIORE MEDICAL CENTER 111 EAST 210TH ST BRONX, NY 10467 Novel enzyme acting on radiation-damaged DNA

R01CA-52040-01A1 (RAD) WALLACE, SUSAN S UNIVERSITY OF VERMONT BURLINGTON, VT 05405 Processing of damage by translesion DNA synthesis

P01CA-52051-01A1 (SRC) HONG, WAUN KI UNIVERSITY OF TEXAS 1515 HOLCOMBE BLVD HOUSTON, TX 77030 Chemoprevention of aerodigestive epithelial cancers

P01CA-52051-01A1 0001 (SRC) HONG, WAUN K Chemoprevention of aerodigestive epithelial cancers Chemoprevention of second primary tumors with 13-cis retinoic acid

P01CA-52051-01A1 0002 (SRC) SCHANTZ, STIMSON Chemoprevention of aerodigestive epithelial cancers Genetic susceptibility to second primary tumors--Risk assessment model

P01CA-52051-01A1 0003 (SRC) LIPPMAN, SCOTT M Chemoprevention of aerodigestive epithelial cancers Chemoprevention trial in oral premalignancy

P01CA-52051-01A1 0004 (SRC) HITTLEMAN, WALTER N Chemoprevention of aerodigestive epithelial cancers Field cancerization--Cellular and molecular tests of hypothesis

P01CA-52051-01A1 0005 (SRC) TAINSKY, MICHAEL A Chemoprevention of aerodigestive epithelial cancers Determinants of growth and differentiation of head and neck tumor

P01CA-52051-01A1 0006 (SRC) LOTAN, REUBEN Chemoprevention of aerodigestive epithelial cancers Retinoic acid receptors in malignant oral mucosa cells with retinoids

P01CA-52051-01A1 9001 (SRC) PAJAK, THOMAS F Chemoprevention of aerodigestive epithelial cancers Core--Biostatistics/data management

P01CA-52051-01A1 9002 (SRC) WINN, RODGER J Chemoprevention of aerodigestive epithelial cancers Core--Biostatistics/data management

P01CA-52051-01A1 9003 (SRC) FRITSCHE, HERBERT A Chemoprevention of aerodigestive epithelial cancers Core--Analytical chemistry

P01CA-52051-01A1 9004 (SRC) LEE, JIN S Chemoprevention of aerodigestive epithelial cancers Core--Histology Lab

P01CA-52051-01A1 9005 (SRC) CHAMBERLAIN, ROBERT M Chemoprevention of aerodigestive epithelial cancers Core--Clinical adherence

P01CA-52051-01A1 9006 (SRC) NICHAMAN, MILTON Z Chemoprevention of aerodigestive epithelial cancers Core--Nutritional epidemiology

P01CA-52066-02 (SRC) DRITSCHILO, ANATOLY GEORGETOWN UNIVERSITY 3800 RESERVOIR ROAD, NW WASHINGTON, DC 20007 Molecular basis of tumor resistance to ionizing radiation

P01CA-52066-02 0001 (SRC) DRITSCHILO, ANATOLY Molecular basis of tumor resistance to ionizing radiation Characterization of differential gene expression in resistant cells

P01CA-52066-02 0002 (SRC) KASID, USHA N Molecular basis of tumor resistance to ionizing radiation Molecular and biochemical mechanisms of radiation resistance

P01CA-52066-02 0003 (SRC) JORGENSON, TIMOTHY J Molecular basis of tumor resistance to ionizing radiation DNA damage and repair

P01CA-52066-02 0004 (SRC) NOTARIO-RUIZ, VINCENTE Molecular basis of tumor resistance to ionizing radiation Genetic modulation of cellular radiation response

P01CA-52066-02 9001 (SRC) HURLEY, CAROLYN K Molecular basis of tumor resistance to ionizing radiation Core--Macromolecular sequencing and synthesis

R01CA-52072-02 (CPA) DER, CHANNING J LA JOLLA CANCER RESEARCH FDN 10901 NORTH TORREY PINES ROAD LA JOLLA, CA 92037 Krev-1 and suppression of ras oncogene transformation

R01CA-52085-02 (CPA) NORRIS, JAMES S MEDICAL UNIV OF SOUTH CAROLINA 171 ASHLEY AVENUE CHARLESTON, SC 29425 Hormonal carcinogenesis--mechanisms

R15CA-52091-01A1 (EVR) LUCHER, LYNNE A ILLINOIS STATE UNIVERSITY NORMAL, IL 61761 Host species influence on adenovirus replication

R01CA-52098-01A1 (VR) LAU, ALAN F UNIVERSITY OF HAWAII 1236 LAUHALA STREET HONOLULU, HI 96813 Connexin43 phosphorylation in RSV-infected cells

R01CA-52102-02 (RAD) CHAPMAN, J DONALD FOX CHASE CANCER CENTER 7701 BURHOLME AVENUE PHILADELPHIA, PA 19111 Preclinical interstitial photodynamic therapy research

R01CA-52108-02 (MEP) MOLDAWER, LYLE L NEW YORK HOSP-CORNELL MED CTR 525 EAST 66TH ST NEW YORK, NY 10021 Cytokines as endogenous mediators of cancer cachexia

R29CA-52112-02 (PTHB) LIN, MING-FONG UNIV OF SOUTHERN CALIFORNIA 2025 ZONAL AVE LOS ANGELES, CA 90033 Biology of human prostate cancer

R01CA-52121-02 (MGN) SCHULTZ, ROGER A UNIVERSITY OF MD SCH OF MED 655 WEST BALTIMORE STREET BALTIMORE, MD 21201 Chromosomal complementation of bloom syndrome cells

R35CA-52127-02 (SRC) ESSIGMANN, JOHN M MASSACHUSETTS INSTITUTE OF TEC CAMBRIDGE, MA 02139 Cellular responses to DNA damage

R29CA-52140-01A1 (EVR) POZZATTI, RUDY O JEROME H HOLLAND LABORATORY 15601 CRABBS BRANCH WAY ROCKVILLE, MD 20855 Transformation properties of the htlv-1 tax gene

R29CA-52142-01A1 (VR) CLARK, STEVEN S UNIV OF WISCONSIN HLTH SCI CTR 600 HIGHLAND AVENUE MADISON, WI 53792 Transformation by BCR-ABL oncogenes

R01CA-52151-02 (SRC) MCCLAY, EDWARD F UNIVERSITY OF CALIF. SAN DIEGO LA JOLLA, CA 92093 Modulation of cisplatin resistance in malignant melanoma
R01CA-52166-02 (SRC) ERNSTOFF, MARC S PITT CAN INST/DIV OF MED ONCO 201 DESOTO STREET PITTSBURGH, PA 15213 Metallothionein and tumor resistance to chemotherapy
R01CA-52168-02 (SRC) SIKIC, BRANIMIR I STANFORD UNIVERSITY MEDICAL CENTER STANFORD, CA 94305-5306 Expression and modulation of multidrug resistance
R01CA-52177-02 (EI) DIAMOND, DON J BECKMAN RESEARCH INSTITUTE 1450 E DUARTE ROAD DUARTE, CA 91010 Analysis of proteins binding to the human gamma interferon promoter
R01CA-52178-02 (SRC) SCHIFFER, CHARLES A UNIVERSITY OF MARYLAND 22 S GREENE STREET BALTIMORE, MD 21201 Mechanisms of drug resistance in acute myeloid leukemia
R01CA-52181-02 (SRC) OZOLS, ROBERT F FOX CHASE CANCER CENTER 7701 BURHOLME AVENUE PHILADELPHIA, PA 19111 Detection and reversal of ovarian cancer drug resistance
R01CA-52182-02 (SRC) ERLICHMAN, CHARLES ONTARIO CANCER INSTITUTE 500 SHERBOURNE STREET TORONTO, ONTARIO CANADA M4X 1K Modulation of multidrug resistance by cyclosporin A
R01CA-52186-02 (SRC) BERMAN, ELLIN MEMORIAL HOSPITAL 1275 YORK AVENUE NEW YORK, NY 10021 Effect of tamoxifen on reversing the MDR phenotype
R01CA-52192-01A1 (EDC) STUKEL, THERESE A DARTMOUTH-HITCHCOCK MEDICAL CT HB 7927 HANOVER, NH 03756 Tumor growth curve analysis
R01CA-52220-02 (CTY) LAU, LESTER F UNIV OF ILLINOIS COLL OF MED 808 SOUTH WOOD STREET CHICAGO, IL 60612 Gene control by growth factor and c-myc
R01CA-52223-02 (EDC) PALMER, JULIE BOSTON UNIVERSITY 1371 BEACON ST BROOKLINE, MA 02146 Gestational trophoblastic disease and oral contraceptives
R01CA-52225-02 (SRC) KLEIN, GEORGE KAROLINSKA INSTITUTE BOX 60400 S-104 01 STOCKHOLM, SWEDEN EB viral strategiesin latency, transformation and immune escape
R01CA-52228-02 (SRC) MILLER, I GEORGE, JR YALE UNIVERSITY SCH OF MED 333 CEDAR ST/PO BOX 3333 NEW HAVEN, CT 06510 Mutants of Epstein-Barr virus
U01CA-52230-02 (SRC) LICHTENSTEIN, EDWARD L OREGON RESEARCH INSTITUTE 1899 WILLAMETTE, SUITE 2 EUGENE, OR 97401 Tobacco policy interventions in northwest indian tribes
U01CA-52237-02 (SRC) BANNER, RICHARD O WAIANAE COAST COMPREHENSIVE 86-260 FARRINGTON HIGHWAY WAIANAE, HI 96792 The Waianae coast cancer control project
R01CA-52241-02 (SRC) COOPER, NEIL R 10666 NORTH TORREY PINES ROAD LA JOLLA, CA 92037 A model for Epstein-Barr virus induced lymphoma
U01CA-52242-02 (SRC) BERNER, JAMES E ALASKA AREA NATIVE HLTH SERVIC 255 GAMBELL STREET ANCHORAGE, AK 99501 Prevention of cervical cancer in Alaska native women
R01CA-52244-02 (SRC) WANG, FREDERICK C S BRIGHAM AND WOMEN'S HOSPITAL 75 FRANCIS STREET BOSTON, MA 02115 Molecular genetic analysis of EBV growth transformation
R01CA-52250-02 (SRC) MOSS, DENIS J QUEENSLAND INST OF MEDICAL RES BRAMSTON TERRACE AUSTRALIA Role of T cell epitopes in tumour surveillance
U01CA-52251-02 (SRC) SCHINKE, STEVEN P COLUMBIA UNIVERSITY 622 WEST 113TH STREET NEW YORK, NY 10025 Reducing cancer risks among Native American adolescents
U01CA-52256-02 (SRC) DIGNAN, MARK B BOWMAN GRAY SCHOOL OF MEDICINE MEDICAL CENTER BLVD. WINSTON-SALEM, NC 27157 Prevention of cervical cancer in Native American women
R01CA-52258-02 (SRC) SIXBEY, JOHN W ST JUDE CHILDREN'S RES HOSP 332 N LAUDERDALE/PO BX 318 MEMPHIS, TN 38101-0318 Epstein-barr virus infection of mucosal epithelium
R01CA-52259-01A2 (PTHA) KITCHINGMAN, GEOFFREY R ST JUDE CHILDREN'S RES HOSP 332 N LAUDERDALE ST/BOX 318 MEMPHIS, TN 38101-0318 Immunoglobulin gene arrangement/expression in leukemia
U01CA-52267-02 (SRC) BAINES, CAROL M AMERICAN INDIAN HLTH CARE ASSO 245 EAST SIXTH ST, SUITE 499 ST. PAUL, MN 55101 Urban Native American women's cancer prevention project
U01CA-52279-02 (SRC) HODGE, FELICIA NORTHERN CALIFORNIA CANCER CTR 1301 SHOREWAY RD- SUITE 425 BELMONT, CA 94002 Smoking cessation for American Indians
U01CA-52283-02 (SRC) DAVIS, SALLY M UNIVERSITY OF NEW MEXICO SURGE BUILDING ALBUQUERQUE, NM 87131 Southwestern cancer prevention project for American Indians
R29CA-52285-03 (RAD) LANGMUIR, VIRGINIA K SRI INTERNATIONAL 333 RAVENSWOOD AVE MENLO PARK, CA 94025 Radioimmunotherapy: isotope and antibody choice
R15CA-52286-01A1 (ET) SCOVELL, WILLIAM M BOWLING GREEN STATE UNIVERSITY BOWLING GREEN, OH 43403-0213 Character and role of HMG 1,2-DNA interactions
R01CA-52298-02 (EI) KAMINSKI, MARK S UNIV OF MICHIGAN MEDICAL CENTE 1500 EAST MEDICAL CENTER DRIVE ANN ARBOR, MI 48109-0374 Anti-tumor effects of anti-idiotype antibodies
R43CA-52304-01A1 (ET) BIGNAMI, GARY S HAWAII BIOTECHNOLOGY GROUP 99193 AIEA HEIGHTS DRIVE AIEA, HI 96701 Bispecific antibody for directed delivery of palytoxin
R01CA-52308-01A1 (EI) PLATSOUCAS, CHRIS D UNIVERSITY OF TEXAS 1515 HOLCOMBE BLVD HOUSTON, TX 77030 Autologous tumor specific TIL in melanoma
R43CA-52323-01A1 (SSS) HUSTON, JAMES S CREATIVE BIOMOLECULES, INC 35 SOUTH STREET HOPKINTON, MA 01748 Humanized antitumor binding sites: framework engineering
R43CA-52331-01A1 (SSS) TOMETSKO, ANDREW M LITRON LABORATORIES LTD 1351 MT HOPE AVENUE ROCHESTER, NY 14620 Rapid production of tumor specific hybridomas
R43CA-52337-01A1 (SSS) MARTIN, RONALD L ACCTEK ASSOCIATES, INC 901 S KENSINGTON AVENUE LAGRANGE, IL 60525 A radiographic aid to proton therapy
R44CA-52342-02 (SSS) MUEHLLEHNER, GERD UGM MEDICAL SYSTEMS 3401 MARKET ST PHILADELPHIA, PA 19104 Positron tomograph using optically coupled detectors
R43CA-52345-01A2 (SSS) GRABOWY, RICHARD S MICROWAVE MEDICAL SYSTEMS, INC 9 GOLDSMITH STREET LITTLETON, MA 10460-0188 Microwave device for detecting air emboli
R29CA-52351-02 (ET) FUQUA, SUZANNE A UNIVERSITY OF TEXAS HLTH SCI C 7703 FLOYD CURL DR SAN ANTONIO, TX 78284-7884 Mutations in individual breast cancers--PCR sequencing
U10CA-52352-02 (SRC) WIESENFELD, MARTIN 788 EIGHTH AVENUE SE CEDAR RAPIDS, IA 52401 Cedar Rapids oncology project--CCOP
R43CA-52365-01A1 (SSP) BECKER, DAVID S I.S. GRUPE, INC. 948 SPRINGER DRIVE LOMBARD, IL 60148 Develop a CD-ROM of the SEER database
R44CA-52370-02 (SSS) ENTINE, GERALD RADIATION MONITORING DEVICES I 44 HUNT STREET WATERTOWN, MA 02172 Intraoperative imaging probe for delineation of tumors
R43CA-52374-01A1 (SSS) FIQUERAS, JOHN APPLIED SYSTEM TECHNOLOGIES, I 8130 BOONE BLVD, SUITE 240 VIENNA, VA 22182 Computer storage and manipulation of chemical structures
R43CA-52378-01A1 (MEP) LAM, LUKE K T LKT LABORATORIES, INC 2010 E. HENNEPIN AVE. MINNEAPOLIS, MN 55413 Proinhibitors of chemical carcinogenesis
U10CA-52384-02 (SRC) DUGAN, WILLIAM M, JR METHODIST HOSPITAL INDIANA INC 1701 N SENATE BLVD PO BOX 1367 INDIANAPOLIS, IN 46206 Methodist Hospital of Indiana, Inc. CCOP
U10CA-52385-02 (SRC) EVERSON, LLOYD COMMUNITY HOSP INDIANAPOLIS 1500 N RITTER INDIANAPOLIS, IN 46219 Indiana regional cancer center
R43CA-52391-01A2 (SSS) COWSERT, LEX M ISIS PHARMACEUTICALS 2280 FARADAY AVENUE CARLSBAD, CA 92008 Oligonucleotides as inhibitors of papillomavirus
R44CA-52401-02 (SSS) YAROSH, DANIEL B APPLIED GENETICS, INC 205 BUFFALO AVENUE FREEPORT, NY 11520 T4N5 liposomes for prevention of skin cancer
R01CA-52405-02 (BIO) RESH, MARILYN D SLOAN-KETTERING INSTITUTE 1275 YORK AVENUE NEW YORK, N Y 10021 Myristylation of proteins in transformed cells
R01CA-52406-02 (ARR) RAAB-TRAUB, NANCY J UNIV OF N C AT CHAPEL HILL 115 LINEBERGER CANCER RES CTR CHAPEL HILL, NC 27599-7295 AIDS-associated leukoplakia--The role of EBV
R43CA-52407-01A1 (SSS) BUNOW, BARRY J CIVILIZED SOFTWARE, INC 7735 OLD GEORGETOWN ROAD BETHESDA, MD 20814 Mlab 3d graphics--Scientific visualization software
R01CA-52408-01A1 (ARRE) VOGEL, JONATHAN AMERICAN RED CROSS 15601 CRABBS BRANCH WAY ROCKVILLE, MD 20855 Biological studies of Kaposi's sarcoma in transgenic mice
R01CA-52410-02 (ARR) ROSENBLATT, JOSEPH D UCLA SCHOOL OF MEDICINE 10833 LE CONTE AVENUE LOS ANGELES, CA 90024 Pathogenesis of HTLV-1 associated myelopathy
R01CA-52412-01A1 (ARRA) WONG-STAAL, FLOSSIE UNIVERSITY OF CALIFORNIA LA JOLLA, CA 92093 HIV Tat protein and Kaposi's sarcoma pathogenesis
R43CA-52419-01A1 (HUD) FREDERIKSEN, LEE W HEALTH INNOVATIONS, INC 12355 SUNRISE VALLEY DR RESTON, VA 22091 Computer-assisted smokeless tobacco cessation
U10CA-52420-02 (SRC) EISENBERG, PETER ROSS KENTFIELD MEDICAL BLDG 1150 SIR FRANCIS DRAKE BLVD KENTFIELD, CA 94904 San Francisco--Bay area community clinical oncology program
R01CA-52421-02 (ARR) YUEN, PICK-HOONG U T MD ANDERSON CANCER CENTER SMITHVILLE, TX 78957 Kaposi's sarcoma associated with AIDS-- A mouse model
R01CA-52443-02 (MBY) BREWER, GARY A BOWMAN GRAY SCH MED/WAKE FORES 300 S HAWTHORNE RD WINSTON SALEM, NC 27103 Post transcriptional regulation of oncogene messenger RNA
R03CA-52447-02 (SRC) HULKA, BARBARA S UNIV. OF NORTH CAROLINA, C.H. CAMPUS BOX #7400 CHAPEL HILL, NC 27599 Rare Ha-ras alleles and breast cancer
R01CA-52457-02 (PTHB) KRIPKE, MARGARET L UNIVERSITY OF TEXAS 1515 HOLCOMBE BLVD HOUSTON, TX 77030 Role of antigen presenting cells in skin cancer immunity
R29CA-52460-02 (ET) O'BRIAN, CATHERINE A U.T. M.D. ANDERSON CANCER CENT 1515 HOLCOMBE BLVD, BOX 173 HOUSTON, TX 77030 Protein phosphorylation in multidrug resistance
R01CA-52462-02 (RAD) FUKS, ZVI SLOAN-KETTERING INST/CNCR RES 1275 YORK AVENUE NEW YORK, NY 10021 FGF induced radiation damage repair in endothelial cells
R01CA-52468-02 (CPA) BUTLER, ANDREW P UNIV OF TX M D ANDERSON CAN CT P O BOX 389 SMITHVILLE, TX 78957 Gene regulation in phorbol sensitive and resistant mice
R29CA-52471-01A1 (ET) WILLIAMS, CAROL L MAYO FOUNDATION 200 FIRST STREET SOUTHWEST ROCHESTER, MN 55905 Regulation of lung cancer growth
R01CA-52475-01 (RAD) GOULD, MICHAEL N UNIVERSITY OF WISCONSIN 600 N HIGHLAND AVENUE MADISON, WI 53792 Radiobiology of synchrotron produced ultrasoft x rays
P01CA-52477-01A1 (SRC) HOSKINS, WILLIAM J MEMORIAL HOSP/CANCER & DISEASE 1275 YORK AVE NEW YORK, NY 10021 Epithelial ovarian cancer program project
P01CA-52477-01A1 0001 (SRC) HAKES, THOMAS B Epithelial ovarian cancer program project Clinical trials project
P01CA-52477-01A1 0002 (SRC) PORTENOY, RUSSELL K Epithelial ovarian cancer program project Evaluation of ovarian pain and quality of life
P01CA-52477-01A1 0003 (SRC) RUBIN, STEPHEN C Epithelial ovarian cancer program project Monoclonal antibody imaging and therapy
P01CA-52477-01A1 0004 (SRC) LLOYD, KENNETH O Epithelial ovarian cancer program project Immunological and biochemical studies
P01CA-52477-01A1 9001 (SRC) LLOYD, KENNETH O Epithelial ovarian cancer program project Core--Monoclonal antibodies and laboratory support
P01CA-52477-01A1 9002 (SRC) WONG, GEORGE Y Epithelial ovarian cancer program project Core--Biostatistics and data management
P01CA-52477-01A1 9003 (SRC) SAIGO, PATRICIA E Epithelial ovarian cancer program project Core--Pathology
R01CA-52481-02 (CBY) MORGAN, DAVID O UNIVERSITY OF CALIFORNIA, PARNASSUS AVE Molecular control of cell proliferation

PROJECT NO., ORGANIZATIONAL UNIT., INVESTIGATOR, ADDRESS, TITLE

R01CA-52491-02 (PTHB) ITZKOWITZ, STEVEN H MOUNT SINAI MEDICAL CENTER 1 GUSTAVE L LEVY PLACE BOX 106 NEW YORK, NY 10029 Pathobiology of colon cancer mucin
R01CA-52498-01A1 (PBC) CARRAWAY, KERMIT L UNIVERSITY OF MIAMI 1600 NW 10TH AVE MIAMI, FL 33136 Structure/biosynthesis of tumor sialomucin complex
R29CA-52499-02 (ET) BELLDEGRUN, ARIE S UCLA SCHOOL OF MEDICINE 10833 LE CONTE AVE LOS ANGELES, CA 90042-1738 Tumor specific tumor infiltrating lymphocytes from renal cancer
R01CA-52500-01A1 (MEP) SCHWARTZ, ARTHUR G TEMPLE UNIV SCHOOL OF MEDICINE 3420 N BROAD ST PHILADELPHIA, PA 19140 Chemoprevention of skin tumors by DHEA analogs
R03CA-52505-02 (SRC) LE MARCHAND, LOIC UNIV OF HAWAII CANCER RES CTR 1236 LAUHALA ST, SUITE 407 HONOLULU, HI 96813 Breath markers of colonic fermentation
R01CA-52506-02 (BBCA) WANG, ANDREW H 407 S GOODWIN URBANA, IL 61801 Molecular mechanisms of anticancer drugs
R01CA-52511-01A1 (EI) KRONENBERG, MITCHELL E 10833 LE CONTE AVENUE LOS ANGELES, CA 90024-1747 Expression and function of the MHC-encoded TL molecule
R01CA-52515-01A1 (ARRC) BALDWIN, ALBERT S, JR UNIV OF N C AT CHAPEL HILL CB #7295 CHAPEL HILL, NC 27599 Inducible HIV and class I MHC enhancer binding proteins
R01CA-52519-01A1 (EI) NAKAMURA, ICHIRO STATE UNIV OF NY AT BUFFALO 232 FARBER HALL BUFFALO, NY 14214 Genetic analysis of hemopoietic histocompatibility
R01CA-52526-01A1 (PTHA) GLICK, MARY C CHILDREN'S HOPITAL OF PHILA 34TH & CIVIC CENTER BLVD PHILADELPHIA, PA 19104 Polysialic acid in pediatric neural tumors/development
R01CA-52527-02 (EI) OSTRAND-ROSENBERG, SUZANNE UNIVERSITY OF MARYLAND BALTIMORE, MD 21228 Enhancing tumor immunity by class II gene transfection
R01CA-52539-01A1 (EI) THEOFILOPOULOS, ARGYRIOS N RES INST OF SCRIPPS CLINIC 10666 NORTH TORREY PINES ROAD LA JOLLA, CA 92037 Antigen receptor genes in T cell malignancies
R01CA-52541-01A1 (PTHB) BAGLIONI, CORRADO SUNY AT ALBANY 1400 WASHINGTON AVE ALBANY, NY 12222 Mechanisms of action of tumor necrosis factor
R01CA-52559-02 (MGN) HAMLIN, JOYCE L UNIVERSITY OF VIRGINIA BOX 440 CHARLOTTESVILLE, VA 22908 Mammalian genome organization and gene amplification
R03CA-52560-01A1 (SRC) HSIEH, CHUNG-CHENG HARVARD SCHOOL OF PUBLIC HLTH 677 HUNTINGTON AVENUE BOSTON, MA 02115 A study of chinese tea and stomach cancer in Shanghai
R25CA-52570-02 (SRC) COOPER, M ROBERT WAKE FOREST UNIVERSITY 300 SOUTH HAWTHORNE ROAD WINSTON-SALEM, N C 27103 Cancer education program--Student research
R01CA-52572-02 (SSS) OAKES, DAVID UNIVERSITY OF ROCHESTER HYLAN 710 ROCHESTER, NY 14627 Statistical analysis of multiple event time data
R01CA-52574-02 (BIO) KENT, CLAUDIA PURDUE UNIVERSITY WEST LAFAYETTE, IN 47907 Phosphatidylcholine metabolism in ras-transfected cells
R29CA-52584-02 (MEP) ROY, DEODUTTA UNIVERSITY OF TEXAS MED BRANCH GALVESTON, TX 77550-2782 Role of non-histone proteins in hormonal carcinogenesis
R01CA-52585-01A1 (RAD) LEAVITT, DENNIS D UNIVERSITY OF UTAH MEDICAL CTR SALT LAKE CITY, UT 84132 Dynamic field shaping/stereotactic radiosurgery doses
R29CA-52592-02 (MEP) YEE, DOUGLAS UNIV OF TEXAS HEALTH SCIENCE C 7703 FLOYD CURL DR SAN ANTONIO, TX 78284 Growth regulation of cancer by IGF-I
R01CA-52596-01A1 (SRC) MEYSKENS, FRANK L JR UCIMC CLINICAL CANCER CTR 101 THE CITY DRIVE ORANGE, CA 92668 Chemoprevention efficacy trial of beta-carotene/retinol
R01CA-52599-01A1 (BCE) GLASS, CHRISTOPHER K UNIV CALIFORNIA, SAN DIEGO 9500 GILMAN DRIVE LA JOLLA, CA 92093-0656 Hormonal regulation of macrophage development
R01CA-52603-02 (ET) LERMAN, STEPHEN P WAYNE STATE UNIVERSITY 550 E CANFIELD DETROIT, MI 48201 Chemo/immunotherapy of a T cell dependent B cell tumor
R01CA-52605-01 (CCG) TILLEY, BARBARA C DIVISION OF BIOSTATISTICS AND 23725 NORTHWESTERN HWY SOUTHFIELD, MI 48075 Colorectal cancer screening and nutrition intervention
R01CA-52607-02 (CPA) ROOP, DENNIS R BAYLOR COLLEGE OF MEDICINE ONE BAYLOR PLAZA HOUSTON, TX 77030 Targeting oncogene expression to skin in transgenic mice
R29CA-52618-01A1 (ET) NUTTER, LOUISE M UNIVERSITY OF MINNESOTA MED SC 435 DELAWARE ST SOUTHEAST MINNEAPOLIS, MN 55455 Mechanism(s) of resistance to menadione
R01CA-52621-02 (MGN) LILLY, FRANK ALBERT EINSTEIN COLLEGE OF MED 1300 MORRIS PARK AVENUE BRONX, NY 10461 Resistance to chemically induced lymphoma in mice
U10CA-52623-02 (SRC) STUCKEY, WALTER J TULANE UNIV SCHOOL OF MED 1430 TULANE AVENUE NEW ORLEANS, LA 70112 Tulane University minority-based CCOP
R01CA-52625-02 (ET) KAMEN, BARTON A U.T. SOUTHWESTERN MEDICAL CENT 5323 HARRY HINES BLVD DALLAS, TX 75235 Folate receptor as marker & target in cancer therapy
R01CA-52626-02 (MEP) THOMPSON, HENRY J AMC CANCER RESEARCH CENTER 1600 PIERCE STREET LAKEWOOD, CO 80214 Exercise and breast cancer prevention
R01CA-52631-01A1 (SSS) DIETRICH, ALLEN J DARTMOUTH MEDICAL SCHOOL HANOVER, NH 03756 A phase IV cancer control project for primary physicians
R01CA-52643-02 (RNM) BARRETT, HARRISON H UNIVERSITY OF ARIZONA ARIZONA HEALTH SCI CENTER TUCSON, AZ 85724 SPECT reconstruction algorithms and parallel computing
U10CA-52650-02 (SRC) VAUGHN, CLARENCE B SOUTHFIELD ONCOLOGY INST, INC 27211 LAHSER ROAD SOUTHFIELD, MI 48034 Community clinical oncology program of Metropolitan Detroit
U10CA-52651-02 (SRC) LAD, THOMAS E UNIVERSITY OF ILLINOIS MED CTR PO BOX 6998 CHICAGO, IL 60680 University of Illinois minority-based CCOP
U10CA-52652-02 (SRC) GOLDSON, ALFRED L HOWARD UNIVERSITY HOSPITAL 2041 GEORGIA AVENUE, N.W. WASHINGTON, D.C. 20060 Metropolitan Washington DC minority-based CCOP
U10CA-52654-02 (SRC) CONRAD, MARCEL E UNIVERSITY OF SOUTH ALABAMA UNIVERSITY BOULEVARD MOBILE, AL 36688 Minority-based community clinical oncology program
R01CA-52656-01A1 (EDC) DALING, JANET R FRED HUTCHINSON CANCER RES CTR 1124 COLUMBIA STREET SEATTLE, WA 98104 The changing epidemiology of thyroid cancer
R01CA-52658-02 (IMB) WORTIS, HENRY H TUFTS UNIVERSITY 136 HARRISON AVENUE BOSTON, MA 02111 Specificity and function of gamma/delta T cells
U10CA-52667-02 (SRC) BAEZ, LUIS SAN JUAN CITY HOSPITAL ONE VETERAN PLAZA SAN JUAN, PR 00927 San Juan City minority-based CCOP
R01CA-52669-02 (EI) IMBODEN, JOHN B VETERANS ADMIN MED CTR-111R SAN FRANCISCO, CA 94121 Characterization of gp35, a signal transducer on NK cells
R01CA-52678-02 (SAT) HARDY, MARK A COLUMBIA UNIVERSITY 630 WEST 168TH STREET NEW YORK, NY 10032 UVB induced adult chimeras for organ transplantation
R01CA-52679-01A1 (RAD) WEBER, CHRISTINE A UNIVERSITY OF CALIFORNIA P.O. BOX 5507 LIVERMORE, CA 94551 Genetic analysis of nucleotide excision repair
R55CA-52681-01A1 (SSS) HARRISON, GEORGE H UNIV OF MD SCHOOL OF MEDICINE 655 W BALTIMORE ST BALTIMORE, MD 21201 Potentiation of chemotherapy by low-level ultrasound
R01CA-52682-02 (ET) BEERMAN, TERRY A HEALTH RES. INC./ROSWELL PK DI 666 ELM STREET BUFFALO, NY 14263 Extrachromosomal DNA, a new target for antitumor drugs
R01CA-52683-01A1 (ET) SEDWICK, W DAVID CASE WESTERN RESERVE UNIVERSIT UCRC #2 - SUITE 200 CLEVELAND, OH 44106 Anthracycline-induced DNA sequence specific mutation
P01CA-52686-02 (SRC) KINSELLA, TIMOTHY J UNIV WISCONSIN CLIN CANCER CTR 600 HIGHLAND AVENUE MADISON, WI 53792 Growth factor alteration of radiation response in tumors
P01CA-52686-02 9001 (SRC) FOWLER, JOHN F Growth factor alteration of radiation response in tumors Core--Laboratory
P01CA-52686-02 0001 (SRC) GOULD, MICHAEL N Growth factor alteration of radiation response in tumors In vitro modification of radiation effects by cytostatic agents
P01CA-52686-02 0002 (SRC) KINSELLA, TIMOTHY J Growth factor alteration of radiation response in tumors Halogenated pyrimidine radiosensitization in tumors
P01CA-52686-02 0003 (SRC) MULCAHY, R TIMOTHY Growth factor alteration of radiation response in tumors: Antiestrogens & cytostatic agents--Radiation response in breast cancer
P01CA-52686-02 0004 (SRC) FOWLER, JOHN F Growth factor alteration of radiation response in tumors Proliferation in tumors during radiotherapy
P01CA-52686-02 0005 (SRC) KINSELLA, TIMOTHY J Growth factor alteration of radiation response in tumors Tumor cell kinetics--Altered proliferation/radiosensitivity
R01CA-52689-01A1 (EDC) WRENSCH, MARGARET R UNIVERSITY OF CALIFORNIA 1699 HSW, UCSF (BOX 0560) SAN FRANCISCO, CA 94143-0560 Genetic epidemiology of malignant glioma
R01CA-52692-02 (RAD) MACKIE, THOMAS R UNIVERSITY OF WISCONSIN 1300 UNIVERSITY AVENUE MADISON, WI 53706 Electron beam dose planning using Monte Carlo simulation
R01CA-52694-02 (MGN) WEAVER, DAVID T DANA FARBER CANCER INSTITUTE 44 BINNEY ST BOSTON, MA 02115 Bloom's syndrome--DNA ligase and immunodeficiency
R01CA-52709-01A1 (RAD) MEYER, CHARLES R UNIVERSITY OF MICHIGAN KRESGE III, BOX 0553 ANN ARBOR, MI 48109-0553 Computed 3d surface and volume estimation in CT and MRI
R01CA-52713-02 (RAD) LING, C CLIFTON MEMORIAL HOSPITAL 1275 YORK AVE NEW YORK, NY 10021 Radiobiology of low-energy and short -lived isotopes
R55CA-52715-01A1 (RAD) ILIAKIS, GEORGE THOMAS JEFFERSON UNIV HOSPITAL 10TH AND WALNUT STREETS PHILADELPHIA, PA 19107 Molecular mechanisms of heat induced radiosensitization
R29CA-52733-02 (SSS) KIM, KYUNGMANN DANA-FARBER CANCER INST 44 BINNEY STREET BOSTON, MA 02115 Sequential methods for clinical trials
U10CA-52735-02 (SRC) MOORE, MELVIN R EMORY UNIV SCHOOL OF MEDICINE 69 BUTLER ST SE ATLANTA, GA 30303 Grady Hospital CCOP
R29CA-52741-02 (PTHB) HASDAY, JEFFREY DAVID UNIVERSITY OF MARYLAND AT BALT 10 S PINE STREET BALTIMORE, MD 21201 Receptor--Ligand events in macrophage tumor recognition
U10CA-52743-02 (SRC) HALL, THOMAS C TECH TRANSFER CTR FOR CANCER 1 BRUCE STREET NEWARK, NJ 07103 Newark inner city community clinical oncology program
R18CA-52748-02 (CCG) CURTIS, PETER UNIV OF NC AT CHAPEL HILL W.B. AYCOCK BLDG. CB #7595 CHAPEL HILL, NC 27599-7595 Increasing pap smear adequacy rates
R01CA-52750-02 (PTHA) BOUCK, NOEL P NORTHWESTERN UNIVERSITY 303 E CHICAGO AVENUE CHICAGO, IL 60611 Tumor suppressor genes and angiogenesis
R01CA-52752-02 (CBY) RYDER, KEVIN INSTITUTE FOR CANCER RESEARCH 7701 BURHOLME AVE PHILADELPHIA, PA 19111 Comparative analysis of jun protein function
R29CA-52754-02 (VR) HOWE, JOHN G YALE UNIVERSITY SCHOOL OF MED 333 CEDAR ST NEW HAVEN, CT 06510 Immortalization of B-lymphocytes by Epstein-Barr virus
R01CA-52756-01A1 (PTHA) BERNARDS, RENE MASSACHUSETTS GENERAL HOSP 13TH STREET CHARLESTOWN, MA 02129 Studies on tumor progression in neuroblastoma
U10CA-52757-02 (SRC) LOPEZ, JOSE A SANTA ROSA HOSPITAL 519 WEST HOUSTON STREET SAN ANTONIO, TX 78207-3108 San Antonio community clinical oncology program
R55CA-52761-01A1 (PTHB) WANG, NANCY UNIV OF ROCHESTER MED/DENTISTR 601 ELMWOOD AVENUE ROCHESTER, NY 14642 Cytogenetic evaluation of tumor cell subpopulations
U10CA-52771-02 (SRC) PARMLEY, RICHARD T UNIVERSITY OF TEXAS

HLTH SCI C 7703 FLOYD CURL DR SAN ANTONIO, TX 78284-7810 South Texas pediatric minority-based community clinical oncology program

U10CA-52772-02 (SRC) ROSENTHAL, CONSTANTIN J SUNY-HEALTH SCI CTR. AT BROOKL 450 Clarkson Avenue BROOKLYN, NY 11203 Kings county minority based-community clinical oncology program

R01CA-52774-02 (REN) PAVLIK, EDWARD J UNIVERSITY OF KENTUCKY GYNECOLOGY Antiestrogen resistance--The role of AESBS

R01CA-52778-02 (ARR) FORD, RICHARD J, JR UT M D ANDERSON CANCER CENTER 1515 HOCOMBE BLVD HOUSTON, TX 77030 Role of human retroviruses in AIDS-related lymphomas

U10CA-52784-02 (SRC) DESCH, CHRISTOPHER E MEDICAL COLLEGE OF VIRGINIA MCV STATION BOX 230 RICHMOND, VA 23298 The MCV/CMH minority-based CCOP of Virginia

R01CA-52790-02 (MCHA) GEORG, GUNDA I UNIVERSITY OF KANSAS LAWRENCE, KS 66045-2506 Semisynthetic taxol derivatives

R01CA-52791-02 (PTHB) VERDERAME, MICHAEL F PENNSYLVANIA STATE UNIVERSITY PO BOX 850 HERSHEY, PA 17033 Genetic & biochemical regulation of pp60-v-src activity

R29CA-52799-01A1 (PTHB) RAY, RATNA UNIV OF ALABAMA AT BIRMINGHAM UAB STATION BIRMINGHAM, AL 35294 Cloning and characterization of c-myc promoter binding protein

R01CA-52800-01A1 (BNP) HANGAUER, DAVID G SUNY AT BUFFALO COOKE-HOCHSTETTER TOWERS BUFFALO, NY 14260 Protein kinase inhibitors

R01CA-52814-02 (ET) NITISS, JOHN L CHILDRENS HOSPITAL OF LA 4560 SUNSET BLVD LOS ANGELES, CA 90027 Analysis of anti-topoisomerase drug action in yeast

P01CA-52823-02 (SRC) REID, JOHN M DREXEL UNIVERSITY 32ND & CHESTNUT STREETS PHILADELPHIA, PA 19104 Developing of ultrasonic tissue characterization methods

P01CA-52823-02 0004 (SRC) SHANKAR, P MOHANA Developing of ultrasonic tissue characterization methods Signal processing for enhanced tissue imaging

P01CA-52823-02 0005 (SRC) ROSE, JOSEPH L Developing of ultrasonic tissue characterization methods Oblique incidence potential in tissue classification

P01CA-52823-02 0006 (SRC) WHEATLEY, MARGARET A Developing of ultrasonic tissue characterization methods New class of ultrasonic contrast agent--Development and evaluation

P01CA-52823-02 0007 (SRC) LEWIN, PETER A Developing of ultrasonic tissue characterization methods Development of wideband transducers

P01CA-52823-02 9001 (SRC) GOLDBERG, BARRY B Developing of ultrasonic tissue characterization methods Clinical core

P01CA-52823-02 9002 (SRC) REID, JOHN M Developing of ultrasonic tissue characterization methods Laboratory core

P01CA-52823-02 0001 (SRC) SOETANTO, KAWAN Developing of ultrasonic tissue characterization methods Intra-operational tissue characterization

P01CA-52823-02 0002 (SRC) COHEN, FERNAND S Developing of ultrasonic tissue characterization methods Texture/attenuation models for soft tissue characterization

P01CA-52823-02 0003 (SRC) BILGUTAY, NIHAT M Developing of ultrasonic tissue characterization methods Two dimensional split-spectrum image analysis

R01CA-52834-02 (BNP) KECK, GARY E UNIVERSITY OF UTAH 309 PARK BLDG SALT LAKE CITY, UT 84112 New synthesis methods for alkaloid synthesis

R29CA-52835-01A1 (EI) NIKAIDO, TOSHIO THE WISTAR INSTITUTE 36TH AND SPRUCE STREETS PHILADELPHIA, PA 19104 Molecular mechanisms of cell growth control

R29CA-52837-01A1 (PTHB) RANGNEKAR, VIVEK M UNIVERSITY OF CHICAGO 5841 SOUTH MARYLAND AVENUE CHICAGO, IL 60637 Study of IL-1 inducible genes in human melanoma cells

R29CA-52853-02 (CPA) KNEPPER, JANICE E VILLANOVA UNIVERSITY VILLANOVA, PA 19085 A new integration locus for mouse mammary tumor virus

R29CA-52855-02 (PTHA) FULTS, DANIEL W UNIV OF UTAH SCHOOL OF MED 50 N MEDICAL DRIVE SALT LAKE CITY, UT 84132 Molecular genetics of human astrocytoma

R01CA-52856-02 (ALY) SHERMAN, LINDA A SCRIPPS CLINIC & RESEARCH FOUN 10666 NORTH TORREY PINES ROAD LA JOLLA, CA 92037 CTL specific for allo-MHC plus self and tumor peptides

U01CA-52857-02 (SRC) BREM, HENRY JOHNS HOPKINS HOSPITAL MEYER 7-113 BALTIMORE, MD 21205 Controlled release polymers for brain tumors

U01CA-52857-02 0001 (SRC) BREM, HENRY Controlled release polymers for brain tumors Controlled release drug delivery--Effectiveness & safety

U01CA-52857-02 0002 (SRC) LANGER, ROBERT Controlled release polymers for brain tumors Development of controlled release polymers

U01CA-52857-02 0003 (SRC) SALTZMAN, MARK Controlled release polymers for brain tumors Modeling of drug transported for brain therapy

U01CA-52857-02 0004 (SRC) COLVIN, MICHAEL Controlled release polymers for brain tumors Development of drugs for use with controlled release polymers

U01CA-52857-02 0005 (SRC) CHASIN, MARK Controlled release polymers for brain tumors New methods for development and testing of polymer drugs

R01CA-52862-01A1 (EDC) THOMAS, DUNCAN C USC SCHOOL OF MEDICINE 2025 ZONAL AVE, PMB-B201 LOS ANGELES, CA 90033 Survival model for genetic epidemiology

R13CA-52872-01 (SRC) BECKER, FREDERICK F UNIVERSITY OF TEXAS 1515 HOLCOMBE BLVD HOUSTON, TX 77030 1990 annual symposium on fundamental cancer research

R01CA-52874-01A1 (BNP) GELB, MICHAEL H UNIVERSITY OF WASHINGTON SEATTLE, WA 98195 Biochemistry of protein prenylation

R01CA-52879-02 (PTHB) BOURDON, MARIO A CALIFORNIA INST OF BIOL RES 11099 NORTH TORREY PINES ROAD LA JOLLA, CA 92037 Tenascin structure and role in neoplasia

R55CA-52880-01A1 (RNM) WAHL, RICHARD L UNIVERSITY OF MICHIGAN MED CTR 1500 EAST MED CTRB1G412-UH ANN ARBOR, MI 48109-0028 Positron emission tomography of breast carcinoma

R01CA-52881-02 (CPA) FISHBEIN, JAMES C WAKE FOREST UNIVERSITY 7486 REYNOLDA STATION WINSTON-SALEM, NC 27109 N-alkyl-N-nitro-nitrosoguanidines and alkane diazotates

U01CA-52903-02 (CCG) FLORES, ESTEVAN T UNIVERSITY OF COLORADO CAMPUS BOX 327 BOULDER, CO 80309-0327 Breast and cervical cancer screening among Hispanic women

R01CA-52915-02 (SRC) STEINBERG, MARK L CITY COLLEGE OF CUNY CONVENT AVE AT 138TH STREET NEW YORK, NY 10031 Protease inhibitor effects in epithelial transformation

R01CA-52926-02 (SRC) GARTE, SEYMOUR J NEW YORK UNIV MEDICAL CENTER 550 FIRST AVENUE NEW YORK, NY 10016 Protease inhibitors suppression of oncogene function

R01CA-52931-01A1 (SSS) HUBBELL, F ALLAN UNIVERSITY OF CALIFORNIA IRVINE, CA 92717 Cancer control among Hispanic women--A research proposal

U01CA-52939-02 (CCG) MC ALISTER, ALFRED L U TEXAS HEALTH SCIENCE CENTER P O BOX 20186 HOUSTON, TX 77225 Salud--Mexican-American participation in the prevention

R01CA-52945-02 (SRC) THRAVES, PETER J GEORGETOWN UNIVERSITY MED CTR 3800 RESERVOIR RD, NW WASHINGTON, DC 20007 Protease inhibitors & radiation transformation

U01CA-52948-02 (CCG) KAPLAN, ROBERT M UNIV OF CALIFORNIA, SAN DIEGO LA JOLLA, CA 92093-0622 Por la vida model in cancer prevention

R01CA-52949-02 (ET) GIBSON, NEIL W UNIV OF SOUTHERN CALIFORNIA 1303 N MISSION ROAD LOS ANGELES, CA 90033 Chronic myelogenous leukemia: A therapeutic approach

U01CA-52955-02 (SRC) CREWS, PHILLIP UNIV OF CALIFORNIA 1156 HIGH STREET SANTA CRUZ, CA 95064 Discovery of antitumor marine products by mechanism base

U01CA-52955-02 0001 (SRC) SCHMITZ, FRANCIS Discovery of antitumor marine products by mechanism base Antitumor agents from microorganisms and invertebrates

U01CA-52955-02 0002 (SRC) GERWICK, WILLIAM Discovery of antitumor marine products by mechanism base Antineoplastic agents from marine microalgae

U01CA-52955-02 0003 (SRC) CREWS, PHILLIP Discovery of antitumor marine products by mechanism base Anticancer leads from marine animals

U01CA-52955-02 9001 (SRC) CREWS, PHILLIP Discovery of antitumor marine products by mechanism base Core project

U01CA-52956-02 (SRC) CORDELL, GEOFFREY A UNIV. OF ILLINOIS AT CHICAGO 833 S. WOOD ST., M/C 781 CHICAGO, IL 60612 Novel strategies for plant-derived anticancer agents

U01CA-52956-02 0001 (SRC) FARNSWORTH, NORMAN R Novel strategies for plant-derived anticancer agents Plant selection and collection

U01CA-52956-02 0002 (SRC) KINGHORN, A DOUGLAS Novel strategies for plant-derived anticancer agents Extraction, fractionation, isolation, structure elucidation

U01CA-52956-02 0003 (SRC) PEZZUTO, JOHN M Novel strategies for plant-derived anticancer agents Biological evaluation

U01CA-52956-02 0004 (SRC) WALL, MONROE E Novel strategies for plant-derived anticancer agents Extraction, fractionation, isolation, structure elucidation, and biological eval

U01CA-52956-02 0005 (SRC) HARRIS, TIMOTHY J Novel strategies for plant-derived anticancer agents Biological evaluation, structure elucidation, large-scale extraction & synthesis

R01CA-52958-02 (SRC) FELDMAN, JUDITH RHODE ISLAND DEPT OF HEALTH 3 CAPITOL HILL PROVIDENCE, RI 02908-5097 Increasing cancer screening in poor and minority women

R01CA-52962-10 (CTY) CABRAL, FERNANDO R UNIV OF TEXAS MED SCHOOL PO BOX 20708 HOUSTON, TEXAS 77225 Genetic approach to microtubule function in CHO cells

R01CA-52977-02 (SRC) SIMPSON, DIANE M TEXAS DEPT OF HEALTH 1100 WEST 49TH STREET AUSTIN, TX 78756 Mujeres protejase/Women protect yourself--Cancer screening in El Paso

R01CA-52994-02 (SRC) SLATER, JONATHAN S MINNESOTA DEPT OF HEALTH 717 S.E. DELAWARE STREET MINNEAPOLIS, MN 55440 Increasing cancer screening among underserved women

U01CA-52995-02 (SRC) POWIS, GARTH MAYO FOUNDATION 200 FIRST STREET SOUTHWEST ROCHESTER, MN 55905 Cancer drugs active against signal transduction targets

U01CA-52995-02 0001 (SRC) ZALKOW, LEON H Cancer drugs active against signal transduction targets Novel compounds from isolation and chemical modifications

U01CA-52995-02 0002 (SRC) POWIS, GARTH Cancer drugs active against signal transduction targets Inhibition of Ca++ signalling mechanisms

U01CA-52995-02 0003 (SRC) ASHENDEL, CURTIS L Cancer drugs active against signal transduction targets Modulation of protein kinase C activity

U01CA-52995-02 0004 (SRC) ABRAHAM, ROBERT T Cancer drugs active against signal transduction targets Inhibition of protein tyrosine kinase activity

U01CA-52995-02 0005 (SRC) POWIN, GARTH Cancer drugs active against signal transduction targets In vitro cytotoxicity testing of potential anticancer drugs

R01CA-52997-02 (ET) KESSEL, DAVID H WAYNE STATE UNIVERSITY DETROIT, MI 48201 Characterization of new photosensitizing dyes

U01CA-53001-02 (SRC) VALERIOTE, FREDERICK A WAYNE STATE UNIVERSITY PO BOX 02188 DETROIT, MI 48201 Discovery of new anticancer agents from natural products

U01CA-53001-02 0001 (SRC) MOORE, RICHARD Discovery of new anticancer agents from natural products Production of natural products and organic synthesis

U01CA-53001-02 0002 (SRC) CORBETT, THOMAS H Discovery of new anticancer agents from natural products Drug discovery--In vitro and in vivo

U01CA-53001-02 0003 (SRC) CORBETT, THOMAS Discovery of new anticancer agents from natural products Secondary evaluation of new anticancer agents

U01CA-53001-02 0004 (SRC) VALERIOTE, FREDERICK A Discovery of new anticancer agents from natural products New anticancer agents--Pharmacologic/biochemical/cellular/molecular action

R01CA-53003-02 (SRC) TROLL, WALTER NEW YORK UNIV MEDICAL CENTER 550 FIRST AVENUE NEW YORK, NY 10016 Anticarcinogenesis by nicotinamide, a protease inhibitor

PROJECT NO., ORGANIZATIONAL UNIT., INVESTIGATOR, ADDRESS, TITLE

R29CA-53005-02 (PTHB) WILCZYNSKI, SHARON P CITY OF HOPE NATIONAL MED CTR 1500 E DUARTE RD DUARTE, CA 91010 Pathologic & molecular study of HPV in cervical cancer

R43CA-53022-01A1 (SSS) DIGIACOMO, ENZO V MEDICAL HORIZONS, INC 66 JONQUIL LANE LONGMEADOW, MA 01106 Better cancer screening by computerizing medical records

R43CA-53030-01A1 (SSS) KOPPEL, LOUIS N ARACOR 425 LAKESIDE DRIVE SUNNYVALE, CA 94086 Novel x-ray mammography system development

R43CA-53035-01A1 (ET) BUNOW, BARRY J CIVILIZED SOFTWARE, INC 7735 OLD GEORGETOWN ROAD BETHESDA, MD 20814 COMBO--Program for analyzing drug combination assays

R43CA-53040-01A1 (SSS) TUCKER, STANLEY D UNIV OF TX MD ANDERSON CA CTR 1515 HOLCOMBE BLVD, BOX 41 HOUSTON, TX 77030 Isolation and expression of cDNA clones for RIF

R01CA-53058-02 (ARR) EWERT, DONALD L THE WISTAR INSTITUTE 36TH AND SPRUCE STREETS PHILADELPHIA, PA 19104 Mechanisms of lymphomagenesis in AIDS patients

R44CA-53060-02 (SSS) GROTHAUS, PAUL G HAWAII BIOTECHNOLOGY GROUP, IN 99-193 AIEA HEIGHTS DRIVE AIEA, HAWAII 96701 Immunoassays for taxol

R13CA-53064-01 (SRC) HOWELL, ROGER W UNIV OF MED & DENT OF NJ 185 S ORANGE AVE MSB F-451 NEWARK, NJ 07103 2nd international symposium on biophysical aspects of Auger processes

R43CA-53068-01A1 (HUD) MITCHELL, HERMAN E NEW ENGLAND RESEARCH INST, INC 9 GALEN STREET WATERTOWN, MA 02172 Microcomputer mortality surveillance system

R29CA-53076-02 (BMT) MASCHARAK, PRADIP K UNIV OF CALIFORNIA THIMANN LABORATORIES SANTA CRUZ, CA 95064 Systematic analogue approach to metallobleomycins

R01CA-53083-02 (SRC) KERNER, JON F MEMORIAL HOSP FOR CANCER AND 1275 YORK AVENUE NEW YORK, NY 10021 Cancer control needs in multi-ethnic communities

R29CA-53085-02 (CBY) WASILENKO, WILLIAM J EASTERN VIRGINIA MEDICAL SCHOO 700 WEST OLNEY ROAD, PO BOX 19 NORFOLK, VA 23501 Inositol tetrakisphosphate control by the src oncogene

R13CA-53089-01S1 (SRC) WARD, JOHN F UNIV OF CALIFORNIA, SAN DIEGO 114 MEDICAL TEACHING FACILITY LA JOLLA, CA 92093 9th international congress of radiation research

R01CA-53091-01 (CBY) ROLLINS, BARRETT J DANA-FARBER CANCER INSTITUTE 44 BINNEY STREET BOSTON, MA 02115 Functional analysis of a PDGF-inducible cytokine

R29CA-53094-02 (HEM) VARTICOVSKI, LYUBA ST ELIZABETH'S HOSP OF BOSTON 736 CAMBRIDGE STREET BOSTON, MA 02135 Role of novel PI-3 kinase in hematopoietic cell growth

R01CA-53105-01 (SSS) MORSE, DANIEL E UNIVERSITY OF CALIFORNIA SANTA, BARBARA, CA 93106 Oncogenes and tumors in marine invertebrate larvae

R01CA-53106-01A1 (CPA) HINES, RONALD N WAYNE STATE UNIVERSITY 540 E CANFIELD DETROIT, MI 48201 Regulation of flavin-monooxygenase gene expression

R01CA-53113-01 (RAD) SANDISON, GEORGE A INDIANA UNIVERSITY SCHOOL OF M 535 BARNHILL DRIVE INDIANAPOLIS, IN 46202-5289 A new dose algorithm for electron radiotherapy

R01CA-53114-01A1 (RAD) KIM, JAE H HENRY FORD HOSPITAL 2799 WEST GRAND BOULEVARD DETROIT, MI 48202 Combined brachytherapy and hyperthermia

R01CA-53123-01 (CPA) CONTI, CLAUDIO J UNIV OF TX M D ANDERSON CA CTR PO BOX 389 HOUSTON, TX 78957 Tumor suppressor genes in two-stage carcinogenesis

U10CA-53127-01 (CCI) BEARDSLEY, GEORGE P YALE UNIV SCHOOL OF MEDICINE 333 CEDAR STREET NEW HAVEN, CT 06510 Yale institutional pediatric oncology group

U10CA-53127-01 0048 (CCI) BEARDSLEY, GEORGE P Yale institutional pediatric oncology group POG9061-Phase II systemic therapy and irradiation for ALL & CNS leukemia

U10CA-53127-01 0049 (CCI) BEARDSLEY, GEORGE P Yale institutional pediatric oncology group POG 9086--Phase I pilot study of therapy for T-cell ALL or NHL

U10CA-53127-01 0050 (CCI) BEARDSLEY, GEORGE P Yale institutional pediatric oncology group POG9071--Phase I trial of fazarabine in children with acute leukemia

U10CA-53127-01 0051 (CCI) BEARDSLEY, GEORGE P Yale institutional pediatric oncology group POG8970--Phase I trial of fazarabine in children with refractory solid tumors

U10CA-53127-01 0052 (CCI) BEARDSLEY, GEORGE P Yale institutional pediatric oncology group POG8973--Etoposide (VP-16) and carboplatin in children with acute leukemia

U10CA-53127-01 0053 (CCI) BEARDSLEY, GEORGE P Yale institutional pediatric oncology group POG8870--Phase I trial of ifosfamide/VP16/MESNA in children with acute leukemia

U10CA-53127-01 0054 (CCI) BEARDSLEY, GEORGE P Yale institutional pediatric oncology group POG8871--Phase I study of rTNF in children with refractory solid tumors

U10CA-53127-01 0055 (CCI) BEARDSLEY, GEORGE P Yale institutional pediatric oncology group POG8671--Phase I immunotherapy with rIL-2 in children with solid tumors

U10CA-53127-01 0056 (CCI) BEARDSLEY, GEORGE P Yale institutional pediatric oncology group POG8494--Phase I study of fludarabine phosphate in pediatric patients

U10CA-53127-01 0057 (CCI) BEARDSLEY, GEORGE P Yale institutional pediatric oncology group POG8930--A comprehensive genetic analysis of brain tumors

U10CA-53127-01 0058 (CCI) BEARDSLEY, GEORGE P Yale institutional pediatric oncology group POG8828--Late effects of Hodgkin's disease

U10CA-53127-01 0059 (CCI) BEARDSLEY, GEORGE P Yale institutional pediatric oncology group POG9046--Molecular genetic analysis of Wilm's tumors

U10CA-53127-01 0060 (CCI) BEARDSLEY, GEORGE P Yale institutional pediatric oncology group POG9153--Rhabdomyosarcoma study/laboratory evaluation of tumor

U10CA-53127-01 0001 (CCI) BEARDSLEY, GEORGE P Yale institutional pediatric oncology group POG9006--6-MP/methotrexate vs. alternating chemotheray for ALL in childhood

PROJECT NO., ORGANIZATIONAL UNIT., INVESTIGATOR, ADDRESS, TITLE

U10CA-53127-01 0016 (CCI) BEARDSLEY, GEORGE P Yale institutional pediatric oncology group POG8653--Phase III study of childhood soft tissue sarcomas

U10CA-53127-01 0017 (CCI) BEARDSLEY, GEORGE P Yale institutional pediatric oncology group POG8625--Phase III combined therapy in childhood Hodgkin's disease

U10CA-53127-01 0018 (CCI) BEARDSLEY, GEORGE P Yale institutional pediatric oncology group POG8451--Intergroup rhabdomyosarcoma study

U10CA-53127-01 0019 (CCI) BEARDSLEY, GEORGE P Yale institutional pediatric oncology group POG9110--Rotational drug therapy after first marrow relapse of non-T, non B ALL

U10CA-53127-01 0020 (CCI) BEARDSLEY, GEORGE P Yale institutional pediatric oncology group POG9107--Phase II pilot study of infant leukemia

U10CA-53127-01 0021 (CCI) BEARDSLEY, GEORGE P Yale institutional pediatric oncology group POG9140--Phase II therapy for recurrent or refractory neuroblastoma

U10CA-53127-01 0022 (CCI) BEARDSLEY, GEORGE P Yale institutional pediatric oncology group POG9048--Phase II study of malignant germ cell tumors in children

U10CA-53127-01 0023 (CCI) BEARDSLEY, GEORGE P Yale institutional pediatric oncology group POG9060--Intensive QOD ifosfamide treatment for CNS tumors in children

U10CA-53127-01 0024 (CCI) BEARDSLEY, GEORGE P Yale institutional pediatric oncology group POG8936--Phase II study of carboplatin treatment for optic pathway tumors

U10CA-53127-01 0025 (CCI) BEARDSLEY, GEORGE P Yale institutional pediatric oncology group POG8935--Phase II study of surgery and/or radiotherapy for optic pathway tumors

U10CA-53127-01 0026 (CCI) BEARDSLEY, GEORGE P Yale institutional pediatric oncology group POG8820--Phase II/III study of VP-16, AMSA +/- 5-azacytidine in childhood ANLL

U10CA-53127-01 0027 (CCI) BEARDSLEY, GEORGE P Yale institutional pediatric oncology group POG8889--Intergroup rhabdomyosarcoma study for clinical group IV disease

U10CA-53127-01 0028 (CCI) BEARDSLEY, GEORGE P Yale institutional pediatric oncology group POG8866--Phase II asparaginase therapy for acute lymphoblastic leukemia

U10CA-53127-01 0029 (CCI) BEARDSLEY, GEORGE P Yale institutional pediatric oncology group POG8862--Combination chemotherapy of acute T-lymphoblastic leukemia

U10CA-53127-01 0030 (CCI) BEARDSLEY, GEORGE P Yale institutional pediatric oncology group POG8863--Phase II study of high dose cytosine arabinoside in childhood tumors

U10CA-53127-01 0031 (CCI) BEARDSLEY, GEORGE P Yale institutional pediatric oncology group POG8827--Phase II treatment of children with Hodgkin's disease in relapse

U10CA-53127-01 0032 (CCI) BEARDSLEY, GEORGE P Yale institutional pediatric oncology group POG8865--Phase II recombinant alpha-interferon in relapsed T-cell disease

U10CA-53127-01 0033 (CCI) BEARDSLEY, GEORGE P Pediatric oncology group--Phase II recombinant A-interferon in chronic myelogenous leukemia

U10CA-53127-01 0034 (CCI) BEARDSLEY, GEORGE P Yale institutional pediatric oncology group POG8832--Combination chemotherapy followed by radiotherapy for brain tumors

U10CA-53127-01 0035 (CCI) BEARDSLEY, GEORGE P Yale institutional pediatric oncology group POG8731--Phase II trial of methotrexate in treatment of brain tumors in children

U10CA-53127-01 0036 (CCI) BEARDSLEY, GEORGE P Yale institutional pediatric oncology group POG8788--Intergroup rhabdomyosarcoma study/pilot study for clinical group III

U10CA-53127-01 0037 (CCI) BEARDSLEY, GEORGE P Yale institutional pediatric oncology group POG8761--Phase II study of homoharringtonine therapy for nonlymphoblastic leukemi

U10CA-53127-01 0038 (CCI) BEARDSLEY, GEORGE P Yale institutional pediatric oncology group POG8739--Phase II immunotherapy with alpha-2 interferon for brain tumors (human)e

U10CA-53127-01 0039 (CCI) BEARDSLEY, GEORGE P Yale institutional pediatric oncology group POG8741--Treatment of patients with stage C and stage D neuroblastoma

U10CA-53127-01 0040 (CCI) BEARDSLEY, GEORGE P Yale institutional pediatric oncology group POG8751--Phase II methotrexate chemotherapy for rhabdomyosarcoma in children

U10CA-53127-01 0041 (CCI) BEARDSLEY, GEORGE P Yale institutional pediatric oncology group POG8633--Postoperative chemotherapy and delayed irradiation for brain tumors

U10CA-53127-01 0042 (CCI) BEARDSLEY, GEORGE P Yale institutional pediatric oncology group POG8617--Therapy for B-cell acute lymphoblastic leukemia and lymphoma

U10CA-53127-01 0043 (CCI) BEARDSLEY, GEORGE P Yale institutional pediatric oncology group POG9139--Phase I study of cisplatin and irradiation in brain stem gliomas

U10CA-53127-01 0044 (CCI) BEARDSLEY, GEORGE P Yale institutional pediatric oncology group POG9079--Phase I study of L-PAM/CTX with ABM rescue for brain tumors in children

U10CA-53127-01 0045 (CCI) BEARDSLEY, GEORGE P Yale institutional pediatric oncology group POG9075--Phase I study of acivicin in children with solid tumors

U10CA-53127-01 0046 (CCI) BEARDSLEY, GEORGE P Yale institutional pediatric oncology group POG9074--Phase I study of xomazyme-H65 in children with T-cell ALL/lymphoma

U10CA-53127-01 0047 (CCI) BEARDSLEY, GEORGE P Yale institutional pediatric oncology group POG9072--Phase I chemotherapy for recurrent/resistant malignant solid tumors

U10CA-53127-01 0002 (CCI) BEARDSLEY, GEORGE P Yale institutional pediatric oncology group POG9005--Dose intensification of methotrexate & 6-mercaptourine in childhood ALL

U10CA-53127-01 0003 (CCI) BEARDSLEY, GEORGE P Yale institutional pediatric oncology group POG9031--Cisplatin/VP-16 therapy of medulloblastoma/pre vs. post irradiation

U10CA-53127-01 0004 (CCI) BEARDSLEY, GEORGE P Yale institutional pediatric oncology group POG8945--Phase III chemotherapy for

PROJECT NO., ORGANIZATIONAL UNIT., INVESTIGATOR, ADDRESS, TITLE

hepatoblastoma & hepatocellular carcinoma

U10CA-53127-01 0005 (CCI) BEARDSLEY, GEORGE P Yale institutional pediatric oncology group POG9049--Phase III study of high-risk malignant germ cell tumors in children

U10CA-53127-01 0006 (CCI) BEARDSLEY, GEORGE P Yale institutional pediatric oncology group POG8844--Bone marrow transplant in children with stage D neuroblastoma

U10CA-53127-01 0007 (CCI) BEARDSLEY, GEORGE P Yale institutional pediatric oncology group POG8850--Phase III treatment of Ewing's sarcoma and neuroectodermal bone tumors

U10CA-53127-01 0008 (CCI) BEARDSLEY, GEORGE P Yale institutional pediatric oncology group POG8821--Phase III chemotherapy +/- autologous BMT in children with AML

U10CA-53127-01 0009 (CCI) BEARDSLEY, GEORGE P Yale institutional pediatric oncology group POG8725--Phase III chemotherapy +/- radiation therapy in pediatric Hodgkins

U10CA-53127-01 0010 (CCI) BEARDSLEY, GEORGE P Yale institutional pediatric oncology group POG8704--Phase III chemotherapy of childhood T cell ALL & lymphoblastic lymphoma

U10CA-53127-01 0011 (CCI) BEARDSLEY, GEORGE P Yale institutional pediatric oncology group POG8719--Phase III chemotherapy for non-Hodgkin's lymphoma in children

U10CA-53127-01 0012 (CCI) BEARDSLEY, GEORGE P Yale institutional pediatric oncology group POG8650--National Wilm's tumor and clear cell sarcoma study

U10CA-53127-01 0013 (CCI) BEARDSLEY, GEORGE P Yale institutional pediatric oncology group POG8616--Phase III chemotherapy for childhood Burkitt and non-Burkitts lymphoma

U10CA-53127-01 0014 (CCI) BEARDSLEY, GEORGE P Yale institutional pediatric oncology group POG8615--Phase III study of large cell lymphomas in children and adolescents

U10CA-53127-01 0015 (CCI) BEARDSLEY, GEORGE P Yale institutional pediatric oncology group POG8651--Phase III study of childhood nonmetastatic osteosarcoma

U10CA-53128-01 0019 (CCI) PATTERSON, RICHARD B Pediatric oncology group studies POG9110--Rotational drug therapy after first marrow relapse of non-T, non B ALL

U10CA-53128-01 (CCI) PATTERSON, RICHARD B WAKE FOREST UNIVERSITY 300 SOUTH HAWTHORNE ROAD WINSTON-SALEM, NC 27103 **Pediatric** oncology group studies

U10CA-53128-01 0001 (CCI) PATTERSON, RICHARD B Pediatric oncology group studies POG9006--6-MP/methotrexate vs. alternating chemotherapy for ALL in childhood

U10CA-53128-01 0002 (CCI) PATTERSON, RICHARD B Pediatric oncology group studies POG9005--Dose intensification of methotrexate & 6-mercaptourine in childhood ALL

U10CA-53128-01 0003 (CCI) PATTERSON, RICHARD B Pediatric oncology group studies POG9031--Cisplatin/VP-16 therapy of medulloblastoma/pre vs. post irradiation

U10CA-53128-01 0004 (CCI) PATTERSON, RICHARD B Pediatric oncology group studies POG8945--Phase III chemotherapy for hepatoblastoma & hepatocellular carcinoma

U10CA-53128-01 0005 (CCI) PATTERSON, RICHARD B Pediatric oncology group studies POG9049--Phase III study of high-risk malignant germ cell tumors in children

U10CA-53128-01 0006 (CCI) PATTERSON, RICHARD B Pediatric oncology group studies POG8844--Bone marrow transplant in children with stage D neuroblastoma

U10CA-53128-01 0007 (CCI) PATTERSON, RICHARD B Pediatric oncology group studies POG8850--Phase III treatment of Ewing's sarcoma and neuroectodermal bone tumors

U10CA-53128-01 0008 (CCI) PATTERSON, RICHARD B Pediatric oncology group studies POG8821--Phase III chemotherapy +/- autologous BMT in children with AML

U10CA-53128-01 0009 (CCI) PATTERSON, RICHARD B Pediatric oncology group studies POG8725--Phase III chemotherapy +/- radiation therapy in pediatric Hodgkins

U10CA-53128-01 0010 (CCI) PATTERSON, RICHARD B Pediatric oncology group studies POG8704--Phase III chemotherapy of childhood T cell ALL & lymphoblastic lymphoma

U10CA-53128-01 0011 (CCI) PATTERSON, RICHARD B Pediatric oncology group studies POG8719--Phase III chemotherapy for non-Hodgkin's lymphoma in children

U10CA-53128-01 0012 (CCI) PATTERSON, RICHARD B Pediatric oncology group studies POG8650--National Wilm's tumor and clear cell sarcoma study

U10CA-53128-01 0013 (CCI) PATTERSON, RICHARD B Pediatric oncology group studies POG8616--Phase III chemotherapy for childhood Burkitt and non-Burkitts lymphoma

U10CA-53128-01 0014 (CCI) PATTERSON, RICHARD B Pediatric oncology group studies POG8615--Phase III study of large cell lymphomas in children and adolescents

U10CA-53128-01 0015 (CCI) PATTERSON, RICHARD B Pediatric oncology group studies POG8651--Phase III study of childhood nonmetastatic osteosarcoma

U10CA-53128-01 0016 (CCI) PATTERSON, RICHARD B Pediatric oncology group studies POG8653--Phase III study of childhood soft tissue sarcomas

U10CA-53128-01 0017 (CCI) PATTERSON, RICHARD B Pediatric oncology group studies POG8625--Phase III combined therapy in childhood Hodgkin's disease

U10CA-53128-01 0018 (CCI) PATTERSON, RICHARD B Pediatric oncology group studies POG8451--Intergroup rhabdomyosarcoma study

U10CA-53128-01 0020 (CCI) PATTERSON, RICHARD B Pediatric oncology group studies POG9107--Phase II pilot study of infant leukemia

U10CA-53128-01 0051 (CCI) PATTERSON, RICHARD B Pediatric oncology group studies POG8970--Phase I trial of fazarabine in children with refractory solid tumors

U10CA-53128-01 0052 (CCI) PATTERSON, RICHARD B Pediatric oncology group studies POG8973--Etoposide (VP-16) and carboplatin in children with acute leukemia

U10CA-53128-01 0053 (CCI) PATTERSON, RICHARD B Pediatric oncology group studies POG8870--Phase I trial of ifosfamide/VP16/MESNA in children with acute leukemia

U10CA-53128-01 0054 (CCI) PATTERSON, RICHARD B Pediatric oncology group studies POG8871--Phase I study of rTNF in children with refractory solid tumors

U10CA-53128-01 0055 (CCI) PATTERSON, RICHARD B Pediatric oncology group studies POG8671--Phase I immunotherapy with rIL-2 in children with solid tumors

U10CA-53128-01 0056 (CCI) PATTERSON, RICHARD B Pediatric oncology group studies POG8494--Phase I study of fludarabine phosphate in pediatric patients

U10CA-53128-01 0057 (CCI) PATTERSON, RICHARD B Pediatric oncology group studies POG8930--A comprehensive genetic analysis of brain tumors

U10CA-53128-01 0058 (CCI) PATTERSON, RICHARD B Pediatric oncology group studies POG8828--Late effects of Hodgkin's disease

U10CA-53128-01 0059 (CCI) PATTERSON, RICHARD B Pediatric oncology group studies POG9046--Molecular genetic analysis of Wilm's tumors

U10CA-53128-01 0060 (CCI) PATTERSON, RICHARD B Pediatric oncology group studies POG9153--Rhabdomyosarcoma study/laboratory evaluation of tumor

U10CA-53128-01 0021 (CCI) PATTERSON, RICHARD B Pediatric oncology group studies POG9140--Phase II therapy for recurrent or refractory neuroblastoma

U10CA-53128-01 0022 (CCI) PATTERSON, RICHARD B Pediatric oncology group studies POG9048--Phase II study of malignant germ cell tumors in children

U10CA-53128-01 0023 (CCI) PATTERSON, RICHARD B Pediatric oncology group studies POG9060--Intensive QOD ifosfamide treatment for CNS tumors in children

U10CA-53128-01 0024 (CCI) PATTERSON, RICHARD B Pediatric oncology group studies POG8936--Phase II study of carboplatin treatment for optic pathway tumors

U10CA-53128-01 0025 (CCI) PATTERSON, RICHARD B Pediatric oncology group studies POG8935--Phase II study of surgery and/or radiotherapy for optic pathway tumors

U10CA-53128-01 0026 (CCI) PATTERSON, RICHARD B Pediatric oncology group studies POG8820--Phase II/III study of VP-16, AMSA +/- 5-azacytidine in childhood ANLL

U10CA-53128-01 0027 (CCI) PATTERSON, RICHARD B Pediatric oncology group studies POG8889--Intergroup rhabdomyosarcoma study for clinical group IV disease

U10CA-53128-01 0028 (CCI) PATTERSON, RICHARD B Pediatric oncology group studies POG8866--Phase II asparaginase therapy for acute lymphoblastic leukemia

U10CA-53128-01 0029 (CCI) PATTERSON, RICHARD B Pediatric oncology group studies POG8862--Combination chemotherapy of acute T-lymphoblastic leukemia

U10CA-53128-01 0030 (CCI) PATTERSON, RICHARD B Pediatric oncology group studies POG8863--Phase II study of high dose cytosine arabinoside in childhood tumors

U10CA-53128-01 0031 (CCI) PATTERSON, RICHARD B Pediatric oncology group studies POG8827--Phase II treatment of children with Hodgkin's disease in relapse

U10CA-53128-01 0032 (CCI) PATTERSON, RICHARD B Pediatric oncology group studies POG8865--Phase II recombinant alpha-interferon in relapsed T-cell disease

U10CA-53128-01 0033 (CCI) PATTERSON, RICHARD B Pediatric oncology group--Phase II recombinant A-interferon in chronic myelogenous leukemia

U10CA-53128-01 0034 (CCI) PATTERSON, RICHARD B Pediatric oncology group studies POG8832--Combination chemotherapy followed by radiotherapy for brain tumors

U10CA-53128-01 0035 (CCI) PATTERSON, RICHARD B Pediatric oncology group studies POG8731--Phase II trial of methotrexate in treatment of brain tumors in children

U10CA-53128-01 0036 (CCI) PATTERSON, RICHARD B Pediatric oncology group studies POG8788--Intergroup rhabdomyosarcoma study/pilot study for clinical group III

U10CA-53128-01 0037 (CCI) PATTERSON, RICHARD B Pediatric oncology group studies POG8761--Phase II study of homoharringtonine therapy for nonlymphoblastic leukemi

U10CA-53128-01 0038 (CCI) PATTERSON, RICHARD B Pediatric oncology group studies POG8739--Phase II immunotherapy with alpha-2 interferon for brain tumors (human)e

U10CA-53128-01 0039 (CCI) PATTERSON, RICHARD B Pediatric oncology group studies POG8741--Treatment of patients with stage C and stage D neuroblastoma

U10CA-53128-01 0040 (CCI) PATTERSON, RICHARD B Pediatric oncology group studies POG8751--Phase II methotrexate chemotherapy for rhabdomyosarcoma in children

U10CA-53128-01 0041 (CCI) PATTERSON, RICHARD B Pediatric oncology group studies POG8633--Postoperative chemotherapy and delayed irradiation for brain tumors

U10CA-53128-01 0042 (CCI) PATTERSON, RICHARD B Pediatric oncology group studies POG8617--Therapy for B-cell acute lymphoblastic leukemia and lymphoma

U10CA-53128-01 0043 (CCI) PATTERSON, RICHARD B Pediatric oncology group studies POG9139--Phase I study of cisplatin and irradiation in brain stem gliomas

U10CA-53128-01 0044 (CCI) PATTERSON, RICHARD B Pediatric oncology group studies POG9079--Phase I study of L-PAM/CTX with ABM rescue for brain tumors in children

U10CA-53128-01 0045 (CCI) PATTERSON, RICHARD B Pediatric oncology group studies POG9075--Phase I study of acivicin in children with solid tumors

U10CA-53128-01 0046 (CCI) PATTERSON, RICHARD B Pediatric oncology group studies POG9074--Phase I study of xomazyme-H65 in children with T-cell ALL/lymphoma

U10CA-53128-01 0047 (CCI) PATTERSON, RICHARD B Pediatric oncology group studies POG9072--Phase I chemotherapy for recurrent/resistant malignant solid tumors

U10CA-53128-01 0048 (CCI) PATTERSON, RICHARD B Pediatric oncology group studies POG9061-Phase II systemic therapy and irradiation for

ALL & CNS leukemia

U10CA-53128-01 0049 (CCI) PATTERSON, RICHARD B Pediatric oncology group studies POG 9086--Phase I pilot study of therapy for T-cell ALL or NHL

U10CA-53128-01 0050 (CCI) PATTERSON, RICHARD B Pediatric oncology group studies POG9071--Phase I trial of fazarabine in children with acute leukemia

R55CA-53136-01A1 (PTHB) SMALL, MICHAEL B UMDNJ-NEW JERSEY MEDICAL SCHOO 185 SOUTH ORANGE AVENUE NEWARK, NJ 07103-2714 Genetic analysis of neoplastic transformation by myc

R01CA-53139-01 (PTHB) CANAANI, DAN TEL AVIV UNIVERSITY RAMAT AVIV, ISRAEL 69978 Molecular basis for xeroderma pigmentosum group C defect

R01CA-53149-01A1 (PTHB) WONG, ALBERT J FOX CHASE CANCER CENTER 7701 BURHOLME AVENUE PHILADELPHIA, PA 19111 The role of phospholipase C in transformation

R13CA-53160-01 (SRC) WILLIAMS, GARY M AMERICAN HEALTH FOUNDATION ONE DANA ROAD VALHALLA, NY 10595 Cancer mechanisms--Implications for risk assessment

R13CA-53161-01 (SRC) PARNES, HOWARD L UNIV OF MARYLAND CANCER CENTER 22 S GREENE STREET BALTIMORE, MD 21201 Symposium--Cancer in the socioeconomically disadvantaged

R01CA-53167-01 (RAD) ARMOUR, ELWOOD P WILLIAM BEAUMONT HOSPITAL 3601 W 13 MILE ROAD ROYAL OAK, MI 48073-6769 Low temperature hyperthermia and LDR irradiation

R01CA-53172-01 (RNM) WAHL, RICHARD L UNIVERSITY OF MICHIGAN MED CTR 1500 E MED CENTER DR ANN ARBOR, MI 48109-0028 Positron emission tomography of genitourinary malignancies

R29CA-53184-01 (ET) LOCK, RICHARD B THE UNIVERSITY OF LOUISVILLE 529 SOUTH JACKSON STREET LOUISVILLE, KY 40292 Cdc2 in G2 arrest and cell death by antitumor agents

R01CA-53191-01A1 (PHRA) STROBEL, HENRY W UNIVERSITY OF TEXAS MED SCHOOL PO BOX 20708 HOUSTON, TX 77030 Reductase/p450 interaction affects carcinogen activation

R01CA-53197-01 (SSS) SIKKA, HARISH C STATE UNIVERSITY OF NEW YORK 1300 ELMWOOD AVENUE BUFFALO, N Y 14222 Metabolism of acetylaminofluorene by rainbow trout

R29CA-53199-01A1 (RAD) VALERIE, KRISTOFFER C MEDICAL COLLEGE OF VIRGINIA BOX 58 - MCV STATION RICHMOND, VA 23298-0058 Radiation-induced gene expression

R01CA-53203-01A1 (END) SHAIN, SYDNEY A UNIV OF TEXAS HLTH SCI CTR 7703 FLOYD CURL DRIVE SAN ANTONIO, TX 78284 Prostate cancer--An in vivo rodent model

R01CA-53246-01 (EVR) LANFORD, ROBERT E SW FOUNDATION FOR BIOMED RES P O BOX 28147 SAN ANTONIO, TX 78228-0147 Model systems for analysis of HBV replication

R01CA-53248-01 (CTY) HOROWITZ, JONATHAN M DUKE UNIV MEDICAL CTR BOX 3686 DURHAM, NC 27710 The rb protein biochemical and functional analysis

R01CA-53250-01 (PBC) PYTELA, ROBERT UNIVERSITY OF CALIFORNIA, S F BOX 0854 SAN FRANCISCO, CA 94143-0854 Integrin distribution and function in tumor cells

R03CA-53267-01 (SRC) WESTBROOK, CAROL A UNIVERSITY OF CHICAGO 5841 S MARYLAND AVE, BOX 420 CHICAGO, IL 60637-1470 Molecular genetic findings in colorectal cancer

R01CA-53271-01 (MBY) OSTROWSKI, MICHAEL C DUKE UNIVERSITY MEDICAL CTR P O BOX 3020 DURHAM, NC 27710 Analysis of ras oncogene-activated gene expression

R03CA-53280-02 (SRC) MUGGIA, FRANCO M USC NORRIS CANCER HOSPITAL 1441 EASTLAKE AVENUE LOS ANGELES, CA 90033-0800 Repair of DNA adducts--Relationships to platinum response

R03CA-53282-02 (SRC) FISHER, BERNARD UNIVERSITY OF PITTSBURGH 3550 TERRACE STREET PITTSBURGH, PA 15261 Correlative laboratory studies and innovative clinical trails

R03CA-53284-02 (SRC) SMITH, R GRAHAM U T SOUTHWESTERN MEDICAL CENTE 5323 HARRY HINES BOULEVARD DALLAS, TX 75235-8852 Immunoglobulin genes as markers for residual ALL

R03CA-53293-02 (SRC) ENSLEY, JOHN F HARPER HOSPITAL 3990 JOHN R DETROIT, MI 48201 Clinical potential of flow cytometry in head and neck cancer

R03CA-53311-02 (SRC) GANDHI, VARSHA UT MD ANDERSON CANCER CENTER 1515 HOLCOMBE BOULEVARD HOUSTON, TX 77030 Biochemical modulation to increase leukemia response

R01CA-53313-01 (SSS) SCHMALE, MICHAEL C 4600 RICKENBACKER CAUSEWAY MIAMI, FL 33149 Cancer in damselfish--Immunology and in vitro models

R03CA-53318-02 (SRC) HANSEN, MARC F UNIVERSITY OF TEXAS 1515 HOLCOMBE BLVD HOUSTON, TX 77030 Correlation of RB1 expression and prognosis in sarcomas

R03CA-53329-02 (SRC) SEEGER, ROBERT C CHILDRENS HOSPITAL LOS ANGELES 4650 SUNSET BOULEVARD LOS ANGELES, CA 90027 Immunocytology of marrow metastases in neuroblastoma

R55CA-53332-01 (EVR) BARKLIS, ERIC OREGON HEALTH SCIENCES UNIVER 3181 S W SAM JACKSON PARK ROAD PORTLAND, OR 97201-3098 Regulation of retrovirus expression in stem cells

R03CA-53336-01 (SRC) HAYES, DANIEL DANA-FARBER CANCER INSTITUTE 44 BINNEY STREET Circulating c-neu protein in breast cancer patients

R03CA-53341-02 (SRC) CUNNINGHAM-RUNDLES, CHARLOTTE MOUNT SINAI MEDICAL CENTER ONE GUSTAVE LEVY PLACE NEW YORK, NY 10029 Effects of PEG-IL-2 in primary immunodeficiency disease

R03CA-53352-01 (SRC) ABBOUD, CAMILLE N UNIV OF ROCHESTER MED CTR 601 ELMWOOD AVENUE, BOX 610 ROCHESTER, NY 14642 In-vitro and in-vivo effects of GM-CSF on adult ANLL

R01CA-53370-01 (VR) WHITE, EILEEN CTR FOR ADVANCED BIOTECH & MED 679 HOES LANE PICATAWAY, NJ 08854-5638 Function of the adenovirus E1B oncogene

R01CA-53371-01 (VR) SCHLEGEL, RICHARD GEORGETOWN UNIVERSITY MED SCHO 3900 RESERVOIR ROAD, NORTHWEST WASHINGTON, DC 20007 Papillomavirus E5 oncoprotein and cell transformation

R03CA-53372-02 (SRC) TAYLOR, CHARLES W 1501 NORTH CAMPBELL AVENUE TUCSON, AZ 85724 In vitro correlations of suramin response in melanoma

R01CA-53394-01 (VR) PRIVALSKY, MARTIN L UNIVERSITY OF CALIFORNIA DAVIS, CA 95616 Mechanism of action of the v-ERB a oncogene of AEV

R01CA-53395-01 (CBY) SOLOMON, FRANK E MASSACHUSETTS INST OF TECH 77 MASSACHUSETTS AVENUE CAMBRIDGE, MA 02139-4307 Molecular analysis of cytoskeletal interactions

R03CA-53398-01 (SRC) ABBRUZZESE, JAMES L UNIVERSITY OF TEXAS 1515 HOLCOMBE BLVD, BOX 78 HOUSTON, TX 77030 Human topoisomerase I--An exploitable anticancer drug target

R03CA-53411-02 (SRC) HERLYN, DOROTHEE WISTAR INSTITUTE 36TH AND SPRUCE STREETS PHILADELPHIA, PA 19104 Phase I clinical trial with monoclonal anti-idiotype antibodies

R03CA-53414-01 (SRC) KUFE, DONALD W DANA-FARBER CANCER INSTITUTE 44 BINNEY STREET BOSTON, MA 02115 Clonality in acute myeloid leukemia and myelodysplasia

R29CA-53440-01 (RAD) LAWRENCE, THEODORE S UNIVERSITY OF MICHIGAN 1331 E ANN STREET, BOX 0582 ANN ARBOR, MI 48109 halogenated pyrimidines and low dose rate irradiation

R03CA-53441-02 (SRC) SONDEL, PAUL M UW CLINICAL CANCER CENTER 600 HIGHLAND AVENUE MADISON, WI 53792 BRM monitoring of pediatric neuroblastoma/osteosarcoma

R03CA-53444-02 (SRC) GRAZIANO, STEPHEN L VA MEDICAL CENTER 800 IRVING AVENUE SYRACUSE, NY 13210 Prognostic factors in non-small cell lung cancer

R01CA-53445-01A1 (IMB) CHORNEY, MICHAEL J PENNSYLVANIA STATE UNIVERSITY PO BOX 850 HERSHEY, PA 17033 Studies on the mouse thymus leukemia genes and antigens

R03CA-53446-02 (SRC) AUGENLICHT, LEONARD H MONTEFIORE MEDICAL CENTER 111 EAST 210TH STREET BRONX, NY 10467 Gene changes and chemotherapy for colon cancer

R29CA-53449-01 (ARRB) EMERSON, SCOTT S UNIVERSITY OF ARIZONA TUCSON, AZ 85724 Group sequential methods for clinical trials

R01CA-53453-01 (CPA) SHINOZUKA, HISASHI UNIVERSITY OF PITTSBURGH 750 SCAIFE HALL PITTSBURGH, PA 15261 Cyclosporine and liver carcinogenesis

R25CA-53459-01A1 (CEC) HARRISON, GAIL G UNIVERSITY OF ARIZONA 1501 N. CAMPBELL AVENUE TUCSON, AZ 85724 Nutrition education in the medical school curriculum

R03CA-53468-01 (SRC) BYSTRYN, JEAN-CLAUDE NEW YORK UNIV MED CTR 560 FIRST AVENUE NEW YORK, NY 10016 Correlation of antibody response to melanoma vaccine

R01CA-53477-01 (MEP) MOODY, TERRY W GEORGE WASHINGTON UNIVERSITY 2300 EYE STREET, NW WASHINGTON, DC 20037 Bombesin & IGF-I receptors in small cell lung cancer

R55CA-53482-01A1 (MEP) BEEZHOLD, DONALD H DONALD GUTHRIE FDN/MEDICAL RES 1 GUTHRIE SQUARE SAYRE, PA 18840-1692 Fibronectin induced tumor necrosis factor secretion

R01CA-53484-02 (MEP) BASERGA, RENATO L THOMAS JEFFERSON UNIVERSITY 1025 WALNUT STREET PHILADELPHIA, PA 19107 Biology of the proliferating cell nuclear antigen

R13CA-53492-01S1 (SRC) DAVIES, KELVIN J UNIV OF SOUTHERN CALIFORNIA 1985 ZONAL AVE, PSC 616 LOS ANGELES, CA 90033 Meeting--"Oxidative damage and repair"

R13CA-53494-01 (SRC) CARUTHERS, MARVIN H UNIV OF COLORADO CAMPUS BOX 215 BOULDER, CO 80309-0215 Antisense DNA therapeutics

R03CA-53503-02 (SRC) FOON, KENNETH ROSWELL PARK CANCER INST ELM & CARLTON STREETS BUFFALO, NY 14263 Validation of an in vitro drug sensitivity assay for CLL

R55CA-53506-01A1 (REN) WIMALASENA, JAYANTHA UNIVERSITY OF NEBRASKA 600 SOUTH 42ND STREET OMAHA, NE 68198-4575 Role of gonadotropins in ovarian cancer

R29CA-53511-01 (PTHB) HOULDSWORTH, JANE SLOAN-KETTERING INST CANCER RE 1275 YORK AVENUE NEW YORK, NY 10021 Isolation of amplified gene in human germ cell tumors

R29CA-53516-01 (RAD) ZEMAN, ELAINE M UNIVERSITY OF NORTH CAROLINA CB7512 MACNIDER CHAPEL HILL, NC 27599-7512 Radiation-induced perturbations of cell cycle transit

R29CA-53517-01 (ET) ANDERSON, PETER M UNIVERSITY OF MINNESOTA BOX 484 UMHC MINNEAPOLIS, MN 55455 Studies of IL-2 liposomes in cancer of the lung

R01CA-53525-01 (EVR) O'DONNELL, MICHAEL E CORNELL UNIV MEDICAL COLLEGE 1300 YORK AVENUE NEW YORK, NY 10021 Biochemical action of ebna1 on EBV replication origin

R03CA-53527-02 (SRC) ROSS, BRIAN D HUNTINGTON MEDICAL RES. INST. 660 SOUTH FAIR OAKS AVE PASADENA, CA 91105 Magnetic resonance spectroscopy in clinical immunotherapy

R03CA-53543-02 (SRC) REAMAN, GREGORY CHILDREN'S HOSP NATL MED CTR 111 MICHIGAN AVENUE, NORTHWEST WASHINGTON, DC 20010 Anti-GD3 monoclonal antibody therapy of T-cell all acute lymphoblastic leukemia

U10CA-53549-01 (CCI) SCHWENN, MOLLY R BOSTON FLOATING HOSPITAL BOX 14, 750 WASHINGTON ST BOSTON, MA 02111 Boston floating hospital/Pediatric Oncology Group

U10CA-53549-01 0001 (CCI) SCHWENN, MOLLY R Boston floating hospital/Pediatric Oncology Group POG9006--6-MP/methotrexate vs. alternating chemotherapy for ALL in childhood

U10CA-53549-01 0002 (CCI) SCHWENN, MOLLY R Boston floating hospital/Pediatric Oncology Group POG9005--Dose intensification of methotrexate & 6-mercaptopurine in childhood ALL

U10CA-53549-01 0027 (CCI) SCHWENN, MOLLY R Boston floating hospital/Pediatric Oncology Group POG8869--Intergroup rhabdomyosarcoma study for clinical group IV disease

U10CA-53549-01 0028 (CCI) SCHWENN, MOLLY R Boston floating hospital/Pediatric Oncology Group POG8866--Phase II asparaginase therapy for acute lymphoblastic leukemia

U10CA-53549-01 0029 (CCI) SCHWENN, MOLLY R Boston floating hospital/Pediatric Oncology Group POG8862--Combination chemotherapy of acute T-lymphoblastic leukemia

U10CA-53549-01 0030 (CCI) SCHWENN, MOLLY R Boston floating hospital/Pediatric Oncology Group POG8863--Phase II study of high dose cytosine arabinoside in childhood tumors

U10CA-53549-01 0031 (CCI) SCHWENN, MOLLY R Boston floating hospital/Pediatric Oncology Group POG8827--Phase II treatment of children with Hodgkin's disease in relapse

U10CA-53549-01 0032 (CCI) SCHWENN, MOLLY R Boston floating

hospital/Pediatric Oncology Group POG8865--Phase II recombinant alpha-interferon in relapsed T-cell disease
U10CA-53549-01 0033 (CCI) SCHWENN, MOLLY R Boston floating hospital/Pediatric Oncology Group--Phase II recombinant A-interferon in chronic myelogenous leukemia
U10CA-53549-01 0034 (CCI) SCHWENN, MOLLY R Boston floating hospital/Pediatric Oncology Group POG8832--Combination chemotherapy followed by radiotherapy for brain tumors
U10CA-53549-01 0035 (CCI) SCHWENN, MOLLY R Boston floating hospital/Pediatric Oncology Group POG8731--Phase II trial of methotrexate in treatment of brain tumors in children
U10CA-53549-01 0036 (CCI) SCHWENN, MOLLY R Boston floating hospital/Pediatric Oncology Group POG8788--Intergroup rhabdomyosarcoma study/pilot study for clinical group III
U10CA-53549-01 0037 (CCI) SCHWENN, MOLLY R Boston floating hospital/Pediatric Oncology Group POG8761--Phase II study of homoharringtonine therapy for nonlymphoblastic leukemi
U10CA-53549-01 0038 (CCI) SCHWENN, MOLLY R Boston floating hospital/Pediatric Oncology Group POG8739--Phase II immunotherapy with alpha-2 interferon for brain tumors (human)e
U10CA-53549-01 0039 (CCI) SCHWENN, MOLLY R Boston floating hospital/Pediatric Oncology Group POG8741--Treatment of patients with stage C and stage D neuroblastoma
U10CA-53549-01 0040 (CCI) SCHWENN, MOLLY R Boston floating hospital/Pediatric Oncology Group POG8751--Phase II methotrexate chemotherapy for rhabdomyosarcoma in children
U10CA-53549-01 0041 (CCI) SCHWENN, MOLLY R Boston floating hospital/Pediatric Oncology Group POG8633--Postoperative chemotherapy and delayed irradiation for brain tumors
U10CA-53549-01 0042 (CCI) SCHWENN, MOLLY R Boston floating hospital/Pediatric Oncology Group POG8617--Therapy for B-cell acute lymphoblastic leukemia and lymphoma
U10CA-53549-01 0043 (CCI) SCHWENN, MOLLY R Boston floating hospital/Pediatric Oncology Group POG9139--Phase I study of cisplatin and irradiation in brain stem gliomas
U10CA-53549-01 0044 (CCI) SCHWENN, MOLLY R Boston floating hospital/Pediatric Oncology Group POG9079--Phase I study of L-PAM/CTX with ABM rescue for brain tumors in children
U10CA-53549-01 0045 (CCI) SCHWENN, MOLLY R Boston floating hospital/Pediatric Oncology Group POG9075--Phase I study of acivicin in children with solid tumors
U10CA-53549-01 0046 (CCI) SCHWENN, MOLLY R Boston floating hospital/Pediatric Oncology Group POG9074--Phase I study of xomazyme-H65 in children with T-cell ALL/lymphoma
U10CA-53549-01 0047 (CCI) SCHWENN, MOLLY R Boston floating hospital/Pediatric Oncology Group POG9072--Phase I chemotherapy for recurrent/resistant malignant solid tumors
U10CA-53549-01 0048 (CCI) SCHWENN, MOLLY R Boston floating hospital/Pediatric Oncology Group POG9061-Phase II systemic therapy and irradiation for ALL & CNS leukemia
U10CA-53549-01 0049 (CCI) SCHWENN, MOLLY R Boston floating hospital/Pediatric Oncology Group POG 9086--Phase I pilot study of therapy for T-cell ALL or NHL
U10CA-53549-01 0050 (CCI) SCHWENN, MOLLY R Boston floating hospital/Pediatric Oncology Group POG9071--Phase I trial of fazarabine in children with acute leukemia
U10CA-53549-01 0051 (CCI) SCHWENN, MOLLY R Boston floating hospital/Pediatric Oncology Group POG8970--Phase I trial of fazarabine in children with refractory solid tumors
U10CA-53549-01 0052 (CCI) SCHWENN, MOLLY R Boston floating hospital/Pediatric Oncology Group POG8973--Etoposide (VP-16) and carboplatin in children with acute leukemia
U10CA-53549-01 0053 (CCI) SCHWENN, MOLLY R Boston floating hospital/Pediatric Oncology Group POG8870--Phase I trial of ifosfamide/VP16/MESNA in children with acute leukemia
U10CA-53549-01 0054 (CCI) SCHWENN, MOLLY R Boston floating hospital/Pediatric Oncology Group POG8871--Phase I study of rTNF in children with refractory solid tumors
U10CA-53549-01 0055 (CCI) SCHWENN, MOLLY R Boston floating hospital/Pediatric Oncology Group POG8671--Phase I immunotherapy with rIL-2 in children with solid tumors
U10CA-53549-01 0056 (CCI) SCHWENN, MOLLY R Boston floating hospital/Pediatric Oncology Group POG8494--Phase I study of fludarabine phosphate in pediatric patients
U10CA-53549-01 0057 (CCI) SCHWENN, MOLLY R Boston floating hospital/Pediatric Oncology Group POG8930--A comprehensive genetic analysis of brain tumors
U10CA-53549-01 0058 (CCI) SCHWENN, MOLLY R Boston floating hospital/Pediatric Oncology Group POG8828--Late effects of Hodgkin's disease
U10CA-53549-01 0003 (CCI) SCHWENN, MOLLY R Boston floating hospital/Pediatric Oncology Group POG9031--Cisplatin/VP-16 therapy of medulloblastoma/pre vs. post irradiation
U10CA-53549-01 0059 (CCI) SCHWENN, MOLLY R Boston floating hospital/Pediatric Oncology Group POG9046--Molecular genetic analysis of Wilm's tumors
U10CA-53549-01 0060 (CCI) SCHWENN, MOLLY R Boston floating hospital/Pediatric Oncology Group POG9153--Rhabdomyosarcoma study/laboratory evaluation of tumor
U10CA-53549-01 0004 (CCI) SCHWENN, MOLLY R Boston floating hospital/Pediatric Oncology Group POG8945--Phase III chemotherapy for hepatoblastoma & hepatocellular carcinoma
U10CA-53549-01 0005 (CCI) SCHWENN, MOLLY R Boston floating hospital/Pediatric Oncology Group POG9049--Phase III study of high-risk malignant germ cell tumors in children
U10CA-53549-01 0006 (CCI) SCHWENN, MOLLY R Boston floating hospital/Pediatric Oncology Group POG8844--Bone marrow transplant in children with stage D neuroblastoma
U10CA-53549-01 0007 (CCI) SCHWENN, MOLLY R Boston floating hospital/Pediatric Oncology Group POG8850--Phase III treatment of Ewing's sarcoma and neuroectodermal bone tumors
U10CA-53549-01 0008 (CCI) SCHWENN, MOLLY R Boston floating hospital/Pediatric Oncology Group POG8821--Phase III chemotherapy +/- autologous BMT in children with AML
U10CA-53549-01 0009 (CCI) SCHWENN, MOLLY R Boston floating hospital/Pediatric Oncology Group POG8725--Phase III chemotherapy +/- radiation therapy in pediatric Hodgkins
U10CA-53549-01 0010 (CCI) SCHWENN, MOLLY R Boston floating hospital/Pediatric Oncology Group POG8704--Phase III chemotherapy of childhood T cell ALL & lymphoblastic lymphoma
U10CA-53549-01 0011 (CCI) SCHWENN, MOLLY R Boston floating hospital/Pediatric Oncology Group POG8719--Phase III chemotherapy for non-Hodgkin's lymphoma in children
U10CA-53549-01 0012 (CCI) SCHWENN, MOLLY R Boston floating hospital/Pediatric Oncology Group POG8650--National Wilm's tumor and clear cell sarcoma study
U10CA-53549-01 0013 (CCI) SCHWENN, MOLLY R Boston floating hospital/Pediatric Oncology Group POG8616--Phase III chemotherapy for childhood Burkitt and non-Burkitts lymphoma
U10CA-53549-01 0014 (CCI) SCHWENN, MOLLY R Boston floating hospital/Pediatric Oncology Group POG8615--Phase III study of large cell lymphomas in children and adolescents
U10CA-53549-01 0015 (CCI) SCHWENN, MOLLY R Boston floating hospital/Pediatric Oncology Group POG8651--Phase III study of childhood nonmetastatic osteosarcoma
U10CA-53549-01 0016 (CCI) SCHWENN, MOLLY R Boston floating hospital/Pediatric Oncology Group POG8653--Phase III study of childhood soft tissue sarcomas
U10CA-53549-01 0017 (CCI) SCHWENN, MOLLY R Boston floating hospital/Pediatric Oncology Group POG8625--Phase III combined therapy in childhood Hodgkin's disease
U10CA-53549-01 0018 (CCI) SCHWENN, MOLLY R Boston floating hospital/Pediatric Oncology Group POG8451--Intergroup rhabdomyosarcoma study
U10CA-53549-01 0019 (CCI) SCHWENN, MOLLY R Boston floating hospital/Pediatric Oncology Group POG9110--Rotational drug therapy after first marrow relapse of non-T, non B ALL
U10CA-53549-01 0020 (CCI) SCHWENN, MOLLY R Boston floating hospital/Pediatric Oncology Group POG9107--Phase II pilot study of infant leukemia
U10CA-53549-01 0021 (CCI) SCHWENN, MOLLY R Boston floating hospital/Pediatric Oncology Group POG9140--Phase II therapy for recurrent or refractory neuroblastoma
U10CA-53549-01 0022 (CCI) SCHWENN, MOLLY R Boston floating hospital/Pediatric Oncology Group POG9048--Phase II study of malignant germ cell tumors in children
U10CA-53549-01 0023 (CCI) SCHWENN, MOLLY R Boston floating hospital/Pediatric Oncology Group POG9060--Intensive QOD ifosfamide treatment for CNS tumors in children
U10CA-53549-01 0024 (CCI) SCHWENN, MOLLY R Boston floating hospital/Pediatric Oncology Group POG8936--Phase II study of carboplatin treatment for optic pathway tumors
U10CA-53549-01 0025 (CCI) SCHWENN, MOLLY R Boston floating hospital/Pediatric Oncology Group POG8935--Phase II study of surgery and/or radiotherapy for optic pathway tumors
U10CA-53549-01 0026 (CCI) SCHWENN, MOLLY R Boston floating hospital/Pediatric Oncology Group POG8820--Phase II/III study of VP-16, AMSA +/- 5-azacytidine in childhood ANLL
R01CA-53559-01 (CBY) MASSAGUE, JOAN SLOAN-KETTERING INSTITUTE FOR 1275 YORK AVENUE NEW YORK, NY 10021 Biosynthesis & action of transforming growth factor-alpha
R01CA-53572-01A1 (PTHB) NEWCOMB, ELIZABETH W NEW YORK UNIV MEDICAL CENTER 550 FIRST AVENUE NEW YORK, NY 10016 Molecular biology of B-cell chronic lymphocytic leukemia
R01CA-53584-01 (MEP) SPINDEL, ELIOT R OREGON REGIONAL PRIMATE RES CT 505 NW 185TH AVENUE BEAVERTON, OR 97006 Bombesin receptors in normal and neoplastic tissues
R44CA-53590-02 (SSS) TICKNER, E GLENN SIERRA BIOMEDICAL CORPORATION PO BOX 155 COULTERVILLE, CA 95311 Magnetic gelatin particles for tumor detection
R01CA-53592-01A1 (MBY) MORAN, ELIZABETH COLD SPRING HARBOR LABORATORY PO BOX 100 COLD SPRING HARBOR, NY 11724 Protein interactions and repression function of the E1A
R01CA-53595-01 (EI) ANDERSON, PAUL J DANA-FARBER CANCER INSTITUTE 44 BINNEY STREET BOSTON, MA 02115 Functional analysis of the CD16--Zeta NK receptor complex
R29CA-53596-01A1 (MEP) WAN, YU-JUI Y HARBOR-UCLA MEDICAL CENTER 1000 WEST CARSON ST TORRANCE, CA 90509 Retinoic acid receptor alpha-fetoprotein and hepatoma
R29CA-53599-01A1 (MEP) SHERMAN, MATTHEW L DANA-FARBER CANCER INSTITUTE 44 BINNEY STREET BOSTON, MA 02115 Pharmacologic and molecular control of C-jun in leukemia
R29CA-53607-01 (SSS) HIGGINS, WILLIAM E PENNSYLVANIA STATE UNIVERSITY 206 ELECTRICAL ENG EAST BLDG UNIVERSITY PARK, PA 16802 Automatic analysis of 3-d and 4-d radiological images
R01CA-53615-01A1 (ALY) HOLERS, V MICHAEL WASHINGTON UNIV SCH OF MED 660 S EUCLID ST LOUIS, MO 63110 Analysis of C3d/EBV receptor (CR2) ligand binding sites
U01CA-53617-02 (SRC) LEVIN, VICTOR A U.T. M.D. ANDERSON CANCER CENT 1515 HOLCOMBE BLVD HOUSTON, TX 77030 Discovery and development of tyrosine kinase inhibitors
R01CA-53619-01 (BBCA) HARRIMAN, ANTHONY M UNIVERSITY OF TEXAS AUSTIN, TX 78712 Photoisomerization of cyanine dyes
R01CA-53624-01A1 (ET) CHEUNG, NAI-KONG V MEM HOSP/CANCER & ALLIED DISEA 1275 YORK AVENUE NEW YORK, NY 10021 Monocyte rhM-CSF and antibodies in cancer treatment
R29CA-53625-01A1 (CPA) SPRATT, THOMAS E AMERICAN HEALTH FOUNDATION ONE DANA ROAD VALHALLA, NY 10595 Mechanism of O(6)-alkylguanine-DNA alkyltransferase
R01CA-53628-01A1 (MEP) CHIAO, JEN W NEW YORK MEDICAL COLLEGE VALHALLA, NY 10595 Human prostate derived growth factor
R01CA-53632-02 (ARR) ROSENBLATT, JOSEPH D UCLA DEPT OF MEDICINE 12-153 FACTOR BUILDING LOS ANGELES, CA 90024-1406 Regulation of gene expression in HTLV type I/II
R01CA-53633-02 (ARR) JAY, GILBERT AMERICAN RED CROSS 15601 CRABBS BRANCH WAY ROCKVILLE, MD 20855 Role of the HIV-1 regulatory

genes in transgenic mice

R13CA-53709-01 (SRC) PIERSCHBACHER, MICHAEL D LA JOLLA CANCER RESEARCH FDN 10901 NORTH TORREY PINES RD LA JOLLA, CA 92037 Gordon conference on fibronectin and related macromolecule

R01CA-53711-01 (SSS) LIBURDY, ROBERT P UNIVERSITY OF CALIFORNIA 1 CYCLOTRON ROAD BEKELEY, CA 94720 High-field NMR bioeffects--Lymphocyte Ca2+ metabolism

R13CA-53712-01 (SRC) HENDERSON, MAUREEN M FRED HUTCHINSON CANCER RES CTR 1124 COLUMBIA STREET SEATTLE, WA 98104 Promoting health related dietary changes in communities

R01CA-53713-01 (MEP) KLEIN-SZANTO, ANDRE J FOX CHASE CANCER CENTER 7701 BURHOLME AVENUE PHILADELPHIA, PA 19111 Tumor suppressor genes in chemically induced skin tumors

R01CA-53717-01 (RNM) FELD, MICHAEL S MASSACHUSETTS INST OF TECH 77 MASSACHUSETTS AVENUE CAMBRIDGE, MA 02139 Real time in vivo diagnosis of dysplasia by fluorescence

R01CA-53765-01 (GMA) NOONAN, FRANCES P GEORGE WASHINGTON UNIV MED CTR 2300 EYE STREET, NW WASH. DC 20037 Strain differences in UVB suppression

R29CA-53782-01 (CBY) HWANG, YU-WEN NYS INST FOR BASIC RESEARCH 1050 FOREST HILL ROAD STATEN ISLAND, NY 10314 Study of ras genes by dominant negative mutants

R01CA-53783-01 (MEDB) TAYLOR, MILTON W INDIANA UNIVERSITY JORDAN HALL 341 BLOOMINGTON, IN 47405 IFN-r resistant mutants of mammalian cells

R29CA-53787-02 (SSS) BECKER, MARK P UNIVERSITY OF MICHIGAN 109 S OBSERVATORY ANN ARBOR, MI 48109 Analysis of repeated categorical measurements

R01CA-53791-01 (CPA) MITRA, SANKAR OAK RIDGE NATIONAL LAB PO BOX 2009 OAK RIDGE, TN 37831-8077 Structure and regulation of DNA repair genes of mammals

R01CA-53793-01 (GMA) DE FABO, EDWARD C GEORGE WASHINGTON UNIV MED CTR ROSS HALL, ROOM 101B WASHINGTON, DC 20037 Urocanic acid, sunlight & immunity--A novel interaction

U01CA-53799-01 (SRC) MOBARHAN, SOHRAB LOYOLA UNIV MEDICAL CENTER 2160 SOUTH FIRST AVENUE MAYWOOD, IL 60153 Effects of beta-carotene on colonic cell proliferation

U01CA-53801-01 (SRC) GIARDIELLO, FRANCIS M THE JOHNS HOPKINS HOSPITAL 600 NORTH WOLFE STREET BALTIMORE, MD 21205 Sulindac chemoprevention in adenomatous polyposis coli

R29CA-53805-01A1 (EI) CHONG, ANITA S RUSH PRESB ST LUKE'S MED CTR 1653 W CONGRESS PARKWAY CHICAGO, IL 60612 Stimulation of TNF-alpha and IFN-gamma production in IL-2 stimulated lymphocytes

U01CA-53807-01 (SRC) MC WHORTER, WILLIAM P UNIVERSITY OF UTAH MEDICAL CTR SALT LAKE CITY, UT 84132 Effect of tamoxifen on proliferative breast disease

R55CA-53812-01A1 (CPA) PACKER, LESTER UNIVERSITY OF CALIFORNIA BERKELEY, CA 94720 UV light skin antioxidant defenses and skin damage

R01CA-53813-02 (ET) STEARNS, MARK E MEDICAL COLLEGE OF PENNSYLVANI 3300 HENRY AVENUE PHILADELPHIA, PA 19129 Association of prostate metastases and drug resistance

U01CA-53818-01 (SRC) ROMNEY, SEYMOUR L ALBERT EINSTEIN COLLEGE OF MED 1300 MORRIS PARK AVENUE BRONX, NY 10461 Beta carotene clinical trial monitoring cervix dysplasia

R01CA-53827-01A1 (EDC) BARON, JOHN A DARTMOUTH-HITCHCOCK MED CTR 2 MAYNARD STREET HANOVER, NH 03756 Rectal mucosal proliferation indices--Effects of calcium

R01CA-53840-01A1 (CBY) TONKS, NICHOLAS K COLD SPRING HARBOR LABORATORY P O BOX 100 COLD SPRING HARBOR, NY 11724 Protein tyrosine dephosphorylation and signal transduction

R01CA-53841-01 (MEDB) JAKEN, SUSAN W ALTON JONES CELL SCI CTR 10 OLD BARN RD LAKE PLACID, NY 12946 Cytoskeletal association of protein kinase C

R01CA-53858-02 (TOX) MULLENIX, PHYLLIS J FORSYTH DENTAL CENTER 140 FENWAY BOSTON, MA 02115 Neurotoxicity of CNS prophylactic therapies in ALL

R01CA-53866-02 (MGN) DURNAM, DIANE M ZYMOGENETICS, INC 4225 ROOSEVELT WAY NE SEATTLE, WA 98105 Molecular dissection of a chromosomal fragile site

R35CA-53867-01 (SRC) WITTE, OWEN N DEPARTMENT OF MICROBIOLOGY 405 HILGARD AVENUE Role of the ABL oncogene in murine and human leukemias

R01CA-53870-01 (SRC) HAWTHORNE, M FREDERICK UNIVERSITY OF CALIFORNIA 405 HILGARD AVENUE LOS ANGELES, CA 90024 Bifunctional antibody mediated neutron capture therapy

R35CA-53874-01 (SRC) TONEGAWA, SUSUMU MASSACHUSETTS INST OF TECH 77 MASSACHUSETTS AVENUE CAMBRIDGE, MA 02139 Development and function of lymphocytes

R35CA-53877-01 (SRC) BARTELS, PETER H UNIVERSITY OF ARIZONA TUCSON, AZ 85721 Knowledge based systems for diagnostic histopathology

R35CA-53887-01 (SRC) WHITLOCK, JAMES P, JR STANFORD UNIVERSITY SCHOOL OF MEDICINE STANFORD, CA 94305-5332 Mechanism of dioxin action

R01CA-53892-01 (SRC) SCHINAZI, RAYMOND F VA MEDICAL CENTER 1670 CLAIRMONT ROAD DECATUR, GA 30033 Boron-containing nucleosides for neutron capture therapy

R01CA-53896-01 (SRC) SOLOWAY, ALBERT H OHIO STATE UNIVERSITY 500 W TWELFTH AVENUE COLUMBUS, OH 43210 Carboranyl nucleotides--Potential DNA probes for BNCT

R01CA-53899-02 (ARR) KIESSLING, ANN A FAULKNER CTR /REPRODUCTIVE MED 1153 CENTRE ST BOSTON, MA 02130 Retroviruses associated with human reproductive tract

R01CA-53901-01 (SRC) KAHL, STEPHEN B UNIVERSITY OF CALIFORNIA SAN FRANCISCO, CA 94143-0446 Design and synthesis of boronated tumor-seeking macrocycles

R29CA-53910-01 (MEDB) TROEN, BRUCE R THE UNIVERSITY OF MICHIGAN 1150 WEST MEDICAL CENTER DRIVE ANN ARBOR, MI 48109-0680 Regulation of cathepsin l gene expression

R35CA-53913-01 (SRC) HECHT, SIDNEY M UNIVERSITY OF VIRGINIA MCCORMICK ROAD CHARLOTTESVILLE, VA 22901 Nucleic acids as therapeutic targets

R29CA-53914-02 (BIO) STUEHR, DENNIS J CLEVELAND CLINIC FOUNDATION CLEVELAND, OH 44195 Biochemistry of macrophage nitric oxide synthesis

PROJECT NO., ORGANIZATIONAL UNIT., INVESTIGATOR, ADDRESS, TITLE

R43CA-53917-01 (SSS) LONGWORTH, JAMES W MCR TECHNOLOGY INST PO BOX 10084 CHICAGO, IL 60610-0084 Three dimensional holographic imaging of tumor cells

R43CA-53925-01 (SSS) HYMAN, EDWARD D SYBTREL BIOTECHNOLOGY 1500 EDWARDS AVENUE HARAHAN, LA 70123 Protein production using a new expression vector system

R43CA-53938-01 (ET) CHIANG, YAWEN L GENETIC THERAPY, INC 19 FIRSTFIELD RD GAITHERSBURG, MD 20878 Retroviral vectors to express alpha-IFN in human TIL

R43CA-53939-01 (SSS) HUANG, CHUN-MING PHARMINGEN 11555 SORRENTO VALLEY RD/SUITE SAN DIEGO, CA 92121 Mabs specific to human tumor suppressor protein P53

R43CA-53941-01 (SSS) KING, RAY J KDC TECHNOLOGY CORPORATION 2011 RESEARCH DRIVE LIVERMORE, CA 94550 Microwave interstitial sensors and hyperthermia probes

R43CA-53944-01 (SSS) ENTINE, GERALD RADIATION MONITORING DEVICES 44 HUNT STREET WATERTOWN, MA 02172 Microdosimetric solid state tissue equivalent detector

R43CA-53950-01 (SSS) HU, FUPEI ADA DIGITAL SYSTEM, INC 10402 46TH AVENUE, #204 BELTSVILLE, MD 20705 Bi-directional fluroscopic imager

R43CA-53951-01 (SSS) CHANDRAN, V C BIO-IMAGING RESEARCH INC 425 BARCLAY BOULEVARD LINCOLNSHIRE, IL 60069 Interactive medical image analysis workstation

R43CA-53952-01 (SSS) STOLLER, MILTON LORAD MEDICAL SYSTEMS INC 262 PRESTIGE PARK RD EAST HARTFORD, CT 06108 High energy photoelectronic-digital mammography

R43CA-53953-01 (SSS) HUGHEY, BARBARA J SCIENCE RESEARCH LAB INC 15 WARD STREET SOMERVILLE, MA 02143 New target technology for PET radionuclide production

R43CA-53956-01 (HEM) BROCKBANK, KELVIN G CRYOLIFE, INC 2211 NEW MARKET PKWY, SUITE 14 MARIETTA, GA 30067 Bone marrow cryopreservation with antifreeze peptides

R43CA-53963-01A2 (ET) FU, XINYU ANTICANCER, INC 5325 METRO STREET SAN DIEGO, CA 92110 Orthotopic human tumor implants in nude mice

R43CA-53964-01 (SSS) SCHONBERG, RUSSELL G SCHONBERG RADIATION CORP 3300 KELLER STREET SANTA CLARA, CA 95054 Intraoperative electron beam therapy with a small LINAC

R43CA-53966-01A1 (SSS) SHLICHTA, PAUL J CRYSTAL RESEARCH 1441 SUNNYSIDE TERRACE SAN PEDRO, CA 90732 Scintillator crystals for improved PET

R43CA-53967-01 (SSP) ERRECART, MICHAEL T MACRO SYSTEMS, INC 8630 FENTON STREET SILVER SPRING, MD 20910 Improving cati using macintosh technology

R43CA-53977-01 (HUD) ROSS, JAMES G MACRO SYSTEMS INC 8630 FENTON STREET SILVER SPRING, MD 20910 Expert system application to cancer prevention

R43CA-53979-01 (HUD) ERRECART, MICHAEL T MACRO SYSTEMS INC 8630 FENTON ST.- SUITE 300 SILVER SPRING, MD 20910 Feasibility of hypermedia for PDQ-P with high risk

R43CA-53980-01 (HUD) KRAUS, LEWIS INFOUSE 1995 UNIVERSITY AVE BERKELEY, CA 94704 Cancer prevention interactive multimedia system

R43CA-53984-01 (HUD) BOUMA, SUSAN Z I S GRUPE, INC 948 SPRINGER DRIVE LOMBARD, IL 60148 Multi-media cancer prevention database

R43CA-53987-01 (SSS) BRENNER, DOUGLAS M COGENT LIGHT TECHNOLOGIES 116 N ROBERTSON BLVD LOS ANGELES, CA 90048 Photodynamic diagnostics as an aid for clinical biopsy

R43CA-53991-01A1 (SSS) GIERHART, DENNIS L APPLIED FOOD BIOTECHNOLOGY INC 300 BILTMORE DR FENTON, MO 63026 Xanthophyll biosynthesis in bacteria

R43CA-53993-02 (SSS) SKEATH, PERRY R INTEGRATED TECHNOLOGIES 1113 DENNIS AVENUE SILVER SPRING, MD 20901 Miniaturized bench-top analytical cell sorter

R43CA-53995-01A1 (ET) LI, LINGNA ANTICANCER, INC 5325 METRO STREET SAN DIEGO, CA 92110 Histoculture of skin for toxicity assay

P01CA-53996-14 (SRC) PRENTICE, ROSS L FRED HUTCHINSON CANCER RES CTR 1124 COLUMBIA STREET SEATTLE, WA 98104 Statistical methods for medical studies

P01CA-53996-14 0001 (SRC) PRENTICE, ROSS L Statistical methods for medical studies Statistical methods for disease prevention trials

P01CA-53996-14 0002 (SRC) MOOLGAVKAR, SURESH Statistical methods for medical studies Statistical methods for epidemiologic studies

P01CA-53996-14 0003 (SRC) CROWLEY, JOHN J Statistical methods for medical studies Statistical methods for therapeutic trials

P01CA-53996-14 0004 (SRC) CROWLEY, JOHN J Statistical methods for medical studies Statistical methods in carcinogenesis testing

R01CA-53997-01 (MEP) BARTLES, JAMES R NORTHWESTERN UNIV MEDICAL SCHO 303 E CHICAGO AVE CHICAGO, IL 60611 Regulation of CE 9 protein by peroxisome proliferators

R43CA-54004-01 (SSS) BUNOW, BARRY J CIVILIZED SOFTWARE, INC 7735 OLD GEORGETOWN RD#410 BETHESDA, MD 20814 Design power software for clinical studies

U01CA-54009-01 (SRC) MOORE, SHEILA G STANFORD UNIVERSITY SCHOOL OF MEDICINE STANFORD, CA 94305 Imaging evaluation of muskuloskeletal tumors

U01CA-54011-01 (SRC) DALLEY, ROBERT W UNIVERSITY OF WASHINGTON SEATTLE, WA 98195 National collaborative diagnostic imaging trial projects

U01CA-54012-01 (SRC) SEEGER, LEANNE UNIV OF CALIFORNIA, LA 405 HILGARD AVENUE LOS ANGELES, CA 90024-1406 Staging and monitoring musculoskeletal sarcomas

U01CA-54016-01 (SRC) CURTIN, HUGH D EYE & EAR HOSPITAL 230 LOTHROP STREET PITTSBURGH, PA 15213 Comparative imaging of cancer metastases to neck nodes

U01CA-54019-01 (SRC) MC NEIL, BARBARA J HARVARD MEDICAL SCHOOL 25 SHATTUCK STREET BOSTON, MA 02115 Radiologic diagnostic oncology group III--Operations and statistics

U01CA-54021-01 (SRC) NEWTON, WILLIAM A, JR CHILDREN'S HOSPITAL 700 CHILDREN'S DRIVE COLUMBUS, OH 43205 Cooperative human tissue network pediatric division

U01CA-54022-01 (SRC) ROSENTHAL, DANIEL I MASSACHUSETTS GENERAL HOSPITAL 15 PARKMAN ST WACC, SUITE 515 BOSTON, MA 02114 Optimized imaging of musculoskeletal tumors

U01CA-54026-01 (SRC) MANCUSO, ANTHONY A UNIV OF FLORIDA COLL OF MED BOX J-374 GAINESVILLE, FL 32610 Comparison of CT, MRI & ultrasound in staging cervical metastases

U01CA-54031-01 (SRC) PRETLOW, THOMAS G, II CASE WESTERN RESERVE UNIV 2085 ADELBERT ROAD CLEVELAND, OH 44106 Cooperative human tissue network

R43CA-54035-01A1 (SB) ZHANG, JILUN LKT LABORATORIES INC 2010 E HENNEPIN AVE MINNEAPOLIS, MN 55413 Bypass colostomy model for carcinogenesis studies

R43CA-54036-01 (SB) VARNER, HUGH H BALTIMORE BIOTECH, INC 7620 YORK ROAD BALTIMORE, MD 21284 Urokinase-specific inhibitors as anti-metastatic agents

R43CA-54037-01A1 (MEP) LAM, LUKE K LKT LABORATORIES, INC. 2010 E. HENNEPIN AVE. MINNEAPOLIS, MN 55413 Rapid screening of inhibitors of colon carcinogenesis

R43CA-54039-01 (NTN) BASEL, RICHARD M LEBENSMITTEL CONSULTING 10760 WEST SENECA CO RD 18 FOSTORIA, OH 44830 A safer flame broil grill to reduce carcinogenesis

R43CA-54040-01 (HUD) LEVITAN, KAREN B KBL GROUP, INC 7100 BALTIMORE, AVE COLLEGE PARK, MD 20740 PDQ-P for college populations

R29CA-54044-02 (RAD) LIEBERMAN, HOWARD B COLUMBIA UNIV, HLTH SCI. 630 WEST 168TH STREET NEW YORK, NY 10032 Repair of DNA damage induced by radiations

U01CA-54046-01 (SRC) PANICEK, DAVID M MEMORIAL HOSPITAL FOR 1275 YORK AVE NEW YORK, NY 10021 Computed tomography & MR imaging in staging of musculoskeletal neoplasms

R01CA-54050-02 (RAD) CROUSE, GRAY F EMORY UNIVERSITY ATLANTA, GA 30322 DNA repair in eukaryots

R01CA-54053-01A1 (ARRD) PALEFSKY, JOEL M UNIV OF CALIFORNIA, S F SAN FRANCISCO, CA 94143-0512 Natural history of anal neoplasia in HIV infected men

R29CA-54079-02 (RAD) NICKOLOFF, JAC A HARVARD SCHOOL OF PUBLIC HEALT 665 HUNTINGTON AVENUE BOSTON, MA 02115 Mammalian models for radiation-induced recombination

R43CA-54089-01 (ET) LUCK, EDWARD E MATRIX PHARMACEUTICAL, INC 1430 O'BRIEN DRIVE MENLO PARK, CA 94025 5-fluorouracil therapeutic implant in kaposi's sarcoma

R01CA-54092-01 (SRC) COLEMAN, R EDWARD DUKE UNIVERSITY MEDICAL CENTER BOX 3808 DURHAM, N C 27710 Specific applications of PET and MRS in brain tumors

R29CA-54093-02 (RAD) MIVECHI, NAHID F STANFORD UNIVERSITY CANCER BIOLOGY RESEARCH LAB STANFORD, CA 94305 Role of hyperthermia in bone marrow transplantation

R13CA-54094-01 (SRC) KOOP, EVERETT C CCCR 555 MADISON AVENUE NEW YORK, NY 10022 International conference on cancer prevention--Facts, maybes & rumor

R01CA-54104-01 (SRC) JUNCK, LARRY UNIVERSITY OF MICHIGAN MED CTR 1500 E MEDICAL CENTER DRIVE ANN ARBOR, MI 48109-0316 PET growth kinetics and neuropathology of brain tumors

R13CA-54109-01 (SRC) LEVINE, ARNOLD J PRINCETON UNIVERSITY PRINCETON, NJ 08544-1014 The P53 workshop

R01CA-54112-01 (SRC) BRYAN, R NICK JOHNS HOPKINS HOSPITAL 600 N WOLFE ST, MEYER 8-140 BALTIMORE, MD 21205 The physiologic imaging of human brain tumors

R01CA-54114-02 (MEP) GROOPMAN, JOHN D HOPKINS U/HYGIENE & PUB HLT SC 615 NORTH WOLFE STREET BALTIMORE, MD 21205 Aflatoxin DNA adducts detected by monoclonal antibodies

R01CA-54116-02 (TOX) FRANKEL, ARTHUR E 616 E ALTAMONTE DR ALTAMONTE SPRINGS, FL 32701 Molecular mechanisms of ricin cytotoxicity

R03CA-54119-01 (SRC) SCHOTTENFELD, DAVID UNIVERSITY OF MICHIGAN 109 S. OBSERVATORY STREET ANN ARBOR, MI 48109-2029 Chronic obstructive pulmonary disease as a risk factor for lung cancer

R13CA-54129-01 (SRC) LIEBERMAN, MICHAEL W BAYLOR COLLEGE OF MEDICINE ONE BAYLOR PLAZA HOUSTON, TX 77030 FASEB conference--Molecular mechanisms of carcinogenesis

R13CA-54130-01 (SRC) SETLOW, RICHARD B BROOKHAVEN NATIONAL LABORATORY UPTON, NY 11973 Gordon research conference on mammalian DNA repair

R01CA-54141-01 (MBC) ROSEN, BARRY P WAYNE STATE UNIVERSITY 540 EAST CANFIELD DETROIT, MI 48201 Substrate recognition in multidrug resistance

R01CA-54149-01 (EVR) KABAT, DAVID 3181 SW SAM JACKSON PARK RD PORTLAND, OR 97201-3098 Erythropoietin receptors in leukemia

R29CA-54152-01 (MEP) HILL, STEVEN M TULANE UNIVERSITY DEPARTMENT OF ANATOMY NEW ORLEANS, LA 70112 Neuroendocrine influences on mammary cancer

R13CA-54155-01 (SRC) KLAGSBRUN, MICHAEL CHILDREN'S HOSPITAL CORP 300 LONGWOOD AVENUE BOSTON, MA 02115 The chemistry and biology of the fibroblast growth factor family

R03CA-54156-01 (SRC) GUESS, HARRY A UNIVERSITY OF NORTH CAROLINA MCGAVRAN-GREENBERG HALL CHAPEL HILL, NC 27599 Prediagnostic serum vitamin D and prostate cancer

R13CA-54157-01 (SRC) BARTSCH, HELMUT INTERNATIONAL AGENCY FOR 150 COURS ALBERT THOMAS 69372 LYON CEDEX 08, FRANCE Conference--Biomonitoring and susceptibility markers in human cancer

R01CA-54168-01 (ET) THORPE, PHILIP E U T SOUTHWESTERN MEDICAL CENTE 5323 HARRY HINES BLVD DALLAS, TX 75235 Immunotoxins for the treatment of Hodgkin's disease

P30CA-54174-01 (CCS) COLTMAN, CHARLES A, JR CANCER THERAPY & RESEARCH CTR 4450 MEDICAL DRIVE SAN ANTONIO, TX 78229 Institute for cancer research and care

P30CA-54174-01 9006 (CCS) BOLDT, DAVID Institute for cancer research and care Flow cytometry --core

P30CA-54174-01 9007 (CCS) MOYER, MARY P Institute for cancer research and care Tissue culture--core

P30CA-54174-01 9001 (CCS) CLARK, GARY Institute for cancer research and care Biostatistics, data management and data processing

P30CA-54174-01 9008 (CCS) JOHNSON, KATHERIN Institute for cancer research and care Common equipment maintenance--core

P30CA-54174-01 9009 (CCS) COLTMAN, CHARLES Institute for cancer research and care Development--core

P30CA-54174-01 9002 (CCS) WOLF, ROBERT Institute for cancer research and care Animal resources

P30CA-54174-01 9003 (CCS) KUHN, JOHN Institute for cancer research and care Pharmacology core

P30CA-54174-01 9004 (CCS) ALLRED, CRAIG Institute for cancer research and care Pathology core

P30CA-54174-01 9005 (CCS) NAYLOR, SUSAN Institute for cancer research and care Molecular biology--core

R13CA-54176-01 (SRC) NISHIOKA, KENJI UT MD ANDERSON CANCER CENTER 1515 HOLCOMBE BLVD HOUSTON, TX 77030 International symposium on polyamines in cancer

R03CA-54179-01 (SRC) HULKA, BARBARA S UNIV OF N.C. AT CHAPEL HILL CAMPUS BOX #7400 CHAPEL HILL, NC 27599-7400 Maternal alpha fetoprotein and subsequent breast cancer rsk

R13CA-54182-01 (SRC) MARSHALL, JAMES R SUNY AT BUFFALO 2211 MAIN STREET BUFFALO, NY 14214 Symposium on future directions of diet and cancer

R01CA-54184-01 (RAD) RAAPHORST, G PETER OTTAWA REGIONAL CANCER CENTRE 190 MELROSE AVE OTTAWA, ONTARIO K1Y 4K7 Low dose irradiation and hyperthermia in human tumours

R01CA-54198-01 (ALY) MURRE, CORNELIS UNIV. OF CALIFORNIA, SAN DIEGO The role of E12 and E47 in B cell development

R01CA-54203-01 (ET) JONES, RICHARD J JOHNS HOPKINS UNIVERSITY 600 NORTH WOLFE STREET BALTIMORE, MD 21205 Antitumor effect of autologous graft-versus-host disease

R29CA-54212-01 (RNM) LU, JIAN-YU MAYO FOUNDATION 200 FIRST STREET SOUTHWEST Medical ultrasonic nondiffracting tranducers

R29CA-54216-01 (RNM) SHULKIN, BARRY L UNIV OF MICHIGAN MEDICAL CENTE 1500 E MEDICAL CENTER DR ANN ARBOR, MI 48109-0028 PET evaluation of neuroendocrine tumors

R29CA-54223-01 (RNM) HEBDEN, JEREMY C UNIVERSITY OF UTAH AC 213 SCHOOL OF MEDICINE SALT LAKE CITY, UT 84132 Breast imaging using picosecond pulses of light

R01CA-54231-01 (MEP) GLAZER, ROBERT I GEORGETOWN UNIVERSITY 3900 RESERVOIR ROAD, NW WASHINGTON, DC 20007 C-fes protein-tyrosine kinase in myeloid differentiation

R01CA-54239-01A1 (EDC) PETRAKIS, NICHOLAS L UNIV OF CALIFORNIA 1699 HSW (BOX 0560) SAN FRANCISCO, CA 94143-0560 Epidemiology and natural history of breast cancer

R55CA-54247-01 (CPA) YASWEN, PAUL LAWRENCE BERKELEY LABORATORY 1 CYCLOTRON RD BERKELEY, CA 94720 Calmodulin-related gene and epithelial transformation

R01CA-54248-01A1 (ET) THOMASSEN, MARY J CLEVELAND CLINIC FOUNDATION 9500 EUCLID AVENUE CLEVELAND, OH 44195 Regulation of macrophage activity--In vitro vs in vivo

R13CA-54258-01 (SRC) WASSERMAN, TODD H WASH UNIV SCHOOL OF MEDICINE 4939 AUDUBON AVENUE ST LOUIS, MO 63110 Meeting travel--Chemical modifiers of cancer therapy

R55CA-54263-01 (PTHB) MC CARTHY, JAMES B UNIVERSITY OF MINNESOTA 420 DELAWARE ST SE ST PAUL, MN 55455 Type IV collagen mediated melanoma cell migration

R29CA-54273-01 (MEP) MIRA-Y-LOPEZ, RAFAEL MOUNT SINAI SCHOOL OF MEDICINE ONE GUSTAVE L LEVY PLACE NEW YORK, NY 10029 Retinoic acid and cyclic AMP in breast cancer

R29CA-54277-01 (ET) HUDSON, M'LISS A BAYLOR COLLEGE OF MEDICINE ONE BAYLOR PLAZA HOUSTON, TX 77030 Urokinase--Effect on efficacy of BCG therapy

R01CA-54284-01 (CPA) CARDIFF, ROBERT D SCHOOL OF MEDICINE DAVIS, CA 95616 Protooncogenes and multistep mammary carcinogenesis

R29CA-54290-01A1 (CBY) LEBOEUF, ROBERT D UNIVERSITY OF ALABAMA UAB STATION BIRMINGHAM, AL 35294-0005 Cell and molecular studies on suppressin-inhibited growth

R01CA-54295-02 (RAD) SCHULTHEISS, TIMOTHY EDWARD FOX CHASE CANCER CENTER 7701 BURHOLME AVENUE PHILADELPHIA, PA 19111 Analysis of radiation injuries in 440 overdosed patients

R01CA-54296-01 (CPA) HANAUSEK-WALASZEK, MARGARET UT MD ANDERSON CANCER CENTER PO BOX 389 SMITHVILLE, TX 78957 An oncofetal protein expression in hepatocarcinogenesis

R01CA-54298-01 (PTHB) JACKSON, JANIS H SCRIPPS CLINIC & RESEARCH FDN 10666 NORTH TORREY PINES ROAD LA JOLLA, CA 92037 Processing, membrane association and activity of K-ras 4B

R01CA-54300-01 (SRC) DIETRICH, ALLEN J DARTMOUTH MEDICAL SCHOOL HANOVER, NH 03756 Improved cancer control for low income/minority patients

R13CA-54318-01 (SRC) LOVE, RICHARD R UNIVERSITY OF WISCONSIN 1300 UNIVERSITY AVENUE MADISON, WI 53706 Conference--American society of preventive oncology

R29CA-54323-01 (EVR) CHANG, LONG-SHENG CHILDREN'S HOSPITAL RES FDN 700 CHILDREN'S DRIVE COLUMBUS, OH 43205 Functional analyses of the retinoblastoma gene product

R13CA-54325-01 (SRC) KLEIN, JOHN P OHIO STATE UNIVERSITY 1958 NEIL AVENUE COLUMBUS, OH 43210 Workshop--Survival analysis and related topics

R13CA-54328-01 (SRC) BUKOWSKI, RONALD M CLEVELAND CLINIC FOUNDATION 9500 EUCLID AVENUE CLEVELAND, OHIO 44195-5236 2nd symposium on immunobiology of renal cell carcinoma

R01CA-54337-01 (MBY) GROUDINE, MARK T FRED HUTCHINSON CANCER RES CTR 1124 COLUMBIA ST, MAIL STOP M7 SEATTLE, WA 98104 C-myc proto-oncogene transcriptional elongation block

R01CA-54343-01 (SRC) KALUZNY, ARNOLD D UNIVERSITY OF NORTH CAROLINA CAMPUS BOX 7490 CHAPEL HILL, NC 27599 North Carolina cancer early detection program

R01CA-54345-01 (SRC) WILLIAMS, ROBERT B MEDICAL COLLEGE OF VIRGINIA PO BOX 251, MCV STATION RICHMOND, VA 23298-0251 Patient-initiated computer system for primary care

R01CA-54346-01 (GNM) SCHIMKE, ROBERT T STANFORD UNIVERSITY STANFORD, CA 94305 Cloning genes with an episomal vector

R01CA-54347-01 (BNP) MACDONALD, TIMOTHY L UNIVERSITY OF VIRGINIA MCCORMICK ROAD CHARLOTTESVILLE, VA 22901 DNA topoisomerase II as a therapeutic target

R13CA-54355-01 (SRC) COLTMAN, CHARLES A, JR UNIV OF TEXAS HLTH SCI CTR 7703 FLOYD CURL DR SAN ANTONIO, TX 78284-7884 13th annual San Antonio breast cancer symposium

PROJECT NO., ORGANIZATIONAL UNIT., INVESTIGATOR, ADDRESS, TITLE

R01CA-54356-01 (RNM) LEWITT, ROBERT M UNIVERSITY OF PENNSYLVANIA 418 SERVICE DRIVE PHILADELPHIA, PA 19104-6021 Digital image representations for tomographic radiology

R01CA-54358-01 (PTHB) FEINBERG, ANDREW P UNIV OF MICHIGAN MEDICAL SCH 1150 W MEDICAL CAMPUS DRIVE ANN ARBOR, MI 48109-0650 Molecular pathology of Wilms'tumor related genes on 11P

R01CA-54362-01 (RNM) ROGERS, W LESLIE UNIV OF MICHIGAN MED CTR ANN ARBOR, MI 48109-0028 Estimation strategies for nuclear medical imaging

R29CA-54363-01 (MEP) CAMPBELL, PHIL G ALLEGHENY-SINGER RES INSTITUTE 320 E NORTH AVE PITTSBURGH, PA 15212 The plasmin system and IGF function in osteosarcoma

R01CA-54364-01 (TOX) DIAMOND, ALAN M UNIVERSITY OF CHICAGO 5841 S MARYLAND AVE, BOX 442 CHICAGO, IL 60637 Translational control of glutathione peroxidase

R13CA-54368-01 (SRC) MAGIN, RICHARD L UNIVERSITY OF ILLINOIS 1406 W. GREET STREET URBANA, IL 61801 Conference--Biological effects and safey aspects of MRI and MRS

R55CA-54380-01 (ET) MILLER, DONALD M UNIVERSITY OF ALABAMA/BIRMINGH 1918 UNIVERSITY BLVD BIRMINGHAM, AL 35294 Specific inhibition of dhfr and mdr1 transcription

R01CA-54384-01 (PTHB) GEWIRTZ, ALAN M UNIVERSITY OF PENNSYLVANIA 133 SOUTH 36TH STREET PHILADELPHIA, PA 19104-3246 Role of proto-oncogenes in malignant hematopoiesis

R29CA-54385-01 (PTHB) CRAIG, RUTH W JOHNS HOPKINS UNIV SCH OF MED 725 NORTH WOLFE STREET BALTIMORE, MD 21205 Genes expressed early in leukemic cell differentiation

R01CA-54396-01 (PTHB) BAYLIN, STEPHEN B 424 N BOND STREET BALTIMORE, MD 21231 DNA methyltransferase gene expression in colon cancer

R01CA-54403-01 (SRC) LACEY, LORETTA F UNIVERSITY OF ILLINOIS 850 W JACKSON BOULEVARD CHICAGO, IL 60607 Prescribe for health--Urban minority primary care

R55CA-54404-01 (PTHB) PASTERNACK, GARY R JOHNS HOPKINS UNIVERSITY 600 N WOLFE STREET BALTIMORE, MD 21205 Novel nuclear proteins in normal and cancer cells

R01CA-54415-01 (PC) WANG, TERESA S STANFORD UNIVERSITY SCHOOL OF MEDICINE STANFORD, CA 94305 Control of DNA replication and cell division

P01CA-54418-01 (SRC) VERMA, INDER M THE SALK INSTITUTE PO BOX 85800 SAN DIEGO, CA 92186-5800 Transcriptional regulation of cell growth

P01CA-54418-01 0001 (SRC) MONTMINY, MARC R Transcriptional regulation of cell growth Developmental regulation of transcription factor CREB

P01CA-54418-01 0002 (SRC) JONES, KATHERINE A Transcriptional regulation of cell growth T-cell specific transcriptional activators and silencers

P01CA-54418-01 0003 (SRC) EMERSON, BEVERLY M Transcriptional regulation of cell growth Transcriptional regulation of T-cell receptor alpha gene

P01CA-54418-01 0004 (SRC) EVANS, RONALD M Transcriptional regulation of cell growth Interaction of nuclear receptors and AP-1 regulating networks

P01CA-54418-01 9001 (SRC) RIVIER, JEAN Transcriptional regulation of cell growth Core--Peptide synthesis and characterization

P01CA-54418-01 9002 (SRC) FISCHER, WOLFGANG H Transcriptional regulation of cell growth Core--Protein sequencing and characterization

P01CA-54418-01 9003 (SRC) VALE, WYLIE W Transcriptional regulation of cell growth Core--Antibody production and evaluation

P01CA-54418-01 9004 (SRC) JONES, KATHERINE A Transcriptional regulation of cell growth Core--Large scale cell culture and extract preparation

R01CA-54421-01 (BNP) TOWNSEND, CRAIG A JOHNS HOPKINS UNIVERSITY CHARLES & 34TH STREETS BALTIMORE, MD 21218 Diynene antibiotics and their DNA cleavage chemistry

R29CA-54428-02 (IMB) WILLIAMS, THOMAS M UNIVERSITY OF NEW MEXICO ALBUQUERQUE, NM 87131 Immunobiology of interleukin-2 regulation

R01CA-54432-01 (MEDB) GABIG, THEODORE G 975 W WALNUT STREET INDIANAPOLIS, IN 46202-5121 Proliferative signals from Il-3 receptors to nucleus

R13CA-54434-01 (SRC) TSICHLIS, PHILIP N FOX CHASE CANCER CTR 7701 BURHOLME AVENUE PHILADELPHIA, PA 19111 Third workshop on the pathogenesis by non-acute retroviruses

R01CA-54436-01 (PTHB) SHACKLEFORD, GREGORY M CHILDRENS HOSPITAL LOS ANGELES 4650 SUNSET BOULEVARD LOS ANGELES, CA 90027 The int-1 proto-oncogene family

R15CA-54443-01 (CPA) KANG, JAE O UNIVERSITY OF NEW HAMPSHIRE HEWITT HALL, ROOM 207 DURHAM, NH 03824-3563 Mechanism of 1,2-dimethylhydrazine (DMH)-induced carcinogenesis

R15CA-54462-01 (RNM) KOZIK, MARIUSZ CANISIUS COLLEGE 2001 MAIN STREET BUFFALO, NY 14208 New contrast agents for magnetic resonance imaging

R55CA-54464-01 (ALY) TEDDER, THOMAS F DANA-FARBER CANCER INSTITUTE 44 BINNEY STREET BOSTON, MA 02115 Regulation of human leukocyte recirculation

R01CA-54484-01 (ET) SILBER, ROBERT NEW YORK UNIV MED CTR 550 FIRST AVE NEW YORK, NY 10016 Novel camptothecin analogs in CLL

R15CA-54488-01 (CPA) BROCKMAN, HERMAN E ILLINOIS STATE UNIVERSITY NORMAL, IL 61761 Are "cryptic mutagens" mutagenic in the ARA test?

R13CA-54489-01 (SRC) FOX, C FRED THE KEYSTONE CENTER PO BOX 606 KEYSTONE, CO 80435 Conference on transgenic animal models

R01CA-54491-01 (PBC) BANKERT, RICHARD B ROSWELL PARK CANCER INST ELM & CARLTON STREETS BUFFALO, NY 14263 Factors affecting human lung tumor growth in scid mice

R01CA-54494-01 (MEP) DMITROVSKY, ETHAN MEM HOSP CANCER & ALLIED DIS 1275 YORK AVE NEW YORK, NY 10021 Growth factors and germ cell tumor differentiation

R01CA-54498-01 (EDC) BRESLOW, NORMAN E FRED HUTCHINSON CANCER RES CTR 1124 COLUMBIA STREET SEATTLE, WA 98104 Late effects in Wilms' tumor survivors and offspring

PROJECT NO., ORGANIZATIONAL UNIT., INVESTIGATOR, ADDRESS, TITLE

R55CA-54502-01 (MEP) KANE, MADELEINE A UNIV OF COLORADO HLTH SCIS CTR 4200 E NINTH AVENUE DENVER, CO 80262 Expression of gastrin releasing peptide receptor

R01CA-54507-01 (MCHA) ANDERSON, WAYNE K STATE UNIV. OF NY AT BUFFALO SCHOOL OF PHARMACY AMHERST, NY 14260 Design, synthesis and study of impd inhibitors

R01CA-54508-01 (MCHA) LEE, KUO-HSIUNG UNIVERSITY OF NORTH CAROLINA CB#7360 BEARD HALL CHAPEL HILL, NC 27599-7360 Novel inhibitors of DNA topoisomerase II

R01CA-54513-01A1 (BBCB) WAGNER, GERHARD HARVARD MEDICAL SCHOOL 25 SHATTUCK ST BOSTON, MA 02115 Anti-folate induced conformational changes in human DHFR

R15CA-54517-01 (BNP) BEHFOROUZ, MOHAMMAD BALL STATE UNIVERSITY 2000 UNIVERSITY AVE MUNCIE, IN 47306-0445 Synthesis and study of ras K specific antitumor drugs

R01CA-54518-01 (SSS) SALZMAN, GARY C UNIVERSITY OF CALIFORNIA PO BOX 1663, MS M882 LOS ALAMOS, NM 87545 Flow cytometry data analysis by expert systems

R29CA-54521-01 (EI) LINDSTEN, TULLIA UNIVERSITY OF MICHIGAN 1301 CATHERINE RD ANN ARBOR, MI 48109-0602 Lymphokine-specific RNA binding proteins

R01CA-54522-01 (EDC) CAMPBELL, T COLIN CORNELL UNIVERSITY N204 MVR HALL ITHACA, NY 14853-4401 Diet and cancer in China

R01CA-54524-01 (SRC) LIANG, T JAKE MASSACHUSETTS GENERAL HOSPITAL 149 13TH STREET 7TH FLOOR CHARLESTOWN, MA 02129 HBV variants and hepatocellular carcinoma

R01CA-54525-01 (SRC) SCHNEIDER, ROBERT J NEW YORK UNIV MEDICAL CENTER 550 FIRST AVENUE NEW YORK, NY 10016 Role of HBV X gene in viral infection and transformation

R01CA-54526-01 (SRC) SELL, STEWART UNIV OF TEX HLTH SCI CTR HOUST PO BOX 20708 HOUSTON, TX 77225 Hepatic co-carcinogenesis in transgenic mice

R01CA-54533-01 (SRC) OU, JING-HSIUNG J UNIV OF SOUTHERN CALIFORNIA 2011 ZONAL AVE, HMR-401 LOS ANGELES, CA 90033 Mechanism of HBV and HCV-induced hepatocellular oncogenesis

R01CA-54547-01 (SRC) STRAIR, ROGER K YALE UNIV SCH OF MED 333 CEDAR STREET NEW HAVEN, CT 06510 Detection of viral transactivators in primary cells

R01CA-54551-01 (SRC) CHEN, IRVIN S UCLA SCHOOL OF MEDICINE 10833 LE CONTE AVENUE LOS ANGELES, CA 90024-1678 HTLV pathogenesis in vivo

R01CA-54552-01 (SRC) LOUGHRAN, THOMAS P, JR FRED HUTCHINSON CANCER RES CTR 1124 COLUMBIA STREET SEATTLE, WA 98104 Retroviral infection in LGL leukemia

R01CA-54557-01 (SRC) SLAGLE, BETTY L BAYLOR COLLEGE OF MEDICINE ONE BAYLOR PLAZA HOUSTON, TX 77030 Hepatitis B virus and hepatocellular carcinoma (human, mice)

R01CA-54559-01 (SRC) WIGDAHL, BRIAN MILTON S HERSHEY MEDICAL CTR PENNSYLVANIA ST UNIV/PO BX 850 HERSHEY, PA 17033 Pathogenesis of HTLV-1 in developing nervous system

R01CA-54560-01 (SRC) CHISARI, FRANCIS V SCRIPPS CLINIC AND RESEARCH FD 10666 NORTH TORREY PINES ROAD LA JOLLA, CA 92037 Molecular pathogenesis of hepatocellular carcinoma

R01CA-54561-01 (ET) CHEEVER, MARTIN A UNIVERSITY OF WASHINGTON SEATTLE, WA 98195 Ras-specific T cell mediated immunotherapy

R01CA-54564-01 (SRC) JAY, GILBERT AMERICAN RED CROSS 15601 CRABBS BRANCH WAY ROCKVILLE, MD 20855 Functional analysis of the human T-lymphotropic viruses

R01CA-54567-01 (SRC) OZTURK, MEHMET MGH CANCER CTR/MGH EAST 149 13TH STREET 7TH FLOOR CHARLESTOWN, MA 02129 Tumor suppressor P53 gene in viral hepatocarcinoma

R01CA-54569-01 (SRC) MC PHEE, STEPHEN J UNIVERSITY OF CALIFORNIA, S.F. 400 PARNASSUS AVENUE, ROOM A-4 SAN FRANCISCO, CA 94143-0320 Promoting cancer prevention among vietnamese immigrants

R01CA-54573-01 (SRC) BURACK, ROBERT C WAYNE STATE UNIVERSITY 4201 ST ANTOINE DETROIT, MI 48201 The Detroit cancer control intervention project

R29CA-54590-02 (CPA) OSTRANDER, GARY K OKLAHOMA STATE UNIVERSITY LSW 430 STILLWATER, OK 74078 Glycolipid changes during chemical hepatocarcinogenesis

R01CA-54605-01 (SRC) HIATT, ROBERT A NORTHERN CALIFORNIA CANCER CTR 1301 SHOREWAY RD, SUITE 425 BELMONT, CA 94002 Breast and cervical cancer intervention study

R43CA-54627-01 (SSS) ARLINGHAUS, HEINRICH F ATOM SCIENCES, INC 114 RIDGEWAY CTR OAK RIDGE, TN 37830 Imaging of boron in tissue at cellular level for bnct

R43CA-54629-01 (SSS) LONGWORTH, JAMES W MCR TECHNOLOGY CORPORATION PO BOX 10084 CHICAGO, IL 60610-0084 3D ultrasonic holography for cardiac and tumor imaging

R01CA-54641-02 (ET) VINIK, AARON I THE DIABETES INSTITUTES 855 WEST BRAMBLETON AVENUE NORFOLK, VIRGINIA 23510 Diagnosis and management of gut/neuroendocrine tumors

R43CA-54646-01 (SSS) EGGERS, PHILIP E EGGARS RIDIHALGH PARTNERS, INC 5366 RESERVE DR DUBLIN, OH 43017 Hospital-based irradiation facility for neutron therapy

R43CA-54647-01 (SSS) REYNOLDS, THOMAS C SOMATIX THERAPY CORPORATION 850 MARINA VILLAGE PARKWAY ALAMODA, CALIFORNIA 94501 Improved packaging cells for recombinant retroviruses

R43CA-54652-01 (ET) BIGNAMI, GARY S HAWAII BIOTECHNOLOGY GROUP 99-193 AIEA HEIGHTS DRIVE AIEA, HI 96701 Palytoxin prodrug activation by antibody-linked enzyme

R43CA-54653-01 (ET) TURNER, NANCY A MOLECULAR ONCOLOGY, INC 19 FIRSTFIELD ROAD GAITHERSBURG, MD 20878 LS-MET-1, a highly metastatic human carcinoma cell line

R43CA-54657-01 (SSS) KHALID, SYED SYNCHROTRONICS, INC 3401 MARKET STREET PHILADELPHIA, PA 19104 Cryostat/detector for X-ray spectroscopy noise compensation

R43CA-54662-01 (SSS) BIRD, ROBERT E MOLECULAR ONCOLOGY, INC 19 FIRSTFIELD ROAD GAITHERSBURG, MD 20878 Human collagenase IV and its inhibitors

R43CA-54670-01 (SSS) DROZDOWICZ, ZBIGNIEW QUANTRONIX CORP 49 WIRELESS BLVD, BOX 9014 SMITHTOWN, NY 11787-9014 Laser-diode-pumped fiber-delivered Tm:YLF surgical laser

R01CA-54672-14A1 (PTHB) BENEDICT, WILLIAM F BAYLOR COLLEGE OF MEDICINE 4000 RESEARCH FOREST DRIVE WOODLANDS, TX 77381 Biochemical and cytogenetic markers in retinoblastoma

R01CA-54676-01 (HCT) NATTINGER, ANN B MILWAUKEE COUNTY MEDICAL COMPL 8700 W WISCONSIN AVE BX 135 MILWAUKEE, WI 53226 Use of breast-conserving surgery in the elderly

R13CA-54684-01 (SRC) YATVIN, MILTON B OREGON HEALTH SCIENCES UNIV 3181 S W SAM JACKSON PARK RD PORTLAND, OR 97201-3098 Experimental radiation oncology conference

R43CA-54685-01 (MEP) NELSON, CHRISTOPHER E KEMIN INDUSTRIES, INC 2100 MAURY ST, PO BOX 70 DES MOINES, IA 50301 Production of an anticarcinogenic protease inhibitor

R43CA-54689-01 (SSS) MORTON, STEVEN G OXFORD COMPUTER INC 39 OLD GOOD HILL ROAD OXFORD, CT 06483 Prototype duplication of cytology specimen

R43CA-54694-01 (SSS) KNAZEK, RICHARD A CELLCO ADVANCED BIOREACTORS, I 5516 NICHOLSON LANE KENSINGTON, MD 20895 Clearing of tumor cells from human bone marrow cultures

R13CA-54695-01 (SRC) SHANKEL, DELBERT M UNIVERSITY OF KANSAS 7035 HAWORTH HALL LAWRENCE, KS 66045 Conference on mechanisms of antimutagenesis/anticarcinogenesis

R01CA-54696-01 (SRC) HARLOW, EDWARD E MASS GENERAL HOSP CANCER CTR 13TH STREET CHARLESTOWN, MA 02129 Investigation of the cellular p300 protein

R01CA-54699-01 (SRC) FIELDS, STANLEY STATE UNIVERSITY OF NEW YORK STONY BROOK, NY 11794-8621 Yeast system to detect oncoprotein-associated proteins

R01CA-54703-01 (SRC) GREEN, MAURICE ST LOUIS UNIVERSITY 3681 PARK AVE ST LOUIS, MO 63110 Cellular proteins involved in adenovirus E1A repression

R01CA-54706-01 (EDC) KLEIN, JOHN P OHIO STATE UNIV 1958 NEIL AVENUE COLUMBUS, OH 43210 Techniques for modeling complex longitudinal studies

R55CA-54718-01 (ARRE) ROSENBLATT, JOSEPH D UCLA SCHOOL OF MEDICINE 10833 LE CONTE AVE LOS ANGELES, CA 90024-1678 Pathogenic mechanisms in htlv-1 linked diseases

R43CA-54719-01 (BIOL) PARMS, CLIFFORD A INTERSYSTEMS INC 820 WEST END AVENUE, STE 15E NEW YORK, NY 10025 Cancer risk reduction among Native American adolescents

R01CA-54722-01 (ARRA) TOMPKINS, WAYNE A NORTH CAROLINA STATE UNIV 4700 HILLSBOROUGH STREET RALEIGH, NC 27606 Pathogenesis of feline immunodeficiency virus -AIDS

R01CA-54726-01 (SRC) MUMBY, MARC C UNIV OF TEX SW MED CTR AT DALL 5323 HARRY HINES BOULEVARD DALLAS, TX 75235-9041 Protein phosphatase 2A in transformation by polyoma/SV40

R13CA-54736-01 (SRC) WILSON, CHARLES B UNIVERSITY OF CALIFORNIA BOX 0112 SAN FRANCISCO, CA 94143 9th International conference on brain tumor research

R01CA-54741-01 (SRC) HIRSCH, MARTIN S MASSACHUSETTS GENERAL HOSPITAL FRUIT ST BOSTON, MA 02114 HIV-CMV interactions

R01CA-54743-01 (SRC) MCGRATH, MICHAEL S SAN FRANCISCO GENERAL HOSPITAL 1001 POTRERO AVENUE SAN FRANCISCO, CA 94110 Antigenic specificity and V region use of AIDS B NHLs

R01CA-54755-01 (SRC) KIPPS, THOMAS J UNIV OF CALIFORNIA, SAN DIEGO LA JOLLA, CA 92093-0945 Mechanisms of AIDS-associated lymphomagenesis

R01CA-54757-01 (SRC) TSAI, CHE-CHUNG UNIVERSITY OF WASHINGTON MEDICAL LAKE, WA 99022-0536 Mechanisms of viral induced AIDS-associated neoplasia

R01CA-54763-01 (SRC) SHARMA, SURENDRA R WILLIAMS GEN HOSP-BROWN UNIV 825 CHALKSTONE AVENUE PROVIDENCE, RI 02908 Pathogenetic evaluation of AIDS associated lymphomas

R13CA-54764-01 (SRC) YOHN, DAVID S 300 W 10TH AVE COLUMBUS, OH 43210 XV International symposium--Comparative leukemia research

R13CA-54767-01 (SRC) TRENT, JEFFREY M UNIVERSITY OF ARIZONA ARIZONA CANCER CENTER TUCSON, AZ 85724 4th International workshop on chromosomes in solid tumor

R01CA-54773-01 (MGN) HOLMQUIST, GERALD P BECKMAN RES INST/CITY OF HOPE 1450 EAST DUARTE ROAD DUARTE, CA 91010 Adduct and repair mapping in oncogenes

R13CA-54775-01 (SRC) SCHANTZ, STIMSON P UT MD ANDERSON CANCER CANCER C 1515 HOLCOMBE BLVD, BOX 69 HOUSTON, TX 77030 R-13 scientific meeting proposal

R13CA-54776-01 (SRC) NEWELL, GUY R UT MD ANDERSON CANCER CENTER 1515 HOLCOMBE BLVD, BOX 189 HOUSTON, TX 77030 Conference--Prevention of aerodigestive tract cancer

R13CA-54777-01 (SRC) FOX, C FRED KEYSTONE CENTER PO BOX 606 KEYSTONE, CO 80435 Conference on genomic instability and dysregulation

R13CA-54779-01 (SRC) FOX, C FRED KEYSTONE SYMPOSIA PO BOX 606 KEYSTONE, CO 80435 Conference on growth factor signal transduction

R13CA-54780-01 (SRC) FOX, C FRED KEYSTONE CENTER PO BOX 606 KEYSTONE, CO 80435 Conference on molecular biology of pathogenic viruses

R13CA-54781-01 (SRC) FOX, C FRED KEYSTONE CENTER PO BOX 606 KEYSTONE, CO 80435 FGF, endothelial cell growth factors and angiogenesis

R29CA-54785-01 (MGN) WINDLE, BRADFORD E CANCER THERAPY & RESEARCH CENT 4450 MEDICAL DRIVE SAN ANTONIO, TX 78229 Repair and recombination of broken chromosomes

R01CA-54786-01 (CBY) COOPER, JONATHAN A FRED HUTCHINSON CANCER RES CTR 1124 COLUMBIA STREET SEATTLE, WA 98104 Signal transduction via receptor tyrosine kinases

R13CA-54787-01 (SRC) SELL, KENNETH W EMORY UNIV SCHOOL OF MEDICINE ATLANTA, GA 30322 International conference series on human cancer--Nutrition and cancer

R13CA-54796-01 (SRC) KERBEL, ROBERT S MT SINAI HOSPITAL 600 UNIV AVE, RM 880 TORONTO, CANADA M5G 1X5 Gordon conference on cancer 1991

R13CA-54798-01 (SRC) BOKOCH, GARY M RES INST OF SCRIPPS CLINIC 10666 N TORREY PINES ROAD LA JOLLA, CA 92037 Faseb conference/low molecular weight GTP bind protiens

R03CA-54801-01 (SRC) RIMM, ALFRED A MEDICAL COLLEGE OF WISCONSIN 8701 W WATERTOWN PLANK RD MILWAUKEE, WI 53226 United States Atlas of cancer incidence

R01CA-54807-01 (MEP) BRATTAIN, MICHAEL G BAYLOR COLLEGE OF MEDICINE ONE BAYLOR PLAZA HOUSTON, TX 77030 Autoactivation of colon cancer cell by intracellular TGF

R29CA-54818-01 (PTHB) AVIGAN, MARK I GEORGETOWN UNIV SCH OF MEDICIN 3900 RESERVOIR ROAD NW WASHINGTON, DC 20007 A regulated protein which stimulates c-myc expression

R01CA-54819-01 (MCHA) SEMMELHACK, MARTIN F PRINCETON UNIVERSITY WASHINGTON ROAD PRINCETON, NJ 08544-1009 Functional analogs of ene-diyne toxins

R01CA-54826-01 (REN) SHYAMALA, GOPALAN LAWRENCE BERKELEY LABORATORY 1 CYCLOTRON ROAD BERKELEY, CA 94720 Normal and neoplastic growth--Role of estrogens and HSP90

R03CA-54838-01 (SRC) SHEARN, ALLEN D JOHNS HOPKINS UNIVERSITY 34TH & CHARLES STREETS BALTIMORE, MD 21218 Invasive neoplasms of drosophila as models of metastasis

R55CA-54849-01 (SRC) JACKSON, MARIAN J 655 WEST BALTIMORE STREET BALTIMORE, MD 21201 Reactive nitrogen and metastatic progression

R03CA-54851-01 (SRC) HERLYN, DOROTHEE M WISTAR INSTITUTE 36TH AND SPRUCE STREETS PHILADELPHIA, PA 19104 Cancer patients immune responses studied in SCID mice

R01CA-54852-01 (SSS) GREENHOUSE, JOEL B CARNEGIE-MELLON UNIVERSITY 5000 FORBES AVENUE PITTSBURGH, PA 15213 Bayesian methods in biostatistics

R03CA-54856-01 (SRC) DONNENBERG, ALBERT D 600 NORTH WOLFE STREET BALTIMORE, MD 21205 Lymphocyte/tumor interactions in SCID/HU chimeric mice

R03CA-54861-01 (SRC) DE CLERCK, YVES A CHILDREN'S HOSPITAL OF L A 4650 SUNSET BLVD, BOX 54 LOS ANGELES, CA 90027 Two step inhibition of invasion and metastasis

R03CA-54873-01 (SRC) TESTA, JACQUELINE E STATE UNIVERSITY OF NEW YORK SCHOOL OF MED BHS T9 140 STONY BROOK, NY 11794-8691 Genes which positively regulate tumor cell metastasis

R03CA-54877-01 (SRC) HIXSON, DOUGLAS C RHODE ISLAND HOSPITAL 593 EDDY STREET PROVIDENCE, RI 02903 Rat model of transplantable hepatocellular carcinoma

R55CA-54885-01 (SRC) LUNA, ELIZABETH J WORCESTER FDN/EXPER BIOLOGY 222 MAPLE AVENUE SHREWSBURY, MA 01545 Actin-binding membrane proteins in invasive cells

R01CA-54886-01 (RNM) BRADY, THOMAS J MGH-NMR CENTER 13TH STREET CHARLESTOWN, MA 02129 MR receptor imaging

R03CA-54889-01 (SRC) BEAMER, WESLEY G 600 MAIN STREET BAR HARBOR, ME 04609-0800 Development of a mouse model for ovarian cancer

R29CA-54891-01 (RAD) HOWELL, ROGER W UMDNJ-NEW JERSEY MEDICAL SCHOO 185 S ORANGE AVE NEWARK, NJ 07103 Effects of radon laden water on mouse testes

R29CA-54892-01 (ET) CARRERA, CARLOS J UNIV OF CALIFORNIA, SAN DIEGO LA JOLLA, CA 92093-0945 Mechanisms of programmed cell death in chemotherapy

R03CA-54906-01 (SRC) BEN DAVID, YAACOV REICHMANN RESEARCH BUILDING 2075 BAYVIEW AVENUE CANADA M4N 3M5 Genetic alterations in progression of human melanoma

R03CA-54926-01 (SRC) MILLER, FRED R MICHIGAN CANCER FOUNDATION 110 EAST WARREN AVENUE DETROIT, MI 48201 A model to sequentially analyze the metastatic cascade

R03CA-54932-01 (SRC) CONDEELIS, JOHN S ALBERT EINSTEIN COLL OF MED 1300 MORRIS PARK AVENUE BRONX, NY 10461 Molecular analysis of chemotaxis in metastatic cells

R03CA-54936-01 (SRC) CANNON-ALBRIGHT, LISA A 420 CHIPETA WAY, RM. 180 SALT LAKE CITY, UT 84108 Analysis of familial clustering of cancer in Utah

R03CA-54942-01 (SRC) ENNIS, BRUCE W VANDERBILT UNIVERSITY C-2310 MCN NASHVILLE, TN 37232-2175 Autocrine stimulated tumor progression of breast cancer

R03CA-54944-01 (SRC) MALATHY-SHEKHAR, PV MICHIGAN CANCER FOUNDATION 110 E WARREN AVENUE DETROIT, MI 48201 Role of metastasis genes at specific steps of metastasis

R55CA-54950-01 (SRC) HELGERSON, SAM L MONTANA STATE UNIVERSITY 108 GAINES HALL BOZEMAN, MT 59717 Structural biology of metastasis determining integrins

R03CA-54952-01 (SRC) BOYD, FREDERICK T UNIV OF MINN/BOX 609 UMHC 420 DELAWARE STREET S.E. MINNEAPOLIS, MN 55455 Growth suppressor genes in metastatic melanoma

R01CA-54957-01 (EI) REED, JOHN C UNIVERSITY OF PENNSYLVANIA 207 JOHN MORGAN BUILDING PHILADELPHIA, PA 19104-6082 Kinase encoding proto-oncogenes in Il-2 signal transduct

R01CA-54959-01 (RNM) OLLINGER, JOHN M WASHINGTON UNIVERSITY 700 S EUCLID AVENUE ST LOUIS, MO 63110 Model-based scatter correction in PET

R03CA-54978-01 (SRC) BRANDSMA, JANET L YALE UNIVERSITY SCHOOL OF MED 333 CEDAR STREET; PO BOX 3333 NEW HAVEN, CT 06510 Studies in vivo of papillomavirus transforming genes

R03CA-54984-01 (SRC) HENDRIX, MARY J UNIVERSITY OF ARIZONA COLLEGE OF MEDICINE TUCSON, AZ 85724 Molecular analysis of cytokeratins during tumor invasion

R03CA-54989-01 (SRC) YU, DIHUA U T M D ANDRSON CANCER CENTER 1515 HOLCOMBE BLVD BOX 79 HOUSTON, TX 77030 Neu oncogene and metastasis

R03CA-54990-01 (SRC) SRIVASTAVA, PRAMOD K MT SINAI SCHOOL OF MEDICINE BOX 1215 NEW YORK, NY 10029 Immune response to tumors of ras and jun transgenic mice

R29CA-54998-01 (ET) VANDEVANTER, DONALD R 409 EKLIND H./SWE HOS MED CTR. 747 SUMMIT AVE SEATTLE, WA 98104 Search for drug resistance genes on extrachromosomal DNA

R29CA-54999-01 (VR) GELINAS, CELINE UMDNJ-ROBT WOOD JOHNSON MED SC 679 HOES LANE PISCATAWAY, NJ 08854-5638 Trans-acting function of the V- and C-rel oncoproteins

R29CA-55003-01 (MEP) CULLEN, KEVIN J LOMBARDI CANCER RESEARCH CENTE 3800 RESERVOIR ROAD, NW WASHINGTON, DC 20007 Stromal-epithelial interactions in breast cancer

PROJECT NO., ORGANIZATIONAL UNIT., INVESTIGATOR, ADDRESS, TITLE

R01CA-55008-01 (PTHB) **DER, CHANNING J** LA JOLLA CANCER RESEARCH FDN 10901 NORTH TORREY PINES ROAD LA JOLLA, CA 92037 Function of ras oncogene protein related rab proteins

R13CA-55013-01 (SRC) **STANCEL, GEORGE M** UNIV OF TEXAS MED SCH AT HOUST HOUSTON, TX 77225 Gordon research conference on hormonal carcinogenesis

R13CA-55015-01 (SRC) **BECKER, FREDERICK F** THE UNIVERSITY OF TEXAS 1515 HOLCOMBE BLVD HOUSTON, TX 77030 1991 annual symposium on fundamental cancer research

R29CA-55017-01 (GMA) **LESSIN, STUART R** UNIVERSITY OF PENNSYLVANIA 422 CURIE BLVD PHILADELPHIA, PA 19104-6142 Molecular characterization of cutaneous T-cell lymphoma

R01CA-55019-01 (RAD) **REYNOLDS, RICHARD J** LOS ALAMOS NATIONAL LABORATORY PO BOX 1663, MS M886 LOS ALAMOS, NM 87545 Repair of bifilar DNA damage induced by radiation

R01CA-55029-01 (PTHB) **CLEARY, MICHAEL L** STANFORD UNIVERSITY MEDICAL CENTER, L-235 STANFORD, CA 94305-5324 Pathology and biology of leukemia oncogenes

R55CA-55035-01 (EVR) **NYBORG, JENNIFER K** COLORADO STATE UNIVERSITY FORT COLLINS, CO 80523 Tax1 regulation of HTLV-I transcription and replication

R01CA-55036-01 (PTHB) **FINLAY, CATHY A** PRINCETON UNIVERSITY PRINCETON, NJ 08544-1014 The role of P53 in cell proliferation

R01CA-55042-01 (CPA) **SAMSON, LEONA D** HARVARD SCHOOL PUBLIC HEALTH 665 HUNGTINGTON AVE BOSTON, MA 02115 Eukarytic DNA alkylation repair

R29CA-55048-01 (VR) **LAMBERT, PAUL F** UNIVERSITY OF WISCONSIN MADISO 1400 UNIVERSITY AVE MADISON, WI 53706 Coordinate regulation in transforming papillomaviruses

R01CA-55056-01 (ET) **BELT, JUDITH A** ST JUDE CHILDREN'S RES HOSP 332 NORTH LAUDERDALE MEMPHIS, TN 38101 Biochemical modulation with transport inhibitors

R29CA-55064-01 (ET) **PIEPER, RUSSELL O** LOYOLA UNIV MEDICAL CENTER 2160 S FIRST AVE MAYWOOD, IL 60153 Control of alkyltransferase expression/DNA methylation

R55CA-55065-01 (CPA) **CORDEIRO-STONE, MARILA** UNIVERSITY OF NORTH CAROLINA 522 BRINKHOUS-BULLITT BLDG CHAPEL HILL, NC 27599-7525 Replication of damaged DNA in human cells

R29CA-55066-01 (CPA) **GILMOUR, SUSAN K** LANKENAU MED RESEARCH CTR LANCASTER AVE, W OF CITY LINE PHILADELPHIA, PA 19151 Ornithine decarboxylase and epidermal carcinogenesis

P01CA-55075-01 (SRC) **WILLETT, WALTER C** HARVARD SCHOOL OF PUBLIC HLTH 677 HUNTINGTON AVENUE BOSTON, MA 02155 Prospective studies of diet and cancer in men and women

P01CA-55075-01 0001 (SRC) **WILLETT, WALTER C** Prospective studies of diet and cancer in men and women Male health professional follow-up study

P01CA-55075-01 0002 (SRC) **STAMPFER, MEIR** Prospective studies of diet and cancer in men and women Prospective study of diet and colorectal polyps

P01CA-55075-01 0003 (SRC) **COLDITZ, GRAHAM** Prospective studies of diet and cancer in men and women Diet and benign breast disease--Prospective study

P01CA-55075-01 0004 (SRC) **HUNTER, DAVID J** Prospective studies of diet and cancer in men and women Pooled analysis of prospective diet and cancer studies

P01CA-55075-01 0005 (SRC) **WILLETT, WALTER C** Prospective studies of diet and cancer in men and women Dietary assessment methods for epidemiologic studies

R13CA-55083-01 (SRC) **MODIANO, MANUEL R** ARIZONA CANCER CENTER 1515 N CAMPBELL AVENUE TUCSON, AZ 85724 North American conference on cancer in hispanics

R13CA-55089-01 (SRC) **ENWONWU, CYRIL O** MEHARRY MEDICAL COLLEGE(A-73) 1005 D.B. TODD BLVD. NASHVILLE, TN 37208 Workshop-- Diet, nutrition and cancer

R13CA-55093-01 (SRC) **NILSEN-HAMILTON, MARIT** IOWA STATE UNIVERSITY AMES, IA 50010 Transforming factor-beta/related proteins in development

R01CA-55095-01 (PBC) **SHIPP, MARGARET A** DANA-FARBER CANCER INSTITUTE 44 BINNEY STREET BOSTON, MA 02115 Neutral proteases in lung cancer

R01CA-55098-01 (SSS) **LAN, KK GORDON** BIOSTATISTICS CENTER 6110 EXECUTIVE BLVD ROCKVILLE, MD 20852 Statistical methods for cancer clinical trials

R13CA-55100-01 (SRC) **COLVIN, O MICHAEL** JOHNS HOPKINS ONCOLOGY CENTER 600 NORTH WOLFE STREET BALTIMORE, MD 21205 Gordon research conference on cancer chemotherapy

R01CA-55102-01 (SRC) **AYNSLEY, JOHN S** ESCAGENETICS CORPORATION 830 BRANSTEN ROAD SAN CARLOS, CA 94070-3305 Production of taxol by plant tissue culture

R01CA-55106-01 (SRC) **ELLIS, DAVID D** UNIVERSITY OF WISCONSIN 1575 LINDEN DRIVE MADISON, WI 53706 Taxol production utilizing a nodule culture system

R13CA-55109-01 (SRC) **LI, JONATHAN J** WASHINGTON STATE UNIVERSITY PULLMAN, WA 99164-6510 1st international symposium on hormonal carcinogenesis

R55CA-55111-01 (SRC) **MACDONALD, TIMOTHY L** UNIVERSITY OF VIRGINIA MC CORMICK ROAD CHARLOTTESVILLE, VA 22901 Taxol interactions with microtubules and tubulin

R01CA-55118-01 (SRC) **CHANG, CHING-JER** PURDUE UNIVERSITY SCH OF PHARMACY/PHARMACAL SCIS WEST LAFAYETTE, INDIANA 47907 Taxol and taxanes from plant tissue culture

R01CA-55127-01 (SRC) **MCCHESNEY, JAMES D** UNIVERSITY OF MISSISSIPPI UNIVERSITY, MS 38677 Development of reliable and economic sources of taxol

R01CA-55131-01 (SRC) **KINGSTON, DAVID G** VIRGINIA POLYTECHNIC INSTITUTE DEPT OF CHEMISTRY BLACKSBURG, VA 24061-0212 Enhancement of taxol's anticancer activity and supply

R01CA-55133-01 (SRC) **ROWINSKY, ERIC K** JOHNS HOPKINS ONCOLOGY CENTER 600 NORTH WOLFE ST, RM 1-121 BALTIMORE, MD 21205 Human metabolism of taxol

R01CA-55138-01 (SRC) **SHULER, MICHAEL L** CORNELL UNIVERSITY ITHACA, NY 14853-5201 Manipulation of T. brevifolia physiology in tissue culture

PROJECT NO., ORGANIZATIONAL UNIT., INVESTIGATOR, ADDRESS, TITLE

R01CA-55139-01 (SRC) **SWINDELL, CHARLES S** BRYN MAWR COLLEGE BRYN MAWR, PA 19010 Chemical studies of taxol and microtubules

R01CA-55148-01 (SRC) **KISHI, YOSHITO** HARVARD UNIVERSITY 12 OXFORD STREET CAMBRIDGE, MA 02138 Synthetic studies towards taxol and related compounds

R01CA-55150-01 (SRC) **WHEELER, NICHOLAS C** WEYERHAEUSER COMPANY 505 NORTH PEARL ST CENTRALIA, WA 98531 Genetic improvement and cultivation of yew for taxol

R01CA-55151-01 (SRC) **KELSEY, RICK G** PACIFIC NW RESEARCH STATION 3200 JEFFERSON WAY CORVALLIS, OR 97331 Culture, physiology, genetics, influencing taxane yields

R13CA-55154-01 (SRC) **MEDINA, DANIEL** BAYLOR COLLEGE OF MEDICINE ONE BAYLOR PLAZA HOUSTON, TEXAS 77030 Gordon research conference on mammary gland biology

R55CA-55159-01 (SRC) **ERLANGER, BERNARD F** COLUMBIA UNIVERSITY 630 W 168TH STREET NEW YORK, NY 10032 Immunologic approaches to studies of taxol

R03CA-55168-01 (SRC) **FITZGERALD, EDWARD F** NEW YORK STATE DEPT OF HEALTH 2 UNIVERSITY PLACE ALBANY, NY 12203 Case control study of osteosarcoma and fluoride exposure

R29CA-55173-01 (PTHA) **SKUSE, GARY R** UNIVERSITY OF ROCHESTER 601 ELMWOOD AVENUE ROCHESTER, NY 14642 Molecular pathogenesis of tumors in neurofibromatosis

R55CA-55178-01 (EI) **WEINER, GEORGE J** UNIVERSITY OF IOWA GENERAL HOSPITAL RM C32-K IOWA CITY, IA 52242 Bispecific antibody therapy of B-cell lymphoma

R29CA-55195-01 (EI) **OWEN-SCHAUB, LAURIE B** UNIVERSITY OF TEXAS 1515 HOLCOMBE BOULEVARD HOUSTON, TX 77030 Analysis of the Fas antigen on human lymphocytes

R29CA-55202-01 (NURS) **HOLLEN, PATRICIA J** UNIVERSITY OF ROCHESTER 601 ELMWOOD AVE ROCHESTER, NY 14642 Cancer surviving adolescents reducing risk behaviors

R01CA-55207-01 (PTHB) **FREEDMAN, ARNOLD S** DANA-FARBER CANCER INSTITUTE 44 BINNEY STREET BOSTON, MA 02115 Germinal center adhesion of normal/neoplastic B cells

R01CA-55211-01 (CPA) **ROBERTSON, FREDIKA M** UMDNJ-ROBERT W JOHNSON MED SCH ONE ROBERT WOOD JOHNSON PLACE NEW BRUNSWICK, NJ 08903 Role of adhesion molecules and cytokines in tumor promotion

R29CA-55212-01 (SSS) **JONES, MICHAEL P** UNIVERSITY OF IOWA 2800 STEINDLER BLDG IOWA CITY, IA 52242 Survival analysis for cancer data

R55CA-55219-01 (BIO) **JOHNSON, EDWARD M** MT SINAI SCHOOL OF MEDICINE ONE GUSTLAVE L LEVY PLACE NEW YORK, NY 10029 Control of initiation of DNA replication in lung cancer

R01CA-55227-01 (PTHB) **ROBBINS, PAUL D** UNIV OF PITTSBURGH SCH OF MED W1256 BST PITTSBURGH, PA 15261 Regulation of transcription-retinoblastoma anti-oncogene

R01CA-55230-01 (ET) **SHACKNEY, STANLEY E** ALLEGHENY-SINGER RES INSTITUTE 320 EAST NORTH AVENUE PITTSBURGH, PA 15212 Genetic staging of breast cancers for adjuvant therapy

R29CA-55231-01 (PTHB) **ISAACS, WILLIAM B** JOHNS HOPKINS HOSPITAL 600 NORTH WOLFE STREET BALTIMORE, MD 21205 Tumor suppressor gene inactivation in prostate cancer

R01CA-55232-01 (CPA) **HENNER, WILLIAM D** OREGON HEALTH SCIENCES UNIV 3181 SW SAM JACKSON PARK RD/L5 PORTLAND, OR 97201-3098 Mutagenesis by the antineoplastic mustards

R01CA-55245-01 (CPA) **NAIRN, RODNEY S** UT MD ANDERSON CANC CTR P O BOX 389 SMITHVILLE, TX 78957 Tumor suppressor genes in heritable melanoma models

R01CA-55251-01 (SRC) **STRAUBINGER, ROBERT M** ST UNIV OF NEW YORK/BUFFALO 539 COOKE HALL BUFFALO, NY 14260 Pharmacology and efficacy of novel taxol formulations

R13CA-55253-01 (SRC) **MC DOUGALL, JAMES K** FRED HUTCHINSON CANCER RES CTR 1124 COLUMBIA STREET SEATTLE, WA 98104 Tenth international papillomavirus workshop

R01CA-55254-01 (SRC) **CROTEAU, RODNEY B** WASHINGTON STATE UNIVERSITY 467 CLARK HALL PULLMAN, WA 99164-6340 Biosynthesis of taxol

R29CA-55266-01 (EI) **STREET, NANCY E** UNIV OF TX SOUTHWESTERN MED CT 5323 HARRY HINES BLVD DALLAS, TX 75235-8576 Role of CD4+ T helper cells in B cell tumor dormancy

R55CA-55274-01 (EI) **SUZUKI, TSUNEO** UNIV OF KANSAS MEDICAL CENTER 39TH AND RAINBOW BLVD KANSAS CITY, KS 66103-8410 Lps-mediated regulation of PKG in macrophage activation

R29CA-55275-01 (PBC) **CHEN, JING-MAY** THOMAS JEFFERSON UNIVERSITY 1020 LOCUST STREET PHILADELPHIA, PA 19107-6799 Matrix degradation in transformed cells

R01CA-55276-01 (BNP) **BOGER, DALE L** RESEARCH INST OF SCRIPPS CLINI 10666 NORTH TORREY PINES ROAD LA JOLLA, CA 92037 Antitumor antibiotics-- Duocarmycin and azinomycin

R01CA-55279-01 (CTY) **RAYCHAUDHURI, PRADIP** UNIV OF ILLINOIS AT CHICAGO 1853 W POLK STREET CHICAGO, IL 60612 Transcription control by the nuclear oncoprotein, E1A

R13CA-55284-01 (SRC) **ROYSTON, IVOR** SAN DIEGO REGIONAL CANCER CENT 8008 FROST STREET SUITE 400 SAN DIEGO, CA 92123 Sixth international conference on monoclonal antibody immunoconjugates for cancer

R01CA-55290-01 (EI) **SYKES, MEGAN** MASSACHUSETTS GENERAL HOSPITAL BUILDING 149, 13TH STREET CHARLESTOWN, MA 02129 Achieving the graft versus leukemia effect without GVHD

R29CA-55293-01 (CBY) **FELDMAN, RICARDO A** UNIVERSITY OF MARYLAND 655 WEST BALTIMORE STREET BALTIMORE, MD 21201 Role of fps/fes proto-oncogene in myeloid cell function

R29CA-55299-01 (SAT) **SONDAK, VERNON K** 1500 E MEDICAL CENTER DR GENERAL SURGERY-TC 2920-0331 ANN ARBOR, MI 48109 Tumor-induced suppression of specific T cell response

R01CA-55305-01 (RAD) **PHIPPS, RICHARD P** UNIV OF ROCHESTER SCH OF MED 601 ELMWOOD AVE BX 704 CAN CTR ROCHESTER, NY 14642 Radiation-induced cytokine synthesis and lung fibrosis

R01CA-55325-01 (SSS) **OLSHEN, RICHARD A** STANFORD UNIVERSITY HRP BUILDING, ROOM 110 STANFORD UNIV, CA 94305-5092 Tree-structured statistical methods

R01CA-55326-01 (ET) **CHANEY, STEPHEN G** UNIVERSITY OF NORTH

CAROLINA CB# 7260, 303A FLOB CHAPEL HILL, NC 27599-7260 Biotransformation studies with ormaplatin

R01CA-55330-01 (CTY) MORAN, ELIZABETH COLD SPRING HARBOR LABORATORY PO BOX 100 COLD SPRING HARBOR, NY 11724 The cell growth control functions of the E1A oncogene

R01CA-55331-01 (MEP) DAVIES, RICHARD J UNIV OF CALIFORNIA, SAN DIEGO 225 DICKINSON ST., H891B SAN DIEGO, CA 92103 Cellular pH homeostasis in colorectal cancer

R01CA-55333-01 (ALY) WRIGHT, TIMOTHY M UNIVERSITY OF PITTSBURGH 965 SCAIFE HALL PITTSBURGH, PA 15261 Molecular basis of gamma interferon-specific gene expression

R55CA-55334-01 (CPA) HANNA, PATRICK E UNIVERSITY OF MINNESOTA 435 DELAWARE STREET SE MINNEAPOLIS, MN 55455 Studies on carcinogen-activating transacetylases

R01CA-55339-01 (CBY) HARLOW, EDWARD E MASS GENERAL HOSP CANCER CTR 13TH STREET/BUILDING 149 CHARLESTOWN, MA 02129 Oncogene-mediated changes in cell cycle control

R01CA-55349-01 (EI) SCHEINBERG, DAVID A SLOAN-KETTERING INST CANCER RE 1275 YORK AVENUE NEW YORK, NY 10021 Recombinant anti-CD33 antibody for AML

R01CA-55356-01 (HEM) MCKEITHAN, TIMOTHY W THE UNIV OF CHICAGO 5841 SOUTH MARYLAND AVENUE CHICAGO, IL 60637 Molecular analysis of the 14;19 translocation

R01CA-55357-01 (RAD) CAIN, CHARLES A THE UNIV OF MICHIGAN 3304 GGB/DOW CONNECTOR ANN ARBOR, MI 48109-2125 Activation of anti-cancer agents with ultrasound

R01CA-55360-01 (CBY) BAR-SAGI, DAFNA COLD SPRING HARBOR LABORATORY PO BOX 100 COLD SPRING HARBOR, NY 11724 Mechanisms of signal transduction by ras proteins

R13CA-55370-01 (SRC) PORTER, CARL W ROSWELL PARK CANCER INST ELM & CARLTON STREETS BUFFALO, N Y 14263 Ninth Gordon Research Conference on polyamines and cancer

R01CA-55372-01 (SRC) BOONE, JOHN M THOMAS JEFFERSON UNIVERSITY 111 SOUTH 11TH STREET PHILADELPHIA, PA 19107 Equalized dual energy/dual phosphor chest radiography

R01CA-55378-01 (SRC) DIBIANCA, FRANK A COLL OF GRADUATE HEALTH SCIENC 899 MADISON AVE, ROOM 801 MEMPHIS, TN 38163 Evaluation and development of a KCD digital chest x-ray

R01CA-55382-01 (SRC) SANDERS, PATRICIA C UNIVERSITY OF ALABAMA UNIVERSITY STATION BIRMINGHAM, AL 35294 Scatter-free dual-energy digital chest radiography

R13CA-55385-01 (SRC) WEINBERG, ROBERT A WHITEHEAD INST FOR BIOMED RES NINE CAMBRIDGE CENTER CAMBRIDGE, MA 02142 Negative controls on cell growth

R01CA-55397-01 (HEM) COLLINS, STEVEN J FRED HUTCHINSON CANCER RES CTR 1124 COLUMBIA STREET SEATTLE, WA 98104 The retinoic acid receptor in myeloid leukemia

R01CA-55406-01 (MEP) LUPU, RUTH GEORGETOWN UNIVERSITY 3800 RESERVOIR ROAD, NW WASHINGTON, DC 20007 Ligands for the ERAB-2: Purification, cloning & bio prop

R43CA-55413-01 (SSS) KAMENTSKY, LOUIS A COMPUCYTE CORPORATION ONE KENDALL SQUARE CAMBRIDGE, MA 02139 Clinical application of a laser scanning cytometer

R01CA-55414-01 (ET) HENTOSH, PATRICIA CHICAGO MEDICAL SCHOOL 3333 GREEN BAY RD NORTH CHICAGO, IL 60064 Functional consequences of 2-chloroadenine in DNA

R43CA-55417-01 (SSS) SUTHANTHIRAN, KRISHNAN BEST INDUSTRIES, INC 7643-B FULLERTON RD SPRINGFIELD, VA 22153 Samarium-145 sources for brachytherapy

R43CA-55418-01 (SSS) POOL, JEREMY D BELMONT RESEARCH INC 315 COMMON STREET BELMONT, MA 02178 Laser graphics visualization tools for clinical research

R43CA-55421-01 (SSS) DELAYRE, JOHN L TECMAG, INC 6006 BELLAIRE BLVD HOUSTON, TX 77081 Desktop magnet for magnetic resonance imaging

R43CA-55422-01 (SSS) CAPELLI, CHRISTOPHER C BIOINTERFACE TECHNOLOGIES, INC 1202 ANN STREET MADISON, WI 53713 Non-protein MR contrast agent for breast cancer imaging

R43CA-55423-01 (ET) LAI, CHEE K REPLIGEN CORPORATION ONE KENDELL SQUARE, BLDG 700 CAMBRIDGE, MA 02139 Generation of PF4 polyethylene glycol conjugates

R43CA-55430-01 (SSS) ALVAREZ, ROBERT E APREND TECHNOLOGY 2369 LAURA LANE MOUNTAIN VIEW, CA 94043 Active energy selective cassette

R43CA-55432-01 (SSS) POWELL, RICHARD D BROOKHAVEN NATIONAL LABORATORY UPTON, NY 11973 Amplification of silver-gold immuno- and DNA probes

R43CA-55433-01 (SSS) YANEZ, LUIS ONCOGENE SCIECES, INC 350 COMMUNITY DR MANHASSET, NY 11030 A novel assay to detect translocation in leukemias

R43CA-55434-01 (SSS) ALBRIGHT, MICHAEL J TECMAG 6006 BELLAIRE BLVD HOUSTON, TX 77081 NMR processing software for macintosh computers

R43CA-55438-01 (SSS) HALEY, JOHN D ONCOGENE SCIENCE INC 350 COMMUNITY DRIVE MANHASSET, NY 11030 Transcriptional control of the EGF receptor gene

R43CA-55446-01 (SSS) DOIRON, DANIEL R LASERTHERAPEUTICS, INC P.O. BOX 1965 BUELLTON, CA 93427 LED light source for photodynamic therapy

R43CA-55449-01 (SSS) RZEDZIAN, RICHARD R ADVANCED NMR SYSTEMS INC 46 JONSPIN ROAD WILMINGTON, MA 01887 Fast low cost MR breast scanner and novel compact magnet

R43CA-55451-01 (SSS) MALAND, LYNN ANESTA CORP 825 NORTH 300 WEST STE 200 SALT LAKE CITY, UT 84103 Buccal drug delivery system for cancer pain management

R43CA-55452-01 (SSS) HEDLUND, BO E BIOMEDICAL FRONTIERS, INC 1095 10TH AVENUE S.E. MINNEAPOLIS, MN 55414 Macromolecular contrast agents for magnetic resonance

R43CA-55456-01 (ET) PRINCE, CHRISTOPHER L PHYTON CATALYTIC 83 BROWN RD ITHACA, NY 14853 Feasibility study--Taxol from plant cell culture

R43CA-55459-01 (ET) TAYLOR, ELLISON H ATOM SCIENCES, INC 114 RIDGEWAY CENTER OAK RIDGE, TN 37830 Ultra sensitive analysis for PT by RIS in tumor therapy

R43CA-55469-01 (ET) KAIGHN, M EDWARD BIOLOGICAL RES FACULTY/FACILIT 10075-20 TYLER PLACE IJAMSVILLE, MD 21754 Toxicity and growth inhibition assays by image analysis

R43CA-55474-01 (SSS) KYLE, DAVID J MARTEK CORPORATION 6480 DOBBIN ROAD COLUMBIA, MD 21045 Producing natural beta-carotene for chemotherapeutic use

R43CA-55478-01 (CMS) BARAFF, DAVID R AMERICAN ARTIFICIAL LARYNX CO 19 EAST CENTRAL AVENUE PAOLI, PA 19301 Development a speech aid to rehabilitate laryngectomees

R01CA-55480-01 (ARRB) HJELLE, BRIAN L UNIV OF NEW MEXICO SCH OF MED ALBUQUERQUE, NM 87131 Prevalence and pathologic burden of HTLV-II infection

R01CA-55487-01 (ARRC) RABSON, ARNOLD B CTR FOR ADVANCED BIOTECH & MED 679 HOES LANE PISCATAWAY, NJ 08854-5638 Effect of NFKB and rel-family proteins on HIV expression

R01CA-55492-01 (ARRA) REDDY, E PREMKUMAR THE WISTAR INSTITUTE 36TH & SPRUCE STREETS PHILADELPHIA, PA 19104 Role of myb in transcriptional-regulation of HIV-1 and H

R01CA-55506-01 (SRC) BYRNES, JOHN J UNIV OF MIAMI HOSPITAL 1475 N W 12 AVE RM 1067A MIAMI, FL 33136 Trial and correlative studies of DDI in AIDS-lymphoma

R01CA-55507-01 (SRC) MURPHY, SHARON B CHILDRENS MEMORIAL HOSPITAL 2300 CHILDRENS PLAZA #30 CHICAGO, IL 60614 Pediatric AIDS/lymphoma network

R01CA-55509-01 (SRC) FISHER, RICHARD I LOYOLA UNIV MED CTR 2160 SOUTH FIRST AVE MAYWOOD, IL 60153 Biology and treatment of AIDS lymphomas

R01CA-55510-01 (SRC) LEVINE, ALEXANDRA M UNIV OF SOUTHERN CALIFORNIA 1975 ZONAL AVE KAM #110F LOS ANGELES, CA 90033 HIV, cytokines and therapeutic result in AIDS lymphoma

R01CA-55513-01 (SRC) FEIGAL, ELLEN G DIVISION OF HEMATOLOGY/ONCOLOG 225 DICKINSON STREET, H-811K SAN DIEGO, CA 92103 Novel therapeutic approaches in HIV-associated lymphomas

R01CA-55514-01 (SRC) KAPLAN, LAWRENCE D SAN FRANCISCO GENERAL HOSP 995 POTRERO AVE SAN FRANCISCO, CA 94110 Novel therapeutic approaches for HIV-associated NHL

R01CA-55518-01 (SRC) GORDON, LEO I NORTHWESTERN UNIVERSITY 303 EAST CHICAGO, 8524 OLSON CHICAGO, IL 60611 AIDS related lymphomas--Clinical and biologic studies

R01CA-55520-01 (SRC) SCADDEN, DAVID T NEW ENGLAND DEACONESS HOSPITAL 185 PILGRIM ROAD BOSTON, MA 02215 Biological approaches to AIDS lymphoma

R01CA-55526-01 (SRC) FORD, RICHARD J, JR UNIV TEXAS/M D ANDERSON CA CTR 1515 HOLCOMBE BOULEVARD HOUSTON, TX 77030 Clinical and molecular studies on AIDS-related lymphomas

R01CA-55529-01 (SRC) AMBINDER, RICHARD F THE JOHNS HOPKINS UNIV 418 N BOND ST BALTIMORE, MARYLAND 21231 EBV as a tumor marker in AIDS CNS lymphoma

R01CA-55531-01 (SRC) STRAUS, DAVID J MEMORIAL HOSPITAL FOR CANCER 1275 YORK AVE NEW YORK, NY 10021 Monoclonal antibody treatment of AIDS-related lymphoma

R44CA-55543-02 (SSS) SPIELVOGEL, BERNARD F BORON BIOLOGICALS, INC 2811 O'BERRY STREET RALEIGH, NC 27607 Oligonucleotides with boronated phosphorus backbones

R13CA-55586-01 (SRC) JONES, LOVELL A UNIVERSITY OF TEXAS 1515 HOLCOMBE BLVD HOUSTON, TX 77030 3rd biennial symposium on minorities and cancer

R01CA-55621-01 (SRC) MATSUDAIRA, PAUL T WHITEHEAD INSTITUTE FOR NINE CAMBRIDGE CENTER CAMBRIDGE, MA 02142 Transmembrane communication in cell function

R03CA-55637-01 (SRC) HERTZ-PICCIOTTO, IRVA UNIVERSITY OF NORTH CAROLINA CB #7400 CHAPEL HILL, NC 27599-7410 The healthy worker survivor effect and cancer mortality

R01CA-55700-01 (SRC) GOODMAN, MARC T UNIVERSITY OF HAWAII 2540 MAILE WAY HONOLULU. HI 96822 Multiethnic study of pre-invasive cervical lesions in Hawaii

R01CA-55728-01 (PTHA) JAMES, CHARLES D EMORY UNIVERSITY 2040 RIDGEWOOD DRIVE, NE ATLANTA, GA 30322 Genetic alterations in CNS tumor development

R01CA-55730-01 (SRC) SAMET, JONATHAN UNIV OF NEW MEXICO MED CTR 900 CAMINO DE SALUD, NE ALBUQUERQUE, NM 87131-5306 Breast cancer epidemiology in New Mexico Hispanics

R01CA-55760-01 (SRC) GODLEY, PAUL A UNIV OF NORTH CAROLINA 3009 OLD CLINIC BLDG CHAPEL HILL, NC 27599-7305 Race, fatty acid exposure, and risk of prostate cancer

R01CA-55763-01 (SRC) HAAS, GABRIEL P 4160 JOHN R SUITE 1017 DETROIT, MI 48201 Racial differences in prostate cancer--An autopsy study

R01CA-55764-01 (SRC) PARSONNET, JULIE STANFORD UNIVERSITY HLTH RES. & POLICY BLDG RM 109 STANFORD, CA 94305 Helicobacter pylori and risk for gastric cancer

R01CA-55766-01 (SRC) PALMER, JULIE R BOSTON UNIVERSITY SCH OF MED 1371 BEACON STREET BROOKLINE, MA 02146 Risk factors for breast, lung and colon cancer in US Blacks

R01CA-55769-01 (SRC) SPITZ, MARGARET R UNIVERSITY OF TEXAS 1515 HOLCOMBE BLVD HOUSTON, TX 77030 Ecogenetics of lung cancer in minority populations

R01CA-55772-01 (SRC) DEMENAIS, FLORENCE M HOWARD UNIVERSITY CANCER CENTE 2041 GEORGIA AVE NW WASHINGTON, DC 20060 Breast cancer among black women--Gene-environment interactions

R01CA-55781-01 (SRC) ROMNEY, SEYMOUR L ALBERT EINSTEIN COLLEGE OF MED 1300 MORRIS PARK AVENUE BRONX, NY 10461 Cervical dysplasias in ethnic/minority subgroups

R01CA-55874-01 (SRC) LE MARCHAND, LOIC CANCER RESEARCH CENTER 2540 MAILE WAY HONOLULU, HI 96822 A multidisciplinary study of lung cancer in Hawaiians

S15CA-55919-01 (NSS) AFIFI, ABDELMONEM A UNIV OF CALIF, LOS ANGELES 405 HILGARD AVENUE LOS ANGELES, CA 90024-1772 Small instrumentation grant

S15CA-55920-01 (NSS) FIELDER, DAVID R MEDICAL RESEARCH INST. OF S.F. 2200 WEBSTER STREET SAN FRANCISCO, CA 94115 Small instrumentation grant

S15CA-55921-01 (NSS) DELEUSE, BETSEY W THE ROCKEFELLER UNIVERSITY 1230 YORK AVENUE NEW YORK, NY 10021 Small instrumentation grant

PROJECT NO., ORGANIZATIONAL UNIT., INVESTIGATOR, ADDRESS, TITLE

S15CA-55922-01 (NSS) RUOSLAHTI, ERKKI I LA JOLLA CANCER RES FOUNDATION 10901 NORTH TORREY PINES ROAD LA JOLLA, CA 92037 Small instrumentation grant

S15CA-55923-01 (NSS) DAY, ROBERT W FRED HUTCHINSON CANCER RES CTR 1124 COLUMBIA STREET SEATTLE, WA 98104 Small instrumentation grant

S15CA-55924-01 (NSS) MC CORMICK, J JUSTIN MICHIGAN STATE UNIVERSITY EAST LANSING, MICHIGAN 48824 Small instrumentation grant

S15CA-55925-01 (NSS) LANSKY, SHIRLEY B ILLINOIS CANCER COUNCIL 200 S MICHIGAN AVENUE CHICAGO, IL 60604 Small instrumentation grant

S15CA-55926-01 (NSS) MINION, F CHRIS IOWA STATE UNIVERSITY ELWOOD DRIVE AMES, IA 50011 Small instrumentation grant

S15CA-55927-01 (NSS) WALDMAN, ROBERT H UNIV OF NEBRASKA MED CENTER 600 SOUTH 42ND STREET OMAHA, NE 68198-6545 Small instrumentation grant

S15CA-55928-01 (NSS) HOLDEN, JOSEPH T BECKMAN RESEARCH INSTITUTE 1450 E DUARTE ROAD DUARTE, CA 91010 Small instrumentation grant

S15CA-55929-01 (NSS) HULL, BARBARA E WRIGHT STATE UNIVERSITY 3640 COLONEL GLENN HIGHWAY DAYTON, OH 45435 Small instrumentation grant

S15CA-55930-01 (NSS) ABDEL-MONEM, MAHMOUD M WASHINGTON STATE UNIVERSITY COLLEGE OF PHARMACY PULLMAN, WA 99164-6510 Small instrumentation grant

S15CA-55931-01 (NSS) PHEMISTER, ROBERT D CORNELL UNIV, COL OF VET MED C114 SCHURMAN HALL ITHACA, N Y 14853 Small instrumentation grant

S15CA-55932-01 (NSS) FARBER, SAUL J NEW YORK UNIV MEDICAL CENTER 550 FIRST AVENUE NEW YORK, N Y 10016 Small instrumentation grant

S15CA-55933-01 (NSS) WILSON, EMERY A UNIV OF KENTUCKY, COM 800 ROSE STREET LEXINGTON, KY 40536-0084 Small instrumentation grant

S15CA-55934-01 (NSS) CULLUM, MALFORD E UNIV OF ILLINOIS AT CHICAGO 801 SOUTH PAULINA CHICAGO, IL 60612 Small instrumentation grant

S15CA-55935-01 (NSS) PAUL, ARA G UNIVERSITY OF MICHIGAN 428 CHURCH STREET ANN ARBOR, MI 48109-1065 Small instrumentation grant

S15CA-55936-01 (NSS) GOZZO, JAMES J NORTHWESTERN UNIVERSITY 360 HUNTINGTON AVE/206 MUGAR BOSTON, MA 02115 Small instrumentation grant

S15CA-55937-01 (NSS) WATANABE, KYOICHI A SLOAN-KETTERING INST/CNCR RES 1275 YORK AVENUE NEW YORK, NY 10021 Small instrumentation grant

S15CA-55938-01 (NSS) WALLACE, ANDREW G DARTMOUTH MEDICAL SCHOOL HANOVER, NH 03756 Small instrumentation grant

S15CA-55939-01 (NSS) SHACKS, SAMUEL J CHARLES R DREW UNIV MED & SCI 1621 EAST 120TH ST LOS ANGELES, CA 90059 Small instrumentation grant

S15CA-55940-01 (NSS) ROSENQUIST, GLENN C CHILDREN'S HOSPITAL 111 MICHIGAN AVE N W WASHINGTON, DC 20010 Small instrumentation grant

S15CA-55941-01 (NSS) MOON, RICHARD C IIT RESEARCH INSTITUTE 10 WEST 35TH ST CHICAGO, IL 60616 Small instrumentation grant

S15CA-55942-01 (NSS) DALEN, JAMES E UNIVERSITY OF ARIZONA 1501 N CAMPBELL AVE, RM 2222 TUCSON, AZ 85724 Small instrumentation grant

S15CA-55943-01 (NSS) WARE, JAMES H HARVARD SCH OF PUBLIC HEALTH 677 HUNTINGTON AVE BOSTON, MA 02115 Small instrumentation grant

S15CA-55944-01 (NSS) DELONG, STEPHEN E UNIV AT ALBANY, SUNY 1400 WASHINGTON AVE ALBANY, NY 12222 Small instrumentation grant

S15CA-55945-01 (NSS) LASKER, LORRAINE NEW YORK MEDICAL COLLEGE VALHALLA, NY 10595 Small instrumentation grant

S15CA-55946-01 (NSS) MAIZEL, ABBY ROGER WILLIAMS MED CTR 825 CHALKSTONE AVENUE PROVIDENCE, RI 02908 Small instrumentation grant

S15CA-55947-01 (NSS) GOLD, DAVID V CTR FOR MOLECULAR MED/IMMUNOLO 1 BRUCE ST NEWARK, NJ 07103 Small instrumentation grant

S15CA-55948-01 (NSS) ANDERSON, WAYNE K UNIVERSITY AT BUFFALO 429A COOKE HALL/SCH OF PHARMAC BUFFALO, NY 14260-0001 Small instrumentation grant

S15CA-55949-01 (NSS) KUMAR, AJIT GEORGE WASHINGTON UNIVERSITY 2300 EYE ST NW WASHINGTON, DC 20037 Small instrumentation grant

S15CA-55950-01 (NSS) HUTCHINSON, WILLIAM B 720 BROADWAY SEATTLE, WA 98122 Small instrumentation grant

S15CA-55951-01 (NSS) WRAY, SUSAN D UNIVERSITY OF FLORIDA 219 GRINTER HALL GAINESVILLE, FL 32611-2037 Small instrumentation grant

S15CA-55952-01 (NSS) GRAVES, DAVID E UNIVERSITY OF MISSISSIPPI UNIVERSITY, MS 38677 Small instrumentation grant

S15CA-55953-01 (NSS) CROSBY, LEANNA J UNIVERSITY OF ARIZONA COLLEGE OF NURSING TUCSON, AZ 85721 Small instrumentation grant

S15CA-55955-01 (NSS) MOOD, DARLENE W WAYNE ST UNIV. COLL OF NURSING 5557 CASS AVENUE DETROIT, MI 48202 Small instrumentation grant

S15CA-55956-01 (NSS) WALLACE, LANE J OHIO STATE UNIVERSITY 500 WEST 12TH AVENUE COLUMBUS, OH 43210 Small instrumentation grant

S15CA-55957-01 (NSS) OVERSTROM, ERIC W 200 WESTBORO ROAD NORTH GRAFTON, MA 01536 Small instrumentation grant

S15CA-55958-01 (NSS) NOELL, JOHN OREGON RESEARCH INSTITUTE 1899 WILLAMETTE EUGENE, OREGON 97401 Small instrumentation grant

S15CA-55959-01 (NSS) SCUTCHFIELD, F DOUGLAS SAN DIEGO STATE UNIV 5300 CAMPANILE DRIVE SAN DIEGO, CA 92182-0405 Small instrumentation grant

S15CA-55960-01 (NSS) YEE, DOUGLAS UNIV OF TEXAS HEALTH SCIENCE C 7703 FLOYD CURL DR SAN ANTONIO, TX 78284-7884 Small instrumentation grant

S15CA-55961-01 (NSS) HELLMAN, SAMUEL 970 EAST 58TH STREET CHICAGO, IL 60637 Small instrumentation grant

S15CA-55963-01 (NSS) KINGHORN, ALAN D UNIV OF ILLINOIS AT CHICAGO 833 SOUTH WOOD ST, M/C 877 CHICAGO, IL 60612 Small instrumentation grant

S15CA-55964-01 (NSS) LAWELLIN, DAVID W CHILDREN'S HOSPITAL 1056 EAST 19TH AVENUE DENVER, CO 80218 Small instrumentation grant

S15CA-55965-01 (NSS) VINCE, ROBERT UNIVERSITY OF MINNESOTA 308 HARVARD ST, SE MINNEAPOLIS, MN 55455 Small instrumentation grant

S15CA-55966-01 (NSS) FUHR, JOSEPH E UNIV OF TENNESSEE MED CTR 1924 ALCOA HIGHWAY KNOXVILLE, TN 37920 Small instrumentation grant

S15CA-55967-01 (NSS) OETTGEN, HERBERT F MEMORIAL HOSPITAL FOR

PROJECT NO., ORGANIZATIONAL UNIT., INVESTIGATOR, ADDRESS, TITLE

CANCER 1275 YORK AVENUE NEW YORK, N Y 10021 Small instrumentation grant

S15CA-55968-01 (NSS) TRANQUADA, ROBERT E UNIV OF SOUTHERN CALIFORNIA 1975 ZONAL AVE, KAM 500 LOS ANGELES, CA 90033 Small instrumentation grant

S15CA-55969-01 (NSS) SUSMAN, MILLARD 1300 UNIVERSITY AVENUE MADISON, WI 53706 Small instrumentation grant

S15CA-55970-01 (NSS) PETERSON, JERRY A JOHN MUIR CANCER & AGING 2055 NORTH BROADWAY WALNUT CREEK, CA 94596 Small instrumentation grant

S15CA-55971-01 (NSS) BURRIS, JAMES F GEORGETOWN UNIVERSITY 3900 RESERVOIR RD NW WASHINGTON, DC 20007 Small instrumentation grant

S15CA-55972-01 (NSS) SCOTCH, NORMAN A BOSTON UNIVERSITY 80 EAST CONCORD STREET BOSTON, MA 02118 Small instrumentation grant

S15CA-55973-01 (NSS) WEI, WEI-ZEN MICHIGAN CANCER FOUNDATION 110 EAST WARREN AVENUE DETROIT, MI 48201 Small instrumentation grant

S15CA-55974-01 (NSS) CHERNIACK, NEIL S CASE WESTERN RESERVE UNIVERSIT 2109 ADELBERT RD CLEVELAND, OH 44106 Small instrumentation grant

S15CA-55975-01 (NSS) SODETZ, JAMES M UNIVERSITY OF SOUTH CAROLINA DEPARTMENT OF CHEMISTRY COLUMBIA, SC 29208 Small instrumentation grant

S15CA-55976-01 (NSS) BUENING, GERALD M UNIV OF MISSOURI-COLUMBIA COLL OF VETERINARY MEDICINE COLUMBIA, MO 65211 Small instrumentation grant

S15CA-55977-01 (NSS) OTTO, DAVID A BAPTIST MEDICAL CENTERS 701 PRINCETON AVENUE BIRMINGHAM, AL 35211 Small instrumentation grant

S15CA-55978-01 (NSS) KISZKISS, DAVID F NEW ENGLAND DEACONESS HOSPITAL 185 PILGRAM RD BOSTON, MA 02215-5399 Small instrumentation grant

S15CA-55979-01 (NSS) LEY, RONALD D LOVELACE MEDICAL FOUNDATION 2425 RIDGECREST DRIVE S E ALBUQUERQUE, NM 87108 Small instrumentation grant

S15CA-55980-01 (NSS) SWARBRICK, JAMES UNIV OF NC AT CHAPEL HILL BEARD HALL CB# 7360 CHAPEL HILL, NC 27599-7360 Small instrumentation grant

S15CA-55981-01 (NSS) KANESHIRO, EDNA S UNIVERSITY OF CINCINNATI 309 BRAUNSTEIN BLDG CINCINNATI, OH 45221-0627 Small instrumentation grant

S15CA-55982-01 (NSS) RODGERS, MICHAEL A J BOWLING GREEN STATE UNIVERSITY BOWLING GREEN, OH 43403 Small instrumentation grant

S15CA-55988-01 (NSS) SATO, GORDON H W ALTON JONES CELL SCI CTR, IN 10 OLD BARN ROAD LAKE PLACID, NY 12946 Small instrumentation grant

S15CA-55989-01 (NSS) LEDLEY, ROBERT S NATIONAL BIOMEDICAL RES FDN 3900 RESERVOIR ROAD, NW WASHINGTON, DC 20007 Small instrumentation grant

S15CA-55990-01 (NSS) CAHALAN, MICHAEL D UNIV OF CALIFORNIA - IRVINE IRVINE, CA 92717 Small instrumentation grant

S15CA-55991-01 (NSS) SIMMONS, DANIEL T SCHOOL OF LIFE/HLT SCIENCES UNIVERSITY OF DELAWARE NEWARK, DE 19716 Small instrumentation grant

S15CA-55992-01 (NSS) BOSMANN, BRUCE H UNIV OF ILLINOIS AT CHICAGO 1853 WEST POLK ST CHICAGO, IL 60612 Small instrumentation grant

S15CA-55993-01 (NSS) COLTMAN, CHARLES A, JR CANCER THERAPY & RESEARCH CTR 4450 MEDICAL DRIVE SAN ANTONIO, TX 28229 Small instrumentation grant

S15CA-55994-01 (NSS) RUDDON, RAYMOND W EPPLEY INSTITUTE FOR RESEARCH 600 SOUTH 42ND STREET OMAHA, NE 68198-6805 Small instrumentation grant

S15CA-55995-01 (NSS) RUBIN, BERISH Y FORDHAM UNIVERSITY LARKIN HALL 160 BRONX, NEW YORK 10458 Small instrumentation grant

S15CA-55996-01 (NSS) SPERLING, MARK A CHILDREN'S HOSP OF PITTSBURGH 3705 FIFTH AVE PITTSBURGH, PA 15213-2583 Small instrumentation grant

S15CA-55997-01 (NSS) SIMONE, JOSEPH V ST JUDE CHILDREN'S RES HOSPITA 332 N LAUDERDALE, P O BOX 318 MEMPHIS, TN 38101 Small instrumentation grant

S15CA-55998-01 (NSS) EISERLING, FREDERICK A UNIVERSITY OF CALIFORNIA 1312 MURPHY HALL LOS ANGELES, CA 90024 Small instrumentation grant

S15CA-55999-01 (NSS) BLAYNEY, KEITH D UNIV OF ALABAMA AT BIRMINGHAM WEBB BUILDING, ROOM 616B BIRMINGHAM, AL 35294 Small instrumentation grant

S15CA-56000-01 (NSS) CORNWELL, DAVID G MEDICINE ADMINISTRATION 260 MEILING HALL/370 W-9TH AVE COLUMBUS, OH 43210 Small instrumentation grant

S15CA-56001-01 (NSS) MISTRETTA, CHARLOTTE M THE UNIVERSITY OF MICHIGAN 400 N INGALLS BLDG ANN ARBOR, MI 48109-0482 Small instrumentation grant

S15CA-56002-01 (NSS) CARLSON, GEORGE A 1625 3RD AVENUE NO GREAT FALLS, MT 59401 Small instrumentation grant

S15CA-56003-01 (NSS) SHAPIRO, JOAN R BARROW NEUROLOGICAL INST 350 W THOMAS RD PHOENIX, AZ 85013-4496 Small instrumentation grant

S15CA-56004-01 (NSS) NEET, KENNETH E 3333 GREEN BAY ROAD NORTH CHICAGO, IL 60064 Small instrumentation grant

S15CA-56006-01 (NSS) ROOSA, ROBERT A WISTAR INSTITUTE 36TH AND SPRUCE STREETS PHILADELPHIA, PA 19104 Small instrumentation grant

S15CA-56007-01 (NSS) YIELDING, K LEMONE UNIV OF TEXAS MEDICAL BRANCH 301 UNIVERSITY BLVD GALVESTON, TX 77550 Small instrumentation grant

S15CA-56008-01 (NSS) BECKER, FREDERICK F UT M.D. ANDERSON CANCER CTR 1515 HOLCOMBE BLVD HOUSTON, TX 77030 Small instrumentation grant

S15CA-56009-01 (NSS) HATCHER, VICTOR B MONTEFIORE MEDICAL CENTER 111 EAST 210TH ST BRONX, NY 10467 Small instrumentation grant

S15CA-56010-01 (NSS) KLEPPER, JOHN RICHARD INST OF APPLIED PHYSIOLOGY & M 701 16TH AVENUE SEATTLE, WA 98122 Small instrumentation grant

S15CA-56011-01 (NSS) DAMBACH, GEORGE E WAYNE STATE UNIVERSITY 540 EAST CANFIELD DETROIT, MI 48201 Small instrumentation grant

S15CA-56012-01 (NSS) EDWARDS, CHARLES UNIV OF SOUTH FLORIDA 12901 BRUCE B DOWNS BLVD TAMPA, FL 33612 Small instrumentation grant

PROJECT NO., ORGANIZATIONAL UNIT., INVESTIGATOR, ADDRESS, TITLE

S15CA-56013-01 (NSS) MORROW, GRANT, III CHILDREN'S HOSPITAL RES FDN 700 CHILDREN'S DRIVE COLUMBUS, OHIO 43205 Small instrumentation grant

S15CA-56014-01 (NSS) DIAMOND, LOUIS UNIVERSITY OF COLORADO CAMPUS BOX 297 BOULDER, CO 80309-0297 Small instrumentation grant

S15CA-56015-01 (NSS) WYNDER, ERNST L ONE DANA RD VALHALLA, NY 10595 Small instrumentation grant

S15CA-56016-01 (NSS) SUTHERLAND, ROBERT M SRI INTERNATIONAL 333 RAVENSWOOD AVENUE MENLO PARK, CA 94025 Small instrumentation grant

S15CA-56017-01 (NSS) JACOBSON, HERBERT I ALBANY MEDICAL COLLEGE 47 NEW SCOTLAND AVENUE ALBANY, NY 12208 Small instrumentation grant

S15CA-56018-01 (NSS) GIBBONS, BARBARA H UNIV OF HAWAII AT MANOA 2540 MAILE WAY, SPALDING 255 HONOLULU, HAWAII 96822 Small instrumentation grant

S15CA-56019-01 (NSS) PARKER, WILLIAM B SOUTHERN RESEARCH INSTITUTE 2000 NINTH AVE SOUTH BIRMINGHAM, AL 35255-5305 Small instrumentation grant

S15CA-56020-01 (NSS) WORTIS, HENRY H TUFTS UNIVERSITY 136 HARRISON AVE BOSTON, MA 02111 Small instrumentation grant

S15CA-56021-01 (NSS) BOLE, GILES G UNIV OF MICHIGAN MED SCHOOL 7321 MED SCI 1, 1301 CATHERINE ANN ARBOR, MI 48109-0624 Small instrumentation grant

S15CA-56022-01 (NSS) SANDBERG, AVERY A SOUTHWEST BIOMEDICAL RES INST 6401 EAST THOMAS ROAD SCOTTSDALE, AZ 85251 Small instrumentation grant

S15CA-56023-01 (NSS) KARR, JAMES P ROSWELL PARK CANCER INST ELM & CARLTON STREETS BUFFALO, NY 14263 Small instrumentation grant

S15CA-56024-01 (NSS) YOUNG, ROBERT C FOX CHASE CANCER CENTER 7701 BURHOLME AVENUE PHILADELPHIA, PA 19111 Small instrumentation grant

S15CA-56025-01 (NSS) STEVENS, JAMES O UNIV OF COLORADO HLTH SCI CTR 4200 EAST 9TH AVE, BOX C-290 DENVER, CO 80262 Small instrumentation grant

S15CA-56026-01 (NSS) DUKES, PETER P CHILDRENS HOSP OF LOS ANGELES 4650 SUNSET BLVD LOS ANGELES, CALIF 90027 Small instrumentation grant

S15CA-56027-01 (NSS) BURGESS, DAVID R UNIVERSITY OF PITTSBURGH PITTSBURGH, PA 15260 Small instrumentation grant

S15CA-56028-01 (NSS) RE, RICHARD N ALTON OCHSNER MEDICAL FDN 1516 JEFFERSON HIGHWAY NEW ORLEANS, LA 70121 Small instrumentation grant

S15CA-56029-01 (NSS) LUZZI, LOUIS A UNIVERSITY OF RHODE ISLAND COLLEGE OF PHARMACY KINGSTON, R I 02881 Small instrumentation grant

S15CA-56030-01 (NSS) NEURATH, A ROBERT NEW YORK BLOOD CENTER 310 E. 67TH STREET NEW YORK, NY 10021 Small instrumentation grant

S15CA-56031-01 (NSS) WEST, DEE W NORTHERN CALIFORNIA CANCER CTR PO BOX 2030 BELMONT, CA 94002-5030 Small instrumentation grant

S15CA-56032-01 (NSS) COOPER, RICHARD A MEDICAL COLLEGE OF WISCONSIN 8701 WATERTOWN PLANK ROAD MILWAUKEE, WI 53226 Small instrumentation grant

S15CA-56033-01 (NSS) THOMPSON, HENRY J AMC CANCER RESEARCH CENTER 1600 PIERCE STREET LAKEWOOD, CO 80214 Small instrumentation grant

R55CA-56041-01 (PTHA) STECK, PETER A UNIVERSITY OF TEXAS 1515 HOLCOMBE BOULEVARD HOUSTON, TX 77030 Differentially expressed gene products in human gliomas

R01CA-56103-01 (ET) FINN, OLIVERA J UNIV OF PITT. SCH OF MED W1143 BIOMED SCI. TWR. PITTSBURGH, PA 15261 Human T cell immunity to epithelial tumor mucins

R13CA-56114-01 (MBY) FOX, C FRED KEYSTONE SYMPOSIA PO BOX 606 KEYSTONE, CO 80435 Conference on gene regulation by antisense RNA and DNA

R01CA-56115-01 (SRC) BIGNER, DARELL D DUKE UNIV MEDICAL CENTER P O BOX 3712 DURHAM, N C 27710 Intrathecal therapy of melanoma neoplastic meningitis

R01CA-56116-01 (SRC) CHOU, CHUNG-KWANG CITY OF HOPE NAT'L MED CTR 1500 E DUARTE RD DUARTE, CA 91010 Intracavitary hyperthermia & radiation of esophageal cancer

R01CA-56117-01 (SRC) LAD, THOMAS E UNIVERSITY OF ILLINOIS MED CTR PO BOX 6998, M/C 787 CHICAGO, IL 60680 Correlates of drug resistance in gastric carcinoma

R01CA-56121-01 (SRC) KREVSKY, BENJAMIN TEMPLE UNIV HOSPITAL 3401 N BROAD STREET PHILADELPHIA, PA 19140 Endoscopic laser therapy for esophageal cancer

R01CA-56125-01 (SRC) KELSEN, DAVID P MEMORIAL HOSPITAL 1275 YORK AVE NEW YORK, NY 10021 Multimodality treatment/ clinical-biological correlates of upper GI cancer

R01CA-56129-01 (SRC) HOCHSTER, HOWARD S NYU MEDICAL CENTER 462 FIRST AVE RM 556 NEW YORK, NY 10016 Topoisomerase-1 inhibitors--Novel therapy of upper GI cancer

R01CA-56130-01 (SRC) YEO, CHARLES J JOHNS HOPKINS UNIVERSITY 600 N WOLFE ST/HALSTED 614 BALTIMORE, MD 21205 Correlates and treatment of pancreatic carcinoma

R01CA-56138-01 (SRC) COLTMAN, CHARLES A, JR SOUTHWEST ONCOLOGY GROUP 5430 FREDERICKSBURG RD SUITE 6 SAN ANTONIO, TX 78229-6197 Pharmacodynamic correlates in advanced gastric cancer

R13CA-56142-01 (AITC) FOX, C FRED KEYSTONE CENTER PO BOX 606 KEYSTONE , CO 80435 Conference on monoclonal antibodies

R01CA-56159-01 (SSS) PEREDNIA, DOUGLAS A OREGON HLTH SCIENCES UNIVERSIT 3181 S W SAM JACKSON PARK ROAD PORTLAND, OR 97201-3098 Melanoma screening by computer detection of skin changes

R43CA-56182-01 (ET) CASTOR, TREVOR P BIO-ENG, INC 216 SYLVIA STREET ARLINGTON, MA 02174 Critical fluid extraction and purification of taxol

R43CA-56263-01 (HUD) WRIGHT, MICHAEL P SCIENTIFIC SOCIAL RESEARCH 811 W. BOYD NORMAN, OK 73069 Software for HIV risk assessment & education

R01CA-56273-01 (SRC) LU, LEE-JANE W UNIV OF TEXAS MED BRANCH 2.102 EWING HALL, J-10 GALVESTON, TX 77550 Pharmacokinetics of soybean anticarcinogens

R29CA-56277-01 (EI) VERCELLI, DONATA CHILDREN'S HOSPITAL 300 LONGWOOD AVENUE BOSTON, MA 02115 Function of the human monocyte antigen CD14

PROJECT NO., ORGANIZATIONAL UNIT., INVESTIGATOR, ADDRESS, TITLE

R01CA-56300-01 (CBY) MACARA, IAN G UNIVERSITY OF VERMONT MEDICAL ALUMNI BUILDING BURLINGTON, VT 05405 Ras-like GTP-binding proteins--Regulation and function

R01CA-56303-01 (SRC) SETCHELL, KENNETH D CHILDREN'S HOSP MEDICAL CTR ELLAND & BETHESDA AVENUE CINCINNATI, OH 45229-2899 Analysis and physiology of isoflavones in soybeans

R01CA-56307-01 (MEP) CHUNG, LELAND W U T M D ANDERSON CANCER CTR 1515 HOLCOMBE BLVD HOUSTON, TX 77030 Sex steroids and growth factors in prostatic growth

R01CA-56308-01 (SRC) MURPHY, PATRICIA A IOWA STATE UNIVERSITY 147 DAIRY INDUSTRY AMES, IA 50011 Quantitation and bioavailability of soyfood isoflavones

P01CA-56309-01 (SRC) BASERGA, RENATO THOMAS JEFF U/ JEFF MED COLL 1025 WALNUT STREE PHILADELPHIA, PA 19104 Cell cycle progression

P01CA-56309-01 0001 (SRC) BASERGA, RENATO Cell cycle progression Studies on the proliferating cell nuclear antigen (PCNA) gene

P01CA-56309-01 0002 (SRC) CALABRETTA, BRUNO Cell cycle progression Role of human c-myb in T-lymphocyte proliferation

P01CA-56309-01 0003 (SRC) LIPSON, KENNETH L Cell cycle progression Gene regulation at the G1/S phase boundary of the cell cycle

P01CA-56309-01 0004 (SRC) SOPRANO, KENNETH J Cell cycle progression The role of c-jun in G1-S

P01CA-56309-01 9001 (SRC) BASERGA, RENATO Cell cycle progression Core--Molecular biology

R43CA-56311-01 (HUD) BARNETT, BETH BARNETT TECHNICAL SERVICES 1004 WOODSIDE PKWY SUITE 1A SILVER SPRING, MD 20910 Cancer prevention on computer for minority children

R43CA-56511-01 (SSS) PRESTON, KENDALL, JR SUITE C214 TUCSON, AZ 85711 Intelligent microscope workstation for cancer diagnosis

R13CA-56580-01 (CBY) STILES, CHARLES D DANA FARBER CANCER INST 44 BINNEY STREET BOSTON, MA 02115 Molecular and genetic basis for cell proliferation--Gordon Research Conference

R01CA-56701-01 (EI) KOHLER, HEINZ SAN DIEGO REGIONAL CANCER CENT 3099 SCIENCE PARK ROAD SAN DIEGO, CA 92121 Structure - function of tumor anti-idiotypic antibodies

R01CA-56728-02 (SRC) WALTER, RONALD B SW TEXAS STATE UNIVERSITY SAN MARCOS, TX 78666 Development of transgenic fish for biomedical research

R29CA-56843-01 (EI) KORETZKY, GARY A UNIVERSITY OF IOWA 540 EMRB IOWA CITY, IA 52242 CD45 regulation of T cell receptor signal transduction

R01CA-56844-01 (SSS) WEI, LEE-JEN HARVARD SCHOOL OF PUBLIC HEALT 677 HUNTINGTON AVENUE BOSTON, MA 02115 Statistical semi-parametric methods for cancer studies

R01CA-56909-01 (RAD) LI, GLORIA C SLOAN KETTERING INST/CANCER RE 1275 YORK AVENUE NEW YORK, NY 10021 Hyperthermia and the functions of HSP70

R01CA-56931-01 (SRC) GOITEIN, MICHAEL MASSACHUSETTS GENERAL HOSPITAL BOSTON, MA 02114 Planning and development for a proton facility at Massachusets General Hospital

R01CA-56932-01 (SRC) ALONSO, JOSE R LAWRENCE BERKELEY LABORATORY 1 CYCLOTRON ROAD BERKELEY, CA 94720 Design study for the UCSF proton facility

R01CA-56960-01 (RNM) NEGENDANK, WILLIAM G FOX CHASE CANCER CENTER 7701 BURHOLME AVENUE PHILADELPHIA, PA 19111 31P MRS for diagnosis of bone and soft tissue lesions

R43CA-56961-01 (ET) MORROW, PHILLIP R LIDAK BIOPHARMACEUTICALS 11077 NORTH TORREY PINES ROAD LA JOLLA, CA 92037 Human B-Lymphocyte tumor xenografts in SCID mice

R01CA-57004-01 (EDC) OLSHAN, ANDREW F SCHOOL OF PUBLIC HEALTH CB# 7400 MCGAVRAN/GREENBERG HA CHAPEL HILL, NC 27599-7400 Case-control study of risk factors for neuroblastoma

R01CA-57034-01 (SRC) HOLLAND, HENRY K EMORY UNIVERSITY BOX AR ATLANTA, GA 30322 Allogeneic bone marrow transplant for HIV-1 lymphoma

R01CA-57035-01 (SRC) OGSTON, CHARLES W KALAMAZOO COLLEGE 1200 ACADEMY STREET KALAMAZOO, MI 49007 Woodchuck hepatitis virus non-structural genes

R55CA-57064-01 (MEP) BOYNTON, ALTON L PACIFIC NORTHWEST RES FDN 720 BROADWAY SEATTLE, WA 98122 Mediators of platelet-derived growth factor actions

R01CA-57111-01 (SRC) SEIGLER, HILLIARD F DUKE UNIVERSITY MEDICAL CENTER ERWIN ROAD DURHAM, NC 27710 Melanoma immunotherapy

R55CA-57134-01 (ET) KEEVER, CAROLYN A MEDICAL COLLEGE OF WISCONSIN 8700 W WISCONSIN AVENUE MILWAUKEE, WI 53226 Anti-leukemia activity following marrow transplantation

U10CA-57137-01 (SRC) RAFLA, SAMEER THE METHODIST HOSPITAL 506 SIXTH STREET BROOKLYN, NY 11215 Brooklyn community clinical oncology program

R01CA-57138-01 (SRC) EISENMAN, ROBERT N FRED HUTCHINSON CANCER RES CTR 1124 COLUMBIA STREET SEATTLE, WA 98104 Myc oncoprotein function

R55CA-57139-01 (SRC) PETERSON, JOHN R PANLABS, INC 11804 NORTH CREEK PKWY S BOTHELL, WA 98011-8805 Taxol molecular mimics and photoreactive analogs

R01CA-57140-01 (SSS) CASTRO, FELIPE G ARIZONA STATE UNIVERSITY TEMPE, AZ 85287-1903 Campaneros in las salud--cancer control among hispanics

R01CA-57155-01 (EDC) SCHANTZ, STIMSON P MEMORIAL HOSPITAL FOR 1275 YORK AVENUE NEW YORK, N.Y. 10021 Multiple primary cancers and mutagen hypersensitivity

R01CA-57156-01 (SRC) GROUDINE, MARK T FRED HUTCHINSON CANCER RES CTR 1124 COLUMBIA ST SEATTLE, WA 98104 Molecular basis of c-myc deregulation in Burkitt lymphoma

R01CA-57156-01 0006 (SRC) GROUDINE, MARK Molecular basis of c-myc deregulation in Burkitt lymphoma Molecular basis of chromosomal alterations--Proviral insertions

R01CA-57157-01 (PTHB) REDDY, E SHYAM P THOMAS JEFFERSON UNIVERSITY 233 LOCUST ST/BLUEMLE LIFE SCI PHILADELPHIA, PA 19107 Functional dissection of human c-ets-1 gene

P01CA-57165-01 (SRC) FOON, KENNETH THE SCRIPPS RESEARCH INSTITUTE 10666 NORTH TORREY PINES ROAD LA JOLLA, CA 92037 Monoclonal antibody therapy of GI cancers

PROJECT NO., ORGANIZATIONAL UNIT., INVESTIGATOR, ADDRESS, TITLE

P01CA-57165-01 9003 (SRC) CHATTERJEE, MALAYA Monoclonal antibody therapy of GI cancers Core--Monoclonal antibody production and toxicology

P01CA-57165-01 0001 (SRC) CHATTERJEE, MALAYA Monoclonal antibody therapy of GI cancers Generation of anti-idiotype tumor vaccines

P01CA-57165-01 0002 (SRC) KOHLER, HEINZ Monoclonal antibody therapy of GI cancers Structure-function of tumor anti-idiotypic antibodies

P01CA-57165-01 0003 (SRC) FOON, KENNETH A Monoclonal antibody therapy of GI cancers Phase I/II study of anti-idiotype vaccine for GI cancer

P01CA-57165-01 9001 (SRC) FOON, KENNETH A Monoclonal antibody therapy of GI cancers Core--General

P01CA-57165-01 9002 (SRC) STEWART, CARLETON Monoclonal antibody therapy of GI cancers Core--Immunopathology

R01CA-57166-01 (ET) SACKS, PETER G SLOAN-KETTERING INSTITUTE 1275 YORK AVENUE NEW YORK, NY 10021 A differentiation therapy model for squamous carcinoma

R01CA-57202-01 (PBC) GEHLSEN, KURT R CALIFORNIA INT OF BIOLOGICAL R 11099 N TORREY PINES RD, S # 3 LA JOLLA, CA 92037 A model system for study of cell-matrix interaction

Z01CB-00366-20 (LB) KUFF, E L NCI, NIH Structure and expression of endogenous retroviral elements

Z01CB-00550-11 (LP) JAFFE, E S NCI, NIH Immunologic characterization of malignant lymphomas

Z01CB-00852-38 (LP) SOLOMON, D NCI, NIH Cytology applied to human diagnostic and research problems

Z01CB-00853-38 (LP) MERINO, M J NCI, NIH Surgical pathology

Z01CB-00855-09 (LP) JAFFE, E S NCI, NIH Pathologic features of viral associated lymphoproliferative disorders

Z01CB-00891-08 (LP) STRACKE, M NCI, NIH Stimulated motility in tumor cells

Z01CB-00892-07 (LP) STEEG, P S NCI, NIH Molecular biology of the metastatic phenotype

Z01CB-00897-06 (LP) SOLOMON, D NCI, NIH Immunocytochemistry as an adjunct to cytopathological diagnosis

Z01CB-00945-18 (LB) PETERKOFSKY, B NCI, NIH Factors regulating synthesis of collagen in normal and transformed cells

Z01CB-03229-23 (CBGY) APPELLA, E NCI, NIH T-cell antigen recognition and tumor antigens

Z01CB-03638-22 (D) ROBBINS, J H NCI, NIH Studies of DNA repair in human degenerative disease

Z01CB-03657-17 (D) KATZ, S I NCI, NIH Immunopathologic mechanisms involved in inflammatory skin diseases

Z01CB-03663-15 (LCO) LOWY, D R NCI, NIH Tumor virus expression in vitro and in vivo

Z01CB-03667-07 (D) STANLEY, J R NCI, NIH Molecules defined by autoantibody - mediated skin diseases

Z01CB-03669-02 (D) UDEY, M NCI, NIH Regulation of cutaneous accessory cell activity in health and disease

Z01CB-04002-22 (MET) WALDMANN, T A NCI, NIH Defects in immunoregulatory cell interactions in patients with immune dysfunction

Z01CB-04015-15 (MET) BLAESE, R M NCI, NIH Development and function of humoral and cellular immune mechanisms

Z01CB-04016-18 (MET) NISSLEY, S P NCI, NIH Mechanism of action of insulin-like growth factors

Z01CB-04017-13 (MET) NELSON, D L NCI, NIH Biology of the immune response

Z01CB-04018-15 (MET) MUCHMORE, A V NCI, NIH Immunoregulatory glycoproteins purification and characterization

Z01CB-04020-14 (MET) BERZOFSKY, J A NCI, NIH Antigen-specific T-cell activation--vaccines for malaria/AIDS

Z01CB-04024-04 (MET) STAUDT, L M NCI, NIH Control of gene expression in lymphoid development

Z01CB-04829-17 (LTIB) CALLAHAN, R NCI, NIH The identification and characterization of human genes associated with neoplasia

Z01CB-04848-19 (LTIB) BASSIN, R H NCI, NIH Anti-oncogenes--The analysis of cellular resistance to transformation

Z01CB-05021-20 (I) SACHS, D H NCI, NIH Antigens determined by the murine major histocompatibility locus

Z01CB-05023-20 (I) SACHS, D H NCI, NIH Transplantation antigens of swine

Z01CB-05148-12 (LTIB) CALLAHAN, R NCI, NIH Mammary tumorigenesis in inbred and feral mice

Z01CB-05190-11 (LTIB) SCHLOM, J NCI, NIH Monoclonal antibodies define carcinoma associated and differentiation antigens

Z01CB-05202-24 (LB) MCBRIDE, O W NCI, NIH Isolation, fractionation, and characterization of native nucleoproteins

Z01CB-05203-23 (LB) MAGE, M G NCI, NIH Immunochemical purification and characterization of immunocytes and components

Z01CB-05214-20 (LB) WILSON, S H NCI, NIH DNA synthesis in mammalian cells--Structure and function of DNA polymerases

Z01CB-05216-20 (LTIB) CHO-CHUNG, Y S NCI, NIH Site-selective cAMP analogs as antineoplastics and chemopreventives

Z01CB-05231-17 (LB) KLEE, C B NCI, NIH Role of subunit interactions in enzyme chemistry and cellular regulation

Z01CB-05244-14 (LB) SINGER, M F NCI, NIH Transposable elements in the human genome

Z01CB-05258-12 (LB) PATERSON, B M NCI, NIH Molecular studies of eukaryotic gene regulation

Z01CB-05262-11 (LB) HAMER, D H NCI, NIH Eukaryotic gene regulation and function--The metallothionein system

Z01CB-05263-10 (LB) WU, C NCI, NIH Eukaryotic chromatin structure and gene regulation

Z01CB-05264-10 (LB) LUEDERS, K K NCI, NIH Intracisternal A-particle (IAP) and growth factor genes in mouse myelomas

Z01CB-05265-09 (LB) WAGNER, P NCI, NIH Regulation of cytoskeletal proteins

Z01CB-05267-07 (LB) YARMOLINSKY, M NCI, NIH Mechanisms of plasmid maintenance

Z01CB-05268-03 (LB) LICHTEN, M NCI, NIH Mechanisms of meiotic recombination

Z01CB-05269-04 (LB) WILSON, S H NCI, NIH DNA synthesis in mammalian cells--Studies of nucleic acid binding proteins

PROJECT NO., ORGANIZATIONAL UNIT., INVESTIGATOR, ADDRESS, TITLE

Z01CB-05270-04 (LB) WILSON, S H NCI, NIH DNA synthesis in mammalian cells--Mechanism of HIV reverse transcriptase

Z01CB-05552-22 (LGN) COON, H G NCI, NIH Mammalian cellular genetics and cell culture

Z01CB-05553-22 (LGN) RUDIKOFF, S NCI, NIH Immunoglobulin structure & diversity--Characterization of cell membrane proteins

Z01CB-05596-22 (LGN) POTTER, M NCI, NIH Pathogenesis of plasma cell neoplasia--Resistance and susceptibility genes

Z01CB-05598-02 (CBGY) GOTTESMAN, M NCI, NIH Genetic analysis of the multidrug resistance phenotype in tumor cells

Z01CB-05599-01 (CBGY) ULLRICH, S NCI, NIH Structural and functional characterization of the p53 gene and protein

N01CB-05689-01 (**) EXPOSITO, LORENZO F Provide computer programming support services for the

Z01CB-08000-21 (LMB) PASTAN, I NCI, NIH Regulation of gene activity

Z01CB-08010-18 (LMB) WILLINGHAM, M C NCI, NIH Morphological mechanisms of organelle function and transformation in culture cell

Z01CB-08212-17 (LB) BERGER, S L NCI, NIH From gene to protein--Structure function and control in eukaryotic cells

Z01CB-08226-15 (LTIB) VONDERHAAR, B K NCI, NIH Hormones and growth factors in development of mammary glands and tumorigenesis

Z01CB-08281-09 (LTIB) CHO-CHUNG, Y S NCI, NIH Role of cAMP in growth control and differentiation--Gene regulation

Z01CB-08300-19 (LMMB) ZECH, L A NCI, NIH SAAM, developing and applications for analogic systems realization

Z01CB-08303-18 (LMMB) BLUMENTHAL, R P NCI, NIH Membrane fusion mediated by viral spike glycoproteins

Z01CB-08320-15 (LMMB) JERNIGAN, R L NCI, NIH Peptide conformations

Z01CB-08341-13 (LMMB) WEINSTEIN, J N NCI, NIH Structure/function relationships in treatment of cancer and AIDS

Z01CB-08363-09 (LMMB) GUY, H R NCI, NIH Membrane protein modeling

Z01CB-08366-08 (LMMB) WEINSTEIN, J N NCI, NIH The pharmacology of monoclonal antibodies and other biological ligands

Z01CB-08370-08 (LMMB) JERNIGAN, R L NCI, NIH Interactions in globular proteins and protein folding

Z01CB-08371-08 (LMMB) JERNIGAN, R L NCI, NIH Conformational variation in DNA and DNA-protein binding

Z01CB-08380-07 (LMMB) MAIZEL, J V NCI, NIH Molecular structure of animal viruses and cells by computational analysis

Z01CB-08381-08 (LMMB) LEMKIN, P NCI, NIH Computer aided two-dimensional electrophoretic gel analysis

Z01CB-08382-08 (LMMB) SHAPIRO, B NCI, NIH Computer analysis of nucleic acid structure

Z01CB-08386-05 (LMMB) QASBA, P K NCI, NIH Primary structure and topology of beta 1-4 galatosyltransferase

Z01CB-08387-04 (LMMB) PINTO DE SILVA, P NCI, NIH Neuroanat. & topochem. of the outer & cytochem.surface of biomembranes

Z01CB-08389-04 (LMMB) QASBA, P K NCI, NIH Structure-function relationship of beta 1-4 galactosyltransferase

Z01CB-08392-03 (LMMB) WEINSTEIN, J N NCI, NIH Combination chemotherapy of AIDS and cancer

Z01CB-08394-03 (LMMB) KONOPKA, A K NCI, NIH Non-contiguous patterns and functional domains in DNA

Z01CB-08396-03 (LMMB) SCHNEIDER, T D NCI, NIH Information theory in molecular biology

Z01CB-08552-25 (LIB) BORSOS, T NCI, NIH Mechanism of complement fixation and action

Z01CB-08575-18 (LIB) LEONARD, E J NCI, NIH Inflammation

Z01CB-08577-06 (LIB) ZBAR, B NCI, NIH Restriction fragment length polymorphisms in normal and neoplastic tissues

Z01CB-08578-02 (LIB) ZBAR, B NCI, NIH Preparation of a high resolution genetic map of human chromosome 3

Z01CB-08705-15 (CBGY) GOTTESMAN, M M NCI, NIH Genetic and biochemical analysis of cell behavior

Z01CB-08710-14 (LMB) WICKNER, S NCI, NIH DNA replication in vitro

Z01CB-08714-14 (LMB) GOTTESMAN, S NCI, NIH Bacterial function involved in cell growth control

Z01CB-08715-13 (CBGY) GOTTESMAN, M M NCI, NIH Synthesis and function of a transformation-dependent secreted lysosomal protease

Z01CB-08727-14 (LGN) MUSHINSKI, J F NCI, NIH Organization and control of genetic material in plasmacytomas

Z01CB-08750-11 (LMB) GARGES, S NCI, NIH Genetic regulatory mechanisms in Escherichia coli and its bacteriophage

Z01CB-08751-11 (LMB) ADHYA, S L NCI, NIH Regulation of the gal operon of Escherichia coli

Z01CB-08752-11 (LMB) CHENG, S-Y NCI, NIH Mechanism of the transport of thyroid hormones into animal cells

Z01CB-08753-09 (LMB) PASTAN, I NCI, NIH Immunotoxin and oncotoxin therapy of cancer cells

Z01CB-08754-06 (LMB) GOTTESMAN, M M NCI, NIH Genetic analysis of the multiple drug resistance phenotype in tumor cells

Z01CB-08756-04 (LMB) MERLINO, G T NCI, NIH The transgenic mouse as a model system to study gene function and regulation

Z01CB-08757-04 (LMB) FITZGERALD, D J NCI, NIH Development of immunotoxins in cancer

Z01CB-08905-10 (LCO) ANDERSON, W B NCI, NIH Role of protein kinases in modulating cell growth and malignant transformation

Z01CB-08907-08 (OD) TING, C C NCI, NIH Regulation of immune response to tumor cells and alloantigens

Z01CB-08950-09 (LGN) SMITH-GILL, S NCI, NIH Molecular recognition by protein effector molecules

Z01CB-08952-06 (LGN) WOLFF, L NCI, NIH Retrovirus-induced acute myeloid leukemias in mice

Z01CB-08953-01 (LGN) DAVIDSON, W NCI, NIH Effects of individual genes on hematopoietic cell differen. and function

Z01CB-09003-09 (LTIB) SALOMON, D S NCI, NIH EGF-related peptides in the etiology and progression of breast and colon cancer

Z01CB-09006-09 (LTIB) COOPER, H L NCI, NIH Studies on the nature and function of the phosphoprotein, prosolin

Z01CB-09008-10 (LTIB) SCHLOM, J NCI, NIH Localization and therapy using labeled monoclonal antibodies--Model systems
Z01CB-09009-10 (LTIB) GREINER, J W NCI, NIH Augmentation of tumor antigen expression
Z01CB-09018-07 (LTIB) SCHLOM, J NCI, NIH Anti-carcinoma monoclonal antibodies clinical trials
Z01CB-09021-05 (LTIB) ROBBINS, P NCI, NIH Isolation and characterization of genes coding for carcinoma-associated antigens
Z01CB-09022-05 (LTIB) COOPER, H L NCI, NIH Cytoskeletal proteins in oncogenic transformation and human neoplasia
Z01CB-09023-05 (LTIB) KASHMIRI, S NCI, NIH Cloning of anti-tumor antigen immunoglobin genes
Z01CB-09025-04 (LTIB) TSANG, K Y NCI, NIH Antibody directed cellular immunotherapy of human carcinoma
Z01CB-09028-01 (LTIB) KANTOR, J NCI, NIH Active immunotherapy to human carcinoma associated antigens
Z01CB-09052-03 (LCO) SCHILLER, J T NCI, NIH Analysis of papillomaviruses
Z01CB-09100-06 (CBGY) HEARING, V J NCI, NIH Immunogenicity of melanoma
Z01CB-09131-07 (LP) SOBEL, M E NCI, NIH Role of laminin-binding proteins in human cancer
Z01CB-09145-07 (LP) KATZ, D A NCI, NIH Neuropathology
Z01CB-09153-04 (LP) SOLOMON, D NCI, NIH Cytophenotypic analysis of tumor suspensions and TIL cultures in immunotherapy
Z01CB-09163-03 (LP) KOHN, E C NCI, NIH Anticancer effects of a novel drug Merck L651582
Z01CB-09164-03 (LP) STETLER-STEVENSON, W G NCI, NIH Role of collagenolytic metalloproteinases in metastases
Z01CB-09165-04 (LP) TRAVIS, W D NCI, NIH Pulmonary and postmortem pathology
Z01CB-09166-02 (LP) TRAVIS, W D NCI, NIH Pathology of interstitial pulmonary fibrosis
Z01CB-09168-03 (LP) LEVENS, D L NCI, NIH Analysis of a multiprotein complex interacting with the gibbon ape leukemia
Z01CB-09170-04 (LP) MACKEM, S NCI, NIH Genes differentially expressed in developing embryonic limb buds
Z01CB-09171-07 (LP) KELLY, K NCI, NIH The regulation of lymphocyte proliferation
Z01CB-09172-03 (LP) ROBERTS, D D NCI, NIH Cell interactions with thrombospondin
Z01CB-09173-03 (LP) ROBERTS, D D NCI, NIH Carbohydrate receptors for human pathogens
Z01CB-09174-03 (LP) ROBERTS, D D NCI, NIH Role of sulfated glycoconjugates in tumor cell adhesion
Z01CB-09175-03 (LP) ROBERTS, D D NCI, NIH Glycolipid antigens expressed in cancer cells
Z01CB-09176-03 (LP) SOLOMON, D NCI, NIH Quality assurance in cervical/vaginal cytopathology
Z01CB-09178-03 (LP) ELWOOD, L NCI, NIH Immunophenotypes of T cells and stromal cells in mouse Peyer's patches
Z01CB-09179-03 (LP) STETLER-STEVENSON, W G NCI, NIH Novel metalloproteinase inhibitors--Role in tumor invasion and metastasis
Z01CB-09181-03 (LP) STETLER-STEVENSON, M NCI, NIH Expression of oncogenes in lymphoproliferative disorders
Z01CB-09182-03 (LP) RAFFELD, M NCI, NIH Molecular biology of human lymphoproliferative diseases
Z01CB-09185-02 (LP) AZNAVOORIAN, S NCI, NIH G proteins and tumor cell motility
Z01CB-09186-02 (LP) ELWOOD, L NCI, NIH Bone marrow effects of interleukin-1 alpha
Z01CB-09187-02 (LP) TSOKOS, M NCI, NIH Transforming growth factor beta in the differentiation of neuroblastoma and PNET
Z01CB-09191-02 (LP) RAFFELD, M NCI, NIH Molecular biology of progression in lymphoproliferative diseases
Z01CB-09192-01 (LP) MERINO, M NCI, NIH Histologic changes in renal cell carcinoma after LAK therapy
Z01CB-09193-02 (LP) MERINO, M NCI, NIH Malignant changes associated with sclerosing adhesions
Z01CB-09194-01 (LP) MERINO, M NCI, NIH P-glycoprotein expression in normal secretory gestational endometrium
Z01CB-09250-25 (E) WUNDERLICH, J NCI, NIH Cell-mediated cytotoxicity
Z01CB-09251-21 (E) HENKART, P A NCI, NIH Target cell damage by immune mechanisms
Z01CB-09254-03 (E) SEGAL, D M NCI, NIH Targeted cellular cytotoxicity
Z01CB-09255-16 (E) SHARROW, S O NCI, NIH Application of flow cytometry to cell biology
Z01CB-09257-16 (E) SHAW, S NCI, NIH Mechanisms of cellular immune responses
Z01CB-09258-13 (E) HODES, R J NCI, NIH Immune response gene regulation of the immune response in vitro
Z01CB-09259-13 (E) SHEARER, G M NCI, NIH Effects of graft vs host reactions on cell-mediated immunity
Z01CB-09263-10 (E) HENKART, P A NCI, NIH mRNA expression and function of cytotoxic T lymphocyte granule components
Z01CB-09264-04 (E) SHEARER, G M NCI, NIH Studies of T lymphocyte function in transplantation
Z01CB-09265-10 (E) HODES, R J NCI, NIH Analysis of the T cell repertoire
Z01CB-09266-09 (E) HODES, R J NCI, NIH T cell regulation of B cell activation
Z01CB-09267-09 (E) SHEARER, G M NCI, NIH Cellular immune function in AIDS and in primary immune deficiencies
Z01CB-09268-04 (E) SINGER, A NCI, NIH Role of CD4 and CD8 accessory molecules in T cell function
Z01CB-09270-06 (E) SINGER, D NCI, NIH Regulation of expression of class I MHC gene
Z01CB-09273-04 (E) SINGER, A NCI, NIH T cell differentiation and repertoire selection
Z01CB-09275-04 (E) SINGER, A NCI, NIH In vivo study of MHC-specific T cells
Z01CB-09279-06 (E) SINGER, D NCI, NIH Isolation and characterization of a novel H-2 class I gene
Z01CB-09281-06 (E) HODES, R J NCI, NIH Receptor mediated T cell activation
Z01CB-09282-05 (E) SHEARER, G M NCI, NIH T cell immune deficiency in mice and humans with autoimmune disease
Z01CB-09285-05 (E) SINGER, D NCI, NIH Responses of MHC class I genes to exogenous stimuli
Z01CB-09287-04 (E) GRESS, R E NCI, NIH Marrow graft failure rejection in allogeneic bone marrow transplantation
Z01CB-09288-04 (E) GRESS, R E NCI, NIH T cell function in T cell depleted bone marrow transplantation
Z01CB-09289-03 (E) SEGAL, D NCI, NIH Single chain bispecific antibodies
Z01CB-09290-01 (E) SEGAL, D NCI, NIH Targeted antigen presentation
Z01CB-09291-01 (E) WEISSMAN, A NCI, NIH Genomic organization, characterization, and regulation of the human zeta gene
Z01CB-09292-01 (E) WEISSMAN, A NCI, NIH Signal transduction in T lymphocytes
Z01CB-09295-02 (E) WEISSMAN, A NCI, NIH The role of HIV gp120 in the immune response
Z01CB-09350-01 (LP) COWAN, K NCI, NIH Immunocytochemistry of glutathione S-transferase-pi in breast and uterine cervix
Z01CB-09351-01 (LP) ELWOOD, L NCI, NIH The revision of proposed federal cytology regulations implementing CLIA '88
Z01CB-09352-01 (LP) BECKNER, M NCI, NIH Motility regulator proteins
Z01CB-09353-01 (LP) CASTRONOVO, V NCI, NIH Differential gene expression in gynecological tumors
Z01CB-09354-01 (LP) TSOKOS, M NCI, NIH The role of transforming growth factor beta in rhabdomyosarcoma
Z01CB-09355-01 (LP) TSOKOS, M NCI, NIH Immunohistochemical detection of wild and mutant p53 gene in rhabdomyosarcoma
Z01CB-09356-01 (LP) KELLY, K NCI, NIH Structural and functional characterization of NF-KB binding transcription factor
Z01CB-09357-01 (LP) KELLY, K NCI, NIH RAI-1--A mitogen-inducible RAS-related protein
Z01CB-09358-01 (LP) KELLY, K NCI, NIH Characterization of a mitogen-inducible tyrosine phosphatase, CAP-1
Z01CB-09359-01 (LP) MERINO, M NCI, NIH Prognostic markers in soft tissue sarcomas
Z01CB-09360-01 (LP) MERINO, M NCI, NIH The role of basement membrane proteins in trophoblast implantation sites
Z01CB-09361-01 (LP) MERINO, M NCI, NIH P-Glycoprotein expression in breast cancerr
N01CB-61005-09 (**) MANDEL, JACK Hemoccult screening techniques for bowel cancef
N01CB-71010-06 (**) BEAUDRY, NORMAN N Radioimmunoassay & enzyme linked immunoassays
N01CB-71085-10 (**) WAX, JUDY Transplantation, induction and preservation of plasma
N01CB-71091-19 (**) BERNARD, DAVID Maintenance and development of inbred and congenic research animals
N01CB-85607-21 (**) DENENNO, LEANNE Maintenance of an animal holding facility and provision
N01CB-85608-09 (**) DIVEN, KINTA Facility for preparing and housing virus infected mice
N01CB-95600-04 (**) DUNSMORE, MARLENE Biomedical computing software services
N01CB-95601-07 (**) DIMAGNO, EUGENE Maintenance of NCI serum bank
N01CB-95613-08 (**) MANDEL, DR JACK Effect of periodic screening for occult stool blood
N01CB-95621-10 (**) HOGG, EVELYN Feral mouse breeding colony and attendant support services
R43CE-00011-01 (SSS) MYERS, DONALD R TRIANGLE RES & DEVELOPMENT COR PO BOX 12696 RES TRIANGLE PARK, NC 27709 Protective headgear employing novel air-cell technology
R43CE-00014-01 (SOH) SERBY, VICTOR M VMS CONSULTING ENGINEERS WOODMERE, NY 11598 Extended-life, non-removable battery for smoke detectors
R43CE-00015-01 (SOH) RATTE, DONNA J COMSIS CORP 8737 COLESVILLE RD SILVER SPRING, MD 20910 Children & non-traffic pedestrian/motor vehicle injuries
R43CE-00016-01 (HUD) BERENHOLZ, GERRY 27 LOCKE LANE LEXINGTON, MA 02173 Accuracy and compatibility of external cause data
R43CI-00004-01 (SSS) FENNEWALD, SUSAN M TRIPLEX PHARMACEUTICAL CORP 9391 GROGANS MILL ROAD THE WOODLANDS, TX 77380 Anti-HSV-1 action of triplex forming oligonucleotides
R43CI-00015-01 (SSS) LEVIN, ANDREW E IMMUNETICS, INC 380 GREEN STREET CAMBRIDGE, MA 02139 A perfusion test for detecting the agent of Lyme disease
R43CI-00017-01 (SOH) HICKS, RICHARD E 108 DEVONSHIRE RD WABAN, MA 02168-2213 An air-purifier for preventing nosocomial infection
R43CI-00020-01 (SSS) WEBER, GEORGE H KASSIA INTERNATIONAL INC. 22422 ESTALLENS MISSION VIEJO, CA 92692 Prevention and treatment of vaginal infections
Z10CL-00007- RASE CC Fleisse
Z01CL-00018-05 (CCMD) SHELHAMER, J H CC, NIH Monoclonal antibodies recognizing respiratory mucous glycoproteins
Z01CL-00020-05 (CCMD) SHELHAMER, J H CC, NIH Protein kinase C activation in feline airway cultures
Z01CL-00024-05 (CCMD) SHELHAMER, J H CC, NIH Activating factor on airway eicosanoid generation
Z01CL-00030-04 (CCMD) SHELHAMER, J H CC, NIH Cytomegalovirus in causing pulmonary disease in AIDS patients
Z01CL-00032-04 (CCMD) PARKER, M M CC, NIH Study of cardiac function in patients with HIV infection
Z01CL-00034-04 (CCMD) KOVACS, J A CC, NIH Screening of drugs for anti-Pneumocystis carinii activity in tissue culture
Z01CL-00035-04 (CCMD) KOVACS, J A CC, NIH Agents for treating T. gondii infection

PROJECT NO., ORGANIZATIONAL UNIT., INVESTIGATOR, ADDRESS, TITLE

Z01CL-00036-04 (CCMD) KOVACS, J A CC, NIH Phase I/II study of AZT and IL-2 in HIV infection
Z01CL-00037-04 (CCMD) KOVACS, J A CC, NIH Isolation and characterization of P. carinii surface antigens
Z01CL-00044-03 (CCMD) NATANSON, C CC, NIH A controlled trial of monoclonal antibodies to endotoxin
Z01CL-00045-03 (CCMD) NATANSON, C CC, NIH A comparison of strains of E. coli to produce septic shock in dogs
Z01CL-00049-03 (CCMD) KOVACS, J A CC, NIH Investigations of the epidemiology of Pneumocystis carinii by PCR
Z01CL-00050-03 (CCMD) OGNIBENE, F P CC, NIH Diagnosis of Pneumocystis carinii by induced sputum in immunosuppressed children
Z01CL-00051-03 (CCMD) FALLOON, J CC, NIH A study of weekly dapsone and dapsone plus pyrimethamine to prevent pcp
Z01CL-00055-02 (CCMD) SHELHAMER, J H CC, NIH Bronchoscopy and bronchoalveolar lavage to study Wegener's granulomatosis
Z01CL-00056-03 (CCMD) SUFFREDINI, A F CC, NIH Cardiopulmonary effects of endotoxin in normal volunteers
Z01CL-00063-03 (CCMD) SUFFREDINI, A F CC, NIH Role of cytokines in the cardiovascular abnormalities of human septic shock
Z01CL-00064-03 (CCMD) DANNER, R L CC, NIH Role of exotoxin A in severe P. aeruginosa infections
Z01CL-00065-03 (CCMD) DANNER, R L CC, NIH Role of neutrophil activating protein in septic shock and ARDS
Z01CL-00067-03 (CCMD) DANNER, R L CC, NIH Therapeutic efficacy of lipid X in a canine model of septic shock
Z01CL-00068-03 (CCMD) DANNER, R L CC, NIH Endotoxemia in human septic shock
Z01CL-00069-03 (CCMD) DANNER, R L CC, NIH Structure-function relationship in LPS binding peptides
Z01CL-00070-03 (CCMD) DANNER, R L CC,NIH Antagonism of endotoxin by analogs of lipid A and lipid X
Z01CL-00073-03 (CCMD) NATANSON, C CC, NIH Investigations of new therapies in septic shock
Z01CL-00075-03 (CCMD) EICHACKER, P Q CC, NIH Oxygen extraction efficiency after endotoxin in a canine model
Z01CL-00076-03 (CCMD) CUNNION, R E CC, NIH Noninvasive determination of left atrial pressure and total vascular resistance
Z01CL-00077-03 (CCMD) CUNNION, R E CC, NIH An in vitro model of vascular relaxation in sepsis
Z01CL-00078-02 (CCMD) EICHACKER, P Q CC, NIH The effects of antibody to leukocyte CD11b/18 adhesion TNF tissue
Z01CL-00080-02 (CCMD) FALLOON, J CC, NIH Phase I/II study of 566C80 for treatment of PCP in AIDS
Z01CL-00081-02 (CCMD) FALLOON, J CC, NIH A randomized double blind study of 566C80 vs septra for treatment of PCP in AIDS
Z01CL-00082-02 (CCMD) ANGUS, C W CC, NIH Identification of P. carinii dihydropteroate synthetase
Z01CL-00083-02 (90MD) ANGUS, C W CC, NIH TNF production in alveolar macrophages
Z01CL-00084-02 (CCMD) CUNNION, R E CC, NIH Forearm blood flow in septic shock
Z01CL-00085-02 (CCMD) CUNNION, R E CC, NIH Retrospective clinical analysis of septic shock
Z01CL-00086-02 (CCMD) OGNIBENE, F P CC, NIH Atypical presentation of Pneumocystis carinii pneumonia in HIV infected patients
Z01CL-00087-02 (CCMD) KOVACS, J A CC, NIH Phase I-II study of ddI plus interferon in HIV infection
Z01CL-00088-02 (CCMD) KOVACS, J A CC, NIH Pilot study of 566C80 in the treatment of toxoplasmosis in HIV-infected patients
Z01CL-00089-02 (CCMD) HOFFMAN, W CC, NIH Interaction of factors to produce the hemodynamic response to anesthetics
Z01CL-00090-02 (CCMD) DANNER, R L CC, NIH The nitric oxide pathway--Its effects on phagocyte function and septic shock
Z01CL-00091-02 (CCMD) PARKER, M CC, NIH Endothelin levels in human septic shock
Z01CL-00092-02 (CCMD) SHELHAMER, J CC, NIH Surfactant metabolism in AIDS patients with Pneumocystis carinii pneumonia
Z01CL-00093-02 (CCMD) SOLOMON, M A CC, NIH Myocardial metabolism in a canine model of human bacterial sepsis
Z01CL-00098-01 (CCMD) KOVACS, J A CC, NIH Investigation of the pathogenesis of Pneumocystis carinii pneumonia in humans
Z01CL-00099-01 (CCMD) KOVACS, J A CC, NIH Characterization of immune responses to Pneumocystis carinii surface antigen
Z01CL-00101-01 (NMMA) NEWMAN, R CC, NIH Myocardial oxidative metabolism in adriamycin-treated dogs--11C-acetate PET study
Z01CL-00102-01 (CCMD) SUSLA, G M CC, NIH Pharmacokinetics of fentanyl in critically ill patients
Z01CL-00103-01 (CCMD) POLIS, M A CC, NIH Pharmacokinetics of clarithromycin with zidovudine in persons with HIV infection
Z01CL-00104-01 (CCMD) POLIS, M A CC, NIH Azithromycin for toxoplasmosis in persons with AIDS
Z01CL-00105-01 (CCMD) OGNIBENE, F P CC, NIH Nebulization technique for aerosolization of pentamidine
Z01CL-00106-01 (CCMD) OGNIBENE, F P CC, NIH Assessment of tolerance of aerosolized pentamidine in pediatric patients
Z01CL-00107-01 (CCMD) OGNIBENE, F P CC, NIH Assessment of ifosfamide-induced cardiovascular dysfunction
Z01CL-00108-01 (CCMD) NATANSON, C CC, NIH Role of complement in endotoxic shock
Z01CL-00109-01 (CCMD) HOFFMAN, W D CC, NIH Therapeutic effects of LPS-reactive antibodies in gram-negative septic shock
Z01CL-00110-01 (CCMD) WAISMAN, Y CC, NIH Cardiopulmonary effect of granulocyte colony stimulating factor in gram-negative
Z01CL-00111-01 (CCMD) EICHACKER, P Q CC, NIH Cardiopulmonary effects of soluble TNF receptor in an endotoxin non-human model
Z01CL-00112-01 (CCMD) SHELHAMER, J CC, NIH The effect of inflammatory mediators on mucin gene expression
Z01CL-00113-01 (CCMD) FALLOON, J CC, NIH 566C80 for treatment of cryptosporidial and microsporidial diarrhea in AIDS
Z01CL-00301-04 (NMPE) BACHARACH, S CC, NIH 3-D image display and registration

PROJECT NO., ORGANIZATIONAL UNIT., INVESTIGATOR, ADDRESS, TITLE

Z01CL-00304-03 (NMPE) BACHARACH, S L CC, NIH Improving quantition in PET myocardial blood flow
Z01CL-00400-04 (RMIP) GREEN, M V CC, NIH Head motion and restraint in PET/other brain imaging
Z01CL-00401-03 (NMIP) GREEN, M V CC, NIH Measurement of stimulus-induced changes in cerebral function
Z01CL-00600-06 (NMMA) CARRASQUILLO, J A CC, NIH Intraperitoneal radiolabeled antibody to treat ovarian and colon cancer
Z01CL-00601-06 (NMMA) CARRASQUILLO, JA CC, NIH The use of radiolabeled monoclonal antibodies to detect adenocarcinomas
Z01CL-00603-07 (NMMA) CARRASQUILLO, J A CC, NIH Intraperitoneal and intra-arterial delivery of I-131 B72.3
Z01CL-00604-01 (NMMA) NEUMANN, R CC, NIH Radioiodine-labelled cpds--Hepatobiliary carcinoma imaging/therapy in guinea pigs
Z01CL-00801-01 (NMPE) CARSON, R E CC, NIH Pixel by pixel equilibrium measurement of the opiate receptor with PET
Z01CL-00802-01 (NMPE) CARSON, R E CC, NIH An approximation formula for the variance of PET region-of-interest values
Z01CL-02005-22 (DTM) ALTER, H J CC, NIH Post-transfusion hepatitis (PTH) in open heart surgery patients
Z01CL-02010-17 (DTM) HOOFNAGLE, J H CC, NIH Chronic sequelae of non-A, non-B hepatitis
Z01CL-02036-08 (DTM) ALTER, H J CC, NIH Safety and immunogenicity studies of a DNA recombinant hepatitis B vaccine
Z01CL-02038-08 (DTM) ALTER, H J CC, NIH Transmission of HIV (AIDS) infection to the chimpanzee
Z01CL-02040-07 (DTM) ALTER, H J CC, NIH Significance of anti-HIV antibody in asymptomatic donors
Z01CL-02045-06 (DTM) LEITMAN, S F CC, NIH Etiology of allergic reactions in plateletpheresis donors
Z01CL-02050-05 (DTM) LEITMAN, S F CC, NIH Survival studies of stored autologous platelets
Z01CL-02055-04 (DTM) LEITMAN, S F CC,NIH Kinetic studies of indium-labeled leukocytes
Z01CL-02056-04 (DTM) LEITMAN, S F CC, NIH Kinetic studies of indium-labeled platelets
Z01CL-02057-04 (DTM) LEITMAN, S F CC, NIH Apheresis in the treatment of polymyositis/dermatomyositis
Z01CL-02058-03 (DTM) LO, S C CC, NIH Characterization of a human pathogenic mycoplasma from HIV infected patients
Z01CL-02061-02 (DTM) SHIH, J CC, NIH Modeling of human HBV infection with a transfected rat hepatoma cell line
Z01CL-02062-02 (DTM) LEITMAN, S CC, NIH Treatment of familial hypercholesterolemia by dextran sulfate apheresis
Z01CL-02063-01 (DTM) LEITMAN, S F CC, NIH Efficacy of recombinant erythropoietin in increasing autologous blood donation
Z01CL-02064-01 (DTM) SHIH, J CC, NIH Quantitative analysis of viral genomes and their clinical correlations
Z01CL-02065-01 (DTM) LEITMAN, S F CC, NIH Immunoabsorption therapy for platelet alloimmunization
Z01CL-03002-01 (NMPE) HERSCOVITCH, P CC, NIH Rapid repeat rCBF measurement with positron emission tomography and O15 water
Z01CL-03003-01 (NMPE) HERSCOVITCH, P CC, NIH Error analysis of PET rCBF measurements under non-steady state conditions
Z01CL-04001-01 (NMPE) DAUBE-WITHERSPOON, M E CC, NIH Unified deadtime correction for positron emission tomography
Z01CL-06014-04 (DRM) OAKLEY, F CC, NIH Occupational role dysfunction in illness--Comparisons with normative data
Z01CL-07002-03 (NMRC) SCHMALL, B CC, NIH Development of high specific activity 11C receptor ligands
Z01CL-08001-04 (NMRC) CHANNING, M A CC, NIH Synthesis of 11C palmitic, arachidonic & docosahexaenoic acid
Z01CL-09002-01 (NMRC) KIESEWETTER, D O CC, NIH Evaluation of NMDA receptor binding radiotracers
Z01CL-10001-17 (CP) ELIN, R J CC, NIH Analytical methodology--Development and interpretative application
Z01CL-10009-17 (CP) ZIERDT, C H CC, NIH Blastocystis hominis--Structure, physiology and pathogenicity
Z01CL-10010-16 (CP) ELIN, R J CC, NIH Magnesium metabolism in human and biological systems
Z01CL-10012-23 (CP) GRALNICK, H R CC,NIH Investigation of hemorrhagic and thrombotic disorders in man
Z01CL-10013-24 (CP) GRALNICK, H R CC, NIH Chemical and structural studies on factor VIII/Von Willebrand factor protein
Z01CL-10035-11 (CP) RICK, M E CC, NIH Factor VIII interaction with other coagulation factors
Z01CL-10058-12 (CP) RICK, M E CC, NIH Investigation of variants of von Willebrand's disease
Z01CL-10085-09 (CP) KROLL, M H CC, NIH Mechanism of Jaffe reaction for creatinine
Z01CL-10106-08 (CP) GRALNICK, H R CC, NIH Platelet antigens and platelet activation
Z01CL-10117-08 (CP) GRALNICK, H R CC, NIH Platelet adhesion on arterial subendothelium
Z01CL-10125-07 (CP) KROLL, M H CC, NIH Binding of magnesium to albumin
Z01CL-10133-03 (CP) ZIERDT, C H CC, NIH Cultivation of mycobacterium leprae
Z01CL-10139-06 (CP) FLEISHER, T A CC, NIH Lymphocyte phenotypes in normal individuals using dual color flow cytometry
Z01CL-10140-06 (CP) FLEISHER, T A CC, NIH Determination of anti-cardiolipin antibodies in SLE
Z01CL-10149-05 (CP) ZWEIG, M H CC, NIH Human anti-mouse immunoglobulin antibodies in IRMAs formulated with mouse MAB
Z01CL-10152-05 (CP) ZWEIG, M CC, NIH Evaluation of free thyroxin techniques
Z01CL-10153-05 (CP) ZWEIG, M H CC, NIH Assessment of the clinical performance of lab tests
Z01CL-10162-04 (CP) FLEISHER, T A CC, NIH Determination of anti-neutrophil cytoplasmic antibodies
Z01CL-10164-04 (CP) FLEISHER, T A CC, NIH Monitoring lymphocytes phenotype during T101/Itrium therapy
Z01CL-10166-04 (CP) TANNENBAUM, S H CC,NIH Regulation of von

PROJECT NUMBER LISTING

PROJECT NO., ORGANIZATIONAL UNIT., INVESTIGATOR, ADDRESS, TITLE

Willebrand factor in human endothelial cells

Z01CL-10170-03 (CP) KROLL, M H CC,NIH Standardization of cholesterol

Z01CL-10172-03 (CP) WITEBSKY, F G CC,NIH Identification of yeast with microscan yeast identification panel

Z01CL-10175-03 (CP) ZIERDT, C H CC,NIH Blastocystis hominis--Axenization of strains dep. on mixed growth bacteria

Z01CL-10176-03 (CP) ZIERDT, C H CC,NIH Blastocystis hominis--Development of monophasic medium for culture

Z01CL-10179-02 (CP) FOWLER, C L CC, NIH Chlamydia pneumonia surveillance

Z01CL-10180-02 (CP) FOWLER, C L CC, NIH Prevalence of vancomycin and gentamicin resistant enterococci

Z01CL-10181-02 (CP) ZIERDT, C H CC, NIH Identification of oxacillin resistant strains of Staphylococcus aureus

Z01CL-10182-02 (CP) HENDERSON, D CC, NIH Staphylococcus aureus epidemiology--Testing index of infections potential

Z01CL-10184-02 (CP) ZISCOVICI, S CC, NIH Evaluation of two enzyme immunoassays for detection of adenovirus in feces

Z01CL-10185-02 (CP) ZISCOVICI, S CC, NIH Comparison of three kits for detection of P. carinii in respiratory specimens

Z01CL-10186-02 (CP) ZISCOVICI, S CC, NIH Evaluation of four enzyme immunoassays for detection of rotavirus in feces

Z01CL-10187-02 (CP) WITEBSKY, F G CC, NIH Evaluation of a calcofluor white stain for pneumocystis carinii

Z01CL-10190-02 (CP) ELIN, R J CC, NIH Biological properties of and assays for bacterial endotoxin

Z01CL-10191-02 (CP) PARKER, R I CC, NIH Use of DDAVP to improve hemostasis in Gaucher's disease

Z01CL-10192-02 (CP) HORNE, M K CC, NIH Heparin binding to platelets

Z01CL-10193-02 (CP) CONNAGHAN, D G CC, NIH Comparative study of thrombolytic therapy in catheter related thrombosis

Z01CL-10194-01 (CP) KROLL, M H CC, NIH Development of flow injection analysis methods

Z01CL-10195-01 (CP) MCNAMARA, A M CC, NIH Comparison of three rapid methods for the detection of herpes simplex virus

Z01CL-10196-01 (CP) MCNAMARA, A M CC, NIH Development of an ELISA test for the detection of Pneumocystis carinii

Z01CL-10197-01 (CP) ENGLER, H D CC, NIH Detection of respiratory syncytial virus in bronchial lavages and sputa

Z01CL-10198-01 (CP) ENGLER, H D CC, NIH Determination of cross-reactivity of a cryptococcal antigen EIA

Z01CL-10199-01 (CP) ENGLER, H D CC, NIH Use of sonication to enhance shell vial culture of specimens for cytomegalovirus

Z01CL-10200-01 (CP) GILL, V J CC, NIH Usefulness of the Diff-Quick stain for diagnosis of infectious agents

Z01CL-10201-01 (CP) WITEBSKY, F G CC, NIH Development of PCR techniques for mycobacterial detection

Z01CL-10202-01 (CP) ZISCOVICI, S CC, NIH Comparison of three kits for detection of P. carinii in respiratory specimens

Z01CL-10203-01 (CP) ZISCOVICI, S CC, NIH Comparison of two cryptoccal antigen detection kits

N01CL-12108-00 (**) OBLITAS, JAIME Donor apheresis services

Z01CL-30002-01 (NMRC) SIMPSON, N CC, NIH Synthesis of 1-[11C] sodium acetate for heart studies

Z01CL-40000-01 (NMRC) ADAMS, R CC, NIH Design of F-18 labeled dopamine receptor ligands

Z01CL-60011-01 (DRM) GERBER, L H CC, NIH Study of effects of discontinuing bracing in children w/ osteogenesis imperfecta

Z01CL-60012-01 (DRM) LEVINSON, S F CC, NIH Sonoelastic determination of skeletal muscle elasticity

Z01CL-60013-01 (DRM) O'CONNELL, P G CC, NIH Study of the effects of forefoot arthroplasty in rheumatoid arthritis

Z01CL-60015-01 (DRM) PICKERING, S CC, NIH The level of occupational functioning of persons with Parkinson's disease

Z01CL-60016-01 (DRM) STANHOPE, S J CC, NIH Rigid body data base on normal gait

N01CL-62104-18 (**) MCCURDY, PAUL R Donor apheresis services

N01CL-72105-07 (**) LEE, JOHN HLA typing and matching services

N01CL-82107-07 (**) PRICE, DAVID Clinical center medical information system

N01CL-92100-04 (**) WEBSTER, WAYNE PET scanner - brain model no. pc2048-15b

Z01CM-00650-36 (RO) GLATSTEIN, E NCI, NIH Service radiation therapy

Z01CM-03024-22 (NMOB) IHDE, D C NCI, NIH Treatment of extensive stage small cell lung cancer

Z01CM-03581-22 (LMC) KELLEY, J A NCI, NIH The analytical chemistry of new anticancer drugs

Z01CM-03800-21 (SURG) ROSENBERG, S A NCI, NIH Surgical consultations and collaborative research in surgical services at NIH

Z01CM-03801-21 (SURG) ROSENBERG, S A NCI, NIH Clinical studies in cancer surgery

Z01CM-03811-17 (SURG) ROSENBERG, S A NCI, NIH The immunotherapy of animal and human cancer

Z01CM-06119-22 (M) WHANG-PENG, J NCI, NIH Cytogenetic studies

Z01CM-06140-15 (LMPH) BONNER, W NCI, NIH Regulation of histone biosynthesis

Z01CM-06150-10 (LMPH) POMMIER, Y NCI, NIH Protein-associated DNA breaks as indicator of topoisomerase inhibition

Z01CM-06161-08 (LMPH) POMMIER, Y NCI, NIH DNA topoisomerases as target of action of anticancer drugs

Z01CM-06163-07 (LBC) CYSYK, R NCI, NIH Pharmacologic aspects of nucleotide metabolism

Z01CM-06167-07 (LBC) FELSTED, R L NCI, NIH Myristoylation-dependent cell transformation and retroviral replication

Z01CM-06170-07 (LMPH) HATCH, C NCI, NIH Study of the histone H2A.Z gene

Z01CM-06172-07 (LMPH) KOHN, K W NCI, NIH Molecular mechanism of action of antitumor alkylating agents

Z01CM-06173-06 (LMC) MARQUEZ, V E NCI, NIH Dideoxynucleosides as potential anti-AIDS drugs

Z01CM-06174-06 (LMC) MARQUEZ, V E NCI, NIH Cyclopentenyl nucleoside isosteres as potential antitumor and antiviral agents

Z01CM-06175-06 (LMC) MARQUEZ, V E NCI, NIH Synthesis and properties of oligonucleotides containing 5-azacytosine residues

Z01CM-06176-07 (LMC) MARQUEZ, V E NCI, NIH Enzyme inhibitors as protential anticancer and antiviral drugs

Z01CM-06177-06 (LMC) KELLEY, J A NCI, NIH The analytical chemistry of anti-AIDS agents

Z01CM-06178-06 (LMC) KELLEY, J A NCI, NIH Applications of new mass spectral techniques

Z01CM-06181-06 (LBC) KAHN, R A NCI, NIH The ARF family as regulators of protein secretion and other cellular processes

Z01CM-06186-05 (LMPH) BOHR, V NCI, NIH DNA damage and repair at the level of the gene

Z01CM-06192-03 (LMPH) BONNER, W NCI, NIH Histone H2A.X

Z01CM-06194-03 (LMC) MILNE, G W NCI, NIH Molecular modelling and drug design by computer

Z01CM-06195-03 (LMC) ROLLER, P P NCI, NIH Polypeptides as potential anti-HIV and antitumor agents

Z01CM-06197-02 (LMC) HARTMAN, N NCI, NIH Preclinical and clinical pharmacology of anti-HIV agents

Z01CM-06198-02 (LMC) BURKE, T R NCI, NIH Inhibitors of tyrosine-specific protein kinases as anticancer agents

Z01CM-06310-12 (RO) STRAUS, K L NCI, NIH Surgery versus radiation therapy in treatment of primary breast cancer

Z01CM-06320-12 (RO) RUSSO, A NCI, NIH Response of mammalian cells to chemotherapy drugs

Z01CM-06321-12 (RO) MITCHELL, J B NCI, NIH Radiosensitization and chemosensitization of aerated and hypoxic mammalian cells

Z01CM-06329-11 (RO) VAN DE GEIJN, J NCI, NIH Clinical radiation physics service

Z01CM-06330-11 (RO) VAN DE GEIJN, J NCI, NIH Radiation field modeling and computerized treatment planning

Z01CM-06351-09 (RO) MITCHELL, J B NCI, NIH Response of mammalian cells to halogenated pyrimidines

Z01CM-06353-09 (RO) GANSOW, O A NCI, NIH Metal chelate conjugated monoclonal antibodies for tumor diagnosis and therapy

Z01CM-06357-08 (RO) GLATSTEIN, E NCI, NIH Clinical studies on intraoperative radiation therapy

Z01CM-06358-08 (RO) RIESZ, P NCI, NIH Radiolysis, photolysis and sonolysis of cells and their constituents

Z01CM-06361-07 (RO) RUSSO, A NCI, NIH Phototherapy of intracavitary spaces

Z01CM-06378-06 (RO) VAN DE GEIGN, J NCI, NIH QA of treatment delivery by means of overlayed digitized stimulator & port films

Z01CM-06379-05 (RO) DELANEY, T F NCI, NIH Phase I study of photodynamic therapy for surface malignancies

Z01CM-06381-05 (RO) VAN DE GEIJN, J NCI, NIH Modeling of time-dose response of human tumors and normal tissues

Z01CM-06382-05 (RO) MILLER, R NCI, NIH Radiation therapy with radiolabelled antibodies--Technical aspects and dosimetry

Z01CM-06383-05 (RO) MILLER, R NCI, NIH Development of an improved treatment chair for radiation therapy

Z01CM-06386-04 (RO) GOFFMAN, T NCI, NIH Radioimmunotherapy of peritoneal cancer with I-131 labeled B72.3

Z01CM-06387-04 (RO) RUSSO, A NCI, NIH Development of superoxide dismutase mimics

Z01CM-06388-04 (RO) DE LANEY, T F NCI, NIH Treatment of superfical carcinoma of the bladder with photoradiation

Z01CM-06390-03 (RO) MCMURRY, T NCI, NIH Bifunctional chelates for gallium

Z01CM-06391-02 (RO) GOFFMAN, T NCI, NIH IUdR as a radiosensitizer in unresectable sarcomas

Z01CM-06392-02 (RO) GOFFMAN, T NCI, NIH IUdR as a radiosensitizer in unfavorable neoplasms

Z01CM-06393-02 (RO) DELANEY, T F NCI, NIH Study of surgery and photodynamic therapy for intraperitoneal malignancies

Z01CM-06394-02 (RO) VAN DE GEIJN, J NCI, NIH Developing insights into radiolabelled antibody dosimetry by computer simulation

Z01CM-06395-02 (RO) PIPPIN, C G NCI, NIH Solution chemistry of metal-ions used in radioimmunotherapy

Z01CM-06396-01 (RO) PIERCE, L NCI, NIH Treatment of invasive carcinoma of the bladder

Z01CM-06513-15 (M) ALLEGA, C NCI, NIH Pharmacology of antimetabolite agents

Z01CM-06516-10 (M) COWAN, K H NCI, NIH Drug resistance in human breast tumor cells

Z01CM-06523-06 (CP) SINHA, B K NCI, NIH Metabolism and mechanism of action of etoposide

Z01CM-06524-01 (CP) MYERS, C E NCI, NIH Role of myeloperoxidases in vincristine resistance

Z01CM-06525-01 (CP) NECKERS, L M NCI, NIH Evaluation of cytotoxicity of ansamycins to defined cell lines

Z01CM-06526-01 (CP) NECKERS, L M NCI, NIH Modulation of cell growth by antisense and antigene reagents

Z01CM-06527-01 (CP) SARTOR, O NCI, NIH Oncologic aspects of tyrosine kinases and epithelial cancer

Z01CM-06528-01 (CP) SAUSVILLE, E NCI, NIH Bacterial and plant-derived cytotoxins as novel antineoplastic agents

Z01CM-06529-01 (CP) SAUSVILLE, E NCI, NIH Preclinical pharmacology of protein kinase antagonists

Z01CM-06530-01 (CP) SAUSVILLE, E NCI, NIH G-proteins and their effectors as targets for cancer therapy

Z01CM-06579-08 (NMOB) KIRSCH, I R NCI, NIH Chromosomal abnormalities that highlight regions of differentiated activity

Z01CM-06581-08 (NMOB) KUEHL, W M NCI, NIH Molecular genetics of differentiation and transformation

Z01CM-06587-07 (NMOB) KIRSCH, I R NCI, NIH Gene rearrangements as tumor specific markers

Z01CM-06589-07 (NMOB) GAZDAR, A NCI, NIH Biology, growth, and

chemosensitivity testing
Z01CM-06594-06 (NMOB) JOHNSON, B E NCI, NIH Molecular genetic events in lung cancer
Z01CM-06595-05 (NMOB) LINNOILA, I NCI, NIH Clinically relevant immunohistochemical markers in lung cancer
Z01CM-06596-05 (NMOB) JOHNSON, B E NCI, NIH In vitro drug testing for limited SCLC and phase I drug development
Z01CM-06597-05 (NMOB) MULSHINE, J L NCI, NIH Non small cell lung cancer therapy project
Z01CM-06598-05 (NMOB) MULSHINE, J L NCI, NIH Diagnostic and therapeutic clinical trials with monoclonal antibodies--Part 1
Z01CM-06654-14 (SURG) SINDELAR, W F NCI, NIH Studies in malignant disease
Z01CM-06657-09 (SURG) NORTON, J A NCI, NIH Metabolic studies with cytokine and clinical studies with endocrine tumors
Z01CM-06659-09 (SURG) LINEHAN, W M NCI, NIH Tumor suppressor genes in genitourinary malignancy
Z01CM-06660-08 (SURG) YANG, J C NCI, NIH The study of interleukin-2 based immunotherapy
Z01CM-06662-05 (SURG) PASS, H I NCI, NIH Studies of phototherapy and free radical lymphokine relationships
Z01CM-06663-02 (SURG) DANFORTH, D N NCI, NIH The effect of IL-1, Il-6, and TNF on breast cancer cell growth and metabolism
Z01CM-06664-02 (SURG) TOPALIAN, S L NCI, NIH Immune recognition of autologous tumor by human tumor infiltrating lymphocytes
Z01CM-06665-02 (SURG) MULE, J J NCI, NIH Preclinical studies of antitumor efficacy of adoptive immunotherapy
Z01CM-06667-01 (SURG) ALEXANDER, R B NCI, NIH Detection of tumor reactive T cells by determination of intracellular calcium
Z01CM-06668-01 (SURG) ETTINGHAUSEN, S E NCI, NIH Cancer immunotherapy with tumor infiltrating lymphocytes and interleukin-2
Z01CM-06716-04 (M) REED, E NCI, NIH Platinum drug resistance in human malignancies
Z01CM-06718-03 (M) ELWOOD, P C NCI, NIH Human folate binding/transport proteins
Z01CM-06719-03 (CP) TREPEL, J B NCI, NIYH Signal transduction events and the regulation of cell growth
Z01CM-06721-04 (CP) TREPEL, J B NCI, NIH Analysis of drug resistance by flow microfluorocytometry
Z01CM-06722-03 (CP) NORDAN, R P NCI, NIH Characterization of IL6-mediated myeloma growth
Z01CM-06723-03 (CP) COLAMONICI, O R NCI, NIH Subunits of the interleukin 2 receptor
Z01CM-06727-02 (M) ZAJAC-KAYE, M NCI, NIH Oncogenes activation in human malignancies
Z01CM-06728-03 (CP) HORAK, I D NCI, NIH Regulation of tyrosine protein kinases in hematopoietic cells
Z01CM-06730-03 (CP) MYERS, C E NCI, NIH Polyanions used as anti-neoplastic and anti-HIV agents
Z01CM-06731-03 (M) BATES, S NCI, NIH Expression and regulation of the mdr1 gene and transforming growth factor alpha
Z01CM-06732-03 (M) FOJO, A T NCI, NIH Modulation of the expression of a multidrug resistance gene
Z01CM-06734-02 (M) ZAJAC-KAYE, M NCI, NIH The role of signal transduction in the regulation of nuclear oncogenes & viruses
Z01CM-06735-01 (M) O'SHAUGHNESSY, J A NCI, NIH Clinical treatment trials in breast cancer
Z01CM-06736-01 (M) REED, E NCI, NIH The clinical therapy of ovarian cancer
Z01CM-06813-09 (PB) THIELE, C J NCI, NIH Molecular biology of pediatric tumors
Z01CM-06830-21 (PB) PIZZO, P NCI, NIH Infectious complications of malignancy and HIV infection in children
Z01CM-06840-16 (PB) POPLACK, D G NCI, NIH Treatment of acute leukemia
Z01CM-06880-13 (PB) POPLACK, D G NCI, NIH Clinical pharmacology
Z01CM-06890-13 (PB) MAGRATH, I T NCI, NIH Biology and treatment of non-Hodgkin's lymphoma
Z01CM-06891-03 (PB) HOROWITZ, M E NCI, NIH Solid tumors
Z01CM-06892-02 (PB) HELMAN, L NCI, NIH Molecular biology of pediatirc tumors
Z01CM-07102-16 (LMPH) HAMEL, E NCI, NIH Tubulin as a site for pharmacologic attack
Z01CM-07156-08 (LBC) BREITMAN, T R NCI, NIH Differentiation of human leukemia cells
Z01CM-07179-06 (LMPH) HAMEL, E NCI, NIH Protein-protein and protein-nucleotide interactions in microtubule assembly
Z01CM-07181-06 (LMC) JOHNS, G NCI, NIH Cellular pharmacology of chemotherapeutic nucleosides
Z01CM-07183-05 (PRB) QUINN, F R NCI, NIH The influence of molecular structure on chemical and biological properties
Z01CM-07184-02 (LMPH) FORNACE, A J NCI, NIH Molecular biology of cellular injury
Z01CM-07186-02 (LMPH) FORNACE, A J NCI, NIH DNA damage by alkylating agents and their repair in human tumor cells
Z01CM-07187-02 (LMPH) FORNACE, A J NCI, NIH Increased expression of stress-induced genes in chemoresistant tumor cells
Z01CM-07188-02 (LMPH) FORNACE, A J NCI, NIH Regulation and cDNA cloning of DNA polymerse beta in Chinese hamster cells
Z01CM-07189-01 (LMPH) RABINOVITZ, M NCI, NIH Molecular, cellular and therapeutic mechanisms in amino acid deficiencies
Z01CM-07190-01 (LBC) FRIEDMAN, S J NCI, NIH Regulation of intercellular junctions
Z01CM-07191-01 (DDRD) MCMAHON, J NCI, NIH Development of assays for stage II evaluations of new anti-HIV compounds
Z01CM-07192-01 (DDRD) SKEHAN, P NCI, NIH In vitro methods for anticancer drug screening and stage II evaluation
Z01CM-07193-01 (DDRD) ALLEY, M NCI, NIH Development and application of agar-based stage II antitumor assays
Z01CM-07194-01 (DDRD) VISTICA, D NCI, NIH In vitro cellular pharmacology of new anti-HIV and antitumor drugs
Z01CM-07195-01 (DDRD) VISTICA, D NCI, NIH Biochemical mechanism(s) of selective cytotoxicity
Z01CM-07196-01 (DDRD) STINSON, S NCI, NIH Preclinical pharmacological/toxicological evaluations of high priority compounds
Z01CM-07197-01 (DDRD) STINSON, S NCI, NIH Characterization of human tumor cell lines for use in NCI antitumor drug screen
Z01CM-07198-01 (DDRD) MALSPEIS, L NCI, NIH Structure-activity optimization strategies
Z01CM-07199-01 (DDRD) SHOEMAKER, R NCI, NIH Molecular approaches to assessment of experimental metastatic tumor burden
Z01CM-07202-08 (BDMS) STEINBERG, S M NCI, NIH Biostatistics and data management section
Z01CM-07209-03 (CO) YARCHOAN, R NCI, NIH Administration of 2',3'-dideoxyinosine (ddl) for severe HIV infection
Z01CM-07210-02 (CO) YARCHOAN, R NCI, NIH Study of non-Hodgkin's lymphoma in the setting of severe HIV infection
Z01CM-07211-02 (CO) YARCHOAN, R NCI, NIH Inhibition and modulation of HIV infection in monocytes
Z01CM-07216-01 (CO) YARCHOAN, R NCI, NIH Treatment of AIDS-related Kaposi's sarcoma
Z01CM-07217-01 (CO) YARCHOAN, R NCI, NIH Combination therapy of HIV infection
Z01CM-07218-01 (CO) MITSUYA, H NCI, NIH The effect of DNA demethylation HIV-1 expression in vitro
Z01CM-07219-01 (CO) MITSUYA, H NCI, NIH Development of resistance of HIV in patients receiving AZT, ddC, or ddl
Z01CM-07220-01 (CO) MATSUYA, H NCI, NIH In vitro inhibition of HIV-1 replication by C2 symmetric HIV protease inhibitors
Z01CM-07221-01 (CO) MITSUYA, H NCI, NIH Plasma HIV-1 viremia in HIV-1 infected individuals assessed by RNA-polymerase
Z01CM-07222-01 (CO) MITSUYA, H NCI, NIH In vitro inhibition of hepatitis B virus replication by dideoxynucleosides
Z01CM-07223-01 (CO) MITSUYA, H NCI, NIH Synthesis and in vitro anti-HIV activity of lipophilic dideoxynucleosides
Z01CM-07250-05 (NMOB) KRAMER, B S NCI, NIH New drug discovery project
Z01CM-07255-03 (NMOB) BIRRER, M J NCI, NIH Biologic properties of nuclear oncogenes and attempts to block their effects
Z01CM-07256-03 (NMOB) KAYE, F J NCI, NIH Mechanisms of oncogene action in tumorigenesis
Z01CM-07257-03 (NMOB) SEGAL, S NCI, NIH Molecular biology of erythroleukemia and F9 teratocarcinoma cell differentiation
Z01CM-07258-03 (NMOB) FOSS, F NCI, NIH Etiology of cutaneous T-cell lymphomas
Z01CM-07259-02 (NMOB) LINNOILA, I NCI, NIH Molecular pathology of pre-malignant lung
N44CM-07261-02 (**) DOIRON, DANIEL R Interstitial NDYAG laser hyperthermia system
Z01CM-07300-01 (DDRD) CARDELLINA, J NCI, NIH Investigation of a link between anti-HIV and phorbol receptor binding activities
N01CM-07301-03 (**) RATAIN, MARK J Phase I and clinical pharmacokinetic studies of anti-cancer agents
Z01CM-07301-01 (DDRD) CARDELLINA, J H NCI, NIH Preparative separation of complex mixtures of priority natural products
N01CM-07302-02 (**) DONEHOWER, ROSS Phase I and pharmacokinetic studies of anticancer agents
Z01CM-07302-01 (DDRD) CARDELLINA, J NCI, NIH Development of chemical characterization/dereplication strategies
N01CM-07303-02 (**) VAN ECHO, DAVID A Phase I and pharmacokinetic studies of anticancer agents
Z01CM-07303-01 (DDRD) BEUTLER, J NCI, NIH Anti-HIV sulfated polysaccharides from a marine sponge and a tunicate
N01CM-07304-01 (**) RICHARDSON, RONALD L Phase I and pharmacokinetic studies of anticancer agents
Z01CM-07304-01 (DDRD) BEUTLER, J NCI, NIH Anti-HIV alkaloids isolated from Buchenavia capitata
N01CM-07305-02 (**) VON HOFF, DANIEL D Phase I and clinical pharmacokinetic studies of anticancer agents
Z01CM-07305-01 (DDRD) MANFREDI, K NCI, NIH Lutein, a xanthophyll with anti-HIV activity
N01CM-07306-03 (**) SPRIGGS, DAVID R Phase I and clinical pharmacokinetic studies of anti-cancer agents
Z01CM-07306-01 (DDRD) MANFREDI, K NCI, NIH Anti-HIV dimeric alkaloids from Ancistrocladus sp.
Z01CM-07307-01 (DDRD) GUSTAFSON, K NCI, NIH AIDS antiviral plant diterpenes
N01CM-07309-01 (**) KOVACH, JOHN S Phase II/III clinical trials of anticancer agents
Z01CM-07309-01 (LMPH) FORNACE, A J NCI, NIH The effects of stress response genes on the regulation of HIV-1 gene expression
N01CM-07310-01 (**) KRAKOFF, IRWIN H Phase II/III clinical trials of anticancer agents
N01CM-07311-04 (**) KELSEN, DAVID Phase II/III clinical trials of anticancer agents
N01CM-07313-02 (**) SWITALSKI, RICHARD Operational systems development in support of developmental therapeutics program
N01CM-07314-04 (**) MELENEY, JANET Logistics and conference support
N01CM-07315-01 (**) GRISWOLD, D P JR Detailed drug evaluation and development of treatment
N01CM-07316-01 (**) GREENHOUSE, DOROTHY Partial support of inst of laboratory animal resources
N01CM-07317-01 (**) GROOVER, KATHLEEN Storage and distribution of chemicals and drugs used in preclinical studies
N01CM-07320-03 (**) MILLER, ROBERT Storage and distribution of clinical drugs
N01CM-07321-03 (**) WILSON, WILLIAM R Synthesis of radiosensitizing agents
N01CM-07322-02 (**) MURPHY, PETER Shallow water marine organism collection
N01CM-07329-01 (**) TEMPLE, CARROLL G Master agreement order for chemical synthesis
N01CM-07330-05 (**) SELTZMAN, H Master agreement order for chemical synthesis

PROJECT NO., ORGANIZATIONAL UNIT., INVESTIGATOR, ADDRESS, TITLE

N01CM-07333-02 (**) TANGA, MARY J Master agreement order for chemical synthesis
N01CM-07335-02 (**) CAINE, DRURY S Master agreement order for chemical synthesis
N01CM-07340-04 (**) FURNEAUX, RICHARD H Master agreement order for chemical synthesis
N01CM-07341-02 (**) HSIAO, LUKE Y Master agreement for chemical synthesis
N01CM-07353-01 (**) PROTEAU, PAUL DTP biological data processing system
N44CM-07601-02 (**) ENTINE, GERALD High contrast, real time portal scanner for radiation therapy
Z01CM-09216-11 (LMI) VARESIO, L NCI, NIH Molecular basis for macrophage activation and immortalization
Z01CM-09247-11 (LEI) ORTALDO, J R NCI, NIH Natural cell-mediated immunity mechanism of lysis
Z01CM-09251-09 (LMI) RUSCETTI, F W NCI, NIH Interactions of human retroviruses with hematopoietic and adherent cells
Z01CM-09254-09 (LMI) FARRAR, W L NCI, NIH Biochemical and molecular mechanisms of growth factor modulated proliferation
Z01CM-09256-09 (LEI) ORTALDO, J R NCI, NIH Natural cell-mediated immunity--Biology and regulation of CD3-LGL
Z01CM-09262-10 (LEI) WILTROUT, R H NCI, NIH Antitumor effects of BRM-stimulated lymphocytes, NK cells, macrophages in mice
Z01CM-09264-09 (LMI) RUSCETTI, F W NCI, NIH Regulation of normal and neoplastic hematopoietic cell growth--Role of BRMs
Z01CM-09283-07 (LEI) YOUNG, H A NCI, NIH Control of human interferon gamma gene expression
Z01CM-09287-07 (LMI) DURUM, S K NCI, NIH Cytokines and the immune response
Z01CM-09288-06 (LEI) PEARSON, J W NCI, NIH Biological and chemotherapeutic modalities against human tumors in nude mice
Z01CM-09289-06 (LMI) OPPENHEIM, J J NCI, NIH Restorative role of cytokines in hematopoiesis and oncogenesis
Z01CM-09290-06 (OAD) ASHWELL, J D NCI, NIH Antigen presentation and T cell activation
Z01CM-09291-06 (CRB) SMITH, J W NCI, NIH Alternating 2'-dCF and recombinant leukocyte A IFN in hairy cell leukemia
Z01CM-09299-04 (LBP) KUNG, H NCI, NIH Characterization of HIV infection in peripheral blood mononuclear cells
Z01CM-09300-05 (LBP) KUNG, H NCI, NIH Intracellular activities of cytokines
Z01CM-09301-05 (LBP) KUNG, H NCI, NIH Transforming properties of eukaryotic initiation factor-4E
Z01CM-09302-05 (LBP) KUNG, H NCI, NIH Studies on the biological functions of human Ras proteins
Z01CM-09303-05 (LEI) YOUNG, H A NCI, NIH Studies of human B cell malignancies
Z01CM-09305-05 (CRB) STEIS, R G NCI, NIH 2' Deoxycoformycin in patients with HCL or T-gamma lymphoproliferative disorder
Z01CM-09306-05 (CRB) STEIS, R G NCI, NIH Phase Ib trial of intraperitoneal GM-CSF
Z01CM-09308-05 (CRB) SMITH, J W NCI, NIH Phase II efficacy study of Roferon A (RO22-8181/002) in hairy cell leukemia
Z01CM-09310-05 (OAD) KRUISBEEK, A M NCI, NIH Early T cell development
Z01CM-09311-05 (OAD) ASHWELL, J D NCI, NIH Antigen-specific receptor structure and function in T lymphocytes
Z01CM-09312-05 (LBP) KUNG, H NCI, NIH Cytokine research--Biochemical studies of interleukin-6 and its receptors
Z01CM-09315-05 (LBP) KUNG, H NCI, NIH Transcriptional regulation of HIV gene expression
Z01CM-09316-04 (LBP) KUNG, H NCI, NIH Studies of signal transduction in Xenopus oocytes
Z01CM-09322-03 (LEI) PILARO, A M NCI, NIH Mechanisms of leukocyte migration following BRM treatment
Z01CM-09323-04 (OAD) KRUISBEEK, A M NCI, NIH Selection of the T cell repertoire
Z01CM-09326-03 (LEI) YOUNG, H A NCI, NIH Induction of cytokine gene expression in vivo by flavone acetic acid
Z01CM-09329-03 (CRB) JANIK, J E NCI, NIH rGM-CSF and high dose carboplatin therapy in refractory ovarian cancer
Z01CM-09331-03 (CRB) CREEKMORE, S P NCI, NIH Phase Ib trial of poly ICIC in combination with IL-2 in patients with cancer
Z01CM-09332-03 (CRB) SMITH, J W NCI, NIH Phase I evaluation of interleukin-1 alpha
Z01CM-09335-03 (CRB) LONGO, D L NCI, NIH MoAb (anti T3) treatment of patients with lymphoproliferative disorders
Z01CM-09336-03 (CRB) LONGO, D L NCI, NIH Short course ProMACE-CytaBOM for stages II-IV diffuse aggressive lymphoma
Z01CM-09337-03 (CRB) LONGO, D L NCI, NIH Dose intense MOPP for patients with poor prognosis Hodgkin's disease
Z01CM-09339-03 (CRB) LONGO, D L NCI, NIH MOPP vs radiotherapy for early stage Hodgkin's disease
Z01CM-09340-03 (CRB) LONGO, D L NCI, NIH Observation vs. intensive chemotherapy for indolent lymphoma
Z01CM-09341-03 (CRB) LONGO, D L NCI, NIH ProMace-CytaBOM treatment for angiocentric immunoproliferative lesions
Z01CM-09342-03 (CRB) LONGO, D L NCI, NIH Treatment of stage I diffuse aggressive lymphomas
Z01CM-09345-02 (LEI) YOUNG, H A NCI, NIH Molecular studies of cellular cytotoxicity
Z01CM-09348-02 (LEI) WILTROUT, R H NCI, NIH Chemoprotective effects of recombinant cytokines
Z01CM-09349-02 (LEI) O'SHEA, J NCI, NIH Comparative study of receptor-mediated signaling in T cells and NK cells
Z01CM-09350-02 (CRB) SMITH, J W NCI, NIH A phase Ib trial of levamisole alone and in combination with rIFN-gamma
Z01CM-09351-02 (CRB) SZNOL, M NCI, NIH Phase Ib study of R24 MoAb given in conjunction with IL-2 and LAK cells
Z01CM-09352-02 (CRB) LONGO, D L NCI, NIH 5FU, leucovorin, AZT & persantine for melanoma, renal, and colorectal cancer
Z01CM-09353-02 (CRB) CREEKMORE, S P NCI, NIH A phase I/II study of a monoclonal antibody & IL-2 & cyclophosphamide
Z01CM-09354-02 (CRB) SMITH, J W NCI, NIH Phase Ib evaluation of IL-1 beta
Z01CM-09355-02 (CRB) SZNOL, M NCI, NIH A phase II study of CIS-platinum/IFN-alfa & IL-2 in malignant melanoma
Z01CM-09356-02 (CRB) SZNOL, M NCI, NIH A phase I trial of concurrent rIL-2 and rIFN-alfa administered subcutaneously
Z01CM-09357-02 (CRB) JANIK, J E NCI, NIH Poly ICLC and alpha interferon in refractory malignancy
Z01CM-09358-01 (LMI) MATIS, L A NCI, NIH Development, function and specificity of T lymphocytes
Z01CM-09359-01 (LMI) COX, G W NCI, NIH Modulation of macrophage gene expression and function
Z01CM-09360-01 (LMI) LINNEKIN, D M NCI, NIH Signal transduction mechanisms of hematopoietic growth factors
Z01CM-09361-01 (CRB) SHARFMAN, W H NCI, NIH Carboplatin, cisplatin, IFN alpha and tamoxifen for metastatic melanoma
Z01CM-09362-01 (CRB) JANIK, J E NCI, NIH Phase 1 evaluation of intratumoral interleukin-1 alpha
Z01CM-09363-01 (CRB) CURTI, B D NCI, NIH Measurement of interstitial pressure in subcutaneous tumor sites
Z01CM-09364-01 (CRB) FENTON, R G NCI, NIH Role of IL-2 in active specific immunotherapy for renal cell carcinoma
Z01CM-09365-01 (CRB) SMITH, J W NCI, NIH Phase I study of high dose carboplatin plus IL-1 alpha.
Z01CM-09366-01 (CRB) SMITH, J W NCI, NIH Phase II trial of IL-1 alpha + indomethacin in melanoma patients
Z01CM-09367-01 (CRB) LONGO, D L NCI, NIH Evaluation of activated killer T cells (T-AK) with anti-CD3 and IL-2
Z01CM-09368-01 (OAD) MURPHY, W J NCI, NIH Acceleration of immune reconstitution and T-cell development following BMT
Z01CM-09369-01 (LMI) KELVIN, D J NCI, NIH Receptor interaction and signal transduction by inflammatory cytokines
N01CM-17501-02 (**) FOWLER, GEORGE Clinical data management
N01CM-17502-00 (**) DAWSON, MARCIA Natural products lead-based synthesis
N01CM-17503-02 (**) DEGRAFFENREID, LINDA Conference and logistical support services
N01CM-17505-01 (**) RANSOM, JANET H Production and testing of lymphokine-activated killer cells
N01CM-17506-01 (**) NOVAK, JOEL W Clinical trials data management support
N01CM-17507-01 (**) GOTAY, CAROLYN C Information management support
N01CM-17508-01 (**) PROTEAU, PAUL R Computer support for the cancer therapy evaluation
N01CM-17509-00 (**) INDRA, PRAKASH Synthesis of bulk chemicals and drugs for preclinical and clinical trials
N01CM-17510-00 (**) MARKOVAC, ANICA Synthesis of chemicals and drugs for preclinical testing
N01CM-17511-00 (**) KEPLER, J A Preparation of radiolabeled anti-AIDS compounds
N01CM-17512-00 (**) CUSHMAN, MARK S Synthesis of congeners and prodrugs
N01CM-17513-00 (**) CUSHMAN, MARK S Synthesis of congeners and prodrugs of antiAIDS compounds
N01CM-17517-00 (**) PRABHAKAR, RISBOOD Resynthesis of compounds for screening
N01CM-17519-00 (**) CHEUNG, ANDREW P Analysis of chemicals and pharmaceutical formulations
N01CM-17528-00 (**) GUZIEC, FRANK Resynthesis of compounds for screening
N01CM-17529-00 (**) MOSS, HOWARD Neuropsychological testing for children and adults with HIV infection
N01CM-17531-00 (**) LEYKO, MARIE A Collection, storage, quality assurance of biological reagents & tumor cell line
N01CM-17532-00 (**) CURTIS, TOMMIE G Computer based searches for chemical structures
N01CM-17533-00 (**) ALTMAN, NORMAN DR Operation of an animal diagnostic laboratory
N01CM-17534-00 (**) WAGNER, JOSEPH E Operation of an animal diagnostic laboratory
N01CM-17535-00 (**) YOSHIO, SAKURAI Information services in support of cancer research
N01CM-17541-01 (**) LEYKO, MARY ANN The preparation of 14G2a MX-DTPA
N01CM-17542-00 (**) HOLLINGSHEAD, MELINDA Detailed drug evaluation of anti-AIDS agents
N01CM-17543-00 (**) NAGARAJAN, SRIDHER Synthesis of chemicals and drugs for preclinical testing
N01CM-17544-00 (**) PARSONS, JACK Synthesis of chemicals and drugs for preclinical testing
N01CM-17545-00 (**) BACKLUND, STEPHEN J Large scale preparation of anti-AIDS and anti-cancer bulk drugs
N01CM-17546-00 (**) DALY, DOUGLAS Plant collection and taxonomy--Central and South America
N01CM-17547-00 (**) FORERO, ENRIQUE Plant collection and taxonomy--Central African Republic
N01CM-17548-00 (**) SOEJARTO, DOEL Plant collection and taxonomy--Southeast Asia
N01CM-17549-00 (**) PHELAN, SAM Maintenance of a rodent production center
N01CM-17550-00 (**) ZALKOW, LEON H Synthesis of congeners and prodrugs of anti-AIDS compounds
N01CM-17551-00 (**) BAKER, DAVID C Synthesis of congeners and prodrugs of anti-AIDS compounds
N43CM-17566-00 (**) MORAVEK, JOSEF Chemical synthesis of C14, H3 and S35 labeled anti-AIDS and anti-cancer agents
N01CM-17568-00 (**) SELTZMAN, HERBERT H Resynthesis of compounds for screening
N01CM-17569-00 (**) ANDERSON, WAYNE K Synthesis of congeners and prodrugs
N01CM-17570-00 (**) ZALKOW, L H Synthesis of congeners and

PROJECT NO., ORGANIZATIONAL UNIT., INVESTIGATOR, ADDRESS, TITLE

prodrugs
N01CM-23911-52 (**) RUSSELL, ROBERT J Animal production at the NCI Frederick Cancer Research Facility
N01CM-25606-16 (**) HURT, MAURE JR NCI conference and logistical support services
N01CM-36011-15 (**) YOSHIO, SAKURAI Information service for cancer treatment research
N01CM-37536-12 (**) WOMACK, JAMES E Biochemical genetic monitoring of rodents
N01CM-47675-01 (**) MITCHELL, MALCOLM Monoclonal antibody in combination with interferon or interleukin-2
N01CM-57775-12 (**) PETERS, LESTER J Neutron therapy clinical trials
N01CM-67810-12 (**) BEACH, JANIS A Cancer therapy evaluation program information system
N01CM-67895-01 (**) BLUM, RONALD Phase 1 clinical trial of GM-CSF
N01CM-67902-01 (**) MASTRANGELO, MICHAEL J Phase IB clinical trial of immunotherapy with interleukin 2
N01CM-73701-06 (**) SUPKO, JEFFREY G Clinical pharmacokinetics of anticancer drugs
N01CM-73709-10 (**) VIT, ROBERT Support services for CTEP
N01CM-73710-11 (**) LEYKO, MARIE ANN Collection, storage, quality assurance and distribution
N01CM-73712-06 (**) PRICE, JAMES C Shelf life evaluation of clinical drugs
N01CM-73713-05 (**) MURRILL, EVELYN Analysis of chemicals and pharmaceuticals formulations
N01CM-73714-05 (**) HINES, JOHN Analysis of chemicals and pharmaceuticals formulations
N01CM-73715-05 (**) LIM, PETER Analysis of chemicals and pharmaceuticals formulations
N01CM-73719-05 (**) SMITH, TIMOTHY D Production of clinical doses of antitumor agents
N01CM-73720-07 (**) SOBERS, CARLTON Computer based searches for chemical structures
N01CM-87202-08 (**) REDMOND, NINFA Performance of protocol toxicology studies
N01CM-87208-03 (**) ROYDS, ROBERT B Clinical trials monitoring service
N01CM-87228-03 (**) MURRILL, EVELYN Analysis of formulations for anti-AIDS agents
N01CM-87236-09 (**) RANSOM, JANET Production and testing of human lymphokine-activated cells
N01CM-87237-03 (**) SHANNON, WILLIAM M Primary screening of HTLV-III/LAV
N01CM-87245-04 (**) SAYLOR, TILLMAN Hyperthermia quality assurance program
N01CM-87249-09 (**) JOHNSON, DAVID L Services in support of the developmental therapeutics
N01CM-87253-02 (**) GILLIES, STEPHEN D Production of chimeric monoclonal antibody R24
N01CM-87256-10 (**) LIAO, JAMES T F Performance of protocol toxicology studies
N01CM-87257-04 (**) MELVOLD, ROGER Iso-antigenic typing of mouse strains
N01CM-87258-09 (**) STEDHAM, MICHAEL A Pathology and veterinary services in support of toxicology studies
N01CM-87259-11 (**) PAGE, JOHN G Performance of protocol toxicology studies
N01CM-87263-09 (**) MOSS, HOWARD Neuropsychological testing for HIV infection
N01CM-87270-04 (**) GABRILOV, JANICE Phase I/II clinical studies of biological response
N01CM-87275-07 (**) HANKS, GERALD E Patterns of care study in radiation oncology
N01CM-87276-06 (**) MILLER, JAMES Maintenance of the NCI drug information system
N01CM-87284-05 (**) NOMEIR, AMIN A Preclinical pharmacology studies of anti-AIDS agents
N01CM-87285-04 (**) HILL, DONALD Preclinical pharmacology studies of anti-AIDS agents
N01CM-87286-04 (**) MCCORMACK, JOHN Preclinical pharmacology studies of anti-AIDS agents
N01CM-97553-05 (**) HARRISON, STEADMAN D JR Quality control/model dev'l in rodents and tumor cells
N01CM-97561-02 (**) KEPLER, JOHN A Preparation of radiolabeled materials
N01CM-97564-03 (**) PURDY, JAMES A Radiotherapy treatment planning tools
N01CM-97565-03 (**) CHANEY, EDWARD Radiotherapy treatment planning tools
N01CM-97566-06 (**) KALET, IRA J Radiotherapy treatment planning tools
N01CM-97567-05 (**) MEHTA, RAJESHWARI R Procurement of human breast cancer cell lines for antineo. drug screening
N01CM-97568-04 (**) STAMEY, THOMAS A Procurement of prostate cancer cell lines
N01CM-97569-03 (**) ROBESON, BONNIE L Acquisition of compounds for anticancer/AIDS screening
N01CM-97570-02 (**) HNATOWICH, DONALD J Single photon radiopharmaceuticals
N01CM-97571-03 (**) DESAI, ASHOK Oral dosage forms of anti-AIDS agents
N01CM-97572-02 (**) CHIN, TING-FONG Development and manufacture of oral dosage forms of anti-AIDS agents
N01CM-97574-06 (**) PAGE, JOHN G Preclinical tox and pharm of drugs developed for AIDS
N01CM-97575-07 (**) CAIL, STEPHEN Primary rodent production centers, task A
N01CM-97576-02 (**) STELLA, VALENTINO Development of dosage forms and delivery systems for anticancer drugs
N01CM-97577-02 (**) CHIN, TING FONG Development and production of pharmaceutical dosage
N01CM-97585-02 (**) ANDERSON, BRADLEY D Dosage from developement of new agents for the treatment of AIDS
N01CM-97587-02 (**) BHAT, VENTATRAMANA Large-scale preparation of anti-Aids drugs
N01CM-97590-02 (**) SAYEED, VILAYAT Large scale preparation of anti-AIDS drugs for phase II
N01CM-97591-03 (**) GEORGIEV, VASSIL S Large scale preparation of anti-AIDS drugs for phase II
N01CM-97592-02 (**) MARKOVAC, ANICA PHD Preparation of anti-AIDS bulk drugs
N01CM-97596-06 (**) PIERCE, JOSEPH F Provision, maintenance and transfer of tumor bearing models
N01CM-97600-04 (**) PROTEAU, PAUL DTP-AIDS screening database support
N01CM-97609-05 (**) HOUGHTON, ALAN Clinical trials of monoclonal antibodies, immunoconjugates
N01CM-97610-07 (**) MURRAY, LEE Clinical trials of monoclonal antibodies, immunoconjugate
N01CM-97611-05 (**) LOBUGLIO, ALBERT F Monoclonal antibodies and other targeting agents
N01CM-97615-03 (**) BEHRENS, PAUL Cultivation of marine protozoa
N01CM-97617-04 (**) PLACKE, MICHAEL E Preclinical toxicology & pharmacology of drugs developed for AIDS
N01CM-97618-02 (**) AMES, MATTHEW M Preclinical pharmacology invest of antitumor agents
N01CM-97619-04 (**) FELLER, DENNIS R Preclinical pharmacology invest of antitumor agents
N01CM-97620-02 (**) CHAN, KENNETH Preclinical pharmacology invest of antitumor agents
N01CM-97623-04 (**) NORBERG, ROBERT Primary rodent production centers, task B
N01CM-97624-03 (**) RUSSELL, JAMES D Primary rodent production centers, task C
N01CM-97626-02 (**) HSIAO, LUKE Y Large scale preparation of anti-AIDS drugs
N01CM-97627-03 (**) RUBINO, JOSEPH T Development of dosage forms and delievery systems
N01CM-97628-04 (**) KOZLOWSKI, JAMES M Procurement of prostate cancer cell lines
N01CM-97637-04 (**) CHRISEY, LINDA A Production of antisense oligodeoxynucleotides
Z01CN-00100-09 (CPSB) ALBANES, D NCI, NIH Alpha-tocopherol, beta-carotene lung cancer prevention study
Z01CN-00101-09 (CPSB) TAYLOR, P R NCI, NIH Human studies of diet and nutrition
Z01CN-00103-09 (CPSB) TANGREA, J A NCI, NIH Use of isotretinoin in prevention of basal cell carcinoma
Z01CN-00104-09 (CPSB) TAYLOR, P R NCI, NIH NHANES I epidemiologic follow-up survey--Chemoprevention/nutrition aspects
Z01CN-00105-09 (BB) PROROK, P C NCI, NIH Research in cancer screening and statistical methodology
Z01CN-00106-08 (BB) PROROK, P C NCI, NIH Studies in cancer screening
Z01CN-00107-09 (BB) PATTERSON, B NCI, NIH Design and analysis of pharmacokinetic studies of selenium
Z01CN-00112-08 (CPSB) TAYLOR, P R NCI, NIH Nutrition intervention study in esophageal cancer in Linxian, China
Z01CN-00113-08 (BB) LOCKE, F B NCI, NIH Cancer in Oriental populations
Z01CN-00115-07 (BB) CONNELLY, R R NCI, NIH Descriptive cancer epidemiology
Z01CN-00116-08 (BB) GREEN, S B NCI, NIH Statistical methodology research
Z01CN-00119-08 (BB) GREEN, S B NCI, NIH Consultation on clinical trials and other studies
Z01CN-00121-07 (BB) BROWN, C C NCI, NIH Research in biostatistical methodology and mathematical modeling
Z01CN-00142-07 (BB) LEVIN, D L NCI, NIH Cancer control objectives and cancer mortality projections
Z01CN-00143-07 (CPSB) TAYLOR, P R NCI, NIH Continued follow-up of the breast cancer detection and demonstration project
Z01CN-00146-03 (CPSB) SCHATZKIN, A NCI, NIH Nutritional factors and cancer in the Framingham heart study
Z01CN-00147-03 (CPSB) SCHATZKIN, A NCI, NIH Nutritional factors and cancer in the Framingham offspring study
Z01CN-00148-03 (CPSB) ALBANES, D NCI, NIH Finland studies of nutrition and cancer
Z01CN-00149-03 (CPSB) TAYLOR, P R NCI, NIH Yunnan tin miners lung cancer studies
Z01CN-00150-03 (CPSB) TAYLOR, P R NCI, NIH Esophageal cancer genetics studies
Z01CN-00151-03 (CPSB) SCHATZKIN, A NCI, NIH A dietary intervention study of the recurrence of large bowel adenomatous polyps
Z01CN-00153-02 (CPSB) DORGAN, J NCI, NIH Evaluation of the effects of fat-modified diet on hormone during adolescent
Z01CN-00154-01 (CPSB) ALBANES, D NCI, NIH Fels early nutrition and growth study
Z01CN-00155-01 (LNMR) YEH, G C NCI, NIH New mechanism for carcinogen resistance--Regulation by diet and nutrients
Z01CN-00156-01 (LNMR) PLOUZEK, C A NCI, NIH Nutritional regulation of carcinogens in placenta-related cells
Z01CN-00157-01 (LNMR) PHANG, J M NCI, NIH Effect of proteins, peptides and amino acids on carcinogenesis
Z01CN-00158-01 (LNMR) WELSH, C J NCI, NIH Dietary lipids and signal transduction in breast cells
Z01CN-00159-01 (LNMR) WANG, T NCI, NIH Regulation of tumor suppressor protein p53
Z01CN-00160-01 (LNMR) PERKINS, S N NCI, NIH Nutritional regulation of ras proto-oncogene activity
Z01CN-00161-01 (LNMR) SATHYAMOORTHY, N NCI, NIH Biological effects of dietary fiber on colon cells

PROJECT NUMBER LISTING

PROJECT NO., ORGANIZATIONAL UNIT., INVESTIGATOR, ADDRESS, TITLE

Z01CN-00162-01 (LNMR) LEWIS, K C NCI, NIH Effects of vitamin A nutriture on retinoid metabolism
N01CN-05220-01 (**) BOWEN, PHYLLIS Large bowel adenomatous polyp dietary intervention study
N01CN-05221-01 (**) CAHILL, JACK Large bowel adenomatous polyp dietary intervention
N01CN-05222-08 (**) MCWHORTER, WILLIAM The surveillance epidemiology and end results
N01CN-05223-06 (**) KOLONEL, LAURENCE N Surveillance epidemiology & end results
N01CN-05224-07 (**) WEST, DEE Surveillance epidemiology & end results program
N01CN-05225-08 (**) SWANSON, MARIE G The surveillance epidemiology and end results
N01CN-05226-06 (**) JANERICH, DWIGHT Surveillance epidemiology and end results
N01CN-05227-09 (**) GREENBERG, RAYMOND Surveillance, epidemiology & end results
N01CN-05228-08 (**) KEY, CHARLES Surveillance, Epidemiology, and end results
N01CN-05229-08 (**) LYNCH, CHARLES Surveillance epidemiology and end results
N01CN-05230-08 (**) THOMAS, DAVID Surveillance epidemiology and end results
N01CN-05241-01 (**) CARAGAY, ALEGRIA F Technical support for experimental food program
N01CN-05243-05 (**) DOTSON, JAMES Management and support services for DCPC
N01CN-05247-04 (**) ZIPPEN, CALVIN Seer/surveillance quality control unit
N01CN-05261-01 (**) WEBB, THOMAS E Special studies facilitating the flow of preclinical
N01CN-05267-01 (**) MIRSALIS, JON C Special studies facilitating the flow of preclinical
N01CN-05270-02 (**) REIST, ELMER Synthesis of 10 grams of 18 alpha loean-12 ene 3 beta 23 28 triol
N01CN-05275-01 (**) AMACHER, RICHARD Support services contract for the smoking,
N01CN-05295-03 (**) MASSEY, MARILYN Coordinating center for american stop smoking
N44CN-05308-03 (**) LEVITAN, KAREN B Evaluation of worksite health promotion materials
N44CN-05310-02 (**) HERNANDEZ, TERESITA Computer-based dietary intervention program for the worksite
N01CN-05316-01 (**) FRIEDMAN, GARY Large bowel adenomatous polyp dietary intervention study
N01CN-05317-01 (**) GLASS, ANDREW Large bowel adenomatous polyp dietary intervention study
N01CN-05318-01 (**) SHIKE, MOSHE Large bowel adenomatous polyp dietary intervention study
N01CN-05319-01 (**) MARSHALL, JAMES Large bowel adenomatous polyp dietary intervention study
N01CN-05320-01 (**) SCHADE, ROBERT Large bowel adenomatous polyp dietary intervention study
N01CN-05321-01 (**) BURT, RANDALL Large bowel adenomatous polyp dietary intervention study
N01CN-05322-01 (**) COOPER, ROBERT Large bowel adenomatous polyp dietary intervention study
N01CN-07344-20 (**) LUANDE, JEFF Chemoprevention of skin cancer in albinos
N01CN-15331-00 (**) MUSEY, PAUL Evaluation of the effect of a fat modified diet on hormones during adolescence
N01CN-15337-01 (**) YOUNG, CHARLES Phase I and pharmacokinetic studies of calcium glucanate
N01CN-15340-01 (**) GRIZZLE, WILLIAM E Early detection research network - tissue collection
N01CN-15343-00 (**) PRENTICE, ROSS Women's health trial -- Feasibility study in minority populations
N01CN-15348-00 (**) NIEMCRYCK, STEVE Support for cancer control science program
N01CN-15352-01 (**) LEVIN, BARRY Oral subchronic toxicity in rats & dogs applied to DFMO with N-acetylcysteine
N01CN-15359-01 (**) PARS, HARRY Synthesis of 10 grams of lycopene
N01CN-15363-01 (**) LIPKIN, MARTIN Key dietary factors in the precancerous and cancerous in colon mucosa
N01CN-15371-00 (**) LAKE, WILLIAM, JR Computing software support for the biometry branch
N01CN-15373-00 (**) REMINGTON, PATRICK American stop smoking intervention study
N01CN-15374-00 (**) BEASLEY, JOHN M American stop smoking intervention study
N01CN-15375-00 (**) FELDMAN, JUDITH American stop smoking intervention study
N01CN-15376-00 (**) SCHWARTZ, RANDY American stop smoking intervention study
N01CN-15377-00 (**) DAVIS, JAMES American stop smoking intervention study
N01CN-15378-00 (**) HARTY, KATHLEEN American stop smoking intervention study
N01CN-15379-00 (**) NOVICK, LLOYD F American stop smoking intervention study
N01CN-15380-00 (**) YOUNG, WALTER F American stop smoking intervention study
N01CN-15381-00 (**) FARRELL, JOHN American stop smoking intervention study
N01CN-15382-00 (**) WHEELER, FRANCES C American stop smoking intervention study
N01CN-15383-00 (**) LANSDALE, SHARON American stop smoking intervention study
N01CN-15384-00 (**) DESCADA, MYRA American stop smoking intervention study
N01CN-15385-00 (**) CONNOLLY, GREGORY American stop smoking intervention study
N01CN-15386-00 (**) STOODT, GEORJEAN American stop smoking intervention study
N01CN-15387-00 (**) MCLAIN, ROGER American stop smoking intervention study
N01CN-15388-00 (**) WADSWORTH, JO American stop smoking intervention study
N01CN-15389-00 (**) FACEY, MARIA R American stop smoking intervention study
N44CN-15392-00 (**) RUDNER, LAWRENCE Software to aid in the meta-analysis of research studies
N01CN-15393-01 (**) WHITESIDE, THERESA Early detection research network - tissue collection
N44CN-15402-00 (**) SCHIMKE, JOEL T Oncologic pain instructional and advisory treatment (OPIAT) system, phase II
N01CN-45165-17 (**) HEINONEN, OLLI P U S-Finland studies of nutrition and cancer
N01CN-45175-11 (**) CHEN, VIVIEN Study of black/white cancer patient survival experience
N01CN-64091-10 (**) OCKENE, JUDITH K Community clinical trial for heavy smokers
N01CN-64092-13 (**) POMREHN, PAUL Community clinical trial for heavy smokers
N01CN-64093-10 (**) BEST, J ALLAN Community clinical trial for heavy smokers
N01CN-64094-09 (**) LICHTENSTEIN, EDWARD Community clinical trial for heavy smokers
N01CN-64095-09 (**) ORLANDI, MARIO Community clinical trial for heavy smokers
N01CN-64096-09 (**) HARTWELL, TYLER D Community clinical trial for heavy smokers
N01CN-64097-11 (**) WALLACK, LAWRENCE Community clinical trial for heavy smokers
N01CN-64098-10 (**) CUMMINGS, K MICHAEL Community clinical trial for heavy smokers
N01CN-64099-11 (**) HYMOWITZ, NORMAN Community clinical trial for heavy smokers
N01CN-64100-11 (**) HENDERSON, MAUREEN Community clinical trial for heavy smokers
N01CN-64101-09 (**) PILAND, NEILL F Community clinical trial for heavy smokers
N01CN-65028-17 (**) DARITY, WILLIAM A Primary prevention (smoking) of cancer in black population
N01CN-65034-19 (**) MICHIELUTTE, ROBERT Avoidable mortality from cancers in black populations
N01CN-65035-18 (**) BRENNAN, MICHAEL J Avoidable mortality from cancers in black populations
N01CN-65048-16 (**) BOTVIN, GILBERT J Prevention (smoking) of cancer in black populations
N01CN-75401-15 (**) RONEY, DAVID Biomedical computing support for cancer prevention and control
N01CN-75405-12 (**) HUGHES, MARY O Support contract for public health agency initiative
N01CN-75406-13 (**) BEACH, JANIS Community clinical trial for heavy smokers
N01CN-75415-19 (**) PHILLIPS, CLYDE Avoidable mortality from cancers in black populations
N01CN-75435-08 (**) KALUZNY, ARNOLD D Assessment of the implementation and impact of the
N01CN-85060-06 (**) STERN, HARRIET Research support service for diet, nutrition and cancer
N01CN-85062-02 (**) GRUBBS, CLINTON Chemoprevention of MNU-induced mammary tumors in rats
N01CN-85095-06 (**) CHUNG, FRANK Chemoprevention of NNK induced lung cancer in rat with isothiocyanate
N01CN-85096-01 (**) PEREIRA, MICHAEL Chemoprevention of MNU induced foci of aberrant crypts
N01CN-85097-11 (**) MOON, RICHARD Chemoprevention of MNU induced mammary tumors in the rat
N01CN-85104-02 (**) DIMITROV, NIKOLAY Phase I and pharmacokinetic studies of oltipraz
N01CN-85109-01 (**) CARBONE, PAUL P Phase I and pharmacokinetics of difluoromethylorinithine
N01CN-85120-04 (**) BASSETT, DANUTA Evaluation cohort survey for community intervention
N01CN-85122-01 (**) CIEMNECKI, ANNE The evaluation of the 1990 medicare legislation
N01CN-85125-02 (**) SCHULMAN, MARK Worksite, school-worksite and religious organizations
N01CN-95127-02 (**) GRIFFEN, CAROL Iso-BCC study coordinating center
N01CN-95151-08 (**) MOON, RICHARD Chemoprevention of pancreatic carcinogenesis in hamsters
N01CN-95156-04 (**) GRUBBS, CLINTON Chemoprevention of DMBA induced mammary tumors with chemopreventive agents
N01CN-95159-05 (**) SIGMAN, CAROLINE Intermediate endpoint markers for cancer risk
N01CN-95162-03 (**) NIEMCRYK, STEVE J Support contract for special populations initiatives
N01CN-95166-04 (**) MILLER, RODNEY Centralized chemopreventive agent repository
N01CN-95168-04 (**) TYSON, CHARLES Toxicity of 4-HPR with tamoxifen in rats and dogs
N01CN-95170-02 (**) PAGE, JOHN Phenexylisothiocyanate toxicity studies on rats and dogs
N01CN-95172-09 (**) SHARMA, SHEELA In vitro screening of chemopreventive agents
N01CN-95173-03 (**) MEHTA, RAJENDRE In vitro screening of chemopreventive agents
N01CN-95175-03 (**) RUDD, COLLETTE In vitro screening of chemopreventive agents
N01CN-95177-05 (**) PETERSEN, BARBARA J Dietary surveys and food composition data

PROJECT NO., ORGANIZATIONAL UNIT., INVESTIGATOR, ADDRESS, TITLE

N01CN-95182-02 (**) AMACHER, RICHARD Smoking and tobacco control monographs
N01CN-95214-01 (**) TICH, NANCY Strategy development by workshop on chemoprevention
N01CO-03851-02 (**) CANDAGE, MELLEN Editorial services for the International Cancer Information Center
N01CO-03852-01 (**) KERN, LAWRENCE Maintenance of NCI files and mail delivery service
N01CO-03859-13 (**) LEFEBVRE, CRAIG Office of cancer communications program support
N01CO-03861-02 (**) DANZEISEN, RICHARD Budget execution and formulation support
N01CO-03862-05 (**) ETTINGER, DAVID S Cancer information service
N01CO-03863-06 (**) RAICH, PETER Cancer information service
N01CO-03864-06 (**) ENGSTROM, P F Cancer information service
N01CO-03865-05 (**) STUYCK, STEPHEN C Cancer information service
N01CO-03866-05 (**) FAHEY, THOMAS J Cancer information service
N01CO-03867-05 (**) SARTORELLI, A Cancer information service
N01CO-03868-04 (**) BROWN, HELENE Cancer information service
N01CO-03869-05 (**) FRIEDELL, GILBERT H Cancer information service
N01CO-03870-05 (**) DAY, ROBERT W Cancer information service
N01CO-03871-06 (**) PATTERSON, BRADFORD W Cancer information service
N01CO-03872-05 (**) MIRAND, EDWIN A Cancer information service
N01CO-03873-07 (**) HARRIS, RANDALL E Cancer information service
N01CO-03874-05 (**) GEORGE, STEPHEN Cancer information service
N01CO-03875-05 (**) TRAPIDO, EDWARD Cancer information service
N01CO-03876-05 (**) ZINN, CHARLES J Cancer information service
N01CO-03877-06 (**) EYRE, HARMON J Cancer information service
N01CO-03878-06 (**) LANSKY, SHIRLEY B Cancer information service
N01CO-03887-47 (**) MATYAS, MICHAEL NCI/NICHD LAN hardware and software
N44CO-05180-01 (**) WALTON, PETER L Clinical oncology workstation
N01CO-05709-01 (**) WEEKS, RICHARD A mammogram-once a year for a lifetime
N01CO-05714-01 (**) KOHLER, BEN Mammography awareness kit
N01CO-05725-01 (**) BOWNS, TIMOTHY Graduate internship in the health communications
N01CO-05733-01 (**) POUDRIER, DON Brochure-- Once a year for a lifetime
N01CO-15603-00 (**) CAMPBELL, DAVID Monthly updating and system maintenance of mumps
N01CO-15624-01 (**) ISSELL, BRIAN F Cancer information service
N01CO-15625-00 (**) KOHLER, BEN Journal of the National Cancer Institute
N01CO-15626-00 (**) KOHLER, BEN Once a year for a lifetime
N01CO-15627-00 (**) KOHLER, BEN Journal of National Cancer Institute
N01CO-15629-00 (**) KATZ, WILLIAM Students with cancer
N01CO-15631-01 (**) POUDRIER, DON Post doctoral research fellowship opportunities
N01CO-15632-00 (**) STRAUS, RICHARD What you need to know about dysplastic nevi
N01CO-15633-00 (**) POUDRIER, DON Cancer patient education video directory
N01CO-15634-00 (**) KOHLER, BEN Journal of National Cancer Institute
N01CO-15635-01 (**) SARRO, TONY A mammogram-- Once a year for a lifetime
N01CO-15636-03 (**) YOUNG, PEGGY Technical support service for the Division of Extramural
N01CO-15637-00 (**) TOTH, FRANK Hospital days-treatment ways
N01CO-15638-00 (**) VINGI, ROBERT Help yourself--Tips for teenagers with cancer
N01CO-15639-00 (**) TOTH, FRANK Breast cancer-- Understanding treatment options
N01CO-15640-00 (**) KOHLER, BEN Radiation therapy and you-- A guide to self help
N01CO-15642-00 (**) BARRON, RICHARD Chemotherapy and you-- A guide to self help during treatment
N01CO-15645-00 (**) KOHLER, BEN Journal of national cancer institute
N01CO-15649-00 (**) FOX, RAYMOND Chemotherapy and you-- A guide to self help during
N01CO-15650-00 (**) TOTH, FRANK Mastectomy-- A treatment for breast cancer
N01CO-15651-00 (**) WEEKS, RICK A mammogram-- Once a year for a lifetime
N01CO-15653-00 (**) POUDRIER, DON How to help your patients stop smoking
N01CO-15654-00 (**) BARRON, RICHARD Chemotherapy and you-- A guide to self help
N01CO-15655-00 (**) LINDENZWEIG, C R Radiation therapy and you-- A guide to self help
N01CO-15656-00 (**) KOHLER, BEN Journal of national cancer institute
N01CO-15658-00 (**) KOHLER, BEN Eating hints
N01CO-15659-00 (**) SILLIMAN, D NCI investigational drugs-- Pharmaceutical data
N01CO-15660-00 (**) HALTERMAN, BARBARA Cancer survivorship
N01CO-15661-00 (**) RAVIDA, MARK Journal of the national cancer institute
N01CO-15662-00 (**) FOX, RAYMOND Eating hints
N01CO-15663-00 (**) MOREY, DAVID Cancer statistics review
N01CO-15664-00 (**) KOHLER, BEN Journal of national cancer institute
N01CO-15666-00 (**) KOHLER, BEN Leadership summit II
N01CO-15668-00 (**) SILLIMAN, DAVID Leadership summit
N01CO-15669-00 (**) VINGI, ROBERT E Chew or snuff is real bad stuff
N01CO-15670-00 (**) TOTH, FRANK Self-guided strategies for smoking cessation
N01CO-15671-00 (**) SILLIMAN, DAVID Conduct of research
N01CO-15684-00 (**) MAXIN, LENORA Skin cancers
N01CO-15685-01 (**) HARTMAN, RAYMOND Talking with your child about cancer
N01CO-15686-01 (**) TOTH, FRANK Taking time
N01CO-15687-00 (**) POUDRIER, DON Postdoctoral research fellowship opportunities
N01CO-15691-00 (**) LINDENZWEIG, C R Breast reconstruction-- A matter of choice
N01CO-15692-00 (**) VINGI, ROBERT Journal of the national cancer institute
N01CO-15693-00 (**) KATZ, BILL The national cancer institute brochure
N01CO-15694-00 (**) KOHLER, BEN Announcement alert
N01CO-15695-00 (**) WEEKS, RICK Do the right thing
N01CO-15696-01 (**) STRAUS, RICHARD R Nutrition posters, receipe cards and letter
N01CO-15697-01 (**) MOREY, DAVID Do the right thing Version: Items 1 thru 20)
N01CO-15698-01 (**) HEYMAN, BARRY Do the right thing
N01CO-15699-00 (**) RAUDENBUSH, BRIAN Do the right thing
N01CO-15700-00 (**) TOTH, FRANK Four national cancer institute pubettes
N01CO-15702-00 (**) REED, MELVIN L Cancer information service
N01CO-15703-00 (**) UNDERWOOD, JEFFREY T Cancer information service
N01CO-15704-00 (**) HENNEY, JANE E Cancer information service
N01CO-15705-00 (**) COSTANZI, JOHN J Cancer information service
N01CO-15706-01 (**) LINDENZWEIG, C R Decade of the brain 1990-2000
N01CO-15710-00 (**) KOHLER, BEN NCI fact book - 1990
N01CO-15711-00 (**) MOREY, DAVID B An integrated oncology workstation
N01CO-15721-00 (**) LINDENZWEIG, C R Decade of the brain 1990-2000
N01CO-15722-01 (**) WECKER, DONALD National cancer advisory board
N01CO-15724-00 (**) MOREY, DAVID NIH glass unit and NIH calendar of events
N01CO-15725-01 (**) KOHLER, BEN Cancer statistics review
N01CO-15726-01 (**) LINDENZWEIG, C R Cancer prevention fellowship program
N01CO-15727-01 (**) WU, PYNG-PYNG Programming and systems maintenance in support of the NCI/ cont.management
N01CO-15728-00 (**) STRAUS, THOMAS F Receipe cards
N01CO-15733-00 (**) KOHLER, BEN Do the right thing
N01CO-15734-00 (**) TOTH, FRANK Brochure 1-- Get a mammogram
N01CO-15735-00 (**) HOSSLI, JOHN Do the right thing pocket folder
N01CO-15736-00 (**) RAY, BRUCE W Choosing a mammography facility
N01CO-15738-00 (**) POUDRIER, DON NCI 1993 budget estimate
N01CO-15740-00 (**) CHALKLEY, NEAL A mammogram - once a year for a lifetime
N01CO-15741-00 (**) KOHLER, BEN Contract contents file
N01CO-15743-00 (**) LAMASTERS, PAUL R Clearing the air
N01CO-15745-00 (**) KOHLER, BEN Do the right thing
N01CO-15746-00 (**) LAMASTERS, PAUL R Do the right thing poster
N01CO-15747-00 (**) TOTH, FRANK Zora brown article
N01CO-15748-00 (**) TOTH, FRANK What you need to know about cancer of the uterus
N01CO-15749-00 (**) LINDENZWEIG, C R What you need to know about cancer of the cervix
N01CO-15753-00 (**) LINDENZWEIG, BOB Polyp prevention trial - what you should know
N01CO-15755-00 (**) KOHLER, BEN DCBDC1991 annual report
N01CO-15756-00 (**) LAMASTERS, PAUL R Get the fax on cancer
N01CO-15758-00 (**) KOHLER, BEN Worksite mammography kit
N01CO-15759-00 (**) STRAUS, THOM You can make healthy choices bookmark
N01CO-15760-00 (**) CHALKLEY, NEAL A mammogram-once a year for a lifetime
N01CO-15762-00 (**) KOOTZ, RUSTY Hagase um mamograma
N01CO-15763-00 (**) CHALKLEY, NEAL Hagalo hay por su salud y su familia
N01CO-15764-00 (**) TOTH, FRANK Brochure 1-- Get a mammogram
N01CO-15765-00 (**) LINDENZWEIG, C R What you need to know about cancer of the cervix
N01CO-15768-00 (**) LINDENZWEIG, C R What you need to know about cancer of the uterus
N01CO-15769-00 (**) LAMASTERS, PAUL R The pap test-- It can save your life
N01CO-15771-01 (**) KATZ, WILLIAM Breast exams-- What you should know
N01CO-15772-00 (**) LINDENZWEIG, C R Polyp prevention trial - what you should know
N01CO-15773-00 (**) TOTH, FRANK Mammography kit mastheads

PROJECT NO., ORGANIZATIONAL UNIT., INVESTIGATOR, ADDRESS, TITLE

N01CO-15774-00 (**) CHALKLEY, NEAL A mammogram - once a year for a lifetime

N01CO-15775-00 (**) TOTH, FRANK Do the right thing - get a mammogram

N01CO-15776-00 (**) LAMASTERS, PAUL R How to help your patients stop using tobacco

N01CO-15777-00 (**) KOHLER, BEN Item 1– Cervical cancer control

N01CO-15778-00 (**) KOHLER, BEN Facts about breast cancer mammography and black women

N01CO-15779-00 (**) CHALKLEY, NEAL Small grants program 1984-1990

N01CO-15780-00 (**) KILBURN, DANNY Do the right thing bookmark

N01CO-15781-00 (**) LINDENZWEIG, C R Scientific information services of the NCI

N01CO-15782-00 (**) LAMASTERS, PAUL R Research training and career development programs

N01CO-23913-33 (**) WILSON, SUSAN W Scientific library services-NCI Frederick facility

N01CO-33858-24 (**) WU, HO-I Support the NCI contracts management system

N01CO-44027-10 (**) GERARDI, DONNA Support of activities

N01CO-54052-16 (**) YOUNG, PEGGY L Support services for the DEA, OD, NCI

N01CO-74101-20 (**) VANDE WOUDE, GEORGE Basic research at the National Cancer Institute Frederick

N01CO-74102-45 (**) GILDEN, RAYMOND V Operations and technical support

N01CO-74103-16 (**) CALLAHAN, LAWRENCE Computer services

N01CO-74115-03 (**) GORDON, CHRISTOPHER Management information systems support services

N01CO-84331-01 (**) PATENAUDE, ANDREA FARKAS Cancer survivor project

N01CO-84338-10 (**) DUNLOP, SILBA CUNNINGHAM Screening, indexing, abstracting and keying of cancer

N01CO-84339-19 (**) STONE, MARY Technical writing, publications distribution

N01CO-84340-06 (**) COLEMAN, M P Clearinghouse for on-going work in cancer epidemiology

N01CO-84343-11 (**) KEARNEY, CHERRI L Support services for the office of the director, NCI

N01CO-84348-11 (**) CREASEY, W Cancer information dissemination and analysis center

N01CO-94381-15 (**) KALANTAR, RAY ADP support services for DEA and the OD, NCI

N01CO-94382-05 (**) DARBY, CHARLES A Cancer communications program evaluation

N01CO-94383-03 (**) PONTEN, JAN Scientist to scientist exchange program

N01CO-94386-11 (**) WALTON, PETER L Computer support for cancer information dissemination

N01CO-94392-11 (**) SALEMI, JOSEPH Support for NCI/NICHD local area networks

N01CO-94393-03 (**) FENNELL, PEARLIE Cancer prevention awareness–The black college as a resource

Z01CP-00543-13 (LTVB) HOWLEY, P M NCI, NIH Characterization of the papillomaviruses

Z01CP-00565-09 (LTVB) MUNGER, K NCI, NIH Structure function studies on the human papillomavirus E7 oncoprotein

Z01CP-00698-08 (LTVB) HOWLEY, P M NCI, NIH Role of human papillomaviruses in human carcinogenesis

Z01CP-03509-26 (OD) THORGEIRSSON, U P NCI, NIH Carcinogenesis, chemotherapy and biological markers in nonhuman primates

Z01CP-04265-26 (BB) GART, J J NCI, NIH Consulting in statistics and applied mathematics

Z01CP-04267-26 (BB) GART, J J NCI, NIH Research in statistics and applied mathematics

Z01CP-04269-20 (BB) STUMP, J M NCI, NIH Biomedical computing – Consultation, research and development service

Z01CP-04377-20 (CEB) PARRY, D M NCI, NIH Familial, congenital, and genetic factors in malignancy

Z01CP-04378-16 (EEB) HOOVER, R N NCI, NIH U S cancer mortality survey and related analytic studies

Z01CP-04400-26 (CEB) LI, F P NCI, NIH Clinical epidemiology of cancer

Z01CP-04410-15 (EEB) TUCKER, M A NCI, NIH Studies of persons at high risk of cancer

Z01CP-04411-15 (EEB) HAYES, H M NCI, NIH Cancer and related conditions in domestic animals–Epidemiologic comparisons

Z01CP-04475-14 (BB) SCOTTO, J NCI, NIH Skin cancer and solar radiation program

Z01CP-04480-16 (EEB) BLAIR, A NCI, NIH Studies of occupational cancer

Z01CP-04481-15 (REB) BOICE, J D NCI, NIH Studies of radiation-induced cancer

Z01CP-04491-15 (LEP) SAFFIOTTI, U NCI, NIH Quantitative studies on concurrent factors in neoplastic transformation

Z01CP-04496-15 (LMC) BUSTIN, M NCI, NIH Chromosomal proteins and chromatin function

Z01CP-04500-14 (BB) GAIL, M H NCI, NIH Methodologic studies in epidemiology

Z01CP-04504-19 (CCTP) YUSPA, S H NCI, NIH Model systems for study of chemical carcinogenesis at the cellular level

Z01CP-04517-15 (LMC) KRAEMER, K H NCI, NIH DNA repair in human cancer-prone genetic diseases

Z01CP-04542-19 (LCC) KEEFER, L K NCI, NIH Chemistry of nitroso compounds & other substances of interest in cancer research

Z01CP-04548-19 (OD) STEWART, H L NCI, NIH Registry of experimental cancers/WHO collab. center for tumors of lab animals

Z01CP-04582-16 (LCC) KASPRZAK, K S NCI, NIH Mechanisms of nickel carcinogenesis

PROJECT NO., ORGANIZATIONAL UNIT., INVESTIGATOR, ADDRESS, TITLE

Z01CP-04629-26 (LB) DIPAOLO, J A NCI, NIH Regulation of stages of carcinogensis induced by chemical or physical agents

Z01CP-04673-20 (LB) EVANS, C H NCI, NIH Immunobiology of carcinogenesis

Z01CP-04779-15 (BB) BLOT, W J NCI, NIH Field studies in high risk areas

Z01CP-04798-21 (CCTP) DELUCA, L M NCI, NIH Retinoids in differentiation and neoplasia

Z01CP-04930-20 (LCMB) ARNSTEIN, P NCI, NIH Biology of natural and induced neoplasia

Z01CP-04940-24 (LCMB) AARONSON, S A NCI, NIH Transforming genes in experimental oncogenesis and human cancer

Z01CP-04941-19 (LCMB) TRONICK, S R NCI, NIH Biochemical characterization of retroviruses

Z01CP-04963-15 (LMO) SHIH, T Y NCI, NIH Toward a molecular description of malignant transformation by ras oncogenes

Z01CP-04976-14 (LCMB) SANFORD, K K NCI, NIH Mechanisms of neoplastic transformation in cultured human cells

Z01CP-04986-15 (LEC) HAGER, G NCI, NIH Molecular basis of steroid hormone action

Z01CP-05051-13 (LC) ROBERTS, A B NCI, NIH Biology and molecular biology of transforming growth factor-beta

Z01CP-05060-13 (LCMB) RHIM, J S NCI, NIH Mechanisms of carcinogenesis–Neoplastic transformation of human cells

Z01CP-05062-13 (LCMB) EVA, A NCI, NIH Transforming genes of naturally occuring and chemically induced tumors

Z01CP-05063-13 (LCMB) ABLASHI, D NCI, NIH Human herpesvirus-6 (HHV-6), Epstein-Barr virus (EBV) and HIV studies

Z01CP-05086-11 (LMC) PARK, S S NCI, NIH Monoclonal antibodies to human EDP-glucunosyltransferase

Z01CP-05092-14 (LCC) RICE, J M NCI, NIH Transplacental carcinogenesis and tumor promotion in nonhuman primates

Z01CP-05093-13 (LCC) PERANTONI, A O NCI, NIH In vitro studies on organ specificity in transplacental carcinogenesis

Z01CP-05120-12 (LMO) LAUTENBERGER, J A NCI, NIH Structural, biochemical, and biological characterization of HIV Nef and Vpu

Z01CP-05125-11 (LMC) PARK, S S NCI, NIH Preparation of monoclonal antibodies to rabbit b5 and rat P-450 3A1

Z01CP-05128-12 (EEB) ZIEGLER, R G NCI, NIH Diet and nutrition in cancer etiology

Z01CP-05139-12 (CEB) PARRY, D M NCI,NIH NIH Interinstitute medical genetics program–The genetics clinic

Z01CP-05146-12 (CEB) BYRNE, J NCI, NIH Morbidity in childhood cancer survivors and their offspring

Z01CP-05164-11 (LCMB) PIERCE, J NCI, NIH Oncogenes, growth factor pathways and hematopoietic cell transformation

Z01CP-05177-10 (CCTP) POIRIER, M C NCI, NIH Use of immunological techniques to study the interaction of carcinogens with DNA

Z01CP-05178-10 (CCTP) STRICKLAND, J NCI, NIH Cellular and tissue determinants of susceptibility to chemical carcinogenesis

Z01CP-05238-10 (LMO) WATSON, D NCI, NIH The transforming genes of acute leukemia viruses and their cellular homologues

Z01CP-05254-10 (LMV) BRADY, J NCI, NIH Regulation of HTLV-I gene expression

Z01CP-05262-10 (LEC) EVARTS, R P NCI, NIH Cellular evolution of chemically induced rat hepatomas

Z01CP-05263-09 (LEC) MILLER, M J NCI, NIH Two-dimensional gel analysis of oncogene-mediated transformation

Z01CP-05270-10 (CCTP) BLUMBERG, P M NCI, NIH Molecular mechanism of action of phorbol ester tumor promoters

Z01CP-05274-10 (LEP) SAFFIOTTI, U NCI, NIH Respiratory carcinogenesis by chemical and physical factors

Z01CP-05276-10 (LEP) SAFFIOTTI, U NCI, NIH Growth control in epithelial cells and its alteration in carcinogenesis

Z01CP-05279-08 (CEB) BEEBE, G W NCI, NIH Development of epidemiologic data resources

Z01CP-05280-08 (CEB) BEEBE, G W NCI, NIH Carcinogenic effects of ionizing radiation

Z01CP-05295-10 (LMO) BLAIR, D G NCI, NIH Studies on the activation of oncogenes in viruses and human tumors

Z01CP-05299-11 (LCC) LUBET, R A NCI, NIH Interspecies differences in transplacental carcinogenesis and tumor promotion

Z01CP-05301-10 (LCC) WARD, J M NCI, NIH Biology and pathology of natural and experimentally induced tumors

Z01CP-05303-10 (LCC) WARD, J M NCI, NIH Pathogenesis and promotion of natural and induced tumors

Z01CP-05317-08 (LEC) HATFIELD, D L NCI, NIH Selenocysteine, the 21st amino acid in the genetic code

Z01CP-05318-09 (LMC) FRIEDMAN, F K NCI, NIH Structure-function of cytochrome P-450

Z01CP-05326-09 (LVC) MANN, D L NCI, NIH HLA antigens–Structure, function and disease association

Z01CP-05328-09 (LVC) MANN, D L NCI, NIH Immunologic studies of human T-cell lymphoma virus

Z01CP-05329-08 (CEB) BEEBE, G W NCI, NIH Hepatitis B virus (HBV) and liver cancer in army veterans of WWII

Z01CP-05352-09 (LCC) ANDERSON, L M NCI, NIH Metabolic and pharmacological determinants in perinatal carcinogenesis

Z01CP-05353-09 (LCC) ANDERSON, L M NCI, NIH Sensitivity factors in special carcinogenesis models

Z01CP-05366-08 (LCMB) KRAUS, M H NCI, NIH erbB-3 Protein reveals structural features of a transmembrane tyrosine kinase

Z01CP-05367-07 (LVC) OBRIEN, S J NCI, NIH The genetic structure of natural populations of past and present

Z01CP-05368-08 (REB) BOICE, J D NCI, NIH Studies of drug-induced cancer and multiple primary cancers

Z01CP-05382-08 (LVC) COLBURN, N H NCI, NIH Genes involved in preneoplastic progression

Z01CP-05383-08 (LVC) COLBURN, N H NCI, NIH Membrane signal transduction in tumor promotion

Z01CP-05384-08 (LVC) OBRIEN, S J NCI, NIH Genetic analysis of human cellular genes in neoplastic transformation

PROJECT NO., ORGANIZATIONAL UNIT., INVESTIGATOR, ADDRESS, TITLE

Z01CP-05385-08 (LVC) OBRIEN, S J NCI, NIH Molecular genetic analysis of feline cellular genes--A comparative approach

Z01CP-05389-08 (LVC) OBRIEN, S J NCI, NIH Reproductive strategies in animal species emphasizing developmental biology

Z01CP-05398-08 (LC) WAKEFIELD, L M NCI, NIH Function and regulation of latent forms of TGF-beta

Z01CP-05399-08 (LCC) RICE, J M NCI, NIH Oncogene expression in chemically induced tumors

Z01CP-05400-08 (EEB) BLATTNER, W A NCI, NIH Epidemiology of human lymphotrophic viruses--ATL, AIDS and cancer

Z01CP-05414-08 (LVC) BENVENISTE, R E NCI, NIH Characterization of retroviruses (TYpe-D and SIVs) isolated from primates

Z01CP-05417-07 (LVC) RAPP, U R NCI, NIH Characterization and expression of raf oncogenes in normal and tumor cells

Z01CP-05434-07 (LVC) MANN, D L NCI, NIH Immunology of AIDS and AIDS-related diseases

Z01CP-05435-07 (LHC) WESTON, A NCI, NIH Development of methods for human molecular dosimetry

Z01CP-05436-07 (LMC) GELBOIN, H V NCI, NIH Reaction phenotyping and monoclonal antibodies and cDNA expressed P-450s

Z01CP-05441-07 (LMO) PAPAS, T S NCI, NIH Characterization of the gene products of the ETS locus

Z01CP-05443-07 (LMO) PAPAS, T S NCI, NIH C-ets gene expression during cell proliferation and differentiation

Z01CP-05445-07 (CCTP) YUSPA, S H NCI, NIH Molecular regulation of epidermal specific differentiation products

Z01CP-05450-07 (LEC) HAGER, G L NCI, NIH Chromatin structure and gene expression

Z01CP-05453-07 (LEC) THORGEIRSSON, S S NCI, NIH Cellular and molecular biology of the hepatic stem cell compartment

Z01CP-05457-07 (LCMB) DIFIORE, P P NCI, NIH Growth factor receptors and mitogenic pathways in transformation

Z01CP-05469-06 (LCMB) KRUH, G NCI, NIH Identification of new tyrosine kinase oncogenes

Z01CP-05480-06 (LHC) WESTON, A NCI, NIH Molecular epidemiology of human lung cancer

Z01CP-05481-06 (LTVB) BOLEN, J B NCI, NIH Biochemical regulation of tyrosine protein kinases

Z01CP-05482-06 (LTVB) BAKER, C C NCI, NIH Control of papillomavirus late transcription

Z01CP-05488-06 (LCC) WAALKES, M P NCI, NIH Mechanisms of inorganic carcinogenesis

Z01CP-05496-07 (LEC) SNYDERWINE, E G NCI, NIH Food-derived arylamine carcinogens--Metabolic processing and DNA repair

Z01CP-05498-06 (BB) GAIL, M H NCI, NIH Consulting on epidemiologic methods

Z01CP-05499-06 (LB) POPESCU, N C NCI, NIH Chromosome alterations and proto-oncogenes transposition in carcinogenesis

Z01CP-05505-07 (LHC) HARRIS, C C NCI, NIH Neoplastic transformation of human epithelial cells by oncogenes

Z01CP-05518-05 (LTVB) BOLEN, J B NCI, NIH Transformation and gene regulation of the hamster papovavirus

Z01CP-05521-05 (LMC) GONZALEZ, F J NCI, NIH Polymorphic drug oxidation--The human CYP2D6 gene

Z01CP-05522-06 (LMC) KIMURA, S NCI, NIH Structure and characterization of human thyroid peroxidase

Z01CP-05526-05 (EEB) BRINTON, L A NCI, NIH Analytical investigations of selected issues in human cancer

Z01CP-05528-05 (LVC) DERSE, D NCI, NIH Mechanisms of the HTLV-1 and BLV rex proteins

Z01CP-05529-05 (LVC) YUHKI, N NCI, NIH Genetic and molecular organization of the MHC in the domestic cat

Z01CP-05531-05 (LVC) RAPP, U R NCI, NIH Characterization of the relationship between raf and growth regulators

Z01CP-05533-05 (LVC) FANNING-HEIDECKER, G NCI, NIH Domains involved in regulation of raf activity

Z01CP-05534-05 (LTCB) GALLO, R C NCI, NIH Mechanisms of HIV-1 pathogenesis--AIDS-associated Kaposi's sarcoma

Z01CP-05535-05 (LTCB) SARIN, P S NCI, NIH Retrovirus infection and treatment

Z01CP-05536-05 (LTCB) ROBERT-GUROFF, M NCI, NIH Humoral and cellular immune response to HIV for vaccine development

Z01CP-05537-05 (LTCB) SAXINGER, W C NCI, NIH Immunopathogenesis of human RNA and DNA viruses

Z01CP-05538-05 (LTCB) REITZ, M NCI, NIH HIV-1 envelope gene variability

Z01CP-05539-05 (LTCB) ARYA, S NCI, NIH Determinants of latency and pathogenicity of human retroviruses in AIDS

Z01CP-05541-04 (LHC) LECHNER, J F NCI, NIH In vitro model for human liver carcinogenesis studies

Z01CP-05543-04 (LHC) HARRIS, C C NCI, NIH Tumor suppression genes in human carcinogenesis

Z01CP-05546-04 (LCMB) LAROCHELLE, W J NCI, NIH Structural and functional characterization of v-sis gene product

Z01CP-05548-04 (LCMB) MIKI, T NCI, NIH Development of expression cloning system for oncogene cDNAs

Z01CP-05550-04 (LC) FLANDERS, K C NCI, NIH Localization of TGF-beta in tissues and its effects on gene expression

Z01CP-05552-04 (LB) EVANS, C H NCI, NIH Lymphokine modulation of human cervical epithelial cell carcinogenesis

Z01CP-05555-04 (LEC) HATFIELD, D L NCI, NIH Aminoacyl-tRNAs in HIV and other retroviral infected cells

Z01CP-05558-04 (LEC) THORGEIRSSON, S S NCI, NIH Negative growth regulators in normal and neoplastic liver

Z01CP-05559-04 (LEC) PARMELEE, D C NCI, NIH Plasma membrane proteins in normal and neoplastic rat hepatocytes

Z01CP-05561-04 (LMC) GONZALEZ, F NCI, NIH Transcriptional regulation of cytochrome P-450 genes

Z01CP-05562-04 (LMC) GONZALEZ, F NCI, NIH Identification and characterization of new human P-450

Z01CP-05564-04 (LMO) LAUTENBERGER, J A NCI, NIH Analysis of HIV gene expression

Z01CP-05565-04 (LMO) SETH, A NCI, NIH Biochemical and functional properties of the ets proto-oncogenes

PROJECT NO., ORGANIZATIONAL UNIT., INVESTIGATOR, ADDRESS, TITLE

Z01CP-05566-04 (LMO) SETH, A NCI, NIH Study of the biological and biochemical functions of ets proto-oncogenes

Z01CP-05569-04 (LMO) SCHWEINFEST, C W NCI, NIH Effect of c-myc on cellular gene expression

Z01CP-05570-04 (LMO) LAUTENBERGER, J A NCI, NIH Scale-up purification of HIV-1 and HIV-2 recombinant env polypeptides

Z01CP-05571-04 (LMO) BLAIR, D G NCI, NIH Studies of E26 avian v-ets and its cellular homologue in mouse cells

Z01CP-05572-04 (LMO) BLAIR, D K NCI, NIH Isolation of potential oncogenes from teleost tumors

Z01CP-05574-04 (LMO) WATSON, D K NCI, NIH Characterization of Drosophila melanogaster--Ets and ets-like genes

Z01CP-05576-04 (OD) THORGEIRSSON, U P NCI, NIH Expression of ras and collagenase in primary tumors vs metastases

Z01CP-05582-04 (LVC) RAPP, U R NCI, NIH Growth modulation and analysis of chemically induced tumors

Z01CP-05583-04 (LVC) DERSE, D NCI, NIH Transcriptional regulatory elements in equine anemia virus

Z01CP-05584-04 (LVC) SEUANEZ, H N NCI, NIH Genomic organization in nonhuman primates & other genet.studies

Z01CP-05585-03 (LMO) SCHWEINFEST, C W NCI,NIH Gene expression in colon carcinoma and polyposis

Z01CP-05587-03 (LMO) LAUTENBERGER, J A NCI,NIH Analysis of ets-related sequences in lower eukaryotes

Z01CP-05588-03 (LMO) SETH, A NCI,NIH Transgenic mouse model system for the Ets-1 and Ets-2 proto-oncogenes function

Z01CP-05591-03 (LMO) PAPAS, T S NCI,NIH Cellular function and regulation of ETS proteins

Z01CP-05593-03 (LMO) MAVROTHALASSITIS, G J NCI,NIH Transcription regulation of the human ETS-2 oncogene

Z01CP-05594-03 (LMO) SHIH, T Y NCI,NIH Suppression of transformation by dominant negative mutants of H-ras oncogene

Z01CP-05595-03 (LMO) BLAIR, D G NCI,NIH DNA topomerase 1 activity in retroviruses

Z01CP-05596-03 (LCMB) RUBIN, J S NCI,NIH Characterization of epithelial cell mitogens and their receptors

Z01CP-05599-03 (LEC) NAKATSUKASA, H NCI, NIH Mechanism of fibrogenesis and cirrhosis in rat liver

Z01CP-05600-03 (LEC) THORGEIRSSON, S S NCI, NIH Cloning of the rat mdr gene family and regulation in normal and neoplastic liver

Z01CP-05601-03 (LEC) HAGER, G L NCI,NIH Analysis of POMC tissue-specific expression and glucocorticoid repression

Z01CP-05605-03 (LMV) BRADY, J NCI,NIH Transformation by human CMV

Z01CP-05607-03 (LMO) GREEN, J E NCI,NIH HTLV-1 transgenic mice

Z01CP-05608-03 (OD) MACKAY, A R NCI, NIH Purification and further characteristics of tumor cell gelatinase

N01CP-05609-02 (**) DRZYZGULA, CATHY Biomedical computing--Design and implementation

Z01CP-05609-03 (OD) MACKAY, A R NCI, NIH Gelatinase / type IV collagenase response in normal and neoplastic cells to TPA

Z01CP-05611-03 (LHC) GERWIN, B I NCI,NIH In vitro studies of human mesothelial cell carcinogenesis

Z01CP-05614-03 (LTCB) NARA, P L NCI,NIH Immunobiology of HIV-1--Antigenic variation and vaccine development

Z01CP-05616-03 (LTCB) NARA, P L NCI,NIH Anti-HIV factors in animal sera and CD4 anti-receptor therapy for HIV-1

Z01CP-05617-03 (LC) ROBERTS, A NCI,NIH Characterization of the promoters of TGF-beta's 1, 2, and 3

N01CP-05618-05 (**) BEACH, JANIS Biomedical computing--Design and implementation

Z01CP-05618-03 (LVC) DEASE, D NCI,NIH Construction of a novel class of retroviral vectors based on BLV and HTLV

N01CP-05619-01 (**) CHEN, ANDY Resource to support the chemical, economic & biological needs of cancer etiology

N01CP-05620-02 (**) SAN, RICHARD In vitro evaluation of chemical candidates for in vivo testing

Z01CP-05620-03 (LVC) BENVENISTE, R E NCI,NIH Develop. of vaccines and antivir. against retrovirus infection in primate

N01CP-05621-06 (**) CLARK, ALICE Chemical carcinogen reference standard repository

N01CP-05622-05 (**) DALGARD, DAN Biological markers and therapy of tumors in primates

Z01CP-05622-02 (LC) JAKOWLEW, S B NCI, NIH Molecular identification of TGF-beta mRNAs

N01CP-05623-05 (**) LAIMING, VIRGINIA DR Support of biochemical epidemiology

Z01CP-05624-02 (LC) FLANDERS, K NCI, NIH Development and application of antibodies specific for isoforms of TGF-beta

N01CP-05625-04 (**) BURTON, ROBERT W Biomedical computing--Design and implementation

Z01CP-05625-02 (LB) WOODWORTH, C D NCI, NIH Regulation of cellular gene expression by human papillomaviruses

N01CP-05626-07 (**) LANNOM, LINDA Support of biostatistical and analytical studies

Z01CP-05626-02 (LCMB) AARONSON, S A NCI, NIH Characterization of the hepatocye growth factor receptor signaling pathways

Z01CP-05627-02 (LCMB) AARONSON, S A NCI, NIH Molecular cloning and characterization of plasminogen-like growth factor

Z01CP-05630-02 (LCMB) DI FIORE, P P NCI, NIH The gp185 erbB-2 and epidermal growth factor receptor signalling pathways

Z01CP-05631-02 (LCMB) FLEMING, T P NCI, NIH Isolation of the B-raf oncogene

Z01CP-05633-02 (LCMB) HEIDARAN, M A NCI, NIH Structural and functional characterization of aPDGFR gene product

N01CP-05634-02 (**) BING, LI DR Nutrition intervention trials in Linxian, China

Z01CP-05634-02 (LCMB) AARONSON, S A NCI, NIH Functional and structural characterization of human PDGF receptors

Z01CP-05641-02 (OD) THORGEIRSSON, U P NCI, NIH Use of nonhuman primates to study progression of hepatocellular carcinoma

Z01CP-05643-02 (LMV) DHAR, R NCI, NIH Yeast as a surrogate

organism to study the function of viral genes
Z01CP-05644-02 (LCMB) AARONSON, S A NCI, NIH Functional characterization of cytoplasmic domain of alphaPDGF receptor
Z01CP-05645-02 (LTCB) FRANCHINI, G NCI, NIH Molecular epidemiology and biological determinants of HTLV-1
Z01CP-05646-02 (ADBC) TABOR, E NCI, NIH Oncogene expression in cell lines derived from human hepatocellular carcinoma
Z01CP-05647-02 (ADBC) TABOR, E NCI, NIH Inhibition of hepatocellular carcinoma by deferoxamine
Z01CP-05651-02 (LMC) GONZALEZ, F J NCI,NIH Structure and function analysis of P-450
Z01CP-05652-02 (LVC) O'BRIEN, S NCI, NIH Mutational analysis of the cystic fibrosis gene
Z01CP-05653-02 (LVC) YUHKI, N NCI, NIH Molecular genetic analysis of homeobox genes in the domestic cat
Z01CP-05654-02 (LVC) FANNING-HEIDECKER, G NCI, NIH The function of the Nef protein of SIV/Mne
Z01CP-05655-02 (LVC) RAPP, U R NCI, NIH Mechanisms involved in Raf-1 activation by growth factors
Z01CP-05656-02 (LVC) RAPP, U R NCI, NIH B-raf protein kinase--Structure, expression and activation in vivo
Z01CP-05657-02 (LMO) RUSCETTI, S K NCI, NIH Molecular basis for the acute erythroleukemias induced by murine retroviruses
Z01CP-05658-02 (LMO) SHIH, T Y NCI, NIH The role of Ras oncogenes in signal transduction
Z01CP-05659-02 (LEC) WIRTH, P J NCI, NIH Detection of polypeptide and genetic alterations during hepatocarcinogenesis
Z01CP-05660-02 (LEC) HAGER, G L NCI, NIH Tissue-specific expression of MMTV and mechanism of protooncogene activation
Z01CP-05661-01 (LC) ANZANO, M A NCI, NIH Mechanism of prostate carcinogenesis and chemoprevention by retinoids
Z01CP-05662-01 (LTVB) MCBRIDE, A A NCI, NIH Characterization of the papillomavirus regulatory proteins
Z01CP-05663-01 (LTVB) SPALHOLZ, B NCI, NIH Papillomavirus transcriptional program
Z01CP-05664-01 (LMO) SCHWEINFEST, C W NCI, NIH Gene expression in ovarian neoplasia
Z01CP-05665-01 (LMO) WATSON, D K NCI, NIH Modulation of ETS function by protein:protein interactions
Z01CP-05666-01 (LMO) BURDETT, L A NCI, NIH Functional analysis of ets-related sequences by microinjection
Z01CP-05667-01 (LMO) PAPAS, T S NCI, NIH Molecular immunology
Z01CP-05668-01 (LMO) SETH, A K NCI, NIH Mechanism of suppressor gene deletions and mutations in breast cancer
Z01CP-05669-01 (LMO) PAPAS, T S NCI, NIH Mechanism of transcriptional activation by the human ETS family protein in vitro
Z01CP-05670-01 (LMO) GREEN, J E NCI, NIH Functional analysis of murine ets-1 and ets-2 genes in transgenic mice
Z01CP-05671-01 (LMO) GREEN, J E NCI, NIH Gene therapy for HIV and HTLV-I
Z01CP-05672-01 (LMO) BLAIR, D G NCI, NIH Analysis of cellular factors affecting retrovirus infection and growth
Z01CP-05673-01 (LCC) KEEFER, L K NCI, NIH Chemistry and biology of nitric oxide
Z01CP-05674-01 (LEP) DANIEL, L N NCI, NIH Gene damage induced by crystalline silica
Z01CP-05675-01 (LEC) MILLER, M J NCI, NIH Plasma proteins as early biomarkers of exposure to carcinogenic aromatic amines
Z01CP-05676-01 (LMC) KORZEKWA, K NCI, NIH Theoretical models for cytochrome P450 mediated oxidations
Z01CP-05677-01 (LMC) KORZEKWA, K NCI, NIH Studies on the active sites and mechanisms of cytochrome P450
Z01CP-05678-01 (LVC) O'BRIEN, S NCI, NIH Developing high resolution RFLPs for human genetic analysis
Z01CP-05679-01 (LVC) O'BRIEN, S NCI, NIH Identification of human genetic loci which influence susc. to HIV
Z01CP-05680-01 (LVC) STEPHENS, J C NCI, NIH Progress towards mapping the human genome
N01CP-05681-03 (**) HOLLY, ELIZABETH "Case study of cutaneous malignant melanoma: (human):
Z01CP-05681-01 (LVC) STEPHENS, J C NCI, NIH Estimation of heterozygosity for single probe, multi. DNA finger.
N01CP-05682-02 (**) HALPERN, ALLEN C Case control study of cutaneous malignant melanoma
Z01CP-05682-01 (LVC) YUHKI, N NCI, NIH Genetic and molecular characterization of nuclear mtDNA in felids
N01CP-05683-01 (**) HANSON, LOUISE Case control study of cutaneous malignant melanoma
Z01CP-05683-01 (LVC) DERSE, D NCI, NIH Structure, function and mechanism of lentivirus TAT proteins
N01CP-05684-02 (**) HAY, ROBERT J Procurement of transformed lymphocytes, lymphoblastoid
Z01CP-05684-01 (LVC) RAPP, U NCI, NIH c-Raf-1 is required for AP-1/Ets-dependent transcription
Z01CP-05685-01 (LVC) RAPP, U NCI, NIH Raf-1 activates transcription from the HIV-long terminal repeat
N01CP-05686-06 (**) STEUER, ANTON F Services in virology, tissue culture, & immunology
Z01CP-05686-01 (LVC) RAPP, U NCI, NIH v-Raf regulation of lineage commitment in hematopoietic cells
Z01CP-05687-01 (LVC) RAPP, U NCI, NIH Role of ras in raf coupling to transmembrane receptor tyrosine kinases
Z01CP-05688-01 (LTCB) RFRANCHINI, G NCI, NIH Molecular approaches for development of an HIV vaccine--Rhesus Macaques model
Z01CP-05689-01 (LTCB) KLOTMAN, M E NCI, NIH HTLV-1 and adult T cell leukemia--Pathophysiology of HTLV-1 infection
Z01CP-05690-01 (LTCB) NARA, P L NCI, NIH Characterization of the neutralization reaction with antibody against HIV-1
Z01CP-05691-01 (LMV) BRADY, J NCI, NIH Soluble HTLV-I Tax1 protein stimulates proliferation of human lymphocytes
Z01CP-05692-01 (LMV) BRADY, J NCI, NIH Induction of NF-kB after exposure of lymphoid cells to soluble Tax1
Z01CP-05693-01 (ADBC) TABOR, E NCI, NIH Development of systems to detect PCR contamination
Z01CP-05694-01 (ADBC) TABOR, E NCI, NIH Immunohistochemical studies of human hepatocellular carcinoma
Z01CP-05695-01 (ADBC) TABOR, E NCI, NIH PCR for detection of hepatitis B virus in sera from patients with HCC
Z01CP-05696-01 (ADBC) TABOR, E NCI, NIH Role of pre-S2 promoter of HBV studied in hepatocellular carcinoma cell line
Z01CP-05697-01 (ADBC) TABOR, E NCI, NIH Inhibition by desferrioxamine of in vitro replication of HIV-1
Z01CP-05698-01 (OD) CHILUKURI, N R NCI, NIH Identification and characterization of new endothelial proteinase inhibitors
Z01CP-05699-01 (OD) MACKAY, A R NCI, NIH The plasmin system basement membrane degradation and tumor invasion
Z01CP-05700-01 (OD) THORGEIRSSON, U P NCI, NIH Tumor-endothelial cell interactions--In vitro and in vivo models
N01CP-05707-03 (**) BARTLETT, KIRBY K Develop and purify monoclonal and polyclonal antibodies
Z01CP-07148-05 (LTCB) GALLO, R C NCI, NIH Studies on T-cell malignacies, lymphomas and AIDS
Z01CP-07149-08 (LTCB) REITZ, M S NCI, NIH Molecular biological studies of human pathogenic viruses
N01CP-15600-00 (**) NORTHRUP, DORIS R Extended evaluation of mortality experience of workers at Hill Air Force Base
N01CP-15602-00 (**) CWI, JOAN S Support services for clinical epidemiologic studies
N01CP-15618-00 (**) ZHENG, YUNKAI Cellular and molecular studies of human hepatocarcinogenesis in China
N01CP-15620-00 (**) XU, GUANG-WEI Precancerous gastric lesions in relation to stomach cancer in china
N01CP-15622-00 (**) BING, LI DR Nutrition intervention trials in Linxian, China
N01CP-15623-00 (**) TRUMP, BENJAMIN F Resource for human esophageal tissues and cells from donors
N01CP-15628-00 (**) IYPE, P THOMAS Biological specimen repository for patients at high risk for cancer
N01CP-15641-00 (**) HART, C Operation of a registry of tumors in lower animals
N01CP-15643-02 (**) SARNGADHARAN, DR M G Purify and characterize HIV viral proteins
N01CP-15644-03 (**) BRADBURY, DR RICHARD P Test the immune response of viral antigens in subhumans
N01CP-15652-00 (**) HOLM, LARS E Thyroid nodularity following exposure to diagnostic I-131
N01CP-15657-00 (**) BRADBURY, RICHARD Transplacental carcinogenesis and tumor promotion
N01CP-15665-00 (**) ROBISON, ALICE Repository for storage and distribution of biological reagents
N01CP-15672-03 (**) ROSENTHAL, JEANNE Support services for epidemiologic studies
N01CP-15673-00 (**) MANDEL, JACK S Cancer risk in X-ray technologists--Second survey for incidence
N01CP-15674-01 (**) SLY, LINDA Laboratory rodent and rabbit facility
N01CP-15690-00 (**) ROBINETTE, C DENNIS Studies of cancer in veteran twin registry
N01CP-15723-00 (**) SIGMAN, CAROLINE C Survey of compounds which have been tested for carcinogenic activity
N01CP-15732-00 (**) WILEY, JAMES Synthesis of derivatives of polynuclear aromatic hydrocarbons
N01CP-15737-00 (**) TANGA, MARY J Synthesis of derivatives of polynuclear aromatic hydrocarbons
N01CP-15750-00 (**) CLARK, MARY Technical and logistical support services
N01CP-31006-25 (**) HANCHARD, BARRIE DR Human T-cell leukemia/lymphoma virus in Jamaica
N01CP-41026-06 (**) REEVES, WILLIAM C Investigations of cervical cancer in Latin America
N01CP-51001-09 (**) RIGGS, JOHN L Breeding and production of 129J and NFR mice
N01CP-61012-08 (**) STEWART, KAREN Support services for clinical epidemiologic studies
N01CP-61022-11 (**) HULL, BARBARA DR Epidemiology of human T-cell leukemia/lymphoma virus
N01CP-71007-07 (**) RUEHLE, PAUL Synthesis of selected chemical carcinogens
N01CP-71018-06 (**) SANDBERG, AVERY A Solid tumor chromosome analysis of persons at high risk
N01CP-71025-09 (**) IYPE, P THOMAS DR Biological speciman repository for patients at high risk
N01CP-71081-05 (**) SPARKES, ROBERT S Genetic factors in persons at high risk of cancer-genetic
N01CP-71096-02 (**) ERZINE, SANDI Case control study, residential exposure to radon
N01CP-71098-01 (**) CADELL, DIANE Baseline survey for community intervention trials
N01CP-71108-06 (**) REIST, ELMER J Synthesis of selected chemical carcinogens
N01CP-71114-05 (**) CAMPBELL, BEVERLY Survey of compounds which have been tested for carcinogenic activity
N01CP-71126-04 (**) JHANWAR, SURESH C Solid tumor chromosome analysis of persons at high risk
N01CP-71127-06 (**) WOOD KLINGER, KATHERINE Genetic factors in persons at high risk of cancer
N01CP-71128-08 (**) LAZEN, AL Epidemiology of cancer among atomic bomb survivors
N01CP-73722-09 (**) SARNGADHARAN, MANGALAS G Provision of tissues and cells
N01CP-73723-13 (**) SARNGADHARAN, MANGALAS G Cell cultures, growth factors and type C virus protein
N01CP-73724-07 (**) TSAI, SHIEN Preparation and supply of fresh and cultured mammalian cells
N01CP-73725-08 (**) MARKHAM, P D Preparation and purification of viral components

PROJECT NO., ORGANIZATIONAL UNIT., INVESTIGATOR, ADDRESS, TITLE

N01CP-85603-07 (**) LEVIN, ARTHUR G Epidemiology survey of human retroviruses
N01CP-85604-06 (**) WILSON, DANNY Support services for radiation and related studies
N01CP-85605-17 (**) CLARK, MARY Support services for the division of cancer etiology
N01CP-85606-03 (**) YEAGER, HENRY Resource for procurement of human tissues from donors
N01CP-85625-02 (**) HOLOWATY, E J Second cancer following treatment for non-Hodgkin's lymphoma
N01CP-85626-02 (**) LYNCH, CHARLES F Second cancer following treatment for cervical cancer
N01CP-85636-03 (**) ADAMI, HANS-OLOV Second cancer following treatment for non-Hodgkin's lymphoma
N01CP-85638-02 (**) TEPPO, LYLY Second cancer following treatment for cervical cancer
N01CP-85639-01 (**) STORM, HANS H Second cancer following treatment for cervical cancer
N01CP-85645-06 (**) PETERSON, WARD D Cell culture identification -- Cytologic/karyotypic
N01CP-85649-09 (**) HARRIS, BENJAMIN S H III Support services for retrovirus epidemiology
N01CP-85651-07 (**) CADELL, DIANE Breast and other cancers following X-rays for scoliosis
N01CP-87213-11 (**) MARKHAM, PHILLIP D DR Provision of animal facilities and performance of routine tests
N01CP-87214-14 (**) SARNGADHARAN, MANGALAS G Provision of purified AIDS virus proteins and nonhuman primate
N01CP-95602-02 (**) KROSS, BURTON C Exposure assessment methods for pesticides
N01CP-95604-07 (**) LIFF, JONATHAN Breast cancer in women under the age of 45 field center
N01CP-95605-05 (**) MAFFEO, CARLA E Breast cancer in women under the age of 45
N01CP-95606-04 (**) HIATT, ROBERT DR Studies of environ can utilizing prepaid health plans
N01CP-95608-03 (**) GARDNER, SUSAN Support services for childhood leukemia and magnetic fields
N01CP-95612-06 (**) BARNETT, MAJORIE Support for studies of HIV and related viruses
N01CP-95614-05 (**) STOVALL, MARILYN Radiation dosimetry for epidemiologic studies
N01CP-95618-08 (**) MORAN, FRANK X Support of occupational studies
N01CP-95624-02 (**) TRUMP, BENJAMIN Resource for collection and evaluation of human tissue
N01CP-95626-08 (**) JOSEPHS, STEVEN F Recombinant viral proteins produced in E Coli
N01CP-95648-01 (**) GLASS, ANDREW Diagnostic x-rays and risk of thyroid cancer and adenomas
N01CP-95651-02 (**) YODER, CRAIG R Dosimetry support for studies of radiation workers
N01CP-95663-06 (**) RINGER, DANIEL C Laboratory support for processing and storage of biological specimens
N01CP-95670-04 (**) MOORE, MICHAEL DR Resource for xenotransplantation & evaluation of tissues
N01CP-95671-03 (**) DALING, JANET R Breast cancer in women under the age of 45 field centers
N01CP-95672-04 (**) SCHOENBERG, JANET B Breast cancer in women under the age of 45 field centers
N01CP-95675-05 (**) GLASS, ANDREW DR Studies on environmental cancer utilizing prepaid health
N01CP-95680-04 (**) ZIEL, HARRY K DR Studies of environmental cancer utilizing prepaid health
Z01CT-00001-21 (LSM) DUNHAM, G DCRT, NIH Automatic data processing of medical language
Z01CT-00002-22 (LSM) BAILEY, J J DCRT, NIH Computer aided analysis of electrocardiography
Z01CT-00003-21 (LAS) DOUGLAS, M A DCRT, NIH Computer systems and applications for nuclear medicine
Z01CT-00004-21 (LAS) POTTALA, E W DCRT, NIH Analysis of physiological signals
Z01CT-00008-18 (LSM) SHAPIRO, M DCRT, NIH Computer graphics and applications
Z01CT-00010-17 (LAS) SHRAGER, R I DCRT, NIH Mathematical and computational methods for solving nonlinear equations
Z01CT-00011-18 (LSM) HUTCHINSON, G DCRT, NIH Discrete mathematics and applications
Z01CT-00013-18 (LSM) MOSIMANN, J E DCRT, NIH Multivariate statistical analysis
Z01CT-00014-25 (PSL) WEISS, G DCRT, NIH Instrumental analysis
Z01CT-00017-19 (PSL) NOSSAL, R DCRT, NIH Biophysical analysis
Z01CT-00024-15 (PSL) WEISS, G DCRT, NIH Studies in applied mathematics and statistics
Z01CT-00026-16 (PSL) PARSEGIAN, V DCRT, NIH Molecular forces in celluar organization and function
Z01CT-00039-15 (LSM) MALLEY, J D DCRT, NIH Algebraic methods in statistics
Z01CT-00042-14 (LAS) DOUGLAS, M A DCRT, NIH Image processing in electron microscopy, x-ray, and EEL spectroscopy
Z01CT-00045-14 (LAS) FLETCHER, J E DCRT, NIH The solution of reaction diffusion systems in biology
Z01CT-00090-12 (CSL) TRUS, B L DCRT, NIH Molecular graphics, computer modeling, and sequence analysis
Z01CT-00092-10 (CSL) TRUS, B L DCRT, NIH Structural biology--Image processing of electron micrographs
Z01CT-00111-10 (LSM) CAMPBELL, G DCRT, NIH Nonparametric statistics
Z01CT-00130-07 (PSL) LEE, B DCRT, NIH Computer graphics
Z01CT-00132-08 (LSM) MOSIMANN, J E DCRT, NIH Consulting services
Z01CT-00137-08 (CSL) VIVINO, M A DCRT, NIH Acquisition and analysis of ophthalmic images
Z01CT-00138-08 (CSL) KEMPNER, K M DCRT, NIH Brain image registration
Z01CT-00139-08 (CSL) GORLEN, K E DCRT, NIH Advanced laboratory workstation
Z01CT-00148-07 (CSL) MARTINO, R L DCRT, NIH Neuromagnetometer computer system
Z01CT-00155-06 (PSL) LEE, B DCRT, NIH Theoretical study of protein stability
Z01CT-00173-05 (LAS) FLETCHER, J E DCRT, NIH Cellular kinetics models of the human immune system
Z01CT-00176-06 (PSL) LEE, B DCRT, NIH Protein folding
Z01CT-00189-01 (LSM) MALLEY, J D DCRT, NIH Quantum statistical interference
Z01CT-00199-02 (CSL) KEMPNER, K M DCRT, NIH Image management and communication system
Z01CT-00200-02 (CSL) MARTINO, R L DCRT, NIH Highly parallel computer system
Z01CT-00201-02 (CSL) TATE, R L DCRT, NIH Molecular disease branch lipid analysis sample tracking system
Z01CT-00203-02 (CSL) FREDRICKSON, H A DCRT, NIH 100 Channel high speed spectrophotometer
Z01CT-00204-02 (CSL) DELEO, J M DCRT, NIH Computer assisted patient interviewing in clinical pharmacy
Z01CT-00206-02 (CSL) POWELL, J I DCRT, NIH Computer support for molecular biology sequencing and genetic mapping
Z01CT-00207-02 (CSL) POWELL, J I DCRT, NIH Laboratory analysis package
Z01CT-00218-02 (OD) CHU, E M DCRT, NIH Information retrieval systems on local area networks
Z01CT-00221-01 (CSL) DELEO, J M DCRT,NIH Breast cancer patient survival prediction--A neural network approach
Z01CT-00222-01 (CSL) VIVINO, M A DCRT,NIH High resolution imaging system
Z01CT-00223-01 (LAS) BAILEY, J J DCRT, NIH Clinical and research use of evoked potentials
Z01CT-00224-01 (LAS) FLETCHER, J E DCRT, NIH Mathematical modeling systems
Z01CT-00225-01 (PSL) LEE, B DCRT, NIH Computing with an artificial neural network
Z01CT-00226-01 (OD) MUNSON, P J DCRT, NIH Computational methods for molecular biology, DNA sequence, and protein structure
Z01CT-00227-01 (OD) MUNSON, P J DCRT, NIH Statistical & computational methods for physiology, pharmacology, & endocrinology
Z01CT-00228-01 (OD) MICHAELS, G DCRT, NIH Logic programing-based query system chromosomal information
Z01CT-00229-01 (OD) MICHAELS, G DCRT, NIH Prototype genome informatics systems
Z01CT-00230-01 (OD) MICHAELS, G DCRT, NIH Understanding protein-nucleic acid interactions
Z01CT-00231-01 (CSL) BARDEN, L K DCRT,NIH Flow cytometry advanced data analysis
Z01CT-00232-01 (OD) BROOKS, B R DCRT, NIH Molecular dynamics simulations of biological macromolecules
Z01CT-00233-01 (OD) BROOKS, B R DCRT, NIH Development of theoretical methods for studying biological macromolecules
Z01CT-00234-01 (OD) BROOKS, B R DCRT, NIH Development of advanced computer hardware and software
Z01CT-00235-01 (OD) FELDMAN, R J DCRT, NIH Simulating the behavior of the electronic grant application process
Z01CT-00236-01 (OD) FELDMAN, R J DCRT, NIH Modeling the mechanisms of protein folding
Z01CT-00237-01 (OD) FELDMAN, R J DCRT, NIH Applying parallelized reasoning to biological problems
Z01DA-00001-06 (BPL) GOLDBERG, S R ARC, NIDA Control of behavior by drug injection
Z01DA-00002-06 (CDM) CONE, E J ARC, NIDA Validity studies of commercial drug screening assays
Z01DA-00003-06 (BPL) GOLDBERG, S R ARC, NIDA Effects of drugs on schedule-controlled behavior of experimental animals
Z01DA-00004-05 (BDL) HENNINGFIELD, J E ARC, NIDA Comparative self-administration (monkeys and human)--Nicotine and cocaine
Z01DA-00005-05 (BDL) HENNINGFIELD, J E ARC, NIDA Abuse liability of smokeless tobacco products
Z01DA-00006-04 (BDL) HENNINGFIELD, J E ARC, NIDA Triazolam self-administration--Effects of yohimbine pretreatment
Z01DA-00007-05 (BDL) HENNINGFIELD, J E ARC, NIDA Effects of commonly used drugs on behavioral performance in normal subjects
K05DA-00008-17 (SRCD) HOLTZMAN, STEPHEN G EMORY UNIVERSITY SCH OF MEDICI ATLANTA, GA 30322 Behavioral pharmacology of opioids and caffeine
Z01DA-00008-04 (BDL) HENNINGFIELD, J E ARC, NIDA Behavioral performance and physiologic effects of drugs--Atropine and diazepam
Z01DA-00009-04 (BPL) SCHINDLER, C W ARC, NIDA Cardiovascular changes induced by cocaine
Z01DA-00010-06 (BDL) HENNINGFIELD, J E ARC, NIDA Behavioral and pharmacologic factors in nicotine replacement for tobacco dependen
Z01DA-00011-06 (BDL) HENNINGFIELD, J E ARC, NIDA Physiologic dependence to tobacco--Cigarette withdrawal and nicotine substitution
Z01DA-00012-02 (BPL) MARLEY, R J ARC, NIDA Genetic factors in response to chronic drug treatment
Z01DA-00013-05 (BDL) HAERTZEN, C A ARC, NIDA Archival data base project
Z01DA-00014-04 (NEI) DAX, E M ARC, NIDA Inhalable nitrites--Immune function and abuse potential
Z01DA-00015-02 (NEI) PILOTTE, N S ARC, NIDA The effects of cocaine on dopamine release from hypothalamic neurons
Z01DA-00016-02 (NEI) PILOTTE, N S ARC, NIDA Effects of cocaine and withdrawal from cocaine on central receptors
K05DA-00017-16 (DAPA) BENTLER, PETER M UNIV OF CALIFORNIA FRANZ HALL, 405 HILGARD AVENUE LOS ANGELES, CA 90024-1563 New psychometric methods for substance abuse research
R01DA-00017-27 (DABR) SIMON, ERIC J NEW YORK UNIV MEDICAL CTR DEPARTMENT OF PSYCHIATRY NEW YORK, N Y 10016 Effects of morphine and

PROJECT NO., ORGANIZATIONAL UNIT., INVESTIGATOR, ADDRESS, TITLE

PROJECT NO., ORGANIZATIONAL UNIT., INVESTIGATOR, ADDRESS, TITLE

analogues on cell metabolism
Z01DA-00017-02 (NEI) DAX, E M ARC, NIDA Cardiac effects of IV cocaine administration
K05DA-00018-16 (SRCD) BRADY, JOSEPH V JOHNS HOPKINS UNIV SCH OF MED 720 RUTLAND AVE BALTIMORE, MD 21205 Environmental-behavioral interactions and drug taking
Z01DA-00018-02 (NEI) DAX, E M ARC, NIDA Effect of metachlorophenylpiperazine on rat brain receptors, neurotransmitters
Z01DA-00019-01 (NEI) DAX, E M ARC, NIDA HIV prevalence--In depth survey of Baltimore
K05DA-00020-14 (SRCD) LEE, NANCY M UNIVERSITY OF MINNESOTA 3-260 MILLARD HALL MINNEAPOLIS, MN 55455 Beta-endorphin receptor and dynorphin receptor
Z01DA-00020-04 (NEI) DAX, E M ARC, NIDA Cannabinoids and their effects on the immune system and cognitive function
Z01DA-00021-04 (NEI) DAX, E ARC, NIDA Neuroendocrine secretion during cocaine withdrawal
Z01DA-00022-04 (NEI) DAX, E ARC, NIDA The effects of cocaine on hormone secretin from the anterior pituitary
Z01DA-00023-05 (CDM) CONE, E J ARC, NIDA Detection of drugs of abuse in human saliva
Z01DA-00024-03 (BDL) HENNINGFIELD, J E ARC, NIDA Opioid self-administration--Humans compared to animals
Z01DA-00025-03 (BDL) HENNINGFIELD, J E ARC, NIDA Acquisition of dependence to cigarettes and smokeless tobacco
Z01DA-00026-02 (BDL) HENNINGFIELD, J E ARC, NIDA Assessment of opioid agonists and antagonists
Z01DA-00028-02 (BDL) HENNINGFIELD, J E ARC, NIDA Assessment of mazindol for abuse liability
Z01DA-00029-02 (BDL) HENNINGFIELD, J E ARC, NIDA Interaction between ethanol and prostaglandin synthetase inhibitors
Z01DA-00030-02 (BDL) HENNINGFIELD, J E ARC, NIDA Passive tobacco smoke--Nicotine absorption, subjective effects and performance
Z01DA-00031-02 (BDL) HENNINGFIELD, J E ARC, NIDA Effects of nicotine in nonsmokers
Z01DA-00032-02 (BDL) UHL, G R ARC, NIDA Dopaminergic lesions and subjective effects of methylphenidate
K05DA-00033-15 (SRCD) DYKSTRA, LINDA A UNIVERSITY OF NORTH CAROLINA DEPARTMENT OF PSYCHOLOGY CHAPEL HILL, N C 27514 Opioid analgesics--pharmacological and behavioral factors
Z01DA-00033-02 (BDL) HENNINGFIELD, J E ARC, NIDA Nicotine patch--Effects on smoking subjective and physiologic functions
Z01DA-00034-02 (BDL) HENNINGFIELD, J E ARC, NIDA Opoid self-administration in humans
Z01DA-00035-02 (BDL) HENNINGFIELD, J E ARC, NIDA Why do substance abusers seek help? What are their worries about that help?
Z01DA-00036-06 (BDL) HENNINGFIELD, J E ARC, NIDA Effects of drugs on cigarette smoking and responses to nicotine
Z01DA-00037-01 (BDL) HENNINGFIELD, J E ARC, NIDA Physiologic, cognitive and subject effects of commonly abused drugs
Z01DA-00038-01 (BDL) PICKWORTH, W B ARC, NIDA Transcranial electrostimulation therapy (TCET) during smoking cessation
Z01DA-00039-01 (BDL) PICKWORTH, W B ARC, NIDA Effects of ethanol and pentobarbital and interactions with indomethacin
Z01DA-00040-01 (BDL) HENNINGFIELD, J E ARC, NIDA Opoid agonist and antagonist sensitivity in opiate-experienced individuals
Z01DA-00041-01 (BDL) HENNINGFIELD, J E ARC, NIDA Discriminative stimulus effects of stimulant drugs
Z01DA-00042-01 (BDL) HENNINGFIELD, J E ARC, NIDA Effect of reinforcement contingencies on human task performance
K05DA-00043-15 (SRCD) BURSTEIN, SUMNER H U OF MASSACHUSETTS MED CENTER 55 LAKE AVENUE NORTH WORCESTER, MASS 01655 Mechanism of action of cannabis
Z01DA-00044-01 (BDL) HENNINGFIELD, J E ARC, NIDA Psychotropic properties of stimulants and sedatives--Discriminative properties
Z01DA-00045-01 (BDL) HENNINGFIELD, J E ARC, NIDA Lobeline and nicotine--Subjective, physiologic and kinetic effects
Z01DA-00046-01 (BDL) HENNINGFIELD, J E ARC, NIDA Arterial kinetics of smoked cocaine
Z01DA-00047-01 (BDL) HENNINGFIELD, J E ARC, NIDA Outpatient drug discrimination
Z01DA-00048-03 (BDL) HENNINGFIELD, J E ARC, NIDA Cholinergic agonists and antagonists
K05DA-00049-14 (DACB) KREEK, MARY J THE ROCKEFELLER UNIVERSITY 1230 YORK AVE NEW YORK, N Y 10021-6399 Addictive drugs--Pharmacology and physiology
Z01DA-00049-02 (NEI) PILOTTE, N S ARC, NIDA The effects of cocaine on prolactin secretion from single cells of the pituitary
K05DA-00050-14 (SRCD) BIGELOW, GEORGE E FRANCIS SCOTT KEY MEDICAL CTR 4940 EASTERN AVENUE BALTIMORE, MD 21224 Human behavioral pharmacology of drug abuse
K05DA-00053-15 (DACB) JONES, REESE T UNIVERSITY OF CALIFORNIA 401 PARNASSUS AVENUE SAN FRANCISCO, CA 94143 Neuropsychopharmacology of altered consciousness
K05DA-00060-12 (DABR) WEINSTEIN, HAREL MT SINANI SCHOOL OF MEDICINE BOX 1218, 1 GUSTAVE L LEVY PLA NEW YORK, NY 10029 Molecular determinants for the action of hallucinogens
K05DA-00064-12 (SRCD) MENDELSON, JACK H MCLEAN HOSPITAL 115 MILL STREET BELMONT, MA 02178 Biobehavioral studies of narcotics abuse in humans
K05DA-00074-12 (DABR) SNYDER, SOLOMON H JOHNS HOPKINS SCHOOL OF MED 725 NORTH WOLFE STREET BALTIMORE, MD 21205 Neurotransmitter receptors
K05DA-00079-19 (DABR) GROVES, PHILIP M UNIV OF CALIFORNIA, SAN DIEGO 9500 GILMAN DRIVE LA JOLLA, CA 92093-0603 Novel modes of actions of abused drugs
K05DA-00081-11 (DAPA) KANDEL, DENISE B COLUMBIA UNIVERSITY 722 W 168TH STREET NEW YORK, NY 10032 Epidemiological/familial aspects of drug use
Z01DA-00081-03 (CTL) COVI, L ARC, NIDA Desipramine, fluoxetine and bromocriptine/cocaine & PCP abuse therapy
R01DA-00085-19 (SRCD) SEIDEN, LEWIS S UNIVERSITY OF CHICAGO 947 EAST 58TH STREET CHICAGO, IL 60637 The effects of chronic methamphetamine administration
K02DA-00088-10 (DABR) SPEALMAN, ROGER D NEW ENG REG PRIMATE RES CENTER ONE PINE HILL SOUTH SOUTHBOROUGH, MASS 01772 Behavioral effects of abused drugs
K05DA-00089-09 (DACB) ROUNSAVILLE, BRUCE J YALE UNIVERSITY 904 HOWARD AVE, SUITE 2 A NEW HAVEN, CT 06519 Diagnosis & treatment of substance use disorders
Z01DA-00090-02 (CTL) JOHNSON, R E ARC, NIDA Buprenorphine/methadone comparison--Maintenance and detoxification
R37DA-00091-21 (DABR) WEI, EDWARD T UNIVERSITY OF CALIFORNIA WARREN HALL BERKELEY, CA 94720 Corticotropin-releasing factor--Anti-inflamatory analgesic
Z01DA-00091-01 (CTL) CHESKIN, L J ARC, NIDA Nalmefene glucuronide as a selective antagonist of gut opioid action
K05DA-00095-09 (DABR) CICERO, THEODORE J WASHINGTON UNIVERSITY ST LOUIS, MO 63110 Substance abuse--Neuroendocrinological aspects
K05DA-00097-06 (DABR) MAINS, RICHARD E JOHNS HOPKINS UNIV SCH OF MED 725 N WOLFE ST, WBSB 914 BALTIMORE, MD 21205 Plasticity and cell biology of peptide production
K05DA-00098-06 (DABR) EIPPER, ELIZABETH A JOHNS HOPKINS U SCH OF MED 725 N. WOLFE STREET BALTIMORE, MD 21205 Regulation of peptidergic neurons & endocrine cells
Z01DA-00098-02 (CTL) COVI, L ARC, NIDA Impact of differing intensities of drug abuse counseling
K05DA-00099-06 (DABR) KORNETSKY, CONAN BOSTON UNIV SCHOOL OF MED 80 EAST CONCORD STREET BOSTON, MA 02118 Brain stimulation models of drug abuse
K02DA-00100-06 (SRCD) SZETO, HAZEL H CORNELL UNIV MEDICAL COLLEGE 1300 YORK AVENUE NEW YORK, N Y 10021 Maternal-fetal pharmacology of the drugs of abuse
Z01DA-00100-01 (CTL) CHESKIN, L J ARC, NIDA Comparison of detoxification treatment for opiate addiction
K05DA-00101-06 (SRCD) MELLO, NANCY K MC LEAN HOSPITAL 115 MILL STREET BELMONT, MASS 02178 Biobehavioral studies of substance abuse
Z01DA-00101-05 (BGL) ELMER, G I ARC, NIDA Pharmacogenetics--Acute responses to drug administration
Z01DA-00102-05 (BGL) ELMER, G I ARC, NIDA Pharmacogenetic factors in drug reinforced behavior
Z01DA-00103-01 (PBL) KATZ, J L ARC, NIDA Basic mechanisms of cocaine effects
Z01DA-00104-01 (PBL) WITKIN, J M ARC, NIDA Drug development
Z01DA-00105-01 (PBL) KATZ, J L ARC, NIDA Behavioral pharmacology of dopamine systems
K02DA-00106-06 (DABR) MILLER, RICHARD J THE UNIVERSITY OF CHICAGO 947 EAST 58TH STREET CHICAGO, IL 60637 Cellular mechanism of opiate action
Z01DA-00106-01 (CTL) BALL, J ARC, NIDA Evaluation of methadone maintenance treatment for opiate dependence
Z01DA-00107-05 (MPL) KUHAR, M J ARC, NIDA Drug receptors in vivo
Z01DA-00108-04 (MPL) KUHAR, M J ARC, NIDA The cocaine receptor
K02DA-00109-07 (SRCD) HUGHES, JOHN R UNIVERSITY OF VERMONT DEPARTMENT OF PSYCHIATRY BURLINGTON, VT 05405 Behavioral/epidemiological/treatment studies of drug use
Z01DA-00110-03 (NEI) DAX, E M ARC, NIDA Development of monoclonal antibodies to drugs and hormones
Z01DA-00111-03 (NEI) DAX, E M ARC, NIDA Neuroendocrine correlates of HIV infection and the development of ARC and AIDS
K02DA-00112-05 (DACB) KOSTEN, THOMAS R APT, FDN 904 HOWARD AVE - SUITE 2 E NEW HAVEN, CT 06519 Agonist to antagonist--new approaches
Z01DA-00112-04 (MPL) KUHAR, M J ARC, NIDA Drug receptors, neurotransmitters and addiction
Z01DA-00113-03 (NEI) DAX, E M ARC, NIDA Neuroendocrine correlates of aggressive/impulsive behavior
K05DA-00114-02 (SRCD) SMITH, JAMES E BOWMAN GRAY SCHOOL OF MEDICINE 300 S HAWTHORNE ROAD WINSTON-SALEM, NC 27103 Neurobiological mechanisms of drug reinforcement
Z01DA-00114-02 (MNL) UHL, G R ARC, NIDA Receptor cDNA expression cloning using ligand autoradiographic screening
K02DA-00115-06 (SRCD) LUKAS, SCOTT E ADARC/MCLEAN HOSPITAL 115 MILL STREET BELMONT, MA 02178 Biobehavioral and pharmacologic analysis of drug abuse
Z01DA-00115-03 (MNL) UHL, G R ARC, NIDA Receptor cDNA expression cloning using Xenopus oocyte expression
K02DA-00116-04 (SRCD) COLLINS, ALLAN C UNIVERSITY OF COLORADO INSTITUTE FOR BEHAVIORAL GENET BOULDER, COLO 80309 Genetic control of nicotinic receptor function
Z01DA-00116-03 (MNL) UHL, G R ARC, NIDA Genes related to drug abuse--Regulation of opioid peptide genes
K02DA-00117-05 (SRCD) WOOD, RONALD W NEW YORK UNIVERSITY MED CTR DEPT OF ENVIRONMENTAL MED NEW YORK, NY 10016 Behavioral pharmacology & toxicology of abused inhalants
Z01DA-00117-02 (MNL) UHL, G R ARC, NIDA Genes related to drug abuse II--Central brain pathways of reinforcement/reward
K02DA-00118-03 (SRCD) MOSBERG, HENRY I UNIVERSITY OF MICHIGAN ANN ARBOR, MI 48109-1065 Conformational analysis of receptor selective opioids
K05DA-00119-04 (SRCD) DEADWYLER, SAMUEL A BOWMAN GRAY SCHOOL OF MEDICNE 300 S HAWTHORNE ROAD WINSTON-SALEM, N C 27103 Hippocampal correlates of drug abuse
K02DA-00124-04 (SRCD) LARSON, ALICE A UNIVERSITY OF MINNESOTA ST PAUL, MN 55108 Nociceptive transmission in the spinal cord
K02DA-00131-04 (DABR) HENRIKSEN, STEVEN J SCRIPPS RESEARCH INSTITUTE RISC, 10666 N TORREY PINES RD LA JOLLA, CA 92037 Cellular neurobiology of endorphins--role in drug abuse
K02DA-00132-03 (DACB) YOUNG, ALICE M WAYNE STATE UNIVERSITY DETROIT, MI 48202 Behavioral pharmacology of tolerance processes
K05DA-00136-03 (EPS) KAPLAN, HOWARD B TEXAS A & M UNIVERSITY COLLEGE STATION, TX 77843 Drug abuse and other deviant adaptations to stress
K02DA-00138-03 (DABR) PASTERNAK, GAVRIL W SLOAN KETTERING INST/CNCR RES 1275 YORK AVENUE NEW YORK, NY 10021 Opiate receptor pharmacology

PROJECT NO., ORGANIZATIONAL UNIT., INVESTIGATOR, ADDRESS, TITLE

K01DA-00139-03 (DAPA) **HSER, YIH-ING** UCLA DRUG ABUSE RESEARCH GROUP 1100 GLENDON AVE, SUITE 763 LOS ANGELES, CA 90024-3511 Innovative statistical application to drug abuse data
Z01DA-00139-01 (PTL) **GORELICK, D A** ARC, NIDA Effects of carbamazepine on cocaine self-administration
K02DA-00140-03 (SRCD) **SPEAR, LINDA P** SUNY AT BINGHAMTON DEPT OF PSYCHOLOGY BINGHAMTON, NY 13901 Neurobehavioral teratogenic studies of cocaine
Z01DA-00140-01 (PTL) **GORELICK, D A** ARC, NIDA HIV infection, high-risk behaviors, and drug abuse treatment
K02DA-00141-02 (SRCD) **WILLIAMS, JOHN T** OREGON HEALTH SCIS UNIVERSITY 3181 SW SAM JACKSON PARK RD PORTLAND, OR 97201 Cocaine--Actions on single isolated central neurons
K05DA-00142-02 (SRCD) **FALK, JOHN L** RUTGERS UNIVERSITY BUSCH CAMPUS NEW BRUNSWICK, NJ 08903 Oral drug abuse--Determinants and consequences
K20DA-00143-02 (SRCD) **MAYER, JOSEPH H** SCRIPPS CLINIC & RESEARCH FDN 10666 NORTH TORREY PINES ROAD LA JOLLA, CA 92037 Endogenous opioid processes--Role in drug abuse
K20DA-00144-02 (SRCD) **CORNISH, JAMES W** ADDICTION RESEARCH CENTER 3900 CHESTNUT STREET PHILADELPHIA, PA 19104-6178 Scientist development award for a clinician
K02DA-00145-02 (SRCD) **WILCOX, GEORGE L** UNIVERSITY OF MINNESOTA 1100 WASHINGTON AVENUE SOUTH MINNEAPOLIS, MN 55415 Cellular mechanisms of spinal analgesia
K02DA-00146-02 (DACB) **ANGLIN, M DOUGLAS** UCLA DRUG ABUSE RESEARCH GROUP 1100 GLENDAN AVENUE LOS ANGELES, CA 90024-3511 Drug abuse treatment--Process, outcomes, & social policy
Z01DA-00147-01 (PTL) **GORELICK, D** ARC, NIDA Esterase actibity in human cocaine abusers
K20DA-00150-02 (DAPA) **BOYD, CAROL J** UNIVERSITY OF MICHIGAN 400 N INGALLS BLDG ANN ARBOR, MI 48109-0482 Factors related to female cocaine abuse
K02DA-00151-02 (DABR) **COMB, MICHAEL J** MASSACHUSETTS GENERAL HOSPITAL BOSTON, MA 02114 Molecular mechanisms of proenkephalin gene regulation
K02DA-00152-02 (DABR) **MAKRIYANNIS, ALEXANDROS** UNIVERSITY OF CONNECTICUT STORRS, CT 06269 Effects of cannabinoids on membranes
K02DA-00153-02 (SRCD) **KALIVAS, PETER W** WASHINGTON UNIVERSITY PULLMAN, WA 99164-6520 Cocaine, opioids, and drug abuse
K20DA-00154-01 (DACB) **NUNES, EDWARD V** 722 WEST 168TH STREET NEW YORK, NY 10032 Drug abuse treatment comorbidity and clinical trials
K02DA-00157-01 (DABR) **NOCK, BRUCE L** WASHINGTON UNIVERSITY 660 SOUTH EUCLID AVENUE ST LOUIS, MO 63110 Brain opiate receptor properties and function
K02DA-00158-01 (DAAR) **HALL, NICHOLAS R** USF PSYCHIATRY CENTER 3515 EAST FLETCHER AVENUE TAMPA, FL 33613 Opioid properties of interferon
K05DA-00159-01 (SRCD) **MEISCH, RICHARD A** UNIVERSITY OF TEXAS 1300 MOURSUND AVENUE HOUSTON, TX 77030 Drug reinforcing effects
K21DA-00160-01 (DABR) **CARDEN, SUSAN E** NEW YORK STATE PSYCHIATRIC INS 722 WEST 168TH ST BOX 40 NEW YORK, NY 10032 Opioid modulation of social isolation responses
K02DA-00161-01 (DACB) **WOOLVERTON, WILLIAM L** 947 EAST 58TH STREET, BOX 271 CHICAGO, IL 60637 Behavioral pharmacology of drug self-administration
K12DA-00167-01 (SRCM) **ROUNSAVILLE, BRUCE J** 27 SYLVAN AVE NEW HAVEN, CT 06519 Physician scientist training in substance abuse research
K12DA-00172-01 (SRCM) **O'BRIEN, CHARLES P** UNIVERSITY OF PENNSYLVANIA 3900 CHESTNUT STREET PHILADELPHIA, PA 19104-6178 Institutional physician scientist development program
Z01DA-00200-06 (NPL) **LONDON, E D** ARC, NIDA Cerebral effects of abused drugs--Brain imaging in humans and laboratory animals
Z01DA-00202-07 (NPL) **LONDON, E D** ARC, NIDA Physiological effects of opioids
Z01DA-00206-06 (NPL) **SU, T P** ARC, NIDA Sigma receptors
Z01DA-00210-05 (NPL) **KIMES, A S** ARC, NIDA HIV infection and drug abuse
Z01DA-00212-03 (NEI) **LANGE, W R** ARC, NIDA HIV sero-status in missionaries from Africa, 1968-1983
Z01DA-00213-07 (BDL) **HENNINGFIELD, J E** ARC, NIDA Factors influencing behavioral and physiologic response to opioids
P50DA-00250-20 (SRCD) **SEIDEN, LEWIS S** UNIVERSITY OF CHICAGO 5841 S MARYLAND AVE CHICAGO, IL 60637 Research center--Studies of drug dependence and abuse
P50DA-00250-20 0022 (SRCD) **WOOLVERTON, WILLIAM L** Research center--Studies of drug dependence and abuse Drug self-administration--Environmental & pharmacological determinants
P50DA-00250-20 0023 (SRCD) **SEIDEN, LEWIS S** Research center--Studies of drug dependence and abuse Mechanism of methamphetamine-induced neurotoxicity
P50DA-00250-20 0026 (SRCD) **WOOLVERTON, WILLIAM** Research center--Studies of drug dependence and abuse Modification of acute and chronic cocaine effects
P50DA-00250-20 0027 (SRCD) **DE WIT, HARRIET** Research center--Studies of drug dependence and abuse Reinstatement of drug-taking
P50DA-00250-20 0028 (SRCD) **CHAIT, LARRY D** Research center--Studies of drug dependence and abuse Reinforcing effects of psychomotor stimulants
P50DA-00250-20 0029 (SRCD) **PERRY, BRUCE D** Research center--Studies of drug dependence and abuse Cocaine effects in reaggregate tissue culture
P50DA-00254-20 (SRCD) **WOODS, JAMES H** UNIVERSITY OF MICH MED SCH ANN ARBOR, MI 48109-0626 Narcotic drug and opiate peptide basic research project
P50DA-00254-20 0009 (SRCD) **MEDZIHRADSKY, FEDOR** Narcotic drug and opiate peptide basic research project: In vitro opioid pharmacology--Novel opioid characterization
P50DA-00254-20 0010 (SRCD) **WOODS, JAMES H** Narcotic drug and opiate peptide basic research project Delta opioid project
P50DA-00254-20 0011 (SRCD) **SMITH, CHARLES B** Narcotic drug and opiate peptide basic research project Opioid agonists & antagonists evaluation at opioid receptor
P50DA-00254-20 0012 (SRCD) **FRANCE, CHARLES P** Narcotic drug and opiate peptide basic research project Opioid discriminative stimulus, analgesia, respiration and dependence
P50DA-00254-20 0013 (SRCD) **WINGER, GAIL D** Narcotic drug and opiate peptide basic research project Reinforcing effects of opioids
P50DA-00254-20 9002 (SRCD) **MOSBERG, HENRY I** Narcotic drug and opiate peptide basic research project Synthetic core
P50DA-00266-20 (SRCD) **SNYDER, SOLOMON H** JOHNS HOPKINS SCHOOL OF MED 720 RUTLAND AVENUE BALTIMORE, MD 21205 Drug abuse research center
P50DA-00266-20 0006 (SRCD) **SNYDER, SOLOMON H** Drug abuse research center Neuronal localization of opiate receptors
P50DA-00266-20 0010 (SRCD) **MAINS, RICHARD E** Drug abuse research center Developmental neurobiology of ACTA/endorphin cells
P50DA-00266-20 0011 (SRCD) **EIPPER, ELIZABETH A** Drug abuse research center Neurons and endocrine cells of the ACTA/endorphin family
P50DA-00266-20 0012 (SRCD) **BARABAN, JAY M.** Drug abuse research center 5-HT2 receptor key role in the hallucinogenic response
R01DA-00289-19 (DABR) **TAKEMORI, AKIRA E** UNIVERSITY OF MINNESOTA MINNEAPOLIS, MINN 55455 Mechanism of narcotic action tolerance and dependence
Z01DA-00302-03 (NBL) **DE SOUZA, E B** ARC, NIDA Neurotoxic effects of MDA and MDMA
Z01DA-00303-03 (NBL) **DE SOUZA, E B** ARC, NIDA CRF in addictive, neuropsychiatric and neurodegenerative disorders
Z01DA-00304-03 (NBL) **DE SOUZA, E B** ARC, NIDA CRF as a stress neurotransmitter in the brain-endocrine-immune axis
Z01DA-00305-03 (NBL) **DE SOUZA, E B** ARC, NIDA Neurotoxicity of selected drugs to monoamine neurons in brain
Z01DA-00306-04 (CDM) **CONE, E J** ARC, NIDA Pharmacokinetics and pharmacodynamics of opiate analgesics
Z01DA-00307-03 (NBL) **YEH, S Y** ARC, NIDA Effects of cocaine on monamines and their metabolites in rat brain
Z01DA-00308-03 (NBL) **DE SOUZA, E B** ARC, NIDA Role of sigma receptors in endocrine organs and immune tissue
Z01DA-00309-03 (NBL) **DE SOUZA, E B** ARC, NIDA Interleukin-1 in the brain-endocrine-immune axis
Z01DA-00310-02 (CDM) **CONE, E J** ARC, NIDA Methodological assessment of the risk of passive inhalation of drugs of abuse
Z01DA-00311-02 (NBL) **DE SOUSA, E B** ARC, NIDA Sigma and PCP receptors in neuropsychiatric disorders
Z01DA-00312-01 (NPL) **LONDON, E D** ARC, NIDA Ligand-gated ion channels
Z01DA-00314-01 (MNL) **UHL, G R** ARC, NIDA D2 receptor gene allelic association with substance use
Z01DA-00327-03 (CDM) **CONE, E J** ARC, NIDA Pharmacokinetics and pharmacodynamics of drugs of abuse in hair
Z01DA-00328-02 (CDM) **CONE, E J** ARC, NIDA Pharmacokinetics and pharmacodynamics of methamphetamine
Z01DA-00329-02 (CDM) **HUESTIS, M A** ARC, NIDA Fast action dynamics of marijuana
R01DA-00346-18 (DABR) **KARLER, RALPH** UNIV OF UTAH SCHOOL OF MED ROOM 2C219, MEDICAL CNTR SALT LAKE CITY, UTAH 84112 Cannabinoids--Drug interactions, mechanisms of action
R01DA-00376-18 (DABR) **ADLER, MARTIN W** TEMPLE UNIVERSITY 3420 N BROAD STREET PHILADELPHIA, PA 19140 Narcotic receptors in nonaddicted and addicted states
R01DA-00451-18 (DABR) **FUJIMOTO, JAMES M** MEDICAL COLLEGE OF WISCONSIN 8701 WATERTOWN PLANK RD MILWAUKEE, WI 53226 Metabolism-response to naloxone and naltrexone
R01DA-00464-16 (SRCD) **ABOOD, LEO G** UNIVERSITY OF ROCHESTER 601 ELMWOOD AVENUE ROCHESTER, NY 14642 Studies on the nicotine receptor in rat brain
R01DA-00490-16 (SRCD) **HARRIS, LOUIS S** VIRGINIA COMMONWEALTH UNIV MCV STATION, BOX 27 RICHMOND, VA 23298-0027 A multidisciplinary study of drugs of abuse
R01DA-00499-17 (DABR) **SPEALMAN, ROGER D** NEW ENGLAND REG PRIMATE RES CT ONE PINE HILL DRIVE SOUTHBOROUGH, MA 01772 Analysis of behavior controlled by drug injections
Z01DA-00500-01 (VL) **NEWLIN, D B** ARC, NIDA Individual differences in cocaine craving--Physiological and affective correlate
Z01DA-00501-01 (VL) **NEWLIN, D B** ARC, NIDA Intravenous morphine produces initial heart rate increases/vagal tone decreases
Z01DA-00502-01 (VL) **NEWLIN, D B** ARC, NIDA Cardiovascular response to naloxone-precipitated withdrawal
Z01DA-00504-01 (VL) **NEWLIN, D B** ARC, NIDA Acute intravenous cocaine reduces cardiac vagal tone in cocaine abusers
Z01DA-00505-01 (VL) **WONG, C J** ARC, NIDA The ARC drug expectancy questionnaire
Z01DA-00506-01 (VL) **NEWLIN, D B** ARC, NIDA Acute effects of various abused drugs on heart rate and cardiac vagal tone
Z01DA-00507-01 (VL) **HICKEY, J E** ARC, NIDA Vagal tone and attention in 8 to 12-year-old males exposed to opiates in utero
Z01DA-00508-01 (CTL) **COVI, L** ARC, NIDA Reasons for seeking drug abuse treatment
Z01DA-00509-01 (VL) **HERNING, R I** ARC, NIDA Neurocognitive status of young boys exposed to opiates in utero
R37DA-00541-18 (SRCD) **HOLTZMAN, STEPHEN G** EMORY UNIV SCH OF MED DEPT OF PHARMACOLOGY ATLANTA, GA 30322 Behavioral pharmacology of narcotic antagonists
R01DA-00564-19 (SRCD) **LOH, HORACE H** UNIVERSITY OF MINNESOTA 435 DELAWARE ST, SE MINNEAPOLIS, MN 55455 Neurochemical basis of narcotic addiction
R01DA-00662-16 (DABR) **KOSTERLITZ, HANS W** UNIVERSITY OF ABERDEEN UNIT/RES ON ADDICTIVE DRUGS ABERDEEN AB9 1AS, SCOTLAND UK Opioid peptides--receptors, biosynthesis and release
R01DA-00869-17 (DABR) **GIBB, JAMES W** UNIVERSITY OF UTAH SALT LAKE CITY, UT 84112 Drug abuse and regulatory enzymes of biogenic amines
R01DA-01015-17 (DACB) **MC KEARNEY, JAMES W** WORCESTER FDN/EXPER BIO 222 MAPLE AVE SHREWSBURY, MA 01545 Pharmacology of narcotics and narcotic antagonists
R01DA-01050-17 (DABR) **YOUNG, GERALD A** UNIV OF MARYLAND @ BALTIMORE 20 NORTH STREET BALTIMORE, MD 21201 Opiate receptors, EEG

spectra, tolerance & dependence

P01DA-01070-18 (SRCD) BENTLER, PETER M UNIV OF CALIFORNIA LOS ANGELES, CA 90024-1563 Adolescent drug abuse etiologies

R01DA-01147-17 (SRCD) GRIFFITHS, ROLAND R JOHNS HOPKINS UNIVERSITY 720 RUTLAND AVENUE BALTIMORE, MD 21205 Abuse liability of benzodiazepines and caffeine

R01DA-01161-16 (SRCD) BYRD, LARRY D EMORY UNIVERSITY ATLANTA, GA 30322 Behavioral and physiological concomitants of drug abuse

R01DA-01411-17 (SRCD) JOHNSTON, LLOYD D UNIVERSITY OF MICHIGAN 426 THOMPSON ANN ARBOR, MI 48109-1248 Drug use and lifestyles of American youth

R01DA-01442-16 (SRCD) BALSTER, ROBERT L VIRGINIA COMMONWEALTH UNIVERSI BOX 568, MCV STATION RICHMOND, VA 23298 The behavioral pharmacology of phencyclidine

R01DA-01451-15 (DAAR) FALEK, ARTHUR GEORGIA MENTAL HEALTH INST 1256 BRIARCLIFF ROAD N E ATLANTA, GA 30306 Cellular genetic aspects of opiate use

R01DA-01457-16 (DABR) INTURRISI, CHARLES E CORNELL UNIV MEDICAL COLLEGE 1300 YORK AVENUE NEW YORK, NY 10021 Regulation of opioid peptide biosynthesis and release

R01DA-01531-07A5 (DABR) DOMINO, EDWARD F UNIVERSITY OF MICHIGAN ANN ARBOR, MI 48109-0626 Neuropsychopharmacology of phencyclidine

R01DA-01533-16 (DABR) PORTOGHESE, PHILIP S UNIVERSITY OF MINNESOTA 308 HARVARD STREET, SE MINNEAPOLIS, MN 55455 Affinity labels as opioid receptor probes

R01DA-01568-15 (SRCD) SEGAL, DAVID S UNIV OF CALIFORNIA, SAN DIEGO LA JOLLA, CALIF 92093 Behavioral pharmacology of acute and chronic amphetamine

R37DA-01583-14 (SRCD) LOH, HORACE H FORSYTH DENTAL CENTER 140 FENWAY BOSTON, MA 02115 Isolation/characterization studies of opiate receptor

R01DA-01642-11 (DABR) GLENNON, RICHARD A VIRGINIA COMMONWEALTH UNIV BOX 540 MCV STATION RICHMOND, VA 23298-0540 Chemical/behavioral studies on hallucinogenic agents

R01DA-01647-15 (SRCD) DEWEY, WILLIAM L MEDICAL COLLEGE OF VIRGINIA BOX 613, MCV STATION RICHMOND, VA 23298-0613 Enkephalin--Neuropharmacology and abuse potential

R01DA-01674-15 (DABR) ARCHER, SYDNEY RENSSELAER POLYTECHNIC INST COGSWELL LABORATORY TROY, NY 12180-3590 Ligands for opiate receptors

P50DA-01696-12 (SRCD) JONES, REESE T UNIVERSITY OF CALIFORNIA 401 PARNASSUS AVENUE SAN FRANCISCO, CA 94143 Drug dependence clinical research program

P50DA-01696-12 0012 (SRCD) BENOWITZ, NEAL L Drug dependence clinical research program The clinical pharmacology of caffeine

P50DA-01696-12 0013 (SRCD) LANNON, RICHARD Drug dependence clinical research program Affective disorders--Treatment and drug abuse

P50DA-01696-12 0014 (SRCD) BATKI, STEVEN L Drug dependence clinical research program Cocaine, opioids and depression --Diagnosis and treatment

P50DA-01696-12 0015 (SRCD) ROWBOTHAM, MICHAEL C Drug dependence clinical research program Neurologic sequelae of cocaine use

P50DA-01696-12 9002 (SRCD) JONES, REESE T Drug dependence clinical research program Core -- Analytical laboratory

R37DA-01720-15 (DABR) WISE, ROY A CONCORDIA UNIVERSITY 1455 DE MAISONNEUVE BLVD WEST MONTREAL QUEBEC CANADA H3G 1M8 Neural substrate of cocaine abuse

R01DA-01880-12 (DABR) SPARBER, SHELDON B UNIVERSITY OF MINNESOTA DEPARTMENT OF PHARMACOLOGY MINNEAPOLIS, MN 55455 Opiate addiction and abstinence during development

R01DA-01883-11 (SRCD) ELLINWOOD, EVERETT H DUKE UNIVERSITY MEDICAL CENTER P O BOX 3870 DURHAM, NC 27710 Sensitivity to driving impairment with drugs of abuse

R01DA-01933-09 (DABR) WILCOX, GEORGE L UNIVERSITY OF MINNESOTA 435 DELAWARE STREET S E MINNAOPOLIS, MN 55455 Nociception--Neuropharmacology of drugs of abuse

R37DA-01949-14 (DABR) FIELDS, HOWARD L UNIVERSITY OF CALIFORNIA DEPARTMENT OF NEUROLOGY, M-794 SAN FRANCISCO, CALIF 94143 The neuronal substrate of opiate analgesia

R01DA-01987-11 (DACB) SMITH, JAMES B MERCER UNIVERSITY 3001 MERCER UNIV DRIVE ATLANTA, GA 30341 Behavioral influences on development of drug tolerance

R37DA-01999-14 (SRCD) SMITH, JAMES E WAKE FOREST UNIVERSITY 300 S HAWTHORNE ROAD WINSTON-SALEM, N C 27103 Drug abuse--neurobiological mechanisms of morphine

Z01DA-02001-05 (VL) HERNING, R I ARC, NIDA Mapping the effects of opioid agonists by EEG

R01DA-02031-12 (DABR) CRAIN, STANLEY M ALBERT EINSTEIN COLL OF MED 1300 MORRIS PARK AVENUE BRONX, N Y 10461 Dual opioid modulation of spinal cord-ganglion activity

R01DA-02043-15 (SRCD) BURSTEIN, SUMNER H UNIV OF MASSACHUSETTS MED CTR 55 LAKE AVE NORTH WORCESTER, MA 01655 Prostaglandins and cannabis

R01DA-02052-15 (SRCD) BURSTEIN, SUMNER H UNIV OF MASSACHUSETTS MED SCH 55 LAKE AVENUE, NORTH WORCESTER, MA 01655 Biological activities of cannabinoids

R01DA-02073-13 (DABR) JOHNSON, KENNETH M, JR UNIVERSITY OF TEXAS MED BRANCH DEPT OF PHARMA & TOXICOLOGY GALVESTON, TEX 77550-2774 Neurochemical pharmacology of phencyclidine

N01DA-02101-00 ( ) INFORMATION DATA SYSTEMS, INC** 8737 COLESVILLE ROAD SUITE 501 SILVER SPRING, MD 20910 International visiting scientists and technical exchange program

Z01DA-02101-05 (VL) HERNING, R I ARC, NIDA Acute abstinence from tobacco--Electrophysiological and cognitive signs

R01DA-02110-13 (DABR) YAKSH, TONY L UNIV OF CALIF, SAN DIEGO LA JOLLA, CA 92093-0618 Spinal action of opiates

R01DA-02121-13 (SRCD) MILLER, RICHARD J THE UNIVERSITY OF CHICAGO 947 EAST 58TH STREET CHICAGO, IL 60637 Neuropharmacology of opiate peptides

R01DA-02163-14 (DABR) BURKS, THOMAS F UNIV OF TEXAS HLTH SCIS CTR P O BOX 20708 HOUSTON, TX 77225 Intestinal actions of narcotic drugs

R01DA-02189-12 (DABR) NICHOLS, DAVID E PURDUE UNIVERSITY R E HEINE PHARMACY BLDG WEST LAFAYETTE, IN 47907 Stereochemical aspects of hallucinogenesis

R01DA-02194-13A1 (DABR) ROSENBERG, HOWARD C MEDICAL COLLEGE OF OHIO PO BOX 10008 TOLEDO, OH 43699 Pharmacology of benzodiazepine tolerance and dependence

R01DA-02195-12 (DABR) MARTIN, WILLIAM R UNIVERSITY OF KENTUCKY RM 212A RESEARCH FACILITY NO 3 LEXINGTON, KY 40536-0216 Study of dependence properties of sedatives

N01DA-02200-00 ( ) ABT ASSOCIATES, INC** 55 WHEELER STREET CAMBRIDGE, MA 02138 Technology transfer support

N01DA-02205-00 ( ) CSR, INCORPORATED** 1400 EYE STREET, N W SUITE 600 WASHINGTON, D C 20005 Technology transfer conference and videotape program development

R01DA-02206-10 (SRCD) GALE, KAREN N GEORGETOWN UNIVERSITY 3900 RESERVOIR ROAD, N W WASHINGTON, D C 20007 Neurochemical effects of chronic stimulant exposure

N01DA-02208-00 ( ) WESTOVER CONSULTANTS, INC** 500 E STREET, N W SUITE 910 WASHINGTON, D C 20024 AIDS training for adolescents and staff

R01DA-02243-14 (DABR) HERSH, LOUIS B UNIV OF TEXAS S W MEDICAL CENT 5323 HARRY HINES BOULEVARD DALLAS, TX 75235 Degradation of opioid peptides

R01DA-02251-13A1 (DACB) MC MILLAN, DONALD E UNIV OF ARKANSAS FOR MED SCI 4301 WEST MARKHAM STREET LITTLE ROCK, AR 72205 Drugs of abuse--Chronic interactions and behavior

R01DA-02254-10 (DABR) BECKMAN, ALEXANDER L CALIFORNIA STATE UNIVERSITY 1250 BELLFLOWER BOULEVARD LONG BEACH, CA 90840-0901 Narcotic action in depressed brain

R01DA-02265-13 (DABR) AKIL, HUDA UNIVERSITY OF MICHIGAN 205 WASHTENAW PLACE ANN ARBOR, MI 4809-0720 Brain beta-endorphin--Role in transmission and addiction

R01DA-02277-13 (DACB) BENOWITZ, NEAL L UNIVERSITY OF CALIFORNIA 1001 POTRERO AVE, BLDG 30 SAN FRANCISCO, CA 94143-0842 Pharmacokinetics and pharmacodynamics of nicotine

R01DA-02285-10 (DABR) BOZARTH, MICHAEL A STATE UNIVERSITY OF NEW YORK BUFFALO, NY 14260 Role of physical dependence in opiate reinforcement

R01DA-02297-12 (DABR) NEALE, JOSEPH H GEORGETOWN UNIVERSITY 37TH & O STREETS, N.W. WASHINGTON, DC 20057 Benzodiazepines and opiates in neuronal cell cultures

R01DA-02326-12 (DABR) KORNETSKY, CONAN BOSTON UNIVERSITY 80 EAST CONCORD STREET BOSTON, MA 02118 Drugs of abuse and brain stimulation reward

R01DA-02338-12 (DABA) WOODWARD, DONALD J SOUTHWESTERN MED CTR @ DALLAS 5323 HARRY HINES BLVD DALLAS, TX 75235 Physiology of CNS monoamines and drugs of abuse

R01DA-02403-12 (DACB) OVERTON, DONALD A TEMPLE UNIVERSITY SCH OF MED WEISS HALL PHILADELPHIA, PA 19122 New behavioral methods for categorizing abused drugs

R01DA-02411-12 (DABR) CHO, ARTHUR K UNIVERSITY OF CALIFORNIA LOS ANGELES, CA 90024-1735 Chemistry of phencyclidine metabolism

R01DA-02429-12 (DABR) FREEDMAN, ROBERT UNIV OF COL HLTH SCIS CTR BOX C268 DENVER, CO 80262 Effects of phencyclidine on neuronal function

R01DA-02451-11 (DABR) REBEC, GEORGE V INDIANA UNIVERSITY BLOOMINGTON, IN 47405 Neuropharmacology of drugs of abuse--Amphetamine

R01DA-02475-12 (SRCD) SZETO, HAZEL H CORNELL UNIVERSITY MED COLL 1300 YORK AVENUE NEW YORK, N Y 10021 Pharmacokinetics and fetal exposure to narcotics

R01DA-02486-12 (SRCD) CARROLL, MARILYN E UNIVERSITY OF MINNESOTA BOX 392 UMHC MINNEAPOLIS, MN 55455 A primate model of drug abuse--Intervention strategies

R01DA-02490-12 (SRCD) HIENZ, ROBERT D JOHNS HOPKINS UNIVERSITY 720 RUTLAND AVE BALTIMORE, MD 21205-2196 Drugs of abuse--Sensory psychophysical effects

R01DA-02497-12 (SRCD) KAPLAN, HOWARD B TEXAS A&M UNIVERSITY COLLEGE STATION, TX 77843 Drug abuse and other deviant adaptations to stress

R01DA-02519-10 (SRCD) MELLO, NANCY K MC LEAN HOSPITAL 115 MILL STREET BELMONT, MASS 02178 Buprenorphine--A behavioral analysis

R01DA-02538-12 (DACB) HALL, SHARON M SAN FRANCISCO VET ADMIN MED CT 4150 CLEMENT ST SAN FRANCISCO, CA 94121 Maintaining nonsmoking

R01DA-02543-18 (DABR) APPEL, JAMES B UNIVERSITY OF SOUTH CAROLINA COLUMBIA, S C 29208 Neurohumoral determinants of sensitivity to drugs

R01DA-02575-12 (DABR) DAWSON, GLYN UNIVERSITY OF CHICAGO 5841 S MARYLAND AVE, HOSP BX 8 CHICAGO, IL 60637 Mechanisms of opiate/opioid peptide action

R01DA-02598-11 (DABR) BHARGAVA, HEMENDRA N UNIVERSITY OF ILLINOIS PO BOX 6998 CHICAGO, IL 60680 Hypothalamus and narcotic effects

R01DA-02615-12 (DABR) PASTERNAK, GAVRIL W SLOAN KETTERING INST/CNCR RES 1275 YORK AVENUE NEW YORK, NY 10021 Biochemical characterization of opiate binding sites

R01DA-02632-13 (SRCD) MICZEK, KLAUS A TUFTS UNIVERSITY DEPARTMENT OF PSYCHOLOGY MEDFORD, MASS 02155 Psychomotor stimulants and aggression

R01DA-02643-11 (SRCD) LEE, NANCY M UNIVERSITY OF MINNESOTA 435 DELAWARE STREET SE MINNEAPOLIS, MN 55455 Characterization and regulation of B-endorphin receptor

R01DA-02659-08 (DABR) PORTOGHESE, PHILIP S UNIVERSITY OF MINNESOTA 308 HARVARD STREET SE MINNEAPOLIS, MN 55455 Bivalent ligands as probes for opioid receptors

R01DA-02665-12 (DACB) ROSE, JED E VA MEDICAL CENTER 508 FULTON STREET DURHAM, NC 27705 Scaling the reinforcing value of cigarette smoke

R01DA-02668-12 (DABR) WESTFALL, THOMAS C ST LOUIS UNIV SCH OF MEDICINE 1402 S GRAND BOULEVARD ST LOUIS, MO 63104 Acute and chronic nicotine on brain amine release

R01DA-02702-12 (DABR) DUNWIDDIE, THOMAS V UNIV OF COLORADO HLTH SCIS CTR DEPARTMENT OF PHARMACOLOGY DENVER, CO 80262 Opiate pharmacology of monoamine pathways

R01DA-02739-10 (SRCD) KUHN, CYNTHIA M DUKE UNIVERSITY MEDICAL

PROJECT NO., ORGANIZATIONAL UNIT., INVESTIGATOR, ADDRESS, TITLE

CENTER BOX 3813 DURHAM, NC 27710 Opiate effects on maturation of endocrine regulation

R37DA-02749-16 (SRCD) DYKSTRA, LINDA A UNIVERSITY OF NORTH CAROLINA DEPARTMENT OF PSYCHOLOGY CHAPEL HILL, N C 27599 Opioid analgesics--pharmacological & behavioral factors

R01DA-02812-11 (DACB) DE WIT, HARRIET UNIVERSITY OF CHICAGO 5841 SOUTH MARYLAND CHICAGO, IL 60637 Determinants of drug preference in humans

R01DA-02845-06 (DABR) ADVOKAT, CLAIRE D LOUISIANA STATE UNIVERSITY 236 AUDUBON HALL BATON ROUGE, LA 70803 Mechanism of conditioned tolerance to morphine

R37DA-02854-12 (DABR) GROVES, PHILIP M UNIV OF CALIFORNIA, SAN DIEGO PSYCHIATRY DEPT, 0603 LA JOLLA, CA 92093-0603 Mechanisms of action of drugs of abuse--Amphetamine

R01DA-02873-11 (DACB) BARRETT, JAMES E UNIFORMED SERVICES UNIVERSITY 4301 JONES BRIDGE ROAD BETHESDA, MD 20814-4799 Determinants of the behavioral effects of abused drugs

R01DA-02879-15 (SRCD) GEBHART, GERALD F UNIVERSITY OF IOWA DEPARTMENT OF PHARMACOLOGY IOWA CITY, IA 52242 Neuropharmacology of opioids and nociception

R01DA-02904-11 (SRCD) CHILDERS, STEVEN R WAKE FOREST UNIV-BOWMAN GRAY 300 S HAWTHORNE ROAD WINSTON-SALEM, N C 27103 Molecular regulatory mechanisms of brain opioid systems

R01DA-02925-10 (DABR) GEYER, MARK A UNIV OF CALIFORNIA SAN DIEGO DEPT OF PSYCHIATRY, 0804 LA JOLLA, CA 92093 Monoamines and hallucinogens' effects on rat behavior

R37DA-03008-09 (SRCD) O'BRIEN, CHARLES P UNIVERSITY OF PENNSYLVANIA 3900 CHESTNUT ST PHILADELPHIA, PA 19104-6178 Integrated addiction treatment--Role of extinction

R01DA-03018-10 (SRCD) TASHKIN, DONALD P UNIVERSITY OF CALIFORNIA, LA LOS ANGELES, CA 90024 Pulmonary effects of habitual, use of marijuana and/ or cocaine

R01DA-03025-08 (DABR) REITH, MAARTEN E NATHAN S KLINE INSTITUTE ORANGEBURG, N Y 10962 Cocaine, vesicles, channels and behavior

R01DA-03062-07 (DACB) HALL, SHARON M SAN FRANCISCO VET ADMIN MED CT 4150 CLEMENT ST SAN FRANCISCO, CA 94121 Relapse to abused drugs

Z01DA-03101-05 (VL) HERNING, R I ARC, NIDA Effects of atropine on cognitive information processing

R37DA-03102-10 (DABR) COX, BRIAN M UNIFORMED SER UNIV HLTH SCIS 4301 JONES BRIDGE ROAD BETHESDA, MD 20814 Opioid receptor mechanisms

R01DA-03112-07 (SRCD) BALSTER, ROBERT L MEDICAL COLLEGE OF VIRGINIA BOX 613, MCV STATION RICHMOND, VA 23298 Behavioral pharmacology of abused solvents

R01DA-03117-10 (DACB) FALK, JOHN L RUTGERS UNIVERSITY PSYCHOLOGY BLDG, BUSCH CAMPUS NEW BRUNSWICK, N J 08903 Benzodiazepine overindulgence and its consequences

R37DA-03160-12 (SRCD) NORTH, RICHARD A OREGON HEALTH SCIENCES UNIV VOLLUM INSTITUTE PORTLAND, OR 97201 Opiate actions and dependence--Single neuron studies

R01DA-03161-11 (SRCD) NORTH, RICHARD A OREGON HEALTH SCIENCES UNIV 3181 S W SAM JACKSON PARK ROAD PORTLAND, OR 97201-3098 Opiate actions on single brain neurons in vitro

R01DA-03166-08 (SRCD) CHEREK, DON R UNIV OF TEXAS HLTH SCI CTR 1300 MOURSUND HOUSTON, TX 77225 Drugs of abuse and aggressive behavior

R01DA-03173-07 (SRCD) MORETON, J EDWARD U OF MD SCHOOL OF PHARMACY 20 NORTH PINE STREET BALTIMORE, MD 21201 PCP analogue self-administration--EEG and behavior

R01DA-03188-09 (DAPA) BROOK, JUDITH S NEW YORK MEDICAL COLLEGE VALHALLA, N Y 10595 Childhood etiologic determinants of adolescent drug use

R01DA-03194-09 (DABR) COLLINS, ALLAN C UNIVERSITY OF COLORADO INSTITUTE FOR BEHAV GENETICS BOULDER, CO 80309 Genetics of nicotine tolerance--Role of receptors

R37DA-03240-09 (SRCD) CARROLL, MARILYN E UNIVERSITY OF MINNESOTA BOX 392 UMHC MINNEAPOLIS, MN 55455 Environmental and pharmacological control of drug abuse

R01DA-03272-08 (DAPS) PRICE, RICHARD H UNIVERSITY OF MICHIGAN 2263 ISR PO BOX 1248 ANN ARBOR, MI 48106-1248 National survey of outpatient drug abuse treatment

R01DA-03277-07 (ALCP) SCHINKE, STEVEN P COLUMBIA UNIVERSITY 622 WEST 113TH STREET NEW YORK, N Y 10025 Drug prevention with American Indian adolescents

R01DA-03365-08 (DABR) MOISES, HYLAN C UNIV OF MICHIGAN SCH OF MEDICI ANN ARBOR, MI 48109-1340 Adrenoreceptor function after chronic opiate treatment

R01DA-03371-09 (DAPA) BEAUVAIS, FREDERICK COLORADO STATE UNIVERSITY DEPARTMENT OF PSYCHOLOGY FT. COLLINS, CO 80523 Drug use among young Indians--Epidemiology and correlates

R01DA-03383-09 (DABR) ZUKIN, STEPHEN R ALBERT EINSTEIN COLL OF MED DEPT OF PSYCH & NEUROSCIENCE BRONX, N Y 10461 Phencyclidine abuse and psychosis--Biomedical mechanisms

R01DA-03385-06 (DACB) WINTER, JERROLD C SUNY AT BUFFALO BUFFALO, NY 14214 Behavioral & pharmacological analysis of drugs of abuse

R01DA-03395-08 (DAPA) PANDINA, ROBERT J RUTGERS STATE UNIVERSITY PO BOX 1089 PISCATAWAY, NJ 08855-1089 Marijuana use and consequences--A developmental study

R01DA-03413-08 (DACB) HOLTZMAN, STEPHEN G EMORY UNIVERSITY SCH OF MEDICI ATLANTA, GA 30322 Chronic caffeine--Behavioral/neurochemical correlates

R01DA-03476-09 (SRCD) FISCHMAN, MARIAN W JOHNS HOPKINS UNIVERSITY 720 RUTLAND AVE BALTIMORE, MD 21205 Drug effects on behavior--Workplace implications

R37DA-03502-08 (SRCD) DEADWYLER, SAMUEL A BOWMAN GRAY SCHOOL OF MEDICINE 300 SOUTH HAWTHORNE ROAD WINSTON-SALEM, NC 27103 Long-term brain-behavior effects of delta-9-tetrahydrocannabinol

R01DA-03517-08 (DACB) CHAIT, LARRY D THE UNIVERSITY OF CHICAGO 5841 S MARYLAND CHICAGO, IL 60637 Marijuana--Effects of repeated smoking in humans

R01DA-03521-06 (DACB) EMMETT-OGLESBY, MICHAEL W TEXAS COLL OF OSTEOPATHIC MED DEPARTMENT OF PHARMACOLOGY FORT WORTH, TX 76107-2690 Characterization of benzodiazepine dependence

R01DA-03544-07 (DABR) HUTCHINGS, DONALD E RES FND FOR MENTAL HYGIENE INC 722 WEST 168TH STREET NEW YORK, N Y 10032 Marijuana during pregnancy--Neurobehavioral effects in offspring

R01DA-03573-09 (DACB) MOERSCHBAECHER, JOSEPH M L S U MEDICAL CENTER 1901 PERDIDO ST NEW ORLEANS, LA 70112-1393 Effects of narcotics on complex operant behavior

R01DA-03574-08 (SRCD) DES JARLAIS, DON C BETH ISRAEL MEDICAL CTR 1ST AVE & 16TH ST NEW YORK, NY 10003 Risk factors for AIDS among intravenous drug users

R01DA-03586-06 (DACB) ROFFMAN, ROGER A UNIVERSITY OF WASHINGTON SCHOOL OF SOCIAL WORK, JH-30 SEATTLE, WA 98115 Relapse prevention in treatment of marijuana dependence

R01DA-03597-06 (DABR) HOEBEL, BARTLEY G PRINCETON UNIVERSITY PRINCETON, NJ 08544 Drugs of abuse, dopamine and control by brain peptides

R01DA-03608-05 (DACB) CUNNINGHAM, CHRISTOPHER L OREG HLTH SCIS UNIV/MED PSYCH 3181 SW SAM JACKSON PARK ROAD PORTLAND, OR 97201 Pavlovian mediation of drug self-administration

R01DA-03616-07 (DABR) PITT, COLIN G AMGEN, INC. 1900 OAK TERRACE LANE THOUSAND OAKS, CA 91320 Subdermal delivery systems for narcotic antagonists

R01DA-03628-08 (SRCD) SMITH, JAMES E BOWMAN GRAY SCHOOL OF MEDICINE MEDICAL CENTER BOULEVARD WINSTON-SALEM, N C 27157 Neurobiological parameters of cocaine reinforcement

R01DA-03637-08 (DABR) LANDFIELD, PHILIP W UNIV OF KENTUCKY RESEARCH FND CHANDLER MEDICAL CENTER LEXINGTON, KY 40536 Long-term effects of delta-9-THC on brain structure

R01DA-03646-08 (DAAR) FRIEDMAN, HERMAN UNIVERSITY OF SOUTH FLORIDA 12901 NORTH BRUCE B DOWNS BLVD TAMPA, FLA 33612 Marijuana effects on immunity-- Nature and mechanisms

R01DA-03647-06 (DAAR) CABRAL, GUY A VIRGINIA COMMONWEALTH UNIV BOX 678, MCV STATION RICHMOND, VA 23298-0568 Effect of cannabinoids on vaginal herpes 2 in

R01DA-03665-09 (DABR) SIGGINS, GEORGE R SCRIPPS CLINIC & RESEARCH FDN 10666 NORTH TORREY PINES ROAD LA JOLLA, CA 92037 Morphine-like brain peptides--Cellular neurobiology

R01DA-03672-08 (DABR) MARTIN, BILLY R VIRGINIA COMMONWEALTH UNIV BOX 613, MCV STATION RICHMOND, VA 23298-0001 Investigation of tetrahydrocannabinol receptors

R01DA-03680-06A1 (SRCD) ELDEFRAWI, MOHYEE E UNIVERSITY OF MARYLAND 655 W BALTIMORE STREET BALTIMORE, MD 21201 Cocaine receptors and addiction

R01DA-03690-08 (DABR) HOWLETT, ALLYN C ST LOUIS UNIVERSITY SCH OF MED 1402 SOUTH GRAND BOULEVARD ST LOUIS, MO 63104 Cannabinoid receptors in neuronal cells and brain

R01DA-03706-08 (DAPA) HOPS, HYMAN OREGON RESEARCH INSTITUTE 1899 WILLAMETTE, SUITE 2 EUGENE, OREG 97401 Family influence on adolescent smoking

R01DA-03721-07 (SRCD) HAWKINS, JOHN D UNIVERSITY OF WASHINGTON SCHOOL OF SOCIAL WORK, JH-30 SEATTLE, WA 98195 Preventing youthful drug abuse--A longitudinal study

R01DA-03742-08 (DABR) BIDLACK, JEAN M UNIVERSITY OF ROCHESTER 601 ELMWOOD AVE ROCHESTER, NY 14642 Molecular aspects of the multiple opioid receptor

R01DA-03766-07 (SRC) NURCO, DAVID N FRIENDS MED SCI RES CTR 1229 W MT ROYAL AVE BALRIMORE, MD 21217 Vulnerability to narcotic addiction--Etiologic aspects

R01DA-03773-06 (SRCD) FLEMING, WILLIAM W WEST VIRGINIA UNIVERSITY HEALTH SCIENCES CENTER, NORTH MORGANTOWN, WV 26506 membrane potential and morphine tolerance

R01DA-03774-07 (DACB) BERGMAN, JACK HARVARD MEDICAL SCHOOL ONE PINE HILL DRIVE SOUTHBOROUGH, MA 01772 Behavioral effects and abuse of dopaminergic drugs

R01DA-03776-06 (DABR) BOWEN, WAYNE D BROWN UNIV DIVISION OF BIOLOGY & MEDICINE PROVIDENCE, RI 02912 Identification and analysis of opiate receptor proteins

R01DA-03796-07 (SRCD) YOUNG, ALICE M WAYNE STATE UNIVERSITY 71 WEST WARREN AVE DETROIT, MI 48202 Behavioral pharmacology of opioid tolerance

R01DA-03801-07 (SRCD) MAKRIYANNIS, ALEXANDROS UNIVERSITY OF CONNECTICUT STORRS, CT 06268 Effects of cannabinoids on membranes

R01DA-03811-07 (SRCD) TSENG, LIANG-FU MEDICAL COLLEGE OF WISCONSIN DEPT OF PHARMACOLOGY & TOXICO MILWAUKEE, WI 53226 Spinal release of endorphins by opioids

R01DA-03816-08 (DABR) HOUGH, LINDSAY B ALBANY MEDICAL COLLEGE DEPT OF PHARMA & TOXICOLOGY ALBANY, NY 12208 Histaminergic mechanisms of non-opiate analgesia

R01DA-03817-07 (SRCD) GLICK, STANLEY D ALBANY MEDICAL COLLEGE 47 NEW SCOTLAND AVE ALBANY, N Y 12208 Neuro-behavioral mechanisms of drug addiction

R37DA-03818-08 (DACB) FISCHMAN, MARIAN W JOHNS HOPKINS UNIV SCH OF MED 720 RUTLAND AVENUE BALTIMORE, MD 21205 Cocaine effects in humans--Physiology and behavior

R01DA-03833-07 (DABR) CICERO, THEODORE J WASHINGTON UNIVERSITY 724 S EUCLID AVENUE ST LOUIS, MO 63110 Opiate-endocrine interactions--Developmental aspects

R01DA-03874-05 (SRCD) DAY, NANCY L WESTERN PSYCHIATRIC INST/CLIN 3811 O'HARA STREET PITTSBURGH, PA 15213 An epidemiological study of prenatal marijuana exposure

R01DA-03876-06 (SRCD) FRENCH, EDWARD D UNIVERSITY OF ARIZONA COLLEGE OF MEDICINE TUCSON, AZ 85724 PCP and midbrain dopamine neurons--Cellular neurobiology

R01DA-03889-08 (SRCD) GRIFFITHS, ROLAND R FRANCIS SCOTT KEY MEDICAL CTR 4940 EASTERN AVENUE BALTIMORE, MD 21224 Experimental analysis of sedative/stimulant abuse

R01DA-03890-08 (SRCD) GRIFFITHS, ROLAND R FRANCIS SCOTT KEY MEDICAL CENT 4940 EASTERN AVE BALTIMORE, MD 21224 Licit and illicit abused drugs--Behavioral interaction

R01DA-03893-08 (SRCD) STITZER, MAXINE L FRANCIS SCOTT KEY MED CENTER 4940 EASTERN AVE BALTIMORE, MD 21224 Behavioral methods for cigarette smoking cessation

R01DA-03906-08 (SRCD) KALIVAS, PETER W WASHINGTON STATE UNIVERSITY PULLMAN, WA 99164-6520 Cocaine, opioids, and drug abuse

R01DA-03910-06 (DABR) MOSBERG, HENRY I UNIVERSITY OF MICHIGAN

428 CHURCH STREET ANN ARBOR, MI 48109-1065 Conformation-selectivity relations of opioid peptides

R01DA-03956-06 (DABR) CARR, KENNETH D NEW YORK UNIVERSITY MED CTR 550 FIRST AVE NEW YORK, N Y 10016 CNS opioid mechanisms that modulate reward and aversion

R01DA-03961-06 (DACB) CROWLEY, THOMAS J UNIVERSITY OF COLORADO 4200 EAST NINTH AVE C268-35 DENVER, CO 80262 Reinforcing smoking reductions in COPD patients

R01DA-03976-07 (DAPA) PENTZ, MARY A UNIV OF SOUTHERN CALIFORNIA 35 NORTH LAKE AVENUE PASADENA, CA 91101 Drug abuse prevention--Adolescence and early adulthood

R01DA-03977-07 (DABR) SHARP, BURT M HENNEPIN COUNTY MEDICAL CENTER 701 PARK AVENUE SOUTH MINNEAPOLIS, MN 55415 Interaction between nicotine and stress

R01DA-03980-10 (SRCD) PROUDFIT, HERBERT K UNIV OF ILLINOIS COLLEGE OF ME CHICAGO, IL 60612 Pharmacologic studies of CNS pain systems

R01DA-03982-08 (DABR) MC GINTY, JACQUELINE F EAST CAROLINA UNIVERSITY GREENVILLE, NC 27858-4354 Telencephalic opioid neurons--Psychostimulant effects

R01DA-03983-05 (DABR) HAN, JI-SHENG BEIJING MED UNIVERSITY BEIJING 100083, P.R. CHINA Neurobiology of acupuncture analgesia

R01DA-03992-04 (DAAR) ANTHONY, JAMES C JOHNS HOPKINS UNIVERSITY 615 NORTH WOLFE STREET BALTIMORE, MD 21205 Epidemiology of adult cocaine use

R01DA-03994-05 (SRCD) LUKAS, SCOTT E ADARC/MCLEAN HOSPITAL 115 MILL STREET BELMONT, MA 02178 Polydrug abuse--EEG and behavior

R01DA-03999-05 (SRCD) LEVINE, ALLEN S VA MEDICAL CENTER ONE VETERANS DRIVE MINNEAPOLIS, MN 55417 Opioid-induced feeding

R01DA-04011-06 (DACB) STITZER, MAXINE L FRANCIS SCOTT KEY MED CENTER 4940 EASTERN AVE BALTIMORE, MD 21224 Antagonist-precipitated effects after opioid exposure

R01DA-04017-06S1 (SRCD) GOLDSTEIN, PAUL J NARCOTIC & DRUG RESEARCH INC 11 BEACH STREET NEW YORK, NEW YORK 10013 Female drug related involvement in violent episodes

R01DA-04029-06 (SRCD) ROUNSAVILLE, BRUCE J APT FOUNDATION, INC 27 SYLVAN AVENUE NEW HAVEN, CT 06519 Psychiatric disorders in cocaine abusers

R01DA-04038-06 (DABR) WILKERSON, ROBERT D MEDICAL COLLEGE OF OHIO CS #10008 TOLEDO, OH 43699 Cocaine use--Acute and chronic cardiovascular effects

R01DA-04043-06 (DABR) KOOB, GEORGE F RES INST OF SCRIPPS CLINIC 10666 NORTH TORREY PINES ROAD LA JOLLA, CA 92037 Central mechanism of opiate reinforcement and dependence

R01DA-04050-05 (DACB) TIFFANY, STEPHEN T PURDUE UNIVERSITY WEST LAFAYETTE, IN 47907-1364 Opiate tolerance--Associative and nonassociative effects

P50DA-04060-06 (SRCD) KOSTEN, THOMAS R YALE UNIV SCHOOL OF MEDICINE 27 SYLVAN AVE NEW HAVEN, CT 05619 Clinical research center for opioid and cocaine abuse

P50DA-04060-06 0005 (SRCD) MARGOLIN, ARTHUR Clinical research center for opioid and cocaine abuse Bupropion for treatment of cocaine dependence in methadone-maintained patients

P50DA-04060-06 0006 (SRCD) KRANZLER, HENRY R Clinical research center for opioid and cocaine abuse Carbamazepine treatment of cocaine dependence

P50DA-04060-06 0007 (SRCD) JATLOW, PETER Clinical research center for opioid and cocaine abuse Cocaine-ethanol--Metabolism and role of cocaethylene

P50DA-04060-06 0008 (SRCD) PRICE, LAWRENCE H Clinical research center for opioid and cocaine abuse Clinical neurobiology of cocaine administration and abstinence

P50DA-04060-06 0009 (SRCD) KOSTEN, THERESE A Clinical research center for opioid and cocaine abuse Neurobehavioral studies of cocaine preference

P50DA-04060-06 0010 (SRCD) INNIS, ROBERT B Clinical research center for opioid and cocaine abuse SPECT and microdialysis measurements of stimulant abuse

P50DA-04060-06 0011 (SRCD) SATEL, SALLY L Clinical research center for opioid and cocaine abuse Serotonin medication of cue-induced cocaine craving

R01DA-04074-05 (DACB) BRANCH, MARC N UNIVERSITY OF FLORIDA GAINESVILLE, FL 32611 Behavioral determinants of cocaine tolerance

R01DA-04075-04A2 (DABR) TIETZ, ELIZABETH I MEDICAL COLLEGE OF OHIO PO BOX 10008 TOLEDO, OH 43699-0008 Chronic benzodiazepine effects on GABA receptor complex

R01DA-04077-05 (DABR) PATRICK, JAMES W BAYLOR COLLEGE OF MEDICINE ONE BAYLOR PLAZA HOUSTON, TX 77030 Monoclonal antibodies to the nicotine receptor site

R01DA-04087-05 (DABR) MEDZIHRADSKY, FEDOR UNIV OF MICHIGAN MEDICAL SCH 6440 MEDICAL SCIENCE I ANN ARBOR, MI 48109-0606 Opioid receptor mechanisms

R01DA-04089-07 (DACB) BIGELOW, GEORGE E FRANCIS SCOTT KEY MEDICAL CTR 4940 EASTERN AVENUE BALTIMORE, MD 21224 Opioid drug discrimination in humans

R01DA-04090-06 (DABR) LARSON, ALICE A UNIVERSITY OF MINNESOTA 295 ANIMAL SCI/VET MED BLDG ST PAUL, MN 55108 Excitatory amino acids--Role in pain and opioid activity

R01DA-04093-07 (DABR) WHITE, FRANCIS J LAFAYETTE CLINIC 951 E LAFAYETTE DETROIT, MI 48207 Cocaine and mesolimbic dopamine electrophysiology

R01DA-04103-05 (SRCD) CHASNOFF, IRA J NAPARE 11 EAST HUBBARD, SUITE 200 CHICAGO, IL 60611 Cocaine use in pregnancy

R01DA-04111-05 (DAPA) COLLINS, LINDA M UNIVER OF SOUTHERN CALIFORNIA LOS ANGELES, CA 90089-1061 Latent path/transition analysis in drug abuse prevention

R01DA-04113-05 (SRCD) PECHNICK, ROBERT UCLA SCHOOL OF MEDICINE LOS ANGELES, CA 90024-1735 Neuroendocrine effects of phencyclidine

R01DA-04118-06 (DABR) DOW-EDWARDS, DIANA L SUNY-HEALTH SCIENCE CENTER 450 CLARKSON AVE/BOX 1189 BROOKLYN, NY 11203 Effects of cocaine on development -- Brain and behavior

R01DA-04120-05 (DABR) GALLOWAY, MATTHEW P NPRU 951 E LAFAYETTE DETROIT, MI 48207 Cocaine and amphetamine--Mesocortical dopamine neurons

PROJECT NO., ORGANIZATIONAL UNIT., INVESTIGATOR, ADDRESS, TITLE

R01DA-04122-06 (DABR) MACDONALD, ROBERT L UNIVERSITY OF MICHIGAN ANN ARBOR, MI 48109 Opioid peptides--receptor - Ion channel coupling

R01DA-04123-04 (DABR) CHAVKIN, CHARLES UNIVERSITY OF WASHINGTON SEATTLE, WA 98195 Endogenous opioid peptide action in the hippocampus

R01DA-04126-03 (DACB) KSIR, CHARLES J, JR UNIVERSITY OF WYOMING DEPT OF PSYCHOLOGY LARAMIE, WY 82071 Behavioral neuropharmacology of nicotine

R01DA-04128-05 (DABR) KREAM, RICHARD M TUFTS UNIVERSITY 136 HARRISON AVENUE BOSTON, MA 02111 Dynamics of neuropeptide processing

R01DA-04130-06 (SRCD) FOLTIN, RICHARD W JOHNS HOPKINS UNIVERSITY 720 RUTLAND AVE BALTIMORE, MD 21205 Anorectic drugs--Abuse and behavioral mechanisms of action

R01DA-04133-06 (SRCD) ATOR, NANCY A JOHNS HOPKINS UNIV SCH OF MED 720 RUTLAND AVENUE BALTIMORE, MD 21205-2196 Analysis of anxiolytics as discriminative stimuli

R01DA-04136-06 (DABR) OWENS, S MICHAEL UNIV OF ARKANSAS MEDICAL SCIS 4301 W. MARKHAM STREET LITTLE ROCK, AR 72205 An immunological model of the PCP receptor and neuroligand

R01DA-04137-05 (DACB) EMMETT-OGLESBY, MICHAEL W TEXAS COL OF OSTEOPATHIC MED 3500 CAMP BOWIE BLVD FOR WORTH, TX 76107-2690 Tolerance to the stimulus properties of cocaine

R01DA-04141-05 (DAAR) SPECTER, STEVEN C UNIV OF SOUTH FLORIDA 12901 BRUCE B DOWNS TAMPA, FL 33612 Marihuana & immunity--suppressive mechanisms in humans

R01DA-04154-06 (DABR) DOUGLASS, JAMES O OREGON HEALTH SCIS UNIVERSITY 3181 SW SAM JACKSON PARK RD PORTLAND, OR 97201-3098 Control of expression of opioid peptide genes

R01DA-04157-07 (SRCD) KUCZENSKI, RONALD T UNIV OF CALIFORNIA, SAN DIEGO 9500 GILMAN DRIVE LA JOLLA, CA 92093-0603 Chronic drugs -- CNS biochemistry and behavior

R01DA-04166-06 (DABR) SADEE, WOLFGANG UNIVERSITY OF CALIFORNIA SAN FRANCISCO, CA 94143-0446 Opioid receptors in neuroblastoma cell lines

R01DA-04174-06 (DACB) PERKINS, KENNETH A WESTERN PSY INST AND CLINIC 3811 O'HARA STREET PITTSBURGH, PA 15213 Nicotine, energy balance, and prevention of weight gain

R01DA-04185-05 (DABR) YOBURN, BYRON C ST JOHN'S UNIVERSITY GRANT CENTRAL & UTOPIA PKWAYS JAMAICA, NY 11439 Pharmacodynamics of upregulation by opioid antagonists

R01DA-04190-05 (SRCD) LARSON, ALICE A UNIVERSITY OF MINNESOTA 1988 FITCH AVENUE ST PAUL, MN 55104 Opioids and desensitization to substance P in the spinal cord

R01DA-04194-03 (DABR) BODNAR, RICHARD J QUEENS COLLEGE OF CUNY 65-30 KISSENA BLVD FLUSHING, NY 11367 Opioid receptor subtype roles in rat feeding behavior

R01DA-04195-05 (SRCD) MARTINEZ, JOE L JR UNIVERSITY OF CALIFORNIA 3210 TOLMAN HALL BERKELEY, CA 94720 Enkephalins and learning

R01DA-04196-06 (DAAR) SHARP, BURT M HENNEPIN COUNTY MEDICAL CTR 701 PARK AVENUE SOUTH MINNEAPOLIS, MN 55415 Opiate receptor-mediated effects of stress on immunity

R01DA-04197-06 (SRCD) TYLOR, JOHN WATSON RUTGERS STATE UNIVERSITY P.O. BOX 939 NEW JERSEY, NJ 08855-0939 The development of peptide models of beta-endorphin

R01DA-04206-05 (DABR) CHO, ARTHUR K UNIV OF CALIFORNIA @ LOS ANGEL LOS ANGELES, CA 90024-1735 Chemical pharmacology of MDA and MDMA

R01DA-04216-04 (DABR) ZAHNISER, NANCY R UNIV OF COLORADO HLTH SCIS CTR 4200 EAST NINTH AVE DENVER, CO 80262 Persistent cocaine induced changes in dopamine release

R01DA-04222-06 (DABR) GIBB, JAMES W UNIVERSITY OF UTAH DEPT. OF PHARMA. & TOXICOLOGY SALT LAKE CITY, UT 84112 Neurochemical alterations by designer drugs

R01DA-04240-06 (DABR) CHANG, KWEN-JEN DUKE UNIV OF MED CTR BOX 3094 DURHAM, NC 27710 Molecular basis of multiple opioid receptors

R01DA-04248-05 (DABR) HRUBY, VICTOR J UNIVERSITY OF ARIZONA TUCSON, AZ 85721 Opioid receptor specific peptides

R01DA-04264-05 (SRCD) HO, ING K UNIV OF MISSISSIPPI MED CTR 2500 NORTH STATE STREET JACKSON, MS 39216 Cocaine--Pharmacodynamic and kinetic study in hypertensive rats

R01DA-04265-05 (DABR) BORNHEIM, LESTER M UNIV OF CALIF, SAN FRANCISCO SAN FRANCISCO, CA 94143 Cannabidiol--Effect on cytochrome P-450 isozymes

R01DA-04268-04S1 (DACB) ANGLIN, M DOUGLAS UCLA DRUG ABUSE RESEARCH GROUP 1100 GLENDON AVENUE, SUITE 763 LOS ANGELES, CA 90024-3511 Cocaine abuse--A prospective evaluation of therapeutic modalities

R01DA-04271-06 (DABR) HOOK, VIVIAN Y H UNIFORMED SRVS UNIV OF HLTH SC 4301 JONES BRIDGE ROAD BETHESDA, MD 20814 Biosynthesis of carboxypeptidase H and opiate peptides

R01DA-04274-05 (DABR) WILCOX, GEORGE L UNIVERSITY OF MINNESOTA 435 DELAWARE STREET, SE MINNEAPOLIS, MN 55455 Nociception, excitatory amino acids and drugs of abuse

R01DA-04275-05 (SRCD) RILEY, EDWARD P SAN DIEGO STATE UNIVERSITY 5300 CAMPANILE DRIVE SAN DIEGO, CA 92182-0350 Behavioral teratology of cocaine in the rat

R01DA-04278-04A2 (DABR) WESSINGER, WILLIAM D UNIV OF ARKANSAS FOR MED SCIS 4301 WEST MARKHAM STREET LITTLE ROCK, AR 72205 Determinants of the behavioral effects of PCP withdrawal

R01DA-04291-04 (DABR) BRIDGES, ROBERT S TUFTS UNIVERSITY 200 WESTBORO RD NORTH GRAFTON, MA 01536-1895 Opiate regulation and involvement in maternal behavior

R01DA-04293-04A2 (DABR) GOEDERS, NICHOLAS E LOUISIANA STATE UNIV MED CTR PO BOX 33932 SHREVEPORT, LA 71130-3932 Neurobiology of chronic cocaine administration

R01DA-04294-04 (DABR) ROBINSON, TERRY E UNIVERSITY OF MICHIGAN 1103 E HURON STREET ANN ARBOR, MI 48104-1687 The neural basis of behavioral sensitization

R01DA-04312-05 (SRCD) JOHNSON, JOHN P UNIVERSITY OF MARYLAND 655 W BALTIMORE STREET BALTIMORE, MD 21201 AIDS risk in pregnant IV drug users and their children

R01DA-04315-06 (DAAR) KARPATKIN, SIMON NEW YORK UNIVERSITY MEDICAL SC 550 FIRST AVENUE NEW YORK, NY 10016 AIDS and

PROJECT NO., ORGANIZATIONAL UNIT., INVESTIGATOR, ADDRESS, TITLE

thrombocytopenia in drug-abusers and homosexuals

R01DA-04331-05 (DAAR) COWAN, MORTON J UNIVERSITY OF CALIFORNIA THIRD & PARNASSUS AVENUES SAN FRANCISCO, CA 94143 HIV infection in children of IV drug abusing women

R01DA-04334-05 (SRCD) VLAHOV, DAVID JOHNS HOPKINS UNIVERSITY 615 NORTH WOLFE STREET The natural history of HTLV-III infection among drug users

R01DA-04337-05 (SRCD) DORUS, WALTER VETERANS ADMIN HOSPITAL DRUG DEPENDENCY TREATMENT CTR HINES, IL 60141 Consequences of HTLV-III infection for IV drug abusers

R01DA-04346-05 (SRCD) NURCO, DAVID N SOCIAL RESEARCH CENTER 1229 W MT ROYAL AVE BALTIMORE, MD 21217 Narcotic addiction, AIDS and intervention

R01DA-04347-05 (SRCD) FRIEDLAND, GERALD H MONTEFIORE MEDICAL CENTER 111 EAST 210TH STREET BRONX, N Y 10467 Natural history of HTLV-III/LAV infection in intravenous drug abusers

R01DA-04355-03 (DAAR) BIDLACK, JEAN M UNIVERSITY OF ROCHESTER 601 ELMWOOD AVE ROCHESTER, NY 14642 Opioid modulation of immunocompetence

R01DA-04363-05A1 (DAAR) MOSS, ANDREW R UNIVERSITY OF CALIFORNIA 995 PORTRERO AVENUE SAN FRANCISCO, CA 94110 HIV and drug use among the homeless in San Franciso

R01DA-04376-05 (DACB) STOLERMAN, IAN P INSTITUTE OF PSYCHIATRY DE CRESPIGNY PARK LONDON, SE5 8AF ENGLAND Comprehensive database of drug discrimination research

R01DA-04381-05 (DAAR) PETERSON, PHILLIP K HENNEPIN COUNTY MED CENTER 701 PARK AVENUE MINNEAPOLIS, MN 55415 Modulation of cell-mediated immune function by opiates

R01DA-04382-04A1 (DABR) CONLEE, ROBERT K BRIGHAM YOUNG UNIVERSITY 116-B RB PROVO, UT 84602 Cocaine and exercise--Role of the adrenergic system

R01DA-04390-03 (DAPA) LEHMAN, WAYNE TEXAS CHRISTIAN UNIVERSITY PO BOX 32880 FT WORTH, TX 76129 Drug use in the workplace--Prevalence, reasons, & impact

R01DA-04392-04 (SRCD) ANTHONY, JAMES C JOHNS HOPKINS UNIVERSITY 624 NORTH BROADWAY, RM 880 BALTIMORE, MD 21205 Etiology and prevention of drug-related behavior

R01DA-04398-05 (SRCD) KOOB, GEORGE F RESEARCH INST. OF SCRIPPS CLIN 10666 N TORREY PINES ROAD LA JOLLA, CA 92037 Neuronal substrates of cocaine reward

R01DA-04400-03S2 (DABR) DONAHOE, ROBERT M GEORGIA MENTAL HEALTH INST 1256 BRIARCLIFF ROAD, NE ATLANTA, GA 30306 AIDS and opiates--Monkey model

R01DA-04403-05 (SRCD) WINGER, GAIL D UNIV OF MICHIGAN MED SCHOOL M6322 MEDICAL SCIENCES BLDG I ANN ARBOR, MI 48109-0626 Pharmacological treatment of cocaine abuse

R01DA-04415-06 (DABR) WOODS, JAMES R, JR UNIVERSITY OF ROCHESTER DEPARTMENT OF OB/GYN ROCHESTER, NY 14642 The effects of cocaine on fetal oxygenation

R01DA-04418-06 (DACB) MC AULIFFE, WILLIAM E CAMBRIDGE HOSPITAL CAMBRIDGE, MA 02139 Recovery training and self help for cocaine addicts

R01DA-04420-05 (DABR) LIGHT, ALAN R UNIV OF N C AT CHAPEL HILL CB# 7545 CHAPEL HILL, N C 27599 Opioid peptide effects on spinal lamina I and II neurons

R01DA-04431-05 (DABR) MOLLIVER, MARK E JOHNS HOPKINS UNIV SCH OF MED 725 NORTH WOLFE STREET BALTIMORE, MD 21205 Neurotoxic effects of drugs on serotonergic neurons

R01DA-04433-05 (DAAR) CHITWOOD, DALE UNIVERSITY OF MIAMI SCH OF MED 1550 NW 10TH AVENUE, SUITE 309 MIAMI, FL 33136 Epidemiology of HTLV-III in intravenous drug abusers

R01DA-04438-06 (DACB) WOOD, RONALD W NEW YORK UNIVERSITY MED CTR 550 FIRST AVE NEW YORK, NY 10016 Drug self-administration by inhalation in the primate

R01DA-04441-05 (DABR) DEADWYLER, SAMUEL A BOWMAN GRAY SCHOOL OF MEDICNE 300 S HAWTHORNE ROAD WINSTON-SALEM, N C 27103 Consequences of THC induced structural changes in CNS

R01DA-04443-05 (SRCD) SCHILLER, PETER W CLINICAL RES INST OF MONTREAL 110 PINE AVE WEST MONTREAL, CANANDA H2W 1R7 Development of receptor-specific opioid peptide analogs

R01DA-04444-05 (DACB) HOLLOWAY, FRANK A UNIV OF OKLA HLTH SCIS CTR OKLAHOMA CITY, OK 73190-3000 Abuse liability of drug adjuncts for cocaine withdrawal

R29DA-04446-05 (DABR) MADHOK, THELMA C MINNEAPOLIS MEDICAL RES FDN 825 SOUTH 8TH ST, MMS D-3 MINNEAPOLIS, MN 55404 Central effects of nicotine on phosphorylation and cAMP

R01DA-04447-06 (DAPA) CURRY, SUSAN J GRP HLTH COOP CTR HLTH ST SUITE 1600 Increasing use of self-help relapse prevention programs

R01DA-04478-05 (SRCD) SPEAR, LINDA P SUNY AT BINGHAMTON DEPT OF PSYCHOLOGY BINGHAMTON, NY 13901 Neurobehavioral teratogenic investigations of cocaine

R01DA-04480-05 (SRCD) HO, ING K 2500 NORTH STATE STREET JACKSON, MS 39216-4505 Barbiturate tolerance-dependence and GABA system

R01DA-04484-05 (DACB) PEREZ-REYES, MARIO UNIV OF N C AT CHAPEL HILL MEDICAL RESEARCH BG CB# 7175 CHAPEL HILL, N C 27599 Psychoactive drugs/ethanol interaction

R01DA-04490-02 (SRCD) MC GIVERN, ROBERT F DEPARTMENT OF PSYCHOLOGY 5300 CAMPANILE DRIVE SAN DIEGO, CA 92182 Cocaine abuse--Effects on brain sexual differentiation

R01DA-04494-05 (DABR) FRICKER, LLOYD D ALBERT EINSTEIN COLL OF MED 1300 MORRIS PARK AVENUE BRONX, NEW YORK 10461 Regulation of carboxypeptidase E

R01DA-04497-04 (DAPA) BUSH, PATRICIA J GEORGETOWN UNIVERSITY 3900 RESERVOIR ROAD, N W WASHINGTON, D C 20007 Black childrens substance use -- Longitudinal influences

R01DA-04498-04A1 (SRCD) DONAHOE, ROBERT M GEORGIA MENTAL HEALTH INST 1256 BRIARCLIFF RD ATLANTA, GA 30306 Drug abuse and AIDS--An in vitro immunological model

R01DA-04507-03 (DABR) GOLDFARB, JOSEPH MOUNT SINAI SCHOOL OF MEDICINE ONE GUSTAVE L LEVY PLACE NEW YORK, NY 10029-6574 Hallucinogens--Serotonergic mechanisms in hippocampus

R01DA-04512-02 (DABR) MAKMAN, MAYNARD H ALBERT EINSTEIN COLLEGE OF MED 1300 MORRIS PARK AVENUE BRONX, NY 10461 Biochemistry of opioid tolerance--Cord-ganglia culture

R29DA-04520-05 (DACB) CINCIRIPINI, PAUL M UNIV OF TEXAS MEDICAL BRANCH DEPARTMENT OF PSYCHIATRY GALVESTON, TEX 77550-2774 Gradual vs abrupt smoking cessation--The effect of schedules

R01DA-04523-05 (DABR) WILLIAMS, JOHN T OREGON HEALTH SCIS UNIVERSITY 3181 SW SAM JACKSON PARK RD PORTLAND, OR 97201-3098 Cocaine--Effects on single neurons

R01DA-04530-04 (ALCP) EGGERT, LEONA L UNIVERSITY OF WASHINGTON DEPT OF PSYCHOSOC NUR SC-76 SEATTLE, WA 98195 Reconnecting at-risk youth: drug users and dropouts

R29DA-04545-05 (SRCD) HIGGINS, STEPHEN T UNIVERSITY OF VERMONT DEPARTMENT OF PSYCHIATRY BURLINGTON, VT 05401 Stimulant-alcohol interactions in humans

R29DA-04551-05 (DABR) WEST, MARK O RUTGERS UNIVERSITY DEPT OF PSYCH - BUSCH CAMPUS NEW BRUNSWICK, NJ 08903 Cocaine--Striatal and accumbens neurons and behavior

R01DA-04582-10 (NLS) POTTER, DAVID D HARVARD MEDICAL SCHOOL 220 LONGWOOD AVE BOSTON, MASS 02115 Synaptic functions in culture--Peptidergic and others

R01DA-04586-03 (DABR) KRISTAL, MARK B SUNY AT BUFFALO DEPARTMENT OF PSYCHOLOGY BUFFALO, NY 14260 Characterization of placental opioid-enhancing factor

R01DA-04592-02 (SRCD) WOLGIN, DAVID L FLORIDA ATLANTIC UNIVERSITY BOCA RATON, FL 33431-0991 Role of instrumental learning in tolerance to stimulants

R29DA-04598-04 (SRCD) MILLINGTON, WILLIAM R UNIV OF MISSOURI @ KANSAS CITY BIOLOGICAL SCIENCE BUILDING KANSAS CITY, MO 64110-2499 The post-translational processing of beta-endorphin

R01DA-04600-03 (DABR) PICKEL, VIRGINIA M 411 EAST 69TH STREET NEW YORK, NY 10021 EM-transmitter interactions of striatal opioid neurons

R01DA-04604-02 (DAPA) TSUANG, MING T BROCKTON-W ROXBURY VA MED CTR 940 BELMONT STREET BROCKTON, MA 02401 Twin study of drug abuse and dependence

R01DA-04722-05 (DAAR) THOMSEN, DONALD L, JR SOCIETAL INST/THE MATH SCIS 97 PARISH ROAD SOUTH NEW CANAAN, CT 06840 Statistical methodology for study of the AIDS epidemic

R01DA-04725-03 (DACB) OVERTON, DONALD A TEMPLE UNIVERSITY 13TH & C B MOORE AVE/WEISS HAL PHILADELPHIA, PA 19122 Modification of drug effects by conditioning procedures

R01DA-04731-04 (SRCD) HIENZ, ROBERT D JOHNS HOPKINS UNIVERSITY BALTIMORE, MD 21205 Cocaine--Sensory/motor psychophysical effects

R01DA-04732-03 (DACB) GLASSMAN, ALEXANDER H NYS PSYCHIATRIC INSTITUTE 722 WEST 168TH STREET NEW YORK, NY 10032 Clinical trial of clonidine for nicotine withdrawal

R29DA-04745-04 (SRCD) LIU-CHEN, LEE-YUAN TEMPLE UNIVERSITY 3420 N BROAD STREET PHILADELPHIA, PA 19140 Purification of mu opioid receptor

R01DA-04746-02 (DABR) ROBINSON, SUSAN E VIRGINIA COMMONWEALTH UNIVERSI BOX 613/MCV STATION RICHMOND, VA 23298-0613 The development neurochemistry of cocaine

R01DA-04750-05 (SRCD) CRAVEN, DONALD E BOSTON CITY HOSPITAL 818 HARRISON AVENUE, BLDG 411 BOSTON, MA 02118 HIV transmission in newborns--Pregnant women at high risk for AIDS

R01DA-04758-04 (DABR) NICHOLS, DAVID E PURDUE UNIVERSITY R.E. HEINE PHARMACY BUILDING WEST LAFAYETTE, IN 47907 Structure activity studies of MDMA-like substances

R01DA-04762-03 (DABR) FROIMOWITZ, MARK MCLEAN HOSPITAL 115 MILL STREET BELMONT, MA 02178 Effect of conformation on opioid agonists/antagonists

R01DA-04775-05 (DACB) MOERSCHBAECHER, JOSEPH M L S U MEDICAL CENTER DEPARTMENT OF PHARMACOLOGY NEW ORLEANS, LA 70112-1393 Benzodiazepine effects on operant behavior

R01DA-04777-05 (SRCD) CHAVEZ, ERNEST L COLORADO STATE UNIVERSITY FORT COLLINS, CO 80523 Mexican-American dropouts and drug abuse

R01DA-04787-05 (SRCD) SHAPSHAK, PAUL UNIVERSITY OF MIAMI 1425 NW 10TH AVE MIAMI, FL 33136 Replication of HIV in brain cell cultures

R29DA-04788-05 (SRCD) KELLEY, ANN E NORTHEASTERN UNIVERSITY 360 HUNTINGTON AVE BOSTON, MA 02115 Peptide modulation of mesolimbic dopamine--Behavior analysis

R29DA-04789-04 (SRCD) KING, ROY J STANFORD UNIVERSITY DEPT OF PSYCHIATRY STANFORD, CA 94305 Monoamine predictors of drug abuse and sociopathy

R01DA-04791-04 (SRCD) KRASINSKI, KEITH M NEW YORK UNIVERSITY DEPT. OF PEDIATRICS NEW YORK, N Y 10016 Natural history of HIV infection in infants of addicted mothers

R01DA-04795-04A1 (DABR) ROSENZWEIG, MARK R UNIVERSITY OF CALIFORNIA BERKELEY, CA 94720 Drugs of abuse studied in chick brain memory system

R29DA-04800-04 (SRCD) HILLARD, CECILIA J MEDICAL COLLEGE OF WISCONSIN 8701 WATERTOWN PLANK RD MILWAUKEE, WI 53226 Neurochemical mechanisms of nicotine action

R01DA-04822-05 (SRC) CHASNOFF, IRA J NATL ASSOC FOR PERINATAL RES/E 11 E HUBBARD ST CHICAGO, IL 60611 Epidemiology of maternal substance abuse in pregnancy

R01DA-04827-03 (DAAR) WATSON, RONALD R UNIVERSITY OF ARIZONA TUCSON, AZ 85724 Drugs, immunomodulation & resistance to retrovirus-AIDS

R18DA-04841-03S1 (SRCD) KOTRANSKI, LYNNE C PHILADELPHIA HLTH MGN CO 260 SO BROAD STREET - 20TH FL PHILADELPHIA, PA 19102 Philadelphia IV/AIDS community outreach demonstration

R01DA-04844-03 (DACB) GELLER, BARBARA WASHINGTON UNIVERSITY 4940 AUDUBON AVENUE ST LOUIS, MO 63110 Lithium in adolescent drug abuse

R01DA-04859-04 (SRCD) MONTI, PETER M PROVIDENCE VA MEDICAL CENTER DAVIS PARK PROVIDENCE, R I 02908 Social skills treatment of cocaine abusers

R01DA-04864-03 (DACB) RIES, RICHARD K UNIVERSITY OF WASHINGTON 325 9TH AVE ZA-99 SEATTLE, WA 98195 Dual diagnosis intervention study

R01DA-04865-03 (DABR) VAN DE KAR, LOUIS D LOYOLA UNIVERSITY OF CHICAGO 2160 SOUTH FIRST AVENUE MAYWOOD, IL 60153 Effects of cocaine on neuroendocrine function

R01DA-04866-04 (DAPA) KANDEL, DENISE B COLUMBIA UNIVERSITY 722 W

PROJECT NO., ORGANIZATIONAL UNIT., INVESTIGATOR, ADDRESS, TITLE

PROJECT NO., ORGANIZATIONAL UNIT., INVESTIGATOR, ADDRESS, TITLE

168TH ST NEW YORK, NY 10032 Epidemiology/family in drug use-- The second generation

R01DA-04870-03 (SRCD) LEX, BARBARA W MC LEAN HOSPITAL 115 MILL STREET BELMONT, MASS 02178 Female marihuana users & familial alcoholism

R01DA-04874-04 (SRCD) FRIED, PETER A CARLETON UNIVERSITY OTTAWA, ONTARIO CANADA K1S 5B6 Cannabis and cigarette exposure--Long term effects

R01DA-04887-03 (DAPA) DONOHEW, ROBERT L UNIVERSITY OF KENTUCKY LEXINGTON, KY 40506-0042 Sensation seeking & drug abuse prevention

R01DA-04905-03 (DABR) OLSEN, GEORGE D OREGON HEALTH SCIENCES UNIV 3181 SW SAM JACKSON PARK ROAD PORTLAND, OR 97201-3098 Fetal cocaine exposure; effect on neonatal breathing

R01DA-04907-03 (DABR) HORITA, AKIRA UNIVERSITY OF WASHINGTON DEPT OF PHARMACOLOGY, SJ-30 SEATTLE, WA 98195 Cholinergic mechanisms in cocaine & amphetamine actions

R01DA-04925-03 (DACB) LATIES, VICTOR G UNIV. OF ROCHESTER ENVIRON. HEALTH SCIENCES CTR. ROCHESTER, NY 14642 Psychomotor stimulants & stimulus control

R01DA-04944-05 (SRCA) HARVEY, JOHN A MEDICAL COLL OF PENNSYLVANIA DEPARTMENT OF PHARMACOLOGY PHILADELPHIA, PA 19129 Neurotoxic hallucinogens--Effects on learning

R01DA-04953-04 (DABR) COX, BRIAN M UNIFORMED SERV UNIV/HEALTH SCI 4301 JONES BRIDGE ROAD BETHESDA, MD 20814 Molecular basis of cocaine action

R01DA-04965-02 (DACB) HURT, HALLAM ALBERT EINSTEIN MED CENTER YORK AND TABOR ROADS PHILADELPHIA, PA 19141 Maternal cocaine abuse--long-term effects on infants

R01DA-04972-03 (DACB) MEISCH, RICHARD A UNIV OF TEXAS HLTH SCI CTR DEPT OF PSYCHIATRY BEHAV SCI HOUSTON, TX 77225 Acquisition of drug reinforcing effects

R01DA-04975-04 (DABR) AIZENMAN, ELIAS UNIVERSITY OF PITTSBURGH 3550 TERRACE STREET PITTSBURGH, PA 15261 Functional properties of a central nicotine receptor

R01DA-04986-04 (SRCD) SACHS, DAVID P PALO ALTO CTR/PULM DIS PREVENT 750 WELCH ROAD, SUITE 200 PALO ALTO, CA 94304-1509 Optimum dose and schedule for nicotine gum treatment

R01DA-04987-03 (DAPA) DANSEREAU, DONALD F TEXAS CHRISTIAN UNIVERSITY FORT WORTH, TX 76129 Tools for improving drug and alcohol education/prevention

R01DA-04988-04 (DABR) WALKER, J MICHAEL BROWN UNIVERSITY-HUNTER LAB 89 WATERMAN STREET, BOX 1853 PROVIDENCE, RI 02912 Sigma opiate receptor pharmacology

R01DA-05002-04A1 (SRCD) MADDEN, JOHN J GEORGIA MENTAL HEALTH INSTI 1256 BRIARCLIFF ROAD, NE ATLANTA, GA 30306 Cellular aspects of opiate binding to human leukocytes

P50DA-05010-05 (SRCD) BARCHAS, JACK D UNIV OF CALIFORNIA @ LOS ANGEL 760 WESTWOOD PLAZA LOS ANGELES, CA 90024-1722 Center for study of neuroregulators and drugs of abuse

P50DA-05010-05 0001 (SRCD) BARCHAS, JACK D Center for study of neuroregulators and drugs of abuse Mechanism of processing of opioid precursors

P50DA-05010-05 0002 (SRCD) BARCHAS, JACK D Center for study of neuroregulators and drugs of abuse Studies on opiate-regulated receptors

P50DA-05010-05 0003 (SRCD) BARCHAS, JACK D Center for study of neuroregulators and drugs of abuse Regulation and interactions between components of the opioid system

R01DA-05013-05 (SRCD) HATSUKAMI, DOROTHY K UNIVERSITY OF MINNESOTA BOX 392 UMHC MINNEAPOLIS, MN 55455 Treatment of smokeless tobacco users

R01DA-05014-02 (DABR) TANK, A WILLIAM UNIVERSITY OF ROCHESTER 601 ELMWOOD AVENUE ROCHESTER, NY 14642 Effects of nicotine on the adrenal medulla

R01DA-05018-04 (DABR) FRANCE, CHARLES P LSU SCHOOL OF DENTISTRY 1100 FLORIDA AVE NEW ORLEANS, PA 70119 Discriminative stimulus effects of opioid withdrawal

R01DA-05031-03 (SRCD) SEIDLER, FREDERIC J DUKE UNIV MEDICAL CENTER DURHAM, N C 27710 Maternal cocaine & neonatal nervous system development

R01DA-05038-06 (SRCD) PIPER, DOUGLAS L PACIFIC INST FOR RES & EVAL 5157 LORUTH TERRACE MADISON, WI 53711 Healthy for life--An efficacy test of two program versions

R01DA-05041-04 (SRCD) ETTENBERG, AARON UNIVERSITY OF CALIFORNIA SANTA BARBARA, CA 93106 Mechanisms of opiate and stimulant drug reinforcement

R01DA-05056-03 (SRCD) REINISCH, JUNE M INDIANA UNIVERSITY THE KINSEY INST FOR RESEARCH BLOOMINGTON, IN 47405 Social deviance & drug abuse--Effects of drugs in utero

R01DA-05066-03 (DABR) GNEGY, MARGARET E UNIVERSITY OF MICHIGAN M6322 MEDICAL SCIENCE I ANN ARBOR, MI 48109-0626 Chronic stimulants and calmodulin

R01DA-05072-05 (SRCD) OLNEY, JOHN W WASHINGTON UNIVERSITY 660 S EUCLIKD AVENUE, BOX 8134 ST LOUIS, MO 63110 PCP, sigma opiates, and glutamergic transmission

R01DA-05073-02 (DABR) BENNETT, BARBARA A BOWMAN GRAY SCHOOL OF MEDICINE 300 SOUTH HAWTHORNE ROAD WINSTON-SALEM, NC 27103 Effects of stimulants on dopaminergic neurons in culture

R01DA-05080-04 (DACB) WOOD, RONALD W NEW YORK UNIVERSITY MED CTR 550 FIRST AVE NEW YORK, NY 10016 Behavioral pharmacology of abused aerosols - "crack"

R01DA-05084-04 (DABR) LINDBERG, IRIS LOUISIANA STATE UNIVERSITY 1901 PERDIDO STREET NEW ORLEANS, LA 70112 Opioid peptide synthesizing enzymes

R01DA-05086-04 (DACB) ROEHRS, TIMOTHY A HENRY FORD HOSPITAL 2921 W GRAND BLVD DETROIT, MI 48202 Determinants of hypnotic self administration

R01DA-05100-03 (DABR) KORNETSKY, CONAN BOSTON UNIV SCHOOL OF MED 80 EAST CONCORD STREET BOSTON, MA 02118 Opiate receptor subtypes & CNS motivational systems

R29DA-05102-04 (SRCD) MOODY, DAVID E UNIVERSITY OF UTAH CTR FOR HUMAN TOXICOLOGY SALT LAKE CITY, UTAH 84112 Polymorphism in the metabolism of drugs of abuse

R01DA-05104-02 (DACB) WINTERS, KEN C UNIVERSITY OF MINNESOTA HARVARD ST @ E RIVER ROAD MINNEAPOLIS, MN 55455 Assessment & treatment of adolescent substance abusers

R01DA-05107-02 (DACB) STEIN, LARRY UNIV OF CALIFORNIA COLL OF MED IRVINE, CA 92717 Reward mechanisms & drug abuse

R01DA-05114-05 (SRCD) LEHMAN, ANTHONY F UNIV OF MARYLAND MEDICAL CENTR 645 W REDWOOD ST BALTIMORE, MARYLAND 21201 Implications of substance abuse in pychiatric patients

R01DA-05117-01A2 (DABR) WATERHOUSE, BARRY D HAHNEMANN UNIVERSITY BROAD AND VINE PHILADELPHIA, PA 19102-1192 Cocaine modulation of sensory cortical function

R01DA-05121-04 (DACB) ELKINS, RALPH L VA MEDICAL CENTER PSYCHOLOGY SERVICE (116BU) AUGUSTA, GA 30910 Aversion therapy of cocaine abuse

R01DA-05126-03 (DAPA) JOHNSON, BRUCE D NARCOTIC AND DRUG RESEARCH INC 11 BEACH STREET NEW YORK, NY 10013 Natural history of crack distribution

P50DA-05130-05 (SRCD) KREEK, MARY J ROCKEFELLER UNIV-ENDOCRIN DEPT 1230 YORK AVE NEW YORK, N Y 10021-6399 Treatment of addictions--Biological correlates

P50DA-05130-05 0001 (SRCD) PASTERNAK, GAVRIL W Treatment of addictions--Biological correlates Long-acting opiate agonists and antagonists

P50DA-05130-05 0002 (SRCD) INTURRISI, CHARLES E Treatment of addictions--Biological correlates Biosynthesis and release of opioid peptides and catecholamines

P50DA-05130-05 0003 (SRCD) ROBERTSON, HUGH D Treatment of addictions--Biological correlates Detection and characterization of causative agent for delta hepatitis

P50DA-05130-05 0004 (SRCD) KREEK, MARY JEANNE Treatment of addictions--Biological correlates Methadone metabolism, drug interactions

P50DA-05130-05 0005 (SRCD) KREEK, MARY JEANNE Treatment of addictions--Biological correlates Neuroendocrine, endocrine effects of addictive drugs--Role of endogenous opioids

P50DA-05130-05 0006 (SRCD) CULPEPPER-MORGAN, JOAN Treatment of addictions--Biological correlates GI effects of opiates & antagonists--Role of endogenous opioids in GI function

P50DA-05130-05 0007 (SRCD) KREEK, MARY JEANNE Treatment of addictions--Biological correlates Immune function of effects of abused drugs and drugs used to treat addiction

P50DA-05130-05 0008 (SRCD) NOVICK, DAVID Treatment of addictions--Biological correlates Treated narcotic addicts--Co-existing major medical problems

R01DA-05142-05 (SRCD) BRUNSWICK, ANN F COLUMBIA UNIVERSITY 60 HAVEN AVENUE, B-4 NEW YORK, NEW YORK 10032 Multidimensional study of AIDS risk in a black community

R01DA-05147-05 (SRCD) LYKKEN, DAVID T UNIVERSITY OF MINNESOTA DEPARTMENT OF PSYCHIATRY MINNEAPOLIS, MN 55455 Twin/family study of vulnerability to substance abuse

R01DA-05152-04 (DAAR) COOLEY, PHILIP C RESEARCH TRIANGLE INSTITUTE P O BOX 12194 RES TRIANGLE PARK, NC 27709 Simulation of IV drug effects on HIV infections and AIDS

R01DA-05154-02 (DACB) CHEREK, DONALD R UNIV OF TEXAS HEALTH SCIENCE C 1300 MOURSUND HOUSTON, TX 77225 Marihuana effects on performance and social behavior

R18DA-05156-03S1 (SRCD) WILLIAMS, MARK L AFFILIATED SYSTEMS CORP 1200 POST OAK BLVD SUITE 540 HOUSTON, TX 77056-3104 AIDS community outreach demonstration project

R01DA-05158-04 (SRCD) KELLY, MARTIN J OREGON HEALTH SCIS UNIVERSITY 3181 S W SAM JACKSON PARK ROAD PORTLAND, OREG 97201 Opioid effects on hypothalamic neuronal excitability

R01DA-05159-03 (SRCD) JOHNSON, KENNETH M, JR UNIVERSITY OF TEXAS MED BRANCH 301 UNIVERSITY BOULEVARD GALVESTON, TEX 77550-2774 Neurochemical pharmacology of chronic cocaine

R01DA-05161-03 (SRCD) PAHWA, SAVITA N SHORE UNIVERSITY HOSPITAL 300 COMMUNITY DRIVE MANHASSET, NY 11030 HIV infection in children of IV drug abusers

R01DA-05167-04 (SRCD) WAMSLEY, JAMES KEVIN THE NEUROPSYCHIATRIC INSTITUTE 700 FIRST AVENUE SOUTH FARGO, ND 58103 Cocaine -- Effects on dopamine receptors and transport

R01DA-05171-05 (SRCD) MORGAN, JAMES P BETH ISRAEL HOSPITAL 330 BROOKLINE AVENUE BOSTON, MA 02215 Cardiac & vascular toxicity of cocaine

R01DA-05175-05 (SRCD) PARSONS, OSCAR A UNIV OF OKLAHOMA HLTH SCI CTR DEPT OF PSYCH & BEHAV SCI OKLAHOMA CITY, OK 73104 Diazepam, alcohol and human information processing

R18DA-05176-03S1 (SRCD) WATSON, DEENA D DARCO DRUG SERVICES, INC 2722 INWOOD RD DALLAS, TEXAS 75235 AIDS and IV drug users--community outreach/education

R01DA-05180-03 (SRCD) KNUEPFER, MARK M ST. LOUIS UNIVERSITY MED CTR 1402 S GRAND BOULEVARD ST. LOUIS, MO 63104 Cardiovascular effects of cocaine

R01DA-05183-04 (DAPA) HUIZINGA, DAVID H UNIVERSITY OF COLORADO CAMPUS BOX 483 BOULDER, CO 80309 Children, youth, and drugs--A longitudinal study

P50DA-05186-05 (SRCD) O'BRIEN, CHARLES P UNIVERSITY OF PENNSYLVANIA DEPARTMENT OF PSYCHIATRY PHILADELPHIA, PA 19104-6021 Treatment and prevention of intravenous drug abuse

P50DA-05186-05 0001 (SRCD) WOODY, GEORGE E Treatment and prevention of intravenous drug abuse Psychotherapy for intravenous opiate dependence

P50DA-05186-05 0002 (SRCD) ALTERMAN, ARTHUR I Treatment and prevention of intravenous drug abuse Treatment of dependence on intravenous or inhaled cocaine

P50DA-05186-05 0003 (SRCD) YOBURN, BYRON C Treatment and prevention of intravenous drug abuse Naltrexone safety

P50DA-05186-05 0004 (SRCD) MCLELLAN, A THOMAS Treatment and prevention of intravenous drug abuse Prevention of relapse to IV opioids in federal probationers

P50DA-05186-05 0005 (SRCD) LUCKI, IRWIN Treatment and prevention of intravenous drug abuse Dependence on prescription medication

P50DA-05186-05 0006 (SRCD) EHRMAN, RONALD N Treatment and prevention of intravenous drug abuse Animal models of stress and IV drug dependence

P50DA-05186-05 0007 (SRCD) TERENIUS, LARS Y Treatment and prevention of intravenous drug abuse Endogenous opioids in tolerance and dependence

R01DA-05192-04 (SRCD) DE LEON, GEORGE INTEGRITY, INC 103 LINCOLN PARK NEWARK, N J 07102 Adolescent drug abusers in TCs: evaluation of effectiveness

R01DA-05195-03 (SRCD) ALDRICH, JANE L OREGON STATE UNIVERSITY PHARMACY BUILDING CORVALLIS, OR 97331-3507 Dynorphin analogues as K opioid receptor antagonists

R01DA-05196-05 (SRCD) PRESTON, KENZIE L FRANCIS SCOTT KEY MEDICAL CTR 4940 EASTERN AVE BALTIMORE, MD 21224 Pharmacological modulation of cocaine effects

R01DA-05220-03 (DAPA) KILPATRICK, DEAN G MEDICAL UNIV OF SOUTH CAROLINA 171 ASHLEY AVENUE CHARLESTON, SC 29425-0742 Risk factors for substance abuse--A longitudinal study

R01DA-05227-05 (SRCD) CHASSIN, LAURIE A ARIZONA STATE UNIVERSITY TEMPE, AZ 85287 Substance use among adolescent children of alcoholics

R01DA-05228-03 (DABR) CRABBE, JOHN C OREGON HEALTH SCIENCES UNIV PORTLAND, OR 97201 Genetic vulnerability to drugs of abuse

R01DA-05253-03 (DACB) KALLMAN, MARY J UNIVERSITY OF MISSISSIPPI UNIVERSITY, MS 38677 Behavioral pharmacology of chronic benzodiazepine use

R01DA-05255-02 (DABR) NAPIER, TAYVE C LOYOLA UNIVERSITY CHICAGO 2160 SOUTH FIRST AVENUE MAYWOOD, IL 60153 Opioid effects on nucleus basalis cholinergic neurons

R01DA-05258-04A1 (DABR) GREENBLATT, DAVID J TUFTS UNIVERSITY 136 HARRISON AVE BOSTON, MA 02111 Chronic benzodiazepines -- Behavior and neurochemistry

R01DA-05259-02 (DAPA) FRIEDMAN, ALFRED S PHILADELPHIA PSYCHIATRIC CTR FORD ROAD AND MONUMENT AVENUE PHILADELPHIA, PA 1913 Drug use or abuse as predictor to school and career failure

R18DA-05271-03S1 (SRCD) MC AULIFFE, WILLIAM E PROJECT OUTREACH 875 MASSACHUSETTS AVE CAMBRIDGE, MA 02139 Boston demonstration of outreach for AIDS prevention

R01DA-05272-04 (SRCD) SMITH, CHARLES B UNIV OF MICHIGAN MEDICAL SCHOO ANN ARBOR, MI 48109-0626 Psychomotor stimulants and adrenergic nerve function

P50DA-05273-04 (SRCD) BIGELOW, GEORGE E FRANCIS SCOTT KEY MEDICAL CTR 4940 EASTERN AVENUE BALTIMORE, MD 21224 Treatment research center--Behavioral pharmacology

P50DA-05274-04 (SRCD) MARTIN, BILLY R MEDICAL COLLEGE OF VIRGINIA BOX 613, MCV STATION RICHMOND, VA 23298-0001 Center for drug abuse research

P50DA-05274-04 0003 (SRCD) ROBINSON, SUSAN Center for drug abuse research The developmental neurochemistry of methadone

P50DA-05274-04 0005 (SRCD) BALSTER, ROBERT L Center for drug abuse research Neural basis for the abuse of cocaine

P50DA-05274-04 0007 (SRCD) ELLIS, EARL F Center for drug abuse research Cocaine and the cerebral circulation

P50DA-05274-04 0008 (SRCD) MARTIN, BILLY R Center for drug abuse research Nicotine agonist and antagonist receptors

P50DA-05274-04 0009 (SRCD) DEWEY, WILLIAM L Center for drug abuse research Opioid tolerance /dependence in neonatal rats

P50DA-05274-04 0010 (SRCD) ABOOD, MARY E Center for drug abuse research Cloning and characterization of cannabinoid receptors

P50DA-05274-04 0011 (SRCD) WELCH, SANDRA P Center for drug abuse research Mechanism Of cannabinoid antinociceptive action

P50DA-05274-04 9001 (SRCD) MARTIN, BILLY R Center for drug abuse research Core -- Drug abuse research

R01DA-05277-02 (DAAR) ROSENBAUM, MARSHA INST FOR SCIENTIFIC ANALYSIS 2235 LOMBARD STREET SAN FRANCISCO, CA 94123 IV drug use methadone maintenance and AIDS

R18DA-05283-03S1 (SRCD) SUFIAN, MERYL NARCOTIC & DRUG RESEARCH, INC. 11 BEACH STREET NEW YORK, NY 10013 Community AIDS-prevention outreach demonstration

R18DA-05285-03S2 (SRCD) WIEBEL, W WAYNE UNIV OF ILLINOIS @ CHICAGO 2121 W TAYLOR CHICAGO, IL 60612 AIDS community outreach demonstration project

R18DA-05286-03S1 (SRCD) FRENCH, JOHN NEW JERSTY STATE DEPT OF HLTH CN 632 TRENTON, NEW JERSEY 08625 Newark AIDS community outreach demonstration project

R18DA-05289-03S1 (SRCD) FRENCH, JOHN NEW JERSEY STATE DEPT OF HLTH CN 362 TRENTON, NEW JERSEY 08625-0362 Jersey City AIDS community outreach demonstration

R01DA-05295-03 (DACB) AZRIN, NATHAN H NOVA UNIV 3301 COLLEGE AVE FORT LAUDERDALE, FL 33314 Behavior therapy for drug abuse

P50DA-05303-03 (SRCD) ELLINWOOD, EVERETT H, JR DUKE UNIVERSITY MEDICAL CENTER DEPARTMENT OF PSYCHIATRY DURHAM, N C 27710 Preclinical sciences center for cocaine treatment

P50DA-05303-03 0006 (SRCD) GUPTA, SAMIR K Preclinical sciences center for cocaine treatment Comparative pharmacokinetics and dynamics of cocaine

P50DA-05303-03 9001 (SRCD) KRISHNAN, H RANGA Preclinical sciences center for cocaine treatment Core--Human recruitment and assessment

P50DA-05303-03 9002 (SRCD) ELLINWOOD, EVERETT H Preclinical sciences center for cocaine treatment Core--Animal preparation and testing

P50DA-05303-03 0001 (SRCD) ELLINWOOD, EVERETT H Preclinical sciences center for cocaine treatment Autoreceptor sensitivities in single unit studies

P50DA-05303-03 0002 (SRCD) KILTS, CLINTON D Preclinical sciences center for cocaine treatment Chronic cocaine administration & withdrawal--Effect on dopamine neuronal function

P50DA-05303-03 0003 (SRCD) NEMEROFF, CHARLES B Preclinical sciences center for cocaine treatment Neuropeptide interctions with chronic cocaine-induced behavior changes

P50DA-05303-03 0004 (SRCD) SLOTKIN, THEODORE Preclinical sciences center for cocaine treatment Interaction of cocaine with biogenic amine uptake sites

P50DA-05303-03 0005 (SRCD) PRITCHETT, EDWARD L C Preclinical sciences center for cocaine treatment Recreational cocaine use and cardiac arrhythmias

PROJECT NO., ORGANIZATIONAL UNIT., INVESTIGATOR, ADDRESS, TITLE

R01DA-05305-05 (SRCD) FALK, JOHN L RUTGERS UNIVERSITY PSYCHOLOGY BLDG, BUSCH CAMPUS NEW BRUNSWICK, N J 08903 Cocaine & behavior--Oral abuse & motor control

R01DA-05311-03 (SRCD) ROSENBERG, NEIL L CTR FOR OCCUPATIONAL NEUROLOGY 701 EAST HAMPDEN AVENUE ENGLEWOOD, CO 80110 Neurological sequelae of chronic toluence inhalation abuse

P50DA-05312-05 (SRCD) CLAYTON, RICHARD R CTR FOR PREVENTION RESEARCH 147 WASHINGTON AVE LEXINGTON, KY 40506-0402 Drug abuse prevention--A life course perspective

P50DA-05312-05 0001 (SRCD) BARDO, MICHAEL T Drug abuse prevention--A life course perspective Novelty, dopamine and drug reward

P50DA-05312-05 0002 (SRCD) CLAYTON, RICHARD R Drug abuse prevention--A life course perspective Evaluation of Project DARE, a primary prevention program

P50DA-05312-05 0003 (SRCD) DONOHEW, ROBERT L Drug abuse prevention--A life course perspective Increasing the effectiveness of televised anti-drug public service announcements

P50DA-05312-05 0004 (SRCD) COLE, HENRY P Drug abuse prevention--A life course perspective Preventing drug abuse in the mining industry

P50DA-05312-05 0005 (SRCD) HENDRICKS, JON A Drug abuse prevention--A life course perspective Drug abuse and its prevention among the elderly

R01DA-05314-03 (DABR) GERMAN, DWIGHT C UNIV OF TEXAS S W MEDICAL CTR 5323 HARRY HINES BLVD DALLAS, TX 75235-9070 Neurobiology of opioid-dopamine interactions

R01DA-05317-05 (SRCD) PEARLSON, GODFREY D JOHNS HOPKINS HOSPITAL 600 NORTH WOLFE STREET BALTIMORE, MD 21205 Cocaine PET effects on brain metabolism and dopaminergic D2 receptors

P50DA-05321-04 (SRCD) SCHINKE, STEVEN P COLUMBIA UNIVERSITY 622 WEST 113TH ST NEW YORK, NY 10025 Research center on AIDS prevention among minority groups

P50DA-05321-04 0001 (SRCD) HEBERT, JAMES R Research center on AIDS prevention among minority groups Epidemiology of HIV infection

P50DA-05321-04 0002 (SRCD) MILLER, SAMUEL O Research center on AIDS prevention among minority groups Black youth and prevention of HIV infection

P50DA-05321-04 0003 (SRCD) SCHINKE, STEVEN P Research center on AIDS prevention among minority groups Hispanic youth and families and prevention

P50DA-05321-04 0004 (SRCD) SCHILLING, ROBERT F Research center on AIDS prevention among minority groups HIV prevention and drug users

P50DA-05321-04 9001 (SRCD) SCHINKE, STEVEN P Research center on AIDS prevention among minority groups Core--Intervention development

P50DA-05321-04 9002 (SRCD) MAHAN, CLAIRE Research center on AIDS prevention among minority groups Core--Program evaluation, data processing, telecommunications

P50DA-05321-04 9003 (SRCD) MILLER, SAMUEL O Research center on AIDS prevention among minority groups Core--social marketing

P50DA-05321-04 9004 (SRCD) NICHOLS, STUART E Research center on AIDS prevention among minority groups Core--Community interaction

R01DA-05324-05 (SRCD) SEIDLIN, MINDELL NYU MED CTR DEPT MEDICINE 550 FIRST AVENUE NEW YORK, NY 10016 Heterosexual transmission of HIV to partners of IV drug abusers

R01DA-05325-04 (SRCD) WOODS, JAMES H UNIVERSITY OF MICH MED SCH ANN ARBOR, MI 48109-0626 Behavioral pharmacology of PCP & related compounds

R01DA-05332-03 (DAPA) ROSENBAUM, MARSHA INST FOR SCIENTIFIC ANALYSIS 2235 LOMBARD STREET SAN FRANCISCO, CA 94123 Women and cocaine--A descriptive study

R01DA-05333-05 (DABR) GILLIS, RICHARD A GEORGETOWN UNIVERSITY 3900 RESERVOIR ROAD, NW WASHINGTON, DC 20007 Neurocardiovascular effects of cocaine

R01DA-05334-05 (SRCD) SZAPOCZNIK, JOSE SPANISH FAMILY GUIDANCE CTR 1425 N W 10TH AVENUE, 3RD FL MIAMI, FL 33136 Engagement and treatment of adolescent drug users

R29DA-05346-03 (DACB) HOWELL, LEONARD L EMORY UNIVERSITY ATLANTA, GA 30322 Behavioral and respiratory effects of methylxanthines

R01DA-05347-05 (DAPA) CONGER, RAND D IOWA STATE UNIVERSITY 107 EAST HALL AMES, IA 50011 Rural family economic stress and adolescent drug use

R01DA-05348-05 (SRCD) MERIKANGAS, KATHLEEN R YALE UNIVERSITY 40 TEMPLE ST LOWER LEVEL NEW HAVEN, CT 06510-3223 Specificity of transmission of drug abuse

R18DA-05349-03S1 (SRCD) MCCOY, CLYDE B UNIV OF MIAMI SCHOOL OF MED 1550 NW 10TH AVE, SUITE 309 MIAMI, FL 33136 Prevention of HIV/related disease among Miami IV drug users

R01DA-05356-04 (DAAR) SCHILLING, ROBERT F COLUMBIA UNIVERSITY 622 WEST 113TH STREET NEW YORK, NY 10025 Reducing relapse and the spread of AIDS in IV drug users

R01DA-05361-03 (DACB) GILBERT, DAVID G SOUTHERN ILLINOIS UNIVERSITY DEPT OF PSYCHOLOGY CARBONDALE, IL 62901-6502 Factors influencing success in cigarette abstinence

R01DA-05365-04 (SRCD) STREISSGUTH, ANN P UNIVERSITY OF WASHINGTON MAILSTOP GG-20 SEATTLE, WA 98195 Cocaine--Pregnancy use and offspring development

R01DA-05366-05 (DABR) CAREY, ROBERT J SUNY HEALTH SCIENCE CENTER 750 EAST ADAMS STREET SYRACUSE, NY 13210 Study of stimulant-induced conditioned drug effects

R44DA-05395-03 (SRCD) GRISSOM, GRANT R INTEGRA, INC 320 KING OF PRUSSIA ROAD RADNOR, PA 19087 Enhancement of the addiction severity index

R01DA-05396-03 (DACB) HANS, SYDNEY L UNIVERSITY OF CHICAGO HOSPITAL 5841 S MARYLAND AVENUE CHICAGO, IL 60637 Behavior of school-age children from drug-using families

R44DA-05400-03 (SRCD) NUWAYSER, ELIE S BIOTEK, INC 21-C OLYMPIA AVENUE WOBURN, MA 01801 One week sustained release methadone microcapsules

R01DA-05412-05 (DABR) COSCIA, CARMINE J ST LOUIS UNIVERSITY SCH OF MED 1402 S GRAND BLVD ST LOUIS, MO 63104 Differential development of opoid receptors

R01DA-05431-01A2 (DABR) BOISSE, NORMAN R NORTHEASTERN UNIVERSITY 360 HUNTINGTON AVE. BOSTON, MA. 02115 Pharmacology of benzodiazepine dependence

R01DA-05433-04 (DACB) MC MAHON, ROBERT C UNIVERSITY OF MIAMI P O BOX 248065 CORAL GABLES, FL 33124 Prediction of relapse among treated cocaine abusers

R01DA-05440-04 (DABR) TEMPEL, ANN HILLSIDE HOSPITAL DIV OF LIJMC 75-59 263RD STREET GLEN OAKS, N Y 11004 Opioid receptor regulation in the developing animal

R29DA-05446-04 (DABR) PECHNICK, ROBERT NELSON UCLA SCHOOL OF MEDICINE LOS ANGELES, CA 90024-1735 Effects of perinatal phencyclidine in the rat

R29DA-05452-03 (DABR) MURPHY, LAURA LYNN SOUTHERN ILLINOIS UNIVERSITY CARBONDALE, IL 62901 Neuroendocrine mechanisms of cannabinoid action

R29DA-05460-04 (SRCD) RICHARDSON, GALE A WESTERN PSYCHIATRIC INST/CLIN 3811 O'HARA STREET PITTSBURGH, PA 15213 The effect of prenatal cocaine use on infant outcome

R01DA-05466-04 (DABR) WESSENDORF, MARTIN W UNIVERSITY OF MINNESOTA DEPT OF CELL BIO & NEUROANA MINNEAPOLIS, MINNESOTA 55455 Pain, opiates, and coexistence of transmitter with 5-ht

R01DA-05471-04 (DACB) GOSNELL, BLAKE A UNIV OF MICHIGAN MED CTR BOX 0116 ANN ARBOR, MI 48109-0116 Opiates, taste and food preferences

R01DA-05477-04 (SRCD) CARROLL, FRANK I RESEARCH TRIANGLE INSTITUTE PO BOX 12194 RES TRIANGLE PARK, NC 27709 Cocaine -- A study of the biochemical mechanism of action

R01DA-05484-05 (EDC) BRACKEN, MICHAEL B YALE UNIVERSITY DEPT OF EPID & PUBLIC HEALTH NEW HAVEN, CT 06510 Environmental tobacco smoke and pregnancy outcome

R01DA-05485-04 (DACB) NADEMANEE, KOONLAWEE DENVER HEALTH AND HOSPITALS 777 BANNOCK STREET DENVER, CO 80204 Cardiovascular effects and toxicities of cocaine

R01DA-05488-04 (DABR) RAZDAN, RAJ K ORGANIX INC 65 CUMMINGS PARK WOBURN, MA 01801 Synthesis of delta-9THC related compounds

R29DA-05490-03 (DABR) NESTLER, ERIC J CONNECTICUT MENTAL HLTH CTR 34 PARK STREET NEW HAVEN, CT 06508 Intracellular mediators of psychotropic drug action

R29DA-05510-04 (SRCD) VARELA, BENIGNO L PONCE SCHOOL OF MEDICINE P O BOX 7004, UNIVERSITY STREE PONCE, PR 00732 HTLV-I infection & ATL in Puerto Rico

R01DA-05512-04 (DAPA) THORNBERRY, TERENCE P S U N Y-ALBANY, DRAPER HALL 135 WESTERN AVENUE ALBANY, N Y 12222 Social network approach to drug use of minority youth

R01DA-05513-03 (DABR) HILL, HARLAN F FRED HUTCHINSON CANCER RES CTR 1124 COLUMBIA STREET SEATTLE, WA 98104 Enhancement of opioid analgesia in human

R01DA-05536-04A2 (DABR) CHURCH, MICHAEL W WAYNE STATE UNIVERSITY 275 EAST HANCOCK DETROIT, MI 48201 Teratogenicity of cocaine -- Sensory disorders

R01DA-05539-02 (SRCD) GOODMAN, MURRAY UNIV OF CALIFORNIA, SAN DIEGO LA JOLLA, CA 92093 Synthesis of selective cyclic opioids

R01DA-05543-04 (DACB) STOLERMAN, IAN PETER INSTITUTE OF PSYCHIATRY LONDON, ENGLAND SE5 8AF The discrimination of abused drug mixtures

R29DA-05548-04 (DACB) SCHENK, SUSAN TEXAS A&M UNIVERSITY DEPARTMENT OF PSYCHOLOGY COLLEGE STATION, TX 77843 Mechanisms of enviromental influences on cocaine reward

R01DA-05565-04 (DAAR) NYAMATHI, ADELINE M UNIV OF CALIFORNIA, L.A. SCHOOL OF NURSING LOS ANGELES, CA 90024-6918 Counseling/HIV testing for at risk minority women

R01DA-05568-02 (DAAR) KLEIN, THOMAS W UNIVERSITY OF SOUTH FLORIDA 12901 N BRUCE B DOWNS BLVD TAMPA, FL 33612 Cocaine and catecholamine effects on T lymphocytes

R01DA-05569-03 (DACB) BROONER, ROBERT K FRANCIS SCOTT KEY MED CTR SEBDTP/DEPT OF PSYCHIATRY DSE BALTIMORE, MD 21224 Antisocial drug abusers--diagnosis and treatment

R01DA-05570-03 (DACB) SPEAR, SHERILYNN NORTHERN ILLINOIS UNIVERSITY DE KALB, IL 60115 Evaluating two approaches to adolescent aftercare

R01DA-05575-04 (DAAR) DJEU, JULIE Y UNIVERSITY OF SOUTH FLORIDA 12901 BRUCE B DOWNS BLVD TAMPA, FL 33612 Effect of cannabinoids on resistance to C. albicans

R01DA-05581-04 (SRCD) BROWN, LAWRENCE S JR ADDIC RES & TREATMENT CORP 22 CHAPEL STREET BROOKLYN, NY 11201 Heterosexual HIV transmission--Minority IVDA and their sexual partners

R18DA-05582-03 (SRCA) HAVASSY, BARBARA E UNIV OF CALIFORNIA @ SAN FRAN SAN FRANCISCO GENERAL HOSPITAL SAN FRANCISCO, CA 94110 Efficacy of cocaine treatments--A collaborative study

R01DA-05583-03 (DAAR) LYMAN, WILLIAM D ALBERT EINSTEIN COLLEGE OF MED BRONX, NY 10461 HIV infection of neural tissue: an organotypic model

R01DA-05585-04 (DACB) COTTLER, LINDA M WASHINGTON UNIVERSITY ST LOUIS, MO 63110 Reliability of DMS & ICD substance use disorders

R01DA-05589-04 (SRCD) ANGLIN, M DOUGLAS UCLA DRUG ABUSE RESEARCH CTR. 1100 GLENDON AVENUE, SUITE 763 LOS ANGELES, CA 90024 HIV infection and transmission risk in homosexual and heterosexual IVDU

R01DA-05592-04 (SRCD) ROUNSAVILLE, BRUCE J APT FOUNDATION, INC 904 HOWARD AVEUE NEW HAVEN, CT 06519 Diagnosis of drug abuse--Clinical implications

R01DA-05593-03 (DAAR) WOODY, GEORGE E VA MEDICAL CENTER UNIVERSITY & WOODLAND AVE PHILADELPHIA, PA 19104 Spread of AIDS in intravenous drug users

R01DA-05602-02 (SRCD) RIVIER, CATHERINE SALK INST FOR BIOLOGICAL STUDI PO BOX 85800 SAN DIEGO, CA 92138-5800 Effect of cocaine on endocrine function

P50DA-05605-03 (SRCD) TARTER, RALPH E WESTERN PSYCHIATRIC INST & CLN 3811 O'HARA STREET PITTSBURGH, PA 15213 Drug abuse vulnerability-mechanisms and manifestations

R01DA-05615-02 (DAAR) LEWIS, BENJAMIN F SPECTRUM HOUSE INC 106 EAST MAIN STREET WESTBORO, MA 01581 Comprehensive surveillance of HIV in intravenous drug users

R01DA-05617-01A1 (DAPA) SU, S SUSAN UNIVERSITY OF MINNESOTA 290 MCNEAL HALL ST. PAUL, MN 55108 Vulnerability to drug abuse in high-risk youth

R01DA-05618-03 (DABR) ZUKIN, RUTH S ALBERT EINSTEIN COLLEGE OF MED 1300 MORRIS PARK AVENUE BRONX, N Y 10461 Molecular characterization of kappa receptor subtypes

R01DA-05619-03 (DAAR) COTTLER, LINDA M WASHINGTON UNIVERSITY 4940 AUDUBON AVE ST LOUIS, MO 63110 Risk factors for HIV infection in drug users and partners

R01DA-05623-03 (DACB) GOLDSTEIN, MICHAEL G MIRIAM HOSPITAL 164 SUMMIT AVE PROVIDENCE, R I 02906 Efficacy of clonidine as an aid to smoking cessation

R01DA-05626-04 (SRCD) KOSTEN, THOMAS R YALE UNIVERSITY 27 SYLVAN AVENUE NEW HAVEN, CT 06519 Buprenorphine maintenance for opioid addicts

R01DA-05634-03 (DAPA) MC LELLAN, A THOMAS UNIVERSITY OF PENNSYLVANIA PHILADELPHIA, PA 19104-6021 Patient-treatment matching strategy for EAP networks

R18DA-05661-05 (SRCA) CASTRO, FELIPE G SAN DIEGO STATE UNIVERSITY 5178 COLLEGE AVENUE SAN DIEGO, CA 92182 Matches and mismatches in treatments for cocaine users

R01DA-05672-03 (DAPA) PETTIWAY, LEON E UNIVERSITY OF DELAWARE NEWARK, DE 19716 Drug use and the spatial patterns of crime

R01DA-05685-03 (DACB) WILKINS, JEFFREY N BRENTWOOD, VAMC (B116A22) LOS ANGELES, CA 90073 Bromocriptine in the treatment of cocaine abuse

R01DA-05688-03 (DACB) LANGENBUCHER, JAMES RUTGERS STATE UNIVERSITY P O BOX 1089 PISCATAWAY, NJ 08855-1089 Multisite study of substance use diagnosis

R01DA-05691-03 (DAPA) COOK, ROYER F CONSAD RESEARCH CORPORATION 121 N HIGHLAND AVE PITTSBURGH, PA 15206 Workplace drug use prevalence estimation methods

P01DA-05695-03 (SRCD) LOH, HORACE H UNIVERSITY OF MINNESOTA DEPARTMENT OF PHARMACOLOGY MINNEAPOLIS, MN 55455 Regulation of neuropeptides and receptor function

P01DA-05695-03 0001 (SRCD) CONTI-TRONCONI, BIANCA Regulation of neuropeptides and receptor function Peptide mapping of neurotransmitter receptors

P01DA-05695-03 0002 (SRCD) LOH, HORACE H Regulation of neuropeptides and receptor function Characterization of delta opioid receptors

P01DA-05695-03 0003 (SRCD) PORTOGHESE, PHILIP Regulation of neuropeptides and receptor function Non-washable binding of opioid azines to brain membranes

P01DA-05695-03 0004 (SRCD) LAW, PING-YEE Regulation of neuropeptides and receptor function Regulation of delta opioid receptor gene--controlling elements

P01DA-05695-03 0005 (SRCD) TAKEMORI, A E Regulation of neuropeptides and receptor function Delta opioid receptors--Development of opioid tolerance & dependence

P01DA-05695-03 0006 (SRCD) ELDE, ROBERT Regulation of neuropeptides and receptor function: Processes involved in storage and release of neuropeptides

P01DA-05695-03 0007 (SRCD) RAFERTY, MICHAEL Regulation of neuropeptides and receptor function Study of voltage-generated sodium channels

P01DA-05695-03 0008 (SRCD) LEE, NANCY M Regulation of neuropeptides and receptor function Role of dynorphin in perception and modulation of pain

P01DA-05695-03 9001 (SRCD) LOH, HORACE H Regulation of neuropeptides and receptor function Core--Scientific

R29DA-05699-03 (DABR) WELDER, ALLISON A UNIV OF OKLAHOMA HEALTH SCIS C COLLEGE OF PHARMACY OKLAHOMA CITY, OK 73190 Effects of exercise training on cocaine cardiotoxicity

R01DA-05702-04 (DAPA) BROOK, JUDITH S NEW YORK MEDICAL COLLEGE VALHALLA, N Y 10595 Drug use and problem behaviors in minority youth

R01DA-05706-03 (DABR) COMB, MICHAEL J MASSACHUSETTS GENERAL HOSPITAL BLDG 149 13TH STREET BOSTON, MA 02129 Molecular mechanisms of proenkephalin gene regulation

R29DA-05707-03 (DABR) RICAURTE, GEORGE A FRANCIS SCOTT KEY MEDICAL CTR. 4940 EASTERN AVENUE BALTIMORE, MD 21224 MDMA neurotoxicity in primates -- Permanent or transient?

R29DA-05708-03 (DABR) CUNNINGHAM, KATHRYN A UNIV OF TEXAS MEDICAL BRANCH GALVESTON, TX 77550-2774 Limbic neuropsychopharmacology of cocaine

R29DA-05712-04 (SRCD) BEARDSLEY, PATRICK M G D SEARLE & COMPANY 4901 SEARLE PKWY, J-1 CNSDR SKOKIE, IL 60077 Stimulus control by drugs of drug self-administration

R29DA-05716-03 (DACB) ROACHE, JOHN D UNIV OF TEXAS MENTAL SCI INST 1300 MOURSUND AVE. HOUSTON, TEXAS 77030 Analysis of performance deficits induced by abused drugs

R01DA-05721-03 (DABR) CARROLL, FRANK I RESEARCH TRIANGLE INSTITUTE PO BOX 12194 RES TRIANGLE PARK, NC 27709 Development of selective sigma receptor ligands

R01DA-05722-03 (DACB) CROWLEY, THOMAS J UNIV OF COLORADO SCH OF MED 4200 EAST NINTH AVENUE DENVER, COLO 80262 Cocaine effects on alcohol drinking and social behavior

R01DA-05723-03 (SRCD) HALL, NICHOLAS R UNIVERSITY OF SOUTH FLORIDA 3515 EAST FLETCHER AVENUE TAMPA, FL 33613 Attenuation of morphine withdrawal by alpha-interferon

R01DA-05724-03 (DACB) BLASS, ELLIOTT M DEPT OF PSYCHOLOGY CORNELL UNIVERSITY ITHACA, NY 14853-7601 Affective development in human infants

R01DA-05728-02 (DABR) MURPHY, RANDALL B NEW YORK UNIVERSITY 4 WASHINGTON PLACE NEW YORK, NY 10003 Isolation and characterization of the sigma-receptor

R01DA-05730-03 (DAPA) NG, STEPHEN K COLUMBIA U - SERGIEVSKY CENTER 630 WEST 168TH STREET NEW YORK, N Y 10032 Cocaine abuse--effects on pregnancy and the newborn

R29DA-05737-02 (DABR) MCCASLIN, PATRICK P UNIV OF MISSISSIPPI MED CENTER 2500 NORTH STATE STREET JACKSON, MS 39216-4505 Acute and chronic barbiturates--in vitro biochemistry

R18DA-05741-03S1 (SRCD) VOGTSBERGER, KENNETH N UNIV OF TEXAS HLTH SCI CENTER 7703 FLOYD CURL DRIVE SAN ANTONIO, TX 78284-7792 AIDS community outreach demonstration project

R18DA-05743-03S1 (SRCD) ROBLES, RAFAELA R PUERTO RICO DEPT ADDICTION SER PO BOX 21414, RIO PIEDRAS STAT RIO PIEDRAS, P R 00928-1474 AIDS community outreach and counseling

PROJECT NO., ORGANIZATIONAL UNIT., INVESTIGATOR, ADDRESS, TITLE

R18DA-05745-03S1 (SRCD) LEWIN, JOHN C HAWAII STATE DEPT OF HEALTH P.O. BOX 3378 HONOLULU, HI 96801 AIDS research & chow project
R18DA-05746-03S1 (SRCD) DEREN, SHERRY NARCOTIC & DRUG RESEARCH, INC 11 BEACH STREET NEW YORK, NY 10013 Harlem AIDS outreach & counseling demonstration project
R18DA-05747-03S1 (SRCD) RHODES, FEN CALIFORNIA STATE UNIV-LONG BEA PSYCHOLOGY DEPT, AIDS ED, 438 LONG BEACH, CA 90840 AIDS outreach to IV drug users, sex partner's, and runaways
R18DA-05748-03S1 (SRCD) GLIDER, PEGGY J AMITY, INC 316 S 6TH AVENUE TUCSON, AZ 85701 Comprehensive community-based AIDS outreach/counseling
R18DA-05750-03S1 (SRCD) SCHENSUL, JEAN INSTITUTE FOR COMMUNITY RES 999 ASYLUM AVENUE HARTFORD, CT 06105 Community outreach prevention effort
R18DA-05751-03S1 (SRCD) BROADNAX, STANLEY E CINCINNATI HEALTH DEPARTMENT 3101 BURNET AVENUE CINCINNATI, OH 45229 Reaching Everyone--Aids and Cincinnati's Health--REACH
R18DA-05752-03S1 (SRCD) WOOD, ROBERT W SEATTLE-KING CTY DEPT OF HLTH 1116 SUMMIT, SUITE 300 SEATTLE, WA 98101 Control of AIDS through community health outreach
R18DA-05753-03S1 (SRCD) ODEGAARD, BILLI OREGON HEALTH DIVISION 1400 SW 5TH, 2ND FLOOR PORTLAND, OR 97201 Outreach & AIDS prevention education to IV drug users
R18DA-05754-03S1 (SRCD) STEPHENS, RICHARD C CLEVELAND STATE UNIVERSITY DEPARTMENT OF SOCIOLOGY CLEVELAND, OH 44115 AIDS education to IV drug users and sexual partners
R18DA-05755-04 (SRCD) FRENCH, JOHN NJ STATE DEPT OF HEALTH CN 362, 129 E HANOVER ST TRENTON, NJ 08625-0362 Paterson AIDS community outreach/counseling project
R18DA-05757-03S1 (SRCD) SIEGAL, HARVEY A WRIGHT STATE UNIVERSITY SUBSTANCE ABUSE INTERVEN PROG DAYTON, OH 45435 Dayton-Columbus AIDS outreach/prevention program
R18DA-05758-03S1 (SRCD) ROUNSAVILLE, BRUCE J APT FOUNDATION, INC 904 HOWARD AVENUE, SUITE 2A NEW HAVEN, CT 06519 AIDS outreach demonstration research project
R18DA-05759-03S1 (SRCD) SHORTY, VERNON DESIRE NARCOTIC REHAB CTR, INC 3307 DESIRE PARKWAY NEW ORLEANS, LA 70126 New Orleans--desire AIDS/IV drug outreach demo research
R18DA-05761-03S1 (SRCD) GREEN, ANNETTE ALLEGHENY COUNTY MH/MR DA PROG 304 WOOD ST., 5TH FLOOR PITTSBURGH, PA 15222 Allegheny County outreach/intervention project
R18DA-05763-03S1 (SRCD) HALIKAS, JAMES A UNIVERSITY OF MINNESOTA BOX 393 UMHC MINNEAPOLIS, MN 55455 A phase II community based AIDS risk reduction project
R44DA-05778-03 (SRCD) RAWSON, RICHARD MATRIX CENTER, INC 8447 WILSHIRE BLVD BEVERLY HILLS, CA 90211 Neurobehavioral model for outpatient cocaine treatment
R01DA-05794-03 (DAAR) LANCZ, GERALD J UNIVERSITY OF SOUTH FLORIDA 12901 BRUCE B DOWNS BLVD/MDC 1 TAMPA, FL 33612 Marijuana, immunity and herpesvirus infection
Z01DA-05801-04 (VL) HERNING, R I ARC, NIDA Mapping the effects of cocaine
R01DA-05807-03 (DACB) PERKINS, KENNETH A WESTERN PSY INST AND CLINIC 3811 O'HARA STREET PITTSBURGH, PA 15213 Chronic and acute tolerance to nicotine in humans
R01DA-05815-03 (DACB) WENGER, GALEN R UNIV OF ARKANSAS FOR MED SCIS 4301 WEST MARKHAM STREET LITTLE ROCK, AR 72205 Drugs of abuse and cognitive behavior
R01DA-05816-02 (DABR) NOCK, BRUCE L WASHINGTON UNIVERSITY 660 SOUTH EUCLID AVENUE ST LOUIS, MO 63110 Properties of kappa and a novel opiate receptor in brain
R01DA-05817-03 (DABR) MUELLER, KATHYRNE J TEXAS CHRISTIAN UNIVERSITY BOX 32878 FORT WORTH, TX 76129 Amphetamine-induced stereotypic locomotions
R01DA-05819-03 (DABR) HOWELLS, RICHARD D UMDNJ-NEW JERSEY MEDICAL SCH 185 SOUTH ORANGE AVENUE NEWARK, NJ 07103-2757 Molecular consequences of tolerance and dependence
R01DA-05821-03 (DAPA) CADORET, REMI J UNIVERSITY OF IOWA IOWA CITY, IA 52242 Gene-environment interaction in etiology of drug abuse
R01DA-05824-02 (DAPA) CATALANO, RICHARD F UNIVERSITY OF WASHINGTON 146 N CANAL STREET, SEATTLE, WA 98103 Risk focused prevention training/methadone maintenance
R01DA-05826-03 (DACB) BAUER, LANCE O UNIV OF CONNECTICUT HLTH CTR FARMINGTON, CT 06032 Cocaine withdrawal--Neuropsychological aspects
R01DA-05828-03 (DABR) HO, ING KANG UNIV OF MISSISSIPPI MED CTR 2500 NORTH STATE STREET JACKSON, MS 39216-4505 Mechanism of action of butorphanol
R29DA-05831-03 (DAPA) SKINNER, WILLIAM F UNIVERSITY OF KENTUCKY DEPARTMENT OF SOCIOLOGY LEXINGTON, KY 40506-0057 Drug abuse among homosexuals--A longitudinal study
R01DA-05832-01A2 (DAAR) CABRAL, GUY A VIRGINIA COMMONWEALTH UNIV BOX 678, MCV STATION RICHMOND, VA 23298-0678 Effect of marijuana on macrophage antigen presentation
R29DA-05833-02 (SRCD) VATHY, ILONA U ALBERT EINSTEIN COLL OF MED 1300 MORRIS PARK AVE BRONX, NEW YORK 10461 Opiates & development of female reproductive behavior
R01DA-05834-03 (DAPA) DEYKIN, EVA Y HARVARD SCHOOL OF PUB HEALTH 677 HUNTINGTON AVE , KRESGE 3 BOSTON, MA 02115 Teen drug dependence--comorbidity and treatment course
R01DA-05850-02 (DACB) MANNO, BARBARA R LOUISIANA STATE UNIV MED CTR 1501 KINGS HIGHWAY SHREVEPORT, LA 71130-3932 Cannabis pharmacokinetics--relation to human performance
R01DA-05852-02 (DAPA) COLLINS, R LORRAINE RES INST ON ALCOHOLISM 1021 MAIN STREET BUFFALO, NY 14203 Nurses' substance abuse--stress, coping and self-efficacy
R01DA-05854-01A2 (SRCD) EYLER, FONDA DAVIS UNIVERSITY OF FLORIDA BOX J-296 GAINESVILLE, FL 32610 Project care
R29DA-05856-03 (DABR) TUNIN MACANESPIE, CAROL JOHNS HOPKINS UNIV SCH OF MED 720 RUTLAND AVE BALTIMORE, MD 21205 Cardiovascular and baroreceptor responses to cocaine
R01DA-05858-02 (SRCD) ALTERMAN, ARTHUR VETRANS ADMIN MEDICAL CENTER UNIVERSITY & WOODLAND AVENUES PHILADELPHIA, PA 19104 Sociopathy and treatment outcome in substance abusers

PROJECT NO., ORGANIZATIONAL UNIT., INVESTIGATOR, ADDRESS, TITLE

R01DA-05860-03 (DABR) FOLTZ, RODGER L UNIVERSITY OF UTAH 417 WAKARA WAY RM 290 SALT LAKE CITY, UT 84108 MDMA--Metabolite indentification and neurotoxicity
R01DA-05874-02 (DAPA) BROOK, JUDITH S NEW YORK MEDICAL COLLEGE VALHALLA, N Y 10595 Drug use: A multigenerational study
R01DA-05876-02 (DAAR) MACGREGOR, ROB R UNIVERSITY OF PENNSYLVANIA PHILADELPHIA, PA 19104 Opiates, immune function, and control of HIV infection
R01DA-05880-07 (DACB) STITZER, MAXINE L FRANCIS SCOTT KEY MED CENTER 4940 EASTERN AVE, D-5-WEST BALTIMORE, MD 21224 Marijuana smoking--behavioral and biological effects
R44DA-05889-02 (SRCD) HINK, ROBERT F EXPERT SYSTEM DESIGN, INC 156 TUNNEL ROAD BERKELEY, CA 94705 An expert system advisor for drug detoxification
R01DA-05899-02 (DAAR) ANDIMAN, WARREN A YALE UNIV SCHOOL OF MEDICINE 333 CEDAR STREET NEW HAVEN, CT 06510 Pathogenetic and virologic aspects of pediatric AIDS
R01DA-05901-02 (DAAR) CHUANG, RONALD Y UNIVERSITY OF CALIFORNIA DEPARTMENT OF PHARMACOLOGY DAVIS, CA 95616 Opioid dependency and AIDS
R01DA-05907-03 (DACB) BAUMEISTER, ALAN A LOUISIANA STATE UNIVERSITY 236 AUDUBON HALL BATON ROUGE, LA 70803 CNS effects of morphine--Role of the ventral midbrain
R01DA-05911-03 (DAAR) NELSON, KENRAD E JOHNS HOPKINS UNIVERSITY 615 N WOLFE STREET BALTIMORE, MD 21205 Incident and sexually transmitted HIV in drug users
R01DA-05912-03 (DAPA) VEGA, WILLIAM A UNIVERSITY OF CALIFORNIA 504 WARREN HALL BERKELEY, CA 94720 Patterns of drug use: hispanic & non-hispanic male teens
R01DA-05917-02 (SRCD) BILLMAN, GEORGE E OHIO STATE UNIVERSITY 333 WEST 10TH AVE COLUMBUS, OH 43210 Cocaine-induced ventricular fibrillation
R01DA-05919-02 (SRCD) WHEELER, DARRELL D MEDICAL UNIV OF SOUTH CAROLINA 171 ASHLEY AVENUE CHARLESTON, SC 29425 Cocaine & monoaminergic systems--in vitro studies
R29DA-05932-03 (DABR) WILSON, MARLENE A UNIVERSITY OF SOUTH CAROLINA COLUMBIA, SC 29208 Hormones, GABA responses and benzodiazepine tolerance
R01DA-05934-02 (DAPA) ERFURT, JOHN C UNIVERSITY OF MICHIGAN 1111 EAST CATHERINE ANN ARBOR, MI 48109-2054 EAP client follow-up and family involvement
R01DA-05938-03 (DACB) RICAURTE, GEORGE A FRANCIS SCOTT KEY MEDICAL CTR 4940 EASTERN AVENUE BALTIMORE, MD 21224 MDMA neurotoxicity in humans--Occurrance and consequences
R01DA-05942-02 (DAAR) MAGURA, STEPHEN NARCOTIC & DRUG RESEARCH 11 BEACH STREET NEW YORK, NY 10013 AIDS prevention in jail for IV drug users and at-risk youth (RAP)
R29DA-05944-03 (DACB) WEISS, ROGER D MC LEAN HOSPITAL 115 MILL STREET BELMONT, MA 02178 Predictors of outcome in cocaine dependence
R01DA-05945-03 (SRC) LAW, PING Y UNIVERSITY OF MINNESOTA MINNEAPOLIS, MN 55455 Cloning at kappa-opiod receptor
R01DA-05950-03 (DAPA) WILLS, THOMAS A ALBERT EINSTEIN COLLEGE OF MED 1300 MORRIS PARK AVE BRONX, NY 10461 Coping and competence in adolescent drug use
P01DA-05951-03 (ALCB) CICERO, THEODORE J WASHINGTON UNIVERSITY DEPARTMENT OF PSYCHIATRY ST LOUIS, MO 63110 Dependence liability of psychotrophic substances
R01DA-05952-02 (DAPA) MEZZICH, ADA C WESTERN PSYCHIATRIC INST & CLI 3811 O'HARA STREET PITTSBURGH, PA 15260 Female adolescent drug abuse--biobehavioral development
R01DA-05964-02 (DABR) JONAKAIT, G MILLER RUTGERS, STATE UNIVERSITY 101 WARREN STREET NEWARK, NJ 07102 Maternal drug abuse--Effects on fetal raphe development
R01DA-05969-03 (DABR) CHANG, SULIE L LSU MEDICAL CTR 1100 FLORIDA AVE NEW ORLEANS, LA 70119 Molecular neurobiology of morphine action
R01DA-05970-02 (DABR) CLARKE, PAUL B MCGILL UNIVERSITY 3655 DRUMMOND STREET QUEBEC, CANADA H3G 1Y6 Quasi-irreversible blockade of nicotine's central action
R01DA-05971-02 (DACB) HANDELSMAN, LEONARD MOUNT SINAI SCHOOL OF MEDICINE ONE GUSTAVE L LEVY PLACE NEW YORK, NY 10029 Amantadine for treatment of cocaine dependence
R43DA-05983-01A2 (SRCD) TIPTON, ARTHUR J ATRIX LABORATORIES, INC 1625 SHARP POINT DR, BOX 20150 FT COLLINS, CO 80522-2501 Biodegradable injectable delivery system for naltrexone
R44DA-05984-02 (SRCD) RAMACHANDRAN, JANAKIRAMAN NEUREX CORPORATION 3760 HAVEN AVENUE MENLO PARK, CA 94025 Cloning and expression of opioid receptor genes
R43DA-05987-01A1 (SRCD) DAY, HARRY R DEVELOPMENT ASSOCIATES, INC 1730 NORTH LYNN STREET ARLINGTON, VA 22209-2009 An EAP managed care and evaluation system
R01DA-05995-02 (DAAR) MANTELL, JOANNE E NEW YORK CITY DEPT OF HEALTH 125 WORTH STREET, BOX A 1 NEW YORK, NY 10013 HIV testing/risk reduction among inner-city women
R01DA-05998-02 (DAAR) LYNCH, THOMAS J TEMPLE UNIVERSITY SCH OF MED 3420 N BROAD STREET PHILADELPHIA, PA 19140 Do immune mediators modify the effects of drugs of abuse
R01DA-06001-01A1 (DAAR) MARMOR, MICHAEL NEW YORK UNIV MEDICAL CENTER 341 EAST 25TH STREET 2ND FLOOR NEW YORK, NY 10010-2508 HIV infection among intravenous drug users
R01DA-06011-02 (SRCD) LEE, NANCY M UNIVERSITY OF MINNESOTA 435 DELAWARE STREET, SE MINNEAPOLIS, MN 55455 Opioid effects on bone marrow and T-cells
R01DA-06013-02 (DACB) GOEDERS, NICHOLAS E LOUISIANA STATE UNIV MED CTR SHREVEPORT, LA 71130-3932 Environmental influences on cocaine self-administration
R01DA-06030-02 (SRCA) JOHANSON, CHRIS E UNIFORMED SERVS UNIV OF THE 4301 JONES BRIDGE RD BETHESDA, MD 20814 Stimulus properties of anxiolytics in humans
R29DA-06031-02 (DABR) WELCH, SANDRA P MEDICAL COLLEGE OF VIRGINIA BOX 613, MCV STATION RICHMOND, VA 23298-0613 Calcium modulation in opiate tolerance and dependence
R01DA-06037-02 (DAAR) YAMAMURA, YASUHIRO PONCE SCHOOL OF

MEDICINE UNIVERSITY ST/PO BOX 7004 PONCE, PR 00732 HTLV-I and AIDS in Puerto Rican intravenous drug users

R01DA-06038-02 (SRCD) WESSON, DONALD R MERRITT PERALTA INSTITUTE 435 HAWTHORNE AVENUE OAKLAND, CA 94609 Controlled study of naltrexone induction with clonidine

R01DA-06039-02 (DABR) KING, THOMAS S UNIV OF TEXAS HLTH SCIS CTR 7703 FLOYD CURL DRIVE SAN ANTONIO, TX 78284 Cocaine and female reproductive dysfunction

R01DA-06047-02 (DABR) VAN VUNAKIS, HELEN BRANDEIS UNIVERSITY 415 SOUTH ST WALTHAM, MA 02254 Toxicological aspects of nicotine metabolism

R29DA-06049-03 (SRCD) BARRON, SUSAN UNIVERSITY OF KENTUCKY 201 KINKEAD HALL LEXINGTON, KY 40506-0044 Third trimester model of prenatal cocaine exposure

R01DA-06076-02 (DAPA) MANSON, SPERO M UNIV OF COLORADO HLTH SCIS CTR 4200 EAST NINTH AVE BOX C249 DENVER, CO 80262 Substance use among indian boarding school students

R18DA-06082-03 (SRCD) LING, WALTER TREATMENT RESEARCH UNIT 8447 WILSHIRE BOULEVARD BEVERLY HILLS, CA 90211 A treatment research unit for intravenous drug users

R01DA-06084-02 (SRCD) SHIFFMAN, SAUL UNIVERSITY OF PITTSBURGH 4015 O'HARA STREET PITTSBURGH, PA 15260 Computerized self-monitoring of smoking relapse process

R18DA-06086-03 (SRCD) BOKOS, PETER J INTERVENTIONS 1234 S. MICHIGAN AVE., ST. 200 CHICAGO, IL 60605 Substance abuse client case management project

R18DA-06094-03 (SRCD) SCHNOLL, SIDNEY H VIRGINIA COMMONWEALTH UNIV BOX 109, MCV STATION RICHMOND, VA 23298-0109 AIDS reduction in pregnant & non-pregnant addicted women

R18DA-06096-03 (SRCD) IGUCHI, MARTIN YONEO HAHNEMANN UNIVERSITY BROAD & VINE STREET PHILADELPHIA, PA 19102-1192 Methadone treatment--Behavioral/pharmacological variable

R18DA-06097-03 (SRCD) SORENSEN, JAMES L UCSF AT SAN FRANCISCO GEN HOSP 1001 POTRERO AVE, BLDG 92 SAN FRANCISCO, CA 94110 Improved outpatient treatment to slow the spread of AIDS

R18DA-06104-03 (SRCD) WREDE, ARNOLD F SEATTLE-KING CTY DEPT/PUB HEAL 1006 SMITH TOWER, 506 SECOND A SEATTLE, WA 98104 Comparison of three levels of methadone intervention

R01DA-06106-03 (DABR) ALLAN, ANDREA M WASHINGTON UNIVERSITY 4940 AUDUBON AVE ST LOUIS, MO 63110 Mechanism of sedative hypnotic tolerance and dependence

R18DA-06107-02 (SRCD) O'BRIEN, CHARLES P UNIVERSITY OF PENNSYLVANIA 3900 CHESTNUT STREET PHILADELPHIA, PA 19104 Treatment research unit--IV drug abuse

R18DA-06113-03 (SRCD) HIGGINS, STEPHEN T IRA ALLEN SCH OF VT 38 FLETCHER PLACE A behavioral treatment for IV cocaine dependence

R18DA-06116-03 (SRCD) MENDELSON, JACK H MCLEAN HOSPITAL ALCOHOL/DRUG ABUSE RES. CTR. BELMONT, MA 02178 Treatment efficacy for drug abuse and AIDS prevention

R18DA-06120-03 (SRCD) BIGELOW, GEORGE E FRANCIS SCOTT KEY MED CTR 4940 EASTERN AVENUE BALTIMORE, MD 21224 TRU--Behavioral pharmacological AIDS prevention in IV drug abusers

R18DA-06122-03 (SRCD) GALANTER, MARC NYU MED. CENTER - PSYCHIATRY 550 FIRST AVE NEW YORK, NY 10016 Buprenorphine treatment of heroin addiction

R18DA-06124-03 (SRCD) INCIARDI, JAMES A UNIVERSITY OF DELAWARE NEWARK, DE 19716 Assertive community treatment for high risk drug users

R18DA-06126-03 (SRCD) MADDUX, JAMES F UNIV OF TEXAS HLTH SCI CTR 7703 FLOYD CURL DRIVE SAN ANTONIO, TX 78284-7792 Improving retention on methadone maintenance

R18DA-06131-03 (SRCD) DE LEON, GEORGE NARCOTIC & DRUG RESEARCH, INC 11 BEACH STREET NEW YORK, NY 10013 Therapeutic community methods in methadone maintenance

R18DA-06140-03 (SRCD) QUITKIN, FREDERIC M RES FOUN MH, NY ST PSY INS 722 WEST 168TH STREET NEW YORK, N Y 10032 AIDS prevention--Imipramine for depressed drug abusers

R18DA-06142-03 (SRCD) BROWN, LAWRENCE S, JR ADDIC RES & TREATMENT CORP 22 CHAPEL STREET BROOKLYN, NY 11201 New therapeutic initiatives in methadone maintenance

R18DA-06143-03 (SRCD) GRABOWSKI, JOHN UNIV OF TEXAS HEALTH SCI CTR 1300 MOURSUND - UTMSI HOUSTON, TX 77030 Behavior-pharm treatments reducing drug abuse and HIV spread

R18DA-06145-03 (SRCD) NEWMEYER, JOHN A HAIGHT-ASHBURY FREE CLINICS, I 529 CLAYTON STREET SAN FRANCISCO, CA 94117 A clinical/behavioral program to fight hiv in drug users

R18DA-06151-03 (SRCD) LEWIS, BENJAMIN F SPECTRUM HOUSE, INC 106 E. MAIN STREET WESTBORO, MA 01581 Aids prevention-- Four residential treatment models

R18DA-06153-03 (SRCD) MILLMAN, ROBERT B CORNELL UNIV MEDICAL COLLEGE 411 EAST 69TH STREET NEW YORK, NY 10021 Comprehensive vocational enhancement program for mmtp's

R18DA-06162-03 (SRCD) SIMPSON, D DWAYNE TEXAS CHRISTIAN UNIVERSITY INST. OF BEHAVIORAL RESEARCH FORT WORTH, TEXAS 76129 Improving drug abuse treatment for AIDS-risk reduction

R18DA-06163-03 (SRCD) COTTLER, LINDA M WASHINGTON UNIVERSITY DEPARTMENT OF PSYCHIATRY ST LOUIS, MO 63110 St Louis' effort to reduce the spread of AIDS in IVDUS

R18DA-06165-03 (SRCD) STITZER, MAXINE L FRANCIS SCOTT KEY MED CENTER 4940 EASTERN AVE, D-5-WEST BALTIMORE, MD 21224 Buprenorphine--Evaluation for IV drug abuse treatment

R18DA-06166-03 (SRCD) GOTTHEIL, EDWARD JEFFERSON MEDICAL COLLEGE DEPT OF PSYCH & HUMAN BEHAVIOR PHILADELPHIA, PA 19107 Cocaine and AIDS--Individual vs group treatments

R18DA-06168-03 (SRCD) HOFFMAN, JEFFREY A KOBA INSTITUTE, INC 1156 15TH ST NW, ST 200 WASHINGTON, DC 20005 Effective treatments for cocaine abuse and HIV risk

R01DA-06169-02 (DABR) KESNER, RAYMOND P UNIVERSITY OF UTAH SALT LAKE CITY, UT 84112 Phencyclidine effects on CNS and memory functions

R01DA-06170-02S1 (SRCD) STREUFERT, SIEGFRIED PENNSYLVANIA STATE UNIV P O BOX 850 HERSHEY, PA 17033 Acute drug effects on simple and complex performance

R01DA-06171-01A2 (SRCD) ROSEN, TOVE S COLUMBIA UNIVERSITY 630 W 168 STREET NEW YORK, NY 10032 Maternal crack use--Perinatal and infancy effects

R01DA-06175-02 (SRCA) JOHANSON, CHRIS-ELLYN UNIFOR. SERVS UNIV OF HLTH SCI 4301 JONES BRIDGE RD BETHESDA, MD 20814 Drug abuse and behavioral experience

R01DA-06176-02 (PCB) DE WIT, HARRIET UNIVERSITY OF CHICAGO 5841 S MARYLAND CHICAGO, IL 60637 Drugs of abuse on regional cerebral metabolism and mood

R01DA-06183-01A2 (DACB) GARVEY, ARTHUR J HARVARD SCHOOL OF DENTAL MED 9 INGERSOLL ROAD WELLESLEY, MA 02181 Nicotine replacement for treatment of tobacco addiction

R18DA-06185-03 (SRCD) RAWSON, RICHARD MATRIX CENTER, INC 9033 WILSHIRE BLVD, SUITE 201 BEVERLY HILLS, CA 90211 Treatment of stimulant users to reduce HIV transmission

R18DA-06190-02 (SRCD) KOSTEN, THOMAS R YALE UNIVERSITY 27 SYLVAN AVENUE NEW HAVEN, CT 06519 Treatment research unit--Reducing AIDS risks by pharmaco & psychotherapy

R01DA-06192-02 (SRCD) MARTINEZ, JOE L UNIV OF CALIFORNIA 3210 TOLMAN HALL BERKELEY, CA 94720 Cocaine studied through a rodent learning model

R01DA-06194-02 (DABR) HARLAN, RICHARD E TULANE UNIVERSITY SCHOOL OF ME 1430 TULANE AVENUE NEW ORLEANS, LA 70112 Neurobiology of androgen abuse

R03DA-06195-02 (MSM) ECCLES, CHRISTINE U UNIV OF MARYLAND @ BALTIMORE 20 NORTH PINE STREET BALTIMORE, MD 21201 Sigma ligand electrophysiology in rat hippocampal slice

R01DA-06199-02 (DABR) KELLER, RICHARD W ALBANY MEDICAL COLLEGE 47 NEW SCOTLAND AVE ALBANY, NY 12208 Effects of prenatal stimulant exposure on brain dopamine

R01DA-06201-01A1 (DABR) RANDALL, PATRICK K UNIV OF TEXAS @ AUSTIN AUSTIN, TX 78712 Cocaine and dopamine--Linked responses

R01DA-06204-02 (DABR) HAUSER, KURT F UNIVERSITY OF KENTUCKY 800 ROSE STREET LEXINGTON, KY 40536-0084 Role of abused opiate drugs in neural development

R01DA-06205-02 (SRCD) BICKEL, WARREN K UNIVERSITY OF VERMONT 1 SOUTH PROSPECT STREET BURLINGTON, VT 05401 Benzodiazepine drug discrimination in humans

R18DA-06212-03 (SRCD) KONEFAL, JANET UNIVERSITY OF MIAMI SCH OF MED P.O. BOX 016960 (D-22) MIAMI, FL 33101 Drug abuse detoxification for risk behah. of AIDS

R01DA-06213-02 (DAPA) URBERG, KATHRYN A WAYNE STATE UNIVERSITY DETROIT, MI 48202 Aspects of peer influence in adolescent substance use

R01DA-06214-03 (DABR) ASTON-JONES, GARY S HAHNEMANN UNIVERSITY BROAD AND VINE PHILADELPHIA, PA 19102-1192 Locus coeruleus, rostral medulla, and morphine abuse

R01DA-06218-02 (DABR) ELDRIDGE, CHARLES J BOWMAN GRAY SCHOOL OF MEDICINE 300 S HAWTHORNE RD WINSTON-SALEM, NC 27103 Cannabinoid interactions with corticosteroid receptors

R01DA-06219-01A2 (DABR) KUHN, DONALD M LAFAYETTE CLINIC 951 E LAFAYETTE DETROIT, MI 48207 Cocaine & serotonin neurochemistry

R01DA-06224-02 (DAPA) PIPER, DOUGLAS L PACIFIC INST FOR RES 5157 LORUTH TERRACE MADISON, WI 53711 Community component for "Healthy for Life"

R01DA-06227-02 (SRCD) MASH, DEBORAH C UNIV OF MIAMI SCH OF MED 1501 N W 9TH AVENUE MIAMI, FL 33136 Limbic and medullary mechanisms in cocaine-related sudden death

R01DA-06230-02 (SRCD) BOTVIN, GILBERT J CORNELL U MEDICAL COLLEGE 411 EAST 69TH STREET NEW YORK, NY 10021 Reducing drug abuse and AIDS risk

R01DA-06234-02 (SRCD) FISCHMAN, MARIAN W JOHNS HOPKINS UNIV SCH OF MED 720 RUTLAND AVENUE BALTIMORE, MD 21205 IV cocaine abuse treatment--A laboratory model

R01DA-06236-02 (SRCD) SONSALLA, PATRICIA K UMDNJ-ROBERT W JOHNSON MED SCH 675 HOES LANE PISCATAWAY, NJ 08854 Excitotoxins and the neurotoxicity of amphetamines

R01DA-06241-02 (DABR) PASTERNAK, GAVRIL W SLOAN KETTERING INST/CNCR RES 1275 YORK AVENUE NEW YORK, NY 10021 Synthesis and pharmacology of novel opiate ligands

R29DA-06244-02 (DABR) ANANTHAN, SUBRAMANIAM SOUTHERN RESEARCH INSTITUTE BIRMINGHAM, AL 35255-5305 Molecular probes and drugs for benzodiazepine dependency

R18DA-06250-03 (SRCD) ANGLIN, M DOUGLAS UCLA DRUG ABUSE RESEARCH GROUP 1100 GLENDON AVE., SUITE 763 LOS ANGELES, CA 90024-3511 Enhanced methadone maintenance program for AIDS containment

R01DA-06251-03 (SRCD) PORTOGHESE, PHILIP S UNIVERSITY OF MINNESOTA 308 HARVARD STREET, SE MINNEAPOLIS, MN 55455 Amino acid conjugates of opioid ligands

R01DA-06252-02 (SRCD) SCHILLER, PETER W CLINICAL RES INST OF MONTREAL 110 PINE AVENUE WEST MONTREAL, QUEBEC, CANADA H2W 1 Peptides as centrally or peripherally acting analgesics

R01DA-06254-03 (SRCD) GOODMAN, MURRAY UNIV OF CALIFORNIA, SAN DIEGO 9500 GILMAN DRIVE LA JOLLA, CA 92093-0343 An intergrated approach to opioid design

R01DA-06258-02 (DABR) HOSS, WAYNE P UNIVERSITY OF TOLEDO 2801 WEST BANCROFT ST TOLEDO, OH 43606 Kappa opioid receptors and turnover in the brain

R01DA-06264-02 (DACB) BYRD, LARRY D EMORY UNIVERSITY ATLANTA, GA 30322 Chronic cocaine exposure during gestation

R01DA-06269-02 (SRCD) SILVERMAN, PETER B UNIV OF TEXAS MEDICAL SCHOOL 1300 MOURSUND HOUSTON, TX 77030 Rotational behavior--Model of conditioned drug effects

R01DA-06271-01A1 (DABR) HUI, KOON-SEA RESEARCH FDN FOR MENTAL HYGIEN ORANGEBURG, NY 10962 Endogenous anti-enkephalinase peptides in brain

R01DA-06272-02 (DABR) FOWLER, FRANK W STATE UNIVERSITY OF NEW YORK STONY BROOK, NY 11794-3400 Thermal reactions of (-)-cocaine and related alkaloids

R01DA-06275-01A2 (SRCD) RICAURTE, GEORGE A JOHNS HOPKINS MEDICAL INST 4940 EASTERN AVENUE BALTIMORE, MD 21224 Studies of N-methylated analogues of MDMA and fenfluramine

R01DA-06278-02 (SRCD) VOLKOW, NORA D ASSOCIATED UNIVERSITIES, INC BROOKHAVEN NATIONAL LABORATORY UPTON, NY 11973 PET studies in

PROJECT NO., ORGANIZATIONAL UNIT., INVESTIGATOR, ADDRESS, TITLE

cocaine abuse
R01DA-06282-03 (SRCD) COOK, CLARENCE EDGAR RESEARCH TRIANGLE INSTITUTE PO BOX 12194 RES TRI PARK, NC 27709-2194 A new prodrug approach to addiction treatment
P01DA-06284-03 (SRCD) HRUBY, VICTOR J UNIVERSITY OF ARIZONA TUCSON, AZ 85721 New modalities for treatment of pain and drug abuse
R01DA-06287-02 (DAPA) ROWE, DAVID C UNIVERSITY OF ARIZONA TUCSON, AZ 85721 Sibling mutual interaction, drug use, and deviance
R01DA-06289-03 (SRCD) GAWIN, FRANK H FRIENDS MED SCIENCE RES CTR WILSHIRE & SAWTELLE BLVDS LOS ANGELES, CA 90073 Flupenthixol decanoate in "crack" cocaine smoking
R01DA-06293-02 (DAPA) CHAVEZ, ERNEST L COLORADO STATE UNIVERSITY FORT COLLINS, CO 80523 Drug use, delinquency and Mexican-American youth
R37DA-06299-02 (SRCD) ELDE, ROBERT P UNIVERSITY OF MINNESOTA 321 CHURCH STREET SOUTHEAST MINNEAPOLIS, MN 55455 Laser confocal imaging of opioid peptides and receptors
R01DA-06301-01A2 (DABR) DAVIES, HUW M WAKE FOREST UNIVERSITY P O BOX 7486 WINSTON-SALEM, NC 27109 Synthesis and evaluation of novel cocaine analogs
R01DA-06302-02 (SRCD) CARROLL, FRANK I RESEARCH TRIANGLE INSTITUTE PO BOX 12194 RES TRIANGLE PARK, NC 27709 Development of selective PCP receptor ligands
R01DA-06303-03 (SRCD) SPEALMAN, ROGER D NEW ENG REG PRIMATE RES CENTER ONE PINE HILL DRIVE SOUTHBOROUGH, MA 01772 Molecular probes for specific cocaine recognition sites
R01DA-06304-03 (SRCD) LOEW, GILDA H MOLECULAR RESEARCH INSTITUTE 845 PAGE MILL ROAD PALO ALTO, CA 94304 Molecular modeling, design and evaluation of BDZ-ligands
R01DA-06305-02 (SRCD) ZALKOW, LEON H GEORGIA INST OF TECHNOLOGY 225 NORTH AVENUE, NW ATLANTA, GA 30332 Irreversible antagonists of cocaine and other stimulants
P01DA-06306-01A1 (SRCD) MORGAN, JAMES P BETH ISRAEL HOSPITAL 330 BROOKLINE AVENUE BOSTON, MA 02215 Clinical cardiovascular toxicity of cocaine
P01DA-06306-01A1 0001 (SRCD) MORGAN, JAMES P Clinical cardiovascular toxicity of cocaine Minipig model of coronary spasm--Effects of cocaine
P01DA-06306-01A1 0002 (SRCD) SHANNON, RICHARD P Clinical cardiovascular toxicity of cocaine Cocaine effect in conscious, chronically instrumented dog
P01DA-06306-01A1 0003 (SRCD) WARE, ANTHONY J Clinical cardiovascular toxicity of cocaine Cocaine and catecholamine-induced platelet activation
P01DA-06306-01A1 0004 (SRCD) GOLDBERGER, ARY L Clinical cardiovascular toxicity of cocaine Clinical predictors of electrical instability due to cocaine toxicity
P01DA-06306-01A1 9001 (SRCD) WAKSMONSKI, CAROL A Clinical cardiovascular toxicity of cocaine Core--Cocaine cardiotoxicity in man databank
P01DA-06306-01A1 9002 (SRCD) ORIOL, NANCY E Clinical cardiovascular toxicity of cocaine Core--Cocaine cardiotoxicity during pregnancy
R01DA-06307-01A1 (DAPA) FLAY, BRIAN R UNIVERSITY OF ILLINOIS 850 W JACKSON BOULEVARD CHICAGO, IL 60607 Etiology of drug use and abuse
R01DA-06310-03 (SRCD) LOVE, BRIAN E AUBURN UNIVERSITY DEPT. OF CHEMISTRY AUBURN, AL 36849-5312 Preparation of b-carbolines via a-lithiated indoles
R01DA-06312-03 (SRCD) HOWLETT, ALLYN C SAINT LOUIS UNIVERSITY 1402 S GRAND BLVD ST LOUIS, MO 63104 Cannabinoid receptor/effector structure-activity
R01DA-06315-03 (SRCD) VOYKSNER, ROBERT D RESEARCH TRIANGLE INST P O BOX 12194 RES TRIANGLE PARK, NC 27709 Determination of opioid peptides by electrospray LC/MS
R01DA-06316-02 (DAPA) HOPS, HYMAN OREGON RESEARCH INSTITUTE 1899 WILLAMETTE EUGENE, OR 97401 Adolescent substance use--multi-method analysis
R01DA-06317-03 (SRCD) BRINE, GEORGE A RESEARCH TRIANGLE INSTITUTE P O BOX 12194 RES TRIANGLE PARK, NC 27709 Treatment drugs and molecular probes for narcotic abuse
R29DA-06319-02 (DABR) SCALZO, FRANK M UNIV OF ARKANSAS FOR MEDICAL S 4301 W MARKHAM STREET JEFFERSON, AR 72079 Cocaine and PCP--Neonatal cardiovascular/behavioral effects
R01DA-06323-02 (DAPA) CHALMERS, THOMAS C HARVARD SCHOOL PUBLIC HEALTH 677 HUNTINGTON AVENUE BOSTON, MA 02115 Meta-analysis of clinical trials in drug abuse
R01DA-06324-02 (SRCD) MEISCH, RICHARD A UNIVERSITY OF TEXAS 1300 MOURSUND AVE HOUSTON, TX 77030 Orally delivered cocaine as a reinforcer
R01DA-06325-02 (SRCM) GEYER, MARK A DEPARTMENT OF PSYCHIATRY LA JOLLA, CA 92093-0804 Drugs of abuse--Complexity measures classify behavior
R01DA-06326-02 (DAAR) MANDELL, WALLACE JOHNS HOPKINS UNIVERSITY 615 NORTH WOLFE STREET BALTIMORE, MD 21205 Prevention of AIDS in IV drug user networks
R01DA-06327-01A2 (DABR) MILLER, LAWRENCE G TUFTS-NEW ENGLAND MEDICAL CENT 171 HARRISON AVENUE BOSTON, MA 02111 Prenatal exposure to benzodiazepines
R01DA-06328-03 (SRCD) CIRAULO, DOMENIC A TUFTS UNIVERSITY 750 WASHINGTON ST BOX 1007 BOSTON, MA 02111 Bz receptor effects of prenatal ethanol/benzodiazepines
R01DA-06331-02 (DAPA) BERKOWITZ, MARVIN W MARQUETTE UNIVERSITY MILWAUKEE, WI 53233 Moral reasoning and adolescent drug and alcohol abuse
R01DA-06333-02 (DABR) ERLANGER, BERNARD F COLUMBIA UNIV HEALTH SCIENCES 630 W 168TH ST NEW YORK, NY 10032 Adenosine receptors, neuromodulators of drug reactions
R44DA-06344-02 (SRCD) SCHRAMM, WILLFRIED BIOQUANT, INC 1919 GREEN ROAD ANN ARBOR, MI 48105 Immunosensor for drug monitoring
R18DA-06360-03 (SRCD) FINE, JAMES SUNY HLTH SCIENCE, BROOKLYN 450 CLARKSON AVE, BOX 1203 BROOKLYN, NY 11203 Communication skills trng for pregnant substance abusers
R18DA-06361-03 (SRCD) STARK, KENNETH DEPT OF SOCIAL & HEALTH SER BUREAU OF ALCOHOL & SUB ABUSE OLYMPIA, WA 98504 Comprehensive treatment approach-Drug addiction & abusing pregnant women
R18DA-06363-03 (SRCD) KALTENBACH, KAROL JEFFERSON MEDICAL COLLEGE 1201 CHESTNUT ST, 11TH FLOOR PHILADELPHIA, PA 19107-4192 Cocaine, pregnancy and progeny--Treatment and evaluation
R18DA-06365-03 (SRCD) BROWN, ELIZABETH R BOSTON CITY HOSP.-NEONATOLOGY 818 HARRISON AVENUE BOSTON, MA 02118 Randomized trial-Comprehensive day treatment-pregnant drug users
R18DA-06369-03 (SRCD) COLETTI, SHIRLEY D OPERATION PAR, INC 10901-C ROOSE BLVD, ST 1000 ST PETERSBURG, FL 33716 Residential trmt of addicted women with their infants
R18DA-06371-02 (SRCD) COOPER, LOUIS ST LUKE'S-ROOSEVELT HOSPITAL C 114TH STREET & AMSTERDAM AVENU NEW YORK, NY 10025 Comprehensive care center for addicted mothers & infants
R18DA-06373-03 (SRCD) CHASNOFF, IRA J N.A.P.A.R.E. 11 E. HUBBARD ST., SUITE 200 CHICAGO, IL 60611 Residential care--Cocaine/polydrug using pregnant women
R18DA-06378-03 (SRCD) SEIDEN, ANNE M COOK COUNTY HOSPITAL 1825 WEST HARRISON STREET CHICAGO, IL 60612 Effects of comprehensive care for pregnant drug abusers
R18DA-06379-03 (SRCD) MARQUES, PAUL R NATIONAL PUB SER RES INST 8201 CORPORATE DR, STE 220 LANDOVER, MD 20785 Drug positive infants--Rreferring mothers for treatment
R18DA-06380-03 (SRCD) HOWARD, JUDY UNIV OF CALIFORNIA, L.A. DEPARTMENT OF PEDIATRICS LOS ANGELES, CA 90024-1797 Pregnant addicts and offspring--Evaluating intervention
R01DA-06385-02 (DAAR) PROSS, SUSAN H UNIVERSITY OF SOUTH FLORIDA 12901 BRUCE B DOWNS BLVD TAMPA, FL 33612 Immune modulation by marihuana--Function of age
R01DA-06387-02 (DAAR) JORDAN, B KATHLEEN RESEARCH TRIANGLE INSTITUTE P O BOX 12194 3040 CORNWALLIS RES TRIANGLE PK, NC 27709 Understanding the AIDS risk behaviors of women prisoners
R43DA-06388-01A1 (SRCD) SWANSON, MELVIN J BIO-METRIC SYSTEMS, INC 9924 WEST 74TH STREET EDEN PRAIRIE, MN 55344 Multiple drug detection in finger prick blood
R01DA-06393-02 (DAAR) COHEN, JUDITH B UNIVERSITY OF CALIFORNIA 995 POTRERO AVE, BLDG 90 WARD SAN FRANCISCO, CA 94110 Peer intervention effect on HIV risk in drug using women
R19DA-06401-03 (SRCD) COMO, DAVID M Grants to states-alc and drug abuse collection systems
R19DA-06402-03 (SRCD) TYBURSKI, ROBERT F Grants to states-alc & drug abuse collection systems
R19DA-06403-03 (SRCD) BRUNO, DARRYL L Grants to states-alc and drug abuse collection system
R19DA-06404-03 (SRCD) KOWALKOWSKI, STAN Grants to states-alc and drug abuse data collection system Washington State
R19DA-06405-03 (SRCD) BEESON, PETER G Grants to states-alc & drug abuse data collection systems
R19DA-06407-03 (SRCD) PATTERSON, KEN Grants to states-drug abuse and alcohol collection systems
R19DA-06408-03 (SRCD) HUSSEIN, CARLESSIA A Grants to states-Alcoholism and drug abuse
R19DA-06409-03 (SRCD) FRENCH, JOHN Grants to states--Drug abuse/alcohol abuse data collection systems
R19DA-06410-03 (SRCD) COLBERT, JACK Grants to states--Alcoholism and drug abuse data collection systems
R19DA-06411-03 (SRCD) TIPPETT, MAURICE L Grants to states--Alcoholism and drug abuse data collection systems
R19DA-06412-03 (SRCD) RANDLE, MICHEL Grants to states--Alcoholism and drug abuse data collection systems
R19DA-06414-03 (SRCD) EVANS, DAN Grants to states--Alcoholism and drug abuse data collection systems
R19DA-06415-03 (SRCD) MAXWELL, JANE C Grants to states--Alcohol and drug abuse data collection systems
R19DA-06416-03 (SRCD) HULL, WALTER J Grants to states-Alcohol and drug abuse data collection systems
R19DA-06417-03 (SRCD) THACKER, WAYNE Grants to states--Alcoholism and drug abuse data collection systems
R19DA-06418-03 (SRCD) HARRIS, JAMES P Grants to states--Alcoholism and drug abuse data collection systems
R19DA-06419-03 (SRCD) TOWNSEND, MICHAEL E Grants to states-Alcoholism and drug abuse data collection systems
R19DA-06420-03 (SRCD) HOLLEY, JEREAL W Grants to states-Alcoholism and drug abuse data collection systems
R19DA-06421-03 (SRCD) SHERWOOD, ALAN CHARLES Grants to states--Alcoholism and drug abuse data collection systems
R19DA-06424-03 (SRCD) KNAPPENBERGER, ROBERT Grants to states--Alcoholism and drug abuse data collection systems
R19DA-06425-03 (SRCD) MCGARRITY, MICHAEL Grants to states-Alcoholism and drug abuse data collection systems
R19DA-06426-03 (SRCD) DICKERSON, DEBORAH Grants to states--Alcoholism and drug abuse data collection systems
R19DA-06427-03 (SRCD) FERGUSON, JAMES M Grants to states--Mental health data collection systems
R19DA-06428-03 (SRCD) SHANELARIS, JAMES Grants to states--Alcoholism and drug abuse data collection systems
R19DA-06429-03 (SRCD) DAVIS, STEVEN P Grants to states- Alcoholism and drug abuse data collection systems
R19DA-06430-03 (SRCD) HINTON, MARY ANN Grants to states--Alcoholism and drug abuse data collection systems
R19DA-06431-03 (SRCD) MC MAHON, MICHAEL J Grants to states--Alcoholism and drug abuse data collection systems
R19DA-06432-03 (SRCD) ZWICK, JANET Grants to states--Alcoholism and drug abuse data collection systems
R19DA-06433-03 (SRCD) MEADOWS, HAROLD L Grants to states-Alcoholism and drug abuse data collection systems
R19DA-06434-03 (SRCD) GOFF, CLINTON Grants to states--Alcoholism and drug abuse data collection systems
R19DA-06435-03 (SRCD) BALL, ROBERT S Grants to states--Alcoholism and drug abuse data collection systems
R19DA-06436-03 (SRCD) MAILLY, TIMOTHY Grants to states--Alcoholism and drug abuse data collection systems
R19DA-06437-03 (SRCD) WARD, WILLIAM L Grants to states--Alcoholism and drug abuse data collection systems

PROJECT NO., ORGANIZATIONAL UNIT., INVESTIGATOR, ADDRESS, TITLE

R19DA-06440-03 (SRCD) ROBERTSON, ANNE D Grants to states--Alcoholism and drug abuse data collection system

R19DA-06442-03 (SRCD) WILSON, ELAINE Grants to states--Alcoholism & drug abuse data collection systems

R19DA-06443-03 (SRCD) CALKINS, RICHARD F Grants to states--Alcoholism and drug abuse data collection systems

R19DA-06444-03 (SRCD) PETERSEN, PAMELA Grants to states to implement uniform alcohol & drug abuse data

R19DA-06445-03 (SRCD) ALLEN, JOHN J Grants to states--Alcoholism and drug abuse data collection systems

R19DA-06446-03 (SRCD) O'DONOVAN, ANDREW Grants to states--Alcoholism and drug abuse data collection systems

R19DA-06447-03 (SRCD) CHAPMAN, ANNIE B Grants to states--Alcoholism and drug abuse data collection systems

R19DA-06448-03 (SRCD) DENNIS, SHANE Grants to states--Alcoholism and drug abuse data collection system

R19DA-06449-03 (SRCD) MCCARTY, DENNIS Grants to states--Alcoholism and drug abuse data collection systems

R19DA-06450-03 (SRCD) BROCKINGTON, KENNETH F Grants to states--Alcoholism and drug abuse data collection systems

R19DA-06451-03 (SRCD) TOPOLSKI, JAMES M Grants to states--Alcoholism and drug abuse data collection systems

R19DA-06452-03 (SRCD) BISHOP, MARK T Grants to states-Alcoholism and drug abuse data collection systems

R19DA-06453-03 (SRCD) LINDSAY, HARRIET A Grants to states--Alcoholism and drug abuse data collection systems

R19DA-06455-03 (SRCD) BIANCONI, JOHN E Grants to states--Alcoholism and drug abuse data collection system

R19DA-06456-03 (SRCD) SMITH, FRED W Grants to states--DA/AA data collection system

R19DA-06457-03 (SRCD) PEZZOLLA, PETER A Grant to states--Alcoholism and drug abuse data collection systems

R01DA-06463-02 (DACB) VAN HAAREN, FRANS UNIVERSITY OF FLORIDA GAINESVILLE, FL 32611 Sex differences in the behavioral effects of cocaine

R01DA-06466-02 (DACB) BURNS, MARCELLINE M SOUTHERN CALIFORNIA RES INST 11912 W WASHINGTON BLVD LOS ANGELES, CA 90066 A study of cocaine effects & symptoms

R01DA-06470-03 (DABR) BANNON, MICHAEL JOHN SINAI HOSPITAL OF DETROIT 6767 WEST OUTER DRIVE DETROIT, MI 48235 Cocaine-binding dopamine transporter--Molecular biology

R03DA-06472-02 (DACB) SVARE, BRUCE B SUNY-ALBANY 1400 WASHINGTON AVE ALBANY, NY 12222 Anabolic steroid abuse--Causes and consequences

R19DA-06474-03 (SRCD) KINNEY, ROOSEVELT L Grants to implement uniform alcohol and drug abuse, data systems

R03DA-06476-02 (DABR) YUTRZENKA, GERALD J UNIV OF SOUTH DAKOTA SCH OF ME 414 EAST CLARK STREET VERMILLION, SD 57069 Benzodiazepine inverse agonists in pentobarbital dependence

R01DA-06481-02 (DABR) MECHOULAM, RAPHAEL HEBREW UNIVERSITY FACULTY OF MEDICINE JERUSALEM 91120, ISRAEL Cannabinoid investigations

R03DA-06482-01A1 (DABR) MORLEY, BARBARA J BOYS TOWN NATIONAL INSTITUTE 555 N 30TH ST OMAHA, NE 68131 Nicotine mediated sodium flux in primary cultures

R01DA-06484-02 (SRCD) WAGERLE, L CRAIG UNIVERSITY OF PENNSYLVANIA B-400 RICHARD BLDG PHILADELPHIA, PA 19104 Microvascular mechanisms and cocaine in the fetal brain

R01DA-06485-03 (DABR) STEIN, ELLIOT A MEDICAL COLLEGE OF WISCONSIN 8701 WATERTOWN PLANK ROAD MILWAUKEE, WI 53226 Endorphins and brain reward mechanisms

R01DA-06486-02 (DABR) KELLAR, KENNETH J GEORGETOWN UNIV MEDICAL CTR 3900 RESEVOIR ROAD, NW WASHINGTON, D C 20007 Antagonist actions of nicotine

R01DA-06487-02 (DAPA) WALDORF, DANIEL INST FOR SCIENTIFIC ANALYSIS 2235 LOMBARD ST SAN FRANCISCO, CA 94123 Crack sales, gangs and violence--An exploration

R29DA-06490-01A2 (DABR) HURD, WILLIAM W UNIVERSITY OF MICHIGAN MED CTR 1550 E MED CTR DR MPB D2202-07 ANN ARBOR, MI 48109-0718 Direct effects of cocaine on the pregnant human uterus

R03DA-06491-02 (SRCD) NASH, J FRANK HANNA PAVILION UNIV HOSP/CLEVL 2040 ABINGTON ROAD CLEVLAND, OH 44106 Role of dopamine in MDMA-induced serotonin depletion

R01DA-06495-01A1 (DABR) MEYER, JERROLD S UNIVERSITY OF MASSACHUSETTS AMHERST, MA 01003 Mechanisms of cocaine action on the developing brain

R29DA-06498-02 (SRCD) HAKAN, ROBERT L UNIVERSITY OF NORTH CAROLINA 601 SOUTH COLLEGE ROAD WILMINGTON, NC 28403-3297 Role of nucleus accumbens in drug abuse

R03DA-06499-02 (DACB) NEWLAND, M CHRISTOPHER AUBURN UNIVERSITY AUBURN UNIVERSITY, AL 36849-51 Caffeine-induced supersensitivity to adenosine agonists

R01DA-06502-03 (DAAR) PRAKASH, OM ALTON OCHSNER MEDICAL FOUNDATI NEW ORLEANS, LA 70121 Molecular determinants of hiv expression by opiates

R01DA-06503-03 (DACB) COLLINS, FRANK L OKLAHOMA STATE UNIVERSITY DEPT OF PSYCHOLOGY STILLWATER, OK 74078 The effect of food deprivation on cigarette smoking

R03DA-06510-02 (DABR) SALLEE, FLOYD R MEDICAL UNIV OF SOUTH CAROLINA 171 ASHLEY AVE CHARLESTON, SC 29425 Photoaffinity labeling of the cocaine receptor

R01DA-06511-02 (SRCD) CUNNINGHAM, KATHRYN A UNIV OF TEXAS MEDICAL BRANCH 301 UNIVERSITY BOULEVARD GALVESTON, TX 77550-2774 Neurobehavioral pharmacology of stimulants

R01DA-06513-02 (DAPA) BLACK, GORDON S GORDON S BLACK CORPORATION 1661 PENFIELD RD ROCHESTER, NY 14625 Attitudes and use of drugs--Efficacy of a media campaign

R01DA-06514-01A1 (DAPA) LEWIS, ROBERT A PURDUE UNIVERSITY 525 RUSSELL STREET WEST LAFAYETTE, IN 47907 Initiation and sequencing of adolescent drug use

R01DA-06519-02 (DABR) ELLINWOOD, EVERETT H DUKE UNIVERSITY MEDICAL CENTER PO BOX 3870 DURHAM, NC 27710 Dopamine cell inhibition--Relation to cocaine treatment

R01DA-06522-01A1 (DACB) POPE, HARRISON G, JR MC LEAN HOSPITAL BELMONT, MA 02178 Neuropsychological effects of marijuana in students

PROJECT NO., ORGANIZATIONAL UNIT., INVESTIGATOR, ADDRESS, TITLE

R03DA-06524-02 (DACB) STRASSMAN, RICK J UNIV OF NEW MEXICO SCHOOL OF M 2400 TUCKER, NE ALBUQUERQUE, NM 87131 Human psychopharmacology & neuroendocrinology of DMT

R01DA-06526-02 (SRCD) BICKEL, WARREN K UNIVERSITY OF VERMONT BURLINGTON, VT 05401 Behavioral economics of human drug self-administration

R01DA-06529-02 (DACB) POMERLEAU, OVIDE F UNIVERSITY OF MICHIGAN 900 WALL STREET ANN ARBOR, MI 48105 Corticosteroids, stress, and nicotine dependence

R01DA-06532-02 (SRCD) FRANK, DEBORAH A TRUSTEES OF HEALTH AND HOSPITA 1010 MASSACHUSETTS AVENUE BOSTON, MA 02118 Cocaine exposure in utero--Two year infant follow-up

R01DA-06534-02 (DAPA) TARDIFF, KENNETH J NEW YORK HOSPITAL 525 EAST 68TH STREET NEW YORK, NY 10021 Cocaine and fatal injuries

R01DA-06539-02 (DACB) CARLSON, KRISTIN R UNIVERSITY OF MASSACHUSETTS 55 LAKE AVENUE NORTH WORCESTER, MA 01655 Selective breeding for opiate self-administration

R01DA-06543-02 (DACB) POPE, HARRISON G, JR MCLEAN HOSPITAL 115 MILL STREET BELMONT, MA 02178 Psychiatric effects of anabolic steroids

R01DA-06551-02 (DACB) WILKINS, JEFFERY N BRENTWOOD V A MEDICAL CENTER 11301 WILSHIRE BLVD LOS ANGELES, CA 90073 Desipramine treatment of schizophrenic cocaine addicts

R01DA-06554-02 (DABR) BURGESS, KEVIN RICE UNIVERSITY PO BOX 1892 HOUSTON, TX 77251 Synthetic analogues of FMRF-nh2 & F-8-F-nh

R01DA-06556-02 (SRCD) BANDSTRA, EMMALEE S DEPARTMENT OF PEDIATRICS UNIVERSITY OF MIAMI MIAMI, FLORIDA 33101 Neurodevelopmental outcome of in utero cocaine exposure

R01DA-06559-03 (DACB) PARKER, LINDA A WILFRID LAURIER UNIVERSITY DEPARTMENT OF PSYCHOLOGY WATERLOO, ONTARIO CAN. N2L 3C5 Abused drugs may produce a different type of CTA

R44DA-06567-02 (SRCD) SACHS, DAVID P PULMONARY DIAGNOSTIC/REHAB 750 WELCH RD, SUITE 200 PALO ALTO, CA 94304-1509 A flexible scheduling program for longitudinal studies

R43DA-06570-01A1 (SRCD) GROSS DE NUNEZ, GAYLE SAVANTES 2409 PERKINS RD DURHAM, NC 27706 Drug education video--A neuroscience approach

R44DA-06573-02 (SRCD) NUWAYSER, ELIE S BIOTEK, INC 21-C OLYMPIA AVENUE WOBURN, MA 01801 Sustained action buprenophine

R44DA-06580-02 (SRCD) KELLY, KATHLEEN J ROCKY MOUNTAIN BEHAV SCI INST 2190 W DRAKE RD FORT COLLINS, CO 80526 Community based media prevention campaign

R01DA-06589-02 (SRCD) WIEBEL, W WAYNE UNIVERSITY OF ILLINOIS 2121 WEST TAYLOR STREET CHICAGO, ILLINOIS 60612 AIDS/IVDU social network panel study

R01DA-06596-02 (DAAR) FOUNG, STEVEN K H STANFORD UNIVERSITY BLOOD CTR 800 WELCH ROAD PALO ALTO, CA 94304 Immunologic response of intravenous drug users to HTLV

R01DA-06597-01A1 (DAAR) SATZ, PAUL CHARLES R DREW UNIVERSITY 1621 E 120TH STREET LOS ANGELES, CA 90059 Neurobehavioral factors in black men at risk for AIDS

R19DA-06599-03 (SRCM) DIEHL, RUTH Grants to states--MH data collection systems - Wisconsin

R01DA-06600-03 (DABR) BARR, GORDON A RES FDN FOR MENTAL HYGIENE INC 722 W 168TH STREET NEW YORK, NY 10032 Development and plasticity of opiate and stimulant reward

R29DA-06605-02 (SRCM) ROMANOSKI, ALAN J JOHNS HOPKINS HOSPITAL 600 NORTH WOLFE STREET BALTIMORE, MD 21205 Mental illness in domiciled and homeless substance abusers

R01DA-06609-01 (DAPA) SIDNEY, STEPHEN KAISER FOUNDATION RESEARCH INS 3451 PIEDMONT AVE OAKLAND, CA 94611 Epidemiological study of marijuana and health

R01DA-06612-02 (DABR) CHURCHILL, LYNN WASHINGTON STATE UNIVERSITY PULLMAN, WA 99164-6520 Dopamine-opioid receptor interactions in basal forebrain

R01DA-06614-02 (DAPA) AQUILINO, WILLIAM S UNIVERSITY OF WISCONSIN 4412 SOCIAL SCIENCE BLDG MADISON, WI 53706 Survey mode effects in epidemiological drug use

R01DA-06615-01 (DAPA) JOHNSON, BRUCE D NARCOTIC AND DRUG RESEARCH INC 11 BEACH STREET NEW YORK, NY 10013 Careers in drug use/distribution, and nondrug criminality

R01DA-06620-02 (DABR) WEINSTEIN, HAREL MOUNT SINAI SCHOOL OF MEDICINE ONE GUSTAVE L LEVY PLACE NEW YORK, NY 10029 Hallucinogens on 5-HT receptors--Mechanisms/drug development

R01DA-06625-01A2 (DAPA) SLOAN, MICHAEL A UNIVERSITY OF MARYLAND HOSPITA 22 SOUTH GREENE STREET BALTIMORE, MD 21201 Case control study of drug use/abuse in stroke

R01DA-06630-01A1 (DAPA) ENSMINGER, MARGARET E JOHNS HOPKINS UNIVERSITY 615 N WOLFE STREET BALTIMORE, MD 21205 A high risk prospective study of drug use and crime

R29DA-06633-02 (DACB) SPIGA, RALPH UNIV OF TX HLTH SCI CTR, HOUST 1300 MOURSUND AVE HOUSTON, TX 77030 Effects of drugs of abuse on cooperative responding

P50DA-06634-01A1 (SRCD) SMITH, JAMES E BOWMAN GRAY SCHOOL OF MEDICINE 300 S HAWTHORNE ROAD WINSTON-SALEM, NC 27103 Center for neurobiological investigation of drug abuse

P50DA-06634-01A1 0001 (SRCD) CHILDERS, STEVEN R Center for neurobiological investigation of drug abuse Cellular mechanisms of tolerance and dependence

P50DA-06634-01A1 0002 (SRCD) DWORKIN, STEVEN I Center for neurobiological investigation of drug abuse Effects of contingent and noncontingent cocaine administration

P50DA-06634-01A1 0003 (SRCD) DEADWYLER, SAMUEL A Center for neurobiological investigation of drug abuse Neurophysiological analysis of self-administration of cocaine

P50DA-06634-01A1 0004 (SRCD) DAVIES, HUW M L Center for neurobiological investigation of drug abuse Synthesis and evaluation of novel cocaine analogs

P50DA-06634-01A1 0005 (SRCD) SMITH, JAMES E Center for neurobiological investigation of drug abuse Drug reinforcement mechanisms

P50DA-06634-01A1 0006 (SRCD) WOOD, FRANK Center for neurobiological investigation of drug abuse Brain glucose utilization in cocaine users

PROJECT NO., ORGANIZATIONAL UNIT., INVESTIGATOR, ADDRESS, TITLE

P50DA-06634-01A1 9001 (SRCD) CHILDERS, STEVEN R Center for neurobiological investigation of drug abuse Core--Receptor mechanisms, cellular neurobiology, and molecular biology
P50DA-06634-01A1 9002 (SRCD) SMITH, JAMES E Center for neurobiological investigation of drug abuse Core--Microdialysis, neurochemistry and neuroendocrinology
P50DA-06634-01A1 9003 (SRCD) BOOZE, ROSEMARIE M Center for neurobiological investigation of drug abuse Core--Neuroanatomy and imaging
P50DA-06634-01A1 9004 (SRCD) DWORKIN, STEVEN I Center for neurobiological investigation of drug abuse Core--Behavioral pharmacology
R03DA-06637-01A1 (DABR) BRONSON, MAUREEN E UNIV OF NORTH CAROLINA DAVIE HALL CHAPEL HILL, NC 27599-3270 Benzodiazepines -- Tolerance and acute/chronic dependence
R01DA-06638-01A1 (DABR) BOOZE, ROSEMARIE M WAKE FOREST UNIVERSITY 300 S HAWTHORNE ROAD WINSTON-SALEM, NC 27103 Mechanisms of stimulant action in nucleus accumbens
R01DA-06643-02 (DACB) STRUVE, FREDERICK A LOUISIANA STATE UNIV MED CTR PO BOX 33932 SHREVEPORT, LA 71130-3932 Persistent CNS EEG-EP sequelae of chronic THC exposure
R01DA-06644-02 (SRCD) KARMEL, BERNARD Z NYS INST FOR BASIC RESEARCH 1050 FOREST HILL ROAD STATEN ISLAND, NY 10314 Cocaine effects on arousal and attention in neonates
R01DA-06645-01 (DABR) HAMMER, RONALD P, JR UNIV OF HAWAII 1960 EAST-WEST ROAD HONOLULU, HI 96822 Nucleus accumbens, cocaine reward and recovery
R01DA-06646-02 (DABR) MORISHIMA, HISAYO O COLUMBIA UNIV HLTH SCIENCES 630 WEST 168TH STREET NEW YORK, N Y 10032 Perinatal cocaine intoxication/ and treatment
R01DA-06650-01 (DAAR) ADLER, MARTIN W TEMPLE UNIVERSITY SCHOOL OF ME 3420 N BROAD STREET PHILADELPHIA, PA 19140 Opioids, opioid receptors, and immune competence
R01DA-06657-02 (DAPA) DEMBO, RICHARD UNIVERSITY OF SOUTH FLORIDA 4202 E FOWLER AVE TAMPA, FL 33620-8100 Drug use and its effects among high risk youths
R01DA-06658-02 (DABR) TRAYSTMAN, RICHARD J JOHNS HOPKINS HOSPITAL 600 N WOLFE STREET BALTIMORE, MD 21205 Cocaine and cerebral blood flow--Fetus, newborn, and adult
R01DA-06662-01A1 (DAAR) SODERBERG, LEE S UNIVERSITY OF ARKANSAS 4301 WEST MARKHAM LITTLE ROCK, AR 72205 Immunotoxicity of abused nitrite inhalants
R03DA-06665-02 (DABR) GOSPE, SIDNEY M JR UNIV OF CALIFORNIA, DAVIS 2315 STOCKTON BLVD SACRAMENTO, CA 95817 Prenatal toluene exposure and development of the CNS
R29DA-06667-01A1 (DABR) WERLING, LINDA L GEORGE WASHINGTON UNIVERSITY 2300 EYE ST NW WASHINGTON, DC 20037 Molecular mechanism of PCP- and sigma-drug actions
R01DA-06668-02 (DABR) DEY, SUDHANSU K UNIV OF KANSAS MEDICAL CTR 39TH & RAINBOW KANSAS CITY, KANS 66103 Effects of marijhuana on early pregnancy
R01DA-06670-01 (DABR) YANAI, JOSEPH HEBREW UNIV HADASSAH MEDICAL S 91010 JERUSALEM, ISRAEL Mechanism of phenobarbital neuroteratogenicity
R01DA-06675-02 (DABR) NELSON, WENDEL L UNIVERSITY OF WASHINGTON SEATTLE, WASH 98195 Ligands for opioid receptor subtypes
R01DA-06676-02 (DACB) HERNANDEZ, LINDA L WJB DORN VETERANS HOSPITAL COLUMBIA, S C 29201 Pavlovian learning following low doses of abused drugs
R29DA-06679-02 (DACB) LEISCHOW, SCOTT J UNIVERSITY OF ARIZONA 1435 NORTH FREMONT STREET TUCSON, AZ 85719 Methods to prevent post-smoking cessation weight gain
R01DA-06680-01 (SRCD) NURCO, DAVID N FRIENDS MEDICAL SCIENCE RES CT 1229 W MT ROYAL AVENUE BALTIMORE, MD 21217 Addicts and their children--data-based intervention trial
R01DA-06681-02 (BPN) FROIMOWITZ, MARK MCLEAN HOSPITAL 115 MILL STREET BELMONT, MA 02178 Study of typical and atypical dopaminergic compounds
R01DA-06682-02 (DABR) TOLL, LAWRENCE SRI INTERNATIONAL 333 RAVENSWOOD AVE MENLO PARK, CA 94025 Biochemical studies into opiate efficacies
R24DA-06686-02 (SRCM) SHOCKLEY, DOLORES C MEHARRY MEDICAL COLLEGE 1005 D.B. TODD BLVD NASHVILLE, TN 37208 Drug abuse--Behavioral and neurochemical studies drug
R01DA-06687-02 (DABR) BEITZ, ALVIN J UNIVERSITY OF MINNESOTA 1988 FITCH AVENUE ST PAUL, MN 55108 Opioids, amino acids, & pag's involvement in analgesia
R43DA-06688-01A1 (SRCD) GRISSOM, GRANT R INTEGRA, INC 320 KING OF PRUSSIA ROAD RADNOR, PA 19087 Development of an item count substance abuse survey
R03DA-06689-01A1 (DACB) VANDENBERGH, JOHN G NORTH CAROLINA STATE UNIVERSIT DEPT OF ZOOLOGY RALEIGH, NC 27695-7617 Effect of cocaine on social regulation of reproduction
R43DA-06698-01A1 (SRCD) FREDERIKSEN, LEE W HEALTH INNOVATIONS, INC 12355 SUNRISE VALLEY RESTON, VA 22091 Computer-assisted smoking cessation for heavy smokers
R01DA-06719-01 (DAAR) NYAMATHI, ADELINE M UNIVERSITY OF CALIFORNIA 10833 LE CONTE AVENUE LOS ANGELES, CA 90024-6918 AIDS program for addicted/homeless minority women
R01DA-06723-02 (DAAR) FRIEDMAN, SAMUEL R NARCOTIC & DRUG RESEARCH, INC. 11 BEACH STREET NEW YORK, NY 10013 Social factors and HIV risk
R01DA-06726-02 (SRCD) WEBER, ECKARD UNIVERSITY OF CALIFORNIA IRVIN IRVINE, CA 92717 PCP receptor characterization with new affinity ligands
R01DA-06728-01A1 (DACB) ROEMER, RICHARD A PHILADELPHIA PSY CTR FORD RD & MONUMENT AVE PHILADELPHIA, PA 19131 Electrophysiological studies of cocaine abstinence
R01DA-06731-02 (DABR) TIUS, MARCUS A UNIVERSITY OF HAWAII AT MANOA 2545 THE MALL HONOLULU, HAWAII 96822 Functionalized cannabinoids
R01DA-06733-01A1 (DABR) VORHEES, CHARLES V CHILDREN'S HOSPITAL MEDICAL CT ELLAND AND BETHESDA AVENUES CINCINNATI, OH 45229-2899 Developmental effects of methamphetamine-like stimulants
R01DA-06735-01 (DABR) LEWIS, DARRELL V DUKE UNIVERSITY MED CTR PO BOX 3430 DURHAM, NC 27710 Endogenous opioids -- Their role in LTP in dentate gyrus
R01DA-06736-01 (SRCD) HAMMOND, DONNA L UNIVERSITY OF CHICAGO 5841 S MARYLAND AVENUE CHICAGO, IL 60637 Opioid mechanisms of analgesia
R01DA-06743-01 (DABR) CHANG, ALBERT S BAYLOR COLLEGE OF MEDICINE 4000 RESEARCH FOREST DRIVE THE WOODLANDS, TX 77381 Molecular analyses of high-affinity serotonin transport
R01DA-06746-02 (SRCD) CRIPPEN, GORDON M UNIVERSITY OF MICHIGAN ANN ARBOR, MI 48109 Mapping of cocaine receptors
R01DA-06753-01 (DAAR) SINGHAL, PRAVIN C LONG ISLAND JEWISH MED CENTER 400 LAKEVILLE ROAD NEW HYDE, NY 11042 Effects of opioids on the glomerular mesangium
R01DA-06775-02 (DABR) MAYERSOHN, MICHAEL UNIVERSITY OF ARIZONA TUCSON, AZ 85721 Methamphetamine disposition kinetics in animals
R01DA-06781-01 (DABR) THAYER, STANLEY A UNIV OF MINNESOTA MEDICAL SCH 435 DELEWARE ST SE MINNEAPOLIS, MN 55455 Opioid regulation of intracellular ion concentrations
R01DA-06784-01 (DABR) CHILDERS, STEVEN R WAKE FOREST UNIVERSITY 300 SOUTH HAWTHORNE ROAD WINSTON-SALEM, NC 27103 Endogenous cannabinoid systems in brain
R01DA-06786-02 (DABR) ARCHER, SYDNEY RENSSELAER POLYTECHNIC INST TROY, NY 12180-3590 Cocaine and heroin antagonists
R03DA-06790-01A1 (DABR) VOOGT, JAMES L UNIV OF KANSAS MEDICAL CENTER 39TH & RAINBOW BLVD/PHYSIOLOGY KANSAS CITY, KS 66103-8410 Neuroendocrine effects of perinatal opiate exposure
R01DA-06791-01 (ALCP) KRAHN, DEAN D UNIV OF MICHIGAN MEDICAL CTR 1500 E MEDICAL CTR DR AN ARBOR, MI 48109-0116 Effect of dieting on alcohol and drug use in young women
R03DA-06792-02 (DABR) PINNICK, HAROLD W BUCKNELL UNIVERSITY LEWISBURG, PA 17837 Synthesis of delta-1-tetrahydrocannabinol-7-oic acid
R03DA-06793-01A1 (DAPA) LABIG, CHALMER E, JR COLLEGE OF BUSINESS ADMIN STILLWATER, OK 74078-0555 Generating referrals and consultations for an EAP
R01DA-06798-01A1 (DACB) PENA, JOSE M TULANE UNIVERSITY SCHOOL OF ME 1430 TULANE AVE NEW ORLEANS, LA 70112 Treatment of cocaine abuse--Psychotherapy of black men
Z01DA-06801-04 (VL) HERNING, R I ARC, NIDA Cognitive neurophysiologic signs of cocaine abstinence
R03DA-06804-01 (SRCD) BAUER, HAROLD R CHILDREN'S HOSPITAL 700 CHILDREN'S DRIVE COLUMBUS, OH 43205 Infant development outcomes of prenatal cocaine exposure
R01DA-06805-01 (DABR) WAHLESTEDT, CLAES CORNELL UNIVERSITY MEDICAL COL 411 EAST 69TH STREET NEW YORK, NY 10021 Cocaine and brain neuropeptide Y
R01DA-06811-01 (DABR) SCHWARTZ-GIBLIN, SUSAN T ROCKEFELLER UNIVERSITY 1230 YORK AVENUE NEW YORK, N Y 10021 Benzodiazepine/sex steroid interactions in brainstem
R01DA-06821-01A1 (SRCD) OSTREA, ENRIQUE M, JR HUTZEL HOSPITAL 4707 ST ANTOINE BOULEVARD DETROIT, MI 48201 Meconium drug screening in newborn infants
R03DA-06822-01A1 (DAAR) STEVEN, WILLIAM M LSU MEDICAL CENTER IN SHREVPOR PO BOX 33932 SHREVPORT, LA 71130-3932 Cocaine and maternal immune transfer to neonates
R01DA-06825-01A1 (DACB) SCHENK, SUSAN TEXAS A&M UNIVERSITY COLLEGE STATION, TX 77843 Sensitization to cocaine
R01DA-06827-02 (SRCD) KRAHN, DEAN D UNIV OF MICHIGAN MEDICAL CTR 1500 E MEDICAL CENTER DRIVE ANN ARBOR, MI 48109-0116 Effect of food/taste preferences on drug intake in rats
R01DA-06828-02 (DACB) BARRETT, JAMES E UNIFORMED SERVICES UNIVERSITY 4301 JONES BRIDGE ROAD BETHESDA, MD 20814-4799 Behavioral and pharmacological antecedents of drug abuse
R01DA-06829-01 (DACB) NADER, MICHAEL A UNIVERSITY OF CHICAGO 5841 S. MARYLAND AVE. CHICAGO, IL 60637 Effects of behavioral history on cocaine self-administration
R01DA-06832-01A1 (DAPA) ROSENBAUM, MARSHA INST FOR SCIENTIFIC ANALYSIS 2235 LOMBARD STREET SAN FRANCISCO, CA 94123 An ethnographic study of pregnancy and drugs
R29DA-06838-01 (DACB) SNODGRASS, SAMUEL H UNIVERSITY OF ARKANSAS MED SCI 4301 WEST MARKHAM STREET LITTLE ROCK, AR 72205 Determinants of the reinforcing efficacy of cocaine
R01DA-06839-01 (SRCD) RICHARDSON, GALE A WESTERN PSYCHIATRIC INST 3811 O'HARA STREET PITTSBURGH, PA 15213 Prenatal cocaine use--a longitudinal epidemiologic study
R03DA-06841-02 (DACB) HUGHES, RICHARD A IOWA STATE UNIVERSITY AMES, IA 50011-3180 An avian model for determinants of drug abuse
R01DA-06844-02 (DAPA) LONDON, PERRY RUTGERS UNIVERSITY FRELINGHUYSEN AVE PISCATAWAY, NJ 08855-0819 Adolescent self-perspectives on problem behavior
R01DA-06853-01 (DAPA) MORGAN, PATRICIA INSTITUTE FOR SCIENTIFIC ANALY 2235 LOMBARD STREET SAN FRANCISCO, CA 94123 Ice and methamphetamine use-- An exploratory study
R01DA-06857-01A1 (DACB) LANE, JAMES D DUKE UNIVERSITY MEDICAL CENTER PO BOX 3926 DURHAM, NC 27710 Caffeine's effects on smoking and nicotine withdrawal
R01DA-06861-01 (DACB) SACHS, DAVID P PALO ALTO CTR/PULM DIS PREVENT 750 WELCH ROAD, SUITE 200 PALO ALTO, CA 94304-1509 Nicotine/caffeine codependence in nicotine withdrawal
R01DA-06863-02 (DABR) POLAND, RUSSELL E HARBOR-U C L A MEDICAL CENTER 1000 W CARSON STREET TORRANCE, CA 90509 Neuroendocrine reflections of MDMA neurotoxicity
R01DA-06866-01 (DABR) BURCHFIELD, DAVID J UNIVERSITY OF FLORIDA BOX J-296, JHMHC GAINESVILLE, FL 32610 Cocaine--Effect on fetal brain metabolism and function
R29DA-06867-01 (SRCD) ABOOD, MARY E VIRGINIA COMMONWEALTH UNIVERSI BOX 524 MCV STATION RICHMOND, VA 23298-0524 Opioid receptors in a model development system
R03DA-06869-01A1 (DABR) SKOLNICK, MALCOLM H UNIV OF TEXAS HLTH SCI CTR 1343 MOURSUND AVENUE HOUSTON, TX 77030 Potentiation of opiate analgesia by electrostimulation

R03DA-06870-01 (DABR) ASHBY, CHARLES R SUNY AT STONY BROOK PUTNAM HALL - SOUTH CAMPUS STONY BROOK, NY 11794-8790 The mode of action of MDMA
P01DA-06871-01 (SRCD) HARVEY, JOHN A MEDICAL COLL OF PENNSYLVANIA 3200 HENRY AVE PHILADELPHIA, PA 19129 Brain structure and function after cocaine exposure
P01DA-06871-01 0001 (SRCD) MURPHY, E HAZEL Brain structure and function after cocaine exposure Prenatal cocaine exposure effect on postnatal neocortex development
P01DA-06871-01 0002 (SRCD) LEVITT, PAT Brain structure and function after cocaine exposure Prenatal cocaine exposure effect on limbic system
P01DA-06871-01 0003 (SRCD) FRIEDMAN, EITAN Brain structure and function after cocaine exposure Prenatal cocaine effect on dopamine and serotonin neurotransmission
P01DA-06871-01 0004 (SRCD) HARVEY, JOHN A Brain structure and function after cocaine exposure Behavioral consequences of fetal cocaine exposure
P01DA-06871-01 0005 (SRCD) ROBERTS, JAY Brain structure and function after cocaine exposure Prenatal cocaine--Cardiovascular/sympathetic nervous system development
P01DA-06871-01 9001 (SRCD) HARVEY, JOHN Brain structure and function after cocaine exposure Core--Animal facility and image analysis
R01DA-06876-01 (DABR) ACETO, MARIO D VIRGINIA COMMONWEALTH UNIV MCV STATION, BOX 613 RICHMOND, VA 23298-0613 Cocaine psychostimulation model and pharmacotherapy
R01DA-06882-02 (SRCD) TRONICK, EDWARD Z CHILDREN'S HOSPITAL CORP 300 LONGWOOD AVENUE BOSTON, MA 02115 Neuromotor functioning in cocaine-exposed infants
R01DA-06886-01 (DABR) WEST, MARK O RUTGERS UNIVERSITY BUSCH CAMPUS NEW BRUNSWICK, NJ 08903 Accumbens neurophysiology & cocaine self-administration
R01DA-06889-01 (DACB) SELLERS, EDWARD M ADDICTION RESEARCH FOUNDATION 33 RUSSELL STREET TORONTO, ONTARIO M5S 2S1 Pharmacogenetic risk factors in drug abuse
R01DA-06890-01 (DABR) SHIVERICK, KATHLEEN T UNIVERSITY OF FLORIDA BOX J-267 JHMHC GAINESVILLE, FL 32610-0267 Effects of cocaine on placental growth factors
R01DA-06891-02 (DABR) VOLKOW, NORA D ASSOCIATED UNIVERSITIES, INC BROOKHAVEN NATIONAL LABORATORY UPTON, NY 11973 PET studies of brain dopamine in cocaine abusers
R01DA-06892-02 (DAPA) DONOHEW, ROBERT L UNIVERSITY OF KENTUCKY 227 GREHAN BUILDING LEXINGTON, KY 40506-0042 Increasing the effectiveness of televised anti-drug PSAS
R01DA-06893-01A1 (DABR) ROBERTS, STEPHEN M UNIVERSITY OF FLORIDA ONE PROGRESS BLVD/BOX 17 ALACHUA, FL 32615 Methamphetamine-potentiated hepatotoxicity
R03DA-06895-02 (DABR) STORK, PHILIP J OREGON HEALTH SCIENCES UNIV 3181 S W SAM JACKSON PARK RD PORTLAND, OR 97201 Cloning of the catecholamine uptake transporter
R18DA-06897-02 (SRCD) MC CAUL, MARY E COMPREHENSIVE WOMEN'S CENTER 708 NORTH BROADWAY BALTIMORE, MD 21205 Female IV drug abusers--Impact of specialized care
R18DA-06900-02 (SRCD) FIELD, TIFFANY M UNIV OF MIAMI SCHOOL OF MEDICI PO BOX 016820 MIAMI, FL 33101 Interventions for cocaine-expo teenage mothers/infants
U01DA-06903-02 (SRCD) ANDERSEN, MARCIA D PERSONALIZED NURSING CORP, PC 100 RENAISSANCE CENTER DETROIT, MI 48243 Light model--Randomized clinical trial with iv DUs
U01DA-06906-02 (SRCD) WILLIAMS, MARK L AFFILIATED SYSTEMS CORP 1200 POST OAK ROAD HOUSTON, TX 77056-3104 Cooperative agreement for AIDS community-based outreach
U01DA-06908-02 (SRCD) WATTERS, JOHN K URBAN HEALTH STUDY SAN FRANCISCO, CA 94143-1304 AIDS community-based outreach/intervention research
U01DA-06910-02 (SRCD) MC COY, CLYDE B UNIVERSITY OF MIAMI SCH OF MED 1550 NORTHWEST 10TH AVENUE MIAMI, FL 33136 Prevention of HIV-related diseases among high risk users
R18DA-06911-02 (SRCD) HALL, JAMES A UCSD MEDICAL CENTER 225 DICKINSON STREET SAN DIEGO, CA 92103 Drug abuse treatment for pregnant and non-pregnant teens
U01DA-06912-02 (SRCD) CROWLEY, THOMAS J UNIVERSITY OF COLORADO 4200 EAST 9TH AVE, BOX C268 DENVER, CO 80262 Community AIDS prevention--A cross-over study
R18DA-06913-02 (SRCD) ALEMI, FARROKH CLEVELAND STATE UNIVERSITY 2121 EUCLID AVENUE CLEVELAND, OH 44115 Extended case management of cocaine addicted pregnancy
R18DA-06915-02 (SRCD) SCHOTTENFELD, RICHARD S APT FOUNDATION, INC 904 HOWARD AVENUE NEW HAVEN, CT 06519 Effectiveness of services for pregnant substance abusers
R18DA-06918-02 (SRCD) MULLEN, ROD AMITY, INC PO BOX 32200 TUCSON, AZ 85751-2200 Addicted mothers and offspring recovery and education
U01DA-06919-02 (SRCD) KOTRANSKI, LYNNE C PHILA HEALTH MGMT CORP 260 SOUTH BROAD STREET PHILADELPHIA, PA 19102 Community-based monitoring and AIDS prevention research
R18DA-06925-02 (SRCD) DRUCKER, ERNEST MONTEFIORE MEDICAL CENTER 111 EAST 210TH STREET BRONX, NY 10467 Family case management for maternal drug users
R18DA-06932-02 (SRCD) LEWIS, ROBERT A PURDUE UNIVERSITY 525 RUSSELL STREET WEST LAFAYETTE, IN 47907 Couple-focused therapy for drug abusing women
R18DA-06941-02 (SRCD) CROWLEY, THOMAS J UNIVERSITY OF COLORADO 4200 EAST 9TH AVENUE, BOX C268 DENVER, CO 80262 Drug-abusing, conduct-disordered youth--Treatment and research
R18DA-06944-02 (SRCD) SIEGAL, HARVEY A WRIGHT STATE UNIVERSITY 3640 COLONEL GLENN HIGHWAY DAYTON, OH 45435 Enhanced treatment through induction and case management
R18DA-06948-02 (SRCD) INCIARDI, JAMES A UNIVERSITY OF DELAWARE NEWARK, DE 19716 A therapeutic community work release center for inmates
R18DA-06949-02 (SRCD) BRADY, JOSEPH V INSTITUTE FOR BEHAVIOR RESOURC TRIAD TECH CENTER, SUITE 2400 BALTIMORE, MD 21224 Enhancing drug abuse treatment by mobile health service
R18DA-06953-02 (SRCD) ABBOTT, PATRICK J UNIV OF NEW MEXICO/MH PROGRAMS 2350 ALAMO SE ALBUQUERQUE, NM 87106 Community/relapse pevention approachs to heroin abuse
R18DA-06954-02 (SRCD) CAMPBELL, JAN L V A MEDICAL CENTER 4801 LINWOOD BOULEVARD KANSAS CITY, MO 64128 Pharmacotherapy and intensive treatment of drug abuse
R18DA-06959-02 (SRCD) MAGURA, STEPHEN NARCOTIC & DRUG RESEARCH, INC 11 BEACH STREET NEW YORK, NY 10013 Neurobehavioral treatment--Cocaine-abusing methadone patients
R18DA-06963-02 (SRCD) ROUNSAVILLE, BRUCE J A P T FOUNDATION, INC 904 HOWARD AVE/SUITE 2A NEW HAVEN, CT 06519 Improving cocaine and opiate abuse treatment
R18DA-06968-02 (SRCD) RAHAV, MICHAEL ARGUS COMMUNITY INC 760 EAST 160TH STREET BRONX, NY 10456 Research and treatment to enhance residential MICA program
R18DA-06969-02 (SRCD) BICKEL, WARREN K UNIV OF VERMONT COLL OF MED 1 SOUTH PROSPECT ST BURLINGTON, VT 05401 Buprenorphine pharmacology related to addiction treatment
R01DA-06971-05 (CMS) ROSENFELD, JOEL P NORTHWESTERN UNIVERSITY 2021 SHERIDAN ROAD EVANSTON, IL 60208 Single neuronal activation by multiple opiate substrates
R18DA-06975-02 (SRCD) HALIKAS, JAMES A UNIVERSITY OF MINNESOTA 420 DELAWARE ST SE, PO BOX 393 MINNEAPOLIS, MN 55455 Carbamazepine in the treatment of cocaine abuse
R18DA-06979-02 (SRCD) WERDEGAR, DAVID INST FOR HLTH POL STUDIES, UCS 1388 SUTTER ST, 11TH FLOOR SAN FRANCISCO, CA 94109 A clinical trial of drug abuse day treatment
R18DA-06983-02 (SRCD) BROWN, VIVIAN B PROTOTYPES 845 EAST ARROW HIGHWAY POMONA, CA 91767 Non-tradional supports for drug abusing women
R18DA-06984-02 (SRCD) SENAY, EDWARD C UNIVERSITY OF CHICAGO 5841 S. MARYLAND AVE CHICAGO, IL 60637 A study of medical maintenance
R18DA-06986-02 (SRCD) PLATT, JEROME J HAHNEMANN UNIVERSITY BROAD & VINE STREETS PHILADELPHIA, PA 19102-1192 Enhancing day treatment for cocaine abusers
R18DA-06988-02 (SRCD) NURCO, DAVID N SOCIAL RESEARCH CENTER 1229 W MT ROYAL AVENUE BALTIMORE, MD 21217 Social support and drug-free living among parolees
R18DA-06989-02 (SRCD) CHENEY, ROSE A PHILADELPHIA HLTH MGMT COR 260 S BROAD ST / 20TH FLOOR PHILADELPHIA, PA 19102-3890 Peer support groups for recovering women
R18DA-06993-02 (SRCD) ROBLES, RAFAELA R DEPT OF ANTI ADDICTION SERVICE BOX 21414 RIO PIEDRAS STATION RIO PIEDRAS, PR 00928-1414 Community support and integration for recovering addicts
R18DA-06994-02 (SRCD) LEVY, JUDITH UNIVERSITY OF ILLINOIS 2121 WEST TAYLOR STREET CHICAGO, ILLINOIS 60612 Community-based service demonstration project
R18DA-06995-02 (SRCD) SONNENSTUHL, WILLIAM J CORNELL UNIVERSITY PO BOX 100 ITHACA, NY 14853 Generating criteria for comparative evaluation of MAPS
R18DA-07003-02 (SRCD) MASON, THERESA H ABT ASSOCIATES INC 55 WHEELER ST CAMBRIDGE, MA 02138-1168 Evaluation of social support services for drug abusers
R01DA-07004-02 (NLS) HAMMOND, DONNA LOUISE THE UNIVERSITY OF CHICAGO 5841 S MARYLAND AVENUE CHICAGO, IL 60637 Control of nociception by GABA
R43DA-07007-01 (SRCD) LYNCH, THOMAS J PHARMAVENE, INC 35 WEST WATKINS MILL RD GAITHERSBURG, MD 20878 Cocaine detoxification by butyrylcholinesterase
R43DA-07010-01 (SRCD) FORGEY, MARY A INTERSYSTEMS INC 820 WEST END AVE NEW YORK, NY 10025 Measuring drug abuse risk in Employee Assistance Programs and workplace settings
R43DA-07014-01 (SRCD) ELBAUM, DANEK BIO-FOCUS, INC BOX 450, AWOSTING ROAD PINE BUSH, NY 12566 Detector for endogenous opioid peptides
R43DA-07017-01 (SRCD) WILSON, OWEN B NEUROMEDICAL TECHNOLOGIES, INC 3131 WEST ALABAMA, SUITE 210 HOUSTON, TX 77098 TCET as an aid to opiate drug withdrawal
R43DA-07018-01 (SRCD) HOUGHTEN, RICHARD A MULTIPLE PEPTIDE SYSTEMS, INC 10955 JOHN JAY HOPKINS DRIVE SAN DIEGO, CA 92121 Large scale synthesis of the opioid peptide DPDPE
R43DA-07020-01 (SRCD) ROGERS, SANDRA A FHAIS/CES 307 PK LKE CIR/BX 536905 ORLANDO, FL 32853-6905 CAI drug abuse curriculum for healthcare personnel
R01DA-07029-01A1 (DAPA) SPOTH, RICHARD L IOWA STATE UNIVERSITY AMES, IA 50011 Rural family and community drug abuse prevention project
R01DA-07030-02 (SRCD) HANSEN, WILLIAM B WAKE FOREST UNIVERSITY 300 S HAWTHORNE RD WINSTON-SALEM, NC 27103 Effective school-based substance abuse prevention
R01DA-07031-01 (SRCD) DISHION, THOMAS J OREGON SOCIAL LEARNING CENTER 207 E 5TH AVE EUGENE, OR 97401 Multi-component prevention for at-risk adolescents
R01DA-07037-02 (SRCD) RINGWALT, CHRISTOPHER L RESEARCH TRIANGLE INSTITUTE PO BOX 12194, 3040 CORNWALLIS RES TRIANGLE PARK, NC 27709 a Process and outcome evaluation of project DARE
R01DA-07041-02 (SRCD) BLACK, GORDON S GORDON S BLACK CORPORATION 1661 PENFIELD RD ROCHESTER, NY 14625 Multi-intervention plan to reduce drug abuse
R43DA-07045-01 (SRCD) FOLTZ, RODGER L NORTHWEST TOXICOLOGY INC 1141 EAST 3900 SOUTH SALT LAKE CITY, UT 84124 Ultra-sensitive MS/MS assay for LSD in urine
R01DA-07047-02 (SRC) WELLS, ELIZABETH A UNIVERSITY OF WASHINGTON 146 N CANAL STREET SEATTLE, WA 98103 Children's conceptions of AIDS and related risky behaviors
R29DA-07050-01A1 (DAAR) COUCH, DAVID B UNIVERSITY OF MISSISSIPPI 2500 NORTH STATE ST JACKSON, MS 39216-4505 Effects of morphine and genotoxicants on lymphocytes
R01DA-07055-01 (DAAR) BERGER, ALAN R MONTEFIORE MEDICAL CENTER 111 EAST 210TH STREET BRONX, NY 10467 Peripheral neuropathy in HIV+ intravenous drug abusers
R01DA-07059-01 (DAAR) SCHILLING, ROBERT F COLUMBIA UNIVERSITY

PROJECT NO., ORGANIZATIONAL UNIT., INVESTIGATOR, ADDRESS, TITLE

622 WEST 113TH STREET NEW YORK, NY 10025 Reducing AIDS and relapse among female offenders
R01DA-07062-01A1 (DAAR) COTTAM, GENE L UNIV OF TX SOUTHWESTERN MED CT 5323 HARRY HINES BLVD DALLAS, TX 75235-9038 Opioid metabolism by immune system membrane peptidases
R01DA-07063-01 (DAAR) MC AULIFFE, WILLIAM E PROJECT OUTREACH 875 MASSACHUSETTS AVE CAMBRIDGE, MA 02139 Evaluation of outreach for prevention of AIDS in intravenous drug users
R03DA-07067-01 (DAAR) MOSS, ANDREW R SAN FRANCISCO GENERAL HOSPITAL 995 POTRERO AVENUE SAN FRANCISCO, CA 94110 Gender and ethnic differences in surrogate markers
R29DA-07068-01 (DAAR) LINNER, KRISTIN M MINNEAPOLIS MEDICAL RESEARCH F 825 S 8TH STREET MINNEAPOLIS, MN 55404 Opioids/opiates in thymocyte maturation and activation
P50DA-07074-02 (SRCD) SUINN, RICHARD M COLORADO STATE UNIVERSITY FORT COLLINS, CO 80523 Tri-ethnic center for study of drug abuse prevention
P50DA-07074-02 0001 (SRCD) BEAUVAIS, FRED Tri-ethnic center for study of drug abuse prevention Correlates of drug use and ethnicity
P50DA-07074-02 0002 (SRCD) CHAVEZ, ERNEST L Tri-ethnic center for study of drug abuse prevention Dropouts and drugs--Cross sectional and longitudinal studies
P50DA-07074-02 0003 (SRCD) DEFFENBACHER, JERRY L Tri-ethnic center for study of drug abuse prevention Behavioral intervention--Anger management training for angry youth
P50DA-07074-02 0004 (SRCD) EDWARDS, RUTH W Tri-ethnic center for study of drug abuse prevention Community-wide action against drugs
P50DA-07074-02 9001 (SRCD) SUINN, RICHARD M Tri-ethnic center for study of drug abuse prevention Core
R01DA-07080-02 (DABR) KELLOGG, CAROL K UNIVERSITY OF ROCHESTER COLLEGE OF ARTS & SCIENCES ROCHESTER, NY 14627 Drug-stress interactions in pregnancy and development
U18DA-07082-02 (SRCD) WISH, ERIC D KOBA ASSOCIATES INC 1156 15TH ST NW WASHINGTON, DC 20005 D C diagnostic referral and data management unit
U18DA-07084-02 (SRCD) BESTEMAN, KARST INST FOR BEHAVIORAL RESOURCES 400 NORTH CAPITOL ST, NW WASHINGTON, DC 20001 Substance treatment and outcome programs--District of Columbia
U18DA-07085-02 (SRCD) LUBORSKY, LESTER B UNIVERSITY OF PENNSYLVANIA 3400 SPRUCE ST PHILADELPHIA, PA 19104-4283 Psychosocial treatment of cocaine use disorder--Collaborative site
U18DA-07090-02 (SRCD) CRITS-CHRISTOPH, PAUL HOSPITAL OF THE UNIV OF PENN 3400 SPRUCE ST PHILADELPHIA, PA 19104-4283 Coordinating center for treatment of cocaine abuse study
R03DA-07100-01 (DABR) VILLAR, HUGO O MOLECULAR RESEARCH INST 845 PAGE MILL ROAD PALO ALTO, CA 94304 CADD of D1/D2 receptor ligands for cocaine abuse therapy
R03DA-07103-01 (DACB) ZACNY, JAMES P UNIVERSITY OF CHICAGO 5841 S MARYLAND AVE CHICAGO, IL 60637 Behavioral effects of nitrous oxide in humans
R01DA-07110-01 (DACB) GABBAY, FRANCES H UNIFORMED SERV UNIV HLTH SCI 4301 JONES BRIDGE ROAD BETHESDA, MD 20814-4799 Stimulant and sedative drug response
R01DA-07111-01A1 (DAPA) SAFFER, HENRY NATL BUREAU OF ECONOMIC RES 269 MERCER STREET NEW YORK, NY 10003 The effect of legal deterrents on drug and alcohol use
R13DA-07113-01 (DABR) HARRIS, LOUIS S VIRGINIA COMMONWEALTH UNIV BOX 613, MED COLL OF VA STATIO RICHMOND, VA 23298-0613 Committee on problems of drug dependence annual meeting
R01DA-07128-01 (DAPA) MOORE, JOAN W UNIV OF WISCONSIN - MILWAUKEE P O BOX 413 MILWAUKEE, WI 53201 Drug posses, gangs and the underclass in milwaukee
R01DA-07130-01A1 (DABR) PRITCHETT, DOLAN B UNIVERSITY OF PENNSYLVANIA 34TH & CIVIC CENTER BLVD PHILADELPHIA, PA 19104 GABA-a receptor subtypes and drug abuse
R01DA-07134-01 (DABR) HYMAN, STEVEN E MASSACHUSETTS GENERAL HOSPITAL FRUIT ST BOSTON, MA 02114 Cocaine-induced plasticity of neural gene expression
U18DA-07160-02 (SRCD) KARSON, SAMUEL SECOND GENESIS, INC 7910 WOODMONT AVE, STE 500 BETHESDA, MD 20814-3048 Second genesis research demonstration
P01DA-07171-01 (SRCD) MCCLEARN, GERALD E THE PENNSYLVANIA STATE UNIV S-211 HENDERSON BLDG UNIVERSITY PARK, PA 16802 Chromosome locations of genes affecting cocaine actions
P01DA-07171-01 0001 (SRCD) JONES, BYRON C Chromosome locations of genes affecting cocaine actions Cocaine related behavior
P01DA-07171-01 0002 (SRCD) ERWIN, V GENE Chromosome locations of genes affecting cocaine actions Cocaine related neurochemistry
P01DA-07171-01 0003 (SRCD) MCCLEARN, GERALD E Chromosome locations of genes affecting cocaine actions Quantitative trait loci (QTL) based selective breeding
P01DA-07171-01 9001 (SRCD) PLOMIN, ROBERT Chromosome locations of genes affecting cocaine actions Quantitative trait loci (QTL) core
R03DA-07175-01 (DABR) JIMENEZ-RIVERA, CARLOS A UNIV CENTRAL DEL CARIBE 156 MUNOZ RIVERA AVE BOX 935 CAYEY, PR 00634 Cocaine's effect on noradrenergic physiology
R01DA-07176-01 (DABR) VASKO, MICHAEL R INDIANA UNIVERSITY SCH OF MED 635 BARNHILL DRIVE INDIANAPOLIS, IN 46202-5120 Tolerance to opioid actions on sensory neurons
R03DA-07181-01 (DABR) BATEMAN, ROBERT C, JR UNIV OF SOUTHERN MISSISSIPPI SOUTHERN STATION/BOX 5043 HATTIESBURG, MS 39406-5043 Enzyme-activated enkephalinase inhibitors
R01DA-07182-01 (DABR) KISH, STEPHEN J CLARKE INSTITUTE OF PSYCHIATRY 250 COLLEGE STREET TORONTO, ONTARIO, CANADA M5T 1 Is chronic cocaine abuse toxic to the human brain?
R01DA-07186-01 (DABR) EISENBERG, RICHARD M UNIVERSITY MINNESOTA DULUTH 10 UNIVERSITY DR DULUTH, MN 55812 Opiate dependence and tolerance
R13DA-07194-01 (DABR) SADEE, WOLFGANG U OF CALIFORNIA, SF 926 MEDICAL SCIENCES BLDG SAN FRANCISCO, CA 94143-0446 22nd annual International Narcotic Research Conference
R01DA-07201-01 (SRCD) WEISSMAN, MYRNA M COLUMBIA UNIVERSITY 630 WEST 168TH STREET NEW YORK, NY 10038 Opiate addicts children-psychopathology/neurodevelopment
R01DA-07203-01 (DACB) WELLS, KAREN C DUKE UNIV MEDICAL CENTER BOX 3320 2213 ELBA STREET DURHAM, NC 27710 Adolescent drug abuse--Controlled trial of family therapy
R01DA-07212-01A1 (DABR) SIREN, ANNA-LEENA K UNIFORMED SER UNIV OF HLTH SCI 4301 JONES BRIDGE RD BETHESDA, MD 20814-4799 Mu-opioid and alpha2-adrenergic mechanisms in analgesia
R01DA-07213-01 (DABR) PIERSON, MARTHA G WADSWORTH CENTER FOR LABS & RE EMPIRE STATE PLAZA, BOX 509 ALBANY, NY 12201-0509 Phencyclinoid-promoted epileptogenesis in developing rat
R01DA-07216-01 (DABR) LYNCH, KEVIN R UNIVERSITY OF VIRGINIA 1300 JEFFERSON PARK AVE, BOX 4 CHARLOTTESVILLE, VA 22908 Alpha2-adrenergic receptor subtypes in the CNS
R01DA-07218-01 (SRCD) MURRAY, THOMAS F OREGON STATE UNIVERSITY COLLEGE OF PHARMACY CORVALLIS, OREG 97331-3507 Dextrorotatory opioids as probes for PCP receptors
R01DA-07223-01 (DABR) SEEMAN, PHILIP 8 TADDLECREEK RD TORONTO, CANADA M5S 1A8 Receptors for cocaine and dopamine
R24DA-07234-01 (SRCM) ZAPATA, JESSE T UNIVERSITY OF TEXAS SAN ANTONIO, TX 78285 Minority research center
R29DA-07239-01A1 (DABR) FINNEGAN, KEVIN T VETERANS ADMIN MEDICAL CENTER 500 FOOTHILL DRIVE SALT LAKE CITY, UT 84148 MDMA-induced neurotoxicity -- Role of glutamate and calcium
R01DA-07240-01 (DABR) LINTHICUM, DARWIN S TEXAS A&M UNIVERSITY COLLEGE STATION, TX 77843 Molecular mimicry of receptors for alkaloid drugs
R01DA-07242-01 (DABR) PASTERNAK, GAVRIL W SLOAN KETTERING INST/CNCR RES 1275 YORK AVENUE NEW YORK, NY 10021 Pharmacology of opioid receptor subtypes
R29DA-07244-01 (DABR) MACLENNAN, ALEXANDER J UNIV OF FLORIDA COLLEGE OF MED BOX J-244 JHMHC GAINESVILLE, FL 32610-0244 Molecular study of nucleus accumbens dopamine receptors
R03DA-07247-01 (DABR) GINGRAS, JEANNINE L DUKE UNIVERSITY MEDICAL CENTER BOX 3179 DURHAM, NC 27710 Cocaine, breathing and neurotransmitters -- SIDS link
R01DA-07250-01 (DAPA) HARTWELL, TYLER D RESEARCH TRIANGLE INSTITUTE PO BOX 12194-3040 CORNWALLIS R RES TRIANGLE PARK, NC 27709 Prevalence and impact of employee assistance programs
R18DA-07262-02 (NSS) RACHAL, J VALLEY RESEARCH TRIANGLE INSTITUTE PO BX 12194/3040 CORNWALLIS RD RES TRIANGLE PK, NC 27709 Enhancing methadone maintenance programs to prevent AIDS
R29DA-07263-02 (DABR) SNOOK, SANDRA S ANIMAL RESOURCES CENTER 5841 SOUTH MARYLAND AVE CHICAGO, IL 60637 In utero methadone exposure in the rhesus monkey
R43DA-07276-01 (SRCD) HINK, ROBERT F EXPERT SYSTEM DESIGN, INC 156 TUNNEL ROAD BERKELEY, CA 94705 Substance abuse treatment manager
U01DA-07286-01 (SRCD) DEREN, SHERRY NARCOTIC & DRUG RESEARCH, INC 11 BEACH STREET NEW YORK, NY 10013 Cooperative agreement for the prevention of AIDS
U01DA-07287-01 (SRCD) ROBLES, RAFAELA R DEPT OF ANTI-ADDICTION SERVICE PO BOX 21414 RIO PIEDRAS, PR 00928-1414 Continuous care for the prevention of HIV risk behaviors
R01DA-07288-01 (DAAR) HARRIS, RUTH M UNIVERSITY OF MARYLAND BALTIMORE COUNTY CAMPUS BALTIMORE, MD 21228 AIDS prevention for black women in a drug user community
U01DA-07290-01 (SRCD) FISHER, DENNIS G UNIVERSITY OF ALASKA 3211 PROVIDENCE DRIVE ANCHORAGE, AK 99508 IVDU's not in treatment in Alaska
R01DA-07292-01 (SRCD) FUCHS, BRUCE A VIRGINIA COMMONWEALTH UNIV BOX 613, MCV STATION RICHMOND, VA 23298-0613 Neuroimmune mechanisms of morphine immunosuppression
R01DA-07293-01 (DAAR) BAYER, BARBARA M GEORGETOWN UNIVERSITY 3900 RESERVOIR RD NW WASHINGTON, DC 20007 Neuroendocrinology of cocaine-induced immunosuppression
U01DA-07295-01 (SRCD) TROTTER, ROBERT T II NORTHERN ARIZONA UNIVERSITY CAMPUS BOX 15200 FLAGSTAFF, AZ 86011 Multicultural outreach for HIV/AIDS/drug risks
R01DA-07296-01 (DAAR) MC AULIFFE, WILLIAM E CAMBRIDGE HOSPITAL 875 MASSACHUSETTS AVENUE CAMBRIDGE, MA 02139 A longitudinal study of the IV-AIDS epidemic
N01DA-07300-00 (**) BIOMETRIC RESEARCH INC 1401 WILSON BLVD SUITE 400 ARLINGTON, VA 22209-2306 Medications development database
U01DA-07302-01 (SRCD) FLEMING, DAVID W OREGON HEALTH DIVISION 1400 SW 5TH AVE PORTLAND, OR 97201 Targeted HIV risk reduction in drug treatment drop-outs
R03DA-07303-01A1 (DAAR) PARADISE, LOIS J UNIV OF SOUTH FLORIDA 12901 N BRUCE B DOWNS BLVD TAMPA, FL 33612 Effect of marijuana on experimental syphilis in rabbits
U01DA-07306-01 (SRCD) SIEGAL, HARVEY A WRIGHT STATE UNIVERSITY 3640 COLONEL GLENN HIGHWAY DAYTON, OH 45435 Enhancing HIV risk reduction through case management
N01DA-07307-00 ( ) UNIV OF CALIFORNIA** 3333 CALIFORNIA STREET, #11 SAN FRANCISCO, CA 94118 Pharmacokinetics of psychoactive drugs
R01DA-07310-02 (DAAR) GIBSON, DAVID R UNIVERSITY OF CALIFORNIA BOX 0886 SAN FRANCISCO, CA 94143-0886 Measurement and prediction of AIDS risk in IV drug users
R18DA-07311-02 (SRCD) STRANTZ, IRMA UNIV OF SOUTHERN CALIFORNIA UNIVERSITY PARK - MC-0411 LOS ANGELES, CA 90089 Evaluation of perinatal cocaine abusers-- A treatment model
R01DA-07313-01 (SAT) HILL, HARLAN F FRED HUTCHINSON CANCER RES CTR 1124 COLUMBIA STREET SEATTLE, WA 98104 Epidural analgesics--In vitro and in vivo studies
R01DA-07315-01 (DABR) LEWIS, JOHN W UNIV OF BRISTOL CANTOCKS COLOSE BRISTOL, ENGLAND BS8 1TS Discovery of new treatments for intravenous drug abuse
R03DA-07316-01 (DABR) MOKLER, DAVID J UNIV NEW ENG/COLL OF OSTEO MED 11 HILLS BEACH ROAD BIDDEFORD, ME 04005 5 hydroxytryptamine mechanisms of hallucinogenic drugs
R03DA-07318-01 (DABR) DEUTSCH, DALE G STATE UNIVERSITY OF NEW YORK LIFE SCIENCES BUILDING STONY BROOK, NY 11794 The cannabinoids and cytochrome P-450 gene expression
R29DA-07327-01 (DACB) PICKER, MITCHELL J UNIVERSITY OF NORTH CAROLINA CB#3270 CHAPEL HILL, NC 27599-3270 Biobehavioral actions of

partial opioid agonists
R03DA-07328-01 (DABR) MC CAMAN, RICHARD E BECKMAN RES INST OF CITY OF HO 1450 EAST DUARTE ROAD DUARTE, CA 91010 Cloning invertebrate neuronal neurotransmitter receptors
R01DA-07339-01 (DABR) LAW, PING Y UNIVERSITY OF MINNESOTA 435 DELAWARE STREET, S E MINNEAPOLIS, MN 55455 G-proteins and opioid receptor functions
R01DA-07348-01 (DACB) WEISS, FRIEDBERT RES INST OF SCRIPPS CLINIC 10666 N TORREY PINES RD, BCR 1 LA JOLLA, CA 92037 Novel treatments for cocaine dependence--An animal model
R29DA-07353-01 (DABR) STORNETTA, RUTH L UNIVERSITY OF VIRGINIA BOX 448, 1300 JEFFERSON PARK A CHARLOTTESVILLE, VA 22908 Opiate actions -- Neuropeptides and brainstem mechanisms
R01DA-07355-01 (DABR) ERICKSON, CARLTON K UNIVERSITY OF TEXAS AUSTIN, TX 78712 Pentobarbital activation in selected mouse lines
R01DA-07359-01 (DABR) NESTLER, ERIC J YALE UNIVERSITY 34 PARK STREET NEW HAVEN, CT 06508 Molecular actions of cocaine in brain reward regions
R01DA-07362-01 (SRCD) COLES, CLAIRE D GEORGIA MENTAL HEALTH INST 1256 BRIARCLIFF ROAD, NE ATLANTA, GA 30306 Maternal substance abuse--Developmental outcome in infancy
R01DA-07364-01 (DABR) WEST, JAMES R UNIVERSITY OF IOWA COLLEGE OF MEDICINE IOWA CITY, IA 52242 Cocaine and brain development
R03DA-07366-01 (DABR) PODUSLO, SHIRLEY E TEXAS TECH UNIVERSITY 3601 4TH ST LUBBOCK, TX 79430 Fire and ice -- Neurons response to illicit drugs
R01DA-07374-01 (SRCD) SPUNT, BARRY J NARCOTIC & DRUG RESEARCH, INC 11 BEACH STREET NEW YORK, NY 10013 Female drug relationships in murder (FEMDREIM)
R29DA-07376-01 (DABR) BERGER, S PAUL 401 PARNASUS AVE BOX GMO SAN FRANCISCO, CA 94143-0984 Molecular mechanisms--Cocaine and other uptake inhibitors
R01DA-07380-01 (DACB) GALIZIO, J MARK UNC-WILMINGTON 601 SOUTH COLLEGE ROAD WILMINGTON, NC 28403-3297 Drugs of abuse and negative reinforcement
R01DA-07381-01 (DACB) KOSS, JOAN D UNIVERSITY OF NEW MEXICO 2400 TUCKER, NE ALBUQUERQUE, NM 87131 Retaining hispanic drug abusing youth in family therapy
R01DA-07382-01 (DAPA) HSER, YIH-ING UCLA DRUG ABUSE RESEARCH GROUP 1100 GLENDON AVENUE LOS ANGELES, CA 90024-3511 Treatment util & effectiveness for drug-dependent users
R01DA-07389-01 (DAPA) ARY, DENNIS V OREGON RESEARCH INSTITUTE 1899 WILLAMETTE EUGENE, OREGON 97401 Community intervention trial to prevent youth drug use
R01DA-07390-01 (DABR) BLAKELY, RANDY D EMORY UNIVERSITY SCH OF MEDICI ATLANTA, GA 30322 Molecular analyses of monoamine reuptake systems
R29DA-07391-01 (DACB) RAMSAY, DOUGLAS S UNIVERSITY OF WASHINGTON SB-26 SEATTLE, WA 98195 Tolerance to nitrous oxide in humans
N01DA-07401-01 (**) BURGESS, ANNE CARLETON UNIVERSITY 1525 DUNTON TOWER OTTAWA, ONTARIO K15 5B6 Animal model for treatment of cocaine addiction
R01DA-07402-01 (DABR) CRAIG, ARTHUR D BARROW NEUROLOGICAL INSTITUTE 350 WEST THOMAS RD PHOENIX, AZ 85013 Opiate analgesia -- The lamina I STT projection
N01DA-07403-00 (**) NEW YORK UNIVERSITY 15 WASHINGTON PLACE NEW YORK, NEW YORK 10003 Designer drug induced neuropathology
N01DA-07405-00 (**) OREGON HLTH SCIENCES UNIV 3181 SW, SAM JACKSON PARK RD MAIL CODE L-106 PORTLAND, OREGON 97201-3098 Molecular genetics of drug-seeking behavior
N01DA-07407-00 (**) SRI INTERNATIONAL 333 RAVENSWOOD AVENUE MENLO PARK, CA 94025 Effects of long term marijuana exposure on CNS of monkeys
N01DA-07408-00 (**) JOHNS HOPKINS UNIV SCHOOL OF MEDICINE 720 RUTLAND AVENUE BALTIMORE, MD 21205-2195 Screening for neurotoxicity of new treatment drugs
R01DA-07415-01 (DABR) MC CLESKEY, EDWIN W WASHINGTON UNIVERSITY 660 S EUCLID AVE BOX 8228 ST LOUIS, MO 63110 Opioid and opiate modulation of calcium in sensory neurons
R01DA-07417-01 (DAPA) BLUM, TERRY C GEORGIA INSTITUTE OF TECHNOLOG GEORGIA INST OF TECHNOLOGY ATLANTA, GA 30332 Employer and employee reactions to drug abuse
R29DA-07418-01 (DABR) SULZER, DAVID COLUMBIA UNIVERSITY 722 WEST 168TH STREET, BOX 62 NEW YORK, NY 10032 Amphetamine action mesolimbic dopamine neuronal culture
R01DA-07425-01 (DABR) LEON, MICHAEL A UNIVERSITY OF CALIFORNIA IRVINE, CALIF 92717 Cocaine and the neurobiology of early learning
R01DA-07426-01 (DACB) BURLING, THOMAS A AMERICAN INSTITUTES FOR RESEAR P O BOX 1113 PALO ALTO, CA 94302 Stop-smoking treatment for drug/alcohol abuse inpatients
R01DA-07428-01 (DACB) ANDERSON, DAVID C HENNEPIN COUNTY MEDICAL CENTER 701 PARK AVE SOUTH MINNEAPOLIS, MN 55415 Human brain atrophy and dysfunction in chronic cocainism
R01DA-07432-01 (SRCD) NAIR, PRASANNA U OF MD SCHOOL OF MEDICINE 22 SOUTH GREENE STREET BALTIMORE, MD 21201 Intervention for drug abusing women and their infants
R43DA-07437-01 (SRCD) PARIKH, INDU RESEARCH TRIANGLE PHARMACEUTIC 4364 SOUTH ALSTON AVE DURHAM, NC 27713 Microdroplet based sustained delivery of naltrexone
R43DA-07438-01 (SRCD) GRISSOM, GRANT R INTEGRA, INC 320 KING OF PRUSSIA ROAD RADNOR, PA 19087 Evaluation of substance abuse treatment programs
R43DA-07445-01 (SRCD) CARD, JOSEFINA J SOCIOMETRICS CORPORATION 170 STATE STREET LOS ALTOS, CA 94022 Data archive on maternal drug abuse
R43DA-07450-01 (SRCD) DUQUETTE, PETER H BIO-METRIC SYSTEMS, INC 9924 WEST 74TH STREET EDEN PRAIRIE, MN 55344 Rapid enzyme immunoassay (EIA) for anabolic steroid abuse
R43DA-07455-01 (SRCD) HARTIG, PAUL R NEUROGENETIC CORPORATION 215 COLLEGE ROAD PARAMUS, NJ 07652 Molecular cloning of opiate receptor subtypes
R03DA-07456-01 (DABR) STRECKER, ROBERT E SUNY AT STONY BROOK PUTNAM HALL, SOUTH CAMPUS STONY BROOK, NY 11794-8790 Dopamine release induced by 4-methylaminorex
R29DA-07458-01 (DAAR) CLAPPER, ROCK L BROWN UNIVERSITY BOX G PROVIDENCE, RI 02912 Deterring preadolescent drug and AIDS-risky behavior
R13DA-07460-01 (DAAR) THOMSEN, DONALD L, JR SIMS 97 PARISH RD, SOUTH NEW CANAAN, CT 06840 Conference-Statistical methodology for study of AIDS epidemic
U01DA-07470-01 (SRCD) STEVENS, SALLY J AMITY INC. COPASA 316 S 6TH AVE TUCSON, AZ 85701 Community outreach project on AIDS in southern Arizona
U01DA-07474-01 (SRCD) RHODES, FEN CALIFORNIA STATE UNIVERSITY 1250 BELLFLOWER BOULEVARD LONG BEACH, CA 90840 AIDS community based outreach/intervention research
U01DA-07475-01 (SRCD) SHORTY, VERNON DESIRE NARCOTIC REHAB CTR, INC 3307 DESIRE PARKWAY NEW ORLEANS, LA 70126 New Orleans Coop agreement for AIDS community outreach/intervention
R03DA-07607-01 (DABR) SCHREIBER, MICHAEL D UNIV OF CHICAGO 5841 S MARYLAND AVE CHICAGO, IL 60637 Cocaine and perinatal cerebral and umbilical vessels
R29DA-07635-01A1 (TDA) CAREY, KATE B SYRACUSE UNIVERSITY 430 HUNTINGTON HALL SYRACUSE, NY 13244-2340 Understanding the mentally ill chemical abuser
R43DA-07641-01 (SRCD) RAWSON, RICHARD A MATRIX CENTER, INC 8447 WILSHIRE BLVD BEVERLY HILLS, CA 90211 A structured manual to facilitate naltrexone treatment
P50DA-07656-01 (SRCD) BOTVIN, GILBERT J CORNELL UNIVERSITY MED COLLEGE 411 EAST 69TH STREET NEW YORK, NY 10021 Multi-ethnic drug abuse prevention among New York youth
P50DA-07656-01 0004 (SRCD) DUSENBURY, LINDA Multi-ethnic drug abuse prevention among New York youth Drug abuse prevention with youth in homeless shelters
P50DA-07656-01 9001 (SRCD) SCHINKE, STEVEN P Multi-ethnic drug abuse prevention among New York youth Core--Intervention development
P50DA-07656-01 0001 (SRCD) BOTVIN, GILBERT J Multi-ethnic drug abuse prevention among New York youth School-based drug abuse prevention among Hispanic youth
P50DA-07656-01 0002 (SRCD) SCHINKE, STEVEN P Multi-ethnic drug abuse prevention among New York youth Preventing drug abuse through community agencies
P50DA-07656-01 0003 (SRCD) ORLANDI, MARIO A Multi-ethnic drug abuse prevention among New York youth Preventing drug abuse in housing projects with African American youth
P50DA-07656-01 9002 (SRCD) NG, STEPHEN Multi-ethnic drug abuse prevention among New York youth Core--Information management, statistics and program evaluation
U01DA-07663-01 (SRCD) FRANK, ARLENE F BROOKSIDE HOSPITAL 11 NORTHWEST BLVD NASHUA, NH 03063 Cost-effectiveness of cocaine abuse treatment
U01DA-07673-01 (SRCD) THASE, MICHAEL E WESTERN PSYCHIATRIC INST 3811 O'HARA STREET PITTSBURGH, PA 15213 Psychosocial treatments for cocaine abuse
U01DA-07693-01 (SRCD) WEISS, ROGER D MC LEAN HOSPITAL 115 MILL STREET BELMONT, MA 02178 Psychosocial treatment of cocaine use disorder
P50DA-07697-01 (SRCD) LIDDLE, HOWARD A TEMPLE UNIVERSITY T U 265-63 PHILADELPHIA, PA 19122 Center for treatment research on adolescent drug abuse
P50DA-07697-01 0001 (SRCD) LIDDLE, HOWARD A Center for treatment research on adolescent drug abuse Family versus individual therapy for adolescent drug abuse
P50DA-07697-01 0002 (SRCD) ALEXANDER, JAMES F Center for treatment research on adolescent drug abuse Family therapist impact on treatment process outcome
P50DA-07697-01 9001 (SRCD) TURNER, RALPH M Center for treatment research on adolescent drug abuse Core--Data management and statistics
P50DA-07697-01 9002 (SRCD) TURNER, RALPH M Center for treatment research on adolescent drug abuse Core--Assessment
P50DA-07699-01 (SRCD) ANGLIN, M DOUGLAS UCLA DRUG ABUSE RESEARCH GROUP 1100 GLENDON AVENUE LOS ANGELES, CA 90024-6913 UCLA center on treatment careers
P50DA-07699-01 0001 (SRCD) HSER, YIH-ING UCLA center on treatment careers Improving the efficacy and efficiency of matching drug user's needs to services
P50DA-07699-01 0002 (SRCD) LONGSHORE, DOUGLAS UCLA center on treatment careers Treatment engagement and referral--A culture-based-approach
P50DA-07699-01 0003 (SRCD) KHALSA, HARI K UCLA center on treatment careers Drug dependence and treatment careers--Short and longterm processes and outcomes
P50DA-07700-01 (SRCD) DE LEON, GEORGE NARCOTIC & DRUG RESEARCH, INC 11 BEACH STREET NEW YORK, NY 10013 Center for therapeutic community evaluation research
P50DA-07700-01 0001 (SRCD) DE LEON, GEORGE Center for therapeutic community evaluation research Modified therapeutic community for dually mentally ill chemical abuser patients
P50DA-07700-01 0002 (SRCD) JAINCHILL, NANCY Center for therapeutic community evaluation research Adolescents in therapeutic community--Client profile and treatment outcome
P50DA-07700-01 0003 (SRCD) WEXLER, HARRY K Center for therapeutic community evaluation research Evaluation of Rightum--Prison-based therapeutic community for substance abusers
P50DA-07700-01 9001 (SRCD) DE LEON, GEORGE Center for therapeutic community evaluation research Core
P50DA-07705-01 (SRCD) MC LELLAN, A THOMAS VA MEDICAL CENTER UNIVERSITY & WOODLAND PHILADELPHIA, PA 19104 Drug abuse treatment evaluation center
P50DA-07705-01 0001 (SRCD) MCLELLAN, A THOMAS Drug abuse treatment evaluation center Addiction severity index--Further studies
P50DA-07705-01 0002 (SRCD) METZGER, DAVID S Drug abuse treatment evaluation center Risk for AIDS behavior questionnaire studies
P50DA-07705-01 0003 (SRCD) EHRMAN, RONALD N Drug abuse treatment evaluation center Cue exposure technique--Possible measure of relapse vulnerability

PROJECT NO., ORGANIZATIONAL UNIT., INVESTIGATOR, ADDRESS, TITLE

P50DA-07705-01 0004 (SRCD) MCLELLAN, A THOMAS Drug abuse treatment evaluation center Treatment services review studies
P50DA-07705-01 0005 (SRCD) METZGER, DAVID S Drug abuse treatment evaluation center Problem severity index studies
P50DA-07705-01 9001 (SRCD) MCLELLAN, A THOMAS Drug abuse treatment evaluation center Core
S15DA-07773-01 (SRCA) SCHWARZ, RICHARD H SUNY HEALTH SCIENCE CENTER 450 CLARKSON AVE, BOX 129 BROOKLYN, N Y 11201 Small instrumentation grant
S15DA-07774-01 (SRCA) KEANE, WILLIAM 825 SOUTH EIGHTH ST MINNEAPOLIS, MN 55404 Small instrumentation grant
S15DA-07776-01 (SRCA) CRUZE, ALVIN M RESEARCH TRIANGLE INSTITUTE PO BOX 12194 RES TRIANGLE PARK, NC 27709 Small instrumentation grant
S15DA-07779-01 (SRCA) FOGEL, BERNARD J UNIV OF MIAMI SCH OF MEDICINE P.O BOX 016960 MIAMI, FL 33101 Small instrumentation grant
S15DA-07780-01 (SRCA) LIPTON, DOUGLAS S NARCOTIC & DRUG RESEARCH INC 11 BEACH STREET NEW YORK, NY 10013 Small instrumentation grant
S15DA-07782-01 (SRCA) PENRY, J KIFFIN BOWMAN GRAY SCHOOL OF MEDICINE MEDICAL CENTER BLVD WINSTON SALEM, NC 27157 Small instrumentation grant
S15DA-07783-01 (SRCA) MUSLOW, IKE LOUISIANA STATE UNIV MED CTR PO BOX 33932 SHREVEPORT, LA 71130-3932 Small instrumentation grant
S15DA-07785-01 (SRCA) BYRNE, JOSEPH J 193 HARRISON AVENUE BOSTON, MA 02111 Small instrumentation grant
S15DA-07786-01 (SRCA) COX, BRIAN M UNIFORMED SERV UNIV OF HLTH SC 4301 JONES BRIDGE ROAD BETHESDA, MD 20814-4799 Small instrumentation grant
S15DA-07787-01 (SRCA) CHUANG, RONALD Y UNIV OF CAL, DAVIS DAVIS, CA 95616 Small instrumentation grant
S15DA-07791-01 (SRCA) CICERO, THEODORE J WASHINGTON UNIVERSITY 4940 AUDUBON AVE ST LOUIS, MO 63110 Small instrumentation grant
S15DA-07792-01 (SRCA) DAVIS, JOSEPH H MCLEAN HOSPITAL 115 MILL STREET BELMONT, MA 02178 Small instrumentation grant
S15DA-07793-01 (SRCA) WESTFALL, THOMAS C 1402 S GRAND BLVD ST LOUIS, MO 63104 Small instrumentation grant
S15DA-07794-01 (SRCA) HOGENKAMP, HENRICUS P UNIV OF MINNESOTA 417 JOHNSTON HALL MINNEAPOLIS, MN 55455 Small instrumentation grant
S15DA-07798-01 (SRCA) SISKIND, GREGORY W CORNELL UNIV MEDICAL COLL 1300 YORK AVE NEW YORK, NY 10021 Small instrumentation grant
S15DA-07800-01 (SRCA) COOPER, RICHARD A MEDICAL COLLEGE OF WISCONSIN MILWAUKEE, WI 53226 Small instrumentation grant
S15DA-07801-01 (SRCA) TASH, WILLIAM R TEMPLE UNIVERSITY BROAD & OXFORD ST PHILADELPHIA, PA 19122 Small instrumentation grant
S15DA-07802-01 (SRCA) DANIELS, ROBERT S LOUISIANA STATE UNIVERSITY 1542 TULANE AVENUE NEW ORLEANS, LA 70112 Small instrumentation grant
S15DA-07805-01 (SRCA) STEVENS, ANN R EMORY UNIV 1462 CLIFTON ROAD, N E ATLANTA, GEORGIA 30322 Small instrumentation grant
S15DA-07816-01 (SRCA) BURROW, GERARD N UNIV OF CAL, SAN DIEGO LA JOLLA, CA 92093-0602 Small instrumentation grant
S15DA-07817-01 (SRCA) MILLER, RICHARD E TEXAS A&M UNIVERSITY COLLEGE STATION, TX 77843-312 Small instrumentation grant
S15DA-07818-01 (SRCA) HO, ING K UNIVERSITY OF MISSISSIPPI 2500 NORTH STATE STREET JACKSON, MS 39216 Small instrumentation grant
S15DA-07819-01 (SRCA) MC COY, KATHERINE O UNIV OF SOUTH CAROLINA COLUMBIA, SC 29208 Small instrumentation grant
S15DA-07835-01 (SRCA) DAMBACH, GEORGE E WAYNE STATE UNIVERSITY 540 EAST CANFIELD DETROIT, MI 48201 Small instrumentation grant
R01DA-07844-01 (DABR) FREEMAN, ARTHUR S SINAI RESEARCH INSTITUTE 6767 W OUTER DRIVE DETROIT, MI 48235 Evaluation of PCP and sigma effects on DA physiology
N01DA-08105-00 (**) THE CIRCLE, INC 8201 GREENSBORO DRIVE SUITE 600 MCLEAN, VA 22102 Development of model plan for a HIV/AIDS and drug abuse program for the workplace
N01DA-08200-00 (**) RESEARCH TRIANGLE INST P O BOX 12194 RESEARCH TRIANGLE PARK NORTH CAROLINA 27709 National laboratory certification program
N01DA-08201-00 (**) RES & EVALUATION ASSOC, INC 100 EUROPA DRIVE SUITE 590 CHAPEL HILL, N C 27514 Drug use and workplace safety in transportation industry
N01DA-08203-00 (**) NATIONAL ACADEMY OF SCIENCES 2101 CONSTITUTION AVENUE, NW WASHINGTON, D C 20418 Drug use in the workplace
N01DA-08401-00 (**) NOVA RESEARCH COMPANY, INC Waiting list community intervention
N01DA-08402-00 (**) UNIV CALIF, SAN FRANCISCO INSTITUTE FOR HLTH POLICY STUD 1326 THIRD AVENUE SAN FRANCISCO, CA 94143-0936 Evaluation of community service for multi-problem street youth at risk for AIDS
N01DA-08405-00 (**) NOVA RESEARCH COMPANY 4600 EAST-WEST HIGHWAY SUITE 700 BETHESDA, MD 20814 Pilot testing--AIDS prevention model--Women at risk
Z01DA-09601-03 (VL) UHL, G ARC, NIDA Antagonist-withdrawal up-regulation of endogenous opiate
N01DA-10002-00 (**) T HEAD & COMPANY, INC 950 HERNDON PARKWAY - SUITE 23 HERNDON, VA 22070 Technical support for expert studies and secondary analysis
N01DA-10004-00 (**) CAPITAL CONSULTING CORPORATION 9300 FOREST POINT CIRCLE MANASSAS, VA 22110 Logistical and technical support for the special populations research
Z01DA-10701-02 (VL) NEWLIN, D B ARC, NIDA Alcohol ingestion increases self-report of cocaine-craving
N01DA-11301-00 (**) TAS CONSULTATION ASSN, INC 4733 BETHESDA AVE, SUITE 725 BETHESDA, MD 20814 Logistics support for NIDA constract proposal review meetings
N01DA-12215-00 (**) SMALL BUSINESS ADMIN 409 3RD ST, SW WASHINGTON, DC 20416 NIDA drug information treatment and referral hotline
N01DA-14305-00 (**) RESEARCH TRIANGLE INST 3040 CORNWALLIS ROAD - BOX 12 RESEARCH TRIANGLE PK, NC 27709 Evaluation of campus treatment demonstration program
N01DA-15302-00 (**) CYGNUS CORPORATION 1400 EYE STREET, NW SUITE 1275 WASHINGTON, D C 20005 Drug use surveillance among native American population
N01DA-15305-00 (**) CSR, INC CSR, INCORPORATED 1400 EYE STREET, N.W. /SUITE 6 WASHINGTON, DC 20005 Analysis of epidemiological study data
N01DA-18104-00 (**) CYGNUS CORPORATION 1400 EYE STREET, NW SUITE 1275 WASHINGTON, DC 20005 Operation of a toll-free drug-free workplace helpline
N01DA-18205-00 (**) CDM GROUP, INC 5530 WISCONSIN AVE - SUITE 1 CHEVY CHASE, MD 20815 Drug abuse research technical support
N01DA-18321-00 (**) NAT'L OPINION RESEARCH CTR 1155 EAST 60TH STREET CHICAGO, ILLINOIS 60637 Services research outcomes study
N01DA-18407-00 (**) NOVA RESEARCH COMPANY 4600 EAST-WEST HIGHWAY STE 700 BETHESDA, MD 20814 Data management and support to cooperative agreements
N01DA-19200-00 (**) UNIV KENTUCKY RES FDN 201 KINKEAD HALL LEXINGTON, KY 40506-0057 Pharmaceutical preparation for addiction treatment
N01DA-19201-00 (**) IIT RESEARCH INST 10 WEST 35TH STREET CHICAGO, IL 60616 Immunomodulatory effects of drugs of abuse and potential medications
N01DA-19205-00 (**) CTR FOR HUMAN TOXICOLOGY UNIV OF UTAH 309 PARK BUILDING SALT LAKE CITY, UTAH 84112 Analytical services center for medications development program
N01DA-19302-00 (**) SOUTHERN RES INST 2000 9TH AVE SOUTH - BOX 55305 BIRMINGHAM, AL 35255-5305 Toxicity testing of potential treatment drugs
N01DA-19400-00 (**) QUINTILES, INC P.O. BOX 13979 RESEARCH TRIANGLE PK, NC 27709 Clinical trial monitoring and integrated study report
N01DA-68113-02 (**) JOHNS HOPKINS UNIVERSITY SCHOOL OF MEDICINE 720 RUTLAND AVENUE BALTIMORE, MD 21205 Evaluation of compounds for abuse potential in baboons
K05DA-70554-19 (SRCD) LOH, HORACE H UNIVERSITY OF MINNESOTA DEPT OF PHARMACOLOGY MINNEAPOLIS, MN 55455 Neurochemical mechanism of narcotic actions
N01DA-88010-00 (**) ROW SCIENCES, INC 5515 SECURITY LANE, SUITE 510 ROCKVILLE, MD 20852 Research analysis and utilization system
N01DA-88227-00 (**) MACRO SYSTEMS, INC 8630 FENTON STREET SUITE 300 SILVER SPRING, MD 20910 AIDS outreach/pregnant women and their children
N01DA-88231-00 (**) NOVA RESEARCH COMPANY 4720 MONTGOMERY LANE SUITE 210 BETHESDA, MD 20814 Central data coordinating system
N01DA-88238-00 (**) NATIONAL CAPITOL SYSTEMS, INC 5205 LEESBURG PIKE SUITE 400 FALLS CHURCH, VIRGINIA 22041-3 AIDS training for drug abuse workers institute
N01DA-88254-00 (**) ABT ASSOCIATES, INC 55 WHEELER STREET CAMBRIDGE, MA 02138-1168 AIDS outreach/pregnant women and their children
N01DA-88310-00 (**) RESEARCH TRIANGLE INSTITUTE P O BOX 12194 RESEARCH TRIANGLE PARK NORTH CAROLINA 27709 National household survey on drug abuse
N01DA-88508-00 (**) ADVERTISING CNCL, INC 825 THIRD AVENUE NEW YORK, N Y 10022 Comprehensive drug abuse and AIDS campaign
N01DA-92009-00 (**) FRANCIS SCOTT KEY MED CTR 4940 EASTERN AVENUE BALTIMORE, MD 21224 Professional medical support services for the addiction research center
N01DA-92010-00 (**) THE BIONETICS CORPORATION 20 RESEARCH DRIVE HAMPTON, VA 23666-1396 Animal care & support services for the addiction research center, NIDA
N01DA-98016-00 (**) ROW SCIENCES, INC 5515 SECURITY LANE SUITE 510 ROCKVILLE, MD 20852 Logistical support and editorial services for research evaluation meetings
N01DA-98146-00 (**) JOHNS HOPKINS UNIV SCHOOL OF MEDICINE 720 RUTLAND AVENUE BALTIMORE, MD 21205 Evaluation of unknown compounds for drug abuse
N01DA-98149-00 (**) RESEARCH TRIANGLE INST P O BOX 12194 RESEARCH TRIANGLE PK, NC 27709 Cannabinoid quantification by radioimmunoassay
N01DA-98155-00 (**) UNIV OF MINNESOTA 1919 UNIVERSITY AVE, 5TH FLOOR ST PAUL, MN 55104-3481 Effects of treatment and abused drugs on immune function
N01DA-98156-00 (**) VA COMMONWEALTH UNIV MEDICAL COLLEGE OF VIRGINIA BOX 568 RICHMOND, VA 23298-0569 Pharmacological and toxicological evaluation of treatment drugs
N01DA-98158-00 (**) RESEARCH TRIANGLE INST P O BOX 12194 RESEARCH TRIANGLE PK, NC 27709 Pharmacokinetic studies of treatment drugs
N01DA-98159-00 (**) SRI INTERNATIONAL 333 RAVENSWOOD AVENUE MENLO PARK, CA 94025 Drug activity determination for new drug development
N01DA-98160-00 (**) RESEARCH TRIANGLE INST P O BOX 12194 RESEARCH TRIANGLE PK, NC 27709 Synthetic peptides as structural probes for drug development
N01DA-98233-00 (**) RESEARCH TRIANGLE INSTITUTE P O BOX 12194 RESEARCH TRIANGLE PARK, N C 27 Drug abuse outcome study
N01DA-98252-00 (**) PACIFIC INST FOR RESEARCH & EV 7101 WISCONSIN AVENUE BETHESDA, MD 20814 Drug activity determination for new drug development
N01DA-98325-00 (**) CSR, INC SUITE A600 Statistical reports of drug abuse
N01DA-98333-00 (**) RESEARCH TRIANGLE INST POST OFFICE BOX 12194 NC 27709-2194 Statistical reports of drug abuse
N01DA-98337-00 (**) COMPUTECH, INC 4800 HAMPDEN LANE SUITE 600 BETHESDA, MD 20814 Analytical, programming and operational support for the client data system
N01DA-98340-00 (**) RESEARCH TRIANGLE INST P O BOX 12194 RESEARCH TRIANGLE PK, NC 27709 Metropolitan area surveys in the Washington, D C area
N01DA-98516-01 (**) BIGEL INST FOR HLTH POLICY THE HELLER SCH, BRANDEIS UNIV 415 SOUTH STREET WALTHAM, MA 0225-9110 Analysis of drug abuse financing
N01DA-98518-00 (**) ACTUARIAL RESEARCH CORP 6928 LITTLE RIVER

TURNPIKE SUITE E ANNANDALE, VA 22003 Evaluation of treatment of substance abuse potential within HMO setting

N01DA-98525-00 ( ) RESARCH/EVALUATION ASSOC, INC** 1030 - 15TH STREET, NW SUITE 750 WASHINGTON, D C 20005 Drug testing laboratories data analysis

N01DA-98532-00 ( ) RESEARCH TRIANGLE INST** P O BOX 12194 RESEARCH TRIANGLE PK, NC 27709 Methadone maintenance quality assurance system

N01DA-98542-00 ( ) RES TRIANGLE INST** P O BOX 12194 RESEARCH TRIANGLE PK, NC 27709 Availabilty, impact, cost and effectiveness of drug abuse treatment program

N01DA-98544-00 ( ) ENTERTAINMENT INDUSTRIES, INC** 1760 RESTON PARKWAY SUITE 101 RESTON, VA 22090 AIDS and drug abuse--Outreach to the entertainment community

K08DC-00001-02 (CDRC) TELIAN, STEVEN A UNIVERSITY OF MICHIGAN 1500 E MEDICAL CENTER DRIVE ANN ARBOR, MI 48109 Habituation therapy for chronic vestibular dysfunction

Z01DC-00001-03 (LMB) FEX, J NIDCD, NIH Molecular biology of the inner ear

K04DC-00002-02 (CMS) DERBY, CHARLES D GEORGIA STATE UNIVERSITY UNIVERSITY PLAZA ATLANTA, GA 30303 Mixture interactions in olfaction: effects & mechanisms

Z01DC-00002-03 (LCB) KACHAR, B NIDCD, NIH Molecular basis of transduction in auditory sensory organs

K08DC-00003-02 (CDRC) CRAIG, CHIE H UNIV OF WISCONSIN PO BOX 413 MILWAUKEE, WI 53201 Speech restoration and real-time understanding

Z01DC-00003-03 (LNC) WENTHOLD, R J NIDCD, NIH Neurochemical mechanisms of hearing

Z01DC-00004-03 (VSS) LUDLOW, C L NIDCD, NIH Normal physiology, pathophysiology, and treatment of voice disorders

Z01DC-00005-03 (VSS) LUDLOW, C L NIDCD, NIH Pathophysiology and treatment of speech disorders

Z01DC-00006-03 (VSS) LUDLOW, C L NIDCD, NIH Central control of speech and voice production and perception

Z01DC-00007-03 (HS) PIKUS, A NIDCD, NIH Audiologic findings in diverse disease processes and therapeutic regimens

Z01DC-00008-04 (HS) PIKUS, A NIDCD, NIH Hearing assessment

K08DC-00009-04 (CDR) WOODSON, GAYLE E VA MEDICAL CENTER 3350 LA JOLLA VILLAGE DR., SAN DIEGO, CA 92161 Cricothyroid reflexes & recurrent laryngeal nerve paralysis

R55DC-00015-01A1 (CMS) FUJIMURA, OSAMU OHIO STATE UNIVERSITY 1070 CARMACK ROAD COLUMBUS, OH 43210-1002 Articulation of glossectomies with intraoral prostheses

R01DC-00017-02 (HAR) BERG, KATHLEEN M UNIVERSITY OF FLORIDA 63 DAUER HALL GAINESVILLE, FL 32611 Auditory temporal and spectral summation in infants

R01DC-00018-02 (HAR) GRAY, LINCOLN C UNIVERSITY OF TEXAS 6431 FANNIN, SUITE 5.003 HOUSTON, TX 77030 Roles of early experience in development of hearing

R29DC-00021-02 (HAR) SININGER, YVONNE S HOUSE EAR INSTITUTE 256 SOUTH LAKE STREET LOS ANGELES, CA 90057 Threshold determination with auditory brainstem response

K08DC-00024-05 (CDR) PALMER, JEFFREY B GSHPOB 303 5601 LOCH RAVEN BLVD BALTIMORE, MD 21239 Neuromuscular activity of the pharynx during swallowing

K04DC-00027-04 (CMS) SCHWARTZ, MYRNA F MOSS REHABILITATION HOSPITAL 12TH STREET AND TABOR ROAD PHILADELPHIA, PA 19141 Studies in applied cognitive neuropsychology

K04DC-00028-04 (CMS) MARSCHARK, MARC E UNIVERSITY OF NORTH CAROLINA AT GREENSBORO GREENSBORO, N C 27412 Study and research on deafness and development

K08DC-00029-04 (NSPA) NEWMAN, ANITA NADINE DIV OF HEAD & NECK SURGERY UCLA SCHOOL OF MEDICINE LOS ANGELES, CA 90024-1624 Regeneration of the eighth cranial nerve

K08DC-00030-04 (CDR) HOIT, JEANNETTE D UNIVERSITY OF ARIZONA SPEECH BUILDING NO 25 TUCSON, AZ 85721 Normal and abnormal speech production biomechanics

K08DC-00031-04 (CDR) CASTRO, DAN J UCLA SCHOOL OF MEDICINE DEPT OF SURGERY LOS ANGELES, CA 90024-1624 Laser phototherapy for the treatment of malignancies

K08DC-00032-04 (CDR) HERDMAN, SUSAN J THE JOHNS HOPKINS HOSPITAL CARNEGIE 485, 600 N. WOLFE ST. BALTIMORE, MD. 21205 Adaptive capabilities of postural stabilizing reflexes

K08DC-00033-02 (CDR) EVANS, W JAMES UNIV OF CALIFORNIA, IRVINE CALIFORNIA COLLEGE OF MEDICINE IRVINE, CA 92717 Electrophysiological testing of olfactory function

R01DC-00033-02 (HAR) MROZ, EDMUND A MASS EYE & EAR INFIRMARY 243 CHARLES STREET BOSTON, MA 02114 Pharmacological analysis of ionic balance in hair cells

K08DC-00034-03 (CDR) HIGGINBOTHAM, D JEFFERY SUNY AT BUFFALO BUFFALO, NY 14260 Communication device effect--conversational performance

K08DC-00035-03 (CDR) COLTRERA, MARC D UNIVERSITY OF WASHINGTON DEPT OF OTOLARYNGOLOGY, RL-30 SEATTLE, WA 98195 Head and neck carcinoma cell kinetics

K08DC-00036-04 (CDRC) GRAY, STEVEN DEAN DIV OF OTOLARYNGOLOGY-HNS SALT LAKE CITY, UT 84132 The basement membrane zone in vocal injury

K04DC-00038-03 (HAR) ZOOK, JOHN M OHIO UNIVERSITY IRVINE HALL ATHENS, OH 45701 Medial nucleus of the trapezoid body: in vitro studies

R01DC-00038-02 (EDC) DIEHL, SCOTT R VIRGINIA COMMONWEALTH UNIVERSI BOX 710 MCV STATION RICHMOND, VA 23298 Linkage studies of Waardenburg syndrome

K08DC-00039-02 (CDR) GROSSMAN, MURRAY UNIVERSITY OF PENNSYLVANIA-HOS 3400 SPRUCE ST PHILADELPHIA, PA 19104 The physiologic basis for neurolinguistic impairments

K08DC-00040-02 (CDR) CAMPBELL, KATHLEEN C M SOUTHERN ILLINOIS UNIVERSITY PO BOX 19230 SPRINGFIELD, IL 62794-9230 Effect of ototoxicity on auditory evoked potentials

K04DC-00042-02 (HAR) SINNOTT, JOAN M UNIVERSITY OF SOUTH ALABAMA MOBILE, AL 36688 Comparative auditory processing

K08DC-00043-01A1 (CDRC) STRAND, EDYTHE A UNIVERSITY OF WASHINGTON 1417 N E 42ND STREET SEATTLE, WA 98195 Studies in dysarthria and intelligibility

R01DC-00043-02 (HAR) DON, MANUEL HOUSE EAR INSTITUTE 256 SOUTH LAKE STREET LOS ANGELES, CA 90057 Quantitative objective analyses of derived ABRS

K08DC-00044-01A1 (CDRC) GRACCO, CAROL HASKINS LABORATORIES 270 CROWN STREET NEW HAVEN, CT 06511-6695 Vocal tract manifestations of Parkinson's disease

K04DC-00045-02 (HUD) BEST, CATHERINE T WESLEYAN UNIVERSITY JUDD HALL MIDDLETOWN, CT 06457 Early ontogeny of attunement to the language enviroment

K04DC-00048-02 (HAR) MANIS, PAUL B JOHN HOPKINS UNIVERSITY 720 RUTLAND AVENUE BALTIMORE, MD 21205 Mechanisms of auditory information processing

K08DC-00051-01 (CDRC) HASHISAKI, GEORGE T UNIVERSITY OF CALIFORNIA 101 CITY DRIVE SOUTH ORANGE, CA 92668 The nature of auditory nerve regeneration

K04DC-00052-01 (HAR) KEVETTER, GOLDA A UNIVERSITY OF TEXAS MED BRANCH GALVESTON, TX 77550-2774 Substrates for vestibular sensory-motor integration

K08DC-00054-01 (CDRC) SMALL, STEVEN L UNIVERSITY OF PITTSBURGH 325 SCAIFE HALL PITTSBURGH, PA 15261 Connectionist models in cognitive neurolinguistics

R29DC-00054-02 (HAR) FUZESSERY, ZOLTAN M UNIVERSITY OF WYOMING LARAMIE, WY 82071 Spatial processing in auditory cortex

K08DC-00055-01 (CDRC) SILVER, KENNETH H THE GOOD SAMARITAN HOSPITAL 5601 LOCH RAVEN BLVD, PO BX 30 BALTIMORE, MD 21239 Scintigraphic quantification of pulmonary aspiration

K04DC-00057-01 (HAR) MC GINN, MICHAEL D UNIVERSITY OF CALIFORNIA 1159 SURGE III DAVIS, CA 95616 Effects of auditory experience on the cochlear nucleus

K04DC-00058-02 (BPO) BOTTJER, SARAH W UNIV OF SOUTHERN CALIFORNIA LOS ANGELES, CA 90089-2520 Neuronal mechanisms underlying vocal learning

R01DC-00058-02 (CMS) FRANK, MARION E UNIV OF CONNECTICUT HLTH CTR 263 FARMINGTON AVENUE FARMINGTON, CT 06032 Peripheral gustatory mechanisms

R01DC-00059-02 (CMS) BRADLEY, ROBERT M UNIVERSITY OF MICHIGAN 1011 NORTH UNIVERSITY ANN ARBOR, MI 48109-1078 Long term recording from afferent taste fibers

R01DC-00060-01A1 (CMS) INGHAM, ROGER J UNIVERSITY OF CALIFORNIA RESEARCH INSTITUTE SANTA BARBARA, CA 93106 Time interval investigations of stuttering measurement

K08DC-00062-01 (CDRC) WACKYM, PHILLIP A UCLA SCHOOL OF MEDICINE LOS ANGELES, CA 90024-1624 Vestibular efferent cell and molecular biology

K08DC-00063-01 (CDRC) GILLAM, RONALD B 303 LEWIS HALL Modality specific memory mechanisms in SLI children

R01DC-00064-02 (CMS) MIYAMOTO, RICHARD T RILEY HOSPITAL 702 BARNHILL DR INDIANAPOLIS, IN 46202-5230 Comparison of sensory aids in deaf children

R01DC-00066-02 (BPO) SMITH, DAVID V UNIV OF CINCINNATI COLL OF MED COLLEGE OF MEDICINE CINCINNATI, OH 45267-0528 Processing of taste mixtures by brainstem neurons

R01DC-00068-02 (HAR) PENNER, MERRILYNN J UNIVERSITY OF MARYLAND COLLEGE PARK, MD 20742 Tinnitus in patients with sensorineural hearing loss

R01DC-00070-35 (HAR) GOLDBERG, JAY M UNIVERSITY OF CHICAGO 947 EAST 58TH STREET CHICAGO, IL 60637 Physiology of the vestibular system

R01DC-00070-35 0001 (HAR) FERNANDEZ, CESAR Physiology of the vestibular system: Morphophysiological studies of the mammalian vestibular end organs

R01DC-00070-35 0002 (HAR) GOLDBERG, JAY M Physiology of the vestibular system Studies of the posterior crista in the turtle

R01DC-00070-35 0003 (HAR) FERNANDEZ, CESAR Physiology of the vestibular system Central projections of vestibular-nerve afferents

R01DC-00070-35 0004 (HAR) GOLDBERG, JAY M Physiology of the vestibular system: Vestibular-nerve inputs in the horizontal vestibulo-ocular reflex

R01DC-00072-26 (CMS) MOZELL, MAXWELL M SUNY 750 EAST ADAMS STREET SYRACUSE, N Y 13210 The electrophysiology of olfactory discrimination

R01DC-00073-30 (HAR) KIMURA, ROBERT S MASSACHUSETTS EYE/EAR INFIRMAR 243 CHARLES STREET BOSTON, MA 02114 Electron microscopy of the inner ear

R01DC-00074-29 (HAR) ZWISLOCKI, JOZEF J SYRACUSE UNIVERSITY MERRILL LANE SYRACUSE, NY 13244-5290 Sensory processes

R01DC-00075-28 (CMS) STEVENS, KENNETH N MASSACHUSETTS INST OF TECH 77 MASSACHUSSETTS AVENUE CAMBRIDGE, MA 02139 Physiological and acoustical studies of speech

R01DC-00076-29 (CMS) CHOLEWIAK, ROGER W PRINCETON UNIVERSITY PRINCETON, NJ 08544-1010 The role of the haptic system in communication

R01DC-00077-26 (HAR) REVOILE, SALLY G GALLAUDET UNIVERSITY 800 FLORIDA AVENUE, NE WASHINGTON, DC 20002 Perception of complex auditory stimuli by the deaf

P01DC-00078-27 (CDRC) SCHACHT, JOCHEN UNIVERSITY OF MICHIGAN 1301 E ANN STREET ANN ARBOR, MI 48109-0506 Perception and processing of complex biological signals

P01DC-00078-27 0038 (CDRC) ALTSCHULER, RICHARD A Perception and processing of complex biological signals Molecular structure of peripheral auditory processes

P01DC-00078-27 0039 (CDRC) CLOPTON, BEN M Perception and processing of complex biological signals Auditory physiology

P01DC-00078-27 0040 (CDRC) STEBBINS, WILLIAM Perception and processing of complex biological signals Behavior

P01DC-00078-27 0041 (CDRC) SCHACHT, JOCHEN Perception and processing of complex biological signals Biochemical regulation of outer hair cells

R01DC-00079-26 (HAR) SCHUKNECHT, HAROLD F MASSACHUSETTES EYE & EAR INF 243 CHARLES STREET BOSTON, MA 02114 Otopathology by light microscopy

R01DC-00080-23 (CMS) FARBMAN, ALBERT I NORTHWESTERN UNIVERSITY

PROJECT NO., ORGANIZATIONAL UNIT., INVESTIGATOR, ADDRESS, TITLE

2153 SHERIDAN ROAD EVANSTON ILLINOIS 60208 Cytological effects of induction during development

P01DC-00081-26 (CDRC) GOODGLASS, HAROLD BOSTON VA MEDICAL CENTER 150 SOUTH HUNTINGTON AVE BOSTON, MA 02130 Boston university aphasia research center

P01DC-00081-26 0001 (CDRC) GOODGLASS, HAROLD Boston university aphasia research center Processing for lexical production

P01DC-00081-26 0007 (CDRC) NAESER, MARGARET A Boston university aphasia research center Studies with magnetic resonance imaging

P01DC-00081-26 0012 (CDRC) HELM-ESTABROOKS, NANCY Boston university aphasia research center Perseveration in aphasia

P01DC-00081-26 0013 (CDRC) GRODZINSKY, YOSEF Boston university aphasia research center Structural representations in aphasia

P01DC-00081-26 0014 (CDRC) ZURIF, EDGAR Boston university aphasia research center Processing for lexical comprehension

P01DC-00081-26 0015 (CDRC) CAPLAN, DAVID Boston university aphasia research center Disorders of sentence production

P01DC-00081-26 0016 (CDRC) ALBERT, MARTIN Boston university aphasia research center Long-term recovery from aphasia

P01DC-00081-26 0017 (CDRC) ALBERT, MARTIN Boston university aphasia research center Nonfluency in aphasia

P01DC-00081-26 0018 (CDRC) KINSBOURNE, MARCEL Boston university aphasia research center Right hemisphere compensation

P01DC-00081-26 0019 (CDRC) NAESER, MARGARET Boston university aphasia research center CT scan correlates of long-term recovery

P01DC-00081-26 9001 (CDRC) GALLAGHER, ROBERTA Boston university aphasia research center Core-- Patient/data management

P01DC-00081-26 9002 (CDRC) NAESER, MARGARET Boston university aphasia research center Core-- Neuroimaging resources

R01DC-00082-26 (BPO) SCHMIDT, ROBERT S LOYOLA MEDICAL CENTER MAYWOOD, IL 60153 Neuroethology

R01DC-00083-25 (CMS) OAKLEY, BRUCE UNIVERSITY OF MICHIGAN 3129 NATURAL SCIENCE BLDG ANN ARBOR, MI 48109-1048 Neural plasticity in taste

R01DC-00084-16 (HAR) SCHARF, BERTRAM NORTHEASTERN UNIVERSITY 360 HUNTINGTON AVENUE BOSTON, MASS 02115 Loudness summation, lateralization, and fusion

R01DC-00086-24 (CMS) SHEPHERD, GORDON M YALE UNIVERSITY 333 CEDAR ST. - NEUROANATOMY NEW HAVEN, CONN 06510 Integrative mechanisms of cortical neurons

R01DC-00087-23 (BPO) HAFTER, ERVIN R UNIVERSITY OF CALIFORNIA DEPARTMENT OF PSYCHOLOGY BERKELEY, CALIF 94720 Psychological studies of binaural hearing and attention

R01DC-00088-22 (HAR) VAN DE WATER, THOMAS R ALBERT EINSTEIN COLL OF MED 1410 PELHAM PARKWAY S BRONX, NY 10461 Embryology of the inner ear

R01DC-00089-21 (HAR) DALLOS, PETER J NORTHWESTERN UNIVERSITY 2299 SHERIDAN ROAD EVANSTON, IL 60208 Studies in cochlear hair cell transduction

R01DC-00090-21 (HAR) DEMARIA, THOMAS OHIO STATE UNIVERSITY 456 W 10TH AVENUE COLUMBUS, OH 43210 Otitis media with effusion--Human studies

R01DC-00092-21 (HAR) CAPRANICA, ROBERT R CORNELL UNIVERSITY W255 SEELEY G. MUDD HALL ITHACA, N Y 14853 Encoding of vocal signals in the auditory system

R01DC-00093-21 (CMS) PRICE, JOSEPH L WASH UNIV SCHOOL OF MED 724 SOUTH EUCLID AVENUE ST LOUIS, MO 63110 Studies on the olfactory cortex

R01DC-00094-17 (HAR) DIRKS, DONALD D AUDIOLOGY RES LAB - 62-132 CHS UCLA SCHOOL OF MEDICINE LOS ANGELES, CA 90024 Suprathreshold auditory behavior

R01DC-00095-21 (HAR) CRAIG, JAMES C DEPARTMENT OF PSYCHOLOGY INDIANA UNIVERSITY BLOOMINGTON, IN 47405 Cutaneous pattern perception

R01DC-00096-21 (BPO) BURTON, HAROLD WASHINGTON UNIV SCH OF MED 660 SOUTH EUCLID AVENUE ST LOUIS, MO 63110 Somatosensory properties of neurons in cortex

P50DC-00097-21 (CDR) HONRUBIA, VICENTE UCLA SCHOOL OF MEDICINE DEPT OF SURGERY LOS ANGELES, CA 90024-1624 Communicative disorders clinical research center

P50DC-00097-21 0001 (CDR) BALOH, ROBERT W Communicative disorders clinical research center Clinical vestibular laboratory

P50DC-00097-21 0009 (CDR) HONRUBIA, VICENTE Communicative disorders clinical research center Vestibular physiology laboratory

R01DC-00098-19 (CMS) VERRILLO, RONALD T SYRACUSE UNIVERSITY MERRILL LANE SYRACUSE, NY 13244-5290 Cutaneous mechanoreceptor systems

R01DC-00099-19 (HAR) SIMMONS, F BLAIR DIVISION OF OTOLARYNGOLOGY R125, STANFORD MEDICAL CENTER STANFORD, CALIFORNIA 94305 Development of a cochlear prosthesis

R01DC-00100-17 (HAR) COLBURN, HARRY S BOSTON UNIVERSITY 44 CUMMINGTON STREET BOSTON, MA 02215 Binaural hearing

R01DC-00103-19 (HAR) HOY, RONALD R CORNELL UNIVERSITY ITHACA, NY 14853 Acoustic behavior--its neural and developmental bases

R01DC-00104-17 (BPO) HALPERN, MIMI N SUNY 450 CLARKSON AVE/BX 5 BROOKLYN, NY 11203 Functional studies of the vomeronasal system

R01DC-00105-17 (HAR) NUTTALL, ALFRED L UNIVERSITY OF MICHIGAN 1301 EAST ANN ST ANN ARBOR, MI 48109-0506 Control of inner ear microcirculation

R01DC-00107-15 (HAR) NABELEK, ANNA K UNIVERSITY OF TENNESSEE KNOXVILLE, TN 37996-0740 Noise and reverberation degradation of acoustic cues

R01DC-00108-16 (HAR) STEELE, CHARLES R STANFORD UNIVERSITY DURAND BUILDING STANFORD, CALIF 94305-4040 Mechanics of the organ of corti

R01DC-00109-17 (HAR) SACHS, MURRAY B THE JOHNS HOPKINS UNIVERSITY CHARLES & 34TH STREETS BALTIMORE, MARYLAND 21218 Stimulus encoding in the auditory system

P50DC-00110-17 (SRC) DUVALL, ARNDT J, III UNIV OF MINNESOTA HOSP & CLINI BX 396, HARVARD ST AT E RIVER MINNEAPOLIS, MN 55455 Mechanisms of auditory and vestibular dysfunction

P50DC-00110-17 0020 (SRC) ANDERSON, JOHN H Mechanisms of auditory and vestibular dysfunction Peripheral and central contributions to vestibular reflex behavior

P50DC-00110-17 0022 (SRC) VAN TASELL, DIANNE J Mechanisms of auditory and vestibular dysfunction Perception of acoustic speech cues

P50DC-00110-17 0023 (SRC) DUVALL, ARNDT J Mechanisms of auditory and vestibular dysfunction Ultrastructural and permeability correlates of hearing loss

P50DC-00110-17 0001 (SRC) WARD, W DIXON Mechanisms of auditory and vestibular dysfunction Growth of noise-induced hearing damage

P50DC-00110-17 0004 (SRC) SANTI, PETER A Mechanisms of auditory and vestibular dysfunction Morphological correlates of auditory dysfunctions

P50DC-00110-17 0005 (SRC) RUGGERO, MARIO A Mechanisms of auditory and vestibular dysfunction Peripheral mechanisms of deafness

P50DC-00110-17 0017 (SRC) NELSON, DAVID A Mechanisms of auditory and vestibular dysfunction Imperception of complex acoustic signals

P50DC-00110-17 0018 (SRC) SPEAKS, CHARLES E Mechanisms of auditory and vestibular dysfunction Central auditory speech tests and sensorineural hearing loss

P50DC-00110-17 0019 (SRC) VIEMEISTER, NEAL F Mechanisms of auditory and vestibular dysfunction Dynamic properties of normal and imparied hearing

R01DC-00111-15 (CMS) PISONI, DAVID B INDIANA UNIVERSITY DEPARTMENT OF PSYCHOLOGY BLOOMINGTON, IND 47405 Speech perception, analysis and synthesis

R01DC-00112-16 (HAR) LEWIS, EDWIN R UNIV OF CALIFORNIA 253 CORY HALL BERKELEY, CA 94720 Morphology and physiology of the inner ear

R01DC-00113-12 (CMS) SCOTT, JOHN W EMORY UNIVERSITY DEPT OF ANATOMY & CELL BIOLOGY ATLANTA, GA 30322 Physiological analysis of the olfactory projections

R01DC-00114-15 (HAR) HENSON, O'DELL W, JR U OF NORTH CAROLINA CHAPEL HIL CB#7090, 108 TAYLOR BUILDING CHAPEL HILL, NC 27599 Mechanisms of acoustic perception and orientation

R01DC-00115-16 (HAR) YOUNG, ERIC D JOHNS HOPKINS UNIV SCH OF MED 720 RUTLAND AV, TRAYLOR BLDG. BALTIMORE, MD 21205 Internal organization of the dorsal cochlear nucleus

P01DC-00116-16 (CDR) BRUGGE, JOHN F 281 MEDICAL SCIENCES BLDG 1300 UNIVERSITY AVENUE MADISON, WI 53706 Research program on the neural basis of hearing

P01DC-00116-16 0013 (CDR) YIN, T C Research program on the neural basis of hearing Neural mechanisms if binaural hearing

P01DC-00116-16 0015 (CDR) HIND, JOSEPH E. Research program on the neural basis of hearing Acoustical properties of the external ear

P01DC-00116-16 0016 (CDR) RHODE, WILLIAM Research program on the neural basis of hearing Mechanical motion in the cochlea

P01DC-00116-16 0017 (CDR) GEISLER, C. DANIEL Research program on the neural basis of hearing Stimulus encoding by eight nerve fibers

P01DC-00116-16 0018 (CDR) RHODE, WILLIAM Research program on the neural basis of hearing Information coding in the cochlear nucleus

P01DC-00116-16 0019 (CDR) BRUGGE, JOHN F. Research program on the neural basis of hearing Functional development of the auditory brainstem

P01DC-00116-16 0020 (CDR) BRUGGE, JOHN F. Research program on the neural basis of hearing Hearing impairment associated with hyperbilirubinemia

P01DC-00116-16 0021 (CDR) DARTEL, DONATA Research program on the neural basis of hearing Studies in vitro of abnormal cochlea nuclei

P01DC-00116-16 0022 (CDR) WIGHTMAN, FREDERIC Research program on the neural basis of hearing Studies of human sound localization

P01DC-00116-16 9001 (CDR) BRUGGE, JOHN F. Research program on the neural basis of hearing Core--Technical support

R01DC-00117-16 (HAR) BRAIDA, LOUIS D MASSACHUSETTS INST OF TECH 77 MASSACHUSETTS AVE RM 36-747 CAMBRIDGE, MASS 02139 Hearing aid research

P01DC-00119-16 (CDR) KIANG, NELSON Y MASS EYE & EAR INFIRMARY 243 CHARLES STREET BOSTON, MASS 02114 Basic and clinical studies of the auditory system

P01DC-00119-16 0001 (CDR) PEAKE, WILLIAM T Basic and clinical studies of the auditory system External and middle ear

P01DC-00119-16 0002 (CDR) WEISS, THOMAS F Basic and clinical studies of the auditory system Cochlea

P01DC-00119-16 0003 (CDR) KIANG, NELSON Y Basic and clinical studies of the auditory system Auditory nerve

P01DC-00119-16 0004 (CDR) RYUGO, DAVID K Basic and clinical studies of the auditory system Cochlear nucleus

P01DC-00119-16 0006 (CDR) GUINAN, JOHN T Basic and clinical studies of the auditory system Central neural pathways

P01DC-00119-16 0007 (CDR) MROZ, EDMUND A Basic and clinical studies of the auditory system Cochlea--Hair cell transmitters

P01DC-00119-16 0008 (CDR) LEVINE, ROBERT A Basic and clinical studies of the auditory system Central neural pathways--Man

P01DC-00119-16 9001 (CDR) KIANG, NELSON Y Basic and clinical studies of the auditory system Core

P01DC-00121-29A1 (CDRC) HARRIS, KATHERINE S HASKINS LABORATORIES, INC 270 CROWN STREET NEW HAVEN, CT 06511-6695 Research program on dynamics of speech articulation

P01DC-00121-29A1 0007 (CDRC) ALFONSO, PETER J Research program on dynamics of speech articulation Studies of disordered speech

P01DC-00121-29A1 0010 (CDRC) SALTZMAN, ELLIOT Research program on dynamics of speech articulation Computational and functional-anatomical investigations of vocal tract behavior

P01DC-00121-29A1 9001 (CDRC) RUBEN, PHILIP Research program on dynamics of speech articulation Core facilities--Instrumentation, techniques and data management

P01DC-00121-29A1 0001 (CDRC) BROWMAN, CATHERINE P Research program on dynamics of speech articulation The spatiotemporal organization of speech

P01DC-00121-29A1 0004 (CDRC) GRACCO, VINCENT L Research program on dynamics of speech articulation The articulatory mechanism as a model motor system

R01DC-00122-14 (CMS) DE SIMONE, JOHN A MEDICAL COLLEGE OF VIRGINIA BOX 551, MCV STATION RICHMOND, VA 23298 A physicochemical investigation of taste

R01DC-00123-15 (CMS) SANDO, ISAMU EYE & EAR INST OF PITTSBURGH 203 LOTHROP STREET PITTSBURGH, PA 15213 Histopathology of temporal bones

R01DC-00124-14 (HAR) SCHACHT, JOCHEN KRESGE HEARING RESEARCH INST 1301 E ANN STREET ANN ARBOR, MI 48109-0506 Mechanisms of antibiotic-induced hearing loss

R01DC-00126-12 (CMS) REED, CHARLOTTE M MASSACHUSETTS INST OF TECHNOLO 77 MASSACHUSETTS AVENUE CAMBRIDGE, MA 02139 Tactile communication of speech

R01DC-00128-13 (CMS) NEVILLE, HELEN J SALK INSTITUTE P O BOX 85800 SAN DIEGO, CALIF 92138 Development of cerebral specializations

R01DC-00129-13 (HAR) RYAN, ALLEN F U OF CALIF, SAN DIEGO MED CTR 225 DICKINSON STREET SAN DIEGO, CA 92103 Middle ear response in serious otitis media

R01DC-00130-14 (CMS) MILLER, JOANNE L NORTHEASTERN UNIV./PSYCHOLOGY 360 HUNTINGTON AVENUE BOSTON, MASS 02115 Some determinants of speech perception

R01DC-00132-15 (HAR) SCHWARTZ, ILSA R YALE UNIVERSITY, SCHOOL OF MED P O BOX 3333 NEW HAVEN, CT 06510 Dynamic aspects of auditory synaptic terminals

P50DC-00133-13 (CDR) GIEBINK, G SCOTT UNIVERSTIY OF MINNESOTA 420 DELAWARE ST SE, BOX 483 MINNEAPOLIS, MN 55455 Otitis media pathogenesis research program

P50DC-00133-13 0005 (CDR) JUHN, STEVEN K Otitis media pathogenesis research program Middle ear inflammation

P50DC-00133-13 0009 (CDR) GIEBINK, G SCOTT Otitis media pathogenesis research program Subcellular bacterial components

P50DC-00133-13 0012 (CDR) CANAFAX, DANIEL Otitis media pathogenesis research program Antimicrobial treatment

P50DC-00133-13 0013 (CDR) MORIZONO, TETSUO Otitis media pathogenesis research program Ototoxicity of topical antimicrobial agents

P50DC-00133-13 0015 (CDR) GIEBINK, G. SCOTT Otitis media pathogenesis research program Risk determination for chronic otitis media

P50DC-00133-13 0016 (CDR) PAPARELLA, MICHAEL M. Otitis media pathogenesis research program Histopathological characterization of the otitis media

P50DC-00133-13 0017 (CDR) GOYCOOLEA, MARCOS Otitis media pathogenesis research program Round window membrane morphology, pathology,and permeability

P50DC-00133-13 9002 (CDR) PAPARELLA, MICHAEL M Otitis media pathogenesis research program Laboratory core

P50DC-00133-13 9003 (CDR) LE, C.T. Otitis media pathogenesis research program Biometry--core

P50DC-00133-13 9004 (CDR) PAPARELLA, M.M. Otitis media pathogenesis research program Otopathology--core

P50DC-00133-13 9005 (CDR) JUHN, S.K. Otitis media pathogenesis research program Biochemistry--core

R01DC-00134-14 (HAR) KONISHI, MASAKAZU CALIFORNIA INST OF TECHNOLOGY PASADENA, CA 91125 Neurophysiology of sound localization

R01DC-00135-13 (CMS) CANT, NELL B DUKE UNIVERSITY MEDICAL CENTER PO BOX 3209 DURHAM, NC 27710 Neuroanatomy of the auditory system

R01DC-00136-14 (HAR) JESTEADT, WALT BOYS TOWN NATIONAL INSTITUTE 555 NORTH 30TH STREET OMAHA, NE 68131 Frequency analysis in normal and impaired listeners

R01DC-00138-11 (HAR) JAVEL, ERIC DUKE UNIVERSITY MEDICAL CENTER BOX 3805 DURHAM, NC 27710 Physiological bases of auditory perceptual performance

R01DC-00139-12 (HAR) RYAN, ALLEN F VETERAN ADMIN MEDICAL CENTER 3350 LA JOLLA VILLAGE DR/V-112 SAN DIEGO, CA 92161 Environment influences upon auditory development

R01DC-00141-12 (HAR) NUTTALL, ALFRED L UNIVERSITY OF MICHIGAN 1301 E ANN ST ANN ARBOR, MI 48109-0506 Efferent influence on cochlear mechanoelectric physiology

R01DC-00142-13 (CMS) BLUMSTEIN, SHEILA E BROWN UNIVERSITY BOX 1978 PROVIDENCE, RI 02912 Acoustic and perceptual invariance in speech

R01DC-00144-13 (CMS) PARKS, THOMAS N UNIVERSTIY OF UTAH COLLEGE OF MEDICINE SALT LAKE CITY, UTAH 84132 Cell interactions in developing auditory system

R01DC-00145-12 (BBCA) KIM, SUNG-HOU UNIVERSITY OF CALIFORNIA DEPT OF CHEMISTRY BERKELEY, CA 94720 Crystallography of sweet receptor binding protein

R01DC-00146-13 (CMS) BELLUGI, URSULA SALK INST FOR BIO STUDIES PO BOX 85800 SAN DIEGO, CA 92186-5800 The acquisition of morphological processes in ASL

R01DC-00147-13 (CMS) FINGER, THOMAS E UNIV OF COLORADO MED CENTER 4200 EAST NINTH AVENUE DENVER, COLORADO 80262 Two gustatory channels-- Pathways and neurotransmitters

R01DC-00149-13 (HAR) NELSON, DAVID A UNIVERSITY OF MINNESOTA 2630 UNIVESITY AVENUE, S.E. MINNEAPOLIS, MINNESOTA 55414 Auditory analysis & sensorineural hearing loss

R01DC-00150-11 (CMS) WHITNEY, GLAYDE D FLORIDA STATE UNIVERSITY TALLAHASSEE, FL 32306-1051 Behavior genetic approach to chemosensory function

R01DC-00151-12 (NEUB) CASPARY, DONALD M SIU SCHOOL OF MEDICINE PO BOX 19230 SPRINGFIELD, IL 62794-9230 Coding in auditory neurons--Effects of amino acids

R01DC-00152-12 (HAR) NADOL, JOSEPH B, JR MASS EYE & EAR INFIRMARY 243 CHARLES STREET BOSTON, MA 02114 Electron microscopy of the human inner ear

R01DC-00153-12 (HAR) MC FADDEN, DENNIS UNIVERSITY OF TEXAS AUSTIN, TX 78712 Auditory adaptation for suprathreshold stimuli

R01DC-00154-13 (HAR) STUDEBAKER, GERALD A MEMPHIS SPEECH & HEARING CENTE 807 JEFFERSON AVENUE MEMPHIS, TN 38105 Hearing aid characteristic selection

R01DC-00155-12 (HAR) KNUDSEN, ERIC I STANFORD UNIVERSITY STANFORD, CA 94305-5401 Analysis of space by the auditory system

R01DC-00156-12 (HAR) DRESCHER, DENNIS G WAYNE STATE UNIV SCH OF MED 540 EAST CANFIELD AVENUE DETROIT, MICH 48201 Indentification of acoustico-lateralis transmitters

R01DC-00157-11 (CMS) TITZE, INGO R 127A S.H.C. UNIVERSITY OF IOWA IOWA CITY, IOWA 52242 Nonintrusive techniques for evaluating

phonatory function

R01DC-00159-12 (CMS) GETCHELL, THOMAS V UNIVERSITY OF KENTUCKY COLLEGE OF MEDICINE LEXINGTON, KY 40536-0084 Odorant-receptor interactions in olfactory neurons

R01DC-00160-10 (HAR) LEAKE, PATRICIA A UNIV OF CALIF., SAN FRANCISCO HSE 871, BOX 0526 SAN FRANCISCO, CA 94143-0526 Morphology & connections of the spiral ganglion

P01DC-00161-11 (CDR) DOTY, RICHARD L UNIVERSITY OF PENNSYLVANIA 3400 SPRUCE ST PHILADELPHIA, PA 19104-4283 University of Pennsylvania smell and taste center

P01DC-00161-11 0001 (CDR) DOTY, RICHARD L University of Pennsylvania smell and taste center Development of clinical olfactory diagnostic tests

P01DC-00161-11 0009 (CDR) DOTY, RICHARD L University of Pennsylvania smell and taste center Endocrine factors, brain mechanisms and olfactory sensitivity

P01DC-00161-11 0011 (CDR) SETTLE, R. GREGG University of Pennsylvania smell and taste center Taste sensitivity and hedonic perceptin in depression

P01DC-00161-11 0012 (CDR) DEEMS, DANIEL A. University of Pennsylvania smell and taste center Medial hypothalamus in chemosensory aversion learning

P01DC-00161-11 0013 (CDR) SPECTOR, ALAN C. University of Pennsylvania smell and taste center Role of the parabrachial nucleus in taste discrimination

P01DC-00161-11 9001 (CDR) SNOW, JAMES B University of Pennsylvania smell and taste center Core facilities

P50DC-00162-10S2 (SRC) ABBS, JAMES H WAISMAN CENTER 1500 HIGHLAND AVE MADISON, WI 53705-2280 Speech movement research with an X-ray microbeam

R01DC-00163-11 (CMS) HECOX, KURT E 1500 HIGHLAND AVENUE MADISON, WI 53705 Electrophysiologic correlates of auditory function

R01DC-00164-12 (CMS) BROWN, CHARLES H UNIVERSITY OF SOUTH ALABAMA MOBILE, AL 36688 Perceptual adaptations for communication

R01DC-00167-11 (CMS) NEWPORT, ELISSA L UNIVERSITY OF ROCHESTER ROCHESTER, NY 14627 Structure and acquisition of American sign language

P01DC-00168-10 (SRC) FRANK, MARION E UNIV OF CONNECTICUT HLTH CTR 263 FARMINGTON AVENUE FARMINGTON, CT 06032 Connecticut chemosensory clinical research center

P01DC-00168-10 0006 (SRC) BARTOSHUK, LINDA M Connecticut chemosensory clinical research center Clinical taste psychophysics

P01DC-00168-10 0013 (SRC) FRANK, MARION E Connecticut chemosensory clinical research center Cranial nerve loss and taste function

P01DC-00168-10 0016 (SRC) RODIN, JUDY Connecticut chemosensory clinical research center Experiential & developmental factors in taste & responsiveness

P01DC-00168-10 0017 (SRC) STEWART, WILLIAM B Connecticut chemosensory clinical research center Topographic organization of the olfactory system

P01DC-00168-10 0018 (SRC) SCOTT, APRIL E Connecticut chemosensory clinical research center Taste and smell clinic

P01DC-00168-10 0019 (SRC) BARRY, MICHAEL A Connecticut chemosensory clinical research center Denervated and regenerated gustatory system

P01DC-00168-10 0020 (SRC) LONDON, JILL A Connecticut chemosensory clinical research center Electrophysiology and anatomy of gustatory cortex

R01DC-00172-11A1 (HAR) GODFREY, DONALD A MEDICAL COLLEGE OF OHIO P O BOX 10008 TOLEDO, OHIO 43699 Microchemistry of the cochlear nucleus

R01DC-00173-10 (HAR) IMIG, THOMAS J UNIV OF KANSAS MEDICAL KANSAS 39TH & RAINBOW BLVD KANSAS CITY, KS 66103-8410 Organization of thalamocortical auditory system

R01DC-00174-09 (HAR) BILGER, ROBERT C UNIVERSITY OF ILLINOIS 901 S SIXTH STREET CHAMPAIGN, IL 61820 Psychoacoustic studies of subjective tinnitus

R01DC-00175-11 (HAR) SUGA, NOBUO WASHINGTON UNIVERSITY LINDELL-SKINKER BOULEVARD ST LOUIS, MO 63130 Neural basis of complex-sound processing

R01DC-00176-10 (HAR) OERTEL, DONATA UNIVERSITY OF WISCONSIN 1300 UNIVERSITY AVENUE MADISON, WI 53706 In vitro studies of the cochlear nucleus

P01DC-00178-10 (CDR) LEVITT, HARRY CUNY GRADUATE SCHOOL & UNIV CT 33 WEST 42ND STREET NEW YORK, NY 10036 Rehabilitation strategies for the hearing impaired

P01DC-00178-10 0001 (CDR) MC GARR, NANCY M Rehabilitation strategies for the hearing impaired Speech perception and production

P01DC-00178-10 0002 (CDR) LEVITT, HARRY Rehabilitation strategies for the hearing impaired A digitally programmable master aid

P01DC-00178-10 0004 (CDR) BOOTHROYD, ARTHUR Rehabilitation strategies for the hearing impaired Tactile supplements to speechreading

P01DC-00178-10 0005 (CDR) BOOTHROYD, ARTHUR Rehabilitation strategies for the hearing impaired Efficacy of cochlear implants

P01DC-00178-10 0010 (CDR) LEVITT, HARRY Rehabilitation strategies for the hearing impaired Signal processing hearing aids

P01DC-00178-10 0011 (CDR) WEISS, MARK Rehabilitation strategies for the hearing impaired Noise reduction techniques for sensory aids

R01DC-00179-10 (HAR) HEFFNER, RICKYE S UNIVERSITY OF TOLEDO 2801 WEST BANCROFT STREET TOLEDO, OH 43606 Comparative study of sound localization

R01DC-00181-10 (HAR) HARTMANN, WILLIAM M MICHIGAN STATE UNIVERSITY EAST LANSING, MI 48824-1116 Human hearing-models of pitch and location

R01DC-00182-09 (BBP) NOTTEBOHM, FERNANDO ROCKEFELLER UNIVERSITY 1230 YORK AVENUE NEW YORK, N Y 10021 Vocal-learning model for neuronal basis of cognition

R01DC-00183-09 (CMS) LILLO-MARTIN, DIANE HASKINS LABORATORIES 270 CROWN STREET NEW HAVEN, CT 06511-6695 Acquisition of literacy by deaf children and adults

R01DC-00184-10 (HAR) DUBNO, JUDY R MED UNIV OF SOUTH CAROLINA 171 ASHLEY AVE CHARLESTON, SC 29425 Auditory analysis and speech recognition

PROJECT NO., ORGANIZATIONAL UNIT., INVESTIGATOR, ADDRESS, TITLE

R01DC-00185-07 (HAR) GRANTHAM, D WESLEY B WILKERSON HEARING/SPEECH CTR 1114 19TH AVENUE SOUTH NASHVILLE, TN 37212 Auditory motion perception

R01DC-00187-08 (HAR) FLORENTINE, MARY NORTHEASTERN UNIVERSITY 360 HUNTINGTON AVE BOSTON, MA 02115 Intensity DLS and masking in normal and impaired hearing

R01DC-00188-10 (HAR) LIBERMAN, M CHARLES MASSACHUSETTS EYE & EAR INFIRM 243 CHARLES STREET BOSTON, MA 02114 Single-neuron marking in the study of abnormal cochleas

R01DC-00189-10 (HAR) OLIVER, DOUGLAS L UNIV OF CONNECTICUT HEALTH CTR FARMINGTON, CT 06032 Synaptic organization of the auditory system

R01DC-00190-11 (BPO) BOTTJER, SARAH W UNIV OF SOUTHERN CALIFORNIA UNIVERSITY PARK LOS ANGELES, CA 90089 Neural mechanisms of vocal learning

R01DC-00191-10 (CMS) SAFFRAN, ELEANOR M TEMPLE UNIV SCH OF MED 3401 NORTH BROAD STREET PHILADELPHIA, PA 19140 Psycholinguistic analysis of aphasic syndromes

R01DC-00193-09 (HAR) HARRIS, JEFFREY P UNIV OF CALIF, SAN DIEGO DEPT OF SURGERY/OTOLARYNGOLOGY SAN DIEGO, CA 92103-8220 Aspects of inner ear immunology

R01DC-00194-09 (HAR) ROSOWSKI, JOHN MASS. INSTITUTE OF TECHNOLOGY 77 MASSACHUSETTS AVENUE CAMBRIDGE, MASS 02139 Structure-function relations in middle ears

R01DC-00197-09 (HAR) GLENDENNING, KAREN FLORIDA STATE UNIVERSITY DEPARTMENT OF PSYCHOLOGY TALLAHASSEE, FLORIDA 32306 Acoustic chiasm--Anatomy and behavior

R01DC-00198-09 (BPO) DOOLING, ROBERT J UNIV OF MD AT COLLEGE PARK COLLEGE PARK, MD 20742 Biological foundations of vocal learning

R01DC-00199-08 (HAR) POTASHNER, STEVEN J UNIV OF CONNECTICUT HLTH CTR 263 FARMINGTON AVENUE FARMINGTON, CT 06030 Neurotransmitters in the auditory system

R01DC-00200-09 (NEUB) CORWIN, JEFFREY T UNIVERSITY OF VIRGINIA BOX 396 CHARLOTTESVILLE, VA 22908 Growth and regeneration in the inner ear

R01DC-00201-09 (CMS) BELLUGI, URSULA SALK INST PO BOX 85800 SAN DIEGO, CA 92138 Brain organization--Clues from sign aphasia

P01DC-00203-09 (CDRC) STEINBERG, BETTIE M LONG ISLAND JEWISH MED CTR 270-05 76TH AVENUE NEW HYDE PARK, NY 11042 Studies of papillomas from the upper respiratory tract

P01DC-00203-09 0004 (CDRC) ABRAMSON, ALLAN L Studies of papillomas from the upper respiratory tract Optimization of photodynamic therapy using dihematoporphyrin ether

P01DC-00203-09 0005 (CDRC) TAICHMAN, LORNE B Studies of papillomas from the upper respiratory tract Latent HPV-11 DNA replication

P01DC-00203-09 0007 (CDRC) SHIKOWITZ, MARK J Studies of papillomas from the upper respiratory tract Use of a new photoactive drug for photodynamic therapy--An animal model

P01DC-00203-09 0008 (CDRC) AUBORN, KAREN J Studies of papillomas from the upper respiratory tract Cellular factors determining the variant behavior of HPV-11

P01DC-00203-09 0001 (CDRC) STEINBERG, BETTIE M Studies of papillomas from the upper respiratory tract Cell virus interactions in activation of latent infection

R01DC-00205-10 (CMS) BLACK, FRANKLIN O GOOD SAMARITAN HOSPITAL 1015 N W 22ND AVENUE PORTLAND, OREG 97210 Control of human postural sway trajectories

R01DC-00206-08S1 (HAR) WEBSTER, DOUGLAS B LOUISIANA STATE UNIV MED CNTR 2020 GRAVIER STREET, SUITE A NEW ORLEANS, LA 70112-2234 Central effects of peripheral hearing impairments

R01DC-00207-09 (CMS) LARSON, CHARLES R NORTHWESTERN UNIVERSITY 2299 SHERIDAN ROAD EVANSTON, IL 60208 Neural mechanisms of laryngeal control

R01DC-00208-07 (CEP) WARREN, RICHARD M UNIVERSITY OF WISCONSIN POST OFFICE BOX 413 MILWAUKEE, WI 53201 Mechanisms underlying perception of speech

R01DC-00210-07A1 (CMS) GREER, CHARLES A YALE UNIVERSITY 333 CEDAR STREET NEW HAVEN, CT 06510 Genetic determinants of local circuit organization

R01DC-00212-09 (HAR) MARCUS, DANIEL C BOYS TOWN NATIONAL RES HOSP 555 NORTH 30TH STREET OMAHA, NE 68131 Cochlear and vestibular ion transport

P50DC-00214-06 (CDR) BEAUCHAMP, GARY K MONELL CHEMICAL SENSES CENTER 3500 MARKET STREET PHILADELPHIA, PA 19104 Chemosensory clinical research center

P50DC-00214-06 0001 (CDR) FRIEDMAN, MARK I Chemosensory clinical research center Chemosensory changes in liver disease

P50DC-00214-06 0002 (CDR) MATTES, RICHARD D Chemosensory clinical research center Effects of antihypertensive agents on taste and smell

P50DC-00214-06 0003 (CDR) WYSOCKI, CHARLES J Chemosensory clinical research center Individual variation in human olfaction

P50DC-00214-06 9001 (CDR) COWART, BEVERLY J Chemosensory clinical research center Sensory core

P50DC-00214-06 9002 (CDR) PRETI, GEORGE Chemosensory clinical research center Analytical core

P50DC-00215-08 (CDR) JESTEADT, WALT BOYS TOWN NATIONAL INSTITUTE 555 NO 30TH STREET OMAHA, NEB 68131 Communication disorders in children

P50DC-00215-08 0001 (CDR) JAVEL, ERIC Communication disorders in children physiological correlates of auditory perception

P50DC-00215-08 0002 (CDR) JAVEL, ERIC Communication disorders in children Neurobiological studies of vocal tract control

P50DC-00215-08 0004 (CDR) JESTEADT, WALT Communication disorders in children Measurement of normal and impaired cochlear function

P50DC-00215-08 0005 (CDR) NETSELL, RONALD Communication disorders in children Quantitative method for assessing speech disorders

P50DC-00215-08 0006 (CDR) KIMBERLING, WILLIAM Communication disorders in children Hereditary hearing loss

P50DC-00215-08 0007 (CDR) FARLEY, GLENN Communication disorders in children Neurobiological studies of vocal tract control

P50DC-00215-08 9001 (CDR) NETSELL, RONALD Communication disorders in children Animal care--Core

P50DC-00215-08 9002 (CDR) NETSELL, RONALD Communication disorders in children Data management and analysis

PROJECT NO., ORGANIZATIONAL UNIT., INVESTIGATOR, ADDRESS, TITLE

R01DC-00216-08 (CMS) BATES, ELIZABETH UNIVERSITY OF CALIFORNIA 0126 LA JOLLA, CA 92093-0126 Cross linguistic studies in aphasia

R01DC-00217-08 (NEUB) ARNOLD, ARTHUR P UNIVERSITY OF CALIFORNIA 405 HILGARD AVENUE LOS ANGELES, CALIF Neural & hormonal bases of vocalization

R01DC-00218-08 (CMS) MARTIN, RANDI C RICE UNIVERSITY P O BOX 1892 HOUSTON, TX 77251 Short term memory and syntactic deficits in aphasia

R01DC-00219-09 (CMS) SAWUSCH, JAMES R STATE UNIV OF NEW YORK PARK HALL AMHERST, NY 14260 Auditory and phonetic coding of speech

P01DC-00220-08 (CDR) MOZELL, MAXWELL M SUNY HEALTH SCIENCE CENTER 750 EAST ADAMS STREET SYRACUSE, NY 13210 The Suny Upstate clinical smell research center

P01DC-00220-08 0003 (CDR) LEOPOLD, DONALD A The Suny Upstate clinical smell research center The effect of the nasal airway on olfactory function

P01DC-00220-08 0004 (CDR) MOZELL, MAXWELL M The Suny Upstate clinical smell research center The effect of laryngectomy upon olfactory ability

P01DC-00220-08 0005 (CDR) RICHMAN, ROBERT A The Suny Upstate clinical smell research center Olfactory maturation during childhood

P01DC-00220-08 0006 (CDR) HORNUNG, DAVID G The Suny Upstate clinical smell research center Nasal airflow patterns

P01DC-00220-08 9001 (CDR) LEOPOLD, DONALD A The Suny Upstate clinical smell research center Core B - Clinical

P01DC-00220-08 0001 (CDR) WRIGHT, HERBERT N The Suny Upstate clinical smell research center Psychophysical evaluation of olfactory dysfunction

P01DC-00220-08 0002 (CDR) YOUNGENTOB, STEVEN L The Suny Upstate clinical smell research center Relation of sniffing strategies to olfactory function

R01DC-00222-08 (HAR) NARINS, PETER M UNIVERSITY OF CALIFORNIA 405 HILGARD AVE LOS ANGELES, CA 90024 Biological constraints on tuning in the inner ear

P01DC-00223-08 (CDR) RUBEN, ROBERT J ALBERT EINSTEIN COLLEGE OF MED 1300 MORRIS PARK AVENUE BRONX, N Y 10461 Clinical reserch center for communicative disorders

P01DC-00223-08 0001 (CDR) GRAVEL, JUDITH S Clinical reserch center for communicative disorders Behavioral & brainstem evoked potential estimates of auditory sensitivity

P01DC-00223-08 0004 (CDR) KURTZBERG, DIANE Clinical reserch center for communicative disorders Cortical electrophysiological indices of speech processing deficits

P01DC-00223-08 0005 (CDR) BERNSTEIN, RICHARD Clinical reserch center for communicative disorders Early auditory discrimination learning & development of language skills

P01DC-00223-08 0006 (CDR) STAPELLS, DAVID Clinical reserch center for communicative disorders Probes of frequency-specific auditory system dysfunction

P01DC-00223-08 0007 (CDR) VAUGHN, HERBERT G Clinical reserch center for communicative disorders Indicators of normal and deviant cortical language processing

P01DC-00223-08 9001 (CDR) RUBEN, ROBERT J Clinical reserch center for communicative disorders Core facilities

R01DC-00228-10 (CMS) KAUER, JOHN S NEW ENGLAND MEDICAL CENTER 750 WASHINGTON STREET BOSTON, MA. 02111 Odor processing and olfactory bulb local circuits

R01DC-00230-07 (CMS) MILLER, INGLIS J, JR WAKE FOREST UNIVERSITY 300 S HAWTHORNE RD WINSTON-SALEM, N C 27103 Quantitative distribution of taste buds on the tongue

R01DC-00231-05 (CMS) MAYBERRY, RACHEL I HUMAN COMMUNICATION DISORDERS 1266 PINE AVENUE WEST MONTREAL, QUEBEC 1A8 CANADA Early language & sign language comprehension

R01DC-00232-07 (HAR) RYUGO, DAVID K JOHNS HOPKINS UNIV-SCH OF MED 720 RUTLAND AVENUE BALTIMORE, MD 21205 Single cell marking studies of the auditory nerve

R01DC-00233-09 (HAR) SCHWEITZER, LAURA F UNIV OF LOUISVILLE 500 SOUTH PRESTON ST LOUISVILLE, KY 40292 Neuroanatomical development of the auditory system

R01DC-00234-09 (HAR) TRAHIOTIS, CONSTANTINE UNIV OF CONNECTICUT HLTH CNTR 263 FARMINGTON AVE FARMINGTON, CT 06032 Spectral and temporal factors in binaural hearing

R01DC-00235-07A2 (CMS) GUINAN, JOHN J, JR MASSACHUSETTS INST TECHNOLOGY 243 CHARLES STREET BOSTON, MA 02114 Olivocochlear efferent systems

R01DC-00236-10 (CMS) MASSARO, DOMINIC W UNIVERSITY OF CALIFORNIA 1156 HIGH STREET SANTA CRUZ, CA 95064 Synthesis, analysis, and perception of visible speech

R01DC-00238-08 (HAR) WEISS, THOMAS F MASSACHUSETTS INST OF TECHNOLO 77 MASSACHUSETTS AVENUE CAMBRIDGE, MA 02139 Experimental-theoretical studies of cochlear mechanisms

R01DC-00239-08 (HAR) GRAF, WERNER M ROCKEFELLER UNIVERSITY 1230 YORK AVENUE NEW YORK, N Y 10021 Adaptive changes in vestibular system

R01DC-00240-09 (BPO) NORGREN, RALPH E MILTON S HERSHEY MEDICAL CNTR P O BOX 850 HERSHEY, PA 17033 Neural systems of ingestive behavior

R01DC-00241-10 (HAR) HUDSPETH, ALBERT JAMES UNIVERSITY OF TEXAS SW MED CTR 5323 HARRY HINES BLVD DALLAS, TX 75235 Transduction mechanism of hair cells

P50DC-00242-07 (CDRC) GANTZ, BRUCE J UNIVERSITY OF IOWA HEAD & NECK SURGERY IOWA CITY, IA 52242 Iowa cochlear implant project

P50DC-00242-07 0001 (CDRC) TYLER, RICHARD S Iowa cochlear implant project Audiology

P50DC-00242-07 0002 (CDRC) KNUTSON, JOHN Iowa cochlear implant project Psychology

P50DC-00242-07 0003 (CDRC) TYE-MURRAY, NANCY Iowa cochlear implant project Rehabilitation

P50DC-00242-07 0005 (CDRC) ABBAS, PAUL A Iowa cochlear implant project Electrophysiology

P50DC-00242-07 0006 (CDRC) TYE-MURRAY, NANCY Iowa cochlear implant project Child rehabilitation and speech production

P50DC-00242-07 9001 (CDRC) GANTZ, BRUCE J Iowa cochlear implant project Patient management and technical support core

R01DC-00243-07 (HAR) GRAY, LINCOLN C UNIVERSITY OF TEXAS P O BOX 20708 HOUSTON, TX 77225 Neonatal development of auditory frequency selectivity

P01DC-00244-07 (CDR) FINGER, THOMAS E UNIVERSITY OF COLORADO 4200 EAST 9TH AVE DENVER, CO 80262 Rocky Mountain taste and smell center

P01DC-00244-07 0001 (CDR) MORAN, DAVID T Rocky Mountain taste and smell center Neurobiology of vertebrate olfactory mucosa

P01DC-00244-07 0002 (CDR) ROPER, STEPHEN D Rocky Mountain taste and smell center Chemosensory transduction in vertebrate taste buds

P01DC-00244-07 0003 (CDR) FINGER, THOMAS E Rocky Mountain taste and smell center Synaptic relationships of chemoreceptor neurons

P01DC-00244-07 0004 (CDR) JAFEK, BRUCE W Rocky Mountain taste and smell center Neurobiology of normal and abnormal gustatory receptors

P01DC-00244-07 0005 (CDR) KINNAMON, SUE C Rocky Mountain taste and smell center Modulation of taste cell function

P01DC-00244-07 9002 (CDR) JAFEK, BRUCE Rocky Mountain taste and smell center Clinical core B

R01DC-00245-07 (CMS) DAVIS, BARRY J UNIVERSITY OF ALABAMA UNIVERSITY STATION BIRMINGHAM, AL 35294 Gustatory zone of the nucleus of the solitary tract

R01DC-00246-07 (CMS) PRITCHARD, THOMAS C PENNSYLVANIA STATE UNIVERSITY DEPT OF BEHAVIORAL SCIENCE HERSHEY, PA 17033 Gustatory neural responses in the forebrain

R01DC-00248-07 (BPO) BERNSTEIN, ILENE L UNIVERSITY OF WASHINGTON SEATTLE, WA 98195 Salt preference: Influence of age and strain

R01DC-00249-08 (HAR) GREEN, BARRY G MONELL CHEMICAL SENSES CENTER 3500 MARKET STREET PHILADELPHIA, PA 19104-3308 Oral somesthesis

R01DC-00250-09 (HAR) WATSON, CHARLES S INDIANA UNIVERSITY DEPT OF SPEECH/HEARING SCIS BLOOMINGTON, IND 47405 Discrimination and identification of auditory patterns

R01DC-00251-06 (HAR) NEELY, STEPHEN T BOYS TOWN NATIONAL INSTITUTE 555 NORTH 30TH STREET OMAHA, NE 68131 Mathematical modeling of cochlear mechanics

R01DC-00253-06 (CMS) GRAZIADEI, PASQUALE P FLORIDA STATE UNIVERSITY DEPT OF BIOL SCI UNIT I TALLAHASSEE, FL 32306 Brain transplantation and olfactory neurons interaction

R01DC-00256-06 (CMS) DIONNE, VINCENT E UNIVERSITY OF CALIFORNIA LA JOLLA, CA 92093 Receptors mechanisms in olfaction

R01DC-00257-08 (HUD) FLEGE, JAMES E 503 UAB STATION BIRMINGHAM, AL 35294 The development of phonetic categories

R01DC-00260-07 (HUD) ELBERT, MARY INDIANA UNIVERSITY BLOOMINGTON, IN 47405 Phonological knowledge and learning

R01DC-00262-07 (CMS) BERNDT, RITA S UNIV OF MARYLAND SCHOOL OF MED 22 S GREENE STREET BALTIMORE, MD 21201 Syntactic deficits in aphasia

R01DC-00263-06 (HAR) CHOLE, RICHARD A UNIV OF CALIFORNIA, DAVIS 1159 SURGE III DAVIS, CA 95616 Mechanisms of tissue destruction in the middle ear

R01DC-00264-07 (HAR) KRAUS, NINA NORTHWSESTERN UNIVERSITY 2299 SHERIDAN ROAD EVANSTON, IL 60208 MLR generators, maturation & hearing assessment

R01DC-00266-07 (CMS) HILLMAN, ROBERT E BOSTON UNIVERSITY 635 COMMONWEALTH AVENUE BOSTON, MA 02215 Object assessment of vocal hyperfunction

R01DC-00267-07 (CMS) O'NEILL, WILLIAM E UNIVERSITY OF ROCHESTER MED SC 601 ELMWOOD AVENUE ROCHESTER, NY 14642 Auditory control of vocalization

R01DC-00268-06 (HAR) POLLAK, GEORGE D UNIVERSITY OF TEXAS AUSTIN, TX 78712 Functional organization of the inferior colliculus

R01DC-00269-06 (HAR) ADAMS, JOE C MASS EYE & EAR INFIRMARY 243 CHARLES STREET BOSTON, MA 02114-3096 Cytology and connections of the auditory system

R01DC-00270-07 (HAR) ZUREK, PATRICK M MASS INST OF TECH/RES ELECTRON 77 MASSACHUSETTS AVE CAMBRIDGE, MASS 02139 Multimicrophone monaural aids for the hearing impaired

R01DC-00271-08 (CMS) MARKS, LAWRENCE E JOHN B PIERCE FOUNDATION LAB 290 CONGRESS AVENUE NEW HAVEN, CT 06519 Commonalities in touch, hearing vision & taste

R01DC-00272-06 (NEUA) MOLLER, AAGE R PRESBYTERIAN UNIV HOSP 230 LOTHROP ST 9402 PITTSBURGH, PA 15213 Studies of the neural brainstem auditory responses

R01DC-00273-09 (HAR) SANTOS-SACCHI, JOSEPH R YALE UNIVERSITY 333 CEDAR STREET NEW HAVEN, CT 06510 Membrane properties of cells comprising the OHC system

P01DC-00274-08 (CDR) MILLER, JOSEF M UNIVERSITY OF MICHIGAN 1301 EAST ANN STREET ANN ARBOR, MI 48109-0506 Studies of the cochlear prosthesis

P01DC-00274-08 0003 (CDR) SUTTON, DWIGHT Studies of the cochlear prosthesis Histology and histopathology

P01DC-00274-08 0004 (CDR) SPELMAN, FRANCIS A Studies of the cochlear prosthesis Biophysics of the inner ear

P01DC-00274-08 0005 (CDR) ALTSCHULER, RICHARD A Studies of the cochlear prosthesis Peripheral effects of stimulation

P01DC-00274-08 0006 (CDR) KILENY, PAUL R Studies of the cochlear prosthesis Subject selection and rehabilitation

P01DC-00274-08 0007 (CDR) WAKEFIELD, GREGORY H Studies of the cochlear prosthesis Human psychophysics

P01DC-00274-08 0001 (CDR) PFINGST, BRYAN E Studies of the cochlear prosthesis Psychophysical studies

P01DC-00274-08 0002 (CDR) CLOPTON, BEN M Studies of the cochlear prosthesis: Neurophysiology

R13DC-00275-08 (CDR) YOST, WILLIAM A LOYOLA UNIV/PARMLY INSTITUTE 6525 NORTH SHERIDAN ROAD CHICAGO, ILL 60626 Symposia for Association for Research in Otolaryngology

R01DC-00276-07 (HAR) FUCHS, PAUL A UNIVERSITY OF COLORADO 4200 EAST NINTH AVENUE DENVER, COLO 80262 Electrical development of cochlear hair cells

R01DC-00277-06 (HAR) MOISEFF, ANDREW UNIVERSITY OF CONNECTICUT 75 NORTH EAGLEVILLE ROAD STORRS, CT 06268 Neural mechanisms of sound localization

R01DC-00281-07 (CMS) HIXON, THOMAS J UNIVERSITY OF ARIZONA SPEECH BUILDING NO 25 TUSCON, ARIZ 85721 Speech breathing kinematics across the human life span

R01DC-00282-07 (HAR) MOLNAR, CHARLES E WASHINGTON UNIVERSITY 660 S EUCLID AVE, BOX 8036 ST LOUIS, MO 63110 Cochlear mechanics and neural encoding

R01DC-00283-07 (CMS) BARTOSHUK, LINDA M YALE UNIV SCH OF MEDICINE PO BOX 3333/333 CEDAR ST NEW HAVEN, CT 06510 Taste psychophysics

R01DC-00284-07 (CMS) CAIN, WILLIAM S JOHN B PIERCE LABORATORY INC 290 CONGRESS AVENUE NEW HAVEN, CT 06519 Clinical olfactory psychophysics

R01DC-00285-06A2 (NEUB) KINNAMON, JOHN C UNIVERSITY OF COLORADO CAMPUS BOX 347 BOULDER, CO 80309-0347 Functional morphology of taste buds

R01DC-00287-07 (HAR) CASSEDAY, JOHN H DUKE UNIVERSITY MEDICAL CENTER P.O. BOX 3209 DURHAM, N C 27710 Parallel auditory pathways in the brain stem

R01DC-00288-06 (BPO) BRADLEY, ROBERT M UNIVERSITY OF MICHIGAN 1011 NORTH UNIVERSITY AVENUE ANN ARBOR, MI 48109 Afferent and efferent interactions in taste

R01DC-00290-05 (HAR) WALL, CONRAD III MASSACHUSETTS EYE/EAR INFIRMAR 243 CHARLES STREET BOSTON, MA 02114 Human vestibular response to horizontal rotation

P50DC-00293-07 (CDR) YOST, WILLIAM A LOYOLA UNIV/PARMLY INSTITUTE 6525 NORTH SHERIDAN ROAD CHICAGO, ILL 60626 Information processing by the auditory system

P50DC-00293-07 0001 (CDR) DYE, RAYMOND Information processing by the auditory system Binaural processing of complex stimuli

P50DC-00293-07 0002 (CDR) FAY, RICHARD R Information processing by the auditory system Temporal processing by a vertebrate auditory system

P50DC-00293-07 0004 (CDR) COOMBS, SHERYL Information processing by the auditory system Lateral line system

P50DC-00293-07 0005 (CDR) YOST, WILLIAM A Information processing by the auditory system Processing of complex auditory signals

R01DC-00296-07 (CMS) MILLER, JAMES D CENTRAL INSTITUTE FOR THE DEAF 818 S EUCLID AVE ST LOUIS, MO 63110 Auditory-perceptual processing of speech

R01DC-00298-07 (CMS) WYSOCKI, CHARLES J MONELL CHEMICAL SENSES CENTER 3500 MARKET STREET PHILADELPHIA, PA 19104 Individual variation in olfaction

R01DC-00299-07 (HAR) JASTREBOFF, PAWEL J UNIVERSITY OF MARYLAND 10 SOUTH PINE STREET BALTIMORE, MD 21201 Mechanism of tinnitus

R01DC-00300-08 (CMS) HAMILTON, KATHRYN ANN LOUISIANA STATE UNIVERSITY 1501 KINGS HIGHWAY SHREVEPORT, LA 711303932 Odor responses and anatomy of olfactory bulb neurons

R01DC-00301-07 (CMS) HINOJOSA, RAUL UNIVERSITY OF CHICAGO 5841 S MARYLAND AV, BOX 412 CHICAGO, IL 60637 Histopathologic studies of the human temporal bones

R01DC-00303-06 (HAR) GUTH, PAUL S TULANE UNIVERSITY SCH OF MED 1430 TULANE AVE NEW ORLEANS, LA 70112 Pharmacology of vestibular neurotransmission

R01DC-00304-06 (HAR) COREY, DAVID P MASSACHUSETTS GENERAL HOSPITAL FRUIT ST BOSTON, MA 02114 Molecular mechanisms of auditory transduction

R01DC-00306-08 (CMS) WEISENBERGER, JANET M OHIO STATE UNIVERSITY 1070 CARMACK ROAD COLUMBUS, OH 43210 Basic and applied studies of tactile perception

R01DC-00307-06 (HAR) LONG, GLENIS R PURDUE UNIVERSITY WEST LAFAYETTE, IN 47907-1353 Cochlear emissions and psychoacoustic microstructure

R01DC-00308-07 (CMS) REMEZ, ROBERT E BARNARD COLLEGE - PSYCHOLOGY 3009 BROADWAY NEW YORK, N Y 10027 Sensory and perceptual factors in spoken communication

R01DC-00309-07 (HAR) MULROY, MICHAEL J MEDICAL COLLEGE OF GEORGIA AUGUSTA, GEORGIA 30912 Changes in auditory stereocilia during deafness

R01DC-00312-06 (CMS) DERBY, CHARLES D GEORGIA STATE UNIVERSITY UNIVERSITY PLAZA ATLANTA, GA 30303 Mixture interactions in olfaction

R01DC-00314-07 (CMS) BLUMSTEIN, SHEILA E BROWN UNIVERSITY BOX 1978 PROVIDENCE, RI 02912 Speech and language processing in aphasia

P01DC-00316-06 (CDR) KHANNA, SHYAM M COLUMBIA UNIVERSITY 630 WEST 168TH STREET NEW YORK, N Y 10032 Interdisciplinary investigation of the auditory system

P01DC-00316-06 0001 (CDR) STINSON, MICHAEL Interdisciplinary investigation of the auditory system Acoustical input to the ear at high frequencies

P01DC-00316-06 0002 (CDR) KHANNA, SHYAM Interdisciplinary investigation of the auditory system Function of the tympanic membrane

P01DC-00316-06 0003 (CDR) KOESTER, CHARLES Interdisciplinary investigation of the auditory system Optical sectioning microscope for inner ear study

P01DC-00316-06 0004 (CDR) DANDLIKER, RENE Interdisciplinary investigation of the auditory system Heterodyne interferometer for inner ear studies

P01DC-00316-06 0005 (CDR) KHANNA, SHYAM Interdisciplinary investigation of the auditory system Inner ear micromechanics at the cellular level

P01DC-00316-06 0006 (CDR) KHANNA, SHYAM Interdisciplinary investigation of the auditory system Vibration patterns and mobile processes in cells of guinea pig cochlea

R01DC-00317-07 (HAR) HUDSPETH, ALBERT J UNIV OF TX SW MED CTR AT DALLA 5323 HARRY HINES BLVD DALLAS, TX 75235 Ionic channels of hair cells

R01DC-00319-07 (CMS) KENT, RAYMOND D UNIVERSITY OF WISCONSIN 1975 WILLOW DRIVE MADISON, WIS 53706 Intelligibility assessment in dysarthria

R01DC-00321-07 (HAR) RYBAK, LEONARD P SOUTHERN ILLINOIS UNIVERSITY P.O. BOX 19230 SPRINGFIELD, IL 62794-9230 Effects of organic acids on loop diuretic ototoxicity

R01DC-00323-07 (CMS) STRANGE, WINIFRED UNIVERSITY OF SOUTH

PROJECT NO., ORGANIZATIONAL UNIT., INVESTIGATOR, ADDRESS, TITLE

FLORIDA 4202 E. FOWLER AVE TAMPA, FL 33620 Studies of vowel perception

R01DC-00327-06 (CMS) BRYANT, BRUCE P MONELL CHEMICAL SENSE CENTER 3500 MARKET STREET PHILDELPHIA, PA 19104-3308 Agonists/antagonists for characterizing chemoreceptors

R01DC-00328-06 (HAR) JEWETT, DON L ABRATECH CORPORATION 150 SHORELINE HWY MILL VALLEY, CA 94941-6610 3-d analysis of auditory brainstem response in humans

R01DC-00333-06 (HAR) MILLER, MICHAEL I WASHINGTON UNIVERSITY 700 SOUTH EUCLID ST LOUIS, MO 63110 Statistical coding of complex stimuli in auditory nerve

R01DC-00334-07 (HAR) GREEN, DAVID M UNIVERSITY OF FLORIDA DEPT OF PSYCHOLOGY GAINESVILLE, FLA 32611 Auditory discrimination and masking

R01DC-00335-06 (HAR) BRUNSO-BECHTOLD, JUDY K BOWMAN GRAY SCHOOL OF MED 300 SOUTH HAWTHORNE ROAD WINSTON-SALEM, NC 27157 Hearing: anatomical development of binaural interaction

R01DC-00337-07 (HAR) DOBIE, ROBERT A UNIVERSITY OF TEXAS HLTH SCI C 7703 FLOYD CURL DR SAN ANTONIO, TX 78274 Analysis of auditory evoked potentials

R01DC-00338-04A2 (CMS) BRUNJES, PETER C UNIVERSITY OF VIRGINIA 102 GILMER HALL CHARLOTTESVILLE, VA 22903 Maturation and plasticity in the olfactory system

R01DC-00341-06 (HAR) SINEX, DONAL G BOYS TOWN NATIONAL INSTITUTE 555 NORTH 30TH STREET OMAHA, NE 68131 Auditory nerve fiber responses to speech

P01DC-00347-06 (SRC) SHIPLEY, MICHAEL T UNIVERSITY OF CINCINNATI 231 BETHESDA AVENUE CINCINNATI, OH 45267-0521 Development and regeneration in vertebrate chemoreception

P01DC-00347-06 0001 (SRC) GESTELAND, ROBERT C Development and regeneration in vertebrate chemoreception Developmental biophysics of olfactory neurons

P01DC-00347-06 0002 (SRC) FARBMAN, ALBERT I Development and regeneration in vertebrate chemoreception Early development of olfactory receptor

P01DC-00347-06 0003 (SRC) SHIPLEY, MICHAEL T Development and regeneration in vertebrate chemoreception Development and regeneration of olfactory nerve

P01DC-00347-06 0006 (SRC) AKESON, RICHARD A Development and regeneration in vertebrate chemoreception Neuronal subclasses in olfactory development

P01DC-00347-06 0007 (SRC) PIXLEY, SARAH K Development and regeneration in vertebrate chemoreception Differentiation of olfactory receptor neurons in culture

P01DC-00347-06 0008 (SRC) SMITH, DAVID Development and regeneration in vertebrate chemoreception Taste bud development and regeneration

R01DC-00348-06 (NEUB) HILDEBRAND, JOHN G UNIVERSITY OF ARIZONA 611 GOULD-SIMPSON BLDG. TUCSON, AZ 85721 Olfactory control of a simple motor system

R01DC-00353-06 (CMS) SMITH, DAVID V UNIV CINCINNATI COLL MEDICINE 231 BETHESDA AVE CINCINNATI, OH 45267-0528 Adaptation and sensory coding in taste

R01DC-00354-06A1 (HAR) BROWNELL, WILLIAM E JOHNS HOPKINS UNIV SCH OF MED 522 TRAYLOR RESEARCH BLDG. BALTIMORE, MD 21205-2196 Intracochlear electro-chemical gradients

R29DC-00355-05 (HAR) BAIRD, RICHARD A RS DOW NEUROLOGICAL SCIENCE IN 1120 NW 20TH AVENUE PORTLAND, OR 97209 Morphophysiology of vestibular endorgans

R01DC-00356-06 (CMS) BRAND, JOSEPH G MONELL CHEMICAL SENSES CENTER 3500 MARKET STREET PHILADELPHIA, PA 19104-3308 Biochemical mechanisms of taste function

R01DC-00357-06 (HUD) LOVELAND, KATHERINE A UNIV OF TEXAS MENTAL SCIS INST 1300 MOURSUND AVENUE HOUSTON, TX 77030 Communication in autism--Pragmatic deficits

R01DC-00360-07A1 (HAR) KIM, DUCK O UNIV OF CONNECTICUT HLTH CTR 263 FARMINGTON AVENUE FARMINGTON, CT 06032-9984 Auditory neurobiology and biophysics

P01DC-00361-05S1 (SRC) NADOL, JOSEPH B, JR MASS EYE & EAR INFIRMARY 243 CHARLES STREET BOSTON, MA 02114 Basic and applied research on cochlear prostheses

P01DC-00361-05S1 0001 (SRC) RABINOWITZ, WILLIAM M Basic and applied research on cochlear prostheses Human perceptual studies

P01DC-00361-05S1 0002 (SRC) LANE, HARLAN L Basic and applied research on cochlear prostheses Speech production

P01DC-00361-05S1 0003 (SRC) THORNTON, AARON R Basic and applied research on cochlear prostheses Human evoked potential studies

P01DC-00361-05S1 0004 (SRC) NADOL, JOSEPH B Basic and applied research on cochlear prostheses Anatomical considerations in cochlear implantation, stimulation

P01DC-00361-05S1 0005 (SRC) DELGUTTE, BERTRAND Basic and applied research on cochlear prostheses Physiology of electrical stimulation of the auditory nerve

P01DC-00361-05S1 9001 (SRC) NADOL, JOSEPH B Basic and applied research on cochlear prostheses Core

R29DC-00364-05 (HAR) SEMPLE, MALCOLM N UNIV OF CALIFORNIA, IRVINE IRVINE, CA 92717 Neural processing of binaural information

R01DC-00365-06A1 (CMS) BARLOW, STEVEN M INDIANA UNIVERSITY 3RD STREET AND JORDAN AVE BLOOMINGTON, IN 47405 Reflex and fine force dynamics of the perioral system

R01DC-00366-05 (CMS) CARAMAZZA, ALFONSO JOHNS HOPKINS UNIVERSITY BALTIMORE, MD 21218 Morphological processing deficits in aphasia

R01DC-00369-05 (HAR) SHAPIRO, STEVEN M MEDICAL COLLEGE OF VIRGINIA BOX 599, MCV STATION RICHMOND, VA 23298-0599 Bilirubin toxicity in the auditory system

R01DC-00372-06 (HAR) WARR, WILLIAM B BOYS TOWN NATIONAL INSTITUTE 555 NORTH 30TH STREET OMAHA, NE 68131 Descending connections of the lower auditory system

R01DC-00374-04 (CMS) ROPER, STEPHEN D COLORADO STATE UNIV FT COLLINS, CO 80523 Chemosensory transduction in taste cells

R01DC-00377-03 (HAR) TURNER, CHRISTOPHER W SYRACUSE UNIVERSITY 805 SOUTH CROUSE AVENUE SYRACUSE, N Y 13244-2280 Models of hearing loss

PROJECT NO., ORGANIZATIONAL UNIT., INVESTIGATOR, ADDRESS, TITLE

P01DC-00379-05 (CDR) BERLIN, CHARLES I LOUISIANA STATE UNIVERSITY 2020 GRAVIER ST SUITE A NEW ORLEANS, LA 70112-2234 Auditory mechanisms

P01DC-00379-05 0001 (CDR) BERLIN, CHARLES I Auditory mechanisms The development of high frequency sensitivity

P01DC-00379-05 0002 (CDR) WEBSTER, DOUGLAS B Auditory mechanisms Age dependent effects of apical cochlear lesions

P01DC-00379-05 0003 (CDR) BOBBIN, RICHARD P Auditory mechanisms Cochlear efferent transmitters and modulators

P01DC-00379-05 0004 (CDR) CULLEN, JOHN K Auditory mechanisms Comparative signal processing measures for basal/apical regions

P01DC-00379-05 9001 (CDR) CULLEN, JOHN K Auditory mechanisms Engineering and shop support--core B

P01DC-00379-05 9002 (CDR) HUGHES, LARRY F Auditory mechanisms Computer and statistical support--core C

P01DC-00380-05 (CDRC) VERRILLO, RONALD T SYRACUSE UNIVERSITY MERRILL LANE SYRACUSE, NY 13244 Intensity effects in the auditory and tactile systems

P01DC-00380-05 0001 (CDRC) ZWISLOCKI, JOZET J Intensity effects in the auditory and tactile systems Behavioral intensity effects

P01DC-00380-05 0002 (CDRC) SMITH, ROBERT L Intensity effects in the auditory and tactile systems Neural intensity effects

P01DC-00380-05 0003 (CDRC) SLEPECKY, NORMA Intensity effects in the auditory and tactile systems Morphological substrates underlying intensity coding

R01DC-00381-06 (HAR) THOMPSON, GLENN C UNIV OF OKLAHOMA HLTH SCIS CTR P O BOX 26901 OKLAHOMA CITY, OK Neurochemical correlates of vestibular compensation

R01DC-00383-05 (HAR) ALTSCHULER, RICHARD A KRESGE HEARING RESEARCH INST 1301 EAST ANN STREET ANN ARBOR, MI 48109-0506 Amino acid neurotransmitters in the auditory brainstem

P01DC-00384-05 (CDR) THALMANN, RUEDIGER R WASHINGTON UNIV SCHOOL OF MED 517 S EUCLID AVENUE ST LOUIS, MO 63110 Inner ear fluid dynamics in health and disease

P01DC-00384-05 0002 (CDR) THALMANN, RUEDIGER R Inner ear fluid dynamics in health and disease Interrelations between fluids of the inner ear

P01DC-00384-05 0003 (CDR) MARCUS, DANIEL C Inner ear fluid dynamics in health and disease Tracer fluxes across the utricle

P01DC-00384-05 0004 (CDR) THALMANN, ISOLDE Inner ear fluid dynamics in health and disease Tectorial membrane--Solid and fluid phase interrelation

P01DC-00384-05 0001 (CDR) SALT, ALEC N Inner ear fluid dynamics in health and disease Endolymph volume and flow

R01DC-00385-04A1 (HAR) PERACHIO, ADRIAN A UNIVERSITY OF TEXAS MED BRANCH JOHN SEALY HOSP 7.316 GALVESTON, TX 77550-2774 Morphophysiological analysis of vestibular neurons

R01DC-00386-05 (HAR) WOOLF, NIGEL K UNIV OF CALIFORNIA, SAN DIEGO 225 DICKINSON STREET SAN DIEGO, CA 92103 A congenital cytomegalovirus model of auditory pathology

R01DC-00387-05 (HAR) TITZE, INGO R DENVER CTR FOR PERFORMING ARTS 1245 CHAMPA STREET DENVER, CO 80204 Toward standards for voice analysis and recording

R01DC-00389-06 (HUD) STARK-SEITZ, RACHEL E PURDUE UNIVERSITY HEAVILON HALL WEST LAFAYETTE, IN 47907 Speech processing in childhood language disorders

R29DC-00394-06 (CMS) ANHOLT, ROBERT R DEPT OF PHYSIOLOGY, BOX 3709 DUKE UNIVERSITY MEDICAL CENTER DURHAM, N C 27710 Primary events in olfactory reception

R01DC-00395-06 (SSS) RUBEL, EDWIN W UNIVERSITY OF WASHINGTON SEATTLE, WA 98195 Ontogeny of vertebrate sensory processes

R01DC-00396-06 (HAR) WERNER, LYNNE A UNIVERSITY OF WASHINGTON CDMRC, WJ-10, BOX 47 SEATTLE, WA 98195 Development of frequency resolution in infancy

R01DC-00397-06 (HAR) HALL, JOSEPH W UNIV OF NORTH CAROLINA 610 BURNET-WOMACK CHAPEL HILL, N C 27599 Binaural hearing before and after middle ear surgery

R01DC-00398-05 (CMS) BRUGGE, JOHN F DEPT OF NEUROPHYSIOLOGY 627 WAISMAN CTR ON MENTAL RET MADISON, WI 53706 Studies on the auditory cortex

R29DC-00399-04 (HAR) BURKARD, ROBERT F BOSTON UNIVERSITY 48 CUMMINGTON STREET BOSTON, MA 02215 Electrophysiologic correlates of auditory masking

R01DC-00400-04 (CMS) MARUNIAK, JOEL A UNIVERSITY OF MISSOURI 213 LEFEVRE HALL COLUMBIA, MO 65211 Etiology of disorders of olfactory epithelia

R29DC-00401-05 (CMS) HERNESS, M SCOTT ROCKEFELLER UNIVERSITY 1230 YORK AVENUE NEW YORK, NY 10021 Electrolyte transduction mechanisms in frog gustation

R29DC-00402-05 (BPO) NOWICKI, STEPHEN DUKE UNIVERSITY 243 BIOLOGICAL SCIENCE BLDG DURHAM, NC 27706 Comparative study of mechanisms of vocal production

R01DC-00403-04A1 (HUD) BEST, CATHERINE T HASKINS LABORATORIES 270 CROWN STREET NEW HAVEN, CT 06511-6695 Early ontogeny of attunement to the language environment

R29DC-00405-05 (HAR) KEITHLEY, ELIZABETH M VA MEDICAL CENTER 3350 LA JOLLA VILLAGE DR SAN DIEGO, CA 92161 The effects of aging on auditory spiral ganglion cells

R01DC-00407-06 (CMS) HILL, DAVID L UNIVERSITY OF VIRGINIA CHARLOTTESVILLE, VA 22903-347 Ontogeny of central neural taste responses

R29DC-00408-04 (HAR) FRISINA, ROBERT D UNIV OF ROCHESTER MED CENTER 601 ELMWOOD AVE ROCHESTER NY 14642 Neural encoding of dynamic features of complex sounds

R29DC-00409-06 (HAR) SHANNON, ROBERT V HOUSE EAR INSTITUTE 256 SOUTH LAKE STREET LOS ANGELES, CA 90057 Temporal processing in cochlear implants

R29DC-00411-04 (CMS) TULLER, BETTY H FLORIDA ATLANTIC UNIVERSITY 500 NW 20TH ST., BLDG. MT9 BOCA RATON, FL 33431 Speech as a self-organized cooperative process

R29DC-00412-04 (HAR) COTANCHE, DOUGLAS A BOSTON UNIV SCHOOL OF MED 80 EAST CONCORD STREET BOSTON, MA 02118 Regulation of hair cell development and regeneration

PROJECT NO., ORGANIZATIONAL UNIT., INVESTIGATOR, ADDRESS, TITLE

R29DC-00414-05 (HAR) EATOCK, RUTH A UNIVERSITY OF ROCHESTER 601 ELMWOOD AVE, BOX 642 ROCHESTER, NY 14642 In vitro studies of inner-ear function

R01DC-00417-05 (BPO) TRAVERS, JOSEPH B OHIO STATE UNIVERSITY 305 WEST TWELFTH AVENUE COLUMBUS, OH 43210-1241 Neural basis of taste elicited ingestion and rejection

R01DC-00418-06 (HAR) HALL, JOSEPH W UNIV OF NC AT CHAPEL HILL CAMPUS BOX #7050 CHAPEL HILL, NC 27599-7070 The effect of cochlear loss on spectro-temporal pattern analysis

R01DC-00419-05 (HAR) RUGGERO, MARIO A UNIVERSITY OF MINNESOTA 2630 UNIVERSITY AVE S E MINNEAPOLIS, MN 55414 Peripheral mechanisms of hearing

R29DC-00420-05 (HAR) MIDDLEBROOKS, JOHN C UNIVERSITY OF FLORIDA BOX J-244, JHMHC GAINESVILLE, FL 32610 Cortical representation of auditory space

R29DC-00421-03 (HAR) JERGER, SUSAN W BAYLOR COLL MED/NEUROSENSORY C 6501 FANNIN/NA200 HOUSTON, TX 77030 Auditory processing in hearing-impaired children

P50DC-00422-05 (CDR) MILLS, JOHN H MEDICAL UNIV OF SOUTH CAROLINA 171 ASHLEY AVENUE CHARLESTON, SC 29425 Experimental and clinical studies of presbyacusis

P50DC-00422-05 0003 (CDR) SCHMIEDT, RICHARD A Experimental and clinical studies of presbyacusis Pathophysiology of presbyacusis

P50DC-00422-05 0004 (CDR) ADAMS, JOE C Experimental and clinical studies of presbyacusis Morphological studies if the aging gerbil cochlea

P50DC-00422-05 0005 (CDR) SCHULE, B Experimental and clinical studies of presbyacusis Histochemical studies of presbyacusis

P50DC-00422-05 9001 (CDR) SCHMIEDT, R A Experimental and clinical studies of presbyacusis Computer and instrumentation support-Core

P50DC-00422-05 9002 (CDR) SCHMIEDT, R A Experimental and clinical studies of presbyacusis Core--Histology support

P50DC-00422-05 0001 (CDR) MILLS, J H Experimental and clinical studies of presbyacusis Animal model of presbyacusis

P50DC-00422-05 0002 (CDR) ADKINS, WARREN Experimental and clinical studies of presbyacusis Clinical studies of presbyacusis

R01DC-00423-05 (HAR) OSBERGER, MARY J RILEY RESEARCH WING 702 BARNHILL DRIVE INDIANAPOLIS, IN 46202-5200 Cochlear-implant & tactile-aid studying with the deaf

R29DC-00424-05 (HAR) BACON, SIDNEY P ARIZONA STATE UNIVERSITY HEARING RESEARCH LABORATORY TEMPE, AZ 85287-0102 Dynamic characteristics of auditory masking

R01DC-00425-04 (HAR) MANIS, PAUL B JOHN HOPKINS UNIVERSITY 720 RUTLAND AVE BALTIMORE, MD 21205 Physiology of dorsal cochlear nucleus molecular layer

R55DC-00426-04A1 (HAR) RAREY, KYLE E UNIVERSITY OF FLORIDA BOX J-235, JHMHC GAINESVILLE, FL 32610 Microhomeostasis of the cochlear duct

R01DC-00427-04 (CMS) DIEHL, RANDY L UNIVERSITY OF TEXAS AUSTIN, TX 78712 Auditory factors in speech perception

R29DC-00428-05 (HAR) KOEHNKE, JANET D UNIVERSITY OF CONNECTICUT BOX U-85 Clinical applications of binaural hearing

R29DC-00429-05 (CMS) TYACK, PETER L WOODS HOLE OCEANOGRAPHIC INST WOODS HOLE, MA 02543 Ontogeny of signature whistles and mimicry

R29DC-00431-04 (CMS) OLSWANG, LESLEY B UNIV OF WASHINGTON, JG-15 1417 N E 42ND STREET SEATTLE, WASH 98195 Predicting the benefits of language treatment

R01DC-00432-04 (CMS) SARNO, MARTHA T NEW YORK UNIVERSITY MED CTR 400 EAST 34TH STREET NEW YORK, NY 10016 Age, linguistic evolution and quality of life in aphasia

R29DC-00433-05 (CMS) GIERUT, JUDITH A INDIANA UNIVERSITY BLOOMINGTON, IN 47402 Learnability of sound systems

R29DC-00436-04 (HAR) CARR, CATHERINE E UNIVERSITY OF MARYLAND COLLEGE PARK, MD. 20742-4415 Cellular mechanisms underlying sound localization

R29DC-00437-04 (HAR) BUUS, SOREN NORTHEASTERN UNIVERSITY 360 HUNTINGTON AVE BOSTON, MASS 02115 Envelope & co-modulation cues in normal & impaired ears

R01DC-00438-03 (CMS) BATES, ELIZABETH A UNIV OF CALIFORNIA C-009 LA JOLLA, CA 92093 Grammatical abilities in Alzheimer's disease

R01DC-00443-04 (CMS) GEERS, ANN E CENTRAL INST FOR THE DEAF 818 SO EUCLID ST LOUIS, MO 63110 Evaluation of cochlear implants with deaf children

R01DC-00445-03 (CMS) JASTREBOFF, PAWEL J UNIVERSITY OF MARYLAND 10 S PINE STREET BALTIMORE, MD 21201 Animal phantom perception

R01DC-00446-04 (NEUB) BURD, GAIL D UNIVERSITY OF ARIZONA BIO SCIS WEST BLDG, RM 308 TUCSON, ARIZ 85721 Development of the olfactory system

R29DC-00447-05 (CMS) KOHN, SUSAN E BRAINTREE HOSPITAL 250 POND STREET BRAINTREE, MA 02184 Evolution of phonological deficits in fluent aphasics

P01DC-00450-04 (CDRC) KITZES, LEONARD M UNIVERSITY OF CALIFORNIA IRVINE, CA 92717 Structure and function of auditory cortex

P01DC-00450-04 0001 (CDRC) SEMPLE, MALCOLM Structure and function of auditory cortex Binaural processing in auditory cortex

P01DC-00450-04 0002 (CDRC) KITZES, LEONARD Structure and function of auditory cortex Intracortical processing of auditory information

P01DC-00450-04 0004 (CDRC) ROBERTSON, RICHARD T. Structure and function of auditory cortex Development of auditory cortex afferents

P01DC-00450-04 0005 (CDRC) LESLIE, FRANCES Structure and function of auditory cortex Autoradiographic localization of receptors in AI cortex

P01DC-00450-04 0006 (CDRC) HENDRY, STEWARD Structure and function of auditory cortex Inhibitory circuits in AI cortex

P01DC-00450-04 9001 (CDRC) KITZES, LEONARD M. Structure and function of auditory cortex Central facilities core

R01DC-00451-04 (CMS) DAVIS, BARRY J UNIVERSITY OF ALABAMA UNIVERSITY STATION BIRMINGHAM, AL 35294 The pontine taste area

R29DC-00452-05 (CMS) WHITEHEAD, MARK C UNIVERSITY OF CALIFORNIA 9500 GILMAN DRIVE LA JOLLA, CA 92093-0934 The gustatory system--Cellular and synaptic organization

R29DC-00453-04 (CMS) TOMPKINS, CONNIE A UNIVERSITY OF PITTSBURGH 1101 CATHEDRAL OF LEARNING PITTSBURGH, PA 15260 Intended meanings and right brain damage

R01DC-00454-04 (HAR) ART, JONATHAN J UNIVERSITY OF CHICAGO 947 EAST 58TH STREET, BOX 271 CHICAGO, IL 60637 Cellular basis of tuning in the cochlea

R01DC-00456-04 (BPO) MISTRETTA, CHARLOTTE M UNIVERSITY OF MICHIGAN 1011 N UNIVERSITY ANN ARBOR, MI 48109 Development of the sense of taste

R01DC-00458-04 (CMS) LEONARD, LAURENCE B PURDUE UNIVERSITY HEAVILON HALL W LAFAYETTE, IN 47907 Morphological deficits in specific language impairment

R01DC-00459-03 (CMS) YAIRI, EHUD UNIVERSITY OF ILLINOIS 901 SOUTH SIXTH STREET CHAMPAIGN, IL 61820 Developmental trends of early childhood stuttering

R29DC-00462-03 (CMS) HILDEBRANDT, NANCY MASSACHUSETTS GENERAL HOSPITAL 15 RIVER STREET BOSTON, MA 02108 Written sentence comprehension in aphasia

R01DC-00464-02 (HUD) OHDE, RALPH N VANDERBILT UNIVERSITY 21ST AVE S NASHVILLE, TN 37232 Variance in children's speech--Acoustics and perception

R29DC-00465-05 (HAR) KENNA, MARGARET A CHILDREN'S HOSPITAL-PITTSBURGH 3705 FIFTH AVE @ DESOTO STREET PITTSBURGH, PA 15213 Pathogenesis of chronic suppurative otitis media

R29DC-00467-03 (CMS) SCHWOB, JAMES E STATE UNIVERSITY OF NEW YORK 750 E ADAMS STREET SYRACUSE, NY 13210 Development of the primary olfactory projection

R29DC-00468-03 (HAR) SIMON, HELEN SMITH-KETTLEWELL EYE RES FDN 2232 WEBSTER STREET SAN FRANCISCO, CA 94115 Unique perceptually balanced binaural hearing aid

R01DC-00473-04 (HAR) WEISS, THOMAS F MASS INSTITUTE OF TECHNOLOGY 77 MASS AVE ROOM 36-857 CAMBRIDGE, MASS 02139 Theory of fluid mechanical stimulation of hair cells

R01DC-00481-04 (CMS) NEVILLE, HELEN J THE SALK INSTITUTE P.O. BOX 85800 SAN DIEGO, CA 92138 Neurobehavioral development in normal and LI/RD children

R29DC-00482-04 (HUD) THAL, DONNA J SAN DIEGO STATE UNIVERSITY 5178 COLLEGE AVENUE SAN DIEGO, CA 92182-1900 Early identification of risk for language disorder

R01DC-00484-04 (CMS) OLLER, D KIMBROUGH MAILMAN CTR/CHILD DEVELOPMENT PO BOX 016820 MIAMI, FL 33101 Vocal development in handicapped infants

R29DC-00485-04 (HUD) RICE, MABEL L UNIVERSITY OF KANSAS 290 HAWORTH LAWRENCE, KANS 66045 Language impaired children's fast mapping of new words

R29DC-00487-05 (BPO) BRENOWITZ, ELIOT A UNIVERSITY OF WASHINGTON DEPARTMENT OF PSYCHOLOGY NI-25 SEATTLE, WA 98195 Neuroendrocine basis of vocal perception and production

R44DC-00489-03 (HAR) SILVERBERG, BARBARA 1909 TUNNEL ROAD BERKELEY, CA 94705 Auditory brainstem response at high stimulus rates

R01DC-00491-04 (CMS) GOLDIN-MEADOW, SUSAN J UNIVERSITY OF CHICAGO 5801 S ELLIS AVE CHICAGO, IL 60637 Spontaneous sign systems in children

R29DC-00493-02 (HAR) ECHTELER, STEPHEN M NORTHWESTERN UNIVERSITY 2299 SHERIDAN ROAD EVANSTON, IL 60208 Cochlear nerve development

R29DC-00494-04 (CMS) SHAPIRO, LEWIS P FLORIDA STATE UNIVERSITY P O BOX 3091 BOCA RATON, LA 33431 Sentence processing in normal and aphasic populations

R01DC-00496-04 (CMS) SHRIBERG, LAWRENCE D WAISMAN CTR. MENTAL RETARDATIO 1500 HIGHLAND AVE. MADISON, WI. 53705 Studies in developmental phonological disorders

R01DC-00498-02 (HAR) CONLEE, JOHN W UNIVERSITY OF UTAH SALT LAKE CITY, UT 84132 Pigment influences on auditory structure & function

R29DC-00502-04 (HAR) GREENBERG, STEVEN UNIVERSITY OF CALIFORNIA BERKELEY, CA 94720 Speech coding in the posteroventral cochlear nucleus

R01DC-00505-04 (CMS) GOLD, GEOFFREY H MONELL CHEMICAL SENSES CENTER 3500 MARKET STREET PHILADELPHIA, PA 19104-3308 Intracellular messengers in olfactory transduction

R01DC-00507-04 (HAR) LEVITT, HARRY CUNY GRADUATE SCHOOL 33 W 42ND ST - RM 902 NEW YORK, NY 10036 Video processing of speech for hearing-impaired persons

R01DC-00508-03 (HUD) NELSON, KEITH E PENNSYLVANIA STATE UNIVERSITY 417 MOORE BLDG/PSYCHOLOGY UNIVERSITY PARK, PA 16802 Experimental studies of language learning processes

R29DC-00510-05 (CMS) GREEN, KERRY P UNIVERSITY OF ARIZONA DEPARMENT OF PSYCHOLOGY TUSCON, AZ 85721 Auditory-visual perception of speech by adults

R01DC-00515-04 (CMS) GANDOUR, JACKSON PURDUE UNIVERSITY WEST LAFAYETTE, IN 47907 Prosodic aspects of speech after brain damage

R29DC-00516-03 (CMS) STATHOPOULOS, ELAINE T SUNY AT BUFFALO 109 PARK HALL BUFFALO, NY 14260 Children's mechanisms for varying vocal intensity

R01DC-00517-04 (CMS) SOBKOWICZ, HANNA M 75 MEDICAL SCIENCE BUILDING 1300 UNIVERSITY AVENUE MADISON, WI 53706 Development of efferent nerve fibers in the cochlea

P01DC-00520-04 (SRC) RUBEL, EDWIN W DEPT OF OTOLARYNGOLOGY RL-30 UNIVERSITY OF WASHINGTON SEATTLE, WA 98195 Hearing development

P01DC-00520-04 0003 (SRC) DURHAM, DIANNE Hearing development Afferent control of central auditory metabolism

P01DC-00520-04 0004 (SRC) FOLSOM, RICHARD C. Hearing development Auditory sensitivity and frequency resolution in infants

P01DC-00520-04 0005 (SRC) KUHL, PATRICIA K. Hearing development Developmental speech perception

P01DC-00520-04 0006 (SRC) OLSHO, LYNNE W. Hearing development Psychoacoustic and A B R measures of infant auditory function

P01DC-00520-04 9001 (SRC) BURNS, EDWARD M. Hearing development Core--biotechnology

P01DC-00520-04 9002 (SRC) KUHL, PATRICK K. Hearing development Core--infant subjects

P01DC-00520-04 0001 (SRC) BURNS, EDWARD M Hearing development Measurements of cochlear development in infants

P01DC-00520-04 0002 (SRC) KEEFE, DOUGLAS H. Hearing development

PROJECT NO., ORGANIZATIONAL UNIT., INVESTIGATOR, ADDRESS, TITLE

Acoustical measures of infant external and middle ears

R29DC-00522-03 (CMS) **CONNINE, CYNTHIA M** UNIVERSITY OF NEW YORK DEPT. PSYCHOLOGY BINGHAMTON, NY 13901 Pre and post perceptual context effects in speech

R01DC-00523-01A2 (HUD) **CONTURE, EDWARD G** SYRACUSE UNIVERSITY 805 S CROUSE AVENUE SYRACUSE, NY 13244-2280 Stuttering and disordered phonology in young children

R29DC-00526-04 (HAR) **RICHARDS, VIRGINIA MARIE** UNIVERSITY OF PENNSYLVANIA 3815 WALNUT STREET PHILADELPHIA, PA 19104-6196 Envelope synchrony perception

R29DC-00527-03 (HAR) **BERNSTEIN, LESLIE R** UNIV OF CONNECTICUT HEALTH CTR 263 FARMINGTON AVE FARMINGTON, CT 06032 Binaural information processing

R29DC-00528-03 (HUD) **LEWIS, BARBARA A** RAINBOW BABIES & CHILDRENS HOS 2101 ADELBERT ROAD CLEVELAND, OH 44106 Familial study of severe phonology disorders

R01DC-00531-03 (HAR) **SAUNDERS, JAMES C** 5 SILVERSTEIN-OTO 3400 SPRUCE STREET PHILADELPHIA, PA 19104 Middle ear development

R01DC-00533-02 (CMS) **BROEN, PATRICIA A** UNIVERSITY OF MINNESOTA 164 PILLSBURY DR, SE MINNEAPOLIS, MN 55455 Cleft palate children's early phonological development

R29DC-00535-03 (HAR) **TAKAHASHI, TERRY T** UNIVERSITY OF OREGON HUESTIS HALL EUGENE, OR 97403 Generation of auditory spatial receptive fields

R01DC-00537-03 (CMS) **MENYUK, PAULA** BOSTON UNIVERSITY 605 COMMONWEALTH AVENUE BOSTON, MA 02215 Improving language processing in impaired children

R29DC-00539-03 (CMS) **REILLY, JUDY S** SAN DIEGO STATE UNIVERSITY DEPARTMENT OF PSYCHOLOGY SAN DIEGO, CA 92182 Acquisition of grammatical facial expression in ASL

R29DC-00540-03 (HAR) **SANES, DAN H** NEW YORK UNIVERSITY MEDICAL CT 550 FIRST AVENUE NEW YORK, NY 10016 Development/influence-inhibition in the auditory system

R29DC-00545-01A3 (HAR) **KIDD, GARY R** INDIANA UNIVERSITY BLOOMINGTON, IN 47405 Dynamic attending and the perception of patterns in time

R01DC-00550-03 (CMS) **LAZAR, RICHARD B** REHAB INSTITUTE OF CHICAGO 345 E SUPERIOR ST CHICAGO, IL 60611 Prognosis for swallowing function recovery following CVA

R29DC-00553-03 (CMS) **WILLIAMS, HEATHER** WILLIAMS COLLEGE DEPT OF BIOLOGY WILLIAMSTOWN, MA 01267 Modulation of auditory and motor modes in vocal learning

R01DC-00559-03 (CMS) **SMITH, ANNE** PURDUE UNIVERSITY HEAVILON HALL W LAFAYETTE, IN 47907 Physiological correlates of stuttering

R01DC-00560-03 (HAR) **PFINGST, BRYAN E** UNIVERSITY OF MICHIGAN 1301 EAST ANN ST, BOX 0506 ANN ARBOR, MI 48109 Nonspectral frequency discrimination

R29DC-00561-03 (HAR) **CHAN, KENNY H** CHILDREN'S HOSP OF PITTSBURGH ONE CHILDREN'S PLACE PITTSBURGH, PA 15213 Otitis medica--An in vivo model

R29DC-00565-03 (CMS) **ETCOFF, NANCY L** MASSACHUSETTS INSTI OF TECH DEPT OF BRAIN/COGNITIVE SCI CAMBRIDGE, MASS 021139 Neuropsychology of the perception of emotion

R01DC-00566-03 (CMS) **TEETER, JOHN H** MONELL CHEMICAL SENSES CENTER 3500 MARKET ST PHILADELPHIA, PA 19104-3308 Peripheral mechanisms of olfactory reception

R01DC-00577-03 (CMS) **CHILDERS, DONALD G** UNIVERSITY OF FLORIDA 405 CSE GAINESVILLE, FL 32611-2024 Modeling vocal disorders

R01DC-00581-02 (HAR) **SKINNER, MARGARET W** WASHINGTON UNIV SCH OF MED 517 SOUTH EUCLID AVE, BOX 8115 ST LOUIS, MO 63110 Strategies to optimize benefit from a cochlear implant

R01DC-00583-04 (CMS) **SCHWARTZ, RICHARD G** CUNY-GRAD SCH & UNIV CTR 33 WEST 42ND STREET NEW YORK, NY 10036-8099 Input-output relationships in speech-language impairment

R01DC-00588-04 (CMS) **VOGT, RICHARD GUPTON** UNIVERSITY OF SOUTH CAROLINA COLUMBIA, SC 29208 Molecular neurobiology of olfactory proteins

R01DC-00589-03 (CMS) **KOHUT, ROBERT I** BOWMAN GRAY SCHOOL OF MEDICINE 300 SOUTH HAWTHORNE RD WINSTON-SALEM, NC 27103 Sensori hearing loss due to perilymphatic fistulas

R29DC-00591-01A1 (CMS) **SAPIR, SHIMON** NORTHWESTERN UNIVERSITY 2299 SHERIDAN ROAD EVANSTON, IL 60208-3570 Trigemino-laryngeal reflexes in stutterers and normals

R01DC-00594-03 (CMS) **GRACCO, VINCENT L** HASKINS LABORATORIES 270 CROWN STREET NEW HAVEN, CT 06511 Mechanisms of speech motor control

R01DC-00597-03 (HAR) **KIDD, GERALD D, JR** BOSTON UNIVERSITY 635 COMMONWEALTH AVE BOSTON, MA 02215 Spectral shape discrimination in hearing

R01DC-00599-03 (HAR) **NORTON, SUSAN J** 4800 SAND POINT WAY NE SEATTLE, WA 98105 Non-invasive measurements of human cochlear mechanics

R01DC-00600-03 (HAR) **WONG, DONALD** INDIANA UNIVERSITY SCH OF MED 635 BARNHILL DRIVE INDIANAPOLIS, IN 46202-5120 Cortical integration underlying auditory perception

R01DC-00601-03 (CMS) **NUSBAUM, HOWARD C** UNIVERSITY OF CHICAGO 5848 S UNIVERSITY AVE CHICAGO, IL 60637 Structure and process in speech perception

R01DC-00607-02 (HAR) **COVEY, ELLEN** DUKE UNIVERSITY MEDICAL CTR 349 MSI-A, PO BOX 3943 DURHAM, NC 27710 Central auditory pathways

R01DC-00612-03 (CMS) **TOMBLIN, JAMES B** UNIVERSITY OF IOWA IOWA CITY, IA 52242 Specific language disorder--Genetic epidemiologic study

R01DC-00613-04 (CMS) **MARTIN, GLEN KAY** UNIVERSITY OF MIAMI SCH OF MED P.O. BOX 016960 MIAMI, FL 33101 Otoacoustic emission cochleography

R01DC-00618-02 (HAR) **PETERSON, ELLENGENE H** OHIO UNIV - IRVINE HALL DEPT OF ZOOLOGICAL-BIOMED SCI ATHENS, OH 45701-2979 Information channels in the vestibular nerve

R44DC-00619-02A1 (HAR) **BROWN, CAROLYN J** BREAKTHROUGH OAKDALE, IA 52319 Computer-aided training for speech perception in the deaf

R44DC-00621-03 (HAR) **FRANKLIN, DAVID** AUDIOLOGICAL ENGINEERING CORP 35 MEDFORD ST SOMERVILLE, MA 02143 A multiple modality assistive listening device

R44DC-00623-03 (BPO) **ROTHENBERG, MARTIN** GLOTTAL ENTERPRISES 719 EAST GENESEE STREET SYRACUSE, NY 13210 A new electroglottograph

R44DC-00624-02A1 (CMS) **BERKOVITZ, ROBERT** SENSIMETRICS CORPORATION ONE KENDALL SQUARE CAMBRIDGE, MA 02139 Speech synthesis work station

R29DC-00625-04 (CMS) **SRINIVASAN, MANDAYAM A** MASS INST OF TECHNOLOGY RES LAB OF ELECTRONICS CAMBRIDGE, MA 02139 Role of skin biomechanics in mechanoreceptor response

R01DC-00626-03 (HAR) **LEEK, MARJORIE R** WALTER REED ARMY MEDICAL CENTE ARMY AUDIOLOGY & SPEECH CTR WASHINGTON, DC 20307-5001 Hearing loss and the perception of complex sounds

R29DC-00633-04 (CMS) **NITTROUER, SUSAN** UNIVERSITY OF NEBRASKA AT OMAH KAYSER HALL 115 OMAHA, NE 68182-0054 Ontogeny of segmental speech organization

R01DC-00642-03 (CMS) **MADDIESON, IAN** UNIVERSITY OF CALIFORNIA 405 HILGARD AVENUE LOS ANGELES, CA 90024-1543 Language-universal sequencing of sounds

R01DC-00646-02 (CMS) **KAHRILAS, PETER J** NORTHWESTERN MEMORIAL HOSPITAL 250 E SUPERIOR STREET CHICAGO, IL 60611 Volitional, bolus, and age effects on human swallowing

R01DC-00652-03 (GMA) **YOO, TAI JUNE** UNIVERSITY OF TENNESSEE 956 COURT AVENUE MEMPHIS, TN 38163 Epitope specificity in collagen induced ear lesions

R29DC-00653-02 (HAR) **WHITLON, DONNA S** MEMORIAL VETERANS ADM HOSPITAL 600 HIGHLAND AVENUE MADISON, WI 53792 Determinants of neuronal connectivity in the cochlea

R01DC-00654-02 (HAR) **DORMAN, MICHAEL F** ARIZONA STATE UNIVERSITY COMMUNITY SERVICES BUILDING TEMPE, AZ 85287-0102 Cochler implant--Auditory function and speech recognition

R29DC-00656-03 (HAR) **HENLEY, CHARLES M** BAYLOR COLLEGE OF MEDICINE ONE BAYLOR PLAZA HOUSTON, TX 77030 Role of polyamines in postnatal cochlear development

R29DC-00657-02 (HAR) **STEINSCHNEIDER, MITCHELL** ALBERT EINSTEIN COLLEGE OF MED 1300 MORRIS PARK AVENUE BRONX, NY 10461 Speech sound processing in auditory cortex

R01DC-00663-02 (HAR) **FENG, ALBERT S** UNIVERSITY OF ILLINOIS 407 SOUTH GOODWIN DRIVE URBANA, IL 61801 Sound direction on neural processing of complex sounds

R01DC-00669-03 (SB) **DODDS, WYLIE J** FROEDTERT MEMORIAL LUTHERAN HO 9200 WEST WISCONSIN AVENUE MILWAUKEE, WI 53226 Esophageal sphincter opening and transphincteric flow

R01DC-00674-01A2 (HAR) **HANTZ, EDWIN C** EASTMAN SCHOOL OF MUSIC 26 GIBBS STREET ROCHESTER, NY 14604 Neural basis of music cognition

R01DC-00676-02 (HUD) **LAHEY, MARGARET** EMERSON COLLEGE 168 BEACON STREET BOSTON, MA 02116 Speech encoding & specific language impairment

R01DC-00677-02 (HAR) **KIMBERLING, WILLIAM J** BOYS TOWN NAT RESEARCH HOSPITA 555 NORTH 30TH STREET OMAHA, NE 68131 A collaborative study of usher syndrome

R01DC-00683-02 (HAR) **VIEMEISTER, NEAL F** UNIVERSITY OF MINNESOTA 75 EAST RIVER ROAD MINNEAPOLIS, MN 55455 Intensity coding and dynamic processes in hearing

R29DC-00690-03 (CMS) **HARRISON, THERESA A** MED COLL OF GEORGIA SCH OF MED AUGUSTA, GA 30912-2000 Neurobiology of gustatory neurons in solitary nucleus

R01DC-00693-02 (HAR) **YATES, BILLY J** ROCKEFELLER UNIVERSITY 1230 YORK AVENUE NEW YORK, NY 10021-6399 Vestibular influences on the sympathetic nervous system

R01DC-00695-04 (CMS) **BERNSTEIN, LYNNE E** MARY THORNBERRY BLDG. B-7C 800 FLORIDA AVE. N.E. WASHINGTON, DC 20002 Cutaneous communication aids for the deaf

R44DC-00697-02 (HAR) **BRUCE, ROBERT D** COLLABORATION SCI & TECH INC 15835 PARK TEN PLACE HOUSTON, TX 77084-5131 A computerized distortion product hearing screener

R01DC-00699-03 (HUD) **BERNDT, RITA S** UNIV. OF MARYLAND HOSPITAL 22 S GREENE STREET BALTIMORE, MD 21201 Cognitive/linguistic factors in acquired dyslexia

R01DC-00706-02 (HAR) **WAKEFIELD, GREGORY H** UNIVERSITY OF MICHIGAN 1301 BEAL AVENUE ANN ARBOR, MI 48109-2122 Binaural localization in complex acoustic environments

R01DC-00708-02 (HAR) **DALLOS, PETER J** NORTHWESTERN UNIVERSITY 2299 SHERIDAN ROAD EVANSTON, IL 60208 In vitro studies of cochlear neurobiology

R01DC-00710-02 (HAR) **SAUNDERS, JAMES C** 5 SILVERSTEIN - ORL 3400 SPRUCE STREET PHILADELPHIA, PA 19104-4283 Hair cell micromechanics

R01DC-00712-02 (HAR) **GUTH, PAUL S** TULANE UNIVERSITY SCH OF MED 1430 TULANE AVE NEW ORLEANS, LA 70112 Histamine storage and release--Role of synaptic body

R01DC-00713-02 (HAR) **SCHULTE, BRADLEY A** MED UNIV OF SOUTH CAROLINA 171 ASHLEY AVENUE CHARLESTON, SC 29425 Histochemical studies of the cochlea

R01DC-00716-02 (HAR) **RAREY, KYLE E** UNIVERSITY OF FLORIDA BOX J-235, JHMHC GAINESVILLE, FL 32610 Inner ear adrenocorticosteroid receptor system

R29DC-00719-02 (HAR) **KLUENDER, KEITH R** UNIVERSITY OF WISCONSIN 1202 WEST JOHNSON ST MADISON, WI 53706 Spectral temporal factors in perception of fluent speech

R01DC-00721-02 (CMS) **VAN HOUTEN, JUDITH L** UNIVERSITY OF VERMONT BURLINGTON, VT 05405 Chemosensory transduction in paramecium

R01DC-00722-01A1 (HAR) **BOBBIN, RICHARD P** LOUISIANNA STATE UNIVERSITY 2020 GRAVIER ST NEW ORLEANS, LA 70112-2234 Pharmacology of isolated outer hair cells

R01DC-00726-02 (HAR) **SAINT MARIE, RICHARD L** UNIV OF CONNECTICUT HEALTH CTR FARMINGTON, CT 06032 Cytochemistry of central auditory pathways

R01DC-00730-02 (CMS) **MENN, LISE** UNIVERSITY OF COLORADO CAMPUS BOX 344 BOULDER, CO 80309-0344 The use of syntax in Japanese and English aphasic speech

R01DC-00732-02 (CMS) **LASITER, PHILLIP S** FLORIDA ATLANTIC UNIVERSITY BIOLOGICAL SCIENCES BUILDING BOCA RATON, FL 33431 Receptor damage effects on central gustatory development

R29DC-00735-02 (CMS) **SWEAZEY, ROBERT D** UNIVERSITY OF MICHIGAN 1011 N UNIVERSITY ANN ARBOR, MI 48109 Neurobiology of solitary nucleus chemosensory neurons

R01DC-00737-02 (HAR) **GOLDSTEIN, JULIUS L** CENTRAL INSTITUTE FOR

PROJECT NO., ORGANIZATIONAL UNIT., INVESTIGATOR, ADDRESS, TITLE

THE DEAF 818 S EUCLID AVE ST LOUIS, MO 63110 Model of nonlinear and active cochlear signal processing
R01DC-00739-02 (HAR) BALABAN, CAREY D EYE & EAR INST OF PITTSBURGH 203 LOTHROP ST, SUITE 500 PITTSBURGH, PA 15213 Vestibulo-cerebellar circuits
R29DC-00741-02 (CMS) NEILS, JEAN M UNIVERSITY OF CINCINNATI MAIL LOCATION #379 CINCINNATI, OH 45221-0379 Dysgraphia in early Alzheimer's disease
R15DC-00760-01A1 (CMS) POSSIDENTE, BERNARD P, JR SKIDMORE COLLEGE SARATOGA SPRINGS, NY 12866 Olfactory bulb role in a circadian system
R01DC-00766-02 (CMS) KINNAMON, SUE C COLORADO STATE UNIVERSITY FORT COLLINS, CO 80523 Electrophysiology of taste transduction
R01DC-00767-01A1 (HAR) SEWELL, WILLIAM F MASS EYE AND EAR INFIRMARY 243 CHARLES STREET BOSTON, MA 02114 Pharmacology of neurotransmitters in hair-cell organs
R01DC-00776-02 (CMS) CAPLAN, DAVID N MASSACHUSETTS GENERAL HOSPITAL FRUIT STREET BOSTON, MA 02114 Acoustic-phonetic disorders & lexical access
R29DC-00783-02 (CMS) FORREST, KAREN UNIVERSITY OF WISCONSIN 1500 HIGHLAND AVENUE MADISON, WI 53705-2280 Sensory-motor interactions in Parkinsonian speech
R01DC-00786-03 (HAR) GILKEY, ROBERT H WRIGHT STATE UNIVERSITY DAYTON, OH 45435 Monaural masking binaural masking and their interrelations
R29DC-00787-02 (CMS) WULFECK, BEVERLY B UNIV OF CALIF, SAN DIEGO M-031P LA JOLLA, CA 92093 Grammatical processing abilities in language disorders
R29DC-00792-01A1 (HAR) GRANT, KENNETH W WALTER REED ARMY MEDICAL CENTE WASHINGTON, DC 20307-5001 Auditory supplements to speechreading
R01DC-00793-02 (HUD) PAUL, RHEA PORTLAND STATE UNIVERSITY P O BOX 751 PORTLAND, OR 97207-0751 Predicting outcomes of early expressive language delay
R44DC-00796-02 (HAR) FRANKLIN, DAVID AUDIOLOGICAL ENGINEERING CORP 35 MEDFORD ST SOMERVILLE, MA 02143 Advanced tactile display for the deaf--Phase II
R01DC-00807-02 (HUD) RESCORLA, LESLIE A BRYN MAWR COLLEGE DEPT OF HUMAN DEVELOPMENT BRYN MAWR, PA 19010 Expressive language delay at 2--Epidemiology and outcome
R29DC-00811-04 (CMS) BAYNES, KATHLEEN DARTMOUTH MEDICAL SCHOOL DEPT OF PSYCHIATRY HANOVER, NH 03756 Components of auditory comprehension in aphasic patients
R01DC-00813-02 (HAR) HENKEL, CRAIG K WAKE FOREST UNIVERSITY 300 S HAWTHORNE RD WINSTON-SALEM, NC 27103 Structural basis of central hearing mechanisms
R01DC-00818-02 (CMS) MARKS, LAWRENCE E JOHN B PIERCE FOUNDATION LAB 290 CONGRESS AVENUE NEW HAVEN, CT 06519 Encoding and judgment of sensory magnitudes
R01DC-00820-02 (CMS) WESTBURY, JOHN R UNIVERSITY OF WISCONSIN RETARDATION & DEVELOPMENT MADISON, WI 53705-2280 X-ray microbeam speech production database
R29DC-00822-01A1 (CMS) MOORE, CHRISTOPHER A UNIVERSITY OF PITTSBURGH 313 SALK HALL PITTSBURGH, PA 15261 Physiological development of speech production
R01DC-00824-01A1 (HAR) MOSCICKI, RICHARD A MASSACHUSETTS GENERAL HOSPITAL FRUIT STREET BOSTON, MA 02114 Idiopathic sensorineural hearing loss-- Diagnosis and treatment
R01DC-00825-01A1 (CMS) WHALEN, DOUGLAS H HASKINS LABORATORIES 270 CROWN STREET NEW HAVEN, CT 06511-6695 Word frequency and the proper/common dimension in speech
R01DC-00848-03 (CMS) GAY, THOMAS J UNIV OF CONNECTICUT HLTH CTR 263 FARMINGTON AVENUE FARMINGTON, CT 06032 Organization of speech--Analysis by synthesis
R01DC-00853-02 (CMS) FRANK, MARION E UNIV OF CONNECTICUT HLTH CTR 263 FARMINGTON AVENUE FARMINGTON, CT 06032 Taste quality representation in the solitary nucleus
R01DC-00855-02 (CMS) BERKE, GERALD S VAMC WEST LOS ANGELES WILSHIRE & SAWTELLE BLVDS LOS ANGELES, CA 90073 Intraoperative measures of vocal fold youngs modulus
R01DC-00856-02 (CMS) WEINRICH, MICHAEL UNIVERSITY OF MARYLAND HOSPITA 22 SOUTH GREENE STREET BALTIMORE, MD 21201 Processing deficits in aphasic patients
R29DC-00858-02 (HAR) HYSON, RICHARD L SEATTLE, WA 98195 RL-30 Transneuronal signals for afferent regulation
R01DC-00865-02 (CMS) LOFQVIST, ANDERS HASKINS LABORATORIES 270 CROWN STREET NEW HAVEN, CT 06511-6695 Sources of sound in speech
R01DC-00866-01A1 (CMS) WILSON, DONALD A UNIVERSITY OF OKLAHOMA 455 WEST LINDSEY NORMAN, OK 73019 Functional consequences of early olfactory deprivation
R01DC-00871-02 (MGN) MORTON, CYNTHIA C BRIGHAM & WOMEN'S HOSP, INC 75 FRANCIS STREET BOSTON, MA 02115 Cloning genes involved in hearing
R29DC-00872-02 (CMS) RONNETT, GABRIELE V THE JOHNS HOPKINS UNIVERSITY 725 N WOLFE STREET BALTIMORE, MD 21205 Mechanisms of olfactory signal transduction
R29DC-00879-02 (CMS) LUCE, PAUL A STATE UNIVERSITY NEW YORK AMHERST, NY 14260 Spoken word recognition and neighborhood activation
R01DC-00880-08 (NEUB) SCHWANZEL-FUKUDA, MARLENE ROCKEFELLER UNIVERSITY 1230 YORK AVENUE NEW YORK, NY 10021 Nervus terminalis relay of chemical signals
R29DC-00881-01A1 (HAR) FRENZ, DOROTHY A ALBERT EINSTEIN COLL OF MED 1410 PELHAM PARKWAY SOUTH BRONX, NY 10461 Role of growth factors in otic capsule formation
R01DC-00882-09 (CMS) BEAUCHAMP, GARY K MONELL CHEMICAL SENSES CENTER 3500 MARKET STREET PHILADELPHIA, PA 19104-3308 Modification of salt taste
R01DC-00885-02 (CMS) REDING, MICHAEL J BURKE REHABILITATION CENTER 785 MAMARONECK AVE WHITE PLAINS, NY 10605 Dysphagia therapy following stroke--A controlled trial
R01DC-00895-02 (CMS) DEACON, DIANA CITY COLLEGE OF CUNY CONVENT AVE & 138TH ST NEW YORK, N Y 10031 Brain potentials, semantic processing & attention
R01DC-00902-01A1 (CMS) LAWLESS, HARRY T CORNELL UNIVERSITY STOCKING HALL ITHACA, NY 14853 Psychophysics of astringent compounds

PROJECT NO., ORGANIZATIONAL UNIT., INVESTIGATOR, ADDRESS, TITLE

R01DC-00906-01 (CMS) MEREDITH, MICHAEL FLORIDA STATE UNIVERSITY TALLAHASSEE, FL 32306 Chemoreceptor systems involved in chemical communication
R13DC-00909-01 (CDRC) MILLER, JAMES D CENTRAL INSTITUTE FOR THE DEAF 818 S EUCLID AVE ST LOUIS, MO 63110 First conference on biological replacement in sensory systems
R29DC-00911-01A1 (HAR) THIBODEAU, LINDA M UNIVERSITY OF TEXAS AUSTIN, TX 78712-1089 Auditory adaptation and speech recognition in noise
R55DC-00918-01A1 (CMS) DUNCAN, GARY E UNIVERSITY OF NORTH CAROLINA CB #7090, 534A TAYLOR HALL CHAPEL HILL, NC 27599-7090 Hearing and vocalization--Brain activity patterns
R01DC-00920-01 (CMS) FIRESTEIN, STUART YALE UNIVERSITY 333 CEDAR ST NEW HAVEN, CT 06510 Molecular mechanisms of adaptation in olfactory neurons
R29DC-00921-01 (CMS) DEPAUL, ROXANNE REGENTS OF UNIV OF WISCONSIN 800 WEST MAIN STREET WHITEWATER, WI 53190 Oral-motor function for speech and swallowing in ALS
R01DC-00922-01A1 (HAR) MOREL, ANNE E VANDERBILT UNIVERSITY PSYCHOLOGY BUILDING NASHVILLE, TN 37240 Organization of auditory cortex
R01DC-00925-01 (HAR) NEFF, DONNA L BOYS TOWN NATIONAL INST 555 N 30TH STREET OMAHA, NE 68131 Auditory processing of uncertain stimuli
R55DC-00926-01A1 (CMS) KLEENE, STEVEN J UNIVERSITY OF CINCINNATI 231 BETHESDA AVE CINCINNATI, OH 45267-0521 Biophysics of olfactory receptor neurons
R29DC-00929-02 (HAR) POTE, KENNETH GENE DEPT OF OTOLARYNGOLOGY COMM DI 300 LONGWOOD AVENUE BOSTON, MA 02115 Otoconial protein expression in vestibular epithelia
R29DC-00937-01 (HAR) WENSTRUP, JEFFREY J NORTHEASTERN OHIO UNIVERSITIES ST RT 44 ROOTSTOWN, OH 44272 Auditory tecto-thalamic pathways--Information processing
R01DC-00942-01 (CMS) CAPLAN, DAVID N MASSACHUSETTS GENERAL HOSPITAL FRUIT STREET BOSTON, MA 02114 Fractionation of disorders of sentence comprehension
R29DC-00945-01 (HAR) ANDREWS, JAMES C UCLA SCHOOL OF MEDICINE LOS ANGELES, CA 90024-1624 Vestibular function and pressure in hydrops
R29DC-00952-01 (CMS) SCHICK, BRENDA S BOYS TOWN NATIONAL INSTITUTE 555 NORTH 30TH STREET OMAHA, NE 68131 The development of phonological organization in ASL
R29DC-00954-01 (HAR) MAY, BRADFORD J JOHNS HOPKINS UNIV SCH OF MED 720 RUTLAND AVENUE BALTIMORE, MD 21205 Spectral cues for sound localization
R01DC-00969-01A1 (HUD) STEFANATOS, GERRY A MEDICAL COLL OF PENNSYLVANIA 3200 HENRY AVENUE PHILADELPHIA, PA 19129 Neurophysiological studies of language disorders in children
R01DC-00970-01 (HAR) PEUSNER, KENNA D GEORGE WASHINGTON UNIVERSITY 2300 I STREET, NW WASHINGTON, DC 20037 Synaptic transmission during neuronal differentiation
P60DC-00976-02 (SRC) TITZE, INGO R UNIVERSITY OF IOWA IOWA CITY, IA 52242 Center for voice and speech communication
P60DC-00976-02 0001 (SRC) TITZE, INGO R Center for voice and speech communication Biomechanics of the larynx
P60DC-00976-02 0002 (SRC) LUSCHEI, ERICH S Center for voice and speech communication Neurophysiology of phonation
P60DC-00976-02 0003 (SRC) FOLKINS, JOHN W Center for voice and speech communication Velopharyngeal structure and function
P60DC-00976-02 0004 (SRC) MOON, JERALD B Center for voice and speech communication Articulatory coordination in speech disorders
P60DC-00976-02 0005 (SRC) BLESS, DIANE M Center for voice and speech communication Assessment and treatment of voice disorders
P60DC-00976-02 0006 (SRC) HORII, YOSHIYUKI Center for voice and speech communication Perception and acoustic analysis of vocal qualities
P60DC-00976-02 0007 (SRC) RAMIG, LORRAINE O Center for voice and speech communication Treatment efficacy in Parkinson's patients
P60DC-00976-02 0008 (SRC) SCHERER, RONALD Center for voice and speech communication Mechanisms of phonation--The trained voice
P60DC-00976-02 0009 (SRC) SCHERER, RONALD C Center for voice and speech communication Dissemination
P60DC-00976-02 0010 (SRC) PINTO, NEAL B Center for voice and speech communication Speech synthesis and analysis
P60DC-00976-02 9001 (SRC) LEMKE, JON H Center for voice and speech communication Core--Biostatistics
P60DC-00976-02 9002 (SRC) DRUKER, DAVID G Center for voice and speech communication Core--Equipment
P60DC-00979-02 (SRC) SACHS, MURRAY B JOHNS HOPKINS SCHOOL OF MED 720 RUTLAND AVENUE BALTIMORE, MD 21205 Research and training center in hearing and balance
P60DC-00979-02 0001 (SRC) YOUNG, ERIC D Research and training center in hearing and balance Somatosensory inputs to the cochlear nucleus
P60DC-00979-02 0002 (SRC) RYUGO, DAVID K Research and training center in hearing and balance Structural basis for stimulus coding in the cochlear nucleus
P60DC-00979-02 0003 (SRC) MANIS, PAUL B Research and training center in hearing and balance Mechanisms of stellate cell function
P60DC-00979-02 0004 (SRC) SACHS, MURRAY B Research and training center in hearing and balance Inhibitory influences on signal processing in the cochlear nucleus
P60DC-00979-02 0005 (SRC) MATTOX, DOUGLAS E Research and training center in hearing and balance Hearing loss from polyamine synthesis inhibition
P60DC-00979-02 0006 (SRC) HERDMAN, SUSAN J Research and training center in hearing and balance Research on the effect of rehabilitation
P60DC-00979-02 0007 (SRC) ZEE, DAVID S Research and training center in hearing and balance Canal, otolith, and visual determinants of VOR adaptation in human beings
P60DC-00979-02 9001 (SRC) SACHS, MURRAY B Research and training center in hearing and balance Core--Research training
P60DC-00979-02 9002 (SRC) FREEMAN, ELAINE K Research and training

PROJECT NO., ORGANIZATIONAL UNIT., INVESTIGATOR, ADDRESS, TITLE

center in hearing and balance Core--Information dissemination
P60DC-00979-02 9003 (SRC) SACHS, MURRAY B Research and training center in hearing and balance Core--Continuing education
P60DC-00982-02 (SRC) BROOKHOUSER, PATRICK E BOYS TOWN NATIONAL RES HOSPITA 55 NORTH 30TH STREET OMAHA, NE 68131 Center for hearing loss in children
P60DC-00982-02 0004 (SRC) WALSH, EDWARD Center for hearing loss in children Development of peripheral auditory non-linearities
P60DC-00982-02 0005 (SRC) MORLEY, BARBARA Center for hearing loss in children Efferent neurotransmitter systems in the developing cochleas
P60DC-00982-02 9001 (SRC) JESTEADT, WALT Center for hearing loss in children Core--Technical support
P60DC-00982-02 9002 (SRC) ING, PAUL Center for hearing loss in children Core--Genetics
P60DC-00982-02 9003 (SRC) BROOKHOUSER, PATRICK E Center for hearing loss in children Core--Clinical services
P60DC-00982-02 0001 (SRC) STELMACHOWICZ, PATRICIA Center for hearing loss in children Early identification and remediation of hearing loss
P60DC-00982-02 0002 (SRC) CARNEY, ARLENE Center for hearing loss in children Speech perception and production in hearing-impaired children
P60DC-00982-02 0003 (SRC) SMITH, SHELLEY D Center for hearing loss in children Genetic analysis of dominant progressive hearing loss
R01DC-00993-01 (CMS) GAY, THOMAS J UNIV OF CONNECTICUT HLTH CTR 263 FARMINGTON AVENUE FARMINGTON, CT 06032 Oral mechanisms in swallowing
R43DC-00998-01 (BPO) BERKOVITZ, ROBERT SENSIMETRICS CORPORATION ONE KENDALL SQUARE CAMBRIDGE, MA 02139 Evoked otoacoustic distortion screening device
R43DC-01000-01 (BPO) CASTRACANE, JAMES INTERSCIENCE, INC 105 JORDAN ROAD TROY, NY 12180 Compact, fiber optic holographic probe for otolaryngology
R43DC-01001-01 (BPO) BIRCK, JONATHAN D VIRTUAL CORPORATION 521 SW 11TH AVE, SUITE 400 PORTLAND, OR 97205 A dual-probe impedance tester
R43DC-01004-01 (BPO) MISKIEL, EDWARD INTELLIGENT HEARING SYSTEMS,CO 1125 NE 125 ST NORTH MIAMI, FL 33161 Development of an improved tactual vocoder
R01DC-01007-02 (HAR) WALSH, EDWARD J BOY'S TOWN NATIONAL INSTITUTE 555 NORTH 30TH STREET OMAHA, NE 68131 Ontogeny of cochlear nucleus responses to amino acids
R43DC-01008-01 (SSS) JAKOBS, THOMAS INVOTEK 700 WEST 20TH STREET FAYETTEVILLE, AR 72701 Laser activated keyboard for accessing personal computer
R43DC-01011-01 (BPO) MOUNTY, JUDITH L A-2 CARVER PL LAWRENCEVILLE, NJ 08648 Signed language acquisition checklist
R03DC-01019-01 (SRC) AKABAS, MYLES H COLUMBIA UNIVERSITY 630 W 168TH STREET NEW YORK, N Y 10032 Molecular cloning of the human sweet taste receptor
R03DC-01028-01 (SRC) HUNKER, CHAUNCEY J WAISMAN CENTER 1500 HIGHLAND AVENUE MADISON, WI 53705-2280 Physiological characteristics of orofacial bradykinesia
R03DC-01031-01A1 (SRC) WALDRON, MANJULA B OHIO STATE UNIVERSITY 270 BEVIS HALL COLUMBUS, OH 43210 Feasibility of using neural networks to study ASL signs
R03DC-01033-01 (SRC) FARBMAN, ALBERT I NORTHWESTERN UNIVERSITY 2153 SHERIDAN ROAD EVANSTON, IL 60208 Development of fungiform papilla and taste buds
R03DC-01038-01 (SRC) TALLAL, PAULA RUTGERS, THE STATE UNIV OF N J 195 UNIVERSITY AVENUE NEWARK, NJ 07102 An animal model for development of cerebral asymmetry
R03DC-01042-01A1 (SRC) ACHE, BARRY W 9505 OCEAN SHORE BLVD ST AUGUSTINE, FL 32086-8623 Labelling of physiologically active olfactory neurons
R03DC-01043-01 (SRC) PARK, JANIE C FLORIDA INSTITUTE OF TECHNOLOG 150 WEST UNIVERSITY BOULEVARD MELBOURNE, FL 32901-6988 Synaptic vesicle isolation from frog saccular hair cells
R03DC-01045-01 (SRC) PUNCH, JERRY L MICHIGAN STATE UNIVERSITY EAST LANSING, MI 48824 A DSP-based approach to the study of hearing aid fitting
R01DC-01049-02 (NEUA) WOODS, DAVID L VA MEDICAL CENTER 150 MUIR ROAD MARTINEZ, CA 94553 Human middle latency auditory evoked potentials
R01DC-01065-01 (CMS) SIMON, SIDNEY A DUKE UNIVERSITY MEDICAL CENTER BOX 3209 DURHAM, NC 27710 Chemical responses of oral trigeminal nerves
R13DC-01069-01 (CDRC) WERNER, LYNNE A UNIVERSITY OF WASHINGTON SEATTLE, WA 98195 Developmental psychoacoustics conference
R01DC-01071-01 (CMS) GRAZIADEI, PASQUALE P FLORIDA STATE UNIVERSITY BIO UNIT I, B-157 TALLAHASSEE, FL 32306-3050 Funtional morphology of the olfactory bulb
R01DC-01076-01 (MGN) KING, MARY C UNIVERSITY OF CALIFORNIA BERKELEY, CA 94720 Mapping a gene for deafness in a large kindred
R01DC-01081-01 (CMS) NORTHCUTT, RICHARD G UNIVERSITY OF CALIFORNIA LA JOLLA, CA 92093 Taste bud development
R13DC-01085-01 (CDRC) DEMARIA, THOMAS OHIO STATE UNIVERSITY 456 W 10TH AVENUE COLUMBUS, OH 43210 Recent advances in otitis media--Research conference
R01DC-01086-01 (HAR) BEITZ, ALVIN J UNIVERSITY OF MINNESOTA 1988 FITCH AVENUE ST PAUL, MN 55108 Neurochemistry of the vestibular complex
R01DC-01089-01 (HAR) BROWN, M CHRISTIAN MASSACHUSETTS EYE & EAR INFIRM 243 CHARLES STREET BOSTON, MA 02114 Descending systems to the cochlea and cochlear nucleus
R01DC-01094-01 (HAR) MC ELLIGOTT, JAMES G TEMPLE UNIV SCHOOL OF MED 3400 N BROAD STREET PHILADELPHIA, PA 19140 Pharmacology of vestibulo-ocular reflex adaptation
R01DC-01099-01 (HAR) VOIGT, HERBERT F BOSTON UNIVERSITY 44 CUMMINGTON STREET BOSTON, MA 02215 Structure/function relations of cochlear nucleus neurons
R29DC-01101-01 (HUD) ELLIS WEISMER, SUSAN UNIVERSITY OF WISCONSIN 1975 WILLOW DRIVE MADISON, WI 53706 Prosodic effects on language impaired children
R55DC-01104-01 (HAR) SHUPERT, CHARLOTTE L GOOD SAMARITAN HOSP & MED CTR 1120 NW 20TH AVE PORTLAND, OR 97209 Stabilization of head position during postural movements
R01DC-01107-01 (CMS) RAMIREZ, ISRAEL MONELL CHEMICAL SENSES CENTER 3500 MARKET STREET PHILADELPHIA, PA 19104-3308 Chemoreception for insoluble substances--Starch and oil
R15DC-01122-01 (CMS) PINKOWSKI, BEN WESTERN MICHIGAN UNIVERSITY KALAMAZOO, MI 49008 Fourier descriptors for sound spectrogrames
R29DC-01125-01 (CMS) KESHNER, EMILY A UNIVERSITY OF ILLINOIS 1919 WEST TAYLOR ST / 4TH FLOO CHICAGO, IL 60612 Regulatory mechanisms subserving postural stability
R15DC-01128-01 (HAR) STRAIN, GEORGE M LOUISIANA STATE UNIVERSITY SCHOOL VETERINARY MEDICINE BATON ROUGE, LA 70803-8420 Postnatal auditory function development
R01DC-01131-02 (SRC) COLTON, RAYMOND H SUNY HEALTH SCIENCE CENTER 750 EAST ADAMS STREET SYRACUSE, NY 13210 Objective studies of the management of voice disorders
R01DC-01139-02 (SRC) BRIN, MITCHELL COLUMBIA UNIVERSITY 710 WEST 168TH STREET NEW YORK, NY 10032 Double-blind botulinum toxin for spasmodic dysphonia
R01DC-01143-02 (SRC) SANDERS, IRA MOUNT SINAI SCHOOL OF MEDICINE 1 GUSTAVE L LEVY PLACE, BOX 11 NEW YORK, NY 10029 Development of a laryngeal pacer
R01DC-01147-02 (SRC) SASAKI, CLARENCE T YALE UNIVERSITY SCH OF MED PO BOX 3333 NEW HAVEN, CT 06510 Comparison of surgical treatments for paralytic dysphonia
R01DC-01149-02 (SRC) ZEALEAR, DAVID L VANDERBILT UNIVERSITY NASHVILLE, TN 37232 Rehabilitation of the paralyzed larynx
R01DC-01150-02 (SRC) RAMIG, LORRAINE O UNIVERSITY OF COLORADO CAMPUS BOX 409 BOULDER, CO 80309-0409 Efficacy of voice treatment for Parkinson's disease
R43DC-01166-01 (HAR) CLACK, WILLIAM F AUDIOLOGICAL ENGINEERING CORP 35 MEDFORD STREET SOMERVILLE, MA 02143 Auditory enhancement devices for the deaf
R43DC-01168-01 (HAR) HILL, CHARLES E, III MEDICAL DEVICES GROUP, INC 3200 WEST END AVENUE NASHVILLE, TN 37203 Powered incus replacement prosthesis
R43DC-01172-01 (CMS) AHMED, WISSAM W AI SYSTEMS INC 504 SOUTH BEACH BLVD ANAHEIM, CA 92804 Stuttering recognition using artificial neural networks
R43DC-01174-01 (CMS) BERKOVITZ, ROBERT A SENSIMETRICS CORPORATION ONE KENDALL SQUARE CAMBRIDGE, MA 02139 Computer based course in acoustic phonetics
R43DC-01175-01 (CMS) ASIMOPOULOS, NIKOS IMAGE PROCESSING TECHNOLOGIES 205 SOUTH MAIN ST, PO BOX 582 BLACKSBURG, VA 24060 Telesign-- Video telecommunication of sign language
R03DC-01182-01 (SRC) ROBIN, DONALD A UNIVERSITY OF IOWA W JOHNSON SPEECH/HEARING CENTE IOWA CITY, IA 52242 Tongue strength and fatigability in relation to speech
R03DC-01192-01 (SRC) LAWLESS, HARRY T CORNELL UNIVERSITY STOCKING HALL ITHACA, NY 14853 Functional significance of specific anosmia
R03DC-01196-01 (SRC) KLEIN, STEVEN L UNIV OF VIRGINIA HLTH SCI CTR BOX 439 JORDAN HALL CHARLOTTESVILLE, VA 22903 Inhibitory and inductive signals of olfactory neurogenesis
R03DC-01198-01 (SRC) CAPLAN, DAVID N MASSACHUSETTS GENERAL HOSPITAL FRUIT STREET BOSTON, MA 02114 Localization of syntactic comprehension by PET scanning
R03DC-01207-01 (SRC) BRAY, NORMAN W, JR UNIVERSITY OF ALABAMA P O BOX 313, UAB STATION BIRMINGHAM, AL 35294 Semantic compaction skills of children with cerebral palsy
R03DC-01210-01 (SRC) MC MULLEN, NATHANIEL T UNIVERSITY OF ARIZONA 1501 N CAMPBELL AVENUE TUCSON, AZ 85724 Excitatory and inhibitory circuits in auditory neocortex
R03DC-01223-01 (SRC) ROSS, CHARLES D UNIV OF OKLAHOMA HLTH SCI CENT P O BOX 26901 OKLAHOMA CITY, OK 73190-3048 Quantitation and localization of amino acids in brain
R43DC-01225-01 (BPO) GOLDHOR, RICHARD S AUDIOFILE, INC 4 MILITIA DRIVE / SUITE 20 LEXINGTON, MA 02173 System for converting speech into synthesis parameters
R13DC-01226-01 (CDRC) NANCE, WALTER E VIRGINIA COMMONWEALTH UNIVERSI 1101 EAST MARSHALL STREET RICHMOND, VA 23298 Hereditary deafness workshop
R01DC-01228-01 (CMS) KALINOSKI, DARLINE L MONELL CHEMICAL SENSES CENTER 3500 MARKET STREET PHILADELPHIA, PA 19104-3308 Characterization of IP3 receptors in olfactory cilia
R13DC-01229-01 (CDRC) COREY, DAVID P MASSACHUSETTS GENERAL HOSPITAL WELLMAN 414 BOSTON, MA 02114 Sensory transduction: a symposium
R13DC-01232-01 (SRC) HARRIS, JEFFREY P UNIVERSITY OF CALIFORNIA 225 DICKINSON STREET SAN DIEGO, CA 92103 Third national conference on research goals and methods
R01DC-01234-01 (HUD) TAGER-FLUSBERG, HELEN B UNIVERSITY OF MASSACHUSETTS HARBOR CAMPUS BOSTON, MA 02125-3393 Language deficit and mental state knowledge in autism
R01DC-01238-01 (CMS) ROPER, STEPHEN D COLORADO STATE UNIVERSITY FORT COLLINS, CO 80523 Neurotransmission in the vertebrate taste bud
R01DC-01240-01 (CMS) MC KOON, GAIL A NORTHWESTERN UNIVERSITY 2029 SHERIDAN ROAD EVANSTON, IL 60208-2710 Intonation and sentence processing
R01DC-01242-01 (EDC) DALY, KATHLEEN A UNIVERSITY OF MINNESOTA HARVARD STREET AT EAST RIVER R MINNEAPOLIS, MN 55455 Epidemiology of early otitis media
R01DC-01243-01 (CMS) VERRILLO, RONALD T SYRACUSE UNIVERSITY MERRILL LANE SYRACUSE, NY 13244-5290 Aging effects on vibrotactile sensation
R13DC-01244-01 (CDRC) HALPERN, MIMI N SUNY 450 CLARKSON AVE/BOX 5 BROOKLYN, NY 11203 Neuroethology of chemical communication--Emerging model
R01DC-01245-01 (HAR) RYALS, BRENDA M JAMES MADISON UNIVERSITY HARRISONBURG, VA 22807 Innervation and function of regenerated hair cells

PROJECT NO., ORGANIZATIONAL UNIT., INVESTIGATOR, ADDRESS, TITLE

R29DC-01247-01 (CMS) MC GOWAN, RICHARD S HASKINS LABORATORIES 270 CROWN STREET NEW HAVEN, CT 06511-6695 Recovering articulatory movement from speech acoustics

R01DC-01250-01 (CMS) TARTTER, VIVIEN C THE CITY COLLEGE OF CUNY CONVENT AVE AND 138TH ST NEW YORK, N Y 10031 Auditory feedback and speech production

R01DC-01251-01 (HAR) MASTERS, W MITCH OHIO STATE UNIVERSITY 1735 NEIL AVE COLUMBUS, OH 43210 Head-phone presented model echo studies of sonar

R29DC-01258-01 (HAR) ASSMANN, PETER F UNIVERSITY OF TEXAS 2601 N FLOYD RD-BOX 830688 RICHARDSON, TX 75083-0688 Perception of speech in the presence of competing voices

R29DC-01259-01 (CMS) NICHOLAS, JOHANNA G CENTRAL INSTITUTE FOR THE DEAF 818 S EUCLID AVE ST LOUIS, MO 63110 Development of communicative functions in deaf children

R01DC-01262-01 (HAR) LUTFI, ROBERT A UNIVERSITY OF WISCONSIN 1500 HIGHLAND AVENUE MADISON, WI 53705 The information in auditory patterns

R01DC-01266-01 (CMS) SLOTNICK, BURTON M THE AMERICAN UNIVERSITY 4400 MASSACHUSETTS AVENUE N W WASHINGTON, D C 20016 Olfactory coding

R01DC-01273-01 (HAR) CORREIA, MANNING J UNIV OF TEXAS MEDICAL BRANCH 301 UNIVERSITY BOULEVARD GALVESTON, TX 77550 Studies of vestibular type I and type II hair cells

R01DC-01282-07 (HAR) CLARK, GRAEME M UNIVERSITY OF MELBOURNE VICTORIA, AUSTRALIA 3052 Improved cochlear implants: psychophysics and engineering

U01DC-01285-01 (SRC) TELIAN, STEVEN A UNIVERSITY OF MICHIGAN 1500 E MEDICAL CENTER DRIVE ANN ARBOR, MI 48109 Development of clinical marker for perilymph fistula

P01DC-01289-01 (CDRC) BATES, ELIZABETH A UNIVERSITY OF CALIFORNIA 9500 GILMAN DR LA JOLLA, CA 92093-0109 Origins of communication disorders

P01DC-01289-01 0001 (CDRC) THAL, DONNA Origins of communication disorders Origins of communication disorders in late talkers

P01DC-01289-01 0002 (CDRC) BATES, ELIZABETH A Origins of communication disorders Origins of communication disorders in infants with focal brain injury

P01DC-01289-01 0003 (CDRC) BELLGUI, URSULA Origins of communication disorders Origins of communication disorders in Williams syndrome infants

P01DC-01289-01 0004 (CDRC) DIXON, SUZANNE Origins of communication disorders Origins of communication disorders in infants of substance abusing

P01DC-01289-01 0005 (CDRC) NEVILLE, HELEN Origins of communication disorders Electrophysiological studies of communication disorders

P01DC-01289-01 9001 (CDRC) TRAUNER, DORIS Origins of communication disorders Core--Biomedical diagnostic

P01DC-01289-01 9002 (CDRC) WOLFECK, BEVERLY Origins of communication disorders Core--Behavioral diagnostic

R01DC-01291-01 (CMS) PERKELL, JOSEPH P MASSACHUSETTS INST OF TECHNOLO 77 MASSACHUSETTS AVENUE CAMBRIDGE, MA 02139 Degradation of speech and hearing from acoustic neuromas

R29DC-01294-01 (CMS) KOBLER, JAMES B MASSACHUSETTS EYE/EAR INFIRMAR 243 CHARLES STREET BOSTON, MA 02114 Cellular basis of pharyngeal motor control

R01DC-01295-01 (HED) DENHARDT, DAVID T RUTGERS, STATE UNIVERSITY PO BOX 1059 PISCATAWAY, NJ 08855-1059 Studies of spp in auditory ontogeny

R43DC-01299-01 (HAR) BERKOVITZ, ROBERT A SENSIMETRICS CORPORATION ONE KENDALL SQUARE CAMBRIDGE, MA 02139 Development of headset hearing aids

R01DC-01303-01 (HAR) ZOOK, JOHN M OHIO UNIVERSITY ATHENS, OH 45701-2979 Superior olive and descending auditory pathways

R43DC-01306-01 (CMS) HERTZ, SUSAN R ELOQUENT TECHNOLOGY, INC 24 HIGHGATE CIRCLE ITHACA, NY 14850 Optimization of speech synthesis software for vocal communication

R29DC-01317-05 (HAR) FURMAN, JOSEPH M THE EAR & EYE INST OF PITTSBUR 203 LOTHROP ST PITTSBURGH, PA 15213 Vestibulocular function in neurological disorders

R03DC-01318-01 (SRC) KOVACS, GREGORY T A STANFORD UNIVERSITY CENTER FOR INTEGRATED SYSTEMS STANFORD, CA 94305 Neural interfaces for multi fiber eighth nerve recording

R03DC-01323-01 (SRC) LORIG, TYLER S WASHINGTON & LEE UNIVERSITY LEXINGTON, VA 24450 Event-related potentials to odors

R03DC-01328-01 (SRC) CAMPBELL, THOMAS F CHILDRENS HOSP OF PITTSBURGH 200 MEYREN AVE PARKVALE BLDG PITTSBURGH, PA 15213 Bone lead level as predictor of speech/language deficits

R03DC-01338-01 (SRC) ARNOS, KATHLEEN S GALLAUDET UNIVERSITY 800 FLORIDA AVE NE WASHINGTON, DC 20002 A population genetic study of hearing loss in adults

R29DC-01387-01 (NEUB) SPIROU, GEORGE A WEST VIRGINIA UNIVERSITY 2222 HSCS MORGANTOWN, WV 26506 Descending projections to the cochlear nuclei

P60DC-01404-01 (SRC) HONRUBIA, VICENTE UCLA SCHOOL OF MEDICINE DEPT OF SURGERY LOS ANGELES, CA 90024-1624 Otoneurologic and vestibular clinical and basic research

P60DC-01404-01 0001 (SRC) BALOH, ROBERT W Otoneurologic and vestibular clinical and basic research Human vestibular laboratory

P60DC-01404-01 0002 (SRC) HONRUBIA, VICENTE Otoneurologic and vestibular clinical and basic research Vestibular nerve function laboratory

P60DC-01404-01 0003 (SRC) HONRUBIA, VICENTE Otoneurologic and vestibular clinical and basic research Vestibulo-ocular function laboratory

P60DC-01404-01 0004 (SRC) HONRUBIA, VICENTE Otoneurologic and vestibular clinical and basic research Research training component

P60DC-01404-01 0005 (SRC) ANDREWS, JAMES Otoneurologic and vestibular clinical and basic research Continuing education component

P60DC-01404-01 0006 (SRC) HARRIS, MARJORIE R Otoneurologic and vestibular clinical and basic research Information dissemination component

P60DC-01409-01 (SRC) HIXON, THOMAS J UNIVERSITY OF ARIZONA SPEECH BUILDING NO 25 TUSCON, ARIZ 85721 Neurogenic communication disorders

PROJECT NO., ORGANIZATIONAL UNIT., INVESTIGATOR, ADDRESS, TITLE

P60DC-01409-01 0001 (SRC) HIXON, THOMAS J Neurogenic communication disorders Normal and abnormal speech production

P60DC-01409-01 0002 (SRC) GREEN, KERRY P Neurogenic communication disorders Studies of speech perception

P60DC-01409-01 0003 (SRC) GARRETT, MERRILL F Neurogenic communication disorders Lexical and syntactic processes

P60DC-01409-01 0004 (SRC) HOLLAND, AUDREY L Neurogenic communication disorders Comparative studies of naming impairments in aphasia and Alzheimer's

P60DC-01409-01 0005 (SRC) HELM-ESTABROOKS, NANCY Neurogenic communication disorders Perseveration in age-related neurologic disease

P60DC-01409-01 0006 (SRC) GLATTKE, THEODORE J Neurogenic communication disorders Research training program

P60DC-01409-01 0007 (SRC) BAYLES, KATHRYN A Neurogenic communication disorders Continuing education

P60DC-01409-01 0008 (SRC) BAYLES, KATHRYN A Neurogenic communication disorders Information dissemination

R01DC-01425-09 (HAR) HIGHSTEIN, STEPHEN M WASHINGTON UNIVERSITY 517 SOUTH EUCLID AVENUE ST LOUIS, MO 63110 Vestibular afferent and efferent activity

P20DC-01433-01 (SRC) HARRIS, JEFFREY P UNIVERSITY OF CALIFORNIA 225 DICKINSON STREET H-895 SAN DIEGO, CA 92103 Research training center in otolaryngology

P20DC-01434-01 (SRC) BEAUCHAMP, GARY K MONELL CHEMICAL SENSES CENTER 3500 MARKET STREET PHILADELPHIA, PA 19104-3308 Development of an RTC for taste and smell

P20DC-01437-01 (SRC) BESS, FRED H VANDERBILT UNIV SCHOOL OF MED UNIVERSITY STATION BOX 552 NASHVILLE, TN 37232-8700 Communication disorders in at-risk children

P20DC-01437-01 0001 (SRC) ASHMEAD, DANIEL H Communication disorders in at-risk children Binaural processing capability development in normal infants

P20DC-01437-01 0002 (SRC) CAMARATA, STEPHEN M Communication disorders in at-risk children Acoustic, phonetic, linguistic measures in normal and at-risk infants

P20DC-01437-01 0003 (SRC) OCHS, MARLEEN T Communication disorders in at-risk children Research training

P20DC-01439-01 (SRC) FINGER, THOMAS E UNIVERSITY OF COLORADO 4200 EAST 9TH AVE DENVER, CO 80262 Mountain-Plains rearch training center for chemosensory disorders

P20DC-01439-01 0001 (SRC) FINGER, THOMAS E Mountain-Plains rearch training center for chemosensory disorders Post-irradiation gustatory dysfunction

P20DC-01439-01 0002 (SRC) LASHER, ROBERT S Mountain-Plains rearch training center for chemosensory disorders Tissue culture of taste buds

P20DC-01439-01 0003 (SRC) GERHARDT, GREG A Mountain-Plains rearch training center for chemosensory disorders Odorant diffusion in olfactory mucus

P20DC-01439-01 0004 (SRC) CALL, RICHARD Mountain-Plains rearch training center for chemosensory disorders Continuing education and outreach

R13DC-01558-01 (CDRC) COHEN, BERNARD MOUNT SINAI SCHOOL OF MEDICINE 1 GUSTAVE L LEVY PLACE NEW YORK, NY 10029 Sensing and controlling motion--Vestibular and sensorimotor

N01DC-02400-01 (**) SUTTON, DWIGHT Cochlear re-implantation--histopathology

N01DC-02401-01 (**) MERZENICH, MICHAEL Design of pediatric cochlear implants

N01DC-12104-00 (**) RICHARD, SHEILA A National Institute on Deafness/Communication Disorders--Information Clearinghouse

N01DC-12107-00 (**) TOMBLIN, BRUCE Epidemiology of specific language impairment

N01DC-12116-00 (**) LEVINE, WILLIAM S Mathematical modeling of laryngeal motion

N01DC-12400-00 (**) LEAKE, PATRICIA A Protective effects of patterned electrical stimulation

N01DC-92400-04 (**) CLARK, GRAEME M Speech processors for auditory prosthesis

Z01DE-00001-39 (LCDO) FOLK, J E NIDR, NIH Transglutaminases--Specificity and control

Z01DE-00012-29 (BRB) FOWLER, B O NIDR, NIH Infrared and raman spectroscopy of teeth, bones and related synthetic compounds

Z01DE-00031-23 (NA) BROWN, F J NIDR, NIH Design and computer interfacing of neurophysiologic instrumentation

Z01DE-00034-23 (LI) SIRAGANIAN, R NIDR, NIH Mechanisms of histamine release

Z01DE-00043-22 (LME) DONKERSLOOT, J A NIDR, NIH Physiological and genetic studies on pathogenic oral microorganisms

Z01DE-00044-21 (MSS) MCMANUS, C NIDR, NIH Handling of microbial strain information by computers

Z01DE-00046-19 (LI) WAHL, S M NIDR, NIH Normal and pathologic mechanisms of inflammation and repair

Z01DE-00049-20 (LCDO) CHUNG, S I NIDR, NIH Physiological function of transglutaminases

Z01DE-00061-20 (LME) SANDBERG, A L NIDR, NIH Complement activation and inflammation

Z01DE-00070-19 (DPHP) DRISCOLL, W S NIDR, NIH Combined self-applied fluorides and sealants for caries prevention

Z01DE-00074-19 (BRB) FISHER, L W NIDR, NIH Bone and tooth matrix biochemistry and metabolism

Z01DE-00088-18 (BRB) EANES, E D NIDR, NIH Chemical, structural, and morphological studies on calcium phosphates

Z01DE-00132-17 (NA) DIONNE, R NIDR, NIH Pharmacological modulation of neuroendocrine responses to stress & inflammation

Z01DE-00133-17 (NA) GRACELY, R H NIDR, NIH Assessment of experimental and clinical pain

Z01DE-00134-17 (BRB) HASCALL, V C NIDR, NIH Structure and biosynthesis of proteoglycans

K16DE-00151-05S2 (SRC) SCHENKEIN, HARVEY A VIRGINIA COMMONWEALTH UNIVERSI BOX 566, MCV STATION RICHMOND, VA 23298 Dentist scientist program award

K16DE-00151-06S2 0001 (SRC) CALIFANO, JOSEPH Dentist scientist program award Antigen-specific human antibody response to periodontal microorganisms

K16DE-00151-06S2 0002 (SRC) HART, THOMAS Dentist scientist program award Genetic basis for susceptibility to juvenile periodontitis

K16DE-00152-07 (SRC) HOLT, STANLEY C UNIV OF TEXAS HLTH SCI CTR 7703 FLOYD CURL DRIVE SAN ANTONIO, TX 78284-7894 Dentist scientist award - institutional

K16DE-00157-06S2 (SRC) KOLLAR, EDWARD J UNIV OF CONN HEALTH CTR 263 FARMINGTON AVENUE FARMINGTON, CT 06030 Dentist/scientist program award

K16DE-00157-06S2 0003 (SRC) HELMS, JILL Dentist/scientist program award Pinpointing neurotransmitters responsible for pain

K16DE-00157-06S2 0004 (SRC) MARUCHA, PHILIP Dentist/scientist program award Migration of white blood cells

K16DE-00157-06S2 0005 (SRC) RICHARDS, DAVID Dentist/scientist program award Effects of interleukin 1 on collagenase, collagen, and collagenase inhibitor

Z01DE-00157-16 (BRB) TORCHIA, D A NIH Biophysical studies on the structure, dynamics and function of proteins

K16DE-00158-07 (SRC) GENCO, ROBERT J SUNY SCHOOL OF DENTAL MEDICINE 3435 MAIN STREET BUFFALO, NY 14214 Dentist scientist award--Institutional

K16DE-00159-07 (SRC) BOWEN, WILLIAM H UNIV OF ROCHESTER MED CTR 601 ELMWOOD AVE/BOX 611 ROCHESTER, NY 14642 Dentist scientist award

K16DE-00161-06S2 (SRC) DALE, BEVERLY A UNIVERSITY OF WASHINGTON SCHOOL OF DENTISTRY SEATTLE, WA 98195 Dentist-scientist program award

K16DE-00165-07 (SRC) BAWDEN, JAMES W UNIVERSITY OF NORTH CAROLINA 440 W FRANKLIN ST CHAPEL HILL, NC 27599-7455 Dentist scientist program award

K15DE-00168-05 (DSR) MEILLER, TIMOTHY F UNIVERSITY OF MARYLAND 666 W BALTIMORE STREET BALTIMORE, MD 21201 Oral viral disease in cancer patients

K16DE-00175-07 (SRC) SQUIER, CHRISTOPHER A UNIV OF IOWA COLL OF DENTISTRY DOWS INSTITUTE FOR DENT RES IOWA CITY, IA 52242 Dentist scientist program award - institutional

K16DE-00199-06S1 (SRC) KENT, JOHN N LOUISIANA STATE UNIV MED CTR 1100 FLORIDA AVE NEW ORLEANS, LA 70119 Dentist scientist program award

K16DE-00199-06S1 0001 (SRC) ARDOIN, ROBIN Dentist scientist program award Predifferentiation of fibroblasts in vivo by BMP

K16DE-00199-06S1 0002 (SRC) MARUCHA, PHILIP Dentist scientist program award

Z01DE-00199-15 (LI) OLIVER, C NIDR, NIH In vitro studies of secretary cell structure and function

K11DE-00203-03 (DSR) GRUNWERG, BARRY UNIV OF MED & DENT OF N J ROBERT WOOD JOHNSON MED SCH PISCATAWAY, N J 08854-5635 Orofacial pain pathways

Z01DE-00204-15 (LCDO) REDDI, A H NIDR, NIH Growth and differentiation factors in bone and cartilage

K15DE-00205-06 (SRC) GERSTNER, GEOFFREY E U OF CALIFORNIA, LOS ANGELES SCHOOL OF DENTISTRY, CHS LOS ANGELES, CA 90024 Correlative constraints of diet, morphology and behavior

K11DE-00208-06 (DSR) FITCHETT, JAMES E, JR HARVARD MEDICAL SCHOOL 25 SHATTUCK STREET BOSTON, MASS 02115 Epithelial mesenchymal transformation/facial development

K11DE-00210-05 (DSR) LOGIN, GARY R BETH ISRAEL HOSPITAL 330 BROOKLINE AVENUE BOSTON, MA 02215 Basophil and mast cell vesicular transport mechanisms

K11DE-00212-05 (DSR) KINDER, SUSAN A UNIV OF TEXAS HEALTH SCI CTR 7703 FLOYD CURL DRIVE SAN ANTONIO, TX 78284-7894 Cell surface in adherence of bacteroides gingivalis

Z01DE-00212-14 (CIPC) WEIFFENBACH, J M NIDR, NIH Taste and its disorders

K11DE-00213-05 (DSR) EDGERTON, MIRA SUNY AT BUFFALO 109 FOSTER HALL - 3435 MAIN ST BUFFALO, N Y 14214 The oral ecology of prosthetic surfaces

K15DE-00214-06 (DSR) CUTLER, CHRISTOPHER W UNIVERSITY OF NC AT CHAPEL HIL CB #7455, ROOM 101 Neutrophil interactions with bacteroides gingivalis

K15DE-00218-04 (DSR) RIDALL, AMY L UNIV OF TEXAS HLTH SCIS CTR P.O. BOX 20068 HOUSTON, TX 77225 Molecular biological studies on a bone phosphoprotein

K11DE-00219-05 (DSR) HENRY, MICHAEL A UNIVERSITY OF WASHINGTON DEPT OF NEUROLOGICAL SURGERY SEATTLE, WA 98195 Immature dental projections

K15DE-00223-05 (SRC) SCIOTE, JAMES J THE UNIVERSITY OF MICHIGAN 6222 DENTAL SCHOOL ANN ARBOR, MI 48109-1078 Lateral pterygoid muscle function and condylar growth

K15DE-00224-05 (DSR) ERICKSON, PAMELA R UNIV OF MINNESOTA 515 DELAWARE STREET S E MINNEAPOLIS, MN 55455 Biochemistry of proline domains on oral proteins

K15DE-00225-03 (DSR) KEHL, LOIS J UNIVERSITY OF MINNESOTA 435 DELAWARE STREET MINNEAPOLIS, MN 55455 Trigeminal studies of nociception

K15DE-00227-05 (DSR) SIROIS, DAVID A UNIVERSITY OF PENNSYLVANIA 4001 SPRUCE ST PHILADELPHIA, PA 19104 Central trigeminal plasticity--Effect of sensory organ damage

K15DE-00228-05 (DSR) TAYLOR, REGINALD W HARVARD MEDICAL SCHOOL 220 LONGWOOD AVENUE BOSTON, MA 02115 Molecular biology of periodontal ligament collagens

K04DE-00229-04 (OBM) LOOMIS, RONALD E S U N Y AT BUFFALO 321 FOSTER HALL BUFFALO, N Y 14214 Conformation of dentally relevant salivary molecules

Z01DE-00230-16 (DB) KLEINMAN, H K NIDR, NIH Proteins in tissue architecture and cell function

K04DE-00231-05 (OBM) MURRAY, PATRICIA A UMDNJ - NEW JERSEY DENT SCH 185 S ORANGE AVE MSB (C-634) NEWARK, NEW JERSEY 07103 Characteriztion of microbial lectins

K11DE-00232-04 (DSR) KATZ, JANNET UNIV OF ALABAMA AT BIRMINGHAM UNIVERSITY STATION BIRMINGHAM, ALABAMA 35294 T cell regulatory mechanisms in periodontal disease

K04DE-00233-04 (OBM) YAMAUCHI, MITSUO UNIVERSITY OF NORTH CAROLINA DENT RES CTR (210H) CB 3 7455 CHAPEL HILL, NC 27599 Structure & function of dentin matrix proteins

K04DE-00234-03 (OBM) KELLER, JOHN C UNIVERSITY OF IOWA COLLEGE OF DENTISTRY IOWA CITY, IA 52242 Wound healing responses to Ti implant surfaces

K04DE-00236-04 (OBM) BROWN, THOMAS A UNIVERSITY OF FLORIDA BOX J-424, JHMHC GAINESVILLE, FL 32610 Anti-S. mutans IgA--Subclasses, IgA proteases

K04DE-00237-04 (OBM) KIYONO, HIROSHI UNIV OF ALABAMA AT BIRMINGHAM UNIVERSITY STATION BIRMINGHAM, AL 35294 T cell regulation of caries immunity/periodontal disease

K04DE-00238-04 (OBM) CHEN, MEEI-SHIA UNIVERSITY OF CHICAGO 1101 E 58TH ST CHICAGO, IL 60637 Dental health--A cross-national analysis of determinants

K11DE-00239-04 (DSR) PAVLIN, DUBRAVKO UNIVERSITY OF CONNECTICUT DEPT. BIOSTRUCTURE & FUNCTION FARMINGTON, CT 06030 Molecular events in collagen gene response to vitamin D

K15DE-00240-04 (DSR) BEBRIN, WILLIAM R HARVARD MEDICAL SCHOOL 250 LONGWOOD AVENUE BOSTON, MA 02115 Functional relatedness of viral DNA polymerases

K15DE-00242-04 (DSR) RAMOS, DANIEL M UNIVERSITY OF CA HSW 604, BOX 0512 SAN FRANCISCO, CA 94143 Lymphatic metastasis of melanoma tumor cells

K11DE-00243-03 (DSR) HARTSFIELD, JAMES K JR UNIVERSITY OF SOUTH FLORIDA BOX 15-G 12901 BRUCE B. DOWNS TAMPA, FL 33612-4799 In vitro murine phenytoin metabolism and oral clefting

K04DE-00247-04 (OBM) PRINCE, CHARLES W UNIV OF ALABAMA AT BIRMINGHAM UNIVERSITY STATION BIRMINGHAM, AL 35294 Proteoglycans & osteopontin in bone formation

K15DE-00249-03 (DSR) SCHMITZ, JOHN P UNIV OF TEXAS HLTH SCI CTR 7703 FLOYD CURL DRIVE SAN ANTONIO, TX 78284 Cellular mechanisms of cranial nonunion formation

Z01DE-00250-14 (MSS) WALCZAK, C A NIDR, NIH Algorithms for microbial systematics

K15DE-00251-04 (DSR) FANNON, LEWIS D, JR UNIVERSITY OF FLORIDA DEPT OF PHYSIOLOGY J-274 JHMHC GAINESVILLE, FL 32610-0274 Autonomic induced immunity impairment in hypertension and periodontal disorders

K15DE-00253-03 (DSR) BINDER, TERRI A HEALTH SCIENCES 630 WEST 168TH STREET Genetic susceptibility to murine experimental allergic encephalomyelitis

K04DE-00254-04 (OBM) GRAVES, DANA T BOSTON UNIV SCH OF DENTISTRY 100 E NEWTON ST, ROOM G-10 BOSTON, MA 02118 Bone-derived cells produce a chemotactic factor

Z01DE-00254-14 (LME) CISAR, J O NIDR, NIH Microbial antigens associated with specific adherence

K04DE-00255-02 (OBM) SHEA, BRIAN T NORTHWESTERN UNIVERSITY 303 EAST CHICAGO AVENUE CHICAGO, IL 60611 Effect of growth hormone on craniofacial proportions

K11DE-00257-03 (DSR) RUBY, JOHN D WEST VIRGINIA UNIVERSITY MORGANTOWN, WV 26506 Periplasmic flagella of Treponema denticola

K11DE-00260-03 (DSR) SPENCER, PAULETTE UNIV OF MISSOURI-KANSAS CITY 650 EAST 25TH STREET KANSAS CITY, MO 64108 Development of a substrate for testing dental adhesion

K15DE-00262-03 (DSR) MORRISON, GRACE M UNIVERSITY OF MICHIGAN 1011 N. UNIVERSITY ANN ARBOR, MI 48109-1078 Dentist scientist award - individual

K11DE-00263-03 (DSR) GARLICK, JONATHAN A ORAL BIOLOGY AND PATHOLOGY STONY BROOK, NY 11794-8700 Tissue specific replication of papillomaviruses

K16DE-00270-02 (SRC) HERZBERG, MARK C UNIVERSITY OF MINNESOTA 1100 WASH. AVE., S., SUITE 201 Institutional Dentist-Scientist Award

Z01DE-00273-13 (LME) KOLENBRANDER, P E NIDR, NIH Cell-cell interaction between oral actinomycetes and other oral bacteria

K16DE-00275-02 (SRC) WILLIAMS, RAY C HARVARD SCHOOL OF DENTAL MED 188 LONGWOOD AVENUE BOSTON, MA 02115 Institutional Dentist Scientist Award

K15DE-00276-03 (DSR) REDFORD-BADWAL, DEBORAH A UNIV OF CONNECTICUT HEALTH CTR 263 FARMINGTON AVENUE FARMINGTON, CT 06030 Mutation identification in heritable chondrodystrophies

K15DE-00277-02 (DSR) ELOVIC, REBECCA P HARVARD SCH OF DENTAL MEDICINE 188 LONGWOOD AVENUE BOSTON, MA 02115 Mechanics and bone remodeling in an osteoporotic mandible

K16DE-00279-02 (SRC) JEFFCOAT, MARJORIE K UNIVERSITY OF ALABAMA BOX 34 UAB STATION BIRMINGHAM, AL 35294 Dentist scientist award--institutional

K11DE-00280-03 (DSR) OHRBACH, RICHARD SUNY AT BUFFALO 355 SQUIRE HALL MED BUFFALO, NY 14214 Psychophysiological assessment of stress in chronic pain

K04DE-00282-03 (OBM) MIYASAKI, KENNETH T UCLA SCHOOL OF MEDICINE CTR FOR THE HLTH. SCI. LOS ANGELES, CA 90024-1668 Control of periodontal bacteria by neutrophils

Z01DE-00282-13 (OPS) MIRTH, D B NIDR, NIH Refinement of the intraoral fluoride releasing device

K15DE-00283-03 (DSR) BODDEN, MARTIN K UNIVERSITY OF ALABAMA UAB STATION BIRMINGHAM, AL 35294 Metalloproteinase inhibitor (TIMP): collagen remodeling

K11DE-00286-03 (DSR) KRONMILLER, JAN E UNIV OF CONNECTICUT HLTH CTR 362 FARMINGTON AVE FARMINGTON, CT 06030 Effects of retinoids and growth factors on branchial arch

Z01DE-00286-12 (NA) DIONNE, R A NIDR, NIH Experimental therapeutics for acute pain

K15DE-00287-04 (DSR) DANIEL, MICHAEL A EASTMAN DENTAL CENTER 625 ELMWOOD AVENUE ROCHESTER, NY 14620 Molecular biology of PMN chemotaxis in LJP

Z01DE-00288-12 (NA) RUDA, M NIDR, NIH Neuropharmacological characterization of synaptic circuitry in the dorsal horn

Z01DE-00290-12 (LI) SIRAGANIAN, R NIDR, NIH Production of hybridomas

K04DE-00291-03 (OBM) HUMPHREYS-BEHER, MICHAEL G UNIVERSITY OF FLORIDA BOX J-424 JHMHC GAINESVILLE, FL 32610 Analysis of parotid gland 4beta-galactosyltransferase

Z01DE-00291-12 (NA) THOMAS, D NIDR, NIH Microinjection of analgesic agents into medullary dorsal horn of monkey

K04DE-00292-02 (OBM) ANN, DAVID K U MINNESOTA MEDICAL SCHOOL 435 DELAWARE STREET, S.E. MINNEAPOLIS, MN 55455 Gene expression of salivary gland specific genes

K11DE-00293-02 (DSR) MAK, GILBERT K UNIV OF SOUTHERN CALIFORNIA UNIVERSITY PARK GER 324,MC-019 LOS ANGELES, CA 90089-0191 Epigenetic growth factors in mandibular morphogenesis

K11DE-00300-01 (DSR) LEVIN, LINDA G UNIVERSITY OF NORTH CAROLINA 405 BRAUER HALL CHAPEL HILL, NC 27599 Mechanisms regulating expression of TGF-alpha mRNA

K11DE-00301-02 (DSR) KATZ, RONALD W UNIVERSITY OF MICHIGAN 1150 W MEDICAL CENTER DRIVE ANN ARBOR, MI 48109-0650 Role of thrombospondin in odontogenesis

K15DE-00302-01A1 (DSR) CHOI, JOHN U UNIV OF SOUTHERN CALIFORNIA LOS ANGELES, CA 90089-0641 Fructosyltransferase from Streptococcus mutans

K15DE-00307-01 (DSR) STERN, MICHAEL UNIVERSITY OF CALIFORNIA HSW 604 SAN FRANCISCO, CA 94143 Hyaluronidase inhibitor in adult and fetal wounds

K15DE-00309-01 (DSR) DEVOLL, ROBERT E UNIV TX HLTH SCIENCE CENTER 6516 JOHN FREEMAN AVENUE HOUSTON, TX 77225 Distribution of osteopontin in neoplastic disease

K11DE-00310-01 (DSR) DAVIS, JACQUELINE K INDIANA UNIVERSITY SCH OF MED 635 BARNHILL DRIVE INDIANAPOLIS, IN 46202-5120 Role of T-cell in pathogenesis of TMJ rheumatoid arthritis

Z01DE-00310-11 (DPHP) DRISCOLL, W S NIDR, NIH Fluoride mouthrinsing and fluoride tablets used separately and in combination

Z01DE-00311-11 (LCDO) PARK, M H NIDR, NIH Hypusine in eIF-4D--Biosynthesis and function

K11DE-00312-01 (DSR) TENCZA, MICHAEL G UNIVERSITY OF NORTH CAROLINA CB #7290, 804 FLOB CHAPEL HILL, NC 27599 The RNase H activity encoded by hepadnaviruses

K15DE-00313-01 (DSR) LINGEN, MARK W NORTHWESTERN UNIVERSITY 303 E CHICAGO AVENUE CHICAGO, IL 60611 Suppressor genes, oncogenes and oral carcinogenesis

K04DE-00318-01 (OBM) WONG, DAVID T HARVARD SCHOOL OF DENTAL MED 188 LONGWOOD AVENUE BOSTON, MA 02115 Molecular determinants of oral carcinogenesis

K11DE-00321-01 (DSR) WERKMEISTER, JAMES R OHIO STATE UNIVERSITY 1925 COFFEY ROAD COLUMBUS, OH 43210 Regulation of parathyroid hormone-related protein

K15DE-00322-01 (DSR) AMALFITANO, JOSEPH UNIVERSITY OF MICHIGAN 1011 N UNIVERSITY, #3209 ANN ARBOR, MI 48109-1078 Effects of periodontopathic bacteria on neutrophils

K11DE-00323-01 (DSR) ELOVIC, ARAM E HARVARD SCHOOL OF DENTAL MED 188 LONGWOOD AVENUE BOSTON, MA 02115 The biology of eosinophil-derived TGF-alpha

K15DE-00325-01 (DSR) COLLINS, JOHN G UNIVERSITY OF NORTH CAROLINA CHAPEL HILL, NC 27599-7450 Neutrophil-platelet interactions in periodontal disease

Z01DE-00329-10 (NA) KENSHALO, D NIDR, NIH Discrimination of thermal stimuli in monkeys

Z01DE-00332-09 (CIPC) ATKINSON, J C NIDR, NIH Clinical investigations and case reports

K04DE-00333-01 (OBM) WIDMER, CHARLES G UNIVERSITY OF FLORIDA BOX J-416, JHMHSC GAINESVILLE, FL 32610-0416 Functional organization and control of human masseters

Z01DE-00336-09 (CIPC) BAUM, B J NIDR, NIH Salivary gland secretory mechanisms during normal and altered functional states

Z01DE-00337-09 (CIPC) FOX, P C NIDR, NIH Oral physiological processes--Normal function and disease perturbation

Z01DE-00341-11 (LME) THOMPSON, J NIDR, NIH Regulation of sugar transport and metabolism in lactic acid bacteria

Z01DE-00366-09 (NA) MAX, M NIDR, NIH Analgesic mechanisms in patients with chronic pain

Z01DE-00379-09 (BRB) YOUNG, M F NIDR, NIH Structure and bone matrix gene expression

Z01DE-00380-08 (BRB) ROBEY, P G NIDR, NIH Metabolism of bone cells in vitro

Z01DE-00382-09 (LMI) ROBRISH, S A NIDR, NIH Growth and interaction of oral microorganisms

Z01DE-00392-08 (LI) SMITH, P D NIDR, NIH Macrophage responses to mucosal microorganisms

Z01DE-00410-07 (EB) LOE, H NIDR, NIH Natural history of periodontal disease in man

Z01DE-00412-06 (CIPC) BRAHIM, J S NIDR, NIH Clinical study of oral endosseous titanium implants in edentulous subjects

Z01DE-00413-06 (NA) BENNETT, G J NIDR, NIH Experimental neuropathy of peripheral nerve in rats

Z01DE-00414-07 (NA) IADAROLA, M J NIDR, NIH CNS neurotransmitter regulation during peripheral inflammatory states

Z01DE-00415-05 (CIPC) TURNER, R J NIDR, NIH Ion transport and fluid secretion in salivary glands

Z01DE-00420-07 (EB) BRUNELLE, J A NIDR, NIH Design and analysis of national survey of oral health in school children

Z01DE-00421-07 (LOM) ROONEY, J F NIDR, NIH Herpes simplex virus and persistent infections

Z01DE-00423-06 (LOM) LAN, M NIDR, NIH Cloning, expression and characterization of human autoantigens

Z01DE-00424-05 (LI) MCCARTNEY-FRANCIS, N L NIDR, NIH Molecular analysis of monocyte phenotype and function

Z01DE-00431-04 (BRB) YANAGISHITA, M NIDR, NIH Metabolism of proteoglycans

Z01DE-00433-05 (LCDO) ROBEY, F A NIDR, NIH Functional aspects of C-reactive protein

Z01DE-00434-05 (LCDO) ROBEY, F A NIDR, NIH HIV-1 targeted drug delivery systems

Z01DE-00437-05 (LCDO) ROBEY, F A NIDR, NIH Peptide polymers as vaccine candidates

Z01DE-00438-04 (CIPC) AMBUDKAR, I S NIDR, NIH Molecular mechanisms regulating calcium flux in salivary glands

Z01DE-00439-05 (DPHP) NOWJACK-RAYMER, R E NIDR, NIH Different approaches to prevent gingivitis in teenage children

Z01DE-00440-05 (91) REN, K NIDR, NIH Dorsal horn circuitry related to pain--Inflammation-induced plasticity

Z01DE-00441-05 (LI) ALLEN, J NIDR, NIH Immunoregulation of experimentally induced immune responses

Z01DE-00454-05 (LME) LONDON, J NIDR, NIH Role of surface molecules in the metabolism and ecology of oral bacteria

Z01DE-00456-04 (LI) WAHL, L M NIDR, NIH Signal transduction in the monocyte-macrophage

Z01DE-00458-03 (CIPC) KOUSVELARI, E NIDR, NIH Beta-adrenoreceptors and gene regulation

Z01DE-00460-04 (NA) NAHIN, R L NIDR, NIH Neuroanatomical mechanisms of pain transmission and modulation

Z01DE-00462-04 (OPS) SHOU-HUA, L NIDR, NIH Methods for estimating age-specific DMFT and DMFS scores in the U.S.

Z01DE-00464-04 (EB) SWANGO, P A NIDR, NIH Natural history of oral manifestations of HIV infection

Z01DE-00467-04 (LOM) HARINDRANATH, N NIDR, NIH Human B cell repertoire and autoantibodies

Z01DE-00471-04 (LOM) FRANKS, R NIDR, NIH Transgenic mice as a model for studies of AIDS and other diseases

Z01DE-00475-04 (ASB) BROWN, L J NIDR, NIH Utilization, treatment needs, cost, and dental disease in veterans

Z01DE-00479-03 (LCDO) ROBBINS, K C NIDR, NIH Molecular mechanisms responsible for oncogenesis

Z01DE-00480-03 (LCDO) ROBBINS, K C NIDR, NIH Physiological roles for nonreceptor protein-tyrosine kinase

Z01DE-00481-03 (DB) BRUGGEMAN, L NIDR, NIH Connective tissue gene expression in development and disease

Z01DE-00482-03 (DB) KLEINMAN, H NIDR, NIH Tumor growth and metastases

Z01DE-00483-03 (DB) YAMADA, Y NIDR, NIH Gene regulation and function of cartilage

Z01DE-00484-03 (DB) YAMADA, Y NIDR, NIH Animal models of connective tissue diseases

Z01DE-00485-03 (DB) YAMADA, Y NIDR, NIH Gene regulation and function of basement membrane

Z01DE-00495-03 (ASB) BROWN, L J NIDR, NIH Relation between dental conditions and utilization of dental services

Z01DE-00496-03 (ASB) BROWN, L J NIDR, NIH Determinants of permanent tooth loss in Connecticut and North Carolina

Z01DE-00497-03 (ASB) BROWN, L J NIDR, NIH Forecasting dental health and utilization using a microsimulation model

Z01DE-00498-02 (LME) LONDON, J P NIDR, NIH Identification and enumeration of oral bacteria from HIV-1 infected subjects

Z01DE-00499-02 (CIPC) ATKINSON, J C NIDR, NIH Oral health and salivary function in HIV-1 infected patients

Z01DE-00500-02 (CIPC) SHIP, J A NIDR, NIH Oral physiology of aging

Z01DE-00501-02 (OPS) LI, S-H NIDR, NIH Surface-specific attack rates in primary teeth from two national surveys

Z01DE-00502-02 (CIPC) BRAHIM, J S NIDR, NIH Maxillofacial surgery--Rigid vs. nonrigid fixation following orthognathic surgery

Z01DE-00503-02 (OPS) MILLER-CHISHOLM, A NIDR, NIH Public use tapes documentation--1986-87 and 1979-80 surveys of school children

Z01DE-00504-02 (OPS) SNOWDEN, C B NIDR, NIH Statistical analyses of the 1986-87 and 1979-80 NIDR surveys of school children

Z01DE-00505-02 (OPS) SNOWDEN, C B NIDR, NIH Public use tape documentation--Survey of oral health in employed adults, 1985-86

Z01DE-00506-02 (OPS) MILLER-CHISHOLM, A NIDR, NIH Public use tape documentation--Survey of oral health in seniors, 1985-86

Z01DE-00507-02 (BRB) TORCHIA, D A NIDR, NIH NMR studies of the structure and interactions of an HIV-inhibitor complex

Z01DE-00508-02 (DB) KLOTMAN, P NIDR, NIH Pathogenesis of Human Immunodeficiency Virus 1 (HIV 1)

Z01DE-00509-02 (NA) BENNET, G J NIDR, NIH Neurosensory mechanisms in painful neuropathy

Z01DE-00510-03 (BRB) MORALES, T I NIDR, NIH Regulation of cartilage matrix metabolism

Z01DE-00512-02 (LME) GENTRY-WEEKS, C R NIDR, NIH Genetic analysis of Bordetella avium pathogenicity

Z01DE-00513-02 (LI) WAHL, S M NIDR, NIH Role of monocytes in AIDS and as targets for antiviral therapy

Z01DE-00514-02 (LME) LEPPLA, S H NIDR, NIH Anthrax toxin--A model for bacterial pathogenesis

Z01DE-00515-02 (ASB) BROWN, L J NIDR, NIH Studies of periodontal health in adult americans

Z01DE-00517-02 (ASB) BROWN, L J NIDR, NIH Alveolar bone loss and aging among healthy U.S. males

Z01DE-00518-02 (LME) KEITH, J M NIDR, NIH Development of detoxified pertussis toxin for acellular whooping cough vaccine

Z01DE-00519-02 (EODP) KINGMAN, A NIDR, NIH Measurement error in assessing periodontal diseases

Z01DE-00520-02 (EODP) KINGMAN, A NIDR, NIH Surface-specific attack rates in Iceland and the U.S.

Z01DE-00521-02 (EODP) KINGMAN, A NIDR, NIH Predictive value of salivary assays in predicting dental caries

Z01DE-00522-02 (EODP) KINGMAN, A NIDR, NIH Statistical issues for gingivitis trials of superiority and equivalence

Z01DE-00523-02 (DPHP) DRISCOLL, W S NIDR, NIH Prevalence of dental caries and dental fluorosis in relation to water fluoride

Z01DE-00524-01 (DB) YAMADA, K NIDR, NIH Function and developmental regulation of matrix receptors

Z01DE-00525-01 (DB) YAMADA, K NIDR, NIH Regulation of cell adhesion, migration, and morphogenesis

Z01DE-00526-01 (NA) DELEON, M NIDR, NIH Cloning of genes regulated during neural injury and nerve regen.

Z01DE-00527-01 (OPS) SNOWDEN, C NIDR, NIH Software for analysing data from complex dental surveys

Z01DE-00528-01 (OPS) SNOWDEN, C NIDR, NIH Statistical methods and software for analysis of geographic ref.data

Z01DE-00529-01 (LOM) LE THI, B-T NIDR, NIH Mechanism regulating polyreactive antibody production

Z01DE-00530-01 (DPHP) GIFT, H NIDR, NIH Improving understanding

PROJECT NO., ORGANIZATIONAL UNIT., INVESTIGATOR, ADDRESS, TITLE

of oral disease prevention strategies

Z01DE-00531-01 (EB) BRUNELLE, J NIDR, NIH Diagnostic criteria manual for epidemiological surveys

Z01DE-00532-01 (NA) REID, K NIDR, NIH Pathophysiology of chronic pain

Z01DE-00533-02 (LI) BRANDES, M NIDR, NIH Regulation of leukocyte recruitment, activation and survival by cytokines

Z01DE-00534-01 (LOM) RANDO, R F NIDR, NIH Cloning of the human immunoglobulin repertoire in E. coli

Z01DE-00535-01 (LOM) DORFMAN, N NIDR, NIH Development of human monoclonal antibodies specific for HIV gP160

Z01DE-00536-01 (LOM) KEARNS, M K NIDR, NIH Transgenic mice containing the CR2 gene for the EBV receptor

Z01DE-00537-01 (LME) LEPPLA, S NIDR, NIH Protein virulence factors of bacterial periodontal pathogens

Z01DE-00538-01 (EB) BHAT, M NIDR, NIH Developmental enamel defects in children with cerebral palsy

Z01DE-00539-01 (ASB) OLDAKOWSKI, R J NIDR, NIH Comparing micro-computers to mainframes in statistical analysis

Z01DE-00540-01 (ASB) MARCUS, S E NIDR, NIH Smoking and oral health

Z01DE-00541-01 (ASB) MARCUS, S E NIDR, NIH The use of smokeless tobacco and oral health

Z01DE-00542-01 (ASB) BROWN, L J NIDR, NIH Analysis of trends in and risk factors for permanent tooth loss

Z01DE-00543-01 (ASB) TREACY, J G NIDR, NIH Optimizing throughput on an IBM RISC 6000 system

Z01DE-00544-01 (ASB) BROWN, L J NIDR, NIH Studies of periodontal health in adolescent americans

Z01DE-00545-01 (ASB) BROWN, L J NIDR, NIH Longitudinal studies of periodontal health in Norwegians and Sri Lankans

R37DE-01374-31 (OBM) VEIS, ARTHUR NORTHWESTERN UNIVERSITY 303 EAST CHICAGO AVENUE CHICAGO, IL 60611 Matrix component interactions in bone and dentin

R01DE-02110-27 (OBM) SCHNEYER, CHARLOTTE A UNIV OF ALABAMA AT BIRMINGHAM UAB STATION BIRMINGHAM, ALA 35294 Salivary gland structure and function

R01DE-02525-25 (OBM) SIMMELINK, JAMES W CASE WESTERN RES UNIV 2123 ABINGTON RD CLEVELAND, OH 44106 Ultrastructural histopathology of dental enamel

N01DE-02578-04 ( ) CALDWELL, STEVEN** Development of a computer forecasting model of tooth loss

N01DE-02579-01 ( ) SEYBOLD, VIRGINIA S** Postmortem studies of painful peripheral neuropathy

N01DE-02580-03 ( ) KLAUS, ROBERT J** Adult oral health promotion initiative

N01DE-02581-02 ( ) DEPAOLA, PAUL F** Self-applied fluoride/root caries/coronal caries

N01DE-02582-03 ( ) HALL, MARGRUETTA** Epidemiologic issues of the oral health of black Americans

P01DE-02847-23 (SSS) SOCRANSKY, SIGMUND S FORSYTH DENTAL CENTER 140 THE FENWAY BOSTON, MA 02115 Microbial ecology and its relation to dental disease

P01DE-02847-23 0024 (SSS) GIBBONS, RONALD Microbial ecology and its relation to dental disease Molecular basis for gingival microbial interactions

P01DE-02847-23 0025 (SSS) GIBBONS, RONALD Microbial ecology and its relation to dental disease Neuraminidases and proteases modulating gingival plaque

P01DE-02847-23 0026 (SSS) GIBBONS, RONALD Microbial ecology and its relation to dental disease Bacterial chemotaxis in subgingival colonization

P01DE-02847-23 0027 (SSS) GIBBONS, RONALD Microbial ecology and its relation to dental disease Bacterial flora in periodontally involved sites

R01DE-02936-23 (OBM) MAHLER, DAVID B OREGON HLTH SCI UNIV 611 S W CAMPUS DRIVE PORTLAND, OREG 97201 Relationship of microstructure to behavior of amalgam

R01DE-03180-20 (OBM) ROSAN, BURTON UNIVERSITY OF PENNSYLVANIA 4001 SPRUCE STREET PHILADELPHIA, PA 19104-6003 Microbiologic studies of human oral streptococci

R37DE-03187-20 (NSS) MORENO, EDGARD C FORSYTH DENTAL CENTER 140 THE FENWAY BOSTON, MASS 02115 Transport in enamel and solubility of enamel

R37DE-03223-21 (OBM) NANCOLLAS, GEORGE H S U N Y AT BUFFALO ACHESON HALL, SOUTH CAMPUS BUFFALO, NY 14214 The kinetics of mineralization of teeth

R37DE-03258-20 (NSS) KURAMITSU, HOWARD K UNIVERSITY OF TEXAS 7703 FLOYD CURL DRIVE SAN ANTONIO, TX 78284-7888 Molecular genetic analysis of S. mutans cariogenicity

R37DE-03420-18 (OBM) TAUBMAN, MARTIN A FORSYTH DENTAL CENTER 140 FENWAY BOSTON, MA 02115 Regulatory cells in experimental periodontal disease

R01DE-03578-18A1 (PC) ROBYT, JOHN F IOWA STATE UNIVERSITY GILMAN HALL AMES, IA 50011 Biosynthetic study of dental plaque polysaccharides

R37DE-03606-22 (MBC) ANDERSON, DWIGHT L UNIV OF MINNESOTA SCHL OF DENT 515 DELAWARE STREET S E MINNEAPOLIS, MN 55455 Morphogenesis of bacteriophage Phi-29

R37DE-03658-27 (OBM) AZEN, EDWIN A UNIVERSITY OF WISCONSIN 1300 UNIVERSITY AVENUE MADISON, WI 53706 Genetic polymorphisms of saliva

R01DE-03739-19 (OBM) MOOSER, GREGORY UNIV OF SOUTHERN CALIFORNIA 925 W 34TH STREET LOS ANGELES, CA 90089-0641 Glycosyltransferases from oral bacteria

R37DE-03915-18 (OBM) HAY, DONALD I FORSYTH DENTAL CENTER 140 FENWAY BOSTON, MA 02115 Tooth-saliva interface phenomena and dental caries

R37DE-03967-17 (OBM) GOLUB, LORNE M SUNY AT STONY BROOK SCHOOL OF DENTAL MEDICINE, HSC STONY BROOK, NY 11794 Gingival collagen metabolism in health & disease

R01DE-04008-16 (OBM) CAPLAN, ARNOLD I CASE WESTERN RESERVE UNIV CLEVELAND, OH 44106 Cellular and developmental control of calcification

PROJECT NO., ORGANIZATIONAL UNIT., INVESTIGATOR, ADDRESS, TITLE

R37DE-04141-17 (OBM) BOSKEY, ADELE L HOSPITAL FOR SPECIAL SURGERY 535 EAST 70TH STREET NEW YORK, N Y 10021 Mechanism of hard tissue mineralization

R37DE-04166-22 (OBM) GOLDBERG, LOUIS J UNIV OF CALIFORNIA, LOS ANGELE SCHOOL OF DENTISTRY LOS ANGELES, CA 90024 Oral pharyngeal reflexes

R37DE-04217-17 (OBM) MC GHEE, JERRY R UNIV OF ALABAMA AT BIRMINGHAM UAB STATION BIRMINGHAM, AL 35294 Caries immunity--Regulation of anti-S. mutans responses

R37DE-04224-17 (NSS) MACRINA, FRANCIS L VIRGINIA COMMONWEALTH UNIV BOX 678, MCV STATION RICHMOND, VA 23298-0678 Studies on the genetics of oral microflora

R01DE-04235-14 (OBM) THOMAS, EDWIN L UNIV OF TENNESSEE, MEMPHIS 894 UNION AVENUE MEMPHIS, TN 38163 Peroxidase in saliva and prevention of oral disease

R01DE-04316-14A2 (HED) WESTON, JAMES A UNIVERSITY OF OREGON EUGENE, OR 97403 Environmenal control of neural crest development

R01DE-04345-16 (OBM) GAY, CAROL V PENNSYLVANIA STATE UNIVERSITY 468A SOUTH FREAR BLDG UNIVERSITY PARK, PA 16802 Cell biology of osteoclasts

R01DE-04358-15 (BEM) GALE, ELLIOT N SUNY AT BUFFALO 3435 MAIN STREET BUFFALO, NY 14214 Treatment of temporomandibular joint pain

R01DE-04385-15 (OBM) VOGEL, GERALD L AMERICAN DENTAL ASSOC HLTH FDN GAITHERSBURG, MD 20899 Mechanism of dental caries

R01DE-04486-11 (OBM) WEFEL, JAMES S UNIV OF IOWA COLL OF DENTISTRY IOWA CITY, IA 52242 Mechanisms of fluoride action--in vitro and in vivo studies

R37DE-04511-16 (OBM) TAICHMAN, LORNE B SUNY AT STONY BROOK SCHOOL OF DENTAL MEDICINE STONY BROOK, NY 11794-8702 Stability of differentiation--Craniofacial study

R01DE-04529-13A2 (OBM) HILLMAN, JEFFREY D FORSYTH DENTAL CENTER 140 FENWAY BOSTON, MA 02115 Replacement therapy of dental caries

R37DE-04531-13 (OBM) HYLANDER, WILLIAM L DUKE UNIVERSITY MEDICAL CENTER BOX 3170 DURHAM, N C 27710 Strain in the facial bones of macaca fascicularis

R37DE-04614-15 (OBM) LILJEMARK, WILLIAM F UNIVERSITY OF MINNESOTA 515 DELAWARE STREET S E MINNEAPOLIS, MINN 55455 Adherence of dental plaque bacteria to hydroxyapatite

R37DE-04660-16 (OBM) DALE, BEVERLY A UNIVERSITY OF WASHINGTON SCHOOL OF DENTISTRY SEATTLE, WASH 98195 Keratohyalin in keratinization of oral mucosa and skin

R01DE-04724-13 (OBM) BARON, ROLAND E YALE UNIVERSITY 333 CEDAR STREET NEW HAVEN, CONN 06510 Cellular events in bone remodeling

R01DE-04733-13 (OBM) TAUBMAN, MARTIN A FORSYTH DENTAL CENTER 140 FENWAY BOSTON, MA 02115 Synthetic peptide vaccines for dental caries

R01DE-04786-14 (CMS) SESSLE, BARRY J UNIVERSITY OF TORONTO 124 EDWARD STREET TORONTO, ONTARIO CANADA M5G 1G Dental and orofacial pain brain stem mechanisms

P50DE-04881-14 (SRC) SOCRANSKY, SIGMUND S FORSYTH DENTAL CENTER 140 THE FENWAY BOSTON, MASS 02115 Clinical research in periodontal diseases

P50DE-04881-14 0004 (SRC) HAFFAJEE, ANNE D Clinical research in periodontal diseases Bone destruction in periodontal disease

P50DE-04881-14 0001 (SRC) SOCRANSKY, SIGMUND S Clinical research in periodontal diseases Diagnosis and treatment of destructive periodontal diseases

P50DE-04881-14 0002 (SRC) SOCRANSKY, SIGMUND S Clinical research in periodontal diseases Relationship of subgingival microbiota to etiology of periodontal disease

P50DE-04881-14 0003 (SRC) HAFFAJEE, ANNE D Clinical research in periodontal diseases Host immunologic response to oral microorganisms

R01DE-04897-11 (OBM) MARTINEZ, J RICARDO LOVELACE MEDICAL FOUNDATION 2425 RIDGECREST DR SE ALBUQUERQUE, N M 87108 Functional development of salivary glands

P50DE-04898-14 (SRC) GENCO, ROBERT J SUNY AT BUFFALO 3435 MAIN STREET BUFFALO, N Y 14214 Periodontal disease research center

P50DE-04898-14 0001 (SRC) ZAMBON, JOSEPH Periodontal disease research center Microbiologic studies

P50DE-04898-14 0002 (SRC) WILSON, MARIE Periodontal disease research center Host response studies

P50DE-04898-14 0003 (SRC) CHRISTERRSON, LARS A Periodontal disease research center Therapy and prevention of periodontal diseases

R01DE-04942-11 (NLS) WESTRUM, LESNICK E UNIVERSITY OF WASHINGTON DEPT. NEUROLOGICAL SURG. RI-20 SEATTLE, WA 98195 Teeth and trigeminal pathways

R01DE-04960-13 (OBM) DENNY, PAUL C UNIV OF SOUTHERN CALIF/SCH DEN SCHOOL OF DENTISTRY LOS ANGELES, CA 90089-0641 Mechanisms of salivary gland development

R01DE-05030-13 (OBM) MATHEW, MATHAI AMERICAN DENTAL ASSOC HLTH FDN NATL INST OF STANDARDS & TECH GAITHERSBURG, MD 20899 Crystal chemistry of calcium phosphates

R37DE-05092-14 (OBM) BUTLER, WILLIAM T UNIVERSITY TEXAS HEALTH SCI CT PO BOX 20068 HOUSTON, TX 77225 Proteins involved in dentinogenesis

R01DE-05102-11A2 (OBM) TAYLOR, K GRANT UNIVERSITY OF LOUISVILLE LOUISVILLE, KY 40292 Potential anti-caries agents

R37DE-05129-14 (OBM) BOWEN, RAFAEL L AMERICAN DENTAL ASSOC HLTH FDN PAFFENBARGER RESEARCH CENTER GAITHERSBURG, MD 20899 Improvement of preventive and restorative materials

R01DE-05159-13 (NLS) BYERS, MARGARET R UNIV OF WASHINGTON SEATTLE, WA 98195 Distribution and ultrastructure of dental innervation

R01DE-05180-10A3 (OBM) DANEO-MOORE, LOLITA TEMPLE UNIVERSITY SCHOOL OF ME 3400 N BROAD ST PHILADELPHIA, PA 19140 Regulation of surface synthesis in Streptococcus mutans

R37DE-05215-13 (OBM) PROFFIT, WILLIAM R UNIVERSITY OF NORTH CAROLINA CHAPEL HILL, NC 27599-7450 Influences on stability following orthognathic surgery

R01DE-05249-12 (OBM) WATSON, EILEEN L UNIVERSITY OF WASHINGTON SEATTLE, WA 98195 Salivary secretion--Role of calcium

R01DE-05253-09A4 (OBM) KASHKET, SHELBY FORSYTH DENTAL CENTER 140 FENWAY BOSTON, MA 02115 Measurements of enamel permeability as related to caries

R01DE-05262-12 (OBM) ANDERSON, HARRISON C UNIVERSITY OF KANSAS MEDICAL C 39TH AND RAINBOW BOULEVARD KANSAS CITY, KS 66103 Mineralization studies related to oral biology

R01DE-05354-14 (OBM) CHOW, LAURENCE C AMER DENTAL ASSOC HLTH FDN NATIONAL INST/STANDARDS & TECH GAITHERSBURG, MD 20899 Prevention of dental caries

R01DE-05395-11 (OBM) MACKENZIE, IAN C U OF TEXAS HLTH SCI CTR/HOUSTO PO BOX 20068 HOUSTON, TX 77225 Stem cells in oral mucosa

R01DE-05404-12 (NLS) DOSTROVSKY, JONATHAN O UNIVERSITY OF TORONTO TORONTO, ONTARIO M5S 1A8 CANAD Neural mechanisms of nociception in the face and mouth

R01DE-05413-12 (GMB) TEITELBAUM, STEVEN L JEWISH HOSP AT WASHINGTON UNIV 216 SOUTH KINGSHIGHWAY ST. LOUIS, MO 63110 Bone resorption in periodontal disease

R01DE-05423-10 (OBM) O'BRIEN, WILLIAM J UNIVERSITY OF MICHIGAN ANN ARBOR, MI 48109-1078 Diffuse reflectance by esthetic dental materials

R01DE-05429-11 (OBM) CLARK, WILLIAM B UNIVERSITY OF FLORIDA BOX J-424 JHMHC GAINESVILLE, FL 32610 Adherence of periodontal disease-associated bacteria

R01DE-05476-10 (BNP) GOODMAN, MURRAY UNIV OF CALIFORNIA, SAN DIEGO LA JOLLA, CA 92093 Novel peptide derived sweeteners

R01DE-05494-11 (OBM) PABST, MICHAEL J UNIV OF TENNESSEE, MEMPHIS 894 UNION AVENUE MEMPHIS, TN 38163 Activation of macrophages in periodontal disease

R01DE-05501-10 (OBM) HERZBERG, MARK C UNIVERSITY OF MINNESOTA 17-164 MOOS TOWER MINNEAPOLIS, MN 55455 Platelet-streptococcal interactions in endocarditis

R01DE-05550-10A2 (OBM) GREENE, ROBERT M JEFFERSON MEDICAL COLLEGE 1020 LOCUST STREET PHILADELPHIA, PA 19107 Signal transduction during craniofacial embryogenesis

R01DE-05606-11 (BM) FIVES-TAYLOR, PAULA M UNIVERSITY OF VERMONT GIVEN MEDICAL BUILDING BURLINGTON, VT 05405 Fimbriae of S. sanguis and their role in adhesion

R01DE-05626-10 (NTN) CERKLEWSKI, FLORIAN L OREGON STATE UNIVERSITY COLLEGE OF HOME ECONOMICS CORVALLIS, OR 97331 Interaction between fluoride and other dietary minerals

R01DE-05666-12 (OBM) SLOMIANY, BRONISLAW L UMDNJ - NEW JERSEY DENTAL SCH 110 BERGEN STREET NEWARK, NJ 07103-2400 Biochemistry of salivary lipids

R37DE-05672-09 (OBM) OPPENHEIM, FRANK G BOSTON UNIVERSITY 100 E NEWTON ST BOSTON, MA 02118 Anionic salivary proteins in dental integuments

R01DE-05764-10 (OBM) RUBIN, RONALD P SUNY AT BUFFALO BUFFALO, NY 14214 Cellular pharmacology of salivary secretion

R01DE-05780-08 (OBM) DEUTSCH, DAN HEBREW UNIVERSITY PO BOX 1172 JERUSALEM, ISRAEL Development and mineralization of enamel in teeth

P01DE-05837-10 (SSS) MORRIS, HUGHLETT L UNIV OF IOWA HOSP & CLINICS THE UNIVERSITY OF IOWA IOWA CITY, IA 52242 Growth, surgical and speech aspects of cleft palate

P01DE-05837-10 0001 (SSS) VAN DEMARK, D R Growth, surgical and speech aspects of cleft palate Speech pathology

P01DE-05837-10 0002 (SSS) KREMENAK, C R Growth, surgical and speech aspects of cleft palate Maxillofacial growth

P01DE-05837-10 0003 (SSS) MOON, JERRY B Growth, surgical and speech aspects of cleft palate Speech physiology

P01DE-05837-10 0004 (SSS) BARDACH, J Growth, surgical and speech aspects of cleft palate Cleft lip and palate surgery

P01DE-05837-10 0005 (SSS) RICHMAN, L C Growth, surgical and speech aspects of cleft palate Developmental neuropsychology project

R01DE-05838-12 (CBY) TOOLE, BRYAN P TUFTS UNIVERSITY 136 HARRISON AVE BOSTON, MA 02111 Morphogenetic role of glycosaminoglycans

R01DE-05932-09 (OBM) BOYAN, BARBARA D UNIV OF TEXAS HLTH SCI CTR 7703 FLOYD CURL DRIVE SAN ANTONIO, TX 78284 Role of lipoproteins in microbial calcification

R01DE-05937-10 (OBM) BOYAN, BARBARA D UNIV OF TEXAS HLTH SCI CTR 7703 FLOYD CURL DRIVE SAN ANTONIO, TX 78284 Role of membranes in mineralization of bones and teeth

R01DE-05978-07A1 (OBM) ALAM, SYED Q LOUISIANA STATE UNIV MED CTR 1100 FLORIDA AVENUE NEW ORLEANS, LA 70119 Lipid nutrition, membrane fluidity and salivary enzymes

R01DE-05989-07A2 (BEM) DOHRENWEND, BRUCE P COLUMBIA UNIVERSITY 600 WEST 168TH STREET NEW YORK, NY 10032 Myofascial pain-dysfunction syndrome and life stress

R01DE-05996-07A2 (OBM) MARKS, SANDY C, JR UNIV OF MASSACHUSETTS MED SCH 55 LAKE AVENUE NORTH WORCESTER, MA 01655 Regulation of tooth eruption

R01DE-06000-10 (OBM) JOHNSON, DORTHEA A UNIV OF TEXAS HLTH SCI CTR 7703 FLOYD CURL DRIVE SAN ANTONIO, TX 78284 Effect of parotid function on saliva and cells

R01DE-06007-09 (OBM) MILLER, SCOTT C UNIVERSITY OF UTAH SALT LAKE CITY, UT 84112 Periodontal tissue changes during pregnancy-lactation

R01DE-06014-10 (OBM) SHENKER, BRUCE J UNIVERSITY OF PENNSYLVANIA 4010 LOCUST STREET PHILADELPHIA, PA 19104-6002 Bacteria and lymphocyte suppression in periodontitis

R01DE-06027-10 (OBM) CAPRA, NORMAN F UNIV OF MARYLAND DENTAL SCHOOL 666 W. BALTIMORE STREET BALTIMORE, MD 21201 Kinesthetic mechanisms in the trigeminal system

R01DE-06065-10 (OBM) SCHNEIDER, GARY B LOYOLA UNIVERSITY OF CHICAGO 2160 SOUTH FIRST AVENUE MAYWOOD, ILL 60153 Natural immunity and bone resorption

R01DE-06070-06 (OBM) WALKER, CLAY B UNIVERSITY OF FLORIDA BOX J424 JHMHC GAINESVILLE, FL 32610 Antibiotic susceptibilities of periodontal bacteria

R01DE-06103-08 (OBM) KALDAHL, WAYNE B UNIV OF NEBRASKA MED CTR COLLEGE OF DENTISTRY LINCOLN, NE 68583-0740 Evaluation of four modalities of periodontal therapy

R55DE-06112-09A1 (OBM) MERTZ-FAIRHURST, EVA J MEDICAL COLLEGE OF GEORGIA 1120 FIFTEENTH STREET AUGUSTA, GA 30912-1260 Filled sealant as a conservative restorative material

R01DE-06115-07 (OBM) DOWD, FRANK J CREIGHTON UNIVERSITY CALIFORNIA AT 24TH ST OMAHA, NE 68178 Parotid ectoATPase purinergic responses and ectokinase

R01DE-06127-09 (OBM) MARQUIS, ROBERT E UNIVERSITY OF ROCHESTER 601 ELMWOOD AVENUE ROCHESTER, N Y 14642 Acid-base physiology of oral streptococci

R01DE-06153-09 (OBM) SMITH, DANIEL J FORSYTH DENTAL CTR 140 FENWAY BOSTON, MA 02115 Antibody to glucosyltransferase in adults and children

R01DE-06159-08 (OBM) SCHLESINGER, DAVID H NEW YORK UNIV MED CTR 550 FIRST AVENUE NEW YORK, NY 10016 Protein inhibitors of calcium phosphate precipitation

R01DE-06179-07 (OBM) CABASSO, ISRAEL STATE UNIVERSITY OF NEW YORK 225 BAKER LABORATORY SYRACUSE, N Y 13210 Radiopaque restorative and prosthetic dental resins

R01DE-06193-09 (NEUB) CHANDLER, SCOTT H U OF CALIFORNIA, LOS ANGELES 405 HILGARD AVE LOS ANGELES, CA 90024-1568 Brain stem mechanisms controlling rhythmical jaw movement

R01DE-06219-08 (SSP) LERESCHE, LINDA UNIVERSITY OF WASHINGTON SEATTLE, WA 98195 Facial behavior related to acute dental pain

R37DE-06374-10 (OBM) FAIRHURST, CARL W MEDICAL COLLEGE OF GEORGIA AUGUSTA, GA 30912-1264 Semi-and nonprecious metal-porcelain systems

R01DE-06425-08 (OBM) SLAVKIN, HAROLD C UNIV OF SOUTHERN CALIFORNIA UNIVERSITY PARK GER 314, MC-01 LOS ANGELES, CA 90089-0191 Nutritional studies of tooth development in vitro

R01DE-06427-10 (OBM) PASHLEY, DAVID H MEDICAL COLLEGE OF GEORGIA SCHOOL OF DENTISTRY AUGUSTA, GA 30912-1129 Permeability characteristics of dentin

R01DE-06429-08 (OBM) WHITFORD, GARY M MEDICAL COLLEGE OF GEORGIA SCHOOL OF DENTISTRY AUGUSTA, GA 30912-1129 Influence of acid-base status on fluoride metabolism

R01DE-06533-09 (OBM) GOLUB, ELLIS E UNIV OF PENNSYLVANIA 4001 SPRUCE STREET PHILADELPHIA, PA 19104 Vesicles and endochondral bone formation

R01DE-06552-07 (OBM) FOX, JEFFREY L UNIVERSITY OF UTAH COLLEGE OF PHARMACY SALT LAKE CITY, UT 84112 Hydroxyapatite remineralization--Role of fluoride

R01DE-06563-08 (OBM) MARSHALL, GRAYSON W UNIV OF CALIFORNIA, SAN FRANCI SAN FRANCISCO, CA 94143-0758 Microstructure vs. deterioration of amalgam restorations

R01DE-06632-08 (OBM) NODEN, DREW M NY STATE COLL OF VETERINARY ME CORNELL UNIVERSITY ITHACA, NY 14853 Development of head nerves, blood vessels, bones, muscle

R01DE-06635-07 (OBM) BALL, WILLIAM D HOWARD UNIVERSITY DEPT. OF ANATOMY WASHINGTON, D C 20059 Tissue interactions and salivary cytodifferentiation

R01DE-06672-09 (OBM) ANUSAVICE, KENNETH J UNIVERSITY OF FLORIDA GAINESVILLE, FL 32610-0446 Optimization of restoration design

R37DE-06673-09 (OBM) CURTISS, ROY, III WASHINGTON UNIVERSITY DEPT. OF BIOLOGY ST. LOUIS, MO 63130 Genetic and biochemical bases for S mutans virulence

R01DE-06682-08 (NLS) BEITZ, ALVIN J UNIVERSITY OF MINNESOTA 1988 FITCH AVENUE ST PAUL, MN 55108 CNS modulation of orofacial input to the nucleus of V

R01DE-06720-08 (OBM) LANG, BRIEN R UNIV OF MICHIGAN 1011 N UNIVERSITY AVENUE ANN ARBOR, MI 48109 In-vivo wear resistance of various restorative materials

R01DE-06739-07 (OBM) PRINCE, CHARLES W UNIV OF ALABAMA AT BIRMINGHAM UAB STATION BIRMINGHAM, AL 35294 Biochemical studies of mineralized tissue proteoglycans

R01DE-06746-08 (OBM) RUSSELL, MICHAEL W UNIV OF ALABAMA AT BIRMINGHAM UAB STATION BIRMINGHAM, AL 35294 Antigens of streptococcus mutans in caries immunity

R01DE-06869-08 (OBM) ARNOLD, ROLAND R UNIVERSITY OF NORTH CAROLINA CHAPEL HILL, NC 27599-7455 Bactericidal activity of lactoferrin on oral flora

R01DE-06881-09 (OBM) VIG, PETER S UNIVERSITY OF PITTSBURGH PITTSBURGH, PA 15261 Oral facial morphology and breathing--Quantitative studies

R01DE-06886-09 (OBM) SYFTESTAD, GLENN T UNIV OF CALIFORNIA, DAVIS ORTHOPAEDIC RES LABS, TB 150 DAVIS, CA 95616 Chondrogenic stimulating factors in adult bone matrix

R01DE-06891-06 (ORTH) OSDOBY, PHILIP A WASHINGTON UNIVERSITY SCHOOL OF DENTAL MEDICINE ST. LOUIS, MO 63110 Cellular basis of craniofacial bone disorders

R01DE-06892-08 (OBM) DENNY, PAUL C UNIV OF SOUTHERN CALIFORNIA LOS ANGELES, CA 90089-0641 Salivary mucin synthesis, processing and secretion

R01DE-06894-04A4 (SAT) QUOCK, RAYMOND M UNIVERSITY OF ILLINOIS 1601 PARKVIEW AVENUE ROCKFORD, IL 61107-1897 Nitrous oxide and endogenous opioid systems

R01DE-06950-03A2 (BEM) MILGROM, PETER M UNIVERSITY OF WASHINGTON SM-35 SEATTLE, WA 98195 Epidemiology of dental fear

R01DE-06954-07 (OBM) WEINER, STEPHEN THE WEIZMANN INST OF SCIENCE REHOVOT, 76100 ISRAEL Structural studies of matrix proteins in teeth and bones

R01DE-06957-08 (OBM) WARREN, DONALD W UNIVERSITY OF NORTH CAROLINA CHAPEL HILL, NC 27599 Nasal airway and respiratory mode in cleft palate

R01DE-06988-07 (OBM) SNEAD, MALCOLM L UNIV OF SOUTHERN CALIFORNIA 2250 ALCAZAR ST CLIN/SCI 1ST F LOS ANGELES, CA 90033 Determination and expression of amelogenin gene products

P50DE-07003-08 (SRC) BOWEN, WILLIAM H UNIVERSITY OF ROCHESTER 601 ELMWOOD AVE ROCHESTER, NY 14642 Rochester caries research center

P50DE-07003-08 0001 (SRC) MARQUIS, ROBERT E Rochester caries research center Implantable ammonia-producing streptococci

P50DE-07003-08 0003 (SRC) QUIVEY, ROBERT Rochester caries research center Regulation of ATPase in oral Streptococci

P50DE-07003-08 0005 (SRC) BOWEN, WILLIAM H Rochester caries research center Effects of age and drug induced hyposalivation on caries

P50DE-07003-08 0009 (SRC) TABAK, LAWRENCE A Rochester caries

PROJECT NO., ORGANIZATIONAL UNIT., INVESTIGATOR, ADDRESS, TITLE

research center Salivary mediated base production in humans

P50DE-07003-08 0010 (SRC) MEYEROWITZ, CYRIL Rochester caries research center Caries experience in renal dialysis patients

P50DE-07003-08 0011 (SRC) MELVIN, JAMES E Rochester caries research center Effect of age and hyposalivation on fluoride transport

P50DE-07003-08 0012 (SRC) CULP, DAVID J Rochester caries research center Mucous cell regulation and changes with hyposalivation

R01DE-07007-06 (OBM) SHILLITOE, EDWARD J UNIV OF TEXAS HEALTH SCI CTR PO BOX 20068 HOUSTON, TX 77225 Multiple factors in the etiology of oral cancer

P50DE-07009-08 (SRC) DEPAOLA, PAUL F FORSYTH DENTAL CENTER 140 FENWAY BOSTON, MA 02115 Specialized caries research center

P50DE-07009-08 0003 (SRC) HAY, DON I Specialized caries research center Bacterial adhesion to enamel and root surfaces

P50DE-07009-08 0004 (SRC) SMITH, DANIEL J Specialized caries research center Effect of immunologic factors on root surface microflora colonization

P50DE-07009-08 0005 (SRC) MORENO, EDGARD C Specialized caries research center: Physical, chemical & microbiological aspects of root caries formation

P50DE-07009-08 0009 (SRC) VAN HOUTE, J Specialized caries research center Microbiology of root surface caries

R01DE-07075-07 (OBM) THOMAS, HUW F UNIV OF CONNECTICUT HLTH CTR 263 FARMINGTON AVENUE FARMINGTON, CT 06032 Tissue interactions in root development

R01DE-07076-06 (OBM) MANSSON-RAHEMTULLA, BRITTA UNIV OF ALABAMA AT BIRMINGHAM UAB STATION BIRMINGHAM, AL 35294 Salivary peroxidase--properties and metabolism

R01DE-07077-04A4 (OBM) MC DOWELL, THOMAS D UNIVERSITY OF NEW MEXICO ALBUQUERQUE, NM 87131 Cell surface regulation in a cariogenic streptococcus

R01DE-07105-07 (OBM) WARREN, DONALD W UNIV OF N CAROLINA/CHAPEL HILL DENT RES CTR/CB#7455 CHAPEL HILL, NC 27599 Speech aerodynamics--regulation and control in cleft palate

P50DE-07117-07 (SRC) CLARK, WILLIAM B UNIVERSITY OF FLORIDA BOX J-424 JHMHC GAINESVILLE, FL 32610 Periodontal disease research center

P50DE-07117-07 0001 (SRC) MAGNUSSON, N INGVAR Periodontal disease research center Diagnosis and treatment of human periodontal disease

P50DE-07117-07 0002 (SRC) WALKER, CLAY B Periodontal disease research center: Microbiologic, pharmacologic, and immunologic studies with periodontal disease

P50DE-07117-07 0003 (SRC) MCARTHUR, WILLIAM P. Periodontal disease research center Modulation of colonization by presumptive periodontopathogens in animal models

P50DE-07118-07 (SRC) TAICHMAN, NORTON S UNIVERSITY OF PENNSYLVANIA 4001 SPRUCE STREET PHILADELPHIA, PA 19104-6292 Periodontal diseases research center

P50DE-07118-07 0001 (SRC) BRIGHTMAN, VERNON J Periodontal diseases research center Clinical management section

P50DE-07118-07 0002 (SRC) SLOTS, JORGEN Periodontal diseases research center Clinical microbiological studies

P50DE-07118-07 0004 (SRC) TAICHMAN, NORTON S Periodontal diseases research center Immune and leukocyte functions

P50DE-07118-07 0006 (SRC) DIRIENZO, JOSEPH M. Periodontal diseases research center Actionobacillus actinomycetemcomitans infections in LJP--molecular probes

P50DE-07118-07 0007 (SRC) ROSAN, BURTON Periodontal diseases research center Actinobacillus factors contributing to mechanisms of microbial colonization

P50DE-07118-07 0008 (SRC) LALLY, EDWARD Periodontal diseases research center Molecular cloning and expression of A. actinomycetemcomitans leukotoxin

P50DE-07118-07 0009 (SRC) OLER, JACQUELINE Periodontal diseases research center Biostatistics and data management section

R01DE-07120-06 (OBM) SHUR, BARRY D UNIVERSITY OF TEXAS 1515 HOLCOMBE BLVD. HOUSTON, TX 77030 Substrate interaction in craniofacial morphogenesis

R01DE-07168-07A1 (BM) CIHLAR, RONALD L GEORGETOWN UNIVERSITY 3900 RESERVOIR ROAD NW WASHINGTON, DC 20007 Membrane function during germination of Candida albicans

R01DE-07199-06 (OBM) DOYLE, RONALD J UNIV OF LOUISVILLE HTH SCI CTR HEALTH SCIENCE CENTER LOUISVILLE, KY 40292 Adherence factors of oral streptococci

R01DE-07201-05 (OBM) QUISSELL, DAVID O UNIV OF COLORADO HLTH SCI CTR 1300 S. POTOMAC ST. #110 AURORA, CO 80012 Rat parotid exocytosis

R01DE-07204-08 (OBM) SUZUKI, JON B UNIVERSITY OF PITTSBURGH 3501 TERRACE ST PITTSBURGH, PA 15261 Family studies of early onset periodontitis

R01DE-07218-06 (OBM) HASTY, DAVID L UNIV OF TENNESSEE-HLTH SCI CTR 800 MADISON AVE MEMPHIS, TN 38163 Mechanisms of bacterial adherence and colonization

R01DE-07220-06 (OBM) CAPLAN, ARNOLD I CASE WESTERN RESERVE UNIVERSIT 2080 ADELBERT RD CLEVELAND, OH 44106 Bioactive factors in skeletal repair

R01DE-07223-04A2 (OBM) LEGEROS, RACQUEL Z NEW YORK UNIV DENTAL CENTER 345 EAST 24TH STREET NEW YORK, NY 10010 Magnesium and formation/stability of calcium phosphates

R01DE-07227-06 (OBM) NISENGARD, RUSSELL J SUNY AT BUFFALO 3435 MAIN STREET BUFFALO, NY 14214 Host-bacterial interactions in periodontal disease

R01DE-07233-06 (OBM) RUDNEY, JOEL D UNIVERSITY OF MINNESOTA MINNEAPOLIS, MN 55455 In vivo studies of saliva antimicrobial proteins

R01DE-07244-06 (OBM) FISHER, SUSAN J UNIV OF CALIFORNIA, SAN FRAN HSW 604, BOX 0512 SAN FRANCISCO, CA 94143 Molecular mechanisms of bacterial adherence to cementum

R01DE-07256-08 (OBM) LANTZ, MARILYN S UNIVERSITY OF ALABAMA UNIVERISTY STATION BOX 34 BIRMINHAM, AL 35294-0007 Fibrinogen binding and virulence of bacteroides species

R01DE-07267-07 (OBM) HOLT, STANLEY C UNIV OF TEXAS HLTH SCI CTR 7703 FLOYD CURL DRIVE SAN ANTONIO, TX 78284-7894 Periodontopathic bacteria--Chemical-biologic nature

PROJECT NO., ORGANIZATIONAL UNIT., INVESTIGATOR, ADDRESS, TITLE

R01DE-07272-07 (OBM) HOCK, JANET M TUFTS UNIVERSITY 136 HARRISON AVENUE BOSTON, MA 02111 Hormonal regulation of bone growth in vivo

R01DE-07341-07 (OBM) HURLEY, THOMAS W UNIVERSITY OF MISSOURI ONE HOSPITAL DRIVE COLUMBIA, MO 65212 Second messenger function in exocrine glands

R01DE-07378-07 (OBM) DEWHIRST, FLOYD E FORSYTH DENTAL CENTER 140 FENWAY BOSTON, MASS 02115 Mechanisms of action of human bone resorptive cytokines

R01DE-07441-06 (OBM) POLLOCK, JERRY J SUNY AT STONY BROOK SCHOOL OF DENTAL MEDICINE STONY BROOK, NY 11794-8702 Histidine-rich polypeptides, oral candidiasis and AIDS

R01DE-07444-06 (OBM) MARKS, SANDY C, JR UNIV OF MASSACHUSETTS MED CTR 55 LAKE AVE NORTH WORCESTER, MA 01655 Bone matrix and bone resorption

R01DE-07457-06 (OBM) DELANEY, JAYNE E UNIV OF TEXAS HLTH SCI CTR 7703 FLOYD CURL DRIVE SAN ANTONIO, TEX 78284 Periodontal microflora acquisition--Mother-infant studies

R01DE-07481-04A2 (OBM) HEFTI, ARTHUR UNIVERSITY OF FLORIDA BOX J-434, JHMHSC GAINESVILLE, FL 32610 Gingival pathology elicited by cyclosporine-A

R01DE-07493-05 (OBM) MARGOLIS, HENRY C FORSYTH DENTAL CENTER 140 THE FENWAY BOSTON, MA 02115 Cariogenic potential of dental plaque fluid

R01DE-07496-06 (OBM) PROGULSKE-FOX, ANN UNIVERSITY OF FLORIDA BOX J-424 JHMHSC GAINESVILLE, FL 32610-0424 Surface antigens of oral bacteroides species

R01DE-07514-06 (BEM) RUDY, THOMAS E PAIN EVAL & TREATMENT INST BAUM BOULEVARD AT CRAIG STREET PITTSBURG, PA 15213 Treatment of TMD--A multiaxial approach

R01DE-07559-08 (OBM) GRAVES, DANA T BOSTON UNIV SCH OF DENTISTRY 100 E NEWTON ST BOSTON, MA 02118 Bone-derived cells produce a chemotactic factor

P01DE-07585-04 (SSS) LEVINE, MICHAEL J SUNY AT BUFFALO 3435 MAIN STREET BUFFALO, NY 14214 Functions of salivary mucins and phosphoproteins

P01DE-07585-04 0001 (SSS) LEVINE, MICHAEL J Functions of salivary mucins and phosphoproteins Functions of salivary mucins and phosphoproteins--Structure-function

P01DE-07585-04 0002 (SSS) BOBEK, LIBUSE Functions of salivary mucins and phosphoproteins Functions of salivary mucins and phosphoproteins--Molecular organization

P01DE-07585-04 0003 (SSS) STINSON, M W Functions of salivary mucins and phosphoproteins Functions of salivary mucins and phosphoproteins--Bacterial adhesions

P01DE-07585-04 0004 (SSS) NANCOLLAS, G H Functions of salivary mucins and phosphoproteins Salivary mucins and phosphoproteins functions--Remineralization-demineralization

R01DE-07606-04A2 (OBM) SCHENKEIN, HARVEY A VIRGINIA COMMONWEALTH UNIV. BOX 566 MCV STATION RICHMOND, VA 23298-0566 Complement and periodontal pathogenic microoganisms

R01DE-07623-06 (OBM) AOBA, TAKAAKI FORSYTH DENTAL CENTER 140 FENWAY BOSTON, MA 02115 Normal and pathological enamel mineralization

R01DE-07644-06 (OBM) OKABE, TORU BAYLOR COLLEGE OF DENTISTRY 3302 GASTON AVENUE DALLAS, TX 75246 Evaluation of mercury release from dental amalgams

R01DE-07652-06 (OBM) OPPENHEIM, FRANK G BOSTON UNIVERSITY 100 E NEWTON ST BOSTON, MA 02118 microbicidal salivary histidine-rich proteins

R01DE-07662-07 (NLS) JACQUIN, MARK F ST LOUIS SCHOOL OF MEDICINE 1402 SOUTH GRAND BOULEVARD ST LOUIS, MO 63104 Trigeminal brainstem circuitry

R01DE-07674-04A1 (OBM) MINKOFF, ROBERT UNIVERSITY OF TEXAS PO BOX 20068 HOUSTON, TX 77225 Analysis of primary palate formation

R01DE-07682-04 (OBM) SHULER, CHARLES F UNIV OF SOUTHERN CALIFORNIA 2250 ALCAZAR ST. CSA 103 LOS ANGELES, CA 90033 In vitro production of oral mucosa for grafting

P01DE-07687-09A1 (SRC) FAULKNER, JOHN A UNIV OF MICHIGAN MED SCHOOL 7775 MEDICAL SCIENCE II BLDG. ANN ARBOR, MI 48109-0622 Regeneration and transplantation of skeletal muscle

P01DE-07687-09A1 0001 (SRC) CARLSON, BRUCE M Regeneration and transplantation of skeletal muscle Morphological studies

P01DE-07687-09A1 0003 (SRC) WHITE, TIMOTHY Regeneration and transplantation of skeletal muscle Contractile and regulatory proteins

P01DE-07687-09A1 0005 (SRC) FAULKNER, JOHN A Regeneration and transplantation of skeletal muscle Functional properties

P01DE-07687-09A1 9001 (SRC) CARLSON, BRUCE M Regeneration and transplantation of skeletal muscle Animal core

P01DE-07687-09A1 9002 (SRC) SCHORK, MICHAEL A Regeneration and transplantation of skeletal muscle Statistics Core

P01DE-07734-06 (SRC) JACQUIN, MARK F ST LOUIS UNIVERSITY SCH OF MED 1402 SOUTH GRAND BLVD. ST LOUIS, MO 63104 Mechanisms of damage-induced trigeminal reorganization

P01DE-07734-06 0002 (SRC) RENEHAN, WILLIAM E Mechanisms of damage-induced trigeminal reorganization Mechanisms of trigeminal primary afferent arbor formation

P01DE-07734-06 0003 (SRC) MILLER, MICHAEL W Mechanisms of damage-induced trigeminal reorganization Plasticity of trigeminal-somatosensory system

P01DE-07734-06 0004 (SRC) JACQUIN, MARK F Mechanisms of damage-induced trigeminal reorganization Deafferation and trigeminal second order neurons

P01DE-07734-06 0005 (SRC) CHIAIA, NICHOLAS L Mechanisms of damage-induced trigeminal reorganization Trigeminothalmic organization and plasticity

P01DE-07734-06 0006 (SRC) ROISEN, FRED J Mechanisms of damage-induced trigeminal reorganization Development of plasticity of thalamocortical axons

P01DE-07734-06 0007 (SRC) HARING, JOHN H Mechanisms of damage-induced trigeminal reorganization Effects of trigeminal injury on monoaminergic ontogeny

P01DE-07734-06 0001 (SRC) RHOADES, ROBERT W Mechanisms of damage-induced trigeminal reorganization Trigeminal primary afferent organization and development

R01DE-07754-06 (OBM) MAREK, MIROSLAV I GEORGIA INST OF TECHNOLOGY SCH OF MATERIALS ENGINEERING ATLANTA, GA 30332-0245 Dissolution of mercury from dental amalgams

R01DE-07755-06 (OBM) BAWDEN, JAMES W UNIV OF NORTH CAROLINA DENTAL RESEARCH CENTER 210H CHAPEL HILL, NC 27599-7455 Placental transfer of fluoride in the guinea pig

R01DE-07760-06 (OBM) LOOMIS, RONALD E SUNY AT BUFFALO SCH DENT MED 129 PARKER HALL BUFFALO, NY 14214 Conformation of dental salivary molecules

R01DE-07761-06 (OBM) DECHOW, PAUL C BAYLOR COLLEGE OF DENTISTRY 3302 GASTON AVENUE DALLAS, TX 75246 Functional effects of masticatory muscle alteration

R01DE-07766-05 (OBM) DURBAN, ELISA M UNIV OF TEXAS DENTAL BRANCH PO BOX 20068 HOUSTON, TX 77225 Salivary epithelial cells -- Behavior and oncogene effects

R01DE-07777-04 (OBM) QUIVEY, ROBERT G, JR UNIVERSITY OF ROCHESTER 601 ELMWOOD AVE BOX 611 ROCHESTER, NY 14642-0002 Dental plaque reduction by genetic engineering

R01DE-07803-05A2 (OBM) BERTOLAMI, CHARLES N UCLA SCHOOL OF DENTIDTRY 10833 LE CONTE AVE LOS ANGELES, CA 90024-1668 Fibroblastic heterogeneity in orofacial scarring

R01DE-07806-06 (OBM) MACKERT, J R, JR MEDICAL COLLEGE OF GEORGIA SCHOOL OF DENTISTRY AUGUSTA, GA 30912-1264 Thermally induced changes in dental porcelain expansion

R01DE-07889-03 (BEM) KIYAK, H ASUMAN UNIVERSITY OF WASHINGTON B-214 HEALTH SCIENCES CENTER SEATTLE, WASH 98195 Cognitive & behavioral methods for geriatric oral health

R01DE-07907-05 (OBM) BOWEN, WILLIAM H UNIVERSITY OF ROCHESTER 601 ELMWOOD AVE BOX 611 ROCHESTER, NY 14642 Saliva-glucosyltransferase interactions on surfaces

R29DE-07926-05 (OBM) DE NARDIN, ERNESTO DEPT OF ORAL BIOLOGY 3435 MAIN STREET BUFFALO, N Y 14214 Neutrophil function in dental disease

P01DE-07946-05 (SRC) GREENSPAN, JOHN S UNIVERSITY OF CALIFORNIA SAN FRANCISCO, CA 94143-0512 Oral manifestations of the acquired immunodeficiency syndrome

P01DE-07946-05 0001 (SRC) FEIGAL, DAVID W Oral manifestations of the acquired immunodeficiency syndrome Epidemiology of oral manifestations of HIV infection

P01DE-07946-05 0002 (SRC) GREENSPAN, JOHN S Oral manifestations of the acquired immunodeficiency syndrome Oral manifestations of HIV infection

P01DE-07946-05 0003 (SRC) ARMITAGE, GARY C Oral manifestations of the acquired immunodeficiency syndrome Oral aspects of simian AIDS

R01DE-07979-02 (OBM) DRUMMOND, JAMES L UNIV OF ILLINOIS AT CHICAGO 801 SOUTH PAULINA STREET CHICAGO, IL 60612 Fracture characteristics of dental composites

R01DE-08000-05 (OBM) MC MANUS, LINDA M UNIV OF TEXAS HLTH SCIENCE CTR 7703 FLOYD CURL DR SAN ANTONIO, TX 78284 Characterization of salivary PAF

R29DE-08003-04 (OBM) JOHNSTON, WILLIAM M OHIO STATE UNIVERSITY 305 W 12TH AVE COLUMBUS, OHIO 43210-1241 Colorant formulation of polymeric prosthetic materials

R37DE-08007-06 (OBM) BLEIWEIS, ARNOLD S UNIVERSITY OF FLORIDA BOX 100424 JHMHSC GAINESVILLE, FL 32610 Membranes of the dental pathogen streptococcus mutans

R29DE-08013-05 (NLS) MAIXNER, WILLIAM UNIVERSITY OF NORTH CAROLINA CHAPEL HILL, NC 27599-7455 Modulation of response to noxious orafacial stimulation

R01DE-08024-06 (OBM) VAIDYANATHAN, TRITALA K UNIV OF MED & DENT OF N J 100 BERGEN STREET NEWARK, N J 07103 Optimization of small particle composites

R29DE-08030-05 (OBM) BABU, JEGDISH P UNIVERSITY OF TENNESSEE 894 UNION AVENUE MEMPHIS, TENN 38163 Mechanism of A. naeslundii adhesion to buccal epithelium

R01DE-08050-04A1 (OBM) YU, JIA-HUEY DEPART OF VET AFFAIRS 50 IRVING STREET NW WASHINGTON, DC 20422 Xerostomia-inducing mechanisms of psychotropic drugs

R01DE-08060-05 (OBM) BLAZER, DAN G, III DUKE UNIVERSITY MEDICAL CTR BOX 3215 DURHAM, NC 27710 Piedmont 65+ dental study

R29DE-08061-05 (OBM) STORTHZ, KAREN A UNIV OF TEXAS DENTAL BRANCH P O BOX 20068 HOUSTON, TX 77225 Etiology of lesions of the oral mucosa

R29DE-08074-04 (OBM) BERGEY, EARL J STATE UNIV OF NY AT BUFFALO 3435 MAIN ST, 109 FOSTER HALL BUFFALO, NY 14214 Salivary-viral interactions in dental disease

R01DE-08108-05A1 (OBM) TABAK, LAWRENCE A UNIVERSITY OF ROCHESTER 601 ELMWOOD AVENUE, BOX 611 ROCHESTER, NY 14642 Regulation of mucin glycoprotein biosynthesis

R01DE-08144-04 (OBM) KLEBE, ROBERT J UNIV OF TEXAS HLTH SCI CTR 7703 FLOYD CURL DRIVE SAN ANTONIO, TX 78284-7762 Initial events in bone and tooth morphogenesis

R29DE-08153-05 (BEM) TOBIASEN, JOYCE M UNIV OF KANSAS MEDICAL CTR 39TH AND RAINBOW BOULEVARD KANSAS CITY, KS 66103 Scaling facial impairment in cleft lip patients

R29DE-08165-02 (OBM) KILLIANY, DENNIS M ST. LOUIS UNIV MEDICAL CTR 3556 CAROLINE ST ST LOUIS, MISSOURI 63104 Reduction of orthognathic surgical relapse

R29DE-08172-04 (OBM) QWARNSTROM, EVA E UNIV OF WASHINGTON DEPT OF PATHOLOGY SM-30 SEATTLE, WA 98195 Regulation of gingival fibroblasts in tissue generation

R29DE-08173-04 (OBM) HILDEBOLT, CHARLES F WASHINGTON UNIVERSITY MALLINCKRODT INST OF RADIOLOGY ST LOUIS, MO 63110 Assessment of peridontal disease by digital imaging

R01DE-08174-05 (MGN) SHAW, PHYLLIS A MT SINAI SCHOOL OF MEDICINE ONE GUSTAVE L. LEVY PLACE NEW YORK, N Y 10029 Age-related response of salivary glands to isoproterenol

R01DE-08178-03 (OBM) COLE, MICHAEL F GEORGETOWN UNIVERSITY 3900 RESERVOIR ROAD N W WASHINGTON, D C 20007 Salivary immune response to commensal oral bacteria

R01DE-08182-04 (OBM) MICHALEK, SUZANNE M UNIV OF ALABAMA AT BIRMINGHAM UAB STATION BIRMINGHAM, ALABAMA 35294 Regulation of immune responses in the oral cavity

R29DE-08185-06 (NLS) CLEMENTS, JANE R TEXAS A & M UNIVERSITY COLLEGE STATION, TX 77843 Glutamate and aspartate in the spinal trigeminal nucleus

R01DE-08188-04A1 (OBM) TERRANOVA, VICTOR P COLUMBIA UNIVERSITY 630 WEST 168TH ST NEW YORK, NY 10032 Biochemical approach to periodontal regeneration

R01DE-08191-05 (OBM) FERRETTI, JOSEPH J UNIV OF OKLAHOMA HEALTH SCI CT 940 STANTON L YOUNG BLVD OKLAHOMA CITY, OK 73104 Genetics of sucrose metabolism in mutans streptococci

R01DE-08199-04 (OBM) GREENE, ROBERT M JEFFERSON MEDICAL COLLEGE 1020 LOCUST STREET PHILADELPHIA, PA 19107 Cellular analysis of orofacial development

R29DE-08207-05 (OBM) FELTON, JEFFREY R UNIVERSITY OF CALIFORNIA SAN FRANCISCO, CALIF 94143 Genetic study of proteases in Bacteroides gingivalis

R01DE-08222-02 (OBM) BUNDY, KIRK J TULANE UNIVERSITY 6823 ST CHARLES AVE NEW ORLEANS, LA 70118 Optimizing corrosion testing of dental alloys

R01DE-08223-04 (OBM) EICK, J DAVID UNIV OF MISSOURI-KANSAS CITY 650 E 25TH STREET KANSAS CITY, MO 64108 Development of new multifunctional dental adhesives

R01DE-08227-03 (HSR) GREMBOWSKI, DAVID E UNIVERSITY OF WASHINGTON SEATTLE, WA 98195 Fluoridation effects on dental demand

P50DE-08228-04 (SRC) BIRKEDAL-HANSEN, HENNING UNIV OF ALABAMA AT BIRMINGHAM UAB STATION BIRMINGHAM, AL 35294 Molecular/Cellular immunoregulation in periodontal disease,

P50DE-08228-04 0001 (SRC) MICHALEK, SUZANNE M Molecular/Cellular immunoregulation in periodontal disease, Molecular/cellular immunoregulation in periodontal disease

P50DE-08228-04 0002 (SRC) MILLER, EDWARD J Molecular/Cellular immunoregulation in periodontal disease, Three novel proteins of the extracellular matrix

P50DE-08228-04 0003 (SRC) BIRKEDAL-HANSEN, HENNING Molecular/Cellular immunoregulation in periodontal disease, Biologic mechanisms of collagenase--Dependent collagen breakdown

P50DE-08229-05 (SRC) PAGE, ROY C UNIVERSITY OF WASHINGTON SM-42 SEATTLE, WA 98195 Support of research center in oral biology

P50DE-08229-05 0001 (SRC) PAGE, ROY C Support of research center in oral biology Complement system regulation of fibroblast function

P50DE-08229-05 0002 (SRC) MORRIS, DAVID R Support of research center in oral biology Growth-associated gene expression in fibroblasts

P50DE-08229-05 0003 (SRC) CLARK, EDWARD A Support of research center in oral biology Down-regulation of B cell activation/differentiation

P50DE-08229-05 0004 (SRC) BORNSTEIN, PAUL Support of research center in oral biology Regulation of thrombospondin and collagen gene expression

P50DE-08229-05 0005 (SRC) ALTMAN, LEONARD C Support of research center in oral biology Junctional epithelial cells

P50DE-08229-05 0006 (SRC) NARAYAMAN, A SAMPATH Support of research center in oral biology Regulation of fibroblasts by cementum components

P50DE-08229-05 0007 (SRC) WIGHT, THOMAS N Support of research center in oral biology Proteoglycan/hyaluronic acid and cell proliferation

P50DE-08239-04 (SRC) ROSENBLOOM, JOEL UNIVERSITY OF PENNSYLVANIA 3451 WALNUT STREET PHILADELPHIA, PA 19104-6002 Research center in oral biology

P50DE-08239-04 0007 (SRC) TAICHMAN, NORTON S Research center in oral biology Pathobiology of actinobacillus leukotoxin

P50DE-08239-04 0008 (SRC) ROSENBLOOM, JOEL Research center in oral biology Molecular cloning, expression and structure of enamel proteins

P50DE-08239-04 0009 (SRC) LEBOY, PHOEBE S Research center in oral biology Gene expression and the mineralization of the epiphyseal growth cartilage

P50DE-08239-04 0010 (SRC) HASELGROVE, JOHN C Research center in oral biology Metabolic control of osteogenesis

P50DE-08239-04 0011 (SRC) CRAIG, RONALD G Research center in oral biology Regeneration of dental cementum

P50DE-08239-04 0005 (SRC) COHEN, GARY H Research center in oral biology Functional analysis of glycoprotein D of herpes simplex

P50DE-08239-04 0006 (SRC) MALAMUD, DANIEL Research center in oral biology Mechanism of saliva mediated bacterial aggregation

P50DE-08239-04 9001 (SRC) GIBSON, CAROLYN Research center in oral biology Molecular biology core

P50DE-08239-04 9002 (SRC) BERTHOLD, PETER Research center in oral biology Electron microscope core

P50DE-08239-04 9003 (SRC) GOLUB, ELLIS Research center in oral biology Computer and imaging core

P50DE-08239-04 9004 (SRC) LALLY, EDWARD Research center in oral biology Immunology core

P50DE-08240-05 (SRC) LEVINE, MICHAEL J SUNY AT BUFFALO 3435 MAIN ST BUFFALO, NY 14214 Modulation of natural defense in oral disease

P50DE-08240-05 0001 (SRC) LEVINE, MICHAEL J Modulation of natural defense in oral disease Synthesis and function of composite salivary molecules

P50DE-08240-05 0002 (SRC) BHANDARY, KRISHNA Modulation of natural defense in oral disease Design and function of salivary cycloneoglycopeptide

P50DE-08240-05 0003 (SRC) DOUGLAS, WILLIAM H Modulation of natural defense in oral disease Lubrication effects of salivary pellicles

P50DE-08240-05 0004 (SRC) STINSON, MURRAY W Modulation of natural defense in oral disease Coaggregation mechanisms of streptococcus sanguis and bacteroides species

P50DE-08240-05 0005 (SRC) ZAMBON, JOSEPH J Modulation of natural defense in oral disease Pathogenic potential of black-pigmented bacteroides species

P50DE-08240-05 0006 (SRC) SHIFFERIE, ROBERT Modulation of natural defense in oral disease Capsular polysaccharide of black-pigmented bacteroides

PROJECT NO., ORGANIZATIONAL UNIT., INVESTIGATOR, ADDRESS, TITLE

P50DE-08240-05 0007 (SRC) DYER, DAVID Modulation of natural defense in oral disease Genetics of virulence determinants of black-pigmented Bacteroides
P50DE-08240-05 0008 (SRC) GENCO, ROBERT J Modulation of natural defense in oral disease Epitope mapping of black-pigmented bacteroides fimbriae
P50DE-08240-05 0009 (SRC) DZIAK, ROSEMARY Modulation of natural defense in oral disease Effects of immune cell factors on bone cell metabolism
P50DE-08240-05 0010 (SRC) CHO, MOON Modulation of natural defense in oral disease Regulatory mechanisms for development and function of periodontium
P50DE-08240-05 0011 (SRC) WILSON, MARK Modulation of natural defense in oral disease Stereochemically constrained ligands to define PMN receptor binding sites
P50DE-08240-05 0012 (SRC) NEIDERS, MIRDZA Modulation of natural defense in oral disease Gene expression and bone metabolism
P50DE-08240-05 0013 (SRC) AGUIRRE, ALFREDO Modulation of natural defense in oral disease Initiatives for underrepresented minorities in biomedical research
P50DE-08240-05 0014 (SRC) HILL, DEBORAH Modulation of natural defense in oral disease Initiatives for underrepresented minorities in biomedical research--II
R01DE-08252-05 (PBC) RODEN, LENNART UNIV OF ALABAMA AT BIRMINGHAM UAB STATION BIRMINGHAM, ALA 35294 Biosynthesis of heparin and heparan sulfate
R01DE-08293-05 (OBM) KURAMITSU, HOWARD K UNIVERSITY OF TEXAS HLTH SCI C 7703 FLOYD CURL DR SAN ANTONIO, TX 78284 B gingivalis collagenase-molecular genetic analysis
R01DE-08295-04 (OBM) WATSON, EILEEN L UNIVERSITY OF WASHINGTON DEPT OF ORAL BIOLOGY, SB-22 SEATTLE, WA 98195 Sugar metabolism in oral actinomyces viscosus
R01DE-08296-02 (BEM) BERGGREN, ULF E UNIVERSITY OF GOTHENBURG BOX 33070 SE-400 33 GOTHENBURG, SWEDEN Etiology and treatment of dental fear
R01DE-08303-03 (OBM) PASTER, BRUCE J FORSYTH DENTAL CENTER 140 FENWAY BOSTON, MASS 02115 Development of DNA probes to periodontal pathogens
R29DE-08412-04 (OBM) BOEHRINGER, HANSRUEDI UNIVERSITY OF PENNSYLVANIA 4001 SPRUCE STREET PHILADELPHIA, PA 19104 Interactions of neutrophils with periodontal spirochetes
R01DE-08414-02 (BEM) GATCHEL, ROBERT J U OF TEXAS SW MED CTR AT DALLA 5323 HARRY HINES BLVD/MED CENT DALLAS, TX 75235 Filmed behavioral intervention and dental anxiety
R01DE-08417-03 (BEM) SADOWSKY, DONALD JACOBI HOSPITAL BRONX, N Y 10461 Predictors of dentists infection control behaviors
R01DE-08428-03 (OBM) DAVIDOVITCH, ZEEV THE OHIO STATE UNIVERSITY 305 WEST TWELFTH AVENUE COLUMBUS, OH 43210-1241 Neurotransmitters and cytokines in tooth movement
R29DE-08448-04 (OBM) COHEN, ROBERT E SUNY AT BUFFALO BUFFALO, N Y 14214 Immunochemistry of salivary mucins in dental disease
R29DE-08455-05 (OBM) REKOW, E DIANNE UNIVERSITY OF MARYLAND 666 W BALTIMORE ST BALTIMORE, MD 21201 Computer-aided design and manufacture of dental restorations
R01DE-08477-04A1 (GMA) BRYSK, MIRIAM M UNIV OF TEXAS MEDICAL BRANCH SCHOOL OF MEDICINE GALVESTON, TX 77550 Glycoproteins in desquamation in skin and oral mucosa
P50DE-08489-04 (SRC) PIHLSTROM, BRUCE L UNIV OF MINNESOTA 515 DELAWARE S.E. MINNEAPOLIS, MN 55455 Clinical research center for periodontal diseases
P50DE-08489-04 0001 (SRC) WOLFF, L Clinical research center for periodontal diseases Bacterial risk assessment for periodontal disease
P50DE-08489-04 0002 (SRC) SMITH, Q Clinical research center for periodontal diseases Crevicular fluid composition and risk for periodontitis
P50DE-08489-04 0003 (SRC) SCHACHTELE, CHARLES F Clinical research center for periodontal diseases Passive immunization--bacteria periodontal disease
R01DE-08505-05 (SRC) RUDNEY, JOEL D UNIVERSITY OF MINNESOTA 515 DELAWARE STREET S E MINNEAPOLIS, MN 55455 Host defense factors in oral ecology
R01DE-08506-05 (SRC) YASBIN, RONALD E UNIVERSITY OF MARYLAND BALTIMORE, MD 21228 Gene regulation in the oral streptococci
R01DE-08507-05 (SRC) KARNOVSKY, MORRIS J HARVARD MEDICAL SCHOOL 25 SHATTUCK STREET BOSTON, MASS 02115 Mechanisms of leukocyte activation
R01DE-08510-05 (SRC) SHIPMAN, CHARLES, JR THE UNIVERSITY OF MICHIGAN 1011 N UNIVERSITY ANN ARBOR, MI 48109 Topical thiosemicarbazones for control of oral herpes
R01DE-08511-05 (SRC) TABAK, LAWRENCE A UNIVERSITY OF ROCHESTER DEPT OF DENTAL RES BOX 611 ROCHESTER, NY 14642 Proline-rich glycoprotein mediated masticatory lubricati
R01DE-08512-05 (SRC) CLARK, VIRGINIA L UNIV OF ROCHESTER BOX 8672 ROCHESTER, NY 14642 Cloning Bacteroides gingivalis collagenase
R01DE-08513-05 (SRC) HERRING, SUSAN W UNIVERSITY OF WASHINGTON SEATTLE, WA 98195 Bone growth, periosteal migration and muscle function
R01DE-08514-05 (SRC) GERMAINE, GREG R UNIVERSITY OF MINNESOTA 515 DELAWARE STREET, S E MINNEAPOLIS, MN 55455 In situ analysis of human plaque formation
R01DE-08515-05 (SRC) ANDERSON, DWIGHT L UNIVERSITY OF MINNESOTA 18-246 MOOS HLTH SCI TOWER MINNEAPOLIS, MINN 55455 Topological modification of viral DNA
R01DE-08518-05 (SRC) LURIE, ALAN G UNIV OF CONNECTICUT HLTH CTR 263 FARMINGTON AVENUE FARMINGTON, CT 06030-1605 Acute vs split dose gamma-ray effects on DNA
R01DE-08519-05 (SRC) HAUSCHKA, PETER HARVARD SCH OF DENTAL MED BOSTON, MA 02115 Chemoattractants & growth factors in mineralized tissues
R01DE-08520-04 (OBM) MILLER, EDWARD J UNIV OF ALABAMA AT BIRMINGHAM UAB STATION BIRMINGHAM, AL 35294 Chemistry/biology of the genetically-distinct collagens
R01DE-08521-05 (SRC) EBERSOLE, JEFFREY L UNIV OF TEXAS HEALTH SCI CTR 7703 FLOYD CURL DRIVE SAN ANTONIO, TX 78284-7894 Cloning and biologic function of leukotoxin from A. actinomycetemcomitans
R01DE-08522-05 (SRC) YAMAUCHI, MITSUO U OF N CAROLINA AT CHAPEL HILL DENTAL RESEARCH CENTER (210H) CHAPEL HILL, NC 27599 Structure and function of dentin matrix proteins
R01DE-08525-05 (SRC) VEIS, ARTHUR NORTHWESTERN UNIVERSITY 303 EAST CHICAGO AVENUE CHICAGO, IL 60611 Osteogenic factors from dentin matri
R01DE-08540-03 (OBM) KELLER, JOHN C UNIVERSITY OF IOWA COLLEGE OF DENTISTRY IOWA CITY, IA 52242 Cell response to modified Ti surfaces
R01DE-08544-04 (OBM) HAUSMANN, ERNEST SUNY AT BUFFALO 3435 MAIN ST SQUIRE HALL SCH/M BUFFALO, NY 14214 Image analysis in periodontics--Estimation of accuracy
P01DE-08555-03 (SSS) PAGE, ROY C UNIVERSITY OF WASHINGTON SEATTLE, WASH 98195 Humoral immunity and periodontal disease
P01DE-08555-03 0001 (SSS) PAGE, ROY C. Humoral immunity and periodontal disease Microbiological antigens and human peridonal disease
P01DE-08555-03 0002 (SSS) ENGLE, L DAVID Humoral immunity and periodontal disease Serum antibodies and human periodontitis
P01DE-08555-03 0003 (SSS) PERSSON, ROGER Humoral immunity and periodontal disease Humoral immunity and periodontitis in nonhuman primate model
P01DE-08555-03 0004 (SSS) MONCLA, BERNARD J. Humoral immunity and periodontal disease Composition of periodontal microflora
P01DE-08555-03 9001 (SSS) PAGE, ROY C. Humoral immunity and periodontal disease Biostatistical support and communications core
R01DE-08558-03 (OBM) WU-YUAN, CHRISTINE D UNIVERSITY OF IOWA COLLEGE OF DENTISTRY IOWA CITY, IOWA 52242 Glucan-induced agglutination/virulence of streptococcus
R01DE-08559-04 (EDC) MURRAY, JEFFREY C UNIVERSITY OF IOWA DEPARTMENT OF PEDIATRICS IOWA CITY, IOWA 52242 Molecular genetic epidemiology of cleft lip and palate
R01DE-08561-03 (OBM) BAYNE, STEPHEN C SCHOOL OF DENTISTRY UNIV OF NORTH CAROLINA CHAPEL HILL, NC 27599-7450 Evaluation of protection hypothesis for composite wear
P01DE-08569-03 (SSS) HOLT, STANLEY C UNIV OF TEXAS HLTH SCI CTR 7703 FLOYD CURL DRIVE SAN ANTONIO, TX 78284-7894 Modulators of bone cell function in oral disease
P01DE-08569-03 0001 (SSS) HOLT, STANLEY C Modulators of bone cell function in oral disease Bacterial cell surface and oral disease
P01DE-08569-03 0002 (SSS) BONEWALD, LYNDA Modulators of bone cell function in oral disease Effects of TGF-beta and related inflammatory cell products on bone cells
P01DE-08569-03 0003 (SSS) POSER, JAMES W Modulators of bone cell function in oral disease Effects of autocrine-paracrine factors produced during bone resorption
P01DE-08569-03 0004 (SSS) CARNES, DAVID Modulators of bone cell function in oral disease Production of autocrine-paracrine factors during bone resorption
P01DE-08569-03 0005 (SSS) YONEDA, TOSHIYUKI Modulators of bone cell function in oral disease Oral cavity tumors--relationship between bone-resorption and colony stimulation
P01DE-08569-03 9001 (SSS) MUNDY, GREGORY R Modulators of bone cell function in oral disease Core laboratory--Cell products and assays
R29DE-08580-03 (OBM) MOORE, WILLIAM G UNIV OF ALABAMA AT BIRMINGHAM DEPT OF DENTISTRY BIRMINGHAM, AL 35294 Biological role of gelatinase
R29DE-08586-03 (OBM) STEFLIK, DAVID E MEDICAL COLLEGE OF GEORGIA SCHOOL OF DENTISTRY - AD 186 AUGUSTA, GA 30912-1110 Comparative experimental evaluations of dental implants
R01DE-08587-03 (OBM) SHENKER, BRUCE J UNIVERSITY OF PENNSYLVANIA 4010 LOCUST ST PHILADELPHIA, PA 19104-6002 Mercury and leukocyte function
R01DE-08589-03 (OBM) BOACKLE, ROBERT J MEDICAL UNIV OF SOUTH CAROLINA 171 ASHLEY AVENUE CHARLESTON, SC 29425-2230 Regulation of the first complement component by saliva
R01DE-08590-02 (OBM) HERZBERG, MARK C UNIV OF MINN SCHOOL OF DENTIST 515 DELAWARE ST., SE MINNEAPOLIS, MN 55455 Streptococcus sanguis adhesion--molecular basis of specificity
R01DE-08601-04 (OBM) HAY, DONALD I FORSYTH DENTAL CENTER 140 FENWAY BOSTON, MA 02115 Salivary proteins and bacterial adhesion to oral surface
R01DE-08603-03 (ORTH) BOYAN, BARBARA D UNIV OF TEXAS HLTH SCI CTR 7703 FLOYD CURL DRIVE SAN ANTONIO, TX 78284-7774 Role of bone factors in endochondral ossification
R01DE-08606-03 (OBM) STOHLER, CHRISTIAN S UNIVERSITY OF MICHIGAN ANN ARBOR, MI 48109-1078 Pain-modulated jaw motor function
R01DE-08641-03 (BEM) GROSS, ALAN M UNIVERSITY OF MISSISSIPPI UNIVERSITY, MS 38677 Oral factors--Impact on dento-facial development and TX
R01DE-08648-04 (OBM) SAUK, JOHN J UNIVERSITY OF MARYLAND 666 W BALTIMORE STREET BALTIMORE, MD 21201 Basis for stress tolerance in osteoligament cells
R01DE-08649-04 (OBM) PAZ, MERCEDES A CHILDREN'S HOSPITAL 300 LONGWOOD AVENUE, G1221 BOSTON, MA 02115 Synthesis and mechanism of secretion of parotid proteins
R01DE-08659-03 (OBM) KING, GREGORY J UNIVERSITY OF FLORIDA BOX J-444, JHMHC GAINESVILLE, FL 32610 Bone turnover studies in orthodontic tooth movement
R01DE-08664-03 (OBM) SYED, SALAM A UNIV OF MICHIGAN DENTAL SCH 1011 N UNIVERSITY ANN ARBOR, MI 48109-1078 Oral treponemes: ecological and biochemical studies
R29DE-08668-01A2 (OBM) SCHIFFMAN, ERIC L UNIVERSITY OF MINNESOTA MOOS TOWER/6-320 MINNEAPOLIS, MN 55455 Craniomandibular disorders--Long term outcome study
R01DE-08670-04 (OBM) AOBA, TAKAAKI FORSYTH DENTAL CENTER 140 FENWAY BOSTON, MA 02115 Carbonatoapatite formation in enamel mineralization
R01DE-08671-03 (OBM) LUNDBLAD, ROGER L UNIVERSITY OF NORTH CAROLINA DENTAL RESEARCH CENTER CHAPEL HILL, NC 27599-7455 Thrombin in wound healing--Multiple functions

PROJECT NO., ORGANIZATIONAL UNIT., INVESTIGATOR, ADDRESS, TITLE

R01DE-08678-03 (OBM) SNEAD, MALCOLM L UNIV OF SOUTHERN CALIFORNIA 2250 ALCAZAR STREET LOS ANGELES, CA 90033 Differential gene expression in ameloblastomas

R29DE-08680-04 (OBM) WONG, DAVID T HARVARD SCHOOL OF DENTAL MED 188 LONGWOOD AVENUE BOSTON, MA 02115 Molecular determinants of oral carcinogenesis

R01DE-08681-02 (ORTH) LAU, KIN-HING W JERRY L PETTIS MEM VETERANS HO 11201 BENTON STREET LOMA LINDA, CA 92357 Bone acid phosphatase and osteogenic action of fluoride

R01DE-08682-04 (OBM) MINA, MINA UNIVERSITY OF CONNECTICUT 263 FARMINGTON AVE FARMINGTON, CT 06030 Developmental and molecular biology of Meckel's cartilage

R01DE-08693-03 (OBM) CHEN, MEEI-SHIA UNIVERSITY OF CHICAGO 1101 E 58TH ST CHICAGO, IL 60637 Analytical and theoretical study of oral health

R01DE-08697-04 (OBM) GERMAN, REBECCA Z UNIVERSITY OF CINCINNATI 821A RIEVESCHL CINCINNATI, OH 45221-0006 Ontogeny of feeding behavior

R29DE-08699-04 (OBM) FIELD, RUTH B ORAL PATHOLOGY RES LAB 151-I 50 IRVING ST WASHINGTON, DC 20422 Lingual serous glands--regulation of enzyme secretion

R01DE-08701-03 (NLS) COOPER, BRIAN Y UNIV OF FLORIDA JHMHC BOX J-244 GAINESVILLE, FL 32610 Properties of high threshold mechanoreceptors in the oral cavity

R01DE-08706-03 (OBM) DENBESTEN, PAMELA K FORSYTH DENTAL CENTER 140 FENWAY BOSTON, MA 02115 Proteinases in developing enamel matrix

R01DE-08708-04 (SRC) PROFFIT, WILLIAM R UNIVERSITY OF NORTH CAROLINA SCHOOL OF DENTISTRY CHAPEL HILL, NC 27599-7450 Early vs late treatment in class II malocclusion

R01DE-08713-04 (SRC) BAUMRIND, SHELDON UNIVERSITY OF CALIFORNIA BOX 0640, C-734 SAN FRANCISCO, CA 94143 Adult orthodontic therapy--Extraction vs non-extraction

R01DE-08715-02 (OBM) KING, GREGORY J UNIVERSITY OF FLORIDA COLLEGE OF DENTISTRY GAINESVILLE, FL 32610 Timing treatment for class II malocclusion in children

R01DE-08716-04 (SRC) JOHNSTON, LYSLE E, JR UNIVERSITY OF MICHIGAN 1011 N UNIVERSITY ANN ARBOR, MI 48109-1078 Comparative analysis of class II treatments

R01DE-08722-04 (SRC) GHAFARI, JOSEPH G UNIVERSITY OF PENNSYLVANIA 4001 SPRUCE ST PHILADELPHIA, PA 19104 Early treatment of distoclusions--Comparison of alternatives

R01DE-08730-04 (OBM) KOWALSKI, CHARLES J UNIVERSITY OF MICHIGAN 1034 KELLOG ANN ARBOR, MI 48109-1078 Methods for analyzing longitudinal data

R01DE-08766-03 (OBM) OPHAUG, ROBERT H UNIV OF MINNESOTA SCH OF DENT 515 DELAWARE ST. MINNEAPOLIS, MN 55455 Fluoride absorption

P01DE-08773-03 (SRC) DWORKIN, SAMUEL F UNIVERSITY OF WASHINGTON SCHOOL OF DENTISTRY SEATTLE, WA 98195 TMD longitudinal studies--Clinical/chronic pain syndrome

P01DE-08773-03 0001 (SRC) DWORKIN, S F TMD longitudinal studies--Clinical/chronic pain syndrome Longitudinal studies of temporomandibular disorders

P01DE-08773-03 0002 (SRC) VON KORFF, M TMD longitudinal studies--Clinical/chronic pain syndrome Longitudinal studies of chronic pain syndrome in TMD

P01DE-08773-03 0003 (SRC) LERESCHE, L A TMD longitudinal studies--Clinical/chronic pain syndrome Dentists' understanding of TMD and chronic pain syndrome

P01DE-08773-03 0004 (SRC) DWORKIN, S F TMD longitudinal studies--Clinical/chronic pain syndrome Early education/cognitive-behavioral intervention in TMD

R01DE-08778-04 (OBM) HUMPHREYS-BEHER, MICHAEL G UNIVERSITY OF FLORDIA BOX J-424 JHMHSC GAINESVILLE, FL 32611 Regulation of acinar cell proliferation

R01DE-08798-03 (ORTH) GREENBERGER, JOEL S UNIV OF MASSACHUSETTS MED CTR 55 LAKE AVENUE NORTH WORCESTER, MA 01655 Role of marrow stroma in osteoclast differentiation

R01DE-08824-01A2 (OBM) CARLSON, DAVID S UNIVERSITY OF MICHIGAN ANN ARBOR, MI 48109-1078 Growth following replacement of the mandibular condyle

P50DE-08845-04 (SRC) HEFT, MARC W UNIVERSITY OF FLORIDA GAINESVILLE, FL 32610 Research center on oral health in aging

P50DE-08845-04 0001 (SRC) DUNCAN, R P Research center on oral health in aging Dental services utilization among Florida's elderly

P50DE-08845-04 0002 (SRC) HEFT, M W Research center on oral health in aging Age differences in oral sensory functioning

P50DE-08845-04 0003 (SRC) CLARK, W B Research center on oral health in aging Host-parasite interactions in the healthy and periodontally diseased elderly

P50DE-08845-04 0004 (SRC) SCARPACE, P Research center on oral health in aging Beta-adrenergic mechanisms in salivary protein secretions

R01DE-08851-01A3 (OBM) BLOCK, MICHAEL S LSU SCHOOL OF DENTISTRY 1100 FLORIDA AVENUE NEW ORLEANS, LA 70119 Prospective evaluation of implant supported bridges

R44DE-08877-02 (SRC) KOEN, JOHN B MO-SCI CORPORATION PO BOX 2 ROLLA, MO 65401 Bioabsorbable glass fiber/polymer composites

R44DE-08878-02A1 (SRC) LYNCH, SAMUEL E INST OF MOLECULAR BIOLOGY, INC 812 HUNTINGTON AVENUE BOSTON, MA 02115 Development of a growth factor product to treat periodontitis

R01DE-08902-03 (OBM) DICKINSON, DOUGLAS P DENTAL BRANCH, UTHSC HOUSTON, TX 77225 Molecular analysis of human salivary cystatin genes

R44DE-08905-03 (SRC) WANG, RONG FAILURE ANALYSIS ASSOCIATES, I 8411 154TH AVE NE REDMOND, WASHINGTON 98052 Low-noble metal content duplex dental alloys

R01DE-08909-03 (OBM) VANNIER, MICHAEL W WASHINGTON UNIVERSITY ST LOUIS, MO 63110 Diagnostic imaging of craniosynostoses

R01DE-08911-01A3 (OBM) WISE, GARY E TEXAS COLLEGE OF OSTEOPATHIC M 3500 CAMP BOWIE BLVD FORT WORTH, TX 76107-2690 Cellular basis of tooth eruption

R01DE-08915-03 (OBM) LEBLANC, DONALD J UNIV OF TEXAS HEALTH SCI CTR 7703 FLOYD CURL DRIVE SAN ANTONIO, TX 78284-7758 Oral streptococcal virulence: new molecular approaches

R01DE-08916-03 (OBM) TUNG, MING S ADAHF PAFFENBARGER RES CTR NATIONAL BUREAU OF STANDARDS GAITHERSBURG, MD 20899 Three approaches to rapid remineralization of the tooth

PROJECT NO., ORGANIZATIONAL UNIT., INVESTIGATOR, ADDRESS, TITLE

P01DE-08917-02 (SRC) FRITZ, MICHAEL E EMORY UNIV SCH OF DENTISTRY 1462 CLIFTON RD, NE ATLANTA, GA 30322 Implant, prosthetic and periodontal studies in monkeys

P01DE-08917-02 0001 (SRC) LEMONS, JACK E Implant, prosthetic and periodontal studies in monkeys Biomaterials

P01DE-08917-02 0002 (SRC) JEFFCOAT, MARJORIE K Implant, prosthetic and periodontal studies in monkeys Radiology

P01DE-08917-02 0003 (SRC) BIDEZ, MARTHA W Implant, prosthetic and periodontal studies in monkeys Biomechanics

P01DE-08917-02 9000 (SRC) FRITZ, MICHAEL E Implant, prosthetic and periodontal studies in monkeys Biomaterials core

P01DE-08917-02 9001 (SRC) ARNOLD, ROLAND R Implant, prosthetic and periodontal studies in monkeys Microbiology core

R01DE-08921-03 (OBM) MELVIN, JAMES E UNIVERSITY OF ROCHESTER 601 ELMWOOD AVE, BOX 611 ROCHESTER, NY 14642 Physiology of mucus-secreting salivary glands

R29DE-08932-03 (OBM) YEUNG, MARIA K UNIV OF TEXAS HLTH SCI CTR 7703 FLOYD CURL DRIVE SAN ANTONIO, TX 78284 Genetic analysis of the fimbrial genes of actinomyces

R01DE-08937-01A2 (BNP) KINGHORN, ALAN D UNIVERSITY OF ILLINOIS CHICAGO 833 SOUTH WOOD ST CHICAGO, IL 60612 Noncariogenic intense natural sweetners

R29DE-08939-02 (OBM) PENDRYS, DAVID G UNIV OF CONNECTICUT HEALTH CTR SCHOOL OF DENTAL MEDICINE FARMINGTON, CT 06030 Risk factors of enamel fluorosis

R01DE-08941-03 (OBM) CASTLE, JOHN D UNIV OF VIRGINIA MED CTR CHARLOTTESVILLE, VA 22908 Sorting of parotid salivary proteins

R01DE-08942-03 (OBM) DANEO-MOORE, LOLITA TEMPLE UNIV SCH OF MEDICINE 3400 NORTH BROAD ST PHILADELPHIA, PA 19140 Chromosome organization in oral streptococci

R01DE-08946-01A2 (OBM) BILLINGS, RONALD J EASTMAN DENTAL CENTER 625 ELMWOOD AVENUE ROCHESTER, NY 14620 Assessment of risk of caries onset in children

R01DE-08948-02 (OBM) SHEA, BRIAN T NORTHWESTERN UNIVERSITY 303 E CHICAGO AVE CHICAGO, IL 60611 Effect of growth hormone on craniofacial proportions

R01DE-08952-02 (OBM) MARKS, SANDY C, JR UNIV OF MASSACHUSETTS MED CTR 55 LAKE AVE NORTH WORCESTER, MA 01655 Mandibular bone augmentation by prostaglandin E1

R01DE-08966-02 (OBM) KLEIN, BRADLEY G VIRGINIA TECH BLACKSBURG, VA 24061 Monoaminergic role in the trigeminal brainstem

R01DE-08971-02 (NLS) CHIAIA, NICOLAS L MEDICAL COLLEGE OF OHIO PO BOX 10008 TOLEDO, OH 43699-0008 Trigeminothalamic organization and plasticity

P01DE-08972-03 (SRC) SCHENKEIN, HARVEY A VIRGINIA COMMONWEALTH UNIV. BOX 566 MCV STATION RICHMOND, VA 23298-0001 Periodontal disease research program project grant

P01DE-08972-03 0001 (SRC) NANCE, W E Periodontal disease research program project grant Family study of adult onset periodontal disease

P01DE-08972-03 0002 (SRC) NANCE, W E Periodontal disease research program project grant Twin study of adult onset periodontal disease

P01DE-08972-03 0003 (SRC) MOORE, L V Periodontal disease research program project grant Bacteriologic studies of adult twins

P01DE-08972-03 0004 (SRC) TEW, J C Periodontal disease research program project grant Immune mechanisms in periodontal diseases

P01DE-08972-03 0005 (SRC) SCHENKEIN, HARVEY A Periodontal disease research program project grant Biostatistical core

P50DE-08973-02 (SRC) LEVINE, JON D UNIVERSITY OF CALIFORNIA U-426, BOX 0724 SAN FRANCISCO, CA 94143-0724 Trigeminal pain, mechanisms and control

P50DE-08973-02 0001 (SRC) RALSTON, HENRY Trigeminal pain, mechanisms and control Anatomical examination of trigeminothalmic organization

P50DE-08973-02 0002 (SRC) BASBAUM, ALLAN Trigeminal pain, mechanisms and control Modulation of noxious stimulus-induced C-FOS expression

P50DE-08973-02 0003 (SRC) CODERRE, TERENCE Trigeminal pain, mechanisms and control Analgesic synergy in animal models

P50DE-08973-02 0004 (SRC) LEVINE, JON Trigeminal pain, mechanisms and control Factors affecting dental postoperative pain

P50DE-08973-02 9000 (SRC) GOLDYNE, MARK Trigeminal pain, mechanisms and control Core--Biochemical pharmacology

R29DE-08994-03 (OBM) WRIGHT, JOHN TIMOTHY UNIVERSITY OF NORTH CAROLINA CB#7450 SCHOOL OF DENTISTRY CHAPEL HILL, N C 27599-7450 Dental analysis of epidermolysis bullosa

R37DE-09002-02 (OBM) SLAVKIN, HAROLD C UNIV OF SOUTHERN CALIFORNIA UNIVERSITY PARK GER 314, MC-01 LOS ANGELES, CA 90089-0191 Molecular phenotype of Hertwig's epithelial root sheath

R01DE-09018-03 (OBM) STASHENKO, PHILIP FORSYTH DENTAL CENTER 140 THE FENWAY BOSTON, MA 02115 Mechanism of bone destruction in periapical lesions

R15DE-09023-01A2 (OBM) MOGHADAM, BEHJAT KH UNIVERSITY OF MISSOURI 650 EAST 25TH STREET KANSAS CITY, KS 64108 Transferrin-receptor in human oral mucosa

R01DE-09035-09 (MBC) MACRINA, FRANCIS L VIRGINIA COMMONWEALTH UNIV BOX 678 MCV STATION RICHMOND, VA 23298-0678 Antibiotic resistance in oral and colonic anaerobes

R44DE-09063-02 (SRC) WEICKMANN, JOACHIM L XOMA CORPORATION 1545 17TH STREET SANTA MONICA, CA 90404 3-D structures of two low-calorie protein sweeteners

R01DE-09065-03 (OBM) ANDERSON, LEIGH C SEATTLE, WA 98195 SB-22 Diabetes and salivary gland function

R29DE-09066-04 (EVR) TURK, STEVEN R UNIVERSITY OF MICHIGAN 1011 N UNIVERSITY ANN ARBOR, MI 48109-1078 Ribonucleotide reductase--Target for oral herpes control

R29DE-09079-03 (OBM) HURWITZ, MARY Y TEXAS CHILDREN'S CLIN CARE CTR 8080 N. STADIUM DRIVE HOUSTON, TX 77054 CD18 mutations in periodontitis

R01DE-09081-02 (OBM) MICHALEK, SUZANNE M UNIVERSITY OF ALABAMA UAB STATION BIRMINGHAM, AL 35294 Genetically engineered oral vaccines and caries immunity

PROJECT NO., ORGANIZATIONAL UNIT., INVESTIGATOR, ADDRESS, TITLE

R01DE-09062-01A2 (OBM) CAUFIELD, PAGE W UNIV OF ALABAMA AT BIRMINGHAM UNIVERSITY STATION BIRMINGHAM, AL 35294 Transpositional mutagenesis and mutacins in S. mutans
R29DE-09063-04 (OBM) RITTMAN, BARRY R UNIV OF TEXAS HLTH SCI CTR P O BOX 20036 HOUSTON, TX 77225 Kinetics of langerhans cells in oral mucosa and skin
R01DE-09065-02 (OBM) KAPUR, KRISHAN K UCLA SCHOOL OF DENTISTRY LOS ANGELES, CA 90024 Efficacy of implant supported dentures in diabetics
R01DE-09066-01A1 (OBM) CORPRON, RICHARD E UNIVERSITY OF MICHIGAN 1011 NORTH UNIVERSITY AVENUE ANN ARBOR, MI 48109-1078 In Vivo enamel remineralizing fluoride-releasing device
R29DE-09068-01A2 (OBM) GARCIA, RAUL I TUFTS UNIV SCH OF DENTAL MED ONE KNEELAND STREET BOSTON, MA 02111 Vascular endothelium and periodontal inflammation
R01DE-09100-03 (OBM) KRUKOWSKI, MARILYN WASHINGTON UNIVERSITY 1 BROOKINGS DR ST LOUIS, MO 63130 Charged beads--Craniofacial reparir and augmentation
R01DE-09109-03 (OBM) LEVERETT, DENNIS H EASTMAN DENTAL CENTER 625 ELMWOOD AVENUE ROCHESTER, NY 14620 Prevalence and incidence of oral conditions in adults
R01DE-09119-03 (OBM) ROSENSTIEL, STEPHEN F OHIO STATE COLLEGE OF DENTISTR 305 WEST 12TH AVENUE COLUMBUS, OH 43210-1241 Fracture properties of dental ceramics
R01DE-09122-03 (OBM) VAN WART, HAROLD E FLORIDA STATE UNIVERSITY DEPT. OF CHEMISTRY TALLAHASSEE, FLA 32306 Inhibition of extracellular matrix metalloproteinases
R01DE-09126-02 (OBM) GOLDBERG, A JON UNIV OF CONNECTICUT HLTH CTR SCHOOL OF DENTAL MEDICINE FARMINGTON, CT 06030 Fiber-reinforced composites in dentistry
R01DE-09137-01A1 (NEUB) NAFTEL, JOHN P UNIV OF MISSISSIPPI MEDICAL CT 2500 NORTH STATE STREET JACKSON, MS 39216 Regulation of dental innervation by trophic factors
P01DE-09142-02 (SRC) LOESCHE, WALTER J UNIVERSITY OF MICHIGAN 1011 NORTH UNIVERSITY ANN ARBOR, MI 48109-1078 Geriatric dental program project
P01DE-09142-02 0001 (SRC) TERPENNING, MARGARET Geriatric dental program project Epidemiology of salivary and oropharyngeal disorders and clinical correlations
P01DE-09142-02 0002 (SRC) LOESCHE, WALTER J Geriatric dental program project Identification of bacterial risk factors in the elderly
P01DE-09142-02 0003 (SRC) LOPATIN, DENNIS Geriatric dental program project Factors predisposing the elderly to gram negative bacillary colonization
P01DE-09142-02 0004 (SRC) LANGMORE, SUSAN Geriatric dental program project Risk factors for aspiration pneumonia in elderly patients with dysphagia
P01DE-09142-02 9001 (SRC) BROMBERG, JUDITH Geriatric dental program project Biostatistical core
R01DE-09155-01A2 (OBM) GUNSOLLEY, JOHN C VIRGINIA COMMONWEALTH UNIVERSI PO BOX 566, MCV STATION RICHMOND, VA 23298-0566 Analysis of site specific periodontal data
R01DE-09161-01A2 (OBM) GENCO, CAROLINE A EMORY UNIVERSITY 1462 CLIFTON ROAD ATLANTA, GA 30322 Iron utilization by bacteroides gingivalis
P50DE-09164-03 (SRC) GASSER, DAVID L UNIVERSITY OF PENNSYLVANIA 37TH & HAMILTON WALK PHILADELPHIA, PA 19104-6072 Craniofacial anomalies research center
P50DE-09164-03 0002 (SRC) BUETOW, KENNETH H Craniofacial anomalies research center H-2 linked control of steroid susceptibilities
P50DE-09164-03 0003 (SRC) GIBSON, C Craniofacial anomalies research center Regulation of gene expression during enamel organ development
P50DE-09164-03 0004 (SRC) STAMBOLIAN, D E Craniofacial anomalies research center Molecular genetic mapping of the Nance Horan syndrome
P50DE-09164-03 0005 (SRC) GASSSER, D L Craniofacial anomalies research center Molecular genetic mapping of Treacher Collins syndrome and orofacial clefts
P50DE-09164-03 9000 (SRC) BUETOW, KENNETH H Craniofacial anomalies research center Molecular biology core
P50DE-09165-03 (SRC) SLAVKIN, HAROLD C UNIV OF SOUTHERN CALIFORNIA UNIVERSITY PARK GER 314 LOS ANGELES, CA 90089-0191 Center for craniofacial molecular biology
P50DE-09165-03 0001 (SRC) MAXON, ROBERT Center for craniofacial molecular biology Identification of genes involved in normal and abnormal craniofacial development
P50DE-09165-03 0002 (SRC) KEDES, LAURENCE Center for craniofacial molecular biology Distribution and mechanism of troponin C gene expression in craniofacial muscles
P50DE-09165-03 0003 (SRC) LAU, EDUARDO Center for craniofacial molecular biology Glucocorticoid receptor gene expression during craniofacial morphogenesis
P50DE-09165-03 0004 (SRC) SLAVKIN, HAROLD C Center for craniofacial molecular biology Autocrine and paracrine factors regulating first branchial arch
P50DE-09165-03 0005 (SRC) SHULER, CHARLES Center for craniofacial molecular biology Epithelial transformation into ectomesenchyme
P50DE-09170-03 (SRC) SOLURSH, MICHAEL UNIVERSITY OF IOWA DEPARTMENT OF BIOLOGY IOWA CITY, IA 52242 Genes important in craniofacial anomalies
P50DE-09170-03 0001 (SRC) HANSON, JAMES Genes important in craniofacial anomalies Genetic and evironmental risk factors for human facial cleft defects
P50DE-09170-03 0002 (SRC) MURRAY, JEFFERY Genes important in craniofacial anomalies Identification of genes involved in craniofacial anomalies
P50DE-09170-03 0003 (SRC) SOLURSH, M Genes important in craniofacial anomalies Cloning and sequencing of genes involved in craniofacial anomalies
P50DE-09170-03 9000 (SRC) RUSSO, A Genes important in craniofacial anomalies Molecular biology--tissue culture core facility
R29DE-09174-03 (OBM) LINDEMANN, ROBERT A UNIV OF CALIFORNIA SCH OF DENT CTR FOR HLTH SCIENCES LOS ANGELES, CA 90024-1668 Natural killer and monocyte regulation in periodontal disease
R29DE-09175-03 (OBM) ANN, DAVID K UNIVERSITY OF MINNESOTA 435 DELAWARE STREET MINNEAPOLIS, MN 55455 Gene expression of salivary gland specific genes
R01DE-09177-01A1 (OBM) HASSELL, THOMAS M UNIVERSITY OF FLORIDA BOX J-434, JHMHSC GAINESVILLE, FL 32610 Human twin studies of periodontal disease susceptibility
R01DE-09178-03 (OBM) BERTOLAMI, CHARLES N UCLA SCHOOL OF DENTISTRY 10833 LE CONTE AVE LOS ANGELES, CA 90024-1668 Hyaluronate catabolism in orofacial scarring
R01DE-09211-01A2 (BEM) LITT, MARK D UNIVERSITY OF CONNECTICUT FARMINGTON, CT 06030 Preparing for oral surgery--Cognitive-behavioral aspects
R01DE-09217-02 (BEM) TINANOFF, NORMAN UNIVER OF CONNECTICUT HLTH CTR 263 FARMINGTON AVE FARMINGTON, CT 06032 Predicting caries from biological and social variables
R01DE-09218-02 (OBM) MOCHAN, EUGENE U OF MED & DENT OF NEW JERSEY 401 HADDON AVENUE CAMDEN, NJ 08103 Interleukin-1 and gingival proteinases in periodontitis
R29DE-09219-02 (OBM) PRICE, RAY M HEALTH SCIENCES 630 WEST 168 STREET NEW YORK, NY 10032 Macrophage control of periodontal wound repair
R01DE-09237-02 (OBM) ROBERTS, W EUGENE INDIANA UNIVERSITY 1121 W MICHIGAN ST INDIANAPOLIS, IN 46202 Bone physiology of endosseous implants
R01DE-09270-06 (OBM) MARTINEZ, J RICARDO LOVELACE MEDICAL FOUNDATION 2425 RIDGECREST DRIVE, SE ALBUQUERQUE, NM 87108 Secretory mechanisms in the salivary glands
R01DE-09271-05A1 (OBM) IZUTSU, KENNETH T UNIVERSITY OF WASHINGTON SEATTLE, WA 98195 Labial salivary glands-autonomic characterization
R01DE-09292-01A1 (OBM) SODERHOLM, KARL-JOHAN M UNIVERSITY OF FLORIDA BOX J-446, JHMHC GAINESVILLE, FL 32610-0446 In vivo/in vitro wear performance of posterior composite
P50DE-09296-03 (SRC) CRAIG, ROBERT G UNIVERSITY OF MICHIGAN 2217 SCHOOL OF DENTISTRY ANN ARBOR, MI 48109-1078 Specialized materials science research center
P50DE-09296-03 0001 (SRC) O'BRIEN, W J Specialized materials science research center Strengthening mechanisms for dental procelain
P50DE-09296-03 0002 (SRC) KORAN, A Specialized materials science research center Silicone block copolymers for soft denture liners and maxillofacial materials
P50DE-09296-03 0003 (SRC) CRAIG, R G Specialized materials science research center Composite group
P50DE-09296-03 0004 (SRC) HANKS, C Specialized materials science research center Biocompatibility of prosthetic materials
P50DE-09307-03 (SRC) ANUSAVICE, KENNETH J UNIVERSITY OF FLORIDA BOX J-446, JHMHC GAINESVILLE, FL 32610-0446 Specialized materials science research center
P50DE-09307-03 0001 (SRC) BATICH, C Specialized materials science research center Controlled release of diagnostic and therapeutic agents
P50DE-09307-03 0002 (SRC) CLARK, A Specialized materials science research center Sol-gel derived powders with surface active properties
P50DE-09307-03 0004 (SRC) ANUSAVICE, K Specialized materials science research center Thermal and chemical control of glass-ceramic color
R01DE-09311-02 (OBM) TALAL, NORMAN UNIV OF TEXAS HEALTH SCIENCE C 7703 FLOYD CURL DRIVE SAN ANTONIO, TX 78284 Interleukin-2 production in Sjogren's syndrome
R29DE-09316-02 (OBM) DRAKE, DAVID R UNIVERSITY OF IOWA COLLEGE OF DENTISTRY IOWA CITY, IA 52242 Glucan-binding lectin of Streptococcus mutans
P50DE-09322-03 (SRC) BOWEN, RAFAEL L AMERICAN DENTAL ASSN HLTH FDN NATL INST OF STANDARDS & TECH GAITHERSBURG, MD 20899 Center of excellence for materials science research
P50DE-09322-03 0002 (SRC) ANTONUCCI, J Center of excellence for materials science research Resin system with minimal dimensional change
P50DE-09322-03 0003 (SRC) JOHSTON, A Center of excellence for materials science research Novel monomers for protective preventive coatings
P50DE-09322-03 0004 (SRC) CHOW, L Center of excellence for materials science research Synthetic dentin
P50DE-09322-03 0007 (SRC) EICHMILLER, F C Center of excellence for materials science research Maxillofacial protective prosthetic materials for radiation therapy
P50DE-09322-03 0008 (SRC) BOWEN, RAFAEL L Center of excellence for materials science research Beta-quartz microcrystalline glass megafilled restorations
R03DE-09373-01A1 (DSR) DRAKE, DAVID R UNIVERSITY OF IOWA DENTAL SCIENCE BLDG IOWA CITY, IA 52242 Bacterial adhesion to titanium implant surfaces
R03DE-09381-01A1 (DSR) FOTOS, PETE G UNIVERSITY OF IOWA COLLEGE OF DENTISTRY IOWA CITY, IA 52242 Genetic relatedness of candida albicans in oral commensa
R01DE-09389-02 (OBM) DENBESTEN, PAMELA K FORSYTH DENTAL CENTER 140 FENWAY BOSTON, MA 02115 Alterations in ameloblast function in enamel fluorosis
R01DE-09393-01A1 (OBM) WOOD, MORTON 666 WEST BALTIMORE STREET BALTIMORE, MD 21201 Bonded bridges--Projected longevity/periodontal response
R01DE-09399-02 (OBM) THESLEFF, IRMA UNIVERSITY OF HELSINKI SF-00300 HELSINKI FINLAND Molecular changes in differentiating dental mesenchyme
R01DE-09401-01A1 (OBM) KAPUR, KRISHAN K UCLA SCHOOL OF DENTISTRY LOS ANGELES, CA 90024 Oral motor and sensory functions in denture wearers
R29DE-09408-01A1 (ARRE) ROWLAND, RANDAL W VIRGINIA COMMONWEALTH UNIVERSI MCV STATION, BOX 566 RICHMOND, VA 23298 HIV infection--Host factors in acute periodontal disease
R01DE-09411-01A1 (OBM) TERRANOVA, VICTOR P COLUMBIA UNIVERSITY 630 WEST 168TH STREET NEW YORK, NY 10032 Periodontal ligament cell autocrine factor

PROJECT NO., ORGANIZATIONAL UNIT., INVESTIGATOR, ADDRESS, TITLE

R29DE-09418-01A1 (OBM) RUEGGEBERG, FREDERICK A MEDICAL COLLEGE OF GEORGIA SCHOOL OF DENTISTRY AUGUSTA, GA 30912-1264 Thermally induced changes in dental resin composites
R01DE-09419-01A2 (BEM) LOGAN, HENRIETTA L UNIVERSITY OF IOWA N334, DSB IOWA CITY, IA 52242 Pain, distress and personal control
R01DE-09420-01A1 (OBM) CLARKSON, BRIAN H UNIVERSITY OF CONNECTICUT 263 FARMINGTON AVE FARMINGTON, CT 06032 Human tooth root phosphoprotein and remineralization
R01DE-09426-01A1 (OBM) FLOOD, PATRICK M UNIVERSITY OF NORTH CAROLINA 308 DENTAL RESEARCH CTR CHAPEL HILL, NC 27599-7455 Immunogenicity of fimbrillin from B. gingivalis
R01DE-09428-02 (OBM) MIRELS, LILY UNIVERSITY OF CALIFORNIA 9500 GILMAN DR LA JOLLA, CA 92093-0322 Regulation of submandibular gland gene expression
R15DE-09434-01A1 (OBM) COHEN, STEPHEN M UMDNJ-NEW JERSEY DENTAL SCHOOL 110 BERGEN STREET NEWARK, NJ 07103-2425 Castability quantification by image analysis
R29DE-09439-01A2 (OBM) LAMONT, RICHARD J UNIVERSITY OF WASHINGTON SEATTLE, WA 98195 Colonization mechanisms of periodontal pathogens
R01DE-09445-03 (OBM) BUSH, C ALLEN UNIV OF MARYLAND BALTIMORE CO. DEPT. OF CHEMISTRY BALTIMORE, MD 21228 Structure of the receptors for oral bacterial adhesins
R13DE-09458-01S1 (SRC) DAVIDOVITCH, ZEEV THE OHIO STATE UNIVERSITY 305 WEST TWELFTH AVENUE COLUMBUS, OH 43210-1241 International conference on biological mechanisms of tooth movement
R01DE-09459-01A1 (OBM) GAY, CAROL V PENNSYLVANIA STATE UNIVERSITY 468A NORTH FREAS BUILDING UNIVERSITY PARK, PA 16802 Functional studies of osteoblasts
R03DE-09463-01A1 (DSR) NUMMIKOSKI, PIRKKA V UNIV TEXAS HEALTH SCIENCE CTR 7703 FLOYD CURL DR SAN ANTONIO, TX 78284 Subtraction radiography in detection of recurrent caries
R43DE-09481-01A1 (SSS) NEMIR, DAVID C 279 SHADOW MOUNTAIN EL PASO, TX 79912 Biofeedback apparatus for home treatment of bruxism
R43DE-09486-01A1 (SSS) CHARETTE, MARC F CREATIVE BIOMOLECULES, INC 35 SOUTH STREET HOPKINTON, MA 01748 Growth factor regeneration of periodontal tissue
R03DE-09488-01A1 (DSR) BAMFORD, OWEN S UNIVERSITY OF MARYLAND HOSP 22 SOUTH GREENE STREET BALTIMORE, MD 21201 Laryngeal EMG impedance and sounds in suckle feeding
R01DE-09496-02 (ARR) BATTERSON, WILLIAM W UNIV OF TEXAS HLTH SCI CENTER PO BOX 20068 HOUSTON, TX 77225 Oral diagnosis of HIV infected hemophiliac children
R01DE-09514-01A2 (OBM) RICHIE, JOHN P, JR AMERICAN HEALTH FOUNDATION ONE DANA ROAD VALHALLA, NY 10595 Nutritional biochemistry and neoplasia in oral tissues
R01DE-09517-02 (OBM) LALLY, EDWARD T UNIVERSITY OF PENNSYLVANIA 4001 SPRUCE ST PHILADELPHIA, PA 19104 Virulence factors in periodontal disease
R01DE-09523-01A1 (OBM) KAUGARS, GEORGE E MEDICAL COLLEGE OF VIRGINIA PO BOX 566 RICHMOND, VA 23298 Vitamin supplementation in the treatment of oral lesions
R01DE-09530-02 (OBM) BARAN, GEORGE R TEMPLE UNIVERSITY 3223 NORTH BROAD STREET PHILADELPHIA, PA 19140 Restorative material wear factors
R01DE-09532-03 (OBM) SOMERMAN, MARTHA J UNIVERSITY OF MICHIGAN 1011 N UNIVERSITY ANN ARBOR, MI 48109 Expression of attachment proteins during cementogenesis
R01DE-09540-01A1 (OBM) GREENE, ROBERT M JEFFERSON MEDICAL COLLEGE 1020 LOCUST STREET PHILADELPHIA, PA 19107 Growth factor regulation of cell differentiation
P01DE-09545-01A1 (SSS) LAMSTER, IRA B COLUMBIA UNIVERSITY 630 WEST 168TH STREET NEW YORK, NY 10032 Oral findings in HIV infection--Different risk groups
P01DE-09545-01A1 0001 (SSS) PHELAN, JOAN A Oral findings in HIV infection-- Different risk groups Epidemiology and clinical studies--Oral findings in HIV
P01DE-09545-01A1 0002 (SSS) LAMSTER, IRA B Oral findings in HIV infection-- Different risk groups Host response--Oral findings in HIV infection
P01DE-09545-01A1 0003 (SSS) ZAMBON, JOSEPH J Oral findings in HIV infection-- Different risk groups Microbiology of subgingival plaque
P01DE-09545-01A1 9001 (SSS) LAMSTER, IRA B Oral findings in HIV infection-- Different risk groups Core--Biostatistics
R01DE-09551-01A1 (OBM) LEVY, STEVEN M UNIVERSITY OF IOWA IOWA CITY, IA 52242 Longitudinal study of fluoride exposure and dental fluorosis
R01DE-09559-01 (NLS) HU, JAMES W UNIVERSITY OF TORONTO 124 EDWARD STREET TORONTO, CANADA M5G 1G6 Brain stem mechanisms of deep craniofacial pain
R01DE-09560-01A1 (OBM) CUTTING, COURT B NYU MEDICAL CENTER 550 FIRST AVENUE NEW YORK, NY 10016 Analysis of biological surface form by ridge curves
R01DE-09562-02 (SRC) BERGEY, EARL J STATE UNIVERSITY OF NEW YORK 3435 MAIN ST BUFFALO, NY 14214 Characterization of saliva-HIV interactions
R01DE-09563-02 (SRC) RESNICK, LIONEL MOUNT SINAI MEDICAL CTR 4300 ALTON RD MIAMI BEACH, FL 33140 HIV inhibitory factors in human saliva
R01DE-09569-02 (SRC) MALAMUD, DANIEL UNIVERSITY OF PENNSYLVANIA 4001 SPRUCE ST PHILADELPHIA, PA 19104 HIV inhibitory factors in human saliva
R03DE-09573-01 (DSR) BADEN, SALLY T CASE WESTERN RESERVE UNIVERSIT 2123 ABINGTON ROAD CLEVELAND, OH 44106 Developing neuronal pathways to the oral epithelium
R01DE-09575-02 (SRC) RICE, WILLIAM G EMORY UNIV SCH OF POSTGRAD DEN 1462 CLIFTON RD N.E. ATLANTA, GA 30322 Nature of inhibitors of HIV in human secretory fluids
R01DE-09576-02 (OBM) RIFKIN, BARRY R NEW YORK UNIVERSITY 345 E 24TH STREET NEW YORK, NY 10010 Effect of tetracyclines on bone cell function in vitro
R01DE-09581-02 (ORTH) GRAVES, DANA T BOSTON UNIV SCH OF DENTISTRY 100 E NEWTON ST BOSTON, MA 02118 Autocrine stimulation of normal bone cells

PROJECT NO., ORGANIZATIONAL UNIT., INVESTIGATOR, ADDRESS, TITLE

R01DE-09588-01A1 (OBM) SPENCER, ANDREW J UNIVERSITY OF ADELAIDE BOX 498 GPO ADELAIDE 5001 ADELAIDE 5001, SOUTH AUSTRALIA The social impact of oral disease in elderly populations
R01DE-09589-02 (SRC) PRASAD, KEDAR N UNIV OF COLORADO HLTH SCI CTR 4200 EAST NINTH AVE/BOX A-031 DENVER, CO 80262 Regulation of synthesis and secretion of salivary proteins
R01DE-09591-02 (SRC) CHOPRA, DHARAM P WAYNE STATE UNIVERSITY 2727 SECOND AVENUE DETROIT, MI 48201 Immortalization of human salivary epithelial cell lines
R55DE-09596-01A1 (OBM) JEFFERSON, DOUGLAS M NEW ENGLAND MEDICAL CENTER 750 WASHINGTON ST, PO BOX 477 BOSTON, MA 02111 Parotid acinar cell physiology--A new cell culture model
R01DE-09598-02 (SRC) SAMUELSON, LINDA C UNIVERSITY OF MICHIGAN 7761 MED SCI II BOX 0622 ANN ARBOR, MI 48109-0622 Salivary amylase expression in parotid cell lines
R01DE-09599-02 (SRC) CULP, DAVID J UNIV OF ROCHESTER MED CENTER 601 ELMWOOD AVENUE ROCHESTER, N Y 14642 Development of cell lines from sublingual glands
R29DE-09602-01A1 (OBM) SCHIFFERLE, ROBERT E SUNY 3435 MAIN STREET BUFFALO, NY 14214 B. gingivalis polysaccharides-- Structure and function
R43DE-09619-01A1 (SSS) HARRELL, WILLIAM E, JR MEDICAL ARTS BLDG 1110 ALLISON DRIVE ALEXANDER CITY, AL 35010 3-D cephalometric appraisal of TMJ/orthodontic patients
R01DE-09630-02 (SRC) RUGH, JOHN D UNIV OF TEXAS HLTH SCIENCE CTR 7703 FLOYD CURL DRIVE SAN ANTONIO, TX 78284-7910 Multisite clinical trial of rigid- vs wire-fixation
R13DE-09648-01A1 (SRC) STANFORD, JOHN W AMERICAN DENTAL ASSOCIATION 211 EAST CHICAGO AVENUE CHICAGO, IL 60611 Symposium--Esthetic restorative materials
R01DE-09653-01A1 (OBM) ENWONWU, CYRIL O MEHARRY MEDICAL COLLEGE 1005 D.B. TODD BLVD/BOX A 73 NASHVILLE, TN 37208 Ascorbate status and salivary gland function
R01DE-09655-01 (OBM) CASTLE, J DAVID UNIVERSITY OF VIRGINIA CHARLOTTESVILLE, VA 22908 Membrane function in parotid secretory mechanisms
R01DE-09658-01A1 (OBM) MONTGOMERY, PAUL C WAYNE STATE UNIVERSITY 540 EAST CANFIELD AVENUE DETROIT, MI 48201 Characterization of salivary-associated lymphoid tissue
R01DE-09659-01 (OBM) BALISH, EDWARD UNIVERSITY OF WISCONSIN 4638 MEDICAL SCIENCES CENTER MADISON, WI 53706 Immunity to oral cavity candidiasis
R29DE-09661-01A1 (OBM) GILLESPIE, M JANE STATE UNIVERSITY OF NEW YORK SCHOOL OF DENTAL MEDICINE BUFFALO, NY 14214 Action of the Wolinella recta lipopolysaccharide
R29DE-09662-01A1 (OBM) DAVIDSON, ROBERT M UNIV OF CONNECTICUT HLTH CENTE 263 FARMINGTON AVENUE FARMINGTON, CT 06030 Ion channels in periodontal connective tissue cells
R01DE-09669-01 (OBM) DIGNAM, JOHN D MEDICAL COLLEGE OF OHIO PO BOX 10008 TOLEDO, OH 43699-0008 Regulation and structure of prolyl-tRNA synthetase
R03DE-09671-01 (DSR) FIVES-TAYLOR, PAULA UNIVERSITY OF VERMONT GIVEN BLDG BURLINGTON, VT 05405 In vitro invasion model for periodontopathogens
R01DE-09677-01 (OBM) PLAUT, ANDREW G NEW ENGLAND MEDICAL CTR HOSP 750 WASHINGTON ST, BOX 006 BOSTON, MA 02111 IgA proteases of mucosal and cariogenic pathogens
R29DE-09678-01 (NLS) SEE, RONALD E WASHINGTON STATE UNIVERSITY PULLMAN, WA 99164-4820 Pharmacology of an animal model of tardive dyskinesia
R01DE-09684-01 (OBM) SHAPIRO, IRVING M UNIVERSITY OF PENNSYLVANIA 4001 SPRUCE STREET PHILADELPHIA, PA 19104 Oxidative metabolism & growth plate mineralization
R55DE-09690-01A1 (OBM) BEDI, GURRINDER S SUNY/BUFFALO SCH DENTAL MEDICI 213 FOSTER HALL BUFFALO, NY 14214 The organization and expression of cystatin genes
R01DE-09691-01 (OBM) RUSSELL, MICHAEL W UNIV OF ALABAMA AT BIRMINGHAM UAB STATION BIRMINGHAM, AL 35294 Salivary IgA antibodies in oral defense
R01DE-09692-01 (OBM) MELVIN, JAMES E UNIVERSITY OF ROCHESTER 601 ELMWOOD AVE, BOX 611 ROCHESTER, NY 14642 Mechanisms of anion transport proteins in salivary cells
P01DE-09696-01 (SRC) EICK, J DAVID UNIV OF MISSOURI-KANSAS CITY 650 E 25TH STREET KANSAS CITY, MO 64108 Improved polymeric restorative through molecular design
P01DE-09696-01 0001 (SRC) CHAPPELOW, CECIL C Improved polymeric restorative through molecular design Development of copolymer dental adhesive
P01DE-09696-01 0002 (SRC) KINZIG, BARBARA J Improved polymeric restorative through molecular design Surface characterization of dental restorative resins
P01DE-09696-01 0003 (SRC) YOURTREE, DAVID M Improved polymeric restorative through molecular design Biocompatibility tests of restorative molecular stability
P01DE-09696-01 9001 (SRC) EICK, J DAVID Improved polymeric restorative through molecular design Core--Statistical support
P01DE-09696-01 9002 (SRC) EICK, J DAVID Improved polymeric restorative through molecular design Core--Surface and interface characterization
P01DE-09696-01 9003 (SRC) EICK, J DAVID Improved polymeric restorative through molecular design Core--Biocompatibility testing
R03DE-09730-01 (DSR) RAWLS, HENRY R UNIV TEXAS HEALTH SCIENCE CTR 7703 FLOYD CURL DRIVE SAN ANTONIO, TX 78284-7890 Oral controlled-release delivery systems
R01DE-09731-01 (OBM) CHAO, LEE MEDICAL UNIV OF SOUTH CAROLINA 171 ASHLEY AVENUE CHARLESTON, SC 29425 Salivary kallikreins--Gene expression and secretion
P30DE-09737-02 (SRC) PIHLSTROM, BRUCE L UNIV OF MINNESOTA SCH OF DENT 515 DELAWARE ST, SE MINNEAPOLIS, MN 55455 Minnesota clinical dental research center
P30DE-09737-02 0002 (SRC) MICHALOWICZ, BRYAN Minnesota clinical dental research center Distribution of bacteria in human gingival plaque

PROJECT NO., ORGANIZATIONAL UNIT., INVESTIGATOR, ADDRESS, TITLE

P30DE-09737-02 0003 (SRC) HINRICHS, JAMES Minnesota clinical dental research center Laser Doppler measurements for periodontal evaluation
P30DE-09737-02 0004 (SRC) PINTADO, MARIA Minnesota clinical dental research center Quantitative wear of enamel at occlusal contacts in vivo
P30DE-09737-02 9000 (SRC) DELONG, RALPH Minnesota clinical dental research center Biophysical analysis core
P30DE-09737-02 9001 (SRC) HERZBERG, MARK Minnesota clinical dental research center Molecular/cell analysis core
P30DE-09737-02 9002 (SRC) BORN, DAVID Minnesota clinical dental research center Clinical research management and analysis core
P30DE-09743-02 (SRC) PAGE, ROY C UNIVERSITY OF WASHINGTON SM-42 SEATTLE, WA 98195 Clinical dental research core centers
P30DE-09743-02 0012 (SRC) KIYAK, ASUMAN Clinical dental research core centers Evaluating informed consent in dentistry
P30DE-09743-02 0014 (SRC) MILGROM, PETER Clinical dental research core centers Benzodiazepines and cognitive behavioral therapy
P30DE-09743-02 0015 (SRC) WILSON, LEANNE Clinical dental research core centers Controlled trial of amitriptyline for temporomandibular dysfunction
P30DE-09743-02 0016 (SRC) WELLS, NORMA Clinical dental research core centers Fissure sealant pilot study
P30DE-09743-02 0017 (SRC) PERSSON, RUTGER Clinical dental research core centers Rapidly progressive periodontitis and preterm childbirth
P30DE-09743-02 0018 (SRC) LAMONT, RICHARD J Clinical dental research core centers DNA probes for Streptococcus mutans and S sobrinus
P30DE-09743-02 9000 (SRC) ENGEL, L DAVID Clinical dental research core centers Laboratory core
P30DE-09743-02 9001 (SRC) DEROUEN, TIMOTHY A Clinical dental research core centers Biometry core
P30DE-09743-02 9002 (SRC) HOLLENDER, LARS Clinical dental research core centers Imaging core
P30DE-09743-02 9003 (SRC) DWORKIN, SAMUEL F Clinical dental research core centers Clinical core
P30DE-09743-02 0003 (SRC) STIEFEL, DORIS J Clinical dental research core centers Use of dental chemoprevention in disabled populations
P30DE-09743-02 0004 (SRC) LERESCHE, LINDA Clinical dental research core centers Analysis of facial movement disorders
P30DE-09743-02 0009 (SRC) SHAPIRO, PETER Clinical dental research core centers Implants for maxillary protraction
P30DE-09743-02 0011 (SRC) ROTHWELL, BRUCE R Clinical dental research core centers Hemostasis for dental extractions in hemophiliacs
R01DE-09761-01A1 (PBC) TRAVIS, JAMES UNIVERSITY OF GEORGIA ATHENS, GA 30602 Bacterial proteinases in periodontal disease
R43DE-09765-01 (SSS) LESIECKI, MICHAEL CANDELA LASER CORPORATION 530 BOSTON POST ROAD WAYLAND, MA 01778 Flash cure light for dental composites
R43DE-09767-01A1 (SSS) DONDERO, RICHARD S CISTRON BIOTECHNOLOGY INC 10 BLOOMFIELD AVE PINE BROOK, NJ 07058 Interleukin-1 beta levels in patients with periodontitis
R03DE-09770-01 (DSR) LEVY, STEVEN M UNIVERSITY OF IOWA COLLEGE OF DENTISTRY IOWA CITY, IA 52242 Fluoride treatment of incipient root surface caries
R13DE-09772-01 (SRC) BAWDEN, JAMES W UNIVERSITY OF NORTH CAROLINA CHAPEL HILL, NC 27599-7455 Workshop--Changing patterns in systemic fluoride intake
R03DE-09773-01 (DSR) DUNIPACE, ANN J INDIANA UNIVERSITY 415 NORTH LANSING ST INDIANAPOLIS, IN 46202 Genotoxicity of glutaraldehyde; safe use in dentistry
R43DE-09787-01A1 (SSS) BOURGELAIS, DONNA B MEDICAL LASER RES & DEV CORP PO BOX 539 MALDEN, MA 02148 Accelerated osseointegration
R03DE-09799-01 (DSR) BAYLES, KENNETH W UNIVERSITY OF MARYLAND BALTIMORE COUNTY BALTIMORE, MD 21228 Regulation of exoenzyme genes in streptococcus mutans
R03DE-09804-01 (DSR) MILGROM, PETER M UNIVERSITY OF WASHINGTON SEATTLE, WA 98195 Benzodiazepines and cognitive behavioral therapy
R03DE-09807-01 (DSR) GRIFFEN, ANN L OHIO STATE UNIVERSITY 305 W 12TH AVE COLUMBUS, OH 43210 Molecular methods for strain identification of A. actinomycetemcomitans
R13DE-09808-01A1 (SRC) RAZZOOG, MICHAEL E UNIVERSITY OF MICHIGAN 1011 NORTH UNIVERSITY ANN ARBOR, MI 48109-1078 National workshop black dentistry in the 21st century
R03DE-09810-01 (DSR) PLESH, OCTAVIA UNIVERSITY OF CALIFORNIA 707 PARNASSUS AVENUE SAN FRANCISCO, CA 94143-0758 Phosphorus MRS of normal human masseter muscle
R01DE-09812-01 (OBM) IZUTSU, KENNETH T UNIVERSITY OF WASHINGTON SEATTLE, WA 98195 Ion channels in salivary gland duct cells
R03DE-09831-01 (DSR) WOLINSKY, LAWRENCE E UNIVERSITY OF CALIFORNIA 405 HILGARD AVE LOS ANGELES, CA 90024-1406 Treponemal interactions with epithelial cell monolayers
R29DE-09832-01 (OBM) LANDESBERG, REGINA UNIVERSITY OF ROCHESTER SCHOOL OF MEDICINE & DENTISTRY ROCHESTER, NY 14642 Temporomandibular joint-- Cellular and molecular biology
P01DE-09835-01A1 (SRC) STOOKEY, GEORGE K INDIANA UNIVERSITY SCH OF DENT 415 NORTH LANSING STREET INDIANAPOLIS, IND 46202 Pharmacological effects of fluoride
P01DE-09835-01A1 0001 (SRC) JACKSON, RICHARD D Pharmacological effects of fluoride Long-term effects of fluoride ingestion
P01DE-09835-01A1 0002 (SRC) DUNIPACE, ANN J Pharmacological effects of fluoride Effects of fluoride in medically compromised animals
P01DE-09835-01A1 0003 (SRC) STOOKEY, GEORGE K Pharmacological effects of fluoride Impact of malnutrition on fluoride pharmacology
P01DE-09835-01A1 9001 (SRC) KATZ, BARRY P Pharmacological effects of fluoride Biostatistics core
P01DE-09835-01A1 9002 (SRC) DUNIPACE, ANN J Pharmacological effects of fluoride Laboratory core
R01DE-09837-01 (OBM) KIYONO, HIROSHI UNIV OF ALABAMA AT BIRMINGHAM UAB STATION BIRMINGHAM, AL 35294 Salivary IgA response--Regulation by TH1 and TH2 cells
R01DE-09839-01 (OBM) LAINE, RICHARD M UNIVERSITY OF WASHINGTON 325 ROBERTS HALL FB-10 SEATTLE, WA 98195 Tailored copolymers as advanced dental restorations
R01DE-09841-01 (OBM) BOYD, NORMAN D UNIVERSITY OF MASSACHUSETTS 55 LAKE AVE NORTH WORCESTER, MASS 01655 Signal transduction in salivary gland
R01DE-09848-01 (OBM) WEI, YEN DREXEL UNIVERSITY 32ND AND CHESTNUT STREETS PHILADELPHIA, PA 19104 Synthesis of molecular composites novel dental materials
R01DE-09851-01 (OBM) WALTERS, JOHN D POSTLE HALL, BOX 5 305 WEST 12TH AVE COLUMBUS, OH 43210 Role of gingival fluid polyamines in PMN modulation
P01DE-09859-01 (SRC) MARSHALL, SALLY J UNIVERSITY OF CALIFORNIA 707 PARNASSUS AVE BOX 0758 SAN FRANCISCO, CA 94143-0758 Dentin characterization and modification
P01DE-09859-01 0001 (SRC) JENDRESEN, MALCOLM D Dentin characterization and modification Effects of postextraction history on dentin
P01DE-09859-01 0002 (SRC) MARSHALL, GRAYSON W Dentin characterization and modification Dentin characterization
P01DE-09859-01 0003 (SRC) KINNEY, JOHN H Dentin characterization and modification X-ray tomographic microscopy of dentin
P01DE-09859-01 0004 (SRC) BHATNAGAR, RAJENDRA Dentin characterization and modification Dentin collagen characterization and grafting
P01DE-09859-01 0005 (SRC) WHITE, JOEL M Dentin characterization and modification Laser modification of dentin
R15DE-09863-01 (OBM) GOODMAN, ALAN H HAMPSHIRE COLLEGE AMHERST, MA 01002 Undernutrition, morbidity, and enamel development
R03DE-09864-01 (DSR) KURAMITSU, HOWARD K UNIVERSITY OF TEXAS 7703 FLOYD CURL DRIVE SAN ANTONIO, TX 78284-7888 Genetic analysis of S. mutans aciduricity
R15DE-09865-01 (OBM) GETTLEMAN, LAWRENCE UNIVERSITY OF LOUISVILLE LOUISVILLE, KY 40292 Phosphazene polymers for dental & biomedical application
R03DE-09866-01 (DSR) GILBERT, JEREMY L NORTHWESTERN UNIVERSITY 311 E CHICAGO AVE CHICAGO, IL 60611 Scanning potential microscope for spatial imaging
R15DE-09872-01 (OBM) WHITSON, S WILLIAM SOUTHERN ILLINOIS UNIVERSITY EDWARDSVILLE, IL 62026 In vitro study of human reparative dentin formation
R15DE-09874-01 (OBM) KASINATHAN, CHINNASWAMY UNIV OF MED/DENT OF NEW JERSEY 110 BERGEN STREET NEWARK, NJ 07103-2400 Protein fatty acylesterase in salivary glands
R29DE-09875-01 (OBM) MACDOUGALL, MARY B UNIVERSITY/SOUTHERN CALIFORNIA 2250 ALCAZAR STREET LOS ANGELES , CA 90033 Dentinogenesis imperfecta
R01DE-09883-02 (OBM) VIG, PETER S UNIVERSITY OF PITTSBURGH SCHOOL OF DENTAL MEDICINE PITTSBURGH, PA 15261 Orthodontic process and outcome--Efficacy studies
R13DE-09884-02 (SRC) SCHROEDER, KATHLEEN LEE WEST VIRGINIA UNIVERSITY MORGANTOWN, WV 26506 First international conference on smokeless tobacco
R03DE-09889-01 (DSR) MILLER, CORINNE E UNIVERSITY OF MINNESOTA 515 DELAWARE MINNEAPOLIS, MN 55455 Use of dental sealants--a diffusion of an innovation
R03DE-09890-01 (DSR) ODA, DOLPHINE UNIVERSITY OF WASHINGTON SEATTLE, WA 98195 Human papilloma virus and oral cancer
R43DE-09906-01 (SSS) SOLTANI, PETER K QUANTEX CORPORATION 2 RESEARCH COURT ROCKVILLE, MD 20850 New storage phosphor imaging media for oral radiography
R03DE-09915-01 (DSR) TATAKIS, DIMITRIS N UNIVERSITY OF LOUISVILLE HEALTH SCIENCES CENTER LOUISVILLE, KY 40292 The role of lipoxins in bone cell metabolism
R13DE-09917-01 (SRC) KIM, SYNGCUK COLUMBIA UNIV DENTAL SCHOOL 630 WEST 168TH STREET NEW YORK, NY 10032 Conference--Pathobiology of the dentin/pulp complex
R03DE-09930-01 (SRC) CHEN, PRISCILLA B SUNY AT BUFFALO 216 FOSTER HALL BUFFALO, NY 14214 Lymphocyte activation by porphyromonas gingivalis
R03DE-09931-01 (DSR) EDGERTON, MIRA SUNY AT BUFFALO 109 FOSTER HALL BUFFALO, N Y 14214 Salivary conditioning of dental acrylic
R03DE-09933-01 (DSR) LEACH, ROBIN J UNIV OF TEXAS HLTH SCI CENTER 7703 FLOYD CURL DRIVE SAN ANTONIO, TX 78284-7762 Genetic basis of oculoauriculovertebral dysplasia
R03DE-09935-01 (DSR) SHROFF, BHAVNA UNIVERSITY OF MARYLAND 666 WEST BALTIMORE ST BALTIMORE, MD 21201 Follicular expression of collagen I during eruption
R29DE-09942-01 (OBM) MARUCHA, PHILLIP T OHIO STATE UNIVERSITY 305 WEST 12TH STREET COLUMBUS, OH 43210 Gene expression in activated human PMN
R29DE-09954-01 (OBM) HECHT, JACQUELINE T UNIV OF TEXAS HLTH SCI CTR P O BOX 20708 HOUSTON, TX 77225 DNA linkage study of cleft lip and palate
R13DE-09956-01 (SRC) BARKMEIER, WAYNE W CREIGHTON UNIVERSITY 24TH & CALIFORNIA OMAHA, NE 68178 International symposium on adhesives in dentistry
R01DE-09978-01 (OBM) AHMED, A RAZZAQUE CENTER FOR BLOOD RESEARCH 800 HUNTINGTON AVENUE BOSTON, MA 02115 Oral vesiculo-bullous diseases-- Mechanism of pathogenes
R55DE-09983-01 (OBM) PHIPPS, KATHY R OREGON HEALTH SCIENCES UNIVERS 611 SW CAMPUS DR, SD 3 PORTLAND, OR 97201-3097 The relationship between fluoridation and osteopenia
R03DE-09998-01 (DSR) VAUGHN, LINDA K MARQUETTE UNIVERSITY 604 N 16TH ST MILWAUKEE, WI 53233 Opioid mechanisms in nitrous oxide dependence
R03DE-10000-02 (DSR) MACCHIARULO, PATRICIA A UNIVERSITY OF MINNESOTA 515 DELAWARE ST. S.E MINNEAPOLIS, MN 55455 Investigation of the receptor for osteocalcin
R03DE-10002-01 (DSR) RUBENSTEIN, LORETTA VIRGINIA COMMONWEALTH UNIV MCV STATION, BOX 566 RICHMOND, VA 23298-0566 Lower arch perimeter preservation using the lingual arch
R03DE-10003-01 (DSR) CHIANG, TAO HARVARD SCH OF DENTAL MEDICINE 188 LONGWOOD AVENUE BOSTON, MA 02115 Cloning of the hamster TGF-alpha 3'untranslated region

PROJECT NO., ORGANIZATIONAL UNIT., INVESTIGATOR, ADDRESS, TITLE

R03DE-10005-01 (DSR) **CULP, DAVID J** UNIVERSITY OF ROCHESTER 601 ELMWOOD AVENUE, BX 611 ROCHESTER, NY 14642-0002 Guinea pig sublingual gland as a mucous cell model

R43DE-10010-01 (SSS) **STEINHOFF, FREDRICK** MEDICAL ELECTRONIC CONSULT ASS 5761 N ALTON INDIANAPOLIS, IN 46208 A replacement X-ray cone to reduce dental X-ray dosage

R43DE-10016-01 (SSS) **SCHETKY, L** MEMRY TECHNOLOGIES 83 KEELER AVENUE NORWALK, CT 06854 Titanium based variable modulus orthodontic wire

R43DE-10018-01 (SSS) **KARUNA-KARAN, ARTHUR** REGENETEC BIOMATRIX INC. 18511 58TH AVE NE SEATTLE, WA 98155 A controlled resorption periodontal collagen membrane

R03DE-10047-01 (DSR) **JOHNSON, ROGER B** UNIV OF MISSISSIPPI MEDICAL CT 2500 NORTH STATE STREET JACKSON, MS 39216-4505 Effects of IGF-1 and cell deformation on bone deposition

R01DE-10066-01 (HED) **BRONNER-FRASER, MARIANNE** UNIVERSITY OF CALIFORNIA IRVINE, CA 92717 Cell adhesion molecules in neural crest ontogeny

S15DE-10068-01 (NSS) **PHIPPS, GRANT** T S U N Y AT BUFFALO BUFFALO, N Y 14214 Small instrumentation grant

S15DE-10069-01 (NSS) **BIRKEDAL-HANSEN, HENNING** UNIV. OF ALAB. AT BIRM. UAB STATION BIRMINGHAM, AL 35294 Small instrumentation grant

S15DE-10070-01 (NSS) **SQUIER, CHRISTOPHER A** UNIV OF IOWA COLL OF DENTISTRY IOWA CITY, IA 52242 Small instrumentation grant

S15DE-10071-01 (NSS) **FRANKL, SPENCER N** BOSTON UNIVERSITY 100 E NEWTON ST RM G-317 BOSTON, MA 02118 Small instrumentation grant

S15DE-10072-01 (NSS) **ASHE, WARREN K** HOWARD UNIVERSITY 520 W ST NW WASHINGTON, DC 20059 Small instrumentation grant

S15DE-10073-01 (NSS) **CLARK, GLENN T** UNIV OF CALIFORNIA LOS ANGELES, CA 90024 Small instrumentation grant

S15DE-10074-01 (NSS) **VAIDYANATHAN, T K** UNIV OF MED & DENT OF N J 110 BERGEN STREET NEWARK, NJ 07103 Small instrumentation grant

S15DE-10075-01 (NSS) **SCHACHTELE, CHARLES F** 515 DELAWARE ST SE MINNEAPOLIS, MN 55455 Small instrumentation grant

S15DE-10076-01 (NSS) **KURAMITSU, HOWARD K** UNIVERSITY OF TEXAS 7703 FLOYD CURL DRIVE SAN ANTONIO, TX 78284-7888 Small instrumentation grant

S15DE-10077-01 (NSS) **GARANT, PHILIAS R** STATE UNIVERSITY OF NEW YORK SCHOOL OF DENTAL MEDICINE STONY BROOK, N Y 11794-8700 Small instrumentation grant

S15DE-10078-01 (NSS) **GIBBONS, RONALD J** FORSYTH DENTAL CENTER 140 THE FENWAY BOSTON, MA 02115 Small instrumentation grant

S15DE-10079-01 (NSS) **LEGEROS, RACQUEL Z** NEW YORK UNIV DENTAL CENTER 345 EAST 24TH STREET RM 1178W NEW YORK, NY 10010 Small instrumentation grant

S15DE-10080-01 (NSS) **HANKS, CARL T** UNIVERSITY OF MICHIGAN 1011 N UNIVERSITY AVENUE ANN ARBOR, MI 48109-1078 Small instrumentation grant

S15DE-10081-01 (NSS) **SCHENKEIN, HARVEY A** P.O. BOX 566 RICHMOND, VA 23298 Small instrumentation grant

S15DE-10082-01 (NSS) **EICHMILLER, FREDERICK C** AMERICAN DENTAL ASSN HEALTH FD 211 EAST CHICAGO AVE CHICAGO, IL 60611 Small instrumentation grant

S15DE-10083-01 (NSS) **FEATHERSTONE, JOHN D** EASTMAN DENTAL CENTER 625 ELMWOOD AVENUE ROCHESTER, NY 14620 Small instrumentation grant

S15DE-10084-01 (NSS) **DIRKSEN, THOMAS R** MEDICAL COLLEGE OF GEORGIA SCHOOL OF DENTISTRY AUGUSTA, GA 30912-1000 Small instrumentation grant

S15DE-10085-01 (NSS) **OMNELL, KARL-AKE** UNIVERSITY OF WASHINGTON SCHOOL OF DENTISTRY SC-62 SEATTLE, WA 98195 Small instrumentation grant

P30DE-10126-01 (SRC) **WEFEL, J S** UNIVERSITY OF IOWA IOWA CITY, IA 52242 Clinical core center for oral health research

P30DE-10126-01 0003 (SRC) **LEVY, STEVEN M** Clinical core center for oral health research Daily fluoride application for root surface caries

P30DE-10126-01 0004 (SRC) **ETTINGER, RONALD** Clinical core center for oral health research Dental care for cognitively impaired elderly patients

P30DE-10126-01 9001 (SRC) **KOHOUT, F** Clinical core center for oral health research Core--Experimental design and biostatistics core

P30DE-10126-01 9002 (SRC) **ETTINGER, RONALD** Clinical core center for oral health research Core--Clinical core

P30DE-10126-01 9003 (SRC) **SQUIER, CHRISTOPHER** Clinical core center for oral health research Core--Laboratory core

P30DE-10126-01 0001 (SRC) **DRAKE, DAVID R** Clinical core center for oral health research Adhesion of periodontal pathogens to titanium implant surfaces

P30DE-10126-01 0002 (SRC) **SQUIER, CHRISTOPHER A** Clinical core center for oral health research Permeability of hyperplastic and hyperkeratotic oral epithelium

R01DE-10130-01 (OBM) **WIDMER, CHARLES G** UNIVERSITY OF FLORIDA BOX J-416, JHMHSC GAINESVILLE, FL 32610-0416 Functional organization and control of human masseters

R01DE-10131-01 (OBM) **ZERNIK, JOSEPH** UNIV OF SOUTHERN CALIFORNIA DEN 4338 LOS ANGELES, CA 90089-0641 Craniofacial skeleton-osteoblastic gene expression

R01DE-10132-01 (OBM) **DESSEM, DEAN** UNIV OF MARYLAND DENTAL SCHOOL 666 W BALTIMORE STREET BALTIMORE, MD 21201 The role of tooth merchanoreceptors in jaw movement

R01DE-10140-01 (OBM) **STANNARD, JAN G** ENDICOTT COLLEGE 376 HALE STREET BEVERLY, MA 01915 Glass transition temperature and wear of dental resins

R01DE-10144-01 (ARRC) **SUNDSTROM, PAULA** TEXAS COLLEGE OSTEOPATHIC MED 3500 CAMP BOWIE BLVD FORT WORTH, TX 76107-2690 Proteins of Candida albicans an AIDS-related pathogen

R03DE-10200-01 (DSR) **SEGHI, ROBERT R** 305 WEST 12TH AVENUE COLUMBUS, OH 43210 Sol-gel derived continuous dual matrix composites

N01DE-12584-00 (**) **STANFORD, JOHN W** Improved dental instruments and materials through standard development

N01DE-12585-00 (**) **ORENSTEIN, JAN M** Opportunistic infections of oral mucosa and other tissue in AIDS

N01DE-12586-00 (**) **KIYAK, H ASUMAN** Cost-effective preventive regimens for high-risk older adults

N01DE-12587-00 (**) **HEFT, MARC W** Biomedical and psychosocial risk factors for tooth loss in older Americans

N01DE-12588-00 (**) **BURT, BRIAN A** Tooth loss and periodontitis in diabetic adults of the Gala River Indian

N01DE-12589-00 (**) **HOLLIS, JACK** Group oral hygiene intervention for older periodontal patients

N01DE-12590-00 (**) **MOORE, PAUL A** Risk factors for oral disease in adult diabetics

N01DE-12591-00 (**) **BEAZOGLOU, TRYPHON** Determinants of loss permanet teeth

N01DE-12592-00 (**) **MASTERS, MARY N** Progression of, and risk markers associated with, early onset periodontitis

N01DE-32441-17 (**) **LEVERETT, DENNIS H** Effect of prenatal fluoride in preventing dental caries

N01DE-62560-10 (**) **JUDKINS, DAVID** Epidemiologic survey of oral health in school children

N01DE-62562-16 (**) **BLAINE, LOIS D** Microbial and hybridoma data base as taxonomic and ecological resources

N01DE-72570-07 (**) **BARMES, DAVID** International collaborative study of oral health outcome

N01DE-82573-05 (**) **BONITO, ARTHUR** International collaborative study of oral health outcomes

N01DE-92574-05 (**) **SWITALSKI, RICHARD N** Program enhancement and maintenance of the NIDR microbiological info system

N01DE-92576-09 (**) **KESSLER, BEATRICE** Conference management documentation and analytical servi

R01DK-00110-40 (BCE) **LIEBERMAN, SEYMOUR** ST LUKE'S-ROOSEVELT INST HTH S 428 W 59TH ST AJA 118 NEW YORK, NY 10019 Application of chemical methods to steroid metabolism

R01DK-00180-40A1 (REB) **MIGEON, CLAUDE J** THE JOHNS HOPKINS HOSPITAL 600 N WOLFE STREET BALTIMORE, MD 21205 Relation of hormones to growth and development

R01DK-00562-37 (PB) **GUNSALUS, IRWIN C** UNIVERSITY OF ILLINOIS 1209 W. CALIFORNIA STREET URBANA, IL 61801 Metabolic mechanisms

R01DK-00709-38 (MCHA) **DAUBEN, WILLIAM G** UNIVERSITY OF CALIFORNIA BERKELEY, CA 94720 Ultraviolet irradiation of natural products

R01DK-01022-36 (BCE) **LUND, PAULINE K** UNIVERSITY OF NORTH CAROLINA CB# 7545 CHAPEL HILL, NC 27599-7545 Role of endocrine secretions in growth and development

R01DK-01107-35 (BIO) **TANG, JORDAN J** OKLAHOMA MEDICAL RES FND 825 N.E. 13TH STREET OKLAHOMA CITY, OKLA 73104 Components of human gastric juice

R01DK-01226-35 (SAT) **LACY, PAUL E** WASHINGTON UNIV SCH OF MEDICIN 660 SOUTH EUCLID AVENUE ST LOUIS, MO 63110 Tissue culture of the islets of Langerhans

R01DK-01237-36 (BCE) **PORTER, JOHN C** UNIV OF TX SOUTHWESTERN MED CT 5323 HARRY HINES BLVD DALLAS, TX 75235-9032 Hormonal control of hypothalamic dopamine secretion

R01DK-01260-36 (BNP) **MERRIFIELD, ROBERT B** ROCKEFELLER UNIVERSITY 1230 YORK AVENUE NEW YORK, NY 10021-6399 Solid phase synthesis of peptides and proteins

K12DK-01295-06S3 (SRC) **CLARK, ROBERT** COLLEGE OF MEDICINE UNIVERSITY OF IOWA IOWA CITY, IOWA 52242 Physician scientist program award

K12DK-01296-07 (DDK) **STOBO, JOHN D** JOHNS HOPKINS HOSPITAL 1830 E MONUMENT STREET BALTIMORE, MD 21205 Physician scientist program award

R37DK-01392-35 (GMA) **ISSELBACHER, KURT J** MASSACHUSETTS GENERAL HOSPITAL 32 FRUIT STREET BOSTON, MA 02114 Intestinal cells, membranes and hexose transport

K12DK-01401-06S2 (SRC) **CHIN, WILLIAM W** BRIGHAM AND WOMEN'S HOSPITAL 75 FRANCIS STREET BOSTON, MASS 02115 Physician scientist program award

K12DK-01408-07 (DDK) **STEINBERG, DANIEL** UNIV OF CALIFORNIA, SAN DIEGO DEPARTMENT OF MEDICINE LA JOLLA, CA 92093 Physician scientist program award

K12DK-01410-07 (DDK) **POTTS, JOHN T, JR** MASSACHUSETTS GENERAL HOSPITAL FRUIT STREET BOSTON, MA 02114 Program Physician Scientist Award

R37DK-01410-33 (NSS) **GRODSKY, GEROLD M** UNIVERSITY OF CALIFORNIA THIRD AND PARNASSUS AVENUES SAN FRANCISCO, CA 94143 Insulin synthesis, storage and secretion in vitro

K12DK-01423-05S2 (SRC) **HARDIN, JOHN A** YALE UNIVERSITY 333 CEDAR STREET NEW HAVEN, CT 06510 Physician scientist program award

R01DK-01447-35 (END) **GREER, MONTE A** OREGON HEALTH SCIENCES UNIV 3181 S W SAM JACKSON PARK ROAD PORTLAND, OR 97201-3098 Neuroendocrine and thyroid physiology

K11DK-01456-04 (ADDK) **KRAGIE, LAURA** 321 HOCHSTETTER HALL SUNYAB BUFFALO, NY 14260 Thyroid hormone and cellular calcium regulation

R01DK-01483-32 (GMB) **SCHACHTER, DAVID** COLUMBIA UNIVERSITY 630 WEST 168TH STREET NEW YORK, NY 10032 Transport of calcium

R01DK-01549-34 (BMT) **METZLER, DAVID E** IOWA STATE UNIVERSITY BIOCHEM. & BIOPHYSICS DEPT AMES, IOWA 50011 Mechanisms and inhibitors of pyridoxal-dependent enzymes

K04DK-01553-06 (MET) **TURK, JOHN W** WASHINGTON UNIV SCHOOL OF MED. 660 SOUTH EUCLID AVENUE ST LOUIS, MO 63110 Phospholipid-derived mediators and insulin secretion

K08DK-01554-06 (ADDK) **DEVLIN, JOHN T** MAINE MEDICAL CENTER 22 BRAMHALL ST PORTLAND, ME 04102 Fuel metabolism during and after exercise in diabetes

K04DK-01589-05 (MBY) **HARDISON, ROSS C** PENNSYLVANIA STATE UNIVERSITY 206 ALTHOUSE LABORATORY UNIVERSITY PARK, PA 16802 Regulation and evolution of rabbit globin genes

K08DK-01603-06 (ADDK) **GROGGEL, GERALD C** UNIVERSITY OF VERMONT D305 GIVEN BLDG BURLINGTON, VT 05405 Heparan sulfate proteoglycan in glomerular injury

K11DK-01660-05 (ADDK) **BREYER, JULIA A** VANDERBILT UNIVERSITY ROOM S-3223 MCN NASHVILLE, TN 37232 Purification & characterization of renal preproEGF

K11DK-01662-05 (ADDK) **TEPPER, ROBERT I** MASSACHUSETTS GENERAL HOSPITAL FRUIT STREET BOSTON, MA 02114 Basic science training in hematology & molecular genetics

PROJECT NO., ORGANIZATIONAL UNIT., INVESTIGATOR, ADDRESS, TITLE

K11DK-01680-06 (ADDK) SACKS, DAVID B BRIGHAM & WOMEN'S HOSPITAL 75 FRANCIS STREET BOSTON, MA 02115 Phosphorylation of the glucose transporter by insulin

K11DK-01682-05 (ADDK) HELPER, DEBRA J INDIANA UNIVERSITY MEDICAL CTR 975 W. WALNUT ST., IB 424 INDIANAPOLIS, IN 46202-5121 Contractile mechanisms in esophageal smooth muscle

K04DK-01690-05 (BIO) DEPAOLI-ROACH, ANNA A INDIANA UNIVERSITY 635 BARNHILL DRIVE INDIANAPOLIS, IN 46202-5122 Structure and regulation of phosphoprotein phosphatases

K04DK-01722-04 (PC) LA PORTE, DAVID C UNIVERSITY OF MINNESOTA 4-225 MILLARD HALL MINNEAPOLIS, MN 55455 Structure and regulation of a protein kinase/phosphatase

K08DK-01726-05 (ADDK) LUHRS, CAROL A SUNY-DOWSTATE MEDICAL CENTER 450 CLARKSON AVENUE BROOKLYN, N Y 11203 Properties and function of folate binding protein

K11DK-01732-05 (ADDK) STEERS, WILLIAM D UNIVERSITY OF VIRGINIA BOX 422 CHARLOTTESVILLE, VA 22908 Effect of bladder outlet obstruction detrusor function

K04DK-01742-05 (MET) PATEL, TARUN B UNIV. OF TENNESSEE, MEMPHIS 874 UNION AV./100 CROWNE BLDG. MEMPHIS, TN 38163 Hormonal regulation of energy metabolism

K04DK-01745-05 (GMB) GOOD, DAVID W UNIVERSITY OF TEXAS MEDICAL BR JOHN SEALY HOSP 4.200 E-62 GALVESTON, TEX 77550 Regulation of thick ascending limb acid-base transport

K08DK-01746-05 (ADDK) TOMPKINS, RONALD G MASSACHUSETTS GENERAL HOSPITAL AMBULATORY CARE CENTER BOSTON, MA 02114 Hybrid artificial liver using immobilized hepatocytes

K08DK-01747-05 (ADDK) ALTSCHULER, STEVEN M CHILDRENS HOSP OF PHILADELPHIA 34TH & CIVIC CENTER BLVD PHILADELPHIA, PA 19104 Esophageal receptor reflexes--Brainstem circuitry

K04DK-01748-05 (EDC) HANIS, CRAIG L DEMOG. & POP. GENETICS CENTER POST OFFICE BOX 20334 HOUSTON, TX 77225 Genetic and epidemiologic approaches to chronic diseases

K08DK-01750-05 (ADDK) CONKLIN, JEFFREY L UNIV OF IOWA HOSP &CLINICS IOWA CITY, IOWA 52242 Muscarinic control of gastrointestinal smooth muscle

K11DK-01751-04 (ADDK) TAKESHITA, KENICHI YALE UNIVERSITY 333 CEDAR STREET NEW HAVEN, CT 06510 Studies on gene expression during granulopoiesis

K11DK-01762-05 (ADDK) SEMENKOVICH, CLAY F WASHINGTON UNIV., SHOOL OF MED 4566 SCOTT AVE., BOX 8046 ST. LOUIS, MO 63110 Regulation of lipoprotein lipase synthesis

K11DK-01777-05 (ADDK) BACALLAO, ROBERT L UCLA SCHOOL OF MEDICINE 405 HILGARD AVENUE LOS ANGELES, CA 90024 Isolation of a component of the bacterial export pathway

K04DK-01782-03 (PC) SHUKLA, SHIVENDRA D UNIV OF MISSOURI SCH OF MED DEPT OF PHARMACOLOGY COLUMBIA, MO 65212 PAF-stimulated phosphoinositide turnover in platelets

K04DK-01787-05 (PHY) ZERWEKH, JOSEPH E U OF TX SW MED CTR AT DALLAS 5323 HARRY HINES BLVD DALLAS, TX 75235 25,26(OH)2D3--Effect on metabolism of 1,25(OH)2D

K08DK-01789-05 (DDK) LLOYD, MARK L WM S MIDDLETON MEM VETS HOSP 2500 OVERLOOK TERRACE MADISON, WI 53705 Biosynthesis of lactase in health and disease

K11DK-01790-05 (DDK) WORMAN, HOWARD J MOUNT SINAI SCHOOL OF MEDICINE ONE GUSTAVE L. LEVY PL, BOX 10 NEW YORK, NY 10029 Characterization of nuclear pore complex proteins

K08DK-01792-05 (DDK) CZAJA, MARK J ALBERT EINSTEIN COL. OF MED. 1300 MORRIS PARK AVENUE BRONX, NY 10461 Cytokines as regulators of hepatic fibrosis

K04DK-01793-04 (BBCB) STARK, RUTH E COLLEGE OF STATEN ISLAND CUNY 50 BAY STREET STATEN ISLAND, NEW YORK 10301 Spectroscopic studies of model digestive systems

K11DK-01799-05 (DDK) LEBWOHL, DAVID SLOAN-KETTERING INST CANCER 1275 YORK AVENUE, BOX 97 NEW YORK, NY 10021 Substrates for the insulin receptor tyrosine kinase

K04DK-01810-05 (NTN) MOCK, DONALD M UNIV OF IOWA HOSP & CLINICS IOWA CITY, IOWA 52242 Human requirement for biotin

K11DK-01811-05 (DDK) MATSUI, SUZANNE M DIVISION OF GASTROENTEROLOGY 3801 MIRANDA AVENUE PALO ALTO, CA 94304 Rotavirus VP3--Molecular determinants of function

K11DK-01815-04 (DDK) KUJUBU, DEAN A UCLA SCHOOL OF MEDICINE 900 VETERAN AVENUE LOS ANGELES, CA 90024 Gene control of cell differentiation and proliferation

K11DK-01816-04 (DDK) REILLY, ROBERT F YALE UNIVERSITY 333 CEDAR STREET NEW HAVEN, CT 06510 Molecular biology of the renal Na/H exchanger

K08DK-01820-04 (DDK) SALOMON, DANIEL R GEORGETOWN UNIVERSITY 37TH AND O STREETS, NW WASHINGTON, DC 20057 Tolerance in experimental kidney transplantation

K04DK-01822-04 (MET) PESSIN, JEFFREY E UNIVERSITY OF IOWA IOWA CITY, IA 52242 Transmembrane activation of the insulin receptor kinase

K08DK-01823-04 (DDK) DELVALLE, JOHN UNIV OF MICHIGAN MEDICAL CTR. 1150 W. MEDICAL CENTER DRIVE ANN ARBOR, MI 48109-0682 Chemistry and biology of gut pancreastatin

K11DK-01825-04 (DDK) ISALES, CARLOS M YALE UNIVERSITY SCH OF MED 3333 CEDAR STREET NEW HAVEN, CT 06510 Critical cellular events in aldosterone synthesis

K04DK-01827-04 (CBY) WILEY, HENRY S THE UNIVERSITY OF UTAH 50 NORTH MEDICAL DRIVE SALT LAKE CITY, UT 84132 A quantitative model of EGF-cell interactions

K11DK-01831-04 (DDK) MA, AVERIL COLUMBIA UNIVERSITY HLTH SCI 630 WEST 168TH STREET NEW YORK, NY 10032 Training in molecular genetics & gastroenterology

K08DK-01832-03 (DDK) MAILLIARD, MARK E UNIVERSITY OF FLORIDA BOX J-214, JHMHC GAINESVILLE, FL 32610 Amino acid control of plasma membrane protein synthesis

K08DK-01836-05 (AMS) SILVERBERG, SHONNI J COLUMBIA UNIVERSITY 630 WEST 168TH STREET NEW YORK, NY 10032 Influence of phosphate upon human skeletal metabolism

K08DK-01839-04 (DDK) KATZKA, DAVID A HOSP OF UNIV OF PENNSYLVANIA 3400 SPRUCE ST PHILADELPHIA, PA 19104 Ionic channel regulation in mammalian visceral myocytes

PROJECT NO., ORGANIZATIONAL UNIT., INVESTIGATOR, ADDRESS, TITLE

K08DK-01840-03 (DDK) SMITH, BRENDA C PENNSYLVANIA STATE UNIVERSITY PO BOX 850 HERSHEY, PA 17033 Control of acid-base balance by liver and kidney

K11DK-01841-04 (DDK) ROTTMAN, GERALD A JOHNS HOPKINS UNIVERSITY 600 NORTH WOLFE STREET BALTIMORE, MD 21205 Spectroscopic studies of iron proteins & metabolism

K11DK-01845-04 (DDK) LANDIS, CLAUDIA UNIV OF CALIF, SAN FRANCISCO S 1212 SAN FRANCISCO, CA 94143-0415 The signaling roles of GI/GO proteins

K08DK-01848-03 (DDK) LENCER, WAYNE I CHILDREN'S HOSPITAL 300 LONGWOOD AVE BOSTON, MA 02115 Transepithelial targeting of cholera toxin

K08DK-01849-04 (DDK) PERR, HILARY A MEDICAL COLLEGE OF VIRGINIA MCV STATION, BOX 529 RICHMOND, VA 23298 Ontogeny of human intestinal smooth muscle cell function

K11DK-01851-04 (DDK) MACIAS, WILLIAM L INDIANA UNIVERSITY FESLER HALL RM. 108, 1120 S DR INDIANAPOLIS, IN 46202-5113 Role of ion transport renal cyst growth

K11DK-01854-04 (DDK) SEALFON, STUART C MOUNT SINAI ONE GUSTAVE LEVY PL. NEW YORK, NY 10029 Regulation of neuro-hormone receptors

K08DK-01856-04 (DDK) LIPKOWITZ, MICHAEL S MT SINAI SCH OF MED-RENAL DIV BOX 1243, 1 GUSTAVE LEVY PLACE NEW YORK, NEW YORK 10029 Regulation of renal membrane permeability

K08DK-01858-03 (DDK) LAKE, JOHN R UNIVERSITY OF CALIFORNIA 3RD & PARNASSUS AVE. SAN FRANCISCO, CA 94143-0538 Role of H+/HCO3- transport in bile formation

K08DK-01859-04 (DDK) HAYS, STEVEN R U OF TX SW MED CEN AT DALLAS 5323 HARRY HINES BLVD DALLAS, TX 75235 Regulation of acidification in the OMCT

K11DK-01860-04 (DDK) LACEY, STEPHEN W UNIV OF TEXAS SWESTERN MED CTR 5323 HARRY HINES BLVD DALLAS, TX 75235-9013 Molecular basis of lactase expression

K08DK-01861-04 (DDK) CLARE-SALZLER, MICHAEL J UCLA CTR FOR THE HLTH SCIENCE DEPT OF MEDICINE LOS ANGELES, CA 90024-1682 Role of the dendritic cells in NOD autoimmune diabetes

K08DK-01863-04 (DDK) THOMPSON, JOHN F NEW ENGLAND MED CENTER BOX 213 750 WASHINGTON ST BOSTON, MA 02111 Role of epidermal growth factor receptor in enterocytes

K04DK-01868-04 (END) LINDBERG, IRIS LOUISIANA STATE UNIVERSITY 1901 PERDIDO STREET NEW ORLEANS, LA 70112 Enkephalin biosynthesis in adrenal medulla

K08DK-01869-03 (DDK) VAN ADELSBERG, JANET S COLUMBIA UNIVERSITY 630 WEST 168TH STR.-P&S 10-421 NEW YORK, NY 10032 Molecular mechanisms of HC03- secretion

K08DK-01870-03 (DDK) LAKSHMANAN, MARK C CASE WESTERN RESERVE SCH OF M 2119 ABINGTON ROAD CLEVELAND, OH 44106 Thyroid hormone transport across CNS plasma membranes

K11DK-01872-04 (DDK) ROBERTSON, DAVID G EMORY UNIVERSITY MED SCHOOL DEPARTMENT OF BIOCHEMISTRY ATLANTA, GA 30322 Insulin signal transduction and insulin resistance

K04DK-01874-03 (END) WEHRENBERG, WILLIAM B UNIVERSITY OF WISCONSIN DPT OF HEALTH SCIENCES MILWAUKEE, WI 53201 Neuroendocrine regulation of growth

K11DK-01877-04 (DDK) PEARCE, DAVID UNIVERSITY OF CALIFORNIA 1065 HSE, BOX 0532 SAN FRANCISCO, CA 94143 Role of gene regulation in renal physiologic responses

K11DK-01878-03 (DDK) SEGAL, ROBERT UNIVERSITY OF CALIFORNIA 405 HILGARD AVENUE LOS ANGELES, CA 90024 Transcription regulation and cell differentiation

K11DK-01879-03 (DDK) ANTON, PETER A THE REGENTS OF THE UNIV OF CA 405 HILGARD AVE. LOS ANGELES, CA 90024-1406 Neuroimmunomodulation in human gut mucosa

K08DK-01883-05 (DDK) SEGERSON, THOMAS PATRICK OREGON HLTH SCIS UNIVERSITY 3181 SW SAM JACKSON PARK ROAD PORTLAND, OR 97201-3098 Regulation of TRH receptor biosynthesis

K08DK-01885-04 (DDK) KONE, BRUCE C 506 GROOM DRIVE TOWSON, MD 21204 Structure-function analysis of na/k-atpase isoforms

K08DK-01886-03 (DDK) BLUMBERG, RICHARD S BRIGHAM AND WOMEN'S HOSPITAL 75 FRANCIS STREET BOSTON, MA 02115 Assembly and function of the T cell receptor/CD3 complex

K08DK-01888-03 (DDK) STAR, ROBERT A UNIV OF TX SWESTERN MED CTR 5323 HARRY HINES BLVD DALLAS, TX 75235 Acid-base transport in inner medullary collecting ducts

K08DK-01893-03 (DDK) BARNARD, JOHN A VANDERBILT UNIVERSITY MEDICAL CTR, D-4130 NASHVILLE, TN 37232 Role of transforming growth factors in the intestine

K08DK-01894-03 (DDK) DANOFF, ANN ALBERT EINSTEIN COL OF MED 1300 MORRIS PK AVENUE BRONX, NY 10461 Translational regulation of preprosomatostatin

K04DK-01897-04 (BPO) GEISELMAN, PAULA J LOUISIANA STATE UNIVERSITY BATON ROUGE, LA 70803-4525 Hunger and satiety produced by simple sugar

K04DK-01898-03 (HED) KELLER-WOOD, MAUREEN E UNIVERSITY OF FLORIDA PHARMACODYNAMICS, BOX J-487 GAINESVILLE, FL 32610-0274 Control of corticotropin during pregnancy

K08DK-01899-04 (DDK) TURKA, LAURENCE A UNIVERSITY OF MICHIGAN MED. CT 1150 W. MEDICAL CENTER DRIVE ANN ARBOR, MI 48109-0676 Suppressor cells in human renal transplantation

K11DK-01900-03 (DDK) ROSENBLUM, NORMAN D HARVARD MEDICAL SCHOOL 25 SHATTUCK STREET BOSTON, MA 02115 Molecular biology of mesangial matrix in health/disease

K08DK-01902-02 (DDK) CHIPKIN, STUART R BOSTON UNIV SCH OF MED 80 EAST CONCORD STREET BOSTON, MA 02118 Glucocorticoids and hexose transport across the blood brain barrier

K08DK-01903-02 (DDK) DICKINSON, CHRIS J UNIV OF MICHIGAN MEDICAL CTR BOX 0800 ANN ARBOR, MI 48109 Regulation of gastrin post-translational processing

K08DK-01904-03 (DDK) FOSTER, MARY H UNIVERSITY OF PENNSYLVANIA 700 CLINICAL RESEARCH BLDG PHILADELPHIA, PA 19104-6144 Genetic origins of nephritogenic autoantibodies

K11DK-01905-03 (DDK) HABER, BARBARA A CHILDREN'S HOSP. OF PHILADELPH 34TH AND CIVIC CENTER BLVD. PHILADELPHIA, PA 19104

PROJECT NO., ORGANIZATIONAL UNIT., INVESTIGATOR, ADDRESS, TITLE

Biogenesis of canalicular membrane glycoproteins

K08DK-01908-03 (DDK) COHEN, MITCHELL B CHILDREN'S HOSPITAL MED CNTR ELLAND & BETHESDA AVENUES CINCINNATI, OH 45229 Regulation of ST action--Human intestinal ST receptor

K08DK-01909-03 (DDK) GUPTA, SANJEEV ALBERT ENSTEIN COLL OF MEDICIN 1300 MORRIS PARK AVE BRONX, NY 10461 Growth factors and liver regeneration

K08DK-01910-03 (DDK) MARINO, CHRISTOPHER R YALE UNIV SCHOOL OF MEDICINE 333 CEDAR ST NEW HAVEN, CT 06510 The secretory granule membrane in regulated exocytosis

K04DK-01918-03 (PC) COBB, MELANIE H UNIV OF TX SW MEDICAL CENTER 5323 HARRY HINES BLVD DALLAS, TX 75235 Insulin-enhanced phosphorylation of ribosomal protein S6

K08DK-01920-03 (DDK) SEAQUIST, ELIZABETH R UNIVERSITY OF MINNESOTA HARVARD ST @ E RIVER RD MINNEAPOLIS, MN 55455 Pge2, g proteins, and insulin secretion

K11DK-01924-03 (DDK) HOLZMAN, LAWRENCE B UNIVERSITY OF MICHIGAN 3914 TAUBMAN CENTER ANN ARBOR, MI 48109-0364 Thrombospondin in crescentic glomerulonephritis

K08DK-01925-03 (DDK) SCHILSKY, MICHAEL ALBERT EINSTEIN COLL OF MED 1300 MORRIS PARK AVE BRONX, NY 10461 Hepatic biosynthesis of ceruloplasmin

K11DK-01927-03 (DDK) SKOLNIK, EDWARD NEW YORK UNIVERSITY MEDICAL CT 550 FIRST AVENUE NEW YORK, NY 10016 Glycosylated proteins in developing diabetic kidney disease

K08DK-01928-03 (DDK) KRAUSE, KURT L BAYLOR COLLEGE OF MEDICINE 6565 FANNIN, MS A-601 HOUSTON, TX 77030 Diffraction methods in biomedical research

K08DK-01929-03 (DDK) SCHEVING, LAWRENCE A STANFORD UNIVERSITY SCH OF MED ROOM S-069 STANFORD, CA 94305-5100 E. coli heat stable entertoxin and intestinal receptor

K11DK-01931-02 (DDK) LEVY, RICHARD S UNIVERSITY OF CALIFORNIA 10833 LE CONTE AVE/44-144 CHS LOS ANGELES, CA 90024-1786 Molecular genetics of gastrointestinal T cell receptors

K08DK-01933-03 (DDK) GRONICH, JOSEPH UNIV HOSPITAL OF CLEVLAND 2074 ABINGTON ROAD CLEVELAND, OH 44106 Phospholipase A2 regulation in the mesangial cell

K08DK-01934-03 (DDK) KOPIN, ALAN S NEW ENGLAND MED CTR HOSPITALS 750 WASHINGTON STREET-233 BOSTON, MA 02111 Biosynthesis of secretin

K11DK-01935-02 (DDK) DUVALL, MICHAEL D UNIVERSITY OF MINNESOTA 1988 FITCH AVE ST PAUL, MN 55108 Regulation of ion transport across porcine gallbladder

K08DK-01936-02 (DDK) ORLOFF, JOHN J WEST HAVEN VA MEDICAL CTR WEST SPRING STREET WEST HAVEN, CT 06516 Receptors for parathyroid hormone-like protein

K08DK-01937-02 (DDK) WANG, TIMOTHY C MASSACHUSETTS GENERAL HOSPITAL FRUIT STREET BOSTON, MA 02114 Development regulation of gastrin gene expression

K08DK-01938-02 (DDK) HEROLD, KEVAN C UNIVERSITY OF CHICAGO 5841 S MARYLAND AVENUE CHICAGO, IL 60637 Islet cell reactive T lymphocytes in murine diabetes

K04DK-01942-02 (HEM) PARKER, CHARLES J VA MEDICAL CENTER 500 FOOTHILL DRIVE SALT LAKE CITY, UT 84148 Characterization of erythrocyte inhibitor of complement

K11DK-01945-02 (DDK) GRABER, MARTHA L UNIVERSITY OF CALIFORNIA 505 PARNASSUS, BOX 0724 SAN FRANCISCO, CA 94143 Identification of a G protein in PI pathway in T cells

K11DK-01946-02 (DDK) MC CONNELL, KEVIN R YALE UNIV SCHOOL OF MEDICINE 333 CEDAR STREET NEW HAVEN, CT 06510 Molecular biology of anion transport in mammalian kidney

K08DK-01948-02 (DDK) COHEN, MITCHELL L STANFORD UNIV SCHOOL OF MED STANFORD, CA 94305-5100 Molecular regulation of intestinal aminooligopeptidase

K08DK-01949-01A1 (DDK) HERMAN-BONERT, VIVIEN S CEDARS-SINAI MEDICAL CENTER 8700 BEVERLY BLVD LOS ANGELES, CA 90048 Pathogenesis of human pituitary adenomas

K08DK-01952-02 (DDK) LIANG, JAKE T MASSACHUSETTS GENERAL HOSPITAL 149 13TH STREET 7TH FLOOR CHARLESTOWN, MA Pathogenesis of idiopathic liver disease

K08DK-01953-03 (DDK) HEILIG, CHARLES W BRIGHAM AND WOMEN'S HOSPITAL 75 FRANCIS ST BOSTON, MA 02115 Homoglogous recombination to inactivate a gt gene

K08DK-01954-02 (DDK) ROBERTS, MICHELLE M UNIVERSITY OF PITTSBURGH 930 SCAIFE HALL PITTSBURGH, PA 15261 Physiology and pathophysiology of vasopressin synthesis

K08DK-01956-02 (DDK) BROSIUS, FRANK C UNIV OF MICHIGAN MEDICAL CTR 1150 WEST MEDICAL CENTER DRIVE ANN ARBOR, MI 48109 Characterization of glomerular glucose transporters

K08DK-01963-02 (DDK) CALLES-ESCANDON, JORGE UNIVERSITY OF VERMONT COLLEGE OF MEDICINE BURLINGTON, VT 05405 Upper body obesity--Thermogenic perspective

K12DK-01964-02 (DDK) BIERMAN, EDWIN L UNIVERSITY OF WASHINGTON MAIL STOP RG-26 SEATTLE, WA 98195 Program physician scientist award

K12DK-01965-02 (DDK) KREDICH, NICHOLAS M PO BOX 3100 DURHAM, NC 27710 Program physician scientist award

K12DK-01977-02 (DDK) LUX, SAMUEL E CHILDREN'S HOSPITAL CORP 300 LONGWOOD AVENUE BOSTON, MA 02115 Program physician scientist award

K04DK-01978-01 (END) TOLLEFSEN, SHERIDA E WASHINGTON UNIV SCH OF MEDICIN 400 SO. KINGSHIGHWAY ST. LOUIS, MO 63110 Structure definition of IGF I receptor functional domain

K08DK-01980-01A1 (DDK) JORGENSEN, E VERENA ALL CHILDRENS HOSPITAL 801 SIXTH ST. SOUTH BOX 690 ST PETERSBURG, FL 33701 Cholinergic regulation of growth hormone secretion

K08DK-01983-01A1 (DDK) ROSENBAUM, MICHAEL ROCKEFELLER UNIVERSITY 1230 YORK AVENUE NEW YORK, NY 10021-6399 The ontogeny and maintenance of regional fat distribution

K08DK-01984-02 (DDK) BRION, LUC P BRONX MUNICIPAL HOSPITAL CENTE PELHAM PARKWAY SOUTH BRONX, NY 10461 Regulation and development of renal acid-base transport

K08DK-01986-02 (DDK) FORCE, THOMAS L MASSACHUSETTS GENERAL HOSPITAL FRUIT STREET BOSTON, MA 02114 Non-cyclooxygenase eicosanoids in renal mesangial cells

K08DK-01987-02 (DDK) LIDOFSKY, STEVEN D UNIVERSITY OF CALIFORNIA HSW 1120 SAN FRANCISCO, CA 94143-0538 Mechanisms of ionic signaling by hepatic growth factors

K04DK-01988-02 (BIO) APPLING, DEAN R UNVI OF TEXAS AT AUSTIN AUSTIN, TX 78712 Regulation of folate-mediated one-carbon metabolism

K04DK-01989-01A1 (BCE) BROOKS, CHARLES L OHIO STATE UNIVERSITY 1925 COFFEY ROAD COLUMBUS, OH 43210-1005 Phosphorylated bovine prolactin and growth hormone

K11DK-01990-02 (DDK) SENDER, LEONARD S UNIVERSITY OF LOUISVILLE LOUISVILLE, KY 40292 Mouse models for genetic diseases

K08DK-01992-02 (DDK) DANNENBERG, ANDREW J CORNELL UNIVERSITY MEDICAL COL 1300 YORK AVENUE NEW YORK, NY 10021 Modulation of xenobiotic toxicity by diet

K11DK-01997-02 (DDK) NAKAMOTO, JON M UCLA MEDICAL CENTER 22-315 MDCC LOS ANGELES, CA 90024-1752 Molecular basis of pseudohypoparathyroidism type Ia

K08DK-01998-02 (DDK) LENZ, HEINZ J UNIV OF CALIF, SAN DIEGO 0648 225 DICKENSON STRET LA JOLLA, CA 92093-0648 Characterization of brain-gut transcription factors

R01DK-02001-34 (MET) BUSE, MARIA G MED. UNIV. OF SOUTH CAROLINA 171 ASHLEY AVENUE CHARLESTON, SC 29425 Factors that modify insulin action

K08DK-02005-02 (DDK) FARWELL, ALAN P UNIVERSITY OF MASS MED CTR 55 LAKE AVE NORTH WORCESTER, MA 01655 Hormone action in the central nervous system

K04DK-02006-02 (PHY) MILANICK, MARK A UNIVERSITY OF MISSOURI MA415 MEDICAL SCIENCES COLUMBIA, MO 65212 Mechanism of the Ca/H exchange pump

K08DK-02007-01 (DDK) EAKER, ERVIN Y UNIVERSITY OF FLORIDA PO BOX J214 JHMHC GAINESVILLE, FL 32610 Study of cytoskeletal proteins in enteric neurons

K11DK-02009-01 (DDK) WOLOSCHAK, MICHAEL MOUNT SINAI SCH OF MEDICINE ONE GUSTAVE L LEVY PLACE NEW YORK, NY 10029 Analysis of human POMC promoter function

K08DK-02010-01 (DDK) RUSSELL, GARY J MASSACHUSETTS GENERAL HOSPITAL BARTLETT EXTENION 4 BOSTON, MA 02114 Defining mucosal lymphocyte subpopulation

K08DK-02011-01A1 (DDK) ROTHSTEIN, DAVID M DANA-FARBER CANCER INSTITUTE 44 BINNEY STREET/MAYER-755 BOSTON, MA 02115 Regulation of T cells by CD45 in renal transplantation

K08DK-02012-02 (DDK) ARAKAKI, RICHARD F UNIVERSITY OF HAWAII 1356 LUSITANA ST., SUITE 718 HONOLULU, HI 96813 Insulin sensitivity in native hawaiians with NIDDM

K08DK-02013-01 (DDK) HECHT, GAIL A UNIVERSITY OF ILLINOIS 840 S WOOD ST CHICAGO, IL 60612 Regulation of intestinal epithelial paracellular flow

K08DK-02014-01 (DDK) DOHANICS, JANOS UNIV OF PITTSBURGH, SCH OF MED E-1140 BIOMEDICAL SCIENCE TOWE PITTSBURGH, PA 15260 Determinants of magnocellular neuron survival after injury

K08DK-02015-01 (DDK) SOMLO, STEFAN YALE UNIV SCHOOL OF MEDICINE 333 CEDAR STREET NEW HAVEN, CT 06510 Cloning of a second locus (PKD2) for polycystic disease

K08DK-02017-01 (DDK) WAYBILL, MARY M PENNSYLVANIA STATE UNIVERSITY P O BOX 850 HERSHEY, PA 17033 Role of intracellular calcium in mesangial cell growth

K11DK-02018-01 (DDK) BOLLEKENS, JACQUES A YALE UNIVERSITY SCH OF MEDICIN 333 CEDAR STREET NEW HAVEN, CT 06510 The role of homeobox genes in hematopoiesis

K04DK-02019-01 (BCE) GREGERSON, KAREN A UNIVERSITY OF MARYLAND 655 WEST BALTIMORE STREET BALTIMORE, MD 21201 Mechanisms in the regulation of prolactin secretion

K08DK-02020-01 (DDK) FAJTOVA, VERA T BRIGHAM & WOMEN'S HOSPITAL 221 LONGWOOD AVE BOSTON, MA 02115 Calcium ion sensing in a calcitonin secreting cell line

K08DK-02022-02 (DDK) BISSONNETTE, BRUCE M THE UNIVERSITY OF CHICAGO 5841 S MARYLAND AVENUE CHICAGO, IL 60637 Roles of actin and myosin in pancreatic secretion

K08DK-02023-01 (DDK) PRAGER, DIANE CEDARS-SINAI MEDICAL CENTER 8700 BEVERLY BOULEVARD LOS ANGELES, CA 90048 Insulin action in the cell nucleus

K11DK-02024-01 (DDK) JONES, JOHN I, III UNIV OF NC AT CHAPEL HILL CB# 7170, MACNIDER BUILDING CHAPEL HILL, NC 27599-7170 Insulinlike growth factor binding protein phosphorylation and matrix association

K04DK-02026-01 (HEM) PICKART, CECILE M STATE UNIVERSITY OF NEW YORK 3435 MAIN STREET BUFFALO, NY 14214 Novel ubiquitin-conjugating enzyme in erythroid cells

K11DK-02030-01 (DDK) FALLON, MICHAEL B YALE UNIVERSITY SCH OF MED 333 CEDAR STREET NEW HAVEN, CT 06520 The tight junction in cholestasis--A molecular approach

K11DK-02031-01 (DDK) LUIDENS, MARY K ALBANY MEDICAL COLLEGE 113 HOLLAND AVENUEE ALBANY, NY 12206 Transcriptional regulation by steroid hormone receptors

K08DK-02035-01 (DDK) STORK, PHILIP J OREGON HEALTH SCIENCES UNIV 3181 SW SAM JACKSON PK RD PORTLAND, OR 97201-3098 Cloning of the catecholamine uptake transporter

K11DK-02040-01 (DDK) BASTIAN-ECHEVARRIA, WILLIAM UNIV OF ROCHESTER 601 ELMWOOD AVE BOX 693 ROCHESTER, NY 14642 Mutant insulin receptors and insulin action

K04DK-02042-01 (BCE) PESCOVITZ, ORA H INDIANA UNIV SCHOOL OF MEDICIN 702 BARNHILL DRIVE INDIANAPOLIS, IN 46202-5225 Characterizing GHRH-like substance in testis and placenta

K11DK-02043-01 (DDK) GIVENS, CAROLYN R UNIV OF CA, SF HSW 1656 BOX 0556 SAN FRANCISCO, CA 94143 Regulation of steroidogenesis

K08DK-02046-01 (DDK) POST, THEODORE W BRIGHAM AND WOMEN'S HOSPITAL 75 FRANCIS STREET BOSTON, MA 02115 Mac-1 and p150,95 avidity changes in transfected cells

K11DK-02047-01 (DDK) ZUCKER, STEPHEN D BRIGHAM & WOMEN'S HOSPITAL 75 FRANCIS STREET BOSTON, MA 02115 Hepatocellular transport of small hydrophobic compounds

K11DK-02053-01 (DDK) WILLENBUCHER, ROBERT F HARBOR-UCLA MEDICAL CENTER 1124 W CARSON ST, C-1 TRAILER TORRANCE, CA 90502-2064 The kinetics of colonic smooth muscle relaxation

PROJECT NO., ORGANIZATIONAL UNIT., INVESTIGATOR, ADDRESS, TITLE

K08DK-02054-01 (DDK) CALLE, ROBERTO A YALE UNIVERSITY 333 CEDAR STREET NEW HAVEN, CT 06510 Time-dependent potentiation of insulin secretion
K08DK-02056-01 (DDK) KAIKAUS, RAJA M UNIVERSITY OF CALIFORNIA GI UNIT RM HSW-1120 SAN FRANCISCO, CA 94143-0538 Mechanisms of induction of peroxisomal beta-oxidation
K08DK-02057-01 (DDK) WEINSTEIN, STEVEN P MOUNT SINAI SCHOOL OF MEDICINE 1 GUSTAVE L LEVY PL/BX 1055 NEW YORK, NY 10029 Hormonal regulation of glucose transporters
K11DK-02067-01 (DDK) BILLUPS, KEVIN UNIVERSITY OF VIRGINIA HEALTH SCIENCES CTR BOX 422 CHARLOTTESVILLE, VA 22908 Microvascular physiology of the lower urogenital tract
K08DK-02094-01 (DDK) LYNN, RICHARD B JEFFERSON MEDICAL COLLEGE 1025 WALNUT STREET PHILADELPHIA, PA 19107 Neuropeptide pathways to the dorsal vagal complex
R01DK-02109-34 (MBC) RABINOWITZ, JESSE C UNIVERSITY OF CALIFORNIA 401 BARKER HALL BERKELEY, CALIF 94720 Purine and pteridine metabolism
K08DK-02115-01 (DDK) GUBA, SUSAN C UNIV OF ARKANSAS/MEDICAL SCI 4301 W MARKHAM - SLOT 508 LITTLE ROCK, AR 72205 CD2-activated T cell lymphokine production
K11DK-02116-01 (DDK) HOWARD, RANDY L INDIANA UNIVERSITY FESLER HALL 108, 1120 S DRIVE INDIANAPOLIS, IN 46202-5116 Cloning and characterization of the vasopressin receptor
N01DK-02251-05 (**) DETRE, KATHERINE M Liver transplantation coordinating center
N01DK-02252-03 (**) ASCHER, NANCY L Liver transplantation centers
N01DK-02253-05 (**) WIESNER, RUSSELL H Liver transplantation centers
N01DK-02254-03 (**) WOOD, R PATRICK Liver transplantation center
N01DK-02255-03 (**) LYON, KAREN S Support services for national information clearinghouses
N01DK-02256-03 (**) PARLOW, ALBERT F Immunoaffinity and purification of human pituitary hormones
R01DK-02375-33 (SAT) TERASAKI, PAUL I UNIVERSITY OF CALIFORNIA 950 VETERAN AVE LOS ANGELES, CA 90024 HLA in disease and transplantation
P01DK-02456-33A1 (DDK) BIERMAN, EDWIN L UNIV OF WASHINGTON RG-26 SEATTLE, WA 98195 Pathobiology of diabetes mellitus
P01DK-02456-33A1 0008 (DDK) BIERMAN, EDWIN L Pathobiology of diabetes mellitus Human arterial cell in diabetes-- Lipoproteins and cell cholesterol regulation
P01DK-02456-33A1 0009 (DDK) BRUNZELL, JOHN D Pathobiology of diabetes mellitus Lipoprotein lipase, lipoproteins, and diabetes mellitus
P01DK-02456-33A1 0013 (DDK) PALMER, JERRY Pathobiology of diabetes mellitus Beta cell function, immune markers and preclinical IDDM
P01DK-02456-33A1 0014 (DDK) LEBOEUF, RENE Pathobiology of diabetes mellitus Gene regulation of atherosclerosis in diabetic animals
P01DK-02456-33A1 0015 (DDK) CHAIT, ALAN Pathobiology of diabetes mellitus Macrophages and atherosclerosis in diabetes
P01DK-02456-33A1 9001 (DDK) ORAM, JOHN Pathobiology of diabetes mellitus Core-- Microchemistry and molecular biology laboratory
R37DK-02700-32 (NSS) UNGER, ROGER H UNIVERSITY OF TEXAS 5323 HARRY HINES BLVD DALLAS, TX 75235 Glucoregulatory peptide hormones
R01DK-03535-32A1 (BCE) MUNCK, ALLAN U DARTMOUTH MEDICAL SCHOOL P O BOX 7 HANOVER, NH 03756 Mode of action of steroid hormones
R01DK-03718-32 (PC) DEKKER, EUGENE E UNIV. OF MICHIGAN MED. SCHOOL MED. SCIENCE BLDG. I, BOX 0606 ANN ARBOR, MI 48109 Enzymic paths, mechanisms and structure/function
R01DK-03787-32 (MCHA) JOHNSON, WILLIAM S STANFORD UNIVERSITY JORDAN QUAD/BIRCH 125 PANAMA S STANFORD, CA 94305 Steroid and terpenoid synthesis and related studies
R01DK-03858-30 (PHY) HAYS, RICHARD M ALBERT EINSTEIN COLLEGE OF MED 1300 MORRIS PARK AVE BRONX, NY 10461 Epithelial transport--A morphological approach
R01DK-03892-32S1 (BCE) WILSON, JEAN D U OF TEX SOUTHWESTERN MED CTR 5323 HARRY HINES BLVD. DALLAS, TX 75235-8857 Action of hormones on protein and RNA metabolism
R37DK-04256-32 (NSS) EDELMAN, GERALD M THE ROCKEFELLER UNIVERSITY 1230 YORK AVENUE NEW YORK, NY 10021-6399 Interaction and energy transfer in biological systems
R37DK-04652-31 (GMB) WASSERMAN, ROBERT H CORNELL UNIVERSITY PHYSIOLOGY DEPARTMENT ITHACA, N Y 14853 Intestinal absorption of mineral ions
R37DK-05195-31 (NSS) YOUNT, RALPH G WASHINGTON STATE UNIVERSITY PULLMAN, WA 99164-4660 Interaction of ATP analogs with myosin
R37DK-05472-30 (BM) ELSBACH, PETER NEW YORK UNIVERSITY MED CENTER 550 FIRST AVENUE NEW YORK, N Y 10016 Microbicidal activity of leukocytes--Membrane factors
R37DK-05736-30 (PHY) WILSON, THOMAS H HARVARD MEDICAL SCHOOL 25 SHATTUCK STREET BOSTON, MA 02115 Comparative physiology of membrane transport
R37DK-05968-31 (SSS) GOODMAN, DE WITT S COLUMBIA UNIVERSITY 630 WEST 168TH STREET NEW YORK, N Y 10032 Studies in metabolism and nutrition
R37DK-05968-31 0001 (SSS) GOODMAN, DE WITT S Studies in metabolism and nutrition Vitamin a transport and retinol-binding protein metabolism
R37DK-05968-31 0003 (SSS) GOODMAN, DE WITT S Studies in metabolism and nutrition Intracellular binding proteins for retinol and retinoic acid
R01DK-06181-30 (MET) MC DANIEL, MICHAEL L WASHINGTON UNIV BOX 8118 660 SOUTH EUCLID AVE ST LOUID, MO 63110 Study of secretion and biosynthesis of insulin
R01DK-06415-30 (CVB) BIGLIERI, EDWARD G S.F. GEN. HOSPITAL, BLDG. 100 1001 POTRERO AVENUE, RM. 321 SAN FRANCISCO, CA 94110 Steroid secretory mixtures of adrenal cortex
R01DK-06725-29 (MET) KONO, TETSURO VANDERBILT UNIVERSITY LIGHT HALL, ROOM 702 NASHVILLE, TN 37232-0615 Insulin-receptor interaction and phosphodiesterase

PROJECT NO., ORGANIZATIONAL UNIT., INVESTIGATOR, ADDRESS, TITLE

R01DK-07140-26 (BIO) HIMES, RICHARD H UNIVERSITY OF KANSAS LAWRENCE, KS 66045-2106 Protein structure and function
R01DK-07141-28 (PC) NORDLIE, ROBERT C UNIV OF NORTH DAKOTA GRAND FORKS, ND 58202 Liver pyrophosphate-phosphotransferase activities
R01DK-07422-28 (PB) TALALAY, PAUL JOHNS HOPKINS UNIVERSITY 725 NORTH WOLFE STREET BALTIMORE, MD 21205 Biochemical pharmacology of steroid hormones
R01DK-07902-29 (PC) FISCHER, EDMOND H UNIVERSITY OF WASHINGTON SEATTLE, WA 98195 Signal transduction by protein phosphorylation
R37DK-08126-28 (PB) HATEFI, YOUSSEF SCRIPPS RESEARCH INSTITUTE 10666 N TORREY PINES RD BCR-7 LA JOLLA, CA 92037-1093 Energy conservation and transfer in mitochondria
R01DK-08465-25 (BBCA) SCHERAGA, HAROLD A CORNELL UNIVERSITY ITHACA, NY 14853-1301 Interactions in synthetic polyamino acids
R37DK-09012-27 (NSS) NORMAN, ANTHONY W UNIVERSITY OF CALOFORNIA RIVERSIDE, CA 92521 Studies on vitamin D and calcium metabolism
R01DK-09070-26 (BMT) COLEMAN, JOSEPH E YALE UNIVERSITY 333 CEDAR ST-BOX 3333 NEW HAVEN, CT 06510 Metalloenzyme synthesis, structure and function
R01DK-09094-24A2 (END) ARIMURA, AKIRA A TULANE UNIVERSITY HERBERT CENTER BELLE CHASSE, LA 70037 Physiology of hypothalamic neurohormones
R37DK-09171-26 (PB) BRUICE, THOMAS C UNIVERSITY OF CALIFORNIA SANTA BARBARA, CA 93106 Biochemical mechanisms -- enzymes, cancer, and models
R01DK-09235-26 (BIO) HERS, HENRI-GERY UCL-LAB/PHYSIOLOGICAL CHEM 75. 75 AVENUE HIPPOCRATE B-1200 BRUSSELS, BELGIUM Inborn errors of carbohydrate metabolism
R01DK-09527-27 (BIO) KALOUSEK, FRANTISEK YALE UNIVERSITY SCHOOL OF MED 333 CEDAR ST BOX 3333 NEW HAVEN, CT 06510 Amino acid metabolism--Enzyme biogenesis and mutation
R01DK-09602-22 (PB) PAIK, WOON K TEMPLE UNIV. SCHOOL OF MED. 3420 NORTH BROAD STREET PHILADELPHIA, PA 19140 Biological methylation of cytochrome C in fungi and plants
R37DK-09765-26 (MBC) KOSHLAND, DANIEL E, JR UNIVERSITY OF CALIFORNIA DIV OF BIOCHEM & MOLECULAR BIO BERKELEY, CA 94720 Regulatory processes in biological systems
R37DK-09765-26 0005 (MBC) KOSHLAND, DANIEL E Regulatory processes in biological systems Structure-function relationships of receptor proteins
R37DK-09765-26 0007 (MBC) KOSHLAND, DANIEL E Regulatory processes in biological systems Feedback relationships in a complex system
R37DK-09765-26 0008 (MBC) KOSHLAND, DANIEL E Regulatory processes in biological systems Principles of regulation
R37DK-09970-26 (PBC) LEE, YUAN C THE JOHNS HOPKINS UNIVERSITY CHARLES AND 34TH STREETS BALTIMORE, MD 21218 Chemistry and biochemistry of glycoconjugates
P01DK-09976-27 (DDK) KLAHR, SAULO THE JEWISH HOSPITAL OF ST. LOU 216 S. KINGSHIGHWAY ST. LOUIS, MO 63110 Pathophysiology of renal disease and uremia
P01DK-09976-27 0016 (DDK) MORRISSEY, JEREMIAH J Pathophysiology of renal disease and uremia Biogenesis of hyperparathyroidism of renal failure
P01DK-09976-27 0017 (DDK) SCHRELNER, GEORGE Pathophysiology of renal disease and uremia Immune modulation of tubular cell transport
P01DK-09976-27 0018 (DDK) HAMM, L LEE Pathophysiology of renal disease and uremia Adaptations in tubule transport functions
P01DK-09976-27 0019 (DDK) GLUCK, STEPHEN Pathophysiology of renal disease and uremia Characterization of H-ion ATPase in urinary acidification
P01DK-09976-27 0020 (DDK) SLATOPOLSKY, EDUARDO Pathophysiology of renal disease and uremia Vitamin D and phosphate in secondary hyperparathyroidism
P01DK-09976-27 0021 (DDK) HAMMERMAN, MARC R Pathophysiology of renal disease and uremia Renal glucose homeostasis in health and disease
P01DK-09976-27 0002 (DDK) MORRISON, AUBREY R Pathophysiology of renal disease and uremia Membrane lipids in renal injury
P01DK-09976-27 0007 (DDK) MARTIN, KEVIN J Pathophysiology of renal disease and uremia PTH--Peripheral metabolism and cellular actions
P01DK-09976-27 0009 (DDK) HRUSKA, KEITH A Pathophysiology of renal disease and uremia Control of renal ion transport by parathyroid hormone
P01DK-09976-27 0014 (DDK) KLAHR, SAULO Pathophysiology of renal disease and uremia Pathophysiology of obstructive nephropathy
P01DK-09976-27 9001 (DDK) KLAHR, SAULO Pathophysiology of renal disease and uremia Core--Chemistry laboratory
P01DK-09976-27 9002 (DDK) SLATOPOLSKY, EDUARDO Pathophysiology of renal disease and uremia Core--RIA, biochemical analysis and tissue culture facilities
R01DK-10073-24 (REB) MC CANN, SAMUEL M UNIV TEXAS SOUTHWESTERN MED CT 5323 HARRY HINES BLVD DALLAS, TX 75235 Neurohumoral control of anterior pituitary
R01DK-10141-25A2 (GMA) FORTE, JOHN G UNIVERSITY OF CALIFORNIA LIFE SCIENCES ADDITION BERKELEY, CA 94720 Mechanisms of HCL transport by gastric mucosa
R01DK-10206-26 (GMB) TASHJIAN, ARMEN H, JR HARVARD SCHOOL OF PUBLIC HEALT 665 HUNTINGTON AVENUE BOSTON, MA 02115 Hormones affecting mineral metabolism
R01DK-10334-26 (PC) LARDY, HENRY A UNIVERSITY OF WISCONSIN 1710 UNIVERSITY AVENUE MADISON, WI 53705 Control processes in mammalian cells
R37DK-10339-26 (NSS) COON, MINOR J UNIVERSITY OF MICHIGAN 5416 MED SCI I ANN ARBOR, MI 48109-0606 Function of hydroxylases and other oxidative enzymes
R01DK-10486-26 (HEM) BAINTON, DOROTHY F UNIVERSITY OF CALIFORNIA SAN FRANCISCO, CA 94143-0506 Maturation and function of bone marrow cells
R01DK-10699-24 (SSS) METZGER, BOYD E NORTHWESTERN UNIV MED SCH 303 E CHICAGO AVENUE CHICAGO, ILL 60611 Control mechanisms in diabetes and normal metabolism
R01DK-11011-24S1 (BCE) TASHJIAN, ARMEN H, JR HARVARD SCHOOL OF

PUBLIC HLTH 665 HUNTINGTON AVENUE BOSTON, MA 02115 Differentiated functions in dispersed cell cultures
R01DK-11043-22 (END) DUNN, JOHN T UNIVERSITY OF VIRGINIA BOX 511 CHARLOTTESVILLE, VA 22908 Thyroglobulin in thyroid disease
R37DK-11242-25 (SB) CHRISTENSEN, JAMES UNIVERSITY OF IOWA IOWA CITY, IOWA 52242 Regulation of the lower esophageal sphincter
R01DK-11270-23S1 (GMA) GRAY, GARY M STANFORD UNIVERSITY MEDICAL CENTER STANFORD, CA 94305-5100 Regulation of carbohydrate digestion
R01DK-11295-25A1 (BBCA) ENGLANDER, S WALTER UNIVERSITY OF PENNSYLVANIA 3451 WALNUT ST PHILADELPHIA, PA 19104 Physical studies of biological macromolecules
R01DK-11313-24 (PC) SRERE, PAUL A U OF TX SW MED CNTR AT DALLAS 5323 HARRY HINES BOULEVARD DALLAS, TX 75235 Structures and mechanisms of citrate enzymes
R01DK-11356-25 (HEM) PARKER, JOHN C UNIV OF N C AT CHAPEL HILL 335 MACNICDER BLDG., CB# 7035 CHAPEL HILL, NC 27599 Ion transfer and metabolism in mammalian red blood cells
R01DK-11489-23A2 (GMB) WINDHAGER, ERICH E CORNELL UNIVERSITY 1300 YORK AVENUE NEW YORK, NY 10021 Ion and water transport across renal tubules
R01DK-11727-20A2 (END) NICOLOFF, JOHN T UNIV OF SOUTHERN CALIFORNIA 2025 ZONAL AVENUE LOS ANGELES, CA 90033 Human thyroid hormone metabolism
P01DK-11794-24 (DDK) POTTS, JOHN T, JR MASSACHUSETTS GENERAL HOSPITAL FRUIT STREET BOSTON, MASS 02114 Hormonal control of calcium metabolism
P01DK-11794-24 0002 (DDK) KRONENBERG, HENRY M Hormonal control of calcium metabolism Structure, function & evolution of parathyroid hormone gene
P01DK-11794-24 0004 (DDK) SERGE, GINO V Hormonal control of calcium metabolism Cellular response to PTH--Receptor structure,function & regulation
P01DK-11794-24 0005 (DDK) NUSSBAUM,SAMUEL R Hormonal control of calcium metabolism Structural basis of the biological action of parathyroid hormone
P01DK-11794-24 0006 (DDK) BRINGHURST,F RICHARD Hormonal control of calcium metabolism Intracellular responses of target cells to parathyroid hormone
P01DK-11794-24 9001 (DDK) POTTS, JOHN T Hormonal control of calcium metabolism Core--Equipment
P01DK-11794-24 9002 (DDK) KEUTMANN,HENRY T Hormonal control of calcium metabolism Core--Peptide and oligonucleotide laboratory
R37DK-12027-24 (END) MELBY, JAMES C UNIVERSITY HOSPITAL 88 EAST NEWTON STREET BOSTON, MA 02118 Mechanisms regulating adrenocortical secretion
R37DK-12034-25 (BIO) MEISTER, ALTON CORNELL UNIV MEDICAL COLLEGE 1300 YORK AVENUE NEW YORK, NY 10021 Amino acid and protein metabolism
R37DK-12121-24 (NSS) AMES, GIOVANNA F UNIVERSITY OF CALIFORNIA 308 BARKER HALL BERKELEY, CA 94720 Membranes and active transport of amino acids
R01DK-12152-23 (PC) HOFFEE, PATRICIA A UNIVERSITY OF PITTSBURGH W1252 BIOMEDICAL SCIENCE TOWER PITTSBURGH, PA 15261 Regulation of nucleotide metabolic enzymes
N44DK-12253-01 (**) LEWICKI, JOHN Inhibitors of atrial naturetic peptide clearance
N44DK-12259-00 (**) ALLNUTT, F C THOMAS Stable isotopically-labeled compounds using microalgae as labeled feedstock
N44DK-12262-01 (**) SQUILLANTE, MICHAEL R Solid state detector for capillary electrophoresis
N01DK-12269-00 (**) PARLOW, ALBERT F Production of polyclonal antibodies directed against rat pituitary hormones
N01DK-12270-00 (**) THOMAS, PAUL R Opportunities in the nutrition and food sciences
N43DK-12271-00 (**) EVANS, DAVID S Software for molecular dynamics simulation on a PC-based processor
N43DK-12272-00 (**) DURAN, LISE W Preparation of microbicidal urinary tract catheters
N43DK-12274-00 (**) KLUG, THOMAS Detection of alteration in estrogen metabolism
R01DK-12274-24 (HEM) ZUCKER-FRANKLIN, DOROTHEA NEW YORK UNIVERSITY MED CENTER 550 FIRST AVENUE NEW YORK, N Y 10016 Ultrastructure of leukocytes and platelets
N43DK-12275-00 (**) SIOSHANSI, PIRAN Infection resistant catheters-- Silver coatings by ion beam assisted deposition
N43DK-12276-00 (**) TAMARKIN, LAWRENCE Development of an enzyme immunoassay for a murine cytokine
N43DK-12277-00 (**) ANDERSON, THOMAS R Monoclonal antibodies against progestin receptor isoforms
N43DK-12278-00 (**) ANDERSON, THOMAS R Monoclonal antibodies against parathyroid hormone related peptide
N43DK-12279-00 (**) KIEFER, DAVID J Enzyme immunoassay for primary biliary cirrhosis
N01DK-12282-00 (**) SEWALL, ASE I Technical support for the NIDDK epidemiology committee
R01DK-12386-24 (NTN) SALTMAN, PAUL D UNIV OF CALIF, SAN DIEGO LA JOLLA, CA 92093 Metabolism and nutrition of iron and other trace metals
R01DK-12401-23 (HEM) RIEDER, RONALD F SUNY HLTH SCI CTR AT BROOKLYN 450 CLARKSON AVENUE BROOKLYN, N Y 11203 Protein synthesis in erythroid precursors
R01DK-12402-23 (PC) RUDNEY, HARRY UNIVERSITY OF CINCINNATI 231 BETHESDA AVE CINCINNATI, OH 45267-0524 Regulation of enzymes in mevalonate synthesis
R37DK-12413-25 (BIO) HOLMES, EDWARD W JR UNIV OF PENNSYLVANIA HOSPITAL 3400 SPRUCE STREET PHILADELPHIA, PA 19104 Pathogenesis of AMP deaminase deficiency
R01DK-12432-23 (NTN) HAMBIDGE, K MICHAEL UNIVERSITY OF COLORADO 4200 EAST 9TH AVE, C233 DENVER, CO 80262 Studies of human zinc deficiency
R01DK-12434-24 (PBC) SWEELEY, CHARLES C MICHIGAN STATE UNIVERSITY 212 BIOCHEMISTRY BUILDING EAST LANSING, MICH 48824 Chemistry and metabolism of sphingolipids & glycoprotein

PROJECT NO., ORGANIZATIONAL UNIT., INVESTIGATOR, ADDRESS, TITLE

R01DK-12579-23 (BIO) FENTON, WAYNE A YALE UNIVERSITY SCH OF MED 333 CEDAR STREET, PO BOX 3333 NEW HAVEN, CT 06510 Inborn errors--Molecular analysis in cultured cells
R01DK-12715-22 (PHY) ARMSTRONG, WILLIAM M INDIANA UNIVERSITY SCH OF MED 635 BARNHILL DRIVE INDIANAPOLIS, IN 46202-5120 Ion transport in small intestine
R37DK-12769-26 (SAT) MALT, RONALD A MASSACHUSETTS GENERAL HOSP FRUIT STREET BOSTON, MASS 02114 Study of nephrectomy at birth and during growth
R01DK-12828-24 (BIO) KREDICH, NICHOLAS M DUKE UNIVERSITY MEDICAL CENTER PO BOX 3100 DURHAM, NC 27710 Regulation of sulfur metabolism
R01DK-12829-23 (MET) PORTE, DANIEL, JR VA MEDICAL CENTER 1660 SOUTH COLUMBIAN WAY SEATTLE, WA 98108 Neural regulation and effects of pancreatic hormones
R01DK-12925-22 (BNP) KATSOYANNIS, PANAYOTIS G MOUNT SINAI SCHOOL OF MEDICINE ONE GUSTAVE L LEVY PLACE NEW YORK, NY 10029-6574 Synthetic insulins and analogs
Z01DK-13001-18 (MRB) RALL, W NIDDK, NIH Mathematical formulations and analysis relevant to experimental neurophysiology
Z01DK-13002-19 (MRB) GONZALES-FERNANDEZ, J M NIDDK, NIH Mathematical description of substrate transport in capillary-tissue structures
Z01DK-13004-18 (MRB) RINZEL, J NIDDK, NIH Mathematical description of cellular neuroelectric signal transmission
Z01DK-13020-02 (MRB) SHERMAN, A NIDDK, NIH Electrical and chemical oscillations in coupled cell systems
R01DK-13048-23 (MEDB) FINKELSTEIN, JAMES D DVA MEDICAL CENTER 50 IRVING ST, NW WASHINGTON, DC 20422 Sulfur amino acid metabolism in mammals
P01DK-13083-24 (DDK) NAJARIAN, JOHN S UNIVERSITY OF MINNESOTA MAYO MEMORIAL BLDG., BOX 195 MINNEAPOLIS, MN 55455 Studies of organ transplantation in animals and man
P01DK-13083-24 0167 (DDK) SIBLEY, RICHARD Studies of organ transplantation in animals and man Immunohistology, prognosis--Cyclosporine vs conventional immunosuppression
P01DK-13083-24 0169 (DDK) BARBOSA, JOSE F Studies of organ transplantation in animals and man Effect of strict diabetic control on diabetic glomerulosclerosis
P01DK-13083-24 0171 (DDK) BALFOUR, HENRY H Studies of organ transplantation in animals and man Prevention and treatment of cytomegalovirus infection in renal allografts
P01DK-13083-24 0174 (DDK) SIMMONS, ROBERTA Studies of organ transplantation in animals and man Quality of life of recipients and donors after kidney transplant
P01DK-13083-24 0183 (DDK) BACH, FRITZ H Studies of organ transplantation in animals and man Characterization of T-cell clones
P01DK-13083-24 0184 (DDK) SUTHERLAND, DAVID E Studies of organ transplantation in animals and man Effects of pancreas transplantation on diabetic nephropathy in man
P01DK-13083-24 0185 (DDK) SUTHERLAND, DAVID E Studies of organ transplantation in animals and man Total lymphoid irradiation versus cyclosporine for retransplantation patients
P01DK-13083-24 0186 (DDK) BALFOUR, HENRY H Studies of organ transplantation in animals and man Immune defects in organ transplant patients with Epstein Barr virus disorders
P01DK-13083-24 0188 (DDK) ASCHER, NANCY L Studies of organ transplantation in animals and man Cellular mechanisms during immunosuppression
P01DK-13083-24 0189 (DDK) BACH, FRITZ H Studies of organ transplantation in animals and man Role of MHC antigens on rejection of islet allografts
P01DK-13083-24 0191 (DDK) SUTHERLAND, DAVID E Studies of organ transplantation in animals and man Cyclosporine vs. conventional immunosuppression in renal transplantation
P01DK-13083-24 0192 (DDK) ASCHER, NANCY L Studies of organ transplantation in animals and man Immune adaption to allograft--Conventional vs. cyclosporine immunosuppression
P01DK-13083-24 9001 (DDK) NAJARIAN, JOHN S Studies of organ transplantation in animals and man Core--Clinical data storage and retrieval system for renal transplantation
R37DK-13149-24 (END) GILL, GORDON N UNIV OF CALF, SAN DIEGO LA JOLLA, CA 92093 Hormonal regulation of control mechanisms
R01DK-13195-19A2 (TOX) CASTRO, JOSE A 1603 VILLA MARTELLI PCIA, DE BUENOS AIRES ARGENTIN Mechanism of carbon tetrachloride hepatotoxicity
R01DK-13309-23 (GMA) LEVITT, MICHAEL D VETERANS ADMIN MEDICAL CENTER ONE VETERANS DRIVE MINNEAPOLIS, MN 55417 Production and absorption of intestinal gas
R37DK-13328-22 (GMA) OCKNER, ROBERT K UNIVERSITY OF CALIFORNIA HSW 1120 SAN FRANCISCO, CA 94143 Lipid metabolism in liver and intestine
R37DK-13332-23 (PC) FRIEDEN, CARL WASHINGTON UNIV SCH OF MEDICIN 660 SOUTH EUCLID AVE BOX 8231 ST LOUIS, MO 63110 Metabolic regulation and interacting enzyme systems
R37DK-13339-23 (BMT) HALPERN, JACK THE UNIVERSITY OF CHICAGO 5735 SOUTH ELLIS AVENUE CHICAGO, IL 60637 Metal complexes related to vitamin B12
R01DK-13377-23 (END) DE GROOT, LESLIE J UNIVERSITY OF CHICAGO 5841 S MARYLAND AVE BOX 138 CHICAGO, IL 60637 Biosynthesis and action of thyroid hormone
R01DK-13448-23 (BIO) HAMILTON, GORDON A PENNSYLVANIA STATE UNIVERSITY 152 DAVEY LABORATORY UNIVERSITY PARK, PA 16802 A mechanistic study of some O2 oxidoreductases
R01DK-13476-22 (GMB) GRANTHAM, JARED J UNIV OF KANSAS MEDICAL CENTER 39TH & RAINBOW BLVD KANSAS CITY, KANSAS 66103 Mechanisms of transport in kidney tubules and cells
R37DK-13499-23 (NSS) JEFFERSON, LEONARD S, JR MILTON S. HERSHEY MEDICAL CNTR P O BOX 850 HERSHEY, PA 17033 Regulation of liver growth and function
R01DK-13531-22 (END) LITWACK, GERALD THOMAS JEFFERSON UNIVERSITY 1025 WALNUT ST PHILADELPHIA, PA 19107 The glucocorticoid receptor

PROJECT NO., ORGANIZATIONAL UNIT., INVESTIGATOR, ADDRESS, TITLE

R01DK-13613-23 (BIO) WALSH, DONAL A UNIV. OF CA SCHOOL OF MEDICINE DAVIS, CA 95616 Regulation of phosphorylase kinase
R01DK-13682-32 (HEM) SCHRIER, STANLEY L STANFORD UNIV MED CTR STANFORD, CA 94305-5112 Metabolism of erythrocyte stroma
R01DK-13711-20 (GMA) MC GUIGAN, JAMES E UNIVERSITY OF FLORIDA DEPARTMENT OF MEDICINE GAINESVILLE, FL 32610 Immunology and diseases of the gastrointestinal tract
R01DK-13894-22 (MBC) MAGASANIK, BORIS MASSACHUSETTS INST OF TECHNOLO 77 MASSACHUSETTS AVENUE CAMBRIDGE, MA 02139 Synthesis of histidine degrading enzymes
R37DK-13897-22 (NTN) DALLMAN, PETER R UNIVERSITY OF CALIFORNIA DEPT OF PEDIATRICS SAN FRANCISCO, CA 94143 Developmental aspects of iron nutrition
R01DK-13912-18S1 (BBCA) ANDERSON, SONIA R OREGON STATE UNIVERSITY CORVALLIS, OR 97331-6503 Fluorescence studies of enzyme structure and function
R37DK-13914-22 (MET) STEINER, DONALD F UNIVERSITY OF CHICAGO BOX 23/5841 S MARYLAND AVENUE CHICAGO, IL 60637 Studies on pancreatic hormones
R01DK-13927-22 (GMA) OLSEN, WARD A WM S MIDDLETON VA HOSP 2500 OVERLOOK TERRACE MADISON, WI 53705 Intestinal mucosal function in diabetes
R01DK-13939-20 (PB) DAVIS, ELDRED J INDIANA U. SCHOOL OF MEDICINE 635 BARNHILL DRIVE INDIANAPOLIS, IN 46202-5122 Regulatory mechanisms in energy metabolism
R37DK-13983-22 (HEM) KAZAZIAN, HAIG H, JR JOHNS HOPKINS HOSPITAL 600 N WOLFE STREET BALTIMORE, MD 21205 Genetic control of hemoglobin synthesis
R37DK-14038-22 (GMA) ALPERS, DAVID H WASHINGTON UNIVERSITY 660 SOUTH EUCLID AVE./BOX 8124 ST. LOUIS, MO 63110 Intestinal protein metabolism and function
R01DK-14184-21 (NTN) GANTHER, HOWARD E UNIV OF TEXAS MEDICAL BRANCH EWING HALL, 700 THE STRAND GALVESTON, TEXAS 77550-2774 Organoselenium compounds--Biosynthesis and function
R01DK-14241-21 (PHY) MAACK, THOMAS M CORNELL UNIVERSITY MED COLL 1300 YORK AVENUE NEW YORK, N Y 10021 Renal transport and metabolism of proteins
R37DK-14334-23 (NSS) LARNER, JOSEPH UNIVERSITY OF VIRGINIA 1300 JEFFERSON PARK AVE CHARLOTTESVILLE, VA 22908 Chemical mechanism of action of insulin
K06DK-14370-30 (NSS) HARRIS, JOHN W CASE WESTERN RESERVE UNIV 3395 SCRANTON ROAD CLEVELAND, OH 44109 A study of nutritional and hemolytic anemias
R37DK-14507-22 (MET) LANDAU, BERNARD R UNIVERSITY HOSPITALS 2074 ABINGTON ROAD CLEVELAND, OHIO 44106 Carbohydrate and lipid metabolic pathways
R37DK-14574-22 (PC) LANE, M DANIEL JOHNS HOPKINS UNIVERSITY 725 NORTH WOLFE STREET BALTIMORE, MD 21205 Mechanism of insulin action
R01DK-14575-23 (MET) LANE, M DANIEL JOHNS HOPKINS UNIVERSITY 725 NORTH WOLFE STREET BALITMORE, MD 21205-2185 Regulation of lipogenesis and VLDL synthesis/assembly
R01DK-14669-20 (GMA) BINDER, HENRY J YALE UNIVERSITY SCH OF MED 333 CEDAR STREET NEW HAVEN, CONN 06510 Intestinal electrolyte transport in health and disease
R01DK-14681-22 (SAT) ROBERTS, JAMES A DELTA REGIONAL PRIMATE RES CTR 3 RIVERS ROAD COVINGTON, LA 70433 Host-parasite interaction in pyelonephritis
R01DK-14729-18 (PB) BENISEK, WILLIAM F UNIVERSITY OF CALIFORNIA DEPT OF BIOLOGICAL CHEMISTRY DAVIS, CA 95616 Steroid binding sites of steroid binding proteins
R37DK-14744-22 (END) ROY, ARUN K UNIVERSITY OF TEXAS HLTH SCI C 7703 FLOYD CURL DRIVE SAN ANTONIO, TX 78284 Hormonal control of alpha 2u globulin synthesis in liver
R01DK-14752-21 (PHY) HERSEY, STEPHEN J EMORY UNIVERSITY 1462 CLIFTON RD NE ATLANTA, GA 30322 Intracellular reactions in gastric mucosa
R01DK-14770-19 (MGN) GANSCHOW, ROGER E CHILDREN'S HOSPITAL RES FDN ELLAND AND BETHESDA AVENUES CINCINNATI, OH 45229-2899 Genetic control of mammalian enzyme expression
P01DK-14881-21 (DDK) DE LUCA, HECTOR F UNIVERSITY OF WISCONSIN 420 HENRY MALL MADISON, WI 53706 Metabolism and function of the fat-soluble vitamins
P01DK-14881-21 0001 (DDK) DE LUCA, HECTOR F Metabolism and function of the fat-soluble vitamins Studies on vitamin D
P01DK-14881-21 0012 (DDK) DE LUCA, HECTOR F Metabolism and function of the fat-soluble vitamins Studies on vitamin A
P01DK-14881-21 0013 (DDK) SUTTIE, JOHN W Metabolism and function of the fat-soluble vitamins Studies on vitamin K
P01DK-14881-21 0014 (DDK) DELUCA, HECTOR F Metabolism and function of the fat-soluble vitamins Vitamin A metabolism and mechanism of action
R01DK-15056-21 (PB) AISEN, PHILIP A EINSTEIN COLLEGE OF MEDICINE 1300 MORRIS PARK AVENUE BRONX, NY 10461 Iron-binding proteins and control of iron metabolism
R01DK-15057-21 (PB) TOLLIN, GORDON UNIVERSITY OF ARIZONA TUCSON, AZ 85721 Flavin-protein interactions in flavoenzyme catalysis
R37DK-15070-20 (END) REFETOFF, SAMUEL UNIVERSITY OF CHICAGO 5841 SOUTH MARYLAND AVE CHICAGO, IL 60637 Studies on regulation and mechanism of hormone action
R37DK-15089-22 (NSS) LEMANN, JACOB JR MEDICAL COLL OF WISCONSIN 9200 WEST WISCONSIN AVE MILWAUKEE, WI 53226 Sugar ingestion, calciuria, crystalluria, and stones
Z01DK-15100-21 (LCDB) SIMPSON, R T NIDDK, NIH Protein-nucleic acid interactions--Chromatin structure and function
Z01DK-15102-31 (LCDB) HARTLEY, R W NIDDK, NIH Ribonuclease and its inhibitor from Bacillus amyloliquefaciens
R01DK-15120-21 (PB) WILLIAMSON, JOHN R UNIVERSITY OF PENNSYLVANIA 37TH & HAMILTON WALK PHILADELPHIA, PA 19104-6089 Control of metabolism in normal and disease states
Z01DK-15200-31 (LCDB) KAUFMAN, B T NIDDK, NIH Studies on folic acid
R37DK-15241-21 (NSS) THOMPSON, JAMES C THE UNIVERSITY OF TEXAS MED BR RT E-27 GALVESTON, TX 77550 Surgical studies on metabolism of GI hormones
R01DK-15289-16 (NTN) WAGNER, CONRAD VANDERBILT UNIVERSITY 21TH AVE SOUTH NASHVILLE, TN 37232 Tissue stores of folate--Dietary control and assay
R01DK-15304-18 (SB) WILLIAMS, LESTER F, JR VANDERBILT UNIVERSITY 21ST AVE SOUTH & GARLAND AVE NASHVILLE, TN 37232 Role of gallbladder in pathogenesis of gallstones
R37DK-15350-21 (GMA) POWELL, DON WATSON UNIVERSITY OF TEXAS 301 UNIVERSITY BLVD GALVESTON, TX 77550 Mechanisms of intestinal secretion
R01DK-15365-20 (CBY) KIMMICH, GEORGE A UNIVERSITY OF ROCHESTER SCHOOL OF MED & DENTISTRY ROCHESTER, NY 14642 Mechanism of Na+-dependent metabolite transport
Z01DK-15401-19 (LCDB) SCOW, R O NIDDK, NIH Synthesis and transport of lipoprotein and hepatic lipases in tissues and cells
Z01DK-15404-07 (LCDB) BLANCHETTE-MACKIE, E J NIDDK, NIH Ultrastructural immunocytochemistry of lipid metabolism in cells and tissue
R01DK-15410-20 (SSS) GOODMAN, MURRAY UNIV. OF CALIFORNIA, SAN DIEGO DEPARTMENT OF CHEMISTRY, 0314 LA JOLLA, CA 92093 Constrained cyclic peptidomimetic hormones
R01DK-15440-19 (PTHA) TRUMP, BENJAMIN F UNIVERSITY OF MARYLAND 10 S. PINE ST. BALTIMORE, MD 21201 Subcellular reaction to injury in the kidney
Z01DK-15500-32 (LCDB) SHILOACH, J NIDDK, NIH Large-scale processing of biological material
Z01DK-15503-10 (LCDB) KIMMEL, A R NIDDK, NIH Regulation of developmental gene expression
Z01DK-15505-14 (LCDB) LONDOS, C NIDDK, NIH Regulation of adipocyte metabolism
Z01DK-15506-08 (LCDB) DEAN, J NIDDK, NIH Control of gene expression in early mammalian development
Z01DK-15508-04 (LCDB) DEAN, A NIDDK, NIH Chromatin structure in regulation of mammalian gene expression
R01DK-15555-20 (HEM) KRANTZ, SANFORD B VANDERVILT UNIVERSITY DIV OF HEMATOLOGY NASHVILLE, TN 37232-2287 Erythropoletin and the regulation of erythropoiesis
R37DK-15556-21 (BCE) KATZENELLENBOGEN, JOHN A UNIVERSITY OF ILLINOIS 1209 CALIFORNIA STREET URBANA, ILL 61801 Uterine estrogen receptor affinity labeling
R37DK-15564-20 (GMA) MAKHLOUF, GABRIEL M VIRGINIA COMMONWEALTH UNIV BOX 711, MCV STATION RICHMOND, VA 23298 Hormonal integration of exocrine and endocrine organs
R01DK-15658-21 (MET) JEFFERSON, LEONARD S, JR MILTON S. HERSHEY MEDICAL CNTR P. O. BOX 850 HERSHEY, PA 17033 Regulation of skeletal muscle metabolism
R37DK-15681-20 (SB) SILEN, WILLIAM BETH ISRAEL HOSPITAL 330 BROOKLINE AVENUE BOSTON, MA 02215 G.I. mucosal barrier in health and surgical disease
R01DK-15708-20 (REB) WARREN, JAMES C WASHINGTON UNIVERSITY 4911 BARNES HOSPITAL PLAZA ST. LOUIS, MO 63110 Binding, biosynthesis, and action of steroids
R01DK-15843-18A2 (CVB) DI BONA, GERALD F UNIVERSITY OF IOWA COLLEGE OF MEDICINE IOWA CITY, IO 52242 The neural control of renal function
R37DK-15847-21 (NTN) ROMSOS, DALE R MICHIGAN STATE UNIVERSITY EAST LANSING, MI 48824-1224 Effect of diet on energy metabolism
R01DK-15851-20 (GMA) SIMON, FRANCIS R UNIVERSITY OF COLORADO 4200 EAST NINTH AVENUE DENVER, CO 80262 Surface membrane regulation of bile acid transport
R01DK-15855-15A1 (NTN) ADIBI, SIAMAK A MONTEFIORE HOSPITAL 3459 FIFTH AVENUE PITTSBURGH, PA 15213 Dietary regulating branched chain amino acid metabolism
R22DK-15856-18 (MEP) YOUNG, VERNON R MASSACHUSETTS INST OF TECH 77 MASSACHUSETTS AVENUE CAMBRIDGE, MA 02139 Dietary protein intake & human protein metabolism
R01DK-15861-17 (NTN) ADIBI, SIAMAK A MONTEFIORE HOSPITAL 3459 FIFTH AVENUE PITTSBURGH, PA 15213 Metabolism & clinical applications of oligopeptides
R37DK-15968-20 (CVB) MARSH, DONALD J UNIV OF SOUTHERN CALIFORNIA 1333 SAN PABLO STREET LOS ANGELES, CA 90033 Regulation of renal circulation
R01DK-16073-17 (BIO) SMITH, STUART CHILDREN'S HOSP MEDICAL CTR 747 FIFTY-SECOND ST. OAKLAND, CA 94609 Structure and specificity of lipogenic enzymes
R01DK-16095-17 (HEM) SHOHET, S B UNIVERSITY OF CALIFORNIA BOX 0128, CRI SAN FRANCISCO, CA 94143 Architecture of erythrocyte skeleton--Bilayer interface
R01DK-16177-20 (END) YOUNG, DONALD A UNIVERSITY OF ROCHESTER 601 ELMWOOD AVENUE ROCHESTER, NY 14642-8693 Mechanism of action of steroid hormones
R01DK-16194-20 (BIO) UYEDA, KOSAKU VETERANS AFFAIRS MEDICAL CENTE 4500 SOUTH LANCASTER ROAD DALLAS, TX 75216 Structure and function of phosphofructokinase
R01DK-16272-19 (HEM) LONDON, IRVING M MASS INST OF TECH, E25-551 77 MASSACHUSETTS AVENUE CAMBRIDGE, MASS 02139 Regulation of protein synthesis and erythropoiesis
R01DK-16294-17 (GMB) DANTZLER, WILLIAM H UNIV OF ARIZONA HEALTH SCIS CT COLLEGE OF MEDICINE TUCSON, AZ 85724 Regulation of individual nephron filtration rates
R37DK-16505-20 (GMA) JOHNSON, LEONARD R UNIVERSITY OF TENNESSEE 894 UNION AVENUE MEMPHIS, TN 38163 GI hormones and other factors on growth of GI mucosa
R01DK-16532-17 (BBCB) BOTHNER-BY, AKSEL A CARNEGIE MELLON UNIVERSITY 5000 FORBES AVENUE PITTSBURGH, PA 15213 New methods in high field NMR spectroscopy
R37DK-16636-19 (END) SAMUELS, HERBERT H NEW YORK UNIV MED CTR 550 FIRST AVE NEW YORK, NY 10016 Metabolic effects of thyroid hormone
R37DK-16666-19 (NSS) KAN, YUET W UNIVESITY OF CALIFORNIA 3RD & PARNASSUS AVE SAN FRANCISCO, CA 94143-0724 Abnormal hemoglobin synthesis-mechanism and detection
R37DK-16684-20 (END) REICHLIN, SEYMOUR NEW ENGLAND MED CTR

HOSPITAL 750 WASHINGTON ST, BOX 275 BOSTON, MA 02111 Neural control mechanisms of metabolic functions

R01DK-16691-19 (HEM) SCHWARTZ, ELIAS CHILDREN'S HOSPITAL 34TH STREET AND CIVIC CENTER PHILADELPHIA, PA 19104 Heme and globin synthesis in infants and children

R37DK-16702-19 (HEM) SPIVAK, JERRY L JOHNS HOPKINS HOSPITAL 600 N WOLFE ST, BLALOCK 1033 BALTIMORE, MD 21205 Role of erythropoietin in transcriptional control

R01DK-16739-19A1 (TOX) COOPER, ARTHUR CORNELL UNIV MEDICAL COLLEGE 1300 YORK AVENUE NEW YORK, N Y 10021 Pathogenesis of hepatic coma

R37DK-16746-19 (NSS) PERMUTT, MARSHALL ALAN WASHINGTON UNIV SCHOOL OF MED 660 SOUTH EUCLID AVENUE ST LOUIS, MO 63110 Control of insulin biosynthesis

R01DK-16816-18 (GMA) FELDMAN, MARK V.A. MEDICAL CENTER 4500 SOUTH LANCASTER ROAD DALLAS, TX 75216 Gastric acid secretion and buffer content after eating

R01DK-16928-16 (GMB) BRODSKY, WILLIAM A MOUNT SINAI SCHOOL OF MEDICINE ANN. 21-26 NEW YORK, N Y 10029 Regulation of urinary acid-base excretion

Z01DK-17001-25 (LBM) ASHWELL, G NIDDK, NIH Role of the carbohydrate moiety glycoproteins in cellular activity

Z01DK-17002-21 (LBM) JAKOBY, W B NIDDK, NIH Enzymatic basis of detoxification

Z01DK-17003-24 (LBM) CABIB, E NIDDK, NIH Polysaccharides in morphogenesis

Z01DK-17004-23 (LBM) MCPHIE, P NIDDK, NIH Thermodynamic and kinetic studies of protein structure and enzyme mechanisms

Z01DK-17009-06 (LBM) HENNIGHAUSEN, L NIDDK, NIH Tissue specific and hormone regulated gene expression

P30DK-17047-15 (DDK) PORTE, DANIEL, JR VA MEDICAL CENTER 1200-12TH AVE. S. SEATTLE, WA 98144 Diabetes-endocrinology research center

P30DK-17047-15 0046 (DDK) GOODNER, CJ Diabetes-endocrinology research center Pilot study--Molecular biology of diabetes

P30DK-17047-15 9001 (DDK) KOERKER, DONNA J Diabetes-endocrinology research center Core--Physiology

P30DK-17047-15 9002 (DDK) KLAFF, LESLIE Diabetes-endocrinology research center Core--Radioimmunoassay

P30DK-17047-15 9003 (DDK) PALMER, JERRY P Diabetes-endocrinology research center Core--Clinical research

P30DK-17047-15 9004 (DDK) BASKIN, DENIS G Diabetes-endocrinology research center Core--Cytohistochemistry

P30DK-17047-15 9006 (DDK) FUJIMOTO, WILFRED Y Diabetes-endocrinology research center Core--Tissue culture

P30DK-17047-15 9007 (DDK) FISHER, LLOYD Diabetes-endocrinology research center Core--Biostatistics

R01DK-17049-19 (BBCB) NOWAK, THOMAS UNIVERSITY OF NOTRE DAME NOTRE DAME, IN 46556 NMR studies of metals in kinases and related enzymes

R37DK-17238-18 (NSS) SZURSZEWSKI, JOSEPH H MAYO FOUNDATION 200 FIRST ST SW ROCHESTER, MN 55905 Gastrointestinal smooth muscle in health and disease

R37DK-17294-18 (GMA) WALSH, JOHN H CURE/VA WADSWORTH WILSHITRE & SAWTELLE BLVDS LOS ANGELES, CA 90073 Hormonal stimulation and inhibition of gastric secretion

R37DK-17335-19 (BBCA) ALLEWELL, NORMA UNIVERSITY OF MINNESOTA 1479 GORTNER AVE ST. PAUL, MN 55108 Structure-energy correlates in aspartate transcarbamylase

R37DK-17389-19 (CBY) JAMIESON, JAMES D YALE UNIVERSITY 333 CEDAR ST, BOX 3333 NEW HAVEN, CT 06510 Cell secretion and membrane formation in the pancreas

R01DK-17420-18 (BNP) HRUBY, VICTOR J UNIVERSITY OF ARIZONA 2030 E SPEEDWAY, SUITE 113 TUCSON, AZ 85721 Peptide hormone structure and function

P01DK-17433-18 (DDK) GIEBISCH, GERHARD H YALE UNIVERSITY 333 CEDAR STREET NEW HAVEN, CT 06510 Cellular and molecular studies of renal transport

P01DK-17433-18 0001 (DDK) GIEBISCH, GERHARD H Cellular and molecular studies of renal transport Mechanisms of solute and water transport across the renala tubule

P01DK-17433-18 0002 (DDK) BOULPAEP, EMILE L Cellular and molecular studies of renal transport Electrophysiology and ion transport of the distal tubule

P01DK-17433-18 0012 (DDK) KASHGARIAN, MICHAEL Cellular and molecular studies of renal transport Cell biology of adaptation of transporting epithelia

P01DK-17433-18 0014 (DDK) BORON, WALTER F Cellular and molecular studies of renal transport mechanism of tubular acidification

P01DK-17433-18 0015 (DDK) ARONSON, PETER S Cellular and molecular studies of renal transport Mechanism of tubular anion transport

P01DK-17433-18 0021 (DDK) FORBUSH, BLISS Cellular and molecular studies of renal transport Plasma membrane Na, C1, K ion co-transport system

P01DK-17433-18 9002 (DDK) KASHGARIAN, MICHAEL Cellular and molecular studies of renal transport Core--Electron microscopy

P01DK-17433-18 9004 (DDK) BOULPAEP, EMILE L Cellular and molecular studies of renal transport Electronic shop--Core

P01DK-17433-18 9005 (DDK) FORREST, JOHN Cellular and molecular studies of renal transport Tissue culture--Core

R01DK-17436-16A2 (NLS) BARNES, EUGENE M, JR BAYLOR COLLEGE OF MEDICINE ONE BAYLOR PLAZA HOUSTON, TX 77030 Regulation of transport in mammalian cells

R37DK-17453-19 (BIO) TANAKA, KAY YALE UNIVERSITY 333 CEDAR STREET NEW HAVEN, CT 06510 Molecular basis disorders of branched chain amino acids metabolism

R01DK-17477-19 (PC) SPIRO, ROBERT G ELLIOT P JOSLIN RESEARCH LAB ONE JOSLIN PLACE BOSTON, MA 02215 Studies on the biosynthesis of glycoproteins

R01DK-17562-18 (GMA) HOLZBACH, R THOMAS CLEVELAND CLINIC FOUNDATION 9500 EUCLID AVENUE CLEVELAND, OH 44195-5218 Biliary cholesterol solubility

R01DK-17593-14 (SSS) TEWARSON, REGINALD P STATE UNIVERSITY OF NEW YORK STONY BROOK, NY 11794-3600 Numerical solution of renal transport equations

R01DK-17609-18 (PTHB) SHAFRITZ, DAVID A ALBERT EINSTEIN COLL OF MED 1300 MORRIS PARK AVE BRONX, NY 10461 Protein synthesis in normal and regenerating liver

R01DK-17632-17A1 (GMA) SZURSZEWSKI, JOSEPH H MAYO FOUNDATION 200 FIRST ST SW ROCHESTER, MN 55905 Extrinsic control of gastrointestinal motility

R01DK-17724-18 (PTHA) FARQUHAR, MARILYN G UNIV OF CALIFORNIA, SAN DIEGO3 9500 GILMAN DRIVE LA JOLLA, CA 92093-0651 Glomerular capillaries--Normal and pathological

R01DK-17776-16A1 (MET) AVRUCH, JOSEPH MASSACHUSETTS GENERAL HOSP 13TH ST MGH E BLDG 149 8TH FL CHARLESTOWN, MA 02129 Phosphopeptide metabolism in adipocytes

R37DK-17780-19 (CBY) FARQUHAR, MARILYN GIST UNIVERSITY OF CA, SAN DIEGO SCHOOL OF MEDICINE LA JOLLA, CA 92093-0651 Secretion and golgi traffic in pituitary and other cells

R37DK-17806-17 (BNP) LIU, ROBERT S UNIVERSITY OF HAWAII 2545 THE MALL HONOLULU, HI 96822 Isomers of vitamin A, carotene and visual pigments

R01DK-17808-18 (BIO) SODERLING, THOMAS R OREGON HEALTH SCIENCES UNIV 3181 SAM JACKSON PARK RD PORTLAND, OR 97201 Molecular mechanisms of insulin--Glycogen synthase

R01DK-17844-16 (BPN) WOODS, STEPHEN C UNIVERSITY OF WASHINGTON NI-25 SEATTLE, WASH 98195 Insulin and control of body weight and food intake

R37DK-17938-18 (GMA) KIM, YOUNG S V.A.M.C., G.I. RESEARCH LAB. 4150 CLEMENT STREET, 151M2 SAN FRANCISCO, CA 94121 Intestinal peptide hydrolases and peptide transport

R01DK-17989-16 (BMT) DOLPHIN, DAVID H UNIVERSITY OF BRITISH COLUMBIA 2036 MAIN HALL CHEMISTRY DEPT VANCOUVER, B.C, CANADA V6T 1Y6 Porphyrin ions and radicals in metabolic processes

Z01DK-18007-12 (LBM) GROLLMAN, E F NIDDK, NIH Electrochemical ion gradients as a mechanism of cellular message transmission

Z01DK-18009-12 (LBM) ROBBIN, A R NIDDK, NIH Endocytosis, secretion and compartmentalization in mutant CHO cells

Z01DK-18013-04 (LBM) PARSEGIAN, V A NIDDK, NIH Physics of ionic channels and other proteins with aqueous cavities

R37DK-18024-16 (BIO) DIXON, JACK E PURDUE UNIVERSITY DEPT OF BIOCHEMISTRY WEST LAFAYETTE, IND 47907 Studies on pancreatic hormones

R01DK-18061-17 (GMB) HAYSLETT, JOHN P YALE UNIVERSITY SCH OF MED 333 CEDAR STREET NEW HAVEN, CT 06510 Mechanism of cellular action of aldosterone

R01DK-18078-18 (GMB) EPSTEIN, FRANKLIN H BETH ISRAEL HOSPITAL 330 BROOKLINE AVENUE BOSTON, MA 02215 Water and electrolytes in health and disease

R01DK-18090-18 (GEN) JONES, ELIZABETH W CARNEGIE-MELLON UNIVERSITY 4400 FIFTH AVENUE PITTSBURGH, PA 15213 Genetic regulation of proteases in yeast

R01DK-18130-18 (END) MERIMEE, THOMAS J UNIVERSITY OF FLORIDA BOX J-226, JHMHC GAINESVILLE, FLA 32610 Insulin & High--Secretion and metabolic actions

R01DK-18141-17 (END) PEDERSEN, ROBERT C STATE UNIVESRSITY OF NEW YORK MAIN STREET CAMPUS BUFFALO, NY 14214 Steroidogenesis in adrenocortical & gonadal tissue

R37DK-18171-17 (PC) WILLIAMS, DAVID L SUNY HLTH SCIS CTR STONY BROOK, NY 11794-8651 Hormonal regulation--Vitellogenin and lipoprotein synthesis

R01DK-18243-17 (END) CHERRINGTON, ALAN D VANDERBILT UNIV SCH OF MED 702 LIGHT HALL NASHVILLE, TN 37232-0615 Gluconeogenesis & glycogenolysis--Role and regulation

R01DK-18269-17 (MET) MILLER, THOMAS B, JR UNIVERSITY OF MASSACHUSETTS 55 LAKE AVENUE NORTH WORCESTER, MA 01655 Regulation of hepatic glycogen synthesis

R37DK-18278-17 (NSS) KELLY, KEITH A MAYO FOUNDATION 200 FIRST STREET, S W ROCHESTER, MN 55905 Motility of the digestive tract in health and disease

R37DK-18347-18 (NSS) TAGER, HOWARD S UNIVERSITY OF CHICAGO 920 EAST 58TH STREET CHICAGO, IL 60637 Biosynthesis and secretion of peptide hormones

R01DK-18381-18 (PTHA) HUDSON, BILLY G UNIVERSITY OF KANSAS MED CTR 39TH AND RAINBOW BLVD KANSAS CITY, KS 66103-8410 Studies on the structure of basement membranes

R01DK-18413-15 (GMB) TOBACK, FREDERICK G UNIVERSITY OF CHICAGO 5841 SOUTH MARYLAND AVENUE CHICAGO, IL 60637 Biochemical regulation of controlled renal growth

R01DK-18427-14 (BIO) BIEBER, LORAN L MICHIGAN STATE UNIVERSITY BIOCHEMISTRY DEPARTMENT EAST LANSING, MI 48824 Short-chain acylcarnitines--function and enzymology

R01DK-18477-16A1 (END) ROSENFELD, MICHAEL G UNIV OF CA, SAN DIEGO LA JOLLA, CA 92093 Hormonal and developmental regulation of gene expression

R01DK-18512-17 (BIO) LEE, ERNEST Y UNIVERSITY OF MIAMI MED SCH BOX 016129/BIOCHEM MOL BIO DPT MIAMI, FL 33136 Phosphoprotein phosphatases--Properties and regulation

R01DK-18532-18 (CTY) SCHEELE, GEORGE A BETH ISRAEL HOSP/HARVARD MED S 330 BROOKLINE AVENUE BOSTON, MA 02215 Molecular basis of secretion in the exocrine pancreas

R01DK-18535-11 (END) DANFORTH, ELLIOT, JR UNIVERSITY OF VERMONT GIVEN BLDG, C-332 BURLINGTON, VT 05405 Effect of over- and undernutrition on thyroid hormone

R37DK-18573-30 (MET) FOSTER, DANIEL W UNIV OF TX SW MED CTR 5323 HARRY HINES BOULEVARD DALLAS, TX 75235 Carnitine palmitoyltransferase and fatty acid metabolism

R01DK-18585-16 (END) JEFCOATE, COLIN R UNIVERSITY OF WISCONSIN 1300 UNIVERSITY AVENUE MADISON, WI 53706 Cholesterol metabolism and mitochondrial cytochrome P450

R37DK-18624-16 (SAT) BELZER, FOLKERT O UNIVERSITY OF WISCONSIN 600 HIGHLAND AVENUE MADISON, WI 53792 Studies in organ preservation

R01DK-18707-15 (GMA) SALEN, GERALD VETERANS ADMINISTRATION HOSP TREMONT AVENUE EAST ORANGE, N J 07019 Metabolism of ursodeoxycholic acid in man

P01DK-18811-17A1 (DDK) BAIRD, ANDREW J THE WHITTER

PROJECT NO., ORGANIZATIONAL UNIT., INVESTIGATOR, ADDRESS, TITLE

INST/DIABETES/ENDO 9894 GENESEE AVENUE LA JOLLA, CA 92037 Brain peptides in pituitary functions and diabetes
P01DK-18811-17A1 0017 (DDK) BAIRD, ANDREW Brain peptides in pituitary functions and diabetes Regulation of fibroblast growth factor activity
P01DK-18811-17A1 0018 (DDK) FLORKIEWICZ, ROBERT Brain peptides in pituitary functions and diabetes Molecular biology of basic fibroblast growth factor
P01DK-18811-17A1 0019 (DDK) MAHER, PAMELA Brain peptides in pituitary functions and diabetes Fibroblast growth factor receptors in embryonic development
P01DK-18811-17A1 0020 (DDK) BAIRD, ANDREW Brain peptides in pituitary functions and diabetes Novel growth factors and inhibitors
P01DK-18811-17A1 9003 (DDK) LING, NICHOLAS C Brain peptides in pituitary functions and diabetes Core--Peptide synthesis
P01DK-18811-17A1 9005 (DDK) BUSCAGLIA, MARINO Brain peptides in pituitary functions and diabetes Core-- Histology and immunotechniques
P01DK-18811-17A1 9006 (DDK) FLORKIEWICZ, ROBERT Brain peptides in pituitary functions and diabetes Core-- Molecular biology and recombinant technology
R01DK-18849-16 (BIO) DIXON, JACK E PURDUE UNIVERSITY WEST LAFAYETTE, IN 47907 Regulation of neuropeptide biosynthesis
R01DK-18899-17 (MET) STERN, JUDITH S UNIVERSITY OF CALIFORNIA/DAVIS DEPARTMENT OF NUTRITION DAVIS, CA 95616 Physical activity, pancreatic function, and obesity
R01DK-18903-15 (NTN) BLACKARD, WILLIAM G VIRGINIA COMMONWEALTH UNIV P O BOX 155, MCV STATION RICHMOND, VA 23298-1001 Pathogenesis of diabetes mellitus
R01DK-18918-15 (GMB) GOLDINGER, JAMES M STATE UNIVERSITY OF NEW YORK 124 SHERMAN HALL BUFFALO, NY 14214 Mechanisms of tubular secretion of organic anions
R01DK-18919-17 (END) BRAVERMAN, LEWIS E UNIV OF MASSACHUSETTS MED CTR 55 LAKE AVENUE NORTH WORCESTER, MA 01655 Regulation of thyroid function T4 and T3 kinetics
R01DK-18951-14A2 (HEM) DALE, DAVID C UNIVERSITY OF WASHINGTON 1959 NE PACIFIC SEATTLE, WA 98195 Marrow regulation in cyclic hematopoiesis
R01DK-18986-15 (RAP) HOLLOSZY, JOHN O WASHINGTON UNIVERSITY 4566 SCOTT AVENUE BOX 8113 ST LOUIS, MO 63110 Carbohydrate and fat metabolism during exercise
R01DK-19038-13 (BMT) GRAY, HARRY B CALIFORNIA INSTITUTE OF TECH 1201 E CALIFORNIA BLVD PASADENA, CA 91125 Electron-transfer processes in iron and copper proteins
R37DK-19155-17 (NSS) LIKE, ARTHUR A UNIVERSITY OF MASSACHUSETTS 55 LAKE AVENUE NORTH WORCESTER, MA 01655 Ultrastructural and physiologic studies of diabetes
R37DK-19155-17 0001 (NSS) LIKE, ARTHUR A Ultrastructural and physiologic studies of diabetes Production of congenic BB-W rats and clarification of genetic basis of diabetes
R37DK-19155-17 0002 (NSS) LIKE, ARTHUR A Ultrastructural and physiologic studies of diabetes Morphology and physiology of diabetes in adult rats and their offspring
R37DK-19155-17 0004 (NSS) LIKE, ARTHUR A Ultrastructural and physiologic studies of diabetes Cell mediated autoimmune mechanisms in diabetes
R37DK-19155-17 0006 (NSS) LIKE, ARTHUR A Ultrastructural and physiologic studies of diabetes Renal glomerular studies
R01DK-19185-14 (PHY) SACHS, JOHN R S U N Y - AT STONY BROOK P.O. BOX 9 STONY BROOK, NY 11794 Physiological aspects of membrane cation transport
R01DK-19212-15A1 (GMA) VESSEY, DONALD A VETERANS ADMINISTRATION MED CT 4150 CLEMENT ST SAN FRANCISCO, CA 94121 Characterization of bile acid conjugation
R01DK-19221-15 (PBC) PUTNAM, FRANK W INDIANA UNIVERSITY DEPARTMENT OF BIOLOGY BLOOMINGTON, IN 47405 Blood plasma proteins--structure and function
R01DK-19259-13A3 (BIO) HARRIS, ROBERT A INDIANA UNIVERSITY SCH OF MED 635 BARNHILL DRIVE INDIANAPOLIS, IN 46223-5122 Regulation of leucine oxidation
R01DK-19289-16 (END) RAPOPORT, BASIL VETERANS ADMIN MED CTR 111T 4150 CLEMENT ST SAN FRANCISCO, CA 94121 Thyroid stimulators in health and disease
P01DK-19300-16 (DDK) COFFEY, DONALD S JOHNS HOPKINS HOSPITAL 600 NORTH WOLFE STREET BALTIMORE, MD 21205 Programmatical studies on benign prostatic hyperplasia
P01DK-19300-16 0003 (DDK) EWING, LARRY L Programmatical studies on benign prostatic hyperplasia Testicular imprinting, estrogens and benign prostatic hyperplasia
P01DK-19300-16 0004 (DDK) BARRACK, EVELYN R Programmatical studies on benign prostatic hyperplasia Receptor studies
P01DK-19300-16 0007 (DDK) COFFEY, DONALD S Programmatical studies on benign prostatic hyperplasia Prostate cell structure and function in BPH
P01DK-19300-16 0008 (DDK) ZIRKEN, BARRY R. Programmatical studies on benign prostatic hyperplasia Cell kinetics in normal and abnormal growth of the prostate
P01DK-19300-16 0010 (DDK) MOSTWIN, JACEL Programmatical studies on benign prostatic hyperplasia Urethral obstruction in guinea pigs
P01DK-19300-16 9001 (DDK) COFFEY, DONALD S Programmatical studies on benign prostatic hyperplasia Core--animal studies
R01DK-19302-16 (BPO) MORAN, TIMOTHY H JOHNS HOPKINS HOSPITAL 600 N WOLFE STREET BALTIMORE, MD 21205 Gastrointestinal integration and feeding
R37DK-19318-15 (NSS) BIRNBAUMER, LUTZ BAYLOR COLLEGE OF MEDICINE ONE BAYLOR PLAZA HOUSTON, TX 77030 Action of hormones on adenyl cyclase systems
R37DK-19394-15 (CTY) LAZAROW, PAUL B MOUNT SINAI SCHOOL OF MEDICINE ONE GUSTAVE L. LEVY PLACE NEW YORK, NY 10029-6574 Biogenesis of liver peroxisomes
R37DK-19406-15 (PHY) AUSIELLO, DENNIS A MASSACHUSETTS GENERAL HOSPITAL RENAL UNIT BOSTON, MASS 02114 Mechanism of action of vasopressin
R01DK-19407-15A3 (PHY) WARNOCK, DAVID G UNIV OF ALABAMA UAB STATION BIRMINGHAM, AL 35294 Na/ion reabsorption and H/ion secretion renal mechanisms
R01DK-19473-16 (PB) OLSON, MERLE S U. OF TX H.S.C. AT SAN ANTONIO 7703 FLOYD CURL DRIVE SAN ANTONIO, TX 78284-7760 Regulatory mechanisms in hepatic metabolism
R01DK-19482-16 (HEM) FORGET, BERNARD G YALE UNIVERSITY SCH OF MEDICIN 333 CEDAR STREET NEW HAVEN, CT 06510 Molecular genetics of the erythroid cell
R01DK-19514-13A1 (MET) RUDERMAN, NEIL B UNIVERSITY HOSPITAL 88 EAST NEWTON STREET BOSTON, MA 02118 Insulin resistance and DAG/PKC signaling in muscle
R01DK-19520-13 (PHY) MACHEN, TERRY E UNIVERSITY OF CALIFORNIA BERKELEY, CA 94720 Transitions and transport in gastric mucosa
P30DK-19525-15 (DDK) MATSCHINSKY, FRANZ M UNIVERSITY OF PENNSYVANIA 36TH & HAMILTON WALK PHILADELPHIA, PA 19104-6015 University of Pennsylvania diabetes center
P30DK-19525-15 9001 (DDK) RONNER, PETER University of Pennsylvania diabetes center Core--Radioimmunoassay
P30DK-19525-15 9002 (DDK) MATSCHINSKY, FRANZ M University of Pennsylvania diabetes center Core-- Pancreatic islet cell culture
P30DK-19525-15 9004 (DDK) JARETT, LEONARD University of Pennsylvania diabetes center Core-- Electron microscopy and morphology
P30DK-19525-15 9005 (DDK) KENNETT, ROGER University of Pennsylvania diabetes center Core-- Antibody production
P30DK-19525-15 9006 (DDK) TUNG, LIM University of Pennsylvania diabetes center Core-- Protein and nucleic acid chemistry
P30DK-19525-15 0018 (DDK) SPIELMAN, RICHARD University of Pennsylvania diabetes center Pilot study-- Genetics of type II diabetes (NIDDM) in family studies
P30DK-19525-15 0019 (DDK) CIVAN, MORTIMER University of Pennsylvania diabetes center Pilot study-- Effects of diabetes on transport by retinal pigment epithelium
P30DK-19525-15 0020 (DDK) TUNG, LIM University of Pennsylvania diabetes center Pilot study-- Biochemistry of insulin-stimulated protein phosphatase
R01DK-19567-15 (PHY) WRIGHT, ERNEST M UNIV OF CA, LOS ANGELES 405 HILGARD AVE. LOS ANGELES, CA 90024-1751 Molecular mechanisms of intestinal transport
R01DK-19577-10 (RAP) BROOKS, GEORGE A UNIVERSITY OF CALIFORNIA 103 HARMON GYMNASIUM BERKELEY, CA 94720 Substrate supply during exercise
R01DK-19645-14 (PTHA) SCHMIDT, ROBERT E WASHINGTON UNIV SCH OF MED 660 SOUTH EUCLID AVENUE ST LOUIS, MO 63110 Experimental diabetic autonomic neuropathy
R01DK-19682-14 (PBC) VIJAY, INDER K UNIVERSITY OF MARYLAND DEPARTMENT OF ANIMAL SCIENCES COLLEGE PARK, MD 20742 Developmental regulation of mammary glycoproteins
R37DK-19691-16 (MET) BOND, JUDITH S VIRGINIA POLYTECH INST/ST UNIV BLACKSBURG, VA 24061-0308 Intracellular protein catabolism in diabetes mellitus
R01DK-19715-14A1 (GMB) KNOX, FRANKLYN G MAYO FOUNDATION 200 FIRST STREET SOUTHWEST ROCHESTER, MN 55905 Intrarenal regulation of phosphate metabolism
R01DK-19743-14A1 (GMB) NUNEZ, ELADIO A COLUMBIA UNIVERSITY 630 WEST 168TH STREET NEW YORK, NY 10032 Studies of the parafollicular cell of the thyroid gland
R01DK-19812-16 (END) OPPENHEIMER, JACK H UNIV OF MINNESOTA 420 DELAWARE ST SE BOX 91 UMHC MINNEAPOLIS, MN 55455 Thyroxine-protein interactions
R37DK-19813-16 (GMB) RASMUSSEN, HOWARD YALE UNIVERSITY P O BOX 3333 NEW HAVEN, CT 06510 Hormonal and ionic control of metabolism
R01DK-19822-14 (GMB) BOURGOIGNIE, JACQUES J UNIVERSITY OF MIAMI P O BOX 061960 MIAMI, FL 33101 Renal failure--Pathophysiology and possible prevention
R01DK-19856-15 (BBCA) DETITTA, GEORGE T MEDICAL FDN OF BUFFALO, INC 73 HIGH STREET BUFFALO, N Y 14203 Diffraction studies of the biotin vitamers
R01DK-19912-15 (PC) KEMP, ROBERT G UNIV OF HLTH SCI/CHIC MED SCHL 3333 GREEN BAY ROAD NORTH CHICAGO, IL 60064 Allosteric properties of phosphofructokinase
R01DK-19920-16 (HEM) WEISS, LEON P UNIVERSITY OF PENNSYLVANIA SUITE 200 PHILADELPHIA, PA 19104-6046 Electron microscopy of the reticuloendothelial system
R01DK-19925-15 (MET) KONO, TETSURO VANDERBILT UNIVERSITY 702 LIGHT HALL NASHVILLE, TN 37232-0615 Action of insulin of sugar transport
P01DK-19928-13 (DDK) SCHRIER, ROBERT W UNIVERSITY OF CO HLTH SCIS CTR 4200 EAST NINTH AVENUE DENVER, CO 80262 Regulation, release and action of vasopressin
P01DK-19928-13 0015 (DDK) SCHRIER, ROBERT W Regulation, release and action of vasopressin Vasopressin action--Potassium, calcium and endoperoxide derivatives
P01DK-19928-13 0016 (DDK) SCHRIER, ROBERT W Regulation, release and action of vasopressin Central mechanisms of arginine vasopressin release
P01DK-19928-13 0017 (DDK) SCHRIER, ROBERT W Regulation, release and action of vasopressin Vascular effects of arginine vasopressin
P01DK-19928-13 0018 (DDK) KIM, JIN K Regulation, release and action of vasopressin Newer methods of vasopressin replacement and antagonism
P01DK-19928-13 9001 (DDK) KIM, JIN K Regulation, release and action of vasopressin Core laboratory
R01DK-19952-15 (MET) GARRISON, JAMES C, II UNIVERSITY OF VIRGINIA MED CTR PO BOX 448, JORDAN HALL CHARLOTTESVILLE, VA 22908 Hormonal control of hepatic metabolism and function
R37DK-19971-15 (NSS) BAYNES, JOHN W UNIVERSITY OF SOUTH CAROLINA PHYSICAL SCIENCES CENTER COLUMBIA, S C 29208 Glycation of protein in diabetes
R01DK-19974-15 (BCE) HINKLE, PATRICIA M UNIVERSITY OF ROCHESTER 601 ELMWOOD AVENUE ROCHESTER, N Y 14642 Modulation of receptor number in cultured cells
R01DK-19984-15 (GMA) SOLL, ANDREW H CTR/ULCER RES/EDC/BLDG 115/RM VA WADSWORTH MD CTR/WILSHIRE/S LOS ANGELES, CA 90073 Physiology of the isolated mammalian parietal cell

PROJECT NO., ORGANIZATIONAL UNIT., INVESTIGATOR, ADDRESS, TITLE

R01DK-20043-14 (PTHA) WILSON, CURTIS B THE SCRIPPS RESEARCH INSTITUTE 10666 NORTH TORREY PINES ROAD LA JOLLA, CALIF 92037 Immunopathology of renal disease in man

R55DK-20129-14A2 (END) LOCKWOOD, DEAN H UNIV OF ROCHESTER MEDICAL CTR PO BOX 693/601 ELMWOOD AVENUE ROCHESTER, NY 14642 Insulin action in normal and resistant states

R37DK-20205-15 (BIO) BELL, ROBERT M DUKE UNIVERSITY MEDICAL CENTER 212 NAN DUKE BLDG RESEARCH DR DURHAM, NC 27710 Regulation of enzymes of lipid metabolism

R37DK-20251-15 (HEM) THEIL, ELIZABETH C NORTH CAROLINA STATE UNIVERSIT 339 POLK HALL, NCSU BOX 7622 RALEIGH, NC 27695-7622 Red cell ferritin--Ontogenetic control

R01DK-20270-13 (CTY) WANG, KUAN UNIV OF TEXAS AT AUSTIN AUSTIN, TEX 78712 Proteins and architecture of an elastic sarcomere matrix

R01DK-20357-11 (BBCB) COWBURN, DAVID A ROCKEFELLER UNIVERSITY 1230 YORK AVE NEW YORK, NY 10021 Conformations of insulin & its receptor complexes

R37DK-20368-14 (GMB) DEEN, WILLIAM M MASSACHUSETTS INST. OF TECH. CAMBRIDGE, MA 02139 Physico-chemical aspects of renal transport processes

R01DK-20378-15 (MET) LANDSBERG, LEWIS NORTHWESTERN UNIVERSITY 250 E SUPERIOR STREET CHICAGO, IL 60611-2950 Carbohydrate metabolism and catecholamines

R01DK-20387-14 (MET) SPRECHER, HOWARD W OHIO STATE UNIVERSITY 333 WEST 10TH AVENUE COLUMBUS, OH 43210 Regulation of (n-3) and (n-6) fatty acid metabolism

R37DK-20407-14 (PC) STRAUSS, ARNOLD W WASHINGTON UNIVERSITY 724 SOUTH EUCLID ST. LOUIS, MO 63110 Protein translocation across organelle membranes

R37DK-20411-16 (NSS) GERICH, JOHN E UNIVERSITY OF PITTSBURGH 230 LOTHROP STREET PITTSBURGH, PA 15261 Alpha and beta cell function in human diabetes

R01DK-20446-09S2 (NTN) SCHNEEMAN, BARBARA O UNIVERSITY OF CALIFORNIA DAVIS, CA 95616 Nutritional effects of plant fiber on digestion

R01DK-20478-12 (MEDB) PATEL, MULCHAND S CASE WESTERN RESERVE UNIV 2119 ABINGTON RD CLEVELAND, OH 44106 Inborn errors of pyruvate metabolism

R01DK-20495-15 (MET) SHERWIN, ROBERT S YALE UNIVERSITY BOX 3333, FITKIN I NEW HAVEN, CONNECTICUT 06510 Glucoregulatory hormone interactions in diabetes

R01DK-20503-14 (HEM) KUSHNER, JAMES P UNIVERSITY OF UTAH MED CENTER 50 NORTH MEDICAL DRIVE SALT LAKE CITY, UTAH 84132 Porphyrin biosynthesis in normal and disease states

P60DK-20541-14 (DDK) FLEISCHER, NORMAN S A. EINSTEIN COLLEGE OF MED. 1300 MORRIS PARK AVENUE BRONX, NY 10461 Diabetes research and training center

P60DK-20541-14 0023 (DDK) WISE, LEIGH S Diabetes research and training center Pilot study--Hormone action and 3T3-L1 cells

P60DK-20541-14 0025 (DDK) SHIELDS,DENNIS Diabetes research and training center Pilot study--Biosynthesis and structure of hormones

P60DK-20541-14 0026 (DDK) RUBIN,CHARLES Diabetes research and training center Pilot study--Cyclic AMP mediation and action

P60DK-20541-14 0027 (DDK) EDER,HOWARD Diabetes research and training center Pilot study--Diabetes and lipids,basement membrane & carbohydrate metabolism

P60DK-20541-14 0028 (DDK) FEIN,FREDERICK Diabetes research and training center Pilot study--Effects of diabetes on heart & kidneys

P60DK-20541-14 0029 (DDK) MAZZE,ROGER Diabetes research and training center Pilot study--Patient care,metabolic control & human physiology

P60DK-20541-14 9001 (DDK) RUBIN, CHARLES S Diabetes research and training center Core--Cell culture and molecular biology laboratory

P60DK-20541-14 9002 (DDK) FLEISCHER, NORMAN S Diabetes research and training center Core--Radioimmunoassay-islet laboratory

P60DK-20541-14 9003 (DDK) EDER, HOWARD A Diabetes research and training center Core--Chemical laboratory

P60DK-20541-14 9004 (DDK) MAZZE, ROGER S Diabetes research and training center Core--Education and training component

P60DK-20542-14 (ADDK) CLARK, CHARLES M, JR INDIANA UNIV SCHOOL OF MED 1001 WEST 10TH STREET INDIANAPOLIS, IN 46202-2859 Diabetes research and training center

P60DK-20542-14 9001 (ADDK) FINEBERG, JAOMI S Diabetes research and training center Core--Biostatistics and epidemiology

P60DK-20542-14 9002 (ADDK) FINEBERG, S EDWIN Diabetes research and training center Core--Immunoassay laboratory

P60DK-20542-14 9004 (ADDK) MAZZUCA, STEVEN A Diabetes research and training center Educational development and evaluation core

P60DK-20542-14 9007 (ADDK) VINICOR, FRANK Diabetes research and training center Core--Diabetes clinical facility

P60DK-20542-14 9009 (ADDK) DIXON, JACK E Diabetes research and training center Core--Molecular biology and protein sequencing

P60DK-20542-14 9010 (ADDK) VINICOR, FRANK Diabetes research and training center Outreach core

P01DK-20543-15 (DDK) PAK, CHARLES Y UNIVERSITY OF TEXAS 5323 HARRY HINES BLVD DALLAS, TEX 75235-8885 Formulation of a rational therapy of nephrolithiasis

P01DK-20543-15 0009 (DDK) ZERWEKH, JOSEPH Formulation of a rational therapy of nephrolithiasis DNA encoding of 1,25-dihydroxycholecalciferol receptor

P01DK-20543-15 0010 (DDK) BRESLAU, NEIL Formulation of a rational therapy of nephrolithiasis Pathogenesis of hypercalciuria

P01DK-20543-15 0011 (DDK) ALPERN, ROBERT Formulation of a rational therapy of nephrolithiasis Renal basis of hypocitraturia

P01DK-20543-15 0012 (DDK) SAKHAEE, KHASHAYAR Formulation of a rational therapy of nephrolithiasis Stone forming risk of calcium supplementation and sodium abuse

P01DK-20543-15 0013 (DDK) PAK, CHARLES Formulation of a rational therapy of nephrolithiasis Intestinal mechanisms for poor citraturic response to potassium citrate

P01DK-20543-15 0014 (DDK) PREMINGER, GLENN Formulation of a rational therapy of nephrolithiasis In vitro and in vivo studies of stone fragmentation and tissue injury

P01DK-20543-15 0015 (DDK) PREMINGER, GLENN Formulation of a rational therapy of nephrolithiasis Alterations in renal tissue induced by extracorporal shock

P01DK-20543-15 0016 (DDK) PAK, CHARLES Formulation of a rational therapy of nephrolithiasis Therapeutic modalities for hypercalciuria

P01DK-20543-15 0017 (DDK) PAK, CHARLES Formulation of a rational therapy of nephrolithiasis Novel treatments for hypocitraturic calcium nephrolithiasis

P01DK-20543-15 9001 (DDK) PAK, CHARLES Y Formulation of a rational therapy of nephrolithiasis Core--Support services

P01DK-20543-15 0008 (DDK) ZERWEKH, JOSEPH Formulation of a rational therapy of nephrolithiasis 1,25-Dihydroxycholecalciferol receptor characterization

P60DK-20572-14 (ADDK) GREENE, DOUGLAS A UNIVERSITY OF MICHIGAN 3920 TAUBMAN CENTER ANN ARBOR, MI 48109-0354 Michigan diabetes research and training center

P60DK-20572-14 0038 (ADDK) JACKSON, CHARLES V Michigan diabetes research and training center Pilot study--Myocardial function in streptozotocin-induced diabetes

P60DK-20572-14 0039 (ADDK) LANDEFELD, THOMAS D Michigan diabetes research and training center Pilot study--Analysis of insulin gene from patients with mutant insulins

P60DK-20572-14 0040 (ADDK) ROSEN, STEPHEN G Michigan diabetes research and training center Pilot study--Evaluation of hypoglycemia unawareness in diabetes mellitus

P60DK-20572-14 0041 (ADDK) FINK, DAVID J Michigan diabetes research and training center Pilot study--Retrograde axonal transport in streptozotocin diabetes

P60DK-20572-14 0043 (ADDK) WILLIAMS, DAVID Michigan diabetes research and training center P-31 NMR spectroscopy of the diabetic forefoot

P60DK-20572-14 0044 (ADDK) VINIK, AARON Michigan diabetes research and training center Improved diabetes control and platelet function in NIDDM

P60DK-20572-14 0045 (ADDK) THOMAS, DAVID Michigan diabetes research and training center Class II MHC antigens in diabetes

P60DK-20572-14 0046 (ADDK) MEISLEER, MIRIAM Michigan diabetes research and training center Insulin dependence of amylase in transgenic mice

P60DK-20572-14 9001 (ADDK) KOSTYO, JACK Michigan diabetes research and training center Core--Research development and research training

P60DK-20572-14 9002 (ADDK) MARTIN, DENNIS Michigan diabetes research and training center Core--Biochemistry facility

P60DK-20572-14 9003 (ADDK) CORNELL, RICHARD G Michigan diabetes research and training center Core--Biostatistics and data systems

P60DK-20572-14 9004 (ADDK) COHEN, BENNETT J Michigan diabetes research and training center Core--Diabetic animal facility

P60DK-20572-14 9005 (ADDK) ENGLAND, BARRY G Michigan diabetes research and training center Core--ligand assay facility

P60DK-20572-14 9007 (ADDK) HALTER, JEFFREY Michigan diabetes research and training center Core--Diabetes center unit

P60DK-20572-14 9008 (ADDK) HISS, ROLAND G Michigan diabetes research and training center Core--Continuing education and outreach

P60DK-20572-14 9009 (ADDK) DAVIS, WAYNE K Michigan diabetes research and training center Core--Educational development and evaluation

P60DK-20579-14 (DDK) KIPNIS, DAVID M WASHINGTON UNIVERSITY 660 SOUTH EUCLID AVENUE ST. LOUIS, MO 63110 Diabetes research and training center

P60DK-20579-14 0033 (DDK) SILBERT, DAVID F Diabetes research and training center Pilot--Membrane lipids and insulin-induced hexose transport

P60DK-20579-14 9001 (DDK) CRYER, PHILIP E Diabetes research and training center Core--clinical research facility and diabetes registry

P60DK-20579-14 9002 (DDK) GINGERICH, RONALD Diabetes research and training center Core--Radioimmunoassay facility

P60DK-20579-14 9003 (DDK) WILLIAMSON, JOSEPH R Diabetes research and training center Core--Pathobiology facility

P60DK-20579-14 9004 (DDK) OSTLUND, RICHARD E Diabetes research and training center Core--Tissue culture facility

P60DK-20579-14 9005 (DDK) SHERMAN, WILLIAM R Diabetes research and training center Core--Mass spectrometry facility

P60DK-20579-14 9006 (DDK) FISHER, EDWIN B Diabetes research and training center Core--Training and information component

P60DK-20579-14 9007 (DDK) GRANT, GREGORY A Diabetes research and training center Core--Molecular biology laboratory

P60DK-20579-14 9008 (DDK) SCHARP, DAVID Diabetes research and training center Core--Human islet isolation

P60DK-20579-14 0029 (DDK) FLAVIN, KAREN Diabetes research and training center Pilot--Assessment of clinical diabetes management by physicians

P60DK-20579-14 0030 (DDK) AUSLANDER, WENDY Diabetes research and training center Pilot--Family coping patterns and control in high risk IDDM

P60DK-20579-14 0031 (DDK) CROUCH, EDMOND C Diabetes research and training center Pilot--basement membrane collagen during wound healing in drug-induced diabetes

P60DK-20579-14 0032 (DDK) MUECKLER, MICHAEL M Diabetes research and training center Pilot--Structure and function of he glucose transporter

P01DK-20586-15 (SRC) HACKETT, RAYMOND L UNIVERSITY OF FLORIDA JHMHC BOX J-275 GAINESVILLE, FL 32610 Protein chemistry core

P01DK-20586-15 0001 (SRC) FINLAYSON, BIRDWELL Protein chemistry core Physical chemistry--Nucleation and aggregation

P01DK-20586-15 0003 (SRC) HACKETT, RAYMOND L Protein chemistry core Tissue-crystal interactions in urolithiasis

P01DK-20586-15 0006 (SRC) BATICH, CHRISTOPHER Protein chemistry core Encrustation

P01DK-20586-15 9001 (SRC) THOMAS, WILLIAM C Protein chemistry core Core--urine chemistry

P01DK-20586-15 9002 (SRC) FINLAYSON, BIRDWELL Protein chemistry core Core B-- Computer services and particle characterization

P60DK-20593-13 (DDK) CROFFORD, OSCAR B VANDERBILT UNIVERSITY 21ST AVE. SOUTH & GARLAND ST. NASHHVILLE, TN 37232 Diabetes research and training center

P60DK-20593-13 0001 (DDK) WASSERMAN, DAVID Diabetes research and training center Regulation of glucose uptake during exercise--pilot/feasibility study

P60DK-20593-13 0002 (DDK) MCGUINNESS, OWEN Diabetes research and training center Hormonal regulation of glucose metabolism in sepsis-pilot/feasibility study

P60DK-20593-13 0003 (DDK) CHALKLEY, ROGER Diabetes research and training center Effect of glucocorticoids,cAMP,insulin on structure of PEPCK gene- pilot study

P60DK-20593-13 9001 (DDK) WILLIAMS, PHILLIP E Diabetes research and training center Animal resources core

P60DK-20593-13 9002 (DDK) CAMPBELL, PETER Diabetes research and training center Hormone assay core

P60DK-20593-13 9003 (DDK) ABUMRAD, NAJI Diabetes research and training center Amino acid core

P60DK-20593-13 9004 (DDK) WEIL, ANTHONY Diabetes research and training center Molecular biology core

P60DK-20593-13 9005 (DDK) WEIL, ANTHONY Diabetes research and training center Media and cell production core

P60DK-20593-13 9006 (DDK) SCHLUNDT, DAVID Diabetes research and training center Model demonstration unit core

P60DK-20593-13 9007 (DDK) PINCHERT, JAMES Diabetes research and training center Education evaluation core

P60DK-20595-14 (DDK) RUBENSTEIN, ARTHUR H THE UNIVERSITY OF CHICAGO 5841 SOUTH MARYLAND AVENUE CHICAGO, IL 60637 Diabetes research and training center

P60DK-20595-14 0024 (DDK) ROBERTSON, GARY L Diabetes research and training center: Pilot study--Role of vasopressin in platelet abnormalities in diabetes

P60DK-20595-14 0025 (DDK) THISTLETHWAITE, J RICHARD Diabetes research and training center Pilot study--Passenger leukocyte depletion from intact pancreas

P60DK-20595-14 9001 (DDK) STEINER, DONALD F Diabetes research and training center Core--Cellular and molecular biology

P60DK-20595-14 9002 (DDK) TAGER, HOWARD S Diabetes research and training center Core--Peptide and protein analysis

P60DK-20595-14 9003 (DDK) RUBENSTEIN, ARTHUR H Diabetes research and training center Core--Radioimmunoassay and clinical studies

P60DK-20595-14 9007 (DDK) MCNABB, WYLIE Diabetes research and training center Core--Educational development unit

P60DK-20595-14 9008 (DDK) LEVITSKY, LYNNE L Diabetes research and training center Core--Pediatric maodel demonstration unit

P60DK-20595-14 0017 (DDK) STECK, THEODORE L Diabetes research and training center Pilot study--band 3 tyrosine kinase in human erythrocyte membranes

P60DK-20595-14 0018 (DDK) PALFREY, CLIVE H Diabetes research and training center Pilot study--Role of calmodulin binding protein in insulin secretion

P60DK-20595-14 0020 (DDK) NAKAO, MARTA S Diabetes research and training center Pilot study--Altered regulation of growth hormone in diabetes

P60DK-20595-14 0022 (DDK) VILLEREAL, MITCHELL L Diabetes research and training center Pilot study--Cell physiology of pancreatic beta cell secretion

P60DK-20595-14 0023 (DDK) BORROW, KENNETH Diabetes research and training center Pilot study--Diabetic LV dysfunction muscle or autonomic abnormality

R01DK-20630-13 (HEM) KUSHNER, JAMES P UNIVERSITY OF UTAH MED CENTER 50 NORTH MEDICAL DRIVE SALT LAKE CITY, UTAH 84132 Hereditary hemochromatosis

R01DK-20678-13 (BIO) LARDY, HENRY A INSTITUTE FOR ENZYME RESEARCH 1710 UNIVERSITY AVENUE MADISON, WI 53705 Regulation of gluconeogenesis in diabetes

R01DK-20827-13A2 (SAT) MULLEN, YOKO S UNIVERSITY OF CALIFORNIA ROOM 4770 LOS ANGELES, CA 90024 Immune aspects in fetal pancreas allografts

R01DK-20902-14 (MEDB) HERSHFIELD, MICHAEL S DUKE UNIVERSITY MEDICAL CENTER BOX 3049 DURHAM, NC 27710 A lymphoblast model for diseases of metabolism

R01DK-20948-13 (MET) AMATRUDA, JOHN M UNIV OF ROCHESTER MED SCHOOL 601 ELMWOOD AVENUE ROCHESTER, N Y 14642 Insulin action in the liver

R37DK-20999-14 (NSS) AL-AWQATI, QAIS COLUMBIA UNIVERSITY 630 W 168TH STREET NEW YORK, NY 10032 Active H+ transport in urinary acidification

Z01DK-21008-25 (LCBG) TJIO, J H NIDDK, NIH Cytogenetics

R55DK-21019-14 (BIO) WALSH, DONAL A UNIVERSITY OF CALIFORNIA DAVIS, CA 95616 Protein inhibitor of the cAMP-dependent protein kinase

Z01DK-21019-09 (LCBG) POLLARD, H B NIDDK, NIH Mechanisms of hormone and transmitter secretion

R37DK-21085-15 (PC) HRUBY, VICTOR J UNIVERSITY OF ARIZONA DEPARTMENT OF CHEMISTRY TUCSON, ARIZONA 85721 Glucagon structure function studies

R01DK-21248-14 (PC) RUBIN, CHARLES S A. EINSTEIN COLLEGE OF MED. 1300 MORRIS PARK AVENUE BRONX, NY 10461 Insulin/IGF-I regulation of adipocyte development

R37DK-21344-15 (CTY) RUTTER, WILLIAM J UNIVERSITY OF CALIFORNIA HORMONE RESEARCH LABORATORY SAN FRANCISCO, CA 94143-0534 Differentiation in the endocrine & exocrine pancreas

R37DK-21365-15 (NSS) ALLEN, ROBERT H UNIV OF COLORADO HLTH SCIS CTR 4200 E 9TH AVE, BX B170 DENVER, CO 80262 Structure and function of B12-binding proteins

R01DK-21397-14 (BPO) GRILL, HARVEY J THE UNIVERSITY OF PENNSYLVANIA 3815 WALNUT STREET PHILADELPHIA, PA 19104-6196 Neural hierarchy in the modulation of ingestive behavior

R01DK-21404-10 (CVB) MORRIS, DAVID J THE MIRIAM HOSPITAL 164 SUMMIT AVENUE PROVIDENCE, RI 02906 Regulation of metabolism and action of aldosterone

R37DK-21474-14 (GMA) MAC DERMOTT, RICHARD P JR UNIVERSITY OF PENNSYLVANIA 3400 SPRUCE STREET PHILADELPHIA, PA 19104-4283 Cell mediated immunity in inflammatory bowel disease

PROJECT NO., ORGANIZATIONAL UNIT., INVESTIGATOR, ADDRESS, TITLE

R01DK-21489-12 (BBCA) LEE, JAMES C UNIVERSITY OF TX MEDICAL BRAMC 617 E BASIC SCIENCE BLDG. F-47 GALVESTON, TX 77550-2774 Physical studies of protein interactions

R37DK-21491-14 (MEDB) MIZIORKO, HENRY M MEDICAL COLLEGE OF WISCONSIN 8701 WATERTOWN PLANK ROAD MILWAUKEE, WI 53226 HMG-CoA cycle control in normal and diabetic liver

R01DK-21505-15 (GMA) NEUTRA, MARIAN R ENDERS PEDIATRICS RESEARCH LAB 300 LONGWOOD AVENUE BOSTON, MA 02115 Epithelial differentiation and intestinal secretion

R01DK-21506-14 (GMA) HOFMANN, ALAN F UNIV OF CA, SAN DIEGO DIV OF GASTROENTEROLOGY T-013 LA JOLLA, CA 92093 Bile acid metabolism in health and disease

R01DK-21536-11 (SSS) SCHWARTZ, MELVIN M RUSH-PRESBYTERIAN MED CENTER 1653 WEST CONGRESS PARKWAY CHICAGO, IL 60612 Study of glomerular epithelial cell injury

R01DK-21576-11 (PHY) MARVER, DIANA U OF TEXAS SOUTHWESTERN MED CT 5323 HARRY HINES BLVD DALLAS, TX 75235-8856 Characterization of hormone target sites on chromatin

R01DK-21594-15 (PC) GOODRIDGE, ALAN G UNIVERSITY OF IOWA BOWEN SCIENCE BUILDING IOWA CITY, IA 52242 Regulation of the synthesis of lipogenic enzymes

R01DK-21614-14 (GMB) ARNAUD, CLAUDE D VA MEDICAL CENTER 1710 SCOTT ST., 3RD FLOOR SAN FRANCISCO, CA 94115 Parathyroid hormone and calcitonin

R01DK-21624-14 (MET) MORTIMORE, GLENN E THE MILTON S HERSHEY MED CTR PO BOX 850 HERSHEY, PA 17033 Mechanism and regulation of protein turnover in liver

R01DK-21633-14 (PB) CINTI, DOMINICK L UNIV. OF CONNECTICUT HLTH. CTR 263 FARMINGTON AVENU / MC-3605 FARMINGTON, CT 06030 Isolation of elongation enzymes & site of synthesis

R01DK-21668-13A2 (GMA) ODELL, GERARD B UNIVERSITY OF WISCONSIN 600 HIGHLAND AVE MADISON, WI 53792 Maturation of liver for the metabolism of bilirubin

R01DK-21684-15 (GMA) SLOMIANY, BRONISLAW L UNIV OF MED & DENT OF NJ 110 BERGEN ST NEWARK, NJ 07103-2400 Biochemistry of glycolipids in gastric secretion

R01DK-21712-12A1 (NTN) MARLETT, JUDITH A UNIVERSITY OF WISCONSIN 1415 LINDEN DRIVE MADISON, WI 53706 Measuring dietary fiber

R01DK-21723-14 (BIO) BEAVO, JOSEPH A UNIVERSITY OF WASHINGTON SEATTLE, WA 98195 Metabolism and function of cyclic nucleotides

R01DK-21737-13 (MBC) SOKATCH, JOHN R UNIV OF OKLAHOMA HLTH SCIS CTR P O BOX 26901 OKLAHOMA CITY, OK 73190 Structure of branched chain keto acid dehydrogenase

R01DK-21739-10 (BMT) WOODWORTH, ROBERT C UNIVERSITY OF VERMONT B401 GIVEN BUILDING BURLINGTON, VT 05405 Iron delivery via blood--Structural role of transferrin

R01DK-21800-15 (PC) ELBEIN, ALAN D UNIV OF AR MEDICAL SCIENCES 4301 W. MARKHAM STREET LITTLE ROCK, AR 72205 Lipid-linked saccharides in glycoprotein synthesis

R37DK-21859-13 (BIO) HANSON, RICHARD W CASE WESTERN RESERVE UNIV 10900 EUCLID AVENUE CLEVELAND, OH 44106-4935 Structure and function of PEP carboxykinase isozymes

R37DK-21860-14 (END) SHIELDS, DENNIS ALBERT EINSTEIN COLL OF MED 1300 MORRIS PARK AVENUE BRONX, N Y 10461 Biosynthesis and processing of peptide hormone precursor

R01DK-21901-13 (END) AGARWAL, KAN L UNIVERSITY OF CHICAGO 920 EAST 58TH STREET CHICAGO, IL 60637 Biosynthesis of gastrin

R37DK-22000-20 (BCE) COFFEY, DONALD S JOHNS HOPKINS HOSPITAL 600 NORTH WOLFE STREET BALTIMORE, MD 21205 Regulation of prostatic growth by androgens

R01DK-22036-13 (GMB) SCHLONDORFF, DETLEF O ALBERT EINSTEIN COLLEGE 1300 MORRIS PARK AVE BRONX, NY 10461 Pathophysiology of cAMP and prostaglandins in the kidney

R01DK-22040-11A2 (PTHA) SAVIN, VIRGINIA J UNIVERSITY OF KANSAS MED CTR 39TH & RAINBOW BOULEVARD KANSAS CITY, KS 66103-8410 Modulation of glomerular ultrafiltration coefficient

R37DK-22042-14 (GMB) SMITH, WILLIAM L MICHIGAN STATE UNIVERSITY DEPARTMENT OF BIOCHEMISTRY EAST LANSING, MI 48824 Prostaglandin synthesis in kidney collecting tubules

R37DK-22122-14 (NSS) MATSCHINSKY, FRANZ M UNIVERSITY OF PENNSYVANIA 36TH & HAMILTON WALK PHILADELPHIA, PA 19104-6015 Metabolism of islets of Langerhans and hormone release

N01DK-22200-14 (**) HENDERSON, LAURA Support services for NIADDK advisory boards

N01DK-22206-37 (**) LACHIN, JOHN M Complications of insulin-dependent diabetes mellitus

R01DK-23026-13 (GMA) WOLKOFF, ALLAN W ALBERT EINSTEIN COLL OF MEDICI 1300 MORRIS PARK AVENUE BRONX, NY 10461 Hepatic organic anion uptake and transport

R01DK-23045-12 (HEM) TAO, MARIANO UNIV. OF ILLINOIS AT CHICAGO 1853 WEST POLK STREET M/C 536 CHICAGO, IL 60612 Phosphorylation & control of red cell cytoskeleton

Z01DK-23140-33 (LBP) BLACK, S NIDDK, NIH Biochemistry of sulfur-containing compounds

Z01DK-23330-13 (LBP) COLEMAN, W G NIFFK, NIH Aldoheptose biosynthesis and its regulation and hepatitis non-A, non-B

Z01DK-23580-28 (LBP) FURANO, A V NIDDK, NIH Mammalian transposons

Z01DK-23750-05 (LBP) HINTON, D M NIDDK, NIH Bacteriophage T4 gene expression

R01DK-24021-13 (EDC) DRASH, ALLAN L CHILDREN'S HOSPITAL 125 DESOTO STREET PITTSBURGH, PA 15213 Juvenile diabetes mellitus epidemiology and etiology

R37DK-24031-13 (GMA) LA RUSSO, NICHOLAS F MAYO FOUNDATION 200 FIRST STREET SOUTHWEST ROCHESTER, MN 55905 Biliary excretion of lysosomal protein

R01DK-24039-14 (PC) MERRIFIELD, ROBERT B THE ROCKEFELLER UNIVERSITY 1230 YORK AVENUE NEW YORK, NY 10021-6399 Synthetic analogs of glucagon for diabetes studies

R01DK-24085-12 (END) HINTZ, RAYMOND L STANFORD UNIVERSITY STANFORD, CA 94305-5119 Plasma somatomedin metabolism and actions

R01DK-24092-12 (MET) DE FRONZO, RALPH A UNIV OF TEXAS HLTH SCIENCE CTR 7703 FLOYDF CURL DRIVE SAN ANTONIO, TX 78284-7886

Regulation of hepatic and peripheral glucose metabolism

Z01DK-24140-25 (LBP) MILES, E W NIDDK, NIH Structure and function of the tryptophan synthase multienzyme complex

Z01DK-24150-20 (LBP) MINTON, A P NIDDK, NIH Noncovalent intermolecular interactions in biochemistry

Z01DK-24260-25 (LBP) NOSSAL, N G NIDDK, NIH Enzymatic mechanisms of DNA replication--The bacteriophage T4 system

Z01DK-24590-21 (LBP) SAROFF, H A NIDDK, NIH Structure and interactions of biologically important macromolecules

Z01DK-24709-10 (LBP) TABOR, C W NIDDK, NIH Polyamine biosynthesis and function

Z01DK-24940-18 (LBP) WICKNER, R B NIDDK, NIH Yeast RNA virology

Z01DK-25011-17 (LCB) TANIUCHI, H NIDDK, NIH Studies of protein folding problem

Z01DK-25016-18 (LCB) SCHECHTER, A N NIDDK, NIH Trans-acting factor(s) controlling globin gene expression in K562 cells & mice

Z01DK-25021-16 (LCB) NOGUCHI, C T NIDDK, NIH Sickle cell anemia--The intracellular polymerization of hemoglobin S

Z01DK-25025-15 (LCB) TANIUCHI, H NIDDK, NIH The mechanism of antigen-antibody interaction

Z01DK-25028-13 (LCB) RODGERS, G P NIDDK, NIH Development of non-invasive methods to assess sickle cell patients

Z01DK-25045-08 (LCB) BERG, P NIDDK, NIH Regulation of beta globin gene expression

Z01DK-25058-08 (LCB) RODGERS, G P NIDDK, NIH Laboratory models of adult globin gene expression

Z01DK-25060-06 (LCB) WADA, Y NIDDK, NIH The epsilon gene silencer--Characterization of trans-acting factor

Z01DK-25061-06 (LCB) NOGUCHI, C T NIDDK, NIH Human erythropoietin receptor gene--Cloning and transcription analysis

Z01DK-25063-05 (LCB) RODGERS, G P NIDDK, NIH Effect of hydroxyurea on fetal hemoglobin synthesis in sickle cell patients

Z01DK-25064-05 (LCB) WHITE, B J NIDDK, NIH Cytogenetic investigations of patients with genetically determined disorders

Z01DK-25066-05 (LCB) YUAN, J NIDDK, NIH AIDS--Transcriptional regulation by TAT-protein and LTR of HIV in vitro

Z01DK-25070-03 (LCB) MEREZHINSKAYA, N NIDDK,NIH Analysis of the epsilon globin gene flanking sequences

Z01DK-25071-04 (LCB) BROYLES, R H NIDDK,NIH Trans-regulation of human globin genes

Z01DK-25073-03 (LCB) Williams, Donna M NIDDK,NIH Erythropoietin receptor and its genetic control in red cell development

Z01DK-25074-04 (LCB) KIM, I H NIDDK,NIH Mechanism(s) of enhanced gamma globin gene expression in patients

Z01DK-25076-02 (LCB) PETERS, B NIDDK, NIH Characterization of transcription factors binding to the epsilon globin silencer

Z01DK-25077-02 (LCB) HUANG, S NIDDK, NIH Beta-globin gene expression in different types of beta-thalassemia mutation

Z01DK-25078-01 (LCB) BURKE, L NIDDK, NIH Globin expression in an erythroid progenitor culture system

R01DK-25141-09 (NTN) MAGGIO, CAROL A ST LUKE'S ROOSEVELT HOSP CENTE AMSTERDAM AVE & 114TH STREET NEW YORK, NY 10025 Behavioral & metabolic correlates of genetic obesity

R01DK-25231-13 (GMB) STOKES, JOHN B, III UNIVERSITY OF IOWA COLLEGE OF MEDICINE IOWA CITY, IOWA 52242 Ion transport by the cortical collecting duct

R01DK-25243-13 (SB) MILLER, JOSHUA UNIVERSITY OF MIAMI P O BOX 016310 MIAMI, FL 33101 Regulatory T and B cell circuits in transplantation

R37DK-25248-15 (NSS) TANNEN, RICHARD L UNIV OF SOUTHERN CALIFORNIA 2025 ZONAL AVE RM 7900 LOS ANGELES, CA 90033 Hydrogen ion regulation by the mammalian nephron

R37DK-25274-26 (HEM) BANK, ARTHUR COLUMBIA UNIVERSITY 701 W 168TH STREET NEW YORK, N Y 10032 Regulation of hemoglobin synthesis in erythroid cells

P30DK-25295-12S1 (DDK) BAR, ROBERT S UNIVERSITY OF IOWA DEPT OF INTERNAL MEDICINE IOWA CITY, IOWA 52240 Core center--Diabetes and endocrinology

P30DK-25295-12S1 0009 (DDK) FELDMAN, ROSS D Core center--Diabetes and endocrinology Lymphocyte beta-receptor regulation--age effects

P30DK-25295-12S1 0014 (DDK) PESSIN, JEFFREY Core center--Diabetes and endocrinology Site specific anti-insulin receptor antibodies

P30DK-25295-12S1 9001 (DDK) BAR, ROBERT S Core center--Diabetes and endocrinology Core--Enrichment program

P30DK-25295-12S1 9002 (DDK) GINSBERG, BARRY H Core center--Diabetes and endocrinology Core--Central facility for peptide iodination

P30DK-25295-12S1 9006 (DDK) GINSBERG, BARRY H Core center--Diabetes and endocrinology Core--Computer center

P30DK-25295-12S1 9007 (DDK) BAR, ROBERT S Core center--Diabetes and endocrinology Core--Tissue culture

P30DK-25295-12S1 9011 (DDK) DONELSON, JOHN E Core center--Diabetes and endocrinology Core--Recombinant DNA

P30DK-25295-12S1 9012 (DDK) FELDBUSH, THOMAS Core center--Diabetes and endocrinology Core--Monoclonal antibody production

P30DK-25295-12S1 9013 (DDK) SANDRA, ALEXANDER Core center--Diabetes and endocrinology Core--Receptor localization

P30DK-25295-12S1 9014 (DDK) WALDER, JOSEPH A Core center--Diabetes and endocrinology Core--DNA synthesis

P30DK-25295-12S1 0011 (DDK) YOREK, MARK A Core center--Diabetes and endocrinology Myo-inositol metabolism in normal and diabetic PNS--Pilot study

P30DK-25295-12S1 0012 (DDK) SPAZIANI, EUGENE Core center--Diabetes and endocrinology Pilot study--Mechanism of neuropeptide control of steroidogenesis

P30DK-25295-12S1 0013 (DDK) TUREK, LUBOMIR Core center--Diabetes and endocrinology Pilot study--Papilloma virus cloning--Role of trans/cis factor in gene regulation

R37DK-25306-14 (NSS) ROSSINI, ALDO A UNIVERSITY OF MASSACHUSETTS 55 LAKE AVENUE NORTH WORCESTER, MA 01655 Experimental juvenile-type diabetes

R01DK-25336-13 (PC) LIENHARD, GUSTAV E DARTMOUTH MEDICAL SCHOOL 7200 VAIL BLDG HANOVER, NH 03755-3844 Insulin regulation of the adipocyte glucose transporter

R01DK-25373-13 (SSS) THORPE, SUZANNE R UNIVERSITY OF SOUTH CAROLINA DEPARTMENT OF CHEMISTRY COLUMBIA, S C 29208 Sites and mechanisms of plasma protein catabolism

R01DK-25377-13 (END) ORLOWSKI, MARIAN MOUNT SINAI SCHOOL OF MEDICINE ONE GUSTAVE L. LEVY PLACE NEW YORK, NY 10029 Pituitary hormones-- Enzymatic formation and degradation

R01DK-25387-13 (CBY) MOOSEKER, MARK S YALE UNIVERSITY 12 PROSPECT PLACE NEW HAVEN, CT 06511 Cytoskeletal structure in the intestinal brush border

R01DK-25409-12 (ORTH) KUMAR, RAJIV MAYO FOUNDATION 200 FIRST STREET SOUTHWEST ROCHESTER, MN 55905 The physiology and metabolism of vitamin D

R01DK-25410-13 (NLS) MALBON, CRAIG C SUNY AT STONY BROOK SCH OF MED HEALTH SCI CENTER STONY BROOK, NY 11794-8651 Hormone regulation of hepatocyte carbohydrate metabolism

R01DK-25412-13 (HEM) LORAND, LASZLO NORTHWESTERN UNIVERSITY EVANSTON, ILLINOIS 60208 Studies of human erythrocytes

R01DK-25421-13 (END) BAR, ROBERT S UNIVERSITY OF IOWA 3E19 VA MEDICAL CENTER IOWA CITY, IA 52246 Action of insulin & growth peptides on endothelium

R01DK-25446-12A1 (EDC) ZIMMET, PAUL Z CAULFIELD GENERAL MED CENTER 260 KOOYON ROAD AUSTRALIA, 3162 Diabetes in Pacific--Environmental/genetic determinants

R01DK-25489-11 (PC) STAROS, JAMES V VANDERBILT UNIVERSITY BOX 1820 STATION B NASHVILLE, TN 37235 Peptide receptors in biological membranes

R01DK-25498-12 (MGN) TAYLOR, MILTON W INDIANA UNIVERSITY JORDAN HALL 343 BLOOMINGTON, IN 47405 Biochemistry and genetics of mammalian/APRT

R01DK-25519-13 (GMB) SCHAFER, JAMES A NEPHROLOGY RES & TRAINING CTR PO BOX 10/SDB/UNIV STN BIRMINGHAM, AL 35294 Renal transport of nonelectrolytes, salt, and water

R01DK-25532-13 (REN) HABENER, JOEL F MASSACHUSETTS GENERAL HOSPITAL FRUIT STREET BOSTON, MASS 02114 Biosynthesis of thyroid-stimulating hormone

R01DK-25541-14 (BIO) HANSON, RICHARD W CASE WESTERN RESERVE UNIV 2119 ABINGTON ROAD CLEVELAND, OHIO 44106 Hormonal regulation of enzyme levels in mammalian tissue

R01DK-25548-10A1 (MEDB) THOENE, JESS G UNIVERSITY OF MICHIGAN 109 OBSERVATORY 2612 SPH I ANN ARBOR, MI 48109-2029 Lysosomal physiology and protein degradation in cystinosis

R01DK-25568-11A1 (BEM) KOVACS, MARIA WESTERN PSYCH, INST, & CLINIC 3811 O'HARA ST PITTSBURGH, PA 15213 Depression in newly diagnosed juvenile diabetics

R01DK-25614-12 (BIO) HERSHKO, AVRAM TECHNION-ISRAEL INST OF TECH PO BOX 9649 HAIFA, ISRAEL 31096 Mechanisms of intracellular protein breakdown

R37DK-25636-15 (GMA) BOYER, JAMES L YALE UNIVERSITY 333 CEDAR STREET PO BOX 3333 NEW HAVEN, CT 06510 Mechanisms of bile secretion and cholestasis

R01DK-25692-13 (END) BARNEA, AYALLA UNIV. OF TX SW MED CTR AT DALL 5323 HARRY HINES BOULEVARD DALLAS, TX 75235 Role of hormones in the processing of neuronal peptides

R01DK-25705-14 (MET) LAYCHOCK, SUZANNE GALE SUNY AT BUFFALO 102 FARBER HALL BUFFALO, NY 14214 Putative mediators of insulin secretion

R01DK-25731-13 (SB) DODDS, WYLIE J FROEDTERT MEMORIAL LUTHERAN HO 9200 WEST WISCONSIN AVENUE MILWAUKEE, WI 53226 Esophageal motor function in health and disease

R01DK-25754-10 (GMA) WEISER, MILTON M S U N Y AT BUFFALO 100 HIGH STREET, KIMBERLY BLDG BUFFALO, N Y 14203 Intestinal cell membranes: structure and function

R01DK-25759-13 (BIO) HASKINS, MARK UNIVERSITY OF PENNSYLVANIA 3800 SPRUCE ST PHILADELPHIA, PA 19104 Animal models of mucopolysaccharidoses

R01DK-25802-12 (SB) MINTZ, DANIEL H UNIVERSITY OF MIAMI 1600 NW 10TH AVENUE MIAMI, FL 33101 Pancreatic transplantation and diabetes mellitus

R01DK-25807-13 (CBY) CARNEY, DARRELL H UNIV OF TEXAS MEDICAL BRANCH 11TH AND MECHANIC GALVESTON, TX 77550 Role of cell surface in regulation cell proliferation

R01DK-25836-12 (CBY) LEVY, DANIEL UNIV. OF SOUTHERN CALIFORNIA 2011 ZONAL AVENUE LOS ANGELES, CA 90033 Structure and function of membrane transport proteins

R55DK-25838-13 (SAT) MILLER, THOMAS A UNIV OF TEXAS MED SCHOOL 6431 FANNIN, MSMB 4.266 HOUSTON, TX 77030 Surgical studies on prostaglandins and gastric ulcers

R37DK-25861-12 (BCE) MARTIN, THOMAS F UNIVERSITY OF WISCONSIN-MADISO 1117 WEST JOHNSON STREET MADISON, WI 53706 The mechanism of action of thyrotropin-releasing hormone

R01DK-25878-13 (GMA) JONES, ALBERT L VETERANS ADMIN MEDICAL CENTER 4150 CLEMENT STREET SAN FRANCISCO, CA 94121 Subcellular study of bile secretion

R01DK-25962-11A1 (SB) CHEY, WILLIAM Y GENESEE HOSPITAL 224 ALEXANDER ST ROCHESTER, NY 14607 The pathophysiology of secretin and cholecystokinin

R01DK-25998-14 (SB) CHEUNG, LAURENCE Y UNIVERSITY OF KANSAS MEDICAL C 39TH AND RAINBOW BOULEVARD KANSAS CITY, KS 66103 Gastric mucosal injury role of inflammatory mediators

R37DK-26007-13 (SAT) BARKER, CLYDE F UNIVERSITY OF PENNSYLVANIA 3400 SPRUCE STREET PHILADELPHIA, PA 19104 Spontaneous rat diabetes--Pathogenesis and treatment

R01DK-26012-11 (GMB) HUGHEY, REBECCA P UNIVERSITY OF PITTSBURGH SCHOOL OF MEDICINE PITTSBURGH, PA 15261 Renal glutathione metabolism--Gamma glutamyltranspeptidase

R01DK-26081-13 (BBCB) FLETTERICK, ROBERT J UNIV. OF CA, SAN FRANCISCO ROOM 1058S SAN FRANCISCO, CA 94143 Structure-function relationships in phosphorylase a

R01DK-26088-12 (END) DEERY, WILLIAM BAYLOR COLLEGE OF MEDICINE ONE BAYLOR PLAZA HOUSTON, TX 77030 Effect of TSH on thyroid metabolism

R01DK-26142-11 (GMB) BERRY, CHRISTINE A UNIVERSITY OF

PROJECT NO., ORGANIZATIONAL UNIT., INVESTIGATOR, ADDRESS, TITLE

CALIFORNIA DIVISION OF NEPHROLOGY SAN FRANCISCO, CA 94143 Water and solute transport in the proximal tubule

R01DK-26190-09 (IMS) **LERNMARK, AKE** UNIVERSITY OF WASHINGTON MAIL STOP RG-20 SEATTLE, WA 98195 Islet cell membrane antibodies in diabetes

R01DK-26206-12 (BIO) **SO, ANTERO G** UNIV OF MIAMI SCH OF MEDICINE P O BOX 016960 MIAMI, FLA 33101 Fidelity of DNA synthesis in hematopoetic tissues

R01DK-26214-13 (BMT) **FINKE, RICHARD G** UNIVERSITY OF OREGON 148 OREGON HALL EUGENE, OR 97403 Mechanistic metallobiochemistry of coenzyme B12

R01DK-26263-13 (HEM) **NARLA, MOHANDAS** LAWRENCE BERKELEY LABORATORY 1 CYCLOTRON RD BERKELEY, CA 94720 Red cell deformability in vitro and survival in vivo

R01DK-26270-12 (GMA) **SCHARSCHMIDT, BRUCE F** UNIV OF CALIFORNIA, SF SAN FRANCISCO, CA 94143-0538 Mechanisms of canalicular bile formation

R01DK-26307-12 (GMA) **MC DONAGH, ANTONY F** UNIVERSITY OF CALIFORNIA 3RD & PARNASSUS AVES RM HSW-11 SAN FRANCISCO, CA 94143-0538 Bilirubin and photobilirubin/metabolism and excretion

R01DK-26317-11 (MET) **HORTON, EDWARD S** UNIVERSITY OF VERMONT BURLINGTON, VT 05405 Effects of exercise on insulin resistance in muscle

R01DK-26341-10 (GMB) **MOORE, LEON C** SUNY HEALTH SCIENCE CTR STONY BROOK, NY 11794-8661 Regulation of glomerular and proximal nephron function

R01DK-26347-10 (PHY) **BIBER, THOMAS U** VIRGINIA COMMONWEALTH UNIV P O BOX 551, MCV STATION RICHMOND, VA 23298 Mechanisms of chloride transport in epithelial cells

R01DK-26356-12 (MET) **ECKEL, ROBERT H** UNIV OF COLORADO HEALTH SCIS C BOX B151/4200 EAST NINTH AVENU DENVER, CO 80262 Tissue specific regulation of lipoprotein lipase

R01DK-26438-11A1 (GMA) **BERK, PAUL D** MOUNT SINAI SCHOOL OF MEDICINE 1 GUSTAVE L LEVY PLACE NEW YORK, NY 10029 Mechanisms of hepatic bilirubin transport

R01DK-26466-13 (GMA) **BLOOMER, JOSEPH R** UNIVERSITY HOSPITALS BOX 172 MINNEAPOLIS, MINN 55455 Enzyme defects in disorders of protoporphyrin metabolism

R01DK-26508-11 (SAT) **LEVIN, ROBERT M** HOSP OF THE UNIV OF PENNSYLVAN 3010 RAVDIN COURTYARD BLDG PHILADELPHIA, PA 19104 Autonomic control of lower urinary tract function

R01DK-26518-12 (GMA) **KING, LLOYD E, JR** V. A. MEDICAL CENTER 1310 24TH AVENUE SOUTH NASHVILLE, TN 37203 Epidermal growth factor & membrane phosphorylation

R01DK-26523-12 (GMA) **DONOWITZ, MARK** JOHNS HOPKINS HOSPITAL 725 NORTH WOLFE STREET BALTIMORE, MD 21205 Diarrheal diseases--A physiologic approach to treatment

R37DK-26546-24 (NSS) **DUAX, WILLIAM L** MEDICAL FDN OF BUFFALO, INC 73 HIGH STREET BUFFALO, NY 14203 Molecular structure of steroids

R01DK-26609-08 (BM) **STRUNK, ROBERT C** WASHINGTON UNIV SCH OF MED 400 S KINGSHIGHWAY BLVD ST LOUIS, MO 63110 Regulation of complement synthesis in inflammation

R01DK-26638-13 (GMA) **SEETHARAM, BELLUR** MEDICAL COLLEGE OF WISCONSIN 8701 WATERTOWN PLANK RD MILWAUKEE, WI 53226 Intestinal brush border memberanes

P30DK-26657-12 (DDK) **GREENE, HARRY L** VANDERBILT UNIVERSITY SCHOOL OF MEDICINE NASHVILLE, TN 37232 Development of clinical nutrition research unit

P30DK-26657-12 0026 (DDK) **SCHULMAN, GERALD** Development of clinical nutrition research unit Pilot--Effect of GH on nitrogen retention during intradialytic hyperalimentation

P30DK-26657-12 0027 (DDK) **VNENCAK-JONES, CINDY** Development of clinical nutrition research unit Pilot study--Molecular basis of GH and CSH tissue specific expression

P30DK-26657-12 0028 (DDK) **HUMMELL, DONNA** Development of clinical nutrition research unit Pilot--Retinoids in promoting the differentiation of B cell subsets in humans

P30DK-26657-12 9003 (DDK) **BLAIR, IAN A** Development of clinical nutrition research unit Core--Mass spectrometry laboratory

P30DK-26657-12 9004 (DDK) **GHISHAN, FAYEZ K** Development of clinical nutrition research unit Core--Intestinal transport laboratory

P30DK-26657-12 9005 (DDK) **COLLINS, JERRY C** Development of clinical nutrition research unit Core--Data management

P30DK-26657-12 9006 (DDK) **SWIFT, LARRY** Development of clinical nutrition research unit Analytical core

P30DK-26657-12 9007 (DDK) **HILL, JAMES** Development of clinical nutrition research unit Energy balance core

R01DK-26667-11 (MET) **GOLDFINE, IRA D** MT ZION HOSPITAL & MEDICAL CTR PO BOX 7921/DIABETES SAN FRANCISCO, CA 94120 Hormonal regulation of insulin receptors

P30DK-26678-12 (DDK) **SITRIN, MICHAEL D** UNIV OF CHICAGO CLIN NUTR RES 5841 SOUTH MARYLAND AVE. BOX 2 CHICAGO, IL 60637 Clinical nutrition research unit

P30DK-26678-12 0004 (DDK) **HARIG, JAMES M** Clinical nutrition research unit Intestinal nutrient transport in brush border membrane vesicles

P30DK-26678-12 0005 (DDK) **DAVIS, BERNARD H** Clinical nutrition research unit Vitamin A metabolism during hepatic Ito cell culture

P30DK-26678-12 0006 (DDK) **GOTTLIEB, LAWRENCE J** Clinical nutrition research unit Energy expenditure in burned patients

P30DK-26678-12 9004 (DDK) **SCHUETTE, SALLY A** Clinical nutrition research unit Core--Vitamin/bone mineral assay laboratory

P30DK-26678-12 9005 (DDK) **SCHOELLER, DALE A** Clinical nutrition research unit Core--Stable isotope/macronutrient metabolism laboratory

P30DK-26678-12 9006 (DDK) **JANGHORBANI, MORTEZA** Clinical nutrition research unit Core--Trace element/mass spectrometry laboratory

P30DK-26678-12 9007 (DDK) **GETZ, GODFREY S** Clinical nutrition research unit Lipid laboratory core

P30DK-26678-12 9011 (DDK) **POLONSKY, KENNETH S** Clinical nutrition research unit Core--radioimmunoassay laboratory

P30DK-26678-12 9012 (DDK) **SITRIN, MICHAEL D** Clinical nutrition research unit Assessment and support core

P30DK-26678-12 9013 (DDK) **BRASITUS, T A** Clinical nutrition research unit Core--Membrane biochemistry

PROJECT NO., ORGANIZATIONAL UNIT., INVESTIGATOR, ADDRESS, TITLE

P30DK-26687-11 (DDK) **PI-SUNYER, F XAVIER** ST LUKE'S-ROOSEVELT HOSP CTR AMSTERDAM AVE AT 114TH STREET NEW YORK, NY 10025 New York obesity research core center

P30DK-26687-11 9001 (DDK) **FAUST, IRVING M** New York obesity research core center Core--Adipose tissue morphology and metabolism

P30DK-26687-11 9003 (DDK) **PI-SUNYER, F XAVIER** New York obesity research core center Core--Hormones and metabolites

P30DK-26687-11 9005 (DDK) **LEIBEL, RUDOLPH L** New York obesity research core center Core-- Inpatient clinical studies

P30DK-26687-11 9007 (DDK) **VAN ITALLIE, THEODORE B** New York obesity research core center Core--Body composition, energy metabolism, and physical performance

P30DK-26687-11 9008 (DDK) **GIBBS, JAMES** New York obesity research core center Core-- Ingestive behavior

P30DK-26687-11 9009 (DDK) **MATTHEWS, DWIGHT** New York obesity research core center Core-- Mass spectroscopy

P30DK-26687-11 9010 (DDK) **HEYMSFIELD, STEVEN** New York obesity research core center Core-- Out-patient research

P01DK-26741-12 (DDK) **VALE, WYLIE W** SALK INST FOR BIOLOGICAL STUDI PO BOX 85800 SAN DIEGO, CA 92138 Biology of neuroendocrine peptides

P01DK-26741-12 0005 (DDK) **ROSENFELD, MICHAEL G** Biology of neuroendocrine peptides Biosynthesis of regulatory peptides

P01DK-26741-12 0001 (DDK) **VALE, WYLIE W** Biology of neuroendocrine peptides Neuroendocrine roles of regulatory peptides

P01DK-26741-12 0004 (DDK) **KOOB, GEORGE F** Biology of neuroendocrine peptides Behavioral significance of neuroendocrine peptides

P01DK-26741-12 0007 (DDK) **SWANSON, LARRY W** Biology of neuroendocrine peptides Anatomy of hypophysiotrophic peptide pathways in brain

P01DK-26741-12 0009 (DDK) **RIVIER, CATHERINE L** Biology of neuroendocrine peptides Hypophysiotropic roles of corticotropin releasing factor

P01DK-26741-12 0010 (DDK) **RIVIER, JEAN** Biology of neuroendocrine peptides Pharmacology of neuroendocrine peptides

P01DK-26741-12 9001 (DDK) **RIVIER, CATHERINE L** Biology of neuroendocrine peptides Core--Radioimmunoassay

P01DK-26741-12 9003 (DDK) **RIVIER, JEAN E** Biology of neuroendocrine peptides Core--High performance liquid chromatography

P01DK-26741-12 9004 (DDK) **FISCHER, WOLFGANG** Biology of neuroendocrine peptides Sequence analysis of peptides

P30DK-26743-11 (DDK) **OCKNER, ROBERT K** UNIVERSITY OF CALIFORNIA BOX 0538 SAN FRANCISCO, CA 94143-0538 Liver core center

P30DK-26743-11 0010 (DDK) **LINGAPPA, VISHWANATH** Liver core center Pilot study-- Molecular mechanisms of apolipoprotein B biogenesis

P30DK-26743-11 0011 (DDK) **GUMBINER, BARRY** Liver core center Pilot study-- Glucocorticoid regulation of epithelial tight junctions

P30DK-26743-11 0012 (DDK) **MOSTOV, KEITH** Liver core center Pilot study-- Rat liver proteins involved in IgA transcytosis

P30DK-26743-11 9002 (DDK) **BISSELL, D MONTGOMERY** Liver core center Core--Liver cell culture

P30DK-26743-11 9004 (DDK) **JONES, ALBERT L** Liver core center Core--Microscopy

P30DK-26743-11 9006 (DDK) **BURLINGAME, A L** Liver core center Core--Mass spectrometry

P30DK-26743-11 9007 (DDK) **CORREIA, M ALMIRA** Liver core center Core--Spectrophotometry and spectrofluorimetry

P30DK-26743-11 9008 (DDK) **LICKO, VOJTECH** Liver core center Core--Biomathematics

P30DK-26743-11 9009 (DDK) **GANEM, DONALD** Liver core center Core--Animal facility

P30DK-26743-11 9010 (DDK) **GIBBS, VERNA** Liver core center Core--Molecular biology

P30DK-26743-11 9011 (DDK) **WEISIGER, RICHARD** Liver core center Core-- Isolated liver perfusion

R37DK-26756-13 (GMA) **SHEFER, SARAH** UMDNJ/NEW JERSEY MED. SCHOOL 185 SOUTH ORANGE AVE. NEWARK, NJ 07103-2757 Inborn errors in bile acid synthesis

R01DK-26758-13 (MGN) **COX, RODY P** U OF TX SW MED CTR AT DALLAS 5323 HARRY HINES BLVD DALLAS, TX 75235 Inborn errors of metabolism in cell culture

R01DK-26816-12 (GMB) **MANDEL, LAZARO J** DUKE UNIVERSITY DURHAM, N C 27710 Oxidative metabolism & transport in renal tubules

R01DK-26824-12 (MGN) **DESNICK, ROBERT J** MOUNT SINAI SCHOOL OF MEDICINE FIFTH AVENUE AND 100TH STREET NEW YORK, N Y 10029 Studies of porphyria and human heme biosynthesis

R01DK-26831-12 (END) **GANN, DONALD S** UNIV. OF MD, DEPT. OF SURGERY 22 SOUTH GREENE STREET BALTIMORE, MD 21201 Hemodynamic control of pituitary adrenal function

R01DK-26844-10 (ALY) **ALPER, CHESTER A** CENTER FOR BLOOD RESEARCH 800 HUNTINGTON AVENUE BOSTON, MA 02115 Genetics of insulin-dependent diabetes mellitus

R01DK-26912-11 (BIO) **GRIFFITH, OWEN W** CORNELL UNIV MEDICAL COLLEGE 1300 YORK AVENUE NEW YORK, N Y 10021 Mammalian cysteine metabolism

R01DK-26956-10 (HEM) **ALTER, BLANCHE P** MOUNT SINAI SCHOOL OF MEDICINE ONE GUSTAVE LEVY PLACE NEW YORK, N Y 10029 Regulation of hemoglobin synthesis

R01DK-26989-12 (MET) **HAYMOND, MOREY W** THE NEMOURS CHILDREN'S CLINIC P. O. BOX 5720 JACKSONVILLE, FL 32247 Control of BCAA metabolism in normal and diabetic man

R01DK-27044-14 (CBY) **ROTHMAN, JAMES E** SLOAN-KETTERING INST 1275 YORK AVENUE NEW YORK, N Y 10021 "Inatracellular" transport in cell-free extracts

R01DK-27071-12 (HEM) **DAINIAK, NICHOLAS** UNIV OF CONNECTICUT HLTH CTR 263 FARMINGTON AVENUE FARMINGTON, CT 06032-9984 Control of erythropoiesis by growth promoting peptides

R01DK-27078-11 (PC) **DAVIES, PETER J** UNIV. OF TX MEDICAL SCHOOL HOUSTON, TX 77225 Role of transglutaminase in hormone internalization

R01DK-27083-13 (CTY) **MAXFIELD, FREDERICK R** COLLEGE OF PHYSICIANS & SURGEO 630 WEST 168TH STREET NEW YORK, NY 10032 Receptor-mediated endocytosis--mechanism and function

PROJECT NUMBER LISTING

PROJECT NO., ORGANIZATIONAL UNIT., INVESTIGATOR, ADDRESS, TITLE

R01DK-27085-11A1 (MET) CRYER, PHILIP E WASHINGTON UNIV SCH OF MEDICIN 660 SOUTH EUCLID AVE/BOX 8127 ST LOUIS, MO 63110 Adrenergic mechanisms in metabolic pathophysiology
R01DK-27097-12 (END) CARDELL, ROBERT R, JR UNIVERSITY OF CINCINNATI 231 BETHESDA AVENUE CINCINNATI, OH 45267-0521 Subcellular effects of metabolic hormones on rat liver
R01DK-27221-13 (BIO) ROACH, PETER J INDIANA UNIVERSITY 635 BARNHILL DRIVE INDIANAPOLIS, IN 46202-5122 Hormonal control of glycogen metabolism
R01DK-27323-12 (MBC) LJUNGDAHL, LARS G UNIVERSITY OF GEORGIA DEPARTMENT OF BIOCHEMISTRY ATHENS, GA 30602 Biochemistry of vitamin B12 & folic acid compounds
R01DK-27373-12 (PB) LAMBETH, JOHN D EMORY UNIVERSITY DEPT OF BIOCHEMISTRY ATLANTA, GA 30322 Adrenal cortex steroidogenesis: enzymology & control
R01DK-27384-11 (IMS) DE GROOT, LESLIE J UNIVERSITY OF CHICAGO 5841 S MARYLAND AVE BOX 138 CHICAGO, IL 60637 Pathogenesis and therapy of autoimmune thyroid disease
R01DK-27389-07A2 (GMA) BEHAR, JOSE RHODE ISLAND HOSPITAL 593 EDDY STREET PROVIDENCE, RI 02902 Muscle contraction in gallbladders
R37DK-27400-11 (CBY) LEVER, JULIA E UNIVERSITY OF TEXAS 6431 FANNIN HOUSTON, TX 77030 Mechanisms and regulation of epithelial transport
R01DK-27424-12 (HEM) QUESENBERRY, PETER J UNIVERSITY OF VIRGINIA SCHOOL OF MEDICINE, BOX 502 CHARLOTTESVILLE, VA 22908 Hemopoietic cellular interaction and lithium
R01DK-27430-12 (MBY) MAC DONALD, RAYMOND J UNIV OF TX SW MED CTR, DALLAS 5323 HARRY HINES BOULEVARD DALLAS, TEX 75235 Organization and expression of pancreatic genes
R01DK-27495-12 (HEM) KNAUF, PHILIP A UNIV OF ROCHESTER MED CENTER 601 ELMWOOD AVENUE ROCHESTER, NY 14642 Ion transport mechanisms in blood cells
R37DK-27600-12 (GMB) HAMMERMAN, MARC R WASHINGTON UNIVERSITY 660 SOUTH EUCLID AVENUE ST LOUIS, MO 63110 Renal membrane phosphorylation and transport
R37DK-27623-12 (GMA) FORKER, E LEE MA415 MEDICAL SCIENCES BLDG. UNIV OF MISSOURI SCHOOL OF MED COLUMBIA, MO 65212 Mechanisms of bile formation
R01DK-27624-12 (GMA) KOLDOVSKY, OTAKAR UNIVERSITY OF ARIZONA TUCSON, AZ 85724 Metabolism of the developing small intestine
R01DK-27626-10S1 (PB) GUIDOTTI, GUIDO HARVARD UNIVERSITY FAIRCHILD BIOCH BLDG/7DIVITY A CAMBRIDGE, MA 02138 Structure and function of the insulin receptor
R01DK-27627-12S1 (BPO) POWLEY, TERRY L PURDUE UNIVERSITY WEST LAFAYETTE, IN 47907 Hypothalamic control of body weight and feeding
R01DK-27635-11 (MBY) HARDISON, ROSS C PENNSYLVANIA STATE UNIVERSITY 206 ALTHOUSE LABORATORY UNIVERSITY PARK, PA 16802 Organization and expression of globin gene loci
P30DK-27651-09 (DDK) DAVIS, PAMELA B RAINBOW BABIES CHILDRENS HOSP 2101 ADELBERT ROAD CLEVELAND, OH 44106 Core center-- Cystic fibrosis
P30DK-27651-09 0009 (DDK) GERKEN, THOMAS Core center-- Cystic fibrosis Pilot study-- Conformational studies of mucin granules
P30DK-27651-09 0010 (DDK) INFELD, MICHAEL Core center-- Cystic fibrosis Pilot study-- Mesenchymal influence on epithelial differentiation
P30DK-27651-09 0011 (DDK) KONSTAN, MICHAEL Core center-- Cystic fibrosis Pilot study-- Antiproteases and the treatment of inflammation of the lung in CF
P30DK-27651-09 9001 (DDK) STERN, ROBERT C Core center-- Cystic fibrosis Core--Patient facilities
P30DK-27651-09 9006 (DDK) TARTAKOFF, ALAN Core center-- Cystic fibrosis Core--Morphology
P30DK-27651-09 9009 (DDK) BERGER, MELVIN Core center-- Cystic fibrosis Core-- Bronchoalveolar lavage and immunology
P30DK-27651-09 9010 (DDK) HOPFER, ULRICH Core center-- Cystic fibrosis Core-- Cell physiology
P30DK-27651-09 9011 (DDK) WALENGA, RONALD Core center-- Cystic fibrosis Core-- Inflammatory mediators
P30DK-27651-09 9012 (DDK) DEARBORN, DORR Core center-- Cystic fibrosis Core-- Epithelial cell culture
P30DK-27685-10 (SRC) GOTTO, ANTONIO M, JR BAYLOR COLLEGE OF MEDICINE ONE BAYLOR PLAZA HOUSTON, TEXAS 77030 Diabetes and endocrinology research center
P30DK-27685-10 9003 (SRC) BIRNBAUMER, LUTZ Diabetes and endocrinology research center Core--Molecular endocrinology
P30DK-27685-10 0008 (SRC) FIELD, JAMES B Diabetes and endocrinology research center Pilot study--Restriction length polymorphism of insulin gene in diabetes
P30DK-27685-10 0009 (SRC) TATE, CHARLOTTE A Diabetes and endocrinology research center Pilot study--Insulin gene expression in pancreas development
P30DK-27685-10 9001 (SRC) BOYD, AUBREY E Diabetes and endocrinology research center Core--Tissue culture
P30DK-27685-10 9002 (SRC) CUNNINGHAM, GLENN R Diabetes and endocrinology research center Core--Hormone radioimmunoassay
R01DK-27695-07A2 (SB) KAMINSKI, DONALD L ST LOUIS UNIVERSITY 3635 VISTA AVE AT GRAND BLVD ST LOUIS, MO 63110-0250 Eicosanoids in gallbladder physiology and disease
R01DK-27722-11 (PTHA) LEITER, EDWARD H THE JACKSON LABORATORY 600 MAIN STREET BAR HARBOR, ME 04609-0800 Pathogenesis of autoimmune diabetes in mice
R01DK-27726-09 (HEM) BARKER, JANE E JACKSON LABORATORY 600 MAIN STREET BAR HARBOR, ME 04609-0800 Genetic engineering of cells from anemic animals
R01DK-27736-11 (BIO) ERLICHMAN, JACK ALBERT EINSTEIN COLLEGE OF MED 1300 MORRIS PARK AVENUE BRONX, N Y 10461 Regulation of cAMP-dependent protein kinases
R01DK-27845-10 (SSP) JACOBSON, ALAN M JOSLIN DIABETES CENTER ONE JOSLIN PLACE BOSTON, MA 02215 Family contexts of outcomes in diabetic adolescents
R01DK-27847-11 (PHY) PALMER, LAWRENCE G CORNELL UNIVERSITY MED COLLEGE 1300 YORK AVENUE NEW YORK, N Y 10021 Membrane processes mediating NaCl reabsorption
R01DK-27857-11 (GMA) SATO, KENZO UNIVERSITY OF IOWA 270 MED LABS IOWA CITY, IOWA 52242 Eccrine sweat gland function and cystic fibrosis
R01DK-27895-09 (SAT) ANDERSON, CHARLES B 4960 AUDUBON AVENUE ST. LOUIS, MISSOURI 63110 Renal transplant enhancement by donor specific blood
R01DK-27959-11 (CBY) HOLZ, RONALD W UNIVERSITY OF MICHIGAN ANN ARBOR, MI 48109-0626 Exocytosis from adrenal chromaffin cells
R01DK-28015-09 (REN) COSTELLO, LESLIE C UNIVERSITY OF MARYLAND 666 W BALTIMORE ST BALTIMORE, MD 21201 Testosterone control of prostate citrate production
R01DK-28029-12 (GMA) RUBIN, RONALD P STATE UNIVERSITY OF NEW YORK 102 FARBER HALL-SCHOOL OF MED BUFFALO, NY 14214 Phospholipid turnover in exocrine pancreas
R01DK-28081-10 (GMB) CORTES, PEDRO HENRY FORD HOSPITAL 2799 WEST GRAND BOULEVARD DETROIT, MI 48202 Diabetic glomerulopathy and pyrimidine metabolism
R01DK-28082-10 (MET) FLIER, JEFFREY S BETH ISRAEL HOSPITAL 330 BROOKLINE AVENUE BOSTON, MA 02215 Insulin and IGF receptors/action in insulin resistance
R01DK-28116-11 (GMA) BIKLE, DANIEL D UNIV OF CA/VA MEDICAL CENTER 4150 CLEMENT ST SAN FRANCISCO, CA 94121 D-stimulated intestinal calcium transport
R01DK-28143-11A1 (MET) JARETT, LEONARD HOSPITAL OF THE UNIV OF PA 3400 SPRUCE ST 6 GATES PHILADELPHIA, PA 19104 Cell biological studies on diabetes and metabolism
R01DK-28144-12 (MET) JARETT, LEONARD UNIVERSITY OF PENNSYLVANIA DEPT OF PATHOLOGY & LAB MED PHILADELPHIA, PA 19104 Mediation of insulin action
R37DK-28172-11 (END) DALLMAN, MARY F UNIVERSITY OF CALIFORNIA PARNASSUS AVENUE SAN FRANCISCO, CA 94143 Brain-pituitary-adrenal interrelationships
R01DK-28195-11 (GMA) LAMONT, JOHN T UNIVERSITY HOSPITAL 88 E NEWTON STREET BOSTON, MA 02118 Structure & function of intestinal mucin
R01DK-28215-11 (CBY) LEFFERT, HYAM L UNIVERSITY OF CA, SAN DIEGO 9500 GILMAN DRIVE LA JOLLA, CA 92093-0636 Isolation and action of adult rat hepatocyte mitogens
R01DK-28229-11 (END) ROSENFELD, RON G STANFORD UNIVERSITY 300 PASTEUR DR STANFORD, CA 94305-5119 Comparative studies of somatomedin and insulin receptors
R01DK-28231-10 (PHY) O'NEIL, ROGER G UNIVERSITY OF TEXAS MED SCHOOL P.O. BOX 20708 HOUSTON, TX 77225 Regulation of renal transport process
R01DK-28288-10 (BEM) COX, DANIEL J UNIVERSITY OF VIRGINIA BLDG 915 DRAWER F CHARLOTTESVILLE, VA 22901 Blood glucose awareness training
R01DK-28300-11 (GMA) MAKHLOUF, GABRIEL M VIRGINIA COMMONWEALTH UNIV BOX 711, MCV STATION RICHMOND, VA 23298-0711 Function of gut peptides in isolated gut muscle cells
R01DK-28305-10 (GMA) BARRETT, KIM E UNIVERSITY OF CALIFORNIA 225 DICKINSON STREET LA JOLLA, CA 92093-1996 Intestinal secretory mechanisms and antidiarrheal drugs
R01DK-28312-11 (PC) LAWRENCE, JOHN C, JR WASHINGTON UNIVERSITY 660 SOUTH EUCLID AVENUE ST LOUIS, MO 63110 Insulin action in muscle and fat cells
R01DK-28330-12 (PTHA) TISHER, C CRAIG UNIVERSITY OF FLORIDA BOX J-224, JHMHC GAINESVILLE, FL 32610-0224 Water & electrolyte movement in renal tubules
R01DK-28348-11 (MET) MAC DONALD, MICHAEL J UNIV. OF WI SCHOOL OF MED 1300 UNIVERSITY AVE MADISON, WI 53706 Glucose metabolism and calcium in pancreatic islets
R01DK-28350-11 (BCE) WATERMAN, MICHAEL R UNIV OF TX SOUTHWESTERN MED CT 5323 HARRY HINES BLVD DALLAS, TX 75235 ACTH induction of cytochrome P-450 in adrenal cells
R01DK-28353-10 (CBY) MALLER, JAMES L THE UNIV. OF COLORADO H.S.C. 4200 EAST NINTH AVENUE DENVER, CO 80262 S6 phosphorylation and tyrosine protein kinases
R01DK-28374-10A1 (MET) KILBERG, MICHAEL S UNIVERSITY OF FLORIDA J HILLIS MILLER HEALTH CENTER GAINESVILLE, FL 32610 Hepatic amino acid transport in diabetic animals
R01DK-28389-08 (GMA) LEIBACH, FREDERICK H MEDICAL COLL OF GEORGIA 1120 - 15TH STREET AUGUSTA, GA 30912-2100 Protein nutrition--peptide transport in gut and kidney
R01DK-28433-11 (PBC) VERTEL, BARBARA M THE CHICAGO MEDICAL SCHOOL 3333 GREEN BAY ROAD NORTH CHICAGO, IL 60064 Biosynthesis of proteoglycan and formation of matrix
R01DK-28477-08A2 (PHY) SPITZER, ADRIAN ROSE F KENNEDY CENTER 1410 PELHAM PARKWAY SOUTH BRONX, N Y 10461 Regulation of renal phosphate transport in development
R01DK-28492-11 (PTHA) KANWAR, YASHPAL S NORTHWESTERN UNIV MED SCHOOL 303 E CHICAGO AVENUE CHICAGO, IL 60611 Glomerular capillary wall--Normal and pathologic
R01DK-28516-11 (CBY) SPECTOR, ARTHUR A UNIVERSITY OF IOWA DEPT OF BIOCHEMISTRY IOWA CITY, IA 52242 Myristic acid and membrane signal transduction
R01DK-28537-10 (MEP) MESTECKY, JIRI F UNIVERSITY OF ALABAMA UAB STATION BIRMINGHAM, AL 35294 Receptor-mediated binding of IgA to hepatocytes
R01DK-28554-11 (BIO) BECKER, MICHAEL A UNIV OF CHICAGO MED CTR 5841 S. MARYLAND, AVE., BOX 74 CHICAGO, IL 60637 Regulation of purine nucleotide synthesis in man
R01DK-28559-11 (END) NILSON, JOHN H CASE WESTERN RESERVE UNIV 2119 ABINGTON ROAD CLEVELAND, OH 44106 Regulation of gonadotropin gene expression
R01DK-28561-10 (GMA) ROTHENBERG, SHELDON P SUNY HLTH SCI CTR 450 CLARKSON AVENUE BROOKLYN, N Y 11203 Kinetics of B12, intrinsic factor and other proteins
R01DK-28565-12 (END) CARRAWAY, ROBERT E UNIVERSITY OF MASSACHUSETTS 55 LAKE AVENUE NORTH WORCESTER, MA 01605 Biochemistry of brain and intestinal neurotensin
R01DK-28602-19 (GMB) BLANTZ, ROLAND C UNIVERSITY OF CALIFORNIA

PROJECT NO., ORGANIZATIONAL UNIT., INVESTIGATOR, ADDRESS, TITLE

9500 GILMAN DR LA JOLLA, CA 92093-9111H Autoregulation of glomerular filtration rate
R37DK-28607-11 (PB) FREY, PERRY A UNIVERSITY OF WISCONSIN 1710 UNIVERSITY AVENUE MADISON, WI 53705 Enzyme catalysis of electron and group transfer
R01DK-28614-11 (GMA) BIANCANI, PIERO RHODE ISLAND HOSPITAL SWP-5TH FL, RM 20--593 EDDY ST PROVIDENCE, RI 02902 Biophysical principles of peristaltic phenomena
R37DK-28616-11 (PB) MILDVAN, ALBERT S JOHNS HOPKINS UNIVERSITY BIOLOGICAL CHEMISTRY DEPT BALTIMORE, MD 21205 Nmr studies of enzyme-metal-substrate interactions
R01DK-28623-10 (GMA) ELSON, CHARLES O UNIV OF ALABAMA AT BIRMINGHAM U A B STATION, DIV/GASTRO BIRMINGHAM, AL 35294 Regulation of intestinal immune responses
R01DK-28640-08 (GMA) ROBINS, SANDER J BOSTON VA MEDICAL CENTER 150 SOUTH HUNTINGTON AVE BOSTON, MA 02130 Mechanism of biliary cholesterol and lecithin secretion
Z01DK-29001-19 (LCP) LEVIN, I W NIDDK, NIH Molecular dynamics and vibrational characteristics of membrane assemblies
Z01DK-29005-17 (LCP) ZIFFER, H NIDDK, NIH Asymmetric synthesis--Structure, stereochemistry and NMR
Z01DK-29006-21 (LCP) CHARNEY, E NIDDK, NIH Structure and dynamic properties of macromolecules
Z01DK-29007-20 (LCP) KON, H NIDDK, NIH Structure and interaction of biomolecules
Z01DK-29008-20 (LCP) MCDIARMID, R NIDDK, NIH Electric and molecular structural investigations
Z01DK-29010-19 (LCP) EATON, W A NIDDK, NIH Dynamics of proteins and studies on sickle cell disease
Z01DK-29011-20 (LCP) HAGINS, W A NIDDK, NIH Physics and chemistry of photoreception
Z01DK-29016-15 (LCP) HOFRICHTER, J NIDDK, NIH Macromolecular dynamics and assembly reactions
Z01DK-29017-12 (LCP) ADAMS, R G NIDDK, NIH Spectroscopic investigation of membrane lipids and models
Z01DK-29019-11 (LCP) SZABO, A NIDDK, NIH Theoretical studies on the dynamic aspects of macromolecular function
Z01DK-29020-07 (LCP) BAX, A NIDDK, NIH Nuclear magnetic resonance--New methods and molecular structure determination
Z01DK-29021-06 (LCP) HENRY, E R NIDDK, NIH Conformation and dynamic of biological macromolecules
Z01DK-29022-04 (LCP) GRONEBORN, A M NIDDK, NIH Structural studies of AIDS proteins by NMR
Z01DK-29023-04 (LCP) CLORE, G M NIDDK, NIH Determination of 3D-dimensional structures of macromolecules in solution by NMR
Z01DK-29025-03 (LCP) GRONENBORN, A M NIDDK, NIH Investigations of macromolecular structures and dynamics in solution by NMR
Z01DK-29026-03 (LCP) BECKER, E D NIDDK, NIH NMR and other spectroscopic studies of molecular structure
Z01DK-29027-03 (LCP) ZWANZIG, R NIDDK, NIH Theoretical studies of dynamical processes in chemical physics and biophysics
Z01DK-29028-01 (LCP) CHEN, Y NIDDK, NIH Free energy conversion in biology
R01DK-29757-11 (BEM) WING, RENA R UNIVERSITY OF PITTSBURGH 3811 O'HARA STREET PITTSBURGH, PA 15213 Behavioral weight loss for adults with diabetes mellitus
R01DK-29786-10 (GMA) DAWSON, DAVID C UNIVERSITY OF MICHIGAN 6811 MEDICAL SCIENCE BLDG II ANN ARBOR, MI 48109-0622 Ion transport by colon and hormonal control
R01DK-29787-10 (PTHA) KREISBERG, JEFFREY I UNIVERSITY OF TEXAS 7703 FLOYD CURL DRIVE SAN ANTONIO, TX 78284-7750 Pathobiology of diabetic glomerulosclerosis
R01DK-29800-11 (MGN) SHEN, CHE-KUN J UNIVERSITY OF CALIFORNIA DAVIS, CA 95616 Evolution and expression of primate alpha-globin gene cluster
R37DK-29808-12 (HEM) BENNETT, GEORGE V DUKE UNIVERSITY MEDICAL CNTR P O BOX 3892 DURHAM, NC 27710 Human erythrocyte membrane cytoskeleton associations
R01DK-29857-10 (PHY) WEINSTEIN, ALAN M CORNELL UNIV MEDICAL COLLEGE 1300 YORK AVENUE NEW YORK, N Y 10021 Theory of solute and water transport across epithelia
R01DK-29867-10 (MET) BERGMAN, RICHARD N UNIV. OF SOUTHERN CALIFORNIA 1410 BIGGY STREET OCD 315 LOS ANGELES, CA 90033 Quantitation of factors regulating glucose tolerance
R01DK-29876-12 (BCE) LEEMAN, SUSAN E UNIV OF MASSACHUSETTS MED CTR 55 LAKE AVE NORTH WORCESTER, MASS 01605 Purification and function of hypothalamic peptides
R01DK-29902-12 (HEM) GINDER, GORDON D UNIVERSITY OF MINNESOTA BOX 236 UMHC/411 MASONIC CTR MINNEAPOLIS, MN 55455 Globin gene regulation during erythroid differentiation
R01DK-29920-11 (GMA) KRIER, JACOB MICHIGAN STATE UNIVERSITY 308 GILTNER HALL EAST LANSING, MI 48824-1101 Extrinsic neural control of colonic motility/defecation
R01DK-29930-11 (NTN) NEURINGER, MARTHA D OREGON HEALTH SCIENCES UNIV 3181 SW SAM JACKSON PARK RD PORTLAND, OR 97201-3098 Essentiality of dietary omega-3 fatty acids in primates
R01DK-29953-10 (END) RIZZA, ROBERT A MAYO FOUNDATION 200 FIRST STREET SOUTHWEST ROCHESTER, MN 55905 Mechanisms of insulin resistance in man
R55DK-29955-11 (GMB) MASSRY, SHAUL G UNIV OF SOUTHERN CALIFORNIA 2025 ZONAL AVENUE LOS ANGELES, CA 90033 Parathyroid hormone and uremia
R37DK-29961-11 (SAT) STARZL, THOMAS E UNIVERSITY OF PITTSBURGH 350 THACKERAY HALL PITTSBURGH, PA 15260 Effects of orthotopic liver transplantation
R01DK-29962-11 (PHY) WILLS, NANCY K UNIV OF TEXAS MEDICAL HOSP 301 UNIVERSITY BLVD. GALVESTON, TX 77550 Regulation of Na+ & K+ transport across epithelia
R01DK-29985-10 (GMB) MYERS, BRYAN D STANFORD UNIVERSITY STANFORD, CA 94305 Pathophysiology of human acute renal failure
R01DK-30002-08A2 (CBY) EARP, H SHELTON, III UNIV OF NC AT CHAPEL HILL LINEBERGER CANCER RES, CTR. CHAPEL HILL, NC 27599-7295 EGF receptor synthesis--Structure and role in liver growth

PROJECT NO., ORGANIZATIONAL UNIT., INVESTIGATOR, ADDRESS, TITLE

R01DK-30025-14 (MCHA) KOREEDA, MASATO UNIVERSITY OF MICHIGAN ANN ARBOR, MI 48109 Synthesis of steroid hormones and acyclic systems
R01DK-30031-09 (NTN) SCHOELLER, DALE A UNIVERSITY OF CHICAGO 5841 SOUTH MARYLAND AVE, BOX 4 CHICAGO, IL 60637 Noninvasive measurement of energy expenditure in man
R01DK-30051-11 (PBC) ENGVALL, EVA S LA JOLLA CANCER RESEARCH FDN 10901 NORTH TORREY PINES ROAD LA JOLLA, CA 92037 Basement membrane glycoprotein laminin
R01DK-30066-10 (MET) LEVIN, BARRY E VA MEDICAL CENTER EAST ORANGE, NJ 07019 Obesity--Neural control of metabolism and weight gain
R01DK-30109-09 (BCE) VICKERY, LARRY E UNIV OF CALIFORNIA, IRVINE COLLEGE OF MEDICINE IRVINE, CA 92715 Molecular mechanisms and control of steroid biosynthesis
R01DK-30110-09 (GMA) TACHE, YVETTE F VA/WADSWORTH MEDICAL CENTER WILSHIRE AND SAWTELLE BLVDS LOS ANGELES, CA 90073 Brain regulating gastric acid function by neuropeptides
R37DK-30118-11 (END) GILBERT, LAWRENCE I UNIVERSITY OF NORTH CAROLINA CB #3280, COKER HALL CHAPEL HILL, NC 27599-3280 Biochemical analysis of the action of hormones
R01DK-30142-11 (HEM) TAVASSOLI, MEHDI 1500 E WOODROW WILSON DRIVE JACKSON, MS 39216 Structure-function relations in hemopoiesis
R01DK-30144-11 (EVR) ESTES, MARY K BAYLOR COLLEGE OF MEDICINE ONE BAYLOR PLAZA HOUSTON, TX 77030 Molecular biology of the rotaviruses
R01DK-30167-10 (MCHA) COY, DAVID H TULANE U. SCHOOL OF MEDICINE 1430 TULANE AVENUE NEW ORLEANS, LA 70112 VIP family peptides-analogs-GH, insulin, glucagon
R01DK-30178-10 (GMB) MORRISSEY, JEREMIAH J WASHINGTON UNIVERSITY 660 SOUTH EUCLID AVE, BOX 8126 ST LOUIS, MO 63110 Regulation of parathyroid function
R01DK-30203-10 (HEM) MULLER-EBERHARD, URSULA CORNELL UNIVERSITY MED COLLEGE 525 EAST 68TH STREET NEW YORK, NY 10021 Hemoglobin metabolism--Clinical and basic approach
R01DK-30239-08 (BBCA) FERRONE, FRANK A DREXEL UNIVERSITY 32ND & CHESTNUT STREETS PHILADELPHIA, PA 19104 Conformational kinetics of biological molecules
R37DK-30241-10 (MGN) STROMINGER, JACK L HARVARD UNIVERSITY 7 DIVINITY AVENUE CAMBRIDGE, MA 02138 Genetic organization of the human MHC
R37DK-30254-09 (ECS) HSUEH, WILLA A UNIV OF SOUTHERN CALIFORNIA 2025 ZONAL AVE LOS ANGELES, CA 90033 Biochemistry of renin secretion
R37DK-30280-10 (PTHB) NEILSON, ERIC G UNIV OF PENNSYLVANIA HOSPITAL 3400 SPRUCE STREET PHILADELPHIA, PA 19104 Immunologic mechanisms in interstitial nephritis
R01DK-30292-10 (CTY) GORDON, JEFFREY I WASHINGTON U SCH OF MED 660 S EUCLID AVE, BOX 8231 ST LOUIS, MO 63110 Regulation of gene expression in the small intestine
R01DK-30297-10 (BIO) ORTIZ DE MONTELLANO, PAUL R UNIVERSITY OF CALIFORNIA 926 MEDICAL SCIENCES BLDG SAN FRANCISCO, CA 94143-0446 Hemolytic anemia and abnormal heme catabolites
R01DK-30312-10 (GMA) KAPLOWITZ, NEIL UNIV SOUTHERN CALIFORNIA 2025 ZONAL AVE LAC 11 221 LOS ANGELES, CA 90033 Physiology of glutathione efflux from the liver
R01DK-30343-10 (BIO) RAUSHEL, FRANK M TEXAS A & M UNIVERSITY DEPARTMENT OF CHEMISTRY COLLEGE STATION, TX 77843 Mechanism & control of urea biosynthesis
R01DK-30344-10 (PHY) BORON, WALTER F YALE UNIV SCHOOL OF MEDICINE 333 CEDAR STREET NEW HAVEN, CT 06510 Regulation of intracellular pH in the renal proximal tubule
R01DK-30399-09 (GMA) FIOCCHI, CLAUDIO CLEVELAND CLINIC FOUNDATION 9500 EUCLID AVENUE RES INSTITU CLEVELAND, OHIO 44106 Mucosal lymphokines in inflammatory bowel disease
R37DK-30410-09 (NSS) BRENNER, BARRY M BRIGHAM AND WOMEN'S HOSP, INC 75 FRANCIS STREET BOSTON, MASS 02115 Renal function in experimental diabetes mellitus
R01DK-30415-09 (GMA) RAYFORD, PHILLIP L UNIVERSITY OF ARKANSAS 4301 WEST MARKHAM, SLOT 505 LITTLE ROCK, AR 72205 Endocrinologic studies of the gastrointestinal tract
R01DK-30425-10 (MET) PILCH, PAUL F BOSTON UNIV SCH OF MEDICINE 80 EAST CONCORD STREET BOSTON, MA 02118 Activation of hexose transport by insulin
R01DK-30444-09A2 (GMA) SOLL, ANDREW H CURE/VA WADSWORTH WILSHIRE & SAWTELLE BLVDS LOS ANGELES, CA 90073 Characterization of fundic mucosal cells in vitro
R01DK-30457-10 (BCE) HABENER, JOEL F MASSACHUSETTS GENERAL HOSPITAL WELLMAN 3 BOSTON, MA 02114 Somatostatin--Endocrine and paracrine biosynthesis
R01DK-30534-10 (HEM) KAPLAN, JERRY UNIVERSITY OF UTAH 50 NORTH MEDICAL DRIVE SALT LAKE CITY, UTAH 84132 Factors regulating cellular uptake of iron
R01DK-30577-10 (NLS) EICHBERG, JOSEPH UNIV OF HOUSTON-UNIV PARK 4800 CALHOUN HOUSTON, TX 77204-5500 Phospholipid metabolism in diabetic neuropathy
R01DK-30579-08 (BBCB) MANDEL, NEIL S VA MEDICAL CTR MILWAUKEE, WI 53295 Crystal interactions in renal stone disease
R01DK-30583-09 (MET) LEIBEL, RUDOLPH L ROCKEFELLER UNIVERSITY 1230 YORK AVENUE NEW YORK, NY 10021-6399 Energy homeostasis in human obesity
U01DK-30590-09 (ADDK) GOLDSTEIN, DAVID E THE UNIVERSITY OF MISSOURI ONE HOSPITAL DRIVE COLUMBIA, MO 65212 Diabetes control and complications trial (DCCT)
U01DK-30598-09 (ADDK) ETZWILER, DONNELL D INTERNATIONAL DIABETES CENTER 5000 WEST 39TH STREET MINNEAPOLIS, MN 55416 Diabetes control and complications trial
R01DK-30603-12 (GMB) DUBOSE, THOMAS D, JR UNIVERSITY OF TEXAS MED SCH 6431 FANNIN SUITE MSB 4.130 HOUSTON, TX 77030 Mechanism of renal acid-base homeostasis
U01DK-30604-09 (ADDK) PALMER, JERRY P VA MEDICAL CENTER, MED SER. 11 1660 S. COLUMBIAN WAY SEATTLE, WA 98108 Diabetes control and complications trial (DCCT)
U01DK-30609-09 (ADDK) SERVICE, F JOHN MAYO FOUNDATION 200 FIRST STREET, S.W. ROCHESTER, MN 55905 Diabetes control and complications

trial (DCCT)
U01DK-30611-09 (ADDK) RASKIN, PHILIP U.T. SOUTHWESTERN MED. CENTER 5323 HARRY HINES BOULEVARD DALLAS, TX 75235 Diabetes control and complications trial (DCCT)
U01DK-30618-09 (ADDK) TAMBORLANE, WILLIAM V, JR YALE UNIVERSITY SCHOOL OF MED. 333 CEDAR ST., P. O. BOX 3333 NEW HAVEN, CT 06510 Diabetes control and complications trial (DCCT)
U01DK-30619-09 (ADDK) BAKER, LESTER CHILDREN'S HOSP., PHILADELPHIA 34TH & CIVIC CENTER BOULEVARD PHILDELPHIA, PA 19104 Diabetes control and complications trial (DCCT)
U01DK-30620-09 (ADDK) LORENZ, RODNEY A VANDERBILT UNIVERSITY 21ST AVE. SOUTH & GARLAND ST. NASHVILLE, TN 37232 Diabetes control and complications trial (DCCT)
U01DK-30625-09 (ADDK) KITABCHI, ABBAS E UNIV. OF TENNESSEE, MEMPHIS 951 COURT AVENUE, ROOM 335 MEMPHIS, TN 38163 Diabetes control and complications trial (DCCT)
U01DK-30626-09 (ADDK) BANTLE, JOHN P THE UNIVERSITY OF MINNESOTA 515 DELAWARE STREET MINNEAPOLIS, MN 55455 Diabetes control and complications trial (DCCT)
U01DK-30627-08 (ADDK) CAMPBELL, ROBERT G CORNELL UNIV. MEDICAL COLLEGE 515 EAST 71ST ST., ROOM S-106 NEW YORK, NY 10021 Diabetes control and complications trial
U01DK-30628-09 (ADDK) GENUTH, SAUL M MOUNT SINAI MEDICAL CENTER 1800 EAST 105TH STREET CLEVELAND, OH 44106 Diabetes control and complications trial (DCCT)
U01DK-30632-09 (ADDK) ZINMAN, BERNARD MOUNT SINAI HOSPITAL 600 UNIVERSITY AVENUE, SUITE 7 TORONTO, ONTARIO M5G 1X5 Diabetes control and complications trial
U01DK-30633-09 (ADDK) JACOBSON, ALAN M JOSLIN DIABETES CENTER, INC. ONE JOSLIN PLACE BOSTON, MA 02215 Diabetes control and complications trial (DCCT)
U01DK-30636-09 (ADDK) WHITEHOUSE, FRED W HENRY FORD HOSPITAL 2799 WEST GRAND BOULEVARD DETROIT, MI 48202 Diabetes control and complications trial (DCCT)
U01DK-30643-09 (ADDK) NATHAN, DAVID M MASSCHUSETTS GENERAL HOSPITAL 32 FRUIT STREET BOSTON, MA 02114 Diabetes control and complications trial
R01DK-30648-11 (MET) CZECH, MICHAEL P UNIV OF MASSACHUSETTS MED SCHL 55 LAKE AVENUE NORTH WORCESTER, MA 01655 Properties of the high affinity insulin receptor
U01DK-30651-09 (ADDK) COLWELL, JOHN A MED. UNIV. OF SOUTH CAROLINA 171 ASHLEY AVENUE CHARLESTON, SC 29425 Diabetes control and complications trial (DCCT)
U01DK-30653-09 (ADDK) SANTIAGO, JULIO V WASHINGTON U./PEDIATRICS DEPT. 400 SOUTH KINGSHIGHWAY ST. LOUIS, MO 63110 Diabetes control and complications trial
U01DK-30659-09 (ADDK) ZEITLER, ROD UNIVERSITY OF IOWA W316 GENERAL HOSPITAL IOWA CITY, IA 52242 Diabetes control and complications trial (DCCT)
R01DK-30664-10A1 (GMA) MULLER-EBERHARD, URSULA CORNELL UNIV MED COLLEGE 525 E 68TH STREET N-804 NEW YORK, NY 10021 Distribution of iron and heme by proteins
U01DK-30665-09 (ADDK) DRASH, ALLAN L ONE CHILDREN'S PLACE 3705 FIFTH AVENUE AT DESOTO PITTSBURGH, PA 15213 Diabetes control and complications trial (DCCT)
U01DK-30666-09 (ADDK) DUPRE, JOHN U. OF W. ONT. - UNIV. HOSPITAL 50P18, P. O. BOX 5339 LONDON, ONT. CANADA N6A 5A5 Diabetes control and complications trial
R37DK-30667-11 (END) FROHMAN, LAWRENCE A UNIVERSITY OF CINCINNATI 231 BETHESDA AVENUE CINCINNATI, OHIO 45267 Neuroendocrine control of anterior pituitary hormones
R37DK-30693-11 (GMB) STEINMETZ, PHILIP R UNIVERSITY OF CONNECTICUT 263 FARMINGTON AVE FARMINGTON, CT 06030 Transport processes of urinary acidification
R01DK-30718-06 (BMT) WILSON, GEORGE S UNIVERSITY OF KANSAS LAWRENCE, KS 66045 Studies of potentially implantable glucose sensors
R01DK-30747-09 (EDC) HAMMAN, RICHARD F UNIV OF COLORADO SCH OF MED 4200 E NINTH AVE, C-245 DENVER, CO 80262 Diabetes mellitus in the San Luis Valley, Colorado
R37DK-30759-10 (NSS) DOUSA, THOMAS P MAYO FOUNDATION 200 FIRST STREET SOUTHWEST ROCHESTER, MN 55901 Cellular regulation of phosphate transport in kidney
R01DK-30770-07 (SB) HORBETT, THOMAS A UNIVERSITY OF WASHINGTON SEATTLE, WA 98195 Glucose sensitive membranes in the delivery of insulin
R01DK-30787-11 (PHRA) MURAD, FERID ABBOTT LABORATORIES DEPT 473 PHARM DISCOVERY ABBOTT PARK, IL 60064 Regulation of cyclic nucleotide formation & action
R01DK-30808-09A1 (SB) UEHLING, DAVID T UNIVERSITY OF WISCONSIN 600 HIGHLAND AVENUE MADISON, WI 53792 Immunization against urinary tract infection
R01DK-30825-08 (SAT) ORLOFF, MARSHALL J UNIV OF CALIFORNIA MED CTR 225 DICKINSON STREET SAN DIEGO, CA 92103 Effect of pancreas transplants on pathology of diabetes
R01DK-30834-09 (PC) HABENER, JOEL F MASSACHUSETTS GENERAL HOSPITAL FRUIT STREET BOSTON, MA 02114 Glucagon biosynthesis and metabolism
R37DK-30852-10 (HEM) PAPAYANNOPOULOU, THALIA UNIVERSITY OF WASHINGTON SEATTLE, WA 98195 Studies of globin switching and erythroid differentiation
R01DK-30879-10 (PTHA) HUMES, H DAVID VA MEDICAL CENTER 2215 FULLER ROAD ANN ARBOR, MI 48105 Pathogenesis of acute renal failure
R01DK-30898-11 (MET) CZECH, MICHAEL P UNIVERSITY OF MASSACHUSETTS 55 LAKE AVENUE NORTH WORCESTER, MA 01655 Insulin action on the fat cell surface membrane
R01DK-30932-09 (PTHB) SALANT, DAVID J UNIVERSITY HOSPITAL 80 EAST CONCORD STREET BOSTON, MA 02118 Mediation of antibody-induced glomerular injury
R01DK-30964-08 (BPO) SCOTT, THOMAS R, JR UNIVERSITY OF DELAWARE 220 WOLF HALL NEWARK, DE 19716 Gustatory involvement in ingestion
R55DK-30992-09A1 (MET) GOODNER, CHARLES J HARBORVIEW MEDICAL CENTER 325 NINTH AVENUE SEATTLE, WA 98104 Metabolic consequences of cyclic secretion by the islets
R01DK-31016-10 (BPO) COLLIER, GEORGE H RUTGERS, THE STATE UNIVERSITY BUSCH CAMPUS NEW BRUNSWICK, N J 08903 Determinants of choice
R01DK-31036-10 (PC) KAHN, C RONALD JOSLIN DIABETES CENTER ONE JOSLIN PLACE BOSTON, MA 02215 Insulin receptor structure and turnover
R01DK-31038-10 (BMT) WALKER, FRANCES A UNIVERSITY OF ARIZONA TUCSON, AZ 85721 Cytochromes B--Models and protein studies
R01DK-31050-09 (MET) CHAN, TIMOTHY M UNV OF SOUTHERN CALIFORNIA 1985 ZONAL AVENUE LOS ANGELES, CALIF 90033 Skeletal muscle metabolism in obese-diabetic mice
R01DK-31056-10 (HEM) SIMONS, ELIZABETH R BOSTON UNIV SCHOOL OF MEDICINE 80 E CONCORD STREET BOSTON, MA 02118 Functional studies of granulocyte membranes
R01DK-31060-08A2 (HEM) DAINIAK, NICHOLAS UNIV OF CONNECTICUT HLTH CTR 263 FARMINGTON AVENUE FARMINGTON, CT 06032 Biology of hematopoietic membrane regulatory molecules
R01DK-31063-10 (SAT) LAWSON, RUSSELL K MEDICAL COLLEGE OF WISCONSIN 9200 W. WISCONSIN AVENUE MILWAUKEE, WIS 53226 Benign prostatic hyperplasia -- Prostate growth factor
R01DK-31091-11 (PHY) FRIZZELL, RAYMOND A UNIVERSITY OF ALABAMA 1918 UNIVERSITY BOULEVARD BIRMINGHAM, AL 35294 Chloride secretion by epithelial tissues
R37DK-31092-11 (NSS) GOYAL, RAJ K BETH ISRAEL HOSPITAL 330 BROOKLINE AVENUE BOSTON, MA 02215 Physiology and pathophysiology of esophageal motility
Z01DK-31100-26 (LBC) DALY, J W NIDDK, NIH Pharmacologically active compounds from amphibians and other natural sources
Z01DK-31101-22 (LBC) CREVELING, C R NIDDK, NIH Pharmacology and metabolism of biogenic amines and related compounds
Z01DK-31102-21 (LBC) DALY, J W NIDDK, NIH Ion Channels--Receptors and Second Messengers in the Nervous System
Z01DK-31104-23 (LBC) JERINA, D M NIDDK, NIH Enzymatic oxidation of drugs to toxic and carcinogenic metabolites
Z01DK-31106-04 (LBC) JERINA, D M NIDDK, NIH Mechanistic enzymology of HIV proteins
Z01DK-31107-04 (LBC) PANNELL, L NIDDK,NIH Mass spectrometry of drugs, metabolites and natural products
Z01DK-31108-03 (LBC) DALY, J W NIDDK,NIH Adenosine receptor agonists and antagonists
Z01DK-31109-02 (LBC) GUSOVSKY, F NIDDK, NIH Interaction between second messengers system
Z01DK-31110-15 (LBC) COHEN, L A NIDDK, NIH Analogues of thyrotropin-releasing hormone
Z01DK-31111-21 (LBC) COHEN, L A NIDDK, NIH Stereopopulation control in drug delivery and enzyme simulation
Z01DK-31112-15 (LBC) COHEN, L A NIDDK, NIH Chemistry of bioimidazoles
Z01DK-31113-15 (LBC) KIRK, K L NIDDK, NIH Halogenated biogenic amines in biochemistry and pharmacology
Z01DK-31114-09 (LBC) COHEN, L A NIDDK, NIH Significance of ligand tautomerism in biorecognition
Z01DK-31115-08 (LBC) JACOBSON, K NIDDK, NIH Functionalized congeners of bioactive compounds
Z01DK-31116-04 (LBC) JACOBSON, K NIDDK, NIH Prosthetic groups for radiolabeling of functionalized drugs and peptides
Z01DK-31117-04 (LBC) JACOBSON, K NIDDK, NIH Development of drugs acting at adenosine receptors
Z01DK-31118-02 (LBC) COHEN, L A NIDDK, NIH Aldose Reductase inhibitors
Z01DK-31119-02 (LBC) COHEN, L A NIDDK, NIH Novel amino acids for conformational and stereochemical constraints in peptides
Z01DK-31120-02 (LBC) COHEN, L A NIDDK, NIH Fluorinated analogues of bioactive peptides
Z01DK-31121-01 (LBC) COHEN, L A NIDDK, NIH Chemistry and biology of novel pyrimidine and purine nucleosides
Z01DK-31122-01 (LBC) COHEN, L A NIDDK, NIH Antimalarial agents based on bioheterocycles
R01DK-31127-10 (NTN) COUSINS, ROBERT J UNIVERSITY OF FLORIDA GAINESVILLE, FL 32611-0163 Zinc and the synthesis of zinc binding protein
R01DK-31135-08 (BPO) SCLAFANI, ANTHONY BROOKLYN COLLEGE OF CUNY BROOKLYN, NY 11210 Carbohydrate appetite and obesity
R01DK-31147-09 (GMA) SNAPE, WILLIAM J, JR HABOR-UCLA MEDICAL CENTER 1000 W CARSON ST., C-1 TRAILER TORRANCE, CA 90509 Neurohormonal regulation of colonic smooth muscle
R01DK-31198-10 (GMA) BISSELL, DWIGHT M, JR SAN FRANCISCO GENERAL HOSPITAL 1001 POTRERO AVE, BLDG 40 SAN FRANCISCO, CA 94110 Cellular pathophysiology of hepatic fibrosis
R01DK-31205-10 (GMA) SCHRON, CHARLES M UNIVERSITY OF CINCINNATI 231 BETHESDA AVENUE (ML594) CINCINNATI, OH 45267 Cellular mechanisms of hepatic ion transport
R01DK-31206-08 (BIO) MENDELSON, CAROLE R UNVI OF TEXAS SW MEDICAL CTR 5323 HARRY HINES BOULEVARD DALLAS, TX 75235-9038 Cellular mechanisms in the induction of aromatase
P01DK-31232-10 (DDK) STAMATOYANNOPOULOS, GEORGE UNIVERSITY OF WASHINGTON 1959 NE PACIFIC ST SEATTLE, WA 98195 Developmental biology of hemoglobin switching
P01DK-31232-10 0003 (DDK) GELINAS, RICHARD Developmental biology of hemoglobin switching Regulatory sequences in human globin loci
P01DK-31232-10 0001 (DDK) STAMATOYANNAPOULOS, GEORGE Developmental biology of hemoglobin switching Studies of human hemoglobin switching
P01DK-31232-10 0002 (DDK) GROUDINE, MARK T Developmental biology of hemoglobin switching Chromatin structure and expression of human globin genes
P01DK-31232-10 0004 (DDK) WEINTRAUB, HAROLD Developmental biology of hemoglobin switching Biochemical analysis of red cell precursor cells
P01DK-31232-10 0005 (DDK) HAKOMORI, SEN-ITIROH Developmental biology of hemoglobin switching Membrane differentiation in erythroid cells
P01DK-31232-10 9001 (DDK) SHEPARD, THOMAS Developmental biology of hemoglobin switching Fetal erythroid tissues--Core
P01DK-31232-10 9002 (DDK) PAPAYANNOPOULOU, THALIA Developmental

biology of hemoglobin switching Tissue culture core

R01DK-31357-11 (BIO) GLEW, ROBERT H UNIV OF NEW MEXICO SCH OF MED 915 STANFORD ST NW ALBUQUERQUE, NM 87131 Beta-Glucosidases in Gaucher disease

R01DK-31370-06 (DDK) CHAN, JAMES C MEDICAL COLLEGE OF VIRGINIA MCV STATION, BOX 498 RICHMOND, VA 23298 Growth failure in children with renal diseases

R37DK-31379-10 (HEM) ROSSE, WENDELL F DUKE UNIVERSITY MEDICAL CENTER DURHAM, NC 27710 Membrane abnormalities in paroxysmal nocturnal hemoglobinura

R01DK-31389-10 (SAT) SNYDMAN, DAVID R NEW ENGLAND MEDICAL CENTER 750 WASHINGTON ST., BOX 238 BOSTON, MA 02111 Liver transplant associated cytomegalovirus prevention

R37DK-31396-09 (SB) STEER, MICHAEL L BETH ISRAEL HOSPITAL 330 BROOKLINE AVENUE BOSTON, MA 02215 Acute pancreatitis

R01DK-31398-07A2 (GMB) POLLOCK, ALLAN S VA MEDICAL CENTER 4150 CLEMENT STREET SAN FRANCISCO, CA 94121 Kidney PEPCK gene expression--pH response

R01DK-31405-10 (PC) SPIEGELMAN, BRUCE M DANA-FARBER CANCER INSTITUTE 44 BINNEY STREET BOSTON, MA 02115 Control of lipogenic enzyme synthesis in adipocytes

R01DK-31428-10 (NEUC) CASKEY, CHARLES T BAYLOR COLLEGE OF MEDICINE ONE BAYLOR PLAZA/TEXAS MED CTR HOUSTON, TX 77030 Genetic alterations in Lesch-Nyhan disease

R01DK-31437-08 (GMB) HOSTETTER, THOMAS H UNIVERSITY OF MINNESOTA 516 DELAWARE ST, S E BOX 736 MINNEAPOLIS, MN 55455 Renal adaptation and injury

R01DK-31450-11 (BMT) SOLOMON, EDWARD I STANFORD UNIVERSITY S G MUDD BUILTDING STANFORD, CA 94305 Spectroscopic studies of copper clusters in proteins

R01DK-31513-09 (HEM) KOURY, MARK J VANDERBILT UNIVERSITY C3101 MED CTR NORTH/HEMATOLOGY NASHVILLE, TN 37232 Erythropoietin--its production and its mechanism of action

R01DK-31550-07 (PHY) STEPHENSON, JOHN L CORNELL UNIVERSITY MED COLL 1300 YORK AVE NEW YORK, N Y 10021 Theoretical analysis of solute and H2O transport in kidney

R01DK-31559-07A3 (PC) TORNHEIM, KEITH BOSTON UNIVERSITY SCHOOL OF ME 80 E CONCORD ST BOSTON, MA 02118 Oscillations and the control of glycolysis

R01DK-31573-10 (END) PRATT, WILLIAM B UNIVERSITY OF MICHIGAN M6322 MEDICAL SCIENCE BLDG I ANN ARBOR, MICH 48109-0010 An endogenous steroid receptor stabilizing factor

R01DK-31580-09 (CBY) KILBERG, MICHAEL S UNIVERSITY OF FLORIDA DEPT/BIOCHEM/MOLEC/BIO J-245 GAINESVILLE, FL 32610 Adaptive processes for amino acid uptake by liver cells

R01DK-31620-09 (PHY) WALSH, JOHN V UNIVERSITY OF MASS MED SCHOOL 55 LAKE AVENUE NORTH WORCESTER, MA 01655 Ionic channels in dissociated smooth muscle cells

R01DK-31623-06 (GMB) HUMPHREYS, MICHAEL H SAN FRANCISCO GNRL HOSP 1001 POTRERO AVE/RM 350 BLDG 1 SAN FRANCISCO, CA 94110 Reflex control of compensatory renal growth & function

R01DK-31642-09 (TMP) BOLLENBACHER, WALTER E UNIV OF NC AT CHAPEL HILL CB# 3280 COKER HALL 010A CHAPEL HILL, NC 27599-3280 Endocrinology of insect diapause

R01DK-31643-11 (CBY) BURGESS, DAVID R UNIVERSITY OF PITTSBURGH PITTSBURGH, PA 15260 Control of brush border motility and microvillus growth

R01DK-31667-09 (GMA) SHARP, GEOFFREY W DEPARTMENT OF PHARMACOLOGY NYS COLLEGE OF VETERINARY MED. ITHACA, NY 14853-6401 Diarrheal diseases--Ca++ -calmodulin phosphorylation

R01DK-31676-07A1 (PC) CHANG, SIMON H LOUISIANA STATE UNIVERSITY BATON ROUGE, LA 70803 Genetics of phosphofructokinase structure and function

R01DK-31683-09 (PC) EARP, H SHELTON, III UNIVERSITY OF NORTH CAROLINA 102 LINEBERGER COMPREHENSIVE CHAPEL HILL, NC 27599 Membrane phosphorylation and hepatic growth

R01DK-31722-05 (BIO) CHATTERJEE, SUBROTO B JOHNS HOPKINS HOSPITAL 600 N WOLFE ST BALTIMORE, MD 21205 Regulation of lactosylceramide synthesis in renal cells

R01DK-31764-09 (GMA) BULKLEY, GREGORY B JOHNS HOPKINS HOSPITAL 600 N WOLFE ST/BLALOCK 685 BALTIMORE, MD 21205 Gut ischemia and MOF syndrome--microvascular transduction

R01DK-31765-09 (GMA) KERN, FRED, JR UNIVERSITY OF COLORADO 4200 EAST NINTH AVENUE DENVER, COLO 80262 Mechanism of estrogen effects on biliary cholesterol

R01DK-31774-09 (SAT) SOLLINGER, HANS W UNIVERSITY OF WISCONSIN 600 HIGHLAND AVENUE MADISON, WI 53792 Kidney transplantation and donor-specific transfusions

R01DK-31775-09 (MGN) GREENBERG, DAVID A MT SINAI MEDICAL CENTER 1 GUSTAV LEVY PLACE NEW YORK, N Y 10029 Two-locus models, heterogeneity and diabetes

R55DK-31813-09 (MGN) HODGE, SUSAN E NY STATE PSYCHIATRIC INSTITUTE BX 14, 722 W 168TH ST NEW YORK, NY 10032 Linkage and segregation in complex genetic diseases

R01DK-31842-09 (MET) POLONSKY, KENNETH S UNIV. OF CHICAGO 5841 S. MARYLAND AVE CHICAGO, IL 60637 The regulation of hepatic insulin extraction

R01DK-31847-07 (GMB) WALTERS, MARIAN R TULANE MEDICAL SCHOOL 1430 TULANE AVENUE NEW ORLEANS, LA 70112 1,25-dihydroxyvitamin D receptor/function in new targets

R01DK-31900-11 (GMA) CHEW, CATHERINE S MOREHOUSE SCHOOL OF MEDICINE 720 WESTVIEW DRIVE SW ATLANTA, GA 30310-1495 Gastric H+ ion transport--Cellular control mechanisms

R01DK-31914-09 (GMA) STEER, MICHAEL L BETH ISRAEL HOSPITAL 330 BROOKLINE AVENUE BOSTON, MA 02215 Stimulus-secretion coupling in the exocrine pancreas

R01DK-31933-09 (NTN) BISTRIAN, BRUCE R NEW ENGLAND DEACONESS HOSPITAL 185 PILGRIM ROAD BOSTON, MA 02215 Nutritional determinants of LEM production

R01DK-31969-09 (GMA) DOBBINS, JOHN W YALE UNIVERSITY SCH OF MEDICIN 333 CEDAR ST PO BOX 3333 NEW HAVEN, CT 06510 Control of ion transport in health and diarrheal disease

R01DK-31988-09 (MET) BRAY, GEORGE A PENNINGTON BIOMEDICAL RES CTR 6400 PERKINS RD BATON ROUGE, LA 70808 Hypothalamic obesity

R01DK-32008-09 (GMB) WALSER, MACKENZIE JOHNS HOPKINS UNIV SCH OF MED 725 NORTH WOLFE STREET BALTIMORE, MD 21205 Ketoacid therapy of renal failure

R01DK-32009-08 (NTN) WALSER, MACKENZIE JOHNS HOPKINS UNIVERSITY 725 NORTH WOLFE STREET BALTIMORE, MD 21205 Keto analogue incorporation into proteins

R01DK-32030-10 (BMT) GUPTA, RAJ K ALBERT EINSTEIN COLL OF MED 1300 MORRIS PARK AVENUE BRONX, NY 10461 NMR studies of metal ions in intact cells and tissues

R01DK-32032-08A2 (GMB) BELL, PHILLIP D UNIVERSITY OF ALABAMA UAB STATION BIRMINGHAM, AL 35294 Cellular mechanism for tubuloglomerular feedback system

R01DK-32034-10 (BMT) SCOTT, A IAN TEXAS A&M UNIVERSITY COLLEGE STATION, TX 77843 Porphyrin and corrinoid biosynthesis

R01DK-32046-10 (BCE) MAHESH, VIRENDRA B MEDICAL COLLEGE OF GEORGIA PHYSIOLOGY/ENDOCRINOLOGY DEPT. AUGUSTA, GA 30912-3000 Regulation of steroid hormone receptor activity

R01DK-32083-10 (IMS) EISENBARTH, GEORGE S JOSLIN DIABETES CENTER, INC. ONE JOSLIN PLACE BOSTON, MA 02215 Diabetes/islet growth probed with monoclonal antibodies

R01DK-32085-08 (MBY) EFSTRATIADIS, ARGIRIS COLUMBIA UNIVERSITY 701 WEST 168TH STREET NEW YORK, N Y 10032 Pre-mRNA splicing factors

R01DK-32088-07 (SAT) CERILLI, G JAMES UNIVERSITY OF ROCHESTER 601 ELMWOOD AVENUE ROCHESTER, NY 14642 Antivascular endothelial antibody--Organ transplantation

R01DK-32089-10 (NTN) BRAY, GEORGE A PENNINGTON BIOMEDICAL RES CTR 6400 PERKINS ROAD BATON ROUGE, LA 70808-4124 Dietary obesity

P01DK-32094-08 (ADDK) SHOHET, STEPHEN B UNIV. OF CA, SAN FRANCISCO 1282 MOFFITT HOSPITAL SAN FRANCISCO, CA 94143 Red cell membrane studies

R01DK-32121-09 (SB) PHILLIPS, SIDNEY F MAYO FOUNDATION 200 FIRST STREET, SW ROCHESTER, MN 55905 Motility and transit across the ileocolonic junction

R01DK-32130-09 (SB) MOORE, EDWARD W MEDICAL COLLEGE OF VIRGINIA BOX 711, MCV STATION RICHMOND, VA 23298 Pathogenesis of calcium containing gallstones

R01DK-32148-10 (GMB) KEMPSON, STEPHEN A INDIANA UNIV SCHOOL OF MED 635 BARNHILL DR-MED BDG RM 374 INDIANAPOLIS, IN 46202-5120 Phosphate transport by kidney cell membranes

R37DK-32157-09 (PTHB) CUNHA, GERALD R UNIVERSITY OF CALIFORNIA SAN FRANCISCO, CA 94143-0452 Benign prostatic hyperplasia--Developmental approach

R01DK-32161-04A3 (MEDB) DI CIOCCIO, RICHARD A ROSWELL PARK MEMORIAL INST ELM & CARLTON STREET BUFFALO, NY 14263 Regulation of alpha-l-fucosidase in health and disease

R01DK-32176-09 (GMA) PUBLICOVER, NELSON G UNIVERSITY OF NEVADA SCH OF ME 105 ANDERSON MED SCIS BLDG RENO, NV 89557 Regulation of G.I. motility patterns

R01DK-32189-08 (NTN) HORNE, DONALD W VA MEDICAL CENTER (151) 1310 24TH AVENUE, SOUTH NASHVILLE, TN 37212-2637 Folate and B12 in nutritional anemias--Dietary control

R01DK-32234-09 (END) SCHONBRUNN, AGNES UNIVERSITY OF TEXAS MEDICAL CT PO BOX 20708 HOUSTON, TX 77225 Somatostatin receptor structure and function

R01DK-32237-09 (SAT) SORENSON, ROBERT L UNIVERSITY OF MINNESOTA 4-135 JACKSON HALL MINNEAPOLIS, MN 55455 In vitro methods for islet isolation and transplantation

R01DK-32239-09 (NEUA) HOELDTKE, ROBERT D WVU SCHOOL OF MEDICINE HEALTH SCIENCES CENTER NORTH MORGANTOWN, WV 26506 Norepinephrine in diabetic autonomic neuropathy

R01DK-32253-09 (SB) MOHANAKUMAR, THALACHALLOUR WASHINGTON UNIVERSITY 4960 AUDUBON AVE-PO BOX 8109 ST LOUIS, MO 63110 Non-MHC antigens--Role in renal, cardiac transplantation

R01DK-32288-08 (GMA) TSO, PATRICK P LOUISIANA STATE UNIV MED CTR 1501 KINGS HIGHWAY SHREVEPORT, LA 71130 Formation and secretion of intestinal lipoproteins

R01DK-32294-09 (HEM) OGAWA, MAKIO V.A.M.C., RESEARCH SERV. (151) 109 BEE STREET CHARLESTON, SC 29403 Hemopoietic stem cells

R01DK-32303-09 (HEM) DAILEY, HARRY A UNIVERSITY OF GEORGIA 621 GRADUATE STUDIES BLDG ATHENS, GA 30602 Characterization of mammalian ferrochelatase

R01DK-32329-09 (IMS) THOMAS, JAMES W VANDERBILT UNIVERSITY T3219 MEDICAL CENTER NORTH NASHVILLE, TN 37232 Immune response to insulin in man

R01DK-32333-08 (ORTH) BILEZIKIAN, JOHN P COLLEGE OF PHYSICIANS & SURGEO 630 W 168TH STREET NEW YORK, NY 10032 Primary hyperparathyroidism

R01DK-32342-08 (SSS) RABKIN, RALPH V A MEDICAL CENTER 3801 MIRANDA AVENUE PALO ALTO, CA 94304 The kidney and insulin

R01DK-32346-08 (SB) SARNA, SUSHIL K MEDICAL COLLEGE OF WISCONSIN 8700 WEST WISCONSIN AVENUE MILWAUKEE, WIS 53226 Control of colonic motility in health and disease

R01DK-32431-08 (DDK) CHINCHILLI, VERNON M MEDICAL COLLEGE OF VIRGINIA BOX 32, MCV STATION RICHMOND, VA 23298 Data coordinating center--Pediatric renal disease study

R01DK-32442-09 (END) CRITCHLOW, B VAUGHN OREGON REGIONAL PRIMATE RES DEPT OF NEUROSCIENCE BEAVERTON, OREG 97006 Neural regulation of anterior pituitary

R01DK-32448-10 (BPO) GEARY, NORCROSS D CORNELL UNIV MED CTR 1300 YORK AVENUE NEW YORK, NY 10021 Neurobehavioral analysis of glucagon satiety

R01DK-32459-10 (END) CIDLOWSKI, JOHN A UNIV OF NC AT CHAPEL HILL CB #7545 CHAPEL HILL, NC 27599-7545 Vitamin B-6 and steroid hormone action

R01DK-32460-09 (END) CIDLOWSKI, JOHN A UNIVERSITY OF NORTH CAROLINA 460 MED SCI RES BLDG CB 7545 CHAPEL HILL, NC 27599-7545 Glucocorticoid action in synchronized cells

R01DK-32465-09A1 (BIO) BRADSHAW, RALPH A UNIVERSITY OF CALIFORNIA, IRVI IRVINE, CA 92717 Co-translational processing and protein turnover

R01DK-32469-09 (GMB) BANK, NORMAN MONTEFIORE MED CTR 111 E 210TH STREET BRONX, N Y 10467 Renal hemodynamic abnormalities in

PROJECT NO., ORGANIZATIONAL UNIT., INVESTIGATOR, ADDRESS, TITLE

early diabetes
R01DK-32471-06 (HEM) SMOLEN, JAMES E THE UNIVERSITY OF MICHIGAN 1150 WEST MEDICAL CENTER DRIVE ANN ARBOR, MICHIGAN 48109 The initiation of granulocyte responses
R01DK-32472-07 (BBCB) HIGUCHI, WILLIAM I UNIVERSITY OF UTAH 301 SKAGGS HALL SALT LAKE CITY, UTAH 84112 Mechanisms of cholesterol gallstone dissolution
R01DK-32493-09 (EDC) HAMMAN, RICHARD F UNIV OF COLORADO SCH OF MED 4200 E NINTH AVE, C-245 DENVER, CO 80262 Colorado insulin-dependent diabetes mellitus registry
P30DK-32520-08 (DDK) MILLER, THOMAS B U. OF MASSACHUSETTS MED. SCHL. 55 LAKE AVENUE, NORTH WORCESTER, MA 01655 Diabetes-endocrinology research center
P30DK-32520-08 9001 (DDK) MOLE, JOHN E Diabetes-endocrinology research center Core facility--Protein chemistry
P30DK-32520-08 9002 (DDK) ENNIS, FRANCES A Diabetes-endocrinology research center Core facility--cell science
P30DK-32520-08 9003 (DDK) APPEL, MICHAEL C Diabetes-endocrinology research center Core facility--morphology
R01DK-32561-06 (GMA) KORC, MURRAY UNIVERSITY OF CALIFORNIA IRVINE, CA 92717 Regulation of pancreatic exocrine function by manganese
R01DK-32640-07 (NTN) CARMEL, RALPH USC SCHOOL OF MEDICINE 2025 ZONAL AVENUE LOS ANGELES, CA 90033 Subtle disturbances of cobalamin status
R01DK-32642-08 (MEP) ONG, DAVID E VANDERBILT UNIVERSITY NASHVILLE, TN 37232 Binding proteins for compounds with vitamin a activity
R01DK-32656-09 (CBY) QUARONI, ANDREA CORNELL UNIVERSITY 724 VET RES TOWER ITHACA, NY 14853 Intestinal cell differentiation in vivo and in culture
R01DK-32658-08 (GMA) GRAND, RICHARD J NEW ENDLAND MEDICAL CENTER 750 WASHINGTON STREET, BOX 213 BOSTON, MA 02111 Development and control of synthesis and secretion
R37DK-32753-09 (GMB) GUGGINO, WILLIAM B JOHNS HOPKINS UNIVERSITY 725 NORTH WOLFE STREET BALTIMORE, MD 21205 Mechanisms of Cl transport in proximal and distal tubule
R01DK-32767-09 (EDC) ACTON, RONALD T UNIV OF ALABAMA AT BIRMINGHAM UAB STATION BIRMINGHAM, AL 35294 Predicting gestational & subsequent overt diabetes
R01DK-32770-09 (BIO) ROTTMAN, FRITZ M CASE WESTERN RESERVE UNIV DEPT MOLECULAR BIO & MICROBIO CLEVELAND, OHIO 44106-4960 Post-transcription regulation-- pituitary gene expression
R01DK-32783-07 (PC) POWERS, CLAUD A NEW YORK MEDICAL COLLEGE DEPARTMENT OF PHARMACOLOGY VALHALLA, N Y 10595 Pituitary kallikrein and prohormone processing
R01DK-32817-08 (END) BERRY, SUSAN MD UNIV OF MINNESOTA HOSPITAL 420 DELAWARE STREET, S.E. ST. PAUL, MINN. 55104 Regulation of hepatocellular function by growth hormone
R01DK-32822-08 (BIO) FLETTERICK, ROBERT J UNIV OF CALIFORNIA SAN FRANCISCO, CA 94143-0448 Primary and tertiary structures of human phosphorylases
R01DK-32838-09 (GMA) OWYANG, CHUNG UNIVERSITY OF MICHIGAN 3912 TAUBMAN CTR ANN ARBOR, MI 48109-0362 Feedback regulation of pancreatic enzyme secretion
R01DK-32839-08 (PHY) WADE, JAMES B UNIV OF MARYLAND AT BALTIMORE 655 WEST BALTIMORE STREET BALTIMORE, MD 21201 Structure-function analysis of vasopressin action
R01DK-32842-08 (GMA) GUMUCIO, JORGE J VA MEDICAL CENTER 2215 FULLER RD ANN ARBOR, MI 48105 Cell differentiation within the liver acinus
R01DK-32878-09 (GMA) MILLER, LAURENCE J MAYO FOUNDATION 200 FIRST STREET SOUTHWEST ROCHESTER, MN 55905 Type A cholecystokinin receptor structure, function and regulation
R01DK-32880-07 (MET) BERHANU, PAULOS UNIVERSITY OF COLORADO 4200 EAST NINTH AVE/BOX B151 DENVER, COLO 80262 Insulin receptor metabolism and insulin action
R01DK-32885-07 (PC) MARIASH, CARY N UNIVERSITY OF MINNESOTA 515 DELAWARE ST., BOX 91--MAYO MINNEAPOLIS, MN 55455 Metabolic regulation of gene expression
R01DK-32890-09 (HEM) SASSA, SHIGERU ROCKEFELLLER UNIVERSITY 1230 YORK AVENUE NEW YORK, N Y 10021 Genetics and development of erythroid heme enzymes
R01DK-32896-09 (GMA) WEISIGER, RICHARD A UNIV OF CALIFORNIA MEDICAL CTR BOX 0538, HSW-1120 SAN FRANCISCO, CA 94143 Role of binding proteins in hepatic organic anion uptake
R01DK-32907-07 (NTN) HORWITZ, BARBARA A UNIVERSITY OF CALIFORNIA DEPT OF ANIMAL PHYSIOLOGY DAVIS, CA 95616 Ontogeny of altered thermogenesis in obesity
R01DK-32910-08 (GMB) ARANT, BILLY S, JR SOUTHWESTERN MED CTR AT DALLAS DALLAS, TX 75235-9063 Mild and moderate vesicoureteric reflux in children
R01DK-32926-07 (MET) BASS, NATHAN M UNIVERSITY OF CALIFORNIA BOX 0538, HSW-1120 SAN FRANCISCO, CA 94143 Function and regulation of fatty acid binding proteins
R37DK-32948-10 (END) MAINS, RICHARD E JOHNS HOPKINS UNIVERSITY 725 NORTH WOLFE STREET BALTIMORE, MD 21205 Cell biology of bioactive peptide secretion
R37DK-32949-09 (END) EIPPER, ELIZABETH A JOHNS HOPKINS UNIV SCHL OF MED 720 RUTLAND AVE BALTIMORE, MD 21205 Biochemistry and physiology of peptide processing
R01DK-32953-10 (PC) CARLSON, GERALD M UNIV OF TENNESSEE, MEMPHIS 800 MADISON AVENUE MEMPHIS, TN 38163 Subunit interactions of phosphorylase kinase
P01DK-32971-08 (DDK) RUBIN, CYRUS E UNIVERSITY OF WASHINGTON DEPT OF MEDICINE RG-24 SEATTLE, WASH 98195 Structural and genome changes in the human GI mucosa
P01DK-32971-08 0004 (DDK) REID, BRIAN Structural and genome changes in the human GI mucosa Barrett's esophagus
P01DK-32971-08 0005 (DDK) LEVINE, DOUGLAS Structural and genome changes in the human GI mucosa Precursors of sporadic colon cancer
P01DK-32971-08 0006 (DDK) RUBIN, CYRUS Structural and genome changes in the human GI mucosa Ulcerative colitis

PROJECT NO., ORGANIZATIONAL UNIT., INVESTIGATOR, ADDRESS, TITLE

P01DK-32971-08 9002 (DDK) RUBIN, CYRUS E Structural and genome changes in the human GI mucosa Core--morphology
P01DK-32971-08 9003 (DDK) RABINOVITCH, PETER Structural and genome changes in the human GI mucosa Flow cytometry core
P01DK-32971-08 9004 (DDK) BURMER, GLENNA Structural and genome changes in the human GI mucosa Molecular genetics core
P01DK-32971-08 9005 (DDK) RASKIND, WENDY Structural and genome changes in the human GI mucosa Clonality, tissue culture and cytogenetics core
R01DK-32972-08 (PBC) STOCKERT, RICHARD J A. EINSTEIN COLLEGE OF MED. 1300 MORRIS PARK AVENUE BRONX, NY 10461 Regulation of hepatic membrane glycoprotein receptor
R01DK-32976-08 (BPO) WADE, GEORGE N UNIVERSITY OF MASSACHUSETTS AMHERST, MA 01003 Environmental control of seasonal weight cycles
R01DK-32995-09 (GMA) JAVITT, NORMAN B NEW YORK UNIVERSITY MED CENTER 550 FIRST AVENUE NEW YORK, NY 10016 Metabolic pathways of bile acid synthesis
R01DK-32999-12 (BMT) RAYMOND, KENNETH N UNIVERSITY OF CALIFORNIA BERKELEY, CA 94720 Ferric ion sequestering agents--iron removal in man
Z01DK-33000-25 (LMB) GELLERT, M NIDDK, NIH Studies of functions involved in genetic recombination
Z01DK-33001-07 (LMB) GELLERT, M NIDDK, NIH Studies of immunoglobulin gene rearrangement
Z01DK-33006-13 (LMB) MIZUUCHI, K NIDDK, NIH Studies on the mechanism of genetic recombination
R01DK-33010-08 (GMA) PANDOL, STEPHEN J UNIVERSITY OF CALIFORNIA V-111H LA JOLLA, CA 92093 Pancreatic secretion and phosphatidylinositol metabolism
R01DK-33022-08 (BIO) WOLF, BARRY MEDICAL COLLEGE OF VIRGINIA P O BOX 33, MCV STATION RICHMOND, VA 23298-0033 Recycling defects of covalently-bound vitamins
R01DK-33054-05 (PTHB) CHATTERJEE, NANDO K NEW YORK STATE DEPT OF HLTH EMPIRE STATE PLAZA ALBANY, NY 12201 Molecular mechanism of virus-induced diabetes mellitus
R01DK-33061-07A1 (GMA) TACHE, YVETTE F CURE/VA WADSWORTH WILSHIRE & SAWTELLE BLVDS LOS ANGELES, CA 90073 Corticotropin releasing factor--Action on gastrointestinal function
R01DK-33062-06 (GMB) GALBRAITH, ROBERT M MEDICAL UNIV OF SOUTH CAROLINA 171 ASHLEY AVE CHARLESTON, S C 29425 Lymphocyte interactions with Gc protein and vitamin D3
R01DK-33069-08 (GMA) YOLKEN, ROBERT H THE JOHNS HOPKINS UNIVERSITY 600 NORTH WOLFE STREET BALTIMORE, MD 21205 Prevention of viral gastroenteritis
R01DK-33100-08 (ALY) GUYRE, PAUL M DARTMOUTH MEDICAL SCHOOL HANOVER, NH 03756 Glucocorticoids,interferon and Fc receptors
R01DK-33139-07 (GMB) ADAMS, JOHN S CEDARS-SINAL MEDICAL CENTER 8700 BEVERLY BLVD LOS ANGELES, CA 90048 Vitamin D metabolism in sarcoidosis and lymphoma
R01DK-33144-08 (BIO) MORRIS, SIDNEY M UNIV OF PITTSBURGH SCH OF MED W 1255 BIOMEDICAL SCIENCE TOWE PITTSBURGH, PA 15261 Regulation of urea cycle enzyme synthesis
R01DK-33151-08 (CBY) CREUTZ, CARL E UNIVERSITY OF VIRGINIA R1300 JEFFERSON PARK AVE CHARLOTTESVILLE, VA 22908 Role of secretory vesicle binding proteins in exocytosis
R01DK-33152-05 (EDC) TURNER, ROBERT C RADCLIFFE INFIRMARY WOODSTOCK ROAD OXFORD, UK OX2 6H3 Prospective study of diabetes control and nephropathy
R01DK-33155-08 (PC) LEE, TERRY BECKMAN RES INST CITY OF HOPE 1450 E DUARTE ROAD DURATE, CA 91010 Characterization of human gastrointestinal hormones
R01DK-33165-08 (GMA) STENSON, WILLIAM F JEWISH HOSPITAL 216 S KINGSHIGHWAY ST LOUIS, MO 63110 Lipoxygenase products and inflammatory bowel disease
R01DK-33201-08 (MET) KAHN, C RONALD JOSLIN DIABETES CENTER, INC. ONE JOSLIN PLACE BOSTON, MA 02215 Insulin receptor phosphorylation and insulin action
R01DK-33209-08 (GMA) GHISHAN, FAYEZ K VANDERBILT UNIVERSITY MED CTR D-4130 MEDICAL CTR NORTH NASHVILLE, TN 37232 Development of intestinal transport of Ca++ and Pi
R01DK-33214-08 (NTN) FLATT, JEAN-PIERRE UNIV OF MASACHUSETTS MED CTR 55 LAKE AVENUE NORTH WORCESTER, MA 01655 Dietary fat, carbohydrate balance and weight maintenance
R01DK-33225-07 (EDC) GOETZ, FREDERICK G UNIVERSITY OF MINNESOTA 516 DELAWARE ST S E MINNEAPOLIS, MN 55455 Insulin C-peptide, youth, age & diabetes--Community study
R01DK-33231-08 (NTN) COHEN, HARVEY J UNIV OF ROCHESTER MED CTR 601 ELMWOOD AVENUE, BOX 777 ROCHESTER, NY 14642 Selenium nutrition - effects on blood cell function
R01DK-33239-08A1 (GMA) LICHTENBERGER, LENARD M UNIV OF TEXAS MED SCH P O BOX 20708 HOUSTON, TX 77225 Role of GI phospholipids in ulcer protection
R01DK-33243-08 (PHY) LEWIS, SIMON A UNIVERSITY OF TEXAS MED BRANCH 301 UNIVERSITY BOULEVARD GALVESTON, TX 77550 Regulation of epithelial transport
R55DK-33248-07 (PYB) GIBBS, JAMES G, JR NEW YORK HOSP CORNELL MED CTR 21 BLOOMINGDALE RD WHITE PLAINS, NY 10605 Peripheral and central satiety actions of bombesin
R01DK-33273-08 (SSS) JENSEN, DENNIS M UNIVERSITY OF CALIFORNIA BUILDING 115 LOS ANGELES, CA 90073-1792 Studies of ulcer hemorrhage and endoscopic hemostasis
R01DK-33289-08 (BIO) RHEAD, WILLIAM J UNIVERSITY OF IOWA 200 HAWKINS DR IOWA CITY, IA 52242 Inherited disorders of oxidative metabolism in man
R01DK-33293-08 (SSS) WEINER, MICHAEL W VA MEDICAL CENTER (11M) 4150 CLEMENT STREET SAN FRANCISCO, CALIF 94121 1H and 31P NMR of human kidney, heart and tumors
R01DK-33301-08 (MET) ABUMRAD, NADA A VANDERBILT U. MEDICAL SCHOOL 602 LIGHT HALL NASHVILLE, TN 37232 Fatty acid transporter--regulation identification
R01DK-33314-08A1 (PBC) ARONSON, NATHAN N, JR PENNSYLVANIA STATE UNIVERSITY 308 ALTHOUSE LABORATORY UNIVERSITY PARK, PA 16802 Glycoprotein degradation by lysosomes

PROJECT NO., ORGANIZATIONAL UNIT., INVESTIGATOR, ADDRESS, TITLE

R01DK-33326-07 (CTY) DUNN, WILLIAM A, JR UNIVERSITY OF FLORIDA J.H.M.H.C., BOX J-235 GAINESVILLE, FL 32610 Studies on the mechanism of autophagy

R01DK-33345-07 (EI) NUGENT, DIANE J UNIVERSITY OF WISCONSIN 1300 UNIVERSITY AVENUE MADISON, WI 53706 Human monoclonal antibodies

R01DK-33349-06 (GMA) RAMASWAMY, KRISHNAMURTHY UNIVERSITY OF ILLINOIS 840 SOUTH WOOD STREET CHICAGO, IL 60612 Transport mechanisms in the human small intestine

R01DK-33351-06 (ORTH) HAUSSLER, MARK R UNIVERSITY OF ARIZONA HLTH CTR DEPT OF BIOCHEMISTRY TUCSON, ARIZ 85724 Vitamin D hormone mechanism of action in cultured cells

R01DK-33352-06 (GMB) RAYSON, BARBARA M CORNELL UNIV MEDICAL COLLEGE 1300 YORK AVENUE NEW YORK, N Y 10021 Regulation of renal Na/K-ATPase activity

R01DK-33357-22 (RNM) MC AFEE, JOHN G GEORGE WASHINGTON UNIVERSITY 901 23RD STREET N W WASHINGTON, D C 20037 Nuclear diagnostic methods for renal disease

R01DK-33436-09 (GMA) ANWER, MOHAMMED S TUFTS UNIVERSITY 200 WESTBORO ROAD NORTH GRAFTON, MA 01536 Mechanism of canalicular bile formation and cholestasis

R01DK-33445-09 (MEDB) MC LACHLAN, ALAN SCRIPPS CLINIC & RES FOUNDATIO 10666 NORTH TORREY PINES ROAD LA JOLLA, CA 92037 Human PFK isozymes-- Biochemical and genetic studies

R01DK-33460-09 (BIO) POWERS-LEE, SUSAN G NORTHEASTERN UNIVERSITY 360 HUNTINGTON AVE BOSTON, MA 02115 Regulation of the activity of the urea cycle

R01DK-33466-11 (SAT) GOZZO, JAMES J NORTHEASTERN UNIV-COLL OF PHAR & ALLIED HEALTH BOSTON, MA 02115 Induction of specific unresponsiveness to allografts

R01DK-33470-08 (SAT) LAFFERTY, KEVIN J UNIVERSITY OF COLORADO 4200 EAST NINTH AVENUE DENVER, COLO 80262 Reversal of diabetes by islet transplantation

P01DK-33487-05 (SRC) ALPERS, DAVID H WASHINGTON UNIVERSITY 660 SOUTH EUCLID, BOX 8124 ST. LOUIS, MO 63110 Gastrointestinal proteins cellular and molecular regulation

P01DK-33487-05 0001 (SRC) SHONFELD, GUSTAV Gastrointestinal proteins cellular and molecular regulation Biosynthesis, expression of apolipoproteins in intestine, liver

P01DK-33487-05 0002 (SRC) STENSON, WILLIAM Gastrointestinal proteins cellular and molecular regulation Lipid-protein in interactions in intestinal membranes

P01DK-33487-05 0003 (SRC) STRAUSS, ARNOLD W Gastrointestinal proteins cellular and molecular regulation Biosynthesis and structure of rat disaccharidases

P01DK-33487-05 0004 (SRC) MACDERMOTT, RICHARD P Gastrointestinal proteins cellular and molecular regulation Antibody secretion by intestinal and bone marrow mononuclear cells

P01DK-33487-05 0005 (SRC) ALPERS, DAVID H Gastrointestinal proteins cellular and molecular regulation Structure and function of bobalamin-binding proteins

P01DK-33487-05 0006 (SRC) ROSENBLUM, JERRY Gastrointestinal proteins cellular and molecular regulation Digestive enzymes--immunoassay and metabolism

P01DK-33487-05 9001 (SRC) GRANT, GREG Gastrointestinal proteins cellular and molecular regulation Core A--Laboratory of biomolecular chemistry

P01DK-33487-05 9002 (SRC) DESCHRYVER, KATHERINE Gastrointestinal proteins cellular and molecular regulation Core B--Morphology

P01DK-33487-05 9003 (SRC) MACDERMOTT, RICHARD Gastrointestinal proteins cellular and molecular regulation Core C--Tissue culture

R01DK-33488-08 (HEM) ESCHBACH, JOSEPH W, JR UNIVERSITY OF WASHINGTON DIVISION OF HEMATOLOGY SEATTLE, WA 98195 Factors suppressing erythropoiesis in renal failure

R01DK-33491-07 (GMA) ISENBERG, JON I UCSD MEDICAL CENTER#8413 225 DICKINSON ST SAN DIEGO, CA 92103-8413 Duodenal mucosal bicarbonate secretion in humans

R01DK-33500-09 (BIO) YAMADA, TADATAKA UNIVERSITY OF MICHIGAN MED CTR 3912 TAUBMAN CENTER ANN ARBOR, MI 48109-0368 Chemistry and biology of gut somatostatin

P01DK-33506-08 (DDK) WALKER, W ALLAN MASSACHUSETTS GENERAL HOSPITAL BOSTON, MA 02114 Barrier functions of the GI tract in health and disease

P01DK-33506-08 0001 (DDK) WALKER, W ALLAN Barrier functions of the GI tract in health and disease Uptake of intestinal macromolecules

P01DK-33506-08 0003 (DDK) BLOCH, KURT J Barrier functions of the GI tract in health and disease Experimental allergic gastroenteropathy

P01DK-33506-08 0006 (DDK) HARMATZ, PAUL Barrier functions of the GI tract in health and disease Dietary antigen interaction with milk cells in the neonate

P01DK-33506-08 0007 (DDK) MADARA, JAMES Barrier functions of the GI tract in health and disease Intestinal disease--Epithelial neutrophil interaction

P01DK-33506-08 0008 (DDK) BHAN, ATUL Barrier functions of the GI tract in health and disease Biology of mucosal lymphocytes

P01DK-33506-08 0009 (DDK) WERSHIL, BARRY Barrier functions of the GI tract in health and disease Mass cells in IgE dependent gastric inflammation and antigen uptake

P01DK-33506-08 0010 (DDK) AUSUBEL, FREDERICK Barrier functions of the GI tract in health and disease Molecular biology of enterobacteria that populate GI tract

P01DK-33506-08 9001 (DDK) MOSCICKI, RICHARD Barrier functions of the GI tract in health and disease Core--Flow cytometry

P01DK-33506-08 9002 (DDK) AUSUBEL, FREDERICK Barrier functions of the GI tract in health and disease Core--Molecular biology

R01DK-33538-08 (BIO) HANAHAN, DONALD J UNIV OF TEXAS HLTH SCI CTR 7703 FLOYD CURL DRIVE SAN ANTONIO, TX 78284-7760 AGEPC--A potent lipid biochemical mediator in liver

R01DK-33547-07 (SB) PORRECA, FRANK F UNIVERSITY OF ARIZONA DEPARTMENT OF PHARMACOLOGY TUCSON, AZ 85724 Spinal and brain modulation of gastrointestinal motility

R01DK-33554-06 (SAT) BELZER, FOLKERT O UNIVERSITY OF WISCONSIN 600 HIGHLAND AVENUE MADISON, WI 53792 Pancreatic preservation for clinical transplantation

PROJECT NO., ORGANIZATIONAL UNIT., INVESTIGATOR, ADDRESS, TITLE

R01DK-33559-07 (SAT) LEVIN, ROBERT M HOSP OF THE UNIV OF PENNSYLVAN 3400 SPRUCE STREET PHILADELPHIA, PA 19104 Metabolic regulation of urinary bladder function

R01DK-33594-07 (GMA) GRANGER, DANIEL N LOUISIANA STATE UNIV MED CTR P O BOX 33932/1501 KINGS HIGHW SHREVEPORT, LA 71130-3932 Intestinal ischemia: role of oxygen radicals

R01DK-33612-08 (GMB) ERLIJ, DAVID J UNIVERSITY OF NEW YORK 450 CLARKSON AVENUE BROOKLYN, N Y 11203 Regulation of transport in epithelia

R01DK-33627-07 (PHY) STONE, DENNIS K U OF TEX SW MED CEN AT DALLAS 5323 HARRY HINES BLVD DALLAS, TX 75235 Reconstitution of renal acidification mechanisms

R01DK-33640-09 (PHY) DUNHAM, PHILIP B SYRACUSE UNIVERSITY 130 COLLEGE PLACE SYRACUSE, NY 13210 Cation transport in erythrocytes

R37DK-33649-09 (MET) OLEFSKY, JERROLD M UNIV OF CA AT SAN DIEGO DEPT OF MED/M-023E LA JOLLA, CA 92093-0934 Mechanisms of insulin resistance in man

R01DK-33651-09 (MET) OLEFSKY, JERROLD M UNIV OF CA, SAN DIEGO LA JOLLA, CA 90293 Insulin receptors and the glucose transport system

R01DK-33655-06 (HED) SORENSON, ROBERT UNIVERSITY OF MINNESOTA 321 CHURCH STREET, SE MINNEAPOLIS, MN 55455 Islet cell coupling and secretion in pregnancy

R01DK-33665-08 (PTHA) ABBOUD, HANNA E UNIV OF TEXAS HLTH SCIENCE CEN 7703 LOYD CURL DRIVE SAN ANTONIO, TEXAS 78284-7882 Inflammatory mediators and glomerular cells in culture

R01DK-33694-08 (PTHA) MADAIO, MICHAEL P RENAL ELECTROLYTE SECTION 422 CURIE BLVD PHILADELPHIA, PA 19104 Immunologic mechanisms in lupus nephritis

R01DK-33727-07 (ECS) JOHNSON, J DAVID PHYSIOLOGICAL CHEMISTRY 333 W. TENTH AVE COLUMBUS, OHIO 43210 Calcium and calmodulin in smooth muscle contraction

R01DK-33729-07 (SSS) MARSH, DONALD J UNIV OF SOUTHERN CALIFORNIA 1333 SAN PABLO STREET LOS ANGELES, CA 90033 Simulation of the renal medulla

R01DK-33749-05 (MET) STUART, CHARLES A UNIVERSITY OF TEXAS MED BRANCH OJSH 4 174, E68 GALVESTON, TX 77550 The insulin resistance of acanthosis nigricans

R01DK-33765-08 (PB) WAXMAN, DAVID J DANA-FARBER CANCER INSTITUTE 44 BINNEY STREET BOSTON, MA 02115 Cytochrome P-450--Endogenous substrate metabolism

R01DK-33790-09 (MET) SOELDNER, JOHN S UNIVERSITY OF CA SCH OF MED 1625 ALHAMBRA PLAZA SUITE 2901 SACRAMENTO, CA 95816 Pathogenesis of type I diabetes in monozygotic twins

R01DK-33793-08 (GMB) ARONSON, PETER S YALE UNIVERSITY SCHOOL MED 333 CEDAR STREET NEW HAVEN, CT 06510 Molecular mechanisms of proximal tubular ion transport

R01DK-33804-08 (MET) SALTIEL, ALAN R THE UNIVERISTY OF MICHIGAN MEDICAL SCHOOL ANN ARBOR, MI 48109-0622 Molecular mechanisms of insulin action

R01DK-33814-06 (GMB) TUNE, BRUCE M STANFORD UNIVERISTY SCHOOL OF MEDICINE STANFORD, CA 94305-5119 Tubular cell metabolism and antibiotic nephrotoxicity

R01DK-33823-08 (MET) PESSIN, JEFFREY E UNIV OF IOWA IOWA CITY, IA 52242 Regulation of the insulin receptor kinase

R01DK-33835-08 (OBM) QUISSELL, DAVID O UNIVERSITY OF COLORADO 1300 S POTOMAC ST AURORA, CO 80012 Primary culture of salivary gland cells

R01DK-33850-06 (GMA) REEVE, JOSEPH R, JR CURE/VA WADSWORTH/RM 203 WILSHIRE AND SAWTELLE BLVDS LOS ANGELES, CA 90073 Gastrointestinal physiology of cholecystokinin

R01DK-33861-07 (PTHA) BROWNLEE, MICHAEL A A. EINSTEIN COLLEGE OF MED. 1300 MORRIS PARK AVENUE BRONX, NY 10461 Glucose-derived cross-links and diabetic pathology

R01DK-33873-07 (IMS) LERNMARK, AKE UNIVERSITY OF WASHINGTON DEPARTMENT OF MEDICINE, RG-20 SEATTLE, WA 98195 Isolation of islet cell autoantigens

R01DK-33880-08 (IMS) MC DEVITT, HUGH O STANFORD UNIV. SCH OF MEDICINE D345 FAIRCHILD BUILDING STANFORD, CALIF 94305 Allele specific prevention of diabetes mellitus

R01DK-33883-07 (GMA) VIERLING, JOHN M CEDARS-SINAI MEDICAL CENTER 8700 BEVERLY BLVD, SUITE 7511 LOS ANGELES, CA 90048 Hepatic lesions in murine chronic graft-vs-host disease

R01DK-33886-06 (MGN) BAUMANN, HEINZ ROSWELL PARK CANCER INST ELM & CARLTON STREETS BUFFALO, NY 14263 Genetic regulation of the hepatic acute phase response

R01DK-33938-08 (MBY) MAQUAT, LYNNE E ROSWELL PARK CANCER INSTITUTE ELM & CARLTON STREETS BUFFALO, NY 14263 Regulation of normal and defective human genes

R01DK-33941-08 (PTHA) MAKKER, SUDESH P UNIVERSITY OF CALIFORNIA DAVIS 2516 STOCKTON BLVD SACRAMENTO, CA 95817 Pathogenesis of membranous glomerulonephropathy

P01DK-33949-09 (ADDK) COE, FREDRIC L UNIVERSITY OF CHICAGO 5481 S MARYLAND AVENUE, BOX 28 CHICAGO, IL 60637 Specialized center of research in urolithiasis

R01DK-33952-08 (SAT) WOLFE, ROBERT R SHRINERS BURNS INSTITUTE 610 TEXAS AVENUE GALVESTON, TX 77550 Glucose metabolism in septic patients

R01DK-33973-08A1 (END) PUETT, J DAVID UNIVERSITY OF MIAMI SCH OF MED PO BOX 016960 MIAMI, FL 33101 HCG structure-function relationships

Z01DK-34001-26 (LMB) FELSENFELD, G NIDDK, NIH Chromatin structure and function

Z01DK-34002-27 (LMB) DAVIES, D R NIDDK, NIH Enzyme structure

Z01DK-34003-23 (LMB) DAVIES, D R NIDDK, NIH Three-dimensional structure of cytokines, receptors and immune system proteins

R01DK-34013-07 (PHRA) LEE, VINCENT H UNIVERSITY OF SOUTHERN CALIF 1985 ZONAL AVENUE LOS ANGELES, CALIF 90033 Cellular uptake and degradation of liposomes in liver

P01DK-34039-06A1 (DDK) GABOW, PATRICIA A UNIV OF COLORADO HEALTH SCIS C 4200 EAST NINTH AVENUE DENVER, CO 80262 Human polycystic kidney disease

P01DK-34039-06A1 0006 (DDK) KIMBERLING, WILLIAM Human polycystic kidney disease Genetic studies in polycystic kidney disease

PROJECT NO., ORGANIZATIONAL UNIT., INVESTIGATOR, ADDRESS, TITLE

P01DK-34039-06A1 0007 (DDK) GABOW, PATRICIA Human polycystic kidney disease Natural history of autosomal dominant polycystic kidney disease
P01DK-34039-06A1 9001 (DDK) GABOW, PATRICIA A Human polycystic kidney disease Core-- Human ADPKD patient population
P01DK-34039-06A1 9002 (DDK) JOHNSON, MICHAEL L Human polycystic kidney disease Core-- Imaging techniques for ADPKD
P01DK-34039-06A1 0002 (DDK) SCHRIER, ROBERT W Human polycystic kidney disease Hypertension in autosomal dominant polycystic kidney disease
P01DK-34039-06A1 0004 (DDK) EVERSON, GREGORY T Human polycystic kidney disease Hormonal regulation of hepatic cystic disease in ADPKD
R01DK-34045-06 (MGN) DESNICK, ROBERT J MOUNT SINAI SCHOOL OF MEDICINE 100TH STREET & FIFTH AVE NEW YORK, NY 10029 Fabry disease--Molecular and model therapeutic studies
R01DK-34049-08 (GMB) NORMAN, JILL UNIVERSITY OF CALIFORNIA UCLA SCHOOL OF MEDICINE LOS ANGELES, CA 90024-1406 Compensatory hypertrophy of the kidney
R37DK-34083-10 (HEM) LUX, SAMUEL E, IV CHILDREN'S HOSPITAL CORP 300 LONGWOOD AVENUE BOSTON, MASS 02115 Pathophysiology of red cell membrane diseases
R01DK-34108-06A1 (EDC) FARRELL, PHILIP M CLINICAL SCIENCE CTR 600 HIGHLAND AVENUE MADISON, WI 53792 Pulmonary benefits of cystic fibrosis neonatal screening
R01DK-34110-06 (GMA) SEIDEL, EDWARD R EAST CAROLINA UNIVERSITY SCHOOL OF MEDICINE GREENVILLE, NC 27858 Polyamines in the regulation of gastrointestinal growth
R01DK-34127-07 (GMB) IVES, HARLAN E UNIVERSITY OF CALIFORNIA 1065 HEALTH SCIENCES E TOWER SAN FRANCISCO, CALIF 94143 Regulation of Na/H exchange in renal and non-renal cells
R01DK-34128-07 (PC) COBB, MELANIE H U T SOUTHWESTERN MEDICAL CENTE 5323 HARRY HINES BLVD DALLAS, TX 75235-9041 Insulin-enhanced phosphorylation of ribosomal protein S6
R01DK-34148-06 (GMA) OUYANG, ANN HOSP OF UNIV OF PENNSYLVANIA 3400 SPRUCE STREET PHILADELPHIA, PA 19104-4283 Receptor pharmacy and physiology of gut peptides
R01DK-34151-08 (GMA) GRAHAM, MARTIN F MEDICAL COLLEGE OF VIRGINIA BOX 529, MCV STATION RICHMOND, VA 23298 Intestinal stricture formation in Crohn's disease
R01DK-34153-06 (GMA) GRIDER, JOHN R MEDICAL COLLEGE OF VIRGINIA BOX 711-MCV STATION RICHMOND, VA 23298-0711 Role of gut peptides in intestinal peristalsis
R01DK-34171-07 (END) CARTER-SU, CHRISTIN UNIVERSITY OF MICHIGAN 1301 CATHERINE ST ANN ARBOR, MI 48109-0622 Growth hormone receptors and action
R37DK-34198-07 (PTHA) COUSER, WILLIAM G UNIVERSITY OF WASHINGTON 1959 NE PACIFIC AVE SEATTLE, WA 98195 Distal complement components in immune renal injury
R01DK-34208-08 (GMB) FORREST, JOHN N YALE UNIVERSITY 333 CEDAR STREET NEW HAVEN, CONN 06510 Adenosine receptors and ion transport in epithelia
R01DK-34232-08 (SB) HARDY, MARK A COLUMBIA UNIVERSITY 630 WEST 168TH STREET NEW YORK, N Y 10032 Pancreatic islet xenograft transplantation with UV
R01DK-34234-07 (PTHA) TROYER, DEAN A U. OF TX H.S.C. AT SAN ANTONIO 7703 FLOYD CURL DRIVE SAN ANTONIO, TX 78284 Phospholipids, diabetes, and glomerular pathology
R01DK-34238-06 (EDC) DICKSON, EDGAR R MAYO FOUNDATION 200 FIRST STREET SOUTHWEST ROCHESTER, MN 55905 Chronic liver diseases: survival models and application
R01DK-34275-07 (PTHA) WEINBERG, JOEL M DIV OF NEPHROLOGY (BOX 0364) 3914 TAUBMAN HEALTH CARE CEN ANN ARBOR, MICHIGAN 48109 Cellular pathophysiology of acute renal failure
R01DK-34281-07 (MEDB) LEVINE, MICHAEL A JOHNS HOPKINS UNIV SCH OF MED 725 N WOLFE STREET BALTIMORE, MD 21205 Nucleotide regulatory unit of adenylate cyclase
R01DK-34286-08 (GMA) RABON, EDD C CURE/VAMC WADSWORTH WILSHIRE & SAWTELLE BLVDS LOS ANGELES, CA 90073 Gastric acid secretion, regulation of K+ transporters
R01DK-34306-08 (GMA) YAMADA, TADATAKA UNIVERSITY OF MICHIGAN MED CTR 3912 TAUBMAN CENTER ANN ARBOR, MI 48109-0362 Gastrointestinal significance of gastrin regulation
R01DK-34316-07 (GMB) MC DONOUGH, ALICIA A UNIV OF SOUTHERN CALIFORNIA 1333 SAN PABLO STREET LOS ANGELES, CA 90033 Regulation of sodium pumps in the kidney
R01DK-34357-08 (BIO) ROY-CHOWDHURY, JAYANTA ALBERT EINSTEIN COLL OF MED 1300 MORRIS PARK AVENUE BRONX, N Y 10461 Inherited disorders of bilirubin glucuronidation
R01DK-34384-08 (MBY) BIRKENMEIER, EDWARD H THE JACKSON LABORATORY 600 MAIN STREET BAR HARBOR, ME 04609-0800 Human and mouse GPDH--Molecular structure and regulation
R01DK-34388-07 (MET) TURK, JOHN W WASHINGTON UNIV SCH OF MED BOX 8118 660 EUCLID AVE ST. LOUIS, MO 63110 Phospholipid-derived mediators and insulin secretion
R01DK-34389-09 (PC) ROSENZWEIG, STEVEN A MEDICAL UNIV OF SOUTH CAROLINA 171 ASHLEY AVENUE CHARLESTON, S C 29425 Structure and function of cholecystokinin receptors
R01DK-34394-08 (GMB) HAMM, L LEE WASHINGTON UNIV SCH OF MED 660 S EUCLID ST LOUIS, MO 63110 Urinary buffer transport and metabolism
R01DK-34397-08 (MET) ENSINCK, JOHN W UNIVERSITY OF WASHINGTON SEATTLE, WA 98195 Pro-somatostatin related peptides
R01DK-34400-08 (SSS) SHACKLETON, CEDRIC H CHILDREN'S HOSP./OAKLAND R. I. 747 52ND STREET OAKLAND, CA 94609 Endocrinological investigations by gas chromatography and mass spectrometry
R01DK-34422-08 (GMA) PODOLSKY, DANIEL K MASSACHUSETTS GENERAL HOSPITAL GASTROINTESTINAL UNIT BOSTON, MASS 02114 Colonic glycoproteins--Role in inflammatory bowel disease
R01DK-34427-06 (END) FUJITA-YAMAGUCHI, YOKO BECKMAN RESEARCH INSTITUTE 1450 EAST DUARTE ROAD DUARTE, CA 91010 Structure and function of peptide hormone receptors
R01DK-34431-07 (HEM) TOROK-STORB, BEVERLY J FRED HUTCHINSON CANCER RES CTR 1124 COLUMBIA STREET SEATTLE, WA 98104 Regulation of hematopoiesis
R01DK-34447-09 (MET) BOYD, AUBREY E, III NEW ENGLAND MEDICAL CENTER 750 WASHINGTON ST, BOX 268 BOSTON, MA 02111 Regulation of insulin release by calcium
R01DK-34449-06 (BCE) CHEN, CHING-LING C THE POPULATION COUNCIL 1230 YORK AVENUE NEW YORK, NY 10021 Intratesticular regulation of inhibin and POMC genes
R01DK-34475-06 (PHRA) BURCKART, GILBERT J UNIVERSITY OF PITTSBURGH 721 SALK HALL PITTSBURGH, PA 15261 Drug disposition in liver transplant patients
U01DK-34495-07 (DDK) HUNSICKER, LAWRENCE G UNIVERSITY OF IOWA HOSPITALS IOWA CITY, IOWA 52242 The modification of diet in renal disease (MDRD) study
U01DK-34513-07 (DDK) KOPPLE, JOEL D HARBOR-UCLA MEDICAL CENTER 1000 W CARSON STREET TORRANCE, CA 90509 The modification of diet in renal disease (MDRD) study
U01DK-34516-07 (DDK) LEVEY, ANDREW S NEW ENGLAND MED CTR HOSPS, INC 750 WASHINGTON STREET BOSTON, MASS 02111 Modification of diet in renal disease (MDRD) study
R01DK-34533-07 (PHY) STANTON, BRUCE A DARTMOUTH MEDICAL SCHOOL HANOVER, N H 03756 Cellular mechanisms of renal distal tubule ion transport
U01DK-34534-07 (DDK) TESCHAN, PAUL E VANDERBILT UNIV MEDICAL CENTER 422 MEDICAL ARTS BUILDING NASHVILLE, TN 37232-1371 Modification of diet in renal disease (MDRD) study
R01DK-34540-07 (END) JACKSON, IVOR M RHODE ISLAND HOSPITAL 593 EDDY STREET PROVIDENCE, RI 02903 Secretion of TRH and other neural peptides
R01DK-34549-07 (TMP) FEYEREISEN, RENE UNIVERSITY OF ARIZONA FORBES BLDG, RM 410 TUCSON, AZ 85721 Regulation of insect juvenile hormone biosynthesis
R01DK-34574-06 (GMA) HSUEH, WEI CHILDREN'S MEMORIAL HOSPITAL 2300 CHILDREN'S PLAZA CHICAGO, IL 60614 Pathogenesis of experimental bowel necrosis
P01DK-34576-06 (DDK) SHULMAN, ROBERT G YALE UNIVERSITY 333 CEDAR STREET NEW HAVEN, CT 06510 Spectroscopic studies of metabolism in humans
P01DK-34576-06 0001 (DDK) PRICHARD, JAMES W Spectroscopic studies of metabolism in humans NMR studies of the human brain
P01DK-34576-06 0002 (DDK) SHULMAN, GERALD Spectroscopic studies of metabolism in humans NMR analysis of glycogen metabolism in human liver
P01DK-34576-06 0003 (DDK) SIEGEL, NORMAN Spectroscopic studies of metabolism in humans NMR studies of orthotopic human kidney
P01DK-34576-06 9001 (DDK) SHULMAN, ROBERT G Spectroscopic studies of metabolism in humans NMR core
R01DK-34583-08 (GMA) LAMONT, JOHN T UNIVERSITY HOSPITAL 88 E NEWTON STREET BOSTON, MA 02118 Intestinal mechanisms of C. difficile toxins
R01DK-34668-05 (GMA) STERNLIEB, IRMIN ALBERT EINSTEIN COLLEGE OF MED 1300 MORRIS PARK AVENUE BRONX, NY 10461 Copper metabolism in human hepatocyte derived cell line
R01DK-34706-07 (RNM) STADALNIK, ROBERT C UNIVERSITY OF CALIFORNIA 4301 X STREET SACRAMENTO, CA 95817 Tc-99m NGA in the evaluation of liver disease
R01DK-34738-08 (MET) HUTSON, SUSAN M BOWMAN GRAY SCHOOL OF MEDICINE MEDICAL CENTER BOULEVARD WINSTON-SALEM, NC 27157 Branched chain amino acid metabolism in skeletal muscle
R01DK-34774-06 (SAT) OROSZ, CHARLES G OHIO STATE UNIVERSITY HOSPITAL 259 MEANS HALL, 1654 UPHAM DRI COLUMBUS, OH 43210 lymphocyte endothelial interactions in rejection
R01DK-34793-07 (PTHA) LIANOS, ELIAS A MEDICAL COLLEGE WISCONSIN 9200 WEST WISCONSIN AVENUE MILWAUKEE, WI 53226 Novel inflammatory mediators in glomerulonephritis
R01DK-34804-06 (PB) JOSEPH, SURESH K UNIVERSITY OF PENNSYLVANIA 601 GODDARD LABS/6089 PHILADELPHIA, PA 19104 Mechanism of action of inositol triphosphate
R01DK-34807-08 (CBY) PEERCE, BRIAN E UNIVERSITY OF TEXAS 301 UNIVERSITY BOULEVARD GALVESTON, TEXAS 77550 Molecular mechanism of Na/glucose cotransport
R01DK-34814-06 (SB) SILVERSTEIN, FRED E UNIVERSITY OF WASHINGTON GASTROENTEROLOGY, RG-24 SEATTLE, WA 98195 Intestinal wall investigation by endoscopic echo probe
R01DK-34817-07 (MET) WOLFE, ROBERT R SHRINERS BURNS INSTITUTE 610 TEXAS AVENUE GALVESTON, TX 77550-2774 The role of substrate cycling in energy metabolism
R01DK-34818-07 (EDC) ORCHARD, TREVOR J UNIVERSITY OF PITTSBURGH 130 DESOTO STREET PITTSBURGH, PA 15261 Epidemiology of diabetic complications
R01DK-34822-06 (GMB) RUSSELL, JOHN ALBERT EINSTEIN COLL OF MED 1300 MORRIS PARK AVENUE BRONX, NY 10461 Vitamin D metabolites and parathyroid hormone production
R01DK-34824-07 (MET) MELMED, SHLOMO CEDARS-SINAI MEDICAL CENTER 8700 BEVERLY BLVD LOS ANGELES, CALIF 90048 Insulin action on polypeptide hormone expression
R01DK-34839-06 (END) DI STEFANO, JOSEPH J, III UNIVERSITY OF CALIFORNIA 4731 BELTER HALL LOS ANGELES, CA 90024 Metabolism and enterohepatic regulation of thyroid hormones
P30DK-34854-08 (DDK) SILEN, WILLIAM BETH ISRAEL HOSPITAL 330 BROOKLINE AVE BOSTON, MA 02215 Structure-function relationships in the alimentary tract
P30DK-34854-08 0011 (DDK) KARNIK, PRATIMA S Structure-function relationships in the alimentary tract Pilot study--regulation of gastrin gene promoter by somatostatin
P30DK-34854-08 0012 (DDK) REINHART, FREDERICK Structure-function relationships in the alimentary tract Pilot study-effects of exocytosis on tight junctions
P30DK-34854-08 9003 (DDK) CAREY, MARTIN C Structure-function relationships in the alimentary tract Core--Membrane preparation and analysis
P30DK-34854-08 9004 (DDK) TRIER, JERRY S Structure-function relationships in the alimentary tract Core--Morphology
P30DK-34854-08 9006 (DDK) WALKER, W. ALLAN Structure-function

PROJECT NO., ORGANIZATIONAL UNIT., INVESTIGATOR, ADDRESS, TITLE

relationships in the alimentary tract Core--immunology
R01DK-34878-06 (SAT) NAJI, ALI UNIVERSITY OF PENNSYLVANIA 3400 SPRUCE ST PHILADELPHIA, PA 19104 Deletion of passenger cells from organ allografts
R01DK-34891-07 (PTHA) AVNER, ELLIS D CHILDREN'S HOSPITAL 4800 SAND POINT WAY, N.E. SEATTLE, WASHINGTON 98105 Pathogenesis of congenital murine cystic nephrogenesis
R01DK-34900-02 (BIO) BUXBAUM, JOEL N NEW YORK VA MEDICAL CTR 408 FIRST AVENUE NEW YORK, NY 10010 Gene expression in familial and senile cardiac amyloid
R01DK-34909-07 (BMT) WRIGHT, PETER E RES INST OF SCRIPPS CLINIC 10666 NORTH TORREY PINES ROAD LA JOLLA, CA 92037 Conformation and dynamics of hemoglobins and myoglobins
P30DK-34914-06 (DDK) SIMON, FRANCIS R UNIVERSITY OF COLORADO 4200 EAST NINTH AVENUE DENVER, CO 80262 Hepatobiliary center
P30DK-34914-06 0008 (DDK) MAPOLES, JOHN Hepatobiliary center Pilot study-- Cloning the sodium-dependent bile acid transporter
P30DK-34914-06 0009 (DDK) EVERSON, GREGORY Hepatobiliary center Pilot study-- Functional characteristics of hepatic cystic epithelium in ADPKD
P30DK-34914-06 0010 (DDK) BROWN, JERRY Hepatobiliary center Pilot study-- Regulation of expression of sets of liver specific genes
P30DK-34914-06 0011 (DDK) FRANZUSOFF, ALEX Hepatobiliary center Pilot study-- Analysis of highly conserved liver Golgi protein function
P30DK-34914-06 0012 (DDK) SARNOW, PETER Hepatobiliary center Pilot study-- Translation of hepatitis B virus pregenomic mRNA in human liver
P30DK-34914-06 0013 (DDK) SIDDIQUI, ALEEM Hepatobiliary center Pilot study-- Induction of viral acute hepatitis by hepatitis B virus genes
P30DK-34914-06 9002 (DDK) DAVIS, ROGER Hepatobiliary center Core--Cell culture laboratory
P30DK-34914-06 9005 (DDK) HOWELL, KATHRYN Hepatobiliary center Core-- Membrane biochemistry and biophysics laboratory
P30DK-34914-06 9006 (DDK) EVERSON, GREGORY Hepatobiliary center Core-- Chromatography and mass spectrometry laboratory
P30DK-34914-06 9007 (DDK) MOORHEAD, JOHN Hepatobiliary center Core-- Immunology laboratory
P30DK-34914-06 9008 (DDK) BROWN, JERRY Hepatobiliary center Core-- Biotechnology laboratory
R37DK-34926-08 (MET) ROTH, RICHARD A STANFORD UNIVERSITY 125 PANAMA ST STANFORD, CA 94305 Insulin degrading enzyme and the insulin receptor
P30DK-34928-07 (DDK) PLAUT, ANDREW G NEW ENGLAND MEDICAL CTR HOSP 750 WASHINGTON ST, BOX 006 BOSTON, MA 02111 GI research on absorptive and secretory processes
P30DK-34928-07 9001 (DDK) PLAUT, ANDREW GI research on absorptive and secretory processes Core--Intestinal microbiology
P30DK-34928-07 9002 (DDK) GOODMAN, RICHARD H GI research on absorptive and secretory processes Core--Molecular biology
P30DK-34928-07 9003 (DDK) DONOWITZ, MARK GI research on absorptive and secretory processes Core--Fluorescent probe
P30DK-34928-07 9004 (DDK) GRAND, RICHARD J GI research on absorptive and secretory processes Core--Cell culture
P30DK-34933-06A1 (DDK) YAMADA, TADATAKA UNIVERSITY OF MICHIGAN MED CTR ANN ARBOR, MI 48109-0362 Gastrointestinal hormone research core center
P30DK-34933-06A1 0009 (DDK) MONSOUR, ALFRED Gastrointestinal hormone research core center Pilot study--Opioid receptor in migrostriatal and hypothalamic-pituitary system
P30DK-34933-06A1 0010 (DDK) MEISLER, MIRIAM Gastrointestinal hormone research core center Site-specific mutagenesis of pancreas specific enhancers
P30DK-34933-06A1 0011 (DDK) HASLER, WILLIAM Gastrointestinal hormone research core center Pilot study--Protein kinase C in gastric smooth muscle contraction
P30DK-34933-06A1 9001 (DDK) MEISLER, MIRIAM H Gastrointestinal hormone research core center Core--Molecular biology
P30DK-34933-06A1 9002 (DDK) AKIL, HUDA Gastrointestinal hormone research core center Core--Biochemistry
P30DK-34933-06A1 9003 (DDK) WATSON, STANLEY J Gastrointestinal hormone research core center Core--histochemistry
P30DK-34933-06A1 9004 (DDK) VINIK, AARON I Gastrointestinal hormone research core center Core--Radioimmunoassay
P30DK-34933-06A1 9005 (DDK) WILSON, BARRY S Gastrointestinal hormone research core center Core--Tissue culture
P30DK-34933-06A1 9006 (DDK) WILLIAMS, JOHN Gastrointestinal hormone research core center Core--Cell biology
P30DK-34933-06A1 9007 (DDK) OWYANG, CHUNG Gastrointestinal hormone research core center Core--In vitro studies
R01DK-34944-07 (CBY) TSUI, LAP-CHEE THE HOSPITAL FOR SICK CHILDREN 555 UNIVERSITY AVENUE TORONTO, ONTARIO CANADA M5G 1X Molecular genetics of cystic fibrosis
R01DK-34949-07 (PBC) MEEZAN, ELIAS UNIV OF ALABAMA AT BIRMINGHAM UAB STATION BIRMINGHAM, AL 35294 Role of sulfation in the pathology of cystic fibrosis
R01DK-34972-07 (PTHA) ABRAHAMSON, DALE R UNIV OF ALABAMA AT BIRMINGHAM UAB STATION BIRMINGHAM, AL 35294 Laminin localization in glomerular basement membranes
P30DK-34987-06 (DDK) POWELL, DON W UNIV OF N C AT CHAPEL HILL CB #7080, 326 BURNETT-WOMACK CHAPEL HILL, N C 27599-7080 Digestive disease research core center
P30DK-34987-06 0006 (DDK) HASKILL, STEPHEN Digestive disease research core center Pilot study--Localization/induction of cytokines in inflammatory bowel disease
P30DK-34987-06 0007 (DDK) PETERS, B Digestive disease research core center Pilot study--Basal lamina biosynthesis by epithelial cells
P30DK-34987-06 0008 (DDK) RHOADS, J Digestive disease research core center Pilot study--Jejunal potassium transport in acute viral enteritis
P30DK-34987-06 9001 (DDK) CARTER, PHILIP B Digestive disease research core center Core--Barrier intact animal facility
P30DK-34987-06 9002 (DDK) GRIZZLE, JAMES E Digestive disease research core center Core--Biostatistics
P30DK-34987-06 9003 (DDK) MCPHERSON, C Digestive disease research core center Core-- Gnotobiotic-transgenic animal facility
P30DK-34987-06 9004 (DDK) LUND, P Digestive disease research core center Core--Molecular biology
P30DK-34987-06 9005 (DDK) PETRUSZ, PETER Digestive disease research core center Core--Immunoassay laboratory
P30DK-34989-08 (DDK) BOYER, JAMES L P O BOX 3333, 1080 LMP NEW HAVEN, CT 96510 Digestive diseases research core center
P30DK-34989-08 9004 (DDK) BOYER, JAMES L Digestive diseases research core center Core--Laboratory for liver cell morphology
P30DK-34989-08 9006 (DDK) RIELY, CAROLINE A Digestive diseases research core center Core--Clinical studies
P30DK-34989-08 0010 (DDK) WEISSMAN, SHERMAN M Digestive diseases research core center Characterization of MHC genes encoding secreted liver specific-antigens
P30DK-34989-08 0011 (DDK) FARQUHAR, MARILYN G Digestive diseases research core center Pilot study--Heparan sulfate proteoglycan traffic in rat liver
P30DK-34989-08 0012 (DDK) GORDON, ELLEN R Digestive diseases research core center Pilot study--Effect of cholestatic & choleratic agents on liver plasma membrane
P30DK-34989-08 0013 (DDK) MELLMAN, IRA Digestive diseases research core center Pilot study--Genetic analysis of the hepatocyte lysosomal membrane
P30DK-34989-08 0014 (DDK) BOYER, JAMES L Digestive diseases research core center Pilot study--Glutathione as primary driving force in bile formation
P30DK-34989-08 0015 (DDK) GORELICK, FRED Digestive diseases research core center Pilot--Identification and function of hepatocyte calmodulin kinase to substrates
P30DK-34989-08 0016 (DDK) SHULMAN, GERALD Digestive diseases research core center Pilot--NMR studies of the functional heterogeneity of hepatocytes
P30DK-34989-08 0017 (DDK) SZTUL, ELIZABETH Digestive diseases research core center Pilot--Reconstitution in vitro of vesicular traffic from the hepatic rough ER
P30DK-34989-08 9001 (DDK) GAUTAM, ANIL Digestive diseases research core center Core--Isolated hepatocyte and cell culture
P30DK-34989-08 9002 (DDK) GORDON, ELLEN R Digestive diseases research core center Core--Perfusion laboratory
P30DK-34989-08 9003 (DDK) BOYER, JAMES L Digestive diseases research core center Core--Liver membrane isolation
Z01DK-35000-27 (LMB) MILES, H T NIDDK, NIH Chemical and structural investigations of nucleic acids and related molecules
R01DK-35008-06 (SAT) KRENSKY, ALAN M STANFORD UNIV MEDICAL CENTER STANFORD, CA 94305-5119 Antigens in CTL mediated transplant rejection
R01DK-35039-03 (NTN) YOUNG, ELEANOR A UNIV OF TEXAS HEALTH SCI CTR 7703 FLOYD CURL DRIVE SAN ANTONIO, TX 78284-7878 Gastrointestinal & cardiac response to semi-starvation and refeeding
R01DK-35047-07 (ALY) SPIELMAN, RICHARD S UNIVERSITY OF PENNSYLVANIA CRB- 422 CURIE BOULEVARD PHILADELPHIA, PA 19104-6145 Type I diabetes & genes of the HLA-D region
R01DK-35065-06 (PHY) FAVUS, MURRAY J UNIVERSITY OF CHICAGO BOX 28/5841 S MARYLAND AVE CHICAGO, IL 60637 Hormonal control of renal 1,25(OH)2d3 biosynthesis
U01DK-35073-07 (DDK) WILLIAMS, GEORGE W CLEVELAND CLINIC FOUNDATION 9500 EUCLID AVE-ONE CLINIC CEN CLEVELAND, OHIO 44195 Central facilities modifying diet in renal disease
R01DK-35081-07 (ALY) PANGBURN, MICHAEL K UNIVERSITY OF TEXAS HLTH CTR P O BOX 2003 TYLER, TEX 75710 Activation of the alternative pathway of complement
R01DK-35083-07 (MBY) PFAHL, MAGNUS LA JOLLA CANCER RESEARCH FDN 10901 NORTH TORREY PINES ROAD LA JOLLA, CA 92037 Cloning and analysis of steroid receptor genes
R01DK-35090-08 (BMT) CHAMPION, PAUL M NORTHEASTERN UNIVERSITY 360 HUNTINGTON AVENUE BOSTON, MA 02115 Near ultraviolet Raman studies of cytochrome P450
P01DK-35098-06A1 (DDK) SCHRIER, ROBERT W UNIV OF COLORADO HLTH SCI CTR 4200 E 9TH AVENUE DENVER, CO 80262 Pathogenesis and prevention of renal cell injury
P01DK-35098-06A1 0006 (DDK) SCHRIER, ROBERT Pathogenesis and prevention of renal cell injury Proximal tubular injury-- Pathogenesis and modes of protection
P01DK-35098-06A1 0007 (DDK) CONGER, JOHN Pathogenesis and prevention of renal cell injury Mechanisms of vasotoxicity as prevention of cyclosporine nephrotoxicity
P01DK-35098-06A1 0008 (DDK) LINAS, STUART Pathogenesis and prevention of renal cell injury Neutrophil mediated injury to vascular smooth muscle and proximal tubule cells
P01DK-35098-06A1 9001 (DDK) BURKE, THOMAS Pathogenesis and prevention of renal cell injury Laboratory core
R37DK-35107-06 (END) GRANNER, DARYL K VANDERBILT UNIV SCH OF MED NASHVILLE, TN 37232-0615 Insulin receptors and insulin action
P01DK-35108-07 (DDK) KAGNOFF, MARTIN F UNIVERSITY OF CALIFORNIA LA JOLLA, CA 92093 Intestinal immune system in host-environment interaction
P01DK-35108-07 0001 (DDK) KAGNOFF, MARTIN F Intestinal immune system in host-environment interaction Pathogenesis of celiac disease
P01DK-35108-07 0002 (DDK) KAGNOFF, MARTIN F Intestinal immune system in host-environment interaction Peyer's patch T-cells and lymphokines
P01DK-35108-07 0003 (DDK) GILLIN, FRANCES Intestinal immune system in host-environment interaction Mucosal immune responses to human protozoa
P01DK-35108-07 0004 (DDK) GIGLI, IRMA Intestinal immune system in host-environment interaction Dermatitis herpetiformis--Immunological studies, complemental and Giardia
P01DK-35108-07 0006 (DDK) FIERER, JOSHUA Intestinal immune system in host-environment interaction Pathogenesis of Salmonella dublin intestinal infections

P01DK-35108-07 9001 (DDK) KAGNOFF, MARTIN F Intestinal immune system in host-environment interaction Tissue culture--Core
P01DK-35108-07 9002 (DDK) KAGNOFF, MARTIN F Intestinal immune system in host-environment interaction Murine breeding core
P01DK-35108-07 9003 (DDK) GUINEY, DONALD Intestinal immune system in host-environment interaction Molecular biology--Core
R01DK-35124-06 (PHY) VERKMAN, ALAN S UNIVERSITY OF CALIFORNIA 1065 HEALTH SCIENCES EAST SAN FRANCISCO, CA 94143 Mechanisms of water transport in renal epithelia
R01DK-35129-05 (RAD) GERACI, JOSEPH P UNIVERSITY OF WASHINGTON RADIOLOGICAL SCIENCES, SB-75 SEATTLE, WA 98195 Radiation - induced hepatic injury in the rat
R01DK-35142-06A2 (PTHA) ABRASS, CHRISTINE K VA MEDICAL CENTER (111A) 1660 SOUTH COLUMBIAN WAY SEATTLE, WA 98108 Immunopathologic studies of Heymann nephritis
R01DK-35143-06 (SAT) SOUTHARD, JAMES H UNIVERSITY OF WISCONSIN 600 HIGHLAND AVENUE MADISON, WI 53792 Liver preservation for clinical transplantation
R01DK-35153-07 (BMT) KINCAID, JAMES R MARQUETTE UNIVERSITY MILWAUKEE, WI 53233 Raman and time-resolved Raman studies of heme proteins
R01DK-35170-06 (PC) SHUKLA, SHIVENDRA D UNIVERSITY OF MISSOURI DEPARTMENT OF PHARMACOLOGY COLUMBIA, MO 65212 PAF stimulated phosphoinositide turnover in platelets
R01DK-35183-06 (GMA) FIELD, MICHAEL COLUMBIA UNIVERSITY 630 WEST 168TH STREET NEW YORK, N Y 10032 Regulation of epithelial fluid transport
R01DK-35187-07 (BBCB) KLEVIT, RACHEL E UNIVERSITY OF WASHINGTON DEPARTMENT OF BIOCHEM., SJ-70 SEATTLE, WA 98195 2D NMR studies of protein structure/function
R01DK-35191-06 (SAT) CHEUNG, LAURENCE Y UNIVERSITY OF KANSAS MEDICAL C 39TH AND RAINBOW BOULEVARD KANSAS CITY, KS 66103 Role of gastric blood flow in acute ulcerogenesis
R01DK-35193-06 (GMA) SELLIN, JOSEPH H UNIV OF TX HLTH SCI CTR/HOUSTO P O BOX 20708 HOUSTON, TX 77225 Cecum and proximal colon:Distinct transport epithelium
R01DK-35199-06 (END) LINDBERG, IRIS LOUISIANA STATE UNIVERSITY 1901 PERDIDO STREET NEW ORLEANS, LA 70112 Enkephalin biosynthesis in adrenal medulla
R01DK-35220-07 (BIO) DALE, GEORGE L UNIV OKLAHOMA HEALTH SCI CEN P.O. BOX 26901 OKLAHOMA CITY, OK 73190 Phosphoinositides in normal & abnormal human red cells
R01DK-35228-06 (SB) HARDY, MARK A COLUMBIA UNIV HEALTH SCIS 630 WEST 168TH STREET NEW YORK, NY 10032 Islet destruction in the etiology of diabetic BB rat
R01DK-35254-08 (BPO) BARTNESS, TIMOTHY J GEORGIA STATE UNIVERSITY UNIVERSITY PLAZA ATLANTA, GA 30303-3083 Photoperiodic control of obesity
R01DK-35275-07 (BIO) BRASH, ALAN R VANDERBILT UNIVERSITY DEPARTMENT OF PHARMACOLOGY NASHVILLE, TENN 37232 Activation of arachidonate metabolism
R01DK-35292-07 (MET) HALBAN, PHILIPPE A LAB DE RECHERCHE LOUIS JEANTET CTR MED U/ 1 RUE MICHEL-SERVET CH-1211 GENEVA 4, SWITZERLAND Processing of proinsulin/insulin by B-cell organelles
R01DK-35306-07 (PC) MATSUDAIRA, PAUL T WHITEHEAD INST FOR BIOMED RES NINE CAMBRIDGE CENTER CAMBRIDGE, MA 02142 Structure and function of the intestine brush border
R01DK-35310-06 (PTHB) MC KEEHAN, WALLACE L W A JONES CELL SCI CTR, INC 10 OLD BARN ROAD LAKE PLACID, N Y 12946 Human hepatocyte growth factors
R01DK-35317-05A2 (OBM) FRANCESCHI, RENNY T UNIVERSITY OF TEXAS DEPT OF BIOLOGICAL CHEMISTRY HOUSTON, TEXAS 77030 Role of the extracellular matrix in osteoblast formation
R01DK-35323-07 (GMB) NISSENSON, ROBERT A UNIVERSITY OF CALIFORNIA 4150 CLEMENT ST/111 N SAN FRANCISCO, CA 94121 Parathyroid hormone receptors in kidney and bone
R01DK-35341-07 (GMB) WATLINGTON, CHARLES O MEDICAL COLLEGE OF VIRGINIA BOX 145 RICHMOND, VA 23298-0145 Corticosteroid regulation of ion transport in renal cell
R01DK-35368-04A2 (EDC) FOXMAN, BETSY UNIVERSITY OF MICHIGAN 109 OBSERVATORY STREET ANN ARBOR, MI 48109-2029 Recurring urinary tract infection--Risk factors
R01DK-35375-07 (NTN) HAYES, KENNETH C BRANDEIS UNIVERSITY FOSTER BIOMEDICAL RESEARCH LAB WALTHAM, MA 02254 Dietary influence on gallstones
R01DK-35385-06 (GMA) RATTAN, SATISH C JEFFERSON MED COLLEGE OF 105 WALNUT ST., RM 901 COLLEGE PHILADELPHIA, PA 19107 Neurohumoral control of internal anal sphincter
R01DK-35393-06 (PC) BROSTROM, CHARLES O UMDNJ-ROBERT WOOD JOHNSON MED SCHOOL, 675 HOES LANE PISCATAWAY, N J 08854 Regulation of protein synthesis by calcium
R01DK-35402-06 (EDC) MORRISON, ALAN S BROWN UNIVERSITY BOX G PROVIDENCE, R I 02912 Hormones in the epidemiology of prostatic hyperplasia
R01DK-35423-05 (GMB) SALUSKY, ISIDRO B UCLA SCHOOL OF MEDICINE 10833 LE CONTE AVE LOS ANGELES, CA 90024-1752 Calcitriol therapy on dialyzed children
R01DK-35446-06A1 (SAT) HULLETT, DEBRA A UNIVERSITY OF WISCONSIN 600 HIGHLAND AVENUE MADISON, WI 53792 Transplantation of endocrine tissues
R01DK-35449-08 (MET) WEIR, GORDON C JOSLIN DIABETES CENTER ONE JOSLIN PLACE BOSTON, MA 02215 Islet function and diabetes
R01DK-35490-07 (SAT) MEYERS, WILLIAM C DUKE UNIVERSITY MEDICAL CENTER DEPARTMENT OF SURGERY DURHAM, NC 27710 Bile secretory studies in the transplanted liver
R01DK-35527-07 (IMS) MULLEN, HELEN B UNIVERSITY OF MISSOURI DEPT OF MEDICINE COLUMBIA, MO 65212 Autoimmune thyroiditis--Mechanisms of induction
R01DK-35543-06A1 (MET) BRUNENGRABER, HENRI MOUNT SINAI MEDICAL CENTER 1800 EAST 105TH STREET CLEVELAND, OH 44106 1,3-diol and ketone body metabolism
R01DK-35566-07 (IMB) KLEIN, JOHN R UNIVERSITY OF TULSA 600 S COLLEGE AVE TULSA, OK 74104 Gut-derived immune effector cells

PROJECT NO., ORGANIZATIONAL UNIT., INVESTIGATOR, ADDRESS, TITLE

R01DK-35592-08 (MGN) PHILLIPS, JOHN A, III VANDERBILT UNIVERSITY 21ST AVENUE AT GARLAND NASVILLE, TN 37232 Genetic analysis--Peptide hormone and collagen disorders
P01DK-35608-06A1 (DDK) THOMPSON, JAMES C THE UNIV OF TEXAS MED BRANCH 301 UNIVERSITY BLVD A-35 GALVESTON, TX 77550 Studies in gastrointestinal endocrinology
P01DK-35608-06A1 0010 (DDK) GREELEY, GEORGE Studies in gastrointestinal endocrinology Chromogranin A-related peptides in the gut and pancreas
P01DK-35608-06A1 0001 (DDK) THOMPSON, JAMES C Studies in gastrointestinal endocrinology Effect of aging on gastrointestinal hormones
P01DK-35608-06A1 0003 (DDK) TOWNSEND, COURTNEY M Studies in gastrointestinal endocrinology GI hormones--Normal and neoplastic gut and pancreas
P01DK-35608-06A1 0008 (DDK) COOPER, CARY W Studies in gastrointestinal endocrinology Actions of calcium regulating hormones in the gut
P01DK-35608-06A1 9001 (DDK) GREELEY, GEORGE H Studies in gastrointestinal endocrinology Radioimmunoassay and biochemistry core
P01DK-35608-06A1 9002 (DDK) TOWNSEND, COURTNEY M Studies in gastrointestinal endocrinology Tissue culture core
P01DK-35608-06A1 9003 (DDK) SINGH, POMILA Studies in gastrointestinal endocrinology Peptide receptors core
P01DK-35608-06A1 9004 (DDK) BEAUCHAMP, R DANIEL Studies in gastrointestinal endocrinology Molecular pathobiology core
R01DK-35612-08 (SAT) STEIN, THOMAS P UNIV OF MED & DENT OF NJ 401 HADDON AVE. CAMDEN, NJ 08103 Nitrogen pools and turnover in surgical patients
R01DK-35642-06 (BNP) TAYLOR, EDWARD C PRINCETON UNIVERSITY WASHINGTON RD PRINCETON, NJ 08544 Synthesis of molybdopterin and the molybdenum cofactor
R37DK-35652-07 (GMA) ARIAS, IRWIN M TUFTS UNIVERSITY 136 HARRISON AVENUE BOSTON, MA 02111 Mechanism of bile pigment excretion
R01DK-35679-05A2 (REN) MARKOFF, EDITH CHILDRENS HOSPITAL MEDICAL CTR ELLAND AND BETHESDA AVENUE CINCINNATI, OH 45229-2899 The physiological role of glycosylated human prolactin
R01DK-35712-07 (PC) WITTERS, LEE A DARTMOUTH MEDICAL SCHOOL REMSEN 417, HINMAN 7515 HANOVER, NH 03756 Regulation of hepatic metabolism by insulin
R01DK-35713-06 (MET) PATEL, TARUN B UNIV. OF TENNESSEE, MEMPHIS 874 UNION AV./100 CROWNE BLDG. MEMPHIS, TN 38163 Hormonal regulation of energy metabolism
R01DK-35740-07 (GMA) WALSH, JOHN H VA WADSWORTH HOSPITAL CENTER BUILDING 115, RM 203 LOS ANGELES, CA 90073 Physiological role of gastric neuropeptidases
P30DK-35747-06 (DDK) HALSTED, CHARLES H UNIVERSITY OF CALIFORNIA DAVIS, CA 95616 Clinical nutrition research unit
P30DK-35747-06 0010 (DDK) TAIT, ROBERT Clinical nutrition research unit Pilot study--Brain insulin receptors and regulation of obesity
P30DK-35747-06 0011 (DDK) LEUNG, PATRICK Clinical nutrition research unit Pilot study--Heat shock proteins,zinc and teratogenicity
P30DK-35747-06 9003 (DDK) GERSHWIN, M ERIC Clinical nutrition research unit Core--Molecular and cell biology laboratory
P30DK-35747-06 9004 (DDK) PHINNEY, STEPHEN D Clinical nutrition research unit Core--Metabolic laboratory
P30DK-35747-06 9005 (DDK) STERN, JUDITH Clinical nutrition research unit Core--Animal models laboratory
P30DK-35747-06 9006 (DDK) HALSTED, CHARLES H Clinical nutrition research unit Core--Clinical nutrition support laboratory
R01DK-35764-06 (END) DAVIES, TERRY F MT SINAI SCH OF MED BOX #1055 ONE GUSTAVE L LEVY PLACE NEW YORK, N Y 10029 Cloning of thyroid-specific human T cells
R01DK-35766-05 (BNP) MARTIN, OLIVIER R STATE UNIVERSITY OF NEW YORK VESTAL PARKWAY EAST BINGHAMTON, NY 13901 Synthesis and biological evaluation of C-disaccharides
R01DK-35804-08 (IMS) SINGH, ASHOK K LOYOLA UNIVERSITY MEDICAL CTR 2160 SOUTH FIRST AVENUE MAYWOOD, IL 60153 Pathogenesis of glomerular subepithelial immune deposits
R01DK-35808-07 (MET) ERECINSKA, MARIA UNIVERSITY OF PENNSYLVANIA 36TH & HAMILTON WALK PHILADELPHIA, PA 19104 Metabolic basis of fuel sensing in pancreatic B-cells
P30DK-35816-06 (DDK) BIERMAN, EDWIN L UNIV OF WASHINGTON DEPT OF MED RAIT HALL RG26 SEATTLE, WA 98195 Clinical nutrition research unit
P30DK-35816-06 0001 (DDK) ELMER, GARY W Clinical nutrition research unit Pilot study--Dietary influences of digoxin on metabolism
P30DK-35816-06 0002 (DDK) FIGLEWICZ, DIANNE Clinical nutrition research unit Pilot study--Role of insulin in the brain of the obese Zucker rat
P30DK-35816-06 0003 (DDK) ROSENFELD, MICHAEL Clinical nutrition research unit Pilot study-- Lipids in the aorta of rabbit model
P30DK-35816-06 9001 (DDK) BIERMAN, EDWIN L Clinical nutrition research unit Core-- Nutrition laboratory
P30DK-35816-06 9002 (DDK) BIERMAN, EDWIN L Clinical nutrition research unit Core-- Clinical nutrition research
R55DK-35830-07 (HEM) PARKER, CHARLES J VA MEDICAL CENTER 500 FOOTHILL DRIVE SALT LAKE CITY, UT 84148 Human erythrocyte membrane regulation of complement
R01DK-35836-07 (REB) HAY, WILLIAM W, JR UNIVERSITY OF COLORADO 4200 E 9TH AVE/BOX B 199 DENVER, CO 80262 Metabolic studies in diabetic pregnancy
R01DK-35853-06 (NTN) STEELE, ROBERT D UNIVERSITY OF WISCONSIN 1415 LINDEN DRIVE MADISON, WI 53706 Control of folic acid metabolism in mammals
R01DK-35898-05 (HEM) DAILEY, HARRY A UNIVERSITY OF GEORGIA ATHENS, GA 30602 Induction of heme biosynthesis in Friend cells
R01DK-35904-07 (BCE) SCHECHTER, JOEL E UNIVERSITY OF SOUTHERN CALIF 1333 SAN PABLO ST LOS ANGELES, CA 90033 Determinants of pituitary development
R01DK-35905-05A1 (EDC) LA PORTE, RONALD E UNIVERSITY OF PITTSBURGH 130 DESOTO STREET PITTSBURGH, PA 15261 Epidemiology of IDDM mortality in seven countries

PROJECT NO., ORGANIZATIONAL UNIT., INVESTIGATOR, ADDRESS, TITLE

R55DK-35911-05A2 (BEM) PI-SUNYER, F XAVIER ST LUKE'S-ROOSEVELT HOSP CTR AMSTERDAM AVE AT 114TH STREET NEW YORK, NY 10025 The effect of exercise on food intake
R01DK-35912-05A2 (GMA) LOGSDON, CRAIG D UNIVERSITY OF MICHIGAN 7713 MEDICAL SCI 11 BLDG ANN ARBOR, MI 48109-0622 Hormonal regulation of cultured pancreatic acinar cells
R37DK-35914-08 (MET) CORKEY, BARBARA E UNIV HOSPITAL 88 E NEWTON ST BOSTON, MA 02118 Calcium, inositides and energy state in insulin release
R01DK-35930-07 (GMB) BRENNER, BARRY M BRIGHAM AND WOMEN'S HOSPITAL 75 FRANCIS STREET BOSTON, MASS 02115 Control of fluid exchanges in mammalian kidney
R01DK-35931-07 (PTHA) RENNKE, HELMUT G BRIGHAM & WOMEN'S HOSPITAL 75 FRANCIS STREET BOSTON, MA 02115 Pathogenesis of experimental glomerulonephritis
R01DK-35932-07 (GMA) MADARA, JAMES L BRIGHAM & WOMEN'S HOSPITAL 75 FRANCIS STREET BOSTON, MA 02115 Functional morphology of intestinal permeability
R01DK-35937-06 (END) LEONG, DENIS A UNIVERSITY OF VIRGINIA BOX 511 CHARLOTTESVILLE, VA 22908 Multifactorial regulation of ACTH secretion
R01DK-35985-06 (GMB) BOURDEAU, JAMES E UNIV OF OKLAHOMA HEALTH SCI CE 921 NORTHEAST 13TH STREET OKLAHOMA CITY, OKLAHOMA 73104 Regulating Ca+2 concentration in calcium transport
Z01DK-36003-07 (LMB) ROSNER, J L NIDDK, NIH Non-heritable antibiotic resistance
R01DK-36013-06 (GMA) ORLANDO, ROY C UNC SCH OF MEDICINE CB# 7080, 324 BURNETT WOMACK CHAPEL HILL, N C 27599-7080 Esophageal cytoprotection--Agents and mechanisms
R01DK-36024-07 (IMS) GREINER, DALE L UNIV OF MASSACHUSETTS MED SCH 55 LAKE AVENUE, NORTH WORCESTER, MA 01655 Prothymocytes and diabetes mellitus in BB/W rats
R01DK-36031-05 (GMB) GULLANS, STEVEN R BRIGHAM AND WOMEN'S HOSPITAL 75 FRANCIS STREET BOSTON, MA 02115 Renal cell solute regulation
R01DK-36054-04A2 (END) HOFFMAN, ANDREW R STANFORD UNIVERSITY SCHOOL OF MEDICINE STANFORD, CA 94305-5103 Somatomedin and insulin regulation of the pituitary
R01DK-36061-07 (SB) O'DORISIO, SUE M CHILDREN'S HOSPITAL 700 CHILDREN'S DRIVE COLUMBUS, OH 43205 Intestinal transplantation in inbred rats
R01DK-36069-06 (BIO) BRASS, ERIC P CASE WESTERN RESERVE UNIV 10900 EUCLID AVE CLEVELAND, OH 44106-4892 Short chain acylcarnitine-acyl CoA interaction in liver
R01DK-36079-06 (CVB) WILCOX, CHRISTOPHER S NEPHROLOGY & HYPERTENSION 111G VA MED CNTR - 1601 ARCHER ROAD GAINESVILLE, FL 32602 Regulation of renal function and BP by thromboxane
R01DK-36081-07 (MET) CARRUTHERS, ANTHONY UNIV OF MASSACHUSETTS MED SCH WORCESTER, MA 01655 Endocrine control of RBC and adipose sugar transport
R01DK-36089-07 (END) MEISLER, MIRIAM H UNIV OF MICHIGAN MEDICAL SCH 1500 EAST MEDICAL CENTER DRIVE ANN ARBOR, MI 48109-0618 Hormonal regulation of amylase gene expression
R01DK-36090-07 (MET) SCHIMMEL, RICHARD J UNIV OF MED & DENT OF NJ 401 SOUTH CENTRAL AVENUE STRAFORD, NJ 08084 Alpha adrenergic regulation of brown adipose tissue
Z01DK-36104-10 (LMB) ROSS, P D NIDDK, NIH Thermal measurements of biomolecular systems
Z01DK-36105-09 (LMB) ZIMMERMAN, S B NIDDK, NIH Influences of macromolecular crowding on biochemical systems
Z01DK-36106-04 (LMB) WOLFFE, A NIDDK, NIH Developmental regulation of differential gene expression
Z01DK-36108-04 (LMB) CRAIGIE, R NIDDK, NIH Studies on the mechanism of retroviral DNA integration
Z01DK-36109-04 (LMB) DAVIES, D R NIDDK, NIH AIDS related proteins--Structure and function
Z01DK-36110-04 (LMB) NICKOL, J NIDDK, NIH Control of gene expression during chicken erythrocyte development
R01DK-36111-04A3 (GMB) HARAMATI, AVIAD GEORGETOWN UNIVERSITY 3900 RESERVOIR ROAD, NW WASHINGTON, DC 20007 Regulation of renal phosphate reabsorption during growth
Z01DK-36111-03 (LMB) NICKOL, J NIDDK, NIH Structural molecular biology
R01DK-36112-06 (HEM) CONRAD, MARCEL E UNIV OF S ALABAMA CANCER CTR (414) MOBILE, AL 36688 Regulators of iron absorption
Z01DK-36113-02 (LMB) MARTIN, R G NIDDK, NIH Channeling in the biosynthesis of histidine
Z01DK-36114-01 (LMB) PADLAN, E A NIDDK, NIH Structural studies of molecular recognition
Z01DK-36115-01 (LMB) PADLAN, E A NIDDK, NIH Study of the potential use of catalytic antibodies against AIDS
R01DK-36119-07 (GMB) SABATINI, SANDRA TEXAS TECH UNIV HEALTH SCI CEN DEPT OF INTERNAL MEDICINE LUBBOCK, TEX 79430 Relationship of PTH, Ca, Na & H20 transport
R01DK-36149-07 (PTHA) KELLEY, VICKI E BRIGHAM & WOMEN'S HOSPITAL 75 FRANCIS STREET BOSTON, MA 02115 Cell mediated renal injury in lupus
R01DK-36175-06A1 (IMS) LEITER, EDWARD H THE JACKSON LABORATORY 600 MAIN STREET BAR HARBOR, ME 04609-0800 Genetics and pathology of non-obese diabetic (NOD) mice
R01DK-36182-07 (END) RAPOPORT, BASIL V.A.M.C., METABOLISM (111F) 4150 CLEMENT STREET SAN FRANCISCO, CA 94121 Studies on Graves' disease and Hashimoto's thyroiditis
P30DK-36200-05S1 (SRC) SNAPE, WILLIAM J, JR HARBOR-UCLA MEDICAL CENTER 1124 WEST CARSON STREET TORRANCE, CA 90502 Center for the study of inflammatory bowel disease
P30DK-36200-05S1 0001 (SRC) SHANAHAN, FERGUS Center for the study of inflammatory bowel disease Neuropeptide immunocyte interactions in inflammatory bowel disease
P30DK-36200-05S1 0002 (SRC) PETERSON, GLORIA M Center for the study of inflammatory bowel disease Genetic predisposition to colonic disease in Cotton-Top-Tamarins
P30DK-36200-05S1 0003 (SRC) KAO, HENRY W Center for the study of inflammatory bowel disease Prostanoids and isolated colonic smooth muscle cells
P30DK-36200-05S1 0004 (SRC) PANG, KAM YEE Center for the study of inflammatory bowel disease Differentiation of colonic epithelial cells in experimental colitis
P30DK-36200-05S1 9001 (SRC) TARGAN, STEPHAN R Center for the study of inflammatory bowel disease Immunology core
P30DK-36200-05S1 9002 (SRC) ZIPSER, ROBERT D Center for the study of inflammatory bowel disease Biochemistry of inflammation core
P30DK-36200-05S1 9003 (SRC) LECHAGO, JUAN Center for the study of inflammatory bowel disease Morphology core
P30DK-36200-05S1 9004 (SRC) ROTTER, JEROME I Center for the study of inflammatory bowel disease Genetic epidemiology core
P30DK-36200-05S1 9005 (SRC) SCHOENFIELD, LESLIE J Center for the study of inflammatory bowel disease Human and animal research core
R01DK-36253-06 (GMB) ARRUDA, JOSE A UNIVERSITY OF ILLINOIS BOX 6998, RM 420-W CHICAGO, IL 60680 Adaptation to metabolic & respiratory acidosis
R01DK-36256-07 (END) LARSEN, PHILIP R BRIGHAM AND WOMEN'S HOSPITAL 75 FRANCIS STREET BOSTON, MA 02115 Physiological role of thyroxine binding proteins
R01DK-36263-07 (PB) WOODRUFF, WILLIAM H INC-4 MAIL STOP C-345 UNIV CA P O BOX 1663 LOS ALAMOS, N MEX 87545 Vibrational spectroscopy of redox metalloproteins
R01DK-36264-07 (PC) SUL, HEI S HARVARD SCH OF PUBLIC HEALTH 665 HUNTINGTON AVENUE BOSTON M A 02115 Hormonal and nutritional control of enzyme biosynthesis
R01DK-36288-19 (BBCA) PARKHURST, LAWRENCE J UNIVERSITY OF NEBRASKA HAMILTON HALL, 525 LINCOLN, NE 68588-0304 Hemoglobin and myoglobin kinetic studies
P01DK-36289-06A1 (DDK) YAMAMURA, HENRY I COLLEGE OF MEDICINE UNIVERSITY OF ARIZONA TUCSON, AZ 85724 Gastrointestinal control by neuropeptides
P01DK-36289-06A1 0003 (DDK) KREULEN, DAVID L Gastrointestinal control by neuropeptides Neuropeptides and abdominal sympathetic ganglia
P01DK-36289-06A1 0004 (DDK) BARBER, WILLIAM D Gastrointestinal control by neuropeptides Neurochemical substrate--Gastric-brainstem interactions
P01DK-36289-06A1 0006 (DDK) HRUBY, VICTOR J Gastrointestinal control by neuropeptides Design and synthesis of receptor selective CCK analogues
P01DK-36289-06A1 0007 (DDK) YAMAMURA, HENRY I Gastrointestinal control by neuropeptides CCK peptide and receptor characterization
P01DK-36289-06A1 0009 (DDK) KRAMER, THOMAS Gastrointestinal control by neuropeptides Neuropeptide control of gastrointestinal motility
P01DK-36289-06A1 0010 (DDK) PORRECA, FRANK Gastrointestinal control by neuropeptides Neuropeptide regulation of intestinal fluid
P01DK-36289-06A1 0011 (DDK) DAVIS, THOMAS Gastrointestinal control by neuropeptides Regulation of CCK and GRP mRNA and metabolism
P01DK-36296-05 (ADDK) CARO, JOSE F EAST CAROLINA UNIV SCH OF MED GREENVILLE, NC 27858 East Carolina University diabetes program project
P01DK-36296-05 0003 (ADDK) SINHA, MADHUR East Carolina University diabetes program project Mechanism of insulin resistance in adipose tissue
P01DK-36296-05 0004 (ADDK) SINHA, MADHUR K East Carolina University diabetes program project Metabolism and lipoprotein subpopulations in diabetes
P01DK-36296-05 9001 (ADDK) SILVERMAN, JAN F East Carolina University diabetes program project Core laboratories
P01DK-36296-05 0001 (ADDK) CARO, JOSE F East Carolina University diabetes program project Effects of insulin on the liver in obesity
P01DK-36296-05 0002 (ADDK) DOHM, GERALD L East Carolina University diabetes program project Mechanisms of insulin resistance in muscle
R01DK-36339-06 (BPO) TORDOFF, MICHAEL G MONELL CHEMICAL SENSE CENTER 3500 MARKET STREET PHILDELPHIA, PA 19104 Hepatic-portal infusions and feeding
P01DK-36350-05S1 (SRC) PODOLSKY, DANIEL K MASSACHUSETTS GENERAL HOSPITAL FRUIT STREET BOSTON, MA 02114 Cotton-top tamarin model for studies of colitis and cancer
P01DK-36350-05S1 0001 (SRC) KING, NORVAL W Cotton-top tamarin model for studies of colitis and cancer Natural history of spontaneous colitis and cancer in the cotton-top tamarin
P01DK-36350-05S1 0002 (SRC) LETVIN, NORMAN L Cotton-top tamarin model for studies of colitis and cancer Studies of basic immune mechanism in cotton-top tamarin
P01DK-36350-05S1 0003 (SRC) PODOLASKY, DAVID K Cotton-top tamarin model for studies of colitis and cancer Colonic glycoproteins in the cotton-top tamarin--Role in colitis and cancer
P01DK-36350-05S1 0004 (SRC) ISSELBACHER, KURT J Cotton-top tamarin model for studies of colitis and cancer Molecular biology--Colitis and colon cancer in the cotton-top tamarin
P01DK-36350-05S1 9001 (SRC) HUNT, RONALD D Cotton-top tamarin model for studies of colitis and cancer Core--New England regional primate research center
R01DK-36351-04A2 (GMB) NORD, EDWARD P STATE UNIVERSITY OF NEW YORK SCHOOL OF MEDICINE STONY BROOK, NY 11794 Modulation of Na+-H+ antiport by catecholamines
R01DK-36398-04 (PHRA) CASHMAN, JOHN R UNIVERSITY OF CALIFORNIA 513 PARNASSUS AVE BOX 0446 SAN FRANCISCO, CA 94143 Fatty acid epoxides as modulators of prolactin release
R01DK-36407-06 (END) MAURER, RICHARD A UNIVERSITY OF IOWA SCIENCES BLDG IOWA CITY, IOWA 52242 Pituitary glycoprotein hormone gene expression
R01DK-36424-06 (PC) PILCH, PAUL F BOSTON UNIV SCHOOL OF MEDICINE 80 EAST CONCORD STREET BOSTON, MA 02118 The chemistry of insulin and IGF-1 receptors
R01DK-36425-06 (PBC) YURCHENCO, PETER D UMDNJ ROBERT W JOHNSON MED CTR MEDICAL SCHOOL, 675 HOES LANE PISCATAWAY, NJ 08854 Basement membrane self-assembly and structure
R01DK-36440-06 (CVB) SCHAFFER, STEPHEN W UNIVERSITY OF SOUTH ALABAMA MSB 3130 COLLEGE OF MED MOBILE, AL 36688 Myocardial

abnormality in noninsulin-dependent diabetes
R01DK-36449-06 (MET) KATZ, JOSEPH CEDARS-SINAI MED CENTER 8700 BEVERLY BOULEVARD LOS ANGELES, CA 90048 Studies on glycogen synthesis & gluconeogenesis
R01DK-36452-06 (BEM) LUSTMAN, PATRICK J WASHINGTON UNIVERSITY SCHOOL OF MEDICINE ST LOUIS, MO 63110 Psychiatric disorder in adults with diabetes mellitus
R01DK-36467-05 (GMB) ROBERTSON, GARY L MEDICAL SCHOOL 303 EAST CHICAGO AVENUE CHICAGO, IL 60611 Endogenous opiates in the regulation of vasopressin
R01DK-36468-06 (BCE) KILPATRICK, DANIEL L WORCESTER FDN FOR EXPER. BIOLO 222 MAPLE AVE SHREWSBURY, MA 01545 Expression of preproenkephalin-like mRNA in the testis
R01DK-36505-05 (MET) LISCUM, LAURA TUFTS UNIVERSITY 136 HARRISON AVENUE BOSTON, MA 02111 Intracellular cholesterol metabolism studies
R01DK-36563-06 (GMA) PAPPO, JACQUES VA ADMINISTRATION MEDICAL CTR CELL BIOL AND AGING SEC (151E) SAN FRANCISCO, CALIF 94121 Isolation & characterization of peyers patch M cells
R01DK-36569-06 (BIO) DEPAOLI-ROACH, ANNA A INDIANA UNIVERSITY 635 BARNHILL DRIVE INDIANAPOLIS, IN 46202-5122 Structure and regulation of type 1 protein phosphatases
R37DK-36588-07 (NSS) CAREY, MARTIN C BRIGHAM AND WOMEN'S HOSPITAL 75 FRANCIS STREET BOSTON, MA 02115 Alimentary tract lipids in health and disease
R01DK-36597-05 (GMB) KRONENBERG, HENRY M MASSACHUSETTS GENERAL HOSPITAL WELLMAN BUILDING/ROOM 5 BOSTON, MA 02114 Regulation of bone cell genes by 1,25-(OH)2 vitamin D
R01DK-36598-06 (SB) KIM, SUNG-WAN UNIVERSITY OF UTAH 421 WAKARA PARK SALT LAKE CITY, UT 84108 Artificial pancreas--a biochemical approach
R01DK-36632-06 (PBC) SAHAGIAN, GARABED G TUFTS UNIVERSITY 136 HARRISON AVENUE BOSTON, MA 02111 Regulation of lysosomal enzyme trafficking
R01DK-36639-06 (MEDB) BEUTLER, ERNEST SCRIPPS RESEARCH INSTITUTE 10666 NORTH TORREY PINES ROAD LA JOLLA, CA 92037 Gaucher disease -- Molecular biology and therapy
R01DK-36659-05 (MET) COOPER, ALLEN D PALO ALTO MEDICAL RESEARCH FDN 860 BRYANT STREET PALO ALTO, CA 94301 Intestinal lipoprotein metabolism
R01DK-36702-07 (GMA) TERKELTAUB, ROBERT UNIV OF CALIFORNIA, SAN DIEGO DEPT OF MEDICINE, V-111 K LA JOLLA, CA 92093 Low density lipoprotein and inflammation
R01DK-36714-05 (END) ROSNER, WILLIAM ST LUKES-ROOSEVELT HOSP CTR 428 W 59TH ST NEW YORK, NY 10019 Testosterone-estradiol-binding globulin receptors
R01DK-36729-06 (BIO) GRABOWSKI, GREGORY A MOUNT SINAI SCHOOL OF MEDICINE BOX 1203, FIFTH AVE & 100TH ST NEW YORK, NY 10029-6574 Studies of Gaucher disease--A prototype lipidosis
R01DK-36734-06 (MEP) JOHNSON, KENNETH H UNIVERSITY OF MINNESOTA DEPT OF VET PATHOBIO, VET MEDI ST. PAUL, MN 55108 Diabetes mellitus and islet amyloid in polypeptide
R01DK-36739-05 (BIO) AHMAD, FAZAL UNIVERSITY OF MIAMI P. O. BOX 016129 MIAMI, FL 33101 Pyruvate carboxylase and biotin holocarboxylase synthase
R01DK-36747-06 (BIO) SUTTLE, DALE P, JR ST JUDE CHILDRENS RES HOSPITAL 332 NORTH LAUDERDALE MEMPHIS, TN 38101 UMP synthase and the molecular basis of orotic aciduria
R01DK-36796-06 (GMB) BROWN, EDWARD M BRIGHAM AND WOMEN'S HOSPITAL 75 FRANCIS STREET BOSTON, MA 02115 Second messengers and the control of PTH secretion
R01DK-36798-07 (EDC) SPEIZER, FRANK E CHANNING LABORATORY 180 LONGWOOD AVENUE BOSTON, MA 02115 Dietary risk factors for diabetes in a cohort of women
R01DK-36803-06 (GMB) HEBERT, STEVEN C BRIGHAM AND WOMEN'S HOSPITAL 75 FRANCIS STREET BOSTON, MA 02115 Salt transport and cell volume regulation in the nephron
R01DK-36807-21 (PTHA) ANDRES, GIUSEPPE A MASSACHUSETTS GENERAL HOSPITAL FRUIT ST BOSTON, MA 02114 Immunopathology of nephritis and renal allograft
R01DK-36812-06 (PC) CARLSON, DON M UNIVERSITY OF CALIFORNIA BIOCHEMISTRY & BIOPHYSICS DAVIS, CA 95616 Tissue-specific gene regulation in parotid glands
R01DK-36822-07 (PHY) SCHOOLWERTH, ANTON C VIRGINIA COMMONWEALTH UNIV 1101 E MARSHALL ST, BOX 160 RICHMOND, VA 23298-0160 Mitochondrial transport and renal ammoniagenesis
R01DK-36823-07 (NTN) MOCK, DONALD M UNIVERSITY OF IOWA 200 HAWKINS DR IOWA CITY, IA 52242-1009 Indices of biotin nutrition
R37DK-36835-07 (GMA) TRIER, JERRY S BRIGHAM & WOMEN'S HOSP, GASTRO 75 FRANCIS STREET BOSTON, MA 02115 Functional morphology of the alimentary tract
P30DK-36836-05 (SRC) KAHN, C RONALD JOSLIN DIABETES CENTER ONE JOSLIN PLACE BOSTON, MA 02215 Diabetes and endocrinology research center
P30DK-36836-05 0001 (SRC) EDGE, ALBERT S Diabetes and endocrinology research center Pilot study--carbohydrate of insulin receptor
P30DK-36836-05 0002 (SRC) GANDA, OM P Diabetes and endocrinology research center Pilot study--Pathogenesis of type II diabetes in monozygotic twins
P30DK-36836-05 0003 (SRC) JACKSON, RICHARD A Diabetes and endocrinology research center Pilot study--Inheritance of diabetes--T cell receptor and MHC genes
P30DK-36836-05 0004 (SRC) LEAHY, JOHN L Diabetes and endocrinology research center Pilot study--Insulin secretion and action in chronic hyperglycemia
P30DK-36836-05 0005 (SRC) MARATOS-FLIER, ELEFTHERIA Diabetes and endocrinology research center Pilot study--Effects of reovirus infection on gene expression
P30DK-36836-05 0006 (SRC) SRIKANTA, SATHYANARAYANA Diabetes and endocrinology research center Pilot study--Islet cell antigens--Molecular biology and function
P30DK-36836-05 0007 (SRC) WHITE, MORRIS F Diabetes and endocrinology research center Pilot study--Relation between insulin receptor and pp60 SRC in hepatoma cells
P30DK-36836-05 9001 (SRC) KING, GEORGE L Diabetes and endocrinology research center Core--Tissue culture media
P30DK-36836-05 9002 (SRC) BONNER-WEIR, SUSAN Diabetes and endocrinology research center Core--Electron microscopy/morphology
P30DK-36836-05 9003 (SRC) CHIN, WILLIAM W Diabetes and endocrinology research center Core--Molecular biology
P30DK-36836-05 9004 (SRC) JACKSON, RICHARD A Diabetes and endocrinology research center Core--Cell sorter/flow cytometer
P30DK-36836-05 9005 (SRC) SPIRO, ROBERT G Diabetes and endocrinology research center Core--Glycoconjugates
P30DK-36836-05 9006 (SRC) RAND, LAWRENCE L Diabetes and endocrinology research center Core--Patient resource center
P30DK-36836-05 9007 (SRC) RAND, LAWRENCE L Diabetes and endocrinology research center Core--Clinical research center
P30DK-36836-05 9008 (SRC) RAND, LAWRENCE L Diabetes and endocrinology research center Core--Diabetes epidemiology and biostatistics center
P30DK-36836-05 9009 (SRC) HOTTORI, MASAKAZU Diabetes and endocrinology research center Core--Animal resource
P30DK-36836-05 9010 (SRC) SOELDNER, J STEWART Diabetes and endocrinology research center Core--Radioligand assay
R01DK-36843-07 (END) RIDGWAY, CHESTER E UNIVERSITY OF COLORADO 4200 EAST NINTH AVE B151 DENVER, CO 80262 Regulation of TSH subunit gene expression
R01DK-36849-05 (BBCB) CAFFREY, MARTIN D OHIO STATE UNIVERSITY 120 WEST 18TH AVENUE COLUMBUS, OH 43210-1173 Kinetics & mechanism of lipid phase transitions
R01DK-36855-05 (CBY) SHANAHAN, MICHAEL F SOUTHERN ILLINOIS UNIVERSITY DEPARTMENT OF PHYSIOLOGY CARBONDALE, IL 62901 Characterization of erythrocyte hexose transporter
R01DK-36870-07 (PC) NAPOLI, JOSEPH L SUNY-AT BUFFALO 3435 MAIN STREET BUFFALO, NEW YORK 14214 Characterization of retinoic acid metabolism
R01DK-36873-06 (PC) FALLER, LARRY D VETERANS ADMINISTRATION CENTER BUILDING 115 LOS ANGELES, CA 90073 Mechanistic studies of the gastric H,K-ATPase
R01DK-36887-07 (GMA) GOLLAN, JOHN L BRIGHAM & WOMEN'S HOSPITAL, IN 75 FRANCIS STREET BOSTON, MA 02115 Hepatic pathways of heme and bilirubin metabolism
R01DK-36888-05 (BBCB) STARK, RUTH E COLLEGE OF STATEN ISLAND--CUNY 50 BAY STREET STATEN ISLAND, NY 10301 Spectroscopic studies of model digestive systems
R01DK-36904-05 (EDC) D'ALESSIO, DONN J UNIVERSITY OF WISCONSIN 504 N WALNUT STREET MADISON, WI 53705-2368 Wisconsin incidence cohort registry of type I diabetes
R01DK-36913-05 (BIO) APPLING, DEAN R UNIV OF TEXAS AT AUSTIN AUSTIN, TX 78712 Regulation of folate-mediated one-carbon metabolism
R01DK-36916-05 (PB) FRIEDMANN, NAOMI K UNIV OF TX H.S.C. AT HOUSTON PO BOX 20708 HOUSTON, TX 77225 Role of Ca2+ fluxes in the gluconeogenic response
R01DK-36969-05 (SAT) SCHLOERB, PAUL R UNIVERSITY OF KANASAS MED CTR 39TH AND RAINBOW BOULEVARD KANSAS CITY, KS 66103 Body composition and nutrition in spinal cord injury
R01DK-37004-06 (MET) FAIN, JOHN N UNIV OF TENNESSEE 800 MADISON AVENUE MEMPHIS, TN 38163 Hormonal regulation of phosphoinositide metabolism
R01DK-37006-07 (MET) GRANNEMAN, JAMES SINAI HOSPITAL OF DETROIT 6767 WEST OUTER DRIVE DETROIT, MI 48235 Regulation of brown fat transmembrane signalling
R01DK-37007-04A3 (BIO) LITOSCH, IRENE UNIV OF MIAMI SCH OF MEDICINE 1600 NW 10TH AVE MIAMI, FL 33136 Hormone regulation of phosphoinositide hydrolysis
R01DK-37016-04A1 (PBC) FUKUDA, MICHIKO N LA JOLLA CANCER RES FNDN 10901 N TORREY PINES RD LA JOLLA, CA 92037 Cell-surface glycoconjugates in hematological disorders
R01DK-37021-06 (NLS) LECHAN, RONALD M NEW ENGLAND MEDICAL CTR HOSP ENDOCRINOLOGY DIV, BOX 268 BOSTON, MA 02111 TRH regulation/biosynthesis in paraventricular nucleus
R01DK-37034-06 (SAT) LEMASTERS, JOHN J UNIV OF NORTH CAROLINA CB #7090, LAB FOR CELL BIOLOGY CHAPEL HILL, NC 27599-7090 Liver preservation for transplantation
R01DK-37050-07 (SB) JACOBSON, EUGENE D UNIV OF COLORADO HLTH SCIS CTR 4200 EAST NINTH AVENUE DENVER, CO 80262 Intestinal ischemia
R01DK-37061-05 (END) NORDEEN, STEVEN K UNIV OF COLORADO HLTH SCIS CTR 4200 EAST NINTH AVE DENVER, CO 80262 Molecular mechanisms of glucocorticoid hormone action
U01DK-37072-06 (DDK) LAZARUS, J MICHAEL BRIGHAM AND WOMEN'S HOSP, INC 75 FRANCIS STREET BOSTON, MASS 02115 The modification of diet in renal disease (MDRD) study
R01DK-37075-05A2 (GMA) WEIKEL, CYNTHIA S JOHNS HOPKINS UNIVERSITY 725 N WOLFE STREET BALTIMORE, MD 21205 Diarrhea--Protein kinase C and secretagogues
R01DK-37080-05 (GMA) MARKS, JAY W CEDARS-SINAI MEDICAL CENTER 8700 BEVERLY BLVD, #7511 LOS ANGELES, CA 90048 Gallstone formation and prevention during weight reduction
R01DK-37094-06 (END) MONDER, CARL POPULATION COUNCIL 1230 YORK AVENUE NEW YORK, NY 10021 Corticosteriod metabolism in juvenile hypertension
R01DK-37097-07 (PHY) JACOBSON, HARRY R VANDERBILT UNIVERSITY MEDICAL CTR. NORTH NASHVILLE, TN 37232 Mechanisms and regulating acidification in kidney tubules
R01DK-37100-05 (PTHA) CALVET, JAMES P UNIV OF KANSAS MED CENTER 39TH & RAINBOW BLVD KANSAS CITY, KS 66103-8410 Gene activity in the development of polycystic kidneys
R01DK-37105-05 (GMB) SCHWARTZ, JOHN H BOSTON CITY HOSPITAL 818 HARRISON AVENUE BOSTON, MA 02118 Pathogenesis of ischemic renal disease
R01DK-37124-06 (BIO) CURTHOYS, NORMAN P COLORADO STATE UNIVERSITY FORT COLLINS , CO 80523 Control of renal glutaminase induction during acidosis
R01DK-37139-05 (PTHB) VENKATACHALAM, MANJERI A UNIVERSITY OF TEXAS 7703 FLOYD CURL DRIVE SAN ANTONIO, TX 78284 Membrane pathology

in renal cell injury

R37DK-37172-07 (GMA) FORDTRAN, JOHN S BAYLOR UNIV MED CTR 3500 GASTON AVE DALLAS, TX 75246 Absorption, secretion, malabsorption and diarrhea

R01DK-37173-06A1 (SB) DEBAS, HAILE T UNIVERSITY OF CALIFORNIA SAN FRANCISCO, CA 94143-0104 Inhibitory mechanisms of the gastric fundus

R01DK-37175-07 (NTN) MITCH, WILLIAM E EMORY UNIVERSITY SCH OF MED 1364 CLIFTON RD, N E ATLANTA, GA 30322 Protein nutrition in experimental uremia

R01DK-37206-07 (PHY) BENOS, DALE J UNIVERSITY OF ALABAMA UNIV STATION, BHSB 706 BIRMINGHAM, AL 35294-0005 Sodium entry into amiloride-sensitive epithelia

R01DK-37219-06 (PC) HILDEBRANDT, JOHN D MEDICAL UNIV OF SOUTH CAROLINA 171 ASHLEY AVENUE CHARLESTON, S C 29425 Hormone-regulated GTP-binding proteins

R01DK-37222-06A1 (MBC) PARKS, LEO W NORTH CAROLINA STATE UNIVERSIT PO BOX 7615 RALEIGH, NC 27695-7615 Analysis of the sterol components of yeast

R01DK-37223-06A1 (GMB) CHESNEY, RUSSELL W LE BONHEUR CHILDRENS MEDICAL C 848 ADAMS AVENUE MEMPHIS, TN 38103 Adaptation of renal taurine transport

R01DK-37227-15 (PTHA) TOBACK, FREDERICK G UNIVERSITY OF CHICAGO 5841 SOUTH MARYLAND AVENUE CHICAGO, IL 60637 Membranes and phospholipids in renal hyperplasia

R01DK-37237-05 (GMA) COOKE, HELEN J OHIO STATE UNIVERSITY 333 WEST 10TH AVENUE COLUMBUS, OH 43210-1239 Neural regulation of small intestinal mucosa

R01DK-37240-07 (GMA) COOKE, HELEN J OHIO STATE UNIVERSITY 1645 NEIL AVE/305D HAMILTON HA COLUMBUS, OH 43210-1238 Neural control of human intestinal mucosa

R01DK-37241-06 (NLS) DE GROAT, WILLIAM C UNIVERSITY OF PITTSBURGH SCHOOL OF MEDICINE PITTSBURGH, PA 15261 Viscerosomatic interactions in lumbosacral spinal cord

R01DK-37249-06 (CBY) BROWN, WILLIAM J CORNELL UNIVERSITY BIOCHEM, MOLECULAR & CELL BIOL ITHACA, NY 14853-8101 Biogenesis of lysosomes

R01DK-37255-06A2 (BMT) NEWTON, WILLIAM E VIRGINIA TECH BLACKSBURG, VA 24061-0308 Role of FeMo-cofactor in nitrogenase catalysis

R01DK-37265-06 (MGN) BERGER, FRANKLIN G UNIVERSITY OF SOUTH CAROLINA COLUMBIA, SC 29208 Genetics of androgen-inducible mRNAs in mouse kidney

R01DK-37273-06 (BPO) KALRA, PUSHPA S UNIV OF FLORIDA COLL OF MED PO BX J-294 JHMHC/DEPT GYN/OBS GAINESVILLE, FL 32610 Neuropeptide Y in feeding

R01DK-37274-06 (END) THOMAS, GARY OREGON HEALTH SCIENCES UNIV 3181 S W SAM JACKSON PARK RD PORTLAND, OR 97201 Cell-type specific processing of opioid precursors

R01DK-37301-03 (BIO) WATFORD, MALCOLM RUTGERS, THE STATE UNIVERSITY P. O. BOX 231 NEW BRUNSWICK, NY 08903 Hepatic glutaminase

R01DK-37312-07 (MET) METZ, STEWART A UNIVERSITY OF WISCONSIN-MADISO 600 HIGHLAND AVE MADISON, WI 53792 Role of phospholipases A2 and D in insulin release

R01DK-37332-06 (CBY) PFEFFER, SUZANNE R STANFORD UNIVERSITY SCHOOL OF MEDICINE STANFORD, CA 94350-5307 Intracellular transport--The mannose-phosphate receptor

R01DK-37340-05 (MEP) FRIEDMAN, SCOTT L USCF LIVER CTR LAB 1001 POTRERO AVE SAN FRANCISCO, CA 94110 The role of lipocytes in hepatic fibrosis

R01DK-37373-04A1 (BIO) CHUANG, DAVID T UNIVERSITY OF TEXAS 5323 HARRY HINES BLVD DALLAS, TX 75235 Mammalian branched-chain keto acid dehydrogenase complex

R01DK-37380-05 (PHY) MISLER, STANLEY THE JEWISH HOSP OF ST LOUIS 216 SOUTH KINGSHIGHWAY BLVD ST LOUIS, MO 63110 Ion channels in pancreatic islet cells

R01DK-37423-05 (PHY) COGAN, MARTIN G UNIVERSITY OF CALIFORNIA 1065 HSE, BOX 0532 SAN FRANCISCO, CA 94143-0532 Axial heterogeneity of proximal tubule anion transport

R01DK-37435-06 (TMP) SMITH, WENDY A NORTHEASTERN UNIVERSITY 360 HUNTINGTON AVE BOSTON, MA 02115 Regulation of endocrine cell response--An insect model

R01DK-37448-06 (GMB) SCHNERMANN, JURGEN B UNIVERSITY OF MICHIGAN 7712 MED SCI II BLDG ANN ARBOR, MI 48109 Cellular function of the juxtaglomerular apparatus

R01DK-37449-06 (END) ROTWEIN, PETER S WASHINGTON UNIVERSITY 724 S EUCLID AVE ST LOUIS, MO 63110 Regulation of insulin-like growth factor I expression

R01DK-37463-06 (GMA) SMITH, ANN UNIVERSITY OF MISSOURI 5100 ROCKHILL ROAD KANSAS CITY, MO 64110-2499 Role of heme-binding proteins in hepatic heme transport

R01DK-37482-04A1 (GMA) GREEN, GARY M UNIV OF TEXAS HLTH SCI CTR 7703 FLOYD CURL DRIVE SAN ANTONIO, TX 78284-7756 Feedback regulation of pancreatic secretion

R01DK-37484-03 (MET) WOLFE, ROBERT R SHRINERS BURNS INSTITUTE 610 TEXAS AVENUE GALVESTON, TX 77550 Assessment of substrate kinetic analysis using tracers

R01DK-37500-04A1 (PC) WHELAN, WILLIAM J UNIV OF MIAMI SCHOOL OF MED P O BOX 016129 (R629) MIAMI, FL 33101 The biogenesis of glycogen

R01DK-37512-06 (PHY) MILANICK, MARK A UNIVERSITY OF MISSOURI MA415 MEDICAL SCIENCES COLUMBIA, MO 65212 Cytosolic modulation of plasma membrane ion transport

R01DK-37513-06 (HEM) SHEFFERY, MICHAEL B SLOAN-KETTERING INSTITUTE 1275 YORK AVE NEW YORK, NY 10021 Characterization of globin gene binding proteins

R01DK-37583-06 (BIO) STEINBERG, ROBERT A UNIV OF OKLAHOMA HLTH SCI CTR P O BOX 26901 OKLAHOMA CITY, OK 73190 Structural studies of protein kinase regulatory subunit

R01DK-37596-04 (GMA) SIEGMAN, MARION J THOMAS JEFFERSON UNIVERSITY 1020 LOCUST STREET PHILADELPHIA, PA 19107 Functional adaptations of intestinal smooth muscle

R55DK-37602-04A1 (MGN) GIGER, URS UNIVERSITY OF PENNSYLVANIA 3850 SPRUCE STREET PHILADELPHIA, PA 19104-6010 Canine muscle type phosphofructokinase deficiency

R01DK-37605-04A1 (GMB) HEBERT, STEVEN C BRIGHAM AND WOMEN'S HOSPITAL 75 FRANCIS STREET BOSTON, MA 02115 Potassium transport and adaptation in the nephron

R01DK-37667-05 (END) GUTIERREZ-HARTMANN, ARTHUR UNIV OF COLORADO HLTH SCIS CTR 4200 E NINTH AVE DENVER, CO 80262 Reconstitution of pituitary-specific transcription

R01DK-37694-06 (REN) LIAO, SHUTSUNG BEN MAY INST 5841 SOUTH MARYLAND AVE CHICAGO, IL 60637 Androgen receptors--Antibodies and gene cloning

R01DK-37706-07 (GMB) PELAYO, JUAN C UCLA SCHOOL OF MEDICINE 10833 LE CONTE AVENUE LOS ANGELES, CALIF 90024-1752 Functional and hormonal adaptations of remnant nephrons

U01DK-37825-06 (ADDK) SCHADE, DAVID S U. OF NEW MEXICO SCHL. OF MED. DEPARTMENT OF MEDICINE ALBUQUERQUE, NM 87131 Diabetes control and complications trial

U01DK-37828-06 (ADDK) KOLTERMAN, ORVILLE G UNIV. OF CALIFORNIA, SAN DIEGO DEPARTMENT OF MEDICINE, H-203 LA JOLLA, CA 92093 Diabetes control and complications trial

U01DK-37834-06 (ADDK) KOWARSKI, ALLEN A UNIV. OF MARYLAND AT BALTIMORE 655 WEST BALTIMORE STREET BALTIMROE, MD 21201 Diabetes control and complications trial

U01DK-37857-06 (ADDK) MALONE, JOHN I UNIV. OF S. FL DIABETES CENTER 12901 NORTH 30TH STREET TAMPA, FL 33612-4799 Diabetes control and complications trial

U01DK-37859-06 (ADDK) MOLITCH, MARK E NORTHWESTERN U. MEDICAL SCHOOL 303 EAST CHICAGO AVENUE CHICAGO, IL 60611 Diabetes control and complications trial (DCCT)

U01DK-37863-06 (ADDK) SHAMOON, HARRY A. EINSTEIN COLLEGE OF MED. 1300 MORRIS PARK AVENUE BRONX, NY 10461 Diabetes control and complications trial

R01DK-37867-06 (MGN) WHITE, PERRIN CORNELL UNIV MEDICAL COLLEGE 1300 YORK AVENUE NEW YORK, NY 10021 molecular genetics of congenital adrenal hyperplasia

R01DK-37868-06 (PTHA) ICHIKAWA, IEKUNI VANDERBILT UNIVERSITY HOSPITAL 21ST AND GARLAND AVENUE NASHVILLE, TN 37232-2584 Immune and non-immune bases for renal diseases

R55DK-37869-06A1 (GMB) ICHIKAWA, IEKUNI VANDERBILT UNIV MED CTR 1161 21ST AVE SOUTH NASHVILLE, TN 37232-2584 Regulatory mechanisms of renal microcirculation

R01DK-37871-10 (CBY) JOHNSON, GARY L NATL JEWISH CENTER FOR IMMUN 1400 JACKSON STREET DENVER, CO 80206 Properties of the NGF receptor

R01DK-37879-05 (PTHA) LEFKOWITH, JAMES A WASHINGTON UNIVERSITY MED SCH 660 SOUTH EUCLID AVENUE ST LOUIS, MO 63110 Role and manipulation of lipid mediators in nephritis

R29DK-37907-01A2 (PHY) GRASSL, STEVEN M SUNY HLTH SCI CTR AT SYRACUSE 750 E ADAMS STREET SYRACUSE, NY 13210 Ion-coupled renal basolateral bicarbonate transport

R01DK-37908-04A2 (SAT) FISCHER, JOSEF E UNIVERSITY OF CINCINNATI 231 BETHESDA AVE CINCINNATI, OH 45267-0558 Muscle protein turnover and amino acid uptake in sepsis

R01DK-37915-04 (PBC) PETERSON, PER A SCRIPPS CLINIC & RSRCH. FNDTN. 10666 NORTH TORREY PINES ROAD LA JOLLA, CA 92037 Studies on retinoid-binding proteins

R01DK-37922-05 (END) MILLER, WALTER L UNIV OF CA, SAN FRANCISCO THIRD & PARNASSUS AVES SAN FRANCISCO, CA 94143-0978 Molecular biology of steroidogenic P450 enzymes

R01DK-37927-05 (BMT) AISEN, PHILIP ALBERT EINSTEIN COLL OF MEDICI 1300 MORRIS PARK AVENUE BRONX, NY 10461 Transferrin and hepatic iron metabolism

R01DK-37948-05 (NTN) SEGAL, KAREN R MOUNT SINAI SCHOOL OF MEDICINE 1 GUSTAVE LEVY PLACE NEW YORK, N Y 10029 Thermogenesis and exercise in lean and obese men

R01DK-37957-04A1 (EDC) TUOMILEHTO, JAAKKO NATIONAL PUBLIC HEALTH INSTITU MANNERHEIMINTIE 166 HELSINKI, FINLAND 00300 Epidemiology and genetics of IDDM in finland

R01DK-37958-05 (CPA) REDDY, JANARDAN K NORTHWESTERN UNIV MEDICAL SCH 303 EAST CHICAGO AVENUE CHICAGO, IL 60611 Hepatocyte differentiation in pancreas

R01DK-37960-05 (CTY) GORDON, JEFFREY I WASHINGTON UNIV SCH OF MED 660 SOUTH EUCLID AVE, BOX 8904 ST LOUIS, MO 63110 Molecular genetics of intestinal development

R01DK-37963-05 (GMB) EATON, DOUGLAS C EMORY UNIVERSITY MEDICAL SCH 1440 CLIFTON RD NE ATLANTA, GA 30322 Regulation of ion transport in tight epithelia

R01DK-37994-06 (PHRA) BRATER, DONALD C WISHARD MEMORIAL HOSPITAL 1001 W 10TH ST INDIANAPOLIS, IN 46202-2879 Pharmacology of NSIADS--Disposition and renal effects

R01DK-38010-04 (NTN) WOLFE, ROBERT R U/OF TX MED BRANCH AT GALVESTO 301 UNIVERSITY BLVD GALVESTON, TX 77550-2774 Effect of exercise on protein metabolism in humans

R01DK-38015-06 (ORTH) DREZNER, MARC K DUKE UNIVERSITY MEDICAL CENTER BOX 3285 DURHAM, N C 27710 Vitamin D metabolism post renal transplantation

R01DK-38016-05 (SAT) KAHAN, BARRY D UNIV OF TEXAS MEDICAL SCHOOL 6431 FANNIN HOUSTON, TX 77030 Cyclosporine pharmacology in clinical transplantation

R01DK-38024-06 (NEUC) BLALOCK, JAMES E UNIVERSITY OF ALABAMA UAB STATION BIRMINGHAM, AL 35294 Lymphocyte-derived hormones and their receptors

R01DK-38026-02 (GMA) DUFFEY, MICHAEL E STATE UNIVERSITY OF NEW YORK 119 SHERMAN HALL BUFFALO, NY 14214 Cholinergic regulation of intestinal potassium transport

P01DK-38030-05 (ADDK) VLAHCEVIC, ZDRAVKO R BOX 711 MCV STATION RICHMOND, VA 23298-0711 Liver and intestinal metabolism of bile acids and lipids

P01DK-38030-05 9001 (ADDK) HYLEMON, PHILLIP B Liver and intestinal metabolism of bile acids and lipids Cell culture and molecular biology core

P01DK-38030-05 0001 (ADDK) VLAHCEVIC, Z. RENO Liver and intestinal metabolism of bile acids and lipids Regulation of bile acid synthesis in the liver

PROJECT NO., ORGANIZATIONAL UNIT., INVESTIGATOR, ADDRESS, TITLE

P01DK-38030-05 0002 (ADDK) SCHWARTZ, CHARLES C. Liver and intestinal metabolism of bile acids and lipids Cholesterol metabolism in plasma lipoprotein and liver
P01DK-38030-05 0003 (ADDK) GROGAN, WILLIAM M. Liver and intestinal metabolism of bile acids and lipids Roles of cholesteryl ester hydrolases in the liver
P01DK-38030-05 0004 (ADDK) HYLEMON, PHILLIP B. Liver and intestinal metabolism of bile acids and lipids Bile acid 7 alpha dehydroxylation by anaerobic bacteria
R01DK-38041-05 (BIO) DODGSON, SUSANNA J UNIVERSITY OF PENNSYLVANIA PHILADELPHIA, PA 19104-6085 Carbon dioxide exchanges in the liver
R01DK-38052-05 (HEM) BOYER, SAMUEL H THE JOHNS HOPKINS UNIVERSITY 720 RUTLAND AVENUE, ROOM 933 BALTIMORE, MD 21205 Molecular genetics of heme biosynthetic enzymes
R01DK-38063-03 (SB) MODLIN, IRVIN M YALE UNIVERSITY SCHOOL OF MED 333 CEDAR ST NEW HAVEN, CT 06510 Secretagogue regulation in parietal cells
R01DK-38088-06 (NTN) HILL, JAMES O VANDERBILT UNIVERSITY D-4130 MEDICAL CENTER NORTH NASHVILLE, TN 37232 Utilization of ingested energy during underfeeding
R01DK-38092-05 (MET) MILES, JOHN M MAYO FOUNDATION 200 FIRST STREET SOUTHWEST ROCHESTER, MN 55905 Regulation of free fatty acids metabolism in normal and diabetic man
R29DK-38101-04 (GMB) BURNATOWSKA-HLEDIN, MARIA MICHIGAN STATE UNIVERSITY EAST LANSING, MI 48824-1101 Vasopressin signaling in collecting tubule cells
P01DK-38108-04 (DDK) COFFMAN, THOMAS M NEPHROLOGY SECTION (111I) VA MEDICAL CEN, 508 FULTON ST. DURHAM, N C 27705 Pathophysiology of renal allograft dysfunction
P01DK-38108-04 0001 (DDK) KLOTMAN, PAUL E Pathophysiology of renal allograft dysfunction Lipid mediators in renal allograft dysfunction
P01DK-38108-04 0002 (DDK) SANFILIPPO, ALFRED P Pathophysiology of renal allograft dysfunction Pathophysiology of renal allograft dysfunction in the rat
P01DK-38108-04 0003 (DDK) HAMILTON, JOHN D Pathophysiology of renal allograft dysfunction Role of cytomegalovirus in renal transplantation
P01DK-38108-04 9001 (DDK) KLOTMAN, PAUL E Pathophysiology of renal allograft dysfunction Core--Animal breeding and surgical facility
P01DK-38111-05 (ADDK) MORRISON, AUBREY WASHINGTON U. MEDICAL SCHOOL 660 SOUTH EUCLID AVENUE ST. LOUIS, MO 63110 Eicosanoid synthesis, function and regulation
P01DK-38111-05 0001 (ADDK) NEEDLEMAN, PHILLIP Eicosanoid synthesis, function and regulation Eicosanoids and renal pathophysiology
P01DK-38111-05 0002 (ADDK) PENTLAND, ALICE P Eicosanoid synthesis, function and regulation Eicosanoid metabolism in epidermal injury
P01DK-38111-05 0003 (ADDK) EVERS, ALEX S Eicosanoid synthesis, function and regulation Brain fatty acid composition and anesthetic effect
P01DK-38111-05 0004 (ADDK) MORRISON, AUBERY R Eicosanoid synthesis, function and regulation Phospholipids, arachidonic acid release, and renal function
P01DK-38111-05 9001 (ADDK) MORRISON, AUBERY R Eicosanoid synthesis, function and regulation Analytical--Core facility
R01DK-38130-06 (MBY) PIKE, JOHN W BAYLOR COLLEGE OF MEDICINE 1 BAYLOR PLAZA HOUSTON, TX 77030 Complementary DNA probes to a steroid receptor gene
R01DK-38138-04A1 (MET) MOONEY, ROBERT A UNIVERSITY OF ROCHESTER 601 ELMWOOD AVENUE, BOX 608 ROCHESTER, NY 14642 Insulin action and lipolysis in permeabilized adipocytes
P01DK-38149-04 (DDK) WIGGINS, ROGER C UNIVERSITY OF MICHIGAN 3914 TAUBMAN MEDICAL CENTER ANN ARBOR, MICHIGAN 48109 Crescentic nephritis
P01DK-38149-04 0001 (DDK) PHAN, SEM H Crescentic nephritis Fibrotic mechanisms in crescentic nephritis
P01DK-38149-04 0002 (DDK) FANTONE, JOSEPH C Crescentic nephritis Phagocytic cells and glomerular injury
P01DK-38149-04 0003 (DDK) WIGGINS, ROGER C Crescentic nephritis Coagulation/fibrinolysis in the crescentic glomerulus
P01DK-38149-04 0004 (DDK) KUNKEL, STEVEN Crescentic nephritis Macrophages function in cresentic nephritis
P01DK-38149-04 9001 (DDK) WIGGINS, ROGER C Crescentic nephritis Core--The model, cell culture, antibody production
P01DK-38149-04 9002 (DDK) JOHNSTON, KENT J Crescentic nephritis Core--Morphology
R01DK-38153-05 (PTHA) NORENBERG, MICHAEL D UNIVERSITY OF MIAMI P O BOX 016960 MIAMI, FL 33101 Astrocyte bendodiazepine receptor in hepatic coma
R01DK-38154-05 (BIO) TANAKA, KAY YALE UNIV SCH OF MEDICINE 333 CEDAR ST PO BOX 3333 NEW HAVEN, CT 06510 Molecular basis of acyl-coA dehydrogenase deficiencies
R01DK-38163-05 (PTHA) JOHNSON, PETER C BARROW NEUROLOGICAL INSTITUTE 350 WEST THOMAS ROAD PHOENIX, AZ 85013 Pathology of diabetic neuropathy
P01DK-38181-05 (DDK) TARTAKOFF, ALAN M CASE WESTERN RESERVE UNIV 2085 ADELBERT ROAD CLEVELAND, OHIO 44106 Glycolipid protein anchors in PNH and thy-1 mutants
P01DK-38181-05 0002 (DDK) ROSENBERRY, TERRONE L Glycolipid protein anchors in PNH and thy-1 mutants Glycolipid anchors of membrane protein
P01DK-38181-05 0003 (DDK) TARTAKOFF, ALAN M Glycolipid protein anchors in PNH and thy-1 mutants Biosynthesis and anchoring of thy-1
P01DK-38181-05 9001 (DDK) GRAY, WESLEY Glycolipid protein anchors in PNH and thy-1 mutants Core facilities
P01DK-38181-05 0001 (DDK) MEDOF, M Glycolipid protein anchors in PNH and thy-1 mutants Analysis of decay accelerating factor (DAF) in affected lymphocytes
R01DK-38201-05 (SAT) CLEMENS, MARK G JOHNS HOPKINS UNIVERSITY 600 NORTH WOLFE ST BALTIMORE, MD 21205 Pharmacologic agents for preservation of donor livers
R01DK-38215-07 (HED) FRAWLEY, LEO S MEDICAL UNIVERSITY OF S CAROLI 171 ASHLEY AVE CHARLESTON, SC 29425-2204 Control of prolactin and GH secretion from single cells

PROJECT NO., ORGANIZATIONAL UNIT., INVESTIGATOR, ADDRESS, TITLE

R01DK-38216-06 (GMA) TAYLOR, IAN L DUKE UNIVERSITY MEDICAL CENTER PO BOX 3913 DURHAM, NC 27710 Peptide YY--The colonic gastric and pancreatic inhibitor
R01DK-38217-05 (GMB) GOOD, DAVID W UNIVERSITY OF TEXAS MEDICAL BR 4.200 JOHN SEALY HOSP E62 GALVESTON, TX 77550 Regulation of thick ascending limb acid-base transport
P01DK-38226-06 (DDK) JACOBSON, HARRY R VANDERBILT UNIV SCHOOL OF MED DIV OF NEPHROLOGY RM S-223 MCN NASHVILLE, TN 37232 Role of eicosanoids in renal function
P01DK-38226-06 0001 (DDK) JACOBSON HARRY R Role of eicosanoids in renal function Transport effects of arachidonate metabolites in perfused tubule
P01DK-38226-06 0002 (DDK) CAPDEVILA JORGE H Role of eicosanoids in renal function Characterization of renal non-cyclooxygenase arachidonate metabolism
P01DK-38226-06 0003 (DDK) BLAIR IAN A Role of eicosanoids in renal function Role of products of arachidonic metabolism in human platelet aggregation
P01DK-38226-06 0004 (DDK) BADR KAMAL F Role of eicosanoids in renal function in vivo studies of cytochrome P-450 generated metabolites of arachidonic acid
P01DK-38226-06 0005 (DDK) HARRIS RAYMOND C Role of eicosanoids in renal function Model cell systems to study cytochrome P450 arachidonate metabolites
P01DK-38226-06 0006 (DDK) FALCK JOHN RUSSELL Role of eicosanoids in renal function Characterization and synthesis of renal eicosanoids
P01DK-38226-06 9001 (DDK) CAPDEVILA JORGE H Role of eicosanoids in renal function Core--analytical biochemistry laboratory
P01DK-38226-06 9002 (DDK) FALCK JOHN RUSSELL Role of eicosanoids in renal function Core--chemical services laboratory
R44DK-38271-03 (SSS) CLAPPER, DAVID L BIO-METRIC SYSTEMS, INC 9924 WEST 74TH STREET EDEN PRAIRIE, MN 55344 Surface modification for improved percutaneous catheters
R01DK-38296-06 (GMB) COHN, DAVID V UNIVERSITY OF LOUISVILLE HEALTH SCIENCES CENTER LOUISVILLE, KY 40292 Parathyroid chromogranin A, pancreastatin, PTH relation
R01DK-38304-06 (PTHA) GREENE, DOUGLAS A UNIVERSITY OF MICHIGAN 5570 MSRB II, BOX 0678 ANN ARBOR, MI 48109-0520 Altered neural myoinositol metabolism in diabetes
R01DK-38305-06 (CPA) FARBER, JOHN L THOMAS JEFFERSON UNIVERSITY ROOM 203A - MAIN BUILDING PHILADELPHIA, PA 19107 Pathogenesis of liver cell necrosis
R01DK-38306-19A1 (NTN) WHANGER, PHILIP D OREGON STATE UNIVERSITY CORVALLIS, OR 97331 Metabolic relationships of selenium in myopathies
R01DK-38308-05 (PTHA) COHEN, MARGO P UNIVERSITY CITY SCIENCE CENTER 3508 MARKET STREET PHILADELPHIA, PA 19104 Matrix interactions and glycation in diabetic nephropathy
R01DK-38309-06 (MBC) JENSEN, ROY A UNIVERSITY OF FLORIDA 1059 MCCARTY HALL GAINESVILLE, FL 32611 Biosynthesis and regulation of aromatics in pseudomonas
R01DK-38310-05 (GMA) APONTE, GREGORY W UNIVERSITY OF CALIFORNIA BERKELEY, CA 94720 Dual packaging and polarized release of GI peptides
R37DK-38311-14 (SB) WEISS, ROBERT M YALE UNIVERSITY 333 CEDAR STREET, P O BOX 3333 NEW HAVEN, CT 06510 Age dependent factors in ureteral-vesical function
R01DK-38313-04 (MEP) TOPHAM, RICHARD W UNIVERSITY OF RICHMOND RICHMOND, VA 23173 Important factors in the regulation of iron absorption
R01DK-38318-06 (MET) COOPER, ALLEN D PALO ALTO MEDICAL RESEARCH FDN 860 BRYANT STREET PALO ALTO, CA 94301 Hepatic metabolism of diet derived lipoproteins
R01DK-38320-06 (BIO) DANNER, DEAN J EMORY UNIVERSITY SCH OF MEDICI 2040 RIDGEWOOD DRIVE ATLANTA, GA 30322 Synthesis/assembly-branched chain ketoacid dehydrogenase
R01DK-38325-06 (MET) ROBERTSON, RODERICK P UNIVERSITY OF MINNESOTA UNIVERSITY HOSPITAL, BOX 91 MINNEAPOLIS, MN 55455 PGE receptor and post-receptor actions in the islet
R01DK-38327-05 (GMA) WEINSTOCK, JOEL V UNIVERSITY OF IOWA HOSPITALS COLLEGE OF MEDICINE IOWA CITY, IA 52242 Immunoregulation of intestinal granulomas
R01DK-38333-04 (GMA) VAN DYKE, REBECCA W UNIVERSITY OF MICHIGAN 3912 TAUBMAN CENTER ANN ARBOR, MI 48109-0362 Liver proton & solute transport & endocytosis
R01DK-38337-04 (END) KATZEFF, HARVEY L NORTH SHORE UNIVERSITY HOSPITA 300 COMMUNITY DRIVE MANHASSET, NY 11030 Catecholamine modulation of thyroid hormone metabolism
R29DK-38342-05 (SAT) MYERS, STUART I UNIVERSITY OF TEXAS SW MED CTR 5323 HARRY HINES BLVD DALLAS, TX 75235 Surgical studies on gallbladder inflammation
R29DK-38348-04 (PC) BULLESBACH, ERIKA E MED. UNIV. OF SOUTH CAROLINA 171 ASHLEY AVENUE CHARLESTON, SC 29403 Studies on the active site of insulin
R37DK-38354-06 (PC) PILKIS, SIMON J SUNY AT STONY BROOK STONY BROOK, NY 11794-8661 Hormonal control of hepatic gluconeogenesis/glycolysis
R29DK-38381-06 (MGN) SMITH, FRANCES I SHRIVER CTR FOR MENT RETARD IN 200 TRAPELO RD WALTHAM, MA 02254 Detection of single base mutations in RNA molecules
R29DK-38383-05 (BIO) MUENZER, JOSEPH UNIV. OF MICHIGAN MED. CENTER F2125 MOTT, BOX 0274 ANN ARBOR, MI 48109 Molecular genetics of iduronate sulfatase deficiencies
R29DK-38389-05 (GMA) STORCH, JUDITH HARVARD SCH OF PUBLIC HEALTH 665 HUNTINGTON AVENUE BOSTON, MA 02115 Fatty acid assimilation in the intestine
R01DK-38392-04 (EDC) PUGH, JACQUELINE A ALMM VA HOSPITAL 7400 MERTON MINTER BLVD SAN ANTONIO, TX 78284 Diabetes related ESRD--Ethnic comparisons
R29DK-38394-05 (PTHA) DIAMOND, JONATHAN R MILTON D. HERSHEY MED CEN DIV OF NEPHROLOGY-P.O. BOX 850 HERSHEY, PA 17033 Mesangial proliferation in progressive glomerulopathy
R29DK-38397-03 (BEM) GREY, MARGARET UNIVERSITY OF PENNSYLVANIA 420 SERVICE DRIVE PHILADELPHIA, PA 19104-6096 Children's responses to

PROJECT NO., ORGANIZATIONAL UNIT., INVESTIGATOR, ADDRESS, TITLE

the stress of chronic ilnes
R01DK-38402-05 (BPO) BERGER, RALPH J UNIVERSITY OF CALIFORNIA 1156 HIGH STREET SANTA CRUZ, CA 95064 Circadian regulation of metabolism in the pigeon
R29DK-38406-05 (GMB) CULPEPPER, ROY M MEDICAL COLLEGE OF VIRGINIA 1101 EAST MARSHALL STREET RICHMOND, VA 23298-0001 Regulation of ion transport in mammalian nephrons
R01DK-38416-05 (RAP) DOHM, GERALD L EAST CAROLINA UNIVERSITY DEPARTMENT OF BIOCHEMISTRY GREENVILLE, NC 27834 Muscle glucose metabolism in diabetes and exercise
R01DK-38418-05 (PC) LANE, M DANIEL JOHNS HOPKINS UNIVERSITY 725 NORTH WOLFE STREET BALTIMORE, MD 21205 Insulin and adipose conversion
R29DK-38422-04 (PC) THOMAS, ANDREW P JEFFERSON MEDICAL COLLEGE 1020 LOCUST STREET PHILADELPHIA, PA 19107 Hormonal calcium mobilization--Regulation in liver
R01DK-38429-06 (MET) MATTHEWS, DWIGHT E CORNELL UNIVERSITY MEDICAL COL 1300 YORK AVENUE NEW YORK, N Y 10021 Dynamic aspects of amino acid metabolism
R01DK-38432-04 (PTHA) ZAGER, RICHARD A HARBORVIEW MEDICAL CEN, ZA-67 325 NINTH AVENUE SEATTLE, WA 98104 Sepsis induced acute renal failure
R01DK-38436-05 (IMS) JONES, ALBERT L CELL BIOLOGY AND AGING SECTION VA MEDICAL CENTER SAN FRANCISCO, CALIF 94121 Development of the secretory immune system
R29DK-38444-05 (CVB) SHENKER, YORAM UNIVERSITY OF WISCONSIN 2500 OVERLOOK TERR MADISON, WI 53705 Effect of atrial natriuretic hormone on aldosterone
R29DK-38446-05 (GMA) SOKOL, RONALD J UNIVERSITY OF COLORADO 1056 E 19TH AVE DENVER, CO 80218 Effect of vitamin E on hepatocyte structure and function
R29DK-38449-05 (END) BARKAN, ARIEL L UNIVERSITY OF MICHIGAN 3920 TAUBMAN CENTER, BOX 0354 ANN ARBOR, MI 48109-0354 Physiopathology of pulsatile GH secretion in
R29DK-38451-04 (PTHA) ADLER, SHARON G HARBOR-UCLA MEDICAL CENTER 1000 W CARSON STREET TORRANCE, CA 90509 The mesangial cell in development of glomerulosclerosis
P01DK-38452-05 (ADDK) AUSIELLO, DENNIS A MASSACHUSETTS GENERAL HOSP 149 13TH STREET CHARLESTOWN, MA 02129 Cellular biology of renal function and disease
P01DK-38452-05 0001 (ADDK) AUSIELLO, DENNIS Cellular biology of renal function and disease Vesicle cycling and function in vasopressin-induced water flow
P01DK-38452-05 0002 (ADDK) HARTWIG, JOHN H Cellular biology of renal function and disease Role of the cytoskeleton in toads vasopressin action
P01DK-38452-05 0003 (ADDK) ZANER, KENNETH S Cellular biology of renal function and disease Osmotic properties of purified cytoskeleton proteins
P01DK-38452-05 0004 (ADDK) BROWN, DENNIS Cellular biology of renal function and disease H+ATPase recycling in epithelial cells
P01DK-38452-05 0005 (ADDK) MCCLUSKEY, ROBERT T Cellular biology of renal function and disease Structure and function of nephritogenic antigens in Heymann nephritis
P01DK-38452-05 0006 (ADDK) BONVENTRE, JOSEPH Cellular biology of renal function and disease Mesangial cell in disease--Role of calcium
P01DK-38452-05 9001 (ADDK) BROWN, DENNIS Cellular biology of renal function and disease Microscopy core
R01DK-38466-05 (SAT) MOSTWIN, JACEK L JOHNS HOPKINS UNIVERSITY MARBURG 401C BALTIMORE, MD 21205 Obstructed bladder muscle - Electrophysiological effects
R01DK-38495-05 (PC) MUECKLER, MIKE M WASHINGTON UNIV/SCHL OF MEDICI 660 S EUCLID AVE BOX 8228 ST LOUIS, MO 63110 Regulation of the glucose transporter
R01DK-38504-02 (GMA) GERBER, JOHN G UNIV OF COLORADO HLTH SCIS CTR 4200 E NINTH AVE, BOX C237 DENVER, CO 80262 Modulators of gastric histamine release in vivo
R01DK-38510-06 (GMA) CHANG, EUGENE B UNIVERSITY OF CHICAGO MED: BOX 400/5841 S MARYLAND CHICAGO, IL 60637 C-kinase and Ca+2 regulation of intestinal ion transport
R29DK-38516-04 (PTHA) SHANLEY, PAUL F UNIVERSITY OF COLORADO 4200 EAST NINTH AVE DENVER, COLORADO 80262 Two types of hypoxic injury in the kidney
R01DK-38517-04A1 (PTHA) DANIEL, THOMAS O VANDERBILT UNIV MEDICAL CTR RM S-3223MCN NASHVILLE, TN 37232-2372 Growth factor expression in renal endothelial cells
P01DK-38518-05 (ADDK) FRIZZELL, RAYMOND A UNIVERSITY OF ALABAMA 1918 UNIVERSITY BOULEVARD BIRMINGHAM, AL 35294 Ion transport regulation in cystic fibrosis
P01DK-38518-05 0001 (ADDK) FRIZZELL, RAYMOND A Ion transport regulation in cystic fibrosis Chloride channel regulation in cystic fibrosis
P01DK-38518-05 0002 (ADDK) WALLACE, ROBERT W Ion transport regulation in cystic fibrosis Molecular mechanisms regulating chloride secretion
P01DK-38518-05 0003 (ADDK) DUBINSKY, WILLIAM P Ion transport regulation in cystic fibrosis Regulation of secretion in normal and cystic fibrosis cells
P01DK-38518-05 0004 (ADDK) KIRK, KEVIN L Ion transport regulation in cystic fibrosis Ion transport and cell volume control in sweat ducts
P01DK-38518-05 9001 (ADDK) BRINKLRY, B R Ion transport regulation in cystic fibrosis Core facility--Cell culture and morphology
R01DK-38527-05 (END) KARIN, MICHAEL UNIV OF CA, SAN DIEGO 9500 GILMAN DRIVE LA JOLLA, CA 92093-0636 Tissue specific expression of human growth hormone gene
R29DK-38529-05 (CBY) PEREZ-ARMENDARIZ, ELIA M A. EINSTEIN COLLEGE OF MED. 1300 MORRIS PARK AVENUE BRONX, NY 10461 Gap junctions between pancreatic beta cells
R01DK-38531-03 (BIO) OSBORNE, WILLIAM R UNIVERSITY OF WASHINGTON DEPT OF PEDIATRICS, RD-20 SEATTLE, WA 98195 Purine nucleoside phosphorylase gene transfer
R01DK-38543-06 (MET) LEAHY, JOHN L JOSLIN DIABETES CENTER ONE JOSLIN PLACE BOSTON, MA 02215 Viability and function of transplanted islet-cells
R29DK-38546-05 (END) SHARP, Z DAVE UNIVERSITY OF TEXAS 7703 FLOYD CURL DRIVE SAN ANTONIO, TX 78284 Pituitary hormone regulation
R01DK-38550-05 (GMA) ERMAK, THOMAS H VA MEDICL CENTER 4150 CLEMENT ST SAN FRANCISCO, CA 94121 M cell uptake and cytoarchitecture in Peyer's patches
R01DK-38558-05 (PTHA) SEDOR, JOHN R UNIVERSITY HOSPITALS 2074 ABINGTON ROAD CLEVELAND, OH 44106 Mechanisms of glomerular immune injury
R29DK-38593-05 (BIO) HANCOCK, LARRY W U OF MN 4-135 JACKSON HALL 321 CHURCH STRET, S E MINNEAPOLIS, MN 55455 Lysosomal transport and metabolism of sialic acid
R55DK-38596-04 (PHY) SACKIN, HENRY J CORNELL UNIVERSITY MEDICAL COL 1300 YORK AVNEUE NEW YORK, N Y 10021 Basolateral K conductance in the proximal tubule
R01DK-38626-05 (GMA) LIDDLE, RODGER A DUKE UNIV MEDICAL CENTER BOX 3083 DURHAM, NC 27710 Second messenger signalling in cholecystokinin cells
P01DK-38639-04 (DDK) SATO, GORDON H W ALTON JONES CELL SCI CTR, IN 10 OLD BARN ROAD LAKE PLACID, NY 12946 Tissue culture/growth factors and metabolic disorders
P01DK-38639-04 0001 (DDK) MCKEEHAN, WALLACE L Tissue culture/growth factors and metabolic disorders Hormonal regulation of hepatoma-derived protease
P01DK-38639-04 0002 (DDK) CHEN, JAN-KAN Tissue culture/growth factors and metabolic disorders Growth and proteoglycan metabolism of human vascular cells
P01DK-38639-04 0003 (DDK) HARRIS, STEPHEN E Tissue culture/growth factors and metabolic disorders The androgen receptor gene in growth and differentiation
P01DK-38639-04 0004 (DDK) HAYASHI, JUN Tissue culture/growth factors and metabolic disorders Thymic stromal cells and T cell differentiation
P01DK-38639-04 0005 (DDK) SERRERO, GINETTE Tissue culture/growth factors and metabolic disorders Mesenchymal cell differentiation
P01DK-38639-04 9001 (DDK) SATO, GORDON Tissue culture/growth factors and metabolic disorders Molecular biology core
P01DK-38639-04 9002 (DDK) SATO, GORDON Tissue culture/growth factors and metabolic disorders Protein chemistry core
R01DK-38644-05 (PTHA) CAVALLO, TITO BROWN UNIVERSITY BIO-MED CENTER PROVIDENCE, RI 02912 Studies on lupus nephritis and proteinuria
R01DK-38649-04 (PTHB) CHUNG, LELAND W UNIV OF TX SYSTEM CANCER CTR M D ANDERSON HSPL & TUMOR INST HOUSTON, TX 77030 cellular interactions and prostate growth
R01DK-38652-05 (MEP) CHOJKIER, MARIO UNIV. OF CALIFORNIA, SAN DIEGO LA JOLLA, CA 92093 Hepatic connective tissue protein production in vivo
R29DK-38660-05 (MET) ROBINSON, MITCHELL E EAST TENNESSEE STATE UNIV QUILLEN-DISHNER COLLEGE OF MED JOHNSON CITY, TN 37614 Metabolism of phospholipid molecular species
R01DK-38664-05 (PHY) DEMAREST, JEFFREY UNIVERSITY OF ARKANSAS 632 SCEN FAYETTEVILLE, AR 72701 Electrophysiology of gastric ion transport salamanders
R29DK-38667-05 (PTHA) BADR, KAMAL F VANDERBILT UNIVERSITY DIV. OF NEPHROLOGY, S-3223 MCN NASHVILLE, TN 37232 Vasoactive lipoxygenase products in glomerular injury
R01DK-38674-05 (BBCA) VINOGRADOV, SERGE N WAYNE STATE UNIVERSITY 540 E CANFIELD DETROIT, MI 48201 Structure and function of annelid hemoglobins
R29DK-38676-04 (BBCB) LIVE, DAVID H CALIFORNIA INST OF TECHNOLOGY 164-30 CR PASADENA, CA 91125 Conformation of mitogenic peptide growth factors
R29DK-38681-05 (PTHA) PARKS, DALE A UNIV OF ALABAMA AT BIRMINGHAM UNIVERSITY STATION BIRMINGHAM, ALA 35294 Liver preservation and reperfusion
R01DK-38682-05 (HEM) LEY, TIMOTHY J UNIV MEDICAL CENTER 216 SO KINGSHIGHWAY BLVD ST LOUIS, MO 63110 Regulation of fetal & adult human hemoglobin production
R01DK-38696-03 (GMB) SILVER, JUSTIN HADASSAH UNIVERSITY HOSPITAL POB 12000, JERUSALEM IL-91120, ISRAEL Regulation of parathyroid hormone and calcitonin genes
R01DK-38699-05 (HEM) KAUFMAN, RUSSEL E DUKE UNIVERSITY MEDICAL CENTER BOX 3250 DURHAM, NC 27710 Control of the hematopoietic developmental program
R29DK-38702-04 (EDC) RAMIREZ, MARIA E UNIVERSITY OF UTAH 50 NORTH MEDICAL DRIVE SALT LAKE CITY, UT 84112 Familial aggregation of fat patterns & disease
R01DK-38704-06 (PHY) BELLO-REUSS, ELSA UNIV OF TEXAS MEDICAL BRANCH GALVESTON, TX 77550 Ion transport in collecting cell cultures
P30DK-38707-05 (ADDK) GRAY, GARY M STANFORD UNIV SCH OF MEDICINE STANFORD, CA 94305-5100 Gastrointestinal membrane receptor
P30DK-38707-05 0001 (ADDK) GRAY, GARY M Gastrointestinal membrane receptor Small intestinal membrane glycoprotein hydrolases and receptors
P30DK-38707-05 0002 (ADDK) BUTCHER, EUGENE C Gastrointestinal membrane receptor Molecular mechanisms of leukocyte homing
P30DK-38707-05 0003 (ADDK) COOPER, ALLEN D Gastrointestinal membrane receptor Cholesterol and lipoprotein metabolism in the liver and GI tract
P30DK-38707-05 0004 (ADDK) GREENBERG, HARRY B Gastrointestinal membrane receptor Molecular mechanisms of viral diarrhea
P30DK-38707-05 0005 (ADDK) SCHOOLNIK, GARY Gastrointestinal membrane receptor Molecular basis of bacterial interaction with host tissues
P30DK-38707-05 0006 (ADDK) BUTCHER, EUGENE C Gastrointestinal membrane receptor Mucosal epithelial factors regulating lymphocyte homing
P30DK-38707-05 0007 (ADDK) COOPER, ALLEN D Gastrointestinal membrane receptor LDL receptors in intestines
P30DK-38707-05 0008 (ADDK) NGUYEN, TOAN D Gastrointestinal membrane receptor VIP receptor in liver plasma membranes
P30DK-38707-05 0009 (ADDK) OFFIT, PAUL A Gastrointestinal membrane receptor Immune protection against rotavirus infection

PROJECT NO., ORGANIZATIONAL UNIT., INVESTIGATOR, ADDRESS, TITLE

P30DK-38707-05 0010 (ADDK) O'HANLEY, PETER Gastrointestinal membrane receptor Epithelial receptor for enteroinvasive E coli phagocytosis

P30DK-38707-05 0011 (ADDK) ROBINSON, WILLIAM S Gastrointestinal membrane receptor Vaccine strategy for producing enteric and systemic immune responses

P30DK-38707-05 0012 (ADDK) SCHOOLNIK, GARY K Gastrointestinal membrane receptor E coli heat-stable enterotoxin and competitive antagonists

P30DK-38707-05 9001 (ADDK) GREENBERG, HARRY B Gastrointestinal membrane receptor Monoclonal antibody and FACS--Core

P30DK-38707-05 9002 (ADDK) KEDES, LAURENCE H Gastrointestinal membrane receptor Genetic engineering--Core

P30DK-38707-05 9003 (ADDK) SCHOOLNIK, GARY K Gastrointestinal membrane receptor Protein structure--Core

R55DK-38712-04A1 (PC) WHITE, MORRIS F JOSLIN DIABETES CENTER ONE JOSLIN PLACE BOSTON, MA 02215 Interaction between insulin receptors and cell proteins

R29DK-38729-04 (GMA) ROBERTS, INGRAM M GEORGE WASHINGTON UNIVERSITY 2150 PENNSYLVANIA AVENUE N W WASHINGTON, D C 20037 Importance of lingual lipase in fat digestion

R01DK-38734-06 (PHY) REUSS, LUIS UNIV OF TEXAS MEDICAL BRANCH 301 UNIVERSITY BOULEVARD GALVESTON, TEXAS 77550 Salt transport mechanisms in gallbladder epithelium

R01DK-38752-05 (END) STERNINI, CATIA CURE/VA WADSWORTH WILSHIRE & SAWTELLE BLVDS LOS ANGELES, CA 90073 Organization and expression of CGRP in the pancreas

R29DK-38757-04 (BPO) GREENBERG, DANIELLE CORNELL MEDICAL CENTER 21 BLOOMINGDALE ROAD WHITE PLAINS, NY 10605 Upper GI tract mediation of the satiety effect of fats

R01DK-38760-05 (GMA) MANSBACH, CHARLES M, II UNIVERSITY OF TENNESSEE 951 COURT AVENUE, RM 555D MEMPHIS, TENNESSEE 38163 Regulation of intestinal lipid transport

R01DK-38761-06 (BIO) IYENGAR, SRINIVAS R MOUNT SINAI SCHOOL OF MEDICINE ONE GUSTAVE L LEVY PLACE NEW YORK, N Y 10029 Structure and function of signal tranducing components

R01DK-38763-06 (SAT) DEMETRIOU, ACHILLES A 1310 24TH AVE, SOUTH NASHVILLE, TN 37212-2637 Hepatocytes--transplantation, extracorporeal support

R29DK-38765-06 (MET) GARVEY, W TIMOTHY INDIANA UNIVERSITY 1481 WEST 10TH ST. VA HOSP.-11 INDIANAPOLIS, IN 46202-2884 Role of glucose transport proteins in diabetes mellitus

R29DK-38767-04 (GMB) NATH, KARL A UNIV OF MINNESOTA HOSPITALS 420 DELAWARE ST, SE MINNEAPOLIS, MINN 55455 Humoral mechanisms of injury in surviving nephrons

R01DK-38772-06 (END) LEONARD, JACK L UNIVERSITY O MASSACUSETTS 55 LAKE AVENUE NORTH WORCESTER, MA 01655 Thyroid hormone metabolism in extrathyroidal tissues

R01DK-38773-06 (GMB) POWELL, DAVID R BAYLOR COLLEGE OF MEDICINE 8080 N STADIUM DR HOUSTON, TX 77054 Growth factors and their inhibitors in renal failure

R01DK-38794-04A2 (MET) MAY, JAMES M VANDERBILT UNIVERSITY 21ST AVENUE SOUTH AND GARLAND NASHVILLE, TN 37232-2230 Affinity labeling of the adipocyte hexose carrier

R01DK-38795-06 (MGN) WENGER, DAVID A JEFFERSON MEDICAL COLLEGE 1100 WALNUT ST/RM 410 PHILADELPHIA, PA 19107 Genetic and biochemical studies on Krabbe's disease

R01DK-38814-05 (END) FERGUSON, DUNCAN C UNIVERSITY OF GEORGIA COLLEGE OF VETERINARY MEDICINE ATHENS, GA 30602 Regulation or renal thyroid hormone uptake and metabolism

R29DK-38821-05 (BIO) TOLAN, DEAN R BOSTON UNIVERSITY 2 CUMMINGTON STREET BOSTON, MA 02215 Aldolase genes in normal and fructose intolerant humans

R01DK-38825-07 (GMA) BONKOVSKY, HERBERT L UNIVERSITY OF MASSACHUSETTS 55 LAKE AVE WORCESTER, MA 01655 Regulation of hepatic heme metabolism

R01DK-38828-05A1 (PHRA) JOHNSON, ROGER A SUNY AT STONY BROOK HSC, BHS, T-6, 140 STONY BROOK, NY 11794-8661 Regulation of adenylyl cyclase

R01DK-38830-06 (PHY) EATON, DOUGLAS C EMORY UNIVERSITY SCHOOL OF MED ATLANTA, GA 30322 Sodium transport in epithelial tissue

R01DK-38841-06 (HEM) SYTKOWSKI, ARTHUR J NEW ENGLAND DEACONESS HOSPITAL 185 PILGRIM RD BOSTON, MA 02215 A new system for the study of erythropoiesis

R01DK-38842-05 (RNM) TAYLOR, ANDREW T, JR EMORY UNIVERSITY HOSPITAL 1364 CLIFTON ROAD ATLANTA, GA 30322 Development of Tc-99m renal tubular agents

R01DK-38847-05 (MET) WEIGLE, DAVID S HARBORVIEW MEDICAL CENTER 325 NINTH AVNEUE SEATTLE, WA 98104 Physiology & therapeutic use of insulin pulses

R01DK-38848-05 (GMB) GLUCK, STEPHEN L JEWISH HOSPITAL OF ST LOUIS 216 SOUTH KINGSHIGHWAY ST LOUIS, MO 63110 H+ATPase in urinary acidification

R01DK-38855-06 (GMB) HEATH, HUNTER, III MAYO FOUNDATION 200 FIRST STREET SOUTHWEST ROCHESTER, MN 55905 Pathogenesis of hypercalcemia

R01DK-38857-06 (MGN) NEUFELD, ELIZABETH F UNIVERSITY OF CALIFORNIA CENTER FOR HEALTH SCIENCES LOS ANGELES, CA 90024-1737 Molecular study of MPS I; gene therapy in a canine model

R29DK-38883-04 (GMA) SMITH, DANIEL J H6/516 CSC 600 HIGHLAND AVENUE MADISON, WI 53792 Membrane fluidity in the pathogenesis of hepatic disease

R29DK-38893-05 (BIO) KOHANSKI, RONALD A MOUNT SINAI SCHOOL OF MEDICINE ONE GUSTAVE L. LEVY PLACE NEW YORK, NY 10029 Insulin receptor/kinase regulation in the intact cells

R01DK-38895-03 (BM) CALLAHAN, HUGH J THOMAS JEFFERSON UNIVERSITY 1025 WALNUT STREET PHILADELPHIA, PA 19107 Antibacterial properties of urinary tract glycoproteins

R29DK-38917-03 (MET) GORRAY, KENNETH C LONG ISLAND JEWISH MEDICAL CTR DEPARTMENT OF MEDICINE NEW HYDE PARK, NY 11042 Alloxan resistance & islet regeneration

R01DK-38925-04 (TOX) STEVENS, JAMES W ALTON JONES CELL SCI CTR, IN 10 OLD BARN ROAD LAKE PLACID, NY 12946 Nephrotoxicity of cysteine conjugates

R01DK-38930-05 (REN) WELTMAN, ARTHUR L UNIVERSITY OF VIRGINIA EXERCISE PHYSIOLOGY LAB CHARLOTTESVILLE, VA 22903 Bone mineral content and reproductive hormones in women runners

R01DK-38932-04 (BIO) ROESSLER, BLAKE J UNIVERSITY OF MICHIGAN 3918 TAUBMAN CENTER, BOX 0358 ANN ARBOR, MI 48109 Molecular mechanisms of prpp-synthetase overactivity

R01DK-38938-06 (GMA) MUALLEM, SHMUEL U T SOUTHWESTERN MED CTR 5323 HARRY HINES BOULEVARD DALLAS, TX 75235-9040 Hormone regulation of [Ca 2+] in pancreatic acinar cells

R01DK-38940-06 (PB) MC CORMICK, DONALD B EMORY UNIVERSITY ROLLINS RESEARCH CENTER ATLANTA, GA 30322 Flavocoenzyme formation--Flavokinase and FAD synthetase

P30DK-38942-04 (DDK) BARRETT, EUGENE UNIVERSITY OF VIRGINIA BOX 448 JORDAN HALL CHARLOTTESVILLE, VA 22908 Diabetes endocrinology research center

P30DK-38942-04 9005 (DDK) LYNCH, KEVIN R Diabetes endocrinology research center Molecular biology core facilities

P30DK-38942-04 9001 (DDK) FREEDLENDER, ARTHUR E Diabetes endocrinology research center Radioassay core facilities

P30DK-38942-04 9002 (DDK) HAMLIN, JOYCE L Diabetes endocrinology research center issue culture core facilities

P30DK-38942-04 9003 (DDK) JOHNSON, MICHAEL L Diabetes endocrinology research center Biomathematics core facilities

P30DK-38942-04 9004 (DDK) BENJAMIN, DAVID C Diabetes endocrinology research center Protein and nucleic core facilities

R29DK-38949-04 (MET) HENRY, ROBERT R UNIV. OF CALIFORNIA, SAN DIEGO DEPT. OF MEDICINE, V-111 G LA JOLLA, CA 92093 Comparative studies of intracellular glucose metabolism

R29DK-38953-03 (GMB) MAY, ROBERT C EMORY UNIVERSITY SCHOOL OF MED 1364 CLIFTON RD, NE ATLANTA, GEORGIA 30322 Uremia--Effects on insulin binding and receptor function

R01DK-38955-05 (SAT) KRIEGER, JOHN N UNIVERSITY OF WASHINGTON SEATTLE, WA 98195 Urological studies of idiopathic lower tract syndromes

R01DK-38961-05 (GMB) CHRISTAKOS, SYLVIA S UNIV OF MED/DENT OF NEW JERSEY 185 SO. ORANGE AVENUE NEWARK, NJ 07103-2714 Ca++ binding proteins and the vitamin D endocrine system

R29DK-38965-05 (END) LOOSE, DAVID S UNIV OF TEXAS HLTH SCI CTR 6431 FANNIN BOX # 20708 HOUSTON, TX 77225 Phosphoenolpyruvate carboxykinase in adipose tissue

R01DK-38972-05 (GMA) FORTE, JOHN G UNIVERSITY OF CALIFORNIA 241 LIFE SCIENCES ANNEX BERKELEY, CA 94720 Development of gastric HCl secretion

R01DK-38980-05 (GMB) GRANTHAM, JARED J UNIVERSITY OF KANSAS MED CENTE 39TH AND RAINBOW KANSAS CITY, KS 66103-8410 Control of epithelial growth in renal cystic disease

R01DK-38995-02 (PTHA) MENDRICK, DONNA L BRIGHAM AND WOMEN'S HOSPITAL 75 FRANCIS STREET BOSTON, MA 02115 Pathobiology of the glomerular epithelial cell

R29DK-39003-06 (REN) LAXMANAN, SEETHALAKSHMI UNIV OF MASS, DIV OF UROLOGY 55 LAKE AVE NORTH WORCHESTER, MA 01655 Effects of cyclosporine on male reproduction

R29DK-39007-06 (GMA) HALM, DAN R OHIO STATE UNIVERSITY 1645 NEIL AVE COLUMBUS, OH 43210 Active potassium transport across colonic epithelium

R01DK-39019-05 (END) CHAE, CHI-BOM UNIVERSITY OF NORTH CAROLINA CB# 7260, 405 FLOB CHAPEL HILL, NC 27599-7260 Hormonal regulation of thyroglobulin gene in thyroids

R29DK-39023-05 (GMB) WILLIAMS, JAMES C JR INDIANA UNIVERSITY 635 BARNHILL DR INDIANAPOLIS, IN 46202-5120 Volume absorption in the renal proximal tubule

R29DK-39024-04 (IMB) LEMIRE, JACQUES M UNIV OF CALIFORNIA, SAN DIEGO LA JOLLA, CA 92093-0609 Immunosuppressive properties of dihydroxyvitamin D3

R01DK-39035-03 (SB) BROLIN, ROBERT E UNDNJ-ROBERT WOOD JOHNSON MED ONE ROBERT WOOD JOHNSON PL. NEW BRUNSWICK, NJ 08903-0019 Quantitative assessment of intestinal ischemic disease

R29DK-39065-04 (HEM) SILBERSTEIN, LESLIE E UNIVERSITY OF PENNSYLVANIA SCHOOL OF MEDICINE PHILADELPHIA, PA 19104-6082 Human B cell repertoire of erythrocyte autoantibodies

R29DK-39068-05 (GMB) JOHNSON, RICHARD J DIV OF NEPHROLOGY R-11 UNIVERSITY OF WASHINGTON SEATTLE, WA 98195 Myeloperoxidase-H2O2-halide system in glomerular injury

R01DK-39074-04 (GMA) LACY, ERIC R MEDICAL UNIV OF SOUTH CAROLINA 171 ASHLEY AVENUE CHARLESTON, S C 29425 Mechanism of gastric protection & epithelial restitution

R01DK-39075-05 (PC) COLMAN, ROBERTA F UNIV OF DELAWARE NEWARK, DE 19716 Active and allosteric site of isocitrate dehydrogenases

R01DK-39078-05 (PC) CHEN, YUAN-TSONG DUKE U. MED. CNTR./DIV. OF GENETICS & METAB./BOX 3028 DURHAM, NC 27710 Molecular mechanism in type III glycogen storage disease

P01DK-39079-05 (DDK) MACLAREN, NOEL K UNIVERSITY OF FLORIDA BOX J100275 JHMHC GAINESVILLE, FL 32610 Genetics & pathogenesis of insulin dependent diabetes

P01DK-39079-05 0001 (DDK) MACLAREO, NOEL K Genetics & pathogenesis of insulin dependent diabetes Identification, characterization & epidemiology of islet autoantigens

P01DK-39079-05 0002 (DDK) JOHNSON, SUZANNE Genetics & pathogenesis of insulin dependent diabetes Psychological correlates of diabetes onset

P01DK-39079-05 0003 (DDK) WAKELANDS, EDWARD Genetics & pathogenesis of insulin dependent diabetes Molecular genetics of HLA-D polymorphism associated with IDD

P01DK-39079-05 0004 (DDK) RILEY, WILLIAM Genetics & pathogenesis of insulin dependent diabetes Disordered cell mediated cell immunity in IDD

P01DK-39079-05 0005 (DDK) PECK, AMON B Genetics & pathogenesis of insulin dependent diabetes Immunogenetics

P01DK-39079-05 0006 (DDK) CLARKE, DERRELL Genetics & pathogenesis of insulin dependent diabetes: Characterization, localization and registration of insulin transcription

P01DK-39079-05 0007 (DDK) BURR, IAN Genetics & pathogenesis of insulin dependent diabetes Superoxide radicals and pancreatic beta

PROJECT NO., ORGANIZATIONAL UNIT., INVESTIGATOR, ADDRESS, TITLE

cell injury
P01DK-39079-05 9001 (DDK) PECK, AMMON Genetics & pathogenesis of insulin dependent diabetes Animal core
P01DK-39079-05 9002 (DDK) KLEIN, PAUL Genetics & pathogenesis of insulin dependent diabetes Laboratory core
R01DK-39080-05 (SAT) SAENZ DE TEJADA, I BOSTON UNIVERSITY 720 HARRISON AVE BOSTON, MA 02118 Physiology of human penile smooth muscle
R01DK-39085-04A1 (GMB) BARAN, DANIEL T UNIV OF MASSACHUSETTS MED CTR 55 LAKE AVE, N WORCESTER, MA 01655 Rapid molecular actions of 1alpha,25-dihydroxyvitamin D3
R01DK-39086-06 (SAT) HANNO, PHILIP M TEMPLE UNIVERSITY MEDICAL CENT 3400 NORTH BROAD STREET PHILADELPHIA, PA 19140 Interstitial cystitis--Human and animal studies
R01DK-39087-03 (SAT) HAYEK, ALBERTO WHITTIER INST FOR DIABETES 9894 GENESEE AVENUE LA JOLLA, CA 92037 Islet transplantation in experimental diabetes
R01DK-39088-01A3 (SAT) WEBER, COLLIN J COLUMBIA UNIVERSITY 630 WEST 168TH ST NEW YORK, NY 10032 Microencapsulated islet xenografts in nod mice
R29DK-39101-04 (GMB) VEHASKARI, V MATTI WASHINGTON UNIVERSITY 400 S KINGSHIGHWAY ST LOUIS, MO 63110 Biology of compensatory adaptation in collecting tubule
R29DK-39110-04 (BIO) LOIKE, JOHN D COLUMBIA UNIVERSITY 630 WEST 168TH STREET NEW YORK, NY 10032 Creatine homeostasis in health and disease
R29DK-39120-03 (BM) MOBASSALEH, MUNIR NEW ENGLAND MED CENTER, INC 750 WASHINGTON ST, BOX 213 BOSTON, MA 02111 Intestinal toxin receptors and pathogenesis of diarrhea
R01DK-39121-05 (MBC) ADLER, JULIUS UNIVERSITY OF WISCONSIN 420 HENRY MALL MADISON, WI 53706 Ion channels & osmotaxis in Escherichia coli
R29DK-39125-05 (EDC) DORMAN, JANICE S UNIVERSITY OF PITTSBURGH 130 DESOTO STREET PITTSBURGH, PA 15261 The familial clustering of diabetes complications
R29DK-39135-04 (PC) FROST, SUSAN C UNIVERSITY OF FLORIDA BOX J-245 JHMHC GAINESVILLE, FL 32610 Insulin action in differentiating 3T3-l1 adipocytes
R01DK-39137-05 (PC) ROY-CHOWDHURY, NAMITA ALBERT EINSTEIN COLLEGE OF MED 1300 MORRIS PARK AVE BRONX, NY 10461 Relation of enzyme processing to hepatic glucuronidation
R29DK-39138-05 (GMB) REDDY, SATYANARAYANA G WOMEN & INFANTS' HOSPITAL 101 DUDLEY STREET PROVIDENCE, R I 02905-2501 Side chain metabolism of vitamin D
R01DK-39144-05 (END) FERIN, MICHEL J COLUMBIA UNIVERSITY 630 WEST 168 STREET NEW YORK, NY 10032 The adrenal axis and the reproductive process
R01DK-39154-06 (PHY) CHASE, HERBERT S, JR COLUMBIA COLLEGE 630 W 168TH STREET NEW YORK, N Y 10032 Renal sodium transport by cellular calcium bufo marinus
R29DK-39157-03 (NTN) VAZQUEZ, JORGE A MONTEFIORE HOSPITAL 3459 FIFTH AVE PITTSBURGH, PA 15213 Protein sparing during treatment of obesity
R29DK-39160-05 (NTN) BEARD, JOHN L PENNSYLVANIA STATE UNIVERSITY S 126 HENDERSON BLDG UNIVERSITY PARK, PA 16802 Iron deficiency anemia and conmpensatory SNS activity
R29DK-39165-05 (GMA) BALLATORI, NAZZARENO UNIV OF ROCHESTER DEPT OF BIOPHYSICS ROCHESTER, NY 14642 Hepatobiliary transport and metabolism of glutathione
R29DK-39167-04 (GMA) MOSELEY, RICHARD H VA MEDICAL CENTER 2215 FULLER ROAD ANN ARBOR, MI 48105 Studies of hepatic membrane transport
R29DK-39168-04 (GMA) GRISHAM, MATTHEW B LSU MEDICAL CENTERH 1501 KINGS HIGHWAY PO BOX 3393 SHREVEPORT, LA 71130-3932 Ulcerative colitis--Role of reactive oxygen metabolites
R01DK-39177-05 (BPO) ROLLS, BARBARA J THE JOHNS HOPKINS HOSPITAL 600 NORTH WOLFE STREET BALTIMORE, MD 21205 Factors affecting caloric regulation in human feeding
R01DK-39178-05 (HED) JACKSON, BENJAMIN T VETERANS AFFAIRS MEDICAL CTR DAVIS PARK PROVIDENCE, RI 02908 Hormonal effects within the fetus in diabetic pregnancy
R01DK-39180-05A1 (BPO) FRANKMANN, SANDRA P NEW YORK HOSP-CORNELL MED CTR 21 BLOOMINGDALE ROAD WHITE PLAINS, NY 10605 Prior history and salt intake of rats
R01DK-39188-05 (GMA) TATEMOTO, KAZUHIKO DEPARTMENT OF PSYCHIATRY STANFORD UNIV SCH OF MED STANFORD, CA 94305 Search for novel gastrointestinal hormones
R01DK-39197-04A1 (TMP) JONES, GRACE M UNIVERSITY OF KENTUCKY S-225 AGRIC SCIENCE CTR NORTH LEXINGTON, KY 40546-0091 Regulatory sequences needed for juvenile hormone action
R01DK-39199-02 (GMA) OWYANG, CHUNG UNIVERSITY OF MICHIGAN BOX 0362 ANN ARBOR, MI 48109-0362 Secretin and gastric motility in health and duodenal ulcers
R29DK-39208-05 (GMA) HELM, JAMES F FROEDTERT MEM LUTHERAN HOSP 9200 W WISCONSIN AVENUE MILUAKEE, WI 53226 Esophageal clearance in health & disease
R29DK-39216-04 (PTHA) TSILIBARY, PHOTINI-EFFIE C UNIV. OF MINNESOTA, BOX 609 420 DELAWARE STREET, S.E. MINNEAPOLIS, MN 55455 Functional importance of domain of type IV collagen
R01DK-39225-05 (TOX) TAPPEL, ALOYS L UNIVERSITY OF CALIFORNIA 1480 CHEMISTRY ANNEX DAVIS, CALIF 95616 Free radical lipid peroxidation damage
R01DK-39233-05 (EDC) SOELDNER, JOHN S ALHAMBRA PLAZA 1625 ALHAMBRA BLVD SACRAMENTO, CA 95816 Pathogenesis of IDDM--The earliest lesion
R01DK-39239-05 (SAT) PARSONS, C L UNIV OF CALIFORNIA, SAN DIEGO 225 DICKINSON ST SAN DIEGO, CA 92103 Interstitial cystitis--Pathogenesis and treatement
R01DK-39246-05 (NTN) COOK, JAMES D UNIV OF KANSAS MED CENTER 39TH & RAINBOW BLVD KANSAS CITY, KS 66103-8410 Regulation of body iron exchange
P50DK-39249-05 (DDK) BRENNER, BARRY M BRIGHAM AND WOMEN'S HOSPITAL 75 FRANCIS STREET BOSTON, MA 02115 Harvard center for the study of kidney disease

PROJECT NO., ORGANIZATIONAL UNIT., INVESTIGATOR, ADDRESS, TITLE

P50DK-39249-05 0002 (DDK) MITCH, WILLIAM E Harvard center for the study of kidney disease Renal cell protein turnover and other relationship in diabetics
P50DK-39249-05 0003 (DDK) ZEIDEL, MARK L Harvard center for the study of kidney disease Glucose metabolism and ion transport in medullary cells
P50DK-39249-05 0004 (DDK) SEIFTER, JULIAN L Harvard center for the study of kidney disease Effects of fructose on renal glucose metabolism
P50DK-39249-05 0005 (DDK) ALPER, SETH L Harvard center for the study of kidney disease Structural analysis of multiple band genes
P50DK-39249-05 0006 (DDK) CANTLEY, LLOYD Harvard center for the study of kidney disease Isolation and characterization of a chloride channel
P50DK-39249-05 0007 (DDK) EPSTEIN, FRANKLIN H Harvard center for the study of kidney disease Diabetes and acute renal failure
P50DK-39249-05 0008 (DDK) COHEN, BRIAN J Harvard center for the study of kidney disease Membrane transport regulation in hepatocytes
P50DK-39249-05 0009 (DDK) CARPENTER, CHARLES B Harvard center for the study of kidney disease Kidney rejection and autoimmune diabetes
P50DK-39249-05 0010 (DDK) STROM, TERRY B Harvard center for the study of kidney disease Immunotherapy to prevent nephropathy in type I diabetes
P50DK-39249-05 0011 (DDK) AXELROD, LLOYD Harvard center for the study of kidney disease Effect of insulin in eicosanoid production
P50DK-39249-05 0001 (DDK) BALLERMANN, BARBARA J Harvard center for the study of kidney disease Cellular basis for glomerular sclerosis in diabetic rats
P50DK-39249-05 0012 (DDK) AVRUCH, JOSEPH Harvard center for the study of kidney disease Lipocortin regulation by phosphorylation in diabetes
P50DK-39249-05 0013 (DDK) ERCOLANI, LOUIS Harvard center for the study of kidney disease Transcriptional regulation of pyruvate carboxylase by insulin
P50DK-39249-05 0014 (DDK) CANTLEY, LEWIS Harvard center for the study of kidney disease Phosphatidylinositol turnover in mesangial cells
P50DK-39249-05 0015 (DDK) STOSSEL, THOMAS P Harvard center for the study of kidney disease Microfilament organization in diabetic glomerular mesangium
P50DK-39249-05 0016 (DDK) WEBER, PETER C Harvard center for the study of kidney disease Effects of fatty acids on cellular pathophysiology in diabetes
P50DK-39249-05 0017 (DDK) KROLEWSKI, ANDRZEJ S Harvard center for the study of kidney disease Genetic predisposition to hypertension in diabetes
P50DK-39250-05 (DDK) GRAYHACK, JOHN T NORTHWESTERN UNIV MEDICAL SCH 303 EAST CHICAGO AVENUE CHICAGO, IL 60611-3008 Cellular and chemical aspects of benign prostatic growth
P50DK-39250-05 0001 (DDK) KOZLOWSKI, JAMES M Cellular and chemical aspects of benign prostatic growth Cell biology
P50DK-39250-05 0002 (DDK) GARNETT, JOHN E Cellular and chemical aspects of benign prostatic growth Biochemical composition of human prostate
P50DK-39250-05 0003 (DDK) GRAYHACK, JOHN T Cellular and chemical aspects of benign prostatic growth Benign prostatic hyperplasia
P50DK-39250-05 0004 (DDK) LEE, CHUNG Cellular and chemical aspects of benign prostatic growth Non-androgenic factors of prostatic growth
P50DK-39250-05 9001 (DDK) LEE, CHUNG Cellular and chemical aspects of benign prostatic growth Core facilities
P50DK-39255-05 (DDK) WIGGINS, ROGER UNIVERSITY OF MICHIGAN 3914 TAUBMAN CENTER ANN ARBOR, MI 48109-0364 Mechanisms of glomerular and tubular injury
P50DK-39255-05 0001 (DDK) PHAN, SEM Mechanisms of glomerular and tubular injury Fibrotic mechanisms in crescentric GN
P50DK-39255-05 0002 (DDK) KUNKEL, STEVEN Mechanisms of glomerular and tubular injury Macrophage function in crescentic GN
P50DK-39255-05 0003 (DDK) FANTONE, JOSEPH Mechanisms of glomerular and tubular injury Phagocytic cells and glomerular injury
P50DK-39255-05 0004 (DDK) JOHNSON, KENT J Mechanisms of glomerular and tubular injury Oxidants and glomerular injury
P50DK-39255-05 0005 (DDK) WEINBERG, JOEL Mechanisms of glomerular and tubular injury Inflammatory cell mediated proximal tubule injury
P50DK-39255-05 9001 (DDK) WIGGINS, ROGER Mechanisms of glomerular and tubular injury GN model and glomerular culture core
P50DK-39255-05 9002 (DDK) JOHNSON, KENT Mechanisms of glomerular and tubular injury Morphology core
P50DK-39255-05 0006 (DDK) SHAYMAN, JAMES Mechanisms of glomerular and tubular injury Determination of inositol phosphate mass in renal epithelium
P50DK-39255-05 0007 (DDK) TANNEN, RICHARD Mechanisms of glomerular and tubular injury Carbohydrate metabolism in cultured proximal tubles
P50DK-39255-05 0008 (DDK) HUMES, DAVID Mechanisms of glomerular and tubular injury Free radical induced mitochondrical dysfunction
P50DK-39255-05 0009 (DDK) BRIGGS, JOSEPHINE Mechanisms of glomerular and tubular injury Role of tubuloglomerular feedback nephrotoxic renal damage
R29DK-39256-05 (VR) PALSSON, BERNHARD O UNIVERSITY OF MICHIGAN 3026 DOW BLDG ANN ARBOR, MI 48109 Metabolic dynamics and the red blood cell
P50DK-39257-05 (DDK) ELBADAWI, AHMAD SUNY HSC AT SYRACUSE 750 EAST ADAMS STREET SYRACUSE, NY 13210 Kidney and urological research centers
P50DK-39257-05 0001 (DDK) MCGUIRE, EDWARD J Kidney and urological research centers In vivo studies on obstructive uropathy
P50DK-39257-05 0002 (DDK) ELBADAWI, AHMED Kidney and urological research centers Morphologic studies on obstructive uropathy
P50DK-39257-05 0003 (DDK) LEVIN, ROBERT M Kidney and urological research centers In vitro studies on obstructive uropathy
P50DK-39258-05 (DDK) WARNOCK, DAVID G UNIVERSITY OF AL AT BIRMINGHAM U.A.B. STATION BIRMINGHAM, AL 35294 Mechanisms and consequences of renal hypertension
P50DK-39258-05 0001 (DDK) SCHAFER, JAMES A Mechanisms and

consequences of renal hypertension Hormone interaction in the cortical collecting tubule
P50DK-39258-05 0002 (DDK) NAVAR, L GABRIEL Mechanisms and consequences of renal hypertension Interactions between angiotensin II and norepinephrine
P50DK-39258-05 0003 (DDK) ABRAHAMSON, DALE Mechanisms and consequences of renal hypertension Structure, function and development of the juxtaglomerular apparatus
P50DK-39258-05 0004 (DDK) RICK, ROGER Mechanisms and consequences of renal hypertension Cellular ion homeostasis in hypertension
P50DK-39258-05 0005 (DDK) SMITH, JEFFREY B Mechanisms and consequences of renal hypertension Ions, endothelium, and vascular reactivity in hypertension
P50DK-39258-05 0006 (DDK) PLOTH, DAVID W Mechanisms and consequences of renal hypertension Tubuloglomerular mechanisms in renal vascular hypertension
P50DK-39258-05 0007 (DDK) WORK, JACK Mechanisms and consequences of renal hypertension Altered NaC1 transport in Henle's loop in--Models of hypertension
P50DK-39258-05 0008 (DDK) CURTIS, JOHN J Mechanisms and consequences of renal hypertension Mechanisms of cyclosporine induced renal hypertension
P50DK-39258-05 9001 (DDK) WORK, JACK Mechanisms and consequences of renal hypertension Radioimmunoassay core
P50DK-39258-05 9002 (DDK) RICK, ROGER Mechanisms and consequences of renal hypertension Microdroplet ion assay by electron microprobe--Core
P50DK-39261-05 (DDK) JACOBSON, HARRY R VANDERBILT UNIV MED CENTER NASHVILLE, TN 37232 The biology of progressive nephron destruction
P50DK-39261-05 0001 (DDK) ICHIKAWA, LEKUNI The biology of progressive nephron destruction Characterization of glomerular sclerosis I
P50DK-39261-05 0002 (DDK) BADR, KAMAL The biology of progressive nephron destruction Functional characterization of renal allograft rejection
P50DK-39261-05 0003 (DDK) DANIEL, THOMAS O The biology of progressive nephron destruction Growth factor expression of the glomerular cell
P50DK-39261-05 0004 (DDK) RAYMOND, C HARRIS The biology of progressive nephron destruction Mechanism of growth and functional capacity in decreased renal mass
P50DK-39261-05 0005 (DDK) BREYER, MATTHEW D The biology of progressive nephron destruction Effects of cytokines, epidermal growth factor andcyclosporin A on kidney tubules
P50DK-39261-05 9001 (DDK) BLAIR, IAN A The biology of progressive nephron destruction Core facilities
R29DK-39263-04 (BIO) PAXTON, RALPH AUBURN UNIVERSITY COLLEGE OF VETERINARY MEDICINE AUBURN, AL 36849-5520 Regulating branched-chain alpha-ketoacid dehydrogenase
R01DK-39264-01A3 (HEM) SASSA, SHIGERU ROCKEFELLLER UNIVERSITY 1230 YORK AVENUE NEW YORK, NY 10021 Heme synthesis in human liver culture
R44DK-39278-02A2 (SSS) SARANGAPANI, SRINIVASAN GINER, INC 14 SPRING STREET WALTHAM, MA 02254-9147 Electrochemical reactor to disinfect reused dialyzers
R01DK-39285-04A3 (MEDB) BRADY, LINDA J UNIVERSITY OF MINNESOTA 1334 ECKLES AVENUE ST PAUL, MN 55108 Carnitine acyltransferase characteristics
R01DK-39286-05 (EVR) GINSBERG-FELLNER, FREDDA V MOUNT SINAI SCHOOL OF MEDICINE ONE GUSTAVE L. LEVY PLACE NEW YORK, NY 10029 Congenital rubella--Pathogenic model for type I diabetes
R01DK-39298-04A1 (GMB) ALPERN, ROBERT J UNIV OF TEXAS SW MED CTR 5323 HARRY HINES BLVD DALLAS, TX 75235-8856 Regulation of renal bicarbonate and chloride absorption
R01DK-39304-04 (BIO) FLETTERICK, ROBERT J UNIV. OF CA, SAN FRANCISCO DEPT. OF BIOCHEMISTRY, S-964 SAN FRANCISCO, CA 94143 Structural analysis of engineered trypsin
R13DK-39306-05 (DDK) FRANK, MARTIN AMERICAN PHYSIOLOGICAL SOCIETY 9650 ROCKVILLE PIKE BETHESDA, MD 20814 Conference fellowship for minority physiologists
R01DK-39308-04A2 (CVB) JOSE, PEDRO A GEORGETOWN UNIVERSITY MED CTR 3800 RESERVOIR ROAD, NW WASHINGTON, DC 20007 Renal dopamine-1 receptor defect in hypertension
R29DK-39311-04 (MGN) ELBEIN, STEVEN C UNIVERSITY OF UTAH 50 N MEDICAL DRIVE SALT LAKE CITY, UT 84132 The genetics of non-insulin dependent diabetes mellitus
R01DK-39326-04 (MET) DI GIROLAMO, MARIO EMORY UNIVERSITY 69 BUTLER STREET S E ATLANTA, GA 30303 Obesity, lactate overproduction and insulin resistance
R01DK-39329-04 (BIO) HARGROVE, JAMES L UNIVERSITY OF GEORGIA DAWSON HALL ATHENS, GA 30602 Selective degradation of tyrosine aminotransferase
R29DK-39331-03 (GMB) GURICH, RICHARD W UNIVERSITY OF TEXAS MED BRANCH 4.200 E-62 GALVESTON, TX 77550 Endosomal proton transport in the renal proximal tubule
R01DK-39337-03 (SB) SARR, MICHAEL G MAYO FOUNDATION 200 FIRST STREET S W ROCHESTER, MN 55905 Enteric physiology and function of the transplanted gut
R29DK-39343-04 (GMB) YARED, AIDA VANDERBILT UNIVERSITY DIV OF PED NEPHROLOGY C4204MCN NASHVILLE, TN 37232-2584 Biology of the maturation of the mammalian glomerulus
R01DK-39348-04 (BIO) NISSIM, ITZHAK CHILDREN'S HOSPITAL 34TH AND CIVIC CENTER BLVD PHILADELPHIA, PA 19104 Hepatic ureagenesis--Studies with 15-N GC-MS and 13C NMR
R01DK-39354-04 (PHY) VERKMAN, ALAN S UNIVERSITY OF CALIFORNIA BOX 0532 SAN FRANCISCO, CA 94143-0532 Development of chloride-sensitive fluorescent indicators
R29DK-39356-05 (GMA) LOUIE, DEXTER STEPHEN UNIVERSITY OF NORTH CAROLINA CB#7400, MCGAVRAN-GREENBERG HA CHAPEL HILL, NC 27599-7400 Protein kinase C mediation of pancreatic secretion
R01DK-39361-04 (BCE) EMANUELE, NICHOLAS V HINES VA HOSPITAL MEDICAL SERVICE 111J HINES, IL 60141 Brain prolactin--Further characterization and studies
U01DK-39366-04 (DDK) BUCKALEW, VARDAMAN M, JR BOWMAN GRAY SCHOOL OF MEDICINE 300 S HAWTHORNE ROAD WINSTON-SALEM, NC 27103 Modification of diet in renal disease (MDRD) study
U01DK-39367-04 (DDK) PORUSH, JEROME G BROOKDALE HOSPITAL MED CENTER LINDEN BLVD AT BROOKDALE PLZ BROOKLYN, NEW YORK 11212 Modification of diet in renal disease (MDRD) study
U01DK-39368-04 (DDK) BOSCH, JUAN P THE GEORGE WASHINGTON UNIVERSI 2150 PENN AVE, NW #4-425 WASHINGTON, D C 20037 Modification of diet in renal disease (MDRD) study
U01DK-39479-04 (DDK) LIFSCHITZ, MEYER D UNIVERSITY OF TEXAS 7703 FLOYD CURL DRIVE SAN ANTONIO, TX 78284 Modification of diet in renal disease (MDRD) study
U01DK-39480-04 (DDK) TISHER, C CRAIG UNIVERSITY OF FLORIDA BOX J-224 GAINESVILLE, FL 32610 Modification of diet in renal disease (MDRD) study
U01DK-39481-04 (DDK) BOURGOIGNE, JACQUES J UNIVERSITY OF MIAMI P O BOX 061960 MIAMI, FL 33101 Modification of diet in renal disease (MDRD) study
U01DK-39485-04 (DDK) HEBERT, LEE A OHIO STATE UNIV RESEARCH FDN 1655 UPHAM DR, RM N210 MEANS COLUMBUS, OHIO 43210 Modification of diet in renal disease (MDRD) study
U01DK-39486-04 (DDK) DENNIS, VINCENT W DUKE UNIVERSITY MEDICAL CENTER BOX 3014 DURHAM, NC 27710 Modification of diet in renal disease (MDRD) study
U01DK-39488-04 (DDK) MITCH, WILLIAM E EMORY UNIVERSITY SCH OF MED 1364 CLIFTON RD, N E ATLANTA, GA 30322 Modification of diet in renal disease (MDRD) study
R01DK-39497-04 (MGN) ATKIN, CURTIS L THE UNIV. OF UTAH MEDICAL CTR. 50 NORTH MEDICAL DRIVE SALT LAKE CITY, UT 84132 Genetic characterization of Alport syndrome
R01DK-39502-03 (PC) LENARD, JOHN UNIV OF MED & DENTISTRY OF NJ ROBERT WOOD JOHNSON MED SCH PISCATAWAY, NJ 08854-5635 Neurospora crassa insulin and insulin receptor
R29DK-39512-03 (GMA) CRAWFORD, JAMES M BRIGHAM AND WOMEN'S HOSPITAL 75 FRANCIS STREET BOSTON, MA 02115 Hepatocellular mechanisms of bile formation
R01DK-39515-04 (GMA) FIELD, MICHAEL COLUMBIA UNIVERSITY 630 WEST 168TH STREET NEW YORK, N Y 10032 Na,K-ATPase regulation in intestine
R01DK-39519-04 (PC) BIRNBAUM, MORRIS J HARVARD MEDICAL SCHOOL 25 SHATTUCK STREET BOSTON, MA 02115 The regulation of glucose transport by insulin
R01DK-39520-04 (BIO) VARSHAVSKY, ALEXANDER J MASSACHUSETTS INST/TECHNOLOGY DEPT OF BIOLOGY, 16-520 CAMBRIDGE, MASS 02139 Studies on selective protein turnover
R01DK-39523-04 (GMB) FEJES-TOTH, GEZA DARTMOUTH MEDICAL SCHOOL 2799 WEST GRAND BLVD HANOVER, NH 03756 Isolated collecting tubule cells--Ion transport
R29DK-39526-04 (BCE) PHILLIPS, JOSEPH T UNIV OF TEXAS SW MED CENTER 5323 HARRY HINES BOULEVARD DALLAS, TX 75235 Prolactin and cyclosporin--Immunoregulatory interactions
R01DK-39532-03 (PHY) AL-AWQATI, QAIS COLUMBIA UNIVERSITY 630 W 168TH STREET NEW YORK, N Y 10032 Epithelial chloride channel
R01DK-39544-04 (SB) KOPECEK, JINDRICH UNIVERSITY OF UTAH 421 WAKARA WAY SALT LAKE CITY, UT 84112 Bioadhesive polymers for treatment of colon disease
R29DK-39546-04 (PHRA) HALL, STEPHEN D WISHARD MEMORIAL HOSPITAL 1001 WEST 10TH STREET INDIANAPOLIS, IN 46202-2879 Factors affecting the renal excretion of drugs
R29DK-39547-04 (CVB) KON, VALENTINA VANDERBILT UNIVERSISTY C-4204 M.C.N. NASHVILLE, TN 37232-2104 Physiology-adrenergic influence on renal fluid transfer
R29DK-39552-03 (PBC) SUSSMAN, NORMAN L BAYLOR COLLEGE OF MEDICINE ONE BAYLOR PLAZA, ROOM 533D HOUSTON, TX 77003 Biosynthesis of liver alkaline phosphatase
R29DK-39565-04 (GMB) ZIYADEH, FUAD N UNIVERSITY OF PENNSYLVANIA 3400 SPRUCE STREET PHILA, PENNA 19104 Effects of benzodiazepines on thick ascending limb
R29DK-39566-03 (HEM) SOLOMON, WILLIAM B STATE UNIVERSITY OF NEW YORK 450 CLARKSON AVENUE/BOX 55 BROOKLYN, NY 11203 Enhancer 10 kb 5' to human epsilon globin
R01DK-39570-02 (GMA) KRAKOWKA, GEORGE S OHIO STATE UNIVERSITY 1925 COFFEY ROAD COLUMBUS, OH 43212 Campylobacter pylori-induced gastric disease
R01DK-39573-03 (GMA) BRASITUS, THOMAS A UNIVERSITY OF CHICAGO 5841 S MARYLAND AVE BOX 400 CHICAGO, IL 60637 Rat intestinal membranes: vitamin D-mediated effects
R37DK-39585-04 (HEM) LINGREL, JERRY B UNIV. OF CINCINNATI MED. CNTR. 231 BETHESDA AVENUE CINCINNATI, OH 45267-0524 Mechanism of the switch from fetal to adult hemoglobin
R01DK-39586-05 (HEM) EMERSON, STEPHEN G UNIVERSITY OF MICHIGAN 1150 WEST MEDICAL CENTER DRIVE ANN ARBOR, MI 48109 T cell CSF regulation and bone marrow transplantation
R01DK-39588-04 (IMS) GERSHWIN, MERRILL E UNIVERSITY OF CALIFORNIA MRAK HALL DAVIS, CA 95616 Mechanisms and pathogenesis of primary biliary cirrhosis
R01DK-39595-04A1 (SAT) HANKS, JOHN B UNIVERSITY OF VIRGINIA BOX 181 HLTH SCIENCES CTR CHARLOTTESVILLE, VA 22908 Glucose homeostasis in the surgically altered pancreas
R01DK-39599-03 (END) DISTELHORST, CLARK W UNIVERSITY HOSPS OF CLEVELAND 2074 ABINGTON ROAD CLEVELAND, OH 44106 Glucocorticoid receptor-heat shock protein interaction
R29DK-39604-04 (NTN) DI SILVESTRO, ROBERT A HUMAN NUTRITION & FOOD MGMT 1787 NEIL AVENUE COLUMBUS, OH 43210-1295 Marginal copper intake effects--SOD & lipid peroxidation
R29DK-39616-04 (EDC) BOYKO, EDWARD J V A MEDICAL CENTER 1660 S COLUMBIAN WAY SEATTLE, WA 98108 Oral contraceptives and inflammatory bowel disease risk
R01DK-39624-04 (BIO) DEYKIN, DANIEL BOSTON V. A. MEDICAL CENTER 150 SOUTH HUNTINGTON AVENUE BOSTON, MA 02130 Arachidonic acid metabolism in diabetes
R01DK-39626-04 (BIO) SHULL, GARY E UNIVERSITY OF CINCINNATI 231

PROJECT NO., ORGANIZATIONAL UNIT., INVESTIGATOR, ADDRESS, TITLE

BETHESDA AVENUE, ML 524 CINCINNATI, OH 45267-0524 Characterization of the H+ K+-ATPase and its genes
R29DK-39628-01A3 (PTHA) MAHAN, JOHN D CHILDREN'S HOSPITAL 700 CHILDREN'S DRIVE COLUMBUS, OH 43205 Glomerular endothelial & mesangial cell-immune complex
R01DK-39629-04 (BEM) RYAN, CHRISTOPHER M W. PSYCHIATRIC INST. & CLINIC 3811 O'HARA STREET PITTSBURGH, PA 15213 Neurobehavioral complications in type I diabetic adults
R29DK-39647-04 (GMA) PALMER, JEFFREY M MEDICAL COLLEGE OF WISCONSIN 8700 WEST WISCONSIN AVE. MILWAUKEE, WI 53226 Mechanism of GI motor disturbances in enteric parasitism
R01DK-39652-02 (PHY) EDDLESTONE, GEOFFREY T CORNELL UNIVERSITY ITHACA, N Y 14853-6401 Neuroendocrine control of K channels in diabetic B-cells
R01DK-39654-04 (GMB) SPIELMAN, WILLIAM S MICHIGAN STATE UNIVERSITY 127B GILTNER HALL EAST LANSING, MI 48824 Regulation of renal function by adenosine
R01DK-39658-03 (CBY) HOPFER, ULRICH CWRU SCHOOL OF MEDICINE 2119 ABINGTON ROAD CLEVELAND, OH 44106 Chloride transport across membranes of zymogen granules
R29DK-39668-05 (GMA) CAREY, HANNAH V UNIVERSITY OF WISCONSIN 2015 LINDEN DRIVE WEST MADISON, WI 53706 Intestinal function in a hibernator--Adaptive changes
R01DK-39669-04 (BIO) MARTINIUK, FRANK T NYU MEDICAL CENTER 550 FIRST AVE / 7N24 NEW YORK, NY 10016 The molecular biology of acid maltase deficiency
R01DK-39671-02 (END) BLACK, VIRGINIA H NEW YORK UNIV MED CTR 550 FIRST AVENUE NEW YORK, NY 10016 Regulation of cytochrome P450's in adrenal
R01DK-39673-04 (BEM) AGRAS, W S DEPT OF PSYCH & BEHAV SCI STANFORD UNIV-MEDICAL SCHOOL STANFORD, CALIF 94305 Study of weight loss maintenance in severe obesity
R01DK-39690-04 (CBY) COLLINS, FRANCIS S UM MEDICAL CENTER 4708 MEDICAL SCIENCES 11 ANN ARBOR, MI 48109-0650 Reverse genetics of CF locus using chromosome jumping
R01DK-39731-05 (DDK) KAO, CHIEN-YUAN S.U.N.Y. H.S.C. AT BROOKLYN 450 CLARKSON AVENUE BROOKLYN, NY 11203-9967 Rurinary tract smooth muscles bioelectric properties
R01DK-39733-04 (MEP) OLSON, JAMES A IOWA STATE UNIVERSITY 125 BEARSHEAR HALL AMES, IOWA 50011 Bioactivity of water-soluble forms of vitamin a
R22DK-39734-02 (EDC) SPURR, G B MEDICAL COLLEGE OF WISCONSIN 8701 WATERTOWN PLANK RD MILWAUKEE, WI 53226 Energy-nutrition of urban women in a developing country
R01DK-39739-03 (END) STRAUS, DANIEL S UNIVERSITY OF CALIFORNIA DIV OF BIOMEDICAL SCIENCES RIVERSIDE, CALIF 92521-0121 Molecular biology of growth regulation by nutrition
R01DK-39740-04 (SAT) CHACKO, SAMUEL K UNIVERSITY OF PENNSYLVANIA 3800 SPRUCE STREET PHILADELPHIA, PA 19104 Intracellular mechanism for urinary bladder function
R01DK-39753-04 (CBY) SUN, TUNG-TIEN NEW YORK UNIVERSITY MED SCHOOL 550 FIRST AVENUE NEW YORK, NY 10016 Biochemistry of urothelial differentiation
R29DK-39755-04 (END) WANG, SAN YOU BETH ISRAEL HOSPITAL 330 BROOKLINE AVENUE BOSTON, MA 02215 Studies of the impairment in insulin synthesis with age
R01DK-39773-07 (PTHA) BONVENTRE, JOSEPH V MASSACHUSETTS GENERAL HOSPITAL 32 FRUIT STREET BOSTON, MA 02114 Nucleotides in anoxic and ischemic cellular injury
R01DK-39776-05 (PTHA) LOVETT, DAVID H UNIVERSITY OF CALIFORNIA 4150 CLEMENT STREET (111J) SAN FRANCISCO, CA 94121 Pathobiology of glomerular matrix metabolism
R01DK-39777-04 (PTHA) BERNSTEIN, KENNETH E EMORY UNIVERSITY SCHOOL OF MED ROOM 703 WMB ATLANTA, GA 30322 Angiotensin-converting enzyme and glomerular pressure
R01DK-39781-05 (DDK) SAWYER, STEPHEN T C3101 MEDICAL CENTER NORTH 21ST AND GARLAND AVENUES NASHVILLE, TN 37232 Studies on the receptor for erythropoietin
R01DK-39786-05 (DDK) KLEIN, DAVID J UNIVERSITY OF MINNESOTA BOX 491 UMHC MINNEAPOLIS, MN 55455 Cell surface & cytoskeletal proteoglycans of glomerulus
R01DK-39789-03 (MEP) VAN THIEL, DAVID H UNIVERSITY OF PITTSBURGH 3550 TERRACE STREET PITTSBURGH, PENNSYLVANIA 15260 Vitamin E and neurologic status in liver disease
R01DK-39796-04 (RNM) CARSTENSEN, EDWIN L UNIVERSITY OF ROCHESTER HOPEMAN 203 ROCHESTER, NY 14627 Role of cavitation in lithotripsy
R01DK-39814-04 (SSS) RUDERMAN, NEIL B UNIVERSITY HOSPITAL 88 EAST NEWTON STREET BOSTON, MA 02118 Vascular metabolism in diabetes
U01DK-39819-04 (DDK) MASSRY, SHAUL G UNIV OF SOUTHERN CALIFORNIA 2025 ZONAL AVENUE LOS ANGELES, CA 90033 Modification of diet in renal disease (MDRD) study
R01DK-39826-05 (DDK) BAIN, RAYMOND BIOSTATISTICS CENTER 6110 EXECUTIVE BLVD, SUITE 750 ROCKVILLE, MD 20852 Angiotensin converting enzyme inhibition in diabetic nephropathy
R01DK-39869-05 (HEM) SEMENZA, GREGG L JOHNS HOPKINS HOSPITAL 600 N WOLFE ST BALTIMORE, MD 21205 Expression of the erythropoietin gene
R01DK-39871-04 (PTHA) ABRASS, CHRISTINE K VA MEDICAL CENTER (111A) 1660 SOUTH COLUMBIAN WAY SEATTLE, WA 98108 Mesangial matrix expansion in diabetes-- Role of insulin-like growth factors
R01DK-39881-03 (HUD) DE CASTRO, JOHN M GEORGIA STATE UNIVERSITY UNIVERSITY PLAZA ATLANTA, GA 30302 Influence of heredity on meal patterns in humans
R01DK-39885-05 (DDK) WALKER, W GORDON JOHNS HOPKINS UNIVERSITY 720 RUTLAND AVE BALTIMORE, MD 21205 Prevention of diabetic nephropathy in IDDM
R01DK-39888-05 (DDK) BOYER, SAMUEL H JOHNS HOPKINS UNIVERSITY 720 RUTLAND AVENUE RM 933 BALTIMORE, MD 21205 Murine erythropoietin--response and receptors
R01DK-39891-04 (BIO) WHITLEY, CHESTER B UNIVERSITY OF MINNESOTA MINNEAPOLIS, MN 55455 Bone marrow transplantation for mucopolysaccharidosis

PROJECT NO., ORGANIZATIONAL UNIT., INVESTIGATOR, ADDRESS, TITLE

R01DK-39908-05 (DDK) LEWIS, EDMUND J RUSH-PRESBY-ST LUKE'S MED CTR 1653 W. CONGRESS PARKWAY CHICAGO, ILL 60612 ACE inhibition in diabetic nephropathy
R29DK-39918-05 (BBCB) GERKEN, THOMAS A CASE WESTERN RESERVE UNIV 2101 ADELBERT RD CLEVELAND, OH 44106 NMR studies of mucous glycoproteins
R01DK-39919-05 (BM) GRAHAM, DAVID Y BAYLOR COLLEGE OF MEDICINE ONE BAYLOR PLAZA HOUSTON, TX 77030 Campylobacter pyloridis in gastroduodenal disease
R44DK-39921-03 (SSS) TAYLOR, ELLISON H ATOM SCIENCES, INC 114 RIDGEWAY CENTER OAK RIDGE, TN 37830 The role of chromium deficiency in insulin resistance
R44DK-39923-03 (SSS) SARANGAPANI, S GINER INCORPORATED 14 SPRING STREET WALTHAM, MA 02254-9147 Glucose sensor with improved stability
R01DK-39944-05 (PHY) PEERCE, BRIAN E UNIV OF TEXAS MEDICAL BRANCH 301 UNIVERSITY BLVD GALVESTON, TX 77550 Structure & regulation of Na/phosphate cotransporter
R37DK-39949-10 (END) ROSENFELD, MICHAEL G UNIV OF CALIFORNIA SAN DIEGO LA JOLLA, CA 92093 Neuroendocrine peptide switching events in cancer
R01DK-39950-03 (SAT) ANDERSEN, DANA K UNIVERSITY OF CHICAGO 5812 SOUTH ELLIS AVENUE CHICAGO, IL 60637 Surgery of the pancreas--Effects on glucose metabolism
R01DK-39957-05 (SB) BUNNETT, NIGEL W UNIVERSITY OF CALIFORNIA BOX 0104 SAN FRANCISCO, CA 94143-0660 Peptide metabolism in human stomach
R01DK-39959-04 (ALY) FATHMAN, CHARLES G STANFORD UNIVERSITY SUMC S-021 STANFORD, CA 94305-5111 Immunotherapy in murine diabetes--The nod mouse
R29DK-39965-05 (MET) OWERBACH, DAVID BAYLOR COLLEGE OF MEDICINE ONE BAYLOR PLAZA HOUSTON, TEXAS 77030 Molecular biology of "diabetogenic haplotypes" diabetes
R01DK-39966-03 (SAT) WAIT, RICHARD B SUNY-HEALTH SCIENCE CTR 450 CLARKSON AVE BROOKLYN, N Y 11203 Characterization of cyclosporine nephrotoxicity
R29DK-39968-04 (END) MORGAN, EDWARD THOMAS EMORY UNIVERSITY SCHOOL OF MED DEPT OF PHARMACOLOGY ATLANTA, GEORGIA 30322 Growth hormone regulation of hepatic gene expression
R01DK-39994-03 (MET) ROBERTSON, RODERICK P UNIVERSITY OF MINNESOTA BOX 101 UMHC MINNEAPOLIS, MN 55455 Pancreatic transplantation in diabetic patients--Endocrine physiology
R29DK-39996-04 (HEM) BRENNER, DAVID A UNIV OF CA, SAN DIEGO DEPT OF MEDICINE, M-023-D LA JOLLA, CA 92093 Molecular defect in protoporphyria
R01DK-39997-04 (END) TOWLE, HOWARD C UNIVERSITY OF MINNEOSTA 4-225 MILLARD HALL MINNEAPOLIS, MN 55455 The thyroid hormone receptor and gene expression
R01DK-39998-03 (END) LAVIN, THOMAS N NY HOSP.-CORNELL UNV MED COLLE 525 EAST 68TH STREET NEW YORK, NY 10021 Thyroid hormone receptor DNA recognition
R29DK-40027-03 (GMA) MITTAL, RAVINDER K UNIVERSITY OF VIRGINIA DEPT OF INTERNAL MED, BOX 145 CHARLOTTESVILLE, VA 22908 Diaphragm: an external lower esophageal sphincter
R01DK-40029-03 (BIO) CORBIN, JACKIE D VANDERBILT UNIV SCHOOL OF MED 702 LIGHT HALL NASHVILLE, TN 37232-0615 Different isozymic form of cGMP-dependent protein kinase
P01DK-40031-03 (DDK) QUESENBERRY, PETER J UNIVERSITY OF VIRGINIA SCHOOL OF MEDICINE, BOX 502 CHARLOTTESVILLE, VA 22908 Hemolymphopoietic growth factors
P01DK-40031-03 0001 (DDK) QUESENBERRY, PETER Hemolymphopoietic growth factors Combination of growth factor on hemolymphopietic stem cells
P01DK-40031-03 0002 (DDK) EMERSON, CHARLES Hemolymphopoietic growth factors Effects of growth factors on expression of transfected troponin I in muscle cells
P01DK-40031-03 0003 (DDK) BALIAN, GARY Hemolymphopoietic growth factors Extracellular matrix & collagen production & growth factor in control
P01DK-40031-03 0004 (DDK) SANDO, JULIANNE Hemolymphopoietic growth factors Interleukin 2 and granulocyte/macrophage colony stimulating factor production
P01DK-40031-03 9001 (DDK) QUESENBERRY, PETER Hemolymphopoietic growth factors Cell culture core
R29DK-40035-03 (SB) SZABO, JOANNE S UNIV OF ARKANSAS FOR MED SCIS 4301 WEST MARKHAM ST SLOT 512 LITTLE ROCK, AR 72205-7199 GI myoelectric activity--Maturation and function
R01DK-40042-04 (GMB) BRIGGS, JOSEPHINE PASHLER UNIVERSITY OF MICHIGAN 3914 TAUBMAN HEALTH CTR ANN ARBOR, MI 48109-0364 Renin release from isolated juxtaglomerular apparatus
R01DK-40045-03 (EDC) STAMM, WALTER E HARBORVIEW MEDICAL CENTER 325 NINTH AVENUE 10TH FLOOR SEATTLE, WASH 98104 Factors predisposing to urinary tract infectious
R29DK-40046-04 (NTN) JEN, KAI-LIN C WAYNE STATE UNIVERSITY 160 OLD MAIN DETROIT, MI 48202 Nutrition, obesity and gestational diabetes
R01DK-40049-02 (END) COPP, RICHARD P NEW YORK UNIV MEDICAL CENTER 550 FIRST AVE NEW YORK, NY 10016 Cyclic nucleotides and growth hormone gene expression
R29DK-40057-04 (GMA) SHANAHAN, FERGUS UCLA SCHOOL OF MEDICINE 24-156 WARREN HALL/900 VETERAN LOS ANGELES, CA 90024 Inflammatory bowel disease; role in vivo primed CTL
R01DK-40061-04 (PC) GREEN, ALLAN UNIV. OF TEXAS MEDICAL BRANCH OJSH 4.174, ROUTE E68 GALVESTON, TX 77550 Adenosine receptor regulation and insulin action
R29DK-40069-03 (PTHA) SCADUTO, RUSSELL C, JR PENNSYLVANIA STATE UNIVERSITY HERSHEY MEDICAL CENTER HERSHEY, PA 17033 Mechanisms of cellular injury in renal ischemia
R29DK-40082-04 (BCE) SANDERS, MICHEL M UNIVERSITY OF MINNESOTA 4-225 MILLARD HALL MINNEAPOLIS, MN 55455 Multihormonal regulation of gene expression
R29DK-40083-05 (MET) MOJSOV, SVETLANA THE ROCKEFELLER UNIVERSITY 1230 YORK AVENUE NEW YORK, N Y 10021 Role of glp-I(7-37)

in insulin secretion
R29DK-40092-04 (SAT) THISTLETHWAITE, JAMES R, JR THE UNIVERSITY OF CHICAGO 5841 SOUTH MARYLAND AVENUE CHICAGO, IL 60637 Ex vivo immunoalteration of pancreas organ transplants
R01DK-40093-02 (HEM) DE SIMONE, JOSEPH UNIV OF ILLINOIS COLL OF MED BOX 6998 CHICAGO, ILL 60680 DNA-binding proteins and fetal hemoglobin regulation
R29DK-40095-03 (BCE) KOENIG, RONALD J UNIVERSITY OF MICHIGAN HOSP. 3920 TAUBMAN CENTER ANN ARBOR, MI 48109-0354 Functional role of multiple thyroid hormone receptors
R01DK-40099-04 (BPO) TORDOFF, MICHAEL G MONELL CHEMICAL SENSE CENTER 3500 MARKET STREET PHILDELPHIA, PA 19104-3308 Calcium and salt intake
R01DK-40117-03 (PTHA) JACKSON, SUSAN UNIVERSITY OF ALABAMA UAB STATION BIRMINGHAM, AL 35294 Idiotypes and immune complexes in IgA nephropathies
R29DK-40121-04 (NTN) BECKMAN, JEFFREY K VANDERBILT MEDICAL CTR NORTH DD-2205 NASHVILLE, TN 37232 Effects of dietary fat on lipid peroxidative injury
R01DK-40127-04 (GMB) TILLOTSON, DOUGLAS L BOSTON UNIV SCHOOL OF MEDCINIE 80 EAST CONCORD STREET BOSTON, MA 02118 Steroid secretion – Role of calcium in adrenal cells
R29DK-40129-04 (GMA) FOSTER, EMILY S MICHAEL REESE HOSP & MED CTR 31ST ST AND LAKE SHORE DRIVE CHICAGO, ILLINOIS 60616 Regulation of colonic potassium transport
R29DK-40131-04 (END) ENYEART, JOHN J OHIO STATE UNIV. RESEARCH FDN 333 WEST TENTH AVE. COLUMBUS, OH 43210-1239 A study of ionic channels in rat pituitary somatotrophs
P01DK-40144-04 (DDK) LAFFERTY, KEVIN J UNIV OF COLORADO HLTH SCIS CTR 4200 EAST 9TH AVENUE DENVER, CO 80262 Immunobiology of type I diabetes
P01DK-40144-04 0001 (DDK) BELLGRAU, DONALD Immunobiology of type I diabetes Biology of the thymus in the Biobreeding rat
P01DK-40144-04 0003 (DDK) LAFFERTY, KEVIN Immunobiology of type I diabetes Pathogenesis of the disease process
P01DK-40144-04 0004 (DDK) MCDUFFIE, MARCIA Immunobiology of type I diabetes Thymic regulation of the peripheral repertoire
P01DK-40144-04 0005 (DDK) KOTZIN, BRIAN L Immunobiology of type I diabetes Genetic control of the disease process
P01DK-40144-04 0006 (DDK) HAYWARD, ANTHONY Immunobiology of type I diabetes Manipulation of the diabetic phenotype
P01DK-40144-04 9001 (DDK) BELLGRAU, DONALD Immunobiology of type I diabetes Core--Animal facilities
P01DK-40144-04 9002 (DDK) HASKINS, KATHRYN Immunobiology of type I diabetes Core--Biological services
P01DK-40144-04 9003 (DDK) MCDUFFIE, MARCIA Immunobiology of type I diabetes EPICS core
P01DK-40144-04 0002 (DDK) HASKINS, KATHRYN Immunobiology of type I diabetes Definition of islet antigens
R01DK-40145-04 (PHY) CIVAN, MORTIMER M UNIVERSITY OF PENNSYLVANIA RICHARDS BUILDING/G4 PHILADELPHIA, PA 19104-6085 Na+ transport regulation by protein kinase C/insulin
R29DK-40154-04 (BBCB) APPLEGATE, DIANNE E MOUNT SINAI SCHOOL OF MEDICINE ONE GUSTAVE L LEVY PLACE NEW YORK, NEW YORK 10029 Dynamic conformational changes of smooth muscle myosin
R01DK-40162-04 (SSS) PUBLICOVER, NELSON G UNIVERSITY OF NEVADA ANERSON MEDICAL BUILDING RENO, NV 89557 Multi-dimensional, mathematical model of GI motility
R01DK-40163-04 (MGN) SLY, WILLIAM S ST LOUIS UNIVERSITY SCH OF MED 1402 S GRAND BLVD ST LOUIS, MO 63104 Biochemical genetics of carbonic anhydrase deficiencies
R01DK-40170-05 (PTHB) MAJZOUB, JOSEPH A THE CHILDREN'S HOSPITAL 300 LONGWOOD AVENUE BOSTON, MA 02115 The endocrine regulation of vasopressin biosynthesis
R29DK-40172-03 (BIO) LI, ELLEN WASHINGTON UNIVERSITY SCH OF M 660 S EUCLID AVE ST LOUIS, MO 63110 A study of intestinal vitamin a binding proteins
R29DK-40189-03 (PBC) KANALAS, JOHN J UNIV TEXAS HEALTH SCIENCE CTR 7703 FLOYD CURL DRIVE SAN ANTONIO, TX 78284 Study of a serum protein which binds the HN autoantigen
R29DK-40192-04 (PC) ZOELLER, RAPHAEL ANDREW BOSTON UNIVERSITY 80 EAST CONCORD STREET BOSTON, MA 02118 Biosynthesis and functions of animal cell phospholipids
R01DK-40202-03 (BCE) BOWERS, CYRIL Y TULANE UNIVERSITY 1430 TULANE AVENUE NEW ORLEANS, LA 70112 Isolation/identification of a new GH releasing peptide
R01DK-40208-03 (PTHA) FALK, RONALD J UNIV OF NC AT CHAPEL HILL 3034 OLD CLINIC BLDG CHAPEL HILL, N C 27599 Neutrophil autoantibodies in vasculitis and nephritis
R29DK-40210-02 (GMA) GALLIGAN, JAMES J MICHIGAN STATE UNIVERSITY EAST LANSING, MI 48824 Intestinal motility--Mechanisms of regulation
R01DK-40218-03 (HEM) YU, JOHN C THE SCRIPPS RESEARCH INSTITUTE 10666 N TORREY PINES ROAD LA JOLLA, CA 92037 The role of inhibin and FRP proteins in erythropoiesis
R29DK-40221-05 (HED) CUTTLER, LEONA RAINBOW BABIES & CHILDREN'S HO 2101 ADELBERT ROAD CLEVELAND, OH 44106 Perinatal maturation of pituitary growth hormone release
R01DK-40222-02 (GMA) LE DUC, LOUISE E HARBOR-UCLA MEDICAL CENTER 1124 WEST CARSON STREET TORRANCE, CA 90502-2064 Inflammatory mediators, eicosanoids, and colitis
R29DK-40223-03 (GMA) DAVIS, BERNARD H UNIVERSITY OF CHICAGO 5841 SOUTH MARYLAND AVE/BOX 40 CHICAGO, IL 60637 Regulation of liver cell function during cirrhosis
R29DK-40242-04 (HEM) WOJCHOWSKI, DON M PENNSYLVANIA STATE UNIVERSITY 408 S. FREAR LABORATORY UNIVERSITY PARK, PA 16802 Biochemistry of the erythropoietin receptor
R01DK-40247-03 (GMA) LUND, PAULINE K UNIVERSITY OF NORTH CAROLINA PHYSIO/CB #7545 MED SCIS BLDG CHAPEL HILL, NC 27599-7545 Intestinal adaptation--Role of hormones & growth factors
R01DK-40249-03 (BM) SARTOR, RYAN B UNIVERSITY OF NORTH CAROLINA CB#7080/465 BURNETT-WOMACK BLD CHAPEL HILL, NC 27599-7080 Bacterial cell wall-induced granulomatous enterocolitis
R01DK-40250-17 (HEM) GOLDWASSER, EUGENE UNIVERSITY OF CHICAGO 920 E 58TH ST ROOM 661 CHICAGO, ILL 60637 Hemopoietic stem cells and induced differentiation
R01DK-40251-04 (MEP) WILSON, CURTIS B SCRIPPS CLINIC & RESEARCH FDN 10666 NORTH TORREY PINES ROAD LA JOLLA, CALIF 92037 Pathophysiology of immune glomerular injury
R01DK-40252-03 (SAT) BISTRIAN, BRUCE R NEW ENGLAND DEACONESS HOSPITAL 185 PILGRIM ROAD BOSTON, MA 02215 Structured lipids in catabolic states
R01DK-40253-04 (ECS) SCHNEIDER, EDWARD G UNIVERSITY OF TENNESSEE MEMPHI 894 UNION AVENUE MEMPHIS, TN 38163 Osmotic and ph modulation of aldosterone secretion
R01DK-40255-04 (BCE) BRUEGGEMEIER, ROBERT W OHIO STATE UNIVERSITY 500 WEST 12TH AVENUE COLUMBUS, OH 43210-1291 Biochemical probes of the active site of aromatase
R29DK-40259-05 (GMA) BARBER, DIANE L UNIVERSITY OF CALIFORNIA 513 PARNASSUS AVE HSW 604 SAN FRANCISCO, CA 94143-0512 Regulation of neurotensin-containing enteric cells
R01DK-40286-10 (PTHA) TAUB, MARY L STATE UNIVERSITY OF NEW YORK BUFFALO, NY 14214 Hormonal regulation of kidney epithelial cell growth
R29DK-40317-04 (END) BACHRACH, LAURA K STANFORD UNIV. MEDICAL CENTER DEPARTMENT OF PEDIATRICS STANFORD, CA 94305 Insulin-like growth factors in thyroid physiology
R01DK-40321-04 (GMB) KLAHR, SAULO THE JEWISH HOSPITAL OF ST. LOU 216 S. KINGSHIGHWAY ST. LOUIS, MO 63110 The role of leukocytes in obstructive nephropathy
R29DK-40323-04 (BIO) PISONI, RONALD L THE UNIVERSITY OF MICHIGAN 2618 SPH I, 109 OBSERVATORY ANN ARBOR, MI 48109-2029 Lysosomal transport of nucleosides and nucleobases
R29DK-40332-04 (BIO) SCHWARZENBERG, SARAH J UNIVERSITY OF MINNESOTA BOX 274 UMHC MINNEAPOLIS, MN 55455 Characterization of two hepatic antiproteases
R29DK-40336-04 (BCE) GREGERSON, KAREN A UNIV OF MARYLAND AT BALTIMORE 655 WEST BALTIMORE STREET BALTIMORE, MD 21201 Mechanisms in the regulation of prolactin secretion
R01DK-40343-02 (BCE) DANNIES, PRISCILLA S YALE UNIVERSITY SCHOOL OF MED PO BOX 3333 NEW HAVEN, CT 06510-8066 Estrogen induction of growth and differentiation
R29DK-40344-04 (END) ARVAN, PETER BETH ISRAEL HOSPITAL 330 BROOKLINE AVE BOSTON, MA 02215 Polarized secretory targeting in cultured thyrocytes
R01DK-40353-04 (BCE) CASEY, M LINETTE UNIV OF TX SW MED CTR AT DALLA BIOLOGY SCIENCES DALLAS, TX 75235-9051 Extraadrenal mineralocorticosteroid formation-metabolism
R29DK-40355-03 (BCE) MENDEL, CARL M UNIVERSITY OF CALIFORNIA 1327 MOFFITT HOPITAL SAN FRANCISCO, CA 94143-0130 Flux of lipophilic hormones between plasma and tissues
R29DK-40372-03 (GMB) WHITFIELD, G KERR UNIVERSITY OF ARIZONA 1501 N CAMPBELL AVENUE TUCSON, AZ 85724 Structure/function studies of the vitamin D receptor
R01DK-40381-03 (SB) HINDER, RONALD A CREIGHTON UNIVERSITY 601 NO 30TH STREET OMAHA, NE 68131 Duodenogastric reflux in health and disease
R01DK-40382-04 (MET) BERRY, GERARD T CHILDREN'S HOSPITAL 34TH & CIVIC CENTER BOULEVARD PHILADELPHIA, PA 19104 Biochemical basis of diabetic angiopathy
R01DK-40393-03 (MGN) DOVE, WILLIAM F UNIVERSITY OF WISCONSIN MCARDLE LAB FOR CANCER RESEARC MADISON, WI 53706 Mouse genetic models for phenylketonuria
R01DK-40394-04 (MET) LIVINGSTON, JAMES N UNIVERSITY OF ROCHESTER 601 ELMWOOD AVENUE ROCHESTER, N Y 14642 Insulin action and mutant insulin receptors
R01DK-40401-02 (BNP) YOUNATHAN, EZZAT S LOUISIANA STATE UNIVERSITY 322 CHOPPIN HALL BATON ROUGE, LA 70803 Fructofuranose modulators--Structural/enzymatic studies
R01DK-40408-04 (MET) BLACKSHEAR, PERRY J DUKE UNIVERSITY MEDICAL CENTER RESEARCH DRIVE, BOX 3897 DURHAM, NC 27710 Insulin regulation of c-fos expression
R01DK-40426-03 (PTHA) BIDANI, ANIL K LOYOLA UNIVERSITY 2160 SOUTH FIRST AVE MAYWOOD, IL 60153 Pathology of hypertensive injury in remnant kidneys
R01DK-40428-04 (BCE) MARTIN, THOMAS F ZOOLOGY RESEARCH BUILDING 1117 WEST JOHNSON STREET MADISON, WI 53706 Calcium regulation of secretion in GH3 pituitary cells
R01DK-40439-04 (NTN) STACPOOLE, PETER W UNIVERSITY OF FLORIDA BOX 100226 GAINESVILLE, FL 32610-0226 Nutritional control of intermediary metabolism
R01DK-40441-04 (BIO) HARRIS, ROBERT A INDIANA UNIVERSITY SCH OF MED 635 BARNHILL DRIVE INDIANAPOLIS, IN 46202-5122 Characterization of enzymes of valine catabolism
R29DK-40445-05 (GMB) BALLERMANN, BARBARA JUTTA JOHNS HOPKINS UNIVERSITY 725 N WOLFE STREET BALTIMORE, MD 21205 ANP receptor-mediated function in glomerular cells
R01DK-40446-04 (RAP) WINDER, WILLIAM W BRIGHAM YOUNG UNIVERSITY DEPT OF ZOOLOGY, 571 WIDB PROVO, UTAH 84602 Physiology of muscle lactate production during exercise
R29DK-40454-04 (SAT) JENDRISAK, MARTIN D WASHINGTON UNIVERSITY 3356 CLINICAL SCI RESEARCH BLD ST. LOUIS, MO 63110 Eicosanoid modulation in rat renal allograft rejection
R01DK-40456-03 (MET) MESSINA, JOSEPH L SUNY HLTH SCI CTR AT SYRACUSE 750 EAST ADAMS STREET SYRACUSE, NY 13210 Insulin's regulation of three hepatic messenger RNAs
R01DK-40457-05 (END) LOW, MALCOLM JAMES OREGON HEALTH SCIENCES UNIV 3181 SW SAM JACKSON PARK RD PORTLAND, OR 97201-3098 Pathobiology of Cushing's disease
R01DK-40465-04 (SAT) SCHARP, DAVID W WASHINGTON UNIVERSITY 4960 AUDUBON AVE/BOX 8109 ST LOUIS, MO 63110 Clinical trials on human islet transplantation
R29DK-40472-04 (GMA) POWERS, ROBERT E YALE UNIV SCHOOL OF MED P.O. BOX 3333/FMB 109 NEW HAVEN, CT 06510 Altered acinar cell function during acute pancreatitis
R29DK-40475-05 (END) ADLER, GAIL K BRIGHAM & WOMEN'S HOSPITAL

221 LONGWOOD AVENUE BOSTON, MA 02115 Endocrine regulation of corticotropin releasing hormone
R29DK-40484-04 (NTN) JENSEN, MICHAEL D MAYO FOUNDATION 200 FIRST ST SOUTHWEST ROCHESTER, MN 55905 Free fatty acid metabolism in different types of human obesity
R01DK-40486-04 (PC) LA PORTE, DAVID C UNIV OF MINNEOSTA 435 DELAWARE ST. S.E. MINNEAPOLIS, MN 55455 Coordination of regulatory mechanisms in metabolism
R01DK-40487-04 (SAT) SAENZ DE TEJADA, INIGO BOSTON UNIVERSITY SCH. OF MED. 720 HARRISON AVE BOSTON, MA 02118 Role of the endothelium in penile erection
R01DK-40498-03 (BPO) RITTER, W SUE WASHINGTON STATE UNIV PULLMAN, WA 99164-6520 Neural substrates of metabolic controls of ingestion
R29DK-40504-04 (PTHA) MANN, RICHARD A DIV OF NEPH, MEB, CN-19 UMDNJ-ROBERT W JOHNSON MED SCH PISCATAWAY, N J 08854-5635 Immunoregulatory defects in lupus nephritis
R29DK-40506-04 (END) NGUYEN, TOAN D V A MEDICAL CENTER 508 FULTON STREET DURHAM, NC 27705 VIP, VIP receptors and the intestinal epithelial cell
U01DK-40509-04 (DDK) CAGGIULA, ARLENE W UNIVERSITY OF PITTSBURGH 130 DESOTO STREET PITTABURGH, PA 15260 Clinical study of modification of diet in renal disease
R01DK-40511-04 (PC) ELLIS, LELAND U T SOUTHWESTERN MEDICAL CTR. 5323 HARRY HINES BLVD/RM Y5224 DALLAS, TX 75235-9050 Insulin receptor tyrosine kinase structure
R01DK-40516-02 (EDC) SEGALL, MIRIAM UNIVERSITY OF MINNESOTA IMMUNOBIO RES CTR/BOX 724 UMHC MINNEAPOLIS, MN 55455 HLA in families with IDD and NIDD--A distinct subset?
R01DK-40518-03 (PC) SUL, HEI S HARVARD SCH OF PUBLIC HEALTH 665 HUNTINGTON AVENUE BOSTON M A 02115 Phosphofructokinase isozyme expression during myogenesis
R29DK-40519-04 (SSS) MONTGOMERY, DAVID W UNIVERSITY OF ARIZONA DEPARTMENT OF PHARMACOLOGY TUCSON, AZ 85724 Immunoregulatory roles of lymphocyte-derived prolactins
R29DK-40527-04 (GMB) YOSHIOKA, TOSHIMASA VANDERBILT UNIVERSITY 21ST AND GARLAND AVENUE NASHVILLE, TN 37232-2584 Reactive oxygen species in glomerular dysfunction
R29DK-40538-03 (BIO) OFFNER, GWYNNETH D BOSTON UNIVERSITY 80 E CONCORD ST DEPT OF BIO BOSTON, MA 02118 Molecular basis for multiple forms of heme oxygenase
R29DK-40543-04 (END) BRAND, STEPHEN J MASSACHUSETTS GENERAL HOSPITAL FRUIT STREET BOSTON, MA 02114 Physiological regulation of gastrin gene expression
P01DK-40555-04 (DDK) SEGAL, STANTON JOSEPH STOKES, JR RESEARCH INS 34TH & CIVIC CTR BLVD PHILADELPHIA, PA 19104 Mechanisms of inherited membrane transport disorders
P01DK-40555-04 0001 (DDK) SEGAL, STANTON Mechanisms of inherited membrane transport disorders Cystinuria and the nature of the renal cystine-lysine transport system
P01DK-40555-04 0002 (DDK) NISSIM, ITZHAK Mechanisms of inherited membrane transport disorders Chemical models of the Fanconi syndrome--15N-GC-MS and 13C-NMR
P01DK-40555-04 0003 (DDK) STATES, BEATRICE Mechanisms of inherited membrane transport disorders Cultured renal epithelial cells as model systems of renal transport mechanisms
P01DK-40555-04 0004 (DDK) BOVEE, KENNETH Mechanisms of inherited membrane transport disorders Animal models of transport disorders
P01DK-40555-04 0005 (DDK) MC NAMARA, PAMELA Mechanisms of inherited membrane transport disorders Examination of human intestinal amino acid transport systems
P01DK-40555-04 0006 (DDK) HSU, BETTY Mechanisms of inherited membrane transport disorders Ontogeny and regulation of transport in renal membranes
P01DK-40555-04 9001 (DDK) MC NAMARA, PAMELA Mechanisms of inherited membrane transport disorders Core--Membrane and tubule preparation
P01DK-40555-04 9002 (DDK) YANDRASITZ, JOHN Mechanisms of inherited membrane transport disorders Core--Analytical chromatography
R29DK-40556-03 (BIO) KAM, WING UNIVERSITY OF CALIFORNIA DEPT OF MEDICINE SAN FRANCISCO, CA 94143-0724 Study of gastrointestinal (and liver) alkaline phosphatases
R01DK-40558-04 (CVB) CHEVALIER, ROBERT L UNIVERSITY OF VIRGINIA DEPT OF PEDIATRICS, BOX 386 CHARLOTTESVILLE, VA 22908 Renin-angiotensin and growth in ureteral obstruction
P30DK-40566-02 (DDK) MC CARRON, DAVID A OREGON HEALTH SCIENCES UNIV 3181 SW SAM JACKSON PARK ROAD PORTLAND, OR 97201 Clinical nutrition research unit
P30DK-40566-02 0002 (DDK) MORRIS, CYNTHIA Clinical nutrition research unit Case control study of senile cataract and hypertension
P30DK-40566-02 0003 (DDK) ULLMAN, DANIEL Clinical nutrition research unit Effect of dietary lipids in human spermatozoa and seminal fluid
P30DK-40566-02 0004 (DDK) ROULLET, JB Clinical nutrition research unit Regulation of calcium metabolism in myocytes and macrophages
P30DK-40566-02 0005 (DDK) HATTON, DANIEL Clinical nutrition research unit Effect of alcohol and calcium on the incidence of stroke
P30DK-40566-02 0006 (DDK) ELZINGA, LAWRENCE Clinical nutrition research unit Cyclosporine nephrotoxicity and hypertension
P30DK-40566-02 0007 (DDK) HALL, JEAN Clinical nutrition research unit Vitamin E absorption in humans
P30DK-40566-02 9001 (DDK) MORRIS, CYNTHIA Clinical nutrition research unit Biostatistics and nutrient assessment core
P30DK-40566-02 9002 (DDK) YOUNG, ERIC Clinical nutrition research unit Hormone and mineral metabolism core
P30DK-40566-02 9003 (DDK) ILLINGSWORTH, ROGER Clinical nutrition research unit Lipid and lipoprotein metabolism core
P30DK-40566-02 9004 (DDK) BUKOSKI, RICHARD Clinical nutrition research unit Cell calcium core
R01DK-40569-04 (GMA) SANDERS, KENTON M UNIVERSITY OF NEVADA SCHOOL OF MEDICINE RENO, NV 89557 Electrical control of pyloric motility
R01DK-40582-04 (ARRE) KAGNOFF, MARTIN F UNIVERSITY OF CALIFORNIA LA JOLLA, CA 92093 HIV infection of intestinal epithelium
R29DK-40593-04 (BCE) SCAMMELL, JONATHAN G UNIVERSITY OF SOUTH ALABAMA COLLEGE OF MEDICINE - MSB 3130 MOBILE, AL 36688 Chromogranins in neuroendocrine tumor cells
R01DK-40605-03 (MET) DUNAIF, ANDREA MOUNT SINAI SCHOOL OF MEDICINE ONE GUSTAVE L LEVY PLACE NEW YORK, NY 10029 Insulin action in the polycystic ovary syndrome
R01DK-40608-04 (PC) ENNS, CAROLINE A OREGON HEALTH SCIENCES UNIV 318 SW SAM JACKSON PARK BLVD PORTLAND, OR 97201-3098 Structure - function of the human transferrin receptor
R01DK-40611-04 (DDK) CHLEBOWSKI, ROWAN T HARBOR-UCLA MEDICAL CENTER 1000 W CARSON STREET TORRANCE, CALIF 90509 Nutrition, gastrointestinal dysfunction and AIDS
R01DK-40615-04 (GMA) SACHS, GEORGE VETERANS ADMINISTRATION HOSP WADSWORTH HOSPITAL CENTER LOS ANGELES, CALIF 90073 Gastric acid secretion
R01DK-40627-02 (EDC) MC CULLOCH, DAVID K VA MEDICAL CENTER 1660 SOUTH COLUMBIA WAY ZB-21 SEATTLE, WA 98108 Prediction of IDDM in the general population
R44DK-40657-02 (SSS) RHODES, RATHBUN K MARKWELL MEDICAL INST 1202 ANN STREET MADISON, WI 53713 Glucose enzyme electrode suitable for implantation
R44DK-40661-02A2 (SSS) MIX, THOMAS W MERIX CORPORATION 77 CHARLES STREET NEEDHAM HEIGHTS, MA 02194 Improved bile acid adsorbents
R44DK-40664-03 (SSS) JOSEPHSON, LEE ADVANCED MAGNETICS INC 61 MOONEY STREET CAMBRIDGE, MASS 02138 Hepatocyte specific NMR contrast agents
R01DK-40698-03 (DDK) WILSON, PATRICIA D UMDNJ-ROBT WOOD JOHNSON MED/S 675 HOES LANE PISCATAWAY, NJ 08854-5635 Mechanism of cyst formation in polycystic kidney disease
R01DK-40700-02 (GMB) WOO, DAVID D UNIVERSITY OF CALIFORNIA 405 HILGARD AVE LOS ANGELES, CA 90024-1689 Differential gene expression in polycystic kidneys
R29DK-40701-04 (GMA) COHN, JONATHAN A DUKE UNIVERSITY MEDICAL CENTER BOX 3913 DURHAM, NC 27710 Secretory diarrhea--Cellular mechanisms
R01DK-40703-03 (DDK) REEDERS, STEPHEN T YALE UNIV SCH OF MEDICINE 333 CEDAR ST PO BOX 3333 NEW HAVEN, CT 06510 Molecular pathology of adult polycystic disease
R01DK-40707-03 (IMS) WODA, BRUCE A UNIVERSITY OF MASSACHUSETTS 55 LAKE AVENUE NORTH WORCESTER, MA 01655 Autoimmune T-Lymphocyte cell lines in diabetes
R29DK-40725-04 (PTHA) LASH, LAWRENCE H WAYNE STATE UNIVERSITY 540 EAST CANFIELD AVE/SCH OF M DETROIT, MI 48201 Glutathione and mitochondria in toxic renal injury
R29DK-40732-04 (MET) SHALWITZ, ROBERT ALAN CHILDREN'S HOSPITAL 455 S MAIN STREET ORANGE, CA 92668 In vivo regulation of hepatic glucose metabolism
R29DK-40734-03 (BIO) NEWGARD, CHRISTOPHER B U OF TX SW MED CTR AT DALLAS 5323 HARRY HINES BLVD DALLAS, TX 75235 Allosteric regulation of tissue-specific phosphorylases
R01DK-40739-03 (CBY) MC KEEHAN, WALLACE L W A JONES CELL SCI CTR, INC 10 OLD BARN ROAD LAKE PLACID, N Y 12946 Human heparin-binding growth factor receptor
R01DK-40747-04 (DDK) KRIEGER, JOHN N UNIVERSITY OF WASHINGTON SEATTLE, WA 98195 GU sites and consequences of HIV infection
R01DK-40751-04 (IMS) SINGER, PAUL A WHITTIER INSTITUTE 9894 GENESEE AVENUE LA JOLLA, CA 92037 T cell receptor genes in autoimmune diabetes
R29DK-40752-03 (REN) LARSEN, JENNIFER L UNIV OF NEBRASKA MEDICAL CENTE 600 SOUTH 42ND STREET OMAHO, NE 68198 Role of G proteins in prolactin signal transduction
R29DK-40753-03 (PC) ROMERO, GUILLERMO G UNIV. OF PITTSBURGH SCH OF MED W1345 BIOMEDICAL SCIENCE TOWER PITTSBRGH, PA 15261 Studies on the generation of insulin mediators
R29DK-40759-03 (END) CARNES, MARY L W S.MIDDLETON MEMORIAL VAMC 2500 OVERLOOK TERRACE MADISON, WI 53705 The phenomenology of ACTH micropulses
R01DK-40788-04 (END) KOENIG, JAMES I GEORGETOWN UNIV MED SCH 3900 RESERVOIR RD, NW WASHINGTON, DC 20007 Integrated neuropeptide regulation of ACTH secretion
R29DK-40790-03 (NTN) PAPPAS, THEODORE N DUKE UNIVERSITY BOX 3479 DURHAM, NC 27710 Regulation of food intake--Brain and gut mediators
R01DK-40800-04 (DDK) MYERS, BRYAN D STANFORD UNIV. SCHOOL OF MED. S215 DIVISION OF NEPHROLOGY STANFORD, CA 94305-5114 Pathophysiology of AIDS glomerulopathy
R01DK-40804-03 (MET) SINENSKY, MICHAEL S ELEANOR ROOSEVELT INSTITUTE 1899 GAYLORD STREET DENVER, CO 80206 Biochemical genetics of cellular cholesterol metabolism
R01DK-40811-03 (DDK) KIMMEL, PAUL L GEORGE WASHINGTON UNIVERSITY 2150 PENNSYLVANIA AVE, NW, 505 WASHINGTON, D C 20037 Affect of HIV on kidney and renal transplants
R01DK-40816-03 (NTN) AMATRUDA, JOHN M UNIVERSITY OF ROCHESTER 601 ELMWOOD AVE ROCHESTER, NY 14642-8693 Metabolic rate and protein turnover in obesity
R29DK-40832-03 (SAT) SAWCZUK, IHOR S COLUMBIA UNIVERSITY 622 W 168TH STREET NEW YORK, NY 10032 Renal growth/during ureteral obstruction
R01DK-40834-03 (GMB) SCHEINMAN, JON I DUKE UNIVERSITY MED CTR ROOM 101, P O BOX 3959 DURHAM, NC 27710 Loss of kidney function by glomerular sclerosis
R01DK-40836-03 (DDK) BOURGOIGNIE, JACQUES J UNIVERSITY OF MIAMI P O BOX 016960 MIAMI, FL 33101 Human immunodeficiency virus infection and the kidney
R01DK-40838-03 (DDK) STRAUSS, JOSE UNIVERSITY OF MIAMI P.O. BOX 016960 MIAMI, FL 33101 HIV associated nephropathy in children
P01DK-40839-03 (DDK) BRENNER, BARRY M BRIGHAM AND WOMEN'S HOSPITAL 75 FRANCIS STREET BOSTON, MASS 02115 Mediators and expression systems in renal injury
P01DK-40839-03 0001 (DDK) BALLERMANN, BARBARA J Mediators and expression systems in renal injury Pathobiology of glomerular endothelial and mesangial cells
P01DK-40839-03 0002 (DDK) RENNKE, HELMUT G Mediators and expression

PROJECT NO., ORGANIZATIONAL UNIT., INVESTIGATOR, ADDRESS, TITLE

systems in renal injury Epithelial cell determinants of glomerulosclerosis

P01DK-40839-03 0003 (DDK) DIAMOND, JONATHAN Mediators and expression systems in renal injury Macrophages & other mediators of injury in experimental nephrotic syndrome

P01DK-40839-03 0004 (DDK) GULLANS, STEVEN R Mediators and expression systems in renal injury Cellular basis of nephrotoxicity

P01DK-40839-03 0005 (DDK) KELLEY, VICKI E Mediators and expression systems in renal injury Pathologic expression of class II MHC molecules in renal injury

P01DK-40839-03 0006 (DDK) ANDERSON, SHARON Mediators and expression systems in renal injury Glomerular adaptations to invivo injury

P01DK-40839-03 0007 (DDK) BRENNER, BARRY M Mediators and expression systems in renal injury Regulation of filtration surface area to glomerular sclerosis and hypertension

R29DK-40890-03 (REN) PRINS, GAIL S MICHAEL REESE HOSP & MED CTR LAKE SHORE DR AT 31ST STREET CHICAGO, IL 60616 Hormonal regulation of prostate steroid receptors

R01DK-40891-03 (PHY) GITELMAN, HILLEL J UNIVERSITY OF NORTH CAROLINA CB #7005, 3035 OLD CLINIC BLDG CHAPEL HILL, NC 27599 Chloride channels in a model epithelium, the gallbladder

R01DK-40895-03 (HEM) BISHOP, DAVID F MOUNT SINAI SCHOOL OF MEDICINE FIFTH AVENUE AT 100TH STREET NEW YORK, NY 10029 Human aminolevulinate synthetase structure and regulation

R01DK-40907-02 (NTN) MITCH, WILLIAM E EMORY UNIVERSITY SCH OF MED 1364 CLIFTON RD, N E ATLANTA, GA 30322 Mechanism of adapting to dietary manipulation in uremia

R29DK-40910-02 (MET) MAY, MICHAEL E VANDERBILT UNIVERSITY 21ST AVE SOUTH & GARLAND ST NASHVILLE, TN 37232-2230 Kinetic analysis of protein turnover in vivo

R01DK-40914-03 (GMA) REUBEN, ADRIAN YALE UNIVERSITY SCH OF MED PO BOX 3333 NEW HAVEN, CT 06510 Intrahepatic bile acid transport in vitro and in vivo

R01DK-40917-02 (PC) HUI, DAVID Y UNIVERSITY OF CINCINNATI 231 BETHESDA AVENUE CINCINNATI, OH 45267-0529 Cholesterol esterases in mammalian tissues

R29DK-40918-03 (GMA) KANOF, MARJORIE E MASSACHUSETTS GENERAL HOSP FRUIT STREET BOSTON, MA 02114 Regulation of mucosal immune systems in Crohn's disease

R01DK-40919-03 (GMA) MAYER, EMERAN A HARBOR-UCLA MEDICAL CENTER 1000 WEST CARSON STREET TORRANCE, CA 90509 Membrane events: activating longitudinal colonic muscle

R01DK-40922-03 (GMA) CHANG, EUGENE B UNIVERSITY OF CHICAGO MED: BOX 400/5841 S MARYLAND CHICAGO, IL 60637 Role of basement membrane in diabetic gut adaptation

R01DK-40923-02 (END) LIPPMAN, STEPHEN S UNIVERSITY OF ARKANSAS/MED SCI 4301 WEST MARKHAM LITTLE ROCK, AR 72205-7199 A glucocorticoid action domain in pituitary tumor cells

R01DK-40930-02 (BIO) WARREN, CHRISTOPHER D MASSACHUSETTS GENERAL HOSPITAL 32 FRUIT STREET BOSTON, MA 02114 Exogenous substrates for glycoprotein biosynthesis

R29DK-40935-03 (NLS) ANDERSON, GREGORY J OREGON HEALTH SCIENCES UNIV 3181 SW SAM JACKSON PARK ROAD PORTLAND, OR 97201 Dietary n-3 fatty acids--Transport and uptake into brain

R01DK-40936-03 (MET) SHULMAN, GERALD I YALE U SCH OF MED FITKIN 104 333 CEDAR ST, P O BOX 3333 NEW HAVEN, CT 06510 In vivo NMR studies of carbohydrate metabolism

R29DK-40939-03 (CBY) VIDRICH, ALDA UNIVERSITY OF CALIFORNIA 900 VETERAN AVENUE LOS ANGELES, CA 90024-1786 Culture adult colonic epithelia--A systematic approach

R01DK-40940-03 (EDC) KRONMAL, RICHARD A UNIVERSITY OF WASHINGTON SEATTLE, WA 98195 Case-control study of vasectomy urolithiasis

R01DK-40945-03 (REN) WEINER, RICHARD I UNIVERSITY OF CALIFORNIA 505 PARNASSUS AVENUE SAN FRANCISCO, CA 94143-0962 Etiology of estrogen induced prolactin tumors

R01DK-40947-03 (END) KLIBANSKI, ANNE MASSACHUSETTS GENERAL HOSPITAL FRUIT STREET BOSTON, MA 02114 Hormone regulation and pathogenesis of pituitary tumors

R01DK-40949-03 (BBCA) WEISS, MICHAEL A MASSACHUSETTS GENERAL HOSPITAL FRUIT STREET BOSTON, MA 02114 NMR studies of mutant insulins associated with diabetes

R01DK-40961-03 (PCB) HALMI, KATHERINE A NEW YORK HOSP-WESTCHESTER DIV 21 BLOOMINGDALE ROAD WHITE PLAINS, NY 10605 Cognitive responses to meals in eating disorders

R01DK-40963-04 (BPO) LATTEMANN, DIANNE F UNIVERSITY OF WASHINGTON 1660 S COLUMBIAN WAY SEATTLE, WA 98108 Behavioral physiology of body weight regulation

R29DK-40964-03 (ALY) KWOK, WILLIAM VIRGINIA MASON RESEARCH CTR 1000 SENECA SEATTLE, WA 98101 Molecular analysis of the IDDM associated HLA-dq3-2 gene

R01DK-40966-02 (SB) CONDON, ROBERT E MEDICAL COLLEGE OF WISCONSIN 8700 WEST WISCONSIN AVE MILWAUKEE, WI 53226 Human colonic myoelectric activity

R01DK-40968-04 (SRC) ROLLS, BARBARA J THE JOHNS HOPKINS HOSPITAL 600 NORTH WOLFE STREET BALTIMORE, MD 21205 Food selection & regulation in eating disorders

R01DK-40973-02 (GMB) YANAGAWA, NORIMOTO SEPULVEDA VA MEDICAL CENTER 16111 PLUMMER STREET SEPULVEDA, CA 91343 Luminal action of angiotensin II on proximal tubule transport

R29DK-40982-03 (NTN) LAUTERIO, THOMAS J V A MEDICAL CTR MEDICAL RESEARCH SERVICE (151) HAMPTON, VA 23667 Obesity--Role nutrition IGF-II and insulin

R01DK-40986-03 (MBC) HYLEMON, PHILLIP B VIRGINIA COMMONWEALTH UNIV BOX 678, MCV STATION RICHMOND, VA 23298-0678 Molecular biology of intestinal bile salt metabolism

R01DK-40990-03 (DDK) GRUNFELD, CARL V. A. MEDICAL CENTER 4150 CLEMENT ST./METAB. (111F) SAN FRANCISCO, CA 94121 Role of cytokines in hyperlipidemia and wasting of AIDS

R01DK-40994-03 (DDK) MC CANN, SAMUEL M UNIV TEXAS SOUTHWESTERN MED CT 5323 HARRY HINES BLVD DALLAS, TX 75235 Monokines in control of hypothalamic-putuitary axis

R01DK-40995-03 (DDK) HELLERSTEIN, MARC SAN FRANCISCO GENERAL HOSPITAL 1001 POTRERO AVE RM 4101 BLDG SAN FRANCISCO, CA 94110 Substrate pathways, monokines, wasting and HIV infection

PROJECT NO., ORGANIZATIONAL UNIT., INVESTIGATOR, ADDRESS, TITLE

R29DK-41004-03 (GMA) RAYBOULD, HELEN CURE/VA WADSWORTH WILSHIRE & SAWTELLE BOULEVARDS LOS ANGELES, CA 90073 Cholecystokinin--Role in postprandial gastric motility

P01DK-41006-03 (DDK) DANTZLER, WILLIAM H UNIV OF ARIZONA COLLEGE OF MED ARIZONA HEALTH SCIENCES CENTER TUCSON, AZ 85724 Renal handling of organic ions

P01DK-41006-03 0001 (DDK) DANTZLER, WILLIAM Renal handling of organic ions Transport of organic ions by renal tubules

P01DK-41006-03 0002 (DDK) WRIGHT, STEPHEN Renal handling of organic ions Mechanisms of renal organic ion transport

P01DK-41006-03 0003 (DDK) GANDOLFI, A JAY Renal handling of organic ions in vitro renal toxicology--Role of transport

P01DK-41006-03 9001 (DDK) BURT, JANIS Renal handling of organic ions Instrumentation core

R01DK-41009-03 (BBCA) CODY, VIVIAN MEDICAL FDN OF BUFFALO INC 73 HIGH STREET BUFFALO, N Y 14203 Protein binding interactions of thyroactive compounds

R29DK-41014-04 (GMA) STOLZ, ANDREW A UNIV OF SOUTHERN CALIFORNIA 2025 ZONAL AVENUE LOS ANGELES, CA 90033 Molecular studies of a key bile acid metabolizing enzyme

R01DK-41015-03 (DDK) FINDLING, JAMES W ST LUKE'S MEDICAL CENTER 2900 W OKLAHOMA AVENUE MILWAUKEE, WI 52315 Adrenocortical control in patients with HIV infection

R01DK-41016-03 (DDK) MELBY, JAMES C UNIVERSITY HOSPITAL 88 EAST NEWTON STREET BOSTON, MA 02118 Immune-adrenal axis in AIDS

R01DK-41022-03 (ARR) MAX, STEPHEN R UNIV OF MARYLAND SCH OF MED 655 W BALTIMORE STREET BALTIMORE, MD 21201 Endocrine aspects of muscle wasting in AIDS

R01DK-41025-03 (DDK) O'GRADY, MAUREEN P USF PSYCHIATRY CENTER 3515 E FLETCHER AVENUE TAMPA, FL 33613 Prenatal viral infection and neuroendocrine development

R01DK-41034-03 (DDK) SMITH, ERIC M UNIV OF TEXAS MEDICAL BRANCH 301 UNIVERSITY BLVD GALVESTON, TX 77550 Effects of HIV on the immune and neuroendocrine axis

R01DK-41035-03 (DDK) MELNER, MICHAEL H OREGON REGN PRIMATE RES CTR 505 N W 185TH AVE BEAVERTON, OR 97006 Regulation of neuro-immuno-endocrine cells

R01DK-41043-03 (DDK) ORTH, DAVID N VANDERBILT UNIVERSITY MED SCH ROOM A-4215 MEDICAL CENTER NOR NASHVILLE, TENN 37232 POMC peptide synthesis by normal and AIDS leukocytes

R01DK-41053-03 (DDK) OLSEN, NANCY J VANDERBILT UNIVERSITY T-3219 MEDICAL CENTER NORTH NASHVILLE, TN 37232 Effect of androgens on the thymus

R01DK-41058-03 (DDK) THOMPSON, E BRAD UNIV OF TEXAS MEDICAL BRANCH BASIC SCIENCE BUILDING GALVESTON, TX 77550-2779 Steroid hormones, HIV-infected cells and HIV genes

R01DK-41059-03 (DDK) MILLS, JOHN SAN FRANCISCO GENERAL HOSP 995 POTRERO STREET, BLDG 80 SAN FRANCISCO, CA 94110 Neuropeptide interactions with HIV-infected macrophages

R01DK-41066-03 (DDK) ROJKO, JENNIFER L OHIO STATE UNIVERSITY DEPARTMENT OF VET PATHOBIOLOGY COLUMBUS, OH 43210-1005 Feline retrovirus associated endocrine dysfunction

R01DK-41075-03 (MET) MANDARINO, LAWRENCE J EYE & EAR INST OF PITTSBURGH 203 LOTHROP ST PITTSBURGH, PA 15213 Pathways of skeletal muscle glucose metabolism in man

R01DK-41077-03 (PC) STURGILL, THOMAS W UNIVERSITY OF VIRGINIA BOX 419 CHARLOTTESVILLE, VA 22908 Regulation and function of insulin stimulated MAP kinase

R01DK-41079-03 (HEM) SHEFFERY, MICHAEL B SLOAN-KETTERING INSTITUTE 1275 YORK AVE NEW YORK, NY 10021 A-globin promotor binding factors -- Structure and cloning

R01DK-41082-03 (BIO) BIRKENMEIER, EDWARD H JACKSON LABORATORY 600 MAIN STREET BAR HARBOR, ME 04609-0800 Characterization and treatment of murine MPS VII

R01DK-41084-02 (BEM) LEVENSTEIN, SUSAN B REPARTO DI GASTROENTEROLOGIA VIA MOROSINI 30 00100 ROME, ITALY Life stressors in duodenal ulcer: two subpopulations

R29DK-41089-03 (NTN) SOPRANO, DIANNE R TEMPLE UNIVERSITY SCH. OF MED 3420 N. BROAD STREET PHILADELPHIA, PA 19140 Biochemical mechanism of action of vitamin A

R01DK-41090-03 (IMS) APPEL, MICHAEL C UNIV OF MA MED SCH 55 LAKE AVE N DEPT OF PATHOLOG WORCESTER, MASS 01655 Experimental insulin dependent diabetes

R01DK-41093-03 (END) SAMUELS, HERBERT H NEW YORK UNIVERSITY MED CTR 550 FIRST AVE NEW YORK, N Y 10016 Glucocorticoid receptors--Structure and function

R01DK-41096-03 (NTN) FRIEDMAN, JEFFREY M ROCKEFELLER UNIVERSITY 1230 YORK AVENUE NEW YORK, NY 10021-6399 The genomic basis of heritable obesity in mice

R01DK-41110-03 (PBC) NEILSON, ERIC G UNIVERSITY OF PENNSYLVANIA 860 GATES PAVILION PHILADELPHIA, PA 19104 Characterization 3m-1 antigen in interstitial nephritis

R01DK-41113-03 (DDK) GABBAY, KENNETH H BAYLOR COLLEGE OF MEDICINE ONE BAYLOR PLAZA HOUSTON, TX 77030 AIDS in infants and children--Endocrine and wasting aspects

R01DK-41116-02 (NTN) GREGER, JANET L UNIVERSITY OF WISCONSIN 1415 LINDEN DR MADISON, WI 53706 Metabolism of dietary aluminum

R01DK-41117-03 (GMB) JOHNS, DEARING W UNIVERSITY OF VIRGINIA BOX 146 CHARLOTTESVILLE, VA 22908 Regulation of renin in isolated kidney cortical cells

R01DK-41122-03 (GMA) WILLIAMS, JOHN A UNIVERSITY OF MICHIGAN DEPARTMENT OF PHYSIOLOGY ANN ARBOR, MI 48109-0622 Calcium and pancreatic stimulus-secretion coupling

R01DK-41126-02 (GMB) MOLITORIS, BRUCE A VETERANS ADMINISTRATION MED CT 1055 CLERMONT ST DENVER, CO 80220 Ischemia-induced loss of epithelial polarity

R01DK-41128-03 (MEP) BISTRIAN, BRUCE R NEW ENGLAND DEACONESS HOSPITAL 185 PILGRIM ROAD BOSTON, MA 02215 Wasting in AIDS--Role of monokines

P50DK-41146-04 (SRC) AL-AWQATI, QAIS COLUMBIA U. DEPT. OF MEDICINE 630 WEST 168TH STREET NEW YORK, NY 10032 Molecular biology

of CL channel in cystic fibrosis
P50DK-41146-04 0001 (SRC) AL-AWQATI, QAIS Molecular biology of CL channel in cystic fibrosis The chloride channel in cystic fibrosis
P50DK-41146-04 0002 (SRC) FIELD, MICHAEL Molecular biology of CL channel in cystic fibrosis Expression cloning of chloride channels is Xenopus oocytes
P50DK-41146-04 0003 (SRC) CHASE, HERBERT Molecular biology of CL channel in cystic fibrosis Role of cell calcium in chloride secretion
P50DK-41146-04 0004 (SRC) GOTTESMAN, MAX E Molecular biology of CL channel in cystic fibrosis Cloning of iodide transport proteins
P50DK-41146-04 0005 (SRC) AKABAS, MYLES Molecular biology of CL channel in cystic fibrosis Reconstitution of epithelial chloride channels in planar lipid bilayers
P50DK-41146-04 0006 (SRC) SEMRAD, CAROL Molecular biology of CL channel in cystic fibrosis Establishment of epithelial line from cystic fibrosis colon mucosa
R44DK-41171-03 (SSS) GUIRE, PATRICK BIO-METRIC SYSTEMS, INC 9924 WEST 74TH STREET EDEN PRAIRIE, MN 55344 Enzyme immobilization for removal of toxic metabolites
R29DK-41178-03 (SB) YEO, CHARLES J JOHNS HOPKINS UNIVERSITY 600 N WOLFE STREET BALTIMORE, MD 21205 Neural and 2nd messenger control of intestinal transport
R01DK-41204-03 (SB) MULHOLLAND, MICHAEL W UNIV OF MICH/DEPT OF SURGERY 1500 E MEDICAL CENTER DRIVE ANN ARBOR, MI 48109 Gastrointestinal autonomic dysfunction
R01DK-41206-04 (END) EBERHARDT, NORMAN L MAYO FOUNDATION 200 FIRST STREET SOUTHWEST ROCHESTER, MN 55905 Structure and function of growth hormone-related genes
R01DK-41212-01A3 (PHY) KURTZ, IRA UNIVERSITY OF CALIFORNIA LOS ANGELES, CA 90024-1689 Confocal microscopy--Collecting duct pH regulation
R01DK-41214-03 (HEM) MULLER-SIEBURG, CHRISTA E MEDICAL BIOLOGY INSTITUTE 11077 N TORREY PINES RD LA JOLLA, CA 92037 Isolation of hematopoietic and stromal cell precursors
R01DK-41215-03 (TOX) WALLIG, MATTHEW A UNIVERSITY OF ILLINOIS 2001 S LINCOLN AVE URBANA, IL 61801 Cyanohydroxybutene toxicity and glutathione
R01DK-41218-02 (PTHA) NOBLE, BERNICE STATE UNIVERSITY OF NEW YORK MAIN STREET CAMPUS BUFFALO, NY 14214 Mononuclear cell function in chronic serum sickness
R01DK-41225-03 (GMA) WILLIAMS, JOHN A UNIVERSITY OF MICHIGAN 7744 MEDICAL SCIENCES 11 ANN ARBOR, MI 48109-0622 Receptors for CCK & other GI hormones
R01DK-41230-03 (MET) ZAWALICH, WALTER S YALE UNIVERSITY SCH OF NURSING 25 PARK STREET, P. O. BOX 9740 NEW HAVEN, CT 06536 Phosphoinositide hydrolysis & beta cell secretion
R01DK-41234-03 (HEM) BUNN, H FRANKLIN BRIGHAM AND WOMEN'S HOSP, INC 75 FRANCIS STREET BOSTON, MA 02115 The regulation of erythropoietin production
R01DK-41235-03 (PTHA) MORDES, JOHN P UNIV OF MASSACHUSETTS MED SCH 55 LAKE AVENUE NORTH WORCESTER, MA 01655 Role of venular endothelium in diabetes
R01DK-41244-02 (BCE) BIRNBAUMER, MARIEL BAYLOR COLLEGE OF MEDICINE ONE BAYLOR PLAZA HOUSTON, TX 77030 Molecular biology and pathology of vasopressin receptors
R01DK-41246-02 (GMB) FELDMAN, DAVID STANFORD UNIVERSITY SCH OF MED STANFORD, CA 94305 Vitamin D receptor in normal and hormone-resistant cells
R01DK-41253-02 (BBCA) HIRSCH, RHODA E ALBERT EINSTEIN COLL OF MEDICI 1300 MORRIS PARK AVENUE BRONX, NY 10461 Conformational aspects of Hb by front-face fluorometry
R01DK-41255-03 (SAT) MAKI, TAKASHI NEW ENGLAND DEACONESS HOSPITAL 185 PILGRIM ROAD BOSTON, MA 02215 Pancreatic islet transplantation in NOD mice
R29DK-41260-04 (END) DONOHOUE, PATRICIA A UNIVERSITY OF IOWA COLLEGE OF MEDICINE IOWA CITY, IA 32242 21-hydroxylase deficiency--Mutations and mechanisms
R01DK-41263-03 (END) WIDMAIER, ERIC P BOSTON UNIVERSITY 881 COMMONWEALTH AVE. BOSTON, MA 02215 Control of stress response by energy substrates
R01DK-41269-04 (MGN) BOWDEN, DONALD WARREN WAKE FOREST UNIVERSITY 300 SOUTH HAWTHORNE ROAD WINSTON-SALEM, N C 27103 Genetic mapping of non-insulin dependent diabetes
R01DK-41274-04 (GMA) GHISHAN, FAYEZ K VANDERBILT UNIVERSITY MED CTR 21ST & GARLAN / D-4130 MCND NASHVILLE, TN 37232 Development of intestinal ion transport
R01DK-41279-03 (SRC) GLASS, JONATHAN LOUISIANA STATE MEDICAL CENTER 1501 KINGS HIGHWAY, BOX 33932 SHREVEPORT, LA 71130-3932 Molecular mechanisms of intestinal iron transport
R01DK-41294-03 (CVB) CONGER, JOHN D UNIV OF COLORADO HLTH SCIS CTR BOX C-281, 4200 EAST 9TH AVE DENVER, CO 80262 Vasculature dynamic abnormalities in acute renal failure
P30DK-41296-03 (DDK) SHAFRITZ, DAVID A ALBERT EINSTEIN COLL OF MED 1300 MORRIS PARK AVENUE BRONX, NY 10461 Liver research core center
P30DK-41296-03 0001 (DDK) KRAUTER, KENNETH Liver research core center Pilot study--Regulation of alpha 1 antitrypsin gene expression
P30DK-41296-03 0002 (DDK) CZAJA, MARK Liver research core center Pilot study--Cytokine modulation of acute liver injury
P30DK-41296-03 0003 (DDK) HORWITZ, SUSAN Liver research core center Pilot study--P-glycoprotein in liver and hepatocellular carcinoma
P30DK-41296-03 0004 (DDK) STANLEY, PAMELA Liver research core center Pilot study--HepG2 mutants defective in endocytosis
P30DK-41296-03 0005 (DDK) SATIR, BRIGIT Liver research core center Pilto study--Parafusin in liver and hepatocytes
P30DK-41296-03 9001 (DDK) ROGLER, CHARLES Liver research core center Core--Molecular biology
P30DK-41296-03 9002 (DDK) REID, LOLA Liver research core center Core--Cell culture/matrix
P30DK-41296-03 9003 (DDK) GOLDFISCHER, SIDNEY Liver research core center Core--Morphology
P30DK-41296-03 9004 (DDK) CHOWDHURY, JAYANTA Liver research core center Core--Animal facility
R29DK-41298-03 (HEM) WONG, PETER M SUNY SCIENCE CENTER 450 CLARKSON AVENUE BROOKLYN, NY 11203 The effect of Il-6 and Il-1 on hemopoietic stem cells
P30DK-41301-02 (DDK) WALSH, JOHN H CURE/VA WADSWORTH WILSHITRE & SAWTELLE BLVDS LOS ANGELES, CA 90073 CURE digestive disease core center
P30DK-41301-02 0001 (DDK) KARNES, WILLIAM CURE digestive disease core center Paracellular resistance across chief cell monolayers
P30DK-41301-02 0002 (DDK) COLLIE, NATHAN CURE digestive disease core center Enteroglucagon and intestinal adaptation
P30DK-41301-02 9001 (DDK) JENSEN, DENNIS CURE digestive disease core center Peptic disease study core
P30DK-41301-02 9002 (DDK) TACHE, YVETTE CURE digestive disease core center Animal core for assessment of gastric function
P30DK-41301-02 9003 (DDK) GUTH, PAUL CURE digestive disease core center Gastrointestinal blood flow and experimental ulcer core
P30DK-41301-02 9004 (DDK) SACHS, GEORGE CURE digestive disease core center Cell biology core
P30DK-41301-02 9005 (DDK) STERNINI, CATIA CURE digestive disease core center Neuroendocrine anatomy core
R01DK-41312-02 (IMS) MILLER, GERALDINE P VANDERBILT UNIVERSITY A3310 MEDICAL CENTER NORTH NASHVILLE, TN 37232 Human T cell repertoire for insulin
P01DK-41315-03 (DDK) SANDERS, KENTON M UNIV OF NEVADA SCHOOL OF MED RENO, NV 89557-6890 Regulatory mechanism in colonic motility-program project
P01DK-41315-03 0003 (DDK) HUME, JOSEPH Regulatory mechanism in colonic motility-program project Regulation of ionic currents in isolated colonic cells
P01DK-41315-03 0004 (DDK) KENYON, JAMES Regulatory mechanism in colonic motility-program project Single ionic channels in colonic muscle cells
P01DK-41315-03 0005 (DDK) BUXTON, IAIN Regulatory mechanism in colonic motility-program project Receptor signal transduction in colonic muscle
P01DK-41315-03 0006 (DDK) PUBLICOVER, NELSON Regulatory mechanism in colonic motility-program project Regulation of calcium during colonic motility
P01DK-41315-03 0001 (DDK) KEEF, KATHLEEN Regulatory mechanism in colonic motility-program project Neural regulation of colonic electrical and mechanical activity
P01DK-41315-03 0002 (DDK) SANDERS, KENTON Regulatory mechanism in colonic motility-program project Electrophysiology and structure of colonic muscles
P01DK-41315-03 0007 (DDK) GERTHOFFER, WILLIAM Regulatory mechanism in colonic motility-program project Regulation of phasic and tonic contraction in colonic muscles
P01DK-41315-03 9001 (DDK) BUXTON, IAIN Regulatory mechanism in colonic motility-program project Core--Tissue culture laboratory
P01DK-41315-03 9002 (DDK) PUBLICOVER, NELSON Regulatory mechanism in colonic motility-program project Core--Imaging and morphology laboratory
P01DK-41315-03 9003 (DDK) KENYON, JAMES Regulatory mechanism in colonic motility-program project Core--Electronics and computing
R01DK-41317-03 (GMB) KOMM, BARRY S UNIVERSITY OF ARIZONA TUCSON, AZ 85724 CaBP gene interaction with vitamin D3 receptor
R29DK-41321-02 (BCE) LEE, STEPHANIE L NEW ENGLAND MED CTR HOSP, INC 750 WASHINGTON ST, BOX 268 BOSTON, MA 02111 Regulation of TRH gene expression in neuroendocrine cell
R01DK-41323-01A2 (SB) MAHER, JAMES W UNIVERSITY OF IOWA DEPT OF SURGERY IOWA CITY, IA 52242 Chemo-nociceptive mechanisms of the distal esophagus
R01DK-41324-02 (CBY) GARDNER, PHYLLIS I STANFORD UNIVERSITY STANFORD, CA 94305-5246 CAMP-regulated chloride channel in t-lymphocytes
R01DK-41326-02 (END) CHOMCZYNSKI, PIOTR UNIVERSITY OF CINCINNATI 231 BETHESDA AVE M L #547 CINCINNATI, OH 45267 Secretory proteins of somatomammotroph cell lines
R01DK-41329-03 (SRC) QUINTON, PAUL M UNIVERSITY OF CALIFORNIA DIV OF BIOMEDICAL SCIENCES RIVERSIDE, CALIF 92521-0121 Immortal sweat gland cells for cystic fibrosis research
R01DK-41330-03 (SRC) FRIZZELL, RAYMOND A UNIVERSITY OF ALABAMA UNIVERSITY STATION BIRMINGHAM, AL 35294 Cystic fibrosis pancreatic adenocarcinoma cell lines
R01DK-41331-03 (SRC) DEARBORN, DORR G CASE WESTERN RESERVE UNIV 2101 ADELBERT ROAD CLEVELAND, OHIO 44106 Human sweat duct--In vitro model
R01DK-41341-01A2 (EDC) FIHN, STEPHAN D SEATTLE VA MEDICAL CENTER 1660 SOUTH COLUMBIAN WAY SEATTLE, WA 98108 Vaginal spermicides and urinary tract infections
R29DK-41347-02 (IMS) CONCANNON, PATRICK J VIRGINIA MASON RESEARCH CTR 1000 SENECA ST, R1-RC SEATTLE, WA 98101 T-cell receptor repertoire in type I diabetes
R01DK-41350-03 (PC) LOGSDON, CRAIG D UNIVERSITY OF MICHIGAN 1301 CATHERINE STREET ANN ARBOR, MI 48109 Molecular analysis of the cholecystokinin receptor
R29DK-41353-02 (RAP) SCHUETTE, SALLY A UNIVERSITY OF CHICAGO 5841 S MARYLAND AVE, BOX 400 CHICAGO, IL 60637 Mg turnover and exchange--Functional significance
R01DK-41368-02 (PHY) SAEZ, JUAN C ALBERT EINSTEIN COLL OF MEDICI 1300 MORRIS PARK AVENUE BRONX, NY 10461 Pineal gap junction--characterizing regulation and function
R01DK-41371-03 (GMA) BARBER, DIANE L YALE UNIVERSITY SURGERY DEPT, 333 CEDAR ST NEW HAVEN, CT 06510 Mechanisms regulating intestinal neurotensin expression
R29DK-41376-03 (NTN) CAMPBELL, PETER J VANDERBILT UNIVERSITY 21ST AVE SOUTH & GARLAND ST NASHVILLE, TN 37232 Role of lipolysis in human obesity and fasting
R29DK-41380-02 (MET) EDENS, NEILE K ROCKEFELLER UNIVERSITY 1230 YORK AVE NEW YORK, NY 10021-6399 Regulation of adipocyte free fatty acid reesterification
R01DK-41383-03 (BPO) HOUPT, THOMAS R CORNELL UNIVERSITY COLLEGE OF VETERINARY MED ITHACA, N Y 14853 Controls of anticipatory,

meal-related water drinking
R01DK-41386-03 (HEM) PATEL, VIKRAM P NORTHWESTERN UNIVERSITY 2153 SHERIDAN RD EVANSTON, IL 60208 Blood cell development--Role of fibronectin receptors
R01DK-41387-03 (BBCA) SMITH, G DAVID MEDICAL FDN OF BUFFALO, INC 73 HIGH STREET BUFFALO, NY 14203 Alpha-helix promotion in insulin hexamers
R29DK-41393-03 (PB) TRABER, PETER G VETERANS ADMIN MED CTR 2215 FULLER RD/GI DIV (111-D) ANN ARBOR, MI 48105 Intestinal and colonic cytochrome P450 gene expression
R29DK-41395-03 (HEM) FELDMAN, LAURIE NEW ENGLAND DEACONESS HOSPITAL 185 PILGRIM ROAD BOSTON, MA 02215 Membrane-derived growth factors in hematopoiesis
R01DK-41399-02 (GMA) KVIETYS, PETER R LOUISIANA STATE UNIV MED CTR PO BOX 33932 SHREVEPORT, LA 71130-3932 Gastric mucosal injury
R01DK-41402-03 (MET) SCHROEDER, FRIEDHELM UNIVERSITY OF CINCINNATI MED C 231 BETHESDA AVENUE CINCINNATI, OH 45267-0004 Fatty acid binding proteins-ligand specificity
R01DK-41415-03 (GMB) BROWN, EDWARD M BRIGHAM AND WOMENS HOSPITAL 75 FRANCIS STREET BOSTON, MA 02115 Pharmacology of bovine parathyroid Ca++ "receptors"
R01DK-41418-03 (END) SCHLEICHER, ROSEMARY L VETS ADMIN MEDICAL CTR 1670 CLAIRMONT ROAD DECATUR, GA 30033 Beta-endorphin in the pancreatic islets
R29DK-41419-02 (END) GWOSDOW, ANDREA R SHRINERS BURNS INSTITUTE 51 BLOSSOM STREET BOSTON, MA 02114 Cytokine regulation of the pituitary-adrenal axis
R01DK-41427-03 (GMB) HUGHES, MARK R BAYLOR COLLEGE OF MEDICINE TAUB RESEARCH BLDG., T921 HOUSTON, TX 77030 Receptor mutants in vitamin D resistant rickets of bone
R29DK-41430-02 (END) UNTERMAN, TERRY G UNIVERSITY OF ILLINOIS PO BOX 6998 CHICAGO, IL 60680 Growth factor binding proteins and inhibitors in diabetes
R29DK-41431-03 (PTHA) SKIDGEL, RANDAL A UNIV OF ILLINOIS AT CHICAGO 835 S WOLCOTT AVE CHICAGO, IL 60612 Structure and function of carboxypeptidase M
R01DK-41434-01A2 (GMB) KHAN, SAEED R UNIVERSITY OF FLORIDA BOX J-275 JHMHC GAINESVILLE, FL 32610 Role of lipids in urolithiasis
R15DK-41460-01A2 (BMT) JEWETT, SANDRA L CA STATE UNIV, NORTHRIDGE 18111 NORDHOFF STREET NORTHRIDGE, CA 91330 Oxidation of superoxide dismutase--Role in red cell aging
R01DK-41479-03 (MEP) ROSS, ALTA C THE MED COLL OF PENNSYLVANIA 3300 HENRY AVENUE, 318R PHILADELPHIA, PA 19129 Vitamin a nutritional status and immune function
R01DK-41480-04 (GMB) SHAH, SUDHIR V UNIV OF ARKANSAS/MED. SCIENCES 4301 W MARKHAM LITTLE ROCK, AR 72205 Oxidant mechanisms in membranous nephropathy
R01DK-41485-02 (DDK) LOGAN, JOY L UNIV OF ARIZONA COLLEGE OF MED 1501 N CAMPBELL TUCSON, AZ 85724 Renal effects of dietary fat in experimental diabetes
R01DK-41487-02 (DDK) SHAYMAN, JAMES A UNIVERSITY OF MICHIGAN 3914 TAUBMAN CENTER, BOX 0364 ANN ARBOR, MI 48109 Renal polyol metabolism
R01DK-41500-02 (DDK) YURCHENCO, PETER D UMDNJ ROBERT W JOHNSON MED CTR MEDICAL SCHOOL, 675 HOES LANE PISCATAWAY, NJ 08854 Glycation-dependent alteration of basement membranes
R01DK-41513-02 (DDK) AVRUCH, JOSEPH MASSACHUSETTS GENERAL HOSPITAL FRUIT STREET BOSTON, MASS 02114 Molecular mediators of diabetic renal hypertrophy
R01DK-41517-03 (PTHA) KASINATH, BALAKUNTALAM S UNIVERSITY OF TEXAS HLTH SCI C 7703 FLOYD CURL DR SAN ANTONIO, TX 78284 Glomerular epithelial cell metabolism in diabetes
R01DK-41526-02 (EDC) KROLEWSKI, ANDRZEJ S JOSLIN DIABETES CENTER ONE JOSLIN PLACE BOSTON, MA 02215 Natural history of microalbuminuria in type I diabetes
R01DK-41527-02 (DDK) ARON, DAVID C VA MEDICAL CTR 151W 10701 EAST BLVD CLEVELAND, OH 44106 Insulin-like growth factor I in diabetic nephropathy
R01DK-41544-03 (CBY) CARRASCO, NANCY ALBERT EINSTEIN COLLEGE OF MED 1300 MORRIS PARK AVE BRONX, NY 10461 Molecular characterization of the iodide carrier
R15DK-41550-01A1 (BMT) STROTHKAMP, KENNETH G DREW UNIVERSITY MADISON, NJ 07940 Binuclear mixed-metal derivatives of tyrosinase
R29DK-41553-04 (NEUB) KLUEBER, KATHLEEN UNIVERSITY OF LOUISVILLE DEPT OF ANATOMICAL SCIENCES LOUISVILLE, KY 40292 Neuromuscular relationships of diabetic muscle and nerve
R01DK-41562-02 (MET) WOODSIDE, WILLIAM F UNIVERSITY OF NEW MEXICO 915 STANFORD NE ALBUQUERQUE, MN 87131-5316 Adrenoceptor role in atherosclerotic serum lipid changes
R01DK-41563-02 (BPO) DAVIS, JOHN D UNIVERSITY OF ILLINOIS BOX 4348 CHICAGO, IL 60680 Analysis of the microstructure of ingestive behavior
R01DK-41566-03 (DDK) SCHLONDORFF, DETLEF O ALBERT EINSTEIN COLLEGE OF MED 1300 MORRIS PARK AVE BRONX, NY 10461 Nonenzymatic glycosylation of the mesangium in diabetes
R55DK-41567-01A1 (PC) BAEKKESKOV, STEINUNN UNIVERSITY OF CALIFORNIA SAN FRANCISCO, CA 94143-0534 Molecular characterization of B-cell membrane antigens
R01DK-41571-03 (SB) HENDERSON, JOHN M EMORY UNIVERSITY 1364 CLIFTON ROAD, N E ATLANTA, GA 30322 Methods of hemodynamic study and regulation in cirrhosis
R01DK-41572-03 (NLS) RAMSAY, RONA R UNIVERSITY OF CALIFORNIA 4150 CLEMENT ST RM 222 SAN FRANCISCO, CA 94121 Mitochondria-enzymes, inhibition, metabolic consequences
R29DK-41573-03 (PTHA) GOLIGORSKY, MICHAEL S SUNY AT STONY BROOK DIV OF NEPHRO & HYPERTENSION STONY BROOKE, NY 11794-8152 Oxidative insult to cultured renal tubular cells
R44DK-41597-03 (SSS) SAUNDERS, ALEX M CHRONOMED, INC 8 TRILLIUM LANE SAN CARLOS, CA 94070 Improved resolution of metabolic control in diabetes
R44DK-41601-03 (SSS) DE CASTRO, AURORA F GDS TECHNOLOGY, INC PO BOX 473 ELKHART, IN 46515 A simple blood test of D-3 hydroxybutyrate for diabetics

R01DK-41606-01A2 (ET) NELSON, J ARLY UNIV TX MD ANDERSON CANCER CTR 1515 HOLCOMBE BLVD HOUSTON, TX 77030 Pleiotropic drug resistance and transport
R01DK-41612-01A2 (GMB) BAUM, MICHEL G UNIVERSITY OF TEXAS 5323 HARRY HINES BOULEVARD DALLAS, TX 75235-9063 Neonatal proximal tubular acidification
R01DK-41625-03 (HEM) NEWBURGER, PETER E UNIV OF MASSACHUSETTS MED SCH 55 LAKE AVENUE NORTH WORCESTER, MA 01655 Leukocyte glutathione peroxidase expression
R01DK-41627-03 (SAT) SOLLINGER, HANS W UNIVERSITY OF WISCONSIN 600 HIGHLAND AVENUE MADISON, WIS 53792 Mechanism of alteration of allograft antigenicity
R01DK-41631-03 (MET) RAY, PAUL D UNIV OF NORTH DAKOTA MED SCH DEPT OF BIOCHEMISTRY GRAND FORKS, ND 58202 Alternative roles for phosphoenolpyruvate carboxykinase
R01DK-41641-01A1 (GMB) DEEN, WILLIAM M MASSACHUSETTS INST. OF TECH. CHEMICAL ENGINEERING/RM 66-509 CAMBRIDGE, MA 02139 Glomerular hypertension and sieving of macromolecules
R29DK-41647-02 (NTN) CHRISTENSEN, MERRILL J BRIGHAM YOUNG UNIVERSITY PROVO, UT 84602 Selenium regulation of the glutathione peroxidase gene
R01DK-41652-03 (BCE) BOOCKFOR, FREDRIC R MEDICAL UNIV OF SOUTH CAROLINA 171 ASHLEY AVENUE CHARLESTON, SC 29425-2204 GH and prolactin release from single and dual secretors
R01DK-41670-03 (REN) LIAO, SHUTSUNG UNIV OF CHICAGO/BEN MAY INST 5841 SOUTH MARYLAND AVE CHICAGO, IL 60637 Steroid 5-alpha reductase--Structures and functions
R01DK-41674-01A2 (END) HABER, RICHARD S MOUNT SINAI SCHOOL OF MED 1 GUSTAVE L LEVY PL/BOX 1055 NEW YORK, NY 10029 Regulation of membrane transport by thyroid hormone
R01DK-41678-02 (GMA) LEE, SUM P UNIVERSITY OF WASHINGTON (111GI) ZB-20 SEATTLE, WA 98195 Cholesterol solubilization in bile
R01DK-41682-03 (NTN) HARRIS, EDWARD D TEXAS A&M UNIVERSITY COLLEGE STATION, TX 77843 The ascorbate copper link in nutrition
R01DK-41684-03 (PTHA) DUNN, MICHAEL J UNIVERSITY HOSPITALS 2074 ABINGTON ROAD CLEVELAND, OH 44106 Eicosanoids and platelet activating factor in renal injury
R29DK-41693-03 (NTN) CHAPKIN, ROBERT S TEXAS A & M UNIVERSITY BOX 3578 COLLEGE STATION TX 77843 Dietary significance of gammalinolenic acid
R29DK-41705-03 (MET) FREAKE, HEDLEY C UNIVERSITY OF CONNECTICUT 3624 HORSEBARN ROAD EXTENSION STORRS, CT 06269-4017 Regulation of lipogenesis by thyroid hormones and diet
R29DK-41706-03 (BCE) PENTECOST, BRIAN T WADSWORTH CTR/LABS & RESEARCH PO BOX 509 EMPIRE STATE PLAZA ALBANY, NY 12201-0509 Estrogen regulation of rat uterine creatine kinase B
R29DK-41707-03 (GMB) SANDS, JEFF M EMORY UNIVERSITY SCHOOL OF MED 1364 CLIFTON ROAD, NE ATLANTA, GA 30322 Regulation of rat renal inner medullary function
R01DK-41709-03 (SB) TOMPKINS, RONALD G MASSACHUSETTS GENERAL HOSPITAL FRUIT STREET BOSTON, MA 02114 Development of hepatic support systems
R01DK-41714-03 (HEM) SCHROIT, ALAN J UNIV OF TX MD ANDERSON CANCER 1515 HOLCOMBE BLVD HOUSTON, TX 77030 Maintenance of lipid asymmetry in the human erythrocyte
R01DK-41720-03 (BCE) VAN ITALLIE, CHRISTINA M YALE UNIVERSITY SCHOOL OF MED 333 CEDAR ST PO BOX 3333 NEW HAVEN, CT 06510 Hormonal regulation of mitochondrial gene expression
R29DK-41725-03 (GMB) WORCESTER, ELAINE M CLEMENT J ZABLOCKI VA MED CENT 5000 W NATIONAL AVENUE MILWAUKEE, WI 53295 Crystal growth inhibitor protein and nephrolithiasis
R29DK-41726-03 (GMB) MILLER, RICHARD T U OF TEXAS SOUTHWESTERN MED CT 5323 HARRY HINES BLVD DALLAS, TX 75235-9030 Renal proximal tubule transport--hormonal regulation
R01DK-41732-03 (NTN) KING, JANET C UNIVERSITY OF CALIFORNIA 119 MORGAN HALL BERKELEY, CA 94720 Zinc absorption in diabetic pregnant women
R01DK-41737-02 (CTY) SUBRAMANI, SURESH UNIVERSITY OF CALIFORNIA 9500 GILMAN DRIVE LA JOLLA, CA 92093-0322 Targeting of proteins into peroxisomes
R01DK-41738-03 (BIO) BAENZIGER, JACQUES U WASHINGTON UNIV SCH OF MEDICIN 660 SOUTH EUCLID AVE ST LOUIS, MO 63110 Glycoprotein hormone oligosaccharides
R01DK-41740-04 (BIO) DEDMAN, JOHN R UNIVERSITY OF CINCINNATI COLLEGE OF MEDICINE CINCINNATI, OH 45267-0576 Calcium regulation of epithelia
R01DK-41755-01A1 (SAT) BRUSKEWITZ, REGINALD C UNIVERSITY OF WISCONSIN 600 HIGHLAND AVENUE MADISON, WI 53792 Effects of the sensory nerve system on bladder function
R01DK-41758-02 (HEM) MATHEY-PREVOT, BERNARD DANA FARBER CANCER INSTITUTE 44 BINNEY ST BOSTON, MA 02115 Gene regulation of the cytokines IL-3 and GM-CSF
R01DK-41762-03 (MET) AVRUCH, JOSEPH MASSACHUSETTS GENERAL HOSP EAS 13TH ST BLDG 149 CHARLESTOWN, MA 02129 Physiologic target of the insulin receptor kinase
R29DK-41764-03 (MET) JAHOOR, FAROOK UNIVERSITY OF TEXAS MED BRANCH 610 TEXAS AVENUE GALVESTON, TX 77550 Glycolytic rate in the regulation of protein synthesis
R01DK-41765-03 (PC) ROTH, RICHARD A STANFORD UNIVERSITY ENCINA HALL, ROOM 40 STANFORD, CA 94305 Substrates for the insulin receptor tyrosine kinase
R01DK-41777-03 (END) KUHN, CYNTHIA M DUKE UNIVERSITY MEDICAL CTR BOX 3813 DURHAM, NC 27710 Integration of stress response in ontogeny--Role of CRF
R01DK-41780-03 (BIO) DAVIES, ALBERT O BAYLOR COLLEGE OF MEDICINE ONE BAYLOR PLAZA HOUSTON, TX 77030 Human adrenergic receptor and G-protein regulation
P01DK-41801-02 (DDK) LERNMARK, AKE UNIVERSITY OF WASHINGTON MAIL STOP RG-20 SEATTLE, WA 98195 Immune response in insulin-dependent diabetes
P01DK-41801-02 0003 (DDK) MILNER, ERIC Immune response in insulin-dependent diabetes Immunoglobulin genes and insulin-dependent diabetes mellitus

PROJECT NO., ORGANIZATIONAL UNIT., INVESTIGATOR, ADDRESS, TITLE

P01DK-41801-02 0004 (DDK) CONCANNON, PATRICK Immune response in insulin-dependent diabetes T-cell receptor genes in insulin-dependent diabetes mellitus

P01DK-41801-02 0005 (DDK) LERNMARK, AKE Immune response in insulin-dependent diabetes Pancreatic islet cell autoantigens in insulin-dependent diabetes mellitus

P01DK-41801-02 0006 (DDK) PALMER, JERRY Immune response in insulin-dependent diabetes Cytokine effects on islet cells

P01DK-41801-02 0007 (DDK) SARVETNICK, NORA Immune response in insulin-dependent diabetes Dissection of the islet inflammatory response

P01DK-41801-02 9001 (DDK) NEPOM, GERALD Immune response in insulin-dependent diabetes DNA and cell bank

P01DK-41801-02 0001 (DDK) PIOUS, DONALD Immune response in insulin-dependent diabetes T-cells and islet molecules in diabetes

P01DK-41801-02 0002 (DDK) NEPOM, GERALD Immune response in insulin-dependent diabetes Genetic and regulatory parameters of IDDM susceptibility genes

P01DK-41822-03 (DDK) HANAHAN, DOUGLAS UNIVERSITY OF CALIFORNIA SAN FRANCISCO, CA 94143-0534 Cell and molecular biology of the pancreatic islet cells

P01DK-41822-03 0001 (DDK) HANAHAN, DOUGLAS Cell and molecular biology of the pancreatic islet cells Transgenic tumors, cell lines, and genes of the four islet cell types

P01DK-41822-03 0002 (DDK) BAEKKESKOV, STEINUNN Cell and molecular biology of the pancreatic islet cells Proteins correlating with islet cell type, organization and function

P01DK-41822-03 0003 (DDK) KELLY, REGIS Cell and molecular biology of the pancreatic islet cells Secretory functions and malfunctions in the pancreatic islet cells

P01DK-41822-03 0004 (DDK) RUTTER, WILLIAM Cell and molecular biology of the pancreatic islet cells Intercellular regulatory networks--Hormones,receptors and transcription

P01DK-41822-03 9001 (DDK) HANAHAN, DOUGLAS Cell and molecular biology of the pancreatic islet cells Scientific core

R01DK-41825-02 (SB) WOOD, JACKIE D 4196 GRAVES HALL COLUMBUS, OH 43210-1239 Colitis and colon cancer in cotton-top tamarins

R01DK-41837-01A2 (EDC) KLAG, MICHAEL J JOHNS HOPKINS HOSPITAL 600 N WOLFE STREET BALTIMORE, MD 21205 A prospective study of blood pressure and ESRD

R01DK-41841-04 (GMB) NARAY-FEJES-TOTH, ANIKO DARTMOUTH MEDICAL SCHOOL 2799 W GRAND BLVD HANOVER, NH 03756 Corticosteroid interactions in ion transport

R01DK-41842-03 (END) BAXTER, JOHN D UNIVERSITY OF CALIFORNIA 3RD & PARNASSUS/HSE 671 SAN FRANCISCO, CA 94143 Thyroid hormone receptor

R01DK-41843-03 (BIO) RIZZO, WILLIAM B MEDICAL COLLEGE OF VIRGINIA BOX 259, MCV STATION RICHMOND, VA 23298-0259 Fatty alcohol metabolism in Sjogren-Larsson syndrome

R01DK-41859-03 (SB) DRAKE, ROBERT E UNIVERSITY OF TEXAS 6431 FANNIN HOUSTON, TX 77030 Circuit analysis of the lymphatic system

R01DK-41868-03 (NTN) HWANG, DANIEL H LOUISIANA STATE UNIVERSITY 6400 PERKINS ROAD BATON ROUGE, LA 70808 Effects of dietary linolenate on arachidonate

R29DK-41869-03 (END) HOENIG, MARGARETHE E UNIVERSITY OF GEORGIA COLLEGE OF VET MED ATHENS, GA 30602 Role of the plasma membrane in stimulus-secretion coupling

R01DK-41872-02 (PC) CHIRALA, SUBRAHMANYAM S BAYLOR COLLEGE OF MEDICINE ONE BAYLOR PLAZA HOUSTON, TX 77030 Genetic regulation of fatty acid biosynthesis in yeast

R29DK-41873-03 (PTHA) QUIGG, RICHARD J, JR MEDICAL COLLEGE OF VIRGINIA 1101 E MARSHALL/BX 160 MCV STN RICHMOND, VA 23298 Complement activation on the glomeruler epithelial cell

R01DK-41875-03 (MEP) ZERN, MARK A ROGER WILLIAMS GENERAL HOSPITA 825 CHALKSTONE AVE PROVIDENCE, RI 02908 Omega-3 fatty acid and CCl4 induced liver disease

R29DK-41876-03 (GMA) GORES, GREGORY J MAYO FOUNDATION 200 FIRST STREET S W ROCHESTER, NY 55905 Intracellular pH in liver cell injury

R01DK-41879-04 (REB) COLLINS, DELWOOD C UNIVERSITY OF KENTUCKY A301 MEDICAL PLAZA LEXINGTON, KY 40536-0223 Androgen glucuronides as markers of androgen action

R01DK-41881-03 (REN) FABER, LEE E MEDICAL COLLEGE OF OHIO CS 10008 TOLEDO, OH 43699 Characterization of P59

R29DK-41889-03 (SB) LILLEMOE, KEITH D JOHNS HOPKINS HOSPITAL 600 N WOLFE STREET BALTIMORE, MD 21205 Role of calcium and caffeine in gallstone disease

R29DK-41891-01A2 (BBCB) NEWCOMER, MARCIA E VANDERBILT UNIVERSITY SCHOOL OF MEDICINE NASHVILLE, TN 37232 X-ray crystallographic study-vitamin A binding proteins

R29DK-41892-02 (BCE) BATEMAN, ROBERT C JR UNIV OF SOUTHERN MISSISSIPPI SOUTHERN STATION/BOX 5043 HATTIESBURG, MS 39406-5043 Mechanistic studies of glutamine cyclotransferase

R29DK-41896-02 (MET) LEWIS, ROBERT E UNIVERSITY OF NEBRASKA 600 SOUTH 42ND STREET OMAHA, NE 68198-6805 Insulin receptor regulation by serine and threonine phosphorylation

R01DK-41898-03 (BIO) NELSON, DANIEL A BAYLOR COLLEGE ONE BAYLOR PLAZA HOUSTON, TX 77030 Sulfonylurea receptor characterization and gene cloning

R01DK-41899-02 (BCE) PESCOVITZ, ORA H INDIANA UNIV SCHOOL OF MEDICIN 702 BARNHILL DRIVE INDIANAPOLIS, IN 46202-5225 Characterization of a GHRH-like substance in rat testis

R01DK-41906-02 (BCE) MELMED, SHLOMO CEDARS-SINAI MEDICAL CENTER 8700 BEVERLY BLVD LOS ANGELES, CA 90048 Pituitary tumor cell cultures

R29DK-41908-02 (MET) MOERLAND, TIMOTHY S FLORIDA STATE UNIVERSITY TALLAHASSEE, FL 32306-3050 Adaptation of skeletal muscle to streptozotocin diabetes

P01DK-41918-02 (DDK) WOLKOFF, ALLAN W ALBERT EINSTEIN COLL OF MEDICI 1300 MORRIS PARK AVENUE BRONX, NY 10461 Liver cell membrane proteins-- Expression and function

P01DK-41918-02 0001 (DDK) WOLKOFF, ALLAN W Liver cell membrane proteins-- Expression and function Control of vesicular trafficking in the hepatocyte

P01DK-41918-02 0002 (DDK) SPRAY, DAVID C Liver cell membrane proteins-- Expression and function Expressions,processing and function of liver gap junctions

P01DK-41918-02 0003 (DDK) ROJKIND, MARCOS Liver cell membrane proteins-- Expression and function Mechanisms of liver cell/matrix interaction

P01DK-41918-02 9001 (DDK) NOVIKOFF, PHYLLIS Liver cell membrane proteins-- Expression and function Molecular cytology core

R01DK-41920-02 (SB) ORLOFF, MARSHALL J UNIVERSITY OF CALIFORNIA 225 DICKINSON STREET SAN DIEGO, CA 92103 San Diego bleeding esophageal varices study

R29DK-41921-04 (END) CONE, ROGER DAVID OREGON HEALTH SCIENCES UNIV 3181 SW SAM JACKSON PARK RD PORTLAND, OR 97201-3098 Molecular basis of thyroidal iodide transport

R01DK-41923-01A1 (PTHA) RUDOFSKY, ULRICH H NEW YORK STATE DEPT OF HEALTH EMPIRE STATE LABS, PO BOX 509 ALBANY, NY 12201-0509 Differential expression of SLE in NZB/NZW RIS mice

R01DK-41927-02 (ARR) STEIN, THOMAS P UNIV OF MED & DENT OF NJ 401 HADDON AVENUE CAMDEN, NJ 08103 Protein and energy metabolism in AIDS patients

R01DK-41931-04A2 (END) SONENBERG, MARTIN SLOAN-KETTERING INSTITUTE 1275 YORK AVENUE NEW YORK, NY 10021 Growth hormone and differentiation

R01DK-41933-03 (SRC) BAGBY, GROVER C OREGON HLTH SCIS UNIVERSITY 3181 S W SAM JACKSON PARK ROAD PORTLAND, OR 97201 Mononuclear phagocytes, HIV, and hematopoiesis

R01DK-41934-03 (SRC) ABKOWITZ, JANIS L UNIV OF WASH - SCHOOL OF MED DIV OF HEMATOLOGY SEATTLE, WA 98195 Marrow suppression from a lentivirus

R01DK-41935-03 (SRC) ZUCKERMAN, KENNETH S UNIV OF ALABAMA AT BIRMINGHAM DIVISION OF HEMATOLOGY/ONCOLOG BIRMINGHAM, AL 35294 HIV and hemopoietic microenvironment

R01DK-41936-03 (SRC) KOEFFLER, PHILLIP H UNIVERSITY OF CALIFORNIA LOS ANGELES, CA 90024 HIV and myeloid hematopoiesis

R01DK-41937-04 (SRC) ADAMSON, JOHN W THE NEW YORK BLOOD CENTER 310 EAST 67TH STREET NEW YORK, N Y 10021 Pathobiology of bone marrow suppression in AIDS or ARC

R01DK-41938-03 (SRC) WEINBERG, RONA S MOUNT SINAI SCHOOL OF MEDICINE ONE GUSTAVE LEVY PLACE NEW YORK, N Y 10029 Hematopoiesis in AIDS

R01DK-41939-03 (SRC) KOCIBA, GARY J OHIO STATE UNIVERSITY 1925 COFFEY ROAD COLUMBUS, OH 43210-1005 Stromal defects in retrovirus-induced myelosuppression

R01DK-41940-02 (NTN) GREGER, JANET L UNIVERSITY OF WISCONSIN 1415 LINDEN DR MADISON, WI 53706 Interactions of dietary manganese and iron

R44DK-41947-02 (SSS) MALOY, W LEE MAGAININ SCIENCES, INC 5110 CAMPUS DRIVE PLYMOUTH MEETING, PA 19462 Novel magainin drugs for pseudomembranous colitis

R44DK-41962-02 (SSS) KYLE, DAVID J MARTEK CORPORATION 6480 DOBBIN RD COLUMBIA, MD 21045 13 C - labeled triolein for diagnostic breath tests

R44DK-41963-02 (SSS) KYLE, DAVID J MARTEK CORPORATION 6480 DOBBIN ROAD COLUMBIA, MD 21045 Docosahexaenoic acid from microalgae

R29DK-41969-03 (BEM) HANSON, CINDY L SAN DIEGO STATE UNIVERSITY 6215 FERRIS SQUARE SUITE 210 SAN DIEGO, CA 92182 Cardiovascular and metabolic health in high risk youth

R01DK-41971-03 (BBCA) SMITH, FRANCINE R UNIV OF NC AT CHAPEL HILL CB# 7260/405 FLOB CHAPEL HILL, NC 27599-7260 Structural studies of modified human hemoglobins

R01DK-41973-03 (MET) NAIR, K SREEKUMRAN UNIVERSITY OF VERMONT COLLEGE OF MEDICINE/GIVEN C-33 BURLINGTON, VT 05405 In vivo regulation of protein turnover by hormones

P50DK-41978-03 (DDK) SMITH, ARNOLD L UNIVERSITY OF WASHINGTON SCH OF MED/INFECTIOUS DIS ZC10 SEATTLE, WA 98195 Metabolism and cystic fibrosis

P50DK-41978-03 0001 (DDK) WILSON, CHRISTOPHER Metabolism and cystic fibrosis Cytokines in cystic fibrosis

P50DK-41978-03 0002 (DDK) MCKNIGHT, G STANLEY Metabolism and cystic fibrosis Chloride channel regulation by cAMP

P50DK-41978-03 0003 (DDK) UNADKAT, JASHVANT Metabolism and cystic fibrosis Hepatic and renal drug clearance in cystic fibrosis

P50DK-41978-03 0004 (DDK) LEE, SUM Metabolism and cystic fibrosis Control of gallbladder mucus secretion

P50DK-41978-03 0005 (DDK) HENDERSON, WILLIAM Metabolism and cystic fibrosis Omega-3 supplementation

P50DK-41980-03 (DDK) RIORDAN, JOHN R HOSPITAL FOR SICK CHILDREN 555 UNIVERSITY AVENUE TORONTO, ONT CANADA M5G 1X8 Molecular and cellular biology of cystic fibrosis

P50DK-41980-03 0001 (DDK) RIORDAN, JOHN Molecular and cellular biology of cystic fibrosis Molecular basis of cystic fibrosis apical chloride permeability defect

P50DK-41980-03 0002 (DDK) DURIE, PETER Molecular and cellular biology of cystic fibrosis Clinical and genetic variations in cystic fibrosis

P50DK-41980-03 0003 (DDK) FOSKETT, JAMES Molecular and cellular biology of cystic fibrosis Optical imaging of ion transport defects in cystic fibrosis

P50DK-41980-03 0004 (DDK) HANRAHAN, JOHN Molecular and cellular biology of cystic fibrosis The role of chloride channels in pancreatic secretion

P50DK-41980-03 0005 (DDK) BEAR, CHRISTINE Molecular and cellular biology of cystic fibrosis Chloride channel regulation in nonepithelial cells

P50DK-41980-03 9001 (DDK) COREY, MARY Molecular and cellular biology of cystic fibrosis Biostatistics core

R01DK-41995-01A2 (REN) YOUNG, CHARLES Y MAYO FOUNDATION 200 FIRST STREET SOUTHWEST ROCHESTER, MN 55905 Kallikrein gene expression in human prostate cells

R29DK-42008-01A2 (END) MORRIS, JOHN C, III MAYO FOUNDATION 200 FIRST STREET SOUTHWEST ROCHESTER, MN 55905 Studies of thyrotropin and its receptor

P50DK-42017-03 (DDK) BENOS, DALE J UNIVERSITY OF ALABAMA 1918 UNIVERSITY BLVD BIRMINGHAM, AL 35294 Cell and molecular biology of

secretory Cl channels
P50DK-42017-03 0001 (DDK) BENOS, DALE J Cell and molecular biology of secretory Cl channels Isolation/reconstitution of secretory Cl channels using antibody probes
P50DK-42017-03 0002 (DDK) FULLER, GERALD Cell and molecular biology of secretory Cl channels Cloning and expression of secretory Cl channels
P50DK-42017-03 0003 (DDK) MARCHASE, RICHARD Cell and molecular biology of secretory Cl channels Immunocytochemistry and intracellular trafficking of Cl channels
P50DK-42017-03 0004 (DDK) BRIDGES, ROBERT Cell and molecular biology of secretory Cl channels Disulfonic stilbenes as probes of reconstituted Cl channels
P50DK-42017-03 9001 (DDK) BRINKLEY, BILL Cell and molecular biology of secretory Cl channels Core--Cell culture and molecular probes
R01DK-42019-01A2 (END) FINN, FRANCES M UNIVERSITY OF PITTSBURGH 3550 TERRACE STREET PITTSBURGH, PA 15261 Site-directed derivatization of insulin receptor
R29DK-42026-03 (HEM) ASCENSAO, JOAO L UNIV OF CONNECTICUT SCH OF MED DIVISION OF HEMATOLOGY-ONCOLOG FARMINGTON, CT 06032-9984 Role of endothelial cells in blood production
R01DK-42027-03 (SAT) MELMAN, ARNOLD MONTEFIORE MEDICAL CENTER 111 EAST 210TH ST BRONX, NY 10467 Pharmacological studies of human erectile tissue
R01DK-42033-02 (NTN) SHANE, BARRY UNIVERSITY OF CALIFORNIA 119 MORGAN HALL BERKELEY, CALIF 94720 Folic acid requirements and one carbon metabolism
R29DK-42056-03 (REB) DUNCAN, MARILYN JEAN UNIVERSITY OF KENTUCKY 800 ROSE STREET MN224 LEXINGTON, KY 40536-0084 Reproductive consequences of neural melatonin receptors
R29DK-42059-03 (END) SPANGELO, BRYAN LEE MEDICAL UNIV OF SOUTH CAROLINA 171 ASHLEY AVENUE CHARLESTON, SC 29425-2258 Immune system hormones as pituitary releasing factors
R01DK-42063-01A1 (MET) SHARP, GEOFFREY W CORNELL UNIVERSITY D101 SCHURMAN HALL ITHACA, NY 14853-6401 Mechanisms of inhibition of insulin release by galanin
R01DK-42069-02 (GMB) LEIBACH, FREDERICK H MEDICAL COLL OF GEORGIA AUGUSTA, GA 30912-2100 Dipeptidylpeptidase IV deficiency--biochemical consequences
R29DK-42081-02 (GMA) FALLON, ROBERT J WASHINGTON UNIVERSITY 400 S KINGSHIGHWAY ST LOUIS, MO 63110 Analysis of receptor regulation of human liver cells
R01DK-42083-01A1 (HEM) HAMMOND, WILLIAM P UNIV OF WASHINGTON/SCH OF MED SEATTLE, WA 98195 Pathophysiology of G-CSF in canine neutropenia
P30DK-42086-02 (DDK) BRASITUS, THOMAS A UNIVERSITY OF CHICAGO 5841 S MARYLAND AVE CHICAGO, IL 60637 Cell and molecular biology of the gastrointestinal tract
P30DK-42086-02 0007 (DDK) REARDON, C Cell and molecular biology of the gastrointestinal tract Apolipoprotein A-II structure and function
P30DK-42086-02 9001 (DDK) CHANG, E Cell and molecular biology of the gastrointestinal tract Cell culture core
P30DK-42086-02 9002 (DDK) DAVIDSON, N Cell and molecular biology of the gastrointestinal tract Molecular biology core
P30DK-42086-02 9003 (DDK) SWIFT, H Cell and molecular biology of the gastrointestinal tract Ultrastructure and cytomorphology core
P30DK-42086-02 9004 (DDK) MEREDITH, S Cell and molecular biology of the gastrointestinal tract Amino acid and peptide analysis core
P30DK-42086-02 9005 (DDK) BRASITUS, T Cell and molecular biology of the gastrointestinal tract Biochemistry and biophysics core
P30DK-42086-02 0001 (DDK) DAVIS, B Cell and molecular biology of the gastrointestinal tract Modulation of Ito cell type I collagen & TGF-beta gene expression
P30DK-42086-02 0002 (DDK) MUSCH, M Cell and molecular biology of the gastrointestinal tract Regulation of arachidonic acid release & metabolism in macrophages
P30DK-42086-02 0003 (DDK) POLONSKY, K Cell and molecular biology of the gastrointestinal tract Regulation of glucose transporter-like proteins in the gastrointestinal tract
P30DK-42086-02 0004 (DDK) STECK, T Cell and molecular biology of the gastrointestinal tract Endocytosis in intestinal macrophages
P30DK-42086-02 0005 (DDK) TENG, B Cell and molecular biology of the gastrointestinal tract Gradients of apolipoprotein gene expression and processing in gut and liver
P30DK-42086-02 0006 (DDK) SITRIN, M Cell and molecular biology of the gastrointestinal tract Effect of 1,25 dihydroxyvitamin D3 on growth and differentiation of Caco-2 cells
R29DK-42091-02 (SSS) LAYTON, HAROLD E DUKE UNIVERSITY DURHAM, NC 27706 Mathematical models of renal dynamics
R01DK-42093-02 (GMB) MEYER, TIMOTHY W STANFORD UNIV MEDICAL CTR DIVISION OF NEPHROLOGY,S215 STANFORD, CA 94305-5114 Glomerular function and structure in diabetic rats
R29DK-42100-02 (GMA) BERSCHNEIDER, HELEN M COLLEGE OF VETERINARY MEDICINE 4700 HILLSBOROUGH ST RALEIGH, NC 27606 Ontogeny of intestinal epithelial electrolyte transport
R01DK-42101-02 (NTN) YOUNG, VERNON R MASSACHUSETTS INST OF TECHNOLO 50 AMES STREET CAMBRIDGE, MA 02142 Human amino acid kinetics and requirements
R01DK-42111-02 (BIO) BENSON, MERRILL D R L ROUDEBUSH VA MEDICAL CTR 1481 WEST TENTH STREET INDIANAPOLIS, IN 46202-2884 Pathogenesis of hereditary transthyretin amyloidosis
R01DK-42118-02 (NTN) SWIFT, LARRY L VANDERBILT UNIVERSITY D-4130 MCN NASHVILLE, TN 37232 Vitamin B2 and B6 in very low birth weight infants
R29DK-42120-02 (PC) LOWE, MARK EVAN WASHINGTON UNIV MEDICAL CENTER 400 S KINGSHIGHWAY ST LOUIS , MO 63110 Human pancreatic lipase and colipase structure and function
R29DK-42122-01A2 (MEDB) PEZACKA, EWA H CLEVELAND CLINIC FOUNDATION 9500 EUCLID AVE, ONE CLINIC CT CLEVELAND, OH 44195-5139 Inborn errors in the metabolic processing of cobalamin
R01DK-42124-02 (BBCB) DUNN, MICHAEL F UNIV OF CALIFORNIA, RIVERSIDE RIVERSIDE, CA 92521 Chemical and structural signatures of insulin function
R01DK-42125-02 (END) REPPERT, STEVEN M MASSACHUSETTS GENERAL HOSPITAL 32 FRUIT ST BOSTON, MA 02114 Melatonin--Sites and mechanisms of hormone action
R29DK-42131-02 (PTHA) FOGO, AGNES B VANDERBILT UNIV SCH OF MED 1161 21ST AVE SOUTH NASHVILLE, TN 37232-2561 Role of circulating cells in glomerular injury
R01DK-42137-01A2 (HED) BARTKE, ANDRZEJ SOUTHERN ILLINOIS UNIVERSITY SCHOOL OF MEDICINE CARBONDALE, IL 62901-6512 Effects of growth hormone in transgenic mice
R01DK-42139-02 (END) SNYDER, PETER J UNIVERSITY OF PENNSYLVANIA 422 CURIE BLVD PHILADELPHIA, PA 19104-6149 Gonadotroph adenomas--Prevalence and pharmacology
R01DK-42144-01A1 (END) JAMESON, JAMES L MASSACHUSETTS GENERAL HOSPITAL FRUIT STREET BOSTON, MA 02114 Steroid receptor interactions with pituitary genes
R01DK-42146-01A1 (GMB) NISSENSON, ROBERT VA MEDICAL CENTER 4150 CLEMENT STREET (111-N) SAN FRANCISCO, CA 94121 Cloning of the parathyroid hormone receptor cDNA
R01DK-42147-02 (END) BRAND, STEPHEN J MASSACHUSETTS GENERAL HOSPITAL FRUIT STREET BOSTON, MA 02114 Gut peptide expression in the endocrine pancreas
R01DK-42154-02 (END) MILLER, WALTER L UNIVERSITY OF CALIFORNIA THIRD & PARNASSUS AVENUES SAN FRANCISCO, CA 94143-0434 Molecular regulation of steroidogenesis
R01DK-42155-02 (PTHA) KELLY, CAROLYN J UNIVERSITY OF PENNSYLVANIA 3400 SPRUCE STREET PHILADELPHIA, PA 19104 Autoimmune T cell mechanisms in interstitial nephritis
R01DK-42159-02 (CVB) KON, VALENTINA VANDERBILT UNIVERSITY SCH OF M 21ST & GARLAND AVE NASHVILLE, TN 37232-2584 Role of endothelin in glomerular dysfunction
R29DK-42161-01A2 (SAT) JOHNSTON, DAVID E NEW ENGLAND MEDICAL CENTER 750 WASHINGTON ST BOX 217 BOSTON, MA 02111 Regulation of hepatocyte prostaglandin metabolism
R01DK-42166-02 (GMA) EBERT, ELLEN C UMDNJ-ROBERT W JOHNSON MED SCH ONE ROBERT W JOHNSON PLACE NEW BRUNSWICK, NJ 08903-0019 Intraepithelial lymphocytes relation to epithelial cells
R01DK-42169-02 (END) WHITE, PERRIN C CORNELL UNIV MEDICAL COLLEGE 1300 YORK AVENUE, S-613 NEW YORK, NY 10021 Molecular genetics of low-renin hypertension
R01DK-42171-02 (PC) WHITTAKER, JONATHAN HEALTH SCIENCES CENTER, T15 SUNY AT STONY BROOK STONY BROOK, NY 11794-8154 Structure & function of binding site of insulin receptor
R01DK-42176-01A1 (MET) MAC DONALD, MICHAEL J UNIVERSITY OF WISCONSIN 1300 UNIVERSITY AVE., RM. 3459 MADISON, WI 53706 Glucose metabolism responsive genes in pancreatic islets
R01DK-42182-02 (GMA) WU, GEORGE Y UNIVERSITY OF CONNECTICUT 263 FARMINGTON AVE. FARMINGTON, CT 06032 Targeted gene delivery and expression in hepatocytes
R29DK-42185-02 (GMB) FELDER, ROBIN A UNIV OF VIRIGNIA HLTH SCIS CTR BOX 168 CHARLOTTESVILLE, VA 22908 Renal tubular dopaminergic mechanisms in hypertension
R29DK-42189-02 (END) KAPLAN, LEE MICHAEL MASSACHUSETTS GENERAL HOSPITAL JACKSON 711 BOSTON, MA 02114 Hormonal regulation of galanin gene expression
R29DK-42191-03 (GMA) COMINELLI, FABIO UNIVERSITY OF SO CALIFORNIA 2025 ZONAL AVENUE LOS ANGELES, CA 90033 Cytokines and inflammatory bowel disease
R01DK-42193-02 (GMA) WILSON, JAMES M UNIVERSITY OF MICHIGAN 4520 MEDICAL SCIENCE RES BLDG ANN ARBOR, MI 48109 Liver-directed gene therapies
N01DK-42201-08 (**) KIRK, DAVID N Steroid reference collection
R01DK-42201-02 (BEM) JEFFERY, ROBERT W UNIVERSITY OF MINNESOTA 611 BEACON STREET SE MINNEAPOLIS, MN 55455 Low fat ad libitum diet and weight loss
R01DK-42202-02 (EDC) MORRISON, ALAN S BROWN UNIVERSITY POST OFFICE BOX G PROVIDENCE, RI 02912 Hormones and risk of prostatic hyperplasia
R01DK-42260-03 (SRC) SIEFF, COLIN A MB BCH DANA-FARBER CANCER INSTITUTE 44 BINNEY ST BOSTON, MA 02115 Human immunodeficiency virus and hematopoiesis
R01DK-42266-02 (NTN) ECKEL, ROBERT H UNIV OF COLORADO HEALTH SCIS C BOX B151/4200 EAST NINTH AVENU DENVER, CO 80262 Nutrition, lipoprotein lipase and body weight regulation
R01DK-42268-02 (SAT) DILLON, PATRICK F MICHIGAN STATE UNIVERSITY 111 GILTNER HALL EAST LANSING, MI 48824 Energy transduction in the urinary bladder
R01DK-42270-02 (MET) PANINI, SANKHAVARAM R ELEANOR ROOSEVELT INSTITUTE 1899 GAYLORD STREET DENVER, CO 80206 Endogenous regulators of isoprenoid biosynthesis
R01DK-42271-02 (END) ST GERMAIN, DONALD L DARTMOUTH MEDICAL SCHOOL HANOVER, NH 03756 Regulation of thyroid hormone metabolism
R01DK-42273-01A2 (EDC) STERN, MICHAEL P UNIVERSITY OF TEXAS 7703 FLOYD CURL DRIVE SAN ANTONIO, TX 78284-7873 Genetic epidemiology of NIDDM in Mexican Americans
R29DK-42274-01A2 (NTN) GIETZEN, DOROTHY W UNIVERSITY OF CALIFORNIA SCHOOL OF VETERINARY MEDICINE DAVIS, CA 95616 Dietary amino acid disproportion--Neural responses
R01DK-42279-01A2 (SAT) PUTNAM, CHARLES W ARIZONA HEALTH SCIENCES CENTER 1501 N CAMPBELL AVENUE TUCSON, AZ 85724 Surgical hepatectomy -- Prolactin initiates mitogenesis
R01DK-42290-01A1 (RNM) CARSON, PAUL L UNIVERSITY OF MICHIGAN HOSPITA KRESGG 111, R 3315 ANN ARBOR, MI 48109-0553 Ultrasonic generation of microbubbles for diagnosis
R01DK-42297-02 (PTHA) KAYSEN, GEORGE A VA MEDICAL CENTER 150 MUIR ROAD MARTINEZ, CA 94553 Regulation of serum protein composition in nephrosis
R01DK-42303-02 (BBCA) SMITH, JANET L PURDUE UNIVERSITY DEPT OF BIOLOGICAL SCIENCES WEST LAFAYETTE, IN 47907 Structure and function of a purine biosynthetic enzyme
R01DK-42304-02 (PTHA) CARONE, FRANK A NORTHWESTERN UNIV MEDICAL SCHO 303 E CHICAGO AVENUE CHICAGO, ILL 60611 Autosomal dominant polycystic kidney disease

PROJECT NO., ORGANIZATIONAL UNIT., INVESTIGATOR, ADDRESS, TITLE

R01DK-42315-01A1 (SSP) JACOBSON, ALAN M JOSLIN DIABETES CENTER ONE JOSLIN PLACE BOSTON, MA 02215 Symptom experiences and glycemic control

R01DK-42316-02 (EDC) DORMAN, JANICE S UNIVERSITY OF PITTSBURGH 130 DESOTO STREET PITTSBURGH, PA 15261 Global epidemiology of IDDM--Host susceptibility

R01DK-42323-02 (BCE) SILVERMAN, ANN J COLUMBIA UNIVERSITY 630 WEST 168TH STREET NEW YORK, N Y 10032 Plasticity of GNRH neuronal systems in the primate CNS

R01DK-42331-01A1 (TOX) PETERSON, DARRYL R UNIV HEALTH SCI/CHIGAGO MED SC 3333 GREEN BAY ROAD NORTH CHICAGO, IL 60064 A mechanism for charged-related nephrotoxicity

R01DK-42346-06 (GMA) TAVOLONI, NICOLA MOUNT SINAI MEDICAL SCHOOL 100TH STREET & MADISON AVENUE NEW YORK, N Y 10029 Postnatal development of bile secretory function

R01DK-42347-01A2 (HEM) BERLINER, NANCY YALE MEDICAL SCHOOL 333 CEDAR STREET NEW HAVEN, CT 06510-8056 Control of transcobalamin 1--Neutrophil granule protein

R01DK-42353-03 (END) LITWACK, GERALD THOMAS JEFFERSON UNIVERSITY 1025 WALNUT ST PHILADELPHIA, PA 19107 Modulator and the glucocorticoid receptor

R01DK-42361-01A2 (BCE) TALAMANTES, FRANK J UNIVERSITY OF CALIFORNIA SINSHEIMER LABORATORIES SANTA CRUZ, CA 95064 Growth hormone receptor and serum binding protein

R01DK-42367-03 (DDK) FELSEN, DIANE CORNELL UNIVERSITY MED. COLLEG 1300 YORK AVENUE/BOX 94 NEW YORK, NY 10021 Interstitial cystitis--inflammatory mediator involvment

R01DK-42369-02 (NLS) DE GROAT, WILLIAM C UNIVERSITY OF PITTSBURGH W1352 BIOMEDICAL SCIENCE TOWER PITTSBURGH, PA 15261 Central and peripheral mechanisms of bladder pain

R44DK-42379-02 (SSS) HALE, PAUL D SUNY/MOLTECH CORPORATION STONY BROOK, NY 11794-3400 Amperometric glucose sensor with redox polymer mediators

R44DK-42396-02 (MEP) DEMPSTER, PHILIP T LIFE MEASUREMENT INSTRUMENTS PO BOX 4456 DAVIS, CA 95617-4456 Apparatus to measure body volume and composition

R01DK-42409-03 (DDK) THEOHARIDES, THEOHARIS C TUFTS UNIVERSITY 136 HARRISON AVE BOSTON, MA 02111 Secretion of bladder mast cell mediators in interstitial cystitis

R01DK-42412-03 (BMT) TORTI, FRANK M VETERANS AFFAIRS MED CENTER 3801 MIRANDA AVE 154-N PALO ALTO, CA 94304 Tumor necrosis factor and iron metabolism

R01DK-42418-02 (ARR) COWDERY, JOHN S UNIV OF IOWA COLLEGE OF MEDICI IOWA CITY, IA 52242 CD4 T cell deficiency and intestinal immune responses

R01DK-42420-09 (CBY) CASTELLOT, JOHN J, JR TUFTS UNIVERSITY 136 HARRISON AVENUE BOSTON, MA 02111 Mechanisms of angiogenesis in adipocyte differentiation

R01DK-42421-03 (SAT) SELAWRY, HELENA P VETERANS ADMIN MEDICAL CENTER 1030 JEFFERSON AVE MEMPHIS, TN 38104 Islet transplantation

R01DK-42424-03 (GMB) CANALIS, ERNESTO M ST FRANCIS HOSPITAL & MED CTR 114 WOODLAND STREET HARTFORD, CONN 06105 Somatomedin, an autologous regulator of bone formation

R01DK-42428-03 (SSS) RICHTER, JOEL E UNIVERSITY OF ALABAMA DIVISION OF GASTROENTEROLOGY BIRMINGHAM, AL 35294 Psychophysiological interactions in non-cardiac chest pain

R01DK-42431-03 (REN) SILVA, JORGE E BETH ISRAEL HOSPITAL 330 BROOKLINE AVENUE BOSTON, MA 02215 Role of thyroid hormone in brown adipose tissue function

R01DK-42433-02 (GMA) DUANE, WILLIAM C VA MEDICAL CENTER ONE VETERANS DRIVE MINNEAPOLIS, MN 55417 Regulation of biliary lipid metabolism

R01DK-42439-01A1 (EDC) SELBY, JOSEPH V KAISER FDN RESEARCH INSTITUTE 3451 PIEDMONT AVENUE OAKLAND, CA 94611 Predictors of complications in a large diabetic cohort

R01DK-42446-01A1 (BPO) CASTONGUAY, THOMAS W UNIVERSITY OF MARYLAND COLLEGE PARK, MD 20742 Adrenal-pancreas interactions--intake and weight control

R01DK-42452-01A1 (PC) PESSIN, JEFFREY E THE UNIVERSITY OF IOWA BOWEN SCIENCE BLDG., RM. 6-430 IOWA CITY, IA 52242 Insulin-responsive glucose transport in adipose tissue

R01DK-42455-01A1 (SAT) REMICK, DANIEL G UNIVERSITY OF MICHIGAN 1301 CATHERINE RD ANN ARBOR, MI 48109-0602 Hepatic ischemia induced TNF and multi-organ injury

R01DK-42457-01A1 (GMA) MONTROSE, MARSHALL H THE JOHNS HOPKINS UNIVERSITY 725 N WOLFE STREET BALTIMORE, MD 21205 Intestinal ion transport in health and diarrheal disease

R01DK-42461-02 (END) HORSEMAN, NELSON D UNIVERSITY OF CINCINNATI CINCINNATI, OH 45267-0576 A lactogen-regulated calpactin gene

R29DK-42469-02 (MET) BARON, ALAIN D INDIANA UNIVERSITY 545 BARNHILL DRIVE INDIANAPOLIS, IN 46202-5124 Role of hemodynamics in in vivo insulin resistance

R01DK-42470-01A1 (NTN) HAMEL, FREDERICK G VETERANS ADMIN MEDICAL CTR 4101 WOOLWORTH AVENUE OMAHA, NE 68105 Effects of vanadium on insulin target tissues

R01DK-42479-02 (PHY) HANDLER, JOSEPH S JOHNS HOPKINS UNIVERSITY 725 N WOLFE ST BALTIMORE, MD 21205 Regulation of the sodium/myo-inositol cotransporter

R01DK-42482-01A1 (GMB) FELDMAN, DAVID STANFORD UNIVERSITY S005 JORDAN QUAD/BIRCH STANFORD, CA 94305 Regulation of vitamin D receptor gene expression

R29DK-42485-02 (SB) RAPER, STEVEN E UNIVERSITY OF MICHIGAN 2922H TAUBMAN HEALTH CARE CTR ANN ARBOR, MI 48109-0331 Antiproliferative effects of somatostatin on the liver

R29DK-42486-02 (PC) GETTYS, THOMAS W DUKE UNIVERSITY MEDICAL CENTER BOX 3913 DURHAM, NC 27710 G-protein function in adipocytes from diabetic rodents

R01DK-42488-02 (MET) WASSERMAN, DAVID H VANDERBILT UNIV SCHOOL OF MED 702 LIGHT HALL NASHVILLE, TN 37232-0615 Regulation of carbohydrate metabolism during exercise

R29DK-42495-02 (GMB) PALLONE, THOMAS L PENNSYLVANIA STATE UNIVERSITY P.O. BOX 850 HERSHEY, PA 17033 Microvascular transport in the renal medulla

P01DK-42502-02 (DDK) CHALKLEY, ROGER VANDERBILT UNIVERSITY MED SCH 702 LIGHT HALL NASHVILLE, TN 37232-0615 DNA protein binding in tissue-specific and endocrinologic control

P01DK-42502-02 0001 (DDK) CHALKLEY, ROGER DNA protein binding in tissue-specific and endocrinologic control Role of upstream binding factors in the control of chromatin structure

P01DK-42502-02 0002 (DDK) GRANNER, DARYL K DNA protein binding in tissue-specific and endocrinologic control Tissue and hormone regulated expression of the glucokinase gene

P01DK-42502-02 0003 (DDK) STEIN, ROLAND W DNA protein binding in tissue-specific and endocrinologic control Positive regulation of insulin gene transcription

P01DK-42502-02 0004 (DDK) WEIL, P A DNA protein binding in tissue-specific and endocrinologic control Structure-function studies of transcription factor TFIID

P01DK-42502-02 0005 (DDK) ANDERSON, WAYNE F DNA protein binding in tissue-specific and endocrinologic control Structure of proteins that regulate transcription

P01DK-42502-02 9001 (DDK) MAGNUSON, M A DNA protein binding in tissue-specific and endocrinologic control Gene expression core

P01DK-42502-02 9002 (DDK) CHALKLEY, ROGER DNA protein binding in tissue-specific and endocrinologic control Transgenic mice core

R01DK-42503-02 (PHY) JAMES, DAVID E WASHINGTON UNIV SCH/ MEDICINE 660 ELUCID AVENUE ST LOUIS, MO 63110 Cell biology of insulin stimulated glucose transport

R01DK-42506-01A2 (GMA) HOROWITZ, BURTON UNIVERSITY OF NEVADA ANDERSON MED SCIENCES BLDG RENO, NV 89557-0046 The role of the sodium pump in colonic motility

R01DK-42509-02 (BIO) SMITH, WILLIAM L MICHIGAN STATE UNIVERSITY EAST LANSING, MI 48824 Catalysis by prostaglandin G/H synthase

R29DK-42514-02 (PTHA) QUINONES, SUSAN R ROBERT WOOD JOHNSON MED SCHOOL 675 HOES LANE PISCATAWAY, NJ 08854 Goodpasture syndrome--New path to diagnosis and therapy

R01DK-42528-02 (BIO) KREBS, EDWIN G UNIVERSITY OF WASHINGTON SEATTLE, WA 98195 Linking of protein tyrosine and serine phosphorylation

R29DK-42530-02 (SAT) LATIFPOUR, JAMSHID YALE UNIVERSITY SCH OF MEDICIN PO BOX 3333 NEW HAVEN, CT 06510 Biochemical & functional changes in diabetic bladder

R29DK-42533-01A1 (NLS) EDWARDS, GAYLEN L UNIVERSITY OF GEORGIA 621 GRADUATE STUDIES BUILDING ATHENS, GA 30602 Hindbrain involvement in water and sodium intake

R29DK-42536-01A1 (MET) HU, CHING Y OREGON STATE UNIVERSITY CORVALLIS, OR 97331-6702 Adipose accretion--Role of adipocytes

R01DK-42539-02 (PC) SPIEGELMAN, BRUCE M DANA-FARBER CANCER INSTITUTE 44 BINNEY STREET BOSTON, MA 02115 Physiology and genetic studies of adipsin in obesity

R01DK-42543-01A1 (GMB) ERCOLANI, LOUIS MASSACHUSETTS GENERAL HOSPITAL 149 13TH STREET CHARLESTOWN, MA 02129 G-protein regulation in the kidney

R01DK-42549-02 (NTN) HILL, JAMES O VANDERBILT UNIVERSITY D-4130 MEDICAL CENTER NORTH NASHVILLE, TN 37232 The influence of diet on nutrient balance in man

R01DK-42552-02 (END) DANIELSEN, MARK GEORGETOWN UNIVERSITY MED SCHO 3900 RESERVOIR ROAD, NW WASHINGTON, DC 20007 The glucocorticoid receptor: Structure and function

R01DK-42562-01A1 (MET) ABUMRAD, NAJI N VANDERBILT UNIVERSITY A-2219 MEDICAL CENTER NORTH NASHVILLE, TN 37232 Proteolysis in hypoglycemia--Impact of CNS

R01DK-42572-03 (GMB) FITZPATRICK, LORRAINE A MAYO FOUNDATION 200 FIRST STREET SOUTHWEST ROCHESTER, MN 55905 Regulation of parathyroid cell secretion

R01DK-42576-01A1 (PC) ROACH, PETER J INDIANA UNIV SCH OF MEDICINE 635 BARNHILL DRIVE INDIANAPOLIS, IND 46202-5122 Glycogen metabolism and signal transduction in yeast

P01DK-42582-02 (DDK) UNGER, ROGER H UNIV OF TX SOUTHWESTERN MED CT 5323 HARRY HINES ROAD DALLAS, TX 75235 Molecular mechanisms of beta-cell impairment-destruction

P01DK-42582-02 0001 (DDK) UNGER, ROGER Molecular mechanisms of beta-cell impairment-destruction Initial beta-cell derangements of autoimmune and nonautoimmune diabetes

P01DK-42582-02 0002 (DDK) NEWGARD, CHRISTOPHER Molecular mechanisms of beta-cell impairment-destruction Glucose sensing apparatus of pancreatic islets

P01DK-42582-02 0003 (DDK) MCGARRY, J DENIS Molecular mechanisms of beta-cell impairment-destruction Role of carnitine palmitoyltransferase in insulin secretion by beta-cells

P01DK-42582-02 0004 (DDK) LUSKEY, KENNETH Molecular mechanisms of beta-cell impairment-destruction Amylin expression in normal and diabetic states

P01DK-42582-02 0005 (DDK) BEUTLER, BRUCE Molecular mechanisms of beta-cell impairment-destruction Role of inflammatory cytokines in islet cell damage

P01DK-42582-02 0006 (DDK) CAPRA, J DONALD Molecular mechanisms of beta-cell impairment-destruction Oligoclonal responses in insulin-dependent diabetes mellitus

P01DK-42582-02 9001 (DDK) CAPRA, J DONALD Molecular mechanisms of beta-cell impairment-destruction Molecular biology core

P01DK-42582-02 9002 (DDK) UNGER, ROGER H Molecular mechanisms of beta-cell impairment-destruction Pancreatic islet core

P01DK-42582-02 9003 (DDK) LECHAGO, JUAN Molecular mechanisms of beta-cell impairment-destruction Morphology core

R01DK-42601-01A1 (NTN) NOY, NOA CORNELL UNIVERSITY 1300 YORK AVE NEW YORK, NY 10021 Uptake of retinoids by target cells

R01DK-42604-01A2 (BCE) BROOKS, CHARLES L OHIO STATE UNIVERSITY 1925 COFFEY ROAD COLUMBUS, OH 43210-1005 Phosphorylated bovine prolactin and growth hormone

R15DK-42609-01A1 (REN) TIMMS, BARRY G USD SCH OF MEDICINE 414 EAST CLARK STREET VERMILLION, SD 57069 Ductal branching patterns in the developing prostate

R01DK-42612-02 (PC) MAGNUSON, MARK A VANDERBILT UNIV SCH OF MED SCHOOL OF MEDICINE NASHVILLE, TN 37232 Glucokinase gene

expression in the pancreatic beta cell
R01DK-42615-01A1 (PC) ROSENTHAL, MIRIAM D EASTERN VIRGINIA MEDICAL SCHOO 700 OLNEY RD PO BOX 1980 NORFOLK, VA 23501 Novel effectors of neutrophil phospholipase A2
P01DK-42618-02 (DDK) PIERSON, RICHARD N, JR ST LUKE'S ROOSEVELT INST 114TH ST & AMSTERDAM AVE NEW YORK, NY 10025 Medical application of high precision neutron activation
P01DK-42618-02 0001 (DDK) ALOIA, JOHN F Medical application of high precision neutron activation Black race, body composition, and osteoporosis
P01DK-42618-02 0002 (DDK) KOTLER, DONALD P Medical application of high precision neutron activation Nutritional and intestinal complications of AIDS
P01DK-42618-02 0003 (DDK) HEYMSFIELD, STEVE Medical application of high precision neutron activation Ethnicity and obesity
P01DK-42618-02 9001 (DDK) DILMANIAN, F AVRAHAM Medical application of high precision neutron activation Neutron activation core
P01DK-42618-02 0004 (DDK) EVANS, WILLIAM J Medical application of high precision neutron activation Strength training and weight reduction--Effects on bone
R01DK-42621-02 (END) RUDERMAN, NEIL B UNIVERSITY HOSPITAL 88 EAST NEWTON STREET BOSTON, MA 02118 Insulin stimulation of phosphatidylinositol-3' kinase
R01DK-42636-01A2 (PC) SMITH, STUART CHILDREN'S HOSP MEDICAL CTR 747 FIFTY-SECOND ST OAKLAND, CA 94609 Dietary regulation of fatty acid synthase expression
R55DK-42643-01A1 (IMS) KRAWITT, EDWARD L UNIVERSITY OF VERMONT GIVEN C-317 BURLINGTON, VT 05405 Immunogenetic studies of chronic active hepatitis
R01DK-42648-02 (SAT) SCHAEFFER, ANTHONY J NORTHWESTERN UNIV MEDICAL SCH 303 EAST CHICAGO AVENUE CHICAGO, IL 60611 Host factors in susceptibility to urinary tract infection
R01DK-42654-01A1 (EDC) LERNMARK, AKE UNIVERSITY OF WASHINGTON MAIL STOP RG-20 SEATTLE, WA 98195 Diabetes in the 15-34 year old
R29DK-42657-02 (BIO) KLUVE-BECKERMAN, BARBARA RL ROUDEBUSH VETERANS MED CTR 1481 WEST 10TH ST INDIANAPOLIS, IN 46202-2884 Differential regulation of human serum amyloid isotype
R01DK-42658-01A1 (END) TOLLEFSEN, SHERIDA E WASHINGTON UNIV SCH OF MEDICIN 400 SO. KINGSHIGHWAY ST. LOUIS, MO 63110 Structure definition of Igf I receptor function domains
R01DK-42671-02 (PB) HARDWICK, JAMES P NORTHEASTERN OHIO UNIVERSITY 4209 STATE ROUTE 44 ROOTSTOWN, OH 44272 Characterization of omega hydroxylase P450 gene family
R01DK-42678-02 (DDK) WILSON, JOHN H BAYLOR COLLEGE OF MEDICINE ONE BAYLOR PLAZA HOUSTON, TEXAS 77030 Targeted gene correction in human cells
R01DK-42693-02 (DDK) MOORE, MALCOLM A SLON-KETTERING INST/CANCER RES 1275 YORK AVENUE NEW YORK, N Y 10021 Retroviral gene transfer into human progenitors
R01DK-42694-01A1 (MEDB) KOHN, DONALD B CHILDRENS HOSPITAL LOS ANGELES 4650 SUNSET BOULEVARD LOS ANGELES, CA 90027 Glucocerebrosidase gene expression in hematopoietic cells
R01DK-42696-02 (DDK) CASKEY, CHARLES T BAYLOR COLLEGE OF MEDICINE ONE BAYLOR PLAZA HOUSTON, TX 77030 Gene replacement therapy-- Human and mouse models
R01DK-42698-01A2 (NTN) BILLINGTON, CHARLES J VA MEDICAL CENTER ONE VETERANS DRIVE 111G MINNEAPOLIS, MN 55417 Neuropeptide Y -- Effects on energy metabolism
R01DK-42701-02 (DDK) SAMULSKI, R JUDE UNIVERSITY OF PITTSBURGH 269 CRAWFORD HALL PITTSBURGH, PA 15260 Adeno-associated virus (AAV) a eucaryotic viral vector
R01DK-42706-02 (DDK) NABEL, ELIZABETH G UNIVERSITY OF MICHIGAN HOSPITA 1500 EAST MEDICAL CENTER DRIVE ANN ARBOR, MI 48109-0022 Site-specific gene expression in vivo
R01DK-42707-02 (DDK) WOLFE, JOHN H UNIVERSITY OF PENNSYLVANIA 3850 SPRUCE STREET PHILADELPHIA, PA 19104-6010 Gene therapy for the CNS in lysosomal storage diseases
R01DK-42709-02 (DDK) WOLFF, JON A UNIVERSITY OF WISCONSIN 1500 HIGHLAND AVE MADISON, WI 53706 Direct gene therapy for inborn errors of metabolism
R29DK-42714-01A2 (GMA) HORNBY, PAMELA J LSU MEDICAL CENTER 1901 PERDIDO STREET NEW ORLEANS, LA 70112-1393 CNS autonomic pathways and gastrointestinal function
R01DK-42716-02 (HEM) STORB, RAINER F FRED HUTCHINSON CANCER RES CTR 1124 COLUMBIA STREET SEATTLE, WA 98104 Hematopoietic growth factor in canine marrow graft model
P01DK-42717-02 (DDK) TAN, ENG M SCRIPPS RESEARCH INSTITUTE 10666 N TORREY PINES RD LA JOLLA, CA 92037 Immune and inflammatory mediators in interstitial cystitis
P01DK-42717-02 0001 (DDK) WILSON, CURTIS Immune and inflammatory mediators in interstitial cystitis Immunopathology of interstitial cystitis
P01DK-42717-02 0002 (DDK) TAN, ENG Immune and inflammatory mediators in interstitial cystitis Autoimmunity and autoantigens of interstitial cystitis
P01DK-42717-02 0003 (DDK) SPIEGELBERG, HANS Immune and inflammatory mediators in interstitial cystitis Secretory IgE mast cells in interstitial cystitis
P01DK-42717-02 0004 (DDK) HUGLI, TONY Immune and inflammatory mediators in interstitial cystitis Humoral and lipid mediators in interstitial cystitis
P01DK-42717-02 0005 (DDK) ZURAW, BRUCE Immune and inflammatory mediators in interstitial cystitis Kallikrein and kinin in interstitial cystitis
P01DK-42717-02 0006 (DDK) LOTZ, MARTIN Immune and inflammatory mediators in interstitial cystitis Peptide regulatory factors in interstitial cystitis
P01DK-42717-02 9001 (DDK) GITTES, RUBEN Immune and inflammatory mediators in interstitial cystitis Clinical core
P01DK-42718-02 (DDK) COLLINS, FRANCIS S UNIV OF MICHIGAN MED CTR 3570 MSRB II ANN ARBOR, MI 48109-0652 Experimental models of gene therapy
P01DK-42718-02 0001 (DDK) WILSON, JAMES M Experimental models of gene therapy Gene therapy of urea cycle disorders
P01DK-42718-02 0002 (DDK) IANNUZZI, MICHAEL C Experimental models of gene therapy Gene transfer to respiratory epithelial progenitor cells
P01DK-42718-02 0003 (DDK) PALELLA, THOMAS D Experimental models of gene therapy Macrophage-mediated retroviral gene transfer into the central nervous system
P01DK-42718-02 0004 (DDK) EMERSON, STEPHEN G Experimental models of gene therapy Evaluation of growth factors for gene transfer into hematopoietic stem cells
P01DK-42718-02 0005 (DDK) KURACHI, KOTOKU Experimental models of gene therapy Development of recombinant retrovirus vector for canine factor IX expression
P01DK-42718-02 0006 (DDK) LEIDEN, JEFFREY M Experimental models of gene therapy Animal model of gene therapy for hemophilia
P01DK-42718-02 9001 (DDK) OXENDER, DALE Experimental models of gene therapy Molecular biology core
P01DK-42718-02 9002 (DDK) WILSON, JAMES M Experimental models of gene therapy Vectors core
P01DK-42718-02 9003 (DDK) CHRISTENSEN, A KENT Experimental models of gene therapy Cell morphology core
P01DK-42718-02 9004 (DDK) WILSON, JAMES M Experimental models of gene therapy Animal models core
R01DK-42722-02 (PTHA) ARNAOUT, M AMIN MASSACHUSETTS GENERAL HOSPITAL 149 13TH ST 8TH FLOOR CHARLESTOWN, MA 02129 Granulocyte cytoplasmic antigens in renal vasculitis
R01DK-42725-03 (MET) ROGNSTAD, ROBERT A WHITTIER INSTITUTE FOR DIABETE 9894 GENESEE AVENUE LA JOLLA, CA 92037 Pathways of liver glycogen synthesis in vivo
R29DK-42730-01A1 (END) SEASHOLTZ, AUDREY F UNIVERSITY OF MICHIGAN 205 ZINA PITCHER PLACE ANN ARBOR, MI 48109 Transcriptional regulation of CRH gene expression
R01DK-42732-02 (IMS) NEPOM, GERALD T VIRGINIA MASON RESEARCH CENTER 1000 SENECA STREET SEATTLE, WA 98101 HLA-DQ class II genes in IDDM
R01DK-42748-01A1 (END) ROTWEIN, PETER S WASHINGTON UNIVERSITY 724 S EUCLID AVE ST LOUIS, MO 63110 Insulin-like growth factors and muscle differentiation
R44DK-42753-02 (HEM) BROWN, RONALD L QUALITY BIOLOGICAL INC 7581 LINDBERGH DRIVE GAITHERSBURG, MD 20879 Serum free medium kit for the culture of human cells
R01DK-42785-02 (SRC) SEGAL, STANTON STOKES, JR RES/CHILDREN'S HOSP 34TH & CIVIC CENTER BLVD PHILADELPHIA, PA 19104 New strategies in galactosemia therapy
R29DK-42786-03 (REN) CROXTON, THOMAS L JOHNS HOPKINS UNIVERSITY 615 NORTH WOLFE STREET BALTIMORE, MD 21205 Pituitary tumors--Pathogenesis and cellular function
R29DK-42787-03 (EDC) SOBAL, JEFFERY CORNELL UNIVERSITY 303 MVR ITHACA, NY 14853 Marital status, marital satisfaction and obesity
P01DK-42788-01 (DDK) THOMPSON, E BRAD UNIV OF TEXAS MEDICAL BRANCH 601 BASIC SCIENCE BLDG, F-45 GALVESTON, TX 77550-2779 Mechanisms of growth control by steroids
P01DK-42788-01 0001 (DDK) THOMPSON, E BRAD Mechanisms of growth control by steroids Growth regulation of leukemic cells by oxysterols
P01DK-42788-01 0002 (DDK) LIEHR, JOACHIM Mechanisms of growth control by steroids Mechanism of estrogen induced cell proliferation
P01DK-42788-01 0003 (DDK) THOMPSON, E AUBREY Mechanisms of growth control by steroids Cell proliferation and oncogene transcription
P01DK-42788-01 9001 (DDK) LIEHR, JOACHIM Mechanisms of growth control by steroids Core-- Chemical synthesis and analysis
P01DK-42792-01A1 (DDK) MELMED, SHLOMO CEDARS-SINAI MEDICAL CENTER 8700 BEVERLY BLVD LOS ANGELES, CA 90048 Endocrine aspects of human neoplasia
P01DK-42792-01A1 0001 (DDK) CLEMENS, THOMAS Endocrine aspects of human neoplasia Endocrinology of PTH-related human tumor protein
P01DK-42792-01A1 0003 (DDK) FAGIN, JAMES Endocrine aspects of human neoplasia Allelotype and linkage analysis of human thyroid neoplasms
P01DK-42792-01A1 0004 (DDK) MELMED, SHLOMO Endocrine aspects of human neoplasia Mechanisms of human pituitary tumorigenesis
P01DK-42792-01A1 0005 (DDK) KOEFFLER, H PHILLIP Endocrine aspects of human neoplasia Human ovarian cancer and p53 gene
P01DK-42792-01A1 9001 (DDK) CLEMENS, THOMAS Endocrine aspects of human neoplasia Laboratory core
P01DK-42792-01A1 9002 (DDK) SCHRECK, RHONA Endocrine aspects of human neoplasia Cytogenetics core
R01DK-42799-02 (END) FIRESTONE, GARY L UNIVERSITY OF CA, BERKELEY 591 LIFE SCIENCE ADDITION BERKELEY, CA 94720 Posttranslation responses of steroid hormones
R55DK-42802-01A1 (GMB) FITZPATRICK, LORRAINE A MAYO FOUNDATION 200 FIRST STREET SOUTHWEST ROCHESTER, MN 55905 Synthesis and secretion of parathyroid hormone
R01DK-42804-01A1 (NTN) SNYDER, FRED L OAK RIDGE ASSOCIATED UNIV P O BOX 117 OAK RIDGE, TN 37831-0117 Dietary ether-linked lipids and n-3 fatty acids
R29DK-42806-01A1 (CTY) SIFERS, RICHARD N BAYLOR COLLEGE OF MEDICINE ONE BAYLOR PLAZA HOUSTON, TX 77030 Pre-Golgi degradation of mutant secretory proteins
R29DK-42807-02 (END) USALA, STEPHEN J EAST CAROLINA UNIVERSITY SCHOOL OF MEDICINE GREENVILLE, NC 27858 TH receptors in kindreds with generalized TH resistance
R01DK-42816-02 (MET) LIENHARD, GUSTAV E DARTMOUTH MEDICAL SCHOOL DEPARTMENT OF BIOCHEMISTRY HANOVER, N H 03756 Phosphotyrosyl proteins in insulin receptor signaling
R01DK-42825-02 (PC) NTAMBI, JAMES M GEORGETOWN UNIVERSITY MED CENT 3900 RESERVOIR RD, NW WASHINGTON, DC 20007 Metabolic regulation of lipid biogenesis
R29DK-42835-02 (NTN) NEY, DENISE M UNIVERSITY OF WISCONSIN SYSTEM 1415 LINDEN DRIVE MADISON, WI 53706 Total parenteral nutrition and somatomedin responses
R29DK-42840-01 (END) MALCHOFF, CARL D UNIV OF CONNECTICUT HLTH CTR 263 FARMINGTON AVE FARMINGTON, CT 06032 Primary cortisol resistance
R01DK-42857-01A1 (IMS) MILLER, JAMES F THE UNIVERSITY OF CHICAGO

920 EAST 58TH STREET CHICAGO, ILLINOIS 60637 Pancreatic islet antigens–Tolerance and autoimmunity
R01DK-42860-02 (NTN) TRAN, ZUNG V UNIV OF NORTHERN COLORADO GREELY, CO 80639 Dietary treatment of diabetes mellitus–A meta analysis
R01DK-42874-01A1 (GMA) MC ROBERTS, JAMES A HARBOR/UCLA MED CENTER 1124 WEST CARSON STREET TORRANCE, CA 90502 Regulation of epithelial permeability by growth factors
R01DK-42876-01A1 (GMA) BITAR, KHALIL N UNIVERSITY OF MICHIGAN 1150 W MEDICAL CENTER DRIVE ANN ARBOR, MI 48109-0658 Myogenic control mechanisms in internal anal sphincter
R01DK-42879-02 (CBY) LYTTON, JONATHAN BRIGHAM AND WOMENS HOSPITAL 75 FRANCIS ST BOSTON, MA 02115 Molecular biology of organellar Ca-ATPase isoforms
R29DK-42880-02 (GMA) STEPHENS, ROBERT L, JR OHIO STATE UNIVERSITY 333 W 10TH AVE COLUMBUS, OH 43210 Gastrointestinal function–Serotonergic control
R29DK-42881-02 (PBC) STOW, JENNIFER L MASSACHUSETTES GENERAL HOSPITA 149 13TH STREET CHARLESTOWN, MA 02129 Regulation of proteoglycan secretion
R01DK-42885-02 (BIO) PATEL, MULCHAND S CASE WESTERN RESERVE UNIV 2119 ABINGTON RD CLEVELAND, OH 44106 Regulation of mammalian dihydrolipoamide dehydrogenase
R01DK-42890-01A1 (SAT) RUGGIERI, MICHAEL R 3400 NORTH BROAD STREET PHILADELPHIA, PA 19140 Antibacterial defense factors of urinary bladder mucosa
R01DK-42892-02 (GMB) LINDSAY, ROBERT HELEN HAYES HOSPITAL ROUTE 9W WEST HAVERSTRAW, NY 10993 Treatment strategies for osteoporosis
R29DK-42907-02 (EDC) FELDMAN, HORALD I UNIVERSITY OF PENNSYLVANIA 332R NURSING EDUCATION BLDG PHILADELPHIA, PA 19104-6095 A risk factor study of hemodialysis vascular access
R01DK-42910-01A1 (MBY) VAN DYKE, TERRY A UNIVERSITY OF PITTSBURGH A234 LANGLEY HALL PITTSBURGH, PA 15260 Molecular basis of different transthyretin gene control
R01DK-42912-01A1 (ORTH) CAVANAGH, PETER R PENNSYLVANIA STATE UNIVERSITY CENTER OF LOCOMOTION STUDIES UNIVERSITY PARK, PA 16802 Objective study of therapeutic footwear in diabetes
R29DK-42917-01A1 (PHY) WEINMAN, STEVEN A UNIV OF TEXAS MEDICAL BRANCH 301 UNIVERSITY BOULEVARD GALVESTON, TX 77550 Electrophysiology of organic ion transport in hepatocyte
R01DK-42921-01A1 (GMB) IGARASHI, PETER YALE SCHOOL OF MEDICINE 333 CEDAR STREET PO BOX 3333 NEW HAVEN, CT 06510 Regulation of renal Na+/H+ exchanger gene expression
R01DK-42923-01A1 (MET) SURWIT, RICHARD S DUKE UNIVERSITY MEDICAL CTR PO BOX 3842 DURHAM, NC 27710 Genetics of a murine model of type 2 diabetes
R01DK-42932-02 (HEM) IHLE, JAMES N ST JUDE CHILDREN'S RES HOSPITA 332 NORTH LAUDERDALE MEMPHIS, TN 38105 Interleukin-3 regulated growth of hematopoietic cells
R01DK-42949-02 (BEM) KUTNER, NANCY G EMORY UNIVERSITY 1441 CLIFTON ROAD, N E ATLANTA, GA 30322 Gender, race, age and survival on chronic dialysis
R01DK-42956-01A1 (GMB) BROWN, DENNIS MASSACHUSETTS GENERAL HOSPITAL FRUIT STREET BOSTON, MA 02114 Cellular regulation of kidney epithelial cell polarity
R01DK-42958-02 (GMB) HAMMERMAN, MARC R WASHINGTON UNIVERSITY 660 SOUTH EUCLID AVENUE ST LOUIS, MO 63110 Insulin-like growth factors and kidney development
R01DK-42971-02 (OBM) KUMAR, RAJIV MAYO FOUNDATION 200 FIRST STREET SOUTHWEST ROCHESTER, MN 55905 Plasma membrane calcium pump in osteoblasts
R01DK-42973-02 (GMA) DIAMOND, JARED M UNIVERSITY OF CALIFORNIA 405 HILGARD AVENUE LOS ANGELES, CA 90024-1751 Enteroglucagon and intestinal adaptation
R29DK-42982-01A1 (ALY) LEBMAN, DEBORAH A VIRGINIA COMMONWEALTH UNIV BOX 678 RICHMOND, VA 23298-0678 Regulation of IgA response in murine B lymphocytes
R01DK-42989-02 (HEM) LEMISCHKA, IHOR R PRINCETON UNVIERSITY PRINCETON, NJ 08544-1014 Clonal and molecular studies of normal hematopoiesis
Z01DK-43002-26 (MD) AURBACH, G D NIDDK, NIH Structure, secretion and mechanism of action of parathyroid hormone
R01DK-43003-02 (BIO) LEYH, THOMAS S ALBERT EINSTEIN COLL OF MEDICI 1300 MORRIS PARK AVENUE BRONX, NY 10461 Sulfate adenylation–Biochemistry and enzymology
Z01DK-43003-26 (MD) MARX, S J NIDDK, NIH Mode of action of thyrocalcitonin
R01DK-43005-02 (NTN) MC CORMICK, DONALD B EMORY UNIVERSITY SCHOOL OF MEDICINE ATLANTA, GA 30322 Vitamins B2 and B6 transport by renal and hepatic cells
Z01DK-43006-16 (MD) AURBACH, G D NIDDK,NIH Hyperparathyroidism–Etiology, diagnosis and treatment
Z01DK-43008-10 (MD) MARX, S J NIDDK, NIH Vitamin D resistance and related disorders
Z01DK-43009-06 (MD) MARX, S J NIDDK, NIH Regulation of mineral metabolism
R29DK-43013-01A1 (MET) CLORE, JOHN N VIRGINIA COMMONWEALTH UNIVERSI PO BOX 111 MCV STATION RICHMOND , VA 23298-0111 Control mechanisms of hepatic glucose output
R01DK-43018-01A1 (NTN) GANNON, MARY C VA MEDICAL CTR ONE VETERANS DR MINNEAPOLIS, MN 55417 Oral protein effects on liver glycogen metabolism
R01DK-43020-01A1 (GMA) PETERS, MARION G WASHINGTON UNIVERSITY 660 SOUTH EUCLID, BOX 8124 ST LOUIS, MO 63110 Intestinal immune response in inflammatory bowel disease
R01DK-43025-02 (HEM) NIMER, STEPHEN D UCLA SCHOOL OF MEDICINE DIV OF HEMATOLOGY-ONCOLOGY LOS ANGELES, CA 90024 Cellular control of hemopoietic growth factor production
R01DK-43026-01A1 (GMA) TARGAN, STEPHEN R UNIVERSITY OF CALIFORNIA 14-231 WARREN HALL LOS ANGELES, CA 90024 IBD: role of antineutrophil cytoplasmic antibodies
R29DK-43029-02 (GMA) LEVIN, MARC S WASHINGTON UNIVERSITY 660 SOUTH EUCLID BOX 8124 ST LOUIS, MO 63110 Gut nutrient metabolism–Molecular cellular approaches
R01DK-43031-02 (ALY) SEED, BRIAN MASSACHUSETTS GENERAL HOSPITAL FRUIT STREET BOSTON, MA 02114 Lymphoid tissue adhesion molecules
R01DK-43036-02 (BCE) GERSHENGORN, MARVIN C CORNELL UNIVERSITY MED COLLEGE 1300 YORK AVE RM A328 NEW YORK, NY 10021 Thyrotropin-releasing hormone receptor molecular biology
R01DK-43039-01A1 (END) NILSON, JOHN H CASE WESTERN RESERVE UNIV 2119 ABINGTON ROAD CLEVELAND, OH 44106 Regulation of equine chorionic gonadotropin expression
R01DK-43042-02 (HEM) WILLMAN, CHERYL L UNIV OF NEW MEXICO SCHOOL OF M ALBUQUERQUE, NM 87131 Function of c-fgr in normal and neoplastic myeloid cells
R29DK-43050-01A1 (IMS) GAUTHIER, VERLENE J UNIVERSITY OF WASHINGTON SEATTLE, WA 98195 Cationic antibody structure in Lupus renal disease
R01DK-43055-02 (BIO) RILLING, HANS C UNIVERSITY OF UTAH 410 CHIPETA WAY SALT LAKE CITY, UT 84108 Prenylated proteins–Structure, biosynthesis
R29DK-43058-01 (HEM) KOURY, STEPHEN T VANDERBILT UNIVERSITY SCH OF M NASHVILLE, TN 37232-2287 Nucleus and cytoskeleton in late erythroid morphogenesis
R01DK-43064-02 (BCE) WHITE, BRUCE A UNVI OF CONNECTICUT HEALTH CTR 263 FARMINGTON AVE FARMINGTON, CT 06030 Calcium control of prolactin mRNA levels
R01DK-43070-02 (BIO) WIGLER, MICHAEL H COLD SPRING HARBOR LABORATORY PO BOX 100 COLD SPRING HARBOR, NY 11724 Molecular characterization of human phosphodiesterases
R01DK-43071-02 (MET) MEANS, ANTHONY R DUKE UNIVERSITY P O BOX 3813 DURHAM, N C 27710 New animal model for early onset nonimmune diabetes
R29DK-43075-01A1 (EI) ROSENBERG, MARK E UNIVERSITY OF MINNESOTA BOX 736, 516 DELAWARE STREET, MINNEAPOLIS, MN 55455 Gene expression in the growing kidney
P01DK-43078-02 (DDK) JANEWAY, CHARLES A, JR YALE UNIVERSITY, SCHOOL OF MED 310 CEDAR ST NEW HAVEN, CT 06510 Cellular and molecular basis of autoimmune diabetes
P01DK-43078-02 0001 (DDK) JANEWAY, CHARLES A Cellular and molecular basis of autoimmune diabetes Effector T cell receptors and ligands in insulin-dependent diabetes mellitus
P01DK-43078-02 0002 (DDK) HAYDAY, ADRIAN Cellular and molecular basis of autoimmune diabetes Pancreatic islet responsive T cell receptors
P01DK-43078-02 0003 (DDK) FLAVELL, RICHARD Cellular and molecular basis of autoimmune diabetes Initiation and prevention of autoimmune diabetes
P01DK-43078-02 0004 (DDK) SHERWIN, ROBERT Cellular and molecular basis of autoimmune diabetes Mechanisms of beta cell injury by T cells
P01DK-43078-02 9001 (DDK) REICH, EVA-PIA Cellular and molecular basis of autoimmune diabetes Animal core
P01DK-43078-02 9002 (DDK) SHERWIN, ROBERT Cellular and molecular basis of autoimmune diabetes Rodent islet isolation core
P01DK-43078-02 9003 (DDK) DECAMILLI, PIETRO Cellular and molecular basis of autoimmune diabetes Immunocytochemistry core
R01DK-43093-02 (MBY) STALLCUP, MICHAEL R UNVI OF SOUTHERN CA HEALTH CTR 2011 ZONAL AVENUE LOS ANGELES, CA 90033 Genetics of hormone binding to glucocorticoid receptor
R01DK-43097-01A1 (NTN) BLANER, WILLIAM S COLUMBIA UNIVERSITY 630 WEST 168TH STREET NEW YORK, NY 10032 Studies of retinoic acid uptake and formation by tissues
R01DK-43098-02 (NTN) CLIFFORD, ANDREW J UNIVERSITY OF CALIFORNIA 275 MRAK HALL DAVIS, CA 95616 Stable isotope labelled vitamins–Key to human nutrition
R29DK-43101-02 (BBCA) LECOMTE, JULIETTE T J PENNSYLVANIA STATE UNIVERSITY 152 DAVEY LABORATORY UNIVERSITY PARK, PA 16802 Mechanisms of stabilization of b-hemeproteins
R01DK-43102-01 (HEM) ROTH, ROBERT I VETERANS ADMININSTRATION MED C 4150 CLEMENT STREET SAN FRANCISCO, CA 94121 Activation of biologic cascades by bacterial endotoxins
R29DK-43104-02 (SB) OTTERSON, MARY F MEDICAL COLLEGE OF WISCONSIN 8700 WEST WISCONSIN AVENUE MILWAUKEE, WI 53226 Gastrointestinal motor effects of ionizing radiation
R01DK-43105-01A1 (HEM) YANG, YU-CHUNG INDIANA UNIVERSITY 975 WEST WALNUT ST INDIANAPOLIS, IN 46202-5121 Gene regulation of human interleukin-9
R01DK-43106-01A1 (BEM) SURWIT, RICHARD S DUKE UNIVERSITY MEDICAL CTR PO BOX 3842 DURHAM, NC 27710 Stress, glycemic reactivity and risk for type 2 diabetes
R29DK-43107-02 (BCE) RAMSDELL, JOHN S MEDICAL UNIV OF SOUTH CAROLINA 171 ASHLEY AVENUE CHARLESTON, SC 29425 Growth-inhibitory factor action on GH4 pituitary cells
R01DK-43109-01A1 (BEM) FOREYT, JOHN P THE METHODIST HOSPITAL 6535 FANNIN HOUSTON, TX 77030 Obesity treatment–Self management vs dependence models
R29DK-43127-02 (END) RIEGEL, ANNA T GEORGETOWN UNIVERSITY 3900 RESERVOIR RD, NW WASHINGTON, DC 20007 Immune regulation of the pro-opiomelanocortin gene
R29DK-43129-02 (END) MOSS, LARRY G BAYLOR COLLEGE OF MEDICINE ONE BAYLOR PLAZA HOUSTON, TX 77030 Glucose regulation of insulin biosynthesis
R01DK-43135-01A1 (PB) ALAM, JAWED ALTON OCHSNER MEDICAL FOUNDATI 1516 JEFFERSON HIGHWAY NEW ORLEANS, LA 70121 Regulatory effects of heme transport into liver cells
R01DK-43138-02 (GMA) SMOLKA, ADAM J MEIDCAL UNIV OF SOUTH CAROLINA 171 ASHLEY AVENUE CHARLESTON, SC 29425 Epithelial H+ transport–Structure of H,K-ATPase
R01DK-43141-01 (HCT) BAME, SHERRY I TEXAS A & M UNIVERSITY COLLEGE STATION, TX 77843 Effect of dialysis unit design on compliance and staffing
R01DK-43142-03 (MET) KINLAW, WILLIAM B DARTMOUTH MEDICAL SCHOOL HINMAN BOX 7515 HANOVER, NH 03756 Physiological function of the s14 protein
R01DK-43146-02 (BBCB) SHULMAN, ROBERT G YALE UNIVERSITY 333 CEDAR STREET NEW HAVEN, CT 06510 In vivo NMR studies of brain liver

and kidney

R01DK-43147-02 (BCE) BROWN, TERRY R JOHNS HOPKINS HOSP 615 N. WOLFE STREET BALTIMORE, MD 21205 Molecular genetics of human androgen insensitivity

R29DK-43148-02 (SAT) LEPOR, HERBERT MEDICAL COLLEGE OF WISCONSIN 9200 W WISCONSIN AVENUE MILWAUKEE, WI 53226 Alternatives to the surgical treatment of BPH

R01DK-43159-02 (BIO) LAPOSATA, MICHAEL MASSACHUSETTS GENERAL HOSPITAL FRUIT STREET BOSTON, MA 02114 Extracellular fatty acid supply and eicosanoid production

R43DK-43166-01A1 (SSS) SCHAFER, MARK E SONIC TECHNOLOGIES 101 GIBRALTAR ROAD HORSHAM, PA 19044 A stone phantom device for lithotripsy quality assurance

R01DK-43171-02 (CBY) HEDIGER, MATTHIAS A BRIGHAM AND WOMEN'S HOSPITAL 75 FRANCIS STREET BOSTON, MA 02115 Molecular biology of brush border transport proteins

R44DK-43174-02 (SSS) BEHRENS, PAUL W MARTEK CORPORATION 6480 DOBBIN ROAD COLUMBIA, MD 21045 Production of stable isotopically labeled glycerol

R01DK-43184-01 (SAT) MENON, MANI UNIVERSITY OF MASSACHUSETTS 55 LAKE AVENUE NORTH WORCESTER, MA 01655 Urolithiasis-- Role of nephron dysfunction and injury

R13DK-43185-01 (DDK) SIMMONDS, HERMIONE A PURINE LABORATORY GUY'S HOSPITAL LONDON, SE1 9RT UNITED KINGDOM Seventh international symposium on purine metabolism in man

R01DK-43186-02 (DDK) HUTCHISON, FLORENCE N V A MEDICAL CENTER 109 BEE STREET CHARLESTON, SC 29403 Hormonal modulation of proteinuria in diabetes mellitus

Z01DK-43200-12 (MD) TSOKOS, G C NIDDK, NIH Disorders of immune regulation in patients with systemic lupus erythematosus

Z01DK-43201-07 (MD) TSOKOS, G C NIDDK,NIH Production and characterization of nephritic factor

Z01DK-43202-08 (MD) TSOKOS, G C NIDDK, NIH Regulation of human immune response by complement

Z01DK-43204-12 (MD) BALOW, J E NIDDK, NIH Immunosuppressive drug therapy in lupus glomerulonephritis

Z01DK-43205-14 (MD) BALOW, J E NIDDK, NIH Renal biopsy pathology in systemic lupus erythematosus

R01DK-43211-01A1 (GMA) TARGAN, STEPHEN R UNIVERSITY OF CALIFORNIA LOS ANGELES, CA 90024 Role of activated T cells in gut injury

Z01DK-43211-07 (MD) STRIKER, L NIDDK,NIH Histopathology of renal lesions in Pima Indians

Z01DK-43214-07 (MD) STRIKER, L NIDDK, NIH Studies of glomerular cells derived from transgenic mice

R01DK-43220-01A1 (NTN) JUMP, DONALD B MICHIGAN STATE UNIVERSITY EAST LANSING, MI 48824-1101 Dietary fat regulation of hepatic gene expression

Z01DK-43221-06 (MD) ELLIOT, S NIDDK, NIH Biology of insulin receptors in glomerular cells

Z01DK-43222-06 (MD) AUSTIN, H A NIDDK, NIH Pathogenesis of murine lupus nephritis

Z01DK-43224-05 (MD) AUSTIN, H A NIDDK, NIH Membranous lupus nephropathy

R01DK-43225-01 (SB) MULHOLLAND, MICHAEL W UNIV OF MICHIGAN 1500 E MEDICAL CENTER DRIVE ANN ARBOR, MI 48109-0331 Neuropeptide regulation of enteropancreatic function

Z01DK-43226-04 (MD) STRIKER, L NIDDK, NIH Glomerular lesions in transgenic mice for GH

R01DK-43227-01A1 (MET) BAGDADE, JOHN D RUSH-PRESBYTERIAN-ST LUKE'S 1653 W CONGRESS PARKWAY CHICAGO, IL 60612-3864 Effects of IDDM on lipoprotein remodeling and function

Z01DK-43227-04 (MD) Elliot, S NIDDK, NIH Role of IGF-I in the biology of mouse glomerular cells

Z01DK-43228-04 (MD) STRIKER, L NIDDK, NIH Biology of human glomerular mesangial cells

R01DK-43229-01 (HEM) MOORE, ROBERT N UNIVERSITY OF TENNESSEE WALTERS LIFE SCIENCE BLDG KNOXVILLE, TN 37996-0845 Bradykinin regulation of m-csf stimulated myelopoiesis

Z01DK-43231-04 (MD) AUSTIN, H A NIDDK, NIH Idiopathic membranous nephropathy

Z01DK-43232-02 (MD) STRIKER, L NIDDK, NIH Renal lesions in the ablation model--Role of growth factors

Z01DK-43233-02 (MD) STRIKER, G NIDDK, NIH Identification of IFG-1 binding proteins by mouse mesangial cells

Z01DK-43234-02 (MD) MACKAY, K NIDDK, NIH Interactions between TGF-beta and glomeruli

Z01DK-43235-02 (MDB) STRIKER, L NIDDK, NIH Glomerular lesions in non-obese diabetic mice

Z01DK-43236-01 (MD) STRIKER, L NIDDK, NIH Advanced glycosylation end products and effect of mesangial cells

Z01DK-43237-01 (MD) CAROME, M NIDDK, NIH Production of metalloproteinases and TIMP1 by glomerular cells

Z01DK-43238-01 (MD) STRIKER, L NIDDK, NIH Gene expression in microdissected mouse glomeri

Z01DK-43239-01 (MD) BOUMPAS, D T NIDDK, NIH Effects of glucocorticoids on T cell activation

Z01DK-43240-01 (MD) BOUMPAS, D T NIDDK, NIH Transcriptional regulation of immunoglobulin genes

R01DK-43250-01 (NTN) ATKINSON, RICHARD L EASTERN VIRGINIA MED SCHOOL HAMPTON, VA 23667 Mechanisms of weight loss with obesity surgery

R29DK-43258-01 (END) CONOVER, CHERYL A MAYO FOUNDATION 200 FIRST STREET SOUTHWEST ROCHESTER, NY 55905 IGF binding proteins--Regulation and biological actions

R29DK-43264-01A1 (GMA) SHIFFMAN, MITCHELL L MEDICAL COLLEGE OF VIRGINA BOX 711, MCV STATION RICHMOND, VA 23298 Effect of mucin hypersecretion on gallbladder physiology

R29DK-43267-01 (GMB) MC DONNELL, DONALD P BAYLOR COLLEGE OF MEDICINE ONE BAYLOR PLAZA HOUSTON, TX 77030 Biological actions of 1-25(OH)2D3

R01DK-43278-01 (GMA) FITZ, JOHN G DUKE UNIVERSITY MED CENTER BOX 3671 DURHAM, NC 27710 Mechanisms of hepatic electrolyte transport

R01DK-43285-01 (HEM) KELLER, GORDON M NATIONAL JEWISH CENTER 1400 JACKSON STREET DENVER, CO 80206 Regulation of hematopoietic stem cell development

R29DK-43290-01 (MET) FLAKOLL, PAUL J VANDERBILT UNIV SCHOOL OF MED NASHVILLE, TN 37232 Amino acid regulation of glucose metabolism in vivo

R29DK-43294-01 (GMA) LOWE, ANSON W STANFORD UNIVERSITY STANFORD, CA 94305-5100 Characterization and sorting of zymogen granule proteins

R01DK-43311-01A1 (HED) ROSS, MICHAEL G HARBOR-UCLA MEDICAL CENTER 1124 WEST CARSON STREET TORRANCE, CA 90502 Fetal swallowing--Ontogeny and regulation

R01DK-43323-01 (BBCA) ROYER, WILLIAM E, JR UNIV OF MASSACHUSETTS MED CTR 373 PLANTATION ST WORCESTER, MA 01655 Structural basis for cooperativity in clam hemoglobins

R01DK-43326-01 (BIO) OSHEROFF, NEIL VANDERBILT UNIVERSITY SCHOOL OF MEDICINE NASHVILLE, TN 37232-0146 Hormonal regulation of casein kinase II in human cells

R29DK-43329-01A1 (GMA) WILSON, JEAN M UNIV OF ARIZONA COLL OF MEDICI 1501 N CAMPBELL TUCSON, AZ 85724 Molecular structure of endosomes in developing intestine

R01DK-43333-01A1 (SAT) RUGGIERI, MICHAEL R TEMPLE UNIVERSITY 3400 NORTH BROAD STREET PHILADELPHIA, PA 19104 Urinary bladder muscarinic receptor subtypes

R55DK-43344-01 (EDC) MEIKLE, A WAYNE UNIVERSITY OF UTAH 50 NORTH MEDICAL DRIVE SALT LAKE CITY, UT 84132 Factors in benign prostatic hyperplasia

R01DK-43346-01A1 (PTHA) NATH, KARL A UNIV OF MINNESOTA 516 DELAWARE ST, SE BOX 736 MINNEAPOLIS, MINN 55455 Mitochondrial adaptation in renal growth and injury

P30DK-43351-01 (DDK) PODOLSKY, DANIEL K MASSACHUSETTS GENERAL HOSPITAL FRUIT STREET BOSTON, MA 02114 Center for the study of inflammatory bowel disease

P30DK-43351-01 0001 (DDK) WATKINS, DAVID Center for the study of inflammatory bowel disease Pilot study-- Immune regulation in the cotton-top tamarin

P30DK-43351-01 0002 (DDK) RUSSELL, GARY Center for the study of inflammatory bowel disease Pilot study--Identification of distinctive markers of intraepithelial lymphocytes

P30DK-43351-01 0003 (DDK) NAGLER-ANDERSON, CATHRYN Center for the study of inflammatory bowel disease Pilot study-- Heat shock proteins and cytolytic T cells in IBD

P30DK-43351-01 0004 (DDK) CHERAYIL, BOBBY Center for the study of inflammatory bowel disease Pilot study--Mac 2 in regulation of intestinal granuloma formation

P30DK-43351-01 9001 (DDK) BRAND, STEPHEN Center for the study of inflammatory bowel disease Core-- Molecular biology

P30DK-43351-01 9002 (DDK) STOW, JENNIFER Center for the study of inflammatory bowel disease Core-- Morphology laboratory

P30DK-43351-01 9003 (DDK) LETVIN, NORMAN Center for the study of inflammatory bowel disease Core-- Immunology and inflammation studies

P30DK-43351-01 9004 (DDK) HUNT, RONALD Center for the study of inflammatory bowel disease Core-- Primate colony

P30DK-43351-01 9005 (DDK) PODOLSKY, DANIEL Center for the study of inflammatory bowel disease Core-- Clinical tissue laboratory

R01DK-43354-01A1 (END) WOLF, BRYAN A UNIVERSITY OF PENNSYLVANIA 36TH & HAMILTON WALK PHILADELPHIA, PA 19104-6082 Role of phospholipases in insulin secretion

R29DK-43356-01 (SB) BASS, BARBARA L VETERANS AFFAIRS MEDICAL CENTE 50 IRVING STREET NW WASHINGTON, DC 20422 Chemosensitive neurons and esophageal blood flow

R55DK-43358-01A1 (END) PAPADOPOULOS, VASSILIOS GEORGETOWN UNIVERSITY 3900 RESERVOIR ROAD, NW WASHINGTON, DC 20007 Mechanisms of regulation of cholesterol transport

R01DK-43377-01A1 (PHY) CUPPOLETTI, JOHN UNIVERSITY OF CINCINNATI 231 BETHESDA AVE/MAIL LOC 576 CINCINNATI, OH 45267-0576 Interactions of peptides and ions with gastric H/K ATPase

R01DK-43382-01A1 (BCE) MOORE, DAVID D MASSACHUSETTS GENERAL HOSPITAL WELLMAN 9 BOSTON, MA 02114 Biochemistry and genetics of thyroid hormone receptors

R03DK-43384-01 (DDK) WINE, JEFFREY J STANFORD UNIVERSITY JORDAN HALL, BUILDING 420 STANFORD, CA 94305-2130 Cystic fibrosis--Molecular and cellular biology

R01DK-43391-01A1 (RNM) CLOUSE, MELVIN E NEW ENGLAND DEACONESS HOSPITAL 185 PILGRIM ROAD BOSTON, MA 02215 Donor liver viability assessment by NMR and microscopy

R29DK-43394-01 (EDC) KRISKA, ANDREA M UNIVERSITY OF PITTSBURGH 130 DESOTO STREET PITTSBURGH, PA 15261 The role of physical activity in NIDDM development

R01DK-43396-01A1 (PC) GOLDSTEIN, BARRY J JOSLIN DIABETES CENTER ONE JOSLIN PLACE BOSTON, MA 02215 Protein tyrosine phosphatases in insulin action

R01DK-43400-01 (GMB) SHOBACK, DOLORES M UNIVERSITY OF CALIFORNIA 4150 CLEMENT STREET SAN FRANCISCO, CA 94121 Regulation of intracellular calcium in parathyroid cells

R29DK-43402-01 (PC) LYNCH, CHRISTOPHER J PENNSYLVANIA STATE UNIVERSITY PO BOX 850 HERSHEY, PA 17033 Regulation of hepatic Na+/K+ -ATPase by protein kinases

R29DK-43405-01 (GMA) GOLDENRING, JAMES R YALE UNIVERSITY 333 CEDAR STREET WEST HAVEN, CT 06516 Cyclic AMP-dependent mediation of parietal cell function

R01DK-43409-01 (MET) ROGNSTAD, ROBERT A THE WHITTIER INSTITUTE FOR 9894 GENESEE AVENUE LA JOLLA, CA 92037 Liver oxygenation and metabolic zonation

R01DK-43422-01A1 (PTHA) JOHNSON, RICHARD J UNIVERSITY OF WASHINGTON 1959 N E PACIFIC AVENUE SEATTLE, WA 98195 Platelets in immune glomerular injury

R01DK-43423-01A1 (GMB) GUGGINO, SANDRA E JOHNS HOPKINS UNIVERSITY 725 N WOLFE STREET BALTIMORE, MD 21205 Ion channels controlling bone remodeling

R01DK-43442-02 (MET) FRIED, SUSAN K RUTGERS, THE STATE UNIV OF NJ NEW BRUNSWICK, NJ 08903 Nutrition and lipoprotein lipase-molecular mechanisms

R29DK-43470-01 (HEM) ROTH, MARK S UNIVERSITY OF MICHIGAN 1150

PROJECT NO., ORGANIZATIONAL UNIT., INVESTIGATOR, ADDRESS, TITLE

W. MEDICAL CTR. DR. ANN ARBOR, MI 48109-0680 Molecular genetic analysis--Bone marrow transplantation
R01DK-43491-02 (NTN) SUNDE, ROGER A UNIVERSITY OF MISSOURI-COLUMBI 10 GWYNN HALL COLUMBIA, MO 65211 Nutritional regulation of selenoenzymes and proteins
R55DK-43494-01A1 (EDC) TELL, GRETHE S BOWMAN GRAY SCH OF MEDICINE MEDICAL CENTER BLVD WINSTON-SALEM, NC 27157-1063 Renal disease epidemiology--Predictors of outcome
R01DK-43495-01 (GMB) ALPER, SETH L BETH ISRAEL HOSPITAL 330 BROOKLINE AVENUE BOSTON, MA 02215 Molecular physiology of band 3-like proteins of kidney
R01DK-43505-01A1 (ECS) SIMONSON, DONALD C JOSLIN DIABETES CENTER ONE JOSLIN PLACE BOSTON, MA 02215 Sodium regulation and response to angiotensin II in IDDM
R01DK-43507-01 (PTHA) HUDSON, BILLY G UNIVERSITY OF KANSAS MED CENTE 3901 RAINBOW BOULEVARD KANSAS CITY, KS 66160-7421 Glycation in the pathogenesis of diabetic nephropathy
R01DK-43509-01A1 (GMA) SUCHY, FREDERICK J YALE UNIVERSITY SCH OF MED 333 CEDAR STREET NEW HAVEN, CT 06510-8064 Ontogenic characterization of ileal bile acid transport
R55DK-43513-01A1 (END) FOSTER, CAROL M UNIVERSITY OF MICHIGAN 1500 EAST MED CENTER DR BOX 07 ANN ARBOR, MI 48109 Regulation of growth hormone secretion and action
R01DK-43517-01A1 (HEM) SNODGRASS, HIRAM R UNIVERSITY OF NORTH CAROLINA 211 LINEBERGER CANCER RES CTR CHAPEL HILL, NC 27599 Embryonic stem cell and in vitro hematopoietic development
R29DK-43518-01A1 (NTN) PERCIVAL, SUSAN S UNIVERSITY OF FLORIDA GAINESVILLE, FL 32611 Regulation of copper and cuzn superoxide dismutase
R01DK-43523-01A1 (MEP) THOMPSON, TIMOTHY C BAYLOR COLLEGE OF MEDICINE ONE BAYLOR PLAZA HOUSTON, TX 77030 Mesenchymal growth factor activities in mouse BPH model
R29DK-43526-02 (MET) MC CLAIN, DONALD A UNIVERSITY OF ALABAMA UAB STATION BIRMINGHAM, AL 35294 Analysis of the alternate forms of the insulin receptor
R29DK-43530-01 (HEM) HICKSTEIN, DENNIS D SEATTLE VA MEDICAL CENTER 1660 SOUTH COLUMBIAN SEATTLE, WA 98108 Molecular regulation of neutrophil adherence receptor
R55DK-43538-01A1 (GMB) WILLIAMS, RICHARD D UNIVERSITY OF IOWA IOWA CITY, IA 52242 Enteral reservoir dialysis for renal insufficiency
R43DK-43556-01 (SSS) FLUSBERG, ALLEN M SCIENCE RESEARCH LABORATORY IN 15 WARD STREET SOMERVILLE, MA 02143 In-vivo resonant-gamma detection/imaging of n and Ca
R43DK-43562-01A1 (SSS) CHRISTENSON, LISA CELLULAR TRANSPLANTS, INC FOUR RICHMOND SQUARE PROVIDENCE, RI 02906 Optimal islet matrix for immunoisolated transplants
R01DK-43569-01 (DDK) CHARONIS, ARISTIDIS S UNIV OF MINNESOTA 420 DELAWARE ST BOX 609 UMHC MINNEAPOLIS, MN 55455 Nonenzymatic glycation of glomerular basement membrane
R01DK-43574-01 (DDK) TSILIBARY, EFFIE C UNIVERSITY OF MINNESOTA 420 DELAWARE ST SE BOX 609 UMH MINNEAPOLIS, MN 55455 Mesangial cell interactions with glucosylated matrix
R01DK-43577-02 (ECS) RAFF, HERSHEL ST LUKES MEDICAL CENTER 2900 W OKLAHOMA AVENUE MILWAUKEE, WI 53215 Role of oxygen in aldosteronogenesis
R01DK-43595-02 (DDK) GRIMSHAW, CHARLES E WHITTIER INST/DIABETES & ENDOC 9894 GENESSEE AVE LA JOLLA, CA 92037 Aldose reductase activation in diabetic complications
R01DK-43597-01 (DDK) MEYER, TIMOTHY W STANFORD UNIV MEDICAL CTR DIVISION OF NEPHROLOGY,S215 STANFORD, CA 94305-5114 Pathobiology of glomerular injury in type II diabetes
R01DK-43605-01 (DDK) STEFFES, MICHAEL W UNIVERSITY OF MINNESOTA MED SC BOX 198, 420 DELAWARE ST, SE MINNEAPOLIS, MN 55455 Pancreas transplantation and diabetic nephropathy
R01DK-43609-02 (DDK) BORDER, WAYNE A UNIVERSITY OF UTAH 50 NORTH MEDICAL DRIVE SALT LAKE CITY, UT 84132 Regulating extracellular matrix in diabetic kidney disease
R01DK-43614-02 (DDK) CATANESE, VERONICA M TISCH HOSPITAL 560 FIRST AVE NEW YORK, NY 10016 Role of renal IGF-1 in diabetic nephropathy
R01DK-43620-02 (DDK) WILLIAMS, STUART K UNIVERSITY OF ARIZONA 1501 N. CAMPBELL AVE TUCSON, AZ 85724 Nonenzymatic glycation in diabetic kidney disease
R01DK-43632-02 (DDK) HEDIGER, MATTHIAS A BRIGHAM & WOMENS HOSPITAL 75 FRANCIS ST BOSTON, MA 02115 Molecular biology of renal glucose transport in diabetes
R01DK-43634-02 (DDK) LU, CHRISTOPHER Y UNIVERSITY OF TEXAS SW MED CTR 5323 HARRY HINES BLVD DALLAS, TX 75235-8856 Regulation of macrophages and mesangial cells by diabetic ECM
R29DK-43649-02 (GMA) LANCE, MICHAEL P VA MEDICAL CENTER/GI UNIT 111G 3495 BAILEY AVENUE BUFFALO, NY 14215 Hepatic and colonic sialyltransferase expression
R03DK-43651-01 (DDK) SARRAS, MICHAEL P, JR UNIVERSITY OF KANSAS MEDICAL C 39TH AND RAINBOW BLVD KANSAS CITY, KS 66103-8410 A model for basement membrane thickening in diabetes
R01DK-43652-01 (REN) KUDLOW, JEFFREY E UNIV OF ALABAMA AT BIRMINGHAM UAB STATION BIRMINGHAM, AL 35294 Growth factor involvement in pituitary function
R29DK-43653-01 (END) WONDISFORD, FREDRIC E CASE WESTERN RESERVE UNIVERSIT 2119 ABINGTON RD CLEVELAND, OH 44106 Human TSH-b gene expression and regulation by TH
R01DK-43675-01 (MET) MC EVOY, ROBERT C MOUNT SINAI MEDICAL SCHOOL ONE GUSTAVE L LEVY PLACE NEW YORK, N Y 10029 New beta cell-specific membrane protein relevant to IDDM
R01DK-43684-01 (CTY) KLIONSKY, DANIEL J UIVERSITY OF CALIFORNIA 275 MRAK HALL DAVIS, CA 95616-8665 Targeting of vacuolar proteins in yeast
R01DK-43687-01 (SAT) KOGAN, BARRY A UNIVERSITY OF CALIFORNIA 533 PARNASSUS SAN FRANCISCO, CA 94143 Consequences of early bladder outlet obstruction
R01DK-43695-01 (CBY) MUECKLER, MIKE M WASHINGTON UNIV/SCHL OF MEDICI 660 SOUTH EUCLID AVENUE ST. LOUIS, MO 63110 Structure and function of the glucose transporter
R01DK-43704-01 (GMB) CURTHOYS, NORMAN P COLORADO STATE UNIVERSITY FORT COLLINS , CO 80523 Mechanism of pH-response in renal PEPCK gene expression
R01DK-43706-01 (MET) CHERRINGTON, ALAN D VANDERBILT UNIV SCH OF MED 702 LIGHT HALL NASHVILLE, TN 37232-0615 Regulation of net hepatic glucose uptake in vivo
R01DK-43709-02 (MGN) BARRANGER, JOHN A UNIV/PITTSBURGH SCH /PUBLIC HL 130 DE SOTO STREET PITTSBURGH, PA 15261 Studies of human lysosomal glucocerebrosidase
R55DK-43721-01 (MGN) TAGGART, R THOMAS WAYNE STATE UNIV MEDICAL SCHOO 540 EAST CANFIELD DETROIT, MI 48201 The multiple endocrine neoplasia type I gene
R29DK-43726-01 (ALY) SMALE, STEPHEN T UNIVERSITY OF CALIFORNIA 405 HILGARD AVE LOS ANGELES, CA 90024 Regulation of TdT expression during lymphopoiesis
R01DK-43736-01 (MET) POWERS, ALVIN C VANDERBILT UNIVERSITY 21ST AVE SO AT GARLAND NASHVILLE, TN 37232-2250 Characterization of pancreatic islet glucose transporter
R29DK-43743-01 (GMA) CARTWRIGHT, CHRISTINE A STANFORD UNIVERSITY STANFORD, CA 94305-5100 Intestinal cell growth control--Role of tyrosine kinase
R01DK-43746-01 (GMA) RAYFORD, PHILLIP L UNIVERSITY OF ARKANSAS 4301 WEST MARKHAM, SLOT 505 LITTLE ROCK, AR 72205 Chronobiology and gastrointestinal endocrinology
R01DK-43747-01 (PB) AMES, GIOVANNA F UNIVERSITY OF CALIFORNIA 401 BARKER HALL BERKELEY, CA 94720 Protein-protein interactions in membrane receptors
R29DK-43778-01 (GMA) TSE, CHUNG MING JOHNS HOPKINS UNIVERSITY 725 N WOLFE ST BALTIMORE, MD 21205 Cloning and regulation of intestinal Na+/H+ exchangers
P01DK-43785-01 (DDK) GRANGER, DANIEL N LOUISIANA STATE UNIV MED CTR P O BOX 33932/1501 KINGS HIGHW SHREVEPORT, LA 71130-3932 Pathophysiology of intestinal ischemia-reperfusion
P01DK-43785-01 0001 (DDK) TSO, PATRICK Pathophysiology of intestinal ischemia-reperfusion Reperfusion injury and lipid absorption
P01DK-43785-01 0002 (DDK) CRISSINGER, KAREN D Pathophysiology of intestinal ischemia-reperfusion Feeding, ischemia, and oxygenation in developing intestine
P01DK-43785-01 0003 (DDK) BENOIT, JOSEPH N Pathophysiology of intestinal ischemia-reperfusion Vascular reactivity following ischemia-reperfusion
P01DK-43785-01 0004 (DDK) GRANGER, DANIEL N Pathophysiology of intestinal ischemia-reperfusion Leukocyte adhesion and emigration in venules
P01DK-43785-01 0005 (DDK) KVIETYS, PETER R Pathophysiology of intestinal ischemia-reperfusion Leukocyte-endothelial cell interactions during anoxia reoxygenation
P01DK-43785-01 0006 (DDK) GRISHAM, MATTHEW B Pathophysiology of intestinal ischemia-reperfusion Neutrophil-mediated mucosal injury
P01DK-43785-01 9001 (DDK) KVIETYS, PETER R Pathophysiology of intestinal ischemia-reperfusion Core--Cell culture facility
P01DK-43785-01 9002 (DDK) GRISHAM, MATTHEW B Pathophysiology of intestinal ischemia-reperfusion Core--Biochemistry facility
P01DK-43785-01 9003 (DDK) SPECIAN, ROBERT D Pathophysiology of intestinal ischemia-reperfusion Core--Morphology facility
R01DK-43794-01 (PHY) IWANIJ, VICTORIA UNIVERSITY OF MINNESOTA 1445 GORTNER AVENUE ST PAUL, MN 55108-1095 Molecular and biochemical properties of glucagon receptor
R01DK-43806-01 (END) LAZAR, MITCHELL A UNIVERSITY OF PENNSYLVANIA 422 CURIE BLVD PHILADELPHIA, PA 19104-6149 Thyroid hormone receptors--Regulation and function
R01DK-43808-01 (PC) WHITE, MORRIS F JOSLIN DIABETES CENTER ONE JOSLIN PLACE BOSTON, MA 02215 Function of the insulin receptor substrate pp185
R01DK-43812-01 (PTHA) MORROW, JON S YALE UNIVERSITY 310 CEDAR ST NEW HAVEN, CT 06510 Topographic spectrin assembly in acute renal failure
R01DK-43816-01 (GMA) CUPPOLETTI, JOHN UNIVERSITY OF CINCINNATI 231 BETHESDA AVE CINCINNATI, OH 45267-0576 Chloride channels and gastric acid secretion
R01DK-43846-01 (GMB) WALTERS, MARIAN R TULANE MEDICAL SCHOOL NEW ORLEANS, LA 70112 Calcium binding protein function and vitamin D
R13DK-43849-01 (DDK) TACHE, YVETTE F CTR FOR ULCER RESEARCH/EDUCATI WILSHIRE & SAWTELLE BLVDS LOS ANGELES, CA 90073 International conference on calcitonin gene-related peptides
R01DK-43850-01 (NTN) LONNERDAL, BO UNIVERSITY OF CALIFORNIA 275 MRAK HALL DAVIS, CA 95616-8669 Receptor-mediated uptake of iron from lactoferrin
R01DK-43859-01 (END) CONE, ROGER D OREGON HEALTH SCIENCES UNIV 3181 SW SAM JACKSON PARK RD PORTLAND, OR 97201-3098 Molecular etiology of Graves' disease
R01DK-43871-01 (BCE) QUINN, PATRICK G MILTON S HERSHEY MED CENTER P O BOX 850 HERSHEY, PA 17033 Molecular endocrinology of PEPCK gene regulation by cAMP
R01DK-43883-01 (PTHA) BADR, KAMAL F VANDERBILT UNIV MED CTR 21ST & GARLAND RM S 3223 MCN NASHVILLE, TN 37232-2372 Lipoxygenase products in glomerular immune injury
R01DK-43884-01 (PTHA) SIMA, ANDERS A UNIVERSITY OF MICHIGAN 1301 CATHERINE RD ANN ARBOR, MI 48109-0602 Pathology of the node of Ranvier in diabetic neuropathy
R01DK-43886-01 (PTHA) COSIO, FERNANDO G OHIO STATE UNIVERSITY 1654 UPHAM DR ROOM N210 COLUMBUS, OH 43210 Adhesion of human glomerular cell to matrix
R55DK-43901-01 (SAT) ILDSTAD, SUZANNE T UNIVERSITY OF PITTSBURGH W1556 BIOMEDICAL TOWER PITTSBURGH, PA 15213 Mixed chimerism to induce tolerance to hepatic allograft
R01DK-43904-01 (HEM) GRIFFIN, JAMES D DANA-FARBER CANCER INSTITUTE 44 BINNEY STREET BOSTON, MA 02115 G1/S cell cycle control in human hematopoietic cells
R15DK-43923-01 (MET) RULFS, JILL WORCESTER POLYTECHNIC INST 100 INSTITUTE RD WORCESTER, MA 01609 Diabetes induced changes in glycogen

synthesis
R15DK-43944-01 (BMT) ERMAN, JAMES E NORTHERN ILLINOIS UNIVERSITY DEKALB, IL 60115 Active site properties of Fe(III) heme proteins
R01DK-43955-01 (GMB) ZEIDEL, MARK L WEST ROXBURY DVAMC 1400 VFW PARKWAY WEST ROXBURY, MA 02132 Mechanisms of water flow across biological membranes
R01DK-43956-01 (DDK) GRAY, MICHAEL A UNIV OF NEWCASTLE UPON TYNE FRAMLINGTON PLACE NEWCASTLE UPON TYNE NE2 4HH, U Anion conductances in ductal epithelial cells and CF
R15DK-43958-01 (GMB) LEE, RICHARD E, JR MIAMI UNIVERSITY OXFORD, OH 45056 Physiological mechanisms of vertebrate freeze tolerance
R01DK-43961-06 (HED) ROBILLARD, JEAN E UNIVERSITY OF IOWA IOWA CITY, IA 52242 Ontogenesis of the sympathetic control of renal function
R01DK-43962-01 (DDK) PEDERSEN, PETER L JOHNS HOPKINS UNIVERSITY 725 NORTH WOLFE STREET BALTIMORE, MD 21205-2185 Molecular and chemical description of CFTR function
R01DK-43973-01 (DDK) KELLEY, KEVIN A MT SINAI SCHOOL OF MEDICINE BOX 1065/ONE GUSTAVE L LEVY PL NEW YORK, NY 10029 Development of mouse cystic fibrosis model and mouse CFTR analysis
R01DK-43974-01 (DDK) KIRK, KEVIN L UNIVERSITY OF ALABAMA AT BIRMI UAB STATION BIRMINGHAM, AL 35294 Vesicle trafficking and CL-transport in CF cells
R01DK-43988-01 (PTHA) ABBOUD, HANNA E U T HEALTH SCIENCES CENTER 7703 FLOYD CURL DRIVE SAN ANTONIO, TX 78284-7882 Mechanisms of glomerular injury
R01DK-43994-01 (DDK) KOPITO, RON R STANFORD UNIVERSITY DEPT OF BIOLOGICAL SCIENCES STANFORD, CA 94305-5020 Molecular and cellular biology of the CFTR
R01DK-43999-01 (DDK) DAVIS, PAMELA B CASE WESTERN RESERVE UNIVERSIT 2101 ADELBERT ROAD CLEVELAND, OH 44106 Targeting genes to cells relevant to cystic fibrosis
R01DK-44003-01 (DDK) CUTTING, GARRY R THE JOHNS HOPKINS HOSPITAL 600 N WOLFE STREET BALTIMORE, MD 21205 Molecular genetics of cystic fibrosis
R01DK-44006-01 (DDK) HANRAHAN, JOHN W MC GILL UNIVERSITY 3655 DRUMMOND STREET MONTREAL, QUE. CANADA H3G 1Y6 Low-conductance chloride channel in cystic fibrosis
R01DK-44015-01 (DDK) MALONEY, PETER C JOHNS HOPKINS UNIVERSITY 725 N WOLF ST BALTIMORE, MD 21205 Functional analysis of CFTR
R01DK-44017-01 (DDK) EATON, DOUGLAS C EMORY UNIVERSITY 1440 CLIFTON RD NE ATLANTA, GA 30322 Regulation of sodium and chloride channels in cystic fibrosis cells
R01DK-44023-01 (DDK) KRASNE, SALLY J UNIV. OF CALIFORNIA, LOS ANGEL 405 HILGARD AVENUE LOS ANGELES, CA 90024-1751 Optical and patch clamp studies of intact sweat ducts
R01DK-44025-01 (DDK) PERALTA, ERNEST G HARVARD UNIVERSITY 7 DIVINITY AVENUE CAMBRIDGE, MA 02138 Structure and regulation of chloride ion channels
R43DK-44046-01 (SSS) SWEET, LAUREL J CALIFORNIA BIOTECHNOLOGY INC 2450 BAYSHORE PARKWAY MOUNTAIN VIEW, CA 94043 Isolation of insulin receptor phosphatases
R43DK-44047-01 (SSS) SIPOS, TIBOR DIGESTIVE CARE INC (DCI) 51 BISSELL RD LEBANON, NJ 08833 Production of ursodiol from turkey bile
R43DK-44049-01 (SSS) SIPOS, TIBOR DIGESTIVE CARE INC (DCI) 51 BISSELL RD LEBANON, NJ 08833 Developing digestizyme microspheres in cystic fibrosis
R43DK-44056-01 (SSS) HALEY, JOHN D ONCOGENE SCIENCE INC 350 COMMUNITY DRIVE MANHASSET, NY 11030 Development of growth hormone releasing factor agonists
R43DK-44057-01 (HEM) MILLER, FREDERICK N MICRO-MED, INC 4350 BROWNSBORO ROAD, SUITE 13 LOUISVILLE, KY 40207 Microphotohemolysis to measure erythrocyte fragility
R01DK-44058-01 (HEM) FORGET, BERNARD G YALE UNIVERSITY SCH OF MEDICIN 333 CEDAR STREET NEW HAVEN, CT 06510 Human globin and erythropoietin receptor gene regulation
R43DK-44064-01 (SSS) MODELL, HAROLD I CONSULTING/MATERRIALS DEVP PO BOX 51187 SEATTLE, WA 98115 Impact of computer simulations on physiology training
R13DK-44067-01 (DDK) EPSTEIN, FRANKLIN H BETH ISRAEL HOSPITAL 330 BROOKLINE AVENUE BOSTON, MA 02215 Symposium on newer aspects of renal injury
R01DK-44070-01 (SRC) LANOUE, KATHRYN F PENNSYLVANIA STATE UNIVERSITY PO BOX 850 HERSHEY, PA 17033 Transmembrane signalling in genetic obesity
R01DK-44072-01 (SRC) TAYLOR, IAN L DUKE UNIV OF MEDICAL CENTER PO BOX 3913 DURHAM, NC 27710 Neuropeptide Y and its role in congenital obesity
R01DK-44073-01 (SRC) PRICE, R ARLEN UNIVERSITY OF PENNSYLVANIA 302 PIERSOL PHILADELPHIA, PA 19104 Genetic studies of human obesity
R01DK-44074-01 (SRC) FIEDOREK, FREDERICK T, JR WASHINGTON UNIVERSITY 660 S EUCLID AVE, BOX 8127 ST LOUIS, MO 63110 Mapping and structural analysis of mouse obesity genes
P01DK-44080-01 (DDK) WOO, SAVIO L BAYLOR COLLEGE OF MEDICINE ONE BAYLOR PLAZA HOUSTON, TX 77030 Somatic gene therapy for hepatic deficiences
P01DK-44080-01 0001 (DDK) WOO, SAVIO Somatic gene therapy for hepatic deficiences Correction of hepatic deficiencies in animal models
P01DK-44080-01 0002 (DDK) DARLINGTON, GRETCHEN Somatic gene therapy for hepatic deficiences Hepatocyte growth and differentiation
P01DK-44080-01 0003 (DDK) BRANDT, MARY Somatic gene therapy for hepatic deficiences Surgical approach to hepatocellular transplantation
P01DK-44080-01 9001 (DDK) LEDLEY, FRED Somatic gene therapy for hepatic deficiences Core-- Virus and tissue laboratory
P01DK-44080-01 9002 (DDK) WHISENNAND, HARTWELL Somatic gene therapy for hepatic deficiences Core-- Surgery facility
P01DK-44080-01 9003 (DDK) FINEGOLD, MILTON Somatic gene therapy for hepatic deficiences Core-- Histology and morphology laboratory
R01DK-44083-01 (BNP) BEGLEY, TADHG P CORNELL UNIVERSITY 120 BAKER LABORATORY ITHACA, NY 14853-1301 The mechanistic enzymology of thiamine biosynthesis
R29DK-44093-01 (MET) GUSTAFSON, THOMAS A UNIV OF MARYLAND AT BALTIMORE 655 W. BALTIMORE STREET BALTIMORE, MD 21201 Mechanisms of insulin and IGFI receptor function
R29DK-44099-01 (HEM) LIM, BING BETH ISRAEL HOSPITAL 330 BROOKLINE AVENUE, DA 601 BOSTON, MA 02215 Hematopoietic differentiation in embryonal stem cells
R13DK-44100-01 (DDK) FOX, C FRED KEYSTONE CENTER PO BOX 606 KEYSTONE, CO 80435 Conference on the adipose cell-- Model of hormone action
R01DK-44107-01 (PTHA) BOLTON, WARREN K UNIV OF VIRGINIA HLTH SCIS CTR BOX 133 CHARLOTTESVILLE, VA 22908 Study of cell mediated glomerulonephritis in a new model
R01DK-44122-01 (GMB) NAGAMI, GLENN T VA MED CTR WEST LA WILSHIRE AND SAWTELLE BLVDS LOS ANGELES, CA 90073 Ammonia production and transport by the nephron
R55DK-44125-01 (BBCB) XUONG, NGUYEN-HUU UNIVERSITY OF CALIFORNIA 9500 GILMAN DRIVE LA JOLLA, CA 92093-0317 Structure of some enzymes from neurotransmitters pathway
R55DK-44130-01 (MGN) GLOVER, THOMAS W UNIVERSITY OF MICHIGAN BOX 0718 ANN ARBOR, MI 48109-0718 Molecular biology of the Menkes syndrome gene
R55DK-44132-01 (IMS) HASKINS, KATHRYN UNIVERSITY OF CALIFORNIA 4200 E 9TH AVE BOX B140 DENVER, CO 80262 Antigen specificity of T cell clones from the NOD mouse
R55DK-44134-01 (HEM) WINKELMANN, JOHN C UNIVERSITY OF MINNESOTA 420 SE DELAWARE ST BOX 480 UMH MINNEAPOLIS, MN 55455 The human erythropoietin receptor
R55DK-44142-01 (END) SHUPNIK, MARGARET A UNIVERSITY OF VIRGINIA BOX 511 CHARLOTTESVILLE, VA 22908 TRH regulation of the rat thyrotropin beta gene
R13DK-44145-01 (DDK) SUCHY, FREDERICK J YALE UNIVERSITY SCHOOL OF MED 333 CEDAR STREET NEW HAVEN, CT 06510 Characterization of membrane transport mechanisms
R13DK-44146-01 (DDK) COATES, PAUL M JOSEPH STOKES JR RESEARCH INST 34TH & CIVIC CENTER BLVD PHILADELPHIA, PA 19104 Second international symposium on fatty acid oxidation
R01DK-44155-01 (END) KOENIG, RONALD J UNIVERSITY OF MICHIGAN 1150 W MEDICAL CTR DR ANN ARBOR, MI 48109-0678 Mechanism of action of thyroid hormone receptors
R01DK-44158-01 (HEM) CLEVELAND, JOHN L ST JUDE CHILDREN'S RESEARCH 332 N LAUDERDALE MEMPHIS, TN 38101-0318 C-myc function in myeloid cell growth and differentiation
R01DK-44167-01 (MBY) EVANS, TODD R UNIVERSITY OF PITTSBURG 350 THACKERAY HALL PITTSBURG, PA 15260 Molecular mechanisms of cell lineage determination
R01DK-44199-01 (CBY) PARSONS, SARAH J UNIVERSITY OF VIRGINIA HEALTH SCIENCES CENTER CHARLOTTESVILLE, VA 22908 P42 and related tyrosine kinase substrates in exocytosis
R13DK-44205-01 (DDK) SMITH, LYNWOOD H MAYO CLINIC ROCHESTER, MN 55905 Gordon conference on calcium oxalate
R01DK-44218-01 (MET) GIL, GREGORIO UNIV OF MASSACHUSETTS MED CENT 55 LAKE AVENUE NORTH WORCESTER, MA 01655 Cholesterol 7alpha-hydroxylase in transgenic mice
R55DK-44219-01 (CTY) ROGERS, JOHN C WASHINGTON UNIV SCH OF MED 660 S EUCLID AVE -BOX 8125 ST LOUIS, MO 63110 Processing of procathepsin H
R01DK-44220-01 (MEDB) JONAS, ADAM J HARBOR-UCLA MEDICAL CENTER 1124 WEST CARSON STREET TORRANCE, CA 90502-2064 Characterization of the lysosomal anion transporter
R13DK-44225-01 (DDK) OLSON, JAMES A IOWA STATE UNIVERSITY AMES, IA 50011 US-Japan conference on molecular and comparative nutrition
R29DK-44233-01 (GMA) LICHTMAN, STEVEN N UNIV OF NORTH CAROLINA AT CH CB #7220 310 BURNETT-WOMACK BL CHAPEL HILL, NC 27599-7220 Kupffer cell activation by intestine bacteria overgrowth
R55DK-44235-01 (MET) CRYER, PHILIP E WASHINGTON UNIV SCH OF MEDICIN 660 SOUTH EUCLID AVE/BOX 8127 ST LOUIS, MO 63110 Hypoglycemia-associated autonomic failure in IDDM
R01DK-44237-01 (CBY) TAUB, REBECCA A UNIVERSITY OF PENNSYLVANIA 422 CURIE BLVD - CRB PHILADELPHIA, PA 19104-6145 Expression of IGFBP-1 in liver regeneration
R01DK-44238-01 (CTY) RINDLER, MICHAEL J NEW YORK UNIVERSITY MED CTR 550 FIRST AVENUE NEW YORK, NY 10016 Biogenesis of exocrine secretory granule membranes
P01DK-44240-01 (DDK) ELSON, CHARLES O UNIV OF ALABAMA U A B STATION BIRMINGHAM, AL 35294 Chronic intestinal inflammation-- Mechanisms and effects
P01DK-44240-01 0001 (DDK) ELSON, CHARLES Chronic intestinal inflammation-- Mechanisms and effects T cell receptors and epitopes in chronic colitis
P01DK-44240-01 0002 (DDK) MCGHEE, JERRY Chronic intestinal inflammation-- Mechanisms and effects Mucosal immunity in inflammatory bowel disease
P01DK-44240-01 0003 (DDK) BEAGLEY, KENNETH Chronic intestinal inflammation-- Mechanisms and effects Role of cytokines in acute and chronic colitis
P01DK-44240-01 9001 (DDK) ELSON, CHARLES Chronic intestinal inflammation-- Mechanisms and effects Animal model core
R13DK-44261-01 (DDK) GERSHON, MICHAEL D 630 WEST 168TH ST NEW YORK, NY 10032 FASEB summer research conference-- Cell and molecular biology
R55DK-44279-01 (SB) PITT, HENRY A JOHNS HOPKINS HOSPITAL 600 NORTH WOLFE STREET BALTIMORE, MD 21205 Biliary glycoproteins in gallstone pathogenesis
R01DK-44282-01 (END) NELSON, CHRISTIAN UNIV OF CA, RIVERSIDE RIVERSIDE, CA 92521-0129 Regulation of insulin and pancreatic gene expression
R55DK-44287-01 (GMA) HAGEN, SUSAN J BRIGHAM AND WOMEN'S HOSPITAL 75 FRANCIS STREET BOSTON, MA 02115 Damage/repair of the intestinal brush border
R13DK-44288-01 (DDK) FRIZZELL, RAYMOND A UNIVERSITY OF ALABAMA 1918 UNIVERSITY BOULEVARD BIRMINGHAM, AL 35294 Mechanisms of membrane

PROJECT NO., ORGANIZATIONAL UNIT., INVESTIGATOR, ADDRESS, TITLE

transport proteins
R13DK-44290-01 (DDK) ROSEN, JEFFREY M BAYLOR COLLEGE OF MEDICINE ONE BAYLOR PLAZA HOUSTON, TX 77030 Gordon research conference on hormone action
R03DK-44292-01 (DDK) HEATH, HUNTER, III MAYO FOUNDATION 200 FIRST STREET SOUTHWEST ROCHESTER, MN 55905 Genetic linkage mapping of familial benign hypercalcemia
R55DK-44299-01 (PC) PRATT, RAYMOND D JOHNS HOPKINS UNIV SCH OF MED 725 N WOLFE STREET BALTIMORE, MD 21205 Structural biology of mitochondrial metabolite transport
R29DK-44305-01 (MEP) FOX, EBEN S NEW ENGLAND DEACONESS HOSPITAL 185 PILGRIM ROAD BOSTON, MA 02215 Mechanisms of Kupffer cell cytokine regulation
R01DK-44309-01 (SAT) NAJI, ALI HOSP OF THE UNIV OF PA 3400 SPRUCE ST PHILADELPHIA, PA 19104 Intrathymic cellular transplantation
R01DK-44314-01 (GMA) DAS, KIRON M UMDNJ-ROB WOOD JOHNSON MED SCH 1 ROBERT WOOD JOHNSON PL-CN 19 NEW BRUNSWICK, NJ 08903 Ulcerative colitis: an animal model with an autoantigen
R01DK-44331-01 (PC) HADDOX, MARI K UNIV OF TEXAS HLTH SCI CTR PO BOX 20708 HOUSTON, TX 77225 Regulation of ornithine decarboxylase metabolism
R29DK-44332-01 (BCE) DARLING, DOUGLAS S BRIGHAM & WOMEN'S HOSPITAL 75 FRANCIS STREET BOSTON, MA 02115 Auxiliary proteins in the response to thyroid hormone
R01DK-44336-01 (GMB) SIEGEL, NORMAN J YALE UNIV SCHOOL OF MEDICINE 333 CEDAR STREET NEW HAVEN, CT 06510 Adenine nucleotide metabolism in renal ischemia
R29DK-44341-01 (MET) BUTLER, PETER C EAST CAROLINA UNIVERSITY BRODY 2N-72 GREENVILLE, NC 27858 Role of pulsatile insulin secretion on insulin action
R01DK-44347-01 (BMT) NOVOTNY, MILOS V INDIANA UNIVERSITY BLOOMINGTON, IN 47405 Biochemical aspects of diabetic neuropathies
R01DK-44350-01 (MEDB) KRISANS, SKAIDRITE SAN DIEGO STATE UNIVERSITY 5300 CAMPANILE DRIVE SAN DIEGO, CA 92182 Peroxisomal cholesterol synthesis--Biochemistry function
R13DK-44376-01 (DDK) COLLINS, FRANCIS S UNIVERSITY OF RHODE ISLAND 1150 W MEDICAL CENTER DRIVE ANN ARBOR, MI 48109-0650 Gordon research conference on molecular genetics
R55DK-44378-01 (SAT) HOPKINS, WALTER J UNIVERSITY OF WISCONSIN 600 HIGHLAND AVENUE MADISON, WI 53792 Urinary tract infections--Immune basis of susceptibility
R29DK-44380-01 (PTHA) BRADY, HUGH R BRIGHAM & WOMEN'S HOSPITAL 75 FRANCIS STREET BOSTON, MA 02115 Phagocyte-glomerular cell interaction
R43DK-44385-01 (HEM) TRANTOLO, DEBRA J CAMBRIDGE SCIENTIFIC, INC 195 COMMON STREET BELMONT, MA 02178 Blood shunt for enzymatic modification of heparin
R43DK-44386-01 (SSS) COHEN, MARGO P EXOCELL INC 3508 MARKET STREET PHILADELPHIA, PA 19104 Measurement of glycated LDL with monoclonal antibodies
R43DK-44393-01 (SSS) CASE, CASEY C ONCOGENE SCIENCE, INC 350 COMMUNITY DRIVE MANHASSET, NY 11030 Transcriptional control of the erythropoietin gene
R43DK-44394-01 (HEM) AMBRUS, CLARA M HEMEX, INC. 143 WINDSOR AVENUE BUFFALO, NY 14209 Blood tissue iron depletion by extracorporeal chelator
R43DK-44399-01 (SSS) WAGNER, DAVID A METABOLIC SOLUTIONS INC 33 NAGOG PARK ACTON, MA 01720 A 13C-xylose breath test for bacterial overgrowth
R43DK-44402-01 (HUD) BROWN, STEPHEN J RAYA SYSTEMS INCORPORATED 2570 WEST EL CAMINO REAL MOUNTAIN VIEW, CA 94040 Computer game for diabetes education
R43DK-44409-01 (NTN) BERGER, PETER E BRIMSON LABORATORIES 1549 HIIRONEN RD BRIMSON, MN 55602 A layperson's dietary data collection/analysis system
R43DK-44411-01 (SSS) SAHNI, SURESH K MOLTECH CORPORATION CHEMISTRY BLDG SUNY STONY BROOK, NY 11794-3400 Fiber optic sensors for oxygen and glucose
R43DK-44414-01 (SSS) LE, DIEM D LE RESEARCH LABORATORY, INC PO BOX 1236 ROLLA, MO 65401 Syntheses of 13C labeled polyunsaturated fatty acids
R29DK-44446-01 (NTN) WEST, DAVID B LOUISIANA STATE UNIVERSITY 6400 PERKINS ROAD BATON ROUGE, LA 70808-4124 Nutrition and hypertension - Role of hyperinsulinemia
R13DK-44447-01 (DDK) ROBERTS, JAMES A DELTA REGIONAL PRIMATE RES CTR 18703 THREE RIVERS ROAD COVINGTON, LA 70433 International workshop on reflux and pyelonephritis
R13DK-44465-01 (DDK) KAPLOWITZ, NEIL USC SCHOOL OF MEDICINE 2025 ZONAL AVE LOS ANGELES, CA 90033 Role of cytokines in inflammation
R13DK-44466-01 (DDK) BARRETT, KIM E UCSD MEDICAL CENTER 225 DICKINSON STREET SAN DIEGO, CA 92103 Neuro-immunophysiology of the gastrointestinal mucosa
R01DK-44557-01 (CBY) RUSSELL, WILLIAM E VANDERBILT UNIV MEDICAL CENTER NASHVILLE, TN 37232-2579 Growth factor modulation of liver growth and repair
R21DK-44560-01 (DDK) CARTER, JANETTE S VA MEDICAL CENTER 2100 RIDGECREST DR SE ALBUQUERQUE, NM 87108 Family-centered education intervention in New Mexico Pueblo Indians
R21DK-44561-01 (DDK) BOYKO, EDWARD J V A MEDICAL CENTER 1660 S COLUMBIAN WAY SEATTLE, WA 98108 Diabetes mellitus in Alaska natives
R21DK-44562-01 (DDK) WALKER, W GORDON JOHNS HOPKINS MEDICAL INST 5601 LOCH RAVEN BLVD BALTIMORE, MD 21239 Planning grant--Diabetes and nephropathy in Apache Indians
R21DK-44564-01 (DDK) NELSON, ROBERT G CLEVELAND CLINIC FOUNDATION 1616 EAST INDIAN SCHOOL RD PHOENIX, AZ 85016 Diabetes prevention study-- Planning phase
R21DK-44565-01 (DDK) BINDON, JAMES R THE UNIVERSITY OF ALABAMA PO BOX 870210 TUSCALOOSA, AL 35487-0210 Diabetes among the Mississippi band of Choctaw
R21DK-44567-01 (DDK) LEE, ELISA T UNIV OF OKLAHOMA HLTH SCI CTR 801 N.E 13TH ST P O BOX 26901 OKLAHOMA CITY, OK 73190 Evaluation of NIDDM risk factors in Cherokees of Oklahoma

PROJECT NO., ORGANIZATIONAL UNIT., INVESTIGATOR, ADDRESS, TITLE

R21DK-44586-01 (DDK) JOE, JENNIE R UNIVERSITY OF ARIZONA 1642 EAST HELEN STREET TUCSON, AZ 85719 Native American community-based diabetes prevention models
R21DK-44587-01 (DDK) KEANE, WILLIAM F HENNEPIN COUNTY MEDICAL CENTER 701 PARK AVENUE MINNEAPOLIS, MN 55415 Diabetic nephropathy in Minnesota American Indians
R21DK-44592-01 (DDK) EBBESSON, SVEN O E UNIV OF ALASKA, ANCHORAGE 3211 PROVIDENCE DR ANCHORAGE, AK 99508 Diabetes risk factors in Alaskan and Siberian Eskimos
R21DK-44594-01 (DDK) SUGARMAN, JONATHAN R SHIPROCK PHS HOSPITAL P O BOX 160 SHIPROCK, NM 87420 Diabetes prevention in Navajo women--Planning phase
R21DK-44595-01 (DDK) LEWIS, CORA E UNIVERSITY OF ALABAMA UAB STATION BIRMINGHAM, AL 35294 Planning for diabetes prevention among Native Americans
R21DK-44596-01 (DDK) STAHN, RUGGLES M PHS INDIAN HOSPITAL 3200 CANYON LAKE DR RAPID CITY, SD 57702 The prevention of diabetes in Northern Plains Indians
R21DK-44597-01 (DDK) ZINMAN, BERNARD MOUNT SINAI HOSPITAL 600 UNIVERSITY AVE TORONTO, ONT CANADA M5G 1X5 A community based Native American diabetes intervention program
R21DK-44598-01 (DDK) HOOD, VIRGINIA L UNIVERSITY OF VERMONT D305 GIVEN BUILDING BURLINGTON, VT 05405 Preventing diabetes-- A Mohawk community initiative
R21DK-44608-01 (DDK) BISHOP, DONALD B MINNESOTA DEPT OF HEALTH 717 S E DELAWARE ST/BOX 9441 MINNEAPOLIS, MN 55440 Planning-- Primary prevention of diabetes mellitus in urban Indian youth
S15DK-44656-01 (NSS) CRAM, L SCOTT LOS ALAMOS NATIONAL LAB MAIL STOP M881 LOS ALAMOS, NM 87545 Small instrumentation grant
S15DK-44657-01 (NSS) WILEY, JOHN D UNIVERSITY OF WISCONSIN 500 LINCOLN DRIVE MADISON, WI 53706 Small instrumentation grant
S15DK-44658-01 (NSS) BOTTJE, WALTER G UNIVERSITY OF ARKANSAS FAYETTEVILLE, AR 72701 Small instrumentation grant
S15DK-44659-01 (NSS) COLEMAN, MARY S UNIVERSITY OF NORTH CAROLINA CB#4000 02 SOUTH BLDG CHAPEL HILL, NC 27599-4000 Small instrumentation grant
S15DK-44660-01 (NSS) FRESCO, JACQUES R PRINCETON UNIVERSITY LEWIS THOMAS LAB PRINCETON, NJ 08544 Small instrumentation grant
S15DK-44661-01 (NSS) ISOM, GARY E PURDUE UNIVERSITY 301 HOVDE HALL WEST LAFAYETTE, IND 47907 Small instrumentation grant
S15DK-44662-01 (NSS) GOLIN, JOHN E CATHOLIC UNIVERSITY OF AMERICA WASHINGTON, D C 20064 Small instrumentation grant
S15DK-44663-01 (NSS) PAINE, PHILIP L ST JOHN'S UNIVERSITY GRAND CENTRAL & UTOPIA PARKWAY JAMAICA, NY 11439 Small instrumentation grant
S15DK-44664-01 (NSS) BEARSE, ROBERT C UNIVERSITY OF KANSAS 226 STRONG HALL LAWRENCE, KS 66045-2904 Small instrumentation grant
S15DK-44665-01 (NSS) LEE, CHING-TSE BROOKLYN COLLEGE OF CUNY BROOKLYN, NY 11210 Small instrumentation grant
R03DK-44666-01 (DDK) LIVE, DAVID H CALIFORNIA INST OF TECHNOLOGY 1201 E CALIFORNIA BLVD PASADENA, CA 91125 3-dimensional nuclear magnetic resonance of dihydrofolate reductase
S15DK-44667-01 (NSS) DANIELS, ROBERT S LOUISIANA STATE UNIVERSITY 1542 TULANE AVENUE NEW ORLEANS, LA 70112 Small instrumentation grant
S15DK-44668-01 (NSS) LACHIN, JOHN M THE BIOSTATISTICS CENTER 6110 EXECUTIVE BOULEVARD, #750 ROCKVILLE, MD 20852 Small instrumentation grant
S15DK-44669-01 (NSS) PIJOAN, CARLOS B 1365 GORTNER AVE ST PAUL, MN 55108 Small instrumentation grant
S15DK-44670-01 (NSS) DETKE, SIEGFRIED UNIVERSITY OF NORTH DAKOTA GRAND FORKS, ND 58202 Small instrumentation grant
S15DK-44671-01 (NSS) SCHIMMEL, RICHARD J UNIV OF MED & DENT OF NJ 401 SOUTH CENTRAL AVENUE STRATFORD, NJ 08084 Small instrumentation grant
S15DK-44672-01 (NSS) MC MILLAN, PAUL N RHODE ISLAND HOSPITAL 593 EDDY STREET PROVIDENCE, RI 02903 Small instrumentation grant
S15DK-44673-01 (NSS) YOUNG, FRANKLIN A MEDICAL UNIV OF SOUTH CAROLINA 171 ASHLEY AVE CHARLESTON, S C 29482 Small instrumentation grant
S15DK-44674-01 (NSS) HAUPTMAN, HERBERT A MEDICAL FDN OF BUFFALO, INC 73 HIGH STREET BUFFALO, N Y 14203-1196 Small instrumentation grant
S15DK-44675-01 (NSS) FARQUHAR, LYNDA J MICHIGAN STATE UNIVERSITY A101 EAST FEE HALL EAST LANSING, MI 44824 Small instrumentation grant
S15DK-44676-01 (NSS) NEAVES, WILLIAM B UT SOUTHWESTERN MED CTR 5323 HARRY HINES BLVD DALLAS, TX 75235-9002 Small instrumentation grant
S15DK-44677-01 (NSS) DALY, WALTER J INDIANA UNIV SCH OF MEDICINE 1120 SOUTH DRIVE INDIANAPOLIS, IN 46202-5114 Small instrumentation grant
S15DK-44678-01 (NSS) LARSON, ELAINE L JOHNS HOPKINS UNIVERSITY 600 NORTH WOLFE STREET BALTIMORE, MD 21205 Small instrumentation grant
S15DK-44679-01 (NSS) WILKERSON, WILLAM R UNIVERSITY OF VIRGINIA PO BOX 9025 CHARLOTTESVILLE, VA 22906-902 Small instrumentation grant
S15DK-44680-01 (NSS) TU, SHIAO-CHUN UNIVERSITY OF HOUSTON 4800 CALHOUN HOUSTON, TX 77204-5500 Small instrumentation grant
S15DK-44681-01 (NSS) HOLTEN, DAROLD D UNIVERSITY OF CALIFORNIA RIVERSIDE, CA 92521-0217 Small instrumentation grant
S15DK-44682-01 (NSS) PECK, WILLIAM A WASHINGTON UNIVERSITY MED SCH 660 SOUTH EUCLID AVENUE ST. LOUIS, MO 63110 Small instrumentation grant
S15DK-44690-01 (NSS) HOCHSTEIN, PAUL UNIVERSITY OF SO CALIFORNIA 1985 ZONAL AVENUE LOS ANGELES, CA 90033 Small instrumentation grant
S15DK-44691-01 (NSS) MUSLOW, IKE LSU MED CTR - SCH OF MED P O BOX 33932 SHREVEPORT, LA 71130-3932 Small instrumentation grant
S15DK-44692-01 (NSS) WILD, JAMES R TEXAS A&M UNIVERSITY OFFICE OF THE DEAN COLLEGE STATION, TX 77843-214 Small instrumentation grant
S15DK-44693-01 (NSS) STEINBERG, BETTIE M LONG ISLAND JEWISH MED CTR 270-05 76TH AVENUE NEW HYDE PARK, NY 11042 Small instrumentation

grant
S15DK-44694-01 (NSS) WATT, GERALD D BRIGHAM YOUNG UNIVERSITY 633 WIDTSOE BLDG PROVO, UT 84602 Small instrumentation grant
S15DK-44695-01 (NSS) KLINENBERG, JAMES R CEDARS-SINAI MEDICAL CENTER 8700 BEVERLY BLVD RM 2211 LOS ANGELES, CALIF 90048 Small instrumentation grant
S15DK-44696-01 (NSS) NEWBOWER, RONALD S MASSACHUSETTS GENERAL HOSPITAL BARTLETT 3 BOSTON, MASSACHUSETTS 02114 Small instrumentation grant
S15DK-44697-01 (NSS) BRYAN, GEORGE T UNIV OF TEXAS MED BRANCH 301 UNIVERSITY BOULEVARD GALVESTON, TX 77550 Small instrumentation grant
S15DK-44698-01 (NSS) WINKELSTEIN, ALAN MONTEFIORE HOSPITAL 3459 FIFTH AVENUE PITTSBURGH, PA 15213 Small instrumentation grant
S15DK-44699-01 (NSS) BERNFIELD, MERTON CHILDREN'S HOSP 300 LONGWOOD AVENUE BOSTON, MA 02115 Small instrumentation grant
S15DK-44700-01 (NSS) BERNSTEIN, SOL LOS ANGELES COUNTY+USC MED CTR 1739 GRIFFIN AVE LOS ANGELES, CA 90031 Small instrumentation grant
S15DK-44701-01 (NSS) MARTINEZ-CARRION, MARINO UNIV OF MISSOURI-KANSAS CITY 5100 ROCKHILL RD KANSAS CITY, MO 64110-2499 Small instrumentation grant
S15DK-44702-01 (NSS) NEEL, JAMES W SAN DIEGO STATE UNIVERSITY SAN DIEGO, CA 82182-1900 Small instrumentation grant
S15DK-44703-01 (NSS) AASLESTAD, HALVOR G YALE UNIVERSITY SCH OF MED 333 CEDAR STREET NEW HAVEN, CT 06510 Small instrumentation grant
S15DK-44704-01 (NSS) COFFMAN, JAY D UNIVERSITY HOSPITAL 88 EAST NEWTON STREET BOSTON, MA 02118 Small instrumentation grant
S15DK-44705-01 (NSS) HAYEK, ALBERTO WHITTIER INSTITUTE 9894 GENESEE AVENUE LA JOLLA, CA 92037 Small instrumentation grant
S15DK-44706-01 (NSS) GOLDBERG, HERBERT S UNIVERSITY OF MISSOURI MA 203 MEDICAL SCIENCES BLDG COLUMBIA, MO 65212 Small instrumentation grant
S15DK-44707-01 (NSS) GOODMAN, RICHARD H OREGON HEALTH SCIENCES UNIV 3181 SW SAM JACKSON PARK ROAD PORTLAND, OR 97201-3098 Small instrumentation grant
S15DK-44708-01 (NSS) ADRIAN, THOMAS E CREIGHTON UNIVERSITY 2500 CALIFORNIA ST OMAHA, NE 68178 Small instrumentation grant
S15DK-44709-01 (NSS) SMITH, STUART CHILDREN'S HOSP MEDICAL CENTER 747 FIFTY-SECOND ST OAKLAND, CA 49609 Small instrumentation grant
S15DK-44710-01 (NSS) HARLAN, RICHARD E TULANE UNIVERSITY SCH OF MED 1430 TULANE AVENUE NEW ORLEANS, LA 70112 Small instrumentation grant
S15DK-44711-01 (NSS) HUMPHREY, DONALD R EMORY UNIVERSITY 1440 CLIFTON ROAD ATLANTA, GA 30322 Small instrumentation grant
S15DK-44712-01 (NSS) MARTIN, OLIVIER R SUNY-BINGHAMTON PO BOX 6000 BINGHAMTON, NY 13902-6000 Small instrumentation grant
S15DK-44713-01 (NSS) EISENBARTH, GEORGE S JOSLIN DIABETES CENTER, INC. ONE JOSLIN PLACE BOSTON, MA 02215 Small instrumentation grant
S15DK-44714-01 (NSS) EISENMAN, JOSEPH S MT SINAI SCHOOL OF MEDICINE 1 GUSTAVE LEVY PL BOX 1075 NEW YORK, N Y 10029-6574 Small instrumentation grant
S15DK-44715-01 (NSS) CLIFTON, JAMES A UNIVERSITY OF IOWA 200E EMRB IOWA CITY, IA 52242 Small instrumentation grant
R29DK-44716-01 (TOX) MAYEUX, PHILIP R UNIV ARKANSAS FOR MEDICAL SCI 4301 WEST MARKHAM, SLOT 501 LITTLE ROCK, AR 72205 Role of calcium in endotoxin-induced tubule cell injury
R13DK-44731-01 (DDK) KARLOWICZ, KAREN A 2628 WIMBLEDON POINT DRIVE VIRGINIA BEACH, VA 23454 National multi-speciality nursing conference on urinary continence
P50DK-44756-01 (DDK) ROBILLARD, JEAN E UNIVERSITY OF IOWA IOWA CITY, IA 52242 Developmental physiology of the kidney and urinary tract
P50DK-44756-01 0001 (DDK) ROBILLARD, JEAN Developmental physiology of the kidney and urinary tract Neuronal regulation of renal function during development
P50DK-44756-01 0002 (DDK) JOSE, PEDRO Developmental physiology of the kidney and urinary tract Maturation of adrenergic receptors and post-receptor mechanisms
P50DK-44756-01 0003 (DDK) GOMEZ, R ARIEL Developmental physiology of the kidney and urinary tract Renin processing in renal development
P50DK-44756-01 0004 (DDK) CHEVALIER, ROBERT Developmental physiology of the kidney and urinary tract Regulation of ANP synthesis and response in early development
P50DK-44756-01 9001 (DDK) ROBILLARD, JEAN Developmental physiology of the kidney and urinary tract Education core
R01DK-44762-01 (DDK) HOLLINGSWORTH, MICHAEL A UNIVERSITY OF NEBRASKA MED CTR 600 SOUTH 42ND STREET OMAHA, NE 68198-6805 Molecular studies of mucin expression in cystic fibrosis
R43DK-44794-01 (HUD) MAGYARI, PATRICIA A MACRO SYSTEMS INC 8630 FENTON ST SILVER SPRING, MD 20910 Cystic fibrosis carrier screening educational materials
R01DK-44804-01 (DDK) LIEBERT, MONICA UNIV OF MICHIGAN MED CTR 1500 E MEDICAL CTR DR ANN ARBOR, MI 48109 Urothelial cell activation in interstitial cystitis
R01DK-44812-01 (DDK) DOMINGUE, GERALD J TULANE UNIVERSITY 1430 TULANE AVE NEW ORLEANS, LA 70112 Buried bacterial genomes in interstitial cystitis
R01DK-44817-01 (DDK) WESTFALL, DAVID P UNIV OF NEVADA SCH OF MED HOWARD MEDICAL SCIENCES BLDG RENO, NV 89557 Role of ATP in bladder neuroeffector function
R01DK-44821-01 (DDK) LEWIS, SIMON A UNIVERSITY OF TEXAS MED BRANCH 301 UNIVERSITY BLVD GALVESTON, TX 77550 Physiology of the mammalian urinary bladder epithelium
R01DK-44830-01 (DDK) TUTTLE, JEREMY B UNIVERSITY VIRGINIA SCH OF MED BOX 230 CHARLOTTESVILLE, VA 22908 Neurotrophic changes induced by inflammation of bladder
R01DK-44833-01 (DDK) WILSON, PATRICIA D UMDNJ-R W JOHNSON MED/SCH 675 HOES LA/PHYSIO & BIOPHYS PISCATAWAY, NJ 08854-5635 Role of NaK-ATPase and polarity defects in ADPKD cyst formation
R01DK-44833-01 9002 (DDK) JOHNSON, MICHAEL L Role of NaK-ATPase and polarity defects in ADPKD cyst formation Core--Imaging techniques for PKD
R01DK-44834-01 (MET) GOLDFINE, IRA D MOUNT ZION MEDICAL CTR OF UCSF PO BOX 7921 SAN FRANCISCO, CA 94120 Insulin receptor signalling
R01DK-44835-01 (DDK) ELGAVISH, ADA UNIVERSITY OF ALABAMA UAB STATION BIRMINGHAM, AL 35294 Pathogenic mechanisms of interstitial cystitis
R01DK-44836-01 (IMB) CALABRETTA, BRUNO THOMAS JEFFERSON UNIVERSITY 1025 WALNUT ST PHILADELPHIA, PA 19107-5083 The role of c-myb in T-lymphocytes proliferation
R01DK-44838-01 (BCE) MELLON, PAMELA L SALK INST/BIOLOGICAL STUDIES POST OFFICE BOX 85800 SAN DIEGO, CA 92138 Neurosecretory gene expression in the hypothalamus
R01DK-44848-01 (DDK) KILLEN, PAUL D UNIVERSITY OF MICHIGAN 1301 CATHERINE RD BOX 0602 ANN ARBOR, MI 48109-0602 Collagen IV gene transcription in cpk/cpk mice
R01DK-44853-01 (DDK) KLINGER, KATHERINE W INTEGRATED GENETICS ONE MOUNTAIN ROAD FRAMINGHAM, MA 01701 The etiology of APKD--Molecular genetics of PKD-1
R01DK-44861-01 (DDK) JEFFERSON, DOUGLAS M NEW ENGLAND MEDICAL CENTER 750 WASHINGTON ST, PO BOX 477 BOSTON, MA 02111 Growth and secretion by liver cysts in ADPKD
R01DK-44863-01 (DDK) TORRES, VICENTE E MAYO FOUNDATION 200 FIRST STREET SOUTHWEST ROCHESTER, MN 55905 Renin angiotensin system in the pathogenesis of ADPKD
R01DK-44875-01 (DDK) AVNER, ELLIS D CHILDREN'S HOSPITAL & MED CENT 4800 SAND POINT WAY, NE SEATTLE, WA 98105 Cellular biology of congenital murine renal cystogenesis
R01DK-44889-01 (RAP) DEVLIN, JOHN T MAINE MEDICAL CENTER 22 BRAMHALL ST PORTLAND, ME 04102 Effects of exercise on protein metabolism in diabetes
R13DK-44904-01 (DDK) COLLINS, FRANCIS S UNIVERSITY OF MICHIGAN 4570 MEDICAL SCI, 11 BOX 0650 ANN ARBOR, MI 48109-0650 Toward new therapeutical treatments for cystic fibrosis
U01DK-44998-01 (DDK) WEIN, ALAN J UNIVERSITY OF PENNSYLVANIA 3010 RAVDIN COURTYARD BLDG PHILADELPHIA, PA 19104 Interstitial cystitis database clinical center
Z01DK-45000-24 (CEB) ROBBINS, J NIDDK, NIH Thyroxine protein interactions
Z01DK-45009-24 (CEB) ROBBINS, J NIDDK, NIH Studies in thyroid disease
U01DK-45013-01 (DDK) DIOKNO, ANANIAS C WILLIAM BEAUMONT HOSPITAL 3601 W 13 MILE RD ROYAL OAK, MI 48073 Interstitial cystitis data collection program
Z01DK-45014-21 (CEB) WOLFF, J NIDDK,NIH Membranes and secretion
Z01DK-45016-21 (CEB) WOLFF, J NIDDK, NIH Thyroid hormone secretion and function of microtubles
Z01DK-45020-15 (CEB) ROBBINS, J NIDDK, NIH Synthesis of thyroxine transport proteins
U01DK-45021-01 (DDK) SCHAEFFER, ANTHONY J NORTHWESTERN UNIV MEDICAL SCH 303 EAST CHICAGO AVENUE CHICAGO, IL 60611 Interstitial cystitis data base clinical center
R13DK-45023-01 (CBY) REED, RANDALL R JOHNS HOPKINS UNIVERSITY 725 NORTH WOLFE ST PCTB 818 BALTIMORE, MD 21205 Conference on 2nd Messengers/Protein Phosphorylation
R29DK-45024-01 (MET) ROSSETTI, LUCIANO ALBERT EINSTEIN COLLEGE OF MED 1300 MORRIS PARK AVENUE BRONX, NY 10461 Insulinomimetic probes--Novel approach to the study of diabetes
U01DK-45026-01 (DDK) PARSONS, C LOWELL UNIV OF CALIF MED CTR 225 DICKINSON ST SAN DIEGO, CA 92103-1990 Interstitial cystitis data base--Clinical center
Z01DK-45028-13 (CEB) ROBBINS, J NIDDK, NIH Thyroid hormones-cell interactions
Z01DK-45033-08 (CEB) NIKODEM, V M NIDDK, NIH Mapping of triiodothyronine responsive genes
Z01DK-45038-04 (CEB) NIKODEM, V M NIDDK, NIH Molecular biology of thyroid hormone receptors
Z01DK-45040-03 (CEB) NIKODEM, VA NIDDK,NIH Effect of thyroid hormone on synthesis of myelin basic proteins
Z01DK-45041-02 (CEB) SATO, S NIDDK, NIH Role of POU-domain genes during Xenopus laevis embryogenesis
Z01DK-45042-02 (CEB) SATO, S NIDDK, NIH The role of Xenopus-posterior (Xpo) in early frog development
R01DK-45066-01 (MGN) FISLER, JANIS S UNIVERSITY OF CALIFORNIA 405 HILGARD AVENUE LOS ANGELES, CA 90024-1406 Identity and nature of genetic loci promoting obesity
R01DK-45213-01 (HEM) MALTER, JAMES S UNIVERSITY OF WISCONSIN 1300 UNIVERSITY AVENUE MADISON, WI 53706 Regulation of hematopoietic growth factor production
R01DK-45218-01 (GMB) HERZLINGER, DORIS A CORNELL UNIVERSITY MED COLLEGE 1300 YORK AVENUE NEW YORK, NY 10021 Generation of renal epithelial cell diversity
R01DK-45227-01 (AMS) CANALIS, ERNESTO M ST FRANCIS HOSPITAL & MED CTR 114 WOODLAND STREET HARTFORD, CT 06105-1299 Mechanisms of cortisol action in bone
R01DK-45242-01 (HEM) PEIPER, STEPHEN C UNIVERSITY OF LOUISVILLE 529 SOUTH JACKSON STREET LOUISVILLE, KY 40292 Molecular basis of hematopoietic growth factor signaling
Z01DK-47001-10 (DB) LEROITH, D NIDDK, NIH Phosphorylation of the insulin and IGF-I receptors
Z01DK-47002-04 (DB) DE PABLO, F NIDDK, NIH Insulin gene expression and insulin action
Z01DK-47005-19 (DB) GORDEN, P NIDDK, NIH Studies of insulin receptors in circulating cells in man
Z01DK-47009-04 (DB) EASTMAN, R NIDDK, NIH Positron emission tomography
Z01DK-47018-14 (DB) LEROITH, D NIDDK, NIH Cellular hormone-like peptides
Z01DK-47019-14 (DB) GORDEN, P NIDDK, NIH Morphological studies of ligand binding to cells
Z01DK-47022-12 (DB) TAYLOR, S I NIDDK, NIH Insulin receptors in syndromes of extreme insulin resistance

PROJECT NO., ORGANIZATIONAL UNIT., INVESTIGATOR, ADDRESS, TITLE

PROJECT NO., ORGANIZATIONAL UNIT., INVESTIGATOR, ADDRESS, TITLE

Z01DK-47024-12 (DB) COLLIER, E NIDDK, NIH Biosynthetic labeling of the insulin receptor
Z01DK-47026-07 (DB) TAYLOR, S I NIDDK, NIH Tyrosine-specific protein kinase activity associated with the insulin receptor
Z01DK-47027-06 (DB) EASTMAN, R NIDDK, NIH Use of SMS 201-995 in hormone secreting tumors
Z01DK-47028-02 (DB) MCKEON, C NIDDK, NIH Insulin gene expression and insulin action
Z01DK-51000-33 (CHB) SHULMAN, N R NIDDK, NIH Immunology of blood cell deficiencies
Z01DK-51001-33 (CHB) SHULMAN, N R NIDDK, NIH Blood coagulation and diseases of hemorrhage and thrombosis
Z01DK-52008-12 (GBB) CAMERINI-OTERO, R D NIDDK, NIH Gene expression and human genetics
Z01DK-52011-07 (GBB) ACKERMAN, E NIDDK, NIH Toxins and DNA repair in Xenopus oocytes
Z01DK-52012-07 (GBB) PROIA, R L NIDDK, NIH Structure-function relationships of lysosomal enzymes
Z01DK-52014-04 (GBB) CAMERINI-OTERO, R D NIDDK, NIH CD4 receptor structure/function project
Z01DK-52015-03 (GBB) HSIEH, P NIDDK,NIH Molecular studies of protein-DNA interactions
Z01DK-53001-21 (DDB) GARDNER, J D NIDDK, NIH Studies of membrane function
Z01DK-53004-19 (DDB) GARDNER, J D NIDDK, NIH Cyclic nucleotide mediated functions
Z01DK-53100-03 (DDB) JENSEN, R T NIDDK, NIH Identification and characterization of receptors for GI peptides
Z01DK-53101-03 (DDB) JENSEN, R T NIDDK, NIH Cellular basis of action of gastrointestinal peptides
Z01DK-53200-02 (DDB) MATON, P N NIDDK, NIH Management of islet cell tumors
Z01DK-53201-02 (DDB) MATON, P N NIDDK, NIH Receptors on gastric smooth muscle cells
Z01DK-53501-18 (DDB) JONES, E A NIDDK, NIH Studies relating to the pathogenesis of hepatic encephalopathy
Z01DK-53503-17 (DDB) JONES, E A NIDDK, NIH Immunologic studies in primary biliary cirrhosis
Z01DK-53509-13 (DDB) HOOFNAGLE, J H NIDDK, NIH Studies of the natural history and treatment of chronic type B hepatitis
Z01DK-53510-12 (DDB) JONES, E A NIADDK, NIH Natural history and treatment of chronic non-A, non-B hepatitis
Z01DK-53511-12 (DDB) JONES, E A NIDDK, NIH Trials of therapies for primary biliary cirrhosis
Z01DK-53514-07 (DDB) JONES, E A NIDDK, NIH Immunological studies in chronic viral hepatitis
Z01DK-53516-02 (DDB) JONES, E A NIDDK, NIH Studies of the opiate system in cholestatic liver disease
Z01DK-55000-19 (MCNE) WEINTRAUB, B D NIDDK, NIH Biosynthesis and glycosylation of thyrotropin
Z01DK-55002-11 (MCNE) WEINTRAUB, B D NIDDK, NIH Molecular biology of pituitary glycoprotein hormones & hypothalamic hormones
Z01DK-55006-18 (MCNE) RECHLER, M M NIDDK, NIH Insulin-like growth factors
Z01DK-55012-09 (MCNE) CUSHMAN, S W NIDDK, NIH Insulin's regulation of hormone binding
Z01DK-55015-02 (MCNE) WEINTRAUB, B D NIDDK, NIH Mutations of the thyroid hormone receptor gene in thyroid hormone resistance
Z01DK-57000-26 (LSB) GINSBURG, V NIDDK, NIH Biology of complex carbohydrates
Z01DK-57002-17 (LSB) FOULDS, J NIDDK, NIH Expression and function of bacterial cell surface components
Z01DK-57501-15 (LMCB) CARTER, B J NIDDK, NIH Function of DNA virus genomes in animal cells
Z01DK-57502-18 (LMCB) OKA, T NIDDK, NIH Hormonal regulation of cell growth and differentiation
Z01DK-57503-18 (LMCB) TIETZE, F NIDDK, NIH Lysosomal transport and storage disease
Z01DK-57504-04 (LMCB) CARTER, B J NIDDK, NIH Regulation of HIV by AAV
Z01DK-58000-47 (LAC) BECKER, E D NIDDK, NIH Analytical services and methodology
Z01DK-58002-16 (RLMC) SIMONS, S S NIDDK, NIH 90 90 Initial intracellular events of steroid hormone action
Z01DK-58003-17 (LAC) FOLTZ, C M NIDDK, NIH Development of methods and materials for the study of medical problems
Z01DK-58004-24 (LAC) FEDER, N NIDDK, NIH Professional practices of biomedical scientists
Z01DK-58007-07 (LAC) BROSSI, A NIDDK, NIH Physostigmine and analogs
Z01DK-58010-06 (LAC) BROSSI, A NIDDK, NIH Mammalian alkaloids
Z01DK-58011-15 (LAC) BROSSI, A NIDDK, NIH Structure-activity relationship of colchicinoids based on tubulin binding
Z01DK-58017-02 (LAC) BROSSI, A NIDDK, NIH Nortropane alkaloids
Z01DK-58018-02 (LAC) BROSSI, A NIDDK, NIH Analytical reagents from dihydrofluorescein
Z01DK-58501-06 (LNS) SKOLNICK, P NIDDK, NIH Receptors for neurotransmitters and drugs in brain and peripheral tissues
Z01DK-59000-04 (MPB) SPIEGEL, A NIDDK, NIH Molecular biologic studies on the cause of parathyroid neoplasia
Z01DK-59001-26 (MPB) SPIEGEL, A NIDDK, NIH Guanine nucleotide binding proteins as receptor-effector couplers
Z01DK-59002-26 (MPB) SPIEGEL, A NIDDK, NIH Studies on pseudohypoparathyroidism and related disorders
Z01DK-59003-01 (MPB) SPIEGEL, A NIDDK, NIH Studies on McCune-Albright Syndrome
Z01DK-59501-06 (LMC) RICE, K C NIDDK, NIH Design and synthesis of drugs acting on central and peripheral tissues
Z01DK-59502-06 (LMC) JACOBSON, A E NIDDK,NIH Design, synthesis and evaluation of medicinal agents and research tools
Z01DK-59601-04 (LMC) TORRENCE, P F NIDDK, NIH Analogues of nucleic acids and their components as potential anti-AIDS agents
Z01DK-59602-18 (LMC) TORRENCE, P F NIDDK, NIH Interferon induction and action-- Antiviral activity of nucleoside analogs
Z01DK-59701-19 (LMC) GLAUDEMANS, C P J NIDDK, NIH Reactions and immunochemistry of carbohydrates
N01DK-62274-06 (**) SHARP, HARVEY L Liver tissue procurement and distribution system
N01DK-62285-10 (**) WILLIAMS, GEORGE W Coordinating center for diabetic renal disease in the Pima Indian population
Z01DK-69000-26 (PECR) KNOWLER, W C NIDDK, NIH Diabetes mellitus and other chronic diseases in the Gila River Indian community
Z01DK-69001-22 (PECR) PETTITT, D J NIDDK, NIH Complications and outcome of diabetic and prediabetic pregnancies
Z01DK-69006-21 (PECR) BENNETT, P H NIDDK, NIH Gila River Indian Community autopsy and mortality study
Z01DK-69009-26 (PECR) BENNETT, P H NIDDK, NIH Natural history of arthritis and rheumatism on the Gila River Indian Community
Z01DK-69015-09 (PECR) BOGARDUS, C NIDDK, NIH Cross-sectional and longitudinal studies of prediabetes in the Pima Indians
Z01DK-69020-08 (PECR) BOGARDUS, C NIDDK, NIH Insulin resistance and the regulation of muscle glycogen synthase activity
Z01DK-69021-10 (PECR) BOGARDUS, C NIDDK, NIH Energy expenditure in Pima Indians--Risk factors for body weight gain
Z01DK-69024-05 (PECR) BENNETT, P H NIDDK, NIH WHO collaborating center for epidemiological/clinical investigations in diabetes
Z01DK-69025-05 (PECR) KNOWLER, W C NIDDK, NIH Treatment of impaired glucose tolerance in Malmohus County, Sweden
Z01DK-69027-03 (PECR) BOGARDUS, C NIDDK, NIH Role of insulin-receptor tyrosine kinase in insulin resistance in Pima Indians
Z01DK-69028-03 (PECR) KNOWLER, W C NIDDK, NIH Genetics of non-insulin dependent diabetes mellitus
Z01DK-69029-03 (PECR) SOMMERCORN, J NIDDK, NIH Regulation of skeletal muscle ribosomal protein S6 kinase by insulin
Z01DK-69030-03 (PECR) SOMMERCORN, J NIDDK,NIH Contribution of protein tyrosine phosphatase to insulin resistance
Z01DK-69031-03 (PECR) SOMMERCORN, J NIDDK,NIH Regulation of phosphorylase phosphatase by insulin
Z01DK-69032-04 (PECR) SOMMERCORN, J NIDDK,NIH Regulation of skeletal muscle casein kinase II by insulin
Z01DK-69033-03 (PECR) BOGARDUS, C NIDDK, NIH Relationship between insulin resistance and blood pressure
Z01DK-69034-03 (PECR) BOGARDUS, C NIDDK,NIH The long Q-T interval syndrome in diabetic mellitus
Z01DK-69035-03 (PECR) BOGARDUS, C NIDDK,NIH Autonomic nervous system activity in obesity
Z01DK-69036-02 (PECR) KNOWLER, W C NIDDK, NIH Epidemiology of complications of non-insulin-dependent diabetes
Z01DK-69037-02 (PECR) BENNETT, P H NIDDK, NIH Kidney function in non-insulin-dependent diabetes mellitus
Z01DK-69038-02 (PECR) KNOWLER, W C NIDDK, NIH Insulin and hypertension in Pima Indians
Z01DK-69039-02 (PECR) KNOWLER, W C NIDDK, NIH Dietary survey of the Pima Indians of the Gila River Indian Community
Z01DK-69040-02 (PECR) KNOWLER, W C NIDDK, NIH Sodium-lithium countertransport and blood pressure
Z01DK-69041-02 (PECR) BOGARDUS, C NIDDK, NIH Insulin resistance in obesity and the association with lymph insulin kinetics
Z01DK-69042-02 (PECR) BOGARDDUS, C NIDDK, NIH Effect of nicotinic acid-induced insulin resistance on B-cell function
Z01DK-69043-02 (PECR) SOMMERCORN, J NIDDK, NIH Regulation of gene expression by insulin
Z01DK-69044-01 (PECR) BOGARDUS, C NIDDK, NIH Insulin resistance in obesity and the associations with membrane phospholipid
N01DK-72289-07 (**) SEWALL, ASE I Analysis of surveys natl center for health statistics
N01DK-72291-09 (**) MYERS, BRYAN D Evaluation diabetic renal disease in the Pima indian population
N01DK-72292-06 (**) WALL, TERESA Center for diabetes, arthritis, renal disease in community
N01DK-82234-06 (**) HELD, PHILIP Coordinating center for consolidated end stage renal disease data system
N01DK-92242-07 (**) MELNICK, ELAINE Support for national advisory boards and committees
N01DK-92244-06 (**) SUTHERLAND, DAVID E R Pancreas and islet transplant data base
N01DK-92250-06 (**) GIACOMINI, JOHN P Provide support services for the office of the director, NIDDK
P30ES-00002-29 (EHS) LITTLE, JOHN B HARVARD UNIVERSITY 665 HUNTINGTON AVENUE BOSTON, MA 02115 Occupational and environmental health center
P30ES-00002-29 0012 (EHS) BRAIN, JOSEPH D Occupational and environmental health center Respiratory biology and inhalation toxicology studies
P30ES-00002-29 0014 (EHS) LITTLE, JOHN B Occupational and environmental health center Radiobiology and experimental studies
P30ES-00002-29 0034 (EHS) MACMAHON, BRIAN Occupational and environmental health center Environmental epidemiology studies
P30ES-00002-29 0038 (EHS) MONSON, RICHARD Occupational and environmental health center Occupational health studies
P30ES-00002-29 0039 (EHS) TASHJIAN, A.H. Occupational and environmental health center Biochemical and environmental toxicology studies
P30ES-00002-29 9002 (EHS) LITTLE, JOHN B Occupational and environmental health center Cell sorter/cytofluorography core
P30ES-00002-29 9004 (EHS) FELDMAN, HENRY Occupational and environmental health center Modelling and statistics core
P30ES-00002-29 9005 (EHS) LITTLE, JOHN B. Occupational and environmental health center Feasibility core
P01ES-00040-27 (EHS) REED, DONALD J OREGON STATE UNIVERSITY WENIGER HALL 317 CORVALLIS, OREG 97331 Toxicology of environmental halocarbons
P01ES-00040-27 0071 (EHS) REED, DONALD J Toxicology of environmental halocarbons Chemical toxicity and glutathione conjugates
P01ES-00040-27 0075 (EHS) DEINZER, MAX L Toxicology of environmental halocarbons Analysis of polychlorinated aromatics by

negative ion mass spectrometry

P01ES-00040-27 0076 (EHS) FREEMAN, PETER K Toxicology of environmental halocarbons Photochemistry of environmentally significant polychloroarenes

P01ES-00040-27 0077 (EHS) MILLER, TERRY L Toxicology of environmental halocarbons Membrane effects of chlorophenolic environmental toxicants

P01ES-00040-27 0078 (EHS) BUHLER, DONALD R Toxicology of environmental halocarbons Characterization of quail and trout mfo systems

P01ES-00040-27 0079 (EHS) NIXON, JOSEPH E Toxicology of environmental halocarbons Mechanisms of inhibition of aflatoxin B1 carcinogenesis

P01ES-00040-27 0080 (EHS) KERKVILIET, NANCY I Toxicology of environmental halocarbons Mechanisms of chlorobiphenyl immunotoxicity

P01ES-00044-26 (EHS) HODGSON, ERNEST N C STATE UNIVERSITY 840 METHOD RD, UNIT IV,BX 7633 RALEIGH, NC 27695 Mechanisms of pesticide toxicity

P01ES-00044-26 0002 (EHS) DAUTERMAN, WALTER Mechanisms of pesticide toxicity Molecular basis for comparative toxicity

P01ES-00044-26 0004 (EHS) HODGSON, ERNEST Mechanisms of pesticide toxicity Pesticides and xenobiotic-metabolizing enzymes

P01ES-00044-26 0007 (EHS) GUTHRIE, FRANK E Mechanisms of pesticide toxicity Absorption and transport of toxicants

P01ES-00044-26 0008 (EHS) LINDERMAN, RUSSELL J. Mechanisms of pesticide toxicity Enzyme specificity and mechanisms at a molecular level

P01ES-00044-26 0009 (EHS) SMART, ROBERT C. Mechanisms of pesticide toxicity Mechanisms of organochloride pesticide induced tumor promotion

P01ES-00049-27 (EHS) CASIDA, JOHN E UNIVERSITY OF CALIFORNIA 114 WELLMAN HALL BERKELEY, CA 94720 Mode of action and metabolism of organic toxicants

P01ES-00049-27 0003 (EHS) CASIDA, JOHN E Mode of action and metabolism of organic toxicants Insecticide chemistry

P01ES-00049-27 0013 (EHS) CASIDA, JOHN E Mode of action and metabolism of organic toxicants Acetylcholinesterase inhibitors and GABA antagonists

P01ES-00049-27 0015 (EHS) CASIDA, JOHN E Mode of action and metabolism of organic toxicants Novel targets

P01ES-00049-27 0029 (EHS) CASIDA, JOHN E Mode of action and metabolism of organic toxicants Toxicology of neuroactive insecticides

P30ES-00159-24S1 (EHS) ALBERT, ROY E UNIVERSITY OF CINCINNATI 3223 EDEN AVENUE CINCINNATI, OH 45267-0056 Environmental health sciences center

P30ES-00159-24S1 0018 (EHS) COOPER, GARY P Environmental health sciences center Neurobehavioral and neurophysiological studies

P30ES-00159-24S1 0040 (EHS) BROOKS, STUART Environmental health sciences center Human studies--Clinical and epidemiological

P30ES-00159-24S1 0041 (EHS) SALTZMAN, BERNARD E Environmental health sciences center Environmental health and analytical studies

P30ES-00159-24S1 9001 (EHS) SUSKIND, RAYMOND R Environmental health sciences center Core facilities

P30ES-00159-24S1 0033 (EHS) FOULKES, ERNEST C Environmental health sciences center Toxic and essential metals

P30ES-00159-24S1 0036 (EHS) WARSHAWSKY, D Environmental health sciences center Environmental carcinogenesis, teratogenesis, mutagenesis

P30ES-00159-24S1 0037 (EHS) VINEGAR, ALLEN Environmental health sciences center Pulmonary and inhalation toxicology

K04ES-00163-04 (CPA) WILLIAMS, MARSHALL V OHIO STATE UNIV COLLEGE OF MED 5072 GRAVES HALL COLUMBUS, OH 43210 Mechanism of mercury toxicity and carcinogenicity cells

K11ES-00170-06 (EHS) RUNGE-MORRIS, MELISSA A WAYNE STATE UNIVERSITY 2727 SECOND AVENUE DETROIT, MI. 48201 Pyridine--Enzyme induction, metabolism, and toxicity

K11ES-00173-05 (EHS) NEWMAN, LEE S NAT JEWISH CTR IMMUNO/RES MED 1400 JACKSON ST DENVER, CO 80206 Immunologic & toxic mechanisms in beryllium disease

K04ES-00174-05 (TOX) YOKEL, ROBERT A UNIVERSITY OF KENTUCKY ROSE STREET LEXINGTON KY 40536 Al+3 toxicity--Contributing factors, Al form & chelation

K04ES-00178-04 (TOX) ATCHISON, WILLIAM D MICHIGAN STATE UNIVERSITY B403 LIFE SCIENCES BLDG EAST LANSING, MICH 48824 Neurotoxic mechanism of methylmercury poisoning

K04ES-00180-04 (SSS) ROBINS, JAMES M HARVARD SCH OF PUBLIC HEALTH 665 HUNTINGTON AVE BOSTON, MASS 02115 The control of bias when risk factors determine exposure

K04ES-00182-03 (TOX) KURTH, MARK J UNIVERSITY OF CALIFORNIA DAVIS, CA 95616 Immunochemistry immunoassays to artificial enzymes

K04ES-00190-03 (TOX) CHAMBERS, JANICE E MISSISSIPPI STATE UNIVERSITY PO DRAWER GY MISSISSIPPI STATE, MS 39762 Research career development in biochemical toxicology

K04ES-00193-03 (TOX) BOEKELHEIDE, KIM BROWN UNIVERSITY BOX G PROVIDENCE, RI 02912 Cytoskeletal targets of neuronal/testicular toxicants

K08ES-00196-02 (EHS) MERCHANT, ROBERT K UNIVERSITY OF IOWA DEPT OF MEDICINE, C33, GH IOWA CITY, IA 52242 Silica induced epithelial injury

K04ES-00202-02 (EDC) GOLD, ELLEN B UNIVERSITY OF CALIFORNIA 275 MRAK HALL DAVIS, CA 95616 Prospective reproductive study in semiconductor workers

K08ES-00203-02 (SRC) SCHWARTZ, DAVID A UNIVERSITY OF IOWA PULMONARY DISEASE DIV IOWA CITY, IA 52242 Epidemiology of vegetable dust-induced airway disease

K07ES-00204-01 (SRC) SOKAS, ROSEMARY K GEORGE WASHINGTON SCHOOL OF ME 2150 PENNSYLVANIA AVENUE, NW WASHINGTON, DC 20037 Environmental/occupational medicine academic award

K07ES-00209-01 (SRC) KEOGH, JAMES P UNIV OF MARYLAND AT BALTIMORE 405 W REDWOOD ST 2ND FL BALTIMORE, MD 21201 Environmental/occupational medicine academic award NIEHS

P30ES-00210-24 (EHS) REED, DONALD J OREGON STATE UNIVERSITY CORVALLIS, OR 97331-6504 Environmental health sciences center

PROJECT NO., ORGANIZATIONAL UNIT., INVESTIGATOR, ADDRESS, TITLE

P30ES-00210-24 9001 (EHS) BAROFSKY, DOUGLAS F Environmental health sciences center Core--Bioanalytical chemistry

P30ES-00210-24 9002 (EHS) HEDSTROM, OLAF R Environmental health sciences center Core--Pathology

P30ES-00210-24 9003 (EHS) REED, DONALD J Environmental health sciences center Core--Technical services

P30ES-00210-24 9004 (EHS) PIERCE, DONALD A Environmental health sciences center Core--Statistics

P30ES-00210-24 9005 (EHS) DEINZER, MAX L Environmental health sciences center Core-- Mass spectrometry

P30ES-00210-24 9006 (EHS) BUHLER, DONALD R Environmental health sciences center Core--Nucleic acids and proteins

P30ES-00210-24 9007 (EHS) HENDRICKS, JERRY D Environmental health sciences center Core--Aquatic toxicology

P30ES-00210-24 9008 (EHS) BARNES, DAVID W Environmental health sciences center Core--Cell culture

P30ES-00210-24 9009 (EHS) KERKVLIET, NANCY I Environmental health sciences center Core--Flow cytometry

K07ES-00214-01 (SRC) KREISS, KATHLEEN NATL JEWISH CTR-IMMUNO/RESP ME 1400 JACKSON STREET DENVER, CO 80206-1997 Environmental/occupational medicine academic award NIEHS

K07ES-00216-01 (SRC) BAKER, DEAN B MOUNT SINAI SCHOOL OF MEDICINE ONE GUSTAVE L LEVY PL/BOX 1057 NEW YORK, NY 10029 Environmental/occupational medicine academic award, NIEH

K07ES-00219-01 (SRC) BALMES, JOHN R SAN FRANCISCO GENERAL HOSPITAL 1001 POTRERO AVENUE SAN FRANCISCO, CA 94110 Academic award in environmental & occupational medicine, NIEHS

K07ES-00220-01 (SRC) UTELL, MARK J UNIVERSITY OF ROCHESTER MED CT 601 ELMWOOD AVENUE ROCHESTER, NY 14642 Academic award in environmental/occupational medicine

K07ES-00227-01 (SRC) CULLEN, MARK R YALE UNIV SCH OF MED 333 CEDAR STREET NEW HAVEN, CT 06510 Academic award in environmental/occupational medicine

K07ES-00237-01 (SRC) ROSENSTOCK, LINDA UNIVERSITY OF WASHINGTON 325 9TH AVENUE SEATTLE, WA 98104 Environmental/occupational medicine academic award, NIEH

K08ES-00239-02 (EHS) SCHAPIRA, RALPH M MEDICAL COLLEGE OF WISCONSIN 8700 WEST WISCONSIN AVENUE MILWAUKEE, WI 53226 Growth factor secretion in dust-induced lung disease

K08ES-00244-01 (CT) DUMENCO, LUBA L UNIVERSITY HOSP OF CLEVELAND 2074 ABINGTON ROAD CLEVELAND, OH 44106 Modulation of leukemogenesis by gene transfer

P30ES-00260-29 (EHS) UPTON, ARTHUR C NEW YORK UNIVERSITY MED CTR 550 FIRST AVENUE NEW YORK, N Y 10016 Research in environmental health sciences

P30ES-00260-29 9005 (EHS) PASTERNACK, BERNARD S Research in environmental health sciences Core--Epidemiology, biometry and risk assessment

P30ES-00260-29 9007 (EHS) GARTE, SEYMOUR Research in environmental health sciences Core--Carcinogenesis

P30ES-00260-29 9008 (EHS) COSTA, MAX Research in environmental health sciences Core--Molecular toxicology

P30ES-00260-29 9009 (EHS) SCHLESINGER, RICHARD Research in environmental health sciences Core--Systemic toxicology

P30ES-00260-29 9010 (EHS) LIPPMANN, MORTON Research in environmental health sciences Core--Exposure and health effects

P30ES-00260-29 9011 (EHS) UPTON, ARTHUR C Research in environmental health sciences Core--Shared resources

P30ES-00267-25 (SRC) GUENGERICH, F PETER VANDERBILT UNIVERSITY SCHOOL OF MEDICINE NASHVILLE, TN 37232 Environmental health sciences center grant

P30ES-00267-25 9001 (SRC) HARRIS, THOMAS M Environmental health sciences center grant Core--NMR

P30ES-00267-25 9003 (SRC) BRIGGS, ROBERT C Environmental health sciences center grant Core--Cell biology

P30ES-00267-25 9005 (SRC) LLOYD, R STEPHEN Environmental health sciences center grant Core--Molecular genetics

P30ES-00267-25 9006 (SRC) BLAIR, IAN A Environmental health sciences center grant Core--Mass spectrometry/analytical chemistry

P30ES-00267-25 9007 (SRC) GUENGERICH, F PETER Environmental health sciences center grant Core--Protein chemistry

P01ES-00628-19 (SRC) PLOPPER, CHARLES G UNIVERSITY OF CALIFORNIA DAVIS, CA 95616 Pulmonary effects of environmental oxidant pollutants

P01ES-00628-19 0003 (SRC) PLOPPER, CHARLES G Pulmonary effects of environmental oxidant pollutants Epithelial antioxidant mechanisms and ozone toxicity

P01ES-00628-19 0009 (SRC) WU, REEN Pulmonary effects of environmental oxidant pollutants Epithelial ozone toxicity and heat shock proteins in vitro

P01ES-00628-19 0010 (SRC) HYDE, DALLAS M Pulmonary effects of environmental oxidant pollutants Neutrophil-induced acute lung injury and ozone exposure

P01ES-00628-19 0011 (SRC) WITSCHI, HANSPETER Pulmonary effects of environmental oxidant pollutants Ozone-induced epithelial cell proliferation and response to a carcinogen

P01ES-00628-19 0012 (SRC) PINKERTON, KENT E Pulmonary effects of environmental oxidant pollutants Effects of ozone and acid aerosols on fate of respired particulates

P01ES-00628-19 9001 (SRC) TYLER, WALTER S Pulmonary effects of environmental oxidant pollutants Core facilities

R01ES-00834-17 (TOX) KUPFER, DAVID WORCESTER FDN/EXPERIMENTAL BIO 222 MAPLE AVENUE SHREWSBURY, MA 01545 Effects of chlorinated hydrocarbons on mammalian systems

R01ES-00881-18 (TOX) LIPPMANN, MORTON NEW YORK UNIVERSITY OF MED CTR 550 FIRST AVENUE NEW YORK, N Y 10016 Regional deposition of inhaled particles

P30ES-00928-18 (EHS) LANDRIGAN, PHILIP J MOUNT SINAI SCHOOL OF MEDICINE ONE GUSTAVE L LEVY PLACE NEW YORK, NY 10029 Environmental Health Sciences Center

P30ES-00928-18 9002 (EHS) BAKER, DEAN Environmental Health Sciences Center Epidemiology and biostatistics core

P30ES-00928-18 9003 (EHS) LILIS, RUTH Environmental Health Sciences

PROJECT NO., ORGANIZATIONAL UNIT., INVESTIGATOR, ADDRESS, TITLE

Center Clinical studies unit
P30ES-00928-18 9006 (EHS) VALCIUKAS, JOSE Environmental Health Sciences Center Clinical studies--Neurotoxicology
P30ES-00928-18 9010 (EHS) NICHOLSON, WILLIAM Environmental Health Sciences Center Epidemiology--Risk assessment
P30ES-00928-18 9014 (EHS) LANDRIGAN, PHILLIP J Environmental Health Sciences Center Industrial hygiene core
P30ES-00928-18 9012 (EHS) SUZUKI, YASUNOSUKE Environmental Health Sciences Center Laboratory sciences--Pathology
P30ES-00928-18 9013 (EHS) WOLF, MARY Environmental Health Sciences Center Laboratory sciences--Chemistry
R37ES-01060-16 (BMT) ROSEN, JOHN F MONTEFIORE MEDICAL CENTER 111 EAST 210TH STREET BRONX, NY 10467 The metabolism of lead in bone
R01ES-01062-15 (HED) BOWMAN, ROBERT E UNIVERSITY OF WISCONSIN 22 NORTH CHARTER STREET MADISON, WI 53715 Cognitive effects of neonatal lead exposure in monkeys
R01ES-01080-17 (TOX) LECH, JOHN J MEDICAL COLLEGE OF WISCONSIN 8701 WATERTOWN PLANK ROAD MILWAUKEE, WIS 53226 Metabolism of environmental contaminants by fish
P01ES-01104-16 (EHS) MAILMAN, RICHARD B UNIVERSITY OF NORTH CAROLINA CB#7250 BDRC CHAPEL HILL, NC 27599-7250 Neurobiology of environmental pollutants
P01ES-01104-16 0003 (EHS) MAILMAN, RICHARD B Neurobiology of environmental pollutants Neuropharmacology section
P01ES-01104-16 0004 (EHS) KRIGMAN, MARTIN R Neurobiology of environmental pollutants Morphology section
P01ES-01104-16 0007 (EHS) MORELL, PIERRE Neurobiology of environmental pollutants Neurochemistry section
P01ES-01104-16 0009 (EHS) MC CARTHY, KEN D Neurobiology of environmental pollutants Tissue culture analysis section
P01ES-01104-16 9001 (EHS) KRIGMAN, MARTIN R Neurobiology of environmental pollutants Animal models core
P01ES-01104-16 9002 (EHS) MUSHAK, PAUL Neurobiology of environmental pollutants Analytic toxicology core
P01ES-01104-16 9003 (EHS) GRIZZLE, JAMES G Neurobiology of environmental pollutants Biostatistics core
R01ES-01108-18 (NSS) DOCKERY, DOUGLAS W 665 HUNTINGTON AVENUE BOSTON, MA 02115 Effects of SO2 and respirable particulates on health
R01ES-01142-17 (TOX) KLAASSEN, CURTIS D UNIV OF KANSAS MEDICAL CENTER 39TH STREET AT RAINBOW BLVD KANSAS CITY, KANS 66103 Cadmium toxicology
P30ES-01247-17 (EHS) CLARKSON, THOMAS W UNIVERSITY OF ROCHESTER PO BOX EHSC ROCHESTER, NY 14642 Trace contaminants as environmental health hazards to man
P30ES-01247-17 9005 (EHS) GATES, ALLEN H Trace contaminants as environmental health hazards to man Core--Lab animals services
P30ES-01247-17 9007 (EHS) COX, CHRISTOPHER Trace contaminants as environmental health hazards to man Core--Biostatistics
P30ES-01247-17 9009 (EHS) GASIEWICZ, THOMAS Trace contaminants as environmental health hazards to man Core--Hazardous substance facility
P30ES-01247-17 9010 (EHS) FINKLESTEIN, JACOB Trace contaminants as environmental health hazards to man Core--Cell and tissue culture
P30ES-01247-17 0030 (EHS) NOTIDES, ANGELO C Trace contaminants as environmental health hazards to man Interaction of estrogenic agents with the estrogen receptors
P30ES-01247-17 0031 (EHS) GASIEWICZ, THOMAS A Trace contaminants as environmental health hazards to man Chlorinated dibenzo-p-dioxins, molecular mechanisms of toxicity
P30ES-01247-17 0039 (EHS) MERIGAN, WILLIAM H Trace contaminants as environmental health hazards to man Functional indices of visual system damage in primates
P30ES-01247-17 0063 (EHS) OBERDOERSTER, GUENTER Trace contaminants as environmental health hazards to man Pulmonary toxicology of metals
P30ES-01247-17 0064 (EHS) UTELL, MARK J Trace contaminants as environmental health hazards to man Effects of environmental pollutants on human lung function
P30ES-01247-17 0069 (EHS) MACARA, IAN G Trace contaminants as environmental health hazards to man Signal transduction in cellular differentiation and transformation
P30ES-01247-17 0079 (EHS) CORY-SLECHTA, DEBORAH A Trace contaminants as environmental health hazards to man Behavioral toxicity of lead--A pharmacological analysis
P30ES-01247-17 0082 (EHS) WEISS, BERNARD Trace contaminants as environmental health hazards to man Neurobehavioral toxicity of metals
P30ES-01247-17 0096 (EHS) HIGGINS, GERALD A Trace contaminants as environmental health hazards to man Gene expression and neuronal plasticity in aging and Alzheimer's disease
P30ES-01247-17 0097 (EHS) FINKELSTEIN, JACOB N Trace contaminants as environmental health hazards to man Molecular and cellular response of lung cells to oxidant stress
P30ES-01247-17 0098 (EHS) LOONEY, J R Trace contaminants as environmental health hazards to man Alveolar macrophage immunoglobulin receptors in host defenses
P30ES-01247-17 0099 (EHS) WILLY, JAMES C Trace contaminants as environmental health hazards to man Mechanisms of bronchogenic carcinogensis
P30ES-01247-17 0100 (EHS) ANDERS, M W Trace contaminants as environmental health hazards to man Metabolism and toxicity of halogenated hydrocarbons
P30ES-01247-17 0101 (EHS) MAINES, MAHIM Trace contaminants as environmental health hazards to man Environmental chemicals and heme metabolism
P30ES-01247-17 0102 (EHS) BALLATORI, NAZZARENO Trace contaminants as environmental health hazards to man Regulation of hepatic glutathione metabolism
P30ES-01247-17 9002 (EHS) TORIBARA, TAFT Y Trace contaminants as environmental health hazards to man Core--Analytical facility
P30ES-01247-17 9003 (EHS) LAPHAM, LOWELL W Trace contaminants as environmental health hazards to man Core--Pathology-morphology
R01ES-01301-16 (HAR) MILLS, JOHN H MEDICAL UNIV OF SOUTH CAROLINA 171 ASHLEY AVENUE CHARLESTON, S C 29425 Auditory effects of long exposures to low-level noise
R01ES-01532-14 (PHRA) KAROL, MERYL H UNIVERSITY OF PITTSBURGH 130 DESOTO STREET PITTSBURGH, PA 15261 Respiratory anaphylaxis to industrial chemicals
P01ES-01566-13 (EHS) HAMMOND, PAUL B UNIVERSITY OF CINCINNATI 3223 EDEN AVENUE CINCINNATI, OH 45267 Health effects of lead on child development
P01ES-01566-13 0001 (EHS) DIETRICH, KIM N Health effects of lead on child development Neurobehavioral effects of lead exposure in children--Ten year follow-up
P01ES-01566-13 0002 (EHS) BHATTACHARYA, AMIT Health effects of lead on child development Childhood lead exposure and maturation of postural stability and control
P01ES-01566-13 0003 (EHS) SUCCOP, P Health effects of lead on child development Methods for analyzing epidemiologic data with incomplete observations
P01ES-01566-13 9001 (EHS) HAMMOND, PAUL B Health effects of lead on child development Core-- Analytical services and research
P01ES-01640-14 (SRC) THILLY, WILLIAM G MASSACHUSETTS INST OF TECH 77 MASS AVE, RM E18-666 CAMBRIDGE, MA 02139 Health effects of fossil fuels utilization program
P01ES-01640-14 0009 (SRC) LONGWELL, JOHN P Health effects of fossil fuels utilization program Mutagen formation in combustion of vaporizable fuels
P01ES-01640-14 0010 (SRC) SAROFIM, ADEL F Health effects of fossil fuels utilization program Mutagen formation by pyrolysis of solid fuels
P01ES-01640-14 0012 (SRC) BIEMANN, KLAUS Health effects of fossil fuels utilization program Analytical chemistry for oxidative pyrolysis products
P01ES-01640-14 0015 (SRC) THILLY, WILLIAM G Health effects of fossil fuels utilization program Mutational spectra of products of incomplete combustion and pyrolysis
P01ES-01640-14 0016 (SRC) TANNENBAUM, STEVEN R Health effects of fossil fuels utilization program Adduct identification and chemical dosimetry of exposure to genetic agents
P01ES-01640-14 0017 (SRC) BEER, JANOS M Health effects of fossil fuels utilization program Polycyclic hydrocarbons in furnace flames
P01ES-01640-14 0018 (SRC) ELLIOTT, JOHN F Health effects of fossil fuels utilization program Toxicity and mutagenicity of combustion generated particles
P01ES-01640-14 0019 (SRC) WOGAN, GERALD N Health effects of fossil fuels utilization program Dosimetry of DNA adducts of fuel combustion products
P01ES-01640-14 9001 (SRC) BRAUN, ANDREW G Health effects of fossil fuels utilization program Core--Genetic toxicology testing
P01ES-01640-14 9002 (SRC) LAFLEUR, ARTHUR L Health effects of fossil fuels utilization program Core--Analytical chemistry
P01ES-01640-14 9003 (SRC) BUSBY, WILLIAM F Health effects of fossil fuels utilization program Core--Tumerigenicity testing
R01ES-01664-15 (CPA) O'BRIEN, THOMAS G THE LANKENAU MEDICAL RES CTR 100 LANCASTER AVE.W CITY LINE WYNNEWOOD, PA 19096 Polyamines & chemical carcinogenesis in vitro
R01ES-01670-14 (MCHA) TOWNSEND, CRAIG A JOHNS HOPKINS UNIVERSITY CHARLES & 34TH STREETS BALTIMORE, MD 21218 Biosynthesis of aflatoxin and related studies
R01ES-01821-35 (TOX) GLENDE, ERIC A, JR CASE WESTERN RESERVE UNIV 2109 ADELBERT ROAD CLEVELAND, OH 44106 Toxic liver injury--Ca2+, PLA2, proteases and eiconsanoids
R01ES-01871-11 (TOX) AHMED, AHMED E UNIVERSITY OF TEXAS MED BRANCH 301 UNIVERSITY BOULEVARD GALVESTON, TX 77550-0605 Chemical pathology of halonitriles biotransformation
R37ES-01884-15 (CPA) POLAND, ALAN P UNIVERSITY OF WISCONSIN 1400 UNIVERSITY AVENUE MADISON, WI 53706 Studies on the halogenated aromatic hydrocarbons
P30ES-01896-13 (EHS) AMES, BRUCE N UNIVERSITY OF CALIFORNIA 401 BARKER HALL BERKELEY, CA 94720 Environmental health sciences center
P30ES-01896-13 9013 (EHS) GOLD, LOIS S Environmental health sciences center Carcinogenic potency database
P30ES-01896-13 9014 (EHS) AMES, BRUCE N Environmental health sciences center Facilities core -- Analytical chemistry support
P30ES-01896-13 9016 (EHS) AMES, BRUCE N Environmental health sciences center Facilities core -- Fermentor/P3 facility
P30ES-01896-13 9017 (EHS) AMES, BRUCE N Environmental health sciences center Facilities core -- Media kitchen
P30ES-01896-13 9018 (EHS) AMES, BRUCE N Environmental health sciences center Facilities core -- Salmonella mutagenicity test resource
P30ES-01896-13 9019 (EHS) AMES, BRUCE N Environmental health sciences center Facilities core -- Shops
P30ES-01896-13 9020 (EHS) AMES, BRUCE N Environmental health sciences center Facilities core -- Storeroom
P30ES-01896-13 9021 (EHS) AMES, BRUCE N Environmental health sciences center Facilities core -- Tissue culture
P30ES-01896-13 9022 (EHS) AMES, BRUCE N Environmental health sciences center Facilities core -- Carcinogenic potency group
P30ES-01896-13 9023 (EHS) AMES, BRUCE N Environmental health sciences center Research core -- Dr. Bruce Ames
P30ES-01896-13 9024 (EHS) BLACKBURN, ELIZABETH H Environmental health sciences center Research core -- Dr. Elizabeth Blackburn
P30ES-01896-13 9025 (EHS) BOTCHAN, MICHAEL R Environmental health sciences center Research core -- Dr. Michael Botchan
P30ES-01896-13 9026 (EHS) COLE, DAVID Environmental health sciences center Research core -- Dr. David Cole
P30ES-01896-13 9027 (EHS) COZZARELLI, NICHOLAS Environmental health sciences center Research core -- Dr. Nicholas Cozzarelli
P30ES-01896-13 9028 (EHS) ECHOLS, HARRISON Environmental health sciences center Research core -- Dr. Harrison Echols
P30ES-01896-13 9029 (EHS) LINN, STUART Environmental health sciences center Research core -- Dr. Stuart Linn
P30ES-01896-13 9030 (EHS) NEILANDS, JOHN B Environmental health sciences center Research core -- Dr. John Neilands
P30ES-01896-13 9031 (EHS) RINE, JASPER D Environmental health sciences center Research core -- Dr. Jasper Rine
P30ES-01896-13 9032 (EHS) SMITH, MARTYN Environmental health

sciences center Research core
P30ES-01896-13 9033 (EHS) WILSON, ALLAN C Environmental health sciences center Research core – Dr. Allan Wilson
P30ES-01896-13 9034 (EHS) AMES, BRUCE N Environmental health sciences center Program enrichment core
P30ES-01896-13 9035 (EHS) AMES, BRUCE N Environmental health sciences center Facilities core – Computer/information retrieval support
P30ES-01896-13 9015 (EHS) AMES, BRUCE N Environmental health sciences center Facilities core – Electron microscopy
R01ES-01900-14 (GMA) BICKERS, DAVID R V A RESEARCH ROOM K-211 10701 E BOULEVARD CLEVELAND, OHIO 44106 Skin metabolism of drugs and carcinogens
P30ES-01908-14 (EHS) BONAVENTURA, JOSEPH DUKE UNIVERSITY MARINE LAB PIVERS ISLAND BEAUFORT, NC 28516 Marine/freshwater biomedical center grant
P30ES-01908-14 9001 (EHS) BONAVENTURA, JOSEPH Marine/freshwater biomedical center grant Core--Facilities and services
R37ES-01978-14 (NSS) REED, DONALD J OREGON STATE UNIVERSITY CORVALLIS, OR 97331-6503 Chemical toxicity and glutathione regulation
R37ES-01984-13 (CPA) MURRAY, ROBERT W UNIVERSITY OF MISSOURI 8001 NATURAL BRIDGE ROAD ST LOUIS, MO 63121 Ozone chemistry and chemical carcinogenesis
N44ES-02001-03 ( ) KAIGHN, ME** Development of defined medium for hamster embryo cells
R37ES-02030-13 (TOX) LA VOIE, EDMOND J RUTGERS STATE UNIVERSITY PO BOX 789 PISCATAWAY, NJ 08855-0789 Environmental polycyclics--Metabolism and activation
P30ES-02109-13 (SRC) THILLY, WILLIAM G MASSACHUSETTS INST OF TECH 77 MASS AVE CAMBRIDGE, MA 02139 MIT center for environmental health sciences
P30ES-02109-13 9004 (SRC) MOREL, FRANCOIS M M MIT center for environmental health sciences Core--Environmental transport and tranformation
P30ES-02109-13 0010 (SRC) WALSH, PETER MIT center for environmental health sciences Pilot--Yield of PAC during pyrolysis of bituminous coal
P30ES-02109-13 9001 (SRC) LONGWELL, JOHN P MIT center for environmental health sciences CORE--Mutagens from combustion sources
P30ES-02109-13 9002 (SRC) BIEMAN, KLAUS MIT center for environmental health sciences Core--Analytical chemistsry
P30ES-02109-13 9003 (SRC) TANNENBAUM, STEVEN R MIT center for environmental health sciences Toxicology core unit
R01ES-02205-13 (TOX) GUENGERICH, F PETER VANDERBILT UNIVRERSITY NASHVILLE, TENN 37232 Bioactivation and covalent binding of toxic haloalkenes
R01ES-02338-11 (TOX) LA VOIE, EDMOND J RUTGERS STATE UNIVERSITY PO BOX 789 PISCATAWAY, NJ 08855-0789 Quinolines and carbazoles--Mutagens and carcinogens
R01ES-02366-11 (TOX) KOENIG, JANE Q UNIVERSITY OF WASHINGTON SEATTLE, WA 98195 Sulfur oxides effects on lung function in asthmatics
R01ES-02370-11 (CPA) MALKINSON, ALVIN M UNIVERSITY OF COLORADO SCHOOL OF PHARMACY BOULDER, CO 80309-0297 Biochemistry of urethane-induced lung tumors
R01ES-02377-10A1 (TOX) SHELTON, KEITH R VIRGINIA COMMONWEALTH UNIVERSI BOX 614, MCV STATION RICHMOND, VA 23298-0614 Proteins in lead-induced nuclear inclusion bodies
R01ES-02380-13 (TOX) GOLDSTEIN, GARY W KENNEDY INSTITUTE 707 N BROADWAY BALTIMORE, MD 21205 Metabolic activity of brain capillaries
R01ES-02388-09 (TOX) WANI, ALTAF A OHIO STATE UNIVERSITY 400 W 12TH AVE, WISEMAN HALL COLUMBUS, OHIO 43210 DNA damage following exposure to genotoxin
R01ES-02424-09 (TOX) PIPER, WALTER N UNIVERSITY OF MICHIGAN 1420 WASHINGTON HEIGHTS ANN ARBOR, MI 48109-2029 Lead and drug toxicity related to heme biosynthesis
P01ES-02429-11 (EHS) AMDUR, MARY O NY UNV MED CTR, INST ENVI MED LONG MEADOW ROAD TUXEDO, NEW YORK 10987 Toxicology of inorganic coal combustion aerosols
P01ES-02429-11 0001 (EHS) AMDUR, MARY O Toxicology of inorganic coal combustion aerosols Toxicological assessment of pulmonary function
P01ES-02429-11 0002 (EHS) ELLIOT, JOHN F Toxicology of inorganic coal combustion aerosols Thermochemistry of inorganic combustion particulates
P01ES-02429-11 0003 (EHS) SAROFIM, ADEL F Toxicology of inorganic coal combustion aerosols Inorganic aerosols produced during coal combustion
P01ES-02429-11 0004 (EHS) ROGERS, ADRIANNE E Toxicology of inorganic coal combustion aerosols Morphology of acute-subacute effect of respiratory toxicants
P01ES-02429-11 9001 (EHS) MC CARTHY, JOHN F Toxicology of inorganic coal combustion aerosols Aerosol characterization--Core laboratory
R01ES-02453-12 (TOX) FOULKES, ERNEST C UNIVERSITY OF CINCINNATI 3223 EDEN AVENUE CINCINNATI, OH 45267-0056 Renal reabsorption of glutamate
R01ES-02470-10 (CPA) STAMATO, THOMAS D LANKENAU MEDICAL RESEARCH CENT LANCASTER AVE WEST OF CITY LIN WYNNEWOOD PA 19096 Delayed mutation and sectoring in mammalian cells
R01ES-02497-13 (NTN) BURK, RAYMOND F, JR VANDERBILT UNIVERSITY C-2104 MEDICAL CENTER NORTH NASHVILLE, TN 37232-2279 Nutritional and metabolic significance of selenium
R01ES-02515-11 (TOX) GASIEWICZ, THOMAS A UNIVERSITY OF ROCHESTER SCHOOL OF MEDICINE ROCHESTER, NY 14642 Molecular toxicity of TCDD
R01ES-02520-09 (TOX) HOLSAPPLE, MICHAEL P VIRGINIA COMMONWEALTH UNIVERSI BOX 613, MCV STATION RICHMOND, VA 23298 Mechanism of action of the toxic effects of TCDD
R01ES-02521-10 (PHRA) NOVAK, RAYMOND F WAYNE STATE UNIVERSITY INST. OF CHEMICAL TOXICOLOGY DETROIT, MI 48202 Hemoglobin hemeoxygenase activity and red cell toxicity
R01ES-02558-08A1 (TOX) WITZ, GISELA UNIV OF MED & DENT OF NEW JERS 675 HOES LANE PISCATAWAY, NJ 08854-5635 Muconaldehyde in relation to benzene hematotoxicity
R01ES-02566-10 (TOX) BROWN, OLEN R UNIV OF MISSOURI, COLUMBIA OFFICE OF SPONSORED PROG ADMIN COLUMBIA, MO 65211 Cellular free radical toxicity mechanisms
R37ES-02581-11 (PHRA) ROTH, ROBERT A, JR MICHIGAN STATE UNIVERSITY DEPT OF PHARM & TOXICOLOGY EAST LANSING, MICH 48824 Platelets and lung injury from monocrotaline
R01ES-02594-16 (TOX) ELDEFRAWI, AMIRA T UNIVERSITY OF MARYLAND 655 WEST BALTIMORE STREET BALTIMORE, MD 21201 Receptors as targets for insecticides
R37ES-02611-11 (TOX) GRAHAM, DOYLE G DUKE UNIVERSITY MEDICAL CENTER BOX 3712 DURHAM, NC 27710 Environmental toxin induced neurofilament neuropathology
R01ES-02614-12 (CPA) SMERDON, MICHAEL J WASHINGTON STATE UNIVERSITY PULLMAN, WA 99164-4660 Repair of carcinogen-damaged in human chromatin
U01ES-02617-12 (SRC) MERCIER, MICHEL WORLD HEALTH ORGANIZATION DIV ENVIRONMENTAL HEALTH 1211 GENEVA, SWITZERLAND 27 International Programme on Chemical Safety
R01ES-02638-11 (TOX) JONES, MARK M VANDERBILT UNIVERSITY BOX 1583 STATION B NASHVILLE, TN 37235 Chelate antidotes for cadmium intoxication
R01ES-02654-10 (GEN) MARONI, GUSTAVO P UNIVERSITY OF NORTH CAROLINA DEPARTMENT OF BIOLOGY CHAPEL HILL, N C 27514 Genetics of thionein and tolerance to metals
R01ES-02662-11 (SSS) MAKI, AUGUST H UNIVERSITY OF CALIFORNIA DAVIS, CALIF 95616 Spectroscopy of heavy atom perturbed biopolymers
R01ES-02679-11 (TOX) UTELL, MARK J UNIVERSITY OF ROCHESTER MED CT 601 ELMWOOD AVENUE ROCHESTER, NY 14642 Toxic effects of particles and oxidants on lung function
R01ES-02698-09 (TOX) DURBIN, PATRICIA W LAWRENCE BERKELEY LABORATORY 1 CYCLOTRON RD BERKELEY, CA 94720 Biological evaluation of new actinide-chelating agents
R01ES-02710-11 (TOX) HAMMOCK, BRUCE D UNIVERSITY OF CALIFORNIA 303 BRIGGS HALL DAVIS, CA 95616 Hydrolytic enzymes in the metabolism of toxins
R01ES-02728-10 (TOX) NELSON, SIDNEY D UNIVERSITY OF WASHINGTON DEPT OF MED CHEMISTRY SEATTLE, WA 98195 Metabolism and toxicity of halogenated alkyl compounds
R01ES-02747-09 (TOX) ALARIE, YVES C UNIVERSITY OF PITTSBURGH 130 DESOTO STREET PITTSBURGH, PA 15261 Methods to detect pneumotoxicity of chemicals
R01ES-02759-10 (TOX) THURMAN, RONALD G UNIV OF NORTH CARLINA AT CH CB# 7365 F L O B CHAPEL HILL, NC 27599-7365 Mechanisms of hepatotoxicity by environmental pollutants
R01ES-02774-09 (TOX) MILLER, RICHARD K UNIVERSITY OF ROCHESTER 601 ELMWOOD AVENUE ROCHESTER, NY 14642 Placental toxicology
R01ES-02852-08 (TOX) FECHTER, LAURENCE D JOHNS HOPKINS UNIVERSITY 615 NORTH WOLFE STREET BALTIMORE, MD 21205 Ototoxicity of chemical asphyxiants and noise
R01ES-02875-07A1 (TOX) BARNETT, JOHN B UNIVERSITY OF ARKANSAS 4301 W MARKHAM STREET LITTLE ROCK, AR 72205 Effect of prenatal chlordane on macrophage function
R01ES-02922-10 (TOX) ADAMS, DOLPH O DUKE UNIVERSITY DURHAM, NC 27710 Immunotoxicology--Environmental agents and macrophages
R01ES-03085-09 (TOX) BERMAN, HARVEY A S U N Y AT BUFFALO 335 HOCHSTETTER HALL BUFFALO, N Y 14260 Sites and mechanisms of organophosphate toxicity
R01ES-03098-07A2 (TOX) HART, BETH A UNIVERSITY OF VERMONT BURLINGTON, VT 05405 Synthesis and role of metallothionein in the lung
R01ES-03124-10 (CPA) TANG, ERIC M UNIVERSITY OF TEXAS P O BOX 389 SMITHVILLE, TX 78957 Repair of DNA damaged by model environmental chemicals
R37ES-03127-10 (NSS) ANDERS, MARION W UNIVERSITY OF ROCHESTER 601 ELMWOOD AVENUE ROCHESTER, NY 14642 Metabolism and toxicity of halogenated hydrocarbons
R01ES-03154-09 (BMT) RUSLING, JAMES F UNIVERSITY OF CONNECTICUT BOX U-60, 215 GLENBROOK RD 06269-3060 Electrocatalytic reduction of halogenated biphenyls
R01ES-03157-09 (TOX) FAUSTMAN, ELAINE M UNIVERSITY OF WASHINGTON ENVIRONMENTAL HEALTH, SC-34 SEATTLE, WASH 98195 In vitro embryotoxicity of N-nitroso compounds
R01ES-03179-09 (TOX) LAWRENCE, DAVID A ALBANY MED COLL OF UNION UNIV 47 NEW SCOTLAND AVENUE ALBANY, N Y 12208 Immunotoxicology of heavy metals
R01ES-03187-07 (PHRA) SHAIKH, ZAHIR A UNIVERSITY OF RHODE ISLAND COLLEGE PHARMACY KINGSTON, RI 02881 Factors affecting cadmium metabolism and toxicity
R01ES-03189-09 (SOH) KANE, AGNES B BROWN UNIVERSITY BOX G PROVIDENCE, RI 02912 Pathogenesis of mineral dust toxicity
R01ES-03192-21 (TOX) KLAASSEN, CURTIS D UNIV OF KANSAS MED CTR 39TH & RAINBOW BOULEVARD KANSAS CITY, KS 66160-0000 Hepatobiliary disposition in toxicology
R01ES-03221-09 (BMT) CARUSO, JOSEPH A UNIVERSITY OF CINCINNATI CINCINNATI, OH 45221-0037 Atomic emission spectrometry for dioxin trace analysis
R01ES-03230-04A2 (TOX) BIGAZZI, PIERLUIGI E UNIV OF CONNECTICUT HEALTH CTR 263 FARMINGTON AVE FARMINGTON, CT 06032 Immune effects of metals-- Mercury-induced autoimmune disease
R01ES-03257-07 (CPA) FIALA, EMERICH S AMERICAN HEALTH FOUNDATION ONE DANA ROAD VALHALLA, NY 10595 Carcinogenicity of 2-nitropropane--A probable mechanism
R01ES-03272-06 (TOX) MEREDITH, MICHAEL J CR OHSU SD CR 3181 SW SAM JACKSON P R PORTLAND OR 97201 Fate of toxic chemicals in hepatocyte and hepatoma cells
R01ES-03298-08 (TMP) GILL, SARJEET S UNIVERSITY OF CALIFORNIA 5419 WEBBER HALL EAST RIVERSIDE, CA 92521 Mode of action of Bacillus thuringiensis endotoxin
R01ES-03299-08 (TOX) ATCHISON, WILLIAM D MICHIGAN STATE UNIVERSITY EAST LANSING, MI 48824 Neurotoxic mechanism of acute methylmercury poisoning
R01ES-03329-07 (SSS) GANDHI, OM P UNIVERSITY OF UTAH SALT LAKE

CITY, UT 84112 Electromagnetic energy absorption and distribution in humans

R01ES-03334-05 (MCHA) WHITE, JAMES D OREGON STATE UNIVERSITY CORVALLIS, OR 97331-4003 Synthesis of macrolactone pyrrolizidine alkaloids

R01ES-03345-11 (TOX) SINSHEIMER, JOSEPH E UNIVERSITY OF MICHIGAN 1028 PHARMACY ANN ARBOR, MI 48109-1065 Epoxide toxicity in alkene metabolism

R01ES-03346-06 (CPA) KUMAR, SUBODH STATE UNIVERSITY OF NEW YORK 1300 ELMWOOD AVENUE BUFFALO, NY 14222 Mechanism of carcinogenesis of dibenzacridine

P01ES-03347-08 (EHS) LEE, WILLIAM R LOUISIANA STATE UNIVERSTY AGRICULTURAL/MECHANICAL COLL S BATON ROUGE, LA 70803-1725 Mechanisms of mutagenesis for environmental mutagens

P01ES-03347-08 0003 (EHS) LEE, WILLIAM R Mechanisms of mutagenesis for environmental mutagens Repair in both competent and repair deficient germ cells

P01ES-03347-08 0005 (EHS) SILVERMAN, HAROLD Mechanisms of mutagenesis for environmental mutagens Characterization of proteins

P01ES-03347-08 0007 (EHS) CHANG, SIMON H Mechanisms of mutagenesis for environmental mutagens Site directed mutagenesis

P01ES-03347-08 9001 (EHS) LEE WILLIAM R Mechanisms of mutagenesis for environmental mutagens Drosophila Core

P01ES-03347-08 0001 (EHS) LEE, WILLIAM R Mechanisms of mutagenesis for environmental mutagens The relation between dose and genetic response

P01ES-03347-08 0002 (EHS) CHANG, SIMON H Mechanisms of mutagenesis for environmental mutagens Distribution of adducts among target sites of DNA

R01ES-03356-08 (TOX) APOSHIAN, H VASKEN UNIVERSITY OF ARIZONA LIFE SCIENCES SOUTH 444 TUCSON, AZ 85721 DMSA, DMPS and other orally active dithiol chelators

R01ES-03358-07 (TOX) PESTKA, JAMES J MICHIGAN STATE UNIVERSITY EAST LANSING, MI 48824 Effect of trichothecene mycotoxins and IgA production

R01ES-03386-05 (TOX) LANGE, DAVID G JOHNS HOPKINS HOSPITAL 600 NORTH WOLFE STREET BALTIMORE, MD 21205 Microwave toxicology and membrane barrier changes

R01ES-03425-14 (TOX) STERN, ARNOLD NEW YORK UNIV MEDICAL CENTER 550 FIRST AVENUE NEW YORK, NY 10016 Oxygen toxicity in the red cell

R01ES-03433-09 (CPA) GOLD, AVRAM UNIVERSITY OF NORTH CAROLINA CHAPEL HILL, NC 27599-7400 Oxoporphinatoiron (v) oxidation of polycyclic aromatics

R01ES-03437-08 (TOX) MOORE, ALBERT L UNIFORMED SERVICES UNIV/HS 4301 JONES BRIDGE ROAD BETHESDA, MD 20814-4799 Cell calcium, calcium pump and toxin action

R01ES-03456-08 (CPA) WILSON, GLENN L UNIVERSITY OF SOUTH ALABAMA 307 UNIVERSITY BLVD MOBILE, AL 36688 Environmental beta cell toxins mechanism of action

R01ES-03460-07 (EDC) GRAZIANO, JOSEPH H COLUMBIA UNIVERSITY COLL OF PHYSICIANS & SURGEONS NEW YORK, NY 10032 Environmental lead, reproduction and infant development (human)

R01ES-03466-06 (TOX) SEVANIAN, ALEX UNIV OF SOUTHERN CALIFRONIA 1985 ZONAL AVENUE LOS ANGELES, CA 90033 Cytotoxicity of cholesterol oxides

R01ES-03484-07 (TOX) FINLAYSON-PITTS, BARBARA J CALIFORNIA STATE UNIVERSITY FULLERTON, CA 92634 Does pulmonary surfactant react with inhaled pollutants?

R01ES-03499-10 (CPA) BLOOM, STEPHEN E CORNELL UNIVERSITY ITHACA, N Y 14853 Chick embryos for detecting environmental mutagens

R01ES-03500-09 (CMS) LONSBURY-MARTIN, BRENDA L UNIVERSITY OF MIAMI SCH OF MED P.O. BOX 016960 MIAMI, FL 33101 The physiological bases of ototraumatic insult

P01ES-03505-07 (EHS) SPANNHAKE, ERNST W JOHNS HOPKINS UNIVERSITY 615 NORTH WOLFE STREET BALTIMORE, MD 21205 Mechanisms of susceptibility in the ozone-exposed lung

P01ES-03505-07 0003 (EHS) SPANNHAKE, ERNST W Mechanisms of susceptibility in the ozone-exposed lung Influence of oxidant on the airway response to antigen

P01ES-03505-07 0005 (EHS) KLEEBERGER, STEVEN R Mechanisms of susceptibility in the ozone-exposed lung Genetic susceptibility to ozone--Biochemical mechanism

P01ES-03505-07 0006 (EHS) WEINMANN, GAIL G Mechanisms of susceptibility in the ozone-exposed lung Mechanism of susceptibility to ozone in humans

P01ES-03505-07 9001 (EHS) BROMBERGER-BARNEA, BARUCH Mechanisms of susceptibility in the ozone-exposed lung Technical core

R01ES-03509-08 (CPA) SWAMINATHA, SANTHANAM UNIV OF WISCONSIN COMP CANCER 600 HIGHLAND AVENUE MADISON, WI 53792 Activation of carcinogens by human urothelium in vitro

R01ES-03521-07 (TOX) BHALLA, DEEPAK K UNIVERSITY OF CALIFORNIA IRVINE, CA 92717-1825 Mechanism of air pollutant induced airway permeability

R01ES-03543-05 (TOX) CHOU, IIH-NAN BOSTON UNIVERSITY 80 EAST CONCORD STREET BOSTON, MASS 02118 Epigenetic mechanisms of toxicity of environmental metal

R01ES-03554-07 (TOX) SAFE, STEPHEN H TEXAS A & M RESEARCH FOUNDATIO BOX 3578 COLLEGE STATION, TX 77843 Characterization of Ah receptor-radioligand interactions

R01ES-03561-07 (TOX) GIERTHY, JOHN F NEW YORK STATE DEPT OF HEALTH WADSWORTH CTR FOR LAB & RES ALBANY, N Y 12201 Dioxin-epithelial cell interactions--mechanism and assay

R01ES-03575-07 (TOX) MATSUMURA, FUMIO UNIVERSITY OF CALIFORNIA IEHR FACILITY DAVIS, CA 95616 Alteration of cell-surface membrane for dioxin toxicity

R01ES-03597-07 (TOX) PUHVEL, S MADLI UCLA SCHOOL OF MEDICINE 175018 LOS ANGELES, CA 90024 Mechanisms of toxicity of dioxin

R01ES-03598-08 (TOX) DAVIES, KELVIN JAMES ANTHONY THE ALBANY MEDICAL COLLEGE NEW SCOTLAND AVENUE ALBANY, NY 12208 Oxygen radical toxicity and red cell protein degradation

R01ES-03606-06 (TOX) RIFKIND, ARLEEN B CORNELL UNIV MEDICAL COLLEGE 1300 YORK AVENUE NEW YORK, NY 10021 Arachidonate products in dioxin and PCB toxicity

R01ES-03614-05 (REB) KATZ, DAVID F UNIVERSITY OF CALIFORNIA SUBER HOUSE DAVIS, CA 95616 Methods for assessment of environmental hazards

R01ES-03619-07 (TOX) HALPERT, JAMES R UNIV OF AR, COLL OF PHARMACY TUCSON, ARIZ 85721 Cytochrome P-450 inhibition by dichloromethyl compounds

R01ES-03628-06 (TOX) WOODS, JAMES S BATTELLE SEATTLE RESEARCH CTR 4000 NORTHEAST 41ST STREET SEATTLE, WA 98105 Trace metal alteration of renal porphyrin metabolism

R01ES-03631-07 (TOX) CORBETT, MICHAEL D UNIVERSITY OF FLORIDA 1500 SW 23RD DR /531 IFAS GAINESVILLE, FL 32611-0531 Metabolic activation of arylamines in leukocytes

R01ES-03647-06 (TOX) LASKIN, JEFFREY D UMDNJ-ROBERT WOOD JOHN MED SCH 675 HOES LANE PISCATAWAY, N J 08854-5635 Phototoxicity of environmental chemicals

R55ES-03648-07 (CPA) HOWARD, PAUL C CASE WESTERN RESERVE UNIVERSIT 2109 ADELBERT ROAD CLEVELAND, OH 44106-4901 Metabolism and DNA adducts of carcinogenic nitroarenes

R01ES-03654-09 (PB) JAFFE, EILEEN K INSTITUTE OF CANCER RESEARCH 7701 BURHOLME AVENUE PHILADELPHIA, PA 19111 Porphobilinogen synthase, probes of the active site

R01ES-03656-05 (PHRA) NOVAK, RAYMOND F WAYNE STATE UNIVERSITY 2727 SECOND AVE DETROIT, MI 48201 Nitrogen heterocycles--Metabolic effects & toxicity

R01ES-03712-07 (RNM) LAI, HENRY C UNIVERSITY OF WASHINGTON SEATTLE, WA 98195 Neural effects of low-level microwaves

R01ES-03719-07 (MEP) WHITLOCK, JAMES P, JR STANFORD UNIVERSITY SCH OF MED STANFORD, CA 94305-5332 Control of gene expression by dioxin

R01ES-03721-07 (PTHB) KANE, AGNES B BROWN UNIVERSITY BOX G PROVIDENCE, RI 02912 Pathogenesis of mesenchymal tumors induced by asbestos

R01ES-03726-07 (TOX) SHANK, RONALD C UNIVERSITY OF CALIFORNIA DEPT OF PHARMACOLOGY IRVINE CA 92717 Environmental hydrazines and methylation of DNA guanine

R01ES-03745-05 (TOX) BURBACHER, THOMAS M SEATTLE, WA 98195 SC-34 Primate developmental effects of methyl mercury

R01ES-03749-07 (TOX) SOKOL, REBECCA Z HARBOR-U C L A MEDICAL CENTER 1000 WEST CARSON ST TORRANCE, CA 90509 Effects of Pb on hypothalamic-pituitary-testicular axis

R01ES-03755-06 (CPA) HARRIS, THOMAS M VANDERBILT UNIVERSITY BOX 1715, STATION B NASHVILLE, TN 37235 Interactions of environmental toxicants with DNA

R01ES-03765-06 (TOX) PARKINSON, ANDREW UNIVERSITY OF KANSAS PHARMACOLOGY/TOXICOLOGY/THERAP KANSAS CITY, KS 66103 Biochemical toxicology of cytochrome P-450

R01ES-03771-07 (PHRA) OKITA, RICHARD T WASHINGTON STATE UNIVERSITY 105 WEGNER HALL PULLMAN, WA 99164-6510 Effects of DEHP on liver

R01ES-03778-07 (PHRA) LAWRENCE, DAVID A ALBANY MEDICAL COLLEGE 47 NEW SCOTLAND AVENUE ALBANY, NY 12208 Cellular thiols--Immunotoxicity

R01ES-03817-10 (PB) WINGE, DENNIS R UNIVERSITY OF UTAH MED CENTER 50 N MEDICAL DR, RM 4C-131 SALT LAKE CITY, UT 84112 Metal chelation in metallothionein

P30ES-03819-06A1 (EHS) CORN, MORTON JOHNS HOPKINS UNIVERSITY 615 NORTH WOLFE ST BALTIMORE, MD 21205 Environmental health sciences core center grant

P30ES-03819-06A1 9001 (EHS) MATANOSKI, GENEVIEVE M Environmental health sciences core center grant Core-- Epidemiology: Exposure assessment

P30ES-03819-06A1 9013 (EHS) BASSETT, DAVID J P Environmental health sciences core center grant Core-- Animal inhalation facility

P30ES-03819-06A1 9014 (EHS) GROOPMAN, JOHN Environmental health sciences core center grant Core-- Molecular dosimetry and biological monitoring

P30ES-03819-06A1 9015 (EHS) YAGER, JAMES Environmental health sciences core center grant Core- Environmental carcinogenesis

P30ES-03819-06A1 9016 (EHS) MITZNER, WAYNE Environmental health sciences core center grant Core-- Physiologic responses to inhaled pollutants

P30ES-03819-06A1 9017 (EHS) ROSE, NOEL R Environmental health sciences core center grant Core-- Cellular and immune mechanisms

P30ES-03819-06A1 9018 (EHS) FECHTER, LAURENCE Environmental health sciences core center grant Neurotoxicology

P30ES-03819-06A1 9019 (EHS) DANNENBERG, A M Environmental health sciences core center grant Core-- Histopathology facility

P30ES-03819-06A1 9020 (EHS) MCMACKEN, R Environmental health sciences core center grant Core-- Oligonucleotide synthesis facility

P30ES-03819-06A1 9021 (EHS) MITZNER, WAYNE A Environmental health sciences core center grant Core-- Machine and electronics shops facility

R13ES-03820-05 (SRC) GOLDSTEIN, BERNARD D UMDNJ-ROBERT W JOHNSON MED SCH 675 HOES LANE PISCATAWAY, NJ 08854 Conference on the safety evaluation of chemicals

P30ES-03828-06 (EHS) EVANS, DAVID H MOUNT DESERT ISLAND BIO LAB OLD BAR HARBOR ROAD SALSBURY COVE, ME 04672 A mfbs SCOR at the Mount Desert Island biological lab

P30ES-03828-06 0003 (EHS) CHARNEY, ALAN N A mfbs SCOR at the Mount Desert Island biological lab Action of copper and zinc on transport of ions in gill and intestinal epithelia

P30ES-03828-06 0004 (EHS) DAWSON, DAVID C A mfbs SCOR at the Mount Desert Island biological lab Heavy metal modification of epithelial potassium transport

P30ES-03828-06 0005 (EHS) GREGER, RAINER F A mfbs SCOR at the Mount Desert Island biological lab Effect of toxins in the isolated in vitro perfused rectal gland tubule

P30ES-03828-06 0006 (EHS) SILVA, PATRICIO A mfbs SCOR at the Mount Desert Island biological lab Isolated rectal gland cells

P30ES-03828-06 0007 (EHS) EPSTEIN, FRANKLIN H A mfbs SCOR at the Mount Desert Island biological lab Studies of intact perfused rectal glands

P30ES-03828-06 0008 (EHS) GOLDSTEIN, LEON A mfbs SCOR at the Mount

Desert Island biological lab Heavy metal effects on nutrient absorption by fish intestine

P30ES-03828-06 0009 (EHS) KINNE, ROLF A mfbs SCOR at the Mount Desert Island biological lab Isolated membranes--Effect of cadmium on renal transport processes

P30ES-03828-06 0010 (EHS) KLEINZELLER, ARNOST A mfbs SCOR at the Mount Desert Island biological lab Effects of mercurials on cell volume regulation in the dogfish rectal gland

P30ES-03828-06 0011 (EHS) SHUTTLEWORTH, TREVOR J A mfbs SCOR at the Mount Desert Island biological lab Effects of cadmium on coupling in ion transporting epithelia

P30ES-03828-06 0012 (EHS) STOKES, JOHN B A mfbs SCOR at the Mount Desert Island biological lab: Effects of cadmium and mercurials on transport properties of the bladder

P30ES-03828-06 0013 (EHS) STOLTE, HILMAR A mfbs SCOR at the Mount Desert Island biological lab Effect of cadmium on the glomerular permeability for proteins in the hagfish

P30ES-03828-06 0014 (EHS) ZADUNAISKY, JOSE A mfbs SCOR at the Mount Desert Island biological lab The epithelia of the eye--Effect of environmental agents

P30ES-03828-06 0001 (EHS) EVANS, DAVID H A mfbs SCOR at the Mount Desert Island biological lab The effects of cadmium on ammonia, H, and HCO3 transport across the fish gill

P30ES-03828-06 0002 (EHS) BOYER, JAMES L A mfbs SCOR at the Mount Desert Island biological lab Biliary transport of methylmercury in elasmobranchs

R01ES-03830-05 (TOX) LOPACHIN, RICHARD M SUNY AT STONY BROOK STONY BROOK, NY 11794 Role of calcium in acrylamide neurotoxicity

R01ES-03832-07 (CPA) HINES, RONALD N WAYNE STATE UNIVERSITY 540 E CANFIELD DETROIT MI 48201 Human cytochrome P450 expression--Environmental effect

R01ES-03843-06 (TOX) SAFE, STEPHEN H TEXAS A&M UNIVERSITY COLLEGE STATION, TX 77843 Mechanism of action of dioxin antagonists

P30ES-03850-07 (EHS) BAILEY, GEORGE S OREGON STATE UNIVERSITY WIEGAND HALL CORVALLIS, OR 97331 NIEHS marine freshwater biomedical sciences center

P30ES-03850-07 0004 (EHS) KAATARRI, STEPHEN L NIEHS marine freshwater biomedical sciences center Pilot--Immunological analysis of hepatocellular carcinomas

P30ES-03850-07 0005 (EHS) MURRAY, THOMAS F NIEHS marine freshwater biomedical sciences center Pilot--Pyrethroid & GABA receptor function in trout brain

P30ES-03850-07 0006 (EHS) SELIVONCHICK, DANIEL P NIEHS marine freshwater biomedical sciences center Pilot--Dietary cyclopropenoid & fatty acid in the insulin receptor

P30ES-03850-07 9002 (EHS) HENDRICKS, JERRY NIEHS marine freshwater biomedical sciences center Aquatic core

R01ES-03863-06 (TOX) ENGER, M DUANE IOWA STATE UNIVERSITY 339 SCIENCE II AMES, IA 50011 Cellular cadmium responses

P01ES-03926-07 (EHS) THILLY, WILLIAM G MASSACHUSETTS INST OF TECHNOLO 77 MASSACHUSETTS AVENUE CAMBRIDGE, MA 02139 Program project grant-- Genetics and toxicology

P01ES-03926-07 0001 (EHS) DEMPLE, BRUCE Program project grant--Genetics and toxicology Biochemical genetics of oxidized DNA repair in yeast

P01ES-03926-07 0003 (EHS) ESSIGMANN, JOHN M Program project grant--Genetics and toxicology Mutagenesis and repair of DNA adducts in mammalian cells

P01ES-03926-07 0004 (EHS) SAMSON, LEONA Program project grant--Genetics and toxicology Inducible responses of human cells to DNA damage

P01ES-03926-07 0005 (EHS) THILLY, WILLIAM G Program project grant--Genetics and toxicology DNA adduct spectrometry

P01ES-03926-07 0006 (EHS) WALKER, GRAHAM C Program project grant--Genetics and toxicology Studies of DNA repair using Rhizobium meliloti

P01ES-03926-07 0007 (EHS) ZARBL, HELMUT Program project grant--Genetics and toxicology In vivo damage, repair, and mutagenesis of cancer genes

R01ES-03928-06 (TOX) BROOKES, NEVILLE UNIVERSITY OF MARYLAND 660 WEST REDWOOD STREET BALTIMORE, MD 21201 Neurotoxic mechanisms in primary CNS cell cultures

R01ES-03933-04 (MEP) EATON, DAVID L UNIVERSITY OF WASHINGTON SEATTLE, WA 98195 Effect of enzyme inducers on liver preneoplastic lesions

R01ES-03938-06 (PHRA) YANG, CHUNG S RUTGERS, THE STATE UNIV OF NJ LABORATORY FOR CANCER RESEARCH PISCATAWAY, N J 08855 Cytochrome P-450ac--Functions and mechanisms of induction

R01ES-03950-04A1 (TOX) JOHNSON, DONALD C UNIV OF KANSAS MEDICAL COLL 39TH & RAINBOW BOULEVARD KANSAS CITY, KS 66103-8410 Environmental toxins and establishment of pregnancy

R01ES-03953-06 (MEP) LOEPPKY, RICHARD N UNIVERSITY OF MISSOURI 123 CHEMISTRY BUILDING COLUMBIA, MO 65211 Carcinogenesis--Highly reactive nitrosamines

R01ES-03954-06 (TOX) GUSTAFSSON, JAN-AKE KAROLINSKA INSTITUTET F60, NOVUM S-141 86 HUDDINGE, SWEDEN Structure and function of the dioxin receptor

R01ES-03966-05 (PHRA) KERKVLIET, NANCY I OREGON STATE UNIVERSITY MAGRUDER HALL CORVALLIS, OR 97331-4802 Immune-endocrine interactions in TCDD toxicity

R01ES-03968-07 (TOX) MAINES, MAHIN D THE UNIVERSITY OF ROCHESTER SCHOOL OF MEDICINE ROCHESTER, N Y 14627 Effect of metals on heme & glutathione metabolism

R01ES-03980-07 (CPA) BRESNICK, EDWARD DARTMOUTH MEDICAL SCHOOL HINMAN BOX 7650 HANOVER, NH 03756 Polycyclic hydrocarbon-induced expression of P450

R29ES-04020-06 (TOX) MUDZINSKI, STANLEY P UNION UNIVERSITY 47 NEW SCOTLAND AVENUE ALBANY, N Y 12208 Immunotoxicologic screening of chemical carcinogens

R01ES-04026-05 (TOX) PETERING, DAVID H UNIVERSITY OF WISCONSIN PO BOX 413 MILWAUKEE, WI 53201 Cadmium, zinc, metallothionein and kidney toxicity

R01ES-04036-07 (BMT) OTVOS, JAMES D NORTH CAROLINA STATE UNIVERSIT PO BOX 7622 RALEIGH, NC 27695 NMR studies of metallothionein structure and reactivity

R01ES-04039-06 (SOH) ROSEN, JOHN F MONTEFIORE MEDICAL CENTER 111 EAST 210TH STREET BRONX, NY 10467 Treatment outcomes in moderately lead toxic children

R01ES-04040-04A1 (PHRA) POUNDS, JOEL G WAYNE STATE UNIVERSITY 2727 SECOND AVE DETROIT, MI 48201 Cellular interactions of lead, calcium, and zinc

R01ES-04041-06 (HED) JUCHAU, MONT R UNIVERSITY OF WASHINGTON SJ-30 SEATTLE, WA 98195 Embryotoxicity of environmental chemicals

R01ES-04050-06 (MBC) CHAKRABARTY, ANANDA M UNIVERSITY OF ILLINOIS MED CTR PO BOX 6998 CHICAGO, IL 60612 Microbial degradation of agent orange

R01ES-04066-06 (TOX) MAINES, MAHIN D UNIVERSITY OF ROCHESTER 601 ELMWOOD AVENUE ROCHESTER, NY 14627 Biliverdin reductase--multiplicity & control by toxins

P01ES-04068-05 (EHS) GROLLMAN, ARTHUR P SUNY AT STONY BROOK SCH OF MED, HLTH SCI CENTER STONY BROOK, N Y 11794-8651 Molecular toxicology of DNA adducts

P01ES-04068-05 0001 (EHS) JOHNSON, FRANCIS Molecular toxicology of DNA adducts Synthesis of oligodeoxynucleotides bearing mutagens as site-specified adducts

P01ES-04068-05 0002 (EHS) GROLLMAN, ARTHUR P Molecular toxicology of DNA adducts Mechanisms of chemical mutagenesis

P01ES-04068-05 0003 (EHS) BOGENHAGEN, DANIEL Molecular toxicology of DNA adducts Effects of DNA adducts on transcription by eukaryotic RNA polymerases

P01ES-04068-05 0004 (EHS) FISHER, PAUL Molecular toxicology of DNA adducts Studies on DNA polymerase alpha and delta

P01ES-04068-05 0006 (EHS) EISENBERG, MOSHE Molecular toxicology of DNA adducts Molecular modeling of DNA adducts and other lesions

P01ES-04068-05 9001 (EHS) IDEN, CHARLES Molecular toxicology of DNA adducts Core--Core component

R01ES-04070-06 (TOX) WOODRUFF, MICHAEL L EAST TENNESSEE STATE UNIV PO BOX BOX 19,960A JOHNSON CITY, TN 37614 Trimethyltin behavioral toxicity and neural grafting

R01ES-04072-06 (TOX) FULLMER, CURTIS S CORNELL UNIVERSITY DEPARTMENT OF PHYSIOLOGY ITHACA, NY 14853 Intestinal interactions of lead and calcium

R01ES-04074-03 (BMT) BROUWER, MARIUS DUKE UNIVERSITY MARINE LAB PIVERS ISLAND BEAUFORT, NC 28516 Biological function of copper-metallothionein

R01ES-04087-06 (BMT) FRENKEL, GERALD D RUTGERS UNIVERSITY 101 WARREN STREET NEWARK, NJ 07102 Interactions of selenium and sulfhydryl compounds

R01ES-04090-04A1 (TOX) SUSZKIW, JANUSZ B UNIVERSITY OF CINCINNATI 231 BETHESDA AVE CINCINNATI, OH 45267-0576 Calcium-surrogate actions of lead ions in secretion

R01ES-04091-05 (BIO) LLOYD, ROBERT S VANDERBILT UNIVERSITY 21ST AVENUE AT GARLAND NASHVILLE, TN 37232-0146 T4 endonuclease V--Structure-function analyses

R01ES-04092-04A1 (CPA) REED, GREGORY A UNIV OF KANSAS MEDICAL CENTER 39TH AND RAINBOW BLVD KANSAS CITY, KS 66103-8410 Genotoxicity of benzo[a]pyrene derivatives and sulfite

R01ES-04099-04 (TOX) HASTINGS, LLOYD UNIVERSITY OF CINCINNATI 3223 EDEN AVENUE CINCINNATI, OH 45267-0056 Sensory neurotoxicology - toxic metals and olfaction

R01ES-04106-05 (RAD) SMERDON, MICHAEL J WASHINGTON STATE UNIVERSITY BIOCHEM/BIOPHYSICS PROGRAM PULLMAN, WA 99164-4660 DNA repair in a hormone-responsive gene

R01ES-04112-05 (SOH) ROSS, DAVID UNIVERSITY OF COLORADO CAMPUS BOX 297 BOULDER, CO 80309-0297 Metabolic basis of benzene-induced myelotoxicity

R01ES-04132-03 (TOX) CHAN, LEE-NIEN L UNIV OF TEXAS MEDICAL BRANCH 301 UNIVERSITY BOULEVARD GALVESTON, TX 77550 Multigeneration effects of paternal mutagen exposure

R01ES-04140-06 (TOX) ISOM, GARY E PURDUE UNIVERSITY DEPT PHARM & TOXICOLOGY W LAFAYETTE, IN 47907 Cyanide-induced neurotoxicity

R01ES-04151-06 (MBY) KARIN, MICHAEL UNIV OF CALIFORNIA, SAN DIEGO DEPT OF PHARMACOLOGY, M-036 LA JOLLA, CA 92093 Interactions of heavy metal ions with the human genome

R01ES-04176-03 (TOX) SAFE, STEPHEN H TEXAS A&M UNIVERSITY COLLEGE STATION, TX 77843 Effects of 2,3,7,8-TCDD on estrogenic responses

P30ES-04184-05 (EHS) PETERING, DAVID H UNIV OF WISCONSIN POST OFFICE BOX 413 MILWAUKEE, WI 53201 Marine and freshwater biomedical core center

R01ES-04187-04A1 (RNM) JOHNSON, G ALLAN DUKE UNIVERSITY MEDICAL CENTER BOX 3302 DURHAM, NC 27710 In vivo assay of environmental toxins with MR microscopy

R01ES-04190-05 (TOX) GOLUB, MARI S UNIVERSITY OF CALIFORNIA DAVIS, CA 95616 A mouse model for chronic oral aluminum toxicity

R01ES-04202-05 (EDC) KRIEBEL, DAVID UNIVERSITY OF LOWELL ONE UNIVERSITY AVENUE LOWELL, MA 01854 Epidemiologic methods for estimating airborne exposures

R01ES-04203-05 (CPA) WARSHAWSKY, DAVID UNIV OF CINCINNATI COLL OF MED 3223 EDEN AVENUE CINCINNATI, OH 45267-0056 Metabolic activation of n-heterocyclic aromatics

R01ES-04214-05 (REN) THOMAS, PETER UNIVERSITY OF TEXAS P O BOX 1267 PORT ARANSAS, TX 78373-1267 Endocrine effects of reproductive toxins in female fish

R01ES-04220-05 (SRC) STEGEMAN, JOHN J WOODS HOLE OCEANOGRAPHIC INST REDFIELD 3 WOODS HOLE, MA 02543 Cytochrome P-450 isozymes in non-mammalian species

R01ES-04244-06 (TOX) PROUGH, RUSSELL A UNIV OF LOUISVILLE MED SCHOOL DEPARTMENT OF BIOCHEMISTRY LOUISVILLE, KY 40292 Effects of toxic chemicals on fetal adrenal and liver

R01ES-04249-05 (TOX) ROTH, JEROME A SUNY AT BUFFALO 102 FARBER HALL BUFFALO, N Y 14214 Effects of 03 and N02 on lung macrophage phagocytosis

R29ES-04262-06 (TOX) WALSH, THOMAS J RUTGERS UNIVERSITY DEPARTMENT OF PSYCHOLOGY NEW BRUNSWICK, N J 08903 Alterations in brain dopamine systems following triethyllead exposure

R01ES-04266-05 (CPA) HARVEY, RONALD G UNIVERSITY OF CHICAGO

PROJECT NO., ORGANIZATIONAL UNIT., INVESTIGATOR, ADDRESS, TITLE

5841 SOUTH MARYLAND AVE CHICAGO, IL 60637 Nonalternant carcinogenic polycyclic hydrocarbons

R29ES-04299-05 (PC) MATTS, ROBERT L OKLAHOMA STATE UNIV STILLWATER, OK 74078-0454 Effect of heavy metal ions on eukaryotic protein synthes is

R29ES-04302-04 (CPA) COONEY, ROBERT V UNIVERSITY OF HAWAII, MANOA 1236 LAUHALA ST HONOLULU, HAWAII 96813 Analysis of carcinogen formation by inhaled nitrogen

R01ES-04311-05 (TOX) BUCKPITT, ALAN R UNIVERSITY OF CALIFORNIA SCHOOL OF VETERINARY MEDICINE DAVIS, CA 95616 Mechanisms of lung injury by napthalenes

R01ES-04312-05 (HED) KLEIN, NORMAN W UNIVERSITY OF CONNECTICUT U-39, 3636 HORSEBARN RD EXT STORRS, CT 06269-4039 Pollutants, laminin antibody and reproductive failure

R01ES-04317-05 (RAP) YEATES, DONOVAN B UNIV OF ILLINOIS AT CHICAGO 1940 W TAYLOR ST CHICAGO, IL 60612 Regulation of ciliary beat

R29ES-04337-06 (TOX) RODGERS, KATHLEEN E LIVINGSTON REPRODUCTIVE LAB 1321 N MISSION RD RM 110 LOS ANGELES, CA 90033 Molecular mechanisms of organophosphate immunotoxicity

R29ES-04344-04 (SOH) BACKES, WAYNE L LOUISIANA STATE UNIVERSITY 1901 PERDIDO ST NEW ORLEANS, LA 70112 Toxicological significance of alkylbenzene metabolism

R01ES-04348-06 (TOX) SCHOOK, LAWRENCE B UNIVERSITY OF ILLINOIS 1201 WEST GREGORY DRIVE URBANA, IL 61801 Dimethylnitrosamine effects on cellular immunity

R01ES-04356-06 (HAR) GREEN, BARRY G MONELL CHEMICAL SENSES CENTER 3500 MARKET STREET PHILADELPHIA, PA 19104 Common chemicals and cutaneous sensitivity

R01ES-04360-06 (TOX) LAMARTINIERE, CORAL A UNIVERSITY OF ALABAMA UAB STATION BIRMINGHAM, AL 35294 Altered metabolism and carcinogenesis by DES

R01ES-04362-05 (TOX) CARLSON, GARY P PURDUE UNIVERSITY SCH OF PHARMACY & PHARMACAL SC WEST LAFAYETTE, IN 47907 Ethanol and xenobiotic metbolism and toxicity in lung

R37ES-04391-05 (TOX) MAINES, MAHIN D THE UNIVERSITY OF ROCHESTER SCHOOL OF MEDICINE ROCHESTER, N Y 14627 Multiple forms of heme oxygenase--Regulation by toxins

R01ES-04394-05 (PHRA) CHAMBERS, JANICE E MISSISSIPPI STATE UNIVERSITY PO DRAWER GY MISSISSIPPI STATE, MS 39762 Phosphorothionate insecticide activation by rat brain

R01ES-04400-05 (TOX) CLARKSON, THOMAS W UNIV OF ROCHESTER SCH OF MED P. O. BOX BPHYS ROCHESTER, NY 14642 Mechanisms of hepatobiliary transport of mercury

R29ES-04402-05 (HED) COLLINS, MICHAEL D CHILDREN'S HOSP RES FDN ELLAND & BETHESDA AVENUE CINCINNATI, OH 45229 Neural tube defects induced by anions via increased intracellular pH

R29ES-04410-05 (TOX) SCHNELLMANN, RICKY G UNIV OF GEORGIA DEPT OF PHYSIOLOGY & PHARMACOL ATHENS, GA 30602 Mechanism of nephrotoxicity of environmental halocarbons

R29ES-04413-04 (TOX) HAZEN-MARTIN, DEBRA J MEDICAL UNIV / SOUTH CAROLINA 171 ASHLEY AVENUE CHARLESTON, S C 29425 Cadmium nephrotoxicity a cell culture approach

R01ES-04422-05 (TOX) DAHL, ALAN R LOVELACE BIOMED/ENVIRON RES IN PO BOX 5890 ALBUQUERQUE, NM 87185 Fate of inhaled vapors in rats, dogs and monkeys

R29ES-04424-05 (REN) CARUSO, RITA L UNIVERSITY OF MICHIGAN 109 S OBSERVATORY ANN ARBOR, MI 48109-2029 Cell-cell communication in myometrial cultures

R29ES-04427-05 (TOX) BOLLA-WILSON, KAREN JOHNS HOPKINS MEDICAL INST 4940 EASTERN AVENUE BALTIMORE, MD 21224 Neurologic effects of environmental aluminum exposure

R29ES-04433-05 (SOH) SODERHOLM, SIDNEY C UNIVERSITY OF ROCHESTER 601 ELMWOOD AVENUE ROCHESTER, NEW YORK 14642 Deposition of volatile aerosols in the respiratory tract

R29ES-04434-05 (SOH) THOMPSON, CHARLES M LOYOLA UNIVERSITY OF CHICAGO 6525 N SHERIDAN ROAD CHICAGO, IL 60626 Stereodependent intoxication by thiophosphorus esters

R01ES-04435-04A1 (TOX) SHIVERICK, KATHLEEN T UNIVERSITY OF FLORIDA BOX J-267 JHMHC GAINESVILLE, FL 32610-0267 Effects of polyaromatic compounds on placental proteins

R01ES-04595-05 (SRC) SPEIZER, FRANK E HARVARD SCH OF PUBLIC HEALTH 665 HUNTINGTON AVENUE BOSTON, MA 02115 Acid aerosol health effects in North American children

R01ES-04612-04S1 (SRC) THURSTON, GEORGE D NEW YORK UNIVERSITY MED CENTER LONG MEADOW RD TUXEDO, NY 10987 Acid aerosol exposure--Effect on respiratory morbidity in New York State

R01ES-04616-04 (TOX) CARTER, DEAN E UNIVERSITY OF ARIZONA COLLEGE OF PHARMACY TUCSON, AZ 85721 Disposition metabolism and toxicity of haloaldehydes

R01ES-04623-04 (TOX) MILO, GEORGE E OHIO STATE UNIV-RESEARCH FDN 1645 NEIL AVE COLUMBUS, OHIO 43210 B(a)p-metabolism & modification of DNA in skin xenograft

R01ES-04628-04 (TOX) SCHUETZ, ERIN VA COMMONWEALTH UNIVERSITY BOX 267, MCV STATION RICHMOND, VA 23298 Regulation of cytochrome P-450b/e in hepatocyte cultures

R01ES-04640-01A2 (TOX) YOKEL, ROBERT A UNIVERSITY OF KENTUCKY ROSE STREET RM 509 LEXINGTON, KY 40536-0082 Aluminum toxicity--Chelator identification and safety

R01ES-04662-05 (TOX) MONKS, TERRANCE J UNIVERSITY OF TEXAS AUSTIN, TX 78712-1074 Toxicology of quinone-thioethers

P42ES-04675-05 (SRC) THILLY, WILLIAM G MASSACHUSETTS INST OF TECHNOLO 77 MASSACHUSETTS AVENUE CAMBRIDGE, MA 02139 MIT superfund hazardous substances basic research program

P42ES-04675-05 0001 (SRC) THILLY, WILLIAM MIT superfund hazardous substances basic research program Measurement of human mutational spectra

P42ES-04675-05 0002 (SRC) WOGAN, G N MIT superfund hazardous substances basic research program Mutational spectra identification in DNA of human tissue

P42ES-04675-05 0003 (SRC) TANNENBAUM, S MIT superfund hazardous substances basic research program Identification of preoncogenic mutations in human tissue

P42ES-04675-05 0004 (SRC) BIEMANN, K MIT superfund hazardous substances basic research program Identification of adducts to cysteine residues in human hemoglobin

P42ES-04696-05 (SRC) EATON, DAVID L UNIVERSITY OF WASHINGTON SC-34 SEATTLE, WA 98195 Effect-related monitors of toxic exposures

P42ES-04696-05 0001 (SRC) EATON, D Effect-related monitors of toxic exposures Glutathione perturbations with toxic exposures

P42ES-04696-05 0002 (SRC) WOODS, J S Effect-related monitors of toxic exposures Porphyrin profiles as biological indicators of trace metal exposure & toxicity

P42ES-04696-05 0003 (SRC) COSTA, L S Effect-related monitors of toxic exposures Peripheral markers of potential neurotoxic chemicals

P42ES-04696-05 0004 (SRC) OMIECINSKI, C I Effect-related monitors of toxic exposures Modeling chemical exposure by fingerprinting of cytochrome P-450 gene expression

P42ES-04696-05 0005 (SRC) FAUSTMAN, E Effect-related monitors of toxic exposures Embryotoxic interactions of toxic waste site chemicals

P42ES-04699-05 (SRC) HAMMOCK, BRUCE D UNIVERSITY OF CALIFORNIA 303 BRIGGS HALL DAVIS, CA 95616 Biomarkers of exposure to hazardous substances

P42ES-04699-05 0001 (SRC) SEIBER, J N Biomarkers of exposure to hazardous substances Analytical assessment of airborne emissions from hazardous waste sites

P42ES-04699-05 0002 (SRC) HINTON, D E Biomarkers of exposure to hazardous substances Genotoxicity screening of chemical wastes

P42ES-04699-05 0004 (SRC) BUCKPITT, A B Biomarkers of exposure to hazardous substances Biomarkers for metabolically activated cytotoxic agents

P42ES-04699-05 0005 (SRC) HAMMOCK, B D Biomarkers of exposure to hazardous substances Immunoassays for human and evironmental exposure

P42ES-04699-05 0006 (SRC) KURTH, M J Biomarkers of exposure to hazardous substances Immunoassays for toxic waste substances

P42ES-04699-05 0007 (SRC) SHIBAMOTO, T Biomarkers of exposure to hazardous substances Metabolism and toxicity of 1,3-dinitrobenzene

P42ES-04699-05 0008 (SRC) KATZ, D J Biomarkers of exposure to hazardous substances Methods for assessment of environmental hazards to male fertility

P42ES-04699-05 0009 (SRC) LASLEY, B Biomarkers of exposure to hazardous substances Biomarkers for assessing environmental hazards to female reproduction

P42ES-04699-05 9001 (SRC) SHULL, L R Biomarkers of exposure to hazardous substances Core--cell culture laboratory

P42ES-04699-05 9002 (SRC) KURTH, M J Biomarkers of exposure to hazardous substances Hybridoma and immunoassay core

P42ES-04699-05 9003 (SRC) SCHENKER, M B Biomarkers of exposure to hazardous substances Biological markers of exposure to hazardous waste among human population--Core

P42ES-04705-05 (SRC) SMITH, MARTYN T UNIVERSITY OF CALIFORNIA 322 WARREN HALL BERKELEY, CA 94720 Health effects of toxic substances

P42ES-04705-05 0001 (SRC) SMITH, MARTYN Health effects of toxic substances Metabolism, toxicokinetics and genotoxicity of benzene and its phenol metabolites

P42ES-04705-05 0002 (SRC) STEPHEN, RAPPAPORT Health effects of toxic substances Exposure-response for airborne genotoxins

P42ES-04705-05 0003 (SRC) BODELL, WILLIAM Health effects of toxic substances DNA adducts as molecular dosimeters of genotoxins

P42ES-04705-05 0004 (SRC) WIENCKE, JOHN Health effects of toxic substances Correlation of cytogenetic damage with DNA adducts in lymphocytes

P42ES-04705-05 0005 (SRC) HAAS, ROBERT Health effects of toxic substances Methods development--Exposure to benzene, styrene, and vinyl chloride

P42ES-04705-05 0006 (SRC) BURLINGAME, A. Health effects of toxic substances Characterization of DNA and protein covalent adducts by LSIMS and GC/MS

P42ES-04705-05 0007 (SRC) DRAPER, WILLIAM Health effects of toxic substances Quantation of chemical exposure by thermospray

P42ES-04705-05 0008 (SRC) TOZER, THOMAS Health effects of toxic substances Toxicokinetics of primary environmental pollutants

P42ES-04705-05 0009 (SRC) SPEAR, ROBERT Health effects of toxic substances Modelling variability in chemical exposure and response

P42ES-04705-05 0010 (SRC) BECKER, CHARLES Health effects of toxic substances Human studies of the effects of halocarbon exposure

P42ES-04705-05 0011 (SRC) WEI, EDWARD Health effects of toxic substances Inhibition of inflammatory response to chemical injury

R01ES-04715-03 (CPA) COSTA, MAX NEW YORK UNIV MEDICAL CENTER 550 FIRST AVE NEW YORK, NY 10016 DNA: Protein crosslinking by the carcinogen chromate

R29ES-04722-04 (TOX) SARAFIAN, THEODORE A UCLA SCHOOL OF MEDICINE 13-385 CHS LOS ANGELES CA 90024-1406 Methyl mercury & neuronal protein phosphorylation /rats/

R55ES-04725-04A1 (HED) ANDREWS, GLEN K UNIVERSITY OF KANSAS MED CTR 39TH AND RAINBOW BLVD KANSAS CITY, KS 66103-8410 Metallothionein--Regulation and role in embryogenesis

R01ES-04728-03 (MGN) SHORT, JAY M STRATAGENE, INC. 11099 NORTH TORREY PINES RD. LA JOLLA, CA 92037 Model for identification of genetic lesions

R01ES-04732-04 (CPA) HARVEY, RONALD G UNIVERSITY OF CHICAGO 5841 S MARYLAND AVE, BOX 424 CHICAGO, ILL 60637 Oligonucleotide adducts of carcinogenic hydrocarbons

R01ES-04738-03 (SOH) LASKIN, DEBRA L RUTGERS UNIV COLL OF PHARMACY PISCATAWAY, N J 08854 Activated macrophages and ozone toxicity

R01ES-04751-03 (TOX) CHOU, IIH-NAN BOSTON UNIVERSITY 80 EAST CONCORD STREET BOSTON, MASS 02118 Cytoskeletal injury & mechanism of herbicide toxicity

R01ES-04757-03 (EDC) VEDAL, SVERRE VANCOUVER GENERAL HOSPITAL 2775 HEATHER STREET VANCOUVER, BC V5Z 3J5 CANADA Inhalable particle pollution and chilhood asthma

R01ES-04758-03 (TOX) BARNETT, JOHN B UNIVERSITY OF ARKANSAS 4301 W MARKHAM STREET LITTLE ROCK, AR 72205 Immunotoxicity of propanil and tetrachloroazobenzene

R01ES-04762-02 (TOX) ANGLE, CAROL R UNIV OF NEBRASKA MED CENTER 600 SOUTH 42ND STREET OMAHA, NE 68198-6055 Childhood blood lead--Air, soil and dust sources

P01ES-04766-04 (EHS) BAILEY, GEORGE S OREGON STATE UNIVERSITY WIEGAND HALL CORVALLIS, OR 97331 Rainbow trout: A model for environmental carcinogenesis

P01ES-04766-04 0001 (EHS) BAILEY, GEORGE S. Rainbow trout: A model for environmental carcinogenesis Carcinogenicity of four aflatoxins: Molecular mechanisms

P01ES-04766-04 0002 (EHS) BUHLER, DONALD R. Rainbow trout: A model for environmental carcinogenesis Development changes in xenobiotic metabolizing enzymes

P01ES-04766-04 0003 (EHS) CURTIS, LAWRENCE R. Rainbow trout: A model for environmental carcinogenesis Temperature-modulated actions of genotoxins

P01ES-04766-04 0004 (EHS) HENDRICKS, JERRY D. Rainbow trout: A model for environmental carcinogenesis Embryonic inhibitor/promotor studies and model development

P01ES-04766-04 0005 (EHS) THORGAARD, GARY H. Rainbow trout: A model for environmental carcinogenesis Generation and analysis of homozygous clones

P01ES-04766-04 0006 (EHS) VAN HOLDE, KENSAL E. Rainbow trout: A model for environmental carcinogenesis Genotoxic agents and chromatin structure

P01ES-04766-04 0007 (EHS) WILLIAMS, DAVID E. Rainbow trout: A model for environmental carcinogenesis Peroxidative pathways of carcinogenesis

R29ES-04787-03 (EDC) MARBURY, MARIAN C MINNESOTA DEPT OF HEALTH 717 DELAWARE ST S E, PO BOX 94 MINNEAPOLIS, MN 55440 Epidemiology of respiratory illness & indoor pollution

R01ES-04802-04 (TOX) HIRATA, FUSAO WAYNE STATE UNIVERSITY 528 SHAPERO HALL DETROIT, MI 48202 Molecular mechanism of immunotoxic action of TCDD & DTT

R01ES-04803-04 (TOX) BERNDT, WILLIAM O UNIVERSITY OF NEBRASKA MED CTR 600 SOUTH 42ND ST OMAHA, NE 68198-6810 Effects of xenobiotics on renal membrane transport

R01ES-04804-03 (TOX) HOLIAN, ANDRIJ UNIV OF TEXAS HEALTH SCI CENTE PO BOX 20036 HOUSTON, TX 77225 Effects of silica and asbestos on macrophage function

R01ES-04814-06 (TOX) HOLICK, MICHAEL F BOSTON UNIVERSITY SCH OF MED 80 EAST CONCORD ST, 10TH FLOOR BOSTON, MA 02118 A new approach for evaluating bone toxicity

R01ES-04840-03 (TOX) FOULKES, ERNEST C UNIVERSITY OF CINCINNATI 3223 EDEN AVENUE CINCINNATI, OH 45267-0056 Reactions of heavy metals with epithelial cells

R01ES-04843-04 (EDC) KREISS, KATHLEEN NATIONAL JEWISH HOSP/RES CTR 1400 JACKSON STREET DENVER, CO 80206-1997 Epidemiology of immunologic lung disease

R01ES-04849-05 (TOX) RAMOS, KENNETH S TEXAS A & M UNIVERSITY COLLEGE STATION, TX 77843 In vivo-in vitro correlates of vascular toxicity

R01ES-04855-04 (EDC) LYON, JOSEPH L UNIVERSITY OF UTAH 50 N MEDICAL DR SALT LAKE CITY, UT 84132 Radon progeny & risk of lung cancer

R29ES-04857-04 (TOX) LERTRATANANGKOON, KHINGKAN THE UNIV OF TEXAS MED BRANCH DEPT OF PHAR & TOXICOLOGY GALVESTON, TX 77550 The glutathione pathway to the formation of phenols

R01ES-04860-01A3 (TOX) LAUGHLIN, NELLIE K HARLOW PRIMATE LABORATORY 22 NORTH CHARTER STREET MADISON, WI 53715 Lead effects on the auditory system in monkeys

R01ES-04862-02 (TOX) GASIEWICZ, THOMAS A UNIVERSITY OF ROCHESTER ROCHESTER, NY 14642 Effect of TCDD on thymic lymphocyte differentiation

R01ES-04863-04 (TOX) CASIDA, JOHN E UNIVERSITY OF CALIFORNIA 114 WELLMAN HALL BERKELEY, CALIF 94720 Reactive intermediates in toxicant action

R29ES-04869-03 (TOX) PERDEW, GARY H PURDUE UNIVERSITY STONE HALL WEST LAFAYETTE, IN 47907 Biochemical characterization of the Ah receptor

R01ES-04872-04 (TOX) OBERDOERSTER, GUENTER UNIVERSITY OF ROCHESTER SCH OF MEDICINE AND DENTISTRY ROCHESTER, N Y 14642 Mechanisms of chronic lung injury by inhaled particles

R55ES-04875-04 (RAD) KRIPKE, MARGARET L UNIVERSITY OF TEXAS 1515 HOLCOMBE BLVD BOX 178 HOUSTON, TX 77030 Effects of UV exposure on the pathogenesis of disease

R01ES-04889-04 (RAD) EISENSTARK, ABRAHAM CANCER RESEARCH CENTER 3501 BERRYWOOD DRIVE COLUMBIA, MO 65201 Environmental effects of near-UV radiation on bacteria

P42ES-04895-03 (SRC) COSTA, MAX NEW YORK UNIV MEDICAL CENTER 550 FIRST AVE NEW YORK, NY 10016 Detect and predict human exposure to toxic chemicals

P42ES-04895-03 9002 (SRC) SNYDER, CARROLL A. Detect and predict human exposure to toxic chemicals Core --Exposure, analytical chemistry and biostatistics

P42ES-04895-03 0001 (SRC) TROLL, WALTER Detect and predict human exposure to toxic chemicals Neutrophil assay of exposure to toxins

P42ES-04895-03 0002 (SRC) SNYDER, CARROL A. Detect and predict human exposure to toxic chemicals Immune function assays as indicators of toxiant exposure

P42ES-04895-03 0003 (SRC) GARTE, SEYMOUR J. Detect and predict human exposure to toxic chemicals Molecular assays for toxicant exposure

P42ES-04895-03 0004 (SRC) COSTA, MAX Detect and predict human exposure to toxic chemicals

P42ES-04895-03 0005 (SRC) CHRISTIE, NELWYN T. Detect and predict human exposure to toxic chemicals Development of genotoxic assays in lymphocytes

P42ES-04895-03 0006 (SRC) ROSSMAN, TOBY G. Detect and predict human exposure to toxic chemicals Mutagens and mutagenic metabolites in blood

P42ES-04895-03 0007 (SRC) EVANS, HUGH Detect and predict human exposure to toxic chemicals Correlations between behavior and CNS-specific proteins

P42ES-04895-03 0008 (SRC) BURNS, FREDERIC J. Detect and predict human exposure to toxic chemicals Hair follicle keratinocytes as indicators of toxic and carcinogenic exposure

P42ES-04895-03 0009 (SRC) O'CONNOR, JOSEPH M. Detect and predict human exposure to toxic chemicals Bioconcentration and bioaccumulation of chemicals in striped bass

P42ES-04895-03 0010 (SRC) YOUNG, LILY Y. Detect and predict human exposure to toxic chemicals Biodegradation of benzene, xylene and toluene

P42ES-04895-03 0011 (SRC) FRENKEL, KRYSTYNA Detect and predict human exposure to toxic chemicals Effect of chemical exposure on macrophage functions of fish

P42ES-04895-03 0012 (SRC) DITORO, DOMINIC M. Detect and predict human exposure to toxic chemicals Predicting toxic metal sorption

P42ES-04895-03 0013 (SRC) THOMANN, ROBERT V. Detect and predict human exposure to toxic chemicals Modeling and control of chemical exposure in water

P42ES-04895-03 9001 (SRC) SHORE, ROY Detect and predict human exposure to toxic chemicals Core -- Human subjects

P42ES-04908-03 (SRC) LOPER, JOHN C UNIVERSITY OF CINCINNATI 3233 EDEN AVE CINCINNATI, OH 45267-0056 Hazardous substances basic research program

P42ES-04908-03 0001 (SRC) LOPER, JOHN C HAZARDOUS SUBSTANCES BASIC RESEARCH PROGRAM Detoxification of recalcitrant wastes by p-450 system

P42ES-04908-03 0002 (SRC) TABOR, M WILSON HAZARDOUS SUBSTANCES BASIC RESEARCH PROGRAM Toxicity of by-products in the aerobic degradation of azo dyes

P42ES-04908-03 0003 (SRC) WARSHAWSKY, DAVID HAZARDOUS SUBSTANCES BASIC RESEARCH PROGRAM Microbial degradation of polycyclic and N-cyclic aromatic hydrocarbons

P42ES-04908-03 0004 (SRC) BISHOP, PAUL HAZARDOUS SUBSTANCES BASIC RESEARCH PROGRAM Use of microbial bioreactors for biodegradation of hazardous substances

P42ES-04908-03 0005 (SRC) CARUSE, JOSEPH A HAZARDOUS SUBSTANCES BASIC RESEARCH PROGRAM Ultratrace methods for environmental samples by plasma mass spectrometry

P42ES-04911-03 (SRC) FISCHER, LAWRENCE J MICHIGAN STATE UNIVERSITY C-231 HOLDEN HALL EAST LANSING, MI 48824-1206 Health hazards from groundwater contamination

P42ES-04911-03 0001 (SRC) TIEDJE, JAMES M Health hazards from groundwater contamination Biodegradation of volatile organic compounds

P42ES-04911-03 0002 (SRC) VOICE, THOMAS Health hazards from groundwater contamination Bio-activated carbon absorption columns for contaminated water supply treatment

P42ES-04911-03 0003 (SRC) BOYD, STEPHEN A Health hazards from groundwater contamination Modified clays for sorption and catalytic degradation of VOCs

P42ES-04911-03 0004 (SRC) WALLACE, ROGER B Health hazards from groundwater contamination Volatile organic contaminants--quantifying their movement in the unsaturated zone

P42ES-04911-03 0005 (SRC) ABRIOLA, LINDA M Health hazards from groundwater contamination Modeling volatilization and vapor transport of contaminants in the subsurface

P42ES-04911-03 0006 (SRC) ABRIOLA, LINDA M Health hazards from groundwater contamination Mass transfer reactions between VOCs, aqueous & vapor phases in the subsurface

P42ES-04911-03 0007 (SRC) ROTH, ROBERT A Health hazards from groundwater contamination Volatile organic chemicals and neutrophil function

P42ES-04911-03 0008 (SRC) DUKELOW, W RICHARD Health hazards from groundwater contamination: Toxic chemical influences on reproduction in vivo & in vitro

P42ES-04911-03 0009 (SRC) TROSKO, JAMES E Health hazards from groundwater contamination Molecular and Cellular mechanisms of carcinogenesis

P42ES-04911-03 9001 (SRC) VOICE, THOMAS Health hazards from groundwater contamination Analytical core

P42ES-04911-03 9002 (SRC) FISCHER, LAWRENCE J Health hazards from groundwater contamination Training core

P42ES-04913-02 (SRC) CARPENTER, DAVID O RESEARCH FOUNDATION OF SUNY TWO UNIVERSITY PLACE ALBANY NY 12203-3399 Multidisciplinary study of PCBs and PCDFs at a waste site

P42ES-04913-02 0001 (SRC) FITZGERALD, EDWARD F Multidisciplinary study of PCBs and PCDFs at a waste site PCBs, PCDDs, and PCDFs from toxic waste in a population of native Americans

P42ES-04913-02 0002 (SRC) SEEGAL, RICHARD F Multidisciplinary study of PCBs and PCDFs at a waste site Developmental neurochemical effects of exposure to PCBs and PCDFs

P42ES-04913-02 0003 (SRC) JAHAN-PARWAR, BEHRUS Multidisciplinary study of PCBs and PCDFs at a waste site Neurobehavioral effects of PCBs

P42ES-04913-02 0004 (SRC) MCDOWELL, WILLIAM H Multidisciplinary study of PCBs and PCDFs at a waste site Degradation of PCBs in an anaerobic digestor

P42ES-04913-02 0005 (SRC) TAVLARIDES, LAWRENCE Multidisciplinary study of PCBs and PCDFs at a waste site Supercritical extraction & wet oxidation elimination of PCBs, PCDDs, and PCDFs

P42ES-04913-02 0006 (SRC) CLEMENCE, SAMUEL P Multidisciplinary study of PCBs and PCDFs at a waste site Transport and fate of organic contaminants through soil/rock systems

P42ES-04913-02 0007 (SRC) BUSH, BRIAN Multidisciplinary study of PCBs and PCDFs at a waste site New PCB, PCDD, PCDF sampling methods for humans

P42ES-04913-02 9001 (SRC) CARPENTER, DAVID Multidisciplinary study of PCBs and PCDFs at a waste site Core--Analytical

P42ES-04917-03 (SRC) SAFE, STEPHEN H TEXAS A & M UNIVERSITY BOX 3578 COLLEGE STATION, TX 77843 Procedures to assess the hazard of a Superfund site

P42ES-04917-03 0004 (SRC) PHILLIPS, T D PROCEDURES TO ASSESS THE HAZARD OF A SUPERFUND SITE Detection of hazards associated with chemical wastes

P42ES-04917-03 0005 (SRC) RANDERATH, K PROCEDURES TO ASSESS THE HAZARD OF A SUPERFUND SITE Halogenated aryl hydrocarbons--Mechanism of carcinogenicity

P42ES-04917-03 0006 (SRC) BROWN, K W PROCEDURES TO ASSESS THE

PROJECT NO., ORGANIZATIONAL UNIT., INVESTIGATOR, ADDRESS, TITLE

HAZARD OF A SUPERFUND SITE Bioassays to assess the hazard of uncontrolled hazardous waste sites

P42ES-04917-03 0001 (SRC) GIAM, C S PROCEDURES TO ASSESS THE HAZARD OF A SUPERFUND SITE Bioassay of hazardous organic chemicals in waste contaminated environments

P42ES-04917-03 0002 (SRC) SAFE, S H PROCEDURES TO ASSESS THE HAZARD OF A SUPERFUND SITE Development of bioassays for toxic halogenated aromatics

P42ES-04917-03 0003 (SRC) BUSBEE, D L PROCEDURES TO ASSESS THE HAZARD OF A SUPERFUND SITE Development of bioassay for hazard assessment at a waste site

P42ES-04922-03 (SRC) AUST, STEVEN D UTAH STATE UNIVERSITY LOGAN UT 84322-4430 Biological hazardous waste management

P42ES-04922-03 0001 (SRC) AUST, STEVEN D Biological hazardous waste management Optimization of biodegradation

P42ES-04922-03 0002 (SRC) BUMPUS, JOHN A Biological hazardous waste management Enzymology of fungal and mammalian peroxides

P42ES-04922-03 0003 (SRC) LI, JOSEPH K Biological hazardous waste management Ligninase production by eukaryote expression vectors

P42ES-04922-03 0004 (SRC) POWERS, LINDA S Biological hazardous waste management Physical-chemical analysis of peroxidases

P42ES-04922-03 0005 (SRC) SIMS, RONALD C Biological hazardous waste management Bioreactor engineering, design and operation

P42ES-04922-03 0006 (SRC) TIEN, MING Biological hazardous waste management Molecular structure and function of lignin peroxidases

P42ES-04922-03 9001 (SRC) AUST, STEVEN D Biological hazardous waste management Graduate training core

R01ES-04926-02 (SOH) AU, WILLIAM W UNIV OF TEXAS MEDICAL BRANCH 24 KEILLER GALVESTON, TX 77550 Genetic and reproductive toxicity of ethylene glycol

P42ES-04940-02 (SRC) CARTER, DEAN E UNIVERSITY OF ARIZONA COLLEGE OF PHARMACY TUCSON, AZ 85721 Interactive toxicity--Superfund hazardous substances

P42ES-04940-02 0001 (SRC) BALES, R C Interactive toxicity--Superfund hazardous substances Effects of cosolutes on hydrophobic contaminant transport

P42ES-04940-02 0002 (SRC) CONKLIN, M H Interactive toxicity--Superfund hazardous substances Humic-facilitated subsurface transport of metals

P42ES-04940-02 0003 (SRC) GERBA, C P Interactive toxicity--Superfund hazardous substances Subsurface transport of biocolloid

P42ES-04940-02 0004 (SRC) FERNANDO, Q Interactive toxicity--Superfund hazardous substances Toxic species in environmental and biological samples

P42ES-04940-02 0005 (SRC) BRENDEL, K Interactive toxicity--Superfund hazardous substances Organ culture in interactive toxicology

P42ES-04940-02 0006 (SRC) APOSHIAN, H V Interactive toxicity--Superfund hazardous substances Detoxification of metals--in vitro and in vivo studies

P42ES-04940-02 0007 (SRC) GOLDBERG, S J Interactive toxicity--Superfund hazardous substances Cardiac teratogenicity of trichloroethylene

P42ES-04940-02 0008 (SRC) SINCLAIR, N A Interactive toxicity--Superfund hazardous substances Gene transfer and the evolution of biodegradation

P42ES-04940-02 0009 (SRC) ISTOCK, C A Interactive toxicity--Superfund hazardous substances Ecological and genetic adaptation of soil populations of Bacillus

P42ES-04940-02 0010 (SRC) PEPPER, I L Interactive toxicity--Superfund hazardous substances Gene probe detection of organisms in hazardous wastes

P42ES-04940-02 0011 (SRC) ARNOLD, R G Interactive toxicity--Superfund hazardous substances In situ bioremediation via sequential treatments

P42ES-04940-02 9001 (SRC) YEH, J Interactive toxicity--Superfund hazardous substances Core--Site selection

P42ES-04940-02 9002 (SRC) FERNANDO, Q Interactive toxicity--Superfund hazardous substances Core--Analytical center

R01ES-04947-03 (RAP) GORDON, TERRY NEW YORK UNIVERSITY MEDICAL CT 550 FIRST AVENUE NEW YORK, NY 10016 Mechanisms of airway responses to organic dusts

R01ES-04951-03 (TOX) MADDEN, MICHAEL C UNC AT CHAPEL HILL CB #7310, MED RES BLDG C CHAPEL HILL, NC 27599-7310 Role of eicosanoids in ozone-induced lung injury

R29ES-04952-03 (TOX) POSTLETHWAIT, EDWARD M UNIVERSITY OF TEXAS MED BRANCH PULMONARY DIVISION, H-76 GALVESTON, TX 77550 Determinants of pulmonary No2 surface interactions

R01ES-04954-02 (TOX) RANKIN, GARY O MARSHALL UNIVERSITY SCH OF MED 1542 SPRING VALLEY DRIVE HUNTINGTON, WV 25755-9310 Chloroaniline-induced nephrotoxicity

R01ES-04976-03 (TOX) REUHL, KENNETH R RUTGERS UNIVERSITY, BUSCH CP DEPT OF PHARMACOLOGY/TOXICOL. PISCATAWAY, NJ 08855-0789 Mechanisms of MeHg neurotoxicity during development

R01ES-04977-03 (TOX) ELDEFRAWI, MOHYEE E UNIVERSITY OF MARYLAND 655 W BALTIMORE STREET BALTIMORE, MD 21201 Insecticidal and neurotoxic actions of philanthotoxins

R01ES-04978-03 (TOX) OMIECINSKI, CURTIS J UNIVERSITY OF WASHINGTON D E H SC - 34 SEATTLE, WA 98195 Molecular toxicology of epoxide hydrolase

R01ES-04979-02 (TOX) FOWLER, BRUCE A UNIVERSITY OF MARYLAND 660 WEST REDWOOD STREET BALTIMORE, MD 21201 Biological indicators of toxicity from semiconductors

R01ES-04989-02 (RAP) KELNER, MICHAEL J UCSD MEDICAL CENTER 225 DICKINSON STREET SAN DIEGO, CA 92103 Investigation into paraquat cytotoxicity

R01ES-04995-03 (TOX) HALPERT, JAMES R UNIV OF ARIZONA COLL OF PHARMA 1703 E MABEL ST TUCSON, AZ 85721 Genes for PCB-detoxifying cytochromes P-450

R01ES-04996-03 (TOX) PARKINSON, ANDREW UNIV OF KANSAS MED CENTER 39TH & RAINBOW BLVD KANSAS CITY, KS 66103 Biochemical toxicology of carboxytesterases

PROJECT NO., ORGANIZATIONAL UNIT., INVESTIGATOR, ADDRESS, TITLE

R01ES-04999-02 (TOX) JOHNSON, DAVID A ETSU, J H QUILLEN COLL OF MED PO BOX 19930A JOHNSON CITY, TN 37614-0002 Effects of O3 and NO2 on human lung proteins

R29ES-05002-03 (TOX) PESSAH, ISAAC N UNIVERSITY OF CALIFORNIA SCHOOL OF VETERINARY MEDICINE DAVIS, CA 95616 Mechanism influencing ligand-gated Ca2+ release channels

R29ES-05003-03 (CPA) WIRGIN, ISAAC I NEW YORK UNIVERSITY MED CTR 550 FIRST AVENUE NEW YORK, NY 10016 Molecular mechanisms of carcinogenesis in feral fish

R29ES-05006-03 (TOX) EELLS, JANIS THANE MED COLL OF WISCONSIN DEPT/PHARMACO/TOXICOLOGY MILWAUKEE, WI 53226 Neurochemical mechanisms of insecticide toxicity

R01ES-05011-03 (TOX) MOTTET, N KARLE UNIVERSITY OF WASHINGTON SCHOOL OF MEDICINE SEATTLE, WA 98195 Long-term organic/inorganic mercury neurotoxicity

R01ES-05015-02 (TOX) NEEDLEMAN, HERBERT L WESTERN PSYCHIATRIC INST & CLI 3811 O'HARA STREET PITTSBURGH, PA 15213 Attention deficit, school dysfunction & lead exposure

R01ES-05017-02 (TOX) CORY-SLECHTA, DEBORAH A UNIVERSITY OF ROCHESTER ENVIRONMENTAL HEALTH SCIS CTR ROCHESTER, NY 14642 Behavioral toxicity of lead--A pharmacological analysis

R01ES-05020-01A3 (PHRA) LAWRENCE, DAVID A ALBANY MEDICAL COLLEGE 47 NEW SCOTLAND AVENUE, A-68 ALBANY, NY 12208 Hematotoxic effects of benzene and doxorubicin

P30ES-05022-04 (EHS) GOLDSTEIN, BERNARD D UNIV OF MED & DENT OF NEW JERS 675 HOES LANE PISCATAWAY, NJ 08854 Research in environmental health sciences

P30ES-05022-04 9001 (EHS) SNYDER, ROBERT Research in environmental health sciences Environmental health sciences

P30ES-05022-04 9002 (EHS) KAUFFMAN, FRED Research in environmental health sciences Cellular mechanisms of toxicity and carcinogenesis core

P30ES-05022-04 9003 (EHS) YANG, CHUNG S Research in environmental health sciences Nutritional impact on toxicity and carcinogenesis core

P30ES-05022-04 9004 (EHS) LIOY, PAUL L Research in environmental health sciences Human environmental exposure core

P30ES-05022-04 9005 (EHS) LOWNDES, HERBERT E Research in environmental health sciences Neurotoxicology core

R01ES-05025-03 (TOX) GRAZIANO, JOSEPH H COLUMBIA UNIVERSITY 630 WEST 168TH STREET NEW YORK, N Y 10032 DMSA--A new oral antidote for childhood lead poisoning

R01ES-05033-07 (TOX) BOEKELHEIDE, KIM BROWN UNIVERSITY BROWN UNIVERSITY, BOX G PROVIDENCE, RI 02912 Environmental/industrial toxicants and testicular injury

R01ES-05046-03 (TOX) WETMUR, JAMES MOUNT SINAI, BOX 1124 ONE GUSTAVE L LEVY PLACE NEW YORK, NY 10029 Lead toxicity and the ALA-dehydratase polymorphism

R01ES-05047-02 (TOX) SINSHEIMER, JOSEPH E UNIVERSITY OF MICHIGAN 1028 PHARMACY ANN ARBOR, MI 48109-1065 Genotoxicity of benzidine analogues

R01ES-05056-03 (TOX) AUST, STEVEN D UTAH STATE UNIVERSITY LOGAN, UT 84322-4430 Role of iron in toxicities and pathologies

R29ES-05064-02 (ORTH) HANSON, DOUGLAS B FORSYTH DENTAL CENTER 140 FENWAY BOSTON, MA 02115 Toxic factors affecting bone quality during growth

R01ES-05071-02 (NLS) ABOU-DONIA, MOHAMED B DUKE UNIVERSITY BOX 3813 DURHAM, NC 27710 Mechanisms of dying back neuropathies

R01ES-05079-03 (EDC) NICHOLSON, WILLIAM J MOUNT SINAI SCHOOL OF MEDICINE ONE GUSTAVE L LEVY PLACE NEW YORK, NY 10029-6754 Radon levels, cigarette smoking exposure & cancer

R01ES-05116-02 (EDC) SANTELLA, REGINA M COLUMBIA UNIVERSITY 650 WEST 168TH STREET NEW YORK, NY 10032 Biological monitoring for exposure to aflatoxin

R01ES-05131-02 (MEP) TRUSH, MICHAEL A JOHNS HOPKINS UNIVERSITY 615 NORTH WOLFE STREET BALTIMORE, MD 21205 Activation & toxicities of phenolic compounds

R01ES-05139-03 (SOH) WAY, JAMES L TEXAS A&M UNIVERSITY MED PHARMACOLOGY/TOXICOLOGY COLLEGE STATION, TX 77843 Antagonism of organophosphorous intoxications

R01ES-05142-03 (TOX) BITTAR, E EDWARD UNIVERSITY OF WISCONSIN 1300 UNIVERSITY AVENUE MADISON, WI 53706 Mechanisms by which chlorophenols act as cytotoxins

R44ES-05151-02 (SOH) PENN, STEPHEN M EXTREL CORPORATION 575 EPSILON DR PO BOX 11512 PITTSBURGH, PA 15238 Preconcentrator/CI source for QMS of trace gases in air

R01ES-05154-07 (SOH) ABOU-DONIA, MOHAMED B DUKE UNIV MEDICAL CENTER BOX 3813 DURHAM, NC 27710 Mechanisms of occupational neuropathies

R44ES-05156-03 (SOH) STETTER, JOSEPH R TRANSDUCER RESEARCH, INC 1228 OLYMPUS DRIVE NAPERVILLE, IL 60540 Development of instruments to measure human exposure

R29ES-05157-04 (TOX) ZALUPS, RUDOLFS K MERCER UNIVERSITY SCH OF MED 1550 COLLEGE STREET MACON, GA 31207 Mercury nephrotoxicity after a reduction of renal mass

R01ES-05172-02 (TOX) DE CAPRIO, ANTHONY P NEW YORK STATE DEPT OF HEALTH EMPIRE STATE PLAZA ALBANY, NY 12201 Environmental neurotoxicants & the axonal cytoskeleton

R01ES-05174-03 (NCR) MCQUEEN, CHARLENE A UNIVERSITY OF ARIZONA 1703 E MABEL STREET TUCSON, AZ 85721 Genetic susceptibility to aromatic amines toxicity

R01ES-05180-03 (RAD) LEY, RONALD D LOVELACE MEDICAL FOUNDATION 2425 RIDGECREST DRIVE S E ALBUQUERQUE, NM 87108 Life-shortening effects of environmental UV exposure

R29ES-05189-02 (TOX) HARVISON, PETER J PHILADELPHIA COLL OF PHARM & S WOODLAND AVENUE AT 43RD ST PHILADELPHIA, PA 19104 Metabolism and nephrotoxicity of agricultural fungicides

R01ES-05194-03 (TOX) FURLONG, CLEMENT EUGENE UNIVERSITY OF WASHINGTON SEATTLE, WA 98195 Human serum paraoxonase--Role in pesticide metabolism

P01ES-05197-01A1 (EHS) CLARKSON, THOMAS W UNIV OF ROCHESTER SCH OF MED BOX EHSC ROCHESTER, NY 14642 Health hazards of methylmercury

P01ES-05197-01A1 0001 (EHS) MYERS, GARY J Health hazards of methylmercury Child development following prenatal methyl mercury

exposure via fish diet
P01ES-05197-01A1 0002 (EHS) CLARKSON, THOMAS W Health hazards of methylmercury Dosimetry
P01ES-05197-01A1 0003 (EHS) BALLATORI, NAZZARENO Health hazards of methylmercury Methylmercury uptake into brain
P01ES-05197-01A1 9001 (EHS) COX, CHRISTOPHER Health hazards of methylmercury Core-- Biostatistics
P01ES-05197-01A1 9002 (EHS) RODIER, PATRICIA M Health hazards of methylmercury Core-- Morphology and histochemistry
P01ES-05197-01A1 9003 (EHS) MILLER, RICHARD Health hazards of methylmercury Core-- Analytical
R01ES-05203-03 (TOX) CARPENTER, DAVID O NYS DEPARTMENT OF HEALTH EMPIRE STATE PLAZA ALBANY, N Y 12237 Mechanisms of lead neurotoxicity
R01ES-05204-03 (CPA) STAMBROOK, PETER J UNIVERSITY OF CINCINNATI 231 BETHESDA AVENUE/ML #521 CINCINNATI, OH 45267-0521 Whole animal detection of genotoxic agents
R29ES-05211-03 (TOX) THOM, STEPHEN R UNIVERSITY OF PENNSYLVANIA 36TH STREET & HAMILTON WALK PHILADELPHIA, PA 19104-6068 Co poisoning in the context of a reperfusion injury
R29ES-05214-03 (TOX) HESS, REX A UNIVERSITY OF ILLINOIS 2001 SOUTH LINCOLN AVENUE URBANA, IL 61801 Mechanisms of pesticide-induced testicular atrophy
R01ES-05216-03 (SOH) JAMES, ROBERT C CENTER FOR ENVIRONMENTAL TOXIC 1 PROGRESS BLVD., BOX 17 ALACHUA, FL 32615 Stress and environmental chemical hazards
R44ES-05220-02 (SOH) STONE, MARCIA J HYBRIVET 32 PINEWOOD ROAD WELLESLEY, MA 02181 Detection of multiple organophosphate residues
R29ES-05223-03 (TOX) ASCHNER, MICHAEL ALBANY MEDICAL COLLEGE 47 NEW SCOTLAND AVENUE ALBANY, NY 12208 Mn transport across the blood-brain barrier
R01ES-05227-02 (REN) RORKE, ELLEN A CASE WESTERN RESERVE UNIVERSIT 2119 ABINGTON ROAD CLEVELAND, OH 44106 Toxicant induced changes in uterine and cervical epithelia
R01ES-05233-02 (TOX) MATSUMURA, FUMIO UNIVERSITY OF CALIFORNIA LEHR DAVIS, CA 95616 Biochemical causes for hypertriglyceridemia
R01ES-05234-02 (TOX) SMITH, JEFFREY B UNIV OF ALABAMA AT BIRMINGHAM UAB STATION BIRMINGHAM, AL 35294 Toxic metals, membrane signaling, and cell growth
R29ES-05235-02 (TOX) HARRIS, CRAIG UNIVERSITY OF MICHIGAN 1420 WASHINGTON HEIGHTS ANN ARBOR, MI 48109-2029 Glutathione interactions in chemical embryotoxicity
R01ES-05252-02 (TOX) NOELLE, RANDOLPH J DARTMOUTH MEDICAL SCHOOL HANOVER, NH 03756 Effect of Hg and Cd on B lymphocyte function
R01ES-05255-02 (TOX) BASSETT, DAVID J JOHNS HOPKINS UNIVERSITY 615 NORTH WOLFE STREET BALTIMORE, MD 21205 Biochemical and cellular determinants of lung ozone injury
R01ES-05257-01A1 (EDC) HU, HOWARD BRIGHAM AND WOMEN'S HOSPITAL MEDICINE BOSTON MA 02115 The epidemiology of lead, diet and blood pressure
R01ES-05261-02 (TOX) ANTHONY, DOUGLAS C DUKE UNIVERSITY MED CENTER BOX 3712 DURHAM, NC 22710 Hemoglobin adducts--A dosimeter of internal exposure
N01ES-05279-02 (**) ALLEN, ANTON Rodent disease diagnostic laboratories
R01ES-05279-02 (NEUC) MAILMAN, RICHARD B UNC AT CHAPEL HILL CAMPUS BOX #7250 BDRC CHAPEL HILL, NC 27599 Lead and development--Immune and brain studies
N01ES-05280-01 (**) LINDSEY, J RUSSELL Rodent disease diagnostic laboratories
N01ES-05284-10 (**) PENNYBACKER, MARGARET Support services for epidemiologic studies
N01ES-05285-07 (**) FRANKLIN, CLAIRE Biokinetics of lead in nonhuman primate pregnancy
N01ES-05286-02 (**) GULATI, DUSHYANT Cytogenetic tests in vitro and in vivo
N01ES-05287-04 (**) CHOU, BILL G Chronic toxicity study of cobaltous sulfate
N01ES-05288-04 (**) MUNSON, ALBERT E Immune response to xenobiotics
N01ES-05289-01 (**) PREJEAN, JD Prechronic and chronic studies of glyoxal
N01ES-05290-01 (**) RAYMER, JAMES H Expired breath analysis in chemical toxicity assessment
N01ES-05291-03 (**) CHOU, BILLY J Chronic study of chloroprene
N01ES-05293-01 (**) KURTZ, PERRY Skin paint studies of diethanolamine and Xylene Sulfonate
N01ES-05294-02 (**) UNDERSOOW, LOUIS E Support services for clinical research projects
P01ES-05294-02 (EHS) PERERA, FREDERICA P COLUMBIA UNIVERSITY 60 HAVEN AVENUE, B-109 NEW YORK, NY 10032 Molecular toxicology of environmental carcinogens
P01ES-05294-02 0001 (EHS) SANTELLA, REGINA M Molecular toxicology of environmental carcinogens Carcinogen adducts measured by immunologic methods
P01ES-05294-02 0002 (EHS) JEFFREY, ALAN M Molecular toxicology of environmental carcinogens: Carcinogen-protein adducts analysis by gas chromatography/mass spectrometry
P01ES-05294-02 0003 (EHS) WEINSTEIN, I BERNARD Molecular toxicology of environmental carcinogens Tumor promotion mechanisms--Development of study methods
P01ES-05294-02 9001 (EHS) PERERA, FREDERICA P Molecular toxicology of environmental carcinogens Molecular epidemiology and biostatistics core
N01ES-05295-04 (**) KURTZ, PERRY Toxicity studies of primaclone and oxymetholone
N01ES-05296-01 (**) ADKINS, BERNIE Animal research on toxicology of environmental chemicals
N01ES-05298-02 (**) COMBES, ROBERT Special mutagenicity studies with Salmonella
R01ES-05298-02 (TOX) BRABEC, MICHAEL J EASTERN MICHIGAN UNIVERSITY YPSILANTI, MI 48197 Heat shock proteins in sertoli cell toxicity
R01ES-05299-02 (TOX) GOODMAN, JAY I MICHIGAN STATE UNIVERSITY EAST LANSING, MI 48824 Threshold mechanisms in environmental toxicology
N01ES-05300-01 (**) BRAUN, ANDREW Chronic toxicity studies of chloropropanol
N01ES-05301-02 (**) FAN, HUNG Y In vitro transformation of oncogene primed cells
N01ES-05302-01 (**) BRAUN, ANDREW Chronic dosed feed study of phenolphthalein
N01ES-05303-02 (**) WENK, MARTIN L Prechronic studies of cyclohexanone oxime & 2-butanone oxime
R29ES-05303-02 (TOX) KURL, RABINDER N ROGER WILLIAMS MEDICAL CENTER 825 CHALKSTONE AVENUE PROVIDENCE, RI 02908 Regulation of rRNA gene expression by 2,3,7,8-TCD dioxin
N01ES-05304-02 (**) POWIS, GARTH Methods to assess metabolism of chemical xenobiotics
R01ES-05304-02 (CPA) PATIERNO, STEVEN R GEORGE WASHINGTON UNIV MED CTR 2300 EYE STREET, NW WASHINGTON, DC 20037 Mechanism of particulate chromate carcinogenesis
N01ES-05305-04 (**) HOZIER, JOHN A study of tumor suppresor genes
R01ES-05307-03 (SOH) JELOVSEK, FREDERICK R EAST TENNESSEE STATE UNIVERSIT P O BOX 19,570A JOHNSON CITY, TN 37614-0002 Knowledge elicitation for developmental risk assessment
R29ES-05311-02 (TOX) MARCUS, CRAIG B PURDUE UNIVERSITY WEST LAFAYETTE, IN 47907 Regulation of cytochrome P-450 by methylenedioxybenzenes
R29ES-05318-03 (TOX) GANDY, JAY UNIVERSITY OF ARKANSAS 4301 WEST MARKHAM ST, SLOT 638 LITTLE ROCK, AR 72205 Role of glutathione in male reproductive toxicity
R01ES-05323-02 (CPA) MURPHY, EDWIN C, JR UNIVERSITY OF TEXAS 1515 HOLCOMBE BLVD HOUSTON, TX 77030 Metal carcinogen-induced mutations in mammalian genes
R01ES-05331-02 (TOX) SUNDERMAN, F WILLIAM, JR UNIV OF CONN HEALTH CENTER FARMINGTON, CT 06032 Zn-finger proteins as targets of metal embryotoxicity
R01ES-05337-03 (HED) SANYAL, MRINAL K YALE UNIVERSITY 333 CEDAR STREET NEW HAVEN, CT 06510-8063 Abnormal fetal development due to toxic exposure
P01ES-05355-01A1 (SRC) HARRIS, THOMAS M VANDERBILT UNIVERSITY BOX 1715, STATION B NASHVILLE, TN 37235 Chemistry and biology of carcinogen-DNA adducts
P01ES-05355-01A1 0001 (SRC) HARRIS, THOMAS M Chemistry and biology of carcinogen-DNA adducts Synthetic approaches to carcinogen-linked oligonucleotides
P01ES-05355-01A1 0002 (SRC) LLOYD, STEPHEN R Chemistry and biology of carcinogen-DNA adducts Biological fate of specific DNA adducts within a bacteriophage vector
P01ES-05355-01A1 0003 (SRC) STONE, MICHAEL P Chemistry and biology of carcinogen-DNA adducts Conformational studies of adducted oligonucleotides
P01ES-05355-01A1 9001 (SRC) HARRIS, THOMAS M Chemistry and biology of carcinogen-DNA adducts Core--DNA synthesis
R01ES-05372-02 (NLS) AUDESIRK, GERALD J UNIVERSITY OF COLORADO AT DENV P O BOX 173364 DENVER CO 80217-3364 Mechanisms of neurotoxicity
R01ES-05379-02 (SSS) TARTER, MICHAEL E UNIVERSITY OF CALIFORNIA 3115 ETCHEVERRY HALL BERKELEY, CA 94720 Efficiency enhanced series curves estimation
R43ES-05381-01 (SSS) TICE, RAYMOND R INTEGRATED LABORATORY SYSTEMS P O BOX 13501 RES TRIANGLE PARK, NC 27709 Mechanisms--Micronuclei induction in mouse marrow
R44ES-05383-02 (SSS) TICE, RAYMOND R INTEGRATED LABORATORY SYSTEMS 801-8 CAPITOLA DR DURHAM, NC 27713 Detection of germ cell damage in rodents
R43ES-05385-01A1 (GMB) DIAMONDIS, PETER J DIVERSIFIED RESEARCH, INC 1155 REDWOOD ROAD MERRITT ISLAND, FL 32952 State of the art radon detection system
R01ES-05400-02 (CPA) DIXON, KATHLEEN UNIVERSITY OF CINCINNATI 3223 EDEN AVENUE CINCINNATI, OH 45267-0056 In vitro analysis of mechanisms of mammalian mutagenesis
R01ES-05405-01A1 (TOX) DAWSON, DOUGLAS A UNIVERSITY OF TENNESSEE PO BOX 1071 KNOXVILLE, TN 37901-1071 Mixture teratogenesis--Relation to mechanisms and QSARS
R01ES-05407-02 (TOX) ANDERS, MARION W UNIVERSITY OF ROCHESTER 601 ELMWOOD AVENUE ROCHESTER, NY 14642 Hydrochlorofluorocarbon metabolism and toxicity
R01ES-05409-01A1 (RAD) WILEY, LYNN M UNIVERSITY OF CALIFORNIA DAVIS, CA 95616 Radiosensitive target in the early mouse embryo
R01ES-05410-02 (EDC) LEADERER, BRIAN P JOHN B PIERCE FDN LABORATORY I 290 CONGRESS AVE NEW HAVEN, CT 06519 Acid aerosol--Respiratory effects in infants and mothers
R01ES-05417-01A1 (SSS) CLEARY, STEPHEN F VIRGINIA COMMONWEALTH UNIVERSI BOX 551, MCV STATION RICHMOND, VA 23298 RF radiation cellular effects mechanisms
R01ES-05423-02 (PB) CADENAS, ENRIQUE UNIV OF SOUTHERN CALIFORNIA 1985 ZONAL AVENUE LOS ANGELES, CA 90033 Modulation of quinone toxicity by two-electron transfers
R01ES-05429-02 (TOX) JAKAB, GEORGE J JOHNS HOPKINS UNIVERSITY 615 NORTH WOLFE STREET BALTIMORE, MD 21205 Particle-bound acrolein and pulmonary defenses
R01ES-05433-02 (TOX) WEISS, BERNARD UNIVERSITY OF ROCHESTER 601 ELMWOOD AVENUE ROCHESTER, NY 14642 Late consequences of prenatal exposure to methyl mercury
R01ES-05436-02 (TOX) JONES, THOMAS W UNIVERSITY OF MARYLAND 10 SOUTH PINE STREET BALTIMORE, MD 21201 Mechanism of cysteine conjugate toxicity
R29ES-05440-02 (TOX) HOUSER, WILLIAM H WEST VIRGINIA UNIVERSITY HEALTH SCIENCES CENTER NORTH MORGANTOWN, WV 26506 Regulation of polycyclic aromatic hydrocarbon toxicity
R01ES-05450-02 (TOX) BILLINGSLEY, MELVIN L MILTON S HERSHEY MEDICAL CTR PO BOX 850 HERSHEY, PA 17033 Molecular neurotoxicology of

PROJECT NO., ORGANIZATIONAL UNIT., INVESTIGATOR, ADDRESS, TITLE

organotin compounds

R01ES-05452-01A1 (TOX) FARISS, MARC W VIRGINIA COMMONWEALTH UNIVERSI BOX 662, MCV STATION RICHMOND, VA 23298-0662 Chemical toxicity--Protective role of vitamin E succinate

R01ES-05483-01 (HUD) JACOBSON, JOSEPH L WAYNE STATE UNIVERSITY 71 W WARREN DETROIT, MI 48202 Human exposure to PCBs--Congeners & developmental effect

R01ES-05504-01 (TOX) CHAN, TIMOTHY M UNIV OF SOUTHERN CALIFORNIA 1985 ZONAL AVE, PSC 620 LOS ANGELES, CA 90033 Mechanisms of growth-promoting action of toxic quinones

R01ES-05509-01 (BNP) HARRIS, THOMAS M VANDERBILT UNIVERSITY BOX 1715, STATION B NASHVILLE, TN 37235 DNA adducts of styrene and other vinyl monomers

R01ES-05511-01 (PTHA) FORMAN, HENRY J CHILDRENS HOSPITAL 4650 SUNSET BLVD, BOX 83 LOS ANGELES, CA 90027 Glutathione synthesis and uptake in antioxidant defense

R01ES-05533-01 (SSS) BUHLER, DONALD R OREGON STATE UNIVERSITY CORVALLIS, OR 97331 Hormonal regulation of carcinogenesis in trout

R01ES-05534-01 (SSS) FAISAL, MOHAMED VIRGINIA INSTITUTE OF MARINE S DIV OF CHEMISTRY AND TOXICOLOG GLOUCESTER POINT, VA 23062 In vitro effects of benzo(a)pyrene on fish cytotoxic leukocytes

R01ES-05536-01 (SSS) ORIS, JAMES T MIAMI UNIVERSITY COLLEGE OF ARTS AND SCIENCES OXFORD, OH 45056 Disposition of benzo(a)pyrene in a sediment-feeding fish

R01ES-05540-01 (RAD) SEDWICK, W DAVID CASE WESTERN RESERVE UNIVERSIT UCRC BLDG #2 - SUITE 200 CLEVELAND, OH 44106 Ionizing radiation induced mutation in endogenous genes

R01ES-05541-01 (SSS) WIRGIN, ISAAC I NEW YORK UNIVERSITY MED CTR 550 FIRST AVENUE NEW YORK, NY 10016 Genetic analysis of cancer in hudson river tomcod

R01ES-05543-01 (SSS) CURTIS, LAWRENCE R OREGON STATE UNIVERSITY OAK CREEK LABORATORY OF BIOLOG CORVALLIS, OR 97331-3803 Induction of carcinogen binding proteins in fish

R01ES-05548-01A1 (PHRA) POUNDS, JOEL G WAYNE STATE UNIVERSITY 2727 SECOND AVE DETROIT, MI 48201 Dimercaptosuccinic acid (DMSA) action on cellular lead metabolism & toxicity

R01ES-05552-01 (TOX) BEASLEY, VAL R 2001 SOUTH LINCOLN AVENUE URBANA, IL 61801 Mechanisms of microcystin-LR hepatotoxicity

R01ES-05561-01A1 (PHRA) CARTER, DEAN E UNIV OF ARIZONA TUCSON, AZ 85721 Lung metabolism and toxicity of environmental arsenicals

P30ES-05605-02 (EHS) MERCHANT, JAMES A UNIVERSITY OF IOWA 124 AMRF/OAKDALE CAMPUS IOWA CITY, IA 52242 Environmental health sciences core center grant

P30ES-05605-02 9001 (EHS) ISACSON, E PETER Environmental health sciences core center grant Core--Epidemiology and biometry

P30ES-05605-02 9002 (EHS) SCHNOOR, JERALD Environmental health sciences core center grant Core--Environmental assessment and control

P30ES-05605-02 9003 (EHS) MERCHANT, JAMES Environmental health sciences core center grant Core--Occupational health research

P30ES-05605-02 9004 (EHS) HUNNINGHAKE, GARY W Environmental health sciences core center grant Core--Pulmonary biology

P30ES-05605-02 9005 (EHS) LYNCH, CHARLES Environmental health sciences core center grant Health registry facility

P30ES-05605-02 9006 (EHS) THORNE, PETER S Environmental health sciences core center grant Core--Environmental measurement facility

P30ES-05605-02 9007 (EHS) RICHERSON, H B Environmental health sciences core center grant Core--Human immunology facility

R29ES-05607-01 (TOX) PETERSON, DANIEL D UNIVERSITY OF CINCINNATI 3223 EDEN AVENUE CINCINNATI, OH 45267-0056 Molecular toxicology-- Nmo-1 gene expression

R01ES-05619-01 (TOX) CASTRO, JOSE A 1603 VILLA MARTELLI PCIA, DE BUENOS AIRES, ARGENTI DNA, proteins and carbon tetrachloride hepatotoxicity

P01ES-05622-02 (EHS) WOGAN, GERALD N MASSACHUSETTS INST OF TECHNOLO 77 MASSACHUSETTS AVENUE CAMBRIDGE, MA 02139 Molecular biomarkers of exposure and environmental carcinogens

P01ES-05622-02 0029 (EHS) WOGAN, GERALD N Molecular biomarkers of exposure and environmental carcinogens Alterations in oncogenes & tumor suppressor genes in chemical carcinogenesis

P01ES-05622-02 0032 (EHS) TANNENBAUM, STEVEN R Molecular biomarkers of exposure and environmental carcinogens Molecular dosimetry of carcinogens and mutagens

P01ES-05622-02 0033 (EHS) THILLY, WILLIAM G Molecular biomarkers of exposure and environmental carcinogens Analysis of the mutational pathways in carcinogenesis

P01ES-05622-02 9001 (EHS) WISHNOK, JOHN S Molecular biomarkers of exposure and environmental carcinogens Core activities and facilities

R01ES-05623-02 (PHRA) FANTEL, ALAN G UNIVERSITY OF WASHINGTON SCHOOL OF MEDICINE SEATTLE, WA 98195 Embryotoxicity of bioreducible compounds

R13ES-05632-01 (EHS) CRAIGHEAD, JOHN E UNIV OF VERMONT COLL OF MEDICI BURLINGTON, VT 05405-0068 Environmental disease curriculum development conference

R01ES-05638-01 (EDC) WOLFF, MARY S MOUNT SINAI SCHOOL OF MEDICINE ONE GUSTAVE L LEVY PL BOX 1057 NEW YORK, NY 10029 DDE and PCBs as potential contributors to breast cancer

R01ES-05641-01 (MET) HSU, WALTER H IOWA STATE UNIVERSITY 2008 VETERINARY MEDICINE AMES, IA 50011 Amitraz-induced inhibition of insulin release

R01ES-05642-01 (TOX) WILLIAMS, GARY M AMERICAN HEALTH FOUNDATION ONE DANA ROAD VALHALLA, NY 10595 Molecular mechanisms of chemical toxicity

R01ES-05650-01 (TOX) LUCHTEL, DANIEL L UNIVERSITY OF WASHINGTON SEATTLE, WA 98195 In vitro toxicity of airborne pollutants and chemicals

P01ES-05652-01 (EHS) STAMBROOK, PETER J UNIVERSITY OF CINCINNATI 231 BETHESDA AVE, ML #521 CINCINNATI, OH 45267-0521 Transgenic reporters of environmental genotoxicants

P01ES-05652-01 0004 (EHS) STRINGER, JAMES Transgenic reporters of environmental genotoxicants Recombination and mutation in transgenic mice

P01ES-05652-01 0005 (EHS) DIXON, KATHLEEN Transgenic reporters of environmental genotoxicants Organ specificity of mutagenesis and carcinogenesis

P01ES-05652-01 9001 (EHS) DOETSCHMAN, THOMAS Transgenic reporters of environmental genotoxicants Core-- ES cell transgenic mouse facility

P01ES-05652-01 9002 (EHS) WARSHAWSKY, DAVID Transgenic reporters of environmental genotoxicants Core-- Mouse mutagenesis facility

P01ES-05652-01 9003 (EHS) KOPCHICK, JOHN Transgenic reporters of environmental genotoxicants Core-- Pronuclear injection transgenic mouse facility

P01ES-05652-01 9004 (EHS) KIER, ANN Transgenic reporters of environmental genotoxicants Core-- Pathology

P01ES-05652-01 0001 (EHS) STAMBROOK, PETER J Transgenic reporters of environmental genotoxicants Detection of mutation by transgene reversion in mice

P01ES-05652-01 0002 (EHS) SINDEN, RICHARD R Transgenic reporters of environmental genotoxicants Genotoxicants, alternate DNA conformations and mutation

P01ES-05652-01 0003 (EHS) DOETSCHMAN, T Transgenic reporters of environmental genotoxicants Tumor suppressor heterozygotes as genotoxicant reporters

R15ES-05656-02 (TOX) PROZIALECK, WALTER CHARLES CHICAGO COLL OF OSTEOPATHIC ME 555 31ST STREET DOWNERS GROVE, IL 60515 Mechanisms of cadmium toxicity in LLC-PK1 cells

R15ES-05657-01 (TOX) ADAMS, JAMES A UNIV OF MARYLAND EASTERN SHORE PRINCESS ANNE, MD 21853 Reproductive toxicology of no 2 diesel fuel

R15ES-05659-01 (TOX) OSWEILER, GARY D IOWA STATE UNIVERSITY AMES, IA 50011 In vitro cytoxicity of fumonisin mycotoxins

R01ES-05660-01 (TOX) HAMMOND, PAUL B UNIVERSITY OF CINCINNATI 3223 EDEN AVENUE CINCINNATI OH 45267-0056 Mechanisms underlying lead-induced depression of growth

R01ES-05670-01 (PTHA) STEVENS, JAMES L W ALTON JONES CELL SCI CTR 10 OLD BARN ROAD LAKE PLACID, NY 12946 Chemical pathology and renal repair

R15ES-05671-01 (TOX) HEASLEY, VICTOR L POINT LOMA NAZARENE COLLEGE 3900 LOMALAND DR SAN DIEGO, CA 92106 Halogenation of compounds related to water contamination

R01ES-05678-02 (TOX) RUNNEGAR, MARIA T UNIVERSITY OF SOUTHERN CALIF MUDD BLDG, ROOM 417 LOS ANGELES, CA 90033 Microcystin environmental toxins--Mode of action

R43ES-05681-01 (SSS) ROSEMEIER, RONALD G BRIMROSE CORP OF AMERICA 5020 CAMPBELL BOULEVARD BALTIMORE, MD 21236 Programmable ultraviolet illuminator using an AOTF

R43ES-05687-01 (SSS) DE ROCHEMONT, L PIERRE RADIATION MONITORING DEVICES I 44 HUNT STREET WATERTOWN, MA 02172 Novel infrared fiber-optic biosensor

R01ES-05694-01 (CPA) SOLOMON, JEROME J NEW YORK UNIVERSITY MEDICAL CT 550 FIRST AVENUE NEW YORK, NY 10016 Significance of epoxide-generated 3-alkyl-uracil in DNA

R01ES-05695-01 (CPA) BASU, ASHIS K UNIVERSITY OF CONNECTICUT 215 GLENBROOK ROAD STORRS, CT 06269-3060 Biological effects of DNA adducts formed by nitropyrenes

R29ES-05703-01 (TOX) BRADFIELD, CHRISTOPHER A NORTHWESTERN UNIV MED SCHOOL 303 EAST CHICAGO AVE CHICAGO, IL 60611 Molecular cloning of Ah-receptor polymorphs

R01ES-05704-01 (TOX) ANDREWS, GLEN K UNIVERSITY OF KANSAS MED CTR 39TH AND RAINBOW BLVD KANSAS CITY, KS 66103-8410 Environmental toxicology using transgenic mouse models

P30ES-05705-01 (SRC) BADEN, DANIEL G UNIVERSITY OF MIAMI 4600 RICKENBACKER CAUSEWAY MIAMI, FL 33149 NIEHS marine/freshwater biomedical sciences center grant

P30ES-05705-01 0001 (SRC) FLEMING, LORA E NIEHS marine/freshwater biomedical sciences center grant Pilot--Epidemiology and human health effects of marine toxins--Ciguatera

P30ES-05705-01 9001 (SRC) BADEN, DANIEL G NIEHS marine/freshwater biomedical sciences center grant Core--Toxin supply

P30ES-05705-01 9002 (SRC) BADEN, DANIEL G NIEHS marine/freshwater biomedical sciences center grant Core--Fish tissue culture

P30ES-05705-01 9003 (SRC) BADEN, DANIEL G NIEHS marine/freshwater biomedical sciences center grant Core--Fish cancer and immunology

P30ES-05705-01 9004 (SRC) BADEN, DANIEL G NIEHS marine/freshwater biomedical sciences center grant Core--Electrophysiology laboratory

P30ES-05705-01 9005 (SRC) BADEN, DANIEL G NIEHS marine/freshwater biomedical sciences center grant Core--Metabolic neurophysiology

P30ES-05705-01 9006 (SRC) BADEN, DANIEL G NIEHS marine/freshwater biomedical sciences center grant Core--Metabolism and analytical biochemistry

P30ES-05705-01 9007 (SRC) BADEN, DANIEL G NIEHS marine/freshwater biomedical sciences center grant Core--Electron microscopy

P30ES-05705-01 9008 (SRC) BADEN, DANIEL G NIEHS marine/freshwater biomedical sciences center grant Core--Biostatistics

P30ES-05705-01 9009 (SRC) BADEN, DANIEL G NIEHS marine/freshwater biomedical sciences center grant Core--Experimental fish and shellfish hatchery

R13ES-05708-01 (EHS) CRANMER, JOAN M UNIV OF ARKANSAS FOR MED SCIS 4301 WEST MARKHAM STREET LITTLE ROCK, AR 72205 New dimensions of lead neurotoxicity-- Conference

R55ES-05712-01 (CPA) KANE, AGNES B BROWN UNIVERSITY BOX G PROVIDENCE, RI 02912 Pleural dosimetry and biologic markers of response to fibers

R29ES-05722-01 (TOX) GANEY, PATRICIA E MICHIGAN STATE UNIVERSITY EAST LANSING, MI 48824 Activated Kupffer cells and hepatotoxicity

R01ES-05727-01 (TOX) D'AMBROSIO, STEVEN M OHIO STATE UNIVERSITY 400 W 12TH AVE/103 WISEMAN HAL COLUMBUS, OH 43210 Genotoxic modulation--Human liver cell differentiation

R01ES-05729-01 (TOX) HOROWITZ, PAUL M UNIVERSITY OF TEXAS 7703 FLOYD CURL DRIVE SAN ANTONIO, TX 78284-7760 Structural & functional correlates of protein oxidation

R01ES-05735-01 (SSS) HENDERSON, ANN S HUNTER COLLEGE OF CUNY 695 PARK AVENUE NEW YORK, NY 10021 Exposure of human cells to electromagnetic fields as a cause of cancer

R01ES-05738-01 (EDC) HERTZ-PICCIOTTO, IRVA UNIVERSITY OF NORTH

CAROLINA CB #7400 CHAPEL HILL, NC 27599-7400 Lead in pregnancy, hypertension and neonatal health

R43ES-05742-01 (SOH) ZHAO, JUNGUO ENZYME TECHNOLOGY RESEARCH GRO 710 WEST MAIN ST DURHAM, NC 27701 Inhibited enzyme electrodes for detection of toxins

R01ES-05744-06 (TOX) GUZELIAN, PHILIP S, JR MEDICAL COLLEGE OF VIRGINIA 1101 E MARSHALL ST RICHMOND, VA 23298 Regulation of microsomal hemoproteins

R01ES-05750-01 (SRC) KUNCL, RALPH W JOHNS HOPKINS HOSPITAL 600 N WOLFE ST BALTIMORE, MD 21205 Mechanisms of AZT-induced myopathy

R01ES-05752-01 (SRC) APFEL, STUART C ALBERT EINSTEIN COLLEGE OF MED 1300 MORRIS PARK AVE BRONX, NY 10461 The study and prevention of DDI and DDC neuropathy

R55ES-05770-01 (TOX) WATKINS, PAUL B UNIV OF MICHIGAN MED CENTER ANN ARBOR, MI 48109-0682 Noninvasive assays of p450IIIA enzymes in man

R01ES-05772-01 (SRC) HARTMAN, PHILIP S TEXAS CHRISTIAN UNIVERSITY BOX 32916 FT WORTH, TX 76129 UV radiation mutagenesis in C elegans

R01ES-05773-01 (SRC) LECH, JOHN J DR. CORYCE O. HAAVIK 8701 WATERTOWN PLANK ROAD MILWAUKEE, WIS 53226 Comparison of rat and trout hepatic P450 induction

R01ES-05774-01 (SRC) BROUWER, KIM L UNIVERSITY OF NORTH CAROLINA CHAPEL HILL, NC 27599-7360 Models of hepatobiliary xenobiotic disposition in aging

R01ES-05780-04 (CPA) EATON, DAVID L UNIVERSITY OF WASHINGTON SEATTLE, WA 98195 Species differences in glutathione-s-transferase

R01ES-05781-05 (SSS) JAMES, MARGARET O UNIVERSITY OF FLORIDA BOX J-485 GAINESVILLE, FL 32610 Carcinogen biotransformation by aquatic invertebrates

R01ES-05782-01 (TOX) AUST, ANN E UTAH STATE UNIVERSITY LOGAN, UT 84322-0300 Role of iron in abestos-induced DNA damage

R01ES-05783-01 (SSS) KAATTARI, STEPHEN L OREGON STATE UNIVERISTY CORVALLIS, OR 97331-3804 Mechanisms of carcinogen-induced immune dysfunction

R43ES-05784-01 (SSS) RUEGG, CHARLES E IN VITRO ALTERNATIVES INC 5202 WESTLAND BLVD BALTIMORE, MD 21227 Predicting nephrotoxic potential in vitro

R01ES-05787-01 (CPA) FOILES, PETER AMERICAN HEALTH FOUNDATION ONE DANA ROAD VALHALLA, NY 10595 Biomarkers of NNK and NNN metabolism in humans

R01ES-05790-05 (TOX) GANDOLFI, A JAY UNIVERSITY OF ARIZONA COLLEGE OF MEDICINE TUCSON, AZ 85724 In vitro toxicology--Precision tissue slice technology

R29ES-05801-01 (RAD) HEI, TOM K COLUMBIA UNIVERSITY, HLTH SCIS 630 W 168TH ST NEW YORK, NY 10032 Radiation, asbestos, and mutagenesis

S15ES-05831-01 (NSS) OSBORN, JUNE E UNIVERSITY OF MICHIGAN 109 S OBSERVATORY ANN ARBOR, MI 48109-2029 Small instrumentation grant

S15ES-05832-01 (NSS) BARNETT, JOHN B UNIV OF ARKANSAS MED SCI 4301 W MARKHAM STREET LITTLE ROCK, AR 72205 Small instrumentation grant

S15ES-05833-01 (NSS) BLAIR, JAMES B OKLAHOMA STATE UNIVERSITY STILLWATER, OK 74078-0454 Small instrumentation grant

S15ES-05834-01 (NSS) SIMS, LESLIE B NORTH CAROLINA STATE UNIV BOX 7003 RALEIGH, NC 27695-7003 Small instrumentation grant

S15ES-05835-01 (NSS) CHAPMAN, A L UNIVERSITY OF KANSAS MED CTR 39TH & RAINBOW BLVD KANSAS CITY, KS 66103-8410 Small instrumentation grant

S15ES-05836-01 (NSS) SOHN, RICHARD J COLUMBIA UNIVERSITY HLTH SCI 630 W 168TH ST NEW YORK, NY 10032 Small instrumentation grant

S15ES-05837-01 (NSS) MORRIS, JOHN B UNIVERSITY OF CONNECTICUT 372 FAIRFIELD RD STORRS, CT 06269 Small instrumentation grant

S15ES-05838-01 (NSS) MEAD, RODNEY A UNIVERSITY OF IDAHO MOSCOW, ID 83843 Small instrumentation grant

S15ES-05839-01 (NSS) MC QUEEN, CHARLENE A UNIVERSITY OF ARIZONA 1703 E MABEL ST TUCSON, AZ 85721 Small instrumentation grant

S15ES-05840-01 (NSS) SHADDUCK, JOHN A TEXAS A&M UNIVERSITY COLLEGE STATION, TX 77843-446 Small instrumentation grant

S15ES-05841-01 (NSS) MURPHY, FREDERICK A UNIVERSITY OF CALIFORNIA 1018 HARING HALL DAVIS, CA 95616 Small instrumentation grant

S15ES-05842-01 (NSS) LASHOF, JOYCE C UNIVERSITY OF CALIFORNIA WARREN HALL BERKELEY, CA 94720 Small instrumentation grant

S15ES-05843-01 (NSS) CHAMBERS, JANICE E MISSISSIPPI STATE UNIVERSITY PO BOX 6156 MISSISSIPPI STATE, MS 39762 Small instrumentation grant

S15ES-05844-01 (NSS) WEYAND, ERIC H RUTGERS STATE UNIVERSITY PO BOX 789 PISCATAWAY, NJ 08855-0789 Small instrumentation grant

S15ES-05845-01 (NSS) MACMAHON, JAMES A UTAH STATE UNIVERSITY LOGAN, UT 84322-4400 Small instrumentation grant

S15ES-05846-01 (NSS) LOUDON, G MARC PURDUE UNIVERSITY 1330 RHPH WEST LAFAYETTE, IN 47907-1330 Small instrumentation grant

S15ES-05847-01 (NSS) RANKIN, GARY O MARSHALL UNIVERSITY SCH OF MED 1542 SPRING VALLEY DRIVE HUNTINGTON, WV 25755 Small instrumentation grant

S15ES-05848-01 (NSS) CHOPRA, DHARAM P WAYNE STATE UNIVERSITY 2727 SECOND AVENUE RM 4000 DETROIT, MI 48201 Small instrumentation grant

S15ES-05849-01 (NSS) PETERING, DAVID H UNIVERSITY OF WISCONSIN PO BOX 413 MILWAUKEE, WI 53201 Small instrumentation grant

R43ES-05872-01 (SSS) LOATS, HARRY L LOATS ASSOCIATES, INC 1004 LITTLESTOWN PIKE WESTMINSTER, MD 21157 Color based automated micronuclei assay

R55ES-05903-01 (TOX) CORY-SLECHTA, DEBORAH A UNIVERSITY OF ROCHESTER PO BOX EHSC ROCHESTER, NY 14642 Behavioral toxicity of lead--Role of the NMDA receptor

R43ES-05904-01 (SOH) WRIGHT, HARVEL A CONSULTEC SCIENTIFIC INC 725 PELLISSIPPI PARKWAY KNOXVILLE, TN 37932-3300 A radon progeny lung dose monitor

Z01ES-10004-12 (LMB) LONDON, R E NIEHS, NIH NMR studies of the mechanisms of cell injury

N43ES-11001-00 (**) MAUL, DIANA M SBIR topic number 030 optical immunoassay

N43ES-11002-00 (**) CRESPI, CHARLES SBIR topic number 021 development of human cell lines

N43ES-11003-00 (**) GRATZNER, H G SBIR topic number 026 assays for DNA methylation

N43ES-11004-00 (**) ANDERSON, THOMAS Nonisotopic immunoassays for cyclic nucleotides

N44ES-12001-00 (**) CRESPI, CHARLES Development of cell lines expressing rat cytochrome

N01ES-15306-00 (**) MURRILL, EVELYN A Chemistry support services for NTP

N01ES-15307-01 (**) HANDY, RW Chemistry support services for the ntp

N01ES-15308-00 (**) KURTZ, PERRY Chronic toxicity study of carisoprodol

N01ES-15311-00 (**) TICE, RAYMOND Rat and mouse in vivo micronucleus test

N01ES-15312-00 (**) EREXSON, GREGORY Rat and mouse in vivo micronucleus tests

N01ES-15313-00 (**) CHOU, BILLY Subchronic and chronic toxicity study of isobutene

N01ES-15314-00 (**) KURTZ, PERRY Chronic studies of coconut oil fatty acids

N01ES-15315-01 (**) CHOU, BILLY Chronic inhalation toxicity study of furfuryl alcohol

N01ES-15317-00 (**) WHISNANT, CAROL C Genetic monitoring of inbred rodents

N01ES-15318-00 (**) CHOU, BILLY Inhalation studies of 2-butoxyethanol

N01ES-15319-00 (**) WENK, MARTIN L Toxicity studies in animals

N01ES-15320-02 (**) KURTZ, PERRY Toxicity studies in animals

N01ES-15321-00 (**) TICE, RAYMOND Model systems evaluation for chemical safety evaluation

N01ES-15322-00 (**) KURTZ, PERRY Chronic study of oxazepam and pentachlorophenol

N01ES-15323-00 (**) BRIGGS, BRUCE C Reproductive toxicity test system

N01ES-15324-00 (**) SEILKOP, STEVEN K Statistical analysis of laboratory animal studies

N01ES-15325-00 (**) TU, ALICE Transformation assay system

N01ES-15326-00 (**) BRAUN, ANDREW Studies of dichloroethylene and tetrachloroethane

N01ES-15327-00 (**) LIU, EDISON T Oncogene analysis for epidemiologic studies

N01ES-15328-00 (**) PREJEAN, JOE Toxicology of AIDS therapeutics

N01ES-15329-00 (**) JEFFCOAT, A ROBERT Studies of chemical disposition in mammals

N01ES-15330-00 (**) MARQUIS, JUDITH Chronic toxicity studies of polyvinyl alcohol

Z01ES-21003-11 (ETB) BIRNBAUM, L S NIEHS, NIH Disposition of halogenated dibenzofurans

Z01ES-21004-11 (ETB) BIRNBAUM, L S NIEHS, NIH Senescent changes in metabolism

Z01ES-21009-10 (STB) CHAPIN, ROBERT E NIEHS, NIH Reproductive effects in males exposed to environmental chemicals

Z01ES-21016-10 (LMG) RESNICK, M A NIEHS, NIH Enzymes involved in DNA repair and meiosis

Z01ES-21024-10 (LBRA) GOLDSTEIN, J A NIEHS, NIH Drug metabolizing enzymes in animal models and human tissue

Z01ES-21031-07 (STB) MOORMAN, M P NIEHS, NIH Computer simulation of inhalation exposures

Z01ES-21038-09 (ETB) MATTHEWS, H B NIEHS, NIH Chemical metabolism and disposition

Z01ES-21046-08 (STB) KARI, F W NIEHS, NIH Postnatal toxicology

Z01ES-21050-08 (ETB) DIETER, M P NIEHS, NIH Evaluation of microencapsulation as a means to administer chemicals in feed

Z01ES-21051-08 (ECMB) MASON, J M NIEHS, NIH Cytogenetic analysis of mutagen-sensitive mutants

Z01ES-21053-08 (ECMB) MASON, J M NIEHS, NIH Genetic control of mutation in Drosophila

Z01ES-21075-08 (ETB) BURKA, L T NIEHS, NIH Xenobiotic metabolism

Z01ES-21080-07 (ECMB) MARONPOT, R R NIEHS, NIH Magnetic resonance imaging facility

Z01ES-21084-06 (ETB) GHANAYEM, B I NIEHS, NIH Association of chemically-cell proliferation and carcinogenesis

Z01ES-21089-05 (STB) HEINDEL, J J NIEHS, NIH Mechanism of action of testicular toxicants

Z01ES-21090-06 (STB) MORGAN, D L NIEHS, NIH Mechanisms of arsine gas and gallium arsenide toxicity

Z01ES-21091-06 (LMG) RESNICK, M A NIEHS, NIH Effects of DNA lesions of untargeted DNA metabolic events

Z01ES-21093-05 (ETB) BIRNBAUM, L S NIEHS, NIH Mechanisms of dioxin toxicity

Z01ES-21094-05 (ETB) ZEIGER, E NIEHS, NIH Mutagenesis and other cellular response to chemicals that generate free radicals

Z01ES-21097-05 (ETB) DIETER, M P NIEHS, NIH Evaluation of chemical myelotoxicity using an in vivo leukemia transplant model

Z01ES-21098-05 (CCB) HONG, H L NIEHS, NIH Adverse effects of lindane in B6C3F1 mice

Z01ES-21103-05 (ETB) ZEIGER, E NIEHS, NIH Evaluations of genetic toxicity test results

Z01ES-21106-04 (ECMB) CASPARY, W NIEHS, NIH In situ protocols for mammalian cell mutagenesis assays

Z01ES-21107-04 (ETB) ABU-SHAKRA, A NIEHS, NIH Mutagenicity studies of hydrogen peroxide and hydrogen peroxide generating system

Z01ES-21109-04 (ETB) GHANAYEM, B I NIEHS, NIH Mechanisms of 2-butoxyethanol induced hematotoxicity

Z01ES-21110-04 (STB) HEINDEL, J J NIEHS, NIH Developmental immunotoxicity studies of inbred mice

Z01ES-21113-04 (CCB) HONG, H L NIEHS, NIH Myelotoxicity in

PROJECT NO., ORGANIZATIONAL UNIT., INVESTIGATOR, ADDRESS, TITLE

mice caused by drinking mixture of groundwater contaminants

Z01ES-21115-04 (CCB) HONG, H L NIEHS, NIH Effects of d-Limonene on alpha 2U-globulin in rat kidney

Z01ES-21117-03 (ETB) GHANAYEM, B I NIEHS, NIH Role of calcium in chemical-induced toxicity

Z01ES-21118-03 (STB) HEINDEL, J J NIEHS, NIH Mechanism of action of ovarian toxicants

Z01ES-21119-03 (ETB) CUNNINGHAM, M NIEHS, NIH Metabolism and genotoxicity of mutagenic noncarcinogens

Z01ES-21121-03 (ECMB) LANGENBACH, R NIEHS, NIH Transfection of cDNAs for drug metabolism into mammalian cells

Z01ES-21122-03 (LMG) RESNICK, M A NIEHS,NIH Genomic stability and recombinational interactions

Z01ES-21123-03 (ETB) JAMESON, C W NIEHS, NIH Investigation of absorption of chemicals physically bound to feed by F344 rats

Z01ES-21124-03 (STB) KARI, F W NIEHS, NIH Development of a model to study the influence of nutrition on F344/n rat leukemia

Z01ES-21125-02 (CCB) HONG, H L NIEHS, NIH Pesticide and fertilizer mixture study

Z01ES-21126-02 (CCB) HONG, H L NIEHS, NIH Evaluation of L-tryptophan toxicity in mice

Z01ES-21127-02 (STB) CHAPIN, R E NIEHS, NIH Short-term comprehensive reproductive and developmental toxicity screen

Z01ES-21128-02 (ETB) THOMPSON, M B NIEHS, NIH Bile acids as indicators and initiators of hepatotoxicity

Z01ES-21129-02 (ECMB) MARONPOT, R R NIEHS, NIH Frozen tissue archives

Z01ES-21130-02 (ETB) DIXON, D NIEHS, NIH Histogenesis of pulmonary neoplasia in mice

Z01ES-21131-02 (ECMB) MARONPOT, R R NIEHS, NIH Chemically induced and spontaneous neoplasms for oncogene activation

Z01ES-21132-02 (ECMB) MARONPOT, R R NIEHS, NIH Image analysis, quantitative morphometrics and cell turnover

Z01ES-21133-02 (ECMB) LANGENBACH, R NIEHS, NIH Comparative genetic toxicology of H.C. Blue 1 and H.C. Blue 2

Z01ES-21135-02 (STB) ROSENTHAL, G J NIEHS, NIH The effects of AIDS therapeutics on the immune system

Z01ES-21136-02 (STB) MORGAN, D L NIEHS, NIH Toxicity studies of styrene and related chemicals

Z01ES-21137-02 (STB) MORGAN, D L NIEHS, NIH Mechanism of tetranitromethane toxicity and carcinogenicity

Z01ES-21138-02 (ETB) GHANAYEM, B I NIEHS, NIH Comparative metabolism and disposition of aliphatic nitriles

Z01ES-21139-02 (ECMB) CASPARY, W NIEHS, NIH Mechanisms of mutagenesis and carcinogenesis

Z01ES-21141-02 (CCB) RAO, G N NIEHS, NIH Growth and tumors of rats and mice fed NIH-07 and NTP-90 diets

Z01ES-21143-02 (ETB) DIETER, M P NIEHS, NIH Toxicology studies of lead

Z01ES-21144-02 (ETB) DIETER, M P NIEHS, NIH Oximes research project

Z01ES-21145-02 (ETB) DIETER, M P NIEHS, NIH Investigation of subchronic oral toxicity of 4-chloro-a,a,a-trifluorotoluene

Z01ES-21147-01 (CCB) HONG, H L NIEHS, NIH The effect of sodium fluoride administration on radiation induced osteosarcomas

Z01ES-21148-01 (STB) ROSENTHAL, G L NIEHS, HIH Lung immunotoxicology

Z01ES-21149-01 (STB) KARI, F NIEHS, NIH Nasal toxicity of glutaraldehyde

Z01ES-21150-01 (ETB) YUAN, J H NIEHS, NIH Bioavailability of microencapsulated cinnamaldehyde

Z01ES-21151-01 (STB) SANDEDERS, V M NIEHS, NIH Neuroimmunomodulation

Z01ES-21152-01 (STB) HUNTER, E S NIEHS, HIH Altered energetics as a mechanism of development toxicity

Z01ES-21153-01 (ATB) HUNTER, E S NIEHS, HIH Mechanisms of developmental toxicity

Z01ES-21154-01 (STB) HARRY, G J NIEHS, NIH Cellular indicators of neuronal insult

Z01ES-21155-01 (STB) HARRY, G J NIEHS, NIH Gene expression as an injury target site of environmental agents

Z01ES-21156-01 (DTRT) SELKIRK, J K NIEHS, NIH Protein analysis on the phenotypic expression of mutation

Z01ES-21157-01 (ECMB) PAULES, R S NIEHS, NIH Molecular analysis of cell cycle control during carcinogenesis

Z01ES-21158-01 (ECMB) LANGENBACH, R NIEHS, NIH Oncogenic activity of retroviral vectors used in human gene therapy

Z01ES-21159-01 (ETB) CHAN, P C NIEHS, NIH Induction of glutathione S-transferase-II in cultured rat liver cells

Z01ES-21160-01 (ETB) ZHU, S NIEHS, NIH Mutagenicity studies in cultured mammalian cells

Z01ES-21161-01 (ECMB) BRISTOL, D W NIEHS, NIH Structure-activity relationship between chemical substructure and organ toxicity

Z01ES-21162-01 (ECMB) FRENCH, J E NIEHS, NIH Oxidative injury to DNA and non-genotoxic carcinogenesis

Z01ES-21163-01 (ETB) DEMBY, K NIEHS, NIH Toxicokinetics and toxicodynamics of xenobiotics

Z01ES-22109-03 (CMB) GOELZ, M F NIEHS, NIH A comparison of tissue response to complete Freund's and RIBI adjuvant

Z01ES-22110-03 (CMB) THIGPEN, J E NIEHS, NIH Alopecia and dermatitis in C57BL/6N mice

Z01ES-23000-05 (LMC) WISEMAN, R W NIEHS, NIH Genetic events in multistep carcinogenesis of mice

Z01ES-23001-02 (90C) BOYD, J A NIEHS,NIH Molecular genetics of human gynecologic pathology

Z01ES-23002-01 (LMC) BARRETT, J C NIEHS, NIH Role of cell and tissue structure in negative growth regulation

Z01ES-23003-01 (LMC) BARRETT, J C NIEHS, NIH Cell senescence, carcinogenesis, and aging

Z01ES-25001-14 (LMC) BARRETT, J C NIEHS, NIH Role of mutagenesis in carcinogenesis

Z01ES-25020-09 (LPP) HOOK, G R NIEHS, NIH Regulation of pulmonary surfactant system and its modification by toxic agents

PROJECT NO., ORGANIZATIONAL UNIT., INVESTIGATOR, ADDRESS, TITLE

Z01ES-25021-08 (LPP) JETTEN, A M NIEHS, NIH Regulation of differentiation of tracheobronchial epithelial cells

Z01ES-25023-08 (LPP) NETTESHEIM, P NIEHS, NIH Cellular and molecular mechanisms of progression of transformed RTE cells

Z01ES-25027-08 (LPP) HOOK, G R NIEHS, NIH The functions of pulmonary epithelial cells and their secretions

Z01ES-25030-05 (LPP) BRODY, A R NIEHS, NIH Cellular and biochemical mechanisms of particle-induced lung disease

Z01ES-25031-05 (LMC) BARRETT, J C NIEHS, NIH Role of tumor suppressor genes and oncogens in chemical carcinogenesis

Z01ES-25032-02 (LPP) NETTESHEIM, P NIEHS, NIH Regulation of proliferation and differentiation in airway epithelium

Z01ES-30003-20 (LMB) ALBRO, P W NIEHS, NIH Development of biochemical methodology

Z01ES-30106-17 (STB) LUSTER, M I NIEHS, NIH Effects of environmental pollutants on the immune system

Z01ES-35005-12 (LMT) ANDERSON, M W NIEHS, NIH Mechanisms of carcinogen-induced DNA damage and cell transformation

Z01ES-40004-14 (SBB) WEINBERG, C NIEHS, NIH Statistical methods in epidemiology

Z01ES-43002-15 (EB) ROGAN, W J NIEHS, NIH Human exposure to halogenated aromatic compounds

Z01ES-43004-14 (EB) SANDLER, D P NIEHS, NIH Environmental exposures and chronic renal and other diseases

Z01ES-43010-06 (DBRA) HOEL, D G NIEHS, NIH Macromolecular modeling and carcinogenesis

Z01ES-44002-15 (SBB) KAPLAN, N L NIEHS, NIH Mathematical modeling of molecular phenomena

Z01ES-44003-14 (EB) WILCOX, A NIEHS, NIH Epidemiologic study of reproductive outcomes and environmental exposures

Z01ES-45001-11 (SBB) HASEMAN, J K NIEHS, NIH Experimental design and data analysis methodology for animal experiments

N01ES-45067-29 (**) PENNYBACKER, MARGARET Services for new efforts in environmental epidemiology

Z01ES-46002-07 (EB) SANDLER, D P NIEHS, NIH Environmental exposures and cancer risk

Z01ES-46004-07 (LBRA) LUCIER, G NIEHS, NIH Receptor interaction for TCDD and its structural analogs--Species comparisons

Z01ES-46005-07 (LMT) REYNOLDS, S NIEHS, NIH Oncogene activation in rodent and human tumors

Z01ES-46007-01 (LBRA) THOMPSON, CLAUDIA NIEHS, NIH Antisecretory drug effects on cell processes of stomach, liver, and lymphocytes

Z01ES-46008-01 (LBRA) BELL, DOUGLAS A NIEHS, NIH Inherited cancer susceptibility and relation to genetic damage

Z01ES-47001-06 (EB) SANDLER, D P NIEHS, NIH Exposure to radon and cancer risk

Z01ES-47002-05 (EB) BAIRD, D D NIEHS, NIH Biological effects of plant estrogens in postmenopausal women

Z01ES-48001-04 (SBB) PIEGORSCH, W W NIEHS, NIH Statistical analysis of data from genotoxicity experiments

Z01ES-48002-04 (SBB) PORTIER, C J NIEHS, NIH Statistical models in toxicology and biochemistry

Z01ES-48005-04 (LBRA) DIAUGUSTINE, R NIEHS, NIH Biochemical mechanisms related to risk factors of mammary carcinogenesis

Z01ES-49001-03 (EB) JOHNSON, E NIEHS,NIH Studies of occupational population exposed to carcinogenic agents

Z01ES-49002-03 (EB) TAYLOR, J NIEHS-NIH Molecular epidemiology of cancer susceptibility and oncogene activation

Z01ES-49003-02 (EB) BAIRD, D D NIES, NIH Environmental effects on fertility

Z01ES-50046-13 (LMB) CHIGNELL, COLIN F NIEHS, NIH Mechanisms of chemically induced photosensitivity

Z01ES-50080-09 (LMB) TOMER, K B NIEHS, NIH Environmental health applications of mass spectrometry

Z01ES-50087-05 (LMB) DABESTANI, R NIEHS, NIH Mechanisms of singlet oxygen-dependent photosensitivity

Z01ES-50088-05 (LMB) MASON, R P NIEHS, NIH Relationship of free radicals to halocarbon-induced toxicity in the liver

Z01ES-50090-05 (LMB) MASON, R P NIEHS, NIH Porphyrin ion radical metabolites and their reactions

Z01ES-50104-05 (LMB) LONDON, R E NIEHS, NIH In vivo studies of cellular magnesium

Z01ES-50106-03 (LMB) TOMER, K B NIEHS, NIH Collaborative projects in environmental health sciences

Z01ES-50107-03 (LMB) TOMER, K B NIEHS, NIH Development of nanoliter capillary LC/MS techniques

Z01ES-50108-03 (LMB) TOMER, K NIEHS, NIH Development of tandem mass spectrometry for structure elucidation

Z01ES-50109-03 (LMB) MASON, R NIEHS, NIH Peroxyl free radical formation by chloroperoxidase and lipoxygenase

Z01ES-50110-03 (LMB) LONDON, R NIEHS, NIH NMR studies of cellular metabolism

Z01ES-50111-03 (LMB) LONDON, R NIEHS, NIH NMR studies of biomolecular structure, function and dynamics

Z01ES-50112-03 (LMB) LONDON, R NIEHS, NIH Magnetic resonance imaging studies of heavy metal distribution

Z01ES-50114-03 (LMB) ALBRO, P NIEHS, NIH Xenobiotic metabolism in lower species

Z01ES-50115-03 (LMB) CHIGNELL, C F NIEHS, NIH A computerized spin trapping data base

Z01ES-50116-02 (LMB) TOMER, K B NIEHS, NIH Microdialysis/mass spectrometry

Z01ES-50117-01 (LMB) MASON, R P NIEHS, NIH Transition-metal mediated free radical formation in vitro and in vivo

Z01ES-50118-01 (LMB) MASON, R P NIEHS, NIH The mechanism of reduction of toxic chemicals and drugs

N01ES-55073-15 (**) RAGAN, HARVEY A Toxicity and carcinogenicity tests of acetonitrile

N01ES-55105-42 (**) RAGAN, HARVEY A Toxicity and carcinogencity studies

N01ES-55109-07 (**) TYSON, CHARLES A Assessment of chemical

xenobiotic metabolism
N01ES-55111-19 (**) LILJA, HERMAN S Toxicity studies of tetrahydrofuran
Z01ES-60102-13 (ETB) ZEIGER, E NIEHS, NIH Testing of chemicals of interest in Salmonella
Z01ES-60147-08 (LMG) SCHAAPER, R M NIEHS, NIH Molecular mechanisms of SOS-mutagenesis in Escherichia coli
Z01ES-61024-09 (LG) VOELKER, R A NIEHS, NIH Genetic and molecular analysis of suppressor-of-sable function in Drosophila
Z01ES-61037-07 (LMG) SUGINO, A NIEHS, NIH Mechanism of DNA replication in eucaryotes--Yeast as a model system
Z01ES-61039-07 (LMG) SUGINO, A NIEHS, NIH Mechanism of DNA recombination and repair in yeast Saccharomyces cerevisiae
Z01ES-61042-05 (LG) ABBOTT, M NIEHS, NIH Gene expression during Drosophila development
Z01ES-61043-01 (LG) LI, S S NIEHS, NIH Mammalian lactate dehydrogenase genes and their encoded isozymes
Z01ES-61044-01 (LG) LI, S S NIEHS, NIH Research services on protein sequencing and peptide synthesis
Z01ES-61045-01 (LG) LI, S S NIEHS, NIH Human prostatic acid phosphatase gene and its encoded enzyme
Z01ES-61046-01 (LG) LI, S S NIEHS, NIH Mammalian protein tyrosine phosphatase genes and their encoded isoenzymes
Z01ES-61047-01 (LG) BURKHART, J G NIEHS, NIH Mutagenesis in in vivo models of deficient xenobiotic metabolism
Z01ES-61048-01 (LG) VOELKER, R A NIEHS, NIH Genetic and molecular analysis of Minute (1) 1B function in Drosophila
Z01ES-61049-01 (LG) SANDER, M NIEHS, NIH Enzymology of homologous recombination and DNA repair in Drosophila melanogaster
Z01ES-61050-01 (LG) JOHNSON, F M NIEHS, NIH Germinal mutation and morphogenesis
Z01ES-65033-08 (LG) MALLING, H V NEIHS, NIH In vivo mammalian mutagenesis
Z01ES-65034-07 (LMG) SCHAAPER, R M NIEHS, NIH The specificity of spontaneous and induced mutation
Z01ES-65036-07 (LG) JUDD, B H NIEHS, NIH Gene organization and regulation in Drosophila melanogaster
Z01ES-65037-07 (LG) JUDD, B H NIEHS, NIH Transposon-mediated chromosomes instabilities in Drosophila
Z01ES-65041-05 (LMG) CLARK, J M NIEHS, NIH DNA repair in mammalian cells
Z01ES-65042-04 (LMG) DRAKE, J W NIEHS, NIH Role of gene uvsW in error-prone repair by bacteriophage T4
Z01ES-65045-05 (LMG) DRAKE, J W NIEHS, NIH Bacteriophage T4 rl mutations
Z01ES-65046-05 (LMG) KUNKEL, T A NIEHS, NIH Accuracy of DNA replication in vitro
Z01ES-65047-05 (LMG) KUNKEL, T A NIEHS, NIH Fidelity of retroviral reverse transcriptases
Z01ES-65050-05 (91MB) TINDALL, K R NIEHS, NIH Molecular analysis of deletion mutations in Chinese hamster ovary cells
Z01ES-65051-05 (ECMB) TINDALL, K R NIEHS, NIH Molecular analysis of point mutations in Chinese hamster ovary cells
Z01ES-65054-04 (LMG) DRAKE, J W NIEHS, NIH Invariant per-genome mutation rates
Z01ES-65056-03 (LMG) KRICKER, M C NIEHS, NIH Evolution of the T-even bacteriophage tRNA genes
Z01ES-65058-02 (LMG) KRICKER, M C NIEHS, NIH Generation of stable gene families
Z01ES-65070-01 (LMG) KUNKEL, T A NIEHS, NIH Probing structure-function relationships with DNA polymerases
Z01ES-65071-01 (LMG) DRAKE, J W NIEHS, NIH Reviews of mutation and DNA repair
Z01ES-65072-01 (LMG) RESNICK, M A NIEHS, NIH Human genome project--Artificial chromosome stability and mapping in yeast
Z01ES-65073-01 (LMG) RESNICK, M A NIEHS, NIH Molecular mechanisms of DNA repair and recombination in yeast
N01ES-65132-13 (**) ARANYI, CATHERINE Chronic toxicity of methylphenidate hydrochloride
N01ES-65137-05 (**) JEFFCOAT, A ROBERT Studies of chemical disposition
N01ES-65141-22 (**) FAIL, PAT Reproductive toxicity testing systems
N01ES-65143-21 (**) ARANYI, CATHERINE Toxicity studies of isobutyl nitrite
N01ES-65147-02 (**) MULLIGAN, LOUIS T Prechronic toxicity studies of acetone
N01ES-65152-11 (**) MCCORMICK, J J Development of mammalian cell assay systems
N01ES-65167-09 (**) PEREIRA, MICHAEL A Oncogene activation & molecular dosimetry
Z01ES-70060-18 (LRDT) MCLACHLAN, J A NIEHS, NIH Developmental biology/toxicology of estrogenic environmental chemicals
Z01ES-70062-04 (LRDT) NELSON, K G NIEHS, NIH Role of growth factors in growth and differentiation of the reproductive tract
Z01ES-70065-15 (LRDT) KORACH, K S NIEHS, NIH Chemical-receptor interactions in reproduction and hormonal toxicity
Z01ES-70067-08 (LRDT) TENG, C T NIEHS, NIH Molecular mechanism of steroid hormone in sex organ development
Z01ES-70069-09 (LBRA) DIAUGUSTINE, R P NIEHS, NIH DNA adducts in human lymphocytes and hormone-dependent cancers
Z01ES-70076-07 (LRDT) EDDY, E M NIEHS, NIH Germ cell-specific molecules of spermatozoa
Z01ES-70077-06 (LRDT) EDDY, E M NIEHS, NIH Expression of heat-shock genes in mouse spermatogenic cells
Z01ES-70090-08 (LMIN) NEGRO-VILAR, A NIEHS, NIH Neuroendocrine and neurochemical regulation of gonadal function
Z01ES-70092-08 (LMIN) NEGRO-VILAR, A NIEHS, NIH Cellular and molecular mechanisms mediating peptide hormone action
Z01ES-70096-07 (LMIN) CULLER, M D NIEHS, NIH Regulation of pulsatile gonadotropin secretion
N01ES-75146-08 (**) LILJA, HERMAN S Prechronic toxicity studies of sodium selenite and selenate

PROJECT NO., ORGANIZATIONAL UNIT., INVESTIGATOR, ADDRESS, TITLE

N01ES-75178-08 (**) MULLIGAN, LOUIS T Chronic toxicity study of codeine rats,mice
N01ES-75185-13 (**) BLOOM, ARTHUR D Genetic risk evaluation and related issues
N01ES-75189-11 (**) CHOU, BILLY J Prechronic and chronic toxicity study of nitromethane
N01ES-75196-04 (**) SORGE, JOSEPH A Cloning and seqencing activated oncogenes
N01ES-75197-10 (**) GLICKMAN, BARRY W Analysis of mutational specificity
Z01ES-80001-19 (LCMP) PHILPOT, R M NIEHS, NIH Microsomal mixed function oxidase system--Structure and function
Z01ES-80008-16 (LMB) ELING, T E NIEHS, NIH Biosynthesis of prostaglandins, hydroxy-fatty acids and leukotrienes
Z01ES-80031-15 (LCMP) PRITCHARD, J B NIEHS, NIH Role of altered membrane function in xenobiotic toxicity
Z01ES-80035-16 (LMB) ELING, T E NIEHS, NIH Cooxidation of xenobiotics by the prostaglandin synthetase
Z01ES-80040-08 (LRDT) NEGISHI, M NIEHS, NIH Developmental pharmacogenetics of microsomal steroid hydroxylases
Z01ES-80042-05 (LCMP) PUTNEY, J W NIEHS, NIH Calcium regulation and signal transduction mechanisms
Z01ES-80043-04 (LCMP) ARMSTRONG, D L NIEHS, NIH Ion channel modulation by signal transduction systems
Z01ES-80044-03 (LCMP) ARMSTRONG, D NIEHS, NIH Mechanisms of embryonic neural induction
Z01ES-80045-03 (LCMP) RODBELL, M NIEHS, NIH GTP-binding proteins and signal transduction--Structure and function
Z01ES-80046-03 (LCMP) SHEARS, S B NIEHS, NIH Regulation of inositol lipid signalling mechanisms
Z01ES-80047-02 (LCMP) MILLER, D S NIEHS, NIH Intracellular receptors and metabolic control
Z01ES-80048-01 (LCMP) MILLER, D S NIEHS, NIH Cellular mechanisms of xenobiotic transport
N01ES-85206-13 (**) CHOU, B J Toxicity studies of 2-, 4-chloronitrobenzene
N01ES-85207-07 (**) CHOU, BILLY J Chronic toxicity studies of tetrafluoroethylene
N01ES-85210-11 (**) CHOU, BILLY J Prechronic toxicity studies of cadmium oxide
N01ES-85211-16 (**) CHOU, BILLY J Prechronic toxicity studies of gallium oxide
N01ES-85212-12 (**) LILJA, HERMAN S Chronic toxicity studies of delta-9-tetrahydrocannabinol
N01ES-85213-12 (**) PETERS, ARTHUR C Subchronic and chronic studies of oxazepam
N01ES-85215-10 (**) STRICOFF, SCOTT R National toxicology program health and safety support
N01ES-85217-09 (**) PREJEAN, J DAVID Chronic toxicity studies of p-nitrobenzoic acid
N01ES-85219-07 (**) PREJEAN, JOE DAVID Toxicity studies of t-butylhydroquinone
N01ES-85222-09 (**) PREJEAN, JD Chronic studies of butyl benzyl phthalate
N01ES-85223-05 (**) THILAGAR, ARULASANAM K In vitro CHO cytogenetics testing
N01ES-85226-08 (**) PETERS, ARTHUR C Chronic toxicity studies of triethanolamine
N01ES-85227-10 (**) PETERS, ARTHUR Chronic toxicity studies of scopolamine hydrobromide
N01ES-85228-08 (**) BHANDARI, JC Ntp quality assurance retrospective audit support
N01ES-85229-11 (**) BHANDARI, JC Ntp quality assurance retrospective audit support
N01ES-85230-04 (**) SIPES, I GLENN Studies of chemical disposition in mammals
N01ES-85232-07 (**) CHOU, BILLY J Prechronic inhalation study of 1-nitropyrene
N01ES-85233-06 (**) PREJEAN, J DAVID Chronic toxicity study of salicylazosulfapyridine
N01ES-85234-06 (**) PREJEAN, JD Chronic toxicity studies of propanediol
N01ES-85235-06 (**) SHALAT, STUART Study of radon levels, cigarette smoking and cancer
N01ES-85236-03 (**) LYON, JOSEPH Study of radon levels, cigarette smoking and cancer
Z01ES-90033-09 (LMIN) WILSON, W E NIEHS, NIH Milk bradykinin and kininogens
Z01ES-90034-08 (LMIN) WILSON, W E NEIHS, NIH Antigenicity of PHLIP-8 and other physiological peptides
Z01ES-90043-06 (LMIN) MITCHELL, C L NIEHS, NIH Role of zinc in synaptic transmission in the hippocampal formation
Z01ES-90044-06 (LMIN) MITCHELL, C L NIEHS, NIH Modulation of neuronal function by neuropeptides and steroid hormones
Z01ES-90049-05 (LMIN) HONG, J S NIEHS, NIH Regulation of gene expression in adrenomedullary chromaffin cells
Z01ES-90053-04 (LMIN) LAZARUS, L H NIEHS, NIH Neuropeptides--Molecular mechanism of action
Z01ES-90054-04 (LMIN) WETSEL, W C NIEHS, NIH Regulation of biosynthesis, processing and secretion of neuropeptides
Z01ES-90055-03 (LMIN) MERCHENTHALER, I NIEHS, NIH Hypothalamic control of the anteriorpituitary--Morphological aspects
Z01ES-90056-03 (LMIN) HONG, J S NIEHS, NIH Regulation of hippocampal opioid peptides by excitatory amino acids and hormones
Z01ES-90057-02 (LMIN) MITCHELL, C L NIEHS, NIH Modulation of epileptiform activity by various excitatory amino acid inhibitors
Z01ES-90058-03 (LMIN) NEGRO-VILAR, A NIEHS, NIH Role of excitotoxins on brain-endocrine function
Z01ES-90059-02 (LMIN) MCMILLIAN, M NIEHS, NIH Biochemical pathways involved in receptor regulation of neurotransmitter levels
Z01ES-90060-02 (LMIN) SUH, H H NIEHS, NIH Neurotransmitter secretion and gene expression regulated by angiotensin system
Z01ES-90061-02 (LMIN) MAR, E C NIEHS, NIH Molecular mechanism

PROJECT NO., ORGANIZATIONAL UNIT., INVESTIGATOR, ADDRESS, TITLE

of gene regulation in adrenal chromaffin cells
Z01ES-90062-02 (LMIN) LOPEZ, F J NIEHS, NIH Hypothalamic control of pulsatile prolactin secretion
Z01ES-90063-02 (LMIN) LOPEZ, F J NIEHS, NIH Role of galanin in the regulation of gonadal functions
Z01ES-90064-02 (LMIN) MANASCO, P K NIEHS, NIH The endocrinology of normal and abnormal puberty
Z01ES-90065-02 (LMIN) MANASCO, P K NIEHS, NIH Isolation of a testis stimulating factor in familial male precocious puberty
Z01ES-90066-01 (LMIN) PENNYPACKER, K R NIEHS, NIH Regulation of AP1 transcription factors and opioid peptides in seizure paradigms
Z01ES-90067-01 (LMIN) MCMILLIAN, M K NIEHS, NIH Receptor regulation of rat enkephalin
Z01ES-90068-01 (LMIN) WILSON, W E NIEHS, NIH Novel mammalian opioid receptor ligands
N44ES-92001-03 (**) YONGJIA, YU Screening and analysis of mammalian mutational risk
N44ES-92003-05 (**) LIECHTY, MELISSA Genetic analysis of thymidine kinase and HPRT gene mutations
N44ES-92004-07 (**) YACOWITZ, HAROLD Development of humane tattoo system for small rodents
N01ES-95238-04 (**) SHOPP, GEORGE M Immunotoxicological evaluation of AIDS therapeutics
N01ES-95239-07 (**) CHOU, BILLY J Prechronic and chronic inhalation study of ozone
N01ES-95240-07 (**) CHOU, BILLY J Chronic inhalation study of molybdenum trioxide
N01ES-95241-07 (**) CHOU, BJ Chronic toxicity studies of isobutyraldehyde
N01ES-95242-06 (**) MULLIGAN, LOUIS T Prechronic studies of diphenylguanidine
N01ES-95249-03 (**) GULATI, DUSHYANT Range finding studies--Developmental toxicity
N01ES-95252-04 (**) PUTMAN, DONALD Development of mutagenesis assay using transgenic mice
N01ES-95253-04 (**) PINKERT, CARL Development of mutagenesis assay using transgenic mice
N01ES-95254-09 (**) HARDISTY, JERRY F Pathology support for the NTP, pathology QA
N01ES-95255-07 (**) PRICE, CATHERINE J Developmental toxicity testing and research--Task II
N01ES-95256-10 (**) LILJA, HERMAN Studies of 1,2-dihydro-2,2,4-trimethylquinoline
N01ES-95258-08 (**) BRAUN, ANDREW Study of transgenic mice using p-cresidine and reserpine
N01ES-95259-03 (**) CHOU, BILLY Pilot and chronic toxicity study of tetrahydrofuran
N01ES-95260-09 (**) HARDISTY, JERRY F National toxicology program archives
N01ES-95262-06 (**) CHOU, BILLY J Chronic cocarcinogenicity study of ozone and NNK
N01ES-95263-02 (**) TOBLER, JACK Review and analysis on environmental mutagenesis
N01ES-95264-03 (**) RUSSELL, JAMES Rodent production centers
N01ES-95265-02 (**) PHELAN, SAMUEL Rodent production centers
N01ES-95266-12 (**) ARANYI, CATHERINE Prechronic inhalation study of vanadium pentoxide
N01ES-95267-02 (**) HERBST, ARTHUR Impact of prenatal exposure to diethylstilbestrol
N01ES-95268-07 (**) BRAUN, ANDREW Subchronic and chronic dosed water studies of pyridine
N01ES-95269-05 (**) LEININGER, JOEL Pathology support for the national toxicology program
N01ES-95270-02 (**) HILDEBRANDT, PAUL Pathology support for the national toxicology program
N01ES-95271-05 (**) PREJEAN, JD Chronic toxicity study of d&c yellow 11
N01ES-95272-04 (**) BRAUN, ANDREW Subchronic study of 1,1,1-trichloroethane
N01ES-95273-03 (**) LEWIS, SUSAN Combined endpoint mouse germ cell mutagenicity assay
N01ES-95274-03 (**) RUSSELL, JAMES D Rodent foundation colonies
N01ES-95276-05 (**) CARDIS, ELIZABETH International epidemiologic studies of cancers
N01ES-95277-04 (**) GRAFFEO, ANTHONY Prechronic dosed water study of dipropylene glycol
N01ES-95278-07 (**) COCKERHAM, LORRIS G NIP technical report preparation services
N01ES-95281-07 (**) CHOU, BILLY J Prechronic toxicity study of styrene
N01ES-95283-04 (**) FOGEL, SEYMOUR Yeast aneuploidy test system
Z01EY-00003-19 (LMOD) KADOR, P NEI, NIH Pharmacology of ocular complications
Z01EY-00011-17 (OGCS) KAISER-KUPFER, M I NEI, NIH Pigment dispersion with and without glaucoma
R01EY-00012-28 (VISA) LIEBMAN, PAUL A UNIVERSITY OF PENNSYLVANIA 37TH AND HAMILTON WALK PHILADELPHIA, PA 19104-6058 Microphotometric studies on retinal rods
R01EY-00014-24 (VISB) DE VALOIS, RUSSELL L UNIV OF CALIFORNIA BERKELEY, CA 94720 Electrophysiology of color vision
R01EY-00031-20S1 (VISA) ANDERSON, DOUGLAS R BASCOM PALMER EYE INSTITUTE PO BOX 016880 MIAMI, FL 33101 Experimental pathology of the optic nerve
R37EY-00033-22 (VISA) PAK, WILLIAM L PURDUE UNIVERSITY LILLY HALL OF LIFE SCIENCES WEST LAFAYETTE, IN 47907 Molecular genetics of photoreceptor excitation
Z01EY-00045-13 (LSR) ROBINSON, D L NEI, NIH Visuomotor properties of neurons in the thalamus
R01EY-00046-22 (VISA) HALL, MICHAEL O UCLA SCHOOL OF MEDICINE JULES STEIN EYE INSTITUTE 90024-7008 Studies on the etiology of retinal degeneration

PROJECT NO., ORGANIZATIONAL UNIT., INVESTIGATOR, ADDRESS, TITLE

Z01EY-00049-13 (LSR) GOLDBERG, M E NEI, NIH Cerebral cortical mechanisms for eye movements and visual attention
R01EY-00053-22 (VISB) DAW, NIGEL W WASHINGTON UNIVERSITY 660 SOUTH EUCLID AVE, BOX 8228 ST LOUIS, MO 63110 Neural mechanisms of vision
Z01EY-00060-14 (OGCS) KAISER-KUPFER, M I NEI, NIH Visual function and ocular pigmentation in albinism
Z01EY-00062-15 (OGCS) DATILES, MB NEI, NIH Irido-corneal-endothelial (ICE) syndrome
Z01EY-00065-14 (IRP) DE MONASTERIO, F NEI,NIH Physiological studies of the primate visual system
Z01EY-00069-14 (LI) GERY, I NEI, NIH Immune responses to ocular antigens
Z01EY-00070-14 (RCMB) WIGGERT, BARBARA NEI, NIH Vitamin A and ocular tissues
Z01EY-00075-13 (LI) NUSSENBLATT, R NEI, NIH Immune functions in ocular diseases of obscure etiology
Z01EY-00083-14 (OGCS) KAISER-KUPFER, M I NEI, NIH Gyrate atrophy of the choroid and retina and other retinal degenerations
Z01EY-00084-13 (OGCS) KUPFER, C NEI, NIH Anterior chamber anomalies associated with glaucoma or ocular hypertension
Z01EY-00105-12 (LMOD) ZIGLER, J S NEI, NIH Structure and composition of lens crystallins with respect to cataractogenesis
Z01EY-00109-11 (LSR) WURTZ, R H NEI, NIH Visuomotor processing in primate brain
Z01EY-00115-13 (91) NUSSENBLATT, R NEI,NIH Cyclosporin therapy in uveitis
Z01EY-00122-11 (IRP) DE MONASTERIO, F NEI,NIH Anatomical studies of the primate visual system
Z01EY-00123-12 (OGCS) CARUSO, R NEI, NIH Clinical psychophysics of the visual system
Z01EY-00124-11 (RCMB) CHADER, GERALD J NEI,NIH Metabolism of the retina and pigment epithelium
R01EY-00126-22 (VISB) SCHNEIDER, GERALD E MASSACHUSETTS INST OF TECHNOLO CAMBRIDGE, MA 02139 Anatomical & functional studies of the visual system
Z01EY-00126-10 (LMDB) PIATIGORSKY, J NEI, NIH Crystallin genes--Structure, organization, expression, and evolution
Z01EY-00132-10 (RCMB) SHINOHARA, TOSHIMICHI NEI, NIH Molecular biology of phototransduction
Z01EY-00135-19 (IRP) HESS, H H NEI, NIH Biochemistry of retina and pigmented epithelium in health and disease
Z01EY-00144-10 (OGCS) CARUSO, R NEI, NIH Clinical electrophysiology of the visual system
R01EY-00146-20 (VISA) KLINTWORTH, GORDON K DUKE UNIVERSITY MEDICAL CENTER BOX 3712 DURHAM, NC 27710 Experimental approach to diseases of the cornea
Z01EY-00148-18 (RCMB) CHADER, GERALD J NEI, NIH Vision control mechanisms
Z01EY-00149-18 (LMOD) ROBISON, W G NEI, NIH Ultrastructure and function of the cells and tissues of the eye
Z01EY-00153-09 (LSR) MILES, F A NEI, INH Visual motion and the stabilization of gaze
Z01EY-00163-09 (OGCS) KAISER-KUPFER, M I NEI, NIH NIH Interinstitute medical genetics program--The genetics clinic
R01EY-00168-22 (VISB) EASTER, STEPHEN S, JR UNIVERSITY OF MICHIGAN 830 N UNIVERSITY AVE ANN ARBOR, MI 48109-1048 Visual system--Order, regeneration, and competition
R01EY-00169-21 (VISA) BERSON, ELIOT L MASSACHUSETTS EYE & EAR INFIRM 243 CHARLES STREET BOSTON, MASS 02114 Electrophysiological studies of retinal degenerations
Z01EY-00184-09 (LI) CASPI, R NEI, NIH Cellular mechanisms in uveitis
Z01EY-00187-08 (OGCS) DATILES, M B NEI, NIH The effects of corneal contact lenses on the cornea
Z01EY-00188-08 (OGCS) DATILES, M B NEI, NIH Documentation and monitoring of opacities in the human lens
Z01EY-00189-07 (LMOD) GARLAND, D L NEI, NIH Oxidation of proteins in cataractogenesis
Z01EY-00196-09 (RCMB) NICKERSON, JOHN M NEI, NIH Molecular genetics of the eye and ocular diseases
R01EY-00197-34 (VISB) ALPERN, MATHEW W. K. KELLOGG EYE CENTER 990 WALL STREET ANN ARBOR, MI 48105 Psychophysiological studies of ocular abnormalities
Z01EY-00201-07 (LMOD) CARPER, D NEI, NIH Structure expression and gene complexity of aldose reductase
Z01EY-00211-06 (OCGS) KAISER-KUPFER, M I NEI, NIH A double-masked controlled randomized clinical trial of topical cysteamine
Z01EY-00212-06 (OGCS) DATILES, M B NEI, NIH Use of human lens material for determining possible causes of cataracts
Z01EY-00218-06 (LI) DE SMET, M D NEI, NIH Ocular manifestations of the acquired immune deficiency syndrome
R01EY-00219-30 (VISA) GRAYSTON, J THOMAS UNIVERSITY OF WASHINGTON SCHOOL OF PUBLIC HEALTH AND SEATTLE, WA 98195 Prevention of trachoma and related infections
R37EY-00220-30 (VISB) WESTHEIMER, GERALD UNIVERSITY OF CALIFORNIA 211 LIFE SCIENCE ADDITION BERKELEY, CALIF 94720 Retinal & central visual functions
R01EY-00222-31 (VISA) GOLDSMITH, TIMOTHY H YALE UNIVERSITY PO BOX 1504A YALE STATION NEW HAVEN, CT 06520 Visual mechanisms
Z01EY-00222-06 (LI) CHAN, C-C NEI, NIH Immunopathology in the eyes with experimental uveitis
Z01EY-00232-06 (LI) HOOKS, J J NEI, NIH Interferon system in cellular function and disease
Z01EY-00233-06 (LI) HOOKS, J J NEI, NIH Studies of the bioregulatory aspects of the retinal pigment epithelial cell
Z01EY-00237-06 (LMOD) RUSSELL, P NEI, NIH Characterization of the lens
Z01EY-00238-06 (LMDB) ZELENKA, P NEI, NIH Proto-oncogene expression during lens differentiation and development
Z01EY-00240-06 (LI) HOOKS, J J NEI, NIH Virus infections in the eye

PROJECT NO., ORGANIZATIONAL UNIT., INVESTIGATOR, ADDRESS, TITLE

Z01EY-00241-05 (LI) CHAN, C-C NEI, NIH Immunopathology of ocular diseases in humans
Z01EY-00243-06 (LMOD) PFEFFER, B A NEI, NIH Ocular cells cultured under normal diabetic conditions
Z01EY-00246-04 (OGCS) GORIN, M B NEI, NIH Molecular genetics of retinal degenerations
Z01EY-00248-04 (LI) LOPEZ, J S NEI, NIH Magainin therapy of infectious keratitis
Z01EY-00250-04 (RCMB) SHINOHARA, T NEI, NIH Molecular biology of experimental autoimmune uveitis
Z01EY-00251-04 (LMDB) CHEPELINSKY, A B NEI, NIH Engineering the lens with the alpha A-crystallin promoter
Z01EY-00252-03 (LMOD) RUSSELL, P NEI, NIH Cataract in th Philly mouse strain
Z01EY-00253-03 (LMDB) CHEPELINSKY, A B NEI, NIH Regulation of expression in lens fiber membrane genes
Z01EY-00255-04 (LMDB) WISTOW, G J NEI, NIH Origins, structures and functions of crystallins
Z01EY-00256-03 (LSR) OPTICAN, L M NEI, NIH Information processing by visual system neurons
Z01EY-00257-03 (OGCS) CARUSO, R NEI, NIH Visual function diagnosis service
R01EY-00258-29 (VISA) COHEN, ADOLPH I WASHINGTON UNIVERSITY MED SCHO 660 SOUTH EUCLID AVENUE ST LOUIS, MO 63110 Cytology and physiology of the retina
Z01EY-00258-03 (LI) CASPI, R R NEI, NIH Experimental autoimmune uveitis in the mouse
Z01EY-00259-02 (LMDB) CUTHBERTSON, R A NEI,NIH Molecular biology of the cornea
Z01EY-00260-02 (RCMB) REDMOND, T M NEI, NIH Molecular biology of outer retina-specific proteins
Z01EY-00262-02 (LI) EGWUAGU, C E NEI, NIH TCR gene usage in experimental autoimmune uveoretinitis
Z01EY-00263-02 (LI) RUBIN, B I NEI, NIH Comparison of surgical treatment in uveitis patients with glaucoma
Z01EY-00264-02 (LI) CHAN, C-C NEI, NIH Cytokines and ocular antigens in the eye
Z01EY-00266-02 (LI) DE SMET, M D NEI, NIH Characterization of immune responses to S-antigen
Z01EY-00267-02 (LI) DE SMET, M D NEI, NIH Modulation of immune functions using the immunotoxin IL2-PE40
Z01EY-00268-01 (LI) WHITCUP, S M NEI, NIH The diagnosis and treatment of human uveitis
Z01EY-00269-01 (LI) WHITCUP, S M NEI, NIH Ocular toxicity of 2',3'-dideoxyinosine
Z01EY-00270-01 (LI) WHITCUP, S M NEI, NIH Cell adhesion molecules in ocular inflammation
Z01EY-00271-01 (LI) CHAN, C C NEI, NIH The evaluation of antiflammins in the anterior uveitis
Z01EY-00272-01 (LMOD) HEJTMANCIK, J F NEI, NIH Inherited ocular diseases
Z01EY-00273-01 (LMDB) CUTHBERTSON, R A NEI, NIH The retinoblastoma-associated gene during lens cell differentiation--Physiology
Z01EY-00274-01 (LMDB) KIM, R Y NEI, NIH Gene expression in retinal pigment epithelium
K11EY-00281-05 (VSN) RIZZO, JOSEPH F III MASSACHUSETTS EYE & EAR INFIRM 220 COMMONWEALTH AVENUE BOSTON, MA 02116 Identification of human ganglion cell sub-populations
K11EY-00282-05 (VSN) WICK, BRUCE C UNIVERSITY OF HOUSTON UNIVERSITY PARK HOUSTON, TX 77004 Determination of human visual resolution
K11EY-00286-05 (VSN) SEMBA, RICHARD D JOHNS HOPKINS HOSPITAL 600 NORTH WOLFE STREET BALTIMORE, MD 21205 Immunology and pathogenesis of ocular onchocerciasis
K11EY-00289-04 (VSN) WEITZ, CHARLES J JOHNS HOPKINS UNIVERSITY SCHOOL OF MEDICINE BALTIMORE, MD 21205 The structure and function of visual pigments
K11EY-00292-05 (VSN) LATINA, MARK A EYE RESEARCH INSTITUTE 20 STANIFORD ST BOSTON, MA 02114 Photochemical targeting of trabecular meshwork cells
K11EY-00296-04 (VSN) RAIZMAN, MICHAEL B MASS EYE & EAR INFIRMARY 243 CHARLES STREET BOSTON, MA 02114 Mast cell membrane glycolipid expression and function
K11EY-00297-04 (VSN) ZACK, DONALD J THE JOHNS HOPKINS HOSPITAL 601 N. BROADWAY BALTIMORE, MD 21205 Analysis of retinal visual pigment gene expression
K11EY-00298-04 (VSN) SCHNUR, RHONDA E CHILDREN'S HOSP OF PHILA 34TH & CIVIC CENTER BLVD PHILADELPHIA, PA 19104 Molecular study of DELXP22 ocular albinism & ichthyosis
R01EY-00300-26 (VISA) ENGERMAN, RONALD L UNIVERSITY OF WISCONSIN 1300 UNIVERSITY AVENUE MADISON, WI 53706 Study of diabetic retinopathy
K11EY-00302-04 (VSN) BRONTE-STEWART, HELEN U OF CALIFORNIA, SAN FRANCISCO PARNASSUS AVE SAN FRANCISCO, CA 94143 Research/training in ocular motor neurophysiology
K11EY-00304-02 (VSN) SCROGGS, MARK W DUKE UNIVERSITY EYE CTR BOX 3802 DURHAM, N C 27710 Mechanisms of radiation suppressed corneal angiogenesis
K11EY-00305-03 (VSN) SZAPIEL, SUSAN V ROCKEFELLER UNIVERSITY 1230 YORK AVENUE NEW YORK, NY 10021-6399 Analysis of connectivity in striate cortex
K11EY-00306-03 (VSN) GIZZI, MARTIN S MOUNT SINAI SCHOOL OF MEDICINE ONE GUSTAVE L LEVY PLACE NEW YORK, NY 10029-6579 Processes of visual tracking
K11EY-00308-03 (VSN) COUSINS, SCOTT W UNIVERSITY OF MIAMI SCH OF MED PO BOX 016960 MIAMI, FL 33101 Characterization of lymphocyte inhibitor in aqueous humor
K11EY-00309-03 (VSN) BRITT, STEVEN G UNIV OF CALIF., SAN DIEGO DEPARTMENT OF BIOLOGY, B-022 LA JOLLA, CA 92093 Molecular genetics of rhodopsin & visual transduction in Drosophila
K11EY-00310-01A1 (VSN) DEAN, DEBORAH A UNIVERSITY OF CALIFORNIA PARNASSUS AVENUE SAN FRANCISCO, CA 94143-0412 Chlamydia ocular infections, molecular epidemiology
K11EY-00311-03 (VSN) KOSTYK, SANDRA K THE CHILDREN'S HOSPITAL 300 LONGWOOD AVENUE BOSTON, MA 02115 FGF in the visual system
K11EY-00313-03 (VSN) SMALL, KENT W MEDICAL UNIV OF SOUTH CAROLINA 171 ASHLEY AVE CHARLESTON, SC 29425 Genetic linkage of North Carolina macular dystrophy
K11EY-00316-01 (VSN) BECK, ROY W UNIV OF SOUTH FLORIDA 13131 MAGNOLIA DRIVE TAMPA, FL 33612 Epidemiology and biostatistics training
K11EY-00317-01 (VSN) SWEARINGEN, BROOKE MASSACHUSETTS GENERAL HOSPITAL FRUIT ST BOSTON, MA 02114 Trophic factors for retinal ganglion cells
K11EY-00318-01 (VSN) POWERS, MICHAEL R OREGON HEALTH SCIENCES UNIV 3181 SW SAM JACKSON PARK ROAD PORTLAND, OR 97201 Growth factors in neonatal hyperoxic eye and lung injury
K11EY-00320-01 (VSN) BORN, RICHARD T HARVARD MEDICAL SCHOOL 220 LONGWOOD AVE BOSTON, MA 02115 Modularity of primate visual area MT
K11EY-00321-01 (VSN) AUSTIN, CHRISTOPHER P HARVARD MEDICAL SCHOOL 25 SHATTUCK ST BOSTON, MA 02115 Effect of FGF's on retinal development and pathology
R01EY-00327-26 (VISA) REFOJO, MIGUEL F EYE RESEARCH INST RETINA FNDN 20 STANIFORD STREET BOSTON, MASS 02114 Synthetic hydrophylic polymers for eye surgery
P30EY-00331-25 (VSN) HORWITZ, JOSEPH UNIVERSITY OF CALIFORNIA JULES STEIN EYE INSTITUTE LOS ANGELES, CA 90024-7008 Vision research center
R01EY-00360-25 (VISB) THOMAS, JAMES P UNIVERSITY OF CALIFORNIA 405 HILGARD AVENUE LOS ANGELES, CA 90024-1563 Mechanisms of spatial pattern vision
R01EY-00362-23 (VISA) REDDAN, JOHN R OAKLAND UNIVERSITY DEPT OF BIOLOGICAL SCIENCES ROCHESTER, MI 48309-4401 Control of cell division in the ocular lens
R01EY-00379-24 (VISA) GREEN, DANIEL G UNIVERSITY OF MICHIGAN 1103 E HURON ANN ARBOR, MICH 48104-1687 Functional organization of the retina
R01EY-00393-24 (VISA) KEAN, EDWARD L CASE WESTERN RESERVE UNIV 2074 ABINGTON ROAD CLEVELAND, OHIO 44106 Glycolipid and glycoprotein metabolism in eye tissue
R01EY-00395-23 (VISA) LOLLEY, RICHARD N UNIVERSITY OF CALIFORNIA 405 HILGARD AVENUE LOS ANGELES, CA 90024-1406 Maturation of metabolism in normal and dystrophic retina
R01EY-00423-23 (SSS) SPECTOR, ABRAHAM COLUMBIA UNIVERSITY 630 W 168TH STREET NEW YORK, N Y 10032 Studies upon the ocular lens
R01EY-00424-19 (VISA) JOHNSON, MARY K TULANE UNIVERSITY 1430 TULANE AVENUE NEW ORLEANS, LA 70112 Role of microbial cytolysins in ocular infections
R37EY-00431-22 (SSS) MAURICE, DAVID M STANFORD UNIVERSITY MED. CTR. DEPT OF OPHTHALMOLOGY, S030 STANFORD, CA 94305 Control of corneal hydration
R37EY-00444-23 (VISB) BOK, DEAN UNIVERSITY OF CALIFORNIA CENTER FOR THE HEALTH SCIENCES LOS ANGELES, CA 90024 Autoradiography and cytochemistry of ocular tissues
R01EY-00459-22 (VISA) ZIGMAN, SEYMOUR UNIV OF ROCHESTER MED CTR BOX 314-601 ELMWOOD AVE ROCHESTER, NY 14642 Near-UV light effects on ocular tissues
R01EY-00460-23 (VISB) BURKHARDT, DWIGHT A UNIVERSITY OF MINNESOTA 75 E RIVER ROAD MINNEAPOLIS, MINN 55455 Vision and intraretinal potentials
R01EY-00463-23 (VISA) BOWNDS, M DERIC UNIVERSITY OF WISCONSIN 1525 LINDEN DRIVE MADISON, WI 53706 Molecular biology of visual receptor outer segments
R01EY-00475-24 (VISA) BILL, ANDERS A UNIVERSITY OF UPPSALA BOX 572 S-751 23 UPPSALA, SWEDEN Nutrition of the eye
R37EY-00484-24 (VISA) REDDY, VENKAT N OAKLAND UNIVERSITY EYE RESEARCH INSTITUTE ROCHESTER, MI 48309-4401 Study of intraocular transport and metabolism
R01EY-00541-22 (VISA) RILEY, MICHAEL V EYE RESEARCH INSTITUTE OAKLAND UNIVERSITY ROCHESTER, MICH 48309 Control of corneal hydration and transparency
R01EY-00548-20 (VISA) LITMAN, BURTON J UNIVERSITY OF VIRGINIA P. O. BOX 9003 CHARLOTTSVILLE, VA 22903 Disk function: rhodopsin substructure and environment
R01EY-00561-22 (VISA) WERBLIN, FRANK S UNIVERSITY OF CALIFORNIA LIFE SCIENCES ADDITION BERKELEY, CA 94720 Neuromodulatory pathways in the retina
R37EY-00598-23 (VISB) ROBINSON, DAVID A WILMER INST/JOHNS HOPKINS HOSP RM355 WOODS RES BUILDING BALTIMORE, MD 21205 Study of oculomotor control system
R37EY-00605-32 (VISB) HUBEL, DAVID H HARVARD MEDICAL SCHOOL 25 SHATTUCK STREET BOSTON, MASS 02115 Organization of the visual system
R01EY-00621-17 (VISB) PEARLMAN, ALAN L WASHINGTON UNIV SCHOOL OF MED 660 S. EUCLID AVENUE, BOX 8228 ST LOUIS, MO 63110 Functional organization of the visual system
R37EY-00634-21 (VISA) BRUBAKER, RICHARD F MAYO FOUNDATION 200 FIRST STREET SOUTHWEST ROCHESTER, MN 55905 Pathophysiology of the blood-ocular barrier
R01EY-00667-19 (VISA) BARLOW, ROBERT B, JR SYRACUSE UNIVERSITY MERRILL LANE SYRACUSE, NY 13244-5290 Functional organization of the visual system
R01EY-00675-19 (VISA) ZIMMERMAN, WILLIAM F AMHERST COLLEGE AMHERST, MA 01002 Phospholipid metabolism in mammalian photoreceptor cells
R37EY-00676-21 (VISB) SCHILLER, PETER H MASSACHUSETTS INST OF TECH 45 CARLETON STREET, E25-634 CAMBRIDGE, MASS 02139 Interaction between eye movement and vision
R01EY-00698-21 (VISA) RAFFERTY, NANCY S NORTHWESTERN UNIVERSITY MEDICAL AND DENTAL SCHOOLS CHICAGO, IL 60611 Etiology of cataract
R01EY-00735-20 (BPO) HODOS, WILLIAM UNIVERSITY OF MARYLAND DEPARTMENT OF PSYCHOLOGY COLLEGE PARK, MD 20742 Morphological correlates--Visual information processing
R37EY-00745-21 (VISA) FUCHS, ALBERT F UNIVERSITY OF WASHINGTON REGIONAL PRIMATE RESEARCH CTR. SEATTLE, WA 98195 Neurophysiology of the oculomotor system

PROJECT NO., ORGANIZATIONAL UNIT., INVESTIGATOR, ADDRESS, TITLE

R37EY-00759-20 (VISA) SPECTOR, ABRAHAM COLUMBIA UNIVERSITY 630 WEST 168TH STREET NEW YORK, NY 10032 Studies of the effect of aging on the ocular lens
R37EY-00811-20 (VISB) DOWLING, JOHN E HARVARD UNIVERSITY 16 DIVINITY AVE CAMBRIDGE, MA 02138 Anatomical and biochemical organization of the retina
R01EY-00824-21 (VISA) DOWLING, JOHN E HARVARD UNIVERSITY 16 DIVINITY AVENUE CAMBRIDGE, MA 02138 Functional organization of vertebrate visual systems
R01EY-00828-20 (VISA) STERLING, PETER UNIVERSITY OF PENNSYLVANIA SCHOOL OF MEDICINE PHILADELPHIA, PA 19104-6058 Microcircuitry of retina: Form, function, development
R01EY-00871-20 (VISA) ANDERSON, ROBERT E BAYLOR COLLEGE OF MEDICINE ONE BAYLOR PLAZA HOUSTON, TEX 77030 Chemistry and metabolism of retina lipids
R37EY-00888-20 (VISB) FISHER, STEVEN K UNIVERSITY OF CALIFORNIA INST OF ENVIRONMENTAL STRESS SANTA BARBARA, CA 93106 The developing and adult visual system
R01EY-00901-18 (VISB) POKORNY, JOEL M UNIVERSITY OF CHICAGO 939 E 57TH STREET CHICAGO, ILL 60637 Psychophysical studies of color-defective observers
R01EY-00933-20 (VISA) EDELHAUSER, HENRY F EMORY UNIVERSITY EYE CENTER 1327 CLIFTON ROAD, NE ATLANTA, GA 30322 Pathogenesis of corneal edema after intraocular surgery
R01EY-00952-20 (VISA) CONRAD, GARY W KANSAS STATE UNIVERSITY ACKERT HALL MANHATTAN, KANS 66506 Fibroblast differentiation during eye development
R01EY-00983-19 (BBCA) KLIGER, DAVID S UNIVERSITY OF CALIFORNIA NATURAL SCIENCES II SANTA CRUZ, CA 95064 Investigation of the bleaching stages of rhodopsin
R01EY-01019-18 (VISA) FARRELL, RICHARD A JOHNS HOPKINS UNIVERSITY JOHNS HOPKINS ROAD LAUREL, MD 20723-6099 Light scattering studies of ocular tissues
R01EY-01055-18 (VISB) KERTESZ, ANDREW E NORTHWESTERN UNIVERSITY 2145 SHERIDAN ROAD EVANSTON, ILL 60208-3107 Functional aspects of Panum's fusional areas
R37EY-01075-18 (VISA) MASLAND, RICHARD H MASSACHUSETTS GENERAL HOSPITAL FRUIT STREET BOSTON, MA 02114 Neurotransmission in mammalian retina
R01EY-01117-19 (VISB) FREEMAN, JOHN A VANDERBILT UNIV SCH OF MED NASHVILLE, TN 37232 Synaptic organization of the optic tectum
R01EY-01139-17 (VISB) HARWERTH, RONALD S UNIVERSITY OF HOUSTON 4800 CALHOUN BLVD HOUSTON, TX 77204-6052 Behavioral measures of binocular vision
R01EY-01156-14 (VISA) FU, S JOSEPH UNIV OF MEDICINE & DENTISTRY 185 SOUTH ORANGE AVENUE NEWARK, N J 07103 Progression of cataractogenesis and possible reversal
R01EY-01157-18 (VISA) CORNWALL, M CARTER BOSTON UNIVERSITY SCHOOL OF ME 80 EAST CONCORD STREET BOSTON, MA 02118 Spectral and metabolic basis of visual responses
R01EY-01175-19 (VISB) FREEMAN, RALPH D UNIV OF CALIFORNIA 360 MINOR HALL BERKELEY, CA 94720 Studies of normal and abnormal binocular vision
R37EY-01189-19 (VISB) SPARKS, DAVID L UNIV OF PENNSYLVANIA 3815 WALNUT STREET PHILADELPHIA, PA 19104-6196 Eye movement control--Role of brain stem neurons
R01EY-01191-18 (VISB) HELD, RICHARD M MASSACHUSETTS INST OF TECHNOLO 79 AMHERST STREET - E10-145 CAMBRIDGE, MA 02139 Vision and visuomotor mechanisms
R01EY-01197-18 (VISA) RATHBUN, WILLIAM B UNIVERSITY OF MINNESOTA BOX 376 MAYO MEMORIAL BUILDING MINNEAPOLIS, MN 55455 Glutathione metabolism in ocular tissues
R01EY-01199-18 (VISA) CINTRON, CHARLES EYE RESEARCH INST OF RETINA FD 20 STANIFORD STREET BOSTON, MA 02114 Macromolecular morphogenesis of corneal tissues
R01EY-01221-19 (VISA) PINTO, LAWRENCE H NORTHWESTERN UNIVERSITY O T HOGAN HALL EVANSTON, IL 60208 Intermediate processes in photoreceptors
R01EY-01244-19 (VISA) AGUIRRE, GUSTAVO D UNIVERSITY OF PENNSYLVANIA 3850 SPRUCE ST RM. 3113 PHILADELPHIA, PA 19104-6010 Progressive rod-cone degeneration: synthesis & renewal
R01EY-01292-15 (VISA) VARMA, SHAMBHU D UNIVERSITY OF MARYLAND 10 S PINE STREET BALTIMORE, MD 21202 Oxidative stress on ocular lens
R01EY-01303-15 (VISA) FEKE, GILBERT T EYE RESEARCH INST 20 STANIFORD STREET BOSTON, MA 02114 Human retinal blood flow and laser velocimetry
R01EY-01311-18 (VISB) MILAM, ANN H UNIVERSITY OF WASHINGTON SEATTLE, WA 98195 Protein transport in retinal photoreceptors and axons
R01EY-01313-16S1 (CLN) SOUTHREN, A LOUIS NEW YORK MEDICAL COLLEGE VALHALLA, NY 10595-1691 The role of abnormal cortisol metabolism in glaucoma
P30EY-01319-17 (VSN) LENNIE, PETER UNIVERSITY OF ROCHESTER 274 MELIORA HALL, RIVER CAMPUS ROCHESTER, NY 14627 Visual science research center support
R01EY-01323-19 (VISA) EBREY, THOMAS G 407 SOUTH GOODWIN URBANA, IL 61801 Studies on the mechanism of visual excitation
R01EY-01331-16 (VISB) KALIL, RONALD E UNIVERSITY OF WISCONSIN 1300 UNIVERSITY AVENUE MADISON, WIS 53706 Development studies of the visual system
R01EY-01340-17 (VISA) ZADUNAISKY, JOSE A NEW YORK UNIV MED CTR DEPT OF PHYSIOLOGY & BIOPHYSIC NEW YORK, NY 10016 Transport mechanisms in ocular cell membranes
R01EY-01344-17 (VISA) RAVIOLA, ELIO HARVARD MEDICAL SCHOOL 25 SHATTUCK STREET BOSTON, MASS 02115 Cell biology of the retina
R01EY-01406-15 (VISA) BASINGER, SCOTT F BAYLOR COLL MED/CULLEN EYE INS 1 BAYLOR PLAZA/RM C-418 HOUSTON, TX 77030 Retina--photoreceptors membrane synthesis and function
R01EY-01417-18 (VISA) MAISEL, HARRY WAYNE STATE UNIVERSITY 540 E CANFIELD DETROIT, MI 48201 A study of structural lens proteins
R01EY-01428-16 (VISB) KNIGHT, BRUCE W, JR ROCKEFELLER UNIVERSITY 1230 YORK AVENUE NEW YORK, N Y 10021-6399 Dynamics of interacting visual neurons

PROJECT NO., ORGANIZATIONAL UNIT., INVESTIGATOR, ADDRESS, TITLE

R37EY-01429-18 (VISA) STEINBERG, ROY H UNIVERSITY OF CALIFORNIA 513 PARNASSUS AVE SAN FRANCISCO, CA 94143 Pigment epithelium interactions with neural retina
R01EY-01472-17 (VISB) SHAPLEY, ROBERT M NEW YORK UNIVERSITY 6 WASHINGTON PLACE NEW YORK, NY 10003 Spatial summation and dynamics of visual neurons
R37EY-01496-18 (VISB) LISMAN, JOHN E BRANDEIS UNIVERSITY 415 SOUTH STREET WALTHAM, MA 02254 Mechanisms of adaptation and excitation
R37EY-01543-18 (VISA) BAYLOR, DENIS A STANFORD UNIVERSITY FAIRCHILD SCIENCE BUILDING STANFORD, CA 94305-5401 Neural signaling in the retina
R01EY-01545-15 (VISA) RYAN, STEPHEN J UNIV OF SOUTHERN CALIFORNIA 1355 SAN PABLO STREET LOS ANGELES, CA 90033 An experimental approach to maculopathy
R01EY-01576-17 (VISA) HAYREH, SOHAN S UNIVERSITY OF IOWA IOWA CITY, IOWA 52242 Experimental ocular vascular occlusive studies
P30EY-01583-17 (VSN) LIEBMAN, PAUL A UNIVERSITY OF PENNSYLVANIA 37TH & HAMILTON WALK PHILADELPHIA, PA 19104 Core grant for vision research
R01EY-01602-17 (VISA) STREETEN, BARBARA W SUNY HEALTH SCI CTR AT SYRACUS 750 E ADAMS STREET SYRACUSE, NY 13210 The fiber-gel structure of the ocular zonule
R01EY-01621-16 (VISA) O'DAY, DENIS M VANDERBILT UNIVERSITY MED CENT 21ST & GARLAND STREETS NASHVILLE, TN 37232-2540 Studies on experimental fungal infections in the eye.
R01EY-01634-16 (VISA) WALLOW, INGOLF H L UNIVERSITY OF WISCONSIN MED SC 600 HIGHLAND AVENUE, F4/3 MADISON, WI 53792 A proposed intraocular renin-angiotensin system
R01EY-01653-15 (VISA) MC REYNOLDS, JOHN S UNIVERSITY OF MICHIGAN DEPARTMENT OF PHYSIOLOGY ANN ARBOR, MICH 48109 Functional organization of the retina
R01EY-01655-14 (VISA) REDBURN, DIANNA A UNIV OF TX HLTH SCI CTR HOUSTO PO BOX 20708 HOUSTON, TX 77225 Biochemical analysis of neurotransmitters in retina
R01EY-01677-17 (VISA) SRIVASTAVA, SATISH K C3-15 CHILD HEALTH CENTER HUMAN BIOLOG CHEM & GENETICS GALVESTON, TEX 77550 Metabolic studies in normal and cataractous lenses
R01EY-01678-16 (VISA) MARMOR, MICHAEL F STANFORD UNIVERSITY MED CTR STANFORD, CA 94305 Interaction between retina and pigment epithelium
R01EY-01680-16 (VISA) UNAKAR, NALIN J OAKLAND UNIVERSITY ROCHESTER, MI 48309-4401 Morphological studies in cataracts
R01EY-01682-16 (VISB) YAZULLA, STEPHEN STATE UNIVERSITY OF NEW YORK DEPARTMENT OF NEUROBIOLOGY STONY BROOK, N Y 11794 Synaptic transmission in the retina
R01EY-01711-16 (VISB) MACLEOD, DONALD I UNIV OF CALIFORNIA, SAN DIEGO LA JOLLA, CALIF 92093 Retinal mechanisms in vision
R01EY-01728-16 (VISB) LEVI, DENNIS M UNIVERSITY OF HOUSTON 4901 CALHOUN BLVD HOUSTON, TX 77004-6052 Limiting factors in normal and amblyopic spatial vision
P30EY-01730-16 (VSN) KALINA, ROBERT E UNIVERSITY OF WASHINGTON SEATTLE, WA 98195 Vision research center
P30EY-01730-16 9001 (VSN) SAARI, JOHN E Vision research center Core--Biochemistry and immunology
P30EY-01730-16 9002 (VSN) MILAM, ANN H Vision research center Core--Electron microscopy
P30EY-01730-16 9003 (VSN) HENDRICKSON, ANITA E Vision research center Core--Histology
P30EY-01730-16 9004 (VSN) MILAM, ANN E Vision research center Core--Research photography
P30EY-01730-16 9005 (VSN) BARLOW, WILLIAM E Vision research center Core--Biostatistics and clinical vision research
R01EY-01746-16 (VISA) YU, NAI-TENG GEORGIA INST OF TECHNOLOGY 225 NORTH AVENUE, N W ATLANTA, GA 30332 Comparative Raman studies of human and animal lenses
P30EY-01765-16 (VSN) GOLDBERG, MORTON F JOHNS HOPKINS HOSPITAL 600 NORTH WOLFE STREET BALTIMORE, MD 21205 Core center grant - Wilmer Ophthalmological Institute
R01EY-01778-15 (VISB) CASAGRANDE, VIVIEN A VANDERBILT UNIV SCHOOL OF MED DEPARTMENT OF CELL BIOLOGY NASHVILLE, TN 37232 Visual system organization and development
R01EY-01791-15A2 (VISA) MASSOF, ROBERT W WILMER VISION RESEARCH CENTER 1631 E BALTIMORE STREET BALTIMORE, MD 21231 Studies of visual impairments in retinitis pigmentosa
P30EY-01792-14 (VSN) CHANDLER, JOHN W UNIVERSITY OF ILLINOIS 1853 WEST POLK STREET CHICAGO, IL 60612 Ophthalmic research center core grant
R01EY-01808-15 (VISB) KRONAUER, RICHARD E HARVARD UNIVERSITY PIERCE HALL 324 CAMBRIDGE, MA 02138 Cone inputs to human spatial detectors
P30EY-01842-15 (VSN) WITKOVSKY, PAUL NYU MEDICAL CENTER 550 FRIST AVENUE NEW YORK, N Y 10016 Visual sciences research center
R37EY-01844-15 (VISA) FAIN, GORDON L UCLA SCHOOL OF MEDICINE LOS ANGELES, CA 90024-7008 Physiology of photoreceptors
R37EY-01849-16 (VISB) ZEE, DAVID S JOHNS HOPKINS HOSPITAL BALTIMORE, MD 21205 Oculomotor disorders: clinical and experimental study
R01EY-01857-15 (VISA) FRANK, ROBERT N KRESGE EYE INSTITUTE 4717 ST. ANTOINE DETROIT, MI 48201 Retinal cells--Tissue culture and cell biology
P30EY-01867-15 (VSN) CANDIA, OSCAR A MOUNT SINAI SCHOOL OF MEDICINE 1 GUSTAVE L LEVY PL BOX/1183 NEW YORK, NY 10029 Interdisciplinary vision research center
R01EY-01869-15 (VISA) COPENHAGEN, DAVID R KORET VISION RES. LAB., K-140 10 KIRKHAM STREET SAN FRANCISCO, CA 94143-0730 Synaptic interaction in the vertebrate retina
R01EY-01894-15 (VISA) EPSTEIN, DAVID L MASS EYE & EAR INFIRMARY 243 CHARLES STREET BOSTON, MASS 02114 Metabolism of the trabecular meshwork
R01EY-01897-14A1 (VISA) CHRISTENSEN, BURGESS N UNIV OF TEXAS MEDICAL BRANCH 301 UNIVERSITY BLVD GALVESTON, TX 77550-2774 Function of neuron network in visual system

PROJECT NUMBER LISTING

PROJECT NO., ORGANIZATIONAL UNIT., INVESTIGATOR, ADDRESS, TITLE

R01EY-01903-16 (VISA) TSO, MARK O UNIVERSITY OF ILLINOIS DEPARTMENT OF OPHTHALMOLOGY CHICAGO, IL 60612 Pathology of retinal dysfunction

R01EY-01916-16 (VISB) SPEAR, PETER D UNIVERSITY OF WISCONSIN 1202 WEST JOHNSON STREET MADISON, WI 53706 Visual integration in the brain

R01EY-01917-16 (VISA) ALBERT, DANIEL M HOWE LABORATORY 243 CHARLES STREET BOSTON, MASS 02114 Molecular biology of retinoblastoma and unveal melanoma

R37EY-01919-15 (VISB) LA VAIL, MATTHEW M UNIVERSITY OF CALIFORNIA DEPARTMENT OF ANATOMY SAN FRANCISCO, CA 94143-0452 Cellular mechanisms of inherited retinal degeneration

P30EY-01931-15 (VSN) BURKE, JANICE M MEDICAL COLLEGE OF WISCONSIN 8700 WEST WISCONSIN AVE MILWAUKEE, WI 53226 Core grant for vision research

R01EY-01935-11 (VISA) BERK, RICHARD S WAYNE STATE UNIV SCH OF MEDICI 540 E CANFIELD AVENUE DETROIT, MI 48201 Pseudomonas eye infection--An experimental model

R01EY-01938-15 (VISB) DRAGER, URSULA C HARVARD MEDICAL SCHOOL 25 SHATTUCK STREET BOSTON, MASS 02115 Normal and abnormal visual system

R01EY-01959-15 (VISB) ORGANISCIAK, DANIEL T WRIGHT STATE UNIVERSITY SCHOOL OF MEDICINE DAYTON, OH 45435 Environmental light and retinal membrane development

R01EY-01990-08 (VISA) LAING, RONALD A BOSTON UNIV SCH OF MEDICINE 80 EAST CONCORD STREET BOSTON, MA 02118 Metabolic studies of corneal tissues

R01EY-02005-15 (VISB) STRYER, LUBERT STANFORD UNIVERSITY FAIRCHILD BUILDING D133 STANFORD, CA 94305 Conformational aspects of visual excitation

U10EY-02014-15 (VSN) BERSON, ELIOT L MASSACHUSETTS EYE & EAR INFIRM 243 CHARLES STREET BOSTON, MASS 02114 Studies of retinitis pigmentosa and allied diseases

U10EY-02014-15 0001 (VSN) BERSON, ELLIOT L Studies of retinitis pigmentosa and allied diseases Module A--Clinical research

U10EY-02014-15 0002 (VSN) SCHMIDT, SUSAN Y Studies of retinitis pigmentosa and allied diseases Module B--Laboratory support

U10EY-02014-15 0003 (VSN) BERSON, ELLIOT L Studies of retinitis pigmentosa and allied diseases Module C--Data management

R01EY-02027-15 (VISA) GIBLIN, FRANK J OAKLAND UNIVERSITY ROCHESTER, MI 48309-4401 Proteins of normal and cataractous lenses

R01EY-02035-15 (VISA) ORTWERTH, BERYL J MASON INST OF OPHTHALMOLOGY ONE HOSPITAL DRIVE COLUMBIA, MO 65212 Lens inhibitor proteins and cataractogenesis

R01EY-02037-13 (VISA) BOURNE, WILLIAM M MAYO FOUNDATION 200 FIRST STREET SOUTHWEST ROCHESTER, MN 55905 Studies of the cornea

R01EY-02048-15 (VISA) DETWILER, PETER B UNIVERSITY OF WASHINGTON SEATTLE, WA 98195 Photoreceptors and second order cells in vertebrate retina

R37EY-02051-15 (BBCA) MATHIES, RICHARD A UNIVERSITY OF CALIFORNIA 310 HILDEBRAND HALL BERKELEY, CA 94720 Raman investigations of the molecular basis of vision

R01EY-02052-12A2 (VISB) JACOBS, GERALD H UNIVERSITY OF CALIFORNIA SANTA BARBARA, CA 93106 Within-species variations in visual capacity

R01EY-02061-14 (VISA) RYAN, STEPHEN J UNIVERSITY OF SOUTHERN CALIF 1355 SAN PABLO STREET LOS ANGELES, CA 90033 Pars plana vitrectomy in penetrating ocular trauma

R01EY-02068-14 (VISA) ALVARADO, JORGE A UNIVERSITY OF CALIFORNIA 10 KIRKHAM ST SAN FRANCISCO, CA 94143-0730 Pathogenesis of primary open-angle glaucoma

R01EY-02091-15 (VISB) VAN ESSEN, DAVID C CALIFORNIA INST OF TECHNOLOGY 1201 E CALIFORNIA BLVD PASADENA, CALIF 91125 Functional organization of extrastriate visual cortex

N01EY-02111-02 ( ) SCHACHAT, ANDREW** Age-related eye disease study

N01EY-02112-02 ( ) SURESH, CHANDRA R** Age related eye disease study

N01EY-02114-02 ( ) ELMAN, MICHAEL J** Age-related eye disease study

N01EY-02115-02 ( ) MARGHERIO, RAYMOND R** Age-related eye disease study

R01EY-02115-15 (VISB) HOOD, DONALD C COLUMBIA UNIVERSITY 406 SCHERMERHORN HALL NEW YORK, N Y 10027 Tests of models of retinal disease and adaptation

N01EY-02116-03 ( ) MEREDITH, TRAVIS** Age related eye disease study

N01EY-02117-02 ( ) SEDDON, JOHANNA M** Age-related eye disease study

N01EY-02119-02 ( ) KASSOFF, AARON** Age related eye disease study

R01EY-02120-15 (VISA) QUIGLEY, HARRY A JOHNS HOPKINS HOSPITAL MAUMENEE B-110, WILMER INSTITU BALTIMORE, MD 21205 Pathogenesis of glaucomatous optic nerve damage

N01EY-02124-02 ( ) ORTH, DAVID H** Age-related eye disease study

N01EY-02125-02 ( ) FRIBERG, THOMAS R** Age-related eye disease study

N01EY-02126-02 ( ) DREYER, RICHARD F** Age related eye disease study

N01EY-02127-02 ( ) EDERERI, FRED** Age related eye diseases study-- Coordinating center

N01EY-02130-01 ( ) DAVIS, MATTHEW D** Age related eye diseases study--Reading center

R13EY-02143-15 (SRC) QUIGLEY, HARRY A ASSOC FOR RES IN VISION & OPHT 9650 ROCKVILLE PIKE BETHESDA, MD 20814-3928 Young scientist support for vision studies

R01EY-02158-11 (VISB) WILSON, HUGH R EYE RESEARCH LABORATORIES 939 E 57TH STREET CHICAGO, IL 60637 The spatiotemporal basis of grating perception

P30EY-02162-14 (VSN) KRAMER, STEVEN G DEPT. OF OPHTHALMOLOGY, K301 UNIV. OF CA, 10 KIRKHAM STREET SAN FRANCISCO, CALIF 94143 Vision research center

P30EY-02180-14 (VSN) KNIGHTON, ROBERT W BASCOM PALMER EYE INSTITUTE P O BOX 016880 MIAMI, FLA 33101 Core grant for vision research

R01EY-02186-14 (VISA) GOSPODAROWICZ, DENIS J UNIVERSITY OF CALIFORNIA MED C THIRD & PARNASSUS SAN FRANCISCO, CA 94143 Regeneration of corneal endothelium

R37EY-02191-14 (VISB) SPENCER, ROBERT F MEDICAL COLLEGE OF VIRGINIA DEPT OF ANATOMY RICHMOND, VA 23298 Anatomy of oculomotor systems

R01EY-02193-14 (VISB) VAN SLUYTERS, RICHARD C UNIVERSITY OF CALIFORNIA 522 MINOR HALL BERKELEY, CA 94720 Central visual pathways

R01EY-02195-13 (VISB) KORETZ, JANE F RENSSELAER POLYTECHNIC INSTITU 3C15 SCIENCE CENTER TROY, NY 12180-3590 Aging of human crystalline lens dynamics

R37EY-02205-14 (VISA) MILLER, SHELDON S UNIVERSITY OF CALIFORNIA 360 MINOR HALL BERKELEY, CA 94720 Homeostatic ability of the retinal pigment epithelium

R01EY-02227-14 (VISA) MAREN, THOMAS H UNIVERSITY OF FLORIDA BOX J-267, JHMHC GAINSVILLE, FL 32610 Glaucoma-new drugs and mechanisms of aqueous secretion

R01EY-02254-12A2 (VISB) BENDER, DAVID B STATE UNIVERSITY OF NEW YORK 4234 RIDGE LEA ROAD BUFFALO, NY 14226 Visual funtions of the pulvinar

R01EY-02267-13 (VISA) POURCHO, ROBERTA G WAYNE STATE UNIVERSITY 540 EAST CANFIELD DETROIT, MI 48201 Retinal neurotransmitters and synaptic circuitry

R01EY-02271-14 (VISB) ADAMS, ANTHONY J UNIVERSITY OF CALIFORNIA BERKELEY, CA 94720 Vision changes in diabetics

R01EY-02294-13 (VISA) BLAZYNSKI, CHRISTINE WASHINGTON UNIVERSITY SCH OF M 660 S EUCLID AVE, BOX 8231 ST LOUIS, MO 63110 Biochemistry and pharmacology of the retina

R01EY-02296-14 (VISB) COHEN, BERNARD MOUNT SINAI SCHOOL OF MEDICINE 1 GUSTAVE L LEVY PLACE NEW YORK, NY 10029 Visual control of the oculomotor system

R01EY-02299-14 (VISA) WAGNER, BETTY J UMDNJ-NEW JERSEY MEDICAL SCH 185 SOUTH ORANGE AVENUE NEWARK, NJ 07103-2714 Proteolytic enzymes and cataractogenesis

R01EY-02305-13 (VISB) SCHLAG-REY, MADELEINE L UNIVERSITY OF CALIFORNIA 405 HILGARD AVENUE LOS ANGELES, CA 90024-1406 Single-unit studies of visuo-oculomotor mechanism

R01EY-02317-15 (VISA) SAARI, JOHN C UNIVERSITY WASHINGTON SEATTLE, WA 98195 Biochemistry of the retina and pigment epithelium

R01EY-02363-15 (VISA) HOLLYFIELD, JOE G BAYLOR COLLEGE OF MEDICINE ONE BAYLOR PLAZA HOUSTON, TX 77030 Development and maintenance of retinal cells

P30EY-02377-13 (VSN) KAUFMAN, HERBERT E LOUSIANA STATE UNIV EYE CTR 2020 GRAVIER STREET, SUITE B NEW ORLEANS, LA 70112 LSU eye center core grant for vision research

R01EY-02414-15 (VISA) BESHARSE, JOSEPH C UNIVERSITY OF KANSAS MED CTR 39TH AND RAINBOW BLVD KANSAS CITY, KS 66103-8410 Studies on disk renewal in retinal visual cells

R01EY-02422-14 (VISA) MOLDAY, ROBERT S UNIVERSITY OF BRITISH COLUMBIA 2146 HEALTH SCIENCES MALL VANCOUVER, BC CANADA V6T 1W5 Molecular properties of rod plasma membrane proteins

R01EY-02423-15 (VISA) LAM, DOMINIC M BAYLOR COLLEGE OF MEDICINE 4000 RESEARCH FOREST DRIVE THE WOODLANDS, TX 77381 Neurotransmitters in the visual system

R01EY-02430-14 (VISA) GOODENOUGH, DANIEL A HARVARD MEDICAL SCHOOL 220 LONGWOOD AVE BOSTON, MA 02115 Lens metabolic cooperation, gap junctions and cataract

R37EY-02440-14 (VISB) SCHWARTZ, ERIC A THE UNIVERSITY OF CHICAGO 947 EAST 58TH STREET CHICAGO, IL 60637 Synaptic function in photorecaptors of a vertebrate eye

R01EY-02477-12 (VISA) POLANSKY, JON R UNIVERSITY OF CALIFORNIA SAN FRANCISCO, CA 94143-0730 Trabecular meshwork cell culture

R01EY-02505-19 (VISB) MC ILWAIN, JAMES T BROWN UNIVERSITY DIV OF BIOLOGY AND MEDICINE PROVIDENCE, R I 02912 Cortical control of superior colliculus

P30EY-02520-13 (VSN) JONES, DAN B BAYLOR COLLEGE OF MEDICINE DEPT OF OPHTHALMOLOGY HOUSTON, TX 77030 Vision research center

R01EY-02545-13 (VISB) SPEAR, PETER D UNIVERSITY OF WISCONSIN DEPARTMENT OF PSYCHOLOGY MADISON, WI 53706 Parallel pathways in visual processing and development

U10EY-02548-13 (VSN) ABRAMS, GARY W EYE INSTITUTE 8700 WEST WISCONSIN AVENUE MILWAUKEE, WI 53226 Macular photocoagulation study

U10EY-02549-13 (VSN) GASS, DONALD M BASCOM PALMER EYE INSTITUTE P O BOX 016880 MIAMI, FLA 33101 Macular photocoagulation study

U10EY-02553-13 (VSN) FOLK, JAMES C UNIVERSITY OF IOWA DEPARTMENT OF OPHTHALMOLOGY IOWA CITY, IOWA 52242 Macular photocoagulation study

U10EY-02554-12 (VSN) SINGERMAN, LAWRENCE J 26900 CEDAR ROAD, SUITE 323 BEACHWOOD, OHIO 44122 Macular photocoagulation study

U10EY-02556-13 (VSN) MURPHY, ROBERT P JOHN HOPKINS HOSPITAL WILMER OPHTHALMOLOGICAL INSTIT BALTIMORE, MD 21205 Macular photocoagulation study

U10EY-02563-12 (VSN) MARGHERIO, RAYMOND R WILLIAM BEAUMONT HOSPITAL 3601 WEST 13 MILE ROAD ROYAL OAK, MI 48073-2793 Macular photocoagulation study

R01EY-02568-14 (VISA) CENEDELLA, RICHARD J COLLEGE OF OSTEOPATHIC MEDICIN 800 W JEFFERSON KIRKSVILLE, MO 63501 Lens cholesterol metabolism and the U18666A cataract

R01EY-02571-14 (VISA) BETTELHEIM, FREDERICK A ADELPHI UNIVERSITY SOUTH AVENUE GARDEN CITY, N Y 11530 Light scattering parameters of cataractous lenses

R01EY-02576-14 (VISA) MARC, ROBERT E UNIVERSITY OF TEXAS 6420 LAMAR FLEMING AVENUE HOUSTON, TX 77030 Structural neurochemistry of retinal circuits

R37EY-02580-14 (VISA) KAUFMAN, HERBERT E LSU EYE CENTER 2020 GRAVIER STREET, SUITE B NEW ORLEANS, LA 70112-2234 Corneal preservation and keratoplasty

R01EY-02597-14 (VISA) WALKENBACH, RONALD J MISSOURI LIONS EYE RESEARCH FD 404 PORTLAND STREET COLUMBIA, MO 65201 Control of corneal physiology by cyclic nucleotides

R01EY-02619-14 (VISA) MITTAG, THOMAS W MOUNT SINAI SCHOOL OF MEDICINE 1 GUSTAVE L LEVY PLACE-BOX 118 NEW YORK, NY 10029 Drug

PROJECT NO., ORGANIZATIONAL UNIT., INVESTIGATOR, ADDRESS, TITLE

effects on ciliary body adenylate cyclase
P30EY-02621-14 (VSN) SCHILLER, PETER H MASSACHUSETTS INST OF TECH 77 MASSACHUSETTS AVENUE CAMBRIDGE, MASS 02139 Central visual processes
R01EY-02648-13 (RAD) WORGUL, BASIL V COLUMBIA UNIVERSITY 630 WEST 168TH STREET NEW YORK CITY, N Y 10032 Radiation cataractogenesis
R37EY-02651-14 (VISB) FARBER, DEBORA B UNIVERSITY OF CALIFORNIA 100 STEIN PLAZA LOS ANGELES, CA 90024-7008 Cyclic nucleotides in cone metabolism and disease
R01EY-02654-13 (VISA) ROSENQUIST, ALAN C UNIVERSITY OF PENNSYLVANIA DEPARTMENT OF ANATOMY PHILADELPHIA, PA 19104-6058 Extrageniculate visual pathways in animals
R01EY-02655-13 (VISA) RICHARDSON, THOMAS M MASS EYE AND EAR INFIRMARY 243 CHARLES ST BOSTON, MA 02114 Elements in the trabecular meshwork
R01EY-02660-13 (VISA) PUGH, EDWARD N, JR UNIVERSITY OF PENNSYLVANIA 3815 WALNUT STREET PHILADELPHIA, PA 19104-6196 Mechanisms of visual transduction
R01EY-02672-14 (VISA) KAUFMAN, HERBERT E LSU EYE CENTER 2020 GRAVIER STREET NEW ORLEANS, LA 70112 Ocular herpes simplex
R37EY-02682-17 (NEUB) WILLARD, MARK B WASHINGTON UNIVERSITY 660 SOUTH EUCLID AVENUE ST LOUIS, MO 63110 Axonally transported proteins in the visual system
R01EY-02686-17 (VISB) KAAS, JON H VANDERBILT UNIVERSITY A & S PSYCHOLOGY BLDG NASHVILLE, TN 37240 Functional organization of the visual system
P30EY-02687-13 (VSN) KAPLAN, HENRY J WASHINGTON UNIV SCHOOL OF MED 660 SOUTH EUCLID AVENUE ST LOUIS, MO 63110 Core grant vision research
R01EY-02688-13 (VISA) GEISLER, WILSON S UNIVERSITY OF TEXAS PSYCHOLOGY DEPARTMENT AUSTIN, TX 78712 Peripheral mechanisms of visual discrimination
R01EY-02695-13 (VISA) MALPELI, JOSEPH G UNIVERSITY OF ILLINOIS DEPT OF PSYCHOLOGY CHAMPAIGN, ILL 61820 Thalamic control of cortical visual processing
R01EY-02698-13 (VISA) KAUFMAN, PAUL L UNIVERSITY OF WISCONSIN 600 HIGHLAND AVENUE MADISON, WI 53792 Anterior ocular segment physiology and pharmacology
R01EY-02708-14 (CLN) COOPER, NIGEL G F UNIVERSITY OF LOUISVILLE SCHOOL OF MEDICINE LOUISVILLE, KY 40292 Photoreceptor synaptogenesis in the retina
R01EY-02715-13S1 (MGN) BENEDICT, WILLIAM F CENTER FOR BIOTECHNOLOGY 4000 RESEARCH FOREST DRIVE THE WOODLANDS, TX 77381 Biochemical and cytogenetic markers in retinoblastoma
R01EY-02727-13 (VISB) WALLMAN, JOSHUA CITY COLLEGE OF CUNY 138TH ST & CONVENT AVE NEW YORK, NY 10031 Role of vision in etiology of axial myopia
R01EY-02853-13A1 (VISA) MC LAUGHLIN, BARBARA J KENTUCKY LIONS EYE RESEARCH IN 301 E MUHAMMAD ALI BLVD LOUISVILLE, KY 40292 Cell biology of inherited retinal degeneration
R01EY-02857-12 (VISB) LEGGE, GORDON E ELLIOTT HALL PSYCHOLOGY DEPARTMENT MINNEAPOLIS, MN 55455 The role of suprathreshold contrast in vision
R01EY-02858-13 (VISA) SHATZ, CARLA J STANFORD UNIVERSITY SCHOOL OF MEDICINE STANFORD, CA 94305 Fetal and postnatal development of visual connections
R01EY-02861-14 (VISA) KULKARNI, PRASAD S UNIVERSITY OF LOUISVILLE LOUISVILLE, KY 40292 role of prostaglandin, thromboxane and related autacoids
R01EY-02866-12 (VISB) GRAYBIEL, ANN M E25-618 77 MASSACHUSETTS AVE CAMBRIDGE, MA 02139 An analysis of extrageniculate visual mechanisms
R01EY-02874-12 (VISB) STRYKER, MICHAEL P UNIV OF CALIFORNIA 513 PARNASSUS AVE/S-762 SAN FRANCISCO, CA 94143-0444 Development and plasticity of the visual system
R01EY-02877-11 (VISB) MONTERO, VICENTE M UNIVERSITY OF WISCONSIN 1500 HIGHLAND AVENUE MADISON, WIS 53706 Neural circuits of the visual thalmus
R01EY-02882-13 (VISA) ALLANSMITH, MATHEA R EYE RESEARCH INSTITUTE 20 STANIFORD STREET BOSTON, MA 02114 The secretory IgA system of the eye
R01EY-02903-14 (VISB) HATCHELL, DIANE L DUKE UNIVERSITY EYE CENTER BOX 3802 DURHAM, NC 27710 Pathogensis of retinal ischemic injury
R01EY-02923-13 (VISB) RODIECK, ROBERT W SEATTLE, WA 98195 RJ-10 Primate color vision
R01EY-02932-13 (VISA) TAKEMOTO, LARRY J KANSAS STATE UNIVERSITY ACKERT HALL MANHATTAN, KS 66506 Lens membrane in relation to human cataractogenesis
R37EY-02934-12 (VISB) LEGGE, GORDON E UNIVERSITY OF MINNESOTA 75 EAST RIVER ROAD MINNEAPOLIS, MN 55455 Psychophysics of reading--Normal and low vision
R01EY-02948-13 (VISA) VALLE, DAVID L JOHNS HOPKINS UNIVERSITY 725 NORTH WOLFE STREET BALTIMORE, MD 21205 Gyrate atrophy--treatment and pathophysiology
R01EY-02949-13 (VISA) WHIKEHART, DAVID R UNIVERSITY OF ALABAMA 924 SOUTH 18TH STREET BIRMINGHAM, AL 35294 Metabolic control of corneal deturgescence
R01EY-02957-13 (VISA) TROUSDALE, MELVIN D DOHENY EYE INSTITUTE 1355 SAN PABLO STREET LOS ANGELES, CA 90033 Ocular herpes simplex infection
R01EY-02966-12 (VISB) POGGIO, GIAN F JOHNS HOPKINS SCHOOL OF MEDICI 725 N WOLFE STREET BALTIMORE, MD 21205 Binocular vision and depth perception
R01EY-02973-11 (VISB) MIZE, RICHARD R UNIV OF TENNESSEE HEALTH SCI C 875 MONROE AVE MEMPHIS, TN 38136 Transmitter specific neural circuits in SC
R01EY-02986-13 (VISA) HAZLETT, LINDA D WAYNE STATE UNIVERSITY 540 EAST CANFIELD DETROIT, MI 48201 Alteration with age of resistance to eye infections
R01EY-02994-13 (VISB) HOWLAND, HOWARD C CORNELL UNIVERSITY W201 SEELEY G MUDD HALL ITHACA, NY 14853 Refractive studies of human and animal eyes

PROJECT NO., ORGANIZATIONAL UNIT., INVESTIGATOR, ADDRESS, TITLE

R01EY-03011-12A1 (VISA) DACHEUX, RAMON F HARVARD MEDICAL SCHOOL 220 LONGWOOD AVENUE BOSTON, MA 02115 Cell communication in retina
R37EY-03014-15 (VISB) MILLER, ROBERT F UNIVERSITY OF MINNESOTA 435 DELAWARE ST S E MINNEAPOLIS, MN 55455 Cell communication in the vertebrate retina
R01EY-03028-14 (VISA) FRANKLIN, RUDOLPH MICHAEL ST JOSEPH HOSPITAL 1919 LABRANCH STREET HOUSTON, TX 77002 Secretory immune system--Relationship to ocular disease
R01EY-03038-12 (VISB) SHERMAN, S MURRAY SUNY AT STONY BROOK STONY BROOK, NY 11794-5230 Effects of visual deprivation on the visual systems
P30EY-03039-13 (VSN) NORTON, THOMAS T UNIV OF ALABAMA AT BIRMINGHAM SCHOOL OF OPTOMETRY BIRMINGHAM, AL 35294 Vision Research Center
P30EY-03040-12 (VSN) OGDEN, THOMAS E ESTELLE DOHENY EYE FOUNDATION 1355 SAN PABLO STREET LOS ANGELES, CALIF 90033 Core grant for vision research
R01EY-03042-11 (VISA) BLANKS, JANET M DOHENY EYE INSTITUTE 1355 SAN PABLO ST LOS ANGELES, CA 90033 Retinal differentiation, cell interactions, and plasticity
R01EY-03083-13 (EDC) KLEIN, RONALD UNIVERSITY OF WISCONSIN DEPARTMENT OF OPHTHALMOLOGY MADISON, WI 53792 An epidemiological study of diabetic retinopathy
R01EY-03142-13 (BBCA) CALLENDER, ROBERT H CITY COLLEGE OF CUNY CONVENT AVENUE & 138TH STREET NEW YORK, NY 10031 Spectroscopic studies of visual transduction
R01EY-03164-13 (VISB) WANDELL, BRIAN A STANFORD UNIVERSITY DEPARTMENT OF PSYCHOLOGY STANFORD, CA 94305 Wavelength discrimination at modulation threshold
R01EY-03168-22 (VISA) HOLTZMAN, ERIC COLUMBIA UNIVERSITY 733 SHERMAN FAIRCHILD CENTER NEW YORK, N Y 10027 Photoreceptor membranes: cycling and sorting
P30EY-03176-11 (VSN) FREEMAN, RALPH D UNIVERSITY OF CALIFORNIA 360 MINOR HALL BERKELEY, CA 94720 Core grant for vision research
R01EY-03177-13 (VISA) MC AVOY, JOHNSTON W UNIVERSITY OF SYDNEY SYDNEY, NSW 2006 AUSTRALIA Studies on lens differentiation--Role of FGF
R01EY-03221-10A1 (VISB) BUCK, STEVEN L UNIVERSITY OF WASHINGTON SEATTLE, WA 98195 Interaction in the visual system
R01EY-03222-13 (VISA) BESHARSE, JOSEPH C UNIV. OF KANSAS MEDICAL CENTER 39TH AND RAINBOW BOULEVARD KANSAS CITY, KS 66103 Visual cell - pigment cell interface and disc turnover
R01EY-03226-11 (VISA) BEYER-MEARS, ANNETTE UMD-NEW JERSEY MEDICAL SCHOOL 185 SOUTH ORANGE AVENUE NEWARK, NJ 07103-2757 Aldose reductase inhibition, myo-inositol regulation of sugar cataract
R01EY-03228-11 (SSS) STERN, WALTER H VA MEDICAL CENTER 4150 CLEMENT STREET SAN FRANCISCO, CA 94121 Experimental massive periretinal proliferation
R01EY-03242-13 (VISA) RIVA, CHARLES E PRESBYTERIAN-UNIVERSITY 51 NORTH 39TH STREET PHILADELPHIA, PA 19104 Noninvasive investigation of the ocular circulation
R01EY-03243-11 (VISA) AUERBACH, ROBERT ZOOLOGY RESEARCH BLDG 215 1117 WEST JOHNSON STREET MADISON, WI 53706 Angiogenesis in the mouse
R01EY-03263-12 (VISA) SUNDAR RAJ, NIRMALA THE EYE AND EAR INSTITUTE 203 LOTHROP STREET PITTSBURGH, PA 15213 Characterization of corneal cell-surface antigens
R01EY-03274-13 (VISA) KATZ, MARTIN L UNIVERSITY OF MISSOURI SCHOOL OF MEDICINE COLUMBIA, MO 65212 Synthesis and phagocytosis in ocular neuroepithelia
R01EY-03279-12 (VISA) ACOTT, TED S OREGON HEALTH SCIENCES UNIV 3181 S W SAM JACKSON PARK ROAD PORTLAND, OR 97201-3098 The vertebrate eye--Studies of aqueous outflow
R37EY-03282-13 (VISA) RAE, JAMES L MAYO FOUNDATION 200 FIRST STREET SOUTHWEST ROCHESTER, MN 55905 Normal and cataractous lens cell bioelectric properties
U10EY-03284-12 (VSN) CHANDRA, SURESH R UNIVERSITY OF WISCONSIN 600 HIGHLAND AVENUE MADISON, WI 53792 Macular photocoagulation study
U10EY-03288-12 (VSN) ORTH, DAVID H INGALLS MEMORIAL HOSPITAL ONE INGALLS DRIVE HARVEY, ILL 60426 Macular photocoagulation study
R37EY-03306-13 (VISA) GIPSON, ILENE K EYE RESEARCH INSTITUTE 20 STANIFORD STREET BOSTON, MA 02114 Cell motility and adhesion in corneal wound healing
R01EY-03311-12S1 (VISA) KLYCE, STEPHEN D LSU EYE CENTER 2020 GRAVIER ST NEW ORLEANS, LA 70112 Transport processes across the corneal epithelium
R01EY-03318-11 (VISA) GREENE, BRUCE M UNIVERSITY OF ALABAMA 1025 18TH ST., SOUTH, ROOM 240 BIRMINGHAM, AL 35205 Onchocerciasis - Immune-mediated eye disease
R01EY-03323-12 (VISB) KOLB, HELGA E UNIVERSITY OF UTAH SCHOOL OF M 410 CHIPETA WAY, RESEARCH PARK SALT LAKE CITY, UT 84108 Neural circuitry of the vertebrate retina
R01EY-03324-11 (VISA) WHITTUM-HUDSON, JUDITH JOHNS HOPKINS HOSPITAL 600 N WOLFE STREET BALTIMORE, MD 21205 Vaccine development and the immune response to trachoma
R01EY-03328-09 (VISA) ALBERT, ARLENE D STATE UNIVERSITY OF NEW YORK 140 FARBER HALL BUFFALO, NY 14214 Rhodopsin structure and environment in vision
R01EY-03347-13 (VISA) STUART, ANN E UNIVERSITY OF NORTH CAROLINA CB 7545 CHAPEL HILL, NC 27599-7545 Neural mechanisms on processing visual information
R01EY-03373-11 (VISA) GILBARD, JEFFREY P EYE RESEARCH INSTITUTE 20 STANIFORD STREET BOSTON, MASS 02114 Drying of the ocular surface
R01EY-03387-11 (VISB) HOTSON, JOHN R SANTA CLARA VALLEY MEDICAL CTR 751 SOUTH BASCOM AVENUE SAN JOSE, CA 95128 Supranuclear control of eye movements
R01EY-03424-11 (VISB) JOHNSON, CHRIS A UNIVERSITY OF CALIFORNIA 1603 ALHAMBRA BLVD SACRAMENTO, CA 95816 Perimetry and clinical psychophysics
R55EY-03446-10A1 (VISA) CHAMBERLAIN, STEVEN C SYRACUSE UNIVERSITY MERRILL LANE SYRACUSE, NY 13244-5290 Adaptive mechanisms that maintain visual sensitivity
R01EY-03463-12 (VISB) MAYS, LAWRENCE E UNIVERSITY OF ALABAMA 1716 UNIVERSITY BLVD BIRMINGHAM, AL 35294 Neural mechanisms of

vergence eye movements

R01EY-03470-12 (VISB) UDIN, SUSAN B STATE UNIVERSITY OF NEW YORK 313 CARY HALL BUFFALO, NY 14214 Effect of visual experience on CNS connectivity

R01EY-03490-08 (VISB) ROBSON, JOHN A SUNY HSC AT SYRACUSE 766 IRVING AVENUE SYRACUSE, N Y 13210 Studies of the visual system

R01EY-03502-11 (VISB) BAUGHMAN, ROBERT W HARVARD MEDICAL SCHOOL 220 LONGWOOD AVENUE BOSTON, MA 02115 Neurotransmitters in the central visual pathway

R01EY-03526-12 (VISA) KARWOSKI, CHESTER J UNIVERSITY OF GEORGIA ATHENS, GA 30602 Physiology of retinal cells in vision

R01EY-03529-11 (VISA) MINKE, BARUCH HEBREW UNIV OF JERUSALEM HADASSAH MEDICAL SCHOOL JERUSALEM, 91010 ISRAEL Genetic dissection of phototransduction

R01EY-03532-10 (VISB) SCHOR, CLIFTON M UNIVERSITY OF CALIFORNIA SCHOOL OF OPTOMETRY BERKELEY, CA 94720 Visual development of sensory and motor functions

R01EY-03552-09 (VISB) SPRINGER, ALAN D NEW YORK MEDICAL COLLEGE VALHALLA, NY 10595 Specificity of regenerated retinal projections

R55EY-03565-11 (VISA) JEDZINIAK, JUDITH A BRIGHAM & WOMEN'S HOSPITAL 75 FRANCIS STREET BOSTON, MA 02115 Properties of pyruvate kinase

R01EY-03570-12 (VISA) WITKOVSKY, PAUL NYU MEDICAL CENTER 550 FRIST AVENUE NEW YORK, NY 10016 Dopamine and retinal adaptation

R37EY-03575-11 (VISA) BURNSIDE, MARY B UNIVERSITY OF CALIFORNIA MOLECULAR & CELL BIOLOGY/ BERKELEY, CALIF 94720 Circadian retinal motility role of cyclic nucleotides

R01EY-03592-11 (VISA) MEINERTZHAGEN, IAN A DALHOUSIE UNIVERSITY HALIFAX, NS B3H 4J1 CANADA Visual system development and synaptogenesis

R01EY-03600-10 (VISA) SHEARER, THOMAS R OREGON HEALTH SCIENCES UNIV 611 S W CAMPUS DRIVE PORTLAND, OR 97201 Mechanism of selenium-induced cataract

R01EY-03604-11 (VISB) SHERMAN, S MURRAY STATE UNIVERSITY OF NEW YORK DEPT OF NEUROBIOLOGY & BEHAV STONY BROOK, NY 11794-5230 Functional ultrastructure of central visual pathways

R01EY-03611-10 (VISA) SMITH, EARL L, III UNIVERSITY OF HOUSTON 4800 CALHOUN BOULEVARD HOUSTON, TX 77204-6052 Optically induced anisometropia in monkeys

R01EY-03621-11 (VISA) OAKES, JOHN E UNIVERSITY OF SOUTH ALABAMA DEPT. OF MICROBIOLOGY MOBILE, ALA 36688 Corneal disease: Mechanism of specific inflammation

R01EY-03624-11 (VISA) RANDO, ROBERT R HARVARD MEDICAL SCHOOL 250 LONGWOOD AVE BOSTON, MA 02115 Molecular mechanisms in visual transduction

R01EY-03635-11 (VISA) MCDONALD, MARGUERITE B LSU EYE CENTER 2020 GRAVIER STREET NEW ORLEANS, LA 70112 Epikeratophakia: the surgical correction of aphakia

R01EY-03650-09A1 (VISA) MC CULLEY, JAMES P U OF TEXAS SOUTHWESTERN MED CT 5323 HARRY HINES BLVD DALLAS, TX 75235-9057 Meibomian keratoconjunctivitis

R01EY-03664-12 (VISA) SARTHY, VIJAY P NORTHWESTERN UNIVERSITY 303 E CHICAGO AVE CHICAGO, IL 60611 Neurotransmitters in the visual system

R01EY-03681-11 (VISA) HIGHTOWER, KENNETH R OAKLAND UNIVERSITY ROCHESTER, MI 48309-4401 The role of cations in cataract development

R01EY-03685-10 (VISA) KEAN, EDWARD L CASE WESTERN RESERVE UNIV 2074 ABINGTON ROAD CLEVELAND, OH 44106 Role of sugars in phagocytosis of rod outer segments

R01EY-03723-11 (VISA) KAPLAN, HENRY J WASHINGTON UNIV SCHOOL OF MED 660 SOUTH EUCLID AVE, BOX 8096 ST LOUIS, MO 63110 Immunologic study of the eye

R01EY-03736-11 (VISB) SCHMIDT, JOHN T UNIVERSITY OF ALBANY 1400 WASHINGTON AVE ALBANY, NY 12222 Activity and trophism in synaptic stabilization

R01EY-03747-09A1 (VISA) TRIPATHI, BRENDA J UNIVERSITY OF CHICAGO 939 EAST 57TH STREET CHICAGO, IL 60637 Cell and molecular biology of aqueous outflow pathway

U10EY-03752-11 (VSN) LYNN, MICHAEL J EMORY UNIVERSITY 1599 CLIFTON RD ATLANTA, GA 30329 Coordinating office for radial keratotomy

R01EY-03754-12 (BBCB) BROWN, MICHAEL F UNIVERSITY OF ARIZONA TUCSON, AZ 85721 Membrane basis of visual excitation

U10EY-03761-11 (VSN) WARING, GEORGE O, III EMORY UNIVERSITY SCH OF MED 1327 CLIFTON ROAD, NE ATLANTA, GA 30322 Prospective evaluation of radial keratotomy (PERK)

R01EY-03778-09A2 (VISB) BONDS, ALFRED B VANDERBILT UNIVERSITY PO BOX 1824/STATION B NASHVILLE, TN 37235 Spatial characteristics of neurons in the striate cortex

R01EY-03785-10 (VISA) OWEN, WILLIAM G UNIVERSITY OF CALIFORNIA BERKELEY, CA 94720 Signal processing in the vertebrate retina

P30EY-03790-11 (VSN) GIPSON, ILENE K EYE RESEARCH INSTITUTE 20 STANIFORD STREET BOSTON, MA 02114 Core grant for vision research

P30EY-03790-11 9004 (VSN) SNODDERLY, MAX Core grant for vision research Core-- Laboratory computer applications module

P30EY-03790-11 9005 (VSN) FEKE, GILBERT T Core grant for vision research Core-- Biostatistics module

P30EY-03790-11 9001 (VSN) GIBSON, ILENE K Core grant for vision research Core-- Morphology module

P30EY-03790-11 9002 (VSN) BARTELS, STEPHEN P Core grant for vision research Core-- Animal resource module

P30EY-03790-11 9003 (VSN) ZIESKE, JAMES Core grant for vision research Core-- Tissue culture /monoclonal antibody module

R01EY-03793-11 (VISA) FEIN, ALAN UNIVERSITY OF CONNECTICUT 263 FARMINGTON AVENUE FARMINIGTON, CT 06032 Mechanisms of visual excitation

R01EY-03816-09 (VISA) LEE, VINCENT H UNIV OF SOUTHERN CALIFORNIA 1985 ZONAL AVENUE LOS ANGELES, CA 90033 Evaluation of esterase activity and prodrugs in the eye

R01EY-03821-11 (VISA) MATTHEWS, GARY G STATE UNIVERSITY OF NEW YORK STONY BROOK, NY 11794-5230 Cellular neurophysiology of the vertebrate retina

R01EY-03829-12 (VISB) LIOU, GREGORY I MEDICAL COLLEGE OF GEORGIA AUGUSTA, GA 30912 Binding protein for retinoids in ocular tissues

R01EY-03841-10 (VISA) ZEIMER, RAN C UNIVERSITY OF ILLINOIS 1855 WEST TAYLOR ST CHICAGO, ILL 60612 Clinical application of a self-tonometer

R01EY-03854-09S2 (VISA) GOURAS, PETER COLUMBIA UNIVERSITY 630 WEST 168TH STREET NEW YORK, NY 10032 Cell biology of human chorioretinal epithelium in vitro

R37EY-03878-11 (VISB) LISBERGER, STEPHEN G UNIVERSITY OF CALIFORNIA PARNASSUS AVENUE SAN FRANCISCO, CALIF 94143 Neural control of eye movement

R01EY-03890-10 (VISA) YUE, BEATRICE Y UNIVERSITY OF ILLINOIS 1855 WEST TAYLOR STREET CHICAGO, IL 60612 Biochemical basis of keratoconus

R01EY-03897-11 (VISA) HORWITZ, JOSEPH UNIVERSITY OF CALIFORNIA JULES STEIN EYE INSTITUTE LOS ANGELES, CA 90024-7008 Analysis of microdissected cataractous human lenses

R01EY-03942-10 (VISA) LORAND, LASZLO NORTHWESTERN UNIVERSITY DEPARTMENT OF BIOCHEMISTRY EVANSTON, IL 60208 Cross-links in diabetic and senile cataract

R01EY-03957-10 (VISB) HAINLINE, LOUISE D BROOKLYN COLLEGE OF CUNY INFANT STUDY CENTER BROOKLYN, NY 11210 Oculomotor development in human infants

R01EY-03980-09 (VISA) POLANSKY, JON R UNIVERSITY OF CALIFORNIA DEPT OF OPHTHALMOLOGY, K-301 SAN FRANCISCO, CA 94143-0730 Adrenergic & cholinergic mechanisms in glaucoma therapy

R01EY-03991-09 (VISA) CHALUPA, LEO M UNIVERSITY OF CALIFORNIA DAVIS, CA 95616 Development and reorganization of prenatal visual system

R01EY-04033-10 (BBCB) SCHLEICH, THOMAS W UNIVERSITY OF CALIFORNIA 1156 HIGH ST SANTA CRUZ, CA 95064 NMR studies of lens transparency and opacification

R01EY-04034-09 (VISA) BAUM, JULES L NEW ENGLAND MEDICAL CENTER 750 WASHINGTON STREET BOSTON, MA 02111 Biochemistry of normal and dystrophic corneas

R01EY-04045-09 (VISB) KING, WILLIAM M UNIV OF ROCHESTER SCH OF MED 601 ELMWOOD AVE, BOX 642 ROCHESTER, NY 14642 Oculomotor system--Neural structure and function

R01EY-04050-10 (VISB) GORDON-LICKEY, BARBARA UNIVERSITY OF OREGON EUGENE, OR 97403 Mechanisms underlying the monocular deprivation effect

R01EY-04063-10 (VISB) NODA, HIROHARU INDIANA UNIVERSITY 800 EAST ATWATER BLOOMINGTON, IN 47405 Neuronal basis of visual perception in eye movements

R01EY-04067-11 (VISA) BRECHA, NICHOLAS C VA WADSWORTH MEDICAL CENTER WILSHIRE & SAWTELLE BLVDS LOS ANGELES, CA 90073 Neurochemical pathways in the inner retina

P30EY-04068-10 (VSN) HAZLETT, LINDA D WAYNE STATE UNIVERSITY 656 WEST KIRBY AVE DETROIT, MI 48202 Core grant for vision research

R01EY-04074-11 (VISA) BEUERMAN, ROGER W LSU EYE CENTER 2020 GRAVIER STREET, SUITE B NEW ORLEANS, LA 70112 Corneal neurobiology

R01EY-04077-11 (VISA) NEWMAN, ERIC A UNIVERSITY OF MINNESOTA 435 DELAWARE ST SE MINNEAPOLIS, MN 55455 Membrane physiology and function of retinal muller cells

R37EY-04096-10 (VISA) RANDO, ROBERT R HARVARD MEDICAL SCHOOL 250 LONGWOOD AVENUE BOSTON, MA 02115 Regeneration of 11-cis retinal in the retina

R01EY-04110-09 (VISA) ZAMPIGHI, GUIDO A UNIVERSITY OF CALIFORNIA 405 HILGARD AVENUE LOS ANGELES, CA 90024-1763 Structure and function of lens communicating channels

R01EY-04112-10 (VISA) WILSON, MARTIN C UNIVERSITY OF CALIFORNIA 2320 STORER HALL DAVIS, CA 95616 Membrane physiology of retinal bipolar cells

R01EY-04131-08 (VISA) KREUTZER, DONALD L UNIV OF CONNECTICUT HLTH CTR 263 FARMINGTON AVENUE FARMINGTON, CONN 06032 Immunologic aspects of ocular injury

R01EY-04138-08 (VISA) GOURAS, PETER COLUMBIA UNIVERSITY 630 W 168TH ST NEW YORK, NY 10032 Clinical electrophysiology of human cone mechanisms

R01EY-04148-09 (HAR) RAPHAN, THEODORE BROOKLYN COLLEGE BEDFORD AVENUE AND AVENUE H BROOKLYN, N Y 11210 Multidimensional dynamics of vestibular-ocular reflex

R01EY-04149-10 (VISA) ANDERSON, ROBERT E BAYLOR COLLEGE OF MEDICINE ONE BAYLOR PLAZA HOUSTON, TX 77030 Role of essential fatty acids in retinal degenerations

R01EY-04158-10 (VISA) BROMBERG, BARRY B UNIVERSITY OF NEW ORLEANS LAKEFRONT NEW ORLEANS, LA 70148 Autonomic control of lacrimal gland function

R01EY-04159-12 (VISB) LYNCH, JAMES C UNIV OF MISSISSIPPI MED CTR 2500 NORTH STATE STREET JACKSON, MS 39216 Oculomotor control mechanisms of the cerebral cortex

R01EY-04161-09A1 (VISA) CHAKRABARTI, BIRESWAR EYE RESEARCH INSTITUTE 20 STANIFORD STREET BOSTON, MA 02114 Lens proteins--Changes due to cataractogenic agents

R01EY-04170-11 (VISB) RHOADES, ROBERT W MEDICAL COLLEGE OF OHIO PO BOX 10008 TOLEDO, OH 43699-0008 Collicular development in hamster

R37EY-04171-10 (VISA) ABDEL-LATIF, ATA A MEDICAL COLLEGE OF GEORGIA AUGUSTA, GA 30912-2100 Lipid & protein PO4 turnover in iris of the eye

R01EY-04318-09 (VISA) RAYMOND, PAMELA A UNIVERSITY OF MICHIGAN DEPT OF ANATOMY & CELL BIOLOGY ANN ARBOR, MI 48109 New neurons and new synapses

R01EY-04366-07 (VISB) GRUBERG, EDWARD R TEMPLE UNIVERSITY BROAD STREET & MONTGOMERY AVE PHILADELPHIA, PA 19122 Studies on the visual inputs to the optic tectum

R01EY-04367-09 (VISB) WILLIAMS, DAVID R UNIVERSITY OF ROCHESTER 274 MELIORA HALL, RIVER CAMPUS ROCHESTER, NY 14627 Retinal mechanisms and visual resolution

R01EY-04368-09 (VISA) ADLER, ALICE J EYE RESEARCH INSTITUTE 20 STANIFORD STREET BOSTON, MA 02114 The interphotoreceptor matrix--Components and functions

R01EY-04377-08S1 (VISA) TURNER, JAMES E WAKE FOREST UNIVERSITY DEPARTMENT OF ANATOMY WINSTON-SALEM, NC 27103 Retinal wound repair--graft and trophic phenomena

PROJECT NO., ORGANIZATIONAL UNIT., INVESTIGATOR, ADDRESS, TITLE

R01EY-04387-10 (VISA) ABDEL-LATIF, ATA A MEDICAL COLLEGE OF GEORGIA 1120 15TH ST AUGUSTA, GA 30912-2100 Glycerolipids and prostaglandins biosynthesis in ocular tissue
R01EY-04395-11 (VISB) BURNS, STEPHEN A EYE RESEARCH INSTITUTE 20 STANIFORD STREET BOSTON, MA 02114 Investigations of human cone pigment kinetics
R55EY-04396-09 (VISA) AWASTHI, YOGESH C UNIV OF TEXAS MEDICAL BRANCH ROUTE F20 GALVESTON, TX 77550-2774 Detoxification of xenobiotics in ocular tissues
R01EY-04424-09 (VISA) CHENG, HONG-MING MASSACHUSETTS EYE & EAR INF 243 CHARLES STREET BOSTON, MA 02114 Activation of the hexosemonophosphate shunt in the lens
R01EY-04428-08 (VISA) BAZAN, NICOLAS G LSU MEDICAL CENTER 2020 GRAVIER STREET NEW ORLEANS, LA 70112-2234 Role of docosahexaenoic acid metabolism in retina
R01EY-04432-09 (VISB) PELLI, DENIS G SYRACUSE UNIVERSITY MERRILL LANE SYRACUSE, NY 13244-5290 The visual requirements of everyday tasks
R01EY-04440-10 (VISA) LENNIE, PETER UNIVERSITY OF ROCHESTER 274 MELIORA HALL, RIVER CAMPUS ROCHESTER, NY 14627 Quantitative studies of visual pathways in primate
R01EY-04444-10 (VISA) LIU, SAMMY H JOHNS HOPKINS HOSPITAL 600 NORTH WOLFE STREET BALTIMORE, MD 21205 mechanisms of ocular inflammation
R01EY-04446-10 (VISA) WU, SAMUEL M BAYLOR COLLEGE OF MEDICINE ONE BAYLOR PLAZA HOUSTON, TX 77030 Physiology and pharmacology of synapses in the retina
R01EY-04460-08 (VISA) DAWSON, WILLIAM W UNIVERSITY OF FLORIDA BOX J-284 JHM HEALTH CENTER GAINESVILLE, FL 32610 Physiology of the pattern-excited retina
R01EY-04470-09 (VISB) TELLER, DAVIDA Y UNIVERSITY OF WASHINGTON NI-25 SEATTLE, WA 98195 Infant spectral sensitivity
R01EY-04478-09 (VISB) BEHAN, MARY UNIVERSITY OF WISCONSIN 2015 LINDEN DRIVE WEST MADISON, WISC 53706 Synaptic organization of the superior colliculus
R01EY-04536-09 (VISA) HENDRICKSON, ANITA E UNIVERSITY OF WASHINGTON SEATTLE, WA 98195 Primate retinal development
R01EY-04542-10 (VISA) CLARK, JOHN I UNIVERSITY OF WASHINGTON SCHOOL OF MEDICINE SEATTLE, WASH 98195 Development and maintenance of transparency in lenses
R01EY-04554-08 (VISA) RAPP, LAURENCE M BAYLOR COLLEGE OF MEDICINE ONE BAYLOR PLAZA HOUSTON, TX 77030 Role of near-UV light in retinal degeneration and aging
R01EY-04558-09 (VISA) GREEN, KEITH MEDICAL COLLEGE OF GEORGIA AUGUSTA, GA 30912-3400 Ion and water movement in ocular tissues
R01EY-04567-09 (VISA) FREDDO, THOMAS F BOSTON UNIV MEDICAL CENTER 80 E CONCORD STREET BOSTON, MA 02118 Mechanisms of recurrence of anterior uveitis of the eye
R01EY-04590-08 (VISA) HARGRAVE, PAUL A UNIVERSITY OF FLORIDA BOX J-284, J H M H C GAINESVILLE, FL 32610 Retinal degeneration--A new animal model
R01EY-04604-06 (VISA) CAVANAGH, H DWIGHT UNIV OF TEXAS S.W. MED CTR 5323 HARRY HINES BLVD DALLAS, TX 75235-9057 Regulation of corneal epithelial RNA polymerase activity
R01EY-04606-10 (VISA) MONDINO, BARTLY J JULES STEIN EYE INSTITUTE UCLA SCHOOL OF MEDICINE LOS ANGELES, CA 90024-7008 Staphylococcal hypersensitivity lesions of the cornea
R01EY-04607-10 (VISB) MONDINO, BARTLY J JULES STEIN EYE INSTITUTE UCLA SCHOOL OF MEDICINE LOS ANGELES, CA 90024-7008 Role of complement in ocular inflammation
R01EY-04609-09 (VISA) SCHANZLIN, DAVID J BETHESDA EYE INSTITUTE 3655 VISTA AVENUE ST LOUIS, MO 63110 Keratocyte function in rabbit eyes after freeze injury
R01EY-04613-09 (VISB) GRAF, WERNER M ROCKEFELLER UNIVERSITY 1230 YORK AVENUE NEW YORK, NY 10021-6399 Spatial coordinats of visuo vestibulo ocular reflexes
R01EY-04694-10 (VISB) SHICHI, HITOSHI WAYNE STATE UNIVERSITY 4717 ST. ANTOINE DETROIT, MI 48201 Drug metabolism & detoxification in the eye
R01EY-04716-08 (VISA) PFISTER, ROSWELL R BROOKWOOD MEDICAL CENTER 2010 BROOKWOOD MED CTR DR BIRMINGHAM, AL 35209 Identification and modulation of inflammatory mediators
R01EY-04722-10 (VISA) SUN, TUNG-TIEN NEW YORK UNIVERSITY MED SCHOOL 560 FIRST AVENUE NEW YORK, N Y 10016 Studies of corneal epithelial differentiation
R01EY-04726-08 (VISB) FERSTER, DAVID L NORTHWESTERN UNIVERSITY 2153 SHERIDAN RD EVANSTON, IL 60208 Intracellular analysis of visual cortical function
R01EY-04740-09 (VISB) BRUCE, CHARLES J YALE UNIVERSITY 333 CEDAR ST NEW HAVEN, CT 06510 Functional organization of primate frontal eye fields
R01EY-04767-09 (GEN) PAK, WILLIAM L PURDUE UNIVERSITY LILLY HALL OF LIFE SCIENCES WEST LAFAYETTE, IN 47907 Isolation of genes involved in photoreceptor function
R01EY-04776-08 (VISA) KLEIN, STANLEY A UNIVERSITY OF CALIFORNIA 360 MINOR HALL BERKELEY, CA 94720 High spatial frequency feature acuity in amblyopia
R01EY-04778-10 (VISB) BARMACK, NEAL H GOOD SAMARITAN HOSP & MED CTR 1120 N W 20TH AVENUE PORTLAND, OR 97209 Central control of eye position
R01EY-04785-10 (VISA) ELDRED, WILLIAM D BOSTON UNIV 2 CUMMINGTON ST/DEPT OF BIO BOSTON, MA 02215 Ultrastructural study of peptidergic retina neurons
R01EY-04795-10 (VISA) REINACH, PETER S MEDICAL COLLEGE OF GEORGIA RESEARCH INSTITUTE INC AUGUSTA, GA 30912-4810 Coupling between metabolism/ionic transport in corneas
R01EY-04799-10 (VISA) BURKE, JANICE M MEDICAL COLLEGE OF WISCONSIN 8700 WEST WISCONSIN AVE MILWAUKEE, WI 53226 Cell biology of vitreoretinal proliferative disease
R01EY-04801-11 (VISA) APPLEBURY, MEREDITHE L EYE RESEARCH LABORATORY 939 EAST 57TH STREET CHICAGO, IL 60637 Photoreception and transduction in vision
R01EY-04802-09 (VISB) SHEVELL, STEVEN K UNIVERSITY OF CHICAGO 5848 S UNIVERSITY AVE CHICAGO, IL 60637 Central and peripheral processes in visual adaptation
R01EY-04810-08 (VISA) CANDIA, OSCAR A MOUNT SINAI SCHOOL OF MEDICINE ONE GUSTAVE L LEVY PLACE NEW YORK, N Y 10029 Solute and fluid transport in the isolated ciliary body
R01EY-04831-09 (VISA) ESSNER, EDWARD S KRESGE EYE INSTITUTE WAYNE STATE UNIVERSITY DETROIT, MICH 48202 Permeability of retinal vessels--Cytochemical studies
R01EY-04847-08 (VISB) SHERK, HELEN A UNIVERSITY OF WASHINGTON SCHOOL OF MEDICINE SEATTLE, WA 98195 Organization of extrastriate visual cortex
R01EY-04853-08 (VISA) BEEBE, DAVID C UNIFORMED SERVS UNIV/HEALTH SC 4301 JONES BRIDGE ROAD BETHESDA, MD 20814-4799 Factors controlling lens epithelial cell differentiation
R01EY-04855-09 (VISB) KOLB, HELGA E UNIVERSITY OF UTAH SCHOOL OF M 410 CHIPETA WAY, RESEARCH PARK SALT LAKE CITY, UT 84108 Synaptic organization of the turtle retina
R01EY-04859-09 (VISA) ADLER, RUBEN JOHNS HOPKINS UNIV SCH OF MED 600 NORTH WOLFE ST. BALITMORE, MD 21205 Visual neurons--Development and regeneration in vitro
R01EY-04863-09 (VISA) MAURICE, DAVID M STANFORD UNIVERSITY MED CTR DEPT. OF OPHTHALMOLOGY -S030 STANFORD, CA 94305 Ocular pharmacokinetics of fluorescent drug analogues
R01EY-04864-09 (VISA) IUVONE, PAUL M EMORY UNIV SCHOOL OF MED ATLANTA, GA 30322 Methoxyindoles in retina--Function and regulation
R01EY-04873-08 (VISA) COCA-PRADOS, MIGUEL YALE UNIVERSITY SCH OF MEDICIN 330 CEDAR ST PO BOX 3333 NEW HAVEN, CT 06510 Biochemical responses of human ciliary epithelial cells
R01EY-04876-08 (VISA) HAROSI, FERENC I MARINE BIOLOGICAL LABORATORY WATER STREET WOODS HOLE, MA 02543 Native and analogue visual pigment studies in situ
R01EY-04885-08 (VISB) MAKOUS, WALTER L UNIVERSITY OF ROCHESTER CENTER FOR VISUAL SCIENCE ROCHESTER, NY 14627 Schematic retina
R01EY-04888-07 (VISB) KAPLAN, EHUD ROCKEFELLER UNIVERSITY 1230 YORK AVENUE NEW YORK, NY 10021 Information transfer and contrast sensitivity in the LGN/monkeys,cats
R01EY-04900-09 (VISA) MC GAHAN, MARY C NORTH CAROLINA STATE UNIVERSIT 4700 HILLSBOROUGH ST-BOX 8401 RALEIGH, NC 27606 Trace element dynamics in the vertebrate eye
R01EY-04914-08 (VISA) BARTELS, STEPHEN P EYE RES INST OF RETINA FDN 20 STANIFORD STREET BOSTON, MA 02114 Pharmacology of aqueous humor formation
R01EY-04919-08 (VISA) SPECTOR, ABRAHAM COLUMBIA UNIVERSITY 630 WEST 168TH STREET NEW YORK, N Y 10032 The effect of oxidation upon lens transport systems
R01EY-04922-08 (VISA) CORLESS, JOSEPH M DUKE UNIVERSITY MEDICAL CENTER RM 445 SANDS BLDG. RESEARCH DR DURHAM, N C 27710 Determinants of retinal photoreceptor morphology
R01EY-04928-09 (VISA) BAZAN, HAYDEE E LSU EYE CENTER 2020 GRAVIER STREET, SUITE B NEW ORLEANS, LA 70112 Corneal lipid metabolism and the response to inflammation
R01EY-04930-06 (VISA) POLSE, KENNETH A UNIVERSITY OF CALIFORNIA 525 MINOR HALL BERKELEY, CA 94720 Corneal hydration control in normal and diseased corneas
R01EY-04939-09 (VISA) CROUCH, ROSALIE K MEDICAL UNIV OF SOUTH CAROLINA 171 ASHLEY AVE CHARLESTON, S C 29425 Synthetic retinal pigments and binding proteins
R01EY-04948-08 (VISB) KING-SMITH, P EWEN OHIO STATE UNIVERSITY 338 WEST TENTH AVENUE COLUMBUS, OH 43210 Physiological analysis of optic nerve disease
R01EY-04950-09 (VISA) BOGENMANN, EMIL CHILDREN'S HOSPITAL OF LA 4650 SUNSET BLVD LOS ANGELES, CA 90027 Tissue specific gene expression in retina-derived cells
R01EY-04951-08 (VISB) LEVENTHAL, AUDIE G UNIVERSITY OF UTAH 50 NORTH MEDICAL DRIVE SALT LAKE CITY, UTAH 84132 Morphology and projection of retinal ganglion cells
R01EY-04976-07 (VISB) WILSON, JAMES R EMORY UNIVERSITY YERKES REGIONAL PRIMATE RESEAR ATLANTA, GA 33022 Morphological/physiological relationships in primate LGN
R01EY-04977-09 (VISB) STANFORD, LAURENCE R UNIVERSITY OF WISCONSIN 1500 HIGHLAND AVENUE MADISON, WIS 53706 Structure/function correlation in retinal ganglion cells
R01EY-05034-09 (VISA) LINSENMEIER, ROBERT A NORTHWESTERN UNIVERSITY 2145 SHERIDAN ROAD EVANSTON, IL 60208-3107 Microenvironment of the mammalian retina
R01EY-05047-08 (VISB) EISNER, ALVIN GOOD SAMARITAN HOSP & MED CENT 1120 NW 20TH AVENUE PORTLAND, OR 97209 Visual function studies of normal and aging human retina
R01EY-05062-07 (VISA) WALL, JACK R MONTREAL GENERAL HOSPITAL 1650 CEDAR AVENUE MONTREAL, QUEBEC H3G 1A4 CANA Antigens and antibodies in Graves' ophthalmopathy
R01EY-05063-09 (VISA) YOUNG, ANTHONY PETER BIOTECHNOLOGY CENTER 1060 CARMACK ROAD COLUMBUS, OH 43212 Regulation of gene expression in the developing retina
R01EY-05068-07 (VISB) BEDELL, HAROLD E UNIVERSITY OF HOUSTON 4800 CALHOUN HOUSTON, TX 77204-6052 Perceptual stability and nystagmus
R01EY-05070-08 (VISA) AMTHOR, FRANKLIN R UNIVERSITY OF ALABAMA UAB STATION BIRMINGHAM, AL 35294 Neural structure function relationships in retina
R01EY-05077-08 (VISA) NATHANSON, JAMES A MASSACHUSETTS GENERAL HOSPITAL 32 FRUIT STREET BOSTON, MA 02114 Regulation of protein phosphorylation in the eye
R01EY-05078-07 (VISA) GREGORY, DOUGLAS S YALE UNIVERSITY 330 CEDAR STREET NEW HAVEN, CT 06510 Animal model for the circadian rhythm of IOP
R01EY-05087-08 (VISB) WOLFE, JEREMY M CENTER FOR CLINICAL CATARACT R 221 LONGWOOD AVENUE BOSTON, MA 02115 Psychophysical structure of human vision
R01EY-05093-08 (VISA) ROUSE, BARRY T UNIVERSITY OF TENNESSEE 1414 WEST CUMBERLAND AVE KNOXVILLE, TN 37996-0845 Keratitis treatment with drug-containing immunoliposomes
R01EY-05095-08 (VISA) DONOSO, LARRY A WILLS EYE HOSPITAL 900 WALNUT STREET PHILADELPHIA, PA 19107 S-antigen--Structure/function

relationships in uveitis

R01EY-05097-08 (VISA) STULTING, ROBERT D EMORY UNIVERSITY 1327 CLIFTON ROAD, N E ATLANTA, GA 30322 Pathologic mechanisms of herpes simplex keratitis

R01EY-05099-08 (VISA) LAUSCH, ROBERT N UNIVERSITY OF SOUTH ALABAMA COLLEGE OF MEDICINE MOBILE, AL 36688 Molecular analysis of herpesvirus corneal infection

R01EY-05100-08 (VISA) WINKLER, BARRY S OAKLAND UNIVERSITY ROCHESTER, MI 48309 Initiating mechanisms of light damage in the retina

R01EY-05102-08 (VISA) MANGEL, STUART C UNIV OF ALABAMA AT BIRMINGHAM UAB STATION BIRMINGHAM, AL 35294 Horizontal cell influences upon ganglion cell properties

R01EY-05109-07 (VISB) THIBOS, LARRY N INDIANA UNIVERSITY 800 EAST ATWATER BLOOMINGTON, IN 47405 Optical and retinal limits to human visual performance

R01EY-05110-08 (VISA) KING, GEORGE L JOSLIN DIABETES CENTER, INC ONE JOSLIN PLACE BOSTON, MASS 02215 Cell biology approach to study diabetic retinopathy

R01EY-05113-08 (VISB) MANNY, RUTH E UNIVERSITY OF HOUSTON 4800 CALHOUN BLVD. HOUSTON, TX 77204-6052 Development of hyperacuity in human infants

R01EY-05118-07 (VISB) JOHNSON, MARY A JOHNS HOPKINS HOSPITAL 601 NORTH BROADWAY BALTIMORE, MD 21205 Studies of visual function in retinal ischemia

R01EY-05121-08 (VISA) BAZAN, NICOLAS G LSU MEDICAL CENTER 2020 GRAVIER STREET NEW ORLEANS, LA 70112-2234 Leukotrienes and prostaglandins in photoreceptor renewal

R37EY-05127-09 (VISA) BENEDEK, GEORGE B MASSACHUSETTS INST OF TECHNOLO 77 MASSACHUSETTS AVENUE CAMBRIDGE, MA 02139 Physical and chemical basis of lens opacity

R01EY-05129-08 (VISA) BIRK, DAVID E ROBERT WOOD JOHNSON MEDICAL SC 675 HOES LANE PISCATAWAY, NJ 08854-5635 Collagen fibrillogenesis and corneal development chick embrkyo,

R01EY-05133-07A2 (VISA) MONTGOMERY, PAUL C WAYNE STATE UNIVERSITY 540 EAST CANFIELD AVENUE DETROIT, MI 48201 Antibody induction and expression in the eye

R01EY-05156-09 (VISB) POLLEN, DANIEL A UNIVERSITY OF MASSACHUSETTS 55 LAKE AVENUE NORTH WORCESTER, MA 01655 Spatial selectivity in visual cortices

R01EY-05166-09 (VISA) BROWN, JOEL E WASHINGTON UNIVERSITY 660 SOUTH EUCLID AVENUE ST LOUIS, MO 63110 Anatomy and physiology of vision

R37EY-05191-09 (PBC) LINSENMAYER, THOMAS F TUFTS UNIVERSITY 136 HARRISON AVENUE BOSTON, MA 02111 Corneal stroma synthesis and assembly of collagen

R01EY-05201-09 (VISA) MACLEISH, PETER R CORNELL UNIVERSITY MED COLL 1300 YORK AVE NEW YORK, NY 10021 Photoreceptor-and retinal synapse physiology

R01EY-05206-09 (VISA) BARNSTABLE, COLIN J YALE UNIVERSITY 330 CEDAR ST, PO BOX 3333 NEW HAVEN, CT 06510 Immunological analysis of the mammalian visual system

R01EY-05212-09 (VISB) SCHECHTER, NISSON SUNY AT STONY BROOK STONY BROOK, NY 11794-8101 Visual system specific proteins--Biochemical studies

R01EY-05213-07 (VISA) KLEINSCHMIDT, JOCHEN NEW YORK UNIVERSITY MED CTR 550 FIRST AVE NEW YORK, NY 10016 Neurotransmitter mechanisms in the distal retina

R37EY-05216-09 (BBCB) HUBBELL, WAYNE L UCLA SCHOOL OF MEDICINE JULES STEIN EYE INSTITUTE LOS ANGELES, CA 90024-1771 Molecular basis of membrane excitation

P30EY-05230-07 (VSN) REDDY, VENKAT N OAKLAND UNIVERSITY EYE RESEARCH INSTITUTE ROCHESTER, MICH 48063 Core grant for vision research

R01EY-05231-05 (VISA) VAN BUSKIRK, E MICHAEL GOOD SAMARITAN HOSPITAL 1040 NW 22ND AVENUE PORTLAND, OR 97210 Uveal vasculature

R01EY-05232-07 (VISA) GORDON, Y JEROLD EYE & EAR INST OF PITTSBURGH 203 LOTHROP STREET PITTSBURGH, PA 15213 HSV 1 latency--Immunization and recurrent ocular disease

R01EY-05235-07 (VISA) BIRCH, DAVID G RETINA FOUNDATION OF SOUTHWEST 8230 WALNUT HILL LANE DALLAS, TX 75231 Retinal pathophysiology in infants and adults

R01EY-05236-08 (VISB) BIRCH, EILEEN E RETINA FOUNDATION OF S W 8230 WALNUT HILL LANE, SUITE 4 DALLAS, TX 75231 Development and maintenance of binocular vision

U10EY-05239-06S1 (SSS) GRAYSTON, J THOMAS UNIVERSITY OF WASHINGTON DEPT OF PATHOBIOLOGY, SC-38 SEATTLE, WA 98195 Clinical trial of eye prophylaxis in the newborn

R01EY-05240-10 (VISA) KRUPIN, THEODORE NORTHWESTERN UNIVERSITY MED SC 303 EAST CHICAGO AVENUE CHICAGO, IL 60611 Electrophysiology of ciliary body transport processes

R01EY-05246-09 (VISA) JUMBLATT, JAMES E UNIVERSITY OF LOUISVILLE KENTUCKY LIONS EYE RES. INST. LOUISVILLE, KY 40202-1511 Prejunctional receptors in the anterior uvea

R01EY-05251-09 (VISB) WIESEL, TORSTEN N ROCKEFELLER UNIVERSITY 1230 YORK AVENUE NEW YORK, N Y 10021 Experimental myopia in primates

R37EY-05253-10 (NSS) WIESEL, TORSTEN ROCKEFELLER UNIVERSITY 1230 YORK AVENUE NEW YORK, NY 10021 Studies of the visual system

R01EY-05262-08 (VISA) DEL CERRO, MANUEL UNIVERSITY OF ROCHESTER 601 ELMWOOD AVE, PO BOX 603 ROCHESTER, NY 14642 Intraocular retinal transplants

R01EY-05272-06 (VISA) TANAKA, TOYOICHI MASS INSTITUTE OF TECHNOLOGY 77 MASSACHUSETTS AVENUE CAMBRIDGE, MASS 02139 Clinical laser spectroscopy of the lens

R01EY-05282-09 (VISB) LUND, JENNIFER S WESTERN PSYCHIATRIC INST 3811 O'HARA STREET PITTSBURGH, PA 15213 Structural basis for processing visual information

R37EY-05283-09 (VISB) LUND, RAYMOND D UNIVERSITY OF PITTSBURGH 3550 TERRACE STREET PITTSBURGH, PA 15261 Transplantation studies of the rat visual system

R01EY-05285-10 (VISA) LEMMON, VANCE P CASE WESTERN RESERVE UNIVERSIT 2040 ADELBERT ROAD CLEVELAND, OH 44106 The growth of retinal ganglion cell axons

R01EY-05289-08 (VISB) BAKER, JAMES F NORTHWESTERN UNIVERSITY 303 EAST CHICAGO AVENUE CHICAGO, IL 60611 Role of cerebellar nodulus and uvula in gaze reflexes

R01EY-05291-06 (VISB) SHUSTER, TERRENCE A CALIFORNIA STATE UNIVERSITY 1250 BELLFLOWER BLVD LONG BEACH, CA 90840-3701 Nucleotide sensitive enzymes in ros and rd retinas

R01EY-05298-08 (VISA) REINER, ANTON J UNIV. OF TENNESSEE, MEMPHIS 875 MONROE AVENUE MEMPHIS, TN 38163 Neural control of choroidal blood flow in the eye

R01EY-05301-07 (VISA) CHAKRABARTI, BIRESWAR EYE RESEARCH INSTITUTE 20 STANIFORD STREET BOSTON, MASS 02114 Hyaluronic acid in the normal aged & diseased vitreous

R01EY-05308-09 (VISB) LUND, RAYMOND D UNIVERSITY OF PITTSBURGH 3550 TERRACE STREET PITTSBURGH, PA 15261 Determinants of optic axon outgrowth

R01EY-05314-09 (VISA) LO, WOO-KUEN MOREHOUSE SCHOOL OF MEDICINE 720 WESTVIEW DRIVE, SW ATLANTA, GA 30310 Studies of cell junctions and cell membranes in the lens

R01EY-05318-09 (VISA) D'AMORE, PATRICIA A CHILDREN'S HOSPITAL CORP 300 LONGWOOD AVENUE BOSTON, MA 02115 Endothelial cell-pericyte interactions in the retina

R01EY-05321-09 (MGN) DRYJA, THADDEUS P MASSACHUSETTS EYE & EAR INF 243 CHARLES STREET BOSTON, MA 02114-3096 Molecular genetics of retinoblastoma and chromosome 13

R01EY-05325-09 (VISA) FULTON, ANNE B CHILDREN'S HOSPITAL 300 LONGWOOD AVENUE BOSTON, MA 02115 Retinal and visual development in the first year

R01EY-05329-09 (VISA) FULTON, ANNE B CHILDREN'S HOSPITAL CORPORATIO 300 LONGWOOD AVENUE BOSTON, MA 02115 The relation of visual pigment and sensitivity

R01EY-05333-09 (VISA) LANGER, ROBERT S CHILDREN'S HOSPITAL MED. CTR. 300 LONGWOOD AVENUE BOSTON, MASS 02115 Inhibition of ocular neovascularization

R44EY-05368-02A4 (VISB) WEINSTEIN, SIDNEY NEUROCOMMUNICATION-RES LABS 36 MILL PLAIN ROAD DANBURY, CT 06811 Corneal aesthesiometer and norms II

R01EY-05371-07 (VISB) MC LOON, STEVEN C UNIVERSITY OF MINNESOTA 321 CHURCH STREET, SE MINNEAPOLIS, MN 55455 Neuronal patterns in the developing visual system

R01EY-05404-07 (VISB) ADLER, RUBEN JOHNS HOPKINS UNIV SCH OF MED 600 NORTH WOLFE ST. BALTIMORE, MD 21205 Survival and maturation of normal and mutant photoreceptors

R01EY-05406-07 (VISA) BEKHOR, ISAAC DOHENY EYE INSTITUTE 1355 SAN PABLO STREET LOS ANGELES, CA 90033 Fiber cell mRNA of normal and cataractous lenses

R01EY-05422-08 (VISB) FRAMBACH, DONALD A DOHENY EYE INSTITUTE 1355 SAN PABLO STREET LOS ANGELES, CA 90033 RPE transepithelial transport

U10EY-05436-07 (VSN) KASS, MICHAEL A WASHINGTON UNIV SCHOOL OF MED 660 SOUTH EUCLID AVENUE ST LOUIS, MO 63110 5-fluorouracil and glaucoma filtering surgery

R01EY-05437-07 (VISB) FU, S JOSEPH NEW JERSEY MEDICAL SCHOOL 185 SOUSTH ORANGE AVE NEWARK, NJ 07103-2714 Characterization of prostaglandins in mammalian lenses

R01EY-05439-05 (VISA) WONG-RILEY, MARGARET T MEDICAL COLLEGE OF WISCONSIN 8701 WATERTOWN PLANK ROAD MILWAUKEE, WI 53226 Metabolic plasticity in adult primate visual cortex

U10EY-05446-07 (VSN) WILENSKY, JACOB T 1855 W TAYLOR STREET CHICAGO, IL 60612 5-Fluorouracil filtering surgery study

R01EY-05454-08 (VISA) STONE, RICHARD A UNIVERSITY OF PENNSYLVANIA D603 RICHARDS BLDG PHILADELPHIA, PA 19104-6075 Innervation of the anterior segment of the eye

U10EY-05473-07 (VSN) PARRISH, RICHARD K BASCOM PALMER EYE INSTITUTE P O BOX 016880 MIAMI, FLA 33101 5-fluorouracil and glaucoma filtering surgery

R01EY-05477-08 (VISB) LIPTON, STUART A CHILDREN'S HOSPITAL CORPORATIO 300 LONGWOOD AVENUE BOSTON, MA 02115 Retinal ganglion cells--Ion channels and transmitters

U10EY-05480-07 (VSN) SCHIFFMAN, JOYCE BASCOM PALMER EYE INSTITUTE P O BOX 016880 MIAMI, FL 33101 5-fluorouracil study--Coordinating center

R01EY-05494-08A1 (VISA) PEPPERBERG, DAVID R UNIVERSITY OF ILLINOIS 1855 W TAYLOR STREET CHICAGO, IL 60612 Visual pigment and photoreceptor adaptation

R01EY-05498-07 (VISA) KORENBROT, JUAN I UNIVERSITY OF CALIFORNIA PARNASSUS AVENUE SAN FRANCISCO, CA 94143 Mechanism of transduction in retinal cone photoreceptors

R01EY-05499-08 (BBCA) ROTHSCHILD, KENNETH J BOSTON UNIVERSITY 590 COMMONWEALTH AVE BOSTON, MA 02215 FTIR study of photoreceptor membrane

R01EY-05503-08 (VISA) KAMM, ROGER D MASSACHUSETTS INST OF TECH 77 MASSACHUSETTS AVENUE CAMBRIDGE, MA 02139 The outflow characteristics of aqueous humor

R01EY-05504-08 (NEUB) JHAVERI, SONAL MASSACHUSETTS INST OF TECHNOLO CAMBRIDGE, MA 02139 Axonal growth stages in the subcortical visual system

R01EY-05508-08 (VISA) PHILP, NANCY J UNIVERSITY OF PENNSYLVANIA PHILADELPHIA, PA 19104-6076 Regulation of cell shape and polarity in RPE cells

R01EY-05522-12 (VISB) ANDERSEN, RICHARD A MASSACHUSETTS INST OF TECHNOLO 77 MASSACHUSETTS AVENUE CAMBRIDGE, MA 02139 Visual-spatial properties of area 7 neurons

R01EY-05551-07 (VISB) LE VAY, SIMON SALK INSTITUTE POST OFFICE BOX 85800 SAN DIEGO, CA 92138 Structure and function of visual corex

R01EY-05570-05 (VISA) CAMMARATA, PATRICK R TEXAS COLL OF OSTEOPATHIC MED 3500 CAMP BOWIE BLVD FORT WORTH, TX 76107 Mechanism of sugar cataract formation in lens cells

U10EY-05571-07 (VSN) AZEN, STANLEY P UNIV OF SOUTHERN CALIFORNIA 1420 SAN PABLO STREET, PMB B-1 LOS ANGELES, CA 90033 Clinical trial of silicone oil in vitreoretinopathy

R01EY-05588-06 (VISA) CANTIN, EDOUARD M CITY OF HOPE NATIONAL MED CTR 1500 EAST DUARTE ROAD DUARTE, CA 91010 Herpes simples keratitis--Models of prevention

PROJECT NO., ORGANIZATIONAL UNIT., INVESTIGATOR, ADDRESS, TITLE

R01EY-05601-06 (VISA) BRANDON, CHRISTOPHER J CHICAGO MEDICAL SCHOOL 3333 GREEN BAY ROAD NORTH CHICAGO, IL 60064 Synaptic circuitry of retinal directional neurons
R01EY-05603-07 (BPO) NEWSOME, WILLIAM T STANFORD UNIVERSITY SHERMAN FAIRCHILD BLDG, D209 STANFORD, CA 94305 Cortical processing of visual motion
U10EY-05604-07 (VSN) SHERWOOD, MARK B UNIVERSITY OF FLORIDA DEPARTMENT OF OPHTHALMOLOGY GAINESVILLE, FL 32610 5-fluorouracil and glaucoma filtering surgery
R01EY-05609-07 (VISA) GEROSKI, DAYLE H EMORY UNIVERSITY 1327 CLIFTON ROAD, N E ATLANTA, GA 30322 Na-K pump function in transporting ocular tissues
R01EY-05612-07 (VISA) SULLIVAN, DAVID A EYE RES INST OF RETINA FDN 20 STANIFORD STREET BOSTON, MASS 02114 Endocrine control of the ocular secretory immune system
R01EY-05622-07 (VISB) WATT, CARL B BAYLOR COLLEGE OF MEDICINE 4000 RESEARCH FOREST DRIVE THE WOODLANDS, TX 77381 Neuroactive peptides in the vertebrate retina
R01EY-05627-06 (VISA) JACOBSON, SAMUEL G BASCOM PALMER EYE INSTITUTE PO BOX 016880 MIAMI, FL 33101 X-linked retinitis pigmentosa--Retinal function phenotypes
R01EY-05628-06 (VISA) YUE, BEATRICE Y UNIVERSITY OF ILLINOIS 1855 W TAYLOR ST B-1 CHICAGO, ILL 60612 Biology of trabecular meshwork in health & disease
R01EY-05629-06 (VISA) KAO, WINSTON W 231 BETHESDA AVE CINCINNATI, OH 45267-0527 Metabolism of extracellular matrix in injured corneas
R01EY-05631-07 (VISB) NIEDERKORN, JERRY Y UNIV OF TEXAS SOUTHWESTERN MEDICAL CENTER AT DALLAS DALLAS, TX 75235-9057 Transplant and tumor rejection processes within the eye
R01EY-05633-07 (VISA) SHIH, VIVIAN E MASSACHUSETTS GENERAL HOSPITAL 32 FRUIT STREET BOSTON, MA 02114 Molecular defect in gyrate atrophy of choroid and retina
R01EY-05640-07 (VISA) UBELS, JOHN L THE EAR & EYE INSTITUTE 203 LOTHROP STREET PITTSBURGH, PA 15213 The tear film and the ocular surface--Vitamin A in tear
R01EY-05653-04S1 (VISA) HYMAN, LESLIE G STATE UNIVERSITY OF NEW YORK STONY BROOK, NY 11787 Risk factors for age related maculopathy
R01EY-05661-07 (SSS) HALL, JAMES E UNIV. OF CALFORNIA, IRVINE MED SCI I D340 IRVINE, CA 92717 Lens connexon structure and function
R01EY-05662-07 (VISA) RAO, NARSING A DOHENY EYE INSTITUTE 1355 SAN PABLO ST LOS ANGELES, CALIF 90033 Protective mechanisms and treatment of uveitis
R01EY-05665-07 (VISA) ZIESKE, JAMES D EYE RESEARCH INSTITUTE 20 STANIFORD ST BOSTON, MA 02114 Corneal stromal-epithelial interactions during repair
R01EY-05675-07 (VISB) MASSOF, ROBERT W JOHNS HOPKINS HOSPITAL 601 NORTH BROADWAY BALTIMORE, MD 21205 Retinal function changes in age-related maculopathy
R37EY-05678-08 (VISA) STREILEIN, J WAYNE UNIV OF MIAMI SCHOOL OF MEDICI PO BOX 016960 R-138 MIAMI, FL 33101 Anterior chamber influence on ocular antigens
R01EY-05684-07 (VISA) LOUIS, CHARLES F UNIVERSITY OF MINNESOTA 1988 FITCH AVENUE ST PAUL, MN 55108 Organization and role of lens membrane proteins
R01EY-05685-07 (VISA) MAYER, D LUISA CHILDREN'S HOSPITAL CORPORATIO 300 LONGWOOD AVENUE BOSTON, MA 02115 Pediatric perimetry
R01EY-05690-12 (NLS) BENOWITZ, LARRY I CHILDREN'S HOSPITAL 300 LONGWOOD AVE BOSTON, MA 02115 Molecular bases of neural connectivity
R01EY-05717-05 (VISA) MARFURT, CARL F INDIANA UNIVERSITY 3400 BROADWAY GARY, IN 46408 Corneal innervation & wound healing
P30EY-05722-06A1 (VSN) KLINTWORTH, GORDON K DUKE UNIVERSITY EYE CENTER BOX 3802 DURHAM, NC 27710 Core grant for vision research
P30EY-05722-06A1 9001 (VSN) HATCHELL, DIANE L Core grant for vision research Core--Animal surgery
P30EY-05722-06A1 9002 (VSN) CORLESS, JOSEPH M Core grant for vision research Core--Ocular morphology
P30EY-05722-06A1 9003 (VSN) WONG, FULTON Core grant for vision research Core--Ocular biochemistry and molecular biology
R01EY-05724-06 (VISB) UPDYKE, BRUCE V LSU MEDICAL SCHOOL 1901 PERDIDO ST NEW ORLEANS, LA 70112 Visual oculomotor integration in striatum
R01EY-05725-08 (VISA) SLAUGHTER, MALCOLM M STATE UNIVERSITY OF NEW YORK 120 CARY HALL BUFFALO, NY 14214 Synaptic mechanisms in the vertebrate retina
R01EY-05729-08 (VISB) HAYHOE, MARY M UNIVERSITY OF ROCHESTER 274 MELIORA HALL, RIVER CAMPUS ROCHESTER, NY 14627 Visual sensitivity regulation and color coding
R01EY-05738-05 (VISA) AKHTAR, RASHID A MEDICAL COLLEGE OF GEORGIA DEPT OF CELL & MOLECULAR BIOL AUGUSTA, GA 30912 Receptors and phosphoinosities metabolism in the cornea
R01EY-05747-07 (VISA) MASLAND, RICHARD H MASSACHUSETTS GENERAL HOSPITAL WELLMAN BUILDING 429 BOSTON, MA 02114 Actions of mammalian amacrine cells
R01EY-05750-07 (VISA) BAYLOR, DENIS A STANDORD UNIVERSITY STANFORD, CA 94305-5401 Visual transduction in primate photoreceptors
R01EY-05758-08 (PTHB) LEE, WEN-HWA UNIVERSITY OF TEXAS HEALTH 7703 FLOYD CURL DRIVE SAN ANTONIO, TX 78284-6250 Molecular mechanisms of the retinoblastoma formation
R01EY-05767-07 (VISA) JOYCE, NANCY C EYE RESEARCH INSTITUTE 20 STANIFORD STREET BOSTON, MA 02114 Pharmacology of the corneal endothelium
R01EY-05775-07 (VISA) GRUNWALD, JUAN E PRESBYTERIAN-UNIV/PENN MED CTR SCHEIE EYE INST - 51 N 39TH ST PHILADELPHIA, PA 19104 Diabetic metabolic control and retinal blood flow
R01EY-05786-06 (VISA) SHEARER, THOMAS R OREGON HEALTH SCIENCES UNIV 611 S W CAMPUS DRIVE PORTLAND, OR 97201 Calcium activated protease in cataract formation
R55EY-05787-07 (VISA) FARNSWORTH, PATRICIA N UMDNJ-NEW JERSEY MEDICAL SCH 185 SOUTH ORANGE AVENUE NEWARK, NJ 07103-2714 Lens NMR--Correlation with lens functional indices
R01EY-05788-05 (VISA) HO, YEE-KIN UNIVERSITY OF ILLINOIS 1853 W POLK STREET - M/C 536 CHICAGO, IL 60612 The retinal cyclic GMP cascade
R01EY-05794-05 (VISA) MEREDITH, TRAVIS A BETHESDA EYE INSTITUTE 3655 VISTA AVE ST. LOUIS, MO 63110 Pathogenesis and treatment of bacterial endophalmitis
R01EY-05798-04A2 (VISA) COTE, RICHARD H UNIVERSITY OF NEW HAMPSHIRE SPAULDING LIFE SCIENCE BLDS DURHAM, NH 03824-3544 Role of cyclic GMP in photoreceptor function
R01EY-05799-06 (VISA) KENYON, KENNETH R EYE RESEARCH INSTITUTE 20 STANIFORD STREET BOSTON, MA 02114 Corneal inflammation and infection in vitamin A deficiency
R01EY-05801-07 (PHY) MIRCHEFF, AUSTIN K UNIV OF SOUTHERN CALIFORNIA 1333 SAN PABLO STREET LOS ANGELES, CALIF 90033 Tear gland fluid formation
R01EY-05803-06 (VISA) LIANG, JACK J MA EYE & EAR INFIRMARY 243 CHARLES ST BOSTON, MA 02114 Age & cataract related changes in lens protein structure
R01EY-05804-07 (VISB) DOBSON, MARGARET V UNIVERSITY OF PITTSBURGH 462 LANGLEY HALL PITTSBURGH, PA 15260 Clinical assessment of visual acuity in human infants
R55EY-05856-08A1 (VISA) PETRASH, J MARK WASHINGTON UNIV SCHOOL OF MED 660 SOUTH EUCLID AVE, BOX 8096 ST LOUIS, MO 63110 Molecular biology of aldose reductase and cataracts
R01EY-05860-10 (CBY) LILIEN, JACK E CLEMSON UNIVERSITY DEPT OF BIOLOGICAL SCIENCES CLEMSON, S C 29634-2903 Retina surface transferase--Properties & function
R01EY-05864-07 (VISB) KIORPES, LYNNE NEW YORK UNIVERSITY 6 WASHINGTON PLACE NEW YORK, NY 10003 Development of visual function in primates
U10EY-05874-07 (VSN) PALMER, EARL A 3181 S W SAM JACKSON PARK RD PORTLAND, OR 97201 Phase II--Cryotherapy for retinopathy of prematurity
R01EY-05879-28 (VISB) SCHLAG, JOHN D UNIVERSITY OF CALIFORNIA LOS ANGELES, CA 90024-1763 Conditioning of pyramidal activity by sensory inflow
R01EY-05883-07 (VISA) PROIA, ALAN D DUKE UNIVERSITY EYE CENTER BOX 3802 DURHAM, N C 27710 Corneal arachidonic acid metabolism
R01EY-05895-07 (VISB) FUNG, BERNARD K JULES STEIN EYE INSTITUTE 100 STEIN PLAZA LOS ANGELES, CA 90024-7008 Phosphodiesterase and GTPase activation in retinal rods
U10EY-05897-07 (VSN) HARDY, ROBERT J UNIV OF TEXAS HLTH SCIENCE CTR 1200 HERMAN PRESSLER HOUSTON, TEX 77030 Cryo-rop follow-up
R01EY-05901-06 (VISB) KRUGER, PHILIP B SUNY STATE COLLEGE OF OPTOMETR 100 EAST 24 STREET NEW YORK, NY 10010 Stimuli for accommodation--Diopatric & non-dioptric cures
R01EY-05910-07 (VISA) STEPHENS, ROBERT J SRI INTERNATIONAL 333 RAVENSWOOD AVE MENLO PARK, CALIF 94025 Mechanisms of retinal phototoxicity
R01EY-05911-06 (VISB) MAUNSELL, JOHN H UNIVERSITY OF ROCHESTER 601 ELMWOOD AVENUE/BOX 642 ROCHESTER, NY 14642 Segregation of visual channel in cerebral cortex
R01EY-05922-06 (VISB) NORTON, THOMAS T UNIVERSITY OF ALABAMA SCHOOL OF OPTOMETRY/MED CTR BIRMINGHAM, AL 35294 Mechanisms of ocular development
R01EY-05926-06 (VISB) LAPPIN, JOSEPH S VANDERBILT UNIVERSITY NASHVILLE, TN 37240 Spatial structure perception in changing optical pattern
R01EY-05945-06 (VISA) HENDRICKS, ROBERT L UNIVERSITY OF ILLINOIS 1855 TAYLOR STREET CHICAGO, IL 60612 Role of cytotoxic lymphocytes in HSV-1 corneal lesions
R01EY-05951-08 (VISA) CAMPOCHIARO, PETER A JOHNS HOPKINS UNIVERSITY 600 NORTH WOLFE STREET BALTIMORE, MD 21205 Mechanisms in retinal pigment epithelial cell migration
R01EY-05957-06 (VISB) PELI, ELIEZER EYE RESEARCH INST 20 STANIFORD STREET BOSTON, MA 02114 Model-based image enhancement for the visually impaired
U10EY-05958-06 (VSN) BRESSLER, NEIL M MPS READING CENTER 5500 N BROADWAY, 9TH FLOOR BALTIMORE, MD 21205 Foveal photocoagulation study reading
R01EY-05972-06 (VISA) LASATER, ERIC M UNIVERSITY OF UTAH 410 CHIPETA WAY, RESEARCH PK SALT LAKE CITY, UT 84108 Membrane properties of vertebrate retinal neurons
R01EY-05975-06 (VISB) BOOTHE, RONALD G EMORY UNIVERSITY YERKS REGIONAL PRIMATE RES CTR ATLANTA, GA 30322 Monkey model for infantile aphakia-amblyopia treatment
R01EY-05978-07 (VISB) ARIEL, MICHAEL UNIVERSITY OF PITTSBURGH 458 CRAWFORD HALL PITTSBURGH, PA 15260 Retinal pharmacology of directional ganglion cells
R01EY-05979-05A1 (VISA) BURNS, MARGARET S UNIVERSITY OF CALIFORNIA 1603 ALHAMBRA BLVD SACRAMENTO, CA 95816 Biochemical alterations in vascular retinopathy
R01EY-05985-07 (VISA) D'AMORE, PATRICIA A CHILDREN'S HOSPITAL CORP 300 LONGWOOD AVENUE BOSTON, MA 02115 Role of FGFS in retinal vascular growth and pathology
R01EY-05990-07 (VISA) WEINREB, ROBERT N UNIV OF CALIFORNIA, SAN DIEGO OPHTHALMOLOGY, T-014 SAN DIEGO, CA 92103 Eicosanoids in the inflow outflow pathways of the eye
U10EY-05995-06 (VSN) HAWKINS, BARBARA S JOHNS HOPKINS UNIVERSITY 550 NORTH BROADWAY BALTIMORE, MD 21205 Foveal photocoagulation study coordinating center
R01EY-05996-05 (VISA) GOLDBAUM, MICHAEL H UNIVERSITY OF CALIFORNIA LA JOLLA, CA 92093 Structured analysis of the retina
R01EY-06000-06 (VISA) TRINKAUS-RANDALL, VICKERY E BOSTON UNIVERSITY MED SCHOOL 80 EAST CONCORD STREET BOSTON, MA 02118 Corneal epithelial adhesion--Morphology and biochemistry
R01EY-06005-07 (VISA) RAE, JAMES L MAYO FOUNDATION 200 FIRST STREET SOUTHWEST ROCHESTER, MN 55905 Ionic channels in epithelia of the eye
R01EY-06006-04 (VISA) WEINREB, ROBERT N UNIVERSITY OF CALIFORNIA 9500 GILMAN DR LA JOLLA, CA 92093-0946 Confocal laser scanning ophthalmoscope/biomicroscope
R01EY-06008-07 (VISA) FOSTER, CHARLES S MASS EYE AND EAR INFIRMARY 243 CHARLES STREET BOSTON, MA 02114 Molecular genetics of herpes simplex-mediated ocular pathology

R01EY-06012-07 (VISA) ATHERTON, SALLY S DEPT OF MICROBIOLOGY & IMM P O BOX 016960 (R-138) MIAMI, FL 33101 Mechanisms of herpes simplex virus retinitis
R37EY-06039-08 (VISB) PATON, MARTHA C YALE UNIVERSITY 12 PROSPECT PLACE NEW HAVEN, CT 06511 Experiments on the development of neural pathways
R01EY-06044-08 (VISA) BHAT, SURAJ P JULES STEIN EYE INSTITUTE UCLA SCHOOL OF MEDICINE LOS ANGELES, CA 90024-7008 Gene expression in the normal and cataractous lens
R01EY-06045-09 (VISA) FLIESLER, STEVEN J BETHESDA EYE INSTITUTE 3655 VISTA AVENUE ST LOUIS, MO 63110 Glycoprotein synthesis and metabolism in retinas
R01EY-06062-07 (VISA) HAMM, HEIDI E UNIVERSITY OF ILLINOIS BOX 6998 CHICAGO, IL 60680 Immunological studies of visual transduction pathways
R01EY-06069-07 (VISA) MUSTARI, MICHAEL J UNIV OF TEXAS MEDICAL BRANCH 200 UNIVERSITY BLVD GALVESTON, TX 77550-2772 Studies of primate smooth eye movements
R01EY-06085-06 (VISA) MC GINNIS, JAMES F UCLA-NPI, ROOM 48-163 760 WESTWOOD PLAZA LOS ANGELES, CA 90024-1759 Biomolecular studies of unique retinal specific proteins
R01EY-06094-06 (VISA) SIEVING, PAUL A KELLOGG EYE CENTER 1000 WALL STREET ANN ARBOR, MI 48109-1994 Inner retinal contributions to the ERG
R01EY-06096-05 (VISB) SCHEIN, STANLEY J UCLA PSYCHOLOGY LOS ANGELES, CA 90024-1563 Mapping from retina to visual cortex
R01EY-06107-06 (CBY) RUTISHAUSER, URS S CASE WESTERN RESERVE UNIV 2119 ABINGTON ROAD CLEVELAND, OH 44106 Cell adhesion in development of the eye
R01EY-06108-05 (VISB) BERSON, DAVID M BROWN UNIVERSITY BOX G PROVIDENCE, RI 02912 Visual circuitry of the superior colliculus
R01EY-06109-07 (VISA) CURCIO, CHRISTINE A UNIVERSITY OF ALABAMA 700 S 18TH STREET BIRMINGHAM, AL 35233 Quantitative analysis of aging primate retina
U10EY-06116-07 (VSN) FOULKS, GARY N DUKE UNIVERSITY EYE CENTER P O BOX 3802-200 DURHAM, NC 27710 Collaborative corneal transplantation studies
U10EY-06121-07 (VSN) STULTING, ROBERT D EMORY UNIVERSITY 1327 CLIFTON ROAD, N E ATLANTA, GA 30322 Collaborative corneal transplantation studies
R01EY-06135-08 (VISA) TOWNES-ANDERSON, ELLEN S CORNELL UNIVERSITY MEDICAL COL 1300 YORK AVE NEW YORK, NY 10021 Biology of isolated retinal cells
U10EY-06146-07 (VSN) MAGUIRE, MAUREEN G JOHNS HOPKINS UNIVERSITY 550 NORTH BROADWAY BALTIMORE, MD 21205 Coordinating center--Corneal transplantation studies
U10EY-06155-07 (VSN) STARK, WALTER J THE JOHNS HOPKINS HOSPITAL 600 NORTH WOLFE STREET BALTIMORE, MD 21205 Clinical center--Corneal transplantation studies (CCTS)
U10EY-06156-07 (VSN) BIAS, WILMA B THE JOHNS HOPKINS UNIVERSITY 2041 E. MONUMENT STREET BALTIMORE, MD 21205 Coordinating laboratory corneal transplantation studies
U10EY-06158-07 (VSN) MEYER, ROGER F UNIVERSITY OF MICHIGAN 1000 WALL STREET ANN ARBOR, MICH 48109 Collaborative corneal transplantation studies
R01EY-06164-05 (VISA) HUNT, RICHARD C UNIVERSITY OF SOUTH CAROLINA SCHOOL OF MEDICINE COLUMBIA, S C 29208 Biochemistry of retinal pigmented epithelium
U10EY-06172-07 (VSN) STARK, WALTER J THE JOHNS HOPKINS HOSPITAL 600 NORTH WOLFE STREET BALTIMORE, MD 21205 Chairman's grant--Corneal transplantation studies
R01EY-06175-06 (VISB) PASTERNAK, TATIANA UNIVERSITY OF ROCHESTER 274 MELIORA HALL, RIVER CAMPUS ROCHESTER, N Y 14627 Neural mechanisms of motion perception
R01EY-06177-07 (VISA) DARTT, DARLENE A EYE RESEARCH INST/RETINA FDN 20 STANIFORD STREET BOSTON, MA 02114 Mechanism of lacrimal gland secretion
R01EY-06178-06 (VISA) FISCHBARG, JORGE COLUMBIA UNIVERSITY 630 WEST 168TH STREET NEW YORK, NY 10032 Transport mechanisms in corneal endothelium
R01EY-06185-05A1 (VISA) THOFT, RICHARD A THE EYE & EAR INST OF PITTSBUR 203 LOTHROP STREET PITTSBURGH, PA 15213 Ocular surface cell culture and replacement
R01EY-06186-07 (VISA) THOFT, RICHARD A EYE & EAR INSTI. OF PITTSBURGH 203 LOTHROP STREET PITTSBURGH, PA 15213 Metabolism of ocular surface epithelium
R01EY-06195-07 (PTHB) BENEDICT, WILLIAM F BAYLOR COLLEGE OF MEDICINE 4000 RESEARCH FOREST DRIVE WOODLANDS, TX 77381 Functional aspects of the retinoblastoma gene
R01EY-06225-07 (VISB) HARGRAVE, PAUL A UNIVERSITY OF FLORIDA BOX J-284, J H M H C GAINESVILLE, FL 32610-0284 Rhodopsin topography in the rod disc membrane
R37EY-06226-07 (VISA) HARGRAVE, PAUL A UNIVERSITY OF FLORDIA DEPT OF OPTHALMOLOGY GAINESVILLE, FL 32610 Rhodopsin structure and function
R01EY-06232-06 (VISB) JACOBY, JEAN NEW YORK UNIVERSITY MED CTR 550 FIRST AVENUE NEW YORK, N Y 10016 Extraocular muscle--Fiber properties and development
R01EY-06234-06 (VISA) LIEBOVITCH, LARRY S COLUMBIA UNIVERSITY 630 WEST 168TH STREET NEW YORK, NY 10032 Ion current analysis in the cornea
U10EY-06237-06 (VSN) GARCIA, CHARLES A HERMANN EYE CENTER 6411 FANNIN HOUSTON, TEXAS 77030 Foveal photocoagulation study clinical center
U10EY-06238-06 (VSN) STERNBERG, PAUL EMORY UNIVERSITY 1327 CLIFTON ROAD, N E ATLANTA, GA 30322 Foveal photocoagulation study clinical center
U10EY-06239-06 (VSN) FISH, GARY E 7150 GREENVILLE AVENUE DALLAS, TX 75231 Foveal photocoagulation study clinical center
U10EY-06253-07 (VSN) ROBERTSON, DENNIS M MAYO FOUNDATION 200 FIRST STREET SOUTHWEST ROCHESTER, MN 55905 Collaborative ocular melanoma study - clinical center
U10EY-06257-07 (VSN) DAVIDORF, FREDERICK H OHIO STATE UNIVERSITY 456 W. TENTH AVE., SUITE 5B COLUMBIA, OHIO 43210 Collaborative ocular melanoma study-clinical center
U10EY-06258-07 (VSN) RUIZ, RICHARD S HERMANN EYE CENTER 6411 FANNIN STREET HOUSTON, TX 77030 Collaborative ocular melanoma study - clinical center
U10EY-06259-07 (VSN) WILSON, DAVID J OREGON HEALTH SCIENCES UNIV 3181 SW SAM JACKSON PARK ROAD PORTLAND, OREGON 97201 Collaborative ocular melanoma study - clinical center
U10EY-06260-07 (VSN) SCHACHAT, ANDREW P JOHNS HOPKINS UNIVERSITY 200 WILMER BALTIMORE, MD 21205 Collaborative ocular melanoma study - clinical center
U10EY-06264-07 (VSN) VAN HEUVEN, WICHARD A UNIV OF TEXAS HEALTH SCIENCE C 7703 FLOYD CURL DRIVE SAN ANTONIO, TX 78284 Collaborative ocular melanoma study-clinical center
U10EY-06265-07 (VSN) TREMPE, CLEMENT L RETINA ASSOCIATES 100 CHARLES RIVER PLAZA BOSTON, MA 02114 Collaborative ocular melanoma study - clinical center
U10EY-06266-07 (VSN) FINE, STUART L SCHEIE EYE INSTITUTE 51 NORTH 39TH STREET PHILADELPHIA, PA 19104 Collaborative ocular melanoma study
U10EY-06268-07 (VSN) STRAATSMA, BRADLEY R JULES STEIN EYE INSTITUTE UCLA SCHOOL OF MEDICINE LOS ANGELES, CA 90024-1771 Collaborative ocular melanoma study - clinical center
U10EY-06269-07 (VSN) WEINGEIST, THOMAS A UNIVERSITY OF IOWA DEPARTMENT OF OPTHAMOLOGY IOWA CITY, IA 52242 Collaborative ocular melanoma study - clinical center
U10EY-06270-07 (VSN) LIGGETT, PETER E USC SCHOOL OF MEDICINE DOHENY EYE INSTITUTE LOS ANGELES, CA 90033 Collaborative ocular melanoma study
U10EY-06274-07 (VSN) STERNBERG, PAUL JR EMORY UNIVERSITY 1327 CLIFTON ROAD, NE ATLANTA, GA 30322 Collaborative ocular melanoma study - clinical center
U10EY-06275-07 (VSN) MURRAY, TIMOTHY G BASCOM PALMER EYE INSTITUTE P O BOX 016880 MIAMI, FLA 33101 Collaborative ocular melanoma study-clinical center
U10EY-06276-07 (VSN) FULLER, DWAIN G TEXAS RETINA ASSOCIATES 7150 GREENVILLE AVENUE DALLAS, TX 75231 Collaborative ocular melanoma study - clinical center
U10EY-06279-07 (VSN) MIELER, WILLIAM F MEDICAL COLLEGE OF WISCONSIN 8700 W WISCONSIN AVENUE MILWAUKEE, WI 53226 Collarborative ocular melanoma study - clinical center
U10EY-06282-07 (VSN) VINE, ANDREW K KELLOGG EYE CENTER 1000 WALL STREET ANN ARBOR, MI 48105 Collaborative ocular melanoma study - clinical center
U10EY-06284-04 (VSN) ALBERT, DANIEL M HOWE LAB OF OPHTHALMOLOGY 243 CHARLES STREET BOSTON, MA 02114 Collaborative ocular melanoma study--Pathology center
U10EY-06287-07 (VSN) HAWKINS, BARBARA S JOHNS HOPKINS UNIVERSITY 550 NORTH BROADWAY, 9TH FLOOR BALTIMORE, MD 21205 Collaborative ocular melanoma study coordinating center
U10EY-06288-07 (VSN) PACKER, SAMUEL NORTH SHORE UNIVERSITY HOSPITA 300 COMMUNITY DRIVE MANHASSET, NY 11030 Collaborative ocular melanoma study - clinical center
U10EY-06289-07 (VSN) MARGHERIO, RAYMOND R WILLIAM BEAUMONT HOSPITAL 3535 WEST 13 MILE ROAD ROYAL OAK, MI 48072 Collaborative ocular melanoma study - clinical center
U10EY-06291-07 (VSN) HANSON, WILLIAM F UNIVERSITY OF TEXAS 1515 HOLCOMBE BOULEVARD HOUSTON, TX 77030 Radiological physics center for collaborative ocular melanomas
R01EY-06311-06 (VISA) HILL, JAMES M LSU EYE CENTER 2020 GRAVIER STREET NEW ORLEANS, LA 70112-2234 Ocular HSV--Latency, reactivation and recurrence
U10EY-06323-07 (VSN) ROGERS, GARY L CHILDRENS HOSPITAL RES FOUND 700 CHILDRENS DRIVE COLUMBUS, OH 43205 Cyro-rop follow-up clinical center
U10EY-06330-07 (VSN) ROTH, ALAN M UNIVERSITY OF CALIFORNIA 1603 ALHAMBRA BOULEVARD SACRAMENTO, CA 95817-7051 Cryo-rop participating center
R01EY-06337-08 (VISA) KNOWLES, DANIEL M COLUMBIA UNIVERSITY 630 WEST 168TH STREET NEW YORK, NY 10032 B and T lymphocyte subpopulations in ocular disease
R01EY-06338-06A1 (VISA) POTTER, DAVID E MOREHOUSE SCHOOL OF MEDICINE 720 WESTVIEW DR., S.W. ATLANTA, GA 30310-1495 Dopamine and alpha 2 agonists--Potential antiglaucoma drugs
U10EY-06354-07 (VSN) PHELPS, DALE L UNIVERSITY OF ROCHESTER P O BOX 651/601 ELMWOOD AVE ROCHESTER, NY 14642 Cryo-rop follow-up clinical center
P30EY-06360-06 (VSN) EDELHAUSER, HENRY F EMORY UNIVERSITY EYE CENTER 1327 CLIFTON ROAD, N E ATLANTA, GA 30322 Core--Department of ophthalmology
P30EY-06360-06 9004 (VSN) STULTING, RD Core--Department of ophthalmology Core--Biostatistics
P30EY-06360-06 9001 (VSN) CHURCH, ROBERT L Core--Department of ophthalmology Core--Analytical biochemistry
P30EY-06360-06 9002 (VSN) GROSSNIKLAUS, H Core--Department of ophthalmology Core--Experimental morphology/research ocular pathology
P30EY-06360-06 9003 (VSN) GEROSKI, D H Core--Department of ophthalmology Core--Tissue culture/immunochemistry
U10EY-06363-07 (VSN) QUINN, GRAHAM E CHILDREN'S HOSPITAL ONE CHILDREN'S CENTER PHILADELPHIA, PA 19104 CRYO-ROP follow-up clinical center
R01EY-06380-06 (VISB) RUBIN, GARY S JOHNS HOPKINS UNIVERSITY SCHOOL OF MED, 720 RUTLAND AVE BALTIMORE, MD 21205 Studies of low vision reading and face recognition
R01EY-06391-07 (VISA) MATHIAS, RICHARD T SUNY AT STONY BROOK STONY BROOK, NY 11794-8661 Volume regulation in normal and cataractous lenses
R01EY-06394-05 (VISB) PORTER, FRANKLIN I UNIVERSITY OF HOUSTON 4901 CALHOUN BLVD HOUSTON, TX 77204-6052 Clinical predictors for successful visual rehabilitation
U10EY-06395-07 (VSN) PALMER, EARL A OREGON HEALTH SCIENCE UNIVERSI 3181 SW SAM JACKSON PARK ROAD PORTLAND, OR 97201 CRYO-ROP participating center-phase II

PROJECT NO., ORGANIZATIONAL UNIT., INVESTIGATOR, ADDRESS, TITLE

U10EY-06396-07 (VSN) SUMMERS, CAROLE G UNIVERSITY OF MINNESOTA 516 DELAWARE ST SE BOX 493 MINNEAPOLIS, MN 55455 CRYO-ROP follow-up clincal center

R01EY-06400-04A3 (VISA) SRIVASTAVA, OM P MISSOURI LIONS EYE RESEARCH FD 404 PORTLAND ST COLUMBIA, MO 65201 Proteinase, inhibitor & crystallin fragments in cataract

R01EY-06409-06 (VISA) WILLIAMS, MARILYN A PURDUE UNIVERSITY WEST LAFAYETTE, IN 47907 Mouse RPE and retina--Cytoskeleton and basement membrane

R01EY-06416-06 (VISA) HERNANDEZ, M ROSARIO EYE RESEARCH INSTITUTE 20 STANIFORD STREET BOSTON, MA 02114 Glaucoma--Connective tissue changes in optic nerve head

R01EY-06429-06 (PC) CERIONE, RICHARD A DEPARTMENT OF PHARMACOLOGY CORNELL UNIV/NYS COLL VET MED ITHACA, NY 14853-6401 Biochemical characterization of signal transduction

R01EY-06431-08 (VISA) KAY, EUNDUCK P DOHENY EYE INSTITUTE 1355 SAN PABLO STREET LOS ANGELES, CA 90033 Studies on mechanism of retrocorneal fibrous membrane

R01EY-06449-07 (VISB) PERRY, GARY W FLORIDA ATLANTIC UNIVERSITY P O BOX 3091 BOCA RATON, LA 33431 Molecular events in optic nerve growth and regeneration

R01EY-06454-07 (VISA) WAGNER, JOHN A CORNELL UNIVERSITY MED COLL 1300 YORK AVENUE NEW YORK, NY 10021 Retina-derived growth factor--A regulator of neural differentiation

R01EY-06457-06 (VISA) PATTERSON, JOHN W UNIV OF CONNECTICUT HEALTH CTR 263 FARMINGTON AVE FARMINGTON, CT 06030 Lens currents observed with a vibrating probe

R01EY-06458-06 (VISA) ELDRED, GRAIG E UNIV OF MISSOURI SCHOOL OF MED DEPT OF OPHTHALMOLOGY COLUMBIA, MO 65212 Lipofuscinogenesis in the retinal pigment epithelium

R01EY-06459-07 (VISB) HUMPHREY, ALLEN L UNIVERSITY OF PITTSBURGH 3550 TERRACE STREET PITTSBURGH, PA 15261 Structure/function relationships in visual cortex

R01EY-06462-05 (VISA) JAMES, ERIC R MEDICAL UNIV OF SOUTH CAROLINA 171 ASHLEY AVENUE CHARLESTON, SC 29425 Retinal binding proteins & autoimmunity in onchocerciasis

R01EY-06463-06 (VISA) HAGEMAN, GREGORY S BETHESDA EYE INSTITUTE DEPT OF OPHTHALMOLOGY ST LOUIS, MO 63110 Retina--Substructure of primate cone photoreceptors

R01EY-06466-07 (BBCA) KOHLER, BRYAN E UNIVERSITY OF CALIFORNIA RIVERSIDE, CA 92521 Spectroscopic studies of visual pigments

R01EY-06469-04A2 (VISA) FRY, KEITH R BAYLOR COLLEGE OF MEDICINE 4000 RESEARCH FOREST DRIVE THE WOODLANDS, TX 77381 Functional organization of the retina

R01EY-06472-05 (VISA) MARSHAK, DAVID W THE UNIV OF TEXAS HEALTH SCI C PO BOX 20708 HOUSTON, TX 77225 Peptidergic neurons of the primate retina

R01EY-06473-06 (VISA) HJELMELAND, LEONARD M UNIVERSITY OF CALIFORNIA DAVIS, CA 95616 Regulation of FGF expression during retinal detachment

R01EY-06477-07 (VISA) ROSENBAUM, JAMES T OREGON HEALTH SCIENCES UNIV 3375 S.W. TERWILLIGER BLVD. PORTLAND, OR 97201-3098 Endotoxin-induced uveitis

R01EY-06482-04 (VISA) SMITH, RONALD E USC SCHOOL OF MEDICINE 1355 SAN PABLO STREET LOS ANGELES, CA 90033 Chronic endophthalmitis complicating cataract surgery

R01EY-06484-06 (VISA) ROSENBAUM, JAMES T OREGON HEALTH SCIENCES UNIV 3181 S W SAM JACKSON PARK ROAD PORTLAND, OR 97201 Chemotactic factors in animal models of uveitis

R01EY-06485-06 (VISB) PETERSON, BARRY W NORTHWESTERN UNIVERSITY 303 E CHICAGO AVENUE CHICAGO, IL 60611-3008 Neuronal organization of the vestibulocular reflex

U10EY-06488-07 (VSN) KLEIN, MICHAEL L CASEY EYE INSTITUTE 3375 SW TERWILLIGER PORTLAND, OR 97201 Macular photocoagulation study

R01EY-06493-06 (VISA) RINTOUL, DAVID A KANSAS STATE UNIVERSITY ACKERT HALL MANHATTAN, KS 66506-4901 Reconstitution of channel-forming proteins

U10EY-06496-07 (VSN) SMITH, RONALD E USC SCHOOL OF MEDICINE 1355 SAN PABLO STREET LOS ANGELES, CA 90033 Collaborative corneal transplantation studies

R01EY-06511-07 (VISB) HOCKFIELD, SUSAN SECTION OF NEUROANATOMY 333 CEDAR STREET NEW HAVEN, CT 06510 Moleular cytoarchitecture of central visual areas

R01EY-06513-05 (VISA) SCHWARTZMAN, MICHAL L NEW YORK MEDICAL COLLEGE VALHALLA, NY 10595 Corneal arachidonate metabolites via cytochrome P450

R01EY-06514-06A1 (VISA) ROOF, DOROTHY J MASS EYE & EAR INFIRMARY 243 CHARLES STREET BOSTON, MA 02114 Rod photoreceptor renewal/cytoskeletal involvement

R55EY-06515-07 (VISA) MASSEY, STEPHEN C UNIV OF TX HLTH SCI CTR HOUSTO 6420 LAMAR FLEMING AVE HOUSTON, TX 77030 Neurotransmitter mechanisms in the retina

R01EY-06516-07 (VISA) RIPPS, HARRIS UNIVERSITY OF ILLINOIS 1855 WEST TAYLOR STREET CHICAGO, IL 60612 Visual adaptation in the vertebrate retina

R01EY-06520-06 (VISA) HARTZER, MICHAEL K EYE RESEARCH INSTITUTE 405 DODGE HALL ROCHESTER, MI 48309 A pharmacologic approach to intraocular proliferation

R01EY-06522-08 (VISB) NAKAYAMA, KEN HARVARD UNIVERSITY WILLIAM JAMES HALL CAMBRIDGE, MA 02138 Visual image motion processing in humans

R01EY-06558-05 (VISB) KANEKO, CHRIS R SEATTLE, WA 98195 SJ-50 Saccadic eye movement studies

R01EY-06562-06 (VISB) STEIN, BARRY E VIRGINIA COMMONWEALTH UNIV BOX 551/MCV STATION RICHMOND, VA 23298-0551 Superior colliculus: development of visual properties

R01EY-06563-05 (VISA) LI, WEIYE HAHNEMANN UNIVERSITY BROAD AND VINE PHILADELPHIA, PA 19102 Diabetic retinopathy--Basic study in pericyte metabolism

R01EY-06564-05 (VISB) CHIAPPINELLI, VINCENT A ST LOUIS UNIVERSITY 1402 SOUTH GRAND BLVD ST LOUIS, MO 63104 Role of peptides in oculomotor neurotransmission

R01EY-06566-05 (MGN) NUSSBAUM, ROBERT L UNIVERSITY OF PENNSYLVANIA 428 CLINICAL RESEARCH BUILDING PHILADELPHIA, PA 19104-6145 Isolating the gene for choroideremia

PROJECT NO., ORGANIZATIONAL UNIT., INVESTIGATOR, ADDRESS, TITLE

R01EY-06579-06 (VISB) NORCIA, ANTHONY SMITH-KETTLEWELL EYE RESEARCH 2232 WEBSTER ST. SAN FRANCISCO, CA 94115 Normal and abnormal spatial development in infants

R01EY-06581-04 (VISA) ROSENZWEIG, STEVEN A MEDICAL UNIV OF SOUTH CAROLINA 171 ASHLEY AVENUE CHARLESTON, SC 29425 Neuropeptide receptors in ocular and peripheral tissues

R01EY-06584-06 (VISA) DUNKEL, EDMUND C EYE RESEARCH INSTITUTE 20 STANIFORD ST BOSTON, MA 02114 Ocular and other varicella/zoster disease in animal models

R01EY-06586-04A2 (VISB) BLASDEL, GARY G HARVARD MEDICAL SCHOOL 220 LONGWOOD AVENUE BOSTON, MA 02115 Voltage sensitive dyes in striate cortex

R29EY-06590-05 (VISA) CHAITIN, MICHAEL H BASCOM PLAMER EYE INSTITUTE P O BOX 016880 MIAMI, FL 33101 Cytoskeletal proteins in retinal photoreceptors

R01EY-06591-04 (VISA) SNODDERLY, D MAX EYE RESEARCH INST OF RETINA FD 20 STANIFORD STREET BOSTON, MA 02114 Retinal circulation and retinal topography

U10EY-06594-05 (EDC) KLEIN, RONALD UNIVERSITY OF WISCONSIN 610 N WALNUT ST-489 WARF MADISON, WI 53705-2397 The epidemiology of age-related ocular disease

R01EY-06595-06 (VISA) MATSUMOTO, HIROYUKI UNIVERSITY OF OKLAHOMA BOX 26901-940 STANTON L YOUNG OKLAHOMA CITY, OK 73190 Molecular mechanism of visual transduction

R01EY-06600-06 (VISA) WILLIAMSON, JOSEPH R WASHINGTON UNIVERSITY 660 S EUCLID AVE-BOX 8118 ST LOUIS, MO 63110 Role of hormones and polyols in diabetic eye disease

R01EY-06603-06 (VISA) CRABB, JOHN W W ALTON JONES CELL SCIS CENTER 10 OLD BARN ROAD LAKE PLACID, NY 12946 Studies of visual cycle proteins

R01EY-06610-06 (VISB) UHLRICH, DANIEL JAMES UNIVERSITY OF WISCONSIN-MADISO 1300 UNIVERSITY AVENUE MADISON, WI 53706 Control of central visual pathways by the brainstem

R55EY-06631-05A1 (VISA) SIDMAN, RICHARD L CHILDREN'S HOSPITAL 320 LONGWOOD AVE BOSTON, MA 02115 New inherited progressive retinal degenerations in mice

R01EY-06635-05 (VISA) BAZAN, HAYDEE E LSU EYE CENTER 2020 GRAVIER ST, SUITE B NEW ORLEANS, LA 70112 Role of protein and lipid phosphorylation in cornea

R01EY-06638-06 (VISB) KRAUSKOPF, JOHN NEW YORK UNIVERSITY 6 WASHINGTON PLACE NEW YORK, NY 10003 Higher order mechanisms in color vision

R01EY-06639-06 (MGN) MC GINNIS, JAMES F UCLA CENTER FOR THE HEALTH SCI 760 WESTWOOD PLAZA, 48-241 LOS ANGELES, CA 90024-1759 Molecular characterization of the rhodopsin gene

R01EY-06640-06 (VISA) TANAKA, JACQUELINE C UNIVERSITY OF PENNSYLVANIA 36TH STREET AND HAMILTON WALK PHILADELPHIA, PA 19104-6089 Photoreceptor light-modulated channel--Molecular studies

R01EY-06641-06 (VISA) HURLEY, JAMES B UNIVERSITY OF WASHINGTON SJ-70 SEATTLE, WA 98195 Determinats of rod and cone response characteristics

R01EY-06642-05S1 (VISA) KUSZAK, JEROME R RUSH-PRESBY ST LUKES' MED CTR 1653 WEST CONGRESS PARKWAY CHICAGO, IL 60612 Electron microscopic studies of crystalline lenses

R01EY-06644-06 (VISB) MC KEE, SUZANNE P SMITH-KETTLEWELL EYE RES INST 2232 WEBSTER STREET SAN FRANCISCO, CA 94115 Stereoacuity and binocular correspondence

R01EY-06656-04A2 (VISA) HURWITZ, RICHARD L TEXAS CHILDREN'S HOSPITAL 6621 FANNIN STREET HOUSTON, TX 77030 Cyclic GMP receptors in the retina

R01EY-06658-04A2 (VISA) GRUNWALD, GERALD B JEFFERSON MEDICAL COLLEGE 1020 LOCUST STREET PHILADELPHIA, PA 19107 The role of cell adhesion in retinal pattern formation

R01EY-06661-06 (VISB) FITZPATRICK, DAVID DUKE UNIVERSITY BOX 3209 MEDICAL CENTER DURHAM, NC 27710 Morphological basic for visual sensation

R01EY-06663-06 (VISA) TWINING, SALLY S MEDICAL COLLEGE OF WISCONSIN 8710 WATERTOWN PLANK RD MILWAUKEE, WI 53226 Role of proteases in corneal ulceration

R01EY-06664-04 (VISA) BURKE, JANICE M MEDICAL COLLEGE OF WISCONSIN 8700 W WISCONSIN AVENUE MILWUKEE, WI 53226 Aging maculopathy--Macular vs extramacular RPE's

R01EY-06671-04A2 (VISA) FRISHMAN, LAURA J UNIVERSITY OF HOUSTON 4901 CALHOUN ROAD HOUSTON, TX 77204-6052 Proximal retinal responses and the ERG

R01EY-06675-06 (VISA) GRAINGER, ROBERT M UNIVERSITY OF VIRGINIA GILMER HALL CHARLOTTESVILLE, VA 22901 Tissue interactions in embryonic lens and eye formation

R01EY-06677-05 (VISB) NEWSOME, DAVID A TOURO INFIRMARY 1401 FOUCHER ST NEW ORLEANS, LA 70115-3593 Biology of human pigment epithelium and bruch's membrane

R01EY-06678-06 (VISA) DACEY, DENNIS M UNIVERSITY OF WASHINGTON DEPT OF BIOLOGICAL STRUCT, SM- SEATTLE, WA 98195 Synaptic inputs to cat retinal ganglion cells

R01EY-06714-06 (CBY) MARCHASE, RICHARD B UNIV OF ALABAMA AT BIRMINGHAM BASIC HEALTH SCIENCES BUILDING BIRMINGHAM, AL 35294 Glycoproteins containing phosphoglucose in neural retina

R01EY-06717-05 (VISB) LEIGH, RICHARD J CLEVELAND VA MEDICAL CENTER 10701 EAST BOULEVARD CLEVELAND, OH 44106 Investigation and treatment of ocular motor disorders

R29EY-06726-05 (VISA) BRAUNHUT, SUSAN J CHILDREN'S HOSPITAL 300 LONGWOOD AVE ENDERS 1061 BOSTON, MA 02115 Retinoids--Modulation of retinal vascular cells in vitro

U10EY-06730-04 (VSN) ORTH, DAVID H INGALLS MEMORIAL HOSPITAL ONE INGALLS DRIVE HARVEY, ILL 60426 Central vein occlusion study -- participating center

R01EY-06733-05 (VISB) KASAMATSU, TAKUJI SMITH-KETTLEWELL EYE RES INST 2232 WEBSTER STREET SAN FRANCISCO, CA 94115 Regulation of neural plasticity in maturing visual cells

R01EY-06746-12 (VISB) MEYER, RONALD L UNIVERSITY OF CALIFORNIA DEVELOPMENTAL AND CELL BIOLOGY IRVINE, CA 92704 Growth of retinotectal connections

U10EY-06749-04 (VSN) CLARKSON, JOHN G BASCOM PALMER EYE INSTITUTE P O BOX 016880 MIAMI, FLA 33101 Collaborative study on central vein occlusion

U10EY-06750-04 (VSN) FINKELSTEIN, DANIEL THE JOHNS HOPKINS HOSPITAL 221 MAUMENEE BUILDING BALTIMORE, MD 21205 Central vein occlusion study -- participating center

U10EY-06751-04 (VSN) CLARKSON, JOHN G BASCOM PALMER EYE INSTITUTE P O BOX 016880 MIAMI, FLA 33101 Collaborative study on central vein occlusion

U10EY-06752-04 (VSN) BRESNICK, GEORGE H UNIVERSITY OF WISCONSIN 600 HIGHLAND AVENUE MADISON, WIS 53792 Central vein occlusion study-participating center

U10EY-06753-04 (VSN) TREMPE, CLEMENT L EYE RES INST OF RETINA FDN 20 STANIFORD STREET BOSTON, MA 02114 Central vein occlusion study - participating center

R01EY-06761-05 (VISA) TSO, MARK O UNIV OF ILLINIOS AT CHICAGO 1855 W TAYLOR ST RM L217 CHICAGO, IL 60612 Amelioration of retinal photic injury

R01EY-06762-05 (VISA) OVERBEEK, PAUL A BAYLOR COLLEGE OF MEDICINE ONE BAYLOR PLAZA HOUSTON, TX 77030 Modification of lens crystallins--Role in cataracts

R01EY-06765-05 (VISA) FERGUSON, THOMAS A WASHINGTON UNIVERSITY 660 S EUCLID AVE BOX 8096 ST LOUIS, MO 63110 Modulation of ACAID by monoclonal antibodies to TsF

R01EY-06769-04 (VISA) LAVKER, ROBERT M UNIVERSITY OF PENNSYLVANIA 422 CURIE BLVD PHILADELPHIA, PA 19104 Corneal epithelial stem cells

R01EY-06776-05 (VISB) BRUNKEN, WILLIAM J BOSTON COLLEGE 140 COMMONWEALTH AVE CHESTNUT HILL, MA 02167 Functional role of indoleamines in retina

U10EY-06777-04 (VSN) KLEIN, MICHAEL L OREGON HEALTH SCIS UNIVERSITY 3181 S W SAM JACKSON PARK ROAD PORTLAND, OR 97201 Central vein occlusion study - participating center

R01EY-06778-06 (VISA) GREENE, MARK I UNIVERSITY OF PENNSYLVANIA 36TH & HAMILTON WALK PHILADELPHIA, PA 19104-6082 Cellular & molecular regulation of ocular immunity

R01EY-06782-04A1 (VISA) MICELI, MICHAEL V TOURO INFIRMARY 1401 FOUCHER ST NEW ORLEANS, LA 70115-3593 Intermediary metabolism of human RPE cells

R01EY-06792-05 (VISB) MC GUIRE, BARBARA A ROCKEFELLER UNIVERSITY 1230 YORK AVEFNUE NEW YORK, N Y 10021 Anatomy of identified cell populations in visual cortex

U10EY-06797-04 (VSN) HILLIS, ARGYE SCOTT & WHITE MEMORIAL HOSPITA 2401 SOUTH 31ST STREET TEMPLE, TX 76508 Central vein occlusion study -- coordination center

R01EY-06800-05 (VISA) BORKMAN, RAYMOND F GEORGIA INSTITUTE OF TECHNOLOG ATLANTA, GA 30332-0400 Photochemistry & spectroscopy of lenses & lens proteins

U10EY-06806-06 (VSN) HEUER, DALE K UNIV OF SOUTHERN CALIF MED SCH 1355 SAN PABLO STREET LOS ANGELES, CA 90033 5-fluorouracil and glaucoma filtering surgery

R01EY-06807-05 (VISA) KENNEY, MARIA C CEDARS-SINAI MEDICAL CENTER 8700 BEVERLY BOULEVARD LOS ANGELES, CA 90048 Metalloproteinases in normal and keratoconus corneas

R01EY-06808-05 (GEN) O'TOUSA, JOSEPH E UNIVERSITY OF NOTRE DAME NOTRE DAME, IN 46556 Genetic analysis of retinal degeneration in Drosophila

R01EY-06810-07 (VISA) WAX, MARTIN B WASHINGTON UNIVERSITY 660 S EUCLID AVE ST LOUIS, MO 63110 G protein effector systems in ciliary epithelial cells

U10EY-06815-03S1 (VSN) COSCAS, GABRIEL J HOSPITAL OF CRETEIL AVENUE VERDUN 40 CRETEIL, 94010 FRANCE Central vein occlusion study participating center

R01EY-06816-06 (VISA) BITENSKY, MARK W UNIVERSITY OF CALIFORNIA PO BOX 1663 LOS ALAMOS, NM 87545 Light-regulated retinal enzymes

R01EY-06818-05 (VISB) WEYAND, THEODORE G UNIVERSITY OF ILLINOIS 603 EAST DANIEL STREET CHAMPAIGN, IL 61820 Corticotectal circuits in visual processing

R01EY-06819-06 (VISA) TSENG, SCHEFFER C BASCOM PALMER EYE INSTITUTE PO BOX 016880 MIAMI, FL 33101 Growth and differntiation of ocular surface epithelia

R01EY-06821-04A1 (VISB) FITZPATRICK, DAVID DUKE UNIVERSITY BOX 3209 MEDICAL CENTER DURHAM, NC 27710 Functional organization of visual cortex

U10EY-06824-05 (VSN) ALLEN, ROBERT C UNIV OF VIRGINIA HEALTH SCIS C BOX 475 CHARLOTTESVILLE, VA 22908 University of Virginia advanced glaucoma intervention

U10EY-06825-05 (VSN) BROWN, H REAY EMORY UNIVERSITY 1327 CLIFTON RD, N E ATLANTA, GA 30322 Advanced glaucoma intervention study clinic

U10EY-06826-05 (VSN) SCHWARTZ, ARTHUR L 5454 WISCONSIN AVE CHEVY CHASE, MD 20815 AGIS clinic Washington Hospital center advanced glaucoma

U10EY-06827-05 (VSN) SKUTA, GREGORY L UNIVERSITY OF MICHIGAN 1000 WALL STREET ANN ARBOR, MI 48105 University of Michigan advanced glaucoma intervention

U10EY-06830-05 (VSN) KATZ, JAY L WILLS EYE HOSPITAL NINTH & WALNUT STREETS PHILADELPHIA, PA 19107 Advanced glaucoma intervention study clinic

U10EY-06831-05 (VSN) WEBER, PAUL A OHIO STATE UNIVERSITY 456 W 10TH AVENUE COLUMBUS, OH 43210 Ohio State Univ advanced glaucoma intervention study

U10EY-06832-05 (VSN) WILENSKY, JACOB T UNIVERSITY OF ILLINOIS 1855 WEST TAYLOR - ROOM 2 78 CHICAGO, IL 60612 University of Illinois advanced glaucoma intervention

U10EY-06833-05 (VSN) CAPRIOLI, JOSEPH YALE EYE CENTER 330 CEDAR ST NEW HAVEN, CT 06510 Advanced glaucoma intervention study

U10EY-06834-05 (VSN) CYRLIN, MARSHALL N AGIS CLINICAL CENTER 29275 NORTHWESTERN HWY, #100 SOUTHFIELD, MI 48034 Advanced glaucoma intervention study clinic

U10EY-06835-05 (VSN) GAASTERLAND, DOUGLAS E GEORGETOWN UNIVERSITY 37TH & O STREETS, NW WASHINGTON, DC 20057 Advanced glaucoma intervention study

R01EY-06837-05 (VISA) YAU, KING-WAI JOHNS HOPKINS UNIVERSITY BALTIMORE, MD 21205 Visual transduction in retinal photoreceptors

U10EY-06839-06 (VSN) SIMPSON, E RAND ONTARIO CANCER INSTITUTE 500 SHERBOURNE STREET TORONTO ONTARIO CANADA M4X 1K9 COMS--Cooperating clinic

U01EY-06842-05S1 (VSN) LA VAIL, MATTHEW M UNIVERSITY OF CALIFORNIA 513 PARNASSUS AVE SAN FRANCISCO, CA 94143-0452 Breeding colony of rats with inherited retinal dystrophy

U10EY-06843-04 (VSN) WEINGEIST, THOMAS A UNIVERSITY OF IOWA DEPARTMENT OF OPHTHALMOLOGY IOWA CITY, IA 52242 COMS--Photograph reading center

U10EY-06844-06 (VSN) JAMPOL, LEE M NORTHWESTERN UNIV MEDICAL SCH 303 EAST CHICAGO AVENUE CHICAGO, IL 60611 Collaborative ocular melanoma study

U10EY-06848-06 (VSN) DUTTON, JONATHAN J DUKE UNIVERSITY EYE CENTER BOX 3802-200 DURHAM, NC 27710 Collaborative ocular melanoma study--Cooperating clinic

U01EY-06855-05S1 (VSN) AGUIRRE, GUSTAVO D UNIVERSITY OF PENNSYLVANIA 3800 SPRUCE ST PHILADELPHIA, PA 19104-6010 Canine models of hereditary retinal degenerations

U01EY-06859-06S1 (VSN) SIDMAN, RICHARD L CHILDREN'S HOSPITAL CORPORATIO 300 LONGWOOD AVENUE BOSTON, MA 02115 Inherited retinal degenerations in mouse mutants

R01EY-06860-06 (VISB) KELLER, EDWARD L SMITH-KETTLEWELL EYE RES FDN 2232 WEBSTER STREET SAN FRANCISCO, CA 94115 Studies of the oculomotor systems of alert primates

R01EY-06861-05 (VISB) SUTTER, ERICH E SMITH-KETTLEWELL EYE RES FDN 2232 WEBSTER STREET SAN FRANCISCO, CA 94115 ERG and VEP--Field topography and source identification

R01EY-06862-06 (VISA) WONG, FULTON DUKE UNIVERSITY EYE CENTER BOX 3802 DUMC DURHAM, N C 27710 Transduction mechanisms of photoreceptors

R01EY-06866-06 (VISA) KALSOW, CAROLYN M UNIVERSITY OF ROCHESTER DEPARTMENT OF OPHTHALMOLOGY ROCHESTER, N Y 14642 Ocular autoimmunity involving retina or uvea

R44EY-06874-03S1 (SSS) KYLE, ANDREW C LIFE-TECH INC P O BOX 36221 HOUSTON, TEXAS 77036 Low-cost computerized clinical eye-movement analysis

P30EY-06883-06 (VSN) MC KEE, SUZANNE P SMITH-KETTLEWELL EYE RES INST 2232 WEBSTER STREET SAN FRANCISCO, CA 94115 Core grant for vision research

P30EY-06883-06 9001 (VSN) SUTTER, ERICH E Core grant for vision research Core--Electronics services module

P30EY-06883-06 9002 (VSN) MILLER, JOEL M Core grant for vision research Core--Computer software services module

R01EY-06888-05 (VISA) JERDAN, JANICE A ST JOESPHS HOSPITAL P O BOX 20000 BALTIMORE, MD 21284 Microscopic examination of vessel regression in vivo

R01EY-06890-07 (VISB) KARTEN, HARVEY J UNIV. OF CALIF., SAN DIEGO M-008 LA JOLLA, CA 92093 Morphological & chemical specificity of ganglion cells

R01EY-06891-04 (VISA) PAPERMASTER, DAVID S UNIVERSITY OF TEXAS DEPT OF PATHOLOGY SAN ANTONIO, TX 78284-7750 Membrane biosynthesis in normal and dystrophic retina

U10EY-06899-06 (VSN) ABRAMSON, DAVID H CORNELL UNIV MEDICAL COLLEGE 1300 YORK AVE NEW YORK, NY 10021 Cooperative ocular melanoma study--Cooperating clinic

R01EY-06913-06 (VISA) DRATZ, EDWARD A MONTANA STATE UNIVERSITY 108 GAINES HALL BOZEMAN, MT 59717 Interactions of lipids with rhodopsin and ros proteins

R01EY-06915-06 (VISA) DELAMERE, NICHOLAS A KENTUCKY LIONS EYE RESEARCH IN 301 E MUHAMMAD ALI BLVD LOUISVILLE, KY 40202 Solute transport mechanisms in the ciliary body

R01EY-06918-05 (VISA) PATERSON, CHRISTOPHER A KY LIONS EYE RES INSTITUTE 301 E MUHAMMAD ALI BLVD LOUISVILLE, KY 40202 Ocular inflammation--Chemical and physiological aspects

R01EY-06926-02 (VISA) MOTICKA, EDWARD J SOUTHERN ILLINOIS UNIVERSITY P O BOX 19230 SPRINGFIELD, IL 62794-9230 Regulation of corneal graft failure

R29EY-06929-05 (VISB) BEAR, MARK F BROWN UNIV CTR FOR NEURAL SCI BOX 1953 PROVIDENCE, RI 02912 Extrathalamic modulation of visual cortical plasticity

R29EY-06931-06 (VISA) PURO, DONALD G UNIVERSITY OF MICHIGAN 1000 WALL STREET ANN ARBOR, MI 48105 Patch clamp studies of mammalian retinal glial cells

R01EY-06958-04 (VISA) MASTERS, BARRY R UNIFORMED SERVICES UNIVERSITY 4301 JONES BRIDGE ROAD BETHESDA, MD 20814-4799 Redox states of normal/pathological cornea

R01EY-06960-05 (VISA) STONE, SUSAN L NEW YORK UNIV MEDICAL CENTER 550 FIRST AVE NEW YORK, NY 10016 Rod-cone interaction in the vertebrate retina

R29EY-06961-05 (VISA) KOH, SHAY-WHEY M UNIVERSITY OF MARYLAND 10 SOUTH PINE ST BALTIMORE, MD 21201 The VIP receptor in the retinal pigment epithelium

R01EY-06969-04 (VISA) FARAHBAKHSH, NASSER A UCLA SCHOOL OF MEDICINE 100 STEIN PLAZA LOS ANGELES, CA 90024-7008 Ion and water transport in ciliary epithelium

R01EY-06973-06 (VISB) MILLER, JOEL M SMITH-KETTLEWELL EYE RES INST 2232 WEBSTER STREET SAN FRANCISCO, CA 94115 Strabismus muscle mechanisms

R01EY-06976-04 (VISA) ZEIMER, RAN C UNIVERSITY OF ILLINOIS 1855 WEST TAYLOR STREET CHICAGO, IL 60612 Application of noninvasive retinal thickness measurement

R29EY-06977-05 (VISB) HUTCHINS, ROBERT J BAYLOR COLLEGE OF DENTISTRY 3302 GASTON AVENUE DALLAS, TEX 75246 Functional organization of the pretectum

R01EY-06979-05 (VISA) ZUKER, CHARLES S UNIVERSITY OF CALIFORNIA LA JOLLA, CA 92093 Molecular biology of vision

R29EY-06989-05 (VISA) SELLNER, PEGGY A UNIV. OF KANSAS MEDICAL CENTER 39TH AND RAINBOW BOULEVARD KANSAS CITY, KS 66103 Fatty acid metabolism in retina and pigment

R01EY-06990-05 (VISA) TAYLOR, JERRY L MEDICAL COLLEGE OF

PROJECT NO., ORGANIZATIONAL UNIT., INVESTIGATOR, ADDRESS, TITLE

WISCONSIN 8701 WATERTOWN PLANK ROAD MILWAUKEE, WI 53226 Interferon's role in antiviral activities
P30EY-07003-05 (VSN) LICHTER, PAUL R UNIVERSITY OF MICHIGAN 1000 WALL ST ANN ARBOR, MI 48105 Core grant for vision research
R01EY-07010-06 (VISA) GARNER, MARGARET H UNIVERSITY OF TEXAS 5323 HARRY HINES BLVD DALLAS, TX 75235-9057 ATP-linked effectors of Na,K-Atpase and cataract
R01EY-07011-06 (VISA) CHANDLER, JOHN W UIC EYE CENTER 1855 W. TAYLOR CHICAGO, IL 60612 Immunopathology and therapy of corneal disease
R01EY-07023-07 (VISA) SUR, MRIGANKA MASSACHUSETTS INST OF TECH E25-618, 45 CARLETON ST CAMBRIDGE, MA 02139 Role of glutamate receptors in the visual pathway
R01EY-07025-06 (VISB) O' LEARY, DENNIS D M SALK INST FOR BIOLOGICAL STUDI PO BOX 85800 SAN DIEGO, CA 92186-5800 Anatomical studies of visual and sensory deprivation
R01EY-07028-06 (RAD) LIVESEY, JOHN C UNIVERSITY OF WASHINGTON 1959 NE PACIFIC ST RC09 SEATTLE, WA 98195 Biochemistry and radioprotection from radiation cataract
R01EY-07043-05 (VISA) FOLBERG, ROBERT UNIVERSITY OF IOWA IOWA CITY, IA 52242 Animal model of primary ocular melanoma
U10EY-07049-05 (VSN) TURNER, ROBERT C RADCLIFFE INFIRMARY WOODSTOCK ROAD OXFORD 0X2 6H3, UK United Kingdom prospective diabetes study
U10EY-07057-05 (VSN) EDERER, FRED THE EMMES CORPORATION 11325 SEVEN LOCKS ROAD POTOMAC, MD 20854 Advanced glaucoma intervention study-coordinating center
R01EY-07058-06 (VISB) ROCKLAND, KATHLEEN S UNIVERSITY OF IOWA COLLEGE OF MEDICINE IOWA CITY, IA 52242 Periodic extrinsic connections in visual cortex
R01EY-07059-05 (VISB) MOTTER, BRAD C SUNY HEALTH SCIS CTR AT SYRACU 750 EAST ADAMS STREET SYRACUSE, NY 13210 Visual attentive processes
R01EY-07060-05 (VISA) HITCHCOCK, PETER F UNIVERSITY OF MICHIGAN 1000 WALL ST ANN ARBOR, MI 48105 Retinal development--Dendritic growth; regeneration
R01EY-07065-05 (VISA) JOHNSON, DOUGLAS H MAYO FOUNDATION 200 FIRST STREET SOUTHWEST ROCHESTER, MN 55905 Cellular biology of the trabecular meshwork
R01EY-07067-05 (VISA) LYNCH, MARY C EMORY UNIVERSITY 1327 CLIFTON ROAD, NE ATLANTA, GA 30322 Class II HLA antigens in the aqueous outflow system
R01EY-07070-05 (VISA) ORTWERTH, BERYL J UNIVERSITY OF MISSOURI ONE HOSPITAL DRIVE COLUMBIA, MO 65212 Ascorbic acid glycation & senile cataract formation
R29EY-07074-05 (VISA) FITZGERALD, PAUL G UNIVERSITY OF CALIFORNIA SCHOOL OF MEDICINE DAVIS, CALIF 95616 Lens membrane domains & epithelial cell differentiation
R01EY-07078-05 (VISB) LINDSEY, DELWIN UNIVERSITY OF WASHINGTON SEATTLE, WASH 98195 Dimensionalizations of color vision
R01EY-07088-05 (VISA) PANJWANI, NOORJAHAN A TUFTS UNIVERSITY 136 HARRISON AVE BOSTON, MA 02111 Corneal epithelial cell surface glycoconjugates
R29EY-07089-05 (VISA) POLANS, ARTHUR S GOOD SAMARITAN HOSPITAL 1120 N W 20TH AVENUE PORTLAND, OREGON 97209 Biochemical studies of rod outer segment plasma membrane
R01EY-07099-05 (VISA) MONNIER, VINCENT M CASE WESTERN RESERVE UNIV 2085 ADELBERT ROAD CLEVELAND, OH 44106 Amino-carbonyl reactions in the aging human lens
R01EY-07103-05 (VISA) HAYES, KENNETH C BRANDEIS UNIVERSITY FOSTER BIOMEDICAL RESEARCH LAB WALTHAM, MA 02254 Nutritional factors in retinal function
R29EY-07107-04 (VISA) WILLIAMS, EDWARD H MANKATO STATE UNIVERSITY BOX 34 MANKATO, MN 56002-8400 Cellular regulation of aldose reductase in cataract lens
R01EY-07111-02 (VISA) SAMPLES, JOHN R OREGON HEALTH SCIENCES UNIV 3375 SW TERWILLINGER BLVD PORTLAND, OR 97201 Regulation of trabecular cell glycoproteins
R01EY-07112-04A1 (VISB) PALMER, LARRY A UNIVERSITY OF PENNSYLVANIA SCHOOL OF MEDICINE PHILADELPHIA, PA 19104-6058 Linear and nonlinear aspects of visual cortical function
R29EY-07113-05 (BPO) PETRY, HEYWOOD M UNIVERSITY OF LOUISVILLE LOUISVILLE, KY 40292 Early visual experience--Role of spectral environment
R01EY-07115-04 (VISA) BAUSHER, LARRY P YALE UNIVERSITY SCH OF MED PO BOX 3333, 333 CEDAR ST NEW HAVEN, CT 06510 Receptor interactions in ciliary processes
R01EY-07119-05 (VISB) BARNSTABLE, COLIN J YALE UNIVERSITY PO BOX 333 NEW HAVEN, CT 06510 Cellular and molecular organization of the visual cortex
R01EY-07125-05 (BM) MARRS, CARL F UNIVERSITY OF MICHIGAN 109 OBSERVATORY STREET ANN ARBOR, MI 48109-2029 Molecular studies of type 4 pili
R29EY-07130-06 (VISB) COLE, GREGORY J MEDICAL UNIVERSITY OF S.C. 171 ASHLEY AVENUE CHARLESTON, S C 29425 Neural retina differentiation
R01EY-07135-05 (VISA) RYAN, JAMES W UNIV OF MIAMI SCH OF MED P O BOX 016960 MIAMI, FL 33101 Ocular functions and peptide hormone systems
R01EY-07142-03 (MGN) DAIGER, STEPHEN P UNIV OF TX HLTH SCI CTR P O BOX 20334 HOUSTON, TX 77225 DNA linkage studies of degenerative retinal diseases
R29EY-07147-05 (BPO) WELLER, ROSALYN E UNIV. OF ALABAMA AT BIRMINGHAM UAB STATION BIRMINGHAM, AL 35294 The organization of inferior temporal cortex of primates
R01EY-07151-05 (VISB) STRAUSFELD, NICHOLAS J UNIVERSITY OF ARIZONA 611 GOULD-SIMPSON SCIENCE BLDG TUCSON, AZ 85721 Neurobiology of a simple oculomotor system
R01EY-07154-05 (VISA) WALDREP, J CLIFFORD BAYLOR COLLEGE OF MEDICINE 4000 RESEARCH FOREST DRIVE WOODLANDS, TX 77381 Intraocular immunoregulation and immune complex disease
R01EY-07158-05 (VISA) ARI, SITARAMAYYA PENNSYLVANIA COLL OF OPTOMETRY 1200 W GODFREY AVE PHILADELPHIA, PA 19141-3399 Kinetics of recovery from photoresponse in rods

PROJECT NO., ORGANIZATIONAL UNIT., INVESTIGATOR, ADDRESS, TITLE

R29EY-07166-05 (VISB) MAY, PAUL J UNIV OF MISSISSIPPI MED CENTER 2500 NORTH STATE STREET JACKSON, MS 39216-4505 Neuronal circuitry controlling the lens and pupil
R01EY-07188-05 (VISA) BIRCH, DAVID G RETINA FDN OF THE SOUTHWEST 8220 WALNUT HILL LANE DALLAS, TEX 75231 Electroretinographic studies in age-related macular degeneration
R29EY-07191-04 (VISA) MATSUMOTO, BRIAN UNIV OF CALIFORNIA SANTA BARBARA, CA 93106 Glutamate stimulated membrane turnover in rods
R01EY-07192-04 (VISA) STARK, WILLIAM S UNIV OF MISSOURI-COLUMBIA 213 LEFEVRE HALL COLUMBIA, MO 65211 Maintenance and function of drosophila visual receptors
R29EY-07206-04 (VISA) FRALEY, SANDRA M NEW YORK MEDICAL COLLEGE MUNGER PAVILLION, SUB-BASEMENT VALHALLA, NY 10595 Factors affecting dendritic elaboration in chick retina
U10EY-07212-05 (VSN) BECK, ROY W UNIV OF SOUTH FLORIDA 12901 BRUCE B DOWNS TAMPA, FL 33612 Optic neuritis treatment trial
R01EY-07213-04 (VISA) MALATY, RAGA UNIVERSITY OF SOUTH ALABAMA 2451 FILLINGIM ST MOBILE, AL 36617 Neural-immune interactions in ocular inflammation
R29EY-07318-05 (VISA) JENSEN, RALPH J SOUTHERN COLLEGE OF OPTOMETRY 1245 MADISON AVENUE MEMPHIS, TN 38104 Function of amacrine cells in mammalian retina
R01EY-07321-03 (VISA) ERICKSON-LAMY, KRISTINE A MASSERSITY EYE & EAR INF 243 CHARLES STREET BOSTON, MA 02114-3096 The perfused trabecular meshwork as a model for outflow
R01EY-07334-05 (VISA) OLSEN, BJORN R HARVARD MEDICAL SCHOOL 220 LONGWOOD AVENUE BOSTON, MA 02115 Extracellular matrix gene expression in cornea
R01EY-07336-05 (VISA) BRANDT, CURTIS R UNIVERSITY OF WISCONSIN 1300 UNIVERSITY AVENUE MADISON, WI 53706-1532 Virus specific factors of HSV related to corneal disease
R01EY-07342-05 (VISB) BAKER, JAMES F NORTHWESTERN UNIVERSITY 303 EAST CHICAGO AVENUE CHICAGO, IL 60611 Otolith vestibulo-ocular reflex
R01EY-07344-04 (VISB) ALBANO, JOANNE E UNIVERSITY OF ROCHESTER ROCHESTER, NY 14627 Adaptive motor learning in the saccadic system
R01EY-07345-01A2 (VISB) HAEGERSTROM-PORTNOY, GUNILLA UNIVERSITY OF CALIFORNIA BERKELEY, CA 94720 Vision of typical rod monochromats
R01EY-07348-05 (VISA) JESTER, JAMES V UNIVERSITY OF TEXAS S.W. MED C 5323 HARRY HINES BLVD DALLAS, TX 75235-9057 Modulation of corneal curvature during wound healing
R01EY-07353-02 (VISA) CAPRIOLI, JOSEPH YALE UNIVERSITY SCH OF MEDICIN 330 CEDAR STREET/P O BOX 3333 NEW HAVEN, CT 06510-8061 Clinical measurements of optic nerve damage in glaucoma
R01EY-07354-02 (VISA) STONE, RICHARD A UNIVERSITY OF PENNSYLVANIA D-603 RICHARDS BUILDING PHILADELPHIA, PA 19104-6075 Myopia and ocular growth--neural mechanisms
R01EY-07360-04 (CLN) BLOOMFIELD, STEWART A NYU MEDICAL CENTER 550 FIRST AVENUE NEW YORK, NY 10016 Amacrine cell function in mammalian retina
R01EY-07361-04 (VISA) KELLER, RONALD K UNIVERSITY SOUTH FLORIDA 12901 BRUCE B DOWNS BLVD TAMPA, FL 33612 Isoprenoid metabolism in the retina
R01EY-07366-04 (SSS) FREEMAN, WILLIAM R UNIV. OF CALIFORNIA, SAN DIEGO SHILEY EYE CENTER 0946 LA JOLLA, CA 92093-0946 Study & treatment of retinopathy associated with AIDS
R01EY-07370-05 (VISA) FITE, KATHERINE V UNIVERSITY OF MASSACHUSETTS TOBIN HALL AMHERST, MA 01003 Experimental analysis of aging in the vertebrate retina
R01EY-07373-03 (VISA) ROSENBAUM, JAMES T OREGON HEALTH SCIENCES UNIV 3181 S W SAM JACKSON PARK ROAD PORTLAND, OR 97201 Growth factors in proliferative vitreoretinopathy
R01EY-07376-05 (VISB) MILLER, ROBERT F UNIVERSITY OF MINNESOTA 435 DELAWARE ST S E MINNEAPOLIS, MN 55455 Electroanatomical studies of retinal neurons
R01EY-07389-04 (VISA) LEE, VINCENT H UNIV OF SOUTHERN CALIFORNIA 1975 ZONAL AVENUE, KAM B-34 LOS ANGELES, CALIF 90033 Minimizing blood to eye ratio of topical eye medications a
R01EY-07390-05 (VISB) SMITH, VIVIANNE C UNIVERSITY OF CHICAGO 939 E 57TH STREET CHICAGO, ILL 60637 Studies of color perception
R01EY-07391-05 (VISB) EVINGER, LESLIE C SUNY - AT STONY BROOK DEPT OF NEUROBIOLOGY/BEHAVIOR STONY BROOK, N Y 11794 Control of the eyelids in normal and pathological states
R01EY-07394-05 (VISA) ABRAHAM, EDATHARA C MEDICAL COLLEGE OF GEORGIA MEDICAL COLLEGE OF GEORGIA AUGUSTA, GA 30912-2100 Lens protein glycation and cataract development
R01EY-07397-06 (NEUC) SKENE, J H PATE DUKE UNIVERSITY BOX 3209 MEDICAL CENTER DURHAM, NC 27710 Control of retinal genes by the optic nerve environment
R01EY-07400-05 (VISA) MITTAG, THOMAS W MOUNT SINAI SCHOOL OF MEDICINE ONE GUSTAVE L LEVY PLACE NEW YORK, NY 10029 Protein phosphatase, vanadate, and intraocular pressure
U10EY-07460-05 (VSN) CLEARY, PATRICIA A BIOSTATISTICS CENTER 6110 EXECUTIVE BOULEVARD ROCKVILLE, MD 20852 Optic neuritis treatment trial - coordinating center
U10EY-07461-04 (VSN) KELTNER, JOHN L UNIV OF CALIFORNIA, DAVIS SCHOOL OF MEDICINE DAVIS, CA 95616 Optic neuritis treatment trial visual field reading center
U10EY-07479-04 (VSN) DAWSON, CHANDLER R UNIVERSITY OF CALIFORNIA F I PROCTOR FDN/RES/OPHTHALM SAN FRANCISCO, CALIF 94143 Herpes eye disease study
U10EY-07480-04 (VSN) JONES, DAN B CULLEN EYE INSTITUTE ONE BAYLOR PLAZA HOUSTON, TX 77030 Herpetic eye disease study
U10EY-07482-04 (VSN) STULTING, ROBERT D EMORY UNIVERSITY 1327 CLIFTON ROAD, N E ATLANTA, GA 30322 Herpes eye disease study clinic
U10EY-07483-04 (VSN) HAUCK, WALTER W FRANCIS I PROCTOR FOUNDATION USCF, S315, BOX 0412 SAN FRANCISCO, CA 94143 Herpetic eye disease study coordinating center
U10EY-07488-04 (VSN) SUGAR, JOEL UNIVERSITY OF ILLINOIS EYE AND EAR INFIRMARY CHICAGO, IL 60612 Herpes eye disease study clinic
U10EY-07489-04 (VSN) BARRON, BRUCE A LSU EYE CENTER 2020 GRAVIER ST, SUITE B NEW ORLEANS, LA 70112 Herpetic eye disease study
R01EY-07492-05 (VISB) ANDERSEN, RICHARD A MASSACHUSETTS INST OF TECHNOLO 77 MASSACHUSETTS AVENUE CAMBRIDGE, MA 02139 Visual motion

processing in the monkey
U10EY-07496-04 (VSN) HYNDIUK, ROBERT A EYE INSTITUTE MED COLL OF WI 8700 WEST WISCONSIN AVE MILWAUKEE, WISCONSIN 53226 Herpes eye disease study clinic
R01EY-07504-04 (RAD) CHAR, DEVRON H UNIV OF CALIF, SAN FRANCISCO 3RD AND PARNASSUS AVENUES SAN FRANCISCO, CALIF 94143 Uveal melanoma cell biology
R01EY-07507-04 (VISA) HESTRIN, SHAUL UNIVERSITY OF CALIFORNIA 3RD & PARNASSUS SAN FRANCISCO, CA 94143-0444 Transduction in vertebrate photoreceptors
R01EY-07511-03 (VISA) CHIOU, GEORGE C TEXAS A&M UNIVERSITY PHARMACOLOGY & TOXICOLOGY COLLEGE STATION, TX 77843 Systemic delivery of peptide drugs through eyes
R01EY-07519-02 (VISB) SEMMLOW, JOHN L RUTGERS STATE UNIVERSITY PO BOX 909 PISCATAWAY, NJ 08855-0909 Control of disparity vergence eye movement
R01EY-07523-04 (VISA) CLACK, JAMES W IUPUI COLUMBUS 4601 CENTRAL AVENUE COLUMBUS, IN 47203 Studies of opsin cGMP-activated single channel activity
U10EY-07525-04 (VSN) BRESNICK, GEORGE H UNIVERSITY OF WISCONSIN 600 HIGHLAND AVENUE MADISON, WIS 53792 ERG-central vein occulsion study-reading center
R01EY-07526-04 (VISA) DOANE, MARSHALL G EYE RESEARCH INSTITUTE 20 STANIFORD STREET BOSTON, MA 02114 Eyelid, tear film, and contact lens interactions
R01EY-07528-03 (VISA) BEEBE, DAVID C UNIFORMED SVCS UNIV OF HLTH SC 4301 JONES BRIDGE RD BETHESDA, MD 20814-4799 Development of the ciliary epithelium
R29EY-07533-05 (VISA) PENN, JOHN S UNIVERSITY OF ARKANSAS 4301 W MARKHAM LITTLE ROCK, AR 72205 An animal model for retinopathy of prematurity
R01EY-07541-03 (VISA) PEYMAN, GHOLAM A LSU EYE CENTER 2020 GRAVIER ST SUITE B NEW ORLEANS, LA 70112 Liposomes for intravitreal drug delivery
R01EY-07543-04 (VISA) CORSON, DAVID WESLEY MED UNIV OF SOUTH CAROLINA 171 ASHLEY AVENUE CHARLESTON, SC 29425 Quantal events in visual transduction
R01EY-07544-04 (VISA) LIU, JOHN H K EYE RESEARCH INSTITUTE 20 STANIFORD STREET BOSTON, MA 02114 Endogenous regulation of aqueous humor dynamics
R01EY-07546-05 (VISA) YAMAZAKI, AKIO WAYNE STATE UNIVERSITY 4717 ST. ANTOINE DETROIT, MI 48201 Guanine nucleotide metabolism in rod photoreceptor
R01EY-07547-03S1 (VISA) SILVERMAN, MARTIN S CENTRAL INSTITUTE FOR THE DEAF 818 S EUCLID AVENUE ST LOUIS, MO 63110 Transplantation of mammalian photoreceptors
P30EY-07551-04 (VSN) FLOM, MERTON C UNIVERSITY OF HOUSTON 4901 CALHOUN HOUSTON, TX 77204 Center for vision research
R01EY-07552-04 (VISB) ZUCKER, CHARLES L EYE RES. INST. OF RETINA FDN. 20 STANIFORD STREET BOSTON, MA 02114 Microcircuitry of identified cells in vertebrate retinas
R29EY-07556-04 (VISB) ZAIDI, QASIM COLUMBIA UNIVERSITY 406 SCHERMERHORN HALL NEW YORK, NY 10027 Mechanisms of color detection, induction and adaptation
R01EY-07557-03 (VISB) MAYER, MELANIE J UNIVERSITY OF CALIFORNIA 435 CLARK KERR HALL SANTA CRUZ, CA 95064 Flicker sensitivity in aging and age-related maculopathy
R01EY-07558-03 (VISB) GAMLIN, PAUL D UNIVERSITY OF ALABAMA DEPT PHYSIOLOGICAL OPTICS BIRMINGHAM, AL 35294 Vergence & ocular accommodation--Role of the cerebellum
R01EY-07559-04 (VISA) NASI, ENRICO BOSTON UNIVERSITY SCH OF MED 80 EAST CONCORD ST BOSTON, MA 02118 Ionic channels and calcium changes in photoreceptors
R01EY-07564-04 (VISA) LAUSCH, ROBERT N UNIVERSITY OF SOUTH ALABAMA COLLEGE OF MEDICINE MOBILE, AL 36688 Protective mechanism of herpes simplex virus antibody
R01EY-07566-04 (VISA) WECHSLER, STEVEN L CEDARS-SINAI MEDICAL CENTER 8700 BEVERLY BOULEVARD LOS ANGELES, CA 90048 Ocular HSV infection - - latency and reactivation
R01EY-07568-04 (VISA) FAIN, GORDON L UNIVERSITY OF CALIFORNIA UCLA SCHOOL OF MEDICINE LOS ANGELES, CA 90024-7008 Physiology and pharmacology of ciliary body epithelium
R01EY-07569-04 (VISB) REGAN, DAVID TORONTO HOSPITAL 399 BATHURST ST TORONTO, ONTARIO M5T 2S8 CANA Visual abnormalities in multiple sclerosis
R29EY-07570-04 (VISA) KASS, LEONARD J UNIVERSITY OF MAINE 100 MURRY HALL ORONO, ME 04469 Efferent control of photoreceptor conductances
R29EY-07573-04 (MGN) YANDELL, DAVID W MASSACHUSETTS EYE & EAR INFIRM 243 CHARLES ST. BOSTON, MA 02114 Retinoblastoma diagnosis using oligonucleotide probes
R01EY-07574-04 (VISA) LEIBOWITZ, HOWARD M BOSTON UNIVERSITY 80 E CONCORD STREET BOSTON, MA 02118 Developing a biopolymeric keratoprosthesis for the eye
R01EY-07576-01A2 (VISA) DE JUAN, EUGENE DUKE UNIVERSITY EYE CENTER PO BOX 3802 DURHAM, NC 27710 Inhibition of angiogenesis and endothelial invasion
R01EY-07577-02 (VISB) SIMONS, KURT JOHNS HOPKINS HOSPITAL 600 NORTH WOLFE STREET BALTIMORE, MD 21205 A prospective study of esotropia development
R29EY-07584-05 (NEUB) JOHNSON, JAMES E BOWMAN GRAY SCHOOL OF MEDICINE WAKE FOREST UNIVERSITY WINSTON-SALEM, NC 27103 Survival factors required by visual system neurons
R01EY-07606-04 (VISB) COHN, THEODORE E UNIVERSITY OF CALIFORNIA 360 MINOR HALL BERKELEY, CALIF 94720 Psychophysical analysis of visual sensory deficity
R01EY-07609-03 (VISA) SMITH, DAVID L PURDUE UNIVERSITY HEINE PHARMACY BUILDING WEST LAFAYETTE, IN 47907 Cataract-related disulfide cross-linkages in crystallins
R01EY-07610-04 (VISA) MERRYMAN, CARMEN F THOMAS JEFFERSON UNIVERSITY 1020 LOCUST STREET PHILADELPHIA, PA 19107 S-antigen--Characterization of T cell clones in uveitis
R55EY-07612-04 (VISA) O'BRIEN, WILLIAM E BAYLOR COLLEGE OF MEDICINE ONE BAYLOR PLAZA HOUSTON, TX 77030 Is avian lens delta-crystallin argininosuccinate lyase?
R01EY-07616-04 (VISA) TYTELL, MICHAEL WAKE FOREST UNIVERSITY BOWMAN GRAY SCHOOL OF MEDICINE WINSTON SALEM, N C 27106 Retinal protection from light damage by hyperthermia
U10EY-07617-04S1 (VSN) SCHACHAT, ANDREW P JOHNS HOPKINS UNIVERSITY 600 NORTH WOLFE ST. BALTIMORE, MD 21205 Barbados eye study reading center
R01EY-07620-04 (RNM) CHENG, HONG-MING HOWE LAB OF OPHTHALMOLOGY 243 CHARLES STREET BOSTON, MA 02114 Regional NMR multinuclear studies of ocular tissues
R29EY-07624-05 (VISB) ELSNER, ANN E EYE RESEARCH INSTITUTE 20 STANIFORD STREET BOSTON, MA 02114 Spatial extent of retinal damage
U10EY-07625-05 (VSN) LESKE, M CRISTINA STATE UNIVERSITY OF NEW YORK STONY BROOK, NY 11794-8275 Barbados eye study
R01EY-07641-04 (VISA) NIEDERKORN, JERRY Y 5323 HARRY HINES BOULEVARD DALLAS, TEX 75235 The immunobiology of corneal allografts
R01EY-07642-04 (VISB) SCHNAPF, JULIE L UNIVERSITY OF CALIFORNIA BOX 0730 SAN FRANCISCO, CA 94143 Signal processing in the primate retina
U10EY-07657-03 (VSN) MC KEE, SUZANNE P SMITH-KETTLEWELL EYE RES INST 2232 WEBSTER STREET SAN FRANCISCO, CA 94115 Cooperative amblyopia classification study
U10EY-07659-04 (VSN) MILLER, NEIL R JOHNS HOPKINS HOSPITAL 600 N. WOLFE STREET BALTIMORE, MD 21205 Ontt cooperating clinic
U10EY-07671-04 (VSN) GUY, JOHN R NEURO-OPHTHALMOLOGY SERVICE BOX J-284 GAINESVILLE, FL 32610-0284 Ontt cooperating clinic
U10EY-07673-04 (VSN) KUPERSMITH, MARK J NEW YORK UNIVERSITY MEDICAL CT 550 FIRST AVENUE NEW YORK, N Y 10016 Ontt cooperating clinic
U10EY-07674-04 (VSN) SAVINO, PETER J WILLS EYE HOSPITAL 9TH AND WALNUT STREETS PHILADELPHIA, PA 19107 Optic neuritis treatment trial cooperating clinic
U10EY-07675-04 (VSN) TROBE, JONATHAN D W K KELLOGG EYE CENTER 1000 WALL STREET ANN ARBOR, MI 48105 ONTT cooperating clinic
U10EY-07676-04 (VSN) CHROUSOS, GEORGIA A GEORGETOWN UNIV MED CENTER 3800 RESERVOIR RD, N W WASHINGTON, D C 20007 Ontt cooperating clinic
U10EY-07678-04 (VSN) BUCKLEY, EDWARD G DUKE UNIVERSITY EYE CENTER BOX 3802 DURHAM, N C 27706 Optic neuritis treatment trial cooperating clinic
U10EY-07679-04 (VSN) MC CRARY, JOHN A, III CULLEN EYE INSTITUTE 6501 FANNIN HOUSTON, TX 77030 Ontt cooperating clinic
U10EY-07680-04 (VSN) KAUFMAN, DAVID I MICHIGAN STATE UNIVERSITY B-309 W FEE HALL EAST LANSING, MI 48824 Ontt cooperating clinic
U10EY-07683-04 (VSN) THOMPSON, H STANLEY UNIVERSITY OF IOWA HOSP & CLIN IOWA CITY, IA 52242 Ontt cooperating clinic
U10EY-07685-04 (VSN) BRODSKY, MICHAEL UNIVERSITY OF ARKANSAS 4301 W MARKHAM (MAIL SLOT 523) LITTLE ROCK, AR 72205-7199 Ontt cooperating clinic
U10EY-07687-04 (VSN) SHULTS, WILLIAM T GOOD SAMARITAN HOSP & MED CTR 1040 N.W. 22ND AVE PORTLAND, OR 97210 ONTT cooperating clinic
U10EY-07689-04 (VSN) GOODWIN, JAMES A UNIV OF IL EYE/EAR INFIRMARY 1855 W TAYLOR ST CHICAGO, IL 60612 Ontt cooperating clinic
U10EY-07694-04 (VSN) SMITH, CRAIG H UNIV OF WASHINGTON SCHOOL OF MEDICINE SEATTLE, W A 98195 ONTT cooperating clinic
U10EY-07695-05 (VSN) KATZ, BARRETT SMITH-KETTLEWELL EYE RES INST 2232 WEBSTER STREET SAN FRANCICSO, CA 94115 Ontt cooperating clinic
R01EY-07705-04 (VISA) AGUIRRE, GUSTAVO D UNIVERSITY OF PENNSYLVANIA 3800 SPRUCE STREET PHILADELPHIA, PA 19104 Extracellular pathways in RPE GAG metabolism
R29EY-07716-01A3 (VISB) SWANSON, WILLIAM H RETINA FOUNDATION/SOUTHWEST 8230 WALNUT HILL LANE DALLAS, TX 75231 Application of psychophysical models to visual disorders
R01EY-07719-03S1 (VISA) SUR, MRIGANKA MASSACHUSETTS INST OF TECHNOLO E25-618 CAMBRIDGE, MA 02139 Plasticity and specificity of visual projections
R21EY-07722-04 (VSN) LESKE, M CRISTINA SUNY AT STONY BROOK STONY BROOK, NY 11794-8036 Clinical vision research development at Stony Brook
R01EY-07728-03 (VISA) POLSE, KENNETH A UNIVERSITY OF CALIFORNIA BERKELEY, CA 94720 Contact lens effects on corneal ph and corneal function
R01EY-07732-02 (VISA) EISENSTEIN, REUBEN SINAI SAMARITAN MEDICAL CENTER 950 NORTH 12 ST MILWAUKEE, WI 53201-0342 Endothelial-lymphocyte interactions in the retina
R01EY-07737-04 (VISA) DONOSO, LARRY A WILLS EYE HOSPITAL 900 WALNUT STREET PHILADELPHIA, PA 19107-5598 Retinoblastoma--clinical/immunopathologic studies/human
R01EY-07738-04 (VISA) NAKA, KEN-ICHI NEW YORK UNIVERSITY MED CENTER 550 FIRST AVENUE NEW YORK, NY 10016 Retinal microcircuitry--Structure and function
R29EY-07739-03 (VISA) GRANT, MARIA B UNIV OF FLORIDA SCHOOL OF MED JHMHC, BOX J-226 GAINESVILLE, FL 32610 Hormones control of neurovascularization in diab. retinopathy
R21EY-07744-04 (VSN) LEMP, MICHAEL A GEORGETOWN UNIVERSITY 3800 RESERVOIR RD, NW WASHINGTON, D C 20057 David M. Worthen center for clinical studies
R01EY-07752-03S1 (VISA) DREYER, WILLIAM J CALIFORNIA INSTITUTE OF TECH 1201 E CALIFORNIA BLVD PASADENA, CA 91125 Cell surface proteins in the visual system
R01EY-07753-03 (VISA) WILLIAMS, THEODORE P FLORIDA STATE UNIVERSITY INSTITUTE OF MOLECULAR BIOPHYS TALLAHASSEE, FLA 32306-3015 Regulation of daily photon-catch
R29EY-07755-03 (VISA) DAVID, LARRY L 611 S W CAMPUS DR PORTLAND, OR 97201 Protein cleavage sites in experimental cataractous lenses
R01EY-07757-04 (BM) STEPHENS, RICHARD S UNIVERSITY OF CA SAN FRANCISCO, CA 94143-0412 Serological evaluation of chlamydial eye infections
R01EY-07760-04 (VISB) BLAKE, R RANDOLPH VANDERBILT UNIVERSITY A & S PSYCHOLOGY BLDG NASHVILLE, TN 37240 Binocular vision and motion

PROJECT NO., ORGANIZATIONAL UNIT., INVESTIGATOR, ADDRESS, TITLE

perception in humans
R21EY-07766-04 (VSN) RICHARDS, RICHARD D UNIVERSITY OF MARYLAND HOSP 22 S. GREENE ST. RMN6W46 BALTIMORE, MD 21201 Maryland biostatistics-epidemiology-clinical trials unit
R01EY-07768-04 (VISA) ZEIMER, RAN C UNIVERSITY OF ILLINOIS 1855 WEST TAYLOR STREET CHICAGO, IL 60612 Targeted drug and dye delivery to the retina
R01EY-07773-04 (VISA) WOLOSIN, JOSE M MOUNT SINAI SCHOOL OF MEDICINE ONE GUSTAVE L LEVY PLACE NEW YORK, N Y 10029 Genesis of cell membrane polarity in corneal epithelium
R01EY-07774-04 (VISB) ZIMMERMAN, ANITA L BROWN UNIVERSITY BOX G PROVIDENCE, RI 02912 Properties of light modulated ion channels in the retina
U10EY-07776-03 (VSN) MAYER, D LUISA CHILDREN'S HOSPITAL CORPORATIO 300 LONGWOOD AVENUE BOSTON, MA 02115 Normative and clinical study of Acuity Cards procedure
U10EY-07788-04 (VSN) SINGERMAN, LAWRENCE J 26900 CEDAR ROAD, SUITE 303 BEACHWOOD, OH 44122 Central vein occlusion study--participating center
R01EY-07794-04 (VISA) BLAIR, NORMAN P UNIV OF ILLINOIS AT CHIC DEPT OF OPHTHALMOLOGY CHICAGO, IL 60612 Vitreoperfusion--A new approach to ocular ischemia
R01EY-07801-02 (VISB) HABER, RALPH N UNIV OF ILLINOIS AT CHICAGO CHICAGO, IL 60680 Measuring the knowledge of spatial layout in blindness
R44EY-07803-03 (SSS) JEFFERS, WILLIAM Q HELIOS, INC 1822 SUNSET PLACE LONGMONT, CO 80501 Laser trephination of the cornea
U10EY-07813-04 (VSN) GUTMAN, FRONCIE A CLEVELAND CLINIC FOUNDATION 9500 EUCLID AVENUE CLEVELAND, OH 44195-5024 Central vein occlusion study, participating center
R29EY-07828-03 (VISA) NATHANS, JEREMY H JOHNS HOPKINS UNIVERSITY 725 N. WOLFE ST BALTIMORE, MD 21203 Molecular biology of visual pigments
R01EY-07832-02 (VISA) MURA, UMBERTO UNIVERSITY OF PISA VIA S MARIA, 55 56100 PISA-ITALY Metabolic regulation of aldose reductase in bovine lens
R01EY-07836-04 (VISA) YABLONSKI, MICHAEL E UNIVERSITY OF NEBRASKA MED CTR 600 SOUTH 42ND STREET OMAHA, NE 68198-5540 Fluorophotometric diagnosis of aqueous humor dynamics
R29EY-07839-03 (VISB) TURANO, KATHLEEN A JOHN HOPKINS HOSP, WILMER B27 601 N. BROADWAY BALTIMORE, MD 21205 Visual perception & orientation/mobility in low vision
R29EY-07840-03 (VISB) EINSTEIN, GILLIAN DUKE UNIVERSITY SCH OF MED BOX 3011 DURHAM, NC 27710 Input/output relationships in visual cortex
R01EY-07845-03 (VISA) KEYSER, KENT T UNIV OF CALIFORNIA SAN DIEGO 9500 GILMAN DRIVE LA JOLLA, CA 92093-0608 Cholinoceptive neurons in the vertebrate retina
R01EY-07846-04 (CPA) FUNG, YUEN K CHILDREN'S HOSPITAL 4650 SUNSET BLVD LOS ANGELES, CA 90027 Function and regulation of the retinoblastoma gene
R01EY-07853-03 (VISB) KORETZ, JANE F RENSSELAER POLYTECHNIC INST DEPARTMENT OF BIOLOGY TROY, N Y 12181 Human accommodation model
R01EY-07860-03 (VISB) LOLLEY, RICHARD N UNIVERSITY OF CALIFORNIA 405 HILGARD AVENUE LOS ANGELES, CALIF 90024 Photoreceptor-phosphoprotein interactions w/transducin
R01EY-07861-03 (VISB) VAINA, LUCIA BOSTON UNIVERSITY 44 CUMMINGTON STREET BOSTON, MA 02215 The effects of lesions on the visual perception of motion
R01EY-07864-03 (VISB) HAUSWIRTH, WILLIAM W UNIVERSITY OF FLORIDA BOX J-284 JHMHC GAINESVILLE, FL 32610-0284 Photoreceptor gene expression in fetal mammalian retina
R01EY-07865-04 (VISA) CAMRAS, CARL B UNIVERSITY OF NEBRASKA 600 SOUTH 42ND STREET OMAHA, NE 68198 Pg-induced reduction of intraocular pressure
R01EY-07883-03 (VISA) SUGRUE, STEPHEN P HARVARD MEDICAL SCHOOL 25 SHATTUCK BOSTON, MA 02115 Epithelial matrix interactions in the cornea
R01EY-07886-02 (VISB) HIGGINS, KENT E PENNSYLVANIA COLL OF OPTOMETRY 1200 WEST GODFREY AVENUE PHILADELPHIA, PA 19141 Information processing & retinal eccentricity
R01EY-07890-01A3 (VISB) TYLER, CHRISTOPHER W SMITH-KETTLEWELL EYE RES INST 2232 WEBSTER STREET SAN FRANCISCO, CA 94115 Contrast, disparity and stereopsis
R29EY-07892-03 (VISA) STERNBERG, PAUL EMORY EYE CTR/UNIV SCH OF MED 1327 CLIFTON ROAD, NE ATLANTA, GA 30322 Antioxdant systems and age-related macular degeneration
R01EY-07924-02 (VISB) GOLDBERG, STEPHEN J VIRGINIA COMMONWEALTH UNIVERSI 1101 E MARSHALL ST, SANGER HAL RICHMOND, VA 23298-0709 The precise control of eye movement and fatigue
R01EY-07935-03 (VISB) MCLOON, LINDA K UNIVERSITY OF MINNESOTA 1100 WASHINGTON AVE S MINNEAPOLIS, MN 55415 Chemomyectomy for eyelid spasms
R01EY-07938-03 (VISA) JERNIGAN, HOWARD M, JR UNIVERSITY OF TENNESSEE 956 COURT, ROOM D222 MEMPHIS, TN 38163 Organic phosphate metabolism in lens stress and cataract
R01EY-07960-03 (VISB) KATZ, LAWRENCE C DUKE UNIVERSITY BOX 3209 MEDICAL CENTER DURHAM, NC 27710 Development of intrinsic circuitry in cat visual cortex
R29EY-07961-04 (VISA) SWAROOP, ANAND UNIVERSITY OF MICHIGAN 1000 WALL STREET ANN ARBOR, MI 48105 X-linked ocular albinism & retinitis pigmentosa
R01EY-07965-03 (VISA) OPRIAN, DANIEL D BRANDEIS UNIVERSITY GRADUATE DEPT OF BIOCHEMISTRY WALTHAM, MA 02254 Structure-function studies of rhodopsin
R01EY-07968-03 (VISB) GILBERT, CHARLES D ROCKEFELLER UNIVERSITY 1230 YORK AVENUE NEW YORK, N Y 10021-6399 Processing mechanisms in monkey visual cortex
R01EY-07975-03 (VISA) BORCHMAN, DOUGLAS KY LIONS EYE RESEARCH INST. 301 E. MUHAMMAD ALI BLVD LOUISVILLE, KY 40202 Spectroscopic and related studies on lens membrane lipid
R01EY-07977-03 (VISB) VICTOR, JONATHAN D CORNELL UNIVERSITY 1300 YORK AVENUE NEW YORK, N Y 10021 Central processing of visual information
R01EY-07980-03 (VISB) TOOTELL, ROGER B HARVARD MEDICAL SCHOOL 220 LONGWOOD AVE BOSTON, MA 02115 Functional anatomy of primate extrastriate visual cortex
R01EY-07981-03 (VISA) WENSEL, THEODORE G BAYLOR COLLEGE OF MEDICINE ONE BAYLOR PLAZA HOUSTON, TX 77030 Transducin interactions with photoreceptor membranes
R01EY-07982-02 (VISB) GUY, JOHN R UNIV OF FLORIDA COLL OF MED BOX J-284 JHMHC GAINESVILLE, FL 32610 Experimental optic neuritis--Oxidative injury
R29EY-07984-03 (VISA) CROOK, RICHARD B UNIVERSITY OF CALIFORNIA, SF DEPT OF OPHTHALMOLOGY SAN FRANCISCO, CA 94143-0730 Glaucoma--Cellular effects of N-G regulators
R01EY-07990-03 (VISB) SIMONS, KURT JOHNS HOPKINS HOSPITAL 600 NORTH WOLFE STREET BALTIMORE, MD 21205 Child vision screening: a case control modality comparison
R29EY-07991-03 (VISB) ROBINSON, FARREL R, JR UNIVERSITY OF WASHINGTON DEPT OF PHYSIOLOGY & BIOPHYSIC SEATTLE, WA 98195 Role of the inferior olive in VOR adaptation
R01EY-07995-03 (VISA) ACOTT, TED S OREGON HEALTH SCIENCES UNIV 3181 SW SAM JACKSON PARK ROAD PORTLAND, OR 97201 Regulation of retinal pigmented epithelial ECMS
R01EY-08001-02 (VISA) LIGGETT, PETER E USC SCHOOL OF MEDICINE DOHENY EYE INSTITUTE LOS ANGELES, CA 90033 Radiation/hyperthermia therapy for choridal melanoma
R01EY-08002-03 (VISA) CHERKSEY, BRUCE D NEW YORK UNIV MEDICAL CENTER 550 FIRST AVENUE NEW YORK, N Y 10016 Aqueous humor inflow mechanisms
R29EY-08006-04 (VISA) WIECHMANN, ALLAN F BOWMAN GRAY SCH OF MEDICINE 300 S HAWTHORNE ROAD WINSTON-SALEM, NC 27103 Regulation and function of melatonin in the retina
R01EY-08012-03 (EDC) KLEIN, BARBARA E UNIVERSITY OF WISCONSIN DEPT OF OPHTHALMOLOGY MADISON, WI 53792 Nutritional factors in age related ocular disorders
R01EY-08015-03 (VISB) MOONEY, RICHARD D MEDICAL COLLEGE OF OHIO DEPT OF ANATOMY/CS #10008 TOLEDO, OH 43699 Visual input to tectofugal neurons
R44EY-08019-03 (SSS) HSIA, JAMES CANDELA LASER CORPORATION 530 BOSTON POST ROAD WAYLAND, MA 01778-1833 Pulsed dye laser Ab-interno sclerotomy
R01EY-08037-03 (VISA) OH, JANG O FRANCES I PROCTOR FOUNDATION UNIVERSITY OF CALIFORNIA SAN FRANCISCO, CA 94143-0412 Eye infection of cytomegalovirus (cmv)
R01EY-08038-03 (VISB) ROWE, MICHAEL H OHIO UNIVERSITY GROSVENOR HALL, ROOM 060 ATHENS, OH 45701-2979 Spatial frequency analysis of cat retina W-cells
R21EY-08039-02 (VSN) BOURNE, WILLIAM M MAYO FOUNDATION 200 FIRST STREET SOUTHWEST ROCHESTER, MN 55905 NEI clinical research development award
R01EY-08041-03 (VISB) MC CREA, ROBERT A UNIVERSITY OF CHICAGO 947 E 58TH STREET CHICAGO, IL 60637 Physiology of oculomotor premotor pathways
R01EY-08043-04 (VISA) TRAVIS, GABRIEL H UNIV. OF TEXAS SOUTHWESTERN 5323 HARRY HINES BLVD DALLAS, TX 75235 Molecular analysis of photoreceptor degeneration
R29EY-08044-02 (VISA) HAY, REGINE E WASHINGTON UNIV SCHOOL OF MED 660 S EUCLID AVE, BOX 8096 ST LOUIS, MO 63110 Transcriptional regulation of eye lens crystallin genes
U10EY-08052-04 (SRC) JABS, DOUGLAS A JOHN HOPKINS HOSPITAL 550 NORTH BROADWAY, SUITE 700 BALTIMORE, MD 21205 Chairmans center--Studies of the ocular complications of AIDS
R01EY-08053-03 (VISA) KOONTZ, MARGARET A UNIVERSITY OF WASHINGTON SEATTLE, WA 98195-0001 Morphology of gabaergic neurons in primate inner retina
R29EY-08055-04 (VISB) AOKI, CHIYE J NEW YORK UNIVERSITY 4 WASHINGTON PLACE NEW YORK, NY 10003 Visual cortex--Cellular basis for noradrenergic actions
U10EY-08057-04 (SRC) MEINERT, CURTIS L JOHNS HOPKINS UNIVERSITY 615 NORTH WOLFE STREET BALTIMORE, MD 21205 Coordinating center--Studies of the ocular complications of AIDS
R01EY-08058-03 (VISA) HYDE, DAVID R UNIVERSITY OF NOTRE DAME NOTRE DAME, IN 46556 Molecular analysis of phototransduction in Drosophila
R29EY-08061-04 (VISA) PALCZEWSKI, KRZYSZTOF R.S DOW NEUROLOGICAL 1120 N.W. 20TH AVENUE PORTLAND, OR 97209-1595 Rhodopsin kinase--Regulation, function and structure
R01EY-08064-03 (VISA) CEPKO, CONSTANCE L HARVARD MEDICAL SCHOOL 25 SHATTUCK STREET BOSTON, MA 02115 Molecular biology of retinal development
U10EY-08067-04 (SRC) DAVIS, MATTHEW D FUNDUS PHOTOGRAPH READING CTR 610 NORTH WALNUT ST, RM 417 MADISON, WI 53705 Ocular complications of AIDS--Fundus photograph reading
R01EY-08076-03 (VISA) OSTRER, HARRY NEW YORK UNIVERSITY MEDICAL CT 550 FIRST AVENUE NEW YORK, NY 10016 Molecular genetic studies of human color vision
R01EY-08079-02 (VISA) SAWHNEY, RAJINDER S RUSH-PRESBY-ST LUKE'S MED CENT 1653 WEST CONGRESS PARKWAY CHICAGO, IL 60612-3864 Regulation of gene expression in lens capsule
R01EY-08082-03 (ARR) QAVI, HAMIDA B BAYLOR COLLEGE OF MEDICINE ONE BAYLOR PLAZA HOUSTON, TX 77030 HIV-1 & HHV-6 in AIDS associated ocular disorders
R29EY-08083-05 (VISB) BROWN, ANGELA M OHIO STATE UNIVERSITY 338 WEST 10TH AVENUE COLUMBUS, OH 43210 Infant chromatic and luminance contrast sensitivity
R01EY-08088-03 (SSS) DRYJA, THADDEUS P MASSACHUSETTS EYE & EAR INFIRM 243 CHARLES STREET BOSTON, MA 02114 Complete genomic sequence of the retinoblastoma gene
R01EY-08089-02 (VISA) OLNEY, JOHN W WASHINGTON UNIVERSITY 660 SOUTH EUCLID AVENUE ST LOUIS, MO 63110 Neuroprotection against retinal ischemia
R01EY-08091-03 (VISA) HETH, CYNTHIA A MASS EYE & EAR INFIRMARY 243 CHARLES STREET BOSTON, MA 02114 Cell biology of retinal pigment epithelium

PROJECT NUMBER LISTING

PROJECT NO., ORGANIZATIONAL UNIT., INVESTIGATOR, ADDRESS, TITLE

R01EY-08097-02 (VISB) BIERSDORF, WILLIAM R JAMES A HALEY VETERANS HOSP 13000 BRUCE B DOWNS BLVD TAMPA, FL 33612 Localization of pattern visual evoked potentials

P30EY-08098-03 (VSN) THOFT, RICHARD A THE EYE & EAR INSTITUTE 203 LOTHROP STREET PITTSBURGH, PA 15213 Core grant for Vision Research

R01EY-08101-03 (VISA) MCDONALD, MARGUERITE B LSU EYE CENTER 2020 GRAVIER ST, SUITE B NEW ORLEANS, LA 70112 Excimer laser ablation to correct refractive error

R29EY-08102-03 (VISA) BAITCH, LAWRENCE WILLIAM UNIV OF MARYLAND SCHOOL OF MED 22 S. GREENE STREET BALTIMORE, MD 21201 Binocular interaction in human visual cortex

R01EY-08103-03 (SSS) ROSNER, BERNARD A CHANNING LABORATORY 180 LONGWOOD AVENUE BOSTON, MA 02115 Statistical methods for ophthalmologic and cluster data

R01EY-08104-03 (VISA) HASSELL, JOHN R EYE & EAR INSTITUTE 203 LOTHROP ST PITTSBURGH, PA 15213 Molecular studies on corneal transparency

R01EY-08106-03 (VISA) SUZUKI, SHINTARO DOHENY EYE INSTITUTE 1355 SAN PABLO STREET LOS ANGELES, CA 90033 The function of the vitronectin receptor of human RPE

R21EY-08107-03 (VSN) DAVIS, MATTHEW D FUNDUS PHOTOGRAPH READING CTR 610 NORTH WALNUT ST, RM 438 MADISON, WI 53705 Development of an ophthalmologic biostatistics program

R01EY-08117-03 (GEN) MONTELL, CRAIG JOHNS HOPKINS UNIVERSITY 725 N WOLFE STREET BALTIMORE, MD 21205 Mutagenesis of ninac--A drosophila neural kinase/myosin

R29EY-08120-03 (VISA) ISHIDA, ANDREW T UNIVERSITY OF CALIFORNIA DAVIS, CA 95616 Pharmacology and physiology of retinal ganglion cells

R01EY-08121-02 (VISA) DOREY, C KATHLEEN EYE RESEARCH INSTITUTE 20 STANIFORD STREET BOSTON, MA 02114 Phagosome dynamics in the retinal pigment epithelium

R29EY-08122-03 (VISA) KSANDER, BRUCE R UNIVERSITY OF MIAMI P O BOX 016960 R-138 MIAMI, FL 33101 Cell-mediated immune response to intraocular tumors

R01EY-08123-02 (VISA) BAEHR, WOLFGANG CULLEN EYE INSTITUTE 6501 FANNIN STREET HOUSTON, TX 77030 Retinal photoreceptor cGMP phosphodiesterases

R01EY-08124-03 (VISB) STERLING, PETER UNIVERSITY OF PENNSYLVANIA SCHOOL OF MED/DEPT OF ANATOMY PHILADELPHIA, PA 19104 Microcircuitry of parallel channels in primate vision

R01EY-08125-03 (VISA) CHUN, LINDA L Y MASSACHUSETTS GENERAL HOSPITAL 32 FRUIT STREET BOSTON, MA 02114 Regulation of retinal ganglion cell development

P30EY-08126-03 (VSN) POWERS, MAUREEN K VANDERBILT UNIVERSITY 301 A & S PSYCHOLOGY NASHVILLE, TN 37240 Core Grant for Vision Research

R01EY-08128-04 (VISA) CHINO, YUZO M UNIVERSITY OF HOUSTON 4800 CALHOUN-COLL OF OPTOMETRY HOUSTON, TX 77204-2163 Amblyopia

R01EY-08131-03 (RAD) CHIU-TSAO, SOU-TUNG HENRY FORD HOSPITAL 2799 W. GRAND BLVD. DETROIT, MI 48202 125I and 60CO Eye plaque dosimetry

R01EY-08132-02 (SOH) LANGE, DAVID G JOHNS HOPKINS HOSPITAL 600 NORTH WOLFE STREET BALTIMORE, MD 21205 Mechanisms of microwave damage in ocular tissue

R01EY-08137-03 (VISA) KHOOBEHI, BAHRAM LOUISIANA STATE UNIV EYE CTR 2020 GRAVIER STREET, SUITE B NEW ORLEANS, LA 70112 Retinal blood flow measurement

R01EY-08143-02 (VISA) PEPOSE, JAY S WASHINGTON UNIVERSITY SCH OF M 660 SOUTH EUCLID AVENUE ST LOUIS, MO 63110 Study of HIV and CMV retinitis

R01EY-08144-03 (ARR) HOFMAN, FLORENCE M DOHENY EYE INSTITUTE 2011 ZONAL AVE, HMR 312 LOS ANGELES, CA 90033 AIDS retinitis - pathogenetic mechanisms

R01EY-08145-03 (ARR) SADUN, ALFREDO A DOHENY EYE INSTITUTE 1355 SAN PABLO STREET LOS ANGELES, CA 90033 AIDS as a cause for primary optic neuropathy

U10EY-08150-04 (VSN) BERNARD, DOFT MONTEFIORE UNIVERSITY HOSPITAL 3459 FIFTH AVENUE PITTSBURGH, PA 15219 Endophthalmitis vitrectomy study

U10EY-08151-03 (VSN) KELSEY, SHERYL F UNIVERSITY OF PITTSBURGH 130 DESOTO STREET PITTSBURGH, PA 15261 Endophthalmitis vitrectomy study coordinating center

R01EY-08152-02 (GEN) BANERJEE, UTPAL UNIVERSITY OF CALIFORNIA 405 HILGARD AVE LOS ANGELES, CA 90024 Genetic and molecular studies of suppressor of sevenless

R44EY-08156-02 (VISB) SPITZBERG, LARRY A L A SPITZBERG, INC 14441 MEMORIAL DRIVE HOUSTON, TX 77079 Ergonomic magnifiers for improved reading and writing

R44EY-08160-03 (SSS) CANTER, JOSEPH CANDELA LASER CORPORATION 530 BOSTON POST ROAD WAYLAND, MA 01778 Infrared fundus videoangiography system

R01EY-08167-03 (ARR) CLEVELAND, PATRICK H V A MEDICAL CENTER (V-151) 3350 LA JOLLA VILLAGE DR SAN DIEGO, CA 92161 Murine model of immunosuppression induced CMV retinitis

R01EY-08168-03 (ARR) NICHOLS, BARBARA A UNIVERSITY OF CALIFORNIA SAN FRANCISCO, CA 94143-0412 Ocular toxoplasmosis in normal & immunosuppressed hosts

R01EY-08172-03 (VISA) DICKINSON, DOUGLAS P UNIV OF TEXAS HLTH SCIS CENTER 6516 J FREEMAN AVE/P O BOX 200 HOUSTON, TX 77225 A recombinant DNA approach to tear protein analysis

U10EY-08176-03 (VSN) DOBSON, MARGARET V UNIVERSITY OF PITTSBURGH 462 LANGLEY HALL PITTSBURGH, PA 15260 CRYO-ROP follow-up visual acuity center

R01EY-08191-06 (EVR) GREENE, MARK I UNIVERSITY OF PENNSYLVANIA RM 252 JOHN MORGAN BLDG PHILADELPHIA, PA 19104 Characterization of the mammalian reovirus receptor

R01EY-08197-03 (VISA) BEAVO, JOSEPH A UNIV. OF WA, SCHOOL OF MED. DEPT. OF PHARMACOLOGY, SJ-30 SEATTLE, WA 98195 Photoreceptor phosphodiesterase structure & function

R01EY-08202-03 (VISA) DE JONG, WILFRIED W UNIVERSITY OF NIJMEGEN PO BOX 9101 6500 HB NIJMEGEN, NETHERLANDS Stability of enzymes as eye lens crystallins

PROJECT NO., ORGANIZATIONAL UNIT., INVESTIGATOR, ADDRESS, TITLE

R01EY-08205-04 (VISA) MCLAUGHLIN, GERALD LEE PURDUE UNIVERSITY SCHOOL OF VETERINARY MEDICINE WEST LAFAYETTE, IN 47907 Use of assays to study acanthamoeba-cornea interactions

R01EY-08206-03 (VISB) PUGH, EDWARD N, JR UNIVERSITY OF PENNSYLVANIA 3815 WALNUT STREET PHILADELPHIA, PA 19104 Polarization contrast--a new kind of vertebrate vision

R01EY-08208-02 (VISB) SAMPLE, PAMELA A UNIVERSITY OF CALIFORNIA LA JOLLA, CA 92093 Color vision in primary open angle glaucoma

U10EY-08210-03 (VSN) DAVIS, MATTHEW D FUNDUS PHOTOGRAPH READING CTR 610 NORTH WALNUT ST, RM 438 MADISON, WI 53705 Endophthalmitis vitrectomy study reading center

R29EY-08212-03 (VISB) SEGRAVES, MARK A NORTHWESTERN UNIVERSITY 2153 SHERIDAN ROAD EVANSTON, IL 60208 Cortical contributions to the control of eye movementsa

R01EY-08213-03 (VISA) LAM, KWOK-WAI UNIV OF TEXAS HEALTH SCIENCE C 7703 FLOYD CURL DRIVE SAN ANTONIO, TX 78284 The function of ascorbate peroxidase in the eye

R01EY-08216-02 (VISB) GUITTON, DANIEL MONTREAL NEUROLOGICAL INSTITUT 3801 UNIVERSITY ST CANADA H3A 2B4 Oculomotor and gaze-motor systems in vision

R01EY-08217-02 (VISB) GNADT, JAMES W STATE UNIVERSITY OF NEW YORK STONY BROOK, NY 11794-0001 Parietal cortex--Ocular vergence and lens accommodation

R29EY-08219-03 (VISA) NISHIMURA, ICHIRO HARVARD SCH OF DENTAL MEDICINE 188 LONGWOOD AVENUE BOSTON, MA 02115 Collagen gene expression in the cornea

U10EY-08221-03 (VSN) REPKA, MICHAEL X JOHNS HOPKINS HOSPITAL 600 NORTH WOLFE STREET BALTIMORE, MD 21205 CRYO-ROP follow-up clinical center

R01EY-08227-01A1 (VISA) GORDON, Y JEROLD EYE & EAR INST OF PITTSBURGH 203 LOTHROP STREET PITTSBURGH, PA 15213 Experimental pathogenesis and therapy of ocular adenovirus

R01EY-08228-02 (VISA) HUTCHINS, JAMES B UNIVERSITY OF MISSISSIPPI 2500 NORTH STATE STREET JACKSON, MS 39216-4505 Retina--Development & neurochemistry

R01EY-08233-03 (VISB) HALL, WILLIAM C DUKE UNIVERSITY BOX 3209 DURHAM, NC 27710 Structural organization of the superior colliculus

R01EY-08239-03 (BMT) KNAPP, DANIEL R MEDICAL UNIV OF SOUTH CAROLINA 171 ASHLEY AVENUE CHARLESTON, SC 29425 Structure and function of rhodopsin by mass spectrometry

R01EY-08240-02 (VISB) TS'O, DANIEL Y ROCKEFELLER UNIVERSITY 1230 YORK AVENUE NEW YORK, NY 10021-6399 Color processing in primate visual cortex

R01EY-08247-03 (VISA) VAN BUSKIRK, E MICHAEL OREGON HLTH SCI UNIVERSITY 3181 SW SAM JACKSON PARK ROAD PORTLAND, OR 97201 Biology of trabecular response to laser trabeculoplasty

R01EY-08249-03 (VISA) KLINTWORTH, GORDON K DUKE UNIVERSITY MEDICAL CENTER BOX 3712 DURHAM, NC 27710 Genetic linkage study macular corneal dystrophy

R01EY-08256-02 (VISB) POWERS, MAUREEN K VANDERBILT UNIVERSITY A & S PSYCHOLOGY BUILDING NASHVILLE, TN 37240 Dynamic retinal structures: influence on visual function

R01EY-08264-02 (VISA) BORGES, LAWRENCE F MASSACHUSETTS GENERAL HOSPITAL FRUIT STREET BOSTON, MA 02114 Effect of intraocular grafting on the cornea

R01EY-08266-03 (VISB) LANDY, MICHAEL S NEW YORK UNIVERSITY 6 WASHINGTON PLACE NEW YORK, NY 10003 Fusion and calibration of multiple depth cues

R01EY-08273-03 (VISA) MACLEISH, PETER R CORNELL UNIVERSITY MED COLLEGE 1300 YORK AVE NEW YORK, NY 10021 Studies of retinal regeneration in vivo & in vitro

R01EY-08277-03 (VISA) CAVANAGH, H DWIGHT UNIV OF TEXAS SW MED CTR 5323 HARRY HINES BLVD DALLAS, TX 75235-9057 In vivo regulation of corneal epithelial RNA polymerase activity

R01EY-08280-03 (VISB) SCOTT, ALAN B SMITH-KETTLEWELL EYE RES INST 2232 WEBSTER STREET SAN FRANCISCO, CA 94115 Ricin reduction of muscle function

R01EY-08281-03 (VISA) TOOTLE, JOHN S UNIVERSITY OF ALABAMA UAB STATION BIRMINGHAM, AL 35294 Development of neuronal structure and function in retina

R01EY-08282-02 (VISA) BATEMAN, JANE B JULES STEIN EYE INSTITUTE 100 STEIN PLAZA LOS ANGELES, CA 90024-7008 Candidate genes in hereditary eye diseases

R01EY-08284-03 (VISA) KORTE, GARY E MONTEFIORE MEDICAL CENTER 111 EAST 210TH STREET BRONX, NY 10467 Plasma membrane reorganization during RPE regeneration

R01EY-08285-03 (VISB) FARBER, DEBORA B JULES STEIN EYE INSTITUTE UCLA SCHOOL OF MEDICINE LOS ANGELES, CA 90024-7008 Molecular mechanisms in retinal degenerations

R01EY-08289-03 (VISA) GILMORE, MICHAEL S UNIV OKLAHOMA HEALTH SCI CTR PO BOX 26901 OKLAHOMA CITY, OK 73190 Streptococcus faecalis endophthalmitis

R01EY-08291-03 (VSN) LESKE, M CRISTINA SUNY @ STONY BROOK SCHOOL OF MEDICINE, HSC STONY BROOK, NY 11974-8036 Natural history of lens opacities study

R01EY-08300-02 (VISA) HAWKEN, MICHAEL J NEW YORK UNIVERSITY 6 WASHINGTON PLACE NEW YORK, NY 10003 Cortical representation of the visual image

R01EY-08301-02 (VISB) ALEXANDER, KENNETH R UNIV. OF ILLINOIS AT CHICAGO 1855 WEST TAYLOR STREET CHICAGO, IL 60612 Studies of visual dysfunction in retinitis pigmentosa

R01EY-08303-02 (SSS) SCOTT, ALAN B SMITH-KETTLEWELL EYE RES INST 2232 WEBSTER STREET SAN FRANCISCO, CA 94115 Dystonia treatment by botulinum toxins

R01EY-08306-03 (VISB) KORENBROT, JUAN I UNIVERSITY OF CALIFORNIA PARNASSUS AVENUE SAN FRANCISCO, CA 94143 Cellular mechanisms of vertebrate photoreceptor renewal

R01EY-08312-03 (HAR) BUDELMANN, BERND U UNIVERSITY OF TEXAS MED BRANCH 200 UNIVERSITY BOULEVARD GALVESTON, TX 77550-2772 Statocyst-oculomotor system/advanced marine invertebrate

R01EY-08313-01A2 (VISB) DEMER, JOSEPH L UNIVERSITY OF CALIFORNIA 100 STEIN PLAZA LOS ANGELES, CA 90024-7002 Biomechanical analysis in strabismus surgery

PROJECT NO., ORGANIZATIONAL UNIT., INVESTIGATOR, ADDRESS, TITLE

R44EY-08316-02 (VISB) SCHWARZBACH, RICHARD J ASSURANCE TECHNOLOGIES INC 495 WEGNER DRIVE WEST CHICAGO, IL 60185-0370 Microcomputer controlled self tonometer for home monitor
R43EY-08320-01A1 (VISB) MUNNERLYN, CHARLES R VISX, INCORPORATED 1150 KIFER ROAD, SUITE 202 SUNNYVALE, CA 94086 Therapeutic correction of astigmatism with excimer PRK
R44EY-08327-02 (VISB) GREENE, HENRY A OCUTECH, INC PO BOX 625 CHAPEL HILL, NC 27515 Autofocus telescope for low vision
R01EY-08338-02 (VISA) YANG, XIONG-LI SHANGHAI INSTITUTE OF PHYSIOLO 320 YO-YANG RD SHANGHAI, CHINA Modulation of retinal function
R01EY-08340-02 (VISA) SEMPLE-ROWLAND, SUSAN L UNIV OF FLORIDA BOX J-244 JHMHC GAINESVILLE, FL 32610-0244 Rd chick model of hereditary blindness: Protein analyses
R01EY-08343-02 (VISA) CIVAN, MORTIMER M UNIVERSITY OF PENNSYLVANIA RICHARDS BUILDING PHILADELPHIA, PA 19104-6085 Transport by ocular ciliary epithelial cells
R01EY-08352-02 (VISB) ULINSKI, PHILIP S UNIVERSITY OF CHICAGO 1025 EAST 57TH STREET CHICAGO, IL 60637 Neural mechanisms of global motion analysis
R01EY-08362-02 (VISA) HUGHES, THOMAS E UNIV OF CALFORNIA, SAN DIEGO 9500 GILMAN DRIVE LA JOLLA, CA 92093-0608 GABA-ceptive neurons in the retina
R01EY-08363-02 (NEUB) FRASER, SCOTT E UNIVERSITY OF CALIFORNIA IRVINE, CA 92717 Dynamic aspects of neuronal patterning
R01EY-08364-02 (VISA) FONG, HENRY K W DOHENY EYE INSTITUTE 1355 SAN PABLO ST LOS ANGELES, CA 90033 G proteins and phospholipase C regulation in RPE cells
R29EY-08368-02 (VISA) BEYER, ERIC C WASHINGTON UNIVERSITY 400 S KINGSHIGHWAY ST LOUIS, MO 63110 Biology of lens intercellular communication
R01EY-08379-02 (VISA) AHMED, A RAZZAQUE CENTER FOR BLOOD RESEARCH 800 HUNTINGTON AVENUE BOSTON, MA 02115 Ocular pemphigoid: mechanism of pathogenesis
R01EY-08384-01A2 (VISB) YOUNG, ROCKEFELLER S TEXAS TECH UNIV HEALTH SCIS CT LUBBOCK, TX 79430-0001 Pupillometric study of a color response
R01EY-08388-02 (VISA) TWINING, SALLY S MEDICAL COLLEGE OF WISCONSIN 8701 WATERTOWN PLANK RD MILWAUKEE, WI 53226 Effect of vitamin A deficiency on leukocyte function
R01EY-08391-01A2 (VISA) MANDARINO, LAWRENCE J EYE AND EAR INSTITUTE 203 LOTHROP STREET PITTSBURGH, PA 15213 Biochemical mechanisms of retinal capillary dysfunction
R01EY-08395-02 (MGN) MOTULSKY, ARNO G UNIVERSITY OF WASHINGTON MAIL STOP RG-25 SEATTLE, WA 98195 Color vision: Molecular and psychophysical studies
R01EY-08396-02 (GEN) REINKE, ROSEMARY ALBERT EINSTEIN COLLEGE OF MED 1300 MORRIS PARK AVENUE BRONX, NY 10461 Genetic and molecular studies on Drosophila eye development
R01EY-08397-02 (VISA) GILBERT, WALTER HARVARD UNIVERSITY 1350 MASSACHUSETTS AVE., RM 44 CAMBRIDGE, MA 02138 Isolation of visual pathway mutants in the fish
R01EY-08398-02 (VISB) SANDBERG, MICHAEL A MASSACHUSETTS EYE & EAR INFIRM 243 CHARLES STREET BOSTON, MA 02114 Functional assessment of macular degenerations
R01EY-08399-02 (VISB) MILLER, JOEL M SMITH-KETTLEWELL EYE RES INST 2232 WEBSTER STREET SAN FRANCISCO, CA 94115 Egocentric localization and saccadic plasticity
R01EY-08406-02 (VISA) DEYOE, EDGAR A, III MEDICAL COLLEGE OF WISCONSIN 8701 WATERTOWN PLANK ROAD MILWAUKEE, WI 53226 Concurrent processing streams in extrastriate visual ctx
R01EY-08408-03 (VISA) FINI, M ELIZABETH MASSACHUSETTS GENERAL HOSPITAL CHARLESTOWN, MA 02129 Molecular mechanisms suppressing comeal ulceration
R01EY-08411-03 (VISB) MCCONNELL, SUSAN K STANFORD UNIVERSITY STANFORD, CA 94305-5020 Determination of neuronal fates in visual cortex
R01EY-08413-02 (VISA) RIVA, CHARLES E PRESBYTERIAN MEDICAL CENTER 51 NORTH 39TH STREET PHILADELPHIA, PA 19104 Oxygenation of the ocular fundus
R01EY-08414-02 (VISA) SZWERGOLD, BENJAMIN FOX CHASE CANCER CENTER 7701 BURHOLME AVENUE PHILADELPHIA, PA 19111 New metabolites & pathways in the mammalian lens
R01EY-08415-01A1 (VISB) REESE, BENJAMIN E UNIVERSITY OF CALIFORNIA OFFICE OF RESEARCH SANTA BARBARA, CA 93106 Fiber reorganization within the mammalian optic pathway
R29EY-08426-02 (VISA) STONE, EDWIN M UNIVERSITY OF IOWA HOSPITALS IOWA CITY, IA 52242 Molecular genetics of age related macular degeneration
R01EY-08427-02 (VISA) HENNEKENS, CHARLES H BRIGHAM & WOMEN'S HOSPITAL 55 POND AVENUE BROOKLINE, MA 02146 Trial of beta-carotene and macular degeneration
R01EY-08459-02 (VISB) GRAHAM, NORMA V COLUMBIA UNIVERSITY NEW YORK, NY 10027 Low-level visual processes in texture segregation
R01EY-08466-02 (NEUB) ELBERGER, ANDREA J THE UNIV OF TENNESSEE, MEMPHIS 875 MONROE AVENUE MEMPHIS, TN 38163 Development of mammalian central nervous system pathways
R01EY-08467-02 (VISA) TAKAHASHI, JOSEPH S NORTHWESTERN UNIVERSITY 2153 SHERIDAN ROAD EVANSTON, IL 60208 Melatonin synthesis in retinal & retinoblastoma cells
R01EY-08468-02 (VISA) PRCHAL, JOSEF T UNIV OF ALABAMA AT BIRMINGHAM 513 TINSLEY HARRISON TOWERS BIRMINGHAM, AL 35294 Isolation & characterization of lens spectrin & ankyrinn
R01EY-08490-02 (CMS) AKESON, RICHARD A CHILDREN'S HOSPITAL MED CENTER ELLAND AND BETHESDA AVNEUES CINCINNATI, OH 45229 Targeted ablation in eye and brain
R01EY-08502-01A1 (VISB) SCHILLER, PETER H MASSACHUSETTS INST OF TECHNOLO E25-634 CAMBRIDGE, MA 02139 The neural control of visually guided eye movements
R01EY-08511-02 (VISA) DELORI, FRANCOIS C EYE RESEARCH INST OF RETINA FN 20 STANIFORD STREET BOSTON, MA 02114 Noninvasive measurement of RPE lipofuscin
R01EY-08512-02 (VISA) STEPP, MARY A EYE RESEARCH INSTITUTE 20 STANIFORD STREET BOSTON, MA 02114 Molecular aspects of corneal epithelial migration

PROJECT NO., ORGANIZATIONAL UNIT., INVESTIGATOR, ADDRESS, TITLE

R01EY-08515-02 (VISB) SREBRO, RICHARD UNIV OF TEXAS SW MED CTR 5323 HARRY HINES BLVD DALLAS, TX 75235-8592 Development of the VEP to luminance modulation
R01EY-08519-01A1 (VISA) ARAMANT, ROBERT B EYE RESEARCH INSTITUTE 20 STANIFORD STREET BOSTON, MA 02114 Transplantation of retina to retina
R01EY-08520-01A1 (VISB) APPLEGATE, RAYMOND A UNIVERSITY OF TEXAS 7703 FLOYD CURL DRIVE SAN ANTONIO, TX 78284-7779 Aberrations of eyes in normal and clinical populations
R01EY-08522-02 (VISA) BARKDOLL, A EDWIN, III PENNSYLVANIA COLL OF OPTOMETRY 1200 WEST GODFREY AVENUE PHILADELPHIA, PA 19141 Mechanisms of vertebrate visual transduction
R01EY-08523-01A1 (VISB) LEVENTHAL, AUDIE G UNIVERSITY OF UTAH SCHOOL OF M SALT LAKE CITY, UT 84132 Mechanisms mediating subcortical orientation sensitivity
R01EY-08535-02 (VISB) FINE, RICHARD E BOSTON UNIVERSITY SCHOOL OF ME 80 EAST CONCORD STREET BOSTON, MA 02118 24 kDa GTP-binding proteins in optic nerve dynamics
R01EY-08538-01A1 (VISA) RODRIGUEZ-BOULAN, ENRIQUE J CORNELL UNIV MEDICAL COLLEGE 1300 YORK AVENUE NEW YORK, NY 10021 Retina--Reversed membrane polarity in RPE
R01EY-08539-02 (VISA) JACOB-LABARRE, JEAN T LOUSIANA STATE UNIV EYE CENTER 2020 GRAVIER STREET NEW ORLEANS, LA 70112 Scleral implants for myopia
R01EY-08540-01A1 (VISA) PETERS, DONNA P UNIVERSITY OF WISCONSIN 1300 UNIVERSITY AVENUE MADISON, WI 53706 Assembly of collagen fibrils in corneal stroma
R21EY-08541-01A1 (VSN) SEDDON, JOHANNA M MASS EYE AND EAR INFIRMARY 243 CHARLES STREET BOSTON, MA 02114 Clinical vision research development at MEEI
R01EY-08544-02 (VISB) LAMBERT, SCOTT R EMORY UNIVERSITY 1327 CLIFTON RD, NE ATLANTA, GA 30322 Correction of monocular aphakia in monkeys with IOLS
R29EY-08547-01A1 (VISA) ANSARI, NASEEM H UNIVERSITY OF TEXAS MED BRANCH C3-14, CHILD HEALTH CTR GALVESTON, TX 77550 Oxidative damage in sugar-induced cataractogenesis
R01EY-08560-02 (VISA) PACKER, SAMUEL NORTH SHORE UNIVERSITY HOSPITA 300 COMMUNITY DRIVE MANHASSET, NY 11030 Boron neutron capture therapy of ocular melanoma
R01EY-08566-01A1 (VISA) TAYLOR, ALLEN TUFTS UNIVERSITY 711 WASHINGTON STREET BOSTON, MA 02111 Mechanisms of cataract delay by caloric restriction
P30EY-08570-02 (VSN) WIESEL, TORSTEN N THE ROCKEFELLER UNIVERSITY 1230 YORK AVENUE NEW YORK, NY 10021-6399 Core grant for vision research
P30EY-08571-02 (VSN) HARGRAVE, PAUL A UNIVERSITY OF FLORDIA BOX J-284, JHMHC GAINESVILLE, FL 32610-0284 Vision research center
R15EY-08572-01A1 (VISA) MEYERTHOLEN, EDWARD P BALL STATE UNIVERSITY 2000 UNIVERSITY AVENUE MUNCIE, IN 47306-0510 Inositol metabolism in rat retinal pigment epithelium
U10EY-08587-02 (VSN) PULIAFITO, CARMEN A MASSACHUSETTS EYE/EAR INFIRMAR 243 CHARLES STREET BOSTON, MA 02114 Endophthalmitis vitrectomy study--clinical center
U10EY-08588-02 (VSN) LAMBERT, H MICHAEL EMORY UNIVERSITY 1327 CLIFTON ROAD, NE ATLANTA, GA 30322 Endophthalmitis vitrectomy study--Clinical center
U10EY-08589-02 (VSN) MARGHERIO, RAYMOND R ASSOCIATED RETINAL CONSULTANTS 3535 WEST 13 MILE ROAD ROYAL OAK, MI 48072 Endophthalmitis vitrectomy study--Clinical center
U10EY-08591-02 (VSN) VINE, ANDREW K UNIVERSITY OF MICHIGAN 1000 WALL STREET ANN ARBOR, MI 48105 Endophthalmitis vitrectomy study--Clinical center
U10EY-08595-02 (VSN) OBER, RICHARD R UNIV OF SOUTHERN CALIFORNIA 1355 SAN PABLO STREET LOS ANGELES, CA 90033 Endophthalmitis vitrectomy study--Clinical center
U10EY-08596-02 (VSN) HAN, DENNIS P EYE INSTITUTE 8700 W. WISCONSIN AVE. MILWAUKEE, WI 53226 Endophthalmitis vitrectomy study--Clinical center
U10EY-08597-02 (VSN) CANTRILL, HERBERT L BOX 493, UNIV. OF MINNESOTA 516 DELAWARD STREET, SE MINNEAPOLIS, MN 55455 Endophthalmitis vitrectomy study (EVS) clinical center
U10EY-08599-02 (VSN) PACKO, KIRK H IRWIN RETINA CENTER ONE INGALLS DRIVE HARVEY, IL 60426 Endophthalmitis vitrectomy study: clinical center
U10EY-08603-02 (VSN) RICE, THOMAS A 26900 CEDAR ROAD CLEVELAND, OH 44122 Endophthalmitis vitrectomy study--Clinical center
U10EY-08605-02 (VSN) PAVAN, PETER R UNIVERSITY OF SOUTH FLORIDA 12901 BRUCE B. DOWNS BLVD. TAMPA, FL 33612-4799 Endophthalmitis vitrectomy study: clinical center
R01EY-08610-01A1 (VISB) AINE, CHERYL J LOS ALAMOS NATIONAL LABORATORY PO BOX 1663 LOS ALAMOS, NM 87545 Neuromagnetic mapping of multiple visual areas in humans
U10EY-08612-02 (VSN) ALWARD, WALLACE L M UNIVERSITY OF IOWA HOSPITALS IOWA CITY, IA 52242 Fluorouracil filtering surgery study
U10EY-08614-02 (VSN) DOFT, BERNARD H RETINA-VITREOUS CONSULTANTS 3501 FORBES AVENUE PITTSBURGH, PA 15219 Endophthalmitis vitrectomy study--Clincal center
R01EY-08616-02 (VISA) CHURCH, ROBERT L EMORY EYE CENTER, EMORY UNIV 1327 CLIFTON ROAD, NE ATLANTA, GA 30322 Characterization of lens membrane proteins
R01EY-08649-03 (VISB) CICERONE, CAROL M UNIV OF CALIFORNIA, IRVINE DEPT OF COGNITIVE SCIENCES IRVINE, CA 92717 Mechanisms of human color vision
R01EY-08654-02 (VISB) FINKELSTEIN, MARCIA A UNIVERSITY OF SOUTH FLORIDA TAMPA, FL 33620 Receptor-related nonlinearities in photopic vision
R01EY-08656-02 (VISB) DEMER, JOSEPH L JULES STEIN EYE INSTITUTE 100 STEIN PLAZA LOS ANGELES, CA 90024-1771 Visual-vestibular interaction with low vision aids
R01EY-08661-01A1 (VISB) BENNETT-CLARKE, CAROL A MEDICAL COLLEGE OF OHIO PO BOX 10008 TOLEDO, OH 43699-0008 Visual cortical development and serotonin

R55EY-08669-01A1 (VISA) JACOB-LABARRE, JEAN T LOUSIANA STATE UNIV EYE CENTER 2020 GRAVIER STREET NEW ORLEANS, LA 70112 Sustained delivery of ocular medications

R01EY-08672-02 (VISA) COCA-PRADOS, MIGUEL YALE UNIVERSITY SCH OF MEDICIN 330 CEDAR ST NEW HAVEN, CT 06510 Na, k-atpase gene expression in the human ciliary body

R01EY-08673-02 (VISA) MATTHEWS, GARY G STATE UNIVERSITY OF NEW YORK STONY BROOK, NY 11794-5230 Cellular physiology of ocular epithelia

R29EY-08676-02 (VISA) WOLANCZYK, JAN P STATE UNIVERSITY OF NEW YORK BINGHAMTON, NY 13901 Biophysical investigations of gamma-crystallins

R01EY-08683-02 (MGN) DRYJA, THADDEUS P MASSACHUSETTS EYE & EAR INFIRM 243 CHARLES STREET BOSTON, MA 02114 Candidate gene study of inherited retinal degenerations

R01EY-08684-02 (VISA) KNIGHTON, ROBERT W BASCOM PALMER EYE INSTITUTE PO BOX 016880 MIAMI, FL 33101 Retinal nerve fiber layer reflectance mechanisms

R29EY-08686-01A1 (VISB) GRAY, CHARLES M SALK INSTITUTE PO BOX 85800 SAN DIEGO, CA 92138-9216 Neuronal mechanisms of visual integration

R01EY-08688-02 (VISA) FLEISHER, LLOYD N NORTH CAROLINA STATE UNIVERSIT 4700 HILLSBOROUGH STREET RALEIGH, NC 27606 Actions and interactions of uveitic mediators

R01EY-08690-02 (MGN) YANDELL, DAVID W MASS EYE AND EAR INFIRMARY 243 CHARLES STREET BOSTON, MA 02114 Direct sequence analysis of the retinoblastoma gene

R01EY-08694-01A1 (VISA) RIZZOLO, LAWRENCE J EMORY UNIVERSITY ATLANTA, GA 30322 Polarity of retinal pigmented epithelium

R01EY-08697-02 (VISA) WECHSLER, STEVEN L CEDARS-SINAI MEDICAL CENTER 8700 BEVERLY BOULEVARD LOS ANGELES, CA 90048 Corneal regulation of the HSV-1 latency (lat) gene

R29EY-08700-01S1 (VISB) BOWNE, SAMUEL F SMITH-KETTLEWELL EYE RES INST 2232 WEBSTER STREET SAN FRANCISCO, CA 94115 Human visual velocity perception in fovea and periphery

R01EY-08701-02 (VISA) GEBHARDT, BRYAN M LOUISIANA STATE UNIV EYE CENTE 2020 GRAVIER STREET NEW ORLEANS, LA 70112 Ocular neuroimmunology

R29EY-08706-02 (MBY) BATEMAN, ERIK A UNIVERSITY OF VERMONT GIVEN BUILDING BURLINGTON, VT 05405 Transcription of Acanthamoeba RNA polymerase II genes

R01EY-08707-02 (VISA) TRIPATHI, RAMESH C THE UNIVERSITY OF CHICAGO 939 EAST 57TH STREET CHICAGO, IL 60637 Aqueous humor growth factors

R01EY-08711-02 (VISA) PFLUGFELDER, STEPHEN C BASCOM PALMER EYE INSTITUTE PO BOX 016880 MIAMI, FL 33101 EBV and ocular pathology in Sjogren's Syndrome

R01EY-08724-02 (VISA) NORK, T MICHAEL WEST VIRGINIA UNIVERSITY MORGANTOWN, WV 26506 Cellular mechanisms of acquired color vision loss

R01EY-08747-02 (VISA) FITZGERALD, PAUL G UNIVERSITY OF CALIFORNIA DAVIS, CA 95616 Molecular analysis of ocular lens beaded filaments

R01EY-08750-01A1 (VISA) KLEIMAN, NORMAN J COLUMBIA UNIVERSITY 630 WEST 168TH STREET NEW YORK, NY 10032 Lens DNA damage and repair

R01EY-08760-02 (VISB) PATON, MARTHA C YALE UNIVERSITY GRANT & CONTRACT ADMIN NEW HAVEN, CT 06520 NMDA effects on developing visual synapses

R55EY-08763-01A1 (VISA) CHALUPA, LEO M UNIVERSITY OF CALIFORNIA 275 MRAK HALL DAVIS, CA 95616 Developmental specificity in primate visual system

R29EY-08765-02 (VISA) EDWARDS, SAMUEL C THE UNIVERSITY OF SOUTH FLORID 4202 E FOWLER AVENUE TAMPA, FL 33620 Role protein phosphates in photoreceptor funtion

R29EY-08768-02 (VISB) COLLEY, NANSI J UNIV OF CALIFORNIA, SAN DIEGO LA JOLLA, CA 92093-0634 Molecular studies of retinal degeneration in drosophila

R01EY-08770-02 (NTN) CARLSON, SUSAN E NEWBORN CENTER 853 JEFFERSON AVE MEMPHIS, TN 38163 The role of dietary n-3 fatty acids in premature infants

R01EY-08772-02 (GEN) ZIPURSKY, STEPHEN L UCLA SCHOOL OF MEDICINE LOS ANGELES, CA 90024-1737 The structure and function of the Drosphila boss gene

R01EY-08773-14 (NEUB) LA VAIL, JENNIFER H UNIVERSITY OF CALIFORNIA SAN FRANCISCO, CA 94143-0452 Axonal transport in the visual system

R01EY-08775-05 (VISB) PETERSEN, STEVEN E WASHINGTON UNIV SCH OF MED 660 S EUCLID, BOX 8111 ST LOUIS, MO 63110 Investigations of human cortical organization with PET--Attentional systems

R01EY-08776-02 (VISA) WEST, SHEILA K JOHNS HOPKINS HOSPITAL 600 N WOLFE STREET BALTIMORE, MD 21205 Eye disease in a cohort of Chesapeake Bay watermen

R01EY-08778-02 (ARR) SHADDUCK, JOHN A TEXAS A & M UNIVERSITY COLLEGE OF VETERINARY MEDICINE COLLEGE STATION, TX 77843 Ocular and systemic microsporidiosis of AIDS patients

R43EY-08791-01A1 (VISB) KILBRIDE, PAUL E VIRTUAL WORLDS, INC PO BOX 8096 ROLLING MEADOWS, IL 60008-809 Driving performance analysis system

R43EY-08794-01A1 (SSS) MOULTON, PETER F SCHWARTZ ELECTRO-OPTICS, INC 45 WINTHROP STREET CONCORD, MA 01742 Tunable-wavelength scanning laser opthalmoscope

R01EY-08805-02 (HSDG) JAVITT, JONATHAN C CENTER FOR SIGHT 3800 RESERVOIR ROAD WASHINGTON, DC 20007 Cost effectiveness of eye research and care

R01EY-08813-01 (VISA) KATZ, MARTIN L UNIVERSITY OF MISSOURI SCHOOL OF MEDICINE COLUMBIA, MO 65212 Retinal pigment epithelial proteolysis and lipofuscin

R01EY-08819-01A1 (VISA) BAHN, REBECCA S MAYO FOUNDATION 200 FIRST STREET SOUTHWEST ROCHESTER, MN 55905 The eye in Graves' disease--Role of orbital fibroblasts

R01EY-08820-01 (VISA) NEWTON, ALEXANDRA C INDIANA UNIVERSITY BLOOMINGTON, IN 47405 Role of protein kinase C in photoreceptors

R01EY-08834-01A1 (VISA) BONANNO, JOSEPH A UNIVERSITY OF CALIFORNIA BERKELEY, CA 94720 Regulation of intracellular pH and fluid flux in corneal endothelium

R01EY-08835-01 (VISA) ALVARADO, JORGE A UNIVERSITY OF CALIFORNIA 10 KIRKHAM STREET SAN FRANCISCO, CA 94143-0730 The use of wound healing retardants in glaucoma surgery

R01EY-08848-01 (VISA) SAKAI, HIROKO M NEW YORK UNIV MEDICAL CENTER 550 FIRST AVENUE NEW YORK, NY 10016 Synaptic organization of vertebrate innner retina

R01EY-08850-01 (VISA) HUGHES, BRET A UNIVERITY OF MICHIGAN 1000 WALL STREET ANN ARBOR, MI 48105 Ion conductances in the retinal pigment epithelium

R55EY-08851-01A1 (VISA) LANGSTON, DEBORAH P EYE RESEARCH INSTITUTE 20 STANIFORD ST BOSTON, MA 02114 Ocular human cytomegalovirus infection in the rabbit

R29EY-08862-01 (VISB) JIANG, BAI-CHUAN UNIVERSITY OF HOUSTON 4901 CALHOUN BLVD HOUSTON, TX 77204-6052 Accomodation convergence and young-adult-onset myopia

R01EY-08868-01 (VISA) WILLIAMS, ROBERT W UNIVERSITY OF TENNESSEE, MEMPH 875 MONROE AVENUE MEMPHIS, TN 38163 Development and clonal structure of mammalian retina

R01EY-08871-01 (VISA) HILL, JAMES M LSU EYE CENTER 2020 GRAVIER STREET NEW ORLEANS, LA 70112-2234 Ocular pathogenesis and therapy of bacterial keratitis

R37EY-08879-01 (VISA) SEARS, MARVIN L YALE UNIVERSITY 330 CEDAR STREET NEW HAVEN, CT 06510 Physiology of the ciliary epithelial bilayer of the eye

R01EY-08882-01 (VISB) SCHOR, CLIFTON M UNIVERSITY OF CALIFORNIA SCHOOL OF OPTOMETRY BERKELEY, CA 94720 Disparity processing in sensory and motor visual systems

R01EY-08883-01 (VISA) DILLON, JAMES P COLUMBIA UNIVERSITY 630 WEST 168TH STREET NEW YORK, NY 10032 Photophysical studies on the constituents of human eye

R01EY-08885-01 (VISA) LARGE, THOMAS H CASE WESTERN RESERVE UNIVERSIT 2040 ADELBERT RD CLEVELAND, OH 44106 Role of nerve growth factor in retinal development

R01EY-08886-01A1 (VISA) SVOBODA, KATHY K BOSTON UNIVERSITY 80 EAST CONCORD STREET BOSTON, MA 02118 Biology of the embryonic corneal epithelium

R01EY-08888-02 (CBY) LILIEN, JACK E CLEMSON UNIVERSITY CLEMSON, SC 29634-2903 Molecular biology of retina cell surface transferase

R01EY-08889-02 (VISA) MCDONNELL, JAN M DOHENY EYE INSTITUTE 1355 SAN PABLO ST LOS ANGELES, CA 90033 Human papillomavirus in conjunctival squamous dysplasia and carcinoma

R01EY-08890-01 (VISB) SCHALL, JEFFREY D VANDERBILT UNIVERSITY 004 DAVID K. WILSON HALL NASHVILLE, TN 37240 Basis of saccade target selection-- Frontal cortex

R01EY-08893-01A1 (VISA) ADAMS, ANTHONY J UNIVERSITY OF CALIFORNIA BERKELEY, CA 94720 Myopia development in children

R01EY-08898-01A1 (VISB) MERIGAN, WILLIAM H UNIV OF ROCHESTER MEDICAL CENT BOX 314 ROCHESTER, NY 14642 Parallel pathways in primate visual cortex

R01EY-08900-01 (NEUC) WORLEY, PAUL F JOHNS HOPKINS UNIVERSITY 725 NORTH WOLFE STREET BALTIMORE, MD 21205 Regulatory gene induction by activity in visual cortex

R01EY-08904-01 (VISA) INANA, GEORGE BASCOM PALMER EYE INSTITUTE PO BOX 016880 MIAMI, FL 33101 Gyrate atrophy-model for molecular study of eye diseases

R01EY-08905-01 (VISA) NGUYEN, THAI D UNIVERSITY OF CALIFORNIA SAN FRANCISCO, CA 94143-0730 HTM steroid inductions by cloning methods

R01EY-08906-01A1 (VISB) CUSICK, CATHERINE G TULANE UNIVERSITY MEDICAL CENT 1430 TULANE AVENUE NEW ORLEANS, LA 70112 Organization of superior temporal polymodal cortex

R01EY-08915-01 (VISA) KAPLAN, HENRY J WASHINGTON UNIV SCHOOL OF MED 660 SOUTH EUCLID AVE, BOX 8096 ST LOUIS, MO 63110 Experimental murine CMV (MCMV) retinitis

R01EY-08921-01A1 (VISB) GRZYWACZ, NORBERTO M SMITH KETTLEWELL EYE RES INST 2232 WEBSTER STREET SAN FRANCISCO, CA 94115 Facilitation and inhibition in directional selectivity

R01EY-08922-01 (VISA) LUKASIEWICZ, PETER D WASHINGTON UNIVERSITY SCH OF M 660 SOUTH EUCLID AVE, BOX 8096 ST LOUIS, MO 63110 Synaptic transmission and its modulation in the retina

R01EY-08969-01 (VISA) SPRAY, DAVID C ALBERT EINSTEIN COLLEGE OF MED 1300 MORRIS PARK AVENUE BRONX, N Y 10461 Lens gap junctions--Identity and properties

R01EY-08972-01 (VISA) FERGUSON, THOMAS A WASHINGTON UNIVERSITY 660 SOUTH EUCLID AVE PO BOX 80 ST LOUIS, MO 63110 the effect of light on the ocular immune response

R01EY-08975-01 (VISA) MANESS, PATRICIA F UNIVERSITY OF NC AT CHAPEL HIL AND BIOPHYSICS CHAPEL HILL, NC 27599-7260 Light-activated tyrosine phosphorylation in the retina

R01EY-08977-01A1 (VISA) MILLER, MICHAEL H MONTEFIORE MEDICAL CENTER 111 EAST 210TH STREET BRONX, NY 10467 Intraocular antibiotic pharmacokinetics

R43EY-09000-01 (VISB) PRESSER, ADOLPH MMTC, INC 12 ROSZEL ROAD PRINCETON, NJ 08540 Improved apparatus for treating intraocular melanomas

R43EY-09002-01 (VISB) SCHLIER, ROBERT CANDELA LASER CORPORATION 530 BOSTON POST ROAD WAYLAND, MA 01778 Laser hemostasis with silicon naphthalocyanines

R43EY-09003-01 (VISB) DOIRON, DANIEL R LASERTHERAPEUTICS INC PO BOX 1965 94 COMMERCE DR BUELLTON, CA 93427 Laser induced hyperthermia of ocular tumors

R43EY-09014-01 (VISB) PARENTAEAU, NANCY L ORGANOGENESIS, INC 83 ROGERS STREET CAMBRIDGE, MA 02142 Construction of a human cornea in vitro

R43EY-09015-01A1 (SSS) WARD, WARREN W FOURWARD TECHNOLOGIES 9932 PROSPECT AVENUE SANTEE, CA 92071 Laser anomaloscope

R43EY-09017-01 (VISB) KLOPOTEK, PETER J SUMMIT TECHNOLOGY INC 150 COOLIDGE AVE WATERTOWN, MA 02172 Beam homogeneizer for excimer laser refractive surgery

R43EY-09021-01A1 (VISB) KELLEHER, PETER J HOUSTON BIOTECHNOLOGY, INC 3608 RESEARCH FOREST DRIVE THE WOODLANDS, TX 77381 PVR-- An

PROJECT NO., ORGANIZATIONAL UNIT., INVESTIGATOR, ADDRESS, TITLE

immunopharmacological approach to treatment
R43EY-09022-01 (VISB) KELLEHER, PETER J HOUSTON BIOTECHNOLOGY INC 3608 RESEARCH FOREST DRIVE THE WOODLANDS, TX 77381 Glaucoma filtering surgery: improved by drug conjugates
R01EY-09024-01 (ARRC) LIPTON, STUART A CHILDREN'S HOSPITAL CORP 300 LONGWOOD AVENUE BOSTON, MA 02115 Ca2+ channel antagonists and AIDS-related neurotoxicity
R01EY-09031-01 (VISA) KAN-MITCHELL, JUNE UNIV OF SOUTHERN CALIFORNIA 2025 ZONAL AVE LOS ANGELES, CA 90033 Cytolytic T cells in uveal melanoma
R29EY-09038-01 (VISB) VAUGHAN, DANA K UNIVERSITY OF UTAH 410 CHIPETA WAY SALT LAKE CITY, UT 84108 Cell biology of teleost horizontal cells
R01EY-09040-01 (MGN) NIKOSKELAINEN, EEVA K UNIVERSITY OF TURKU KIINAMYLLYNKATU 4-8 20520 TURKU FINLAND Gene defects and clinical variation in Leber disease
R01EY-09041-01 (VISB) SREBRO, RICHARD UNIV OF TEXAS SOUTHWEST MED CT 5323 HARRY HINES BLVD DALLAS, TX 75235-9057 Localizing brain activity with visually evoked potentials (VEP's)
R01EY-09045-05 (NEUC) ZIPURSKY, STEPHEN L UCLA SCHOOL OF MEDICINE CTR FOR HEALTH SCIENCES LOS ANGELES, CA 90024-1737 Molecular genetics of a Drosophila retinal antigen
R13EY-09046-01 (VSN) FUNG, BERNARD K UNIVERSITY OF CALIFORNIA 100 STEIN PLAZA LOS ANGELES, CA 90024-7008 1991 FASEB conference--Biology and chemistry of vision
R01EY-09051-01 (VISA) SUZUKI, SHINTARO DOHENY EYE INSTITUTE 1355 SAN PABLO STREET LOS ANGELES, CA 90033 Structure and function of ocular proteoglycans
R01EY-09056-01 (VISA) GORDON, MARION K TUFTS UNIVERSITY SCHOOL OF MED 136 HARRISON AVE BOSTON, MA 02111 Regulation of fibril-associated collagens in cornea
R01EY-09057-01 (VISA) DARTT, DARLENE A EYE RESEARCH INSTITUTE 20 STANIFORD STREET BOSTON, MA 02114 Control of conjunctival goblet cell mucous production
R01EY-09065-01 (VISA) FURCHT, LEO T UNIVERSITY OF MINNESOTA 420 DELAWARE STREET SE MINNEAPOLIS, MN 55455 Type IV collagen peptides-receptors in corneal function
R01EY-09074-01 (VISA) WOLOSIN, JOSE M MOUNT SINAI SCHOOL OF MEDICINE ONE GUSTAVE L LEVY PLACE NEW YORK, NY 10029 Fluorophotometry of ion transport in ciliary body
R01EY-09076-01 (VISB) HOOD, DONALD C COLUMBIA UNIVERSITY 406 SCHERMERHORN NEW YORK, NY 10027 A measure of human receptor and post-receptor activity
R29EY-09081-02 (VISA) SANDELL, JULIE H BOSTON UNIVERSITY 80 EAST CONCORD ST BOSTON, MA 02118 Anatomy of the human inner nuclear layer
R01EY-09088-01 (VISA) RAO, NARSING A DOHENY EYE INSTITUTE 1355 SAN PABLO ST LOS ANGELES, CA 90033 Selective immune therapy of uveitis
R01EY-09092-01 (VISA) BLAKE, DIANE A MEHARRY MEDICAL COLLEGE 1005 D B TODD BLVD NASHVILLE, TN 37208 In vitro model of corneal wound healing--Role of matrix
R29EY-09112-01 (VISA) LEREA, CONNIE L NEW YORK MEDICAL COLLEGE BASIC SCIENCES BLDG VALHALLA, NY 10595 Study of transducin expression in human retinal cones
R01EY-09114-01 (VISA) CAPRIOLI, JOSEPH YALE UNIV SCHOOL OF MED 330 CEDAR ST, PO BOX 3333 NEW HAVEN, CT 06510 Molecular mechanisms of retinal ganglion cell damage
R01EY-09117-01 (VISA) MORRISON, JOHN C OREGON HEALTH SCIENCES UNIV 3181 SW SAM JACKSON PARK ROAD PORTLAND, OR 97201 Extracellular matrix composition of the optic nerve head
R01EY-09120-01 (VISB) HESTRIN, SHAUL UNIVERSITY OF CALIFORNIA 3RD & PARNASSUS SAN FRANCISCO, CA 94143-0444 Physiology and plasticity of visual cortical synapses
R01EY-09122-06 (MET) LORENZI, MARA EYE RESEARCH INSTITUTE 20 STANIFORD ST BOSTON, MA 02114 High glucose, DNA, and diabetic complications
R01EY-09129-01 (VISB) STEINMETZ, MICHAEL A JOHNS HOPKINS UNIVERSITY 725 NORTH WOLFE STREET BALTIMORE, MD 21205 Neurophysiology of posterior parietal cortex
R13EY-09132-01 (VSN) HALL, JAMES E UNIVERSITY OF CALIFORNIA COLLEGE OF MEDICINE IRVINE, CA 92715 International conference on gap junction
R01EY-09139-01 (VISB) JAHR, CRAIG E OREGON HEALTH SCIENCES UNIV 3181 SAM JACKSON PARK ROAD PORTLAND, OR 97201 Synaptic conductances of retinal bipolar cells
U10EY-09152-02 (VSN) MEINERT, CURTIS L JOHNS HOPKINS UNIVERSITY 615 NORTH WOLFE STREET BALTIMORE, MD 21205 Glaucoma laser trial followup study
R43EY-09154-01 (SSS) MOULTON, PETER F SCHWARTZ ELECTRO-OPTICS, INC 45 WINTHROP STREET CONCORD, MA 01742 Solid-state laser source for corneal ablation
R43EY-09155-01 (SSS) CAUGHEY, THOMAS A INRAD, INC 181 LEGRAND AVENUE NORTHVALE, NJ 07647 A solid state light source for corneal sculpting
R43EY-09156-01 (SSS) HSIA, JAMES C CANDELA LASER CORPORATION 530 BOSTON POST ROAD WAYLAND, MA 01778 Laser trabecular ablation
R43EY-09160-01 (VISB) BUDD, RONALD MIRA, INC 87 RUMFORD AVENUE WALTHAM, MA 02154 Electrocycloablation-a new treatment for glaucoma
R43EY-09166-01 (VISB) LAWTON, TERI A NANO TECH SERVICES 1775 WEST 25TH STREET EUGENE, ORGEON 97405 Low vision aid for observers with central vision losses
R43EY-09168-01 (VISB) DRUZGALA, PASCAL J XENON VISION, INC ONE PROGRESS BLVD, #36 ALACHUA, FL 32615 Novel CAI derivatives for topical application
R01EY-09169-01 (ARRC) ATHERTON, SALLY S UNIV OF MIAMI SCH OF MEDICINE PO BOX 016960 (R-138) MIAMI, FL 33101 Virologic and immunologic studies of murine CMV retinitis
R03EY-09183-01 (VSN) BRIGELL, MITCHELL G LOYOLA UNIVERSITY OF CHICAGO 2160 SOUTH FIRST AVENUE MAYWOOD, IL 60153 The pattern VEP--A multi-center pilot study
R03EY-09186-01 (VSN) KAMINSKI, HENRY J CLEVELAND VA MEDICAL CENTER 10701 EAST BLVD CLEVELAND, OH 44106 Expression of AChR mRNA in extraocular muscle

PROJECT NO., ORGANIZATIONAL UNIT., INVESTIGATOR, ADDRESS, TITLE

R01EY-09192-01 (VISA) GORIN, MICHAEL B EYE & EAR INST OF PITTSBURGH 203 LOTHROP ST PITTSBURGH, PA 15213 Mammalian inherited retinal disease--Molecular genetics
R01EY-09193-01 (VISA) THOMPSON, DEBRA A UNIVERSITY OF MICHIGAN 1000 WALL STREET ANN ARBOR, MI 48105 Signal transduction by G-proteins in the retinal pigment epithelium
R03EY-09198-01 (VSN) ZORN, MARK B NEW ENGLAND COLL OF OPTOMETRY 424 BEACON STREET BOSTON, MA 02115 Collagen gene expression during scleral maturation
R03EY-09202-01 (VSN) SNYDER, ROBERT W UNIVERSITY OF ARIZONA TUCSON, AZ 85724 TPA activity in steroid response glaucoma
R01EY-09207-01 (VISA) GREGERSON, DALE S UNIVERSITY OF MINNESOTA PO BOX 493 UMHC MINNEAPOLIS, MN 55455 Autoimmune uveoretinitis--Antigen presenting cells
R29EY-09210-01 (VISB) SCUDDER, CHARLES A EYE & EAR INST OF PITTSBURGH 203 LOTHROP STREET PITTSBURGH, PA 15213 Control of saccade size by cerebellar neurons
R01EY-09213-01 (VISA) WINDLE, JOLENE J CANCER THERAPY & RESEARCH CENT 4450 MEDICAL DRIVE SAN ANTONIO, TX 78229 Rb protein inactivation in the retina of transgenic mice
R03EY-09217-01 (VSN) EPSTEIN, LEON G UNIVERSITY OF ROCHESTER MED CT 601 ELMWOOD AVE, BOX 631 ROCHESTER, NY 14642 HIV infection of neural xenograft in rat eye
R03EY-09243-01 (VSN) HYDE, JAMES S MEDICAL COLLEGE OF WISCONSIN 8701 WATERTOWN PLANK RD MILWAUKEE, WI 53226 MRI of the eye at high spacial resolution
R03EY-09244-01 (VSN) MASUR, SANDRA K MOUNT SINAI SCHOOL OF MEDICINE ONE GUSTAVE L. LEVY PLACE NEW YORK, NY 10029 Keratocyte collagenase induced via fibronectin receptor
R01EY-09252-01 (VISA) KIM, KYUNGMANN DANA-FARBER CANCER INSTITUTE 44 BINNEY STREET BOSTON, MA 02115 Regression models for analysis of ophthalmological data
R29EY-09256-01 (VISA) MC MAHON, DOUGLAS G UNIVERSITY OF KENTUCKY COLLEGE OF MEDICINE LEXINGTON, KY 40536-0084 Mechanisms of retinal synaptic plasticity
R01EY-09258-01 (VISB) CAVANAGH, PATRICK HARVARD UNIVERSITY CAMBRIDGE, MA 02138 Processing streams in early vision
R55EY-09260-01 (VISB) HEINEN, STEPHEN J SMITH-KETTLEWELL EYE RES INST 2232 WEBSTER STREET SAN FRANCISCO, CA 94115 Oculomotor prediction in dorsomedial frontal cortex
R03EY-09266-01 (VSN) FLEISCHMAN, JULIAN B WASHINGTON UNIVERSITY SCH OF M 660 SOUTH EUCLID AVE, BOX 8093 ST LOUIS, MO 63110 Characterization of a plasma protein in pars planitis
R01EY-09268-01 (VISA) KRUPIN, THEODORE NORTHWESTERN UNIVERSITY MED SC 303 EAST CHICAGO AVENUE CHICAGO, IL 60611 Peptide and probe modulation of aqueous dynamics
R01EY-09275-01 (VISA) KARPEN, JEFFREY W UNIV OF COLORADO HEALTH SCI CT 4200 EAST NINTH AVE DENVER, CO 80262 Function and regulation of ion channels in retinal rods
R01EY-09278-01 (VISA) BENZER, SEYMOUR CALIFORNIA INSTITUTE OF TECH 1201 E CALIFORNIA BLVD PASADENA, CA 91125 Human retinal homologs of Drosophila eye genes
R01EY-09284-01 (VISA) PINSKY, PETER M STANFORD UNIVERSITY TERMAN ENGINEERING CENTER STANFORD, CA 94305-4020 Mechanical modelling of keratoplasty
R03EY-09287-01 (VSN) CINER, ELISE PENNSYLVANIA COLL OF OPTOMETRY 1200 WEST GODFREY AVE PHILADELPHIA, PA 19141 Enhancing stereotesting in children from 6 months to 5 years
R55EY-09289-01 (VISB) TUSA, RONALD J JOHNS HOPKINS HOSPITAL 600 NORTH WOLFE STREET BALTIMORE, MD 21205 Development of ocular motor control
R01EY-09296-01 (VISA) NOY, NOA CORNELL UNIVERSITY 1300 YORK AVE NEW YORK, NY 10021 Mechanisms of retinoid movement in the eye
R01EY-09298-01 (NEUC) KATZ, FLORA UT SOUTHWESTERN MEDICAL CENTER 5323 HARRY HINES BOULEVARD DALLAS, TX 75235-9050 Genes that influence neural connectivity in drosophila
R01EY-09299-01 (VISA) MOSES, KEVIN UNIV OF SOUTHERN CALIFORNIA UNIVERSITY PARK LOS ANGELES, CA 90089-1340 Retina--Developmental switch to photoreceptor cell fate
R01EY-09300-01 (VISA) DE PINHO, RONALD A ALBERT EINSTEIN COLL OF MED 1300 MORRIS PARK AVENUE BRONX, NY 10461 Molecular genetics of lens and cataract development
R01EY-09303-01 (VISA) NEITZ, MAUREEN E MEDICAL COLLEGE OF WISCONSIN 8700 W WISCONSIN AVE MILWAUKEE, WI 53226 Genes and visual pigments of red-green color vision
R29EY-09311-01 (VISA) KOTARSKI, MICHAEL A WEST VIRGINIA UNIVERSITY 311 BROOKS HALL MORGANTOWN, WV 26505-6057 Asteroid gene function in Drosophila eye development
R01EY-09314-01 (SRCM) VICTOR, JONATHAN D CORNELL UNIVERSITY 525 E 68TH ST RM STARR 604 NEW YORK, NY 10021 Neural computations in visual cortex
R43EY-09315-01 (SSS) FREDIN, LEIF G ANTROPIX CORPORATION 46 WEST WEDGEWOOD GLEN WOODLANDS, TX 77381 Laser system for photothermal intrastromal keratoplasty
R43EY-09324-01 (VISB) KELLEHER, PETER J HOUSTON BIOTECHNOLOGY, INC 3608 RESEARCH FOREST DRIVE THE WOODLANDS, TX 77381 IOL-immobilized immunotoxins to prevent secondary catara
R43EY-09325-01 (VISB) YEN, DUEN H MULTIPATH SYSTEMS, INC 1255 NUUANU AVE HONOLULU, HI 96817-4017 Rangefinder system for the blind
R01EY-09331-01 (NLS) GOLDMAN, JAMES E COLUMBIA UNIVERSITY 630 WEST 168TH STREET NEW YORK, NY 10032 Studies of the lens protein alpha-crystallin B chain
R01EY-09332-06 (IMB) GREENE, MARK I UNIVERSITY OF PENNSYLVANIA 36TH & HAMILTON WALK PHILADELPHIA, PA 19104-6082 Immunobiology of antireceptor-receptor interactions
R29EY-09355-01 (PHRA) REGAN, JOHN W UNIVERSITY OF ARIZONA COLLEGE OF PHARMACY TUCSON, AZ 85721 Cloning and mutagenesis of alpha adrenergic receptors
S15EY-09443-01 (NSS) TOWNS, LEX C KIRKSVILLE COLLEGE OF 800 WEST JEFFERSON KIRKSVILLE, MO 63501 Small instrumentation grant
S15EY-09444-01 (NSS) EBENHOLTZ, SHELDON M SUNY/COLLEGE OF OPTOMETRY 100 EAST 24TH STREET NEW YORK, NY 10010 Small instrumentation grant

PROJECT NUMBER LISTING

PROJECT NO., ORGANIZATIONAL UNIT., INVESTIGATOR, ADDRESS, TITLE

S15EY-09445-01 (NSS) GAMLIN, PAUL D R UNIVERSITY OF ALABAMA 512 WORRELL BLDG BIRMINGHAM, AL 35294 Small instrumentation grant
S15EY-09446-01 (NSS) ZIESKE, JAMES D EYE RESEARCH INSTITUTE 20 STANIFORD ST BOSTON, MA 02114 Small instrumentation grant
S15EY-09447-01 (NSS) WINKLER, BARRY S OAKLAND UNIVERSITY ROCHESTER, MI 48309-4401 Small instrumentation grant
S15EY-09448-01 (NSS) LEAVITT, JOHN CALIF INSTITUTE FOR MED RESEAR 2260 CLOVE DRIVE SAN JOSE, CA 95128 Small instrumentation grant
S15EY-09449-01 (NSS) ENOCH, JAY M UNIVERSITY OF CALIFORNIA 350 MINOR HALL BERKELEY, CA 94720 Small instrumentation grant
S15EY-09450-01 (NSS) WONG, DAVID T W HARVARD SCHOOL OF DENTAL MED 188 LONGWOOD AVENUE BOSTON, MA 02115 Small instrumentation grant
S15EY-09451-01 (NSS) OKABE, TORU BAYLOR COLLEGE OF DENTISTRY 3302 GASTON AVENUE DALLAS, TX 75246 Small instrumentation grant
S15EY-09452-01 (NSS) BARMACK, NEAL H R S DOW NEUROL SCI INST 1120 N W 20TH AVENUE PORTLAND, OR 97209 Small instrumentation grant
S15EY-09453-01 (NSS) DE VOE, ROBERT D INDIANA UNIVERSITY 800 EAST ATWATER BLOOMINGTON, IN 47405 Small instrumentation grant
S15EY-09454-01 (NSS) TYLER, CHRISTOPHER W SMITH-KETTLEWELL EYE RES INST 2232 WEBSTER STREET SAN FRANCISCO, CA 94115 Small instrumentation grant
S15EY-09455-01 (NSS) MARGHERIO, RAYMOND R WILLIAM BEAUMONT HOSPITAL 3601 WEST 13 MILE ROAD ROYAL OAK, MI 48073-2793 Small instrumentation grant
S15EY-09456-01 (NSS) HALVORSON, HARLYN O MARINE BIOLOGICAL LABORATORY WATER STREET WOODS HOLE, MA 02543 Small instrumentation grant
S15EY-09457-01 (NSS) NEDEAU, JOHN G MASS. EYE & EAR INFIRMARY 243 CHARLES ST BOSTON, MA 02114 Small instrumentation grant
S15EY-09458-01 (NSS) BIRCH, DAVID G RETINA FDN OF THE SOUTHWEST 8220 WALNUT HILL LANE DALLAS, TX 75231-4170 Small instrumentation grant
S15EY-09459-01 (NSS) OGDEN, THOMAS E DOHENY EYE INSTITUTE 1355 SAN PABLO STREET LOS ANGELES, CA 90033 Small instrumentation grant
S15EY-09460-01 (NSS) DONOSO, LARRY A WILLS EYE HOSPITAL NINTH & WALNUT STREETS PHILADELPHIA, PA 19107 Small instrumentation grant
S15EY-09461-01 (NSS) LITSTER, J DAVID MASSACHUSETTS INST OF TECHNOLO 77 MASSACHUSETTS AVE CAMBRIDGE, MA 02139 Small instrumentation grant
S15EY-09462-01 (NSS) MILLER, JAMES D CENTRAL INSTITUTE FOR THE DEAF 818 S EUCLID AVE ST LOUIS, MO 63110 Small instrumentation grant
S15EY-09463-01 (NSS) BROWN, ARTHUR C OHSU SCHOOL OF DENTISTRY 611 SW CAMPUS DRIVE PORTLAND, OR 97201-3098 Small instrumentation grant
S15EY-09464-01 (NSS) GALLETTI, PIERRE M BROWN UNIVERSITY BOX G A117 PROVIDENCE, R I 02912 Small instrumentation grant
S15EY-09465-01 (NSS) BUSE, MARIA G MED. UNIV. OF SOUTH CAROLINA 171 ASHLEY AVENUE CHARLESTON, SC 29425 Small instrumentation grant
S15EY-09466-01 (NSS) FRISHMAN, LAURA J UNIVERSITY OF HOUSTON 4901 CALHOUN ROAD HOUSTON, TX 77204-6052 Small instrumentation grant
S15EY-09467-01 (NSS) THOFT, RICHARD A EYE & EAR INST. OF PITTSBURGH 203 LOTHROP STREET PITTSBURGH, PA 15213 Small instrumentation grant
S15EY-09468-01 (NSS) WILLIAMS, HIBBARD E UNIVERSITY OF CALIFORNIA DAVIS, CA 95616 Small instrumentation grant
S15EY-09469-01 (NSS) CONSIGLI, RICHARD A KANSAS STATE UNIVERSITY MANHATTAN, KS 66506 Small instrumentation grant
S15EY-09470-01 (NSS) ORIAS, EDUARDO UNIVERSITY OF CALIFORNIA DEPT OF BIOLOGICAL SCIENCES SANTA BARBARA, CA 93106 Small instrumentation grant
S15EY-09471-01 (NSS) NEWKOME, GEORGE R UNIVERSITY OF SOUTH FLORIDA 4202 E FOWLER AVE TAMPA, FL 33620-7900 Small instrumentation grant
S15EY-09472-01 (NSS) REED, PETER W VANDERBILT UNIVERSITY 411 KIRKLAND HALL NASHVILLE, TN 37240 Small instrumentation grant
S15EY-09473-01 (NSS) FRANK, JOY S UCLA SCHOOL OF MEDICINE LOS ANGELES, CA 90024-1722 Small instrumentation grant
S15EY-09474-01 (NSS) FELEPPA, ERNEST J RIVERSIDE RESEARCH INSTITUTION 330 WEST 42ND STREET NEW YORK, NY 10036 Small instrumentation grant
S15EY-09475-01 (NSS) STEVENS, C E N C STATE UNIV-VET MED 4700 HILLSBOROUGH STREET RALEIGH, NC 27606 Small instrumentation grant
S15EY-09476-01 (NSS) CRAWFORD, MORRIS L UNIV OF TEXAS HEALTH SCI CTR 6420 LAMAR FLEMING AVENUE HOUSTON, TX 77030 Small instrumentation grant
S15EY-09477-01 (NSS) ZIMMERMAN, WILLIAM F AMHERST COLLEGE AMHERST, MA 01002 Small instrumentation grant
R43EY-09483-01 (VISB) TUCKETT, ROBERT P TOPICAL TESTING, INC 1141 EAST 3900 SOUTH SALT LAKE CITY, UT 84124 A model of ocular irritancy
R01EY-09498-01 (VISA) RAPOPORT, BASIL UNIVERSITY OF CALIFORNIA 4150 CLEMENT STREET SAN FRANCISCO, CA 94121 Pathogenesis of Graves' opthalmopathy
R01EY-09511-01 (VISB) VIMAL, RAM L NEW ENGLAND COLLEGE OF OPTOMET 424 BEACON STREET BOSTON, MA 02115 Spatiotemporal characteristics of visual channels
R01EY-09521-01 (VISA) PANDE, AJAY K BOSTON BIOMEDICAL RESEARCH INS 20 STANIFORD STREET BOSTON, MA 02114 Protein glycation--Structure and stability of products
R01EY-09631-01 (VISA) YAMAZAKI, AKIO WAYNE STATE UNIVERSITY 4717 ST ANTOINE DETROIT, MI 48201 G-protein-effector interaction in rod photoreceptors
R03EY-09635-01 (VSN) WU, GLORIA RETINA ASSOCIATES 100 CHARLES RIVER PLAZA BOSTON, MA 02114 The electroretinogram in background diabetic retinopathy
R29EY-09636-01 (VISA) COOPER, KIM E ARIZONA STATE UNIVERSITY TEMPE, AZ 85287-1501 Inwardly rectifying potassium current in rabbit lens
R03EY-09667-01 (VSN) PETROLL, WALTER M UNIV OF TX SOUTHWESTERN MED CT 5323 HARRY HINES BLVD DALLAS, TX 75235-9057 In vivo analysis of corneal endothelial wound healing
N01EY-72145-21 ( ) AIELLO, LLOYD M** Evaluate early treatment of diabetic retinopathy
N01EY-92103-24 ( ) THYLETORS, BJORN** WHO program for the prevention of blindness
N01EY-92108-03 ( ) GIOVANNI, MARAINI** Collaborative Italian-American study of age-related cataract
N01EY-92109-04 ( ) WOLF, PHILIP A** Framingham offspring eye study
R01GM-00091-46 (PC) RAJAGOPALAN, K V DUKE UNIVERSITY MEDICAL CENTER BOX 3711 DURHAM, NC 27710 Structure and function of enzymes--Role of metals
K04GM-00517-04 (SAT) DUNN, DAVID L UNIVERSITY OF MINNESOTA BOX 242, MAYO BUILDING MINNEAPOLIS, MINN 55455 Immunotherapy during gram-negative bacterial sepsis
K04GM-00521-04 (MBY) WICKENS, MARVIN P UNIV OF WISCONSIN-MADISON DEPT OF BIOCHEM/420 HENRY MALL MADISON, WI 53706 Cleavage, polyadenylation, and transport of mRNA precurs
K04GM-00522-04 (GEN) MC KEE, BRUCE D UNIVERSITY OF TENNESSEE M313 WALTERS LIFE SCI BLDG KNOXVILLE, TN 37996 Stimulation of chromosome pairing and exchange by rDNA
K04GM-00527-04 (BMT) FRIESNER, RICHARD A COLUMBIA UNIVERSITY NEW YORK, NEW YORK 10027 Theoretical studies of metalloprotein chromophores
K04GM-00528-03 (GEN) FITZGERALD-HAYES, MOLLY UNIVERSITY OF MASSACHUSETTS DEPARTMENT OF BIOCHEMISTRY AMHERST, MA 01003 Analysis of components involved in centromere function
K04GM-00536-03 (BBCA) SCHENCK, CRAIG C COLORADO STATE UNIVERSITY DEPT OF BIOCHEMISTRY FORT COLLINS, CO 80523 Bacterial reaction center dynamics
K04GM-00546-03 (MBY) ARES, MANUEL UNIVERSITY OF CALIFORNIA 1156 HIGH STREET SANTA CRUZ, CA 95064 Structure & function of yeast SNRNPS
K04GM-00550-02 (BNP) KOHN, JOACHIM B RUTGERS, STATE UNIV OF NJ PO BOX 939 PISCATAWAY, NJ 08855-0939 New biopolymers derived from alpha-l-amino acids
K04GM-00559-02 (BNP) LIU, HUNG-WEN UNIVERSITY OF MINNESOTA 207 PLEASANT STREET, SE MINNEAPOLIS, MN 55455 Mechanistic study of radicals in biology catalysis
K04GM-00562-02 (PC) GELB, MICHAEL H UNIVERSITY OF WASHINGTON SEATTLE, WA 98195 RCDA in enzymology and protein isoprenylation
K04GM-00563-02 (ALY) SEN, RANJAN BRANDEIS UNIVERSITY PO BOX 9110 WALTHAM, MA 02254-9110 Regulation of receptors on T-lymphocytes
K04GM-00570-02 (MET) VARY, THOMAS C PENNSYLVANIA STATE UNIVERSITY PO BOX 850 HERSHEY, PA 17033 Regulation of protein synthesis in sepsis
K04GM-00575-02 (MCHA) CHA, JIN K UNIVERSITY OF ALABAMA BOX 87036 TUSCALOOSA, AL 35487-0336 Total synthesis of mycotoxins and related compounds
K04GM-00581-01 (SAT) BUCHMAN, TIMOTHY G JOHNS HOPKINS HOSPITAL 600 N WOLFE ST/HALSTED 612 BALTIMORE, MD 22105 Liver gene expression in multiple organ system failure
S14GM-02716-05 (MPRC) HAMMONS, GEORGE J PHILANDER SMITH COLLEGE 812 W 13TH ST LITTLE ROCK, AR 72202 MBRS program at Philander Smith College
S14GM-02716-05 0001 (MPRC) HAMMONS, GEORGE J MBRS program at Philander Smith College Brain glutamate dehydrogenase--Characterization in young and old rats
S14GM-02716-05 0002 (MPRC) WOODS, WILLIAM H MBRS program at Philander Smith College Influence of chronic alcohol administration on neuronal morphology in rats
S06GM-02721-07 (SRC) CIMADEVILLA, JOSE M ST MARY'S UNIVERSITY ONE CAMINO SANTA MARIA SAN ANTONIO, TEXAS 78228 Multidisciplinary minority biomedical research program
S06GM-02721-07 0001 (SRC) ALVARES, FREDERICK Multidisciplinary minority biomedical research program Enrichment program
S06GM-02721-07 0002 (SRC) CIMADEVILLA, JOSE M Multidisciplinary minority biomedical research program Identification of target genes for Pit-1 & related POU domain proteins
S06GM-02721-07 0003 (SRC) GOLDBERG, IRWIN S Multidisciplinary minority biomedical research program Turbulence during high frequency ventilation
S06GM-02721-07 0004 (SRC) MAGHSOUDI, RAHBAR Multidisciplinary minority biomedical research program Anesthesia monitoring/control system using feedback/expert system
S06GM-02721-07 0005 (SRC) REZAIE, BAHMAN Multidisciplinary minority biomedical research program Carpal scaphoid fracture detection by image processing techniques
S06GM-02721-07 0006 (SRC) TRANKINA, MICHELE Multidisciplinary minority biomedical research program Effects of diet/food restriction on insulin processing by hepatocytes
S14GM-02866-07 (MPRC) ARAFAT, ELSAYED S RUST COLLEGE 150 RUST AVENUE HOLLY SPRINGS, MS 38635 Minority biomedical research support program at Rust College
S14GM-02866-07 0001 (MPRC) WATSON, EDNA S Minority biomedical research support program at Rust College Research enrichment plan
S14GM-02866-07 0002 (MPRC) ARAFAT, EL SAYED Minority biomedical research support program at Rust College Steroid metabolites in plasma of patients with premenstral syndrome
S14GM-02867-05 (MPRC) SINGH, JARNAIL STILLMAN COLLEGE P O BOX 1430 TUSCALOOSA, AL 35403 MBRS program at Stillman College
K06GM-03874-28 (NCR) GARTLER, STANLEY M UNIVERSITY OF WASHINGTON SEATTLE, WASH 98195 Mammalian somatic cell genetics
S14GM-04303-03 (GRS) JOHNSON, DAVID W COLLEGE OF SANTA FE ST MICHAEL'S DRIVE SANTA FE, NM 87501 MBRS undergraduate program at the College of Santa Fe
S14GM-04531-03 (GRS) JORDAN, CHESTER L GRAMBLING STATE UNIVERSITY DEPT OF BIOLOGICAL SCIENCES GRAMBLING, LA 71245 MBRS program at Grambling State University
S14GM-04564-03 (GRS) MAHAJAN, SATISH C LANE COLLEGE 545 LANE AVENUE JACKSON, TN 38301 MBRS program at Lane College
R01GM-04725-35 (BBCA) STURTEVANT, JULIAN M YALE UNIVERSITY DEPT OF CHEM, BOX 6666 NEW HAVEN, CT 06511 Physicochemical studies of biochemical reactions
R01GM-04842-36 (BIO) HESS, GEORGE P CORNELL UNIVERSITY 216 BIOTECHNOLOGY BUILDING ITHACA, NEW YORK 14853-2703 Relationships

PROJECT NO., ORGANIZATIONAL UNIT., INVESTIGATOR, ADDRESS, TITLE

between protein structure and function
R01GM-05147-35 (MCHA) STORK, GILBERT COLUMBIA UNIVERSITY BOX 666 NEW YORK, NY 10027 Synthesis of biologically active natural products
S14GM-05231-04 (MPRC) KOCHHAR, TEJINDER S KENTUCKY STATE UNIVERSITY FRANKFORT, KY 40601 Kentucky State University Research Support Programs
S14GM-05231-04 0001 (MPRC) JIANG, K S Kentucky State University Research Support Programs Enrichment activities
S14GM-05231-04 0002 (MPRC) KOCHHAR, T S Kentucky State University Research Support Programs Induction of chromosome changes in mammalian cells
S14GM-05364-03 (GRS) WILMER, LEONARD SOUTHERN UNIV/NATURAL SCIENCE 3050 MARTIN LUTHER KING SHREVEPORT, LA 71107 Development of MBS program for a two-year community college
R37GM-05472-33 (BMT) BIEMANN, KLAUS MASSACHUSETTS INST OF TECHNOLO 77 MASSACHUSETTS AVENUE CAMBRIDGE, MA 02139 Mass spectrometric sequencing of proteins
S14GM-05966-02 (MPRC) BACON, ARTHUR L TALLADEGA COLLEGE 627 WEST BATTLE STREET TALLADEGA, AL 35160 Talladega college biomedical research
R01GM-06048-33 (MBC) MAAS, WERNER K NEW YORK UNIV MEDICAL CTR 550 FIRST AVENUE NEW YORK, N Y 10016 Molecular mechanisms of regulation in bacteria
R37GM-06196-33 (PC) LEHMAN, I R STANFORD UNIVERSITY DEPARTMENT OF BIOCHEMISTRY STANFORD, CA 94305-5307 DNA replication in eukaryotes
R01GM-06590-32A1 (BIO) REED, LESTER J UNIVERSITY OF TEXAS CHEMISTRY DEPARTMENT AUSTIN, TX 78712 Biochemistry of alpha-keto acid dehydrogenase complexes
R37GM-06920-32 (NSS) LIPSCOMB, WILLIAM N HARVARD UNIVERSITY 12 OXFORD STREET CAMBRIDGE, MA 02138 Structure and function of biologically active molecules
R01GM-07261-31 (BIO) LOWENSTEIN, JOHN M BRANDEIS UNIVERSITY WALTHAM, MA 02254 Regulation and function of adenosine production in heart
R01GM-07446-33 (MBC) MAGASANIK, BORIS MASSACHUSETTS INST OF TECHNOLO 77 MASSACHUSETTS AVENUE CAMBRIDGE, MA 02139 Regulation and function of glutamine synthetase
R37GM-07581-31 (BIO) KORNBERG, ARTHUR STANFORD UNIVERSITY DEPARTMENT OF BIOCHEMISTRY STANFORD, CALIF 94305-5307 Mechanism and control of initiation of DNA replication
R01GM-07768-32 (BIO) HAGER, LOWELL P UNIVERSITY OF ILLINOIS 1209 W. CALIFORNIA URBANA, ILL 61801 Enzymatic activation mechanisms
R01GM-07816-32 (MBC) STRAUSS, BERNARD S CUMMINGS LIFE SCIENCE CENTER 920 E 58TH ST, CLSC 955 CHICAGO, ILL 60637 A study of the mode of action of chemical mutagens
R01GM-07874-27 (MCHA) WASSERMAN, HARRY H YALE UNIVERSITY 12 PROSPECT PLACE NEW HAVEN, CT 06511-3516 Methods applicable to beta-lactam and alkoid syntheses
S06GM-08003-21 (SRC) ROBINSON, JACK L SOUTHEASTERN OKLAHOMA ST UNIV STATION A, BOX 4133 DURANT, OK 74701 Southeastern Oklahoma biomedical sciences program
S06GM-08003-21 0006 (SRC) EGGLETON, GORDON L Southeastern Oklahoma biomedical sciences program Heterocyclic thione inhibitors of dopamine beta-hydroxylase
S06GM-08003-21 0007 (SRC) WRIGHT, JOHN R Southeastern Oklahoma biomedical sciences program Inorganic antibody labels for biomedical applications
S06GM-08003-21 0008 (SRC) FIETKAU, RONALD Southeastern Oklahoma biomedical sciences program Rapid ultratrace analysis of biological slurries
S06GM-08003-21 0009 (SRC) WASMUND, LOIDE M Southeastern Oklahoma biomedical sciences program Polypeptide derivatives synthesis and testing as collagenase inhibitors
S06GM-08005-20 (SRC) KONDO, NORMAN S UNIV OF DISTRICT OF COLUMBIA 4200 CONNECTICUT AVE N W WASHINGTON, D C 20008 UDC biomedical research program
S06GM-08005-20 0003 (SRC) KONDO, NORMAN S UDC biomedical research program Alkylated nucleotides as antiviral prodrugs and models
S06GM-08005-20 0005 (SRC) COUSIN, CAROLYN E UDC biomedical research program Nervous system development of Schistosomes
S06GM-08005-20 0007 (SRC) THORSTENSON, PATRICIA C UDC biomedical research program Potential precursors of phosphorus-based amino acids analogs
S06GM-08005-20 0008 (SRC) VAUGHN-COOKE, ANNA F UDC biomedical research program Emergence of semantic categories in the language of Black children
S06GM-08005-20 0009 (SRC) POSEY, ISADORA UDC biomedical research program Lariat ether-mediated cation transport
S06GM-08005-20 0010 (SRC) PROUTY, MURIEL UDC biomedical research program Intermolecular forces in hemoglobin S assembly and gelation
S06GM-08008-21 (SRC) KLEIN, CHERYL L XAVIER UNIVERSITY 7325 PALMETTO STREET NEW ORLEANS, LA 70125 MBRS biomedical research at Xavier University
S06GM-08008-21 0016 (SRC) KISHORE, VIMAL MBRS biomedical research at Xavier University Drug activity modification in copper deficiency
S06GM-08008-21 0017 (SRC) KLEIN, CHERYL L MBRS biomedical research at Xavier University X-ray and structural studies of tricyclic neuroleptics
S06GM-08008-21 0021 (SRC) O'CONNOR, SALLY E MBRS biomedical research at Xavier University Role of cysteine proteinases in glomerulonephritis
S06GM-08012-21 (MPRC) RAEL, EPPIE D UNIVERSITY OF TEXAS EL PASO, TX 79968 MBRS Program at the University of Texas at El Paso
S06GM-08012-21 0008 (MPRC) PANNELL, KEITH H MBRS Program at the University of Texas at El Paso Physiological studies with ionophores
S06GM-08012-21 0011 (MPRC) GOGGIN, JUDITH P MBRS Program at the University of Texas at El Paso Cognitive performance as a function of bilingualism
S06GM-08012-21 0012 (MPRC) RAEL, EPPI D MBRS Program at the University of Texas at El Paso Rattlesnake proteases that affect blood coagulation and complement
S06GM-08012-21 0013 (MPRC) ARENAZ, PABLO MBRS Program at the University of Texas at El Paso Temporal modulation of DNA repair processes
S06GM-08012-21 0014 (MPRC) DAVIS, MICHAEL I MBRS Program at the University of Texas at El Paso Thermodynamic studies of amphiphile + water systems
S06GM-08012-21 0015 (MPRC) MUGANDA-OJIKAU, PERPETUA MBRS Program at the University of Texas at El Paso Role of protein kinases in cytomegalovirus induced neoplasa
S06GM-08012-21 0016 (MPRC) ROJO, JAVIER MBRS Program at the University of Texas at El Paso Estimating life distributions after exposure to hazardous environments
S06GM-08016-21 (MPRC) LITTLETON, GEORGE K HOWARD UNIVERSITY FOURTH AND COLLEGE STREETS, SW WASHINGTON, DC 20059 Biomedical interdisciplinary project
S06GM-08016-21 0027 (MPRC) DUFFIELD, RICHARD M Biomedical interdisciplinary project Chemical releasers in hymenoptera
S06GM-08016-21 0035 (MPRC) HURDLIK, PAUL F Biomedical interdisciplinary project Organosilicon intermediates for the synthesis of organic compounds
S06GM-08016-21 0039 (MPRC) LEWIS, MICHAEL I Biomedical interdisciplinary project Neurobehavioral studies of alcohol reinforcement and tolerance--A continuation
S06GM-08016-21 0044 (MPRC) ROSENBERG, ROBERT C Biomedical interdisciplinary project DBH inhibition by antihypertensive and other compounds
S06GM-08016-21 0048 (MPRC) YUN, JOHN C H Biomedical interdisciplinary project Prostacyclin and muscarinic receptors in the renal response to acetylcholine
S06GM-08016-21 0052 (MPRC) HARRELL, JULES P Biomedical interdisciplinary project Physiological stress in an African American population
S06GM-08016-21 0056 (MPRC) TROUTH, C OVID Biomedical interdisciplinary project Role of superficial chemosensitive brainstem neurons in infant apnea
S06GM-08016-21 0062 (MPRC) SMITH, THOMAS E Biomedical interdisciplinary project Chemistry of enzymatic carboxylation reactions
S06GM-08016-21 0071 (MPRC) PAYNE-JOHNSON, JOAN C Biomedical interdisciplinary project Functional communication of normal aged from institutional and community settings
S06GM-08016-21 0072 (MPRC) ANDERSON, WINSTON A Biomedical interdisciplinary project Subcellular localization of estrogen receptor activity
S06GM-08016-21 0073 (MPRC) CARPENTIER, ROBERT G Biomedical interdisciplinary project Mechanisms of the cardiac arrhythmogenic actions of substances of abuse
S06GM-08016-21 0074 (MPRC) DAVIS, ELAINE J Biomedical interdisciplinary project Factors involved in bacterial conjugal transfer replication
S06GM-08016-21 0075 (MPRC) ECKBERG, WILLIAM R Biomedical interdisciplinary project C-kinase as a regulator of meiotic maturation
S06GM-08016-21 0076 (MPRC) FRANKEL, JACK S Biomedical interdisciplinary project Allelic expression during the development of interspecific hybrids
S06GM-08016-21 0077 (MPRC) GEORGE, MATTHEW Biomedical interdisciplinary project Genetic variability as revealed by mitochondrial DNA analysis
S06GM-08016-21 0078 (MPRC) ISON-FRANKLIN, ELEANOR L Biomedical interdisciplinary project Modulators of left ventricular responses to hypertension
S06GM-08016-21 0079 (MPRC) MOORE, DEXTER S Biomedical interdisciplinary project Binding of antitumor compounds to DNA
S06GM-08016-21 0080 (MPRC) MOSS, SHARON E Biomedical interdisciplinary project Dissociation of lexical and semantic knowledge in Alzheimer's disease
S06GM-08016-21 0081 (MPRC) OVERBY, LYNNETTE Y Biomedical interdisciplinary project Developmental differences in the recall and performance of a motor skill sequence
S06GM-08016-21 0082 (MPRC) WALKER-JONES, DOROTHY G Biomedical interdisciplinary project TGF-beta and oncogene regulation of human mammary epithelial antigens
S06GM-08016-21 0083 (MPRC) DUTTA, SISIR K Biomedical interdisciplinary project Bioeffects of electropollution on expression of neuron and fetal globin genes
S06GM-08016-21 0025 (MPRC) BUTCHER, RAYMOND J Biomedical interdisciplinary project Iron III model complexes with intermediate spin states
S06GM-08019-21 (MPRC) WILLIAMSON, ALEX N NORTH CAROLINA A&T STATE UNIV 1601 EAST MARKET STREET GREENSBORO, NC 27411-0001 Development of a program in biomedical sciences
S06GM-08019-21 0003 (MPRC) WILLIAMSON, ALEX N Development of a program in biomedical sciences Synthesis and characterization of models for hemocyanin
S06GM-08019-21 0005 (MPRC) FOUSHEE, DORETHA B Development of a program in biomedical sciences Characterization and isolation of receptors for IPN virus
S06GM-08019-21 0006 (MPRC) GOLISZEK, ANDREW G Development of a program in biomedical sciences Prenatal and prepubertal stress or salt on cardiovascular function
S06GM-08019-21 0007 (MPRC) HICKS, KENNETH W Development of a program in biomedical sciences Redox studies of some bioinorganic Mo(VI) and (Mo(V))2-amino acid complexes
S06GM-08019-21 0008 (MPRC) JORDAN, LYNDA M Development of a program in biomedical sciences Inhibition of phospholipase A2 by lipocortin
S06GM-08019-21 0009 (MPRC) SCHUMACHER, SUSAN J Development of a program in biomedical sciences Behavioral and neuroendocrine differences in hypertensive and normotensive rats
S06GM-08022-20 (GRS) CHOPRA, BALDEO K JOHNSON C SMITH UNIVERSITY 100 BEATTIES FORD ROAD CHARLOTTE, NC 28216 Research methods for pre-professional students
S06GM-08022-20 0009 (GRS) LITTAU, L W Research methods for pre-professional students Amphibian notochord and its matrix during metamorphosis

PROJECT NO., ORGANIZATIONAL UNIT., INVESTIGATOR, ADDRESS, TITLE

S06GM-08022-20 0010 (GRS) GREENE, R L Research methods for pre-professional students Coping strategies--behavioral patterns of the black elderly in the south
S06GM-08022-20 0005 (GRS) CHOPRA, B K Research methods for pre-professional students Evaluation of 4-quinolones for antimicrobial susceptibility analysis
S06GM-08022-20 0007 (GRS) RHODES, R K Research methods for pre-professional students Biochemistry and distribution of invertebrate fibronectins
S06GM-08022-20 0008 (GRS) RUSSELL, H F Research methods for pre-professional students Synthesis of biologically significant indoles
S06GM-08023-20 (GRS) SMITH, CLIFFORD L ALBANY STATE COLLEGE 504 COLLEGE DRIVE ALBANY, GA 31705 Interdisciplinary biomedical science development
S06GM-08023-20 0002 (GRS) SMITH, CLIFFORD L Interdisciplinary biomedical science development Organosilicon biomedical research
S06GM-08023-20 0004 (GRS) FORT, BRUCE H Interdisciplinary biomedical science development Blood brain barrier and hypothalmic arcuate nucleus
S06GM-08023-20 0005 (GRS) LOCKLEY, ORA Interdisciplinary biomedical science development Effect of taurine and calcium supplemented diets on hypertension
S06GM-08025-21 (MPRC) CHRISTIAN, FREDERICK A SOUTHERN UNIV SOUTHERN BRANCH POST OFFICE BATON ROUGE, LA 70813 Minority biomedical research support program at Southern University
S06GM-08025-21 0003 (MPRC) ECHOLS, RICHARD E Minority biomedical research support program at Southern University Pesticides in lipid synthesis and organ damage
S06GM-08025-21 0009 (MPRC) CHRISTIAN, FRED A Minority biomedical research support program at Southern University Biological characteristics of Fasciola hepatica and it's snail hosts
S06GM-08025-21 0010 (MPRC) DOOMES, EARL Minority biomedical research support program at Southern University Fluorescent carcinogen-like bridged annulenes
S06GM-08025-21 0014 (MPRC) THOMPSON, DOROTHY P Minority biomedical research support program at Southern University Toxicity of phenolic antioxidants of toxigenic fungi
S06GM-08025-21 0015 (MPRC) NAQVI, SYED M Minority biomedical research support program at Southern University Bioaccumulation in selected tissues of laboratory exposed crayfish
S06GM-08025-21 0016 (MPRC) SPENCER, FITZGERALD Minority biomedical research support program at Southern University Uterine metabolism and body temperature rhythm during pseudopregnancy
S06GM-08025-21 0018 (MPRC) METEVIA, LOUIS A Minority biomedical research support program at Southern University Animal model--Influence of drugs and pollutants on Stenostomum microanatomy
S06GM-08025-21 0019 (MPRC) OWENS, JOHN W Minority biomedical research support program at Southern University Characterization of the fluorescent properties of zinc porphyrins
S06GM-08025-21 0020 (MPRC) SAINT-COME, CLAUDE Minority biomedical research support program at Southern University Biochemical transformation of muscle fibers and recovery of motor unit activation
S06GM-08025-21 0021 (MPRC) SISTLER, AUDREY B Minority biomedical research support program at Southern University The ongoing process of caring for a mentally-impaired spouse
S06GM-08025-21 0022 (MPRC) TILLOTSON, LACEY M Minority biomedical research support program at Southern University Type II diabetes coping--Sociocultural and behavioral aspects
S06GM-08033-21 (MPRC) TAYLOR, DONALD F NORFOLK STATE UNIVERSITY 2401 CORPREW AVENUE NORFOLK, VA 23504 MBRS program at Norfolk State University
S06GM-08033-21 0001 (MPRC) BEMPONG, MAXWELL A MBRS program at Norfolk State University Phenotypic reversion of murine cells in culture
S06GM-08033-21 0003 (MPRC) ROSENTHAL, MIRIAM D MBRS program at Norfolk State University Polyunsaturated fatty acids and endothelial signal transduction
S06GM-08033-21 0006 (MPRC) ROWE, H. ALAN MBRS program at Norfolk State University Proteoglycan biochemistry in arterial and ocular tissue
S06GM-08033-21 0007 (MPRC) COLLINS, JIMMY H MBRS program at Norfolk State University Non-muscle myosin activity and assembly
S06GM-08033-21 0008 (MPRC) GRANT, GEORGE C MBRS program at Norfolk State University Redox properties of DIDOX and related molecules
S06GM-08033-21 0009 (MPRC) NWEKE, ANRHONY C MBRS program at Norfolk State University Characterization of oxidants in wastewater chlorination of peptide-N
S06GM-08037-20 (SRC) TOWNSEL, JAMES G MEHARRY MEDICAL COLLEGE 1005 DB TODD BOULEVARD NASHVILLE, TN 37208 Development and expansion of biomedical sciences VI
S06GM-08037-20 0036 (SRC) RUCKER, HUBERT K. Development and expansion of biomedical sciences VI Acetylcholine and acoustic stimulus processing in cortex
S06GM-08037-20 0037 (SRC) SANDER, LINDA D. Development and expansion of biomedical sciences VI Feeding & GI peptide effect on hypothalamic-pituitary-adrenal axis
S06GM-08037-20 0038 (SRC) TOWNSEL, JAMES G Development and expansion of biomedical sciences VI Molecular characterization of high affinity choline transport
S06GM-08037-20 0040 (SRC) VILLALTA, FERNANDO Development and expansion of biomedical sciences VI Host cell invasion by Trypanosoma cruzi
S06GM-08037-20 0041 (SRC) RUSSELL, JAMES Development and expansion of biomedical sciences VI Keloids--An in vitro model of tumor growth regulation
S06GM-08037-20 0043 (SRC) CHARLTON, CLIVEL G Development and expansion of biomedical sciences VI Excess biological methylation and Parkinson's disease
S06GM-08037-20 0044 (SRC) CHONG, PARKSON L Development and expansion of biomedical sciences VI Physio-chemical characterization of spontaneous transfer sterols
S06GM-08037-20 0045 (SRC) CLARK, JOHN T Development and expansion of biomedical sciences VI Adrenergic-neuropeptide interactions in behavior
S06GM-08037-20 0046 (SRC) FREDMAN, STEVEN M Development and expansion of biomedical sciences VI Regulation of synaptic depression
S06GM-08037-20 0047 (SRC) HATCHER, FRANK M Development and expansion of biomedical sciences VI Antibody specific to antigen marker on normal/keloid fibroblast
S06GM-08037-20 0048 (SRC) TALBORT, PAUL A Development and expansion of biomedical sciences VI Ions and transmitter release
S06GM-08037-20 0049 (SRC) BHORJEE, JASWANT S Development and expansion of biomedical sciences VI Cardiac muscle cell development and nuclear proteins
S06GM-08037-20 0050 (SRC) HILL, GOERGE Development and expansion of biomedical sciences VI Purification of GPO and molecular cloning of GPO genes
S06GM-08037-20 0051 (SRC) WILSON, DONELLA J Development and expansion of biomedical sciences VI Characterization of mouse glycophorin gene
S06GM-08037-20 0052 (SRC) MCGINNIS, ETHELENE Development and expansion of biomedical sciences VI The molecular basis of Bartonella bacilliformis pathogenicity
S06GM-08037-20 0013 (SRC) TRUPIN, JOEL S Development and expansion of biomedical sciences VI Regul. of growth/matrix synthesis in atherosclerotic smooth muscle cells
S06GM-08037-20 0025 (SRC) BHATTACHARYYA, MOHIT L Development and expansion of biomedical sciences VI Electrophysiology of hypoxic myocardial tissue and cells
S06GM-08037-20 0027 (SRC) HOLT, ROBERT G Development and expansion of biomedical sciences VI Molecular analysis of surface proteins of cariogenic streptococci
S06GM-08037-20 0029 (SRC) RUSSELL, SHIRLEY B Development and expansion of biomedical sciences VI Role of TGF-beta in the regulation of growth and collagen production
S06GM-08037-20 0030 (SRC) THOMAS, WILLIAM E Development and expansion of biomedical sciences VI Acetylcholine and vasoactive intestinal peptide in the cerebral cortex
S06GM-08037-20 0034 (SRC) MALEQUE, MOHAMMED A. Development and expansion of biomedical sciences VI Effect of tetrahydroisoquinline on cholinergic activity
S06GM-08038-21 (MPRC) ALDRIDGE, JAMES W UNIV OF TEXAS-PAN AMERICAN 1201 W. UNIVERSITY EDINBURG, TX 78539 MBRS program at Pan American university
S06GM-08038-21 0005 (MPRC) ALDRIDGE, JAMES W MBRS program at Pan American university Phonetic storage in speech perception
S06GM-08038-21 0007 (MPRC) ARNOLD, BILL R MBRS program at Pan American university Validation of neuropsychological tests for disabled Mexican Americans
S06GM-08038-21 0008 (MPRC) FAROOQUI, MOHAMMED Y MBRS program at Pan American university Toxicokinetics and biotransformation of allylnitrile
S06GM-08038-21 0009 (MPRC) GUNN, SCOTT J MBRS program at Pan American university Cytogenetic analysis of disease vectoring tick species
S06GM-08038-21 0010 (MPRC) JUAREZ, RUMALDO MBRS program at Pan American university Longitudinal study of Mexican American elderly
S06GM-08038-21 0011 (MPRC) MONTGOMERY, GARY T MBRS program at Pan American university Followup studies of graduates of neonatal intensive care
S06GM-08038-21 0012 (MPRC) VILLARREAL, JOHN R MBRS program at Pan American university Synthesis and structure of antithrombotic organosulfur ring compounds
S06GM-08040-21 (GRS) ATKINSON, WILVERIA B WINSTON-SALEM STATE UNIVERSITY 601 MARTIN LUTHER KING DRIVE WINSTON-SALEM, NC 27110 Biomedical sciences
S06GM-08040-21 0007 (GRS) BENNET, RICHARD Biomedical sciences Chemical and biochemical composition of mucus
S06GM-08040-21 0008 (GRS) BERRY, CAROLYNN Biomedical sciences Determination and modification of health risk factors in black subjects
S06GM-08040-21 0005 (GRS) HELLER, MORTON A Biomedical sciences Visual guidance and imagery in tactual perception and braille
S06GM-08040-21 0006 (GRS) ADAMS, NELSON Biomedical sciences Cardiovascular response to social stress in rats
S06GM-08040-21 0007 (GRS) BENNET, RICHARD Biomedical sciences Chemical and biochemical composition of mucus
S06GM-08040-21 0008 (GRS) BERRY, CAROLYNN Biomedical sciences Determination and modification of health risk factors in black subjects
S06GM-08043-21 (MPRC) SHERMAN, WARREN V CHICAGO STATE UNIVERSITY 95TH STREET AT KING DRIVE CHICAGO, IL 60628 Faculty and student research development
S06GM-08043-21 0010 (MPRC) HENRY, CAROLL E Faculty and student research development The genetics, variability, and pathogenicity of Ustilago hordei
S06GM-08043-21 0011 (MPRC) BEIL, RICHARD E Faculty and student research development Regulation of an androgen-dependent gene expressed by rat bulbourethral glands
S06GM-08043-21 0012 (MPRC) BANKS, FLOYD W Faculty and student research development The effects of exercise hypertrophy on neuromuscular transmission
S06GM-08043-21 0005 (MPRC) FORD, SUSAN H Faculty and student research development Biosynthesis of vitamin B-12
S06GM-08043-21 0013 (MPRC) SHERMAN, WARREN V Faculty and student research development Design and function of sensitizers for photodynamic therapy
S06GM-08047-20S1 (GRS) MACK, ROBERT W JACKSON STATE UNIVERSITY 1400 JR LYNCH ST PO BOX 19750 JACKSON, MS 39217 Interdisciplinary biomedical research program
S06GM-08047-20S1 0013 (GRS) MOHAMED, ABDUL Interdisciplinary biomedical research program Host feeding pattern of Mississippi mosquitoes
S06GM-08047-20S1 0014 (GRS) NELSON, FRED R S Interdisciplinary biomedical research program Turbellaria and planarians as bio-control

for culicidae
S06GM-08047-20S1 0015 (GRS) NOE, ERIC A Interdisciplinary biomedical research program Conformational study by dynamic NMR spectrometry
S06GM-08047-20S1 0018 (GRS) TROTTMAN, CHARLES Interdisciplinary biomedical research program Calmodulin and neurotoxicity of chlordecone & chlordecone alcohol
S06GM-08047-20S1 0024 (GRS) CAMERON, JOSEPH A Interdisciplinary biomedical research program Hormones and age in milk fat synthesis during mammary gland development
S06GM-08047-20S1 0025 (GRS) CHAN, LAI-MAN Interdisciplinary biomedical research program Interaction of pyruvate kinase isozymes with actin-containing filaments
S06GM-08047-20S1 0026 (GRS) DALHOUSE, DERICK A Interdisciplinary biomedical research program Dietary calcium and Na+ transport
S06GM-08047-20S1 0027 (GRS) HUSSEIN, WEDAD R Interdisciplinary biomedical research program Glutamic oxalacetic transaminase activity assay in flow systems
S06GM-08047-20S1 0028 (GRS) JACHIKAWA, HIROYASU Interdisciplinary biomedical research program Redox proteins and their model
S06GM-08047-20S1 0030 (GRS) BHATNAGER, RAVI Interdisciplinary biomedical research program Nitrogen pumped dye laser in ophthalmic surgery
S06GM-08047-20S1 0031 (GRS) CHIGBO, FRANCIS Interdisciplinary biomedical research program Acetylpolyamines as early cancer markers
S06GM-08047-20S1 0032 (GRS) KARVALY, BELA Interdisciplinary biomedical research program Mechanism of charge transfer in biopolymers
S06GM-08047-20S1 0033 (GRS) SULLIVAN, RICHARD H Interdisciplinary biomedical research program Intact sickle cells
S06GM-08047-20S1 0034 (GRS) UZODINMA, JOHN Interdisciplinary biomedical research program Modulation of the GABA-ergic system by pesticides in rats of different ages
S06GM-08049-20 (GRS) PATTILLO, WALTER H, JR NORTH CAROLINA CENTRAL UNIV DURHAM, NC 27707 Minority biomedical research support program
S06GM-08049-20 0007 (GRS) MYERS, JOHN A Minority biomedical research support program Synthesis of nitrogen heterocyclics for the therapeutic treatment of cancer
S06GM-08049-20 0008 (GRS) EVERETT, JAMES Minority biomedical research support program Menkes syndrome--Biochemical and biophysical studies
S06GM-08049-20 0009 (GRS) BOYD, LILLIE Minority biomedical research support program Effects of menhaden/mackerel/herring oil on cardiac parameters in the rat
S06GM-08049-20 0010 (GRS) DAVIS, ELAINE J Minority biomedical research support program Factors involved in conjugal transfer replication
S06GM-08049-20 0011 (GRS) IZYDORE, ROBERT Minority biomedical research support program Synthesis of hydroxamates and hydrazides as antitumor agents
S06GM-08049-20 0012 (GRS) MAYFIELD, JOHN E Minority biomedical research support program Clinical significance of airborne pollen grains and fungal spores
S06GM-08060-21 (MPRC) DATTA-GUPTA, NIRMALENDU SOUTH CAROLINA STATE COLLEGE P O BOX 1731 ORANGEBURG, S C 29117 Minority biomedical research support program
S06GM-08060-21 0001 (MPRC) DATTA-GUPTA, NIRMALENDU Minority biomedical research support program Oxygen carrying porphyrin-protein complexes
S06GM-08060-21 0005 (MPRC) STUKES, JAMES B Minority biomedical research support program Determination of the factors which regulate the partition of r6 in E coli
S06GM-08060-21 0006 (MPRC) SCOTT, DAVID G Minority biomedical research support program Genetic analysis of production and preparation of pheromones
S06GM-08061-17 (MPRC) MC DONALD, CURTIS W TEXAS SOUTHERN UNIVERSITY 3100 CLEBURNE HOUSTON, TX 77004 Minority biomedical research support program
S06GM-08061-17 0002 (MPRC) BHANSALI, KANTI G Minority biomedical research support program Synthesis of 1,2-benzophenoxazone derivatives as antiviral/anticancer agents
S06GM-08061-17 0003 (MPRC) ENIGBOKAN, MOFOLRUNSO A Minority biomedical research support program Epithelial transport of nucleosides
S06GM-08061-17 0004 (MPRC) FELDER, TYRONE B Minority biomedical research support program Chemically induced alterations in pulmonary metabolism
S06GM-08061-17 0001 (MPRC) BATES, THEODORE R Minority biomedical research support program Blood protein binding and disposition kinetics of potential antisickling agents
S06GM-08061-17 0005 (MPRC) HARRELL, WILLIAM B Minority biomedical research support program Drug design--Synthesis and testing of idolizines with biphasic activity
S06GM-08061-17 0006 (MPRC) JADHAV, ARUN L Minority biomedical research support program Membrane sodium transport mechanisms and the pathogenesis of hypertension
S06GM-08061-17 0007 (MPRC) ROBBINS, TERRY J Minority biomedical research support program Anti-HIV drug investigation
S06GM-08061-17 0008 (MPRC) HOGAN, YVONNE H Minority biomedical research support program Ganglionic and renal vascular adenosine receptors in hypertensive rats
S06GM-08061-17 0009 (MPRC) HOWZE, GWENDOLYN B Minority biomedical research support program Cell biology of periosteum
S06GM-08061-17 0010 (MPRC) EDWARDS, KIAH Minority biomedical research support program Genomic arrangement and nucleotide sequence of sex-related repetitive DNA
S06GM-08061-17 0011 (MPRC) HILLAR, MARIAN Minority biomedical research support program Isolation and structure of the gene for glutamate dehydrogenase
S06GM-08061-17 0012 (MPRC) FENNELL, PEARLIE M Minority biomedical research support program Drug metabolism in human uterine microsomes
S06GM-08061-17 0013 (MPRC) MCDONALD, CURTIS W Minority biomedical research support program Determination of sulfur containing biomolecules
S06GM-08061-17 0014 (MPRC) GUILFORD, JAMES Minority biomedical research support program Effects of cadmium on hepatic enzyme activity
S06GM-08061-17 0015 (MPRC) HAYES, BARBARA E Minority biomedical research support program Serum semicarbazide sensitive amine oxidase activity in diabetic nephropathy
S06GM-08061-17 0016 (MPRC) GHOSH, DEBABRATA Minority biomedical research support program Effects of L-tryptophan on indole and catecholamine metabolites in hypertension
S06GM-08061-17 0017 (MPRC) FADULU, SUNDAY O Minority biomedical research support program Biophysical properties of red cell membrane during sickling process
S06GM-08061-17 0018 (MPRC) LEUCHTAG, H R Minority biomedical research support program Phase transitions in sodium channels under patch clamp
S06GM-08061-17 0019 (MPRC) WATKINS, HALCYON O Minority biomedical research support program Effect of dietary salts on hypertension in the rat
S06GM-08062-21 (MPRC) ELLIOTT, I WESLEY FISK UNIVERSITY 1000 - 17TH AVE, NORTH NASHVILLE, TN 37208 MBRS Program at Fisk University
S06GM-08062-21 0001 (MPRC) ELLIOTT, IRVIN W MBRS Program at Fisk University Synthesis of analogs and derivatives of an anti-AIDS compound
S06GM-08062-21 0002 (MPRC) EVANS, PRINCILLA S MBRS Program at Fisk University Effects of interferons on keloid and normal fibroblasts
S06GM-08062-21 0003 (MPRC) MORGAN, STEVEN H MBRS Program at Fisk University Vibrational spectroscopy of protein nucleation and growth
S06GM-08062-21 0004 (MPRC) SPILLER, HART MBRS Program at Fisk University Inorganic carbon uptake in the marine cyanobacterium Synechococcus species
S06GM-08066-20 (GRS) SVEUM, LARRY K NEW MEXICO HIGHLANDS UNIVERSIT LAS VEGAS, NM 87701 Coordinated research and training program
S06GM-08066-20 0005 (GRS) SPENCER, JOHN W Coordinated research and training program An interesting pathogen Yersinia enterocolitica
S06GM-08066-20 0006 (GRS) MISHLER, R Coordinated research and training program Chemical analysis of bone -- Individualization, nutrition, health
S06GM-08073-20 (GRS) SCOTT, JOHN F UNIVEIRSITY OF HAWAII 523 W LANIKAULA ST HILO, HI 96720-4091 Biomedical research at the University of Hawaii at Hilo
S06GM-08073-20 0005 (GRS) HEMMES, DON E Biomedical research at the University of Hawaii at Hilo Calcium binding sites microfilaments and microtubules in Hyphal tips
S06GM-08073-20 0009 (GRS) SEVERENCE, CRAIG J Biomedical research at the University of Hawaii at Hilo Infant growth development and health risk factors in Hawaii
S06GM-08073-20 0010 (GRS) DUDLEY, WALTER C Biomedical research at the University of Hawaii at Hilo Sewage pollution: Health hazards and environmental factors
S06GM-08073-20 0011 (GRS) SCOTT, JOHN F Biomedical research at the University of Hawaii at Hilo Molecular genetic analysis of nuclear DNA replication in yeast
S06GM-08073-20 0012 (GRS) TAKEMOTO-CHOCK, NAOMI K Biomedical research at the University of Hawaii at Hilo Stressors, moderators and outcomes in native Hawaiian adolescents
S06GM-08091-20 (MPRC) THOMAS, JULIAN E TUSKEGEE UNIVERSITY TUSKEGEE, AL 36088 Research opportunities offered to Tuskegee students
S06GM-08091-20 0007 (MPRC) PHAIRE-WASHINGTON, LINDA Research opportunities offered to Tuskegee students Cytoskeletons of neurons exposed to drugs which induce schizophrenia
S06GM-08091-20 0010 (MPRC) DALVI, RAMESH R Research opportunities offered to Tuskegee students Comparative studies of toxicology of captan, captafol and folpet
S06GM-08091-20 0011 (MPRC) DIXON, EARL Research opportunities offered to Tuskegee students Calcium and sodium metabolism in erythrocytes from hypertensive dogs
S06GM-08091-20 0016 (MPRC) LUDWICK, ADRIANE G Research opportunities offered to Tuskegee students Therapeutic value of polynucleotide analogs from water soluble polymers
S06GM-08091-20 0018 (MPRC) VERMA, OM P Research opportunities offered to Tuskegee students Prostacyclin release and uterine motility
S06GM-08091-20 0019 (MPRC) DATTA, MUKUL C Research opportunities offered to Tuskegee students Reverse hemoglobin switching in adult life
S06GM-08091-20 0022 (MPRC) RICHARDSON, VELMA B Research opportunities offered to Tuskegee students Cytogenetic and cytokinetic assessment of alkyl imidates
S06GM-08091-20 0024 (MPRC) DAVIDSON, JOHN P Research opportunities offered to Tuskegee students Function of the his U gene in salmonella typhimurium
S06GM-08091-20 0026 (MPRC) BENFORD, HELEN H Research opportunities offered to Tuskegee students Protein pattern changes preceding vitellogenin gene activation in fat body
S06GM-08091-20 0027 (MPRC) GARG, RAMESH C Research opportunities offered to Tuskegee students Immunosuppressants and penetration of antibiotics into walled-off soft tissue
S06GM-08091-20 0028 (MPRC) GOYAL, HARI O Research opportunities offered to Tuskegee students Ductuli efferentes and epididymis in sperm maturation
S06GM-08091-20 0029 (MPRC) STEVENS, CLAUZELL Research opportunities offered to Tuskegee students Arthropod-borne spiroplasmas--Potential mammalian pathogenic agents
S06GM-08091-20 0030 (MPRC) WILLIAMS, JOHN W Research opportunities offered to Tuskegee students Chromosome rearrangements--Neoplasia and metastasis in rana Pipiens
S06GM-08091-20 0031 (MPRC) WEBSTER, JAMES E Research opportunities offered to Tuskegee students Effects of hormones and electrolytes in hypertensive dogs
S06GM-08091-20 9001 (MPRC) PHAIRE-WASHINGTON, LINDA Research opportunities offered to Tuskegee students Core - in vitro

multidisciplinary research facility
S06GM-08092-18 (GRS) NEWKIRK, ROBERT G TENNESSEE STATE UNIVERSITY 3500 JOHN MERRIT BLVD NASHVILLE, TN 37209-1561 A biomedical research program with student participation
S06GM-08092-18 0012 (GRS) ADAMS, JAMES A. A biomedical research program with student participation Dexriptive reproductive toxicology of selected developing systems
S06GM-08092-18 0013 (GRS) BARRETT, HELEN R. A biomedical research program with student participation Racial comparisons in stress reactivity and modification with biofeedback
S06GM-08092-18 0014 (GRS) CHANG, TAE GYU A biomedical research program with student participation Sleep data analyzing expert system
S06GM-08092-18 0015 (GRS) CHEN, FU-MING A biomedical research program with student participation Kinetic and thermodynamic studies of drug binding to DNA
S06GM-08092-18 0016 (GRS) HUSAINI, BAQAR A. A biomedical research program with student participation Therapeutic program and health changes among the elderly
S06GM-08092-18 0017 (GRS) LINN, JAMES G. A biomedical research program with student participation Mental distress and coping behaviors of HIV infected adults
S06GM-08092-18 0018 (GRS) NEWKIRK, ROBERT F. A biomedical research program with student participation Neurotransmitters in the horse shoe crab
S06GM-08092-18 0019 (GRS) OLLAPALLY, PHILIP J. A biomedical research program with student participation Computer system for localization of arrhythmogenic foci
S06GM-08092-18 0020 (GRS) TOMLINSON, GUS A biomedical research program with student participation Acanthamoeba castellanii--growth encystment
S06GM-08094-17 (GRS) WASHINGTON, ARTHUR C PRAIRIE VIEW A&M UNIVERSITY PRAIRIE VIEW, TEXAS 77446 Support for study of biomedical sciences
S06GM-08094-17 0002 (GRS) DOCTOR, VASANT M Support for study of biomedical sciences Effect of sulfated xylans on coagulation of human plasma
S06GM-08094-17 0005 (GRS) BALLARD, HENRY H Support for study of biomedical sciences New potential tumor inhibitory triazenes
S06GM-08094-17 0006 (GRS) THOMAS, RICHARD G Support for study of biomedical sciences Cadmium and lead uptake and distribution in Vigna sinensis
S06GM-08094-17 0007 (GRS) CHETTY, KOTHAPA N Support for study of biomedical sciences Calcium metabolism changes from chlordecone in calcium deficient rats
S06GM-08094-17 0008 (GRS) WASHINGTON, ARTHUR Support for study of biomedical sciences Isolation, purification and characterization of succinic dehydrogenase
S06GM-08101-20 (GRS) ANDREOLI, ANTHONY J CALIFORNIA STATE UNIVERSITY 5151 STATE UNIVERSITY DRIVE LOS ANGELES, CALIFORNIA 90032 MBRS program at California State University, Los Angeles
S06GM-08101-20 0004 (GRS) ANDREOLI, ANTHONY J MBRS program at California State University, Los Angeles Nicotinamide adenine dinucleotide metabolism in bacteria
S06GM-08101-20 0007 (GRS) BROWN, COSTELLO L MBRS program at California State University, Los Angeles Negative ionization of bioorganic molecules
S06GM-08101-20 0008 (GRS) CURRELL, DOUGLAS L MBRS program at California State University, Los Angeles Synthetic allosteric effectors of hemoglobin
S06GM-08101-20 0011 (GRS) FRATIELLO, ANTHONY MBRS program at California State University, Los Angeles Metal ion complexation
S06GM-08101-20 0014 (GRS) ONAK, THOMAS P MBRS program at California State University, Los Angeles Biologically active small cage boron compounds
S06GM-08101-20 0015 (GRS) PAULSON, DONALD R MBRS program at California State University, Los Angeles Metallo-sulfur complexes as models for electron transfer proteins
S06GM-08101-20 0018 (GRS) SETO, JOSEPH T MBRS program at California State University, Los Angeles Biological properties of the envelope proteins of Sendai virus
S06GM-08101-20 0020 (GRS) PINE, STANLEY H MBRS program at California State University, Los Angeles CIDNP as a probe for free-radical pathways in biochemical reactions
S06GM-08101-20 0021 (GRS) DEA, PHOEBE K MBRS program at California State University, Los Angeles NMR studies of chlorophyll A in photosynthetic membrane
S06GM-08101-20 0023 (GRS) GUTIERREZ, CARLOS MBRS program at California State University, Los Angeles Highly substituted crown ether compounds as selective ionophores
S06GM-08101-20 0025 (GRS) JEFFERSON, MARGARET C MBRS program at California State University, Los Angeles Genetic analysis of olfactory behavior
S06GM-08101-20 0028 (GRS) MARHSALL, ROSEMARIE MBRS program at California State University, Los Angeles Antibiotic sensitivity testing of anaerobic bacteria
S06GM-08101-20 0029 (GRS) PEITZ, BETSY MBRS program at California State University, Los Angeles Role of the seminal vesicles in fertility in the house mice
S06GM-08101-20 0030 (GRS) BOWERS, ROGER R MBRS program at California State University, Los Angeles Mechanism of genetic hypomelanosis (vitiligo) in the fowl
S06GM-08101-20 0031 (GRS) GARCIA, RAYMOND E MBRS program at California State University, Los Angeles Dietary cholesterol as high density lipoprotein metabolism regulator in rabbits
S06GM-08101-20 0032 (GRS) GROVER, SCOTT D MBRS program at California State University, Los Angeles Effect of regulatory ligands and their binding sites on PEP carboxylases
S06GM-08101-20 0033 (GRS) KEYS, RICHARD T MBRS program at California State University, Los Angeles Magnetic resonance investigation of potential spin labels
S06GM-08101-20 0034 (GRS) LOPEZ, GENARO A MBRS program at California State University, Los Angeles Regulation of renin release in the hibernator--Biochemistry and ultrastructure
S06GM-08101-20 0035 (GRS) PEARSON, DAVID MBRS program at California State University, Los Angeles Control of vertebrate neuropeptide synthesis and release
S06GM-08101-20 0036 (GRS) TAM, CHICK R MBRS program at California State University, Los Angeles Priming of the immunodeficiency of Down's syndrome and aging
S06GM-08101-20 0037 (GRS) PERROTT, DAVID R MBRS program at California State University, Los Angeles Auditory localization performance with sources outside the visual field
S06GM-08101-20 0039 (GRS) GOLDWHITE, HAROLD MBRS program at California State University, Los Angeles Analogs of cyclic phosphates
S06GM-08101-20 0040 (GRS) MUCHLINSKI, ALAN E. MBRS program at California State University, Los Angeles Fever response--Physiological/ecological aspects
S06GM-08101-20 0041 (GRS) PHINNEY, JEAN S MBRS program at California State University, Los Angeles Identity development in adolescents from four ethnic groups
S06GM-08101-20 0042 (GRS) SHARP, SANDRA B MBRS program at California State University, Los Angeles Regulatory protein binding sequences in coexpressed muscle
S06GM-08101-20 0043 (GRS) TIKKANEN, WAYNE R MBRS program at California State University, Los Angeles Binuclear metal-polypyridyl molybdenum oxo-thiolates as model for oxotransferases
S06GM-08102-20 (SRC) ESCALONA DE MOTTA, GLADYS UNIVERSITY OF PUERTO RICO P O BOX 23341 RIO PIEDRAS, P R 00931 Support for University Biomedical Education
S06GM-08102-20 0020 (SRC) RODRIGUEZ-DEL VALLE, NURI Support for University Biomedical Education Dimorphism in Sporothrix schenckii ion channels
S06GM-08102-20 0001 (SRC) HILLYER, GEORGE V Support for University Biomedical Education Schistosome-specific worm and egg antigens for immunodiagnosis
S06GM-08102-20 0007 (SRC) MUIR, MARIEL M Support for University Biomedical Education Potential anti-tumor transition metal complexes
S06GM-08102-20 0018 (SRC) RENAUD, FERNANDO L Support for University Biomedical Education Hormonal mechanisms in non-vertebrates
S06GM-08102-20 0019 (SRC) MORALES, REGINALD Support for University Biomedical Education Regulation of specific phenotypes in liver development and neoplasia
S06GM-08102-20 0022 (SRC) RAMIREZ-RONDA, CARLOS H Support for University Biomedical Education Bacterial adherence to endothelial cells and polymers
S06GM-08102-20 0033 (SRC) BAEZ, ADRIANA Support for University Biomedical Education Antitumor activity of fagaronine and analogues
S06GM-08102-20 0034 (SRC) ARCE, RAFAEL Support for University Biomedical Education Reactive intermediates in photocemical reactions of biologically relevant purines
S06GM-08102-20 0037 (SRC) CANDELAS, GRACIELA C Support for University Biomedical Education Regulation of protein synthesis modulation by tRNA
S06GM-08102-20 0046 (SRC) ROSARIO, OSVALDO Support for University Biomedical Education Bioaccumulation of environmental carcinogens--methodology and characterization
S06GM-08102-20 0047 (SRC) BARNES, CHARLES L Support for University Biomedical Education Peptide mycotoxins
S06GM-08102-20 0048 (SRC) SIMMONS, CHARLES J Support for University Biomedical Education X-ray study of synthetic oxygen carriers related to biological systems
S06GM-08102-20 0049 (SRC) GUADALUPE, ANA R Support for University Biomedical Education Interfacial dynamics of electron transfer reactions of proteins
S06GM-08102-20 0050 (SRC) PRIETO, JOSE A Support for University Biomedical Education Synthetic methodology towards the preparation of ansamycin antibiotics
S06GM-08102-20 0051 (SRC) SODERQUIST, JOHN A Support for University Biomedical Education Anti-inflammatory agents, antibiotics and pheromones via vinyl metalloids
S06GM-08102-20 0052 (SRC) FETCHER, NED Support for University Biomedical Education Controls on production of artemisinin and its use in schistosomal infections
S06GM-08102-20 0053 (SRC) GARCIA-ARRARAS, JOSE E Support for University Biomedical Education Environmental regulation of sympathoadrenal phenotypic expression
S06GM-08102-20 0054 (SRC) PEREZ-CHIESA, YVETTE Support for University Biomedical Education Mutagenicity of anticancer drugs in somatic and germ cells of D melanogaster
S06GM-08102-20 0055 (SRC) VOLTZOW, JANICE Support for University Biomedical Education Universality of the morphological correlations of striated muscle function
S06GM-08102-20 0056 (SRC) CANGIANO, JOSE Support for University Biomedical Education Evaluation of cataracts in genetically hypertensive rats
S06GM-08102-20 0057 (SRC) ZUAZAGA, CONCHITA Support for University Biomedical Education Ionic conductance changes in muscle membranes mediated by membrane proteins
S06GM-08102-20 0058 (SRC) CARBALLEIRA, NESTER M Support for University Biomedical Education Isolation of new marine natural products from burrowing sponges
S06GM-08103-18 (MPRC) HERNANDEZ-AVILA, MANUEL L UNIVERSITY OF PUERTO RICO BOX 5000 MAYAGUEZ, PR 00709 Support for studies of biomedical sciences
S06GM-08103-18 0011 (MPRC) RAMIREZ, CARLOS A Support for studies of biomedical sciences Hybrid artificial pancreas for glucose regulation
S06GM-08103-18 0013 (MPRC) SOUTO, FERNANDO A Support for studies of biomedical sciences Electrochemical detection of aflatoxins and other trichothecene mycotoxins
S06GM-08103-18 0015 (MPRC) BALLANTINE, DAVID L Support for studies of biomedical sciences Production/regulation of antibiotic and icosanoid metabolites by red algae
S06GM-08103-18 0016 (MPRC) DIAZ, EMILIO Support for studies of biomedical sciences Characterization and inhibition studies of toxins produced by R. phaseoli
S06GM-08103-18 0017 (MPRC) LOPEZ-GARRIGA, JUAN Support for studies

of biomedical sciences HEME proteins ligand dynamics--The CO poison threshold

S06GM-08103-18 0018 (MPRC) MARTINEZ-CRUZADO, J C Support for studies of biomedical sciences Molecular evolutionary genetics of Hawaiian Drosophila chorion

S06GM-08103-18 0021 (MPRC) VERA, MARSIOL Support for studies of biomedical sciences NMR studies of oligopeptide-nucleic acid complexes

S06GM-08103-18 0022 (MPRC) SHAPIRO, DOUGLAS Y Support for studies of biomedical sciences Sperm availability and environmental influences on sex differentiation

S06GM-08107-18 (GRS) PEREZ, JOHN C TEXAS A&I UNIVERSITY KINGSVILLE, TX 78363 Texas A&I University biomedical support program

S06GM-08107-18 0002 (GRS) PEREZ, JOHN C Texas A&I University biomedical support program Venom neutralization

S06GM-08107-18 0007 (GRS) GRAHAM, JOE S Texas A&I University biomedical support program Mexican American herbal remedies--an evaluation

S06GM-08107-18 0008 (GRS) HAYS, THOMAS R Texas A&I University biomedical support program Structure-function relationships in C. atrox antihemorrhagic factors

S06GM-08107-18 0009 (GRS) TORRES-RAINES, ROSARIO Texas A&I University biomedical support program Social, cultural and psychological influences on overweight and obese women

S06GM-08110-20 (GRS) SRINIVASAN, ASOKA TOUGALOO COLLEGE TOUGALOO, MS 39174 Biomedical research program

S06GM-08110-20 0001 (GRS) SRINIVASAN, ASOKA Biomedical research program Regulation of sex pheromone gland cells in insects

S06GM-08110-20 0004 (GRS) OSWALD, THOMAS H Biomedical research program Herbicide injury to vital functions of cultured cells

S06GM-08110-20 0005 (GRS) KANG, YOHN S Biomedical research program Charge transfer photochemistry and photophysics of organochromium III complexes

S06GM-08110-20 0008 (GRS) MEHROTRA, BAM D Biomedical research program Role of glutamate and GABA receptors in the neurotoxicity of cyclodienes

S06GM-08110-20 0009 (GRS) BRUNO, GERALD VINCENT Biomedical research program Conformation between electron transfer sites involving cytochrome P-450

S06GM-08110-20 0010 (GRS) LIAW, YUN-LONG Biomedical research program Dopaminergic system in paraoxon-induced toxicity

S06GM-08111-19 (GRS) REDDA, KEN FLORIDA A & M UNIVERSITY TALLAHASSEE, FL 32307 Electro-oxidation studies of pyrimidine nucleosides and their analogs

S06GM-08111-19 0023 (GRS) DHANARAJAN, ZACHARIAH Electro-oxidation studies of pyrimidine nucleosides and their analogs Mechanisms of thyroid hormone induced muscle protein synthesis

S06GM-08111-19 0024 (GRS) OLLAPALLY, ABRAHAM Electro-oxidation studies of pyrimidine nucleosides and their analogs Ketodeoxyenohexosyl halouracil analogs as anticancer agents

S06GM-08111-19 0025 (GRS) REDDA, KINFE Electro-oxidation studies of pyrimidine nucleosides and their analogs Synthesis and biological activity of some N-aminotetrahydropyridines

S06GM-08111-19 0026 (GRS) SOLIMAN, KARAM Electro-oxidation studies of pyrimidine nucleosides and their analogs Calcitonin control of calcium metabolism during weightlessness

S06GM-08111-19 0027 (GRS) SOLIMAN, MAGDI Electro-oxidation studies of pyrimidine nucleosides and their analogs Neurochemical basis of beneficial effects of chronobiotic drugs

S06GM-08111-19 0028 (GRS) BLYDEN, GERSHWIN Electro-oxidation studies of pyrimidine nucleosides and their analogs Drug polymorphysims amoung ethnic populations of Florida

S06GM-08111-19 0025 (GRS) REDDA, KINFE Electro-oxidation studies of pyrimidine nucleosides and their analogs Synthesis and biological activity of some N-aminotetrahydropyridines

S06GM-08111-19 0026 (GRS) SOLIMAN, KARAM Electro-oxidation studies of pyrimidine nucleosides and their analogs Calcitonin control of calcium metabolism during weightlessness

S06GM-08111-19 0027 (GRS) SOLIMAN, MAGDI Electro-oxidation studies of pyrimidine nucleosides and their analogs Neurochemical basis of beneficial effects of chronobiotic drugs

S06GM-08111-19 0028 (GRS) BLYDEN, GERSHWIN Electro-oxidation studies of pyrimidine nucleosides and their analogs Drug polymorphysims amoung ethnic populations of Florida

S06GM-08117-18 (SRC) FINLAY, MARY F BENEDICT COLLEGE HARDEN & BLANDING STREETS COLUMBIA, SC 29204 Biomedical science research program

S06GM-08119-18 (GRS) RAHMANI, MUNIR A BETHUNE-COOKMAN COLLEGE 640 SECOND AVENUE DAYTONA BEACH, FL 32115 Bethune-Cookman College support program

S06GM-08119-18 0008 (GRS) CHEEMA, IJAZ R. Bethune-Cookman College support program

S06GM-08119-18 0009 (GRS) GREEN, TERRY J. Bethune-Cookman College support program Micro-computer molecular analysis and information display system

S06GM-08119-18 0010 (GRS) KUO, WU-NAN Bethune-Cookman College support program Phospholipid-regulated protein-kinase and t-RNA regulated kinase

S06GM-08119-18 0011 (GRS) NAYER, RAM Bethune-Cookman College support program Genetics of expression of isozymes in xenotropic virus expressing mice

S06GM-08119-18 0012 (GRS) RAHMANI, MUNIR A. Bethune-Cookman College support program Alpha-adrenergic regulation in hypertension, thyroid state and aging

S06GM-08119-18 0013 (GRS) SHOOK, MICHAEL R. Bethune-Cookman College support program Synthesis and antibacterial activity of thieno [3,4-b] pyridine derivatives

S06GM-08119-18 0014 (GRS) SEN, SHUKDEB Bethune-Cookman College support program Effects of buthionine sulfoximine on chicken embryos

S06GM-08119-18 0015 (GRS) THOMPSON, HERBERT W. Bethune-Cookman College support program Effects of DY3 on fertility and fecundity in female C57BL/6J mice

S06GM-08125-18 (GRS) GREENWOOD, FREDERICK C UNIVERSITY OF HAWAII 1993 EAST-WEST ROAD HONOLULU, HI 96822 Functional homology between monemal dyneins of tetrahymena and sea urchin

S06GM-08125-18 0038 (GRS) DUNLAP, MARILYN R. Functional homology between monemal dyneins of tetrahymena and sea urchin Hormonal control of gametogenesis in a hermaphrodite

S06GM-08125-18 0041 (GRS) AHEARN, GREGORY A. Functional homology between monemal dyneins of tetrahymena and sea urchin Na/H antiport by invertebrate epithelial brush border membrane vesicles/lobsters

S06GM-08125-18 0042 (GRS) BAILEY, LESLIE E. Functional homology between monemal dyneins of tetrahymena and sea urchin Preservation of hearts for transplant by gas perfusion

S06GM-08125-18 0043 (GRS) BITTERMAN, M. E. Functional homology between monemal dyneins of tetrahymena and sea urchin Crustaceau learning

S06GM-08125-18 0044 (GRS) BLANCHARD, CAROLINE D. Functional homology between monemal dyneins of tetrahymena and sea urchin Ethopharmacological approach to the study of anxiety

S06GM-08125-18 0045 (GRS) BLANCHARD, ROBERT J. Functional homology between monemal dyneins of tetrahymena and sea urchin Alcohol,social stress and emotional behavior

S06GM-08125-18 0046 (GRS) BOYNTON, ALTON L. Functional homology between monemal dyneins of tetrahymena and sea urchin Second messengers and neoplastic development

S06GM-08125-18 0047 (GRS) CHING, CLARA Y. Functional homology between monemal dyneins of tetrahymena and sea urchin Natural killer cell system and biological rsponse modification

S06GM-08125-18 0048 (GRS) FOK, AGNES K. Functional homology between monemal dyneins of tetrahymena and sea urchin Control of the digestive lysosomal system

S06GM-08125-18 0049 (GRS) HAMMER, RONALD P., JR. Functional homology between monemal dyneins of tetrahymena and sea urchin Sex hormone-dependent changes of opiate systems in rat brain

S06GM-08125-18 0050 (GRS) HOKAMA, YOSHITSUGI Functional homology between monemal dyneins of tetrahymena and sea urchin C-reactive protein functions in cancer patients

S06GM-08125-18 0051 (GRS) KINZIE, ROBERT A. Functional homology between monemal dyneins of tetrahymena and sea urchin Symbiosis of dinoflagellate with marine invertebrates

S06GM-08125-18 0052 (GRS) NEWCOMB, ROBERT Functional homology between monemal dyneins of tetrahymena and sea urchin Rates of evolution of peptide processing

S06GM-08125-18 0053 (GRS) RADTKE, RICHARD L. Functional homology between monemal dyneins of tetrahymena and sea urchin Gerontological studies of poikilothermic origins

S06GM-08125-18 0049 (GRS) HAMMER, RONALD P., JR. Functional homology between monemal dyneins of tetrahymena and sea urchin Sex hormone-dependent changes of opiate systems in rat brain

S06GM-08125-18 0050 (GRS) HOKAMA, YOSHITSUGI Functional homology between monemal dyneins of tetrahymena and sea urchin C-reactive protein functions in cancer patients

S06GM-08125-18 0051 (GRS) KINZIE, ROBERT A. Functional homology between monemal dyneins of tetrahymena and sea urchin Symbiosis of dinoflagellate with marine invertebrates

S06GM-08125-18 0052 (GRS) NEWCOMB, ROBERT Functional homology between monemal dyneins of tetrahymena and sea urchin Rates of evolution of peptide processing

S06GM-08125-18 0053 (GRS) RADTKE, RICHARD L. Functional homology between monemal dyneins of tetrahymena and sea urchin Gerontological studies of poikilothermic origins

S06GM-08125-18 0039 (GRS) IWAOKA, WAYNE Functional homology between monemal dyneins of tetrahymena and sea urchin Occurrence and analysis of ciquatoxin and related polyethers in Hawaiian fishes

S06GM-08125-18 0040 (GRS) REIMER, NEIL S. Functional homology between monemal dyneins of tetrahymena and sea urchin Sea anemone toxin derivatives as heart sti mulants

S06GM-08132-17 (MPRC) BOWMAN, BARRY J UNIVERSITY OF CALIFORNIA 1156 HIGH STREET SANTA CRUZ, CA 95064 UC Santa Cruz MBRS basic research program

S06GM-08132-17 0009 (MPRC) ORTIZ, CHARLES L UC Santa Cruz MBRS basic research program Developmental physiology of elephant seal pups during natural, prolonged fasts

S06GM-08132-17 0011 (MPRC) ROCHA, VICTOR UC Santa Cruz MBRS basic research program Role of 70kDa calelectrin in mammary secretory differentiation

S06GM-08132-17 0016 (MPRC) BOWMAN, BARRY J UC Santa Cruz MBRS basic research program Structure and function of the vacuolar ATPase

S06GM-08132-17 0017 (MPRC) CREWS, PHILLIP UC Santa Cruz MBRS basic research program Structure and conformation of novel antitumor agents from marine animals

S06GM-08132-17 0018 (MPRC) MASCHARAK, PRADIP K UC Santa Cruz MBRS basic research program Radical-induced DNA damage by metal-bleomycin analogues

S06GM-08132-17 0019 (MPRC) POODRY, CLIFTON A UC Santa Cruz MBRS basic research program Genetic control of cell interactions in development

S06GM-08132-17 0020 (MPRC) TALAMANTES, FRANK J UC Santa Cruz MBRS basic research program Structural and functional characterization of hamster PL-II

S06GM-08132-17 0021 (MPRC) ZUNIGA, MARTHA C UC Santa Cruz MBRS basic research program Mechasnisms and pathways for membrane glycoproteins--Exocytosis and endocytosis

S06GM-08136-18 (SRC) KUEHN, GLENN D NEW MEXICO STATE UNIVERSITY BOX 30001/DEPARTMENT 3C LAS CRUCES, NM 88003-0001 Biomedical research for ethnic minority students

S06GM-08136-18 0015 (SRC) GUZIEC, FRANK S Biomedical research for ethnic minority students Synthesis and testing of potential collagenase inhibitors

S06GM-08136-18 0016 (SRC) HERMAN, CEIL ANN Biomedical research for ethnic minority students Action and metabolism of eicosanoids

S06GM-08136-18 0017 (SRC) BIRNBAUM, EDWARD R Biomedical research for ethnic minority students Lanthanide ions as probe of calcium binding to peptides

S06GM-08136-18 0018 (SRC) LAMMERS, PETER J Biomedical research for ethnic minority students Rearrangement of nif genes during

Cyanobacterial heterocyst differentiation
S06GM-08136-18 0019 (SRC) VELTON, JEFF Biomedical research for ethnic minority students Eukaryotic transcription regulation using T7 RNA polymerase
S06GM-08136-18 0022 (SRC) GOPALAN, ARAVAMUDAN S Biomedical research for ethnic minority students Chiral biologically active molecule synthesis--Microbial reduction
S06GM-08136-18 0023 (SRC) SENGUPTA-GOPALAN, CHAMPA Biomedical research for ethnic minority students Promoter analysis of soybean genes in symbiotic N2 fixation
S06GM-08136-18 0002 (SRC) HAGEMAN, JAMES H Biomedical research for ethnic minority students Proteolysis regulation in sporulating Bacillus subtilis cells
S06GM-08136-18 0003 (SRC) BERNSTEIN, MARVIN H Biomedical research for ethnic minority students Avian cardiopulmonary and cerebrovascular function
S06GM-08136-18 0006 (SRC) KUEHN, GLENN D Biomedical research for ethnic minority students Functional roles for intracellular transglutaminase
S06GM-08136-18 0010 (SRC) CASILLAS, EDMUND R Biomedical research for ethnic minority students Biochemical processes in male animals
S06GM-08136-18 0028 (SRC) O'CONNELL, MARY ANN Biomedical research for ethnic minority students Tomato somatic hybrids and cybrids--Construction and characterization
S06GM-08136-18 0029 (SRC) SERRANO, ELBA E Biomedical research for ethnic minority students Inner ear hair cells--Physiology and anatomy
S06GM-08139-17 (GRS) ATENCIO, ALONZO C UNIV OF NEW MEXICO SCH OF MED BASIC SCIENCES BLDG RM 106 ALBUQUERQUE, NM 87131 Minority biomedical research support program
S06GM-08139-17 0073 (GRS) SMITH, KENNETH S K Minority biomedical research support program Purified testis antigens and testicular autoimmunity
S06GM-08139-17 0006 (GRS) OMDAHL, JOHN L Minority biomedical research support program Renal 25-(OH)D-hydroxylases--Isolation and molecular aspects
S06GM-08139-17 0008 (GRS) SCALLEN, TERENCE J Minority biomedical research support program Regulation by HMG-CoA reductase
S06GM-08139-17 0014 (GRS) REYES, EDWARD Minority biomedical research support program Effect of prenatal alcohol exposure on gamma-GTP
S06GM-08139-17 0018 (GRS) PRIOLA, DONALD V Minority biomedical research support program Intrinsic innervation of the heart
S06GM-08139-17 0027 (GRS) MORROW, CARY J Minority biomedical research support program Synthesis of potential inhibitors of cholesterol biosynthesis
S06GM-08139-17 0035 (GRS) BEAR, DAVID G Minority biomedical research support program Rho-dependent transcription termination of E coli
S06GM-08139-17 0038 (GRS) DAIL, WILLIAM G Minority biomedical research support program Innervation of penile erectile tissue
S06GM-08139-17 0039 (GRS) DAVIS, LARRY E Minority biomedical research support program Influenza B virus model of Reye's syndrome: Pathogenesis
S06GM-08139-17 0041 (GRS) YEATES, TERRY L Minority biomedical research support program: Host genetic factors affecting specificity on the coccidia of small mammals
S06GM-08139-17 0042 (GRS) FEENEY, DENNIS M Minority biomedical research support program Drug therapy for recovery from brain injury
S06GM-08139-17 0047 (GRS) MCDOWELL, THOMAS D Minority biomedical research support program Cell surface regulation in a cariogenic streptococci
S06GM-08139-17 0048 (GRS) MCGUFFEE, LINDA J Minority biomedical research support program Localization of calcium in smooth muscle
S06GM-08139-17 0050 (GRS) ONDRIAS, MARK R Minority biomedical research support program Time resolved and low temperature raman investigation of heme proteins
S06GM-08139-17 0057 (GRS) SALAND, LINDA C Minority biomedical research support program Ultrastructure and control of endorphin cells
S06GM-08139-17 0058 (GRS) SAVAGE, DANIEL D Minority biomedical research support program Effect of fetal ethanol exposure in hippocampal neurotransmission
S06GM-08139-17 0059 (GRS) SMITH, BRIAN R Minority biomedical research support program Mechanisms of bioactivation of drugs and other agents under hypoxia and normoxia
S06GM-08139-17 0062 (GRS) VOGEL, KATHRYN G Minority biomedical research support program Fibroblast proteoglycans and collagen in extracellular matrix
S06GM-08139-17 0063 (GRS) WALLACE, JAMES A Minority biomedical research support program Developmental regulation of neurotransmitter phenotype expression
S06GM-08139-17 0064 (GRS) WEISS, GERALD K Minority biomedical research support program How the locus coeruleus regulates the spread of seizures
S06GM-08139-17 0067 (GRS) VANDER JAGT, DAVID L Minority biomedical research support program Biological properties of gossypol and derivatives
S06GM-08139-17 0068 (GRS) ANDERSON, WILLIAM L Minority biomedical research support program Chemical modifications of antibodies
S06GM-08139-17 0072 (GRS) ROGERS, SHERRY L Minority biomedical research support program Laminin and fibronectin in neural crest differentiation
S06GM-08140-17 (GRS) SHACKS, SAMUEL J CHARLES R DREW UNIVERSITY 1621 E 120TH ST/MAIL PT #27 LOS ANGELES, CA 90059 Minority Biomedical Research Support Program
S06GM-08140-17 0001 (GRS) ALFRED, LAWRENCE J Minority Biomedical Research Support Program Human lymphocyte responses to carcinogenic chemicals
S06GM-08140-17 0010 (GRS) CARR, DAISY M Minority Biomedical Research Support Program In vivo effects of hallucinogens on sister chromatid exchanges
S06GM-08140-17 0015 (GRS) BLOOM, RONALD S Minority Biomedical Research Support Program Thyroid function and fetal pulmonary enzyme activity

PROJECT NO., ORGANIZATIONAL UNIT., INVESTIGATOR, ADDRESS, TITLE

S06GM-08140-17 0016 (GRS) COHN, MAJOR L Minority Biomedical Research Support Program Morphine--A new hypothesis of action
S06GM-08140-17 0017 (GRS) PATEL, RAMON Minority Biomedical Research Support Program T-cell subpopulations in renal disease and systemic lupus erythematosus
S06GM-08140-17 0018 (GRS) TAYLOR, STEPHEN C Minority Biomedical Research Support Program Cell mediated immune functions in Sickle Cell disease
S06GM-08140-17 0019 (GRS) WOJDANI, ARISTO Minority Biomedical Research Support Program Effects of environmental chemicals on cell-mediated immunity
S06GM-08153-16 (GRS) LEWIS, LESLIE A YORK COLLEGE OF THE CITY OF NY 94-20 GUY R BREWER BLVD JAMAICA, NY 11451 Research and training for biomedical career development
S06GM-08153-16 0003 (GRS) COHN, DEIRDRE A Research and training for biomedical career development Androgen sensitivity as factor in immunocompetence
S06GM-08153-16 0005 (GRS) LEWIS, LESLIE A Research and training for biomedical career development Gentamycin – Induced variant cell information in bacteria
S06GM-08153-16 0006 (GRS) YOUNG, PAUL E Research and training for biomedical career development Uniquely labeled amino acids for protein NMR
S06GM-08153-16 0007 (GRS) SCHEINER, PETER Research and training for biomedical career development New approach to antiviral nucleoside analogues
S06GM-08153-16 0008 (GRS) JOHNSON, LAWRENCE W Research and training for biomedical career development Electronic spectroscopy of simple porphyrims and bacteriorhodopsin
S06GM-08153-16 0009 (GRS) BARILE, FRANK A. Research and training for biomedical career development Properties of alveolar epithelial cells from injured lung
S06GM-08156-15 (GRS) ROBLES, LAURA J CALIFORNIA STATE UNIVERSITY 1000 E VICTORIA STREET CARSON, CA 90747 Minority biomedical research
S06GM-08156-15 0008 (GRS) SEELY, OLIVER, JR Minority biomedical research Analysis, comparison and alignment of protein sequences
S06GM-08156-15 0005 (GRS) MORAFKA, DAVID J Minority biomedical research Phylogenetics of moccasins (pit vipers)--improving antivenin specificity
S06GM-08156-15 0007 (GRS) ROBERTS, JOHN W Minority biomedical research Repetitive DNA sequence involvement in genomic rearrangements
S06GM-08156-15 0008 (GRS) SEELY, OLIVER, JR Minority biomedical research Analysis, comparison and alignment of protein sequences
S06GM-08159-13 (MPRC) FRAME, ANNE D INTER AMERICAN UNIV/PUERTO RIC P O BOX 1293 HATO REY, PUERTO RICO 00919 Advancing biomedical research and training in Puerto Rico
S06GM-08159-13 0001 (MPRC) ALZERRECA, ARNALDO Advancing biomedical research and training in Puerto Rico Stereoselective routes of O2 and N2 spirocycles with biomedical potential
S06GM-08159-13 0002 (MPRC) MIRANDA, MARIA Advancing biomedical research and training in Puerto Rico Neuroimmunomodulation patch clamp studies
S06GM-08159-13 0003 (MPRC) OQUENDO, CARMEN A Advancing biomedical research and training in Puerto Rico Vibrio species in market level seafood and coastal waters in Puerto Rico
S06GM-08159-13 0004 (MPRC) MEDINA, FREDDY R Advancing biomedical research and training in Puerto Rico Therapeutic plants for schistosomiasis and molluscicides
S06GM-08167-13 (MPRC) DUNBAR, JOSEPH C WAYNE STATE UNIVERSITY 5275 SCOTT HALL DETROIT, MI 48201 MBRS program at Wayne State University
S06GM-08167-13 0035 (MPRC) JACOBSON, JOSEPH L MBRS program at Wayne State University Effects of prenatal alcohol exposure on infant cognitive functioning
S06GM-08167-13 0036 (MPRC) JAY, JAMES M MBRS program at Wayne State University L forms of Listeria monocytogenes
S06GM-08167-13 0037 (MPRC) JEN, KAI-LIN CATHERINE MBRS program at Wayne State University Fructose feeding--Long term effect on carbohydrate and lipid metabolism in rats
S06GM-08167-13 0038 (MPRC) KUMAR, GYANENDRA MBRS program at Wayne State University Characterization of RNA polymerase II transcription protein
S06GM-08167-13 0039 (MPRC) LAWSON, DAVID M MBRS program at Wayne State University Diethylstibestrol and prolactin bioactivity in rats
S06GM-08167-13 0040 (MPRC) MAISEL, HARRY MBRS program at Wayne State University A study of structural lens proteins
S06GM-08167-13 0041 (MPRC) HIROSHI, MIZUKAMI MBRS program at Wayne State University Macromolecular interactions
S06GM-08167-13 0042 (MPRC) NANNA, IFENDU A MBRS program at Wayne State University Dietary fiber and nutrient interactions--In vitro assessment
S06GM-08167-13 0043 (MPRC) NORMILE, HOWARD J MBRS program at Wayne State University Animal models of dementia--Neurotransmitter interactions
S06GM-08167-13 0044 (MPRC) RAFOLS, JOSE MBRS program at Wayne State University Synaptic plasticity in aged neurons following deafferentation
S06GM-08167-13 0045 (MPRC) RAM, JEFFREY L MBRS program at Wayne State University Regulation of contraction in Aplysia smooth muscle
S06GM-08167-13 0046 (MPRC) RAUCH, HELENE C MBRS program at Wayne State University CNS cell targets in experimental allergic encephalomyelitis
S06GM-08167-13 0047 (MPRC) RILLEMA, JAMES A MBRS program at Wayne State University Hormonal regulation of metabolism in the mammary gland
S06GM-08167-13 0048 (MPRC) SIEGEL, ALBERT MBRS program at Wayne State University Development of RNA virus vector and model system for blocking viral infection
S06GM-08167-13 0049 (MPRC) SMITH, DAVID I MBRS program at Wayne State University Construction of a physical map for human chromosome 3
S06GM-08167-13 0050 (MPRC) SODJA, ANN MBRS program at Wayne State University Actin genes--Evolution of their structure and regulation

PROJECT NO., ORGANIZATIONAL UNIT., INVESTIGATOR, ADDRESS, TITLE

S06GM-08167-13 0051 (MPRC) STEPHENSON, ROBERT S MBRS program at Wayne State University Photoreceptor function--A genetic approach
S06GM-08167-13 0030 (MPRC) ALBIZATI, KIM F MBRS program at Wayne State University Chemistry of heterosubstituded oxyallyl cations and related substances
S06GM-08167-13 0031 (MPRC) BARRACO, ROBIN A MBRS program at Wayne State University Neuropeptide Y neuromodulation of CV central mechanisms
S06GM-08167-13 0032 (MPRC) BERMAN, ROBERT F MBRS program at Wayne State University Role of adenosine in experimental epilepsy--A1 and A2 receptors
S06GM-08167-13 0033 (MPRC) BROOKS, S C MBRS program at Wayne State University Estrogen structure-receptor relationship
S06GM-08167-13 0034 (MPRC) DUNBAR, JOSEPH C MBRS program at Wayne State University CNS nutrient sensing and pathogenesis of diabetes
S06GM-08167-13 0052 (MPRC) WALSH, MARY F MBRS program at Wayne State University Altered adrenergic control of ANP secretion in diabetes
S06GM-08167-13 0053 (MPRC) YOUNG, ALICE M MBRS program at Wayne State University Behavioral pharmacology of opioid tolerance
S06GM-08168-13 (GRS) FISHMAN, MYER M COLLEGE UNIVERSITY OF NEW YORK CONVENT AVE @ 138TH STREET NEW YORK, NY 10031 Enhanced raman effect at the electrode solution-interface
S06GM-08168-13 0021 (GRS) AXENROD, T Enhanced raman effect at the electrode solution-interface Spin-coupling between directely bonded 15N-15N nuclei
S06GM-08168-13 0022 (GRS) BALOGH-NAIR, V Enhanced raman effect at the electrode solution-interface Synthetic compounds to probe molecular events in biology
S06GM-08168-13 0007 (GRS) RUSSELL, CHARLOTTE S Enhanced raman effect at the electrode solution-interface Lipids and lipoproteoglycan hemagglutinins from Nereis
S06GM-08168-13 0008 (GRS) SCHULZ, HORST H Enhanced raman effect at the electrode solution-interface Fatty acid metabolism in heart
S06GM-08168-13 0009 (GRS) SLOAN, DONALD L Enhanced raman effect at the electrode solution-interface Enzymic phosphoribosyl transfer reactions in yeast
S06GM-08168-13 0011 (GRS) COSLOY, SHARON D Enhanced raman effect at the electrode solution-interface Molecular mechanism of genetic recombination in escherichia coli
S06GM-08168-13 0012 (GRS) WALLMAN, JOSHUA Enhanced raman effect at the electrode solution-interface Role of vision in the etiology of axial myopia
S06GM-08168-13 0013 (GRS) WOODWARD, ARTHUR E Enhanced raman effect at the electrode solution-interface Carbon-13-nuclear magnetic resonance studies of trans-1,4-polyisoprene
S06GM-08168-13 0014 (GRS) BIRKE, RONALD L Enhanced raman effect at the electrode solution-interface Redox chemistry of vitamin B12 derivatives
S06GM-08168-13 0015 (GRS) CALLENDER, ROBERT H Enhanced raman effect at the electrode solution-interface Resonance raman studies of rhodopsin and related pigments
S06GM-08168-13 0020 (GRS) AKINS, DANIEL L Enhanced raman effect at the electrode solution-interface Raman scattering by sensitizer dyes on surfaces
S06GM-08168-13 0021 (GRS) AXENROD, T Enhanced raman effect at the electrode solution-interface Spin-coupling between directely bonded 15n-15n nuclei
S06GM-08168-13 0022 (GRS) BALOGH-NAIR, V Enhanced raman effect at the electrode solution-interface Synthetic compounds to probe molecular events in biology
S06GM-08168-13 0016 (GRS) GREEN, MICHAEL E Enhanced raman effect at the electrode solution-interface Ion transport in the membrane solution-interface
S06GM-08168-13 0018 (GRS) MC KENNA, OLIVIA C Enhanced raman effect at the electrode solution-interface Functional anatomy of accessory optic system/pretectum
S06GM-08169-13 (SRC) RAJANNA, BETTAIYA SELMA UNIVERSITY 1501 LAPSLEY ST SELMA, AL 36701 MBRS Program at Selma University
S06GM-08169-13 0002 (SRC) RAJANNA, BETTAIYA MBRS Program at Selma University Biomechanism of heavy metal toxicity
S06GM-08169-13 0003 (SRC) CHAPATWALA, KIRIT D MBRS Program at Selma University Mycobacteria--Drug suceptibility, pathogenicity, immunogenicity
S06GM-08169-13 0004 (SRC) HOBSON, MARVIN MBRS Program at Selma University Research enrichment activities in biomedical sciences
S06GM-08169-13 0005 (SRC) SHOBHA, SRIHARAN MBRS Program at Selma University Larvicide effects against mosquitoes and non-target organisms
S06GM-08170-11A2 (MPRC) HAMILL, DELPHIA F INCARNATE WORD COLLEGE 4301 BROADWAY SAN ANTONIO, TX 78209 MBRS program at Incarnate Word College
S06GM-08170-11A2 0001 (MPRC) HAYE, KEITH R MBRS program at Incarnate Word College Developmental regulation of endocytosis during myogenesis
S06GM-08170-11A2 0002 (MPRC) YOUNG, ELEANOR A MBRS program at Incarnate Word College GI and cardiac adaptation to semi-starvation and refeeding
S06GM-08171-11 (MPRC) JOHNSON, ROBERT H MEDGAR EVERS COLLEGE 1150 CARROLL STREET BROOKLYN, NY 11225 The biomedical research training program
S06GM-08171-11 0008 (MPRC) FERDINAND, PATRICA E The biomedical research training program Effect of IL-3 and hemin on chick yolk sac primitive erythroid cells
S06GM-08171-11 0009 (MPRC) JOHNSON, ROBERT H The biomedical research training program The synthesis and characterization of melanocyte stimulating hormone analogs
S06GM-08171-11 0010 (MPRC) LEWIS, ARTHUR S The biomedical research training program Isolation, purification, and characterization of a peptide carrier for coenzyme Q
S06GM-08174-13 (MPRC) HELLER, RICHARD F BRONX COMMUNITY COLLEGE UNIVERSITY AVE & W 181 ST BRONX, NY 10453 Minority biomedical research support program at BCC
S06GM-08174-13 0003 (MPRC) HELLER, RICHARD F Minority biomedical research support program at BCC Molecular mechanisms of taurine prophylaxsis in oxidant lung injury
S06GM-08174-13 0005 (MPRC) DAVIS, JOHN W Minority biomedical research support program at BCC Microbal urease--A potential antigen mimic of HLA-B27
S06GM-08174-13 0007 (MPRC) SQUITIERI, LOUISE Minority biomedical research support program at BCC BCC research environment activities program
S06GM-08176-12 (GRS) FLEISSNER, ERWIN HUNTER COLLEGE OF CUNY 695 PARK AVENUE NEW YORK, N Y 10021 Minority biomedical research support program
S06GM-08176-12 0004 (GRS) COHEN, WILLIAM D Minority biomedical research support program Marginal band system of erythrocytes
S06GM-08176-12 0014 (GRS) TOMASZ, MARIA Minority biomedical research support program Effects of adducts of mitomycinn C on DNA structure and function
S06GM-08176-12 0018 (GRS) HARDING, CHERYL F Minority biomedical research support program Hormonal activation of male social behavior
S06GM-08176-12 0019 (GRS) LIPKE, PETER N Minority biomedical research support program Cell adhesion in saccaromyces cerevisiae
S06GM-08176-12 0022 (GRS) DIEM, MAX Minority biomedical research support program Solution conformation of biomolecules via infrared circular dichroism
S06GM-08176-12 0023 (GRS) FRANCK, RICHARD W Minority biomedical research support program Synthesis of aureolic acid antibiotics family
S06GM-08176-12 0024 (GRS) GOSS, DIXIE Minority biomedical research support program Biophysical studies of the regulation of mRNA translation
S06GM-08176-12 0025 (GRS) LAVALLEE, DAVID K Minority biomedical research support program Porphyrin studies--DNA interactions and radionuclide binding
S06GM-08176-12 0026 (GRS) RUDNER, RIVKA Minority biomedical research support program Redundancy and function of ribosomal RNA genes in Bacillus subtilis
S06GM-08176-12 0027 (GRS) SWEENEY, WILLIAM Minority biomedical research support program PH dependent properties of Azotobacter vinelandii
S06GM-08177-12 (MPRC) CHAN, CARCY L EAST LOS ANGELES COLLEGE 1301 E BROOKLYN AVENUE MONTEREY PARK, CA 91754 Biomedical research training program for two year college students
S06GM-08180-12 (MPRC) HOYTE, ROBERT M SUNY/COLL AT OLD WESTBURY PO BOX 210 OLD WESTBURY, NY 11568 Minority biomedical research support program
S06GM-08180-12 0001 (MPRC) HOYTE, ROBERT M Minority biomedical research support program Synthesis and purification of biologically important steroid analogs
S06GM-08180-12 0002 (MPRC) COLON-URBAN, RITA Minority biomedical research support program Biologically active substances from bryozoans
S06GM-08180-12 0009 (MPRC) PRYOR, STEPHEN C Minority biomedical research support program Biochemical genetics of arthropod disease vectors
S06GM-08182-12 (MPRC) OFOSU, MILDRED D DELAWARE STATE COLLEGE 1200 NORTH DUPONT HIGHWAY DOVER, DE 19901 Cancer, lipid, stress and thyroid research
S06GM-08182-12 0001 (MPRC) HELMY, FATMA M Cancer, lipid, stress and thyroid research Lipolytic enzymes & substrates in pancreas, intestine, kidney
S06GM-08182-12 0002 (MPRC) MILLER, ALBERT B Cancer, lipid, stress and thyroid research Detection versus control of stress-related physiological variables
S06GM-08182-12 0003 (MPRC) OFOSU, GUSTAV A Cancer, lipid, stress and thyroid research Platinum-thymine for combination chemotherapy of cancer
S06GM-08182-12 0005 (MPRC) OFOSU, MILDRED D Cancer, lipid, stress and thyroid research HLA molecular typing of Blacks with Graves' disease
S06GM-08182-12 0006 (MPRC) WASFI, SADIQ H Cancer, lipid, stress and thyroid research Heteropolymetalate anions as anticancer agents
S06GM-08182-12 0007 (MPRC) WILKINSON, DONALD R Cancer, lipid, stress and thyroid research Synthesis of toxic amino acids hypoglycine A and hypoglycine B
S06GM-08192-12 (MPRC) HICKS, ROBERT A SAN JOSE UNIVERSITY ONE WASHINGTON SQUARE SAN JOSE, CA 95192 Interdisciplinary biomedical research program
S06GM-08192-12 0006 (MPRC) BRANZ, STEPHEN E. Interdisciplinary biomedical research program Intramolecular hydride transfer--Prephenic acid to para hydroxyphenyllactic acid
S06GM-08192-12 0007 (MPRC) FOWLER, ROBERT G. Interdisciplinary biomedical research program Molecular mechanisms of mutagenesis
S06GM-08192-12 0008 (MPRC) HICKS, ROBERT A. Interdisciplinary biomedical research program Sleep, and health related behaviors
S06GM-08192-12 0009 (MPRC) KELLMAN, RAYMOND Interdisciplinary biomedical research program Synthesis of new polymeric biomaterials
S06GM-08192-12 0012 (MPRC) SILBER, HERBERT B. Interdisciplinary biomedical research program Metallo-biochemistry
S06GM-08192-12 0014 (MPRC) VEREGGE, SYLVIA ANN Interdisciplinary biomedical research program Mechanisms by which gonadal steroids modulate neuronal activity
S06GM-08192-12 0016 (MPRC) ASHLEY, KEVIN E Interdisciplinary biomedical research program Interfacial electrochemistry of biomolecules and relate species
S06GM-08192-12 0017 (MPRC) BOOTHBY, JOHN T Interdisciplinary biomedical research program Borrelia burgdorferi HSP-1 in Lyme disease
S06GM-08192-12 0018 (MPRC) BRADEN, JEFFERY P Interdisciplinary biomedical research program Intelligence, speed of information processing, and deafness
S06GM-08192-12 0019 (MPRC) GERMERAAD, SUSAN E Interdisciplinary biomedical research program Sodium channel genes in Drosophila
S06GM-08192-12 0020 (MPRC) SINGMASTER-HERNANDEZ, KAREN A Interdisciplinary biomedical research program Matrix and gas phase reactions of nitrosyl halides and ozone
S06GM-08192-12 0021 (MPRC) KERR, JOANNE T Interdisciplinary biomedical research program Alcohol metabolism, cytotoxicity, and alcoholism

S06GM-08194-12 (MPRC) TSIN, ANDREW UNIV OF TEXAS AT SAN ANTONIO SAN ANTONIO, TX 78285 Minorities in research and science achievement program

S06GM-08194-12 0004 (MPRC) RENTHAL, ROBERT D Minorities in research and science achievement program Purple membrane proton pump

S06GM-08194-12 0022 (MPRC) CLAIBORNE, BRENDA J Minorities in research and science achievement program Structural changes in adult mammalian neurons

S06GM-08194-12 0026 (MPRC) CHAMBERS, JAMES P Minorities in research and science achievement program Changes in Ca homeostasis during aging and Alzheimer's disease

S06GM-08194-12 0028 (MPRC) LEWIS, JAMES A Minorities in research and science achievement program Molecular genetics of nematode acetylcholine receptor

S06GM-08194-12 0029 (MPRC) MARTINEZ, ANDREW O Minorities in research and science achievement program Genetic analysis of MTS-CAM1.2--A WI38SV40 surface antigen

S06GM-08194-12 0033 (MPRC) LONGBOTHAM, HAROLD G Minorities in research and science achievement program Modeling of visual loss via Gabor transforms and morphological shape analysis

S06GM-08194-12 0030 (MPRC) SENSEMAN, DAVID M Minorities in research and science achievement program Information processing in vertebrate olfactory bulb

S06GM-08194-12 0031 (MPRC) TSIN, ANDREW T C Minorities in research and science achievement program Retinal ester hydrolase

S06GM-08194-12 0032 (MPRC) WALMSLEY, JUDITH A Minorities in research and science achievement program Cation dependent aggregation of guanine dinucleotide

S06GM-08197-10 (GRS) SCHNUR, PAUL UNIV OF SOUTHERN COLORADO 2200 BONFORTE BOULEVARD PUEBLO, CO 81001-4901 MBRS program at the University of Southern Colorado

S06GM-08197-10 0010 (GRS) DRUELINGER, MELVIN L MBRS program at the University of Southern Colorado Organofluorine compounds of biological interest via selective fluorinations

S06GM-08197-10 0006 (GRS) HERRMANN, SCOTT J MBRS program at the University of Southern Colorado Anodonta grandis--Biomonitor of aquatic lead pollution

S06GM-08197-10 0007 (GRS) KULKOSKY, PAUL J MBRS program at the University of Southern Colorado Motivation by neuropeptides--Ethanol consumption and behavior

S06GM-08197-10 0008 (GRS) MAHAN, KENT I MBRS program at the University of Southern Colorado Metals in particulate, biological materials, and water

S06GM-08197-10 0009 (GRS) SCHNUR, PAUL MBRS program at the University of Southern Colorado Effects of opiods on hamster locomotor activity

S06GM-08197-10 0010 (GRS) DRUELINGER, MELVIN L MBRS program at the University of Southern Colorado Organofluorine compounds of biological interest via selective fluorinations

S06GM-08198-10 (SRC) FOSTER, HENRY W MEHARRY MEDICAL COLLEGE 1005 DR D B TODD BLVD NASHVILLE, TN 37208 Minority biomedical support

S06GM-08198-10 0001 (SRC) TALLEY, PAUL ALEXIS Minority biomedical support Pulmonary function standards in black Americans

S06GM-08198-10 0009 (SRC) DAS, SALIL Minority biomedical support Physical stress & deoxygenation on membrane lipid peroxidation of rbc/sickle cell

S06GM-08198-10 0010 (SRC) HARA, SABURO Minority biomedical support Response of infants with sickle cell disease to Hemophilus influenza B vaccine

S06GM-08198-10 0011 (SRC) HARDY, ROBERT E Minority biomedical support Steroid hormone receptors in leiomyomas of black and white females

S06GM-08198-10 0012 (SRC) HARGREAVES, MARGARET Minority biomedical support Comparison of the body fat and lean body mass of black and white females

S06GM-08198-10 0013 (SRC) NEVELS, HAROLD Minority biomedical support Determinants of coronary artery disease in black medical students and residents

S06GM-08198-10 0014 (SRC) SOUTH, MARY ANN Minority biomedical support Complement activation in sickle cell disease

S06GM-08198-10 0015 (SRC) TURNER, ERNEST A Minority biomedical support Cell line to support production of infectious B19 virus particles

S06GM-08202-11 (GRS) COOK, NATHAN H LINCOLN UNIVERSITY 820 CHESTNUT STREET JEFFERSON CITY, MO 65102-0029 Research participation in the biomedical sciences

S06GM-08202-11 0003 (GRS) MILLER, HERMAN T Research participation in the biomedical sciences Hyper-responsiveness factor from hog kidney

S06GM-08202-11 0006 (GRS) HANCOCK, ROBERT Research participation in the biomedical sciences Effect of aspartame ingestion on radial-arm maze

S06GM-08202-11 0007 (GRS) MEREDITH, STEVEN Research participation in the biomedical sciences Control of growth of primordial follicles

S06GM-08206-10 (GRS) EDWARDS, MATTHEW E FAYETTEVILLE STATE UNIVERSITY FAYETTEVILLE, NC 28301-4297 Restriction endonuclease analysis of repeated DNA in the genome of avians

S06GM-08206-10 0005 (GRS) HIGGINS, ROBERT H Restriction endonuclease analysis of repeated DNA in the genome of avians Mechanism of ring opening of azetidines and azetidine-3-ols

S06GM-08206-10 0006 (GRS) WILLIAMS, P I Restriction endonuclease analysis of repeated DNA in the genome of avians Proteins--magnetization, vortices, semiconductivity and superconductivity

S06GM-08206-10 0004 (GRS) WADDLE, FLOYD R Restriction endonuclease analysis of repeated DNA in the genome of avians Genetics of segregation distortion

S06GM-08206-10 0005 (GRS) HIGGINS, ROBERT H Restriction endonuclease analysis of repeated DNA in the genome of avians Mechanism of ring opening of azetidines and azetidine-3-ols

S06GM-08206-10 0006 (GRS) WILLIAMS, P I Restriction endonuclease analysis of repeated DNA in the genome of avians Proteins--magnetization, vortices, semiconductivity and superconductivity

S06GM-08211-09 (GRS) WILLINGHAM, WILLIAM M UNIVERSITY OF ARKANSAS BOX 4055 PINE BLUFF, AR 71601 Antineoplastic and radioprotectant copper (II) and manganese (II) salicylates

S06GM-08211-09 0007 (GRS) ORR, CLIFTON Antineoplastic and radioprotectant copper (II) and manganese (II) salicylates Alterations in anticancer drug activity by anguidine

S06GM-08211-09 0008 (GRS) OWASOYO, JOSEPH Antineoplastic and radioprotectant copper (II) and manganese (II) salicylates Effect of diabetes on rat brain cholinergic system and memory

S06GM-08211-09 0010 (GRS) MCCONNELL, ROSE Antineoplastic and radioprotectant copper (II) and manganese (II) salicylates Synthesis and biochemical assay of novel proteinase

S06GM-08211-09 0007 (GRS) ORR, CLIFTON Antineoplastic and radioprotectant copper (II) and manganese (II) salicylates Alterations in anticancer drug activity by anguidine

S06GM-08211-09 0008 (GRS) OWASOYO, JOSEPH Antineoplastic and radioprotectant copper (II) and manganese (II) salicylates Effect of diabetes on rat brain cholinergic system

S06GM-08211-09 0010 (GRS) MCCONNELL, ROSE Antineoplastic and radioprotectant copper (II) and manganese (II) salicylates Synthesis and biochemical assay of novel proteinase

S06GM-08211-09 0006 (GRS) WILLINGHAM, WILLIAM M Antineoplastic and radioprotectant copper (II) and manganese (II) salicylates Antineoplastic and radioprotectant copper (II) and manganese (II) salicylates

S06GM-08212-08 (MPRC) PEACOCK, THOMAS D FOND DU LAC RESERVATION 105 UNIVERSITY ROAD CLOQUET, MN 55720 NI-SHOU-GABAWAG-FDL-UMD Biomedical Research Project

S06GM-08212-08 0011 (MPRC) PEACOCK, THOMAS D NI-SHOU-GABAWAG-FDL-UMD Biomedical Research Project Enrichment activities

S06GM-08212-08 0012 (MPRC) BRADBURY, STEPHEN P NI-SHOU-GABAWAG-FDL-UMD Biomedical Research Project Assessment of metabolic activation in Rainbow Trout

S06GM-08212-08 0013 (MPRC) MCKIM, JAMES M NI-SHOU-GABAWAG-FDL-UMD Biomedical Research Project Predicting aquatic toxicity of hazard waste constituents and exposure

S06GM-08212-08 0014 (MPRC) JOHNSON, RODNEY D NI-SHOU-GABAWAG-FDL-UMD Biomedical Research Project Medaka carcinogenesis model

S06GM-08215-09 (GRS) SPEIDEL, HAROLD K NORTHERN ARIZONA UNIVERSITY PO BOX 5640 FLAGSTAFF, AZ 86011-5640 MBRS program at Northern Arizona University

S06GM-08215-09 0003 (GRS) CAPLE, G MBRS program at Northern Arizona University Templated biosensors in semiconducting systems

S06GM-08215-09 0004 (GRS) EASTMAN, M MBRS program at Northern Arizona University NMR of free radical-cyclodextrin complexes

S06GM-08215-09 0005 (GRS) HUTTLINGER, K MBRS program at Northern Arizona University Diabetes mellitus in Navajo and Hopi men and women

S06GM-08215-09 0006 (GRS) NYE, C MBRS program at Northern Arizona University Parameters and nature of language acquisition in young Navajo children

S06GM-08215-09 0007 (GRS) PRIOR, D MBRS program at Northern Arizona University Hormonal control of neural and cardiac responsiveness

S06GM-08215-09 0008 (GRS) SPEIDEL, H MBRS program at Northern Arizona University Characteristics of antimicrobials from algae

S06GM-08215-09 0009 (GRS) WEEMS, L MBRS program at Northern Arizona University Language acquisition of native American children with fetal alcohol syndrome

S06GM-08216-09 (MPRC) ALEGRIA, ANTONIO E HUMACAO UNIVERSITY COLLEGE CUH STATION HUMACAO, PR 00661 Humacao University College biomedical research improvement program

S06GM-08216-09 0011 (MPRC) ALEGRIA, ANTONIO E Humacao University College biomedical research improvement program Thermodynamic stability of semiquinones as a function of their environment

S06GM-08216-09 0012 (MPRC) BONILLA-ALVAREZ, MARISSA Humacao University College biomedical research improvement program Development of an automated analysis of lipids

S06GM-08216-09 0013 (MPRC) DEL LLANO, ANA M Humacao University College biomedical research improvement program Nuclear events and cytokine production in mixed lymphocyte cultures

S06GM-08216-09 0014 (MPRC) MARRERO-CORLETTO, ROBERTO Humacao University College biomedical research improvement program Olefin oxidation by hybrid model monoxygenase systems

S06GM-08216-09 0015 (MPRC) NIEVES, ILEANA Humacao University College biomedical research improvement program Vanadium interaction studies in relation to the inhibition of Na+-K+-ATPase

S06GM-08216-09 0016 (MPRC) ORTIZ-MARCALES, MARGARITA Humacao University College biomedical research improvement program Stereochemical controlled synthesis of biologically active amines

S06GM-08216-09 0017 (MPRC) REYES-CINTRON, ZELIDETH E Humacao University College biomedical research improvement program Elucidation of the factors affecting electrofacilitation for gaseous detection

S06GM-08218-08 (GRS) YOUNG, DAVID M MONTANA STATE UNIVERSITY MARSH LABORATORY BOZEMAN, MONT 59717 Montana American Indian biomedical program

S06GM-08218-08 0018 (GRS) PADEN, CHARLES M Montana American Indian biomedical program Monoclonal antibodies to neurosecretory cells

S06GM-08218-08 0019 (GRS) PHILLIPS, DWIGHT E Montana American Indian biomedical program Alcohol induced effects in the developing CNS--Glial cells and myelin

S06GM-08218-08 0020 (GRS) ROGERS, BARBARA P Montana American Indian biomedical program Effect of insulin and EGF on keratinocytes from diabetic mice

S06GM-08218-08 0021 (GRS) SANDS, DAVID C Montana American Indian biomedical program Biotechnical approach to weed control on Indian reservations

S06GM-08218-08 0024 (GRS) FEVOLD, H RICHARD Montana American Indian biomedical program Control of P-450I7a gene expression

S06GM-08218-08 0025 (GRS) KNAPP, STUART E Montana American Indian biomedical program Biological control of fascioliasis

S06GM-08218-08 0026 (GRS) MADSEN, ROBERT R Montana American Indian biomedical program Survey of important invertebrates on the Crow and Cheyenne reservations

PROJECT NO., ORGANIZATIONAL UNIT., INVESTIGATOR, ADDRESS, TITLE

S06GM-08218-08 0027 (GRS) MUNDY, BRADFORD P Montana American Indian biomedical program New approaches to oxepanes
S06GM-08218-08 0004 (GRS) MC MILLAN, JAMES A Montana American Indian biomedical program Organization of spinal reflexes
S06GM-08218-08 0009 (GRS) WARREN, GUYLYN R Montana American Indian biomedical program Rapid bioassays as monitors of potentially toxic chemicals
S06GM-08218-08 0011 (GRS) WORLEY, DAVID E Montana American Indian biomedical program Susceptibility of swine to sylvatic Trichinella spiralis isolates
S06GM-08218-08 0012 (GRS) CUTLER, JIMMY E Montana American Indian biomedical program Morphogenesis of Candida albicans
S06GM-08218-08 0014 (GRS) CROWLE, PATRICIA K Montana American Indian biomedical program Mast cells and tumor-associated angiogenesis
S06GM-08218-08 0015 (GRS) HILL, WALTER E Montana American Indian biomedical program Probing ribosomal function
S06GM-08218-08 0017 (GRS) NEWMAN, ROSEMARY K Montana American Indian biomedical program Effect of soluble grain fiber on lipoprotein metabolism
S06GM-08223-08 (MPRC) KOMISARUK, BARRY R RUTGERS UNIVERSITY 360 MARTIN LUTHER KING JR BLVD NEW BRUNSWICK, NJ 08903 MBRS Program at Rutgers-Newark
S06GM-08223-08 0020 (MPRC) JORDAN, FRANK MBRS Program at Rutgers-Newark Enzymes that decarboxylate pyruvate
S06GM-08223-08 0021 (MPRC) KOMISARUK, BARRY R. MBRS Program at Rutgers-Newark Analgesia produced by birth canal stimulation
S06GM-08223-08 0022 (MPRC) MENDELSOHN, RICHARD MBRS Program at Rutgers-Newark Lipid control of membrane protein organization
S06GM-08223-08 0024 (MPRC) ROSENBLATT, JAY S. MBRS Program at Rutgers-Newark Steroid hormone and prolactin in the maternal behavior of rats and hamsters
S06GM-08223-08 0026 (MPRC) BUZSAK1, GYORGI MBRS Program at Rutgers-Newark Suppression of epilepsy by fetal tissue grafts
S06GM-08223-08 0027 (MPRC) CHENG, MEI-FANG MBRS Program at Rutgers-Newark Vocalization--Self stimulation and opioid system
S06GM-08223-08 0028 (MPRC) FEDER, HARVEY H MBRS Program at Rutgers-Newark Taurine in hypertension
S06GM-08223-08 0029 (MPRC) FRYER, RODNEY I MBRS Program at Rutgers-Newark Drug binding site interactions at the central GABA/BZR receptor
S06GM-08223-08 0030 (MPRC) GILCHRIST, ALAN L MBRS Program at Rutgers-Newark Processing of luminance gradients for determining surface lighttness
S06GM-08223-08 0031 (MPRC) GULICK, ELSIE E MBRS Program at Rutgers-Newark MS patient self assessment of health
S06GM-08223-08 0032 (MPRC) SWANN, JENNIFER M MBRS Program at Rutgers-Newark Neuroanatomy of tachykinins in the mating behavior pathway
S06GM-08223-08 0033 (MPRC) JERMMOTT, LORETTA SWEET MBRS Program at Rutgers-Newark Social and cognitive theory and AIDS prevention amoung minority college students
S06GM-08224-07 (GRS) BAEZ, ADRIANA U P R MEDICAL SCIS CAMPUS PO BOX 36-5067 SAN JUAN, PR 00936-5067 UPR medical sciences campus MBRS program
S06GM-08224-07 0011 (GRS) HENTALL, IAN D UPR medical sciences campus MBRS program Neuronal co-operativity in brainstem inhibitory actions
S06GM-08224-07 0012 (GRS) HINE, A BROMFIELD UPR medical sciences campus MBRS program Abused drug effects and interactions on intracranial reward
S06GM-08224-07 0013 (GRS) KOZEK, WIESLAW J UPR medical sciences campus MBRS program Immune humoral responses in human onchocerciasis
S06GM-08224-07 0014 (GRS) KRABELBURD, EDMUNDO N UPR medical sciences campus MBRS program Antiviral agents against human immunodeficiency virus and herpes
S06GM-08224-07 0015 (GRS) LAVERGNE, JULIO A UPR medical sciences campus MBRS program Ultrasound and the structural and functional integrity of immunological cells
S06GM-08224-07 0017 (GRS) ORTIZ, JOSE G UPR medical sciences campus MBRS program Pipecolic acid transport, metabolism and function
S06GM-08224-07 0018 (GRS) PRESTON, ALAN M UPR medical sciences campus MBRS program Gestation diabetes mellitus--Animal model development
S06GM-08224-07 0019 (GRS) SILLAU, ALBERTO H UPR medical sciences campus MBRS program Mitochondrial function and distribution in hypoxic cells
S06GM-08224-07 0020 (GRS) OPAVA-STITZER, SUSAN C UPR medical sciences campus MBRS program Action of ADH on renin secretion in isolated glomeruli
S06GM-08224-07 0021 (GRS) TORRES-BAUZA, LUIS J UPR medical sciences campus MBRS program Cellular events, nuclear proteins & transcription & c. albicans morphogenesis
S06GM-08224-07 0022 (GRS) VARGAS, FERNANDO F UPR medical sciences campus MBRS program Factors mediating albumin effect on vascular permeability
S06GM-08224-07 0023 (GRS) ZLOTNIK, HINDA UPR medical sciences campus MBRS program Nocardia antigens
S06GM-08224-07 0001 (GRS) BANERJEE, DIPAK K UPR medical sciences campus MBRS program Regulation of dolichol-cascade in endothelial cells by cAMP-related stimuli
S06GM-08224-07 0002 (GRS) BASILIO, CARLOS M UPR medical sciences campus MBRS program Influence of nicotinic acid on ethanol effects
S06GM-08224-07 0003 (GRS) BERNSTEIN, JAIME UPR medical sciences campus MBRS program Pulmonary metabolism of ethanol
S06GM-08224-07 0004 (GRS) BOLAMOS, BENJAMIN UPR medical sciences campus MBRS program Role of cell mediated immunity in pulmonary cryptococcosis
S06GM-08224-07 0005 (GRS) CHAVEZ, PEDRO I UPR medical sciences campus MBRS program Bioactive compounds from tropical forests
S06GM-08224-07 0006 (GRS) DEMELLO, WALMOY C UPR medical sciences campus MBRS program Cell to cell communication in the heart
S06GM-08224-07 0007 (GRS) EBERHARDT, MANFRED K UPR medical sciences campus MBRS program Aromatic hydroxylation and radical cations

PROJECT NO., ORGANIZATIONAL UNIT., INVESTIGATOR, ADDRESS, TITLE

S06GM-08224-07 0008 (GRS) ESCOBALES, NELSON UPR medical sciences campus MBRS program Biochemical characterization on Na/H exchange in vascular endothelial cells
S06GM-08224-07 0009 (GRS) FERNANDEZ-REPOLLET, EMMA D UPR medical sciences campus MBRS program Deep nephron function and structure
S06GM-08224-07 0010 (GRS) HABEEB, AHMED UPR medical sciences campus MBRS program Monoclonal antibodies to chemically attemted cercaria of S mansoni
S06GM-08225-07 (MPRC) SWARTZ, KARYL B LEHMAN COLLEGE 250 BEDFORD PARK BLVD, WEST BRONX, NY 10468 Minority biomedical research support at Lehman College
S06GM-08225-07 0003 (MPRC) BASILE, DOMINICK Minority biomedical research support at Lehman College Cell-surface glycoproteins and place-dependent suppression of cell proliferation
S06GM-08225-07 0006 (MPRC) JAKINOVICH, WILLIAM Minority biomedical research support at Lehman College Specificity of mammalian sweet taste response
S06GM-08225-07 0007 (MPRC) JENSEN, THOMAS E Minority biomedical research support at Lehman College Target sites and compartmentalization in heavy metal exposed cells
S06GM-08225-07 0008 (MPRC) KINCAID, DWIGHT T Minority biomedical research support at Lehman College Morphometrics of biological images--Boundry method automation
S06GM-08225-07 0010 (MPRC) PHILLIPP, MANFRED Minority biomedical research support at Lehman College Boronic acid inhibitors of beta-lactamases
S06GM-08225-07 0011 (MPRC) RACHLIN, JOSEPH Minority biomedical research support at Lehman College pH and the heavy metals aluminum, copper, lead, and zinc
S06GM-08225-07 0012 (MPRC) SWARTZ, KARYL B Minority biomedical research support at Lehman College Cognitive components of social perception in nonhuman primates
S06GM-08225-07 0013 (MPRC) BORGESE, THOMAS A Minority biomedical research support at Lehman College Mechanisms of hemoglobin polymerization and red cell aggregation in goosefish
S06GM-08225-07 0014 (MPRC) HAMBRICK-DIXON, PRISCELLA J Minority biomedical research support at Lehman College Subway noise--Black and Latino child health and physiological responses
S06GM-08225-07 0015 (MPRC) WURTZEL, ELEANORE T Minority biomedical research support at Lehman College Molecular biology of carotenoid biosynthesis
S06GM-08225-07 0016 (MPRC) DIBENNARDO, ROBERT Minority biomedical research support at Lehman College Age variation of the lumbosacral laminae--Relation to spina bifida occulta
S06GM-08225-07 0017 (MPRC) YATES, SUZANNE M Minority biomedical research support at Lehman College Determinants of stress resilience among urban minority college students
S06GM-08225-07 0018 (MPRC) DAYAN, JEAN Minority biomedical research support at Lehman College Sulfur-containing DNAs useful for sequencing by scanning/tunneling microscopy
S06GM-08225-07 0019 (MPRC) DOUGHERTY, CHARLES Minority biomedical research support at Lehman College Peptide sulfonamides--Synthesis and enzymatic evaluation
S06GM-08232-06 (GRS) BOWER, ANNETTE MOUNT ST MARYS COLLEGE 12001 CHALON RD LOS ANGELES, CA 90049 MBRS program at Mount St. Mary's College
S06GM-08232-06 0010 (GRS) SIEBERT, ELEANOR D MBRS program at Mount St. Mary's College Dynamics of phase separation in model biological systems
S06GM-08232-06 0008 (GRS) BOWER, ANNETTE MBRS program at Mount St. Mary's College Effects of pro-opiomelanocortin derived peptides on osmoregulation
S06GM-08232-06 0009 (GRS) REAMS, R RENEE MBRS program at Mount St. Mary's College Calorimetric measurement of the thermal unfolding of carbonic anhydrase
S06GM-08232-06 0010 (GRS) SIEBERT, ELEANOR D MBRS program at Mount St. Mary's College Dynamics of phase separation in model biological systems
S06GM-08232-06 0009 (GRS) REAMS, R RENEE MBRS program at Mount St. Mary's College Calorimetric measurement of the thermal unfolding of carbonic anhydrase
S06GM-08238-05 (MPRC) JENSEN, JAMES L CALIFORNIA STATE UNIVERSITY 1250 BELLFLWOER BLVD LONG BEACH, CA 90840-3903 Mbrs program at california state university long beach
S06GM-08238-05 0004 (MPRC) COHLBERG, JEFFREY A Mbrs program at california state university long beach Structure, assembly, and function of intermediate filaments
S06GM-08238-05 0005 (MPRC) JENSEN, JAMES L Mbrs program at california state university long beach Reactivity of heavy metal ions with organosulfur moieties
S06GM-08238-05 0006 (MPRC) KINGSFORD, LAURA Mbrs program at california state university long beach Structure and function of La Crosse virus G1 glycoprotein
S06GM-08238-05 0008 (MPRC) ACEY, ROGER A Mbrs program at california state university long beach Trace metal metabolism in developing Artemia Salina
S06GM-08238-05 0009 (MPRC) ANJO, DENNIS M Mbrs program at california state university long beach Activation of carbon electrodes for catecholamine analysis
S06GM-08238-05 0010 (MPRC) HARTLEY, JOELLEN T Mbrs program at california state university long beach Behavioral and physiological correlates of cognitive aging
S06GM-08238-05 0011 (MPRC) KHATRA, BALWANT S Mbrs program at california state university long beach Glycogen synthase phosphatase in diabetes
S06GM-08238-05 0012 (MPRC) LOPEZ, MARCO A Mbrs program at california state university long beach Factor analytical deconvolution of multicomponent heme-ligand uv-vis spectra
S06GM-08238-05 0013 (MPRC) MASON, ANDREW Z Mbrs program at california state university long beach Processes of metal selection by metal accumulating cells
S06GM-08238-05 0014 (MPRC) MERRYFIELD, MARGARET Mbrs program at california state university long beach Regulation of protein

phosphorylation by polyamines
S06GM-08238-05 0015 (MPRC) PO, HENRY N Mbrs program at california state university long beach Single and multi-electron transfer reactions
S06GM-08238-05 0016 (MPRC) SANDERS, BRENDA Mbrs program at california state university long beach The role of stress proteins in adaptation to thermal stress
S06GM-08238-05 0017 (MPRC) SHUSTER, TERRENCE A Mbrs program at california state university long beach Nucleotide sensitive enzymes in ROS and rd retinas
S06GM-08238-05 0018 (MPRC) STANTON, TONI L Mbrs program at california state university long beach CNS action of melatonin on brain arousal state
S06GM-08239-06 (GRS) CERAME-VIVAS, MAXIMO PONCE SCHOOL OF MEDICINE PO BOX 7004 PONCE, PR 00732 MBRS program at the Ponce School of Medicine
S06GM-08239-06 0001 (GRS) SOLTERO-HARRINGTON, FRED V MBRS program at the Ponce School of Medicine Aging of T lymphocytes
S06GM-08239-06 0004 (GRS) FRAZER DE LLADO, TERESA MBRS program at the Ponce School of Medicine Epidemology of insulin dependent diabetes mellitus in Puerto Rico
S06GM-08239-06 0005 (GRS) MASS, HOWARD MBRS program at the Ponce School of Medicine Myocardial beta-blockade and adjustments to exercise
S06GM-08239-06 0006 (GRS) MERCADO, CARMEN M MBRS program at the Ponce School of Medicine Interaction of nitrofurans with nucleic acids
S06GM-08239-06 0007 (GRS) MONTEALEGRE, FEDERICO J MBRS program at the Ponce School of Medicine Purification of thermoactinomyces vulgaris antigens
S06GM-08239-06 0008 (GRS) PUIZ, JAIME MBRS program at the Ponce School of Medicine Isolation and characterization of morphine UDP-glucuronosyl transferase
S06GM-08239-06 0009 (GRS) TORRES-RUIZ, JOSE A MBRS program at the Ponce School of Medicine RuBisCO putative binding proteins in prokaryotes
S06GM-08239-06 0009 (GRS) TORRES-RUIZ, JOSE A MBRS program at the Ponce School of Medicine RuBisCO putative binding proteins in prokaryotes
S06GM-08241-07 (MPRC) THOMPSON, ALBERT N JR SPELMAN COLLEGE BOX 281 ATLANTA, GEORGIA 30314-4399 Biomedical research improvement program
S06GM-08241-07 0010 (MPRC) BHATIA, SUBHASH C Biomedical research improvement program Vibrational spectroscopic investigation on non-Watson-Crick base pairs
S06GM-08241-07 0004 (MPRC) MCCLURE, SHEILA A Biomedical research improvement program Regulation of fibroid tumor cells
S06GM-08241-07 0005 (MPRC) MULDROW, LYCURGUS L Biomedical research improvement program Molecular biology of Clostridium difficile
S06GM-08241-07 0006 (MPRC) THOMPSON, ALBERT N Biomedical research improvement program Synthesis and characterization of water soluble mesotetraphenylporphyrins
S06GM-08241-07 0007 (MPRC) BOSE, NRIPENDRA K Biomedical research improvement program Molecular cloning and sequencing of chicken liver fructose-1,6 bisphosphatase
S06GM-08241-07 0008 (MPRC) HIBBARD, LISA B Biomedical research improvement program Spectroscopic investigation of UV irridated ocular lens proteins
S06GM-08241-07 0009 (MPRC) CARDELINO, BEATRIZ H Biomedical research improvement program Effect of metal bonding on the stability of DNA base pairing
S06GM-08244-05 (SRC) ASHE, WARREN K HOWARD UNIVERSITY 2400 6TH STREET, NW WASHINGTON, DC 20059 Howard University Center for the Health Sciences
S06GM-08244-05 0012 (SRC) LEFFALL JR, LASALLE D Howard University Center for the Health Sciences Human colonic neoplastic epithelium--Modulation of growth & differentiation
S06GM-08244-05 0017 (SRC) SCOTT, KENNETH R Howard University Center for the Health Sciences Inhibition kinetics of valproic acids and their spiro analogs
S06GM-08244-05 0020 (SRC) CANADA, ROBERT G Howard University Center for the Health Sciences Interactions of adriamycin with a calcium binding site
S06GM-08244-05 0021 (SRC) CRAWFORD-GREEN, CYNTHIA Howard University Center for the Health Sciences Utility of thallium scintigraphy in asymptomatic diabetic patients
S06GM-08244-05 0022 (SRC) DENNIS, GARY C Howard University Center for the Health Sciences Somatosensory evoked potentials in cervical spinal cord compression
S06GM-08244-05 0023 (SRC) PANG, KEUM Y Howard University Center for the Health Sciences Depression, somatization, and Korean elderly immigrants
S06GM-08244-05 0024 (SRC) REECE, ELENA R Howard University Center for the Health Sciences Fetal-Maternal histocompatiblity interactions
S06GM-08244-05 0025 (SRC) SAXENA, SUNITA B Howard University Center for the Health Sciences Gender differences in Black Americans
S06GM-08244-05 0026 (SRC) SMOOT, DUANE T Howard University Center for the Health Sciences Direct cytopathic effects of Campylobacter pylori on human gastric epithelium
S06GM-08244-05 0027 (SRC) TING, PAULINE Howard University Center for the Health Sciences Mediators for postischemic cerebral infarction
S06GM-08244-05 0028 (SRC) WINTER, WALTER P Howard University Center for the Health Sciences Ligand-dependent binding of human hemoglobins to erythrocyte membranes
S06GM-08244-05 9001 (SRC) ASHE, WARREN K Howard University Center for the Health Sciences Core--Biostatistics
S06GM-08245-05 (MPRC) BOWMAN, ARTHUR W HAMPTON UNIVERSITY HAMPTON, VA 23668 Cellular and molecular approach to biomedical research
S06GM-08247-04 (MPRC) BROWNE, JOHN M CLARK ATLANTA UNIVERSITY J P BRAWLEY DR/AT FAIR ST ATLANTA, GA 30314 Research impetus in the biomedical sciences at Clark Atlanta University
S06GM-08247-04 0001 (MPRC) BROWN, IRENE Research impetus in the biomedical sciences at Clark Atlanta University Anti-carcinogenesis properties of retinoids
S06GM-08247-04 0002 (MPRC) BROWNE,JOHN Research impetus in the biomedical sciences at Clark Atlanta University Galactosyltransferase biosynthesis and mammary gland tumors
S06GM-08247-04 0005 (MPRC) MARIAM, YITBAREK Research impetus in the biomedical sciences at Clark Atlanta University Theoretical and QSAR studies of anthracyclines and their analogs
S06GM-08247-04 0006 (MPRC) MICKENS, RONALD Research impetus in the biomedical sciences at Clark Atlanta University Mathematical approaches to cardiac, renal & other bio-systems
S06GM-08247-04 0010 (MPRC) STEWART, JUARINE Research impetus in the biomedical sciences at Clark Atlanta University Differential induction of GST subunits by 3-MC and BHA
S06GM-08247-04 0012 (MPRC) WILLIAMS, ARTHUR Research impetus in the biomedical sciences at Clark Atlanta University Molecular regulation of E. coli adenyl cyclase and cAMP production
S06GM-08247-04 0014 (MPRC) JIDEAMA, NATHAN Research impetus in the biomedical sciences at Clark Atlanta University Identification and cloning of epoxide hydrolase genes forms in liver
S06GM-08247-04 0015 (MPRC) MINTZ, ERIC A Research impetus in the biomedical sciences at Clark Atlanta University Pure entantiomer group IV transition metal complexes for ethical drug synthesis
S06GM-08247-04 0017 (MPRC) THEDFORD, ROOSEVELT Research impetus in the biomedical sciences at Clark Atlanta University Enrichment plan--Alkylated (poly) ribonucleotides synthesis and biological act
S06GM-08247-04 9001 (MPRC) MINTZ, ERIC A Research impetus in the biomedical sciences at Clark Atlanta University Core--NMR center
S06GM-08248-05 (MPRC) SULLIVAN, WALTER W MOREHOUSE SCHOOL OF MEDICINE 720 WESTVIEW DR, SW ATLANTA, GA 30310-1495 Morehouse School of Medicine MBRS Program
S06GM-08248-05 0012 (MPRC) URSO, PAUL Morehouse School of Medicine MBRS Program Cell competence after exposure to carcinogens
S06GM-08248-05 0013 (MPRC) WILLIAMS, EVAN Morehouse School of Medicine MBRS Program Nucleotide transport in cardiovascular function
S06GM-08248-05 0014 (MPRC) DAVIDSON, SANDRA Morehouse School of Medicine MBRS Program Function of nonstructural viral protein E3 in Sindbis virus
S06GM-08248-05 0015 (MPRC) PAULSEN, DOUGLAS Morehouse School of Medicine MBRS Program Mechanisms of retinoid effects on skeletogenesis
S06GM-08248-05 0016 (MPRC) SCANLON, MARY Morehouse School of Medicine MBRS Program Mechanism of tumor necrosis factor induced cell death
S06GM-08248-05 0017 (MPRC) SUNG, JOHN Morehouse School of Medicine MBRS Program Socioeconomic status,cancer screening and stage of colon cancer at diagnosis
S06GM-08248-05 0018 (MPRC) THIERRY-PALMER, MYRTLE Morehouse School of Medicine MBRS Program Function and metabolism of vitamin K in liver mitochondria
S06GM-08248-05 0019 (MPRC) TROTTIER, RALPH Morehouse School of Medicine MBRS Program Pharmacoimmunology of prednisolone derivatives
S06GM-08248-05 0020 (MPRC) WINESKI, LAWRENCE Morehouse School of Medicine MBRS Program Neural organization of facial muscles
S06GM-08248-05 0021 (MPRC) SANFORD, GARY Morehouse School of Medicine MBRS Program Regulation of galaptin gene expression during postnatal lung development
S06GM-08248-05 0001 (MPRC) BAILEY, GORDON B Morehouse School of Medicine MBRS Program Molecular mechanisms of amebiasis
S06GM-08248-05 0002 (MPRC) BAYORH, MOHAMED Morehouse School of Medicine MBRS Program PCP and cocaine induced cardiovascular and hemodynamic responses
S06GM-08248-05 0003 (MPRC) DUTT, KAMLA Morehouse School of Medicine MBRS Program Tissue culture model for retinitis pigmentosa-- A molecular approach
S06GM-08248-05 0004 (MPRC) HARRIS-HOOKER, SANDRA Morehouse School of Medicine MBRS Program Mediators of vascular cell injury-- Modulation by extracellular matrices
S06GM-08248-05 0008 (MPRC) NAVALKAR, RAMCHANDRA Morehouse School of Medicine MBRS Program Reactivity of molecularly defined mycobacterial antigens
S06GM-08250-04 (MPRC) KALE, PURUSHOTTAM G ALABAMA A&M UNIV NORMAL, AL 35762 MBRS Program at Alabama A and M University
S06GM-08250-04 0001 (MPRC) GIBSON, GAIL S MBRS Program at Alabama A and M University A biopsychosocial approah to the treatment of hypertension
S06GM-08250-04 0002 (MPRC) JOHNSON, JACQULINE U MBRS Program at Alabama A and M University Sex hormone/Ig role in mediating antibacterial defense mechanisms
S06GM-08250-04 0003 (MPRC) KALE, PURUSHOTTAM G MBRS Program at Alabama A and M University The utility of Drosophila mosaic mutation test in screening
S06GM-08250-04 0004 (MPRC) KALE, RANJINI P MBRS Program at Alabama A and M University Chromosome studies on lymphocytes of two North Alabama populations
S06GM-08250-04 0005 (MPRC) RAO, DAMANNA R MBRS Program at Alabama A and M University Oral lactic culture supplementation--Fecal bile acids and mutagen
S06GM-08256-03 (GRS) COLLIER, ROBERT E TEXAS WOMAN'S UNIVERSITY PO BOX 22939, TWU STATION DENTON, TX 76204 Minority biomed res support at the Texas women univ.
S06GM-08256-03 0001 (GRS) HSUEH, ANDIE Minority biomed res support at the Texas women univ. Effects of menhaden oil on carcinogenesis.
S06GM-08256-03 0002 (GRS) RUDICK, MICHAEL Minority biomed res support at the Texas women univ. Polarized secretion from epithelial cells.
S06GM-08256-03 0003 (GRS) STEWART, GEORGE Minority biomed res support at the Texas women univ. Gonadal hormones, neurotransmitters, and eating behavior.
S06GM-08256-03 0004 (GRS) DROGE, MICHAEL Minority biomed res support at the Texas women univ. Central pattern generating in spinal cord
S06GM-08256-03 0005 (GRS) JOHNSON, JAMES Minority biomed res support at the Texas women univ. Mechanisms of nucleophilic substitution at C-N bond.

PROJECT NO., ORGANIZATIONAL UNIT., INVESTIGATOR, ADDRESS, TITLE

S06GM-08256-03 0006 (GRS) SABBAHI, MOHAMED Minority biomed res support at the Texas women univ. Kinesthetic sensation in distal thumb joints
S06GM-08256-03 0007 (GRS) UPHOUSE, LYNDA Minority biomed res support at the Texas women univ. Neuroreproductive effects of chlorinated pestisides
S06GM-08258-02 (MPRC) WEBER, BRUCE H CALIFORNIA STATE UNIVERSITY 800 NORTH STATE COLLEGE BLVD FULLERTON, CA 92634 MBRS program at California State University, Fullerton Foundation
S06GM-08258-02 0001 (MPRC) FINLAYSON-PITTS, BARBARA J MBRS program at California State University, Fullerton Foundation Interactions of air pollutants with pulmonary surfactant
S06GM-08258-02 0002 (MPRC) LINDER, MARIA C MBRS program at California State University, Fullerton Foundation Structure, function, and regulation of copper and iron proteins
S06GM-08258-02 0003 (MPRC) NAGEL, GLENN M MBRS program at California State University, Fullerton Foundation Active sites of glycyl-tRNA synthetase--Extracellular sea urchin embryo proteins
S06GM-08258-02 0004 (MPRC) ONO, JOYCE K MBRS program at California State University, Fullerton Foundation Roles of co-localized peptides in convergent neural networks in Aplysia
S06GM-08258-02 0005 (MPRC) WILLIAMS, GREGORY M MBRS program at California State University, Fullerton Foundation Iron polyolefin complexes applied to organic synthesis
S06GM-08266-04 (MPRC) GOVINDAN, MELEDATH UNIVERSITY VIRGIN ISLANDS CHARLOTTE AMALIE ST THOMAS, VI 00802 Biomedical research in the Caribbean environment
S06GM-08266-04 0002 (MPRC) BROWN, DAVID R Biomedical research in the Caribbean environment Leas as a health hazard in St Thomas, VI
S06GM-08266-04 0005 (MPRC) BATTEY, JAMES F Biomedical research in the Caribbean environment Lipid metabolism in symbiotic Coelentrates
S06GM-08266-04 0006 (MPRC) GOVINDAN, MELEDATH Biomedical research in the Caribbean environment Isolation, characterization, and bioassay of marine natural products
S06GM-08266-04 0007 (MPRC) TODMAN, PATRICIA R Biomedical research in the Caribbean environment Predictors of psychiatric patient outcomes
S06GM-08266-04 0001 (MPRC) WATLINGTON, ROY A Biomedical research in the Caribbean environment Enrichment project
S06GM-08267-04 (MPRC) ROSS, ROBERT G CAYEY UNIVERSITY COLLEGE CAYEY, PUERTO RICO 00633 Cayey University College--Biomedical research program
S06GM-08267-04 0001 (MPRC) RIVERA-COLON, MARITZA Cayey University College--Biomedical research program Limb regeneration in Newt Notophalmus viridescens
S06GM-08267-04 0002 (MPRC) VELAZQUEZ-LOZADA, JOSE M Cayey University College--Biomedical research program The distribution of HSP 70 during the life cycle of Tetrahymena
R01GM-08521-31 (BBCB) GRANT, DAVID M UNIVERSITY OF UTAH 1320 HEB SALT LAKE CITY, UTAH 84112 Carbon-13 magnetic resonance - Methods and theory
R01GM-08963-29 (PB) RAY, WILLIAM J, JR PURDUE UNIVERSITY DEPT. OF BIOLOGICAL SCIENCES WEST LAFAYETTE, IND 47907 The mechanism of the group transfer process
R37GM-08995-30 (GEN) METZENBERG, ROBERT L, JR UNIVERSITY OF WISCONSIN DEPT OF PHYSIOLOGICAL CHEM MADISON, WISC 53706 Genetic control of protein synthesis
R01GM-09587-29A2 (BIO) GRAVES, DONALD J IOWA STATE UNIVERSITY 397 GILMAN HALL AMES, IA 50011 Interconversion and regulation of glycogen metabolism
R01GM-09706-26 (BNP) CARPINO, LOUIS A UNIVERSITY OF MASSACHUSETTS DEPARTMENT OF CHEMISTRY AMHERST, MASS 01003 New amino-protecting group
R37GM-09738-29 (MBC) YANOFSKY, CHARLES STANFORD UNIVERSITY DEPT OF BIOLOGICAL SCIENCES STANFORD, CA 94305-5020 Attenuation control of gene expression in bacteria
R01GM-09886-30 (GEN) CHOVNICK, ARTHUR UNIVERSITY OF CONNECTICUT U-131, 354 MANSFIELD RD STORRS, CONN 06268 Genetic studies in Drosophila melanogaster
R37GM-09966-30 (MGN) RUDDLE, FRANK H YALE UNIVERVITY BOX 1504A, YALE STATION NEW HAVEN, CT 06520 Genetic analysis of somatic cell population
R01GM-10040-28 (BMT) BUSCH, DARYLE H UNIVERSITY OF KANSAS LAWRENCE, KS 66045 Biomimetic metal complexes of macrocyclic ligands
R37GM-10265-29 (NSS) LETSINGER, ROBERT L NORTHWESTERN UNIVERSITY 2145 SHERIDAN ROAD EVANSTON, IL 60208-3113 New methods for synthesis of polynucleotides
R01GM-10422-29 (NLS) SALPETER, MIRIAM M CORNELL UNIVERSITY W113 SEELEY G. MUDD HALL ITHACA, NY 14853 High resolution autoradiography
R01GM-10452-28 (GEN) KARLIN, SAMUEL STANFORD UNIVERSITY DEPT OF MATHEMATICS STANFORD, CA 94305-2125 Theory and applied studies in evolutionary genetics
R01GM-10452-28 0001 (GEN) KARLIN, SAMUEL Theory and applied studies in evolutionary genetics Linkage, selection interaction and modifier theory in genetic systems
R01GM-10452-28 0002 (GEN) KARLIN, SAMUEL Theory and applied studies in evolutionary genetics Population division, migration, selection and spatial gene frequency
R01GM-10452-28 0003 (GEN) CAVALLI-SFORZA, LUIGI L Theory and applied studies in evolutionary genetics Cultural evolution and non-mendelian transmission
R01GM-10704-29 (BBCB) SMITH, THOMAS J PURDUE UNIVERSITY WEST LAFAYETTE, IN 47907 Structural studies of protein subunits
R01GM-10831-32 (BBCA) LASKOWSKI, MICHAEL, JR PURDUE UNIV 1393 BROWN CHEMISTRY BLDG WEST LAFAYETTE, IN 47907 Protein proteinase inhibitors
R37GM-10840-33 (BBCA) TINOCO, IGNACIO, JR UNIVERSITY OF CALIFORNIA DEPT OF CHEMISTRY BERKELEY, CA 94720 Structure and function of nucleic acids
R01GM-10851-34 (BMT) GIDDINGS, J CALVIN UNIVERSITY OF UTAH SALT LAKE CITY, UT 84112 Biomedical separations--Field-flow fractionation
R01GM-10880-32 (BBCA) YANG, JEN T UNIV OF CALIF-SAN FRANCISCO 1327 MOFFITT HOSPITAL SAN FRANCISCO, CA 94143-0130 Optical rotatory power of biopolymers

PROJECT NO., ORGANIZATIONAL UNIT., INVESTIGATOR, ADDRESS, TITLE

R01GM-10928-29 (BBCB) KRAUT, JOSEPH UNIV OF CALIFORNIA, SAN DIEGO DEPARTMENT OF CHEMISTRY, B-017 LA JOLLA, CA 92093 Crystallographic study of biological molecules
R01GM-11094-29 (PB) BOYER, PAUL D UNIVERSITY OF CALIFORNIA 405 HILGARD AVENUE LOS ANGELES, CA 90024 The mechanism of ATP synthase and related enzymes
R37GM-11106-29 (PB) MASSEY, VINCENT UNIVERSITY OF MICHIGAN 3441 MEDICAL SCIENCE BLDG I ANN ARBOR, MICH 48109 Biological oxidation mechanisms
R01GM-11223-29 (BBCA) WEBER, GREGORIO UNIVERSITY OF ILLINOIS 1209 WEST CALIFORNIA STREET URBANA, ILLINOIS 61801 Pressure dissociation of oligomeric proteins & viruses
R01GM-11518-26 (BNP) GILHAM, PETER T PURDUE UNIVERSITY WEST LAFAYETTE, IN 47907 Fine structure of nucleic acids
R01GM-11632-29 (BBCB) BRAND, LUDWIG JOHNS HOPKINS UNIVERSITY CHARLES & 34TH STS BALTIMORE, MD 21218 Fluorescence probes in studies of proteins and membranes
R01GM-11726-28 (MBY) ATTARDI, GIUSEPPE CALIFORNIA INST OF TECHNOLOGY DIVISION OF BIOLOGY 156-29 PASADENA, CA 91125 Gene expression and content in cell differentiation
R01GM-11741-24 (BBCA) LOACH, PAUL A NORTHWESTERN UNIVERSITY DEPT OF BIOCHEM/MOLEC BIOLOGY EVANSTON, IL 60208-3500 Reconstitution of bioenergetic membrane system -- The PRC
R01GM-11916-28 (BBCA) ZIMM, BRUNO H UNIV OF CALIF., SAN DIEGO DEPARTMENT OF CHEMISTRY, B-017 LA JOLLA, CA 92093 Nucleic acids and chromosomal DNA
R01GM-11983-28 (MBC) LIN, EDMUND C HARVARD MEDICAL SCHOOL 200 LONGWOOD AVE BOSTON, MA 02115 Glycerol dissimilation and its regulation in bacteria
R37GM-12010-28 (MBC) CHAMBERLIN, MICHAEL J UNIVERSITY OF CALIFORNIA 610 BARKER HALL BERKELEY, CA 94720 Selectivity of bacterial transcription
R01GM-12152-27 (BMT) MARGERUM, DALE W PURDUE UNIVERSITY DEPARTMENT OF CHEMISTRY WEST LAFAYETTE, IND 47907 Metal ion transfer and catalysis in peptide complexes
R37GM-12159-28 (BIO) SCHACHMAN, HOWARD K UNIVERSITY OF CALIFORNIA 229 WENDELL M STANLEY HALL BERKELEY, CA 94720 Structures-interactions of biological macromolecules
R01GM-12522-27 (MBC) UMBARGER, H EDWIN PURDUE UNIVERSITY WEST LAFAYETTE, IN 47907 Enzymic mechanisms in biosynthetic pathways
R01GM-12573-27 (PC) GOLDBERG, IRVING H HARVARD MEDICAL SCHOOL DEPT OF CHEM & MOLECULAR PHARM BOSTON, MA 02115 Molecular pharmacology of anticancer drugs
R01GM-12592-27 (BBCA) HOCHSTRASSER, ROBIN M UNIVERSITY OF PENNSYLVANIA PHILADELPHIA, PA 19104-6323 Photoprocesses in the organic solid state
R01GM-12607-27 (PC) KONIGSBERG, WILLIAM H YALE SCHOOL OF MEDICINE 333 CEDAR STREET NEW HAVEN, CT 06510 Relation of protein structure to biological function
R37GM-12633-28 (BIO) ABELES, ROBERT H BRANDEIS UNIVERSITY 415 S STREET WALTHAM, MA 02254 Enzyme mechanisms and enzyme inhibitors
R37GM-12640-27 (MCHA) CRAM, DONALD J UNIVERSITY OF CALIFORNIA 405 HILGARD AVENUE LOS ANGELES, CA 90024-1406 Host molecules that complex and catalyze
R01GM-12702-27 (GEN) SHERMAN, FRED UNIVERSITY OF ROCHESTER DEPARTMENT OF BIOCHEMISTRY ROCHESTER, N Y 14642 Regulation and gene expression of cytochrome C.
R01GM-12934-27 (MBC) HAYASHI, MASAKI DEPT OF BIOLOGY, B-022 UNIV OF CALIF., SAN DIEGO LA JOLLA, CALIF 92093 Synthesis of infectious bacteriophage particles
R37GM-13191-27 (NSS) FEHER, GEORGE UNIVERSITY OF CALIFORNIA LA JOLLA, CA 92093 Spectroscopic investigations of biological systems
R01GM-13221-27 (MBC) MOSIG, GISELA VANDERBILT UNIVERSITY DEPT OF MOLECULAR BIOLOGY NASHVILLE, TENN 37235 DNA replication and recombination in bacteriophage
R37GM-13235-25 (MGN) BERG, PAUL STANFORD UNIVERSITY STANFORD, CA 94305-5307 Mechanisms and regulation of gene expression
R01GM-13246-32A3 (BNP) LEETE, EDWARD UNIVERSITY OF MINNESOTA 207 PLEASANT STREET SE MINNEAPOLIS, MN 55455 Biosynthesis of cocaine and related tropane alkaloids
R01GM-13306-26 (PB) BENKOVIC, STEPHEN J PENNSYLVANIA STATE UNIVERSITY 152 DAVEY LABORATORY UNIVERSITY PARK, PA 16802 Phosphate activation mechanisms
R01GM-13326-24 (BMT) PARDUE, HARRY L PURDUE UNIVERSITY WEST LAFAYETTE, IN 47907 Instrumentation for fast clinical analyses
R37GM-13453-26 (BNP) KEMP, DANIEL S MASS INSTITUTE OF TECHNOLOGY 77 MASS AVE CAMBRIDGE, MA 02139 Synthesis and reactions of peptides
R37GM-13498-26 (BMT) SPIRO, THOMAS G PRINCETON UNIVERSITY WASHINGTON ROAD/FRICK LAB PRINCETON, NJ 08544-1009 Metal centers in biological systems
R01GM-13511-26 (MBC) GOLDBERG, EDWARD B TUFTS UNIVERSITY 136 HARRISON AVE BOSTON, MA 02111 Viral-host recognition and penetration
R37GM-13598-26 (MCHA) TROST, BARRY M STANFORD UNIVERSITY DEPT OF CHEMISTRY STANFORD, CA 94305-5080 Synthesis of macrolides, steroids, cyclopentanoids etc.
R01GM-13626-25 (MBC) GALLANT, JONATHAN A UNIVERSITY OF WASHINGTON SEATTLE, WA 98195 Control of cell growth
R37GM-13638-26 (BMT) TAUBE, HENRY STANFORD UNIVERSITY JORDAN QUAD/BIRCH STANFORD, CA 94305 Biochemically significant molecules as ligands
R01GM-13684-24 (BBCA) APPLEQUIST, JON B IOWA STATE UNIVERSITY AMES, IA 50011 Theory of molecular optical properties
R01GM-13745-26 (CBY) NICKLAS, R BRUCE DUKE UNIVERSITY DEPARTMENT OF ZOOLOGY DURHAM, N C 27706 Analysis and control of chromosome movement
R37GM-13854-22 (MCHA) WASSERMAN, HARRY H YALE UNIVERSITY DEPARTMENT OF CHEMISTRY NEW HAVEN, CT 06520 Singlet oxygen in the synthesis of bioactive molecules
R01GM-13914-27 (BBCB) SCHUMAKER, VERNE N UNIVERSITY OF CALIFORNIA 405 HILGARD AVENUE LOS ANGELES, CA 90024-1569 Macromolecules of circulatory and genetic importance
R01GM-13925-27 (BBCB) BANASZAK, LEONARD J UNIVERSITY OF

MINNESOTA 435 DELAWARE ST, SE MINNEAPOLIS, MN 55455 Structural studies of lipid:protein systems

R01GM-13956-26 (BNP) COATES, ROBERT M UNIVERSITY OF ILLINOIS 1209 W CALIFORNIA ST URBANA, ILL 61801 Specificity in terpene and sterol biosynthesis

K06GM-13981-30 (NSS) HALBERG, FRANZ UNIVERSITY OF MINNESOTA 420 WASHINGTON AVE SOUTHWEST MINNEAPOLIS, MINN 55455 Temporal parameters of physiological functions in health/disease

R01GM-14108-24 (PC) GANESAN, ADAYAPALAM T STANFORD UNIVERSITY SCH OF MED STANFORD, CA 94305 DNA synthesis and genetic recombination in bacillus

R01GM-14276-27 (BBCA) GIBSON, QUENTIN H CORNELL UNIVERSITY BIOTECHNOLOGY BUILDING ITHACA, NY 14853 Kinetics of enzymes and hemoglobin-ligand reactions

R01GM-14312-36 (BBCA) SCHERAGA, HAROLD A CORNELL UNIVERSITY BAKER LABORATORY OF CHEMISTRY ITHACA, NY 14853-1301 Internal bonding in proteins

R01GM-14372-25 (MBC) NOVICK, RICHARD P PUBLIC HEALTH RESEARCH INST 455 FIRST AVENUE NEW YORK, NY 10016 Molecular biology of bacterial plasmids

R01GM-14603-25 (BBCA) TIMASHEFF, SERGE N BRANDEIS UNIVERSITY 415 SOUTH STREET WALTHAM, MA 02254-9110 Structure and interactions of proteins in solution

R01GM-14628-26 (BBCB) THOMPSON, THOMAS E UNIVERSITY OF VIRGINIA DEPARTMENT OF BIOCHEMISTRY CHARLOTTESVILLE, VA 22908 A study of phospholipid bilayer membranes

R01GM-14642-24 (CTY) ROSENBAUM, JOEL L YALE UNIVERSITY PO BOX 1504A YALE STATION NEW HAVEN, CT 06520 Synthesis and assembly of flagellar proteins

R01GM-14652-24 (MBC) LEE, NANCY L UNIVERSITY OF CALIFORNIA DEPT OF BIOLOGICAL SCIENCES SANTA BARBARA, CALIF 93106 Genetic control of protein synthesis in E coli

R01GM-14711-25 (MBC) INMAN, ROSS B UNIVERSITY OF WISCONSIN 1525 LINDEN DRIVE MADISON, WI 53706 Structure and replication of DNA

R37GM-14772-24 (GMA) DIAMOND, JARED M UNIVERSITY OF CALIFORNIA 405 HILGARD AVENUE LOS ANGELES, CA 90024-1751 Adaptive regulation of nutrient transport by the gut

R01GM-14931-25 (MGN) SCHIMKE, ROBERT T STANFORD UNIVERSITY STANFORD, CA 94305-5020 Enzyme synthesis and degradation in metabolic control

R01GM-15000-22 (BBCA) RICHARDSON, DAVID C DUKE UNIVERSITY DEPT OF BIOCHEMISTRY DURHAM, NC 27710 Crystallographic analysis of protein structures

R01GM-15102-24 (BIO) KOHLHAW, GUNTER B PURDUE UNIVERSITY 1153 BIOCHEMISTRY DEPT WEST LAFAYETTE, IN 47907 Regulation of leucine biosynthesis

K06GM-15129-28 (NCR) MAAS, WERNER K NEW YORK UNIV MED CTR 550 FIRST AVENUE NEW YORK, N Y 10016 Enzyme repression, plasmids genetics, E coli enterotoxin

R01GM-15188-23 (BIO) FISHER, HARVEY F VETERAN ADMIN MEDICAL CENTER 4801 LINWOOD BOULEVARD KANSAS CITY, MO 64128 Mechanisms of enzymatic catalysis

R37GM-15225-24 (BBCB) SIGLER, PAUL B YALE UNIVERSITY PO BOX 6666/260 WHITNEY AVE NEW HAVEN, CT 06511 Structural analysis of biological macromolecules

R01GM-15399-21 (MBY) MAITRA, UMADAS ALBERT EINSTEIN COLLEGE OF MED 1300 MORRIS PARK AVENUE BRONX, N Y 10461 Initiation factors in eukariotic protein biosynthesis

P50GM-15431-24 (SRC) OATES, JOHN A VANDERBILT UNIVERSITY DEPARTMENT OF PHARMACOLOGY NASHVILLE, TENN 37232 Research center for pharmacology and drug toxicology

P50GM-15431-24 0128 (SRC) ROBERTS, L JACKSON Research center for pharmacology and drug toxicology Biochemical pharmacology of prostaglandin D2

P50GM-15431-24 0129 (SRC) BRASH, ALAN R Research center for pharmacology and drug toxicology Pathways and mechanisms of oxygenation of arachidonic acid

P50GM-15431-24 0130 (SRC) KNAPP, HOWARD R Research center for pharmacology and drug toxicology Aspirin-evoked syndromes--Systematic mast cell activation and asthma

P50GM-15431-24 0131 (SRC) FITZGERALD, GARRET A Research center for pharmacology and drug toxicology Allergic asthma

P50GM-15431-24 0134 (SRC) FITZGERALD, GARRET A Research center for pharmacology and drug toxicology Eicosanoid biosynthesis, platelet function and cigarette smoking

P50GM-15431-24 9001 (SRC) BLAIR, IAN A Research center for pharmacology and drug toxicology Analytical core

R01GM-15438-22 (BIO) O'BRIEN, THOMAS W UNIVERSITY OF FLORIDA DEPT OF BIOCHEM & MOL BIOLOGY GAINESVILLE, FLA 32610-0245 Characterization of mammalian mitochondrial ribosomes

R37GM-15539-24 (PC) SCHIMMEL, PAUL MASSACHUSETTS INST OF TECH 77 MASSACHUSETTS AVE, DEPT BIO CAMBRIDGE, MA 02139 Investigations of reactions of physiological importance

R01GM-15547-25 (BBCA) PETICOLAS, WARNER L UNIVERSITY OF OREGON CHEMISTRY DEPARTMENT EUGENE, OREG 97403 Laser Raman scattering from biological macromolecules

R01GM-15590-25A1 (MBC) KAPLAN, SAMUEL UNIV OF TEXAS HLTH CTR P O BOX 20708 HOUSTON, TX 77225 Induction and biogenesis of subcellular organelles

R37GM-15591-24 (TOX) TU, ANTHONY T COLORADO STATE UNIVERSITY FORT COLLINS, CO 80523 Hemorrhagic and necrotic toxins in snake venoms

R01GM-15691-24 (MGN) LUCCHESI, JOHN C EMORY UNIVERSITY O W ROLLINS RESEARCH CENTER ATLANTA, GA 30322 Genetic regulation in Drosophila--Dosage compensation

R37GM-15761-23 (PB) SLAYMAN, CAROLYN W YALE UNIVERSITY SCHOOL OF MED DEPT/HUMAN GENETICS, I-310 SHM NEW HAVEN, CT 06510 Genetic study of ion transport in Neurospora

R37GM-15792-25 (BBCA) VON HIPPEL, PETER H UNIVERSITY OF OREGON EUGENE, OR 97403 Structure and relations of proteins and nucleic acids

R37GM-15847-22 (BMT) KARGER, BARRY L NORTHEASTERN UNIVERSITY 360 HUNTINGTON AVENUE BOSTON, MA 02115 Fluorescence studies of protein adsorption in HPLC

P50GM-15904-24 (SRC) MILLER, KEITH W MASSACHUSETTS GENERAL HOSPITAL BOSTON, MA 02114 Anesthesiology center for research and teaching

P50GM-15904-24 0014 (SRC) MILLER, KEITH W Anesthesiology center for research and teaching General anesthetic & pressure action mechanism on cholinergic receptors

P50GM-15904-24 0023 (SRC) STRICHARTZ, GARY Anesthesiology center for research and teaching Molecular mechanisms of local anesthesia

P50GM-15904-24 0024 (SRC) MAGGIO, JOHN E Anesthesiology center for research and teaching Tachykinins in nociception

P50GM-15904-24 0025 (SRC) BERDE, CHARLES Anesthesiology center for research and teaching Spinal mechanisms of local anesthesia

P50GM-15904-24 9002 (SRC) HUSAIN, S S Anesthesiology center for research and teaching Chemistry core

P50GM-15904-24 9003 (SRC) BERDE, CHARLES Anesthesiology center for research and teaching Tissue culture core

R01GM-15924-24 (PB) STRITTMATTER, PHILIPP UNIV OF CONNECTICUT HLTH CTR DEPT OF BIOCHEMISTRY FARMINGTON, CT 06032 Structure-function studies on microsomal membranes

R01GM-15971-24 (CBY) SINGER, S JONATHAN UNIV OF CALIFORNIA - SAN DIEGO DEPT OF BIOLOGY B-022 LA JOLLA, CA 92093 Molecular approaches to cell ultrastructure

R01GM-15997-21 (MCHA) HART, HAROLD MICHIGAN STATE UNIVERSITY EAST LANSING, MI 48824 Organic synthesis--tandem aryne reactions

R01GM-16317-24 (PC) DEUTSCHER, MURRAY P UNIV OF CONNECTICUT HLTH CTR DEPARTMENT OF BIOCHEMISTRY FARMINGTON, CT 06030 Enzymology and control of amino acid activation

R01GM-16329-24 (MBC) HILL, CHARLES W MILTON S HERSHEY MEDICAL CENTE PO BOX 850 HERSHEY, PA 17033 Genetics and biochemistry of missense suppression

R01GM-16389-22 (BIO) BLUMENFELD, OLGA O ALBERT EINSTEIN COLLEGE OF MED 1300 MORRIS PARK AVENUE BRONX, NY 10461 Proteins of the cell membrane

R01GM-16406-22 (PB) DEBRUNNER, PETER G LOOMIS LABORATORY OF PHYSICS 1110 WEST GREEN STREET URBANA, ILL 61801 Resonance spectroscopy of metalloproteins

R01GM-16424-21 (BIO) RICHARDS, JOHN H CALIFORNIA INST OF TECHNOLOGY DIV OF CHEMISTRY 147-75 PASADENA, CA 91125 Biophysical studies of enzyme systems

R01GM-16609-23 (BMT) MC LAFFERTY, FRED W CORNELL UNIVERSITY DEPARTMENT OF CHEMISTRY ITHACA, N Y 14853-1301 Mass spectrometry in biomedical research

R01GM-16620-22 (RAD) DEERING, REGINALD A PENNSYLVANIA STATE UNIVERSITY 201 ALTHOUSE LABORATORY UNIVERSITY PARK, PA 16802 DNA repair in slime mold

R01GM-16974-22 (PB) ALLISON, WILLIAM S UNIVERSITY OF CALIFORNIA LA JOLLA, CA 92093-0601 Structural studies on the energy transducing ATPase

R01GM-16995-22 (BIO) SCHULMAN, LA DONNE H ALBERT EINSTEIN COLLEGE OF MED 1300 MORRIS PARK AVENUE BRONX, N Y 10461 Protein-nucleic acid interactions

R01GM-17020-23 (GEN) CHAMPE, SEWELL P RUTGERS STATE UNIVERSITY OF NJ WAKSMAN INSTITUTE/PO BOX 759 PISCATAWAY, NJ 08855-0759 Genetic control of development in model systems

R01GM-17078-23 (MBC) ECHOLS, HARRISON UNIVERSITY OF CALIFORNIA 401 BARKER HALL BERKELEY, CA 94720 Genetic and chemical studies of phage lambda development

R37GM-17129-21 (PC) NOLLER, HARRY F, JR UNIVERSITY OF CALIFORNIA SANTA CRUZ, CA 95064 Ribosome structure and function

R01GM-17132-22 (CTY) LUCK, DAVID J L ROCKEFELLER UNIVERSITY 1230 YORK AVENUE NEW YORK, N Y 10021 Biochemical genetics of microtubules

R01GM-17151-22 (PC) RAJBHANDARY, UTTAM L MASS INST OF TECHNOLOGY BLDG 18, ROOM 561 CAMBRIDGE, MASS 02139 Structure and function of transfer ribonucleic acids

R01GM-17152-22 (MBC) FREUNDLICH, MARTIN STATE UNIVERSITY OF NEW YORK STONY BROOK, NY 11794 Operon control by interacting regulatory elements

R01GM-17317-22 (GEN) FOGEL, SEYMOUR UNIVERSITY OF CALIFORNIA BERKELEY, CALIF 94720 Recombination--DNA synthesis and development in yeast

R01GM-17378-23 (BBCA) SUNDARALINGAM, MUTTAIYA OHIO STATE UNIVERSITY 120 W EIGHTEENTH AVE COLUMBUS, OH 43210 X-ray studies on nucleic acid constituents

R01GM-17452-20 (BBCB) HUANG, CHING-HSIEN UNIVERSITY OF VIRGINIA PO BOX 440-HLTH SCIENE CENTER CHARLOTTESVILLE, VA 22908 Phospholipid vesicles--Model for biological membranes

R01GM-17528-34 (BBCA) BRESLOW, ESTHER M CORNELL UNIVERSITY MED COLLEGE 1300 YORK AVENUE NEW YORK, N Y 10021 Interaction of proteins

R01GM-17534-21 (PBC) NISHIMURA, JONATHAN S UNIV OF TEXAS HLTH SCIS CTR 7703 FLOYD CURL DRIVE SAN ANTONIO, TX 78284-7760 Study of succinyl-CoA synthetase & related enzymes

R37GM-17709-22 (GEN) HARTWELL, LELAND H UNIVERSITY OF WASHINGTON SEATTLE, WA 98195 Genetic analysis of the eukaryotic cell cycle

R37GM-17880-21 (PB) COLLMAN, JAMES P STANFORD UNIVERSITY STANFORD, CA 94305-5080 Models for cytochrome P-450 hydroxylases

R01GM-17892-22 (MBC) NEIDHARDT, FREDERICK C UNIVERSITY OF MICHIGAN MICROBIOLOGY & IMMUNOLOGY DEPT ANN ARBOR, MICHIGAN 48109-0620 Regulation of bacterial metabolism

R01GM-17924-21 (PC) TRAUT, ROBERT R UNIV OF CALIFORNIA SCH OF MED DEPT OF BIOLOGICAL CHEMISTRY DAVIS, CA 95616 Ribosome structure and function

R01GM-17959-19 (SAT) MERYMAN, HAROLD T AMERICAN RED CROSS 15601 CRABBS BRANCH WAY ROCKVILLE, MD 20855 Cryopreservation of organs

R37GM-17980-22 (MBC) KING, JONATHAN A MASSACHUSETTS INST OF TECH DEPARTMENT OF BIOLOGY CAMBRIDGE, MASS 02139 Bacteriophage assembly and its genetic control

R01GM-18051-20 (BBCA) FRAUENFELDER, HANS UNIV ILLINOIS/URBANA 1110 WEST GREEN STREET URBANA, IL 61801 Protein dynamics and protein reactions

R01GM-18243-20 (MBC) PETTIJOHN, DAVID E UNIV OF COLORADO HLTH

SCIS CTR 4200 EAST NINTH AVE/B-121 DENVER, COLO 80262 DNA packaging in chromosomes

R01GM-18277-22 (MBC) SCHLEIF, ROBERT FERBER JOHNS HOPKINS UNIVERSITY 34TH AND CHARLES STREETS BALTIMORE, MD 21218 Regulatory mechanisms of the E coli arabinose operon

R01GM-18278-22 (BIO) KOLATTUKUDY, P E 1060 CARMACK ROAD COLUMBUS, OH 43210 Biochemistry of natural products

R01GM-18305-20 (MBC) WEBSTER, ROBERT E DUKE UNIVERSITY 157B NANALINE DUKE BLDG DURHAM, N C 27710 Biosynthesis of membrane proteins

R37GM-18325-21 (BIO) WOLFENDEN, RICHARD V U OF NORTH CAROLINA, CHAPEL HI CB#7260, 413 FLOB CHAPEL HILL, NC 27599-7260 Chemical mechanisms of biosynthesis

R01GM-18360-20 (PC) TAYLOR, PALMER W UNIV OF CALIFORNIA SAN DIEGO 9500 GILMAN DRIVE, 0636 LA JOLLA, CA 92093 Kinetics of drug macromolecule complex formation

R01GM-18375-20 (MBY) WOLSTENHOLME, DAVID R UNIVERSITY OF UTAH DEPARTMENT OF BIOLOGY SALT LAKE CITY, UT 84112 Structure of mitochondrial DNA

R37GM-18386-22 (MBC) GEIDUSCHEK, E PETER UNIV OF CALIF, SAN DIEGO 9500 GILMAN DRIVE LA JOLLA, CA 92093 Nucleic acids and nucleoproteins

R01GM-18457-20 (BBCB) CRAMER, WILLIAM A PURDUE UNIVERSITY WEST LAFAYETTE, IN 47907 Structure and function of the colicin E1 channel

R01GM-18519-21 (MCHA) COREY, ELIAS J HARVARD UNIVERSITY 12 OXFORD STREET CAMBRIDGE, MA 02138 Computer assisted analysis of chemical synthesis

R37GM-18539-21 (MBC) SIMONI, ROBERT D STANFORD UNIVERSITY DEPT. OF BIOLOGICAL SCIENCES STANFORD, CA 94305-5020 Membrane function and cellular energetics

R01GM-18541-20 (GEN) BYERS, BRECK E UNIVERSITY OF WASHINGTON 1959 NE PACIFIC ST SEATTLE, WA 98195 Molecular cytology of the cell cycle

R37GM-18568-19 (MBC) LOSICK, RICHARD M HARVARD UNIVERSITY 16 DIVINITY AVENUE CAMBRIDGE, MASS 02138 Role of RNA polymerase in bacterial differentiation

R01GM-18639-18 (CTY) STAEHELIN, L ANDREW UNIVERSITY OF COLORADO CAMPUS BOX 347 BOULDER, CO 80309-0347 Structure-function studies of Golgi organization

R01GM-18649-33 (PC) BESSMAN, MAURICE J JOHNS HOPKINS UNIVERSITY 34TH & CHARLES STREETS BALTIMORE, MD 21218 Enzymatic synthesis of nucleotides and DNA

R01GM-18684-20 (MGN) TAYLOR, BENJAMIN A JACKSON LABORATORY 600 MAIN STREET BAR HARBOR, ME 04609-0800 Genetic analysis of complex infirmities

R01GM-18694-16 (BNP) GOODMAN, MURRAY UNIV OF CALIFORNIA, SAN DIEGO LA JOLLA, CA 92093 Peptide design--syntheses, spectroscopy and simulations

R01GM-18711-20 (CBY) BROKAW, CHARLES J CALIFORNIA INST OF TECHNOLOGY 1201 E CALIFORNIA BLVD PASADENA, CALIF 91125 Mechanisms of movement of simple sperm flagella

R37GM-18754-30 (NSS) BRESLOW, RONALD C COLUMBIA UNIVERSITY DEPARTMENT OF CHEMISTRY NEW YORK, N Y 10027 Biochemical model reactions

R01GM-18835-21 (MGN) SCHEFFLER, IMMO E UNIV OF CALIFORNIA SAN DIEGO 9500 GILMAN DRIVE LA JOLLA, CA 92093-0322 Molecular characterization of a human centromere

R01GM-18842-18 (MBC) KARAM, JIM D MEDICAL UNIV OF SOUTH CAROLINA 171 ASHLEY AVE CHARLESTON, S C 29425 Genetic control of phage t4 DNA replication

R01GM-18874-20 (MCHA) BEAK, PETER A UNIVERSITY OF ILLINOIS 1209 WEST CALIFORNIA STREET URBANA, IL 61801 New synthetic methods useful for chemotherapeutics

R01GM-18894-21 (BMT) YU, NAI-TENG GEORGIA INST OF TECH 225 NORTH AVE NW ATLANTA, GA 30332 Laser-excited Raman spectroscopy of biopolymers

R01GM-18926-20 (CTY) FANGMAN, WALTON L UNIVERSITY OF WASHINGTON 1959 PACIFIC ST SEATTLE, WA 98195 Eukaryotic chromosome replication

R37GM-18938-20 (BIO) CLELAND, WILLIAM W UNIVERSITY OF WISCONSIN 1710 UNIVERSITY AVENUE MADISON, WI 53705 Determination of enzyme mechanisms by kinetic studies

R37GM-18974-20 (CBY) GOODENOUGH, DANIEL A HARVARD MEDICAL SCHOOL 25 SHATTUCK STREET BOSTON, MASS 02115 Molecular biology of intercellular communication

R37GM-19020-23 (MBC) LINN, STUART M UNIVERSITY OF CALIFORNIA BIOCHEM & MOLEC BIOLOGY BERKELEY, CA 94720 Studies of DNA restriction, damage and repair

R37GM-19043-20 (MBC) INOUYE, MASAYORI UMDNJ-ROBERT WOOD JOHNSON MED 675 HOES LANE, P O BOX 101 PISCATAWAY, N J 08854-5635 Cell division and membrane proteins

R01GM-19060-19 (BBCA) GRAY, DONALD M UNIVERSITY OF TEXAS AT DALLAS BOX 830688 MAIL STOP F031 RICHARDSON, TX 75083-0688 Polynucleotide and polynucleotide-protein structures

R01GM-19078-19 (MBC) KADNER, ROBERT J UNIVERSITY OF VIRGINIA BOX 441/SCHOOL OF MEDICINE CHARLOTTESVILLE, VA 22908 Transport of vitamin B12 in E coli

R01GM-19091-21 (PC) WAKIL, SALIH J BAYLOR COLLEGE OF MEDICINE ONE BAYLOR PLAZA HOUSTON, TX 77030 The metabolism and control of fatty acids

R01GM-19121-21 (PB) MARGOLIASH, EMANUEL UNIVERSITY OF ILLINOIS P O BOX 4348 MAIL CODE 066 CHICAGO, IL 60680 Mitochondrial membrane metabolic role of cytochrome C

R01GM-19179-19 (GEN) LAIRD, CHARLES D UNIVERSITY OF WASHINGTON DEPARTMENT OF ZOOLOGY, NJ-15 SEATTLE, WA 98195 Chromosome structure and function

R01GM-19199-19A1 (CTY) PRESCOTT, DAVID M UNIVERSITY OF COLORADO CAMPUS BOX 347 BOULDER, CO 80309-0347 Processing of DNA by Hypotrichous ciliates

R01GM-19242-20 (GEN) WRIGHT, THEODORE R UNIVERSITY OF VIRGINIA GILMER HALL CHARLOTTESVILLE, VA 22901 Ontogeny and genetic control of enzyme activity

R01GM-19261-19 (RAD) PRAKASH, LOUISE UNIV OF ROCHESTER SCH OF MED 601 ELMWOOD AVENUE ROCHESTER, NY 14642 Repair of DNA damaged by UV irradiation in yeast

PROJECT NO., ORGANIZATIONAL UNIT., INVESTIGATOR, ADDRESS, TITLE

R01GM-19301-20 (PB) TAYLOR, SUSAN S UNIVERSITY OF CALIFORNIA DEPT OF CHEMISTRY LA JOLLA, CA 92093-0654 Protein kinase--Primary structure and cAMP interaction

R01GM-19351-19 (PC) FOURNIER, MAURILLE J, JR UNIVERSITY OF MASSACHUSETTS LEDERLE GRADUATE RES CTR AMHERST, MA 01003 Biochemistry of novel small RNAs in E coli and yeast

R01GM-19363-28 (CBY) GERHART, JOHN C UNIVERSITY OF CALIFORNIA BERKELEY, CA 94720 Studies of cellular regulatory mechanisms

R01GM-19395-20 (BNP) GILHAM, PETER T PURDUE UNIVERSITY WEST LAFAYETTE, IN 47907 Synthesis of polyribonucleotides of defined sequence

R01GM-19398-16 (MBC) BRAMBL, ROBERT M UNIVERSITY OF MINNESOTA 220 BSC/1445 GORTNER AVENUE SAINT PAUL, MN 55108 Fungal spore germination and mitochondrial biogenesis

R01GM-19416-20 (MBC) HOCH, JAMES A SCRIPPS CLINIC & RESEARCH FDN 10666 NORTH TORREY PINES ROAD LA JOLLA, CALIF 92037 Genetic control of development

R01GM-19420-20 (TOX) TEPHLY, THOMAS R UNIVERSITY OF IOWA BOWEN SCIENCE BUILDING IOWA CITY, IA 52242-1109 Methanol poisoning

R37GM-19422-20 (MBC) ALTMAN, SIDNEY YALE UNIVERSITY BOX 1504A, YALE STATION NEW HAVEN, CT 06520 TRNA--Precursors, mutants, and function

R01GM-19427-20 (GEN) BOYNTON, JOHN E DUKE UNIVERSITY DURHAM, NC 27706 Hereditary control of organelle structure and function

R01GM-19511-20 (BM) DE MOSS, JOHN A U OF TEXAS HEALTH SCI CTR HOUSTON, TX 77025 Assembly of a membrane-bound multi-enzyme complex

R01GM-19536-17 (SSS) HASTINGS, JOHN W HARVARD UNIVERSITY 16 DIVINITY AVE CAMBRIDGE, MA 02138 Molecular and cellular mechanisms of circadian rhythms

R01GM-19559-19 (MBC) PARKINSON, JOHN S UNIVERSITY OF UTAH BIOLOGY DEPARTMENT SALT LAKE CITY, UTAH 84112 Genetics of chemotactic behavior in Escherichia coli

R37GM-19629-20 (GEN) HENRY, SUSAN A CARNEGIE-MELLON UNIVERSITY 4400 FIFTH AVENUE PITTSBURGH, PA 15213 Genetic regulation of phospholipid synthesis in yeast

R01GM-19656-20 (MGN) RODERICK, THOMAS H THE JACKSON LABORATORY 600 MAIN STREET BAR HARBOR, MAINE 04609-0800 Mammalian chromosomal inversions

R01GM-19693-17 (MBC) SMITH, ISSAR PUBLIC HEALTH RESEARCH INST 455 FIRST AVENUE NEW YORK, NY 10016 Regulatory mechanisms in Bacillus sporulation

R01GM-19698-20 (MBC) SETLOW, PETER UNIV. OF CONNECTICUT HEALTH CT 263 FARMINGTON AVENUE FARMINGTON, CT 06030 Degradation reactions in spore germination

R01GM-19756-20 (PC) DAHLBERG, ALBERT E DIV OF BIOLOGY & MEDICINE BOX G, BROWN UNIVERSITY PROVIDENCE, R I 02912 Polysomes & subunites--Structure-function relationships

R01GM-19770-18A1 (GEN) HIRAIZUMI, YUICHIRO UNIV OF TEXAS AT AUSTIN PATTERSON LABORATORIES BLDG AUSTIN, TX 78712 Male recombination - mutator system in Drosophila

R37GM-19822-32 (MBC) KENNEDY, EUGENE P HARVARD MEDICAL SCHOOL 25 SHATTUCK STREET BOSTON, MASS 02115 Metabolism and function of complex lipids

R01GM-19906-14A1 (BMT) DOWD, PAUL UNIVERSITY OF PITTSBURGH 219 PARKMAN AVENUE PITTSBURGH, PA 15260 Synthesis of vitamin B12 models

R01GM-19937-19 (GEN) FRISTROM, JAMES W UNIVERSITY OF CALIFORNIA 581 LIFE SCIENCE ADDITION BERKELEY, CALIF 94720 Genic/molecular basis of imaginal disc morphogenesis

R01GM-19957-19 (MBC) DWORKIN, MARTIN UNIV OF MINNESOTA/MEDICAL SCHO 420 DELAWARE STREET, SE MINNEAOLIS, MN 55455 Cell interactions and development in Myxococcus xanthus

R37GM-19963-19 (MBC) GOLD, LAWRENCE M UNIVERSITY OF COLORADO CAMPUS BOX 347 BOULDER, CO 80309 An investigation of the bacteriophage T4 replisome

R37GM-19988-31 (BBCB) BALDWIN, ROBERT L STANFORD UNIVERSITY DEPARTMENT OF BIOCHEMISTRY STANFORD, CALIF 94305 Physical studies of nucleic acids and proteins

R37GM-20011-20 (NSS) WALSH, CHRISTOPHER T HARVARD MEDICAL SCHOOL 240 LONGWOOD AVE BOSTON, MA 02115 Enzymatic reaction mechanisms

R01GM-20015-18 (MBC) BELL, ROBERT M DUKE UNIV MED CTER 212 NANALINE DUKE BLDG/RESCH D DURHAM, NC 27710 Regulation of membrane phospholipid synthesis

R01GM-20056-19 (GEN) HABER, JAMES E BRANDEIS UNIVERSITY 415 SOUTH STREET WALTHAM, MA 02254-9110 Recombination mechanisms in yeast cell differentiation

R01GM-20064-17 (BBCB) HOLTZER, ALFRED M WASHINGTON UNIVERSITY ONE BROOKINGS DRIVE ST LOUIS, MO 63130 Properties of alpha-helix-forming substances

R37GM-20066-19 (BBCA) MATTHEWS, BRIAN W UNIVERSITY OF OREGON EUGENE, OREGON 97403 X-ray structural studies of proteins

R37GM-20069-20 (MGN) SMITHIES, OLIVER UNIVERSITY OF NORTH CAROLINA 701 BRINKHOUS-BULLITT CHAPEL HILL, NC 27599-7525 Genetic control of protein structure and synthesis

R01GM-20080-18 (BBCA) FOOTE, CHRISTOPHER S UNIVERSITY OF CALIFORNIA 405 HILGARD AVENUE LOS ANGELES, CA 90021-1569 Reactive oxygen species in model biological systems

R01GM-20113-18 (CBY) PERACCHIA, CAMILLO UNIVERSITY OF ROCHESTER 601 ELMWOOD AVENUE ROCHESTER, N Y 14642 Structure-function in low resistance junctions

R01GM-20117-28 (BBCA) GROSSWEINER, LEONARD I ILL INSTITUTE OF TECHNOLOGY DEPT OF PHYSICS CHICAGO, ILL 60616 Fast photosensitized reactions of aromatic compounds

R37GM-20168-19 (NSS) REDFIELD, ALFRED G BRANDEIS UNIVERSITY 415 SOUTH STREET WALTHAM, MA 02254 Structural kinetic studies by nuclear magnetic resonance

R01GM-20194-19 (PB) CHASTEEN, NORMAN D UNIVERSITY OF NEW HAMPSHIRE DEPT OF CHEM/PARSONS HALL DURHAM, N H 03824 Iron deposition & mobilization in ferritin

R01GM-20195-34 (BBCA) SCHELLMAN, JOHN A UNIVERSITY OF OREGON INSTITUTE OF MOLECULAR BIO. EUGENE, OREGON 97403 Interactions of nucleotides and proteins

PROJECT NO., ORGANIZATIONAL UNIT., INVESTIGATOR, ADDRESS, TITLE

R01GM-20198-17 (BIO) SCHOWEN, RICHARD L UNIVERSITY OF KANSAS DEPARTMENT OF CHEMISTRY LAWRENCE, KS 66045-0046 Enzyme effector design
R01GM-20261-18 (MBY) GERBI, SUSAN A BROWN UNIVERSITY PO BOX G-J323 PROVIDENCE, RI 02912 Fine structure of ribosomal RNA
R01GM-20277-19 (CBY) SABATINI, DAVID D NEW YORK UNIVERSITY MED CTR 550 FIRST AVENUE NEW YORK, N Y 10016 Attachment of ribosomes to microsomal membranes
R01GM-20293-20 (GEN) NEI, MASATOSHI PENN STATE UNIVERSITY 328 MUELLER LABORATORY UNIVERSITY PARK, PA 16802 Theoretical popluation genetics and its applications
R01GM-20298-18 (SAT) COHEN, IRWIN K MEDICAL COLLEGE OF VIRGINIA BOX 154, MCV STATION RICHMOND, VA 23298-0514 Collagen metabolism in wound repair and keloid
R01GM-20338-24 (PC) COLE, ROGER D UNIVERSITY OF CALIFORNIA MCB - 229 STANLEY HALL BERKELEY, CALIF 94720 Histone biochemistry and the influence of hormone
R01GM-20379-18 (PB) TRUMPOWER, BERNARD L DEPARTMENT OF BIOCHEMISTRY DARTMOUTH MEDICAL SCHOOL HANOVER, NH 03756 Mechanism of respiration and energy transduction
R01GM-20467-19 (MGN) CAVALLI-SFORZA, LUIGI L STANFORD UNIVERSITY DEPT OF GENETICS S337 STANFORD, CA 94305-5120 Human population genetics
R01GM-20478-19 (MBC) DOWHAN, WILLIAM UNIV OF TEXAS MED SCHOOL P O BOX 20708 HOUSTON, TX 77225 Structure and function of membrane proteins
R01GM-20483-18 (MBY) CEDAR, HOWARD HEBREW UNIVERSITY PO BOX 1172 JERUSALEM, ISRAEL 91010 Transcription and modification of chromatin DNA
R01GM-20488-19 (PB) MILLETT, FRANCIS S UNIVERSITY OF ARKANSAS FAYETTEVILLE, AR 72701 Studies of electron transfer proteins
R01GM-20501-17 (PC) DENNIS, EDWARD A UNIVERSITY OF CALIFORNIA LA JOLLA, CA 92093-0601 Action of lipolytic enzymes
R01GM-20509-19 (MBC) ZUSMAN, DAVID R UNIVERSITY OP CALIFORNIA 401 BARKER HALL BERKELEY, CA 94720 Biochemical studies of development in bacteria
R01GM-20530-19 (BBCB) MATHEWS, F SCOTT WASHINGTON UNIV/SCHOOL OF MED 660 S. EUCLID AVENUE/BOX 8228 ST LOUIS, MO 63110 Structural studies of cytochromes b562 and b2
R01GM-20571-18 (PB) MALKIN, RICHARD UNIVERSITY OF CALIFORNIA 111 GEN & PLANT BIO BLDG BERKELEY, CA 94720 Iron - sulfur proteins as bound electron carriers
R01GM-20644-19 (CBY) STEPHENS, RAYMOND E MARINE BIOLOGICAL LABORATORY WOODS HOLE, MASS 02543 The formation and function of microtubules
R01GM-20726-13 (PB) DIWAN, JOYCE J RENSSELAER POLYTECHNIC INST SCIENCE CENTER TROY, NY 12180-3590 Mitochondrial cation transport mechanisms
R01GM-20737-18 (CBY) OXENDER, DALE L UNIVERSITY OF MICHIGAN DEPT OF BIOLOGICAL CHEMISTRY ANN ARBOR, MICH 48109 Transport components from eukaryotes
R01GM-20784-17 (MBC) BRADLEY, DOUGLAS R UNIVERSITY OF WASHINGTON SEATTLE, WA 98195 Bacillus thuringiensis crystal proteins
R01GM-20818-17 (PC) RHOADS, ROBERT E UNIVERSITY OF KENTUCKY 800 ROSE STREET LEXINGTON, KY 40536-0084 Regulation of ovalbumin synthesis in chick oviducts
R37GM-20861-18 (BBCA) OLSON, WILMA K RUTGERS UNIVERSITY DEPT OF CHEMISTRY NEW BRUNSWICK, NJ 08903 Nucleic acid conformation properties and interactions
R37GM-20888-34 (BIO) JENCKS, WILLIAM P BRANDEIS UNIVERSITY DEPT OF BIOCHEMISTRY WALTHAM, MA 02254 Chemistry and biochemistry of energy transfer
R01GM-20919-18 (MGN) EICHER, EVA M THE JACKSON LABORATORY 600 MAIN STREET BAR HARBOR, MAINE 04609-0800 Cytogenetics of the mouse
R37GM-20940-28 (BIO) ROSE, IRWIN A INSTITUTE/CANCER RESEARCH 7701 BURHOLME AVENUE PHILADELPHIA, PA 19111 Mechanisms of proton and phosphoryl transfer
R37GM-20964-18 (ALY) WEIGERT, MARTIN G INSTITUTE FOR CANCER RESEARCH 7701 BURHOLME AVE PHILADELPHIA, PA 19111 Genetic control of antibody structure
R37GM-20993-17 (SSS) HORVATH, CSABA G YALE UNIVERSITY PO BOX 2159/YALE STATION NEW HAVEN, CT 06520 Liquid chromatography of biological substances
R01GM-21020-15 (MBY) MILLER, OSCAR L UNIVERSITY OF VIRGINIA DEPARTMENT OF BIOLOGY CHARLOTTESVILLE, VA 22903 Ultrastructural studies of genetic activity
R01GM-21083-16 (PC) SCHRAMM, VERN L ALBERT EINSTEIN COLL OF MED 1300 MORRIS PK AVE,BIOCHEM DPT BRONX, N Y 10461 Regulation of adenine nucleotide pools
R01GM-21098-18 (MBC) FRAENKEL, DAN G HARVARD MEDICAL SCHOOL 200 LONGWOOD AVENUE BOSTON, MA 02115 Microbial glycolysis mutants
R37GM-21119-18 (MBY) GUTHRIE, CHRISTINE UNIVERSITY OF CALIFORNIA DEPT OF BIOCHEMISTRY & BIOP SAN FRANCISCO, CA 94143-0448 Biosynthesis of RNAs
R01GM-21120-17 (MBC) CARUTHERS, MARVIN H UNIV OF COLO/CAMPUS BOX 215 DEPT OF CHEMISTRY & BIOCHEM BOULDER, COLO 80309-0215 Studies on DNA regulatory regions of chromosomes
R01GM-21135-18 (GEN) EWENS, WARREN J UNIVERSITY OF PENNSYLVANIA PENNSYLVANIA, PA 19104 Stochastic processes in population genetics
R01GM-21156-15A2 (BMT) EATON, GARETH R UNIVERSITY OF DENVER DENVER, CO 80208 Interaction of spin labels with transition metals
R01GM-21168-18 (MGN) CAPECCHI, MARIO R UNIVERSITY OF UTAH SALT LAKE CITY, UT 84112 The control, assembly and termination of proteins
R01GM-21179-18 (GEN) LEWONTIN, RICHARD C HARVARD UNIVERSITY 26 OXFORD STREET CAMBRIDGE, MASS 02138 Genetic variation of proteins in natural populations
R01GM-21199-23 (BIO) SIGMAN, DAVID S UCLA SCHOOL OF MEDICINE LOS ANGELES, CA 90024-1737 Nuclease activity of 1,10-phenanthroline-copper ion
R01GM-21215-16 (SSS) EFRON, BRADLEY STANFORD UNIVERSITY STANFORD, CA 94305-4065 Adaptation of new statistical ideas for medicine
R01GM-21220-15 (PC) WELLS, JACK N VANDERBILT UNIVERSITY SCHOOL OF MEDICINE NASHVILLE, TN 37232-6600 Tissue specific inhibitors of phosphodiesterase
R01GM-21248-16 (BMT) FENSELAU, CATHERINE C UNIVERSITY OF MARYLAND BALTIMORE, MD 21228 Applications of mass spectrometry in pharmacology
R01GM-21277-16 (PB) CUSANOVICH, MICHAEL A UNIVERSITY OF ARIZONA TUCSON, AZ 85721 Biological electron transfer
R01GM-21313-17 (MGN) HUTCHISON, CLYDE A, III UNIV OF N C AT CHAPEL HILL DEPT-MICRBIO & IMMUN -CB#7290 CHAPEL HILL, NC 27599 Eukaryotic gene organization
R01GM-21328-17 (BNP) POULTER, CHARLES D UNIVERSITY OF UTAH SALT LAKE CITY, UT 84112 Terpene condensation reactions
R37GM-21337-17 (BMT) PALMER, GRAHAM A RICE UNIVERSITY P O BOX 1892 DEPT BIOCHEMISTRY HOUSTON, TX 77251 Molecular mechanisms of biological redox reactions
R01GM-21342-18 (PHY) ANDERSEN, OLAF S CORNELL UNIVERSITY MED COLLEGE 1300 YORK AVENUE NEW YORK, N Y 10021 Channel mediated ion movement across lipid bilayers
R01GM-21346-18 (MGN) SCHMID, CARL W UNIVERSITY OF CALIFORNIA DAVIS, CA 95616 Repetitive DNA sequences in the human genome
R01GM-21363-17A2 (PC) BREW, KEITH UNIV OF MIAMI SCH OF MED PO BOX 016129 MIAMI, FL 33101 Structure and function of lactose synthase
R01GM-21363-17A2 0002 (PC) BREW, KEITH Structure and function of lactose synthase Transferrin and its receptors
R01GM-21363-17A2 0004 (PC) BREW, KEITH Structure and function of lactose synthase Inhibitors of the N-glycosylation of proteins
R01GM-21363-17A2 0001 (PC) BREW, KEITH Structure and function of lactose synthase Lactose synthase
R01GM-21371-17 (BBCB) QUIOCHO, FLORANTE A BAYLOR COLLEGE OF MEDICINE ONE BAYLOR PLAZA HOUSTON, TX 77030 Binding proteins for active transport & chemotaxis
R01GM-21422-15 (CPA) GOODMAN, MYRON F UNIV OF SOUTHERN CALIFORNIA UNIVERSITY PARK LOS ANGELES, CA 90089-1340 Error correction in DNA synthesis--A biochemical study
R01GM-21424-16 (PC) TRAUGH, JOLINDA A UNIVERSITY OF CALIFORNIA RIVERSIDE, CA 92521 Effects of ribosomes phosphorylation on translation
R01GM-21436-17 (MBC) DATTA, PRASANTA K UNIVERSITY OF MICHIGAN 4326 MEDICAL SCIENCE I ANN ARBOR, MICH 48109-0606 Allosteric enzymes and metabolic regulation
K06GM-21444-28 (NCR) GOLDTHWAIT, DAVID A CASE WESTERN RESERVE UNIV 2119 ABINGTON ROAD CLEVELAND, OH 44106 Pyridine nucleotide-disulfide oxidoreductases
R01GM-21444-26 (PB) WILLIAMS, C H JR UNIVERSITY OF MICHIGAN ANN ARBOR, MI 48109-0606 Structure and mechanism of flavoenzymes
R01GM-21447-17 (SAT) SABA, THOMAS M ALBANY MEDICAL COLLEGE 47 NEW SCOTLAND AVE ALBANY, NY 12208 Systemic host defense following trauma
R01GM-21457-15 (BNP) MENGER, FREDRIC M EMORY UNIVERSITY ATLANTA, GA 30322 Bio-organic studies of synthetic lipids
R01GM-21473-17 (GEN) HALL, JEFFREY C BRANDEIS UNIVERSITY DEPARTMENT OF BIOLOGY WALTHAM, MASS 02254 Neurogenetics of drosphila reproduction
R01GM-21479-17 (BBCB) JOHNSON, WALTER C, JR OREGON STATE UNIVERSITY WENIGER 535 CORVALLIS, OR 97331-6503 Factors affecting the secondary structure in proteins
R01GM-21499-15 (PC) MURGOLA, EMANUEL J UNIV OF TEXAS MD ANDERSON 1515 HOLCOMBE BOULEVARD HOUSTON, TEXAS 77030 Missense suppression and codon recognition
R37GM-21509-17 (MGN) WILSON, ALLAN C UNIVERSITY OF CALIFORNIA AND BIOLOGY BERKELEY, CA 94720 Regulation as a basis for organismal differences
R01GM-21584-17 (SSS) MC CLOSKEY, JAMES A UNIVERSITY OF UTAH DEPARTMENT OF MEDICINAL CHEM SALT LAKE CITY, UTAH 84112 Mass spectrometry of nucleic acid constituents
R01GM-21589-17 (BBCA) BERMAN, HELEN M RUTGERS UNIVERSITY PO BOX 939 PISCATAWAY, NJ 08855 Nucleic acid structure and interactions
R01GM-21595-17 (MBY) PEDERSON, THORU WORCESTER FDN FOR EXP BIOLOGY 222 MAPLE AVE SHREWSBURY, MA 01545 RNA processing and ribonucleoprotein
R01GM-21626-17 (GEN) WENSINK, PIETER C ROSENSTIEL RESEARCH CENTER BRANDEIS UNIVERSITY WALTHAM, MA 02254 Sequence arrangement in eukaryotic DNA & chromosomes
R01GM-21643-18 (BIO) WALSH, CHRISTOPHER T HARVARD MED SCH/BIOL CHEM DEPT 25 SHATTUCK STREET BOSTON, MA 02115 Mechanistic probes of flavoenzyme catalysis
R37GM-21659-17 (BIO) KNOWLES, JEREMY R HARVARD UNIVERSITY 12 OXFORD STREET CAMBRIDGE, MASS 02138 Mechanisms of enzyme catalysis
P50GM-21681-27 (SRC) BAXTER, CHARLES R UNIV OF TEXAS SOUTHWESTERN MED CENTER AT DALLAS DALLAS, TEX 75235 Pathophysiologic and biochemical changes of thermal injury
P50GM-21681-27 0001 (SRC) DILLER, KENNETH R Pathophysiologic and biochemical changes of thermal injury Microvascular responses to thermal injury
P50GM-21681-27 0004 (SRC) HORTON, JURETA Pathophysiologic and biochemical changes of thermal injury Cardiac responses to thermal injury
P50GM-21681-27 0005 (SRC) VEGA, GLORIA Pathophysiologic and biochemical changes of thermal injury Hypertriglyceridemia pathogenesis during thermal injury
P50GM-21681-27 0008 (SRC) GRINNELL, FREDERICK Pathophysiologic and biochemical changes of thermal injury New methods for cutaneous wound repair
P50GM-21681-27 9001 (SRC) BAXTER, CHARLES R Pathophysiologic and biochemical changes of thermal injury Scientific core
P50GM-21700-15 (SRC) BURKE, JOHN F MASSACHUSETTS GENERAL HOSPITAL FRUIT STREET BOSTON, MA 02114 Burn trauma center
P50GM-21700-15 0008 (SRC) BURKE, JOHN F Burn trauma center Burn injury--Amino acid and energy metabolism
P50GM-21700-15 0011 (SRC) GELFAND, JEFFREY A Burn trauma center Burn injury, inflammation, and the acute phase response
P50GM-21700-15 0012 (SRC) TOMPKINS, RONALD G Burn trauma center Liver gut reaction in burn injury
P50GM-21700-15 9001 (SRC) BURKE, JOHN F Burn trauma center

PROJECT NO., ORGANIZATIONAL UNIT., INVESTIGATOR, ADDRESS, TITLE

CORE--Burn trauma center
R01GM-21737-26 (PB) PENEFSKY, HARVEY S SUNY HEALTH SCIENCE CTR 750 EAST ADAMS STREET SYRACUSE, N Y 13210 Mitochondrial membrane and oxidative phosphorylation
R01GM-21747-16 (BNP) WRIGHT, GEORGE E UNIV OF MASSACHUSETTS MED SCH 55 LAKE AVENUE NORTH WORCESTER, MA 01655 Design of selective inhibitors of DNA polymerases
R01GM-21769-17 (PC) WOOL, IRA G UNIVERSITY OF CHICAGO 920 EAST 58TH ST CHICAGO, IL 60637 Proteins of eukaryotic ribosomes
R01GM-21784-17 (TOX) HANZLIK, ROBERT P UNIVERSITY OF KANSAS LAWRENCE, KS 66045-2506 The role of epoxides in metabolism and drug toxicity
R01GM-21788-17 (RAD) BOCKRATH, RICHARD C INDIANA UNIVERSITY SCH OF MED DPT MICROBIOLOGY & IMMUNOLOGY INDIANAPOLIS, IN 46202-5120 Radiation induced cellular mutagenesis and DNA repair
R01GM-21822-17 (BBCA) VAN DER HELM, DICK UNIVERSITY OF OKLAHOMA NORMAN, OK 73019 Structure and function of siderophores
R01GM-21823-17 (MBC) HASELKORN, ROBERT THE UNIVERSITY OF CHICAGO 920 EAST 58TH STREET CHICAGO, ILL 60637 Differentiation in nitrogen-fixing blue-green algae
K06GM-21839-28 (BIO) CRANE, FREDERICK L PURDUE UNIVERSITY LILLY HALL OF LIFE SCIENCES WEST LAFAYETTE, IN 47907 Organization and function of subcellular particles
R37GM-21841-17 (GEN) THORNER, JEREMY W UNIVERSITY OF CALIFORNIA ROOM 401, BARKER HALL BERKELEY, CA 94720 Yeast peptide hormone synthesis and signal transduction
R01GM-21858-17 (RAD) LAWRENCE, CHRISTOPHER W UNIVERSITY OF ROCHESTER 601 ELMWOOD AVENUE ROCHESTER, NY 14642 Radiation mutagenesis and repair in Saccharomyces
R01GM-21872-17 (MBC) STUDIER, F WILLIAM BROOKHAVEN NATIONAL LABORATORY BIOLOGY DEPARTMENT UPTON, N Y 11973 Replication of T7 DNA
R01GM-21874-17 (GEN) PARDUE, MARY LOU MASSACHUSETTS INST TECHNOLOGY 16-717 CAMBRIDGE, MA 02139 Gene expression in Drosophila
R01GM-21882-16 (PBC) ETZLER, MARILYNN E UNIVERSITY OF CALIFORNIA BIOCHEM & BIOPHYSICS DEPT DAVIS, CALIF 95616 Structure, development, and modifications of lectins
R01GM-21900-16 (BBCB) MAKINEN, MARVIN W UNIVERSITY OF CHICAGO 920 E 58TH STREET CHICAGO, IL 60637 Enzyme reaction intermediates--A new approach
R01GM-21919-17 (BIO) COLEMAN, JOSEPH E YALE UNIVERSITY BOX 3333 NEW HAVEN, CT 06510 Structure and function of DNA binding proteins
R01GM-21941-17 (MBC) ROBERTS, JEFFREY W CORNELL UNIVERSITY BIOTECHNOLOGY BUILDING ITHACA, NY 14853 Gene control in infection & lysogeny by phage lambda
R01GM-21960-16 (MBC) HUANG, WAI M UNIV OF UTAH MEDICAL CENTER SALT LAKE CITY, UTAH 84132 DNA topoisomerase--Structure and function
R01GM-21966-17 (PB) CROTHERS, DONALD M YALE UNIVERSITY 12 PROSPECT PL NEW HAVEN, CT 06511-3516 DNA conformation and dynamics
R01GM-21967-17 (BBCB) MATTHEWS, BRIAN W UNIVERSITY OF OREGON EUGENE, OR 97403 Structure, function and stability of T4 phage lysozyme
R01GM-21971-17 (CBY) KREIBICH, GERT NEW YORK UNIVERSITY MED CTR 550 FIRST AVENUE NEW YORK, N Y 10016 Organization and biosynthesis of ER membrane proteins
R01GM-22057-17 (MBC) KENNEDY, EUGENE P HARVARD MEDICAL SCHOOL 300 LONGWOOD AVE BOSTON, MA 02115 Biogenesis and function of membranes
R01GM-22079-15A2 (CTY) GUPTA, NABA K UNIVERSITY OF NEBRASKA HAMILTON HALL LINCOLN, NE 68588-0304 Protein synthesis initiation in red blood cells
R01GM-22086-15 (PB) NAIDER, FRED R COLLEGE OF STATE ISLAND 50 BAY ST STATEN ISLAND, NY 10301 Peptide-cell interactions in Saccharomyces cerevisiae
R01GM-22087-15 (PB) BECKER, JEFFREY M UNIVERSITY OF TENNESSEE WALTERS LIFE SCIENCES BLDG KNOXVILLE, TN 37996-0845 Peptide-cell interactions in Saccharomyces cerevisiae
R01GM-22092-16 (MBC) KOGOMA, TOKIO UNIV OF MEXICO SCHOOL OF MED 900 CAMINO DE SALUD, NE ALBUQUERQUE, N M 87131 DNA replication in E coli--Regulatory mutants
R01GM-22109-16 (BBCA) STELLWAGEN, EARLE C UNIVERSITY OF IOWA DEPT OF BIOCHEM, 4-612 BSB IOWA CITY, IOWA 52242 The refolding of the dinucleotide fold
R01GM-22131-15 (MBC) SOMERVILLE, RONALD L PURDUE UNIVERSITY 1153 BIOCHEMISTRY BLDG WEST LAFAYETTE, IN 47907-1153 Regulatory mechanisms in tryptophan biosynthesis
R01GM-22135-17 (BIO) HERSHEY, JOHN W DEPT OF BIOLOGICAL CHEM UNIVERSITY OF CALIFORNIA DAVIS, CALIF 95616 Mechanism of initiation of protein biosynthesis
P01GM-22167-16 (SSS) KING, RICHARD A UNIVERSITY OF MINNESOTA 420 DELAWARE STREET S E MINNEAPOLIS, MN 55455 Albinism
P01GM-22167-16 0006 (SSS) WITKOP, CARL J Albinism Clinical and epidemiologic studies of albinism & hermansky-pudlak syndrome
P01GM-22167-16 0007 (SSS) YANZ, JERRY L Albinism Role of melanin in auditory form and function
P01GM-22167-16 0008 (SSS) HORDINSKY, MARIA Albinism Thioredoxin reductase in oxygen radical defense & tyrosinase activity
P01GM-22167-16 0009 (SSS) SUMMERS, GAIL C Albinism Visual function studies in albinism
P01GM-22167-16 9001 (SSS) WITKOP, CARL J Albinism Core--Electron microscopy
P01GM-22167-16 0001 (SSS) WITKOP, CARL J Albinism Melanosome functional morphology and clinical considerations
P01GM-22167-16 0003 (SSS) WITKOP, CARL J Albinism The keratinocyte-melanocyte messenger
P01GM-22167-16 0004 (SSS) KING, RICHARD A Albinism diagnosis & biochemical & molecular mechanisms of oculocutaneous albinism
P01GM-22167-16 0005 (SSS) WHITE, JAMES G Albinism Hermansky-pudlak, chediak-higashi syndrome, other pigmentation defects
R01GM-22172-17 (BNP) CANE, DAVID E BROWN UNIVERSITY DEPARTMENT OF CHEMISTRY PROVIDENCE, RI 02912 Biosynthesis of antibiotic natural products
R01GM-22201-17 (CTY) GARRARD, WILLIAM T UNIV OF TEXAS HLTH SCI CTR 5323 HARRY HINES BLVD. DALLAS, TEX 75235 Structure of the subunits of eukaryotic chromosomes
R01GM-22214-16 (CBY) OLMSTED, JOANNA B UNIVERSITY OF ROCHESTER RIVER CAMPUS ROCHESTER, NY 14627 Cellular control of cytoskeleton assembly
P01GM-22220-15 (SRC) MURPHY, MICHAEL B UNIVERSITY OF CHICAGO 947 EAST 58TH STREET CHICAGO, ILL 60637 Clinical pharmacology center
P01GM-22220-15 0006 (SRC) HORN, PATRICK Clinical pharmacology center Structure and function of dopamine receptors
P01GM-22220-15 0007 (SRC) WOOLVERTON, WILLIAM L Clinical pharmacology center Behavioral analysis of central nervous system dopamine receptors
P01GM-22220-15 0008 (SRC) MURPHY, MICHAEL B Clinical pharmacology center Role of endogenous dopamine in renal function
R01GM-22240-16 (BBCB) WISNIESKI, BERNADINE J UNIV OF CALIFORNIA LOS ANGELES 405 HILGARD AVE LOS ANGELES, CA 90024-1489 Physical structure of animal cell membranes
R01GM-22274-16A1 (MBY) MESELSON, MATTHEW S HARVARD UNIVERSITY 7 DIVINITY AVENUE CAMBRIDGE, MA 02138 Nuclear and messenger RNA of Drosophila
R01GM-22289-17 (CBY) LIN, SHIN JOHNS HOPKINS UNIVERSITY 3400 N CHARLES ST BALTIMORE, MD 21218 Cytochalasin & proteins that affect ends of f-actin
R01GM-22299-17 (MBC) NEWTON, AUSTIN PRINCETON UNIVERSITY DEPT OF MOLECULAR BIOLOGY PRINCETON, N J 08544-1014 Regulation of development in Caulobacter
R01GM-22300-15 (BBCA) BOLEN, DAVID W SOUTHERN ILLINOIS UNIVERSITY DEPARTMENT OF CHEMISTRY CARBONDALE, IL 62901 Elementary steps in enzyme catalysis
R01GM-22323-17 (MBC) EPSTEIN, WOLFGANG UNIVERSITY OF CHICAGO 920 EAST 58TH STREET CHICAGO, ILL 60637 Biochemical studies of ATP-driven bacterial transport
R01GM-22387-16 (GEN) HERMAN, ROBERT K UNIVERSITY OF MINNESOTA 250 BIOSCIENCE CENTER ST PAUL, MN 55108 Developmental genetics of Caenorhabditis elegans
R01GM-22395-17 (MBY) BROWN, DONALD D CARNEGIE INST OF WASHINGTON 115 W UNIVERSITY PARKWAY BALTIMORE, MD 21210 Amphibian metamorphosis--A developmental program
R37GM-22432-17 (BMT) CHAN, SUNNEY I CALIFORNIA INSTITUTE OF TECH 1201 E CALIFORNIA BLVD PASADENA, CA 91125 Membrane proteins--Structure and function
R01GM-22441-16 (BBCA) MATTHEWS, KATHLEEN S RICE UNIVERSITY HOUSTON, TX 77251 Physical and genetic studies of repressor proteins
R01GM-22479-16 (BMT) VOLLHARDT, K PETER C UNIVERSITY OF CALIFORNIA DEPARTMENT OF CHEMISTRY BERKELEY, CALIF 94720 Novel routes to physiologically active compounds
R01GM-22490-17 (BBCA) BHANDARY, KRISHNA K SUNY AT BUFFALO 3435 MAIN ST, 109 FOSTER HALL BUFFALO, N Y 14214 Cyclic peptides, structure, and function
R01GM-22523-16 (MGN) WADE, MICHAEL J UNIVERSITY OF CHICAGO 1101 EAST 57TH STREET CHICAGO, IL 60637 Genetic consequences of population structure
R01GM-22525-16 (BIO) BUTOW, RONALD A UNIVERSITY OF TEXAS 5323 HARRY HINES BLVD DALLAS, TX 75235 Regulation of mitochondrial biogenesis in yeast
R37GM-22526-15 (MBC) PTASHNE, MARK S FAIRCHILD BIOCHEMICAL LABS HARVARD UNIV/7 DIVINITY AVE CAMBRIDGE, MASS 02138 Bacteriophage repressors
R01GM-22580-16 (MBY) PAULE, MARVIN R COLORADO STATE UNIVERSITY FORT COLLINS, CO 80523 Gene selection by multiple eukaryotic RNA polymerases
R01GM-22619-15A1 (MBC) KRAKOW, JOSEPH S HUNTER COLLEGE OF CUNY 695 PARK AVENUE NEW YORK, NY 10021 Studies on the cyclic AMP receptor protein of E coli
R01GM-22629-17 (MGN) CHASIN, LAWRENCE A COLUMBIA UNIVERSITY 912 FAIRCHILD CTR/BIO SCIENCES NEW YORK, NY 10027 Analysis of dihydrofolate reductase gene expression
R01GM-22701-16 (PB) MUNCK, ECKARD CARNEGIE MELLON UNIVERSITY 4400 FIFTH AVENUE PITTSBURGH, PA 15213-3890 Studies of O2 activation by Mossbauer spectroscopy
R01GM-22714-17 (GEN) KUNG, CHING UNIVERSITY OF WISCONSIN 1525 LINDEN DRIVE MADISON, WI 53706 Genetic and biochemical studies of Paramecium behavior
R01GM-22737-13 (PC) OLIVERA, BALDOMERO M UNIVERSITY OF UTAH DEPARTMENT OF BIOLOGY SALT LAKE CITY, UTAH 84112 A biochemical characterization of Conus toxins
R01GM-22749-16 (BIO) DICKSON, ROBERT C UNIVERSITY OF KENTUCKY MED CTR 800 ROSE ST LEXINGTON, KY 40536-0084 Eucaryotic enzyme induction--Beta-galactosidase in yeast
R01GM-22760-16 (MCHA) COHEN, THEODORE UNIV OF PITTSBURGH/DEPT CHEM PITTSBURGH, PA 15260 New methods for synthesis and modification of rings
P01GM-22778-16 (SSS) RICHARDS, FREDERIC M YALE UNIVERSITY 260 WHITNEY AVENUE, BOX 6666 NEW HAVEN, CT 06511 Program in macromolecular structure, motion, control
P01GM-22778-16 0002 (SSS) ENGELMAN, DONALD M Program in macromolecular structure, motion, control Molecular structure of biological membranes
P01GM-22778-16 0003 (SSS) WYCKOFF, HAROLD W Program in macromolecular structure, motion, control X-ray analysis of protein structure and function
P01GM-22778-16 0004 (SSS) RICHARDS, FREDERIC M Program in macromolecular structure, motion, control Study of proteins in solutions, interfaces and solids
P01GM-22778-16 0005 (SSS) STEITZ, THOMAS H Program in macromolecular structure, motion, control Structure basis of enzyme action, specificity and control
P01GM-22778-16 0007 (SSS) MOORE, PETER B Program in macromolecular structure, motion, control Crystallography of ribosomal RNAs and proteins
P01GM-22778-16 9001 (SSS) RICHARDS, FREDERIC M Program in macromolecular structure, motion, control Core facilities --Diffraction and computing
R01GM-22792-14 (BIO) RUBIN, CHARLES S ALBERT EINSTEIN COLL OF

PROJECT NUMBER LISTING

PROJECT NO., ORGANIZATIONAL UNIT., INVESTIGATOR, ADDRESS, TITLE

MEDICI 1300 MORRIS PARK AVENUE BRONX, NY 10461 Cyclic AMP and protein kinases in cell regulation
R01GM-22807-16 (BBCA) ZIMMERMANN, ROBERT A UNIV OF MASSACHUSETTS DEPT OF BIOCHEMISTRY AMHERST, MA 01003 Chemical and genetic probes of ribosome architecture
R01GM-22825-12 (SAT) TURINSKY, JIRI ALBANY MEDICAL COLLEGE 47 NEW SCOTLAND AVENUE ALBANY, NY 12208 Mechanisms of insulin resistance after trauma
R01GM-22827-13 (BBCA) BLAKE, RICHARD D UNIVERSITY OF MAINE HITCHNER HALL ORONO, MAINE 04469 Structure and interactions of DNA
R37GM-22846-17 (BIO) GROSSMAN, LAWRENCE JOHNS HOPKINS UNIVERSITY 615 NORTH WOLFE STREET BALTIMORE, MD 21205 Enzymatic excision and repair mechanisms
R37GM-22854-16 (BIO) SOLL, DIETER G YALE UNIVERSITY 260 WHITNEY AVENUE NEW HAVEN, CT 06511 Studies on transfer RNA
R01GM-22912-15 (CTY) STAEHELIN, L A UNIVERSITY OF COLORADO CAMPUS BOX 347 BOULDER, CO 80309-0347 Membrane protein complexes and morphogenesis
R01GM-22916-16 (MBY) VAN HOLDE, KENSAL E OREGON STATE UNIVERSITY CORVALLIS, OR 97331-6503 Subunit structure of chromatin
R37GM-22923-16 (BBCB) HYDE, JAMES S MEDICAL COLLEGE OF WISCONSIN DEPARTMENT OF RADIOLOGY MILWAUKEE, WI 53226 Nitroxide radical spin label methods
R01GM-22939-16 (BBCA) TURNER, DOUGLAS H UNIVERSITY OF ROCHESTER ROCHESTER, NY 14627-0216 Kinetic and spectroscopic studies of nucleic acids
R37GM-22942-16 (CTY) PAGANO, RICHARD E CARNEGIE INST OF WASH 115 W. UNIVERISTY PARKWAY BALTIMORE, MD 21210 Intracellular translocation and metabolism of lipids
R01GM-22982-16 (BIO) OPPENHEIMER, NORMAN J UNIVERSITY OF CALIFORNIA 513 PARNASSUS AVE BOX 0446 SAN FRANCISCO, CA 94143 Structure/function relations in pyridine coenzymes
R01GM-22994-16 (BBCA) WOODY, ROBERT W COLORADO STATE UNIVERSITY 316 MRB BLDG FORT COLLINS, CO 80523 Optical properties of biological macromolecules
R37GM-23000-16 (NSS) SHIRES, GEORGE T TEXAS TECH UNIVERSITY 3601 4TH STREET LUBBOCK, TX 79430 Evaluation of saline solution in therapy of shock
R01GM-23013-13 (MGN) ROUFA, DONALD J KANSAS STATE UNIVERSITY ACKERT HALL MANHATTAN, KS 66506 Molecular genetics of human ribosomal proteins
R01GM-23105-16 (PB) FILLINGAME, ROBERT H UNIVERSITY OF WISCONSIN MED SC 1215 LINDEN DRIVE MADISON, WI 53706 Proton-translocating sector of E coli H+-ATPase
R01GM-23152-14 (PB) CROSS, RICHARD L SUNY HEALTH SCIENCE CENTER 750 E ADAMS ST SYRACUSE, NY 13210 Mechanism of ATP synthesis by the respiratory chain
R01GM-23167-16 (CTY) TOBIN, ELAINE M UNIVERSITY OF CALIFORNIA 405 HILGARD AVENUE LOS ANGELES, CA 90024 Phytochrome regulation of specific gene expression
R01GM-23200-16 (SSS) CARSON, DENNIS A UNIVERSITY OF CALIFORNIA 9500 GILMAN DRIVE LA JOLLA, CA 92093-0945 Immunodeficiency and adenine nucleotide metabolism
R01GM-23238-16 (CBY) CANDE, WILLIAM Z UNIVERSITY OF CALIFORNIA 341 LIFE SCIENCE ADDITION BERKELEY, CALIF 94720 Functional model for mitosis in cell lines
R01GM-23244-17 (CBY) HORWITZ, ALAN F UNIVERSITY OF ILLINOIS 505 S GOODWIN AVENUE URBANA, IL 61801 Determinants of myogenic membrane phenomena
R01GM-23289-16 (BBCA) GRIFFIN, ROBERT G MASSACHUSETTS INST OF TECH 77 MASSACHUSETTS AVENUE CAMBRIDGE, MA 02139 Solid state NMR studies of membrane proteins
R01GM-23303-16 (BBCA) MATTHEWS, CHARLES R PENNSYLVANIA STATE UNIVERSITY 152 DAVEY LABORATORY UNIVERSITY PARK, PA 16802 Mutagenesis as a probe of the folding of TRP synthase
R01GM-23367-15 (GEN) MARZLUF, GEORGE A 484 WEST TWELFTH AVE COLUMBUS, OH 43210-1292 Regulation of the gene expression in neurospora
R37GM-23377-16 (MBC) WICKNER, WILLIAM T UNIVERSITY OF CALIFORNIA 33-257 CENTER FOR HLTH SCIENCE LOS ANGELES, CA 90024-1737 The assembly of proteins into biological membranes
R37GM-23403-15 (BBCB) GRIFFIN, ROBERT G MASSACHUSETTS INST OF TECH 77 MASS AVE/NW14-5113 CAMBRIDGE, MA 02139 Solid state NMR studies of peptides and proteins
R37GM-23408-15 (MBC) ROTH, JOHN R UNIVERSITY OF UTAH 224 SOUTH BIOLOGY BUILDING SALT LAKE CITY, UT 84112 Transfer RNA production and role in gene regulation
R01GM-23441-15 (MBC) KAISER, A DALE STANFORD UNIVERSITY STANFORD, CA 94305-5307 Control of multicellular development in Myxobacteria
R01GM-23467-15 (BBCA) RECORD, M THOMAS, JR UNIV OF WISCONSIN DEPT OF CHEMISTRY MADISON, WIS 53706 Ion effects on interactions of RNA polymerase and DNA
R01GM-23468-15 (GEN) CLINE, THOMAS W UNIVERSITY OF CALIFORNIA DIVISION OF GENETICS BERKELEY, CA 94720 Regulation of sex-specific genes in Drosophila
R01GM-23476-11 (CTY) LUDUENA, RICHARD F UNIV OF TEXAS HLTH SCIS CTR 7703 FLOYD CURL DRIVE SAN ANTONIO, TX 78284-7760 Control of microtubule assembly in vitro and in vivo
R01GM-23509-13 (BBCA) BRESLAUER, KENNETH J RUTGERS UNIVERSITY PO BOX 939 PISCATAWAY, NJ 08855-0939 DNA stability and flexibility--A thermodynamic study
R01GM-23526-14 (RAD) SHETLAR, MARTIN D UNIVERSITY OF CALIFORNIA 513 PARNASSUS AVE SAN FRANCISCO, CA 94143 Photoinduced DNA protein crosslinkig in chromatin
R01GM-23529-15 (BIO) VILLAFRANCA, JOSEPH J PENNSYLVANIA STATE UNIVERSITY UNIVERSITY PARK, PA 16802 Structure and mechanism of regulatory enzymes
R01GM-23534-15 (MCHA) GUTSCHE, C DAVID TEXAS CHRISTIAN UNIVERSITY FORT WORTH, TX 76129 Calixarenes as enzyme mimics
R01GM-23547-15 (CBY) ROSEN, STEVEN D UNIVERSITY OF CALIFORNIA BOX 0452 SAN FRANCISCO, CA 94143-0452 Cell surface lectins & intercellular adhesion

PROJECT NO., ORGANIZATIONAL UNIT., INVESTIGATOR, ADDRESS, TITLE

R01GM-23549-15 (CTY) ROSBASH, MICHAEL M BRANDEIS UNIVERSITY DEPARTMENT OF BIOLOGY WALTHAM, MASS 02254 Organization of yeast ribosomal protein genes
R01GM-23562-15 (MBC) SCHIMMEL, PAUL MASSACHUSETTS INST OF TECHNOLO 77 MASSACHUSETTS AVE CAMBRIDGE, MA 02139 Genetic approaches to protein-nucleic acid interactions
R01GM-23567-14 (BBCA) NAFIE, LAURENCE A SYRACUSE UNIVERSITY 1-014 CNT FOR SCIENCE/TECHNOLO SYRACUSE, NY 13244-4100 Vibrational optical activity in biological molecules
R37GM-23573-14 (BBCB) THOMPSON, THOMAS E UNIVERSITY OF VIRGINIA DEPT OF BIOCHEMISTRY CHARLOTTESVILLE, VA 22908 Phospholoipid bilayers containing glycosphinogolipids
R01GM-23599-15 (BMT) HORROCKS, WILLIAM D, JR PENNSYLVANIA STATE UNIVERSITY EBERLY COLLEGE OF SCIENCE UNIVERSITY PARK, PA 16802 New lanthanide probes of protein structure
R01GM-23635-13 (SSS) DI BERARDINO, MARIE A MED COLLEGE OF PENNSYLVANIA DEPT OF PHYSIOLOGY & BIOCHEM PHILADELPHIA, PA 19129 Normal differentiation and carcinogenesis
R01GM-23638-14 (VR) GOORHA, RAKESH M ST JUDE CHILDREN'S RES HOSP 332 N LAUDERDALE, P O BOX 318 MEMPHIS, TENN 38101-0318 DNA replication of frog virus 3 and its methylation
R01GM-23656-14 (BMT) BIELSKI, BENON H J BROOKHAVEN NATIONAL LABORATORY UPTON, NY 11973 Biological superoxide radical mechanisms
R01GM-23674-15 (MBY) GRUNSTEIN, MICHAEL UNIVERSITY OF CALIFORNIA 405 HILGARD AVENUE LOS ANGELES, CALIF 90024 Control of histone synthesis and function in yeast
R01GM-23697-14 (BBCB) WOODY, ROBERT W COLORADO STATE UNIVERSITY FORT COLLINS, COLO 80523 Spectroscopic studies of RNA polymerase mechanism
R37GM-23719-16 (NSS) MODRICH, PAUL L DUKE UNIVERSITY MEDICAL CENTER BOX 3711 DURHAM, N C 27710 Molecular mechanisms of DNA - protein interaction
R37GM-23750-16 (CPA) REDDY, JANARDAN K NORTHWESTERN UNIV MEDICAL SCH 303 EAST CHICAGO AVENUE CHICAGO, IL 60611 Biologic studies with liver peroxisome proliferators
R01GM-23822-12 (GEN) LOOMIS, WILLIAM F UNIV OF CALIFORNIA, SAN DIEGO CTR FOR MOLECULAR GENE LA JOLLA, CA 92093-0322 Biochemical basis of development in Dictyostelium
R01GM-23851-11 (BBCA) REED, CHRISTOPHER A UNIV OF SOUTHERN CALIFORNIA LOS ANGELES, CA 90089-0744 Cytochrome oxidase and H-bonded oxyhemoglobin models
R01GM-23858-13 (PB) HOLLOWAY, PETER W UNIVERSITY OF VIRGINIA BOX 440 / JORDAN HALL CHARLOTTESVILLE, VA 22908 The dynamic state of cytochrome B5 in membranes
R01GM-23875-12A1 (SAT) NELSON, THOMAS E UNIV OF TEXAS HEALTH SCIENCE C 6431 FANNIN HOUSTON, TX 77030 Skeletal muscle lesion in malignant hyperthermia
R37GM-23883-15 (GEN) WATERSTON, ROBERT H WASHINGTON UNIV SCH OF MED 660 SOUTH EUCLID, BOX 8232 ST LOUIS, MO 63110 Molecular genetics of muscle assembly in C elegans
R01GM-23900-14 (PC) TRIMBLE, ROBERT B NEW YORK STATE DEPT OF HEALTH P.O. BOX 509 ALBANY, N Y 12201-0509 Glycoprotein biosynthesis in yeast
R01GM-23913-14 (PB) FULCO, ARMAND J UNIVERSITY OF CALIFORNIA 900 VETERAN AVE LOS ANGELES, CA 90024-1786 Soluble cytochrome P 450 hydroxylases from bacteria
R37GM-23917-15 (MBC) GEORGOPOULOS, CONSTANTINE P UNIVERSITY OF UTAH MEDICAL CEN SALT LAKE CITY, UTAH 84132 Bacterial functions in phage development
R01GM-23922-13 (PBC) BEREZNEY, RONALD STATE UNIV OF N Y AT BUFFALO DEPT OF BIOLOGICAL SCIENCES BUFFALO, NEW YORK 14260 Nuclear matrix structure and DNA replication
R01GM-23928-14 (CTY) ALBERTS, BRUCE M UNIVERSITY OF CALIFORNIA SAN FRANCISCO, CA 94143-0448 Biochemistry of gene regulation in higher eukaryotes
R01GM-23999-13 (MBC) SYPHERD, PAUL S UNIVERSITY OF CALIFORNIA DEPT MICROBIO & MOLE GEN IRVINE, CA 92717 Gene structure and ef-1alpha in the fungus Mucor
R01GM-24009-13 (MBC) TORRIANI-GORINI, ANNAMARIA MASS INSTITUTE OF TECHNOLOGY 77 MASSACHUSETTS AVENUE CAMBRIDGE, MA 02139 Phosphate metabolism in E. coli--Regulatory genes function
R37GM-24020-16 (PC) ALBERTS, BRUCE M UNIV OF CALIFORNIA/ BOX 0448 DEPT-BIOCHEMISTRY & BIOPHYSICS SAN FRANCISCO, CA 94143 DNA protein interactions in DNA replication control
R37GM-24032-15 (BBCA) STRYER, LUBERT STANFORD UNIVERSITY FAIRCHILD BUILDING D135 STANFORD, CA 94305-5400 Optical studies of protein structure and function
R01GM-24034-15 (PC) LAKE, JAMES A UNIVERSITY OF CALIFORNIA 405 HILGARD AVENUE LOS ANGELES, CA 90024 Mapping ribosomal functional sites
R01GM-24054-13 (BNP) GANEM, BRUCE CORNELL UNIVERSITY DEPARTMENT OF CHEMISTRY ITHACA, N Y 14853 Synthesis and biosynthesis in the shikimate pathway
R01GM-24110-15 (GEN) PETES, THOMAS D UNIVERSITY OF NORTH CAROLINA CHAPEL HILL, NC 27599-3280 Recombination in yeast
R37GM-24129-15 (PB) BENKOVIC, STEPHEN J PENNSYLVANIA STATE UNIVERSITY 152 DAVEY LABORATORY UNIVERSITY PARK, PA 16802 Transformylase enzymes/dihydrofolate reductase
R01GM-24178-14A1 (MBC) LITTLE, JOHN W UNIVERSITY OF ARIZONA BIOSCIENCES WEST BUILDING TUCSON, AZ 85721 Biochemical analysis of lexA and hk022 repressors
R01GM-24195-15 (PB) MALONEY, PETER C JOHNS HOPKINS MEDICAL SCHOOL 725 N WOLFE ST BALTIMORE, MD 21205 Ion gradients and energy coupling in bacteria
R01GM-24211-15 (PHRA) JUSKO, WILLIAM J S U N Y AT BUFFALO HOCHSTETTER HALL 565 SCH/PHARM AMHERST, N Y 14260 Corticosteroid pharmacokinetics/dynamics
R01GM-24212-15 (MBC) POLISKY, BARRY A INDIANA UNIVERSITY BLOOMINGTON, IN 47405 Molecular basis of ColEI replication control
R01GM-24235-14 (BBCA) RODGERS, MICHAEL A BOWLING GREEN STATE UNIVERSITY CTR FOR PHOTOCHEMICAL SCIENCES BOWLING GREEN, OH 43403 Singlet oxygen in biological systems
R01GM-24266-15 (BBCB) OPELLA, STANLEY J UNIVERSITY OF

PROJECT NO., ORGANIZATIONAL UNIT., INVESTIGATOR, ADDRESS, TITLE

PENNSYLVANIA DEPARTMENT OF CHEMISTRY PHILADELPHIA, PA 19104 NMR studies of biological supramolecular structures

R01GM-24270-13S1 (MBC) PATO, MARTIN L NATL JEWISH CTR FOR IMMUNOLOGY 1400 JACKSON STREET DENVER, CO 80206-1997 Excision and replication of MU virus DNA

R01GM-24279-15 (CTY) FIRTEL, RICHARD A UNIV OF CALIFORNIA, SAN DIEGO 9500 GILMAN DRIVE LA JOLLA, CALIF 92093-0634 Gene structure and transcriptional regulation

R01GM-24299-15 (GEN) KAUFMAN, THOMAS C INDIANA UNIVERSITY DEPARTMENT OF BIOLOGY BLOOMINGTON, IND 47405 The genetic control of morphogenesis in Drosophila

R01GM-24314-15 (BMT) MORRISON, GEORGE H CORNELL UNIVERSITY BAKER LABORATORY ITHACA, N Y 14853-1301 Ion microscopy in biology and medicine

R01GM-24337-14A1 (NLS) TAYLOR, PALMER W UNIV OF CALIFORNIA, SAN DIEGO BASIC SCI BLDG, M-036 LA JOLLA, CA 92093 Pharmacology of membrane association receptors

R01GM-24349-12 (BMT) NOVOTNY, MILOS V INDIANA UNIVERSITY 7TH STREET BLOOMINGTON, IN 47405 Improvements in biochemical high-performance LC

R01GM-24364-13 (CTY) SALMON, EDWARD D UNIV OF NORTH CAROLINA CB #3280 CHAPEL HILL, NC 27599-3280 Mechanisms of mitotic spindle assembly and function

R01GM-24365-15 (MBC) SERWER, PHILIP UNIVERSITY OF TEXAS 7703 FLOYD CURL DRIVE SAN ANTONIO, TX 78284-7760 Biophysics and genetics of viral DNA packaging

R01GM-24375-14A1 (MGN) SHIMIZU, NOBUYOSHI UNIVERSITY OF ARIZONA LIFE SCIENCES SOUTH RM 429 TUCSON, AZ 85721 Genetic control of mammalian cell surface functions

R01GM-24417-12 (HEM) LOW, PHILIP S PURDUE UNIVERSITY WEST LAFAYETTE, IND 47907 Studies of erythrocyte membrane band 3

R01GM-24441-12A2 (PC) BAMBARA, ROBERT A UNIVERSITY OF ROCHESTER 601 ELMWOOD AVENUE ROCHESTER, N Y 14642 Enzymatic mechanisms of DNA synthesis

P01GM-24483-12A1 (SRC) MARSHALL, GARLAND R WASHINGTON UNIVERSITY 660 S EUCLID AVE ST LOUIS, MO 63110 Computer-aided drug design

P01GM-24483-12A1 0013 (SRC) BEUSEN, DENISE Computer-aided drug design Experimental determination of the receptor-bound conformation of ligands

P01GM-24483-12A1 0014 (SRC) NOCK, BRUCE Computer-aided drug design Ligands for the putative opioid receptor

P01GM-24483-12A1 0015 (SRC) MARSHALL, GARLAND Computer-aided drug design Receptor bound conformation of angiotensin II and bradykinin

P01GM-24483-12A1 0016 (SRC) MARSHALL, GARLAND Computer-aided drug design Conformation of cyclosporin and immunosuppression and nephrotoxicity

P01GM-24483-12A1 0017 (SRC) MOELLER, KEVIN D Computer-aided drug design Novel approaches to rigid peptide analogs

P01GM-24483-12A1 0010 (SRC) DAMMKOEHLER, R A Computer-aided drug design Computation and algorithm development

P01GM-24483-12A1 0012 (SRC) PONDER, JAY Computer-aided drug design Potential energy functions for peptides and proteins

R01GM-24485-15 (BBCB) STROUD, ROBERT M UNIVERSITY OF CALIFORNIA BIOCHEM/BIOPHYSICS S-964 SAN FRANCISCO, CA 94143-0448 Structure and function of proteins at molecular level

R37GM-24486-15 (BBCA) ACKERS, GARY K WASHINGTON U SCH OF MEDICINE 660 S EUCLID AVE., BOX 8231 ST LOUIS, MO 63110 Regulatory interactions in protein/nucleic acid systems

R01GM-24492-14 (BBCA) WARSHEL, ARIEH UNIVERSITY OF SOUTHERN CALIF DEPARTMENT OF CHEMISTRY LOS ANGELES, CA 90089-1062 Theoretical studies of enzymatic reactions

R01GM-24496-14 (MBC) MOUNT, DAVID W UNIVERSITY OF ARIZONA TUCSON, AZ 85721 Mechanism of induction of viral and cellular function

R01GM-24497-14 (BIO) TABITA, FRED R OHIO STATE UNIVERSITY 484 W 12TH AVE COLUMBUS, OH 43210 Function and assembly of CO2 assimilatory enzymes

R37GM-24544-15 (BIO) WANG, JAMES C HARVARD UNIVERSITY 7 DIVINITY AVENUE CAMBRIDGE, MA 02138 DNA topoisomerases--Biological functions & mechanisms

R01GM-24658-21 (MBC) ZALKIN, HOWARD PURDUE UNIVERSITY WEST LAFAYETTE, IN 47907 Glutamine amidotransferase structure/function/regulation

R37GM-24663-14 (GEN) HORVITZ, H ROBERT MASSACHUSETTS INST OF TECH 77 MASSACHUSETTS AVENUE CAMBRIDGE, MA 02139 Genetic analysis of nematode egg-laying

R01GM-24681-14 (MGN) TASHIAN, RICHARD E UNIVERSITY OF MICHIGAN DEPARTMENT OF HUMAN GENETICS ANN ARBOR, MICH 48109 Biochemical genetics of the carbonic anhydrases

R01GM-24689-14 (PB) LIPSCOMB, JOHN D UNIVERSITY OF MINNESOTA DEPARTMENT OF BIOCHEMISTRY MINNEAPOLIS, MN 55455 Oxygenase enzyme mechanism

R01GM-24711-14 (CPA) MOSES, ROBB E OREGON HEALTH SCIENCE UNIV 3181 S W SAM JACKSON PARK ROAD PORTLAND, OR 97201-3098 Cellular DNA repair mechanisms and mutagenesis

R01GM-24749-22 (PHY) EISENMAN, GEORGE UCLA SCHOOL OF MEDICINE 405 HILGARD AVENUE LOS ANGELES, CA 90024-1751 Ion permeation through channels, carriers and nerve

R01GM-24751-14 (MBC) SQUIRES, CATHERINE L COLUMBIA UNIVERSITY 701 FAIRCHILD CENTER NEW YORK, NY 10027 Fusion of the ribosomal promotor to other operons

R01GM-24756-13 (GEN) RUBENSTEIN, IRWIN 220 BIOSCIENCE CENTER UNIVERSITY OF MINNESOTA ST PAUL, MN 55108 Genomic organization of zein gene subfamilies

R01GM-24784-15 (PB) SCARBOROUGH, GENE A UNIVERSITY OF NORTH CAROLINA CB#7365, FACULTY LAB OFFICE BL CHAPEL HILL, NC 27599-7365 Energy transduction in Neurospora plasma membranes

R01GM-24795-14 (BBCB) ROBINSON, NEAL C UNIV OF TEXAS HLTH SCIENCE CTR 7703 FLOYD CURL DRIVE SAN ANTONIO, TX 78284-7760 Hydrophobic associations of mitochondrial proteins

R01GM-24797-14 (CBY) HERSCHMAN, HARVEY R UCLA SCHOOL OF MEDICINE CENTER FOR HEALTH SCIENCES LOS ANGELES, CA 90024 Initiation of cellular proliferation

PROJECT NO., ORGANIZATIONAL UNIT., INVESTIGATOR, ADDRESS, TITLE

R01GM-24825-13 (PC) LEVIN, DANIEL H MASSACHUSETTS INST OF TECH 77 MASSACHUSETTS AVENUE CAMBRIDGE, MA 02139 Control of protein synthesis by double-stranded RNA

R01GM-24832-14 (BMT) OLAH, GEORGE A UNIV OF SOUTHERN CALIFORNIA DEPT. OF CHEMISTRY LOS ANGELES, CA 90089-1661 Carbocations and bio-related reactions

R01GM-24872-14 (CTY) MEISLER, MIRIAM H UNIVERSITY OF MICHIGAN MEDICAL SCHOOL II M4708 ANN ARBOR, MI 48109-0618 Genetic regulation of mouse enzymes

R01GM-24891-14 (SAT) HECHTMAN, HERBERT B BRIGHAM AND WOMEN'S HOSPITAL 75 FRANCIS STREET BOSTON, MA 02115 Cardiopulmonary failure following shock and trauma

R37GM-24908-14 (BIO) MATTHEWS, ROWENA G UNIVERSITY OF MICHIGAN 2200 BONISTEEL BLVD ANN ARBOR, MI 48109-2099 Regulation of folate metabolism

R37GM-24913-14 (NSS) WOOD, HARLAND G CASE WESTERN RESV UNIVERSITY 2119 ABINGTON ROAD CLEVELAND, OHIO 44106 Mechanism of autotrophic growth with CO or C02 and H2

R01GM-24963-14 (PC) SPREMULLI, LINDA L UNIVERSITY OF NORTH CAROLINA CB# 3290 CHAPEL HILL, NC 27599-3290 Mechanism of protein biosynthesis in chloroplasts

R01GM-24971-14 (PHY) MC LAUGHLIN, STUART G DEPT. PHYSIOLOGY, HSC SUNY, STONY BROOK STONY BROOK, N Y 11794-8661 Electrostatic potentials and biological membranes

R01GM-24979-14 (ARRD) HOSTETLER, KARL Y UNIVERSITY OF CALIFORNIA LA JOLLA, CA 92093 Antiviral lipid prodrugs in AIDS and hepatitis B

R01GM-25052-15 (BMT) LOBRUTTO, RUSSELL ARIZONA STATE UNIVERSITY TEMPE, AZ 85287-1601 Structures of membrane-bound & soluble metalloproteins

R37GM-25062-13 (CBY) BORISY, GARY G UNIVERSITY OF WISCONSIN 1525 LINDEN DRIVE MADISON, WI 53706 Mechanism and control of microtubule assembly

R01GM-25064-12 (SAT) ATLEE, JOHN L, III MEDICAL COLLEGE OF WISCONSIN 8701 W WATERTOWN PLANK ROAD MILWAUKEE, WI 53226 Mechanisms for cardiac arrhythmias during anesthesia

R01GM-25101-14 (BBCB) SEDAT, JOHN W UNIVERSITY OF CALIFORNIA DEPT OF BIOCHEMISTRY & BIO SAN FRANCISCO, CA 94143-0554 Structure of polytene chromosome bands and interbands

R01GM-25103-14 (GEN) YOUNG, MICHAEL W ROCKEFELLER UNIVERSITY 1230 YORK AVENUE NEW YORK, N Y 10021 Gene organization and function in D melanogaster

R01GM-25154-14 (PB) SILVERMAN, DAVID N UNIVERSITY OF FLORIDA BOX J-267 HEALTH CENTER GAINESVILLE, FL 32610 Catalytic mechanism of carbonic anhydrase

R01GM-25158-13 (BMT) SPIRO, THOMAS G PRINCETON UNIVERSITY WASHINGTON ROAD PRINCETON, NJ 08544-1009 Ultraviolet Raman studies of proteins and nucleic acids

R01GM-25172-14 (BMT) KADISH, KARL M UNIVERSITY OF HOUSTON DEPARTMENT OF CHEMISTRY HOUSTON, TEX 77004 Redox reactions of iron porphyrins

R01GM-25177-12A3 (PB) HOROWITZ, PAUL M UNIV OF TEXAS HEALTH SCI CTR 7703 FLOYD CURL DRIVE SAN ANTONIO TX 78284-7760 Detergent aided protein folding of rhodanese

R01GM-25203-14 (MBY) HERRICK, GLENN A UNIV OF UTAH MEDICAL CENTER 50 NORTH MEDICAL DRIVE SALT LAKE CITY, UT 84132 Somatic genome alterations in Oxytricha fallax

R01GM-25232-14 (MBY) LIS, JOHN T CORNELL UNIVERSITY BIOTECHNOLOGY BUILDING ITHACA, NY 14853 Coordinate gene regulation in animal cells

R01GM-25243-14 (CBY) WARD, SAMUEL UNIVERSITY OF ARIZONA BIOSCIENCES WEST BLDG TUCSON, ARIZONA 85721 Genetic specification of cell morphology

R01GM-25271-13A1 (SSS) GEISSER, SEYMOUR UNIVERSITY OF MINNESOTA 206 CH ST S E/270 VINCENT HALL MINNEAPOLIS, MN 55455 Predictive methods

R01GM-25280-20 (BNP) MANNING, MAURICE MEDICAL COLL OF OHIO PO BOX 10008 TOLEDO, OH 43699-0008 Design and synthesis of neurohypophysial peptides

R37GM-25326-14 (MBC) KLECKNER, NANCY E HARVARD UNIVERSITY 7 DIVINITY AVENUE CAMBRIDGE, MA 02138 Illegitimate recombination by drug resistance elements

R37GM-25349-14 (PB) SENIOR, ALAN E UNIV. OF ROCHESTER MED. CTR. BOX 607 ROCHESTER, N Y 14642 Characterization of E. coli F1F0-ATP synthase

R01GM-25386-14 (CTY) SPRAGUE, KAREN U UNIVERSITY OF OREGON EUGENE, OR 97403 Control of tRNA gene expression in Bombyx mori

R01GM-25418-13 (TOX) NELSON, SIDNEY D UNIV OF WASHINGTON DEPT OF MED CHEM/BG-20 SEATTLE, WA 98195 Alteration of metabolism by structural modification

R01GM-25431-14 (BMT) REGNIER, FRED E PURDUE UNIVERSITY DEPT OF BIOCHEMISTRY WEST LAFAYETTE, IN 47907 High performance liquid chromatography of proteins

R01GM-25434-11 (PC) SLOBIN, LAWRENCE I UNIV OF MISSISSIPPI MED CTR 2500 NORTH STATE STREET JACKSON, MISS 39216 Control of polypeptide chain elongation in eucaryotes

R01GM-25451-12 (BIO) WAHBA, ALBERT J UNIV. OF MISSISSIPPI MED CTR 2500 N STATE ST JACKSON, MS 39216-4505 Protein synthesis in prokaryotes and eukaryotes

R37GM-25459-14 (MCHA) BERGMAN, ROBERT G UNIVERSITY OF CALIFORNIA 213B LEWIS HALL BERKELEY, CA 94720 C-O and C-N bond formation using metal-based reagents

R01GM-25480-13 (BMT) BABCOCK, GERALD T MICHIGAN STATE UNIVERSITY EAST LANSING, MI 48824-1322 Bioenergetic mechanisms in multicenter enzymes

R01GM-25498-13 (BBCA) REVZIN, ARNOLD MICHIGAN STATE UNIVERSITY DEPARTMENT OF BIOCHEMISTRY EAST LANSING, MICH 48824 Regulatory protein-DNA interactions-- Physical studies

R01GM-25505-14 (BBCA) GRIFFIN, ROBERT G MASSACHUSETTS INST OF TECH 77 MASSACHUSETTS AVENUE CAMBRIDGE, MA 02139 NMR studies of the dynamic structure of lipid bilayers

R01GM-25508-14 (BIO) CAMPBELL, JUDITH L CALIFORNIA INST OF TECHNOLOGY 1201 EAST CALIFORNIA BOULEVARD PASADENA, CA 91125 Enzymatic mechanisms of DNA replication

R37GM-25515-14 (PHRA) ORTIZ DE MONTELLANO, PAUL R UNIVERSITY OF CALIFORNIA 926 MEDICAL SCIENCES BUILDING SAN FRANCISCO, CA 94143-0446 Selective destruction of cytochrome P-450 by drugs
R01GM-25521-12 (BNP) POULTER, CHARLES D UNIVERSITY OF UTAH SALT LAKE CITY, UT 84112 Sterol biosynthesis
R01GM-25532-14 (MBY) WARNER, JONATHAN R ALBERT EINSTEIN COLL OF MED 1300 MORRIS PARK AVENUE BRONX, N Y 10461 Ribosomal genes of yeast and their regulation
R01GM-25553-13 (MBY) ANGERER, ROBERT C UNIVERSITY OF ROCHESTER RIVER STATION ROCHESTER, N Y 14627 In situ localization of informational embryo mas
R01GM-25621-12 (MBC) GUMPORT, RICHARD I UNIVERSITY OF ILLINOIS 1209 WEST CALIF ST, 415 RAL URBANA, IL 61801 Studies with T4 RNA ligase
R37GM-25654-13 (BIO) OLIVERA, BALDOMERO M UNIVERSITY OF UTAH DEPT OF BIOLOGY SALT LAKE CITY, UT 84112 NAD and DNA
R01GM-25661-14 (CBY) SNELL, WILLIAM J UNIV OF TEXAS SOUTHWESTERN CELL BIOLOGY & NEUROSCIENCE DALLAS, TEX 75235 Cell surface recognition and cell interactions
R37GM-25662-15 (CBY) ROTHMAN, JAMES E SLOAN-KETTERING INSTITUTE 1275 YORK AVENUE NEW YORK, N Y 10021 Biochemistry of clathrin-coated vesicles
R01GM-25663-14 (BBCA) SMALL, ENOCH W EASTERN WASHINGTON UNIVERSITY MAIL STOP 74 CHENEY, WA 99004 Fluorescence studies of nucleosome structural changes
R01GM-25671-14 (BBCA) ROSENBERG, JOHN M UNIVERSITY OF PITTSBURGH PITTSBURGH, PA 15260 Structure and function of EcoRI endonuclease
R01GM-25680-13 (BNP) CARUTHERS, MARVIN H UNIVERSITY OF COLORADO CAMPUS BOX 215 BOULDER, CO 80309-0215 Chemical and enzymatic studies on gene control regions
R01GM-25690-13 (PC) CHUNG, ALBERT E UNIVERSITY OF PITTSBURGH DEPT OF BIOLOGICAL SCIENCES PITTSBURGH, PA 15260 Characterization of basement membrane glycoproteins
R01GM-25693-13 (BBCA) MAUZERALL, DAVID C ROCKEFELLER UNIVERSITY 1230 YORK AVENUE NEW YORK, N Y 10021 Charge transfer across interfaces of biological systems
R01GM-25698-25 (BBCB) GRIFFITH, O HAYES UNIVERSITY OF OREGON INSTITUTE OF MOLECULAR BIOLOGY EUGENE, OREG 97403 Lipid-protein interactions
R01GM-25716-10 (SAT) UEDA, ISSAKU UNIVERSITY OF UTAH DEPT OF ANESTHESIA SALT LAKE CITY, UTAH 84132 Interfacial action of inhalation anesthetics
R37GM-25765-14 (BIO) KLINMAN, JUDITH P UNIVERSITY OF CALIFORNIA 239B HILDEBRAND HALL BERKELEY, CA 94720 Dopamine monooxygenase--Molecular mechanisms
R37GM-25766-31 (PC) HILL, ROBERT L DUKE UNIVERSITY MEDICAL CENTER DURHAM, N C 27710 Glycosyltransferases, mucins & macrophage receptors
R01GM-25799-12 (MBC) HUTCHINSON, CHARLES R UNIVERSITY OF WISCONSIN 425 NO CHARTER STREET MADISON, WI 53706 Biosynthesis of polyether antibiotics
R01GM-25810-13 (SAT) LANGER, ROBERT S MASSACHUSETTS INST OF TECH 77 MASSACHUSETTS AVENUE CAMBRIDGE, MA 02139 A system for heparin removal
R01GM-25813-13 (CBY) CONDEELIS, JOHN S ALBERT EINSTEIN COLL OF MED 1300 MORRIS PARK AVENUE BRONX, N Y 10461 Interactions of actin cytoskeleton with plasma membrane
R01GM-25821-13 (MBY) RINGOLD, GORDON M SYNTEX (U.S.A.) INC 3401 HILLVIEW AVE S3-1 PALO ALTO, CA 94304 Molecular biology of steroid hormone action
R01GM-25845-12A1 (BMT) MILLER, MARVIN J UNIVERSITY OF NOTRE DAME NOTRE DAME, IN 46556 Siderophores, analogs and bioconjugates: Synthesis and study
R01GM-25846-12 (PB) LUSTY, CAROL J PUBLIC HLTH RES INST OF N Y 455 FIRST AVENUE NEW YORK, N Y 10016 Gene structure of carbamyl phosphate synthetase
R01GM-25848-10 (PC) YANG, DAVID C GEORGETOWN UNIVERSITY DEPARTMENT OF CHEMISTRY WASHINGTON, D C 20057 Mammalian aminoacyl-tRNA synthetase complexes
R01GM-25862-13A1 (BBCB) FREED, JACK H CORNELL UNIVERSITY ITHACA, N Y 14853 Electron-spin relaxation in model membranes
R01GM-25871-13 (MBC) HOLMES, WALTER M VIRGINIA COMMONWEALTH UNIV BOX 678, MCV STATION RICHMOND, VA 23298-0678 Gene organization and expression of tRNA
R01GM-25874-13 (MBY) LINDQUIST, SUSAN L UNIVERSITY OF CHICAGO 5841 SOUTH MARYLAND AVE CHICAGO, IL 60637 The function of heat shock response in Drosophila
R01GM-25909-13 (BIO) MEARES, CLAUDE F UNIVERSITY OF CALIFORNIA DEPARTMENT OF CHEMISTRY DAVIS, CA 95616 Photochemical and spectroscopic probes of RNA polymerase
R01GM-25912-14 (MCHA) REBEK, JULIUS JR MASSACHUSETTS INST OF TECH DEPT OF CHEMISTRY/RM 18-207 CAMBRIDGE, MA 02139 Catalysis and mechanism
R01GM-25953-13 (PB) TU, SHIAO-CHUN UNIVERSITY OF HOUSTON 4800 CALHOUN HOUSTON, TX 77204-5934 Structure and mechanism of flavoprotein hydroxylases
R01GM-25975-10A2 (BBCB) GERIG, JOHN T UNIVERSITY OF CALIFORNIA SANTA BARBARA, CA 93106 Structural studies of proteins by fluorine NMR
R01GM-25976-13 (GEN) SCHEDL, PAUL PRINCETON UNIVERSITY PRINCETON, NJ 08544 Gene expression in D melanogaster embryogenesis
R01GM-26017-13 (MBC) KOLODNER, RICHARD D DANA FARBER CANCER INSTITUTE 44 BINNEY STREET BOSTON, MA 02115 Enzymatic mechanisms of genetic recombination
R01GM-26020-13 (PC) CLARKE, STEVEN G UNIVERSITY OF CALIFORNIA LOS ANGELES, CA 90024-1569 Control of eucaryotic membrane function by methylation
R01GM-26059-12 (CTY) PAULE, MARVIN R COLORADO STATE UNIVERSITY FORT COLLINS, CO 80523 RNA polymerase iii transcription regulation mechanism
R01GM-26061-12 (GEN) ZITOMER, RICHARD S STATE UNIV OF NEW YORK 1400 WASHINGTON AVE ALBANY, NY 12222 Regulation of yeast cytochrome C genes

R01GM-26079-13 (GEN) YOUNG, ELTON T, II UNIVERSITY OF WASHINGTON DEPT OF BIOCHEMISTRY, SJ-70 SEATTLE, WA 98195 Genetic regulation of alcohol metabolism in yeast
R01GM-26091-13 (CBY) BRYAN, JOSEPH BAYLOR COLLEGE OF MEDICINE ONE BAYLOR PLAZA HOUSTON, TX 77030 Chemistry and localization of actin gelling proteins
R01GM-26096-14 (BMT) MACFARLANE, RONALD D TEXAS A&M UNIVERSITY DEPARTMENT OF CHEMISTRY COLLEGE STATION, TEXAS 77843 Biomedical use of plasma desorption mass spectrometry
R01GM-26102-12 (SAT) LOEGERING, DANIEL J ALBANY MEDICAL COLLEGE 47 NEW SCOTLAND AVENUE ALBANY, NY 12208 Hemolysis and phagocytic dysfunction during shock
R01GM-26108-13 (CTY) HAMLIN, JOYCE L UNIVERSITY OF VIRGINIA BOX 440, JORDAN MEB CHARLOTTESVILLE, VA 22908 Control of eukaryotic DNA synthesis
R01GM-26114-14 (PHRA) SCHENKMAN, JOHN B UNIV OF CONN HEALTH CENTER DEPARTMENT OF PHARMACOLOGY FARMINGTON, CONN 06032 Induction and mode of action of hepatic drug oxidase
R37GM-26132-14 (CBY) POLLARD, THOMAS D JOHNS HOPKINS MEDICAL SCHOOL 720 RUTLAND AVENUE BALTIMORE, MD 21205 Actomyosin-microtubule interactions in cell division
P50GM-26145-13 (SRC) GOODWIN, CLEON W CORNELL UNIV MEDICAL COLLEGE NEW YORK, N Y 10021 Burn and trauma research center
P50GM-26145-13 0006 (SRC) GOODWIN, CLEON W Burn and trauma research center Mitochondrial function in postburn hypermetabolism
P50GM-26145-13 0009 (SRC) STAIANO-COICO, LISA Burn and trauma research center Skin grafting of cultured allografts on dermal substitutes
P50GM-26145-13 0010 (SRC) PERRY, SAMUEL W Burn and trauma research center Psychobiological response to stress and loss
P50GM-26145-13 0013 (SRC) MATTHEWS, DWIGHT E Burn and trauma research center Protein and energy metabolism in burn injury
P50GM-26145-13 9002 (SRC) SHIRES, G. TOM Burn and trauma research center CORE--Burn and trauma center
R01GM-26150-12 (CTY) GOODENOUGH, URSULA W WASHINGTON UNIVERSITY BIOLOGY DEPARTMENT ST LOUIS, MO 63130 Flagellar membrane adhesion and sexual signaling
R37GM-26154-21 (MBY) STEITZ, JOAN A YALE UNIVERSITY P O BOX 3333, 333 CEDAR ST NEW HAVEN, CONN 06510 Autoantibody probes for mammalian gene expression
R01GM-26156-12 (MBC) CRONAN, JOHN E, JR UNIVERSITY OF ILLINOIS 407 S GOODWIN/131 BURRILL HALL URBANA, ILLINOIS 61801 Protein lipid interaction
R01GM-26165-11 (CBY) JULIANO, RUDOLPH L UNIVERSITY OF NORTH CAROLINA DEPARTMENT OF PHARMACOLOGY CHAPEL HILL, NC 27599-7365 Molecular bases of cell adhesion
R01GM-26166-13 (BNP) PARRY, RONALD J RICE UNIVERSITY P O BOX 1892 HOUSTON, TX 77251 Biosynthesis and metabolism of nucleosides
R01GM-26176-13 (CTY) WEINTRAUB, HAROLD M FRED HUTCHINSON CANCER RES CTR 1124 COLUMBIA ST/M723 GENETICS SEATTLE, WA 98104 The complexity of chromosomal structure and assembly
R01GM-26178-13 (BMT) HEGEDUS, LOUIS S COLORADO STATE UNIVERSITY DEPARTMENT OF CHEMISTRY FORT COLLINS, CO 80523 Organimetallic syntheses of bioactive compounds
R01GM-26210-12 (MBC) YAO, MENG-CHAO FRED HUTCHINSON CANCER RES CTR 1124 COLUMBIA STREET SEATTLE, WA 98104 Gene amplification and elimination in Tetrahymena
R01GM-26217-12 (GEN) CULBERTSON, MICHAEL R UNIVERSITY OF WISCONSIN 1525 LINDEN DRIVE MADISON, WI 53706 Molecular basis of translational fidelity
R01GM-26226-13 (BMT) BALCH, ALAN L UNIVERSITY OF CALIFORNIA DAVIS, CA 95616 Iron porphyrin activation of dioxygen/small molecules
R01GM-26234-12 (CBY) TILLACK, THOMAS W UNIVERSITY OF VIRGINIA DEPT OF PATHOLOGY, BOX 214 CHARLOTTESVILLE, VA 22908 Glycolipid organization in liposomes and membranes
R01GM-26237-13 (BIO) KANTROWITZ, EVAN R BOSTON COLLEGE CHESTNUT HILL, MA 02167 The molecular basis of cellular control mechanisms
R01GM-26242-13 (BBCA) WOODWARD, CLARE K UNIVERSITY OF MINNESOTA 1479 GORTNER AVE ST PAUL, MN 55108 Single proton exchange kinetics in proteins
R37GM-26259-14 (GEN) BLACKBURN, ELIZABETH H UNIV OF CALIF AT SAN FRANCISCO 3RD & PARNASSUS AVENUE SAN FRANCISCO, CA 94143-0414 Structure and formation of telomeres in Tetrahymena
R01GM-26290-13 (BIO) PEGG, ANTHONY E MILTON S HERSHEY MED CTR PO BOX 850 HERSHEY, PA 17033 Investigations of mammalian aminopropyltransferases
R01GM-26295-11 (BMT) ELLIS, PAUL D UNIVERSITY OF SOUTH CAROLINA COLUMBIA, SC 29208 Cadmium-113 NMR of systems of biological interest
R01GM-26305-13 (PB) CROFTS, ANTONY R UNIVERSITY OF ILLINOIS 407 S GOODWIN, 524 BURRILL URBANA, ILL 61801 The proton pumps of photosynthetic bacteria
R01GM-26338-14 (CBY) POLLARD, THOMAS D JOHNS HOPKINS MEDICAL SCHOOL 725 N WOLFE ST BALTIMORE, MD 21205 Molecular mechanism of cellular motility
R01GM-26351-13 (PB) OZOLS, JURIS B UNIVERSITY OF CONNECTICUT 263 FARMINGTON AVE FARMINGTON, CT 06030 Isolation and structure of microsomal membrane proteins
R01GM-26355-11A3 (TMP) COHEN, STANLEY N STANFORD UNIVERSITY SCHOOL OF MEDICINE STANFORD, CA 94305-5120 Propagation and inheritance of plasmids
R01GM-26357-13 (CBY) DEROSIER, DAVID J BRANDIES UNIVERSITY PO BOX 9110 WALTHAM, MA 02254-9110 Structural studies of cellular assemblies of actin
R01GM-26390-11 (BMT) CLARKE, MICHAEL J BOSTON COLLEGE CHESTNUT HILL, MA 02167-3809 Metal complexes of nucleic acids and related bases
R01GM-26429-26 (MBC) HELMSTETTER, CHARLES E FLORIDA INST OF TECHNOLOGY 150 W UNIVERSITY BLVD MELBOURNE, FL 32901 Biochemistry and radiation effect during the cell cycle
R37GM-26444-13 (BCE) EVANS, RONALD M THE SALK INSTITUTE P O BOX 85800 SAN DIEGO, CALIF 92138 Hormonal regulation of mammalian gene expression
R01GM-26449-14 (MGN) FOURNIER, RAYMOND E FRED HUTCHINSON CANCER

PROJECT NO., ORGANIZATIONAL UNIT., INVESTIGATOR, ADDRESS, TITLE

RES CTR 1124 COLUMBIA STREET SEATTLE, WA 98104 Genetic analysis of cell-type-specific functions
R01GM-26453-12A1 (MBY) GOTTESFELD, JOEL M MEDICAL BIOLOGY INSTITUTE 11077 NORTH TORREY PINES ROAD LA JOLLA, CA 92037 Isolation of 5S gene chromatin
R01GM-26486-13 (BMT) KOLHOUSE, J FRED UNIV OF COLORADO HLTH SCI CTR 4200 E 9TH AVE DENVER, CO 80262 Metabolic role of folate and cobalamin in mammals
R01GM-26494-13 (BBCA) JOHNSON, ARTHUR E UNIVERSITY OF OKLAHOMA 620 PARRINGTON OVAL NORMAN, OK 73019 Protein translocation across the ER membrane
R01GM-26517-11 (MBC) SARKAR, NILIMA BOSTON BIOMEDICAL RES INST 20 STANIFORD STREET BOSTON, MA 02114 Function of polyadenylate sequences in bacterial RNA
R01GM-26568-13 (BNP) SCHULTZ, ARTHUR G RENSSELAER POLYTECHNIC INST DEPARTMENT OF CHEMISTRY TROY, NY 12180-3590 2, 5-cyclohexadienones in natural products synthesis
R01GM-26569-12 (BNP) PARRY, RONALD J RICE UNIVERSITY P O BOX 1892 HOUSTON, TX 77251 Biosynthesis of cyclopentanoids
R01GM-26624-13 (CTY) REEDER, RONALD H HUTCHINSON CANCER RESEARCH CTR 1124 COLUMBIA STREET SEATTLE, WA 98104 Control of ribosomal gene transcription
R01GM-26643-13 (PB) THORPE, COLIN UNIVERSITY OF DELAWARE NEWARK, DE 19716 Flavoproteins in fatty acid metabolism
R01GM-26666-13 (SSS) DESIDERIO, DOMINIC M UNIVERSITY OF TENNESSEE 956 COURT AVE/RM A218 MEMPHIS, TN 38163 Mass spectral analysis of trigeminal sensory peptides
R01GM-26676-13 (PHRA) SHEINER, LEWIS B UNIVERSITY OF CALIFORNIA SF CLINIC BLDG / ROOM C-255 SAN FRANCISCO, CA 94143-0626 Pharmacokinetic/pharmacodynamic data analysis
P50GM-26691-13 (SRC) BENET, LESLIE Z UNIV OF CALIFORNIA 513 PARNASSUS AVE SAN FRANCISCO, CA 94143 Pharmacokinetics/pharmacodynamics
P50GM-26691-13 0004 (SRC) BENET, LESLIE Z Pharmacokinetics/pharmacodynamics Immunopharmacokinetics-immunopharmacodynamics
P50GM-26691-13 0011 (SRC) RUDOLPH, ABRAHAM M Pharmacokinetics/pharmacodynamics Pharmacokinetics and pharmacodynamics--Development considerations
P50GM-26691-13 0015 (SRC) SHEINER, LEWIS B Pharmacokinetics/pharmacodynamics New models for pharmacokinetics/pharmacodynamics
P50GM-26691-13 0016 (SRC) GIACOMINI, KATHLEEN M Pharmacokinetics/pharmacodynamics Cimetidine elimination from cerebrospinal fluid
P50GM-26691-13 0017 (SRC) BRODSKY, FRANCES M Pharmacokinetics/pharmacodynamics Drug delivery via receptor-mediated endocytosis
R01GM-26698-12 (SB) LANGER, ROBERT S MASSACHUSETTS INST OF TECH 77 MASSACHUSETTS AVENUE CAMBRIDGE, MA 02139 Controlled release of macromolecules
R01GM-26701-13 (CTY) VALLEE, RICHARD B WORCHESTER FOUNDATION 222 MAPLE AVENUE SHREWSBURY, MASS 01545 Structure, phosphorylation and function of MAPs
R01GM-26715-13 (BBCA) SNYDER, GRAYSON H STATE UNIVERSITY OF NEW YORK BUFFALO, N Y 14260 Strategies for directing disulfide pairing in proteins
R01GM-26726-13 (CTY) JOHNSON, KENNETH A PENNSYLVANIA STATE UNIVERSITY 301 ALTHOUSE LABORATORY UNIVERSITY PARK, PA 16802 Kinetic analysis of microtubule-dependent ATPases
R01GM-26738-12 (BIO) TRAUGH, JOLINDA A UNIVERSITY OF CALIFORNIA RIVERSIDE, CA 92521 Cyclic nucleotide independent phosphorylation
R01GM-26743-12 (CTY) MALLER, JAMES L UNIV OF COLORADO HLTH SCI CTR 4200 EAST NINTH AVENUE DENVER, CO 80262 Control of cell division in Xenopus oocytes
R01GM-26755-13 (CBY) SCHEKMAN, RANDY W UNIVERSITY OF CALIFORNIA 401 BARKER HALL BERKELEY, CALIF 94720 Biological studies of eukaryotic cell surface growth
R01GM-26758-07S1 (GEN) WATT, WARD B STANFORD UNIV STANFORD, CA 94305-5020 Natural genetic variation in vivo metabolic impact
R01GM-26762-12 (BBCB) ROBERTS, MARY F BOSTON COLLEGE CHESTNUT HILL, MA 02167 Interfacial activation of soluble lipolytic enzymes
R01GM-26782-13 (MCHA) ROUSH, WILLIAM R INDIANA UNIVERSITY BLOOMINGTON, IND 47405 Intramolecular Diels-Alder reactions
R01GM-26788-12 (BBCB) PETSKO, GREGORY A BRANDEIS UNIVERSITY 415 S ST/ ROSENSTIEL-652 WALTHAM, MA 02254-9110 Crytallographic studies of protein structure/function
R01GM-26796-12 (PC) MERRICK, WILLIAM C CASE WESTERN RESERVE UNIV CLEVELAND, OH 44106 Mechanism of protein synthesis inititiation
R01GM-26832-11 (PC) BODLEY, JAMES W UNIVERSITY OF MINNESOTA 435 DELAWARE STREET SE MINNEAPOLIS, MN 55455 The structure and function of elongation factor 2
R01GM-26843-12 (MBC) INOUYE, SUMIKO UNIVERSITY OF MED & DENTISTRY 675 HOES LANE PISCATAWAY, NJ 08854-5635 Gene expression during development of myxobacteria
R01GM-26861-13 (PB) JENNINGS, MICHAEL L UNIVERSITY OF TEXAS MED BRANCH 301 UNIVERSITY BOULEVARD GALVESTON, TX 77550-2774 Biochemical studies of erythrocyte anion transport
R01GM-26874-13 (BBCB) HO, CHIEN CARNEGIE MELLON UNIVERSITY 4400 FIFTH AVENUE PITTSBURGH, PA 15213 NMR and biochemical studies of biological membranes
R37GM-26875-13 (NSS) KIRSCHNER, MARC W UNIVERSITY OF CALIFORNIA SAN FRANCISCO, CA 94143-0448 Biochemical studies of mitosis
R01GM-26878-13 (MBC) STAUFFER, GEORGE V UNIVERSITY OF IOWA IOWA CITY, IA 52242 Regulation of one carbon metabolism
R01GM-26879-12 (MCHA) NICOLAOU, KYRIACOS C UNIV OF CALIFORNIA/SAN DIEGO LA JOLLA, CA 92093-0314 Total synthesis of macrolides
R01GM-26895-10 (SSS) JURNAK, FRANCES A UNIVERSITY OF CALIFORNIA DEPARTMENT OF BIOCHEMISTRY RIVERSIDE, CALIF 92521 Biochemical and structural studies of elongation factors
R01GM-26901-11 (MBY) BRADBURY, EDWIN M UNIVERSITY OF CALIFORNIA DEPARTMENT OF BIOLOGICAL CHEM DAVIS, CA 95616 Chromatin structure and function histone modifications and HMG proteins
R01GM-26916-13 (BBCA) FERGUSON-MILLER, SHELAGH M F MICHIGAN STATE UNIVERSITY EAST LANSING, MICH 48824 Organization and control of electron transfer chains
R01GM-26937-13 (CTY) BOURQUE, DON P UNIVERSITY OF ARIZONA BIOLOGICAL SCIS WEST #537 TUCSON, ARIZ 85721 Molecular biology of chloroplast ribosomes
R01GM-26938-12A1 (MBC) ZAKIAN, VIRGINIA A FRED HUTCHINSON CANCER RES CTR 1124 COLUMBIA STREET SEATTLE, WA 98104 DNA replication and chromosome structure in yeast
R01GM-26939-13 (MGN) MARCU, KENNETH B DEPARTMENT OF BIOCHEMISTRY SUNY AT STONY BROOK STONY BROOK, N Y 11794 Expression of immunoglobulin heavy chain genes
R01GM-26973-13 (CTY) GOROVSKY, MARTIN A UNIVERSITY OF ROCHESTER ROCHESTER, N Y 14627 Control of gene activity and organelle biogenesis
R01GM-26976-09 (PHY) RUDY, BERNARDO NEW YORK UNIV MED CENTER 550 FIRST AVENUE NEW YORK, N Y 10016 K channel diversity--Biophysical and molecular studies
R01GM-27003-22 (BIO) VAN ETTEN, ROBERT L PURDUE UNIVERSITY WEST LAFAYETTE, IN 47907 The active sites of acid phosphatases
R01GM-27014-10 (MGN) GREENBAUM, IRA F TEXAS A&M UNIVERSITY COLLEGE STATION, TX 77843 Chromosomal rearrangement incorporation in mammals
R01GM-27029-20A1 (BMT) RINEHART, KENNETH L UNIVERSITY OF ILLINOIS 1209 W CALIFORNIA ST/BOX 45-5 URBANA, IL 61801 High resolution mass spectra of bioorganic compounds
R01GM-27068-12 (MBC) ROTH, JOHN R UNIVERSITY OF UTAH 309 PARK BUILDING SALT LAKE CITY, UT 84112 Genetic analysis of bacterial chromosome structure
R01GM-27099-12 (MBC) YOUNG, RYLAND F TEXAS A&M UNIVERSITY COLLEGE STATION, TX 77843 Control of virus induced lysis
R01GM-27113-11 (MBC) WOLF, RICHARD E, JR UNIVERSITY OF MARYLAND BALTIMORE, MD 21228 Growth rate-dependent control of gene expression
R01GM-27120-12 (GEN) LANDE, RUSSELL S UNIVERSITY OF OREGON EUGENE, OR 97403 Correlated characters in complex genetic systems
R01GM-27137-12 (BNP) KEANA, JOHN F UNIVERSITY OF OREGON EUGENE, OR 97403 New probes and reagents for biological studies
R01GM-27159-12 (CTY) RECHSTEINER, MARTIN C UNIVERSITY OF UTAH 50 NORTH MEDICAL DRIVE SALT LAKE CITY, UT 84132 Microinjection studies on protein degradation
R01GM-27203-10 (CBY) WANG, JOHN L MICHIGAN STATE UNIVERSITY DEPARTMENT OF BIOCHEMISTRY EAST LANSING, MICH 48824 Molecular analysis of growth regulatory factor
R01GM-27215-12 (GEN) KIRK, DAVID L WASHINGTON UNIVESITY DEPT OF BIO CAMPUS BOX 1137 ST LOUIS, MO 63130 Analysis of control gene action in volvox development
R01GM-27241-10 (MBC) COHEN, STANLEY N STANFORD UNIV SCHOOL OF MEDICI STANFORD, CA 94305-5120 Gene expression in heterospecific environments
R01GM-27242-12 (MBC) SALAS, MARGARITA UNIVERSIDAD AUTONOMA INSTITUTO DE BIOLOGIA MOL CANTO BLANCO, 28049 MADRID DNA-protein complex of Bacillus subtilis phage 029
R01GM-27250-36 (MGN) GLUECKSOHN-WAELSCH, SALOME ALBERT EINSTEIN COLLEGE OF MED 1300 MORRIS PARK AVENUE BRONX, N Y 10461 Genetic control of mammalian differentiation
R01GM-27251-12 (MCHA) MARIANO, PATRICK S UNIVERSITY OF MARYLAND DEPARTMENT OF CHEMISTRY COLLEGE PARK, MD 20742 Photochemistry in natural product synthesis
R01GM-27276-10A2 (BMT) VAN WART, HAROLD E FLORIDA STATE UNIVERSITY TALLAHASSEE, FL 32306 Metalloenzyme dynamics and mechanism
R01GM-27278-10 (BBCB) MC INTOSH, THOMAS J DUKE UNIVERSITY BOX 3011 DURHAM, N C 27710 Short- and long-range forces between membrane surfaces
R01GM-27307-10A1 (MBC) ARTZ, STANLEY W UNIVERSITY OF CALIFORNIA DAVIS, CA 95616 Gene regulatory mechanisms in amino acid biosynthesis
R37GM-27309-13 (PB) DUTTON, P LESLIE UNIVERSITY OF PENNSYLVANIA 358 ANATOMY-CHEM BLDG/G3 PHILADELPHIA, PA 19104 Electron and proton translocation in energy conversion
R01GM-27310-13 (CBY) DOTTIN, ROBERT P HUNTER COLLEGE/CUNY 695 PARK AVENUE NEW YORK, N Y 10021 Developmental control of Dictyostelium gene expression
R01GM-27318-12 (NEUC) HIRSH, JAY UNIVERSITY OF VIRGINIA GILMER HALL CHARLOTTESVILLE, VA 22901 Regulation of the DOPA decarboxylase gene
P50GM-27345-11 (SRC) HUNT, THOMAS K UNIVERSITY OF CALIFORNIA 839 HSE, BOX 0522 SAN FRANCISCO, CA 94143-0522 A study of wound healing and wound infection
P50GM-27345-11 0010 (SRC) HUNT, THOMAS K A study of wound healing and wound infection Oxygenation, healing and infectability
P50GM-27345-11 0012 (SRC) SPENCER, MARTIN A study of wound healing and wound infection Insulin-like growth factors in wound healing
P50GM-27345-11 0013 (SRC) HUSSAIN, ZAMIRUL M A study of wound healing and wound infection Control of collagen synthesis in wounds
P50GM-27345-11 0014 (SRC) ADZICK, SCOTT N A study of wound healing and wound infection Fetal wound healing
P50GM-27345-11 9001 (SRC) HUNT, THOMAS K A study of wound healing and wound infection Core facilities
R01GM-27367-11 (PHY) COHEN, FREDRIC S RUSH PRESBY ST LUKE'S MED CTR 1653 WEST CONGRESS PARKWAY CHICAGO, IL 60612 A model system for physiological exocytosis
R01GM-27589-10 (MGN) CHAN, TEH-SHENG UNIVERSITY OF TEXAS MED BRANCH GALVESTON, TX 77550-2782 Molecular pathology of inherited immunodeficiency
R01GM-27597-14 (BIO) MARTIN, NANCY C UNIVERSITY OF LOUISVILLE LOUISVILLE, KY 40292 Transcription and organization of mitochondrial genes
R37GM-27608-23 (BIO) ENGLUND, PAUL T JOHNS HOPKINS UNIVERSITY 725 N WOLFE STREET BALTIMORE, MD 21205 Structure and synthesis of DNA
R01GM-27611-13 (GEN) STORTI, ROBERT V UNIV OF ILLINOIS AT CHICAGO CHICAGO, IL 60612 Expression and isolation of Drosophila muscle genes
R01GM-27616-12 (BNP) GIERASCH, LILA M UT SOUTHWESTERN MEDICAL

CENTER 5323 HARRY HINES BOULEVARD DALLAS, TX 75235-9041 Peptide conformations & interactions with membranes
R01GM-27647-12 (MCHA) HART, DAVID J OHIO STATE UNIVERSITY 120 W 18TH AVENUE COLUMBUS, OH 43210 Synthesis of biologically active alkaloids
R01GM-27659-12 (PB) DOOLEY, DAVID M AMHERST COLLEGE MERRILL SCIENCE CENTER AMHERST, MASS 01002 Structure and reactivity of copper amine oxidases
R01GM-27665-13 (SSS) HYDE, JAMES S MEDICAL COLLEGE OF WISCONSIN 8701 WATERTOWN PLANK RD MILWAUKEE, WI 53226 National biomedical ESR center
R01GM-27673-11 (SAT) COOK, JAMES A MEDICAL UNIV OF SOUTH CAROLINA 171 ASHLEY AVENUE CHARLESTON, SC 29425 Role of eicosanoids in shock
R01GM-27690-12 (BBCB) STRAUSS, HERBERT L UNIVERSITY OF CALIFORNIA DEPARTMENT OF CHEMISTRY BERKELEY, CALIF 94720 Vibrations, structure and dynamics of biomacromolecules
R01GM-27711-11 (MBC) GOLDMAN, EMANUEL UMDNJ-NEW JERSEY MED SCHOOL 185 SOUTH ORANGE AVE NEWARK, NJ 07103-2714 Analysis of trna coding in protein in synthesis
R01GM-27720-12 (MBY) SOLLNER-WEBB, BARBARA T JOHNS HOPKINS UNIVERSITY 725 N WOLFE STREET BALTIMORE, MD 21205-2185 Transcription of Xenopus and mouse ribosomal RNA genes
R01GM-27731-12 (GEN) LIU, LEROY F JOHNS HOPKINS UNIVERSITY 725 N WOLFE STREET BALTIMORE, MARYLAND 21205 Functional and mechanistic studies of DNA topoisomerases
R01GM-27738-12 (BBCA) BOXER, STEVEN G STANFORD UNIVERSITY DEPARTMENT OF CHEMISTRY STANFORD, CA 94305 Electrostatics and dynamics in myoglobin mutants
R01GM-27739-10 (BPO) MISELIS, RICHARD R UNIVERSITY OF PENNSYLVANIA 3800 SPRUCE STREET PHILADELPHIA, PA 19104-6046 The visceral neuraxis in homeostasis
R01GM-27750-12 (MBC) SPUDICH, JOHN L UNIV OF TEXAS HLTH SCIS 6431 FANNIN HOUSTON, TX 77030 Structure and function of bacterial sensory rhodopsins
R01GM-27754-12 (CTY) WAHL, GEOFFREY M SALK INST/BIOLOGICAL STUDIES P O BOX 85800 SAN DIEGO, CALIFORNIA 92138 Drug resistance and gene amplification in eukaryotes
R01GM-27757-12 (MBY) JACOBSON, ALLAN S UNIVERSITY OF MASSACHUSETTS 55 LAKE AVENUE, NORTH WORCESTER, MA 01655 Messenger RNA metabolism in Dictyostelium discoideum
R01GM-27789-12 (MBY) MARZLUFF, WILLIAM F, JR FLORIDA STATE UNIVERSITY DEPARTMENT OF CHEMISTRY TALLAHASSEE, FLA 32306-3006 Small nuclear RNA synthesis in development
R37GM-27800-12 (PC) BOURNE, HENRY R UNIVERSITY OF CALIFORNIA 1210-MEDICAL SCIENCES BUILDING SAN FRANCISCO, CA 94143 Molecular basis of receptor-cyclase coupling
R01GM-27870-12 (MBC) CRAIG, ELIZABETH A UNIV OF WISCONSIN MED CTR 1300 UNIVERSITY AVE. MADISON, WIS 53706 Characterization of transcriptionally regulated genes
R01GM-27875-12 (GEN) SPRADLING, ALLAN C CARNEGIE INST OF WASHINGTON 115 WEST UNIVERSITY PARKWAY BALTIMORE, MD 21210 Normal and mutant chorion genes of Drosphila
R01GM-27904-13 (PC) PAULSON, JAMES C CYTEL CORPORATION 3525 JOHNS HOPKINS COURT SAN DIEGO, CA 92121 Mammalian sialytransferases
R01GM-27906-12 (PB) THOMAS, DAVID D 435 DELAWARE STREET SE MINNEAPOLIS, MN 55455 Biophysical studies of membrane molecular dynamics
R01GM-27925-12 (MBY) HOPPER, JAMES E MILTON S HERSHEY MEDICAL CTR DEPT OF BIO CHEM/P.O. BOX 850 HERSHEY, PA 17033 Molecular basis of interchromosomal gene regulation
R01GM-27930-12 (MBY) HOPPER, ANITA K MILTON S HERSHEY MEDICAL CTR DEPT OF BIOLOGICAL CHEMISTRY HERSHEY, PA 17033 Mutations affecting the production of mature RNAS
R01GM-27932-11 (MCHA) REBEK, JULIUS, JR MASSACHUSETTS INST OF TECHNOLO 77 MASSACHUSETTS AVE CAMBRIDGE, MA 02139-4307 Molecular recognition
R01GM-27939-11 (BMT) VAN WART, HAROLD E FLORIDA STATE UNIVERSITY TALLAHASSEE, FL 32306 Metalloenzymes and connective tissue metabolism
R01GM-27943-10A2 (BBCA) LOEW, GILDA H MOLECULAR RESEARCH INSTITUTE 845 PAGE MILL ROAD PALO ALTO, CA 94304 Theory of physical properties and reactivity in P450
R01GM-27945-12 (BBCA) FIXMAN, MARSHALL COLORADO STATE UNIVERSITY FORT COLLINS, CO 80523 Theoretical chemistry & polymers
R01GM-27946-13 (SAT) GANN, DONALD S UNIVERSITY OF MARYLAND 22 SOUTH GREENE STREET BALTIMORE, MD 21201 Hormonal and cardiovascular responses to trauma
R01GM-27997-12 (MBC) KUSHNER, SIDNEY R UNIVERSITY OF GEORGIA ATHENS, GA 30602 A biochemical analysis of genetic recombination
R01GM-28007-12 (BIO) DEVREOTES, PETER N JOHNS HOPKINS UNIVERSITY 725 NORTH WOLFE STREET BALTIMORE, MD 21205 Role of signal transduction in Dictyostelium development
R01GM-28016-12 (GEN) FELDMAN, MARCUS W STANFORD UNIVERSITY DEPT OF BIOLOGICAL SCIENCES STANFORD, CALIF 94305-5020 Population genetics theory
R01GM-28017-11 (IMB) EGOROV, IGOR K JACKSON LAB 600 MAIN STREET BAR HARBOR, ME 04609-0800 Mutations of GMAD loci in murine chromosome 17
R01GM-28035-12 (MBC) ROCK, CHARLES O ST JUDE CHILDREN'S RES HOSP 332 N LAUDERDALE MEMPHIS, TN 38105 Regulation of membrane phospholipid structure
R37GM-28039-12 (MBY) CECH, THOMAS R UNIVERSITY OF COLORADO BOULDER, COLO 80309 Splicing of a ribosomal RNA precursor
R01GM-28078-12 (BIO) GREENLEAF, ARNO L DUKE UNIVERSITY BOX 3711 DURHAM, N C 27710 RNA polymerase II subunits and transcription factors
R01GM-28093-11 (BBCA) BLOOMFIELD, VICTOR A UNIVERSITY OF MINNESOTA 1479 GORTNER AVENUE ST PAUL, MN 55108 DNA interactions with polyamines and proteins
R01GM-28117-10A1 (BBCB) PAPAHADJOPOULOS, P DEMETRIOS UNIVERSITY OF CALIFORNIA BOX 0128, M-1282 SAN FRANCISCO, CA 94143 Mechanism of membrane fusion
R01GM-28120-11 (BBCA) HUI, SEK-WEN ROSWELL PARK MEMORIAL INST 666 ELM STREET BUFFALO, N Y 14263 Effects of bilayer defects on membrane activities
R01GM-28139-12 (BBCA) LEE, JOHN W UNIVERSITY OF GEORGIA ATHENS, GA 30602 Structure and interactions of lumazine proteins
R01GM-28140-11 (BIO) CARMAN, GEORGE M RUTGERS UNIVERSITY DEPT OF FOOD SCIENCE NEW BRUNSWICK, NJ 08903 Phospholipid metabolism & membrane function
R01GM-28143-12 (PB) SCHIRCH, VERNE G MEDICAL COLLEGE OF VIRGINIA DEPARTMENT OF BIOCHEMISTRY RICHMOND, VA 23298 Structural studies on enzymes of one carbon metabolism
R01GM-28157-11 (PHRA) WEINSHILBOUM, RICHARD M MAYO FOUNDATION 200 FIRST ST SOUTHWEST ROCHESTER, MN 55905 Inherited variations in drug metabolizing enzymes
R01GM-28173-11 (PB) ROTTENBERG, HAGAI HAHNEMANN UNIVERSITY BROAD AND VINE PHILADELPHIA, PA 19102 Membrane regulation of mitochondrial metabolism
R01GM-28190-12 (BBCA) SCHUSTER, GARY B UNIVERSITY OF ILLINOIS 1209 W CALIFORNIA STREET URBANA, IL 61801 Study of photoaffinity labels by laser spectroscopy
R01GM-28211-12 (MBC) SUMMERS, ANNE O UNIVERSITY OF GEORGIA DEPARTMENT OF MICROBIOLOGY ATHENS, GA 30602 Regulation and structure of the mercury operon
R01GM-28216-16 (GEN) MICHELS, CORINNE A QUEENS COLLEGE 65-30 KISSENA BOULEVARD FLUSHING, N Y 11367 The regulation of maltose fermentation in Saccharomyces
R01GM-28220-12 (MBY) STERNGLANZ, ROLF STATE UNIVERSITY OF NEW YORK DEPT OF BIOCHEMISTRY/CELL BIOL STONY BROOK, NY 11794-5215 DNA topoisomerases and other enzymes affecting chromatin
R01GM-28222-12 (BMT) VALENTINE, JOAN S UNIVERSITY OF CALIFORNIA DEPT OF CHEMISTRY LOS ANGELES, CA 90024 Histidyl imidazole ligand in metalloproteins
R01GM-28226-09 (MBC) JACOBSON, GARY R BOSTON UNIVERSITY DEPT OF BIOLOGY BOSTON, MA 02215 Structure and mechanism of E coli D-mannitol permease
R01GM-28262-11 (GEN) SOKAL, ROBERT R S U N Y - AT STONY BROOK DEPT OF ECOLOGY & EVOLUTION STONY BROOK, N Y 11794-5245 Spatial analysis of human variation
R01GM-28273-11A1 (MCHA) DANHEISER, RICK L MASS INSTITUTE OF TECHNOLOGY CAMBRIDGE, MA 02139 Pericyclic reactions for organic synthesis
R37GM-28289-11 (NSS) KHORANA, HAR G MASSACHUSETTS INST OF TECH 77 MASSACHUSETTS AVENUE CAMBRIDGE, MA 02139 Synthetic and biological studies of nucleic acids
R01GM-28293-12 (BBCA) HAGERMAN, PAUL J UNIV OF COLORADO HEALTH SCIS C 4200 EAST NINTH AVE #B-121 DENVER, CO 80262 Flexibility of DNA
R01GM-28301-12 (BIO) WOOLFORD, JOHN L, JR CARNEGIE-MELLON UNIVERSITY 4400 FIFTH AVE/616 MELLON INST PITTSBURGH, PA 15213 Biosynthesis and function of yeast ribosomes
R01GM-28321-10 (MCHA) BURKE, STEVEN D UNIV OF WISCONSIN 1101 UNIVERSITY AVE MADISON, WI 53706 Synthesis of hormonal, antibiotic and antifungal agents
R01GM-28356-12 (SSS) ELSTON, ROBERT C LOUISIANA ST UNIV MED CTR DEPT OF BIOMETRY AND GENETICS NEW ORLEANS, LA 70112 Genetic analysis of multifactorial traits
R01GM-28358-12 (PB) ORME-JOHNSON, WILLIAM H, III MASSACHUSETTS INST OF TECHNOLO 77 MASSACHUSETTS AVENUE CAMBRIDGE, MA 02139 Structures and mechanisms of electron transfer enzymes
R01GM-28364-11 (SSS) TURNBULL, BRUCE W CORNELL UNIVERSITY ITHACA, NY 14853-7501 Statistical methods for health studies
R01GM-28370-12 (MBC) WULFF, DANIEL L STATE UNIV OF NEW YORK AT ALBA DEPT OF BIOLOGICAL SCIENCES ALBANY, N Y 12222 Control of phage lambda cII gene function
R37GM-28384-11 (MCHA) SHARPLESS, K BARRY MASS INSTITUTE OF TECHNOLOGY 77 MASSACHUSETTS AVE CAMBRIDGE, MASS 02139 New asymmetric processes for use in organic synthesis
P01GM-28428-11 (SSS) CAVALLI-SFORZA, LUIGI L STANFORD UNIVERSITY DEPARTMENT OF GENETICS STANFORD, CALIF 94305 Genetics research project
P01GM-28428-11 0001 (SSS) CAVALLI-SFORZA, LUIGI L Genetics research project Mapping selected human chromosome regions
P01GM-28428-11 0007 (SSS) DAVIS, RONALD W Genetics research project Human disease isolation using genetic linkage and molecular cloning techniques
P01GM-28428-11 0008 (SSS) KING, MARY-CLAIRE Genetics research project Genetic analysis of systemic lupus erythematosus
P01GM-28428-11 0009 (SSS) STEINMAN, LAWRENCE Genetics research project Ethnic variation and autoimmunity
P01GM-28428-11 9001 (SSS) CAVALLI-SFORZA, LUIGI L Genetics research project Core facilities
R01GM-28454-10 (MBC) KRULWICH, TERRY A MOUNT SINAI SCHOOL OF MEDICINE 1 GUSTAVE L LEVY PL; BOX 1020 NEW YORK, NY 10029 ATP synthesis at low protonmotive forces
R01GM-28468-12 (BNP) PAQUETTE, LEO A OHIO STATE UNIVERSITY 120 WEST 18TH AVENUE COLUMBUS, OH 43210-1173 Synthetic elaboration of polyquinane natural products
R37GM-28470-12 (BM) GRINDLEY, NIGEL D YALE UNIVERSITY 333 CEDAR ST/PO BOX 3333 NEW HAVEN, CT 06510 Mechanism of insertion sequence translocation
R37GM-28485-11 (SAT) ULEVITCH, RICHARD J SCRIPPS CLINIC & RESEARCH FDN 10666 NORTH TORREY PINES ROAD LA JOLLA, CA 92037 Molecular pathology of lps-induced shock and DIC
R01GM-28521-12 (CTY) GERACE, LARRY R SCRIPPS CLINIC & RESEARCH FDN. 10666 NORTH TORREY PINES ROAD LA JOLLA, CA 92037 Structure and functions of the nuclear envelope
R01GM-28550-12 (MBC) GRINDLEY, NIGEL D YALE UNIVERSITY 333 CEDAR ST/PO BOX 3333 NEW HAVEN, CT 06510 Structure and function of E.coli polA gene
R01GM-28553-11 (CBY) ERICKSON, HAROLD P DUKE UNIVERSITY MEDICAL CENTER DURHAM, NC 27710 Structure and assembly of cytoskeletal filaments
R01GM-28572-10 (MBY) MARMUR, JULIUS ALBERT EINSTEIN COLL OF MED 1300 MORRIS PARK AVENUE BRONX, N Y 10461 Structure and organization

PROJECT NO., ORGANIZATIONAL UNIT., INVESTIGATOR, ADDRESS, TITLE

of yeast MAL loci

R01GM-28575-11A1 (MBC) BURGESS, RICHARD R UNIVERSITY OF WISCONSIN 1400 UNIVERSITY AVENUE MADISON, WI 53706 RNA polymerase sigma subunit--Structure and function

R01GM-28619-09 (BBCA) DIEM, MAX HUNTER COLL OF CUNY 695 PARK AVENUE NEW YORK, NY 10021 Solution conformation via vibrational optical activity

R01GM-28630-11 (GEN) BENDER, WELCOME W HARVARD MEDICAL SCHOOL DEPT OF BIO CHEM/25 SHATTUCK BOSTON, MA 02115 Molecular genetics of the bithorax complex

R01GM-28643-11 (PHY) JORDAN, PETER C BRANDEIS UNIVERSITY P O BOX 9110 WALTHAM, MA 02254-9110 Electrostatic modeling of ion pores

R01GM-28663-12 (MCHA) FUNK, RAYMOND L PENNSYLVANIA STATE UNIVERSITY DEPARTMENT OF CHEMISTRY UNIVERSITY PARK, PA 16802 New cyclization methods for natural products synthesis

R01GM-28669-11 (GEN) GELBART, WILLIAM M HARVARD UNIVERSITY BIOLOGY CAMBRIDGE, MA 02138 Pattern formation and gene organization in Drosophila

R01GM-28673-10 (PB) FARLEY, ROBERT A UNIV OF SOUTHERN CALIFORNIA 2025 ZONAL AVENUE LOS ANGELES, CA 90033 The structure of Na,K ATPase

R01GM-28685-11 (MBC) GOLD, LAWRENCE M UNIVERSITY OF COLORADO CAMPUS BOX 347 BOULDER, CO 80309-0347 Translation in E. coli--mRNAs, ribosomes and repressors

R01GM-28688-11 (BIO) DUNAWAY-MARIANO, DEBRA UNIVERSITY OF MARYLAND DEPT OF CHEMISTRY/BIOCHEMISTRY COLLEGE PARK, MD 20742 Investigations of phosphoryl transfer reactions

R01GM-28703-11 (PB) BOWMAN, BARRY J UNIVERSITY OF CALIFORNIA 1156 HIGH STREET SANTA CRUZ, CA 95064 Eukaryotic H+ ATPases of plasma membranes & vacuoles

R55GM-28704-10A1 (PB) HACKENBROCK, CHARLES R UNIVERSITY OF NORTH CAROLINA CB#7090, 108 TAYLOR HALL CHAPEL HILL, NC 27599-7090 Structural and functional engineering of a biomembrane

R01GM-28717-11 (MBC) GARDNER, JEFFREY F UNIVERSITY OF ILLINOIS 131 BURRILL HALL URBANA, ILL 61801 Regulatory mutations in the threonine operon

R01GM-28719-12 (MGN) RAO, DABEERU C WASHINGTON UNIV/SCH OF MED 660 S EUCLID AVE/BOX 8067 ST LOUIS, MO 63110 A research project in genetic epidemiology

R37GM-28754-16 (BNP) SHIMIZU, YUZURU UNIVERSITY OF RHODE ISLAND COLLEGE OF PHARMACY KINGSTON, R I 02881 Chemistry and biochemistry of aquatic toxins

R01GM-28755-11 (MBC) STORMO, GARY D UNIV OF CO / CAMPUS BOX 347 MOLECULAR, CELLULAR & DEV BIOL BOULDER, CO 80309 Nucleic acid sequence analysis

R01GM-28760-10 (MBC) KUSHNER, SIDNEY R UNIVERSITY OF GEORGIA ATHENS, GA 30602 Analysis of mRNA turnover in E. coli

R01GM-28791-12 (GEN) SOFER, WILLIAM H RUTGERS STATE UNIV OF N J PO BOX 759 PISCATAWAY, N J 08854 A system for analysis of gene control in

R01GM-28810-11 (CBY) WU, HENRY C HENRY M. JACKSON FOUNDATION 4301 JONES BRIDGE ROAD BETHESDA, MD 20814-4799 Mammalian cell surface genetics and biochemistry

R01GM-28811-12 (MBC) WU, HENRY C UNIFORMED SERVS UNIV HLTH SCIS 4301 JONES BRIDGE RD BETHESDA, MD 20814-4799 Bacterial cell surface structure functions & biogenesis

R01GM-28818-25 (BIO) GOLDBERG, NELSON D UNIVERSITY OF MINNESOTA 435 DELAWARE STREET, SE MINNEAPOLIS, MN 55455 Krebs cycle and cyclic nucleotide control

R01GM-28831-11 (SSS) GOFF, HAROLD M UNIVERSITY OF IOWA IOWA CITY, IA 52242 High oxidation state hemoproteins and halide activation

R01GM-28835-11 (PB) PENNISTON, JOHN T MAYO FOUNDATION 200 FIRST STREET SOUTHWEST ROCHESTER, MN 55905 Purification and properties of Ca2+ pumping ATPase

R01GM-28840-11 (PBC) ADAMS, SHERRILL L UNIV OF PA SCH OF DENTAL MED 4001 SPRUCE STREET PHILADELPHIA, PA 19104 Analysis of human collagen gene expression

R01GM-28842-10A1 (CTY) KAUFMAN, STEPHEN J UNIVERSITY OF ILLINOIS 506 MORRILL HALL/505 S GOODWIN URBANA, IL 61801 Immunochemical analysis of myoblast differentiation

R01GM-28844-11 (PHY) GUTKNECHT, JOHN W DEPT. OF CELL BIOLOGY DUKE UNIVERSITY MARINE LAB. BEAUFORT, NC 28516 Acid/base transport through lipid bilayer membranes

R37GM-28856-12 (BMT) HOLM, RICHARD H HARVARD UNIVERSITY 12 OXFORD STREET CAMBRIDGE, MA 02138 Biologically related iron-sulfur chemistry

R01GM-28882-10A1 (BMT) MEYERHOFF, MARK E UNIVERSITY OF MICHIGAN ANN ARBOR, MI 48109-1055 Polymer membrane based gas and anion sensors

R01GM-28896-08 (MGN) ENGEL, JAMES D NORTHWESTERN UNIVERSITY 2153 SHERIDAN RD EVANSTON, IL 60208-3500 Developmental regulation of avian erythroid genes

R01GM-28904-11 (GEN) ROEDER, G S YALE UNIVERSITY PO BOX 1504A, YALE STATION NEW HAVEN, CT 06520 Molecular mechanisms of genetic recombination in yeast

R01GM-28911-10 (SAT) KNIGHT, PAUL R, III UNIV OF MICHIGAN MEDICAL CTR 1500 E. MEDICAL CENTER DRIVE ANN ARBOR, MICHIGAN 48109 Anesthetic action and virus replication

R01GM-28920-11 (GEN) SMITH, MALCOLM M UNIVERSITY OF VIRGINIA BOX 441 JORDAN BUILDING CHARLOTTESVILLE, VA 22908 Histone gene expression in yeast

R01GM-28924-10A2 (MBC) GUINEY, DONALD G UCSD MEDICAL CENTER 225 DICKINSON STREET SAN DIEGO, CA 92103 Mechanism of plasmid DNA transfer in bacteria

R01GM-28932-11 (CBY) GOODENOUGH, DANIEL A HARVARD MEDICAL SCHOOL DEPT OF ANATOMY/CELLULAR BIOLO BOSTON, MA 02115 Molecular biology of zonulae occludentes

R01GM-28938-11 (BMT) BROOKHART, MAURICE S UNIVERSITY OF NORTH CAROLINA CHAPEL HILL, N C 27599-3290 Development and use of manganese in organic synthesis

R01GM-28946-11 (MBC) DAS, ASIS K UNIVERSITY OF CONNECTICUT 263 FARMINGTON AVE FARMINGTON, CT 06030 Gene regulation by transcription antitermination

PROJECT NO., ORGANIZATIONAL UNIT., INVESTIGATOR, ADDRESS, TITLE

R01GM-28961-11 (MCHA) KECK, GARY E UNIVERSITY OF UTAH DEPARTMENT OF CHEMISTRY SALT LAKE CITY, UTAH 84112 Chiral approaches to natural product synthesis

R01GM-28962-11 (BMT) KARLIN, KENNETH D JOHNS HOPKINS UNIVERSITY CHARLES & 34TH STREETS BALTIMORE, MD 21218 Bioinorganic copper coordination chemistry

R01GM-28965-09 (BNP) BARTLETT, PAUL A UNIVERSITY OF CALIFORNIA BERKELEY, CA 94720 Studies in the shikimate-chorismate pathway

R01GM-28983-11 (MBY) MANLEY, JAMES L COLUMBIA UNIV NEW YORK, NY 10027 Control of mRNA synthesis in mammalian cells

R01GM-28994-10 (BIO) RAPOPORT, HENRY UNIVERSITY OF CALIFORNIA DEPARTMENT OF CHEMISTRY BERKELEY, CALIF 94720 Structure of protein-bound bile pigments

R01GM-29001-11 (PB) MARGOLIASH, EMANUEL UNIVERSITY OF ILLINOIS 4289 SEL (M/C 067) CHICAGO, IL 60680 Cytochrome C mechanism by recombinant DNA technique

R01GM-29006-11 (BIO) HSIEH, TAO-SHIH DUKE UNIVERSITY MED CENTER DURHAM, N C 27710 DNA topoisomerase--Function and mechanism

R01GM-29009-11 (GEN) HENIKOFF, STEVEN FRED HUTCHINSON CANCER RES CTR 1124 COLUMBIA STREET SEATTLE, WA 98104 Gene regulation of the purine synthetic pathway

R01GM-29028-11 (MCHA) SMITH, AMOS B, III UNIVERSITY OF PENNSYLVANIA PHILADELPHIA, PA 19104-6323 Synthesis of bioactive natural products

R01GM-29048-11 (BBCA) DRAPER, DAVID E THE JOHNS HOPKINS UNIVERSITY CHARLES AND 34TH STREETS BALTIMORE, MD 21218 Ribosomal RNA structure and interactions

R01GM-29065-11 (SAT) COLLINS, J G DEPT OF ANESTHESIOLOGY YALE UNIV SCH OF MED NEW HAVEN, CT 06510 Anesthesia-analgesia of awake cat spinal neurons

R01GM-29072-10 (SSS) KOLLMAN, PETER A UNIVERSITY OF CALIFORNIA 926 MEDICAL SCIENCES BLDG SAN FRANCISCO, CA 94143-0446 Modeling protein-small molecule interactions

R01GM-29076-09 (BBCB) KIM, JUNG-JA P MEDICAL COLLEGE OF WISCONSIN 8701 WATERTOWN PLANK ROAD MILWAUKEE, WI 53226 Structure and mechanism of a flavoprotein dehydrogenase

R01GM-29079-10 (BBCA) PACK, GEORGE R UNIVERSITY OF ILLINOIS 1601 PARKVIEW AVENUE ROCKFORD, ILL 61107 Theory of cation induced conformation changes in DNA

R01GM-29085-11 (MBC) FIGURSKI, DAVID H COLUMBIA UNIVERSITY 701 W 168TH ST NEW YORK, NY 10032 Gene regulation in broad host range plasmids

R01GM-29090-11 (CTY) LEINWAND, LESLIE A ALBERT EINSTEIN COLLEGE OF MED 1300 MORRIS PARK AVENUE BRONX, N Y 10461 Mammalian gene organization--Structure-function relation

R01GM-29093-11 (GEN) ARTAVANIS-TSAKONAS, SPYRIDON YALE UNIVERSITY BOX 1504A YALE STATION NEW HAVEN, CT 06520 Gene expression in eukaryotic development

R01GM-29109-11 (BBCA) PTASHNE, MARK S HARVARD UNIVERSITY DEPT OF BIOCHEM & MOL BIO CAMBRIDGE, MASS 02138 Structural study of repressor-operator interactions

R01GM-29123-12 (SSS) OTHMER, HANS G UNIVERSITY OF UTAH SALT LAKE CITY, UT 84112 Dynamic pattern in chemically reacting systems

R01GM-29127-11 (CBY) JACOBSON, BRUCE S UNIVERSITY OF MASSACHUSETTS AMHERST, MA 01003 Plasma-membrane regions as cells grow in monolayers

R01GM-29135-09 (CBY) LEIBOVICH, SAMUEL J NORTHWESTERN UNIVERSITY 303 E CHICAGO AVE CHICAGO, IL 60611 Macrophage derived angiogenic activity

R01GM-29139-11 (BIO) VILLAFRANCA, JOSEPH J PENNSYLVANIA STATE UNIVERSITY 152 DAVEY LABORATORY UNIVERSITY PARK, PA 16802 Mechanistic studies of hydroxylases

R01GM-29158-10S1 (MBC) VON HIPPEL, PETER H UNIVERSITY OF OREGON EUGENE, OR 97403 Molecular interaction in T4 DNA replication complex

R01GM-29169-10 (BBCB) FRANK, JOACHIM N Y STATE DEPT OF HEALTH EMPIRE STATE PLAZA ALBANY, N Y 12201 Structural analysis of macromolecular assemblies

R01GM-29177-11 (MGN) FALK, CATHERINE T NEW YORK BLOOD CENTER 310 EAST 67TH STREET NEW YORK, N Y 10021 Linkage and association of genetic markers and disease

R01GM-29182-11 (GEN) ESPOSITO, ROCHELLE E UNIVERSITY OF CHICAGO 1103 EAST 57TH STREET CHICAGO, IL 60637 Meiotic recombination and segregation in yeast

R01GM-29185-12 (CBY) HUBBARD, ANN L JOHNS HOPKINS UNIVERSITY 725 N WOLFE ST BALTIMORE, MD 21205 Biology of differentiated surface domains in hepatocytes

R01GM-29207-10 (BBCA) JEN-JACOBSON, LINDA UNIV OF PITTSBURGH DEPT OF BIOLOGICAL SCIENCES PITTSBURGH, PA 15260 Sequence-specific DNA protein interactions

R01GM-29210-14 (PHY) FINKELSTEIN, ALAN ALBERT EINSTEIN COLLEGE OF MED 1300 MORRIS PARK AVENUE BRONX, N Y 10461 Gating of protein channels in lipid bilayer membranes

R01GM-29222-11 (BMT) MARZILLI, LUIGI G EMORY UNIVERSITY 1515 PIERCE DRIVE ATLANTA, GA 30322 Synthesis of nucleic acid and nucleotide metal complexes

R01GM-29227-20 (PC) HATTMAN, STANLEY M UNIVERSITY OF ROCHESTER DEPT OF BIOLOGY ROCHESTER, N Y 14627 DNA modification restriction in pro and eukaryotes

R01GM-29228-11 (CBY) MORRIS, N RONALD UNIV MEDICINE DENTISTRY NJ 675 HOES LAND PISCATAWAY, NJ 08854 Genetics of microtubule assembly and function

R01GM-29231-10A1 (MBC) VOLD, BARBARA S SYVA COMPANY 900 ARASTRADERO ROAD PALO ALTO, CA 94303 Role of tRNA in cellular regulatory mechanisms

R01GM-29238-11 (TMP) LAW, JOHN H UNIVERSITY OF ARIZONA LIFE SCIENCES SOUTH 227 TUCSON, AZ 85721 Study of lipid metabolism in insects

R01GM-29265-11 (BIO) SCHWARTZ, IRA S NEW YORK MEDICAL COLLEGE DEPARTMENT OF BIOCHEMISTRY VALHALLA, N Y 10595 Molecular mechanism of protein synthesis initiation

R01GM-29290-11 (MCHA) BOECKMAN, ROBERT K, JR UNIVERSITY OF ROCHESTER ROCHESTER, NY 14627 Methodology for the construction of complex molecules

PROJECT NO., ORGANIZATIONAL UNIT., INVESTIGATOR, ADDRESS, TITLE

P01GM-29301-11 (GEN) KAFATOS, FOTIS C HARVARD UNIVERSITY 16 DIVINITY AVENUE CAMBRIDGE, MA 02138 Molecular and developmental genetics of Drosophila

P01GM-29301-11 0005 (GEN) KAFATOS, FOTIS C Molecular and developmental genetics of Drosophila Molecular and genetic analysis of choriogenesis in Drosophila

P01GM-29301-11 0006 (GEN) LEWONTIN, RICHARD C Molecular and developmental genetics of Drosophila Polymorphism and evolution of DNA sequences in Drosophila

P01GM-29301-11 0007 (GEN) MESELSON, MATTHEW S Molecular and developmental genetics of Drosophila RNA polymerase II mutants and homologous transformation of Drosophila

P01GM-29301-11 0008 (GEN) MANIATIS, THOMAS P Molecular and developmental genetics of Drosophila Homeobox-containing gene in early Drosophila development

P01GM-29301-11 0009 (GEN) GOLDSTEIN, LAWRENCE S Molecular and developmental genetics of Drosophila Structure-function of 205K microtubule-associated protein in Drosophila

P01GM-29301-11 0010 (GEN) MANTIATIS, THOMAS P Molecular and developmental genetics of Drosophila Genetic analysis of nautilus--Presumptive regulatory gene in Drosophila

P01GM-29301-11 9001 (GEN) KAFATOS, FOTIS C Molecular and developmental genetics of Drosophila Core facilities

P01GM-29301-11 0002 (GEN) GELBART, WILLIAM M Molecular and developmental genetics of Drosophila Mobile elements and transformation in Drosophila melanogaster

R01GM-29323-09 (CTY) DEDMAN, JOHN R UNIVERSITY OF CINCINNATI CINCINNATI, OH 45267 Biological role of intracellular CA2+-binding proteins

R01GM-29332-18 (BNP) BORCHARDT, RONALD T UNIVERSITY OF KANSAS 3006 MALOTT HALL LAWRENCE, KS 66045 Structural analogs of s-adenosylmethionine

R01GM-29344-10 (BIO) STANKOVICH, MARIAN T UNIVERSITY OF MINNESOTA 207 PLEASANT STREET, S E MINNEAPOLIS, MINN 55455 A spectroelectrochemical study of selected flavoproteins

R01GM-29356-11 (MBY) JOHNSON, LEE F OHIO STATE UNIVERSITY 484 W 12TH AVE/876 BIO SCIS COLUMBUS, OH 43210 Mouse thymidylate synthase gene expression

R01GM-29357-11 (CTY) FYRBERG, ERIC A JOHNS HOPKINS UNIVERSITY CHARLES & 34TH STREETS BALTIMORE, MD 21218 Gene expression during Drosophila myogenesis

R01GM-29361-12 (MGN) CALAME, KATHRYN L COLUMBIA UNIVERSITY 701 WEST 168TH ST NEW YORK, N Y 10032 Transcription of immunoglobulin heavy chain genes

R01GM-29362-11 (GEN) FOX, THOMAS D CORNELL UNIVERSITY SEC OF GENETICS & DEVELOPMENT ITHACA, N Y 14853-2703 Coding and regulation of yeast mitochondrial genes

R01GM-29379-11 (GEN) MANIATIS, THOMAS P HARVARD UNIVERSITY 7 DIVINITY AVENUE CAMBRIDGE, MA 02138 Mechanisms of tissue-specific gene expression

R01GM-29383-09 (MBC) KOLODNER, RICHARD D DANA FARBER CANCER INSTITUTE 44 BINNEY STREET BOSTON, MA 02115 Enzymatic mechanisms of genetic recombination in yeast

R01GM-29391-11 (BBCA) SCHEINER, STEVE SOUTHERN ILLINOIS UNIVERSITY CARBONDALE, IL 62901 Proton transfers in proteins

R01GM-29433-10 (BIO) EDMONDSON, DALE E EMORY UNIVERSITY ROLLINS RESEARCH CENTER ATLANTA, GA 30322 Covalent flavin coenzymes in flavoenzyme catalysis

R01GM-29456-10 (MBC) GUNSALUS, ROBERT P UNIVERSITY OF CALIFORNIA DEPARTMENT OF MICROBIOLOGY LOS ANGELES, CA 90024 Coordinate regulation of the trp regulon in E. coli

R01GM-29458-11 (BBCA) ROSE, GEORGE D UNIVERSITY OF NORTH CAROLINA CB# 7260, 303 FLOB CHAPEL HILL, NC 27599-7260 Self-recognition in globular proteins

R01GM-29466-11 (MBC) TURNBOUGH, CHARLES L, JR UNIVERSITY OF ALABAMA UAB STATION BIRMINGHAM, AL 35294 Regulation of pyrimidine gene expression in bacteria

R01GM-29470-26 (PBC) GOLDSTEIN, IRWIN J UNIVERSITY OF MICHIGAN 4320 MEDICAL SCIENCE I ANN ARBOR, MI 48109-0606 Protein-carbohydrate interaction

R01GM-29475-11 (MCHA) MARSHALL, JAMES A UNIVERSITY OF SOUTH CAROLINA COLUMBIA, SC 29208 Synthesis of tumor inhibitory compounds

R01GM-29480-10 (GEN) FARABAUGH, PHILIP JAMES UNIVERSITY OF MARYLAND DEPT OF BIOLOGICAL SCIENCES BALTIMORE, MD 21228 Molecular analysis of site specific translational frame shifting

R01GM-29481-09 (MBC) TAYLOR, BARRY L LOMA LINDA UNIVERSITY LOMA LINDA, CA 92350 Sensory transduction in bacteria

R01GM-29487-11 (MBY) LUSE, DONAL S UNIVERSITY OF CINCINNATI CINCINNATI, OH 45267-0524 Control of transcription in eukaryotic cells

R01GM-29495-11 (CTY) GALAU, GLENN A UNIVERSITY OF GEORGIA DEPARTMENT OF BOTANY ATHENS, GA 30602 Regulation of synthesis of a hormone induced protein

R01GM-29496-09 (CBY) TASH, JOSEPH S UNIV. OF KANSAS MEDICAL CENTER 39TH & RAINBOW BLVD. KANSAS CITY, KS 66103-8410 Protein phosphorylation in sperm flagellar motility

R01GM-29498-11 (MBC) LANYI, JANOS K UNIVERSITY OF CALIFORNIA CHENEY HALL RM D340 MED SCI I IRVINE, CA 92717 Mechanism of chloride transport by halorhodopsin

R37GM-29507-10 (SAT) WARD, PETER A UNIVERSITY OF MICHIGAN 1301 CATHERINE ST ANN ARBOR, MI 48109-0602 Lung injury produced by oxygen metabolites

R01GM-29513-11 (CTY) CLEVELAND, DON W JOHNS HOPKINS UNIVERSITY 725 NORTH WOLFE STREET BALTIMORE, MD 21205 Microtubule regulation

R01GM-29536-14 (PHRA) HARDEN, T KENDALL UNIV OF N C AT CHAPEL HILL DEPT. OF PHARMACOLOGY CB#7365 CHAPEL HILL N C 27599 Regulation of phospholipase C

R01GM-29549-09 (MCHA) NELSEN, STEPHEN F UNIVERSITY OF WISCONSIN 1101 UNIVERSITY AVENUE MADISON, WI 53706 Electron transfer reactions of amino nitrogen compounds

R01GM-29554-10 (BBCA) SEEMAN, NADRIAN C DEPARTMENT OF CHEMISTRY NEW YORK UNIVERSITY NEW YORK, NEW YORK 10003 Physical chemistry of recombinational intermediates

PROJECT NO., ORGANIZATIONAL UNIT., INVESTIGATOR, ADDRESS, TITLE

R01GM-29558-10 (MBC) MC ENTEE, KEVIN UNIVERSITY OF CALIFORNIA ENVIRONMENTAL SCIENCES LOS ANGELES, CA 90024-1786 Biochemistry of RecA protein structure and function

R01GM-29569-11 (MBC) WOOD, HARLAND G CASE WESTERN RESERVE UNIV 2119 ABINGTON ROAD CLEVELAND, OH 44106 Role of inorganic polyphosphates in metabolism

R37GM-29595-13 (PB) STUBBE, JO ANNE MASS INSTITUTE OF TECHNOLOGY 77 MASSACHUSETTS AVENUE CAMBRIDGE, MA 02139 Mechanism and inhibition of ribonucleotide reductase

R01GM-29628-10 (SAT) MARSHALL, BRYAN E UNIVERSITY OF PENNSYLVANIA 3400 SPRUCE STREET PHILADELPHIA, PA 19104 Anesthesia and hypoxic pulmonary vasoconstriction

R01GM-29647-11 (CBY) HEUSER, JOHN E WASHINGTON UNIVERSITY 660 S EUCLID AVE ST LOUIS, MO 63110 Structural analysis of clathrin-mediated endocytosis

R01GM-29681-11 (CTY) BOGENHAGEN, DANIEL F SUNY AT STONY BROOK STONY BROOK, NY 11794-8651 Development control of mitochondrial genetic activity

R01GM-29690-11 (BBCA) STELLWAGEN, NANCY C UNIVERSITY OF IOWA BOWEN SCIENCE BUILDING IOWA CITY, IOWA 52242 Electric birefringence of DNA restriction fragments

R01GM-29707-09 (VISB) LIPSON, EDWARD D SYRACUSE UNIVERSITY SYRACUSE, NY 13244-1130 System analysis of phycomyces photoresponses

R01GM-29713-11 (GEN) JONES, ELIZABETH W CARNEGIE-MELLON UNIVERSITY 4400 FIFTH AVENUE PITTSBURGH, PA 15213 Genetic analysis of enzyme processing and localization

R01GM-29721-11 (MBC) LACKS, SANFORD A BROOKHAVEN NATIONAL LABORATORY UPTON, NY 11973 DNA methylation and the regulation of gene function

R01GM-29723-11 (CTY) CLARKE, MARGARET OKLAHOMA MEDICAL RESEARCH FDN 825 N E 13TH STREET OKLAHOMA CITY, OK 73104 Chemistry and function of Dictyostelium calmodulin

R01GM-29736-09 (GEN) HABER, JAMES E BRANDEIS UNIVERSITY WALTHAM, MASS 02254 Physical monitoring of meiotic DNA recombination

R01GM-29745-11 (SSS) LAIRD, NAN M HARVARD UNIV/PUBLIC HEALTH 677 HUNTINGTON AVENUE BOSTON, MA 02115 Statistical methods for longitudinal studies

R01GM-29754-10 (SSS) OPELLA, STANLEY J UNIVERSITY OF PENNSYLVANIA DEPARTMENT OF CHEMISTRY PHILADELPHIA, PA 19104 Solid state NMR of peptides

R01GM-29764-11 (MBC) LUTKENHAUS, JOSEPH F UNIV OF KANSAS MED CENTER KANSAS CITY, KS 66103 Regulation of expression of cell division genes

R01GM-29765-11 (CBY) MELLMAN, IRA S YALE UNIVERSITY SCH OF MED 333 CEDAR ST, PO BOX 3333 NEW HAVEN, CT 06510 Endocytosis & plasma membrane function

R01GM-29787-18 (CTY) SARMA, RAMASWAMY H SUNY/INST BIOMOLEC STEREODYNAM 1400 WASHINGTON AVE ALBANY, NY 12222 Magnetic resonance studies of biological interactions

R01GM-29795-04A4 (BIO) CHAKRABURTTY, KALPANA MEDICAL COLLEGE OF WISCONSIN 8701 WATERTOWN PLANK RD MILWAUKEE, WI 53226 Regulation of ribosomal reactions

R01GM-29798-11 (MBC) RANDALL, LINDA L WASHINGTON STATE UNIVERSITY BIOPHYSICS PULLMAN, WA 99164-4660 Export of proteins in Escherichia coli

R01GM-29812-17 (BMT) MC CLOSKEY, JAMES A UNIVERSITY OF UTAH DEPT. OF MEDICINAL CHEMISTRY SALT LAKE CITY, UT 84112 Structural studies of nucleic acid constituents

R01GM-29818-10 (BBCA) BUNICK, GERARD J UNIVERSITY OF TENNESSEE PO BOX 2009 OAK RIDGE, TN 37831-8077 Stuctural studies of nucleosomes

R01GM-29829-11 (BBCB) MAKOWSKI, LEE BOSTON UNIVERSITY 590 COMMONWEALTH AVE BOSTON, MA 02215 Structural studies of viruses and membranes

R01GM-29831-10 (ALY) OGATA, RONALD T MEDICAL BIOLOGY INSTITUTE 11077 NORTH TORREY PINES ROAD LA JOLLA, CA 92037 Structure and expression of complement genes

R01GM-29832-15 (CTY) MARZLUFF, WILLIAM F, JR FLORIDA STATE UNIVERSITY TALLAHASSEE, FL 32306-3006 Control of histone mRNA synthesis

R01GM-29836-10A1 (NLS) LESTER, HENRY A CALIFORNIA INST OF TECHNOLOGY 1201 EAST CALIFORNIA BLVD PASADENA, CA 91125 Intracellular messengers biophysical studies

R01GM-29840-22 (PHRA) FLEMING, WILLIAM W WEST VIRGINIA UNIV MEDICAL CTR PHARMACOLOGY/TOXICOLOGY MORGANTOWN, WV 26506 Mechanism of nonspecific supersensitivity to drugs

R01GM-29843-10 (MBC) HONG, JEN-SHIANG BOSTON BIOMEDICAL RES INST 20 STANIFORD STREET BOSTON, MASS 02114 Biochemistry and genetics of membrane functions

R01GM-29860-11 (CTY) BURRIDGE, KEITH W UNIV OF N C AT CHAPEL HILL TAYLOR HALL CB# 7090 CHAPEL HILL, NC 27599 Actin-membrane interaction

R01GM-29864-10 (BBCB) MENDELSOHN, RICHARD RUTGERS STATE UNIVERSITY 73 WARREN STREET NEWARK, NJ 07102 Lipid control of membrane protein organization

R01GM-29909-11 (MBC) GIBSON, DAVID T UNIVERSITY OF IOWA BOWEN SCIENCE BLDG/ RM 3-669 IOWA CITY, IA 52242 Mechanisms of enzymatic oxygen fixation

R01GM-29935-10 (MBY) GARRARD, WILLIAM T UNIV OF TEXAS SW MEDICAL CTR 5323 HARRY HINES BLVD DALLAS, TX 75235 Function of the subunits of eukaryotic chromosomes

R01GM-29963-10 (MBC) HAZELBAUER, GERALD L WASHINGTON STATE UNIVERSITY BIOCHEMISTRY/BIOPHYSICS DEPT. PULLMAN, WASH 99164 Molecular studies of chemoreception

R01GM-29994-10 (CBY) ROBERTS, THOMAS M DEPT OF BIOLOGICAL SCIENCES FLORIDA STATE UNIVERSITY TALLAHASSEE, FLORIDA 32306 Amoeboid motility--A cellular and genetic approach

R01GM-30027-10 (GEN) SPRAGUE, GEORGE F, JR UNIVERSITY OF OREGON EUGENE, OREG 97403 Genetic regulation of yeast cell type

R01GM-30048-13 (BBCB) ROBERTUS, JON D UNIVERSITY OF TEXAS/AUSTIN AUSTIN, TEXAS 78712 Structure, action and engineering of plant toxins

R01GM-30052-09 (BNP) POSNER, GARY H JOHNS HOPKINS UNIVERSITY 3300 N CHARLES ST, DEPT/CHEM BALTIMORE, MD 21218 Asymmetric synthesis of physiologically active compounds

PROJECT NO., ORGANIZATIONAL UNIT., INVESTIGATOR, ADDRESS, TITLE

R01GM-30054-09 (MGN) SAVAGEAU, MICHAEL A UNIVERSITY OF MICHIGAN 6730 MEDICAL SCIENCE BLDG II ANN ARBOR, MI 48109-0620 Analysis of molecular networks and control systems

R01GM-30095-08 (SAT) PEARCE, FREDERICK J USUHS 4301 JONES BRIDGE RD BETHESDA, MD 20814-4799 Energy homeostasis by specific organs in shock

R01GM-30105-09 (BBCB) HACKERT, MARVIN L UNIVERSITY OF TEXAS AUSTIN, TX 78712 Structure-function of pyruvoyl and PLP-dependent enzymes

R01GM-30132-09 (CTY) ANDERSON, ROBERT P UNIVERSITY OF WISCONSIN 445 HENRY MALL MADISON, WI 53706 The genetic specification of nematode muscle

R01GM-30140-10 (MGN) WEAVER, STEVEN G UNIV OF ILL AT CHICAGO P.O. BOX 4348, MC 066 CHICAGO, ILL 60680 The maintenance of sequence homology by gene conversion

R01GM-30147-10 (BBCA) KEIDERLING, TIMOTHY A UNIV OF ILLINOIS-CHICAGO DEPARTMENT OF CHEMISTRY CHICAGO, ILL 60680 Vibrational optical activity--Biochemical applications

R01GM-30163-08 (TOX) SZOKA, FRANCIS C, JR UNIVERSITY OF CALIFORNIA SAN FRANCISCO, CA 94143-0446 Controlled disposition of liposomes

R01GM-30179-10 (NLS) SCHULMAN, HOWARD STANFORD UNIVERSITY STANFORD, CA 94305-5332 Regulation of Ca2+/calmodulin kinase by neurotransmitter

R01GM-30186-10 (MBY) STRUHL, KEVIN HARVARD MEDICAL SCHOOL BOSTON, MASS 02115 Molecular mechanisms of yeast transcriptional initiation

R01GM-30204-10 (MBY) KELLEMS, RODNEY E BAYLOR COLLEGE OF MEDICINE ONE BAYLOR PLAZA HOUSTON, TX 77030 The organization of mammalian transcription units

R01GM-30220-09 (MBY) DAHLBERG, JAMES E UNIVERSITY OF WISCONSIN DEPT OF PHYSIOLOGICAL CHEMISTR MADISON, WIS 53706 Structure, organization and expression of sn RNA genes

R01GM-30232-07 (SAT) MAZE, MERVYN V A MEDICAL CENTER 3801 MIRANDA AVENUE PALO ATLO, CA 94304 Adrenergic action during anesthesia with volatile agents

R01GM-30301-10 (BNP) CANE, DAVID E BROWN UNIVERSITY DEPARTMENT OF CHEMISTRY PROVIDENCE, RI 02912 Stereochemical studies of isoprenoid biosynthesis

R01GM-30307-11 (GEN) HOLLAND, MICHAEL J UNIVERSITY OF CALIFORNIA DAVIS, CA 95616 Control of transcription of isolated eucaryotic genes

R01GM-30308-10 (PC) WILKINSON, KEITH D EMORY UNIV SCH OF MED WOODRUFF MEMORIAL BUILDING ATLANTA, GA 30322 Ubiquitin dependent proteolysis--Specificity and mechanism

R01GM-30312-10 (SB) SPITZER, JUDY A LOUISIANA STATE UNIVERSITY 1901 PERDIDO STREET NEW ORLEANS, LA 70112 Altered Ca2+ homeostasis and signal transduction in sepsis

R01GM-30317-11 (PC) KEY, JOE L UNIVERSITY OF GEORGIA A416 LIFE SCIENCES BLDG ATHENS, GA 30602 RNA metabolism in development and hormonal regulation

R01GM-30324-11 (PHRA) JOHNSON, GARY L NATL JEWISH CENTER FOR IMMUN 1400 JACKSON STREET DENVER, CO 80206 Receptor interaction with GTP-regulatory proteins

R01GM-30327-10 (PB) TSAI, MING-DAW OHIO STATE UNIVERSITY 120 W 18TH AVENUE COLUMBUS, OH 43210 Stereochemistry of enzyme reactions at phosphorus

R01GM-30333-10 (MBY) CHILDS, GEOFFREY J ALBERT EINSTEIN COLLEGE OF MED 1300 MORRIS PARK AVENUE BRONX, N Y 10461 Mechanisms generating temporal embryonic gene expression

R13GM-30337-12 (GBD) GRODZICKER, TERRI I COLD SPRING HARBOR LABORATORY P O BOX 100 COLD SPRING HARBOR, N Y 11724 Cold spring harbor advanced bacterial genetics course

R01GM-30353-05 (BBCA) FRANK, HARRY A UNIVERSITY OF CONNECTICUT 215 GLENBROOK RD STORRS, CT 06269-3060 Structure and function of carotenoids

R01GM-30355-11 (BIO) ROSS, ELLIOTT M UNIV OF TEXAS SW MEDICAL CENTE 5323 HARRY HINES BLVD DALLAS, TX 75235-9041 Effect of membrane structure on adenylate cyclase

R37GM-30365-17 (CBY) HIRSCHBERG, CARLOS B UNIV OF MASSACHUSETTS MED CTR 55 LAKE AVENUE NORTH WORCESTER, MA 01655 Glycosylation mechanisms of cell lipids and proteins

R37GM-30367-10 (BNP) WHITESIDES, GEORGE M HARVARD UNIVERSITY 12 OXFORD ST CAMBRIDGE, MA 02138 Enzymes as catalysts in the synthesis of carbohydrates

R01GM-30369-10 (MCHA) STREITWIESER, ANDREW UNIVERSITY OF CALIFORNIA BERKELEY, CA 94720 Ion pair carbon acidity

R01GM-30375-11 (BM) MC CLURE, WILLIAM R MELLON INSTITUTE 4400 FIFTH AVENUE PITTSBURGH, PA 15213 Mechanism and regulation of E. coli RNA polymerase

R01GM-30376-11 (PHY) BEZANILLA, FRANCISCO J U OF CALIFORNIA/SCH. OF MEDICI 405 HILGARD AVENUE LOS ANGELES, CA 90024-1751 Electrophysiological studies of voltage gated channels

R55GM-30377-10 (PHY) NONNER, WOLFGANG F UNIVERSITY OF MIAMI PO BOX 016430 MIAMI, FL 33101 Molecular mechanisms of gating in ionic channels

R01GM-30385-10 (CBY) BORISY, GARY G UNIVERSITY OF WISCONSIN 1525 LINDEN DRIVE MADISON, WIS 53706 Molecular analysis of mitotic spindle components

P01GM-30387-10 (SSS) LEVITT, MICHAEL STANFORD UNIVERSITY STANFORD, CA 94305-5400 Protein structure and function

P01GM-30387-10 0004 (SSS) SPUDICH, JAMES A Protein structure and function Structure of myosin subfragment-1

P01GM-30387-10 0008 (SSS) PARHAM, PETER Protein structure and function Promiscuous peptide binding proteins

P01GM-30387-10 0009 (SSS) LEVITT, MICHAEL Protein structure and function Experimental and theoretical determination of protein structure

P01GM-30387-10 0010 (SSS) MCKAY, DAVID Protein structure and function Substrate recognition by a 70K heat shock protein

P01GM-30387-10 9001 (SSS) SPUDICH, JAMES A Protein structure and function Core--Protein structure

R01GM-30401-15 (CBY) GIBBONS, IAN R PACIFIC BIOMEDICAL RESCH CTR 41 AHUI STREET HONOLULU, HI 96813 Properties of dynein isoenzymes

R01GM-30415-10 (PC) LINN, STUART M UNIVERSITY OF CALIFORNIA 401 BARKER HALL BERKELEY, CA 94720 Studies of DNA polymerases

R01GM-30428-08A1 (MBC) SOKATCH, JOHN R UNIV OF OKLAHOMA HLTH SCIS CTR P O BOX 26901 OKLAHOMA CITY, OK 73190 Biochemistry and genetics of lipoamide dehydrogenase

R01GM-30439-10 (GEN) KLEIN, HANNAH L NEW YORK UNIVERSITY MED CENTER 550 FIRST AVENUE NEW YORK, N Y 10016 Genetic behavior of repeated sequences

R01GM-30452-10 (BBCA) ROSSKY, PETER J UNIVERSITY OF TEXAS DEPT OF CHEMISTRY AUSTIN, TEXAS 78712 Ionic distributions in polynucleotide solutions

R01GM-30454-10 (MBY) GUARENTE, LEONARD P MASS INSTITUTE OF TECHNOLOGY 77 MASSACHUSETTS AVENUE CAMBRIDGE, MA 02139 Molecular analysis of transcriptional activators HAP1-4

R01GM-30471-09 (PC) PLUMMER, T H, JR N Y STATE DEPT OF HEALTH EMPIRE ST PLAZA/PO BOX 509 ALBANY, N Y 12201 Characterization of oligosaccharide chain-releasing enzymes

R01GM-30480-11 (PB) FREY, PERRY A UNIVERSITY OF WISCONSIN 1710 UNIVERSITY AVENUE MADISON, WI 53705 Mechanisms of enzymatic reactions

R01GM-30498-10 (SSS) LOHMAN, TIMOTHY M WASHINGTON UNIV SCHL. OF MED. 660 SOUTH EUCLID AVE. ST. LOUIS, MO 63110 E coli SSB protein-DNA interactions

R01GM-30518-10 (BBCA) HONIG, BARRY H COULUMBIA UNIVERSITY 630 WEST 168TH STREET NEW YORK, N Y 10032 Computer studies of protein structure and function

R13GM-30579-07 (CTY) MATHEWS, MICHAEL B COLD SPRING HARBOR LABORATORY PO BOX 100 COLD SPRING HARBOR, NY 11724 RNA processing

R01GM-30580-10 (BBCA) LEVY, RONALD M RUTGERS UNIVERSITY NEW BRUNSWICK, NJ 08903 Computer simulations of protein structure and dynamics

R01GM-30598-08A1 (BBCB) TAYLOR, KENNETH A DUKE UNIVERSITY MEDICAL CENTER BOX 3011 DURHAM, N C 27710 Electron miscroscope studies on muscle

R01GM-30614-09 (PC) KOWALSKI, DAVID ROSWELL PARK MEMORIAL INST 666 ELM STREET BUFFALO, N Y 14263 Enzymatic probes for open regions in supercoiled DNA

R01GM-30619-10 (MBC) ERREDE, BEVERLY J UNIV OF N.C. AT CHAPEL HILL DEPT OF CHEMISTRY CHAPEL HILL, N C 27599-3290 Regulation of gene expresion by transposable elements

R01GM-30626-10A1 (CBY) WITMAN, GEORGE B, III WORCESTER FOUNDATION 222 MAPLE AVENUE SHREWSBURY, MASS 01545 Molecular mechanism of flagellar motility

R01GM-30637-10 (MBY) KORNBERG, THOMAS B UNIVERSITY OF CALIFORNIA SAN FRANCISCO, CA 94143-0554 Molecular mechanisms in development

R01GM-30667-11 (CBY) HERTZBERG, ELLIOT L ALBERT EINSTEIN COLL OF MED 1300 MORRIS PARK AVENUE BRONX, NY 10461 Probes for the study of gap junctional communication

R01GM-30669-08 (PHRA) CORNETT, LAWRENCE E UNIV OF ARKANSAS FOR MED SCIS 4301 WEST MARKHAM STREET LITTLE ROCK, AR 72205 Adrenergic receptors in a smooth muscle cell line

R01GM-30693-10 (MBY) FIRTEL, RICHARD A UNIVERSITY OF CALIF, SAN DIEGO CTR FOR MOL GENETIC, M-034 LA JOLLA, CALIF 92093-0634 Analysis of developmentally regulated genes

R55GM-30701-09A2 (MBY) ADESNIK, MILTON B NEW YORK UNIVERSITY MEDICAL CT 550 FIRST AVE NEW YORK, NY 10016 Structure and regulation of cytochrome p-45011 genes

R01GM-30702-11 (GEN) MEYER, BARBARA J UNIVERSITY OF CALIFORNIA 401 BARKER HALL BERKELEY, CA 94720 Analysis of nematode sex determination

R01GM-30721-10 (PB) YU, CHANG-AN OKLAHOMA STATE UNIVERSITY STILLWATER, OKLA 74078-0454 Reaction mechanism of myocardial ubiquinone-proteins

R01GM-30731-12 (MBC) ROWND, ROBERT H WAYNE STATE UNIVERSITY 520 BIOLOGICAL SCIENCES BLDG DETROIT, MI 48202 The control of the replication of bacterial episomes

R01GM-30736-09 (PB) OHNISHI, TOMOKO UNIVERSITY OF PENNSYLVANIA DEPT OF BIOCHEM & BIOPHYSICS PHILADELPHIA, PA 19104 Proton & electron transfer & energy coupling

R01GM-30741-10 (BBCA) ASHER, SANFORD A UNIVERSITY OF PITTSBURG DEPARTMENT OF CHEMISTRY PITTSBURGH, PA 15260 UV resonance Raman studies of protein structure

R01GM-30755-11 (GMA) KOCHEVAR, IRENE E MASSACHUSETTS GENERAL HOSPITAL WELLMAN LABORATORY BOSTON, MA 02114 Ultraviolet light induced phenomena in biomembranes

R01GM-30758-10 (CBY) SLUDER, GREENFIELD WORCESTER FDN FOR EXPER BIO 222 MAPLE AVENUE SHREWSBURY, MA 01545 Centrosome formation, function and reproduction

R37GM-30759-16 (BNP) BARTLETT, PAUL A UNIVERSITY OF CALIFORNIA BERKELEY, CA 94720 Design & synthesis of peptide mimics

R01GM-30771-07A3 (MCHA) RIGBY, JAMES H WAYNE STATE UNIVERSITY DETROIT, MI 48202 Synthesis of cytotoxic guaianolides and other terpenoids

R37GM-30787-09 (MCHA) BERSON, JEROME A YALE UNIVERSITY BOX 6666 NEW HAVEN, CT 06511-8118 Mechanistic basis of synthetic design

R01GM-30799-10 (SSS) BLANCK, THOMAS J THE JOHNS HOPKINS HOSPITAL 601 NORTH BROADWAY BALTIMORE, MD 21205 Anesthetic depression of the myocardium

R37GM-30804-21 (BBCA) KARPLUS, MARTIN HARVARD UNIVERSITY 12 OXFORD STREET CAMBRIDGE, MA 02138 Theoretical studies of biomolecules

R01GM-30822-10 (BBCA) WELLS, ROBERT D TEXAS A&M UNIVERSITY 2121 HOLCOMBE AVE HOUSTON, TX 77030 DNA structure and gene regulation

R01GM-30827-09 (MCHA) PAQUETTE, LEO A OHIO STATE UNIVERSITY 120 WEST 18TH AVENUE COLUMBUS, OH 43210-1173 Synthesis of unusual biologically active terpenes

R01GM-30859-10 (MCHA) OVERMAN, LARRY E UNIV OF CALIFORNIA, IRVINE IRVINE, CA 92717 General methods for synthesis of bioactive heterocycles

R01GM-30861-10 (CBY) WATTERSON, DANIEL M VANDERBILT UNIVERSITY 1161 21ST AVENUE SOUTH NASHVILLE, TN 37232-6600 Molecular basis of calcium action in cell processes

R01GM-30870-10 (GEN) BLUMENTHAL, THOMAS INDIANA UNIVERSITY

BLOOMINGTON, IN 47405 Regulation C. elegans vitellogenin genes
R37GM-30881-10 (PC) YARUS, MICHAEL J UNIVERSITY OF COLORADO CAMPUS BOX 347 BOULDER, CO 80309 tRNA structure/function studies via gene construction
R01GM-30902-10 (BBCA) KARLE, ISABELLA L NAVAL RESEARCH LABORATORY CODE 6030 WASHINGTON, D C 20375 X-ray diffraction studies of oligopeptides
R01GM-30910-10 (PB) ARMSTRONG, RICHARD N UNIVERSITY MARYLAND DIV AGRICULTURE & LIFE SCIENCE COLLEGE PARK, MD 20742 Glutathione transferase--Defining and altering catalysis
R01GM-30938-10 (MCHA) DENMARK, SCOTT E UNIV OF ILLINOIS 1209 W CALIFORNIA ST/BOX 18 URBANA, IL 61801 The cycloaddition chemistry of nitroalkenes
R01GM-30943-09 (BIO) ORME-JOHNSON, WILLIAM H, III MASSACHUSETTS INSTITUTE 77 MASSACHUSETTS AVENUE CAMBRIDGE, MA 02139 Enzymes and dinitrogen reduction
R01GM-30948-09 (GEN) ENGELS, WILLIAM R UNIV OF WISCONSIN - MADISON MADISON, WI 53706 Behavior of P factors--Movable elements in Drosophila
R01GM-30959-08 (GEN) ADAMS, JULIAN P UNIV OF MICHIGAN 830 N UNIVERSITY ANN ARBOR, MI 48109-1048 Evolution in yeast--Population structure and genetics
R01GM-30962-10 (MBC) LONG, SHARON R STANFORD UNIVERSITY DEPT OF BIOLOGICAL SCIENCES STANFORD, CALIF 94305-5020 Regulation of nodulation genes in Rhizobium meliloti
R01GM-30969-09 (BBCA) HUI, SEK-WEN ROSWELL PARK MEMORIAL INST 666 ELM ST BUFFALO, NY 14263 Polyethylene-glycol and electric induced membrane fusion
R01GM-30971-07 (TOX) WESTLEY, JOHN L UNIVERSITY OF CHICAGO DEPT OF BIOCHEMISTRY CHICAGO, ILL 60637 Biochemistry of cyanide detoxication with sulfane sulfur
R01GM-30985-09 (CTY) EARNSHAW, WILLIAM C JOHNS HOPKINS UNIVERSITY 725 N WOLFE STREET BALTIMORE, MD 21205 Chromosome structure and condensation mechanisms
R01GM-30990-08 (RAD) MORTIMER, ROBERT K LAWRENCE BERKELEY LABORATORY 1 CYCLOTRON RD/MS 1-213 BERKELEY, CA 94720 Yeast rad genes in DNA repair and recombination
R01GM-30997-10 (NEUC) CHALFIE, MARTIN COLUMBIA UNIVERSITY 1012 FAIRCHILD CENTER NEW YORK NEW YORK 10027 Genetic analysis of nematode cell differentiation
R01GM-30998-08 (GEN) LI, WEN-HSIUNG UNIVERSITY OF TEXAS PO BOX 20334 HOUSTON, TX 77225 Statistical studies of DNA evolution
R01GM-31001-10 (PHRA) JOHNSON, ERIC F SCRIPPS CLINIC & RESEARCH FDN 10666 NORTH TORREY PINES ROAD LA JOLLA, CA 92037 Cytochrome P-450 polymorphism
R01GM-31006-09 (GEN) PRINGLE, JOHN R UNIVERSITY OF MICHIGAN ANN ARBOR, MI 48109-1048 Genetic study of the yeast cell cycle
R01GM-31030-10 (MBC) WALKER, GRAHAM C MASSACHUSETTS INST OF TECHNOLO 77 MASSACHUSETTS AVENUE CAMBRIDGE, MA 02139 Molecular genetics of Rhizobium nodulation plasmids
R01GM-31073-10 (MBY) WEINER, ALAN M YALE MEDICAL SCHOOL 333 CEDAR STREET NEW HAVEN, CT 06510 Transcription and function of human small RNA species
R01GM-31077-07A2 (MCHA) MARTIN, STEPHEN F UNIVERSITY OF TEXAS AUSTIN, TX 78712 Strategies for the synthesis of bioactive targets
R01GM-31082-09 (RAD) SANCAR, AZIZ UNIVERSITY OF NORTH CAROLINA CHAPEL HILL, NC 27599 Structure and function of DNA photolyase
R01GM-31083-07 (PB) MURPHY, ALEXANDER J UNIVERSITY OF PACIFIC 2155 WEBSTER STREET SAN FRANCISCO, CALIF 94115 Sarcoplamic reticulum ATPase--Structure and mechanism
R01GM-31105-10 (GEN) RINE, JASPER D UNIVERSITY OF CALIFORNIA 401 BARKER HALL BERKELEY, CA 94720 Analysis of the genes controlling a position effect
R01GM-31107-10 (MBC) CRAIG, ELIZABETH A UNIVERSITY OF WISCONSIN MED SC 1300 UNIVERSITY AVENUE MADISON, WI 53706 Regulation and function of the yeast heat shock response
R01GM-31110-10 (BIO) GROSSMAN, LAWRENCE JOHNS HOPKINS UNIVERSITY 615 NORTH WOLFE STREET BALTIMORE, MD 21205 DNA repair gene expression in mammalian cells
R01GM-31125-10 (GEN) VOELLMY, RICHARD W UNIV OF MIAMI SCH OF MED DEPT OF BIOCHEM & MOL BIO MIAMI, FLA 33101 Mechanism of regulation of heat shock gene expression
R13GM-31136-12 (CMBD) HALVORSON, HARLYN O MARINE BIOLOGICAL LABORATORY WATER ST WOODS HOLE, MA 02543 Physiology--Cellular and molecular biology
R01GM-31138-08 (MBY) LEE, AMY S USC SCHOOL OF MEDICINE 1441 EASTLAKE AVE LOS ANGELES, CA 90033 Cell cycle regulation of mammalian genes
R01GM-31144-07A1 (SAT) LYNCH, CARL, III UNIVERSITY OF VIRGINIA PO BOX 238 CHARLOTTESVILLE, VA 22908 Calcium current depression by volatile anesthetics
R01GM-31159-09 (CTY) SILFLOW, CAROLYN D UNIVERSITY OF MINNESOTA 1445 GORTNER AVENUE ST PAUL, MN 55108 Characterization and expression of tubulin genes
R01GM-31184-09 (CPA) SANDO, JULIANNE J 1300 JEFFERSON PARK AVE CHARLOTTESVILLE, VA 22908 Cellular mechanism of action of phorbol ester promoters
R01GM-31186-10 (PB) MARKHAM, GEORGE D INSTITUTE FOR CANCER RESEARCH 7701 BURHOLME AVENUE PHILADELPHIA, PA 19111 Enzymatic mechanisms of sulfur-nucleoside metabolism
R01GM-31208-07 (PC) CLARK, RICHARD B UNIV OF TX HLTH SCI CTR-HOUST P O BOX 20334 HOUSTON, TX 77225 Beta-adrenergic receptor structure and desensitization
R01GM-31244-10 (CBY) KEENAN, THOMAS W VPI & STATE UNIVERSITY DEPT OF BIOCHEM & NUTRITION BLACKSBURG, VA 24061 Intracellular origin and growth of milk lipid globules
R01GM-31253-09A1 (MBC) SUBRAMANI, SURESH UNIV OF CALIFORNIA, SAN DIEGO LA JOLLA, CA 92093 Mechanism for DNA recombination and repair in eukaryotes
R01GM-31256-15 (MCHA) SCHLESSINGER, RICHARD H UNIVERSITY OF ROCHESTER DEPARTMENT OF CHEMISTRY ROCHESTER, N Y 14627 Synthetic and mechanistic studies of urethane enolates
R01GM-31265-09 (PC) HERSCOVICS, ANNETTE A MC GILL CANCER CENTRE 3655 DRUMMOND ST MONTREAL, QUEBEC CAN H3G IY6 Mannoprotein biosynthesis in Saccharomyces cerevisiae
R01GM-31278-08 (BNP) FALCK, JOHN R UNIV OF TEXAS SW MEDICAL CENTE 5323 HARRY HINES BLVD DALLAS, TX 75235-9046 Eicosanoid synthesis
P01GM-31286-09 (SSS) KIRSCHNER, MARC W UNIV OF CALIFORNIA 3RD & PARNASSUS AVES SAN FRANCISCO, CA 94143-0448 Molecular biology of cellular growth control
P01GM-31286-09 0004 (SSS) HERSKOWITZ, IRA Molecular biology of cellular growth control Molecular mechanisms of signal transduction--Cell cycle regulator
P01GM-31286-09 0005 (SSS) KIRSCHNER, MARC W Molecular biology of cellular growth control Pattern formation & translational control at gastrulation in Xenopus
P01GM-31286-09 0006 (SSS) KORNBERG, THOMAS B Molecular biology of cellular growth control Patterning genes and oncogenes in Drosophila
P01GM-31286-09 0007 (SSS) ALBERTS, BRUCE M Molecular biology of cellular growth control Detecting chromatin heterogeneity in early Drosophila
P01GM-31286-09 0008 (SSS) KENYON, CYNTHIA Molecular biology of cellular growth control Gene control of cell differentiation in C elegans
P01GM-31286-09 0009 (SSS) O'FARRELL, PATRICK Molecular biology of cellular growth control Regulation of cell cycle in Drosophila embryos
P01GM-31286-09 9001 (SSS) KIRSCHNER, MARC W Molecular biology of cellular growth control Core support
R55GM-31289-09A2 (BIO) FOX, JAY W UNIV OF VIRGINIA HLTH SCIS CTR PO BOX 441/JORDAN HALL CHARLOTTESVILLE, VA 22908 Characterization and inhibition of snake hemorrhagic toxin
R01GM-31296-11 (PHRA) MASTERS, BETTIE S UNIVERSITY OF TEXAS HLTH SCI C 7703 FLOYD CURL DR SAN ANTONIO, TX 78284-7760 Prostaglandin 19-& 20-hydroxylation by cytochrome P-450
P01GM-31299-09 (SSS) DICKERSON, RICHARD E UNIVERSITY OF CALIFORNIA 405 HILGARD AVE LOS ANGELES, CA 90024-1570 Biological structure and recognition
P01GM-31299-09 0001 (SSS) DICKERSON, RICHARD E Biological structure and recognition Structure and interactions of DNA complexes with antitumor drugs and proteins
P01GM-31299-09 0002 (SSS) EISENBERG, DAVID Biological structure and recognition Protein structure and design
P01GM-31299-09 0003 (SSS) YEATES, TODDS Biological structure and recognition Crystallographic and computational studies of proteins
P01GM-31299-09 9001 (SSS) DICKERSON, RICHARD E Biological structure and recognition Core facility
P01GM-31304-09 (SRC) WILKINSON, GRANT R VANDERBILT UNIV SCHOOL OF MEDICINE NASHVILLE, TN 37232-6602 Determinants of individual responsiveness to drugs
P01GM-31304-09 0006 (SRC) WILKINSON, GRANT R Determinants of individual responsiveness to drugs Polymorphic metabolism of mephenytoin and debrisoquine in man
P01GM-31304-09 0008 (SRC) WOOSLEY, RAYMOND L Determinants of individual responsiveness to drugs Evaluation of the antiarrhythmic efficacy of propafenone
P01GM-31304-09 0013 (SRC) BRANCH, ROBERT A Determinants of individual responsiveness to drugs Oxidative polymorphisms in disease states
P01GM-31304-09 0014 (SRC) WOOD, ALASTAIR J J Determinants of individual responsiveness to drugs Drug interactions--Clinical and mechanistic agents
P01GM-31304-09 9001 (SRC) BLAIR, IAN A Determinants of individual responsiveness to drugs Analytical core
R01GM-31305-10 (BIO) WOLD, FINN UNIVERSITY OF TEXAS MED. SCH. DEPT OF BIOCHEM & MOL BIOLOGY HOUSTON, TEX 77225 Protein structure and function
R37GM-31318-29 (PBC) ROBBINS, PHILLIPS W MASSACHUSETTS INST TECH 77 MASSACHUSETTS AVE CAMBRIDGE, MA 02139-4307 Glycosylation and glycosidases--Cell and molecular biology
R01GM-31321-08A1 (SAT) GRINNELL, FREDERICK L UNIV OF TEXAS HLTH SCI CTR 5323 HARRY HINES BOULEVARD DALLAS, TX 75235-9039 Developmental of an in vitro wound healing model
R01GM-31349-09A1 (MCHA) JUNG, MICHAEL E UNIVERSITY OF CALIFORNIA LOS ANGELES, CA 90024-1569 Synthesis of biologically active natural products
R01GM-31352-12A2 (MCHA) SEMMELHACK, MARTIN F PRINCETON UNIVERSITY WASHINGTON ROAD PRINCETON, NJ 08544-1009 Natural product syntheses
R01GM-31354-07A1 (BNP) CROTEAU, RODNEY B WASHINGTON STATE UNIVERSITY 467 CLARK HALL PULLMAN, WA 99164-6340 Enzymatic cyclization of terpenoid natural products
R01GM-31382-08 (SAT) LOUIS, CHARLES F 1988 FITCH AVENUE ST PAUL, MN 55108 Anesthetic reactions in surgery
R01GM-31398-10 (BMT) NICOLAOU, KYRIACOS C SCRIPPS CLINIC AND RES FDN 10666 NORTH TORREY PINES RD LA JOLLA, CA 92037 Total synthesis of brevetoxin B
R01GM-31399-09 (MBC) RUPP, W DEAN YALE UNIV SCHOOL OF MEDICINE 333 CEDAR STREET NEW HAVEN, CONN 06510 Characterization of the UVRABC endonuclease of E coli
R37GM-31409-09 (GEN) HOGNESS, DAVID S STANFORD UNIVERSITY BECKMAN CENTER B300 STANFORD, CA 94305-5427 Molecular basis for genetic control of development
R01GM-31449-09 (BBCB) BUSH, C ALLEN UNIVERSITY OF MARYLAND BALTIMORE, MD 21228 Conformations of glycopeptides and glycoproteins
R01GM-31471-09 (BBCA) PABO, CARL O MASS. INSTITUTE OF TECHNOLOGY CAMBRIDGE, MA 02139 Crystallographic study of homeodomain/DNA complexes
R01GM-31475-09 (BBCA) BALDWIN, ROBERT L STANFORD UNIVERSITY BECKMAN CENTER B400 STANFORD, CA 94305-5307 Rules for alpha-helix formation
R01GM-31480-09 (MBY) PERLMAN, PHILIP UNIV OF TX SW MED CTR AT DALLA 5323 HARRY HINES BLVD DALLAS, TX 75235 Genetic and molecular studies of RNA splicing
R01GM-31483-09 (BNP) JONES, ROGER A RUTGERS UNIVERSITY PO BOX 939 PISCATAWAY, NJ 08855-0939 Synthesis of specifically modified oligonucleotides

PROJECT NO., ORGANIZATIONAL UNIT., INVESTIGATOR, ADDRESS, TITLE

R01GM-31489-09 (MGN) STILES, CHARLES D DANA FARBER CANCER INST 44 BINNEY ST MAYER BLDG RM 830 BOSTON, MA 02115 Trans-dominant suppressor genes for the PDGFs and TGF-b

R01GM-31497-09A1 (BBCA) KUNTZ, IRWIN D, JR UNIVERSITY OF CALIFORNIA 926 MEDICAL SCIENCES BLDG SAN FRANCISCO, CA 94143-0446 Theoretical studies of macromolecules

R01GM-31506-09 (BBCB) BENTZ, JOSEPH E DREXEL UNIVERSITY 32ND AND CHESTNUT STREETS PHILADELPHIA, PA 19104 Membrane fusion

R01GM-31528-08 (MBY) NILSEN, TIMOTHY W CASE WESTERN RESERVE UNIV 10900 EUCLID AVE CLEVELAND, OH 44106-4960 In vitro processing of eukaryotic ribosomal RNA

R01GM-31530-09 (BIO) VARSHAVSKY, ALEXANDER J MASSACHUSETTS INST OF TECH 77 MASSACHUSETTS AVENUE CAMBRIDGE, MA 02139 Functions of ubiquitin-containing proteins

R01GM-31532-09 (CTY) ELGIN, SARAH C WASHINGTON UNIVERSITY DEPARTMENT OF BIOLOGY ST LOUIS, MO 63130 Structural and genetic studies of chromosomal proteins

R01GM-31539-09 (BIO) WILLIAMS, KENNETH R YALE UNIVERSITY 333 CEDAR ST/ PO BOX 3333 NEW HAVEN, CT 06510 Structure/function of eukaryotic RNA binding proteins

R01GM-31540-08 (BBCB) LEVINTHAL, FRANCOISE COLUMBIA UNIVERSITY 1011 SHERMAN FAIRCHILD CENTER NEW YORK, N Y 10027 Structure-function studies of a switchable ion channel

R01GM-31546-10 (MBY) ROBINS, DIANE M UNIVERSITY OF MICHIGAN DEPARTMENT OF HUMAN GENETICS Molecular control of hormonally responsive genes

R01GM-31555-09 (PHRA) BOYER, THOMAS DAVID EMORY UNIVERSITY P O BOX 23206 ATLANTA, GA 30322 Factors in the prevention of toxic liver injury

R01GM-31569-08 (SAT) MARTYN, J JEEVENDRA MASSACHUSETTS GENERAL HOSPITAL DEPARTMENT OF ANESTHESIA BOSTON, MA 02114 Alteration in neuromuscular function following burns

R01GM-31571-08S1 (MGN) TEMPLETON, ALAN R WASHINGTON UNIVERSITY ST LOUIS, MO 63130 Use of recombinant DNA in population genetics

R01GM-31574-09 (BIO) WALSH, CHRISTOPHER T HARVARD MEDICAL SCHOOL 25 SHATTUCK STREET BOSTON, MA 02115 Nickel-dependent enzymes in methanogenesis

R01GM-31575-09 (EDC) MACCLUER, JEAN W SOUTHWEST FOUNDATION P O BOX 28147 SAN ANTONIO, TX 78228-0147 Genetic analysis of common diseases--An evaluation

R01GM-31611-09 (BBCB) MATHEWS, F SCOTT WASHINGTON UNIVERSITY 660 S. EUCLID AVE., BOX 8228 ST LOUIS, MO 63110 Structural studies of complex iron-sulfur flavoproteins

R37GM-31617-10 (NSS) INOUE, SHINYA MARINE BIOLOGICAL LABORATORY WOODS HOLE, MA 02543 Mitosis and related motility directly in living cells

R01GM-31625-09 (MBC) BRYANT, DONALD A PENN ST UNIV/S-101 FREAR BLDG DEPT-MOLECULAR & CELL BIOLOGY UNIVERSITY PARK, PA 16802 Regulation of biliprotein biosynthesis in cyanobacteria

R01GM-31627-09 (CBY) AGARD, DAVID A UNIV OF CALIFORNIA, SF 513 PARNASSUS BOX 0448 SAN FRANCISCO, CA 94143-0448 3-d structure of mitotic chromosomes

R01GM-31651-08A3 (PC) SCHROEDER, FRIEDHELM UNIVERSITY OF CINCINNATI MED C 3223 EDEN AVENUE / M L #004 CINCINNATI, OH 45267-0004 Asymmetric distibution of cholesterol in membranes

R01GM-31655-09 (MBC) COZZARELLI, NICHOLAS R UNIVERSITY OF CALIFORNIA 401 BARKER HALL BERKELEY, CALIF 94720 RNA ligase function and use in DNA synthesis

R37GM-31657-09 (MBC) COZZARELLI, NICHOLAS R UNIVERSITY OF CALIFORNIA BERKELEY, CA 94720 Enzymological and genetic studies of DNA polymerases

R01GM-31660-06S1 (BMT) FENN, JOHN B 9 HILLHOUSE AVE/PO BOX 2159 NEW HAVEN, CT 06520-2159 Ion source for LC-MS analysis of bio-materials

R01GM-31662-09 (SAT) DEMLING, ROBERT H BETH ISRAEL HOSPITAL 330 BROOKLINE AVE BOSTON, MA 02215 Pathophysiology of lungs after thermal injury

R01GM-31664-07 (SAT) LIU, MAW-SHUNG ST LOUIS UNIV SCHOOL OF MED DEPT OF PHARM & PHYSIOLOGICAL ST LOUIS, MO 63104 Hepatic glucose metabolism in shock

R01GM-31667-09 (MBC) KAPLAN, SAMUEL THE UNIV OF TEXAS MED SCH 6431 FANNIN HOUSTON, TX 77030 Genetic analysis of bacterial photosynthesis

R01GM-31678-07A2 (MCHA) CURRAN, DENNIS P UNIVERSITY OF PITTSBURGH PITTSBURGH, PA 15260 Asymmetric thermal addition and cycloaddition reactions

R01GM-31683-08A1 (SSS) MARSHALL, ALAN G OHIO STATE UNIVERSITY 120 W 18TH AVE/100 CHEM BLDG COLUMBUS, OH 43210-1173 FT mass spectrometry for biomolecule analysis

R01GM-31685-10 (MBC) KHAN, SALEEM A UNIVERSITY OF PITTSBURGH SCHOOL OF MEDICINE PITTSBURGH, PA 15261 Plasmid pt181 DNA replication in Staphylococcus aureus

P01GM-31689-08 (SSS) CAPRA, J DONALD UNIVERSITY OF TEXAS SOUTHWESTE 5323 HARRY HINES BOULEVARD DALLAS, TX 75235 Structure-activity relationships among proteins

P01GM-31689-08 0001 (SSS) CAPRA, J DONALD Structure-activity relationships among proteins Organization, polymorphism and expression of human antibody genes

P01GM-31689-08 0002 (SSS) TUCKER, PHILLIP W Structure-activity relationships among proteins Expression and in vitro mutagenesis of membrane Ig DNA

P01GM-31689-08 0003 (SSS) GARRARD, WILLIAM T Structure-activity relationships among proteins Biology and function of DNA methylation

P01GM-31689-08 0004 (SSS) MACDONALD, RAYMOND J Structure-activity relationships among proteins Expression of kallikrein gene family

P01GM-31689-08 9001 (SSS) CAPRA, J DONALD Structure-activity relationships among proteins Core--cell culture

P01GM-31689-08 9002 (SSS) CAPRA, J DONALD Structure-activity relationships among proteins Core--Macromolecular synthesis

R01GM-31693-10 (MBC) SMITH, GERALD R FRED HUTCHINSON CANCER RES CTR 1124 COLUMBIA ST SEATTLE, WA 98104 Molecular analysis of hotspots of genetic recombination

R01GM-31704-10 (PB) JORNS, MARILYN S HAHNEMANN UNIVERSITY BROAD AND VINE PHILADELPHIA PA 19102 Flavoenzyme mechanism--Redox and non-redox reactions

PROJECT NO., ORGANIZATIONAL UNIT., INVESTIGATOR, ADDRESS, TITLE

R01GM-31708-09 (BM) STORM, DANIEL R UNIVERSITY OF WASHINGTON SEATTLE, WA 98195 Calmodulin regulation of B pertussis adenylate cyclase

R01GM-31709-25 (MBC) MINDICH, LEONARD E PUBLIC HEALTH RESEARCH INST 455 FIRST AVENUE NEW YORK, NY 10016 Cell membrane synthesis in the control of growth

R01GM-31710-07A1 (SAT) FINK, B RAYMOND UNIVERSITY OF WASHINGTON SEATTLE, WA 98195 Axonal study for improved selective nerve anesthesia

R01GM-31715-09 (BNP) GOULD, STEVEN J OREGON STATE UNIVERSITY CORVALLIS, OR 97331-4003 Mutasynthetic and bioorganic studies of antibiotics

R01GM-31745-08 (GEN) POLISKY, BARRY A INDIANA UNIVERSITY DEPARTMENT OF BIOLOGY BLOOMINGTON, IN 47405 Structure and function of serotype genes in Paramecium

R01GM-31749-09 (SSS) MC CAMMON, JAMES A UNIVERSITY OF HOUSTON HOUSTON, TX 77204-5641 Theory of biomolecular diffusion

R01GM-31754-09 (SAT) SOLOMKIN, JOSEPH S UNIV OF CINCINNATI COLL OF MED 231 BETHESDA AVENUE CINCINNATI, OH 45267-0558 Mechanisms of neutrophil dysfunction in burns and trauma

R01GM-31756-10 (PB) SLIGAR, STEPHEN G UNIVERSITY OF ILLINOIS 1209 WEST CALIFORNIA ST URBANA, IL 61801 Heme protein reductases

R37GM-31768-09 (END) MILLER, CHRISTOPHER BRANDEIS UNIVERSITY 415 SOUTH ST WALTHAM, MA 02254-9110 Basic mechanisms of ion channel function

R01GM-31770-08 (BBCA) ADMAN, ELINOR T UNIVERSITY OF WASHINGTON SEATTLE, WA 98195 Electron transfer pathways/blue copper proteins

R01GM-31782-09 (PB) FORBUSH, BLISS, III YALE UNIV/SCH OF MED P O BOX 3333 NEW HAVEN, CONN 06510 Physiology of ion transport mechanism of the NA pump

R01GM-31785-09 (MBC) BOYER, HERBERT W UNIV OF CALIFORNIA DEPT OF BIOCHEMISTRY/HSE 1556 SAN FRANCISCO, CA 94143-0554 Genetic analysis of halobacteria/bacterio-opsin gene

R01GM-31808-08 (MBC) DE HASETH, PIETER L CASE WESTERN RESERVE UNIVERSIT 2119 ABINGTON ROAD CLEVELAND, OH 44106 Structure-function relationships of promoter DNA

R01GM-31816-09 (GEN) KIMBLE, JUDITH E UNIVERSITY OF WISCONSIN 1525 LINDEN DRIVE MADISON, WI 53706 Genetic analysis of nematode development

R01GM-31828-06 (SAT) LANZA-JACOBY, SUSAN JEFFERSON MEDICAL COLLEGE 1025 WALNUT STREET PHILDELPHIA, PA 19107 Effect of sepsis on lipid metabolism

R01GM-31837-09 (CBY) OAKLEY, BERL R OHIO STATE UNIVERSITY 484 WEST 12TH AVENUE COLUMBUS, OH 43210 Molecular biology of microtubule-interacting proteins

R01GM-31841-08 (ALY) PATERSON, YVONNE UNIV OF PA SCHOOL OF MEDICINE DEPT OF MICROBIOLOGY PHILADELPHIA, PA 19104-6076 Conformational constraints of antigenic determinants

R01GM-31847-08 (BBCA) ENGLANDER, S WALTER UNIVERSITY OF PENNSYLVANIA BIOCHEM & BIOPHYS DEPARTMENT PHILADELPHIA, PA 19104 Functional labeling of cytochrome c by H-exchange and NMR

R01GM-31859-07A2 (CBY) GOODMAN, JOEL M U OF TEXAS SW MEDICAL CENTER 5323 HARRY HINES BOULEVARD DALLAS, TX 75235-9041 Induction of an organelle--The yeast peroxisome

R01GM-31867-08 (GEN) EICKBUSH, THOMAS H UNIVERSITY OF ROCHESTER HUTCHISON HALL ROCHESTER, N Y 14627 Mutigene families--Structure, expression and evolution

R01GM-31888-09 (MBY) DREYFUSS, GIDEON UNIVERSITY OF PENNSYLVANIA DEPARTMENT OF BIOCHEMISTRY PHILADELPHIA, PA 19104-6059 Ribonucleoproteins, mRNA and cytoskeletal structures

R01GM-31907-09 (CBY) KUCZMARSKI, EDWARD R UNIVERSITY OF HEALTH SCIENCES 3333 GREEN BAY ROAD NORTH CHICAGO, IL 60064 Regulation of myosin heavy chain phosphorylation

R01GM-31910-06 (PB) HANZLIK, ROBERT P UNIVERSITY OF KANSAS 4070 MALOTT HALL LAWRENCE, KS 66045-2506 Mechanisms of P-450 catalyzed C-oxidations

R01GM-31925-07 (MBC) HUTCHINSON, CHARLES R UNIVERSITY OF WISCONSIN DEPT OF PHARMACY MADISON, WISC 53706 Biosynthesis of macrolide antibiotics

R01GM-31935-08 (GEN) GOLDBERG, MICHAEL L CORNELL UNIVERSITY ITHACA, NY 14853-2703 Molecular genetics of the Drosophila zeste locus

R01GM-31944-07A2 (MBC) CSONKA, LASZLO N PURDUE UNIVERSITY WEST LAFAYETTE, IN 47907 Analysis of osmoregulation in Salmonella typhimurium

R01GM-31954-09 (PHRA) STERNWEIS, PAUL C UNIV OF TEXAS SOUTHWESTERN 5323 HARRY HINES BLVD DALLAS, TEX 75235 Transmembrane signaling via receptors and G proteins

R01GM-31958-09 (MCHA) BERCHTOLD, GLENN A MASSACHUSETTS INST/TECHNOLOGY CAMBRIDGE, MA 02139 Investigations of the chorismate pathway

R01GM-31973-09 (BIO) LEE, MARIETTA Y UNIVERSITY OF MIAMI PO BOX 016960 MIAMI, FL 33101 Biochemical studies of human polymerase delta

R01GM-31986-08 (PB) LONDON, ERWIN STATE UNIVERSITY OF NEW YORK DEPARTMENT OF BIOCHEMISTRY STONY BROOK, NY 11794-5215 Diphtheria toxin structure and membrane interaction

R01GM-31987-09 (CBY) INSEL, PAUL A UNIVERSITY OF CALIFORNIA 9500 GILMAN DR LA JOLLA, CA 92093 Cellular actions of catecholamine receptors

R01GM-32003-08 (MBY) BINGHAM, PAUL M STATE UNIVERSITY OF NEW YORK DEPARTMENT OF BIOCHEMISTRY STONY BROOK, NY 11794-5215 Regulation of gene expression in Drosophila melanogaster

R01GM-32007-07 (CBY) ESTES, JAMES E ALBANY MEDICAL COLLEGE 47 NEW SCOTLAND AVE ALBANY, NY 12208 A comparison of Mg-actin and Ca-actin

R01GM-32010-10 (PC) STEIN, GARY S UNIV OF MASSACHUSETTS MED CTR 55 LAKE AVENUE NORTH WORCESTER, MA 01655 Identification of human histone gene regulatory sequences

R01GM-32017-08 (ALY) RASCHKE, WILLIAM C LA JOLLA BIOLOGICAL LABORATORI P O BOX 85350 SAN DIEGO, CA 92138 Gene structure of the murine T200 lymphocyte antigens

R01GM-32018-08 (CTY) ORDAHL, CHARLES P UNIVERSITY OF CALIFORNIA BOX 0452 SAN FRANCISCO, CA 94143 Transcription of muscle-specific genes in myogenesis

R01GM-32022-08 (CBY) MARGOLIS, ROBERT LEWIS UNIVERSITY OF WASHINGTON SEATTLE, WA 98195 Characterization of kinetochore components

R01GM-32035-08 (GMB) COOKE, NANCY E UNIV OF PENNSYLVANIA SCH OF ME 422 CURIE BLVD PHILADELPHIA, PA 19104-6144 Characterization of human vitamin D binding protein gene

R01GM-32079-09 (BBCB) STROUD, ROBERT M UNIVERSITY OF CALIFORNIA DEPT OF BIOCHEM/BIOPHYSICS SAN FRANCISCO, CALIF 94143 Structure and function of bacteriorhodopsin

R01GM-32095-09 (MBC) MOLINEUX, IAN J UNIVERSITY OF TEXAS AUSTIN, TEX 78712-1095 Mechanisms of phage exclusion system

R01GM-32096-12 (MGN) YAMAZAKI, KUNIO MONELL CHEMICAL SENSES CENTER 3500 MARKET ST PHILADELPHIA, PA 19104-3308 Genetics of self-identification in mammalian species

P01GM-32099-09 (NEUA) KUPFERMANN, IRVING RESEARCH FDN FOR MENTAL HYGIEN 722 WEST 168TH STREET NEW YORK, NY 10032 Cellular analysis of behavior

P01GM-32099-09 0009 (NEUA) KUPFERMANN, IRVING Cellular analysis of behavior Scope B--Modulation of sensorimotor synapase

P01GM-32099-09 0010 (NEUA) KUPFERMANN, IRVING Cellular analysis of behavior Scope C--plasticity at synapse underling

P01GM-32099-09 0011 (NEUA) KUPFERMANN, IRVING Cellular analysis of behavior Scope D--Synaptic responses and electropotentials in sub gelatinosa

P01GM-32099-09 0015 (NEUA) MARTIN, J H Cellular analysis of behavior Scope F--Red nucleus in targeting limb movement

P01GM-32099-09 0017 (NEUA) KUPFERMANN, IRVING Cellular analysis of behavior Scope A--Functions of proteins in neuron

R01GM-32110-09 (BNP) GOULD, STEVEN J OREGON STATE UNIVERSITY DEPT OF CHEMISTRY CORVALLIS, OR 97331-4003 Biosynthetic studies using 15N-I3C NMR spectroscopy

R01GM-32111-10 (MGN) DARLINGTON, GRETCHEN J BAYLOR COLLEGE OF MEDICINE ONE BAYLOR PLAZA HOUSTON, TX 77030 Activation and regulation of hepatic genes

R01GM-32117-09 (BMT) AVERILL, BRUCE A UNIVERSITY OF VIRGINIA MCCORMICK RD CHARLOTTESVILLE, VA 22901 Synthetic and physical approaches to metalloproteins

R01GM-32125-08 (BBCB) SPRINGER, CHARLES S, JR STATE UNIVERSITY NEW YORK STONY BROOK, NY 11794-3400 NMR studies of cation transport across biomembranes

R01GM-32130-09 (GEN) HASTINGS, ALAN M UNIVERSITY OF CALIFORNIA 2132 WICKSON HALL DAVIS, CA 95616 New approach to multilocus population genetic models

R37GM-32134-10 (BMT) LIPPARD, STEPHEN J MASS INSTITUTE OF TECH ROOM 18-290 CAMBRIDGE, MA 02139 Ligand-bridged binuclear metal complexes and proteins

R01GM-32136-09 (BBCA) JORGENSEN, WILLIAM L YALE UNIVERSITY 12 PROSPECT PL GRANT/CONTRACT/ NEW HAVEN, CT 06511-3516 Biophysical interactions and dynamics of polypetides

P01GM-32165-09 (SRC) TRAGER, WILLIAM F UNIVERSITY OF WASHINGTON SCHOOL OF PHARMACY, BG-20 SEATTLE, WA 98195 Drug interactions

P01GM-32165-09 0002 (SRC) TRAGER, WILLIAM F Drug interactions Stereoselective drug interactions--In vivo-in vitro correlations

P01GM-32165-09 0003 (SRC) LEVY, RENE H Drug interactions Drug interactions with valproic acid

P01GM-32165-09 0004 (SRC) NELSON, SIDNEY D Drug interactions Drug interactions with acetaminophen

P01GM-32165-09 0005 (SRC) SHEN, DANNY Drug interactions Calcium channel blocker & beta adrenoreceptor antagonist interaction

P01GM-32165-09 9001 (SRC) TRAGER, WILLIAM F Drug interactions Analytical core

R01GM-32184-09 (CPA) MILLER, JEFFREY H UNIVERSITY OF CALIFORNIA 405 HILGARD AVENUE LOS ANGELES, CA 90024 Spontaneous and carcinogen-induced mutagenesis

R01GM-32187-08 (BMT) HUYNH, BOI H EMORY UNIVERSITY DEPARTMENT OF PHYSICS ATLANTA, GA 30322 Mossbauer and EPR studies of hydrogenase

R01GM-32191-10 (BIO) STUBBE, JOANNE MASSACHUSETTS INST OF TECHNGY 77 MASSACHUSETTS AVENUE CAMBRIDGE, MA 02139 Purine biosynthetic enzymes--Mechanism and regulation

R01GM-32192-09 (MCHA) NICOLAOU, KYRIACOS C RESEARCH INST OF SCRIPPS CLINI 10666 NORTH TORREY PINES ROAD LA JOLLA, CA 92037 Total synthesis of aurodox

R01GM-32194-09 (MBC) SMITH, GERALD R FRED HUTCHINSON CANCER RES CTR 1124 COLUMBIA STREET SEATTLE, WA 98104 Molecular mechanisms of genetic recombination

R01GM-32224-08 (SAT) CALDWELL, MICHAEL D UNIV OF MINNESOTA MINNEAPOLIS, MN 55455 Biological priority and regulatory mechanisms of wound healing

R01GM-32238-09 (MBY) BLOOM, KERRY S UNIVERSITY OF NORTH CAROLINA WILSON HALL, CB #3280 CHAPEL HILL, N C 27599-3280 Structural analysis of a eukaryotic centromere

R01GM-32243-09 (BBCB) PRESTEGARD, JAMES H YALE UNIVERSITY 12 PROSPECT PLACE NEW HAVEN, CT 06511-3516 NMR studies of acyl-carrier protein

R01GM-32253-09 (BIO) MC MACKEN, ROGER L JOHNS HOPKINS UNIVERSITY 615 NORTH WOLFE STREET BALTIMORE, MD 21205 Initiation of bacteriophage DNA replication in vitro

R01GM-32257-09 (GEN) FITZGERALD-HAYES, MOLLY UNIVERSITY OF MASSACHUSETTS AMHERST, MA 01003 Yeast centromere structure and function

R01GM-32263-10 (MBC) DONAHUE, THOMAS F INDIANA UNIVERSITY DEPARTMENT OF BIOLOGY BLOOMINGTON, IN 47405 Control of translation initiation in yeast

R01GM-32281-07 (TOX) OMIECINSKI, CURTIS J UNIVERSITY OF WASHINGTON D E H SC - 34 SEATTLE, WA 98195 Molecular mechanisms of expression of cytochrome P-450

R01GM-32286-07 (PHY) KARLISH, STEVEN J WEIZMANN INSTITUTE OF SCIS PO BOX 26 REHOVOT 76100 ISRAEL Mechanisms of cation transport by the Na/K pump

R01GM-32288-05A2 (SAT) SAYEED, MOHAMMED M LOYOLA UNIV MEDICAL CTR 2160 SOUTH FIRST AVENUE MAYWOOD, IL 60153 Calcium antagonists-skeletal muscle nutrient transport

R01GM-32296-09 (BMT) MEYER, THOMAS J UNIVERSITY OF NORTH CAROLINA DEPARTMENT OF CHEMISTRY CHAPEL HILL, N C 27514 Models for biological redox processes

R01GM-32299-13A1 (BNP) WEINREB, STEVEN M PENNSYLVANIA STATE UNIVERSITY 152 DAVEY LABORATORY UNIVERSITY PARK, PA 16802 Studies in alkaloid total synthesis

R01GM-32304-07 (TOX) AWASTHI, YOGESH C UNIV OF TEXAS MEDICAL BRANCH ROUTE F20 GALVESTON, TX 77550 Detoxication of xenobiotics in erythrocytes

R01GM-32308-09 (MBC) PTASHNE, MARK S HARVARD UNIVERSITY 7 DIVINITY AVENUE CAMBRIDGE, MASS 02138 Regulation of the GAL genes in yeast

R01GM-32318-09 (GEN) DUNCAN, IAN W WASHINGTON UNIVERSITY ST LOUIS, MO 63130 Genetic analysis of body segmentation

R01GM-32333-09 (MCHA) FLOSS, HEINZ G UNIVERSITY OF WASHINGTON DEPT. OF CHEMISTRY, BG-10 SEATTLE, WA 98195 Stereochemistry of enzyme reactions

R01GM-32335-09 (MBC) COX, MICHAEL M UNIVERSITY OF WISCONSIN 420 HENRY MALL MADISON, WI 53706 Biochemistry of genetic recombination/recA protein

R01GM-32350-09 (BIO) MASARACCHIA, RUTHANN A UNIVERSITY OF NORTH TEXAS NT STATION BOX 13048 DENTON, TX 76203 Regulation and reactivity of the H4 protein kinase

R01GM-32355-07 (MGN) SUTCLIFFE, J GREGOR 10666 NORTH TORREY PINES ROAD LA JOLLA, CA 92037 Gene expression in rat brain

R01GM-32356-06S1 (PHY) JAKOBSSON, ERIC G U OF ILLINOIS 407 S GOODWIN AVE URBANA, IL 61801 Theoretical chemical physics of ion flux in membranes

R01GM-32367-09 (BMT) DRYHURST, GLENN UNIVERSITY OF OKLAHOMA 620 PARRINGTON OVAL NORMAN, OK 73019 Oxidation chemistry of indoles

R01GM-32373-09 (PC) VARKI, AJIT UNIV OF CALIFORNIA 9500 GILMAN DR 303 MAAC 0063 LA JOLLA, CA 92093-0063 Biology of sialic acid substitutions

R01GM-32375-09 (ALY) STOLLAR, BERNARD D TUFTS UNIVERSITY 136 HARRISON AVE BOSTON, MA 02111 Antibody model for recognition of DNA helical diversity

R01GM-32384-09 (CBY) WALTER, PETER UNIVERSITY OF CALIFORNIA DEPT BIOCHEM & BIOPHYSICS SAN FRANCISCO, CA 94143-0448 Mechanism of protein translocation across membranes

R01GM-32394-08 (BMT) DAY, EDMUND P EMORY UNIVERSITY ATLANTA, GA 30322 Magnetization studies of metalloproteins

R01GM-32414-09 (SAT) DUNN, DAVID L UNIVERSITY OF MINNESOTA 515 DELEWARE ST, SE BOX 242 MINNEAPOLIS, MN 55455 Immunotherapeutic protection during bacterial sepsis

R01GM-32415-10 (BIO) PETSKO, GREGORY A BRANDEIS UNIVERSITY 415 SOUTH STREET WALTHAM, MA 02254-9110 Site-specific mutagenesis of isomerases

R01GM-32422-09 (GEN) WALBOT, VIRGINIA E STANFORD UNIVERSITY DEPT OF BIOLOGICAL SCIENCES STANFORD, CA 94305-5020 Gene isolation and transformation of maize

R01GM-32431-08 (PC) BURGERS, PETER M WASHINGTON UNIV SCH OF MEDICIN 724 SOUTH EUCLID BOX 8231 ST LOUIS, MO 63110 Enzymology of replication of yeast chromosomal DNA

R01GM-32441-09 (MBC) VAN ETTEN, JAMES L UNIVERSITY OF NEBRASKA LINCOLN, NE 48583-0722 DNA replication and gene expression of chlorella viruses

R01GM-32443-09 (CTY) BERNSTEIN, SANFORD I SAN DIEGO STATE UNIVERSITY DEPARTMENT OF BIOLOGY SAN DIEGO, CA 92182-0057 Genetics and molecular biology of myosin

R01GM-32448-09 (MBC) STEVENS, TOM H UNIVERSITY OF OREGON EUGENE, OR 97403 Cell biological study of eukaryotic organelle assembly

R01GM-32453-09 (PC) VOELKER, DENNIS R NAT'L JEWISH IMMUN CTR/RES MED 1400 JACKSON ST DENVER, CO 80206 Phospholipid dynamics in membrane assembly

R01GM-32458-08 (CBY) PARDEE, JOEL D CORNELL UNIVERSITY MED COLL 1300 YORK AVENUE NEW YORK, NY 10021 Cortical regulation of myosin assembly

R01GM-32476-07 (CTY) WANG, YU-LI WORCESTER FOUNDATION 222 MAPLE AVENUE SHREWSBURY, MA 01545 Dynamics of actin structures during cell transformation

R01GM-32488-09 (TOX) ORTIZ DE MONTELLANO, PAUL R UNIV OF CALIFORNIA 513 PARNASSUS AVE BOX 0446 SAN FRANCISCO, CA 94143 Biochemistry and hepatic toxicity of carbon radicals

R01GM-32506-10 (MBC) SHAPIRO, LUCILLE STANFORD UNIVERSITY BECKMAN CENTER, B300 STANFORD, CA 94305-5427 Regulation of differentiation in caulobacter

R01GM-32508-07A2 (CTY) MURPHY, ROBERT F CARNEGIE MELLON UNIVERSITY 4400 FIFTH AVENUE PITTSBURGH, PA 15213 Control of receptor and NA,K-ATPase traffic in mammalian

R01GM-32518-08 (GEN) WEIR, BRUCE S NORTH CAROLINA STATE UNIV BOX 8203 RALEIGH, N C 27695-8203 Theoretical population genetics

R01GM-32525-09 (MBY) SCARPULLA, RICHARD C NORTHWESTERN UNIVERSITY 303 E CHICAGO AVENUE CHICAGO, ILL 60611 Structure and expression of mammalian cytochrome C genes

R01GM-32527-10 (MCHA) SCHREIBER, STUART L HARVARD UNIVERSITY 12 OXFORD STREET CAMBRIDGE, MA 02138 Furan-carbonyl photocycloadditions in organic synthesis

R01GM-32528-09 (GEN) WESSLER, SUSAN R UNIVERSITY OF GEORGIA DEPARTMENT OF BOTANY ATHENS, GA 30602 Molecular analysis of the waxy mutants of maize

R01GM-32540-08 (GEN) JOHNSTON, HENRY M WASHINGTON UNIVERSITY 660 SOUTH EUCLID BOX 8232 ST. LOUIS, MO 63110 Gentic analysis of yeast GAL gene regulation

R01GM-32543-10 (BBCA) BUSTAMANTE, CARLOS J UNIVERSITY OF OREGON EUGENE, OR 97403 The physical chemistry of nucleic acids

R01GM-32544-08S1 (MBY) HEINTZ, NATHANIEL ROCKEFELLER UNIVERSITY LAB OF BIOCHEM & MOL BIOLOGY NEW YORK, NY 10021-6399 Gene expression during the mammalian cell cycle

R01GM-32556-09 (CBY) DENTLER, WILLIAM L UNIVERSITY OF KANSAS DEPT OF PHYSIOLOGY & CELL BIO. LAWRENCE, KS 66045 Function of

PROJECT NO., ORGANIZATIONAL UNIT., INVESTIGATOR, ADDRESS, TITLE

microtubule capping structures
R01GM-32558-07 (MBC) NEEDLEMAN, RICHARD B WAYNE STATE UNIVERSITY SCHOOL OF MEDICINE DETROIT, MI 48201 Control of maltase synthesis in yeast
R01GM-32565-09 (CTY) BLACKBURN, ELIZABETH H UNIV OF CALIFORNIA, S.F. 3RD & PARNASSUS AVE SAN FRANCISCO, CA 94143-0414 RDNA amplification and replication in Tetrahymena
R01GM-32569-07 (MCHA) FRASER-REID, BERTRAM O DUKE UNIVERSITY 101 GROSS CHEMICAL LAB DURHAM, NC 27706 Avermectin, tetrodotoxin, and radical-aldehyde cyclization
R01GM-32596-09 (SSS) SCOTT, A IAN TEXAS A&M UNIVERSITY DEPARTMENT OF CHEMISTRY COLLEGE STATION, TEX 77843 NMR studies of metabolic pathways in vivo and in vitro
R01GM-32606-08 (BMT) HUANG, P C JOHNS HOPKINS UNIVERISTY 615 NORTH WOLFE STREET BALTIMORE, MD 21205 Site specific mutation in metallothionein
R01GM-32614-12 (BBCB) GRUNER, SOL M PRINCETON UNIVERSITY JADWIN HALL BOX 708 PRINCETON, NJ 08544 X-ray diffraction studies of membranes
R01GM-32618-20 (MBC) NESTER, EUGENE W UNIVERSITY OF WASHINGTON DEPT OF MICROBIOLOGY, SC-42 SEATTLE, WASH 98195 Molecular basis of crown gall tumorigenesis
R01GM-32634-12 (PB) SILVERMAN, RICHARD B NORTHWESTERN UNIVERSITY 2145 SHERIDAN RD EVANSTON, IL 60208-3113 Chemistry of drug action of some MAO inhibitors
R37GM-32637-09 (BIO) ABELSON, JOHN N CALIFORNIA INST OF TECHNOLOGY 1201 EAST CALIFORNIA BLVD PASADENA , CA 91125 Structure and function of ribonucleic acids
R01GM-32651-09 (MBC) SMITH, ISSAR PUBLIC HEALTH RESEARCH INST 455 FIRST AVENUE NEW YORK, N Y 10016 Genetics of development in Bacillus subtilis
P01GM-32654-08 (SRC) SPITZER, JOHN J LSU MEDICAL CENTER 1901 PERDIDO STREET NEW ORLEANS, LA 70112 Mechanisms mediating metabolic changes in sepsis and burns
P01GM-32654-08 0001 (SRC) SPITZER, JOHN J Mechanisms mediating metabolic changes in sepsis and burns Dynamics of carbohydrate metabolism in sepsis
P01GM-32654-08 0002 (SRC) BAGBY, GREGORY J Mechanisms mediating metabolic changes in sepsis and burns Cytokine mediation of metabolic adjustments to sepsis
P01GM-32654-08 0004 (SRC) SPITZER, JUDY A Mechanisms mediating metabolic changes in sepsis and burns Hepatic intracellular signalling in endotoxemia and sepsis
P01GM-32654-08 0005 (SRC) NELSON, S Mechanisms mediating metabolic changes in sepsis and burns Sepsis-induced dysfunction of lung host defences
P01GM-32654-08 9001 (SRC) BAGBY, G Mechanisms mediating metabolic changes in sepsis and burns Experimental core
P01GM-32681-08 (SSS) REID, BRIAN R UNIVERSITY OF WASHINGTON DEPT OF CHEMISTRY BG-10 SEATTLE, WA 98195 Dynamic aspects of DNA recognition
P01GM-32681-08 0006 (SSS) DROBNY, GARY Dynamic aspects of DNA recognition Applications of 2-D NMR methods to the study of DNA duplexes
P01GM-32681-08 0009 (SSS) ROBINSON, BRUCE Dynamic aspects of DNA recognition Site-specific DNA dynamics
P01GM-32681-08 9001 (SSS) REID, BRIAN R Dynamic aspects of DNA recognition Core--Chemical synthesis of short DNA duplexes
P01GM-32681-08 0001 (SSS) SCHURR, J MICHAEL Dynamic aspects of DNA recognition Flexibility and recognition of DNA--Optical and NMR studies
P01GM-32681-08 0002 (SSS) REID, BRIAN R Dynamic aspects of DNA recognition DNA structure and dynamics in solution
P01GM-32681-08 0005 (SSS) KLEVIT, RACHEL Dynamic aspects of DNA recognition Drug-DNA interactions by NMR
R01GM-32690-08 (BBCA) ARORA, SATISH K UNIVERSITY OF PITTSBURGH PITTSBURGH, PA 15260 Structural investigations of mode of action of drugs
R01GM-32691-06 (BBCB) BORER, PHILIP N SYRACUSE UNIVERSITY 0-221 CTR FOR SCI & TECHNOLOGY SYRACUSE, NY 13244-4100 NMR analysis of RNA structure and dynamics
R01GM-32693-08 (MCHA) FUCHS, PHILIP L PURDUE UNIVERSITY WTHR WEST LAFAYETTE, IN 47907 Synthesis of bioactive molecules via vinyl sulfones
R01GM-32696-07 (PB) BARBER, MICHAEL J UNIVERSITY OF SOUTH FLORIDA 12901 BRUCE B DOWNS BLVD TAMPA, FL 33612 Thermodynamic properties of NADH:nitrate reductase
R01GM-32703-08 (CBY) EMR, SCOTT D CALIFORNIA INST OF TECHNOLOGY 1201 E CALIFORNIA BLVD PASADENA, CA 91125 Genetics of organelle protein delivery in yeast
R01GM-32705-07 (SAT) EHRLICH, H PAUL SHRINER BURNS INSTITUTE MASSACHUSETTS GENERAL HOSPITAL BOSTON, MASS 02114 A model for studying the contractile process in healing
R01GM-32707-08 (BBCB) LENTZ, BARRY R UNIVERSITY OF NORTH CAROLINA CB#7260 CHAPEL HILL, NC 27599-7260 Microstructural heterogeneity in membranes
R01GM-32715-08 (BBCA) BRUDVIG, GARY W YALE UNIVERSITY 12 PROSPECT PLACE NEW HAVEN, CT 06511-3516 Structure/function relations in intergral membrane proteins
R01GM-32718-10 (MCHA) MAGNUS, PHILIP D UNIVERSITY OF TEXAS AUSTIN, TX 78712-1167 Methodology for the synthesis of nitrogen heterocycles
R01GM-32734-08 (PC) SPREMULLI, LINDA L UNIVERSITY OF NORTH CAROLINA CB # 3290 VENABLE HALL CHAPEL HILL, NC 27599-3290 Mechanism of protein biosynthesis in animal mitochondria
R01GM-32741-08 (MGN) LISKAY, ROBERT M YALE UNIV SCHOOL OF MEDICINE 333 CEDAR STREET NEW HAVEN, CT 06510 Intrachromosomal recombination in mammalian cells
R01GM-32767-08 (CTY) SATIR, BIRGIT H ALBERT EINSTEIN COLLEGE OF MED 1300 MORRIS PARK AVENUE BRONX, N Y 10461 Regulation of stimulus secretion coupling
R01GM-32769-06 (BIO) GLITZ, DOHN G UCLA SCHOOL OF MEDICIME CENTER FOR THE HEALTH SCIENCES LOS ANGELES, CA 90024 Immunoelectron microscopy of modified ribosomal proteins
R01GM-32776-07 (TOX) SPECTOR, ILAN SUNY AT STONY BROOK DEPT OF PHYSIOLOGY STONY BROOK, N Y 11794 Latrunculins--Chemical and biological aspects
R01GM-32777-04A2 (BBCA) SULKES, MARK A TULANE UNIVERSITY NEW ORLEANS, LA 70118 ANS and tryptophan photophysics--Supersonic jet studies
R01GM-32785-08 (BBCB) SANDS, RICHARD H UNIVERSITY OF MICHIGAN 2200 BONISTEEL BLVD ANN ARBOR, MICHIGAN 48109-209 Structure and mechanism of redox proteins
R01GM-32812-08 (BBCA) DUAX, WILLIAM L MEDICAL FDN OF BUFFALO, INC 73 HIGH STREET BUFFALO, NY 14203-1196 Selectivity and mechanism of action of ionophores
R01GM-32821-07 (PC) SLAMA, JAMES T UNIVERSITY OF TOLEDO 2801 W. BANCROFT STREET TOLEDO, OH 43606 New chemical approacheS to ADP-ribosyl transfer
R01GM-32823-09 (BIO) MOSBAUGH, DALE W OREGON ST UNIVERSITY DEPT OF AGRICULTURAL CHEMISTRY CORVALLIS, OR 97331 Uracil-DNA repair in liver nuclei and mitochondria
R01GM-32833-08 (BIO) SANCAR, AZIZ UNIVERSITY OF NORTH CAROLINA CHAPEL HILL, NC 27599 Structure and function of UVRABC excision nuclease
R01GM-32843-08 (GEN) DUTCHER, SUSAN K UNIVERSITY OF COLORADO CAMPUS BOX 347 BOULDER, CO 80309-0347 Genetic analysis of basal body function
R01GM-32851-07 (CTY) SPRAGUE, KAREN U UNIVERSITY OF OREGON EUGENE, OR 97403 Mechanism of selective expression of tRNA genes
R01GM-32866-09 (CBY) GLENNEY, JOHN R UNIVERSITY OF KENTUCKY 800 ROSE STREET LEXINGTON, KY 40536-0084 Membrane-microfilament connections
R01GM-32875-08 (MBY) MC KNIGHT, GEORGE S UNIVERSITY OF WASHINGTON DEPT OF PHARMACOLOGY, SJ-30 SEATTLE, WA 98195 Regulation of cAMP-dependent protein kinase genes
R01GM-32877-08 (MBY) CORUZZI, GLORIA M ROCKEFELLER UNIVERSITY 1230 YORK AVENUE NEW YORK, NEW YORK 10021-6399 Plant gene regulation during N-assimilation/fixation
R01GM-32885-08 (MBC) LAWRENCE, CHRISTOPHER W UNIVERSITY OF ROCHESTER 601 ELMWOOD AVENUE ROCHESTER, NY 14642 DNA sequencing of UV-induced chromosomal mutations
R01GM-32909-08 (TMP) TELFER, WILLIAM H UNIVERSITY OF PENNSYLVANIA BIOLOGY DEPARTMENT PHILADELPHIA, PA 19104-6018 Endocytosis of blood proteins in insect development
R01GM-32910-08 (BNP) FLOSS, HEINZ G UNIVERSITY OF WASHINGTON DEPT. OF CHEMISTRY, BG-10 SEATTLE, WA 98195 Biosynthesis of riboflavin and related compounds
R01GM-32920-06A1 (SAT) GOLUB, MARI S UNIVERSITY OF CALIFORNIA DAVIS, CA 95616 Obstetric analgesia and infant outcome
R01GM-32921-08 (MBY) MELTON, DOUGLAS A HARVARD UNIVERSITY 7 DIVINITY AVENUE CAMBRIDGE, MA 02138 RNA localization and gene activation in frog development
R01GM-32937-06 (BMT) BELL, THOMAS W STATE UNIVERSITY OF NEW YORK STONY BROOK, NY 11794-3400 Large-ring and helical complexing agents for metal ions
R01GM-32955-07 (PB) MARINETTI, TIMOTHY D ROCKEFELLER UNIVERSITY 1230 YORK AVE NEW YORK, N Y 10021 Proton and ion movements in photoactive membrane proteins
R01GM-32964-09 (GEN) SOGIN, MITCHELL L MARINE BIOLOGICAL LABORATORY WATER STREET WOODS HOLE, MA 02543 Molecular phylogeny of eukaryotes
R01GM-32967-08 (GEN) WINSTON, FRED M HARVARD MEDICAL SCHOOL 25 SHATTUCK STREET BOSTON, MA 02115 Analysis of insertion mutation suppressors in yeast
R01GM-32968-08 (MBC) KUEMPEL, PETER L UNIVERSITY OF COLORADO CAMPUS BOX 347 BOULDER, CO 80309-0347 Functions of the terminus region of the chromosome
R01GM-32977-08 (CBY) VALLEE, RICHARD B WORCESTER FOUNDATION FOR 222 MAPLE AVENUE SHREWSBURY, MASS 01545 Protein components of the mitotic spindle
R01GM-32980-08 (BBCA) NALL, BARRY T UNIV OF TEX HLTH SCIENCE CTR 7703 FLOYD CURL DR SAN ANTONIO, TX 78284-7760 Folding of yeast cytochrome c
R55GM-32987-07A1 (BBCA) LU, PONZY UNIVERSITY OF PENNSYLVANIA 231 SOUTH 34TH STREET PHILADELPHIA, PA 19104-6323 Spectroscopic approaches to gene expression
R01GM-32988-07 (BBCA) PERSON, WILLIS B DEPT OF CHEMISTRY UNIVERSITY OF FLORIDA GAINESVILLE, FL 32611-2046 Vibrational spectroscopy of biochemical molecules
R01GM-32994-08A1 (MBY) KOLE, RYSZARD UNIVERSITY OF NORTH CAROLINA CB# 7295, 313 LCRC CHAPEL HILL, NC 27599 Studies on splicing of human mRNA in vitro
R01GM-33023-08 (BNP) ORGEL, LESLIE E SALK INST FOR BIOL STUDIES P O BOX 85800 SAN DIEGO, CA 92186-5800 Aqueous solution derivatization of unprotected RNA/DNA
R01GM-33048-09 (CBY) LUNA, ELIZABETH J WORCESTER FDN FOR EXPER BIOLOG 222 MAPLE AVE SHREWSBURY, MA 01545 Cytoskeleton-membrane interactions
R01GM-33049-15 (MCHA) TROST, BARRY M STANFORD UNIVERSITY MUDD BUILDING/ROOM 330 STANFORD, CA 94305-5080 Novel synthetic approaches to antitumor compounds
R01GM-33061-13 (MCHA) SCHULTZ, ARTHUR G RENSSELAER POLYTECHNIC INST TROY, NY 12180-3590 Enantioselective synthesis of natural products
R01GM-33062-08 (BBCB) BRANT, DAVID A UNIVERSITY OF CALIFORNIA IRVINE, CA 92717 Conformation and dynamics of polysaccharides
R01GM-33063-08 (PBC) ESKO, JEFFREY D UNIV OF ALABAMA BIRMINGHAM, AL 35294-0005 Genetic control of proteoglycan metabolism
R01GM-33080-09 (BMT) COUCOUVANIS, DIMITRI N UNIVERSITY OF MICHIGAN ANNA RBOR, MI 48109-1055 Iron and molybdenum complexes--Enzyme active sites
R37GM-33088-21 (PC) CLAYTON, DAVID A STANFORD UNIVERSITY DEPT. OF DEVELOPMENTAL BIOLOGY STANFORD, CA 94305-5427 Mitochondrial gene expression in malignant cells
R01GM-33132-07 (CTY) FISHER, PAUL A SUNY AT STONY BROOK STONY

PROJECT NUMBER LISTING

PROJECT NO., ORGANIZATIONAL UNIT., INVESTIGATOR, ADDRESS, TITLE

BROOK, NY 11794-8651 Molecular biology of the nuclear envelope

R37GM-33135-09 (GEN) RUBIN, GERALD M UNIVERSITY OF CALIFORNIA DEPT OF MOLECULAR & CELL BIOLO BERKELEY, CA 94720 Control of gene expression in animal cells

R01GM-33136-09 (CBY) KESSIN, RICHARD H COLUMBIA UNIVERSITY 630 WEST 168TH STREET NEW YORK, NY 10032 Control of development in Dictyostelium by cAMP

R01GM-33138-17 (PHRA) RUOHO, ARNOLD E UNIV OF WISCONSIN MED SCHOOL DEPARTMENT OF PHARMACOLOGY MADISON, WI 53706 Structure of the beta-adrenergic receptor-cyclase system

R01GM-33149-11 (BNP) SIH, CHARLES J UNIV OF WISC/SCH OF PHARMACY 425 N CHARTER STREET MADISON, WI 53706 Biocatalytic system in organic synthesis

R01GM-33160-09 (MGN) CHAPMAN, VERNE M ROSWELL PARK MEMORIAL INST ELM & CARLTON STREETS BUFFALO, NY 14263 Wild derived genetic variation

R01GM-33171-08 (CTY) MURPHY, DOUGLAS B JOHNS HOPKINS MEDICAL SCHOOL 725 NORTH WOLFE STREET BALTIMORE, MD 21205 Structure and function of tubulin variants

R01GM-33180-11 (MCHA) ZIEGLER, FREDERICK E YALE UNIVERSITY DEPT OF CHEMISTRY NEW HAVEN, CT 06520 Synthesis of macrolides and related natural products

R01GM-33184-08 (PBC) LENNARZ, WILLIAM J STATE UNIVERSITY OF NEW YORK DEPT OF BIOCHEMISTRY STONY BROOK, N Y 11794-5215 Lipid carriers in membrane glycoprotein synthesis

R37GM-33185-10 (PBC) LENNARZ, WILLIAM J SUNY AT STONY BROOK LIFE SCIENCES BUILDING STONY BROOK, NEW YORK 11794-52 Enzymatic conversion of proteins to glycoproteins

R01GM-33191-07 (MBC) WILD, JAMES R TEXAS A & M UNIVERSITY COLLEGE STATION, TX 77843-2128 Organization and regulation of the atcase cistrons

R01GM-33192-08 (BBCB) EDWARDS, BRIAN F WAYNE STATE UNIVERSITY 540 E CANFIELD DETROIT, MI 48201 Structural studies on proteins involved in hemostasis

R01GM-33200-08 (MCHA) MEYERS, ALBERT I COLORADO STATE UNIVERSITY FORT COLLINS, CO 80523 Biologically active compounds via chiral aromatics

P01GM-33205-08 (SSS) ROSBASH, MICHAEL M BRANDEIS UNIVERSITY 415 S ST/ 235 BASSINE BLDG WALTHAM, MA 02254-9110 Molecular genetics of drosophila development and behavior

P01GM-33205-08 0001 (SSS) HALL, JEFFREY C Molecular genetics of drosophila development and behavior Biological clocks--Genes, behavior and neurobiology

P01GM-33205-08 0003 (SSS) WHITE, KALPANA P Molecular genetics of drosophila development and behavior Analysis of genes essential for neurogenesis

P01GM-33205-08 0005 (SSS) ROSBASH, MICHAEL M Molecular genetics of drosophila development and behavior Molecular biology of rhythym genes

P01GM-33205-08 0006 (SSS) TULLY, TIM Molecular genetics of drosophila development and behavior Molecular cloning of Drosophila memory mutants

P01GM-33205-08 9001 (SSS) ROSBASH, MICHAEL M Molecular genetics of drosophila development and behavior Core facility

R01GM-33216-08 (BIO) REINHART, GREGORY D UNIVERSITY OF OKLAHOMA 620 PARRINGTON OVAL NORMAN, OK 73019 Mechanism of allosteric influence on enzyme activity

R01GM-33218-07 (BIO) MC ALISTER-HENN, L LEE UNIVERSITY OF CALIFORNIA IRVINE, CALIF 92717 Molecular genetics in malate dehydrogenase isozymes

R01GM-33223-07 (CTY) EPSTEIN, HENRY F BAYLOR COLLEGE OF MEDICINE ONE BAYLOR PLAZA HOUSTON, TX 77030 Genetic analysis of thick filament assembly

R01GM-33225-07 (BBCB) PRESTEGARD, JAMES H YALE UNIVERSITY 1504A YALE STATION NEW HAVEN, CT 06520 Nmr investigation of cell surface oligosaccharides

R01GM-33233-07 (MBC) MARINUS, MARTIN G UNIV OF MASS MEDICAL SCHOOL WORCESTER, MA 01655 Specificity of mismatch repair in Escherichia coli

R01GM-33237-08 (BIO) GLOVER, CLAIBORNE V UNIVERSITY OF GEORGIA ATHENS, GA 30602 Casein kinase II of Drosophila

R01GM-33247-08 (MBC) HARSHEY, RASIKA M UNIVERSITY OF TEXAS AT AUSTIN AUSTIN, TX 78712 Studies on bacteriophage Mu DNA transposition

R01GM-33265-09 (BBCB) STUBBS, GERALD J VANDERBILT UNIVERSITY BOX 1820 STA B NASHVILLE, TN 37235 Structure and assembly of helical plant viruses

R01GM-33277-07A1 (GEN) KLOBUTCHER, LAWRENCE A UNIVERSITY OF CONNECTICUT FARMINGTON, CT 06030 Genome reorganization in hypotrichous ciliated protozoa

R01GM-33279-08 (CTY) FORBES, DOUGLASS J UNIVERSITY OF CALIFORNIA 9500 GILMAN DR LA JOLLA, CA 92093-0322 A functional study of native and synthetic nuclei

R01GM-33281-08 (GEN) SANDMEYER, SUZANNE B UNIV OF CALIFORNIA IRVINE, CA 92717 Function of a transposable element in yeast

R01GM-33289-08 (CTY) SPUDICH, JAMES A STANFORD UNIV STANFORD, CA 94305 Myosin movement in vitro--Molecular characterization

R01GM-33291-08 (GEN) MUSKAVITCH, MARC A T INDIANA UNIVERSITY JORDAN HALL A504 BLOOMINGTON, IN 47405 Molecular genetics of neurogenesis

R01GM-33300-05 (MBY) DAHMUS, MICHAEL E UNIVERSITY OF CALIFORNIA DAVIS, CA 95616 Structure/function of mammalian RNA polymerase

R01GM-33301-09 (CBY) BALCH, WILLIAM E RESEARCH INST/SCRIPPS CLINIC 10666 TORREY PINES RD LA JOLLA, CA 92037 Analysis of endoplasmic reticulum export in vitro

R01GM-33309-09 (BNP) BARTON, JACQUELINE K CALIFORNIA INSTITUTE OF TECH CHEM/CHEMICAL ENG MC 164-30 PASADENA, CA 91125 Metal probes and drug binding to DNA

R01GM-33321-08 (MBY) BOGENHAGEN, DANIEL F SUNY HSC, T-8, ROOM 140 STONY BROOK, NY 11794 Mechanism of 5s RNA synthesis

R37GM-33328-09 (MCHA) EVANS, DAVID A HARVARD UNIVERSITY 12 OXFORD STREET CAMBRIDGE, MA 02138 Synthesis of amino acid derived natural products

R01GM-33330-08 (PB) ONDRIAS, MARK R UNIVERSITY OF NEW MEXICO ALBUQUERQUE, NM 87131 Heme-protein dynamics in multi-center systems

PROJECT NO., ORGANIZATIONAL UNIT., INVESTIGATOR, ADDRESS, TITLE

R01GM-33349-08 (MBC) STEEGE, DEBORAH A DUKE UNIV MEDICAL CENTER BOX 3711 DURHAM, NC 27710 Nucleic acid structure-function in gene expression

R01GM-33357-08 (PB) WOHLRAB, HARTMUT BOSTON BIOMEDICAL RES INST 20 STANIFORD STREET BOSTON, MA 02114 Pi (H+) and homologous mitochondrial anion transporters

R01GM-33369-07 (PC) MERRILL, ALFRED H, JR DEPARTMENT OF BIOCHEMISTRY EMORY UNIVERSITY SCH OF MED ATLANTA, GA 30322 Regulation of long-chain base metabolism

R01GM-33372-08 (MCHA) CURRAN, DENNIS P UNIVERSITY OF PITTSBURGH DEPARTMENT OF CHEMISTRY PITTSBURGH, PA 15260 Synthesis via sequential free radical reactions

R01GM-33376-07 (BNP) SPATOLA, ARNO F UNIVERSITY OF LOUISVILLE LOUISVILLE, KY 40292 Properties of constrained cyclic pseudopeptides

R01GM-33385-07 (BIO) JARDETZKY, OLEG STANFORD MGN RESONANCE LAB STANFORD UNIVERSITY STANFORD, CA 94305-5055 NMR studies of the mechanism of action of trp-repressor

R37GM-33397-08 (MBY) GALL, JOSEPH G CARNEGIE INSTITUTION OF WA 115 W UNIVERSITY PARKWAY BALTIMORE, MD 21210 Organization of animal cell nuclei

R01GM-33410-09 (MBY) NORDSTROM, JEFFREY L FORDHAM UNIVERSITY 441 EAST FORDHAM ROAD BRONX, NY 10458-5153 Signals for polyadenylation of globin and other RNAs

R01GM-33422-06 (GEN) WILSON, THOMAS G UNIVERSITY OF VERMONT DEPARTMENT OF ZOOLOGY BURLINGTON, VT 05405 Genetics of a hormone-resistant Drosophila mutant

R01GM-33436-07 (MBC) GROSSMAN, ARTHUR R CARNEGIE INST OF WASHINGTON DEPT OF PLANT BIOLOGY STANFORD, CA 94305 Genetic and biochemical analysis of phycobilisomes

R01GM-33449-07 (BIO) BLANCHARD, JOHN S ALBERT EINSTEIN COLLEGE OF MED 1300 MORRIS PARK AVENUE BRONX, N Y 10461 Mechanism of action of flavoprotein reductases

R01GM-33464-07 (BIO) PENNING, TREVOR M UNIVERSITY OF PENNSYLVANIA 37TH & HAMILTON WALK PHILADELPHIA, PA 19104-6084 Inhibition of 3alpha hsd by anti-inflammatory drugs

R01GM-33471-07 (MBC) HULETT, F MARION UNIVERSITY OF ILLINOIS PO BOX 4348, M/C 066 CHICAGO, IL 60680 Characterization of the B. subtilis APase gene family

R01GM-33476-07 (MBC) MATSON, STEVEN W UNIVERSITY OF NORTH CAROLINA DEPARTMENT OF BIOLOGY CHAPEL HILL, N C 27514 The enzymatic mechanisms of the E. coli helicases

R01GM-33484-07 (MCHA) SHEA, KENNETH J UNIVERSITY OF CALIFORNIA IRVINE, CA 92717 Organic synthesis

R01GM-33504-08 (MBC) RADDING, CHARLES M YALE UNIV SCHOOL OF MED 333 CEDAR ST/P.O. BOX 3333 NEW HAVEN, CT 06510 Recombination in vitro--Enzymology and intermediates

R01GM-33512-07 (MBY) STUMPH, WILLIAM E SAN DIEGO STATE UNIVERSITY SAN DIEGO, CA 92182 Transcription and processing of small nuclear RNAs

R01GM-33523-08 (CTY) NEWPORT, JOHN W UNIV OF CALIFORNIA, SAN DIEGO 9500 GILMAN DR LA JOLLA, CA 92093-0322 Biochemical analysis of nuclear structure

R01GM-33525-08 (PB) BLASIE, J KENT UNIV OF PENNSYLVANIA 231 S 34TH STREET PHILADELPHIA, PA 19104-6323 electron and proton translocation in energy coversion--structure studies

R01GM-33536-07 (BIO) KELLEHER, JOANNE K GEORGE WASHINGTON UNIVERSITY 2300 EYE ST N W WASHINGTON, D C 20037 Metabolic flux patterns in hepatoma cells

R01GM-33537-06 (MGN) LAIPIS, PHILIP J UNIVERSITY OF FLORIDA BOX J-245 JHM HEALTH CENTER GAINESVILLE, FLA 32610 Genetic analysis of mammalian mitochondrial inheritance

R01GM-33551-09 (BIO) WELCH, WILLIAM J UNIVERSITY OF CALIFORNIA SF BOX 0854 SAN FRANCISCO, CA 94143-0854 Function of the mammalian stress proteins

R01GM-33559-06A2 (CTY) SWANK, RICHARD T ROSWELL PARK MEMORIAL INST CARLTON & ELM ST BUFFALO, N Y 14263 Genetic control of the microsomal glucuronidase complex

R01GM-33571-06 (BBCB) KOSSIAKOFF, ANTHONY A UNIVERSITY OF CALIFORNIA DEPT PHARMACEUTICAL CHEMISTRY SAN FRANCISCO, CA 94143-0446 Neutron studies of protein dynamics and solvation

R01GM-33576-22 (BMT) SPIRO, THOMAS G PRINCETON UNIVERSITY DEPT OF CHEMISTRY PRINCETON, NJ 08544 Heme protein structure and dynamics

R01GM-33577-09 (MBY) NADAL-GINARD, BERNARDO CHILDREN'S HOSPITAL 300 LONGWOOD AVENUE BOSTON, MA 02115 Myosin heavy chain expression in muscle cell line

R01GM-33589-07A2 (MCHA) WULFF, WILLIAM D UNIVERSITY OF CHICAGO 5735 SOUTH ELLIS AVE CHICAGO, IL 60637 Synthetic applications of carbene complexes

R01GM-33604-07 (MCHA) KRAUS, GEORGE A IOWA STATE UNIVERSITY AMES, IA 50011 Bridgehead intermediates in synthesis

R01GM-33605-12 (MCHA) GRIECO, PAUL A INDIANA UNIVERSITY BLOOMINGTON, IN 47405 Bio-active compounds via aqueous organic chemistry

R01GM-33631-08 (CTY) JAGUS, ROSEMARY UNIVERSITY OF MARYLAND 600 EAST LOMBARD STREET BALITMORE, MD 21202 Translational control of gene expressioin by mRNA

R01GM-33656-08 (GEN) SCHUBIGER, GEROLD A UNIVERSITY OF WASHINGTON SEATTLE, WA 98195 Control of pattern formation in Drosophila

R01GM-33677-08 (MBC) STAHL, FRANKLIN W UNIVERSITY OF OREGON EUGENE, OR 97403 Genetic recombination in phage and fungi

R01GM-33683-07 (PC) HOWELL, NEIL UNIV OF TEXAS MEDICAL BRANCH 310 GAIL BORDEN BLDG, F56 GALVESTON, TX 77550-2774 Mitochondrial genetics of mammalian cells

R01GM-33688-07 (BBCB) POULOS, THOMAS L 9600 GUDELSKY DRIVE ROCKVILLE, MD 20850 Crystallographic studies on cytochrome P450

R01GM-33689-07 (CTY) RUBENSTEIN, PETER A UNIVERSITY OF IOWA COLLEGE OF MEDICINE IOWA CITY, IA 52242 Actin NH2-terminal processing and its significance

R01GM-33694-08 (CBY) BASERGA, RENATO L THOMAS JEFFERSON UNIVERSITY 1025 WALNUT STREET PHILADELPHIA, PA 19107 Biology of P53 protein

R01GM-33702-06 (PC) WOOL, IRA G UNIVERSITY OF CHICAGO 920 EAST

PROJECT NO., ORGANIZATIONAL UNIT., INVESTIGATOR, ADDRESS, TITLE

58TH STREET CHICAGO, IL 60637 The cytotoxic nuclease a-sarcin and ribosome structure
R01GM-33708-07 (BIO) STORM, DANIEL R UNIVERSITY OF WASHINGTON SEATTLE, WA 98195 Characterization of p57 -- A novel calmodulin binding protein
R01GM-33712-05 (PB) YAGI, TAKAO SCRIPPS CLINIC & RESEARCH FDN 10666 NORTH TORREY PINES ROAD LA JOLLA, CA 92037 NADH-ubiquinone reductase of Paracoccus denitrificans
R01GM-33716-05 (MBC) LEONG, SALLY A 1630 LINDEN DR MADISON, WI 53706 High affinity iron transport in Ustilago maydis
R01GM-33725-07 (CTY) TEWARI, KRISHNA K UNIVERSITY OF CALIFORNIA MOLECULAR BIOLOGY & BIOCHEM IRVINE, CA 92717 Replication of chloroplast DNA
R01GM-33741-08 (GEN) HARTL, DANIEL L WASHINGTON UNIV SCHOOL OF MED DEPT OF GENETICS/BOX 8232 ST LOUIS, MO 63110 Genetics and evolution of transposable elements
R01GM-33752-07 (MGN) SCHEFFLER, IMMO E UNIV OF CALIF, SAN DIEGO LA JOLLA, CA 92093 Molecular genetics of respiration-deficient cells
R01GM-33754-04A2 (ET) CHANG, TA-MIN GENESEE HOSPITAL 224 ALEXANDER ST ROCHESTER, NY 14607 Mechanism of cell intoxication by hybrid toxins
R01GM-33770-08 (SAT) MONAFO, WILLIAM W WASHINGTON UNIVERSITY BOX 8109 ST. LOUIS, MO 63110 Peripheral neuropathy following thermal injury
R01GM-33775-07 (PB) SLIGAR, STEPHEN G UNIVERSITY OF ILLINOIS 1209 WEST CALIFORNIA ST BOX B4 URBANA, IL 61801 Metalloenzyme mechanisms
R01GM-33776-08 (BIO) HOGENKAMP, HENRICUS P UNIVERSITY OF MINNESOTA 435 DELAWARE STREET, S E MINNEAPOLIS, MINN 55455 Ribonucleotide reductase system, active site analysis
R01GM-33778-07 (MBC) VILLAREJO, MERNA R UNIVERSITY OF CALIFORNIA DAVIS, CA 95616 Molecular mechanisms of adaptation to osmotic stress
R01GM-33779-08 (MBC) YOUNG, ELTON T, II UNIVERSITY OF WASHINGTON DEPT OF BIOCHEMISTRY, SJ-70 SEATTLE, WA 98195 Genetic analysis of protein transport into mitochondria
R01GM-33780-05 (BMT) RUSSELL, DAVID H TEXAS A&M UNIVERSITY DEPARTMENT OF CHEMISTRY COLLEGE STATION, TX 77843 Cesium ion desorption ionization-FTMS for biolocules
R01GM-33782-07 (GEN) LEVIN, BRUCE R UNIVERSITY OF MASSACHUSETTS DEPARTMENT OF ZOOLOGY AMHERST, MASS 01003-0027 Population biology of bacterial viruses and plasmids
R01GM-33783-08 (GEN) CLARKE, LOUISE B UNIV OF CALIFORNIA SANTA BARBARA, CA 93106 Chromosome segregation in Schizosaccharomyces pombe
R01GM-33787-07 (CTY) MC INTOSH, JOHN R UNIV OF COLORADO AT BOULDER DEVELOPMENTAL BIOLOGY BOULDER, CO 80309 Microtubule polymerization and dynamics in vivo
R01GM-33804-07 (PB) MAUK, ARTHUR G UNIVERSITY OF BRITISH COLUMBIA COPP BLDG VANCOUVER, BC V6T 1W5 CANADA Mutagenesis-assisted functional studies of cytochrome C
R01GM-33806-09 (PB) JOHNSON, MICHAEL K UNIVERSITY OF GEORGIA SCHOOL OF CHEMICAL SCIENCES ATHENS, GA 30602 Mitochondrial iron-sulfur proteins
R01GM-33808-08 (BIO) HEFFRON, FRED L OREGON HEALTH SCIS UNIV 3181 SW SAM JACKSON PARK RD PORTLAND, OR 97201-3098 The role of nucleases in recombination in yeast
R01GM-33825-07 (BBCB) PETICOLAS, WARNER L UNIVERSITY OF OREGON CHEMISTRY DEPARTMENT EUGENE, OREG 97403 Laser Raman probe of molecular structure in living cells
R01GM-33830-08 (CTY) KIEHART, DANIEL P HARVARD UNIVERSITY 16 DIVINITY AVENUE CAMBRIDGE, MA 02138 Cytoplasmic myosin function in vitro and in vivo
R01GM-33841-07 (BIO) MITCHELL, JOHN L NORTHERN ILLINOIS UNIVERSITY DEPT OF BIOLOGICAL SCIENCES DEKALB, ILL 60115 Ornithine decarboxylase modification and inactivation
R01GM-33842-06 (BIO) ANDERSON, PAUL M UNIV OF MINNESOTA SCH OF MED 10 UNIVERSITY DRIVE DULUTH, MN 55812 Cyanase and the cyanase operon
R01GM-33850-08 (PB) HOKIN, LOWELL E 1300 UNIVERSITY AVENUE MADISON, WI 53706 (Na,K)-ATPase--Structure, biosynthesis, and regulation
R01GM-33851-07 (PB) KURZ, LINDA C WASHINGTON UNIVERSITY SCH OF M 660 SOUTH EUCLID AVE, BX 8094 ST LOUIS, MO 63110 Direct observation of enzymatic catalytic strategies
R01GM-33868-08 (NEUC) EVANS, GLEN A SALK INST/BIOLOGICAL STUDIES P O BOX 85800 SAN DIEGO, CALIF 92138 Regulation of gene expression in neural tissue
R01GM-33881-05 (BMT) MC LENDON, GEORGE L UNIVERSITY OF ROCHESTER HUTCHISON HALL ROCHESTER, NY 14627 Electron transfer in proteins
R01GM-33882-07 (BMT) STOLZENBERG, ALAN M WEST VIRGINIA UNIVERSITY MORGANTOWN WV 26506 Model studies of hydroporphyrin-containing enzymes
R01GM-33894-07 (BIO) RAUSHEL, FRANK M TEXAS A&M UNIVERSITY DEPARTMENT OF CHEMISTRY COLLEGE STATION, TEX 77843 Isotopic probes of enzymatic reaction mechanisms
R01GM-33904-07 (CBY) MELLMAN, IRA S YALE UNIVERSITY SCH OF MED 333 CEDAR STREET NEW HAVEN, CT 06510 Acidification of the endocytic pathway
R01GM-33915-09 (MBY) KOZAK, MARILYN S UNIVERSTIY OF MED & DENT OF NJ 675 HOES LANE PISCATAWAY, N J 08854-5635 Translational control mediated by mrna structure
R01GM-33922-08 (PB) MERTES, KRISTIN B UNIVERSITY OF KANSAS 2099 CONSTANT AVE CAMPUS WEST LAWRENCE, KS 66047 Polyammonium macrocycle catalysis of phosphoryl transfer
R01GM-33927-07S1 (PC) LA PORTE, DAVID C UNIVERSITY OF MINNESOTA 4-225 MILLARD HALL MINNEAPOLIS, MINN 55455 Structure regulation of a protein kinase/phosphatase
R01GM-33928-07 (GEN) LANDY, ARTHUR BROWN UNIVERSITY PROVIDENCE, R I 02912 Recombination intermediates--Formation, properties and resolution
R01GM-33943-08 (CTY) KUCHERLAPATI, RAJU S ALBERT EINSTEIN COLLEGE OF MED 1300 MORRIS PARK AVENUE BRONX, NY 10461 Gene replacement in mammalian cells

PROJECT NO., ORGANIZATIONAL UNIT., INVESTIGATOR, ADDRESS, TITLE

R01GM-33944-08 (BIO) OSHEROFF, NEIL VANDERBILT UNIVERSITY SCH OF M 621 LIGHT HALL NASHVILLE, TN 37232-0146 Function and biology of eukaryotic DNA topoisomerases
R01GM-33956-07 (BM) CLEWELL, DON B UNIVERSITY OF MICHIGAN ANN ARBOR, MI 48109-0402 Sex pheromone-induced plasmid transfer
R01GM-33959-06A1 (GEN) SHEARN, ALLEN D JOHNS HOPKINS UNIVERSITY 34TH & CHARLES STREETS BALTIMORE, MD 21218 Genes which regulate growth of Drosophila imaginal discs
R01GM-33962-07 (PB) KYTE, JACK E UNIV OF CALIFORNIA, SAN DIEGO LA JOLLA, CA 92093-0506 Structure of a protein catalyzing active transport
R01GM-33965-07 (BMT) HALES, BRIAN J LOUISIANA STATE UNIVERSITY DEPT OF CHEMISTRY BATON ROUGE, LA 70803 Vanadium-containing nitrogenase
R01GM-33967-07 (SSS) COTTER, ROBERT J JOHNS HOPKINS SCHOOL OF MEDICI 725 N WOLFE STREET BALTIMORE, MD 21205 A versatile TOF MS/MS instrument
R01GM-33976-08 (BIO) MEANS, ANTHONY R DUKE UNIVERSITY MEDICAL CENTER PO BOX 3813 DURHAM, NC 27710 Structure/function of genetic engineered calmodulins
R01GM-33977-08 (VR) GREEN, MICHAEL R 373 PLANTATION STREET WORCESTER, MA 01605 Adenovirus transcriptional regulation & transformation
R01GM-33984-06 (MBY) NELSON, TIMOTHY M YALE UNIVERSITY 12 PROSPECT PLACE NEW HAVEN, CT 06511 Expression of c4 genes in development of maize leaf cell types
R01GM-33992-08 (MBC) KAGUNI, JON M MICHIGAN STATE UNIVERSITY EAST LANSING, MI 48824-1319 Mechanisms of Escherichia coli chromosomal replication
R01GM-33995-08 (TMP) JONES, DAVY UNIVERSITY OF KENTUCKY 204 FUNKHOUSER BLDG LEXINGTON, KY 40506 Parasite manipulation of host insect endocrinology
R01GM-33998-07 (MBY) COLE, CHARLES N DARTMOUTH MEDICAL SCHOOL DEPARTMENT OF BIOCHEMISTRY HANOVER, N H 03756 Regulation of the metabolism of eucaryotic mRNA
R01GM-34001-07 (PBC) KNAUER, DANIEL J UNIVERSITY OF CALIFORNIA IRVINE, CA 92717 Nexin-I in the regulation of extracellular proteases
R01GM-34005-13 (BMT) SCHWARTZ, JEFFREY PRINCETON UNIVERSITY DEPARTMENT OF CHEMISTRY PRINCETON, N J 08544 Stabilized prostacyclins to treat vascular disease
R01GM-34009-08 (BIO) HAAS, ARTHUR L MEDICAL COLLEGE OF WISCONSIN 8701 WATERTOWN PLANK ROAD MILWAUKEE, WI 53226 Atp, ubiquitin-dependent proteolysis
R01GM-34014-07 (MCHA) DAVIS, FRANKLIN A DREXEL UNIVERSITY 32ND AND CHESTNUT ST PHILADELPHIA, PA 19104 Synthesis of alpha-hydroxycarbonyl compounds
R01GM-34015-07 (BBCA) HARVEY, STEPHEN C BIOCHEMISTRY DEPARTMENT UAB, UNIVERSITY STATION BIRMINGHAM, AL 35294 Conformation and dynamics of deoxyribonucleic acids
R01GM-34023-06 (GEN) NOVOTNY, CHARLES P UNIVERSITY OF VERMONT MOLECULAR GENETICS BURLINGTON, VT 05405 Mating type in schizophyllum
R01GM-34028-08 (GEN) AMBROS, VICTOR R HARVARD UNIVERSITY CELLULAR & DEVELOPMENTAL BIO CAMBRIDGE, MA 02138 Genetic control of nematode development
R01GM-34035-06A1 (TMP) ARONSON, ARTHUR I PURDUE UNIVERSITY WEST LAFAYETTE, IN 47907 Bacillus thuringiensis protoxin structure and synthesis
R01GM-34036-08 (VR) BROWN, JAY C UNIV OF VIRGINIA HLTH SCI CTR BOX 441 CHARLOTTESVILLE, VA 22908 Virus structure determination by ion etching
R01GM-34059-06 (CTY) STROME, SUSAN INDIANA UNIVERSITY JORDAN HALL BLOOMINGTON, IN 47405 Control of early development C. elegans
R01GM-34073-07 (BBCA) BLESSING, ROBERT H MED. FOUND. OF BUFFALO, INC. 73 HIGH STREET BUFFALO, NY 14203 Structural chemical studies of metabolic phosphates
R01GM-34077-07A1 (SSS) WEAVER, JAMES C MASSACHUSETTS INST OF TECHNOLO 77 MASSACHUSETTS AVE CAMBRIDGE, MA 02139 Measurement of growth and secretion of single cells
R01GM-34081-08 (BBCA) DAVIDSON, ERNEST R DEPARTMENT OF CHEMISTRY INDIANA UNIVERSITY BLOOMINGTON, IN 47405 Electronic structure of biocarbonyls
R01GM-34090-08 (PBC) KURKINEN, MARKKU T UNIV OF MED & DENT OF N J 675 HOES LANE PISCATAWAY, N J 08854 Developmental control of type IV collagen synthesis
R01GM-34095-08 (GEN) CARLSON, MARIAN B HAMMER HEALTH SCIENCES CENTER 701 WEST 168TH STREET NEW YORK, N Y 10032 Regulation of yeast invertase gene expression
R01GM-34102-08 (BBCA) HENDRICKSON, WAYNE A COLUMBIA UNIVERSITY BIOCHEM & MOLECULAR BIOPHYSICS NEW YORK, N Y 10032 Anomalous-scattering studies of macromolecular structure
R01GM-34107-08 (CBY) RODRIGUEZ-BOULAN, ENRIQUE J CORNELL UNIV MEDICAL COLLEGE 1300 YORK AVENUE NEW YORK, NY 10021 Sorting of plasma membrane proteins in epithelial cells
R01GM-34127-15 (MBC) KENNELL, DAVID E WASHINGTON UNIV SCH OF MED DEPT OF MICROBIO & IMMUNOLOGY ST LOUIS, MO 63110 Messenger RNA metabolism in bacteria
R01GM-34132-20 (MBC) SCHAECHTER, MOSELIO TUFTS UNIVERSITY 136 HARRISON AVENUE BOSTON, MA 02111 Bacterial cell membrane--Growth and cell division
R01GM-34150-08S1 (MBC) YOUDERIAN, PHILIP A CALIF INST OF BIOLOG RESEARCH 11099 NORTH TORREY PINES ROAD LA JOLLA, CA 92037 Genetic analysis of repressor/DNA recognition
R37GM-34167-17 (MCHA) COREY, ELIAS J HARVARD UNIVERSITY 12 OXFORD STREET CAMBRIDGE, MA 02138 Antiviral/bioactive compounds--synthesis and chemistry
R01GM-34170-07 (GEN) CAVENER, DOUGLAS R VANDERBILT UNIVERSITY NASHVILLE, TENN 37235 Evolution of gene regulation in Drosophila
R01GM-34171-08 (BBCA) SHORTLE, DAVID R JOHNS HOPKINS UNIVERSITY 725 N WOLFE ST BALTIMORE, MD 21205-2185 Biophysical studies of folding mutants of staph nuclease
R01GM-34180-05 (MBC) MENDELSON, NEIL H UNIVERSITY OF ARIZONA BIOSCIENCES WEST 308 TUCSON, AZ 85721 Biomechanics of bacteria

R37GM-34182-08 (PBC) SLY, WILLIAM S ST LOUIS UNIVERSITY SCH OF MED 1402 S GRAND BLVD ST LOUIS, MO 63104 Receptor mediated transport of lysosomal enzymes
R01GM-34190-12 (MBY) TYE, BIK-KWOON CORNELL UNIVERSITY BIOCHEM, MOLEC & CELL BIO ITHACA, N Y 14853 DNA replication in yeast
R01GM-34205-07 (MBC) CROTHERS, DONALD M YALE UNIVERSITY P O BOX 6666 NEW HAVEN, CT 06511 Mechanism of transcription initiation
R01GM-34218-09 (VISA) FOSTER, KENNETH W SYRACUSE UNIVERSITY 201 PHYSICS BUILDING SYRACUSE, NY 13244-1130 Analysis of rhodopsin-like photoreceptors
R01GM-34220-07 (BBCA) JOHNSON, JOHN E PURDUE UNIVERSITY WEST LAFAYETTE, IN 47907 High resolution structural studies of insect viruses
R01GM-34225-07 (HEM) FOWLER, VELIA M INSTITUTE OF SCRIPPS CLINIC 10666 NORTH TORREY PINES RD. LA JOLLA, CA 92037 Actin organization in normal and abnormal red cells
R01GM-34231-07 (CTY) SOLLNER-WEBB, BARBARA T JOHNS HOPKINS UNIVERSITY 725 N WOLFE STREET BALTIMORE, MD 21205 Specificity of eukaryotic RNA production
R01GM-34236-07 (BIO) SIMON, MELVIN I CALIFORNIA INST OF TECHNOLOGY PASADENA, CALIFORNIA 91125 Molecular basis of signal transduction
R01GM-34238-07 (BCE) LINZER, DANIEL I NORTHWESTERN UNIVERSITY 2153 SHERIDAN ROAD EVANSTON, IL 60208 Proliferin--action and expression of a new prolactinoid
R01GM-34248-05 (SSS) NORTHRUP, SCOTT H TENNESSEE TECHNOLOGICAL UNIV BOX 5055 COOKEVILLE, TN 38505 Protein-protein and protein-DNA association in solution
R01GM-34250-06 (SSS) SWARTZ, HAROLD M UNIVERSITY OF ILLINOIS 506 S MATHEWS-190 MED SCI BLDG URBANA, ILLINOIS 61801 Measurement of intracellular oxygen by ESR
R01GM-34275-07 (MCHA) MEYERS, ALBERT I COLORADO STATE UNIVERSITY FORT COLLINS, COLORADO 80523 Approaches to complex chiral quaternary carbon compounds
R01GM-34277-07 (MBY) SHARP, PHILLIP A MASS INSTITUTE OF TECHNOLOGY 77 MASSACHUSETTS AVENUE CAMBRIDGE, MA 02139-4307 Regulation of mRNA processing
R37GM-34296-08 (GEN) FEDOROFF, NINA V CARNEGIE INST OF WASHINGTON 115 WEST UNIVERSITY PARKWAY BALTIMORE, MD 21210 Transposition and developmental regulation of spm
R01GM-34297-06A2 (CBY) DRAPER, ROCKFORD K UNIV OF TEXAS @ DALLAS 2601 N. FLOYD ROAD RICHARDSON, TX 75083-0688 Mutants with defects in endocytic function
R01GM-34310-07 (TOX) LASKIN, DEBRA L RUTGERS UNIVERSITY COLLEGE OF PHARMACY PISCATAWAY, N J 08854 Role of kupffer cells in chemical toxicity
R01GM-34324-07 (MBC) CHAMBLISS, GLENN H UNIVERSITY OF WISCONSIN 1550 LINDEN DRIVE MADISON, WISCONSIN 53706 Genetic analysis of Bacillus subtilis amylase synthesis
R01GM-34341-06 (BBCB) EVANS, D FENNELL UNIVERSITY OF MINNESOTA MATERIALS SCIENCE MINNEAPOLIS, MN 55455 Direct measurement of bio-colloidal interaction forces
R01GM-34343-07 (BBCB) MAKOWSKI, LEE BOSTON UNIVERSITY 590 COMMONWEALTH AVE BOSTON, MA 02215 Neutron diffraction studies of viruses
R01GM-34351-07 (BBCB) RECORD, M THOMAS JR UNIVERSITY OF WISCONSIN 1101 UNIVERSITY AVE MADISON, WI 53706 NMR and Monte Carlo studies of cation-DNA interactions
R01GM-34352-06A2 (MBC) MINDICH, LEONARD E PUBLIC HEALTH RESEARCH INST 455 FIRST AVENUE NEW YORK, NY 10016 Packaging of the segmented genome of bacteriophage phi6
R01GM-34360-07 (BBCB) YONATH, ADA WEIZMANN INSTITUTE OF SCIENCE REHOVOT 76100 ISRAEL Crystallographic studies on ribosomal particles
R01GM-34365-07 (GEN) YOUNG, RICHARD A WHITEHEAD INST FOR BIOMED RES 9 CAMBRIDGE CENTER CAMBRIDGE, MA 02142 Genetic and biochemical analysis of yeast RNA polymerase
R01GM-34396-08 (CBY) HIRSCHBERG, CARLOS B UNIV OF MASSACHUSETTS MED CTR 55 LAKE AVENUE NORTH WORCESTER, MA 01655 Membrane topology and biosynthesis of glycosaminoglycans
R01GM-34399-07 (GMB) FRIEDMAN, PETER A DARTMOUTH MEDICAL SCHOOL HANOVER, NH 03756 Cellular calcium transport in urinary epithelia
R01GM-34431-08 (MBY) LEVINE, MICHAEL S UNIV OF CALIF, SAN DIEGO 9500 GILMAN DRIVE LA JOLLA, CA 92093-0322 Spatial realms of homeotic gene expression in Drosophila
R01GM-34432-07 (CTY) MERRILL, GARY F OREGON STATE UNIVERSITY DEPT OF BIOCHEMISTRY & BIOPHYS CORVALLIS, OR 97331 Developmentally-regulated inhibition of DNA replication
R01GM-34433-07 (CBY) HORWICH, ARTHUR L YALE UNIVERSITY DEPT. OF HUMAN GENETICS NEW HAVEN, CT 06510 Targeting of human OTC to the mitochondrial matrix
R01GM-34436-07 (PB) GARGUS, JOHN J EMORY UNIVERSITY ATLANTA, GA 30322 Isolation of the gene encoding the NA-K-CL cotransporter
R01GM-34437-06 (GEN) LEFEBVRE, PAUL A 250 BIOLOGICAL SCIENCES CTR UNIVERSITY OF MINNESOTA ST PAUL, MN 55108 Genetic analysis of flagellar gene expression
R01GM-34442-08 (MCHA) COMINS, DANIEL L NORTH CAROLINA STATE UNIV RALEIGH, N C 27695-8204 Synthesis and synthetic utility of 1-acyldihydropyridines
R01GM-34443-07 (BMT) TERNER, JAMES VIRGINIA COMMONWEALTH UNIV 1001 WEST MAIN STREET RICHMOND, VA 23284-2006 Resonance raman spectroscopy of chemical transients
R01GM-34454-07 (BMT) KOZARICH, JOHN W UNIVERSITY OF MARYLAND DEPT CHEM & BIOCHEMISTRY COLLEGE PARK, MD 20742 Mechanisms of drug-induced DNA degradation
R01GM-34468-07 (BMT) LOEHR, THOMAS M OREGON GRADUATE INSTITUTE 19600 N W VON NEUMANN DRIVE BEAVERTON, OR 97006-1999 Spectroscopy of biological saturated porphyrins
R01GM-34469-07 (BBCA) BRESLAUER, KENNETH J RUTGERS UNIVERSITY DEPT OF CHEMISTRY NEW BRUNSWICK, NJ 08903 Drug-DNA interactions--Thermodynamics of recognition
R01GM-34478-07 (PB) FORGAC, MICHAEL D TUFTS UNIVERSITY SCHOOL OF MED DEPARTMENT OF PHYSIOLOGY BOSTON, MA 02111 Characterization of the coated vesicle proton pump
R01GM-34492-06 (MCHA) HOYE, THOMAS R UNIVERSITY OF MINNESOTA 207 PLEASANT STREET, SE MINNEAPOLIS, MN 55455 2, 5-linked tetrahydrofurans--uVaricin-related synthesis
R01GM-34496-07 (MBC) ROCK, CHARLES O ST JUDE CHILDREN'S RES HOSP 332 N LAUDERDALE MEMPHIS, TN 38105 Regulation of fatty acid biosynthesis
R37GM-34497-11 (PHRA) GILMAN, ALFRED G UNIV OF TEXAS SW MEDICAL CENTE 5323 HARRY HINES BLVD DALLAS, TX 75235 Regulation of cyclic nucleotide metabolism
R01GM-34500-08 (PHRA) TOEWS, MYRON L UNIV OF NEBRASKA MED CTR DEPT OF PHARM, POYNTER HALL OMAHA, NEBRASKA 68105-1065 Mechanisms of desensitization of adrenergic receptors
R01GM-34504-07 (BBCA) PATEL, DINSHAW J COLUMBIA UNIVERSITY 630 WEST 168TH STREET NEW YORK, NY 10032 DNA architecture and chemotherapeutic recognition
R01GM-34507-04A2 (PHRA) SOINE, WILLIAM H VIRGINIA COMMONWEALTH UNIV BOX 540/MCV STATION RICHMOND, VA 23298-0540 N-glucosylation of barbiturates and related drugs
R37GM-34509-22 (BBCA) NAKANISHI, KOJI COLUMBIA UNIVERSITY DEPARTMENT OF CHEMISTRY NEW YORK, N Y 10027 Structural and biological studies of bioactive compounds
R01GM-34517-07 (BIO) BEACH, DAVID H COLD SPRING HARBOR LABORATORY P O BOX 100 COLD SPRING HARBOR, N Y 11724 Control of meiosis in fission yeast
R01GM-34527-08 (MBC) PACE, NORMAN R DEPARTMENT OF BIOLOGY INDIANA UNIVERSITY BLOOMINGTON, IN 47405 Function and metabolism of RNA
R01GM-34534-11 (EVR) GLORIOSO, JOSEPH C UNIVERSITY OF PITTSBURGH 3550 TERRACE STREET PITTSBURGH, PA 15261 Genetic variation and immuobiology of HSV glycoprotein C
R01GM-34537-06 (MBY) FOLK, WILLIAM R UNIVERSITY OF MISSOURI 117 SCHWEITZER - 65211 COLUMBIA, MO 65212 Expression of pol 3 transcribed genes
R01GM-34541-07 (SSS) BRYANT, ROBERT G UNIVERSITY OF ROCHESTER 601 ELMWOOD AVE ROCHESTER, NY 14642 Biophysical dynamics--Magnetic resonance approaches
R01GM-34548-07 (BBCB) BIRGE, ROBERT R SYRACUSE UNIVERSITY DEPARTMENT OF CHEMISTRY SYRACUSE, N Y 13244 Photophysics of visual chromophores and rhodopsin
R01GM-34557-08 (BIO) MARIANS, KENNETH J SLOAN-KETTERING INST/CNCR RES NEW YORK, N Y 10021 Initiation of lagging strand DNA synthesis
R01GM-34558-08 (MBC) MARIANS, KENNETH J SLOAN-KETTERING INST/CNCR RES NEW YORK, N Y 10021 Role of topoisomerases in DNA metabolism
R37GM-34559-08 (NSS) HURWITZ, JERRAD SLOAN-KETTERING INST/CANCER RE 1275 YORK AVENUE NEW YORK, NY 10021 Studies on procaryotic and eucaryotic DNA replication
R01GM-34561-06 (CBY) KLEIN, CLAUDETTE ST LOUIS UNIV SCHL OF MED 1402 S GRAND BOULEVARD ST LOUIS, MO 63104 Cell specific cohesion in D discoideum
R01GM-34572-08 (BIO) GERLT, JOHN A UNIVERSITY OF MARYLAND COLLEGE PARK, MD 20742 Mechanisms of enzymatic reactions in dark DNA repair
R01GM-34573-08 (BIO) GERLT, JOHN A UNIVERSITY OF MARYLAND COLLEGE PARK, MD 20742 Mechanism of the staphylococcal nuclease reaction
R01GM-34587-08 (GEN) ROTHSTEIN, RODNEY J COLUMBIA UNIV., COLLEGE OF P&S 701 WEST 168TH ST-HHSC 1516 NEW YORK, NY 10032 Mechanisms of genetic recombination
R01GM-34596-08 (MGN) BROACH, JAMES R PRINCETON UNIVERSITY DEPT OF MOLECULAR BIOLOGY PRINCETON, N J 08544 Gene expression of the yeast plasmid 2 micron circle
R01GM-34607-06 (MBC) BEACH, DAVID H COLD SPRING HARBOR LABORATORY PO BOX 100 COLD SPRING HARBOR, NY 11724 Control of cell division in fission yeast
R01GM-34614-08 (MBC) MASKER, WARREN E TEMPLE UNIV SCHOOL OF MEDICINE DEPARTMENT OF BIOCHEMISTRY PHILADELPHIA, PA 19140 The fidelity of in vitro DNA repair and replication
R01GM-34615-06 (MBY) OSTROWSKI, MICHAEL C DUKE UNIVERSITY MEDICAL CTR POST OFFICE 3020 DURHAM, N C 27710 Analysis of regulated promoters isolated as chromatin
R01GM-34622-07 (MBC) KREUZER, KENNETH N DUKE UNIV MED CTR/BOX 3020 DEPT OF MICROBIO & IMMUNOLOGY DURHAM, NORTH CAROLINA 27710 Initiation of DNA replication in the phage t4 system
R01GM-34630-07 (GEN) PIRROTTA, VINCENZO BAYLOR COLLEGE 1 BAYLOR PLAZA HOUSTON, TX 77030 Position dependent gene expression in Drosophila
R01GM-34635-07 (CBY) BRAELL, WILLIAM A HARVARD MEDICAL SCHOOL 240 LONGWOOD AVENUE BOSTON, MA 02115 Biochemistry of endocytosis and recycling
R01GM-34685-07 (BBCA) HOLTEN, DEWEY WASHINGTON UNIVERSITY ONE BROOKINGS DRIVE ST LOUIS, MO 63130 Excited state dynamics of transition metal porphyrins
R01GM-34687-05 (BBCA) HINGERTY, BRIAN E MARTIN MARIETTA SYS INC OAK RIDGE NATIONAL LABORATORY OAK RIDGE, TENN 37831 Hydrogen bond studies of cyclodextrins
R01GM-34690-07 (SAT) MC INTOSH, TRACY K UNIV OF CONNECTICUT HLTH CTR DEPT OF SURGERY FARMINGTON, CT 06030 Endorphins in shock and trauma
R01GM-34695-07 (SAT) LOWRY, STEPHEN F 525 EAST 68 STREET, F2016 NEW YORK, N Y 10021 Muscle protein response--immobility, injury and depletion
R01GM-34710-07 (MCHA) GRAY, GARY R UNIVERSITY OF MINNESOTA 207 PLEASANT ST S E MINNEAPOLIS, MINN 55455 Reductive cleavage method for glycan structural analysis
R01GM-34711-07 (GEN) MORRIS, N RONALD UMDNJ/ROBERT W JOHNSON MED SCH 675 HOES LANE PISCATAWAY, N J 08854 Molecular biology of mitosis in Aspergillus nidulans
R01GM-34715-07 (MBC) MALOY, STANLEY R UNIVERSITY OF ILLINOIS 407 SOUTH GOODWIN AVENUE URBANA, ILL 61801 Genetics of flavin dehydrogenase-membrane interactions
R01GM-34719-07 (GEN) JENNESS, DUANE D UNIV OF MASSACHUSETTS MED

PROJECT NO., ORGANIZATIONAL UNIT., INVESTIGATOR, ADDRESS, TITLE

SCH 55 LAKE AVENUE NORTH WORCESTER, MA 01655 Control of alpha-factor receptor activity in yeast a cells

R01GM-34740-07 (MBY) SACHS, MARTIN M UNIVERSITY OF MISSOURI-COLUMBI COLUMBIA, MO 65211 Analysis of the anaerobic-stress response in maize

R01GM-34765-06A1 (MBC) ELY, BERT UNIVERSITY OF SOUTH CAROLINA COLUMBIA, SC 29208 Gene regulation and promoter sequences in caulobacter

R01GM-34766-08 (MBC) TAI, PHANG C GEORGIA STATE UNIVERSITY UNIVERSITY PLAZA ATLANTA, GA 30303 Protein translocation across Escherichia coli membranes

R01GM-34767-06 (SAT) LITT, LAWRENCE UNIVERSITY OF CALIFORNIA C-450 SAN FRANCISCO, CA 94143 Brain metabolism during anesthesia, low pHi, and hypoxia

R01GM-34770-07 (CBY) MAXFIELD, FREDERICK R COLUMBIA UNIV./SCH. OF MEDICIN 630 WEST 168 STREET NEW YORK, NY 10032 Cytosolic free calcium and cell motility

R01GM-34775-04 (NEUC) CHALFIE, MARTIN COLUMBIA UNIVERSITY 1012 FAIRCHILD CENTER NEW YORK, NY 10027 Genetic analysis of neuronal degeneration in C. elegans

P01GM-34781-07 (SRC) MOLINOFF, PERRY B UNIVERSITY OF PENNSYLVANIA PHILADELPHIA, PA 19104-6084 Pharmacology of receptor/effector systems

P01GM-34781-07 0002 (SRC) MCGONIGLE, PAUL Pharmacology of receptor/effector systems Regulation of dopamine receptors

P01GM-34781-07 0004 (SRC) MANNING, DAVID R Pharmacology of receptor/effector systems Regulation of effector mechanisms

P01GM-34781-07 0005 (SRC) MOLINOFF, PERRY B Pharmacology of receptor/effector systems Regulation of excitatory animo acid receptors

P01GM-34781-07 9002 (SRC) EBERWINE, JAMES H Pharmacology of receptor/effector systems Core--Molecular biology

P01GM-34781-07 9003 (SRC) CHESSELET, MARIE-FRANCOISE Pharmacology of receptor/effector systems Core--Image analysis

R01GM-34788-06 (SAT) GANDOLFI, A JAY UNIVERSITY OF ARIZONA DEPARTMENT OF ANESTHESIOLOGY TUCSON, AZ 85724 Immune mechanisms in halothane hepatitis

R01GM-34799-06 (BMT) NICHOLAS, KENNETH M UNIVERSITY OF OKLAHOMA 620 PARRINGTON OVAL NORMAN, OK 73019 Chemistry and synthetic utility of cobalt-diene and acetylene complexes

R01GM-34804-07 (MBC) ROTH, JOHN R UNIVERSITY OF UTAH SALT LAKE CITY, UT 84112 Biosynthesis of vitamin B12 and anaerobic metabolism

R01GM-34809-07 (BBCA) OLSON, WILMA K RUTGERS UNIVERSITY DEPARTMENT OF CHEMISTRY NEW BRUNSWICK, N J 08903 Theoretical aspects of DNA supercoiling

R01GM-34812-07 (PB) BEINERT, HELMUT MEDICAL COLLEGE OF WISCONSIN MILWAUKEE, WISCONSIN 53226 New aspects of structure-function of iron-sulfur proteins

R01GM-34821-07 (MBC) SILHAVY, THOMAS J PRINCETON UNIVERSITY PRINCETON, NJ 08544 Genetic analysis of protein export

R01GM-34823-06 (PB) PLATZ, MATTHEW S OHIO STATE UNIVERSITY 140 WEST 18TH ST COLUMBUS, OH 43210-1173 Application of low temperature chemistry and kinetics--Photo affinity labelling

R01GM-34825-07 (PC) HAUSWIRTH, WILLIAM W UNIVERSITY OF FLORIDA COLLEGE OF MED/BOX J-266/JHMHC GAINESVILLE, FLA 32610-0266 Molecular biology and variation in mammalian mtDNA

R01GM-34838-05 (MBC) DIEDRICH, DANA L IDAHO STATE UNIVERSITY CAMPUS BOX 8334 POCATELLO, ID 83209-8334 Membrane interactions between Bdellovibrio and its prey

R01GM-34841-06 (BMT) BURROWS, CYNTHIA J STATE UNIVERSITY OF NEW YORK STONY BROOK, NY 11794-3400 Synthetic metalloenzymes as regioselective reagents

R01GM-34846-07 (BNP) WILCOX, CRAIG S UNIVERSITY OF PITTSBURGH DEPARTMENT OF CHEMISTRY PITTSBURGH, PA 15260 Synthetic receptors and functional group arrays

R01GM-34847-07 (BBCA) PRENDERGAST, FRANKLYN G MAYO CLINIC/FOUNDATION 200 FIRST STREET SOUTHWEST ROCHESTER, MN 55905 Structure-luminescence correlations in proteins

R01GM-34850-07 (MBY) BENYAJATI, CHEEPTIP UNIVERSITY OF ROCHESTER ROCHESTER, NEW YORK 14627 Gene control in development transcription and chromatin

R01GM-34852-06 (NLS) MAAYANI, SAUL MOUNT SINAI SCHOOL OF MEDICINE NEW YORK, N Y 10029 5-HT receptors and their effectors

R01GM-34862-06 (MCHA) CURRAN, DENNIS P UNIVERSITY OF PITTSBURGH DEPARTMENT OF CHEMISTRY PITTSBURGH, PA 15260 Substituent effects on the Claisen rearrangement

R01GM-34869-06 (MBY) ENGELKE, DAVID R UNIV OF MICHIGAN MED SCH MED SCI I-RM 4424 ANN ARBOR, MI 48109-0606 Eukaryotic tRNA maturation

R01GM-34873-07 (CTY) HUTCHISON, NANCY J AC 136 GENETICS 1124 COLUMBIA STREET SEATTLE, WASH 98104 Cytogenetic analysis of lampbrush chromosomes

R01GM-34883-07 (PB) AVADHANI, NAVAYAN G UNIVERSITY OF PENNSYLVANIA 3800 SPRUCE STREET PHILADELPHIA, PA 19104-6046 Evolution and functions of hepatic mitochondrial P-450

R01GM-34888-07 (MBY) REYNOLDS, WANDA F LA JOLLA CANCER RES FDN 10901 NORTH TORREY PINES ROAD LA JOLLA, CA 92037 Conformation of the RNA polymerase III promoter

R01GM-34893-06 (MBY) DIECKMANN, CAROL L UNIVERSITY OF ARIZONA TUCSON, AZ 85721 Complex locus involved in cytochrome b mRNA maturation

R01GM-34902-07 (EVR) IMPERIALE, MICHAEL J UNIVERSITY OF MICHIGAN 6714 MEDICAL SCIENCE BLDG II ANN ARBOR, MICH 48109 Post-transcriptional regulation of ad2 mRNA synthesis

R01GM-34903-06A1 (MBC) PECK, HARRY D JR UNIVERSITY OF GEORGIA ATHENS, GA 30602 Desulfovibrio hydrogenase -- Molecular biology

R01GM-34906-06 (CBY) NELSON, DAVID L UNIV OF WISCONSIN 420 HENRY MALL MADISON, WI 53706 Regulation of ciliary motion by cyclic nucleotides

R01GM-34908-05 (CBY) LANDRETH, GARY E CASE WESTERN RESERVE UNIVERSIT 2116 ABINGTON ROAD CLEVELAND, OH 44106 EGF activation of map2 kinase

R01GM-34917-07 (MCHA) BUCHWALD, STEPHEN L MASSACHUSETTS INST OF TECH 77 MASSACHUSETTS AVENUE CAMBRIDGE, MA 02139 Organometallic reagents for carbon-carbon bond formation

PROJECT NO., ORGANIZATIONAL UNIT., INVESTIGATOR, ADDRESS, TITLE

R01GM-34921-07 (BIO) TAYLOR, SUSAN S UNIV OF CALIFORNIA, SAN DIEGO DEPT OF CHEMISTRY LA JOLLA, CALIF 92093 Protein kinase regulatory subunit I--Directed mutagens

R01GM-34925-07 (TOX) BIEBER, ALLAN L ARIZONA STATE UNIVERSITY DEPARTMENT OF CHEMISTRY TEMPE, ARIZONA 85287-1604 Chemical/immunochemical studies of myotoxic proteins

R01GM-34930-06 (VR) PARRIS, DEBORAH S OHIO STATE UNIVERSITY 410 WEST 12TH AVENUE COLUMBUS, OH 43210 Functional domains of the HSV-1 65K DNA binding protein

R01GM-34933-05 (CBY) DEVREOTES, PETER N JOHNS HOPKINS UNIVERSITY 725 NORTH WOLFE STREET BALTIMORE, MD 21205 CAMP receptor subtypes and Dictyostelium development

R01GM-34938-06 (BBCA) KUPKE, DONALD W UNIVERSITY OF VIRGINIA HEALTH SCI CENTER BOX 440 CHARLOTTESVILLE, VA 22908 Sequential volume changes of calcium-binding proteins

R01GM-34939-06 (PB) GARGUS, JOHN J EMORY UNIVERSITY SCH OF MED DEPARTMENT OF PHYSIOLOGY ATLANTA, GA 30322 Isolation and characterization of a mammalian K+ channel

R01GM-34962-08 (BBCB) GIERASCH, LILA M SOUTHWESTERN GRADUATE SCHOOL 5323 HARRY HINES BOULEVARD DALLAS, TX 75235 Targeting sequences--conformation and interactions

R01GM-34963-06 (MBY) CHAMBERLIN, MICHAEL J UNIVERSITY OF CALIFORNIA 606 BARKER HALL BERKELEY, CA 94720 Chain elongation and termination by RNA polymerase II

R01GM-34968-11 (BBCB) KOEPPE, ROGER E, II UNIVERSITY OF ARKANSAS 103 CHEMISTRY BLDG FAYETTEVILLE, AR 72701 Mechanism of ion transport through membrane channels

R01GM-34985-06 (MBY) DUNLAP, JAY C DARTMOUTH MEDICAL SCHOOL DEPARTMENT OF BIOCHEMISTRY HANOVER, NH 03756 Genetic and molecular dissection of the neurospora clock

R01GM-34991-06A1 (IMB) PARNES, JANE R STANFORD UNIV SCHOOL OF MED STANFORD, CA 94305-5111 The Leu-2 T/8 T cell differentiation antigen gene

R01GM-34993-06 (BBCA) DILL, KEN A UNIVERSITY OF CALIFORNIA BOX 0446/513 PARNASSUS AVE SAN FRANCISCO, CA 94143 Combinatorial statistical mechanics of protein folding

R37GM-35010-08 (NSS) FINK, GERALD R WHITHEAD INST FOR BIOMEDI RES 9 CAMBRIDGE CENTER CAMBRIDGE, MA 02142 Regulation of histidine biosynthesis in yeast

R01GM-35012-07 (CBY) LODISH, HARVEY F WHITEHEAD INST FOR BIOMED RES 9 CAMBRIDGE CENTER CAMBRIDGE, MA 02142-1401 Structure and biosynthesis of an hepatic receptor

R01GM-35063-08 (CBY) LOEW, LESLIE M UNIVERSITY OF CONNECTICUT 263 FARMINGTON AVENUE FARMINGTON, CT 06032 Potentiometric dyes and membrane permeability

R01GM-35066-08 (BNP) KOZARICH, JOHN W UNIVERSITY OF MARYLAND DEPT OF CHEMISTRY & BIOCHEMIST COLLEGE PARK, MD 20742 Mechanisms of enzyme action

R01GM-35072-07 (VR) AHLQUIST, PAUL G UNIV OF WISCONSIN SYSTEM 1525 LINDEN DRIVE MADISON, WI 53706 Gene functions and molecular genetics of RNA viruses

R01GM-35078-06 (MBC) SCLAFANI, ROBERT A UNIV OF COLORADO HEALTH SCI CT 4200 EAST NINTH AVE., B-121 DENVER, CO 80262 Genetic and molecular analysis of yeast DNA replication

R01GM-35087-08 (GEN) PALMER, JEFFREY DONALD INDIANA UNIVERSITY DEPARMENT OF BIOLOGY BLOOMINGTON, IN 47405 Organization and expression of organelle genomes

R01GM-35103-17 (BMT) SCHOLES, CHARLES P STATE UNIV OF NEW YORK, ALBANY ALBANY, NY 12222 EPR and ENDOR of paramagnetic biomolecules

R01GM-35108-09 (BMT) COTTON, THERESE M IOWA STATE UNIVERSITY DEPT OF CHEM/A111 GILMAN HALL AMES, IA 50011 Surface enhanced Raman studies of biomolecules

R01GM-35120-07 (MBC) DAVIS, ROWLAND H UNIVERSITY OF CALIFORNIA DEPT OF MOLECULAR BIOL/BIOCHEM IRVINE, CA 92717 Regulation of polyamine biosynthesis

R01GM-35123-07 (RAD) SANCAR, GWENDOLYN B BIOCHEM & BIOPHYSICS-CB#7260 UNIV OF N C AT CHAPEL HILL CHAPEL HILL, NC 27599-7260 Function of the S cerevisiae phri gene and photolyase

R01GM-35126-19 (CBY) BAMBURG, JAMES R COLORADO STATE UNIVERSITY FORT COLLINS, CO 80523 Structure/function of actin depolymerizing factor

R01GM-35132-07 (MBC) CHANG, A-LIEN L UNIV. OF MARYLAND AT BALTIMORE DEPT OF BIOLOGICAL CHEMISTRY BALTIMORE, MD 21201 Mechanistic studies of DNA mismatch repair

R01GM-35135-06 (SAT) KISSIN, IGOR UNIV OF ALABAMA/BIRMINGHAM UAB STATION BRIMINGHAM, AL 35294 Opioid-benzodiazepine interactions

R01GM-35141-06 (SAT) HECHTMAN, HERBERT B BRIGHAM AND WOMEN'S HOSPITAL 75 FRANCIS STREET BOSTON, MA 02115 Local and systemic consequences of ischemia

R01GM-35143-06 (CBY) DOWHAN, WILLIAM UNIV OF TEXAS MED SCHOOL P O BOX 20708 HOUSTON, TX 77225 Synthesis and assembly of membrane phospholipids

R01GM-35153-06 (MCHA) RIEKE, REUBEN D UNIV OF NEBRASKA - LINCOLN 14TH AND R STREETS LINCOLN, NE 68588-0304 New synthetic methods using highly reactive metals

R01GM-35154-07 (BBCA) LAKOWICZ, JOSEPH R UNIV OF MARYLAND AT BALTIMORE 660 WEST REDWOOD STREET BALTIMORE, MD 21201 Distance distributions and dynamics of macromolecules

R01GM-35158-07 (BBCB) KLIGER, DAVID S UNIVERSITY OF CALIFORNIA NATURAL SCIENCES II SANTA CRUZ, CA 95064 Transient circular dichroism spectroscopy

R01GM-35170-07 (MBC) ROTHMAN-DENES, LUCIA B UNIVERSITY OF CHICAGO 920 E 58TH ST CHICAGO, IL 60637 Mechanism of replication of linear DNA

R01GM-35171-07 (BBCB) LATTMAN, EATON E JOHNS HOPKINS UNIVERSITY DEPARTMENT OF BIOPHYSICS BALTIMORE, MD 21205 Structure and interactions of actins and actin-binding proteins

R01GM-35174-06 (ALY) MONGINI, PATRICIA K HOSPITAL FOR JOINT DISEASES 301 EAST 17TH STREET NEW YORK, N Y 10003 Monoclonal anti-Igm regulation of human B cell function

R01GM-35177-06 (BBCA) KEARNS, DAVID R UNIVERSITY OF CALIFORNIA DEPARTMENT OF CHEMISTRY LA JOLLA, CA 92093-0314 Nmr studies of polynucleotide dynamics

R01GM-35183-07 (BBCA) CALLENDER, ROBERT H CITY COLLEGE OF CUNY CONVENT AVENUE @ 138TH STREET NEW YORK, NY 10031 Raman vibrational studies of enzymes

R01GM-35192-07 (PHRA) OIE, SVEIN UNIVERSITY OF CALIFORNIA SF 513 PARNASSUS AVE BOX 0446 SAN FRANCISCO, CA 94143 Modulation of drugs by plasma proteins

R01GM-35208-06 (BNP) HAMILTON, ANDREW D UNIVERSITY OF PITTSBURGH 234 CHEVRON SCIENCE CENTER PITTSBURGH, PA 15260 Molecular recognition in biomimetic receptors

R01GM-35212-07 (CTY) EARNSHAW, WILLIAM C JOHNS HOPKINS UNIVERSITY 725 N WOLFE STREET BALTIMORE, MD 21205 Analysis of the human kinetochore with scleroderma sera

R01GM-35215-06 (BBCB) CAFISO, DAVID S UNIVERSITY OF VIRGINIA DEPARTMENT OF CHEMISTRY CHARLOTTESVILLE, VA 22901 Molecular basis for ion-transport in biological membrane

R01GM-35239-07 (CBY) MOORE, HSIAO-PING H UNIVERSITY OF CALIFORNIA MOLECULAR AND CELL BIOLOGY BERKELEY, CALIF 94720 Sorting of proteins in regulated secretory cells

R01GM-35247-07 (MBC) WEINSTOCK, GEORGE M UNIV OF TX HLTH SCI CTR PO BOX 20708 HOUSTON, TX 77225 Genetic analysis of the RecA protein of E coli

R01GM-35249-07 (MCHA) MOLANDER, GARY A UNIVERSITY OF COLORADO DEPT CHEMISTRY AND BIOCHEM BOULDER, CO 80309-0215 Intramolecular reductive coupling reactions

R01GM-35252-07 (CBY) GOLDSTEIN, LAWRENCE S HARVARD UNIVERSITY 16 DIVINITY AVE/ RM 222 CAMBRIDGE, MA 02138 Genetic and immunologic analysis of microtubule proteins

R01GM-35253-07 (BBCB) WARREN, WARREN S PRINCETON UNIVERSITY PRINCETON, NJ 08544-1009 NMR pulse shaping for biomolecules and imaging

R01GM-35258-07 (CTY) SALISBURY, JEFFREY L MAYO FOUNDATION 200 FIRST STREET SOUTHWEST ROCHESTER, MN 55905 Molecular cytology of a CA-binding contractile protein

R01GM-35266-04A2 (BIO) BRAUTIGAN, DAVID L BROWN UNIVERSITY BOX G-J223 PROVIDENCE, RI 02912 Structure and function of protein tyr(P) phosphatases

R01GM-35268-07 (MBC) REVEL, HELEN R UNIVERSITY OF CHICAGO DEPT OF MOLECULAR GEN/CELL BIO CHICAGO, IL 60637 Rna-protein interactions in bacteriophage development

R01GM-35269-05 (BBCB) EGELMAN, EDWARD H UNIV MINNESOTA, MEDICAL CTR 321 CHURCH ST SE MINNEAPOLIS, MN 55455 Structural studies of recA filaments

R01GM-35305-07 (BBCA) HAGERMAN, PAUL J UNIV OF COLORADO HEALTH SCIS C 4200 EAST NINTH AVE #B-121 DENVER, CO 80262 Protein-dna interactions

R01GM-35308-08 (MBC) HOWELL, ELIZABETH E UNIVERSITY OF TENNESSEE WALTERS LIFE SCIENCE BLDG KNOXVILLE, TN 37996-0840 Second site reversion studies of dihydrofolate reductase

R01GM-35318-07 (BNP) TRAMONTANO, ALFONSO THE SCRIPPS RESEARCH INSTITUTE 10666 NORTH TORREY PINES ROAD LA JOLLA, CALIF 92037 Catalytic antibodies

R01GM-35322-07 (MBC) SIMONS, ROBERT W UNIVERSITY OF CALIFORNIA 405 HILGARD AVE LOS ANGELES, CA 90024 Regulation of is1o gene expression

R01GM-35325-06 (CBY) JACOBSON, KENNETH A U OF NORTH CAROLINA, CHAPEL HI CB# 7090 CHAPEL HILL, N C 27599-7090 Membrane and cytoskeletal dynamics during cell movement

R01GM-35326-06 (MGN) THOMSON, GLENYS J UNIVERSITY OF CALIFORNIA 4079 LSB BERKELEY, CA 94720 Population genetics of the HLA region

R01GM-35332-05 (MBC) LUDDEN, PAUL W UNIVERSITY OF WISCONSIN 420 HENRY MALL MADISON, WI 53706 Biosynthesis of iron-molybdenum cofactor of nitrogenase

R01GM-35342-07 (PB) FEE, JAMES A LOS ALAMOS NATIONAL LABORATORY INC-4, C-345 LOS ALAMOS, NM 87545 Mechanisms in respiration

R01GM-35370-07 (CBY) NOVICK, PETER J YALE UNIV SCHOOL OF MEDICINE 333 CEDAR STREET/BOX 3333 NEW HAVEN, CT 06510 Genetics of secretion in yeast

R01GM-35393-07 (PB) KIRSCH, JACK F UNIVERSITY OF CALIFORNIA 401 BARKER HALL BERKELEY, CA 94720 Active-site directed mutagenesis of aspartate aminotransferase

R01GM-35394-07 (PB) CLAIBORNE, H ALEXANDER, JR WAKE FOREST UNIVERSITY 300 SOUTH HAWTHORNE ROAD WINSTON-SALEM, N C 27103 Mechanisms involved in flavin-linked oxygen metabolism

R01GM-35399-07 (BBCB) MOHRAZ, MANIJEH NEW YORK UNIV MEDICAL CENTER 550 FIRST AVENUE NEW YORK, N Y 10016 Structure determination of the Na/K-ATPase

R01GM-35401-07 (PHY) WANG, GING K BRIGHAM AND WOMEN'S HOSPITAL 75 FRANCIS STREET BOSTON, MA 02115 Molecular basis of ligand-sodium channel interactions

R01GM-35423-13 (BIO) GOLDIN, STANLEY M CAMBRIDGE NEUROSCIENCE RES INC ONE KENDALL SQ, BUILDING 700 CAMBRIDGE, MA 02139 Molecular properties of a cgmp-activated ca channel

R37GM-35433-07 (BBCB) DEROSIER, DAVID J BRANDEIS UNIVERSITY PO BOX 9110 WALTHAM, MA 02254-9110 Structural studies of bacterial flagella

R01GM-35437-07 (GEN) ANDERSON, KATHRYN V UNIVERSITY OF CALIFORNIA BERKELEY, CA 94720 The dorsal-ventral pattern of the Drosophila embryo

R01GM-35438-06 (PB) CROFTS, ANTONY R UNIVERSITY OF ILLINOIS 407 SOUTH GOODWIN AVENUE URBANA, IL 61801 Molecular architecture of UQH2--Cyt C2 oxidoreductase

R01GM-35447-06 (CTY) THEOLOGIS, ATHANASIOS UNIVERSITY OF CALIFORNIA 111 GPBB BERKELEY, CA 94720 Structure and expression of hormonally regulated genes

R01GM-35463-06 (GEN) CORCES, VICTOR G ASSOCIATE PROFESSOR JOHNS HOPKINS UNIVERSITY BALTIMORE, MD 21218 Molecular basis of suppression in Drosophila

R01GM-35490-07 (MBY) GREEN, MICHAEL R UNIV OF MASS MEDICAL SCHOOL 373 PLANTATION STREET WORCESTER, MA 01605 Splicing of mRNA precursors

R01GM-35495-07 (MBC) YOUNGMAN, PHILIP J UNIVERSITY OF GEORGIA DEPARTMENT OF GENETICS ATHENS, GA 30602 Regulation of developmental genes in Bacillus subtilis

R01GM-35501-05 (CTY) BOWEN-POPE, DANIEL F UNIVERSITY OF WASHINGTON SCHOOL OF MEDICINE SM-30 SEATTLE, WA 98195 Regulation of PDGF receptors

R01GM-35510-06A1 (GEN) BUTOW, RONALD A UNIVERSITY OF TEXAS SOUTHWESTE 5323 HARRY HINES BLVD DALLAS, TX 75235 Yeast mitochondrial DNA recombination

R01GM-35523-06A1 (SAT) EISENACH, JAMES C WAKE FOREST UNIVERSITY 300 S HAWTHORNE ROAD WINSTON-SALEM, NC 27103 Spinal alpha2-adrenergic analgesia

R01GM-35527-07 (CBY) NELSON, W JAMES STANFORD UNIV/SCH OF MEDICINE B121 BECKMAN CENTER STANFORD, CA 94305-5426 Regulation of Na+, K+ -ATPase topogenesis in MDCK cells

R01GM-35533-06 (PHRA) WASKELL, LUCY A VETERANS ADMIN MEDICAL CENTER DEPT OF ANESTHESIA (129) SAN FRANCISCO, CA 94121 Participation of cytochrome b5 in anesthetic metabolism

R01GM-35535-07 (MBY) BURCH, JOHN B INSTITUTE FOR CANCER RESEARCH 7701 BURHOLME AVENUE PHILADELPHIA, PA 19111 Chromatin structure and vitellogenin gene expression

R01GM-35556-07 (ALY) GOLDSTEIN, BYRON B UNIVERSITY OF CALIFORNIA P.O. BOX 1663/MAIL STOP K710 LOS ALAMOS, N M 87545 Receptor aggregation and its effects

R01GM-35557-06 (MCHA) GARNER, PHILIP P CASE WESTERN RESERVE UNIVERSIT 2074 ADELBERT RD CLEVELAND, OH 44106-7078 Stereospecific synthesis of aminosugar antibiotics

R01GM-35572-07 (MCHA) PEARSON, WILLIAM H UNIVERSITY OF MICHIGAN 930 N UNIVERSITY ANN ARBOR, MI 48109-1055 New methods for alkaloid synthesis

R01GM-35625-07 (MBY) HALLICK, RICHARD B UNIVERSITY OF ARIZONA TUCSON, AZ 85721 Organization and expression of chloroplast tRNA genes

R01GM-35633-07 (SAT) MANNICK, JOHN A BRIGHAM AND WOMENS HOSPITAL 75 FRANCIS ST BOSTON, MA 02115 Immunologic studies of patients after traumatic injury

R01GM-35642-07 (PC) COOPER, TERRANCE G UNIVERSITY OF TENNESSEE 858 MADISON AVE MEMPHIS, TN 38163 Synthesis and assembly of eucaryotic membranes

R01GM-35647-07 (SAT) STRICHARTZ, GARY R ANESTHESIA RES LABORATORIES 75 FRANCIS STREET BOSTON, MASS 02115 Local anesthesia of peripheral and central nerve pathways

R01GM-35648-07 (CBY) LINCK, RICHARD W UNIVERSITY OF MINNESOTA DEPT OF CELL BIOLOGY/NEUROANAT MINNEAPOLIS, MN 55455 molecular structure and function of tektins in microtubules

R01GM-35649-17A1 (BBCA) OLSON, JOHN S RICE UNIVERSITY PO BOX 1892 HOUSTON, TX 77251 Functional properties of hemoglobins and myoglobins

R01GM-35654-06 (MBC) JAYARAM, MAKKUNI UNIVERSITY OF TEXAS DEPT OF MICROBIOLOGY AUSTIN, TX 78712 Site specific recombination in the yeast plasmid 2 micron circle

R01GM-35655-06 (MBC) CARMAN, GEORGE M RUTGERS UNIVERSITY DEPT OF FOOD SCIENCE NEW BRUNSWICK, N J 08903 Regulation of phosphatidylinositol metabolism

R01GM-35658-07 (MBC) PLATT, TERRY UNIVERSITY OF ROCHESTER 601 ELMWOOD AVENUE ROCHESTER, N Y 14642 RNA transcription termination and 3'end processing

R01GM-35665-07 (MBY) HALLICK, RICHARD B UNIVERSITY OF ARIZONA DEPARTMENT OF BIOCHEMISTRY TUCSON, ARIZ 85721 Gene expression in cell organelles

R01GM-35679-07 (GEN) NEWLON, CAROL S UMDNJ-NEW JERSEY MEDICAL SCH 185 SOUTH ORANGE AVE NEWARK, N J 07103-2757 DNA replication in Saccharomyces cerevisiae

R01GM-35682-09A1 (GNM) DANIELS, DONNA L UNIVERSITY OF WISCONSIN 445 HENRY MALL MADISON, WI 53706 Complete dissection of the Escherichia coli genome

R01GM-35687-07 (CBY) GILMORE, JAMES R UNIV OF MASSACHUSETTS MED CTR 55 LAKE AVENUE NORTH WORCESTER, MASS 01655 Protein translocation across the endoplasmic reticulum

R01GM-35690-06 (GEN) SELKER, ERIC U UNIVERSITY OF OREGON EUGENE, OR 97403 Genetic aspects of DNA methylation

R01GM-35695-06A1 (MBC) MCHENRY, CHARLES S UNIV OF COLORADO HLTH SCIS CTR CB B121/4200 E 9TH AVENUE DENVER, CO 80262 Structure of a replicative complex

R01GM-35710-25 (BNP) MABRY, TOM J UNIVERSITY OF TEXAS AT AUSTIN AUSTIN, TX 78713-7640 Function and systematic role of natural products

R01GM-35712-06A1 (BNP) GANEM, BRUCE CORNELL UNIVERSITY ITHACA, NY 14853 Inhibition of complex carbohydrate biosynthesis

R01GM-35717-06 (PC) HILL, WALTER E UNIVERSITY OF MONTANA DIV OF BIOLOGICAL SCIENCES MISSOULA, MT 59812 Probing ribosomal function

R01GM-35719-06 (BBCB) LAI, CHING-SAN MEDICAL COLLEGE OF WISCONSIN 8701 WATERTOWN PLANK ROAD MILWAUKEE, WI 53226 ESR spin label studies of fibronectin

R01GM-35720-06 (PHRA) WEINSHILBOUM, RICHARD M MAYO FOUNDATION DEPT OF PHARMACOLOGY ROCHESTER, MINN 55905 Sulfate conjugation and drug metabolism

R01GM-35723-06 (VR) MUZYCZKA, NICHOLAS STATE UNIVERSITY OF NEW YORK STONY BROOKS, NY 11794-8621 Genetic studies of adeno-associated virus

R01GM-35724-06 (BNP) DERVAN, PETER B CALIFORNIA INST OF TECHNOLOGY DEPT OF CHEMISTRY PASADENA, CA 91125 Oligonucleotide-directed modification of DNA and RNA

R01GM-35751-06 (PBC) BOURGEOIS-COHN, SUZANNE SALK INST FOR BIOL STUDIES P O BOX 85800 SAN DIEGO, CA 92186-5800 Regulation of extracellular matrix biosynthesis

R01GM-35752-06 (PB) REED, GEORGE H UNIVERSITY OF WISCONSIN 1710 UNIVERSITY AVE MADISON, WI 53705 Spectroscopic studies of enzyme-substrate complexes

R01GM-35754-06 (MBC) GRALLA, JAY D UNIVERSITY OF CALIFORNIA DEPARTMENT OF CHEMISTRY LOS ANGELES, CA 90024-1569 Mechanisms of repression in bacteria

R01GM-35755-06 (MBY) INOUE, TAN SALK INST FOR BIOLOGICAL STUDI PO BOX 85800 SAN DIEGO, CA 92186-5800 Minimum requirement for RNA-mediated reactions

R01GM-35759-06 (CBY) FORTE, MICHAEL A OREGON HEALTH SCIENCES

UNIV 3181 SW SAM JACKSON PARK ROAD PORTLAND, OR 97201-3098 Molecular genetic dissection of the vdac ion channel

R01GM-35766-07A1 (BNP) HALEY, BOYD E THE UNIVERSITY OF KENTUCKY DEPT OF BIOCHEMISTRY LEXINGTON, KY 40536-0084 Application of photoaffinity nucleotide analogs

R01GM-35769-06 (MBC) BELASCO, JOEL G HARVARD MEDICAL SCHOOL 200 LONGWOOD AVENUE BOSTON, MA 02115 Prokaryotic RNA metabolism

R01GM-35774-05 (PBC) ESSELMAN, WALTER J MICHIGAN STATE UNIVERSITY EAST LANSING, MI 48824-1101 Glycoproteins in differentiation

R01GM-35791-06 (MBC) SILHAVY, THOMAS J PRINCETON UNIVERSITY MOLECULAR BIOLOGY DEPARTMENT PRINCETON, NJ 08544 Regulation of the major outer membrane porin proteins

R01GM-35803-07 (BIO) CHAU, VINCENT WAYNE STATE UNIVERSITY 540 E CANFIELD DETROIT, MI 48201 Control of cellular proteolysis

R01GM-35827-06 (GEN) RINE, JASPER D UNIVERSITY OF CALIFORNIA BERKELEY, CA 94720 Regulation of the sterol biosynthetic pathway in yeast

R01GM-35837-05 (MBY) ANNUNZIATO, ANTHONY T BOSTON COLLEGE 140 COMMONWEALTH AVENUE CHESTNUT HILL, MA 02167 Histone-DNA interactions during chromatin biosynthesis

R01GM-35847-06 (BIO) RIGGS, AUSTEN F, II UNIVERSITY OF TEXAS AUSTIN, TX 78712 Biochemistry of invertebrate hemoglobins

R01GM-35850-07 (MBC) TESSMAN, IRWIN PURDUE UNIVERSITY LILLY HAL WEST LAFAYETTE, IN 47907 DNA damage, repair, and mutagenesis

R01GM-35866-06 (BIO) DYNAN, WILLIAM S UNIVERSITY COLORADO DEPT OF CHEM& BIOCHEM CAMPUS BOULDER, COLO 80309 Molecular mechanism of transcriptional activation

R01GM-35873-07 (PBC) LOW, MARTIN G COLUMBIA UNIVERSITY 630 W 168TH ST NEW YORK, NY 10032 Phosphatidylinositol anchor of alkaline phosphase

R01GM-35874-06 (MBC) SQUIRES, CATHERINE L COLUMBIA UNIVERSITY NEW YORK, N Y 10027 Antitermination and cellular gene expression

R01GM-35879-06 (MCHA) MASAMUNE, SATORU MASSACHUSETTS INST OF TECH 77 MASSACHUSETTS AVE CAMBRIDGE, MA 02139 Asymmetric synthesis and its applications

R01GM-35880-07 (ALY) HEDRICK, STEPHEN M U OF CALIFORNIA, SAN DIEGO DEPT OF BIOLOGY 0063 LA JOLLA, CA 92093-0934 T cell recognition analyzed by gene transfection

R01GM-35894-07 (BIO) NEVINS, JOSEPH R DUKE UNIVERSITY MEDICAL CENTER PO BOX 3054 DURHAM, NC 27710 Post-transcriptional mechanisms of gene control

R01GM-35897-06 (PB) KEMPER, BYRON W UNIVERSITY OF ILLINOIS 407 S GOODWIN AVE, 524 BURRILL URBANA, ILL 61801 Structural determinants of functional cytochromes p450

R29GM-35900-06 (SAT) FIRESTONE, LEONARD L UNIV OF PITTSBURGH MED SCHOOL DEPT OF ANESTHESIOLOGY PITTSBURGH, PA 15261 Effects of general anesthetics on nicotinic membranes

R01GM-35906-06 (BNP) LIU, HUNG-WEN UNIVERSITY OF MINNESOTA 207 PLEASANT STREET, SE MINNEAPOLIS, MN 55455 Mechanisms of biosynthetic formation of deoxy sugars

R01GM-35926-07 (BBCA) RODER, HEINRICH INSTITUTE FOR CANCER RESEARCH 7701 BURHOLME AVENUE PHILADELPHIA, PA 19111 Two-dimensional NMR studies of cytochrome C folding

R01GM-35929-03 (CTY) GERBI, SUSAN A BROWN UNIVERSITY DIVISION OF BIO & MED, BOX G PROVIDENCE, R I 02912 Gene amplification--Sciara DNA puffs

R01GM-35940-06 (BBCA) WAND, ANDREW J UNIVERSITY OF ILLINOIS 1209 W CALIFORNIA ST URBANA, IL 61801 Structure and dynamics of free & complexed cytochrome C

R37GM-35949-07 (MBC) NOMURA, MASAYASU UNIV OF CALIFORNIA IRVINE, CA 92717-1700 Genetics and biochemistry of ribosome biosynthesis

R01GM-35955-06 (MBY) GREER, CHRISTOPHER L UNIVERSITY OF CALIFORNIA DEPT OF BIOLOGICAL CHEMISTRY IRVINE, CA 92717 RNA splicing mechanisms

R01GM-35956-06 (MCHA) CHA, JIN K UNIVERSITY OF ALABAMA BOX 870336 TUSCALOOSA, AL 35487-0336 Total synthesis of mycotoxins and related compounds

R01GM-35962-06 (MCHA) GASSMAN, PAUL G UNIVERSITY OF MINNESOTA MINNEAPOLIS, MINN 55455 Cycloaddition reactions of allyl and related cations

R01GM-35971-06 (GEN) CHANDLER, VICKI L UNIVERSITY OF OREGON INSTITUTE OF MOLECULAR BIOLOGY EUGENE, OREG 97403 Isolation of the B gene--A regulatory locus maize

R37GM-35976-07 (BBCB) MARKLEY, JOHN L UNIVERSITY OF WISCONSIN 420 HENRY MALL MADISON, WI 53706-1569 Nmr spectroscopy in protein chemistry

R01GM-35978-06A1 (PBC) WEIGEL, PAUL H UNIV OF TEXAS MED BRANCH GALVESTON, TX 77550 Structure & function of hyaluronate binding proteins/receptors

R01GM-35981-06 (PHY) LATORRE, RAMON C E C S CASILLA 16443, SANTIAGO 9 CHILE Function and modulation of ion channels in muscle

R01GM-35982-06 (BMT) WILLIARD, PAUL G BROWN UNIVERSITY PROVIDENCE, RI 02912 Investigation of intermediates for organic synthesis

R01GM-35998-06 (GEN) SHILO, BEN-ZION WEIZMANN INSTITUTE OF SCIENCE REHOVOT 76100, ISRAEL Drosphila EGF receptor--Genetics and signal transduction

R01GM-36002-05 (PC) BISWAS, SUBHASIS B UNIVERSITY OF MARYLAND 655 WEST BALTIMORE ST BALTIMORE, MD 21201 Mechanism of DNA-protein interaction in DNA replication

R01GM-36044-04A3 (PHY) HARRIS, ANDREW L JOHNS HOPKINS UNIVERSITY 3400 NORTH CHARLES STREET BALTIMORE, MD 21218 Physiology of reconstituted connexin channels

R01GM-36054-06 (BMT) TAKAYAMA, KUNI K W S MIDDLETON MEM VA HOSPITAL 2500 OVERLOOK TERRACE MADISON, WI 53705 Structural analysis of lipopolysaccharides and lipid A

R01GM-36064-06 (ALY) BRODEUR, PETER H TUFTS UNIVERSITY 136 HARRISON AVENUE BOSTON, MA 02111 Organization and expression of V-gene families

R01GM-36065-06 (NEUC) WAECHTER, CHARLES J UNIVERSITY OF KENTUCKY MED CTR 800 ROSE STREET LEXINGTON, KY 40536-0084 Induction of N-glycosylation activity in B lymphocytes

R01GM-36133-07 (PB) CANTLEY, LEWIS C, JR TUFTS UNIVERSITY 136 HARRISON AVENUE BOSTON, MA 02111 Mechanism of cation transport regulation

R01GM-36143-05A2 (BMT) ABRAMSON, FRED P GEORGE WASHINGTON UNIVERSITY 2300 EYE STREET NW WASHINGTON, D C 20037 Reaction interface/MS--Tool for pharmacologic assays

R01GM-36192-04A2 (MBC) MCEWEN, JOAN E UNIVERSITY OF CALIFORNIA 405 HILGARD AVENUE LOS ANGELES, CA 90024 Genetic analysis of cytochrome C oxidase biogenesis

R01GM-36214-06 (SAT) MILLER-GRAZIANO, CAROL L UNIV OF MASS MEDICAL CTR DEPT OF SURGERY WORCESTER, MA 01655 Analysis of immune status of trauma and surgical patient

R01GM-36230-06 (GNM) WATERMAN, MICHAEL S UNIV OF SOUTHERN CALIFORNIA 1042 W 36TH PL DRB 306 MC-1113 LOS ANGELES, CA 90089-1113 Pattern recognition for analysis of molecular sequences

R01GM-36232-06 (BBCB) GAFFNEY, BETTY J JOHNS HOPKINS UNIVERSITY CHARLES AND 34TH STREETS BALTIMORE, MD 21218 Lipid-lipoxygenase interactions

R01GM-36238-05 (BMT) LINDSEY, JONATHAN S CARNEGIE-MELLON UNIVERSITY 4400 FIFTH AVENUE PITTSBURGH, PA 15213 Porphyrin synthetic methods for bioorganic applications

R01GM-36243-06 (BBCA) BOCIAN, DAVID F UNIVERSITY OF CALIFORNIA RIVERSIDE, CA 92521-0403 Raman studies of porphyrins and related macrocycles

R01GM-36255-07 (BIO) MCHENRY, CHARLES S UNIV OF COLO HEALTH SCI CTR 4200 EAST NINTH AVENUE DENVER, CO 80262 Regulation of the synthesis of replication proteins

R01GM-36258-07 (SAT) LANSER, MARC E BETH ISRAEL HOSPITAL DEPARTMENT OF SURGERY BOSTON, MA 02215 Neutrophil bactericidal activity following trauma

R37GM-36259-07 (PHRA) NEER, EVA J BRIGHAM & WOMEN HOSPITAL 75 FRANCIS STREET BOSTON, MA 02115 Adenylate cyclase and the plasma membrane

R01GM-36260-06 (BIO) DUNAWAY-MARIANO, DEBRA UNIVERSITY OF MARYLAND AND BIOCHEMISTRY COLLEGE PARK, MD 20742 Investigation of pyruvate phosphate dikinase

R01GM-36261-10 (IMS) ASHMAN, ROBERT F UNIV OF IOWA HOSPS & CLINICS DEPARTMENT OF MEDICINE IOWA CITY, IOWA 52242 Early activation events in normal and immune deficient B cells

R01GM-36262-06 (BMT) GOKEL, GEORGE W UNIVERSITY OF MIAMI CORAL GABLES, FL 33124 Synthesis of a cation-conducting channel

R01GM-36263-07 (GEN) FOE, VICTORIA E UNIVERSITY OF WASHINGTON SEATTLE, WA 98195 Cell determination in Drosophila embryos

R01GM-36277-08 (CTY) SHEETZ, MICHAEL P DUKE UNIVERSITY BOX 3709 DURHAM, NC 27710 Myosin movement in vitro--Physiological characterization

R01GM-36278-06 (MBC) GROSS, CAROL A UNIVERSITY OF WISCONSIN 1550 LINDEN DRIVE MADISON, WI 53706 Regulation of the heat shock response in E. coli

R01GM-36284-06 (BBCA) MANNING, GERALD S RUTGERS UNIVERSITY P O BOX 939 PISCATAWAY, NJ 08855-0939 Elastic and ionic instabilities of DNA

R01GM-36286-05A1 (BNP) SCHWAB, JOHN M PURDUE UNIVERSITY WEST LAFAYETTE, IN 47907 Structure and function of allylic rearrangement enzymes

R01GM-36292-05A2 (BMT) ARMSTRONG, DANIEL W UNIV OF MISSOURI-ROLLA ROLLA, MO 65401 Chiral recognition and separations via ordered media

R01GM-36296-07 (BM) LIDSTROM, MARY E CALIFORNIA INST OF TECHNOLOGY 1201 EAST CALIF BOULEVARD PASADENA, CA 91125 Regulation of C-1 metabolism in methylotrophs

R01GM-36298-06 (PB) GROVES, JOHN T PRINCETON UNIVERSITY WASHINGTON ROAD PRINCETON, NJ 08544 Molecular probes of the mechanism of cytochrome P-450

R01GM-36306-06 (IMB) RAVETCH, JEFFREY V SLOAN-KETTERING INST/CANCER RE 1275 YORK AVE NEW YORK, NY 10021 IFN-gamma activation of macrophages--Inducible genes

R01GM-36307-05 (PBC) MODAK, MUKUND J UMDNJ-NEW JERSEY MEDICAL SCHOO 185 SOUTH ORANGE AVENUE NEWARK, NJ 07103-2757 Molecular effectors of enzymatic DNA synthesis

R01GM-36308-06 (BMT) MILLAR, MICHELLE M SUNY AT STONY BROOK STONY BROOK, NY 11784-3400 Synthetic analogs for metal-cysteine containing proteins

R01GM-36312-05 (MCHA) MOORE, HAROLD W UNIVERSITY OF CALIFORNIA IRVINE, CA 92717 Chemistry of conjugated ketones--bioreductive alkylation

R01GM-36325-07 (BMT) STOUT, CHARLES D SCRIPPS CLINIC & RESEARCH FDN 10666 NORTH TORREY PINES RD LA JOLLA, CA 92037 Structure and function of aconitase and ferredoxin

R01GM-36326-06 (CTY) HITCHCOCK-DEGREGORI, SARAH E UMDNJ-R W JOHNSON MED SCH 675 HOES LANE PISCATAWAY, N J 08854-5635 Regulation of contraction in muscle and non-muscle cells

R01GM-36336-06 (MCHA) HUA, DUY H KANSAS STATE UNIVERSITY WILLARD HALL MANHATTAN, KS 66506 Synthesis and antitumor activity of alkaloids

R01GM-36339-06 (MBC) FREUNDLICH, MARTIN S U N Y STONY BROOK, NY 11794-5215 Autoregulation and global control of the CRP operon

R01GM-36343-05A2 (BBCA) BEHE, MICHAEL J LEHIGH UNIVERSITY MOUNTAIN TOP CAMPUS BETHLEHEM, PA 18015 Biophysical studies of oligopurine tracts

R01GM-36344-06 (IMB) OSBORNE, BARBARA A UNIV OF MASSACHUSETTS PAIGE LABORATORY AMHERST, MA 01003 Evolutionary mechanisms of Vh and Ch diversity

R01GM-36353-10A1 (IMB) BOURGUIGNON, LILLY Y W UNIVERSITY OF MIAMI SCH OF MED 1600 NW 10TH AVENUE (R-124) MIAMI, FL 33136 Biochemical and cytochemical studies on lymphoid membranes

R01GM-36358-05 (BBCB) LATTMAN, EATON E JOHNS HOPKINS UNIVERSITY 725 N WOLFE STREET BALTIMORE, MD 21205 Structural studies of staphylococcal nuclease

R01GM-36365-04A1 (SAT) HOUSMANS, PHILIPPE R MAYO FOUNDATION 200 FIRST STREET SOUTHWEST ROCHESTER, MN 55905 Volatile anesthetics and cardiac function

R01GM-36373-06 (CBY) SILVER, PAMELA A PRINCETON UNIVERSITY

PRINCETON, NEW JERSEY 08544 Assembly of proteins into the nucleus
R01GM-36376-05 (SB) DEITCH, EDWIN A LOUISIANA ST UNIV MEDICAL CTR PO BOX 33932 SHREVEPORT, LA 71130 Burns and trauma induced infections from the gut
R01GM-36386-06 (PHY) KUNG, CHING UNIVERSITY OF WISCONSIN 1525 LINDEN DRIVE MADISON, WI 53706 Molecular physiology of calmodulin-dependent channels
R01GM-36387-05 (PHY) DUBYAK, GEORGE R CASE WESTERN RESERVE UNIVERSIT 2109 ADELBERT RD CLEVELAND, OH 44106 Transmembrane signalling in smooth muscle cell lines
R01GM-36393-05 (BBCA) VANDERKOOI, JANE M UNIV OF PENNSYLVANIA SCHOOL OF MEDICINE PHILADELPHIA, PA 19104 New oxygen sensor--Use in studying biological systems
R01GM-36397-06 (CTY) MEAGHER, RICHARD B UNIVERSITY OF GEORGIA ATHENS, GA 30602 Differential expression of the diverse plant actin genes
R01GM-36410-06 (GEN) MICHOD, RICHARD E UNIVERSITY OF ARIZONA TUCSON, AZ 85721 Evolutionary genetics of DNA repair and recombination
R01GM-36414-05 (MBC) GAYDA, RANDALL C LOUISIANA STATE UNIVERSITY BATON ROUGE, LA 70803 Regulation of cell septation in Escherichia coli
R01GM-36415-06 (MBC) KUMAMOTO, CAROL A TUFTS UNIVERSITY 136 HARRISON AVENUE BOSTON, MA 02111 Mechanism of action of E coli protein export factors
R01GM-36419-06 (CBY) LAMPPA, GAYLE K UNIVERSITY OF CHICAGO 920 E 58TH STREET CHICAGO, IL 60637 Mechanism of protein transport into chloroplasts
P50GM-36428-07 (SRC) WILMORE, DOUGLAS W BRIGHAM AND WOMEN'S HOSPITAL 75 FRANCIS STREET BOSTON, MA 02115 Trauma--Regulators and modulators of the catabolic state
P50GM-36428-07 0001 (SRC) SMITH, ROBERT J Trauma--Regulators and modulators of the catabolic state Anabolic peptide hormones and post-injury metabolism
P50GM-36428-07 0003 (SRC) WILMORE, DOUGLAS W Trauma--Regulators and modulators of the catabolic state Modulating injury responses
P50GM-36428-07 0005 (SRC) DEMLING, ROBERT H Trauma--Regulators and modulators of the catabolic state Oxidants, post-traumatic sepsis and organ failure
P50GM-36428-07 0006 (SRC) MANNICK, JOHN A Trauma--Regulators and modulators of the catabolic state Trauma and the immune response
P50GM-36428-07 0007 (SRC) JACOBS, DANNY O Trauma--Regulators and modulators of the catabolic state Skeletal muscle energy metabolism in sepsis
P50GM-36428-07 9001 (SRC) WILMORE, DOUGLAS W Trauma--Regulators and modulators of the catabolic state Core - Laboratories
R01GM-36431-06 (GEN) AQUADRO, CHARLES F CORNELL UNIVERSITY 401 BIOTECHNOLOGY BLDG ITHACA, N Y 14853-2703 Comparative molecular population genetics of Drosophila
R01GM-36433-04A2 (BBCB) DEUTSCH, CAROL J UNIVERSITY OF PENNSYLVANIA 37TH AND HAMILTON WALK PHILADELPHIA, PA 19104-6085 Cellular/organelle pH in biological systems
R01GM-36442-05A1 (BMT) BRUDVIG, GARY W YALE UNIVERSITY 12 PROSPECT PLACE NEW HAVEN, CT 06511-3516 Distance measurements in metalloproteins
R01GM-36452-06 (BBCB) MOFFAT, JOHN K BIOCHEMISTRY/MOLECULAR/BIOLOGY 920 E. 58TH STREET Time-resolved macromolecular crystallography
R01GM-36474-05 (MBC) SONNEBORN, DAVID R UNIVERSITY OF WISCONSIN 1117 W JOHNSON STREET MADISON, WI 53706 Analyses of cell development in Blastocladiella
R01GM-36477-06 (MBY) ZARET, KENNETH S BROWN UNIVERSITY DEPT OF BIO & MED, BOX G PROVIDENCE, R I 02912 Trans-acting factors causing cell-specific gene control
R01GM-36481-06 (GEN) BOEKE, JEF D JOHNS HOPKINS UNIVERSITY 725 N WOLFE STREET BALTIMORE, MD 21205-2185 Transposition mechanisms
R01GM-36489-05 (PB) PLATZ, MATTHEW S OHIO STATE UNIVERSITY 120 WEST 18TH AVE COLUMBUS, OH 43210-1073 A study of DNA intercalating aromatic amino azides
R01GM-36490-03 (MBC) SWENSON, RICHARD P THE OHIO STATE UNIVERSITY 484 WEST 12TH AVENUE COLUMBUS, OH 43210-1292 Redox and electron-transfer properties of flavodoxins
R01GM-36494-06 (CBY) SNYDER, MICHAEL P YALE UNIVERSITY BOX 1504A, YALE STATION NEW HAVEN, CT 06520 Analysis of mitotic components in yeast and humans
R01GM-36510-06 (MBY) HOLM, CONNIE HARVARD UNIVERSITY 16 DIVINITY AVE CAMBRIDGE, MA 02138 Genetic analysis of chromosome segregation in yeast
R01GM-36516-06 (BIO) BRYANT, FLOYD R JOHNS HOPKINS UNIVERSITY SCH OF HYGIENE & PUBLIC HLTH BALTIMORE, MD 21205 Enzymatic transformation of the DNA helix
R01GM-36520-06 (BMT) CHANG, CHI K MICHIGAN STATE UNIVERSITY DEPARTMENT OF CHEMISTRY EAST LANSING, MI 48824 Dioneheme, cytochrome CD and nitrite reductions
R01GM-36526-06 (MBC) MC MACKEN, ROGER L JOHNS HOPKINS UNIVERSITY SCHOOL OF HYGIENE/PUBLIC HEALT BALTIMORE, MD 21205 Host-virus interactions in initiation of DNA replication
R01GM-36536-08 (PB) DOUGLAS, MICHAEL G UNIVERSITY OF NORTH CAROLINA CB #7260/ 405 FLOB CHAPEL HILL, NC 27599-7260 Structure -Function analysis of energy transduction
R01GM-36537-07 (CBY) DOUGLAS, MICHAEL G UNIVERSITY OF NORTH CAROLINA DEPT. OF BIOCHEM. & BIOPHYSICS CHAPEL HILL, N C 27599-7260 Analysis of the mithochondrial import system
R01GM-36548-05 (PC) KIRCHHAUSEN, TOMAS HARVARD MEDICAL SCHOOL 220 LONGWOOD AVENUE BOSTON, MA 02115 Structural chemistry of clathrin and associated proteins
R01GM-36549-05 (GEN) MC KEOWN, MICHAEL B SALK INSTITUTE PO BOX 85800 SAN DIEGO, CA 92138 Regulation of sex differentiation in Drosophila
R01GM-36552-06 (PB) WEISS, RICHARD L UNIVERSITY OF CALIFORNIA AND BIOCHEMISTRY LOS ANGELES, CA 90024-1569 Vacuole function in neurospora
R01GM-36562-06 (PB) ANDERSON, VERNON E BROWN UNIVERSITY BOX H PROVIDENCE, RI 02912 Strained intermediates in enzyme catalyzed reactions
R01GM-36564-18 (BNP) NAKANISHI, KOJI COLUMBIA UNIVERSITY NEW YORK, NY 10027 Chemical and bio-organic studies of vision and phototaxis
R01GM-36565-06 (CTY) KUCHERLAPATI, RAJU S ALBERT EINSTEIN COLLEGE OF MED 1300 MORRIS PARK AVENUE BRONX, N Y 10461 Homologous recombination in human cell extracts
R01GM-36570-04A1 (PC) KRAG, SHARON S JOHNS HOPKINS UNIVERSITY 615 NORTH WOLFE STREET BALTIMORE, MD 21205 Two regulatory enzymes of dolichol-linked glycosylation
R01GM-36578-06 (BBCA) HUDSON, BRUCE S UNIVERSITY OF OREGON DEPT OF CHEMISTRY EUGENE, OR 97403 Tryptophan photophysics and protein dynamics
R01GM-36579-05 (GEN) BELOTE, JOHN MADDOX SYRACUSE UNIVERSITY 130 COLLEGE PLACE SYRACUSE, NY 13244-1220 Molecular study of a sex transformer gene in Drosophila
R01GM-36590-06 (PB) TUKEY, ROBERT H UNIV OF CALIFORNIA, SAN DIEGO CANCER CENTER, T-012 LA JOLLA, CA 92093 Human cytochrome P450 genes and their regulation
R01GM-36592-04 (MCHA) SWENTON, JOHN S OHIO STATE UNIVERSITY 120 WEST 18TH AVE COLUMBUS, OH 43210 Chemistry of biologically relevant quinone imines
R01GM-36594-04A1 (SSS) HANSEN, ERIC W DARTMOUTH COLLEGE P O BOX 7 HANOVER, NH 03755 Laser scanning fluorescent microscope
R01GM-36598-06 (BBCA) SCHIFFER, MARIANNE ARGONNE NATIONAL LABORATORY 9700 SOUTH CASS AVENUE ARGONNE, IL 60439-4833 Crystallographic study of photosynthetic reaction center
R01GM-36605-06 (VR) VILLARREAL, LUIS P UNIVERSITY OF CALIFORNIA IRVINE, CA 92717 Tissue specific gene expression--Analysis with polyoma
R01GM-36610-07 (BBCB) SUDDATH, FRED L, JR GEORGIA INSTITUTE OF TECHNOLOG 225 NORTH AVENUE, N W ATLANTA, GA 30332-0400 High resolution structure of Pisum sativum lectin
R01GM-36619-06 (PB) COLEMAN, PETER S NEW YORK UNIVERSITY NEW YORK, NY 10003 ATP binding site photoaffinity probes for F1-ATPase
R01GM-36624-06 (PB) CANTLEY, LEWIS C TUFTS UNIVERSITY 136 HARRISON AVENUE BOSTON, MA 02111 Characterization of phosphatidylinositol kinases
R01GM-36633-04A2 (PHRA) BENET, LESLIE Z UNIVERSITY OF CALIFORNIA SCHOOL OF PHARMACY SAN FRANCISCO, CA 94143-0446 Acyl glucuronides--Covalent binding and pharmacokinetics
R01GM-36643-06 (BBCB) WRIGHT, PETER E RES INST OF SCRIPPS CLINIC 10666 NORTH TORREY PINES ROAD LA JOLLA, CA 92037 NMR studies of the structure and function of proteins
R01GM-36652-06 (CBY) BRETSCHER, ANTHONY P CORNELL UNIVERSITY ITHACA, NY 14853 Microfilament organization and regulation
R01GM-36659-06 (MBY) KORNBERG, ROGER D STANFORD UNIV/FAIRCHILD BLDG D DEPT OF CELL BIOLOGY STANFORD, CA 94305 RNA polymerase II transcription system for yeast
R01GM-36663-06 (CBY) MC INTOSH, JOHN R UNIVERSITY OF COLORADO CAMPUS BOX 347 BOULDER, CO 80309-0347 Mitotic motors
R01GM-36675-06 (MBY) CUMSKY, MICHAEL G UNIVERSITY OF CALIFORNIA MOLECULAR BIOLOGY & BIOCHEMIST IRVINE, CA 92717 Biology and regulation of the COX5 gene family in yeast
R01GM-36688-06 (BNP) HOUK, KENDALL N UNIVERSITY OF CALIFORNIA 405 HILGARD AVE LOS ANGELES, CA 90024 Intramolecular cycloadditions as synthetic methods
R01GM-36692-07 (MBY) JAEHNING, JUDITH A INDIANA UNIVERSITY DEPARTMENT OF BIOLOGY BLOOMINGTON, IN 47405 Mechanisms of yeast mitochondrial transcription
R01GM-36700-06 (BNP) HOUK, KENDALL N UNIVERSITY OF CALIFORNIA DEPT OF CHEMISTRY & BIOCHEM LOS ANGELES, CA 90024 Stereoselectivities of synthetic organic reactions
R01GM-36716-06 (CBY) PFEFFER, LAWRENCE M UNIVERSITY OF TENNESSEE 899 MADISON AVE, BAPTIST MAIN MEMPHIS, TN 38163 Interferon action on cell structure and proliferation
R29GM-36722-04 (MBC) MISRA, TAPAN K UNIVERSITY OF ILLINOIS DEPT OF MICROBIO & IMMUN CHICAGO, ILLINOIS 60680 Evolution and regulation of mercurial resistance genes
R01GM-36734-22 (BIO) CHEUNG, WAI Y ST JUDE CHILDREN'S RES HOSP 332 NORTH LAUDERDALE MEMPHIS, TENN 38101 Regulatory mechanisms in CNS
R01GM-36745-06 (MGN) ARNHEIM, NORMAN UNIV OF SOUTHERN CALIFORNIA 825 WEST 37TH ST LOS ANGELES, CA 90089-1340 Genetic & molecular studies of human and mouse rdna
R01GM-36780-06 (PHRA) GIACOMINI, KATHLEEN M UNIVERSITY OF CALIFORNIA 926 MEDICAL SCIENCES BLDG SAN FRANCISCO, CA 94143-0446 Cellular mechanisms of drug elimination
R01GM-36792-05 (BMT) NEGISHI, EI-ICHI PURDUE UNIVERSITY DEPARTMENT OF CHEMISTRY W. LAFAYETTE, IN 47907 Organometallic cyclization reactions
R01GM-36799-08 (PB) COOK, PAUL F TEXAS COLL OF OSTEOPATHIC MED 3500 CAMP BOWIE BOULEVARD FORT WORTH, TX 76107-2690 Study of kinetic and chemical mechanisms of enzymes
R01GM-36802-06 (CBY) ROGALSKI, ADRIENNE A UNIVERSITY OF ILLINOIS 808 S WOOD STREET CHICAGO, IL 60612 Study of plasma memrane actin-associated glycoproteins
R01GM-36804-09 (ALY) MC MILLAN, MINNIE NORRIS CANCER CENTER 1441 EASTLAKE AVENUE LOS ANGELES, CA 90033-0800 Molecular characterization of immune-related proteins
R01GM-36806-06 (CBY) GOLDMAN, ROBERT D NORTHWESTERN UNIV MED SCH 303 E CHICAGO AVE/WARD 11-145 CHICAGO, IL 60611 Intermediate filament /cell surface interactions
R01GM-36810-07 (BBCA) HERZFELD, JUDITH BRANDEIS UNIVERSITY WALTHAM, MA 02254-9110 NMR studies of biological membranes
R01GM-36811-07 (MBC) SUSSKIND, MIRIAM M UNIV OF SOUTHERN CALIFORNIA UNIVERSITY PARK LOS ANGELES, CA 90089-1340 Interacting regulators of gene expression
R01GM-36812-05 (PBC) VANDEWATER, LIVINGSTON BETH ISRAEL HOSPITAL 330 BROOKLINE AVENUE BOSTON, MA 02215 Pathobiology of macrophage-fibronectin interactions
R01GM-36827-04 (GEN) LYNCH, MICHAEL R UNIVERSITY OF OREGON EUGENE, OREGON 97403 Mutation, drift, & the rate of phenotypic

PROJECT NO., ORGANIZATIONAL UNIT., INVESTIGATOR, ADDRESS, TITLE

evolution

R01GM-36844-06 (MCHA) MARTIN, JAMES C VANDERBILT UNIVERSITY DEPT OF CHEMISTRY, BOX 1822 NASHVILLE, TN 37235 Synthetic and physical studies of anticancer agents

R01GM-36846-06 (GEN) MALONE, ROBERT E UNIVERSITY OF IOWA DEPARTMENT OF BIOLOGY IOWA CITY, IOWA 52242 Isolation & analysis of recombination genes in yeast

R01GM-36847-06 (BCE) BANCROFT, F CARTER MOUNT SINAI SCHOOL OF MEDICINE 1 GUSTAVE L LEVY PLACE/BOX 12 NEW YORK, NY 10029 Growth hormone and prolactin gene regulatory mechanisms

R01GM-36852-07 (PHY) CORONADO, ROBERTO UNIVERSITY OF WISCONSIN 1300 UNIVERSITY AVENUE MADISON, WI 53706 Reconstitution of calcium channels in planar bilayers

R01GM-36862-06 (NEUC) CARLSON, JOHN R YALE UNIVERSITY P O BOX 6666 NEW HAVEN, CT 06511-8112 Genetic and molecular analysis of Drosophila olfaction

R01GM-36877-06 (MBC) STEWART, VALLEY J CORNELL UNIVERSITY ITHACA, NY 14853 Genetic control of nitrate respiration in E. coli

P01GM-36884-06 (SSS) GLAESER, ROBERT M UNIV OF CALIFORNIA/LIFE SCIENC 1 CYCLOTRON ROAD BERKELEY, CA 94720 Membrane proteins--High resolution electron microscopy

P01GM-36884-06 0001 (SSS) DOWNING, KENNETH H Membrane proteins--High resolution electron microscopy High resolution imaging

P01GM-36884-06 0002 (SSS) GLAESER,ROBERT M Membrane proteins--High resolution electron microscopy Bacteriorhodopsin photocycle intermediates

P01GM-36884-06 0004 (SSS) JAP, BING K Membrane proteins--High resolution electron microscopy Molecular structure of outer membrane channels

P01GM-36884-06 9001 (SSS) GLAESER, ROBERT M Membrane proteins--High resolution electron microscopy Core--imaging

R01GM-36887-04 (CBY) WEISMAN, GARY A UNIV OF MISSOURI - COLUMBIA 322A CHEMISTRY BUILDING COLUMBIA, MO 65211 Plasma membrane properties of mammalian cells

R01GM-36890-06 (MBC) GOLDEN, JAMES W TEXAS A & M UNIVERSITY COLLEGE STATION,TX 77843 Developmental genome rearrangement of NIF genes

R01GM-36894-04A1 (CTY) HEIDEMANN, STEVEN R MICHIGAN STATE UNIVERSITY GILTNER HALL EAST LANSING, MI 48824-1101 Tension and compression in the cytoskeleton

R01GM-36912-05 (BBCA) SCHEINER, STEVE SOUTHERN ILLINOIS UNIVERSITY DEPT CHEMISTRY/BIOCHEMISTRY CARBONDALE, IL 62901 Contribution of electron correlation to H-bonds

R01GM-36922-06 (PB) TRAGER, WILLIAM F UNIVERSITY OF WASHINGTON BG-20 SEATTLE, WA 98195 Isotope effects cytochrome P-450 catalyzed oxidations

R01GM-36925-04A2 (MCHA) PEARSON, ANTHONY J CASE WESTERN RESERVE UNIV 2074 ADELBERT RD CLEVELAND, OH 44106 Arene activation by transition metals

R01GM-36927-06 (PHRA) BROWN, JOAN H UNIV OF CALIFORNIA, SAN DIEGO SCHOOL OF MEDICINE LA JOLLA, CA 92093-0636 Phosphoinositides and muscarinic desensitization

R01GM-36936-06 (MBC) KHAN, SHAHID M ALBERT ENSTEIN COLL OF MED 1300 MORRIS PARK AVENUE BRONX, N Y 10461 Motility and chemosensing in bacteria

R37GM-36944-06 (BBCA) UHLENBECK, OLKE C UNIVERSITY OF COLORADO CAMPUS BOX 215 BOULDER, CO 80309-0215 Structure and function of ribonucleic acid

R01GM-36956-06 (BBCA) SONG, PILL-SOON UNIVERSITY OF NEBRASKA INST FOR CELL/MOLECULAR PHOTOB LINCOLN, NE 68588-0304 Structure and function of the photosensor phytochrome

R01GM-36960-05A1 (ALY) OGATA, RONALD T MEDICAL BIOLOGY INSTITUTE 11077 NORTH TORREY PINES ROAD LA JOLLA, CA 92037 Genetic engineering of short consensus repeat elements

R01GM-36970-06 (CTY) LARKINS, BRIAN A UNIVERSITY OF ARIZONA FORBES BLDG #36, ROOM 303C TUCSON, AZ 85721 Analysis of zein gene expression in maize

R01GM-36981-05A2 (MBY) BURKE, JOHN M UNIVERSITY OF VERMONT GIVEN MEDICAL BUILDING BURLINGTON, VT 05405 Self-splicing RNA--The 3' splice site

R01GM-37000-06 (BMT) RABENSTEIN, DALLAS L UNIVERSITY OF CALIFORNIA RIVERSIDE, CA 92521 Biological chemistry of sulfur and selenium

R01GM-37005-06 (BBCB) DRAPER, DAVID E THE JOHNS HOPKINS UNIVERSITY CHARLES AND 34TH STREETS BALTIMORE, MD 21218 Physical studies of RNA structural motifs

R01GM-37006-06 (BMT) MORRIS, MICHAEL D UNIVERSITY OF MICHIGAN 930 NORTH UNIVERSITY AVENUE ANN ARBOR, MI 48109-1055 Electro-optic measurements in electrophoresis

R01GM-37007-06 (BIO) KNOWLES, JEREMY R HARVARD UNIVERSITY 12 OXFORD STREET CAMBRIDGE, MA 02138 Structure and function in enzyme catalysis

R01GM-37039-06 (BBCA) PACE, CARLOS N TEXAS A&M UNIVERSITY COLLEGE STATION, TX 77843 Energetics and mechanism of folding of ribonuclease T1

R01GM-37040-06 (MBC) GOLDEN, SUSAN S TEXAS A&M RESEARCH FOUNDATION COLLEGE STATION, TX 77843 Multiple active genes for a cyanobacterial qb protein

R01GM-37044-04 (TOX) PARKINSON, ANDREW UNIVERSITY OF KANSAS MED CTR DEPT OF PHARM/TOX/THER KANSAS CITY, KAN 66103 Catatoxic steroids--Molecular mechanism of action

R01GM-37045-05 (SAT) ILLNER, HANA P TEX TECH UNIV HLTH SCIEN CTR DEPARTMENT OF SURGERY LUBBOCK, TX 79430 Calcium and magnesium changes in trauma and shock

R01GM-37048-05 (MBC) GOURSE, RICHARD L UNIVERSITY OF WISCONSIN 1550 LINDEN DRIVE MADISON, WI 53706 Medchanism, activation, & control of rRNA transcription

R01GM-37049-06 (MBY) JOHNSON, ALEXANDER D UNIVERSITY OF CALIFORNIA DEPT OF MICROBIO & IMMUN SAN FRANCISCO, CA 94143-0414 Mechanisms of action of yeast transcriptional regulators

R01GM-37052-04A3 (MBC) VOLKERT, MICHAEL R UNIV OF MASSACHUSETTS MED SCH 55 LAKE AVENUE NORTH WORCESTER, MA 01655 Genetic regulation of Escherichia coli aidB gene

PROJECT NO., ORGANIZATIONAL UNIT., INVESTIGATOR, ADDRESS, TITLE

R01GM-37053-06 (GEN) KENYON, CYNTHIA J DEPT OF BIOCHEMISTRY & BIOPHYS UNIVERSITY OF CALIFORNIA, S.F. SAN FRANCISCO, CA 94143 Genetic analysis of antero-posterior pattern formation in C. elegans

R01GM-37060-05 (SAT) RUSH, BENJAMIN F, JR UNIV OF MED & DENTISTRY OF NJ 185 SOUTH ORANGE AVENUE NEWARK, N J 07103 The link between hemorrhagic and septic shock

R01GM-37065-06 (BNP) MC LAUGHLIN, LARRY W BOSTON COLLEGE CHESTNUT HILL, MA 02167 Fluorescent labelling of nucleic acids

R01GM-37120-07 (MBY) REINBERG, DANNY F UNIV OF MED & DENT OF NJ 675 HOES LANE PISCATAWAY, NJ 08854-5635 Initiation of transcription of protein coding genes

R01GM-37123-07 (BBCA) CRIPPEN, GORDON M COLLEGE OF PHARMACY UNIVERSITY OF MICHIGAN ANN ARBOR, MI 48109 Conformational analysis by energy embedding

R01GM-37127-04 (SAT) CHAUDRY, IRSHAD H MICHIGAN STATE UNIVERSITY B424 CLINICAL CENTER EAST LANSING, MI 48824-1315 Immunological aspects of hemorrhage

R01GM-37145-06 (BBCB) THOMPSON, NANCY L UNIVERSITY OF NORTH CAROLINA CB #3290 CHAPEL HILL, NC 27599-3290 Molecular dynamics in receptor-mediated phagocytosis

R01GM-37161-07 (SSS) IWANCZYK, JAN S XSIRIUS INC 4640 ADMIRALTY WAY STE 214 MARINA DEL REY, CA 90292 Detector arrays for synchrotron radiation research

R01GM-37163-06 (GEN) ADLER, PAUL N UNIVERSITY OF VIRGINIA CHARLOTTESVILLE, VA 22901 Molecular genetics of the fz locus

R01GM-37187-04 (MGN) CHINAULT, ALAN C BAYLOR COLLEGE OF MEDICINE ONE BAYLOR PLAZA HOUSTON, TX 77030 X chromosome replication

R01GM-37188-06 (PHRA) AMIDON, GORDON L UNIVERSITY OF MICHIGAN 428 CHURCH STREET ANN ARBOR, MI 48109-1065 Use of muccosal cell carriers/eyzymes in oral absorption

R01GM-37193-06 (MBY) O'FARRELL, PATRICK H UNIVERSITY OF CALIFORNIA DEPT OF BIOCHEM & BIOPHYSICS SAN FRANCISCO, CA 94143 Molecular determinants of developmental fate

R01GM-37210-06 (BNP) KOZARICH, JOHN W UNIVERSITY OF MARYLAND COLLEGE PARK, MD 20742 Enzymes of aromatic acid metabolism

R01GM-37216-06 (RAD) KOW, YOKE W UNIVERSITY OF VERMONT BURLINGTON, VT 05405 Mechanism of action of radiation repair enzymes

R01GM-37219-06 (MBC) GOTTESMAN, MAX COLUMBIA UNIVERSITY 701 WEST 168TH ST NEW YORK, NY 10032 Control of transcription termination in E coli

R01GM-37223-06 (CBY) GROTENDORST, GARY ROBERT UNIVERSITY OF MIAMI 1600 N.W. 10TH AVENUE MIAMI, FL 33136 Cellular and molecular pathobiology of wound repair

R01GM-37233-04 (BBCA) TAKUSAGAWA, FUSAO UNIVERSITY OF KANSAS LAWRENCE, KS 66045-0046 Structural studies of methyl cycle enzymes

R01GM-37251-06 (SSS) BOOKSTEIN, FRED L UNIVERSITY OF MICHIGAN 300 NORTH INGALLS BUILDING ANN ARBOR, MI 48109 Landmark based methods for biometric analysis of shape

R01GM-37254-05 (BBCA) FEIGON, JULI F UNIVERSITY OF CALIFORNIA 405 HILGARD AVE LOS ANGELES, CA 90024-1569 Conformational variability of DNA

R01GM-37279-06 (CBY) SLAYMAN, CAROLYN W YALE UNIVERSITY 333 CEDAR STREET NEW HAVEN, CONN 06510 Regulation of intracellular pH in cultured kidney cell

R01GM-37289-06 (PC) CLAPP, CHARLES H BUCKNELL UNIVERSITY LEWISBURG, PA 17837 Inactivators of lipoxygenase

R01GM-37300-06 (BMT) BABCOCK, GERALD T MICHIGAN STATE UNIVERSITY EAST LANSING, MI 48824-1322 Free radicals in biological redox reactions

R01GM-37307-06 (BBCA) CHANDLER, DAVID UNIVERSITY OF CALIFORNIA DEPT OF CHEMISTRY BERKELEY, CA 94720 Statistical mechanics of amphiphiles in solution

R01GM-37387-06 (PBC) DAVIDSON, JEFFREY M VANDERBILT UNIV/SCH OF MEDICIN 21ST AND GARLAND AVENUES NASHVILLE, TN 37232-2561 Chemistry and biology of the elastin gene

R01GM-37396-06 (PHY) BULLOCK, JAMES O UNIVERSITY OF MISSOURI COLUMBI MA415 MEDICAL SCIENCE BLDG. COLUMBIA, MISSOURI 65212 Physiology of ion channel formation by type E1 colicins

R01GM-37408-05A1 (BBCA) SKOLNICK, JEFFREY SCRIPPS CLINIC & RESEARCH FDN 10666 NORTH TORREY PINES ROAD LA JOLLA, CA 92037 Computer simulations and theory of globular protein folding dynamics

R01GM-37432-05 (CBY) GUMBINER, BARRY M UNIV OF CALIFORNIA 513 PARNASSUS AVE SAN FRANCISCO, CA 94143-0450 Functions of cadherins in epithelial biogenesis

R01GM-37462-05 (MBC) MEYER, RICHARD J UNIVERSITY OF TEXAS 226 EXPERIMENTAL SCI BUILDING AUSTIN, TEX 78712 Conjugative mobilization of plasmid R1162

R01GM-37485-05 (CBY) WALTER, PETER UNIVERSITY OF CALIFORNIA DEPT BIOCHEM & BIOPHYSICS SAN FRANCISCO, CA 94143-0448 Protein translocation in yeast - biochemical & genetic analysis

R01GM-37498-06 (PB) LECH, JOHN J MEDICAL COLLEGE OF WISCONSIN 8701 WATERTOWN PLANK ROAD MILWAUKEE, WI 53226 The characterization of liver cytochromes p-450

R01GM-37504-01A4 (SSS) GUPTA, NABA K UNIVERSITY OF NEBRASKA HAMILTON HALL LINCOLN, NE 68588-0304 Protein synthesis initiation in yeast

R01GM-37508-05 (PC) MATHEWS, CHRISTOPHER K OREGON STATE UNIVERSITY CORVALLIS, OR 97331-6503 DNA precursor dynamics in animal cells

R01GM-37509-04 (MBC) DONOHUE, TIMOTHY J UNIVERSITY OF WISCONSIN 1550 LINDEN DRIVE MADISON, WI 53706 Pathway and regulation of cytochrome biosynthesis

R01GM-37513-02 (BMT) FALLER, JOHN W YALE UNIVERSITY 1504A YALE STATION NEW HAVEN, CT 06520 Organometallic reagents for stereocontrolled synthesis

R01GM-37525-05 (BBCA) BAUER, WILLIAM R STATE UNIVERSITY OF NEW YORK STONY BROOK, N Y 11794-8621 Topology geometry and energetics of closed circular DNA

R01GM-37537-05 (BMT) HUNT, DONALD F UNIVERSITY OF VIRGINIA MCCORMICK RD CHARLOTTESVILLE, VA 22901 Protein sequencing by tandem mass spectrometry

R01GM-37543-04 (CBY) BAJER, ANDREW S UNIVERSITY OF OREGON DEPT OF BIOLOGY EUGENE, OR 97403 Particle transport during mitosis

PROJECT NO., ORGANIZATIONAL UNIT., INVESTIGATOR, ADDRESS, TITLE

R01GM-37547-05 (PBC) ROTH, MICHAEL G UNIVERSITY OF TEXAS 5323 HARRY HINES BLVD DALLAS, TX 75235 Recognition and sorting of glycoproteins
R01GM-37552-07 (BIO) UHLENBECK, OLKE C UNIVERSITY OF COLORADO CAMPUS BOX 215 BOULDER, CO 80309-0215 Nucleotide substitution in tRNA
R01GM-37554-05 (BBCA) BROOKS, CHARLES L, III CARNEGIE MELLON UNIVERSITY 4400 FIFTH AVE PITTSBURGH, PA 15213 Theoretical studies of protein ligand interactions
R01GM-37555-04A2 (MBC) DAS, ANATH UNIVERSITY OF MINNESOTA 1479 GORTNER AVENUE ST PAUL, MN 55108 Function and regulation of A. tumefaciens virulence genes
R01GM-37556-04A1 (CBY) MOOSEKER, MARK S YALE UNIVERSITY 12 PROSPECT PLACE NEW HAVEN, CT 06511 Molecular characterization of the tight junction
R01GM-37561-06 (MBC) WINKLER, MALCOLM E UNIVERSITY OF TEXAS MED SCHOOL 6431 FANNIN, JFB 1 765 HOUSTON, TX 77030 Regulation of pyridoxal phosphate biosynthesis in E.col
R01GM-37567-06 (MGN) MAEDA, NOBUYO UNIVERSITY OF NORTH CAROLINA DEPARTMENT OF PATHOLOGY CHAPEL HILL, NC 27599-7525 History and control of the haptoglobin gene cluster
R01GM-37573-04 (BIO) WILLIAMS, KENNETH R MOLECULAR BIOPHYSICS/BIOCHEM. 333 CEDAR ST PO BOX 333 NEW HAVEN, CT 06510 Single-stranded nucleic acid binding proteins
R01GM-37575-04A1 (GEN) STEPONKUS, PETER L CORNELL UNIVERSITY ITHACA, NY 14853 Cryopreservation of Drosophila melanogaster embryos
R01GM-37590-04 (CBY) ZANER, KEN S BOSTON UNIVERSITY SCH OF MED BLDG S-3E, 80 E CONCORD ST BOSTON, MA 02118 Mechanical properties of purified cytoskeletal proteins
R01GM-37602-05 (GEN) GREENWALD, IVA S PRINCETON UNIVERSITY PRINCETON, NJ 08544-1003 Molecular and genetic studies of the nematode lin-12 gene
R01GM-37621-04A1 (BMT) EWING, ANDREW G PENNSYLVANIA STATE UNIVERSITY 152 DAVEY LABORATORY UNIVERSITY PARK, PA 16802 Subcellular analysis by capillary electrophoresis
R29GM-37631-05 (SAT) FINK, MITCHELL P UNIVERSITY OF MASSACHUSETTS 55 LAKE AVE NORTH WORCESTER, MA 01655 Complement-dependent prostaglandin synthesis in sepsis
R01GM-37639-05 (MBC) KENDALL, DEBRA A UNIVERSITY OF CONNECTICUT 75 NORTH EAGLEVILLE ROAD STORRS, CT 06269 Redesign of structural regions of alkaline phosphatase
P01GM-37641-05 (SSS) SCHIMMEL, PAUL MASSACHUSETTS INST OF TECH 77 MASS AVE / RM 16-437 CAMBRIDGE, MA 02139 Protein structure, function, and engineering at M I T
P01GM-37641-05 0001 (SSS) SCHIMMEL, PAUL Protein structure, function, and engineering at M I T Dissection & manipulation of enzyme structure & activity
P01GM-37641-05 0002 (SSS) GEFTER, MALCOLM L Protein structure, function, and engineering at M I T Isolation & physical chemical analysis of mutant antibody molecules
P01GM-37641-05 0003 (SSS) SAUER, ROBERT T Protein structure, function, and engineering at M I T Protein stability and determinants of antigen structure
P01GM-37641-05 0004 (SSS) FREDERICK, CHRISTIN Protein structure, function, and engineering at M I T Structural studies of protein recognition
P01GM-37641-05 0005 (SSS) RICH, ALEXANDER Protein structure, function, and engineering at M I T Molecular basis of protein-nucleic acid recognition
P01GM-37641-05 9001 (SSS) SCHIMMEL, PAUL Protein structure, function, and engineering at M I T Laboratory - core
R01GM-37650-05 (MCHA) WIBERG, KENNETH B YALE UNIVERSITY 225 PROSPECT STREET NEW HAVEN, CT 06511 Rotational barriers, molecular models & stereoselection
R01GM-37658-04A1 (BBCB) BILTONEN, RODNEY L UNIV OF VIRGINIA HLTH SCI CTR CHARLOTTESVILLE, VA 22908 Anesthetic alteration of protein lipid interactions
R01GM-37661-05 (GEN) JAHN, CAROLYN L DEPT OF BIOLOGICAL SCIENCES P O BOX 4348, MAIL CODE 066 CHICAGO, IL 60680 Genome reorganization during macronuclear development
R01GM-37664-05A1 (PHRA) BYLUND, DAVID B UNIV OF NEBRASKA MED CTR 600 SOUTH 42ND STREET OMAHA, NE 68198-6260 Regulation of alpha-2 adrenergic receptors
R01GM-37666-05 (BIO) COHEN, ROBERT E UNIV OF CALIFORNIA 405 HILGARD AVENUE LOS ANGELES, CA 90024-1569 Specificity of intracellular proteolysis in eukaryotes
R01GM-37674-01A3 (BBCB) SOWADSKI, JANUSZ M UNIV OF CALIFORNIA, SAN DIEGO LA JOLLA, CA 92093 The first crystal structure of protein kinase
R01GM-37677-04A1 (MBY) SINDEN, RICHARD R UNIVERSITY OF CINCINNATI 231 BETHESDA AVE CINCINNATI, OH 45267-0524 Existence of torsional tension in eukaryotic DNA in vivo
R01GM-37684-05 (BBCB) GETZOFF, ELIZABETH D SCRIPPS CLINIC & RESEARCH FDN 10666 N TORREY PINES RD LA JOLLA, CA 92037 Structural analyses of chromatically active proteins
P01GM-37696-05 (SRC) ULEVITCH, RICHARD J SCRIPPS CLINIC & RES FDN 10666 NORTH TORREY PINES ROAD LA JOLLA, CA 92037 Biochemical mechanisms of cellular injury in trauma
P01GM-37696-05 0001 (SRC) ULEVITCH, RICHARD J Biochemical mechanisms of cellular injury in trauma Metabolism of bacterial lipopolysaccharides
P01GM-37696-05 0002 (SRC) COCHRANE, CHARLES G Biochemical mechanisms of cellular injury in trauma Biochemistry of trauma-induced inflammation
P01GM-37696-05 0004 (SRC) SKLAR, LARRY A Biochemical mechanisms of cellular injury in trauma Physiologic modulation of neutrophil function
P01GM-37696-05 0005 (SRC) GINSBERG, MARK H Biochemical mechanisms of cellular injury in trauma Molecular analysis of adhesion receptor dysfunction
P01GM-37696-05 9001 (SRC) ULEVITCH, RICHARD J Biochemical mechanisms of cellular injury in trauma Core--Monoclonal antibody facility
R01GM-37699-05 (MGN) WABL, MATTHIAS R UNIVERSITY OF CALIFORNIA 1855 FOLSOM ST SAN FRANCISCO, CA 94143-0670 Genetic variation in B-Lymphocyte ontogeny
R01GM-37701-05 (CTY) GROSSCHEDL, RUDOLF UNIVERSITY OF CALIFORNIA BOX 0414 SAN FRANCISCO, CA 94143 Developmental regulation of gene expression
R01GM-37704-05 (HEM) TAYLOR, FLETCHER B, JR OKLAHOMA MEDICAL RESEARCH FDN 825 NORTHEAST 13TH STREET OKLAHOMA CITY, OK 73104 Suppression of anticoagulant factors by inflammatory agents
R01GM-37705-05 (EVR) FLINT, SARAH J PRINCETON UNIVERSITY PRINCETON, N J 08544-1014 Factors influencing transcription of Ad2 genes in vitro
R01GM-37706-05 (GEN) FIRE, ANDREW Z CARNEGIE INST OF WASHINGTON 115 WEST UNIVERSITY PARKWAY BALTIMORE, MD 21210 Gene regulation during early development of C elegans
R01GM-37715-05 (BIO) MAS, MARIA T BECKMAN RESEARCH INSTITUTE 1450 EAST DUARTE ROAD DUARTE, CA 91010 Mechanism of domain movement in phosphoglycerate kinase
R01GM-37723-05 (PC) GREENBERG, MIRIAM L UNIV OF MICHIGAN MEDICAL SCH MEDICAL SCIENCE I RM 4412 ANN ARBOR, MI 48109-0606 Genetic regulation of mitochondrial membrane biogenesis
R37GM-37731-07 (GEN) BAKER, BRUCE S STANFORD UNIVERSITY DEPT OF BIOLOGICAL SCIENCES STANFORD, CA 94305-5020 Genetics of meiosis and development in drosophila
R01GM-37734-05 (PTHA) BUTCHER, EUGENE C STANFORD UNIVERSITY MAIL STOP 5324 STANFORD, CA 94305-5324 Endothelial cell biology in inflammation
R01GM-37739-05 (GEN) ROSE, MARK D PRINCETON UNIVERSITY DEPT OF MOLECULAR BIOLOGY PRINCETON, N J 08544-1014 Mechanism of nuclear fusion in yeast
R01GM-37743-08 (EI) YUAN, DOROTHY C U OF TEXAS SOUTHWESTERN MED CT 5323 HARRY HINES BLVD DALLAS, TX 75235 Regulation of C-mu genes and C-delta genes in lymphocytes
R01GM-37745-14 (VR) MORRISON, TRUDY G UNIVERSITY OF MASSACHUSETTS 55 LAKE AVENUE NORTH WORCESTER, MA 01655 Assembly of viral membranes
R01GM-37746-05 (MBC) SHUB, DAVID A SUNY ALBANY 1400 WASHINGTON AVE ALBANY, N Y 12222 Genetics and regulation of RNA splicing in phage T4
R01GM-37751-05 (CBY) PAUL, DAVID L HARVARD MEDICAL SCHOOL 25 SHATTUCK STREET BOSTON, MA 02115 Cloning & expression of gap junction channels
R01GM-37753-05 (SAT) SIMMONS, RICHARD L UNIVERSITY OF PITTSBURGH 497 SCAIFE HALL PITTSBURGH, PA 15261 Hepatocyte--Kupffer cell interactions in surgical sepsis
R01GM-37759-05 (ALY) HAYDAY, ADRIAN C YALE UNIVERSITY BOX 1504A, YALE STATION NEW HAVEN, CT 06520 Regulation of T cell gamma gene expression
R01GM-37762-04A1 (HED) HOWE, CHIN C WISTAR INSTITUTE 36TH & SPRUCE STREETS PHILADELPHIA, PA 19104 Gene expression and mammalian development
R01GM-37774-04A1 (BNP) BUYNAK, JOHN D SOUTHERN METHODIST UNIVERSITY DALLAS, TX 75275 Allenes of synthetic and biochemical importance
R01GM-37778-05 (TMP) RIFKIN, MARY R ROCKEFELLER UNIVERSITY 1230 YORK AVENUE NEW YORK, N Y 10021-6399 Trypanosome surface glycoprotein interaction with lipid
R01GM-37795-03 (SAT) FISHER, DENNIS M UNIVERSITY OF CALIFORNIA SAN FRANCISCO, CA 94143-0648 Maturational changes in response to IV anesthetic drugs
R01GM-37803-05 (CBY) SCHATZ, GOTTFRIED UNIVERSITY OF BASEL KLINGELBERGSTRASSE 70 CH-4056 BASEL, SWITZERLAND Genetic analysis of mitochondrial assembly
R01GM-37812-05 (SSS) BURKS, CHRISTIAN LOS ALAMOS NATIONAL LABORATORY PO BOX 1663 MAIL STOP K710 LOS ALAMOS, NM 87545 Pattern recognition in nucleic acid sequence databases
R01GM-37813-06 (MBY) CHERBAS, PETER T INDIANA UNIVERSITY BLOOMINGTON, IN 47405 Structure and regulation of ecdysone-responsive genes
R01GM-37816-05 (BNP) JENDEN, DONALD J UNIVERSITY OF CALIFORNIA CENTER FOR HEALTH SCIENCES LOS ANGELES, CA 90024 Selective muscarinic and antimuscarinic agents
R01GM-37823-06 (MBY) HIRSH, DAVID I COLUMBIA UNIVERSITY HEALTH SCI 630 W 168TH STREET NEW YORK, NY 10032 Structure and expression of eucaryotic genes
R01GM-37828-05 (BIO) MONTMINY, MARC R SALK INSTITUTE PO BOX 85800 SAN DIEGO, CA 92186-5800 Regulation of somatostatin gene expression
R01GM-37829-06 (CTY) SAMBROOK, JOSEPH F UNIVERSITY OF TEXAS 5323 HARRY HINES BOULEVARD DALLAS, TX 75235-9038 Studies of proteins resident in the ER
R01GM-37830-06 (CBY) FIRTEL, RICHARD UNIV OF CALIFORNIA 9500 GILMAN DR LA JOLLA, CA 92093-0634 Analysis of signalling processes in Dictyostelium
R01GM-37835-05 (MBC) COX, MICHAEL M UNIVERSITY OF WISCONSIN 420 HENRY MALL MADISON, WI 53706 The biochemistry of genetic recombination by flp protein
R01GM-37841-09 (GEN) UYENOYAMA, MARCY K DUKE UNIVERSITY DURHAM, NC 27706 Mathematical population genetics
R01GM-37845-05 (CBY) DAVIS, ROGER J UNIV OF MASSACHUSETTS MED SCH 55 LAKE AVENUE NORTH WORCESTER, MA 01655 Regulation of transferrin receptor cycling
R01GM-37846-05 (SAT) EVERS, ALEX S 660 S EUCLID AVE ST LOUIS, MO 63110 Brain fatty acid composition and the anesthetic effect
R01GM-37886-06 (GEN) TIMBERLAKE, WILLIAM E UNIVERSITY OF GEORGIA ATHENS, GA 30602 Gene regulation during fungal development
R37GM-37904-05 (CTY) GILULA, NORTON B SCRIPPS CLINIC & RESEARCH FDN 10666 N TORREY PINES ROAD LA JOLLA, CA 92037 Gap junctions and cell-cell communication
R01GM-37905-05 (IMB) CLARK, EDWARD A UNIVERSITY OF WASHINGTON DEPT OF MICROBIOLOGY/SC-42 SEATTLE, WA 98195 Structure/function human B cell differentiation antigens
R01GM-37907-03 (CBY) GILULA, NORTON B RES INST OF SCRIPPS CLINIC 10666 N TORREY PINES ROAD LA JOLLA, CA 92037 Gap junction

PROJECT NO., ORGANIZATIONAL UNIT., INVESTIGATOR, ADDRESS, TITLE

expression--Molecular & genetic analysis
R37GM-37909-06 (BBCA) BEVERIDGE, DAVID L WESLEYAN UNIVERSITY CHEMISTRY DEPARTMENT MIDDLETOWN, CT 06459 Studies of DNA structure, dynamics and solvation
R01GM-37911-06A1 (PB) FREIRE, ERNESTO I JOHNS HOPKINS UNIVERSITY 34TH & CHARLES STREETS BALTIMORE, MD 21218 Statistical thermodynamic studies of membranes
R01GM-37922-05 (BIO) CAPDEVILA, JORGE H VANDERBILT UNIV SCH OF MED NEPHROLOGY, RM S-3223 MCN NASHVILLE, TN 37232 NADPH-dependent metabolism of arachidonic acid
R01GM-37934-06 (BNP) KOHN, HAROLD L UNIVERSITY OF HOUSTON 4800 CALHOUN BOULEVARD HOUSTON, TX 77204-5641 Mode of action of bicyclomycin
R29GM-37939-05 (MCHA) DITTAMI, JAMES P WORCESTER POLYTECHNIC INST GODDARD HALL WORCESTER, MA 01609 Approaches to gelsemium alkaloids: synthesis of koumine
R01GM-37942-05 (PB) WATERMAN, MICHAEL R UNIV OF TX SOUTHWESTERN MED CT 5323 HARRY HINES BLVD DALLAS, TX 75235-9016 Steroidogenic P-450 enzymes--Structural mutagenesis
R01GM-37943-05 (MCHA) BARTON, DEREK H TEXAS A & M UNIVERSITY DEPARTMENT OF CHEMISTRY COLLEGE STATION, TX 77843 Invention of general and useful chemical reactions
R01GM-37947-04A2 (MGN) FLAHERTY, LORRAINE A WADSWORTH CTR FOR LAB & RESEAR PO BOX 509 ALBANY, NY 12201-0509 Molecular immunogenetics of the murine MHC
R01GM-37949-06 (GEN) LAMBOWITZ, ALAN M OHIO STATE UNIVERSITY RES FDN 484 WEST 12TH AVES COLUMBUS, OH 43210 Mitochondrial bigenesis and reverse trascriptases
R01GM-37950-06 (CTY) GUILFOYLE, THOMAS J UNIV OF MISSOURI-COLUMBIA DEPT OF BIOCHEMISTRY COLUMBIA, MO 65211 Plant transcription factors and RNA polymerases
R01GM-37951-06 (MBY) LAMBOWITZ, ALAN M OHIO STATE UNIVERSITY RES FDN DEPARTMENT OF GENETICS COLUMBUS, OH 43210 RNA splicing in mitochondria
R01GM-37971-05 (GEN) MANLEY, JAMES L COLUMBIA UNIVERSITY 713 FAIRCHILD CENTER NEW YORK, NY 10027 Transcriptional control of homeo box gene expression
R01GM-37977-04 (CTY) MC KEON, FRANK D HARVARD MEDICAL SCHOOL 25 SHATTUCK ST BOSTON, MASS 02115 Functional domains in the nuclear lamin proteins
R01GM-37985-03 (BNP) GAWLEY, ROBERT E P O BOX 249118 CORAL GABLES, FL 33124-0431 Asymmetric synthesis of biologically important alkaloids
R01GM-37987-05 (CTY) MULLET, JOHN E TEXAS A&M UNIVERSITY COLLEGE STATION, TEXAS 77843 Regulation of chlorophyll-apoprotein synthesis
R01GM-37990-06 (MBC) STEWART, GEORGE C UNIVERSITY OF SOUTH CAROLINA MICROBIOLOGY & IMMUNOLOGY COLUMBIA, SC 29208 Cell division gene products of Bacillus subtilis
R01GM-37991-04A1 (GEN) MOUNT, STEPHEN M COLUMBIA UNIVERSITY 922A FAIRCHILD CENTER NEW YORK, NY 10027 Transposable elements and RNA processing in Drosophila
R29GM-37996-05 (MCHA) MACKENZIE, PETER B NORTHWESTERN UNIVERSITY DEPARTMENT OF CHEMISTRY EVANSTON, IL 60201 New catalysts for asymmetric Diels-Alder reactions
R01GM-37997-05 (MBY) GILBERT, WALTER HARVARD UNIVERSITY 16 DIVINITY AVE CAMBRIDGE, MA 02138 Gene structure and sequence
R29GM-37999-06 (MGN) KILLARY, ANN M UNIV OF TEXAS/M D ANDERSON CTR 1515 HOLCOMBE BLVD HOUSTON, TX 77030 Tissue-specific gene regulation in plasmacytoma cells
R01GM-38006-05 (CBY) STEVENS, TOM H UNIVERSITY OF OREGON EUGENE, OR 97403 Sorting and transport of membrane proteins
R01GM-38008-04 (BMT) CALDWELL, KARIN D UNIVERSITY OF UTAH DEPT OF BIOENGINEERING SALT LAKE CITY, UT 84112 Field-flow fractionation in biochemical analysis
R29GM-38010-05 (BIO) ZIMMERMAN, STEVEN C UNIV OF ILLINOIS 1209 WEST CALIFORNIA ST URBANA, IL 61801 Host-guest chemistry--A rigid DNA bis-intercalator
R29GM-38032-05 (SAT) LANG, CHARLES H LSU MEDICAL CENTER 1901 PERDIDO ST NEW ORLEANS, LA 70112 Sepsis induced insulin resistance in diabetes
R01GM-38035-05 (MBC) WRIGHT, ANDREW TUFTS UNIVERSITY 136 HARRISON AVE BOSTON, MA 02111 Activation and regulation of the bgl operon in E coli K-12
R29GM-38040-05 (BNP) OKUDA, ROY K SAN JOSE STATE UNIVERSITY ONE WASHINGTON SQUARE SAN JOSE, CALIFORNIA 95192 Haloperoxidases & halogenated marine natural products
R01GM-38045-01A2 (BBCA) WARTELL, ROGER M GEORGIA INSTITUTE OF TECHNOLOG ATLANTA, GA 30332 Thermodynamics of base pair opening in DNA
R29GM-38047-05 (BMT) PENNER-HAHN, JAMES E UNIVERSITY OF MICHIGAN 930 N UNIVERSITY AVENUE ANN ARBOR, MI 48109-1055 Structural investigations of metalloprotein metal sites
R01GM-38060-04 (PBC) LINHARDT, ROBERT J UNIVERSITY OF IOWA COLLEGE OF PHARMACY IOWA CITY, IA 52242 Sequencing the polysaccharide component of proteoglycans
R01GM-38070-04 (MBY) WISE, JO ANN UNIVERSITY OF ILLINOIS 1209 W CALIFORNIA STREET URBANA, IL 61801 SnRNP-substrate interactions in S pombe splicing
R01GM-38073-04 (PB) COAN, CAROL R UNIVERSITY OF THE PACIFIC 2155 WEBSTER STREET SAN FRANCISCO, CALIF 94115 Transport mechanism of sarcoplasmic reticulum ATPase
R01GM-38079-04A1 (MCHA) THORNTON, EDWARD R UNIVERSITY OF PENNSLYVANIA PHILADELPHIA, PA 19104-6323 Aldol stereocontrol--Strategies, methods and mechanisms
R01GM-38093-04 (CBY) BRODSKY, FRANCES M UNIV. OF CALIFORNIA, SF 926 MEDICAL SCIENCES BLDG SAN FRANCISCO, CA 94143-0446 The molecular mechanism of clathrin assembly
R01GM-38094-05 (CBY) SIMCHOWITZ, LOUIS WASHINGTON UNIVERSITY 660 S EUCLID AVENUE, BOX 8045 ST LOUIS, MO 63110 Chloride movements in human neutrophils
R01GM-38097-05 (CTY) ROME, LEONARD H U C L A SCHOOL OF MEDICINE 405 HILGARD AVENUE LOS ANGELES, CA 90024-1737 A novel cytoplasmic large ribonucleoprotein particle
R01GM-38101-05 (MBY) JAEHNING, JUDITH A INDIANA UNIVERSITY BLOOMINGTON, IN 47405 A molecular analysis of yeast transcription
R29GM-38104-03 (MBC) DI RUSSO, CONCETTA C UNIVERSITY OF TENNESSEE, MEM DEPT OF BIOCHEMISTRY MEMPHIS, TN 38163 FadR, multifunctional regulator of lipid metabolism
R01GM-38109-05 (MBY) MORIMOTO, RICHARD I NORTHWESTERN UNIVERSITY EVANSTON, IL 60208 Regulation and expression of the human HSP70 gene family
R01GM-38113-04 (CBY) HUANG, BESSIE P RES INST OF SCRIPPS CLINIC 10666 NORTH TORREY PINES ROAD LA JOLLA, CA 92037 Structure/function of a basal body-associated CA2+ -BP
R01GM-38114-05 (BBCA) TEETER, MARTHA M BOSTON COLLEGE DEPARTMENT OF CHEMISTRY CHESTNUT HILL, MA 02167 Prediction methods--Hemolytic toxins and plasmin kringles
P01GM-38125-04 (SSS) SILVERSTEIN, SAUL J COLUMBIA UNIVERSITY 701 WEST 168TH STREET NEW YORK, N Y 10032 Genetics of animal virus replication
P01GM-38125-04 0001 (SSS) GOFF, STEPHEN P Genetics of animal virus replication Targetting of proteins into assembling virions
P01GM-38125-04 0002 (SSS) RACANIELLO, VINCENT R Genetics of animal virus replication Molecular genetics of poliovirus RNA synthesis
P01GM-38125-04 0003 (SSS) SILVERSTEIN, SAUL J Genetics of animal virus replication Early gene products & regulation of herpes simplex expressiom
P01GM-38125-04 0004 (SSS) YOUNG, CHARLES SH Genetics of animal virus replication Divergent transcription in promoter region of adenovirus
P01GM-38125-04 9001 (SSS) SILVERSTEIN, SAUL J Genetics of animal virus replication Tissue culture/media core
R29GM-38130-04 (BMT) BUTLER, ALISON UNIVERSITY OF CALIFORNIA DEPARTEMENT OF CHEMISTRY SANTA BARBARA, CA 93106 Investigations of the biochemistry of vanadium
R01GM-38133-04 (BBCA) SAXTON, MICHAEL J UNIVERSITY OF CALIFORNIA DAVIS, CA 95616 Lateral diffusion in an Archipelago--Monte Carlo studies
R29GM-38137-05 (BBCA) MORDEN, KATHLEEN M LOUISIANA STATE UNIVERSITY DEPT. OF BIOCHEMISTRY BATON ROUGE, LA 70803 NMR studies of perturbed nucleic acid helices
R01GM-38142-04 (BBCB) TEINTZE, MARTIN CORNELL UNIVERSITY 1300 YORK AVENUE NEW YORK, N Y 10021 The mechanism of protein insertion into lipid bilayers
R01GM-38147-05 (MBC) MC ALLISTER, WILLIAM T SUNY AT BROOKLYN 450 CLARKSON AVENUE BROOKLYN, N Y 11203 RNA polymerase structure and function
R01GM-38148-06 (GEN) DELLAPORTA, STEPHEN L YALE UNIVERSITY DEPARTMENT OF BIOLOGY NEW HAVEN, CT 06520 Molecular genetics of the maize controlling element activator
R01GM-38149-06 (PHRA) WATKINS, PAUL B UNIVERSITY OF MICHIGAN MED SCH 3912 TAUBMAN CENTER ANN ARBOR, MI 48109-0362 The environmental and genetic factors regulating HLP
R01GM-38155-04A1 (BIO) POLLACK, RALPH M UNIVERSITY OF MARYLAND BALTIMORE, MD 21228 Mechanism of steroid isomerase
R29GM-38156-05 (IMB) ARCECI, ROBERT J DANA-FARBER CANCER INST 44 BINNEY ST BOSTON, MA 02115 Lineage commitment of t-lymphocytes during development
R01GM-38157-05 (GEN) SPRAGUE, GEORGE F, JR UNIVERSITY OF OREGON INST OF MOLECULAR BIOLOGY EUGENE, OREG 97403 Biochemical analysis of the yeast A-factor receptor
R29GM-38161-05 (BBCB) WAGENKNECHT, TERENCE C NEW YORK STATE DEPT OF HEALTH EMPIRE STATE PLAZA-PO BOX 509 ALBANY, NY 12201-0509 Structural studies of alpha-ketoacid dehydrogenase complex (E coli, rabbits)
R01GM-38166-05 (SSS) JONES, KATHERINE A SALK INST FOR BIOLOGICAL STUDY PO BOX 85800 SAN DIEGO, CA 92186-5800 Molecular mechanisms of gene expression in animal cells
R01GM-38174-05 (GEN) EMMONS, SCOTT W ALBERT EINSTEIN COLLEGE OF MED DEPT OF MOLECULAR GENETICS BRONX, N Y 10461 Transposable elements in Caenorhabditis elegans
R01GM-38177-04 (SAT) BEATTIE, CHARLES THE JOHNS HOPKINS HOSPITAL 600 N WOLFE ST., TOWER 711 BALTIMORE, MD 21205 Regional vs general anesthesia in peripheral vascular surgery
R29GM-38178-05 (PHY) MC CLESKEY, EDWIN W WASHINGTON UNIVERSITY 660 S EUCLID AVE ST LOUIS, MO 63110 Calcium channels--Permeation and regulation
R01GM-38184-04 (BIO) MARTINEZ-CARRION, MARINO UNIVERSITY OF MISSOURI 5100 ROCKHILL RD KANSAS CITY, MO 64110-2499 Pyridoxal as aprobe of molecular function
R01GM-38193-05 (PC) LAU, JOSEPH T ROSWELL PARK MEMORIAL INST 666 ELM STREET BUFFALO, N Y 14263 Regulated synthesis of sialyltransferases
R29GM-38200-05 (BIO) HUBER, PAUL W UNIVERSITY OF NOTRE DAME NOTRE DAME, IN 46556 Protein binding domains on eukaryotic 5S r-RNA and r-DNA
R01GM-38212-05A1 (MBY) SAWADOGO, MICHELE UNIVERSITY OF TEXAS 1515 HOLCOMBE BLVD HOUSTON, TX 77030 Control of cellular & viral gene expression by USF
R01GM-38213-05 (PHRA) HARDEN, T KENDALL UNIVERSITY OF NORTH CAROLINA CB # 7365/FAC LAB OFF BLDG CHAPEL HILL, NC 27599-7365 Muscarinic receptor subtypes on cultured cells
R29GM-38214-04 (BBCA) SCHENCK, CRAIG C COLORADO STATE UNIVERSITY DEPT OF BIOCHEMISTRY FORT COLLINS, CO 80523 Reaction center dynamics
R01GM-38219-05 (MGN) WILSON, JOHN H BAYLOR COLLEGE OF MEDICINE ONE BAYLOR PLAZA HOUSTON, TX 77030 Targeted recombination in mammalian cells
R01GM-38221-07 (BBCA) HAVEL, TIMOTHY F HARVARD MEDICAL SCHOOL 25 SHATTUCK ST BOSTON, MA 02115 Determination and refinement of protein solution structure
R01GM-38225-05 (PB) PERLIN, DAVID S PUBLIC HEALTH RESEARCH INSTITU 455 FIRST AVE NEW YORK, NY 10016 Energy coupling by the yeast plasma membrane-ATPase
R29GM-38228-06 (EVR) KUMAR, GYANENDRA 540 E CANFIELD DETROIT, MI 48201 Characterization of RNA pol II transcription proteins

R29GM-38230-05 (BMT) BERG, JEREMY M JOHNS HOPKINS UNIVERSITY CHARLES & 34TH STREETS BALTIMORE, MD 21218 Metal binding domains from nucleic acid binding proteins

R01GM-38234-04 (EVR) ENGLER, JEFFREY A UNIV OF ALABAMA UAB STATION BIRMINGHAM, AL 35294 Transport and processing of the adenovirus fiber protein

R01GM-38237-06 (MBC) DALDAL, FEVZI UNIVERSITY OF PENNSYLVANIA 204 MUDD BLDG / #6019 PHILADELPHIA, PA 19104-6019 A genetic analysis for the functional sites of the bc complex

R01GM-38242-06 (MBY) FRENDEWEY, DAVID ALLYN NEW YORK UNIVERSITY MEDICAL CT 550 FIRST AVENUE NEW YORK, NY 10016 Pre-mRNA splicing in Schizosaccharomyces pombe

R01GM-38243-03 (MCHA) ALBIZATI, KIM F WAYNE ST UNIV 221 CHEMISTRY DETROIT, MI 48202 New methods of oxygen heterocycle synthesis

R01GM-38244-04 (BBCB) MACDONALD, ROBERT C NORTHWESTERN UNIVERSITY 2153 SHERIDAN RD EVANSTON, IL 60208 Membrane surface pressure--Measurement and significance

R01GM-38250-04 (PHRA) PANG, K SANDY UNIVERSITY OF TORONTO 19 RUSSELL STREET TORONTO, ONTARIO CANADA M5S 1A Hepatic formation and handling of drug metabolites

R01GM-38259-04A2 (GEN) LEVIS, ROBERT W FRED HUTCHINSON CANCER RES CTR 1124 COLUMBIA STREET SEATTLE, WA 98104 Chromosomal telomeres in Drosophila

R01GM-38260-04 (BNP) KAHN, MICHAEL S UNIVERSITY OF ILLINOIS P O BOX 4348 (M/C 111) CHICAGO, ILL 60680 Synthetic approaches to peptide and protein mimetics

R29GM-38261-04 (PB) BLACK, SHAUN D OHIO STATE UNIVERSITY 500 WEST 12TH AVE COLUMBUS, OHIO 43210 Structure, function, and dynamics of P-450 cytochromes

R01GM-38273-06 (BNP) HILVERT, DONALD M THE SCRIPPS RESEARCH INSTITUTE 10666 N TORREY PINES RD LA JOLLA, CA 92037 Antibodies as catalysts

R29GM-38275-05 (BMT) ARMSTRONG, WILLIAM H UNIVERSITY OF CALIFORNIA BERKELEY, CA 94720 Metal-dioxygen chemistry of biological interest

R01GM-38276-07 (CBY) MC DONALD, JOHN A MAYO CLINIC SCOTTSDALE 13400 E SHEA BOULEVARD SCOTTSDALE, AZ 85259 Fibronectin's role in pericellular matrix organization

R01GM-38277-05 (BCE) SCHOENBERG, DANIEL R UNIFORMED SERVICES UNIVERSITY 4301 JONES BRIDGE RD BETHESDA, MD 20814-4799 Estrogen action in xenopus liver cells

R01GM-38278-04 (MBC) GURLEY, WILLIAM B UNIVERSITY OF FLORIDA DEPT OF MICROBIO & CELL SCI GAINESVILLE, FL 32611 Cis & trans-acting components of T-DNA promoter function

R29GM-38280-05 (PC) HORTIN, GLEN L WASHINGTON UNIV SCH OF MED 400 S KINGSHIGHWAY BLVD ST LOUIS, MO 63110 Sulfation of plasma proteins

R01GM-38284-06 (CBY) SCHWARTZ, ALAN L WASHINGTON UNIVERSITY 400 S KINGSHIGHWAY ST LOUIS, MO 63110 Receptor mediated endocytosis in liver

R01GM-38287-03 (SSS) JOHNSTON, ROGER G LOS ALAMOS NATIONAL LABORATORY BIOCHEMISTRY / MS M880 LOS ALAMOS, NM 87545 Phase flow cytometry

R01GM-38318-05 (CBY) CHEN, LAN B DANA-FARBER CANCER INSTITUTE 44 BINNEY ST/ MAYER 840 BOSTON, MA 02115 Studies on proteins involved in cell interaction

R01GM-38320-04 (MBY) REDDY, RAMACHANDRA R BAYLOR COLLEGE OF MEDICINE ONE BAYLOR PLAZA HOUSTON, TX 77030 Factors involved in the synthesis of U6 snRNA

R01GM-38323-04A1 (PB) CRAMER, WILLIAM A PURDUE UNIVERSITY WEST LAFAYETTE, IN 47907 Structure/function of photosynthetic cytochrome complex

R01GM-38328-05 (GEN) REED, STEVEN I SCRIPPS RESEARCH INSTITUTE 10666 N TORREY PINES RD LA JOLLA, CA 92037 Studies on the control of cell division in yeast

R01GM-38330-05 (ALY) BROWN, ERIC J WASHINGTON UNIV SCH OF MEDICIN 660 SOUTH EUCLID AVE ST LOUIS, MO 63110 Extracellular matrix protein enhancement of phagocytosi

R01GM-38341-05 (BBCB) MARTINEZ-CARRION, MARINO UNIVERSITY OF MISSOURI 5100 ROCKHILL ROAD KANSAS CITY, MO 64110-2499 Effectors of organization of transmembrane proteins

R01GM-38346-10 (CBY) HELENIUS, ARI H 333 CEDAR STREET NEW HAVEN, CT 06510 Endocytosis and membrane fusion

R01GM-38351-07 (MBY) GREENBERG, JAY R UNIVERSITY OF ROCHESTER HUTCHISON HALL/RIVER CAMPUS ROCHESTER, NY 14627 Interactions of proteins with mrna and hnRNA

R01GM-38352-05 (SSS) GRIFFIN, ROBERT G MASSACHUSETTS INST OF TECH 77 MASSACHUSETTS AVENUE CAMBRIDGE, MA 02139-4307 High field DNP and EPR in biological systems

R44GM-38355-03 (SSP) SCHNEIDER, MARTIN J WESTCHESTER DISTRIBUTION SYSTE PO BOX 324 SCARSDALE, NY 10583 Hand-held computers to facilitate clinical trials

R01GM-38361-06 (MBC) KUSTU, SYDNEY G UNIVERSITY OF CALIFORNIA BERKELEY, CA 94720 Genetic studies of glutamine synthetase in bacteria

R01GM-38401-19 (BBCA) SCHEIDT, W ROBERT UNIVERSITY OF NOTRE DAME CHEMISTRY & BIOCHEMISTRY NOTRE DAME, IND 46556 X-ray and chemical studies of metalloporphyrins

R01GM-38409-06 (MBY) CASHMORE, ANTHONY R UNIVERSITY OF PENNSYLVANIA DEPARTMENT OF BIOLOGY PHILADELPHIA, PA 19104-6018 Photoregulated gene expression

R01GM-38416-05 (MGN) ROTHMAN-DENES, LUCIA B UNIVERSITY OF CHICAGO 920 E 58TH ST CHICAGO, IL 60637 Regulation of eukaryotic gene expression

R01GM-38419-04A1 (BBCB) WILSON, IAN A THE SCRIPPS RESEARCH INSTITUTE 10666 N TORREY PINES RD/MB-13 LA JOLLA, CA 92037 Crystallographic studies of antibody-steroid interaction

R01GM-38424-05 (CPA) ZARLING, DAVID A SRI INTERNATIONAL 333 RAVENSWOOD AVENUE MENLO PARK, CA 94025 Monoclonal antibody probes of double-helix structure/function

R01GM-38433-06 (PB) BEATTIE, DIANA S WEST VIRGINIA UNIVERSITY DEPT OF BIOCHEMISTRY MORGANTOWN, W VA 26506 Bioenergetics of the cytochrome bc1 complex

PROJECT NO., ORGANIZATIONAL UNIT., INVESTIGATOR, ADDRESS, TITLE

R01GM-38434-05 (BMT) WINEFORDNER, JAMES D UNIVERSITY OF FLORIDA DEPARTMENT OF CHEMISTRY GAINESVILLE, FL 32611 Development of trace atomic spectrometric methods

R01GM-38436-04 (MCHA) ROUSH, WILLIAM R INDIANA UNIVERSITY P O BOX 1847 BLOOMINGTON, IN 47405 Chiral crotylboronates--Methodology and synthesis

R01GM-38456-05 (MBC) MC ENTEE, KEVIN UNIV OF CALIFORNIA, LOS ANGELE ENVIRONMENTAL SCIENCES LOS ANGELES, CA 90024-1786 Molecular mechanisms of DDR gene regulation in yeast

R01GM-38462-05 (GEN) COYNE, JERRY A THE UNIV OF CHICAGO 1103 EAST 57TH STREET CHICAGO, IL 60637 Genetic basis of species differences in Drosophila

R29GM-38464-05 (MBC) JINKS-ROBERTSON, SUE EMORY UNIVERSITY 1510 CLIFTON ROAD, NE ATLANTA, GA 30322 Recombination between repeated sequence in yeast

R01GM-38470-04 (CBY) JONES, JONATHAN C R NORTHWESTERN UNIVERSITY MED SC 303 EAST CHICAGO AVENUE CHICAGO, IL 60611 Dynamics of hemidesmosome assembly

R29GM-38475-05 (CBY) GARD, DAVID L UNIVERSITY OF UTAH SALT LAKE CITY, UT 84112 Microtubule assembly factors from Xenopus eggs

R29GM-38483-05 (GEN) CHRISTENSEN, ALAN C THOMAS JEFFERSON UNIVERSITY 233 SOUTH 10TH ST PHILADELPHIA, PA 19107-5541 Molecular genetics of gene dosage compensation and sex

R01GM-38499-04 (CBY) VALE, RONALD D UNIVERSITY OF CALIFORNIA BOX 0450, S-1210 SAN FRANCISCO, CA 94143-0450 Microtubule-based organelle transport

R29GM-38501-04 (CBY) GREEN, REZA C U N Y MT SINAI SCH OF MED ONE GUSTAVE L LEVY PLACE NEW YORK, N Y 10029 Sorting and processing of peptide hormone precursors

R01GM-38509-05 (MBC) JOHNSON, REID C UNIVERSITY OF CALIFORNIA ROOM 33-257 CHS LOS ANGELES, CA 90024-1737 Molecular analysis of site-specific DNA recombination

R01GM-38511-04 (CBY) CONDEELIS, JOHN S ALBERT EINSTEIN COLL OF MED 1300 MORRIS PARK AVENUE BRONX, N Y 10461 Signal transduction & actin during amoeboid chemotaxis

R01GM-38515-04 (IMB) ROCK, KENNETH L DANA FARBER CANCER INSTITUTE 44 BINNEY STREET BOSTON, MA Immunobiology and structure of TAP and related molecules

R29GM-38516-05 (GEN) BEDINGER, PATRICIA A UNIVERSITY OF NORTH CAROLINA CB #3280 / 010A COKER HALL CHAPEL HILL, NC 27599-3280 Male gametophyte development in maize

R01GM-38519-05 (SSS) JONES, RICHARD H UNIV OF COLORADO HLTH SCIS CTR 4200 EAST NINTH AVE/BOX B119 DENVER, CO 80262 Time series analysis and longitudinal data

R01GM-38526-04 (CTY) BERGET, SUSAN M BAYLOR COLLEGE OF MEDICINE ONE BAYLOR PLAZA HOUSTON, TX 77030 Processing of premessenger RNA

P50GM-38529-04 (SRC) MOODY, FRANK G UNIV OF TEXAS MED SCHOOL 6431 FANNIN, SUITE 4020 HOUSTON, TX 77025 Pathogenesis of multiple organ failure

P50GM-38529-04 0001 (SRC) MOODY, FRANK G Pathogenesis of multiple organ failure

P50GM-38529-04 0003 (SRC) MYERS, STUART I Pathogenesis of multiple organ failure Role of eicosanoids in splanchnic circulation in normal and shock states

P50GM-38529-04 0004 (SRC) MILLER, THOMAS A Pathogenesis of multiple organ failure Intestinal injury--Source of sepsis in hemorrhagic shock

P50GM-38529-04 9001 (SRC) MILLER, THOMAS A Pathogenesis of multiple organ failure Core A--Animal surgery and maintenance

R29GM-38530-04 (BIO) KOTB, MALAK VA MEDICAL CENTER 1030 JEFFERSON AVENUE MEMPHIS, TN 38104 T lymphocyte differentiation--Role of adenosylmethionine

R01GM-38538-05 (CBY) MEYER, DAVID I UCLA SCHOOL OF MEDICINE LOS ANGELES, CA 90024-1737 A molecular analysis of secretory protein translocation

R01GM-38540-05 (CTY) SILBERT, DAVID F WASHINGTON UNIVERSITY 724 S EUCLID, BOX 8231 ST LOUIS, MO 63110 Sphingolipid and phosphatidylinositide mutants

R01GM-38542-03 (CTY) COOPER, JOHN A WASHINGTON UNIV SCH OF MED 660 S. EUCLID AVE, BOX 8228 ST LOUIS, MO 63110 Actin capping protein of the Z line of muscle

R01GM-38543-05 (SSS) KOPITO, RON R STANFORD UNIVERSITY STANFORD, CA 94305-5020 Molecular biology of mammalian anion transport

R29GM-38544-05 (PBC) GREENSPAN, DANIEL S PATHOLOGY DEPT SCH OF MED 470 NORTH CHARTER ST MADISON, WI 53706 Molecular biology of procollagen transport and secretion

R01GM-38545-05 (PBC) LEHRMAN, MARK A UNIV. OF TEXAS SOUTHWESTERN DEPT. OF PHARMACOLOGY DALLAS, TX 75235-9041 Molecular biology of asparagine-linked glycosylation

R01GM-38549-05 (BMT) KLIGER, DAVID S UNIVERSITY OF CALIFORNIA SINSHEIMER HALLS SANTA CRUZ, CA 95064 Transient magnetic circular dichroism

R29GM-38555-05 (BBCB) YUE, KWOK T EMORY UNIVERSITY ROLLINS RESEARCH CENTER ATLANTA, GA 30322 Raman studies of sulfite reductases and other enzymes

R01GM-38556-05 (CBY) BURKE, BRIAN E HARVARD MEDICAL SCHOOL 25 SHATTUCK STREET BOSTON, MA 02115 The nuclear envelope during mitosis

R29GM-38566-05 (CTY) BAKER, RICHARD E UNIVERSITY OF MASS MED SCHOOL 55 LAKE AVENUE NORTH WORCESTER, MA 01655 Kinetochore proteins of yeast

R01GM-38575-05 (BBCA) CLARK, LEIGH B UNIV OF CALIF., SAN DIEGO LA JOLLA, CA 92093-0342 Optical properties of nucleic acid constituents

R29GM-38601-04 (BNP) BALASUBRAMANIAM, AMBIKAIPAKAN UNIV OF CINCINNATI MED CTR DEPARTMENT OF SURGERY CINCINNATI, OH 45267-0558 Synthesis of peptides related to APY, NPY & PYY

R01GM-38608-05 (BBCB) WAGNER, GERHARD HARVARD MEDICAL SCHOOL 25 SHATTUCK ST BOSTON, MA 02115 NMR spectroscopy for protein molecular design

R29GM-38610-05 (CBY) STEWART, STANFORD J VA MEDICAL CENTER 1310-24TH AVE SOUTH NASHVILLE, TN 37203 Molecular mechanisms of T lymphocyte activation

PROJECT NO., ORGANIZATIONAL UNIT., INVESTIGATOR, ADDRESS, TITLE

R01GM-38613-05 (BMT) GEORGE, T ADRIAN UNIVERSITY OF NEBRASKA DEPARTMENT OF CHEMISTRY LINCOLN, NE 68588-0304 Investigations of biomimetic nitrogen fixation

R29GM-38624-05 (BNP) PAUL, VALERIE J UNIV OF GUAM UOG STATION MANGILAO, GUAM 96923 Chemical interactions of coral reef invertebrates

R29GM-38626-04 (MBC) BERMAN, JUDITH G UNIVERSITY OF MINNESOTA DEPARTMENT OF PLANT BIOLOGY ST PAUL, MN 55108 Characterization of a yeast telomere binding activity

R01GM-38627-06 (MCHA) SCHREIBER, STUART L HARVARD UNIVERSITY 12 OXFORD STREET CAMBRIDGE, MA 02138 Synthesis of materials with physiological properties

R01GM-38642-05 (MBY) JACOBSON, ALLAN S UNIV OF MASS MEDICAL SCHOOL 55 LAKE AVENUE, NORTH WORCESTER, MA 01655 Post-transcriptional regulation of r-protein synthesis

R01GM-38643-05 (PC) SCHUTZBACH, JOHN S UNIV OF ALABAMA UAB STATION BIRMINGHAM, ALA 35294 The role of membranes in proteoglycan biosynthesis

R01GM-38649-05 (IMB) STORB, URSULA B UNIVERSITY OF CHICAGO 920 EAST 58TH STREET CHICAGO, ILL 60637 Mutation of Ig genes in myeloma tumors and mice

R29GM-38650-05 (SAT) BARBUL, ADRIAN SINAI HOSPITAL OF BALTIMORE DEPARTMENT OF SURGERY BALTIMORE, MD 21215 T lymphocyte-wound interactions in trauma

R29GM-38652-04 (MBY) KATULA, KAREN S WEST VIRGINIA UNIVERSITY P O BOX 6057 MORGANTOWN, W V 26506-6057 Regulation of actin gene expression in the sea urchin

R01GM-38656-05 (IMB) LITMAN, GARY W BOX 968 ST. PETERSBURG, FL 33701 Developmental control of Xenopus immunoglobulin genes

R01GM-38657-05 (MBC) SILVERMAN, PHILIP M OKLAHOMA MEDICAL RESEARCH FDN 825 N E 13TH STREET OKLAHOMA CITY, OK 73104 Cell-plasmid interactions in bacterial conjugation

R29GM-38659-05 (MBC) MILLER, ERIC S NORTH CAROLINA STATE UNIV RALEIGH, NC 27695-7615 Genetic analysis of bacteriophage t4 regA protein-RNA

R29GM-38660-05 (MBC) LANDICK, ROBERT C WASHINGTON UNIVERSITY ONE BROOKINGS DR ST LOUIS, MO 63130 Structure/function of transcription complex RNA hairpins

R29GM-38663-05 (VR) GRAVES, BARBARA J UNIV OF UTAH SCHOOL OF MEDICIN 5C334 MEDICAL CENTER SALT LAKE CITY, UT 84132 Retroviral transcriptional control mechanisms

R29GM-38671-04 (MBC) PAIETTA, JOHN V WRIGHT STATE UNIVERSITY DEPT OF BIOLOGICAL CHEMISTRY DAYTON, OH 45435 Molecular genetics of sulfur metabolism in neurospora

R01GM-38679-05 (NEUC) RAND, JAMES B OKLAHOMA MEDICAL RES FDN 825 N E 13TH STREET OKLAHOMA CITY, OK 73104 Genetic regulation of acetylcholine synthesis

R01GM-38681-05 (MBC) KADNER, ROBERT J UNIVERSITY OF VIRGINIA BOX 441/SCHOOL OF MEDICINE CHARLOTTESVILLE, VA 22908 Exogenous induction of the E. coli uhpT gene

R29GM-38696-05 (NEUC) LEWIS, ELAINE J OREGON HEALTH SCIENCES UNIV 3181 SW SAM JACKSON PARK ROAD PORTLAND, OR 97201-3098 Regulated expression of catecholamine biosynthesis genes

R01GM-38714-05 (BIO) TERWILLIGER, THOMAS C UNIVERSITY OF CHICAGO 920 EAST 58TH STREET CHICAGO, ILLINOIS 60637 Folding & stability of the gene V protein of phage F1

R29GM-38722-04 (BBCA) DOUGHTY, MICHAEL B UNIV OF KANSAS DEPT OF MEDICINAL CHEMISTRY LAWRENCE, KS 66045-2500 Protein-DNA interactions--An affinity labeling approach

R29GM-38727-06 (MGN) WICHMAN, HOLLY A UNIV OF IDAHO DEPT OF BIOLOGICAL SCIENCES MOSCOW, IDAHO 83843 Mammalian genomes: Stasis and change

R01GM-38731-05 (HED) CHADA, KIRAN K UNIV OF MED & DENTISTRY OF N J 675 HOES LANE PISCATAWAY, NJ 08854 Gene introduction and expression in the developing mouse

R01GM-38735-04 (MCHA) PEDERSEN, STEVEN F UNIVERSITY OF CALIFORNIA BERKELEY, CA 94720 Transition metal radicals in organic synthesis

R01GM-38737-05 (PC) BELL, ROBERT M DUKE UNIV MED CTER 212 NANALINE DUKE BLDG/RESCH D DURHAM, NC 27710 Mechanism of protein kinase C regulation

R29GM-38738-03 (BMT) KHALEDI, MORTEZA G NORTH CAROLINA ST UNIVERSITY DEPT/CHEMISTRY, PO BOX 8204 RALEIGH, NC 27695-8204 Physicochemical & bioanalytical studies using MLC

R01GM-38740-04 (PBC) WANG, JOHN L MICHIGAN STATE UNIVERSITY DEPARTMENT OF BIOCHEMISTRY EAST LANSING, MI 48824 Carbohydrate binding protein 35

R01GM-38743-05 (VR) KIELIAN, MARGARET C ALBERT EINSTEIN COLLEGE OF MED 1300 MORRIS PARK AVENUE BRONX, NY 10461 Membrane fusion and the endocytic pathway

R37GM-38759-05 (MBC) ROSEMAN, SAUL JOHN HOPKINS UNIVERSITY 34TH & CHARLES STS BALTIMORE, MD 21218 The phosphoenolpyruvate--Glycose phosphotransferase syste

R01GM-38760-04A1 (MBY) EMERSON, BEVERLY M SALK INSTITUTE PO BOX 85800 SAN DIEGO, CA 92138 Function of beta-globin DNA binding proteins

R29GM-38765-05 (HEM) SERHAN, CHARLES N BRIGHAM & WOMEN'S HOSPITAL 221 LONGWOOD AVE BOSTON, MA 02115 Blood cell lipoxygenase products--formation & action

R01GM-38767-04A1 (BMT) QUE, LAWRENCE, JR UNIVERSITY OF MINNESOTA 207 PLEASANT ST SE MINNEAPOLIS, MN 55455 Synthetic approaches for modelling metal-oxo proteins

R29GM-38769-04 (MBY) GANTT, JAMES S UNIVERSITY OF MINNESOTA DEPT OF PLANT BIOLOGY ST PAUL, MN 55108 Maize ribosomal protein gene structure and expression

R29GM-38774-05 (IMB) MONACO, JOHN J VIRGINIA COMMONWEALTH UNIVERSI BOX 678, MCV STATION RICHMOND, VA 23298-0678 Cellular and molecular studies of LMP antigens and genes

R01GM-38778-03 (MBC) FONZI, WILLIAM A UNIVERSITY OF CALIFORNIA CALIFORNIA COLLEGE OF MEDICINE IRVINE, CA 92717 Polyamine synthesis in microbial cells

R01GM-38779-04 (BBCB) LE MASTER, DAVID M NORTHWESTERN UNIVERSITY 2153 SHERIDAN ROAD EVANSTON, IL 60208 Protein NMR structure and dynamics via isotopic labeling

R01GM-38782-05 (BIO) WOOLFORD, JOHN L, JR CARNEGIE-MELLON UNIVERSITY 4400 FIFTH AVENUE PITTSBURGH, PA 15213 Role of PRP gene products in yeast pre-mRNA splicing

R29GM-38784-05 (BMT) O'HALLORAN, THOMAS V NORTHWESTERN UNIVERSITY 2145 SHERIDAN ROAD EVANSTON, IL 60208-3113 Mechanistic study of the MeRR metalloregulatory protein

R29GM-38785-05 (PHY) KAPLAN, RONALD S UNIVERSITY OF SOUTH ALABAMA MEDICAL SCIENCES BLDG 3130 MOBILE, AL 36688 Mitochondrial pyruvate & tricarboxylate transporters

R29GM-38788-06 (BIO) UHLER, MICHAEL D UNIVERSITY OF MICHIGAN 205 ZINA PITCHER PL ANN ARBOR, MI 48109-0720 Cylic AMP regulation of protein seretion

R29GM-38791-05 (MBY) EPSTEIN, LLOYD M FLORIDA STATE UNIVERSITY BIO UNIT I B-157 RTALLAHASSEE, FL 32306-3050 Self-cleaving transcripts of satellite DNA from the newt

R29GM-38793-05 (PC) HANKS, STEVEN K VANDERBILT UNIVERSITY SCHOOL OF MEDICINE, C-2310 MCN Characterization of newly-identified protein kinases

P01GM-38794-05 (SSS) OLSON, ARTHUR J THE SCRIPPS RESEARCH INSTITUTE 10666 N. TORREY PINES RD. LA JOLLA, CA 92037 Protein folding and macromolecular assembly

P01GM-38794-05 0001 (SSS) CASE, DAVID A Protein folding and macromolecular assembly Molecular dynamics of hydrogen bonds

P01GM-38794-05 0002 (SSS) HOGLE, JAMES M Protein folding and macromolecular assembly Structural studies of viruses and related virus particles

P01GM-38794-05 0003 (SSS) OLSON, ARTHUR J Protein folding and macromolecular assembly Protein-protein interfaces

P01GM-38794-05 0004 (SSS) SINGH, U. C Protein folding and macromolecular assembly Conformations of metallothionein

P01GM-38794-05 0005 (SSS) WILSON, IAN A Protein folding and macromolecular assembly Protein antigen structure

P01GM-38794-05 0006 (SSS) WRIGHT, PETER E Protein folding and macromolecular assembly Protein folding and assembly

P01GM-38794-05 9001 (SSS) OLSON, ARTHUR J Protein folding and macromolecular assembly Computer-instrumentation core

R01GM-38810-05 (MBY) HERNANDEZ, NOURIA COLD SPRING HARBOR LAB P O BOX 100 COLD SPRING HARBOR, N Y 11724 Expression of snRNA genes

R01GM-38811-04 (PB) TAYLOR, JOHN WATSON RUTGERS, THE STATE UNIVERSITY P.O. BOX 939 PISCATAWAY, NJ 08855-0939 Protein engineering-peptide hormone design

R01GM-38819-05 (PC) NELSESTUEN, GARY L UNIVERSITY OF MINNESOTA 1479 GORTNER AVENUE ST PAUL, MN 55108 Protein kinase C--In vitro studies

R29GM-38823-05 (BBCB) EALICK, STEVEN E UNIV OF ALABAMA, BIRMINGHAM UAB STATION BIRMINGHAM, ALA 35294 3-d structures of uridine & thymidine phosphorylases

R29GM-38827-06 (SAT) ROBINSON, JOSEPH P PURDUE UNIVERSITY VETERINARY PHYS., LYNN HALL WEST LAFAYETTE, IN 47907 Leukocyte defects associated with thermal injury

R29GM-38829-05 (BBCB) MARONEY, MICHAEL J UNIVERSITY OF MASSACHUSETTS AMHERST, MA 01003 Biological metal clusters--Biophysical and model studies

R01GM-38838-05 (CTY) ELSON, ELLIOT L WASHINGTON UNIVERSITY 660 S EUCLID AVE, BOX 8094 SAINT LOUIS, MO 63110 Biophysical studies of cytoskeletal function

R01GM-38839-04 (MBC) O'DONNELL, MICHAEL E CORNELL UNIVERSITY MEDICAL COL DEPT OF MICROBIOLOGY, B-308 NEW YORK, NY 10021 Biochemical mechanism of DNA polymerase III holoenzyme

R29GM-38857-05 (CBY) FERNANDEZ, JULIO M MAYO FOUNDATION 200 FIRST STREET SOUTHWEST ROCHESTER, MN 55905 Stimulus-secretion coupling in mast cells

R29GM-38859-05 (CTY) ROWE, THOMAS C UNIV OF FLORIDA COLLEGE OF MED BOX J-267 JHMHC GAINESVILLE, FLA 32610 DNA topoisomerases in heat shock gene expression

R01GM-38860-01A2 (PBC) SALVESEN, GUY S DUKE UNIVERSITY MEDICAL CENTER BOX 3712 DURHAM, NC 27710 Activation of neutrophil serine proteinase zymogens

R29GM-38866-05 (SAT) KASS, IRA S SUNY HEALTH SCIENCE CENTER BOX 6, 450 CLARKSON AVENUE BROOKLYN, NY 11203-2098 Anesthetic protection of hypoxic brain tissue

R01GM-38872-04 (PC) YARBROUGH, LYNWOOD R UNIV. OF KANSAS MEDICAL CTR 39TH AND RAINBOW BLVD KANSAS CITY, KS 66103 Structural and genetic aspects of tubulin interactions

R29GM-38877-05 (MBC) REITZER, LAWRENCE J UNIVERSITY OF TEXAS P O BOX 830688 RICHARDSON, TX 75083-0688 Activation of transcription by NRI-phosphate in E coli

R01GM-38886-05 (MBY) GERARD, ROBERT D UT SOUTHWESTERN MED CTR 5323 HARRY HINES BOULEVARD DALLAS, TX 75235-9038 Initiation proteins for eukaryotic DNA replication

R29GM-38894-05 (CTY) ECKER, JOSEPH R UNIVERSITY OF PENNSYLVANIA 415 S UNIVERSITY AVE PHILADELPHIA, PA 19104-6018 Molecular genetics of stress-responses in Arabidopsis

R01GM-38895-05 (CTY) WICKNER, WILLIAM T UNIVERSITY OF CALIFORNIA 33-257 CENTER FOR HLTH SCIENCE LOS ANGELES, CA 90024-1737 Vacuole division/segregation during yeast cell cycle

R01GM-38903-05 (PBC) HEMLER, MARTIN E DANA-FARBER CANCER INSTITUTE 44 BINNEY STREET BOSTON, MA 02115 Cell adhesion functions & cloning of VLA proteins

R01GM-38904-07A1 (MCHA) CRIMMINS, MICHAEL T UNIVERSITY OF NORTH CAROLINA VENABLE HALL CHAPEL HILL, NC 27599-3290 Synthesis of cyclopentanoids by photocycloadditions

R29GM-38906-05 (HEM) ANDERSON, RICHARD A UNIVERSITY OF WISCONSIN 1300 UNIVERSITY AVENUE MADISON, WI 53706 Phosphoinositide regulation of erythrocyte cytoskeleton

R01GM-38907-04 (BNP) ROUSH, WILLIAM R INDIANA UNIVERSITY P O BOX 1847 BLOOMINGTON, IN 47402 Synthesis of olivomycin A and polyhydroxylated compounds

R01GM-38912-04 (MBC) STAUFFER, GEORGE V UNIVERSITY OF IOWA DEPARTMENT OF MICROBIOLOGY IOWA CITY, IOWA 52242 Positive regulation of methionine biosynthesis

R01GM-38920-03 (SSS) PRESSMAN, BERTON C UNIV OF MIAMI SCH OF

MEDICINE PO BOX 016189 MIAMI, FL 33136 Uptake of organic cations by cells and mitochondria

R37GM-38922-05 (MBC) BECKWITH, JONATHAN R HARVARD MEDICAL SCHOOL 25 SHATTUCK STREET BOSTON, MASS 02115 Genetic approaches to analyzing the insertion and topology

R29GM-38925-05 (ALY) SEN, RANJAN BRANDEIS UNIVERSITY 415 SOUTH STREET WALTHAM, MA 02254 Factors regulating Ig gene expression in B-cells

R01GM-38927-05 (CBY) ROSEMAN, SAUL JOHNS HOPKINS UNIVERSITY 34TH & CHARLES STS BALTIMORE, MD 21218 Molecular mechanisms of specific intercellular adhesion

R01GM-38931-01A3 (NEUC) VRANA, KENT E WEST VIRGINIA UNIVERSITY WEST VIRGINIA HEALTH SCIENCE C MORGANTOWN, WV 26506 Molecular characterization of tyrosine hydroxylase

R01GM-38932-05 (MGN) ROUFA, DONALD J KANSAS STATE UNIVERSITY ACKERT HALL MANHATTAN, KS 66506 Somatic genetics of a cloned human ribosomal protein

R29GM-38953-06 (PHRA) FALANY, CHARLES N UNIVERSITY OF ALABAMA UAB STATION BOX 600 BIRMINGHAM, AL 35294 Human platelet phenol sulfotransferases

R29GM-38970-06 (IMB) SHAPIRO, DAVID N ST JUDE CHILDREN'S RES HOSP 332 NO LAUDERDALE, P O BOX 318 MEMPHIS, TN 38101 Receptor induced activation in lymphoid cells

R01GM-38984-04 (SSS) NOLL, HANS BIOMEDICAL SCIS. BLDG. #A-110 1960 EAST WEST ROAD HONOLULU, HI 96822 Molecular genetics of toposomes in eucaryotes

R44GM-39005-03 (SSS) ODOM, ROBERT W CHARLES EVANS & ASSOCIATES 301 CHESAPEAKE DRIVE REDWOOD CITY, CA 94063 Development of molecular SIMS imaging for biomolecules

R01GM-39014-06 (TMP) FEYEREISEN, RENE' UNIVERSITY OF ARIZONA TUCSON, AZ 85721 Insect cytochrome P450 genes

R01GM-39015-03 (SSS) CARROLL, RAYMOND J TEXAS A&M UNIVERSITY DEPARTMENT OF STATISTICS COLLEGE STATION, TX 77843 Generalized linear measurement error models

R55GM-39018-01A3 (MBC) FOSTER, JOHN W UNIV OF SOUTH ALABAMA COLLEGE OF MEDICINE/2118 MSB MOBILE, AL 36688 The bifunctional NADR regulatory locus of Salmonella

R01GM-39023-04 (CTY) KIRSCHNER, MARC W UNIV OF CALIFORNIA 3RD & PARNASSUS AVES SAN FRANCISCO, CA 94143-0448 Cell cycle regulation

R01GM-39025-04 (MBY) SCHULER, MARY A UNIVERSITY OF ILLINOIS DEPT-PLANT BIO/505 S. GOODWIN URBANA, IL 61801 The regulation of gene expression in plants

R01GM-39032-04 (MBC) REDDY, CHILEKAMPALLI A MICHIGAN STATE UNIVERSITY DEPT OF MICROBIO & PUBLIC HLTH EAST LANSING, MI 48824-1101 Lignin biodegradaton--Ligninase and glucose oxidase genes

R29GM-39035-03 (PC) SLEIGHT, RICHARD G UNIVERSITY OF CINCINNATI 231 BETHESDA AVENUE CINCINNATI, OH 45267-0524 Metabolic signaling by intracellular lipid translocation

R01GM-39040-04 (MBC) PAYNE, GREGORY S UNIVERSITY OF CALIFORNIA 405 HILGARD AVE LOS ANGELES, CA 90024 Molecular studies of clathrin-coated membrane function

R55GM-39052-04 (MBC) WEST, ROBERT W, JR SUNY HLTH SCI CTR AT SYRACUSE 750 EAST ADAMS STREET SYRACUSE, NY 13210 Repression, derepression and positive control in yeast

R29GM-39056-04 (IMB) BRIAN, ADRIENNE A DEPARTMENT OF CHEMISTRY 0063 UNIVERSITY OF CALIF, SAN DIEGO LA JOLLA, CA 92093-0063 Fluorescence studies of T-cell recognition

R01GM-39063-02 (MCHA) MATTESON, DONALD S WASHINGTON STATE UNIVERSITY PULLMAN, WA 99164-4630 Synthesis of leuconolide via boronic esters

R01GM-39066-04 (CBY) BRETSCHER, ANTHONY P CORNELL UNIVERSITY BIOTECH BUILDING ITHACA, N Y 14853 Microfilaments in the yeast Saccharomyces cerevisiae

R01GM-39067-04 (MBY) STILLMAN, DAVID J THE UNIVERSITY OF UTAH SALT LAKE CITY, UT 84132 Molecular mechanisms in mother specific transcription

R29GM-39068-04 (CTY) SULLIVAN, KEVIN F SCRIPPS CLINIC & RES FDN 10666 NORTH TORREY PINES RD LA JOLLA, CA 92037 Molecular analysis of mammalian kinetochore structure

R29GM-39071-04 (BBCA) HARBISON, GERARD S RES FDN OF S U N Y DEPT OF CHEMISTRY STONY BROOK, N Y 11794 Solid-state 2D-NMR investigation of DNA & its complexes

R29GM-39082-05 (PB) HOLDEN, HAZEL UNIVERSITY OF WISCONSIN 1710 UNIVERSITY AVENUE MADISON, WI 53705 Structural studies of electron transport proteins

R01GM-39087-05 (MBC) SCHNAITMAN, CARL A ARIZONA STATE UNIVERSITY TEMPE, AZ 85287-2701 Genetic analysis of the rfa locus in escherichia coli

R29GM-39092-04 (PHY) EHRLICH, BARBARA E UNIV OF CONNECTICUT HLTH CTR 263 FARMINGTON AVE FARMINGTON, CT 06030 Function and regulation of paramecia calcium channels

R01GM-39102-04 (SAT) CHANG, YI-HAN UNIVERSITY OF CALIFORNIA 1000 VETERAN AVE LOS ANGELES, CA 90024 Cellular mechanisms of hemorrhaged-induced suppression

R29GM-39106-04 (MBC) KRANZ, ROBERT G WASHINGTON UNIVERSITY DEPARTMENT OF BIOLOGY ST LOUIS, MO 63130 Transcriptional regulation in Rhodobacter capsulatus

R01GM-39226-04 (BNP) OJIMA, IWAO SUNY STONY BROOK, NY 11794-3400 New synthesis of biochemicals with homogeneous catalysts

R01GM-39227-01A2 (SAT) KNIGHT, PAUL R, III UNIV OF MICHIGAN MEDICAL SCHOO ANN ARBOR, MI 48109-0572 Volatile anesthetic action and Ca2+ homeostasis

R55GM-39234-04 (MBY) TAYLOR, WILLIAM L VANDERBILT UNIV SCHOOL OF MED 702 LIGHT HALL NASHVILLE, TN 37232-0615 TFIIIA gene expression in oocytes and somatic cells

R29GM-39236-03 (BNP) CHEN, CHING-SHIH UNIVERSITY OF RHODE ISLAND PHARMACOG/ENVIRONMTL HLTH SCI KINGSTON, RI 02881-0809 Metabolic stereoisomeric inversion of chiral drugs

R01GM-39247-04 (SSS) JAMES, THOMAS L UNIV CALIFORNIA/SAN FRANCISCO DEPT OF PHARM/CHEMISTRY SAN FRANCISCO, CA 94143 Two-dimensional NMR studies--AT-containing nucleic acids

R29GM-39254-04 (MBC) MYERS, ALAN M IOWA STATE UNIVERSITY DEPT. OF BIOCHEM. & BIOPHYSICS AMES, IA 50011 Function of the evolutionarily conserved rho gene family

R01GM-39255-04 (GEN) HARTE, PETER J CASE WESTERN RESERVE UNIV 2119 ABINGTON ROAD CLEVELAND, OH 44106 Molecular basis of Drosophila homeotic gene

R01GM-39256-04 (ALY) RAVETCH, JEFFREY V SLOAN-KETTERING INSTITUTE 1275 YORK AVENUE NEW YORK, NEW YORK 10021 Study of Fc receptor genes--Macrophages and lymphocytes

R29GM-39257-04 (MBY) STEIN, ROLAND W VANDERBILT UNIV SCH OF MEDICIN AND BIOPHYSICS NASHVILLE, TN 37232-0615 Negative regulation of rat insulin II gene transcription

R29GM-39261-04 (SSS) LIANG, KUNG-YEE THE JOHNS HOPKINS UNIVERSITY 615 NORTH WOLFE STREET BALTIMORE, MD 21205-3179 Statistical methods for non standard data

R01GM-39264-04 (CBY) CHISHOLM, REX L NORTHWESTERN UNIV MED SCHOOL 303 EAST CHICAGO AVENUE CHICAGO, IL 60611 Molecular genetic analysis of motility--Myosin LCS

R01GM-39271-04 (MBY) BEYER, ANN L UNIVERSITY OF VIRGINIA BOX 441 CHARLOTTESVILLE, VA 22908 RNA processing and nuclear ribonucleoprotein

R01GM-39275-04 (ALY) BRAUNSTEIN, NED S COLUMBIA UNIVERSITY 630 WEST 168TH STREET NEW YORK, NY 10032 Analysis of the mouse MHC abeta2 and ebeta2 molecules

R01GM-39277-03 (MET) VARY, THOMAS C PENNSYLVANIA STATE UNIVERSITY MILTON S HERSHEY MEDICAL CENTE HERSHEY, PA 17033 Regulation of protein turnover in sepsis

R01GM-39287-04 (BMT) DAWSON, JOHN H UNIVERSITY OF SOUTH CAROLINA DEPARTMENT OF CHEMISTRY COLUMBIA, SC 29208 Chemical models for biological electron transfer

R29GM-39290-05 (BIO) BLUMENTHAL, DONALD K, II UNIVERSITY OF UTAH 112 SKAGGS HALL SALT LAKE CITY, UT 84112 Molecular interactions of calmodulin with target enzymes

R01GM-39296-04 (BIO) KLINMAN, JUDITH P UNIVERSITY OF CALIFORNIA 530 BANWAY BLDG BERKELEY, CA 94720 Probes of structure and mechanism in copper amine

R29GM-39300-04 (CBY) LEE, GLORIA BRIGHAM AND WOMEN'S HOSPITAL 75 FRANCIS STREET BOSTON, MA 02115 Structure and function of mouse tau protein

R55GM-39309-04 (BBCB) BRYANT, ROBERT G UNIV OF ROCHESTER MED CTR BOX BPHYS ROCHESTER, NY 14642 Magnetic relaxation control

R29GM-39312-04 (ALY) WEAVER, DAVID T DANA FARBER CANCER INSTITUTE 44 BINNEY ST BOSTON, MA 02115 Regulation of DNA rearrangement in B lymphocytes

R01GM-39324-01A4 (PB) POYTON, ROBERT O UNIVERSITY OF COLORADO CAMPUS BOX 347 BOULDER, CO 80309-0347 Function of subunit isoforms in cytochrome C oxidase

R01GM-39329-03 (SAT) BIRKHAHN, RONALD H MEDICAL COLLEGE OF OHIO PO BOX 10008 TOLEDO, OHIO 43699 Fat metabolism in sepsis and trauma

R29GM-39334-05 (BIO) IMPERIALI, BARBARA CALIFORNIA INST. OF TECHNOLOGY DIVISION OF CHEMISTRY PASADENA, CA 91125 Specificity in co and post translation modification

R29GM-39338-04 (TOX) LAU, SERRINE S THE UNIV OF TEXAS AT AUSTIN COLLEGE OF PHARMACY AUSTIN, TEXAS 78712 Glutathione conjugation--Mediator of organ toxicity

R01GM-39339-01A3 (MCHA) HOYE, THOMAS R UNIVERSITY OF MINNESOTA 207 PLEASANT STREET SE MINNEAPOLIS, MN 55455 C2-symmetric macrocyclic dimer synthesis

R29GM-39341-04 (GEN) ORR-WEAVER, TERRY L WHITEHEAD INST/BIOMEDICAL RES NINE CAMBRIDGE CENTER CAMBRIDGE, MA 02142 Replication and polytenization in Drosophila

R01GM-39343-04 (BBCA) ACKERS, GARY K WASHINGTON U SCH OF MEDICINE 660 S EUCLID AVE., BOX 8231 ST LOUIS, MO 63110 Site-specific energetics of protein-DNA interactions

R01GM-39344-03 (SAT) KISSIN, IGOR UNIV OF ALABAMA-BIRMINGHAM UAB STATION BIRMINGHAM, AL 35294 Modulation of anesthetic action of benzodiazepines

R01GM-39345-04 (BBCB) TAINER, JOHN A THE SCRIPPS RESEARCH INSTITUTE 10666 NORTH TORREY PINES ROAD LA JOLLA, CA 92037 Structure and redesign of human superoxide dismutase

R01GM-39354-04 (MCHA) ANGLE, STEVEN R UNIVERSITY OF CALIFORNIA RIVERSIDE, CA 92521 Synthesis and chemistry of quinone and semiquinone methides

R01GM-39355-04 (GEN) KREITMAN, MARTIN E PRINCETON UNIVERSITY WASHINGTON ROAD PRINCETON, NJ 08544-1003 A test of neutral molecular evolution in Drosophila

R01GM-39359-04 (BMT) IKEDA-SAITO, MASAO CASE WESTERN UNIVERSITY 2119 ABINGTON ROAD CLEVELAND, OH 44106 Cytochrome oxidase intermediates

R01GM-39360-04 (PB) KEMPER, BYRON W UNIVERSITY OF ILLINOIS DEPT OF PHYSIOLOGY/BIOPHYSICS URBANA, IL 61801 Regulation of cytochrome P-450 biosynthesis

R01GM-39390-05 (ALY) MCQUEEN, CHARLENE A UNIVERSITY OF ARIZONA 1703 E MABEL ST TUCSON, AZ 85721 Pharmacogenetic factors and adverse drug reactions

R01GM-39393-04 (MBC) KODADEK, THOMAS J UNIVERSITY OF TEXAS AUSTIN, TX 78712 Biochemistry of T4 homologous recombination

R01GM-39398-03 (TMP) KARP, RICHARD D UNIV OF CINCINNATI DEPT OF BIOLOGICAL SCIENCES CINCINNATI, OH 45221 Origins of inducible humoral immunity

R29GM-39402-04 (MCHA) AUBE, JEFFREY UNIVERSITY OF KANSAS DEPT. OF MEDICINAL CHEMISTRY LAWRENCE, KS 66045-2500 Asymmetric reactions of prochiral ketones

R01GM-39406-04 (BMT) PECORARO, VINCENT L UNIVERSITY OF MICHIGAN 930 N UNIVERSITY AVE ANN ARBOR, MI 48109-1055 Structural models for multinuclear manganese enzyme

R01GM-39415-02 (MBC) AMES, GIOVANNA F UNIVERSITY OF CALIFORNIA 308 BARKER HALL BERKELEY, CA 94720 Function of rep sequences in E coli and S. typhimurium

R29GM-39417-05 (BMT) LANDIS, CLARK UNIVERSITY OF WISCONSIN 750 UNIVERSITY AVENUE MADISON, WI 53706 Understanding and developing asymmetric catalysis

R01GM-39418-04 (MBC) GEIDUSCHEK, E PETER UNIV OF CALIFORNIA, SAN DIEGO DEPT OF BIOLOGY, 0322 LA JOLLA, CALIF 92093 Prokaryotic chromatin & transcriptional regulation

PROJECT NO., ORGANIZATIONAL UNIT., INVESTIGATOR, ADDRESS, TITLE

R01GM-39420-03S1 (MBC) BENNETT, GEORGE N RICE UNIVERSITY P O BOX 1892 HOUSTON, TEX 77251 Regulation of amino acid decarboxylase genes
R01GM-39422-04 (MBC) BELFORT, MARLENE NEW YORK STATE DEPT OF HEALTH EMPIRE STATE PLAZA ALBANY, N Y 12201 Self-splicing introns in the phage t4/e coli system
R01GM-39429-04 (GEN) REED, STEVEN I SCRIPPS CLINIC & RES FDN 10666 NORTH TORREY PINES RD LA JOLLA, CA 92037 Genetics of pheromone transduction in yeast
R01GM-39434-04 (BIO) BOKOCH, GARY M RES INST OF SCRIPPS CLINIC 10666 N TORREY PINES ROAD LA JOLLA, CA 92037 Regulation of neutrophil receptor/G protein interactions
R29GM-39436-03 (PC) JONG, AMBROSE Y CHILDRENS HOSP OF LOS ANGELES DIVISION OF HEMATOLOGY/ONCOLOG LOS ANGELES, CA 90027 Mechanism of action of yeast CDC8 protein in DNA replication
R01GM-39447-01A1 (MBC) MAGUIRE, MICHAEL E CASE WESTERN RESERVE UNIVERSIT 2109 ADELBERT ROAD CLEVELAND, OH 44106-4965 Magnesium transport in Salmonella typhimurium
R01GM-39451-05 (BMT) RAGSDALE, STEPHEN W UNIVERSITY OF NEBRASKA LINCOLN, NEBRASKA 68583-0718 Mechanism of methyl transfers in acetyl-CoA synthesis
R29GM-39455-04 (BNP) KOHN, JOACHIM B RUTGERS, STATE UNIV OF NJ PISCATAWAY, NJ 08855-0939 Structurally new biopolymers derived from amino acids
R01GM-39458-05 (MBY) BALTIMORE, DAVID ROCKEFELLER UNIVERSITY 1230 YORK AVENUE NEW YORK, N Y 10021 Lymphocyte and HIV transcription
R29GM-39471-04 (BBCA) BENIGHT, ALBERT S UNIVERSITY OF ILLINOIS AT CHIC P O BOX 4348 CHICAGO, IL 60680 Thermal denaturation studies of self-complementary DNA loops
R29GM-39476-04 (ALY) GASCOIGNE, NICHOLAS R SCRIPPS CLINIC & RES FOUN 10666 NORTH TORREY PINES RD LA JOLLA, CA 92037 Soluble T cell receptor studies on MHC restriction
R29GM-39478-01A3 (BBCA) POST, CAROL B PURDUE UNIVERSITY HEINE PHARMACY BUILDING WEST LAFAYETTE, IN 47907 NMR structure of band 3 peptide-enzyme complexes
R29GM-39479-05 (MBC) ZUBER, PETER A LOUISIANA STATE UNIV MED CTR DEPT OF BIOCHEM & MOL BIO SHREVEPORT, LA 71130-3932 Regulation of sporulation-associated gene transcription
R29GM-39484-04 (MBC) HAMPSEY, D MICHAEL LSU SCH OF MED IN SHREVEPORT DEPT OF BIOCHEM & MOL BIO SHREVEPORT, LA 71130-3932 Genetic analysis of translation initiation in yeast
R01GM-39492-09 (BMT) IKEDA-SAITO, MASAO CASE WESTERN RESERVE UNIV 2119 ABINGTON ROAD CLEVELAND, OH 44106 Structure and function of myeloperoxidase
R29GM-39494-04 (MCHA) DOXSEE, KENNETH M UNIVERSITY OF OREGON DEPARTMENT OF CHEMISTRY EUGENE, OR 97403 Metallacyclobutenes; synthesis and reactivity
R01GM-39496-04 (MBC) CALVO, JOSEPH M CORNELL UNIVERSITY - ITHACA & CELL BIOLOGY, 211 WING HALL ITHACA, NY 14853 Unusual region controlling ilvIH expression in E. coli
R29GM-39498-04 (CBY) BREITENBERGER, CAROLINE A THE OHIO STATE UNIVERSITY 484 WEST TWELFTH AVENUE COLUMBUS, OH 43210-1292 Targeting of organellar protein synthesis factors
R01GM-39500-04 (PHY) KAPLAN, JACK H D301 RICHARDS BLDG 37TH & HAMILTON WK PHILADELPHIA, PA 19104-6085 :Localization of ligand interactions with the sodium pump/dogs
R29GM-39501-04 (GEN) COHAN, FREDERICK M WESLEYAN UNIVERSITY SHANKLIN LAB/DEPT OF BIOLOGY MIDDLETOWN, CT 06457 The evolutionary effects of major mutations
R01GM-39503-03 (PHY) RASH, JOHN E COLORADO STATE UNIVERSITY DEPT OF ANATOMY & NEUROBIOLOGY FORT COLLINS, CO 80523 Labeling of sodium channel IMPs in freeze-fracture replicas
R29GM-39505-03 (SAT) TAIT, ALAN R UNIV OF MICHIGAN HOSPITAL 1500 E MEDICAL CENTER DRIVE ANN ARBOR, MI 48109 Anesthesia and upper respiratory tract infections
R29GM-39512-04 (BNP) ARMSTRONG, ROBERT W UNIV OF CALIFORNIA 405 HILGARD AVE LOS ANGELES, CA 90024 Synthesis of DNA-binding protein mimics
R01GM-39513-04 (BBCA) CRAVEN, BRYAN M UNIVERSITY OF PITTSBURGH DEPARTMENT OF CRYSTALLOGRAPHY PITTSBURGH, PA 15260 Nucleic acid electrostatic properties from crystals
R29GM-39516-04 (MBC) BECHHOFER, DAVID H MT SINAI SCH OF MEDICINE ONE GUSTAVE L LEVY PLACE NEW YORK, NEW YORK 10029 Regulation of ermC mRNA stability
R01GM-39519-04 (SB) CHAUDRY, IRSHAD H MICHIGAN STATE UNIVERSITY B424 CLINICAL CENTER EAST LANSING, MI 48824-1315 Maintenance of organ function following injury
R01GM-39520-04 (PHY) ALMERS, WOLFHARD UNIVERSITY OF WASHINGTON SEATTLE, WA 98195 Electric studies of exo- and endocytosis
P01GM-39526-05 (SRC) CARR, STEVEN A SMITH KLINE BEECHAM PHARM 709 SWEDELAND ROAD KING OF PRUSSIA, PA 19406 Macromolecular structure studies of HIV-encoded proteins
P01GM-39526-05 0001 (SRC) MEYERS, CHESTER A Macromolecular structure studies of HIV-encoded proteins Structure-function studies of recombinant HIV proteins
P01GM-39526-05 0002 (SRC) DIXON, J SCOTT Macromolecular structure studies of HIV-encoded proteins Development and application of inhibitor design methods
P01GM-39526-05 0003 (SRC) LEWIS, MITCHELL Macromolecular structure studies of HIV-encoded proteins X-ray crystallographic studies of AIDS proteins and inhibitors
P01GM-39526-05 0004 (SRC) MUELLER, LUCIANO Macromolecular structure studies of HIV-encoded proteins Structure and dynamics of proteins by NMR
P01GM-39526-05 0005 (SRC) CARR, STEVEN A Macromolecular structure studies of HIV-encoded proteins Structural characterization of AIDS-related glycoproteins by spectrometry
R01GM-39531-04 (MBC) MITCHELL, AARON P COLUMBIA UNIVERSITY INSTITUTE OF CANCER RESEARCH NEW YORK, N Y 10032 Genetic control of entry into meiosis in yeast
R29GM-39541-05 (MBC) SCHREIER, HAROLD J CENTER OF MARINE BIOTECHNOLOGY 600 EAST LOMBARD STREET BALTIMORE, MD 21202 Regulation of glnA in Bacillus subtilis
P01GM-39546-05 (SRC) ENGELMAN, DONALD M YALE UNIVERSITY 260 WHITNEY AVNUE P O BOX 6666 NEW HAVEN, CT 06511 Structure and function of HIV proteins
P01GM-39546-05 0001 (SRC) ENGELMAN, DONALD M Structure and function of HIV proteins Structural studies of HIV glycoprotein anchor peptides
P01GM-39546-05 0002 (SRC) RICHARDS, FREDERIC M Structure and function of HIV proteins Locating fusion peptides; design of peptide binding sites
P01GM-39546-05 0003 (SRC) STEITZ, THOMAS A Structure and function of HIV proteins Structure of reverse transcriptase and other HIV proteins
P01GM-39546-05 0004 (SRC) SUMMERS, WILLIAM Structure and function of HIV proteins Expression of HIV proteins in prokaryotes and eukaryotes
P01GM-39546-05 9001 (SRC) ENGELMAN, DONALD M Structure and function of HIV proteins Core facilities for protein chemistry and computations
R01GM-39548-03 (CBY) FUKUI, YOSHIO NORTHWESTERN UNIV MEDICAL SCH 303 E CHICAGO, AVE/WARD 7-315 CHICAGO, IL 60611 Cell biological studies of disctyostelium cytoskeleton
R29GM-39549-04 (BIO) CRAMER, CAROLE L VIRGINIA POLYTECHNIC INST AND STATE UNIVERSITY BLACKSBURG, VA 24061 HMG-CO A reductase regulation in plant disease resistance
R01GM-39550-04 (BBCB) GARAVITO, R MICHAEL UNIVERSITY OF CHICAGO 920 E 58TH STREET CHICAGO, ILLINOIS 60637 The structure of bacterial membrane proteins
P01GM-39552-05 (SRC) KENYON, GEORGE L UNIVERSITY OF CALIFORNIA SAN FRANCISCO, CA 94143-0446 Structural biology and targeted drug design for AIDS
P01GM-39552-05 0001 (SRC) ORTIZ DE MONTELLANO, PAUL R Structural biology and targeted drug design for AIDS Synthesis, enzymology and drug design
P01GM-39552-05 0002 (SRC) KUNTZ, IRWIN D Structural biology and targeted drug design for AIDS Molecular modeling and drug design
P01GM-39552-05 0003 (SRC) CRAIK, CHARLES S Structural biology and targeted drug design for AIDS Site-directed mutagenesis of HIV-encoded proteins
P01GM-39552-05 0004 (SRC) STROUD, ROBERT M Structural biology and targeted drug design for AIDS Crystallography and other structural methods
R01GM-39553-04 (IMB) WEISS, ARTHUR UNIV OF CALIFORNIA 3RD & PARNASSUS AVES SAN FRANCISCO, CA 94143 T cell antigen receptor in signal transduction
R01GM-39555-04 (CTY) DEAN, GARY E UNIVERSITY OF CINCINNATTI 231 BETHESDA AVENUE CINCINNATI, OH 45267-0524 The chromaffin granule membrane--Proteins and cDNAs
P01GM-39558-05 (SRC) EISENBERG, DAVID UNIVERSITY OF CALIFORNIA 405 HILGARD AVENUE LOS ANGELES, CA 90024-1570 Structure-based targeting of drugs to HIV proteins
P01GM-39558-05 0001 (SRC) EISENBERG, DAVID Structure-based targeting of drugs to HIV proteins X-ray crystallography studies
P01GM-39558-05 0002 (SRC) EISERLING, FREDERICK A Structure-based targeting of drugs to HIV proteins Electron microscopic studies
P01GM-39558-05 0003 (SRC) DICKERSON, RICHARD E Structure-based targeting of drugs to HIV proteins Crystal structure analysis of HIV reverse transcriptase and related enzymes
P01GM-39558-05 0004 (SRC) REES, DOUGLAS C Structure-based targeting of drugs to HIV proteins Target zones on proteins and energetics of interactions between surfaces
P01GM-39558-05 0005 (SRC) SIGMAN, DAVID S Structure-based targeting of drugs to HIV proteins Antiviral drugs--Nuclease activity of 1,10-phenanthroline-copper ion
P01GM-39558-05 9001 (SRC) CASCIO, DUILIO Structure-based targeting of drugs to HIV proteins Laboratory core
R01GM-39561-03 (PHRA) NEUBIG, RICHARD R UNIV OF MI/1301 E CATHERINE ST M6322 MED SCIENCE BLDG I ANN ARBOR, MI 48109-0626 Rapid kinetics of alpha 2 adrenergic receptor activation
R01GM-39565-04 (CTY) MITCHISON, TIMOTHY J UNIVERSITY OF CALIFORNIA 513 PARNASSUS AVENUE SAN FRANCISCO, CA 94143-0450 Microtubule dynamics and mitotic mechanism
R29GM-39568-04 (SAT) WHEELER, DAVID M JOHNS HOPKINS HOSPITAL 600 N WOLFE STREET BALTIMORE, MD 21205 Volatile anesthetics & rat heart cell contractility
R29GM-39573-05 (SSS) BONNEY, GEORGE E HOWARD UNIVERSITY CNCR CTR 2041 GEORGIA AVE, N W WASHINGTON, D C 20060 Statistical modeling for genetic epidemiology
R29GM-39576-04 (BBCA) KUKI, ATSUO CORNELL UNIVERSITY DEPT OF CHEMISTRY ITHACA, NY 14853-1301 Electronically active Aib helices
R01GM-39578-03 (MGN) WAKELAND, EDWARD K UNIVERSITY OF FLORIDA BOX J-275, JHMHC GAINESVILLE, FLA 32610 Selective mechanisms maintaining H-2 polymorphism
R01GM-39583-05A1 (MBC) CARLSON, RUSSELL W UNIVERSITY OF GEORGIA 220 RIVERBEND ROAD ATHENS, GA 30602 Structural determination of the LPS from Rhizobium
R29GM-39586-04 (ALY) WILKINSON, MILES F OREGON HEALTH SCIENCES UNIV 3181 S W SAM JACKSON PARK RD PORTLAND, OR 97201 Regulation of T-cell receptor gene expression
R29GM-39588-05 (PHRA) BRADFORD, PETER G UNIVERSITY OF BUFFALO-SUNY 102 FARBER HALL BUFFALO, NY 14214 Characterization of the leukocyte INS (1,4,5)p3 receptor
P01GM-39589-05 (SRC) WILEY, DON C HARVARD UNIVERSITY 7 DIVINITY AVENUE CAMBRIDGE, MA 02138 Structural foundations of antiviral drug design
P01GM-39589-05 0001 (SRC) WHITESIDES, GEORGE M Structural foundations of antiviral drug design Synthetic strategies for anti-viral drug design
P01GM-39589-05 0002 (SRC) WILEY, DON C Structural foundations of antiviral drug design Viral glycoprotein-receptor interactions
P01GM-39589-05 0003 (SRC) KARPLUS, MARTIN Structural foundations of antiviral drug design Structural basis for T4/gp120 interaction
R29GM-39593-05 (MGN) ROGERS, ALAN RAY UNIVERSITY OF UTAH SALT LAKE CITY, UTAH 84112 Structured emigration and genetic population differences
P01GM-39599-05 (SRC) MATTHEWS, DAVID A AGOURON PHARMACEUTICALS, INC. 11025 NORTH TORREY PINES RD LA JOLLA, CA 92037 Protein structure

based design of anti-HIV drugs
P01GM-39599-05 0002 (SRC) BELTZ, GERALD Protein structure based design of anti-HIV drugs Production and purification of HIV-encoded proteins
P01GM-39599-05 0003 (SRC) HASELTINE, WILLIAM Protein structure based design of anti-HIV drugs Structural analysis of proteins essential for the replication of HIV
P01GM-39599-05 0001 (SRC) MATTHEWS, DAVID A Protein structure based design of anti-HIV drugs Protein structure based design of anit-HIV drugs
R01GM-39610-03 (BBCB) JENSEN, LYLE H UNIV OF WASHINGTON SM-20 SEATTLE, WA 98195 Crystallographic studies of iron sulfur proteins
R29GM-39612-04 (BBCB) BUNKER, GRANT B ILLINOIS INST OF TECHNOLOGY 3301 S. DEARBORN EXAFS studies of the iron site of ribonucleotide reductase
R29GM-39615-04 (BBCA) NELSON, JEFFREY W LOUISIANA STATE UNIVERSITY DEPT OF BIOCHEMISTRY BATON ROUGE, LA 70803 Influence of alpa-helices on the folding of apamin
R01GM-39617-04 (BBCA) LAKOWICZ, JOSEPH R UNIVERSITY OF MARYLAND DEPT OF BIO/CHEMISTRY BALTIMORE, MARYLAND 21201 Transient effects in fluorescence quenching
R01GM-39620-04 (CBY) BEACH, DAVID H COLD SPRING HARBOR LABORATORY P O BOX 100 COLD SPRING HARBOR, N Y 11724 Biochemical characterization of p34, a human homology
R01GM-39622-04 (TMP) STRINGER, JAMES R UNIVERSITY OF CINCINNATI 231 BETHESDA AVENUE CINCINNATI, OH 45267 Leishmania proton pump--Genes and proteins
R44GM-39641-03 (SB) HAMILTON, ARCHIE C ACH PROJECT MANAGEMENT TEAMS 3422 ROLLING HILLS DRIVE EAGAN MN 55121 Electronic cryogenic surgical probe
R01GM-39686-04 (CBY) BRANTON, DANIEL HARVARD UNIVERSITY 16 DIVINIITY AVENUE CAMBRIDGE, MA 02138 Genetic studies of non-erythroid spectrin
R01GM-39693-04 (MBC) LIN, EDMUND C HARVARD MEDICAL SCHOOL 25 SHATTUCK STREET BOSTON, MASS 02115 Evolution of novel metabolic pathways in bacteria
R01GM-39695-05 (MBY) GRABOWSKI, PAULA J UNIVERSITY OF PITTSBURGH 5TH AVE & RUSKIN ST PITTSBURGH, PA 15213-9910 Regulated splicing of messenger RNA precursors
R29GM-39696-04 (CBY) KOHORN, BRUCE D DEPT OF BOTANY DUKE UNIVERSITY DURHAM, N C 27706 Sorting of nuclear coded chloroplast proteins
R29GM-39698-04 (ALY) LEE, JANET S SLOAN-KETTERING INST CANC RES 1275 YORK AVENUE NEW YORK, N Y 10021 HLA class II genes; regulation of expression
R55GM-39699-05 (IMS) THOMPSON, LINDA F OKLAHOMA MEDICAL RESEARCH FDN 825 N E 13TH STREET OKLAHOMA CITY, OK 73104 Phosphatidylinositol-linked membrane proteins
R29GM-39718-04 (CBY) SPIEGEL, SARAH GEORGETOWN UNIVERSITY 3900 RESERVOIR ROAD WASHINGTON, D.C. 20007 Gangliosides as modulators of cell growth
R29GM-39723-03 (SAT) SESSLER, DANIEL I UNIV OF CALIFORNIA DEPT OF ANESTHESIA C-450 SAN FRANCISCO, CA 94143-0648 Perianesthetic tremor and thermoregulation
R55GM-39724-04 (BBCA) MYERS, ANNE B UNIVERSITY OF ROCHESTER RIVER CAMPUS ROCHESTER, NY 14627 Polyene photophysics--Raman and picosecond spectroscopy
R29GM-39731-03 (PHY) BLATZ, ANDREW L UNIV OF TEXAS SW MEDICAL CENTE DEPT OF PHYSIOLOGY DALLAS, TX 75235-9040 Calcium-activated potassium channels in skeletal muscle
R01GM-39732-04 (MBY) GURLEY, WILLIAM B UNIVERSITY OF FLORIDA DEPT OF MICROBIO & CELL SCI GAINESVILLE, FL 32611 Transcriptional regulation of plant heat shock genes
R01GM-39736-04 (MBC) MANSON, MICHAEL D TEXAS A&M UNIVERSITY DEPT OF BIOLOGY COLLEGE STATION, TX 77843 Function and evolution of periplasmic chemoreceptors
R01GM-39739-03 (MBC) HABER, JAMES E BRANDEIS UNIVERSITY DEPT OF BIOCHEMISTRY & BIOLOGY WALTHAM, MASS 02254 Structure function & regulation of yeast membrane ATPase
R01GM-39740-03 (BNP) MOCK, WILLIAM L UNIV OF ILLINOIS PO BOX 4348 CHICAGO, IL 60680 Enzyme mechanisms; selective protease inactivators
R29GM-39746-04 (PHY) MERCER, ROBERT W WASHINGTON UNIVERSITY SCHOOL OF MEDICINE ST. LOUIS, MO 63110 Molecular physiology of the Na, K-ATPase
R01GM-39750-04 (BBCA) ROSS, J B ALEXANDER MOUNT SINAI SCH OF MEDICINE ONE GUSTAVE L LEVY PLACE NEW YORK, N Y 10029 Intrinsic fluorescence decay mechanisms of proteins
R29GM-39754-04 (PB) RICHARD, JOHN P UNIVERSITY OF KENTUCKY DEPARTMENT OF CHEMISTRY LEXINGTON, KY 40506-0055 Studies on reactive intermediates of enzymatic reactions
R29GM-39756-03 (SAT) BUCHMAN, TIMOTHY G JOHNS HOPKINS HOSPITAL HALSTED BLDG. RM 612 BALTIMORE, MD 21205 Traumatic shock--Related changes in gene expression
R29GM-39758-04 (BNP) HANSEN, DAVID E AMHERST COLLEGE DEPARTMENT OF CHEMISTRY AMHERST, MA 01002 Sequence-specific antibody proteases
R01GM-39764-03 (MCHA) COLLUM, DAVID B CORNELL UNIVERSITY ITHACA, NY 14853 Chemistry of lithium amides
R29GM-39771-04 (SAT) WARNER, DAVID S UNIV OF IOWA HOSPITALS/CLINICS DEPT OF ANESTHESIA IOWA CITY, IA 52242 Cerebral ischemia--Minimizing damage during anesthesia
R29GM-39777-03 (BIO) JULIN, DOUGLAS A UNIVERSITY OF MARYLAND DEPT/CHEMISTRY & BIOCHEMISTRY COLLEGE PARK, MD 20742 Mechanism of the recBCD enzyme from Escherichia coli
R01GM-39783-03 (BNP) HANNA, PATRICK E UNIV OF MN/DEPT PHARMACOLOGY 1100 WASHINGTON AVE. S. MINNEAPOLIS, MN 55415 N-hydroxybenzolactams as protease inhibitors
R01GM-39785-04 (MBC) LEIGH, JOHN A UNIVERSITY OF WASHINGTON MICROBIOLOGY DEPT, SC-42 SEATTLE, WA 98195 Rhizobium exopolysaccharides and nodulation
R01GM-39799-04 (MGN) MAIZELS, NANCY YALE UNIVERSITY DEPT. OF MB&B; RM C-10A NEW HAVEN, CT 06510 Molecular mechanisms of isotype switch recombination

P01GM-39813-04 (SSS) KANKEL, DOUGLAS R YALE UNIVERSITY KLINE BIOLOGY TOWER NEW HAVEN, CT 06520 Nervous system development--Genetic and molecular studies
P01GM-39813-04 0001 (SSS) ARTAVANIS-TSAKONAS, SPYRIDON Nervous system development--Genetic and molecular studies Cell biology and functional domains of notched gene product
P01GM-39813-04 0002 (SSS) CARLSON, JOHN Nervous system development--Genetic and molecular studies Molecular genetics of olfactory system development
P01GM-39813-04 0003 (SSS) GAREN, ALAN Nervous system development--Genetic and molecular studies Molecular genetics of filaentous protein in nerves
P01GM-39813-04 0004 (SSS) KANNEL, DOUGLAS Nervous system development--Genetic and molecular studies Role of neurotransmitters in nervous system development
P01GM-39813-04 0005 (SSS) KESHISHIAN, HAIG Nervous system development--Genetic and molecular studies Development and maintenance of synaptic connections
P01GM-39813-04 0006 (SSS) MC GINNIS, WILLIAM Nervous system development--Genetic and molecular studies Biochemical and genetic functions of homeoitic proteins
P01GM-39813-04 0007 (SSS) WYMAN, ROBERT Nervous system development--Genetic and molecular studies Neural connectivity mutants--Molecular analysis
P01GM-39813-04 9001 (SSS) KANNEL, DOUGLAS Nervous system development--Genetic and molecular studies Core facility
R01GM-39815-03 (MCHA) DE SHONG, PHILIP R UNIVERISTY OF MARYLAND COLLEGE PARK, MD 20742 Organomanganese reagents in organic synthesis
R01GM-39820-03 (MCHA) ENGLER, THOMAS A UNIVERSITY OF KANSAS 2010 MALOTT HALL LAWRENCE, KS 66045-2112 Synthesis of biologically important dihydrobenzofurans
R01GM-39821-03 (MCHA) WAGNER, PETER J MICHIGAN STATE UNIVERSITY EAST LANSING, MI 48824-1322 Ortho photocycloaddition of alkenes to triplet benzenes
R29GM-39822-02 (BNP) NAMBIAR, KRISHNAN P UNIVERSITY OF CALIFORNIA DAVIS, CA 95616 Sequence specific DNA-binding peptides and proteins
R01GM-39825-04 (MCHA) DOWD, PAUL UNIVERSITY OF PITTSBURGH DEPT OF CHEMISTRY PITTSBURGH, PA 15260 Novel ring-enlargement chain-extension reaction
R01GM-39826-04 (PC) SEALY, LINDA J VANDERBILT UNIVERSITY 702, LIGHT HALL NASHVILLE, TN 37232-0615 Cellular trans-acting factors mediating RSV enhancer activity
R29GM-39831-04 (CBY) PARKER, IAN UNIVERSITY OF CALIFORNIA DEPARTMENT OF PSYCHOBIOLOGY IRVINE, CA 92717 Intracellular messenger functions of inositol phosphates
R01GM-39832-04 (GEN) PETERSON, THOMAS A COLD SPRING HARBOR LABORATORY P.O. BOX 100 COLD SPRING HARBOR, NY 11724 Developmental regulation of the maize P gene
R01GM-39835-04 (PHY) ISMAIL-BEIGI, FARAMARZ COLUMBIA UNIVERSITY 630 WEST 168TH STREET NEW YORK CITY, N Y 10032 Physiological regulation of Na, K-ATPase
R01GM-39844-03 (BMT) WARNER, ISIAH M EMORY UNIVERSITY ATLANTA, GA 30322 Bioanalytical studies of drug/protein interactions
R01GM-39852-04 (BIO) ERREDE, BEVERLY J UNIV OF N.C. AT CHAPEL HILL DEPT OF CHEMISTRY CHAPEL HILL, N C 27514 Kinases and control of cell-type specialization
R01GM-39860-04 (RAD) SUBJECK, JOHN R ROSWELL PARK MEMORIAL INST 666 ELM STREET BUFFALO, NY 14263 Interaction of thermotolerance & rRNA transcription
R29GM-39862-04 (GMA) MORRIS, NICHOLAS P OREGON HEALTH SCIS UNIVERSITY 3181 SW SAM JACKSON PARK ROAD PORTLAND, OR 97201 Self assembly of type IX collagen
R29GM-39867-04 (PC) ROBISHAW, JANET D WEIS CENTER FOR RESEARCH GEISINGER CLINIC DANVILLE, PA 17822 G proteins:significance of B and y subunit heterogeneity
R01GM-39868-04 (GEN) THOMAS, JAMES H DEPT. OF GENETICS, SK-50 UNIVERSITY OF WASHINGTON SEATTLE, WASHINGTON 98195 Genetic analysis of cell interactions in C elegans
R01GM-39892-04 (MBC) ARNDT, KIM T COLD SPRING HARBOR LABORATORY P.O. BOX 100 COLD SPRING HARBOR, NY 11724 Multiple global regulations control the yeast HIS4 gene
R29GM-39895-04 (MBY) BEALE, ELMUS G TEXAS TECH UNIV HLTH SCI CTR DEPT OF CELL BIO & ANATOMY LUBBOCK, TX 79430 Regulation of tissue-specific gene expression
R01GM-39900-03 (SSS) COHEN, FRED E UNIVERSITY OF CALIFORNIA 513 PARNASSUS AVE SAN FRANCISCO, CA 94143-0446 Computer analysis prediction of protein structure
R01GM-39901-04 (MBY) PAULE, MARVIN R COLORADO STATE UNIVERSITY DEPARTMENT OF BIOCHEMISTRY FORT COLLINS, COLO 80523 Ribosomal RNA transcription factor functional analysis
R01GM-39902-05 (GEN) WU, CHUNG-I UNIVERSITY OF CHICAGO 1101 E. 57TH STREET CHICAGO, IL 60637 Molecular and evolutionary genetics of segregation
R29GM-39906-03 (SAT) SHIRES III, GEORGE T UNIVERSITY OF TEXAS SW MED CTR 5323 HARRY HINES BLVD DALLAS, TX 75235 Mediators of cell dysfunction in shock and trauma
R01GM-39914-04 (BMT) CASE, DAVID A RESEARCH INST OF SCRIPPS CLINI 10666 N TORREY PINES ROAD LA JOLLA, CA 92037 Electronic structure of iron-sulfur and related proteins
R01GM-39917-04 (MBC) MORAN, CHARLES P, JR EMORY UNIV SCHOOL OF MEDICINE 560 WOODRUFF MEM BLDG, RM 560 ATLANTA, GA 30322 Role of the sigma subunit in bacterial RNA polymerase
R29GM-39924-05 (BBCB) SCARLATA, SUZANNE FRANCES SUNY AT STONY BROOK STONY BROOK, NY 11794-8661 Effects of pressure on membrane-component interactions
R01GM-39928-05 (BBCA) MC KAY, DAVID B STANFORD UNIVERSITY FAIRCHILD BLDG STANFORD, CA 94305 Structure-function studies of 70 kD heat shock proteins
R29GM-39929-04 (BBCA) BRENOWITZ, MICHAEL DAVID ALBERT EINSTEIN COLL OF MED 1300 MORRIS PARK AVE BRONX, NEW YORK 10461 Mechanisms of cooperative protein-DNA interactions
R01GM-39931-04 (MBC) ANDERSON, DWIGHT L UNIV OF MINN

PROJECT NO., ORGANIZATIONAL UNIT., INVESTIGATOR, ADDRESS, TITLE

SCH-DENTISTRY 18-246 HLTH SCI MOOS TOWER MINNEAPOLIS, MINN 55455 RNA in DNA virus assembly
R01GM-39932-04 (BMT) DISMUKES, GERARD C PRINCETON UNIVERSITY FRICK LABORATORY/WASHINGTON RD PRINCETON, NJ 08544 Magnetic characterization of the water oxidizing enzyme
R29GM-39969-05 (BBCA) ROYER, CATHERINE A UNIVERSITY OF WISCONSIN 425 NO CHARTER ST MADISON, WI 53706 Subunit interactions in DNA binding proteins
R01GM-39978-04 (MBC) FUTCHER, BRUCE A COLD SPRING HARBOR LABORATORY P.O. BOX 100 COLD SPRING HARBOR, NY 11724 Size control & commitment to division in S. cerevisiae
R01GM-39990-02 (MCHA) KALLMERTEN, JAMES L SYRACUSE UNIVERSITY SYRACUSE, NY 13244-4100 Synthesis of antitumor ansamycins
R29GM-39993-04 (CTY) WALKER, JOHN C UNIVERSITY OF MISSOURI 105 TUCKER HALL COLUMBIA, MO 65211 Regulatory mechanisms of an inducible gene
R01GM-39998-04 (MCHA) IRELAND, ROBERT E UNIVERSITY OF VIRGINIA MCCORMICK ROAD CHARLOTTESVILLE, VA 22901 Synthesis of polyether antibiotics--Monesin & analogs
R29GM-40024-04 (GEN) SPOEREL, NIKOLAUS A UNIV OF CONN HEALTH CENTER DEPARTMENT OF BIOCHEMISTRY FARMINGTON, CT 06032 Molecular mechanisms of chorion gene regulation
R01GM-40036-04 (MCHA) LAROCK, RICHARD C IOWA STATE UNIVERSITY CHEMISTRY AMES, IA 50011 Palladium-catalyzed alkylation of cycloalkenes
R29GM-40037-05 (GMB) WALKER, PATRICK D 4301 WEST MARKHAM SLOT 517 LITTLE ROCK, AR 72205 Oxy-radicals in gentamicin and other toxic nephropathies
R15GM-40056-01A3 (BIO) JOHNSON, ERIC R BALL STATE UNIVERSITY 2000 UNIVERSITY AVE MUNCIE, IN 47306-0445 Stability and specificity of proteases in denaturant
R01GM-40061-03 (CTY) FERL, ROBERT J UNIVERSITY OF FLORIDA FIFIELD HALL GAINESVILLE, FL 32611 Trans-acting factors regulating ADH gene expression
R01GM-40062-04 (PHY) ANDERSEN, OLAF S CORNELL UNIVERSITY 1300 YORK AVENUE NEW YORK, N Y 10021 Voltage dependent sodium channels in planar lipid bilayers
R01GM-40067-04 (MBC) MORTENSON, LEONARD E UNIVERSITY OF GEORGIA 400 BIOLOGICAL SCIENCES BLDG ATHENS, GA 30602 Energy transduction--Role of atp in nitrogen fixation
R29GM-40071-03 (BBCA) JOHNSON, CAREY K UNIVERSITY OF KANSAS DEPT OF CHEMISTRY LAWRENCE, KS 66045-2112 Protein dynamics in bacteriorhodopsin and rhodopsin
R01GM-40079-04 (MBC) MAIER, ROBERT J JOHNS HOPKINS UNIVERSITY CHARLES AND 34TH STREETS BALTIMORE, MD 21218 Physiology of bacterial nickel metabolism
R01GM-40082-04 (MBC) HERSHEY, JOHN W UNIVERSITY OF CALIFORNIA DAVIS, CALIF 95616 Function of initiation factors in bacterial translation
R01GM-40083-03 (PC) LOW, MARTIN G COLLEGE OF PHYSICIANS & SURG COLUMBIA UNIVERSITY NEW YORK, NY 10032 Phosphatidylinositol membrane protein anchors
R01GM-40086-05 (CBY) BURGESS, DAVID R UNIVERSITY OF PITTSBURGH PITTSBURGH, PA 15260 Biochemistry and biology of a myosin binding protein
R29GM-40087-03 (MBC) MARCH, PAUL E R WOOD JOHNSON MED SCHOOL DEPT OF BIOCHEMISTRY PISCATAWAY, NJ 08854-5635 Analysis of E coli GTP-binding proteins and their genes
R01GM-40089-04 (BBCB) RANCE, MARK A SCRIPPS CLINIC & RESEARCH FDN 10666 NORTH TORREY PINES ROAD LA JOLLA, CA 92037 Development of 2d and 3d NMR for studies of biomolecules
R01GM-40092-04 (BNP) RICH, DANIEL H 2320 CHAMBERLIN HALL 425 N CHARTER STREET MADISON, WI 53706 Design and synthesis of cysteine proteinase inhibitors
R01GM-40111-04 (SAT) HOFFMAN, ALLAN S UNIVERSITY OF WASHINGTON SEATTLE, WA 98195 Non fouling coatings on gas discharge treated surfaces
R01GM-40115-03 (CTY) WARD, DAVID C YALE UNIV/ DEPT. OF HUMAN GENE 333 CEDAR STREET,P.O. BOX 3333 NEW HAVEN, CONN 06510 Chromosome domains in interphase cells
R29GM-40117-05 (BBCB) DLUHY, RICHARD A UNIVERSITY OF GEORGIA ATHENS, GA 30602 In-situ infrared analysis of biomembrane monolayers
R01GM-40118-04 (MBC) OSLEY, MARY A SLOAN-KETTERING INST FOR DEPT OF MOLECULAR BIOLOGY NEW YORK, NY 10021 Genetic analysis of cell cycle-dependent transcription
R29GM-40120-04 (BBCB) CHAZIN, WALTER J RES INST OF SCRIPPS CLINIC MB2 10666 N TORREY PINES RD LA JOLLA, CA 92037 Structure and dynamics of calbindin 9K by 2d NMR
R29GM-40125-04 (NEUC) LEFF, STUART E DEPT OF PHARMACOLOGY STANFORD UNIV SCH OF MEDICINE STANFORD, CA 94305-5332 Control of neuroendocrine gene expression
R29GM-40162-03 (BBCB) NEEDHAM, DAVID DUKE UNIVERSITY DEPT OF MECH & MATERIALS SCI DURHAM, NC 27706 Electropermeabilization/fusion of lipid vesicles and cells
R01GM-40165-04 (SSS) FRANK, JOACHIM NEW YORK DEPT OF HEALTH EMPIRE STATE PLAZA ALBANY, N Y 12201 Three-dimensional reconstruction-- Subcellular structure
R37GM-40168-29 (BMT) PEISACH, JACK ALBERT EINSTEIN COLL OF MED 1300 MORRIS PARK AVENUE BRONX, N Y 10461 Heme protein structure and function
R01GM-40179-02 (PB) LEUSSING, DANIEL L OHIO STATE UNIVERSITY 120 W 18TH AVE COLUMBUS, OH 43210 Metal ion catalysis in group and proton transfer
R01GM-40185-04 (ALY) WALL, RANDOLPH UNIVERSITY OF CALIFORNIA MOLECULAR BIOLOGY INSTITUTE LOS ANGELES, CALIF 90024 Control of lymphocyte development
R29GM-40196-04 (BMT) WHITE, ROBERT L UNIVERSITY OF OKLAHOMA NORMAN, OK 73019 Matrix isolation infrared spectroscopy of mass ions
R01GM-40198-07 (SSS) RIEDER, CONLY L NEW YORK STATE DEPT OF HEALTH EMPIRE STATE PLAZA ALBANY, N Y 12201 Collaborations on mitosis using the Albany HVEM resource
R01GM-40205-04A1 (PBC) MACHER, BRUCE A SAN FRANCISCO STATE UNIVERSITY 1600 HOLLOWAY AVENUE SAN FRANCISCO, CA 94132

PROJECT NO., ORGANIZATIONAL UNIT., INVESTIGATOR, ADDRESS, TITLE

Gal-alpha-1-3galglycoconjugates--Biochemistry and evolution
R01GM-40219-03 (PC) HAGEDORN, CURT H VANDERBILT UNIVERSITY C 2104 MEDICAL CENTER NORTH NASHVILLE, TN 37232 Covalent modifications of eIF-4F/translational control
R01GM-40263-13 (GEN) SIMMONS, MICHAEL J UNIVERSITY OF MINNESOTA 250 BIOLOGICAL SCIENCES CTR ST. PAUL, MINN 55108 Mutation in hybrids of Drosophila
R01GM-40266-08 (GEN) FINK, GERALD R WHITEHEAD INST FOR BIOMEDI RES 9 CAMBRIDGE CENTER CAMBRIDGE, MASS 02142 Chemical carcinogens and frameshift mutation in yeast
R01GM-40282-04 (GEN) SLATKIN, MONTGOMERY W UNIVERSITY OF CALIFORNIA DEPT OF ZOOLOGY, 4079 LSB BERKELEY, CA 94720 Gene flow in natural populations
R01GM-40283-04 (BBCA) WARSHEL, ARIEH UNIVERSITY OF SOUTHERN CALIF LOS ANGELES, CALIF 90089-0482 Computer simulation of electron transfer reactions
R01GM-40287-01A3 (BMT) LIPSHUTZ, BRUCE H UNIVERSITY OF CALIFORNIA SANTA BARBARA, CA 93106 Novel organometallic routes to polyenes and derivatives
R01GM-40289-03 (PB) WALZ, FREDERICK G, JR KENT STATE FOUNDATION INC KENT, OH 44242 Polymorphism and genetic linkage of rat cytochromes P-450
R01GM-40304-04 (MGN) SIBLEY, CHARLES G SAN FRANCISCO STATE UNIVERSITY P O BOX 855 TIBURON, CA. 94920 Molecular evolution in mammals
R29GM-40306-04 (MBC) FASSLER, JAN S UNIVERSITY OF IOWA DEPARTMENT OF BIOLOGY IOWA CITY, IA 52242 Genetic analysis of yeast transcription factors
R29GM-40308-04 (MBY) WEEKS, DANIEL L DEPARTMENT OF BIOCHEMISTRY UNIV OF IOWA COLL OF MED IOWA CITY, IOWA 52242 The study of localized mRNA in Xenopus development
R01GM-40310-04 (GEN) CULBERTSON, MICHAEL R UNIVERSITY OF WISCONSIN LAB OF MOLECULAR BIOLOGY MADISON, WI 53706 TRNA splicing endonuclease in yeast
R01GM-40313-04 (MBC) ESCALANTE-SEMERENA, JORGE C 1550 LINDEN DRIVE MADISON, WI 53706-1567 B12 biosynthesis and anaerobic metabolism in Salmonella
R01GM-40314-03 (MBC) FILUTOWICZ, MARCIN S UNIVERSITY OF WISCONSIN 1550 LINDEN DR/ E B FRED HALL MADISON, WI 53706 Role of nucleoprotein structures in genome duplication
R29GM-40326-04 (BIO) CANNON, JOHN F UNIV OF MISSOURI-COLUMBIA M642 SCHOOL OF MEDICINE COLUMBIA, MO 65212 Analysis of yeast cAMP-dependent protein kinase
R29GM-40334-04 (GEN) BURKE, D J UNIVERSITY OF VIRGINIA DEPARTMENT OF BIOLOGY CHARLOTTESVILLE, VA 22901 A genetic analysis of regulated tubulin synthesis in yeast
R01GM-40335-04 (MBC) MACNAB, ROBERT M YALE UNIVERSITY, SCH OF MED P. O. BOX 3333 NEW HAVEN, CT 06510 Sequence analysis of the bacterial flagellar motor
R01GM-40338-02 (CPA) DIX, THOMAS A UNIVERSITY OF CALIFORNIA IRVINE, CA 92717 Mechanistic studies of oxygen pathology
R29GM-40362-04 (CTY) GOLDFARB, DAVID S UNIVERSITY OF ROCHESTER BIOLOGY DEPT/RIVER CAMPUS ROCHESTER, NY 14627 Nucleocytoplasmic trafficking
R01GM-40366-01A2 (NLS) DESHMUKH, DIWAKAR S INSTITUTE FOR BASIC RESEARCH 1050 FOREST HILL ROAD STATEN ISLAND, NY 10314 Brain phosphoinositides and barbiturates
R29GM-40367-04 (MGN) MARTIN, SANDRA L UNIV. OF COLORADO HEALTH SCI. 4200 E. NINTH AVENUE, B-111 DENVER, CO 80262 Genetic and biochemical analysis of a murine retroposon
R29GM-40375-04 (TOX) ELFARRA, ADNAN A UNIV OF WISCONSIN-MADISON 2015 LINDEN DRIVE WEST MADISON, WI 53706 Metabolic basis of conjugated dienes toxicity
R01GM-40379-04 (BIO) GILBERT, HIRAM F BAYLOR COLLEGE OF MEDICINE ONE BAYLOR PLAZA HOUSTON, TEX 77030 Catalysis of thiol disulfide exchange
R01GM-40392-04 (BMT) SOLOMON, EDWARD I STANFORD UNIVERSITY STANFORD, CA 94305-5080 Spectroscopic studies of non-heme iron enzymes
R01GM-40401-04 (MCHA) BRESLOW, RONALD C COLUMBIA UNIVERSITY DEPARTMENT OF CHEMISTRY NEW YORK, N Y 10027 Selective catalytic functionalizations
R01GM-40403-04 (MBC) ELLIOTT, THOMAS A UNIV OF ALABAMA UNIVERSITY STATION BIRMINGHAM, AL 35294 Genetic control of heme synthesis in S. typhimurium
R55GM-40404-04 (MBC) NIXON, B TRACY PENNSYLVANIA STATE UNIVERSITY 108 ALTHOUSE LABORATORY UNIVERSITY PARK, PA 16802 Functional domains of Rhizobium dct genes
R01GM-40419-01A2 (MBC) GOLDSTEIN, RICHARD BOSTON UNIVERSITY SCHOOL OF ME 774 ALBANY STREET BOSTON, MA 02118 Regulation of expression and assembly by satellite P4
R29GM-40423-04 (CTY) ATKINSON, MARK A L UNIVERSITY OF TEXAS P.O. BOX 2003 TYLER, TX 75710 The regulation of macrophage myosin
R01GM-40426-04 (BBCB) OLDFIELD, ERIC UNIVERSITY OF ILLINOIS 505 SOUTH MATHEWS AVENUE URBANA, ILL 61801 NMR studies of myelin membrane structure
R01GM-40437-04 (SAT) NANNEY, LILLIAN B VANDERBILT MEDICAL CENTER 21ST AND GARLAND AVENUES NASHVILLE, TN 37232 Epidermal growth factor stimulates wound healing in vivo
R01GM-40440-04 (PHRA) FALANY, CHARLES N UNIVERSITY OF ALABAMA BOX 402 BIRMINGHAM, AL 35294 Structure and regulation of rat aryl sulfotransferases
R01GM-40441-03 (BNP) ENGEL, ROBERT R QUEENS COLLEGE OF C U N Y DEPARTMENT OF CHEMISTRY FLUSHING, N Y 11367 Phosphoinositide & inositol phosphate analog synthesis
R01GM-40451-04 (GEN) LASKI, FRANK A UNIVERSITY OF CALIFORNIA DEPT-BIOLOGY/405 HILGARD AVE LOS ANGELES, CA 90024-1606 Developmental regulation in Drosophila
R01GM-40452-04 (GEN) DAWSON, DEAN S TUFTS UNIVERSITY AND MICROBIOLOGY BOSTON, MA 02114 Meiotic chromosome segregation in yeast
R01GM-40457-04 (PHY) SHUTTLEWORTH, TREVOR J UNIVERSITY OF ROCHESTER 601 ELMWOOD AVENUE ROCHESTER, NY 14642 Receptor-regulated calcium entry in exocrine secretion

PROJECT NO., ORGANIZATIONAL UNIT., INVESTIGATOR, ADDRESS, TITLE

R01GM-40458-04 (CTY) SCHWARTZ, LAWRENCE M UNIVERSITY OF MASSACHUSETTS AMHERST, MA 01003 Molecular mechanisms controlling programmed cell death

R01GM-40463-03 (PB) ZWIZINSKI, CRAIG W UNIV OF MINN, HORMEL INSTITUTE 801 16TH AVENUE NE AUSTIN, MN 55912 Cytoplasmic enzymology of mitochondrial protein import

R01GM-40466-04 (PB) LIPSCOMB, JOHN D UNIVERSITY OF MINNESOTA 435 DELAWARE ST,SE/4-225 MILLA MINNEAPOLIS, MN 55455 Methane monooxygenase structure and mechanism

R01GM-40468-04 (MBC) STEINMAN, HOWARD M ALBERT EINSTEIN COLL OF MED 1300 MORRIS PARK AVENUE BRONX, N Y 10461 Molecular mechanisms of oxygen toxicity

R01GM-40478-04 (MBY) ARES, MANUEL UNIVERSITY OF CALIFORNIA THIMANN LABORATORIES SANTA CRUZ, CA 95064 Structure and function of yeast small nuclear RNPS

R01GM-40479-04 (GEN) HUFFAKER, TIM C CORNELL UNIVERSITY BIOTECHNOLOGY BLDG. ITHACA, NY 14853 Molecular analysis of microtubule function in yeast

R01GM-40489-04 (GEN) MC KEE, BRUCE D UNIVERSITY OF TENNESSEE M313 WALTERS LIFE SCI BLDG KNOXVILLE, TN 37996 Stimulation of chromosome pairing & exchange by rDNA

R01GM-40498-03 (BNP) BEGLEY, TADHG P CORNELL UNIVERSITY 120 BAKER LABORATORY ITHACA, NY 14853-1301 Mechanistic studies on DNA photolyase

P01GM-40499-04 (SSS) BENZER, SEYMOUR CALIFORNIA INST OF TECHNOLOGY DIVISION OF BIOLOGY 156-29 PASADENA, CA 91125 Genetic basis of developmental patterns in Drosophila

P01GM-40499-04 0001 (SSS) LIPSHITZ, HOWARD Genetic basis of developmental patterns in Drosophila Localization of pattern determination in Drosophila egg

P01GM-40499-04 0002 (SSS) PARKER, CARL Genetic basis of developmental patterns in Drosophila Patterns of gene activation in Drosophila embryo

P01GM-40499-04 0003 (SSS) LEWIS, EDWARD Genetic basis of developmental patterns in Drosophila Biothorax complex as a microgenome

P01GM-40499-04 0004 (SSS) BENZER, SEYMOUR Genetic basis of developmental patterns in Drosophila Genetic specification of cell type in Dorosophila nervous system

P01GM-40499-04 0005 (SSS) TANOUYE, MARK Genetic basis of developmental patterns in Drosophila Specification of neuronal shape and connectivity in Drosophila

P01GM-40499-04 9001 (SSS) LEWIS, EDWARD Genetic basis of developmental patterns in Drosophila Drosophila culture facility

P01GM-40499-04 9002 (SSS) LIPSHITZ, HOWARD Genetic basis of developmental patterns in Drosophila Mass culture facility

R01GM-40506-04 (CTY) DAVIS, TRISHA N DEPT. OF BIOCHEMISTRY, SJ-70 UNIVERSITY OF WASHINGTON SEATTLE, WA 98195 Molecular analysis of calmodulin function in cell growth

R01GM-40508-04 (MBC) VIK, STEVEN B SOUTHERN METHODIST UNIVERSITY DEPARTMENT OF BIOLOGICAL SCI DALLAS, TX 75275 Structure-function studies of E coli F F-ATPase

R01GM-40509-04 (GEN) SPUDICH, JAMES A STANFORD UNIVERSITY DEPT OF CELL BIOLOGY STANFORD, CALIF 94305 Homologuos recombination in Dictyostelium

R29GM-40510-04 (BIO) BACHAS, LEONIDAS G UNIVERSITY OF KENTUCKY DEPARTMENT OF CHEMISTRY LEXINGTON, KY 40506 Mono-substituted conjugates in enzymeimmunoassays

R01GM-40517-04 (MBY) WEIL, PETER A VANDERBILT UNIV SCH OF MED DEPT OF MOL PHYS & BIOPHYS NASHVILLE, TN 37232-0615 Mechanism of RNA polymerase III transcription

R29GM-40521-03 (BIO) NORCUM, MONA T UNIV OF MISSISSIPPI/MED CTR 2500 NORTH STATE STREET JACKSON, MS 39216-4505 Structure of aminoacyl-tRNA synthetase complexes

R29GM-40525-03 (BMT) CRANS, DEBBIE C COLORADO STATE UNIVERSITY DEPARTMENT OF CHEMISTRY FORT COLLINS, CO 80523 Metallobiochemistry of vanadium(v)

R01GM-40526-04 (BMT) FRIESNER, RICHARD A COLUMBIA UNIVERSITY 116TH & BROADWAY NEW YORK, NY 10027 Theoretical studies of metalloprotein chromophores

R01GM-40528-04 (BBCB) TREWHELLA, JILL UNIVERSITY OF CALIFORNIA LOS ALAMOS NATIONAL LABORATORY LOS ALAMOS, NM 87545 Structural changes and signalling in calcium regulators

R01GM-40536-01A4 (BIO) NISHIKURA, KAZUKO THE WISTAR INSTITUTE 36TH AND SPRUCE STREETS PHILDELPHIA, PA 19104 RNA duplex unwindase

R01GM-40541-03 (BNP) LIU, HUNG-WEN UNIVERSITY OF MINNESOTA 207 PLEASANT STREET, SE MINNEAPOLIS, MN 55455 Mechanisms of enzyme inactivation by cyclopropyl groups

R01GM-40544-04 (PB) HOUK, KENDALL N UNIVERSITY OF CALIFORNIA 405 HILGARD AVE LOS ANGELES, CA 90024 Theory and modeling of macrocyclization reactions

R01GM-40546-04 (MCHA) MACKENZIE, PETER B NORTHWESTERN UNIVERSITY DEPARTMENT OF CHEMISTRY EVANSTON, IL 60208 Absolute stereocontrol via 2-alkenyl-1,3-dioxolanones

R01GM-40547-04 (BNP) KEMP, DANIEL S MASSACHUSETTS INST TECHNOLOGY 77 MASSACHUSETTS AVE/18-584 CAMBRIDGE, MA 02139 Synthesis and study of templates for beta-structure

R29GM-40551-03 (PHRA) MORRIS, MARILYN E S U N Y AT BUFFALO 527 HOCHSTETTER HALL AMHERST, N Y 14260 Pharmacologic alterations of sulfate homeostasis

R29GM-40553-04 (GEN) OLSZEWSKI, NEIL E UNIVERSITY OF MINNESOTA ST. PAUL, MN 55108 Molecular study of gibberellin regulated gene expression

R01GM-40558-04 (GEN) SCHUPBACH, GERTRUD M PRINCETON UNIVERSITY PRINCETON, NJ 08544-1014 Spatial pattern of the egg chamber in Drosophila

R29GM-40560-04 (CBY) ITTMANN, MICHAEL M MANHATTAN VA MEDICAL CENTER 24TH ST & FIRST AVE NEW YORK, N Y 10010 Cloning & characterization of cell proliferation genes

R01GM-40565-03 (MBC) MC INTOSH, MARK A UNIVERSITY OF MISSOURI COLUMBIA, MO 65212 Molecular analysis of ferric enterobactin transport

R29GM-40568-04 (CBY) BOWEN, JESSE W UNIV OF MISSOURI-COLUMBIA DEPT. OF PHARMACOLOGY COLUMBIA, MO 65212 Regulation of Na, K-ATPase expression in kidney cells

R01GM-40570-03 (BIO) GERLT, JOHN A UNIVERSITY OF MARYLAND DEPARTMENT OF CHEMISTRY COLLEGE PARK, MD 20742 Restructuring catalysis in the mandelate pathway

R01GM-40576-03 (BIO) BHAGWAT, ASHOK S WAYNE STATE UNIVERSITY 437 CHEMISTRY BLDG DETROIT, MI 48202 Structure-function analysis of the ECORII methylase

R01GM-40580-04 (CBY) LIN, JIM JUNG-CHING UNIVERSITY OF IOWA IOWA CITY, IA 52242 Tropomyosin isoforms and microfilaments

R01GM-40583-02 (PHY) WERNER, RUDOLF K UNIV OF MIAMI-SCHOOL OF MEDICI PO BOX 016129 MIAMI, FL 33101 Functional analysis of cell-cell channel protein

R01GM-40585-05 (GEN) KURJAN, JANET ANN UNIVERSITY OF VERMONT BURLINGTON, VERMONT 05405-0068 Pheromone response and G proteins in yeast

R01GM-40586-04 (SAT) MOLDAWER, LYLE L NEW YORK HOSP-CORNELL MED CTR 525 E 68TH ST - F2016 NEW YORK, NY 10021 Regulation on monokine production in trauma and surgery

R01GM-40599-04 (CBY) KNECHT, DAVID A U-125 UNIVERSITY OF CONNECTICUT STORRS, CT 06269-3125 The molecular genetics of development in Dictyostelium

R01GM-40600-04 (PC) SCHULMAN, HOWARD STANFORD UNIVERSITY DEPT OF PHARMACOLOGY STANFORD, CALIF 94305 Multifunctional calcium/calmodulin-dependent protein kinase

R29GM-40602-04 (PB) FIERKE, CAROL A DUKE UNIVERSITY MEDICAL CTR BOX 3711 DURHAM, N C 27710 Mutagenesis to probe catalysis by carbonic anhydrase ii

R01GM-40605-04 (CBY) POENIE, MARTIN F UNIVERSITY OF TEXAS AT AUSTIN DEPT OF ZOOLOGY 140 PAT AUSTIN, TX 78712-1064 Local signals mediating T cell activation

R01GM-40613-02 (GEN) THOMAS, JOHN B SALK INST FOR BIOL STUDIES PO BOX 85800 SAN DEIGO, CA 92138 Molecular genetics of Drosophila neural development

R01GM-40614-03 (MBC) VOLKERT, FREDRIC C ST UNIV OF NEW YORK HLTH SCI C DEPT OF MICROBIO & IMMUNOLOGY BROOKLYN, NY 11203 Control of yeast plasmid inheritance and gene expression

R29GM-40623-04 (BIO) JOHNSON, DEBORAH L UNIV OF SOUTHERN CALIFORNIA DEPT OF BIOMED CHEM & BIOCHEM LOS ANGELES, CA 90033 Characterization of the DNA binding function of S cerevisiae RNA polymerase

R01GM-40630-04 (BBCA) EDWARDS, BRIAN F WAYNE STATE UNIVERSITY 540 E CANFIELD DETROIT, MI 48201 Structural analysis of synthetically engineered RNAses

R29GM-40632-04 (MBY) ELLIS, STEVEN R UNIVERSITY OF LOUISVILLE DEPARTMENT OF BIOCHEMISTRY LOUISVILLE, KY 40292 Expression of mitochondrial ribosomal proteins in yeast

R01GM-40634-04 (BBCB) SCHAEFER, JACOB WASHINGTON UNIVERSTIY 1 BROOKINGS DR/CAMPUS BOX 1134 ST. LOUIS, MI 63130 Characterization of protein binding sites by solids NMR

R01GM-40635-04 (BBCA) KEARNS, DAVID R UNIV OF CALIF, SAN DIEGO DEPT OF CHEMISTRY LA JOLLA, CA 92093 Type II DNA-binding proteins--Structure and DNA binding

R01GM-40648-02 (MCHA) HUDLICKY, TOMAS VIRGINIA POLYTECHNIC INST CHEMISTRY DEPARTMENT BLACKSBURG, VA 24061 New (2 + 3) annulation protocol for natural product synthesis

R29GM-40650-04 (MBC) HENKIN, TINA M LOUISIANA STATE UNIV MED CTR DEPT OF BIOCHEM & MOL BIO SHREVEPORT, LA 71130-3932 Regulation of ribosome protein synthesis in B. subtilis

R01GM-40654-04 (CBY) CERIONE, RICHARD A CORNELL UNIVERSITY DEPT OF PHARMACOLOGY ITHACA, NY 14853-6401 Reconstitution of growth factor receptor/tyrosine kinase

R29GM-40658-04 (CTY) LOHKA, MANFRED J UNIV OF COLORADO DEPT OF C & S BIOLOGY DENVER, CO 80262 Characterization of metaphase-promoting factor

P01GM-40660-03 (SRC) HANDSCHUMACHER, ROBERT E YALE UNIV SCHOOL OF MED 333 CEDAR STREET/PO BOX 3333 NEW HAVEN, CT 06510 Analysis of cyclosporin-receptor interaction

P01GM-40660-03 0001 (SRC) SCHREIBER, STUART L. Analysis of cyclosporin-receptor interaction Synthesis of semi-peptide and non-peptide analogs of cyclosporin A

P01GM-40660-03 0002 (SRC) HANDSHUMACHER, ROBERT E. Analysis of cyclosporin-receptor interaction Chemical characterization of cyclophilin isoforms and responsible genes

P01GM-40660-03 0003 (SRC) ARMITAGE, IAN M. Analysis of cyclosporin-receptor interaction NMR analysis of cyclosporin-cyclophilin interaction

R29GM-40670-04 (BIO) HANAS, JAY S UNIV OF OKLA HLTH SCI CTR P O BOX 26901 OKLAHOMA CITY, OK 73190 Transcription factor IIIA structure, function, evolution

R29GM-40672-04 (CTY) CRAWFORD, NIGEL M UNIV OF CALIF, SAN DIEGO 0116 LA JOLLA, CA 92093-0116 Molecular genetics of nitrate reductase in Arabidopsis

R01GM-40676-02 (PC) HIGASHIJIMA, TSUTOMU UNIV OF TEXAS SW MEDICAL CTR 5323 HARRY HINES BLVD DALLAS, TX 75235-9041 Regulation of G proteins by mastoparan

R01GM-40681-03 (MBC) KENDRICK, KATHLEEN E OHIO STATE UNIVERSITY 484 W 12TH AVE/376 BIOSCIENCE COLUMBUS, OH 43210-1292 Regulation of histidine utilization in streptomyces

R29GM-40684-04 (BBCA) OLVERA DE LA CRUZ, MONICA NORTHWESTERN UNIVERSITY 2145 SHERIDAN RD EVANSTON, ILL 60208 Linear and circular polymer gel electrophoresis studies

R01GM-40685-03S1 (MBC) HASELKORN, ROBERT THE UNIVERSITY OF CHICAGO 920 EAST 58TH STREET CHICAGO, ILL 60637 Gene rearrangement in cyanobacterial heterocyst differntiation

R29GM-40689-04 (MBY) BEEN, MICHAEL D DUKE UNIV MEDICAL CENTER DEPARTMENT OF BIOCHEMISTRY DURHAM, N C 27710 RNA catalyzed splicing & nucleotide polymerization

R01GM-40692-04 (BBCB) DILL, KEN A UNIVERSITY OF CALIFORNIA SCHOOL OF PHARMACY SAN FRANCISCO, CA 94143-0446 Head group interactions in membranes & micelles

R29GM-40693-04 (MCHA) KRAFFT, MARIE E FLORIDA STATE UNIVERSITY DEPARTMENT OF CHEMISTRY TALLAHASSEE, FL 32306-3006 Alkaloid synthesis

using organorhodium chemistry
R29GM-40697-04 (GEN) L'HERNAULT, STEVEN W EMORY UNIVERSITY 1510 CLIFTON RD., NE ATLANTA, GA 30322 Genetics of Caenorhabditis elegans sperm morphogenesis
R29GM-40698-04 (BBCA) ELBER, RON UNIV OF ILLINOIS-CHICAGO PO BOX 4348 CHICAGO, IL 60680 Calculations of reaction paths in proteins
R01GM-40700-05 (MBY) JOHNSTON, STEPHEN A UNIVERSITY OF TEXAS SW MED CTR 5323 HARRY HINES BLVD DALLAS, TX 75235-8573 Molecular mechanisms of transcriptional regulation
R01GM-40704-04 (GEN) LEHMANN, RUTH E WHITEHEAD INST-BIOMED RES NINE CAMBRIDGE CENTER CAMBRIDGE, MA 02142 Maternal control of development
R01GM-40705-02 (SSS) APPLE, THOMAS M RENSSELAER POLYTECHNIC INSTITU COGSWELL LAB TROY, NY 12180-3590 Vapor grown carbon fibers for biomedical applications
R01GM-40706-04 (BBCA) MC PHERSON, ALEXANDER UNIVERSITY OF CALIFORNIA DEPARTMENT OF BIOCHEMISTRY RIVERSIDE, CALIF 92521 Diffraction analyses of ss DNA complexes with proteins
R01GM-40708-01A2 (MBY) BURTON, ZACHARY F MICHIGAN STATE UNIVERSITY EAST LANSING, MI 48824-1319 Transcription factors that bind to RNA polymerase II
R01GM-40711-04 (PTHA) SAGE, E HELENE SEATTLE, WA 98195 SM-20 Extracellular proteins as signals in endothelial growth
R01GM-40712-04 (BBCB) KLEIN, MICHAEL UNIVERSITY OF PENNSYLVANIA 300 MELLON BLDG 133 S 36ST ST PHILADELPHIA, PA 19104-3246 Computer simulation of amphiphilic aggregates
R01GM-40713-04 (MEDB) DEWITT, DAVID L MICHIGAN STATE UNIVERSITY EAST LANSING, MI 48824 Regulation of the PGH synthase gene
R01GM-40714-04 (GEN) HOYT, MYLES A THE JOHNS HOPKINS UNIVERSITY CHARLES & 34TH STREETS BALTIMORE, MD 21218 Genetics of chromosomes segregation in yeast
R01GM-40725-03 (GEN) SIGNER, ETHAN R MASSACHUSETTS INST/TECHNOLOGY 77 MASSACHUSETTS AVENUE CAMBRIDGE, MA 02139 Homologous recombination in Arabidopsis thaliana
R01GM-40731-04 (BBCB) FALKE, JOSEPH J UNIVERSITY OF COLORADO AND BIOCHEMISTRY BOULDER, CO 80309-0215 Biophysical studies of protein structure and dynamics
R01GM-40732-03 (CTY) EISSENBERG, JOEL C ST. LOUIS UNIVERSITY 1402 SOUTH GRAND BLVD. ST. LOUIS, MO 63104 Molecular cytogenetics of heterochromatin
R29GM-40735-04 (BBCB) LYON, MARY K UNIVERSITY OF COLORADO CAMPUS BOX 390 BOULDER, CO 80309-0390 Crystal studies of light-harvesting chlorophyll a/b complex
R01GM-40738-04 (END) MIESFELD, ROGER L UNIVERSITY OF ARIZONA 1515 N. CAMPBELL AVE. TUCSON, AZ 85724 Molecular biology of hormone-regulated cytolysis
R01GM-40746-03 (BBCA) KALLENBACH, NEVILLE R NEW YORK UNIVERSITY 4 WASHINGTON PLACE, RM 509 NEW YORK, NY 10003 Determinants of tertiary structure in myoglobins
R01GM-40751-04 (GEN) BRANDRISS, MARJORIE C UMDNJ-NEW JERSEY MEDICAL SCH 185 SOUTH ORANGE AVENUE NEWARK, N J 07103 Regulation & compartmentation in proline metabolism
P01GM-40761-01A2 (SRC) KAPLAN, JOHN E ALBANY MEDICAL COLLEGE 47 NEW SCOTLAND AVENUE ALBANY, N Y 12208 Tissue injury and repair--Fibronectin and macrophages
P01GM-40761-01A2 0001 (SRC) KAPLAN, JOHN E Tissue injury and repair--Fibronectin and macrophages Fibronectin in macrophage-fibrin binding and degradation
P01GM-40761-01A2 0002 (SRC) MOON, DUDLEY J Tissue injury and repair--Fibronectin and macrophages Adhesive glycoproteins in platelet-leukocyte contacts
P01GM-40761-01A2 0003 (SRC) BLUMENSTOCK, FRANK A Tissue injury and repair--Fibronectin and macrophages Post-injury ligands--Binding to fibronectin
P01GM-40761-01A2 0004 (SRC) GUDEWICZ, PAUL W Tissue injury and repair--Fibronectin and macrophages Surface contact modulation of macrophage function
P01GM-40761-01A2 0005 (SRC) MCKEOWN-LONGO, PAULA J Tissue injury and repair--Fibronectin and macrophages Organization of subendothelial fibronectin matrix
P01GM-40761-01A2 9001 (SRC) KAPLAN, JOHN E Tissue injury and repair--Fibronectin and macrophages Core--Scientific
R29GM-40767-05 (BIO) BENEDICT, STEPHEN H UNIVERSITY OF KANSAS LAWRENCE, KS 66045 Regulation of c-fos expression during T cell activation
R01GM-40768-04 (MBC) PARK, JAMES T TUFTS UNIVERSITY BOSTON, MA 02111 Biochemical approaches to the cell division problem
R01GM-40775-04 (MBC) FUCHS, JAMES A UNIVERSITY OF MINNESOTA DEPARTMENT OF BIOCHEMISTRY ST PAUL, MN 55108 Deoxyribonucleotide metabolism in Escherichia coli
R01GM-40778-06 (PB) BERLINER, LAWRENCE J OHIO STATE UNIVERSITY 120 WEST 18TH AVENUE COLUMBUS, OH 43210-1173 The role of alpha-lactalbumin in lactose biosynthesis
R01GM-40781-04 (PHRA) INSEL, PAUL A UNIV OF CALIF/SAN DIEGO SCHOOL OF MEDICINE LA JOLLA, CA 92093-0636 Beta-adrenergic receptors in S49 lymphoma cells
R01GM-40784-07 (PHRA) BYLUND, DAVID B UNIVERSITY OF NEBRASKA 600 SOUTH 42ND STREET OMAHA, NE 68198 Heterogeneity of alpha-2 adrenergic receptors
R01GM-40786-04 (BIO) WOOD, HARLAND G CASE WESTERN RESERVE UNIV 2119 ABINGTON ROAD CLEVELAND, OHIO 44106 Subunits & quaternary structure of transcarboxylase
R01GM-40791-03 (CBY) DETMERS, PATRICIA A ROCKEFELLER UNIVERSITY 1230 YORK AVENUE NEW YORK, NY 10021-6399 Regulation of receptor-ligand interactions
R44GM-40794-03 (SSS) SHATTUCK-EIDENS, DONNA AGRIDYNE TECHNOLOGIES INC. 417 WAKARA WAY SALT LAKE CITY, UT 84108 An improved replacement technology for RFLP analysis
R44GM-40825-03 (SSS) WINDELER, ALFRED S BIOMEDICAL DEVELOPMENT CORP 737 ISOM ROAD SAN ANTONIO, TX 78213 Culture dishes with unique surfaces
R01GM-40852-17 (BBCB) ARNONE, ARTHUR UNIVERSITY OF IOWA DEPARTMENT OF BIOCHEMISTRY IOWA CITY, IOWA 52242 X-ray studies of hemoglobin and other proteins
R01GM-40857-02 (MBY) PELLEGRINI, MARIA C UNIV OF SOUTHERN CALIFORNIA UNIVERSITY PARK, MC 1340 LOS ANGELES, CA 90089-1340 RRNA metabolism in mitotic and nonmitotic cells
R01GM-40858-04 (TOX) HOFFMAN, DOUGLAS W DARTMOUTH MEDICAL SCHOOL SCHOOL OF MEDICINE HANOVER, NH 03756 Endogenous modulation of oto- and nephrotoxicity
R01GM-40859-03 (MBC) LIDSTROM, MARY E CALIFORNIA INST OF TECHNOLOGY KECK LABORATORIES 138-78 PASADENA, CA 91125 Methane oxidation by methanotrophs
R01GM-40894-07 (BMT) TULLIUS, THOMAS D THE JOHNS HOPKINS UNIVERSITY CHARLES AND 34TH STREETS BALTIMORE, MARYLAND 21218 Metal complexes and enzymes as probes of DNA structure
R29GM-40905-03 (GEN) THUMMEL, CARL S UNIV OF UTAH SCH OF MEDICINE 501 WINTROBE BLDG-DEPT H GENE SALT LAKE CITY, UTAH 84132 Ecdysone regulated genes in drosophila
R01GM-40907-03 (GEN) CURTSINGER, JAMES W DEPT OF ECOLOGY-BEHAVORIAL BIO 318 CHURCH STREET S.E. Genetic correlation of quan characters in drosophila
R29GM-40909-03 (SAT) WARNER, DAVID O MAYO FOUNDATION 200 FIRST STREET SOUTHWEST ROCHESTER, MN 55905 Anesthesia and the respiratory muscles
R01GM-40916-03 (PC) LODISH, HARVEY F WHITEHEAD INST FOR BIOMED RES 9 CAMBRIDGE CENTER, ROOM 567 CAMBRIDGE, MASS 02142 Multiple glucose transporter proteins
R29GM-40917-03 (SAT) CHESTNUT, DAVID H UNIVERSITY OF IOWA HOSPITAL DEPT. OF ANTHES., OB & GYN IOWA CITY, IA 52242 Obstetric anesthesia--Tocolysis and hemorrhage
R01GM-40918-03 (MBY) LIS, JOHN T CORNELL UNIVERSITY BIOTECHNOLOGY BUILDING ITHACA, NEW YORK 14853-8101 Molecular dissection of transcription active chromatin
R01GM-40919-03 (PC) EXTON, JOHN H VANDERBILT UNIVERSITY 831 LIGHT HALL NASHVILLE, TN 37232 -0295 Cell signalling by phosphatidylcholine breakdown
R01GM-40922-04 (CTY) ALLIS, CHARLES D SYRACUSE UNIVERSITY 130 COLLEGE PLACE SYRACUSE, NY 13244 Influence of histone H1 and HMGs on gene expression
R01GM-40924-03 (ALY) BOTHWELL, ALFRED L M YALE UNIV SCHOOL OF MEDICINE P.O. BOX 3333 NEW HAVEN, CT 06510 Characterization of the Ly6 multigene family
R29GM-40941-03 (MBC) BAUER, CARL E INDIANA UNIVERSITY DEPARTMENT OF BIOLOGY BLOOMINGTON, IN 47405 Regulation of procaryotic gene expression by molecular oxygen
R01GM-40947-03 (MBC) YOUNG, KEVIN D UNIVERSITY OF NORTH DAKOTA SCHOOL OF MEDICINE GRAND FORKS, ND 58202 Membrane substructure and cell division in E. coli
R01GM-40949-03 (BNP) BARRETT, ANTHONY G COLORADO STATE UNIVERSITY DEPARTMENT OF CHEMISTRY FORT COLLINS, CO 80523 Redox glycosidation
R01GM-40958-03 (BBCA) CONNOLLY, MICHAEL L NEW YORK UNIVERSITY DEPT OF CHEM/WASHINGTON SQUARE NEW YORK, NY 10003 Molecular conformation, comparison and interaction
R01GM-40967-03 (BNP) CAVA, MICHAEL P UNIVERSITY OF ALABAMA PO BOX 870336 TUSCALOOSA, AL 35487-0336 Synthesis of tropoloisoquinoline alkaloids
R01GM-40972-03 (BBCA) ROSS, JOHN STANFORD UNIVERSITY DEPARTMENT OF CHEMISTRY STANFORD, CA 94305-5080 Thermodynamic efficiency of biological pumps
R01GM-40974-03 (BMT) CRABTREE, ROBERT H YALE UNIVERSITY 12 PROSPECT PLACE NEW HAVEN, CT 06511-3516 Some bioinorganic chemistry of nickel
R01GM-40983-03 (BIO) LOW, PHILIP S PURDUE UNIVERSITY DEPARTMENT OF CHEMISTRY WEST LAFAYETTE, IND 47907 Red cell tyrosine kinases and regulation of metabolism
R01GM-40988-03 (MCHA) WILLIAMS, ROBERT M COLORADO STATE UNIVERSITY DEPARTMENT OF CHEMISTRY FORT COLLINS, COLO 80523 Asymmetric synthesis of alpha-amino acids
R01GM-40989-03 (BMT) DIEDERICH, FRANCOIS N UNIVERSITY OF CALIFORNIA 405 HILGARD AVE LOS ANGELES, CA 90024-1569 Chiral molecular recognition and carbohydrate binding
R01GM-40993-03 (MBC) LIN, EDMUND C HARVARD MEDICAL SCHOOL 25 SHATTUCK STREET BOSTON, MASS 02115 Global regulation of aerobic metabolism in bacteria
R01GM-40995-03 (GEN) OCHMAN, HOWARD WASHINGTON UNIV SCH OF MED BOX 8232 660 SO EUCLID ST. LOUIS, MO 63110 Mapping organization and evolution of bacterial genomes
R29GM-41000-03 (GEN) PALTER, KAREN B TEMPLE UNIVERSITY 12TH & BERKS STREET PHILADELPHIA, PA 19122 Role of drosophila hsp70-related cognate proteins
R01GM-41003-11 (PBC) ADAIR, WINSTON L, JR UNIVERSITY OF SOUTH FLORIDA 12901 BRUCE B DOWNS BOULEVARD TAMPA, FL 33612 Biosynthesis of dolichyl phosphate
R01GM-41005-03 (GEN) CHAO, LIN UNIVERSITY OF MARYLAND ZOOLOGY/PSYCHOLOGY BLDG COLLEGE PARK, MD 20742 Evolution of sex & gene coadaptation in the RNA phage 6
R29GM-41009-03 (MBY) WARING, RICHARD B TEMPLE UNIVERSITY DEPT. OF BIOLOGY PHILADELPHIA, PA 19122 Three splice-site of a self-splicing group I intron
R29GM-41023-03 (MBY) HENDERSON, ERIC R IOWA STATE UNIVERSITY DEPARTMENT OF ZOOLOGY AMES, IOWA 50011 Structure & function of non-Watson-Crick telomeric DNA
R01GM-41026-03 (BIO) FITZPATRICK, FRANK A UNIV OF COLORADO HLTH SCI CTR DEPT OF PHARMACOLOGY(C236) DENVER, CO 80262 Biochemical pharmacology of epoxygenase eicosanoids
R01GM-41032-03 (BMT) TONG, WILLIAM G SAN DIEGO STATE UNIVERSITY 5300 CAMPANILE DR SAN DIEGO, CA 92182 Stable isotopes as biotracer by novel laser methods
R01GM-41034-03 (BBCA) MOULT, JOHN CTR FOR ADV RESEARCH IN BIOTEC 9600 GUDELSKY DRIVE ROCKVILLE, MD 20850 Computer algorithm for modeling protein structure
R01GM-41037-03 (PHRA) JUSKO, WILLIAM J S U N Y AT BUFFALO COOKE HALL 319 SCH OF PHARM BUFFALO, N Y 14260 Pharmacokinetics of reversible metabolic systems

PROJECT NUMBER LISTING

PROJECT NO., ORGANIZATIONAL UNIT., INVESTIGATOR, ADDRESS, TITLE

R01GM-41043-03 (BMT) BOSNICH, BRICE UNIVERSITY OF CHICAGO 5735 SOUTH ELLIS AVENUE CHICAGO, IL 60637 Metal catalysed asymmetric Diels-Alder reactions
R01GM-41048-03 (PB) DUTTON, PETER L UNIVERSITY OF PENNSYLVANIA B501 RICHARDS BUILDING PHILADELPHIA, PA 19104 Electron transfer mechanisms in reaction centers
R29GM-41049-03 (BMT) GOODIN, DAVID B SCRIPPS CLINIC DEPT. OF MOLECULAR BIOLOGY LA JOLLA, CA 92037 Determinants of functional diversity in heme enzymes
R01GM-41050-03 (CBY) ROTH, MICHAEL G UNIVERSITY OF TEXAS 5323 HARRY HINES BLVD DALLAS, TX 75235-9038 Isolation of cells defective in sorting glycoproteins
R01GM-41052-03 (ALY) KRANGEL, MICHAEL S DUKE UNIVERSITY P.O. BOX 3010 Human gamma delta T cell receptor
R01GM-41053-03 (MCHA) SCHULTZ, ARTHUR G RENSSELAER POLYTECHNIC INST DEPARTMENT OF CHEMISTRY TROY, N Y 12180-3590 Synthesis of medicinally important natural products
R01GM-41064-03 (BBCA) CHIU, WAH BAYLOR COLLEGE OF MEDICINE ONE BAYLOR PLAZA HOUSTON, TX 77030 Structural studies of rotaviruses
R01GM-41068-02 (TOX) SCHUMACHER, MICHAEL J UNIV OF ARIZONA HLTH SCI CTR 1501 N CAMPBELL TUCSON, AZ 85724 Immunotherapy of africanized bee venom intoxication
R01GM-41071-02 (MCHA) FRASER-REID, BERTRAM O DUKE UNIVERSITY PAUL M GROSS CHEMICAL LAB DURHAM, NC 27706 Pentenyl glycosides in transformations at anomeric center
R29GM-41073-03 (MBC) BREEDEN, LINDA L FRED HUTCHINSON CANCER RES CTR 1124 COLUMBIA STREET SEATTLE, WA 98104 Cell cycle regulation of the yeast HO gene
R01GM-41076-04A1 (CBY) ROSOFF, PHILIP M NEW ENGLAND MEDICAL CTR, INC 750 WASHINGTON ST, BOX 14 BOSTON, MA 02111 Isolation of the human T lymphocyte pertussis toxin
R01GM-41080-03 (GEN) BOGORAD, LAWRENCE HARVARD UNIVERSITY 16 DIVINITY AVE/BIO LAB CAMBRIDGE, MA 02138 Integration of organelle and nuclear gene expression
R29GM-41082-01A1 (SB) GIORGIO, TODD D VANDERBILT UNIVERSITY BOX 60, STATION B NASHVILLE, TN 37235 Shear stress enhanced solute transport across membranes
R01GM-41085-03 (MBC) LEVY , H RICHARD SYRACUSE UNIVERSITY 130 COLLEGE PLACE SYRACUSE, NY 13244-1220 Acetobacter xylinum glucose 6-phosphate dehydrogenases
R01GM-41086-03 (MBC) GOLDBERG, IVAN D UNIV. OF KANSAS MEDICAL CENTER 39TH & RAINBOW BOULEVARD KANSAS CITY, KS 66103 Molecular bases of enzyme thermostability in bacillus
R01GM-41089-03 (NTN) WOLFE, ROBERT R SHRINERS BURNS INSTITUTE 610 TEXAS AVENUE GALVESTON, TEXAS 77550 Energy expenditure in burned patients
R01GM-41097-03 (HEM) DIPERSIO, JOHN F UNIVERSITY OF ROCHESTER 601 ELMWOOD AVE ROCHESTER, NY 14642 The Na+/H+ exchanger in human granulocytic cells
R01GM-41100-04 (GEN) POSAKONY, JAMES W DEPT OF BIOLOGY, 0322 UNIV OF CALIF, SAN DIEGO LA JOLLA, CALIF 92093-0322 The regulated expression of the Drosophila ADH gene
R01GM-41102-05 (SAT) DUCH, DANIEL S CORNELL UNIV MED COLL 1300 YORK AVENUE NEW YORK, NY 10021 Anesthetic actions on single human brain sodium channels
R01GM-41105-03 (MCHA) SUNDBERG, RICHARD J UNIVERSITY OF VIRGINIA MCCORMICK ROAD CHARLOTTESVILLE, VA 22901 Analogs of antineoplastic indole alkaloids
R01GM-41113-03 (MCHA) THORNTON, EDWARD R UNIVERSITY OF PENNSLYVANIA PHILADELPHIA, PA 19104-6323 Asymmetric Diels-Alder reactions--New model
R29GM-41116-04 (HEM) JOHNSON, KEITH R UNIVERSITY OF TOLEDO 2801 W BANCROFT ST TOLEDO, OH 43606 Myleoperoxidase--Analysis of normal & deficient states
R01GM-41117-03 (BMT) CORREIA, JOHN J UNIV OF MISS MED CTR 2500 NORTH STATE STREET JACKSON, MS 39216-4505 Dynamics of microtubule assembly/disassembly
R29GM-41121-02 (TOX) BAKER, MAX T UNIVERSITY OF IOWA IOWA CITY, IA 52242 Flourinated ethene metabolism and hepatoxicity
R01GM-41131-03 (TOX) PETERSON, RICHARD E UNIV OF WIS, SCH OF PHARMACY 425 N CHARTER ST MADISON, WISCONSIN 53706 Toxicology of perfluorinated fatty acid-lipid conjugates
R01GM-41141-03 (PHRA) WALLE, THOMAS MEDICAL UNIV OF SOUTH CAROLINA 171 ASHLEY AVENUE CHARLESTON, SC 29425 Sex steroid hormones--Effects on drug clearance in man
R01GM-41215-02 (MBY) DENIS, CLYDE L UNIVERSITY OF NEW HAMPSHIRE DURHAM, NH 03824 Yeast genes involved in general transcriptional control
R01GM-41216-01A3 (CTY) LINZ, JOHN E MICHIGAN STATE UNIVERSITY EAST LANSING, MI 48824-1224 Ras genes and regulation of cellular morphogenesis
R29GM-41220-04 (CBY) WOLFMAN, ALAN S CLEVELAND CLINIC FDN. 9500 EUCLID AVENUE CLEVELAND, OH 44195 Role of multiple g-proteins in signal transduction
R01GM-41223-03 (CBY) MICHAELIS, SUSAN D JOHNS HOPKINS UNIVERSITY 725 WOLFE STREET BALTIMORE, MD 21205 Biogenesis and function of yeast a-factor
R01GM-41226-03 (CBY) PRYSTOWSKY, MICHAEL B UNIVERSITY OF PENNSYLVANIA 422 CURIE BLVD/545A CLINICAL R PHILADELPHIA, PA 19104-6142 Regulation of cellular proliferation
R55GM-41227-01A2 (NEUC) SALTON, STEPHEN R MT SINAI SCHOOL OF MEDICINE ONE GUSTAVE LEVY PLACE NEW YORK, NY 10029 Rapid selective regulation of NGF 33.1 gene expression B
R01GM-41232-03 (BIO) ROSEVEAR, PAUL R UNIV OF TEXAS HEALTH SCI CTR P O BOX 20708 HOUSTON, TX 77225 Structure-activity--Aminoacyl-trna synthetases
R29GM-41235-03 (BIO) WACKETT, LAWRENCE P THE UNIVERSITY OF MINNESOTA P.O. BOX 100 NAVARRE, MN 55392 Mechanistic studies on bacterial dehalogenase
R29GM-41239-03 (BNP) WHITMAN, CHRISTIAN P UNIVERSITY OF TEXAS PHR 4.220, MED CHEMISTRY DIV AUSTIN, TX 78712 Enzymes of the meta-fission pathway
R01GM-41243-03 (MBY) VOLLOCH, VLADIMIR Z BOSTON BIOMED RESEARCH INST 20 STANIFORD STREET BOSTON, MA 02114 Antisense intron RNA as modulator of gene expression
R29GM-41247-03 (TMP) KANOST, MICHAEL R KANSAS STATE UNIVERSITY WILLARD HALL MANHATTAN, KS 66506 Serine proteinase inhibitors in insects
R01GM-41249-03 (MBY) KADONAGA, JAMES T UNIV OF CALIFORNIA, SAN DIEGO LA JOLLA, CA 92093-0322 Mechanisms of transcriptional regulation in eukaryotes
R01GM-41257-03 (BIO) LIARAKOS, CHARLES D UNIVERSITY OF TENNESSEE 800 MADISON AVENUE MEMPHIS, TN 38163 Ovalbumin mRNA structure-function relationships
R01GM-41258-03 (GEN) POWERS, R SCOTT UMDNJ-R W JOHNSON MED SCHOOL 675 HOES LANE PISCATAWAY, NJ 08854-5635 Genetic analysis of the upstream control of yeast RAS
R01GM-41260-05 (IMB) WETTSTEIN, PETER J MAYO FOUNDATION 200 FIRST STREET S W ROCHESTER, MN 55905 Immunoregulatory gene family diversity and divergence
R01GM-41265-03 (TOX) HOLOHAN, PETER D SUNY HLTH SCI CTR AT SYRACUSE 750 EAST ADAMS STREET SYRACUSE, NY 13210 Nephrotoxicity--In vitro model
R01GM-41269-03 (PC) CORBIN, JACKIE D VANDERBILT UNIV SCH OF MED 702 LIGHT HALL NASHVILLE, TN 37232-0615 cGMP-binding phosphodiesterase--Regulatory mechanisms
R01GM-41281-03 (CBY) RUSSELL, PAUL R SCRIPPS CLINIC & RESEARCH FDN 10666 NORTH TORREY PINES RD LA JOLLA, CA 92037 Regulation of mitosis in fission yeast
R29GM-41283-03 (BIO) NICHOLSON, ALLEN W WAYNE STATE UNIVERSITY DEPT OF BIOLOGICAL SCIENCES DETROIT, MI 48202 Structure and function of an RNase III processing signal
R29GM-41286-03 (GEN) SCHMIDT, ROBERT J UNIV OF CALIF, SAN DIEGO 9500 GILMAN DRIVE LA JOLLA, CALIF 92093-0116 Role of opaque-2 regulating zein expression in maize
R01GM-41292-04 (PC) SODERLING, THOMAS R OREGON HEALTH SCIENCES UNIV 3181 SAM JACKSON PARK RD PORTLAND, OR 97201 Calcium/calmodulin-dependent protein kinase II
R01GM-41293-03 (SAT) CALDWELL, FRED T UNIVERSITY OF ARKANSAS MED CTR 4301 WEST MARKHAM, SLOT 520 LITTLE ROCK, ARKANSAS 72205 Neurohormonal control of postburn hypermetabolism
R01GM-41296-03 (GEN) YANOFSKY, CHARLES STANFORD UNIVERSITY DEPT OF BIOLOGICAL SCIENCES STANFORD, CALIF 94305-5020 Mechanisms of gene regulation in neurospora
R01GM-41297-02 (BIO) LUBLIN, DOUGLAS M WASHINGTON UNIV SCHOOL OF MED BOX 8118, 660 S EUCLID AVE ST LOUIS, MO 63110 Glycosyl-phosphatidylinositol-anchored membrane proteins
R01GM-41300-04 (BBCB) ALLEN, JAMES P ARIZONA STATE UNIVERSITY TEMPE, ARIZONA 85287 Crystallization and characterization of membrane proteins
R01GM-41302-03 (PC) DICKSON, ROBERT C UNIV OF KENTUCKY MED CTR 800 ROSE ST. LEXINGTON, KY 40536-0084 Molecular genetic analysis of yeast sphingolipids
R29GM-41303-04 (SAT) MUSTOE, THOMAS NORTHWESTERN UNIVERSITY 250 EAST SUPERIOR ST CHICAGO, IL 60611 Promotion of surgical wound healing by growth factors
R01GM-41304-04 (MBY) GREEN, MICHAEL R UNIV OF MASSACHUSETTS PROGRAM IN MOLECULAR MEDICINE WORCESTER, MA 01605 MRNA nuclear export
R01GM-41307-03 (BBCB) KIM, PETER S WHITEHEAD INSTITUTE NINE CAMBRIDGE CENTER CAMBRIDGE, MA 02142 Synthetic subdomains of BPTI as protein folding models
R29GM-41314-04 (MGN) HODGSON, CLAGUE P CREIGHTON UNIVERSITY CALIFORNIA AT 24TH STREET OMAHA, NE 68178 Recombinant pharmaceutical protein production in eggs
R29GM-41325-03 (PC) TAMKUN, MICHAEL M VANDERBILT UNIVERSITY SCH OF MEDICINE, 702 LIGHT HL NASHVILLE, TN 37232-0615 Na-k ATPase isoforms--Function and localization
R29GM-41330-03 (MBC) BAKER, HENRY V, II UNIVERSITY OF FLORIDA J-266 JHMHC GAINESVILLE, FL 32610 Molecular biology of glycolytic gene expression
R01GM-41332-03 (BBCA) HYNES, JAMES T UNIVERSITY OF COLORADO CAMPUS BOX 215 BOULDER, CO 80309-0215 Theory of proton and hydride transfer reaction rates
R29GM-41336-03 (BBCB) SOWERS, LAWRENCE C CITY OF HOPE NATL MED CTR 1500 EAST DUARTE ROAD DUARTE, CA 91010 Base pairing and mutagenesis--An NMR study
R01GM-41337-03 (BIO) BARANY, FRANCIS CORNELL UNIVERSITY 1300 YORK AVENUE, BOX 62 NEW YORK, N Y 10021 Mechanism of restriction endonuclease action
R01GM-41343-03 (SAT) KRUMMEL, THOMAS M PENNSYLVANIA STATE UNIV P O BOX 850 HERSHEY, PA 17033 Fetal wound repair--Cellular and biochemical mechanisms
R01GM-41347-04 (BIO) KOWALCZYKOWSKI, STEPHEN C UNIVERSITY OF CALIFORNIA DAVIS, CA 95616-8665 Biochemical mechanism and function of DNA helicases
R01GM-41350-03 (CBY) KURIYAMA, RYOKO UNIVERSITY OF MINNESOTA 321 CHURCH STREET S.E. MINNEAPOLIS, MN 55455 Molecular analysis of a novel MAP/MTOC component
R01GM-41353-03 (MBY) MAYFIELD, STEPHEN P RES INST OF SCRIPPS CLINIC LA JOLLA, CA 92037 Nuclear genes regulating translation of organelles MRNAs
R01GM-41359-03 (BBCA) QUIGLEY, GARY JOSEPH HUNTER COLLEGE OF CUNY 695 PARK AVENUE NEW YORK, NY 10021 Nucleic acid structure and environment
R01GM-41360-03 (BBCA) MAS, MARIA T BECKMAN RESEARCH INSTITUTE 1450 EAST DUARTE ROAD DUARTE, CA 91010 Folding and dynamics of a bi-domain enzyme
R01GM-41363-03 (BNP) FLOSS, HEINZ G UNIVERSITY OF WASHINGTON DEPARTMENT OF CHEMISTRY BG-10 SEATTLE, WA 98195 Biosynthesis of ergot alkaloids
R29GM-41365-03 (BIO) KUKURUZINSKA, MARIA A BOSTON UNIV DEPT OF ORAL BIO 100 E. NEWTON STREET BOSTON, MA 02118 N-glycosylation and controls of ALG7 expression
R01GM-41371-03 (BBCA) HONIG, BARRY H COULUMBIA UNIVERSITY DEPT/BIOCHEMISTRY, 630 W 168 S NEW YORK, N Y 10032 Electrostatic interactions in DNA

PROJECT NO., ORGANIZATIONAL UNIT., INVESTIGATOR, ADDRESS, TITLE

R01GM-41373-03 (BBCA) WEINSTEIN, HAREL MOUNT SINAI SCH OF MEDICINE DEPT OF PHYS/BIO BOX #1218 NEW YORK, NY 10029 Structure-function relations in calcium binding protein
R01GM-41376-03 (MBC) EBRIGHT, RICHARD H RUTGERS, STATE UNIV OF N J WAKSMAN INST OF MICROBIOLOGY PISCATAWAY, NJ 08855-0759 DNA sequence recognition by CAP
R29GM-41385-03 (GEN) SEDENSKY, MARGARET M CASE WESTERN RESERVE UNIVERSIT 2074 ABINGTON ROAD CLEVELAND, OH 44106 Molecular pharmacology of anesthetics in C elegans
R29GM-41388-04 (CBY) DE LISLE, ROBERT C UNIV OF KANSAS MEDICAL CENTER 39TH AND RAINBOW BLVD KANSAS CITY, KS 66103 Pancreatic acinar secretion--Reconstituted exocytosis
R01GM-41394-03 (PBC) DODGSON, JERRY B MICHIGAN STATE UNIVERSITY EAST LANSING, MICH 48824-1101 In vitro mutagenesis of histone and HMG genes
R01GM-41399-02 (MGN) CHAKRABORTY, RANAJIT UNIVERSITY OF TEXAS PO BOX 20334 HOUSTON, TX 77225 Effects of population mixtures on genetic variation
R01GM-41400-03 (CBY) VILLEREAL, MITCHEL L UNIVERSITY OF CHICAGO 947 EAST 58TH STREET CHICAGO, ILL 60637 Cell physiology of the bradykinin receptor
R01GM-41402-03 (BBCB) JACOBSON, KENNETH A UNIVERSITY OF NORTH CAROLINA 108 TAYLOR HALL CHAPEL HILL, N C 27599-7090 Lateral mobility of plasma membrane proteins
R29GM-41409-03 (MBC) WALLIS, JOHN W, JR ST LOUIS UNIVERSITY SCH OF MED 1402 SOUTH GRAND BOULEVARD ST LOUIS, MO 63104 Genetics of recombination between repeated elements
R01GM-41412-03 (BBCA) SMITH, STEVEN O YALE UNIVERSITY P O BOX 6666, 260 WHITNEY AVE NEW HAVEN, CT 06511 Solid-state NMR of membrane proteins and coenzymes
R01GM-41413-04 (BBCB) BROWN, MICHAEL F UNIVERSITY OF ARIZONA TUCSON, AZ 85721 Nmr studies of membrane structure and dynamics
R29GM-41415-04 (BBCA) SMALL, JEANNE RUDZKI EASTERN WASHINGTON UNIVERSITY MAIL STOP 74 CHENEY, WA 99004 Photoacoustic measurements of protein dynamics
R55GM-41421-01A2 (BNP) COSCIA, CARMINE J ST LOUIS UNIVERSITY SCH OF MED 1402 S GRAND BLVD ST LOUIS, MO 63104 Regulation of alkaloid metabolism
R29GM-41423-03 (PC) JOHNSTON, BRIAN H SRI INTERNATIONAL 333 RAVENWOOD AVENUE MENLO PARK, CA 94025 DNA structure and recombinational intermediates
R01GM-41426-03 (GEN) BUTOW, RONALD A UNIV-TEXAS SW MED CTR-DALLAS DALLAS, TEX 75235 Biolistic transformation of yeast mitochondria
R13GM-41434-03 (CTY) MURPHY, DOUGLAS B JOHNS HOPKINS SCHOOL OF MEDICINE BALTIMORE, MD 21205 Program for US/Soviet participation in cell biology
R01GM-41449-03 (BBCB) UNWIN, PETER N MED RES COUNCIL/LAB MOLEC BIO HILLS ROAD CAMBRIDGE CB2 2QH, ENGLAND 3-d design and action of cell membrane channels
R01GM-41452-02 (BNP) HAJDU, JOSEPH CALIFORNIA STATE UNIVERSITY 18111 NORDHOFF STREET NORTHRIDGE, CA 91330 Synthesis of modulator phospholipids
R01GM-41454-03 (BBCA) LEONTIS, NEOCLES B BOWLING GREEN STATE UNIVERSITY DEPT OF CHEMISTRY BOWLING GREEN, OH 43403 Structure and function of 5s RNA flexibility
R01GM-41455-03 (BBCA) LEVITT, MICHAEL STANFORD UNIVERSITY STANFORD, CA 94305 Simulation of protein dynamics and unfolding in solution
R01GM-41460-03 (SSS) TOZEREN, AYDIN CATHOLIC UNIV OF AMERICA WASHINGTON, DC 20064 Micro-mechanics of cell adhesion
R29GM-41465-03 (BBCA) SENEAR, DONALD F UNIVERSITY OF CALIFORNIA DEPT OF MOLECULAR BIOLOGY IRVINE, CA 92717 Coupling mechanisms--Site-specific protein-DNA assembly
R01GM-41467-12 (HEM) DEUTSCH, CAROL J UNIVERSITY OF PENNSYLVANIA D201 RICHARDS BLDG PHILADELPHIA, PA 19104 Cellular physiology of the lymphocyte
R29GM-41470-04 (PHRA) BROWN, ROBERT D UNIV OF ILLINOIS, CHICAGO 835 S WOLCOTT AVE CHICAGO, IL 60612 Alpha 1-adrenergic receptors & smooth muscle responses
R01GM-41476-04 (SSS) LAUFFENBURGER, DOUGLAS A UNIVERSITY OF ILLINOIS 1209 W. CALIFORNIA STREET URBANA, IL 61801 Analysis of microvessel endothelial cell migration
R01GM-41477-03 (CTY) SOLOMON, FRANK E MASSACHUSETTS INST OF TECH 77 MASS AVE, E17-220 CAMBRIDGE, MA 02139-4307 Function of the cytoskeletal proteins in vivo
R01GM-41478-03 (ALY) SMITH, GEORGE P UNIVERSITY OF MISSOURI 110 TUCKER HALL COLUMBIA, MO 65211 Filamentous fusion phage
R01GM-41482-03 (BMT) LE GALL, JEAN UNIVERSITY OF GEORGIA DEPARTMENT OF BIOCHEMISTRY ATHENS, GA 30602 Synthesis of novel iron & mixed metal-sulfur clusters
R55GM-41484-04A2 (BBCA) ROSE, GEORGE D UNIVERSITY OF N. CAROLINA CB# 7260, 303 FLOB CHAPEL HILL, NC 27599-7260 Stability of native and altered proteins
R01GM-41489-03 (BMT) MASLAK, PRZEMYSLAW PENNSYLVANIA STATE UNIV CHEMISTRY, 152 DAVEY LAB UNIVERSITY PK, PA 16802 Near diffusion-limited reactions
R29GM-41496-04 (TOX) BABSON, JOHN R UNIVERSITY OF RHODE ISLAND DEPT OF PHARM & TOXICOLOGY KINGSTON, RI 02881-0809 Toxicological significance of Ca2+-activated proteolysis
R01GM-41497-03 (IMS) TUCKER, PHILIP W U OF TX S W MED CTR AT DALLAS 5323 HARRY HINES BLVD. MICROBI DALLAS, TEX 75235 Expression of T cell receptor gamma and delta chains
R43GM-41504-01A1 (SSS) WALTERS, GLENN A D2C 917 SEPH WAY ESCONDIDO, CA 92027 Large time-bandwidth ultrasound echography
R01GM-41513-03 (GEN) STEPHENSON, EDWIN CLARK UNIVERSITY OF ALABAMA BOX 870344 TUSCALOOSA, AL 35487-0344 Role of the swallow gene in Drosophila development
R01GM-41514-07 (PHY) CAHALAN, MICHAEL D UNIVERSITY OF CALIFORNIA MEDICAL SCI. I, D340 IRVINE, CALIF 92717 The role of ion channels in T lymphocyte activation
R44GM-41523-02 (SSS) BOSSINGER, JUNE A COACT TECHNOLOGIES 135 FENNERTON ROAD PAOLI, PA 19301 Protein purification knowledge base

PROJECT NO., ORGANIZATIONAL UNIT., INVESTIGATOR, ADDRESS, TITLE

R44GM-41539-03 (SSS) SCHROEDER, JOHN L DNASTAR, INC 1228 SOUTH PARK STREET MADISON, WI 53715 Artificial intelligence system for analysis of proteins
R44GM-41547-03 (SSS) KOBAYASHI, KAZUMI CAMBRIDGE NEUROSCIENCE RES, IN ONE KENDALL SQUARE CAMBRIDGE, MA 02139 Novel neuroprotection compounds from spider venoms
R44GM-41558-02A1 (SSS) WESTENSKOW, DWAYNE R ROCKY MOUNTAIN RESEARCH INC 2715 EAST 3300 SOUTH SALT LAKE CITY, UT 84109 Development of an anesthesia workstation
R01GM-41560-09 (MCHA) WILLIAMS, DAVID R INDIANA UNIVERSITY DEPARTMENT OF CHEMISTRY BLOOMINGTON, IN 47405 Chemical synthesis of novel natural products
R44GM-41565-03 (SSS) WHITEHOUSE, CRAIG M ANALYTICA OF BRANFORD INC 29 BUSINESS PARK DRIVE BRANFORD, CT 06405 Electrospray ion source for quadrupole mass spectrometer
R01GM-41571-03 (VR) CONKLIN, KATHLEEN F UNIVERSITY OF MINNESOTA HARVARD ST AT E RIVER RD/BOX 2 MINNEAPOLIS, MN 55455 Retrovirus regulation in vitro and during development
R01GM-41574-04 (PB) DAVIDSON, VICTOR L UNIV OF MISSISSIPPI MED CENTER 2500 NORTH STATE STREET JACKSON, MS 39216-4505 Structure function & biosynthesis of respiratory enzymes
R01GM-41587-03 (MBC) KONISKY, JORDAN U OF ILLINOIS, MICROB DEPT 407 S. GOODWIN AVE URBANA, IL 61801 Characterization of methanococcus voltae ATPase
R01GM-41592-03 (MCHA) JUNG, MICHAEL E UNIVERSITY OF CALIFORNIA LOS ANGELES, CA 90024-1569 Synthesis of biologically active marine natural products
R01GM-41598-03 (BMT) BOSNICH, BRICE UNIVERSITY OF CHICAGO 5735 SOUTH ELLIS AVENUE CHICAGO, IL 60637 Metal mediated asymmetric intramolecular hydrosilation
R01GM-41602-03 (CBY) GREEN, MICHAEL 1402 S GRAND BLVD ST LOUIS, MO 63104 Regulation of ER synthesis in lymphocyte differentiation
R01GM-41605-15 (CBY) CRAIG, SUSAN W JOHNS HOPKINS UNIVERSITY 725 NORTH WOLFE STREET BALTIMORE, MD 21205 Cell surface control of lymphocyte physiology
R01GM-41609-03 (BBCB) FRANKS, PETER N IMPERIAL COLLEGE OF SCI/TECH PRINCE CONSORT RD/BLACKETT LAB LONDON SW7 2BZ, UK Biophysical mechanisms of general anaesthsia
R01GM-41610-03 (PB) WANG, JUI H STATE UNIVERSITY OF NEW YORK 170 ACHESON HALL BUFFALO, NY 14214-3094 New affinity reagents for the active sities of kinases
R01GM-41612-02 (BBCA) WANG, ANDREW H UNIVERSITY OF ILLINOIS DEPT OF PHYSIOLOGY/BIOPHYSICS URBANA, IL 61801 X-ray diffraction studies of nucleic acid structures
R01GM-41617-03 (BMT) TODD, PETER J MARTIN MARIETTA ENERGY SYS,INC PO BOX 2008/BLDG 5510/MS 6365 OAK RIDGE, TN 37831-6365 Organic secondary ion imaging
R01GM-41620-04 (MBY) BERGMAN, LAWRENCE WILLIAM HANEMANN UNIVERSITY BROAD AND VINE PHILADELPHIA, PA 19102-1192 Yeast transcription factors
R01GM-41624-03 (MGN) WEINER, ALAN M YALE UNIV SCHOOL OF MEDICINE 333 CEDAR STREET NEW HAVEN, CT 06510 Genomic plasticity in the human U2 snRNA gene cluster
R01GM-41626-03 (CTY) MAY, GREGORY S BAYLOR COLLEGE OF MEDICINE ONE BAYLOR PLAZA HOUSTON, TX 77030 Mutation affecting kinetochore microtubules in A. nidulans
R01GM-41628-04 (BIO) CONAWAY, RONALD C OKLAHOMA MEDICAL RES FDN 825 N E 13TH STREET OKLAHOMA CITY, OK 73104 Biochemistry of eukaryotic messenger RNA synthesis
R01GM-41635-03 (BMT) FENDER, DEREK H CALIFORNIA INST OF TECHNOLOGY 1201 E CA BLVD/CALTECH 286-80 PASADENA, CA 91125 Problems of human brain magnetite & high magnetic fields
R01GM-41637-03 (BBCA) OKAMURA, MELVIN Y UNIVERSITY OF CALIFORNIA DEPT OF PHYSICS, B-019 LAJOLLA, CA 92093 Quinone binding sites in bacterial reaction centers
R01GM-41639-01A1 (BBCA) JAMES, THOMAS L UNIVERSITY OF CALIFORNIA 926 MEDICAL SCIENCES BUILDING SAN FRANCISCO, CA 94143-0446 Protein structure via analysis of 2d NMR spectra
R01GM-41645-03 (BMT) GRUTZNER, JOHN B PURDUE UNIVERSITY WEST LAFAYETTE, IN 47907-1393 Electrophoretic separations in free solution
R01GM-41650-02 (BMT) HILLHOUSE, GREGORY L UNIVERSITY OF CHICAGO 5735 SOUTH ELLIS AVENUE CHICAGO, IL 60637 Chemistry of NH=NR prepared from transition metals
R01GM-41651-03 (BBCA) MOORE, PETER B YALE UNIVERSITY 12 PROSPECT PLACE NEW HAVEN, CT 06511-3516 The structure & physical properties of RNAs
R01GM-41657-03 (BMT) SESSLER, JONATHAN L UNIVERSITY OF TEXAS AT AUSTIN DEPARTMENT OF CHEMISTRY AUSTIN, TX 78712 Models for the bacterial photosynthetic reaction centers
R29GM-41659-04 (PHRA) LEEB-LUNDBERG, L M UNIV OF TEXAS HLTH SCI CNTR 7703 FLOYD CURL DRIVE SAN ANTONIO, TX 78284-7760 Kinin receptors: molecular properties and regulation
R29GM-41667-03 (SAT) BERNANKE, DAVID H UNIV MISSISSIPPI MEDICAL CTR 2500 NORTH STATE STREET JACKSON, MS 39216-4505 Matrix mediated mechanisms in delayed wound healing
R01GM-41669-03 (GEN) SHIH, MING-CHE UNIVERSITY OF IOWA CHEMISTRY-BOTANY BUILDING IOWA CITY, IA 52242 Regulation of glycolytic genes in Arabidopsis
R01GM-41679-03 (BIO) SCHULTZ, PETER G DEPT OF CHEMISTRY UNIVERSITY OF CALIFORNIA BERKELEY, CA 94720 Generation of sequence specific nucleases
R01GM-41681-01 (CTY) WANG, YU-LI WORCESTER FDN-EXPERIMENTAL BIO 222 MAPLE AVENUE SHREWSBURY, MA 01545 Structural assembly in muscle and non-muscle cells
R01GM-41690-02 (MGN) SEDIVY, JOHN M YALE UNIVERSITY SCHOOL OF MED 333 CEDAR ST, PO BOX 3333 NEW HAVEN, CT 06510 Gene disruption by homologous recombination in mammals
R01GM-41694-03 (SAT) CALDWELL, FRED T UNIVERSITY OF ARKANSAS MED CTR 4301 WEST MARKHAM, SLOT 520 LITTLE ROCK, ARKANSAS 72205 Etiology and control of postburn hypermetabolism
R01GM-41708-03 (MBY) ANDERSON, JOHN N PURDUE UNIVERSITY DEPT OF BIOLOGICAL SCIENCES WEST LAFAYETTE, IN 47907 An artificial origin of

replication

R01GM-41712-02 (MGN) MAIZELS, NANCY YALE MEDICAL SCHOOL 333 CEDAR STREET NEW HAVEN, CT 06510 Mechanisms of somatic mutation of immunoglobulin genes

R01GM-41716-03 (GEN) FELSENSTEIN, JOSEPH UNIVERSITY OF WASHINGTON 1959 N E PACIFIC ST SEATTLE, WA 98195 Methods for inferring molecular genalogies

R01GM-41718-01A1 (CTY) KOSHLAND, DOUGLAS E CARNEGIE INST OF WAHINGTON 115 W UNIVERSITY PARKWAY BALTIMORE, MD 21210 Centromere function of yeast

R29GM-41729-03 (CBY) PIKE, LINDA J HOWARD HUGHES MEDICAL INSTITUT 4940 PARKVIEW BOX 8045 ST. LOUIS, MO 63110 Cloning of a phosphatidylinositol kinase

R01GM-41734-02 (SAT) SIMMONS, RICHARD L UNIVERSITY OF PITTSBURGH DEPT OF SURGERY PITTSBURGH, PA 15261 Trauma, infection, and prosthetic biomaterials

R01GM-41738-03 (PB) BREEN, GAIL A UNIVERSITY OF TEXAS PO BOX 830688 RICHARDSON, TX 75083-0688 Biogenesis of the mammalian mitochondrial ATP synthase complex

R29GM-41745-03 (SAT) OLDHAM, KEITH T DUKE UNIVERSITY MEDICAL CENTER P O BOX 3814 DURHAM, NC 27710 Thermal injury, oxygen radicals and complement activation

R01GM-41746-03 (MGN) WARD, R H UNIVERSITY OF UTAH SALT LAKE CITY, UT 84112 DNA polymorphisms in north american indians

R01GM-41751-03 (CTY) FARRELL, KEVIN W UNIVERSITY OF CALIFORNIA SANTA BARBARA, CA 93106 Molecular analysis of beta-tubulin GTP-binding domains

R01GM-41752-03 (MBY) MOORE, CLAIRE L TUFTS UNIV SCH OF MEDICINE 136 HARRISON AVE BOSTON, MA 02111 Molecular mechanism of mRNA 3' end formation in yeast

R01GM-41753-03 (TMP) DUNN, PETER E PURDUE UNIVERSITY DEPT OF ENTOMOLOGY WEST LAFAYETTE, IN 47907 Regulation of cecropin and attacin gene expression

R01GM-41758-04 (CBY) DOUGLAS, MICHAEL G UNIVERSITY OF NORTH CAROLINA CB #7260/ 405 FLOB CHAPEL HILL, NC 27599-7260 The yeast nuclear pore complex

R01GM-41766-02 (TMP) WOLFERSBERGER, MICHAEL G TEMPLE UNIVERSITY 12TH & NORRIS STREETS PHILADELPHIA, PA 19122 Molecular mode of action of Bacillus thuringiensis toxin

R01GM-41771-02 (CBY) RODRIGUEZ-BOULAN, ENRIQUE J CORNELL UNIV MEDICAL COLLEGE 1300 YORK AVENUE NEW YORK, NY 10021 Targeting and membrane domains in epithelial cells

R01GM-41784-03 (MBC) SYMINGTON, LORRAINE S COLUMBIA UNIVERSITY 701 WEST 168TH STREET NEW YORK, NY 10032 Biochemical analysis of genetic recombination in yeast

R01GM-41786-02 (MGN) LAFUSE, WILLIAM P OHIO STATE UNIVERSITY 333 W 10TH AVENUE COLUMBUS, OH 43210 Characterization of a mouse recombination hot spot

R01GM-41788-03 (BIO) TSAI, MING-DAW OHIO STATE UNIVERSITY 120 W 18TH AVENUE COLUMBUS, OH 43210 Mechanism of phospholipase A2

R29GM-41790-02 (BBCB) MEERS, PAUL R BOSTON UNIV SCHOOL OF MEDICINE 80 EAST CONCORD STREET BOSTON, MA 02118 Annexin-membrane interaction & neutrophil activation

R01GM-41792-02 (CTY) REEDER, RONALD H FRED HUTCHINSON CANCER RES CTR 1124 COLUMBIA STREET SEATTLE, WA 98104 Termination of transcription by RNA polymerase I

R01GM-41796-03 (SAT) WANG, HOWARD H UNIVERSITY OF CALIFORNIA 1156 HIGH ST/SINSHEIMER LAB SANTA CRUZ, CALIF 95064 Action of inhaled anesthetics on synaptic receptors

R01GM-41797-03 (SAT) RORIE, DUANE K MAYO FOUNDATION 200 FIRST STREET SOUTHWEST ROCHESTER, MN 55905 Anesthesia and norepinephrine/neuropeptide interactions

R29GM-41803-03 (CTY) PRICE, CAROLYN M UNIVERSITY OF NEBRASKA-LINCOLN HAMILTON HALL LINCOLN, NE 68588-0304 Telomere structure in euplotes crassus

R01GM-41804-03 (SAT) BRENNER, DAVID A UNIV OF CA, SAN DIEGO LA JOLLA, CA 92093-0623 Role of tnf in the impaired wound healing of cachexia

R01GM-41807-03 (GEN) ANDERSON, ROBERT P UNIVERSITY OF WISCONSIN DEPT OF GENETICS MADISON, WI 53706 Transposable genetic elements of the nematode

R01GM-41815-03 (GEN) KALDERON, DANIEL D COLUMBIA UNIVERSITY DEPT OF BIOLOGICAL SCIENCES NEW YORK, NY 10027 Functions of CAMP-dependent protein kinase in Drosophila

R01GM-41821-02 (BNP) HIRSCHMANN, RALPH F UNIVERSITY OF PENNSYLVANIA DEPT OF CHEMISTRY PHILADELPHIA, PA 19104-3246 Non-peptide peptidomimetics

R01GM-41822-03 (BMT) KORSZUN, Z RICHARD UNIVERSITY OF WISCONSIN BOX NO 2000 KENOSHA, WI 53141-2000 Peroxidases, catalases, and cytochrome P-450

R29GM-41825-02 (BNP) GELLMAN, SAMUEL H UNIVERSITY OF WISCONSIN 1101 UNIVERSITY AVENUE MADISON, WI 53706 Conformational amphiphiles

R29GM-41828-03 (PHRA) SMITH, PHILIP C UNIVERSITY OF TEXAS COLLEGE OF PHARMACY AUSTIN, TX 78712 Disposition of acyl glucuronides & their protein adducts

R01GM-41829-03 (BBCA) SPICER, LEONARD D DUKE UNIVERSITY MED CTR BOX 3711 DURHAM, NC 27710 NMR studies of proteins and protein-DNA binding

R01GM-41840-03 (MBC) THIELE, DENNIS J UNIVERSITY OF MICHIGAN ANN ARBOR, MI 48109-0606 Copper homeostasis in yeast

R29GM-41841-03 (MBC) PAKRASI, HIMADRI B WASHINGTON UNIVERSITY ONE BROOKINGS DRIVE/BOX 1137 ST LOUIS, MO 63130 Use of mutants to study cyanobacterial membrane proteins

R01GM-41845-04 (MBC) TAI, PHANG C GEORGIA STATE UNIVERSITY UNIVERSITY PLAZA ATLANTA, GA 30303 Lipoprotein--Membrane insertion,modification and processing

R01GM-41849-02 (PBC) RAMIREZ, FRANCESCO MT SINAI SCHOOL OF MEDICINE 1 GUSTAVE L LEVY PL, BOX 1128A NEW YORK, N Y 10029 Structure and expression of invertebrate collagens

R01GM-41883-03 (MBC) BECKWITH, JONATHAN R HARVARD MEDICAL SCHOOL 25 SHATTUCK STREET BOSTON, MA 02115 The mechanism of protein secretion in E coli

R01GM-41885-03 (SSS) DEMENAIS, FLORENCE M HOWARD UNIV CANCER CTR EPIDEMIOLOGY WASHINGTON D. C. 20060 Simulation experiments of models in genetic epidemiology

R01GM-41889-01A2 (MBC) ROSENKRANTZ, MARK S VIRGINIA COMMONWEALTH UNIV BOX 678 MCV STATION RICHMOND, VA 23298-0678 Control of citrate synthase expression in yeast

R01GM-41890-02 (PB) CANTLEY, LEWIS C TUFTS UNIVERSITY 136 HARRISON AVENUE BOSTON, MA 02111 Role of phosphatidylinositol-3-P in growth regulation

R01GM-41895-03 (GEN) GILBERT, WALTER HARVARD UNIVERSITY 16 DIVINITY AVE CAMBRIDGE, MA 02138 The role of G4-DNA in the pairing of chromosomes

R29GM-41899-03 (MBY) LARSON, DRENA D IOWA STATE UNIVERSITY DEPARTMENT F ZOOLOGY AMES, IOWA 50011 Regulation of rDNA replication in Tetrahymena

R01GM-41905-03 (BBCA) ELBER, RON UNIVERSITY OF ILLINOIS CHEMISTRY DEPT/PO BOX 4348 CHICAGO, IL 60680 LES--A new method for computer simulation of proteins

R01GM-41908-03 (BMT) KNOCHEL, PAUL UNIVERSITY OF MICHIGAN 930 NORTH UNIVERSITY AVE ANN ARBOR, MI 48109-1055 New highly functionalized copper and zinc reagents

R01GM-41909-02 (BBCA) MILLER, R DWAYNE UNIVERSITY OF ROCHESTER DEPARTMENT OF CHEMISTRY ROCHESTER, NY 14627 Picosecond optical studies of vibrational energy relaxation in proteins

R01GM-41911-03 (BBCA) HEARST, JOHN E UNIVERSITY OF CALIFORNIA DEPARTMENT OF CHEMISTRY BERKELEY, CA 94720 Dynamics of DNA motion at physiological concentrations

R01GM-41913-03 (PB) JAFFE, EILEEN K INSTITUTE OF CANCER RESEARCH 7701 BURHOLME AVENUE PHILADELPHIA, PA 19111 Chorismate mutase--Mechanism of a novel enzymic reation

R01GM-41915-04 (MBY) WIDOM, JONATHAN NORTHWESTERN UNIVERSITY 2153 SHERIDAN ROAD EVANSTON, IL 60208-3500 Biochemical and genetic studies of yeast chromosomes

R01GM-41916-03 (BIO) SCHRAMM, VERN L ALBERT EINSTEIN COLL OF MED 1300 MORRIS PARK AVENUE BRONX, N Y 10461 Transition state analysis of enzymatic reactions

R01GM-41930-03 (BMT) TULLIUS, THOMAS D JOHNS HOPKINS UNIVERSITY DEPARTMENT OF CHEMISTRY BALTIMORE, MARYLAND 21218 Footprinting with iron(II)-generated hydroxyl radical

R01GM-41934-03 (MBC) GROSSMAN, ALAN D MASS INST OF TECHNOLOGY RM 56-510, 77 MASS. AVE. CAMBRIDGE, MA 02139 Initiation of sporulation in bacillus subtilis

R29GM-41935-01A3 (PHRA) BROUWER, KIM L UNIVERSITY OF NORTH CAROLINA CB #7360, BEARD HALL CHAPEL HILL, NC 27599-7360 Altered hepatic disposition of anionic drugs--Mechanisms

R01GM-41936-03 (BBCB) WANG, BI-CHENG UNIVERSITY OF PITTSBURGH DEPARTMENT OF CRYSTALLOGRAPHY PITTSBURGH, PA 15260 Structure-function relationships of RNA polymerases

R01GM-41942-02 (BBCA) SIMON, JOHN D UNIV OF CALIFORNIA, SAN DIEGO LA JOLLA, CA 92093-0314 Picosecond circular dichroism studies of protein motion

R01GM-41955-02 (CTY) GERACE, LARRY R SCRIPPS CLINIC & RESEARCH FDN. 10666 NORTH TORREY PINES ROAD LA JOLLA, CA 92037 Mechanisms of nuclear protein import

R01GM-41961-04 (SAT) BESSEY, PALMER Q BOX 8109/DEPT OF SURGERY 4949 BARNES HOSPITAL PLAZA ST LOUIS, MO 63110 Effects of insulin on the catabolic response to trauma

R01GM-41965-03 (ALY) BUTCHER, EUGENE C STANFORD UNIV MED CTR DEPT OF PATHOLOGY, L235 STANFORD, CA 94305 Molecular biology of human leukocyte homing receptor

R01GM-41967-02 (MBY) FALCK-PEDERSEN, ERIK CORNELL UNIVERSITY MEDICAL COL 1300 YORK AVENUE, BOX 62 NEW YORK, NY 10021 Biochemistry of RNA polII poly(A) site choice and 3' termination

R01GM-41978-03 (MBC) ROTHFIELD, LAWRENCE I 263 FARMINGTON AVE FARMINGTON, CT 06030 Studies of bacterial minicell mutants

R01GM-41980-03 (MBC) DAS SARMA, SHILADITYA UNIVERSITY OF MASSACHUSETTS DEPARTMENT OF MICROBIOLOGY AMHERST, MA 01003 Regulation of gene expression in Halobacterium halobium

R01GM-41983-02 (MCHA) IRELAND, ROBERT E UNIVERSITY OF VIRGINIA MCCORMICK RD CHARLOTTESVILLE, VA 22901 Immunosuppressants--synthesis of FK-506

R29GM-41984-03 (MCHA) HARVEY, DANIEL F UNIV OF CALIF. SAN DIEGO DEPARTMENT OF CHEMISTRY LA JOLLA, CA 92093-0506 Synthesis and study of tumor promoters and inhibitors

R01GM-42010-01A2 (BNP) PANKIEWICZ, KRYSTOF W SLOAN-KETTERING INSTITUTE 1275 YORK AVENUE NEW YORK, NY 10021 Pyridine nucleosides, nucleotides of biological interest

R01GM-42012-03 (BBCA) PLEASS, CHARLES M UNIVERSITY OF DELAWARE COLLEGE MARINE NEWARK, DE 19716 Holographic characterization of microbes

R01GM-42016-02 (BNP) GANDOUR, RICHARD D LOUISIANA STATE UNIVERSITY BATON ROUGE, LA 70803-1804 Reaction intermediate analogs of carnitine acyl transfer

R29GM-42017-03 (BNP) ASHLEY, GARY W NORTHWESTERN UNIVERSITY 2145 SHERIDAN ROAD EVANSTON, IL 60208 Studies of the biosyntheses of biotin and lipoic acid

R01GM-42025-03 (PB) SCOTT, ROBERT A UNIVERSITY OF GEORGIA CEDAR DRIVE ATHENS, GA 30602 X-ray absorption spectroscopy of metalloenzymes

R01GM-42026-03 (CBY) GUNDERSEN, GREGG G COLUMBIA UNIVERSITY 630 WEST 168TH STREET NEW YORK, NY 10032 The generation of cellular asymmetry

R01GM-42031-03 (BNP) ERICKSON, BRUCE W UNIVERSITY OF NORTH CAROLINA DEPARTMENT OF CHEMISTRY CHAPEL HILL, NC 27599-3290 Engineering of nongenetic beta proteins

R01GM-42033-03 (MBC) OLIVER, DONALD B STATE UNIVERSITY OF NEW YORK DEPT. OF MICROBIOLOGY STONY BROOK, NY 11794 Mechanism of protein localization in Escherichia coli

R01GM-42045-01A2 (SAT) KIM, YOUNG D GEORGETOWN UNIVERSITY HOSPITAL 3800 RESERVOIR ROAD, NW WASHINGTON, DC 20007 Anesthesia and regional myocardial function

R01GM-42056-03 (BMT) ROBERTS, L JACKSON VANDERBILT UNIVERSITY DIV OF CLINICAL PHARMACOLOGY NASHVILLE, TN 37232 Structural identification of prostaglandin conjugates

PROJECT NO., ORGANIZATIONAL UNIT., INVESTIGATOR, ADDRESS, TITLE

R01GM-42058-02 (TOX) **BLOUIN, ROBERT A** UNIVERSITY OF KENTUCKY ROSE STREET LEXINGTON, KY 40536-0082 Enzyme induction defect--Implication for toxicity
R01GM-42071-04 (IMB) **MILLER, JAMES F** THE UNIVERSITY OF CHICAGO 920 EAST 58TH STREET CHICAGO, ILLINOIS 60637 Role of intracellular Ia in antigen presentation
R01GM-42077-07 (MBC) **PRICE, CHESTER W** UNIVERSITY OF CALIFORNIA DEPT OF FOOD SCI & TECHNOLOGY DAVIS, CALIF 95616 Molecular genetics of bacillus subtilis RNA polymerase
R15GM-42078-01A2 (BIO) **LIBBY, R DANIEL** COLBY COLLEGE WATERVILLE, ME 04901 Chloroperoxidase as a probe for heme enzyme mechanisms
R15GM-42080-01A2 (MBC) **WILKINSON, BRIAN J** ILLINOIS STATE UNIVERSITY NORMAL, IL 61761 Osmoregulation in staphylococcus aureus
R01GM-42095-03 (SAT) **DILGER, JAMES P** SUNY DEPARTMENT OF ANESTHESIOLOGY STONY BROOK, N Y 11794-8480 General anesthetic mechanisms in excitable membranes
R01GM-42101-03 (BBCA) **BARKLEY, MARY D** LOUISIANA STATE UNIVERSITY DEPARTMENT OF CHEMISTRY BATON ROUGE, LA 70803-1804 Fluorescence studies of peptide structure and dynamics
R01GM-42123-19 (PC) **MC CLAIN, WILLIAM H** UNIVERSIT OF WISCONSIN 1550 LINDEN DRIVE MADISON, WI 53706-1521 Genetic and statistical analyses of tRNA
R01GM-42136-03 (CBY) **CAPLAN, MICHAEL J** YALE UNIVERSITY SCH OF MED 333 CEDAR ST/CELL MOLEC PHYSIO NEW HAVEN, CT 06510 Ion pumps in polarized epithelia--Sorting and function
R29GM-42138-03 (BIO) **KOUDELKA, GERALD B** ST UNIV OF NEW YORK AT BUFFALO NORTH CAMPUS, DEPT/BIO SCIS BUFFALO, NY 14260 DNA sequence recognition--The role of DNA flexibility
R29GM-42140-03 (BIO) **CHANDRASEGARAN, SRINIVASAN** JOHNS HOPKINS UNIVERSITY 615 NORTH WOLFE STREET BALTIMORE, MD 21205 Studies on FOK I (a type IIS) restriction enzyme
R29GM-42143-03 (BIO) **MERCHANT, SABEEHA** UNIVERSITY OF CALIFORNIA 405 HILGARD AVE LOS ANGELES, CA 90024-1569 Cu-dependent transcriptional regulation
R01GM-42146-01A1 (MBC) **POSTLE, KATHLEEN** WASHINGTON STATE UNIVERSITY PULLMAN, WA 99164-4233 Energy transduction between membranes
R01GM-42148-03 (BNP) **ETTER, MARGARET C** UNIVERSITY OF MINNESOTA 207 PLEASANT ST S E MINNEAPOLIS, MN 55455-0431 Hydrogen-bond rules for organic compounds
R15GM-42153-01S1 (BMT) **MILLER, DAVID A** CALIFORNIA STATE UNIVERSITY DEPT OF CHEMSITRY NORTHRIDGE, CA 91330 Development of a 118Te/118Sb radionuclide generator
R01GM-42159-03 (MBC) **MATIN, ABDUL** STANFORD UNIVERSITY D317 FAIRCHILD BLDG STANFORD, CA 94305-5402 Carbon starvation gene expression in Escherichia coli
R01GM-42178-03 (MBY) **TYLER, BRETT M** UNIVERSITY OF CALIFORNIA PLANT PATHOLOGY DEPT DAVIS, CA 94616 Co-regulation of N. crassa ribosomal RNA & protein genes
R01GM-42188-03 (PC) **STUART, KENNETH D** SEATTLE BIOMEDICAL RES. INST. 4 NICKERSON STREET, #100 SEATTLE, WA 98109-1651 RNA editing
R15GM-42206-01A2 (MBC) **JURGENSON, JAMES E** DICKINSON COLLEGE CARLISLE, PA 17013 Isolation of developmental genes of Aspergillus nidulans
R01GM-42208-02 (RNM) **CLARKSON, ROBERT B** UNIVERSITY OF ILLINOIS COLLEGE OF VETERINARY MEDICINE URBANA, IL 61801 Characterization of MRI contrast agents by EPR methods
R01GM-42212-02 (EI) **HUDIG, DOROTHY** UNIVERSITY OF NEVADA RENO, NV 89557 Lymphocyte protease inhibitors as probes of cytolysis
R01GM-42219-03 (MBC) **SONENSHEIN, ABRAHAM L** TUFTS UNIVERSITY 136 HARRISON AVENUE BOSTON, MA 02111 Isolation of early sporulation genes
R01GM-42223-03 (BBCA) **MARKY, LUIS A** NEW YORK UNIV 4 WASHINGTON PLACE/ RM 14 NEW YORK, NY 10003 Thermodynamics of DNA conformation & interactions
R29GM-42224-03 (SAT) **JACOBS, DANNY O** 75 THE ARBORWAY JAMAICA PLAIN, MA 02130 Skeletal muscle energy metabolism in surgical patients
R01GM-42230-01A2 (PHRA) **GIACOMINI, KATHLEEN M** UNIVERSITY OF CALIFORNIA 926 MEDICAL SCIENCES BLDG SAN FRANCISCO, CA 94143-0446 Cellular mechanisms of drug transport in choroid plexus
R01GM-42231-11 (MBY) **MANIATIS, THOMAS P** HARVARD UNIVERSITY 7 DIVINITY AVENUE CAMBRIDGE, MA 02138 Globin gene transcription and mRNA splicing
R44GM-42233-02 (SSS) **CLAPPER, DAVID L** BIO-METRIC SYSTEMS, INC 9924 WEST 74TH STREET EDEN PRAIRIE, MN 55344 Use of ECM peptides to improve cell culture surfaces
R44GM-42247-03 (SSS) **SQUILLANTE, MICHAEL R** RADIATION MONITORING DEVICES 44 HUNT STREET WATERTOWN, MA 02172 New, high Z semiconductor sensor for positron tomography
R01GM-42259-20 (CBY) **STAHL, PHILIP D** WASHINGTON UNIVERSITY 660 S. EUCLID AVE., BOX 8228 ST LOUIS, MO 63110 Lysosome biogenesis--Normal and tumor cells
R44GM-42268-03 (PSF) **FRITZ, LAWRENCE C** ATHENA NEUROSCIENCES, INC 800F GATEWAY BLVD SO SAN FRANCISCO, CA 94080 An in vitro model of the blood-brain barrier
R44GM-42278-03 (SB) **POLAREK, JAMES W** TELIOS PHARMACEUTICALS, INC 2909 SCIENCE PARK RD SAN DIEGO, CA 92121 Development of an arg-gly-asp-based wound healing agent
R01GM-42286-23 (BBCB) **DAY, LOREN A** PUBLIC HEALTH RESEARCH INST 455 FIRST AVENUE NEW YORK, NY 10016 Physical chemistry of viruses and their components
R01GM-42287-04 (BBCB) **STUBBS, GERALD J** VANDERBILT UNIVERSITY BOX 1820 STA B NASHVILLE TN 37235 Electron crystallography of neurotoxins
R44GM-42291-02 (SSS) **SHORT, JAY M** STRATAGENE CLONING SYSTEMS 11099 NORTH TORREY PINES RD LA JOLLA, CA 92037 Gene expression switch mechanism in transgenic animals
R01GM-42295-13 (MCHA) **FUCHS, PHILIP L** PURDUE UNIV DEPT OF CHEMISTRY/WTHR WEST LAFAYETTE, IN 47907 Total synthesis of quassinoidal anticancer agents
R44GM-42312-03 (SSS) **MAY, STERLING R** LIFECELL CORPORATION 3606-A RESEARCH FOREST DRIVE THE WOODLANDS, TX 77381 Freezing, drying, and rehydration of mammalian cells

PROJECT NO., ORGANIZATIONAL UNIT., INVESTIGATOR, ADDRESS, TITLE

R44GM-42322-02 (SSS) **ZHANG, MOE-ZHU** NIM INCORPORATED 3401 MARKET ST SUITE 100 PHILADELPHIA, PA 19104 Construction and test of 200 MHz phase modulation system
R44GM-42331-03 (SSS) **ZACHARY, WAYNE W** CHI SYSTEM, INC BETHLEHEM PIKE AT SHEBLE LANE SPRING HOUSE, PA 19477 Chi systems, inc
R01GM-42336-02 (CTY) **BALCH, WILLIAM E** RES INST OF SCRIPPS CLINIC 10666 N TORREY PINES RD LA JOLLA, CA 92037 Role of rab proteins and Ca2+ in vesicular transport
R01GM-42337-14 (GEN) **LARK, KARL G** UNIVERSITY OF UTAH DEPT OF BIOLOGY SALT LAKE CITY, UT 84112 Use of plant cell culture to study genetic variation
R01GM-42339-03 (MBC) **OSBORN, MARY J** UNIVERSITY OF CONNECTICUT 263 FARMINGTON AVE FARMINGTON, CT 06030 Isolation of mutants in lipopolysaccharide translocation
R01GM-42340-03 (NLS) **MONTAL, S MAURICIO** UNIVERSITY OF CALIFORNIA, SD 9500 GILMAN DRIVE LA JOLLA, CA 92093-0319 Molecular action of local anesthetic on channel peptides
R01GM-42341-07 (CBY) **HARLAND, RICHARD M** UNIVERSITY OF CALIFORNIA 401 BARKER HALL BERKELEY, CA 94720 Gene expression in amphibian development
R01GM-42342-03 (ARR) **GRIFFITH, JACK** UNIV OF N C AT CHAPEL HILL 119 LINEBERGER CANCER RES CTR CHAPEL HILL, N C 27599 DNA-protein interactions in AIDS virus DNA
R01GM-42375-03 (PHY) **DUNN, SUSAN M J** UNIVERSITY OF ALBERTA EDMONTON, ALBERTA CANADA T6G 2 Molecular studies of voltage-dependent calcium channels
R01GM-42376-03 (PHY) **SCHWARZ, THOMAS L** DEPT MOLECULAR/CELLULAR PHY STANFORD UNIV/SCH OF MEDICINE STANFORD, CA 94305 Localization and structure of a cloned k+ channel
R01GM-42379-02 (MGN) **YOKOYAMA, SHOZO** SYRACUSE UNIVERSITY BIOLOGICAL RESEARCH LABS SYRACUSE, N Y 13244-1220 Molecular evolution of visual pigment genes in astyanax
R01GM-42383-03 (PTHB) **BASERGA, RENATO L** THOMAS JEFFERSON UNIVERSITY 1025 WALNUT STREET PHILADELPHIA, PA 19107 The biology of cell cycle mutants
R01GM-42387-03 (MBY) **BIGGIN, MARK D** YALE UNIVERSITY 260 WHITNEY AVENUE NEW HAVEN, CT 06511 Transcription of genes controlling development
R01GM-42388-02 (ALY) **APGAR, JOHN R** MEDICAL BIOLOGY INSTITUTE 11077 NORTH TORREY PINES RD LA JOLLA, CA 92037 IgE receptor interactions in stimulus and secretion
P01GM-42397-01A2 (SSS) **AYALA, FRANCISCO J** UNIVERSITY OF CALIFORNIA IRVINE, CA 92717 Evolutionary genetics of a model system
P01GM-42397-01A2 0001 (SSS) **FITCH, WALTER M** Evolutionary genetics of a model system Evolutionary genetics of SOD and four other genes
P01GM-42397-01A2 0002 (SSS) **HUDSON, RICHARD R** Evolutionary genetics of a model system Population genetics of SOD, ADH, and GPDH
P01GM-42397-01A2 9001 (SSS) **AYALA, FRANCISCO J** Evolutionary genetics of a model system Core--Cell culture facility
R01GM-42399-01A1 (PHY) **PALLOTTA, BARRY S** UNIVERSITY OF NORTH CAROLINA CB# 7365, FAC LAB OFFICE BLDG CHAPEL HILL, NC 27599-7365 Properties of acetylcholine-activated ion channels
R29GM-42403-02 (GEN) **FRANK, STEVEN A** UNIVERSITY OF CALIFORNIA IRVINE, CA 92717 Theory of genetic transmission and genomic conflict
R29GM-42406-03 (MBC) **HEIDEMAN, WARREN** UNIVERSITY OF WISCONSIN 425 N CHARTER STREET MADISON, WI 53706 Regulation of adenylate cyclase activity in yeast
R01GM-42413-03 (MBY) **BARON, MARGARET H** HARVARD UNIVERSITY THE BIOLOGICAL LABORATORIES CAMBRIDGE, MA 02138 Developmental regulation of human b-like globin genes
R01GM-42415-03 (MGN) **ATCHISON, MICHAEL L** UNIVERSITY OF PENNSYLVANIA 3800 SPRUCE ST PHILADELPHIA, PA 19104-6048 Developmental control of immunoglobulin transcription
R01GM-42421-03 (GEN) **GRUNSTEIN, MICHAEL** UNIVERSITY OF CALIFORNIA 405 HILGARD AVENUE LOS ANGELES, CA 90024 Chromosomal repression of the yeast silent mating loci
R01GM-42428-03 (MBC) **BALDWIN, THOMAS O** TEXAS A & M UNIVERSITY COLLEGE STATION, TX 77843 Molecular mechanism of regulation of the lux regulon
R01GM-42437-03 (IMB) **MARCHALONIS, JOHN J** UNIVERSITY OF ARIZONA 1501 N CAMPBELL AVENUE TUCSON, AZ 85724 Immune-like proteins of invertebrates
R01GM-42447-03 (GEN) **HUDSON, RICHARD R** UNIVERSITY OF CALIFORNIA IRVINE, CA 92717 Mathemaqtical analysis of DNA variation within natural Populations
R01GM-42452-03 (BBCB) **JONAS, JIRI** UNIVERSITY OF ILLINOIS 1209 WEST CALIFORNIA/BOX 53-5 URBANA, IL 61801 High pressure NMR studies of proteins and membranes
R01GM-42454-03 (CBY) **MARTIN, NANCY C** UNIVERSITY OF LOUISVILLE LOUISVILLE, KY 40292 Mitochondria and cell sharing of enzymes
R01GM-42455-03 (CBY) **SCHMID, SANDRA L** RESEARCH INST OF SCRIPPS CLINI 10666 NORTH TORREY PINES ROAD LA JOLLA, CA 92037 Analysis of early steps in receptor-mediated endocytosis
R01GM-42461-03 (SAT) **STAIANO-COICO, LISA** CORNELL UNIV MEDICAL COLLEGE 1300 YORK AVENUE NEW YORK, NY 10021 Cultured epidermal grafts for burn patients
R29GM-42465-03 (MBY) **WU, BARBARA** NORTHWESTERN UNIVERSITY EVANSTON, IL 60208 Analyses of E1A dependent transriptional stimulation
R01GM-42466-03 (SAT) **CROSBY, GREGORY** MASSACHUSETTS GENERAL HOSPITAL BOSTON, MA 02114 Anesthetic action on opiate peptide gene expression
R01GM-42469-03 (BIO) **SINNOTT, MICHAEL L** UNIVERSITY OF ILLINOIS BOX 4348 (MC111) CHICAGO, IL 60680 Enzymic and non-enzymic glycosyl transfer.
R29GM-42472-03 (GEN) **SCHAEFFER, STEPHEN W** PENNSYLVANIA STATE UNIVERSITY UNIVERSITY PARK, PA 16802 Molecular population genetics of ADH in Drosphila
R01GM-42474-03 (PBC) **BROWER, DANNY L** UNIVERSITY OF ARIZONA LIFE SCIENCES SOUTH 444 TUCSON, AZ 85721 Structure-function studies of the PS integrins
R29GM-42476-03 (MBY) **RYMOND, BRIAN C** UNIVERSITY OF KENTUCKY T H MORGAN BUILDING LEXINGTON, KY 40506-0225 The function of snRNP

particles in pre-MRNA splicing
R01GM-42482-03 (GEN) HOLLOMAN, WILLIAM K CORNELL UNIVERSITY MED COLLEGE 1300 YORK AVE BOX 62 NEW YORK, NY 10021 Rec1 gene controlling recombination in Ustilago
R01GM-42490-03 (NEUC) AMARA, SUSAN G OREGON HEALTH SCIS UNIV 3181 SW SAM JACKSON PARK RD PORTLAND, OR 97201-3098 Alternative RNA processing in the nervous system
R01GM-42494-03 (BBCA) GOLDENBERG, DAVID P UNIVERSITY OF UTAH DEPARTMENT OF BIOLOGY SALT LAKE CITY, UT 84112 Mutational study of the mechanism of protein folding
R01GM-42495-03 (CBY) RESTREPO, DIEGO MONELL CHEMICAL SENSES CENTER 3500 MARKET STREET PHILADELPHIA, PA 19104-3308 pH regulatory exchange kinetics in HL60 cells
R01GM-42498-03 (EVR) SHUMAN, STEWART H SLOAN-KETTERING INST/CAN RES DEPT OF MOLECULAR BIOLOGY NEW YORK, NY 10021 Vaccinia virus mRNA transcription termination
R29GM-42501-03 (PB) PIELAK, GARY J UNIVERSITY OF NORTH CAROLINA DEPT OF CHEMISTRY CHAPEL HILL, NC 27599-3290 Genetic reversion and NMR as probes of protein structure
R01GM-42504-03 (BIO) GEHRKE, LEE MASSACHUSETTS INST OF TECHNOLO HST DIV, BLDG E25-545 CAMBRIDGE, MA 02139 Control of cell function via selective mRNA translation
P01GM-42508-03 (SSS) CLARK, EDWARD A UNIVERSITY OF WASHINGTON SEATTLE, WA 98195 Lymphocyte activation
P01GM-42508-03 0005 (SSS) FISCHER, E. Lymphocyte activation Protein, tyrosine phosphatases in T and B-cell activation
P01GM-42508-03 0006 (SSS) LEDBETTER, JEFFREY Lymphocyte activation Molecular interactions of T-cell surface receptors
P01GM-42508-03 0007 (SSS) MORRIS, DAVID Lymphocyte activation Elements regulating the c-myc gene
P01GM-42508-03 0008 (SSS) SIBLEY, CAROL Lymphocyte activation Genetic analysis of B-cell activation
P01GM-42508-03 0001 (SSS) CLARK, EDWARD Lymphocyte activation Structure/function murine B-cell surface molecules
P01GM-42508-03 0002 (SSS) BOMSZTYK, KAROL Lymphocyte activation Cytokine-mediated signaling in B lineage cell lines
P01GM-42508-03 0003 (SSS) KREBS, EDWIN Lymphocyte activation Protein tyrosine kinases of lymphocytes
P01GM-42508-03 0004 (SSS) MEIER, KATHRYN Lymphocyte activation B-cell membrane substrates for protein kinases
R29GM-42516-02 (CTY) BELMONT, ANDREW S UNIVERSITY OF ILLINOIS 505 SOUTH GOODWIN AVENUE URBANA, IL 61801 Nuclear and chromosome decondensation during G1-S
R01GM-42522-03 (CBY) MACHAMER, CAROLYN E JOHNS HOPKINS UNIVERSITY MED S 725 NORTH WOLFE STREET BALTIMORE, MD 21205 Membrane insertion and targeting of viral glycoproteins
R01GM-42535-03 (PC) KING, MARITA M OHIO STATE UNIVERSITY 120 W EIGHTEENTH AVE COLUMBUS, OH 43210-1173 Catalytic sites of two calmodulin-dependent enzymes
R01GM-42539-01A2 (GEN) GEYER, PAMELA K UNIVERSITY OF IOWA IOWA CITY, IA 52242 Regulation of tissue-specific gene expression
R01GM-42546-03 (GEN) O'CONNOR, MICHAEL B UNIV OF CALIFORNIA IRVINE, CA 92717-3900 Regulatory organization of the biothorax complex
R01GM-42548-02 (GEN) HOLLOMAN, WILLIAM K CORNELL UNIV MEDICAL COLLEGE 1300 YORK AVENUE/BOX 62 NEW YORK, NY 10021 Analysis of recombination in transformation of Ustilago
R29GM-42549-02 (BIO) MACDONALD, MARNIE L SW BIOMED RESEARCH INST 6401 EAST THOMAS ROAD SCOTTSDALE, AZ 85251 Cellular role of an arachidonoyl-diacylclycerol kinase
R29GM-42550-03 (IMB) BOOTHBY, MARK R HARVARD SCHOOL OF PUBLIC HEALT 665 HUNTINGTON AVENUE BOSTON, MA 02115 An IL-4 inducible protein in lymphocyte gene expression
R01GM-42551-03 (MBY) HAHN, STEVEN M FRED HUTCHINSON CANCER RES CTR 1124 COLUMBIA STREET SEATTLE, WA 98104 Molecular analysis of RNAPII transcription initiation
R01GM-42554-03 (MBC) GOODMAN, MYRON F UNIV OF SOUTHERN CALIFORNIA BIO SCIENCES, ACBR ROOM 239 LOS ANGELES, CA 90089-1340 The biochemical basis of SOS-induced mutagenesis
R01GM-42555-01A2 (EVR) SCHAACK, JEROME B UNIV OF COLORADO HLTH SCI CTR 4200 E 9TH AVE/CAMPUS B175 DENVER, CO 80262 The role of adenovirus DNA-nuclear matrix binding
R01GM-42557-03 (CTY) DAS, ANATHBANDHU UNIVERSITY OF MINNESOTA DEPARTMENT OF BIOCHEMISTRY ST PAUL, MN 55108 Molecular analysis of flowering genes of Pharbitis nil
R01GM-42560-02 (BBCA) BRYAN, PHILIP N CTR FOR ADVANCED RES IN BIOTEC 9600 GUDELSKY DRIVE ROCKVILLE, MD 20850 Protein folding and stability of subtilisin
R29GM-42561-03 (BBCA) SUMMERS, MICHAEL F UNIV OF MARYLAND, BALTI COUNTY CHEMISTRY DEPARTMENT BALTIMORE, MD 21228 NMR studies of retroviral nucleic acid binding proteins
R01GM-42563-03 (MGN) PUMO, DOROTHY E HOFSTRA UNIVERSITY 1000 FULTON AVENUE HEMPSTEAD, NY 11550 Nucleotide sequence divergence in mammalian mtDNA
R01GM-42564-03 (CBY) OSMANI, STEPHEN A BAYLOR COLLEGE OF MEDICINE ONE BAYLOR PLAZA HOUSTON, TX 77030 The role of the nim-A gene in mitotic regulation
R29GM-42569-01A2 (BMT) GIEDROC, DAVID P TEXAS A & M UNIVERSITY COLLEGE STATION, TX 77843 Zinc domain structure and function in t4 gene 32 protein
R01GM-42571-02 (ARR) VOET, DONALD H UNIVERSITY OF PENNSYLVANIA 133 SOUTH 36TH STREET PHILADELPHIA, PA 19104-3246 X-ray structure of GM-CSF
R01GM-42577-03 (SAT) GAMELLI, RICHARD L LOYOLA UNIVERSITY MEDICAL CENT 2160 SOUTH FIRST AVENUE MAYWOOD, IL 60153 Myelopoietic stimulation following burn injury
R01GM-42581-03 (HEM) STRICKLAND, DUDLEY K AMERICAN RED CROSS 15601 CRABBS BRANCH WAY ROCKVILLE, MD 20855 Structure and function of the a2-macroglobulin receptor
R01GM-42584-02 (SSS) HEWETT, JOHN E UNIVERSITY OF MISSOURI MATHEMATICAL SCIENCES BLDG COLUMBIA, MO 65211 Order restricted inference from longitudinal data
R01GM-42588-03 (BNP) PHILLIPS, ROBERT S UNIVERSITY OF GEORGIA ATHENS, GA 30602 Mechanisms of carbon-carbon lyases and kynureninase
R01GM-42597-04 (MGN) ROBINS, DIANE M UNIVERSITY OF MICHIGAN ANN ARBOR, MI 48109 Proviral role in mouse gene regulation and diversity
R01GM-42604-03 (CBY) GOMER, RICHARD H RICE UNIVERSITY DEPARTMENT OF BIOCHEMISTRY HOUSTON, TX 77251 A eukaryotic tissue density sensor
R29GM-42609-03 (CBY) HOFFMAN, NEIL F CARNEGIE INST OF WASHINGTON 290 PANAMA STREET STANFORD, CA 94305 Studies on the assembly of CAB polypeptides
R01GM-42610-03 (GEN) FREELING, MICHAEL R UNIVERSITY OF CALIFORNIA DEPT OF PLANT BIOLOGY BERKELEY, CA 94720 Development biology and genetics of the maize leaf
R01GM-42612-03 (GEN) MACDONALD, PAUL M STANFORD UNIVERSITY STANFORD, CA 94305 Molecular biology of morphogen localization in embryos
R01GM-42614-03 (BMT) POULOS, THOMAS L CTR FOR ADVANCED RES IN BIOTEC 9600 GUDELSKY DRIVE ROCKVILLE, MD 20850 Heme enzyme protein engineering
R01GM-42615-01A1 (TOX) HOTTENDORF, GIRARD H MEDICAL UNIV OF SOUTH CAROLINA 171 ASHLEY AVENUE CHARLESTON, SC 29425 Multifactorial comparison--aminoglycoside nephrotoxicity
R01GM-42618-01A1 (BBCB) REMINGTON, STEPHEN J UNIVERSITY OF OREGON EUGENE, OR 97403 Structure, mechanism and regulation of glycerol kinase
R01GM-42620-03 (TOX) NOVAK, RAYMOND F WAYNE STATE UNIVERSITY 2727 SECOND AVENUE DETROIT, MI 48201 Glutathione S-transferase induction by toxicants
R01GM-42621-01A2 (GEN) COULTER, DOUGLAS E ST LOUIS UNIV/SCH OF MED 1402 S GRAND BLVD ST LOUIS, MO 63104 Structure and expression of the odd-skipped gene
R01GM-42626-01A2 (CBY) GAULTON, GLEN N UNIVERSITY OF PENNSYLVANIA 36TH & SPRUCE STREET PHILADELPHIA, PA 19104-6082 Regulation of T cell growth by glycosyl-pi
R01GM-42628-03 (PC) DRICKAMER, KURT COLUMBIA UNIVERSITY 630 WEST 168TH STREET NEW YORK, NY 10032 Molecular mechanisms of complex carbohydrate recognition
R01GM-42629-02 (CBY) HOWELL, KATHRYN E UNIVERSITY OF COLORADO 4200 EAST NINTH AVENUE, B-111 DENVER, CO 80262 Targeting of vesicles from the trans golgi network
R01GM-42636-03 (BBCB) BRANDTS, JOHN F UNIVERSITY OF MASSACHUSETTS DEPARTMENT OF CHEMISTRY AMHERST, MA 01003 Domain interaction in globular and transmembrane protein
R01GM-42637-01A2 (BMT) RICHARDSON, DAVID E UNIVERSITY OF FLORIDA GAINESVILLE, FL 32611 Monoclonal antibodies as metalloenzymes
R01GM-42641-03 (MCHA) DONALDSON, WILLIAM A MARQUETTE UNIVERSITY 535 N 14TH STREET MILWAUKEE, WI 53233 Iron complexes in acyclic polyene synthesis
R01GM-42642-02 (CTY) NEWMEYER, DONALD D LA JOLLA CANCER RESEARCH FDN 10901 NORTH TORREY PINES ROAD LA JOLLA, CA 92037 Mechanisms of nuclear protein import--Analysis in vitro
R29GM-42644-03 (PC) DUNCAN, ROGER F UNIV OF SOUTHERN CALIFORNIA DEPARTMENT OF PHARMACY LOS ANGELES, CA 90033 Heat stress effects on protein synthesis and prot. phosphorylation
R01GM-42645-03 (BBCA) YOUVAN, DOUGLAS C MASSACHUSETTS INST OF TECHNOLO 77 MASSACHUSETTS AVENUE CAMBRIDGE, MA 02139 Spectroscopic screening of isomorphic protein sequences
R01GM-42647-01A3 (MEDB) APPERT, HUBERT E MEDICAL COLLEGE OF OHIO PO BOX 10008 TOLEDO, OH 43699 Structure-function studies of galactosyltransferase
R01GM-42651-02 (PC) WORLAND, STEPHEN T AGOURON INSTITUTE 505 COAST BLVD SOUTH LA JOLLA, CA 92037-4696 DNA topoisomerase II--Domains, binding sites and functions
R01GM-42652-03 (PHY) CHAUDHARI, NIRUPA COLORADO STATE UNIVERSITY FORT COLLINS, CO 80523 Physiology of calcium channel genes
R29GM-42661-02 (BBCB) SERPERSU, ENGIN H UNIVERSITY OF TENNESSE KNOXVILLE, TN 37996-0840 Nmr studies of phosphoryl transfer enzymes
R01GM-42671-02 (MBY) PARKER, CARL S CALIFORNIA INST OF TECHNOLOGY DIVISION OF CHEMISTRY 147-75 PASADENA, CALIFORNIA 91125 Control of spatial expression of the Drosophila FTZ gene
R01GM-42672-03 (SAT) KRIEGER, NEIL R BRIGHAM & WOMEN'S HOSPITAL 75 FRANCIS ST BOSTON, MA 02115 Molecular target for steriod anesthesia
R29GM-42673-03 (PHY) MOYER, MARY S YALE UNIVERSITY SCHOOL OF MED 333 CEDAR STREET; PO BOX 3333 NEW HAVEN, CT 06510-8064 Ontogeny of intestinal and placental taurine transport
R01GM-42680-03 (BMT) WHITTAKER, JAMES W CARNEGIE MELLON UNIVERSITY 4400 FIFTH AVE PITTSBURGH, PA 15213 Active site spectral studies on manganese metalloenzymes
R01GM-42685-03 (BNP) STAMMER, CHARLES H UNIVERSITY OF GEORGIA ATHENS, GA 30602 Stabilized TRH analogs
R01GM-42686-02 (SAT) RICE, CHARLES L HARBORVIEW MEDICAL CENTER 325 9TH AVENUE, ZA-16 SEATTLE, WA 98104 Neutrophils in ischemia reperfusion injury in shock
R01GM-42694-02 (CTY) SPECTOR, DAVID L COLD SPRING HARBOR LABORATORY PO BOX 100 COLD SPRING HARBOR, NY 11724 Spatial organization of gene expression
R01GM-42697-01A2 (BNP) DAY, RICHARD A UNIVERSITY OF CINCINNATI CINCINNATI, OH 45221-0172 Salt bridge conversion to amide bonds with C2N2
R29GM-42698-03 (PBC) YOUNG, WILLIAM W, JR UNIVERSITY OF LOUISVILLE LOUISVILLE, KY 40292 Glycosphingolipid metabolism and trafficking
R01GM-42699-03 (MBY) KRAINER, ADRIAN R COLD SPRING HARBOR LABORATORY PO BOX 100 COLD SPRING HARBOR, NY 11724 Biochemistry of pre-MRNA splicing
R01GM-42703-02 (BMT) PECORARO, VINCENT L UNIVERSITY OF MICHIGAN ANN ARBOR, MI 48109-1055 Biological vanadium--Models of structure and reactivity
R29GM-42704-03 (BMT) YANG, GILBERT K UNIV OF SOUTHERN CALIFORNIA UNIVERSITY PARK/LJS #358 LOS ANGELES, CA 90089-0744 Energetics and dynamics of organometallic reactions
R01GM-42706-01A2 (BNP) CHAMBERLIN, ARTHUR R UNIVERSITY OF CALIFORNIA IRVINE, CA 92717 Introduction of non-natural amino acids

into proteins
R01GM-42715-03 (BIO) PALFREY, HUGH C UNIVERSITY OF CHICAGO 947 EAST 58TH STREET CHICAGO, IL 60637 Cell physiology of calcium effects on protein synthesis
R01GM-42720-03 (MBY) BELASCO, JOEL G HARVARD MEDICAL SCHOOL 200 LONGWOOD AVENUE BOSTON, MA 02115 Messenger RNA decay in mammalian cells
R01GM-42722-03 (BNP) BARANY, GEORGE UNIVERSITY OF MINNESOTA 207 PLEASANT STREET SE MINNEAPOLIS, MI 55455 Improved handles for solid-phase peptide synthesis
R01GM-42725-02 (BEM) PATTERSON, DAVID R HARBORVIEW MEDICAL CTR 325 9TH AVE SEATTLE, WA 98104 Optimizing the control of pain from severe burns
R01GM-42728-03 (BIO) WILLIS, IAN M ALBERT EINSTEIN COL OF MEDICIN 1300 MORRIS PARK AVENUE BRONX, NY 10461 Structure and function of pol III transcription factors
R29GM-42732-01A2 (BMT) ROSKAMP, ERIC J NORTHWESTERN UNIVERSITY 2145 SHERIDAN ROAD EVANSTON, IL 60208-3113 Divalent germanium and tin in organic synthesis
R01GM-42733-02 (MCHA) KAHNE, DANIEL E PRINCETON UNIVERSITY WASHINGTON ROAD PRINCETON, NJ 08544 Glycosylation strategies for oligosaccharide synthesis
R29GM-42735-02 (MCHA) HALTERMAN, RONALD L BOSTON UNIVERSITY 590 COMMONWEALTH AVENUE BOSTON, MA 02215 Catalytic asymmetric epoxidation
R29GM-42746-03 (MBC) BIEK, DONALD P UNIV OF KENTUCKY MN-375 MEDICAL CENTER LEXINGTON, KY 40536-0084 Inheritance of genetic material in prokaryotes
R01GM-42751-03 (IMB) BUCY, R P UNIVERSITY OF ALABAMA UAB STATION BIRMINGHAM, AL 35294 Studies of chicken T cell sublineages
R29GM-42752-03 (GEN) WEIR, MICHAEL P WESLEYAN UNIVERSITY MIDDLETOWN, CT 06457 Developmental studies of segmentation gene function
R01GM-42759-03 (CBY) DRUBIN, DAVID G UNIVERSITY OF CALIFORNIA 451 LIFE SCIENCE ADDITION BERKELEY, CA 94720 Molecular analysis of the yeast actin cytoskeleton
R01GM-42760-03 (MBY) MOORE, CLAIRE L TUFTS UNIVERSITY BOSTON, MA 02111 Factors which recognize mammalian polyadenylation signal
R01GM-42762-03 (CTY) VIERLING, ELIZABETH UNIVERSITY OF ARIZONA BIOLOGICAL SCIENCES WEST TUCSON, AZ 85721 Expression & function of organelle heat shock proteins
R01GM-42763-01A2 (BNP) MARTIN, STEPHEN F UNIVERSITY OF TEXAS 201 MAIN BUILDING AUSTIN, TX 78712 Design of chemical probes to study phospholipase C
R01GM-42770-03 (CTY) EVANS, ROBERT M UNIV OF COLORADO HEALTH SCI CT 4200 EAST 9TH AVENUE/ #B-216 DENVER, CO 80262 Phosphorylation of intermediate filaments during mitosis
R01GM-42774-02 (BMT) TSE-DINH, YUK-CHING NEW YORK MEDICAL COLLEGE VALHALLA, NY 10595 Zinc binding domains in E. coli DNA topoisomerase I
R01GM-42780-03 (PC) KELLY, THOMAS J JOHNS HOPKINS UNIVERSITY 725 NORTH WOLFE STREET BALTIMORE, MD 21205 Regulation of thymidine kinase in the cell cycle
R29GM-42786-03 (CTY) ROTH, MARK B FRED HUTCHINSON CANCER RES CTR 1124 COLUMBIA STREET SEATTLE, WA 98104 Chromosomal ribonucleoproteins--Structure and assembly
R01GM-42791-03 (BIO) WHITE, MICHAEL W MONTANA STATE UNIVERSITY VETERINARY RESEARCH LABORATORY BOZEMAN, MT 59717 Translational control of ribosomal proteins
R01GM-42796-03 (BBCB) RAMAKRISHNAN, VENKATRAMAN R BROOKHAVEN NATIONAL LABORATORY UPTON, NY 11973 Neutron scattering studies on chromatin
R01GM-42798-02 (BNP) OJIMA, IWAO SUNY STONY BROOK, NY 11794-3400 Asymmetric synthesis of non-protein amino acids
R01GM-42813-01A2 (CTY) JAMES, THARAPPEL C WESLEYAN UNIVERSITY HALL-ATWATER/SHANKLIN LAB MIDDLETOWN, CT 06457-0175 Developmental expression of a heterochromatin protein
R01GM-42816-03 (BIO) KURET, JEFFREY A COLD SPRING HARBOR LABORATORY P O BOX 100 COLD SPRING HARBOR, NY 11724 Structure and biological function of yeast casein kinase 1
R01GM-42817-01A1 (SSS) DEAN, PHILLIP N UNIVERSITY OF CALIFORNIA PO BOX 5507 L-452 LIVERMORE, CA 94550 Three-dimensional image processing and analysis
R01GM-42824-04 (PHY) TANOUYE, MARK A UNIV. OF CA. BERKELEY 201 WELLMAN HALL Ion channels: molecular and biophysical aspects
R01GM-42829-01A1 (PHY) BRANTON, W DALE UNIVERSITY OF MINNESOTA 435 DELAWARE ST SE MINNEAPOLIS, MN 55455 Potent Ca channel blockers from spider venon
R01GM-42833-03 (PB) KANTROWITZ, EVAN R BOSTON COLLEGE DEVLIN 224 CHESTNUT HILL, MA 02167 New insights into enzyme structure and function
R01GM-42843-03 (NLS) PERALTA, ERNEST G HARVARD UNIVERSITY 7 DIVINITY AVENUE CAMBRIDGE, MA 02138 Signal transduction mechanisms of muscarinic receptors
R01GM-42850-03 (SRC) FUNG, HO-LEUNG SUNY COOKE-HOCHSTETTER COMPLEX DEPARTMENT OF PHARMACEUTICS BUFFALO, NY 14260 Vasodilator kinetics and dynamics in heart failure
R01GM-42859-03 (SAT) ALBINA, JORGE E RHODE ISLAND HOSPITAL 593 EDDY STREET PROVIDENCE, RI 02903 Arginine regulation of cell function in healing wounds
R29GM-42878-03 (BIO) WASHABAUGH, MICHAEL W JOHNS HOPKINS UNIVERSITY 615 NORTH WOLFE STREET BALTIMORE, MD 21205 Mechanisms of enzymic and nonenzymic thiamin reactions
R29GM-42893-03 (MBC) WINANS, STEPHEN C DEPT OF MICROBIOLOGY W315 WING HALL/CORNELL UNIV ITHACA, NY 14853-8101 Interactions between agrobacterium and host plants
R01GM-42896-03 (BNP) REID, BRIAN R UNIVERSITY OF WASHINGTON BG-10 SEATTLE, WA 98195 Helical RNA, RNA:DNA hybrids and DNA-RNA junctions
R01GM-42897-10A2 (MCHA) WILLIAMS, DAVID R INDIANA UNIVERSITY BLOOMINGTON, IN 47405 Investigations of interesting bioactive substances
R01GM-42898-03 (ALY) SODETZ, JAMES M UNIVERSITY OF SOUTH CAROLINA COLUMBIA, S C 29208 Structure and function of terminal complement proteins
R01GM-42901-01A1 (MBC) PEABODY, DAVID S UNIV OF NEW MEXICO SCHOOL OF M UNM CANCER CENTER ALBUQUERQUE, NM 87131 Genetic analysis of a translational repressor
R01GM-42912-02 (CBY) ARGRAVES, W SCOTT AMERICAN RED CROSS 15601 CRABBS BRANCH WAY ROCKVILLE, MD 20855 Fibronectin receptor-cytoplasmic interaction
R29GM-42913-01A2 (BBCA) KING, GARRY C RICE UNIVERSITY 6100 SOUTH MAIN STREET HOUSTON, TX 77005 Nmr studies of protein-nucleic acid interactions
R29GM-42921-03 (SSS) PRUITT, RONALD C UNIVERSITY OF MINNESOTA 206 CHURCH STREETS, SE MINNEAPOLIS, MN 55455 Multivariate survival curve analysis
R01GM-42925-03 (MBC) LOVETT, PAUL S DEPT OF BIOLOGICAL SCIENCES UNIVERSITY OF MARYLAND BALTIMORE, MD 21228 Translational attenuation as a gene regulator
R01GM-42935-03 (SRC) NEWELL, JONATHAN C RENSSELAER POLYTECHNIC INSTITU BIOMEDICAL ENGINEERING TROY, N Y 12180-3590 Monitoring lung water by electrical impedance imaging
R01GM-42936-03 (BBCA) FRESCO, JACQUES R PRINCETON UNIVERSITY PRINCETON UNIVERSITY PRINCETON, NJ 08544-1014 Sequence-specific triple-stranded nucleic acid helices
R01GM-42938-03 (BBCB) MC KAY, DAVID B STANFORD UNIV SCH OF MEDICINE SHERMAN FAIRCHILD BLDG STANFORD, CA 94305 Interleukin-2 and alpha interferon structural studies
R29GM-42957-03 (PHRA) JAESCHKE, HARTMUT W BAYLOR COLLEGE OF MEDICINE ONE BAYLOR PLAZA HOUSTON, TX 77030 Pharmacological interventions in hepatic ischemic injury
R01GM-42969-02 (MGN) WIGINTON, DAN A CHILDREN'S HOSP RESEARCH FDN ELLAND AND BETHESDA AVE CINCINNATI, OH 45229-2899 Adenosine deaminase--Mechanisms of tissue expression
R01GM-42975-08 (ALY) GEARHART, PATRICIA J JOHNS HOPKINS UNIVERSITY 615 NORTH WOLFE STREET BALTIMORE, MD 21205 Rearrangement of vk genes during ontogeny
R29GM-42977-02 (BBCB) GARRELL, ROBIN L UNIVERSITY OF CALIFORNIA 405 HILGARD AVENUE LOS ANGELES, CA 90024 Characterization of peptide-surface interactions
R01GM-42987-03 (MCHA) BROKA, CHRIS A SYNTEX (U.S.A.) INC. 3401 HILLVIEW AVE PALO ALTO, CA 94303 Synthetic studies on cytotoxic and antiviral marine natural products
R43GM-43004-01A1 (PSF) CHIANG, CHIA-MING CYGNUS RESEARCH CORP 400 PENOBSCOT DRIVE REDWOOD CITY, CA 94063 Ultrasonically mediated transdermal delivery
R01GM-43023-03 (BIO) HARDY, LARRY W UNIVERSITY OF MASSACHUSETTS 55 LAKE AVE NORTH WORCESTER, MA 01655 Mechanisms of DTMP synthase and DCMP hydroxymethylase
R29GM-43037-03 (BNP) BEDNARSKI, MARK D UNIVERSITY OF CALIFORNIA 713-LATIMER HALL BERKELEY, CALIFORNIA 94720 Enzymatic methods in natural product synthesis
R44GM-43039-02 (SSS) PAGRATIS, NIKOS C THERMOGEN, INC 2201 W CAMPBELL PARK DRIVE CHICAGO, IL 60612 Thermophilic gene transfer system
R01GM-43043-03 (PB) O'LEARY, MARION H UNIVERSITY OF NEBRASKA LINCOLN, NE 68583 Heavy-atom isotope effects on enzymatic reactions
R01GM-43046-03 (BBCB) GILLIES, ROBERT J UNIVERSITY OF ARIZONA DEPT OF BIOCHEMISTRY TUCSON, AZ 85724 NMR analysis of cations and the proliferative response
R01GM-43049-06 (CTY) HELFMAN, DAVID M COLD SPRING HARBOR LABORATORY PO BOX 100 COLD SPRING HARBOR, NY 11724 Tropomyosin in normal and transformed cells
R01GM-43065-06 (CTY) FELDHERR, CARL M UNIVERSITY OF FLORIDA BOX 100235 JHMHC GAINESVILLE, FL 32611 The transport and accumulation of karyophilic proteins in oocytes
R01GM-43074-01A2 (SAT) BUFFINGTON, CHARLES W 3471 5TH AVE/KAUFMANN BLDG RM9 PITTSBURGH, PA 15213 Myocardial ischemia induced by inhaled anesthetics
R01GM-43080-02 (BIO) GREIDER, CAROL W COLD SPRING HARBOR LABORATORY P O BOX 100 COLD SPRING HARBOR, NY 11724 Characterization of the Tetrahymena telomerase RNP
R29GM-43094-02 (BBCA) KURIYAN, JOHN ROCKEFELLER UNIVERSITY 1230 YORK AVE, BOX 3 NEW YORK, NY 10021 Dynamics disorder in X-ray refinement of proteins
R01GM-43098-02 (MBC) PARKINSON, JOHN S UNIVERSITY OF UTAH 201 BIOLOGY BUILDING SALT LAKE CITY, UT 84112 Communication modules in bacterial signaling proteins
R01GM-43100-02 (NEUC) GANETZKY, BARRY S UNIVERSITY OF WISCONSIN 445 HENRY MALL MADISON, WI 53706 The drosophila para locus:genetic and molecular studies
R01GM-43102-02 (NEUC) SADEE, WOLFGANG UNIVERSITY OF CALIFORNIA 926 MEDICAL SCIENCES BUILDING SAN FRANCISCO, CA 94143-0446 Mutations of muscarinic cholinergic receptor genes
R01GM-43107-02 (BMT) LIEBESKIND, LANNY S EMORY UNIVERSITY DEPT OF CHEMISTRY ATLANTA, GA 30322 Heterocycle-metal pi-complexes in organic synthesis
R01GM-43108-02 (CTY) THOMPSON, WILLIAM F NORTH CAROLINA STATE UNIV BOX 7612 RALEIGH, NC 27695-7612 Developmental regulation of ferredoxin gene expression
R01GM-43111-02 (PC) LUCAS, JOHN J SUNY HEALTH SCIENCE CTR 750 E ADAMS STREET SYRACUSE, NY 13210 Carbohydrate determinants in transferrin receptor action
R01GM-43129-02 (BBCA) WEMMER, DAVID E UNIVERSITY OF CALIFORNIA DEPT OF CHEMISTRY BERKELEY, CA 94720 Structural & dynamic aspects of drug-DNA recognition
R01GM-43133-02 (BBCB) JOHNSON, WALTER C, JR OREGON STATE UNIVERSITY WENIGER 535 CORVALLIS, OR 97331-6503 Base tilts in polynucleotides from flow linear dichroism
R29GM-43134-02 (GEN) LAST, ROBERT L BOYCE THOMPSON INS FOR PLT RES TOWER ROAD ITHACA, NY 14853-1801 Molecular genetics of Arabidopsis tryptophan biosynthesis
R01GM-43140-02 (TOX) SENS, MARY A MEDICAL UNIV OF SOUTH CAROLINA 171 ASHLEY AVENUE CHARLESTON, SC 29425 Aminoglycoside nephrotoxicity and cellular transport
R01GM-43144-02 (BMT) BURGESS, BARBARA K UNIVERSITY OF

CALIFORNIA DEPT MOLECULAR BIO & BIOCHEM IRVINE, CA 92717 Structural organization and function of the Mo/Fe protein
R01GM-43149-02 (MBC) HUGHES, KELLY T UNIVERSITY OF WASHINGTON SEATTLE, WA 98195 Salmonella phase variation--Regulation and DNA recognition
R01GM-43153-02 (SAT) MATUSCHAK, GEORGE M UNIVERSITY HOSPITAL 3635 VISTA AVE/PO BOX 15250 ST LOUIS, MO 63110-0250 Liver-lung interactions during gram-negative endotoxemia
R01GM-43154-02 (PC) NEWTON, ALEXANDRA C INDIANA UNIVERSITY BLOOMINGTON, IN 47405 Protein-lipid interactions in signal transduction
R29GM-43164-02 (MBY) SACHS, ALAN BRUCE WHITEHEAD INST FOR BIOMED RES NINE CAMBRIDGE CENTER CAMBRIDGE, MA 02142 Poly(A) function and metabolism in Saccharomyces cerevisiae
R29GM-43165-02 (PC) MUCHMORE, ELAINE A VETERAN'S ADMIN. MED. CENTER 3350 LA JOLLA VILLAGE DRIVE SAN DIEGO, CA 92161 Characterization of N-acetylneuraminic acid hydroxylase
R01GM-43167-03 (CBY) WEBER, LEE A UNIV. OF NEVADA, RENO RENO, NV 89557 Heat shock proteins and cell resistance to hyperthermia
R01GM-43169-02 (CTY) ANDERSON, RICHARD G UNIVERSITY OF TEXAS 5323 HARRY HINES BLVD DALLAS, TEX 75235 Molecular cytology of the folate receptor
R29GM-43178-02 (RAD) KRONENBERG, AMY LAWRENCE BERKELEY LABORATORY 1 CYCLOTRON ROAD BERKELEY, CA 97420 Heavy-ion mutagenesis: Let effects and locus specificity
R01GM-43181-02 (PHRA) HIGUCHI, WILLIAM I UNIVERSITY OF UTAH DEPT OF PHARMACEUTICS SALT LAKE CITY, UT 84112 Transdermal iontophoresis--basic studies and polypeptides
R29GM-43186-02 (CBY) FIELDS, ALAN P CASE WESTERN RESERVE UNIVERSIT 2119 ABINGTON RD CLEVELAND, OH 44106 Role of nuclear protein kinase C in cell growth
R29GM-43187-01A1 (BBCA) MONDRAGON, ALFONSO NORTHWESTERN UNIVERSITY 2153 SHERIDAN ROAD EVANSTON, IL 60208 Structural studies of E. coli DNA topoisomerase I
R01GM-43189-01A1 (PB) LIN, SUE-HWA U OF TEXAS/ANDERSON CANCER CTR HOUSTON, TX 77030 Studies on liver ecto-ATPase as a cell adhesion molecule
R29GM-43193-02 (MBC) HILL, THOMAS M DREXEL UNIVERSITY 32ND & CHESTNUT STREETS PHILADELPHIA, PA 19104 Termination of DNA replication in Escherichia coli
R29GM-43196-02 (MBC) MCCARTER, LINDA L THE AGOURON INSTITUTE 505 COAST BOULEVARD, SOUTH LA JOLLA, CA 92037-4696 Surface-dependent gene regulation in V. parahaemolyticus
R01GM-43199-02 (MBC) BERNLOHR, DAVID A UNIVERSITY OF MINNESOTA 1479 GORTNER AVENUE ST PAUL, MN 55108 Yeast lipid binding protein--Identification and analysis
R01GM-43210-02 (BIO) KRESGE, ALEXANDER J UNIVERSITY OF TORONTO 80 ST GEORGE STREET TORONTO,ONTARIO M5S 1A1 CANADA Biologically important enols
R01GM-43214-01A1 (MCHA) JACOBSEN, ERIC N UNIVERSITY OF ILLINOIS 1209 W CALIFORNIA ST URBANA, IL 61801 Chiral complexes designed to catalyze organic reactions
R01GM-43215-01A2 (PB) EVANS, JEREMY N WASHINGTON STATE UNIVERSITY PULLMAN, WA 99164-4660 Enzyme-intermediate structures by NMR
R01GM-43236-02 (ALY) LIEBER, MICHAEL R STANFORD UNIVERSITY MED CTR 300 PASTEUR DRIVE STANFORD, CA 94305 Normal and mutant lymphoid VDJ recombinase
R01GM-43237-02 (BIO) WOLLENZIEN, PAUL L ST LOUIS UNIVERSITY SCH OF MED 1402 SOUTH GRAND BOULEVARD ST LOUIS, MO 63104 Structure and mechanism of ribosomal RNA in the ribosome
R01GM-43238-01A2 (BBCB) DYSON, HELEN J SCRIPPS CLINIC & RESEARCH FDN 10666 NORTH TORREY PINES ROAD LA JOLLA, CA 92037 Structure and mechanisms of thioredoxin
R01GM-43239-02 (SSS) THOMAS, LEWIS J WASHINGTON UNIVERSITY 700 SOUTH EUCLID AVENUE ST LOUIS, MO 63110 Improved analysis of electron-microscopic autoradiograms
R01GM-43241-02 (PC) COSTA, ROBERT H UNIVERSITY OF ILLINOIS/CHICAGO 1853 W POLK STREET - M/C 536 CHICAGO, IL 60612 Regulation of transthyretin in the liver
R29GM-43251-02 (BIO) MURRAY, CHRISTOPHER J UNIVERSITY OF ARKANSAS CHEMISTRY BUILDING FAYETTEVILLE, AR 72701 Proton tunneling in enzyme reactions
R01GM-43257-02 (ALY) STAMENKOVIC, IVAN MASSACHUSETTS GENERAL HOSPITAL 149 13TH STREET CHARLESTOWN, MA 02129 Genetic analysis B cell surface receptors
R01GM-43261-02 (CTY) MESSING, JOACHIM W RUTGER - THE STATE UNIV OF N J WAKSMAN INST/P O BOX 759 PISCATAWAY, NJ 08855 Cell and site specific DNA rearrangements
R01GM-43264-02 (CTY) PALAZZO, ROBERT E MARINE BIOLOGICAL LABORATORY WOODS HOLE, MA 02543 Centrosome maturation in vitro
R01GM-43265-02 (MBC) ZAKIAN, VIRGINIA A FRED HUTCHINSON CANCER RES CTR 1124 COLUMBIA STREET SEATTLE, WA 98104 Structure and behavior of yeast telomeres
R01GM-43273-02 (BBCA) BARRY, BRIDGETTE A UNIVERSITY OF MINNESOTA 140 GORTNER LAB ST PAUL, MN 55108 Spectroscopic studies of light-driven electron transfer
R01GM-43278-01A1 (BMT) NOODLEMAN, LOUIS RES INST OF SCRIPPS CLINIC 10666 N TORREY PINES ROAD LA JOLLA, CA 92037 Electronic structure of Fe-oxo and Mn-oxo complexes
R01GM-43292-01 (BBCB) TIMKOVICH, RUSSELL UNIVERSITY OF ALABAMA BOX 870336 TUSCALOOSA, AL 35487-0336 Structure of cytochromes
R29GM-43299-03 (BBCB) SHINE, NANCY MEDICAL RESEARCH INSTITUTE 2200 WEBSTER STREET SAN FRANCISCO, CA 94115 Analysis of lectin--Carbohydrate interactions using NMR
R01GM-43301-02 (GEN) COOLEY, LYNN YALE UNIVERSITY SCH OF MEDICIN 333 CEDAR STREET NEW HAVEN, CT 06510 Oocyte development in Drosophila
R29GM-43307-02 (BIO) KIICK, DENNIS M UNIVERSITY OF TENNESSEE 800 MADISON AVE MEMPHIS, TN 38163 Studies of enzyme catalyzed beta-elimination
R01GM-43309-02 (GEN) AKINS, ROBERT A WAYNE STATE UNIVERSITY 540 EAST CANFIELD DETROIT, MI 48201 Molecular genetics of heterokaryon

PROJECT NO., ORGANIZATIONAL UNIT., INVESTIGATOR, ADDRESS, TITLE

incompatibility in Neurospora
R01GM-43315-01 (BMT) QUE, LAWRENCE, JR UNIVERSITY OF MINNESOTA MINNEAPOLIS, MN 55455 Iron and manganese in biocatalysis--A dioxygenase model
R01GM-43327-02 (MCHA) MYERS, ANDREW G CALIFORNIA INSTITUTE OF TECHNO 1201 EAST CALIFORNIA BOULEVARD PASADENA, CA 91125 Synthesis of chemically activated DNA-cleaving agents
R01GM-43328-02 (BNP) HECHT, SIDNEY M UNIVERSITY OF VIRGINIA CHARLOTTESVILLE, VA 22901 Synthetic polypeptides via in vitro protein biosynthesis
R29GM-43333-04 (GEN) TRENT, CAROL WESTERN WASHINGTON UNIVERSITY 355 HAGGARD HALL BELLINGHAM, WA 98225 A molecular analysis of sex determination in C elegans
R29GM-43334-03 (MBY) AWGULEWITSCH, ALEXANDER MEDICAL UNIVERSITY OF SC 171 ASHLEY AVENUE CHARLESTON, SC 29425 Analysis of a murine homeo box locus
R01GM-43337-02 (SB) PEPPAS, NIKOLAOS A PURDUE UNIVERSITY SCHOOL OF CHEMICAL ENGINEERING WEST LAFAYETTE, IN 47907 Ph-sensitive hydrogels for drug release
R01GM-43340-01A1 (BBCB) BERNE, BRUCE J COLUMBIA UNIVERSITY BOX 755, HAVEMEYER NEW YORK, NY 10027 On modeling hydrophobic and hydrophilic interactions
R01GM-43345-02 (MCHA) FLOSS, HEINZ G UNIVERSITY OF WASHINGTON SEATTLE, WA 98195 Biosynthesis of 2,6 dideoxyhexoses
R29GM-43357-02 (GEN) FORNEY, JAMES D PURDUE UNIVERSITY DEPARTMENT OF BIOCHEMISTRY WEST LAFAYETTE, IN 47907 Non-mendelian inheritance of macronuclear traits in paramecium tetraurelia
R01GM-43365-02 (MBC) MARSH, LORRAINE ALBERT EINSTEIN COLLEGE OF MED 1300 MORRIS PARK AVE BRONX, NY 10461 Genetics of yeast G protein - coupled a factor receptor
R01GM-43369-01A1 (CTY) GELLES, JEFF BRANDEIS UNIVERSITY 415 SOUTH STREET WALTHAM, MA 02254-9110 Biophysics and enzymology of kinesin movement
R01GM-43374-02 (SSS) LANGE, CHRISTOPHER S SUNY, HEALTH SCIENCES CENTER 450 CLARKSON AVE/BOX 1212 BROOKLYN, NY 11203 Tests of the unineme model for mammalian chromosome
R01GM-43375-02 (MBY) REED, ROBIN E HARVARD UNIVERSITY 25 SHATTUCK ST BOSTON, MA 02115 Mechanism of pre-mRNA splicing in higher eukaryote
R01GM-43378-02 (CTY) MELANCON, PAUL R UNIVERSITY OF COLORADO DEPT OF CHEM & BIOCHEM BOULDER, CO 80309-0019 Role of GTP-binding proteins in intracellular transport
R29GM-43422-02 (PC) REBECCHI, MARIO J STATE UNIVERSITY OF NEW YORK DEPT OF PHYSIOLOGY & BIOPHYS STONY BROOK, NY 11794-8661 Regulation of phosphoinositide-specific phospholipase C
R29GM-43424-02 (MBC) FORMOSA, TIMOTHY G UNIVERSITY OF UTAH 50 NORTH MEDICAL DRIVE SALT LAKE CITY, UT 84132 DNA polymerase accessory proteins from eukaryotic cells
R01GM-43432-02 (MBY) SCHEDL, PAUL PRINCETON UNIVERSITY PRINCETON, NJ 08544 Molecular analysis of high order chromosomal domains
R01GM-43459-02 (PHY) PAPAZIAN, DIANE M UNIVERSITY OF CALIFORNIA PHYSIOLOGY DEPARTMENT LOS ANGELES, CA 90024-1751 Shaker K+ channels--function of S4 and biochemistry
R01GM-43473-01A2 (BNP) MARTIN, STEPHEN F UNIVERSITY OF TEXAS 201 MAIN BUILDING AUSTIN, TX 78712 Design and synthesis of novel pseudopeptides
R01GM-43475-02 (EDC) VOGLER, GEORGE P WASH UNIV MEDICAL SCHOOL 660 S EUCLID AVE BOX 8067 ST LOUIS, MO 63110 Multivariate genetic analysis of hormone levels in twins
R01GM-43479-02 (PB) PETERSON, JULIAN A UNIV OF TEXAS SW MEDICAL CTR 5323 HARRY HINES BLVD DALLAS, TEX 75235 P450BM-3--Mechanism of electron transfer 02 activation
R01GM-43487-02 (CBY) WITTENBERG, CURT RESEARCH INST OF SCIPPS CLINIC DEPT OF MOLECULAR BIOLOGY LA JOLLA, CA 92037 The role of cyclins in control of the yeast cell cycle
R01GM-43495-02 (PB) CAIN, BRIAN D UNIVERSITY OF FLORIDA DEPT OF BIOCHEM & MOL BIO GAINESVILLE, FL 32610 Proton translocation through F1F0 ATP synthase
R01GM-43496-02 (BBCA) DEBUS, RICHARD J DEPARTMENT OF BIOCHEMISTRY UNIVERSITY OF CALIFORNIA RIVERSIDE, CA 92521 Directed mutagenesis of photosynthetic oxygen evolution
R55GM-43500-01A1 (BBCA) MEZEI, MIHALY HUNTER COLLEGE OF CUNY 695 PARK AVENUE NEW YORK, NY 10021 Computer simulation studies of aqueous systems
R01GM-43501-02 (BNP) SHEPARTZ, ALANNA YALE UNIVERSITY 225 PROSPECT STREET NEW HAVEN, CT 06511 Oligonucleotides as probes of RNA and ribozyme structure
R29GM-43507-02 (BMT) ELLIS, WALTHER R, JR UNIVERSITY OF UTAH DEPT OF CHEMISTRY SALT LAKE CITY, UT 84112 Redox chemistry of bacterial nonheme iron oxygenases
R29GM-43511-02 (TOX) RETTIE, ALLAN E UNIVERSITY OF WASHINGTON DEPT MEDICINAL CHEMISTRY BG 20 SEATTLE, WA 98195 Human flavin-containing monooxygenases
R01GM-43514-02 (MBC) STADER, JOAN A UNIV OF MISSOURI-KANSAS CITY SCHOOL OF BASIC LIFE SCIENCES KANSAS CITY, MO 64110-2499 Multiple functions of the LamB signal sequence
R01GM-43518-02 (CTY) RICHARDS, ERIC J COLD SPRING HARBOR LAB PO BOX 100 COLD SPRING HARBOR, NY 11724 Characterization of Arabidopsis telomeres
R29GM-43528-02 (IMB) HUNT, STEPHEN W, III UNIVERSITY OF NORTH CAROLINA 932 FLOB CB 7280 CHAPEL HILL, NC 27599-7280 Murine Tla genes-- Organization, expression, regulation
R01GM-43548-02 (PB) VICKERY, LARRY E UNIVERSITY OF CALIFORNIA IRVINE, CA 92717 Function and structure of human ferredoxin
R01GM-43552-02 (BNP) BARANY, GEORGE UNIVERSITY OF MINNESOTA 207 PLEASANT STREET SE MINNEAPOLIS, MI 55455 Sulfur-sulfur bridging in solid-phase peptide synthesis
R29GM-43556-02 (MBC) CAREY, JANETTE PRINCETON UNIVERSITY PRINCETON, NJ 08544 Molecular studies of trp repressor structure and function
R01GM-43560-01A2 (NLS) FOX, AARON P UNIVERSITY OF CHICAGO 947 EAST 58TH STREET CHICAGO, IL 606037 Chromaffin cells--Ca

PROJECT NO., ORGANIZATIONAL UNIT., INVESTIGATOR, ADDRESS, TITLE

channels-stimulus secretion coupling
R01GM-43564-08 (MBC) BUCHANAN, CHRISTINE E SOUTHERN METHODIST UNIVERSITY BIOLOGICAL SCIENCES DALLAS, TX 75275 Penicillin-binding proteins of bacillus subtilis
R01GM-43565-02 (MBY) BESTOR, TIMOTHY H HARVARD MEDICAL SCHOOL 45 SHATTUCK ST BOSTON, MA 02115 Role of DNA methyltransferase in mammalian development
R01GM-43566-01A1 (ARRD) KARPLUS, PAUL A CORNELL UNIVERSITY 223 BIOTECHNOLOGY BUILDING ITHACA, NY 14853-2703 Structure determination on the lymphokine GM-CSF
R29GM-43569-02 (BIO) HOCKENSMITH, JOEL W UNIV OF VIRGINIA/SCHOOL OF MED DEPT OF BIOCHEMISTRY/BOX 440 CHARLOTTESVILLE, VA 22908 Eucaryotic DNA-dependent ATPases
R29GM-43572-02 (ALY) TYCKO, BENJAMIN DEPT. OF PATHOLOGY 630 W 168TH STREET Chimeric T cell receptor gene rearrangements
R01GM-43574-06 (MGN) PARSLOW, TRISTRAM G U OF CALIF SCH OF MED DEPT OF PATHOLOGY HSW-501 SAN FRANCISCO, CA 94143 Regulatory elements in the immunoglobulin kappa genes
R01GM-43576-07 (CBY) HENDERSHOT, LINDA M ST JUDE CHILDREN'S RES HOSP 332 N LAUDERDALE MEMPHIS, TN 38105 Biochemical and functional characterization of BIP/GRP78
R01GM-43577-05 (MBC) PIGGOT, PATRICK J TEMPLE UNIV SCHOOL OF MEDICINE 3400 NORTH BROAD STREET PHILADELPHIA, PA 19140 Gene expression during sporulation
R29GM-43582-03 (PHRA) WEISS, ELLEN R UNIV NORTH CAROLINA/CHAPEL HIL 108 TAYLOR HALL CHAPEL HILL, NC 27599-7090 Regulatory domains of G-protein-coupled receptors
R01GM-43583-11A1 (CTY) SABATINI, DAVID D NEW YORK UNIVERSITY MEDICAL CT 550 FIRST AVENUE NEW YORK, NY 10016 Synthesis and distribution of proteins in membranes
R29GM-43585-02 (MBC) KROOS, LEE R MICHIGAN STATE UNIVERSITY DEPARTMENT OF BIOCHEMISTRY EAST LANSING, MI 48824 Temporal and spatial gene regulation in Bacillus subtilis
R01GM-43601-02 (MBC) FINLEY, DANIEL J HARVARD MEDICAL SCHOOL DEPT OF CELL & MOL PHYSIOLOGY BOSTON, MA 02115 Studies of ubiquitin-protein conjugates and fusions
R29GM-43607-02 (CTY) MILLER, KATHRYN G WASHINGTON UNIVERSITY DEPARTMENT OF BIOLOGY ST LOUIS, MO 63130 Function analysis/Actin-binding proteins/Drosophila embryos
R01GM-43609-04 (BMT) JARRETT, HARRY W UNIV OF TENNESSEE 800 MADISON AVENUE MEMPHIS, TN 38163 Polynucleotide high performance affinity chromatography
R01GM-43612-01A1 (MBC) DRAPER, ROCKFORD K UNIVERSITY OF TEXAS P O BOX 830-688 RICHARDSON, TX 75083-0688 Studies on Pseudomonas aeruginosa exotoxin A
R29GM-43617-02 (PB) TOMICH, JOHN M CHILDREN'S HOSP OF LOS ANGELES DIVISION OF MEDICAL GENETICS LOS ANGELES, CA 90027 Role of ordered helical segments in membrane proteins
R44GM-43638-02 (SSS) FUERST, THOMAS R MEDIMMUNE INC 19 FIRSTFIELD ROAD GAITHERSBURG, MD 20878 Novel system for regulated high level gene expression
R01GM-43644-03 (CTY) ESTELLE, MARK A INDIANA UNIVERSITY JORDAN HALL 142 BLOOMINGTON, IN 47405 Characterization of a dominant auxin-resistant mutant of Arabidopsis
R44GM-43669-02 (SSS) VESTAL, MARVIN L VESTEC CORPORATION 9299 KIRBY DRIVE HOUSTON, TX 77054 Element and isotope specific detection for HPLC
R44GM-43675-02 (SSS) WARBURTON, WILLIAM K X-RAY INSTRUMENTATION ASSOCIAT 1300 MILLS STREET MENLO PARK, CA 94025-3210 150 nsec encoding SR protein crystallography detectors
R43GM-43676-01A1 (SSS) ROSEN, DAVID I PHYSICAL SCIENCES INC 20 NEW ENGLAND BUSINESS CENTER ANDOVER, MA 01810 TEA-CO2 debridement of burn eschar
R43GM-43697-01A1 (SSS) MOIR, DONALD T COLLABORATIVE RESEARCH, INC TWO OAK PARK BEDFORD, MA 01730 Allele-specific multiplex DNA diagnostic test
R01GM-43701-10 (TOX) TRUDELL, JAMES R STANFORD UNIVERSITY SCHOOL OF MEDICINE STANFORD, CA 94305 Human metabolism of halothane--Mechanisms of toxicity
R01GM-43724-11 (BM) JARVIS, BRUCE B UNIVERSITY OF MARYLAND COLLEGE PARK, MD 20742 Chemistry of the macrocyclic trichothecene antibiotics
R44GM-43725-02 (SSS) FEIN, HARRY WORLD PRECISION INSTRUMENTS IN 175 SARASOTA CENTER BLVD SARASOTA, FL 34240 A new technique for picoliter injection
R01GM-43751-01A1 (GMA) ECKERT, RICHARD L CASE WESTERN RESERVE UNIVERSIT 2119 ABINGTON ROAD CLEVELAND, OH 44106 Involucrin and cornified envelope formation
R01GM-43753-02 (BIO) RUSSELL, DAVID W UNIV OF TX SOUTHWESTERN MED CT 5323 HARRY HINES BLVD DALLAS, TX 75235 Molecular genetics of steroid 5 alpha-reductase
R01GM-43756-01 (MBC) DUBNAU, DAVID A PUBLIC HLTH RES INST CUNY INC 455 FIRST AVENUE NEW YORK, NY 10016 Genetic competence apparatus of Bacillus subtilis
R01GM-43762-02 (MBC) LIPKE, PETER N HUNTER COLLEGE OF CUNY 695 PARK AVENUE NEW YORK, NY 10021 Cell-cell adhesion in saccharomyces cerevisiae
R01GM-43763-01A1 (NEUC) MORGAN, WILLIAM W THE UNIV OF TEXAS HLTH SCI CTR 7703 FLOYD CURL DRIVE SAN ANTONIO, TX 78284 Cell specific tyrosine hydroxylase gene transcription
R01GM-43768-02 (CBY) GILMORE, JAMES R UNIV OF MASSACHUSETTS MED CTR 55 LAKE AVENUE NORTH WORCESTER, MA 01655 Assembly and transfer of n-linked oligosaccharide
R01GM-43776-01A1 (SAT) AVRAM, MICHAEL J NORTHWESTERN UNIV MEDICAL SCH 303 E CHICAGO AVE CHICAGO, IL 60611-3008 Determinants of drug disposition during anesthesia
R01GM-43778-01A1 (CTY) BENFEY, PHILIP N ROCKEFELLER UNIVERSITY 1230 YORK AVENUE NEW YORK, NY 10021 Developmental regulation of the EPSP synthase gene
R01GM-43783-02 (BMT) CAPRIOLI, RICHARD M UNIVERSITY OF TEXAS PO BOX 20708 HOUSTON, TX 77225 On-line mass spectrometry of biological processes
R01GM-43786-02 (CTY) WOODCOCK, CHRISTOPHER L UNIVERSITY OF MASSACHUSETTS AMHERST, MA 01003 3d Structure of chromatin
R01GM-43787-02 (BBCB) REGEN, STEVEN L LEHIGH UNIVERSITY BETHLEHEM, PA 18015 Molecular-level approach to the study of lipid domains
R01GM-43796-02 (SAT) STOREY, KENNETH B CARLETON UNIVERSITY OTTAWA, ONT K1S 5B6 CANADA Organ preservation studies on a freeze tolerant frog
R01GM-43799-01A1 (MBC) FARR, SPENCER B HARVARD SCHOOL OF PUBLIC HLTH 665 HUNTINGTON AVENUE BOSTON, MA 02115 Genetic responses to oxidative stress in E.coli
R29GM-43803-02 (ALY) AHEARN, JOSEPH M THE JOHNS HOPKINS UNIVERSITY 725 NORTH WOLFE STREET BALTIMORE, MD 21205 Structural requirements for ligand binding to CR2
R01GM-43814-01 (MBY) CHAE, CHI-BOM UNIV OF NC AT CHAPEL HILL CHAPEL HILL, N C 27599-7260 Structure and function of yeast H1 histones
R01GM-43816-01A1 (BNP) PIRRUNG, MICHAEL C DUKE UNIVERSITY DURHAM, NC 27706 Molecular metaphors in bioorganic chemistry
R01GM-43824-02 (SSS) AGRESTI, ALAN UNIVERSITY OF FLORIDA 507 NUCLEAR SCIENCES CENTER GAINESVILLE, FLA 32611 Statistical inference sparse ordered categorical data
R01GM-43825-01A1 (PC) HANNUN, YUSUF A DUKE UNIVERSITY MEDICAL CENTER PO BOX 3355 DURHAM, NC 27710 Sphingomyelin turnover and cellular regulation
R01GM-43827-01A1 (MBC) MILLER, JEFFREY H UNIVERSITY OF CALIFORNIA 405 HILGARD AVENUE LOS ANGELES, CA 90024 Protein structure-function studies using UAG suppressors
R01GM-43840-03 (GEN) BRILLIANT, MURRAY H INSTITUTE FOR CANCER RESEARCH 7701 BURHOLME AVENUE PHILADELPHIA, PA 19111 Genetic and molecular analyses of mouse mutations
R01GM-43844-02 (BMT) MALLOUK, THOMAS E UNIVERSITY OF TEXAS AUSTIN, TX 78712 Chiral molecular sieves for enantiomer separations
R01GM-43847-02 (GEN) FANGMAN, WALTON L UNIVERSITY OF WASHINGTON SEATTLE, WA 98195 Genetic dissection of replication initiation in yeast mtDNA
R01GM-43854-02 (MCHA) RYCHNOVSKY, SCOTT D UNIVERSITY OF MINNESOTA 207 PLEASANT ST SE MINNEAPOLIS, MN 55455-0431 Does specific recognition control ion channel assembly
R29GM-43858-02 (PB) JANDA, KIM D RESEARCH INST OF SCRIPPS CLINI 10666 N TORREY PINES RD LA JOLLA, CA 92037 Catalytic antibodies
R01GM-43873-02 (SB) SALTZMAN, WILLIAM M THE JOHNS HOPKINS UNIVERSITY 34TH & CHARLES STREETS BALTIMORE, MD 21218 Molecular and cellular transport in mucus
R01GM-43874-02 (ALY) SEN, RANJAN BRANDEIS UNIVERSITY PO BOX 9110 WALTHAM, MA 02254 Regulation of receptors on T-lymphocytes
R01GM-43880-02 (PBC) SPIEGEL, SARAH GEORGETOWN UNIVERSITY 3900 RESERVOIR ROAD WASHINGTON, D.C. 20007 Sphingosine as a modulator of cellular proliferation
R55GM-43884-01A1 (GEN) KAY, STEVE A ROCKEFELLER UNIVERSITY 1230 YORK AVE NEW YORK, NY 10021-6399 In vivo structure - function analysis of phytochrome
R01GM-43889-02 (MBC) LOVETT, SUSAN T BRANDEIS UNIVERSITY PO BOX 9110/ROSENSTIEL CENTER WALTHAM, MA 02254-9110 Rec J protein interaction
R01GM-43893-01A1 (CTY) GOTTSCHLING, DANIEL E UNIVERSITY OF CHICAGO 920 EAST 58TH STREET CHICAGO, IL 60637 Dissection of telomere attributes in S. cerevisiae
R01GM-43901-01A1 (MBY) KINGSTON, ROBERT E MASSACHUSETTS GENERAL HOSPITAL FRUIT STREET BOSTON, MA 02114 Characterization of human heat shock factor
R01GM-43910-01A1 (BMT) MC IVER, ROBERT T, JR UNIVERSITY OF CALIFORNIA IRVINE, CA 92717 Photodissociation and metastable decay of high mass ions
R01GM-43911-02 (BBCA) KAY, CHRISTOPHER J GENERAL ATOMICS P O BOX 85608 SAN DIEGO, CA 92186-9784 Long-range electron transfers in flavocytochrome B2
R01GM-43912-02 (MCHA) EVANS, DAVID A HARVARD UNIVERSITY 12 OXFORD STREET CAMBRIDGE, MA 02138 Asymmetric synthesis of vancomycin antibiotics
R29GM-43930-02 (RAD) ZOLAN, MIRIAM E INDIANA UNIVERSITY BLOOMINGTON, IN 47405 Radiation repair & meiosis in Coprinus cinereus
R01GM-43936-02 (BNP) DOUGHERTY, DENNIS A CALIFORNIA INST OF TECHNOLOGY PASADENA, CA 91125 Biomimetic catalysis through molecular recognition
R01GM-43940-03 (MGN) HUGHES, AUSTIN L PENNSYLVANIA STATE UNIVERSITY 208 MUELLER LABORATORY UNIVERSITY PARK, PA 16802 Polymorphism & evolution of MHC genes
R01GM-43949-02 (PHY) MACKINNON, RODERICK HARVARD MEDICAL SCHOOL 25 SHATTUCK STREET BOSTON, MA 02115 Molecular study of potassium channel function
R01GM-43966-03 (BBCB) RAO, B D NAGESWARA INDIANA UNIVERSITY (IUPUI) 1125 EAST 38TH STREET INDIANAPOLIS, IN 46205-2810 Active-site structures of ATP-utilizing enzymes
R29GM-43972-03 (HEM) HARRINGTON, MAUREEN A INDIANA UNIV SCH OF MED 975 W WALNUT ST, RM 549 INDIANAPOLIS, IN 46202-5121 Regulation of the colony stimulating factor-1 gene
R01GM-43974-02 (CBY) DUNPHY, WILLIAM G CALIFORNIA INST OF TECHNOLOGY 1201 E CALIFORNIA BLVD PASADENA, CA 91125 Enzymology of mitosis-promoting factor (MPF)
R55GM-43975-01A2 (BIO) JOHNSON, JERRY D UNIVERSITY OF WYOMING DEPT OF MOLECULAR BIOLOGY LARAMIE, WY 82071 DNA-protein interactions in class III genes
R01GM-43976-03 (CBY) MISKIMINS, WILSON KEITH UNIVERSITY OF SOUTH DAKOTA 414 E CLARK VERMILLION, SD 57069 Regulation of mitogen induced late events
R01GM-43977-01A1 (CTY) KIM, STUART K STANFORD UNIV SCH OF MEDICINE STANFORD, CA 94305-5427 Genetic control of vulval cell fates in C elegans
R01GM-43979-02 (MBC) ZAHLER, STANLEY A CORNELL UNIVERSITY ITHACA, NY 14853-2703 Acetoin production by Bacillus subtilis
R01GM-43982-02 (CBY) SLOBODA, ROGER D DARTMOUTH COLLEGE HANOVER, NH 03755 Calcium, protein phosphorylation, and cell cycle control

PROJECT NO., ORGANIZATIONAL UNIT., INVESTIGATOR, ADDRESS, TITLE

R01GM-43987-02 (CTY) MURRAY, ANDREW W UNIV/CALIFORNIA SAN FRANCISCO PARNASSUS AVENUE SAN FRANCISCO, CA 94143 Feedback control of the cell cycle
R01GM-44001-01A1 (BBCB) STAUFFACHER, CYNTHIA V PURDUE UNIVERSITY WEST LAFAYETTE, IN 47907 Structure of the pore forming fragment of colicin E1
R01GM-44006-02 (BBCA) AGGARWAL, ANEEL K COLUMBIA UNIVERSITY 630 WEST 168TH STREET NEW YORK, NY 10032 Recognition and cleavage of DNA by restriction enzymes
R01GM-44012-02 (MBC) INOUYE, MASAYORI UMDNJ-R W JOHNSON MEDICAL SCHO 675 HOES LANE PISCATAWAY, NJ 08854-5635 Reverse transcriptases in the prokaryotes
R01GM-44022-01A1 (MBC) COOPER, STEPHEN UNIVERSITY OF MICHIGAN ANN ARBOR, MI 48109-0620 Cell wall synthesis during growth and division of bacteria
R01GM-44025-02 (MBC) HOCHSCHILD, ANN HARVARD MEDICAL SCHOOL 200 LONGWOOD AVE BOSTON, MA 02115 Protein-protein interactions in prokaryotic gene control
R01GM-44037-02 (TOX) CORREIA, MARIA A UNIV OF CALIFORNIA BOX 0450, S-1210 SAN FRANCISCO, CA 94143 Hepatic degradation of P-450p isozymes
R01GM-44038-06 (BBCB) SCHUTT, CLARENCE E PRINCETON UNIVERSITY NEW SOUTH BUILDING, 2ND FLOOR PRINCETON, NJ 08544 Crystallography of actin and actin-binding proteins
R01GM-44055-02 (BIO) GUARINO, LINDA A TEXAS A&M UNIVERSITY COLLEGE STATION, TX 77843 Baculovirus ubiquitin and the host ubiquitin system
R15GM-44071-01A1 (CTY) MORRIS, STEPHEN J UNIVERSITY OF MISSOURI 5100 ROCKHILL RD BSB 109 KANSAS CITY, MO 64110-2499 Real time dual fluorescence imaging of living cells
R01GM-44073-02 (MBY) BASS, BRENDA L UNIVERSITY OF UTAH MEDICAL CTR 50 NORTH MEDICAL DRIVE SALT LAKE CITY, UT 84132 Molecular biology of an RNA unwinding/modifying activity
R29GM-44074-01A1 (GEN) LEARNED, ROBERT M UNIVERSITY OF CALIFORNIA DAVIS, CA 95616 Molecular genetics of HMG CoA reductase in Arabadopsis
R01GM-44077-01A1 (SSS) ENKE, CHRISTIE G MICHIGAN STATE UNIVERSITY EAST LANSING, MI 48824-1322 Dual time-of-flight mass spectrometer--High speed MS/MS
R01GM-44086-02 (BIO) NELSON, HILLARY C UNIVERSITY OF CALIFORNIA BERKELEY, CA 94720 Structure of heat shock transcription factor from yeast
R01GM-44088-02 (CBY) KIDD, VINCENT J ST. JUDE CHILDREN'S RES HOSPIT 332 N. LAUDERDALE MEMPHIS, TN 38101 Characterization of a cell division control related gene
R15GM-44097-01A1 (MBC) HIRSHFIELD, IRVIN N ST JOHN'S UNIVERSITY GRAND CENTRAL & UTOPIA PKWYS JAMAICA, NY 11439 Lysyl-tRNA synthetase & apxn synthesis in E coli
R29GM-44100-02 (SAT) BILLIAR, TIMOTHY R UNIVERSITY OF PITTSBURGH PITTSBURGH, PA 15261 Nitric oxide and hepatic function in sepsis and trauma
R15GM-44101-01A1 (MBC) GORDON, ANDREW S OLD DOMINION UNIVERSITY NORFOLK, VA 23529-0266 Bacterial metal detoxification-- Extracellular chelators
R01GM-44112-01A1 (BMT) KUHR, WERNER G UNIVERSITY OF CALIFORNIA RIVERSIDE, CA 92521 Electrochemical methods for in vivo measurements
P01GM-44119-02 (SSS) HUBERMAN, JOEL A ROSWELL PARK MEMORIAL INST 666 ELM STREET BUFFALO, N Y 14263 Regulation of DNA replication & cell growth
P01GM-44119-02 0001 (SSS) HUBERMAN, JOEL Regulation of DNA replication & cell growth Initiation of DNA replication near the c-myc gene
P01GM-44119-02 0002 (SSS) KOWALSKI, DAVID Regulation of DNA replication & cell growth Structure and activity of eukaryotic DNA replication origins
P01GM-44119-02 0003 (SSS) PRUITT, STEVEN Regulation of DNA replication & cell growth Cell type specific growth regulation
P01GM-44119-02 0004 (SSS) YATES, JOHN Regulation of DNA replication & cell growth Cis and trans-acting determinants of extrachromosomal plasmids
R01GM-44127-01A1 (BNP) FRYE, LEAH L RENSSELAER POLYTECH INSTITUTE 332 COGSWELL BUILDING TROY, NY 12180-3590 Synthetic ion channels
R01GM-44140-01A1 (PC) COBB, MELANIE H U T SOUTHWESTERN MEDICAL CENTE 5323 HARRY HINES BOULEVARD DALLAS, TX 75235-9041 Regulation and properties of casein kinase I
R01GM-44154-03 (BNP) WONG, CHI-HUEY SCRIPPS RESEARCH INSTITUTE 10666 N TORREY PINES ROAD LA JOLLA, CA 92037 Enzyme in organic synthesis: construction of polyhydroxy
R01GM-44158-01A1 (BNP) YANG, NIEN-CHU C UNIVERSITY OF CHICAGO 5735 SOUTH ELLIS AVENUE CHICAGO, IL 60637 Photochemistry of aryl halides and its applications
R01GM-44162-02 (BBCA) KIM, PETER S WHITEHEAD INST FOR BIOMED RES CAMBRIDGE, MA 02142 Structure and function of the leucine zipper motif
R29GM-44163-02 (MCHA) STILLE, JOHN R MICHIGAN STATE UNIVERSITY EAST LANSING, MI 48824 Selective intramolecular carbon-carbon bond formation
R01GM-44171-01A1 (BBCB) KLEINFELD, ALAN M MEDICAL BIOLOGY INSTITUTE 11077 NORTH TORREY PINES ROAD LA JOLLA, CA 92037 Transport of free fatty acids across model membranes
R01GM-44173-02 (MBC) MARTIN, G STEVEN UNIVERSITY OF CALIFORNIA 401 BARKER HALL BERKELEY, CA 94720 Protein-tyrosine kinases in yeast
R29GM-44191-02 (BMT) POCHAPSKY, THOMAS C BRANDEIS UNIVERSITY WALTHAM, MA 02254-9110 Structure and dynamics of metal-containing proteins by NMR
R01GM-44199-02 (MBC) NICHOLS, BRIAN P UNIVERSITY OF ILLINOIS PO BOX 4348, MAIL CODE 066 CHICAGO, IL 60680 Enzymes & genes of p-aminobenzoate biosynthesis
R01GM-44200-02 (SAT) FORSE, ROBERT A NEW ENGLAND DEACONESS HOSPITAL 194 PILGRIM ROAD BOSTON, MA 02215 Re-esterification and lipogenesis in septic patients
R01GM-44211-02 (CBY) COLUCCIO, LYNNE M EMORY UNIVERSITY SCHOOL OF MED ATLANTA, GA 30322 Microvillar cytoskeletal-membrane interactions
R01GM-44223-02 (MBY) MILLER, DENNIS L UNIV OF TEXAS AT DALLAS P.O. BOX 830688, F03.1 RICHARDSON, TX 75083-0688 Mitochondrial gene expression in physarum polycephalum
R01GM-44228-02 (CTY) MITCHELL, DAVID R SUNY HEALTH SCIENCE CENTER 750 EAST ADAMS STREET SYRACUSE, NY 13210 Molecular and genetic analysis of flagellar dyneins
R29GM-44246-01A2 (CBY) SEGALL, JEFFREY E ALBERT EINSTEIN COLL OF MED 1300 MORRIS PARK AVENUE BRONX, NY 10461 Mutational analysis of amoeboid chemotaxis
R15GM-44260-01A1 (MCHA) GUNG, BENJAMIN W MIAMI UNIVERSITY OXFORD, OH 45056 Acyclic stereocontrol by double asymmetric synthesis
R01GM-44263-02 (TOX) SMITH, CHARLES V BAYLOR COLLEGE OF MEDICINE ONE BAYLOR PLAZA HOUSTON, TX 77030 Oxidant mechanisms in drug-induced hepatic necrosis
R01GM-44276-02 (BBCB) GILL, STANLEY C UNIVERSITY OF COLORADO CAMPUS BOX 215 BOULDER, CO 80309-0215 Protein interactions from solid model compound studies
R01GM-44283-02 (BMT) RAJAGOPALAN, K V DUKE UNIVERSITY BOX 3711 DURHAM, N C 27710 Molybdenum and the molybdenum cofactor in human health
R01GM-44286-01A1 (MGN) YANG, THOMAS P UNIVERSITY OF FLORIDA BOX J-245 GAINESVILLE, FL 32610 Gene regulation by x chromosome inactivation
R01GM-44288-01A1 (CTY) QUATRANO, RALPH S UNIV OF N CAROLINA/CHAPEL HILL CHAPEL HILL, NC 27599 Elucidation of a hormonal response pathway
R01GM-44292-01 (BBCB) WESTBROOK, EDWIN M ARGONNE NATIONAL LABORATORY 9700 SOUTH CASS AVENUE ARGONNE, IL 60439-4833 Laue diffraction study of bovine pancreatic ribonuclease
R01GM-44295-01A1 (PHRA) MAYER, STEVEN E VANDERBILT UNIVERSITY 1161 21TH AVE SOUTH NASHVILLE, TN 37232-6600 Biochemical mechanisms of drug action on choroid plexus
R15GM-44296-01A1 (PHRA) TARLOFF, JOAN B PHILADELPHIA COLL OF PHARMACY/ 43RD ST AT WOODLAND AVENUE PHILADELPHIA, PA 19104 Role of cytochromes P450 in acetaminophen nephrotoxicity
R01GM-44298-02 (NEUC) JULIUS, DAVID J UNIVERSITY OF CALIFORNIA 513 PARNASSUS AVE SAN FRANCISCO, CA 94143-0450 Molecular analysis of serotonin receptor function
R01GM-44300-01A1 (ALY) CALAME, KATHRYN L COLUMBIA UNIVERSITY 701 WEST 168TH ST NEW YORK, NY 10032 T-cell receptor beta chain gene regulation
R15GM-44309-01A1 (BIO) THURLOW, DAVID L CLARK UNIVERSITY 950 MAIN STREET WORCESTER, MA 01610 Synthetic substrates for nucleotidyltransferase
R15GM-44335-01A1 (BMT) CLELAND, WALTER E, JR UNIVERSITY OF MISSISSIPPI UNIVERSITY, MS 38677 Structural models for nickel enzymes
R15GM-44341-01A1 (BMT) WESDEMIOTIS, CHRYS UNIVERSITY OF AKRON AKRON, OH 44325-3601 Mass spectrometry of free radicals
R29GM-44344-02 (BBCB) WILLSON, RICHARD C UNIVERSITY OF HOUSTON 4800 CALHOUN AVENUE HOUSTON, TX 77204-4792 Thermodynamic basis of antibody-antigen affinity
R15GM-44353-01A1 (PBC) TILLINGHAST, EDWARD K UNIVERSITY OF NEW HAMPSHIRE SPAULDING LIFE SCIS BLDG DURHAM, NH 03824 Characterization of a spider mucin and associated compound
R01GM-44360-02 (BMT) GLUSKER, JENNY P INSTITUTE FOR CANCER RESEARCH 7701 BURHOLME AVENUE PHILADELPHIA, PA 19111 Intermolecular interactions of functional groups
R01GM-44373-02 (PHY) TAKEYASU, KUNIO UNIV OF VIRGINIA/SCH OF MED 1300 JEFFERSON PARK AVE/BX 449 CHARLOTTESVILLE, VA 22908 Biogenesis and function of the (Na++K+)-ATPase subunits
R01GM-44380-02 (BMT) CRAMER, STEPHEN P UNIVERSITY OF CALIFORNIA 228 WALKER HALL DAVIS, CA 95616 Soft X-ray spectroscopy of metalloproteins
R01GM-44390-03 (CBY) PAINE, PHILIP L ST JOHN'S UNIVERSITY GRAND CENTRAL & UTOPIA PARKWAY JAMAICA, NY 11439 Mechanisms of nuclear proein accumulation
R01GM-44400-01A1 (MBC) DITTA, GARY S UNIVERSITY OF CALIFORNIA CTR FOR MOLECULAR GENETICS LA JOLLA, CA 92093 Oxygen regulation of symbiotic genes in Rhizobium
R01GM-44403-01A2 (MBY) LANGMORE, JOHN P UNIVERSITY OF MICHIGAN INST OF SCIENCE & TECHNOLOGY ANN ARBOR, MI 48109-2099 Biochemical study of embryonically regulated histone
R44GM-44418-02 (SSS) KLAUSNER, MITCHELL MATTEK CORPORATION 200 HOMER AVENUE ASHLAND, MA 01721 Improved microporous membranes in mammalian cell culture
R43GM-44424-01A1 (SSS) PRESTON, KENDALL, JR KENSAL CONSULTING 5701 EAST GLENN STREET TUCSON, AZ 85712 Real-time visi chip for 3-d surface rendering for ct & M
R01GM-44427-03 (BIO) SCOTT, JOHN D OREGON HEALTH SCI UNIVERSITY 3181 SW SAM JACKSON PK RD, L47 PORTLAND, OR 97201-3098 Molecular analysis of camp-dep kinase inhibitor proteins
R01GM-44428-01A2 (BIO) BOKOCH, GARY M RESEARCH INST OF SCRIPPS CLINI 10666 N TORREY PINES ROAD LA JOLLA, CA 92037 Role of low MW G protein (rap) in neutrophil activation
R43GM-44437-01A1 (SB) WARD, ROBERT S POLYMER TECHNOLOGY GROUP, INC 4561-A HORTON STREET EMERYVILLE, CA 94608 Shape-memory thermoplastic catheter/insertion sheath
R43GM-44461-01A1 (SSS) WALLACE, DAVID B MICROFAB TECHNOLOGIES, INC 1104 SUMMIT AVENUE PLANO, TX 75074 Measurement of fast enzyme kinetics via droplet merging
R01GM-44467-02 (CBY) PIPERNO, GIANNI MOUNT SINAI SCH OF MEDICINE ONE GUSTAVE L LEVY PL NEW YORK, N Y 10029 Molecular interactions in moving axonemes
R01GM-44470-02 (ARR) KELLY, T ROSS BOSTON COLLEGE CHESTNUT HILL, MA 02167 Synthesis of pradimincin A and related anti-HIV agents
R01GM-44473-02 (ARR) ANDERSON, JOHN E COLD SPRING HARBOR LABRATORY P. O. BOX 100 BUNGTOWN ROAD COLD SPRING HARBOR, NY 11724 Stuctural studies of the fos/jun transcription factor
R01GM-44486-01A1 (SAT) MICHENFELDER, JOHN D MAYO FOUNDATION 200 FIRST STREET SOUTHWEST ROCHESTER, MN 55905 Cerebral effects of anesthesia-related interventions

PROJECT NO., ORGANIZATIONAL UNIT., INVESTIGATOR, ADDRESS, TITLE

R01GM-44500-02 (PBC) PARODI, ARMANDO J INSTITUTO DE INVESTIGACIONES ANTONIO MACHADO 151 1405 BUENOS AIRES, ARGENTINA Transient glucosylation of glycoproteins
R01GM-44507-02 (MBC) ZISSLER, JAMES F UNIV OF MINNESOTA MED SCHOOL 420 DELEWARE ST SE MINNEAPOLIS, MN 55455-0312 Genetic analysis of cell cell signaling in myxococcus
R01GM-44511-02 (TMP) WILLIS, JUDITH H UNIVERSITY OF GEORGIA ATHENS, GA 30602 The metamorphosis of chromatin
R29GM-44520-02 (BIO) MITSIALIS, ALEX S UNIVERSITY HOSPITAL-EVANS 6 88 EAST NEWTON STREET BOSTON, MA 02118 Transcription factors regulating chorion gene promoters
R01GM-44522-02 (CTY) COUREY, ALBERT J UNIVERSITY OF CALIFORNIA 405 HILGARD AVENUE LOS ANGELES, CA 90024-1569 Biochemical analysis of promoters regulating development
R01GM-44525-02 (MCHA) STILL, WILLIAM C, JR COLUMBIA UNIVERSITY DEPT OF CHEMISTRY NEW YORK, NY 10027 Theoretical and experimental studies of complexation
R01GM-44529-01 (MCHA) HOFFMAN, ROBERT V NEW MEXICO STATE UNIVERSITY BOX 30001 DEPT 3C LAS CRUCES, NM 88003-001 Azacyclic synthesis using n-sulfonyloxy amines
R01GM-44530-01A1 (CTY) BANKAITIS, VYTAS A UNIVERSITY OF ILLINOIS 407 S GOODWIN AVE/131 BURRIL H URBANA, IL 61801 The role of phospholipids in Golgi secretory function
R01GM-44532-01A1 (CTY) JOHNSON, ALEXANDER D UNIVERSITY OF CALIFORNIA 401 HEALTH SCIENCE EAST SAN FRANCISCO, CA 94143-0502 Meiotic pairing of chromosomes in yeast
R01GM-44546-02 (PC) VOLINI, MARGUERITE UNIVERSITY OF HAWAII 2538 THE MALL HONOLULU, HI 96822 The regulatory role of the rhodaneses
R01GM-44547-01A1 (MBC) TABER, HARRY W ALBANY MEDICAL COLLEGE, A-68 47 NEW SCOTLAND AVE ALBANY, NY 12208 Molecular genetics of Bacillus subtilis cytochrome aa3
R29GM-44554-02 (BBCB) SEATON, BARBARA A BOSTON UNIV SCHOOL OF MEDICIN 80 EAST CONCORD STREET BOSTON, MA 02118 Annexin crystal structure and phospholipid interaction
R01GM-44557-02 (BBCA) WOLYNES, PETER G UNIVERSITY OF ILLINOIS 505 SOUTH MATHEWS AVE URBANA, IL 61801 Conceptual aspects of the protein folding problem
R01GM-44558-02 (BBCB) GERIG, J T UNIVERSITY OF CALIFORNIA SANTA BARBARA, CA 93106 Simulation of NMR experiments
R29GM-44573-02 (PBC) FRISCH, STEVEN M WASHINGTON UNIV SCHOOL OF MED 660 S EUCLID AVE, BOC 8123 ST LOUIS, MO 63110 E1A control of protease gene transcription
R01GM-44582-02 (CBY) TREVOR, KATRINA T WAYNE STATE UNIVERSITY 540 EAST CANFIELD DETROIT, MI 48201 Intermediate filaments in simple epithelial cells
R01GM-44585-02 (PBC) MARCANTONIO, EUGENE E COLUMBIA UNIVERSITY 630 WEST 168TH STREET NEW YORK, NY 10032 Structure and function of the integrin alpha1 beta1
R55GM-44586-01A1 (GEN) DREESEN, THOMAS D LOUISIANA STATE UNIVERSITY BATON ROUGE, LA 70803-1725 Molecular interactions of Drosophila membrane proteins
R01GM-44588-01A1 (CTY) ELICEIRI, GEORGE L ST LOUIS UNIVERSITY 1402 S GRAND BLVD ST LOUIS, MO 63104 Human small nuclear RNAs with novel nucleotide sequences
R01GM-44589-02 (CBY) SCHROER, TRINA A JOHNS HOPKINS UNIVERSITY CHARLES & 34TH ST BALTIMORE, MD 21218 Regulation of cytoplasmic dynein-based vesicle transport
R01GM-44592-02 (PC) BLUMER, KENDALL J WASHINGTON UNIV SCHOOL OF MEDI 660 S EUCLID AVENUE ST LOUIS, MO 63110 Mechanism and regulation of receptor-G protein signalling
R01GM-44606-01A1 (BMT) WILKINS, CHARLES L UNIVERSITY OF CALIFORNIA RIVERSIDE, CA 92521 Laser-assisted FTMS analysis of high mass biomolecules
R01GM-44613-01A1 (PB) JOHNSON, KENNETH A PENNSYLVANIA STATE UNIVERSITY 108 ALTHOUSE LABORATORY UNIVERSITY PARK, PA 16802 Mechanism and fidelity of DNA replication
R01GM-44617-02 (BBCA) LEWIS, MITCHELL UNIVERSITY OF PENNSYLVANIA SCHOOL OF MEDICINE PHILADELPHIA, PA 19104-6059 Crystallographic studies of the lactose repressor
R01GM-44619-01A1 (GEN) RUVKUN, GARY B MASSACHUSETTS GENERAL HOSPITAL FRUIT STREET BOSTON, MA 02113 Control of the C elegans lineage by heterochronic genes
R01GM-44634-01A1 (MBY) YEE, AMY S TUFTS UNIVERSITY 136 HARRISON AVENUE BOSTON, MA 02111 Regulation of E2F transcription factor function
R01GM-44638-01A1 (MEDB) RAIJMAN, LUISA J UNIV OF SOUTHERN CALIFORNIA 2011 ZONAL AVE / HMR #413 LOS ANGELES, CA 90033 Organization of the pathway of urea synthesis in situ
R01GM-44640-01A1 (CTY) CHUA, NAM-HAI ROCKEFELLER UNIVERSITY 1230 YORK AVENUE NEW YORK, NY 10021-6399 Light-responsive genes
R01GM-44651-02 (PBC) VIJAY, INDER K UNIVERSITY OF MARYLAND COLLEGE PARK, MD 20742 Glucosyltransferase in mammary gland
R01GM-44653-02 (CBY) MELTON, DOUGLAS A HARVARD UNIVERSITY 7 DIVINITY AVENUE CAMBRIDGE, MA 02138 Embryonic induction of mesoderm and neural tissue
R01GM-44655-02 (MBC) NORMARK, STAFFAN WASHINGTON UNIVERSITY ST. LOUIS, MO 63110 Tropisms and interactive surfaces of bacterial adhesins
R01GM-44656-01A1 (CTY) NEWPORT, JOHN W UNIV OF CALIFORNIA DEPT OF BIOLOGY, B-022 LA JOLLA, CA 92093 Biochemical pathways linking DNA replication & mitosis
R01GM-44659-01A1 (GEN) WOLFNER, MARIANA F CORNELL UNIVERSITY 423 BIOTECHNOLOGY BLDG ITHACA, NY 14853-2703 Molecular genetics of pronuclear functions in drosophila
R01GM-44664-02 (MBC) ELLEDGE, STEPHEN J BAYLOR COLLEGE OF MEDICINE ONE BAYLOR PLAZA HOUSTON, TX 77030 Genetics of cell cycle and DNA damage regulation in yeast
R01GM-44665-02 (MBY) BROW, DAVID A UNIV OF WISCONSIN 1300 UNIVERSITY AVENUE MASISON, WI 53706 Characterization of a yeast U6 snRNA gene promoter
R01GM-44666-01A1 (MBC) GARRETT, STEPHEN DUKE UNIVERSITY MEDICAL CTR PO BOX 3686 DURHAM, NC 27710 Genetic analysis of growth and cell cycle in yeast
R01GM-44669-01A1 (MBY) CEDAR, HOWARD HEBREW UNIVERSITY MEDICAL CTR P O BOX 1172 JERUSALEM, 91010, ISRAEL DNA replication in animal cells
R29GM-44671-01A1 (MBC) FORST, STEVEN A UNIVERSITY OF WISCONSIN PO BOX 413 MILWAUKEE, WI 53201 Molecular study of adaptive responses in E.coli
R01GM-44675-02 (ARR) MORRE, D JAMES PURDUE UNIVERSITY WEST LAFAYETTE, IN 47907 Endomembrane trafficking of FIV envelope glycoproteins
R55GM-44685-01A1 (CBY) DUMONT, MARK E UNIVERSITY OF ROCHESTER 601 ELMWOOD AVE/PO BOX 607 ROCHESTER, NY 14642 Import of cytochrome C into yeast mitochondria
R01GM-44700-03 (BBCA) SOYFER, VALERY N GEORGE MASON UNIVERSITY 4400 UNIVERSITY DRIVE FAIRFAX, VIRGINIA 22030 Photofootprinting of triplexes in DNA
R01GM-44713-01 (BNP) CAVA, MICHAEL P UNIVERSITY OF ALABAMA PO BOX 870336 TUSCALOOSA, AL 35487-0336 Synthesis of novel marine heterocycles
R29GM-44720-01A1 (MCHA) WEST, FREDERICK UNIVERSITY OF UTAH SALT LAKE CITY, UT 84112 Polycycle synthesis via 4-pyrone photochemistry
R01GM-44721-02 (MBY) WOLD, MARC S UNIVERSITY OF IOWA 51 NEWTON RD IOWA CITY, IA 52242 Functional roles of cellular proteins in DNA replication
R01GM-44724-01A1 (BNP) VEDEJS, EDWIN UNIVERSITY OF WISCONSIN 1101 UNIVERSITY AVENUE MADISON, WI 53706 Asymmetric memory at heteroatoms
R01GM-44757-02 (CBY) HAYS, THOMAS S BIOSCIENCE CENTER 1445 GORTNER ST PAUL, MN 55108 The structure and function of cytoplasmic dynein
R29GM-44764-02 (SAT) WEST, MICHAEL A HENNEPIN COUNTY MEDICAL CENTER 701 PARK AVENUE MINNEAPOLIS, MN 55415 Regulation of macrophage function in surgical sepsis
R01GM-44772-01A1 (MBC) KNIGHT, KENDALL L UNIV OF MASSACHUSETTS MED CTR 55 LAKE AVENUE NORTH WORCESTER, MA 01655 Functional organization of the RecA protein
S14GM-44779-02 (MPRC) POWELL, ALICE M ALCORN STATE UNIVERSITY PO BOX 1259 LORMAN, MS 39096 MBRS undergraduate program at Alcorn State University
S14GM-44780-02 (MPRC) WATKINS, NELLOUISE D BENNETT COLLEGE 900 E WASHINGTON ST/PO BOX 22 GREENSBORO, N C 27401 Minority biomedical research support program
S14GM-44780-02 0001 (MPRC) LINSTER, MICHELLE L Minority biomedical research support program Impact of race on treatment outcome for black female alcoholics
S14GM-44780-02 0002 (MPRC) RAO, SEKHARA B Minority biomedical research support program Relationship of hypertension to aortic and carotid artery atherosclerosis
S14GM-44780-02 0003 (MPRC) BLAKE, BARBARA H Minority biomedical research support program Metabolic cost and thermogenic potential of crying in hypothermic infants
S14GM-44780-02 0004 (MPRC) BOYD, ROBERT E Minority biomedical research support program A search for active components of medicinal plants
R01GM-44783-02 (PB) RAINES, RONALD T DEPARTMENT OF BIOCHEMISTRY 420 HENRY MALL MADISON, WI 53706 Protein engineering to study ribonuclease A catalysis
R01GM-44794-02 (GEN) KLECKNER, NANCY E HARVARD UNIVERSITY 7 DIVINITY AVENUE CAMBRIDGE, MASS 02138 Meiotic chromosome synapsis and recombination in yeast
S06GM-44796-02 (MPRC) PAUL, VALERIE J UNIV OF GUAM UOG STATION MANGILAO, GUAM 96923 Biomedical research on coral-reef organisms of Guam
S06GM-44796-02 0001 (MPRC) LOBBAN, CHRISTOPHER S Biomedical research on coral-reef organisms of Guam Relationships of ciguatera-producing dinoflagellates to seaweeds
S06GM-44796-02 0002 (MPRC) RICHMOND, ROBERT H Biomedical research on coral-reef organisms of Guam The reproductive biology and population genetics of corals
S06GM-44796-02 0003 (MPRC) PAUL, VALERIE J Biomedical research on coral-reef organisms of Guam Chemical interactions of coral-reef invertebrates
R01GM-44801-02 (BBCA) MATHIES, RICHARD A UNIVERSITY OF CALIFORNIA BERKELEY, CA 94720 Raman studies of light transduction in halobacteria
R01GM-44806-01A1 (BBCB) KURET, JEFFREY A COLD SPRING HARBOR LABORATORY PO BOX 100 COLD SPRING HARBOR, NY 11724 3d-structure of the camp-dependent protein kinase
R01GM-44809-02 (IMS) NEMAZEE, DAVID NATIONAL JEWISH CENTER 1400 JACKSON STREET DENVER, CO 80206 B lymphocyte tolerance in health and autoimmunity
R29GM-44810-02 (BIO) BJORNSTI, MARY-ANN THOMAS JEFFERSON UNIV/MED COLL 1020 LOCUST STREET PHILADELPHIA, PA 19107 Functional analysis of eukaryotic DNA topoisomerase I
S14GM-44814-02 (MPRC) EPPS, THOMAS H VIRGINIA STATE UNIVERSITY PETERSBURG, VA 23803 Virginia State University minority biomedical research program
R01GM-44821-02 (MBY) COCHRAN, BRENT H MASS INSTITUTE TECHNOLOGY 77 MASS AVENUE CAMBRIDGE, MA 02139 Molecular analysis of alpha cell specific UAS function
R01GM-44823-01A1 (CTY) PURICH, DANIEL L UNIVERSITY OF FLORIDA J HILLIS MILLER HEALTH CENTER GAINESVILLE, FL 32610 Neuronal MAP interactions with microtubules
R01GM-44824-02 (GEN) LAHUE, ROBERT S UNIV OF MA MEDICAL SCHOOL 55 LAKE AVE NORTH WORCESTER, MA 01655 Gene conversion and DNA mismatch correction in yeast
R01GM-44828-02 (PB) FORGAC, MICHAEL D TUFTS UNIVERSITY 136 HARRISON AVE BOSTON, MA 02111 Structure and properties of the coated vesicle Cl channel
R29GM-44829-01A1 (PB) FETROW, JACQUELYN S UNIVERSITY AT ALBANY SUNY 1400 WASHINGTON AVE ALBANY, NY 12222 Structural modularity and protein function in cytochrome C
R01GM-44840-02 (PHY) PAPPONE, PAMELA A UNIVERSITY OF CALIFORNIA DEPT OF ANIMAL PHYSIOLOGY DAVIS, CA 95616 Ion channels in brown fat

PROJECT NO., ORGANIZATIONAL UNIT., INVESTIGATOR, ADDRESS, TITLE

R29GM-44841-02 (BMT) MC REE, DUNCAN E RESEARCH INSTITUTE OF SCRIPPS 10666 N TORREY PINES ROAD LA JOLLA, CA 92037 Ligand controlled dissociation of a dimeric protein

R01GM-44842-01A1 (BMT) WEBER, STEPHEN G UNIVERSITY OF PITTSBURGH 219 PARKMAN AVENUE PITTSBURGH, PA 15260 Sensitive and selective detection of peptides

R01GM-44844-02 (MBC) BELFORT, MARLENE WADSWORTH CENTER FOR LABS & RE EMPIRE STATE PLAZA ALBANY, N Y 12201 Expression of an interrupted prokaryotic gene

R01GM-44853-02 (BNP) VERDINE, GREGORY L HARVARD UNIVERSITY 12 OXFORD ST CAMBRIDGE, MA 02138 Functionally tethered oligonucleotides

R01GM-44855-01 (GEN) RYKOWSKI, MARY C UNIVERSITY OF ARIZONA 1501 NORTH CAMPBELL AVENUE TUCSON, AZ 85724 High resolution interphase chromosome structure

R01GM-44865-01A1 (BMT) DARENSBOURG, MARCETTA Y TEXAS A & M UNIVERSITY COLLEGE STATION, TX 77843 Assessing roles of nickel hydrides in hydrogenases

R29GM-44876-01A1 (TMP) VAN HEUSDEN, MIRANDA C UNIVERSITY OF ARIZONA BIOSCIENCES WEST 351 TUCSON, AZ 85721 Study of lipid transfer processes using an insect model

R01GM-44881-03 (BBCA) RODER, HEINRICH INSTITUTE FOR CANCER RESEARCH 7701 BURHOLME AVENUE PHILADELPHIA PA 19111 Studies of protein folding by NMR and mutagenesis

R01GM-44884-01 (SAT) LANGER, ROBERT S MASSACHUSETTS INST OF TECH 77 MASSACHUSETTS AVENUE CAMBRIDGE, MASS 02139 Ultrasonic polymeric drug delivery

R01GM-44885-02 (BMT) FRECHET, JEAN M J CORNELL UNIVERSITY BAKER LABORATORY ITHACA, NY 14853-1301 Polymeric separation media for liquid chromatography

R01GM-44887-02 (PHRA) LA DU, BERT N JR UNIVERSITY OF MICHIGAN ANN ARBOR, MI 48109-0572 DNA polymorphic forms of human serum cholinesterase

R01GM-44889-02 (GEN) SAWYER, STANLEY WASHINGTON UNIVERSITY SCH OF M 4566 SCOTT BOX 8232 ST LOUIS, MO 63110 Statistical tests for detection of gene conversion

R01GM-44900-01A1 (BMT) LUNTE, CRAIG E UNIVERSITY OF KANSAS LAWRENCE, KS 66045 In vivo investigations using microdialysis sampling

R01GM-44901-01A1 (CTY) MELESE, TERI COLUMBIA UNIVERSITY 702A FAIRCHILD CTR NEW YORK, NY 10027 Biochemical and genetic analysis of nuclear transport

R01GM-44902-01A1 (SB) GREEN, PHILIP S SRI INTERNATIONAL 333 RAVENSWOOD AVENUE MENLO PARK, CA 94025 Telepresence for intra-abdominal and endoscopic surgery

R01GM-44918-02 (SAT) REMICK, DANIEL G UNIVERSITY OF MICHIGAN 1301 CATHERINE ROAD ANN ARBOR, MI 48109-0602 The role of cytokines in sepsis and trauma

R55GM-44919-01A1 (PB) COPELAND, ROBERT A UNIVERSITY OF CHICAGO 920 E 58TH STREET CHICAGO, IL 60637 Biophysical studies of bacterial cytochrome oxidase

R29GM-44931-01A1 (BMT) HAGE, DAVID S UNIVERSITY NEBRASKA-LINCOLN 738 HAMILTON HALL LINCOLN, NE 68588-0304 Chromatographic automation of immunoassays

R01GM-44944-02 (PHRA) BENOVIC, JEFFEREY L THOMAS JEFFERSON UNIVERSITY 1025 WALNUT STREET PHILADELPHIA, PA 19107-5083 Cloning and expression of bark related cDNAs

R01GM-44947-02 (PC) SCOTTO, ANTHONY W CORNELL UNIV MEDICAL COLLEGE 1300 YORK AVENUE NEW YORK, NY 10021 The proteoliposome--A membrane model

R01GM-44954-01A1 (SAT) COLLINS, J G YALE UNIVERSITY SCH OF MEDICIN 333 CEDAR ST/PO BOX 3333 NEW HAVEN, CT 06510 Inhalation anesthetic effects on the spinal dorsal horn

R01GM-44965-02 (PHRA) WEBER, WENDELL W UNIVERSITY OF MICHIGAN ANN ARBOR, MI 48109-0626 Recombinant DNA study of rapid/slow n-acetyltransferases

R55GM-44966-01A1 (BBCB) BLOUGH, NEIL V WOODS HOLE OCEANOGRAPHIC INST WOODS HOLE, MA 02543 Fluorescence detection of radical/redox reactions

R01GM-44973-02 (BBCA) WHITE, STEPHEN W DUKE UNIV MED CTR PO BOX 3020 DURHAM, NC 27710 Structural studies on ribosomal components

R29GM-44974-01A1 (BBCA) MERZ, KENNETH M, JR PENNSYLVANIA STATE UNIVERSITY UNIVERSITY PARK, PA 16802 Theoretical study of metalloenzyme structure and function

R01GM-44976-02 (BBCB) NAGLE, JOHN F CARNEGIE-MELLON UNIVERSITY 4400 FIFTH AVE PITTSBURGH, PA 15213 Structure of lipid bilayers

R01GM-44982-01A1 (CPA) THOMAS, PAUL E RUTGERS, THE STATE UNIV OF NJ P O BOX 789 PISCATAWAY, NJ 08855-0789 Regulation and function of P450III gene family isozymes

R01GM-44986-02 (SRC) WIEMER, DAVID F UNIVERSITY OF IOWA IOWA CITY, IA 52242 Synthesis of novel nucleoside phosphonates

R01GM-44993-02 (SRC) SCHREIBER, STUART L HARVARD UNIVERSITY 12 OXFORD STREET CAMBRIDGE, MA 02138 Design of ligands to biological receptors

R01GM-44995-02 (SRC) MATTESON, DONALD S WASHINGTON STATE UNIVERSITY PULLMAN, WA 99164-4630 Boradeoxyribonucleosides

R01GM-45002-02 (SRC) REBEK, JULIUS, JR MASSACHUSETTS INST OF TECHNOLO 77 MASSACHUSETTS AVE CAMBRIDGE, MA 02139 Carriers for membrane transport of AIDS-targeted drugs

R01GM-45011-02 (SRC) OTVOS, LASZLO WISTAR INSTITUTE 36TH & SPRUCE STREETS PHILADELPHIA, PA 19104 Synthesis and conformation of glycopeptides

R01GM-45012-02 (SRC) MILLER, PAUL S JOHNS HOPKINS UNIVERSITY 615 NORTH WOLFE STREET BALTIMORE, MD 21205 DNA-specific oligonucleotide analogs

R01GM-45015-02 (SRC) KONOPELSKI, JOSEPH P UNIVERSITY OF CALIFORNIA THINMAN LABS SANTA CRUZ, CA 95064 Novel asymmetric synthesis of anti-AIDS compounds

R01GM-45027-01A1 (SB) PEPPAS, NIKOLAOS A PURDUE UNIVERSITY WEST LAFAYETTE, IN 47907 Mucoadhesive polymers for nasal and buccal drug delivery

R43GM-45061-01A1 (SSS) HOKE, GLENN D ISIS PHARMACEUTICALS 2280 FARADAY AVENUE CARLSBAD, CA 92008 Synthesis of chiral phosphorothioate oligonucleotides

PROJECT NO., ORGANIZATIONAL UNIT., INVESTIGATOR, ADDRESS, TITLE

R43GM-45075-01A1 (SSS) LEVIN, KENNETH H INFRARED FIBER SYSTEMS, INC 2301-A BROADBIRCH DR SILVER SPRING, MD 20904 Fiber coupled spectroscopic airway gas monitor

R43GM-45087-01 (SSS) GUEBELI, THOMAS P ALITEA USA PO BOX 26 MEDINA, WA 98039 Novel pump for flow injection analysis and chromatography

R01GM-45109-02 (ARR) GILHAM, PETER T PURDUE UNIVERSITY WEST LAFAYETTE, IN 47907 Mechanism of synthetic ribozyme action

R01GM-45129-01A1 (SAT) HARRISON, NEIL L UNIVERSITY OF CHICAGO 5841 S MARYLAND AVE/BOX 428 CHICAGO, IL 60637 Volatile anesthetic interactions with GABA-A receptors

R01GM-45134-01A1 (CTY) BOMSZTYK, KAROL UNIVERSITY OF WASHINGTON SEATTLE, WA 98195 Interleukin 1 induced kinases and transcriptional factors

R01GM-45141-01 (MGN) MOORE, PETER D UNIVERSITY OF ILLINOIS 808 S WOOD STREET CHICAGO, IL 60612 Minisatellite sequences and homologous recombination

R01GM-45144-01 (GEN) CLEGG, MICHAEL T UNIVERSITY OF CALIFORNIA RIVERSIDE, CA 92521 Processes of plant molecular evolution

R01GM-45146-01 (GEN) MACKAY, TRUDY F NORTH CAROLINA STATE UNIVERSIT BOX 7614 RALEIGH, NC 27695-7614 Quantitative trait loci in drosophila

R01GM-45162-01 (BBCB) REES, DOUGLAS C CALIFORNIA INST OF TECHNOLOGY 1201 E CALIFORNIA BLVD PASADENA, CA 91125 Crystallographic studies of electron transfer proteins

R01GM-45179-01 (MBC) ARNDT, KIM T COLD SPRING HARBOR LABORATORY P.O. BOX 100 COLD SPRING HARBOR, NY 11724 Progression from G1 to S requires the SIT4 phosphatase

R01GM-45185-01 (GEN) CHAN, CLARENCE S UNIVERSITY OF TEXAS 24TH AND SPEEDWAY AUSTIN, TX 78712 Molecular analysis of chromosome segregation in yeast

R01GM-45188-01 (CTY) ROBBINS, PHILLIPS W MASSACHUSETTS INST TECH BLDG E17-233 CAMBRIDGE, MA 02139 Glycoprotein processing systems of ER and golgi

R01GM-45190-01 (BIO) MODRICH, PAUL L DUKE UNIVERSITY MEDICAL CENTER BOX 3711 DURHAM, N C 27710 Enzymology of eukaryotic DNA mismatch repair

S06GM-45199-02 (MPRC) CLARK, CLARENCE W MOREHOUSE COLLEGE 830 WESTVIEW DRIVE, S W ATLANTA, GA 30314 Biomedical sciences research improvement program

S06GM-45199-02 0001 (MPRC) ARCHIBOLD, ERROL R Biomedical sciences research improvement program Angiotensin and angiotensin receptor(s) on the growth and proliferation of cells

S06GM-45199-02 0002 (MPRC) CLARK, CLARENCE W Biomedical sciences research improvement program R-plasmid maintenance in gram negative and positive bacteria

S06GM-45199-02 0003 (MPRC) CLARK, VERNESSA Biomedical sciences research improvement program The effects of stress on physiological responding

S06GM-45199-02 0004 (MPRC) COOKE, DAVID B Biomedical sciences research improvement program Genotypic characteristics of prostate cancer affected by differentiation agents

S06GM-45199-02 0005 (MPRC) HAN, GRACE Biomedical sciences research improvement program Oxidized liver fructose 1,6-bisphosphatase--Formation, properties, significance

S06GM-45199-02 0006 (MPRC) HAYNES, JOHN K Biomedical sciences research improvement program Biochemical characterization of sickle cell membranes

S06GM-45199-02 0007 (MPRC) MCCRAY, JOSEPH W Biomedical sciences research improvement program Neutraliztion of human rhinovirus by antipeptide antibodies

S06GM-45199-02 0008 (MPRC) PATTERSON, ROSALYN M Biomedical sciences research improvement program Free radical modification of DNA methylation patterns in vitro

S06GM-45199-02 0009 (MPRC) ROSENMAN, MARTIN F Biomedical sciences research improvement program Amalgam, urine mercury levels, and cognative functioning in children

R01GM-45200-01 (PBC) HO, SIU-CHEONG MICHIGAN STATE UNIVERSITY EAST LANSING, MI 48824 Carbohydrate binding protein of Bradyrhizobium japonicum

R01GM-45201-01 (PC) LEIBOLD, ELIZABETH A UNIVERSITY OF UTAH 50 NORTH MEDICAL DRIVE SALT LAKE CITY, UTAH 84132 Iron regulation of gene expression

R01GM-45205-01A1 (BMT) PENNER-HAHN, JAMES E UNIVERSITY OF MICHIGAN 930 N UNIVERSITY ANN ARBOR, MI 48109-1055 Structure and reactivity studies of Mn catalase

R01GM-45209-01 (BMT) BURGESS, BARBARA K UNIVERSITY OF CALIFORNIA IRVINE, CA 92717 Site directed mutagenesis of azotobacter ferredoxin I

R01GM-45214-01 (MCHA) SIEBURTH, SCOTT M STATE UNIVERSITY OF NEW YORK STONY BROOK, NY 11794-3400 Intramolecular pyrone/pyridone (4+4) photocycloadditions

R55GM-45226-01 (GEN) KIRKPATRICK, MARK A UNIVERSITY OF TEXAS AUSTIN, TX 78712 Genetic models of evolutionary processes

R55GM-45237-01 (TMP) VOLLOCH, VLADIMIR Z BOSTON BIOMED RESEARCH INST 20 STANIFORD STREET BOSTON, MA 02114 Mechanism of RNA editing

R01GM-45244-01 (CTY) ZAMBRYSKI, PATRICIA C UNIVERSITY OF CALIFORNIA 111 GENETICS/ PLANT BIOLOGY BL BERKELEY, CA 94720 Plant virus proteins to probe plasmadesmata function

R01GM-45247-01A1 (GEN) EANES, WALTER F STATE UNIVERSITY OF NEW YORK STONY BROOK, NY 11794 Detecting balanced selection with DNA sequence variation

R01GM-45248-01 (GEN) BERG, CELESTE A UNIVERSITY OF WASHINGTON 1959 NE PACIFIC STREET SEATTLE, WA 98195 Cell-cell interactions during Drosophila oogenesis

R29GM-45250-01 (CTY) DRESSER, MICHAEL E OKLAHOMA MEDICAL RESEARCH FDN 825 NE 13TH STREET OKLAHOMA CITY, OK 73104 Structure and function of the synaptonemal complex

R01GM-45252-01A1 (MBC) ADAMS, THOMAS H TEXAS A&M UNIVERSITY COLLEGE STATION, TX 77843 Molecular mechanisms initiating fungal development

R29GM-45253-01A1 (MBY) SPEAR, BRETT T UNIVERSITY OF KENTUCKY MS-401 MEDICAL CTR LEXINGTON, KY 40536-0084 Genetic schemes to clone mammalian transcription factors

R29GM-45258-01 (MBY) HORIKOSHI, MASAMI THE ROCKEFELLER UNIVERSITY 1230 YORK AVENUE NEW YORK, NY 10021-6399 Structural and functional analysis of yeast TATA factor

R01GM-45260-01 (SSS) RUZICKA, JAROMIR UNIVERSITY OF WASHINGTON SEATTLE, WA 98195 Flow injection cytometry in analytical biology

R01GM-45262-01 (PB) UNKEFER, CLIFFORD J LOS ALAMOS NATIONAL LABORATORY PO BOX 1663 LOS ALAMOS, NM 87545 Mechanism of the PQQ-dependent methanol dehydrogenase

R01GM-45276-01 (GEN) WEINERT, TED A UNIVERSITY OF ARIZONA TUCSON, AZ 85721 Genetic control of cell cycle arrest after DNA damage

R29GM-45282-01 (GEN) SCHMIDHAUSER, THOMAS J SOUTHERN ILLINOIS UNIVERSITY CARBONDALE, IL 62901-4409 Blue light regulation of gene expression in fungi

R01GM-45288-01 (CBY) ADAMS, ALISON E M UNIVERSITY OF ARIZONA BIOSCIENCES WEST TUCSON, AZ 85721 Molecular analysis of the yeast actin cytoskeleton

R01GM-45290-01 (BIO) WEISS, MICHAEL A HARVARD MEDICAL SCHOOL 240 LONGWOOD AVENUE BOSTON, MA 02115 Oct2--Lymphoma-related transcription regulatory factor

R01GM-45295-01 (BIO) KAGUNI, LAURIE S MICHIGAN STATE UNIVERSITY EAST LANSING, MI 48824 Mitochondrial DNA polymerase--Mechanism and structure

R01GM-45299-01A1 (BIO) JOHNSON, DEBORAH L UNIV OF SOUTHERN CALIFORNIA 1985 ZONAL AVE LOS ANGELES, CA 90033 Regulation of Drosophila RNA polymerse I and III gene expression

R29GM-45302-01A1 (BBCA) BAUM, JEAN S RUTGERS UNIVERSITY PISCATAWAY, NJ 08855-0939 NMR approaches to the protein folding problem

R01GM-45311-01 (PTHB) GEISSLER, EDWIN N BETH ISRAEL HOSPITAL 330 BROOKLINE AVE BOSTON, MA 02215 Analysis of the role of c-kit in mast cell development

R01GM-45312-01A1 (BNP) BERGMAN, ROBERT G UNIVERSITY OF CALIFORNIA 213B LEWIS HALL BERKELEY, CA 94720 Fundamental studies of 1,4-dehydrobenzene diradicals

R01GM-45314-01A1 (BIO) GONDA, DAVID K YALE UNIV SCHOOL OF MED 333 CEDAR STREET PO BOX 3333 NEW HAVEN, CT 06510 Ubiquitin-dependent proteolysis in mammalian cells

R01GM-45315-01A1 (BIO) SZOSTAK, JACK W MASSACHUSETTS GENERAL HOSPITAL WELLMAN 9 BOSTON, MA 02114 Ribozyme-substrate interactions

R01GM-45316-01 (BBCA) FINK, ANTHONY L UNIVERSITY OF CALIFORNIA 101 SINSHEIMER LABORATORIES SANTA CRUZ, CA 95064 The role of heat shock proteins in protein folding

R29GM-45322-01 (BBCA) OAS, TERRENCE G DUKE UNIVERSITY MEDICAL CENTER DURHAM, NC 27710 Structural studies of BPTI folding mutants

R01GM-45330-01A1 (BIO) BROWN, NEAL C UNIV OF MASSACHUSETTS MED SCH 55 LAKE AVENUE NORTH WORCESTER, MA 01655 Structure of DNA polymerase III and its HPUra binding site

R01GM-45335-01 (MEDB) COFFINO, PHILIP UNIVERSITY OF CALIFORNIA THIRD AND PARNASSUS AVENUE SAN FRANCISCO, CA 94143-0414 Product mediated regulation of ornithine decarboxylase

R01GM-45343-01A1 (PB) ANDERSON, KAREN S YALE UNIVERSITY SCH OF MED P O BOX 3333 NEW HAVEN, CT 06510 Substrate channeling in tryptophan synthase

P01GM-45344-01 (GEN) WEIR, BRUCE S NORTH CAROLINA STATE UNIV DEPT OF STATISTICS/ BOX 8203 RALEIGH, N C 27695-8203 Statistical and quantitative genetics

P01GM-45344-01 0001 (GEN) COCKERHAM, ZENG Statistical and quantitative genetics Theoretical quantitative genetics

P01GM-45344-01 0005 (GEN) GOODMAN, MAJOR M Statistical and quantitative genetics Quantitative genetics of maize

P01GM-45344-01 0002 (GEN) WEIR, BRUCE S Statistical and quantitative genetics Statistical methods in gentics

P01GM-45344-01 0003 (GEN) ATCHLEY, HALL Statistical and quantitative genetics Developmental quantitative genetics

P01GM-45344-01 0004 (GEN) MACKAY, LANGLEY Statistical and quantitative genetics Drosophila quantitative genetics

R01GM-45351-01 (PB) FESIK, STEPHEN W ABBOTT LABORATORIES ABBOTT PARK, IL 60064 Structure of peptidyl-prolyl isomerase/ligand complexes

R01GM-45355-01 (GEN) HOGNESS, DAVID S STANFORD UNIV SCH. MED. BECKMAN CENTER B300 STANFORD, CA 94305-5427 Hormonal control of genetic hierarchies in development

R01GM-45356-01A1 (SAT) BJORNSON, ANN B JAMES N GAMBLE INST OF MED RES 2141 AUBURN AVENUE CINCINNATI, OH 45219 Biochemistry of neutrophil dysfunction in thermal injury

R29GM-45367-01 (PB) APPLEMAN, JAMES R ST JUDE CHILDREN'S RES HOSP 332 N LAUDERDALE MEMPHIS, TN 38101-0318 Relation of thymidylate synthase structure to function

R29GM-45368-01 (CTY) KENNELLY, PETER J VIRGINIA POLY TECHNIC INST DEPT OF BIOCHEM & NUTRITION BLACKSBURG, VA 24061-0308 Phosphorylation of histones on n-amino acids

R01GM-45371-01 (MBY) PADGETT, RICHARD A UNIV OF TEXAS SW MED CTR DEPT OF BIOCHEMISTRY DALLAS, TX 75235-9038 Analysis of early events in pre-mRNA splicing

R01GM-45372-01A1 (BMT) GLISH, GARY L OAK RIDGE NATIONAL LABORATORY P O BOX 2008/BLDG 5510 OAK RIDGE, TN 37831-6365 Instrumentation for analysis of high mass biomolecules

R01GM-45374-01A1 (CBY) LEWIS, RICHARD S STANFORD UNIVERSITY B105A BECKMAN CENTER STANFORD, CA 94305-5426 Ion channels and signaling mechanisms in T lymphocytes

R01GM-45377-01 (BBCB) AKEY, CHRISTOPHER W BOSTON UNIVERSITY SCH OF MED 80 EAST CONCORD STREET BOSTON, MA 02118-2394 The structural basis of nucleocytoplasmic transport

R55GM-45379-01 (MBC) LOW, DAVID A UNIVERSITY OF UTAH 50 NORTH MEDICAL DRIVE SALT LAKE CITY, UT 84132 Thermoregulatory mechanisms in Escherichia coli

R01GM-45380-02 (PBC) HASSELL, JOHN R EYE & EAR INSTITUTE 203 LOTHROP ST PITTSBURGH, PA 15213 Structure and regulation of basement membrane proteoglycan

R29GM-45396-01 (GEN) HOOPER, JOAN E UNIVERSITY OF COLORADO 4200 E NINTH AVE B-111 DENVER, CO 80262 Cell interactions organizing the insect segment

R01GM-45398-01 (MGN) KAZAZIAN, HAIG H, JR JOHNS HOPKINS HOSPITAL 600 N WOLFE ST/CMSC 10-110 BALTIMORE, MD 21205 A human transposable element

R01GM-45402-01A1 (GEN) MORGAN, PHILIP G 2078 ABINGTON ROAD CLEVELAND, OH 44106 Mechanism of action of volatile anesthetics

R01GM-45410-01 (MBC) FUTCHER, BRUCE A COLD SPRING HARBOR LABORATORY P.O. BOX 100 COLD SPRING HARBOR, NY 11724 Twin cell cycle clocks in S. cerevisiae

R01GM-45413-01 (MGN) LISKAY, ROBERT M YALE UNIV SCHOOL OF MEDICINE 333 CEDAR STREET NEW HAVEN, CT 06510 Homologous recombination in mammalian cells

R01GM-45431-01 (CBY) FERRO-NOVICK, SUSAN S YALE UNIVERSITY SCH OF MED 333 CEDAR ST, BOX 3333 NEW HAVEN, CT 06510 Defining components required for transport from ER

R01GM-45434-01A1 (SAT) LEFER, ALLAN M 1020 LOCUST STREET PHILADELPHIA, PA 19107-6799 Endothelial injury in trauma and ischemia-reperfusion

R01GM-45436-01A1 (CTY) STILLMAN, BRUCE W COLD SPRING HARBOR LABORATORY P O BOX 100 COLD SPRING HARBOR, NY 11724 Regulation of DNA replication

R01GM-45441-01 (MGN) WILLARD, HUNTINGTON F STANFORD UNIVERSITY DEPARTMENT OF GENETICS STANFORD, CA 94305 Molecular genetics of human x chromosome inactivation

R01GM-45443-01 (MBY) PARKER, ROY R UNIVERSITY OF ARIZONA BIOSCIENCES WEST 308 TUCSON, AZ 85721 Regulation of mRNA turnover in yeast

R13GM-45446-01 (MEDB) KORNFELD, ROSALIND H WASHINGTON UNIV MED SCHOOL 660 SOUTH EUCLID AVE, BOX 8125 ST LOUIS, MO 63110 Gordon conference--Glycoproteins and glycolipids

R01GM-45448-01 (MBC) MULLER, ERIC G UNIVERSITY OF WASHINGTON SJ-70 SEATTLE, WA 98195 The role of thioredoxin in cell growth and division

S06GM-45455-01 (MPRC) FREI, JOHN K, SR BARRY UNIVERSITY 11300 NE 2ND AVE MIAMI, FL 33161-6695 Biomedical research at Barry University

S06GM-45455-01 0001 (MPRC) FISHER, GEORGE H Biomedical research at Barry University Altered asparate in dysfunctional proteins

S06GM-45455-01 0002 (MPRC) GANTER, PHILLIP F Biomedical research at Barry University Causes of phenotype variation in natural yeast

S06GM-45455-01 0003 (MPRC) HAYS, ELIZABETH T Biomedical research at Barry University Theophylline/skeletal muscle contraction and energy balance

S06GM-45455-01 0004 (MPRC) SUAREZ, PEDRO Biomedical research at Barry University Modeling the AIDS epidemic in South Florida

R29GM-45460-01 (MBC) GOEBL, MARK G MEDICAL SCIENCE BUILDING 635 BARNHILL DRIVE/RM 417 INDIANAPOLIS, IN 46202-5122 Analysis of cell cycle ubiquitin conjugation in yeast

R01GM-45532-01 (MCHA) DENMARK, SCOTT E UNIV OF ILLINOIS 1209 W CALIFORNIA ST/BOX 18 URBANA, IL 61801 Structure and reactions of chiral phosphorus-stabilized carbanions

R29GM-45535-01 (RAD) MELLON, ISABEL UNIVERSITY OF KENTUCKY 800 ROSE STREET LEXINGTON, KY 40536-0093 Mechanisms of DNA repair in active genes

R01GM-45540-01A1 (BBCB) AMZEL, L MARIO JOHNS HOPKINS SCH OF MEDICINE 725 N WOLFE STREET BALTIMORE, MD 21205 Structure and mechanisms of NAD(P) H:quinone reductase

R55GM-45542-01 (MEP) HAMILTON, GORDON A PENNSYLVANIA STATE UNIVERSITY 152 DAVEY LABORATORY UNIVERSITY PARK, PA 16802 Role of oxalins in cell proliferation and regulation

R29GM-45543-01 (EDC) SEGAL, MARK R THE UNIVERSITY OF CALIFORNIA SAN FRANCISCO, CA 94143-0560 Tree-structured methods for longitudinal and survival data

R01GM-45546-01 (BBCA) HOROWITZ, JACK IOWA STATE UNIV AMES, IA 50011 Transfer ribonucleic acid structure and function

R01GM-45547-01 (BBCA) KURIYAN, JOHN ROCKEFELLER UNIVERSITY 1230 YORK AVE, BOX 3 NEW YORK, NY 10021 Structures of trypanothione and thioredoxin reductases

R01GM-45550-21A1 (MBC) KADO, CLARENCE I UNIVERSITY OF CALIFORNIA DAVIS, CA 95616 Tumor-inducing substance of Agrobacterium tumefaciens

R01GM-45551-01 (BNP) BERGSTROM, DONALD E PURDUE UNIVERSITY SCHOOL OF PHARMACY WEST LAFAYETTE, IN 47907 In search of the universal nucleic acid base

R01GM-45557-01 (CBY) TAMM, SIDNEY L BOSTON UNIVERSITY MARINE BIOLOGICAL LABORATORY WOODS HOLE, MA 02543 Control of ciliary motility

R01GM-45566-01 (BMT) LUNTE, CRAIG E UNIVERSITY OF KANSAS LAWRENCE, KS 66045 In vivo microdialysis sampling for metabolism studies

R01GM-45568-01A1 (PHRA) GOY, MICHAEL F UNIVERSITY OF NORTH CAROLINA 61 MED SCI BLDG/CB #7545 CHAPEL HILL, NC 27599-7545 Peptide regulation of guanylate cyclase

R29GM-45570-01 (GEN) DAVIS, KEITH R OHIO STATE UNIVERSITY 1060 CARMACK RD/207 RIGHTMIRE COLUMBUS, OH 43210 Genetic approaches for identifying plant defense genes

R29GM-45571-01A1 (BNP) DUSSAULT, PATRICK H UNIVERSITY OF NEBRASKA 835 HAMILTON HALL LINCOLN, NE 68588-0304 New synthetic approaches to unsaturated hydroperoxides

R01GM-45572-01A1 (BNP) WIDLANSKI, THEODORE S INDIANA UNIVERSITY BLOOMINGTON, IN 47405 Sulfonyl analogues of sulfates and phosphates

R01GM-45574-01 (MBY) LAM, ERIC RUTGERS STATE UNIVERSITY BOX 759 PISCATAWAY, NJ 08855 Developmentally-regulated DNA-binding proteins

R01GM-45578-01A1 (ALY) DRESKIN, STEPHEN C UNIVERSITY OF COLORADO 4200 EAST NINTH AVENUE DENVER, CO 80262 Signal transduction by the high affinity IgE receptor

R01GM-45579-01 (BBCA) LEE, JAMES C UNIVERSITY OF TEXAS MED BRANCH GALVESTON, TX 77550-2779 Thermodynamic linkages in the control of transcription

R01GM-45597-01 (PB) ADAMS, MICHAEL W UNIVERSITY OF GEORGIA ATHENS, GA 30602 Site-specific properties of a unique iron-sulfur protein

R29GM-45607-01 (BBCA) BASHFORD, DONALD E RES INSTITUTE OF SCRIPPS CLINI 10666 NORTH TORREY PINES RD LA JOLLA, CA 92037

Theoretical studies of protein electrostatics
R01GM-45611-01 (BNP) HIRSCHMANN, RALPH F UNIVERSITY OF PENNSYLVANIA 133 SOUTH 36TH STREET PHILADELPHIA, PA 19104-3246 Catalytic antibodies for peptide synthesis
R29GM-45614-01A1 (BBCB) CHRISTIANSON, DAVID W UNIVERSITY OF PENNSYLVANIA 231 SOUTH 34TH STREET PHILADELPHIA, PA 19104-3623 Structure and function of carbonic anhydrase
R29GM-45616-01 (BBCA) BRIGGS, MARTHA S GEORGIA INSTITUTE OF TECHNOLOG ATLANTA, GA 30332-0400 Peptide models of protein structure and folding
R01GM-45617-01 (MCHA) SINGLETON, DANIEL A TEXAS A&M UNIV COLLEGE STATION, TX 77843 Free-radical mediated annulations and additions
R43GM-45639-01 (SSS) SQUILLANTE, MICHAEL R RADIATION MONITORING DEVICES 44 HUNT STREET WATERTOWN, MA 02172 Large area high resolution x-ray detector for biomedical research
R43GM-45640-01 (SSS) BURRILL, PETER H MERIDIAN INSTRUMENTS INC 2310 SCIENCE PARKWAY OKEMOS, MI 48864 Use of a CCD camera for low-cost confocal microscopy
R43GM-45644-01 (SSS) ROSSER, ROY J PRINCETON X-RAY LASER INC 1-H DEER PARK DRIVE MONMOUTH JUNCTION, NJ 08852 Novel soft x-ray imaging microscope diffraction plate
R43GM-45646-01 (SSS) BROTZMAN, RICHARD W TPL, INC 1549 GLORIETA NE ALBUQUERQUE, NM 87112 Improved dye laser pump source for photodynamic therapy
R43GM-45651-01 (SSS) FINE, RICHARD M BIOSYM TECHNOLOGIES, INC PARSIPPANY, NJ 07054 Computer simulation method for calculating free energy of polypeptides & proteins
R43GM-45656-01 (SSS) MAHONEY, JOHN F PHRASOR SCIENTIFIC, INC 1536 HIGHLAND AVENUE DUARTE, CALIF 91010 Heavy cluster impact desorption of large molecules
R43GM-45658-01A1 (SSS) LIBERTI, PAUL A IMMUNICON CORPORATION 1310 MASONS MILL II HUNTINGDON VALLEY, PA 19006 Bioprocessing using bioreceptor ferrofluids and HGMS
R43GM-45660-01A1 (SSS) DUIGNAN, MICHAEL T POTOMAC PHOTONICS INC 4720-E BOSTON WAY LANHAM, MD 20706 New untrasensitive detector for micro-separations
R43GM-45661-01 (SSS) HSIA, JAMES CANDELA LASER CORPORATION 530 BOSTON POST ROAD WAYLAND, MA 01778 Resonance ionization mass spectrometry solid state laser
R55GM-45670-01 (GNM) LI, WEN-HSIUNG UNIVERSITY OF TEXAS PO BOX 20334 HOUSTON, TX 77225 Origins of the CG-rich isochores of the human genome
R43GM-45674-01 (SSS) STORTI, GEORGE M QUANTEX CORPORATION 2 RESEARCH COURT ROCKVILLE, MD 20850 ET recording media for protein crystallography
R43GM-45677-01 (SSS) SU, YU MICROMATH INC PO BOX 21550 SALT LAKE CITY, UT 84121 Microcomputer software for differential equations
R01GM-45678-20 (SAT) BROWN, BURNELL R, JR UNIVERSITY OF ARIZONA TUCSON, AZ 85724 Studies on inhalation anesthetic hepatotoxicity
R01GM-45687-01A1 (ARRB) ZULL, JAMES E CASE WESTERN RESERVE UNIV 2080 ADELBERT RD CLEVELAND, OH 44106 Immunosensor for HIV antibodies
R01GM-45697-01 (GEN) MEYEROWITZ, ELLIOT M CALIFORNIA INST OF TECHNOLOGY 1201 E CALIFORNIA BLVD PASADENA, CA 91125 Genetics of agamous action in arabisopsis development
R01GM-45718-01 (IMB) KENTER, AMY L UNIVERSITY OF ILLINOIS 835 SOUTH WOLCOTT CHICAGO, IL 60612 Developmentally regulated exonuclease in B lymphocytes
R01GM-45720-01 (MBC) WINSTON, FRED M ASSOCIATE PROFESSOR OF GENETIC HARVARD MEDICAL SCHOOL BOSTON, MA 02115 Analysis of general transcription factors in yeast
R01GM-45726-01 (MBC) WRIGHT, ROBIN L UNIVERSITY OF WASHINGTON SEATTLE, WA 98195 Membrane dynamics and sterol biosynthesis in yeast
R01GM-45727-01 (MBC) WHITELEY, JOHN M SCRIPPS CLINIC & RESEARCH FDN 10666 NORTH TORREY PINES ROAD LA JOLLA, CA 92037 Bacterial regulatory switches--structure and mechanism
R01GM-45737-01 (PC) JACKOWSKI, SUZANNE ST JUDE CHILDREN'S RESEARCH HO 332 NORTH LAUDERDALE MEMPHIS, TN 38105 Regulation of membrane biosynthesis by csf-1
R01GM-45739-01 (MBC) GABER, RICHARD F NORTHWESTERN UNIVERSITY 2153 SHERIDAN ROAD EVANSTON, IL 60208 Transcriptional modulation in yeast
R01GM-45744-01 (GEN) KURODA, MITZI I BAYLOR COLLEGE OF MEDICINE ONE BAYLOR PLAZA HOUSTON, TX 77030 Molecular genetics of dosage compensation in Drosophila
R55GM-45745-01 (CTY) MURPHY, DOUGLAS B THE JOHNS HOPKINS UNIV 725 NORTH WOLFE ST BALTIMORE, MD 21205 Mechanisms of intracellular motility
R01GM-45756-01 (BIO) DAVISSON, V JO PURDUE RESEARCH FOUNDATION PHARMACY BUILDING WEST LAFAYETTE, IN 47907 Enzymes of the histidine biosynthetic pathway
R13GM-45759-01 (CTY) GRUNSTEIN, MICHAEL UNIVERSITY OF CALIFORNIA 405 HILGARD AVENUE LOS ANGELES, CA 90024 Chromatin and transcription -- FASEB Summer conference
S06GM-45765-01 (SRC) AVILA, VERNON L SAN DIEGO STATE UNIVERSITY SAN DIEGO, CA 92182-0057 San Diego State University MBRS program
S06GM-45765-01 0001 (SRC) BERNSTEIN, STANFORD I San Diego State University MBRS program Myosin isoform structure and function
S06GM-45765-01 0003 (SRC) DAHMS, A STEPHEN San Diego State University MBRS program T-tubule membrane structure and function
S06GM-45765-01 0004 (SRC) LOVATO, CHRIS Y San Diego State University MBRS program Lung risk reduction intervention model for painters
S06GM-45765-01 0006 (SRC) REILLY, JUDY S San Diego State University MBRS program The intersection of language and affect
S06GM-45765-01 0007 (SRC) THAL, DONNA J San Diego State University MBRS program Early identification of risk for language disorder
S06GM-45765-01 0008 (SRC) TSOUKAS, CONSTANTINE San Diego State University MBRS program Analysis of Epstein-Barr/virus C3d receptors in T lymphocytes
S06GM-45765-01 0010 (SRC) ZYSKIND, JUDITH W San Diego State University MBRS program Initiation of DNA replication--DnaA, RNA polymerase, & coupling to cell cycle
R01GM-45772-01 (MBY) WINTER, EDWARD P THOMAS JEFFERSON UNIVERSITY 1020 LOCUST STREET PHILADELPHIA, PA 19107-6799 Analysis of an oligo(da) oligo(dt) binding protein
R01GM-45773-01 (VR) ALWINE, JAMES C UNIVERSITY OF PENNSYLVANIA 422 CURIE BLVD/CLIN RES BLDG#5 PHILADELPHIA, PA 19104-6142 Mechanisms of polyadenylation in viral systems
R55GM-45774-01 (MBC) GENNARO, MARIA L PUBLIC HEALTH RESEARCH INST 455 FIRST AVENUE NEW YORK, NY 10016 In vitro studies on DNA replication enhancement
R01GM-45781-01 (BMT) REINHOLD, VERNON N 665 HUNTINGTON AVENUE BOSTON, MA 02115 Glycan sequencing at the femtomole level
R01GM-45783-01 (BMT) BUCHANAN, ROBERT M UNIVERSITY OF LOUISVILLE LOUISVILLE, KY 40292 Polyimidazole oxo-iron complexes
R29GM-45795-01 (BMT) MC CRACKEN, JOHN L MICHIGAN STATE UNIVERSITY EAST LANSING, MI 48824-1322 Pulsed EPR studies of nickel model complexes
R01GM-45797-01 (MBC) PAKRASI, HIMADRI B WASHINGTON UNIVERSITY BOX 1137 ST LOUIS, MO 63130 Molecular biology and biochemistry of photosystem II
R01GM-45804-01 (BNP) HOPKINS, PAUL B UNIVERSITY OF WASHINGTON CHEMISTRY BG-10 SEATTLE, WA 98195 Structure and mechanism of DNA interstrand crosslinking
R01GM-45807-01 (BMT) WOODRUFF, WILLIAM H UNIVERSITY OF CALIFORNIA LOS ALAMOS, NM 87545 Infrared study of oxidase dynamics
R01GM-45811-01 (SSS) CASE, DAVID A RESEARCH INST OF SCRIPPS CLINI 10666 N TORREY PINES ROAD LA JOLLA, CA 92037 Determination of solution structures from NMR
R29GM-45815-01 (CBY) STEINBERG, THOMAS H WASHINGTON UNIVERSITY 660 S EUCLID AVE/BOX 8051 ST LOUIS, MO 63110 ATP-induced gap junction pores in macrophages
R01GM-45820-01 (GEN) MC KEARIN, DENNIS M UNIVERSITY OF TEXAS 5323 HARRY HINES BLVD DALLAS, TX 75235 Germ cell differentiation in drosophila
R29GM-45831-01 (BNP) DRUECKHAMMER, DALE G STANFORD UNIVERSITY HARVARD MEDICAL SCHOOL STANFORD, CA 94305 New technology in enzymatic synthesis
R01GM-45842-01 (CTY) GROSS, DAVID S LOUISIANA STATE UNIV SCH OF ME 1501 KINGS HIGHWAY/PO BOX 3393 SHREVEPORT, LA 71130-3932 Structure and regulation of the yeast hsp90 genes
R01GM-45843-01 (MBY) NAGOSHI, RODNEY N UNIVERSITY OF IOWA IOWA CITY, IA 52242 Regulation of sex-specific RNA splicing in Drosophila
R01GM-45844-01 (MBC) KILEY, PATRICIA J UNIVERSITY OF WISCONSIN 1300 UNIVERSITY AVENUE MADISON, WI 53706 Regulation of gene expression by oxygen
R01GM-45859-01A1 (BBCB) SACCHETTINI, JAMES C ALBERT EINSTEIN COLLEGE OF MED 1300 MORRIS PARK AVENUE BRONX, NY 10461 Tertiary structure studies on lipid binding proteins
R29GM-45872-01 (BCE) HOEFFLER, JAMES P UNIVERSITY OF COLORADO 4200 EAST 9TH AVENUE DENVER, CO 80262 Protein/protein interactions of creb/atf proteins
R01GM-45873-01 (SAT) MAIER, RONALD V HARBORVIEW MEDICAL CENTER 325 9TH AVENUE/ZA-16 SEATTLE, WA 98104 Immunomodulation of macrophages following trauma
R55GM-45879-01 (MBC) PAULUS, HENRY P BOSTON BIOMEDICAL RES INST 20 STANIFORD ST BOSTON, MA 02114 Control of the aspartokinase isozymes in bacillus
R01GM-45883-01 (GNM) CASADABAN, MALCOLM J UNIVERSITY OF CHICAGO 920 EAST 58TH STREET CHICAGO, IL 60637 New reporter genes
R01GM-45891-01 (CTY) HEINTZ, NICHOLAS H UNIVERSITY OF VERMONT COL OF MED/MED ALUMNI BLDG BURLINGTON, VT 05405 Regulation of DNA synthesis in mammalian cells
R29GM-45902-01 (MBC) WILLIAMS, JOANN C ARIZONA STATE UNIVERSITY TEMPE, AZ 85287-1604 Structure-function relations in photosynthetic systems
S06GM-45913-01 (MPRC) JONES, BETTY R MORRIS BROWN COLLEGE 643 MARTIN LUTHER KING, JR, DR ATLANTA, GA 30314 Morris Brown College biomedical research improvement program
S06GM-45913-01 0001 (MPRC) JONES, BETTY R Morris Brown College biomedical research improvement program Putative neurotransmitter substances and enzymes in Schistosoma
S06GM-45913-01 0002 (MPRC) STAHL, JEANNE M Morris Brown College biomedical research improvement program Environmental stimulation as prevention/therapy for brain injuries
S06GM-45913-01 0003 (MPRC) DUROJAIYE, MUSTAPHA A Morris Brown College biomedical research improvement program Recovery of Tetrahymena thermophila from narcotic drugs--Phagocytosis study
R01GM-45914-01 (MEDB) SMITH, DAVID F UNIVERSITY OF GEORGIA BOYD GRADUATE STUDIES RES CTR ATHENS, GA 30602 Controlled expression of neoglycans in animal cells
R29GM-45916-01 (BBCA) HANSEN, JEFFREY C UNIVERSITY OF TEXAS HLTH SCI C 7703 FLOYD CURL DRIVE SAN ANTONIO, TX 78284-7760 Chromatin structure and stability in the solution state
R15GM-45937-01 (MBC) BRUIST, MICHAEL F VASSAR COLLEGE BOX 368 POUGHKEEPSIE, NY 12601 Attachment site recognition in phage lambda integration
R15GM-45938-01 (MBC) FOWLER, ROBERT G SAN JOSE STATE UNIVERSITY ONE WASHINGTON SQUARE SAN JOSE, CA 95192 Oxygen and spontaneous mutagenesis in Escherichia coli
R15GM-45942-01 (MBC) PHILLIPS, GREGORY J COLLEGE OF WILLIAM & MARY WILLIAMSBURG, VA 23185 Genetic analysis of heat shock protein function
R01GM-45948-01 (BIO) LOHMAN, TIMOTHY M WASHINGTON UNIVERSITY 660 S EUCLID AVE ST LOUIS, MO 63110 Helicase--Catalyzed DNA unwinding
R01GM-45952-01 (PB) CLARKE, CATHERINE F UNIVERSITY OF CALIFORNIA LOS ANGELES, CA 90024 Functional roles of ubiquinone in yeast and human cells
R15GM-45959-01 (MBC) BARD, MARTIN INDIANA UNIV-PURDUE UNIVERSITY 1125 EAST 38TH STREET INDIANAPOLIS, IN 46205 Seeking the yeast sparking sterol
R15GM-45966-01 (MBC) AARONSON, LAWRENCE R UTICA COLLEGE OF SYRACUSE UNIV 1600 BURRSTONE RD UTICA, NY 13502 Sphingolipids and omeoviscous adaptation in Neurospora
R15GM-45967-01 (MBC) JOHNSTON, TIMOTHY C MURRAY STATE UNIVERSITY BLACKBURN SCIENCE BUILDING MURRAY, KY 42071 Molecular

characterization of bacterial luciferase
R55GM-45968-01 (BIO) GARCIA, GEORGE A 428 CHURCH ST ANN ARBOR, MI 48109-1065 Kinetics and mechanism of tRNA-quanine transglycolase
R13GM-45969-01 (BIO) GOLDBERG, ALFRED L HARVARD MEDICAL SCHOOL 25 SHATTUCK ST BOSTON, MA 02115 Conference--Ubiquitin and intracellular protein
R01GM-45971-01 (PB) KARLIN, KENNETH D JOHNS HOPKINS UNIVERSITY 34TH & CHARLES STREETS BALTIMORE, MD 21218 Nitrogen oxide (NOX) redox chemistry with copper ion
R01GM-45972-01 (BMT) O'HALLORAN, THOMAS V NORTHWESTERN UNIVERSITY 2145 SHERIDAN ROAD EVANSTON, IL 60208 Metal responsive gene regulation and detoxification
R15GM-45976-01 (MBC) MARTIN, KATHY A CENTRAL CONNECTICUT STATE UNIV NEW BRITAIN, CT 06050 Chromosome segregation in bacteria
R01GM-45985-01 (PHRA) IM, MIE-JAE CLEVELAND CLINIC FOUNDATION 9500 EUCLID AVE /FF3-15A CLEVELAND, OH 44195 G-protein and phospholipase C in hormone signaling
R01GM-45988-01 (BMT) CARR, PETER W UNIVERSITY OF MINNESOTA 207 PLEASANT ST SE MINNEAPOLIS, MN 55455 Base stable and composite ceramic supports for HPLC
R01GM-45989-01 (BIO) LAWRENCE, DAVID S STATE UNIVERSITY OF NEW YORK BUFFALO, NY 14214 Probes of camp-dependent protein kinase specificity
R01GM-45990-01 (BBCA) BEECHEM, JOSEPH M VANDERBILT UNIVERSITY 702 LIGHT HALL NASHVILLE, TN 37232-0615 Time-resolved fluorescence studies of protein folding
R15GM-45991-01 (MBC) NIEUWKOOP, ANTHONY J HOPE COLLEGE HOLLAND, MI 49423 Characterization of the hut genes of Rhizobium fredii
R01GM-46000-01 (PHRA) WALLE, THOMAS MEDICAL UNIV OF SOUTH CAROLINA 171 ASHLEY AVENUE CHARLESTON, SC 29425 Stereospecific sulfation of chiral drugs in humans
R15GM-46004-01 (TOX) SPALL, RICHARD D IDAHO STATE UNIVERSITY BOX 8007 POCATELLO, ID 83209 Organ culture technology for in vitro toxicology
P01GM-46006-01 (SSS) REED, STEVEN I SCRIPPS CLINIC & RES FDN 10666 NORTH TORREY PINES RD LA JOLLA, CA 92037 Cell division cycle control
P01GM-46006-01 0001 (SSS) REED, STEVEN I Cell division cycle control G1 regulatory elements
P01GM-46006-01 0002 (SSS) FOWLER, VELIA M Cell division cycle control Membrane skeleton reorganization in mitosis
P01GM-46006-01 0003 (SSS) GERACE, LARRY Cell division cycle control Analysis of mitosis-specific phosphoproteins
P01GM-46006-01 0004 (SSS) RUSSELL, PAUL R Cell division cycle control M-phase induction by cdc25
P01GM-46006-01 0005 (SSS) SULLIVAN, KEVIN F Cell division cycle control Regulation of centromere protein B in the cell cycle
P01GM-46006-01 0006 (SSS) WITTENBERG, CURT Cell division cycle control Transcriptional control of cell cycle inducers
P01GM-46006-01 9001 (SSS) REED, STEVEN I Cell division cycle control Core--PCR facility
P01GM-46006-01 9002 (SSS) REED, STEVEN I Cell division cycle control Core--Tissue culture facility
R29GM-46009-01 (MBY) CHRISTIANSON, THOMAS W SOUTHERN ILLINOIS UNIVERSITY CARBONDALE, IL 62901-6508 Transcription termination in yeast mitochondria
R15GM-46014-01 (GEN) ZIMMERER, EDMUND J MURRAY STATE UNIVERSITY MURRAY, KY 42071 Characteristics of a murine MHC hotspot of recombination
R15GM-46016-01 (GEN) ROGERS, DUKE S BRIGHAM YOUNG UNIVERSITY PROVO, UT 84602 Molecular and somatic cell mapping of deer mouse genes
R15GM-46024-01 (CTY) JACOBS, MARK SWARTHMORE COLLEGE SWARTHMORE, PA 19081 G-protein function in plant hormone transport
R15GM-46025-01 (CTY) ESSANI, KARIM WESTERN MICHIGAN UNIVERSITY KALAMAZOO, MI 49008 Transcription of methylated DNA
R15GM-46030-01 (CTY) LEVINGER, LOUIS F YORK COLLEGE OF CUNY JAMAICA, NY 11451 Proteins involved in Drosophila melanogaster 5s RNA processing
R15GM-46039-01 (CTY) MA, DIN-POW MISSISSIPPI STATE UNIVERSITY PO BOX 6156 MISSISSIPPI STATE, MI 39762 Termini of the Chlamydomonas reinhardtii mitochondrial genome
R15GM-46045-01 (MBC) POND, FINN R WHITWORTH COLLEGE SPOKANE, WA 99251 Mechanisms of toxicity on killer paramecia
R01GM-46051-01 (PBC) VAN WART, HAROLD E FLORIDA STATE UNIVERSITY TALLAHASSEE, FL 32306 Extracellular regulation of matrix metalloproteinases
R29GM-46052-01 (SB) TRANQUILLO, ROBERT T UNIVERSITY OF MINNESOTA 421 WASHINGTON AVE SE MINNEAPOLIS, MN 55455 Model in vitro assay of wound healing and contraction
R15GM-46067-01 (BBCA) GANNETT, PETER M WEST VIRGINIA UNIVERSITY MORGANTOWN, WV 26506 Base-pairing and stacking properties of 8-hydroxyguanine
R15GM-46068-01 (BNP) HARROLD, MARC W DUQUESNE UNIVERSITY PITTSBURGH, PA 15282 Substrate-based inhibitors of myo-inositol 1-phosphatase
R15GM-46075-01 (MCHA) GARNER, CHARLES M BAYLOR UNIVERSITY WACO, TX 76798 New ligands for metal mediated asymmetric synthesis
R15GM-46086-01 (MCHA) GUTIERREZ, CARLOS G CALIFORNIA STATE UNIVERSITY LOS ANGELES, CA 90032 Enterobactin derivatives--Building a better ferric trap
R15GM-46090-01 (BBCA) KARUKSTIS, KERRY K HARVEY MUDD COLLEGE 301 E TWELFTH ST CLAREMONT, CA 91711 Lanthanide binding to chloroplast thylakoid membranes
R15GM-46098-01 (BMT) FAWCETT, NEWTON C UNIVERSITY OF SOUTHERN MISSISS BOX 5043 HATTIESBURG, MS 39406-5043 A quantitative way to detect nucleic acid hybrids
R15GM-46102-01 (BBCB) FUSON, MICHAEL M DENISON UNIVERSITY GRANVILLE, OH 43023 Chain dynamics in lipid bilayers and micelles
R15GM-46107-01 (BBCB) VOLD, TERJE G SWARTHMORE COLLEGE 500 COLLEGE AVE SWARTHMORE, PA 19081-1397 Scanning tunneling microscopy of organic molecules
R13GM-46112-01 (BBCA) FOX, C FRED KEYSTONE SYMPOSIA PO BOX 606 KEYSTONE, CO 80435 Conference on protein folding and design
R01GM-46116-01 (BIO) CHENG, CHI-LIEN UNIVERSITY OF IOWA IOWA CITY, IA 52242 Transcriptional control of arabidopsis nitrate reductase
R15GM-46123-01 (BNP) FINK, MARY L BAYLOR UNIVERSTIY B.U 7348 WACO, TX 76798-7348 Transglutaminase inhibitors and solid phase substrates
R15GM-46126-01 (BCE) CHAET, ALFRED B UNIVERSITY OF WEST FLORIDA 11000 UNIVERSITY PARKWAY PENSACOLA, FL 32514 Shedhibin-inhibitor to the shedding substance hormone
R01GM-46127-01 (BIO) ROBERTS, RICHARD J COLD SPRING HARBOR LABORATORY POST OFFICE BOX 100 COLD SPRING HARBOR, NY 11724 Studies of m5-cytosine methylases
R15GM-46131-01 (GEN) RICKOLL, WAYNE L UNIVERSITY OF PUGET SOUND 1500 N WARNER TACOMA, WA 94816 Cell suface function in morphogenesis in Drosophila
R15GM-46137-01 (BMT) COX, JAMES A MIAMI UNIVERSITY DEPT OF CHEMISTRY OXFORD, OH 45056 Membrane-based preconcentrators for biomolecules
R15GM-46141-01 (MCHA) MEAD, KEITH T MISSISSIPPI STATE UNIVERSITY PO BOX 6156 MISS STATE, MS 39762 Stereocontrolled approach to pamamycin-607
R43GM-46143-01 (SSS) REED, MICHAEL W MICROPROBE CORPORATION 1725 220TH ST SE, #104 BOTHELL, WA 98021 Novel, specific nucleic acid cleavage agents
R43GM-46154-01 (SSS) ROSEMEIER, RONALD G BRIMROSE CORP OF AMERICA 5020 CAMPBELL BLVD BALTIMORE, MD 21236 Acousto-optic devices for time-resolved fluorescence
R43GM-46156-01 (SSS) SCHMITT, EDWARD E LANDEC LABS 3603 HAVEN AVE MENLO PARK, CA 94025 Thermal generation system for a novel TTS
R43GM-46160-01 (SSS) RINGNALDA, MURCO N 1250 S MARENGO #0 PASADENA, CA 91106 Pseudospectral methods for quantum biochemistry
R43GM-46161-01 (SSS) PUTNAM, DAVID L PACIFIC TECHNOLOGIES, INC 21806 NORTHEAST 1ST STREET REDMOND, WA 98053 Microbial metabolism assay system
R43GM-46163-01 (SSS) ANVIA, FREDERICK MOLECULAR SOLVOMETRICS INC PAUMA VALLEY, CA 92061 A structure activity workstation for drug design
R43GM-46164-01 (SSS) NAVIA, MANUEL A VERTEX PHARMACEUTICALS INC 40 ALLSTON STREET CAMBRIDGE, MA 02139-4211 Novel enzyme immobilization for biosensor applications
R43GM-46166-01 (GMA) ABRAHAM, JUDITH A CALIFORNIA BIOTECHNOLOGY INC 2450 BAYSHORE PARKWAY MOUNTAIN VIEW, CA 94043 Wound repair with heparin-binding EGF-like growth factor
R43GM-46169-01 (SSS) VESTAL, MARVIN L VESTEC CORPORATION 9299 KIRBY DRIVE HOUSTON, TX 77054 Automated protein sequencing by micro-LC/electrospray MS
R13GM-46188-01 (CTY) FOX, C FRED KEYSTONE CENTER PO BOX 606 KEYSTONE, CO 80435 Conference on regulation of transcription elongation & termination
R01GM-46192-01 (ARRD) WILSON, IAN A RESEARCH INST/SCRIPPS CLINIC 10666 N TORREY PINES RD/MB-13 LA JOLLA, CA 92037 X-ray structure of the HIV-1 major neutralizing epitope
R01GM-46193-01 (ARRE) STABEN, CHARLES A UNIVERSITY OF KENTUCKY 101 T H MORGAN BLDG LEXINGTON, KY 40506-0225 Genetic approach to understanding pneumocystis therapy
R43GM-46208-01 (SSS) ORTABASI, ILSE M SPARTA INC 23041 AVENIDA DE LA CARLOTA LAGUNA HILLS, CA 92653-1507 An ultra-thin diamond wire saw for histology
R29GM-46218-01 (MBY) HAI, TSONWIN THE OHIO STATE UNIVERSITY 210 RIGHTMIRE HALL COLUMBUS, OH 43210 Mechanisms of transcriptional regulation by ATF
R01GM-46220-01 (MBC) ORLEAN, PETER A UNIVERSITY OF ILLINOIS 1209 WEST CALIFORNIA STREET URBANA, IL 61801 Glycolipid anchoring and o-glycosylation in yeast
R29GM-46221-01 (MBC) WOLFE, ALAN J LOYOLA UNIVERSITY MEDICAL CTR 2160 S FIRST AVENUE MAYWOOD, IL 60153 CheAs role in regulating chemotactic signal transduction
R01GM-46224-01 (CBY) MALHOTRA, VIVEK UNIVETSITY OF CALIFORNIA, S D 9500 GILMAN DRIVE LA JOLLA, CA 92093-0322 The mechanism of golgi breakdown during mitosis
R01GM-46225-01 (CTY) ENDOW, SHARYN A DUKE UNIV MEDICAL CTR DURHAM, NC 27710 Chromosome movement in meiosis and mitosis
R29GM-46226-01 (GEN) HOFFMAN, CHARLES S BOSTON COLLEGE 140 COMMONWEALTH AVE CHESNUT HILL, MA 02167 Characterization of the S pombe cAMP signal pathway
R01GM-46227-01 (ALY) RAO, ANJANA DANA-FARBER CANCER INSTITUTE 44 BINNEY STREET BOSTON, MA 02115 Signal transduction and gene induction in T lymphocytes
R01GM-46232-01 (MBY) PECK, LAWRENCE J UNIVERSITY OF CALIFORNIA 1156 HIGH STREET SANTA CRUZ, CA 95064 Regulation of transcription by RNA polymerase III in Xenopus
R55GM-46233-01 (GEN) STEPHAN, WOLFGANG H UNIVERSITY OF MARYLAND COLLEGE PARK, MD 20742 Potential mechanisms of epistatic fitness interactions
R01GM-46237-01 (GEN) WENSINK, PIETER C BRANDEIS UNIVERSITY 415 SOUTH STREET WALTHAM, MA 02254-9110 Sex-specific regulation of transcription in Drosophila
R01GM-46255-01 (EDC) THOMPSON, ELIZABETH A UNIVERSITY OF WASHINGTON SEATTLE, WA 98185 Methods for the genetic epidemiology of complex traits
R01GM-46257-01 (BMT) BERG, JEREMY M JOHNS HOPKINS UNIVERSITY 725 NORTH WOLFE STREET BALTIMORE, MD 21205 Multi-domain metalloproteins
R55GM-46258-01 (BBCB) HICKS, JANICE M GEORGETOWN UNIVERSITY 37TH & O STREETS NW WASHINGTON, DC 20057 Nonlinear optical studies of protein-ice interaction
R13GM-46260-01 (MEDB) CORBIN, JACKIE D VANDERBILT UNIVERSITY 702 LIGHT HALL NASHVILLE, TN 37232-0615 FASEB summer research conference--Protein kinases
R29GM-46271-01 (CBY) BENDER, ALAN D INDIANA UNIVERSITY BLOOMINGTON, IN 47405 Control of bud emergence in yeast
R01GM-46272-01 (MBY) SWANSON, MAURICE S UNIVERSITY OF FLORIDA

BOX J266 JHMHC GAINESVILLE, FL 32610 Function of hnRNA binding proteins

R55GM-46277-01 (CBY) JOHNSON, ROSS G UNIVERSITY OF MINNESOTA 1445 GORTNER AVE/250 BIOSCI CT ST PAUL, MN 55108 Gap junction assembly--Mechanisms and regulations

R01GM-46278-01 (BBCB) STOOPS, JAMES K UNIVERSITY OF TEXAS HLTH SCI C PO BOX 20708 HHOUSTON, TX 77225 Structure-function studies of yeast fatty acid synthase

R55GM-46290-01 (BIO) SIH, CHARLES J UNIVERSITY OF WISCONSIN 425 N CHARTER STREET MADISON, WI 53706 Enzymatic modification of proteins and polypeptides

R01GM-46295-01 (CBY) SAXTON, WILLIAM M INDIANA UNIVERSITY BLOOMINGTON, IN 47405 Mechanisms and functions of subcellular motility

R01GM-46297-01 (GNM) WIDGER, WILLIAM R UNIVERSITY OF HOUSTON 4800 CALHOUN SR#1 RM 12 HOUSTON, TX 77004-550 The genomic organization of photosynthetic genes

R01GM-46300-01 (BMT) CORMIER, MILTON J UNIVERSITY OF GEORGIA BOYD GRADUATE STUDIES RES CENT ATHENS, GA 30602 Bioluminescent proteins as labels in diagnostic assays

R01GM-46302-01 (CBY) HALLBERG, RICHARD L SYRACUSE UNIVERSITY 130 COLLEGE PLACE SYRACUSE, NY 13244-1220 Molecular analysis of a mitochondrial assembly factor

R29GM-46309-01 (CTY) OKAMURO, JACK K UNIV OF CALIFORNIA, SANTA CRUZ SINSHEIMER LABORATORIES SANTA CRUZ, CA 95064 Molecular control of flower development in Arabidopsis

R01GM-46312-01 (BMT) TAINER, JOHN A SCRIPPS CLINIC AND RES FDN 10666 NORTH TORREY PINES ROAD LA JOLLA, CA 92037 Structure and function of metalloenzymes for DNA repair

R13GM-46322-01 (CTY) HINRICHSEN, ROBERT D FRED HUTCHINSON CANCER RES CTR 1124 COLUMBIA STREET SEATTLE, WA 98104 International meeting on ciliate molecular biology

R29GM-46324-01 (SAT) SOMERS, SCOTT D JAMES N GAMBLE INST OF MED RES 2141 AUBURN AVENUE CINCINNATI, OH 45219 Effects of thermal injury on macrophage function

R01GM-46330-01 (VR) SHUMAN, STEWART H SLOAN-KETTERING INSTITUTE DEPT OF MOLECULAR BIOLOGY NEW YORK, NY 10021 Vaccinia virus DNA topoisomerase I

R01GM-46331-01 (MBY) REINES, DANIEL EMORY UNIVERSITY SCHOOL OF MED ATLANTA, GA 30322 RNA polymerase II elongation complex

R01GM-46333-01 (BIO) REICH, NORBERT O UNIVERSITY OF CALIFORNIA SANTA BARBARA, CA 93106 Structure-function analysis of mammalian DNA methylase

R01GM-46352-01 (MBY) REEVES, RAYMOND WASHINGTON STATE UNIVERSITY PULLMAN, WA 99164-4660 A.T-specific DNA-binding properties of a human protein

R55GM-46354-01 (SAT) AYALA, ALFRED MICHIGAN STATE UNIVERSITY B-424 CLINICAL CENTER EAST LANSING, MI 48824 Differential effects of sepsis on macrophage function

R13GM-46361-01 (BIO) SARMA, RAMASWAMY H STATE UNIVERSITY OF NEW YORK 1400 WASHINGTON AVE ALBANY, NY 12222 Seventh conversation--Biomolecular stereodynamics

R01GM-46368-01 (PC) MERRILL, ALFRED H, JR EMORY UNIV SCH OF MED 4113 ROLLINS RES BUILDING ATLANTA, GA 30322 Structure/function studies of long-chain bases

R01GM-46370-01 (PHRA) NEER, EVA J BRIGHAM & WOMEN HOSPITAL 75 FRANCIS STREET BOSTON, MA 02115 Regulation of cellular levels of G protein subunits

R01GM-46376-01 (CBY) SCHOLEY, JONATHAN M UNIVERSITY OF CALIFORNIA DAVIS, CA 95616 Kinesin phosphorylation

R01GM-46383-01 (CBY) FERRELL, JAMES E UNIV OF WISCONSIN 1117 WEST JOHNSON STREET MADISON, WI 53706 The role of MAP kinase in the cell cycle

R29GM-46391-01 (IMB) DOYLE, CAROLYN F DUKE UNIVERSITY MEDICAL CENTER PO BOX 3010 DURHAM, NC 27710 Molecular characterization of the CD4 class II interaction

R29GM-46395-01 (PHRA) KRUPINSKI, JOHN WEIS CENTER FOR RESEARCH NORTH ACADEMY AVE DANVILLE, PA 17822-2610 Structural diversity in the adenylyl cyclase family

R01GM-46400-01 (EI) WILLIAMS, WILLIAM V HOSPITAL OF THE UNIVERSITY OF 3600 SPRUCE ST/570 MALONEY BLD PHILADELPHIA, PA 19104 Development of GM-CSF antogonists

R29GM-46402-01 (PBC) NORTON, PAMELA A ROGER WILLIAMS GENERAL HOSPITA 825 CHALKSTONE AVENUE PROVIDENCE, RI 02908 Fibronectin regulation and function in transgenic mice

R37GM-46406-01 (GEN) BOTSTEIN, DAVID STANFORD UNIVERSITY STANFORD , CA 94305 Genetics of functional interactions in yeast

R55GM-46408-01 (SAT) ARONSTAM, ROBERT S MEDICAL COLLEGE OF GEORGIA AUGUSTA, GA 30912-2300 Volatile anesthetics and NMDA receptors

R29GM-46409-01 (GEN) SULLIVAN, WILLIAM T UNIVERSITY OF CALIFORNIA SANTA CRUZ, CA 95064 Drosophila embryonic nuclear division mutations

R01GM-46411-01 (ALY) PETERSON, PER A RES INST OF SCRIPPS CLINIC 10666 NORTH TORREY PINES RD LA JOLLA, CA 92037 Invariant chain and antigen presentation

R55GM-46412-01 (ALY) FERRICK, DAVID A UNIVERSITY OF CALIFORNIA DAVIS, CA 95616 Characterization of self reactive gamma delta T lymphocyte

R13GM-46419-01 (BIO) PABO, CARL O JOHNS HOPKINS UNIV SCH OF MED 725 N WOLFE STREET BALTIMORE, MD 21205 1991 Gordon research conference on nucleic acids

R13GM-46420-01 (PB) RAUSHEL, FRANK M TEXAS A&M UNIVERSITY COLLEGE STATION, TX 77843 Gordon Conference--Enzymes, coenzymes and metabolism

R55GM-46422-01 (MBY) FEDOR, MARTHA J UNIV OF MASSACHUSETTS MED CENT 55 LAKE AVENUE NORTH WORCESTER, MA 01655 Optimization of intermolecular hairpin RNA catalysis

R01GM-46424-01 (BIO) CAREY, MICHAEL F UCLA SCH OF MEDICINE 10833 LE CONTE AVE LOS ANGELES, CA 90024-1737 Transcriptional activation by GAL4 derivatives

R29GM-46425-01 (GEN) MONTELL, DENISE J CARNEGIE INSTITUTE 115 WEST UNIVERSITY PARKWAY BALTIMORE, MD 21210 Molecular genetics of cell migration in Drosophila

R13GM-46427-01 (MBY) GRODZICKER, TERRI I COLD SPRING HARBOR LABORATORY P O BOX 100 COLD SPRING HARBOR, NY 11724 Ribosome synthesis conference

R13GM-46434-01 (BBCB) FRANK, JOACHIM NEW YORK STATE DEPT OF HEALTH ALBANY, NY 12201-0509 Conference--Three dimensional electron microscopy of macromolecules

R01GM-46436-01 (BMT) OHLENDORF, DOUGLAS H UNIVERSITY OF MINNESOTA 435 DELAWARE STREET, SE MINNEAPOLIS, MN 55455 Structural studies of dioxygenases

R29GM-46438-01 (CTY) BAIRD, SCOTT E UNIVERSITY OF PITTSBURGH 213 CLAPP HALL PITTSBURGH, PA 15260 Ray identity specification in Caenorhabditis elegans

R29GM-46443-01 (MBY) SCHMIDT, MARTIN C UNIVERSITY OF PITTSBURGH SCHOOL OF MEDICINE PITTSBURGH, PA 15261 DNA binding activity of recombinant TFII D proteins

R13GM-46446-01 (CBY) BUCK, CLAYTON A 3601 SPRUCE ST PHILADELPHIA, PA 19104 Gordon Conference--Cell contact and adhesion

R29GM-46451-01 (CTY) INNES, ROGER W INDIANA UNIVERSITY BLOOMINGTON, IN 47405 Genetics of disease resistance in Arabidopsis thaliana

R01GM-46453-01 (CBY) BALCZON, RONALD D UNIVERSITY OF SOUTH ALABAMA MSB 2042-COLLEGE OF MEDICINE MOBILE, AL 36688 Cloning of the cDNA encoding a centrosome autoantigen

R01GM-46454-01 (MBY) SHYU, ANN-BIN UNIV OF TX HEALTH SCIENCES DEPT OB BIOCHEM &MOLE BIOLOGY HOUSTON, TEXAS 77225 Messenger RNA decay of immediate early genes

R13GM-46458-01 (BIO) ROSS, ELLIOTT M UNIV OF TEXAS SW MEDICAL CENTE 5323 HARRY HINES BLVD DALLAS, TX 75235-9041 Gordon research conference on molecular pharmacology

R01GM-46459-01 (CTY) VISHWANATHA, JAMBOOR K UNIV OF NEBRASKA MEDICAL CENTE 600 SOUTH 42ND STREET OMAHA, NE 68198-4525 Ap4a in cell proliferation, DNA replication and repair

R55GM-46462-01 (ALY) WEBB, CAROL FRANCES OKLAHOMA MEDICAL RESEARCH FDN 825 NE 13TH ST OKLAHOMA CITY, OK 73104 B cell regulation by interleukin 5 + antigen

R29GM-46467-01 (IMB) WANECK, GERALD L MASSACHUSETTS GENERAL HOSPITAL 13TH STREET CHARLESTOWN, MA 02129 Function and trafficking of GPI-anchored MHC-1 molecules

R01GM-46470-01 (MCHA) SNIDER, BARRY B BRANDEIS UNIVERSITY WALTHAM, MA 02254-9110 Manganese (III) based oxidative free radical cyclization

R55GM-46474-01 (MBY) GARCIA-BLANCO, MARIANO A DUKE UNIVERSITY REGULATION DURHAM, NC 27710 Regulation of pre-mRNA splicing by pPTB

R13GM-46482-01 (MGN) CALAME, KATHRYN L COLUMBIA UNIVERSITY 701 WEST 168TH ST NEW YORK, N Y 10032 FASEB Conference on cellular and molecular genetics

R01GM-46486-01 (CBY) TITUS, MARGARET A DUKE UNIVERSITY MED CENTER BOX 3709 DURHAM, NC 27710 The role of actin-based motors in organelle motility

R01GM-46493-01 (MBC) MANOIL, COLIN C UNIVERSITY OF WASHINGTON SEATTLE, WA 98195 Determinants of a simple membrane protein topology

R01GM-46495-01 (MBC) DUNN, TERESA M UNIFORMED SVCS UNIV OF HLTH SC 4301 JONES BRIDGE ROAD BETHESDA, MD 20889-4799 Biochemistry and genetics of calcium regulation in yeast

R29GM-46498-01 (MBY) BURATOWSKI, STEPHEN WHITEHEAD INST FOR BIOMED RES CAMBRIDGE, MA 02142 The RNA polymerase II transcription initiation complex

R01GM-46503-01 (MCHA) DOYLE, MICHAEL P TRINITY UNIVERSITY 715 STADIUM DRIVE SAN ANTONIO, TX 78212 Chiral catalysts for enantioselective syntheses

R01GM-46506-01 (BMT) HAGEN, KARL S EMORY UNIV 1515 PIERCE DR ATLANTA, GA 30322 Synthetic models of iron sites in biological systems

R13GM-46515-01 (BNP) PETROSKI, RICHARD J NORTHERN REGIONAL RES CENTER 1815 N UNIVERSITY ST PEORIA, IL 61604 Secondary metabolite biosynthesis and metabolism

R55GM-46516-01 (BBCA) ALLISON, STUART A GEORGIA STATE UNIVERSITY ATLANTA, GA 30303 DNA flexibility probes by model physical studies

R01GM-46520-01 (PC) BECKER, JEFFREY M UNIVERSITY OF TENNESSEE KNOXVILLE, TN 37996-0845 Lipopeptide structure and function

R29GM-46524-01 (ALY) JUSTEMENT, LOUIS B UNIVERSITY OF TEXAS MEDICAL BR GALVESTON, TX 77550 Regulation of membrane immunoglobulin-mediated signal transduction

R01GM-46526-01 (ALY) HEMLER, MARTIN E DANA-FARBER CANCER INSTITUTE 44 BINNEY STREET BOSTON, MA 02115 The function and regulation of VLA molecules on T cells

R29GM-46539-01 (BMT) MORROW, JANET R STATE UNIVERSITY OF NEW YORK BUFFALO, NY 14214 Artificial RNA restriction enzymes

R55GM-46540-01 (SAT) DARLINGTON, DANIEL N UNIVERSITY OF MARYLAND 10 S PINE ST/RM 400 BALTIMORE, MD 21201 Death and shock from adrenal insufficiency

R37GM-46551-01 (CBY) SPUDICH, JAMES A STANFORD UNIVERSITY FAIRCHILD BUILDING D-141 STANFORD, CA 94305 Regulation of Dictyostelium myosin by phosphorylation

R01GM-46555-01 (BIO) STRUHL, KEVIN HARVARD MEDICAL SCHOOL 240 LONGWOOD AVENUE BOSTON, MASS 02115 Dimerization and DNA-binding specificity of bZIP proteins

R29GM-46563-01 (CPA) WINEGAR, RICHARD A SRI INTERNATIONAL 333 RAVENSWOOD AVE MENLO PARK, CA 94025 DNA double strand break induced damage and repair

R01GM-46566-01 (NEUC) STERN, MICHAEL RICE UNIVERSITY PO BOX 1892 HOUSTON, TX 77251 Genetic dissection of synaptic transmission in Drosophila

R01GM-46567-01 (GEN) JONES, RICHARD S SOUTHERN METHODIST UNIVERSITY DALLAS, TX 75275 The polycomb-group genes and gene regulation

R01GM-46569-01 (CTY) TARTAKOFF, ALAN M CASE WESTERN RESERVE UNIVERSIT 2085 ADELBERT ROAD CLEVELAND, OH 44106 mRNA export from the nucleus of Saccharomyces cerevisiae

R01GM-46570-01 (MBC) WINKLER, MALCOLM E UNIVERSITY OF TEXAS MED SCHOOL 6431 FANNIN, JFB 1.765 HOUSTON, TX 77030 Regulation of a "mutation frequency switch" in E. coli

R29GM-46572-01 (ALY) YE, RICHARD D SCRIPPS CLINIC & RESEARCH

PROJECT NO., ORGANIZATIONAL UNIT., INVESTIGATOR, ADDRESS, TITLE

FDN 10666 NORTH TORREY PINES RD LA JOLLA, CA 92037 Signal transduction through chemoattractant receptors
R13GM-46575-01 (MBC) BROACH, JAMES R PRINCETON UNIVERSITY DEPT OF MOLECULAR BIOLOGY PRINCETON, N J 08544 Gordon research conference on extrachromosomal elements
R29GM-46577-01 (BIO) KYRIAKIS, JOHN M MASSACHUSETTS GENERAL HOSP BLDG 149, 8TH FL CHARLESTOWN, MA 02129 The regulation and function of pp54 MAP-2 kinase
R43GM-46584-01 (SSS) COLANERI, NICHOLAS F UNIAX CORPORATION 5375 OVERPASS RD SANTA BARBARA, CA 93111 Conducting polymer anode wires for X-ray detectors
R43GM-46585-01 (SSS) SHORT, JAY M STRATAGENE, INC 11099 NORTH TORREY PINES RD LA JOLLA, CA 92037 Combinatorial-splicing vectors for peptide screening
R01GM-46588-01 (NEUC) EVINGER, MARIAN J SUNY HSC LEVEL 11-045 STONY BROOK, NY 11794-8111 Neural regulation of gene expression
R43GM-46592-01 (SSS) DAVIS, EDWARD M SYMBIOTECH INCORPORATED 8 FAIRFIELD BOULEVARD WALLINGFORD, CT 06492 Southern blotting following capillary electrophoresis
R43GM-46600-01 (SSS) DEMIRJIAN, DAVID C THERMOGEN, INC 2201 W CAMPBELL PARK DRIVE CHICAGO, IL 60612 Transposon based tools for thermophilic organisms
R43GM-46605-01 (SSS) NEUMEYER, JOHN L RESEARCH BIOCHEMICALS, INC 1 STRATHMORE ROAD NATICK, MA 01760 Probes of the imidazoline/guanidinium receptor
R43GM-46614-01 (SSS) MEIROVITCH, EVA BIOSYM TECHNOLOGIES, INC 10065 BARNES CANYON RD SAN DIEGO, CA 92121 Scientific testing of NMR structure determination scheme
R37GM-46622-13 (PHRA) WILKINSON, GRANT R VANDERBILT UNIVERSITY NASHVILLE, TN 37232-6602 Effects of aging process on drug responsiveness in man
R01GM-46623-01 (ARRD) LE GRICE, STUART F CASE WESTERN RESERVE UNIVERSIT 2109 ADELBERT ROAD CLEVELAND, OH 44106 Structure/function studies with HIV ribonuclease H
R01GM-46625-01 (ARRD) KOOL, ERIC T UNIVERSITY OF ROCHESTER ROCHESTER, NY 14627 Antisense binding of HIV-1 by circular oligonucleotides
R01GM-46627-14 (BIO) BARTLETT, PAUL A UNIVERSITY OF CALIFORNIA 2111 BANCROFT WAY BERKELEY, CA 94720 Phosphorus-containing transition state analogs
R01GM-46628-01 (BBCA) DILL, KEN A UNIVERSITY OF CALIFORNIA BOX 1204 SAN FRANCISCO, CA 94143 Protein stability theory
R01GM-46631-01 (ARRD) WIEMER, DAVID F UNIVERSITY OF IOWA IOWA CITY, IA 52242 Syntheses of sesquiterpenoid anti-viral agents
R01GM-46638-01 (CBY) LEVINE, MICHAEL S UNIVERSITY OF CALIFORNIA 9500 GILMAN DRIVE LA JOLLA, CA 92093-0322 Molecular characterization of the dorsal morphogen
R13GM-46640-01 (GEN) ROTHMAN-DENES, LUCIA B UNIVERSITY OF CHICAGO 920 EAST 58TH STREET CHICAGO, IL 60637 Gordon Conference on Biological Regulatory Mechanisms
R01GM-46641-13 (GNM) PASSMORE, HOWARD C RUTGERS UNIVERSITY DEPT. OF BIOLOGICAL SCIENCES PISCATAWAY, N J 08854 Recombination analysis of the mouse H-2 complex
R13GM-46652-01 (MBY) HERR, WINSHIP COLD SPRING HARBOR LABORATORY P O BOX 100 COLD SPRING HARBOR, N Y 11724 Regulation of eukaryotic mRNA transcription
R01GM-46773-22 (CBY) CAPLOW, MICHAEL UNIVERSITY OF NORTH CAROLINA BIOCHEMISTRY/BIOPHYSICS CHAPEL HILL, NC 27599-7260 Dynamic properties of the cytoskeleton
R01GM-46938-01 (BIO) LABHART, PAUL SCRIPPS CLINIC & RESEARCH FOUN 10666 NORTH TORREY PINES ROAD LA JOLLA, CA 92037 Ribosomal gene transcription in Xenopus laevis
R13GM-46944-01 (CPA) EATON, JOHN W UNIVERSITY OF MINNESOTA BOX 198 UMHC MINNEAPOLIS, MN 55455 Gordon Research Conference on oxygen radicals in biology
S15GM-47025-01 (NSS) ADAMS, DAVID S WORCESTER POLYTECHNIC INST 100 INSTITUTE ROAD WORCESTER, MA 01609 Small instrumentation grant
S15GM-47026-01 (NSS) RICH, ROBERT R BAYLOR COLLEGE OF MEDICINE ONE BAYLOR PLAZA RM S103 HOUSTON, TX 77030 Small instrumentation grant
S15GM-47027-01 (NSS) SCHOENBERG, DANIEL R UNIFORMED SERVICES UNIVERSITY 4301 JONES BRIDGE RD BETHESDA, MD 20814-4799 Small instrumentation grant
S15GM-47028-01 (NSS) JONES, GRACE M UNIVERSITY OF KENTUCKY 101 T H MORGAN BLDG LEXINGTON,KY 40506 Instrumentation for detection and separation of molecule
S15GM-47029-01 (NSS) ADELBERG, EDWARD A YALE UNIVERSITY 12 PROSPECT PLACE NEW HAVEN, CT 06511-3516 Small instrumentation grant
S15GM-47030-01 (NSS) KLIGER, DAVID S UNIVERSITY OF CALIFORNIA 1156 HIGH ST SANTA CRUZ, CA 95064 Small instrumentation grant
S15GM-47031-01 (NSS) SRIVASTAVA, D K NORTH DAKOTA STATE UNIVERSITY BIOCHEMISTRY DEPARTMENT FARGO, ND 58105 Small instrumentation grant
S15GM-47032-01 (NSS) GRAY, DONALD M UNIVERSITY OF TEXAS P O BOX 830688 M/S FO3.1 RICHARDSON, TX 75083-0688 Small instrumentation grant
S15GM-47033-01 (NSS) COOPERMAN, BARRY S UNIVERSITY OF PENNSYLVANIA 106 COLLEGE HALL PHILADELPHIA, PA 19104-6381 Small instrumentation grant
S15GM-47034-01 (NSS) TERNER, JAMES VIRGINIA COMMONWEALTH UNIV 1001 WEST MAIN STREET RICHMOND, VA 23284-2006 Small instrumentation grant
S15GM-47035-01 (NSS) STUART, W DORSEY UNIVERSITY OF HAWAII 1960 EAST WEST RD HONOLULU, HI 96822 Small instrumentation grant
S15GM-47036-01 (NSS) DIEM, MAX HUNTER COLL OF CUNY 695 PARK AVENUE NEW YORK, NY 10021 Small instrumentation grant
S15GM-47037-01 (NSS) RUTHERFORD, CHARLES L VA POLYTECHNIC INST & STATE UN 2031 DERRING HALL BLACKSBURG, VA 24061-0406 Small instrumentation grant
S15GM-47038-01 (NSS) BECK, DAVID P PUBLIC HEALTH RESEARCH INST 455 FIRST AVENUE NEW YORK, N Y 10016 Small instrumentatin grant
S15GM-47039-01 (NSS) ROBERTS, RICHARD J COLD SPRING HARBOR LABORATORY POST OFFICE BOX 100 COLD SPRING HARBOR, N Y 11724 Small instrumentation grant
S15GM-47040-01 (NSS) RICH, DANIEL H UNIV OF WISCONSIN/SCH OF PHARM 425 NORTH CHARTER STREET MADISON, WI 53706 Small instrumentation grant
S15GM-47041-01 (NSS) YOPP, JOHN H SOUTHERN ILLINOIS UNIVERSITY CARBONDALE, IL 62901 Small instrumentation program
S15GM-47042-01 (NSS) HILLMAN, RALPH TEMPLE UNIVERSITY PHILADELPHIA, PA 19122 Small instrumentation grant
S15GM-47043-01 (NSS) ARGON, JUDITH K DUKE UNIVERSITY 01 ALLEN BLDG DURHAM, NC 27706 Small instrumentation grant
S15GM-47044-01 (NSS) JENSEN, JAMES L CALIFORNIA STATE UNIVERSITY LONG BEACH, CA 90840-3903 Small instrumentation grant
S15GM-47045-01 (NSS) RUDCZYNSKI, ANDREW B RUTGERS UNIVERSITY ADMIN BLDG RM 123, BOX 1089 PISCATAWAY, NJ 08855-1089 Small instrumentation grant
S15GM-47046-01 (NSS) MICHELS, CORINNE A QUEENS COLLEGE OF CUNY 65-30 KISSENA BOULEVARD FLUSHING, N Y 11367 Small instrumentation grant
S15GM-47047-01 (NSS) STRAND, FLEUR 100 WASHINGTON SQUARE EAST NEW YORK, NY 10003 Small instrumentation grant
S15GM-47048-01 (NSS) ABELE, LAWRENCE G FLORIDA STATE UNIVERSITY 212 CONRADI BLDG B-142 TALLAHASSEE, FL 32306 Small instrumentation grant
S15GM-47049-01 (NSS) BOND, LYNNE A UNIVERSITY OF VERMONT BURLINGTON, VT 05405 Small instrumentation grant
S15GM-47050-01 (NSS) PERKINS, JOHN P UT SOUTHWESTERN MED CTR 5323 HARRY HINES BLVD DALLAS, TX 75235-9004 Small instrumentation grant
S15GM-47051-01 (NSS) BUCHANAN, CHRISTINE E SOUTHERN METHODIST UNIVERSITY DALLAS, TX 75275 Small instrumentation grant
S15GM-47052-01 (NSS) EYLAR, EDWARD H PONCE SCHOOL OF MEDICINE UNIVERISTY ST, PO BOX 7004 PONCE, PUERTO RICO 00732-7004 Small instrumentation grant
S15GM-47053-01 (NSS) WAYNER, MATTHEW J UNIVERSITY OF TEXAS SAN ANTONIO, TX 78285 Small instrumentation grant
S15GM-47054-01 (NSS) PAPLAUSKAS, LEONARD P UNIV OF CONNECTICUT HLTH CTR 263 FARMINGTON AVE FARMINGTON, CT 06030-9984 Small instrumentation grant
S15GM-47055-01 (NSS) WURSTER, DALE E UNIVERSITY OF IOWA IOWA CITY, IA 52242 Small instrumentation grant
S15GM-47056-01 (NSS) YASBIN, RONALD E UNIV OF MARYLAND BALTIMORE, MD 21228 Small instrumentation grant
S15GM-47057-01 (NSS) FELDBUSH, THOMAS L NORTHWESTERN UNIVERSITY 303 E CHICAGO AVE CHICAGO, IL 60611-3008 Small instrumentation grant
S15GM-47058-01 (NSS) JARON, DOV DREXEL UNIVERSITY 32ND & CHESTNUT STREETS PHILADELPHIA, PA 19104 Small instrumentation grant
S15GM-47059-01 (NSS) MICHAELIS, ELIAS K UNIVERSITY OF KANSAS MALOTT HALL LAWRENCE, KS 66045 Small instrumentation grant
S15GM-47060-01 (NSS) PURPURA, DOMINICK P ALBERT EINSTEIN COLL OF MED 1300 MORRIS PARK AVENUE BRONX, N Y 10461 Small instrumentation grant
S15GM-47061-01 (NSS) BARKLEY, MARY D LOUISIANA STATE UNIVERSITY BATON ROUGE, LA 70803 Small instrumentation grant
S15GM-47062-01 (NSS) DE FRIES, JOHN C UNIVERSITY OF COLORADO CAMPUS BOX 447 BOULDER, CO 80309 Small instrumentation grant
S15GM-47063-01 (NSS) THOMPSON, BRIAN J UNIVERSITY OF ROCHESTER 200 ADMINISTRATION BUILDING ROCHESTER, NY 14627 Small instrumentation grant
S15GM-47064-01 (NSS) STEVENS, ANN R 1462 CLIFTON RD ATLANTA, GA 30322 Small instrumentation grant
S15GM-47065-01 (NSS) JONES, CLINTON J UNIVERSITY OF NEBRASKA-LINCOLN LINCOLN, NB 68583-0905 Small instrumentation grant
S15GM-47066-01 (NSS) NEVILLE, JAMES A UNIVERSITY OF ALABAMA PO BOX 870326 TUSCALOOSA, AL 35487 Small instrumentation grant
S15GM-47067-01 (NSS) CULLIS, CHRISTOPHER CASE WESTERN RESERVE UNIVERSIT 7080 CRAWFORD HALL CLEVELAND, OH 44106-2699 Small intrumentation grant
S15GM-47068-01 (NSS) FORMICOLA, ALLAN J COLUMBIA UNIVERSITY 630 WEST 168 STREET NEW YORK, N Y 10032 Small instrumentation program
S15GM-47069-01 (NSS) VIJAY, INDER K UNIVERSITY OF MARYLAND ANIMAL SCIENCES BUILDING COLLEGE PARK, MD 20742 Small instrumentation grant
S15GM-47070-01 (NSS) KNOWLES, JEREMY R HARVARD UNIVERSITY UNIVERSITY HALL 5 CAMBRIDGE, MA 02138 Small instrumentation grant
S15GM-47071-01 (NSS) LOWE, JACK W CORNELL UNIVERSITY ITHACA, NY 14853 Small instrumentation grant
S15GM-47072-01 (NSS) SCHAFER, ROLLIE R UNIVERSITY OF NORTH TEXAS PO BOX 5396 UNT STATION DENTON, TX 76203-5396 Small instrumentation grant
S15GM-47073-01 (NSS) BAUN, MARA M UNIVERSITY OF NEBRASKA 600 S 42ND ST OMAHA, NE 68198-5330 Small instrumentation grant
S15GM-47074-01 (NSS) IRIARTE, ANA J UNIVERSITY OF MISSOURI 5100 ROCKHILL RD KANSAS CITY, MO 64110-2499 Small instrumentation grant
S15GM-47075-01 (NSS) BENJAMIN, STEPHEN A COLORADO STATE UNIVERSITY 208 ADMINISTRATION ANNEX FT COLLINS, CO 80523 Small instrumentation grant
S15GM-47076-01 (NSS) GOLDBERG, ALAN M JOHNS HOPKINS UNIVERSITY 615 NORTH WOLFE STREET BALTIMORE, MD 21205 Small instrumentation grant
S15GM-47077-01 (NSS) MEISEL, MARTIN COLUMBIA UNIVERSITY 209 LOW LIBRARY NEW YORK, NY 10027 Small instrumentation program
S15GM-47078-01 (NSS) PEDERSON, THORU WORCESTER FDN/EXPERIMENTAL BIO 222 MAPLE AVENUE SHREWSBURY, MA 01545 Small instrumentation grant
S15GM-47079-01 (NSS) FUNK, MAX O UNIVERSITY OF TOLEDO 2801 W BANCROFT STREET TOLEDO, OH 43606 Small instrumentation program
S15GM-47080-01 (NSS) KONISKY, JORDAN UNIVERSITY OF ILLINOIS 505 S GOODWIN/393 MORRILL HALL URBANA, IL 61801 Small instrumentation grant
S15GM-47081-01 (NSS) KOUDELKA, GERALD B ST UNIV OF NEW YORK AT BUFFALO 607 COOKE HALL BUFFALO, NY 14260 Small instrumentation grant
S15GM-47082-01 (NSS) TROWBRIDGE, IAN S SALK INSTITUTE PO BOX 85800 SAN DIEGO, CA 92186-5800 Small instrumentation grant
S15GM-47083-01 (NSS) ALLEN, MARY M WELLESLEY COLLEGE WELLESLEY,

MA 02181 Small instrumentation grant
S15GM-47084-01 (NSS) SCHWARTZ, JANICE B UNIVERSITY OF CALIFORNIA 513 PARNASSUS AVE BOX 0446 SAN FRANCISCO, CA 94143 Small instrumentation grant
S15GM-47085-01 (NSS) WOJCHOWSKI, DON M PENNSYLVANIA STATE UNIVERSITY 408 S. FREAR LABORATORY UNIVERSITY PARK, PA 16802 Small instrumentation grant
S15GM-47086-01 (NSS) NEWELL, JONATHAN C RENSSELAER POLYTECHNIC INST 110 EIGHTH STREET TROY, NY 12180 Small instrumentation grant
S15GM-47087-01 (NSS) BROWN, DONALD D CARNEGIE INST OF WASHINGTON 1530 P ST NW WASHINGTON, DC 20005 Small instrumentation grant
S15GM-47088-01 (NSS) WEIR, MICHAEL WESLEYAN UNIVERSITY MIDDLETOWN, CT 06459-6032 Small instrumentation grant
S15GM-47089-01 (NSS) BURRIS, JAMES F GEORGETOWN UNIVERSITY 3900 RESERVOIR RD NW WASHINGTON, DC 20007 Small instrumentation grant
S15GM-47090-01 (NSS) COHEN, JOEL M BRANDEIS UNIVERSITY PO BOX 9110 WALTHAM, MA 02254-9110 Small instrument grant
S15GM-47091-01 (NSS) LU, RENNE C BOSTON BIOMEDICAL RESEARCH INS 20 STANIFORD STREET BOSTON, MA 02114 Small instrumentation program
S15GM-47092-01 (NSS) MORSE, DOUGLASS H BROWN UNIVERSITY BOX G-A101 PROVIDENCE, RI 02912 Small instrumentation grant
S15GM-47093-01 (NSS) ROBINSON, NORMAN E MICHIGAN STATE UNIVERSITY G-321 VETERINARY CLINICAL CENT EAST LANSING, MI 48824-1314 Small instrumentation grant
S15GM-47094-01 (NSS) LAUMANN, EDWARD O 1126 E 59TH STREET CHICAGO, IL 60637 Small instrumentation grant
S15GM-47095-01 (NSS) KRESHECK, GORDON C NORTHERN ILLINOIS UNIVERSITY DEKALB, ILL 60115 Small instrumentation grant
S15GM-47096-01 (NSS) SWAN, PATRICIA B IOWA STATE UNIVERSITY 211 BEARDSHEAR HALL AMES, IA 50011 Small instrumentation grant
S15GM-47097-01 (NSS) WELT, CAROL UNIVERSITY OF MEDICINE DENTIST 185 SOUTH ORANGE AVENUE NEWARK, NJ 07103-2714 Small instrumentation grant
S15GM-47098-01 (NSS) MORRISON, JAMES D THE UNIVERSITY OF IOWA 201 GILMORE HALL IOWA CITY, IA 52242 Small instrumentation grant
S15GM-47099-01 (NSS) BEER, MICHAEL THE JOHNS HOPKINS UNIVERSITY 3400 NORTH CHARLES STREET BALTIMORE, MD 21218 Small instrumentation grant
S15GM-47100-01 (NSS) ACKERMAN, JOSEPH J WASHINGTON UNIVERSITY ONE BROOKINGS DR/CAMPUS BOX 11 ST LOUIS, MO 63130-4899 Small instrumentation grant
S15GM-47102-01 (NSS) KEANE, WILLIAM F 825 SOUTH EIGHTH ST MINNEAPOLIS, MN 55404 Small instrumentation grant
S15GM-47103-01 (NSS) ROBERTS, MARY F BOSTON COLLEGE 140 COMMONWEALTH AVENUE CHESTNUT HILL, MA 02167 Small instrumentation grant
S15GM-47104-01 (NSS) JOHNSON, ARTHUR E UNIVERSITY OF OKLAHOMA NORMAN, OK 73019 Small instrumentation grant
R01GM-47111-09 (MBC) MAURER, RUSSELL A CASE WESTERN RESERVE UNIV 2109 ADELBERT RD CLEVELAND, OH 44106 Genetics of DNA replication in bacteria
R01GM-47112-19 (MBC) SWITZER, ROBERT L UNIVERSITY OF ILLINOIS 1209 WEST CALIFORNIA URBANA, IL 61801 Novel control mechanisms in endospore formation
S15GM-47114-01 (NSS) MARTIN, JOSEPH B UNIVERSITY OF CALIFORNIA 513 PARNASSUS AVE SAN FRANCISCO, CA 94143-0410 Small instrumentation grant
S15GM-47115-01 (NSS) GROOTHUIS, DENNIS R 2650 RIDGE AVENUE EVANSTON, IL 60201 Small instrumentation grant
R01GM-47124-01 (TOX) BRANCH, ROBERT A UNIV OF PITTSBURGH MEDICAL CTR 623 SCAIFE HALL PITTSBURGH, PA 15261 Mechanisms of amphotericin B nephrotoxicity
R01GM-47145-01 (SAT) LEVITT, ROY C JOHNS HOPKINS UNIVERSITY 600 NORTH WOLFE STREET BALTIMORE, MD 21205 Malignant hyperthermia susceptibility -- Molecular studies
R01GM-47156-12 (MBC) BENDER, ROBERT A UNIVERSITY OF MICHIGAN ANN ARBOR, MI 48109-1048 Regulation of microbial nitrogen metabolism
R01GM-47157-01 (PBC) TAKADA, YOSHIKAZU SCRIPPS CLINIC & RESEARCH FDN 10666 N TORREY PINES ROAD LA JOLLA, CA 92037 Function of lymphocyte B1 integrins
R43GM-47164-01 (SB) JOHNSON, DONALD G METAL SAMPLES COMPANY PO BOX 8 MUNFORD, AL 36268 Aseptic precisely cut macro/micro slices of live tissues
S06GM-47165-01 (MPRC) ATTIYEH, RICHARD UNIV OF CALIFORNIA SAN DIEGO 9500 GILMAN DRIVE LA JOLLA, CA 92093-0003 University of California San Diego MBRS program
S06GM-47165-01 0004 (MPRC) MCMORRIS, TREVOR C University of California San Diego MBRS program Chemistry of some natural products
S06GM-47165-01 0014 (MPRC) MIYAI, KATSUMI University of California San Diego MBRS program Pathology of cholestasis and hepatic injury
S06GM-47165-01 0017 (MPRC) GAGE, FRED H University of California San Diego MBRS program Embryonic nerve cell transplantation in aged rats
S06GM-47165-01 0021 (MPRC) CHOJKIER, MARIO University of California San Diego MBRS program Hepatic connective tissue protein production in vivo
S06GM-47165-01 0003 (MPRC) FORTES, P A GEORGE University of California San Diego MBRS program Cardiac glycoside receptor structure and conformational dynamics
S06GM-47165-01 0022 (MPRC) ELLISMAN, MARK H University of California San Diego MBRS program Cytoskeletal and endomembrane organization in Alzheimer's disease
S06GM-47165-01 0023 (MPRC) GROVES, PHILIP M University of California San Diego MBRS program Monoaminergic axons and synapses in the neostriatum
S06GM-47165-01 0024 (MPRC) HARVEY, DANIEL F University of California San Diego MBRS program Synthesis and study of tumor promoters and inhibitors
S06GM-47165-01 0025 (MPRC) KELNER, MICHAEL J University of California San Diego MBRS program Construction of catalase expression vectors and cloning of cysteine-beta-lyase
S06GM-47165-01 0026 (MPRC) MATHIEU-COSTELLO, ODILE A University of California San Diego MBRS program Structure-function correlations in peripheral tissue
S06GM-47165-01 0027 (MPRC) MILLER, JEFFERY O University of California San Diego MBRS program Discrete versus continuous models of visual perception
S06GM-47165-01 0028 (MPRC) O'CONNOR, JOSEPH M University of California San Diego MBRS program New methods for preparation of biologically active cyclopentanoids
S06GM-47165-01 0029 (MPRC) SIMON, JOHN D University of California San Diego MBRS program Picosecond circular dichroism studies of protein motion
S06GM-47165-01 0030 (MPRC) TROGLER, WILLIAM C University of California San Diego MBRS program Catalysts for hydrolysis of phosphate diesters and DNA
R13GM-47169-01 (PB) COLEMAN, JOSEPH E YALE UNIVERSITY 333 CEDAR ST, BOX 3333 NEW HAVEN, CT 06510 1992 Gordon Research Conference on metals in biology
R01GM-47176-01 (GEN) KURJAN, JANET A UNIVERSITY OF VERMONT GIVIN BUILDING BURLINGTON, VT 05405 Molecular genetics of yeast sexual agglutinins
R01GM-47214-01 (CBY) SCHWARTZ, MARTIN A SCRIPPS CLINIC & RES FOUNDATIO 10666 NORTH TORREY PINES ROAD LA JOLLA, CA 92037-1093 Cell growth and transmembrane signaling by an integrin
R43GM-47226-01 (SSS) MICHAELS, DAN F CEARA CENTERS, INC 1777 SOUTH HARRISON STREET DENVER, CO 80210 Archival and compression of EEG records
R01GM-47227-04 (MCHA) HELQUIST, PAUL UNIVERSITY OF NOTRE DAME NOTRE DAME, IN 46556 Synthesis and activity of streptogramins A and analogues
R01GM-47228-04 (ARRD) JUNG, MICHAEL E UNIVERSITY OF CALIFORNIA LOS ANGELES, CA 90024-1569 Synthesis of potentially antiviral modified nucleosides
R01GM-47399-12 (BIO) EVANS, DAVID R WAYNE STATE UNIV MED SCH 540 EAST CANFIELD DETROIT, MI 48201 Control of pyrimidine biosynthesis in mammalian cells
R29GM-47466-01 (PHRA) JAISWAL, ANIL K FOX CHASE CANCER CENTER 7701 BURHOLME AVENUE PHILADELPHIA, PA 19111 Regulation of NAD(P)H-quinone oxidoreductases
R01GM-47493-01 (MBC) HANNA, MICHELLE M THE UNIV OF OKLAHOMA 770 VAN VLEET OVAL NORMAN, OK 73019 Mechanisms of transcription elongation and termination
R29GM-47607-01 (CBY) TURNER, CHRISTOPHER E SUNY HEALTH SCI CTR, AT SYRACU 750 EAST ADAMS ST SYRACUSE, NY 13210 Structure and function of paxillin
R01GM-47615-01 (PB) PORTER, TODD D UNIVERSITY OF KENTUCKY ROSE STREET LEXINGTON, KY 40536-0082 Heterologous expression of cytochrome P-450
R01GM-47638-01 (BM) TAI, PHANG C GEORGIA STATE UNIVERSITY UNIVERSITY PLAZA ATLANTA, GA 30303 Protein export by an accessory protein-specified pathway
R01GM-47680-01 (BIO) DAVIS, RONALD L COLD SPRING HARBOR LABORATORY PO BOX 100 COLD SPRING HARBOR, NY 11724 Structure and function of nucleotide phosphodiesterases
R01GM-47735-01 (SSS) KRASNOW, MARK A STANFORD UNIVERSITY B400 BECKMAN CENTER STANFORD, CA 94305-5307 Cellular communication in morphogenesis
R01GM-47795-17 (MBC) HENDRIX, ROGER W UNIVERSITY OF PITTSBURGH PITTSBURGH, PA 15260 Assembly and structure of bacteriophage lambda
N01GM-72110-20 (**) KELLY, MICHAEL J Nucleic acid sequence data bank
N01GM-92102-09 (**) MULIVOR, RICHARD A Human genetic mutant cell repository
N01HB-07085-01 (**) DOSIK, HARVEY Cooperative study of sickle cell disease--Clinical center
N01HB-07086-02 (**) MANCI, ELIZABETH A. Centralized pathology unit for sickle cell disease
N01HB-17087-02 (**) STERN, SUSAN Maintenance of a blood specimen repository
N01HB-17088-00 (**) KASULE, OMAR M. Screening and treatment of sickle cell disease
N01HB-17089-00 (**) SHAW, DOUGLAS National marrow donor program
N01HB-67020-11 (**) VYAS, GIRISH N Screening tests for HTLV-III antigens, antibodies, or nucleic acids
N01HB-73005-21 (**) STEINBERG, MARTIN H Cooperative study of the clinical course of sickle cell disease
N01HB-77029-07 (**) GOODWIN, WILLIAM J. Maintenance of chimpanzees for hepatitis/AIDS research
N01HB-77030-08 (**) VICHINSKY, ELLIOTT Prophylactic penicillin in sickle cell disease
N01HB-77031-09 (**) SCHWARTZ, ALAN L. Prophylactic penicillin in sickle cell disease
N01HB-77032-08 (**) BUCHANAN, GEORGE Prophylactic penicillin in sickle cell disease
N01HB-77033-07 (**) HOLBROOK, C TATE Prophylactic penicillin in sickle cell disease
N01HB-77034-07 (**) BECTON, DAVID Prophylactic penicillin in sickle cell disease
N01HB-77035-07 (**) MILLER, SCOTT Prophylactic penicillin in sickle cell disease
N01HB-77036-07 (**) KINNEY, THOMAS R Prophylactic penicillin in sickle cell disease
N01HB-77037-09 (**) WANG, WINFRED Prophylactic penicillin in sickle cell disease
N01HB-77038-07 (**) BRAY, GORDON L Prophylactic penicillin in sickle cell disease
N01HB-77039-07 (**) PEGELOW, CHARLES H Prophylactic penicillin in sickle cell disease
N01HB-77040-07 (**) GROSSMAN, NEIL J Prophylactic penicillin in sickle cell disease
N01HB-77042-06 (**) WETHERS, DORIS L Prophylactic penicillin in sickle cell disease
N01HB-77043-07 (**) IYER, RATHYI V Prophylactic penicillin in sickle cell disease

PROJECT NO., ORGANIZATIONAL UNIT., INVESTIGATOR, ADDRESS, TITLE

N01HB-77044-07 (**) WOODS, GERALD M Prophylactic penicillin in sickle cell disease
N01HB-77045-06 (**) KALINYAK, KAREN Prophylactic penicillin in sickle cell disease
N01HB-87046-08 (**) THOMAS, MARILYN Management center for prophylactic penicillin in sickle cell diseases
N01HB-87047-04 (**) SEEFF, LEONARD Natural history of posttransfusion non-A, non B hepatitis
N01HB-87049-05 (**) MAURER, HELEN Prophylactic penicillin in sickle cell disease
N01HB-87050-06 (**) BJORNSON, ANN B Prophylactic penicillin study
N01HB-97051-03 (**) CLASTER, SUSAN Cooperative study of sickle cell disease
N01HB-97053-05 (**) SUBRAMANIAN, UMA Cooperative study of sickle cell diseases
N01HB-97054-04 (**) VICHINSKY, ELLIOTT Cooperative study of sickle cell disease
N01HB-97055-03 (**) BRAY, GORDON L Cooperative study of sickle cell disease
N01HB-97056-03 (**) OHENE-FREMPONG, KWAKU Cooperative study of sickle cell disease
N01HB-97058-03 (**) KHAKOO, YUSUF Cooperative study of sickle cell disease
N01HB-97059-03 (**) ROSSE, WENDELL Cooperative study of sickle cell disease
N01HB-97060-04 (**) MILNER, PAUL F. Cooperative study of sickle cell disease
N01HB-97061-03 (**) SCOTT, ROLAND B. Cooperative study of sickle cell disease
N01HB-97062-03 (**) KOSHY, MABEL Cooperative study of sickle cell disease
N01HB-97066-04 (**) WANG, WINFRED Cooperative study of sickle cell disease
N01HB-97067-03 (**) WETHERS, DORIS Cooperative study of sickle cell disease
N01HB-97068-03 (**) GILLETTE, PETER N Cooperative study of sickle cell disease
N01HB-97069-03 (**) MILLER, SCOTT Cooperative study of sickle cell disease
N01HB-97070-04 (**) MAUER, ALVIN M Cooperative study of sickle cell disease
N01HB-97071-04 (**) SCHWARTZ, ALAN L. Cooperative study of sickle cell disease
N01HB-97072-04 (**) PEARSON, HOWARD A Cooperative study of sickle cell disease
N01HB-97073-08 (**) MCKINLAY, SONJA M Statistical service center for cooperative study of sickle cell disease
N01HB-97074-09 (**) MOSLEY, JAMES W. The transfusion safety study
N01HB-97075-11 (**) CONFER, DENNIS National marrow donor program
N01HB-97077-03 (**) MURPHY, EDWARD Blood centers for epidemiological studies of human retroviruses in blood donors
N01HB-97078-03 (**) GILCHER, RONALD Blood centers for epidemiologic studies of human retroviruses among blood donors
N01HB-97079-04 (**) WILLIAMS, ALAN E Blood ctrs, epidem studies, human retroviruses, vol donors
N01HB-97080-04 (**) KLEINMAN, STEVEN Blood ctr for epidemiology study of human retrovirus in vol blood donors
N01HB-97081-04 (**) SHAFER, A W Blood centers for epidemiological study of human retrovirus blood donors
N01HB-97082-03 (**) SCHREIBER, GEORGE Epidemiologic studies of retroviruses in blood donors
N01HC-05102-07 (**) CURB, J. DAVID Honolulu heart program
N01HC-15103-00 (**) BRYAN, NICK R MRI reading center for the cardiovascular health study
N01HC-38038-19 (**) WOLF, PHILIP A. Physical examination/testing the Framingham offspring
N01HC-48051-10 (**) GYARFAS, IVAN Monica project coordinating center
N01HC-48052-18 (**) HAWKINS, C MORTON Systolic hypertension in the elderly
N01HC-48053-11 (**) ALLMAN, RICHARD M. Systolic hypertension in the elderly
N01HC-48054-16 (**) BORHANI, NEMAT O. Systolic hypertension in the elderly program
N01HC-48055-11 (**) BLAUFOX, MORTON D Systolic hypertension in the elderly
N01HC-48056-12 (**) HALL, W DALLAS Systolic hypertension in the elderly
N01HC-48057-12 (**) VOGT, THOMAS M. Systolic hypertension in the elderly
N01HC-48058-13 (**) GUTHRIE, GORDON JR. Systolic hypertension in the elderly
N01HC-48059-08 (**) PRICE, THOMAS R. Systolic hypertension in the elderly program
N01HC-48060-12 (**) SMITH, W MCFATE systolic hypertension in the elderly program
N01HC-48061-12 (**) WALBURN, FRED Systolic hypertension in the elderly
N01HC-48062-10 (**) GRIMM, RICHARD H JR Systolic hypertension in the elderly
N01HC-48063-11 (**) BERKSON, DAVID M Systolic hypertension in the elderly
N01HC-48064-11 (**) PETROVITCH, HELEN Systolic hypertension in the elderly
N01HC-48065-10 (**) KULLER, LEWIS H. Systolic hypertension in the elderly
N01HC-48066-11 (**) KOSTIS, JOHN B. Systolic hypertension in the elderly
N01HC-48067-11 (**) APPLEGATE, WILLIAM B. Systolic hypertension in the elderly

PROJECT NO., ORGANIZATIONAL UNIT., INVESTIGATOR, ADDRESS, TITLE

N01HC-48068-13 (**) PERRY, MITCHELL H JR Systolic hypertension in the elderly
N01HC-48069-11 (**) BLACK, HENRY R. Systolic hypertension in the elderly
N01HC-55000-16 (**) DAVIS, CLARENCE E Studies of left ventricular dysfunction
N01HC-55001-13 (**) ROGERS, WILLIAM J. Studies of left ventricular dysfunction
N01HC-55002-10 (**) LEJEMTEL, THIERRY H. Studies of left ventricular dysfunction
N01HC-55004-13 (**) YOUNG, JAMES B Studies of left ventricular dysfunction
N01HC-55005-11 (**) JOHNSTONE, DAVID E. Studies of left ventricular dysfunction
N01HC-55006-07 (**) BROZENA, SUSAN Studies of left ventricular dysfunction
N01HC-55007-11 (**) RICH, STUART Studies of left ventricular dysfunction
N01HC-55008-10 (**) WILLIS, PARK W Studies of left ventricular dysfunction
N01HC-55009-09 (**) COHN, JAY N Studies of left ventricular dysfunction
N01HC-55010-09 (**) SALEM, DEEB Studies of left ventricular dysfunction
N01HC-55011-11 (**) GREENBERG, BARRY H Studies of left ventricular dysfunction
N01HC-55012-11 (**) KOHN, ROBERT Studies of left ventricular dysfunction
N01HC-55013-10 (**) CAPONE, ROBERT J Studies of left ventricular dysfunction
N01HC-55014-10 (**) HOOD, WILLIAM B JR Studies of left ventricular dysfunction
N01HC-55015-14 (**) WILLIAMS, DALE O Community and cohort surveillance program
N01HC-55016-10 (**) PATSCH, WOLFGANG P Community and cohort surveillance program
N01HC-55018-11 (**) HEISS, GERARDO CCSP - field center and ultrasound reading center
N01HC-55019-10 (**) FOLSOM, AARON R. Community and cohort surveillance program field center
N01HC-55020-11 (**) SZKLO, MOYSES cCSP - field center
N01HC-55021-13 (**) HUTCHINSON, RICHARD G. CCSP - field center
N01HC-55022-13 (**) WU, KENNETH K Community and cohort surveillance program--Hemostatasis laboratory
N01HC-55023-19 (**) BARTON, BRUCE A Development of obesity in young black and white females
N01HC-55024-10 (**) SABRY, Z I Development of obesity in young black and white females
N01HC-55026-09 (**) SCHREIBER, GEORGE B Development of obesity in young black and white females
N01HC-65030-10 (**) POULEUR, HUBERT Studies of left ventricular dysfunction
N01HC-65031-09 (**) PEPINE, CARL J Studies of left ventricular dysfunction-clinical center
N01HC-65032-07 (**) KOSTIS, JOHN B Studies of left ventricular dysfunction-clinical center
N01HC-65033-10 (**) NICHOLAS, JOHN M. Studies of left ventricular dysfunction- clinical center
N01HC-65034-08 (**) BOURASSA, MARTIAL G Studies of left ventricular dysfunction--Clinical center
N01HC-65035-09 (**) HERMAN, MICHAEL V Studies of left ventricular dysfunction--Clinical center
N01HC-65037-10 (**) FRIESINGER, GOTTLIEB Studies of left ventricular dysfunction--Clinical center
N01HC-65038-08 (**) STEWART, DOUGLAS K Studies of left ventricular dysfunction--Clinical center
N01HC-65045-07 (**) HECHT, SUSAN Cardiac arrhythmia treatment study -
N01HC-65046-10 (**) WYSE, D GEORGE Cardiac arrhythmia treatment study
N01HC-65047-08 (**) WALDO, ALBERT L Cardiac arrhythmia treatment study
N01HC-65049-14 (**) SCHLANT, ROBERT C. Cardiac arrhythmia treatment study
N01HC-65052-09 (**) GOLDSTEIN, SIDNEY Cardiac arrhythmia treatment study
N01HC-65053-13 (**) PETERS, ROBERT W Cardiac arrhythmia treatment study
N01HC-65055-10 (**) RICHARDSON, DAVID Cardiac arrhythmia treatment study
N01HC-65056-08 (**) HODGES, MORRISON Cardiac arrhythmia treatment study
N01HC-65057-11 (**) ROY, DENIS Cardiac arrhythmia treatment study
N01HC-65059-15 (**) BEANLANDS, DONALD S Cardiac arrhythmia treatment study
N01HC-65060-08 (**) CAPONE, ROBERT J. Cardiac arrhythmia treatment study
N01HC-65061-07 (**) AKIYAMA, TOSHIO . Cardiac arrhythmia treatment study
N01HC-65062-09 (**) SCHOENBERGER, JAMES A Cardiac arrhythmia treatment study
N01HC-65063-15 (**) BARKER, ALLAN H Cardiac arrhythmia treatment study
N01HC-65064-11 (**) COHEN, JEROME Cardiac arrhythmia treatment study
N01HC-65065-09 (**) RODEN, DAN M Cardiac arrhythmia treatment study
N01HC-65066-11 (**) PLATIA, EDWARD V. Cardiac arrhythmia treatment study
N01HC-65067-09 (**) EL-SHERIF, NABIL E Cardiac arrhythmia treatment study

PROJECT NO., ORGANIZATIONAL UNIT., INVESTIGATOR, ADDRESS, TITLE

N01HC-65068-10 (**) KATZ, RICHARD J Cardiac arrhythmia treatment study
N01HC-65069-12 (**) DEMARIA, ANTHONY N Cardiac arrhythmia treatment study
N01HC-75071-06 (**) HERD, J ALAN Host CABG (coronary artery bypass graft) study
N01HC-75072-06 (**) GRAY, RICHARD J Post CABG (coronary artery bypass graft) study
N01HC-75073-07 (**) HOOGWERF, BYRON J. Post CABG (coronary artery bypass graft) study
N01HC-75074-07 (**) HUNNINGHAKE, DONALD B. Post cabg coronary artery bypass graft study
N01HC-75075-08 (**) CAMPEAU, LUCIEN Post coronary artery bypass graft study
N01HC-75076-13 (**) KNATTERUD, GENELL L Post coronary artery bypass graft study
N01HC-85079-10 (**) KRONMAL, RICHARD Coronary heart disease and stroke in the aged
N01HC-85080-08 (**) FURBERG, CURT D Coronary heart disorder and stroke in the aged
N01HC-85081-06 (**) FRIED, LINDA P Coronary heart disease and stroke in the aged
N01HC-85082-09 (**) KULLER, LEWIS H Coronary heart disease and stroke in the aged
N01HC-85083-09 (**) JOHN, ROBBINS Coronary heart disease and stroke in the aged
N01HC-95095-10 (**) PERKINS, LAURA Coronary artery disease risk development in young adults
N01HC-95100-02 (**) GARDIN, JULIUS M CARDIA--Echocardiography reading center
Z01HD-00035-19 (ERRB) CHEN, H C NICHD, NIH The structure and function of biologically active molecules
Z01HD-00040-16 (LTPB) MUNSON, P J NICHD, NIH Statistical and mathematical studies of molecular interactions
Z01HD-00047-22 (LDN) BRENNEMAN, D E NICHD, NIH Biochemical studies of neurons and other cell types
Z01HD-00054-17 (LCE) BIBEN, M NICHD, NIH Structural behavioral analysis of vocal communication in squirrel monkeys
Z01HD-00056-16 (LDN) LOH, Y P NICHD, NIH Biosynthesis, processing & secretion of neuropeptides & pituitary peptide hormone
Z01HD-00064-15 (LDN) NELSON, P G NICHD, NIH Neurobiologic studies of neurons and glia in cell culture
Z01HD-00066-21 (LMG) WEISBERG, R NICHD, NIH Control mechanisms in temperate bacteriophage lambda
Z01HD-00067-23 (LMG) CASHEL, C M NICHD, NIH Integration of macromolecular synthesis in E coli
Z01HD-00068-20 (LMG) CROUCH, R NICHD, NIH Factors influencing genetic transcription-- Initiation and termination
Z01HD-00069-19 (LMG) LEVIN, J G NICHD, NIH Molecular genetics of mammalian retrovirus replication
Z01HD-00071-19 (LMGD) WESTPHAL, H NICHD, NIH Gene and transgene regulation in the developing mouse
R01HD-00072-28 (END) NEW, MARIA I N Y HOSP-CORNELL MED CTR 525 EAST 68TH STREET NEW YORK, N Y 10021 Androgen metabolism in childhood
Z01HD-00093-17 (OSD) GUROFF, G NICHD, NIH The mechanism of action of nerve growth factor
Z01HD-00094-21 (LDN) KLEIN, D C NICHD, NIH Pineal regulation--Environmental and physiological factors
Z01HD-00095-21 (LDN) KLEIN, D C NICHD, NIH Pineal regulation--Transsynaptic and intracellular mechanisms
Z01HD-00131-17 (HGB) GAHL, W A NICHD, NIH Human biochemical genetics
Z01HD-00133-14 (HGB) SIDBURY, J B NICHD, NIH Study of glycogen storage disease
Z01HD-00137-17 (HGB) OWENS, I S NICHD, NIH Regulation and expression of the UDP glucuronosyltransferase gene family
R01HD-00143-31A1 (HED) HAY, ELIZABETH D HARVARD MEDICAL SCHOOL 220 LONGWOOD AVENUE BOSTON, MA 02115 Role of extracellular matrix in morphogenesis
Z01HD-00146-17 (ERRB) CHEN, H C NICHD, NIH Structural studies of proteins
Z01HD-00147-16 (ERRB) DUFAU, M L NICHD, NIH Mechanism of action of peptide hormones in steroidogenic cells
Z01HD-00150-16 (ERRB) DUFAU, M L NICHD, NIH Characterization of gonadal receptors and gonadotropin biological activity
Z01HD-00151-16 (ERRB) CATT, K J NICHD, NIH Regulation of gonadal function
Z01HD-00171-15 (LTPB) CHRAMBACH, A NICHD, NIH Electrophoretic methodology
Z01HD-00184-13 (ERRB) CATT, K J NICHD, NIH Regulation of pituitary hormone secretion
Z01HD-00187-13 (ERRB) HUANG, K-P NICHD, NIH Hormonal regulation of cellular metabolism
Z01HD-00193-06 (ERRB) CATT, K J NICHD, NIH Angiotensin II receptors and activation mechanisms
Z01HD-00194-03 (ERRB) STROTT, C A NICHD, NIH Steroid biosynthesis and metabolism in the adrenal cortex
Z01HD-00323-12 (EB) BERENDES, H W NICHD, NIH District of Columbia perinatal study
Z01HD-00325-10 (EB) MILLS, J L NICHD, NIH Neural tube defects and folate
Z01HD-00329-10 (ESPR) BERENDES, H W NICHD, NIH Evaluation of an intervention trial to prevent low birth weight in D. C.
Z01HD-00331-08 (EB) MILLS, J L NICHD, NIH Diabetes in early pregnancy project
Z01HD-00334-09 (EB) KLEBANOFF, M A NICHD, NIH Low birth weight across generations
Z01HD-00340-08 (EB) COOPER, L C NICHD, NIH Ethnic differences in birth weight and length of gestation
Z01HD-00343-08 (ESPR) BERENDES, H W NICHD, NIH Westernization effects on infant feeding patterns among Negev Bedouins
Z01HD-00344-08 (EB) MALLOY, M H NICHD, NIH Long term health effects of infant formulas deficient in chloride
Z01HD-00346-07 (EB) KLEBANOFF, M A NICHD, NIH Time trends in the incidence of biliary atresia
Z01HD-00361-05 (EB) OVERPECK, M D NICHD, NIH Child health supplement to the 1988 national health interview survey
Z01HD-00363-04 (EB) COOPER, L C NICHD, NIH NICHD smoking trial of pregnant women
Z01HD-00365-05 (EB) MALLOY, M H NICHD, NIH A randomized clinical trial of umbilical artery catheter placement
Z01HD-00366-04 (EB) KLEBANOFF, M A NICHD, NIH Survey of pregnancy outcomes among medical residents
Z01HD-00368-05 (EB) MALLOY, M H NICHD, NIH Vaginal delivery of very low birth weight infnats--Associated with day 1 deaths
Z01HD-00369-03 (EB) KLEBANOFF, M A NICHD, NIH Adverse perinatal events and subsequent injury-related death
Z01HD-00370-03 (EB) KLEBANOFF, M A NICHD, NIH Ethnic differences in hematocrit levels during pregnancy and preterm delivery
Z01HD-00373-03 (EB) LEVINE, R J NICHD, NIH Calcium supplementation in pregnancy to prevent preeclampsia
Z01HD-00378-03 (EB) OVERPECK, M D NICHD, NIH Evaluation of mortality of infants weighing less than 750 grams
Z01HD-00379-02 (EB) KLEBANOFF, M A NICHD, NIH Data analysis from the vaginal infections and prematurity (VIP) study
Z01HD-00380-02 (EB) HERMAN, A A NICHD, NIH A population-based active information system on perinatal drug abuse
Z01HD-00381-02 (EB) MALLOY, M H NICHD, NIH Methods for analyzing prenatal care--Cohort versus conditional analysis
Z01HD-00382-01 (EB) KLEBANOFF, M A NICHD, NIH Cocaine and marijuana use during pregnancy and pregnancy outcome
Z01HD-00383-01 (EB) KLEBANOFF, M A NICHD, NIH Analyses of data from the Collaborative Perinatal Project
Z01HD-00404-09 (HGB) BUTLER, J D NICHD, NIH Cell and sulfur metabolism in fibroblasts of genetic diseases
Z01HD-00408-08 (HGB) MARINI, J C NICHD, NIH Heritable disorders of connective tissue
Z01HD-00412-04 (LMGR) MARAIA, R J NICHD, NIH Molecular regulation of gene expression
Z01HD-00414-02 (HGB) CHARNAS, L R NICHD, NIH Neurogenetics and neural development
Z01HD-00415-01 (HGB) MUKHERJEE, A B NICHD, NIH Physiology of arachidonic acid metabolism and CFTR mutation in cystic fibrosis
Z01HD-00416-01 (HGB) MUKHERJEE, A B NICHD, NIH Inhibition of HIV-1 aspartic protease
R01HD-00596-29 (REB) GREENWALD, GILBERT S UNIV OF KANSAS MED CTR 39TH AND RAINBOW BOULEVARD KANSAS CITY, KS 66103 Follicular regulation in the mammalian ovary
Z01HD-00610-11 (DEB) CUTLER, G B NICHD, NIH Growth, puberty, & their disorders--Physiology, pathophysiology & molecular biol.
Z01HD-00615-11 (DEB) CHROUSOS, G P NICHD, NIH Steroid antagonists
Z01HD-00616-11 (DEB) NISULA, B C NICHD, NIH Structure, function, and physiology of glycoprotein hormones
Z01HD-00618-10 (DEB) CHROUSOS, G P NICHD, NIH Physiology and pathophysiology of the hypothalamic-pituitary-adrenal axis
Z01HD-00621-09 (DEB) CASSORLA, F NICHD, NIH Diagnosis and treatment of growth disorders
Z01HD-00623-08 (DEB) CUTLER, G B NICHD, NIH Adrenal physiology, pathophysiology, and molecular biology
Z01HD-00626-03 (DEB) NIEMAN, L K NICHD, NIH Progesterone action in reproduction
Z01HD-00627-02 (DEB) BLITHE, D L NICHD, NIH Glycoprotein hormones--Oligosaccharide structure and function
Z01HD-00628-02 (DEB) BONDY, C NICHD, NIH Paracrine and autocrine roles of insulin-like growth factors
Z01HD-00629-02 (DEB) BONDY, C A NICHD, NIH Polyol pathways in health and disease
Z01HD-00631-02 (DEB) AGUILERA, G NICHD, NIH Mechanisms of neuroendocrine regulation
Z01HD-00632-02 (DEB) AGILERA, G NICHD, NIH Physiological actions of the renin-angiotensin system
Z01HD-00633-01 (DEB) NELSON, L M NICHD, NIH Ovarian folliculogenesis
K04HD-00652-05 (CTY) MANESS, PATRICIA F UNIV OF N CAROLINA AT CHAPEL H CHAPEL HILL, NC 27599 Pp60c-src in the developing nervous system
R01HD-00700-28 (CBY) COHEN, STANLEY VANDERBILT UNIVERSITY DEPT OF BIOCHEM/507 LIGHT HALL NASHVILLE, TN 37232 Epidermal growth factor
Z01HD-00704-07 (LDN) NEALE, E A NICHD, NIH Tetanus toxin effects and localization in neurons
Z01HD-00705-10 (LDN) RUSSELL, J NICHD, NIH Functional organization of the nerve terminal
Z01HD-00707-06 (LDN) MAYER, M L NICHD, NIH Pharmacological studies of synaptic transmission in vitro
Z01HD-00708-07 (LDN) NEALE, E A NICHD, NIH Morphologic studies of neuronal and non-neuronal cells in CNS cell cultures
Z01HD-00709-05 (LDN) BRENNEMAN, D NICHD, NIH Prevention of neuronal deficits associated with AIDS
Z01HD-00710-03 (LDN) BUONANNO, A NICHD, NIH Molecular characterization of glutamate receptor expression in brain
Z01HD-00711-02 (LDN) BUONANNO, A NICHD,NIH Transcriptional regulation of synapse-specific genes in skeletal muscle
K04HD-00718-05 (BCE) KELLY, MARTIN J OREGON HEALTH SCIS UNIVERSITY 3181 S W SAM JACKSON PARK ROAD PORTLAND, OREG 97201 Neurophysiological effects of estrogen on neurons
K11HD-00728-05 (SRC) ROMERO, ROBERTO J YALE UNIVERSITY 333 CEDAR STREET PO BOX 3333 NEW HAVEN, CONN 06510-8063 Interleukin-1 in human pregnacy
K04HD-00743-05 (GEN) CLARK, ANDREW G PENNSYLVANIA STATE UNIVERSITY 208 MUELLER LABORATORY UNIVERSITY PARK, PA 16802 Population genetics of the Y chromosome
K04HD-00769-05 (HUD) TREIMAN, REBECCA A WAYNE STATE UNIVERSITY 71 W WARREN AVE DETROIT, MI 48202 Phonology and orthography
K11HD-00772-04 (SRC) JACKSON, REBECCA D OHIO STATE UNIVERSITY

PROJECT NO., ORGANIZATIONAL UNIT., INVESTIGATOR, ADDRESS, TITLE

MED CTR 410 W 10TH AVENUE COLUMBUS, OH 43210 Regulation of human decidual prolactin
K04HD-00774-05 (MGN) CHAKRAVARTI, ARAVINDA UNIVERSITY OF PITTSBURGH ROOM A310 CRABTREE HALL PITTSBURGH, PA 15261 Genetic studies of linkage and recombination
K11HD-00777-06 (SRC) FALLS, DOUGLAS L 220 LONGWOOD AVENUE BOSTON, MA 02115 Molecular basis of trophic interaction in synaptogenesis
P01HD-00781-27S1 (HDMC) BATTAGLIA, FREDERICK C UNIV OF COLO HLTH SCIS CTR 4200 EAST NINTH AVENUE DENVER, CO 80262 Studies on prematurity
P01HD-00781-27S1 0031 (HDMC) HAY, WILLIAM W Studies on prematurity Fetal and maternal carbohydrate metabolism
P01HD-00781-27S1 0032 (HDMC) BATTAGLIA, FREDERICK C Studies on prematurity Carbohydrate and amino acid metabolism in neonatal lambs
P01HD-00781-27S1 0033 (HDMC) BATTAGLIA, FREDERICK C Studies on prematurity Protein synthesis and amino acid turnover during fetal life
P01HD-00781-27S1 0035 (HDMC) MESCHIA, GIACOMO Studies on prematurity Experiments in early fetal life
P01HD-00781-27S1 0039 (HDMC) SPARKS, JOHN W Studies on prematurity Hepatic/hindlimb studies
P01HD-00781-27S1 0041 (HDMC) BATTAGLIA, FREDERICK C Studies on prematurity The metabolic implications of labor
P01HD-00781-27S1 0042 (HDMC) SPARKS, JOHN W Studies on prematurity Intrauterine growth retardation
K11HD-00798-05 (HDPR) HEINECKE, JAY W UNIVERSITY OF WASHINGTON RG-26 DIVISION OF METABOLISM SEATTLE, WA 98195 Reactive oxygen species and the biology fertilization
K11HD-00799-05 (HDMC) HELMS, SHERRON R UNIVERSITY HOSPITALS OF CLEVEL 2074 ABINGTON ROAD CLEVELAND OHIO 44106 Development of a tissue-specific expression system
K04HD-00801-04 (HUD) CECI, STEPHEN J CORNELL UNIVERSITY MARTHA VAN RENSSELAER HALL ITHACA, NY 14853 Contextual constraints on intellectual competence
Z01HD-00801-16 (ESPR) HOFFMAN, H J NICHD, NIH Medical birth registries of Norway and Sweden
Z01HD-00802-16 (ESPR) HOFFMAN, H J NICHD, NIH Linked live births-infant deaths and fetal death from U.S. states
Z01HD-00803-07 (ESPR) HOFFMAN, H J NICHD, NIH Analysis of sudden infant death syndrome (SIDS) risk factors
K04HD-00806-05 (HUD) DODGE, KENNETH A VANDERBILT UNIVERSITY DEPT. OF PSYCHOLOGY NASHVILLE, TN 37203 Social information processing in children
K11HD-00807-05 (HDMR) JENSEN, FRANCES E CHILDREN'S HOSPITAL 300 LONGWOOD AVENUE BOSTON, MASS 02115 Postischemic mental retardation--Reversing neuron damage
K11HD-00810-05 (HDMC) HO, TIMOTHY W UNIVERSITY OF CALIFORNIA DIV OF BIOMEDICAL SCIENCES RIVERSIDE, CA 92521 Isoforms of prolactin
K11HD-00815-05 (HDPR) HILL, JOSEPH A FEARING RESEARCH LABORATORY 250 LONGWOOD AVE RM 225 BOSTON, MA 02115 Cellular immune mechanisms in recurrent spontaneous abortion
K04HD-00816-05 (REB) SALING, PATRICIA M DUKE UNIVERSITY MEDICAL CTR BOX 3648 DURHAM, NC 27710 Sperm components involved in fertilization
K11HD-00819-04 (HDMC) MAST, JOELLE CORNELL UNIV MEDICAL COLLEGE 435 E 70TH ST APT 3-C NEW YORK, NY 10021 Visual testing of infants reared in neonatal ICUS
K11HD-00824-06 (HDMR) SIMS, KATHERINE B MASSACHUSETTS GENERAL HOSPITAL 149 13TH STREET CHARLESTOWN, MA 02129 Molecular genetic study of chromosome 21 gene expression
K11HD-00826-05 (HDMC) LAWRENCE, ROBERT M NEW YORK UNIV MEDICAL CENTER 550 FIRST AVE NEW YORK, NY 10016 Molecular biology of virulence factors
K08HD-00827-05 (HDMC) YOUNG, ROGER C MED UNIV OF SOUTH CAROLINA 171 ASHLEY AVENUE CHARLESTON, S C 29425-2810 Electrophysiology of human reproductive smooth muscle
K11HD-00828-05 (SRC) GHAZZI, MAHMOUD N THE UNIVERSITY OF MICHIGAN 300 NORT INGALLS BLDG ANN ARBOR, MICHIGAN 48109-0404 Nutritional influence on hypothamalamic control of reproduction
K04HD-00829-04 (REB) MC CARREY, JOHN R SOUTHWEST FOUNDATION FOR P. O. BOX 28147 SAN ANTONIO, TX 78228-0147 Gene regulation in spermatogenesis
Z01HD-00832-08 (EB) OVERPECK, M D NICHD, NIH Changes in perinatal and infant mortality by race in selected U.S. cities
R01HD-00836-27 (HED) SHEPARD, THOMAS H UNIVERSITY OF WASHINGTON RD-20 SEATTLE, WA 98195 Laboratory for the study of human embryos and fetuses
K11HD-00837-04 (HDMC) BROWN, ALICE B VANDERBILT UNIV SCHOOL OF MED 21ST AVENUE SOUTH NASHVILLE, TN 37232 Nerve growth factor modulation of the EGF receptor
Z01HD-00841-10 (BB) YU, K F NICHD, NIH Methods for comparing and analyzing data from several complex surveys
K04HD-00845-04 (REN) GEORGE, FREDRICK W U OF TX S W MED CTR AT DALLAS 5323 HARRY HINES BOULEVARD DALLAS, TX 75235 Factors influencing testicular descent
K12HD-00849-04 (HDMC) LONGO, LAWRENCE D LOMA LINDA UNIVERSITY SCHOOL OF MEDICINE LOMA LINDA, CALIF 92350 Reproductive scientist training program
K12HD-00850-05 (SRC) BATTAGLIA, FREDERICK C UNIV OF COLO HLTH SCIS CTR 4200 EAST NINTH AVENUE DENVER, COLO 80262 Pediatric physician scientist program award
Z01HD-00850-16 (BB) BRYLA, D A NICHD, NIH Randomized, controlled study of phototherapy for neonatal hyperbilirubinemia
Z01HD-00854-07 (BB) BRYLA, D A NICHD, NIH Analysis of MCH data from the national longitudinal youth survey
K08HD-00855-03 (HDMR) HEIDENREICH, RANDALL A CHILDREN'S HOSPITAL 34TH & CIVIC CENTER BLVD PHILADELPHIA, PA 19104 Recombinant DNA investigation of galactosemia
K11HD-00858-03 (SRC) FORTENBERRY, JAMES D CHILDREN'S HOSPITAL OKLAHOMA 940 N E 13TH OKLAHOMA CITY, OK 73104 Behavioral epidemiology of adolescence
Z01HD-00860-11 (ESPR) HOFFMAN, H J NICHD, NIH Analysis of

PROJECT NO., ORGANIZATIONAL UNIT., INVESTIGATOR, ADDRESS, TITLE

biomedical time series data
Z01HD-00861-09 (ESPR) HOFFMAN, H J NICHD, NIH In-utero fetal growth patterns in relation to outcome at birth
K04HD-00862-04 (EI) LU, CHRISTOPHER Y UNIVERSITY OF TEXAS SW MED CTR 5323 HARRY HINES BLVD DALLAS, TX 75235-8856 Docosahexanenoic acid & regulation of fetal host defense
K04HD-00865-03 (HED) LIECHTY, EDWARD A INDIANA UNIVERSITY SCH OF MED 702 BARNHILL DRIVE, RM RR-208 INDIANAPOLIS, IN 46202-5225 Fetal branched chain amino acid & ketoacid metabolism
K04HD-00867-01A2 (HUD) WALLANDER, JAN L UNIVERSITY OF ALABAMA 1720 SEVENTH AVENUE SOUTH BIRMINGHAM, AL 35233 Mentally retarded adolescents' stress and coping
K08HD-00868-04 (HDMC) MARTHA, PAUL M JR BAYSTATE MED CTR/PEDIATRC DEPT 759 CHESTNUT STREET SPRINGFIELD, MA 01107 Effect of androgens on growth hormone secretion
K08HD-00869-03 (HDPR) HANSEN, JAMES R UNIV OF IOWA COLLEGE OF MED IOWA CITY, IOWA 52242 Regulation of LH release from ovine gonadotropes
Z01HD-00871-07 (ESPR) HOFFMAN, H J NICHD, NIH Clinical trial of new drug therapy for cystinosis
K04HD-00872-03 (HUD) RAUH, VIRGINIA A CTR FOR POPULATION & FAM HLTH 60 HAVEN AVE, B-3 NEW YORK, N Y 10032 Social influences on child development
Z01HD-00872-07 (ESPR) HOFFMAN, H J NICHD, NIH Factors associated with premature births--Missouri follow-back survey
K11HD-00874-03 (SRC) VIK, TERRY A INDIANA UNIVERSITY 702 BARNHILL DRIVE INDIANAPOLIS, IN 46202-5167 S6 kinase activation, regulation, and organization
Z01HD-00876-01 (ESPR) MAIMAN, L A NICHD, NIH Determinants of childhood poison ingestions
Z01HD-00877-01 (ESPR) MAIMAN, L A NICHD, NIH Prevention and education in coronary heart disease reduction
K11HD-00878-03 (HDMR) WEXLER, ISAIAH D CASE WESTERN RESERVE UNIVERSIT 2074 ABINGTON ROAD CLEVELAND, OH 44106 Inborn errors of the pyruvate dehydrogenase complex
K04HD-00879-03 (REN) LEVINE, JON E NORTHWESTERN UNIVERSITY 2153 SHERIDAN ROAD EVANSTON, IL 60208 Neuroendocrine regulation of in vivo LHRH release
K11HD-00880-01A1 (SRC) LARSON, JANET E OCHSNER MEDICAL FDN 1516 JEFFERSON HWY NEW ORLEANS, LA 70121 Reverse genetic analysis in tissue injury
K08HD-00882-02 (HDMC) MC CRAE, KEITH R HOSP OF UNIV OF PENNSYLVANIA 3400 SPRUCE STREET PHILADELPHIA, PA 19104-4283 Immune trophoblast injury
K08HD-00883-02 (HDMC) FEIGENBAUM, SETH L UNIVERSITY OF CALIFORNIA 505 PARNASSUS; BOX 0556/HSW-16 SAN FRANCISCO, CA 94143 Interleukin-1 mediation of fetal neuroendocrine response
K08HD-00885-03 (HDMC) CHURCH, SUSAN L WASHINGTON UNIVERSITY SCH OF M 400 SOUTH KINGSHIGHWAY ST LOUIS, MO 63110 Regulation of the manganese superoxide dismutase gene
K08HD-00886-02 (HDMC) LITZINGER, MARCIA J UNIVERSITY OF UTAH SALT LAKE CITY, UT 84112 Calcium channel types in the developing human brain
K11HD-00888-03 (HDMR) LEIFER, DANA CHILDREN'S HOSPITAL CORPORATIO 300 LONGWOOD AVENUE BOSTON, MA 02115 THY-1 in mental retardation and CNS regeneration
K08HD-00890-02 (HDPR) BAGATELL, CARRIE J VA MEDICAL CTR 1660 S COLUMBIAN WAY SEATTLE, WA 98108 Testosterone effects on gonadotropins and lipids in men
K08HD-00891-02 (HDMR) RHINE, WILLIAM D STANFORD UNIVERSITY SCH OF MED STANFORD, CA 94305 Bilirubin encephalopathy--Models and metabolic studies
K04HD-00900-01 (PC) KRAMER, JAMES M UNIVERSITY OF ILLINOIS PO BOX 4348 CHICAGO, IL 60680 Molecular genetic studies of Caenorhabditis elegans morphogenesis
K04HD-00901-02 (HED) FREEMARK, MICHAEL S DUKE UNIVERSITY BOX 3080 DURHAM, NC 27710 The role of placental lactogen in fetal development
K08HD-00903-02 (HDPR) MONFORT, STEVEN L CONSERVATION AND RES CENTER ROUTE 522 SOUTH FRONT ROYAL, VA 22630 Endocrine control of testis function
K04HD-00907-01 (BCE) HOYER, PATRICIA B UNIVERSITY OF ARIZONA ARIZONA HEALTH SCIENCES CENTER TUCSON, AZ 85724 Functional regulation in ovine large luteal cells
K11HD-00908-02 (HDPR) NORTON, JOHN N VANDERBILT UNIVERSITY NASHVILLE, TN 37232-6600 Investigation of a testis paracrine factor, P-Mod-S
Z01HD-00910-12 (HGB) MUKHERJEE, A B NICHD, NIH Biochemistry, molecular biology and physiology of phospholipase A2
K08HD-00912-02 (HDMR) FILLOUX, FRANCIS M WESTERN INST NEUROPSYCHIATRY 501 CHIPETA WAY SALT LAKE CITY, UT 84108 Dopamine in neonatal hypoxic-ischemic brain injury
Z01HD-00912-12 (HGB) CHOU, J Y NICHD, NIH Gene regulation and cellular differentiation
Z01HD-00913-01 (HGB) BRANTLY, M NICHD, NIH Molecular basis of alpha1-antitrypsin deficiency
K08HD-00914-02 (HDMR) NYGAARD, TORBJOERN G COLUMBIA U/NY STATE PSYCH INST 710 WEST 168TH STREET NEW YORK, NY 10032 Molecular genetics of dopa-responsive dystonia
K11HD-00916-02 (HDMR) BROWN, STEPHEN A COLUMBIA UNIVERSITY 630 WEST 168TH STREET NEW YORK, NY 10032 Physical map of human chromosome 13 Q32
K04HD-00920-01 (BCE) MAYO, KELLY E NORTHWESTERN UNIVERSITY 2153 SHERIDAN RD EVANSTON, IL 60208 Molecular biology of hormones that regulate reproduction
K04HD-00921-02 (HUD) SORACI, SALVATORE A, JR UNIVERSITY OF ALABAMA BOX 870348 TUSCLOOSA, AL 35487-0348 Facilitating relational learning in MR children
K08HD-00923-02 (HDPR) SANTORO, NANETTE F UMDNJ-NEW JERSEY MEDICAL SCHOO 185 SOUTH ORANGE AVENUE NEWARK, NJ 07103-2757 The reproductive physiology of ovarian failure
K08HD-00924-02 (HDMC) RIVKEES, SCOTT A MASSACHUSETTS GENERAL HOSPITAL JACKSON 1226 BOSTON, MA 02114 Neurobiology of melatonin

action
K08HD-00926-02 (HDMC) KERRIGAN, JAMES R UNIVERSITY OF VIRGINIA HLTH SC BOX 386 CHARLOTTESVILLE, VA 22908 Mechanisms subserving opiatergic control of puberty
K11HD-00929-01 (HDMR) NELSON, STANLEY F STANFORD UNIVERSITY MEDICAL CT STANFORD, CA 94305 Localization of the Wilm's tumor susceptibility gene(s)
K08HD-00933-02 (HDMC) RIDER, EVELYN D HARBOR-UCLA MEDICAL CTR 1000 W CARSON ST TORRANCE, CA 90509 Surfactant catabolism at subcellular levels in the lung
K11HD-00936-02 (HDMC) LANGSTON, AMELIA A FRED HUTCHINSON CANCER RES CTR 1124 COLUMBIA STREET SEATTLE, WA 98104 Molecular and genetic analysis of albumin extinction
K08HD-00938-01 (HDMC) ISRAEL, ESTHER J MASSACHUSETTS GENERAL HOSPITAL FRUIT STREET BOSTON, MA 02114 The Fc receptor of the human intestine
K11HD-00939-01 (HDMC) FOUSER, LAURIE S UNIVERSITY OF WASHINGTON SM-20 SEATTLE, WA 98195 Matrix proteins in metanephric development
K11HD-00940-01 (HDMR) PTACEK, LOUIS J 50 NORTH MEDICAL DR SALT LAKE CITY, UT 84132 Genetic linkage and ion channels in periodic paralyses
K08HD-00943-01 (HDPR) KOLP, LISA A UNIV OF VIRGINIA HLTH SCI CTR BOX 387 CHARLOTTESVILLE, VA 22908 Mechanisms subserving the preovulatory LH surge
K08HD-00945-02 (DDK) RHOADS, JON M UNIVERSITY OF NORTH CAROLINA 310 BURNETT-WOMACK BLDG CB-722 CHAPEL HILL, NC 27599-7220 Glutamine and intestinal transport and mucosal growth
K08HD-00946-02 (DDK) RUBIN, DEBORAH C WASHINGTON UNIVERSITY MED SCH 660 SOUTH EUCLID AVENUE ST LOUIS, MO 63110 Molecular and cell biology of gut differentiation
K11HD-00947-01 (HDMC) SNYDER, SCOTT W UNIVERSITY OF MISSOURI COLUMBIA, MO 65212 Premature labor, endotoxemia and cytokine mechanisms
K04HD-00950-01 (BCE) SISK, CHERYL L MICHIGAN STATE UNIVERSITY 302 ADMINISTRATION BLDG EAST LANSING, MI 48824 Neural and hormonal interactions during puberty
K08HD-00954-02 (HDMC) SIPPEL, C JEFFREY WASHINGTON UNIV SCH OF MED 400 S KINGSHIGHWAY BLVD ST. LOUIS, MO 63110 Mechanisms of canaliculus bile acid transport
K08HD-00955-01 (HDMC) HAUFT, SHERRIE M WASHINGTON UNIV SCH OF MED 660 S EUCLID AVE BOX 8231 ST LOUIS, MO 63110 Molecular biology of gut development/differentiation
K11HD-00960-01 (HDMC) MATZUK, MARTIN M BAYLOR COLLEGE OF MEDICINE ONE BAYLOR PLAZA HOUSTON, TX 77030 Developmental and functional roles of activin and inhibin
K08HD-00963-01 (HDPR) KUPFER, STUART R UNIV OF N C AT CHAPEL HILL MAC NIDER BLDG, UNC-CH/CB #750 CHAPEL HILL, NC 27599 Molecular analysis of androgen insensitivity
K08HD-00964-01 (HDMC) DUDLEY, DONALD J UNIVERSITY OF UTAH 50 N MEDICAL DRIVE SALT LAKE CITY, UTAH 81432 Role of interleukin-6 in preterm labor
K08HD-00966-01 (HDMR) WAGSTAFF, JOSEPH CHILDRENS HOSPITAL 300 LONGWOOD AVE BOSTON, MA 02115 Analysis of an imprinted region of human chromosome 15
K11HD-00983-01 (HDMR) DURE, LEON S MASSACHUSETTS GENERAL HOSPITAL FRUIT STREET BOSTON, MA 02114 Striatal glutamate receptors in developing rat and cat
Z01HD-01001-09 (LMG) DAWID, I B NICHD, NIH Gene organization and expression in Drosophila
Z01HD-01002-10 (LMG) DAWID, I B NICHD, NIH Gene expression during embryonic development of Xenopus laevis
Z01HD-01004-08 (LMG) HINNEBUSCH, A G NICHD, NIH Regulation of amino acid biosynthetic gene in Saccharomyces cerevisiae
Z01HD-01005-04 (LMG) KENNISON, J NICHD, NIH Regulation of cellular proliferation and diversity in Drosophila
Z01HD-01006-03 (LMG) SARGENT, T NICHD, NIH Protein-nucleic acid interactions in vertebrate embryogenesis
Z01HD-01007-02 (NICH) DAWID, I B CC, NIH Structure, function, and genetics of nucleic acid binding proteins
Z01HD-01008-02 (LMG) HAYNES, S NICHD, NIH Molecular genetics of protein/nucleic acid interactions in Drosophila
Z01HD-01106-08 (LCE) SUOMI, S J NICHD, NIH Developmental continuity of individual differences in Rhesus monkey reactivity
Z01HD-01107-08 (LCE) SUOMI, S J NICHD, NIH Adaptation of laboratory reared monkeys to field environments
Z01HD-01108-07 (LCE) BIBEN, M NICHD, NIH Comparative studies of play behavior
Z01HD-01111-01 (LCE) SUOMI, S J NICHD, NIH Factors affecting nuturant behavior toward infants
Z01HD-01112-05 (LCE) LAMB, M E NICHD, NIH Effects of home and out-of-home care in child development
Z01HD-01113-05 (LCE) LAMB, M E NICHD, NIH Antecedents, correlates, consequences of adolescent pregnancy and parenthood
Z01HD-01114-04 (LCE) LAMB, M E NICHD, NIH Individual differences in physical and affective functioning in infancy
Z01HD-01115-04 (LCE) LAMB, M E NICHD, NIH Effects of domestic violence and evaluation of children's testimony
Z01HD-01116-04 (LCE) LAMB, M E NICHD, NIH Pattern of childrearing across cultures and ecologies
Z01HD-01118-04 (LCE) BORNSTEIN, M H NICHD, NIH Latent behavioral effects of diverse form of caretaking in the first year of life
Z01HD-01119-04 (LCE) BORNSTEIN, M H NICHD, NIH Specificity of mother-infant interaction
Z01HD-01120-04 (LCE) BORNSTEIN, M H NICHD, NIH Observations of parenting and infant activity in different societies
Z01HD-01122-04 (LCE) BORNSTEIN, M H NICHD, NIH Assessment of children's mental and social abilities
Z01HD-01123-01 (LCE) NEWMAN, J D NICHD, NIH Physiological correlates and neural mechanisms of the infant cry
Z01HD-01124-01 (LCE) NEWMAN, J D NICHD, NIH Genetic and experiential influences on the development of primate vocal behavior
R01HD-01182-29 (END) GORSKI, ROGER A UNIVERSITY OF CALIFORNIA 10833 LE CONTE AVE LOS ANGELES, CA 90024-1406 Studies on the ovarian-hypothalamic-hypophyseal axis
Z01HD-01202-04 (LDN) LOH, Y P NICHD, NIH Regulation of expression and function of neuropeptides during development
Z01HD-01203-01 (LDN) RUSSELL, J T NICHD, NIH Intracellular signalling in astrocytes
Z01HD-01204-01 (LDN) CHIN, G J NICHD, NIH Characterization of receptors for FMRFamide-related neuropeptides
R01HD-01287-28 (IMB) HERZENBERG, LEONORE A STANFORD UNIVERSITY SCH OF MED STANFORD, CA 94305-5125 Fetal-maternal immunological interactions
Z01HD-01301-08 (LDMI) SCHNEERSON, R NICHD, NIH Human immune response to polysaccharide-protein conjugate vaccines
Z01HD-01303-08 (LDMI) SZU, S C NICHD, NIH Conjugate induced polysaccharide antibodies
Z01HD-01304-09 (LDMI) ROBBINS, J B NICHD, NIH Protective effect of VI and LPS Antibodies against Salmonellae and Shigellae
Z01HD-01310-04 (LDMI) OZATO, K NICHD, NIH Developmental gene regulation of the immune system
Z01HD-01400-09 (LTPB) YERGEY, A L NICHD, NIH Clinical applications of metal stable isotopes
Z01HD-01401-09 (LTPB) YERGEY, A L NICHD, NIH Biological applications of thermospray liquid chromatography/mass spectrometry
Z01HD-01407-02 (LTPB) COSTA, T NICHD, NIH Mechanisms of receptor mediated signal transduction
Z01HD-01408-01 (LTPB) GARNER, M M NICHD, NIH Stability and specificity of DNA-protein interactions
Z01HD-01409-06 (LTPB) ZIMMERBERG, J NICHD, NIH Membrane transport and fusion
Z01HD-01413-01 (LTPB) RAMPINO, N J NICHD, NIH Microscopic analysis of drug induced alterations in DNA
Z01HD-01415-01 (LTPB) ZIMMERBERG, J NICHD, NIH Exocytotic membrane fusion
Z01HD-01500-09 (OSD) LEVINE, A S NICHD, NIH DNA replication, repair, and mutagenesis in eukaryotic and prokaryotic cells
Z01HD-01600-07 (CBMB) SAMELSON, L E NICHD, NIH Biochemical basis of T cell activation
Z01HD-01601-07 (CBMB) HARFORD, J B NICHD, NIH Molecular aspects of regulation of human transferrin receptors
Z01HD-01602-07 (CBMB) KLAUSNER, R D NICHD, NIH Regulation of intracellular iron metabolism
Z01HD-01604-06 (CBMB) LEONARD, W J NICHD, NIH Interleukin-2 receptor structure, function, and regulation
Z01HD-01605-05 (CBMB) KLAUSNER, R D NICHD, NIH T cell antigen receptor--Structure, biosynthesis and cell biology
Z01HD-01606-04 (CBMB) KLAUSNER, R D NICHD, NIH Biology of early organelles of the secretory pathway
Z01HD-01607-01 (CBMB) BONIFACINO, J S NICHD, NIH Regulation of the fate of newly synthesized proteins
Z01HD-01608-01 (CBMB) STORZ, G NICHD, NIH Gene regulation in response to environmental signals
Z01HD-01700-04 (ESPR) BERENDES, H W NICHD, NIH Study of the efficacy of IVIG in HIV infected children
Z01HD-01701-04 (ESPR) BERENDES, H W NICHD,NIH Evaluation of the impact of a model prenatal and followup program in Baltimore
Z01HD-01702-02 (ESPR) BERENDES, H W NICHD, NIH Infant feeding practices among North African Jews
Z01HD-01703-03 (ESPR) BERENDES, H W NICHD, NIH Study of pregnancy outcome, maternal death and child health in Pakistan
Z01HD-01704-01 (ESPR) BERENDES, H W NICHD, NIH Stunting among Bedouin Arab children in the Negev, Israel
R01HD-01743-26 (NTN) KEEN, CARL L UNIVERSITY OF CALIFORNIA DEPARTMENT OF NUTRITION DAVIS, CALIF 95616 Nutritional factors in development
P30HD-01799-27 (HDMR) VAUGHAN, HERBERT G, JR ALBERT EINSTEIN COLLEGE OF MED 1300 MORRIS PARK AVENUE BRONX, N Y 10461 Support for mental retardation research center
P30HD-01799-27 9001 (HDMR) MCCARTON, CECELIA Support for mental retardation research center Core--Longitudinal infant follow-up and evaluation
P30HD-01799-27 9002 (HDMR) WALKLEY, STEVEN Support for mental retardation research center Core--Morphology
P30HD-01799-27 9006 (HDMR) KESSLER, JOHN Support for mental retardation research center Core--Audio-visual facility
P30HD-01799-27 9009 (HDMR) AREZZO, JOSEPH C Support for mental retardation research center Core--Electronic and mechanical facility
P30HD-01799-27 9010 (HDMR) KESSLER, JOHN A Support for mental retardation research center Core--Tissue culture facility
P30HD-01799-27 9011 (HDMR) KUTZBERG, DIANE Support for mental retardation research center Core--Human neurophysiology
P30HD-01799-27 9012 (HDMR) GOLDEN, ROBERT Support for mental retardation research center Core--Biometrics
P30HD-01799-27 9013 (HDMR) VAUGHAN, HERBERT G Support for mental retardation research center Core--Dynamic brain activity imaging
Z01HD-01800-03 (LMGD) DRESSLER, G R NICHD, NIH Functional analysis of murine Pax genes
Z01HD-01801-02 (LMGD) MAHON, K A NICHD, NIH The molecular analysis of development
R37HD-01866-26 (REB) MESCHIA, GIACOMO UNIVERSITY OF COLORADO 4200 EAST NINTH AVENUE C240 DENVER, COLO 80262 Physiological study of the placenta
Z01HD-01900-01 (LME) WOLFFE, A NICHD, NIH Developmental regulation of differential gene expression
P01HD-01994-26A1 (HDMC) STUDDERT-KENNEDY, MICHAEL HASKINS LABORATRIES 270 CROWN STREET NEW HAVEN, CT 06511-6695 Nature and acquisition of the speech code and reading
P01HD-01994-26A1 0007 (HDMC) STUDDERT-KENNEDY, MICHAEL Nature and acquisition of the speech code and reading The speech mode and its early development
P01HD-01994-26A1 0010 (HDMC) SHANKWEILER, DONALD P Nature and acquisition of the speech code and reading Phonological processes in sentence comprehension
P01HD-01994-26A1 0012 (HDMC) FOWLER, CAROL A Nature and acquisition

PROJECT NO., ORGANIZATIONAL UNIT., INVESTIGATOR, ADDRESS, TITLE

of the speech code and reading Gestural timing and linguistic organization
P01HD-01994-26A1 0013 (HDMC) TURVEY, MICHAEL T Nature and acquisition of the speech code and reading Phonological processes in reading individual words
P01HD-01994-26A1 0014 (HDMC) BRADY, SUSAN Nature and acquisition of the speech code and reading Role of phonological representation in phonological awarness and literacy
R01HD-02138-30 (BCE) BARRACLOUGH, CHARLES A UNIVERSITY OF MARYLAND 655 WEST BALTIMORE STREET BALTIMORE, MD 21201 Central nervous system regulation of reproduction
P30HD-02274-24 (HDMR) GURALNICK, MICHAEL J UNIVERSITY OF WASHINGTON CDMR CENTER (WJ-10) SEATTLE, WA 98195 Research in mental retardation and child development
P30HD-02274-24 9002 (HDMR) SACK, ANDREW Research in mental retardation and child development Core instrument development laboratory
P30HD-02274-24 9003 (HDMR) MC DONALD, R H Research in mental retardation and child development Core media services
P30HD-02274-24 9004 (HDMR) RUPPENTHAL, GERALD C Research in mental retardation and child development Core infant primate research laboratory
P30HD-02274-24 9006 (HDMR) WESTRUM, LESNICK Research in mental retardation and child development Electron microscopy--Core
P30HD-02274-24 9007 (HDMR) ELLSWORTH, ALVORD Research in mental retardation and child development Neuropathology core
P30HD-02274-24 9008 (HDMR) SCOTT, RONALD Research in mental retardation and child development Core--Genetics
R01HD-02335-26 (END) GRUMBACH, MELVIN M DEPARTMENT OF PEDIATRICS UNIVERSITY OF CALIFORNIA SAN FRANCISCO, CALIF 94143 Hormonal effects on growth and maturation
P30HD-02528-25A1 (HDMR) SCHROEDER, STEPHEN R UNIVERSITY OF KANSAS 1052 DOLE LAWRENCE, KS 66045 Program for a research center in mental retardation
P30HD-02528-25A1 0001 (HDMR) TARR, CHARLES M Program for a research center in mental retardation Reactive oxygen species in neuronal tissue
P30HD-02528-25A1 9014 (HDMR) GREENWOOD, CHARLES R Program for a research center in mental retardation Core--Computer, statistics, and electronics
P30HD-02528-25A1 9015 (HDMR) COLUMBO, JOHN Program for a research center in mental retardation Core--Communications and graphics
P30HD-02528-25A1 9016 (HDMR) KITOS, PAUL Program for a research center in mental retardation Core--Tissue culture and monoclonal antibodies
P30HD-02528-25A1 9017 (HDMR) TERRANOVA, PAUL Program for a research center in mental retardation Core--Histology and image analysis
R01HD-02871-21 (BIO) WEINHOLD, PAUL A UNIVERSITY OF MICHIGAN DEPT OF BIOLOGICAL CHEMISTRY ANN ARBOR, MI 48109 Phospholipid metabolism during lung development
N01HD-02900-02 (**) BEAUDRY, NORMAN N Radioiodinations of proteins, peptides, nucleotides and antigens
N01HD-02901-03 (**) KAPPS, ATTALLAH Clinical trials of heme-oxygenase inhibitors of hyperbilirubinemia
N01HD-02907-03 (**) BEAUDRY, NORMAN N Polyclonal antibody production
N44HD-02909-02 (**) LERNER, NEIL Residential swimming pool child protective system
N44HD-02910-02 (**) CARD, JOSEFINA J Establishment of a family data archive
N01HD-02911-02 (**) SWANSON, MARK National transgenic mouse facility
N01HD-02912-02 (**) BERNFIELD, MERTON R Hyaluronic acid metabolism and cell proliferation in curly tail mice
N01HD-02913-01 (**) DAVISSON, MURIEL T Distribution of mouse models for neutral tube defects
N01HD-02914-01 (**) MARMOT, MICHAEL G Case control study of oral contraceptives and cardiovascular disease
N01HD-02915-01 (**) LAND, GARLAND Repetition of low birth weight in successive pregnancy
N01HD-02916-01 (**) BROCKERT, JOHN E Low birth weight in successive pregnancy outcomes in Utah
N01HD-02919-01 (**) RAITI, SALVATORE Store, package, and distribute hormones
R01HD-02982-25 (BPO) ZUCKER, IRVING UNIVERSITY OF CALIFORNIA BERKELEY, CA 94720 Photoperiod, behavior and brain function
P01HD-03008-24 (SRC) ZIGLER, EDWARD F YALE UNIVERSITY BOX 11A YALE STATION NEW HAVEN, CONN 06520 Mental retardation and developmental psychopathology
P01HD-03008-24 0041 (SRC) ZIGLER, EDWARD F Mental retardation and developmental psychopathology Developmental approach to psychopathology--Normal and retarded intelligence
P01HD-03008-24 0049 (SRC) SEITZ, VICTORIA Mental retardation and developmental psychopathology A longitudinal study of teenage mothers and their firstborn children
P01HD-03008-24 0050 (SRC) VOLKMAR, FRED R Mental retardation and developmental psychopathology Autism and pervasive developmental disorders
P01HD-03008-24 0060 (SRC) COHEN, DONALD J Mental retardation and developmental psychopathology Tourette's syndrome and neuropsychiatric disorders of childhood
P01HD-03008-24 0062 (SRC) HODAPP, ROBERT M Mental retardation and developmental psychopathology The developmental approach to mental retardation
P01HD-03008-24 9001 (SRC) SPARROW, SARA Mental retardation and developmental psychopathology Core--Assessment and diagnostic
P01HD-03008-24 9002 (SRC) SEITZ, VICTORIA Mental retardation and developmental psychopathology Core--Statistics and methodology
P30HD-03110-24 (HDMR) SUZUKI, KUNIHIKO UNIVERSITY OF N CAROLINA 311 BSRC, CB# 7220 CHAPEL HILL, NC 27599 North Carolina mental retardation research program
P30HD-03110-24 9003 (HDMR) MAILMAN, RICHARD North Carolina mental retardation research program Computer-electronics support unit--Core
P30HD-03110-24 9004 (HDMR) HELMS, RONALD North Carolina mental retardation research program Deign and statistical computing unit--Core
P30HD-03110-24 9005 (HDMR) RAMEY, CRAIG North Carolina mental retardation research program Longitudinal studies--Core
P30HD-03110-24 9006 (HDMR) SUZUKI, KUNIHIKO North Carolina mental retardation research program Nucleic acid laboratory--Core
R37HD-03132-23 (NSS) EPSTEIN, CHARLES J UNIVERSITY OF CALIFORNIA 3RD AVENUE & PARNASSUS SAN FRANCISCO, CA 94143-0106 Biochemistry of early mammalian development
P01HD-03144-24 (SRC) GREENWOOD, CHARLES R UNIV OF KANSAS 1052 DOLE LAWRENCE, KS 66045 Development of children from depriving environments
P01HD-03144-24 0027 (SRC) RISLEY, TODD R Development of children from depriving environments Language component interaction research
P01HD-03144-24 0028 (SRC) HALL, R VANCE Development of children from depriving environments Academic component academic interaction research
P01HD-03144-24 0029 (SRC) GREENWOOD, CHARLES R Development of children from depriving environments Risk control
P01HD-03144-24 9001 (SRC) SEARS, DAVIDA Development of children from depriving environments core--Computer applications
P30HD-03352-25 (HDMR) DOLAN, TERRENCE R WAISMAN CTR ON MENTAL RERARDAT 1500 HIGHLAND AVENUE MADISON, WI 53705-2280 Wisconsin center on mental retardation--Core support
P30HD-03352-25 0001 (HDMR) GREGG, RON G Wisconsin center on mental retardation--Core support Mapping the Prader-Willi Syndrome locus
P30HD-03352-25 9001 (HDMR) STANFORD, LAURENCE R Wisconsin center on mental retardation--Core support Core--Instrumentation
P30HD-03352-25 9002 (HDMR) WIGHTMAN, FREDERIC L Wisconsin center on mental retardation--Core support Core--Computer, statistics and electronics
P30HD-03352-25 9004 (HDMR) BRUER, LLOYD H Wisconsin center on mental retardation--Core support Core--Animal care and breeding
P30HD-03352-25 9011 (HDMR) SIEGEL, FRANK L Wisconsin center on mental retardation--Core support CORE--CELL BIOLOGY
P30HD-03352-25 9012 (HDMR) MILLER, JON F Wisconsin center on mental retardation--Core support Core--Assessment
R01HD-03402-24 (REB) YANAGIMACHI, RYUZO UNIVERSITY OF HAWAII 1960 EAST-WEST ROAD HONOLULU, HAWAII 96822 Analysis of fertilization mechanisms in mammals
R01HD-03807-22 (HED) LONGO, LAWRENCE D LOMA LINDA UNIVERSITY SCHOOL OF MEDICINE LOMA LINDA, CA 92350 Fetal oxygenation and placental gas exchange
R37HD-03820-22 (REB) ORGEBIN-CRIST, MARIE-CLAIRE VANDERBILT UNIVERSITY NASHVILLE, TN 37232-2633 Male reproductive physiology
P30HD-04024-23 (HDMR) GOODMAN, STEPHEN I UNIVERSITY OF COLORADO 4200 EAST NINTH AVENUE DENVER, CO 80262 NICHD mental retardation research core grant
P30HD-04024-23 0014 (HDMR) MC CABE, EDWARD R NICHD mental retardation research core grant Developmental impact of glycerol kinase deficiency
P30HD-04024-23 9002 (HDMR) GOODMAN, STEPHEN NICHD mental retardation research core grant Core--Cell biology
P30HD-04024-23 9003 (HDMR) FENNESSEY, PAUL NICHD mental retardation research core grant Core--Mass spectrometry
P30HD-04024-23 9004 (HDMR) FENNINGTON, BRUCE NICHD mental retardation research core grant Core--Developmental neuropsychology
P30HD-04024-23 9005 (HDMR) CRNIC, LINDA NICHD mental retardation research core grant Core--Animal facility
P30HD-04024-23 9006 (HDMR) WELCH, NOREEN NICHD mental retardation research core grant Core--Glassware washing
R01HD-04134-23 (MGN) GERMAN, JAMES L, III NEW YORK BLOOD CENTER 310 EAST 67TH STREET NEW YORK, N Y 10021 Cytological studies in human genetics
P30HD-04147-22A1 (HDMR) MCCLUER, ROBERT H EUNICE KENNEDY SHRIVER CENTER 200 TRAPELO ROAD WALTHAM, MA 02254 Research in mental retardation
P30HD-04147-22A1 9009 (HDMR) LEES, MARJORIE Research in mental retardation Core--Animal facility
P30HD-04147-22A1 9012 (HDMR) JUNGALWALA, FIROZE Research in mental retardation Core--Molecular analysis
P30HD-04147-22A1 9013 (HDMR) HERRUP, KARL Research in mental retardation Core--Morphological analysis
P30HD-04147-22A1 9014 (HDMR) MCILVANE, WILLIAM J Research in mental retardation Core--Specialist services
P30HD-04147-22A1 9016 (HDMR) SCHWARTING, GERALD Research in mental retardation Core--Molecular and cell biology
R01HD-04229-22 (MBY) SMITH, L DENNIS UNIVERSITY OF CALIFORNIA DEPT OF DEVELOPMENTAL & CELL B IRVINE, CALIF 92717 Cytoplasmic regulation in early cell differentiation
R01HD-04248-22 (PHY) BENNETT, MICHAEL V ALBERT EINSTEIN COLL OF MED 1300 MORRIS PARK AVE BRONX, NY 10461 Function of electrical coupling in embryonic tissues
R37HD-04270-23 (HED) FISHER, DELBERT A HARBOR-UCLA MEDICAL CENTER 1124 WEST CARSON STREET TORRANCE, CA 90509 Thyroid function in the fetus and newborn
R37HD-04358-31 (REB) GROSVENOR, CLARK E PENNSYLVANIA STATE UNIVERSITY 108 ALTHOUSE LABORATORY UNIVERSITY PARK, PA 16802 Neural and hormonal regulation of lactation
R01HD-04367-30 (MBY) NEMER, MARTIN J 7701 BURHOLME AVENUE PHILADELPHIA, PA 19111 Differential gene expression in sea urchin embryogenesis
R37HD-04445-22 (TOX) JOHNSON, ERIC F SCRIPPS CLINIC & RESEARCH FDN 10666 NORTH TORREY PINES ROAD LA JOLLA, CA 92037 Perinatal mechanisms of detoxification
R01HD-04466-21 (REB) FRENCH, FRANK S UNIV OF NORTH CAROLINA MACNIDER BLDG CB#7500 CHAPEL HILL, N C 27599 Development of male reproductive function
R01HD-04467-20 (BPO) FEDER, HARVEY H RUTGERS STATE UNIVERSITY 101 WARREN STREET NEWARK, NJ 07102 Hormonal regulation of behavior
R01HD-04484-20 (BPO) BARFIELD, RONALD J RUTGERS UNIVERSITY BUILDING 4087 NEW BRUNSWICK, N J 08903 Endocrine and neural bases of

behavior
P30HD-04612-21 (HDMR) BUCHWALD, NATHANIEL A UNIVERSITY OF CALIFORNIA 405 HILGARD AVE LOS ANGELES, CA 90024-1759 Mental retardation research center
P30HD-04612-21 9002 (HDMR) BUCHWALD, NATHANIEL Mental retardation research center Core--New program development
P30HD-04612-21 9003 (HDMR) CAMPAGNONI, A Mental retardation research center Core--Molecular biology
P30HD-04612-21 9004 (HDMR) DE VELLIS, JEAN Mental retardation research center Core--Neural cell culture
P30HD-04612-21 9005 (HDMR) FISHER, R Mental retardation research center Core--Neurohistology
P30HD-04612-21 9006 (HDMR) ROME, L Mental retardation research center Core--Microcomputer and media
P30HD-04612-21 9007 (HDMR) GUTHRIE, DONALD Mental retardation research center Core--Statistics
R01HD-04906-22 (REB) HEDRICK, JERRY L UNIVERSITY OF CALIFORNIA DEPARTMENT OF BIOCHEM & BIOPHY DAVIS, CALIF 95616 A molecular approach to fertilization
R37HD-04945-21 (BCE) OSAWA, YOSHIO MEDICAL FDN OF BUFFALO, INC 73 HIGH STREET BUFFALO, N Y 14203-1196 Human development and estrogen biosynthesis
P50HD-05077-21 (HDPR) JAGIELLO, GEORGIANA M COLLEGE-PHYSICIANS & SURGEONS 630 WEST 168TH STREET NEW YORK, NY 10032 Reproductive biochemistry and medicine
P50HD-05077-21 0002 (HDPR) ASSOSIAN, RICHARD Reproductive biochemistry and medicine Control of cell proliferation by TGF beta
P50HD-05077-21 0022 (HDPR) FERIN, MICHEL Reproductive biochemistry and medicine The GnRH pulse generator
P50HD-05077-21 0029 (HDPR) BELLVE, ANTHONY Reproductive biochemistry and medicine Cellular and molecular analysis of mammalian spermatogenesis
P50HD-05077-21 0030 (HDPR) COHEN, ROBERT Reproductive biochemistry and medicine Regulation and role of HSP26 expression in Drosophila
P50HD-05077-21 0031 (HDPR) PINTAR, JOHN Reproductive biochemistry and medicine Prenatal expression of growth factor genes and receptors
P50HD-05077-21 0032 (HDPR) ALLERAND, DOMINIQUE Reproductive biochemistry and medicine Steroid/growth factor interactions in neurodevelopment and aging
P50HD-05077-21 0033 (HDPR) WARDLAW, SHARON Reproductive biochemistry and medicine Steroid regulation of brain POMC and LH secretion in primates
P50HD-05077-21 0034 (HDPR) WOLGEMUTH, DEBRA Reproductive biochemistry and medicine Proto-oncogene expression during mammalian gametogenesis
P50HD-05077-21 9001 (HDPR) HEMBREE, WYLIE Reproductive biochemistry and medicine Radioimmunnoassay core
P50HD-05077-21 9002 (HDPR) FERIN, MICHEL Reproductive biochemistry and medicine Core--Primate colony
P50HD-05077-21 9003 (HDPR) WOLGEMUTH, DEBRA Reproductive biochemistry and medicine Molecular cytology/histology--Core
P50HD-05077-21 9004 (HDPR) BELLVE, ANTHONY Reproductive biochemistry and medicine Cell and Hybridoma--Core
R01HD-05196-20 (MGN) SHOWS, THOMAS B ROSWELL PARK MEMORIAL INST 666 ELM STREET BUFFALO, N Y 14263 genetics of human development & metabolic disease
R01HD-05291-19 (REN) JEFFREY, JOHN J ALBANY MEDICAL COLLEGE 47 NEW SCOTLAND AVENUE ALBANY, N Y 12208 Regulation of collagenase activity in the uterus
R01HD-05331-21 (HUD) EIMAS, PETER D BROWN UNIVERSITY P O BOX 1978 PROVIDENCE, RI 02912 Developmental studies of speech perception
R01HD-05465-21 (MGN) MIGEON, BARBARA R JOHNS HOPKINS HOSPITAL 600N WOLFE ST BALTIMORE, MD 21205 Genetic studies of human somatic cells
R01HD-05505-19 (CBY) SOLURSH, MICHAEL UNIVERSITY OF IOWA IOWA CITY, IA 52242 Cell diversification in the developing limb
R37HD-05506-20 (END) LOEB, JOHN N COLUMBIA UNIVERSITY 630 WEST 168TH ST NEW YORK, N Y 10032 Hormonal regulation of growth and differentiation
P01HD-05515-21 (HDMR) MC CLUER, ROBERT H EUNICE KENNEDY SHRIVER CENTER 200 TRAPELO ROAD WALTHAM, MA 02254 Biochemical & genetic aspects of mental retardation
P01HD-05515-21 0049 (HDMR) MC CLUER, ROBERT H Biochemical & genetic aspects of mental retardation Complex neutral glycosphingolipids in fetal brain
P01HD-05515-21 0051 (HDMR) JUNGALWALA, FIROZE B Biochemical & genetic aspects of mental retardation Neolacto series of glycolipids in developing nervous system
P01HD-05515-21 0052 (HDMR) SCHWARTING, GERALD A Biochemical & genetic aspects of mental retardation Expression of galactosyl-glycoconjugates in rodent olfactory bulb
P01HD-05515-21 9001 (HDMR) MC CLUER, ROBERT H Biochemical & genetic aspects of mental retardation Central core facility
R01HD-05751-19S1 (BPO) PFAFF, DONALD W ROCKEFELLER UNIVERSITY 1230 YORK AVENUE NEW YORK, NY 10021 Brain mechanisms of reproductive behavior
R37HD-05753-22 (SSS) DAVIDSON, ERIC H CALIFORNIA INST OF TECHNOLOGY DIVISION OF BIOLOGY PASADENA, CA 91125 Oogenesis and gene control in animal reproduction
P30HD-05797-20 (SRC) ORGEBIN-CRIST, MARIE-CLAIRE VANDERBILT SCH OF MEDICINE RM D-2303 MCN NASHVILLE, TN 37232-2633 Center for reproductive biology research
P30HD-05797-20 9006 (SRC) GARBERS, DAVID L Center for reproductive biology research protein phosphorylation / cyclic nucleotides core
P30HD-05797-20 9007 (SRC) BRASH, ALAN R Center for reproductive biology research Organic chemistry /prostaglandins core
P30HD-05797-20 9009 (SRC) SMITH, HOWARD E Center for reproductive biology research Organic chemistry core
P30HD-05797-20 9010 (SRC) KUNIO, MISONO Center for reproductive biology research Protein chemistry core
P30HD-05797-20 0001 (SRC) TAYLOR, WILLIAM Center for reproductive biology research Oocyte specificity of the TFIIIA gene of Xenopus
P30HD-05797-20 9001 (SRC) ORTH, DAVID N Center for reproductive biology research Hormone assay core
P30HD-05797-20 9002 (SRC) OLSON, GARY E Center for reproductive biology research Histology and photomicroscopy core
P30HD-05797-20 9003 (SRC) HOFFMAN, LOREN H Center for reproductive biology research Electron microscope core
P30HD-05797-20 9004 (SRC) CARPENTER, GRAHAM Center for reproductive biology research Tissue culture core
P30HD-05798-17 (SRC) UDRY, J RICHARD UNIVERSITY OF NORTH CAROLINA CB# 8120, UNIVERSITY SQUARE CHAPEL HILL, NC 27516-3997 Carolina population center
R01HD-05863-20 (REB) GOLDBERG, ERWIN NORTHWESTERN UNIVERSITY DEPT / BIOCHEM&MOLECULAR&CELL EVANSTON, ILL 60208 Reproductive biochemistry of testes specific ldh-x
P30HD-05876-21 (HDPR) MARE, ROBERT D UNIVERSITY OF WISCONSIN 1180 OBSERVATORY DRIVE MADISON, WIS 53706 NICHD population research core grant
P30HD-05876-21 9001 (HDPR) WINSBOROUGH, HALLIMAN NICHD population research core grant Core--Data processing
P30HD-05876-21 9002 (HDPR) COOPER, ANNE LIGHTFOOT NICHD population research core grant Core--Data library
P30HD-05876-21 9003 (HDPR) HAUSER, ROBERT M NICHD population research core grant Core--Library
P01HD-05958-20 (SRC) BUCHWALD, NATHANIEL A UNIVERSITY OF CALIFORNIA 760 WESTWOOD PLAZA LOS ANGELES, CA 90024-1759 Neurophysiology and neuropsychology in mental retardation
P01HD-05958-20 0001 (SRC) LEVINE, MICHAEL S Neurophysiology and neuropsychology in mental retardation Developmental electrophysiology of intact and decorticated basal ganglia
P01HD-05958-20 0002 (SRC) WOODY, CHARLES D Neurophysiology and neuropsychology in mental retardation Cellular mechanisms of learned motor performance
P01HD-05958-20 0008 (SRC) VILLABLANCA, JAIME R Neurophysiology and neuropsychology in mental retardation Developmental analysis of prenatal cortical damage
P01HD-05958-20 0012 (SRC) DUDEK, F EDWARD Neurophysiology and neuropsychology in mental retardation Developmental electrophysiology of neocortex
P01HD-05958-20 0013 (SRC) FISHER, R S Neurophysiology and neuropsychology in mental retardation Structural development of normal neuronal communication in the cerebral cortex
P01HD-06016-21 (HDMC) RUMBAUGH, DUANE M EMORY UNIVERSITY YERKES REGIONAL PRIMATE RES CT ATLANTA, GA 30322 Language formation studies
P01HD-06016-21 0001 (HDMC) ROMSKI, MARY ANN Language formation studies The Georgia State University Mental Retardation Project
P01HD-06016-21 0004 (HDMC) RUMBAUGH, SUE S Language formation studies Language acquisition in Pan paniscus
P01HD-06016-21 0008 (HDMC) RUMBAUGH, DUANE M Language formation studies Cognitive studies with Pan troglodytes
P01HD-06016-21 0009 (HDMC) MORRIS, ROBIN Language formation studies Neuropsychological foundations project
R37HD-06159-19 (HED) NOVY, MILES J OREG REGIONAL PRIMATE RES CTR 505 N W 185TH AVENUE BEAVERTON, OR 97006 Endocrine and vascular relationships in parturition
P30HD-06160-20S1 (SRC) GALLE, OMER R UNIVERSITY OF TEXAS 1800 MAIN BUILDING AUSTIN, TEX 78712-1088 Population research center
P30HD-06160-20S1 0001 (SRC) BRADSHAW, BENJAMIN S Population research center Mortality of hispanic populations of the United States
P30HD-06160-20S1 0002 (SRC) BRADSHAW, BENJAMIN S Population research center Infant mortality amoung Mexican American, 1935-1985
P30HD-06160-20S1 0003 (SRC) KELLY, WILLIAM R Population research center Nonmarital fertility patterns
P30HD-06160-20S1 0004 (SRC) LANGOIS, JUDITH H Population research center Infant perception of faces and developmental status
P30HD-06160-20S1 0005 (SRC) PULLMAN, THOMAS W Population research center Effects of contextual factors on fertility regulation and fertility
P30HD-06160-20S1 9001 (SRC) BEAN, FRANK D Population research center Population research center
P30HD-06268-18 (HDPR) NATHANSON, CONSTANCE A JOHNS HOPKINS UNIVERSITY 615 N WOLFE STREET BALTIMORE, MD 21205 Hopkins population center
P30HD-06268-18 9004 (HDPR) KIMBALL, ALLYN W Hopkins population center Math/statistical core
P30HD-06268-18 9005 (HDPR) ZIRKIN, BARRY R Hopkins population center Electron microscopy lab core
P30HD-06268-18 9006 (HDPR) ZACUR, HOWARD Hopkins population center Radioimmunoassay core laboratory
P30HD-06268-18 9002 (HDPR) SONNTAG, EDITH E Hopkins population center Information core
P30HD-06268-18 9003 (HDPR) SU, SOL I Hopkins population center Data processing control--Core
P01HD-06274-20 (HDPR) STRAUSS, JEROME F, III UNIV OF PENNSYLVANIA/SCH OF ME 36TH & HAMILTON WALK PHILADELPHIA, PA 19104 A coordinated program in reproductive biology
P01HD-06274-20 0001 (HDPR) STOREY, BAYARD T A coordinated program in reproductive biology Reactions leading to fertilization
P01HD-06274-20 0009 (HDPR) FLICKINGER, GEORGE L A coordinated program in reproductive biology A role for macrophages in corpus luteum
P01HD-06274-20 0010 (HDPR) STRAUSS, JEROME F A coordinated program in reproductive biology Corpus luteum lipoprotein and sterol metabolism
P01HD-06274-20 9001 (HDPR) MASTROIANNI, LUIGI A coordinated program in reproductive biology Electron microscopy core
R01HD-06308-19 (REN) ROSENFIELD, ROBERT L UNIVERSITY OF CHICAGO 5841 SOUTH MARYLAND AVENUE CHICAGO, IL 60637 Free plasma sex hormones and androgen action
R01HD-06331-20 (GEN) LEWIS, EDWARD B CALIFORNIA INSTITUTE OF TECH 1201 E CALIFORNIA BLVD PASADENA, CA 91125 Genetic control of developmental pathways
R01HD-06335-18 (HED) FISHER, DELBERT A HARBOR-UCLA MEDICAL CENTER 1124 WEST CARSON STREET TORRANCE, CA 90502-2064 Vasopressin physiology in the fetus and newborn

PROJECT NO., ORGANIZATIONAL UNIT., INVESTIGATOR, ADDRESS, TITLE

PROJECT NO., ORGANIZATIONAL UNIT., INVESTIGATOR, ADDRESS, TITLE

R01HD-06380-18 (REB) ROSAZZA, JOHN P UNIVERSITY OF IOWA OBSTETRICS & GYNECOLOGY DEPT IOWA CITY, IA 52242 Catechols and prostaglandins--Uterine vascular function
R01HD-06426-20 (NLS) DAWSON, GLYN UNIVERSITY OF CHICAGO 5841 S MARYLAND AVE CHICAGO, IL 60637 Glycosphingolipid metabolism and mental retardation
R01HD-06556-19 (REB) MEAD, RODNEY A UNIVERSITY OF IDAHO MOSCOW, IDAHO 83843 Hormonal control of delayed implantation
R01HD-06565-25 (CBY) GIBBONS, BARBARA H PACIFIC BOMEDICAL RES CENTER 41 AHUI STREET HONOLULU, HAWAII 96813 Structural basis of spermatozoan motility
R01HD-06571-20 (REN) RILLEMA, JAMES A WAYNE STATE UNIVERSITY 540 E CANFIELD DETROIT, MI 48201 Hormonal control of metabolism in the mammary gland
P01HD-06576-18 (HDMR) DE VELLIS, JEAN UNIVERSITY OF CALIFORNIA 760 WESTWOOD PLAZA, RM 68-225 LOS ANGELES, CA 90024-1759 Molecular aspects of mental retardation
P01HD-06576-18 0008 (HDMR) CEDERBAUM, STEPHEN D Molecular aspects of mental retardation The expression and control of mammalian arginase
P01HD-06576-18 0014 (HDMR) HAGGERTY, DONALD F Molecular aspects of mental retardation Phenylalanine hydroxylase--Gene structure and function
P01HD-06576-18 0016 (HDMR) EDMOND, JOHN Molecular aspects of mental retardation Control of metabolites by developing brain
P01HD-06576-18 0017 (HDMR) ROME, LEONARD H Molecular aspects of mental retardation Lysosome biogenesis and function
P01HD-06576-18 0018 (HDMR) DE VELLIS, JEAN Molecular aspects of mental retardation Glial cell development and function
P30HD-06645-20 (HDPR) RYAN, KENNETH J HARVARD MEDICAL SCHOOL 45 SHATTUCK STREET BOSTON, MASS 02115 Center for population research
P30HD-06645-20 9001 (HDPR) VILLEE, CLAUDE A Center for population research Amino acids analysis core
P30HD-06645-20 9002 (HDPR) HUNT, RONALD D Center for population research Animal core
P30HD-06645-20 9004 (HDPR) ANDERSON, EVERETT Center for population research Morphology core
P30HD-06645-20 9005 (HDPR) ANDERSON, EVERETT Center for population research Photography core
P30HD-06645-20 9006 (HDPR) TODD, ROBERTA B Center for population research Radioimmunoassay core
P30HD-06645-20 9007 (HDPR) VILLEE, CLAUDE A Center for population research Seminar core
P30HD-06645-20 9009 (HDPR) MILLETTE, CLARKE F Center for population research Glasswashing core
P30HD-06645-20 9010 (HDPR) BEGG, DAVID A Center for population research Machine shop core
R01HD-06656-17A1 (REN) MENON, JAIRAM K UNIVERSITY OF MICHIGAN 1500 EAST MEDICAL CENTER DRIVE ANN ARBOR, MI 48109-0278 Regulation of ovarian function by gonadotropin
R01HD-06707-19 (BCE) NOTIDES, ANGELO C UNIVERSITY OF ROCHESTER 575 ELMWOOD AVE. ROCHESTER, N Y 14642 The uterine estrogen binding proteins
R37HD-06763-19 (PBC) BERNFIELD, MERTON R CHILDREN'S HOSP CORP/DEPT PED 300 LONGWOOD AVENUE BOSTON, MA 02115 Extracellular materials and embryonic organ formation
R01HD-06770-18 KOVACH, JOSEPH K MENNINGER FOUNDATION BOX 829 TOPEKA, KANS 66601 Development and mediation of a behavioral phenotype
R01HD-06773-20 (PBC) WOESSNER, J FREDERICK, JR UNIVERSITY OF MIAMI PO BOX 016960 MIAMI, FL 33101 Tissue collagenase and its control by steroids
R37HD-06864-18 (HUD) BROWN, ANN L UNIVERSITY OF CALIFORNIA 4533 TOLMAN HALL BERKELEY, CA 94720 Learning and transfer processes in knowledge acquisition
R01HD-06910-17 (HED) BACHVAROVA, ROSEMARY F CORNELL UNIVERSITY MED COLLEGE 1300 YORK AVENUE NEW YORK, NY 10021 Small RNAs and mRNA regulation in mouse oocytes and embryos
R13HD-07098-15 (HDMC) HALVORSON, HARLYN O LABORATORY OF DEVELOPMTL GENET MARINE BIOLOGICAL LABORATORY WOODS HOLE, MA 02543 Embryology
R01HD-07197-19 (BCE) GURPIDE, ERLIO MOUNT SINAI SCH OF MED 100TH STREET AND FIFTH AVENUE NEW YORK, N Y 10029 Steroid dynamics in endocrinology
R01HD-07204-19 (REB) ZIRKIN, BARRY R JOHNS HOPKINS UNIVERSITY 615 N WOLFE STREET BALTIMORE, MD 21205 Regulation of androgen secretion in mammalian testes
R01HD-07447-17 (HED) HANDWERGER, STUART CHILDRENS HOSPITAL MED CTR ELLAND AND BETHESDA AVE CINCINNATI, OH 45229 The physiology of placental lactogen
R01HD-07464-18 (MET) VOLPE, JOSEPH J THE CHILDREN'S HOSPITAL 300 LONGWOOD AVENUE BOSTON, MA 02115 Regulation of fatty acid synthesis during development
P30HD-07495-19 (HDPR) O'MALLEY, BERT W BAYLOR COLLEGE OF MEDICINE HOUSTON, TEX 77030 Cen for pop research and study in reproductive biology
P30HD-07495-19 9009 (HDPR) GLASSER, STANLEY R Cen for pop research and study in reproductive biology Animal resource--Core
P30HD-07495-19 9011 (HDPR) BIRNBAUMER, LUTZ Cen for pop research and study in reproductive biology Molecular probes--Core
P30HD-07495-19 9012 (HDPR) WOO, SAVIO L Cen for pop research and study in reproductive biology Molecular biology--Core
P30HD-07495-19 9015 (HDPR) MEANS, ANTHONY R Cen for pop research and study in reproductive biology Cell and organ culture--Core
P30HD-07495-19 9016 (HDPR) BORDELON, CASSIUS Cen for pop research and study in reproductive biology Histology, radioautography, and photography--Core
P30HD-07495-19 9017 (HDPR) HEATH, JULIAN Cen for pop research and study in reproductive biology Electron microscopy--Core
P30HD-07495-19 9018 (HDPR) WEIGEL, NANCY Cen for pop research and study in reproductive biology Protein analysis--Core
P30HD-07495-19 9019 (HDPR) DUNBAR, BONNIE Cen for pop research and study in reproductive biology Antibody production and distribution--Core
P30HD-07495-19 9020 (HDPR) O'MALLEY, BERT Cen for pop research and study in reproductive biology Sequencing and analysis--Core
P30HD-07495-19 9021 (HDPR) OVERBEEK, PAUL Cen for pop research and study in reproductive biology Transgenic animal--Core
R01HD-07504-17A2 (BCE) SCHWARTZ, NEENA B NORTHWESTERN UNIVERSITY 2153 SHERIDAN RD EVANSTON, IL 60208-3520 Environmental and hormonal interplay of ovulation
R01HD-07562-18 (HED) SMITH, CARL H WASHINGTON UNIVERSITY 600 SOUTH EUCLID AVENUE ST LOUIS, MO 63110 Placental mechanisms of cellular transport
R01HD-07796-19 (PC) EMERSON, CHARLES P, JR INSTITUTE OF CANCER RESEARCH 7701 BURHOLME AVENUE PHILADELPHIA, PA 19111 Control of muscle protein synthesis during myogenesis
R01HD-07841-14 (REN) NETT, TERRY M COLORADO STATE UNIVERSITY FORT COLLINS, CO 80523 Factors regulating synthesis and secretion of LH and FSH
R01HD-07843-16A1 (BCE) FRIESEN, HENRY G UNIVERSITY OF MANITOBA 770 BANNATYNE AVE WINNIPEG, R3E OW3 CANADA Placental protein and polypeptide hormones
R37HD-07857-20 (BCE) O'MALLEY, BERT W BAYLOR COLLEGE OF MEDICINE ONE BAYLOR PLAZA HOUSTON, TX 77030 Sex hormone receptor components & the cell genome
R01HD-07901-24 (IMB) COHEN, NICHOLAS Comparative and developmental immunobiology
P30HD-08008-15S3 (HDPR) WESTOFF, CHARLES F PRINCETON UNIVERSITY 21 PROSPECT AVENUE PRINCETON, N J 08544 Population research center
R01HD-08086-18 (CBY) BODE, HANS R UNIVERSITY OF CALIFORNIA DEVELOPMENT BIOLOGY CENTER IRVINE, CA 92717 Regulation of multipotent stem cell differentiation
R01HD-08129-13A2 (REB) MC CRACKEN, JOHN A WORCESTER FOUNDATION 222 MAPLE AVENUE SHREWSBURY, MA 01545 Hormone receptor regulation of PGF2 alpha secretion
R01HD-08188-20 (REB) O'MALLEY, BERT W BAYLOR COLLEGE OF MEDICINE 1200 MOURSUND AVENUE HOUSTON, TEX 77030 Reproductive hormones--Biological and molecular actions
R37HD-08192-19 (NSS) GORSKI, JACK UNIVERSITY OF WISCONSIN 420 HENRY MALL MADISON, WI 53706 Estrogen regulation of growth and function
R01HD-08299-18 (END) D'ERCOLE, A JOSEPH UNIVERSITY OF NORTH CAROLINA 509 BURNETT-WOMACK BLDG CHAPEL HILL, NC 27599-7220 The hormonal control of developmental growth
P01HD-08315-16 (SRC) GOODMAN, STEPHEN I UNIV OF COLORADO HLTH SCI CTR 4200 EAST NINTH AVE/C233 DENVER, CO 80262 Genetic biochemical disorders in mental retardation
P01HD-08315-16 0020 (SRC) GOODMAN, STEPHEN I. Genetic biochemical disorders in mental retardation Glutaric acidemia – Mutant glutaryl-coA dehydrogenase
P01HD-08315-16 0021 (SRC) FRERMAN, FRANK E. Genetic biochemical disorders in mental retardation Electron transfer domains and complexes of flavoproteins
P01HD-08315-16 0023 (SRC) HOWELL, NEIL Genetic biochemical disorders in mental retardation Molecular & biochemical analysis of mitochondrial diseases
P01HD-08315-16 0024 (SRC) GOODMAN, STEPHEN Genetic biochemical disorders in mental retardation Glutaric acidemia type II – Mutant electron transfer flavoprotein
P01HD-08315-16 0025 (SRC) KRAUS, JAN Genetic biochemical disorders in mental retardation Molecular analysis of inherited metabolic diseases
R01HD-08358-15 (BCE) PAYNE, ANITA H UNIVERSITY OF MICHIGAN ANN ARBOR, MI 48109-0278 Regulation of steroidogenic enzymes in leydig cells
R01HD-08406-14 (HED) SOLOFF, MELVYN S MEDICAL COLLEGE OF OHIO P O BOX 10008 TOLEDO, OH 43699-0008 Mechanisms of oxytocin action
R01HD-08431-17 (MGN) KOZAK, LESLIE P JACKSON LABORATORY 600 MAIN STREET BAR HARBOR, ME 04609-0800 Molecular genetics of thermogenesis
R01HD-08436-18 (BCE) CLARK, JAMES H BAYLOR COLLEGE OF MEDICINE ONE BAYLOR PLAZA HOUSTON, TX 77030 Estrogen receptors and reproductive functions
R01HD-08478-17 (END) JAFFE, ROBERT B UNIVERSITY OF CALIFORNIA 505 PARNASSUS AVENUE SAN FRANCISCO, CA 94143 Primate endocrine regulation in the perinatal period
R37HD-08485-17 (CBY) FRANKEL, JOSEPH UNIVERSITY OF IOWA DEPARTMENT OF BIOLOGY IOWA CITY, IA 52242 Analysis of spatial patterning in a unicellular organism
P30HD-08610-17 (HDPR) PLANT, TONY M UNIVERSITY OF PITTSBURGH W1451 BST PITTSBURGH, PA 15261 Center for research in reproductive physiology
P30HD-08610-17 9001 (HDPR) PLANT, TONY M Center for research in reproductive physiology The primate core
P30HD-08610-17 9003 (HDPR) POHL, CLIFFORD R Center for research in reproductive physiology Core--Radioimmunoassay reagents
P30HD-08610-17 9004 (HDPR) RYAN, KATHLEEN D Center for research in reproductive physiology Core--Histology
P30HD-08610-17 9005 (HDPR) ATTARDI, BARBARA J AND DEFRANC Center for research in reproductive physiology Core--Molecular endocrinology
R01HD-08615-17A1 (BCE) STANCEL, GEORGE M UNIVERSITY OF TEXAS MED SCH POST OFFICE BOX 20708 HOUSTON, TX 77225 Estrogen control of uterine growth and cell division
R01HD-08634-15 (REB) KALRA, SATYA P UNIV OF FLORIDA COLLEGE OF MED GAINESVILLE, FL 32610 Brain-gut peptides in female reproduction-ovulation
R01HD-08662-16 (IMB) GILL, THOMAS J, III UNIV OF PITTSBURGH PITTSBURGH, PA 15261 Maternal fetal interactions and the immune response
R01HD-08700-17 (HED) SHERWOOD, ORRIN D UNIVERSITY OF ILLINOIS DEPT OF PHYSIOLOGY & BIOPHYSIC URBANA, ILL 61801 Relaxin--Biochemical and physiological studies
Z01HD-08719-11 (LMGR) HOWARD, B H NICHD, NIH Development and uses of eukaryotic vectors
R01HD-08766-25 (END) BAHL, OM P STATE UNIV NEW YORK AT BUFFAL COOKE HALL 347 BUFFALO, NY 14260 Chemistry & biology of human & other gonadotropins

PROJECT NO., ORGANIZATIONAL UNIT., INVESTIGATOR, ADDRESS, TITLE

R01HD-08783-17 (HED) ROSENFELD, CHARLES R UNIVERSITY OF TEXAS SW MED CTR 5323 HARRY HINES BLVD DALLAS, TX 75235-9063 Studies of utero-placental circulation
R01HD-08924-16 (END) WEINER, RICHARD I UNIV OF CALIFORNIA/BOX 0556 SAN FRANCISCO, CA 94143 Role of brain monoamines in luteinizing hormone and prolactin release
R01HD-08933-16 (BPO) SACHS, BENJAMIN D UNIVERSITY OF CONNECTICUT 406 BABBIDGE ROAD STORRS, CT 06269-1020 Analysis of masculine behavior
R01HD-09020-16 (END) GALTON, VALERIE A DARTMOUTH MEDICAL SCHOOL HANOVER, NH 03756 Mechanisms of thyroid hormone action in development
R01HD-09046-15 (PC) LUCAS, JOHN J SUNY HLTH SCIS CTR AT SYRACUSE 750 E ADAMS STREET SYRACUSE, NY 13210 Membrane glycoprotein changes during differentiation
P50HD-09140-16 (HDPR) SPELSBERG, THOMAS C MAYO FOUNDATION 200 FIRST STREET SOUTHWEST ROCHESTER, MN 55905 Mode of action of reproductive hormones--SPRCG
P50HD-09140-16 0001 (HDPR) SPELSBERG, THOMAS C Mode of action of reproductive hormones--SPRCG Chromatin acceptor sites for progesterone
P50HD-09140-16 0008 (HDPR) MCCORMICK, DANIEL J Mode of action of reproductive hormones--SPRCG Structure/function of human gonadotropins and receptors
P50HD-09140-16 0012 (HDPR) TOFT, DAVID O Mode of action of reproductive hormones--SPRCG Isolation and characterization of progesterone receptor
P50HD-09140-16 0013 (HDPR) WIEBEN, ERIC D Mode of action of reproductive hormones--SPRCG Androgen action--Control of individual cell growth
P50HD-09140-16 0014 (HDPR) PENNISTON, JOHN T Mode of action of reproductive hormones--SPRCG Intracellular Ca++ control in reproductive cells
P50HD-09140-16 0015 (HDPR) TINDALL, DONALD J Mode of action of reproductive hormones--SPRCG The molecular biology of androgen receptor
P50HD-09140-16 9003 (HDPR) DAVID, CHELLA S Mode of action of reproductive hormones--SPRCG Core--Monoclonal antibody
R37HD-09172-17 (NEUC) PALMITER, RICHARD D UNIVERSITY OF WASHINGTON DEPT OF BIOCHEMISTRY SL-15 SEATTLE, WA 98195 Transgenic approaches to nervous system development
R01HD-09195-16 (HED) CHYTIL, FRANK VANDERBILT UNIVERSITY SCH OF M NASHVILLE, TN 37232 Vitamin A in growth and development
P01HD-09402-16 (HDMR) SCHWARTZ, NANCY B UNIVERSITY OF CHICAGO 5841 S MARYLAND AVE/BOX 426 CHICAGO, IL 60637 Biological basis of mental retardation
P01HD-09402-16 0002 (HDMR) SCHWARTZ, NANCY B Biological basis of mental retardation Structure and synthesis of proteoglycans
P01HD-09402-16 0007 (HDMR) SMALHEISER, NEIL Biological basis of mental retardation Molecular and cellular basis of laminin
P01HD-09402-16 0008 (HDMR) PERLMAN, ROBERT Biological basis of mental retardation Proliferation and differentiation of PC12 cells
P01HD-09402-16 0009 (HDMR) DAWSON, GLYN Biological basis of mental retardation The molecular basis of B-mannosidosis
R01HD-09421-15 (REN) IMPERATO-MCGINLEY, JULIANNE L CORNELL UNIVERSITY MED COLLEGE 1300 YORK AVENUE NEW YORK, NY 10021 Male pseudohermaphroditism--The biology of androgens
R01HD-09490-15 (REB) TURNER, TERRY T UNIVERSITY OF VIRGINIA BOX 422 CHARLOTTESVILLE, VA 22908 The epididymal androgen microenvironment
R01HD-09581-14 (BCE) BIRNBAUMER, LUTZ BAYLOR COLLEGE OF MEDICINE ONE BAYLOR PLAZA HOUSTON, TX 77030 Gonodotrophin and prostaglandin action in the ovary
R01HD-09613-15 (HUD) HARTER, SUSAN UNIV OF DENVER UNIVERSITY PARK DENVER, CO 80208 Self-concept, affect and motivation in children
R01HD-09618-14 (REB) SANBORN, BARBARA M UNIVERSITY OF TEXAS P O BOX 20708 HOUSTON, TEX 77225 Uterine relaxing factors--Molecular aspects of action
R37HD-09635-16 (CBY) EDELMAN, GERALD M ROCKEFELLER UNIVERSITY 1230 YORK AVENUE NEW YORK, N Y 10021 Cell-cell adhesion among embryonic cells
P01HD-09690-18 (HDPR) LING, NICHOLAS CHI-KWAN WHITTIER INSTITUTE 9894 GENESEE AVENUE LA JOLLA, CA 92037 Neuroendocrinology of reproduction and growth
P01HD-09690-18 0001 (HDPR) LING, NICHOLAS Neuroendocrinology of reproduction and growth Growth factors in follicular fluid
P01HD-09690-18 0002 (HDPR) BICSAK, THOMAS Neuroendocrinology of reproduction and growth Regulation and intragonadal action of IGF-binding proteins
P01HD-09690-18 0003 (HDPR) DEPAOLO, LOUIS Neuroendocrinology of reproduction and growth Physiological role of follistatin in reproduction
P01HD-09690-18 0004 (HDPR) SHIMASAKI, SHUNICHI Neuroendocrinology of reproduction and growth Regulation of gonadal polypeptide gene expression
P01HD-09690-18 9002 (HDPR) LING, NICHOLAS C Neuroendocrinology of reproduction and growth Peptide synthesis-Core
P01HD-09690-18 9003 (HDPR) DEPAOLO, LOUIS Neuroendocrinology of reproduction and growth Radioimmunoassays-Core
P01HD-09690-18 9006 (HDPR) SHIMASKI, SHUNICHI Neuroendocrinology of reproduction and growth Core--DNA sequencing and oligonucleotide synthesis
R01HD-09713-15 (NLS) SLOTKIN, THEODORE A DUKE UNIVERSITY BOX 3813 DURHAM, N C 27710 Drugs and development of adrenergic nervous system
R01HD-09800-15 (IMS) STIEHM, E RICHARD UCLA SCHOOL OF MEDICINE 405 HILGARD LOS ANGELES, CA 90024-1752 Cellular immunity in sick and malnourished infants
R01HD-09880-14 (HED) GILL, THOMAS J, III UNIVERSITY OF PITTSBURGH 776 SCAIFE HALL PITTSBURGH, PA 15261 Maternal-fetal interactions and the immune response
R01HD-09885-16 (BCE) TUREK, FRED W NORTHWESTERN UNIVERSITY 2153 SHERIDAN ROAD EVANSTON, IL 60208 Photoperiodic control of neuroendocrine-gonadal activity
R01HD-09921-14 (REN) ZIRKIN, BARRY R JOHNS HOPKINS UNIVERSITY 615 N WOLFE STREET BALTIMORE, MD 21205 Regulation of spermatogenesis in mammals
R01HD-09948-15 (GEN) LENGYEL, JUDITH A UNIVERSITY OF CALIFORNIA 405 HILGARD AVE LOS ANGELES, CA 90024 Analysis of steps controlling gene expression in Drosophila
P30HD-10003-16 (HDPR) ANDERSON, BARBARA A POPULATION STUDIES CENTER 1225 SOUTH UNIV AVENUE ANN ARBOR, MI 48104-2590 Population studies center
P30HD-10003-16 9001 (HDPR) ANDERSON, ALBERT F Population studies center Core--Data processing
P30HD-10003-16 9002 (HDPR) BOUND, JOHN Population studies center Core--Statistical consulting
P30HD-10003-16 9003 (HDPR) HOUSH, CYNTHIA H Population studies center Core--Publication
P30HD-10003-16 9004 (HDPR) GROESBECK, LOIS J Population studies center Core--Library
P30HD-10003-16 9005 (HDPR) COBLE, MICHAEL J Population studies center Core--Data archive
R01HD-10032-15 (HUD) ROBINSON, ARTHUR NATL JEWISH CTR/IMMUN & RES ME 1400 JACKSON STREET DENVER, CO 80206 Sex chromosomal abnormalities--a prospectiv study
P30HD-10202-15 (HDPR) PAUERSTEIN, CARL J UNIV OF TEXAS HLTH SCI CTR 7703 FLOYD CURL DRIVE SAN ANTONIO, TX 78284 Center for research in reproductive biology
P30HD-10202-15 9002 (HDPR) SILER-KHOR, THERESA M Center for research in reproductive biology Radioimmunoassay core facility
P30HD-10202-15 9005 (HDPR) CHAMNESS, GARY C Center for research in reproductive biology Steroid hormone receptor core facility
P30HD-10202-15 9006 (HDPR) KING, THOMAS S Center for research in reproductive biology Neuroendocrine core
P30HD-10202-15 9008 (HDPR) BOWMAN, BARBARA H Center for research in reproductive biology Developmental genetics core
R01HD-10254-16 (BCE) GARBERS, DAVID L UNIV TEXAS SW MEDICAL CENTER 5323 HARRY HINES BLVD. DALLAS, TX 75235 Regulation of sperm cyclic nucleotide metabolism
R01HD-10333-15 (HUD) DE FRIES, JOHN C UNIVERSITY OF COLORADO CAMPUS BOX 447 BOULDER, CO 80309 Determinants of behavioral development in children
R01HD-10342-16 (HED) ENDERS, ALLEN C UNIVERSITY OF CALIFORNIA DEPARTMENT OF HUMAN ANATOMY DAVIS, CALIF 95616 Mechanisms of implantation of the blastocyst
P30HD-10379-15 (HDPR) MENKEN, JANE UNIVERSITY OF PENNSYLVANIA 3718 LOCUST WK, POPUL ST CTR PHILADELPHIA, PA 19104 Population studies center
R01HD-10463-09 (REB) MORRILL, GENE A ALBERT EINSTEIN COLLEGE OF MED 1300 MORRIS PARK AVENUE BRONX, N Y 10461 Steroid action at the oocyte plasma membrane
R01HD-10580-13 (BIO) KENT, CLAUDIA M PURDUE UNIVERSITY WEST LAFAYETTE, IN 47907 Regulation of mammalian phospholipid metabolism
R01HD-10665-16 (BCE) SILVERMAN, ANN J COLUMBIA UNIVERSITY 630 WEST 168TH STREET NEW YORK, N Y 10032 Organization of the endocrine hypothalamus
R01HD-10668-16 (IMB) ARTZT, KAREN UNIVERSITY OF TEXAS DEPARTMENT OF ZOOLOGY AUSTIN, TX 78712 Immunogenetics of spermatozoa, eggs, and embryos
P01HD-10699-15 (HDMC) ALFORD, CHARLES A, JR UNIV OF ALABAMA AT BIRMINGHAM DEPARTMENT OF PEDIATRICS BIRMINGHAM, ALA 35294 Perinatal infections, immunity, and maldevelopment
P01HD-10699-15 0001 (HDMC) STAGNO, SERGIO Perinatal infections, immunity, and maldevelopment Type of maternal CMV infection in relation to infection of the offspring
P01HD-10699-15 0004 (HDMC) PASS, ROBERT F Perinatal infections, immunity, and maldevelopment Central nervous system sequelae of congenital CMV
P01HD-10699-15 0013 (HDMC) PASS, ROBERT F Perinatal infections, immunity, and maldevelopment Cellular immune responses to CMV in cogneital and perinatal infections
P01HD-10699-15 0015 (HDMC) PASS, ROBERT Perinatal infections, immunity, and maldevelopment Sources of maternal and fetal CMV infection
P01HD-10699-15 0016 (HDMC) BRITT, WILLIAM Perinatal infections, immunity, and maldevelopment Host immunity and CMV infection in mothers/offspring
R01HD-10718-15 (REB) BEHRMAN, HAROLD R YALE UNIVERSITY 333 CEDAR ST, PO BOX 3333 NEW HAVENS, CT 06510 Ovarian endocrine control by purines and prostaglandins
R01HD-10793-14 (REB) KISTLER, W STEPHEN UNIVERSITY OF SOUTH CAROLINA COLUMBIA, S C 29208 Role of specific proteins in spermatogenesis
R01HD-10808-14 (REN) GRISWOLD, MICHAEL D WASHINGTON STATE UNIVERSITY PULLMAN, WA 99164-4660 Hormonal regulation of sertoli cell maturation
R01HD-10823-13 (HED) HAMOSH, MARGIT GEORGETOWN UNIVERSITY 3900 RESERVOIR ROAD, N W WASHINGTON, D C 20007 Perinatal fat digestion, role of oro-pharyngeal lipase
R01HD-10907-13A2 (BCE) GOLDSMITH, PAUL C UNIVERSITY OF CALIFORNIA 3RD & PARNASSUS AVENUES SAN FRANCISCO, CA 94143-0556 Control and integration of GNRH neural pathways
P01HD-10981-14 (HDMR) MOSER, HUGO W KENNEDY RESEARCH INSTITUTE, IN 707 NORTH BROADWAY BALTIMORE, MD 21205 Genetic causes of mental retardation
P01HD-10981-14 0001 (HDMR) THOMAS, GEORGE H Genetic causes of mental retardation Sialic acid and sialidase abnormalities in mucolipidosis II and III
P01HD-10981-14 0007 (HDMR) KISHIMOTO, YASUO Genetic causes of mental retardation Adrenoleukodystrophy--enzyme defect study in vitro
P01HD-10981-14 0008 (HDMR) CHEN, WINSTON W Genetic causes of mental retardation Adrenoleukodystrophy
P01HD-10981-14 0009 (HDMR) MOSER, HUGO W Genetic causes of mental retardation Adrenoleukodystrophy--Studies in patients and experimental animals
P01HD-10981-14 0010 (HDMR) THOMAS, GEORGE H Genetic causes of mental retardation Sialidase and the degradation of sialocompounds

PROJECT NO., ORGANIZATIONAL UNIT., INVESTIGATOR, ADDRESS, TITLE

P01HD-10981-14 0011 (HDMR) BATSHAW, MARK L Genetic causes of mental retardation Asymptomatic hyperammonemia--A cause of cortical dysfunction

P01HD-10981-14 9001 (HDMR) VALLE, DAVID L Genetic causes of mental retardation "CORE" shared clinical research and laboratory facility

R37HD-10993-15 (HED) THACH, BRADLEY T WASHINGTON UNIVERSITY 400 S KINGSHIGHWAY BOULEVARD ST LOUIS, MO 63110 Control of breathing in recovery from apnea

P50HD-11089-14 (SRC) KALHAN, SATISH C UNIVERSITY HOSPITALS 2074 ABINGTON ROAD CLEVELAND, OHIO 44106 Perinatal studies of disorders of fetal metabolism

P50HD-11089-14 0019 (SRC) HERTZ, ROGER H. Perinatal studies of disorders of fetal metabolism Geastational diabetes-- Detection and clinical intervention

P50HD-11089-14 0020 (SRC) PHILIPSON, ELLIOT H. Perinatal studies of disorders of fetal metabolism Carbohydrate metabolism in pregnancy -- Effect of gestational diabetes

P50HD-11089-14 0021 (SRC) KALHAN, SATISH C Perinatal studies of disorders of fetal metabolism Protein and fat metabolism in pregnancy and newborn

P50HD-11089-14 0022 (SRC) CLAPP, JAMES F. Perinatal studies of disorders of fetal metabolism Metabolic and cardiopulmonary adaptions in the initial pregnancy

P50HD-11089-14 0023 (SRC) WOLFSON, ROBERT N. Perinatal studies of disorders of fetal metabolism Maternal hyperglycemia -- Effect on neonatal cardiovascular system

P50HD-11089-14 0024 (SRC) MOORE, JOHN J. Perinatal studies of disorders of fetal metabolism Control of human estrogen production by AMP dependent processes

P50HD-11089-14 0025 (SRC) ROBERTSON, STEVEN S. Perinatal studies of disorders of fetal metabolism The coupling behavior and metabolism in the human newborn

P50HD-11089-14 0026 (SRC) KERR, DOUGLAS S. Perinatal studies of disorders of fetal metabolism The metabolic role of epinephrine around birth and in childhood

P50HD-11089-14 0027 (SRC) PATEL, MULCHAND S. Perinatal studies of disorders of fetal metabolism Long term metabolic consequences of early nutritional modification

P50HD-11089-14 9002 (SRC) SAVIN, SAMUEL M Perinatal studies of disorders of fetal metabolism Core metabolism laboratories

P50HD-11089-14 9003 (SRC) ADAM, PETER A Perinatal studies of disorders of fetal metabolism Data Unit

R01HD-11109-13 (HED) CHARLTON, VALERIE E UNIV OF CA, SAN FRAN., 587U 3RD AND PARNASSUS AVENUES SAN FRANCISCO, CALIF 94143 Fetal nutrient therapy--Effects on growth retardation

R37HD-11119-14 (REB) GIBORI, GEULA UNIVERSITY OF ILLINOIS P O BOX 6998 CHICAGO, IL 60680 Regulation of luteal function

R01HD-11134-14S1 (BIO) BRUSILOW, SAUL W JOHNS HOPKINS HOSPITAL 600 NORTH WOLFE STREET BALTIMORE, MD 21205 Urea cycle enzymopathies

P50HD-11149-14 (HDMC) MACDONALD, PAUL C UNIV OF TX HLTH SCI CTR 5323 HARRY HINES BOULEVARD DALLAS, TEXAS 75235-9051 Initiation of human labor--Prevention of prematurity

P50HD-11149-14 0004 (HDMC) JOHNSTON, JOHN M Initiation of human labor--Prevention of prematurity Arachidonic acid and platelet activating factor during birth

P50HD-11149-14 0009 (HDMC) SIMPSON, EVAN R Initiation of human labor--Prevention of prematurity Regulation of steroidogenesis in the human fetal adrenal

P50HD-11149-14 0011 (HDMC) CASEY, M LINNETTE Initiation of human labor--Prevention of prematurity Regulation of myometrial contractile response

P50HD-11149-14 0012 (HDMC) PORTER, JOHN C Initiation of human labor--Prevention of prematurity Cervical softening--Antecedent of labor

P50HD-11149-14 0013 (HDMC) SYNDER, JEANNE Initiation of human labor--Prevention of prematurity Paracrine regulation of decidual function

P50HD-11149-14 0014 (HDMC) MAC DONALD, PAUL Initiation of human labor--Prevention of prematurity Maintenance of pregnancy and the initiation of parturition

R37HD-11210-12 (HED) ROSE, JAMES C BOWMAN GRAY SCHOOL OF MEDICINE 300 SOUTH HAWTHORNE ROAD WINSTON-SALEM, N C 27103 Prenatal and neonatal pituitary adrenal function

R01HD-11239-15 (CTY) RIDDLE, DONALD L UNIVERSITY OF MISSOURI DIV OF BIOLOGICAL SCIENCES COLUMBIA, MO 65211 Developmental genetics of the C. elegans dauer larva

P50HD-11343-14A1 (SRC) OH, WILLIAM WOMEN & INFANTS HOSPITAL 101 DUDLEY STREET PROVIDENCE, R I 02905-2401 Diabetes during pregnancy -- Effects on the offspring

P50HD-11343-14A1 0014 (SRC) STONESTREET, BARBARA S Diabetes during pregnancy -- Effects on the offspring Fetal circulatory adjustment in diabetic pregnancy

P50HD-11343-14A1 0018 (SRC) CARPENTER, MARSHALL W Diabetes during pregnancy -- Effects on the offspring Exercise and glucose homeostasis in gestational diabetes

P50HD-11343-14A1 0019 (SRC) VOHR, BETTY Diabetes during pregnancy -- Effects on the offspring Infants of gestational diabetic mothers -- Birth to seven years

P50HD-11343-14A1 0020 (SRC) OH, WILLIAM Diabetes during pregnancy -- Effects on the offspring Behavioral intervention and growth in infants with prenatal growth retardation

P50HD-11343-14A1 0021 (SRC) GRUPPUSO, PHILIP Diabetes during pregnancy -- Effects on the offspring Regulation of fetal hepatic development by insulin

P50HD-11343-14A1 9002 (SRC) SUSA, JOHN Diabetes during pregnancy -- Effects on the offspring Core B -- Laboratory

R01HD-11355-13 (REN) TERASAWA, EI UNIVERSITY OF WISCONSIN 1223 CAPITOL COURT MADISON, WIS 53715 Hypothalamic control of puberty

R01HD-11362-11 (REB) KALRA, PUSHPA S UNIV OF FLORIDA COLL OF MED PO BOX J-294 JHMHC GAINESVILLE, FL 32610 Steroids and hypothalamic interactions in male rats

R01HD-11487-14A1 (END) DANNIES, PRISCILLA S YALE UNIVERSITY SCHOOL OF MED 333 CEDAR STREET NEW HAVEN, CT 06510 Regulation of hormone synthesis and secretion

PROJECT NO., ORGANIZATIONAL UNIT., INVESTIGATOR, ADDRESS, TITLE

R01HD-11489-15 (BCE) MARSHALL, JOHN C UNIVERSITY OF VIRGINIA BOX 466 CHARLOTTESVILLE, VA 22908 Regulation of gonadotrope function by pulsatile GNRH

R37HD-11590-13 (REB) NISWENDER, GORDON D COLORADO STATE UNIVERSITY DEPARTMENT OF PHYSIOLOGY FORT COLLINS, CO 80523 Regulation of LH receptors and progesterone secretion

R01HD-11658-15 (REB) KING, BARRY F DEPARTMENT OF HUMAN ANATOMY DAVIS, CA 95616 Functional cytology of the placenta and fetal membranes

R01HD-11669-13 (REB) FREEMAN, MARC E FLORIDA STATE UNIVERSITY DEPARTMENT OF BIOLOGICA SCIS TALLAHASSEE, FLA 32306 Control of prolactin secretion

P01HD-11725-13 (SRC) TSANG, REGINALD C UNIV. OF CINCINNATI MED CTR 231 BETHESDA AVENUE CINCINNATI, OH 45267-0541 Diabetes in pregnancy

P01HD-11725-13 0001 (SRC) MIODOVNIK, MENACHEM Diabetes in pregnancy Strict glycemic control of diabetes in pregnancy

P01HD-11725-13 0004 (SRC) MIMOUNI, FRANCIS Diabetes in pregnancy Magnesium deficiency--Neonatal hypocalcemia in diabetic mothers' infants

P01HD-11725-13 0005 (SRC) ROSS, RICHARDUS Diabetes in pregnancy Induction and maintenance of diabetes in the pregnant sheep

P01HD-11725-13 0006 (SRC) WHITSETT, JEFFREY A Diabetes in pregnancy Lung apoprotein studies

P01HD-11725-13 0007 (SRC) BERK, MICHAEL A Diabetes in pregnancy Hypoglycemia, maternal and perinatal mortality

P01HD-11725-13 0008 (SRC) CUPPOLETTI, JOHN Diabetes in pregnancy Regulation of myocardial D-glucose transport--Fetus of diabetic sheep

P01HD-11725-13 0009 (SRC) SPERLING, MARK A Diabetes in pregnancy Pancreatic beta-cell function & body composition in diabetic pregnancy offspring

P01HD-11725-13 0010 (SRC) BERK, MICHAEL Diabetes in pregnancy Effects of pregnancy on diabetic microvascular disease

P01HD-11725-13 0011 (SRC) ROSS, RICHARDUS Diabetes in pregnancy Maternal-fetal mineral metabolism in diabetic pregnancy

P01HD-11725-13 0012 (SRC) SPERLING, MARK Diabetes in pregnancy Glucose kinetics in alloxan diabetic pregnant sheep

P01HD-11725-13 9001 (SRC) HERTZBERG, VICKI Diabetes in pregnancy Core--Biostatistics

R01HD-11762-14 (GEN) WOOD, WILLIAM B UNIVERSITY OF COLORADO CAMPUS BOX 0347 BOULDER, COLORADO 80309 Genetic control of embryogenesis in C elegans

R01HD-11840-13 (BNP) ROBINSON, CECIL H JOHNS HOPKINS UNIV SCH OF MED 725 NORTH WOLFE STREET BALTIMORE, MD 21205 Selective inhibitors of placental steroid aromatase

R01HD-11878-13 (REB) HECHT, NORMAN B TUFTS UNIVERSITY MEDFORD, MA 02155 RNA synthesis in spermatozoa

R01HD-11884-13 (REB) KIERSZENBAUM, ABRAHAM L CITY COLLEGE CUNY 138TH ST & CONVENT AVE NEW YORK, NY 10031 Bioregulation of spermatogenesis

R37HD-11932-13 (HED) JOBE, ALAN H HARBOR-UCLA MEDICAL CENTER 1124 W CARSON ST RB-1 TORRANCE, CA 90502 Lung phospholipid appearance and stability

P01HD-11944-12 (HDMR) EDGERTON, ROBERT B UNIVERSITY OF CALIFORNIA 760 WESTWOOD PLAZA LOS ANGELES, CA 90024-1759 The community adaptation of mildly retarded persons

P01HD-11944-12 0003 (HDMR) KERNAN, KEITH T The community adaptation of mildly retarded persons Linguistic, communicative, and cognitive competence

P01HD-11944-12 0004 (HDMR) EDGERTON, ROBERT The community adaptation of mildly retarded persons Lives and needs of aging mentally retarded

P01HD-11944-12 0005 (HDMR) LANGNESS, LEWIS The community adaptation of mildly retarded persons Life histories of the mildly mentally retarded

P01HD-11944-12 0006 (HDMR) NIHIRA, KAZUO The community adaptation of mildly retarded persons Asian-American families with mentally retarded children

P01HD-11944-12 0007 (HDMR) GALLIMORE, RONALD The community adaptation of mildly retarded persons Performance of Hispanic children at risk for development/education delay

P01HD-11944-12 0008 (HDMR) BROWNER, CAROLE The community adaptation of mildly retarded persons Reproductive decision making for genetic reasons

P01HD-11944-12 0009 (HDMR) WILLIAMS, DOUGLAS The community adaptation of mildly retarded persons Behavior in interpersonal situations among the emotionally disturbed

R01HD-11959-11 (HUD) MITCHELL, MARVIN L STATE LABORATORY INSTITUTE 305 SOUTH STREET JAMAICA PLAIN, MA 02130 New England hypothyroidism collaborative follow-up study

R01HD-11962-13 (REB) HAMILTON, DAVID W UNIVERSITY OF MINNESOTA 321 CHURCH ST S E MINNEAPOLIS, MINN 55455 Structure and function of epididymis and vas deferens

P30HD-11979-13 (HDPR) JAFFE, ROBERT B UNIV OF CALIFORNIA/REP ENDO CT HSW 1656, BOX 0556 SAN FRANCISCO, CA 94143 Reproductive endocrinology center core facilities

P30HD-11979-13 9001 (HDPR) MONROE, SCOTT E Reproductive endocrinology center core facilities Radioimmunoassay core

P30HD-11979-13 9003 (HDPR) GOLDSMITH, PAUL C Reproductive endocrinology center core facilities Morphology--Core

P30HD-11979-13 9004 (HDPR) MONROE, SCOTT E Reproductive endocrinology center core facilities Primate core

P30HD-11979-13 9005 (HDPR) KUHN, ROBERT W Reproductive endocrinology center core facilities Analytical separation

R01HD-12011-13A1 (BCE) LUINE, VICTORIA N HUNTER COLLEGE OF CUNY 695 PARK AVENUE NEW YORK, NY 10021 Serotonergic systems and hormone dependent sexual behavior

R01HD-12014-13 (REB) ZELEZNIK, ANTHONY J MAGEE WOMENS HOSPITAL 300 HALKET STREET PITTSBURGH, PA 15213 Control of folliculogenesis

R01HD-12046-12 (BCE) JUNGMANN, RICHARD A 303 E CHICAGO AVENUE CHICAGO, IL 60611 Gonadotropin regulation of ovarian differentiation

R01HD-12137-10 (REB) TURGEON, JUDITH L UNIVERSITY OF CALIFORNIA DAVIS, CA 95616 Gonadotropin secretion in vitro

PROJECT NO., ORGANIZATIONAL UNIT., INVESTIGATOR, ADDRESS, TITLE

R01HD-12178-13 (MGN) SHAPIRO, LARRY J HARBOR-UCLA MEDICAL CENTER 1000 WEST CARSON STREET TORRANCE, CA 90509 Genetics & biochemical studies of steroid sulfatase

R01HD-12252-14 (SSS) SIERVOGEL, ROGER M THE FELS RESEARCH INSTITUTE 1005 XENIA AVENUE YELLOW SPRINGS, OH 45387 Subcutaneous fat, blood lipids and subsequent outcome

P50HD-12303-13 (HDPR) YEN, SAMUEL S UNIV OF CALIF, SAN DIEGO DEPT OF REPRO MED 0802 LA JOLLA, CA 92093-0802 Control of the hypothalamic-hypophyseal-ovarian system

P50HD-12303-13 0001 (HDPR) YEN, SAMUEL S Control of the hypothalamic-hypophyseal-ovarian system Neuroendocrine control of gonadotropin secretion in women

P50HD-12303-13 0004 (HDPR) MORTOLA, JOSEPH Control of the hypothalamic-hypophyseal-ovarian system Pathophysiology of premenstrual syndrome

P50HD-12303-13 0005 (HDPR) RASMUSSEN, DENNIS D Control of the hypothalamic-hypophyseal-ovarian system POMC peptides in the neuroendocrinology of reproduction

P50HD-12303-13 0006 (HDPR) LIU, JAMES H Control of the hypothalamic-hypophyseal-ovarian system Postpartum hypothalamic amenorrhea

P50HD-12303-13 0007 (HDPR) NY, TOR Control of the hypothalamic-hypophyseal-ovarian system Hormone regulation of tissue plasminogen activator

P50HD-12303-13 9001 (HDPR) YEN, SAMUEL S Control of the hypothalamic-hypophyseal-ovarian system Radioiassay and neuroendocrine laboratory core

R01HD-12304-11 (REB) DEY, SUDHANSU K UNIV OF KANSAS MEDICAL CTR 39TH & RAINBOW KANSAS CITY, KANS 66103 Aspects of blastocyst implantation

R01HD-12308-07A2 (HED) WILSON, DORIS B UNIV OF CALIFORNIA, SAN DIEGO DIVISION OF ANATOMY, M-004 LA JOLLA, CA 92093-0023 Growth and differentiation of the pituitary gland

R55HD-12335-13A1 (GMB) BRUNS, MARY E UNIVERSITY OF VIRGINIA BOX 214 CHARLOTTESVILLE, VA 22908 Developmental aspects of mammalian calcium transport

R01HD-12356-10A1 (REB) GIBORI, GEULA UNIVERSITY OF ILLINOIS 901 SOUTH WOLCOTT AVE M/C 901 CHICAGO, IL 60680 Function of the decidual tissue

R22HD-12437-12 (GMA) WALKER, W ALLAN MASSACHUSETTS GENERAL HOSPITAL PEDIATRIC GASTN & NTN UNIT BOSTON, MA 02114 Effect of colostrum on gut maturation and host defense

R01HD-12496-09S1 (GMB) TOVERUD, SVEIN U UNIVERSITY OF NORTH CAROLINA CHAPEL HILL, NC 27599-7455 Vitamin D and calcium in lactating and suckling rats

R01HD-12625-13 (BCE) STEINER, ROBERT A UNIVERSITY OF WASHINGTON SCHOOL OF MEDICINE RH-20 SEATTLE, WASH 98195 Control of gnrh gene expression in the primate brain

P50HD-12629-12 (HDPR) BREMNER, WILLIAM J VETERANS AFFAIRS MEDICAL CENTE 1660 SOUTH SOLUMBIAN WAY SEATTLE, WA 98108 NICHD population research center grant

P50HD-12629-12 0001 (HDPR) BREMNER, WILLIAM J NICHD population research center grant Hormonal control of human spermatogenesis

P50HD-12629-12 0008 (HDPR) STEINER, ROBERT A NICHD population research center grant Neuroendocrine genes governing reproduction

P50HD-12629-12 0009 (HDPR) MCKNIGHT, G STANLEY NICHD population research center grant Role of cAMP-dependent protein kinases in spermatogenesis

P50HD-12629-12 0010 (HDPR) HILLE, BERTE NICHD population research center grant Control of peptidergic cells in the reproductive axis

P50HD-12629-12 0011 (HDPR) SAGE, HELENE NICHD population research center grant Regulation of testis cell differentiation by extracellular matrix

P50HD-12629-12 9002 (HDPR) BREMNER, WILLIAM J NICHD population research center grant Core--Hormone assay

P50HD-12629-12 9004 (HDPR) IDZERDA, REJEAN NICHD population research center grant Core--Molecular biology

P50HD-12629-12 9005 (HDPR) STEINER, ROBERT NICHD population research center grant Core-Histology

R01HD-12637-12 (NTN) GREENWOOD, MARY R UNIVERSITY OF CALIFORNIA DAVIS, CA 95616 Nutrition and adipocyte growth and development

P50HD-12639-12 (SRC) SMITH, JAMES P RAND CORPORATION 1700 MAIN STREET, PO BOX 2138 SANTA MONICA, CA 90406-2138 Population research center

P50HD-12639-12 0012 (SRC) LEIBOWITZ, ARLEEN Population research center Women's work near childbirth

P50HD-12639-12 0013 (SRC) LILLARD, LEE Population research center Marital fertility--Relative income and business cycle effects

P50HD-12639-12 0014 (SRC) WAITE, LINDA J Population research center Cohabitation, marriage, fertility, and disruption

P50HD-12639-12 0015 (SRC) GOLDSCHEIDER, FRANCIS K Population research center Leaving and returning home in the twentieth century

P50HD-12639-12 0016 (SRC) WAITE, LINDA J Population research center Higher education and family formation of men and women

P50HD-12639-12 0017 (SRC) GERTLER, PAUL Population research center Family consumption and intergenerational time transfers

P50HD-12639-12 0018 (SRC) SMITH, JAMES P Population research center Black-white differences in income and employment

P50HD-12639-12 0019 (SRC) KAROLY, LYNN Population research center Demographic change and earnings inequality

P50HD-12639-12 0020 (SRC) STRAUSS, JOHN Population research center Human capital accumulation and intergenerational mobility

P50HD-12639-12 9001 (SRC) LILLARD, LEE Population research center Core--Data management, computing, and statistical services

R01HD-12714-13 (HED) JOBE, ALAN H HARBOR-UCLA MEDICAL CENTER 1000 W CARSON STREET TORRANCE, CA 90509 Developmental lung phospholipid metabolism

R01HD-12731-13 (MGN) THOMSON, GLENYS J UNIVERSITY OF CALIFORNIA 345 MULFORD HALL BERKELEY, CA 94720 Models in population genetics

R37HD-12806-10 (SSP) UDRY, J RICHARD 123 W FRANKLIN ST. UNIVERSITY SQUARE EAST CHAPEL HILL, NC 27514-3997 Pubertal and social factors of adolescent behavior

R01HD-12851-12 (BCE) KEUTMANN, HENRY T MASSACHUSETTS GENERAL HOSPITAL 5TH FLOOR WELLMAN BLDG BOSTON, MA 02114 Peptide hormones of reproduction--Chemistry and assay

R01HD-12863-13 (REB) POLAKOSKI, KENNETH L WASHINGTON UNIVERSITY 4911 BARNES HOSPITAL PLAZA ST LOUIS, MO 63110 Regulation of sperm proacrosin conversion to acrosin

R01HD-12986-14 (CBY) VACQUIER, VICTOR D UNIVERSITY OF CALIFORNIA 0202 SCRIPPS INST OF OCEANOLOG LA JOLLA, CA 92093 Biochemistry--Sperm-egg interaction, fertilization

P01HD-13021-12 (HDMC) PICKERING, LARRY K UNIVERSITY OF TEXAS 6431 FANNIN STREET HOUSTON, TX 77030 Role of human milk in infant nutrition and health

P01HD-13021-12 0002 (HDMC) KOHL, STEVE Role of human milk in infant nutrition and health Antibody secretion, cytotoxicity, immune regulation

P01HD-13021-12 0009 (HDMC) CLEARY, THOMAS G Role of human milk in infant nutrition and health Role of soluble milk factors in shigellosis

P01HD-13021-12 0010 (HDMC) BUESCHER, STEPHEN E Role of human milk in infant nutrition and health The relationship of human milk phagocytes to infant health

P01HD-13021-12 0011 (HDMC) PICKERING, LARRY E Role of human milk in infant nutrition and health The role of secretory immune system in rotavirus

P01HD-13021-12 0012 (HDMC) RUIZ-PALACIOIS, GUILLERMO Role of human milk in infant nutrition and health The role of human milk in Campylobacter infection

P01HD-13021-12 9002 (HDMC) PICKERING, LARRY K Role of human milk in infant nutrition and health Biochemistry--Core

P01HD-13021-12 9003 (HDMC) PICKERING, LARRY K Role of human milk in infant nutrition and health Epidemiology--Core

R01HD-13037-13 (REB) JACKSON, GARY L 2001 S. LINCOLN URBANA, IL 61801 Neural pathways from photoreceptors to the pituitary

P50HD-13063-12 (HDMC) JAMES, L STANLEY COLUMBIA UNIVERSITY 630 WEST 168TH STREET NEW YORK, NY 10032 Fetal activity/responses to hypoxia during development

P50HD-13063-12 0001 (HDMC) GOLAND, ROBIN Fetal activity/responses to hypoxia during development Placental CRH-pituitary-adrenal axis-fetal development

P50HD-13063-12 0002 (HDMC) STARK, RAYMOND I Fetal activity/responses to hypoxia during development Fetal activity & response to hypoxia during development

P50HD-13063-12 0004 (HDMC) DANILO, PETER Fetal activity/responses to hypoxia during development Chronic hypoxia and the developing heart

P50HD-13063-12 0008 (HDMC) STARK, RAYMOND I Fetal activity/responses to hypoxia during development Fetal hypoxia and the hypothalamohypophyseal system

P50HD-13063-12 0010 (HDMC) DANIEL, SALHA Fetal activity/responses to hypoxia during development Fetal responses to chronic hypoxia

P50HD-13063-12 0011 (HDMC) TIMOR, ILAN Fetal activity/responses to hypoxia during development Fetal activity and the prediction of premature labor

P50HD-13063-12 0012 (HDMC) SCHULZE, KARL Fetal activity/responses to hypoxia during development Activity and response to hypoxia in fetus/immature infant

P50HD-13063-12 9002 (HDMC) JAMES, L STANLEY Fetal activity/responses to hypoxia during development Computer core

N01HD-13100-01 ( ) RIVIER, JEAN E** Peptide antagonists of LHRH as gonadotropin inhibitors

N01HD-13101-01 ( ) FOLKERS, KARL** Peptide antagonists of LHRH as gonadotropin inhibitors

N01HD-13102-00 ( ) ROESKE, ROGER W** Peptide antagonists of LHRH as gonadotropin inhibitors

N01HD-13103-00 ( ) FLOURET, GEORGE R** Peptide antagonists of LHRH as gonadotropin inhibitors

N01HD-13104-00 ( ) MARSHALL, GARLAND R** Peptide antagonists of LHRH as gonadotropin inhibitors

N01HD-13105-01 ( ) FISCHER, KENNETH** Conference--Design of more acceptable foods for orphan diseases

N01HD-13106-00 ( ) BEAUDRY, NORMAN N** Preparation of gonadal cells and cell fractions

N01HD-13107-00 ( ) SISCOVICK, DAVID S** Low-dose oral contraceptives and cardiovascular disease

N01HD-13108-00 ( ) PETITTI, DIANA** Low-dose oral contraceptives and cardiovascular disease

N01HD-13109-00 ( ) BERNSTEIN, GERALD S** Developing and testing a polyurethane condom

N01HD-13110-00 ( ) MCGLOTHIN, MARK W** Developing and testing a polyurethane condom

N01HD-13111-00 ( ) DELSON, DAVID A** Developing and testing a male condom

N01HD-13112-00 ( ) BERNSTEIN, GERALD S** Antibiotic prophylaxis at time of IUD insertion

N01HD-13113-00 ( ) JACKSON, THOMAS E** Spermicidal-Releasing vaginal barrier contraceptive

N01HD-13114-00 ( ) ZELDIN, SHEPHERD** Study of high risk youth behavior

N01HD-13115-01 ( ) BEAUDRY, NORMAN** Performance of radioimmunoassays and radioiodinations

N01HD-13116-00 ( ) GOLDENBERG, ROBERT L** Follow-up study of mental, physical and behavioral development in children

N01HD-13118-00 ( ) MAKLAN, DAVID** Smoking cessation intervention for pregnant women

N01HD-13119-00 ( ) SEXTON, MARY** Smoking cessation intervention for pregnant women

N01HD-13120-00 ( ) COULTER, STEPHEN L** Development of a modified latex condom

N01HD-13121-00 ( ) KNOKE, JAMES** NICHD trial of calcium supplementation in pregnancy

N01HD-13122-00 ( ) HAUTH, JOHN C** Clinical center for NICHD trial of calcium supplement

N01HD-13123-00 ( ) MORRIS, CYNTHIA** Clinical center for NICHD trial of calcium supplement

N01HD-13124-00 ( ) CURET, LUIS** Clinical center for NICHD

PROJECT NO., ORGANIZATIONAL UNIT., INVESTIGATOR, ADDRESS, TITLE

trial of calcium supplement
N01HD-13125-00 ( ) CATALANO, PATRICK M** Clinical center for NICHD trial of calcium supplement
N01HD-13126-00 ( ) SIBAI, BAHA M** Clinical center for NICHD trial of calcium supplement
N01HD-13127-00 ( ) BAKKETEIG, LEIV S** Mental, physical, and behavioral development in children
N01HD-13128-00 ( ) CHIEN, YIE W** Spermicidal-releasing vaginal barrier contraceptive
N01HD-13129-00 ( ) BROWN, BRUCE** Preparation and analysis of pituitary and adrenal cells
N01HD-13130-01 ( ) NAQVI, REHAN H** Biological testing facility
N01HD-13131-00 ( ) DAVISSON, MURIEL T** A repository of mouse models for cytogenetic disorders
N01HD-13132-01 ( ) NIERMAN, WILLIAM** Repository of DNA probes and libraries
N43HD-13133-00 ( ) CARD, JOSEFINA J** Establishment of an AIDS/STD data archive
N01HD-13134-00 ( ) VAN DEN BERG, BARBARA J** Maintenance of child health and development studies
N01HD-13135-01 ( ) SLENKER, SUZANNE** Barrier contraception for prevention of sexually transmitted diseases
N01HD-13136-00 ( ) WERTZ, DOROTHY C** Ethics and human genetics-- A survey of approaches in the USA and Canada
N01HD-13137-00 ( ) RAO, PEMMARAJU N** Maintenance and operation of a synthetic chemical facility
N01HD-13138-00 ( ) ZIELKE, H RONALD** Brain and tissue bank for developmental disorders
N01HD-13139-00 ( ) BIRD, EDWARD** Brain and tissue bank for developmental disorders
N01HD-13140-00 ( ) EXPOSITO, LORENZA** Computer programming support for research in diabetes
R01HD-13162-11 (BPO) MENAKER, MICHAEL UNIVERSITY OF VIRGINIA GILMER HALL CHARLOTTESVILLE, VA 22901 Rhytmms, reproduction and photoreception
R01HD-13232-13 (GMB) SCHWARTZ, GEORGE J ALBERT EINSTEIN COLL OF MED 1300 MORRIS PARK AVE BRONX, N Y 10461 Bicarbonate transport by the maturing renal tubule
R01HD-13234-13 (BCE) SIMPSON, EVAN R UNIV OF TEXAS SW MEDICAL CTR 5323 HARRY HINES BOULEVARD DALLAS, TEX 75235 Regulation of ovarian steroidogenesis
R37HD-13249-12 (CMS) BELLUGI, URSULA SALK INSTITUTE P O BOX 85800 SAN DIEGO, CA 92138 Psycholinguistics of American sign language morphology
R01HD-13250-13 (PHRA) VORE, MARY E UNIVERSITY OF KENTUCKY 800 ROSE STREET LEXINGTON, KY 40536 Hepatic drug elimination in pregnancy
R01HD-13294-11 (HED) ALBRECHT, EUGENE D UNIVERSTIY OF MARYLAND 655 W BALTIMORE STREET BALTIMORE, MD 21201 Maternal-fetal steroid regulation in pregnant baboons
R01HD-13449-11 (DAPA) SHERMAN, STEVEN J INDIANA UNIVERSITY BLOOMINGTON, IN 47405 Social psychological factors in teen and adult smoking
P01HD-13527-12 (SRC) VALE, WYLIE W SALK INST/BIOLOGICAL STUDIES POST OFFICE BOX 85800 SAN DIEGO, CA 92138 Peptides and reproduction
P01HD-13527-12 0001 (SRC) VALE, WYLIE W Peptides and reproduction Peptides and their receptors regulating gonadotrophs
P01HD-13527-12 0002 (SRC) RIVIER, CATHERINE Peptides and reproduction Gonadal & hypothalamic hormones roles in reproduction regulation
P01HD-13527-12 0005 (SRC) RIVIER, JEAN E Peptides and reproduction Synthetic substances controlling reproduction
P01HD-13527-12 0006 (SRC) PLOTSKY, PAUL M Peptides and reproduction GnRH and oxytocin secretion modulation by amines and peptides
P01HD-13527-12 0007 (SRC) HSUEH, AARON Peptides and reproduction Gonadal production and action of inhibin and growth factors
P01HD-13527-12 9001 (SRC) RIVIER, JEAN E Peptides and reproduction Core--High performance liquid chromatography and capillary zone electrophoresis
P01HD-13527-12 9002 (SRC) FISCHER, WOLFGANG Peptides and reproduction Core--Sequence analysis of peptides
P01HD-13527-12 9003 (SRC) RIVIER, CATHERINE Peptides and reproduction Core--Hypothalamic, pituitary, gonadal hormone radioimmunoassay
P50HD-13541-12 (HDPR) BARDIN, CLYDE W THE POPULATION COUNCIL 1230 YORK AVENUE NEW YORK, N Y 10021 Specialized population research center
P50HD-13541-12 0001 (HDPR) JANNE, OLLI A Specialized population research center Androgen regulation of ornithine decarboxylase genes
P50HD-13541-12 0002 (HDPR) MUSTO, NEAL A Specialized population research center Cell biology of the seminiferous tubules
P50HD-13541-12 0004 (HDPR) CHENG, C Y Specialized population research center The biology of the sertoli cell proteins
P50HD-13541-12 0005 (HDPR) CATTERALL, JAMES F Specialized population research center Hormonal and genetic regulation of b-glucuronidase gene
P50HD-13541-12 9002 (HDPR) ASCOLI, MARIO Specialized population research center Tissue culture core
P50HD-13541-12 9003 (HDPR) PHILLIPS, DAVID M Specialized population research center Electron microscopy core
P50HD-13541-12 9004 (HDPR) THAU, ROSEMARIE B Specialized population research center Radioimmunoassay core
P50HD-13541-12 9005 (HDPR) CATTERALL, JAMES F. Specialized population research center Recombinant DNA core
R01HD-13563-12 (PBC) HART, GERALD W JOHNS HOPKINS UNIVERSITY 725 N WOLFE ST BALTIMORE, MD 21205 Glycoconjugates in develoment and immunity
R01HD-13587-11 (BCE) NAFTOLIN, FREDERICK YALE UNIVERSITY 333 CEDAR STREET NEW HAVEN, CT 06510 Metabolism and mechanism of action of estrogens
R01HD-13703-12 (END) CROWLEY, WILLIAM R UNIVERSITY OF TENNESSEE 874 UNION AVENUE MEMPHIS, TN 38163 Brain monoamines and luteinizing hormone secretion

PROJECT NO., ORGANIZATIONAL UNIT., INVESTIGATOR, ADDRESS, TITLE

R01HD-13748-13 (MGN) WARNER, CAROL M NORTHEASTERN UNIVERSITY 360 HUNTINGTON AVENUE BOSTON, MA 02115 Role of the MHC in early mammalian development
R01HD-13810-08A2 (HUD) ROSE, SUSAN A ALBERT EINSTEIN COLL OF MED 1300 MORRIS PARK AVENUE BRONX, NY 10461 cognitive deficits in high risk infants
R01HD-13820-10 (BEM) JOHNSON, SUZANNE B UNIVERSITY OF FLORIDA 1600 SW ARCHER RD SHANDS HOSP GAINESVILLE, FL 32610-0234 Compliance an control in childhood diabetes
R01HD-13909-11 (BCE) BRODIE, ANGELA M UNIVERSITY OF MARYLAND 660 W REDWOOD STREET BALTIMORE, MD 21201 Biologic actions of 4-hydroxyandrostene-3,17-dione
P01HD-13912-12 (HDMC) JOHNSTON, JOHN M UNIVERSITY OF TEXAS 5323 HARRY HINES BOULEVARD DALLAS, TX 75235-9051 Fetal lung maturation--Prevention of RDS
P01HD-13912-12 0001 (HDMC) JOHNSTON, JOHN M Fetal lung maturation--Prevention of RDS Surfactant glycerophospholipids in developing lung
P01HD-13912-12 0003 (HDMC) MENDELSON, CAROLE R Fetal lung maturation--Prevention of RDS Hormonal regulation of surfactant biosynthesis
P01HD-13912-12 0004 (HDMC) ODOM, M JANELLE Fetal lung maturation--Prevention of RDS Adrenergic system in developing fetal lung
P01HD-13912-12 0006 (HDMC) SNYDER, JEANNE M Fetal lung maturation--Prevention of RDS Hormonal regulation of fetal lung maturation
P01HD-13912-12 0007 (HDMC) ROSENFELD, CHARLES R Fetal lung maturation--Prevention of RDS Fetal hormonal adaptation to intrauterine stress
R01HD-13938-13 (BCE) REICHERT, LEO E, JR ALBANY MEDICAL COLLEGE A-10 ALBANY, N Y 12208 Testicular receptors of follicle stimulating hormone
R01HD-13956-11 (END) PETRA, PHILIP H UNIVERSITY OF WASHINGTON DEPARTMENT OF OB/GYN SEATTLE, WASH 98195 structure-function of plasma sex steriod-binding protein
R01HD-13970-12 (MBY) JEFFERY, WILLIAM R UNIVERSITY OF CALIFORNIA BODEGA BAY, CA 94923 Maternal mRNA localizations in determinate egg
R01HD-14010-12 (CBY) SCHNAAR, RONALD L THE JOHNS HOPKINS UNIV SCH MED 725 N. WOLFE STREET BALTIMORE, MARYLAND 21205 Cell surface carbohydrates in neuronal cell function
R37HD-14094-13 (GMA) HENNING, SUSAN J BAYLOR COLLEGE OF MEDICINE ONE BAYLOR PLAZA HOUSTON, TX 77030 Regulation of intestinal development
R01HD-14122-10A1 (HUD) LOZOFF, BETSY CASE WESTERN RESERVE UNIV 2074 ABINGTON RD CLEVELAND, OH 44106 Iron deficiency anemia and infant behavior
R01HD-14193-08 (HUD) ORNITZ, EDWARD M UNIVERSITY OF CALIFORNIA 760 WESTWOOD PLAZA/RM A7 372A LOS ANGELES, CA 90024-1759 Normal development of startle responses
R01HD-14198-15 (GMA) LESTER, ROGER G UNIVERSITY OF ARKANSAS 4301 W MARKHAM ST, BOX 640 LITTLE ROCK, AR 72205 Neonatal nutrition--Development of fat absorption
R01HD-14235-09A1 (REB) BAVISTER, BARRY D UNIVERSITY OF WISCONSIN 1655 LINDEN DRIVE MADISON, WI 53706 Studies on sperm fertilizing ability
R01HD-14388-11 (HED) GERSHWIN, MERRILL E UNIVERSITY OF CALIFORNIA TB 192 DAVIS, CA 95616 Zinc deprivation and teratogenesis
R01HD-14427-11 (HED) REPPERT, STEVEN M MASSACHUSETTS GENERAL HOSPITAL 32 FRUIT ST/JACKSON 1226 BOSTON, MA 02114 Maternal influence on developing 24-hour periodicity
R01HD-14474-12 (CBY) TILNEY, LEWIS G UNIVERSITY OF PENNSYLVANIA PHILADELPHIA, PA 19104-6018 Pattern generation of actin filaments
R01HD-14483-12 (HED) MC CLAY, DAVID R, JR DUKE UNIVERSITY DURHAM, N C 27706 Embryonic cell recognition--Specificity determinants
R01HD-14490-12 (NEUB) HARRIS, WILLIAM A UNIV OF CALIF, SAN DIEGO CTR FOR MOLECULA GENET, B-022 LA JOLLA, CA 92093 Formation of neural pathways in the embryo
R01HD-14501-10A1 (REN) AMANN, RUPERT P COLORADO STATE UNIVERSITY FORT COLLINS, CO 80523 Function of the epididymal epithelium
R01HD-14504-11 (REB) TUNG, KENNETH S UNIVERSITY OF VIRGINIA CHARLOTESVILLE, VA 22903 Purified testis antigens and testicular autoimmunity
R01HD-14574-12 (REB) ANDERSON, EVERETT HARVARD MEDICAL SCHOOL 45 SHATTUCK STREET BOSTON, MA 02115 An analysis of mammalian oogenesis and folliculogenesis
R01HD-14595-12 (PYB) ZUCKER, IRVING UNIVERSITY OF CALIFORNIA BERKELEY, CA 94720 Circannual rhythms behavior and reproduction
R55HD-14625-10A1 (END) RAMIREZ, VICTOR D 407 SOUTH GOODWIN AVE URBANA, IL 61801 Non-genomic action of progesterone on dopamine transmission
R01HD-14643-11 (BCE) SMITH, M SUSAN UNIVERSITY OF PITTSBURGH 3550 TERRACE STREET PITTSBURGH, PA 15261 Control of gonadotropin secretion during lactation
R01HD-14661-10 (END) NICOLL, CHARLES S UNIVERISTY OF CALIFORNIA 2549 LIFE SCIENCE BUILDING BERKELEY, CALIF 94720 Hormonal control of growth
R37HD-14772-09 (HUD) SIPERSTEIN, GARY N UNIVERSITY OF MASSACHUSETTS DOWNTOWN CENTER BOSTON, MA 02125-3393 The social acceptability of mentally retarded children
R01HD-14820-10 (HED) LEMONS, JAMES A INDIANA UNIV SCH OF MED 702 BRANHILL DRIVE INDIANAPOLIS, IN 46202-5225 Fetal amino acid and gluconeogenesis
R01HD-14846-11 (REB) KINSEY, WILLIAM H UNIVERSITY OF KANSAS MEDICAL C 39TH AND RAINBOW BLVD KANSAS CITY, KS 66103-8410 Modification of egg plasma membrane
R01HD-14886-11 (NEUC) MORRISON, MARCELLE R UNIVERSITY OF TEX HLTH SCI CTR 5323 HARRY HINES BLVD DALLAS, TX 75235 Gene expression in brain development
R01HD-14888-08 (HED) MAGUIRE, M HELEN UNIV OF KANSAS MEDICAL CTR 39TH AND RAINBOW BLVD KANSAS CITY, KS 66103 Adenosine and

vasoactive autacoids in the placenta
R01HD-14907-08 (BCE) MOYLE, WILLIAM R UMDNJ-ROBERT W JOHNSON MED SCH 675 HOES LANE PISCATAWAY, N J 08854 Gonadotropin action
R01HD-14939-10 (REB) JAFFE, LAURINDA A UNIV OF CONNECTICUT HEALTH CTR 263 FARMINGTON AVENUE FARMINGTON, CT 06030 Signal transduction at fertilization
R01HD-14947-09 (REB) SRIVASTAVA, PRAKASH N UNIVERSITY OF GEORGIA 626 BOYD GRADUATE STUDIES BLDG ATHENS, GA 30602 Acrosomal enzymes and their role in fertilization
R37HD-14958-11 (NSS) WOOD, WILLIAM B UNIVERSITY OF COLORADO CAMPUS BOX 347 BOULDER, CO 80309 Immunologic studies of C elegans early development
R37HD-14966-11 (REN) TALAMANTES, FRANK J THIMANN LABORATORIES UNIVERSITY OF CALIFORNIA SANTA CRUZ, CA 95064 Placental lactogens--Regulation and bioactivity
R01HD-15021-11 (NEUB) ARNOLD, ARTHUR P UNIVERSITY OF CALIFORNIA 405 HILGARD AVE LOS ANGELES, CA 90024-1563 Steroid influences on neurons involved in behavior
R37HD-15043-11 (MBY) WILT, FRED H UNIVERSITY OF CALIFORNIA 371 LIFE SCIENCE ADDITION BERKELEY, CA 94720 Gene expression in early embryonic development
R01HD-15045-09 (REB) OLDS-CLARKE, PATRICIA J TEMPLE UNIVERSITY 3400 NORTH BROAD STREET PHILADELPHIA, PA 19140 Sperm function in mammalian fertilization
P01HD-15051-11A1 (HDMR) BAUMEISTER, ALFRED A VANDERBILT UNIVERSITY BOX 154, PEABODY STA NASHVILLE, TN 37203 Research program on retarded intellectual development
P01HD-15051-11A1 0174 (HDMR) BRANSFORD, JOHN D Research program on retarded intellectual development New approaches for helping children who are at-risk of school failure
P01HD-15051-11A1 0175 (HDMR) FOX, ROBERT Research program on retarded intellectual development Assessment and analysis of perceptual capacities
P01HD-15051-11A1 0177 (HDMR) KAISER, ANN P Research program on retarded intellectual development Parent implemented language intervention on MR children's communication
P30HD-15052-11 (HDMR) WARREN, STEVEN F VANDERBILT UNIVERSITY BOX 40, PEABODY COLLEGE NASHVILLE, TN 37203 Mental retardation and human development research center
P30HD-15052-11 9001 (HDMR) ROSEMERGY, JANET Mental retardation and human development research center Communication services--Core
P30HD-15052-11 9004 (HDMR) BROWN, WILLIAM Mental retardation and human development research center Behavioral science services--Core
P30HD-15052-11 9010 (HDMR) TAPP, JON Mental retardation and human development research center Computer and statistical Services
P30HD-15052-11 9011 (HDMR) BAUMEISTER, ALFRED Mental retardation and human development research center Neurosciences laboratory--Core
R01HD-15080-09A1 (REN) CROWLEY, WILLIAM F, JR MASSACHUSETTS GENERAL HOSPITAL FRUIT STREET BOSTON, MA 02114 Neuroendocrine control of reproduction in the female
R01HD-15191-09 (BPO) HARDING, CHERYL F AMERICAN MUSEUM OF NAT HISTORY CENTRAL PARK WEST AT 79TH NEW YORK, N Y 10024 Hormonal activation of social behavior
R37HD-15201-12 (HED) HANDWERGER, STUART CHILDRENS HOSPITAL MED CTR ELLAND AND BETHESDA AVE CINCINNATI, OH 45229 Decidual prolactin in normal and pathologic pregnancies
R01HD-15269-11 (REB) MILLETTE, CLARKE F UNIVERSITY OF SOUTH CAROLINA SCHOOL OF MEDICINE COLUMBIA, SC 29208 Glycoprotein metabolism in mammalian spermatogenesis
R01HD-15433-09 (BCE) TERASAWA, EI UNIVERSITY OF WISCONSIN 1223 CAPITOL COURT MADISON, WI 53715-1299 Hypothalmic control of gonadotropin secretion
R01HD-15434-11 (SB) BARTLETT, ROBERT H UNIVERSITY OF MICHIGAN MED CTR 1500 E MEDICAL CTR DR ANN ARBOR, MI 48109-0331 ECMO in pediatric respiratory failure
P01HD-15454-11 (HDPR) CANFIELD, ROBERT E COLUMBIA UNIVERSITY 630 WEST 168TH STREET NEW YORK, NY 10032 Studies of gonadotropins
P01HD-15454-11 0001 (HDPR) BIRKEN, STEVEN Studies of gonadotropins Protein chemistry of gonadotropins and fragments
P01HD-15454-11 0003 (HDPR) MOYLE, WILLIAM R Studies of gonadotropins Glycoprotein hormone structure-funtion
P01HD-15454-11 0004 (HDPR) O'CONNOR, JOHN F Studies of gonadotropins Clinical applications of gonadotropin measurement
P01HD-15454-11 0005 (HDPR) CANFIELD, ROBERT E Studies of gonadotropins Biophysical and immunochemical studies of gonadotropins
P01HD-15454-11 9002 (HDPR) KRICHEVSKY, ALEXANDER Studies of gonadotropins Core--Tissue culture and hybridoma facility
R01HD-15472-10 (END) CHILDS, GWEN V 200 UNIVERSITY BOULEVARD GALVESTON, TX 77550-2772 Hormone storage and secretion in gonadotropes
R01HD-15510-10 (REB) LONGO, FRANK J UNIVERSITY OF IOWA IOWA CITY, IA 52242 Regulation of pronuclear development
R01HD-15527-11 (CBY) BRONNER-FRASER, MARIANNE E UNIV OF CALIFORNIA 4238 BIO SCI II BLDG IRVINE, CA 92717 Cell surface interactions in neural crest development
R01HD-15563-11 (REB) ORTH, JOANNE M TEMPLE UNIVERSITY SCH OF MED 3400 NORTH BROAD STREET PHILADELPHIA, PA 19140 Fertility and sertoli cell development
R37HD-15587-11 (GEN) WIESCHAUS, ERIC F PRINCETON UNIVERSITY GUYOT HALL PRINCETON, NJ 08544-1003 Oogenesis and early embryogenesis in Drosophila
R01HD-15631-08A1 (HED) HAMOSH, MARGIT GEORGETOWN UNIV MED CENTER 3800 RESERVOIR ROAD, N.W. WASHINGTON, DC 20007 Lipid clearing in the parenterally fed preterm infant
R01HD-15736-11 (RAP) HADDAD, GABRIEL G YALE UNIVERISTY SCH/MEDICINE 333 CEDAR STREET NEW HAVEN, CT 06510 Endorphins, sleep and maturation of hypoxic response
R01HD-15788-09S1 (REN) CROWLEY, WILLIAM F, JR MASSACHUSETTS GENERAL HOSPITAL REPRODUCTIVE ENDOCRINE UNIT BOSTON, MASS 02114 LHRH physiology in man--in vivo and in vitro approaches
R01HD-15795-11 (CMS) JUSCZYK, PETER W DEPARTMENT OF PSYCHOLOGY STATE UNIV. OF N.Y. @ BUFFALO The development of speech perception capacities
R01HD-15799-08 (HED) ANTCZAK, DOUGLAS F CORNELL UNIVERSITY NYS COLLEGE OF VETERINARY MED ITHACA, NY 14853 Comparative studies of pregnancy and histocompatibility
R01HD-15842-09 (BCE) STOREY, BAYARD T UNIVERSITY OF PENNSYLVANIA 36TH & HAMILTON WALK PHILADELPHIA, PA 19104-6080 Peroxide reactions in mammalian spermatozoa
R01HD-15955-09 (REN) WISE, PHYLLIS M UNIV OF MARYLAND AT BALTIMORE 655 WEST BALTIMORE STREET BALTIMORE, MD 21201 The effect of hyperprolactinemia on LH release
R01HD-16000-10 (REB) KELCH, ROBERT P UNIVERSITY OF MICHIGAN 1500 E MED CTR ANN ARBOR, MI 48109-0718 Maturational roles of GnRH pulse frequency
R01HD-16022-10 (HED) RESKO, JOHN A OREGON HEALTH SCIENCES UNIV 3181 S W SAM JACKSON PARK RD PORTLAND, OR 97201 Steroid hormones and fetal development
R01HD-16080-09S1 (VR) PROBER, CHARLES G STANFORD UNIV MEDICAL CENTER STANFORD, CA 94305 Herpes simplex, pregnancy neonatal risk, host defense
R01HD-16102-10 (SSS) SMOTHERMAN, WILLIAM P SUNY - BINGHAMTON DEPT OF PSYCHOLOGY BINGHAMTON, N Y 13901 Behavioral biology of the fetus
R01HD-16195-10 (HUD) BERTENTHAL, BENNETT I UNIVERSITY OF VIRGINIA DEPARTMENT OF PSYCHOLOGY CHARLOTTESVILLE, VA 22903 Infants' sensitivity to kinematic information
R01HD-16229-10 (REB) RICHARDS, JOANNE S BAYLOR COLLEGE OF MEDICINE 1 BAYLOR PLAZA HOUSTON, TEX 77030 LH action in ovarian cell differentiation
R01HD-16236-10 (REB) BARKER, KENNETH L TEXAS TECH UNIVERSITY DEPT OF BIOCHEMISTRY LUBBOCK, TX 79430 Specificity of uterine response to ovarian hormones
R01HD-16259-10 (CTY) ALLIS, CHARLES D SYRACUSE UNIVERSITY 130 COLLEGE PLACE SYRACUSE, NY 13244 Nuclear determination and differentiation in development
R01HD-16260-09A2 (REN) DYM, MARTIN GEORGETOWN UNIVERSITY 3900 RESERVOIR ROAD NW WASHINGTON, DC 20007 Role of the Sertoli cell in spermatogenesis
R01HD-16272-10 (BCE) RICHARDS, JOANNE S BAYLOR COLLEGE OF MEDICINE 1 BAYLOR PLAZA HOUSTON, TX 77030 Ovarian follicular development and hormone action
R01HD-16287-08 (HED) MIRKES, PHILIP E UNIVERSITY OF WASHINGTON MED SCH/DEPT PEDIATRICS RD-20 SEATTLE, WA 98195 Molecular mechanisms of cyclophosphamide teratogenesis
R01HD-16305-09 (REN) WILSON, MARK E YERKES PRIMATE RES CNTR EMORY 2409 TAYLOR ROAD LAWRENCEVILLE, GA 30243 Common neuroendocrine mechanisms for growth and puberty
R01HD-16480-06 (HAR) CLARKSON, MARSHA G GEORGIA STATE UNIVERSITY UNIVERSITY PLAZA ATLANTA, GA 30303 Development of infants' auditory perception
R01HD-16484-10 (MET) ROSS, ALTA C THE MED COLL OF PENNSYLVANIA 3300 HENRY AVENUE, 318R PHILADELPHIA, PA 19129 Vitamin A transport during lactation
R01HD-16494-10 (HUD) GUNNAR, MEGAN R UNIVERSITY OF MINNESOTA 51 E RIVER RD - CHILD DEV INST MINNEAPOLIS, MN 55455-0345 Behavioral and hormonal responses to stress in infants
R01HD-16535-08 (REB) DAMASSA, DAVID A TUFTS UNIVERSITY 136 HARRISON AVENUE BOSTON, MASS 02111 Sex steroid binding protein and androgen action
R01HD-16550-09 (CBY) CUNNINGHAM, BRUCE A ROCKEFELLER UNIVERSITY 1230 YORK AVENUE NEW YORK, N Y 10021-6399 Chick cell surface glycoproteins in embryogenesis
R01HD-16580-10 (REB) MYLES, DIANA G UNIV OF CONNECTICUT HEALTH CTR DEPARTMENT OF PHYSIOLOGY FARMINGTON, CONN 06032 Mammalian sperm surface organization and function
P01HD-16596-08 (HDMR) TILDON, J TYSON UNIVERSITY OF MARYLAND 655 W BALTIMORE STREET BALTIMORE, MD 21201 Metabolism and developmental aspects of mental retardation
P01HD-16596-08 0001 (HDMR) TILDON, J Metabolism and developmental aspects of mental retardation Ketone body metabolism and developmental homeostasis in the brain
P01HD-16596-08 0002 (HDMR) ZIELKE, H Metabolism and developmental aspects of mental retardation Glutamine and glutamate metabolism in brain
P01HD-16596-08 0006 (HDMR) STERNBERGER, NANCY Metabolism and developmental aspects of mental retardation Brain endothelial antigens in development
P01HD-16596-08 0007 (HDMR) HILT, DANA Metabolism and developmental aspects of mental retardation Molecular mechanisms of S100 beta/neurite extension factor expression
P01HD-16596-08 0008 (HDMR) MAX, STEPHEN Metabolism and developmental aspects of mental retardation Regulation of ChAT expression in cholinergic neurons
R01HD-16631-09 (BCE) SPIES, HAROLD G OREGON REG PRIMATE RES CENTER 505 N W 185TH AVENUE BEAVERTON, OREG 97006 Neural influence on hypophyseal-gonadal function
R01HD-16634-07 (NTN) STURMAN, JOHN A INST FOR BASIC RESEARCH 1050 FOREST HILL ROAD STATEN ISLAND, NY 10314 Nutritional taurine and feline pregnancy and outcome
R01HD-16640-08 (HUD) TULJAPURKAR, SHRIPAD D STANFORD UNIVERSITY DEPARTMENT OF BIOLOGICAL SCIS STANFORD, CA 94305-5020 Extrinsic and intrinsic dynamics in demography
R37HD-16659-09 (MGN) GARTLER, STANLEY M UNIVERSITY OF WASHINGTON SEATTLE, WA 98195 Dosage compensation in mammals--X-inactivation
R01HD-16666-07 (HED) DUNAWAY, GEORGE A SOUTHERN ILLINOIS UNIVERSITY P.O. BOX 19230 SPRINGFIELD, ILL 62708 Developmental changes in heart and muscle PFK isozymes
R01HD-16688-10 (REB) MAHESH, VIRENDRA B MEDICAL COLLEGE OF GEORGIA AUGUSTA, GA 30912-3000 Effect of progesterone on gonadotropin secretion
R01HD-16715-10 (BCE) CALLARD, GLORIA V BOSTON UNIVERSITY 5 CUMMINGTON ST BOSTON, MA 02215 Testicular steroidogenesis in selected models
R01HD-16720-10 (END) SHAPIRO, DAVID J UNIVERSITY OF ILLINOIS

PROJECT NO., ORGANIZATIONAL UNIT., INVESTIGATOR, ADDRESS, TITLE

1209 W CALIFORNIA URBANA, IL 61801 Gene transcription in estrogen dependent differentiation
R01HD-16739-09A1 (CTY) RAFF, ELIZABETH C INDIANA UNIVERSITY BLOOMINGTON, IN 47405 Genetic control of microtubule function in development
R01HD-16806-08 (REB) VELDHUIS, JOHANNES D UNIVERSITY OF VIRGINIA SCHOOL OF MEDICINE CHARLOTTESVILLE, VA 22908 Hormone action in the ovary--Role of calcium ions
R01HD-16827-09 (REB) POWER, GORDON G LOMA LINDA UNIV SCHL OF MED DIVISION OF PERINATAL BIOLOGY LOMA LINDA, CALIF 92350 Fetal heat production and temperature regulation
R01HD-16842-07A2 (REN) ZELEZNIK, ANTHONY J MAGEE WOMENS HOSPITAL 300 HALKET STREET PITTSBURGH, PA 15213 Regulation of the primate corpus luteum
R01HD-16843-08 (REB) MEISTRICH, MARVIN L UNIVERSITY OF TEXAS 1515 HOLCOMBE BLVD HOUSTON, TX 77030 Nucleoproteins in mammalian spermatogenesis
R01HD-16851-08 (BCE) PLANT, TONY M UNIVERSITY OF PITTSBURGH SCHOOL OF MEDICINE PITTSBURGH, PA 15261 Testicular control of LH and FSH secretion
R01HD-16910-10 (BCE) WILSON, ELIZABETH M UNIVERSITY OF NORTH CAROLINA AT CHAPEL HILL CHAPEL HILL, N C 27599 Androgen receptor regulation of reproductive function
R01HD-16915-07 (HUD) KENNELL, JOHN H CASE WESTERN RESERVE UNIV 2074 ABINGTON ROAD CLEVELAND, OH 44106 Perinatal effects of support during labor
R01HD-16936-08 (PB) APRILLE, JUNE R TUFTS UNIVERSITY MEDFORD, MASS 02155 Metabolic adaptations of neonate to extrauterine life
R01HD-16973-07 (HUD) ROGOFF, BARBARA UNIVERSITY OF UTAH SALT LAKE CITY, UT 84112 The development of planning skills
R01HD-17121-07 (REB) WELSH, MICHAEL J UNIV OF MICHIGAN MEDICAL SCHOO ANN ARBOR, MI 48109-0616 Biochemical mechanisms in sertoli-germ cell interactions
R01HD-17246-06 (HUD) RAYNER, KEITH UNIVERSITY OF MASSACHUSETTS TOBIN HALL AMHERST, MASS 01003 Language processing during reading
R01HD-17269-09 (BCE) BETHEA, CYNTHIA L OREGON REGIONAL PRIMATE RES CT 505 N W 185TH AVENUE BEAVERTON, OREG 97006 Regulation of monkey prolactin
R01HD-17332-08 (PC) SCHWARTZ, NANCY B UNIVERSITY OF CHICAGO 5841 S MARYLAND AVE/BOX 413 CHICAGO, IL 60637 Proteoglycan synthesis in mutant mouse systems
R01HD-17337-09 (REB) PARR, MARGARET B SOUTHERN ILLINOIS UNIVERSITY CARBONDALE, IL 62901 Secretory immunity in the female mouse genital tract
R01HD-17379-08 (PC) TSAI, MING-JER BAYLOR COLLEGE OF MEDICINE ONE BAYLOR PLAZA HOUSTON, TEXAS 77030 In vitro expression of hormone regulated genes--Insulin
R01HD-17427-25 (IMS) OCHS, HANS D UNIVERSITY OF WASHINGTON SEATTLE, WA 98195 Developmental and genetic defects of immunity
R01HD-17437-10 (REB) WEITLAUF, HARRY M TEXAS TECH UNIVERSITY LUBBOCK, TX 79430 Metabolic changes in preimplantation mouse embryos
R37HD-17438-10 (BCE) KNOBIL, ERNST UNIVERSITY OF TEXAS P O BOX 20708 HOUSTON, TX 77225 Studies on reproductive physiology in the macaque
P01HD-17449-08 (HDMR) PATTERSON, DAVID ELEANOR ROOSEVELT INSTITUTE 1899 GAYLORD STREET DENVER, CO 80206 Somatic cell genetic studies of Down's syndrome
P01HD-17449-08 0001 (HDMR) PATTERSON, DAVID Somatic cell genetic studies of Down's syndrome Cytogenetics and molecular characterization of chromosome 21
P01HD-17449-08 0002 (HDMR) LAW, MARTHA Somatic cell genetic studies of Down's syndrome Expression and location of DNA sequences on chromosome 21
P01HD-17449-08 0003 (HDMR) JONES, CAROL Somatic cell genetic studies of Down's syndrome Chromosome 21 associated cell surface antigens
P01HD-17449-08 0004 (HDMR) KAO, FA-TEN Somatic cell genetic studies of Down's syndrome Mapping and microdissection of chromsome 21
P01HD-17449-08 0005 (HDMR) GARDINER, KATHELEEN Somatic cell genetic studies of Down's syndrome Cloning large fragments of chromosome 21 DNA
P01HD-17449-08 0006 (HDMR) DRABKIN, HARRY Somatic cell genetic studies of Down's syndrome Rearrangement in human leukkemia and physical mapping
P01HD-17449-08 9001 (HDMR) PATTERSON, DAVID Somatic cell genetic studies of Down's syndrome Gene transfer Core
P01HD-17449-08 9002 (HDMR) PATTERSON, DAVID Somatic cell genetic studies of Down's syndrome Cytogenetics Core
P01HD-17449-08 9003 (HDMR) PATTERSON, DAVID Somatic cell genetic studies of Down's syndrome Tissue culture--Core
P01HD-17461-08 (SRC) ROSEN, FRED S THE CENTER FOR BLOOD RESEARCH 800 HUNTINGTON AVENUE BOSTON, MASS 02115 Chromosome 6P and developmental defects
P01HD-17461-08 0001 (SRC) ROSEN, FRED S Chromosome 6P and developmental defects Vasoactive peptide from second complement component
P01HD-17461-08 0002 (SRC) ALPER, CHESTER A Chromosome 6P and developmental defects MHC determinants of susceptibility to myasthenia gravis
P01HD-17461-08 0003 (SRC) CARROLL, MICHAEL C Chromosome 6P and developmental defects Molecular genetics of complement C4
P01HD-17461-08 0004 (SRC) STROMINGER, JACK L Chromosome 6P and developmental defects Linkage of TNF genes to HLA-B locus--Ankylosing spondylitis
P01HD-17461-08 0005 (SRC) COLTEN, HARVEY R Chromosome 6P and developmental defects Molecular regulation of MHC class III genes
P01HD-17461-08 9001 (SRC) DAVIS, ALVIN E Chromosome 6P and developmental defects Core--Amino acid analysis, sequencing, peptide synthesis
R01HD-17463-08 (MGN) HASSTEDT, SANDRA J UNIVERSITY OF UTAH MED CENTER 50 NORTH MEDICAL DRIVE SALT LAKE CITY, UTAH 84132 Models for the genetic epidemiology of chronic diseases
R01HD-17484-09 (REB) LEE, HON C UNIV OF MINNESOTA /PHYSIOLOGY 435 DELAWARE STREET, SE MINNEAPOLIS, MN 55455 Calcium regulation systems in sea urchin eggs
R01HD-17491-10 (REN) CUNHA, GERALD R UNIVERSITY OF CALIFORNIA 513 PARNASSUS AVE SAN FRANCISCO, CA 94143-0452 Normal and abnormal utero-vaginal development
R01HD-17553-06 (BSR) ECCLES, JACQUELYNNE S UNIVERSITY OF MICHIGAN PO BOX #1248 ANN ARBOR, MI 48106-1248 Ontogeny of self and task concepts and activity choice
R37HD-17557-10 (NSS) NEUTRA, MARIAN R ENDERS PEDIATRICS RESEARCH LAB 300 LONGWOOD AVENUE BOSTON, MA 02115 Transport of protein in neonatal ileum Peyer's patch
R01HD-17607-11 (GEN) MAHOWALD, ANTHONY P 920 EAST 58TH STREET CHICAGO, IL 60637 Ultrastructural studies of Drosophila development
R01HD-17608-09S1 (GEN) MAHOWALD, ANTHONY P 920 EAST 58TH STREET CHICAGO, IL 60637 Mechanism of cellular determination by germ plasm
R37HD-17664-09 (GMA) HOLBROOK, KAREN A UNIV OF WASHINGTON SCHOOL OF M DEPT OF BIO STRUCTURE SM-20 SEATTLE, WA 98195 Fetal skin biology
R01HD-17665-10 (SSS) GRAY, JOE W LABORATORY FOR CELL ANALYSIS 1855 FOLSOM ST SAN FRANCISCO, CA 94143-0808 Flow karyotyping--Optimization and clinical evaluation
R01HD-17678-08 (HED) WOOD, GARY W UNIVERSITY OF KANSAS MED CTR 39TH AND RAINBOW BLVD KANSAS CITY, KS 66103-8410 Immunoregulation in pregnancy
R01HD-17691-10 (MBY) WORMINGTON, W MICHAEL UNIVERSITY OF VIRGINIA CHARLOTTESVILLE, VA 22901 Development regulation of Xenopus ribosomal protein gene
R01HD-17704-09 (HEM) COSTANTINI, FRANKLIN D COLUMBIA UNIVERSITY NEW YORK, NY 10032 Gene regulation in hemopoiesis--Transgenic approaches
R37HD-17711-09 (MGN) WOO, SAVIO L BAYLOR COLLEGE OF MEDICINE 1200 MOURSUND AVENUE HOUSTON, TEX 77030 Phenylketonuria & the phenylalanine hydroxylase gene
R01HD-17736-08 (HED) TENNYSON, VIRGINIA M COLUMBIA UNIVERSITY 630 WEST 168TH STREET NEW YORK, N Y 10032 Congenital megacolon--Tissue interaction in development
R01HD-17779-09 (GMA) LIGHTNER, DAVID A UNIVERSITY OF NEVADA RENO, NV 89557-0020 Understanding phototherapy for neonatal jaundice
R01HD-17790-07 (HUD) MACWHINNEY, BRIAN J CARNEGIE-MELLON UNIVERSITY DEPARTMENT OF PSYCHOLOGY PITTSBURGH, PA 15213 Cross-linguistic studies of language processes
R01HD-17795-07 (BCE) SANBORN, BARBARA M UNIVERSITY OF TEXAS MED SCHOOL PO BOX 20708 HOUSTON, TX 77225 Molecular aspects of the role of androgens in the testis
R01HD-17802-08 (REB) STEINBERGER, ANNA UNIV OF TEXAS MED SCH 6431 FANNIN, SUITE 3.204 HOUSTON, TX 77030 Spermatogenesis--Sertoli-germ cell interaction
P01HD-17812-09 (HDMC) GRAY, BARRY M UAB UNIVERSITY STATION BIRMINGTON, ALA 35294 Natural history studies--GCS and pneumococcal infection
P01HD-17812-09 0001 (HDMC) BRILES, DAVID Natural history studies--GCS and pneumococcal infection Pneumococcal surface proteins in human disease
P01HD-17812-09 0002 (HDMC) GRAY, BARRY M Natural history studies--GCS and pneumococcal infection Immunity and host defense against streptococci
P01HD-17812-09 0003 (HDMC) PRITCHARD, DAVID G Natural history studies--GCS and pneumococcal infection Immunochemistry of group B streptococci
P01HD-17812-09 9001 (HDMC) GRAY, BARRY M Natural history studies--GCS and pneumococcal infection Core facilities
R01HD-17860-06 (HUD) MOLFESE, DENNIS L SOUTHERN ILLINOIS UNIVERSITY CARBONDALE, IL 62901 Neonatal predictors of language performance
R01HD-17864-07A1 (REB) GOODMAN, ROBERT L WEST VA UNIV HLTH SCI CTR 3051 HEALTH SCI NORTH MORGANTOWN, WV 26506 Neuroendocrine control of seasonality in the ewe
R01HD-17875-08 (MGN) STRICKLAND, SIDNEY SUNY AT STONY BROOK HEALTH SCIENCES CTR BST T-8 STONY BROOK, N Y 11794-8651 Gene regulation in teratocarcinoma and embryonic cells
R01HD-17899-07 (CEP) FOX, NATHAN A UNIVERSITY OF MARYLAND COLLEGE PARK, MD 20742 Affect and cerebral asymmetry: a developmental approach
R01HD-17916-09 (END) PAYNE, ANITA H UNIVERSITY OF MICHIGAN WOMENS HOSPITAL ANN ARBOR, MI 48109-0278 Genetic determinants of steroid hormone biosynthesis
R01HD-17966-09 (EDC) PASS, ROBERT F UNIV OF ALABAMA AT BIRMINGHAM UNIVERSITY STATION BIRMINGHAM, ALA 35294 Epidemiology of cytomegalovirus in day care centers
R01HD-17989-07 (REB) WRIGHT, WILLIAM W THE JOHNS HOPKINS UNIV 615 N WOLFE ST/POP DYNAMICS BALTIMORE, MD 21205 Stage-specific proteins
R01HD-18014-08 (HED) PADBURY, JAMES F HARBOR-UCLA MEDICAL CTR 1124 W. CARSON ST RB-1 TORRANCE, CA 90502 Catecholamine physiology and newborn adaptation
R01HD-18018-06 (REB) MIDGLEY, A REES, JR UNIVERSITY OF MICHIGAN 300 N. INGALLS/11TH FLOOR ANN ARBOR, MI 48109-0404 Gonadotropin - control of the ovary
R01HD-18055-07A1 (CBY) STEWARD, RUTH PRINCETON UNIVERSITY PRINCETON, NJ 08544 Genetic analysis of polarity
R01HD-18066-08 (CTY) SINGER, ROBERT H UNIV OF MASSACHUSETTS MED CTR 55 LAKE AVE NORTH WORCESTER, MA 01655 In situ hybridization visualized using biotinated probes
R01HD-18120-07 (REN) WILSON, MARK E YERKES REGIONAL PRIMATE RES 2409 TAYLOR ROAD LAWRENCE, GA 30245 Prolonged lactational infertility during adolescence
R01HD-18122-08 (REB) WOLGEMUTH, DEBRA J COLUMBIA UNIVERSITY 630 W 168TH ST NEW YORK, NY 10032 Structures of DNA and protein in male germ cells
R01HD-18123-08 (REN) HOFFMAN, LOREN H VANDERBILT UNIV SCH OF MED NASHVILLE, TN 37232 Properties of uterine epithelium related to implantation
R01HD-18127-09 (GEN) FULLER, MARGARET T BECKMAN CENTER STANFORD UNIVERSITY STANFORD, CA 94305 Genetic analysis of tubulin and

interacting proteins

R01HD-18133-07A1 (REN) KATOVICH, MICHAEL J UNIVERISTY OF FLORIDA BOX J-487 COLLEGE OF PHARMACY GAINESVILLE, FL 32610 Animal model for the mechanisms of hot flush

R01HD-18163-09 (GEN) SCOTT, MATTHEW P STANFORD UNIVERSITY SCH OF MED BECKMAN B300 STANFORD, CA 94305-5427 Molecular analysis of development regulating genes

R01HD-18169-09 (REN) CROWLEY, WILLIAM F, JR MASSACHUSETTS GENERAL HOSPITAL 32 FRUIT STREET, BHX-5 BOSTON, MA 02114 Neuroendocrine-gonadal function in puberty

R01HD-18179-08 (CTY) BLAU, HELEN M STANFORD UNIVERSITY ENCINA HALL ROOM 40 STANFORD, CA 94305 Developmental regulation of human muscle proteins

R37HD-18184-12 (BM) WILSON, CHRISTOPHER B UNIVERSITY OF WASHINGTON 3935 UNIVERSITY WAY N.E. SEATTLE, WA 98195 Macrophage/lymphokines in neonatal host defenses

P30HD-18185-08 (SRC) SPIES, HAROLD G OREGON REG PRIMATE RES CENTER 505 N W 185TH AVENUE BEAVERTON, OREG 97006 NICHD population research center core grant

P30HD-18185-08 9001 (SRC) HESS, DAVID L NICHD population research center core grant Core– Radioimmunoassay

P30HD-18185-08 9002 (SRC) BRENNER, ROBERT M NICHD population research center core grant Morphology core

P30HD-18185-08 9003 (SRC) BETHEA, CYNTHIA L NICHD population research center core grant Cell culture core

P30HD-18185-08 9004 (SRC) WOLF, DON P NICHD population research center core grant In vitro fertilization and experimental embryology core

R01HD-18196-08 (REB) RESKO, JOHN A OREGON HEALTH SCIENCES UNIV 3181 S W SAM JACKSON PARK RD PORTLAND, OREG 97201 Brain aromatase activity and reproductive function

R01HD-18201-07 (REB) SALING, PATRICIA M DUKE UNIVERSITY MEDICAL CTR BOX 3143 DURHAM, NC 27710 Function of sperm membrane antigens in fertilization

R01HD-18252-08 (REB) TURNER, TERRY T UNIVERSITY OF VIRGINIA POST OFFICE BOX 422 CHARLOTTESVILLE, VA 22908 Effect of experimental varicocele on the testis

P30HD-18258-08 (SRC) MIDGLEY, A REES, JR UNIVERSITY OF MICHIGAN 300 N. INGALLS/11TH FLOOR ANN ARBOR, MI 48109 Center for the study of reproduction

P30HD-18258-08 9005 (SRC) MIDGLEY, A. REES, JR. Center for the study of reproduction Core--Standards and reagents

P30HD-18258-08 9006 (SRC) CHRISTENSEN, A KENT Center for the study of reproduction Core--Morphology

P30HD-18258-08 9007 (SRC) FOSTER, DOUGLAS L. Center for the study of reproduction Core--Sheep facility

P30HD-18258-08 9008 (SRC) WELSH, MICHAEL J Center for the study of reproduction Core--laboratory animal facility

P30HD-18258-08 9009 (SRC) BROWN, MORTON B. Center for the study of reproduction Core--Data analysis and computing

P30HD-18258-08 9010 (SRC) ERICKSON, ROBERT P. Center for the study of reproduction Core--Molecular biology

R01HD-18269-07 (EDC) SCHOLL, THERESA O UMDNJ-SOM 401 HADDON AVENUE CAMDEN, NJ 08103-1505 Adolescent pregnancy--Nutrition, growth, and outcome

R01HD-18271-06 (END) ILAN, JUDITH CASE WESTERN RESERVE UNIVERSIT 2074 ABINGTON RD/REPRO BIOLOGY CLEVELAND, OH 44106 IGF expression in embryos of normal and diabetic pregnancy

R01HD-18280-07 (HED) SOHAL, GURKIRPAL S MEDICAL COLLEGE OF GEORGIA AUGUSTA, GA 30912 Neuromuscular junction development in vivo

R01HD-18281-07 (EDC) SPRECHER, DENNIS L UNIV OF CINCINNATI MEDICAL CTR 231 BETHESDA AVENUE CINCINNATI, OH 45267 Genetic epidemiology of sex hormones and lipoproteins

R01HD-18287-09 (BCE) TOFT, DAVID O MAYO FOUNDATION 200 FIRST STREET SOUTHWEST ROCHESTER, MN 55905 Progesterone receptor phosphorylation/dephosphorylation

P30HD-18288-08 (HDPR) HOTZ, V JOSEPH POPULATION RESEARCH CENTER 1155 EAST 60TH STREET CHICAGO, IL 60637 Social and economic analysis of demographic change

P30HD-18288-08 9003 (HDPR) MICHAEL, ROBERT T Social and economic analysis of demographic change Computer--Core

P30HD-18288-08 9004 (HDPR) MASSEY, DOUGLAS S Social and economic analysis of demographic change Library--Core

P30HD-18288-08 9005 (HDPR) MASSEY, DOUGLAS S Social and economic analysis of demographic change Survey methodology--Core

R01HD-18337-08 (BCE) KARSCH, FRED J UNIVERSITY OF MICHIGAN 300 NORTH INGALLS BLDG ANN ARBOR, MI 48109-0404 Neuroendocrine regulation of ovarian cyclicity

R01HD-18369-08 (CBY) RUTISHAUSER, URS S CASE WESTERN RESERVE UNIV 2119 ABINGTON ROAD CLEVELAND, OHIO 44106 Cell-cell adhesion molecules in development

R01HD-18370-07 (HED) CLARK, KENNETH E UNIV OF CINCINNATI 231 BETHESDA AVENUE ML #526 CINCINNATI, OHIO 45267 Mechanisms of fetal growth retardation

R01HD-18381-09 (HUD) PINKER, STEVEN MASSACHUSETTS INST OF TECH BRAIN & COGNITIVE SCIENCE DEPT CAMBRIDGE, MA 02139 Language learnability and language development

R01HD-18394-08 (REB) FOSTER, DOUGLAS L UNIVERSITY OF MICHIGAN 300 N INGALLS BLDG, 11TH FLOOR ANN ARBOR, MI 48109-2007 Neuroendocrinology of puberty

R01HD-18426-08 (HUD) FULKER, DAVID W UNIVERSITY OF COLORADO BOULDER, CO 80309-0047 An adoption study of development in middle childhood

R01HD-18447-08 (HED) MARTIN, ROY J UNIVERSITY OF GEORGIA DEPT OF FOODS NUTRITION ATHENS, GA 30602 In utero regulation of adipose tissue development

R01HD-18448-05 (BPO) GINTZLER, ALAN R SUNY HLTH SCI CTR AT BROOKLYN 450 CLARKSON AVENUE BROOKLYN, N Y 11203 Neurochemistry of gestation-produced analgesia

K06HD-18454-30 (NCR) FORBES, GILBERT B DEPT OF PEDIATRICS BX 777 601 ELMWOOD AVENUE ROCHESTER, N Y 14642 Chemical studies in growth and development

R01HD-18478-06 (RAP) KOOS, BRIAN J UNIVERSITY OF CALIFORNIA HEALTH SCIENCES, 22-132 LOS ANGELES, CA 90024-1740 Hypoxia and the control of fetal breathing movements

R01HD-18506-07 (TOX) SHIVERICK, KATHLEEN T UNIVERSITY OF FLORIDA BOX J-267 JHM HEALTH CENTER GAINESVILLE, FLA 32610 Xenobiotic metabolism in fetal hematopoietic cells

R01HD-18511-06A1 (HUD) LEWIS, MICHAEL L UMDNJ/ROBERT W JOHNSON MED SCH NEW BRUNSWICK, NJ 08903-0019 Effects of intraventricular hemorrhage on development

P01HD-18577-08 (HDMC) SOLL, DAVID R UNIVERSITY OF IOWA IOWA CITY, IA 52242 The developmental biology of cell motility

P01HD-18577-08 0001 (HDMC) SOLL, DAVID R The developmental biology of cell motility Chemotaxis and chemokinesis in Dictyostelium

P01HD-18577-08 0002 (HDMC) SOLURSH, MICHAEL The developmental biology of cell motility Cell-matrix interactions in cell migration

P01HD-18577-08 0003 (HDMC) WU,CHUN-FANG The developmental biology of cell motility Growth cone activity and neuronal plasticity in Drosophila

P01HD-18577-08 0004 (HDMC) LIN, JIM JUNG-CHIN The developmental biology of cell motility Molecular basis for vertebrate cell motility

P01HD-18577-08 9001 (HDMC) SOLL, DAVID R The developmental biology of cell motility Core - Laboratory for quantitative analysis of cell behavior

R01HD-18582-09 (MBY) MAXSON, ROBERT E, JR UNIV OF SOUTHERN CALIFORNIA 2025 ZONAL AVENUE NOR533 LOS ANGELES, CA 90033 Temporal regulation of gene expression in development

R01HD-18590-10 (REB) LENNARZ, WILLIAM J STATE UNIVERSITY OF NEW YORK NICOLLS RD STONY BROOK, NY 11794-5215 Plasma membrane changes in fertilization

R01HD-18591-08 (REB) NORMAN, REID L TEXAS TECH UNIV HLTH SCI CTR DEPT OF CELL BIO & ANATOMY LUBBOCK, TX 79430 Central regulation of fertility in primates

R01HD-18592-09 (HED) PINTAR, JOHN E INSULIN GENE EXPRESSION IN EXT 630 WEST 168TH STREET NEW YORK, NY 10032 Prenatal differentiation of the pituitary gland

R01HD-18633-07 (BEM) FREEMAN, ELLEN W HOSPITAL OF THE UNIV OF PA 3400 SPRUCE STREET PHILADELPHIA, PENN 19104 Treatment evaluation in premenstrual syndrome patients

R01HD-18642-08 (MGN) WASMUTH, JOHN J UNIVERSITY OF CALIFORNIA D240, MED SCI I IRVINE, CA 92717 Molecular genetic study of the CRI DU CHAT syndrome

P30HD-18655-10 (HDMR) VOLPE, JOSEPH J CHILDREN'S HOSPITAL 300 LONGWOOD AVENUE BOSTON, MA 02115 Mental retardation & developmental disabilities research

P30HD-18655-10 0183 (HDMR) SYNDER, EVAN Y Mental retardation & developmental disabilities research Use of retroviral vectors to study neural plasticity

P30HD-18655-10 9002 (HDMR) KIRSCHNER, DANIEL A Mental retardation & developmental disabilities research Core--Electron microscopy laboratory

P30HD-18655-10 9004 (HDMR) KUNKEL, LOUIS M Mental retardation & developmental disabilities research Core--Photography and computer graphics laboratory

P30HD-18655-10 9006 (HDMR) KUNKEL, LOUIS M Mental retardation & developmental disabilities research Core--Mouse facility

P30HD-18655-10 9007 (HDMR) KINNEY, HANNAH C Mental retardation & developmental disabilities research Core--Histology laboratory

P30HD-18655-10 9008 (HDMR) MCCALLIE, DAVID Mental retardation & developmental disabilities research Core--Image graphics

P30HD-18655-10 9009 (HDMR) LALANDE, MARC Mental retardation & developmental disabilities research Core--Cell sorter facility

P30HD-18655-10 9010 (HDMR) VILLA-KOMAROFF, LYDIA Mental retardation & developmental disabilities research Core--Transgenic mouse facility

P30HD-18655-10 9011 (HDMR) KORF, BRUCE Mental retardation & developmental disabilities research Core--Molecular diagnosis laboratory

P30HD-18655-10 9012 (HDMR) KUNKEL, LOUIS M Mental retardation & developmental disabilities research Core--DNA sequencer laboratory

P01HD-18658-09 (HDMR) KUNKEL, LOUIS M CHILDREN'S HOSP. CORPORATION 300 LONGWOOD AVENUE BOSTON, MASS 02115 Genetic and cytogenetic studies of mental retardation

P01HD-18658-09 0012 (HDMR) LA LANDE, MARC Genetic and cytogenetic studies of mental retardation Metaphase chromosome flow sorting

P01HD-18658-09 0013 (HDMR) BRUNS, GAIL Genetic and cytogenetic studies of mental retardation Loci for x-linked eye disorders and autosomal tetrasomy

P01HD-18658-09 0014 (HDMR) NEVE, RACHAEL L. Genetic and cytogenetic studies of mental retardation Genes on chromosome 21 and down syndrome

P01HD-18658-09 0015 (HDMR) KUNKEL, LOUIS Genetic and cytogenetic studies of mental retardation Molecular characterization of x chromosome

R37HD-18661-09 (HEM) ORKIN, STUART H CHILDREN'S HOSPITAL 300 LONGWOOD AVENUE BOSTON, MA 02115 Structure function analysis of specific human genes

R01HD-18678-07A1 (NTN) STURMAN, JOHN A INST FOR BASIC RESEARCH 1050 FOREST HILL ROAD STATEN ISLAND, NY 10314 Test of taurine as an essential nutrient: primate model

R01HD-18686-06 (BPN) DAVIS, FREDERICK C NORTHEASTERN UNIVERSITY 360 HUNTINGTON AVENUE BOSTON, MA 02115 Development of mammalian circadian rhythms

R01HD-18702-15 (BCE) JI, TAE H UNIVERSITY OF WYOMING LARAMIE, WY 82071-3944 The structure and functions of the lutropin receptor

R01HD-18708-11 (CMS) CLIFTON, CHARLES E, JR UNIVERSITY OF MASSACHUSETTS AMHERST, MA 01003 Language comprehension

R01HD-18717-05 (HED) HEAD, JUDITH R UNIV OF TX SOUTHWESTERN MED CT 5323 HARRY HINES BOULEVARD DALLAS, TX 75235 Immune processes in the pregnant and non-pregnant uterus

R01HD-18735-08 (REB) JAGIELLO, GEORGIANA M COLUMBIA UNIVERSITY 630 WEST 168TH STREET NEW YORK, NY 10032 Studies on mammalian oocytes and spermatocytes

R01HD-18737-08 (REB) HOSKINS, DALE D OREGON REGIONAL PRIMATE RES CT 505 NW 185TH AVE BEAVERTON, OR 97006 The epididymal initiation of sperm motility

R01HD-18825-07A1 (REB) HOWARDS, STUART S UNIV OF VIRGINIA

PROJECT NO., ORGANIZATIONAL UNIT., INVESTIGATOR, ADDRESS, TITLE

HOSPITAL BOX 422 HEALTH SCIENCES CTR CHARLOTTESVILLE, VA 22908 Vasovasostomy – Morphology physiology and immunology

R01HD-18942-06S1 (HUD) RICHARDS, JOHN E UNIVERSITY OF SOUTH CAROLINA COLUMBIA, SC 29208 The development of sustained attention in infants

P01HD-18955-07 (SRC) SHERMAN, JAMES A BUREAU OF CHILD RESEARCH UNIVERSITY OF KANSAS LAWRENCE, KANSAS 66045 Communication of people with mental retardation

P01HD-18955-07 0002 (SRC) SPRADLIN, J E Communication of people with mental retardation Development, structure, stability of stimulus and classes among retarded persons

P01HD-18955-07 0003 (SRC) BAER, D M Communication of people with mental retardation Generalization characteristics of self-instruction by children

P01HD-18955-07 0004 (SRC) HART, B Communication of people with mental retardation Longitudinal study of language of mentally retarded children reared at home

P01HD-18955-07 0005 (SRC) SHERMAN, J A Communication of people with mental retardation Social skills of retarded adults in the community

P01HD-18955-07 0006 (SRC) MCLEAN, J E Communication of people with mental retardation Pre-linguistic communicative abilities in mentally retarded children

P01HD-18955-07 9001 (SRC) SEARS, DAVIDA Communication of people with mental retardation Core--Computer applications

R01HD-18957-13 (EVR) STARR, STUART E JOSEPH STOKES, JR RESEARCH INS 34TH STREET & CIVIC CENTER BLV PHILADELPHIA, PA 19104 Prevention of CMV disease

R01HD-18967-07 (REN) SOULES, MICHAEL R UNIVERSITY OF WASHINGTON SEATTLE, WA 98195 Gonadotropin patterns and ovarian function

P30HD-18968-08 (HDPR) FRENCH, FRANK S UNIV OF NORTH CAROLINA 375 MED SCI RES BLDG CHAPEL HILL, NC 27599 The laboratories for reproductive biology

P30HD-18968-08 9001 (HDPR) STUMPF, WALTER The laboratories for reproductive biology Histochemistry and microscopy - Core

P30HD-18968-08 9002 (HDPR) PETRUSZ, PETER The laboratories for reproductive biology Radioimmunoassay core

P30HD-18968-08 9004 (HDPR) TRES, LAURA L The laboratories for reproductive biology Tissue culture/hybridoma - core

P30HD-18968-08 9005 (HDPR) JOSEPH, DAVID The laboratories for reproductive biology Recombinant DNA core

R01HD-18999-07 (REN) BULLEN, BEVERLY A BOSTON UNIVERSITY 635 COMMONWEALTH AVENUE BOSTON, MASS 02215 Exercise stimulus in pituitary hormone regulation

R01HD-19011-07 (HUD) SIEGLER, ROBERT S CARNEGIE-MELLON UNIVERSITY 5000 FORBES AVENUE PITTSBURGH, PA 15213 The development of strategy choice procedures

R01HD-19018-08 (REB) BRINSTER, RALPH L UNIVERSITY OF PENNSYLVANIA DEPT ANIMAL BIO SCH VET MED PHILADELPHIA, PA 19104 Introduction of new genes into large animals

R01HD-19054-06 (REB) NISHIOKA, DAVID J GEORGETOWN UNIVERSITY WASHINGTON, DC 20057 The sperm surface in spermatogenesis and fertilization

R01HD-19068-08 (MET) COLEMAN, ROSALIND A UNIVERSITY OF NORTH CAROLINA CHAPEL HILL, NC 27599-7400 Metabolism of glycerolipids liver

R55HD-19077-07 (REB) GIBSON, MARIE J MOUNT SINAI SCHOOL OF MEDICINE 1 GUSTAVE LEVY PLACE, BOX 1055 NEW YORK, NY 10029 Preoptic area brain grafts and the control of ovulation

R01HD-19089-08 (HED) LIECHTY, EDWARD A INDIANA UNIVERSITY SCH OF MED 702 BARNHILL DRIVE, RM RR-208 INDIANAPOLIS, IN 46202-5225 Fetal branched chain amino acid and keto-acid metabolism

R01HD-19124-06 (HUD) GALLIMORE, RONALD G UNIVERSITY OF CALIFORNIA 760 WESTWOOD PLAZA LOS ANGELES, CA 90024-1759 Ecocultural opportunity and family accommodation

R01HD-19126-07 (REB) CHAMBERS, EDWARD L UNIV OF MIAMI SCHOOL OF MED P O BOX 016430 MIAMI, FL 33101 Sperm-egg interaction--Excitation-activation coupling

R01HD-19143-07 (HUD) KAPLAN, PETER S UNIVERSITY OF COLORADO PO BOX 173364 DENVER, CO 80217-3364 A dual-process analysis of infant visual attention

R01HD-19145-08 (SSP) KIM, YOUNG J JOHNS HOPKINS UNIVERSITY 615 NORTH WOLFE STREET BALTIMORE, MD 21205 Generalized population dynamics with changing rates

R01HD-19182-07 (REB) BRENNER, ROBERT M OREGON REGIONAL PRIMATE RES CT 505 NW 185TH AVENUE BEAVERTON, OR 97006 Hormonal control of macaque female reproductive tract

R01HD-19236-05A2 (REB) KREY, LEWIS C ROCKEFELLER UNIVERSITY 1230 YORK AVENUE NEW YORK, NY 10021 Biochemistry of progesterone action in the gonadotroph

R01HD-19247-05 (REB) TSENG, LINDA SUNY HEALTH SCIENCE CENTER SCHOOL OF MEDICINE STONY BROOK, NY 11794 Progestin and relaxin effects on endometrial prolactin

R01HD-19252-08 (GEN) ELDER, ROBERT T TEXAS A & M UNVERSITY COLLEGE STATION, TX 77843 Molecular analysis of gene in meiosis

R01HD-19302-07 (BCE) SLUSS, PATRICK M UNIV OF ROCHESTER MED CTR 601 ELMWOOD AVE, BOX 656 ROCHESTER, NY 14642 Purification of FSH binding inhibitors

R01HD-19342-07 (BEM) THORNTON, ARLAND D UNIVERSITY OF MICHIGAN 426 THOMPSON ST ANN ARBOR, MI 48106 Intergenerational panel study of parents and children

R01HD-19375-08 (SSP) MCLANAHAN, SARA S OFFICE OF POPULATION RES PRINCETON UNIVERSITY PRINCETON, N. J. 08544-2091 Intergenerational consequences of family disruption

R01HD-19383-06A1 (SSP) BRAVER, SANFORD L ARIZONA STATE UNIVERSITY TEMPE, AZ 85287-1104 Noncustodial parents - Parents without children

R01HD-19393-07 (HED) MEYERS-WALLEN, VICKI N CORNELL UNIVERSITY 429 VETERINARY RESEARCH TOWER ITHACA, NY 14853-6401 Defects in mullerian duct regession

R01HD-19426-06 (HUD) BRAY, NORMAN W, JR UNIV OF ALABAMA UAB STATION/PO BOX 313 BIRMINGHAM, AL 35294 Memory skills of mentally retarded children

R01HD-19430-07 (REB) WALLACH, EDWARD E JOHNS HOPKINS UNIVERSITY 600 NORTH WOLFE STREET BALTIMORE, MD 21205 Ovulation--Studies using in vitro perfused ovaries

PROJECT NO., ORGANIZATIONAL UNIT., INVESTIGATOR, ADDRESS, TITLE

P30HD-19445-05S1 (HDPR) SWERDLOFF, RONALD S HARBOR-UCLA MEDICAL CENTER 1124 W CARSON STREET TORRANCE, CA 90502 Population research center

P30HD-19445-05S1 0001 (HDPR) BHASIN, SHALENDER Population research center Synthesis and secretion of alpha and beta subunits of luteinizing hormone

P30HD-19445-05S1 9001 (HDPR) SWERDLOFF, RONALD S Population research center Core--Biostatistics

P30HD-19445-05S1 9002 (HDPR) RAUM, WILLIAM J Population research center Core--Hormone assays

P30HD-19445-05S1 9003 (HDPR) PARLOW, ALBERT F Population research center Core--Tissue banking, peptide chemistry, and antibody production

P30HD-19445-05S1 9004 (HDPR) SHAPIRO, LARRY J Population research center Core--Recombinant DNA

P30HD-19445-05S1 9005 (HDPR) ZAMBONI, LUCIANO Population research center Core--Morphology

R01HD-19469-08 (EDC) MACLAREN, NOEL K UNIVERSITY OF FLORIDA PO BOX J275 JHMHC GAINESVILLE, FL 32610 Islet cell autoantibodies & the natural history of IDDM

R01HD-19505-04A2 (REB) HUSZAR, GABOR B YALE UNIVERSITY SCH OF MEDICIN 333 CEDAR STREET, PO BOX 3333 NEW HAVEN, CT 06510 Factors affecting sperm fertility

R01HD-19521-06 (REB) BENSON, BRYANT UNIVERSITY OF ARIZONA COLLEGE OF MEDICINE TUCSON, AZ 85724 Pineal peptides and reproduction

R01HD-19530-05 (REN) MORRIS, JOHN E OREGON STATE UNIVERSITY CORVALLIS, OR 97331-2132 Cell surface of uterine epithelium in culture

R01HD-19546-05 (REN) WINTERS, STEPHEN J MONTEFIORE HOSPITAL 3459 FIFTH AVENUE PITTSBURGH, PA 15213 Testis hormones and gonadotropins in male infertility

R01HD-19547-07 (REN) NEVILLE, MARGARET C UNIV OF COLORADO HEALTH SCI CT 4200 E NINTH AVE DENVER, CO 80262 Physiological factors affecting human lactation

R01HD-19555-08 (REN) ZANEVELD, LOURENS J RUSH-PRESBY-ST LUKE'S MED CTR 1653 WEST CONGRESS PARKWAY CHICAGO, IL 60612 Human sperm enzymes, inhibitors and fertilization

R01HD-19584-06 (REB) SUAREZ, SUSAN S UNIVERSITY OF FLORIDA 013 BOX J-144, JHMHC GAINESVILLE, FL 32610-0144 Studies of sperm capacitation and hyperactivation

R01HD-19593-07 (REB) SADLER, THOMAS W UNIVERSITY OF NORTH CAROLINA CB#7090, 108 SWING BLDG CHAPEL HILL, NC 27599-7090 Mechanisms of diabetes-induced congenital malformations

R01HD-19679-06 (HAR) FADEN, HOWARD S CHILDREN'S HOSPITAL, BUFFALO 219 BRYANT ST BUFFALO, NY 14222 Natural history and immunology of otitis media due to NTHI

R01HD-19724-03 (EDC) BROWN, JUDITH E UNIV OF MINN SCH/PUBLIC HEALTH 420 DELAWARE/197 MAYO MEM BLDG MINNEAPOLIS, MN 55455 Epidemiological study of risks to reproductive outcomes

R01HD-19735-06 (REB) DEPHILIP, ROBERT M OHIO STATE UNIVERSITY 333 W 10TH AVE/4072 GRAVES HAL COLUMBUS, OH 43210 Sertoli cell-germ cell surface membrane interactions

R01HD-19739-05 (HUD) FAGOT, BEVERLY I OREGON SOCIAL LEARNING CENTER 207 E 5TH AVE, SUITE 202 EUGENE, OR 97401 Process of fathering--Effects on his child's competence

R01HD-19746-04 (BNP) COVEY, DOUGLAS F WASHINGTON UNIVERSITY LINDELL & SKINKER BLVDS ST LOUIS, MO 63130 Mechanisms and chemistry of dehydrogenase inactivators

R01HD-19752-07 (HUD) BIRCH, LEANN L UNIVERSITY OF ILLINOIS 1105 WEST NEVADA URBANA, IL 61801 Associative conditioning of children's food preferences

R01HD-19764-08 (REN) SINGER, ALAN G MONELL CHEMICAL SENSES CENTER 3500 MARKET STREET PHIALADELPHIA, PA 19104-3308 Identification of pheromones regulating reproduction

R01HD-19773-08 (NTN) KIEN, CRAIG L CHILDREN'S HOSPITAL RES FDN 700 CHILDREN'S DRIVE COLUMBUS, OH 43205 Carbohydrate energy absorption in premature infants

R01HD-19789-08 (BPO) BRIDGES, ROBERT S 200 WESTBORO RD NORTH GRAFTON, MA 01536-1895 Endocrine regulation of maternal behavior

R01HD-19802-06 (HUD) FULKER, DAVID W UNIVERSITY OF COLORADO CAMPUS BOX 447 BOULDER, COLO 80309 Infant predictors of adult IQ

R01HD-19803-05 (BCE) KING, JOAN C TUFTS UNIV SCH OF MED 136 HARRISON AVENUE BOSTON, MA 02111 Afferents to LHRH neurons and mammalian reproduction

R01HD-19821-07 (PBC) JONES, PETER USC COMPREHENSIVE CNACER CTR 2025 ZONAL AVE - ROOM 610 LOS ANGELES, CA 90033 Gene regulation in embryonal carcinoma cell differentiation

R01HD-19837-05 (HED) RIZZINO, ARNOLD A UNIVERSITY OF NEBRASKA 42ND & DEWEY AVE OMAHA, NE 68105 Regulation of growth factors and mammalian embryogenesis

U01HD-19897-07 (SRC) BAIN, RAYMOND P BIOSTATISTICS CENTER 6110 EXECUTIVE BLVD ROCKVILLE, MD 20852 Chorion villus sampling vs amniocentesis--Data center

R01HD-19899-08 (END) CONN, PAUL M UNIVERSITY OF IOWA IOWA CITY, IA 52242 Gonadotropin releasing hormone action--role of calcium

R01HD-19913-05A1 (PTHA) VANNUCCI, ROBERT C PENNSYLVANIA STATE UNIVERSITY PO BOX 850 HERSHEY, PA 17033 Pathogenesis of perinatal hypoxic-ischemic brain damage

R01HD-19914-04A2 (HUD) DECI, EDWARD L UNIVERSITY OF ROCHESTER ROCHESTER, NY 14627 The motivational basis of children's self-regulation

R01HD-19915-09 (SSP) ANDERSON, BARBARA A POPULATION STUDIES CENTER 1225 SOUTH UNIVERSITY AVENUE ANN ARBOR, MI 48104-2590 Comparative demographic patterns (USSR)

R01HD-19919-08 (BIO) HUTTON, JOHN J CHILDREN'S HOSP MED CTR ELLAND & BETHESDA AVENUE CINCINNATI, OH 45229-2899 Biochemical genetics of childhood immunodeficiency

R01HD-19927-07 (VISA) BANKS, MARTIN S UNIVERSITY OF CALIFORNIA SCHOOL OF OPTOMETRY BERKELEY, CA 94720 Development of form perception in infancy

P01HD-19937-06 (HDMC) GEHRZ, RICHARD C BIOMEDICAL RES INST/CHILD HOSP 345 NORTH SMITH AVENUE ST PAUL, MN 55102 Mechanisms of immune response to human Cytomegalovirus

P01HD-19937-06 0001 (HDMC) STINSKI, MARK F Mechanisms of immune response to human Cytomegalovirus Human Cytomegalovirus genes involved in immune response to the virus

P01HD-19937-06 0002 (HDMC) LIU, YUNG-NAN Mechanisms of immune response to human Cytomegalovirus Characterization of HCMV-specific T-cell immune response

P01HD-19937-06 0003 (HDMC) GEHRZ, RICHARD C Mechanisms of immune response to human Cytomegalovirus Cellular immunity in congenital HCMV infection

P01HD-19937-06 0005 (HDMC) BACH, FRITZ H Mechanisms of immune response to human Cytomegalovirus Immunogenetic regulation of HCMV-specific T Cells

P01HD-19937-06 0006 (HDMC) KARI, BRUCE Mechanisms of immune response to human Cytomegalovirus Structural and functional analysis of MCMV glycoproteins

P01HD-19937-06 9001 (HDMC) KARI, BRUCE E Mechanisms of immune response to human Cytomegalovirus Biochemistry--Core

P01HD-19937-06 9002 (HDMC) LIU, YUNG-NAN Mechanisms of immune response to human Cytomegalovirus Cell culture/immunology--Core

P01HD-19937-06 9004 (HDMC) GEHRZ, RICHARD Mechanisms of immune response to human Cytomegalovirus Monoclonal antibody--Core

R01HD-19938-08 (BCE) CHIN, WILLIAM W BRIGHAM & WOMEN'S HOSPITAL 75 FRANCIS ST BOSTON, MA 02115 Reproductive physiology of gonadotropin synthesis

R01HD-19947-07 (HUD) KAIL, ROBERT PURDUE UNIVERSITY WEST LAFAYETTE, IN 47907 Developmental change in speed of processing

R01HD-19949-07 (GEN) MICHOD, RICHARD E UNIVERSITY OF ARIZONA TUCSON, AZ 85721 Population genetics of interactions

R01HD-19950-07 (NEUB) LETOURNEAU, PAUL C UNIVERSITY OF MINNESOTA 321 CHURCH STREET SE MINNEAPOLIS, MN 55455 Mechanisms of nerve growth cone turning and branching

R01HD-19966-06 (REB) NUCCITELLI, RICHARD L UNIVERSITY OF CALIFORNIA DEPT. OF ZOOLOGY DAVIS, CA 95616 Ionic regulation in the activation of development

R01HD-19983-06 (SSP) POPKIN, BARRY M UNIVERSITY OF NORTH CAROLINA 123 W FRANKLIN ST CHAPEL HILL, NC 27516-3997 Infant mortality--Underlying and intermediate determinants

R01HD-19998-06 (BCE) ADASHI, ELI Y 655 WEST BALTIMORE STREET ROOM 11-007, BRB BALTIMORE, MD 21201 Somatomedin-C--Novel regulator of granulosa cell function

R01HD-20001-08 (REB) BARTKE, ANDRZEJ SOUTHERN ILLINOIS UNIVERSITY CARBONDALE, IL 62901 Hyperprolactinemia and male reproductive functions

R01HD-20025-07 (BCE) LYTTLE, CECIL R UNIVERSITY OF PENNSYLVANIA 422 CURIE BOULEVARD PHILADELPHIA, PA 19104 Peroxidase and eosinophils in uterine estrogen action

R01HD-20026-05 (HUD) HAITH, MARSHALL M DEPT OF PSYCHOLOGY UNIVERSITY OF DENVER DENVER, CO 80208 Visual anticipation and expectation in early infancy

R01HD-20033-08 (REB) BARTKE, ANDRZEJ SOUTHERN ILLINOIS UNIVERSITY SCHOOL OF MEDICINE CARBONDALE, ILL 62901 Physiological role of growth hormone in the male

R01HD-20034-07 (MGN) FRIEDMANN, THEODORE UNIVERSITY OF CALIFORNIA LA JOLLA, CA 92093 Models for CNS gene therapy

R01HD-20054-07 (GMA) HILLEMEIER, ALFRED C UNIV OF MICHIGAN MEDICAL CTR 1150 W MED CTR DR/15100E MSRB ANN ARBOR, MI Development aspects of upper gastrointestinal motility

R01HD-20055-06 (BCE) STRICKLER, RONALD C JEWISH HOSPITAL 216 S KINGSHIGHWAY ST LOUIS, MO 63110 Placental 3-beta hydroxysteroid dehydrogenase delta 4-5 isomerase

R01HD-20068-07 (REB) ALBERTINI, DAVID F TUFTS UNIVERSITY 136 HARRISON AVENUE BOSTON, MASS 02111 Oocyte maturation--Vital stain-video microscopy analysis

R01HD-20074-07 (REN) CROWLEY, WILLIAM R UNIV. OF TENNESSEE, MEMPHIS DEPARTMENT OF PHARMACOLOGY MEMPHIS, TN 38163 Neural and hormonal regulation of lactation

R01HD-20084-07 (HED) ABRAMS, ROBERT M UNIVERSITY OF FLORIDA BOX J-294, JHMHC GAINESVILLE, FL 32610-0294 Sound in utero--Effects on fetal brain

R01HD-20129-07 (REN) CHILTON, BEVERLY S TEXAS TECH UNIV HLTH SCIS CTR HEALTH SCIENCES CENTER LUBBOCK, TX 79430 Mechanism of estrogen action in the endocervix

R01HD-20136-07 (REN) CHAE, CHI-BOM UNIVERSITY OF NORTH CAROLINA CB#7260 CHAPEL HILL, NC 27599-7260 Role of testis specific histones in spermatogenesis

R01HD-20209-08 (CBY) EICHELE, GREGOR BAYLOR COLLEGE OF MEDICINE ONE BAYLOR PLAZA HOUSTON, TX 77030 Mechanism of pattern formation in the vertebrate limb

R01HD-20275-08 (MGN) SILVER, LEE M PRINCETON UNIVERSITY PRINCETON, NJ 08544 Organization and expression of the mouse T complex

R01HD-20286-08 (CEP) ASLIN, RICHARD N UNIVERSITY OF ROCHESTER MELIORA HALL ROCHESTER, N Y 14627 Perceptual segmentation of speech by human infants

P01HD-20290-06A1 (SRC) LONGCOPE, CHRISTOPHER UNIV OF MASS MED SCHOOL 55 LAKE AVENUE NORTH WORCESTER, MA 01605 Uterus-cyclic hormonal control mechanisms

P01HD-20290-06A1 0001 (SRC) PADYKULA, HELEN A Uterus-cyclic hormonal control mechanisms Hormonal control of uterine proliferation

P01HD-20290-06A1 0002 (SRC) OKULICZ, WILLIAM C Uterus-cyclic hormonal control mechanisms Steroid receptor regulation in the primate endometrium

P01HD-20290-06A1 0003 (SRC) LONGCOPE, CHRISTOPHER L Uterus-cyclic hormonal control mechanisms Uterine uptake and metabolism of estrogens

P01HD-20290-06A1 0004 (SRC) MC CRACKEN, JOHN A Uterus-cyclic hormonal control mechanisms Endocrine physiology of primate endometrium and myometrium

P01HD-20290-06A1 9001 (SRC) MCCRACKEN, JOHN Uterus-cyclic hormonal control mechanisms Core project

R01HD-20295-07A2 (REB) BRACE, ROBERT A UNIVERSITY OF CALIFORNIA U OF CALIFORNIA, SAN DIEGO LA JOLLA, CA 92093-0802 Fetal blood volume dynamics and control

R01HD-20299-07 (HED) CHEUNG, CECILIA Y UNIV OF CALIFORNIA, SAN DIEGO DEPT OF REPR MED, T-002 LA JOLLA, CALIF 92093 Endocrine control of fetal cardiovascular dynamics

R01HD-20337-06 (HED) DELIVORIA-PAPADOPOULOS, MARIA UNIVERSITY OF PENNSYLVANIA B-400 RICHARDS BLDG. PHILADELPHIA, PA 19104-3246 In-vivo cerebral oxidative metabolism in hypoxic newborn

R01HD-20347-06 (HED) HSU, YU-CHIH JOHNS HOPKINS UNIVERSITY 615 NORTH WOLFE STREET BALTIMORE, MD 21205 MRNA in developing mouse embryos

R01HD-20377-07 (BCE) MELLON, PAMELA L SALK INSTITUTE POST OFFICE BOX 85800 SAN DIEGO, CA 92186-5800 Pituitary gonadotropin gene regulation

R01HD-20414-04 (HUD) PORTER, FRAN L WASHINGTON UNIVERSITY 400 SOUTH KINGSHIGHWAY ST LOUIS, MO 63110 Physiological & behavioral responses to pain in infants

R01HD-20419-07 (REB) OLSON, GARY E VANDERBILT UNIVERSITY DEPARTMENT OF ANATOMY NASHVILLE, TENN 37232 Sperm function in fertilization events

R01HD-20469-07 (HED) WANDS, JACK R MASSACHUSETTS GENERAL HOSPITAL 149 13TH ST 7TH FL CHARLESTOWN, MA 02129 First trimester AFP screening for congenital defects

R01HD-20470-05 (NEUB) ROTHMAN, TAUBE P COLUMBIA UNIVERSITY 630 WEST 168TH STREET NEW YORK, N Y 10032 Developmental potential of cells from the neural crest

R01HD-20484-06 (HED) GORDON, JON W MT SINAI SCHOOL OF MEDICINE ONE GUSTAVE L LEVY PLACE NEW YORK, NY 10029 Insertional mutagenesis in transgenic mice

R01HD-20491-05 (SSP) THOMSON, ELIZABETH J CTR FOR DEMOGRAPHY & ECOLOGY 1180 OBSERVATORY DRIVE MADISON, WI 53706 Fertility agreement and conflict resolution

R01HD-20497-07 (CBY) SALE, WINFIELD S EMORY UNIVERSITY SCHOOL OF MED DEPT OF ANATOMY & CELL BIOLOGY ATLANTA, GA 30322 Functional substructure of flagellar dynein

R01HD-20521-06 (MGN) WARREN, STEPHEN T EMORY UNIVERSITY SCH OF MED ROLLINS RESEARCH CENTER ATLANTA, GA 30322 Molecular cloning of the Fragile X site

R01HD-20553-06 (REN) BUHI, WILLIAM C UNIV OF FLORIDA COLLEGE OF MED PO BOX 100294 GAINESVILLE, FL 32610-0294 Hormonal control of oviductal secretory proteins

R01HD-20559-05 (HUD) TAMIS-LEMONDA, CATHERINE NEW YORK UNIVERSITY 6 WASHINGTON PL 7TH FLOOR NEW YORK, N Y 10003 Cognitive assessment in high-risk and normal infants

R01HD-20571-05A1 (REB) VERHAGE, HAROLD G UNIVERSITY OF ILLINOIS 840 S WOOD STREET CHICAGO, IL 60612 Secretions of the mammalian oviduct

R01HD-20575-07 (REB) EPPIG, JOHN J JACKSON LABORATORY 600 MAIN STREET BAR HARBOR, ME 04609-0800 Regulation of mammalian oocyte development

R01HD-20581-06 (HED) BABIARZ, BRUCE S RUTGERS UNIVERSITY DPT OF BIOLOGICAL SCIENCES PISCATAWAY, N J 08855-1059 Analysis of cell surface during mammalian development

R01HD-20583-06 (BCE) SKINNER, MICHAEL K UNIVERSITY OF CALIFORNIA SAN FRANCISCO, CA 94143-0556 Cellular functions and interactions in the testis

R01HD-20601-07 (SSS) LEARY, JAMES F UNIV OF ROCHESTER MEDICAL CTR 601 ELMWOOD AVENUE ROCHESTER, N Y 14642 Isolation of human fetal cells from maternal blood

R01HD-20618-06 (HED) JOBE, ALAN H HARBOR UCLA MEDICAL CENTER BLDG A-17 1000 W CARSON ST TORRANCE, CA 90509 Corticosteroid and thyroid effects on lung maturation

R01HD-20619-06 (MGN) LEDBETTER, DAVID H BAYLOR COLLEGE OF MEDICINE ONE BAYLOR PLAZA HOUSTON, TX 77030 Molecular analysis of human chromosomes 17

R01HD-20632-06 (GMA) SUCHY, FREDERICK J YALE UNIVERSITY SCH OF MED 333 CEDAR STREET NEW HAVEN, CT 06510 Ontogeny of hepatic ion transport

R01HD-20670-06 (MGN) ERICKSON, ROBERT P DEPARTMENT OF PEDIATRICS 1501 N. CAMPBELL AVENUE Biochemical genetics of male sexual determination

R01HD-20676-05 (HED) SOARES, MICHAEL J UNIV OF KANSAS MEDICAL CTR 39TH AND RAINBOW BLVD KANSAS CITY, KS 66103-8410 Trophoblast differentiation

R01HD-20677-06 (REN) LEVINE, JON E NORTHWESTERN UNIVERSITY DPT OF NEUROBIOLOGY & PHYSIOLO EVANSTON, IL 60208 Neuroendocrine regulation of in vivo GnRH release

R01HD-20691-05A1 (GMA) HORTON, WILLIAM A UNIV OF TEXAS P O BOX 20708 HOUSTON, TX 77225 Growth plate studies in the chondrodystrophies

P01HD-20743-05 (SRC) MARKWALD, ROGER R MEDICAL COLLEGE OF WISCONSIN 8701 WATERTOWN PLANK ROAD MILWAUKEE, WI 53226 Extracellular molecular interaction in limb development

P01HD-20743-05 0001 (SRC) MARKWALD, ROGER R Extracellular molecular interaction in limb development Extracellular proteins in limb mesenchyme development(chicks,mice,rabbits,quail)n

P01HD-20743-05 0003 (SRC) GODFREY, EARL W Extracellular molecular interaction in limb development Cell-ECM interactions in limb muscle development

P01HD-20743-05 0004 (SRC) FALLON, JOHN D Extracellular molecular interaction in limb development Role of the ectoderm in limb pattern formation

P01HD-20743-05 9002 (SRC) YORDE, DONALD E Extracellular molecular interaction in limb development Monoclonal core

P01HD-20743-05 9003 (SRC) BOLENDER, DAVID L Extracellular molecular interaction in limb development Primary culture core

P01HD-20743-05 9004 (SRC) RILEY, DANNY A Extracellular molecular interaction in limb development Electron microscopy core

R01HD-20747-07 (HED) MITCHELL, MURRAY D UNIV OF UTAH SCH OF MEDICINE 50 NORTH MEDICAL DRIVE SALT LAKE CITY, UTAH 84132 Arachidonate lipoxygenase activities in human pregnancy

P50HD-20748-06A1 (SRC) TSANG, REGINALD C UNIVERSITY OF CINCINNATI 231 BETHESDA AVENUE CINCINNATI, OH 45267-0541 Perinatal emphasis research center grant

P50HD-20748-06A1 0005 (SRC) KORFHAGEN, THOMAS R Perinatal emphasis research center grant Growth of distal respiratory epithelium during

PROJECT NO., ORGANIZATIONAL UNIT., INVESTIGATOR, ADDRESS, TITLE

branching morphogenesis
P50HD-20748-06A1 0006 (SRC) WEAVER, TIMOTHY Perinatal emphasis research center grant Regulation of pulmonary glycogen in developing rat lung
P50HD-20748-06A1 0007 (SRC) LIEBERMAN, MICHAEL Perinatal emphasis research center grant FGF expression in an IUGR rat model
P50HD-20748-06A1 0008 (SRC) HOATH, STEVEN Perinatal emphasis research center grant Metabolic adaptation in the postnatal rat -- Epidermal growth factor
P50HD-20748-06A1 0009 (SRC) CHERNAUSEK, STEVEN D Perinatal emphasis research center grant IGF binding proteins in perinatal growth
P50HD-20748-06A1 0010 (SRC) IWAMOTO, HARRIET Perinatal emphasis research center grant Regulation of circulating IGF-I during fetal life
P50HD-20748-06A1 0011 (SRC) CLARK, KENNETH E Perinatal emphasis research center grant Systemic metabolism and nutritional supplementation in IUGR
P50HD-20748-06A1 9003 (SRC) WHITSETT, JEFFREY A Perinatal emphasis research center grant Molecular core
P50HD-20761-06A1 (SRC) HAY, WILLIAM W, JR UNIVERSITY OF COLORADO 4200 EAST NINTH AVENUE DENVER, CO 80262 Metabolic regulation of fetal growth
P50HD-20761-06A1 0001 (SRC) HAY, WILLIAM W Metabolic regulation of fetal growth Fetal effects of insulin and glucose deprivation
P50HD-20761-06A1 0005 (SRC) WILKENING, RANDALL B Metabolic regulation of fetal growth Spontaneous placental insufficiency--A model of fetal growth retardation
P50HD-20761-06A1 0006 (SRC) BATTAGLIA, FREDERICK C Metabolic regulation of fetal growth Amino acid and carbohydrate metabolism in growth retarded pregnancies
P50HD-20761-06A1 9002 (SRC) FENNESSEY, PAUL V Metabolic regulation of fetal growth Core--Research Laboratory
P50HD-20761-06A1 9003 (SRC) ZERBE, GARY Metabolic regulation of fetal growth Core--Statistics
P01HD-20805-05A1 (HDMC) BIER, DENNIS M WASHINGTON UNIVERSITY 660 S EUCLID AVENUE ST LOUIS, MO 63110 Program project in the pathophysiology of human growth
P01HD-20805-05A1 0001 (HDMC) BIER, DENNIS M Program project in the pathophysiology of human growth Growth hormone, insulin, energy metabolism and protein homeostasis
P01HD-20805-05A1 0002 (HDMC) DAUGHADAY, WILLIAM H Program project in the pathophysiology of human growth Disorders of growth hormone and IGF structure and action
P01HD-20805-05A1 0004 (HDMC) ROTWEIN, PETER Program project in the pathophysiology of human growth Human insulin-like growth factor I--Gene structure and function
P01HD-20805-05A1 0005 (HDMC) TOLLEFSEN, SHERIDA Program project in the pathophysiology of human growth Signal transduction by insulin-like GFI receptor
P01HD-20805-05A1 9001 (HDMC) HEATH-MONNIG, ELLEN Program project in the pathophysiology of human growth Core--Special procedures
P01HD-20806-05 (HDMC) GALABURDA, ALBERT M BETH ISRAEL HOSPITAL 330 BROOKLINE AVENUE BOSTON, MA 02215 Animal models for developmental dyslexia
P01HD-20806-05 0001 (HDMC) GALABURDA, ALBERT M Animal models for developmental dyslexia Anatomy component research project
P01HD-20806-05 0002 (HDMC) GLICK, STANLEY D Animal models for developmental dyslexia Pharmacology component research project
P01HD-20806-05 0003 (HDMC) DENENBERG, VICTOR H Animal models for developmental dyslexia Behavior component research project--Fragile-X syndrome
P01HD-20806-05 0004 (HDMC) BEHAN, PETER O Animal models for developmental dyslexia Immunology component research project
R01HD-20829-06 (SSP) EPSTEIN, LEONARD H WESTERN PSYCHIATRIC INSTITUTE 3811 O'HARA STREET PITTSBURGH, PA 15213 Follow-up of behavioral childhood obesity treatment
R01HD-20839-06 (REN) CHAN, WALTER Y CORNELL UNIVERSITY 1300 YORK AVENUE NEW YORK, NY 10021 Arachidonic acid metabolites and uterine contractions
R01HD-20851-04A3 (HED) KLIEGMAN, ROBERT M RAINBOW BABIES 2074 ABINGTON ROAD CLEVELAND, OH 44106 Neonatal insulin sensitivity and responsiveness
R01HD-20859-05 (BBCB) BAKER, EDWARD N PALMERSTON NORTH NEW ZEALAND X-ray structural studies of lactoferrin
R01HD-20869-06 (BCE) STOUFFER, RICHARD L OREGON REG PRIMATE RES CTR 505 N W 185TH AVENUE BEAVERTON, OR 97006 Gonadotropin receptors of the primate corpus luteum
R01HD-20876-02A2 (ECS) DESJARDINS, CLAUDE UNIVERSITY OF VIRGINIA BOX 449/SCH OF MED CHARLOTTESVILLE, VA 22908 Regulation of testicular blood flow
R01HD-20919-06 (HED) LACY, ELIZABETH H SLOAN-KETTERING CANCER CTR 1275 YORK AVENUE NEW YORK, NY 10021 Insertional mutations affecting mammalian development
R37HD-20925-06 (TOX) KOCHHAR, DEVENDRA M THOMAS JEFFERSON UNIVERSITY 1020 LOCUST ST PHILADELPHIA, PA 19107 Developmental toxicity of retinoids and mode of action
R01HD-20928-05 (BM) CASSELL, GAIL H UNIVERSITY OF ALABAMA UAB STATION BIRMINGHAM, AL 35294 Role of ureaplasma intra-amniotic infection in IUGR
R01HD-20939-06 (HUD) GUILARTE, TOMAS R JOHNS HOPKINS UNIVERSITY 615 NORTH WOLFE STREET BALTIMORE, MD 21205 Maternal B6 deficiency--Effects on offspring development
R01HD-20954-05 (NEUC) MACAGNO, EDUARDO R COLUMBIA UNIVERSITY NEW YORK, NY 10027 Characterization of homeo box genes in the leech
R01HD-20988-04 (HUD) HOWIE, VIRGIL M UNIV OF TEXAS MED BRANCH RM C41-70, RT C-19 GALVESTON, TX 77550 Impact on child development of early otitis media
R01HD-20991-06 (SSS) KINNEY, HANNAH C CHILDRENS HOSPITAL 300 LONGWOOD AVE BOSTON, MA 02115 Brainstem maturation in the sudden infant death syndrome
R01HD-21009-06 (SSP) BUMPASS, LARRY L UNIVERSITY OF WISCONSIN 1180 OBSERVATORY DR MADISON, WI 53706 The health & well-being of families in transition

PROJECT NO., ORGANIZATIONAL UNIT., INVESTIGATOR, ADDRESS, TITLE

U01HD-21017-05 (SRC) FRIGOLETTO, FREDRIC D BRIGHAM AND WOMEN'S HOSPITAL 75 FRANCIS STREET BOSTON, MA 02115 Ultrasound screening and risk assessment of pregnancy
R01HD-21018-06 (NEUB) EDWARDS, MICHAEL A EUNICE KENNEDY SHRIVER CTR 200 TRAPELO RD WALTHAM, MA 02254 Genesis of cell pattern in mouse cerebellum and striatum
R01HD-21032-06 (NEUB) ROTHMAN, TAUBE P COLUMBIA UNIVERSITY 630 WEST 168TH STREET NEW YORK, N Y 10032 The abnormal terminal bowel of the 1s/1s mutant mouse
R01HD-21033-06 (NEUB) DE VOOGD, TIMOTHY J CORNELL UNIVERSITY 206 URIS HALL ITHACA, NY 14853-7601 Hormonal modulation of avian neuroanatomy
R01HD-21047-05 (GMA) RYAN, JAMES P TEMPLE UNIVERSITY 3420 N BROAD STREET PHILADELPHIA, PA 19140 Gastric motility in the newborn
R01HD-21049-06 (SSS) GARZA, CUTBERTO CORNELL UNIVERSITY 127 SAVAGE HALL ITHACA, N Y 14853-6301 Novel evaluation of lactation performance
R01HD-21056-04 (HUD) EYMAN, RICHARD K UNIVERSITY OF CALIFORNIA RIVERSIDE, CA 92521 Life expectancy of mentally retarded people
R01HD-21065-05 (NLS) AKESON, RICHARD A CHILDREN'S HOSPITAL MED CENTER ELLAND AND BETHESDA AVNEUES CINCINNATI, OH 45229-2899 NCAM-like protein structural and functional diversity
R01HD-21104-06 (HUD) BAILLARGEON, RENEE L UNIVERSITY OF ILLINOIS DEPARTMENT OF PSYCHOLOGY CHAMPAIGN, IL 61820 Object knowledge in young infants
U01HD-21140-05 (SRC) EWIGMAN, BERNARD G DEP OF FAMILY/COMMUNITY MED MA 303-J MEDICAL SCIS BLDG COLUMBIA, MO 65212 Randomized trial of routine prenatal ultrasound
R55HD-21204-04A2 (REN) KLIBANSKI, ANNE MASSACHUSETTS GENERAL HOSPITAL FRUIT STREET BOSTON, MA 02114 Long-term consequences of hypogonadism
R01HD-21212-04A1 (HUD) NEWELL, KARL M UNIVERSITY OF ILLINOIS 906 S GOODWIN AVENUE URBANA, IL 61801 Tardive dyskinesia and stereotypic movement disorders
R01HD-21229-06 (MGN) GRONER, YORAM WEIZMANN INST OF SCIENCE REHOVOT, ISRAEL 76100 Cloning of human genes involved in Down's syndrome
R01HD-21240-05 (SSP) ANDREWS, FRANK M UNIVERSITY OF MICHIGAN 475 EAST JEFFERSON RM 1301 ANN ARBOR, MI 448109-1248 Life quality, psychosocial factors, and infertility -2
R01HD-21244-07 (HED) OBER, CAROLE 5481 S. MARYLAND AVE CHICAGO, IL 60637 Immuno-and molecular genetic of Hutterite fertility
R01HD-21269-06 (ECS) BRACE, ROBERT A UNIVERSITY OF CALIFORNIA SCHOOL OF MEDICINE LA JOLLA, CA 92093-0802 Fetal lymph flow dynamics and control
R37HD-21294-07 (NSS) GOODMAN, COREY S UNIVERSITY OF CALIFRONIA 519 LIFE SCIENCE ADDITION BERKELEY, CA 94720 Cell recognition during neuronal development
R29HD-21295-05 (GMA) MURRAY, ROBERT D CHILDRE'S HOSP RES FOUNDATION 700 CHILDREN'S DRIVE COLUMBUS, OH 43205 Absorption in the neonatal colon
R01HD-21324-05 (HUD) BLACHER, JANET B SCHOOL OF EDUCATION UNIVERSITY OF CALIFORNIA RIVERSIDE, CA 92521-0128 Placement of severely handicapped children--Correlates and consequences
R01HD-21332-06 (HUD) LANGLOIS, JUDITH H UNIVERSITY OF TEXAS MEZES 330 AUSTIN, TX 78712 Infant perception of faces and developmental status
R01HD-21337-06 (MBY) RAFF, RUDOLF A INDIANA UNIVERSITY BLOOMINGHAM, IN 47405 Molecular basis of evolutionary change in development
R01HD-21338-06 (HUD) COWAN, NELSON UNIVERISTY OF MISSOURI, COLUMB 210 MCALESTER HALL COLUMBIA, MO 65211 The development of memory for speech
R01HD-21341-07 (MGN) HASSOLD, TERRY J DIVISION OF MEDICAL GENETICS 2040 RIDGEWOOD DRIVE ATLANTA, GA 30322 A program of research in population cytogenetics
P01HD-21350-05 (HDMC) NATHANIELSZ, PETER W CORNELL UNIVERSITY ITHACA, NY 14853-6401 Fetal neuroendocrinology, parturition and the myometrium
P01HD-21350-05 0001 (HDMC) NATHANIELSZ, PETER W Fetal neuroendocrinology, parturition and the myometrium Factors in the initiation and maintenance of labor
P01HD-21350-05 0002 (HDMC) REIMERS, THOMAS Fetal neuroendocrinology, parturition and the myometrium CF-41, fetal PVN, stress and parturition in sheep
P01HD-21350-05 0003 (HDMC) NATHANIELSZ, PETER W Fetal neuroendocrinology, parturition and the myometrium Parturition and fetal hypothalmic function
P01HD-21350-05 9001 (HDMC) NATHANIELSZ, PETER W Fetal neuroendocrinology, parturition and the myometrium Biochemical core
P01HD-21350-05 9002 (HDMC) POORE, E ROBIN Fetal neuroendocrinology, parturition and the myometrium Computer core
R01HD-21351-10A2 (BCE) SELMANOFF, MICHAEL K UNIV OF MD SCHOOL OF MED 655 WEST BALTIMORE STREET BALTIMORE, MD 21201 Neuroendocrine regulation of LH and prolactin secretion
P01HD-21354-05 (HDMR) THOMSON, ROBERT J, JR DUKE UNIV MEDICAL CENTER P. O. BOX 3362 DURHAM, NC 27710 Development follow-up of very low birth weight infants
P01HD-21354-05 0001 (HDMR) THOMPSON, ROBERT J. Development follow-up of very low birth weight infants Growth
P01HD-21354-05 0002 (HDMR) VILEISIS, RITA A. Development follow-up of very low birth weight infants Effect of parenteral nutrition components in growth
P01HD-21354-05 0003 (HDMR) ECKERMAN, CAROL O. Development follow-up of very low birth weight infants Very low birth weight infants as early social partners
P01HD-21355-04 (HDPR) KNOWLES, BARBARA B WISTAR INSTITUTE 36TH & SPRUCE STREET PHILADELPHIA, PA 19104 Controlling mechanisms in mammalian reproduction
P01HD-21355-04 0001 (HDPR) SOLTER, DAVOR Controlling mechanisms in mammalian reproduction Gene expression in nuclear transfer embryos
P01HD-21355-04 0002 (HDPR) KNOWLES, B B Controlling mechanisms in mammalian reproduction Growth control in early stages of embryogenesis

P01HD-21355-04 0003 (HDPR) LO, CECILIA Controlling mechanisms in mammalian reproduction Cell lineage and gene expression in mouse embryo

P01HD-21355-04 0004 (HDPR) SCHULTZ, RICHARD Controlling mechanisms in mammalian reproduction Transcriptional regulation in preimplantation embryo

P01HD-21355-04 0005 (HDPR) DAMJANOV, IVAN Controlling mechanisms in mammalian reproduction Trophoblast differentiation and its control

P01HD-21355-04 0006 (HDPR) TAUN, ROCKY S Controlling mechanisms in mammalian reproduction Trophectoderm Ca binding protein

P01HD-21355-04 9001 (HDPR) SOLTER, DAVOR Controlling mechanisms in mammalian reproduction Core--Genetic control of mammalian reproduction and development

U01HD-21363-06S1 (SRC) DEPP, RICHARD, III THOMAS JEFFERSON UNIVERSITY 1025 WALNUT ST, RM 310 PHILADELPHIA, PA 19107 Multicenter network of maternal-fetal medicine units

U10HD-21364-06 (SRC) FANAROFF, AVROY A RAINBOW BABIES & CHILDREN HOSP 2074 ABINGTON ROAD CLEVELAND, OH 44106 Cooperative multicenter network of NICUs

U10HD-21366-06 (SRC) ROMERO, ROBERTO J YALE UNIVERSITY 333 CEDAR STREET NEW HAVEN, CT 06510 Coop multicenter network of maternal fetal medicine unit

U10HD-21373-06 (SRC) TYSON, JON E UNIV OF TEXAS SOUTHWESTERN 5323 HARRY HINES BLVD DALLAS, TX 75235-9063 Cooperative multicenter neonatal intensive care unit network

R01HD-21379-07 (CBY) GLABE, CHARLES G UNIVERSITY OF CALIFORNIA MOLECULAR BIOLOGY & BIOCHEM IRVINE, CA 92717 Structure, organization, and function of bindin

U10HD-21385-06 (SRC) SHANKARAN, SEETHA CHILDREN'S HOSPITAL OF MI 3901 BEAUBIEN BLVD., RM. 405 DETROIT, MI 48201 Multicenter network of neonatal intensive care units

U01HD-21386-05S1 (SRC) WITTER, FRANK R JOHNS HOPKINS HOSPITAL 600 N WOLFE ST, HOUCK 228 BALTIMORE, MD 21205 Multicenter network of maternal-fetal medicine units

R01HD-21395-05 (HUD) MATHENY, ADAM P, JR UNIVERSITY OF LOUISVILLE LOUISVILLE, KY 40292 Behavorial-developmental trends in childhood injuries

U10HD-21397-06 (SRC) BAUER, CHARLES R UNIVERSITY OF MIAMI P O BOX 016960 MIAMI, FL 33101 Cooperative multicenter network of neonatal intensive care units

U10HD-21410-06 (SRC) CARITIS, STEVE N MAGEE-WOMENS HOSPITAL FORBES AND HALKET STREETS PITTSBURGH, PA 15213 A multi-center network of maternal-fetal medicine units

U10HD-21414-06 (SRC) SIBAI, BAHA M UNIVERSITY OF TENNESSEE 853 JEFFERSON AVE MEMPHIS, TENN 38103 Coop multicenter network of maternal-fetal medicine units

U10HD-21415-06 (SRC) KORONES, SHELDON B UNIVERSITY OF TENNESSEE 853 JEFFERSON AVE / RM 201 MEMPHIS, TENN 38163 Multicenter network of neonatal intensive care units

R01HD-21423-07 (HED) SIEBER-BLUM, MAYA F MEDICAL COLLEGE OF WISCONSIN 8701 WATERTOWN PLANK RD MILWAUKEE, WI 53226 Differentiation of avian neural crest cells in vitro

U10HD-21434-06 (SRC) PAUL, RICHARD H 1240 NORTH MISSION ROAD LOS ANGELES, CA 90033 Network of maternal-fetal medicine units (MFMUS)

R01HD-21453-03 (HUD) GRAZIANI, LEONARD J JEFFERSON MEDICAL COLLEGE 1025 WALNUT STREET PHILADELPHIA, PA 19107 Ultrasound and ventilator studies in preterm infants

R01HD-21478-04A3 (BPO) MEISEL, ROBERT L PURDUE UNIVERSITY DEPT OF PSYCHOLOGICAL SCIENCE WEST LAFAYETTE, IN 47907 Sociosexual behavior--Cellular basis of hormone action

R01HD-21502-06 (CBY) DE ROBERTIS, EDWARD M UNIVERSITY OF CALIFORNIA 405 HILGARD AVENUE LOS ANGELES, CA 90024-1406 Homeoboxes in Xenopus development

R01HD-21546-06 (REN) HALME, JOUKO K UNIV OF N C AT CHAPEL HILL CB# 7570, MACNIDER CHAPEL HILL, NC 27599 Cell interactions in endometriosis

R01HD-21581-05 (REB) BIGGERS, JOHN D HARVARD MEDICAL SCHOOL 45 SHATTUCK ST BOSTON, MA 02115 Assessing the viability of preimplantation embryos

R01HD-21678-05 (HED) GOLDBERG, BARRY B THOMAS JEFFERSON UNIVERSITY 1015 WALNUT STREET PHILADELPHIA, PA 19107 Effects of prenatal ultrasound on postnatal development

R01HD-21687-04 (RNM) SIDDIQI, TARIQ A UNIVERSITY OF CINCINNATI 231 BETHESDA AVENUE CINCINNATI, OH 45267 Ultrasound dosimetry in human OB/GYN examination

R01HD-21692-04A1 (RNM) DUNN, FLOYD UNIVERSITY OF ILLINOIS 1406 WEST GREEN STREET URBANA, IL 61801 Effects of ultrasonic radiation on fetal gonads

R01HD-21709-05 (HED) SMOLEN, ANDREW UNIVERSITY OF COLORADO CAMPUS BOX 447 BOULDER, CO 80309-0447 The genetics of pregnancy-induced seizures in mice

R01HD-21713-03A2 (SSP) WELCH, FINIS R UNICON RESEARCH CORPORATION 10801 NATIONAL B1 LOS ANGELES, CA 90064 Interrelationship of birthrate and economic factors

R01HD-21735-06 (HED) SHANKLAND, S MARTIN HARVARD MEDICAL SCHOOL 220 LONGWOOD AVE, DEPT/ANATOMY BOSTON, MA 02115 Determination of cell fate by positional cues

R01HD-21736-04 (BEM) HOUTS, ARTHUR C MEMPHIS STATE UNIVERSITY MEMPHIS, TN 38152 Pharmacological and behavioral treatment for enureisis

R01HD-21744-05 (REB) JOSEPH, DAVID R UNIV OF N C AT CHAPEL HILL CB#7500, MACNIDER BLDG CHAPEL HILL, NC 27599 Hormonal regulation of gene expression in Sertoli cells

R01HD-21765-05 (BIO) OKITA, RICHARD T WASHINGTON STATE UNIVERSITY WEGNER HALL RM 105 PULLMAN, WA 99164-6510 Characterization of the lung PGDH from pregnant rabbits

R01HD-21784-07 (HUD) GARDNER, JUDITH M NYS INST BASIC RES 1050 FOREST HILL RD STATEN ISLAND, NY 10314 Arousal and attention in high-risk neonates

R01HD-21785-05 (REN) ROBERTS, JAMES M UNIVERSITY OF CALIFORNIA 3RD & PARNASSUS, 1480 MOFFIT SAN FRANCISCO, CA 94143 Myometrial adrenergic mechanisms--Post receptor modulation

PROJECT NO., ORGANIZATIONAL UNIT., INVESTIGATOR, ADDRESS, TITLE

R01HD-21793-05 (HED) CHAN, WAI-YEE GEORGETOWN UNIVERSITY 3800 RESERVOIR ROAD N W WASHINGTON, D C 20007 Genetic studies of pregnancy specific B1 glycoprotein

R01HD-21801-06 (HED) VAN WINKLE, LON J CHICACO COLL / OSTEOPATHIC MED 555 31ST STREET DOWNERS GROVE, IL 60515 Development of amino acid transport in early embryos

R01HD-21802-06 (BPO) ERSKINE, MARY S BOSTON UNIVERSITY 5 CUMMINGTON STREET BOSTON, MA 02215 Psychoendocrine control of estrous behavior

R01HD-21806-05 (RNM) VORHEES, CHARLES V CHILDREN'S HOSPITAL MEDICAL CT ELLAND AND BETHESDA AVENUES CINCINNATI, OH 45229 Biobehavioral assessment of prenatal ultrasound in rats

R01HD-21823-06 (CBY) WHITTAKER, J RICHARD MARINE BIOLOGICAL LABORATORY WATER STREET WOODS HOLE, MA 02543 Egg cytoplasmic information in cell differentiation

R44HD-21856-03 (REN) JESSEN, JOHN W AVATAR DESIGN DEVELOPMENT, INC 1205 NORTH 145TH STREET SEATTLE, WA 98133-6202 A simple, reliable, low-cost vasovasostomy system

R01HD-21881-07 (PBC) RAPRAEGER, ALAN C UNIVERSITY OF WISCONSIN 1300 UNIVERSITY AVENUE MADISON, WI 53706 Proteoglycans of the plasma membrane

P01HD-21885-05 (HDMC) LUBS, HERBERT A UNIV OF MIAMI SCHOOL OF MED P O BOX 016820 / D-820 MIAMI, FL 33101 Dyslexia subtypes: genetics, behavior and brain imaging

P01HD-21888-04 (HDMC) SHAYWITZ, BENNETT A YALE UNIV SCHOOL OF MEDICINE PO BOX 3333 NEW HAVEN, CT 06510 Psycholinguistic & biological mechanisms in dyslexia

P01HD-21888-04 0001 (HDMC) SHAYWITZ, B Psycholinguistic & biological mechanisms in dyslexia Distribution and typology of reading problems in a learning-disabled population

P01HD-21888-04 0002 (HDMC) SHAYWITZ, B Psycholinguistic & biological mechanisms in dyslexia Neuroimaging analysis

P01HD-21888-04 0003 (HDMC) SALTZBERG, BERNARD Psycholinguistic & biological mechanisms in dyslexia EEG coherence analysis of learning disability classification

P01HD-21888-04 0004 (HDMC) SHAYWITZ, SALLY Psycholinguistic & biological mechanisms in dyslexia Connecticut longitudinal study

P01HD-21888-04 0005 (HDMC) PAULS, DAVID L Psycholinguistic & biological mechanisms in dyslexia Family genetic study of reading disability

P01HD-21888-04 9001 (HDMC) FLETCHER, JACK M Psycholinguistic & biological mechanisms in dyslexia Methodology--Core

R37HD-21896-06 (BCE) ROBERTS, ROBERT M UNIVERSITY OF MISSOURI ASHLAND ROAD COLUMBIA, MO 65211 Interaction between blastocyst and uterine endometrium

P01HD-21921-04 (HDPR) SCHWARTZ, NEENA B NORTHWESTERN UNIVERSITY 2153 SHERIDAN RD EVANSTON, IL 60208-3520 Follicle stimulating hormone--Control and action

P01HD-21921-04 0001 (HDPR) HUNZICKER-DUNN, MARY Follicle stimulating hormone--Control and action Stimulation of immature porcine granulose cells by FSH

P01HD-21921-04 0002 (HDPR) SCHWARTZ, NEENA B Follicle stimulating hormone--Control and action Regulation of FSH secretion by the perifused pituitary gland

P01HD-21921-04 0003 (HDPR) TUREK, FRED W Follicle stimulating hormone--Control and action Photoperiodic control FSH secretion

P01HD-21921-04 0004 (HDPR) LEVINE, JON E Follicle stimulating hormone--Control and action Neural regulation of FSH--GnRH release and feedback mechanisms

P01HD-21921-04 0005 (HDPR) REBAR, ROBERT W Follicle stimulating hormone--Control and action Stress and reproductive function

P01HD-21921-04 0006 (HDPR) MAYO, KELLY E Follicle stimulating hormone--Control and action Genes encoding gonadal FSH--Regulatory hormones

P01HD-21921-04 9001 (HDPR) CHATTERTON, ROBERT T Follicle stimulating hormone--Control and action Radioimmunoassay--Core

R01HD-21926-05 (REB) TEUSCHER, CORY BRIGHAM YOUNG UNIVERSITY PROVO, UT 84602 Infertility and testicular autoimmunity

U01HD-21937-06 (SRC) PETTERS, ROBERT M NORTH CAROLINA STATE UNIV BOX 7621 RALEIGH, N C 27695 Development of rat and porcine embryos in vitro

U01HD-21939-07 (SRC) FOOTE, ROBERT H CORNELL UNIVERSITY 204 MORRISON HALL ITHACA, N Y 14853 Control of oocyte maturation, IVF and embryo development

U01HD-21942-06 (SRC) ZIOMEK, CAROL A GENZYME CORPORATION ONE MOUNTAIN ROAD FRAMINGHAM, MA 01701 In vitro culture of preimplantation mouse embryos

R01HD-21957-06 (HED) ADAMSON, EILEEN D LA JOLLA CANCER RESEARCH FDN 10901 NORTH TORREY PINES ROAD LA JOLLA, CA 92307 Fos oncogene in development

R01HD-21961-06 (HED) SIMMEN, ROSALIA C UNIVERSITY OF FLORIDA 459 SHEALY DRIVE/RM 125 GAINESVILLE, FL 32611 Uteroferrin gene expression during development

R01HD-21966-04A1 (REN) GEORGE, FREDRICK W U OF TX S W MED CTR 5323 HARRY HINES BOULEVARD DALLAS, TX 75235-9039 Gonadal and phenotypic sex differentiation

R01HD-21968-07 (BCE) LEHMAN, MICHAEL N UNIV OF CINICNNATI MED CTR 231 BETHESDA AVE, ML 521 CINCINNATI, OHIO 45267-0521 Neuroendocrine basis of seasonal breeding

U01HD-21970-07 (SRC) EPPIG, JOHN J THE JACKSON LABORATORY 600 MAIN STREET BAR HARBOR, ME 04609-0800 Oocyte culture conditions that promote embryogenesis

R01HD-21973-05A1 (SSP) RODGERS, JOSEPH L UNIVERSITY OF OKLAHOMA 455 WEST LINDSEY NORMAN, OK 73019 Adolescent behavior--Family and non family influences

R01HD-21980-07 (PBC) ROBERTS, ROBERT M UNIVERSITY OF MISSOURI-COLUMBI 158 ANIMAL SCIENCE RESEARCH CT COLUMBIA, MISSOURI 65211 Lysosomal and secreted iron containing phosphatases

U01HD-21988-07 (SRC) BIGGERS, JOHN D HARVARD MEDICAL SCHOOL 45 SHATTUCK ST BOSTON, MA 02115 Culture media for preimplantation development

R01HD-21989-06 (SRC) PRIMAKOFF, PAUL UNIV OF CONN HEALTH CENTER 263 FARMINGTON AVENUE FARMINGTON, CT 06032 Immune response in sperm

PROJECT NO., ORGANIZATIONAL UNIT., INVESTIGATOR, ADDRESS, TITLE

surface antigens
R01HD-21991-06 (BCE) FAZLEABAS, ASGERALLY T UNIVERSITY OF ILLINOIS 840 S WOOD STREET CHICAGO, IL 60612 Uterine secretary activity in the primate
R01HD-22016-07 (PBC) GOETINCK, PAUL F LA JOLLA CANCER RES FOUNDATION 10901 NORTH TORREY PINES ROAD LA JOLLA, CA 92037 Molecular basis of normal and mutant limb development
U01HD-22023-07 (SRC) BAVISTER, BARRY D UNIVERSITY OF WISCONSIN 1655 LINDEN DRIVE MADISON, WI 53706 Normal fertilization and preimplantation growth in vitro
R01HD-22025-06 (MBY) PERRY, WILLIAM M UNIV OF TEXAS/MD ANDERSON CENT BOX 117/1515 HOLCOMBE BLVD HOUSTON, TX 77030 Regulation of Xenopus histone gene transcription
R01HD-22028-07 (PC) KRAMER, JAMES M NORTHWESTERN UNIVERSITY MED SC 303 E. CHICAGO AVENUE CHICAGO, IL 60611 Molecular genetic studies of C. elegans morphogenesis
R01HD-22050-06 (CBY) GOETINCK, PAUL F LA JOLLA CANCER RES FDN 10901 NORTH TORREY PINES RD LA JOLLA, CA 92037 Proteoglycans in avian skin morphogenesis
R01HD-22052-05 (OBM) LAUDER, JEAN M UNIVERSITY OF NORTH CAROLINA CB #7090 CHAPEL HILL, NC 27599-7090 Site-specific malformations in the mouse embryo
R37HD-22054-06 (NSS) BECKER, GARY S ECONOMICS RES CENTER/NORC 1155 EAST 60TH STREET CHICAGO, ILL 60637 Altruism, fertility, and population growth
R01HD-22055-04A2 (MBY) FLYTZANIS, CONSTANTIN N BAYLOR COLLEGE OF MEDICINE ONE BAYLOR PLAZA HOUSTON, TX 77030 Gene regulation during early embryonic development
R01HD-22061-04A3 (BCE) WEIGEL, NANCY L BAYLOR COLLEGE OF MEDICINE ONE BAYLOR PLAZA HOUSTON, TX 77030 Regulation of progesterone receptors by phosphorylation
R01HD-22070-03 (HUD) POULSON, CLAIRE L QUEENS COLLEGE OF CUNY 65-30 KISSENA BLVD FLUSHING, N Y 11367 Operant analysis of immitation in infants
R01HD-22082-06 (ALY) DAVIS, ALVIN E, III CHILDREN'S HOSPITAL RESEARCH F ELLAND AND BETHESDA AVE CINCINNATI, OH 45229-2899 The C1 inhibitor gene and hereditary angioneurotic edema
R01HD-22085-04A1 (REB) LONGO, FRANK J UNIVERSITY OF IOWA IOWA CITY, IA 52242 Sperm-egg fusion--Structural-electrical correlations
R01HD-22095-04 (HED) MIRKES, PHILIP E UNIVERSITY OF WASHINGTON DEPT OF PEDIATRICS, RD-20 SEATTLE, WA 98195 Hyperthermia, heat shock response, and birth defects
R01HD-22103-05 (HED) GANAPATHY, VADIVEL MEDICAL COLLEGE OF GEORGIA AUGUSTA, GA 30912-2100 Human placental Na+-H+ exchanger--Function and regulation
R01HD-22136-06 (SOH) MURPH, JODY R UNIV OF IOWA HOSP & CLINICS DEPARTMENT OF PEDIATRICS IOWA CITY, IA 52242 Occupational risk of cytomegalovirus infection
R01HD-22149-05 (HUD) WELLMAN, HENRY M UNIVERSITY OF MICHIGAN 300 NORTH INGALLS BUILDING ANN ARBOR, MI 48109 The child's theory of mind
R01HD-22163-01A2 (CTY) SHAW, JOCELYN E UNIVERSITY OF MINNESOTA 1445 GORTNER AVENUE ST PAUL, MN 55108 C. elegans embryonic development
R01HD-22171-06 (REB) WARREN, MICHELLE P ST LUKE'S ROOSEVELT HOSP CTR 428 W 59TH STREET NEW YORK, N Y 10019 Estrogen replacement and complications of amenorrhea
R01HD-22190-05 (REB) GILBERT, RAYMOND D LOMA LINDA UNIVERSITY LOMA LINDA, CA 92350 Fetal responses to long-term hypoxemia
R01HD-22196-07 (BCE) SEGALOFF, DEBORAH L UNIVERSITY OF IOWA IOWA CITY, IA 52242 The structure and regulation of the LH/CG receptor
R01HD-22210-06 (CBY) DAMSKY, CAROLINE H UNIVERSITY OF CALIFORNIA 513 PARNASSUS AVE HSW 604 SAN FRANCISCO, CA 94143-0512 Adhesive interactions of human trophoblast cells
R01HD-22211-05 (SSP) WILLIS, ROBERT J ECONOMICS RESEARCH CTR/NORC 1155 E 60TH ST CHICAGO, IL 60637 Implications of marital dissolution
R01HD-22223-05 (CMS) OLSON, RICHARD K UNIVERSITY OF COLORADO CAMPUS BOX 447 BOULDER, CO 80309 Computer-speech feedback in text for dyslexic children
P30HD-22224-05S1 (SSS) KRETCHMER, NORMAN U OF CA; COL OF NATURAL RES DEPT NUTRTN SCI/ MORGAN HALL BERKELEY, CALIF 94720 Nutrition and chronic disease
P30HD-22224-05S1 0001 (SSS) KING, JANET C Nutrition and chronic disease Branched chain amino acid use in obese pregnant women
P30HD-22224-05S1 0002 (SSS) SHACKLETON, CEDRIC H Nutrition and chronic disease Analysis of carnitine and acyl carnitines
P30HD-22224-05S1 9001 (SSS) KRETCHMER, NORMAN Nutrition and chronic disease Core--Nutrition-Metabolism
P30HD-22224-05S1 9002 (SSS) KRETCHMER, NORMAN Nutrition and chronic disease Core-Tissue culture facility
P30HD-22224-05S1 9003 (SSS) KRETCHMER, NORMAN Nutrition and chronic disease Core-Radioimmunoassay
P30HD-22224-05S1 9004 (SSS) KRETCHMER, NORMAN Nutrition and chronic disease Core-Biochemical analysis
R01HD-22248-05A2 (BCE) DAVIS, JOHN S WOMEN'S RESEARCH INSTITUTE 2903 E CENTRAL WICHITA, KS 67214 Hormonal control of C-kinase and corpus luteum function
R01HD-22338-07 (REN) WEISS, GERSON UMDNJ NEW JERSEY MED SCHOOL 185 SOUTH ORANGE AVE NEWARK, NJ 07103-2714 Physiology of human relaxin
R01HD-22380-04A1 (GMA) TYSON, JON E UNIV OF TEXS HLTH SCIS CTR 5323 HARRY HINES BOULEVARD DALLAS, TX 75235-9063 Are omega-3 fatty acids essential for normal development
R01HD-22393-04 (HUD) MILLER, JON F WAISMAN CTR ON MENTAL 1500 HIGHLAND AVENUE MADISON, WI 53705 Early lexical acquisition in children with Down syndrome
R01HD-22400-05 (ORTH) GERSTENFELD, LOUIS C CHILDREN'S HOSPITAL CORPORATIO 300 LONGWOOD AVENUE BOSTON, MA 02115 Expression and regulation of bone-specific genes
R01HD-22415-03A1 (HUD) THOMPSON, TRAVIS I UNIVERSITY OF MINNESOTA 2221 UNIV AVE SE/SUITE 145 MINNEAPOLIS, MN 55414 Behavioral and opioid mechanisms in self-injury
R01HD-22416-04A2 (MGN) MAXSON, ROBERT E, JR UNIV OF SOUTHERN CALIFORNIA 1441 EASTLAKE AVE/NOR-610 LOS ANGELES, CA 9003 Expression and function of mammalian homeobox genes
R22HD-22440-04 (EDC) MARTORELL, REYNALDO STANFORD UNIVERSITY FOOD RESEARCH INSTITUTE STANFORD, CA 94305 Early malnutrition and status in adolescence
R01HD-22448-05 (GEN) GERGEN, JOHN P S U N Y AT STONY BROOK STONY BROOK, N Y 11794-5215 Regulation of the Drosophila segmentation gene runt
P01HD-22486-05 (HDMC) WESTON, JAMES A UNIVERSITY OF OREGON EUGENE, OR 97403 Cellular, molecular and genetic analysis of neuronal development
P01HD-22486-05 0001 (HDMC) EISEN, JUDITH Cellular, molecular and genetic analysis of neuronal development Cell lineage and environment in neural crest cell deversification
P01HD-22486-05 0002 (HDMC) WESTERFIELD, MONTE Cellular, molecular and genetic analysis of neuronal development Molecular mechanisms of neuronal specificity
P01HD-22486-05 0003 (HDMC) KIMMEL, CHARLES Cellular, molecular and genetic analysis of neuronal development Genetic analysis of neural crest development
P01HD-22486-05 9000 (HDMC) SCHABTACH, E Cellular, molecular and genetic analysis of neuronal development Core electron microscope facility
P01HD-22486-05 9001 (HDMC) KIMMEL, CHARLES Cellular, molecular and genetic analysis of neuronal development Core animal facilities
P01HD-22486-05 9002 (HDMC) MARUSICH, MICHAEL Cellular, molecular and genetic analysis of neuronal development Monoclonal antibody core
P01HD-22486-05 9003 (HDMC) BREMILLER, RUTH Cellular, molecular and genetic analysis of neuronal development Core histology facility
P01HD-22486-05 9004 (HDMC) WESTERFIELD, MONTE Cellular, molecular and genetic analysis of neuronal development Core image processing facility
R01HD-22496-04 (EDC) SAAH, ALFRED J THE JOHNS HOPKINS UNIVERSITY 615 NORTH WOLFE STREET BALTIMORE, MD 21205 Hiv infection in African mothers and their children
R01HD-22506-05 (HED) HARPER, RONALD M UNIVERSITY OF CALIFORNIA 10833 LE CONTE AVE LOS ANGELES, CA 90024-1761 Cardiorespiratory patterns during sleep and SIDS risk
R01HD-22514-05 (HUD) MELTZOFF, ANDREW N UNIV OF WASHINGTON (WJ-10) CHILD DEVEL & MENT RTDN CTR SEATTLE, WA 98195 Development of gestural and vocal imitation in infancy
R01HD-22532-05 (MGN) PAGE, DAVID C WHITEHEAD INST FOR BIOMED RES NINE CAMBRIDGE CENTER CAMBRIDGE, MA 02142 Human sex chromosomes and gonadal sex determination
P01HD-22539-04 (SRC) GALLER, JANINA R BOSTON UNIV SCHOOL OF MEDICINE 85 E NEWTON ST, MENT HLTH CTR BOSTON, MASS 02118 Fetal protein malnutrition and mental retardation
P01HD-22539-04 0001 (SRC) GALLER, JANINA R Fetal protein malnutrition and mental retardation Fetal protein malnutrition and mental retardation--Behavioral division
P01HD-22539-04 0002 (SRC) MORGANE, PETER J Fetal protein malnutrition and mental retardation Fetal protein malnutrition and mental retardation--Neurophysiology
P01HD-22539-04 0003 (SRC) KEMPER, THOMAS A Fetal protein malnutrition and mental retardation Fetal protein malnutrition and mental retardation--Neuroanatomy division
P01HD-22539-04 0004 (SRC) ROSENE, DOUGLAS L Fetal protein malnutrition and mental retardation Fetal protein malnutrition and mental retardation--Immunocytochemistry
P01HD-22539-04 0005 (SRC) VOLICER, LADISLAV Fetal protein malnutrition and mental retardation Fetal protein malnurition and mental retardation--Neurochemistry division
P01HD-22539-04 9001 (SRC) RESNICK, OSCAR Fetal protein malnutrition and mental retardation Core--Animal care facility
R01HD-22543-05 (BEM) FRICKE, THOMAS E UNIVERSITY OF MICHIGAN 426 THOMPSON STREET ANN ARBOR, MI 48106 Economy, family change and fertility in Nepal
R29HD-22551-05 (MET) BLACK, DENNIS D UNIVERSITY OF CHICAGO 5841 S MARYLAND AVENUE CHICAGO, IL 60637 Intestinal lipoproteins in the neonatal piglet
R01HD-22559-04A2 (HED) REYNOLDS, LAWRENCE P NORTH DAKOTA STATE UNIVERSITY BOX 5727 FARGO, ND 58105 Role of placental angiogenesis in the fetus
R01HD-22560-04 (RNM) NEEDLEMAN, LAURENCE THOMAS JEFFERSON UNIVERSITY 10TH & SANSOM STREETS PHILADELPHIA, PA 19107 Doppler screening for pregnancy induced hypertension
R01HD-22563-04 (MGN) MC CABE, EDWARD R BAYLOR COLLEGE OF MEDICINE ONE BAYLOR PLAZA HOUSTON, TX 77030 Molecular genetic studies of glycerol kinase deficiency
R01HD-22564-04A2 (HED) NEWMAN, STUART A NEW YORK MEDICAL COLLEGE VALHALLA, NY 10595 Cell-matrix interactions during morphogenesis
R01HD-22590-05 (HED) SHUR, BARRY D UNIVERSITY OF TEXAS BOX 117, 1515 HOLCOMBE BLVD HOUSTON, TX 77030 Molecular control of cell interactions
P01HD-22610-04 (HDMC) ROWE, DAVID W UNIVERSITY OF CONNECTICUT 263 FARMINGTON AVENUE FARMINGTON, CT 06030 Genetic control of limb development
P01HD-22610-04 0001 (HDMC) KOSHER, ROBERT Genetic control of limb development Cartilage differentiation/pattern formation during limb development
P01HD-22610-04 0002 (HDMC) TANZER, MARVIN L Genetic control of limb development Hexabrachion proteins in limb development
P01HD-22610-04 0003 (HDMC) LICHTLER, ALEX Genetic control of limb development Introduction of DNA into chick embryo
P01HD-22610-04 0004 (HDMC) CLARK, STEPHEN H Genetic control of limb development Linkage studies in the chicken
P01HD-22610-04 0005 (HDMC) TSIPOURAS, PETROS Genetic control of limb development Genetic linkage studies in skeletal dysplasias
P01HD-22610-04 0006 (HDMC) ROWE, DAVID W Genetic control of limb development Location of mutations in limb development
P01HD-22610-04 9001 (HDMC) CARMICHAEL, G Genetic control of limb

development Molecular biology – Core

P01HD-22610-04 9002 (HDMC) PIERRO, LOUIS Genetic control of limb development Core-- Chicken colony

R01HD-22614-05 (CMS) KUTAS, MARTA UNIV OF CALIFORNIA 9500 GILMAN DR LA JOLLA, CA 92093-0515 Electrophysiology of linguistic processing

R29HD-22615-05 (REB) FLORMAN, HARVEY M WORCESTER FOUNDATION EXPER BIO 222 MAPLE AVENUE SHREWSBURY, MA 01545 Induction and regulation of acrosome reactions

R01HD-22619-07 (CTY) KLEIN, WILLIAM H UNIVERSITY OF TEXAS 1515 HOLCOMBE BLVD. HOUSTON, TX 77030 Gene family expressed in sea urchin embryonic ectoderm

R01HD-22628-07 (HUD) PORGES, STEPHEN W UNIVERSITY OF MARYLAND HUMAN DEVELOPMENT DEPARTMENT COLLEGE PARK, MD 20742 Neonatal assessment--a psychophysiological approach

P01HD-22634-05 (SRC) WISNIEWSKI, HENRYK M NYS INSTITUTE FOR BASIC RES 1050 FOREST HILL ROAD STATEN ISLAND, N Y 10314 Changes in functioning among mentally retarted adults

R01HD-22637-05 (HUD) MATHENY, ADAM P, JR UNIVERSITY OF LOUISVILLE LOUISVILLE, KY 40292 Developmental trends in infant temperament

R01HD-22642-05 (HUD) BRAY, JAMES H BAYLOR COLLEGE OF MEDICINE 5510 GREENBRIAR/FAMILY MED D HOUSTON, TX 77005 A longitudinal study of stepfamily development

P01HD-22657-05 (HDMC) RIMOIN, DAVID L CEDARS SINAI MEDICAL CENTER 8700 BEVERLY BLVD LOS ANGELES, CA 90048 The skeletal dysplasias

P01HD-22657-05 0001 (HDMC) RIMOIN, DAVID L The skeletal dysplasias Skeletal dysplasias

P01HD-22657-05 0002 (HDMC) RAMIREZ, FRANCESCO The skeletal dysplasias Molecular studies of collagen in the skeletal dysplasias

P01HD-22657-05 0003 (HDMC) MURRAY, LOUANN The skeletal dysplasias Biochemistry of chondrodystrophies

P01HD-22657-05 9001 (HDMC) RIMOIN, DAVID L The skeletal dysplasias Core facility activities

R01HD-22681-05 (REB) SCHULTZ, RICHARD M UNIVERSITY OF PENNSYLVANIA 38TH AND HAMILTON WALK PHILADELPHIA, PA 19104 Protein phosphorylation in preimplantation development

R01HD-22687-05 (REB) BLAKE, CHARLES A UNIVERSITY OF SOUTH CAROLINA COLUMBIA, SC 29208 Mechanisms of cyclic LH and FSH release

R01HD-22695-06 (HED) HARPER, RONALD M UNIVERSITY OF CALIFORNIA 405 HILGARD AVE LOS ANGELES, 90024-1406 Development of sleep states and SIDS risk

R01HD-22696-03 (HED) KEENS, THOMAS G CHILDRENS HOSP OF LOS ANGELES 4650 SUNSET BLVD LOS ANGELES, CA 90027 Hypoxic arousal reponses and increased risk for SIDS

R01HD-22703-07 (RAP) CAMERON, WILLIAM E UNIVERSITY OF PITTSBURGH 446 CRAWFORD HALL PITTSBURGH, PA 15260 Developmental control of the diaphragm and upper airway

R01HD-22712-05 (SRC) SUNDELL, HAKAN W VANDERBILT UNIVERSTIY DEPT. OF PEDIATRICS NASHVILLE, TN 37232 An animal model for sudden infant death syndrome

R01HD-22713-05 (SRC) BECKER, LAURENCE E HOSPITAL FOR SICK CHILDREN 555 UNIVERSITY AVENUE TORONTO, ONTARIO M5G 1X8 Neurochemical control of respiration in SIDs

R01HD-22720-05S1 (BIO) PATTERSON, DAVID ELEANOR ROOSEVELT INST 1899 GAYLORD STREET DENVER, CO 80206 Genetic and biochemical study of human chromosome 21

R01HD-22732-05 (REB) KOPF, GREGORY S UNIV OF PENNSYLVANIA 36TH HAMILTON WALK/RM 313 PHILADELPHIA, PA 19104-6080 Mechanisms of mammalian fertilization/polyspermy block

R29HD-22735-04 (BCE) ROCHE, PATRICK C MAYO FOUNDATION 200 FIRST STREET S W ROCHESTER, MN 55905 Hormonal activation of corpus luteum adenylate cyclase

R29HD-22738-05 (REN) PORETSKY, LEONID CARBRINI MEDICAL CENTER 227 EAST 19TH STREET NEW YORK, N Y 10003 Role of insulin and insulin-like growth factors

R29HD-22746-05 (BCE) WATSON, CHERYL S THE UNIV OF TEXAS MED BRANCH GALVESTON, TX 77550 Hormone induced gene expression--Oocyte reconstitution

R29HD-22747-04 (REN) WISE, MARK E UNIVERSITY OF ARIZONA 228 SHANTZ (BLDG 38) TUCSON, AZ 85721 Regulation of GnRH secretion during sexual maturation

R29HD-22751-04 (GEN) MOHLER, JAMES P BARNARD COLLEGE 3009 BROADWAY NEW YORK, NY 10027 Genetics of hedgehog & adjacent loci of Drosophila

P01HD-22766-05 (HDMC) MC CRACKEN, GEORGE H DEPT. OF PED. & MICROBIOLOGY 5323 HARRY HINES BLVD DALLAS, TX 75235-9063 Immunobiology and pathogenesis of infections

P01HD-22766-05 0001 (HDMC) MUNFORD, ROBERT S Immunobiology and pathogenesis of infections Susceptibility to fulminant meningococcemia

P01HD-22766-05 0002 (HDMC) EIDELS, LEON Immunobiology and pathogenesis of infections Identification of the Pseudomonas aeruginosa exotoxin A receptor

P01HD-22766-05 0003 (HDMC) HANSEN, ERIC J Immunobiology and pathogenesis of infections Haemophilus influenzae lipopolysaccharide and meningitis

P01HD-22766-05 0004 (HDMC) KUPERSZTOCH, YANKEL Immunobiology and pathogenesis of infections Fusion between heat stable and labile enterotoxins of E. coli

P01HD-22766-05 9001 (HDMC) MCCRACKEN, GEORGE H Immunobiology and pathogenesis of infections Core immunobiology laboratory facility

P01HD-22766-05 9002 (HDMC) MCCRACKEN, GEORGE H Immunobiology and pathogenesis of infections Clinical core

R01HD-22780-05 (GEN) WIESCHAUS, ERIC F PRINCETON UNIVERSITY PRINCETON, NJ 08544-1014 Molecular analysis of segmentation in Drosophila

R01HD-22781-05A1 (BCE) GUPTA, CHHANDA CHILDRENS HOSPITAL PITTSBURGH 3705 FIFTH AVE AT DESOTO ST PITTSBURGH, PA 15213-3417 Biochemical mechanism of sexual differentiation

R01HD-22785-04A1 (REN) GLASSER, STANLEY R BAYLOR COLLEGE OF MEDICINE ONE BAYLOR PLAZA HOUSTON, TX 77030 Progesterone regulation of uterine stromal cell sensitization

R01HD-22786-03 (REB) TAYLOR, MICHAEL J IOWA STATE UNIVERSITY DEPT OF PHYSIOLOGY & PHARMACOL AMES, IA 50011 Control of relaxin secretion from single luteal cells

R01HD-22791-03 (BCE) MCILROY, PATRICK J RUTGERS UNIVERSITY 311 N 5TH ST CAMDEN, NJ 08102 Mechanisms of luteal regulation by gonadotropins

R01HD-22798-01A2 (SSP) POTTER, JOSEPH E UNIVERSITY OF TEXAS AT AUSTIN 1800 MAIN BLDG AUSTIN, TX 78712 Contraception, breastfeeding, and the use of health care

R29HD-22799-05 (HUD) HRNCIR, ELIZABETH J UNIVERSITY OF VIRGINIA 405 EMMET STREET CHARLOTTESVILLE, VA 22903 Affect and competence in handicapped infants

R55HD-22806-04A1 (REB) COATES, PENELOPE W TEXAS TECH UNIV HLTH SCI CTR LUBBOCK, TX 79430 Sex hormones and the single neuron

R29HD-22812-04 (HUD) YODER, PAUL J VANDERBILT UNIVERSITY BOX 154 PEABODY COLLEGE NASHVILLE, TN 73203 Recruitment of retarded children's conversation

R01HD-22830-06 (HUD) THELEN, ESTHER INDIANA UNIVERSITY BLOOMINGTON, IN 47405 Dynamical factors in the development of motor skills

R29HD-22831-05 (EDC) ALDERMAN, BETH W UNIVERSITY OF WASHINGTON DEPARTMENT OF EPIDEMIOLOGY SEATTLE, WA 98195 Epidemiologic study of craniosynostosis occurrence

R01HD-22839-04 (HUD) CECI, STEPHEN J CORNELL UNIVERSITY MARTHA VAN RENSSELAER HALL ITHACA, NY 14853 Contextual constraints on intellectual competence

U01HD-22847-06 (SRC) MANES, COLE UNIVERSITY OF SAN DIEGO ALCALA PARK SAN DIEGO, CA 92110 Oxidative damage and iron requirements of the blastocyst

R29HD-22857-05 (GEN) RIO, DONALD C WHITEHEAD INSTITUTE FOR BIOMED NINE CAMBRIDGE CENTER CAMBRIDGE, MA 02142 Regulation of gene expression during animal development

R29HD-22869-04 (BCE) AKESSON, THOMAS R WASHINGTON STATE UNIVERSITY PULLMAN, WA 99164-6520 Organization of steroid regulated hypothalamic substance

R01HD-22871-04 (HUD) GUSTAFSON, GWEN E UNIVERSITY OF CONNECTICUT 406 CROSS CAMPUS RD STORRS, CT 06268 Infant cries--Perception, development, and function

R29HD-22873-05 (HED) TAYLOR, ROBERT N UNIVERSITY OF CALIFORNIA MOFFITT HOSPITAL M-1489 SAN FRANCISCO, CA 94143-0132 Trophoblast proliferation and growth factor expression

R29HD-22879-05 (CBY) BUSA, WILLIAM B JOHNS HOPKINS UNIVERSITY BALTIMORE, MD 21218 Regulation of morphogenesis by ions, camp & inositides

R29HD-22880-05 (IMS) BELMONT, JOHN W BAYLOR COLLEGE OF MEDICINE ONE BAYLOR PLAZA HOUSTON, TEXAS 77030 Molecular biology of T lymphocyte progenitor cells

R01HD-22891-07 (MET) LEVITSKY, LYNNE L PEDIATRIC ENDOCRINE UNIT 15 PARKMAN ST BOSTON, MA 02114 Metabolism in the nonhuman primate and ovine fetus

R29HD-22893-04 (NEUA) PHILLIPS, NONA K UNIVERSITY OF WASHINGTON DEPT OF PSYCHOLOGY (NI-25) SEATTLE, WA 98195 Valproate, phenytoin and infant outcome

R01HD-22896-05 (PBC) KOSHER, ROBERT A UNIV OF CONNECTICUT HLTH CTR 263 FARMINGTON AVE FARMINGTON, CT 06030 Gene expression during limb cartilage differentiation

R01HD-22899-04 (REB) GERTON, GEORGE L UNIVERSITY OF PENNSYLVANIA 306 JOHN MORGAN BLDG/SCH OF ME PHILADELPHIA, PA 19104-6080 Acrosomal enzyme biosynthesis by mammalian spermatids

R01HD-22902-05 (REB) SCHATTEN, GERALD P UNIVERSITY OF WISCONSIN 1117 W JOHNSON ST MADISON, WI 53706 Architectural changes during mouse fertilization

R29HD-22912-05 (GMA) HYMAN, PAUL E HARBOR-UCLA MEDICAL CENTER 1000 W CARSON ST J-4 TORRANCE, CA 90509 Control of isolated gastric muscle cell contraction

R29HD-22913-05 (HED) NELSON, DONALD M THE JEWISH HOSP OF ST LOUIS 216 S KINGSHIGHWAY ST LOUIS, MO 63110 Differentiation in human placental trophoblast

R29HD-22914-05 (HED) ERVIN, M GORE HARBOR-UCLA MEDICAL CENTER 1000 WEST CARSON STREET A-17 TORRANCE, CA 90509 Arginine vasotocin in the ovine fetus and newborn

R01HD-22918-04A1 (REN) KHAN, SOHAIB A UNIVERSITY OF CINCINNATI 231 BETHESDA AVE CINCINNATI, OH 45267-0521 Estrogen control of uterine cell proliferation

R01HD-22924-04 (HED) GLEICH, GERALD J MAYO FOUNDATION 200 FIRST STREET SW ROCHESTER, MN 55905 Eosinophil major basic protein in human pregnancy

R01HD-22929-04 (HUD) KATZ, PHYLLIS A INST FOR RES ON SOCIAL PROBLEM 520 PEARL STREET BOULDER, CO 80302 Development of gender and race stereotypes in children

R01HD-22952-05 (HUD) SCOTT, MARCIA S MAILMAN CTR FOR CHILD DEVELP 1601 N W 12TH AVE (D-820) MIAMI FLORIDA 33101 Early detection of mild mental retardation

R55HD-22953-05 (HUD) WIDAMAN, KEITH F UNIVERSITY OF CALIFORNIA RIVERSIDE, CA 92521 Life-span theory of adaptive behavior of retarded people

R01HD-22954-01A3 (MET) MC NAMARA, DONALD J UNIVERSITY OF ARIZONA TUCSON, AZ 85721 Premature weaning and adult cholesterol homeostasis

R29HD-22965-06 (HED) CATALANO, PATRICK M CASE WESTERN RESERVE UNIVERSIT 3395 SCRANTON ROAD CLEVELAND, OHIO 44109 Insulin resistance and glucose metabolism in pregnancy

R01HD-22969-05 (HED) PARKER, CHARLES R, JR UNIVERSITY OF ALABAMA UAB STATION BIRMINGHAM, AL 35294 Control of lipoprotein and steroid levels in the fetus

R01HD-22970-04 (REB) NAFTOLIN, FREDERICK YALE UNIVERSITY SCH OF MED P O BOX 3333 NEW HAVEN, CT 06510-8063 The ovarian renin-angiotens in system and reproduction

R01HD-22973-05 (REB) BABCOCK, DONNER F UNIVERSITY OF WASHINGTON SEATTLE, WA 98195 Ionic mediators and metaregulation on sperm capacitation

R01HD-22983-05A2 (BCE) MORRELL, JOAN I RUTGERS UNIVERSITY 101 WARREN STREET NEWARK, NJ 07102 Characterization of steroid hormone-concentrating neuron

PROJECT NO., ORGANIZATIONAL UNIT., INVESTIGATOR, ADDRESS, TITLE

R29HD-22993-03 (HED) FANT, MICHAEL E UNIV OF TX DEPT OF PEDIATRICS 5323 HARRY HINES BLVD. DALLAS, TX 75235-9063 Regulation of human placental growth by IGFs
R01HD-23000-04A2 (PHRA) KNUTSON, KRISTINE UNIVERSITY OF UTAH RESEARCH PARK, 421 WAKARA WAY SALT LAKE CITY, UT 84108 Contraceptive steroid transdermal transport/metabolism mechanism
R01HD-23012-05 (HUD) RICHARDSON, STEPHEN A ALBERT EINSTEIN COLLEGE OF MED 1300 MORRIS PARK AVENUE BRONX, N Y 10461 Biosocial histories of mentally retarded young adults
R29HD-23014-04 (HUD) KRAHN, GLORIA L OREGON HLTH SCIENCES UNIV P O BOX 574 PORTLAND, OR 97207 Family adjustment to child handicap
R01HD-23038-05 (SRC) DUNST, CARL J WESTERN CAROLINA CENTER 300 ENOLA ROAD MORGANTON, NC 28655 Social support in families of infants having poor developmental outcomes
R13HD-23040-05 (HDMR) BERKSON, GERSHON B UNIVERSITY OF ILLINOIS PO BOX 4348 CHICAGO, IL 60680 Gatlinburg conference on mental retardation
P01HD-23042-03 (SRC) BREESE, GEORGE R UNIVERSITY OF NORTH CAROLINA CB# 7250, BSRC CHAPEL HILL, N C 27599 Neurobiology of mental retardation--SIB and dopamine
P01HD-23042-03 0007 (SRC) LAUDER, JEAN M Neurobiology of mental retardation--SIB and dopamine Neural growth mechanisms of serotonin and dopamine containing neurons
P01HD-23042-03 0001 (SRC) NYHAN, WILLIAM L Neurobiology of mental retardation--SIB and dopamine Self-injurious behavior and perinatal dopamine functional
P01HD-23042-03 0002 (SRC) GUALTIERI, C THOMAS Neurobiology of mental retardation--SIB and dopamine Clinical neuropsychiatry and psychopharmacology
P01HD-23042-03 0003 (SRC) DOUG, DEAN F Neurobiology of mental retardation--SIB and dopamine PET scanning section--Dopamine integrity and dopamine receptor
P01HD-23042-03 0004 (SRC) KRAMER, GARY W Neurobiology of mental retardation--SIB and dopamine Developmental neurobiology of dopamine systems
P01HD-23042-03 0005 (SRC) BREESE, GEORGE R Neurobiology of mental retardation--SIB and dopamine Neuropharmacology of D1 dopamine receptors and modulatory systems
P01HD-23042-03 0006 (SRC) MUELLER, ROBERT A Neurobiology of mental retardation--SIB and dopamine Biochemical pharmacology of D1 dopamine receptors
R44HD-23052-03 (SSS) BARRETT, JACK C P. O. BX 1810 WILLIAMSBURG, VA 23185 Microcomputer software for census demographic techniques
R01HD-23089-06 (IMB) STORB, URSULA B UNIVERSITY OF CHICAGO 920 EAST 58TH STREET CHICAGO, ILL 60637 Expression of immunoglobulin genes in transgenic mice
R29HD-23093-05 (REB) SCOFIELD, VIRGINIA L UNIVERSITY OF CALIFORNIA LOS ANGELES, CA 90024-1406 Studies of sperm-lymphocyte interaction structures
R01HD-23098-02 (REB) MEIZEL, STANLEY UNIVERSITY OF CALIFORNIA DAVIS, CA 95616 Steroid initiated exocytosis in human sperm
R01HD-23103-06 (HUD) SPELKE, ELIZABETH S CORNELL UNIVERSITY URIS HALL ITHACA, N Y 14853 Perceptual knowledge in infancy
R29HD-23130-05 (MBY) ROSENTHAL, ERIC T PACIFIC BIOMEDICAL RESRCH CTR 41 AHUI STREET HONOLULU, HI 96813 Mechanisms controlling selective translation of mRNA
R01HD-23158-04 (HUD) DUNN, JUDITH F PENNSYLVANIA STATE UNIV S-120B HENDERSON BLDG UNIVERSITY PARK, PA 16802 Development of social understanding in the family
R01HD-23160-03 (SSP) MOTT, FRANK L CENTER FOR HUMAN RESOURCE RES 650 ACKERMAN ROAD, SUITE A COLUMBUS, OHIO 43202 Effects of father's absence--sociodemographic analyse
R29HD-23191-04 (HUD) ASHMEAD, DANIEL H VANDERBILT UNIVERSITY A & S PSYCHOLOGY BLDG. NASHVILLE, TENN 37240 Motion information and infants' coordinated behavior
R29HD-23195-03 (REB) CURRY, THOMAS E, JR UNIV OF KENTUCKY MEDICAL CTR 800 ROSE STREET LEXINGTON, KY 40536-0084 The role of metalloproteinases in ovarian function
R01HD-23223-04 (BIO) WOLF, BARRY MEDICAL COLLEGE OF VIRGINIA P O BOX 33, MCV STATION RICHMOND, VA 23298 Characterization of biotinidase deficiency
R01HD-23229-03 (HUD) LERNER, RICHARD M PENNSYLVANIA STATE UNIVERSITY BEECHER/DOCK HOUSE UNIVERSITY PARK, PA 16802 Early adolescent school achievement--organismic bases
R29HD-23236-05 (REB) ROESS, DEBORAH A COLORADO STATE UNIVERSITY FT COLLINS, CO 80523 Membrane events following hormone binding to L H receptor
R29HD-23243-04 (BPO) PEREIRA, MICHAEL E DUKE UNIV PRIMATE CENTER 3705 ERWIN RD DURHAM, NC 27705 Social structure and development of behavior
R29HD-23244-06 (REN) BIGSBY, ROBERT M INDIANA UNIVERSITY SCH OF MED 926 WEST MICHIGAN STREET INDIANAPOLIS, IN 46202-5167 Hormonal control of female reproductive tract growth
R01HD-23245-05 (MGN) NUSSBAUM, ROBERT L UNIVERSITY OF PENNSYLVANIA 422 CURIE BLVD PHILADELPHIA, PA 19104-6145 Molecular genetic analysis of Lowe's syndrome
R01HD-23247-05 (VISB) DANNEMILLER, JAMES L UNIVERSITY OF WISCONSIN MADISON, WI 53706 Development of motion perception
R29HD-23250-03 (MBY) BIEKER, JAMES J MOUNT SINAI SCHOOL OF MEDICINE 1 GUSTAVE L LEVY PL/BOX 1020 NEW YORK, NY 10029 Xenopus gene expression--Differentiation and development
R29HD-23261-05 (HUD) HAZEN-SWANN, NANCY L UNIVERSITY OF TEXAS DEPT. OF HOME ECONOMICS AUSTIN, TX 78712 Family interaction and young children's peer competence
R01HD-23264-05 (BEM) WALKER, LYNN S VANDERBILT UNIV SCH MEDICINE DEPT OF PEDIATRICS/STATION 17 NASHVILLE, TN 37232 Illness behavior and somatization in children
R01HD-23273-06 (BCE) HSUEH, AARON J W STANFORD UNIV STANFORD, CA 94305-5317 Role of bioactive FSH in reproduction
R29HD-23275-05 (CBY) JAVOIS, LORETTE C CATHOLIC UNIVERSITY OF AMERICA WASHINGTON, DC 20064 Monoclonal antibodies and pattern formation in hydra

PROJECT NO., ORGANIZATIONAL UNIT., INVESTIGATOR, ADDRESS, TITLE

R01HD-23291-05 (HED) GILLIGAN, ANN WISTAR INSTITUTE 36TH & SPRUCE STREET PHILADELPHIA, PA 19104 Cell lineages in development
R29HD-23293-05 (BCE) ROSELLI, CHARLES E OREGON HEALTH SCIENCE UNIVERSI 3181 S W SAM JACKSON PARK ROAD PORTLAND, OR 97201-3098 Cellular mechanisms of androgen action in brain
R01HD-23294-05 (REB) WOLF, DAVID E WORCESTER FDN / EXPER BIOL INC 222 MAPLE AVENUE SHREWSBURY, MASS 01545 Membrane domains and the control of fertilization
R01HD-23295-04A1 (REN) MANN, DAVID R MOREHOUSE SCHOOL OF MEDICINE 720 WESTVIEW DRIVE SW ATLANTA, GA 30310-1495 Mechanism of stress-induced hyposensitivity to luteinizing hormone
P01HD-23315-05 (HDMR) BLACK, IRA B UNIV OF MEDICINE & DENTISTRY-N 675 HOES LANE PISCATAWAY, NJ 08854-5635 Growth & development of the nervous system--Molecular mechanisms
P01HD-23315-05 0005 (HDMR) DREYFUS, CHERYL Growth & development of the nervous system--Molecular mechanisms Role of growth factors in brain development
P01HD-23315-05 9001 (HDMR) CHAO, MOSES Growth & development of the nervous system--Molecular mechanisms Molecular and biochemistry--Core
P01HD-23315-05 0001 (HDMR) ABLACK, IRA B Growth & development of the nervous system--Molecular mechanisms Title regulation of neuronal mitosis
P01HD-23315-05 0002 (HDMR) CHAO, MOSES Growth & development of the nervous system--Molecular mechanisms Developmental regulation of athe NGF receptor gene
P01HD-23315-05 0003 (HDMR) SCHLEIFER, LEONARD S Growth & development of the nervous system--Molecular mechanisms Regulation of cell-specific expression of neurotransmitter receptoars
P01HD-23315-05 0004 (HDMR) ADLER, JOSHUA Growth & development of the nervous system--Molecular mechanisms Membrane factaors regulating transmitter expression
R29HD-23324-05 (CBY) KLEIN, STEVEN L UNIVERSITY OF VIRGINIA BOX 439 JORDAN HALL CHARLOTTESVILLE, VA 22908 Determinative events in cleavage stage frog embryos
R29HD-23325-05 (HUD) MERRILL, EDWARD C UNIVERSITY OF ALABAMA P O BOX 2968 TUSCALOOSA, AL 35487-2968 Resource allocation and mental retardation
R01HD-23327-05 (NTN) LEWIS, DOUGLAS S SOUTHWEST FDN FOR BIOMEDICAL P O BOX 28147 SAN ANTONIO, TX 78228-0147 Nutritional programming of obesity
R29HD-23328-05 (NEUC) WEISBLAT, DAVID A UNIVERSITY OF CALIFORNIA 385 LIFE SCIENCE ADDITION BERKELEY, CA 94720 Cell lineage and segmentation in leech nervous system
R01HD-23333-03 (HAR) WIGHTMAN, FREDERIC L UNIVERSITY OF WISCONSIN 1500 HIGHLAND AVE /RM 315 MADISON, WI 53705-2280 Hearing assessment in preschool and school-aged children
R01HD-23340-04 (HUD) WAGNER, RICHARD K FLORIDA STATE UNIVERSITY DEPT OF PSYCHOLOGY TALLAHASSEE, FL 32306-1051 Reading-related phonological processes
R01HD-23343-05 (SSP) ROSENZWEIG, MARK R UNIVERSITY OF PENNSYLVANIA 3718 LOCUST WALK PHILADELPHIA, PA 19104-6297 Parent demographic behavior--Child health and development
R01HD-23347-02 (REB) LEGAN, SANDRA J UNIVERSITY OF KENTUCKY DEPT. OF PHYSIOLOGY/BIOPHYSICS LEXINGTON, KY 40536-0084 Neuroendocrine regulation of ovine estrous cycles
R29HD-23351-05 (HUD) MEBERT, CAROLYN J UNIVERSITY OF NEW HAMPSHIRE CONANT HALL DURHAM, NH 03824 Antecedents and consequences of cesarean birth
R01HD-23353-04A1 (HUD) CHAPMAN, ROBIN S UNIVERSITY OF WISCONSIN 1500 HIGHLAND AVE MADISON, WI 53705 Language development in Down syndrome children
R01HD-23383-04A1 (REN) BARNES, BRIAN M UNIVERSITY OF ALASKA FAIRBANKS, AK 99775-0180 Endocrine responsiveness in heterothermic mammals
R29HD-23385-05 (HUD) KELLY, MICHAEL UNIVERSITY OF PENNSYLVANIA 3815 WALNUT ST PHILADELPHIA, PA 19104 The coordination of words, syntax and rhythm in speech
P01HD-23388-04 (SRC) SNOW, CATHERINE E HARVARD GRAD SCH OF EDUCATION LARSEN HALL 313 CAMBRIDGE, MA 02138 Foundations for language assessment in spontaneous speech
R01HD-23397-05 (HUD) COHEN, LESLIE B UNIVERSITY OF TEXAS AUSTIN, TX 78712 Infant visual information processing
R01HD-23398-05 (BIO) BOIME, IRVING WASHINGTON UNIVERSITY 660 SOUTH EUCLID ST. LOUIS, MISSOURI 63110 Structure-function studies of gonadotropins
R01HD-23402-03 (HED) MC CORMICK, PAULETTE J STATE UNIVERSITY OF NEW YORK 1400 WASHINGTON AVENUE ALBANY, NY 12222 Biochemical and genetic analyses of an embryonic antigen
R01HD-23412-04 (SRC) HOLMES, KING K HARBORVIEW MEDICAL CENTER 325 NINTH AVENUE SEATTLE, WA 98104 AIDS virus and maternal and child health in Africa
R01HD-23416-02 (SSP) POPKIN, BARRY M UNIV OF N C AT CHAPEL HILL 123 W FRANKLIN/CAROLINA POP CT CHAPEL HILL, NC 27516-3997 Infant feeding, women's nutrition, and birth spacing
R44HD-23420-02 (SSS) READ, PAGE F PAGE READ & COMPANY PO BOX 17824 SEATTLE, WA 98107 Reliable non-invasive uterine activity monitor
R44HD-23432-02 (CMS) FOSTER, KELLI C ONTRACK INCORPORATED 560 SO STATE STREET OREM, UT 84058 Computerized testing/training of phonological awareness
R01HD-23454-03 (SSP) UDRY, J RICHARD UNIV OF NORTH CAROLINA/POPUL C 123 W FRANKLIN STREET CHAPEL HILL, NC 27516-3997 Biosocial models of women's gender role behavior
R01HD-23467-03 (SSP) PARCEL, TOBY L 341 BRICKER HALL 190 N OVAL MALL COLUMBUS, OH 43201 Linking maternal employment and child care arrangements
R01HD-23468-02 (CMS) SCHAUB, DEBORAH L STATE UNIVERSITY OF NEW YORK STONY BROOK, NY 11794 Event-related potentials and language function in dyslexia
R01HD-23472-03 (PC) WANG, CHI-SUN OKLAHOMA MEDICAL RESEARCH FDN 825 NE 13TH STREET OKLAHOMA CITY, OK 73104 Human milk BAL--Structure and physiological function
R01HD-23479-04 (REB) SHUR, BARRY D U T M D ANDERSON CANCER CTR

1515 HOLCOMBE BLVD HOUSTON, TX 77030 Glycosyltransferase function during fertilization

R29HD-23481-03 (HED) RENEGAR, RANDALL H EAST CAROLINA UNIVERSITY DEPT ANATOMY CELL BIO/SCH MED GREENVILLE, NC 27858 Hamster placental relaxin--Structure and secretion

R29HD-23483-05 (REN) OLSTER, DEBORAH H HARBOR/UCLA MEDICAL CENTER 1000 WEST CARSON STREET TORRANCE, CA 90509 Sexual differentiation of behavior and LH secretion

R29HD-23484-04 (REB) SUAREZ-QUIAN, CARLOS A GEORGETOWN UNIVERSITY 3900 RESERVOIR RD, N W WASHINGTON, D C 20007 Characterization of sertoli cell endocytic organelles

R01HD-23492-04 (EDC) WARD, RICHARD H UNIV OF UTAH MEDICAL SCHOOL 50 NORTH MEDICAL DRIVE SALT LAKE CITY, UT 84132 Genetic epidemiology of human fetal growth

R01HD-23498-04 (HED) ILLSLEY, NICHOLAS P UNIVERSITY OF CALIFORNIA BOX 0556 SAN FRANCISCO, CA 94143-0556 Ion transport in the human placenta

R01HD-23511-05A1 (REB) HEYNER, SUSAN UNIVERSITY OF PENNSYLVANIA 36TH & HAMILTON WALK PHILADELPHIA, PA 19104 Ontogeny and function of insulin binding to early embryo

R01HD-23512-04 (SRC) ENDICOTT, JEAN N Y STATE PSYCHIATRIC INST 722 WEST 168TH STREET NEW YORK, N Y 10032 Severe premenstrual syndromes--Risk/course/mechanisms

R01HD-23519-04 (END) JAMESON, JAMES L MASSACHUSETTS GENERAL HOSP FRUIT STREET BOSTON, MA 02114 Regulation of chorionic gonadotropin gene expression

R01HD-23539-04 (SRC) WERB, ZENA UNIVERSITY OF CALIFORNIA 3RD AND PARNASSUS, LR-102 SAN FRANCISCO, CA 94143-0750 Metalloproteinases in peri-implantation development

R37HD-23657-04 (REB) BRINSTER, RALPH L UNIV OF PENNSYLVANIA LAB OF REPRODUCTIVE PHYSIOLOGY PHILADELPHIA, PA 19104 Male germ cell development in transgenic mice

R01HD-23661-03 (EDC) CRAMER, DANIEL W BRIGHAM & WOMEN'S HOSPITAL 221 LONGWOOD AVENUE BOSTON, MA 02115 Epidemiologic and biologic correlates of early menopause

R01HD-23668-05 (SRC) ZIOMEK, CAROL A GENZYME CORPORATION ONE MOUNTAIN ROAD FRAMINGHAM, MA 01701 Alkaline phosphatase in the preimplantation mouse embryo

R01HD-23679-04 (MGN) PUCK, JENNIFER M JOSEPH STOKES JR RESEARCH INST 34TH STREET & CIVIC CTR BLVD PHILADELPHIA, PA 19104 Genetic analysis of immunodeficiency diseases

P01HD-23681-04 (HDMC) TOOLE, BRYAN P TUFTS UNIVERSITY 136 HARRISON AVENUE BOSTON, MA 02111 Cell-matrix interactions in limb development

P01HD-23681-04 0001 (HDMC) TOOLE, BRYAN P. Cell-matrix interactions in limb development Control of hyaluronate synthesis and cell proliferation

P01HD-23681-04 0002 (HDMC) LINSENMAYER, THOMAS Cell-matrix interactions in limb development Limb developement cartilage hypertrophy

P01HD-23681-04 0004 (HDMC) OLIVER, NOELYNN Cell-matrix interactions in limb development Matrix gene expresion in limb developement

P01HD-23681-04 0005 (HDMC) SARKAR, SATYAPRIYA Cell-matrix interactions in limb development Translation inhibitory RNA species

R55HD-23684-04 (GEN) PERRIMON, NORBERT HARVARD MEDICAL SCHOOL 25 SHATTUCK ST BOSTON, MA 02115 The int-1 signal transduction pathway in Drosophila

R01HD-23690-04 (GEN) STERNBERG, PAUL W CALIFORNIA INSTIT OF TECHNOLOY 1201 E CALIFORNIA BLVD PASADENA, CALIFORNIA 91125 Genetic control of nematode vulval development

R01HD-23696-05 (CBY) RUDERMAN, JOAN V HARVARD MEDICAL SCHOOL 220 LONGWOOD AVE BOSTON, MA 02115 Regulation of the cell cycle in early embryos

R01HD-23697-04 (HED) ROTE, NEAL S WRIGHT STATE UNIVERSITY 409 OELMAN HALL DAYTON, OH 45435 Antiphospholipid antibodies & recurrent pregnancy loss

R01HD-23698-04 (SSS) O'SULLIVAN, MARY J UNIVERSITY OF MIAMI P O BOX 016960 MIAMI, FL 33101 The impact of HIV infection in pregnancy

R01HD-23713-03 (SSP) EPSTEIN, LEONARD H WESTERN PSYCHIATRIC INSTITUTE 3811 O'HARA STREET PITTSBURGH, PA 15213 Effectiveness of enhanced family-based obesity treatment

R29HD-23718-04 (EDC) GOLDMAN, MARLENE B HARVARD SCHOOL OF PUBLIC HLTH 677 HUNTINGTON AVE BOSTON, MA 02115 Epidemiologic investigations of human infertility

R01HD-23724-04 (HED) BRACE, ROBERT A UNIV OF CA, SAN DIEGO DEPT. OF REPROD MEDICINE LA JOLLA, CA 92093-0802 Regulation of amniotic fluid volume

R01HD-23736-04 (END) MARSHALL, JOHN C UNIVERSITY OF VIRGINIA BOX 466 CHARLOTTESVILLE, VA 22908 Intracellular mechanisms regulating LH subunit MRNA expression

R01HD-23738-04 (HUD) ENTWISLE, DORIS R JOHN HOPKINS UNIVERSITY CHARLES & 34TH STREETS BALTIMORE, MD 21218 Social structure and development through mid-adolescence

R01HD-23755-04 (SRC) O'RAND, MICHAEL G UNIV OF N C AT CHAPEL HILL TAYLOR HALL CB#7090 CHAPEL HILL, NC 27599 A sperm recombinant antigen as an immunocontraceptive

R01HD-23771-04 (SRC) GOLDBERG, ERWIN NORTHWESTERN UNIVERSITY DEPT / BIOCHEM&MOLECULAR&CELL EVANSTON, IL 60208 Immunosuppression of fertility by human LDH-C4

R01HD-23789-04A1 (REB) HERR, JOHN C UNIVERSITY OF VIRGINIA CHARLOTTESVILLE, VA 22908 Baboon infertility testing of recombinant SP-10 vaccine

R01HD-23799-03 (NEUB) FERNALD, RUSSELL D STANFORD UNIVERSITY DEPARTMENT OF PSYCHOLOGY STANFORD, CA 94305-2130 Social and physiological regulation of maturation

R29HD-23800-05 (HUD) LANDRY, SUSAN H UNIVERSITY OF TEXAS MED SCHOOL 6431 FANNIN - MSB 3.136 HOUSTON, TX 77030 Joint attention and preterm infant competence

R01HD-23818-04 (BCE) MELLON, PAMELA L SALK INST/BIOLOGICAL STUDIES POST OFFICE BOX 85800 SAN DIEGO, CALIF 92138 Glycoprotein hormone a subunit gene transcription

R01HD-23826-04 (MGN) DRABKIN, HARRY A UNIV OF COLORADO HLTH SCI CTR 4200 EAST 9TH AVE, BOX B171 DENVER, CO 80262 Characterization of the chromosome 3p14 3p21.1 region

R01HD-23830-03 (NLS) LERANTH, CSABA YALE UNIV SCHOOL OF MEDICINE 333 CEDAR ST PO BOX 3333 NEW HAVEN, CT 06510 Synaptology of neurons involved in reproduction

R01HD-23839-04 (REB) EPPIG, JOHN J THE JACKSON LABORATORY 600 MAIN STREET BAR HARBOR, ME 04609-0800 Development of mammalian oocyte-granulosa cell complex

R01HD-23844-04 (CTY) ELGIN, SARAH C WASHINGTON UNIVERSITY ONE BROOKINGS DRIVE ST LOUIS, MO 63130 Formation, structure and function in heterochromatin

R29HD-23847-04 (ECS) BLOCK, STEVEN M BOWMAN GRAY SCHOOL OF MEDICINE 300 SOUTH HAWTHRONE RD WINSTON-SALEM, N C 27103 Control of local vascular resistance in newborns

R29HD-23848-02 (IMS) BEAMAN, KENNETH D UHS/CHICAGO MEDICAL SCHOOL 3333 GREEN BAY/MICROBIO-IMMUNO NORTH CHICAGO, IL 60064 Fetal specific immune suppression during pregnancy

R01HD-23853-03 (REB) WILDT, DAVID E SMITHSONIAN INSTITUTION NATIONAL ZOOLOGICAL PARK WASHINGTON, D C 20008 Gamete interaction and in vitro fertilization

R01HD-23854-04A1 (HUD) TRAUNER, DORIS A UNIV OF CALIFORNIA, SAN DIEGO 225 DICKINSON STREET SAN DIEGO, CA 92103 Neurobehavioral phenotypes of the cystionsis gene

R01HD-23855-04 (NTN) HAMBIDGE, K MICHAEL UNIVERSITY OF COLORADO HEALTH SCIENCES CENTER 4200 EAST NINTH AVENUE Zink absorption in pregnant and lactating women

R01HD-23858-04 (CBY) WITMAN, GEORGE B, III WORCESTER FOUNDATION 222 MAPLE AVENUE SHREWSBURY, MASS 01545 Sperm motility control during maturation and capacitation

R29HD-23862-04 (EDC) SAVITZ, DAVID A UNIV OF NC AT CHAPEL HILL SCHOOL OF PUBLIC HEALTH CHAPEL HILL, NC 27599-7400 Epidemiology of pregnancy outcome in a textile community

R01HD-23880-04 (SRC) ADLER, NANCY E UNIVERSITY OF CALIFORNIA 401 PARNASSUS AVENUE SAN FRANCISCO, CALIF 94143 Conscious/preconscious motivation in teenage pregnancy

R01HD-23891-04 (NEUC) KINTNER, CHRIS R SALK INSTITUTE PO BOX 85800 SAN DIEGO, CA 92186-5800 Molecular basis of neurogenesis in vertebrate embryos

R29HD-23896-03 (REB) RIDER, VIRGINIA C TUFTS UNIV SCHL OF VET MED 200 WESTBORO ROAD NORTH GRAFTON, MA 01536 Progesterone regulation of gene expression

R01HD-23898-04 (SRC) THOMSON, ELIZABETH J UNIVERSITY OF WISCONSIN 1180 OBSERVATORY DRIVE MADISON, WI 53706 Gender and fertility motivation

R01HD-23900-04 (SRC) MILLER, WARREN B TRANSNATIONAL FAMILY RES INST 669 GEORGIA AVENUE PALO ALTO, CA 94306 Husbands' and wives' childbearing motivation

R01HD-23915-04 (SRC) KALMUSS, DEBRA COLUMBIA UNIVERSITY 60 HAVEN AVENUE NEW YORK, N Y 10032 Parenting expectations, experiences and fertility plans

R29HD-23921-04 (CBY) MUNEOKA, KEN TULANE UNIVERSITY BIOLOGY DEPARTMENT NEW ORLEANS, LA 70118 Analysis of growth control in developing mouse limbs

R01HD-23922-04 (HUD) KEIL, FRANK C CORNELL UNIVERSITY 228 URIS HALL ITHACA, NY 14853-7601 Concepts, causation and cognitive development

R01HD-23925-04 (REN) HUSAIN, AHSAN THE CLEVELAND CLINIC FND 9500 EUCLID AVE CLEVELAND, OH 44106 Angiotensin II – An introvarian regulatory peptide

R01HD-23943-04 (SRC) ENTWISLE, DORIS R JOHN HOPKINS UNIVERSITY CHARLES & 34TH STREETS BALTIMORE, MD 21218 Black/white families and children's development

R01HD-23968-04 (SRC) BARBARIN, OSCAR A UNIVERSITY OF MICHIGAN ANN ARBOR, MI 48109-1285 Illness, family life and development of Black children

R01HD-23991-04 (SRC) COUSINS, JENNIFER H BAYLOR COLLEGE OF MEDICINE ONE BAYLOR PLAZA, RM 176B HOUSTON, TX 77030 Development of health behaviors in Mexican Americans

R01HD-23998-04 (HUD) MACWHINNEY, BRIAN J CARNEGIE-MELLON UNIVERSITY 5000 FORBES AVENUE PITTSBURGH, PA 15213 Computational analysis of child language transcript data

R44HD-24009-03 (HUD) HUNTER, ROBERT M YELLOWSTONE ENVIRONMENTAL SCI 320 S WILLSON AVE BOZEMAN, MT 59715 Cognitive skill based child-resistant medicine container

R44HD-24023-03 (HUD) ZENO, SUSAN M TOUCHSTONE APPLIED SCI ASSOC FIELDS LANE, PO BOX 382 BREWSTER, NY 10509 Effectiveness measures of vocabulary knowledge

R44HD-24034-03 (REN) HU, CHIA-LING STANDARD SCIENTIFICS, INC PO BOX 322 CAMBRIDGE, MA 02238 A new luteinizing hormone test for ovulation detection

R37HD-24047-05 (BEM) MASSEY, DOUGLAS S NATIONAL OPINION RESEARCH CENT 1155 EAST 60TH STREET CHICAGO, IL 60637 Public use data on mexican immigration

P30HD-24051-03 (HDMR) THOMPSON, TRAVIS I UNIVERSITY OF MINNESOTA 2221 UNIV AVE SE, SUITE 145 MINNEAPOLIS, MN 55414 Center for research on developmental disabilities

P30HD-24051-03 9001 (HDMR) FORBUSH, MARI CENTER FOR RESEARCH ON DEVELOPMENTAL DISABILITIES Transportation--Core

P30HD-24051-03 9002 (HDMR) DIRKX, PATIENCE CENTER FOR RESEARCH ON DEVELOPMENTAL DISABILITIES Communication, media, and information--Core

P30HD-24051-03 9003 (HDMR) KLEBE, KELLY CENTER FOR RESEARCH ON DEVELOPMENTAL DISABILITIES Quantitative and computer unit--Core

P30HD-24051-03 9007 (HDMR) LESTER, BRUCE CENTER FOR RESEARCH ON DEVELOPMENTAL DISABILITIES Scientific apparatus and electronics unit--Core

P30HD-24051-03 9008 (HDMR) LESTER, BRUCE CENTER FOR RESEARCH ON DEVELOPMENTAL DISABILITIES Animal laboratories--Core

P30HD-24051-03 9004 (HDMR) FORBUSH, MARI CENTER FOR RESEARCH ON DEVELOPMENTAL DISABILITIES Participant recruitment and data base management--Core

P30HD-24051-03 9005 (HDMR) MCLOON, LINDA CENTER FOR RESEARCH ON DEVELOPMENTAL DISABILITIES Biomedical laboratories--Core

P30HD-24051-03 9006 (HDMR) KIM, CHRISTINE CENTER FOR RESEARCH ON DEVELOPMENTAL DISABILITIES Psychological laboratories--Core

R29HD-24056-04 (HUD) CAUCE, ANA M UNIVERSITY OF WASHINGTON SEATTLE, WA 98195 Ecological model of well-being in minority adolescents
P30HD-24061-04 (HDMR) MOSER, HUGO W KENNEDY RES INSTITUTE, INC. 707 NORTH BROADWAY/NEUROLOGY BALTIMORE, MD 21205 NICHD mental retardation research center core grant
P30HD-24064-04 (HDMR) MC CABE, EDWARD R BAYLOR COLLEGE OF MEDICINE ONE BAYLOR PLAZA HOUSTON, TX 77030 Baylor mental retardation research center
P30HD-24064-04 9001 (HDMR) BEAUDET, ARTHUR L. Baylor mental retardation research center Biomedical assessment--core
P30HD-24064-04 9002 (HDMR) WILLIAMSON, DANIEL Baylor mental retardation research center Neurodevelopmental assessment--core
P30HD-24064-04 9003 (HDMR) PATEL, PRAGNA Baylor mental retardation research center Tissue culture--core
P30HD-24064-04 9004 (HDMR) OVERBEEK, PAUL Baylor mental retardation research center Transgenic mice--core
P30HD-24064-04 9005 (HDMR) CASKEY, C. THOMAS Baylor mental retardation research center Nucleic acid--core
P30HD-24064-04 9006 (HDMR) COOK, RICHARD G. Baylor mental retardation research center Protein chemistry--core
P30HD-24064-04 9007 (HDMR) LAWRENCE, CHARLES B. Baylor mental retardation research center Sequence analysis--Core
P30HD-24064-04 9008 (HDMR) NOEBELS, JEFFREY L. Baylor mental retardation research center Neurocytology image analysis--core
R01HD-24086-02 (REN) PEDERSEN, CORT A UNIVERSITY OF NORTH CAROLINA BIOLOGICAL SCIS RESEARCH CTR CHAPEL HILL, NC 27599 CNS oxytocin changes associated with mating
R29HD-24094-03 (REN) SHEFFIELD, LEWIS G UNIVERSITY OF WISCONSIN 1675 OBSERVATORY DRIVE MADISON, WI 53706 Role of EGF in mammary gland development
R01HD-24106-03 (SSP) HAINES, MICHAEL R COLGATE UNIVERSITY 19 OAK DRIVE HAMILTON, N Y 13346 A study of mortality decline
R01HD-24112-03 (NTN) DEWEY, KATHRYN G UNIVERSITY OF CALIFORNIA DAVIS, CA 95616 Effects of exercise on lactation performance in humans
R01HD-24114-03 (HUD) CAMPBELL, FRANCES A FRANK PORTER GRAHAM CENTER 105 SMITH LEVEL ROAD CHAPEL HILL, NC 27599-8180 Preventive interventions
R01HD-24116-04 (HUD) REID, MARY K UNIVERSITY OF WASHINGTON SEATTLE, WA 98195 Mental retardation--Family effects on school success
R01HD-24119-04 (BIO) HORWITZ, ALLEN L UNIVERSITY OF CHICAGO 5841 S MARYLAND AVE-HOSP B 413 CHICAGO, IL 60637 Biochemical basis of sulfatase activity
R01HD-24122-04 (SSP) GERONIMUS, ARLINE T UNIV OF MICHIGAN/SCH OF PH 1420 WASHINGTON HGTS ANN ARBOR, MI 48109-2029 Proximate determinants of low birth weight and infant mortality
R01HD-24130-04 (MBY) LINNEY, ELWOOD A DUKE UNIV MEDICAL CENTER P O BOX 3020 DURHAM, N C 27710 Developmental regulation of the glucocorticoid response
R01HD-24149-04 (SRC) SHAIN, ROCHELLE N UNIVERSITY OF TEXAS 7703 FLOYD CURL DRIVE SAN ANTONIO, TEX 78284 Racial/ethnic differences in adverse pregnancy outcomes
R29HD-24167-04 (HUD) OSBORNE, SUSAN S NORTH CAROLINA STATE UNIVERSIT BOX 7801, 402 POE HALL RALEIGH, NC 27695-7801 Reciprocal interaction between teachers and LD students
R29HD-24170-04 (HUD) ZIGMAN, WARREN B NYS INST.DEVELOP. DISABILITIES 1050 FOREST HILL RD. STATEN ISLAND, NY 10314 Functional regression in mentally retarded adults
R01HD-24177-04 (BPO) BRONSON, FRANKLIN H UNIVERSITY OF TEXAS ZOOLOGY DEPARTMENT AUSTIN, TEXAS 78712 Photoperiodism and seasonal breeding in the tropics
P01HD-24180-04 (HDMC) ROBERTS, JAMES M UNIVERSITY OF CALIFORNIA SAN FRANCISCO, CA 94143-0550 Preeclampsia linkage to placental implantation-perfusion
P01HD-24180-04 0001 (HDMC) FISHER, SUSAN Preeclampsia linkage to placental implantation-perfusion Cytotrophoblast in placentation
P01HD-24180-04 0002 (HDMC) MAIN, DENISE Preeclampsia linkage to placental implantation-perfusion Maternal-placental immune interactions in preeclampsia
P01HD-24180-04 0003 (HDMC) ROBERTS, JAMES Preeclampsia linkage to placental implantation-perfusion Endothelial injury in preeclampsia
P01HD-24180-04 9001 (HDMC) LAROS, RUSSEL Preeclampsia linkage to placental implantation-perfusion Clinical data--Core
P01HD-24180-04 0004 (HDMC) GUY, RICHARD Preeclampsia linkage to placental implantation-perfusion Cutaneous vascular reactivity predicting preeclampsia
P01HD-24180-04 0005 (HDMC) KITZMILLER, JOHN Preeclampsia linkage to placental implantation-perfusion Placental ischemia in pregnant monkeys
R29HD-24186-04 (BIO) LEDLEY, FRED D BAYLOR COLLEGE OF MEDICINE ONE BAYLOR PLAZA HOUSTON, TEXAS 77030 Molecular genetic studies on methylmalonyl CoA mutase
R29HD-24189-03 (BCE) SHULL, JAMES D UNIVERSITY OF NEBRASKA 600 SO. 42ND ST OMAHA, NE 68198-6805 Steroid hormone control of prolactin gene expression
R01HD-24190-04 (REN) VOOGT, JAMES L UNIV OF KANSAS MEDICAL CENTER 39TH & RAINBOW BLVD KANSAS CITY, KS 66103-8410 Hypothalamic control of prolactin
R01HD-24192-04 (HED) FREEMARK, MICHAEL S DUKE UNIVERSITY BOX 3080 308 BELL BLDG DURHAM, NC 27710 The role of placental lactogen in fetal development
R01HD-24199-04 (CBY) MC CLAY, DAVID R, JR DUKE UNIVERSITY DEPARTMENT OF ZOOLOGY DURHAM, N C 27706 Extracellular matrix proteins and differentiation
R01HD-24205-04 (SRC) FLOYD, FRANK J MICHIGAN STATE UNIVERSITY 129 PSYCHOLOGY BLVD EAST LANSING, MI 48824-1117 Family interactions with mentally retarded children
R29HD-24212-03 (HED) HUNT, JOAN S UNIV OF KANSAS MED CTR 39TH ST & RAINBOW BLVD KANSAS CITY, KS 66103 Decidual cell/placental interactions
R15HD-24224-01A3 (REN) SNYDER, ANN C UNIVERSITY OF WISCONSIN PO BOX 413 MILWAUKEE, WI 53201 Menstrual cyclicity and physical activity--Role of diet
P01HD-24234-04 (HDMR) PERCY, ALAN K BAYLOR COLLEGE OF MEDICINE ONE BAYLOR PLAZA HOUSTON, TX 77030 Rett syndrome--A program project
P01HD-24234-04 0001 (HDMR) PERCY, ALAN Rett syndrome--A program project Clinical assessment of Rett syndrome
P01HD-24234-04 0002 (HDMR) STACH, BRAD Rett syndrome--A program project Communication skills in Rett syndrome
P01HD-24234-04 0003 (HDMR) GLAZE, DANIEL G Rett syndrome--A program project Clinical neurophysiology of Rett syndrome
P01HD-24234-04 0004 (HDMR) JONES, THOMAS M Rett syndrome--A program project Epidemiology of Rett syndrome
P01HD-24234-04 0005 (HDMR) ZOGHBI, HUDA Y Rett syndrome--A program project Molecular genetics in Rett syndrome
P01HD-24234-04 0006 (HDMR) ARMSTRONG, DAWNA L Rett syndrome--A program project Neuropathology of Rett syndrome
P01HD-24234-04 9001 (HDMR) PERCY, ALAN K Rett syndrome--A program project Patient and data management--Core
P01HD-24236-03 (SRC) LEON, MICHAEL A UNIVERSITY OF CALIFORNIA OF LEARNING & MEMORY IRVINE, CA 92717 The neurobiology of early learning
P01HD-24236-03 0001 (SRC) LEON, MICHAEL The neurobiology of early learning Structure-function relationships in early learning
P01HD-24236-03 0002 (SRC) GALL, CHRISTINE The neurobiology of early learning Neurotransmitter expression in the olfactory bulb
P01HD-24236-03 0003 (SRC) COTMAN, CARL The neurobiology of early learning NMDA receptors and developmental plasticity
P01HD-24236-03 0004 (SRC) LYNCH, GARY The neurobiology of early learning Development of olfactory memory mechanisms
P01HD-24236-03 9001 (SRC) LEON, MICHAEL A The neurobiology of early learning Core--Group facility for neuroanatomical research
R01HD-24301-04 (CBY) CHUONG, CHENG-MING UNIV OF SOUTHERN CA SCH OF MED DEPT PATH/2011 ZONALL AVE LOS ANGELES, CA 90033 Limb chondrogenesis
R29HD-24306-04 (MGN) OVERBEEK, PAUL A HOWARD HUGHES MEDICAL INST ONE BAYLOR PLAZA HOUSTON, TEXAS 77030 A gene essential for normal foot morphogenesis
R01HD-24308-03 (NTN) MOTT, GLEN E UNIV OF TEXAS HLTH SCI CTR DEPT OF PATHOLOGY SAN ANTONIO, TX 78284 Programming of cholesterol metabolism by infant diet
R01HD-24310-02 (GEN) WERREN, JOHN H UNIVERSITY OF ROCHESTER HUTCHINSON HALL ROCHESTER, NY 14627 Genetics of the paternal sex ratio chromosome
R29HD-24312-03 (REB) URBANSKI, HENRYK F OREGON REGIONAL PRIMATE RES. C 505 N.W. 185TH AVENUE BEAVERTON, OR 97006 Neuroendocrine control of seasonal reproduction
R01HD-24314-03 (REN) BRYANT-GREENWOOD, GILLIAN D UNIVERSITY OF HAWAII 1960 EAST WEST ROAD HONOLULU, HAWAII, 96822 Human decidua and fetal membranes as a paracrine system
R01HD-24315-02 (RAP) ARIAGNO, RONALD L STANFORD UNIV SCH OF MED STANFORD, CA 94305 Modulation of circadian rhythmicity in preterm infants
R01HD-24319-05 (MBY) GUDAS, LORRAINE J CORNELL UNIVERSITY 1300 YORK AVENUE NEW YORK, NY 10021 Regulation of laminin genes by retinoids
R01HD-24324-02 (GEN) MENEELY, PHILIP M FRED HUTCHINSON CANCER CTR. 1124 COLUMBIA ST. SEATTLE, WA 98104 The sex determination signal in C. elegans
R01HD-24325-04 (SSP) RINDFUSS, RONALD R UNIVERSITY OF NORTH CAROLINA 123 W FRANKLIN STREET CHAPEL HILL, N C 27514 Disorder in the life course and family formation timing
R01HD-24349-03 (HUD) FERNALD, ANNE STANFORD UNIVERSITY DEPARTMENT OF PSYCHOLOGY STANFORD, CA 94305-2130 Prosodic universals in mothers' speech to infants
R01HD-24360-04 (REN) PANG, SONGYA UNIVERSITY OF ILLINOIS 840 SOUTH WOOD STREET CHICAGO, IL 60612 Hirsutism, ovarian dysfunction--Genetic defects
R01HD-24374-04 (SRC) SCHIMENTI, JOHN C CASE WESTERN RESERVE UNIV CLEVELAND, OHIO 44106 Molecular analysis of T complex genes in spermatogenesis
R01HD-24383-04 (SRC) SILVER, LEE M PRINCETON UNIVERSITY DEPT OF MOLECULAR BIOLOGY PRINCETON, N J 08544 Human t complex testes expressed genes and male sterility
R01HD-24384-04 (SRC) LAU, YUN-FAI C UNIVERSITY OF CALIFORNIA 3RD & PARNASSUS SAN FRANCISCO, CA 94143-0724 Molecular biology of the male-enhanced antigen genes
R44HD-24403-03 (SSS) HALL, HAROLD E ELECTRONIC MED INSTRUMENTS, IN 1800 112TH AVE NE BELLEVUE, WA 98004 Therapy & equipment for those with cerebral palsy
R29HD-24425-03 (REB) NAZ, RAJESH K ALBERT EINSTEIN COLLEGE OF MED 1300 MORRIS PARK AVE. BRONX, NEW YORK 10461 Immunobiological role of fertilization antigen
R29HD-24426-05 (REN) CLOUGH, RICHARD W SOUTHERN ILLINOIS UNIVERSITY LINDEGREN HALL CARBONDALE, IL 62901 Puberty and the neural control of LHRH
R01HD-24427-02 (GMA) DUVIC, MADELEINE UNIVERSITY OF TEXAS MEDICAL SC 6431 FANNIN HOUSTON, TX 77030 Genetic heterogeneity--Ehlers Danlos syndromes VII and IV
R01HD-24438-04 (SRC) MILLER, LEO UNIVERSITY OF ILLINOIS P.O. BOX 4348, MAIL CODE 066 CHICAGO, IL 60680 Keratin gene expression during Xenopus development
R01HD-24442-03 (SRC) KURKINEN, MARKKU T UNIV OF MED & DENT OF N J 675 HOES LANE PISCATAWAY, N J 08854 Matrix degrading proteinases in human skin disorders
P01HD-24448-04 (HDMR) MOSER, HUGO W THE KENNEDY RESEARCH INSTITUTE 707 NORTH BROADWAY BALTIMORE, MD 21205 Pathogenesis of Rett syndrome
P01HD-24448-04 0001 (HDMR) SAKKUBAI, NAIDU Pathogenesis of Rett syndrome Clinical and epidemiological studies
P01HD-24448-04 0002 (HDMR) KITT, CHERYL A Pathogenesis of Rett syndrome Neuropathology of Rett syndrome
P01HD-24448-04 0003 (HDMR) BAUMAN, MARGARET L Pathogenesis of Rett syndrome Gapless serial section survey of Rett Syndrome brain
P01HD-24448-04 0004 (HDMR) WENK, GARY L Pathogenesis of Rett

syndrome Biochemical studies in postmortem brain tissue
P01HD-24448-04 0005 (HDMR) WONG, DEAN F Pathogenesis of Rett syndrome Neurotransmitter alterations in Rett Syndrome brain
P01HD-24448-04 0006 (HDMR) BRYAN, NICK Pathogenesis of Rett syndrome Quantitative magnetic resonance imaging studies in Rett Syndrome
R01HD-24450-03 (HED) PARR, EARL L SOUTHERN ILLINOIS UNIV SCHOOL OF MEDICINE CARBONDALE, IL 62901-6503 Granulated metrial gland cells--Identity and function
R01HD-24451-03 (HED) GANAPATHY, VADIVEL MEDICAL COLLEGE OF GEORGIA DEPT OF CELL & MOLEC BIOLOGY AUGUSTA, GA 30912-2100 Human placental amino acid transport-- Molecular aspects
R01HD-24455-03 (HED) GRUPPUSO, PHILIP A RHODE ISLAND HOSPITAL 593 EDDY STREET PROVIDENCE, RI 02903 Regulation of fetal hepatic growth
R01HD-24459-02 (BCE) HILF, RUSSELL UNIVERSITY OF ROCHESTER BOX 607/607 ELMWOOD AVE ROCHESTER, NY 14642 Estrogen receptor interaction with DNA
R01HD-24462-02 (HED) MAGNUSON, TERRY R CASE WESTERN RESERVE UNIV 2119 ABINGTON ROAD CLEVELAND, OH 44106 The albino-deletion complex and early mouse development
R01HD-24488-02 (REB) MAHESH, VIRENDRA B MEDICAL COLLEGE OF GEORGIA AUGUSTA, GA 30912-3000 Granulosa cell function during folliculogenesis
R29HD-24489-04 (MBY) KONIECZNY, STEPHEN F PURDUE UNIVERSITY LILLY HALL WEST LAFAYETTE, I N 47907 Isolation & characterization of lineage-specific genes
R01HD-24490-04 (SRC) ROTE, NEAL S WRIGHT STATE UNIVERSITY 409 OELMAN HALL DAYTON, OH 45435 Antiphospholipid antibody and hypertension in pregnancy
R01HD-24491-04 (SRC) KING, BARRY F UNIVERSITY OF CALIFORNIA DEPT H A, MSI-A ROOM 3415 DAVIS, CALIF 95616 Post-implantation modification of the spiral arteries
R01HD-24494-04 (SRC) WEINER, CARL P UNIVERSITY OF IOWA DEPT OF OBSTETRICS/GYNECOLOGY IOWA CITY, IOWA 52242 Role of serotonin in pregnancy related hypertension
R01HD-24495-05 (SRC) MAIN, ELLIOTT K MEDICAL RESEARCH INSTITUTE 2200 WEBSTER STREET SAN FRANCISCO, CA 94115 HLA regulation in normal & preeclamptic trophoblasts
R01HD-24496-04 (SRC) HAUTH, JOHN C UNIVERSITY OF AL AT BIRMINGHAM BIRMINGHAM, AL 35294 Low-dose ASA and prevention of pregnancy hypertension
R01HD-24497-04 (MET) SOWERS, JAMES R WAYNE STATE UNIVERSITY 4201 ST ANTOINE DETROIT, MI 48201 Insulin resistance and altered cellular calcium metabolism in pregnancy
R01HD-24499-04 (SRC) GRAVES, STEVEN W BRIGHAM & WOMEN'S HOSPITAL 75 FRANCIS STREET BOSTON, MA 02115 Abnormal sodium homeostasis in hypertensive pregnancy
R01HD-24511-04 (MBY) BODE, HANS R UNIVERSITY OF CALIFORNIA DEVELOPMENT BIOLOGY CENTER IRVINE, CA 92717 Stem cell differentiation in hydra
R01HD-24517-04 (HED) POTTER, STANLEY S CHILDREN'S HOSP RES FDN ELLAND AND BETHESDA AVENUE CINCINNATI, OHIO 45229 Embryology and development studied in transgenic mice
R01HD-24518-04 (BCE) LINZER, DANIEL I NORTHWESTERN UNIVERSITY 2153 SHERIDAN ROAD EVANSTON, IL 60208 Molecular analysis of mouse placental lactogens
R29HD-24529-04 (NTN) MC NAMARA, JOHN P WASHINGTON STATE UNIVERSITY 223 CLARK HALL PULLMAN, WA 99164-6320 Adipose metabolism in support of lactation
R01HD-24538-03 (SRC) GILCHREST, BARBARA A USDA HUMAN NUTRITION RES. CTR 711 WASHINGTON STREET BOSTON, MA 02111 Sequential activation of melanocyte differentiation gene
R01HD-24542-02 (BPO) HINES, MELISSA M UNIVERSITY OF CALIFORNIA 760 WESTWOOD PLAZA LOS ANGELES, CA 90024-1759 Hormonal influences on neural-behavioral development
R01HD-24553-04 (BPO) COHEN, ROCHELLE S UNIVERSITY OF ILLINOIS 808 SOUTH WOOD STREET CHICAGO, IL 60612 Cell biology of estrogen effects on lordosis behavior
R01HD-24554-04 (HUD) RIESER, JOHN J VANDERBILT UNIVERSITY BOX 512 PEABODY COLLEGE NASHVILLE, TN 37203 Young children's perception of self-movement and action
R29HD-24556-04 (REB) BUTLER, JAMES E UNIVERSITY OF IDAHO MOSCOW, ID 83843 Metabolic tests of viability in preimplantation embryos
R01HD-24562-03 (BCE) ADELMAN, JOHN P OREGON HEALTH SCIENCE UNIV. 3181 S.W. SAM JACKSON PARK RD. PORTLAND, OR 97201 Characterization and function of the gnrh-sh gene locus
R01HD-24563-04 (REN) BARBIERI, ROBERT L SUNY AT STONY BROOK DEPT OF OB/GYN STONY BROOK, N Y 11794-8091 Hyperandrogenism and insulin resistence in women
R01HD-24565-04 (REN) HAMMOND, JAMES M PENNSYLVANIA STATE UNIVERSITY DEPT. OF MEDICINE PO BOX 850 HERSHEY, PA 17033 Ovarian growth factors
R01HD-24570-04 (HED) COLEMAN, ROSALIND A UNIVERSITY OF NORTH CAROLINA-C 2203 MCGAVRAN-GREENBERG HALL CHAPEL HILL, NC 27599-7400 Trophoblasts cells--Pathways of lipid release
R01HD-24571-03 (SSP) SELTZER, JUDITH A CENTER FOR DEMOGRAPHY & ECOLOG 1180 OBSERVATORY DRIVE MADISON, WI 53706 Demographic and social issues in child support
R01HD-24575-04 (BPO) LEE, THERESA M UNIVERSITY OF MICHIGAN 1103 E HURON STREET ANN ARBOR, MI 48104-1687 Perinatal determinants of development
R29HD-24599-04 (BCE) KWOK, SIMON C UNIV OF KANSAS MEDICAL CENTER 39TH AND RAINBOW BLVD KANSAS CITY, KS 66103 Porcine prorelaxin converting enzyme
P01HD-24605-03 (SRC) GEARHART, JOHN D JOHNS HOPKINS UNIV SCH OF MED 725 NORTH WOLFE STREET BALTIMORE, MD 21205-2195 Genes, aneuploidy, and mammalian development
P01HD-24605-03 0001 (SRC) HIETER, PHILIP Genes, aneuploidy, and mammalian development Approaches in yeast to study of aneuploidy
P01HD-24605-03 0002 (SRC) REEVES, ROGER H Genes, aneuploidy, and mammalian development Genetic studies of mouse chromosome 16 and human 21
P01HD-24605-03 0003 (SRC) ANTONARAKIS, STYLIANOS E Genes, aneuploidy, and mammalian development Molecular studies on etiology & phenotype of Down syndrome
P01HD-24605-03 0004 (SRC) GEARHART, JOHN D Genes, aneuploidy, and mammalian development Utilization of transgenic and transomic mice in the study of Down syndrome
R01HD-24610-04 (SSS) COX, DAVID R UNIVERSITY OF CALIFORNIA 3RD AVE & PARNASSUS SAN FRANCISCO, CA 94143 The molecular genetics of down syndrome
R01HD-24613-02 (MGN) BRADLEY, ALLAN BAYLOR COLLEGE OF MEDICINE ONE BAYLOR PLAZA HOUSTON, TX 77030 Directed mutagenesis of the hox 2 and AFP genes in mice
R01HD-24617-04 (BCE) HARO, LUIS S WHITTIER INSTITUTE 9894 GENESSEE AVENUE LA JOLLA, CA 92037 Structural studies of receptors for lactogenic hormones
R01HD-24618-03 (EDC) MARCUS, MICHELE MOUNT SINAI SCHOOL OF MEDICINE ONE GUSTAVE L LEVY PLACE NEW YORK, NY 10029 Early pregnancy loss among female office workers
R01HD-24628-02 (REB) HALL, SUSAN H UNIVERSITY OF NORTH CAROLINA CB #7500, MACNIDER BLDG CHAPEL HILL, NC 27599 Mechanisms of FSH-regulated gene expression in the sertoli cell
R29HD-24637-03 (NEUB) FAHRBACH, SUSAN E UNIV OF IL/DEPT OF ENTOMOLOGY 505 S GOODWIN AVE/320MORRILL H URBANA, IL 61801 Mechanisms of neuronal death in manduca sexta
P01HD-24640-03 (SRC) SWEET, RICHARD L SAN FRANCISCO GENERAL HOSPITAL 1001 POTRERO AVENUE, WARD 6D14 SAN FRANCISCO, CA 94110 Bay area perinatal AIDS center
P01HD-24640-03 9001 (SRC) DATTELL, RONNIE Bay area perinatal AIDS center Patient accrual/Epidemiology research core
P01HD-24640-03 9002 (SRC) LEVY, JAY Bay area perinatal AIDS center Virology core
P01HD-24640-03 9003 (SRC) WARA, D. Bay area perinatal AIDS center Pediatric core
P01HD-24640-03 9004 (SRC) COWAN, MORTON Bay area perinatal AIDS center Obsteric immunology
P01HD-24640-03 9005 (SRC) BECKSTEAD, JAY Bay area perinatal AIDS center Immunohistochemistry core
P01HD-24640-03 0001 (SRC) GOLBUS, MITCHELL S. Bay area perinatal AIDS center Effect of HIV infection on the fetus
P01HD-24640-03 0002 (SRC) MAIN, ELLIOTT K. Bay area perinatal AIDS center HIV infection of the placenta
P01HD-24640-03 0003 (SRC) SWEET, RICHARD L. Bay area perinatal AIDS center Natural History -- Material and infant AIDS
R01HD-24643-04 (SSP) FRISBIE, W PARKER UNIVERSITY OF TEXAS 1800 MAIN BUILDING AUSTIN, TX 78712 Infant mortality among Mexican Americans, 1935-1985
R01HD-24644-04 (SSP) BRADSHAW, BENJAMIN S UNIVERSITY OF TEXAS 7703 FLOYD CURL DRIVE SAN ANTONIO, TX 78284 Infant mortality among Mexican Americans, 1935-1985
R01HD-24649-03 (CBY) BONDER, EDWARD M RUTGERS UNIVERSITY DEPT OF BIOLOGICAL SCIENCES NEWARK, NJ 07102 Actin in embryogenesis-- Mechanisms of regulation
R01HD-24650-03 (BCE) MOYLE, WILLIAM R UMDNJ-ROBERT W JOHNSON MED SCH 675 HOES LANE PISCATAWAY, N J 08854 Structure/function of glycoprotein hormone beta subunits
R29HD-24653-04 (NLS) BOYD, SUNNY K UNIV OF NOTRE DAME NOTRE DAME, IN 46556 Sexual dimorphism in neuropeptide systems
R01HD-24659-02S1 (EDC) HATCH, MAUREEN C COLUMBIA UNIVERSITY 600 WEST 168TH STREET NEW YORK, NY 10032 An epidemiologic study of stress in pregnancy
R01HD-24663-04 (GEN) KIMBLE, JUDITH E UNIVERSITY OF WISCONSIN 1525 LINDEN DRIVE MADISON, WI 53706 Molecular analyses of sex determination in C. elegans
R01HD-24669-03 (RNM) TAYLOR, KENNETH J YALE UNIVERSITY 333 CEDAR ST, TE-2; POB 3333 NEW HAVEN, CT 06510 New techniques for diagnosis of ectopic pregnancy
R29HD-24673-03 (MBY) ANDREWS, MATTHEW T NORTH CAROLINA STATE UNIVERSIT BOX 7614 RALEIGH, NC 27695-7614 A developmental switch in embryonic gene expression
R01HD-24676-03 (HUD) SLADE, ARIETTA CITY COLLEGE OF C U N Y PSYCHOLOGICAL CTR, NAC 8/130 NEW YORK, NY 10031 Infants and their mothers: pathways to secure attachment
R01HD-24684-03 (NTN) HIMES, JOHN H UNIVERSITY OF MINNESOTA 420 DELAWARE STEET SE MINNEAPOLIS, MN 55455 Early malnutrition and later bone development
R29HD-24690-03 (CBY) ETTENSOHN, CHARLES A CARNEGIE MELLON UNIVERSITY 4400 FIFTH AVE/BIOLOGICAL SCIS PITTSBURGH, PA 15213 Mechanisms of primary mesenchyme morphogenesis
R01HD-24697-03 (NLS) JENNES, LOTHAR H UNIVERSITY OF KENTUCKY MN 224 MEDICAL CENTER LEXINGTON, KY 40536 Identification and characterization of brain GnRH receptors
R01HD-24700-02 (HUD) LEON, GLORIA R UNIVERSITY OF MINNESOTA 75 EAST RIVER ROAD MINNEAPOLIS, MN 55455 Prospective analysis of adolescent eating practices
R01HD-24701-03 (REB) MCDONALD, JOHN K MEDICAL UNIV OF SOUTH CAROLINA 171 ASHLEY AVENUE CHARLESTON, SC 29425 Lysosomal proteases of spermatozoa
R01HD-24704-03 (HED) MAJZOUB, JOSEPH A CHILDREN'S HOSPITAL 300 LONGWOOD AVENUE BOSTON, MA 02115 Placental corticotropin releasing hormone regulation
R01HD-24710-02 (NEUB) DESMOND, MARY E VILLANOVA UNIVERSITY VILLANOVA, PA 19085 Fluid transport & pressure in embryonic brain growth
R01HD-24714-03 (BM) LINDSAY, JAMES A UNIVERSITY OF FLORIDA GAINESVILLE, FL 32611 Activation of bacterial toxins in sudden infant death
R01HD-24717-03 (REB) WELSH, MARCIA G UNIVERSITY OF SOUTH CAROLINA DEPARTMENT OF ANATOMY COLUMBIA, SC 29208 Reproduction--Pineal grafts, LH, FSH, and prolactin
R01HD-24718-03 (BEM) BOYCE, W THOMAS UNIVERSITY OF CALIFORNIA 400 PARNASSUS AVENUE SAN FRANCISCO, CA 94143-0314 Stress reactivity and health in preschool children
R01HD-24727-02 (NURS) SHERMAN, JACQUELINE B UNIVERSITY OF

PROJECT NO., ORGANIZATIONAL UNIT., INVESTIGATOR, ADDRESS, TITLE

ARIZONA MABEL & MARTIN STREETS TUCSON, ARIZONA 85721 Obesity in Mexican-American children

R01HD-24730-04 (SRC) FERNSTROM, JOHN D WESTERN PSYCHIATRIC INST & CLN 3811 O'HARA STREET PITTSBURGH, PA 15213 Diet, aromatic amino acids, and cns neurotransmitters

R01HD-24737-04 (SRC) NICHTER, MARK UNIVERSITY OF ARIZONA TUCSON, AZ 85721 Food intake, smoking, & diet among adolescent girls

R01HD-24770-03 (SRC) BROOKS-GUNN, JEANNE EDUCATIONAL TESTING SERVICE ROSEDALE ROAD PRINCETON, N J 08541 Nutrition & behavior in adolescent girls

R29HD-24773-02 (GMA) MULVIHILL, SEAN J UNIVERSITY OF CALIFORNIA BOX 0788 SAN FRANCISCO, CA 94143 Fetal gastric epithelial cellular development

R01HD-24775-02 (HUD) CECI, STEPHEN J CORNELL UNIVERSITY ITHACA, NY 14853 The veracity and durability of early memories

R01HD-24777-04 (SRC) HSU, L K GEORGE WEST PSYCHIATRIC INST/CLINIC 3811 O'HARA STREET PITTSBURGH, PA 15212 Bulimia nervosa--Nutritional versus cognitive treatment

R01HD-24797-04 (EI) LU, CHRISTOPHER Y UNIVERSITY OF TEXAS SW MED CTR 5323 HARRY HINES BLVD DALLAS, TX 75235-8856 Docosahexaenoic acid & regulation of fetal host defenses

R01HD-24816-04 (SRC) FADEN, RUTH R JOHNS HOPKINS UNIVERSITY 615 NORTH WOLFE STREET BALTIMORE, MD 21205 Risk of HIV infection and fertility-related behaviors

R44HD-24848-03 (CMS) HUTCHINS, SANDRA E EMERSON & STERN ASSOCIATES, IN 10150 SORRENTO VALLEY ROAD SAN DIEGO, CA 92121 Writing software for the deaf

R01HD-24869-03 (TMP) HAGEDORN, HENRY H UNIVERSITY OF ARIZONA ENTOMOLOGY/FORBES BLDG RM 410 TUCSON, AZ 85721 Homologous gene transfer systems for the mosquito

R01HD-24870-04 (REB) OJEDA, SERGIO R OREGON REG PRIMATE RES CTR 505 NW 185TH AVENUE BEAVERTON, OR 97006 Neural control of the prepubertal ovary

R01HD-24875-03 (HED) SORIANO, PHILIPPE M BAYLOR COLLEGE OF MEDICINE ONE BAYLOR PLAZA HOUSTON, TX 77030 Retroviruses as probes for development

R01HD-24884-03 (HUD) KOZLOWSKI, PIOTR NYS INSTITUTE FOR BASIC RES.. 1050 FOREST HILL ROAD STATEN ISLAND, NY 10314 Neuropathology and brain development in pediatric AIDS

R01HD-24901-02 (BEM) HOBFOLL, STEVAN E KENT STATE UNIVERSITY APPLIED PSYCHOLOGY CENTER KENT, OH 44242 Depression and medical complications among pregnant women

R01HD-24908-03 (BIO) ROE, CHARLES R DUKE UNIVERSITY MED CTR BOX 3028 DURHAM, NC 27710 Characterization & therapy of new fat oxidation defects

R01HD-24915-04 (ECS) WOODS, LORI L OREGON HEALTH SCI UNIVERSITY 3181 SW SAM JACKSON PARK ROAD PORTLAND, OR 97201 Control of blood pressure & body fluids in pregnancy

R01HD-24921-03 (SRC) JEMMOTT, JOHN B, III PRINCETON UNIVERSITY PRINCETON, NJ 08544-1010 Reducing the risk of sexually transmitted HIV infection

P01HD-24926-03 (SRC) STILES, CHARLES D DANA FARBER CANCER INST 44 BINNEY STREET BOSTON, MA 02115 Molecular analysis of cell and animal development

P01HD-24926-03 0001 (SRC) STILES, CHARLES Molecular analysis of cell and animal development Function of PDGF in early embryogenesis

P01HD-24926-03 0002 (SRC) GUDAS, LORRAINE Molecular analysis of cell and animal development Retinoic acid in Drosophila and Xenopus development

P01HD-24926-03 0003 (SRC) ROBERTS, THOMAS Molecular analysis of cell and animal development Molecular analysis of signal transduction melated through csf-1 receptor

P01HD-24926-03 0004 (SRC) SPIEGELMAN, BRUCE Molecular analysis of cell and animal development FOS protein complexes and developmental gene control

P01HD-24926-03 0005 (SRC) CHEN, LAN BO Molecular analysis of cell and animal development Endoplasmic reticulum in living cells

P01HD-24926-03 9001 (SRC) KOLODNER, RICHARD Molecular analysis of cell and animal development Molecular biology core

R01HD-24928-03 (REB) KHAN-DAWOOD, FIRYAL S UNIV OF TEXAS MEDICAL SCHOOL 6431 FANNIN 3110 HOUSTON, TX 77030 Regulation of the primate corpus luteum

R01HD-24934-03 (SRC) COATES, THOMAS J UNIV OF CALIFORNIA, SAN FRAN 400 PARNASSUS AVE, ROOM A405 SAN FRANCISCO, CA 94143 Aids prevention for sexually active adolescents

R01HD-24959-03 (SRC) STYNE, DENNIS M UNIVERSITY OF CALIFORNIA 275 MRAK HALL DAVIS, CA 95616 Mechanisms of egf action in fetal and neonatal monkeys

R01HD-24960-03 (SRC) PARKS, JOHN S EMORY UNIVERSITY DEPARTMENT OF PEDIATRICS ATLANTA, GA 30322 Placental growth hormone axis and human fetal growth

R01HD-24971-04 (SRC) MAGNESS, RONALD R U OF TX SW MED CTR @ DALLAS 5323 HARRY HINES BOULEVARD DALLAS, TX 75235-9063 Vascular reactivity in normal & hypertensive pregnancies

R01HD-24976-03 (REB) CREWS, DAVID P UNIVERSITY OF TEXAS AT AUSTIN AUSTIN, TX 78712 Environmental sex determination and differentiation

R29HD-24979-03 (REN) SILVIA, WILLIAM J UNIVERSITY OF KENTUCKY 405 AG. SCI. SOUTH LEXINGTON, KY 40546-0215 Cellular mechanisms in uterine prostaglandin synthesis

R01HD-24982-03 (BEM) LEE, RONALD D UNIVERSITY OF CALIFORNIA 2232 PIEDMONT AVE BERKELEY, CALIF 94720 Modeling and forecasting demographic time series

R01HD-24990-03 (SRC) HAMILTON, RICHARD T IOWA UNIVERSITY AMES, IOWA 50011 Growth factors and cathepsin l in placental development

R01HD-24995-03 (SRC) NAQVI, ALI M WAYNE STATE UNIVERSITY 71 WEST WARREN DETROIT, MI 48202 AIDS education for children and their parents

R29HD-24998-01A3 (BCE) MURRAY, MARY K TUFTS UNIVERSITY 136 HARRISON AVENUE BOSTON, MA 02111 Steroid control of oviduct differentiation

R01HD-25004-03 (SRC) ILAN, JOSEPH CASE WESTERN RESERVE UNIV 2119 ABINGTON ROAD CLEVELAND, OHIO 44106 Effects of igfs expression on fetal growth

R01HD-25005-04 (SRC) MAHER, PAMELA A WHITTIER INSTITUTE 9894 GENESEE AVENUE LA JOLLA, CA 92037 Developmentally regulated tyrosine kinase substrates

R01HD-25021-03 (SRC) HOVELL, MELBOURNE F SAN DIEGO STATE UNIVERSITY 5300 CAMPANILE DRIVE SAN DIEGO, CA 92182 Teaching youth social skills--An AIDS prevention trial

R29HD-25024-03 (SRC) DEVASKAR, SHERIN U CARDINAL GLENNON CHILDREN'S HO 1465 S GRAND BLVD ST LOUIS, MO 63104 Developmental regulation of neuronal insulin-like peptide

R01HD-25026-03 (SRC) MCKINLAY, JOHN B NEW ENGLAND RESEARCH INST 9 GALEN STREET WATERTOWN, MA 02172 Community AIDS prevention for inner city hispanic youth

R01HD-25034-02 (REB) HAMMOND, JAMES M PENNSYLVANIA STATE UNIVERSITY BOX 850 HERSHEY, PA 17033 Ovarian catecholestrogens

R01HD-25059-03 (REB) VERNON, ROBERT B UNIV OF WASHINGTON SCH OF MED SEATTLE, WA 98195 Regulation and function of SPARC in male reproduction

R01HD-25066-03 (HUD) CAMPOS, JOSEPH J INSTITUTE OF HUMAN DEVELOPMENT UNIVERSITY OF CA. @ BERKELEY Locomotion and psychological development in infancy

R01HD-25069-03 (IMS) ROSSE, CORNELIUS UNIVERSITY OF WASHINGTON DPT OF BIOLOGICAL STRUCTURE SEATTLE, WASH 98195 Postnatal hematogenous & intrathymic T cell progenitors

R01HD-25074-03 (SRC) POLLARD, JEFFREY W ALBERT EINSTEIN COLLEGE OF MED 1300 MORRIS PARK AVE BRONX, NY 10461 Role of colony stimulating factor-1 in placental growth

R01HD-25078-03 (HED) HOWE, CHIN C WISTAR INSTITUTE 36TH & SPRUCE STREETS PHILADELPHIA, PA 19104 Transcriptional regulation in development

R01HD-25090-03 (REB) BOOCKFOR, FREDRIC R MEDICAL UNIV OF SOUTH CAROLINA 171 ASHLEY AVENUE CHARLESTON, SC 29425 Secretory function of individual sertoli cells

R29HD-25094-03 (REB) KIM, KWAN H WASHINGTON STATE UNIVERSITY DEPT OF BIOCHEMISTRY/BIOPHYSIC PULLMAN, WA 99164-4660 Retinol-medicated regulation of spermatogenesis

R01HD-25109-03 (MGN) KUEHN, MICHAEL R UNIVERSITY OF ILLINOIS 808 S WOOD ST/M/C 669 CHICAGO, IL 60612 Developmental insertional mutants in transgenic mice

R01HD-25114-03 (EDC) BELLINGER, DAVID C CHILDREN'S HOSPITAL 300 LONGWOOD AVENUE BBOSTON, MA 02115 Environmental lead and children's psychologic function

R01HD-25123-02 (BCE) OJEDA, SERGIO R OR REGIONAL PRIMATE RES CTR 505 NW 185TH AVENUE BEAVERTON, OR 97006 Neuroendocrinology of puberty and sexual development

R29HD-25126-04 (LCR) ANISFELD, ELIZABETH COLUMBIA UNIVERSITY 630 W 168TH STREET NEW YORK, N Y 10032 Early carrying of prematures as a preventive

R01HD-25128-01A3 (HUD) LANDRY, SUSAN H UNIVERSITY OF TEXAS MED. SCHOO 6431 FANNIN-3.140 HOUSTON, TX 77030 Medical complications and parenting

R01HD-25135-03 (REN) RORKE, ELLEN A CASE WESTERN RESERVE UNIV 10900 EUCLID AVE/SCH OF MED CLEVELAND, OH 44106-4940 Steriod & retinoid effects on female reproductive tract

R01HD-25136-02 (REB) GORDON, JON W MT SINAI SCHOOL OF MEDICINE 1 GUSTAVE L LEVY PLACE NEW YORK, NY 10029 Rapid prenatal sexing of cleaving mouse embryos

R01HD-25137-03 (HUD) NEWCOMBE, NORA S TEMPLE UNIVERSITY-WEISS HALL DEPARTMENT OF PSYCHOLOGY PHILADELPHIA PENN 19122 Development of spatial coding

R01HD-25138-03 (CBY) BRONNER-FRASER, MARIANNE E UNIVERSITY OF CALIFORNIA DEVELOPMENTAL BIOLOGY CENTER IRVINE, CALIF 92717 Cell lineage analysis of the neural crest

R29HD-25143-04 (HED) KNUDSEN, THOMAS B DEPARTMENT OF ANATOMY 1020 LOCUST ST. Adenosine deaminase, a target in molecular teratogenesis

R01HD-25145-01A3 (BPO) POMERANTZ, STEVEN M UNIV OF PITTSBURGH SCH OF MED 3550 TERRACE STREET PITTSBURGH, PA 15262 Biopsychology of primate male sexual behavior

R01HD-25147-03 (BCE) COOKE, NANCY E UNIVERSITY OF PENNSYLVANIA 475 CRB - 422 CURIE BOULEVARD PHILADELPHIA, PA 19104-6145 Somatogenic and lactogenic hormones of the placenta

R01HD-25150-01A2 (HUD) THOMPSON, TRAVIS I UNIVERSITY OF MINNESOTA 2221 UNIVERSITY AVENUE SOUTHEA MINNEAPOLIS, MN 55414 Behavioral architecture and mental retardation

R01HD-25154-02 (NEUB) BIXBY, JOHN L UNIV OF MIAMI SCHOOL OF MED P.O. BOX 016189 MIAMI, FL 33101 Molecular analysis of nerve terminal differentiation

R29HD-25175-04 (HED) FIGUEROA, JORGE P BOWMAN GRAY SCHOOL OF MEDICINE WINSTON-SALEM, NC 27157-1066 Systemic and local regulation of myometrial activity

R01HD-25179-02 (MBY) KREIG, PAUL A UNIVERSITY OF TEXAS AUSTIN, TX 78712 Regulation of gene activity in Xenopus early development

R01HD-25189-03 (SRC) GLASSER, STANLEY R BAYLOR COLLEGE OF MEDICINE ONE BAYLOR PLAZA HOUSTON, TX 77030 In vitro implantation on polarized uterine epithelia

R01HD-25206-02 (BCE) ONG, DAVID E VANDERBILT UNIVERSITY DEPARTMENT OF BIOCHEMISTRY NASHVILLE, TN 37232 Vitamin A and reproduction

R01HD-25208-03 (MGN) ROBERTSON, ELIZABETH J COLUMBIA UNIVERSITY 701 WEST 168TH STREET NEW YORK, NY 10032 Analysis of mouse development using cell lines

R01HD-25211-02 (HUD) KLAHR, DAVID CARNEGIE-MELLON UNIVERSITY 5000 FORBES AVENUES PITTSBURHG, PA 15213 Scientific discovery processes of adults & children

R01HD-25212-02 (NEUB) LI, CHRISTINE BOSTON UNIVERSITY 2 CUMMINGTON STREET BOSTON, MA 02215 Assembly of a neuromuscular unit in C elegans

R29HD-25220-02 (HED) GIUDICE, LINDA C STANFORD UNIVERSITY MEDICAL CT 300 PASTEUR DRIVE STANFORD, CA 94305-4125 Gene expression in human endometrium

R01HD-25224-03 (SRC) HARPER, MICHAEL J UNIV OF TEXAS HEALTH SCI CTR 7703 FLOYD CURL DRIVE SAN ANTONIO, TEX 78284 PAF and

PROJECT NO., ORGANIZATIONAL UNIT., INVESTIGATOR, ADDRESS, TITLE

pre-implantation/implantation phenomena

R01HD-25225-03 (SRC) PAPAIOANNOU, VIRGINIA E TUFTS UNIVERSITY DEPT OF PATHOLOGY BOSTON, MA 02111 Role of trophectoderm subpopulations in implantation

R01HD-25230-03 (EDC) MUELLER, BETH A FRED HUTCHINSON CANCER RES CTR 1124 COLUMBIA STREET SEATTLE, WA 98104 Epidemiology of placenta previa and abruptio placenta

R01HD-25235-03 (SRC) CARSON, DANIEL D UNIV OF TEX/M D ANDERSON CAN C 1515 HOLCOMBE BLVD HOUSTON, TX 77030 Biochemistry of uterine heparan sulfate receptors

R01HD-25236-03 (SRC) NIEDER, GARY L WRIGHT STATE UNIVERSITY SCHOOL OF MEDICINE DAYTON, OH 45435 Embryo protein secretion during implantation

R01HD-25241-02 (HED) WENNBERG, RICHARD P UNIVERSITY OF CALIFORNIA DAVIS, CA 95616 Bilirubin encephalopathy--Role of monovalent anion

R01HD-25250-02 (BEM) ALBA, RICHARD D SUNY-ALBANY ALBANY, NY 12222 Suburbanization patterns of racial and ethnic groups

R01HD-25251-03 (NEUC) CREWS, STEPHEN T UNIVERSITY OF CALIFORNIA 405 HILGARD AVE LOS ANGELES, CA 90024 Molecular biology of neurogenesis

R01HD-25255-02 (HED) PEDERSEN, CORT A UNIVERSITY OF NORTH CAROLINA CHAPEL HILL, NC 27599 CNS oxytocin--Pregnancy, nursing and maternal behavior

R01HD-25256-01A2 (GMA) NOWICKI, PHILIP T CHILDRENS HOSPITAL 700 CHILDRENS DRIVE COLUMBUS, OH 43205 Control of intestinal oxygenation during postnatal life

R01HD-25257-03 (HUD) FALBO, TONI UNIVERSITY OF TEXAS AUSTIN, TX 78712 China's one child policy and children's outcomes

R01HD-25258-02 (HUD) LEPPER, MARK R STANFORD UNIVERSITY STANFORD, CA 94305 Motivational & cognitive strategies of expert tutors

R29HD-25262-03 (END) GOROSPE, WILLIAM C MEDICAL UNIV OF SOUTH CAROLINA 171 ASHLEY AVENUE CHARLESTON, SC 29425-2204 Regulation of granulosa cell function by cytokines

R01HD-25271-03 (HUD) DELOACHE, JUDY S UNIVERSITY OF ILLINOIS 603 E DANIEL CHAMPAIGN, IL 61820 Representational functioning in young children

R01HD-25272-03 (BCE) KEEPING, HUGH S RHODE ISLAND HOSPITAL 593 EDDY STREET PROVIDENCE, RI 02903 Inhibin gene expression in testis and sertoli cells

R01HD-25274-02 (SSP) TEACHMAN, JAY D UNIVERSITY OF MARYLAND ART SOCIOLOGY BUILDING COLLEGE PARK, MD 20742-1315 Family and socioeconomic consequences of military service

R29HD-25275-03 (REN) WIERMAN, MARGARET E UNIV OF COLORADO HEALTH SCIS C 4200 EAST 9TH AVENUE DENVER, CO 80262 Pretranslational regulation of FSH and LH in the rat

R01HD-25277-03 (SRC) YUDKOFF, MARC JOSEPH STOKES JR RSRCH INST CHILDRENS HOSP OF PHILADELPHIA PHILADELPHIA, PA 19104 Stable isotope studies of glutamic acid metabolism

R01HD-25286-03 (SRC) ONG, DAVID E VANDERBILT UNIVERSITY DEPARTMENT OF BIOCHEMISTRY NASHVILLE, TN 37232 Vitamin A transport systems

R01HD-25291-03 (REB) DOWNS, STEPHEN M MARQUETTE UNIVERSITY 530 NORTH 15TH ST. MILWAUKEE, WI 53233 Purines and the maintenance of meiotic arrest

R29HD-25299-04 (SRC) ROSS, NATHAN S DEPT OF VETERANS AFFAIRS MED C WILSHIRE AND SAWTELLE BLVDS. LOS ANGELES, CA 90073 Riboflavin and flavoprotein gene expression

R01HD-25306-03 (SRC) CLEARY, MARGOT P UNIVERSITY OF MINNESOTA 801 16TH AVENUE N E AUSTIN, MN 55912 The "fa" gene, adipocyte lipogenesis and dietary fatty acids

R01HD-25310-01A2 (HUD) WALLANDER, JAN L UNIVERSITY OF ALABAMA 1720 SEVENTH AVENUE SOUTH BIRMINGHAM, AL 35233 Mentally retarded adolescents' stress and coping

R01HD-25323-03 (SRC) WOYCHIK, RICHARD P MARTIN MARIETTA ENERGY SYSTEMS OAK RIDGE NATL LAB BX 2009 OAK RIDGE, TN 37831 Insertional mutagenesis in transgenic mice

R01HD-25326-03 (SRC) BRADLEY, ALLAN BAYLOR COLLEGE OF MEDICINE 1 BAYLOR BLAZA - ROOM T-921 HOUSTON, TX 77030 Insertional mutagenesis and mouse development

R01HD-25329-03 (SRC) TYNER, ANGELA UNIVERSITY OF ILLINOIS 808 S WOOD ST CHICAGO, IL 60612 Retroviral insertional mutagenesis in ES cells & mice

R01HD-25331-03 (SRC) MARTIN, GAIL R UNIVERSITY OF CALIFORNIA DEPT OF ANATOMY BOX 0452 SAN FRANCISCO, CA 94143-0962 Mutatin specific genes in mice by altering ES cells

R01HD-25334-03 (SRC) ROSSANT, JANET MOUNT SINAI HOSP RES INST 600 UNIVERSITY AVE, RM 884 TORONTO ONTARIO, CA M5G 1X5 Genetic control of early mammalian development

R01HD-25335-03 (SRC) ROBERTSON, ELIZABETH J COLUMBIA UNIVERSITY 701 WEST 168TH ST, DEPT OF GEN NEW YORK, NY 10032 Generation of developmental mutants in mice

R01HD-25340-03 (SRC) OVERBEEK, PAUL A HOWARD HUGHES MEDICAL INST ONE BAYLOR PLAZA HOUSTON, TEXAS 77030 Transgenic mice with developmental disorders

R29HD-25345-03 (HUD) ACKLES, PATRICK K UNIVERSITY OF ILLINOIS AT CHIC 1640 WEST ROOSEVELT ROAD CHICAGO, ILL 60608 Information processing and long-latency ERPS in infants

R01HD-25346-03 (SSP) GAGE, TIMOTHY B STATE UNIVERSITY OF NEW YORK 1400 WASHINGTON AVENUE ALBANY, NY 12222 Mortality and nutritional status--A demographic analysis

R44HD-25348-03 (SSS) HORN, GLENN T INTEGRATED GENETICS, INC ONE MOUNTAIN ROAD FRAMINGHAM, MA 01701 DNA amplification for the diagnosis of genetic disease

R44HD-25349-02A1 (SSS) REDDY, VEMURI B TRANSGENIC SCIENCES, CORP. ONE INNOVATION DRIVE WORCESTER, MA 01605 Human growth hormone production in transgenic rabbit milk

R44HD-25354-03 (SSS) MIZE, SUSAN G MIZE INFORMATION ENTERPRISE P O BOX 670847 DALLAS, TX 75367-0847 Registers of inherited metabolic diseases

R44HD-25355-03 (CMS) BRYANT, BRIAN R PRO-ED 8700 SHOAL CREEK BLVD AUSTIN, TX 78758 Screening and training phonological awareness

PROJECT NO., ORGANIZATIONAL UNIT., INVESTIGATOR, ADDRESS, TITLE

R44HD-25357-02 (SSS) DUQUETTE, PETER H BIO-METRIC SYSTEMS, INC 9924 WEST 74TH STREET EDEN PRAIRIE, MN 55344 Rapid EIA for cotinine in biological fluids

R43HD-25382-01A3 (HUD) STOPPEL, DAVID A LEAD FREE KIDS INC 2001 5TH AVE SOUTH MINNEAPOLIS, MN 55404 The evaluation of lead prevention education

R01HD-25387-02 (SRC) PEDERSEN, ROGER A UNIV OF CA, BOX 0750, LR-102 LAB/RADIOBIOLOGY & ENVIR HLTH SAN FRANCISCO, CA 94143-0750 Analysis of cell lineage in marsupial embryos

R01HD-25389-03 (SRC) NADEAU, JOSEPH H JACKSON LABORATORY 600 MAIN STREET BAR HARBOR, ME 04609-0800 Genetics of lineage determination during embryogenesis

R01HD-25390-03 (SSS) JACOBS, RUSSELL E CALIFORNIA INSTITUTE OF TECHNO 1201 E. CALIFORNIA BLVD PASADENA, CA 91125 Cell lineage studies using magnetic resonance imaging

R01HD-25394-03 (SRC) MILLER, JEFFREY B MASSACHUSETTS GENERAL HOSPITAL 149 13TH STREET CHARLESTOWN, MA 02129 Cell lineage commitment in mammalian myogenesis

R01HD-25395-03 (SRC) CAPECCHI, MARIO R UNIVERSITY OF UTAH 50 NORTH MEDICAL DRIVE SALT LAKE CITY, UT 84132 Mouse developmental mutants derived by gene targeting

R01HD-25412-03 (SRC) CHRISTOFFEL, KATHERINE K CHILDRENS MEMORIAL HOSPITAL 2300 CHILDRENS PLAZA CHICAGO, IL 60614 Development and behavior of child pedestrian victims

R01HD-25414-03 (SRC) PETERSON-HOMER, LIZETTE UNIV OF MISSOURI-COLUMBIA 210 MC ALESTER HALL COLUMBIA, MO 65211 Process analysis of children's injury and near injury

R01HD-25419-03 (SRC) PRUITT, STEVEN C ROSWELL PARK CANCER INST ELM & CARLTON ST BUFFALO, NY 14263 Lineage specific cdna markers during mouse embryogenesis

U10HD-25420-02 (SRC) BELSKY, JAY UNIVERSITY OF PITTSBURGH DEPARTMENT OF PSYCHOLOGY PITTSBURGH, PA 15260 The impact of day care and family process on development

U10HD-25430-02 (SRC) HUSTON, ALETHA C UNIVERSITY OF KANSAS 1034 HAWORTH HALL/HUMAN DEV LAWRENCE, KS 66045 Effects of early child-care experiences on childrens soc

U10HD-25445-03 (SRC) COX, MARTHA J WESTERN CAROLINA CENTER RESEARCH DEPT, 300 ENOLA ROAD MORGANTON, NC 28655 Effects of day care on infants--Interrelations with work

U10HD-25447-02 (SRC) BOOTH, CATHRYN L CHILD DEVEL & MENTAL RETARD CT 212 SOUTH BLDG, CDMRC, WJ-10 SEATTLE, WA 98195 Nonmaternal care & mother-child mutual adaptation

U10HD-25449-03 (SRC) PHILLIPS, DEBORAH A UNIVERSITY OF VIRGINIA DEPT/PSYCHOLOGY, GILMER HALL CHARLOTTESVILLE, VA 22903 Quality and stability of infant child care

U10HD-25451-03 (SRC) MC CARTNEY, KATHLEEN UNIVERSITY OF NEW HAMSPHIRE DEPT/PSYCHOLOGY, CONANT HALL DURHAM, NH 03824 The social ecology of infant child care

U10HD-25455-03 (SRC) WEINRAUB, MARSHA TEMPLE UNIVERSITY 13TH & CECIL B MOORE AVE PHILADELPHIA, PA 19122 Effects of non-parental infant day care on children

U10HD-25456-02 (SRC) CLARKE-STEWART, K ALISON UNIVERSITY OF CALIFORNIA PUBLIC POLICY RES ORGANIZATION IRVINE, CA 92717 How maternal employment harms or helps infants

U10HD-25460-03 (SRC) CALDWELL, BETTYE UNIVERSITY OF ARKANSAS 2801 SOUTH UNIVERSITY AVE LITTLE ROCK, AR 72204 An ecological study of infant care

R01HD-25476-03 (HUD) ACREDOLO, LINDA P UNIVERSITY OF CALIFORNIA 149 YOUNG HALL DAVIS, CA 95616 Impact of symbolic gesturing on infant development

R01HD-25479-03 (GMA) ROOP, DENNIS R BAYLOR COLLEGE OF MEDICINE ONE BAYLOR PLAZA HOUSTON, TX 77030 Regulation and function of keratins in the epidermis

R13HD-25480-01A2 (HDMC) HAREL, SHAUL EQUAL OPPORTUNITY FUND BITON 26 TEL HASHOMER, 52621 ISRAEL Third International Workshop on the At-Risk infant

R29HD-25488-01A2 (HUD) DUBE, WILLIAM V E K SHRIVER CENTER 200 TRAPELO ROAD WALTHAM, MA 02254 Programming discriminiation and one-trial learning

R01HD-25492-03 (BEM) AGRAS, W STEWART STANFORD UNIV-MEDICAL SCHOOL DEPT OF PSYCHIATRY/BEHAV SCIS STANFORD, CA 94305-5490 Behaviors influencing adiposity in infancy and childhood

R01HD-25493-03 (REB) KASAHARA, MASANORI UNIV OF MIAMI SCH OF MEDICINE PO BOX 016960/R-138 MIAMI, FL 33101 Male germcell-affecting genes on mouse chromosome 17

R01HD-25498-02 (BCE) SUMMY-LONG, JOAN Y PENNSYLVANIA STATE UNIVERSITY MILTON S. HERSHEY MEDICAL CTR HERSHEY, PA 17033 Lactation--Biology and gene expression of oxytocin neurons

R01HD-25505-02 (HED) HARRISON, MICHAEL R UNIVERSITY OF CALIFORNIA 3RD & PARNASSUS AVE SAN FRANCISCO, CA 94143-0510 Fetal wound healing--The role of the extracellular matrix

R01HD-25510-02 (REN) RAO, CH V UNIVERSITY OF LOUISVILLE SCHOOL OF MEDICINE LOUISVILLE, KY 40292 Action of gonadotropins and eiconsanoids in luteal cells

R01HD-25518-03 (CTY) KONIECZNY, STEPHEN F PURDUE UNIVERSITY LILLY HALL WEST LAFAYETTE, IN 47907 Regulatory elements controlling troponin I expression

R01HD-25522-02 (SSP) JACCARD, JAMES J SUNY AT ALBANY DEPT OF PSYCHOLOGY/CAPR ALBANY, NY 12222 Social psychological adjustment to infertility

R01HD-25524-04 (REB) MOSS, STUART B TEMPLE UNIVERSITY 3400 N BROAD STREET PHILADELPHIA, PA 19140 Mammalian spermatogenesis--histones and DNA reorganization

R29HD-25527-03 (BCE) PANDEY, KAILASH N MEDICAL COLLEGE OF GEORGIA AUGUSTA, GA 30912 Testicular atrial natriuretic factor receptor

R01HD-25528-02 (HED) HENDRICKX, ANDREW G UNIVERSITY OF CALIFORNIA DAVIS, CA 95616 Bioeffects of prenatal ultrasound exposure in Macaques

R01HD-25539-02 (NEUA) YIP, JOSEPH W UNIVERSITY OF PITTSBURGH DEPARTMENT OF PHYSIOLOGY PITTSBURGH, PA 15261 Nuclear magnetic resonance on embryonic development

R01HD-25543-03 (REB) MOBBS, CHARLES V ROCKEFELLER UNIVERSITY

PROJECT NO., ORGANIZATIONAL UNIT., INVESTIGATOR, ADDRESS, TITLE

1230 YORK AVENUE, BOX 275 NEW YORK, NY 10021 Heat-shock-like gene regulation by reproductive hormones

R29HD-25557-03 (CTY) WAY, JEFFREY C RUTGERS, THE STATE UNIVERSITY P.O. BOX 1059, BUSCH CAMPUS PISCATAWAY, NJ 08855-1059 Genetic control of cell type in C. elegans

R01HD-25574-01A1 (SSP) DAVID, HENRY P TRANSNATIONAL FAMILY RES INST 8307 WHITMAN DRIVE BETHESDA, MD 20817 Young adults born of unwanted pregnancies

R01HD-25579-03 (NTN) DIETZ, WILLIAM H, JR NEW ENGLAND MED CTR HOSP, INC 750 WASHINGTON STREET BOSTON, MA 02111 Energy expenditure and the incidence of obesity

R01HD-25580-03 (SSS) HOGAN, BRIGID L VANDERBILT UNIVERSITY SCHOOL OF MEDICINE NASHVILLE, TN 37232 Developmental regulation of matrix-modeling genes

R01HD-25588-02 (BEM) TIENDA, MARTA OGBURN-STOUFFER CENTER/NORC 1155 EAST 60TH STREET CHICAGO, IL 60637 The demography of minority underemployment

R01HD-25592-02 (BEM) WILSON, FRANKLIN D UNIVERSITY OF WISCONSIN 1180 OBSERVATORY DR - #4412 MADISON, WI 53706-1393 Demography of minority underemployment

R01HD-25594-03 (NEUB) KELLER, RAYMOND E UNIVERSITY OF CALIFORNIA LIFE SCI ADDITION/RM 311 BERKELEY, CA 94720 Tissue interactions controlling Xenopus neurulation

R01HD-25614-03 (GEN) SCHEDL, TIM B WASHINGTON UNIV SCH OF MED 660 SO. EUCLID, BX 8232 STOP Analysis of germline sex determination in C. elegans

R01HD-25616-03 (PHY) STEFANI, ENRICO BAYLOR COLLEGE OF MEDICINE ONE BAYLOR PLAZA HOUSTON, TX 77030 Hormonal regulation of ion channels in myometrial cells

R01HD-25620-02 (CBY) BRYANT, SUSAN V UNIVERSITY OF CALIFORNIA IRVINE, CA 92717 Experimental analysis of growth & pattern formation

R01HD-25624-03 (MBY) KRASNOW, MARK A STANFORD UNIVERSITY MED CENTER DEPT OF BIOCHEMISTRY STANFORD, CA 94305 Mechanisms of gene regulation in Drosophila development

R01HD-25629-03 (HED) SMITH, JACKSON B JEFFERSON MEDICAL COLLEGE 1015 WALNUT STREET PHILADELPHIA, PA 19107 First trimester maternal-fetal immunology

R01HD-25630-02 (HED) ONTELL, MARCIA B UNIVERSITY OF PITTSBURGH 3550 TERRACE STREET PITTSBURGH, PA 15261 Mammalian myogenesis subsequent to fetal denervation

R01HD-25641-03 (REB) LIN, TU UNIV OF SOUTH CAROLINA SCH/MED ADMIN BLDG VA CAMPUS COLUMBIA, SC 29208 Modulation of leydig cell function by interleukin-1

R01HD-25669-02 (HUD) BAHRICK, LORRAINE E FLORIDA INTERNATIONAL UNIVERSI UNIVERSITY PARK MIAMI, FL 33199 Intermodal learning in infancy

R01HD-25676-03 (NEUB) LANCE-JONES, CYNTHIA UNIVERSITY OF PITTSBURGH 3550 TERRACE ST PITTSBURGH, PA 15261 Motoneuron axon guidance in the embryonic limb

R01HD-25681-03 (NLS) LANDIS, STORY C CASE WESTERN RESERVE UNIV 2119 ABINGTON ROAD CLEVELAND, OH 44106 Developmental regulation of neuropeptide expression

R01HD-25714-03 (SRCD) LANDESMAN, SHELDON H SUNY-HLTH SCI CTR 450 CLARKSON AVE BROOKLYN, NEW YORK 11203 HIV infection in drug and non-drug using women

R01HD-25718-01A3 (PCB) SHUCARD, DAVID W BUFFALO GENERAL HOSPITAL 100 HIGH STREET BUFFALO, NY 14203 Sex hormones in neurocognitive development

R01HD-25719-03 (END) SHUPNIK, MARGARET A UNIVERSITY OF VIRGINIA BOX 511 - INTERNAL MEDICINE CHARLOTTESVILLE, VA 22908 Estrogen regulation of the rat LH beta gene

R01HD-25742-03 (SRC) TRABASSO, THOMAS R UNIVERSITY OF CHICAGO 5848 SOUTH UNIVERSITY AVENUE CHICAGO, IL 60637 Development of personal and social planning knowledge

R01HD-25748-03 (SSP) WINSHIP, CHRISTOPHER NORTHWESTERN UNIVERSITY CTR/URBAN AFFAIRS & POLICY RES EVANSTON, IL 60208 Demographic influences on family and school transitions

R01HD-25749-03 (SSP) MARE, ROBERT D UNIVERSITY OF WISCONSIN 4412 SOCIAL SCIENCE BUILDING MADISON, WI 53706 Demographic influences on family and school transitions

R01HD-25752-03 (NEUC) PARYSEK, LINDA M UNIVERSITY OF CINCINNATI DEPT/ANATOMY AND CELL BIOLOGY CINCINNATI, OHIO 45267-0521 Intermediate filaments in neural development

R01HD-25754-03 (SRC) ORR, SUEZANNE T JOHNS HOPKINS UNIVERSITY 615 NORTH WOLFE STREET BALTIMORE, MD 21205 Race, psychosocial factors and low birthweight

R01HD-25757-04 (IMS) BALLOW, MARK CHILDREN'S HOSP OF BUFFALO 219 BRYANT STREET BUFFALO, NY 14222 Ontogeny and B-cell development in VLBW premature infant

R01HD-25785-03 (ARR) SAAH, ALFRED J JOHNS HOPKINS SCH HYGIENE/P H 615 NORTH WOLFE STREET BALTIMORE, MD 21205 Natural history of vertically transmitted HIV infection

R01HD-25787-02 (ARR) ZANETTI, MAURIZIO UNIV OF CALIFORNIA, SAN DIEGO 225 DICKINSON STREET SAN DIEGO, CA 92103-1990 Engineered CD4-like antibodies in neonatal HIV infection

R01HD-25792-03 (ARR) KING, MARY C UNIVERSITY OF CALIFORNIA 140 WARREN HALL BERKELEY, CA 94720 Genetic epidemiology of in utero HIV transmission

R01HD-25795-02 (REB) ARMANT, DAVID R WAYNE STATE UNIVERSITY 275 E HANCOCK AVENUE DETROIT, MI 48201 Trophoblast interactions with fibronectin

R44HD-25796-02 (SSS) VON STRANDTMANN, MAXIMILLIAN MEDEA RESEARCH LABORATORIES IN 200 WILSON STREET PORT JEFFERSON, NY 11776 Anticystinotic agents research and development

P50HD-25802-02 (SRC) SHAYWITZ, BENNETT A YALE UNIVERSITY 155 WHITNEY AVENUE NEW HAVEN, CT 06510 Center for the study of learning and attention disorders

P50HD-25806-02 (SRC) DENCKLA, MARTHA B KENNEDY RESEARCH INSTITUTE, IN 707 NORTH BROADWAY BALTIMORE, MD 21205 Neurodevelopmental pathways to learning disabilities

R01HD-25826-03 (CMS) GLUCKSBERG, SAM PRINCETON UNIVERSITY PSYCHOLOGY DEPARTMENT PRINCETON, NJ 08544-1010 Understanding and using non-literal language

PROJECT NO., ORGANIZATIONAL UNIT., INVESTIGATOR, ADDRESS, TITLE

P01HD-25831-01A1 (SRC) CAMPAGNONI, ANTHONY T NEUROPSYCHIATRIC INSTITUTE 760 WESTWOOD PLAZA LOS ANGELES, CA 90024-1759 Regulation of neural gene expression

P01HD-25831-01A1 0001 (SRC) WATSON, JOSEPH B Regulation of neural gene expression Gene expression in the neostriatum

P01HD-25831-01A1 0002 (SRC) MACKLIN, WENDY B Regulation of neural gene expression Regulatory element controlling myelin protein gene expression and assembly

P01HD-25831-01A1 0003 (SRC) CAMPAGNONI, ANTHONY T Regulation of neural gene expression Transcriptional and translational regulation of myelination

P01HD-25831-01A1 0004 (SRC) MERRILL, JEAN E Regulation of neural gene expression Characterization of an oligodendrocyte growth factor

P01HD-25831-01A1 0005 (SRC) GORSKI, ROGER A Regulation of neural gene expression Mechanism of steroid action in the developing rat hypothalamus

R01HD-25839-02 (SSP) RUGGLES, STEVEN UNIVERSITY OF MINNESOTA 267 19TH AVE SOUTH/614 SOC SCI MINNEAPOLIS, MN 55455 Public use sample of the 1880 census

R01HD-25841-02 (BEM) HAMMEL, EUGENE A UNIVERSITY OF CALIFORNIA 2232 PIEDMONT AVENUE BERKELEY, CA 94720 Fertility decline

R01HD-25842-03 (SSP) MANSKI, CHARLES F INSTITUTE FOR RESEARCH/POVERTY 1180 OBSERVATORY DR MADISON, WI 53706 Dynamic choice analysis of schooling behavior

R01HD-25846-03 (REB) GRISWOLD, MICHAEL D WASHINGTON STATE UNIVERSITY PULLMAN, WA 99164-4660 Study of the seminiferous epithelium

R01HD-25849-01A1 (HUD) HERMAN, BARBARA H CHILDREN'S HOSP NAT'L MED CTR 111 MICHIGAN AVENUE, N W WASHINGTON, D C 20010 Role of opioids in autistic mentally retarded children

R01HD-25850-03 (MGN) BERNSTEIN, ALAN SAMUEL LUNENFELD RES INST 600 UNIVERSITY AVE TORONTO, CANADA M5G 1X5 The c-kit proto-oncogene in normal and W mutant mice

R01HD-25857-03 (BPO) EPSTEIN, ALAN N UNIVERSITY OF PENNSYLVANIA LEIDY LABORATORIES PHILADELPHIA, PA 19104-6018 The ontocology of salt intake

R01HD-25858-03 (HUD) BERNINGER, VIRGINIA W UNIVERSITY OF WASHINGTON 322J MILLER DQ-12 SEATTLE, WA 98195 Component processes in writing disabilities

R29HD-25859-03 (SSP) LANDALE, NANCY S PENNSYLVANIA STATE UNIVERSITY 22 BURROWES BUILDING UNIVERSITY PARK, PA 16802 The demography of Puerto Rican household structure

R01HD-25860-03 (BCE) BRESLAU, NEIL A UNIV TEXAS SOUTHWESTERN MED CT 5323 HARRY HINES BOULEVARD DALLAS, TX 75235 Ovarian steroids and calcium homeostasis

R01HD-25863-03 (HED) GEARHART, JOHN D JOHNS HOPKINS UNIV SCH OF MED 725 NORTH WOLFE STREET BALTIMORE, MD 21205 Differential gene expression in early mouse embryos

R01HD-25867-02 (SRC) STOREY, BAYARD T UNIVERSITY OF PENNSYLVANIA 36TH & HAMILTON WALK PHILADELPHIA, PA 19104-6080 Oxidative damage to cryopreserved sperm

R01HD-25869-02 (REB) TULSIANI, DAULAT R VANDERBILT UNIVERSITY/SCH OF M RM D-2303 MCN NASHVILLE, TN 37232-2633 Role of mammalian sperm surface mannosidase

R29HD-25889-03 (CMS) HOLCOMB, PHILLIP J TUFTS UNIVERSITY 490 BOSTON AVENUE MEDFORD, MA 02155 Cross-modality language processing

R01HD-25902-03 (NEUB) JACOBSON, ANTONE G UNIVERSITY OF TEXAS AT AUSTIN DEPARTMENT OF ZOOLOGY AUSTIN, TX 78712 How do tissue boundaries shape the early nervous system?

R01HD-25907-03 (SRC) OVERSTREET, JAMES W THE UNIVERSITY OF CALIFORNIA 275 MRAK HALL DAVIS, CA 95616 Basic and applied research on sperm cryopreservation

R01HD-25908-03 (SRC) HOSKINS, DALE D OREG REGIONAL PRIMATE RES CTR 505 NW 185TH AVENUE BEAVERTON, OR 97006 Regulation and control of human sperm motility

R01HD-25909-02 (PHY) BOYLE, MARY B UNIVERSITY OF IOWA IOWA CITY, IA 52242 Hormonal control of uterine muscle K-channel mRNA

R01HD-25922-03 (REB) STRICKLAND, SIDNEY SUNY AT STONY BROOK HEALTH SCIENCES CENTER STONY BROOK, N Y 11794 Molecular biology of the mouse oocyte

R01HD-25924-01A2 (REB) GOETZ, FREDERICK W, JR UNIVERSITY OF NOTRE DAME NOTRE DAME, IN 46556 Involvement of phosphatidylinositol cycling/protein kinase C in ovulation

R01HD-25926-02 (HED) BIKOFF, ELIZABETH K CITY UNIVERSITY OF NEW YORK ONE GUSTAVE L LEVY PLACE NEW YORK, NY 10029 Manipulating MHC gene expression in ES cells chimeras

R01HD-25929-03 (REN) CAMERON, JUDY L WESTERN PSYCHIATRIC INST/CLIN 3811 O'HARA STREET PITTSBURGH, PA 15213 The etiology of exercise-induced amenorrhea

R01HD-25934-01 (SRC) RINDFUSS, RONALD R UNIVERSITY OF NORTH CAROLINA UNIVERSITY SQ/123 W FRANKLIN CHAPEL HILL, NC 27514-3997 The American teenage study

R01HD-25936-03 (SSP) CHERLIN, ANDREW J JOHNS HOPKINS UNIVERSITY CHARLES & 34TH STS BALTIMORE, MD 21218 The effects of divorce on children

P01HD-25938-02 (SRC) GOETINCK, PAUL F LA JOLLA CANCER RES FDN 10901 NORTH TORREY PINES RD LA JOLLA, CA 92037 Interactions of cell surface proteins in vertebrate development

P01HD-25938-02 0001 (SRC) STALLCUP, WILLIAM B. Interactions of cell surface proteins in vertebrate development Structure, function and expression of NILE glycoprotein

P01HD-25938-02 0002 (SRC) RANSCHT, BARBARA Interactions of cell surface proteins in vertebrate development Structure and role of GP90 in nerve and muscle development

P01HD-25938-02 0003 (SRC) GOETINCK, PAUL F. Interactions of cell surface proteins in vertebrate development Cell surface macromolecules and tissue morphogenesis

P01HD-25938-02 0004 (SRC) MILLAN, JOSE L. Interactions of cell surface proteins in vertebrate development Role of alkaline phosphatase in bone mineralization

P01HD-25938-02 9001 (SRC) GOETINCK, PAUL F. Interactions of cell surface proteins in vertebrate development Core --Molecular biology

P01HD-25938-02 9002 (SRC) GOETINCK, PAUL F. Interactions of cell

surface proteins in vertebrate development Core --Cell behavior analysis
R01HD-25941-02 (BCE) SCHNEYER, ALAN L MASSACHUSETTS GENERAL HOSPITAL FRUIT STREET BOSTON, MA 02114 Role of a gonadal FSH binding competitor in FSH action
R01HD-25949-02 (SRC) CRITSER, JOHN K METHODIST HOSPITAL OF INDIANA 1701 NORTH SENATE BOULEVARD INDIANAPOLIS, IN 46202 Fundamental cryobiology of human spermatozoa
R01HD-25957-03 (SSP) TSUI, AMY O UNIVERSITY OF NORTH CAROLINA CB# 8120, UNIVERSITY SQUARE CHAPEL HILL, NC 27516-3997 A model of pregnancy avoidance
R29HD-25958-03 (HUD) MERRIMAN, WILLIAM E KENT STATE UNIVERSITY KENT, OH 44242-0001 The mutual exclusivity bias in children's word learning
R01HD-25959-02 (EDC) DALING, JANET R FRED HUTCHINSON CANCER RES CTR 1124 COLUMBIA STREET SEATTLE, WA 98104 Ovarian cysts/neoplasms and oral contraceptive use
R01HD-25961-03 (REN) ORLICKY, DAVID J UNIV OF COLORADO HEALTH SCI CT 4200 EAST NINTH AVENUE DENVER, CO 80262 Characterization of the prostaglandin F2alpha receptor
R01HD-25969-01A1 (NEUC) RUSSO, ANDREW F UNIVERSITY OF IOWA IOWA CITY, IA 52242 Glucocorticoid regulation of the calcitonin/CGRP gene
R01HD-25970-02 (BCE) DOUGLASS, JAMES O OREGON HEALTH SCIS UNIVERSITY 3181 SW SAM JACKSON PARK RD PORTLAND, OR 97201-3098 Testicular regulation of epididymal gene expression
R01HD-25973-02 (REN) LLOYD, THOMAS A PA STATE U/HERSHEY MED CTR P.O. BOX 850/DEPT OB GYN HERSHEY, PA 17033 Reproductive development and bone accretion in young women
R01HD-25975-01A1 (HUD) SAGI, ABRAHAM UNIVERSITY OF HAIFA HAIFA, ISRAEL 31999 Israeli infants and daycare--An ecological study
R01HD-25983-01A3 (GMA) MARINO, LUCYNDIA R UNIVERSITY OF MICHIGAN MED CTR C6105 OPB, BOX 0800 ANN ARBOR, MI 48109-0800 Regulation of carbonic anhydrase II gene expression
R01HD-25987-03 (HUD) SPELTZ, MATTHEW L CHILDRENS HOSPITAL & MEDICAL C PO BOX C-5371 SEATTLE, WA 98105 Development of infants with craniofacial anomalies
P01HD-25995-03 (SRC) STODDARD, LAWRENCE T E K SHRIVER CENTER 200 TRAPELO ROAD WALTHAM, MA 02254 Studies of stimulus control in mental retardation
P01HD-25995-03 0001 (SRC) DUBE, WILLIAM V Studies of stimulus control in mental retardation Conditional discrimination and learning set formations
P01HD-25995-03 0002 (SRC) MCILVANE, WILLIAM J Studies of stimulus control in mental retardation Programming conditioned discrimination and production
P01HD-25995-03 0003 (SRC) STROMER, ROBERT Studies of stimulus control in mental retardation Studies of control by complex and compound stimuli
P01HD-25995-03 0004 (SRC) MACKAY, HARRY A Studies of stimulus control in mental retardation Stimulus equivalence in rudimentally reading and spelling
P01HD-25995-03 0005 (SRC) STODDARD, LAWRENCE T Studies of stimulus control in mental retardation Stimulus equivalence and rudimentary monetary and numerical skills
P01HD-25995-03 0006 (SRC) STOPPARD, LAWRENCE T Studies of stimulus control in mental retardation Emergent behavior in severely retarded individuals
P01HD-25995-03 0007 (SRC) STROMER, ROBERT Studies of stimulus control in mental retardation Stimulus control methods and specific reading dysfunction
P01HD-25995-03 9001 (SRC) MCILVANE, WILLIAM J Studies of stimulus control in mental retardation Shared research support
P01HD-25995-03 9002 (SRC) MCILVANE, WILLIAM J Studies of stimulus control in mental retardation Shared research support
R01HD-25997-03 (SSP) EPSTEIN, LEONARD H WESTERN PSYCHIATRIC INSTITUTE 3811 O'HARA STREET PITTSBURGH, PA 15213 Exercise in the long term control of childhood obesity
R01HD-26004-02 (HUD) SUSMAN, ELIZABETH J PENNSYLVANIA STATE UNIVERSITY 314 HEALTH & HUMAN DEVELOPMENT UNIVERSITY PARK, PA 16802 Hormones and emotional development in teenage pregnancy
R01HD-26006-02 (BCE) JOHNSON, HOWARD M UNIVERSITY OF FLORIDA 1059 MC CARTY HALL GAINESVILLE, FL 32611 Structure/function of pregnancy recognition hormone
P01HD-26013-01A2 (SRC) KOLDOVSKY, OTAKAR ARIZONA HEALTH SCIENCES CTR TUCSON, AZ 85724 Role of milk borne hormones for the suckling
P01HD-26013-01A2 0002 (SRC) DAVIS, THOMAS P Role of milk borne hormones for the suckling Metabolism of milk-borne peptides by the suckling
P01HD-26013-01A2 0004 (SRC) MCCUSKEY, ROBERT Role of milk borne hormones for the suckling Role of milk-borne substances in developing liver
P01HD-26013-01A2 0005 (SRC) PHILLIPS, ANTHONY F Role of milk borne hormones for the suckling Nutrition and milk-borne insulin-like growth factor
P01HD-26013-01A2 9001 (SRC) LEBOUTON, ALBERT V Role of milk borne hormones for the suckling Morphological core
P01HD-26013-01A2 9002 (SRC) KOLDOVSKY, OTAKAR Role of milk borne hormones for the suckling Animal core
R01HD-26022-02 (CMS) BELLUGI, URSULA SALK INST PO BOX 85800 SAN DIEGO, CA 92138 Fractionations between language and cognition
R01HD-26024-03 (MBY) HARVEY, RICHARD P ROYAL MELBOURNE HOSPITAL POST OFFICE VICTORIA, AUSTRALIA 3050 The role of Xhox homeobox genes in Xenopus development
R01HD-26026-01A2 (HUD) PARADISE, JACK L CHILDREN'S HOSPITAL 3705 FIFTH AVENUE AT DESOTO ST PITTSBURGH, PA 15213-3417 Child development in relation to early otitis media
R01HD-26031-03 (HUD) BOCK, R DARRELL UNIVERSITY OF CHICAGO 5848 S UNIVERSITY AVENUE CHICAGO, IL 60637 Description and prediction of human growth in stature
R01HD-26032-04 (REB) KLINE, DOUGLAS W KENT STATE UNIVERSITY KENT, OH 44242 Cellular messengers at fertilization in mammalian eggs
R01HD-26047-02 (SRC) MENAGHAN, ELIZABETH G OHIO STATE UNIVERSITY 190 NORTH OVAL MALL COLUMBUS, OH 43210 Effects of parental occupations & child care on child outcome
R01HD-26066-03 (SRC) BROOKS-GUNN, JEANNE EDUCATIONAL TESTING SERVICE ROSEDALE ROAD PRINCETON, NJ 08541 Outcomes of multigenerational child care arrangements
R01HD-26070-02 (SRC) HOGAN, DENNIS P PENNSYLVANIA STATE UNIVERSITY UNIVERSITY PARK, PA 16802 Intergenerational exchanges in families with children
R01HD-26073-03 (NEUC) CULOTTI, JOSEPH G MT SINAI HOSP RESEARCH INST 600 UNIVERSITY AVE, ROOM 840 TORONTO, CANADA M5G 1X5 Longitudinal nerve guidance genes of C. elegans
R01HD-26076-03 (REB) GOULD, KENNETH G EMORY UNIVERSITY ATLANTA, GA 30322 Endocrine control of epididymal function in primates
R29HD-26087-03 (CTY) LINK, CHRISTOPHER D UNIVERSITY OF DENVER S G MUDD BUILDING DENVER, CO 80208 Genetic analysis of bursal morphogenesis in C. elegans
R01HD-26089-02 (SRC) ROSENZWEIG, MARK R UNIVERSITY OF PENNSYLVANIA 3718 LOCUST WALK PHILADELPHIA, PA 19104-6297 Intergenerational financial assistance over adult life-cycles--Parents & children
R01HD-26122-03 (SRC) THOMSON, ELIZABETH J UNIVERSITY OF WISCONSIN 1180 OBSERVATORY DRIVE MADISON, WI 53706-1393 Family structure, socialization and child well-being
R01HD-26144-02 (PTHA) VANNUCCI, ROBERT C PENNSYLVANIA STATE UNIVERSITY P.O. BOX 850 HERSHEY, PA 17033 Hypothermic cardiac arrest and perinatal brain damage
R01HD-26152-03 (SRC) RIEMER, ROBERT K UNIVERSITY OF CALIFORNIA BOX 0550 SAN FRANCISCO, CA 94143-0550 Cellular mechanisms of oxytocin action
R01HD-26164-03 (SRC) STULL, JAMES T UNIVERSITY OF TEXAS 5323 HARRY HINES BLVD DALLAS, TX 75235-9040 Cellular mechanisms regulating myometrial function
R01HD-26167-03 (SRC) MYATT, LESLIE UNIVERSITY OF CINCINNATI 231 BETHESDA AVENUE CINCINNATI, OH 45267-0526 Signal transduction mechanisms and amnion PGE2 synthesis
R01HD-26168-03 (SRC) SOLOFF, MELVYN S MEDICAL COLLEGE OF OHIO CS 10008 TOLEDO, OH 43699 Oxytocin-receptor-mediated prostaglandin release
R01HD-26169-03 (SRC) SCHWARTZ, ALAN L WASHINGTON UNIVERSITY 400 S KINGSHIGHWAY ST LOUIS, MO 63110 Biology of the uterine oxytocin receptor
R01HD-26170-02 (SRC) SPERELAKIS, NICHOLAS UNIVERSITY OF CINCINNATI CINCINNATI, OH 45267-0576 Ion channels of uterine muscle during pregnancy
R01HD-26171-03 (SRC) DENNIS, EDWARD A UNIV OF CALIFORNIA, SAN DIEGO LA JOLLA, CA 92093-0601 Regulation of prostagladin biosynthesis in parturition
R01HD-26173-03 (SRC) RAO, CH V UNIVERSITY OF LOUISVILLE LOUISVILLE, KY 40292 Eicosanoids and pregnant human myometrium
R29HD-26175-03 (NEUB) MESCE, KAREN A UNIVERSITY OF MINNESOTA 1980 FOLWELL AVE/219 HODSON HA ST PAUL, MN 55108 Development of adult-specific behavior in Manduca sexta
R01HD-26180-03 (SRC) BOYLE, MARY B UNIVERSITY OF TEXAS MED BRANCH 300 UNIVERSITY BLVD GALVESTON, TX 77550 Regulation of human myometrial ion channels
R01HD-26182-03 (SRC) BURGHARDT, ROBERT C TEXAS A&M UNIVERSITY COLLEGE OF VETERINARY MEDICINE COLLEGE STATION, TX 77843 Structural and functional studies of uterine smooth muscle cells
R29HD-26186-02 (HUD) HANDEN, BENJAMIN L CHILDREN'S HOSP OF PITTSBURGH 3705 FIFTH AVENUE PITTSBURGH, PA 15213-2583 Mental retardation--Description & treatment of ADHD
R01HD-26200-01A3 (HUD) STROMER, ROBERT L, JR E K SHRIVER CENTER 200 TRAPELO RD WALTHAM, MA 02254 Ordinal relations and transitivity in mental retardation
R01HD-26202-02 (HUD) LUBS, HERBERT A UNIV OF MIAMI SCHOOL OF MEDICI PO BOX 016820 MIAMI, FL 33101 X-linked mental retardation--Linkage and clinical studies
R01HD-26203-02 (HED) NATHANIELSZ, PETER W CORNELL UNIVERSITY ITHACA, NY 14853-6401 Mechanisms of term and preterm labor
R44HD-26205-02 (SSS) VOYTA, JOHN C TROPIX, INC 47 WIGGINS AVENUE BEDFORD, MA 01730 Chemiluminescent detection of luteinizing hormone
R44HD-26209-02A1 (CMS) POTTS, ALBERT M BAHILL INTELLIGENT COMPUTER SY 1622 W MONTENEGRO TUCSON, AZ 85704-1822 Second opinion--An expert system for incipient stuttering
R44HD-26217-02 (REN) FERNANDEZ, SALVADOR M SCIENTIFIC RES ASSOCIATES, INC 50 NYE ROAD, PO BOX 1058 GLASTONBURY, CT 06033 Immunofluorometric assay for reproductive hormones
R01HD-26227-03 (SRC) BUXTON, IAIN L O UNIVERSITY OF NEVADA RENO, NV 89557-0046 The role of adenyl purines in myometrial function
R29HD-26228-04 (HUD) CALLANAN, MAUREEN A UNIVERSITY OF CALIFORNIA CLARK KERR HALL SANTA CRUZ, CA 95064 Parent--child interaction and conceptual development
R55HD-26239-01A2 (ARRF) LEVISON, MATTHEW E MEDICAL COLL OF PENNSYLVANIA 3300 HENRY AVE PHILADELPHIA, PA 19129 Condom use in std and family planning clinic populations
R01HD-26243-01A2 (ARRF) FORREST, KATHERINE A AMERICAN INSTITUTES RESEARCH PO BOX 1113 PALO ALTO, CA 94302 Condom use decision-making by California Hispanic men
R01HD-26245-01A2 (ARRF) WULFERT, EDELGARD UNIVERSITY OF ALBANY STATE UNIVERSITY OF NEW YORK ALBANY, NY 12222 Condom use a cognitive social learning perspective
R01HD-26249-02 (ARR) BIGLAN, ANTHONY OREGON RESEARCH INSTITUTE 1899 WILLAMETTE EUGENE, OR 97401 Social context for adolescent high-risk sexual behavior
R01HD-26250-02 (ARR) FORD, KATHLEEN UNIVERSITY OF MICHIGAN ANN ARBOR, MI 48109-2029 A multiethnic study of condom use
R01HD-26282-02 (SRC) WALDORF, DANIEL O INST FOR SCIENTIFIC ANALYSIS 2235 LOMBARD STREET SAN FRANCISCO, CA 94123 Condom use in a high-risk population
R01HD-26288-02 (SRC) TANFER, KORAY BATTELLE HUMAN AFFAIRS RES CTR 4000 NE 41ST STREET SEATTLE, WA 98105 Condom use by adult men to prevent AIDS
R01HD-26298-02 (REB) GRISWOLD, MICHAEL D WASHINGTON STATE

PROJECT NO., ORGANIZATIONAL UNIT., INVESTIGATOR, ADDRESS, TITLE

UNIVERSITY PULLMAN, WA 99164-4660 Regulation of sertoli cells by germinal cells
R01HD-26321-01A1 (SSP) LICHTER, DANIEL T PENNSYLVANIA STATE UNIVERSITY 22 BURROWES BLDG UNIVERSITY PARK, PA 16802 The demography of local marriage markets
R01HD-26324-01A1 (BIO) WILSON, GOLDER N UNIV OF TEXAS SOUTHWESTERN 5323 HARRY HINES BLVD DALLAS, TX 75235 Ontogeny and phylogeny of human peroxisomal function
R01HD-26330-02 (BEM) HIRSCHMAN, CHARLES UNIVERSITY OF WASHINGTON SEATTLE, WA 98195 A socioeconomic analysis of fertility
R29HD-26339-02 (BCE) EVANS, MARILYN I WEST VIRGINIA UNIVERSITY MORGANTOWN, WV 26506 Regulation of estrogen responsive genes
R29HD-26341-02 (HUD) WOLFSON, MARLA R TEMPLE UNIVERSITY 3420 N BROAD ST PHILADELPHIA, PA 19140 Neonatal brainstem function; chemical /perfusion affairs
R01HD-26349-02 (HUD) BUTTERFIELD, EARL C UNIVERSITY OF WASHINGTON MILLER 322F, DQ-12 SEATTLE, WA 98195 Writing processes & their development
R29HD-26351-03 (CBY) PASPUALE, ELENA B LA JOLLA CANCER RESEARCH FDN. 10901 N. TORREY PINES ROAD LA JOLLA, CA 92032 Developmental biology of protein tyrosine kinases
R01HD-26358-02 (SRC) BRUSILOW, SAUL W JOHNS HOPKINS HOSPITAL 600 NORTH WOLFE ST/CMSC 301 BALTIMORE, MD 21205 Nutritional therapy of urea cycle enzymopathies
R01HD-26360-02 (SRC) BUIST, NEIL R M OREGON HEALTH SCIENCES UNIV PORTLAND, OR 97201 A better organoleptic nutritional product for PKU
R01HD-26371-02 (SRC) MOSER, HUGO W KENNEDY RESEARCH INSTITUTE, IN 707 NORTH BROADWAY BALTIMORE, MD 21205 Glycerol-trierucate therapy of adrenoleukodystrophy
R29HD-26377-02 (EDC) KROHN, MARIJANE A UNIVERSITY OF WASHINGTON SEATTLE, WA 98195 Spontaneous abortion and amniotic fluid infection
R01HD-26384-02 (SSP) ROSENZWEIG, MARK R UNIVERSITY OF PENNSYLVANIA PHILADELPHIA, PA Effects of fertility and mortality on child health
R01HD-26392-02 (HED) ILLSLEY, NICHOLAS P UNIVERSITY OF CALIFORNIA 1462 HSE SAN FRANCISCO, CA 94143-0550 Molecular basis of placental water and solute transport
R01HD-26401-02 (SRC) KAUFMAN, FRANCINE R CHILDRENS HOSP OF LOS ANGELES 4650 SUNSET BLVD LOS ANGELES, CA 90027 The effect of oral uridine in classical galactosemia
R01HD-26402-02 (CBY) DE SIMONE, DOUGLAS W UNIVVERSITY OF VIRGINIA BOX 439, SCHOOL OF MEDICINE CHARLOTTESVILLE, VA 22908 Cell-matrix interactions in amphibian development
R01HD-26421-02 (REN) HANSEN, PETER J UNIVERSITY OF FLORIDA IFAS-0701 GAINESVILLE, FL 32611 Progesterone-induced uterine immunoregulatory proteins
R01HD-26423-02 (REN) MANN, DAVID R MOREHOUSE SCHOOL OF MEDICINE 720 WESTVIEW DRIVE SW ATLANTA, GA 30310-1495 Neonatal testosterone and primate sexual development
R01HD-26429-02 (HED) HUNT, JOAN S UNIV OF KANSAS MED CTR 39TH ST & RAINBOW BLVD KANSAS CITY, KS 66103-8410 Class I MHC genes expressed by human trophoblast cells
R01HD-26454-03 (HED) ERICKSON, ROBERT P UNIVERSITY OF ARIZONA 1501 N. CAMPBELL AVE TUCSON, AZ 85724 Manipulating mammalian development with antisense RNA
R13HD-26455-01A1 (HDMR) SNOW, CATHERINE E HARVARD GRAD SCH OF EDUCATION LARSEN 7 CAMBRIDGE, MA 02138 CHILDES 91--Workshop on automated transcript analysis
R01HD-26456-01A2 (HUD) BORKOWSKI, JOHN G UNIVERSITY OF NOTRE DAME NOTRE DAME, IN 46556 Precursors of retardation in children with teen mothers
R29HD-26458-02 (HED) GOLOS, THADDEUS G UNIVERSITY OF WISCONSIN 1223 CAPITOL CT MADISON, WI 53715-1299 Placental expression of Rhesus gonadotropin alpha gene
R01HD-26460-02 (NEUC) JACOBSON, MARCUS UNIVERSITY OF UTAH 50 NORTH MEDICAL DRIVE SALT LAKE CITY, UT 84132 Neural induction: Analysis using monoclonal antibodies
R01HD-26465-02 (BBCA) WEISS, MICHAEL A HARVARD MEDICAL SCHOOL 240 LONGWOOD AVE BOSTON, MA 02115 Structural NMR studies of the testis determining factor
R01HD-26471-02 (MGN) DOETSCHMAN, THOMAS C UNIVERSITY OF CINCINNATI 231 BETHESDA AVE (ML 524) CINCINNATI, OH 45267-0524 Targeted mutation of TGF-B in es cells
R01HD-26482-02 (NEUC) HARRELSON, ALLAN L UNIVERSITY OF MISSOURI TUCKER HALL COLUMBIA, MO 65211 Molecular studies of fasciclin 2 in neural development
R01HD-26483-02 (BCE) SISK, CHERYL L MICHIGAN STATE UNIVERSITY DEPT PSYCHOLOGY/NEU SCI EAST LANSING, MI 48824 Puberty onset--Behavior, neural and hormonal interactions
R01HD-26485-01A2 (REB) O'BRIEN, DEBORAH A UNIV OF NC AT CHAPEL HILL LAB REPRODUCTIVE BIOLOGY CHAPEL HILL, NC 27599 Spermatogenesis--Roles of mannose 6-phosphate receptors
R01HD-26492-02 (EDC) STEIN, ZENA A COLUMBIA UNIVERSITY 630 WEST 168 STREET NEW YORK, NY 10032 Reproductive outcomes in Dutch famine birth cohort
R01HD-26553-03 (MET) ZEISEL, STEVEN H UNIVERSITY OF NORTH CAROLINA CHAPEL HILL, NC 27599-7400 Choline and formation and secretion of milk
R01HD-26554-02 (HUD) HACK, MAUREEN RAINBOW BABIES & CHILDRENS HOS 2101 ADELBERT ROAD CLEVELAND, OH 44106 School age consequences of 750 gram birthweight
R01HD-26555-01A2 (SSP) PETERS, H ELIZABETH UNIVERSITY OF COLORADO CENTER FOR ECONOMIC ANALYSIS BOULDER, CO 80309-0257 Child custody and monetary transfers in divorce negotiations
R01HD-26556-01A3 (TOX) LOCKARD, JOAN S UNIVERSITY OF WASHINGTON SEATTLE, WA 98195 Polytherapy mechanisms in pregnancy
R01HD-26574-01A1 (HUD) HOLDEN, GEORGE W UNIVERSITY OF TEXAS MEZES HALL 330 AUSTIN, TX 78712 Social cognition and mother's responses to misbehavior
R01HD-26579-02 (HUD) STARKEY, PRENTICE UNIVERSITY OF CALIFORNIA BERKELEY, CA 94720 Temporal segmentation of speech by infants
R01HD-26594-03 (CTY) COOPER, GEOFFREY M DANA-FARBER CANCER INST 44 BINNEY STREET BOSTON, MA 02115 Proto-oncogenes in gametogenesis and early development
R29HD-26595-02 (HUD) NAIGLES, LETITIA G YALE UNIVERSITY 2 HILLHOUSE AVE NEW HAVEN, CT 06520 The use of syntax in verb acquisition
R29HD-26600-02 (HUD) CHAO, CONRAD R COLUMBIA UNIVERSITY 622 W 168TH STREET NEW YORK, NY 10032 Fetal cerebral response to sound stimulation
R01HD-26603-02 (SRC) SHEARER, WILLIAM T BAYLOR COLLEGE OF MEDICINE ONE BAYLOR PLAZA HOUSTON, TX 77030 Improved methods of detecting HIV in high-risk neonates
R29HD-26604-02 (REB) SCHOFF, PATRICK K UNIVERSITY OF WISCONSIN 1675 OBSERVATORY DRIVE MADISON, WI 53706 Characterization of bovine sperm adenylate kinase
R01HD-26606-02 (SRC) PAHWA, SAVITA NORTH SHORE UNIVERSITY HOSPITA 300 COMMUNITY DRIVE MANHASSET, NY 11030 Early diagnosis of HIV infection in neonates and infants
R01HD-26613-02 (SRC) BORKOWSKY, WILLIAM NEW YORK UNIV MEDICAL CTR 550 FIRST AVENUE NEW YORK, NY 10016 Improved methods for early diagnosis of HIV in neonates
R01HD-26619-02 (SRC) HUTTO, SUSAN C UNIVERSITY OF MIAMI SCH OF MED P0 BOX 016960 MIAMI, FL 33101 Early diagnosis of perinatal HIV-1 infection
R01HD-26621-02 (SRC) BRYSON, YVONNE J UNIVERSITY OF CALIFORNIA 10833 LECONTE AVENUE LOS ANGELES, CA 90024-1752 Methods for early HIV infection diagnosis
R01HD-26630-02 (CMS) WOLFF, PETER H CHILDREN'S HOSPITAL 300 LONGWOOD AVENUE BOSTON, MA 02115 Impaired temporal resolution in familial dyslexia
R01HD-26631-03 (SRC) TANFER, KORAY BATTELLE HUMAN AFFAIRS RES CTR 4000 NE 41ST STREET SEATTLE, WA 98105 STDS and fertility-related behavior--A follow-up study
R01HD-26634-02 (ARR) NAHMIAS, ANDRE J EMORY UNIVERSITY 69 BUTLER ST, SE ATLANTA, GA 30303 Perinatal HIV--Clonal lymphoid cell analyses and diagnosis
R01HD-26635-03 (REN) YING, SHAO-YAO UNIV OF SOUTHERN CALIFORNIA 1333 SAN PABLO STREET LOS ANGELES, CA 90033 Follistatin, a novel protein inhibits FSH release
R01HD-26636-01A2 (HUD) KULIN, HOWARD E PENNSYLVANIA STATE UNIVERSITY PO BOX 850 HERSHEY, PA 17033 Sex hormone replacement therapy & adolescent behavior
R01HD-26637-02 (SRC) STEIN, LEONARD D UNIVERSITY OF NORTH CAROLINA 509 BURNETT-WOMACK BLDG, CB 72 CHAPEL HILL, NC 27599 Early diagnosis of HIV-1 infection in neonates and infants
R01HD-26638-02 (REB) HOVERSLAND, ROGER C INDIANA UNIVERSITY 2101 COLISEUM BLVD, EAST FORT WAYNE, IN 46805 Immunosuppression at time of embryo implantation
R29HD-26639-03 (REB) ENDERS, GEORGE C UNIVERSITY OF KANSAS MED CTR 39TH AND RAINBOW BOULEVARD KANSAS CITY, KANSAS 66103-8410 Spermatogenesis--A study of dynamic adhesion events
R29HD-26640-03 (BCE) EYSTER, KATHLEEN M UNIVERSITY OF SOUTH DAKOTA 414 EAST CLARK VERMILLION, SD 57069 Protein kinase C of the rhesus monkey corpus luteum
R01HD-26651-03 (BIO) KRAUS, JAN P UNIV OF COLORADO HLTH SCI CTR 4200 EAST NINTH AVENUE DENVER, CO 80262 Expression of cystathionine synthase and human disease
R01HD-26652-03 (OBM) OFFENBACHER, STEVEN THE UNIVERSITY OF NORTH CAROLI SCHOOL OF DENTISTRY CHAPEL HILL, NC 27599-7450 Effects of oral and enteric endotoxins on pregnancy
R43HD-26690-01A1 (SSS) STOTTLER, RICHARD H STOTTLER HENKE ASSOCIATED 2205 HASTINGS DR. #38 BELMONT, CA 94002 Artificial intelligence aids for communication
R01HD-26691-03 (ARR) KOTLOFF, KAREN L UNIVERSITY OF MARYLAND 10 SOUTH PINE STREET, MSTF BLD BALTIMORE, MD 21201 GI dysfunction in children born to HIV-infected women
R01HD-26706-02 (SSP) CASTERLINE, JOHN B BROWN UNIVERSTIY BOX 1916 PROVIDENCE, RI 02912 The diffusion of fertility control
R01HD-26707-02 (ARR) HENDERSON, GEORGE I UNIVERSITY OF TEXAS HLTH SCI C 7703 FLOYD CURL DR SAN ANTONIO, TX 78284-7878 Placental transfer/cellular effects/drugs used in AIDS
R01HD-26715-02 (NTN) CANFIELD, LOUISE M UNIVERSITY OF ARIZONA BIO SCIENCES WEST TUCSON, AZ 85721 Beta-carotene in human milk--Quantitation and transport
R01HD-26722-02 (MGN) MAGNUSON, TERRY R CASE WESTERN RESERVE UNIV 2119 ABINGTON ROAD CLEVELAND, OH 44106 Mutagenesis of genes expressed during mouse development
P01HD-26732-01A1 (HDPR) PEDERSEN, ROGER A UNIVERSITY OF CALIFORNIA BOX 0750 SAN FRANCISCO, CA 94143-0750 Developmental biology of the implanting mammalian embryo
P01HD-26732-01A1 0001 (HDPR) DAMSKY, CAROLINE H Developmental biology of the implanting mammalian embryo Extracellular matrix receptors in implantation development
P01HD-26732-01A1 0002 (HDPR) FISHER, SUSAN J Developmental biology of the implanting mammalian embryo Mechanisms of trophoblast invasion during placentation
P01HD-26732-01A1 0003 (HDPR) WERB, ZENA Developmental biology of the implanting mammalian embryo Role of growth factors in peri-implantation development
P01HD-26732-01A1 0005 (HDPR) EPSTEIN, CHARLES J Developmental biology of the implanting mammalian embryo Genetic control of peri-implantation development
P01HD-26732-01A1 0006 (HDPR) PEDERSEN, ROGER A Developmental biology of the implanting mammalian embryo Cellular and molecular analysis of imprinting
P01HD-26732-01A1 9001 (HDPR) CALARCO, PATRICIA Developmental biology of the implanting mammalian embryo Core--Morphology/in situ localiaztion
P01HD-26732-01A1 9002 (HDPR) EPSTEIN, CHARLES Developmental biology of the implanting mammalian embryo Core--Transgenesis/cell culture
R01HD-26733-02 (REB) HUTSON, JAMES C TEXAS TECH UNIV HTH SCIS CTR LUBBOCK, TX 79430 Development and regulation of testicular macrophages
R01HD-26746-02 (EDC) COREY, LINDA A VIRGINIA COMMONWEATLH UNIV

PROJECT NO., ORGANIZATIONAL UNIT., INVESTIGATOR, ADDRESS, TITLE

PO BOX 33/MCV STATION RICHMOND, VA 23298-0033 Genetic effects on pregnancy complications and outcome
R01HD-26758-01A1 (PBC) UNDERHILL, CHARLES B GEORGETOWN UNIVERSITY 3900 RESERVOIR RD, NW WASHINGTON, DC 20007 Role of hyaluronate receptors in embryonic development
R01HD-26762-01A1 (HED) DAVIS, DUANE L KANSAS STATE UNIVERSITY MANHATTEN, KS 66506 Embryo-uterine interactions during early pregnancy
R01HD-26765-02 (HUD) RAYNER, KEITH UNIVERSITY OF MASSACHUSETTS AMHERST, MA 01003 Reading & scene perception--Foveal and parafoveal codes
R01HD-26766-01A1 (HUD) BRETHERTON, INGE WAISMAN CENTER ON MENTAL 1500 HIGHLAND AVENUE MADISON, WI 53705-2280 Attachment organization in single parent families
R01HD-26768-01A2 (HUD) FOX, NATHAN A UNIVERSITY OF MARYLAND COLLEGE PARK, MD 20742 Infant cognitive and EEG development--Basic processes
R01HD-26773-02 (HUD) KOPP, CLAIRE B UNIVERSITY OF CALIFORNIA LOS ANGELES, CA 90024-1563 Self-regulation--Developmentally delayed young children
R01HD-26777-02 (NTN) KEEN, CARL L UNIVERSITY OF CALIFORNIA DAVIS, CA 95616 Copper nutrition and development
R01HD-26778-01A2 (BCE) HOYER, PATRICIA B UNIVERSITY OF ARIZONA ARIZONA HEALTH SCIENCES CENTER TUCSON, AZ 85724 Functional regulation in ovine large luteal cells
R01HD-26810-01A1 (NEUC) CHIU, ARLENE Y BECKMAN RES INST CITY OF HOPE 1450 E DUARTE RD DUARTE, CA 91010 Biochemical differentiation of somatic motor neurons
R01HD-26813-02 (EDC) FRIGOLETTO, FREDRIC D BRIGHAM AND WOMEN'S HOSPITAL 75 FRANCIS STREET BOSTON, MA 02115 Cesarean section reduction in primigravid patients
R01HD-26823-01A1 (BPO) BRONSON, FRANKLIN H UNIVERSITY OF TEXAS AUSTIN, TX 78712 Alternative reproductive strategies in Microtus
R01HD-26833-01A1 (END) MCDONALD, JOHN K EMORY UNIVERSITY SCHOOL OF MEDICINE ATLANTA, GA 30322 NPY biosynthesis and secretion in the hypothalamus
R01HD-26841-01A1 (IMS) STAERZ, UWE D NATIONAL JEWISH CTR/IMMUNOLOGY 1400 JACKSON ST K405 DENVER, CO 80206 Accessory cells for immature T lymphocytes
R01HD-26842-01A1 (MBY) TABIN, CLIFFORD J HARVARD MEDICAL SCHOOL 25 SHATTUCK ST BOSTON, MA 02115 Homeobox genes and the molecular control of limb pattern
R29HD-26854-02 (CBY) TALMAGE, DAVID A COLUMBIA UNIVERSITY 630 W 168TH STREET NEW YORK, NY 10032 Vitamin A, signal transduction and cell differentiation
R15HD-26867-01A1 (GEN) IRELAND, ROBERT C CONNECTICUT COLLEGE 270 MOHEGAN AVE BOX 5408 NEW LONDON, CT 06320 Characterization of a putative mouse embryonic GPDH gene
R01HD-26871-01A1 (NTN) UNDERWOOD, LOUIS E UNIVERSITY OF NORTH CAROLINA CB# 7220 509 BURNETT-WOMACK BL CHAPEL HILL, NC 27599-7220 Nutritional control of IGF-I and growth
R01HD-26872-01A1 (SSS) ZIEGLER, EKHARD E UNIVERSITY OF IOWA COLLEGE OF MEDICINE IOWA CITY, IA 52242 Zinc absorption in infancy--stable isotope studies
R15HD-26887-01A1 (REN) CAMPBELL, PAUL S UNIVERSITY OF ALABAMA BOX 311 HUNTSVILLE, AL 35899 Estrogen regulation of EGF secretion
R01HD-26888-02 (BCE) CAMERON, JUDY L WESTERN PSYCH INST & CLINIC 3811 O'HARA ST PITTSBURGH, PA 15213 Control of the GNRH pulse generator by nutrient intake
R01HD-26892-03 (HUD) MERVIS, CAROLYN B EMORY UNIVERSITY PSYCHOLOGY DEPT ATLANTA, GA 30322 Children with down syndrome--Early communicative development
R55HD-26893-01A1 (REN) WILD, ROBERT A UNIV OF OKLAHOMA HLTH SCIS CTR 920 STANTON L YOUNG BLVD OKLAHOMA CITY, OK 73190 Gnrha + estraderm: effect of lipoprotein lipids in pcos
R01HD-26899-02 (SSP) JONES, ROBERT E CENTER FOR DEMOGRAPHY & ECOLOG 1180 OBSERVATORY DRIVE MADISON, WI 53706-1393 Nutrition--On postpartum amenorrhea and waiting-time to conception
R01HD-26911-02 (HUD) MARVIN, ROBERT S KLUGE CHILDRENS REHAB CENTER 2270 IVY ROAD CHARLOTTESVILLE, VA 22901 Attachment in young children with motor impairments
P01HD-26927-01A1 (SRC) SPRADLIN, JOSEPH E UNIVERSITY OF KANSAS LAWRENCE, KS 66045 Severe aberrant behavior among persons with retardation
P01HD-26927-01A1 0001 (SRC) SAUNDERS, RICHARD Severe aberrant behavior among persons with retardation Factors in daily routine effect on behavior in mental retardation
P01HD-26927-01A1 0002 (SRC) BAER, DONALD M Severe aberrant behavior among persons with retardation Tolerance training for severely self-injurious aggressive persons
P01HD-26927-01A1 0003 (SRC) RAST, JAMES Severe aberrant behavior among persons with retardation Neuroleptic & antiseizure drug effect on behavior in mental retardation
P01HD-26927-01A1 0004 (SRC) TESSEL, RICHARD Severe aberrant behavior among persons with retardation Aberrant behavior development--Genetic /prenatal factors & susceptibility
P01HD-26927-01A1 9001 (SRC) SAUNDERS, RICHARD Severe aberrant behavior among persons with retardation Core--Computer
R15HD-26929-01A1 (REN) DIGGINS, MAUREEN R AUGUSTANA COLLEGE 29TH & SUMMIT SIOUX FALLS, SD 57197 Obesity and infertility in the lethal yellow mouse
R01HD-26939-01A1 (NTN) COOPER, DAN M HARBOR-UCLA MED CTR 1124 WEST CARSON STREET TORRANCE, CA 90502-2064 Mechanisms of exercise modulation of human growth
R15HD-26942-01A1 (NEUB) CONWAY, KEVIN M AMERICAN UNIVERSITY 4400 MASSACHUSETTS AVENUE WASHINGTON, DC 20016 Embryonic origins of neurosecretory cells
R01HD-26945-01A1 (HED) NELSON, RALPH A CARLE FOUNDATION 611 WEST PARK STREET URBANA, IL 61801 Infant heat loss determined by infrared thermography
R01HD-26956-01A1 (NEUB) HAMMERSCHLAG, RICHARD BECKMAN RESEARCH INSTITUTE 1450 EAST DUARTE ROAD DUARTE, CA 91010 Thyroid hormone regulation of neuronal development

PROJECT NO., ORGANIZATIONAL UNIT., INVESTIGATOR, ADDRESS, TITLE

R01HD-26962-03 (HED) SAMOLLOW, PAUL B SOUTHWEST FDN FOR BIOMED RES P O BOX 28147 SAN ANTONIO, TX 78228-0147 X-chromosome inactivation in opossum development
R01HD-26971-02 (EDC) SIERVOGEL, ROGER M WRIGHT STATE UNIVERSTITY 1005 XENIA AVENUE YELLOW SPRINGS, OH 45387 The genetic epidemiology of patterns of human growth
U10HD-26975-02 (SRC) DECHERNEY, ALAN H YALE UNIVERSITY 333 CEDAR STREET PO BOX 3333 NEW HAVEN, CT 06510 Cooperative multicenter reproductive medicine network
P30HD-26979-02 (HDMR) BATSHAW, MARK L CHILDREN'S HOSPITAL 34TH AND CIVIC CENTER BLVD PHILADELPHIA, PA 19104 NICHD mental retardation research center core grant
P30HD-26979-02 9001 (HDMR) ZASLOFF, MICHAEL NICHD mental retardation research center core grant Core--Genetics
P30HD-26979-02 9002 (HDMR) ZIMMERMAN, ROBERT NICHD mental retardation research center core grant Core--Neuroimaging
P30HD-26979-02 9003 (HDMR) RORKE, LUCY NICHD mental retardation research center core grant Core--Neuropathology
P30HD-26979-02 9004 (HDMR) PLEASURE, DAVID NICHD mental retardation research center core grant Core--Neuroscience
P30HD-26979-02 9005 (HDMR) PARRISH, JOHN NICHD mental retardation research center core grant Core--Behavior
P30HD-26979-02 9006 (HDMR) STOLLEY, PAUL NICHD mental retardation research center core grant Core--Epidemiology and biostatistics
U10HD-26981-02 (SRC) CHANG, R JEFFREY UNIVERSITY OF CALIFORNIA SCH/M DIVISION OF REPRODUCTIVE BIOLO DAVIS, CA 95616 Cooperative multicenter reproductive medicine network
R01HD-27003-01A1 (HUD) FIELD, TIFFANY M UNIVERSITY OF MIAMI PO BOX 016820 MIAMI, FL 33101 Prematurity and maternal depression effects on infants
U10HD-27006-02 (SRC) CANFIELD, ROBERT E COLUMBIA UNIVERSITY 630 WEST 168TH STREET NEW YORK, NY 10032 Data coordinating center reproductive medicine network
U10HD-27009-02 (SRC) GUZICK, DAVID S MAGEE-WOMENS HOSPITAL 300 HALKET STREET PITTSBRUGH, PA 15213 Cooperative multicenter reproductive medicine network
U10HD-27011-02 (SRC) CARSON, SANDRA A 956 COURT AVE MEMPHIS, TN 38163 Cooperative multicenter RMU--Randomized treatment of recurrent pregnancy loss
R01HD-27020-02 (SRC) SIEGEL, DAVID 74 NEW MONTGOMERY ST SAN FRANCISCO, CA 94105 AIDS knowledge and beliefs in multiethnic school children
R01HD-27035-02 (SRC) HENKER, BARBARA A UNIVERSITY OF CALIFORNIA 405 HILGARD AVENUE LOS ANGELES, CA 90024 Children and health--Concept, concerns, and communication
U10HD-27040-03 (SRC) VANDELL, DEBORAH L WISCONSIN CENTER FOR ED RESEAR 1025 W JOHNSON ST MADISON, WI 53706 Infant child care and family processes
R01HD-27042-03 (HUD) MERVIS, CAROLYN B EMORY UNIVERSITY PSYCHOLOGY DEPT ATLANTA, GA 30322 Category development: the acquisition of expertise
R15HD-27043-01A1 (HUD) TURNER, LISA A UNIVERSITY OF ORLEANS NEW ORLEANS, LA 70148 Memory strategy use in mentally retarded students
R01HD-27044-01A1 (NLS) JOHN, A MEREDITH PRINCETON UNIVERSITY 21 PROSPECT AVE PRINCETON, NJ 08544-2091 Demographic dynamics of childhood diseases and mortality
U10HD-27049-02 (SRC) MASTROIANNI, LUIGI JR HOSPITAL OF THE UNIV OF PA 3400 SPRUCE STREET PHILADELPHIA, PA 19104 Evaluation of treatments of male factor infertility
R01HD-27056-02 (GEN) DOE, CHRIS Q UNIVERSITY OF ILLINOIS 505 S GOODWIN AVENUE URBANA, IL 61801 Genetic and molecular studies of neurogenesis
R01HD-27061-02 (NTN) MOCK, DONALD M UNIVERSITY OF IOWA HOSPITALS JESSUP HALL, ROOM 4 IOWA CITY, IA 52242 The biotin requirements of infants
R29HD-27063-02 (EDC) GUO, SHUMEI WRIGHT STATE UNIV SCHOOL OF ME 1005 XENIA AVE YELLOW SPRINGS, OH 45387-1695 Statistical analysis of body composition, risk factors
R01HD-27068-02 (NTN) OBERKOTTER, LINDA V FLORIDA INST OF TECHNOLOGY 150 WEST UNIVERSITY BLVD MELBOURNE, FL 32901-6988 Maternal iodine deficiency, lactation and infant growth
R01HD-27107-03 (ARR) KOZBOR, DANUTA B THOMAS JEFFERSON UNIVERSITY 233 LOCUST STREET PHILADELPHIA, PA 19107 Cellular activation in primary perinatal HIV infection
R01HD-27110-02 (ARR) UNADKAT, JASHVANT D UNIVERSITY OF WASHINGTON BG-20, 303 BAGLEY HALL SEATTLE, WA 98195 Fetal toxicity of zidovudine
R01HD-27114-02 (ARR) STANTON, BONITA F UNIVERSITY OF MARYLAND 700 W LOMBARD STREET BALTIMORE, MD 21201 Decision making by youths regarding AIDS risk behaviors
R29HD-27116-02 (NEUC) FEDEROFF, HOWARD J ALBERT EINSTEIN COLLEGE OF MED 1300 MORRIS PARK AVE BRONX, NY 10461 A molecular approach to regulation of synapse formation
R01HD-27119-03 (SRC) SONENSTEIN, FREYA L URBAN INSTITUTE 2100 M ST, NW WASHINGTON, DC 20037 1990 follow-up survey of young men
R01HD-27120-03 (HUD) CARON, ALBERT J BOSTON UNIVERSITY 64 CUMMINGTON STREET BOSTON, MA 02215 Development of person-object distinctions in infancy
R01HD-27122-01A1 (REB) JONES, RICHARD E UNIVERSITY OF COLORADO BOULDER, CO 80309-0334 Control of ovarian alternation--Brain studies
R13HD-27123-02 (HDMR) COHEN, MAIMON M AMERICAN SOCIETY/HUMAN GENETIC 9650 ROCKVILLE PIKE BETHESDA, MD 20814 8th international congress of human genetics
R01HD-27125-01A1 (HED) FISHER, RACHEL A MICHIGAN STATE UNIVERSITY EAST LANSING, MI 48824-1317 A prospective study of prenatal Down syndrome screening
R01HD-27139-02 (SSP) BECKER, STAN R JOHNS HOPKINS UNIVERSITY 615 NORTH WOLFE STREET BALTIMORE, MD 21205 Modeling cause specific mortality in infants and toddler
R01HD-27143-01A1 (REB) MALLEY, ARTHUR OREGON REGIONAL PRIM RES CTR 505 NW 185TH AVENUE BEAVERTON, OR 97006 Studies on the immunological basis of fetal tolerance
R01HD-27150-03 (SSP) MICHAEL, ROBERT T UNIVERSITY OF CHICAGO

PROJECT NO., ORGANIZATIONAL UNIT., INVESTIGATOR, ADDRESS, TITLE

1155 E 60TH ST CHICAGO, IL 60637 Children, families and cultures--A US-UK comparison
R01HD-27157-01A1 (HUD) FIELD, TIFFANY M UNIVERSITY OF MIAMI PO BOX 016820 MIAMI, FL 33101 Biological correlates of growth in massaged preterm infants
R01HD-27167-01A1 (BCE) DYER, CHERYL A RESEARCH INST OF SCRIPPS CLINI 10666 NORTH TORREY PINES ROAD LA JOLLA, CA 92037 Cell biology of ovarian apolipoprotein E
R01HD-27171-02 (HUD) TANGNEY, JUNE P GEORGE MASON UNIVERSITY 4400 UNIVERSITY DR FAIRFAX, VA 22030 Constructive anger, shame & empathy--A lifespan study
R01HD-27176-01 (HUD) MORRISON, FREDERICK J UNIVERSITY OF NORTH CAROLINA GREENSBORO, NC 27412-5001 Schooling and cognitive development--A natural experiment
R01HD-27183-02 (CTY) EVANS, RONALD M THE SALK INSTITUTE P O BOX 85800 SAN DIEGO, CA 92186-5800 Spatial regulation of developmental gene expression
R01HD-27184-01 (HUD) BERKSON, GERSHON B UNIVERSITY OF ILLINOIS PO BOX 4348 CHICAGO, IL 60680 Control of abnormal stereotyped behaviors
R01HD-27194-02 (BCE) HIRSHFIELD, ANNE N UNIVERSITY OF MARYLAND 655 WEST BALTIMORE STREET BALTIMORE, MD 21201 Early aspects of follicular development
R01HD-27198-02 (SRC) GOLDFARB, MITCHELL P COLUMBIA UNIVERSITY 630 WEST 168TH STREET NEW YORK, NY 10032 Genetic analysis of FGF-5 proto-oncogene function
R01HD-27200-02 (SRC) MARTIN, MARK E UNIVERSITY OF MISSOURI M-121 COLUMBIA, MO 65211 Role of enhancer factor PEA3 in mammalian development
R01HD-27202-02 (SRC) PEARSON-WHITE, SONIA H UNIVERSITY OF VIRGINIA GILMER HALL, ROOM 042 CHARLOTTESVILLE, VA 22901 The ski proto-oncogene family in early development
R01HD-27206-01A1 (CMS) TANENHAUS, MICHAEL K UNIVERSITY OF ROCHESTER RIVER STATION ROCHESTER, NY 14627 Coordinating information in sentence processing
R01HD-27211-02 (PBC) KRAMER, JAMES M UNIVERSITY OF ILLINOIS P.O. BOX 4348, MAIL CODE 066 CHICAGO, IL 60680 Molecular genetics of basement membranes in C elegans
R01HD-27215-02 (REB) BRAUN, ROBERT E UNIVERSITY OF WASHINGTON SEATTLE, WA 98195 Translational regulation of the mouse protamine 1 gene
R01HD-27233-01A1 (HED) WILKINSON, MILES F OREGON HEALTH SCIENCES UNIV 3181 S W SAM JACKSON PARK RD PORTLAND, OR 97201-3098 Pem-a novel gene expressed in embryos and tumor cells
R29HD-27242-02 (IMB) MOORE, MARK W UNIVERSITY SOUTHERN CALIFORNIA 1441 EASTLAKE AVE/PO BOX 33800 LOS ANGELES, CA 90033-0800 Developmental immunology using I-A beta mutation in ES cells
R55HD-27244-01A1 (REB) CARDULLO, RICHARD A WORCESTER FDN FOR EXP BIOLOGY 222 MAPLE AVENUE SHREWSBURY, MA 01545 Receptor dynamics during fertilization in the mouse
R01HD-27246-02 (CTY) PERRY, WILLIAM M UNIV OF TEXAS/MD ANDERSON CENT 1515 HOLCOMBE BLVD HOUSTON, TX 77030 Function of myogenic factors in early frog development
R01HD-27248-02 (SSP) MOFFITT, ROBERT A BROWN UNIVERSITY PO BOX B PROVIDENCE, RI 02912 Testing theories of female headship
R29HD-27252-02 (GMA) MC HUGH, KIRK M JEFFERSON MEDICAL COLLEGE 1020 LOCUST STREET PHILADELPHIA, PA 19107 Developmental signaling of smooth muscle differentiation
R29HD-27258-02 (HED) MOE, AARON J WASHINGTON UNIVERSITY 400 S KINGSHIGHWAY BLVD ST LOUIS, MO 63110 Glutamate metabolism in cultured human trophoblast
R01HD-27262-02 (CBY) KIMELMAN, DAVID UNIVERSITY OF WASHINGTON SEATTLE, WA 98195 Molecular regulation of early Xenopus development
R01HD-27274-02 (ARR) SIGELMAN, CAROL K UNIVERSITY OF ARIZONA TUCSON, AZ 85721 Development of AIDS understanding and attitudes
R01HD-27275-01A1 (REN) TEUSCHER, CORY BRIGHAM YOUNG UNIVERSITY PROVO, UT 84602 Infertility and ovarian autoimmunity
R01HD-27276-01A1 (HUD) ROBERTS, KENNETH R BOYS TOWN NATIONAL INSTITUTE 555 N 30TH ST OMAHA, NE 68131 Language-cognition interactions in early word learning
R01HD-27289-02 (NTN) GOLDENBERG, ROBERT L UNIVERSITY OF ALABAMA UAB STATION BIRMINGHAM, AL 35294 Randomized trial of zinc supplementation in pregnancy
R01HD-27295-02 (SRC) PAPAIOANNOU, VIRGINIA E TUFTS UNIVERSITY 136 HARRISON AVE BOSTON, MA 02111 Expression/function of C fos and C jun in development
R01HD-27299-02 (CBY) MC CLAY, DAVID R, JR DUKE UNIVERSITY DURHAM, NC 27706 Teratocarcinoma cells--Cell adhesion & differentiation
R01HD-27303-01 (SSP) SMITH, JAMES P RAND CORPORATION PO BOX 2138, 1700 MAIN ST SANTA MONICA, CA 90406-2138 Black-white differences in income and employment
R29HD-27306-02 (REB) CHAREST, NANCY J YALE UNIVERSITY 333 CEDAR STREET NEW HAVEN, CT 06510 Regulation of gene expression in the epididymis
R01HD-27328-03 (CBY) RENDER, JOANN UNIVERSITY OF ILLINOIS 505 S GOODWIN AVE URBANA, IL 61801 Lineage and cell fate specification in early embryos
R01HD-27331-02 (BPO) PHILIPP, DAVID P UNIVERSITY OF ILLINOIS 607 E PEABODY DR CHAMPAIGN, IL 61820 Hormonal control of alternative reproductive strategies
R01HD-27334-01 (BPO) BLOCH, GEORGE J BRIGHAM YOUNG UNIVERSITY 1001 SWKT PROVO, UT 84602 Neuropeptides, sex dimorphism and reproductive behavior
R01HD-27336-02 (HUD) BAUMEISTER, ALFRED A VANDERBILT UNIVERSITY BOX 40/PEABODY COLLEGE NASHVILLE, TN 37203 Induction of relational learning in MR children
R01HD-27344-01A1 (HUD) MC CARTON, CECELIA M ALBERT EINSTEIN COLL OF MED 1410 PELHAM PARKWAY SOUTH BRONX, NY 10461 Early intervention for LBW infants ages 6 to 8
R29HD-27347-02 (EDC) ABRAMS, BARBARA F UNIVERSITY OF CALIFORNIA 419 WARREN HALL BERKELEY, CA 94720 Maternal weight gain and fetal outcome

PROJECT NO., ORGANIZATIONAL UNIT., INVESTIGATOR, ADDRESS, TITLE

R01HD-27351-01A1 (HUD) COHEN, SARALE E UNIVERSITY OF CALIFORNIA 1000 VETERAN AVENUE LOS ANGELES, CA 90024-1797 Biosocial development-- Preterm birth to 18 years
R29HD-27354-02 (BCE) ASEM, ELIKPLIMI K PURDUE UNIVERSITY WEST LAFAYETTE, IN 47907 Granulosa cell-control of Na+/H+ antiport and K+ channel
R01HD-27361-02 (BEM) PEBLEY, ANNE R PRINCETON UNIVERSITY 21 PROSPECT AVENUE PRINCETON, NJ 08544-2091 Social determinants of child mortality
R43HD-27367-01A1 (SSS) VARMA, MADHU ADEZA BIOMEDICAL CORPORATION 1240 ELKO DR SUNNYVALE, CA 94089 Early predictive immunoassay for preeclampsia
R43HD-27380-01A1 (SSS) NUWAYSER, ELIE S BIOTEK, INC 21-C OLYMPIA AVENUE WOBURN, MA 01801 An estrogen-progestin patch for estrogen replacement
R01HD-27383-03 (LCR) SCARR, SANDRA W UNIVERSITY OF VIRGINIA 102 GILMER HALL CHARLOTTESVILLE, VA 22903-2477 The socioemotional effects of center-based child care
R43HD-27387-01A1 (REN) NUWAYSER, ELIE S BIOTEK, INC 21-C OLYMPIA AVENUE WOBURN, MA 01801 Development and testing of new spermicide suppository
R01HD-27392-02 (HED) LAU, YUN-FAI C UNIVERSITY OF CALIFORNIA PARNASSUS AVE VAMC-111C5 SAN FRANCISCO, CA 94143 Functions of zinc finger genes on sex chromosomes
R29HD-27393-02 (HED) HUNT, PATRICIA A WINSHIP CANCER CENTER 1327 CLIFTON RD, NE ATLANTA, GA 30322 Development in murine sex chromosome abnormalities
R43HD-27411-01 (ARR) GEORGE, CINDY L ACADEMIC SOFTWARE, INC 331 WEST SECOND STREET LEXINGTON, KY 40507 The control interface assessment system
R01HD-27433-01 (SRC) PHILLIPS, DAVID M THE POPULATION COUNCIL 1230 YORK AVE NEW YORK, NY 10021 Transplacental transmission of HIV--An in vitro model
R01HD-27438-01 (SRC) UNADKAT, JASHVANT D UNIVERSITY OF WASHINGTON BG-20, 303 BAGLEY HALL SEATTLE, WA 98195 Transplacental pharmacokinetics of anti-HIV drugs
R01HD-27444-01 (SRC) GOUSTIN, ANTON S WAYNE STATE UNIVERSITY 540 E CANFIELD-1201 SCOTT HALL DETROIT, MI 48201 HIV infection of developing placenta
R03HD-27446-02 (SRC) CHAMBERS, SETSUKO K YALE UNIVERSITY 333 CEDAR STREET NEW HAVEN, CT 06510 CSF-1 and drug resistance in reproductive cancers
R03HD-27448-02 (SRC) NARKEWICZ, MICHAEL R UNIVERSITY OF COLORADO 4200 EAST 9TH AVENUE DENVER, CO 80262 Studies of lipogenesis in TNP induced hepatic steatosis
R03HD-27449-01A1 (HDMC) MUSCI, THOMAS J UNIVERSITY OF CALIFORNIA SAN FRANCISCO, CA 94143 Fibroblast growth factor receptor in early development
R01HD-27452-01A1 (HED) FABER, J JOB OREGON HEALTH SCIENCES UNIV 3181 S W SAM JACKSON PARK ROAD PORTLAND, OR 97201-3098 Molecular size selectivity of immature placenta
R01HD-27453-01 (REB) JACKSON, GARY L 2001 S. LINCOLN URBANA, IL 61801 Control of LHRH secretion in the male
R01HD-27455-01 (HED) MILLEY, JOHN R UNIVERSITY OF UTAH 50 N MEDICAL DR SALT LAKE CITY, UT 84132 Oxidation-reduction effects on fetal protein metabolism
R01HD-27468-01A1 (NLS) MAY, VICTOR UNIVERSITY OF VERMONT BURLINGTON, VERMONT 05405 Regulation of peptide expression in neuronal cells
R55HD-27482-01 (HUD) MOSKO, SARAH S UNIV OF CALIFORNIA MED CENTER 101 CITY DRIVE SOUTH ORANGE, CA 92668 Infant-parent co-sleeping: implications for SIDS
R01HD-27485-01 (SSP) MCDANIEL, ANTONIO UNIVERSITY OF PENNSYLVANIA 3718 LOCUST WALK 239 MCNEIL PHILADELPHIA, PA 19104-6298 African-american immigration and mortality
R01HD-27491-01 (BCE) MAYO, KELLY E NORTHWESTERN UNIVERSITY 2153 SHERIDAN RD EVANSTON, IL 60208 Expression of ovarian inhibin and activin genes
R29HD-27503-01 (MET) ARSLANIAN, SILVA CHILDREN'S HOSP OF PITTSBURGH 3705 FIFTH AVE AT DESOTO STREE PITTSBURGH, PA 15213 Energy metabolism and insulin resistance during puberty
R55HD-27506-01A1 (REN) MICHAEL, SANDRA D STATE UNIVERSITY OF NEW YORK PO BOX 6000 BINGHAMTON, NY 13902-6000 Experimental & spontaneous polycystic ovarian syndrome
R01HD-27525-01 (MBY) MOON, RANDALL T UNIV OF WASHINGTON SCH OF MED SEATTLE, WA 98195 Int-1-related genes in xenopus embryos
R29HD-27528-02 (GMA) CRISSINGER, KAREN D LOUISIANA STATE UNIV MEDICAL C PO BOX 33932 SHREVEPORT, LA 71130-3932 Feeding, ischemia, and oxygenation in developing intestine
R29HD-27529-01 (SSP) MONT, DANIEL M CORNELL UNIVERSITY ITHACA, NY 14853 Public agency adoption in New York state
R01HD-27533-01 (SRC) HORWICH, ARTHUR L YALE UNIVERSITY SCH OF MED 333 CEDAR STREET NEW HAVEN, CT 06510 Nuclear transfer and genomic imprinting
R01HD-27546-01 (SRC) BUSA, WILLIAM B JOHNS HOPKINS UNIVERSITY 34TH & CHARLES STREETS BALTIMORE, MD 21218 Exogenous receptor probes of signalling in embryogenesis
R01HD-27549-01 (SRC) LEHMANN, RUTH E WHITEHEAD INST-BIOMED RES NINE CAMBRIDGE CENTER CAMBRIDGE, MA 02142 Genetic and molecular analysis of germline determinants
R01HD-27555-01 (SRC) STUART, GARY W INDIANA STATE UNIVERSITY TERRE HAUTE, IN 47802-1202 Zebrafish genes involved in early embryonic development
R55HD-27556-01A1 (HED) SOPRANO, DIANNE R TEMPLE UNIVERSITY SCH OF MED 3420 N BROAD STREET PHILADELPHIA, PA 19140 B-rar – A model gene to study retinoid teratogenicity
R01HD-27557-01A1 (REN) SCHACHTER, BETH S MT SINAI MEDICAL SCHOOL 1 GUSTAVE LEVY PL/BOX 1175 NEW YORK, NY 10029 Heterogeneity of estrogen receptor structure and action
R01HD-27560-01A1 (SSP) STRAUSS, JOHN THE RAND CORPORATION 1700 MAIN ST/PO BOX 2138 SANTA MONICA, CA 90406-2138 Income economic shocks infrastructure and child growth
R55HD-27570-01 (HUD) RUFF, HOLLY A ALBERT EINSTEIN COLL OF MED

1300 MORRIS PARK AVENUE BRONX, NY 10461 Preschool neurobehavioral assessment -- Reaction time task

R01HD-27581-01 (REB) MILLETTE, CLARKE F UNIVERSITY OF SOUTH CAROLINA SCHOOL OF MEDICINE COLUMBIA, S C 29208 Fucosyltransferase during mammalian spermatogenesis

R01HD-27583-01A1 (HUD) KAISER, ANN P VANDERBILT UNIVERSITY BOX 328 PEABODY COLLEGE NASHVILLE, TN 37203 Generalized effects of naturalistic language teaching

R01HD-27584-01A1 (MGN) BISHOP, COLIN E UNIVERSITY OF TENNESSEE 711 JEFFERSON AVENUE MEMPHIS, TN 38105 The molecular biology of the mouse Y chromosome

R29HD-27592-01A1 (HUD) DIPIETRO, JANET A JOHNS HOPKINS UNIVERSITY 624 N BROADWAY BALTIMORE, MD 21205 Fetal neurobehavioral development and postnatal continuity

R01HD-27597-01 (BEM) FLETCHER, JACK M UNIVERSITY OF TEXAS HLTH SCIS 6431 FANNIN, MSB 3 136 HOUSTON, TX 77225 Neuropsychological sequelae pediatric head injury

R01HD-27598-01 (SSP) MARINI, MARGARET M UNIVERSITY OF MINNESOTA 267 19TH AVENUE SOUTH MINNEAPOLIS, MN 55455 Family and labor market behavior

R29HD-27603-01A1 (HED) EVERSON, WILLIAM V UNIVERSITY OF CINCINNATI 4361 MSB 231 BETHESDA AVE CINCINNATI, OH 45267-0526 Lipocortins and arachidonic acid release in parturition

R01HD-27610-01 (SSP) LARSEN, ULLA M SUNY STONY BROOK STONY BROOK, NY 11794-4356 Sterility in sub-Saharan Africa

R01HD-27620-01A1 (SSP) BILLY, JOHN O HUMAN AFFAIRS RESEARCH CENTERS 4000 N E 41ST STREET SEATTLE, WASH 98105 Contextual effects on reproductive behavior in the U.S.

R01HD-27628-01 (HUD) SALOMON, GAVRIEL UNIVERSITY OF ARIZONA TUCSON, AZ 85721 Cultivating metacognitions using computer tools

R01HD-27638-01 (SSP) TOWNSEND, ROBERT M ECONOMICS RESEARCH CENTER/NORC 1155 E 60TH STREET CHICAGO, IL 60637 Risk, insurance, and the family

R29HD-27684-02 (HED) TSONIS, PANAGIOTIS A THE UNIVERSITY OF DAYTON 300 COLLEGE PARK DAYTON, OH 45469 Role of vitamin D in chondrogenesis

R01HD-27689-01 (SRC) KEMPHUES, KENNETH J CORNELL UNIVERSITY ITHACA, NY 14853-2703 Genetic analysis of early embryogenesis in C elegans

R01HD-27690-01 (SSP) RINDFUSS, RONALD R UNIVERSITY OF NORTH CAROLINA 123 W FRANKLIN STREET CHAPEL HILL, N C 27514 Teen contraceptive behavior in a changing environment

R01HD-27691-01 (ALY) SIMISTER, NEIL E BRANDEIS UNIVERSITY WALTHEM, MA 02254-9110 Intestinal and placental Fc-receptors for immunoglobulin G

R29HD-27692-01A1 (EVR) ABZUG, MARK J THE CHILDREN'S HOSPITAL 1056 EAST 19TH AVENUE DENVER, CO 80218 Enterovirus infections of the placenta and fetus

R01HD-27694-01A1 (HUD) PLOMIN, ROBERT PENNSYLVANIA STATE UNIVERSITY UNIVERSITY PARK, PA 16802 Cognitive development in children--Genetic markers

R01HD-27699-01 (HUD) ACREDOLO, CURT R UNIVERSITY OF CALIFORNIA DAVIS, CA 95616 Cognitive uncertainty and cognitive development

R01HD-27700-01A1 (CBY) DE ROBERTIS, EDWARD M UNIVERSITY OF CALIFORNIA 405 HILGARD AVENUE LOS ANGELES, CA 90024-1406 Xenopus egg ligand-activated transcription factors

R01HD-27706-02 (END) GALTON, VALERIE A DARTMOUTH MEDICAL SCHOOL HANOVER, NH 03756 Thyroid hormone receptors in development

R01HD-27709-01 (HUD) LUKATELA, GEORGIJE L UNIVERSITY OF BELGRADE BULEVAR REVOLUCIJE 73 BEOGRAD, YUGOSLAVIA 11000 Word recognition in English and Serbo-Croatian

R01HD-27712-14A1 (CBY) FRAZIER, WILLIAM A, III WASHINGTON UNIVERSITY 660 SOUTH EUCLID AVE ST LOUIS, MO 63110 Alternative splicing of the human thrombospondin gene

R01HD-27714-04A1 (CEP) CLIFTON, RACHEL K UNIV OF MASSACHUSETTES TOBIN HALL AMHERST, MA 01003 Reaching and cognition in infancy

R55HD-27715-01 (SSP) MAULDON, JANE UNIVERSITY OF CALIFORNIA BERKELEY, CA 94720 Children's health and use of medical care

R01HD-27716-01A1 (HUD) FOX, ROBERT VANDERBILT UNIVERSITY 301 A&S PSYCHOLOGY BLDG NASHVILLE, TN 37240 Mental retardation and perceptual processing

R01HD-27724-01 (HUD) SIMONS, RONALD L IOWA STATE UNIVERSITY 107 EAST HALL AMES, IA 50011 Economic strain and social support in single parents

R29HD-27729-01A1 (REN) PATINO, REYNALDO TEXAS TECH UNIVERSITY RESEARCH UNIT LUBBOCK, TEXAS 79409-2125 Gonadotropic control of oocyte maturational competence

R43HD-27738-01 (REN) ZAVA, DAVID T AERON BIOTECHNOLOGY INC 1933 DAVIS ST., SUITE 310 SAN LEANDRO, CA 94577 An in vitro bioassay for estrogens and antiestrogens

P30HD-27748-02 (SRC) MORRISS, FRANK H, JR UNIVERSITY OF IOWA HOSPITALS & CLINICS IOWA CITY, IA 52242 University of Iowa child health research center

P30HD-27757-02 (SRC) WARSHAW, JOSEPH B YALE UNIVERSITY SCHOOL OF MED 333 CEDAR ST NEW HAVEN, CT 06510 Developmental adaptation

R43HD-27764-01A1 (HUD) VANBIERVLIET, ALAN LEARNING EXPRESS, INC 8029 DANWOOD DR LITTLE ROCK, AR 72204-8311 Rate enhancement for graphic-based communication aids

R43HD-27771-01 (HUD) GIRSON, ANDREW D DVP, INC 2401 RESEARCH BLVD ROCKVILLE, MD 20850 A generic controller for the developmentally disabled

R43HD-27777-01 (HUD) KELLEHER-WALSH, BARBARA J HARTLEY ASSOCIATES INC P O BOX 362 BUFFALO, NY 14225 Development of a child biomechanic data base

R43HD-27781-01 (HUD) LEDDO, JOHN M RESEARCH DEVELOPMENT CORP 11835 COOPERS CT RESTON, VA 22091 Knowledge elicitation tools for educational evaluation

R43HD-27784-01A1 (SSS) CAHN, FREDERICK BIOMAT CORPORATION 57 RALEIGH RD BELMONT, MA 02178 Spermatogenic cells on defined substrates for toxicology

P30HD-27799-02 (SRC) OSKI, FRANK A JOHNS HOPKINS UNIV SCH OF MED 720 RUTLAND AVENUE BALTIMORE, MD 21205 Child health research center--Johns Hopkins Medcal School

R01HD-27801-01 (MGN) SHERMAN, STEPHANIE L EMORY UNIVERSITY 2040 RIDGEWOOD DRIVE ATLANTA, GA 30322 Genetic epidemiology of the fragile x syndrome

P50HD-27802-01S1 (SRC) DE FRIES, JOHN C UNIVERSITY OF COLORADO BOULDER, CO 80309-0447 Differential diagnosis is learning disabilities

P50HD-27802-01S1 0001 (SRC) DE FRIES, JOHN C Differential diagnosis is learning disabilities Psychometric assessment/twin study

P50HD-27802-01S1 0002 (SRC) OLSON, RICHARD K Differential diagnosis is learning disabilities Reading and language processes

P50HD-27802-01S1 0003 (SRC) PENNINGTON, BRUCE F Differential diagnosis is learning disabilities ADHD and executive functions--Relation to learning disabilities

P50HD-27802-01S1 0004 (SRC) SMITH, SHELLY D Differential diagnosis is learning disabilities Genetic linkage analysis

P50HD-27802-01S1 0005 (SRC) OLSON, RICHARD K Differential diagnosis is learning disabilities Computer-based remediation of reading disabilities

R01HD-27806-05 (HUD) BOOTH, CATHRYN L UNIVERSITY OF WASHINGTON MAIL STOP: WJ-10 SEATTLE, WA 98195 Social competence risk assessment--Mother-child factors

R43HD-27815-01A1 (SSS) SWETTE, LARRY GINER, INC 14 SPRING STREET WALTHAM, MA 02254-9147 Unheated transcutaneous pCO2 sensor for neonates

R43HD-27816-01 (REN) SHI, WEIMIN MARTIN GOFFMAN ASSOCIATES 3 DELLVIEW DRIVE EDISON, NJ 08820-2545 Instrument for decreasing the failure rate of condoms

P30HD-27823-02 (SRC) FEIGIN, RALPH D BAYLOR COLLEGE OF MEDICINE ONE BAYLOR PLAZA HOUSTON, TX 77030 Baylor child health research center

P30HD-27827-02 (SRC) SIMMONS, MICHAEL A UNIVERSITY OF UTAH 50 NORTH MEDICAL DRIVE SALT LAKE CITY, UT 84132 Rocky Mountain center for the biology of development

R01HD-27839-02 (PHRA) GUY, RICHARD H UNIVERSITY OF CALIFORNIA 926 MEDICAL SCIENCES BUILDING SAN FRANCISCO, CA 94143-0446 Mechanisms of iontophoretic drug delivery across skin

P30HD-27841-02 (SRC) OGRA, PEARAY L UNIVERSITY OF TEXAS MED BRANCH 301 UNIVERSITY BLVD GALVESTON, TX 77550 Child health research center in developmental immunobiology

R01HD-27845-05 (CBY) DANIEL, CHARLES W UNIVERSITY OF CALIFORNIA 1156 HIGH STREET SANTA CRUZ, CA 95064 Mammary growth regulation by transforming growth factor

R55HD-27847-01 (REB) BLEIL, JEFFREY D SCRIPPS CLINIC & RESEARCH FDN 10666 N TORREY PINES RD LA JOLLA, CA 92037 The role of sperm proteins in zona pellucida recognition

U10HD-27851-01 (SRC) STOLL, BARBARA J EMORY UNIVERSITY SCHOOL OF MED 80 BUTLER STREET ATLANTA, GA 30335 Proposal to participate in multicenter network of NICUs

U10HD-27853-01 (SRC) TSANG, REGINALD C THE PERINATAL INSTITUTE 231 BETHESDA AVENUE CINCINNATI, OH 45267-0541 Cooperative multicenter network of NICUS

U10HD-27856-01 (SRC) LEMONS, JAMES A INDIANA UNIV SCH OF MED 702 BRANHILL DRIVE INDIANAPOLIS, IN 46202-5210 COOP multicenter network of neonatal intensive care unit

U10HD-27860-01 (SRC) MEIS, PAUL J BOWMAN GRAY SCHOOL OF MEDICINE 300 SOUTH HAWTHORNE ROAD WINSTON-SALEM, NC 27103 Maternal-fetal medicine unit cooperative agreement application

U10HD-27861-01 (SRC) MOAWAD, ATEF H UNIVERSITY OF CHICAGO 5841 S MARYLAND AVE CHICAGO, IL 60637 Maternal fetal medicine unit at the University of Chicago

U10HD-27869-01 (SRC) HAUTH, JOHN C UNIVERSITY OF ALABAMA 619 SOUTH 20TH STREET BIRMINGHAM, AL 35294 Coop multicenter network of maternal fetal medicine care

U10HD-27871-01 (SRC) EHRENKRANZ, RICHARD A YALE UNIVERSITY SCH OF MED P O BOX 3333 NEW HAVEN, CT 06510 Multicenter network of neonatal intensive care units

U10HD-27880-01 (SRC) STEVENSON, DAVID K STANFORD UNIVERSITY STANFORD, CA 94305-5119 Coop multicenter network of neonatal intensive care units

U10HD-27881-01 (SRC) PAPILE, LU-ANN UNIVERSITY NEW MEXICO DIV OF NEONATOLOGY ALBUQUERQUE, NM 87131 Cooperative multicenter network of neonatal intensive care units

U10HD-27883-01 (SRC) VANDORSTEN, J PETER MEDICAL COLLEGE OF VIRGINIA BOX 34 MCV STATION RICHMOND, VA 23298-0034 Coop multicenter network of maternal fetal medicine unit

U10HD-27889-01 (SRC) THURNAU, GARY R UNIVERSITY OF OKLAHOMA COLL/ME PO BOX 26901 OKLAHOMA CITY, OK 73190 MFMU cooperative agreement application

U10HD-27904-01 (SRC) OH, WILLIAM WOMEN AND INFANTS HOSP 101 DUDLEY STREET PROVIDENCE, RI 02905 Multicenter neonatal network

U10HD-27905-01 (SRC) MIODOVNIK, MENACHEM UNIVERSITY OF CINCINNATI 4561 MSB 231 BETHESDA AVE CINCINNATI, OH 45267-0526 Coop multicenter network of maternal-fetal medicine unit

U10HD-27917-01 (SRC) BOTTOMS, SIDNEY F WAYNE STATE UNIVERSITY DETROIT, MI 48202-3489 Wayne State University maternal-fetal medicine (MFMU) network center

R13HD-27920-01 (HDMC) KENT, CLAUDIA M PURDUE UNIVERSITY WEST LAFAYETTE, IN 47907 1991 gordon research conference on lipid metabolism

R01HD-27938-01 (REB) SEIDEL, GEORGE E, JR COLORADO STATE UNIVERSITY FORT COLLINS, CO 80523 Regulation of oTP-1 and hCG genes in ovine trophoblast

R13HD-27947-01 (HDMC) NADEAU, JOSEPH H JACKSON LABORATORY 600 MAIN STREET BAR HARBOR, ME 04609-0800 Mammalian developmental genetics workshop

R13HD-27948-01 (HDPR) ROBAIRE, BERNARD MC GILL UNIVERSITY 3655 DRUMMOND STREET MONTREAL QUEBEC, CANADA H3G 1Y 1991 Testis workshop

R13HD-27952-01 (HDMC) SCHUPBACH, TRUDI M WASHINGTON UNIVERSITY PRINCETON, NJ 08544-1003 Gordon Research Conference on developmental biology

R01HD-27955-01 (SSP) OPPENHEIMER, VALERIE K UNIVERSITY OF CALIFORNIA 405 HILGARD AVENUE LOS ANGELES, CA 90024-1484 The career-entry process and young mens marital behavior

PROJECT NO., ORGANIZATIONAL UNIT., INVESTIGATOR, ADDRESS, TITLE

R55HD-27965-01 (NTN) CONNEELY, ORLA M BAYLOR COLLEGE OF MEDICINE ONE BAYLOR PLAZA HOUSTON, TX 77030 Biological functions of lactoferrin in nutrition
R01HD-27970-01 (REN) MELLON, SYNTHIA H UNIVERSITY OF CALIFORNIA BOX 0556 SAN FRANCISCO, CA 94143-0556 Regulation of reproduction in the rat
R01HD-27994-01 (SRC) OLSON, JAMES A IOWA STATE UNIVERSITY AMES, IA 50011 New indicators of marginal status for vitamins A and E
R01HD-28015-01 (SRC) DONLON, TIMOTHY A STANFORD UNIV MED CENTER 300 PASTEUR DR/H1517 STANFORD, CA 94305 Identification of genetic markers for obesity
R01HD-28016-01 (SRC) CAPRIO, SONIA YALE UNIVERSITY SCH OF MEDICIN 333 CEDAR ST NEW HAVEN, CT 06510 Metabolic predictors and markers of childhood obesity
R01HD-28020-01 (SRC) BRAY, GEORGE A PENNINGTON BIOMED RESEARCH CTR 6400 PERKINS ROAD BATON ROUGE, LA 70808 Reduced energy expenditure--A marker for obesity?
R01HD-28025-01 (HED) ADAMSON, EILEEN D LA JOLLA CANCER RES FOUNDATION 10901 NORTH TORREY PINES RD LA JOLLA, CA 92037 The role of PDGF in development
R01HD-28031-01 (EI) POLLACK, SYLVIA B SCHOOL OF MEDICINE UNIVERSITY OF WASHINGTON SEATTLE, WA 98195 NK cells and pregnancy
R01HD-28033-01 (SRC) MOSER-VEILLON, PHYLIS B UNIVERSITY OF MARYLAND COLLEGE PARK, MD 20742 Vitamin B-6 status in pregnancy, lactation and infancy
R03HD-28034-01 (SRC) FABER, LEE E MEDICAL COLLEGE OF OHIO CS 10008 TOLEDO, OH 43699 Growth factors and steroid receptor transformation
R03HD-28038-01 (SRC) RIDER, VIRGINIA C TUFTS UNIVERSITY 136 HARRISON AVENUE BOSTON, MA 02111 Remodelling of the uterine matrix at implantation
R01HD-28047-01 (SRC) LEIBEL, RUDOLPH L ROCKEFELLER UNIVERSITY 1230 YORK AVENUE NEW YORK, NY 10021-6399 Molecular genetic analysis of human obesity
P30HD-28048-01 (HDPR) TUREK, FRED W NORTHWESTERN UNIVERSITY 2153 SHERIDAN ROAD EVANSTON, IL 60208 Center for research on fertility and infertility
P30HD-28048-01 9001 (HDPR) LINZER, DANIEL I Center for research on fertility and infertility Core--Molecular technology
P30HD-28048-01 9002 (HDPR) CHUNG, LEE Center for research on fertility and infertility Core--Protein analysis
P30HD-28048-01 9003 (HDPR) MAYO, KELLY E Center for research on fertility and infertility Core--In situ hybridization
P30HD-28048-01 9004 (HDPR) GOLDBERG, ERWIN Center for research on fertility and infertility Core--Monoclonal antibody and cell culture
P30HD-28048-01 9005 (HDPR) SCHWARTZ, NEENA B Center for research on fertility and infertility Core--Hormone and neurotransmitter measurements
R03HD-28055-01 (SRC) KOOS, ROBERT D UNIVERSITY OF MARYLAND BALTIMORE, MD 21201 Estrogen-induced growth factor expression in the uterus
R01HD-28062-01 (CBY) WRIGHT, CHRISTOPHER V VANDERBILT UNIVERSITY SCHOOL OF MED C-2310 MCN NASHVILLE, TN 37232-2175 Homeobox genes in vertebrate embryonic endoderm
R01HD-28063-01 (MBY) RIO, DONALD C WHITEHEAD INST FOR BIOMED RES CAMBRIDGE, MA 02142 Biochemistry of regulated pre-mRNA splicing in Drosophila
R01HD-28070-01 (SRC) SCHWARZ, KATHLEEN B JOHNS HOPKINS HOSPITAL 600 NORTH WOLFE STREET BALTIMORE, MD 21205 Breath ethane, biomarker of vitamin A and E deficiency
R03HD-28072-01 (SRC) CARSON, DANIEL D UNIVERSITY OF TEXAS 1515 HOLCOMBE BOULEVARD HOUSTON, TX 77030 Growth factor control of uterine cell function in vitro
R03HD-28074-01 (SRC) HENDRY, WILLIAM J, III UNIVERSITY OF ARKANSAS 4301 WEST MARKHAM LITTLE ROCK, AR 72205 Estrogen-induced normal and dysplastic uterine growth
P01HD-28076-01 (SRC) POPKIN, BARRY M UNIV OF NORTH CAROLINA 123 W FRANKLIN STREET CHAPEL HILL, NC 27516-3997 Health and reproduction dynamics and social change
P01HD-28076-01 0001 (SRC) POPKIN, BARRY M Health and reproduction dynamics and social change Longitudinal data collection and dissemination
P01HD-28076-01 0002 (SRC) AKIN, JOHN Health and reproduction dynamics and social change Modeling the health transition
P01HD-28076-01 0003 (SRC) ENTWISLE, BARBARA Health and reproduction dynamics and social change Reproductive behavior, health and role dynamics
P01HD-28076-01 0004 (SRC) BLAU, DAVID Health and reproduction dynamics and social change Infant feeding and female labor supply
P01HD-28076-01 0005 (SRC) AKIN, JOHN Health and reproduction dynamics and social change Demand for contraception
P01HD-28076-01 0006 (SRC) ADAIR, LINDA Health and reproduction dynamics and social change Reproduction cycling and maternal depletion
P01HD-28076-01 0007 (SRC) ADAIR, LINDA Health and reproduction dynamics and social change Infant growth dynamics
P01HD-28076-01 9001 (SRC) LYERLY, AMANDA Health and reproduction dynamics and social change Data core
P01HD-28076-01 9002 (SRC) GUILKEY, DAVID K Health and reproduction dynamics and social change Statistical core
R03HD-28079-01 (SRC) GIUDICE, LINDA C STANFORD UNIVERSITY 300 PASTEUR DRIVE/S317 STANFORD, CA 94305-4125 The insulin-like growth factor system in human oviduct
R01HD-28081-01 (SRC) CLEMMONS, DAVID R UNIVERSITY OF NORTH CAROLINA CB #7005 CHAPEL HILL, NC 27599-7005 IGF's and IGF binding proteins--indices of nutritional status
R01HD-28088-01 (MGN) CHAKRAVARTI, ARAVINDA UNIV OF PITTSBURGH/PUBLIC HEAL 130 DESOTO STREET PITTSBURGH, PA 15261 Genetic analysis of Hirschsprung disease
R03HD-28095-01 (SRC) KACINSKI, BARRY M YALE UNIVERSITY SCHOOL OF MED 333 CEDAR STREET/136 HRT NEW HAVEN, CT 06510 CSF-1, CSF-1 receptor, and steroids in the endometrium
R01HD-28114-01 (SRC) SMOLEN, ANDREW UNIVERSITY OF COLORADO CAMPUS BOX 447 BOULDER, CO 80309-0447 Vitamin B-6 nutritional status assessment in pregnancy
R01HD-28119-01 (SRC) TAMURA, TSUNENOBU UNIVERSITY OF ALABAMA UAB STATION BIRMINGHAM, AL 35294 Functional test of Zn nutriture by Zn stimulation of ACE
R03HD-28122-01 (SRC) MULHOLLAND, JOY I BAYLOR COLLEGE OF MEDICINE ONE BAYLOR PLAZA HOUSTON, TX 77030 TGFB expression during embryo receptivity and cell death
R03HD-28128-01 (SRC) OSTEEN, KEVIN G VANDERBILT UNIV MEDICAL CTR 1116 21ST AVE S-OB/GYN DEPT NASHVILLE, TN 37232-2516 Transforming growth factor-beta in endometrium
R13HD-28134-01 (HDMC) MIZE, SUSAN G MIZE INFORMATION ENTERPRISE PO BOX 670847 DALLAS, TX 75367-0847 Int'l register workshop--Inherited metabolic disorders
P30HD-28138-01 (HDPR) CROWLEY, WILLIAM F, JR MASSACHUSETTS GENERAL HOSPITAL BOSTON, MA 02114 Reproductive endocrine sciences center
P30HD-28138-01 9001 (HDPR) JAMESON, JAMES L Reproductive endocrine sciences center Core--Molecular biology
P30HD-28138-01 9003 (HDPR) DONAHOE, PATRICIA K Reproductive endocrine sciences center Core--Cell culture
P30HD-28138-01 9004 (HDPR) KEUTMANN, HENRY T Reproductive endocrine sciences center CORE--Peptide synthesis/protein sequencing
P30HD-28138-01 9005 (HDPR) CROWLEY, WILLIAM F Reproductive endocrine sciences center Core--Radioimmunoassay
R01HD-28141-01 (HUD) MC ILVANE, WILLIAM J E K SHRIVER CTR 200 TRAPELO ROAD WALTHAM, MA 02254 Frequency analyses of stimulus control in the mentally retarded
R29HD-28152-01 (CBY) WESSEL, GARY M BROWN UNIVERSITY BOX G PROVIDENCE, RI 02912 Ontogeny of the sea urchin endoderm lineage
R15HD-28173-01 (HUD) LEVITT, ANDREA G WELLESLEY COLLEGE WELLESLEY, MA 02181 "Motherese" prosody & speech perception/production
R15HD-28177-01 (HUD) GALOTTI, KATHLEEN M CARLETON COLLEGE ONE NORTH COLLEGE ST NORTHFIELD, MN 55057 Adolescents making a real-life decision
R01HD-28181-01 (HUD) MC CONKIE, GEORGE W CENTER FOR THE STUDY OF READIN 51 GERTY DRIVE CHAMPAIGN, IL 61820 Eye fixation times during reading
R55HD-28184-01 (HED) HOWARD, MARTHE J COLUMBIA UNIVERSITY 630 WEST 168TH ST NEW YORK, NY 10032 Regulation of neural crest development by growth factors
R01HD-28187-01 (PBC) GETTINS, PETER VANDERBILT UNIVERSITY SCHOOL OF MED 670 MRB NASHVILLE, TN 37232-0146 Protease and growth factor-alpha-2 macroglobulin mapping
R15HD-28198-01 (HUD) FINE, MARK A UNIVERSITY OF DAYTON 300 COLLEGE PARK DAYTON, OH 45469-1430 Work/family roles and child adjustment in stepfamilies
R15HD-28210-01 (PBC) BAME, KAREN J UNIVERSITY OF MISSOURI 5100 ROCKHILL RD/RM 109 SCI BL KANSAS CITY, MO 64110-2499 Membrane proteoglycans of Chinese hamster ovary cells
R15HD-28216-01 (HED) PERRY, EDWARD H MEMPHIS STATE UNIVERSITY MEMPHIS, TN 38152 Transepidermal water loss in premature infants
R15HD-28223-01 (HED) STEPHENS, TRENT D IDAHO STATE UNIVERSITY POCATELLO, ID 83209 Source of limb-forming ability in the chick embryo flank
R01HD-28231-01 (SRC) SMOTHERMAN, WILLIAM P STATE UNIVERSITY OF NEW YORK BINGHAMTON, NY 13901 Behavioral effects of milk in the fetus
R01HD-28245-01 (SRC) BLASS, ELLIOTT M CORNELL UNIVERSITY ITHACA, NY 14853 Mechanisms underlying maternal calming and analgesia
R01HD-28246-01 (SRC) ALBERTS, JEFFREY R INDIANA UNIVERSITY BLOOMINGTON, IN 47405 Thermal imaging of perinatal behavior and physiology
R01HD-28247-01 (SRC) BEKOFF, ANNE C UNIVERSITY OF COLORADO CAMPUS BOX 334 BOULDER, CO 80309-0334 Perinatal transitions in motor behavior
P30HD-28251-01 (HDPR) GOLDSCHEIDER, FRANCES K BROWN UNIVERSITY BOX 1916 PROVIDENCE, RI 02912 Population center
P30HD-28251-01 9001 (HDPR) PITT, MARK M Population center Core--Computing and statistical services
P30HD-28251-01 9002 (HDPR) WHITE, MICHAEL J Population center Core--Library services
R01HD-28253-01 (REB) SPEAROW, JIMMY L UNIVERSITY OF CALIFORNIA DAVIS, CA 95616 Genetic control of ovarian steroidogenesis
R13HD-28258-01 (HDPR) WOLF, DOUGLAS A THE URBAN INSTITUTE 2100 M STREET NW WASHINGTON, DC 20037 Us-ussr population symposium
R01HD-28259-01 (TOX) SHARMA, RAGHUBIR P UTAH STATE UNIVERSITY UMC 5600 LOGAN, UT 84322-5600 Anticancer retinoids and birth defects
R01HD-28261-01 (SRC) GRAY, LINCOLN C UNIVERSITY OF TEXAS 6431 FANNIN HOUSTON, TX 77030 Perinatal influences on developing auditory perception
P30HD-28263-01 (HDPR) HOGAN, DENNIS P PENNSYLVANIA STATE UNIVERSITY UNIVERSITY PARK, PA 16802 NICHD population research center core grant
P30HD-28263-01 9001 (HDPR) CLOGG, CLIFFORD C NICHD population research center core grant Core--Statistical
P30HD-28263-01 9002 (HDPR) BRAULT, MARGO NICHD population research center core grant Core--Information
P30HD-28263-01 9003 (HDPR) HENDRICKSON-SMITH, JANET NICHD population research center core grant Core--Computer
R01HD-28296-01 (AFL) GROTEVANT, HAROLD D UNIVERSITY OF MINNESOTA 1985 BUFORD AVENUE ST PAUL, MN 55108 Openness in adoptive family relationships
R13HD-28300-01 (HDPR) STOREY, BAYARD T UNIVERSITY OF PENNSYLVANIA PHILADELPHIA, PA 19104-6080 Gordon Research Conference on fertilization
R01HD-28305-02 (ARRF) TOLBERT, KATHRYN THE POPULATION COUNCIL ALEJANDRO DUMAS #50 MEXICO, D.F. 11560 Influencing risk behaviors of bisexual males in Mexico
R01HD-28306-02 (ARRF) WAWER, MARIA J COLUMBIA UNIVERSITY 60 HAVEN AVE NEW YORK, NY 10032 Behavioral research for AIDS prevention in Thailand
R13HD-28311-01 (SRC) PAYNE, ANITA H UNIVERSITY OF MICHIGAN ANN ARBOR, MI 48109-0278 Symposium and state of the art lectures-Steroid

hormone receptors in reproduction

R01HD-28315-01 (GEN) MC GINNIS, WILLIAM J YALE UNIVERISTY 260 WHITNEY AVE/PO BOX 6666 NEW HAVEN, CT 06511 Genes and cis-elements regulated by homeotic selectors

R01HD-28317-01 (MGN) DE PINHO, RONALD A ALBERT EINSTEIN COLL OF MED 1300 MORRIS PARK AVENUE BRONX, N Y 10461 N-myc expression and activity in cancer and development

R29HD-28330-01 (REB) HORACEK, MARK J UNIVERSITY OF SOUTH CAROLINA COLUMBIA, SC 29208 Pituitary differentiation--Role of extracellular matrix

R01HD-28333-01 (MGN) BALLABIO, ANDREA BAYLOR COLLEGE OF MEDICINE ONE BAYLOR PLAZA HOUSTON, TX 77030 Cloning of disease genes from the human Xp22.3 region

R29HD-28336-01 (NEUB) WAYNE, NANCY L UNIVERSITY OF VIRGINIA GILMER HALL CHARLOTTESVILLE, VA 22901 Neural basis for environmental control of reproduction

R01HD-28342-01 (MGN) EFSTRATIADIS, ARGIRIS COLUMBIA UNIVERSITY 701 WEST 168TH STREET NEW YORK, NY 10032 Parental imprinting in mice

R01HD-28367-01 (BCE) LOW, MALCOLM J OREGON HEALTH SCIENCES UNIV 3181 SW SAM JACKSON PARK RD PORTLAND, OR 97201-3098 Pituitary specific regulation of gonadotropin genes

P01HD-28372-01 (SRC) DAVANZO, JULIE S RAND CORPORATION 1700 MAIN STREET SANTA MONICA, CA 90406 Family decision-making and demographic change

P01HD-28372-01 0001 (SRC) DAVANZO, JULIE Family decision-making and demographic change Indonesian family life survey

P01HD-28372-01 0002 (SRC) DAVANZO, JULIE Family decision-making and demographic change Determinants of infant feeding patterns

P01HD-28372-01 0003 (SRC) STRAUSS, JOHN Family decision-making and demographic change Household resources, seasons, prices and child growth

P01HD-28372-01 0004 (SRC) GERTLER, PAUL Family decision-making and demographic change Content of prenatal care and child health

P01HD-28372-01 0005 (SRC) STRAUSS, JOHN Family decision-making and demographic change Economic causes of adult ill health

P01HD-28372-01 0006 (SRC) STRAUSS, JOHN Family decision-making and demographic change Income, economic shocks, infrastructure and child growth

P01HD-28372-01 0007 (SRC) GERTLER, PAUL Family decision-making and demographic change Effect of health care prices & quality on utilization & outcome

P01HD-28372-01 0008 (SRC) DAVANZO, JULIE Family decision-making and demographic change Socioeconomic and policy influence on fertility decline

P01HD-28372-01 0009 (SRC) THOMAS, DUNCAN Family decision-making and demographic change Economic determinants of migration in Malaysia

P01HD-28372-01 0010 (SRC) LILLARD, LEE Family decision-making and demographic change Intergenerational transfers in Indonesia

P01HD-28372-01 9001 (SRC) GERTLER, PAUL Family decision-making and demographic change Data management and computing core

R55HD-28374-01 (HED) WOLGEMUTH, DEBRA J COLUMBIA UNIV/COLL OF PHYSICIA 630 W 168TH STREET NEW YORK, NY 10032 Role of homeoxbox genes in development of the gut

R01HD-28375-01 (REB) HANKS, STEVEN K VANDERBILT UNIVERSITY SCHOOL OF MEDICINE, C-2310 MCN NASHVILLE, TN 37232-2175 Role of protein-tyrosine kinases in spermatogenesis

R55HD-28376-01 (EDC) BUNIN, GRETA CHILDREN'S HOSP OF PHILA 34TH & CIVIC CTR BLVD PHILADLEPHIA, PA 19104 Paternal exposures and risk of new germinal mutations

R01HD-28409-01 (SSP) FLINN, CHRISTOPHER J C V STARR CTR/APPLIED ECONOMIC 269 MERCER STREET NEW YORK, NY 10003 Compliance with child support orders

R01HD-28410-01 (GNM) BUCAN, MARIJA UNIVERSITY OF PENNSYLVANIA 422 CURRIE BOULEVARD PHILADELPHIA, PA 19104 Physical map of the Ph, W, and Rw region in the mouse

R01HD-28411-01 (SSP) HILL, KENNETH H JOHNS HOPKINS UNIVERSITY 615 N WOLFE STREET BALTIMORE, MD 21205 Child mortality estimation by time since first birth

R01HD-28419-01 (BPO) UPHOUSE, LYNDA L TEXAS WOMAN'S UNIVERSITY P O BOX 23971 DENTON, TX 76204 Reduced lordosis behavior after intracerebral 8-OH DPAT

R55HD-28422-01 (MGN) SOARES, MARCELO B 722 WEST 168TH ST BOX #41 NEW YORK, NY 10032 Subtractive cloning of cDNAs deleted in the 13q syndrome

R29HD-28425-01 (HUD) BAUER, PATRICIA J UNIVERSITY OF MINNESOTA 51 E RIVER RD MINNEAPOLIS, MN 55455-03454 Effects of temporal structure on memory for events

R55HD-28427-01 (BEM) KLEPINGER, DANIEL H BATTELLE HUMAN AFFAIRS RES CTR 4000 NE 41ST SEATTLE, WA 98105 Reproductive behaviors as joint decisions

R01HD-28430-01 (REB) SMITH, ERIC P CHILDRENS HOSPITAL RES FDN ELLAND & BETHESDA AVE CINCINNATI, OH 45229 Testicular insulin-like growth factor binding proteins

R01HD-28434-01 (SSP) JACCARD, JAMES J STATE UNIVERSITY OF NEW YORK UNIVERSITY OF ALBANY, SUNY ALBANY, NY 12222 Parent-teen communication about premarital pregnancy

R01HD-28443-01 (SSP) SCHOEN, ROBERT JOHNS HOPKINS UNIVERSITY 615 NORTH WOLFE STREET BALTIMORE, MD 21205 The dynamics of observed populations

R29HD-28447-01 (HED) DAVENPORT, MARSHA L UNIVERSITY OF NORTH CAROLINA CHAPEL HILL, NC 27599-7220 IGF-I and IGF binding proteins in pregnancy

R01HD-28460-01 (CBY) MERCOLA, MARK K HARVARD MEDICAL SCHOOL 25 SHATTUCK ST BOSTON, MA 02115 PDGF function and head-tail axis formation in embryos

R29HD-28467-01 (BPO) SWANN, JENNIFER M RUTGERS UNIVERSITY NEWARK, NJ 07102 Neuroanatomy of peptides regulating male mating behavior

R29HD-28475-01 (PTHB) SILVERMAN, GARY A WASHINGTON UNIVERSITY 400 S KINGSHIGHWAY, BOX 8116 ST LOUIS, MO 63110 Molecular analysis of the 18q-syndrome

R29HD-28478-01 (NEUB) MACKLIS, JEFFREY D CHILDREN'S HOSPITAL 300 LONGWOOD AVE BOSTON, MA 02115 Neocortical neuron grafting into laser lesioned mental retardation model

U01HD-28484-01 (SRC) WOLF, DON P OREGON REGNL PRIMATE RES CTR 505 N W 185TH AVENUE BEAVERTON, OR 97006 Reproduction and development in the rhesus monkey

R01HD-28500-01 (BPO) PAINTER, SHERRY D MARINE BIOMEDICAL INSTITUTE 200 UNIVERSITY BLVD GALVESTON, TX 77550-2781 Characterization of sexual pheromones in Aplysia

R29HD-28501-01 (REB) WARD, WILLIAM S ROBERT WOOD JOHNSON MED SCHOOL 1 ROBERT WOOD JOHNSON P1 NEW BRUNSWICK, NJ 08903-0019 The organization of DNA in the mammalian sperm nucleus

U01HD-28514-01 (SRC) SCHULTZ, RICHARD M UNIV OF PENNSYLVANIA 415 SOUTH UNIV AVE PHILADELPHIA, PA 19104 Molecular markers for preimplantation development

R01HD-28523-01 (SRC) BIJUR, POLLY E ROSE KENNEDY CENTER 1410 PELHAM PARKWAY SOUTH BRONX, NY 10461 Minor sports injuries as proxy measures of major injury

R29HD-28525-01 (MGN) HAUSER, CRAIG A LA JOLLA CANCER RESEARCH FDN 10901 NORTH TORREY PINES ROAD LA JOLLA, CA 92037 Function and targets of human homeodomain proteins

R13HD-28530-01 (HDMC) FINGERMAN, MILTON TULANE UNIVERSITY NEW ORLEANS, LA 70118 Symposium--Hormonal Control of Growth and Reproduction In Arthropoda

R43HD-28542-01 (SSS) FONTANA, EDUARDO ADELPHI TECHNOLOGY INC 285 HAMILTON AVE STE 430 PALO ALTO, CA 94301 The surface plasmon immunoassay for measurement of HCG

R01HD-28549-01 (ARRB) ABRAMOWSKY, CARLOS R UNIV OF TEXAS SW MEDICAL CTR 5323 HARRY HINES BLVD DALLAS, TX 75235-9023 Pathologic virology studies of placentas from HIV infected women

R03HD-28583-01 (HDMR) TENDLER, CRAIG L MOUNT SINAI MEDICAL CENTER 1 GUSTAVE L LEVY PLACE, BOX 12 NEW YORK, NY 10029-6574 Regulation of beta-polymerase in premalignant conditions

R03HD-28584-01 (HDPR) YEH, JOHN BRIGHAM AND WOMENS HOSPITAL 75 FRANCIS ST BOSTON, MA 02115 Peptide growth factors in polycystic ovarian disease

R03HD-28585-01 (HDMR) GROMPE, MARKUS INSTITUTE FOR MOLECULAR GENETI ONE BAYLOR PLAZA HOUSTON, TX 77030 Creation of a mouse model of tyrosinemia, type 1

R03HD-28586-01 (HDMC) KAHN, STUART J UNIVERSITY OF WASHINGTON SEATTLE, WA 98195 Analysis of the 85-kd sialidase family of T cruzi

R01HD-28632-01 (SOH) O'CONNOR, JOHN F COLUMBIA UNIVERSITY, HLTH SCIS 630 WEST 168TH ST NEW YORK, NY 10032 Urinary HCG expression in pregnancy loss

R13HD-28647-01 (NSPB) RAKIC, PASKO T YALE UNIVERSITY 333 CEDAR STREET NEW HAVEN, CT 06510 Travel award program for the Third IBRO World Congress

S15HD-28735-01 (NSS) CATTERALL, JAMES F POPULATION COUNCIL 1230 YORK AVENUE NEW YORK, NY 10021 Small instrumentation grant

S15HD-28736-01 (NSS) ADELSTEIN, STANLEY J HARVARD MEDICAL SCHOOL 25 SHATTUCK ST BOSTON, MA 02115 Small instrumentation grant

S15HD-28737-01 (NSS) PINKEL, DANIEL LAWRENCE LIVERMORE NATIONAL LA PO BOX 5507 L-452 LIVERMORE, CA 94550 Small instrumentation grant

S15HD-28738-01 (NSS) THOMAS, EWART A C STANFORD UNIVERSITY STANFORD, CA 94305-2070 Small instrumentation grant

S15HD-28739-01 (NSS) CAPRA, NORMAN F UNIV OF MARYLAND DENTAL SCHOOL 666 W BALTIMORE STREET BALTIMORE, MD 21201 Small instrumentation grant

S15HD-28740-01 (NSS) CAMERON, WILLIAM E MAGEE-WOMEN'S HOSPITAL 300 HALKET STREET PITTSBURGH, PA 15213-3180 Small instrumentation grant

S15HD-28741-01 (NSS) SINENSKY, MICHAEL S ELEANOR ROOSEVELT INSTITUTE 1899 GAYLORD STREET DENVER, CO 80206 Small instrumentation grant

S15HD-28742-01 (NSS) PITTMAN, JAMES A, JR UNIVERSITY OF ALABAMA UAB STATION BIRMINGHAM, AL 35294 Small instrumentation grant

S15HD-28743-01 (NSS) BROWN, MARY B UNIVERSITY OF FLORIDA COLLEGE OF VETERINARY MED GAINESVILLE, FL 32611-0633 Small instrumentation grant

S15HD-28744-01 (NSS) YUILL, THOMAS M UNIVERSITY OF WISCONSIN 2015 LINDEN DRIVE WEST MADISON, WI 53706 Small instrumentation grant

S15HD-28745-01 (NSS) WALKER, GEORGE E INDIANA UNIVERSITY PO BOX 1847 BLOOMINGTON, IN 47402 Small instrumentation grant

S15HD-28746-01 (NSS) BEHE, MICHAEL J LEHIGH UNIVERSITY MOUNTAIN TOP CAMPUS #111 BETHLEHEM, PA 18015 Small instrumentation grant

S15HD-28747-01 (NSS) HOGENKAMP, HENRICUS P UNIVERSITY OF MINNESOTA 101 PLEASANT STREET SE MINNEAPOLIS, MN 55455 Small instrumentation grant

S15HD-28748-01 (NSS) SCHNEIDER, ROBERT F STATE UNIVERSITY OF NEW YORK STONY BROOK, NY 11794-0001 Small instrumentation grant

S15HD-28749-01 (NSS) ZUCKER, IRVING UNIVERSITY OF CALIFORNIA 317 UNIVERSITY HALL BERKELEY, CA 94720 Small instrumentation grant

S15HD-28750-01 (NSS) BARTSCHAT, DIETER K EASTERN VIRGINIA MEDICAL SCHOO 700 OLNEY RD PO BOX 1980 NORFOLK, VA 23501 Small instrumentation grant

S15HD-28751-01 (NSS) TOPPINO, THOMAS C VILLANOVA UNIVERSITY VILLANOVA, PA 19085 Small instrumentation grant

S15HD-28752-01 (NSS) KOPPENHEFFER, THOMAS L TRINITY UNIVERSITY 715 STADIUM DR SAN ANTONIO, TX 78212 Small instrumentation grant

S15HD-28753-01 (NSS) FINE, SAMUEL NORTHEASTERN UNIVERSITY 360 HUNTINGTON AVENUE BOSTON, MASS 02115 Small instrumentation grant

S15HD-28754-01 (NSS) GIAMMARA, BEVERLY L UNIV OF LOUISVILLE GRAD PROG/RES JOUETT HALL LOUISVILLE, KY 40292 Small instrumentation grant

S15HD-28755-01 (NSS) BERNIER, GEORGE M, JR UNIVERSITY OF PITTSBURGH 3550 TERRACE ST PITTSBURGH, PA 15261 Small instrumentation grant

S15HD-28756-01 (NSS) JAENISCH, RUDOLF WHITEHEAD INST/BIOMEDICAL RES NINE CAMBRIDGE CENTER CAMBRIDGE, MA 02142 Small instrumentation grant

S15HD-28757-01 (NSS) GOLDSTEIN, GARY W KENNEDY INST 707 N BROADWAY BALTIMORE, MD 21205 Small instrumentation grant

S15HD-28758-01 (NSS) GRACCO, VINCENT L HASKINS LABORATORIES 270 CROWN STREET NEW HAVEN, CT 06511-6695 Small instrumentation grant

S15HD-28759-01 (NSS) PERRY, NATHAN W UNIVERSITY OF FLORIDA BOX

PROJECT NO., ORGANIZATIONAL UNIT., INVESTIGATOR, ADDRESS, TITLE

J-165 HSC GAINESVILLE, FL 32610 Small instrumentation grant
S15HD-28760-01 (NSS) LEIBACH, FREDERICK H MED COLLEGE OF GEORGIA RES INS 1120 15TH STREET AUGUSTA, GA 30912-4810 Small instrumentation grant
S15HD-28761-01 (NSS) CRITCHLOW, B VAUGHN OREG REGIONAL PRIMATE RES CTR 505 NORTHWEST 185TH AVENUE BEAVERTON, OR 97006 Small instrumentation grant
S15HD-28762-01 (NSS) DE SANTIS, FRANK J RESEARCH & EDUCATION INSTITUTE 1124 WEST CARSON STREET TORRANCE, CA 90502-2064 Small instrumentation grant
S15HD-28763-01 (NSS) REID, JOHN B OREGON SOCIAL LEARNING CENTER 207 EAST 5TH AVENUE EUGENE, OR 97401 Small instrumentation grant
S15HD-28764-01 (NSS) HOTZ, V JOSEPH NATIONAL OPINION RES CENTER 1155 E 60TH STREET CHICAGO, IL 60637 Small instrumentation grant
S15HD-28765-01 (NSS) DIPIETRO, JOSEPH A UNIV OF ILLINOIS/COLL OF VET M 2001 SOUTH LINCOLN AVE URBANA, IL 61801 Small instrumentation grant
S15HD-28766-01 (NSS) RESCH, RICHARD I COLLEGE OF STATEN ISLAND 130 STUYVESANT PLACE STATEN ISLAND, NY 10301 Small instrumentation grant
S15HD-28767-01 (NSS) MILLER, DOROTHY L SCIENTIFIC ANALYSIS CORPORATIO 2235 LOMBARD STREET SAN FRANCISCO, CA 94123 Small instrumentation grant
S15HD-28768-01 (NSS) OLDHAM, JOHN M NEW YORK STATE PSYCH INST 722 WEST 168 STREET NEW YORK, N Y 10032 Small instrumentation grant
S15HD-28769-01 (NSS) GRISWOLD, MICHAEL D WASHINGTON STATE UNIVERSITY PULLMAN, WA 99164-4660 Small instrumentation grant
S15HD-28770-01 (NSS) MOSIER, STEPHEN R UNIVERSITY OF NORTH CAROLINA MCIVER BUILDING/RM 100 GREENSBORO, NC 27412-5001 Small instrumentation grant
S15HD-28771-01 (NSS) NEWMAN, SARAH W UNIVERSITY OF MICHIGAN 503 THOMPSON STREET ANN ARBOR, MI 48109-1340 Small instrumentation grant
S15HD-28772-01 (NSS) ROSENFIELD, ALLAN COLUMBIA UNIVERSITY 600 WEST 168TH STREET NEW YORK, NY 10032 Small instrumentation grant
S15HD-28773-01 (NSS) KSIR, CHARLES J, JR UNIVERSITY OF WYOMING PO BOX 3355 LARAMIE, WY 82071-3355 Small instrumentation grant
S15HD-28774-01 (NSS) HEGYVARY, SUE T UNIVERSITY OF WASHINGTON SEATTLE, WA 98195 Small instrumentation grant
S15HD-28775-01 (NSS) MC CARTHY, CHARLOTTE M NEW MEXICO STATE UNIVERSITY BOX 30001/3AF LAS CRUCES, NM 88003-0001 Small instrumentation grant
S15HD-28776-01 (NSS) WARE, BENJAMIN R SYRACUSE UNIVERSITY 304 ADMIN BLDG SYRACUSE, NY 13244-1100 Small instrumentation grant
S15HD-28777-01 (NSS) ADAMS, WALTER C KENT STATE UNIVERSITY 107 AUDITORIUM BLDG KENT, OHIO 44242 Small instrumentation grant
S15HD-28778-01 (NSS) HO, SHUK-MEI TUFTS UNIVERSITY DANA LABORATORY MEDFORD, MA 02155 Small instrumentation grant
R01HD-28779-01 (EDC) ALDERMAN, BETH W FRED HUTCHINSON CANCER RES CTR 124 COLUMBIA STREET SEATTLE, WA 98104 Epidemiology of clubfoot
R01HD-28792-01 (BPO) DAVIDSON, TERRY L PURDUE UNIVERSITY WEST LAFAYETTE, IN 47907-1364 Signals to feed--Biological and associative mechanisms
R01HD-28796-01 (HUD) FABRICIUS, WILLIAM V ARIZONA STATE UNIVERSITY TEMPE, AZ 85287-1104 The development of concepts of mental activities
P30HD-28819-01 (SRC) BURR, IAN M VANDERBILT UNIV/SCH OF MEDICIN 21ST AVENUE AT GARLAND NASHVILLE, TN 37232 Molecular regulation of growth and development
P30HD-28819-01 9001 (SRC) PHILLIPS, JOHN A III Molecular regulation of growth and development Central laboratory core
P30HD-28819-01 9002 (SRC) WATTERSON, MARTIN Molecular regulation of growth and development Protein analysis extended core
P30HD-28819-01 9003 (SRC) DANIEL, THOMAS Molecular regulation of growth and development RNA extended core
P30HD-28819-01 9004 (SRC) TAYLOR, WILLIAM L Molecular regulation of growth and development Laboratory reagents extended core
P30HD-28819-01 9005 (SRC) CONARY, JON T Molecular regulation of growth and development Cloning extended core
P30HD-28819-01 9006 (SRC) TIBBETTS, CLARK Molecular regulation of growth and development DNA sequence analysis extended core
P30HD-28820-01 (SRC) KELCH, ROBERT P UNIVERSITY OF MICHIGAN 1500 EAST MEDICAL CENTER DRIVE ANN ARBOR, MI 48109-0718 Advancing child health through cell/molecular biology--Pediatric Core Facility
P30HD-28822-01 (SRC) HIRSCHHORN, KURT MOUNT SINAI SCHOOL OF MEDICINE ONE GUSTAVE L LEVY PLACE NEW YORK, NY 10029 Molecular genetics and child health
P30HD-28827-01 (SRC) SCHUBERT, WILLIAM K CHILDREN'S HOSPITAL RES. FOUND ELLAND & BETHESDA AVENUES CINCINNATI, OH 45229-2899 Pediatric center for gene expression and development
P30HD-28827-01 9001 (SRC) WHITSELL, JEFFREY A Pediatric center for gene expression and development Molecular biology core
P30HD-28827-01 9002 (SRC) DAVIS, ALVIN E Pediatric center for gene expression and development Protein purification and analysis core
P30HD-28827-01 9003 (SRC) LESSARD, JAMES Pediatric center for gene expression and development Monoclonal antibody / hybridoma core
P30HD-28827-01 9004 (SRC) POTTER, S STEVEN Pediatric center for gene expression and development Transgenic mouse core
P30HD-28831-01 (SRC) STAGNO, SERGIO UNIV OF ALABAMA AT BIRMINGHAM UAB STATION BIRMINGHAM, AL 35294 Molecular cell biology in pediatric research
R01HD-28832-12 (REN) HECHT, NORMAN B TUFTS UNIVERSITY TUFTS UNIVERSITY MEDFORD, MA 02155 Gene expression during spermatogenesis
R29HD-28841-01 (BCE) SHABANOWITZ, ROBERT B GEISINGER MEDICAL CENTER NORTH ACADEMY AVE DANVILLE, PA 17822-1329 Human sperm-zona pellucida interactions
R01HD-28929-01 (SRC) PICKOFF, ARTHUR S TULANE MEDICAL SCHOOL 1430 TULANE AVENUE NEW ORLEANS, LA 70112 Maturation of autonomic control of the newborn heart
R01HD-28931-01 (SRC) GOOTMAN, PHYLLIS M SUNY HLTH & SCI CNTR AT BROOKL 450 CLARKSON AVENUE BOX 31 BROOKLYN, N Y 11203 Modeling of sudden infant death syndrome in neonatal swine
R01HD-28938-01 (SRC) MOISE, NANCY S CORNELL UNIVERSITY NYS COLLEGE OF VETERINARY MED ITHACA, NY 14853 Sudden death in young dogs with ventricular arrhythmias
R01HD-28940-01 (SRC) HADDAD, GABRIEL G YALE UNIV/SCH OF MED 333 CEDAR ST NEW HAVEN, CT 06510 Prenatal hypoxia--Cellular brainstem maturation
R01HD-28942-01 (SRC) SHAIR, HARRY N RES FDN FOR MENTAL HYGIENE, IN 722 WEST 168TH STREET NEW YORK, NY 10032 The psychobiology of early cardio-respiratory control
R01HD-28948-01 (SRC) MILLHORN, DAVID E UNIVERSITY NORTH CAROLINA CB #7545 CHAPEL HILL, NC 27599-7545 Regulation of neuronal phenotype during development
U01HD-28971-01 (SRC) WEESE-MAYER, DEBRA E Event recordings of high risk infants on apnea monitors
R01HD-29003-01 (NLS) TULJAPURKAR, SHRIPAD D STANFORD UNIVERSITY DEPARTMENT OF BIOLOGICAL SCIS STANFORD, CA 94305-5020 Demographic dynamics of childhood disease and mortality
R03HD-29027-01 (BRC) BRENNA, JAMES T CORNELL UNIVERSITY 116 SAVAGE HALL ITHACA, NY 14853 Novel water isotope determination by mass spectrometry
U01HD-29056-01 (SRC) HUNT, CARL E Event recording of high risk infants on apnea monitors
U01HD-29060-01 (SRC) HOPPENBROUWERS, TOKE T Home apnea monitoring in infants at risk for SIDS
U01HD-29067-01 (SRC) CORWIN, MICHAEL J Event recordings of high risk infants on apnea monitors
U01HD-29071-01 (SRC) BAIRD, TERRY M Event recordings of high risk infants on apnea monitors
U01HD-29073-01 (SRC) CROWELL, DAVID H Event recordings of high risk infants on apnea monitors
U54HD-29099-01 (SRC) HERR, JOHN C UNIV OF VIRGINIA/SCH OF MED BOX 439 HEALTH SCI CENTER CHARLOTTESVILLE, VA 22908 Center for recombinant gamete contraceptive vaccinogens
U54HD-29099-01 0001 (SRC) O'RAND, MICHAEL G Center for recombinant gamete contraceptive vaccinogens A human sperm antigen as an immunocontraceptive
U54HD-29099-01 0002 (SRC) GOLDBERG, ERWIN Center for recombinant gamete contraceptive vaccinogens Human testis cDNAs identified by infertility sera
U54HD-29099-01 0003 (SRC) HERR, JOHN Center for recombinant gamete contraceptive vaccinogens Avirulent Salmonella SP-10 vaccine for secretory immunity
U54HD-29099-01 0004 (SRC) TUNG, KENNETH Center for recombinant gamete contraceptive vaccinogens Autoimmune oophoritis--Consequence of gamete vaccines
U54HD-29099-01 9001 (SRC) FLICKINGER, CHARLES J Center for recombinant gamete contraceptive vaccinogens Core--Tissue specificity
U54HD-29099-01 9002 (SRC) WRIGHT, RICHARD M Center for recombinant gamete contraceptive vaccinogens Core--Bioprocess and purification core
U54HD-29099-01 9003 (SRC) CURTISS, ROY Center for recombinant gamete contraceptive vaccinogens Core--Oral recombinant Salmonella antifertility vaccines core
U54HD-29099-01 9004 (SRC) GOLDBERG, ERWIN Center for recombinant gamete contraceptive vaccinogens Core--Preclinical animal models
U54HD-29125-01 (SRC) PRIMAKOFF, PAUL UNIV OF CONN HEALTH CENTER 263 FARMINGTON AVENUE FARMINGTON, CT 06032 Development of immunocontraceptives
U54HD-29125-01 0001 (SRC) PRIMAKOFF, PAUL Development of immunocontraceptives PH-20 vaccine for contraception in women
U54HD-29125-01 0002 (SRC) MYLES, DIANA G Development of immunocontraceptives Male contraception by active and passive immunization
U54HD-29125-01 0003 (SRC) BIGAZZI, PIERLUIGI Development of immunocontraceptives Vaccination with PH-20 in male primate and mouse models
U54HD-29125-01 0004 (SRC) BLEIL, JEFFREY D Development of immunocontraceptives An immunocontraceptive directed against human sperm
U54HD-29125-01 0005 (SRC) SALING, PATRICIA Development of immunocontraceptives Evaluation of the contraceptive potential of p95
U54HD-29125-01 0006 (SRC) LANGER, ROBERT Development of immunocontraceptives Immunization vehicles for sperm antigens
U54HD-29125-01 9001 (SRC) OVERSTREET, JAMES W Development of immunocontraceptives Core--Primate core
U54HD-29164-01 (SRC) CROWLEY, WILLIAM F, JR MASSACHUSETTS GENERAL HOSPITAL BOSTON, MA 02114 Infertility--Defects in LH/FSH synthesis-secretion-action
U54HD-29164-01 0001 (SRC) CROWLEY, WILLIAM F Infertility--Defects in LH/FSH synthesis-secretion-action Neuroendocrine control of reproduction in the female
U54HD-29164-01 0002 (SRC) HALL, JANET E Infertility--Defects in LH/FSH synthesis-secretion-action Treatment of infertility due to ovulatory dysfunction
U54HD-29164-01 0003 (SRC) WHITCOMB, RANDALL W Infertility--Defects in LH/FSH synthesis-secretion-action Control of LH and FSH secretion in normal and infertile men
U54HD-29164-01 0004 (SRC) JAMESON, J LARRY Infertility--Defects in LH/FSH synthesis-secretion-action Regulation of gonadotropin biosynthesis and secretion
U54HD-29164-01 0005 (SRC) SLUSS, PATRICK M Infertility--Defects in LH/FSH synthesis-secretion-action Hypergonadotropic hypogonadism--Physiology and treatment
U54HD-29164-01 0006 (SRC) SCHNEYER, ALAN L Infertility--Defects in LH/FSH synthesis-secretion-action Inhibin physiology in health and disease
U54HD-29184-01 (SRC) REAME, NANCY E UNIVERSITY OF MICHIGAN 300 NORTH INGALLS/11TH FLOOR ANN ARBOR, MI 48109-0482 National Center for Infertility Research
U54HD-29184-01 0001 (SRC) MOGHISSI, KAMRAN National Center for Infertility Research Neuroendocrinology of unexplained infertility
U54HD-29184-01 0002 (SRC) DEMITRACK, MARK National Center for Infertility Research Dieting effects on ovulation in college women
U54HD-29184-01 0003 (SRC) PADMANABHAN, VASANTHA National Center for

Infertility Research Existence of FSH-releasing factor in the portal circulation
U54HD-29184-01 0004 (SRC) MILLER, WILLIAM National Center for Infertility Research Ovulatory disfunction--Gonadotropin releasing hormone receptor regulation
U54HD-29184-01 0005 (SRC) MIDGLEY, A REES National Center for Infertility Research Gonadotrope response to ovulation--Controlling signals
U54HD-29184-01 0006 (SRC) GHAZZI, MAHMOUD National Center for Infertility Research Neuroelectric patterns with gonadotropin-releasing hormone release
U54HD-29184-01 0007 (SRC) FOSTER, CAROL M National Center for Infertility Research E2 modulation of growth hormone action in human granulosa cells
R01HD-29304-01 (NEUB) FRASER, SCOTT E CALIFORNIA INSTITUTE OF TECHNO 1201 E CALIFORNIA BLVD PASADENA, CA 91125 Vital dye analysis of hindbrain development
R01HD-29337-01 (SRC) GRODY, WAYNE W UCLA SCHOOL OF MEDICINE 10833 LE CONTE AVENUE LOS ANGELES, CA 90024-1732 Cystic fibrosis mutation screening and counseling
N01HD-42808-14 ( ) MATALON, REUBEN** Effects of maternal PKU on pregnancy outcome
N01HD-42809-21 ( ) LEVY, HARVEY L** Effects of maternal PKU on pregnancy outcome
N01HD-42811-09 ( ) GOLDENBERG, ROBERT L** Small for gestational age births--Fetal growth
N01HD-43807-14 ( ) KOCH, RICHARD** Effects of maternal PKU of pregnancy outcome
N01HD-43810-12 ( ) ROUSE, BOBBY M** Effects of maternal PKU on pregnancy outcome
N01HD-52901-09 ( ) THOMAS, DAVID B** Steroid contraceptives and neoplasia
N01HD-52917-10 ( ) DAVISSON, MURIEL T** Model for cytogenetic disorders
N01HD-52934-16 ( ) LUBORSKY, JUDITH L** Operation and maintenance of a biological testing facility
N01HD-52944-19 ( ) NIERMAN, WILLIAM C** Repository of human DNA probes and libraries
N01HD-62905-16 ( ) BROWN, BRUCE** Preparation of adrenal and pituitary cells
N01HD-62906-14 ( ) HAY, ROBERT J** Low temperature storage of trophoblastic & liver cells
N01HD-62914-05 ( ) KOEPSELL, THOMAS D** Rheumatoid arthritis in relation to oral contraceptives
N01HD-62915-08 ( ) AUGUST, J THOMAS** Monoclonal antibodies for developmental studies
N01HD-62916-07 ( ) LAND, GARLAND** Factors associated with premature births derived from records
N01HD-62927-11 ( ) SCHNEIDER, JERRY A** New drug therapy in treatment of nephropathic cystinosis
N01HD-62930-07 ( ) GOLUB, HOWARD L** Identify infants at greatest risk for mental retardation
N01HD-62931-08 ( ) SHEPHERD, PATRICIA A** Identify infants at greatest risk for mental retardation
N01HD-62941-12 ( ) DOUGLAS, RICHARD** Production gonadotropins and prolactin
N01HD-72901-07 ( ) WESTOFF, CHARLES F** Annotation of population literature as research resource
N01HD-72909-09 ( ) KATZ, SOLOMON H** Preterm and small for gestational age delivery across generation
N01HD-72913-14 ( ) TACEY, RICHARD** Performance of radioimmunoassays and radioidinations
N01HD-72918-05 ( ) EXPOSITO, LORENZO F** Research for diabetes mellitus in pregnancy and youth
N01HD-72922-09 ( ) THANANART, PAT** Intervention trial to prevent low birth weight
N01HD-72925-28 ( ) DURAKO, STEVEN** Study of IV IgG in treatment of HIV infected children
N01HD-82903-07 ( ) FISHER, SUSAN J** Prenatal diagnosis using fetal cells obtained from maternal blood
N01HD-82904-07 ( ) ELIAS, SHERMAN** Prenatal diagnosis using fetal cells obtained from maternal circulation
N01HD-82908-10 ( ) MCKINLAY, SONJA M** Coordinating center for study of the history of HIV infection
N01HD-82909-07 ( ) HENDRICKS, ANDREW G** Maintenance of a non-human primate breeding colony
N01HD-82913-13 ( ) DURAKO, STEPHEN J** Studies of perinatal transmission of HIV infection
N01HD-82917-07 ( ) GRADY, GEORGE F** Seroepidemiologic study of HIV antibody prevalence
N01HD-92905-03 ( ) TARANGER, JOHN** Immunogenicity of pertussis toxiod-NICHD
N01HD-92907-04 ( ) HASSOLD, TERRY J** Non-disjunction of chromosome 21
N01HD-92908-11 ( ) MATES, SHARON** Production of acellular pertussis vaccine
N01HD-92909-03 ( ) CHIEN, YIE W** Transdermal delivery systems for fertility regulation
N01HD-92912-03 ( ) HARTZ, STUART C** Data bases/risks/benefit/of contraception and hormone use
N01HD-92913-03 ( ) COLDITZ, GRAHAM A** Long term mortality study of men who have undergone vasectomy
N01HD-92914-04 ( ) CONLEY, MARY** Diabetes in early pregnancy project data analysis
N01HD-92919-04 ( ) MOORE, KRISTIN A** Consequences of early childbearing in the 1980's
N01HD-92920-04 ( ) CUTTER, GARY R** Umbilical artery catheter placement associate with hemorrhage
N01HD-92921-02 ( ) COOK, C E** Development and testing of non-steroidal male contraceptive agents
N01HD-92925-04 ( ) ELLIS, GARY** Conference on steroid hormones and breast cancer
N01HD-92927-02 ( ) PARKE, JAMES C, JR** Evaluation of the safety and immunogenicity of an investigational vaccine
K04HG-00001-02 (SSS) GARDINER, KATHELEEN ELEANOR ROOSEVELT INSTITUTE 1899 GAYLORD STREET DENVER, COLORADO 80206 Molecular analysis of human chromosome 21 and 3
K04HG-00002-02 (SSS) LAWRENCE, JEANNE B UNIV OF MASSACHUSETTS MED CENT 55 LAKE AVENUE NORTH WORCESTER, MA 01655 Fluorescence gene mapping within nuclei & chromosomes
K04HG-00004-01 (BIO) BHAGWAT, ASHOK S WAYNE STATE UNIVERSITY 437 CHEMISTRY DETROIT, MI 48202 DNA cytosine methylation--Mechanism and consequences
K04HG-00005-03 (GEN) WU, CHUNG-I UNIVERSITY OF CHICAGO 1101 E. 57TH STREET CHICAGO, IL 60637 Molecular & evolutionary genetics of segregation distorter
R01HG-00008-02 (SSS) OTT, JURG COLUMBIA UNIVERSITY HEALTH SCI 722 WEST 168TH STREETS NEW YORK, NY 10032 Linkage analysis methods for human gene mapping
R01HG-00013-02 (SSS) WILLARD, HUNTINGTON F STANFORD UNIVERSITY STANFORD, CA 94305 Pushmi-pullyu hybrid mapping of the human x chromosome
R01HG-00017-02 (SSS) BEACH, DAVID H COLD SPRING HARBOR LABORATORY P O BOX 100 COLD SPRING HARBOR, N Y 11724 Fission yeast genome mapping
R01HG-00022-02 (SSS) LITT, MICHAEL OREGON HEALTH SCIENCES UNIV 3181 S W SAM JACKSON PARK ROAD PORTLAND, OR 97201-3098 Highly polymorphic microsatellite sequences in the human
R01HG-00023-02 (SSS) KARGER, BARRY L BARNETT INSTITUTE 360 HUNTINGTON AVENUE BOSTON, MA 02115 DNA sequencing using capillary electrophoresis
R01HG-00024-02 (SSS) LEDBETTER, DAVID H BAYLOR COLLEGE OF MEDICINE ONE BAYLOR PLAZA HOUSTON, TX 77030 High-resolution physical map of human chromosome 17
R01HG-00026-02 (SSS) HOLTZMAN, NEIL A THE JOHNS HOPKINS HOSPITAL 600 N WOLFE STREET BALTIMORE, MD 21205 Ethical & legal issues in the diffusion of genetic tests
R01HG-00029-01A1 (GNM) GIESE, ROGER W NORTHEASTERN UNIVERSITY 360 HUNTINGTON AVENUE BOSTON, MA 02115 Electrophore labels for DNA probes
R29HG-00037-02 (SSS) KORENBERG, JULIE R CEDARS-SINAI MEDICAL CENTER 8700 BEVERLY BLVD LOS ANGELES, CA 90048 A retroposon map of the human genome
R01HG-00038-02 (SSS) WARREN, STEPHEN T EMORY UNIVERSITY SCH OF MED WOODRUFF MEMORIAL BUILDING ATLANTA, GA 30322 Molecular genetic analysis of xq28
R01HG-00042-02 (SSS) KILLARY, ANN M UNIVERSITY OF TEXAS DIVISION OF LAB MEDICINE HOUSTON, TX 77030 High efficiency mapping with a human microcell panel
R29HG-00044-02 (SSS) JACKSON, CYNTHIA L RHODE ISLAND HOSPITAL 593 EDDY ST PROVIDENCE, RI 02903 Radiation hybrids from a marked human chromosome 9
R13HG-00049-02 (GEN) ROBERTS, RICHARD J COLD SPRING HARBOR LABORATORY POST OFFICE BOX 100 COLD SPRING HARBOR, NY 11724 Genome Mapping and Sequencing Conference
R44HG-00057-02 (SSS) SCHROEDER, JOHN L DNASTAR, INC 1228 SOUTH PARK STREET MADISON, WI 53715 A film scanner for high throughput DNA sequencing
R01HG-00079-02 (SSS) DOBKIN, CARL S NYS INST BASIC RESEARCH IN DD 1050 FOREST HILL RD STATEN ISLAND, NY 10314 Construction of an SFI I jumping library
R01HG-00081-02 (SSS) JOHNSON, DANIEL H UNIVERSITY OF MIAMI 1600 NW 10TH AVE MIAMI, FL 33101-9990 Sequence-independent amplification of dissected DNA
R01HG-00084-02 (SSS) HOOD, LEROY E CALIFORNIA INST OF TECHNOLOGY PASADENA, CA 91125 New approach to genetic mapping with DNA polymorphisms
R01HG-00096-02 (GEN) LOOMIS, WILLIAM F UNIV OF CALIFORNIA, SAN DIEGO 9500 GILMAN DRIVE LA JOLLA, CA 92093-0322 A physical map of the dictyostelium gonome
P50HG-00098-02 (SRC) LANDER, ERIC S WHITEHEAD INSTITUTE 9 CAMBRIDGE CENTER CAMBRIDGE, MA 02142 Center for genome research
R01HG-00099-02 (SSS) WALLACE, R BRUCE BECKMAN RES INST/CITY OF HOPE 1450 EAST DUARTE ROAD DUARTE, CA 91010 Gene mapping with amplified sequence polymorphisms-ASPS
R01HG-00100-02 (SSS) DONIS-KELLER, HELEN WASHINGTON UNIV SCHOOL OF MED 660 SOUTH EUCLID, BOX 8232 ST LOUIS, MO 63110 Linkage mapping human telomeres and centromeres
R01HG-00101-02 (SSS) SELDIN, MICHAEL F DUKE UNIVERSITY MEDICAL CTR BOX 3380 DURHAM, NC 27710 Genetic analysis of the mouse genome
R01HG-00106-02 (SRC) MC CLELLAND, MICHAEL CALIFORNIA INST OF BIO RESEARC 11099 NORTH TORREY PINES ROAD LA JOLLA, CA 92037 Enzymes involved in methylase/DPNI cleavage strategies
R01HG-00107-05 (GNM) WILLARD, HUNTINGTON F STANFORD UNIVERSITY STANFORD, CA 94305 Mapping centromeric regions of human chromosomes
R13HG-00119-02 (GNM) TEICH, ALBERT H AAAS 1333 H ST, NW WASHINGTON, DC 20005 Ethical and legal implications of genetic testing
R01HG-00122-01A1 (GNM) MAO, JEN-I COLLABORATIVE RESEARCH, INC TWO OAK PARK BEDFORD, MA 01730 A physical and refined genetic map of human chromosome 10
R01HG-00124-02 (SSS) GILBERT, WALTER BIOLOGICAL LABORATORIES 16 DIVINITY AVE CAMBRIDGE, MA 02138 Direct genome sequencing--Mycoplasma capricolum
R01HG-00126-02 (SSS) GRAY, MARK R TUFTS UNIV SCHOOL OF MED 136 HARRISON AVENUE BOSTON, MA 02111 Mouse genetic markers using denaturing gradient gels
R01HG-00130-02 (MGN) GERT, BERNARD DARTMOUTH COLLEGE HANOVER, NH 03755 Ethical issues arising from the human genome project
R01HG-00131-01A1 (GNM) HERMAN, GAIL E BAYLOR COLLEGE OF MEDICINE ONE BAYLOR PLAZA HOUSTON, TX 77030 Physical and genetic mapping of the mouse X chromosome
R01HG-00136-02 (SSS) WATERSTON, ROBERT H WASH UNIV SCHOOL OF MEDICINE 660 SOUTH EUCLID AVENUE ST LOUIS, MO 63110 Sequencing the C. elegans genome
R13HG-00160-01S1 (MGN) ROTHSTEIN, MARK A UNIVERSITY OF HOUSTON LAW CTR 104 TU2 HOUSTON, TX 77204-6381 Legal and ethical issues raised

by the genome project

R29HG-00167-03 (SSS) OVERHAUSER, JOAN M THOMAS JEFFERSON UNIVERSITY DEPT OF BIOCHEM & MOL BIO PHILADELPHIA, PA 19107 Molecular analysis of dosage syndromes of chromosome 18

R01HG-00169-09 (SSS) GUSELLA, JAMES F MASSACHUSETTS GENERAL HOSPITAL FRUIT STREET BOSTON, MA 02114 Ordered overlapping cosmid clones for human chr 21 & 22

R01HG-00170-01 (SSS) CHAPMAN, VERNE M ROSWELL PARK MEMORIAL INST ELM & CARLTON STREETS BUFFALO, N Y 14263 Cumulative multilocus map of mouse chromosome 5

R55HG-00172-01A1 (GNM) WELLS, DAN E UNIVERSITY OF HOUSTON 4800 CALHOUN HOUSTON, TX 77204-5513 Deletion syndromes as tools for mapping chromosome 8

R01HG-00174-02 (SSS) BECKER, CHRISTOPHER H SRI INTERNATIONAL 333 RAVENSWOOD AVE MENLO PARK, CA 94025-3493 Sequencing of DNA by laser ionization

R01HG-00175-01 (SRC) MILLER, PERRY L YALE UNIVERSITY SCHOOL OF MED PO BOX 3333/333 CEDAR ST NEW HAVEN, CT 06510 Representation and retrieval of physical mapping data

R55HG-00177-01 (SSS) LALANDE, MARC E CHILDREN'S HOSPITAL 300 LONGWOOD AVE BOSTON, MA 02115 A physical map of chromosome 13q

R01HG-00180-02 (SRC) GILLETT, WILL D WASHINGTON UNIVERSITY CAMPUS BOX 1045/ONE BROOKINGS ST LOUIS, MO 63130-4899 Computer management of high-resolution physical DNA maps

R01HG-00186-06 (SSS) BRUNS, GAIL A P CHILDREN'S HOSPITAL CORP 300 LONGWOOD AVENUE BOSTON, MASS 02115 Glycolytic and peroxisomal genes on chromosome 11 and 12

R01HG-00189-04 (MGN) NADEAU, JOSEPH H JACKSON LABORATORY 600 MAIN STREET BAR HARBOR, ME 04609-0800 Gene mapping and genome organization in mammals

R01HG-00190-04A1 (GNM) HARDIES, STEPHEN C UNIV OF TEXAS 7703 FLOYD CURL DR SAN ANTONIO, TX 78284-7760 Mammalian repetitive sequences as a genetic tool

R43HG-00191-01A1 (SSS) FULLER, CARL W US BIOCHEMICAL CORPORATION-RES 26111 MILES ROAD CLEVELAND, OH 44128 Intensity encoded DNA sequencing

R37HG-00198-17 (GEN) DAVIS, RONALD W STANFORD UNIVERSITY DEPARTMENT OF BIOCHEMISTRY STANFORD, CALIF 94305 Cell regulation--Biochemically isolated DNA segments

P30HG-00199-01 (SRC) GESTELAND, RAYMOND F UNIVERSITY OF UTAH 743 WINTROBE BLDG SALT LAKE CITY, UT 84132 Utah center for human genome research

P30HG-00199-01 0001 (SRC) WEISS, ROBERT B Utah center for human genome research Multiplex sequencing

P30HG-00199-01 0002 (SRC) DOVICHI, NORMAN J Utah center for human genome research Capillary sequencing

P30HG-00199-01 0003 (SRC) WHITE, RAYMOND Utah center for human genome research Marker development

P30HG-00199-01 9001 (SRC) LEPPERT, MARK F Utah center for human genome research Linkage technology access core

P30HG-00199-01 9002 (SRC) CARTWRIGHT, PETER Utah center for human genome research Informatics lab core

P30HG-00199-01 9003 (SRC) CARTWRIGHT, PETER Utah center for human genome research Computer core

P30HG-00199-01 9004 (SRC) GESTELAND, RAYMOND F Utah center for human genome research Engineering and design core

P30HG-00199-01 9005 (SRC) GESTELAND, RAYMOND F Utah center for human genome research DNA synthesizer core

P50HG-00201-02 (SRC) SCHLESSINGER, DAVID WASHINGTON UNIVERSITY 660 SOUTH EUCLID, BOX 8232 ST LOUIS, MO 63110 Yeast artificial chromosome-based genome mapping

P01HG-00202-02 (SRC) EVANS, GLEN A THE SALK INSTITUTE PO BOX 85800 SAN DIEGO, CA 92186-5800 Structural studies of human chromosome 11

P01HG-00202-02 0001 (SRC) EVANS, GLEN A Structural studies of human chromosome 11 Physical mapping of the long arm of chromosome 11

P01HG-00202-02 0002 (SRC) SUKUMAR, SARASWATI Structural studies of human chromosome 11 Physical mapping of the short arm of chromosome 11

P01HG-00202-02 0003 (SRC) HOEKSTRA, MERL F Structural studies of human chromosome 11 Yeast artificial chromosome clones and libraries for chromosome 11

P01HG-00202-02 0004 (SRC) WAHL, GEOFFREY M Structural studies of human chromosome 11 Somatic cell techniques for mapping chromosome 11

P01HG-00202-02 9001 (SRC) MCELLIGOTT, DAVID Structural studies of human chromosome 11 Core--Microscopy

P01HG-00202-02 9002 (SRC) MCELLIGOTT, DAVID L Structural studies of human chromosome 11 Clone archive and screening laboratory

P01HG-00202-02 9003 (SRC) MCELLIGOTT, DAVID Structural studies of human chromosome 11 Core--DNA synthesis and sequencing

P01HG-00202-02 9004 (SRC) EVANS, GLEN A Structural studies of human chromosome 11 Core--Database

P01HG-00202-02 9005 (SRC) EVANS, GLEN Structural studies of human chromosome 11 Core--Developmental activities

R01HG-00203-01A1 (MGN) MARR, THOMAS G COLD SPRING HARBOR LABORATORY P O BOX 100 COLD SPRING HARBOR, N Y 11724 Database and computer tools for genome mapping

P01HG-00205-02 (SRC) BOTSTEIN, DAVID STANFORD UNIVERSITY STANFORD, CA 94305 Sequence of the yeast genome

P01HG-00205-02 0001 (SRC) DAVIS, RONALD Sequence of the yeast genome DNA sequencing

P01HG-00205-02 0002 (SRC) BOTSTEIN, DAVID Sequence of the yeast genome Genetic structure and function

P01HG-00205-02 9001 (SRC) BOTSTEIN, DAVID Sequence of the yeast genome Core--Oligonucleotide synthesis

P01HG-00205-02 9002 (SRC) BOTSTEIN, DAVID Sequence of the yeast genome Computer core

P01HG-00205-02 9003 (SRC) DAVIS, RONALD Sequence of the yeast genome Automation core

P01HG-00205-02 9004 (SRC) BOTSTEIN, DAVID Sequence of the yeast genome Laboratory services core

P50HG-00206-01S1 (SRC) MYERS, RICHARD M UNIVERSITY OF CALIFORNIA 513 PARNASSUS AVENUE SAN FRANCISCO, CA 94143-0444 Fine-structure mapping of human chromosome 4

P50HG-00206-01S1 0001 (SRC) MYERS, RICHARD M Fine-structure mapping of human chromosome 4 Characterization of DNA probes from human chromosome 4

P50HG-00206-01S1 0002 (SRC) COX, DAVID R Fine-structure mapping of human chromosome 4 Radiation hybrid mapping of human chromosome 4

P50HG-00206-01S1 0003 (SRC) RIDER, SUSAN H Fine-structure mapping of human chromosome 4 Large insert physical mapping of human chromosome 4

P50HG-00206-01S1 0004 (SRC) MURRAY, JEFFREY C Fine-structure mapping of human chromosome 4 Linkage and heterozygosity studies on chromosome 4

P50HG-00206-01S1 0005 (SRC) BUETOW, KENNETH H Fine-structure mapping of human chromosome 4 Quantitative aspects in high resolution meiotic mapping

P50HG-00206-01S1 9001 (SRC) MYERS, RICHARD M Fine-structure mapping of human chromosome 4 Core--Technical core

P30HG-00209-02 (SRC) COLLINS, FRANCIS S UNIV OF MICHIGAN MEDICAL CTR 3570 MSRB II BOX 0652/INT MED ANN ARBOR, MI 48109-0650 Genomic technology and genetic disease

P30HG-00209-02 0001 (SRC) CHAMBERLAIN, JEFFREY Genomic technology and genetic disease Generation of variable number short tandem repeat-specific libraries

P30HG-00209-02 0002 (SRC) COLLINS, FRANCIS Genomic technology and genetic disease Identifying transcripts encoded within yeast artificial chromosomes

P30HG-00209-02 0003 (SRC) ENGELKE, DAVID Genomic technology and genetic disease Expanded PCR for use in genetic mapping

P30HG-00209-02 0004 (SRC) LUBMAN, DAVID Genomic technology and genetic disease DNA sequencing via Maxam-Gilbert cleavage--Mass spectrometry rapid detection

P30HG-00209-02 0005 (SRC) PASYK, KRYSTYNA Genomic technology and genetic disease Linkage analysis of familial vascular malformations

P30HG-00209-02 0006 (SRC) SWAROOP, ANAND Genomic technology and genetic disease Region and chromosome-specific cDNA libraries

P30HG-00209-02 9001 (SRC) MARKEL, DORENE Genomic technology and genetic disease Family collection core

P30HG-00209-02 9002 (SRC) CHAMBERLAIN, JEFFREY S Genomic technology and genetic disease Genetic marker core

P30HG-00209-02 9003 (SRC) BOEHNKE, MICHAEL L Genomic technology and genetic disease Statistical genetics core

P30HG-00209-02 9004 (SRC) GLOVER, THOMAN Genomic technology and genetic disease Somatic cell genetics core

P30HG-00209-02 9005 (SRC) COLLINS, FRANCIS Genomic technology and genetic disease Library core

P30HG-00209-02 9006 (SRC) ENGELKE, DAVID Genomic technology and genetic disease DNA sequencing core

P30HG-00210-01 (SRC) CASKEY, CHARLES T BAYLOR COLLEGE OF MEDICINE ONE BAYLOR PLAZA HOUSTON, TX 77030 Baylor College of Medicine human genome program center

P30HG-00210-01 0001 (SRC) BEATTIE, KENNETH L Baylor College of Medicine human genome program center Pilot--Oligonucleotide synthesis for high throughput genomic sequencing

P30HG-00210-01 0002 (SRC) SMITH, LOUIS C Baylor College of Medicine human genome program center Pilot--In situ hybridization of human chromosome X

P30HG-00210-01 0003 (SRC) GIBBS, RICHARD A Baylor College of Medicine human genome program center Pilot--Methods for rapid determination of sequence tagged segments

P30HG-00210-01 9001 (SRC) LEDBETTER, DAVID H Baylor College of Medicine human genome program center Core--Mapping

P30HG-00210-01 9002 (SRC) CHINAULT, A CRAIG Baylor College of Medicine human genome program center Core--Cloning

P30HG-00210-01 9003 (SRC) GIBBS, RICHARD A Baylor College of Medicine human genome program center Core--Sequencing

P30HG-00210-01 9004 (SRC) LAWRENCE, CHARLES B Baylor College of Medicine human genome program center Core--Computation

P30HG-00210-01 9005 (SRC) MCCABE, EDWARD Baylor College of Medicine human genome program center Core--Molecular medicine

R01HG-00220-01 (GNM) BERGET, SUSAN M BAYLOR COLLEGE OF MEDICINE ONE BAYLOR PLAZA HOUSTON, TX 77030 Exon detection in vertebrate DNA

R01HG-00223-01 (GNM) FRISSE, MARK E WASHINGTON UNIV SCH OF MEDICIN 660 SOUTH EUCLID AVENUE ST LOUIS , MO 63110 A human yeast artificial chromosome library database

R01HG-00225-01 (GNM) SCHWARTZ, DAVID C NEW YORK UNIVERSITY 4 WASHINGTON PLACE 514 NEW YORK, NY 10003 New physical methodologies for genomic analysis

R01HG-00233-01 (GNM) PUCK, JENNIFER M JOSEPH STOKES JR RESEARCH INST 34TH STREET & CIVIC CTR BLVD PHILADELPHIA, PA 19104 Xcen-xq21.3 in overlapping yeast artificial chromosomes

R01HG-00236-01A1 (GNM) OVERHAUSER, JOAN M THOMAS JEFFERSON UNIV 1020 LOCUST ST PHILADELPHIA, PA 19107 Deletion analysis of the short arm of chromosome 5

R01HG-00243-27 (MGN) PIOUS, DONALD A UNIVERSITY OF WASHINGTON PEDIATRICS DEPT, RD-20 SEATTLE, WA 98195 Genetic structure and function in human cells

R01HG-00244-07 (MGN) COLLINS, FRANCIS S UNIVERSITY OF MICHIGAN 4708 MEDICAL SCIENCE II ANN ARBOR, MI 48109-0618 Chromosome hopping by a DNA circularization technique

R01HG-00246-03 (SSS) WARD, DAVID C YALE UNIVERSITY SCH OF MED 333 CEDAR STREET, PO BOX 3333 NEW HAVEN, CT 06510 New methods for analyzing human genes & their defects

R01HG-00247-03 (MGN) SCHLESSINGER, DAVID WASHINGTON UNIVERSITY SCH OF M BOX 8230 ST LOUIS, MO 63110-1093 Human distal q DNA--Analysis with YACs

R01HG-00248-04 (SSS) WEBER, JAMES L MARSHFIELD MED RES & EDUC FDN 1000 NORTH OAK AVENUE MARSHFIELD, WI 54449-5790 Analysis of an abundant class of human DNA polymorphisms

R01HG-00249-03 (SSS) STORMO, GARY D UNIVERSITY OF COLORADO CAMPUS BOX 347 BOULDER, CO 80309-0347 DNA pattern identification and analysis

R01HG-00250-04 (SSS) YOUDERIAN, PHILIP A CALIF INST OF BIOLOG RESEARCH 11099 NORTH TORREY PINES ROAD LA JOLLA, CA 92037 Directed rearrangement of the mammalian genome in vivo

PROJECT NUMBER LISTING

PROJECT NO., ORGANIZATIONAL UNIT., INVESTIGATOR, ADDRESS, TITLE

R01HG-00251-03 (SSS) LAWRENCE, JEANNE B UNIV OF MASSACHUSETTS MED CTR 55 LAKE AVE NORTH WORCESTER, MA 01655 Fluorescent gene mapping at interphase & metaphase

R01HG-00255-01 (BIO) SIGMAN, DAVID S UCLA SCHOOL OF MEDICINE CENTER FOR HEALTH SCIENCES LOS ANGELES, CA 90024-1737 Sequence-specific chemical nucleases for genome analysis

R01HG-00256-01 (GNM) TRASK, BARBARA J LAWRENCE LIVERMORE NATIONAL LA PO BOX 5507/L452 LIVERMORE, CA 94550 Chromatin mapping by fluorescence in situ hybridization

R01HG-00257-01 (GNM) PAGE, DAVID C WHITEHEAD INST FOR BIOMED RES NINE CAMBRIDGE CENTER CAMBRIDGE, MA 02142 Mapping and sequencing the human Y chromosome

R13HG-00262-02 (SRC) MURRAY, JEFFREY C UNIVERSITY OF IOWA IOWA CITY, IA 52242 CEPH consortium linkage maps

R01HG-00263-01 (GNM) KING, MARY C UNIVERSITY OF CALIFORNIA SCHOOL OF PUBLIC HEALTH-BEHS BERKELEY, CA 94720 Sequencing mtDNA for human identification

R13HG-00265-01 (GNM) KARJALA, DENNIS S ARIZONA STATE UNIVERSITY TEMPE, AZ 85287-0604 A legal research agenda for the human genome initiative

R13HG-00270-01 (GNM) BROWN, R STEVEN COUNCIL STATE GOVERNMENTS PO BOX 11910 LEXINGTON, KY 40578-1910 State governments and the human genome project

R01HG-00272-02 (SRC) WARD, DAVID C YALE UNIV SCH OF MEDICINE 333 CEDAR STREET NEW HAVEN, CT 06510 High resolution of gene mapping by in situ hybridization

R13HG-00275-02 (SRC) BODMER, WALTER F IMPERIAL CANCER RESEARCH FUND PO BOX 123 LINCOLNS INN FIELDS LONDON WC2A 3PX, U.K Human gene mapping workshops 10.5/11 -- Travel from USA

R01HG-00277-15 (MGN) CHAPMAN, VERNE M ROSWELL PARK MEMORIAL INST ELM & CARLTON STREETS BUFFALO, NY 14263 Genetic ox x-chromosome regulation in mammals

R43HG-00293-01 (SSS) MACCONNELL, WILLIAM P MACCONNELL RESEARCH 11408 SORRENTO VALLEY RD SAN DIEGO, CA 92121 Universal contamination-preventing pipet tips for PCR

R43HG-00295-01 (SSS) MAO, JEN-I COLLABORATIVE RESEARCH, INC TWO OAK PARK BEDFORD, MA 01730 Use of human polymorphic alu loci as genetic markers

R43HG-00296-01 (SSS) MILLER, GERALD DNASTAR, INC 1228 SOUTH PARK ST MADISON, WI 53715 A reaction robot for high throughput DNA sequencing

R01HG-00298-14 (MGN) FRANCKE, UTA STANFORD UNIV SCH OF MEDICINE DEPARTMENT OF GENETICS STANFORD, CA 94305-4125 Intrachromosomal gene mapping

R01HG-00299-12 (MGN) HOUSMAN, DAVID E MASSACHUSETTS INSTITUTE 77 MASS AVENUE, E17-543 CAMBRIDGE, MA 02139 Genetic mapping and DNA structure of human chromosome 11

R01HG-00300-09 (MGN) D'EUSTACHIO, PETER G NYU MEDICAL CENTER 550 FIRST AVE NEW YORK, NY 10016 Molecular genetics of mouse chromosome 12

R01HG-00301-04 (GRRC) BLATTNER, FREDERICK R UNIVERSITY OF WISCONSIN 445 HENRY MALL MADISON, WI 53706 Determination of complete sequence of E coli

R01HG-00303-04 (SSS) ROBERTS, RICHARD J COLD SPRING HARBOR LABORATORY POST OFFICE BOX 100 COLD SPRING HARBOR, N Y 11724 A search for new restriction endonucleases

R01HG-00304-04S1 (SSS) DONIS-KELLER, HELEN WASH UNIV SCH-MED 660 S EUCLID ST LOUIS, MO 63110 A complete genetic linkage map of the human genome

R01HG-00305-04 (SSS) KOLODNER, RICHARD D DANA FARBER CANCER INSTITUTE 44 BINNEY STREET BOSTON, MA 02115 Enzymology of mismatch repair in yeast

R01HG-00307-04 (SSS) WARD, DAVID C YALE UNIV/ DEPT. OF HUMAN GENE 155 WHITNEY AVEUNE NEW HAVEN, CT 06520 Affinity purification of large fragments of human DNA

R01HG-00309-03 (SSS) FRIEDMANN, THEODORE UNIVERSITY OF CALIFORNIA DEPT OF PEDIATRICS M-034 LA JOLLA, CA 92093 Physical map of the human x chromosome

R01HG-00311-03 (SSS) PIRROTTA, VINCENZO BAYLOR COLLEGE OF MEDICINE DEPT OF CELL BIOLOGY HOUSTON, TX 77030 Microcloning of the Drosophila genome

R01HG-00312-03 (SSS) JUKES, THOMAS H UNIVERSITY OF CALIFORNIA 6701 SAN PABLO AVE OAKLAND, CA 94608 Coding & noncoding regions in DNA sequences

R01HG-00313-03 (SSS) ROE, BRUCE A UNIVERSITY OF OKLAHOMA DEPARTMENT OF CHEMISTRY NORMAN, OK 73019 Automated methods for sequencing the human c-abl gene

R01HG-00314-03 (SRC) FRANCKE, UTA STANFORD UNIVERSITY 125 PANAMA STREET/BIRCH STANFORD, CA 94305-4125 A physical map of human chromosome 18

R01HG-00315-03 (SRC) NAYLOR, SUSAN L UNIV OF TEXAS HEALTH SCI CTR 7703 FLOYD CURL DRIVE SAN ANTONIO, TX 78284 Physical map of human chromosome 3

R01HG-00316-03 (SRC) FRIEDMAN, JEFFREY M ROCKEFELLER UNIVERSITY 1230 YORK AVENUE NEW YORK, NY 10021-6399 Molecular mapping of the mouse genome

R01HG-00317-03 (SRC) GUSELLA, JAMES F MASS GENERAL HOSPITAL 32 FRUIT STREET BOSTON, MA 02114 Ordered overlapping cosmid clones for human chr 21 & 22

R01HG-00318-03 (SRC) LANE, MICHAEL J SUNY HEALTH SCIENCE CTR 750 EAST ADAMS STREET SYRACUSE, NY 13210 A human restriction map derived from genomic insertion data

R01HG-00319-03 (SRC) TARTOF, KENNETH D INSTITUTE FOR CANCER RESEARCH 7701 BURHOLME AVENUE PHILADELPHIA, PA 19111 Genomic mapping

R01HG-00320-03 (SRC) WASMUTH, JOHN J UNIV OF CALIF, IRVINE DEPT OF BIOLOGICAL CHEMISTRY IRVINE, CA 92717 High resolution physical maps of 4P and 5q

R01HG-00321-03 (SRC) SMITH, LLOYD M UNIVERSITY OF WISCONSIN DEPT OF CHEM/1101 UNIV AVENUE MADISON, WI 53706 A system for large-scale automated DNA sequencing

R01HG-00322-03 (SSS) ECKER, JOSEPH R UNIVERSITY OF PENNSYLVANIA 415 S UNIVERSITY AVE PHILADELPHIA, PA 19104-6018 Development of large DNA methods for arabidopsis

PROJECT NO., ORGANIZATIONAL UNIT., INVESTIGATOR, ADDRESS, TITLE

R01HG-00323-03 (GNM) BRENNAN, THOMAS M GENOMYX, INC 460 POINT SAN BRUNO BLVD SOUTH SAN FRANCISCO, CA 94080 New methods to sequence DNA by mass spectrometry

R01HG-00324-03 (SSS) HAINES, JONATHAN L MASSACHUSETTS GENERAL HOSPITAL 13TH STREET BOSTON, MA 02114 Fine structure genetic linkage map of chromosome 21 & 22

R01HG-00325-03 (SRC) COHEN, STANLEY N STANFORD UNIVERSITY SCH OF MED DEPT OF GENETICS/ROOM S-337 STANFORD, CA 94305 Novel approaches for genomic DNA cloning and analysis

R01HG-00326-03 (SRC) MAGLOTT, DONNA R AMERICAN TYPE CULTURE COLLECTI 12301 PARKLAWN DRIVE ROCKVILLE, MD 20852-1776 Developing procedures for a genomic repository

R01HG-00328-03 (SRC) ARNHEIM, NORMAN UNIV OF SOUTHERN CALIFORNIA MOLECULAR BIO/SHS 172, MC 1340 LOS ANGELES, CA 90089-1340 Genetic and molecular studies of mouse and human RDNA

R01HG-00329-03 (SRC) DERVAN, PETER B DEPARTMENT OF CHEMISTRY CALIFORNIA INST OF TECHNOLOGY PASADENA, CA 91125 Site specific chemical methods for cleaving genomic DNA

P01HG-00330-03 (SRC) NADEAU, JOSEPH H JACKSON LABORATORY 600 MAIN STREET BAR HARBOR, ME 04609-0800 Multi-level analysis and display of mouse genome data

P01HG-00330-03 0001 (SRC) NADEAU, JOSEPH H Multi-level analysis and display of mouse genome data Comparative gene mapping--HMDP and DUPLIGENE

P01HG-00330-03 0002 (SRC) EPPIG, JANAN T Multi-level analysis and display of mouse genome data Regional and molecular mapping

P01HG-00330-03 0003 (SRC) MOBRAATEN, LARRY E Multi-level analysis and display of mouse genome data Genetic data sharing and display

P01HG-00330-03 9001 (SRC) NADEAU, JOSEPH H Multi-level analysis and display of mouse genome data Core

R01HG-00331-03 (SRC) THOMAS, LEWIS J, JR BIOMEDICAL COMPUTER LAB 700 SOUTH EUCLID ST LOUIS, MO 63110 Advanced quantitative imaging for DNA physical mapping

R01HG-00332-03 (NEUC) SUTCLIFFE, J G THE SCRIPPS RESEARCH INSTITUTE DEPT OF MOLECULAR BIOLOGY LA JOLLA, CA 92037 Physical approach to genetics of cerebellum development

R01HG-00333-19 (GNM) SHOWS, THOMAS B ROSWELL PARK MEMORIAL INST 666 ELM STREET BUFFALO, N Y 14263 Mapping molecular disease and cancer-related genes

R01HG-00335-04 (SSS) KARLIN, SAMUEL STANFORD UNIVERSITY STANFORD, CALIF 94305 Analysis of molecular sequence data

R01HG-00336-03 (SSS) MACCLUER, JEAN W SOUTHWEST FDN FOR BIOMED RES DEPARTMENT OF GENETICS SAN ANTONIO, TX 78228-0147 Genetic mapping in baboons

R01HG-00337-03 (SRC) TIMBERLAKE, WILLIAM E UNIVERSITY OF GEORGIA ATHENS, GA 30602 Developing procedures for a genomic repository

R01HG-00338-03 (SRC) RADDING, CHARLES M YALE UNIVERSITY SCH OF MED 333 CEDAR STREET NEW HAVEN, CT 06510 RNA-DNA hybridization by E. coli recA protein

R01HG-00339-03 (SRC) STERNBERG, NAT L DU PONT MERCK PHARMACEUTICAL C P.O. BOX 80328 WILMINGTON, DE 19880-0328 Bacteriophage P1 cloning system for high molecular weight

R01HG-00340-10 (MGN) DEININGER, PRESCOTT L DEPT-BIOCHEM & MOLECULAR BIO LSU MED CTR/1901 PERDIDO ST NEW ORLEANS, LA 70112 Human interspersed repeated DNA sequences

R01HG-00343-07 (SSS) KEATS, BRONYA J L S U MEDICAL CENTER DEPT OF BIOMETRY & GENETICS NEW ORLEANS, LA 70112 Maximum likelihood mapping of the human chromosomes

R01HG-00344-07 (MGN) CHAKRAVARTI, ARAVINDA SCHOOL OF PUBLIC HEALTH UNIVERSITY OF PITTSBURGH PITTSBURGH, PA 15261 Genetic heterogeneity in human disease

R37HG-00345-07 (SSS) LERMAN, LEONARD S MASSACHUSETTS INST OF TECH DEPARTMENT OF BIOLOGY CAMBRIDGE, MA 02139 Strategy for the characterization of the human genome

R01HG-00346-12 (ALY) MC DEVITT, HUGH O STANFORD UNIVERSITY D345 FAIRCHILD BUILDING STANFORD, CA 94305 Restriction fragment analysis of hla-d haplotypes

R01HG-00348-04 (SSS) RISCH, NEIL J YALE UNIVERSITY SCHOOL OF MED 60 COLLEGE STREET NEW HAVEN, CT 06510 Statistical methods and applications in human genetics

R29HG-00349-04 (MBC) HACKETT, NEIL R CORNELL UNIVERSITY MED COLLEGE 1300 YORK AVENUE NEW YORK, N Y 10021 Physical mapping of an archaebacterial genome

R01HG-00350-04 (GEN) ALTSCHULER, MARSHA I WILLIAMS COLLEGE DEPARTMENT OF BIOLOGY WILLIAMSTOWN, MA 01267 Cloning and analysis of Tetrahymena somatic chromosomes

R01HG-00355-04 (SRC) MURRAY, JEFFREY C UNIVERSITY OF IOWA DEPARTMENT OF PEDIATRICS IOWA CITY, IOWA 52242 Detailed mapping and recombination of chromosome four

R01HG-00356-04 (SRC) HOOD, LEROY E CALIFORNIA INST OF TECHNOLOGY BIOLOGY DIVISION PASADENA, CA 91125 Characterization of the genomes

R01HG-00357-04 (SRC) HARTL, DANIEL L WASHINGTON UNIV/SCHOOL OF MED DEPT OF GENETICS ST. LOUIS, MO 63110 Drosophila genome mapping using yac vectors

R01HG-00358-04 (GNM) DRABKIN, HARRY A UNIV OF COLORADO HLTH SCI CTR 4200 EAST 9TH AVE DENVER, CO 80262 Physical map and contigs for human chromosome 3

R01HG-00359-04 (SRC) SHOWS, THOMAS B ROSWELL PARK MEMORIAL INST 666 ELM STREET BUFFALO, N Y 14263 Mapping human chromosome 11

R01HG-00360-04 (MGN) FAIN, PAMELA R UNIVERSITY OF UTAH 420 CHIPETA WAY SALT LAKE CITY, UT 84108 High resolution genetic mapping--Strategy-based approach

R01HG-00362-04 (SRC) EFSTRATIADIS, ARGIRIS COLUMBIA UNIVERSITY DEPT OF GENETICS & DEVELOPMENT NEW YORK, N Y 10032 CDNA probes for exon mapping of the human genome

P01HG-00365-04 (SRC) RUDDLE, FRANK H YALE UNIVERSITY DEPT OF BIOLOGY/BOX 1504A NEW HAVEN, CT 06520 High resolution genetic analysis of complex genomes

P01HG-00365-04 0001 (SRC) RUDDLE, FRANK H High resolution genetic analysis of complex genomes Macromapping of mammalian genomes

P01HG-00365-04 0002 (SRC) KIDD, KENNETH K High resolution genetic

PROJECT NO., ORGANIZATIONAL UNIT., INVESTIGATOR, ADDRESS, TITLE

analysis of complex genomes Mendelian fine structure mapping of the human genome
P01HG-00365-04 0003 (SRC) SNYDER, MICHAEL High resolution genetic analysis of complex genomes Cloning and mapping large segments of eukaryotic DNA
P01HG-00365-04 0004 (SRC) SCHREIBER, STUART L High resolution genetic analysis of complex genomes Dual domain reagents for sequence selective DNA cleavage
P01HG-00365-04 0005 (SRC) ARTAVANIS-TSAKONAS, SPYROS High resolution genetic analysis of complex genomes Rapid DNA sequencing
P01HG-00365-04 9001 (SRC) RUDDLE, FRANK H High resolution genetic analysis of complex genomes Core--DNA service laboratory
R55HG-00366-04 (MGN) WARBURTON, DOROTHY P COLUMBIA UNIVERSITY 701 WEST 168TH STREET NEW YORK, NY 10032 Monochromosomal hybrids by retroviral marker transfer
R01HG-00367-04 (SRC) WHITE, RAYMOND L UNIVERSITY OF UTAH DEPARTMENT OF HUMAN GENETICS SALT LAKE CITY, UT 84132 Tools for high resolution linkage mapping of human genes
R01HG-00368-04 (SRC) LOVETT, MICHAEL GENELABS INCORPORATED DEPARTMENT OF HUMAN GENETICS REDWOOD CITY, CA 94063 New methods for producing chromosome-specific libraries
R01HG-00370-04 (SRC) RINCHIK, EUGENE M MARTIN MARIETTA ENERGY SYSTEM OAK RIDGE NAT LAB, PO BOX 2009 OAK RIDGE, TN 37831 Saturation mutagenesis of mouse genomic regions
R01HG-00371-04 (SSS) SUTHERLAND, JOHN C BROOKHAVEN NATIONAL LABORATORY BIOLOGY DEPT, ASSOC UNIV, INC UPTON, N Y 11973 New approaches to DNA mapping--Electronic imaging
R01HG-00372-04 (SSS) BURR, BENJAMIN BROOKHAVEN NATIONAL LABORATORY BIOLOGY DEPT/ASSO UNIV, INC. UPTON, N Y 11973 Mapping and characterizing quantitative traits in maize
P01HG-00373-04 (SSS) MCKUSICK, VICTOR A JOHNS HOPKINS HOSPITAL 600 NORTH WOLFE STREET BALTIMORE, MD 21205 Mapping the chromosomes of man
P01HG-00373-04 0005 (SSS) HURKO, OREST Mapping the chromosomes of man Mapping selected neurologic disorders
P01HG-00373-04 0006 (SSS) ANTONARAKIS, STYLIANOS E Mapping the chromosomes of man Mapping the Norrie disease locus
P01HG-00373-04 9001 (SSS) SCOTT, ALAN F Mapping the chromosomes of man Core facility--Genetics resource
P01HG-00373-04 9002 (SSS) BIAS, WILMA B Mapping the chromosomes of man Core--Amish population genetics resource
P01HG-00373-04 9003 (SSS) MEYERS, DEBORAH A Mapping the chromosomes of man Core--Data management and analysis
P01HG-00373-04 0001 (SSS) HEITER, PHILIP Mapping the chromosomes of man Analysis of DNA on yeast artificial chromosomes
P01HG-00373-04 0002 (SSS) SCOTT, ALAN F Mapping the chromosomes of man New methods for detection of DNA polymorphisms
P01HG-00373-04 0003 (SSS) JABS, ETHYLIN W Mapping the chromosomes of man Centromere mapping and recombination interference
P01HG-00373-04 0004 (SSS) FRANOMANO, CLAIR A Mapping the chromosomes of man Mapping selected skeletal dysplasias
R29HG-00374-04 (SSS) GEORGE, VARGHESE T LSU MED CTR/1901 PERDIDO ST DEPT OF BIOMETRY NEW ORLEANS, LA 70112-1393 Estimation & test of marker association in family data
R01HG-00375-04 (SSS) WATERSTON, ROBERT H WASHINGTON UNIVERSITY DEPT OF GENETICS, BOX 8031 ST LOUIS, MO 63110 Physical map of the C. elegans genome
R29HG-00376-04 (EDC) BOEHNKE, MICHAEL L UNIVERSITY OF MICHIGAN DEPARTMENT OF BIOSTATISTICS ANN ARBOR, MI 48109 Design issues in genetic linkage and segregation studies
R29HG-00377-03 (SSS) BARSH, GREGORY S STANFORD UNIV SCHOOL OF MED DEPARTMENT OF PEDIATRICS STANFORD, CA 94305 Physical and genetic analysis of the mouse agouti locus
R01HG-00378-04 (SRC) GARDINER, KATHELEEN ELEANOR ROOSEVELT INSTITUTE 1899 GAYLORD STREET DENVER, COLORADO 80206 Cloning large fragments of chromosome three DNA
R01HG-00379-01 (GNM) SZYBALSKI, WACLAW UNIVERSITY OF WISCONSIN 1400 UNIVERSITY AVENUE MADISON, WI 53706 Creation of very rare cut sites for genome mapping
R01HG-00380-01 (GNM) KUCHERLAPATI, RAJU S ALBERT EINSTEIN COLLEGE OF MED 1300 MORRIS PARK AVENUE BRONX, NY 10461 Human genome dissection by homologous recombination
R01HG-00385-01 (GNM) RIGAS, BASIL CORNELL UNIVERSITY MED COLLEGE 1300 YORK AVENUE NEW YORK, NY 10021 RecA-assisted rapid physical mapping of the human genome
R01HG-00395-01 (GNM) DRACOPOLI, NICHOLAS C MASSACHUSETTS INST OF TECH 77 MASSACHUSETTS AVENUE CAMBRIDGE, MA 02139 Genetic map of human chromosome 1
R13HG-00401-01A1 (GNM) EUNPU, DEBORAH L ALBERT EINSTEIN MEDICAL CENTER 5501 OLD YORK ROAD PHILADELPHIA, PA 19141-3098 Conference on The Human Genome Project--A Public Forum
R01HG-00402-01 (GNM) MOSELEY, RAY E UNIVERSITY OF FLORIDA BOX J-222, JHMHC GAINESVILLE, FL 32610 Insurance implications of a complete human genome map
R01HG-00405-01 (GNM) REEVES, ROGER H JOHNS HOPKINS UNIVERSITY 725 N WOLFE STREET/RM 205 BALTIMORE, MD 21205 Genetic physical and comparative mapping
R01HG-00406-01 (GNM) PATTERSON, DAVID ELEANOR ROOSEVELT INST FOR CNC 1899 GAYLORD STREET DENVER, CO 80206 The chromosome 21 joint YAC screening effort
R43HG-00410-01 (SSS) FROST, JAMES D, III GENOSYS BIOTECHNOLOGIES, INC. 8701A NEW TRAILS DRIVE THE WOODLANDS, TX 77381 Development of an automated segmented DNA synthesizer
R01HG-00411-01 (GNM) FINE, BETH A NORTHWESTERN UNIVERSITY 333 E SUPERIOR ST #1564 CHICAGO, IL 60611 Genetic counselors as educators on human genome issues
R01HG-00417-01 (GNM) HILGARTNER, STEPHEN COLUMBIA UNIVERSITY 630 WEST 168TH ST NEW YORK, NY 10032 Organizing the HGI--Social impact and technology design
R01HG-00418-01 (GNM) CALLAHAN, DANIEL THE HASTINGS CENTER 255 ELM ROAD BRIARCLIFF MANOR, NY 10510 Ethical priorities for clinical uses of genome research
P20HG-00424-01 (GRRC) EFSTRATIADIS, ARGIRIS COLUMBIA UNIVERSITY 701 WEST 168TH STREET NEW YORK, NY 10032 Physical and genetic mapping of human chromosome 13
P20HG-00424-01 0001 (GRRC) EFSTRATIADIS, ARGIRIS Physical and genetic mapping of human chromosome 13 Physical mapping of human chromosome 13
P20HG-00424-01 0002 (GRRC) WARBURTON, DORTHY Physical and genetic mapping of human chromosome 13 Regional mapping of chromosome 13 probes
P20HG-00424-01 0003 (GRRC) OTT, JURG Physical and genetic mapping of human chromosome 13 Construction on a high resolution genetic map of chromosome 13
P20HG-00424-01 0004 (GRRC) SCHON, ERIC Physical and genetic mapping of human chromosome 13 Informatics--Genome Information Management System GIMS
P20HG-00424-01 9001 (GRRC) EFSTRATIADIS, ARGIRIS Physical and genetic mapping of human chromosome 13 Technical service core
P50HG-00425-01 (GRRC) EMANUEL, BEVERLY S CHILDRENS HOSP OF PHILADELPHIA 34TH & CIVIC CENTER BLVD PHILADELPHIA, PA 19104 Human genome center for chromosome 22
P50HG-00425-01 9001 (GRRC) BIEGEL, JACLYN Human genome center for chromosome 22 Cell culture/cytogenetics core
P50HG-00425-01 0001 (GRRC) TAUB, REBECCA Human genome center for chromosome 22 Anchor marker project
P50HG-00425-01 0002 (GRRC) EMANUEL, BEVERLY Human genome center for chromosome 22 Maping project
P50HG-00425-01 0003 (GRRC) NUSSBAUM, ROBERT Human genome center for chromosome 22 Genomic cloning project
P50HG-00425-01 9002 (GRRC) SURREY, SAUL Human genome center for chromosome 22 Sequencing/oligonucletide synthesis core
P50HG-00425-01 9003 (GRRC) NUSSBAUM, ROBERT L Human genome center for chromosome 22 Clone and library storage core
P50HG-00425-01 9004 (GRRC) OVERTON, G CHRISTIAN Human genome center for chromosome 22 Informatics core
R13HG-00427-01 (GRRC) PATTERSON, DAVID ELEANOR ROOSEVELT INST 1899 GAYLORD STREET DENVER, CO 80206 International workshop on chromosome 21
R13HG-00428-01 (GRRC) GEMMILL, ROBERT M ELEANOR ROOSEVELT INSTITUTE 1899 GAYLORD STREET DENVER, CO 80206 International workshop on chromosome 3
R13HG-00431-01S1 (SRC) WIKLER, DANIEL I UNIVERSITY OF WISCONSIN 1420 MEDICAL SCIENCE CTR MADISON, WI 53706 Human genome research in an interdependent world
R13HG-00436-01 (GRRC) WITKOWSKI, JAN A COLD SPRING HARBOR LABORATORY PO BOX 534 COLD SPRING HARBOR, NY 11724 Workshop on The Genome of E Coli
R43HG-00440-01 (SSS) ANDERSON, NORMAN G LARGE SCALE BIOLOGY CORPORATIO 9620 MEDICAL CENTER DR ROCKVILLE, MD 20850 Automatic multiple-parallel DNA probe synthesizer
R43HG-00441-01 (SSS) SHAPIRO, HOWARD M HOWARD M SHAPIRO, MD PC 283 HIGHLAND AVE WEST NEWTON, MA 02165 New approaches to flow sorting of chromosomes
R01HG-00446-01 (GNM) WETMUR, JAMES G MOUNT SINAI SCHOOL OF MEDICINE BOX 1124 NEW YORK, NY 10029 The branch capture reaction in physical mapping
R01HG-00447-01 (GNM) NELKIN, DOROTHY NEW YORK UNIVERSITY 269 MERCER STREET/RM 404 NEW YORK, NY 10003 Human heredity in american popular culture
R13HG-00448-01 (GRRC) EMANUEL, BEVERLY S CHILDRENS HOSP OF PENNSYLVANIA 34TH & CIVIC CENTER BLVD PHILADELPHIA, PA 19104 Second International Workshop on Chromosome 22
R13HG-00449-01 (GNM) SAMUELS, SHELDON W WORKPLACE HEALTH FUND 815 16TH STREET, N.W., RM 301 WASHINGTON, D.C. 20006 Labor Conference on The Workplace and the Human Genome
R21HG-00450-01 (GNM) BROWN, PATRICK O STANFORD UNIVERSITY 255 BECKMAN CENTER STANFORD, CA 94305 Efficient gene mapping by whole genome mismatch scanning
R01HG-00452-01 (GNM) ROTHSTEIN, RODNEY J COLUMBIA UNIV, COLLEGE OF P&S 701 WEST 168TH ST-HHSC 1516 NEW YORK, NY 10032 Identifying YAC contigs by recombination
R55HG-00456-01 (GNM) MC CLELLAND, MICHAEL CALIFORNIA INST OF BIO RESCH 11099 N TORREY PINES RD LA JOLLA, CA 92037 Genetic mapping in the mouse by PCR fingerprinting
R01HG-00457-01 (GNM) SHEFFIELD, VAL C UNIVERSITY OF IOWA 2615 JCP IOWA CITY, IA 52242 Identification of polymorphisms in sequenced tagged site
R01HG-00460-01 (GRRC) KEITH, TIM P COLLABORATIVE RESEARCH, INC TWO OAK PARK BEDFORD, MA 01730 Framework linkage maps of human chromosomes 10 and 20
R01HG-00461-01 (GRRC) BOWCOCK, ANNE M UNIV OF TEXAS SW MEDICAL CENTE 5323 HARRY HINES BLVD DALLAS, TX 75235-9063 Framework linkage maps of human chromosomes 13q and 15q
R01HG-00462-01 (GRRC) GILLIAM, THOMAS C COLUMBIA UNIVERSITY 722 W 168TH ST, BOX 58 NEW YORK, NY 10032 Construction of a framework map of chromosome 18
R21HG-00463-01 (GNM) ELLEDGE, STEPHEN J BAYLOR COLLEGE OF MEDICINE ONE BAYLOR PLAZA HOUSTON, TX 77030 Genetic manipulation of yeast artificial chromosomes
R01HG-00464-01 (GRRC) NICKERSON, DEBORAH A CALIFORNIA INST OF TECHNOLOGY PASADENA, CA 91125 A framework linkage map for human chromosome 14
R01HG-00469-01 (GRRC) DONIS-KELLER, HELEN WASHINGTON UNIV SCHOOL OF MED 660 SOUTH EUCLID, BOX 8232 ST LOUIS, MO 63110 Framework linkage maps for chromosomes 2, 6, 7, 8, 12, and 14
R01HG-00477-01 (GNM) JONSEN, ALBERT R UNIVERSITY OF WASHINGTON SEATTLE, WA 98195 A paradigm approach to ethical problems in genetics
R01HG-00481-01 (GNM) HOLTZMAN, NEIL A THE JOHNS HOPKINS HOSPITAL 600 N WOLFE STREET BALTIMORE, MD 21205 Ethical and policy issues in cystic fibrosis screening
R21HG-00482-01 (GNM) COX, EDWARD C PRINCETON UNIVERSITY WASHINGTON ROAD PRINCETON, NJ 08544-1014 DNA sequencing by AF and ST microscopy
R01HG-00485-01 (GNM) LEVIS, ROBERT J WAYNE STATE UNIVERSITY 75 CHEMISTRY DETROIT, MI 48202 Rapid low cost DNA sequencing by mass

PROJECT NUMBER LISTING

PROJECT NO., ORGANIZATIONAL UNIT., INVESTIGATOR, ADDRESS, TITLE

spectrometry

R01HG-00487-01 (GNM) PETERS, THEODORE F CTR/THEOLOGY & NATURAL SCIS 2400 RIDGE RAOD BERKELEY, CA 94709 Theological questions raised by human genome initiative

R01HG-00490-01 (GRRC) NAYLOR, SUSAN L UNIV OF TEXAS HEALTH SCI CTR 7703 FLOYD CURL DRIVE SAN ANTONIO, TX 78284-7762 Consortium to construct chromosome 3 framework map

R43HG-00491-01 (SSS) MAO, JEN-I COLLABORATIVE RESEARCH, INC TWO OAK PARK BEDFORD, MA 01730 Develop PCRs to detect polymorphisms at mapped RFLP loci

R01HG-00503-01 (GNM) MURRAY, THOMAS H CASE WESTERN RESERVE UNIVERSIT 2109 ADELBERT/SCH OF MED T-402 CLEVELAND, OH 44106-4901 The human genome initiative and access to health care

R01HG-00504-01 (GRRC) SZYBALSKI, WACLAW UNIVERSITY OF WISCONSIN 420 HENRY MALL MADISON, WI 53706 University of Wisconsin Genome Center

R01HG-00504-01 0001 (GRRC) BLATTNER, FREDERICK R University of Wisconsin Genome Center Pilot study--Use of E coli as a vector

R01HG-00504-01 0002 (GRRC) BLATTNER, FREDERICK R University of Wisconsin Genome Center Feasibility study--Use of E coli as a vector

R01HG-00504-01 0003 (GRRC) SZYBALAKI, WACLAW University of Wisconsin Genome Center Pilot study--Amplification of megabase DNA fragments in E coli

R01HG-00504-01 0004 (GRRC) SZYBALSKI, WACLAW University of Wisconsin Genome Center Pilot study--DNA sequencing by primer elongation using ligation of hexamers

R01HG-00504-01 0005 (GRRC) LIVNY, MIRON University of Wisconsin Genome Center Computer center for genome research--Drosophila database

R01HG-00504-01 9001 (GRRC) ENGLES, WILLIAM University of Wisconsin Genome Center Molecular/genetic dissection of Drosophila genome by transposon tagging--Core

R13HG-00505-01 (GRRC) FAIN, PAMELA R 410 CHIPETA SALT LAKE CITY, UT 84108 Chromosome 17 mapping workshop

R44HG-00508-02 (SSS) LOVETT, MICHAEL GENELABS INCORPORATED 505 PENOBSCOT DRIVE REDWOOD CITY, CA 94063 Study of linked growth factor genes on chromosome 5

R01HG-00517-01 (GRRC) WEISS, ROBERT B UNIVERSITY UTAH 6160 ECCLES GENETICS BLDG SALT LAKE CITY, UT 84112 Megabase sequencing in the NF1 and FAP regions

R13HG-00518-01 (SRC) EVANS, GLEN A THE SALK INSTITUTE PO BOX 85800 SAN DIEGO, CA 92186-5800 Second international workshop on chromosome 11

R01HG-00520-01 (GRRC) MAO, JEN-I COLLABORATIVE RESEARCH, INC TWO OAK PARK BEDFORD, MA 01730 High throughput multiplex sequencing

R13HG-00521-01 (GRRC) NADEAU, JOSEPH H JACKSON LABORATORY 600 MAIN STREET BAR HARBOR, ME 04609-0800 Fifth International Mouse Genome Conference

R43HG-00524-01 (SSS) KOURI, RICHARD E 291 WHITNEY AVENUE NEW HAVEN, CT 06511 Coupled amplification and sequencing of DNA

R43HG-00528-01 (SSS) NAPPI, BRUCE FOSTER-MILLER, INC 350 SECOND AVENUE WALTHAM, MA 02154-1196 Automated high speed sequencing of DNA

R43HG-00532-01 (SSS) ARLINGHAUS, HEINRICH F ATOM SCIENCES, INC 114 RIDGEWAY CTR OAK RIDGE, TN 37830 Optimization of electrophoresis gels for RIS analysis

R13HG-00546-01 (GRRC) HOOD, LEROY CALIFORNIA INST OF TECHNOLOGY PASADENA, CA 91125 Genome Sequencing Conference III

R01HG-00563-01 (MBC) BERG, DOUGLAS E WASHINGTON UNIVERSITY PO BOX 8230 660 S EUCLID AVE ST LOUIS, MO 63110 Analysis of the essential genes of E coli

R01HG-00567-01 (GNM) RIETHMAN, HAROLD WISTAR INSTITUTE 36TH & SPRUCE STREETS PHILADELPHIA, PA 19104 Physical mapping of human telomeric DNA

R13HG-00580-01 (GNM) GRABER, GLENN C UNIVERSITY OF TENNESSEE 801 MCCLUNG TOWER KNOXVILLE, TN 37996-0480 Societal impact of human genetic engineering

P41HG-00586-01 (SRC) PEARSON, PETER L JOHNS HOPKINS UNIVERSITY 1830 E MONUMENT ST 3RD FLOOR BALTIMORE, MD 21205 A human genome data base

P41HG-00586-01 0001 (SRC) PEARSON, PETER REES A human genome data base Map storage, integration, and representation

P41HG-00586-01 0002 (SRC) FRANCOMANO, CLAIR A A human genome data base Online Mendelian Inheritance in Man (OMIM) restructuring and integration

P41HG-00586-01 0003 (SRC) MCKUSICK, VICTOR A human genome data base Maintenance of Online Mendelian Inheritance in Man

P41HG-00586-01 9001 (SRC) MATHESON, N W A human genome data base Core--Informatics

P41HG-00586-01 9002 (SRC) PEARSON, PETER REES A human genome data base Core--Acquisition, validation and maintenance of data

R01HG-00598-01 (GRRC) KWIATKOWSKI, DAVID J BRIGHAM AND WOMEN'S HOSPITAL 75 FRANCIS STREET BOSTON, MA 02115 Map of human chromosome 9

R01HG-00616-01 (SRC) ASCH, DAVID UNIV OF PENNSYLVANIA 3615 CHESTNUT ST/INTERNAL MED PHILADELPHIA, PA 19104-2683 How much information about the risk of cystic fibrosis do couples want?

R01HG-00621-01 (SRC) ASCH, DAVID UNIVERSITY OF PENNSYLVANIA 3615 CHESNUT ST M 317 PHILADELPHIA, PA 19104-2683 Prescriptive decision modeling for cystic fibrosis screening

R01HG-00638-01 (SRC) PHILLIPS, JOHN A, III VANDERBILT UNIVERSITY 21ST AVENUE AT GARLAND NASVILLE, TN 37232 Cystic fibrosis screening--An alternative paradigm

R01HG-00639-01 (SRC) FANOS, JOANNA H CHILDREN'S HOSP OAKLAND RES IN 747 52ND ST OAKLAND, CA 94609 Perception of carrier status by cystic fibrosis siblings

R01HG-00643-01 (SRC) SORENSON, JAMES R UNIV OF NORTH CAROLINA 302 ROSENAU HALL/CB 7400 CHAPEL HILL, NC 27599 An evaluation of testing and counseling for cystic fibrosis carriers

R13HG-00692-01 (SRC) NAYLOR, SUSAN L UNIV OF TEXAS HEALTH SCI CTR 7703 FLOYD CURL DRIVE SAN ANTONIO, TX 78284-7762 International workshop on human chromosome 2

N02HI-09501-06 (**) WALLACE, ROBERT B Cardiac surgery services for the cardiology program

N02HI-09502-05 (**) LEFRAK, EDWARD A Cardiac surgery services for the cardiology program

PROJECT NO., ORGANIZATIONAL UNIT., INVESTIGATOR, ADDRESS, TITLE

N02HI-09503-08 (**) CORSO, PAUL J Coronary angioplasty services for the cardiology program

N01HI-19054-00 (**) SACHS, DAVID H Tolerance induction to a class I antigen by retro.trans.

N02HI-19505-00 (**) PISARRA, VIRGINIA Cardiac surgery services for the cardiology branch

N01HI-79500-09 (**) RANSOM, JANET H. Isolate charactelzation of plasma lipoprotein apoliprotein

Z01HL-00009-17 (LBG) NIRENBERG, M NHLBI, NIH Cell recognition and synapse formation

Z01HL-00018-14 (LBG) SABOL, S L NHLBI, NIH Regulation of neuropeptide gene expression

R01HL-00082-43 (PHY) ROOS, ALBERT WASHINGTON UNIVERSITY 660 S. EUCLID AVE., BOX 8228 ST. LOUIS, MO 63110 Transmembrane movements

Z01HL-00151-21 (LBG) PETERKOFSKY, A NHLBI, NIH The biology of cyclic nucleotides in E coli

Z01HL-00153-04 (LBG) DANIELS, M P NHLBI, NIH Differentiation of excitable membranes

Z01HL-00202-20 (LB) CHOCK, P B NHLBI, NIH Kinetics, regulation and mechanisms of biochemical reactions

Z01HL-00204-24 (LB) GINSBURG, A NHLBI, NIH Protein structure--Enzyme action and control and gene regulation

Z01HL-00205-36 (LB) STADTMAN, T C NHLBI, NIH Biosynthesis and biochemical roles of selenoenzymes and seleno-tRNAs

Z01HL-00206-32 (LB) TSAI, L NHLBI, NIH Stereochemical studies of enzymatic reactions

Z01HL-00211-18 (LB) STADTMAN, E R NHLBI, NIH Ozone mediated oxidation of proteins and tripeptides

Z01HL-00224-14 (LB) HUANG, C Y NHLBI, NIH Calcium-regulated phosphorylation-dephosphorylation and enzyme mechanisms

Z01HL-00225-14 (LB) LEVINE, R L NHLBI, NIH Metal-catalyzed oxidation of proteins

Z01HL-00261-06 (LB) GRAHAME, D A NHLBI, NIH CO Dehydrogenase and Acetoclastic Methanogenesis in Methanosarcina barkeri

Z01HL-00263-06 (LB) RHEE, S G NHLBI, NIH Signal transduction mechanism involving phosphoinositides

Z01HL-00265-05 (LB) AXLEY, M J NHLBI, NIH Factors Affecting Expression of a Selenium-Containing Enzyme

Z01HL-00266-03 (LB) GARCIA, G E NHLBI, NIH Cloning of Selenoprotein A Gene from Clostridium sticklandii

Z01HL-00267-05 (LB) COOK, J C NHLBI, NIH Regulation of ubiquitination

Z01HL-00268-05 (LB) POSTON, J M NHLBI, NIH Biochemical changes in isolated perfused hearts

Z01HL-00272-03 (LB) YIM, M B NHLBI, NIH EPR study of free radicals in biology

Z01HL-00273-02 (LB) FISHER, M T NHLBI, NIH Chaperone assisted protein renaturation using GroEL/ES from E coli

Z01HL-00274-02 (LB) VERES, Z NHLBI, NIH In vitro incorporation of selenium into tRNAs of Salmonella typhimurium

Z01HL-00275-02 (LB) POLITINO, M NHLBI, NIH Biosynthesis and characterization of seleno-tRNAs from Methanococcus vannielii

Z01HL-00276-01 (LB) UCHIDA, K NHLBI,NIH Covalent modification of protein oxidative stress

Z01HL-00277-01 (LB) SZWEDA, L I NHLBI,NIH Oxidative modification of glucose-6-phosphate dehydrogenase

Z01HL-00401-25 (LCB) HENDLER, R W NHLBI, NIH Thermodynamic and kinetic studies of cytochrome C oxidase

Z01HL-00418-11 (LCB) HENDLER, R W NHLBI, NIH Energetic and stoichiometric relationships involving respiration, H, and ATP

Z01HL-00419-11 (LCB) BOWERS, B NHLBI, NIH Structure-Function relationships in eukaryotic cells

Z01HL-00501-18 (LCB) KORN, E D NHLBI, NIH Actin polymerization

Z01HL-00506-16 (LCB) KORN, E D NHLBI, NIH Acanthameba myosins

Z01HL-00514-08 (LCB) HAMMER, J A NHLBI, NIH The structure and sequence of non-muscle myosin

Z01HL-00516-05 (LCB) Eisenberg, E NHLBI, NIH 70 kDa heat shock proteins and the homologous uncoating ATPase

Z01HL-00517-01 (LCB) FLAVIN, M NHLBI, NIH Ultrastructural characterization of new protistan species

Z01HL-00622-14 (CM) MOSS, J NHLBI, NIH Regulation of cyclic nucleotide metabolism

Z01HL-00627-13 (CM) TSAI, S-C NHLBI, NIH GTP binding proteins and adenylate cyclase

Z01HL-00634-11 (CM) MANGANIELLO, V C NHLBI, NIH Characterization of cGMP-stimulated cyclic nucleotide phosphodiesterase

Z01HL-00636-10 (CM) SMITH, C NHLBI, NIH Regulation of the low Km cAMP phosphodiesterase in rat adipocytes

Z01HL-00638-09 (CM) MURTAGH, J NHLBI, NIH Genes for GTP-binding proteins

Z01HL-00643-05 (CM) AVIGAN, J NHLBI, NIH Structure-Function relationships of Go alpha mutants expressed in E. coli

Z01HL-00652-02 (CM) MEACCI, E NHLBI, NIH Regulation of cAMP phosphodiesterase in human platelets and myocardium

Z01HL-00654-01 (CM) TAIRA, M NHLBI, NIH Cloning of cDNA for the rat adipocyte hormone-sensitive cAMP phosphodiesterase

Z01HL-00655-01 (CM) MCDONALD, L J NHLBI, NIH ADP-ribosylation of cysteine in animal cells

Z01HL-00656-01 (CM) PRICE, S R NHLBI, NIH Characterization of native and recombinant ADP-ribosylation factors

Z01HL-00657-01 (CM) WALKER, M NHLBI, NIH Nucleotide-dependent association of ARF with membranes and phospholipids

K06HL-00733-28 (HT) WITTENBERG, JONATHAN B ALBERT EINSTEIN COLL OF MED 1300 MORRIS PARK AVENUE BRONX, N Y 10461 Oxygen metabolism

K06HL-00734-30 (NSS) KRITCHEVSKY, DAVID WISTAR INSITUTE 36TH & SPRUCE STREETS PHILIDELPHIA, PA 19104 Cholesterol metabolism

Z01HL-00937-09 (90P) BEAVEN, M NHLBI, NIH Mechanisms of mast cell degranulation

Z01HL-00962-09 (LCP) PUMFORD, N R NHLBI, NIH Mechanisms of drug-induced toxicities

Z01HL-00967-09 (LCP) OSAWA, Y NHLBI, NIH Regulation of hemoproteins

PROJECT NO., ORGANIZATIONAL UNIT., INVESTIGATOR, ADDRESS, TITLE

Z01HL-00990-05 (LCP) BAUMGARTNER, RUDOLF NHLBI, NIH Secretion of mediators from mast cells
Z01HL-00993-05 (LCP) CHOI, OKSOON NHLBI, NIH Phosphorylation of myosin heavy and light chains in stimulated mast cells
Z01HL-01002-17 (LBC) SOKOLOSKI, E A NHLBI, NIH Structural investigations by nuclear magnetic resonance
Z01HL-01003-19 (LBC) FALES, H M NHLBI, NIH Structure of natural products using instrumental methods
Z01HL-01005-20 (LBC) SILVERTON, J V NHLBI, NIH Solid state and computer studies of physiologically-important molecules
Z01HL-01006-20 (LBC) HIGHET, R J NHLBI, NIH The characterization of natural materials and metabolic products
Z01HL-01027-09 (LBC) FERRETTI, J A NHLBI, NIH Three-dimensional structures of biological macromolecules
Z01HL-01029-04 (LBC) JONES, T NHLBI, NIH Bioorganic chemistry of natural amines and other compounds
Z01HL-01030-03 (LBC) FALES, H M NHLBI, NIH Investigations of mass spectral techniques and processes
Z01HL-01031-02 (LBC) ITO, Y NHLB, NIH Preparative high-speed countercurrent chromatograph with three multilayer coils
Z01HL-01032-01 (LBC) ITO, Y NHLBI, NIH Mechanism on sharp peak formation of bromoacetyl T3 fractionation in CCC
Z01HL-01033-01 (LBC) BERGER, R L NHLBI, NIH Development of Raman spectroscopy for enzyme-substrate reactions
Z01HL-01034-01 (LBC) BERGER, R L NHLBI, NIH Development of NIR for monitoring enzyme-substrate reactions
Z01HL-01035-01 (LBC) FALES, H M NHLBI, NIH Mass spectral approaches to protein analysis
K06HL-01173-28 (NCR) GAENSLER, EDWARD A BOSTON UNIVERSITY 80 EAST CONCORD STREET BOSTON, MASS 02118 Applied pulmonary physiology
Z01HL-01266-09 (KE) SPRING, K R NHLBI, NIH Control of epithelial cell volume, shape, and composition
Z01HL-01282-05 (KE) KNEPPER, M A NHLBI, NIH Solute and water transport in renal epithelia
Z01HL-01283-04 (KE) BURG, M NHLBI, NIH Role of organic osmolytes in renal cells
Z01HL-01404-23 (LCB) KOLOBOW, T NHLBI, NIH Membrane lungs for long term respiratory, cardiac and cardiorespiratory assist
Z01HL-01407-28 (LCB) CHEN, R F NHLBI, NIH Fluorescence spectroscopic studies
Z01HL-01413-29 (LBC) BERGER, R L NHLBI, NIH Development of biophysical methods for studying biochemical reactions
Z01HL-01414-19 (LBC) BERGER, R L NHLBI, NIH Development of microcalorimeters for the study of biological reactions
Z01HL-01452-08 (LCB) KNUTSON, J R NHLBI, NIH Time resolved fluorescence spectroscopy
Z01HL-01462-05 (LBC) ITO, Y NHLBI, NIH Cross-axis synchronous flow-through coil planet centrifuge
Z01HL-01463-05 (LBC) ITO, Y NHLBI, NIH Evaluation of analytical countercurrent chromatographs
Z01HL-01470-03 (LCB) BOWMAN, R L NHLBI, NIH Surrogate host for testing genetically altered cell grafts
K11HL-01596-05 (MR) SMITH, SHIRLEY H UNIV OF ALABAMA IN BIRMINGHAM DEPT OF PATHOLOGY VH GO23 BIRMINGHAM, AL 35294 Humoral mechanisms in cardiac hypertrophy
K04HL-01615-05 (HEM) SCHMAIER, ALVIN H TEMPLE UNIVERSITY SCH OF MED 3400 NORTH BROAD STREET PHILADELPHIA, PA 19140 Interaction of high MW kininogen and platelets
K07HL-01631-05 (SRC) GOTTSCHALL, JEROME L BLOOD CTR/SOUTHEASTERN WIS 1701 WEST WISCONSIN AVENUE MILWAUKEE, WIS 53233 Transfusion medicine academic award, NHLBI
K08HL-01642-05 (MR) SIETSEMA, KATHY E HARBOR-UCLA MED CENTER A-15 ANNEX 1000 CARSON STREET TORRANCE CA 90509 Cardiovascular determinants of gas exchange dynamics
R01HL-01648-44 (HEM) BRINKHOUS, KENNETH M UNIVERSITY OF NORTH CAROLINA CB #7525 CHAPEL HILL, NC 27599-7525 Blood coagulation and hemophilia
K11HL-01650-05 (MR) BREITBART, ROGER E CHILDREN'S HOSP CORPORATION 300 LONGWOOD AVENUE BOSTON, MA 02115 Mechanisms of alternative RNA splicing in troponin T
K11HL-01654-05 (MR) RIVERS, RICHARD J UNIVERSITY OF ROCHESTER 601 ELMWOOD AVENUE ROCHESTER, NEW YORK 14642 Endothelial control of the peripheral circulation
K04HL-01658-05 (ECS) CAFFREY, JAMES L TEXAS COLL OF OSTEOPATHIC MED 3500 CAMP BOWIE BLVD FORT WORTH, TEX 76107 Opiate/autonomic interactions in the circulatory system
R01HL-01661-40A1 (HEM) RATNOFF, OSCAR D UNIVERSITY HOSPITALS CLEVELAND 2074 ABINGTON RD CLEVELAND, OH 44106 Hemostatic mechanisms
Z01HL-01665-16 (MC) KAWAMOATO, S NHLBI, NIH Growth and differentiation of smooth muscle and nonmuscle cells
K11HL-01674-05 (MR) LURIE, KEITH G VETERANS ADMIN MEDICAL CENTER 4150 CLEMENT STREET SAN FRANCISCO, CA 94121 Quantitative histrochemistry of Purkinje cell metabolism
K04HL-01683-05 (PTHA) STEIN-STREILEIN, JOAN E UNIVERSITY OF MIAMI SCH OF MED P O BOX 016960 MIAMI, FL 33101 Immunological mechanisms in lung defense and disease
K08HL-01687-05 (MR) ETINGIN, ORLI R CORNELL UNIVERSITY 1300 YORK AVENUE NEW YORK, N Y 10021 Prostaglandins mediators in arterial lipid metabolism
K07HL-01717-05 (MR) LIMACHER, MARIAN C UNIVERSITY OF FLORIDA BOX J-277, JHMHC GAINESVILLE, FL 32610 Preventive cardiology academic award
K14HL-01730-06 (SRC) MIA, ABDUL J JARVIS CHRISTIAN COLLEGE P O BOX DRAWER G HAWKINS, TX 75765 Minority school faculty development award
K08HL-01744-05 (MR) SINOWAY, LAWRENCE I MILTON S HERSHEY MED CENTER P O BOX 850 HERSHEY, PA 17033 Peripheral blood flow characteristics
K11HL-01749-05 (MR) HAMILTON, KAREN K U OF OKLAHOMA HLTH SCI CENTER DEPT OF MED., P. O. BOX 26901 OKLAHOMA CITY, OK 73190 von Willebrand factor, fibrinolysis, and the endothelium
K04HL-01768-05 (ECS) CREAGER, MARK A BRIGHAM AND WOMEN'S HOSPITAL 75 FRANCIS STREET BOSTON, MA 02115 The effect of sodium on baroreflex function

PROJECT NO., ORGANIZATIONAL UNIT., INVESTIGATOR, ADDRESS, TITLE

K04HL-01770-05 (CVB) BELLONI, FRANCIS L NEW YORK MEDICAL COLLEGE BASIC SCIENCES BUILDING VALHALLA, N Y 10595 Control of sinoatrial node by adenosine
Z01HL-01785-12 (MC) SELLERS, J R NHLBI, NIH Myosin and caldesmon phosphorylation in nonmuscle cells
Z01HL-01786-12 (MC) SELLERS, J R NHLBI, NIH Role of phosphorylation as a regulatory mechanism in muscle contraction
K04HL-01818-05 (RAP) GROTBERG, JAMES B MD PHD NORTHWESTERN UNIVERSITY BIOMED ENGINEERING DEPT. EVANSTON, ILL 60201 Pulmonary mass and heat transport
K11HL-01822-05 (SRC) TAYLOR, BONNIE J UNIVERSITY OF ARKANSAS 4301 WEST MARKHAM STREET LITTLE ROCK, AR 72205 Mast cells and perinatal pulmonary vascular tone
K08HL-01828-05 (SRC) CALHOUN, WILLIAM J CLINICAL SCIENCE CENTER 600 HIGHLAND AVENUE MADISON, WI 53792 Pathogenic roles of the alveolar macrophage in asthma
K11HL-01829-05 (MR) RICH, ELIZABETH A UNIVERSITY HOSPITALS 2074 ABINGTON ROAD CLEVELAND, OH 44106 Alveolar macrophage - surfactant interactions
K11HL-01835-05 (SRC) LEE, RICHARD T BRIGHAM AND WOMEN'S HOSPITAL 75 FRANCIS STREET BOSTON, MA 02115 The sensitivity of the calcium channel to ischemia
K11HL-01839-05 (SRC) CASCIO, WAYNE E UNIV OF NC AT CHAPEL HILL 349 BURNETT-WOMACK Interaction of ischemia, drugs, and rate on conduction
K08HL-01842-05 (MR) KAISER, LANA MICHIGAN STATE UNIVERSITY GILTNER HALL EAST LANSING, MI 48824 Flow dependent dilation--Mechanisms and significance
K11HL-01853-05 (MR) KNOWLTON, ANNE A BOSTON UNIVERSITY 80 EAST CONCORD STREET BOSTON, MA 02118 Role of fatty acid binding protein in cardiac ischemia
K04HL-01862-05 (EDC) FORDYCE, MARIANNA K UNIVERSITY OF MIAMI P O BOX 016069 MIAMI, FLA 33101 Effect of a low-fat diet on CHD risk factors
K08HL-01867-05 (SRC) SPRAGUE, RANDY S ST LOUIS UNIVERSITY 1402 SOUTH GRAND BLVD ST LOUIS, MO 63104 Role of leukotrienes in acute lung injury
K04HL-01870-05 (HEM) SCHWARTZ, BRADFORD S UNIVERSITY OF WISCONSIN 750 UNIVERSITY AVENUE MADISON, WI 53706 Human monocyte modulation of coagulation/fibrinolysis
K08HL-01888-06 (MR) BIGBY, TIMOTHY D UNIV. OF CALIFORNIA, SD DEPARTMENT OF MEDICINE LA JOLLA, CA Macrophage lipoxygenase pathway--Possible role in asthma
K04HL-01890-05 (CVA) WEISS, JAMES N UCLA SCHOOL OF MEDICINE 405 HILGARD AVENUE LOS ANGELES, CA 90024 Cardiac function during impaired metabolism
K08HL-01893-05 (MR) BROADDUS, COURTNEY SAN FRANCISCO GENERAL HOSPITAL 22ND AND POTERO STREETS SAN FRANCISCO, CA 94110 Comparative physiology of the normal and inflamed pleura
K04HL-01899-05 (EDC) KAPOOR, WISHWA N 190 LOTHROP ST, ROOM 100 PITTSBURGH, PA 15261 Identifying high risk patients with syncope
K11HL-01900-05 (MR) KILLINGSWORTH, CHERYL R HARVARD UNIVERSITY 665 HUNTINGTON AVENUE BOSTON, MA 02115 Viral-autonomic interactions in the trachea
K04HL-01901-05 (SAT) BOSNJAK, ZELJKO J CLEMENT J ZABLOCKI VA MED CTR RESEARCH SERVICE 151 MILWAUKEE, WI 531983 General anesthesia and cardiovascular regulation
K08HL-01902-06 (MR) GRANT, JAMES W WASHINGTON UNIV SCHOOL OF MED 500 SOUTH KINGSHIGHWAY ST LOUIS, MO 63110 Gene regulation of the smooth muscle regulatory light chain
K08HL-01907-05 (SRC) LEWIS, MICHAEL I CEDARS-SINAI MEDICAL CENTER 8700 BEVERLY BLVD LOS ANGELES, CA 90048 Emphysema--Influences on diaphragm fatigue resistance
K04HL-01909-05 (CVA) VATNER, DOROTHY E MASSACHUSETTS GENERAL HOSPITAL FRUIT STREET, JACKSON 13 BOSTON, MA 02114 Autonomic receptor function in lv hypertrophy & failure
K04HL-01910-06 (RAP) IWAMOTO, GARY A COLLEGE OF VETERINARY MEDICINE 2001 SOUTH LINCOLN AVENUE URBANA, IL 61801 Exercise pressor responses and the brainstem
K04HL-01913-05 (BM) CUNNINGHAM, MADELEINE W UNIVERSITY OKLAHOMA HLTH SCI C P O BOX 26901 OKLAHOMA CITY, OK 73190 Autoimmune determinants of rheumatic carditis
K08HL-01916-05 (MR) FISHMAN, JAY A FRUIT STREET BOSTON, MA 02114 Pulmonary-parasite interactions--Pneumocystis
K08HL-01917-05 (MR) ZELDIS, JEROME B UNIVERSITY OF CALIFORNIA 4301 X STREET SACRAMENTO, CA 95817 Hepatitis B virus infection of hematopoietic cells
K04HL-01919-05 (PTHA) STECENKO, ARLENE A UNIVERSITY OF FLORIDA BOX J-296 JHMHC GAINESVILLE, FL 32610 Respiratory syncytial virus bronchiolitis in sheep
K08HL-01920-05 (SRC) AITKEN, MOIRA L UNIVERSITY OF WASHINGTON SEATTLE, WA 98195 Cellular differentiation of airway epithelium
K08HL-01922-05 (MR) HIGH, KATHERINE A UNIV NORTH CAROLINA/CHAPEL HIL 416 BURNETT-WOMACK BLDG CB 703 CHAPEL HILL, NC 27599 Factor IX--Molecular defects and regulation of expression
K08HL-01924-04 (SRC) JACOBS, ELIZABETH R MEDICAL COLLEGE OF WISCONSIN 8700 WEST WISCONSIN AVENUE MILWAUKEE, WI 53226 Pulmonary type II epithelial cells: Role of ion channels
K04HL-01928-05 (PTHA) DE COURSEY, THOMAS E RUSH-PRESBYT-ST LUKE'S UNIV 1753 WEST CONGRESS PARKWAY CHICAGO, ILL 60612 Pulmonary type II epithelial cells--Role of ion channels
K04HL-01929-05 (PC) WILKINSON, KEITH D EMORY UNIVERSITY ROOM 255 ATLANTA, GA 30322 Structure and function of ubiquitin
K08HL-01930-05 (MR) GRUM, CYRIL M UNIVERSITY OF MICHIGAN MED SCH 3916 TAUBMAN CENTER ANN ARBOR, MI 48109 The ATP degradation system in acute tissue injury
K08HL-01931-05 (MR) OHAR, JILL A ST LOUIS UNIVERSITY 1325 SOUTH GRAND BLVD ST LOUIS, MO 63104 Agepc-induced pulmonary hypertension - a chronic animal
K08HL-01932-05 (MR) ABMAN, STEVEN H UNIV OF COLORADO HLTH SCIS CTR 4200 E NINTH AVENUE DENVER, CO 80262 Perinatal oxidant pulmonary vascular injury

PROJECT NO., ORGANIZATIONAL UNIT., INVESTIGATOR, ADDRESS, TITLE

K07HL-01934-05 (MR) WILLIAMS, CHRISTINE L NEW YORK MEDICAL COLLEGE MUNGER PAVILLION VALHALLA, N Y 10595 Preventive cardiology academic award

K07HL-01936-05 (MR) MC BRIDE, PATRICK E UNIVERSITY OF WISCONSIN SYSTEM 777 S MILLS STREET MADISON, WI 53715 Preventive cardiology academic award

K07HL-01940-05 (MR) BRICKER, JOHN T TEXAS CHILDREN'S HOSPITAL 6621 FANNIN AVENUE HOUSTON, TX 77030 Preventive cardiology academic award

K07HL-01942-03 (SRC) AMSTERDAM, EZRA A UNIVERSITY OF CALIFORNIA OFFICE OF RESEARCH, MRAK HALL DAVIS, CA 95616 Preventive cardiology academic award, NHLBI

K07HL-01943-05 (MR) OCKENE, IRA S UNIV OF MASSACHUSETTS MED CTR 55 LAKE AVENUE, NORTH WORCESTER, MA 01655 Preventive cardiology academic award

K07HL-01944-05 (MR) PACOLD, IVAN V HINES VETERANS ADMIN HOSPITAL HINES, IL 60141 Preventive cardiology academic award

K11HL-01950-05 (MR) OLIVIER, N B MICHIGAN STATE UNIVERSITY GILTNER HALL EAST LANSING, MI 48824 Blood pressure control in experimental heart disease

K08HL-01954-05 (MR) KRELL, WILLANE S HARPER HOSPITAL 3990 JOHN R DETROIT, MI 48201 Alterations in respiratory system mechanics with pleural effusions

K08HL-01959-05 (MR) GLEESON, KEVIN THE M S HERSHEY MEDICAL SCH P O BOX 850 HERSHEY, PA 17033 Chemosensitivity, the upper airway--Breathing

K04HL-01962-05 (PTHA) FALCONE, DOMENICK J CORNELL UNIV MEDICAL COLLEGE 1300 YORK AVENUE NEW YORK, N Y 10021 Pathobiology of foam cells in atherosclerosis

K11HL-01963-05 (MR) GIBSON, KEVIN F UNIV OF PITTSBURGH SCH OF MED 440 SCAIFE HALL PITTSBURGH, PA 15261 Uptake of lipids in macrophages and type II cells

K04HL-01965-07 (RAP) MURLAS, CHRISTOPHER G RUSH-PRESBYTERIAN 1653 W CONGRESS PARKWAY CHICAGO, IL 60612 Leukotriene-mediated airway cholinergic hyperresponsiveness

K08HL-01966-05 (MR) CHANG, SHIH-WEN NORTHWESTERN MEMORIAL HOSPITAL 250 E SUPERIOR STREET RM 456 CHICAGO, IL 60611 Mechanisms of endotoxin induced lung injury

K11HL-01967-05 (MR) HERRERA, VICTORIA L BOSTON UNIVERSITY 80 E CONCORD STREET BOSTON, MA 02118 Na, K-ATPase--Molecular genetics and role in hypertension

K14HL-01978-04 (SRC) WATKINS, HALCYON O TEXAS SOUTHERN UNIVERSITY 3100 CLEBURNE AVE HOUSTON, TX 77004 Minority school faculty development award

K14HL-01983-05 (SRC) SCHUMACHER, SUSAN J N C A & T STATE UNIVERSITY 302 G GIBBS HALL GREENSBORO, N C 27411 NHLBI minority school faculty development award

K14HL-01984-05 (SRC) LEWIS, JANNET F HOWARD UNIVERSITY HOSPITAL 2041 GEORGIA AVENUE, N W WASHINGTON, DC 20060 Minority school faculty development award

K14HL-01986-05 (SRC) RAO, SEKHARA B BENNETT COLLEGE 900 E WASHINGTON ST GREENBORO, NC 27401-3239 Minority school faculty development award

K14HL-01988-03 (SRC) STRICKLAND, TONY L CHARLES DREW UNIV MED & SCI 1621 EAST 120TH STREET LOS ANGELES, CA 90059 Minority school faculty development award

K14HL-01989-05 (SRC) OHI, SEIGO MEHARRY MEDICAL COLLEGE 1005 D B TODD, JR BLVD NASHVILLE, TN 37208 Minority school faculty development award

K14HL-01991-04 (SRC) ASHLINE, HERBERT C CLAFLIN COLLEGE Minority school faculty development award

K14HL-01994-04 (SRC) DIXON, EARL TUSKEGEE UNIVERSITY DEPT OF PHYSIOLOGY TUSKEGEE, AL 36083 Shape recovery in ss erythrocytes

K08HL-01996-05 (SRC) MIRRO, ROBERT UNIV OF TENNESSEE, MEMPHIS 853 JEFFERSON AVE, RM 201 MEMPHIS, TN 38163 Perinatal cerebral hemodynamics

K08HL-01998-05 (SRC) LEITER, JAMES C DARTMOUTH MEDICAL SCHOOL HANOVER, NEW HAMPSHIRE 03756 Reflex control of upper airway function in humans

K08HL-01999-05 (SRC) ALLEN, STEVEN J UNIV OF TEXAS MEDICAL SCHOOL 6431 FANNIN, MSMB 5-020 HOUSTON, TX 77030 Pleural effusion and pulmonary edema formation

K08HL-02001-05 (SRC) FISCHELL, TIM A STANFORD UNIVERSITY 300 PASTEUR DRIVE, CVRC STANFORD, CALIF 94305-5246 Arterial vasoreactivity following injury

K08HL-02002-05 (SRC) MAZANEC, MARY B UNIVERSITY HOSP OF CLEVELAND 2074 ABINGTON RD CLEVELAND, OH 44106 Neutralization of respiratory viruses by secretory IgA

K11HL-02009-04 (SRC) ROKEY, ROXANN BAYLOR COLLEGE OF MEDICINE ONE BAYLOR PLAZA RM 512 D HOUSTON, TX 77030 In vivo NMR metabolic study of regional cardiac ischemia

K08HL-02010-06 (SRC) MANN, DOUGLAS HOUSTON VA MEDICAL CENTER 2002 HOLCOMBE BLVD HOUSTON, TX 77030 Contractile performance of hypertrophied cardiocytes

Z01HL-02010-20 (MDB) BREWER, H B NHLBI, NIH Structure and function of plasma lipoproteins and apolipoproteins

K04HL-02011-05 (RAP) STROHL, KINGMAN P UNIVERSITY HOSPITALS 2074 ABINGTON ROAD CLEVELAND, OHIO 44106 Electromechanical function of the upper airway in humans

Z01HL-02012-16 (MDB) BEG, Z NHLBI, NIH Regulation of 3-hydroxy-3-methylglutaryl coenzyme A reductase

K11HL-02014-05 (SRC) ZIMMER, STEVAN UNIVERSITY OF MINNESOTA BOX 508 MAYO MINNEAPOLIS, MN 55455 Bioenergetic mechanisms in normal and pathologic intact

K11HL-02015-05 (SRC) WARE, RUSSELL E DUKE UNIVERSITY MEDICAL CENTER P O BOX 2916 DURHAM, NC 27710 Biology of the bone marrow derived 3A1 (+) stem cell

K11HL-02016-05 (SRC) CROWELL, RICHARD E VA MEDICAL CENTER 2100 RIDGECREST DR SE ALBUQUERQUE, NEW MEXICO 87108 Lung vascular & cellular actions of C3a, C5a, & FMLP

K08HL-02018-05 (SRC) BRESLOW, MICHAEL J JOHNS HOPKINS HOSPITAL 600 N WOLFE ST, TOWER 711 BALTIMORE, MD 21205 Regulation of adrenal medullary and cortial blood flow

PROJECT NO., ORGANIZATIONAL UNIT., INVESTIGATOR, ADDRESS, TITLE

Z01HL-02019-13 (MDB) RADER, DANIEL NHLBI, NIH Peptide chemistry section

K08HL-02022-05 (SRC) BRUNKEN, RICHARD C UCLA SCHOOL OF MEDICINE DIV OF NUCLEAR MED & BIO LOS ANGELES, CA 90024 Flow, glucose metabolism and myocardial viability by PET

Z01HL-02022-11 (MDB) HOEG, J M NHLBI, NIH Cellular lipid and lipoprotein biochemistry

K08HL-02024-05 (SRC) CHAPPELL, DAVID A UNIVERSITY OF IOWA IOWA CITY, IOWA 52242 . Apolipoprotein E binding to receptors in vitro and in vivo

Z01HL-02028-07 (MDB) FOJO, S S NHLBI, NIH Molecular biology of the ApoC-II and Lipoprotein gene

K08HL-02030-05 (SRC) SIMMONS, CHARLES F CHILDREN'S HOSPITAL 300 LONGWOOD AVE BOSTON, MA 02115 Cell & molecular biology of (Na+ + K+) ATPase

K08HL-02031-04 (SRC) SCHWARTZ, ALAN R JOHNS HOPKINS MEDICAL INST 4940 EASTERN AVENUE BALTIMORE, MD 21224 Human upper airway critical pressures during sleep

K07HL-02032-03 (SRC) MORRISON, FRANCIS S UNIV OF MISSISSIPPI MEDICAL CT 2500 NORTH STATE STREET JACKSON, MS 39216 Transfusion medicine academic award, NHLBI, Univ Mississippi

K07HL-02033-05 (SRC) KRUSKALL, MARGOT S BETH ISRAEL HOSPITAL 330 BROOKLINE AVENUE BOSTON, MA 02215 Transfusion medicine academic award

Z01HL-02033-01 (MDB) EGGERMAN, THOMAN L NHLBI, NIH Modulation and differential tissue expression of apolipoproteins

K08HL-02034-05 (SRC) BRINTON, ELIOT A 1230 YORK AVENUE NEW YORK, NY 10021 Molecular genetic control of HDL apoprotein metabolism

Z01HL-02034-01 (MDB) PATTERSON, A P NHLBI, NIH Modulation of apolipoprotein B gene expression

K07HL-02035-05 (SRC) SNYDER, EDWARD L YALE UNIVERSITY 20 YORK STREET RM 459-CB NEW HAVEN, CT 06504 Transfusion medicine academic award, NHLBI

Z01HL-02035-02 (MDB) FOJO, S S NHLBI, NIH Modulation of expression of the human LPL gene

K07HL-02036-02 (SRC) AMBRUSO, DANIEL R BONFILS MEMORIAL BLOOD CTR 4200 EAST NINTH AVENUE DENVER, CO 80262 Transfusion medicine academic award

Z01HL-02036-01 (MDB) FOJO, S S NHLBI, NIH Molecular defects in the lecithin cholesterol acyltransferase gene

Z01HL-02037-01 (MDB) FOJO, S S NHLBI, NIH Structure and function analysis of important structural domains of LPL

Z01HL-02038-01 (MDB) RADER, D J NHLBI, NIH Metabolism of apoA-IV in humans

Z01HL-02039-01 (MDB) RADER, D J NHLBI, NIH Metabolism of Lp(a) in humans

Z01HL-02040-01 (MDB) RADER, D J NHLBI, NIH Apolipoprotein metabolism in CETP deficiency and hyperalphalipoproteinemia

K07HL-02043-05 (SRC) SCHWARTZ, KENNETH A DEPARTMENT OF MEDICINE B220 LIFE SCIENCE BUILDING EAST LANSING, MICHIGAN 48824 Transfusion medicine academic award

K08HL-02047-03 (MR) SIGAL, ELLIOTT MD PHD UNIVERSITY OF CALIFORNIA 500 PARNASSUS AVE, BOX 0130 SAN FRANCISCO, CA 94143 Eosinophil in asthma--Potential role for lipoxygenase

K11HL-02054-04 (MR) FINN, PATRICIA THE CHILDREN'S HOSPITAL 320 LONGWOOD AVENUE BOSTON, MA 02115 Basic sciences training in pulmonary and molecular

K04HL-02055-04 (TOX) OLSON, JACK W UNIV OF KENTUCKY ROSE STREET LEXINGTON, KY 40536-0082 Polyamines & monocrotaline pneumotoxicity

K11HL-02060-04 (MR) CURTIN, PETER T UNIVERSITY OF CALIFORNIA 521 PARNASSUS AVENUE SAN FRANCISCO, CA 94143-6630 Structure and function of a unique b-thalassemia deletion

K04HL-02063-04 (PHRA) HAMILTON, SUSAN L BAYLOR COLLEGE OF MEDICINE ONE BAYLOR PLAZA HOUSTON, TX 77030 Dihydropyridine binding sites and calcium channels

K11HL-02064-05 (MR) FOSTER, PAUL A THE BLOOD CTR FOR SE WISCONSIN 1701 W WISCONSIN AVENUE MILWAUKEE, WI 53233 Structural basis of the interaction of vWF and factor VIII

K04HL-02071-04 (RAP) HEMPLEMAN, STEVEN C UNIVERSITY OF CALIFORNIA DEPT OF MEDICINE M-023A LA JOLLA, CA 92093 Discharge patterns of carotid body chemoreceptors

K04HL-02072-05 (HEM) CARSON, STEVEN D UNIV OF NEBRASKA MED CENTER 42ND AND DEWEY AVENUE OMAHA, NE 68105 Control of tissue factor activity

K11HL-02076-04 (MR) JOHNS, JAMES A VANDERBILT MEDICAL CENTER MEDICAL CENTER NORTH D2217 NASHVILLE, TN 37232 Ionic currents and ca++ in coronary smooth muscle

K07HL-02078-02 (SRC) KAVEY, RAE-ELLEN W SUNY HEALTH SCIENCE CENTER 725 IRVING AVENUE SYRACUSE, NY 13210 Preventive cardiology academic award NHLBI

K07HL-02079-04 (SRC) TOUCHON, ROBERT C MARSHALL UNIVERSITY SCH OF MED 1542 SPRING VALLEY DRIVE HUNTINGTON, WV 25704 Preventive cardiology academic award, NHLBI

K07HL-02083-04 (SRC) BLACK, HENRY R YALE UNIVERSITY, SCH OF MED P O BOX 3333 NEW HAVEN, CT 06510-8056 Preventive cardiology academic award

K07HL-02086-04 (SRC) LAWSON, WILLIAM E SUNY AT STONY BROOK HEALTH SCIENCES CENTER 16T-080 STONY BROOK, NY 11794 Preventive cardiology academic award

K07HL-02087-04 (SRC) SUSKIND, ROBERT M LSU MEDICAL CENTER 1542 TULANE AVE NEW ORLEANS, LA 70112 Preventive cardiology academic award, NHLBI

K07HL-02091-04 (SRC) FANTA, CHRISTOPHER H BRIGHAM AND WOMENS HOSPITAL 75 FRANCIS STREET BOSTON, MASS 02115 Prevention of life-threatening and fatal asthma

K07HL-02095-05 (SRC) REICHMAN, LEE B UMDNJ-UNIVERSITY HOSPITAL 150 BERGEN STREET NEWARK, N J 07103 Preventive pulmonary academic award

K07HL-02096-05 (SRC) BOEHLECKE, BRIAN A UNIVERSITY OF NORTH CAROLINA 724 BURNETT-WOMACK, CB#7020 CHAPEL HILL, NC 27599 Preventive pulmonary medical education and research plan

K07HL-02097-01A4 (SRC) BRAUN, SHELDON R UNIVERSITY OF MISSOURI

PROJECT NO., ORGANIZATIONAL UNIT., INVESTIGATOR, ADDRESS, TITLE

ONE HOSPITAL DR, MA419 HSC COLUMBIA, MO 65212 Preventive pulmonary program

K07HL-02098-05 (SRC) GEPPERT, EUGENE F UNIVERSITY OF CHICAGO 5841 S MARYLAND AVE CHICAGO, ILL 60637 Preventive pulmonary academic award

K07HL-02099-05 (SRC) KLEINHENZ, MARY E CASE WESTERN RESERVE UNIV 2074 ABINGTON ROAD CLEVELAND, OH 44106 Curriculum development in pulmonary preventive medicine

K07HL-02100-02 (SRC) BRESNITZ, EDDY A MEDICAL COLLEGE OF PENNSYLVANI 3300 HENRY AVE PHILADELPHIA, PA 19129 Preventive pulmonary academic award program

K07HL-02102-04 (SRC) OWENS, GREGORY R UNIVERSITY OF PITTSBURGH 440 SCAIFE HALL PITTSBURGH, PA 15260 Preventive pulmonary academic award

K07HL-02104-05 (SRC) WALL, MICHAEL A OREGON HEALTH SCIENCES UNIV 3181 S W SAM JACKSON PARK ROAD PORTLAND, OREG 97201 Preventive pulmonary academic award

K11HL-02107-04 (SRC) PION, PAUL D DEPT OF PHYSIOLOGICAL SCIENCE DAVIS, CA 95616 Taurine deficiency myocardial failure

K11HL-02109-04 (SRC) CROUSE, DENNIS T 525 NEW HILLMAN BUILDING BIRMINGHAM, ALABAMA 35294 02 potentiation of urealplasmal pneumonia in newborns

K11HL-02111-04 (SRC) METUS-SNYDER, MICHELE CHILDREN'S HOSPITAL CORPORATIO 300 LONGWOOD AVENUE BOSTON, MA 02115 Apolipoprotein genes in atherosclerosis

K11HL-02112-02 (MR) RUTLEDGE, JOHN C UNIVERSITY OF CALIFORNIA TB 172 DAVIS, CA 95616 Extracellular transport of LDL

K04HL-02113-04 (HEM) STRICKLAND, DUDLEY K AMERICAN RED CROSS 15601 CRABBS BRANCH WAY ROCKVILLE, MD 20855 Regulation of protease activity by alpha 2-macroglobulin

K04HL-02114-04 (PTHA) GUYTON, JOHN R METHODIST HOSPITAL A-601 6565 FANNIN ST HOUSTON, TEX 77030 Arterial wall and lipid deposition

K04HL-02117-04 (CVB) ADAIR, THOMAS H UNIVERSITY OF MISSISSIPPI 2500 NORTH STATE STREET JACKSON, MISS 39216 Microvascular control--Vascularity and fluid environment

K04HL-02119-05 (TOX) YOST, GAROLD S UNIVERSITY OF UTAH COLLEGE OF PHARMACY SALT LAKE CITY, UT 84112 Mechanisms of chemical pneumotoxicity

K04HL-02122-04 (RAP) OLSON, LYNNE E OHIO STATE UNIVERSITY 1900 COFFEY RD, 309 SISSON HAL COLUMBUS, OH 43210-1092 Mediastinal effects on pulmonary function

K11HL-02123-04 (SRC) LEONE, PETER A WAKE FOREST UNIVERSITY 300 SOUTH HAWTHORNE ROAD WINSTON-SALEM, NC 27103 Neutrophils and lung injury in the pathogenesis of ARDS

K04HL-02124-05 (NEUB) MAYHAN, WILLIAM GERARD UNIVERSITY OF NEBRASKA 42ND AND DEWEY AVENUE OMAHA, NE 68105 Microvascular permeability of the cerebral circulation

K04HL-02126-04 (RAP) DEY, RICHARD D WEST VIRGINIA UNIVERSITY MEDICAL CENTER MORGANTOWN, W V 26506 Origin and distribution of peptidergic nerves in airways

K08HL-02128-05 (MR) MORRIS, CHRISTOPHER L CHILDREN'S HOSP RES FOUNDATION ELLAND & BETHESDA AVENUES CINCINNATI, OHIO 45229 Red cell adhesion of sickle and polycythemia vera blood

K08HL-02129-05 (MR) YEAGER, MARK J RES INST OF SCRIPPS CLINIC 10666 NORTH TORREY PINES ROAD LA JOLLA, CA 92037 Structure analysis of cardiac gap junctions

K08HL-02131-05 (SRC) SCHAEFER, SAUL UNIVERSITY OF CALIFORNIA 410 MRAK HALL DAVIS, CA 95616-8671 NMR assessment of regional myocardial perfusion

K08HL-02133-04 (SRC) HASSOUN, PAUL M NEW ENGLAND MEDICAL CENTER 750 WASHINGTON ST BOSTON, MA 02111 NHLBI clinical investigator award program

K14HL-02134-03 (SRC) OLUBADEWO, JOSEPH O XAVIER UNIV OF LOUISIANA 7325 PALMETTO STREET NEW ORLEANS, LA 70125 Thyroid status vascular and other smooth muscle function

K14HL-02137-04 (SRC) TWENTYMAN, CRAIG T UNIVERSITY OF HAWAII MANOA 2430 CAMPUS ROAD HONOLULU, HI 96822 Psychosocial factors and cardiovascular disease

K14HL-02138-04 (SRC) BANERJEE, MUKUL R MEHARRY MEDICAL COLLEGE 1005 D.B. TODD, JR., BLVD. NASHVILLE, TN 37208 Lung vascular effects of high frequency ventilation

K14HL-02140-01A3 (SRC) ERNST, FREDERICK A MEHARRY MEDICAL COLLEGE 1005 D B TODD BOULEVARD NASHVILLE, TN 37208 Minority school faculty development award

K04HL-02142-03 (CVA) CANTINO, MARIE E UNIVERSITY OF CONNECTICUT 75 N EAGLEVILLE RD BOX U-42 STORRS, CT 06269 Calcium regulation of myocardial contraction

K07HL-02143-04 (SRC) WOODSON, ROBERT D H4/548 - CLINICAL SCIENCE CTR 600 HIGHLAND AVENUE MADISON, WI 53792 Transfusion medicine academic award

K07HL-02146-04 (SRC) MEYERS, KENNETH M WASHINGTON STATE UNIVERSITY PULLMAN, WA 99164 Transfusion medicine academic award

K07HL-02147-04 (SRC) SZYMANSKI, IRMA O UNIVERSITY OF MASSACHUSETTS 55 LAKE AVENUE NORTH WORCESTER, MA 01655 Transfusion medicine academic award NHLBI

K07HL-02151-03 (SRC) PETZ, LAWRENCE D UCLA MEDICAL CENTER 10833 LE CONTE AVENUE LOS ANGELES, CA 90024 Transfusion medicine academic award-NHLBI, UCLA

K08HL-02154-03 (SRC) MENDELSOHN, MICHAEL EDWARD BRIGHAM & WOMEN'S HOSPITAL 75 FRANCIS STREET BOSTON, MA 02115 Endothelial-derived relaxing factor & platelet function

K11HL-02155-04 (SRC) SCHWARTZ, GREGORY G UNIV OF CALIFORNIA 4150 CLEMENT ST. 11D SAN FRANCISCO, CA 94121 Metabolic control of coronary flow: 31P NMR spectroscopy

K08HL-02157-04 (SRC) PIAN, MARK S UNIVERSITY OF CALIFORNIA 1327 MOFFITT HOSPITAL SAN FRANCISCO, CA 94143-0130 Regulation of exocytosis in alveolar type II cells

K11HL-02158-04 (SRC) GORLIN, JED B BRIGHAM AND WOMEN'S HOSPITAL 75 FRANCIS STREET BOSTON, MA 02115 Molecular biology of actin-binding protein

K11HL-02162-04 (SRC) NEVIN, DAVID N UNIVERSITY OF WASHINGTON NUTRITION, RG-26 Hypercholesterolemia and mutations in apolipoprotein-B

PROJECT NO., ORGANIZATIONAL UNIT., INVESTIGATOR, ADDRESS, TITLE

K08HL-02165-04 (SRC) PREZANT, DAVID J MONTEFIORE HOSPITAL EAST 210TH STREET BRONX, NY 10467 Diaphragm adaptations to respiratory training and disuse

K04HL-02166-04 (GMA) DAVIDSON, NICHOLAS O UNIVERSITY OF CHICAGO 5841 S MARYLAND AVE, BOX 400 CHICAGO, IL 60637 Enterohepatic lipid flux and apoprotein biosynthesis

K08HL-02167-02 (MR) SCHUSTER, STEPHEN J JEFFERSON MEDICAL COLLEGE 1025 WALNUT STREET PHILADELPHIA, PA 19107 Renal erythropoietin gene expression

K04HL-02174-04 (RAP) GILLESPIE, MARK N UNIVERSITY OF KENTUCKY COLLEGE OF PHARMACY LEXINGTON, KY 40536 Polyamines in hypoxic pulmonary hypertension

K06HL-02182-29 (NCR) LEWIS, BENJAMIN M HARPER HOSPITAL 3990 JOHN R/PULMONARY DIS DIV DETROIT, MICH 48201 Physiological and pathological reactions of pulmonary capillary bed

K04HL-02183-04 (EDC) WILLIAMS, PAUL T LAWRENCE BERKELEY LABORATORY 1 CYCLOTRON ROAD BERKELEY, CA 94720 Effects of exercise, diet and fat loss on lipoproteins

K08HL-02188-04 (SRC) ZEITLIN, PAMELA L THE JOHNS HOPKINS HOSPITAL 600 NORTH WOLFE STREET BALTIMORE, MD 21205 Development of ion transport in fetal tracheal epithelium

K04HL-02189-03 (EDC) TREVISAN, MAURIZIO STATE UNIVERSITY OF NEW YORK DEPT OF SOCIAL/PREVENTIVE MED BUFFALO, NY 14214-2699 Intracellular sodium metabolism and hypertension

K08HL-02194-04 (SRC) FESSLER, HENRY E JOHNS HOPKINS MED INST 4940 EASTERN AVENUE BALTIMORE, MD 21224 Positive intrathoracic pressure and coronary perfusion

K11HL-02195-04 (SRC) HARDING, SUSAN M UNIVERSITY OF ALABAMA 215 TINSLEY HARRISON TOWER BIRMINGHAM, AL 35294 Endothelial cell cytoskeleton in hyperoxia

K08HL-02196-03 (MR) GREENWALD, JAMES E 660 S EUCLID AVENUE ST. LOUIS, MO 63110 Regulation of myocardial synthesis, release and processing of atriopeptin

K11HL-02197-04 (SRC) BALDWIN, H S JOSEPH STOKES JR. RES. INST. 34TH ST & CIVIC CENTER BLVD. Precardiac cell matrix interactions in heart development

K08HL-02198-03 (SRC) DELLSPERGER, KEVIN C UNIVERSITY OF IOWA E 318-5; GENERAL HOSPITAL IOWA CITY, IA 52242 The effects of hypertension on the coronary circulation

K08HL-02201-04 (SRC) HANLEY, MICHAEL E UNIVERSITY OF COLORADO HLTH. S 4200 EAST NINTH AVENUE DENVER, CO 80262 Xanthine oxidase mediated lung injury

K08HL-02202-04 (SRC) HUANG, ADA J COLUMBIA UNIVERSITY 630 W 168TH STREET NEW YORK, N Y 10032 Mechanism of human transendothelial leukocyte migration

K04HL-02204-04 (RAP) SMITH, JEFFREY C UNIVERSITY OF CALIFORNIA 405 HILGARD AVENUE LOS ANGELES, CA 90024-1568 In vitro studies of neural control of breathing

K04HL-02205-04 (RAP) SOLWAY, JULIAN UNIVERSITY OF CHICAGO 5841 S MARYLAND AVENUE CHICAGO, IL 60637 Mechanisms of airflow obstruction

K04HL-02207-04 (BBCB) KURTZ, DONALD M, JR UNIVERSITY OF GEORGIA DEPARTMENT OF CHEMISTRY ATHENS, GEORGIA 30602 Iron and oxygen chemistries in sipuncular blood

Z01HL-02208-17 (CHB) NIENHUIS, A W NHLBI, NIH Iron chelation and transfusional hemochromatosis

R01HL-02212-36 (HEM) LORAND, LASZLO NORTHWESTERN UNIVERSITY 633 CLARK STREET EVANSTON, IL 60208 Coagulation of blood

K04HL-02213-04 (HEM) LEVITT, LEE J STANFORD UNIVERSITY DIVISION OF HEMATOLOGY STANFORD, CALIF 94305 Regulatory effect of 02 tension on human erythropoiesis

Z01HL-02213-15 (MH) SAFER, B NHLBI, NIH Elements regulating expression of the adenovirus 2 major late promoter

K07HL-02215-04 (SRC) RIES, ANDREW L UNIV OF CALIFORNIA, SAN DIEGO 225 DICKINSON ST, MED CTR H-77 SAN DIEGO, CA 92103-1990 Preventive pulmonary academic award at UCSD

K11HL-02216-04 (MR) SYMINGTON, BANU ERHAN FRED HUTCHINSON CANCER RES. CT 1124 COLUMBIA STREET SEATTLE, WA 98104 Role of the fibronectin receptor in cell localization

Z01HL-02216-12 (MH) ANDERSON, W F NHLBI, NIH Correction of genetic defects by gene transfer

K04HL-02217-03 (BIO) PAUL, SUDHIR NEBRASKA UNIV MED CNTR 42ND AND DEWEY AVENUE OMAHA, NE 68105-1065 Characterization of VIP receptors and VIP autoantibodies

Z01HL-02218-03 (MH) MORGAN, R NHLBI, NIH Development of gene therapy for the treatment of AIDS

Z01HL-02219-03 (MH) DICHEK, D NHLBI, NIH Gene transfer for cardiovascular disease

Z01HL-02220-91 (MHDD) BALTRUCKI, L NHLBI, NIH Gene transfer into liver and hemapoietic/thymic stem cells

K11HL-02221-03 (MR) DRANOFF, GLENN MASSACHUSETTS GENERAL HOSPITAL FRUIT ST. BOSTON, MA 02114 Molecular genetics and hematopoiesis

Z01HL-02221-91 (MH) COUTURE, L NHLBI, NIH Tissue specific and inducible vectors for use in gene therapy

Z01HL-02223-02 (MH) NUSSBAUM, O NHLBI, NIH Targeting of retroviral envelopes for gene transfer to specific cells

Z01HL-02224-02 (MH) DICHEK, D NHLBI, NIH Endothelial cell seeding of intravascular prostheses

K08HL-02225-02 (MR) FERGUSON, GARY T NATIONAL JEWISH CENTER FOR 1400 JACKSON STREET DENVER, CO 80206 Respiratory muscle dysfunction and respiratory failure

Z01HL-02225-02 (MH) MORGAN, R NHLBI, NIH Functional analysis of murine retroviral envelope proteins

K08HL-02226-03 (MR) KULIK, THOMAS J THE CHILDRENS HOSPITAL 300 LONGWOOD AVE BOSTON, MA 02115 Stretch as a growth stimulus in vascular smooth muscle

Z01HL-02226-02 (MH) MIYAMOTO, S NHLBI, NIH Translation factors and T-cell activation

Z01HL-02227-02 (MH) CHIORINI, J A NHLBI, NIH Identification of regulatory elements that modulate the translational efficiency

K11HL-02228-03 (MR) ROSENZWEIG, ANTHONY MASSACHUSETTS GENERAL HOSP FRUIT STREET BOSTON, MA 02114 Molecular immunology & the heart

Z01HL-02228-02 (MH) NOGUICHI, M NHLBI, NIH Regulatory

elements that control expression of the human eIF-2 alpha gene
K11HL-02229-04 (MR) ALBITAR, MAHER U.T.M.D. ANDERSON CANCER CTR 1515 HOLCOMBE BLVD HOUSTON, TEXAS 77030 Hemoglobin synthesis in the human erythrocyte
Z01HL-02229-02 (MH) SAFER, B NHLBI, NIH Isolation and cloning of transacting factors that regulate human eIF-2 alpha
K04HL-02233-03 (HEM) TELEN, MARILYN J DUKE UNIVERSITY MEDICAL CENTER POST OFFICE BOX 3387 DURHAM, N C 27710 Erythrocyte protein antigens regulated by In-Lu
K08HL-02234-03 (MR) TOSI, MICHAEL F RAINBOW BABIES & CHILD HOSP 2101 ADELBERT ROAD CLEVELAND, OH 44106 Elastase cleavage of pseudomonas opsonins in CF
K11HL-02240-02 (SRC) MARTIN, THOMAS R BETH ISRAEL HOSPITAL 330 BROOKLINE AVENUE BOSTON, MA 02215 IgE/mast cell-dependent effects on pulmonary function
K08HL-02244-04 (MR) VELAZQUEZ, MARISSEL ST. LOUIS UNIVERSITY 221 NORTH GRAND BOULEVARD ST. LOUIS, MO 63103 Structure-function correlations during acute lung injury
K08HL-02246-02 (MR) PERRY, STANTON B HARVARD MED SCH-MNR LABORATORY 221 LONGWOOD AVE, RM 209 BOSTON, MA 02115 Ischemia and reperfusion in the immature myocardium
K08HL-02253-03 (MR) DINAUER, MARY C THE CHILDREN'S HOSPITAL 300 LONGWOOD AVENUE BOSTON, MA 02115 Molecular studies of phagocyte oxidase B-cytochrome
K08HL-02254-02 (MR) WENZEL, SALLY E NATIONAL JEWISH CENTER 1400 JACKSON STREET DENVER, CO 80206 Macrophages, mast cells and the late asthmatic response
K07HL-02263-03 (SRC) MILLER, MICHAEL UNIVERSITY OF MARYLAND HOSP DIVISION OF CARDIOLOGY BALTIMORE, MD 21201 Preventive cardiology academic award
K07HL-02268-03 (SRC) FARQUHAR, JOHN W CTR FOR RES IN DIS PREVENTION 1000 WELCH RD STANFORD, CA 94305 Preventive cardiology academic award, NHLBI
K07HL-02269-02 (SRC) RANDALL, OTELIO S HOWARD UNIVERSITY HOSPITAL 2041 GEORGIA AVE, N W WASHINGTON, D C 20060 Preventive cardiology academic award NHLBI
K04HL-02271-02 (HEM) WARE, J ANTHONY HARVARD MEDICAL SCHOOL 330 BROOKLINE AVENUE BOSTON, MA 02215 Platelet intracellular mediators
K04HL-02272-03 (HEM) GONIAS, STEVEN L UNIVERSITY OF VIRGINIA BOX 214 CHARLOTTESVILLE, VA 22908 Proteinase in fibrinolysis and thrombolytic therapy
K04HL-02273-02 (HEM) LOSCALZO, JOSEPH BRIGHAM AND WOMEN'S HOSPITAL 75 FRANCIS STREET BOSTON, MA 02115 Platelets, platelet thrombi, and plasminogen activation
K06HL-02276-03 (SRC) PERKETT, ELIZABETH A VANDERBILT UNIVERSITY B-1308, MEDICAL CENTER NORTH NASHVILLE, TN 37232 Smooth muscle cells and pulmonary hypertension
K11HL-02277-03 (SRC) YOUSSOUFIAN, HAGOP MASSACHUSETTS GENERAL HOSP HEMOTOLOGY-ONCOLOGY UNIT BOSTON, MA 02114 Biogenesis of the red cell membrane and cytoskeleton
K11HL-02288-03 (SRC) ROSENBERG, HELENE F BETH ISRAEL HOSPITAL 330 BROOKLINE AVENUE, DA 617 BOSTON, MA 02215 Cardiotoxicity of eosinophil granule cationic proteins
K08HL-02289-03 (SRC) WIEGAND, LAUREL MILTON S HERSHEY MEDICAL CTR PULMONARY DIVISION, PO BOX 850 HERSHEY, PA 17033 Sleep apnea--The muscular control of pharyngeal patency
K08HL-02292-03 (SRC) OELBERG, DAVID G UNIVERSITY OF TEXAS PEDIATRICS DEPT, 6431 FANNIN HOUSTON, TX 77030 Ion transport by pulmonary epithelial membrane vesicles
K04HL-02297-03 (RAP) MICHAEL, JOHN R UNIV OF UTAH HEALTH SCI CENTER 50 N MEDICAL DRIVE SALT LAKE CITY, UT 84132 Regulation of pulmonary vascular tone
K11HL-02303-02 (MR) COREY, SETH J TUFTS UNIVERSITY 136 HARRISON AVENUE BOSTON, MA 02111 Biochemical mechanisms of GM-CSF priming of neutrophils
K04HL-02305-03 (PHRA) PRESSLEY, THOMAS A UNIVERSITY OF TEXAS DPT OF PHYSIOLOGY & CELL BIOLO HOUSTON, TX 77225 Analysis of cardiac glycoside affinity in cultured cells
K04HL-02307-03 (CVB) GOMEZ, ROBERTO A UNIV OF VIRGINIA SCH OF MED CHARLOTTESVILLE, VA 22908 Regulation of renin synthesis and release in the kidney
Z01HL-02307-12 (CHB) BODINE, D M NHLBI, NIH Retroviral mediated gene transfer into hematopoietic stem cells
K11HL-02309-02 (MR) PETERS, KEVIN UNIVERSITY OF CALIFORNIA BOX 0724 SAN FRANCISCO, CA 94143-0724 Biology of fibroblast growth factor receptors
Z01HL-02310-11 (CHB) SHIMADA, T NHLBI, NIH Characterization of the gene for human dihydrofolate reductase
K08HL-02311-04 (PTHB) KROLL, MICHAEL HOWARD BAYLOR COLLEGE OF MEDICINE 6565 FANNIN ROOM 930 HOUSTON, TX 77030 Mechanisms of von Willebrand factor-induced platelet activation
K08HL-02312-04 (MR) GARCIA, JOE G INDIANA UNIV SCHOOL OF MED 1001 WEST 10TH STREET, OPW 425 INDIANAPOLIS, IN 46202-2879 Cytoskeletal control of endothelial permeability
Z01HL-02313-09 (CHB) NIENHUIS, A W NHLBI, NIH Identification of regulatory elements that modulate globin gene expression
K04HL-02314-03 (ECS) DEKIN, MICHAEL S UNIVERSITY OF KENTUCKY SCHOOL OF BIOLOGICAL SCIENCES LEXINGTON, KY 40506-0225 Role of neurochemicals in respiratory pattern formation
Z01HL-02315-09 (CHB) YOUNG, N NHLBI, NIH Pathogenesis and treatment of aplastic anemia
K07HL-02316-03 (SRC) BECKETT, WILLIAM S YALE UNIV SCH OF MED 333 CEDAR ST/OCCUPATIONAL MED NEW HAVEN, CT 06510 Preventive pulmonary academic award program
K07HL-02318-02 (SRC) MAGUIRE, GEORGE P WESTCHESTER COUNTY MED CTR VALHALLA, NY 10595 Preventive pulmonary academic award
Z01HL-02319-07 (CHB) YOUNG, N NHLBI, NIH Parovirus (human) B19
Z01HL-02320-06 (CHB) NIENHUIS, A W NHLBI, NIH Pharmacologic manipulation of HbF synthesis
K07HL-02321-02 (SRC) BARNHART, SCOTT UNIVERSITY OF WASHINGTON 325 9TH AVENUE SEATTLE, WA 98104 Preventive pulmonary academic award
K07HL-02322-03 (SRC) PHILLIPS, BARBARA A UNIV OF KENTUCKY COLL OF MED DEPT OF MED 800 ROSE STREET LEXINGTON, KY 40536-0084 Preventive pulmonary academic award
K07HL-02327-03 (SRC) BAILEY, WILLIAM C UNIVERSITY OF ALABAMA UAB STATION BIRMINGHAM, AL 35294 Preventive pulmonary academic award program
K08HL-02328-04 (MR) BENDER, JEFFREY R YALE UNIVERSITY SCH OF MEDICIN 333 CEDAR STREET NEW HAVEN, CT 06510 Lymphocyte--endothelial cell molecular interactions
K11HL-02329-03 (SRC) COHEN, ROBERT L UNIV OF CALIFORNIA MED CENTER 3RD AVENUE & PARNASSUS SAN FRANCISCO, CA 94143-0128 Plasminogen activators and PA inhibitors in malignancy
Z01HL-02330-05 (CHB) EPSTEIN, N D NHLBI, NIH Mapping of hypertrophic of cardiomyopathy locus
Z01HL-02331-05 (CHB) SHIMADA, T NHLBI, NIH Development of strategies of genetic therapy of AIDS
K14HL-02332-03 (SRC) TRUPIN, JOEL S MEHARRY MEDICAL COLLEGE 1005 D B TODD BOULEVARD NASHVILLE, TN 37208 Minority school faculty development award
Z01HL-02333-04 (CHB) LEE, A W NHLBI, NIH Structure and function of the murine CS1F-1 receptor
K14HL-02334-03 (SRC) MCGINNIS, ETHELEEN MEHARRY MEDICAL COLLEGE 1005 D B TODD BOULEVARD NASHVILLE, TN 37208 Cloning of the invasiveness gene from bartonella bacilliformis
Z01HL-02335-04 (CHB) BODINE, D NHLBI, NIH Expression of growth genes and oncogenes in primary hematopoietic cells
Z01HL-02336-04 (CHB) NIENHUIS, A W NHLBI, NIH Production and mechanism of action of hematopoietic growth factors
K14HL-02338-03 (SRC) JORDAN, LYNDA M NORTH CAROLINA A&T UNIVERSITY 1601 E MARKET ST GREENSBORO, NC 27411 Characterization of placental phospholipase A2 isozymes
Z01HL-02338-01 (CHB) DONAHUE, R NHLBI, NIH Retroviral mediated gene transfer into primate hematopoietic stem cells
K07HL-02339-02 (SRC) SIMPSON, MARCUS B GEORGE WASHINGTON UNIV HOSPITA 901 23RD STREET, NW WASHINGTON, DC 20037 Transfusion medicine academic award, NHLBI
K07HL-02341-03 (SRC) WARKENTIN, PHYLLIS I UNIVERSITY OF NEBRASKA 600 SOUTH 42ND STREET OMAHA, NE 68198 Transfusion medicine academic award - seventh announcement, Univ Nebraska
K07HL-02342-02 (SRC) BULL, ROBERT W MICHIGAN STATE UNIVERSITY EAST LANSING, MI 48824-1317 Transfusion medicine academic award
K11HL-02346-02 (MR) CONNUCK, DAVID M MEDICAL COLLEGE OF GEORGIA 1120 FIFTEENTH ST AUGUSTA, GEORGA 30912 Aortic arch selection in the chick embryo
K11HL-02347-03 (MR) ZON, LEONARD I CHILDREN'S HOSPITAL CORPORATIO 300 LONGWOOD AVENUE BOSTON, MA 02115 The erythropoietin ligand-receptor interaction
K08HL-02348-03 (MR) REED, GUY L MASSACHUSETTS GENERAL HOSPITAL BOSTON, MA 02114 Enhancing thrombolysis by inhibition of a2-antiplasmin
K11HL-02351-03 (MR) BELL, LEONARD 59 TUMBLEBROOK ROAD WOODBRIDGE, CT 06525 Mechanisms of vascular cell migration
K08HL-02352-03 (MR) HAYNES, JOHNSON, JR UNIV OF SOUTH ALABAMA MED CTR 2451 FILLINGIM STREET MOBILE, AL 36617 Mechanisms of sickle cell induced lung injury
K04HL-02353-03 (RAP) KUNA, SAMUEL T UNIV OF TEXAS MEDICAL BRANCH 301 UNIVERSITY BLVD GALVESTON, TX 77550-2774 Laryngeal function in respiration
K07HL-02355-03 (SRC) GIGER, URS UNIV OF PENNSYLVANIA SCH VET M 3850 SPRUCE STREET PHILADELPHIA, PA 19104-6010 Transfusion medicine academic award, Univ Pennsylvania Veterinary Med
K04HL-02356-03 (RAP) ALTIERE, RALPH J UNIVERSITY OF COLORADO CAMPUS BOX 297 BOULDER, CO 80309-0297 Inhibitory nervous regulation of airway smooth muscle
K11HL-02358-03 (MR) COLLMAN, RONALD G UNIV OF PENNSYLVANIA HOSPITAL 3600 SPRUCE STREET PHILADELPHIA, PA 19104 HIV lung disease and macrophages--Molecular cell biology
K11HL-02361-02 (MR) KINDMAN, L ALLEN STANFORD UNIVERSITY 300 PASTEUR DRIVE STANFORD, CA 94305-5246 Calcium spiking in neuroendocrine signaling
K11HL-02363-02 (MR) MURRAY, KATHERINE T VANDERBILT UNIVERSITY SCH OF M CC-2209 MEDICAL CENTER NORTH NASHVILLE, TN 37232 Metabolic regulation of the cardiac sodium channel
K08HL-02369-02 (MR) BEEHLER, CONNIE J UNIV OF CO HLTH SCIENCES CTR 4200 EAST NINTH AVENUE DENVER, CO 80262 Pulmonary antioxidants affect on ischemia-reperfusion injury
K08HL-02370-03 (MR) MARSHALL, BRUCE C UNIV OF UTAH HEALTH SCIENCE CTR 50 NORTH MEDICAL DRIVE SALT LAKE CITY, UT 84132 Human lung neutral metalloendopeptidase
K08HL-02371-02 (SRC) JARCHO, JOHN A BRIGHAM AND WOMEN'S HOSPITAL 75 FRANCIS STREET BOSTON, MA 02115 A genetic study of familial hypertrophic cardiomyopathy
K04HL-02372-02 (ECS) SKALAK, THOMAS C UNIVERSITY OF VIRGINIA CHARLOTTESVILLE, VA 22901 Microcirculatory network in growth and hypertension
K11HL-02373-02 (SRC) BOZEMAN, PAULA M ST JUDE CHILDREN'S RESEARCH HO 332 N LAUDERDALE MEMPHIS, TN 38101-0318 Anti-inflammatory activity of dapsone
K11HL-02374-03 (MR) FREVERT, CHARLES E HARVARD SCHOOL OF PUBLIC HEALT 665 HUNTINGTON AVENUE BOSTON, MA 02115 Lung macrophage function in endotoxin-induced injury
K08HL-02375-02 (MR) TERADA, LANCE S UNIVERSITY OF COLORADO 4200 EAST 9TH AVENUE DENVER, CO 80262 Xanthine oxidase induced lung injury from intestinal ischemia
K08HL-02376-04 (MR) RAY, DANIEL W EVANSTON HOSPITAL 1301 CENTRAL STREET EVANSTON, IL 60201 Neuropeptides in hyperpnea-induced bronchoconstriction
K04HL-02377-03 (ECS) FABER, JAMES E UNIV OF NC AT CHAPEL HILL CB# 7545, 265 MED SCI RES BLDG CHAPEL HILL, NC 27599 Receptor-effector coupling in microvascular smooth muscle
K11HL-02379-03 (MR) KESSLER, PAUL D JOHNS HOPKINS UNIVERSITY 600 N WOLFE ST BALTIMORE, MD 21205 Cardiac ion pumps--A molecular genetic approach
K08HL-02380-02 (MR) SAUL, JEROME P MASSACHUSETTS INSTITUTE OF TEC 77 MASSACHUSETTS AVENUE CAMBRIDGE, MA 02139 Short-term modulation

PROJECT NO., ORGANIZATIONAL UNIT., INVESTIGATOR, ADDRESS, TITLE

of autonomic function
K08HL-02383-03 (MR) DEFFEBACH, MARK E PACIFIC MEDICAL CENTER 1200 12TH AVE SOUTH SEATTLE, WA 98144 Air conditioning by the trachea--Stimuli and mechanisms
K11HL-02385-02 (MR) LIESVELD, JANE L UNIV OF ROCHESTER MEDICAL CTR 601 ELMWOOD AVENUE ROCHESTER, NY 14642 Study of progenitor cell-microenvironment interactions
K08HL-02387-04 (MR) CUNNINGHAM, MICHAEL J UNIVERSITY OF ROCHESTER 601 ELMWOOD AVENUE ROCHESTER, N Y 14642 Influence of myocardial hypertrophy on diastolic function
K11HL-02388-03 (MR) GUNN, MICHAEL D UNIVERSITY OF CALIFORNIA PO BOX 0724 SAN FRANCISCO, CA 94143 Endothelin receptor--purification and characterization
K11HL-02391-02 (MR) FISHMAN, GLENN I ALBERT EINSTEIN COLLEGE OF MED 1300 MORRIS PARK AVE BRONX, NY 10461 Molecular biology of cardiac gap junctions
K08HL-02394-03 (MR) KOUREMBANAS, STELLA DANA FARBER CANCER INSTITUTE 44 BINNEY STREET BOSTON, MA 02115 Regulation of pdgf production by endothelial cells
K08HL-02395-02 (MR) ARNOLD, LUCY W THE CHILDREN'S HOSPITAL 320 LONGWOOD AVENUE BOSTON, MA 02115 Analysis of rat nonmuscle myosin heavy chain gene
K08HL-02396-03 (MR) LINENBERGER, MICHAEL L UNIV OF WASHINGTON SCHOOL OF M HEMATOLOGY DIVISION SEATTLE, WA 98195 Hemopoietic environment of retroviral infected marrow
K11HL-02397-02 (MR) MC DONALD, THOMAS V STANFORD UNIVERSITY 300 PASTEUR DRIVE STANFORD, CA 94305-5246 Second-messenger regulation of calcium ion channels
K08HL-02401-02 (MR) STRIETER, ROBERT M UNIVERSITY OF MICHIGAN 3916 TAUBMAN CENTER ANN ARBOR, MI 48109-0360 Role of a novel neutrophil chemotaxin in lung injury
K08HL-02407-03 (MR) SPORN, PETER H NORTHWESTERN UNIVERSITY 250 E SUPERIOR ST CHICAGO, IL 60611-2950 Oxidant-induced macrophage arachidonic acid metabolism
Z01HL-02407-17 (PB) CRYSTAL, R G NHLBI, NIH Hereditary lung disease
K08HL-02408-02 (MR) BADESCH, DAVID B UNIVERSITY OF COLORADO 4200 E NINTH AVE, BOX B-133 DENVER, CO 80262 Hypertensive pulmonary vascular remodeling--Role of IGF
K11HL-02410-02 (MR) KAVANAUGH, WILLIAM M UNIV OF CALIFORNIA BOX 0724 SAN FRANCISCO, CA 94143 PDGF & PDGF receptor gene expression in vascular cells
K04HL-02411-02 (GMB) DE LANEROLLE, PRIMAL UNIV OF ILLINOIS AT CHICAGO P O BOX 6998 CHICAGO, ILL 60680 Myosin and smooth muscle regulation
K04HL-02412-02 (HEM) KORNECKI, ELIZABETH H STATE UNIVERSITY OF NEW YORK 450 CLARKSON AVE BROOKLYN, NEW YORK 11203 Molecular mechanisms of platelet activation
K04HL-02414-02 (HEM) RUNGE, MARSCHALL S EMORY UNIVERSITY POST OFFICE DRAWER LL ATLANTA, GA 30322 Fibrin binding sites and plasminogen activator catalysis
K08HL-02415-02 (MR) PAINE, ROBERT, III UNIVERSITY OF MICHIGAN MED SCH 3916 TAUBMAN CENTER ANN ARBOR, MI 48109 Cytokeratin expression in alveolar epithelial cells
K11HL-02417-02 (MR) LINDEMAN, KAREN S JOHNS HOPKINS HOSPITAL 600 NORTH WOLFE STEET BALTIMORE, MD 21205 Mechanisms of calcium chelator-induced airway constriction
K08HL-02419-02 (SRC) KELLER, MARK W UNIVERSITY OF VIRGINIA PO BOX 158 CHARLOTTESVILLE, VA 22908 Microcirculatory studies of reperfusion injury
K08HL-02421-02 (MR) TOMASELLI, GORDON F JOHNS HOPKINS MEDICAL INST 600 NORTH WOLFE STREET BALTIMORE, MD 21205 Molecular physiology of cloned ion channels
K08HL-02423-02 (MR) MC CORMACK, FRANCIS X NATIONAL JEWISH CENTER 1400 JACKSON STREET DENVER, CO 80206 Structure/function relationships of surfactant protein A
K08HL-02424-02 (MR) MURRAY, RICHARD K HOSP OF UNIV OF PENNSYLVANIA 3600 SPRUCE ST PHILADELPHIA, PA 19104 Post receptor changes in signal transduction in airway smooth muscle
K11HL-02425-02 (MR) BOTNEY, MITCHELL D JEWISH HOSPITAL OF ST LOUIS 216 S KINGSHIGHWAY ST LOUIS, MO 63110 Role of growth factors in pulmonary hypertension
K08HL-02426-02 (MR) NYHAN, DANIEL THE JOHNS HOPKINS HOSPITAL 600 N WOLFE ST TOWER 711 BALTIMORE, MD 21205 Pulmonary vascular changes after cardiopulmonary bypass
K08HL-02428-02 (SRC) BIRKENMEIER, THOMAS M WASHINGTON UNIVERSITY PO BOX 8052, 660 S EUCLID ST LOUIS, MO 63110 Regulation of fibronectin receptor expression
K08HL-02429-03 (MR) HIRSCH, ALAN T ORTTA, UNIVERSITY OF MINNESOTA 1100 WASHINGTON AVENUE MINNEAPOLIS, MN 55415-1226 Tissue renin-angiotensin in normal and heart failure rat
K08HL-02430-02 (MR) ALPERT, STEPHEN E CASE WESTERN RESERVE UNIV 2101 ADELBERT RD CLEVELAND, OHIO 44106 Modulation of arachidonate cascade in airway epithelium
K08HL-02431-03 (MR) BAHOU, WADIE F STATE UNIVERSITY OF NEW YORK DIVISION OF HEMATOLOGY STONY BROOK, N Y 11794 Molecular biology of hemonectin
K08HL-02433-02 (MR) GEORGE, SAMUEL E DUKE UNIVERSITY ERWIN ROAD DURHAM, NC 27710 Calcium & myosin light chain kinase in human aorta
K07HL-02435-02 (SRC) FUENTES, FRANCISCO UNIV OF TEXAS HEALTH SCIENCE C 6431 FANNIN HOUSTON, TX 77030 Preventive cardiology academic award
K07HL-02440-02 (SRC) WOLF, WENDY J UNIV OF TEXAS MEDICAL BRANCH C2-40 CHILD HEALTH CENTER GALVESTON, TX 77550-2774 Preventive cardiology academic award NHLBI
K11HL-02444-02 (MR) PEARCE, T ELDER 432 WEST 58TH STREET NEW YORK, NY 10019 Infection of bone marrow by HIV-1--Role in pathogenesis
K11HL-02445-02 (SRC) LOSE, EDWARD J CHILDREN'S HOSPITAL 300 LONGWOOD AVENUE BOSTON, MA 02115 Proteoglycans in pulmonary vascular tissue interactions
K08HL-02447-01A1 (MR) VALANTINE, HANNAH A STANFORD UNIVERSITY 300 PASTEUR DR STANFORD, CA 94305-5246 Immune mediators of acute cardiac allograft dysfunction

PROJECT NO., ORGANIZATIONAL UNIT., INVESTIGATOR, ADDRESS, TITLE

K08HL-02448-02 (SRC) CAMACHO, S ALBERT UNIVERSITY OF CALIFORNIA 505 PARNASUSS, M-1186 SAN FRANCISCO, CA 94143 Metabolic regulation of myocardial contractility
K04HL-02449-02 (PTHA) LIAU, GENE AMERICAN RED CROSS 15601 CRABBS BRANCH WAY ROCKVILLE, MD 20855 Vessel wall injury and repair
K11HL-02451-02 (SRC) LOWENSTEIN, CHARLES J JOHNS HOPKINS UNIVERSITY 725 NORTH WOLFE ST BALTIMORE, MD 21205 Beta-globin gene transfer into hematopoietic stem cells
K04HL-02453-01A1 (EDC) BOERWINKLE, ERIC UNIVERSITY OF TEXAS HLTH SCI C PO BOX 20334 HOUSTON, TX 77225 Epidemiology of genotype by environment interaction
K08HL-02455-02 (SRC) HUNTER, JAMES H UNIVERSITY OF IOWA IOWA CITY, IA 52242 Growth regulation by a type II epithelial cell factor
K08HL-02456-02 (SRC) DENKE, MARGO A UNIVERSITY OF TEXAS 5323 HARRY HINES BLVD DALLAS, TX 75235-9052 Diet and drug responsiveness in hypercholesterolemic women
K08HL-02457-02 (SRC) MATHERNE, GAYNELL P, JR UNIVERSITY OF VIRGINIA HEALTH SCIENCES CENTER CHARLOTTESVILLE, VA 22908 Coronary blood flow during development--Role of adenosine
K08HL-02460-02 (SRC) MADTES, DAVID K FRED HUTCHINSON CANCER RES CTR 1124 COLUMBIA STREET SEATTLE, WA 98104 Mechanism of lung repair--Role of TGF-alpha, TGF-beta and PDGF
K08HL-02463-02 (SRC) LOPEZ, JOSE A GLADSTONE FOUNDATION LABORATOR PO BOX 40608 SAN FRANCISCO, CA 94140-0608 Structure and function of the platelet GP Ib-IX complex
K11HL-02464-02 (SRC) ABRAMS, CHARLES S UNIVERSITY OF PENNSYLVANIA 3400 SPRUCE STREET PHILADELPHIA, PA 19104-4283 Molecular analysis of fibrinogen/GP IIb-IIIa intreraction
K11HL-02466-02 (SRC) BALKE, C WILLIAM UNIV OF MARYLAND AT BALTIMORE 660 WEST REDWOOD STREET BALTIMORE, MD 21201 Cellular mechanisms of delayed afterdepolarizations
K08HL-02467-03 (MR) HOLCOMBE, RANDALL F LSU MEDICAL CENTER SCH OF MED 1501 KINGS HIGHWAY SHREVEPORT, LA 71130-3932 Isolation of the gene for Chediak-Higashi syndrome
K07HL-02474-02 (SRC) COULTAS, DAVID B UNIVERSITY OF NEW MEXICO 2211 LOMAS BLVD, NE ALBUQUERQUE, NM 87131 Preventive pulmonary academic award
K07HL-02479-01A1 (SRC) HAPONIK, EDWARD F BOWMAN GRAY SCHOOL MEDICINE 300 SOUTH HAWTHORNE RD WINSTON-SALEM, NC 27103 Preventive pulmonary academic award
K14HL-02480-02 (SRC) BHATTACHARYYA, MOHIT L MEHARRY MEDICAL COLLEGE 1005 D B TODD BOULEVARD NASHVILLE, TN 37208 Reperfusion induced changes in myocardial tissue and cell
K14HL-02482-02 (SRC) CLARK, JOHN T MEHARRY MEDICAL COLLEGE 1005 DR D B TODD, JR BLVD NASHVILLE, TN 37208 Minority school faculty development award
K08HL-02483-02 (SRC) BHATTACHARYA, SUNITA ST LUKES-ROOSEVELT HOSPITAL CT 428 WEST 59TH ST NEW YORK, NY 10019 Micropuncture studies of lung segmental vasoactivity
K08HL-02484-02 (SRC) WHITE, STEVEN R UNIVERSITY OF CHICAGO 5841 SOUTH MARYLAND AVENUE CHICAGO, IL 60637 Epithelial modulation of respiratory smooth muscle
K08HL-02485-02 (SRC) TOWBIN, JEFFREY A BAYLOR COLLEGE OF MEDICINE 6621 FANIN STREET HOUSTON, TX 77030 Molecular linkage and cloning of X-linked cardiomyopathy
K11HL-02487-02 (MR) HUNG, DAVID T UNIVERSITY OF CALIFORNIA PO BOX 0128 SAN FRANCISCO, CA 94143 Molecular mechanisms of thrombin action
K11HL-02488-03 (MR) ROTTMAN, JEFFREY N JEWISH HOSPITAL OF ST LOUIS 216 KINGSHIGHWAY ST LOUIS, MO 63110 Nuclear hormone receptor in cardiac function/development
K08HL-02490-02 (SRC) SCHWINN, DEBRA A DUKE UNIVERSITY MEDICAL CENTER BOX 3094 DURHAM, NC 27710 Molecular characterization of alpha 1-adrenergic receptors
K08HL-02491-02 (SRC) WATCHKO, JON F MAGEE-WOMENS HOSPITAL FORBES AVENUE AND HALKET STREE PITTSBURGH , PA 15213 Postnatal development of expiratory muscle
K11HL-02492-02 (MR) BRUECKNER, MARTINA YALE UNIVERSITY SCH OF MEDICIN 333 CEDAR STREET NEW HAVEN, CT 06510 IV, a gene that controls cardiac and visceral asymmetry
K11HL-02498-02 (MR) KELLER, BRADLEY B UNIVERSITY OF ROCHESTER MED CT 601 ELMWOOD AVE BOX 631 ROCHESTER, NY 14642 Ventricular mechanics in the chick embryo
K11HL-02504-02 (MR) LIMENTANI, STEVEN A NEW ENGLAND MEDICAL CENTER 750 WASHINGTON ST BOSTON, MA 02111 The gla domain in blood clotting proteins
K08HL-02505-01A1 (MR) STARK, JAMES M UNIVERSITY OF WISCONSIN 600 HIGHLAND AVE H4/434 MADISON, WI 53792 Respiratory virus infection and airway inflammation
K08HL-02507-02 (SRC) DOMINO, KAREN B HARBORVIEW MED CTR 325 NINTH AVE SEATTLE, WA 98104 Ventilation perfusion heterogeneity
K11HL-02508-02 (MR) LIAO, JAMES K BRIGHAM AND WOMEN'S HOSPITAL 75 FRANCIS STREET BOSTON, MA 02115 Role of GTP-binding proteins in mediating EDRF release
K11HL-02514-02 (MR) LOH, EVAN BRIGHAM AND WOMENS HOSPITAL 75 FRANCIS STREET BOSTON, MA 02115 Receptors, G proteins, and cardiac transplantation
K08HL-02515-02 (SRC) NOVOTNY, WILLIAM F UNIVERSITY OF CALIFORNIA 225 DICKINSON ST SAN DIEGO, CA 92103 Lipoprotein and heparin interactions of LACI
K08HL-02519-02 (SRC) STEIN, MICHAEL A EMORY UNIVERSITY 1369 PIERCE DRIVE ATLANTA, GA 30322 Coronary vascular permeability and endothelial dysfunction
K04HL-02520-02 (PHRA) CLARKSON, CRAIG W TULANE UNIVERSITY 1430 TULANE AVE NEW ORLEANS, LA 70112 Mechanisms of cocaine cardiotoxicity
K04HL-02521-02 (HEM) FISCHER, THOMAS H UNIVERSITY OF NORTH CAROLINA 416 BURNETT WOMACK CHAPEL HILL, NC 27599 Mechanisms of platelet inhibition by cAMP
K08HL-02522-02 (SRC) CHEN, CHARLES S NEW ENGLAND DEACONESS HOSPITAL 185 PILGRIM ROAD BOSTON, MA 02215 Platelet-endothelial dysfunction by fibrin(ogen) peptide

K07HL-02530-01A1 (SRC) JETER, ELAINE K MEDICAL UNIV OF SOUTH CAROLINA 171 ASHLEY AVENUE CHARLESTON, SC 29425-0701 Transfusion medicine academic award NHLBI

K07HL-02532-01A1 (SRC) SPENCE, RICHARD K THREE COOPER PLAZA CAMDEN, NJ 08103 Transfusion medicine

Z01HL-02533-07 (PB) CRYSTAL, R G NHLBI, NIH Lung inflammation

K04HL-02536-02 (MEP) KHOO, MICHAEL C UNIV OF SOUTHERN CALIFORNIA OHE-500 LOS ANGELES, CA 90089-1451 Dynamics of respiratory instability in humans in sleep

Z01HL-02536-01 (PB) CRYSTAL, R G NHLBI, NIH Gene therapy

K08HL-02537-02 (SRC) BALLANTYNE, CHRISTIE M BAYLOR COLLEGE OF MEDICINE ONE BAYLOR PLAZA HOUSTON, TX 77030 Molecular studies of endothelial adhesion molecules

K08HL-02539-01 (MR) SILVERMAN, HOWARD S JOHNS HOPKINS UNIV SCHOOL OF M 600 NORTH WOLFE STREET BALTIMORE, MD 21205 Cellular mechanism of post-hypoxic cardiac dysfunction

K04HL-02541-01 (HEM) ASCH, ADAM S CORNELL UNIV MEDICAL COLLEGE 1300 YORK AVE NEW YORK, NY 10021 Structure and function of the TSP-GPIV system

K08HL-02542-01 (MR) ERBAN, JOHN K NEW ENGLAND MEDICAL CENTER 750 WASHINGTON ST BOX 832 BOSTON, MA 02111 The receptor for fibrin on endothelial cells

K08HL-02543-01 (MR) CARROLL, JOHN L JOHNS HOPKINS HOSPITAL 600 NORTH WOLFE STREET BALTIMORE, MD 21205 The carotid body in development of breathing control

K08HL-02547-01 (MR) FLAMM, MICHAEL COLUMBIA UNIVERSITY HLTH SCIS 701 WEST 168TH STREET NEW YORK, NY 10032 Regulation of human globin gene expression

K08HL-02553-01A1 (MR) RABY, KHETHER E BRIGHAM & WOMENS HOSPITAL 75 FRANCIS ST BOSTON, MA 02115 Multivariate stratification of asymptomatic ischemia

K08HL-02554-01 (MR) REILLY, JOHN J BRIGHAM AND WOMENS HOSPITAL 75 FRANCIS STREET BOSTON, MA 02115 Elastases of human alveolar macrophages

K11HL-02555-01 (SRC) CONKLIN, BRUCE R UNIV OF CALIFORNIA SAN FRANCIS 513 PARNASSUS AVENUE SAN FRANCISCO, CA 94143 Mutant G proteins reveal signaling pathways

K08HL-02558-01 (MR) ROSEN, GLENN D WASHINGTON UNIVERSITY SCH OF M 660 S EUCLID/BOX 8052 ST LOUIS, MO 63110 Characterization of different forms of alpha 4 beta 1 integrin

K11HL-02563-01 (SRC) MOULTON, KAREN UNIV OF CALIFORNIA SAN DIEGO LA JOLLA, CA 92093 Regulation of macrophage development

K08HL-02564-01 (MR) FREDERICH, ROBERT C BETH ISRAEL HOSPITAL 330 BROOKLINE AVE BOSTON, MA 02215 Fat-derived angiotensinogen & hypertension of the obese

K04HL-02566-01 (CVB) GANZ, PETER BRIGHAM & WOMEN'S HOSPITAL 75 FRANCIS STREET BOSTON, MA 02115 Endothelial dysfunction in coronary atherosclerosis

K11HL-02568-01 (SRC) CALHOUN, DAVID A UNIVERSITY OF ALABAMA 520 ZEIGLER RES BLDG BIRMINGHAM, AL 35294 Baroreflex in NaCl-sensitive hypertension

K11HL-02574-01 (MR) ROTH, DAVID A NEW ENGLAND MEDICAL CENTER 750 WASHINGTON ST, BOX 832 BOSTON, MA 02111 Kringle domains in blood coagulation proteins

K11HL-02578-01 (MR) RABBANI, LEROY E BRIGHAM & WOMEN'S HOSPITAL 75 FRANCIS STREET BOSTON, MA 02115 Lipids, mitogens, and endothelial fibrinolysis

K08HL-02582-01 (SRC) STAMLER, JONATHAN S BRIGHAM AND WOMEN'S HOSPITAL 75 FRANCIS STREET BOSTON, MA 02115 EDRF, nitrosthiols, and platelet function

K08HL-02583-01 (SRC) LAMURAGLIA, GLENN M MASSACHUSETTS GENERAL HOSP 32 FRUIT STREET BOSTON, MA 02114 Characterization of vascular response to laser injury

K08HL-02584-01 (SRC) DEPALO, LOUIS R ALBERT EINSTEIN COLLEGE OF MED 1300 MORRIS PARK AVENUE BRONX, NY 10461 Cell-cell interactions regulate airway smooth muscle

K08HL-02587-01 (SRC) GILBERT, GARY E BROCKTON-WEST ROXBURY 1400 VFW PARKWAY WEST ROXBURY, MA 02132 Coordinate function of enzyme complexes in hemostasis

K08HL-02588-01 (SRC) BADR, M SAFWAN UNIVERSITY OF WISCONSIN 600 HIGHLAND AVE MADISON, WI 53792 Chemical influences on upper airway obstruction in sleep

K04HL-02590-01 (HEM) LELLA, VIJAYA M UNIVERSITY OF CALIFORNIA 225 DICKINSON STREET SAN DIEGO, CA 92103 Regulation of tissue factor expression on cell surfaces

K11HL-02592-01 (MR) HUMPHRIES, JOHN E UNIVERSITY OF VIRGINIA BOX 34, HEALTH SCIENCES CENTER CHARLOTTESVILLE, VA 22908 Hepatic mechanisms in the regulation of fibrinolysis

K08HL-02595-01 (SRC) ELLIOTT, STEPHEN J BAYLOR COLLEGE OF MEDICINE ONE BAYLOR PLAZA HOUSTON, TX 77030 Oxidant stress and endothelial cell Ca2+ signaling

K11HL-02601-01 (MR) WATTS, RAYMOND G UNIVERSITY OF ALABAMA 1600 7TH AVE, SOUTH BIRMINGHAM, AL 35233 The microfilamentous cytoskeleton and neutrophil shape

K07HL-02603-01 (SRC) TAYLOR, HERMAN A UNIVERSITY OF ALABAMA UNIVERSITY STATION BIRMINGHAM, AL 35294 Preventive cardiology academic award, NHLBI

K07HL-02605-01 (SRC) CAMILLI, ANTHONY E UNIVERSITY OF ARIZONA 1501 N CAMPBELL AVENUE TUCSON, AZ 85724 Preventive pulmonary academic award program

K07HL-02606-01 (SRC) SOCKRIDER, MARIANNA M 2201 W HOLCOMBE, #310 HOUSTON, TX 77030 Preventive pulmonary academic award program

K07HL-02607-01 (SRC) THOMAS, ALVIN V, JR HOWARD UNIVERSITY 520 W STREET NORTHWEST WASHINGTON, DC 20059 Howard University program for preventive pulmonary medicine

K08HL-02611-02 (SRC) LARSEN, ERIC C DARTMOUTH HITCHCOCK MED CTR 2 MAYNARD ST HANOVER, NH 03756 Molecular basis of platelet-leukocyte binding

K08HL-02618-01 (MR) KNOWLTON, KIRK U UNIVERSITY OF CALIFORNIA LA JOLLA, CA 92093 Regulation of the ANF gene during ventricular hypertrophy

K08HL-02620-01 (MR) STEELE, MARK P VA MEDICAL CENTER 508 FULTON STREET DURHAM, NC 27705 Isolation of genes expressed in pulmonary type 2 cells

K08HL-02621-01 (MR) SIEGEL, DONALD L UNIVERSITY OF PENNSYLVANIA 3400 SPRUCE STREET PHILADELPHIA, PA 19104 Biology of human warm autoimmune hemolytic anemia

K08HL-02622-01 (MR) BEATY, CHRISTOPHER D UNIVERSITY OF WASHINGTON SEATTLE, WA 98195 LPS induced signal transduction in macrophages

K11HL-02623-01 (MR) RUSSELL, J ERIC UNIVERSITY OF PENNSYLVANIA 422 CURIE BLVD CRB PHILADELPHIA, PA 19104-6145 Nucleocytoplasmic transport alpha-globin-derivative mRNA

K08HL-02625-01 (MR) GLENNY, ROBB W UNIVERSITY OF WASHINGTON SEATTLE, WA 98195 Fractal and spatial distribution of pulmonary blood flow

K08HL-02626-01 (MR) WELTY, FRANCINE K USDA HNRCA AT TUFTS UNIVERSITY 711 WASHINGTON STREET BOSTON, MA 02111 Apolipoprotein B mutations and lipoprotein metabolism

K08HL-02627-01 (MR) GANNON, DAVID E UNIVERSITY OF VERMONT BURLINGTON, VT 05405 Regulation of oxidant production in lung endothelium

K04HL-02629-01 (TOX) HOLM, BRUCE A CHILDREN'S HOSPITAL 219 BRYANT STREET BUFFALO, NY 14222 Pulmonary oxygen toxicity--Mechanisms and interventions

K08HL-02630-01 (MR) RYAN, RITA M UNIVERSITY OF ROCHESTER 601 ELMWOOD AVENUE ROCHESTER, NY 14642 TGF-beta interactions with the neonatal type II cell

K08HL-02637-01 (MR) BACK, ANTHONY L SEATTLE VA MEDICAL CENTER 1660 SOUTH COLUMBIAN WAY SEATTLE, WA 98108 Neutrophil adherence receptor structure-function

K11HL-02639-01 (MR) LAWRENCE, JOHN H JOHNS HOPKINS UNIVERSITY 725 N WOLFE STREET BALTIMORE, MD 21205 Molecular basis of sodium channel inactivation

K08HL-02641-01 (MR) GREENBERG, STEVEN M COLUMBIA UNIVERSITY 630 WEST 168TH STREET NEW YORK, NY 10032 Phagocytosis in pulmonary alveolar macrophages

K11HL-02643-01 (MR) DECASTRO, CARLOS M DUKE UNIVERSITY MEDICAL CENTER POST OFFICE BOX 3250 DURHAM, NC 27710 Role of c-kit in early hematopoiesis

K11HL-02646-01 (MR) ZIMRIN, ANN B AMERICAN RED CROSS 15601 CRABBS BRANCH WAY ROCKVILLE, MD 20855 The biology of endothelial cell differentiation

K08HL-02647-01 (MR) PANETTIERI, REYNOLD A UNIVERSITY OF PENNSYLVANIA 3600 SPRUCE ST PHILADELPHIA, PA 19104-4283 Cellular mechanisms regulating airway smooth muscle growth

K11HL-02655-01 (MR) GHIO, ANDREW J VA MEDICAL CENTER MAIL STOP 1111 DURHAM, NC 27710 The silicato-iron complex and interstitial lung injury

K08HL-02656-01 (MR) BECKER, PAMELA S YALE UNIVERSITY SCHOOL OF MED 333 CEDAR ST NEW HAVEN, CT 06510 Cytoskeletal regulation by extracellular matrix adhesion

K07HL-02660-01 (SRC) COOKE, JOHN P STANFORD UNIVERSITY 300 PASTEUR DRIVE STANFORD, CA 94305-5246 Vascular disease academic award, NHLBI

K07HL-02663-01 (SRC) CREAGER, MARK A BRIGHAM AND WOMEN'S HOSPITAL 75 FRANCIS STREET BOSTON, MA 02115 Vascular disease academic award NHLBI

K07HL-02669-01 (SRC) WILD, ROBERT A UNIVERSITY OF OKLAHOMA HLTH SC 920 S L YOUNG BLVD OKLAHOMA CITY, OK 73104 Preventive cardiology academic award NHLBI OUHSC

K07HL-02671-01 (SRC) VELEZ, ROMAN UPR, MEDICAL SCIENCES CAMPUS PO BOX 365067 SAN JUAN, PR 00936-5097 Transfusion medicine academic award NHLBI

K07HL-02673-01 (SRC) JEFFERIES, LEIGH C UNIV OF PENNSLYVANIA HOSPITAL 3400 SPRUCE STREET PHILADELPHIA, PA 19104 Transfusion medicine academic award NHLBI

K07HL-02677-01 (SRC) ABRAMS, JONATHAN UNIVERSITY OF NEW MEXICO HOSP 2211 LOMAS, NE ALBUQUERQUE, NM 87131 Preventive cardiology academic award

K07HL-02678-01 (SRC) HINDS, JOSEPH E MEHARRY MEDICAL COLLEGE 1005 D B TODD BOULEVARD NASHVILLE, TN 37208 Preventive cardiology academic award

K07HL-02680-01 (SRC) GRIM, CLARENCE E CHARLES R DREW UNIV OF MEDICIN 1621 E 120TH STREET LOS ANGELES, CA 90059 Preventive cardiology academic award

K08HL-02681-01 (MR) DE LA CADENA, RAUL A TEMPLE UNIVERSITY 3400 NORTH BROAD STREET PHILADELPHIA, PA 19140 Platelet thrombospondin binding domain(s) on hmw-kininogen

K07HL-02682-01 (SRC) STOUDEMIRE, BEVERLY A MOREHOUSE SCHOOL OF MEDICINE 720 WESTVIEW DR SW ATLANTA, GA 30310-1495 Preventive cardiology academic award

K08HL-02686-01 (SRC) SELDIN, DAVID C BRIGHAM AND WOMEN'S HOSPITAL 75 FRANCIS STREET BOSTON, MA 02115 In vitro and in vivo studies of the human IL-4 receptor

K08HL-02712-01 (SRC) MILLER-HANCE, WANDA C UNIVERSITY OF CALIFORNIA LA JOLLA, CA 92093 Commitment factors in developmental cardiogenesis

Z01HL-02714-11 (LAMS) JONES, M NHLBI, NIH Evaluations of prosthetic cardiac valves--In vivo studies

Z01HL-02777-05 (OD) PARENTEAU, G L NHLBI, NIH Monoclonal antibody and IL2 as immunosuppression for cardiac allografts

Z01HL-02832-01 (MDB) SKARLATOS, S I NHLBI, NIH Cholesterol efflux from human monocyte-derived macrophages

Z01HL-02833-01 (MDB) CHAD, F-F NHLBI, NIH Solubilization of aortic cholesterol-rich lipid particles by HDL

Z01HL-02834-01 (MDB) KRUTH, H S NHLBI, NIH Relationship of cholesterol and calcium deposition in atherosclerosis

R01HL-02835-34 (PHY) HOLOHAN, PETER D S U N Y HSC AT SYRACUSE 750 E ADAMS STREET SYRACUSE, N Y 13210 Renal transport carrier for organic compounds

Z01HL-02835-01 (MDB) KRUTH, H S NHLBI, NIH Cholesterol deposition in human cornea

Z01HL-02836-01 (MDB) LILLY, K NHLBI, NIH Cholesterol trafficking in human monocyte-derived macrophages

R01HL-02942-34 (PBC) BERENSON, GERALD S LOUISIANA STATE UNIV

PROJECT NO., ORGANIZATIONAL UNIT., INVESTIGATOR, ADDRESS, TITLE

MED CTR 1542 TULANE AVE NEW ORLEANS, LA 70112 Proteoglycans in the pathogenesis of atherosclerosis
P01HL-03174-36 (HLBB) SCHWARTZ, STEPHEN M UNIVERSITY OF WASHINGTON SEATTLE, WASH 98195 Mechanisms of acute vascular reaction to injury
P01HL-03174-36 0021 (HLBB) HEIMARK, RONALD L. Mechanisms of acute vascular reaction to injury Endothelial assembly
P01HL-03174-36 0022 (HLBB) DAVIE, EARL W. Mechanisms of acute vascular reaction to injury Coagulation factors in endothelial cells
P01HL-03174-36 9001 (HLBB) REIDY, MICHAEL A Mechanisms of acute vascular reaction to injury Core--morphology
P01HL-03174-36 9002 (HLBB) HEIMARK, RONALD L. Mechanisms of acute vascular reaction to injury Core--tissue culture
P01HL-03174-36 9003 (HLBB) YONGMIN, KIM Mechanisms of acute vascular reaction to injury Core--Image analysis
P01HL-03174-36 0001 (HLBB) SCHWARTZ, STEPHEN M Mechanisms of acute vascular reaction to injury Smooth muscle heterogeneity
P01HL-03174-36 0014 (HLBB) BENDITT, EARL P Mechanisms of acute vascular reaction to injury Origins of human atherosclerotic plaques
P01HL-03174-36 0015 (HLBB) HARLAN, JOHN M Mechanisms of acute vascular reaction to injury Septic shock response and human endothelial cells
P01HL-03174-36 0017 (HLBB) DACEY, RALPH C Mechanisms of acute vascular reaction to injury Structure-function in vasular smooth muscle
P01HL-03174-36 0018 (HLBB) REIDY, MICHAEL A. Mechanisms of acute vascular reaction to injury Stimulation of smooth muscle cell growth in vivo
P01HL-03174-36 0019 (HLBB) ROSS, RUSSELL Mechanisms of acute vascular reaction to injury The macrophage and fibroproliferative responses
P01HL-03174-36 0020 (HLBB) SAGE, HELENE Mechanisms of acute vascular reaction to injury Regulation of novel genes by homotypic matrices
R01HL-03290-35 (ECS) GAYESKI, THOMAS UNIVERSITY OF ROCHESTER 601 ELMWOOD AVENUE, BOX 642 ROCHESTER, N Y 14642 Controls of oxygen transport in heart and skeltal muscle
R37HL-03341-35 (NSS) HAMES, CURTIS G EVANS COUNTY HEALTH DEPT PO BOX 308 CAXTON, GA 30417 Epidemiological study of atherosclerosis
K06HL-03512-29 (NCR) LORAND, LASZLO NORTHWESTERN UNIVERSITY BIOCHEM, MOLECULAR BIOL DEPT EVANSTON, ILL 60201 Blood, muscle and prostate chemistry
Z01HL-03563-05 (LCP) HANBAUER, I NHLBI, NIH Endogenous calcium channel modulator
Z01HL-03567-04 (LCP) HANBAUER, I NHLBI, NIH Regulation of the dopamine reuptake system
Z01HL-03585-02 (HE) BOGDANSKI, D F NHLBI, NIH Sodium-dependent secretion and retention of NE in adrenergic terminals
Z01HL-03590-01 (HE) ABASSI, Z NHLBI, NIH Metabolism of endothelin
Z01HL-03591-01 (HE) GOLOMB, E NHLBI, NIH Cellular mechanisms in hypertension
Z01HL-03592-01 (HE) GOLOMB, E NHLBI, NIH Growth factors & their receptors in the cardiac response to hemodynamic overload
Z01HL-03593-01 (HE) KEISER, H R NHLBI, NIH Pheochromocytomas
Z01HL-03994-01 (PA) ROBERTS, W C NHLBI, NIH Mitral motion in hypertrophic cardiomyopathy
Z01HL-03995-01 (PA) ROBERTS, W C NLHBI, NIH Atherosclerotic plaques in sudden death and in myocardial infarction
Z01HL-03996-01 (PA) ROBERTS, W C NHLBI, NIH Atherosclerotic plaques in coronary arteries in women
Z01HL-03997-01 (PA) ROBERTS, W C NHLBI, NIH Coronary atherosclerotic plaques in patients greater than or equal to 90 years
Z01HL-03998-01 (PA) ROBERTS, W C NHLBI, NIH Atrial endocardial lipid deposits in familial hyperchylomicronemia
Z01HL-03999-01 (PA) ROBERTS, W C NHLBI, NIH Sudden death behind the wheel from natural disease
Z01HL-04000-01 (PA) ROBERTS, W C NHLBI, NIH Age at death and sex distribution in age decade in fatal coronary artery disease
Z01HL-04207-06 (MC) YAMAKAWA, K NHLBI, NIH Cloning of cDNAs encoding T lymphocyte myosin heavy chains
Z01HL-04208-05 (MC) TAKAHASHI, M NHLBI, NIH Cloning of the cDNAs for neuronal myosin heavy chains
Z01HL-04210-04 (MC) KELLEY, C A NHLBI, NIH Myosin phosphorylation and the regulation of contractile activity
Z01HL-04212-03 (MC) SELLERS, J R NHLBI, NIH Characterization of vertebrate myosin I
Z01HL-04213-02 (MC) WANG, F NHLBI, NIH Interaction of invertebrate myosins with actin
Z01HL-04214-02 (MC) PHILLIP, C NHLBI, NIH The effect of retroviral infection on myosin heavy chain expression
Z01HL-04215-01 (MC) HOMSHER, E NHLBI, NIH Correlation between in vitro motility and muscle mechanics
Z01HL-04216-01 (MC) MOUSSAVI, M NHLBI, NIH Myosin phosphorylation in human t lymphocytes
Z01HL-04217-01 (MC) CUDA, G NHLBI, NIH Structure and function of cardiac myosin
Z01HL-04218-01 (MC) ELSON, H F NHLBI, NIH Expression of nonmuscle myosin heavy chain cDNA in vertebrate cells
Z01HL-04219-01 (MC) ADELSLEIN, R S NHLBI, NIH Site-directed mutagenesis of nonmuscle myosin heavy chains
Z01HL-04401-02 (LCP) SUGIYAMA, KATSUMI NHLBI, NIH Mechanisms of cytochrome P-450 enzymes
Z01HL-04408-01 (LCP) SASAME, HENRY NHLBI, NIH Development of data bases of the properties of p450 enzymes
Z01HL-04409-01 (LCP) KUTTY, R K NHLBI, NIH Role of heme oxygenase in protecting retina against oxidative stress
Z01HL-04410-01 (LCP) KRISHNA, G NHLBI, NIH Expression of mRNA for guanlate cyclase-A in rat retina
Z01HL-04411-01 (LCP) KRISHNA, G NHLBI, NIH Physical dependence of morphine--Test based on ability to inhibit c-AMP formation
K06HL-04418-28 (NSS) SPARGO, BENJAMIN H UNIVERSITY OF CHICAGO 5841 S MARYLAND AVE BOX 414 CHICAGO, ILL 60637 Ultrastructural renal changes--clinical/experimental

PROJECT NO., ORGANIZATIONAL UNIT., INVESTIGATOR, ADDRESS, TITLE

R01HL-04442-33 (MBY) GETZ, GODFREY S UNIVERSITY OF CHICAGO 5841 SOUTH MARYLAND AVENUE CHICAGO, ILL 60637 Transcription of yeast mitochondrial DNA
Z01HL-04601-04 (CE) BALABAN, R S NHLBI, NIH Control of cellular energy metabolism
Z01HL-04602-04 (CE) BALABAN, R S NHLBI, NIH Non-Invasive techniques for monitoring cellular function and structure
Z01HL-04603-01 (CE) TURNER, R NHLBI, NIH Application of ultra-fast MRI to physiological studies
Z01HL-04823-03 (CB) CANNON, R O NHLBI, NIH Myocardial ischemia and hypertrophic cardiomyopathy
Z01HL-04825-03 (CB) CANNON, R NHLBI, NIH Endocardial sensitivity in patients with chest pain and normal coronary arteries
Z01HL-04827-03 (CB) BONOW, R O NHLBI, NIH Myocardial viability in coronary artery disease and left ventricular dysfunction
Z01HL-04836-01 (CB) CANNON, R O NHLBI, NIH Impact of operation on thallium perfusion defects in cardiomyopathy
Z01HL-04840-01 (CB) CANNON, R NHLBI, NIH Airways hyperresponsiveness in microvascular angina
Z01HL-04842-02 (CB) CANNON, R NHLBI, NIH Left ventricular performance in asymptomatic aortic stenosis
Z01HL-04852-02 (CB) UNGER, E NHLBI, NIH A model of arterial smooth muscle cell proliferation to study restenosis
Z01HL-04853-02 (CB) UNGER, E NHLBI, NIH Promotion of myocardial angiogenesis via direct application of FGF to heart
Z01HL-04856-02 (CB) PEACOCK, J NHLBI, NIH Hemodynamics of coronary artery stents
Z01HL-04860-02 (CB) MARON, B NHLBI, NIH Middle-aged asymptomatic patients with hypertrophic cardiomyopathy
Z01HL-04864-01 (CB) QUYYUMI, A A NHLBI, NIH Effects of myocardial ischemia on signal-averaged electrogram
Z01HL-04865-01 (CB) QUYYUMI, A A NHLBI, NIH Endothelial dysfunction in patients with microvascular angina
Z01HL-04866-01 (CB) QUYYUMI, A A NHLBI, NIH Endothelial dysfunction of the coronary microvasculature in hypertension
Z01HL-04867-01 (CB) QUYYUMI, A A NHLBI, NIH Prognosis of ambulatory silent ischemia
Z01HL-04868-01 (CB) QUYYUMI, A A NHLBI, NIH Angiogenic effects of heparin fragments in coronary artery disease
Z01HL-04869-01 (CB) DILSIZIAN, V NHLBI, NIH Assessment of myocardial viability by thallium scintigraphy
Z01HL-04870-01 (CB) FANANAPAZIR, L NHLBI, NIH Management of symptoms and arrhythmias in hypertrophic cardiomyopathy
Z01HL-04871-01 (CB) DIODATI, J G NHLBI, NIH Mental stress and platelet activation in coronary artery disease
Z01HL-04872-01 (CB) DIODATI, J G NHLBI, NIH Effect of nitroglycerin on platelet activation in coronary artery disease
Z01HL-04873-01 (CB) DIODATI, J G NHLBI, NIH Antithrombotic effects of complexes of nitric oxide
Z01HL-04874-01 (CB) ARRIGHI, J A NHLBI, NIH Assessment of myocardial perfusion with positron emission tomography
Z01HL-04875-01 (CB) ARRIGHI, J A NHLBI, NIH Effect of verapamil on left ventricular diastolic function in elderly subjects
Z01HL-04876-01 (CB) CANNON, R O NHLBI, NIH Hyperinsulinemia in patients with chest pain and normal coronary arteries
Z01HL-04877-01 (CB) CANNON, R O NHLBI, NIH Exercise stress and coronary flow reserve on microvascular angina
Z01HL-04878-01 (CB) CANNON, R O NHLBI, NIH Exercise hemodynamics and cardiac risk in hypertrophic cardiomyopathy
Z01HL-04879-01 (CB) CANNON, R O NHLBI, NIH Atrial-Ventricular pacing in non-obstructive hypertrophic cardiomyopathy
Z01HL-04880-01 (CB) FLUGELMAN, M Y NHLBI, NIH In Vivo gene transfer to proliferating vascular tissue
Z01HL-04881-01 (CB) FLUGELMAN, M Y NHLBI, NIH Vascular smooth muscle prevalence in coronary atherectomy specimens
Z01HL-04882-01 (CB) FLUGELMAN, M Y NHLBI, NIH In Vivo deployment of stents seeded with autologous, genetically modified cells
Z01HL-04883-01 (CB) PANZA, J A NHLBI, NIH Effect of treatment on endothelium-dependent vascular relaxation in hypertension
Z01HL-04884-01 (CB) CHOI, R W NHLBI, NIH Exercise induced diastolic volume changes in coronary artery disease
Z01HL-04885-01 (CB) MARON, B J NHLBI, NIH Determinants of mitral systolic anterior motion in hypertrophic cardiomyopathy
Z01HL-04886-01 (CB) MARON, B J NHLBI, NIH Mitral valve prolapse in patients with hypertrophic cardiomyopathy
Z01HL-04887-01 (CB) MARON, B J NHLBI, NIH Patients with hypertrophic cardiomyopathy surviving competitive athletics
Z01HL-04888-01 (CB) MARON, B J NHLBI, NIH Predictors of athlete's heart in a population of 947 elite athletes
Z01HL-04889-01 (CB) MARON, B J NHLBI, NIH Doppler in athlete heart and hypertrophic cardiomyopathy
Z01HL-04890-01 (CB) MARON, B J NHLBI, NIH Reduction in wall thickness following deconditioning in Olympic athletes
Z01HL-04891-01 (CB) MARON, B J NHLBI, NIH Hypertrophic cardiomyopathy with hypertrophy of the posterior free wall
Z01HL-04892-01 (CB) MARON, B J NHLBI, NIH Atrial fibrillation in hypertrophic cardiomyopathy
Z01HL-04893-01 (CB) SPEIR, E NHLBI, NIH Antisense strategies to inhibit smooth muscle cell proliferation
Z01HL-04894-01 (CB) SPEIR, E NHLBI, NIH Fibroblast growth factors in adult cardiocytes and vascular cells
Z01HL-04895-01 (CB) BRINKMAN, E NHLBI, NIH Cloning and sequencing early and late response involved in SMC proliferation
Z01HL-04896-01 (CB) BIRO, S NHLBI, NIH Antisense targeted to c-myc mRNA inhibits smooth muscle cell proliferation
Z01HL-05001-02 SIEGMAN, M G NHLBI, NIH Barbiturates and cerebral metabolism during hypothermic circulatory arrest
Z01HL-05010-02 (90) ANDERSON, R V NHLBI, NIH Brain protection during hypothermic circulatory arrest--Effect of hypoglycemia
Z01HL-05201-01 (PA) ROBERTS, W C NHLBI, NIH Morphologic findings in mitral valve prolapse
Z01HL-05202-01 (PA) ROBERTS, W C NHLBI, NIH Valve replacement

for pure mitral regurgitation
Z01HL-05203-01 (PA) ROBERTS, W C NHLBI, NIH Mitral valve alterations in hypertrophic cardiomyopathy
Z01HL-05204-01 (PA) ROBERTS, W C NHLBI, NIH Insertion of papillary muscle into mitral leaflets
Z01HL-05205-01 (PA) ROBERTS, W C NHLBI, NIH Infective endocarditis in hypertrophic cardiomyopathy
Z01HL-05206-01 (PA) ROBERTS, W C NHLBI, NIH Mitral regurgitation after myotomy-myectomy in hypertrophic cardiomyopathy
Z01HL-05207-01 (PA) ROBERTS, W C NHLBI, NIH Hypertrophic cardiomyopathy and bicuspid aortic valve
Z01HL-05208-01 (PA) ROBERTS, W C NHLBI, NIH Aortic dissection with the entrance tear in the abdominal aorta
Z01HL-05209-01 (PA) ROBERTS, W C NHLBI, NIH Combined thoracic aortic dissection and abdominal fusiform aneurysm
Z01HL-05210-01 (PA) ROBERTS, W C NHLBI, NIH Effects of recombinant desulphatohirudin (CGP 39393) on restenosis
Z01HL-05211-01 (PA) ROBERTS, W C NHLBI, NIH Subaortic diameter for normalizing cardiac dimensions
Z01HL-05212-01 (PA) FERRANS, V J NHLBI, NIH Structural remodeling in pulmonary Langerhans cell granulomatosis
Z01HL-05213-01 (PA) FERRANS, V J NHLBI, NIH Prevention of bleomycin-induced pulmonary fibrosis by ICRF-187
Z01HL-05214-01 (PA) FERRANS, V J NHLBI, NIH Anthracycline cardiomyopathy
Z01HL-05215-01 (PA) FERRANS, V J NHLBI, NIH Cardiotoxicity of interleukin-2
Z01HL-05216-01 (PA) FERRANS, V J NHLBI, NIH Lesions of selenium-vitamin E deficiency in different strains of mice
Z01HL-05217-01 (PA) FERRANS, V J NHLBI, NIH The cardiotoxicity of liposomal doxorubicin
Z01HL-05218-01 (PA) FERRANS, V J NHLBI, NIH Dendritic cells of rat heart in experimental myocardial infarction
Z01HL-05219-01 (PA) FERRANS, V J NHLBI, NIH Collagen crimping and fixation pressure in porcine aortic valves
Z01HL-05220-01 (PA) FERRANS, V J NHLBI, NIH Pathologic changes in implanted heart valves fabricated of dura mater
Z01HL-05221-01 (PA) FERRANS, V J NHLBI, NIH Cardiac pathologic findings in Weber Christian's disease
Z01HL-05222-01 (PA) ROBERTS, W C NHLBI, NIH Mitral and tricuspid valve replacement with mitral stenosis
R37HL-05791-31 (NSS) BENESCH, RUTH E COLUMBIA UNIVERSITY 630 WEST 168TH STREET NEW YORK, N Y 10032 Structure and function in hemoglobins
R37HL-05806-31 (PHRA) LUCCHESI, BENEDICT R UNIVERSITY OF MICHIGAN 6322 MEDICAL SCIENCE BLDG I ANN ARBOR, MI 48109-0626 Analysis of antiarrhythmic agents
R37HL-05949-31 (NSS) GERGELY, JOHN BOSTON BIOMEDICAL RES INST 20 STANIFORD STREET BOSTON, MA 02114 Biochemistry of muscle contraction
P01HL-06296-31 (SRC) MITCHELL, JERE H UNIV OF TEX SW MED CTR 5323 HARRY HINES BLVD DALLAS, TX 75235-9034 Response and adaptation to exercise
P01HL-06296-31 0007 (SRC) MITCHELL, JERE H Response and adaptation to exercise Peripheral neural regulatory mechanisms in the response to exercise
P01HL-06296-31 0009 (SRC) STULL, JAMES T Response and adaptation to exercise Regulation of myosin phosphorylation in striated muscle
P01HL-06296-31 0012 (SRC) LEWIS, STEVEN F Response and adaptation to exercise Cardiovascular control/adaptation to exercise--Muscle metabolism disorders
P01HL-06296-31 0015 (SRC) DEMARTINO, GEORGE N Response and adaptation to exercise Biochemical mechanisms of intracellular proteolysis
P01HL-06296-31 0016 (SRC) WALDROP, TONY G Response and adaptation to exercise Central neural regulatory mechanisms in response to exercise
P01HL-06296-31 0017 (SRC) VICTOR, RONALD G Response and adaptation to exercise Reflex control of sympathetic nerve activity by muscle afferents in humans
P01HL-06296-31 9001 (SRC) JOHNSON JR, ROBERT L Response and adaptation to exercise Computer facility and biostatistical analysis core
P01HL-06296-31 9002 (SRC) ORDWAY, GEORGE A Response and adaptation to exercise Core--Blood chemistry
P01HL-06296-31 9006 (SRC) STULL, JAMES T Response and adaptation to exercise Core--Monoclonal antibody and recombinant DNA
P01HL-06296-31 9007 (SRC) BERTOCCI, LOREN Response and adaptation to exercise Core--Cell structure and metabolism
P01HL-06308-31 (SRC) HATHAWAY, DAVID R INDIANA UNIVERSITY SCH OF MED 1001 W. 10TH STREET INDIANAPOLIS, IN 46202-2859 Mechanisms and therapy of circulatory disease
P01HL-06308-31 0043 (SRC) LINDEMANN, JON P Mechanisms and therapy of circulatory disease Membrane protein phosphorylation in intact myocardium
P01HL-06308-31 0044 (SRC) DE PAOLI- ROACH, ANNA A. Mechanisms and therapy of circulatory disease Structure and function of type 2A phosphoprotein phosphatase
P01HL-06308-31 9002 (SRC) JONES, LARRY R Mechanisms and therapy of circulatory disease Core--Protein chemistry and molecular biology
P01HL-06308-31 0039 (SRC) WATANABE, AUGUST M Mechanisms and therapy of circulatory disease Muscarinic inhibitors of protein phosphorylation in cardiac muscle
P01HL-06308-31 0040 (SRC) JONES, LARRY R Mechanisms and therapy of circulatory disease Regulation of ion transport in cardiac sarcolemma by phosphorylation
P01HL-06308-31 0041 (SRC) HATHAWAY, DAVID R Mechanisms and therapy of circulatory disease Biochemical mechanisms in regulation of VSM contractility
P01HL-06350-30 (HLBB) ROBERTS, HAROLD R UNIVERSITY OF NORTH CAROLINA CHAPEL HILL, NC 27599 Structure, function and genetics of coagulation factors
P01HL-06350-30 0015 (HLBB) GRAHAM, JOHN B Structure, function and genetics of coagulation factors Structure-Function and genetic studies of factor's VIII and IX
P01HL-06350-30 0018 (HLBB) ROBERTS, HAROLD R Structure, function and genetics of coagulation factors Studies of normal and abnormal factor IX
P01HL-06350-30 0022 (HLBB) EDGELL, CORA-JEAN S Structure, function and genetics of coagulation factors Somatic cell genetics and morphogenesis of factor VIII
P01HL-06350-30 0023 (HLBB) STAFFORD, DARREL W. Structure, function and genetics of coagulation factors Isolation and characterization of the gene for factor IX
P01HL-06350-30 9001 (HLBB) NOYES, CLAUDIA M Structure, function and genetics of coagulation factors Protein/Peptide structural analysis facility
P01HL-06835-30 (SRC) FERRARIO, CARLOS M CLEVELAND CLINIC FOUNDATION 9500 EUCLID AVENUE CLEVELAND, OHIO 44106 Neurohormonal mechanisms in hypertension
P01HL-06835-30 0085 (SRC) BARNES, KAREN Neurohormonal mechanisms in hypertension Neuronal actions of angiotensins II and congener peptides in the medulla
P01HL-06835-30 0086 (SRC) DIZ, DEBRA I Neurohormonal mechanisms in hypertension Functional anatomy of medullary and vagal angiotensin receptors
P01HL-06835-30 0087 (SRC) AVERILL, DAVID B Neurohormonal mechanisms in hypertension Action of angiotensin II in ventrolateral medulla
P01HL-06835-30 0088 (SRC) BROSNIHAN, K BRIDGET Neurohormonal mechanisms in hypertension Expression and regulation of angiotensins in CNS
P01HL-06835-30 0089 (SRC) KHOSLA, MAHESH C Neurohormonal mechanisms in hypertension Synthesis of angiotensin sequences with selective actions
P01HL-06835-30 0090 (SRC) FERRARIO, CARLOS M Neurohormonal mechanisms in hypertension Physiologic role of biologically active angiotensin peptides
P01HL-06835-30 0091 (SRC) BRAVO, EMMANUEL L Neurohormonal mechanisms in hypertension Hypertension induced by intraventricular administered aldosterone
P01HL-06835-30 9003 (SRC) BLOCK, CHRISTINE H Neurohormonal mechanisms in hypertension Core--Neuroanatomy
P01HL-06835-30 9004 (SRC) JACOBSEN, DAVID W Neurohormonal mechanisms in hypertension Core--Biochemistry
P01HL-06835-30 9005 (SRC) FERRARIO, CARLOS M Neurohormonal mechanisms in hypertension Core--Animal surgery
P01HL-06835-30 9006 (SRC) AVERILL, DAVID B Neurohormonal mechanisms in hypertension Core--Bioengineering
R37HL-06975-31 (END) BROWNIE, ALEXANDER C STATE UNIVERSITY NEW YORK 140 FARBER HALL BUFFALO, NY 14214 Pathogenesis of hypertension
K06HL-07064-31 (HTA) SUBIN, SIDNEY S UNIV OF SOUTHERN CALIFORNIA 1200 NORTH STATE ST, BOX 1800 LOS ANGELES, CALIF 90033 Studies of the microcirculation
R01HL-07451-29 (HEM) BRIEHL, ROBIN W ALBERT EINSTEIN COLL OF MEDICI 1300 MORRIS PARK AVENUE BRONX, NY 10461 Sickle hemoglobin--Physical chemistry and pathogenesis
R37HL-07723-28 (NSS) ROTHE, CARL F INDIANA UNIVERSITY 635 BARNHILL DR MS 374 INDIANAPOLIS, IN 46202-5120 Reflex control of vascular capacitance
R01HL-08311-26A2 (PHRA) GROSS, GARRETT J MEDICAL COLLEGE OF WISCONSIN 8701 WATERTOWN PLANK RD MILWAUKEE, WI 53226 Effect of drugs upon myocardial hypoxia
R01HL-08506-28 (MET) REAVEN, GERALD M VA MEDICAL CENTER (182B) 3801 MIRANDA AVENUE PALO ALTO, CA 94304 Lipemia-carbohydrate & glyceride metabolism
R37HL-08508-28 (NSS) HOFFMAN, BRIAN F COLUMBIA UNIVERSITY 630 WEST 168TH STREET NEW YORK, N Y 10032 Cardiac conductivity and automaticity
R01HL-08893-27 (BIO) GUIDOTTI, GUIDO HARVARD UNIVERSITY 7 DIVINITY AVENUE CAMBRIDGE, MA 03128 Structure and function of membrane proteins
R37HL-09163-26 (HEM) SHAPIRO, SANDOR S JEFFERSON MEDICAL COLLEGE 1015 WALNUT STREET PHILADELPHIA, PA 19107 Control mechanisms in hemostasis
R01HL-09315-27A1 (SB) SABISTON, DAVID C JR DUKE UNIVERSITY MED CTR BOX 3704 DURHAM, NC 27710 Coronary insufficiency and myocardial revascularization
R01HL-09364-27 (CBY) BRIERLEY, GERALD P OHIO STATE UNIV MED CENTER GRAVES HALL COLUMBUS, OH 43210 Ion transport by heart mitochondria
R01HL-09562-27 (CVB) SCHREIBER, SIDNEY S VETERANS AFFAIRS MEDICAL CTR 423 EAST 23 ST NEW YORK, NY 10010 Cardiac protein synthesis, overload, alcohol and anoxia
R01HL-09610-27 (MET) DIETSCHY, JOHN M UNIV OF TEXAS SW MEDICAL CENTE 5323 HARRY HINES BLVD DALLAS, TX 75235-8887 Control of cholesterol metabolism--Bile acid transport
R01HL-09902-26A1 (HEM) DODDS, W JEAN NYS DEPARTMENT OF HEALTH EMPIRE STATE PLAZA ALBANY, NY 12201-0509 Comparative study of coagulation and vascular disease
R01HL-09906-26 (PHY) HOFFMAN, JOSEPH F YALE UNIVERSITY SCH OF MED 333 CEDAR STREET NEW HAVEN, CT 06510 Membrane transport processes in red blood cells
P01HL-10342-26 (HLBA) MITZNER, WAYNE A JOHNS HOPKINS UNIVERSITY 615 NORTH WOLFE STREET BALTIMORE, MD 21205 The integrated function of respiration and circulation
P01HL-10342-26 0008 (HLBA) PERMUTT, SOLBERT The integrated function of respiration and circulation Mechanical interaction of respiration and circulation
P01HL-10342-26 0023 (HLBA) SYLVESTER, JIMMIE T The integrated function of respiration and circulation Pulmonary vascular responses to hypoxia
P01HL-10342-26 0028 (HLBA) HIRSHMAN, CAROL The integrated function of respiration and circulation Local regulation of air and blood flow in the lungs
P01HL-10342-26 0029 (HLBA) MITZNER, WAYNE A. The integrated function of respiration and circulation Mechanical and contractile

properties of pulmonary tissue
P01HL-10342-26 0032 (HLBA) WAGNER, ELIZABETH M. The integrated function of respiration and circulation Bronchial circulation and lung function
P01HL-10342-26 0033 (HLBA) FITZGERALD, ROBERT S. The integrated function of respiration and circulation Neurotransmitters and the control of ventilation
P01HL-10342-26 9001 (HLBA) MITZNER, WAYNE A. The integrated function of respiration and circulation Core--Technical and consultation
R01HL-10384-26 (ECS) BERNE, ROBERT M UNIVERSITY OF VIRGINIA BOX 449, JORDAN HALL CHARLOTTESVILLE, PA 22908 Blood flow and adenine nucleotide metabolism
R37HL-10503-26 (CVB) PAGE, ERNEST UNIV OF CHICAGO/MEDICINE 5841 SOUTH MARYLAND AVENUE CHICAGO, IL 60637-1470 Cardiac ion transport and ultrastructure
R01HL-10608-25 (PHRA) BUTLER, VINCENT P, JR COLUMBIA UNIVERSITY 630 WEST 168TH ST NEW YORK, NY 10032 Digoxin-specific antibodies
R01HL-10612-25 (ECS) FREEMAN, RONALD H UNIVERSITY OF MISSOURI MA415 MEDICAL SCIENCES COLUMBIA, MO 65212 Humoral factors in hypertension and heart failure
R01HL-10834-21 (HED) CASSIN, SIDNEY PHD MA UNIVERSITY OF FLORIDA BOX J-274 JHMHC GAINESVILLE, FLA 32610 Control of fetal lung blood flow and lung liquid
R01HL-10881-26 (CVB) SCHMID-SCHOENBEIN, GEERT W UNIVERSITY OF CALIFORNIA LA JOLLA, CA 92093-0412 Structure and function of microcirulation
R37HL-10951-24 (NSS) LEVY, MATTHEW N MT SINAI MEDICAL CENTER ONE MT SINAI DRIVE CLEVELAND, OH 44106 Neural control of the heart
P01HL-11307-25 (HLBA) SPACH, MADISON S DUKE MEDICAL CENTER BOX 3090 DURHAM, NC 27710 Biophysical studies in pediatric cardiology
P01HL-11307-25 0002 (HLBA) SPACH, MADISON S Biophysical studies in pediatric cardiology Propagation and repolarization by extracellular potentials
P01HL-11307-25 0004 (HLBA) SPACH, MADISON S Biophysical studies in pediatric cardiology Body surface potentials based on heart potentials
P01HL-11307-25 0005 (HLBA) BARR, ROGER C Biophysical studies in pediatric cardiology Heart and body electrical events electrocardiography
P01HL-11307-25 0006 (HLBA) SPACH, MADISON S Biophysical studies in pediatric cardiology Body surface and epicardial potential
P01HL-11307-25 0007 (HLBA) PILKINGTON, THEO C Biophysical studies in pediatric cardiology Inverse mathematical models of cardiac phenomena
P01HL-11307-25 0008 (HLBA) SPACH, MADISON S. Biophysical studies in pediatric cardiology Propagation and depolarization in cardiac muscle
P01HL-11307-25 9001 (HLBA) GALLIE, THOMAS M Biophysical studies in pediatric cardiology Core--Computer science
P01HL-11307-25 9002 (HLBA) DOLBER, PAUL C. Biophysical studies in pediatric cardiology Core--Morphology
R37HL-11551-24 (CTY) FLORINI, JAMES R SYRACUSE UNIVERSITY 130 COLLEGE PLACE SYRACUSE, NY 13244-1220 RNA and protein synthesis in repair of heart injury
P01HL-11678-24 (HLBA) HALL, JOHN UNIV. OF MISSISSIPPI MEDICAL C 2500 NORTH STATE STREET JACKSON, MISS 39216 Cardiovascular dynamics and their control
P01HL-11678-24 0058 (HLBA) COLEMAN, THOMAS G Cardiovascular dynamics and their control Overall control of the circulation--Renal mechanisms
P01HL-11678-24 0064 (HLBA) HALL, JOHN E Cardiovascular dynamics and their control Hypertension--Renal excretion of water and electrolytes
P01HL-11678-24 0068 (HLBA) COLEMAN, THOMAS G Cardiovascular dynamics and their control Basic hemodynamics
P01HL-11678-24 0069 (HLBA) NORMAN, ROGER A Cardiovascular dynamics and their control Nervous control of the cirulation and neurogenic hypertension
P01HL-11678-24 0070 (HLBA) MANNING, R DAVIS Cardiovascular dynamics and their control Dynamics of tissue fluids
P01HL-11678-24 9001 (HLBA) COLEMAN, THOMAS G Cardiovascular dynamics and their control CORE--Computer services
P01HL-11678-24 9002 (HLBA) LOHMEIER, THOMAS E Cardiovascular dynamics and their control Core--Radioimmunoassay and chemical laboratory
P01HL-11678-24 9003 (HLBA) GUYTON, ARTHUR C Cardiovascular dynamics and their control CORE--Instrumentation and machine shop
P01HL-11678-24 0001 (HLBA) MANNING, R DAVIS Cardiovascular dynamics and their control Body fluid volumes in the genesis of hypertension
P01HL-11678-24 0027 (HLBA) LOHMEIER, THOMAS E Cardiovascular dynamics and their control Endocrinology of the body fluids
R01HL-11802-23 (SAT) HYMAN, ALBERT L TULANE UNIVERSITY SCH OF MED 1430 TULANE AVENUE NEW ORLEANS, LA 70112 Cardiopulmonary surgical research
R37HL-11876-24 (CVA) GRIGGS, DOUGLAS M, JR UNIVERSITY OF MISSOURI SCHOOL OF MEDICINE COLUMBIA, MO 65212 Coronary collateral function
R37HL-11880-23 (HEM) WHITE, JAMES G UNIVERSITY OF MINNESOTA 420 DELAWARE ST SE/BOX 490 MINNEAPOLIS, MN 55455 Structural physiology and pathology of blood platelets
R01HL-11907-19 (RAP) WASSERMAN, KARLMAN HARBOR-UCLA MEDICAL CENTER 1000 W CARSON ST, A-15 ANNEX CARSON, CA 90509 Coupling of external to cellular respiration during exericise
R37HL-12174-23 (NSS) HLASTALA, MICHAEL P UNIVERSITY OF WASHINGTON MAIL STOP RM-12 SEATTLE, WA 98195 Ventilation perfusion distribution in the lung
R37HL-12186-22 (PHY) BLINKS, JOHN R UNIV OF WASHINGTON 620 UNIVERSITY RD FRIDAY HARBOR, WA 98250 Calcium transients in striated muscle and other cells
R37HL-12415-21 (ECS) BISHOP, VERNON S UNIV OF TEXAS HLTH SCI CTR 7703 FLOYD CURL DRIVE SAN ANTONIO, TX 78284-7764 Regulation of the circulation in conscious dogs
R01HL-12486-22 (CVA) SOMMER, JOACHIM R DUKE UNIVERSITY MED CTR BOX 3712 DURHAM, NC 27710 Structure-function correlation in the atrium
R37HL-12792-22 (ECS) DULING, BRIAN R UNIV OF VIRGINIA SCHOOL OF MED BOX 449/PHYSIO DEPT CHARLOTTESVILLE, VA 22908 Local regulation of microvascular function
R01HL-12839-22 (SB) SUTERA, SALVATORE P WASHINGTON UNIVERSITY BOX 1185 ONE BROOKINGS DRIVE ST LOUIS, MO 63130 Microrheologic mechanisms in vascular pathophysiology
R01HL-12944-22 (HEM) PAGLIA, DONALD E UNIVERSITY OF CALIFORNIA SCHOOL OF MEDICINE LOS ANGELES, CA 90024-1732 Enzymatic and biochemical studies on blood cells
P01HL-13108-22 (HLBA) STINSON, EDWARD B STANFORD UNIVERSITY STANFORD, CALIF 94305 Clinical heart-lung and lung transplantation
P01HL-13108-22 0003 (HLBA) BILLINGHAM, MARGARET T Clinical heart-lung and lung transplantation Pathology--Heart and heart-lung transplantation
P01HL-13108-22 0029 (HLBA) THEODORE, JAMES Clinical heart-lung and lung transplantation Physiology--Heart/lung transplantation
P01HL-13108-22 0031 (HLBA) PEARL, RONALD G. Clinical heart-lung and lung transplantation Pulmonary vascular pathophysiology
P01HL-13108-22 0032 (HLBA) BALDWIN, JOHN C. Clinical heart-lung and lung transplantation Heart-Lung transplantation in cystic firosis
P01HL-13108-22 9001 (HLBA) BALDWIN, JOHN C. Clinical heart-lung and lung transplantation CORE--Clinical
R01HL-13157-21 (BMT) IBERS, JAMES A NORTHWESTERN UNIVERSITY CHEMISTRY DEPARTMENT EVANSTON, ILL 60201 Modeling of ligand binding of hemoproteins
R01HL-13160-21 (HEM) FENTON, JOHN W, II NEW YORK STATE DEPT OF HLTH EMPIRE STATE PLAZA/P O BOX 509 ALBANY, N Y 12201-0509 Human thrombins
R01HL-13164-19 (BBCA) BUCCI, ENRICO UNIV OF MARYLAND-BALTOMORE OFFICE OF SPON PROG ADMIN BALTIMORE, MD 21201 Interaction of a and B chains of hemoglobin
R37HL-13187-22 (ECS) GEBBER, GERARD L MICHIGAN STATE UNIVERSITY EAST LANSING, MICH 48824 Central neural control of cardiovascular function
P01HL-13262-19 (HLBB) HOLLANDER, WILLIAM BOSTON UNIV SCHOOL OF MEDICINE 80 EAST CONCORD STREET BOSTON, MASS 02118 Role of the arterial wall in atherosclerosis
P01HL-13262-19 0028 (HLBB) KAGAN, HERBERT M Role of the arterial wall in atherosclerosis Molecular mechanisms of control of aortic fibrosis
P01HL-13262-19 0026 (HLBB) HOLLANDER, WILLIAM Role of the arterial wall in atherosclerosis Role of hypertension in atherosclerosis
P01HL-13262-19 0027 (HLBB) FRANZBLAU, CARL Role of the arterial wall in atherosclerosis Smooth matrices as a model for injury in atherosclerosis
P01HL-13262-19 0034 (HLBB) SONENSHEIN, GAIL E Role of the arterial wall in atherosclerosis Control of collagen synthesis and proliferation in aortic smooth muscle cells
P01HL-13262-19 0035 (HLBB) MOSS, MARK Role of the arterial wall in atherosclerosis Cerebrovascular diseases behavioral and neuropathological study
P01HL-13262-19 9001 (HLBB) HOLLANDER, WILLIAM Role of the arterial wall in atherosclerosis Core--animal facility
P01HL-13262-19 9002 (HLBB) FRANZBLAU, CARL Role of the arterial wall in atherosclerosis Core--tissue culture facility
P01HL-13262-19 9003 (HLBB) TROXLER, ROBERT F Role of the arterial wall in atherosclerosis Core--protein analytical laboratory
R01HL-13315-21 (RAP) GILLIS, C NORMAN YALE UNIVERSITY 333 CEDAR STREET NEW HAVEN, CT 06510 Disposition of vasoactive hormones in mammalian lung
R37HL-13339-21 (NSS) PAPPANO, ACHILLES J UNIVERSITY OF CONNECTICUT 263 FARMINGTON AVENUE FARMINGTON, CT 06032 Pharmacology of developing cardiac tissues
R37HL-13405-22 (NSS) LONGMORE, WILLIAM J ST LOUIS UNIVERSITY SCHOOL OF MEDICINE ST LOUIS, MO 63104 Regulation of lipid metabolism in the lung
R37HL-13423-21 (HEM) CASTELLINO, FRANCIS J UNIVERSITY OF NOTRE DAME NOTRE DAME, IND 46556 Structure-function studies on plasminogen and plasmin
R01HL-13426-22 (SB) PIERCE, WILLIAM S PENNSYLVANIA STATE UNIVERSITY POST OFFICE BOX 850 HERSHEY, PA 17033 Left ventricular bypass for myocardial infarction
R37HL-13437-22 (NSS) GORE, ROBERT W UNIVERSITY OF ARIZONA COLLEGE OF MEDICINE TUCSON, AZ 85724 Physical determinants of microvascular function
R37HL-13531-19 (BMT) HOFFMAN, BRIAN M NORTHWESTERN UNIV EVANSTON, IL 60208 Coboglobins--Cobalt substituted myo-and hemoglobins
R01HL-13581-24 (BBCA) TRAYLOR, TEDDY G UNIVERSITY OF CALIFORNIA 9500 GILMAN DR LA JOLLA, CA 92093-0506 Mechanisms of reactions of oxygen with heme proteins
R37HL-13629-22 (HEM) ASTER, RICHARD H BLOOD CENTER OF SE WISCONSIN 1701 WEST WISCONSIN AVENUE MILWAUKEE, WI 53233 Hemorrhagic diseases
R01HL-13645-21 (TOX) YOST, GAROLD S UNIVERSITY OF UTAH SALT LAKE CITY, UT 84112 3-methylindole-induced lung injury
R37HL-13652-21 (NSS) HENDRICKSON, DAVID N UNIVERSITY OF CALIFORNIA LA JOLLA, CA 92093-0506 Metal sites in metalloproteins
R01HL-13754-21 (SB) SALZMAN, EDWIN W BETH ISRAEL HOSPITAL 330 BROOKLINE AVENUE BOSTON, MA 02215 Post-operative thromboembolism in surgical patients
P01HL-13851-29 (HLBA) TER-POGOSSIAN, MICHEL M WASHINGTON UNIVERSITY-MED SCHO 510 S KINGSHIGHWAY ST LOUIS, MO 63110 Cyclotron produced isotopes in biology and medicine
P01HL-13851-29 0001 (HLBA) WELCH, MICHAEL J Cyclotron produced isotopes in biology and medicine Chemistry
P01HL-13851-29 0004 (HLBA) RAICHLE, MARCUS E Cyclotron produced isotopes in biology and medicine Neurological studies
P01HL-13851-29 0007 (HLBA) SOBEL, BURTON E. Cyclotron produced isotopes in biology and medicine Cardiovascular studies
P01HL-13851-29 0008 (HLBA) SCHUSTER, DANIEL P. Cyclotron produced isotopes in biology and medicine Pulmonary blood flow during respiratory failure
P01HL-13851-29 9001 (HLBA) TER-POGOSSIAN, MICHEL M Cyclotron produced isotopes in biology and medicine Cyclotron--Core

PROJECT NO., ORGANIZATIONAL UNIT., INVESTIGATOR, ADDRESS, TITLE

R37HL-13870-22 (PHRA) ENTMAN, MARK L THE METHODIST HOSPITAL 6516 BERTNER BOULEVARD HOUSTON, TX 77030 Control of myocardial sarcotubular calcium stores

R01HL-13936-18 (ECS) HUTCHINS, PHILLIP M WAKE FOREST UNIVERSITY 300 S HAWTHORNE ROAD WINSTON-SALEM, NC 27103 Microvascular responses in hypertension

R01HL-14020-18 (HEM) STRACHER, ALFRED SUNY HEALTH SCI CTR AT BROOKLY 450 CLARKSON AVE, BOX 8 BROOKLYN, N Y 11203 Role of cytoskeletal proteins in platelet function

R01HL-14127-29 (TOX) SMITH, ROGER P DARTMOUTH MEDICAL SCHOOL HANOVER, N H 03756 Toxicology of vasoactive-heme reactive compounds

R01HL-14133-21 (GMB) KNOX, FRANKLYN G MAYO FOUNDATION 200 FIRST STREET SOUTHWEST ROCHESTER, MN 55905 Intrarenal electrolyte metabolism

P50HL-14136-20 (SRC) BURROWS, BENJAMIN ARIZONA HEALTH SCIENCES CENTER 1501 NORTH CAMPBELL AVENUE TUCSON, AZ 85724 SCOR--Chronic diseases of the airways

P50HL-14136-20 0017 (SRC) TAUSSIG, LYNN M SCOR--Chronic diseases of the airways Pediatric airways obstructive disease

P50HL-14136-20 0018 (SRC) LEMEN, RICHARD J SCOR--Chronic diseases of the airways Physiology, immunology--acute and recurrent viral bronchiolitis

P50HL-14136-20 0001 (SRC) KNUDSON, RONALD J SCOR--Chronic diseases of the airways Lung structure and function in airways obstructive disease

P50HL-14136-20 0009 (SRC) BURROWS, BENJAMIN SCOR--Chronic diseases of the airways Tucson epidemiological study of airways obstructive disease

P50HL-14136-20 0019 (SRC) LEBOWITZ, MICHEAL D SCOR--Chronic diseases of the airways Host characteristics and airways obstructive disease in adults

P50HL-14136-20 9001 (SRC) LEBOWITZ, MICHAEL D SCOR--Chronic diseases of the airways Biometrics core

P50HL-14136-20 9002 (SRC) KNUDSON, RONALD J SCOR--Chronic diseases of the airways Core--Physiology

P50HL-14136-20 9003 (SRC) HALHONEN, MARILYN J SCOR--Chronic diseases of the airways Pathology/immunology core

P50HL-14136-20 9005 (SRC) RAY, C GEORGE SCOR--Chronic diseases of the airways Core--Microbiology

P50HL-14136-20 9006 (SRC) BURROWS, BENJAMIN SCOR--Chronic diseases of the airways Core--Clinical

P50HL-14147-21 (SRC) MAJERUS, PHILIP W WASHINGTON UNIV SCHOOL OF MED 660 S EUCLID AVENUE ST LOUIS, MO 63110 Specialized center of research in thrombosis

P50HL-14147-21 0019 (SRC) MAJERUS, PHILIP W Specialized center of research in thrombosis Cellular biochemistry laboratory

P50HL-14147-21 0020 (SRC) DEUEL, THOMAS F Specialized center of research in thrombosis Biochemistry of platelet function in thrombosis and cell growth

P50HL-14147-21 0022 (SRC) TOLLEFSEN, DOUGLAS M Specialized center of research in thrombosis Heparin cofactor II/glycosaminoglycan interactions

P50HL-14147-21 0023 (SRC) SADLER, J EVAN Specialized center of research in thrombosis Endothelial cell proteins in hemostasis

P50HL-14147-21 0024 (SRC) FRAZIER, WILLIAM A Specialized center of research in thrombosis Structure and function of human thrombospondin

P50HL-14147-21 0025 (SRC) BROZE, GEORGE J Specialized center of research in thrombosis Regulation of coagulation

P50HL-14147-21 0026 (SRC) MILETICH, JOSEPH P Specialized center of research in thrombosis Autosomal clotting factor deficiency

P50HL-14164-20 (SRC) ST CLAIR, RICHARD WAKE FOREST UNIVERSITY 300 S HAWTHORNE ROAD WINSTON-SALEM, N C 27103 A/S SCOR--Comparative and experimental atherosclerosis

P50HL-14164-20 9008 (SRC) ANTHONY, MARY S A/S SCOR--Comparative and experimental atherosclerosis Core--Comparative clinical studies

P50HL-14164-20 9010 (SRC) LEWIS, JON C A/S SCOR--Comparative and experimental atherosclerosis Core--Electron microscopy

P50HL-14164-20 9011 (SRC) ALEXANDER, NANCY J A/S SCOR--Comparative and experimental atherosclerosis Core--Immunology

P50HL-14164-20 0029 (SRC) WAGNER, WILLIAM D A/S SCOR--Comparative and experimental atherosclerosis Molecular biology of arterial proteoglycans in atherosclerosis

P50HL-14164-20 0033 (SRC) RUDEL, LAWRENCE L A/S SCOR--Comparative and experimental atherosclerosis Low density lipoprotein metabolism

P50HL-14164-20 0035 (SRC) ST CLAIR, RICHARD W A/S SCOR--Comparative and experimental atherosclerosis Cellular mechanisms of atherosclerosis

P50HL-14164-20 0044 (SRC) LEWIS, JON C A/S SCOR--Comparative and experimental atherosclerosis Endothelial surface in coronary atherosclerosis

P50HL-14164-20 0046 (SRC) CLARKSON, THOMAS B A/S SCOR--Comparative and experimental atherosclerosis Pathogenic mechanisms in atherosclerosis

P50HL-14164-20 0047 (SRC) KAPLAN, JAY R A/S SCOR--Comparative and experimental atherosclerosis Biobehavioral studies in atherosclerosis

P50HL-14164-20 0049 (SRC) CROUSE, JOHN R A/S SCOR--Comparative and experimental atherosclerosis Risk factors in coronary artery atherosclerosis

P50HL-14164-20 0050 (SRC) SORCI-THOMAS, MARY A/S SCOR--Comparative and experimental atherosclerosis Molecular genetics of lipoprotein metabolism

P50HL-14164-20 0051 (SRC) ADAMS, MICHAEL R A/S SCOR--Comparative and experimental atherosclerosis Sex steroids and atherosclerosis

P50HL-14164-20 9001 (SRC) ST CLAIR, RICHARD W A/S SCOR--Comparative and experimental atherosclerosis Core--Lipid analytic laboratory

P50HL-14164-20 9002 (SRC) RUDEL, LAWRENCE L A/S SCOR--Comparative and experimental atherosclerosis Core--Lipoprotein laboratory

P50HL-14164-20 9003 (SRC) MOYER, CAROLYN F A/S SCOR--Comparative and experimental atherosclerosis Core--Pathology

P50HL-14164-20 9004 (SRC) LUSSO, FRANCES M A/S SCOR--Comparative and experimental atherosclerosis Core--Data management

P50HL-14164-20 9006 (SRC) WAGNER, WILLIAM D A/S SCOR--Comparative and experimental atherosclerosis Core--Pigeon resource

PROJECT NO., ORGANIZATIONAL UNIT., INVESTIGATOR, ADDRESS, TITLE

P50HL-14164-20 9007 (SRC) KORITNIK, DONALD R A/S SCOR--Comparative and experimental atherosclerosis Core--Endocrine assay laboratory

P50HL-14192-21 (SRC) INAGAMI, TADASHI VANDERBILT UNIVERSITY DEPARTMENT OF BIOCHEMISTRY NASHVILLE, TENN 37232 Hypertension specialized center of research

P50HL-14192-21 0004 (SRC) INAGAMI, TADASHI Hypertension specialized center of research Tissue renin and angiotensin--Formation and function

P50HL-14192-21 0016 (SRC) JACKSON, EDWIN K Hypertension specialized center of research Enhanced slow-pressor response to angiotensin II in spontaneous hypertensive rat

P50HL-14192-21 0017 (SRC) BIAGGIONI, ITALO Hypertension specialized center of research Adenosine and neural mechanisms of cardiovascular control

P50HL-14192-21 0018 (SRC) ROBERTSON, DAVID Hypertension specialized center of research Dopamine beta-hydroxylase and blood pressure regulation

P50HL-14192-21 0019 (SRC) NADEAU, JOHN H Hypertension specialized center of research Angiotensin II modulation mechanism in essential hypertension

P50HL-14192-21 9001 (SRC) NADEAU, JOHN H Hypertension specialized center of research Clinical core

P50HL-14192-21 9002 (SRC) HOLLISTER, ALAN S Hypertension specialized center of research Laboratory core

P50HL-14197-20 (SRC) STEINBERG, DANIEL UNIVERSITY OF CALIFORNIA LA JOLLA, CA 92093-0613 A/S SCOR--Lipoprotein and sterol metabolism

P50HL-14197-20 0006 (SRC) WITZTUM, JOSEPH L A/S SCOR--Lipoprotein and sterol metabolism Clinical studies of lipoprotein metabolism

P50HL-14197-20 0010 (SRC) PARTHASARATHY, SAMPATH A/S SCOR--Lipoprotein and sterol metabolism Cellular mechanisms of lipoprotein metabolism

P50HL-14197-20 0014 (SRC) PITTMAN, RAY C A/S SCOR--Lipoprotein and sterol metabolism Regulation of lipoprotein metabolism

P50HL-14197-20 0018 (SRC) WITZTUM, JOSEPH L A/S SCOR--Lipoprotein and sterol metabolism Lipoprotein structure and function--role of autoantibodies

P50HL-14197-20 0019 (SRC) CAREW, THOMAS E A/S SCOR--Lipoprotein and sterol metabolism Mechanisms of atherogenesis--arterial wall studies

P50HL-14197-20 9001 (SRC) PITTMAN, RAY C A/S SCOR--Lipoprotein and sterol metabolism Core--Lipoprotein preparation

P50HL-14197-20 9002 (SRC) WITZTUM, JOSEPH L A/S SCOR--Lipoprotein and sterol metabolism Core--Immunology

P50HL-14197-20 9003 (SRC) PARTHASARATHY, SAMPATH A/S SCOR--Lipoprotein and sterol metabolism Core--cell culture

P50HL-14197-20 9004 (SRC) BELTZ, W F A/S SCOR--Lipoprotein and sterol metabolism Core--computerized data analysis

P50HL-14197-20 9005 (SRC) CAREW, THOMAS E A/S SCOR--Lipoprotein and sterol metabolism Core--morphology

P50HL-14197-20 9006 (SRC) CAREW, THOMAS E A/S SCOR--Lipoprotein and sterol metabolism Core--WHHL rabbit colony

P50HL-14212-20 (SRC) LOW, ROBERT B UNIVERSITY OF VERMONT BURLINGTON, VT 05405 Scor--Occupational and immunologic lung diseases

P50HL-14212-20 0036 (SRC) BELL, DIANNE Y Scor--Occupational and immunologic lung diseases BAL and serum markers for activity in sarcoidosis

P50HL-14212-20 0037 (SRC) BELL, DIANNE Y Scor--Occupational and immunologic lung diseases Immune mechanism in asbestosis

P50HL-14212-20 0038 (SRC) MOSSMAN, BROOKE T Scor--Occupational and immunologic lung diseases Oxidant injury in asbestos related lung injury and fibrosis

P50HL-14212-20 9001 (SRC) ASHIKAGA, TAKAMARU Scor--Occupational and immunologic lung diseases Core--biometry

P50HL-14212-20 9006 (SRC) LESLIE, KEVIN O Scor--Occupational and immunologic lung diseases Core--morphology

P50HL-14212-20 9007 (SRC) DAVIS, GERALD S Scor--Occupational and immunologic lung diseases Core--bronchoalveolar lavage

P50HL-14212-20 9008 (SRC) HEMENWAY, DAVID R Scor--Occupational and immunologic lung diseases Core--pulmonary SCOR animal care and inhalation studies

P50HL-14212-20 9009 (SRC) ABSHER, MARLENE Scor--Occupational and immunologic lung diseases Core--cell culture

P50HL-14212-20 0028 (SRC) ABSHER, MARLENE Scor--Occupational and immunologic lung diseases Lymphocyte and macrophage function in the evolution of silicosis

P50HL-14212-20 0029 (SRC) DAVIS, GERALD S Scor--Occupational and immunologic lung diseases Macrophage interleukin-1 production in evolving silicosis

P50HL-14212-20 0030 (SRC) HEMENWAY, DAVID R Scor--Occupational and immunologic lung diseases Biological response to silicon dioxide polymorphs

P50HL-14212-20 0031 (SRC) DAVIS, GERALD S Scor--Occupational and immunologic lung diseases Recovery of silica by bronchoalveolar lavage

P50HL-14212-20 0032 (SRC) LOW, ROBERT B Scor--Occupational and immunologic lung diseases Epithelial cell transition in normal and abnormal lung remodeling

P50HL-14212-20 0033 (SRC) MITCHELL, JOHN J Scor--Occupational and immunologic lung diseases The myofibroblast and pulmonary fibrosis

P50HL-14212-20 0034 (SRC) KELLEY, JASON Scor--Occupational and immunologic lung diseases Role of monokines in pulmonary remodeling

P50HL-14212-20 0035 (SRC) DAVIS, GERALD S Scor--Occupational and immunologic lung diseases Mechanism of injury and inflammation in fibrotic lung disease

P50HL-14214-20 (SRC) STAHLMAN, MILDRED T VANDERBILT UNIVERSITY S-4311 MEDICAL CENTER NORTH NASHVILLE, TN 37232-2370 Scor-lung biology and diseases in infants and children

P50HL-14214-20 0023 (SRC) CHYTIL, FRANK Scor-lung biology and diseases in infants and children Regulation of lung maturation--Effects of vitamin A status

P50HL-14214-20 0038 (SRC) HARALSON, MICHAEL A Scor-lung biology and diseases in infants and children Extracellular matrix biosynthesis in cultured fetal lung epithelial cells

P50HL-14214-20 0039 (SRC) STAHLMAN, MILDRED T Scor-lung biology and diseases in infants and children Neuroendocrine cells in developing

and regenerating lung
P50HL-14214-20 0040 (SRC) ORTH, DAVID N Scor-lung biology and diseases in infants and children Secretion of hormone contents of pulmonary neuroendocrine cells
P50HL-14214-20 0044 (SRC) CARPENTER, GRAHAM Scor-lung biology and diseases in infants and children Growth regulation of respiratory epithelia in vitro
P50HL-14214-20 0045 (SRC) SUNDELL, HAKAN W Scor-lung biology and diseases in infants and children Pathogenesis and therapy of hyaline membrane disease
P50HL-14214-20 0046 (SRC) HAZINSKI, THOMAS A Scor-lung biology and diseases in infants and children Prevention of oxygen toxicity in newborn lambs
P50HL-14214-20 0047 (SRC) COTTON, ROBERT B Scor-lung biology and diseases in infants and children Clinical and experimental studies of high frequency ventilation
P50HL-14214-20 9001 (SRC) COTTON, ROBERT B Scor-lung biology and diseases in infants and children Core--Clinical research
P50HL-14214-20 9002 (SRC) SUNDELL, HAKAN W Scor-lung biology and diseases in infants and children Core--Animal laboratory
P50HL-14214-20 9003 (SRC) LINDSTROM, DANIEL P Scor-lung biology and diseases in infants and children Core--Biomedical engineering
P50HL-14214-20 9004 (SRC) LEQUIRE, VIRGIL S Scor-lung biology and diseases in infants and children Core--Histopathology laboratory
P50HL-14230-20 (SRC) SPECTOR, ARTHUR A UNIVERSITY OF IOWA IOWA CITY, IA 52242 Specialized center of research in arteriosclerosis
P50HL-14230-20 9005 (SRC) CLARKE, WILLIAM R Specialized center of research in arteriosclerosis Core--Biostatistics
P50HL-14230-20 0088 (SRC) LAUER, RONALD M Specialized center of research in arteriosclerosis Coronary risk factors in school children--The Muscatine study
P50HL-14230-20 0092 (SRC) SPECTOR, ARTHUR A Specialized center of research in arteriosclerosis Polyunsaturated fatty acids and endothelial function
P50HL-14230-20 0094 (SRC) ARMSTRONG, MARK L Specialized center of research in arteriosclerosis Experimental atherosclerosis--Early lesion formation, progression
P50HL-14230-20 0095 (SRC) CHAPPELL, DAVID A Specialized center of research in arteriosclerosis Endothelial cells--Lipoproteins, smooth muscle cells, monocyte/macrophages
P50HL-14230-20 0099 (SRC) HART, MICHAEL N Specialized center of research in arteriosclerosis Morphology, immunology and cytochemistry of normal and altered endothelium
P50HL-14230-20 0100 (SRC) SANDO, GLORIA N Specialized center of research in arteriosclerosis Lysosomal enzyme in lipid metabolism
P50HL-14230-20 0101 (SRC) HEISTAD, DONALD D Specialized center of research in arteriosclerosis Hemodynamic effects of experimental atherosclerosis
P50HL-14230-20 0102 (SRC) FIELD, F JEFFREY Specialized center of research in arteriosclerosis Eicosanoid production in macrophage-derived foam cells
P50HL-14230-20 9001 (SRC) FIELD, F JEFFREY Specialized center of research in arteriosclerosis Core lipid laboratory
P50HL-14230-20 9003 (SRC) SHASBY, D MICHAEL Specialized center of research in arteriosclerosis Core-Endothelial cell culture laboratory
P50HL-14237-20 (SRC) HAVEL, RICHARD J UNIVERSITY OF CALIFORNIA 505 PARNASSUS AVENUE SAN FRANCISCO, CA 94143 Specialized center of research in arteriosclerosis
P50HL-14237-20 0001 (SRC) HAVEL, RICHARD J Specialized center of research in arteriosclerosis Role of apolipoproteins in lipoprotein catabolism
P50HL-14237-20 0002 (SRC) FIELDING, CHRISTOPHER J Specialized center of research in arteriosclerosis Structure-function relationship of LCAT and cholesteryl ester transfer protein
P50HL-14237-20 0003 (SRC) KANE, JOHN P Specialized center of research in arteriosclerosis Structure of lipoproteins
P50HL-14237-20 0004 (SRC) HAMILTON, ROBERT L Specialized center of research in arteriosclerosis Subcellular origins of nascent plasma lipoproteins in liver
P50HL-14237-20 0005 (SRC) HAVEL, RICHARD J Specialized center of research in arteriosclerosis Genetic disorders of plasma lipoproteins
P50HL-14237-20 0006 (SRC) KANE, JOHN P Specialized center of research in arteriosclerosis Effect of normalization of plasma lipoprotein levels
P50HL-14237-20 0008 (SRC) FIELDING, PHOEBE E Specialized center of research in arteriosclerosis Regulation of cholesteryl ester transfer between lipoprotein species
P50HL-14237-20 0009 (SRC) FIELDING, CHRISTOPHER J Specialized center of research in arteriosclerosis Plasma lipoprotein metabolism--Diabetes, renal disease, hypercholesteremia
P50HL-14237-20 9001 (SRC) KANE, JOHN P Specialized center of research in arteriosclerosis Core--Lipid clinic
P50HL-14237-20 9002 (SRC) HAVEL, RICHARD J Specialized center of research in arteriosclerosis Core laboratories
R01HL-14262-20 (PTHA) SIMON, SANFORD R SUNY AT STONY BROOK STONY BROOK, NY 11794-8691 Proteases and antiproteases in lung--effects of smoking
P01HL-14388-20 (HLBA) ABBOUD, FRANCOIS M UNIVERSITY OF IOWA IOWA CITY, IA 52242 Regulation of the circulation in pathological states
P01HL-14388-20 0243 (HLBA) THAMES, MARC Regulation of the circulation in pathological states Autonomic control in cardiac hypertrophy and failure
P01HL-14388-20 0244 (HLBA) ABBOUD, FRANCOIS M Regulation of the circulation in pathological states Cardiovascular reflexes in hypertension and heart failure
P01HL-14388-20 0168 (HLBA) HERMSMEYER, KENT Regulation of the circulation in pathological states Trophic influence of sympathetic NS--Vascular muscle
P01HL-14388-20 0180 (HLBA) HEISTAD, DONALD D Regulation of the circulation in pathological states Regulation of cerebral blood flow
P01HL-14388-20 0183 (HLBA) SCHMID, PHILLIP G Regulation of the circulation in pathological states Vasopressin in cardiovascular regulation
P01HL-14388-20 0184 (HLBA) MARK, ALLYN L Regulation of the circulation in pathological states Circulatory control in hypertension--Reflex and vascular mechanisms
P01HL-14388-20 0185 (HLBA) ABBOUD, FRANCOIS M Regulation of the circulation in pathological states Autonomic control of circulation
P01HL-14388-20 0191 (HLBA) STEINMETZ, PHILIP R Regulation of the circulation in pathological states Electrolyte transport in the urinary epithelium
P01HL-14388-20 0197 (HLBA) BRODY, MICHAEL J Regulation of the circulation in pathological states Monoamines in physiological functions mediated through the AV3V region
P01HL-14388-20 0198 (HLBA) BRODY, MICHAEL J Regulation of the circulation in pathological states Neural pathways and substrate subserving functions of the AV3V region
P01HL-14388-20 0199 (HLBA) BRODY, MICHAEL J Regulation of the circulation in pathological states Role of the AV3V in experimental hypertension
P01HL-14388-20 0201 (HLBA) BRODY, MICHAEL J Regulation of the circulation in pathological states The role of the AV3V in body fluid balance
P01HL-14388-20 0208 (HLBA) MARK, ALLYN L Regulation of the circulation in pathological states Renal/humoral effects on baroreflex control of sympathetic NS
P01HL-14388-20 0209 (HLBA) ABBOUD, FRANCOIS M Regulation of the circulation in pathological states Determinants of baroreceptor activity
P01HL-14388-20 0216 (HLBA) MARCUS, MELVIN L Regulation of the circulation in pathological states Coronary circulation and myocardial ischemia
P01HL-14388-20 0222 (HLBA) DI BONA, GERALD F Regulation of the circulation in pathological states Neural control of renal function in edema forming states
P01HL-14388-20 0235 (HLBA) MARVIN, WILLIAM J Regulation of the circulation in pathological states Trophic influences of sympathetic NS--Cardiac muscle
P01HL-14388-20 0236 (HLBA) RUBENSTEIN, PETER A Regulation of the circulation in pathological states Differentiation of BC3H-1 smooth muscle cells
P01HL-14388-20 0238 (HLBA) ROBILLARD, JEAN E Regulation of the circulation in pathological states Ontogeny of the renal kallikrein-kinin system
P01HL-14388-20 0242 (HLBA) LAWTON, WILLIAM Regulation of the circulation in pathological states Regulation of renal kallikrein
P01HL-14388-20 0247 (HLBA) STELLWAGEN, EARLE Regulation of the circulation in pathological states Folding and stability of proteins
P01HL-14388-20 0248 (HLBA) MARK, ALLYN L Regulation of the circulation in pathological states Circulatory control in hypertension--Reflex and vascular mechanisms
P01HL-14388-20 0249 (HLBA) PRESSIN, J Regulation of the circulation in pathological states D Glucose transport system in cultured BC3H-1 smooth muscle cells
P01HL-14388-20 0250 (HLBA) MAURER, R Regulation of the circulation in pathological states CAMP dependent protein kinase gene expression
P01HL-14388-20 0251 (HLBA) JOHNSON, A K Regulation of the circulation in pathological states Neural control of body fluid, CV homeostasis and basal forebrain systems
P01HL-14388-20 0252 (HLBA) SCHMID, PHILLIP Regulation of the circulation in pathological states Vasopressin ganglionic sympathetic and parasympathetic function
P01HL-14388-20 0253 (HLBA) DOLE, W P Regulation of the circulation in pathological states Hypertension--Coronary/femoral vascular response to neurohumoral stimuli
P01HL-14388-20 0254 (HLBA) CAMPBELL, K Regulation of the circulation in pathological states Dihydropyridine receptor of cardiac calcium ion channel
P01HL-14388-20 9002 (HLBA) FARLEY, DONNA Regulation of the circulation in pathological states CORE--Radioimmunoassay
P01HL-14388-20 9004 (HLBA) LACHENBRUCH, PETER A Regulation of the circulation in pathological states CORE--Biostatistics
P01HL-14388-20 9005 (HLBA) CAMPBELL, K Regulation of the circulation in pathological states CORE--Hybridoma
P01HL-14388-20 9006 (HLBA) BRODY, MICHAEL J Regulation of the circulation in pathological states CORE--Hypertensive animal colony
P01HL-14388-20 9007 (HLBA) INGRAM, D Regulation of the circulation in pathological states CORE--Electron probe laboratory
R01HL-14456-20 (RAP) FANBURG, BARRY L NEW ENGLAND MED CTR 750 WASHINGTON ST BOX 257 BOSTON, MA 02111 Lung metabolism--Enzymes in the pulmonary circulation
R37HL-14508-23 (BBCB) YONETANI, TAKASHI UNIVERSITY OF PENNSYLVANIA C601 RICHARDS BUILDING/6089 PHILADELPHIA, PA 19104-6089 Structure and function of respiratory hemoproteins
R37HL-14523-20 (PHY) FAY, FREDRIC S UNIV OF MASSACHUSETTS MED SCHO 55 LAKE AVENUE NORTH WORCESTER, MA 01655 Generation and regulation of force in smooth muscle
R01HL-14529-20 (CVB) SHOUKAS, ARTIN A JOHNS HOPKINS UNIVERSITY 720 RUTLAND AVENUE BALTIMORE, MD 21205 Systems analysis of baroreceptor reflex
R01HL-14614-20 (PHY) GIBBONS, WALTER R UNIV OF VERMONT COLLEGE OF MED GIVEN MEDICAL BUILDING E205 BURLINGTON, VT 05405 Voltage control of contraction in heart
R01HL-14637-17 (HEM) MC DONALD, TED P UNIVERSITY OF TENNESSEE P.O. BOX 1071 KNOXVILLE, TN 37901-1071 Thrombopoietin--Immunoassay and characterization
R01HL-14799-18 (SAT) REEMTSMA, KEITH COLUMBIA UNIVERSITY 630 WEST 168TH STREET NEW YORK, NY 10032 Cardiac transplantation-Immunologic modification
R37HL-14899-19 (CVA) CRANEFIELD, PAUL F THE ROCKEFELLER UNIVERSITY 1230 YORK AVENUE NEW YORK, N Y 10021 Mechanism and prevention of cardiac arrhythmias
P01HL-14985-20 (HLBA) WEIL, JOHN V UNIV OF COLO HLTH SCI CTR 4200 EAST NINTH AVENUE BOX B1 DENVER, CO 80262 Adaptations to hypoxia
P01HL-14985-20 0029 (HLBA) MOORE, LORNA G Adaptations to hypoxia Sex

hormones and ventilatory control
P01HL-14985-20 0030 (HLBA) REEVES, JOHN T. Adaptations to hypoxia Tissue adaptation to high altitude
P01HL-14985-20 0002 (HLBA) MOORE, LORNA G Adaptations to hypoxia Pregnancy and systemic vascular control
P01HL-14985-20 0031 (HLBA) MOORE, LORNA G. Adaptations to hypoxia Pregnancy and systemic vascular control
P01HL-14985-20 9003 (HLBA) GROVER, ROBERT F Adaptations to hypoxia CORE--Bioengineering
P01HL-14985-20 9004 (HLBA) O'BRIEN, RICHARD F. Adaptations to hypoxia Core--Tissue culture
P01HL-14985-20 9005 (HLBA) VOELKEL, NOBERT F. Adaptations to hypoxia Core--Eicosanoids
P01HL-14985-20 0016 (HLBA) WEIL, JOHN V Adaptations to hypoxia Endothelium and smooth muscle in pulmonary hypertension response
P01HL-14985-20 0017 (HLBA) REEVES, JOHN T Adaptations to hypoxia Arterial compliance in pulmonary hypertension
P01HL-14985-20 0024 (HLBA) REEVES, JOHN T Adaptations to hypoxia Mechanisms in acclimatization to high altitude
P01HL-14985-20 0025 (HLBA) MCMURTY , IVAN F. Adaptations to hypoxia Role of endothelium in pulmonary vasoregulation
P01HL-14985-20 0026 (HLBA) VOEIKEL, NORBERT F. Adaptations to hypoxia Role of leukotrienes in hypoxic vasoconstriction
P01HL-14985-20 0027 (HLBA) STENMARK, KURT R Adaptations to hypoxia Vascular resistance and compliance in pulmonary hypertension
P01HL-14985-20 0028 (HLBA) WEIL, JOHN V Adaptations to hypoxia Pulmonary vascular permeability in hypoxia
P50HL-15062-20 (SRC) GETZ, GODFREY S UNIVERSITY OF CHICAGO 5841 S MARYLAND AVE CHICAGO, IL 60637 A/S SCOR-Molecular mechanism of hyperlipemia and atherogenesis
P50HL-15062-20 0007 (SRC) MEREDITH, STEPHEN C A/S SCOR-Molecular mechanism of hyperlipemia and atherogenesis Apolipoproteins and lipid exchange
P50HL-15062-20 0009 (SRC) GETZ, GODFREY S A/S SCOR-Molecular mechanism of hyperlipemia and atherogenesis Apo E/LDL receptor biosynthesis--Cholesterol/fatty acids
P50HL-15062-20 0020 (SRC) GLAGOV, SEYMOUR A/S SCOR-Molecular mechanism of hyperlipemia and atherogenesis Reactive and adaptive changes in the artery wall
P50HL-15062-20 0024 (SRC) GETZ, GODFREY S A/S SCOR-Molecular mechanism of hyperlipemia and atherogenesis Apoprotein E domains and VLDL structure and function
P50HL-15062-20 0025 (SRC) MAZZONE, THEODORE A/S SCOR-Molecular mechanism of hyperlipemia and atherogenesis Mechanism of PDGF regulation of the low density lipoprotein receptor
P50HL-15062-20 0027 (SRC) HAY, RICK A/S SCOR-Molecular mechanism of hyperlipemia and atherogenesis Early events in VLDL assembly and secretion
P50HL-15062-20 0028 (SRC) MEREDITH STEPHEN C A/S SCOR-Molecular mechanism of hyperlipemia and atherogenesis Synthetic amphiphilic beta strand peptides as probes of lipoprotein structure
P50HL-15062-20 0029 (SRC) SCHREIBER, JAMES R A/S SCOR-Molecular mechanism of hyperlipemia and atherogenesis Interaction of lipoproteins with gonadal steroidogenic cells
P50HL-15062-20 0030 (SRC) FITCH, FRANK W A/S SCOR-Molecular mechanism of hyperlipemia and atherogenesis Lymphoid proliferation and lipoprotein interactions
P50HL-15062-20 0031 (SRC) GIDDENS, DON P A/S SCOR-Molecular mechanism of hyperlipemia and atherogenesis Hemodynamic determinants of vulnerability to atherogenesis
P50HL-15062-20 0032 (SRC) ZARINS, CHRISTOPHER K A/S SCOR-Molecular mechanism of hyperlipemia and atherogenesis Heart rate, hypertension and flow modulation on coronary atherosclerosis
P50HL-15062-20 0033 (SRC) LANGE, YVONNE A/S SCOR-Molecular mechanism of hyperlipemia and atherogenesis Disposition of intracellular cholesterol
P50HL-15062-20 9002 (SRC) HAY, RICK A/S SCOR-Molecular mechanism of hyperlipemia and atherogenesis Core--antigen and antibody preparation
P50HL-15062-20 9003 (SRC) GETZ, GODFREY S A/S SCOR-Molecular mechanism of hyperlipemia and atherogenesis Core--Chemistry and lipid analysis
P50HL-15062-20 9004 (SRC) MAZZONE, THEODORE A/S SCOR-Molecular mechanism of hyperlipemia and atherogenesis Core--cell culture
P50HL-15092-20 (SRC) WEILL, HANS TULANE UNIVERSITY SCH OF MED 1700 PERDIDO STREET NEW ORLEANS, LA 70112 Scor--Occupational and immunologic lung diseases
P50HL-15092-20 0018 (SRC) JONES, ROBERT N Scor--Occupational and immunologic lung diseases Respiratory effects of exposure to irritant gases and vapors
P50HL-15092-20 0019 (SRC) HAMMAD, YEHIA Y Scor--Occupational and immunologic lung diseases Pulmonary deposition and clearance of man-made mineral fibers
P50HL-15092-20 0020 (SRC) DESHAZO, RICHARD D Scor--Occupational and immunologic lung diseases Neutrophil and macrophage mediated lung damage--Toxic gases
P50HL-15092-20 0021 (SRC) BOZELKA, BRIAN E Scor--Occupational and immunologic lung diseases Intrapulmonary cell mechanisms in asbestos-induced fibrotic lung disease
P50HL-15092-20 9002 (SRC) O'NEIL, CAROL E Scor--Occupational and immunologic lung diseases Immunology core
P50HL-15092-20 9003 (SRC) HUGHES, JANET M Scor--Occupational and immunologic lung diseases Biometry core
P50HL-15092-20 9004 (SRC) HAMMAD, YEHIA Y Scor--Occupational and immunologic lung diseases Core--Environmental characterization
P50HL-15092-20 9005 (SRC) GLINDMEYER, HENRY W Scor--Occupational and immunologic lung diseases Physiology core
R01HL-15104-18 (BMT) GLASS, RICHARD S UNIVERSITY OF ARIZONA DEPT OF CHEMISTRY TUCSON, ARIZ 85721 Redox chemistry and biochemistry of organosulfur compounds
P60HL-15157-20 (SRC) MC MAHON, LILLIAN BOSTON SICKLE CELL CENTER 818 HARRISON AVENUE BOSTON, MA 02118 A comprehensive center for sickle cell disease
P60HL-15157-20 0001 (SRC) MC MAHON, LILLIAN A comprehensive center for sickle cell disease Testing program
P60HL-15157-20 0002 (SRC) MC MAHON, LILLIAN A comprehensive center for sickle cell disease Central data bank and research file
P60HL-15157-20 0003 (SRC) MC MAHON, LILLIAN A comprehensive center for sickle cell disease Public education
P60HL-15157-20 0020 (SRC) PLATT, ORAH S A comprehensive center for sickle cell disease Pathophysiology of red cell membranes in sickle cell disease
P60HL-15157-20 0023 (SRC) PALEK, JIRI A comprehensive center for sickle cell disease Hemin mediated red cell membrane injury
P60HL-15157-20 0024 (SRC) WEINSTEIN, ROBERT A comprehensive center for sickle cell disease Endothelial cell adhesion of sickle cell erythrocytes
P60HL-15157-20 0025 (SRC) GOLAN, DAVID E A comprehensive center for sickle cell disease Mobility and distribution of sickle membrane components
P60HL-15157-20 0026 (SRC) BRUGNARA, CARLO A comprehensive center for sickle cell disease Intracellular determinants of red cell sickling
P60HL-15157-20 9001 (SRC) MC MAHON, LILLIAN A comprehensive center for sickle cell disease Clinical core
P01HL-15194-20 (HLBA) MATES, ROBERT E SUNY AT BUFFALO 462 GRIDER STREET BUFFALO, NY 14215 Coronary circulatory control and pathophysiology
P01HL-15194-20 0001 (HLBA) KLOCKE, FRANCIS J Coronary circulatory control and pathophysiology Mechanisms underlying coronary pressure-flow behavior
P01HL-15194-20 0026 (HLBA) MATES, ROBERT E Coronary circulatory control and pathophysiology Impedance to coronary blood flow
P01HL-15194-20 0027 (HLBA) CANTZ, JOHN Coronary circulatory control and pathophysiology Modulation of coronary autoregulatory responses
P01HL-15194-20 9001 (HLBA) KLOCKE, FRANCIS J Coronary circulatory control and pathophysiology Animal laboratory core
P01HL-15194-20 9002 (HLBA) KLOCKE, FRANCIS J Coronary circulatory control and pathophysiology Analytical laboratory core
P01HL-15194-20 9003 (HLBA) MATES, ROBERT E Coronary circulatory control and pathophysiology Data processing laboratory core
P01HL-15194-20 9004 (HLBA) MATES, ROBERT E Coronary circulatory control and pathophysiology Electonics laboratory core
R01HL-15226-19 (HEM) NIEWIAROWSKI, STEFAN TEMPLE UNIVERSITY SCH OF MED 3420 N BROAD ST DEPT OF PHYSIO PHILADELPHIA, PA 19140 Interaction of cells with polymerizing fibrin
R01HL-15265-19 (SRC) BUCHWALD, HENRY UNIVERSITY OF MINNESOTA BOX 290 420 DELAWARE ST, S E MINNEAPOLIS, MINN 55455 Surgical control of the hyperlipidemias
R01HL-15390-23 (ECS) JOHNSON, PAUL C UNIVERSITY OF ARIZONA ARIZONA HLTH SCIENCES CTR TUCSON, AZ 85724 Regulation of blood flow in the microcirculation
R01HL-15448-18 (SAT) HAGEN, PER-OTTO F DUKE UNIVERSITY MED SCHOOL P O BOX 3473 DURHAM, NC 27710 Surgical and metabolic aspects of venous grafts
R37HL-15469-19 (RAP) DEMPSEY, JEROME A JOHN RANKIN LAB. OF PULMO.MEDI 504 N. WALNUT STREET MADISON, WI 53705 Human ventilatory adaption
R37HL-15473-17 (RAP) BISGARD, GERALD E UNIVERSITY OF WISCONSIN 2015 LINDEN DRIVE WEST MADISON, WI 53706 Peripheral and central ventilatory control
R01HL-15498-19 (RAP) SCHEUER, JAMES MONTEFIORE HOSPITAL & MED CTR 111 EAST 210TH STREET BRONX, N Y 10467 The effects of physical training on the heart
R01HL-15580-15 (RAP) KADOWITZ, PHILIP J TULANE UNIVERSITY 1430 TULANE AVENUE NEW ORLEANS, LA 70112 Humoral control of pulmonary and systemic circulation
R01HL-15647-18 (HEM) LOTHROP, CLINTON D, JR COLLEGE OF VETERINARY MED P O BOX 1071 KNOXVILLE, TN 37901-1071 The molecular biology of cyclic hematopoiesis
R01HL-15690-19 (HEM) DONALDSON, VIRGINIA H CHILDREN'S HOSPITAL RES FDN ELLAND & BETHESDA AVENUES CINCINNATI, OH 45229 Hydrolytic enzymes of blood in health and disease
R37HL-15696-19 (NSS) KUO, JYH-FA EMORY UNIVERSITY 1639 PIERCE DRIVE ATLANTA, GA 30322 Mechanism and role of cyclic GMP and calcium in heart
R37HL-15722-19 (CVB) MEISELMAN, HERBERT J USC SCHOOL OF MEDICINE 2025 ZONAL AVE/PHYSIO BIOPHY LOS ANGELES, CA 90033 Hemorrheology studies related to in vivo blood flow
R01HL-15728-19 (HEM) NELSESTUEN, GARY L UNIVERSITY OF MINNESOTA 1479 GORTNER AVENUE ST PAUL, MN 55108 Vitamin K-dependent plasma proteins
R01HL-15764-18 (CVA) KIRCHBERGER, MADELEINE A MOUNT SINAI SCHOOL OF MEDICINE ONE GUSTAVE L LEVY PLACE NEW YORK, N Y 10029 C-AMP dependent protein kinase in cardiac contraction
P01HL-15835-19 (HLBA) GOLDMAN, YALE E UNIVERSITY OF PENNSYLVANIA 37TH & HAMILTON WALK PHILADELPHIA, PA 19104-6085 Study of muscles related to heart disease
P01HL-15835-19 0001 (HLBA) WEBER, ANNEMARIE A Study of muscles related to heart disease Action assembly of actin filaments
P01HL-15835-19 0004 (HLBA) NACHMIAS, VIVIANNE T Study of muscles related to heart disease Actomyosin systems and cell motility
P01HL-15835-19 0007 (HLBA) LEVINE, RHEA J Study of muscles related to heart disease Structure and function of limulus striated and cardiac muscle
P01HL-15835-19 0009 (HLBA) HOLTZER, HOWARD Study of muscles related to heart disease Aspects of cardiac and skeletal myogenesis
P01HL-15835-19 0010 (HLBA) KELLY, ALAN M Study of muscles related to heart disease Muscle growth and differentiation and injury
P01HL-15835-19 0019 (HLBA) SOMLYO, ANDREW P Study of muscles related to heart disease Vascular smooth muscle
P01HL-15835-19 0029 (HLBA) SANGER, JOSEPH W Study of muscles related to heart disease Fluorescent tracers to study cell motility
P01HL-15835-19 0030 (HLBA) BUTLER, THOMAS M Study of muscles related to heart disease Mechanochemical transduction in whole muscle
P01HL-15835-19 0031 (HLBA) FRANZINI-ARMSTRONG, CLARA Study of muscles related to heart disease Contraction and E-C coupling in

PROJECT NO., ORGANIZATIONAL UNIT., INVESTIGATOR, ADDRESS, TITLE

striated muscle
P01HL-15835-19 0032 (HLBA) GOLDMAN, YALE Study of muscles related to heart disease Correlation of muscle physiology and biochemistry
P01HL-15835-19 0037 (HLBA) TRENTHAM, DAVID R Study of muscles related to heart disease Correlation of muscle physiology and biochemistry
P01HL-15835-19 9001 (HLBA) PEPE, FRANK A Study of muscles related to heart disease Core--Intermediate voltage EM of muscle
R37HL-15852-18 (NSS) JONES, ALLAN W UNIVERSITY OF MISSOURI MA415 MEDICAL SCIENCE BLDG COLUMBIA, MO 65212 Hypertension mechanisms and vascular ion exchange
R01HL-15965-18 (PBC) RUCKER, ROBERT B UNIVERSITY OF CALIFORNIA DAVIS, CALIF 95616 Elastin metabolism
P60HL-15996-19 (SRC) RUCKNAGEL, DONALD L CHILDREN'S HOSPITAL MEDICAL CN ELLAND AND BEHTESDA AVE CINCINNATI, OH 45229-2899 Cincinnati comprehensive sickle cell center
P60HL-15996-19 0006 (SRC) JENKINS, ALVERNA Cincinnati comprehensive sickle cell center Education program
P60HL-15996-19 0007 (SRC) CLARK, JEANETTE A Cincinnati comprehensive sickle cell center Neonatal diagnostic programs for sickle cell anemia in Ohio
P60HL-15996-19 0019 (SRC) DUNCAN, CRAIG H Cincinnati comprehensive sickle cell center Genetic control of fetal globin synthesis
P60HL-15996-19 0020 (SRC) LINGREL, JERRY B Cincinnati comprehensive sickle cell center Mechanism of switch from fetal to adult hemoglobin
P60HL-15996-19 0021 (SRC) LUSE, DONAL S Cincinnati comprehensive sickle cell center Investigation of hemoglobin gene regulation
P60HL-15996-19 0023 (SRC) BURLEW, ANN K Cincinnati comprehensive sickle cell center Sickle cell disease impact on family dynamics and school adjustment
P60HL-15996-19 0025 (SRC) KALINYAK, KAREN Cincinnati comprehensive sickle cell center Pulmonary function studies and nocturnal hypoxemia in sickle cell disease
P60HL-15996-19 0027 (SRC) RUCKNAGEL, DONALD L Cincinnati comprehensive sickle cell center Physiological and genetic varibles affecting severity of sickle cell anemia
P60HL-15996-19 0028 (SRC) FRANCO, ROBERT S Cincinnati comprehensive sickle cell center Modification of sickle cell to prevent sickling
P60HL-15996-19 0029 (SRC) RUCKNAGEL, DONALD L Cincinnati comprehensive sickle cell center Prenatal diagnosis of sickle cell anemia--A model program
P60HL-15996-19 9001 (SRC) KALINYAK, KAREN A Cincinnati comprehensive sickle cell center Patient services core--Pediatric clinical care
P60HL-15996-19 9002 (SRC) PALASCAK, JOSEPH E Cincinnati comprehensive sickle cell center Patient services core--Adult clinical care
P60HL-15996-19 9003 (SRC) HUFFMAN, ANN Cincinnati comprehensive sickle cell center Patient services core--Social services
P60HL-15996-19 9004 (SRC) SMITH, DIANE B Cincinnati comprehensive sickle cell center Core--Electrophoresis laboratory
P60HL-15996-19 9005 (SRC) POTTER, S STEVEN Cincinnati comprehensive sickle cell center Core--Transgenic mice facility
P60HL-15996-19 9006 (SRC) HARRIS, EVETTE Cincinnati comprehensive sickle cell center Core--Genetic counseling
R01HL-16003-20 (PHRA) TRIGGLE, DAVID J SUNY AT BUFFALO 126 COOKE HALL BUFFALO, NY 14260 Calcium and calcium antagonism in smooth and cardiac muscle
P60HL-16008-19 (SRC) WHITTEN, CHARLES F CHILDREN'S HSPT'L OF MICHIGAN 3901 BEAUBIEN DETROIT, MI 48201 Comprehensive sickle cell center support
P60HL-16008-19 0011 (SRC) WHITTEN, CHARLES F Comprehensive sickle cell center support Education, testing, counseling and supportive services
P60HL-16008-19 0017 (SRC) MIZUKAMI, HIROSHI Comprehensive sickle cell center support Transient state of sickle cells and their interaction with ligands
P60HL-16008-19 0019 (SRC) KAPLAN, JOSEPH Comprehensive sickle cell center support Immune response in sickle cell anemia
P60HL-16008-19 0024 (SRC) HANASH, SAMIR M Comprehensive sickle cell center support Fetal hemoglobin synthesis in sickle cell anemia
P60HL-16008-19 0025 (SRC) JOHNSON, ROBERT M Comprehensive sickle cell center support Membrane control of cellular dehydration in sickle cell disease
P60HL-16008-19 0027 (SRC) ATWAH, GEORGE Comprehensive sickle cell center support Clinical and molecular correlation in Sickle-Thalassemia
P60HL-16008-19 9001 (SRC) SING, CHARLES F Comprehensive sickle cell center support Core--Data management
R01HL-16010-28 (CVA) WINEGRAD, SAUL UNIVERSITY OF PENNSYLVANIA SCHOOL OF MEDICINE PHILADELPHIA, PA 19104-6085 Cellular basis of cardiac contractility
R37HL-16022-18 (RAP) EDELMAN, NORMAN H UNIVERSITY OF MEDICINE/DENTIST ONE ROBERT WOOD JOHNSON PLACE NEW BRUNSWICK, NJ 08903-0019 Determinants of the ventilatory response to hypoxia
R37HL-16029-17 (NSS) PRYOR, WILLIAM AUSTIN LOUISIANA STATE UNIVERSITY 711 CHOPPIN HALL BATON ROUGE, LA 70803-1800 Chemistry and toxicology of nitrogen dioxide
R37HL-16037-19 (NSS) LEFKOWITZ, ROBERT J DUKE UNIVERSITY MEDICAL CENTER BOX 3821 DURHAM, N C 27710 Molecular properties of cardiac adrenergic receptors
R01HL-16059-18 (MET) JONAS, ANA UNIVERSITY OF ILLINOIS 506 SOUTH MATHEWS AVENUE URBANA, IL 61801 High density lipoprotein structure-function correlations
R37HL-16066-18 (ECS) HEISTAD, DONALD D UNIVERSITY OF IOWA CARDIOVASCULAR DIVISION IOWA CITY, IOWA 52242 Neurogenic control of the circulation
R37HL-16087-18 (BMT) LA MAR, GERD N UNIVERSITY OF CALIFORNIA 275 MRAK HALL DAVIS, CA 95616 Structural and dynamic study of model heme complexes
R01HL-16101-18 (MBC) GENNIS, ROBERT B UNIVERSITY OF ILLINOIS 505 SOUTH MATHEWS STREET URBANA, IL 61801 Protein-lipid interactions
R01HL-16152-19 (CVA) MORAD, MARTIN UNIVERSITY OF PENNSYLVANIA 37TH & HAMILTON WALK PHILADELPHIA, PA 19104-6085 Electrophysiology of neonatal and adult hearts
P01HL-16251-18 (HLBA) SINGER, THOMAS P VETERANS ADMIN MEDICAL CTR 4150 CLEMENT ST SAN FRANCISCO, CA 94121 Membrane bound enzymes in heart and other tissues
P01HL-16251-18 0002 (HLBA) ACKRELL, BRIAN A Membrane bound enzymes in heart and other tissues Membrane bound enzymes in heart and other tissues
P01HL-16251-18 0003 (HLBA) KEARNEY, EDNA B Membrane bound enzymes in heart and other tissues Complex II of heart mitochondria and related complexes
P01HL-16251-18 0004 (HLBA) KEARNEY, EDNA B Membrane bound enzymes in heart and other tissues Dehydrogenase complexes--Q reduction and reconstitution
P01HL-16251-18 0007 (HLBA) SINGER, THOMAS P Membrane bound enzymes in heart and other tissues Flavoproteins and other enzymes
P01HL-16251-18 0013 (HLBA) SINGER, THOMAS P Membrane bound enzymes in heart and other tissues Flavoproteins and covalently bound flavin and coenzymes
P01HL-16251-18 0014 (HLBA) SINGER, THOMAS P Membrane bound enzymes in heart and other tissues Flavocytochrome p-cresol methylhydroxylase
P01HL-16251-18 0015 (HLBA) RAMSAY, RONA R Membrane bound enzymes in heart and other tissues Structure, function and membrane association fatty acid oxidation enzyme
P01HL-16251-18 0016 (HLBA) SINGER, THOMAS P Membrane bound enzymes in heart and other tissues Cardiac NADH dehydrogenase
P01HL-16251-18 0017 (HLBA) STEENKAMP, DANIEL J Membrane bound enzymes in heart and other tissues Selected aspects of microbial respiration
P01HL-16251-18 9001 (HLBA) ACKRELL, BRIAN A Membrane bound enzymes in heart and other tissues CORE
R01HL-16292-18 (SAT) BUCKBERG, GERALD D UNIV OF CA/CTR FOR HLTH SCIS 10833 LE CONTE AVE LOS ANGELES, CA 90024 Surgical reperfusion of ischemic myocardium
R37HL-16315-18 (ECS) SCHRAMM, LAWRENCE P JOHNS HOPKINS UNIVERSITY 720 NORTH RUTLAND AVENUE BALTIMORE, MD 21205 Analysis of interaction between CNS vasomotor systems
R01HL-16318-33 (PC) HOKIN, LOWELL E 1300 UNIVERSITY AVENUE MADISON, WI 53706 Phosphoinositides--Meatobolism, signaling regulation
R37HL-16346-21 (HEM) LORAND, LASZLO NORTHWESTERN UNIVERSITY BIOCHEM & MOLEC BIOLOGY DEPT EVANSTON, IL 60208 Molecular defects of fibrin stabilization
R01HL-16390-18 (RAP) YAMASHIRO, STANLEY M UNIV OF SOUTHERN CALIFORNIA UNIVERSITY PARK LOS ANGELES, CA 90089-1451 Cardiopulmonary control coupling in exercise
P01HL-16411-18 (HLBB) EDGINGTON, THOMAS S SCRIPPS CLINIC & RESEARCH FDN 10666 NORTH TORREY PINES ROAD LA JOLLA, CA 92037 Vascular molecular and cells biology
P01HL-16411-18 0003 (HLBB) EDGINGTON, THOMAS S Vascular molecular and cells biology Cellular initiation of coagulation
P01HL-16411-18 0004 (HLBB) GINSBERG, MARK H Vascular molecular and cells biology Structure and function of a novel endothelial cell protein
P01HL-16411-18 0005 (HLBB) HUGLI, TONY E Vascular molecular and cells biology Complement factors associated with coagulation and inflammation
P01HL-16411-18 0012 (HLBB) PLOW, EDWARD F Vascular molecular and cells biology Fibrinogen an thrombospondin receptors on platelets
P01HL-16411-18 0013 (HLBB) LOSKUTOFF, DAVID J Vascular molecular and cells biology Endothelial cell blood interface
P01HL-16411-18 0016 (HLBB) WRIGHT, PETER E Vascular molecular and cells biology NMR structural studies of tissue factor
P01HL-16411-18 0017 (HLBB) MORRISSEY, JAMES H Vascular molecular and cells biology Tissue factor gene expression in vascular cells
P01HL-16411-18 9004 (HLBB) EDGINGTON, THOMAS S Vascular molecular and cells biology CORE--Hybridoma
P01HL-16411-18 9005 (HLBB) LOSKUTOFF, DAVID J Vascular molecular and cells biology CORE--Endothelial cell culture
R01HL-16496-17 (ECS) ROMERO, JUAN C MAYO FOUNDATION 200 FIRST STREET SOUTHWEST ROCHESTER, MN 55905 Renal humoral factors in renal function and hypertension
R37HL-16512-17 (NTN) CHAN, LAWRENCE C BAYLOR COLLEGE OF MEDICINE ONE BAYLOR PLAZA HOUSTON, TX 77030 Lipoprotein metabolism and hormonal regulation
R01HL-16549-16 (PHRA) YODA, ATSUNOBU 1300 UNIVERSITY AVENUE MADISON, WI 53706 Interaction of palytoxin with NaK-atpase proteoliposomes
R37HL-16634-26 (HEM) MAJERUS, PHILIP W WASHINGTON UNIVERSITY MED SCH HEMATOLOGY DIV/660 S EUCLID AV ST LOUIS, MO 63110 Function of platelets and coagulation factors
R37HL-16660-18 (NSS) BITTMAN, ROBERT QUEENS COLLEGE OF CUNY 65-30 KISSENA BOULEVARD FLUSHING, NY 11367 Structural properties of membranes
R01HL-16855-14A2 (RAP) HEMMINGSEN, EDVARD A UNIV OF CALIFORNIA, SAN DIEGO 8602 LA JOLLA SHORES DR LA JOLLA, CA 92093 Studies of cavitation in biological systems
P01HL-16910-18 (HLBA) SCHER, ALLEN M UNIVERSITY OF WASHINGTON DEPT OF PHYSIOLOGY/BIOPHYSICS SEATTLE, WASH 98195 Regulation of the peripheral circulation
P01HL-16910-18 0002 (HLBA) FEIGL, ERIC O Regulation of the peripheral circulation Coronary circulation
P01HL-16910-18 0005 (HLBA) SCHER, ALLEN M Regulation of the peripheral circulation Control of circulation by baroreceptor reflexes
P01HL-16910-18 0006 (HLBA) ROWELL, LORING B Regulation of the peripheral circulation Regulation of blood flow distribution
P01HL-16910-18 0007 (HLBA) SMITH, ORVILLE A Regulation of the peripheral circulation Cns--behavioral influences on circulation
P01HL-16910-18 0008 (HLBA) BRENGELMANN, GEORGE L. Regulation of the peripheral circulation Regulation of the cutaneous circulation
P01HL-16910-18 9001 (HLBA) BRENGELMANN, GEORGE L Regulation of the peripheral circulation Electronics and machine CORE
P01HL-16910-18 9002 (HLBA) FEIGL, ERIC O Regulation of the

peripheral circulation Central laboratory CORE

R01HL-16919-18 (HEM) DAVIE, EARL W UNIVERSITY OF WASHINGTON DEPT OF BIOCHEMISTRY SEATTLE, WA 98195 Proteins of blood coagulation

R01HL-16919-18 0020 (HEM) DAVIE, EARL Proteins of blood coagulation Structure and function of human factor XIII

R01HL-16919-18 0021 (HEM) DAVIE, EARL Proteins of blood coagulation Abnormal genes for factor X and expression of factor X in cell culture

R01HL-16919-18 0009 (HEM) DAVIE, EARL W Proteins of blood coagulation Structure and function of human plasminogen and its gene

R01HL-16919-18 0016 (HEM) DAVIE, EARL Proteins of blood coagulation Abnormal genes for factor XI and expression of factor XI in cell culture

R01HL-16919-18 0017 (HEM) DAVIE, EARL Proteins of blood coagulation Placental coagulant protein

R01HL-16919-18 0018 (HEM) DAVIE, EARL Proteins of blood coagulation Structure and function of platelet glycoprotein IV

R01HL-16919-18 0019 (HEM) DAVIE, EARL Proteins of blood coagulation Structure and function of several placental anticoagulant proteins

R01HL-16919-18 0022 (HEM) DAVIE, EARL Proteins of blood coagulation Domain structures in plasma proteins as studied by NMR

R01HL-16955-18 (HEM) DANISHEFSKY, ISIDORE NEW YORK MED COLLEGE VALHALLA, NY 10595 Heparin and blood coagulation

R37HL-17080-18 (PTHA) PALADE, GEORGE E UNIVERSITY OF CALIFORNIA 9500 GILMAN DRIVE LA JOLLA, CA 92093-0934 Location of pore systems in capillary walls

R01HL-17335-17 (RAP) OSOL, GEORGE UNIVERSITY OF VERMONT DEPT OF PHYSIOLOGY/BIOPHYSICS BURLINGTON, VT 05405 Myogenic properties of cerebral arteries in hypertension

R01HL-17371-16 (BBCB) BROCKMAN, HOWARD L, JR UNIVERSITY OF MINNESOTA 801 16TH AVENUE N E AUSTIN, MINN 55912 Regulation of cholesteryl ester levels in mammalian tissues

R55HL-17376-16 (CVA) GOLDSTEIN, MARGARET A BAYLOR COLLEGE OF MEDICINE ONE BAYLOR PLAZA HOUSTON, TX 77030-3498 Role of Z band in cardiac sarcomere

R01HL-17411-17 (CBY) BRANTON, DANIEL HARVARD UNIVERSITY 16 DIVINITY AVENUE CAMBRIDGE, MA 02138 Molecular studies of red blood cell spectrin

P01HL-17421-18 (HLBA) JOHNSON, PAUL C UNIVERSITY OF ARIZONA COLLEGE OF MEDICINE TUCSON, AZ 85724 Regulation and exchange in the microcirculation

P01HL-17421-18 0002 (HLBA) GROSS, JOSEPH F Regulation and exchange in the microcirculation Vasomotion and nonlinear flow behavior

P01HL-17421-18 0014 (HLBA) JOHNSON, PAUL C Regulation and exchange in the microcirculation Oxygen delivery by microvascular networks

P01HL-17421-18 0015 (HLBA) BALDWIN, ANN Regulation and exchange in the microcirculation Structural determinants of fluid exchange in vivo

P01HL-17421-18 9002 (HLBA) SCHAFFER, RICHARD Regulation and exchange in the microcirculation Core--Cell culture

R01HL-17576-15A1 (BBCB) BARENHOLZ, YECHEZKEL UNIVERSITY OF VIRGINIA CHARLOTTESVILLE, VA 22908 Role of sphingomyelin in biomembranes and bilayers

R37HL-17597-18 (MET) NISHIDA, TOSHIRO UNIVERSITY OF ILLINOIS 1208 W. PENNSYLVANIA AVE URBANA, IL 61801 Role of plasma lipoproteins in atherosclerosis

R01HL-17623-17A1 (SB) KIM, SUNG W UNIVERSITY OF UTAH 421 WAKARA WAY, SUITE 318 SALT LAKE CITY, UT 84108 Initial events in thrombus formation on surfaces

P50HL-17646-17 (SRC) SOBEL, BURTON E WASHINGTON UNIVERSITY 660 SOUTH EUCLID AVENUE ST LOUIS, MO 63110 Specialized center of research in ischemic heart disease

P50HL-17646-17 9001 (SRC) SOBEL, BURTON E Specialized center of research in ischemic heart disease Core--Clinical investigation unit

P50HL-17646-17 9002 (SRC) MARKHAM, JOANNE Specialized center of research in ischemic heart disease Core--data management and biostatistics

P50HL-17646-17 9003 (SRC) SAFFITZ, JEFFREY E Specialized center of research in ischemic heart disease Core--Pathology and tissue culture

P50HL-17646-17 0007 (SRC) STRAUSS, ARNOLD W Specialized center of research in ischemic heart disease Regulation of cardiac energy-producing enzymes

P50HL-17646-17 0009 (SRC) SOBEL, BURTON E Specialized center of research in ischemic heart disease Potentiation of coronary thrombolysis

P50HL-17646-17 0015 (SRC) JAFFE, ALLAN S Specialized center of research in ischemic heart disease Thrombosis, thrombolysis & myocardial injury detection--Plasma biomarkers

P50HL-17646-17 0017 (SRC) CORR, PETER B Specialized center of research in ischemic heart disease Arrhythmogenesis biochemistry in ischemic myocardium--Prevention

P50HL-17646-17 0024 (SRC) MILLER, JAMES G Specialized center of research in ischemic heart disease Acoustic properties of cardiovascular tissue--Diagnostic implication

P50HL-17646-17 0025 (SRC) SAFFITZ, JEFFREY E Specialized center of research in ischemic heart disease Arenergic receptors and cardiac pathophysiology

P50HL-17646-17 0026 (SRC) CAIN, MICHAEL E Specialized center of research in ischemic heart disease Determinants of altered frequency components in electrocardiography

P50HL-17646-17 0027 (SRC) LUDBROOK, PHILIP A Specialized center of research in ischemic heart disease Myocardial perfusion in ischemic heart disease--Quantitative analysis

P50HL-17646-17 0032 (SRC) BERGMANN, STEVEN R Specialized center of research in ischemic heart disease Myocardial perfusion,oxidative metab & function after recanalization

P50HL-17646-17 0033 (SRC) SCHWARTZ, ALAN L Specialized center of research in ischemic heart disease Cellular biology of t-PA catabolism

P50HL-17646-17 0034 (SRC) ABENDSCHEIN, DANA R Specialized center of research in ischemic heart disease Prompt, noninvasive recanalization detection after coronary thrombolysis

P50HL-17646-17 0035 (SRC) EISENBERG, PAUL R Specialized center of research in ischemic heart disease Pharmacologic activation of plasminogen--Procoagulant effects

P50HL-17646-17 0036 (SRC) GELTMAN, EDWARD M Specialized center of research in ischemic heart disease Biological determinants of acute coronary syndromes delineated by PET

P50HL-17646-17 0038 (SRC) PEREZ, JULIO E Specialized center of research in ischemic heart disease: Ultrasound backscatter--Ischemic heart disease & atherosclerosis diagnosis

P50HL-17646-17 9006 (SRC) STRAUSS, ARNOLD M Specialized center of research in ischemic heart disease Core--Molecular biology and immunology

P50HL-17655-17 (SRC) WEISFELDT, MYRON L JOHNS HOPKINS HOSPITAL 600 NORTH WOLFE STREET BALTIMORE, MD 21205 SCOR in coronary and vascular disease

P50HL-17655-17 0030 (SRC) BECKER, LEWIS C SCOR in coronary and vascular disease Vascular mediators of reperfusion injury

P50HL-17655-17 0031 (SRC) MARBAN, EDUARDO SCOR in coronary and vascular disease Calcium mediators

P50HL-17655-17 0032 (SRC) HALPERIN, HENRY R SCOR in coronary and vascular disease Mechanical properties of reperfused myocardium

P50HL-17655-17 0033 (SRC) GERSTENBLITH, GARY SCOR in coronary and vascular disease Metabolism of reperfused myocardium

P50HL-17655-17 0034 (SRC) GUERCI, ALLAN D SCOR in coronary and vascular disease Circulatory support with a pneumatic vest for cardiac arrest

P50HL-17655-17 0035 (SRC) GOTTLIEB, SIDNEY O SCOR in coronary and vascular disease Delayed PTCA after MI--Effect on regional ventricular function

P50HL-17655-17 0036 (SRC) ZWEIER, JAY L SCOR in coronary and vascular disease Free radical mediators

P50HL-17655-17 0037 (SRC) HALPERIN, HENRY R SCOR in coronary and vascular disease Mechanical properties of reperfused myocardium

P50HL-17655-17 9010 (SRC) STERN, MICHAEL D SCOR in coronary and vascular disease Core--Myocardial cell pathology

P50HL-17655-17 9011 (SRC) SIU, CYNTHIA O SCOR in coronary and vascular disease Core--Statistics

P50HL-17655-17 9012 (SRC) GOTTLIEB, SIDNEY O SCOR in coronary and vascular disease

P50HL-17655-17 9013 (SRC) GOTTLIEB, SIDNEY O SCOR in coronary and vascular disease Core--Clinical trials

P50HL-17655-17 9014 (SRC) BECKER, LEWIS C SCOR in coronary and vascular disease Core--Animal

P50HL-17667-17 (SRC) POHOST, GERALD M UNIV OF ALABAMA IN BIRMINGHAM BIRMINGHAM, ALA 35294 SCOR in coronary and vascular diseases

P50HL-17667-17 0056 (SRC) KU, DAVID D SCOR in coronary and vascular diseases Endothelial regulation of coronary artery and platelet reactivity

P50HL-17667-17 0062 (SRC) POHOST, GERALD M SCOR in coronary and vascular diseases Lipid changes by 1-H NMR to assess myocardial ischemia

P50HL-17667-17 0069 (SRC) UMEDA, PATRICK K SCOR in coronary and vascular diseases Ischemic alterations in lipid regulation--Molecular biology of CPT

P50HL-17667-17 0070 (SRC) ELGAVISH, GABRIEL A SCOR in coronary and vascular diseases NMR studies of intracellular sodium in myocardial ischemia

P50HL-17667-17 0071 (SRC) URTHALER, FERDINAND SCOR in coronary and vascular diseases Pi, differential myocardial responsiveness to calcium--Early contractile failure

P50HL-17667-17 0072 (SRC) BOOYSE, FRANCOIS M SCOR in coronary and vascular diseases Coronary artery endothelial cell mediated fibrinolysis

P50HL-17667-17 0073 (SRC) KIRKLIN, JOHN W SCOR in coronary and vascular diseases Controlled reperfusion of ischemic myocardium

P50HL-17667-17 9004 (SRC) KIRK, KATHERINE A SCOR in coronary and vascular diseases Core--Statistics and data management

P50HL-17667-17 9005 (SRC) EVANOCHKO, WILLIAM SCOR in coronary and vascular diseases Core--NMR

P50HL-17667-17 9006 (SRC) BISHOP, SANFORD P SCOR in coronary and vascular diseases Core--Pathology/microsphere blood flow

P50HL-17669-17 (SRC) SAMBROOK, JOSEPH UNIVERSITY OF TEXAS 5323 HARRY HINES BOULEVARD DALLAS, TEX 75235 SCOR in coronary and vascular diseases

P50HL-17669-17 0032 (SRC) PESHOCK, RONALD M SCOR in coronary and vascular diseases NMR imaging of perfusion, function and atherosclerosis plaque

P50HL-17669-17 0033 (SRC) MALLOY, CRAIG SCOR in coronary and vascular diseases Diagnosis of reversible myocardial injury by NMR spectroscopy

P50HL-17669-17 0034 (SRC) CORBETT, JAMES R SCOR in coronary and vascular diseases Nuclear cardiology evaluations with SPECT in coronary heart disease

P50HL-17669-17 0035 (SRC) WILLERSON, JAMES T SCOR in coronary and vascular diseases Conversion from chronic to acute CHD syndromes in relevant animal models

P50HL-17669-17 0036 (SRC) CHILIAN, WILLIAM M SCOR in coronary and vascular diseases Pathophysiological disturbances in the coronary circulation

P50HL-17669-17 0038 (SRC) MUNTZ, KATHRYN H SCOR in coronary and vascular diseases Adrenergic system alterations in progression of myocardial injury

P50HL-17669-17 0039 (SRC) CAMPBELL, WILLIAM B SCOR in coronary and vascular diseases Eicosanoid synthesis in coronary vessels and myocardial ischemia

P50HL-17669-17 0040 (SRC) REYNOLDS, GARY A SCOR in coronary and vascular diseases Cellular uncoupling during myocardial ischemia and reperfusion

P50HL-17669-17 0041 (SRC) SAMBROOK, JOSEPH F SCOR in coronary and vascular diseases Molecular genetics of tissue-type plasminogen activator

P50HL-17669-17 0042 (SRC) SAMBROOK, JOSEPH F SCOR in coronary and vascular diseases Control of TPA and PAI-1 gene expression in coronary thrombosis

P50HL-17669-17 0043 (SRC) LIMUMBY, MARC C SCOR in coronary and vascular diseases Mechanisms of cardiac regulation--phosphorylation

and dephosphorylation
P50HL-17669-17 9003 (SRC) HAGLER, HERBERT K SCOR in coronary and vascular diseases Core--pathology laboratory
P50HL-17669-17 0030 (SRC) GRUNDY, SCOTT M SCOR in coronary and vascular diseases Fish oil protection against restenoses after angioplasty--in vitro assessment
P50HL-17669-17 0031 (SRC) EICHHORN, ERIC J SCOR in coronary and vascular diseases: Serotonin evaluation--accumulation at sites of coronary injury in stenoses
P50HL-17670-17 (SRC) STRAUSS, HAROLD C DUKE UNIVERSITY PO BOX 3845 DURHAM, N C 27710 SCOR in coronary and vascular diseases
P50HL-17670-17 0015 (SRC) JONES, ROBERT H SCOR in coronary and vascular diseases Radionuclide studies after coronary artery bypass grafting /human/
P50HL-17670-17 0027 (SRC) IDEKER, RAYMOND E SCOR in coronary and vascular diseases Electrical therapy of cardiac arrythmias /dog/
P50HL-17670-17 0028 (SRC) COBB, FREDERICK R SCOR in coronary and vascular diseases Coronary artery vasomotor activity in conscious dogs
P50HL-17670-17 0030 (SRC) RANKIN, J SCOTT SCOR in coronary and vascular diseases Myocardial energetic performance during ischemia and reperfusion /dog/
P50HL-17670-17 0032 (SRC) STILES, GARY L SCOR in coronary and vascular diseases Signal transduction in vascular smooth muscle /rat, rabbit/
P50HL-17670-17 0033 (SRC) KOBLIKA, BRIAN K SCOR in coronary and vascular diseases Molecular basis for alpha-2 adrenergic receptor function /human, rabbit/
P50HL-17670-17 0034 (SRC) WILLIAMS, R SANDERS SCOR in coronary and vascular diseases Stress-inducible promotor elements in myocytes /tissue culture/
P50HL-17670-17 0035 (SRC) GRANT, AUGUSTUS O SCOR in coronary and vascular diseases Cellular mechanisms of arrhythmias occuring during myocardial ischemia /rabbit/
P50HL-17670-17 0036 (SRC) SWAIN, JUDITH L SCOR in coronary and vascular diseases Proto-oncogenes in cardiac development /mice/
P50HL-17670-17 0037 (SRC) STACK, RICHARD S SCOR in coronary and vascular diseases Development of peripheral and coronary vascular stent prostheses /dog, rabbit/
P50HL-17670-17 0038 (SRC) COLEMAN, R EDWARD SCOR in coronary and vascular diseases F-18 FDG accumulation in ischemia and infarction /dog/
P50HL-17670-17 0039 (SRC) STRAUSS, HAROLD C SCOR in coronary and vascular diseases Arrhythmogenic factors post myocardial infarction--Effect of early reperfusion
P50HL-17670-17 0040 (SRC) COBB, FREDERICK R SCOR in coronary and vascular diseases Central and peripheral limitations to exercise in heart failure /human/
P50HL-17670-17 9001 (SRC) COLEMAN, R EDWARD SCOR in coronary and vascular diseases Core--Radiology laboratory
P50HL-17670-17 9002 (SRC) REIMER, KEITH A SCOR in coronary and vascular diseases Core--Pathology
P50HL-17670-17 9004 (SRC) LEE, KERRY L SCOR in coronary and vascular diseases Core--Biostatistics, data management and patient follow-up
P50HL-17682-17 (SRC) ROSS, JOHN, JR UNIV OF CALIFORNIA, SAN DIEGO BASIC SCIENCE BLDG, ROOM 2022 LA JOLLA, CALIF 92093 Specialized center of research in ischemic heart disease
P50HL-17682-17 0041 (SRC) DILLMAN, WOLFGANG H Specialized center of research in ischemic heart disease: Ischemia induced changes in specific cardiac proteins & mRNA
P50HL-17682-17 0042 (SRC) INSEL, PAUL A Specialized center of research in ischemic heart disease Beta-adrenergic receptors & post-receptor components in myocardial ischemia
P50HL-17682-17 0015 (SRC) ROSS, JOHN Specialized center of research in ischemic heart disease Alpha-adrenergic responses in ischemia--Regional contraction reverse
P50HL-17682-17 0039 (SRC) COVELL, JAMES W Specialized center of research in ischemic heart disease Transmural deformation and stress distribution in ischemic myocardium
P50HL-17682-17 0043 (SRC) CHIEN, KENNETH R Specialized center of research in ischemic heart disease Alterations in NA+ channels during myocardial ischemia & hypertrophy
P50HL-17682-17 0044 (SRC) SCHMID-SCHONBEIN, G W Specialized center of research in ischemic heart disease Leukocyte kinetics in peripheral and coronary microcirculation
P50HL-17682-17 0045 (SRC) MARTIN, JOEL F Specialized center of research in ischemic heart disease In vivo MRI--Detection & quantification of acute & chronic ischemia
P50HL-17682-17 0046 (SRC) NICOD, PAUL Specialized center of research in ischemic heart disease Coronary reactivity after cholesterol lowering regimen in coronary patients
P50HL-17682-17 9001 (SRC) COVELL, JAMES W Specialized center of research in ischemic heart disease Core--Computing, statistics and instrumentation
P50HL-17682-17 9004 (SRC) BLOOR, COLIN M Specialized center of research in ischemic heart disease Core--Pathology laboratory
P50HL-17682-17 9007 (SRC) BOSS, GERRY R Specialized center of research in ischemic heart disease Core--Biochemistry
P50HL-17682-17 9008 (SRC) CHIEN, KENNETH R Specialized center of research in ischemic heart disease Core--Myocardial cell biology
R37HL-17689-19 (RAP) ELDRIDGE, FREDERIC L UNIVERSITY OF NORTH CAROLINA 52 MED SCI RESEARCH BLDG CHAPEL HILL, NC 27599 Neurophysiological studies of respiratory control
R01HL-17705-17 (CVB) MARGOLIUS, HARRY S MED UNIV OF SOUTH CAROLINA 171 ASHLEY AVENUE CHARLESTON, SC 29425 Kallikreins and kinins in hypertension
P01HL-17731-17 (HLBA) WAGNER, PETER D UNIV OF CALIFORNIA, SAN DIEGO DIVISION OF PHYSIOLOGY, M-023A LA JOLLA, CA 92093 Physiological basis of pulmonary disease
P01HL-17731-17 0001 (HLBA) WEST, JOHN B Physiological basis of pulmonary disease Oxygen enrichment on neuropsychological function at 415m altitude
P01HL-17731-17 0003 (HLBA) KOOYMAN, GERALD L Physiological basis of pulmonary disease Exercise physiology to maximum lung volume in aquatic mammals
P01HL-17731-17 0006 (HLBA) WAGNER, PETER D Physiological basis of pulmonary disease Determinants of maximum oxygen uptake
P01HL-17731-17 0010 (HLBA) HILL, ESTHER P Physiological basis of pulmonary disease Oxygen transport and utilization during hypothermia
P01HL-17731-17 0015 (HLBA) WAGNER, PETER D Physiological basis of pulmonary disease Pulmonary gas exchange
P01HL-17731-17 0016 (HLBA) HILL, ESTHER P Physiological basis of pulmonary disease Oxygen transport and critical oxygen tension during hypothermia
P01HL-17731-17 0017 (HLBA) POWELL, FRANK L Physiological basis of pulmonary disease Mechanisms of chemosensitivity
P01HL-17731-17 0019 (HLBA) MATHIEU-COSTELLO, ODILE Physiological basis of pulmonary disease Structure-Function correlations in tissue gas exchange
P01HL-17731-17 9001 (HLBA) MATHIEU-COSTELLO, ODILE Physiological basis of pulmonary disease Histology--core
P01HL-17731-17 9002 (HLBA) EVANS, JOHN W Physiological basis of pulmonary disease Core--statistics and computing
R37HL-17747-17 (PTHA) KARNOVSKY, MORRIS J HARVARD MEDICAL SCHOOL 240 LONGWOOD AVENUE Endothelial injury and regeneration
R01HL-17783-18 (PC) ELBEIN, ALAN D UNIVERSITY OF ARKANSAS 4301 W MARKHAM STREET LITTLE ROCK, AK 72205 Complex carbohydrates--Structure, function, synthesis
R01HL-17809-14 (RAP) COHEN, MICHAEL V MONTEFIORE MEDICAL CENTER 111 EAST 210TH STREET BRONX, N Y 10467 Effects of exercise on the coronary vasculature
R37HL-17818-18 (MET) SALEN, GERALD VETERANS ADMINISTRATION HOSP TREMONT AVENUE EAST ORANGE, NJ 07019 Metabolism of cholestanol and cholesterol in man
R01HL-17921-17 (MCHA) PORTER, NED A DUKE UNIVERSITY DURHAM, N C 27706 Free radicals, membranes, and enzyme photoactivation
R01HL-17964-17 (HEM) PLOW, EDWARD F SCRIPPS CLINIC & RES FNDN 10666 NORTH TORREY PINES ROAD LA JOLLA, CA 92037 Classical and alternative pathways of fibrinolysis
R01HL-18010-17 (CVB) RENKIN, EUGENE M UNIVERSITY OF CALIFORNIA DAVIS, CA 95616 Capillary transport of large molecules
R01HL-18089-16 (PC) SCHULZ, HORST H CITY COLLEGE OF CUNY CONVENT AVE AT 138TH ST NEW YORK, NY 10031 Fatty acid metabolism in heart and its regulation
R01HL-18094-15A3 (MET) NESS, GENE C UNIV OF SOUTH FLORIDA 12901 BRUCE B DOWNS BLVD TAMPA, FL 33612 Regulation of cholesterol biosynthesis and degradation
P01HL-18208-17 (HLBB) LA CELLE, PAUL L UNIVERSITY OF ROCHESTER 601 ELMWOOD AVENUE ROCHESTER, N Y 14642 Properties and vascular relations of blood cells and protein
P01HL-18208-17 0001 (HLBB) LICHTMAN, MARSHALL A Properties and vascular relations of blood cells and protein Cell maturation and activation--Cytoskeleton and membrane
P01HL-18208-17 0010 (HLBB) COKELET, GILES R Properties and vascular relations of blood cells and protein Physical laws for blood flow through small networks
P01HL-18208-17 0012 (HLBB) WAUGH, RICHARD E Properties and vascular relations of blood cells and protein Mechanical aspects of erythroid maturation and survival
P01HL-18208-17 0013 (HLBB) KNAUF, PHILIP A Properties and vascular relations of blood cells and protein Blood cell volume control and circulation
P01HL-18208-17 0014 (HLBB) ABBOUD, CAMILLE E Properties and vascular relations of blood cells and protein Maturation of human marrow cells
P01HL-18208-17 0015 (HLBB) OLBRIGHT, WILLIAM Properties and vascular relations of blood cells and protein Model studies of microcirculatory flow
P01HL-18208-17 0016 (HLBB) FRANK, R. S. Properties and vascular relations of blood cells and protein White cell mechanics--Activation and maturation
P01HL-18208-17 0017 (HLBB) SARELIUS, I. H. Properties and vascular relations of blood cells and protein Determinants of microvascular flow in vivo
P01HL-18208-17 9001 (HLBB) LICHTMAN, MARSHALL A Properties and vascular relations of blood cells and protein Core--common services
P01HL-18208-17 9002 (HLBB) LICHTMAN, MARSHALL A Properties and vascular relations of blood cells and protein Core--Electron microscope
P01HL-18208-17 9003 (HLBB) BRENNAN, JAMES K Properties and vascular relations of blood cells and protein Core--Tissue culture
P01HL-18208-17 9004 (HLBB) LICHTMAN, MARSHALL A Properties and vascular relations of blood cells and protein Core--cell sorting
P01HL-18208-17 9005 (HLBB) WAUGH, RICHARD E Properties and vascular relations of blood cells and protein Core--Video image analysis
R01HL-18255-16 (BBCB) FEIGENSON, GERALD W CORNELL UNIVERSITY ITHACA, NY 14853 Lipid-protein interactions and calcium transport
R01HL-18292-16A1 (ECS) PITTMAN, ROLAND N MEDICAL COLLEGE OF VIRGINIA 1101 E MARSHALL STREET RICHMOND, VA 23298-0551 Vasodilation and microvascular oxygen delivery
P50HL-18323-17 (SRC) LARAGH, JOHN H CORNELL UNIVERSITY 1300 YORK AVENUE NEW YORK, N Y 10021 SCOR in hypertension
P50HL-18323-17 0012 (SRC) ALDERMAN, MICHAEL H SCOR in hypertension Clinical strategies to improve treatment in mild hypertension
P50HL-18323-17 0038 (SRC) ULICK, STANLEY SCOR in hypertension Adrenocortical hypertensive mechanisms
P50HL-18323-17 0045 (SRC) SEALEY, JEAN SCOR in hypertension Prorenin
P50HL-18323-17 0051 (SRC) AUGUST, PHYLLIS SCOR in hypertension Hypertensive & normal pregnancy--Calcium metabolism & renin-angiotensin
P50HL-18323-17 0052 (SRC) PICKERING, THOMAS G SCOR in hypertension White coat hypertension & antihypertensive treatment effect
P50HL-18323-17 0055 (SRC) DEVEREUX, RICHARD B SCOR in hypertension Hypertension, the renin-angiotensin system, and the heart
P50HL-18323-17 0063 (SRC) ATLAS, STEVEN A SCOR in hypertension Renin, ANF, and calcium hormones--Relation to sodium and potassium

PROJECT NO., ORGANIZATIONAL UNIT., INVESTIGATOR, ADDRESS, TITLE

intake
P50HL-18323-17 0064 (SRC) CAMARGO, MARIA J SCOR in hypertension End organ damage in hypertension genetic models
P50HL-18323-17 0065 (SRC) MAACK, THOMAS SCOR in hypertension Angiotensin II renal and vascular receptor functional heterogeneity
P50HL-18323-17 0066 (SRC) BLUMENFELD, JON SCOR in hypertension Renal hemodynamics during exercise
P50HL-18323-17 9004 (SRC) MUELLER, FRANCO B SCOR in hypertension Core--Data management and analysis
P50HL-18323-17 9005 (SRC) PICKERING, THOMAS G SCOR in hypertension Core--Blood pressure measurements
P50HL-18323-17 0067 (SRC) KUMAR, ASHOK SCOR in hypertension Regulation of renin gene expression
P50HL-18323-17 0068 (SRC) RESNICK, LAWRENCE M SCOR in hypertension Calcium and calcium regulating hormones in hypertension
P50HL-18323-17 9001 (SRC) SEALEY, JEAN E SCOR in hypertension Core--Biochemical and molecular biology laboratory
P50HL-18323-17 9002 (SRC) GERBER, LINDA M SCOR in hypertension Core--Human resources
P50HL-18323-17 9003 (SRC) VAUGHN, E DARRACOTT SCOR in hypertension Core--Animal facility
R37HL-18340-17 (PTHA) BARAJAS, LUCIANO HARBOR-UCLA MEDICAL CENTER 1000 WEST CARSON STREET TORRANCE, CA 90509 Studies on the functional anatomy of the kidney
R37HL-18426-18 (GMB) NAVAR, L GABRIEL TULANE UNIVERSITY SCH OF MED 1430 TULANE AVENUE NEW ORLEANS, LA 70112 Regulation of renal hemodynamics
R37HL-18468-16 (NSS) GREENFIELD, JOSEPH C, JR DUKE UNIVERSITY MEDICAL CENTER BOX 3246 DURHAM, N C 27710 Factors affecting distribution of myocardial flow
P01HL-18574-16 (HLBB) KRAUSS, RONALD M LAWRENCE BERKELEY LABORATORY 1 CYCLOTRON ROAD BERKELEY, CA 94720 Metabolic and genetic origins of lipoprotein subclasses
P01HL-18574-16 0004 (HLBB) FORTE, GERTRUDE M Metabolic and genetic origins of lipoprotein subclasses Cellular origins of lipoprotein subclasses
P01HL-18574-16 0005 (HLBB) NICHOLS, ALEX V Metabolic and genetic origins of lipoprotein subclasses Apolipoprotein specific HDL and cholesterol transport
P01HL-18574-16 0006 (HLBB) KRAUSS, RONALD M Metabolic and genetic origins of lipoprotein subclasses Characterization of lipoprotein subclass phenotypes
P01HL-18574-16 0007 (HLBB) MUSLINER, THOMAS A Metabolic and genetic origins of lipoprotein subclasses Intravascular transformations of lipoproteins
P01HL-18574-16 0008 (HLBB) RUBIN, E M Metabolic and genetic origins of lipoprotein subclasses In Vivo effects of human apolipoprotein genes in mice
P01HL-18574-16 9001 (HLBB) LINDGREN, FRANK T Metabolic and genetic origins of lipoprotein subclasses CORE--Liprotein subclass analysis
P01HL-18574-16 9002 (HLBB) SHORE, VIRGIE S Metabolic and genetic origins of lipoprotein subclasses CORE--Apolipoprotein analysis
P01HL-18575-16A1 (HLBB) WEBB, R CLINTON UNIV OF MICHIGAN 1301 CATHERINE ST ANN ARBOR, MI 48109-0622 Altered ion metabolism in hypertension
P01HL-18575-16A1 0008 (HLBB) COYLE, PETER Altered ion metabolism in hypertension Altered mechanisms of cerebral collaterals in hypertension
P01HL-18575-16A1 0012 (HLBB) GREKIN, ROGER J Altered ion metabolism in hypertension Central regulation of aldosterone secretion
P01HL-18575-16A1 0016 (HLBB) BETZ, A LORRIS Altered ion metabolism in hypertension Blood-Brain barrier ion transport in hypertension
P01HL-18575-16A1 0017 (HLBB) FURSPAN, PHILIP Altered ion metabolism in hypertension Abnormality of the ATP-sensitive potassium channel in hypertension
P01HL-18575-16A1 0018 (HLBB) WEBB, R CLINTON Altered ion metabolism in hypertension Altered blood vessel function in hypertension
P01HL-18575-16A1 0019 (HLBB) WEDER, ALAN B Altered ion metabolism in hypertension Cellular and genetic markers of salt sensitivity
P01HL-18575-16A1 9001 (HLBB) BOHR, DAVID F Altered ion metabolism in hypertension CORE--Animal facility
P01HL-18575-16A1 9002 (HLBB) GREKIN, ROGER J Altered ion metabolism in hypertension CORE--Chemistry laboratory facility
P01HL-18577-16 (HLBB) SCANU, ANGELO M UNIVERSITY OF CHICAGO 5841 S MARYLAND AVE, BOX 231 CHICAGO, IL 60637 Lipoproteins--Cell surface interactions
P01HL-18577-16 0005 (HLBB) KAISER, EMIL T Lipoproteins--Cell surface interactions Synthetic peptides and lipid modifying enzymes
P01HL-18577-16 0014 (HLBB) FLESS, GUNTHER M Lipoproteins--Cell surface interactions Examination of lipoprotein heterogeneity
P01HL-18577-16 0016 (HLBB) GORDON, JEFFREY I Lipoproteins--Cell surface interactions Proteases responsible for proapolipoprotein A-I and A-II processing
P01HL-18577-16 0017 (HLBB) SCANU, ANGELO M Lipoproteins--Cell surface interactions Genetic dyslipoproteinemia in Rhesus monkey family
P01HL-18577-16 9001 (HLBB) SCANU, ANGELO M Lipoproteins--Cell surface interactions CORE--Chemistry of lipoproteins and apoproteins
P01HL-18577-16 9002 (HLBB) WOHL, ROBERT Lipoproteins--Cell surface interactions CORE--Protein structure
P01HL-18577-16 9003 (HLBB) DAWSON, GLYN Lipoproteins--Cell surface interactions Core--Cell culture and hybridoma facility
R37HL-18579-17 (CVB) NASJLETTI, ALBERTO NEW YORK MEDICAL COLLEGE VALHALLA, NY 10595 Vasoactive hormones and blood pressure regulation
R37HL-18584-15 (NSS) HELLUMS, JESSE D RICE UNIVERSITY POST OFFICE BOX 1892 HOUSTON, TX 77251 Effects of physical forces on platelets
R01HL-18601-12A3 (NEUB) WAKADE, ARUN R WAYNE STATE UNIVERSITY 540 E CANFIELD AVE/SCOTT HALL DETROIT, MI 48201 Trophism and transmitter release in sympathetic neurons
R01HL-18606-16 (RAP) EFFROS, RICHARD M MEDICAL COLLEGE OF WISCONSIN 8700 WEST WISCONSIN AVENUE MILWAUKEE, WI 53226 Pathogenesis and measurement of pulmonary edema

PROJECT NO., ORGANIZATIONAL UNIT., INVESTIGATOR, ADDRESS, TITLE

P01HL-18645-17 (HLBB) ROSS, RUSSELL UNIVERSITY OF WASHINGTON SEATTLE, WA 98195 Biology of the artery wall and atherosclerosis
P01HL-18645-17 0001 (HLBB) ROSS, RUSSELL Biology of the artery wall and atherosclerosis Growth factors--Characterization and mechanism of action
P01HL-18645-17 0006 (HLBB) ROSS, RUSSELL Biology of the artery wall and atherosclerosis Experimentally induced atherosclerosis and metabolism in vivo
P01HL-18645-17 0008 (HLBB) WIGHT, THOMAS N Biology of the artery wall and atherosclerosis Proteoglycans, glycosaminoglycans an atherosclerosis
P01HL-18645-17 0009 (HLBB) BORNSTEIN, PAUL Biology of the artery wall and atherosclerosis Secreted proteins and regulation of vascular cell growth
P01HL-18645-17 0010 (HLBB) BIERMAN, EDWIN L Biology of the artery wall and atherosclerosis Regulation of cholesterol trafficking in arterial wall cells
P01HL-18645-17 0011 (HLBB) SCHWARTZ, STEPHEN M Biology of the artery wall and atherosclerosis Endothelial regeneration
P01HL-18645-17 0012 (HLBB) CLOWES, ALEXANDER Biology of the artery wall and atherosclerosis Regulation of smooth muscle cell growth by heparin
P01HL-18645-17 0013 (HLBB) HARLAN, JOHN Biology of the artery wall and atherosclerosis Monocyte-endothelial interactions
P01HL-18645-17 0014 (HLBB) BOEWN-POPE, DANIEL Biology of the artery wall and atherosclerosis Structure and function of the PDGF receptor
P01HL-18645-17 9001 (HLBB) BOWEN-POPE, DANIEL F Biology of the artery wall and atherosclerosis CORE--Tissue culture/growth factor
P01HL-18645-17 9002 (HLBB) WIGHT, THOMAS N Biology of the artery wall and atherosclerosis CORE--Morphology
P01HL-18646-15 (SRC) COSIMI, BENEDICT A MASSACHUSETTS GENERAL HOSPITAL FRUIT STREET BOSTON, MASSS 02114 Studies basic to heart transplanation
P01HL-18646-15 0001 (SRC) COSIMI, A BENEDICT Studies basic to heart transplanation Monoclonal antibody monitoring and immunosuppression
P01HL-18646-15 0002 (SRC) COSIMI, A BENEDICT Studies basic to heart transplanation Evaluation of monoclonal antibody immunosuppression in animals
P01HL-18646-15 0011 (SRC) FULLER, THOMAS C Studies basic to heart transplanation Immunogenetics of MHC public epitopes
P01HL-18646-15 9001 (SRC) COLVIN, ROBERT B Studies basic to heart transplanation Core A - Flow cytometry
P01HL-18646-15 9002 (SRC) BHAN, ATUL K Studies basic to heart transplanation Core B - Immunopathology
P01HL-18646-15 9003 (SRC) SCHOOLEY, ROBERT Studies basic to heart transplanation Core C-Human Virology
R37HL-18672-14 (SB) MC INTIRE, LARRY V RICE UNIVERSITY P O BOX 1892 HOUSTON, TX 77251 Dynamic studies of coagulation and thrombosis
R01HL-18676-16 (CVA) POLLACK, GERALD H UNIVERSITY OF WASHINGTON SEATTLE, WA 98195 Myocardial sarcomere mechanics
P01HL-18708-16 (HLBA) SCARPA, ANTONIO CASE WESTERN RESERVE UNIV 2119 ABINGTON RD CLEVELAND, OH 44106 Cardiac bioenergetics
P01HL-18708-16 0009 (HLBA) CHANCE, BRITTON Cardiac bioenergetics Carbon monoxide and oxygen binding to mutant myoglobin
P01HL-18708-16 0017 (HLBA) BLASIE, J KENT Cardiac bioenergetics Structural-functional studies on sarcoplasmic reticulum
P01HL-18708-16 0018 (HLBA) MAGUIRE, MICHAEL E Cardiac bioenergetics Structure-functure of MgtB--Mg transporting P-type ATPase
P01HL-18708-16 0019 (HLBA) SCARPA, ANTONIO Cardiac bioenergetics Magnesium transport and ATP receptors of cardiac cells
P01HL-18708-16 0020 (HLBA) RADDA, GEORGE Cardiac bioenergetics Skeletal and cardiac muscle MRS and biochemistry in hypertension
R37HL-18819-20 (VR) MANNING, JAMES M ROCKEFELLER UNIVERSITY 1230 YORK AVENUE NEW YORK, N Y 10021 Chemical studies on sickle cell hemoglobin
P50HL-18828-16 (SRC) NACHMAN, RALPH L CORNELL UNIVERSITY MED COLLEGE 1300 YORK AVENUE NEW YORK, NY 10021 SCOR in thrombosis
P50HL-18828-16 0001 (SRC) NACHMAN, RALPH L SCOR in thrombosis Lipoprotein (a)--Plasminogen like modulator of vascular function
P50HL-18828-16 0002 (SRC) JAFFE, ERIC A SCOR in thrombosis Endothelial cell surface membrane glycoproteins
P50HL-18828-16 0003 (SRC) HARPEL, PETER C SCOR in thrombosis IgG and lipoprotein (a)--Surface oriented modulators of the plasmin system
P50HL-18828-16 0005 (SRC) WEKSLER, BABETTE B SCOR in thrombosis Heparin-binding growth factors in proliferation and thrombosis
P50HL-18828-16 0006 (SRC) HAJJAR, DAVID P SCOR in thrombosis Vascular cell interactions--Implications in atherosclerosis
P50HL-18828-16 0008 (SRC) MARCUS, AARON J SCOR in thrombosis Control of blood cell and vascular reactivity in thrombosis
P50HL-18828-16 0009 (SRC) ASCH, ADAM S SCOR in thrombosis Thrombospondin--Correlation of structure and function
P50HL-18828-16 0010 (SRC) SILVERSTEIN, ROY L SCOR in thrombosis Activation-dependent platelet surface glycoproteins--Molecular and cell biology
P50HL-18828-16 9001 (SRC) HARPEL, PETER C SCOR in thrombosis Core--Instrumentation facility
R37HL-18834-17 (HEM) FURIE, BARBARA C NEW ENGLAND MED CENTER HOSP 750 WASHINGTON STREET BOSTON, MASS 02111 Metal-dependent complexes in blood coagulation
R37HL-18848-16 (CVA) PATTERSON, DONALD F UNIV OF PA SCH/VET MEDICINE 3800 SPRUCE STREET PHILADELPHIA, PA 19104-6051 Etiology and development of congenital heart disease
R01HL-18912-12 (CVA) HUNTER, WILLIAM C JOHN HOPKINS SCH OF MEDICINE 720 RUTLAND AVENUE BALTIMORE, MD 21205 Mechanics of cardiac chamber contraction
R01HL-18976-12 (BEM) LIGHT, KATHLEEN C UNIVERSITY OF NORTH CAROLINA CB #7175 CHAPEL HILL, NC 27599 Blood pressure control--Relation to behavioral stress
R01HL-18995-16 (SB) KAUFFMAN, GORDON L JR, MD PENNSYLVANIA STATE UNIVERSITY P O BOX 850 HERSHEY, PA 17033 Cardiovascular determinants of catecholamine release
R37HL-19039-15 (CVB) SHOUKAS, ARTIN A JOHNS HOPKINS UNIVERSITY

PROJECT NO., ORGANIZATIONAL UNIT., INVESTIGATOR, ADDRESS, TITLE

720 RUTLAND AVENUE BALTIMORE, MD 21205 Capacity of systemic and cardiopulmonary compartments

R01HL-19044-15 (CVA) BASSETT, ARTHUR L UNIVERSITY OF MIAMI MIAMI, FLA 33101 Effect of drugs on development of cardiac failure

R01HL-19055-16 (SB) EDMUNDS, L HENRY, JR HOSP OF THE UNIVERSITY OF PENN 3400 SPRUCE ST, 4 SILVERSTEIN PHILADELPHIA, PA 19104 Physiology of blood elements during extracorporeal bypas

R37HL-19134-17 (ECS) MALIK, KAFAIT U UNIVERSITY OF TENNESSEE 874 UNION #100, M MEMPHIS, TN 38163 Angiotensins, prostaglandins, adrenergic interactions

R37HL-19139-16 (NSS) BASSINGTHWAIGHTE, JAMES B UNIVERSITY OF WASHINGTON SEATTLE, WA 98195 Dispersion of diffusible indicators in the body

P50HL-19153-15 (SRC) BRIGHAM, KENNETH L VANDERBILT UNIVERSITY 21ST AVENUE AT GARLAND STREET NASHVILLE, TN 37232 SCOR-- Pulmonary vascular diseases

P50HL-19153-15 0004 (SRC) ROSELLI, ROBERT J SCOR-- Pulmonary vascular diseases Mechanism for blood-tissue-lymph exchange of fluid, macromolecules in lung

P50HL-19153-15 0005 (SRC) HARRIS, THOMAS R SCOR-- Pulmonary vascular diseases Mechanisms of small molecule exchange in normal & abnormal lung

P50HL-19153-15 0006 (SRC) BERNARD, GORDON R SCOR-- Pulmonary vascular diseases Pathogenesis and therapy of acute lung injury in humans

P50HL-19153-15 0009 (SRC) BRIGHAM, KENNETH L SCOR-- Pulmonary vascular diseases Endotoxin induced lung injury

P50HL-19153-15 0013 (SRC) MEYRICK, BARBARA O SCOR-- Pulmonary vascular diseases Inflammation of the lung and chronic pulmonary hypertension

P50HL-19153-15 0015 (SRC) BERNARD, GORDON R SCOR-- Pulmonary vascular diseases Lung mechanics in patients with acute respiratory failure

P50HL-19153-15 9001 (SRC) BRIGHAM, KENNETH L SCOR-- Pulmonary vascular diseases Core--Experimental laboratories and support facilities

P50HL-19153-15 9002 (SRC) HARRIS, THOMAS R SCOR-- Pulmonary vascular diseases Core--biomedical engineering

P50HL-19153-15 9003 (SRC) MEYRICK, BARBARA O SCOR-- Pulmonary vascular diseases Core--Pathology

P50HL-19155-15 (SRC) MURRAY, JOHN F SAN FRANCISCO GENERAL HOSPITAL 1001 POTRERO AVENUE SAN FRANCISCO, CA 94110 Cytokine and cell adhesion molecules in acute lung injury

P50HL-19155-15 9001 (SRC) GOLDSTEIN, IRA M Cytokine and cell adhesion molecules in acute lung injury Core - Biochemistry laboratory

P50HL-19155-15 0001 (SRC) MURRAY, JOHN F Cytokine and cell adhesion molecules in acute lung injury Clinical study of pulmonary edema--Early diagnosis of acute lung injury

P50HL-19155-15 0012 (SRC) STAUB, NORMAN C Cytokine and cell adhesion molecules in acute lung injury Mechanism of acute pleural and lung injury

P50HL-19155-15 0013 (SRC) GOLDSTEIN, IRA M Cytokine and cell adhesion molecules in acute lung injury Complement, leukocytes and lung injury

P50HL-19170-15 (SRC) BRAIN, JOSEPH D HARVARD SCH OF PUBLIC HLTH 665 HUNTINGTON AVENUE BOSTON, MA 02115 SCOR--chronic diseases of the airways

P50HL-19170-15 0004 (SRC) BRAIN, JOSEPH D SCOR--chronic diseases of the airways Exercise, increased ventilation effect on pulmonary exposure response

P50HL-19170-15 0012 (SRC) WEINBERGER, STEVEN SCOR--chronic diseases of the airways Characterization and mechanics of dyspnea

P50HL-19170-15 0014 (SRC) WEISS, SCOTT T SCOR--chronic diseases of the airways Prospective evaluation of airways reactivity

P50HL-19170-15 0016 (SRC) DRAZEN, JEFFREY M. SCOR--chronic diseases of the airways Models of chronic airway irritation

P50HL-19170-15 0017 (SRC) LORING, STEPHEN SCOR--chronic diseases of the airways Interaction of respiratory and nonrespiratory acts

P50HL-19170-15 0018 (SRC) BANZETT, ROBERT B. SCOR--chronic diseases of the airways Respiratory perceptions from lungs and chemoreceptors

P50HL-19170-15 0019 (SRC) BRAIN, JOSEPH D. SCOR--chronic diseases of the airways Physiologic, diagnostic and therapeutic implications in airway size

P50HL-19170-15 0020 (SRC) CHAPMAN, HAROLD A. SCOR--chronic diseases of the airways Role of pulmonary macrophages in airway and parenchymal injury

P50HL-19170-15 9002 (SRC) FELDMAN, HENRY A. SCOR--chronic diseases of the airways Core--Experimental design, math modeling, statistical analysis

P50HL-19171-15 (SRC) CLYDE, WALLACE A, JR UNIVERSITY OF NORTH CAROLINA 535 BURNETT-WOMACK BLDG 229H CHAPEL HILL, N C 27514 SCOR--Respiratory disorders of neonates and children

P50HL-19171-15 0001 (SRC) COLLIER, ALBERT M SCOR--Respiratory disorders of neonates and children Acquired ciliary defects in conducting airway epithelium

P50HL-19171-15 0004 (SRC) HENDERSON, FREDERICK W SCOR--Respiratory disorders of neonates and children Respiratory infection, host factors and air pollution--Lung function in children

P50HL-19171-15 0013 (SRC) HELMS, RONALD W SCOR--Respiratory disorders of neonates and children Analysis of incomplete and multivariate data

P50HL-19171-15 0014 (SRC) TIDWELL, RICHARD R SCOR--Respiratory disorders of neonates and children Amidines in respiratory syncytial virus and Pneumocystis carinii infections

P50HL-19171-15 0015 (SRC) HU, PING-CHUAN SCOR--Respiratory disorders of neonates and children Molecular pathogenesis of respiratory infections--Mycoplasma pneumoniae

P50HL-19171-15 0016 (SRC) HENDERSON, FREDERICK W SCOR--Respiratory disorders of neonates and children Protective immune responses in common respiratory infections

P50HL-19171-15 0017 (SRC) WOOD, ROBERT W SCOR--Respiratory disorders of neonates and children Evolution of lung infection & injury in infants & children with cystic fibrosis

PROJECT NO., ORGANIZATIONAL UNIT., INVESTIGATOR, ADDRESS, TITLE

P50HL-19171-15 0018 (SRC) BOAT, THOMAS F SCOR--Respiratory disorders of neonates and children Infection and development of mucociliary mechanisms in airways

P50HL-19171-15 9001 (SRC) HELMS, RONALD W SCOR--Respiratory disorders of neonates and children Core--biometry

P50HL-19171-15 9002 (SRC) CARSON, JOHNNY L SCOR--Respiratory disorders of neonates and children Core--Morphology/ultrastructure

P50HL-19171-15 9004 (SRC) HU, PING-CHUAN SCOR--Respiratory disorders of neonates and children Core--Microbiology/immunology

R37HL-19209-16 (CVB) SHARE, LEONARD UNIV. OF TENNESSEE, MEMPHIS 894 UNION AVENUE MEMPHIS, TN 38163 Role of ADH in experimental renal hypertension

R37HL-19216-16 (NSS) STRAUSS, HAROLD C DUKE UNIVERSITY P O BOX 3845 DURHAM, N C 27710 Characterization of cardiac pacemaker activity

P01HL-19242-15 (HLBA) MURPHY, RICHARD A UNIV OF VIRGINIA MEDICAL CTR BOX 449 CHARLOTTESVILLE, VA 22908 Regulation of vascular muscle growth and function

P01HL-19242-15 0018 (HLBA) SOMLYO, A V Regulation of vascular muscle growth and function Regulation of calcium ion and contraction

P01HL-19242-15 9004 (HLBA) OWENS, G K Regulation of vascular muscle growth and function Core--VSM and endothelial cell cultures

P01HL-19242-15 9005 (HLBA) FORBES, M S Regulation of vascular muscle growth and function Core--Electron microscopy and histology

P01HL-19242-15 0008 (HLBA) PEACH, MICHAEL J Regulation of vascular muscle growth and function Endothelium-Vascular smooth muscle cell interactions

P01HL-19242-15 0012 (HLBA) DULING, BRIAN R Regulation of vascular muscle growth and function Mechanics, anatomy and reactivity of arterioles

P01HL-19242-15 0013 (HLBA) OWENS, G K Regulation of vascular muscle growth and function Mechanisms of vascular smooth muscle growth

P01HL-19242-15 0014 (HLBA) CAREY, R M Regulation of vascular muscle growth and function Juxtaglomeruler cells and regulation of renin release

P01HL-19242-15 0016 (HLBA) MURPHY, RICHARD A Regulation of vascular muscle growth and function Regulation of crossbridge interactions in smooth muscle

P01HL-19242-15 0017 (HLBA) LYNCH, KEVIN R Regulation of vascular muscle growth and function Characterization of vasoactive receptors

R37HL-19278-16 (HEM) COLLER, BARRY S SUNY-STONY BROOK DIVISION OF HEMATOLOGY STONY BROOK, N Y 11794 Biochemistry/physiology of platelet membrane receptors

R37HL-19298-16 (RAP) DAWSON, CHRISTOPHER A ZABLOCKI VA MEDICAL CENTER 5000 W NATIONAL AVENUE MILWAUKEE, WI 53295-1000 Pulmonary hemodynamics

R01HL-19299-15 (ECS) WITTENBERG, BEATRICE A ALBERT EINSTEIN COLL OF MED 1300 MORRIS PARK AVE BRONX, NY 10461 Energy balance in isolated adult heart cells

R01HL-19325-15 (PHRA) WELLS, JACK N VANDERBILT UNIVERSITY SCHOOL OF MEDICINE NASHVILLE, TN 37232-6600 Regulation of smooth muscle contraction

R01HL-19379-14 (PTHA) HOYT, RICHARD F, JR BOSTON UNIVERSITY 80 EAST CONCORD STREET BOSTON, MASS 02118 Characterization of small-granule cells in the lung

R01HL-19414-14 (CVA) GARDNER, TIMOTHY J JOHNS HOPKINS HOSPITAL 600 N WOLFE ST, BLALOCK 618 BALTIMORE, MD 21205 Protection of the myocardium during cardiac surgery

R01HL-19419-15A1 (SB) HORBETT, THOMAS A UNIVERSITY OF WASHINGTON SEATTLE, WA 98195 Cell and protein reactions with foreign materials

R37HL-19429-16 (HEM) STOSSEL, THOMAS P BRIGHAM AND WOMEN'S HOSPITAL 75 FRANCIS STREET BOSTON, MA 02115 Phagocytosis--ingestion in alveolar macrophages

R01HL-19454-16 (CVB) CHIEN, SHU UNIVERSITY OF CALIFORNIA 9500 GILMAN DRIVE/RM 0412 LA JOLLA, CA 92093 Studies of endothelium in relation to atherogenesis

R01HL-19680-13 (BPO) LAWLER, JAMES E DEPT. OF PSYCHOLOGY UNIVERSITY OF TENNESSEE KNOXVILLE, TN 37996 Neurobehavioral bases of stress-induced hypertension

P01HL-19717-15 (HLBA) FRANZBLAU, CARL BOSTON UNIVERSITY SCH OF MED 80 EAST CONCORD STREET BOSTON, MA 02118 Response of the lung to injury

P01HL-19717-15 0001 (HLBA) FRANZBLAU, CARL Response of the lung to injury Lung elastic tissue

P01HL-19717-15 0003 (HLBA) STONE, PHILIP J Response of the lung to injury Interactions of neutrophils with lung elastic fibers

P01HL-19717-15 0004 (HLBA) KAGAN, HERBERT M Response of the lung to injury Control of crosslinking in the injured lung

P01HL-19717-15 0008 (HLBA) SNIDER, GORDON L Response of the lung to injury Animal models of chronic airway injury

P01HL-19717-15 0023 (HLBA) BRODY, JEROME S Response of the lung to injury Matrix control of lung development and repair

P01HL-19717-15 0047 (HLBA) GOLDSTEIN, RONALD H. Response of the lung to injury Control of fibroblast functions by prostaglandins

P01HL-19717-15 0048 (HLBA) NILES, RICHARD Response of the lung to injury In vitro studies of airway epithelium

P01HL-19717-15 0049 (HLBA) FARBER, HARRISON Response of the lung to injury Lipid neutrophil chemoattractants from endothelial cells

P01HL-19717-15 0050 (HLBA) CENTER, DARIT M. Response of the lung to injury Mechanisms of T lymphocyte activation and chemotaxis

P01HL-19717-15 0051 (HLBA) SIMONS, ELIZABETH R Response of the lung to injury Monocyte and alveolar macrophage differentiation and activation mechanism

P01HL-19717-15 9001 (HLBA) VACCARO, CHARLES A. Response of the lung to injury CORE--Histology and electron microscopy

R01HL-19721-16 (PTHA) WEISSMANN, GERALD NEW YORK UNIV MEDICAL CENTER 550 FIRST AVENUE NEW YORK, NY 10016 Lung inflammation

P01HL-19737-15 (HLBA) FORSTER, ROBERT E, II UNIVERSITY OF PENNSYLVANIA PHILADELPHIA, PA 19104-6085 Cellular and molecular aspects of respiratory physiology

P01HL-19737-15 0012 (HLBA) CHANDER, AVINASH Cellular and molecular aspects of respiratory physiology Regulation of lung surfactant secretion

P01HL-19737-15 9001 (HLBA) FORSTER, ROBERT E Cellular and molecular

aspects of respiratory physiology CORE--Instrumentation facility
P01HL-19737-15 9004 (HLBA) ALBERTINE, KURT H. Cellular and molecular aspects of respiratory physiology Core--Morphology laboratory
P01HL-19737-15 0001 (HLBA) FISHER, ARON B Cellular and molecular aspects of respiratory physiology Uptake and reutilization of surfactant components
P01HL-19737-15 0002 (HLBA) COBURN, RONALD F Cellular and molecular aspects of respiratory physiology Pharmacomechanical coupling in airway smooth muscle
P01HL-19737-15 0004 (HLBA) FORSTER, ROBERT E Cellular and molecular aspects of respiratory physiology Carbon dioxide exchange kinetics in muscle, lung and blood
P01HL-19737-15 0009 (HLBA) COBURN, RONALD F Cellular and molecular aspects of respiratory physiology Oxygen chemoreception in vascular smooth muscle
P01HL-19737-15 0011 (HLBA) LAHIRI, SUKHAMAY Cellular and molecular aspects of respiratory physiology Chemoreception in the peripheral chemoreceptors
R01HL-19741-16 (PTHA) CASSELL, GAIL H UNIV OF ALABAMA AT BIRMINGHAM VOLKER HALL - 530 BIRMINGHAM, ALA 35294 Murine CRD--A model of chronic pulmonary inflammation
R01HL-19782-13 (CVA) LUCCHESI, BENEDICT R UNIVERSITY OF MICHIGAN 6322 MEDICAL SCIENCE BLDG I ANN ARBOR, MI 48109-0626 Pharmacologic studies on the ischemic heart
R01HL-19824-13 (SB) HELLUMS, JESSE D RICE UNIVERSITY POST OFFICE BOX 1892 HOUSTON, TX 77251 Mass transfer in the microcirculation
R01HL-19827-15 (ECS) BARTLETT, DONALD, JR DARTMOUTH MEDICAL SCHOOL HANOVER, N H 03756 Role of the upper airways in the control of breathing
R01HL-19982-15 (HEM) CASTELLINO, FRANCIS J UNIVERSITY OF NOTRE DAME DEPARTMENT OF CHEMISTRY NOTRE DAME, IND 46556 Blood coagulation protein-metal ion-lipid interactions
R01HL-20092-15 (HEM) MARTINEZ, JOSE THOMAS JEFFERSON UNIVERSITY 1015 WALNUT STREET PHILADELPHIA, PA 19107 Glycoproteins of blood coagulation
R01HL-20122-14 (RAP) SANT'AMBROGIO, GIUSEPPE UNIV OF TEXAS MEDICAL BRANCH 301 UNIVERSITY BOULEVARD GALVESTON, TX 77550 Operational mechanisms of airway receptors
R01HL-20142-15 (HEM) JONES, RICHARD T OREGON HLTH SCIS UNIVERSITY 3181 S W SAM JACKSON PARK ROAD PORTLAND, OR 97201-3098 Functional studies of abnormal human hemoglobins
R37HL-20161-15 (BNP) HISKEY, RICHARD G UNIVERSITY OF NORTH CAROLINA CONTRACT ADMINISTRATOR CHAPEL HILL, NC 27599 Role of gamma carboxyglutamic acid in blood coagulation
R01HL-20176-15 (CVB) RAPP, JOHN P MEDICAL COLLEGE OF OHIO C S 10008 TOLEDO, OHIO 43699 Biochemistry and genetics of hypertension
R37HL-20190-15 (NSS) BLOOR, COLIN M UNIV OF CALIFORNIA, SAN DIEGO DEPT OF PATHOLOGY, M-012 LA JOLLA, CA 92093 Pathogenesis of cardiac hypertrophy
R01HL-20197-15 (PTHA) GOSPODAROWICZ, DENIS J UNIVERSITY OF CALIFORNIA MED C THIRD & PARNASSUS, BOX 0128 SAN FRANCISCO, CA 94143 Maintenance and repair of vascular endothelium
R01HL-20251-14 (SAT) KIM, SUNG-WAN UNIVERSITY OF UTAH 421 WAKARA PARK SUITE 318 SALT LAKE CITY, UT 84108 A novel approach to nonthrombogenic polymer surfaces
R01HL-20344-15 (RAP) RANNELS, D EUGENE, JR PENNSYLVANIA STATE UNIVERSITY PO BOX 850 HERSHEY, PA 17033 Protein turnover in lung tissue
R01HL-20350-14 (BBCA) CRAVEN, BRYAN M UNIVERSITY OF PITTSBURGH PITTSBURGH, PA 15260 Lipid crystallography
R01HL-20356-15 (SAT) PIERCE, WILLIAM S PENNSYLVANIA STATE UNIVERSITY POST OFFICE BOX 850 HERSHEY, PA 17033 Development and evaluation of an artificial heart
R37HL-20366-16 (RAP) MASSARO, DONALD J GEORGETOWN UNIV. MEDICAL CTR PRECLINICAL SCIENCE BLDG WASHINGTON, D.C. 20007 Physiology of lung tolerance and adaptation
R37HL-20476-15 (MET) MILLER, THOMAS B, JR UNIVERSITY OF MASSACHUSETTS 55 LAKE AVENUE NORTH WORCESTER, MA 01655 Diabetes and regulation of cardiac glycogen metabolism
R37HL-20558-15 (CVA) COHEN, IRA S MD PHD S U N Y AT STONY BROOK HEALTH SCIENCES CENTER STONY BROOK, N Y 11794 Cardiac electrophysiology--Effects of ions and drugs
R01HL-20574-14A2 (RAP) ST JOHN, WALTER M DARTMOUTH MEDICAL SCHOOL HANOVER, NH 03756 Brain stem integration of chemoreceptor activity
P01HL-20592-15 (HLBA) FOZZARD, HARRY A HOSPITAL BOX 249 5841 SOUTH MARYLAND AVENUE CHICAGO, ILL 60637 Cell biology of cardiac and skeletal muscle
P01HL-20592-15 9001 (HLBA) PAGE, ERNEST Cell biology of cardiac and skeletal muscle Electron microscope facility--Core
P01HL-20592-15 9002 (HLBA) FORD, LINCOLN E Cell biology of cardiac and skeletal muscle CORE--Machine and electronic
P01HL-20592-15 0001 (HLBA) TAYLOR, EDWIN W Cell biology of cardiac and skeletal muscle Molecular mechanism of muscle contraction
P01HL-20592-15 0004 (HLBA) FOZZARD, HARRY A Cell biology of cardiac and skeletal muscle Excitation, conduction and contraction in heart
P01HL-20592-15 0006 (HLBA) PAGE, ERNEST Cell biology of cardiac and skeletal muscle Permeability and ultrastructure of cardiac nexuses
P01HL-20592-15 0015 (HLBA) ZAK, RADOVAN Cell biology of cardiac and skeletal muscle Turnover of myosin isoenzymes in cardiac muscle
P01HL-20592-15 0017 (HLBA) HANCK, DOROTHY A Cell biology of cardiac and skeletal muscle Kinetics of cardiac sodium channel
P01HL-20592-15 0018 (HLBA) ROGART, RICHARD Cell biology of cardiac and skeletal muscle Molecular studies of skeletal muscle sodium channels
P01HL-20592-15 0019 (HLBA) MAKIELSKI, JONATHAN C Cell biology of cardiac and skeletal muscle Drug interaction with the cardiac sodium channel
P01HL-20592-15 0020 (HLBA) JANUARY, CRAIG Cell biology of cardiac and skeletal muscle Calcium ion and cardiac contraction
R37HL-20598-16 (CVB) BACHE, ROBERT J UNIVERSITY OF MINNESOTA BOX 508 MAYO MINNEAPOLIS, MN 55455 The coronary vascular response to ischemia

PROJECT NO., ORGANIZATIONAL UNIT., INVESTIGATOR, ADDRESS, TITLE

R01HL-20605-14 (CVB) BOHLEN, HAROLD G INDIANA UNIV. SCH. OF MEDICINE 635 BARNHILL DRIVE INDIANAPOLIS, IN 46223 Microvascular behavior during intestinal absorption
R01HL-20634-14 (RAP) NADEL, ETHAN R JOHN B PIERCE LABORATORY, INC 290 CONGRESS AVENUE NEW HAVEN, CT 06519 Blood volume and venous return in thermal strain
R01HL-20648-12A2 (CVA) DOWNEY, JAMES M UNIVERSITY OF SOUTH ALABAMA MSB 3024 MOBILE, AL 36688 Physical factors and coronary flow
R01HL-20663-13 (RAP) JOHNSON, JOHN M UNIV OF TEXAS HLTH SCI CTR 7703 FLOYD CURL DRIVE SAN ANTONIO, TX 78284 Regulation of skin blood flow in man
R01HL-20749-12 (CVA) ANDERSON, PAGE A DUKE UNIV MEDICAL CENTER DURHAM, NC 27710 Developing heart--Biophysical aspects
R01HL-20754-14 (SAT) SU, JUDY Y UNIVERSITY OF WASHINGTON DEPT OF ANESTHESIOLOGY, RM-10 SEATTLE, WASH 98195 Mechanisms of anesthetic-induced myocardial depression
R01HL-20787-15 (BIO) NEEDLEMAN, PHILIP WASHINGTON UNIV MED SCH 660 SOUTH EUCLID AVENUE ST LOUIS, MO 63110 Eicosanoids in cellular function and disease
R01HL-20827-14 (CVA) DELLSPERGER, KEVIN C MD PHD UNIVERSITY OF IOWA HOSP & CLIN IOWA CITY, IA 52242 Effects of hypertrophy on the coronary circulation
R37HL-20899-15 (HEM) STAMATOYANNOPOULOS, GEORGE UNIVERSITY OF WASHINGTON DIV OF MEDICAL GENETICS, RG-25 SEATTLE, WA 98195 Cellular mechanisms of Hb F regulation
P01HL-20948-15 (HLBB) GOLDSTEIN, JOSEPH L UT SOTHWESTERN MEDICAL CTR 5323 HARRY HINES BLVD DALLAS, TX 75235-9046 Molecular basis of cholesterol metabolism
P01HL-20948-15 0008 (HLBB) BROWN, MICHAEL S Molecular basis of cholesterol metabolism Biochemical and characterization of the LDL receptor pathway
P01HL-20948-15 0009 (HLBB) BROWN, MICHAEL S Molecular basis of cholesterol metabolism Mevalonate metabolism, polyisoprenoid synthesis and cell growth
P01HL-20948-15 0010 (HLBB) BROWN, MICHAEL S Molecular basis of cholesterol metabolism Scavenger cell pathway for lipoprotein degradation
P01HL-20948-15 0011 (HLBB) GOLDSTEIN, JOSEPH L Molecular basis of cholesterol metabolism Genetic analysis of the LDL receptor pathway
P01HL-20948-15 9001 (HLBB) GOLDSTEIN, JOSEPH L Molecular basis of cholesterol metabolism Tissue culture core laboratory
P01HL-20948-15 9002 (HLBB) ANDERSON, RICHARD G Molecular basis of cholesterol metabolism Microscopy core laboratory
P01HL-20984-15 (HLBA) MORKIN, EUGENE MS BS UNIVERSITY OF ARIZONA 1501 NORTH CAMPBELL AVENUE TUCSON, ARIZ 85724 Cellular mechanisms in cardiac hypertrophy
P01HL-20984-15 0001 (HLBA) MORKIN, EUGENE Cellular mechanisms in cardiac hypertrophy Contractile proteins in cardiac hypertrophy
P01HL-20984-15 0005 (HLBA) ROESKE, WILLIAM R Cellular mechanisms in cardiac hypertrophy Neurohumoral receptors in cardiac growth, hypertension, hypertrophy
P01HL-20984-15 0006 (HLBA) HARTSHORNE, DAVID J Cellular mechanisms in cardiac hypertrophy Mechanisms of contraction of arterial smooth muscle
P01HL-20984-15 0007 (HLBA) GOLDMAN, STEVEN Cellular mechanisms in cardiac hypertrophy Regulation of cardiac performance in normal and failing hearts
P01HL-20984-15 9003 (HLBA) GOLDMAN, STEVEN Cellular mechanisms in cardiac hypertrophy Autonomic and reflex control of peripheral circulation in hyperthyroidism--Core
P01HL-20984-15 9004 (HLBA) BAHL, JOSEPH Cellular mechanisms in cardiac hypertrophy Mice, hearts, and cells culture core
P60HL-20985-14 (SRC) MENTZER, WILLIAM C, JR SAN FRANCISCO GENERAL HOSPITAL 1001 POTRERO AVENUE SAN FRANCISCO, CA 94110 Northern California comprehensive sickle cell center
P60HL-20985-14 0017 (SRC) CLASTER, SUSAN Northern California comprehensive sickle cell center
P60HL-20985-14 0018 (SRC) PERRINE, SUSAN Northern California comprehensive sickle cell center The fetal to sickle hemoglobin switch in infancy
P60HL-20985-14 0019 (SRC) VICHINSKY, ELLIOT Northern California comprehensive sickle cell center Blood transfusion program
P60HL-20985-14 0020 (SRC) GAD, MARSHA Northern California comprehensive sickle cell center Family functioning and management of sickle cell disease
P60HL-20985-14 9001 (SRC) MENTZER, WILLIAM C. Northern California comprehensive sickle cell center Core--Testing program
P60HL-20985-14 9002 (SRC) MENTZER, WILLIAM C. Northern California comprehensive sickle cell center Core--Counseling program
P60HL-20985-14 9003 (SRC) HURST, DEBORAH Northern California comprehensive sickle cell center Core--Education program
P60HL-20985-14 9004 (SRC) MENTZER, WILLIAM C. Northern California comprehensive sickle cell center Core-Patient services
P60HL-20985-14 0002 (SRC) WARA, DIANE W Northern California comprehensive sickle cell center The immune response in patients with sickle cell disease
P60HL-20985-14 0004 (SRC) CLARK, MARGARET R Northern California comprehensive sickle cell center Red cell volume maintenance in sickle cell disease
P60HL-20985-14 0005 (SRC) EMBURY, STEPHEN H Northern California comprehensive sickle cell center Thallasemic hemoglobin synthesis and sickle pathophysiology
P60HL-20985-14 0015 (SRC) RUBIN, EDWARD M. Northern California comprehensive sickle cell center Construction of transgenic mouse model of sickle cell disease
P60HL-20985-14 0016 (SRC) LUBIN, BERTRAM H. Northern California comprehensive sickle cell center Critical responses of sickle red blood cell to specific organ environments
R01HL-20989-14 (RAP) WANNER, ADAM MOUNT SINAI MEDICAL CENTER 4300 ALTON ROAD MIAMI, FL 33140 Pathophysiology of bronchial asthma
P50HL-21006-15 (SRC) GOODMAN, DE WITT S COLUMBIA UNIVERSITY 630 WEST 168TH ST., RM 9-510 NEW YORK, N Y 10032 Specialized center of research in atherosclerosis

PROJECT NO., ORGANIZATIONAL UNIT., INVESTIGATOR, ADDRESS, TITLE

P50HL-21006-15 0003 (SRC) GOODMAN, DE WITT S Specialized center of research in atherosclerosis Vitamin A transport and retinol-binding protein metabolism
P50HL-21006-15 0007 (SRC) TALL, ALAN R Specialized center of research in atherosclerosis Cholesteryl ester metabolism in hyperlipidemia and atherosclerosis
P50HL-21006-15 0008 (SRC) GLICKMAN, ROBERT M Specialized center of research in atherosclerosis The intestine and HDL metabolism
P50HL-21006-15 0009 (SRC) KAPLAN, KAREN L Specialized center of research in atherosclerosis Relation between hemostatic system and atherosclerosis
P50HL-21006-15 0010 (SRC) GINSBERG, HENRY N Specialized center of research in atherosclerosis heterogeneity of VLDL metabolism
P50HL-21006-15 0011 (SRC) GOLDBERG,IRA J Specialized center of research in atherosclerosis Human lipoprotein lipase
P50HL-21006-15 0012 (SRC) DECKELBAUM, RICHARD J Specialized center of research in atherosclerosis Plasma LDL remodeling--Effects on lipid transfer and apoprotein b
P50HL-21006-15 0013 (SRC) CANNON, PAUL J Specialized center of research in atherosclerosis Vascular eicosanoids and atherosclerosis
P50HL-21006-15 0014 (SRC) WITTE, LARRY D Specialized center of research in atherosclerosis Mitogens and cell biology of the arterial wall
P50HL-21006-15 9001 (SRC) GINSBERG, HENRY N Specialized center of research in atherosclerosis Clinical core
P50HL-21006-15 9002 (SRC) GINSBERG, HENRY N Specialized center of research in atherosclerosis Lipid laboratory core
P50HL-21006-15 9003 (SRC) DELL, RALPH B Specialized center of research in atherosclerosis Biomathematics/biostatistics core
P50HL-21006-15 9004 (SRC) WITTE, LARRY D Specialized center of research in atherosclerosis Tissue culture core
P50HL-21006-15 9005 (SRC) ALLAN, MAGGI Specialized center of research in atherosclerosis Core--Molecular biology
R01HL-21010-15 (EDC) STAMLER, JEREMIAH NORTHWESTERN UNIVERSITY MED SC 680 N LAKE SHORE DR CHICAGO, IL 60611 Epidemiology of cardiovascular and non-cardiovascular risks
P01HL-21016-15 (HLBB) NAGEL, RONALD L ALBERT EINSTEIN COLLEGE OF MED 1300 MORRIS PARK AVENUE BRONX, N Y 10461 Sickle cell anemia and other hemoglobinopathies
P01HL-21016-15 9003 (HLBB) KAUL, D K Sickle cell anemia and other hemoglobinopathies CORE--Microcirculatory techniques
P01HL-21016-15 9004 (HLBB) EISINGER, JOSEF Sickle cell anemia and other hemoglobinopathies CORE--Fluorescence laboratory
P01HL-21016-15 0017 (HLBB) NAGEL, RONALD L Sickle cell anemia and other hemoglobinopathies Malaria and the red cell
P01HL-21016-15 0018 (HLBB) KAUL, D K Sickle cell anemia and other hemoglobinopathies Sickle cell adhesion during shear flow
P01HL-21016-15 0019 (HLBB) FABRY, M Sickle cell anemia and other hemoglobinopathies Vasoocclusion and sickle cell anemia
P01HL-21016-15 0020 (HLBB) COSTANTINI, F Sickle cell anemia and other hemoglobinopathies Identification of enhancer 3 for adult beta globin gene
P01HL-21016-15 0021 (HLBB) BOOKCHIN, R M Sickle cell anemia and other hemoglobinopathies Membrane transport and lipid structure-dynamics in red cells
P01HL-21016-15 9001 (HLBB) NAGEL, RONALD L Sickle cell anemia and other hemoglobinopathies CORE--Hereditary clinic
R01HL-21066-15 (ECS) CAMPBELL, WILLIAM B UNIVERSITY OF TEXAS 5323 HARRY HINES BLVD DALLAS, TX 75235-9041 Angiotensin and eicosanoid control of aldosterone
R01HL-21159-13 (PTHA) OU, LO-CHANG DARTMOUTH MEDICAL SCHOOL HANOVER, NH 03756 Pathophysiological effects of hypoxia
R01HL-21179-13 (PHY) CALA, PETER M UNIVERSITY OF CALIFORNIA DEPARTMENT OF HUMAN PHYSIOLOGY DAVIS, CALIF 95616 Fundamental and functional aspects of Na/H exchange
R37HL-21195-15 (PHY) HARTZELL, H CRISS, JR EMORY UNIVERSITY ATLANTA, GA 30322 Mechanisms of action of acetylcholine in heart
R01HL-21257-15 (RAP) OREM, JOHN M TEXAS TECH HEALTH SCIS CENTER LUBBOCK, TX 79430 Behavioral control of breathing
R01HL-21276-13 (RNM) DEUTSCH, EDWARD A UNIVERSITY OF CINCINNATI CINCINNATI, OH 45221-0172 Development of 99-mtc myocardial imaging agents
R01HL-21370-13 (BM) CALDERONE, RICHARD A GEORGETOWN UNIV SCH OF MED 3900 RESERVOIR RD N W/MED/DENT WASHINGTON, DC 20007 Pathogenesis of endocarditis caused by candida albicans
R01HL-21403-12 (HEM) SHUMAN, MARC A UNIVERSITY OF CALIFORNIA 1282 MOFFITT BOX 0128 SAN FRANCISCO, CALIF 94143 Cellular regulation of blood clotting
R01HL-21429-14 (PTHA) COLTON, CLARK K MASSACHUSETTS INST OF TECH 77 MASSACHUSETTS AVENUE CAMBRIDGE, MASS 02139 Transport of LDL in arterial wall
R01HL-21435-13 (CVB) YOUNG, DAVID B UNIV OF MISSISSIPPI MED CTR 2500 NORTH STATE STREET JACKSON, MISS 39216-4505 Control cardiovascular and renal effects of potassium
R01HL-21462-13A1 (CVA) CAMPBELL, KENNETH B WASHINGTON STATE UNIVERSITY PULLMAN, WA 99164-6520 Ventricle artery interaction--Measurement/prediction
R37HL-21498-15 (ECS) GRANGER, HARRIS J TEXAS A & M UNIVERSITY BOX 3578 COLLEGE STATION, TX 77843 Pathophysiology of edema
R01HL-21544-15 (HEM) GRIFFIN, JOHN H SCRIPPS CLINIC & RES FDN 10666 NORTH TORREY PINES ROAD LA JOLLA, CALIF 92037 Proteins of coagulation pathways
R37HL-21568-15 (NSS) RYAN, UNA S WASHINGTON UNIV SCHOOL OF MED 4960 AUDUBON AVENUE ST. LOUIS, MO 63110 Cell biology of pulmonary endothelium
R01HL-21644-14 (PBC) MOSHER, DEANE F, JR MEDICAL SCIENCES CTR 4459 1300 UNIVERSITY AVENUE MADISON, WI 53706 Studies of fibronectin and related glycoproteins
K06HL-21670-28 (NSS) COMSTOCK, GEORGE W JOHNS HOPKINS UNIVERSITY 615 NORTH WOLFE STREET BALTIMORE, MD 21205 Follow-up studies of cardiorespiratory disease
R37HL-21676-15 (NSS) GOLDWASSER, EUGENE UNIVERSITY OF CHICAGO 920 EAST 58TH STREET CHICAGO, IL 60637 Erythropoietin--Purification, properties, biogenesis

PROJECT NO., ORGANIZATIONAL UNIT., INVESTIGATOR, ADDRESS, TITLE

R37HL-21788-12 (PHRA) ARNSDORF, MORTON F UNIVERSITY OF CHICAGO 970 E 58TH ST CHICAGO, IL 60637 Electropharmacologic actions of antiarrhythmic drugs
R01HL-21791-14 (BBCA) INGHAM, KENNETH C AMERICAN RED CROSS HOLLAND LAB 15601 CRABBS BRANCH WAY ROCKVILLE, MD. 20855 Physical chemistry of therapeutic plasma proteins
R37HL-21851-14 (NSS) KONTOS, HERMES A VIRGINIA COMMONWEALTH UNIVERSI BOX 281, MCV STATION RICHMOND, VA 23298-0001 Cerebral microcirculation in experimental hypertension
R37HL-21860-31 (PHRA) FURCHGOTT, ROBERT F SUNY HLTH SCI CTR AT BROOKLYN 450 CLARKSON AVE, BOX 29 BROOKLYN, N Y 11203 Mechanisms of action of vasodilator agents
R01HL-21872-14 (CVB) BACHE, ROBERT J UNIVERSITY OF MINNESOTA BOX 508 MINNEAPOLIS, MN 55455 Myocardial perfusion in the hypertrophied heart
R01HL-21906-14 (SRC) FARQUHAR, JOHN W STANFORD CENTER 1000 WELCH RD PALO ALTO, CA 94304 Stanford five city multifactor risk reduction study
R01HL-21922-14 (PHY) KASS, ROBERT S UNIV OF ROCHESTER 601 ELMWOOD AVE BOX 642 ROCHESTER, NY 14627-8642 Modulation of ion channels in the heart
R01HL-22050-14 (PB) CAPALDI, RODERICK A UNIVERSITY OF OREGON EUGENE, OR 97403 Organization of succinic oxidase in heart
R01HL-22149-14 (PTHA) BAUMBACH, GARY L UNIVERSITY OF IOWA 120 MEDICAL LABS IOWA CITY, IA 52242 Morphological examination of brain vessels
R01HL-22170-12 (NLS) WAKADE, ARUN R WAYNE STATE UNIVERSITY 540 E CANFIELD AVE/SCOTT HALL DETROIT, MI 48201 Mechanism of catecholamine secretion
R37HL-22174-14 (GEN) TZAGOLOFF, ALEXANDER A COLUMBIA UNIVERSITY NEW YORK, N Y 10027 Assembly of membranes in heart and yeast mitochondria
R01HL-22231-14 (PHY) SOLARO, R JOHN UNIVERSITY OF ILLINOIS PO BOX 6998, M/C 901 CHICAGO, IL 60680 Modulation of calcium control of cardiac myofibrils
R01HL-22236-12 (SB) GOLLAMUDI, RAMACHANDER UNIVERSITY OF TENNESSEE 26 SOUTH DUNLAP ST MEMPHIS, TN 38163 Surface-active antithrombotic agents for prostheses
R01HL-22242-14 (PBC) WILSON, IRWIN B UNIVERSITY OF COLORADO CAMPUS BOX 215 BOULDER, CO 80309-0215 The angiotensin I converting enzyme
R01HL-22252-14 (BMT) SMITH, KEVIN M UNIVERSITY OF CALIFORNIA 275 MRAK HALL DAVIS, CA 95616 Syntheses of labeled hemes for protein NMR studies
R37HL-22273-14 (TOX) FUNG, HO-LEUNG S U N Y AT BUFFALO PO BOX 9 AMHERST, N Y 14260 Nitrovasodilator pharmacokinetics and vascular action
R01HL-22289-13 (HEM) LOSKUTOFF, DAVID J RESEARCH INST / SCRIPPS CLINIC 10666 NORTH TORREY PINES ROAD LA JOLLA, CA 92037 Endothelial cell mediated fibrinolysis
R01HL-22325-14 (BBCB) PETERS, KEVIN UNIVERSITY OF COLORADO CAMPUS BOX 215 BOULDER, CO 80309-0215 Thermodynamics of binding reactions in respiratory proteins
R01HL-22418-14 (RAP) HARPER, RONALD M UNIVERSITY OF CALIFORNIA 405 HILGARD AVE LOS ANGELES, 90024-1763 Neural control of cardiorespiratory function
R01HL-22461-12 (BBCB) LEHRER, SHERWIN S BOSTON BIOMEDICAL RESEARCH INS 20 STANIFORD STREET BOSTON, MA 02114 Tropomyosin and myosin interaction in muscle
R01HL-22469-13 (HEM) CLEMONS, GISELA K UNIVERSITY OF CALIFORNIA LAWRENCE BERKELEY LABORATORY BERKELEY, CALIF 94720 Radioassay of erythropoietin
R01HL-22484-14 (CVA) MARTIN, PAUL J MT SINAI MEDICAL CENTER ONE MT SINAI DRIVE CLEVELAND, OH 44106 Neural control of cardiac conduction and excitation
R37HL-22512-14 (RNM) HARTLEY, CRAIG J METHODIST HOSPITAL 6535 FANNIN ST HOUSTON, TX 77030 Ultrasonic instrumentation for cardiovascular studies
R01HL-22544-13 (CVB) OPARIL, SUZANNE UNIV OF ALABAMA AT BIRMINGHAM 1012 ZEIGLER RESEARCH BUILDING BIRMINGHAM, ALA 35294 Mechanisms of angiotensin generation and metabolism
R37HL-22549-15 (RAP) TAYLOR, AUBREY E UNIVERSITY OF SOUTH ALABAMA COLLEGE OF MEDICINE MOBILE, AL 36688 Transport across alveolar capillary membrane
R01HL-22559-11 (SB) ENGELMAN, RICHARD M UNIVERSITY OF CONNECTICUT 263 FARMINGTON AVE FARMINGTON, CT 06030 Myocardial preservation during ischemic arrest
R01HL-22562-10A2 (CVA) JOYNER, RONALD W EMORY UNIVERSITY 2040 RIDGEWOOD DRIVE, N E ATLANTA, GA 30322 Mechanisms of cardiac action potential propagation
R37HL-22563-15 (ECS) DUNN, MICHAEL J UINIVERSITY HOSPITALS 2074 ABINGTON ROAD CLEVELAND, OH 44106 Prostaglandins, the kidney and hypertension
R01HL-22573-14 (NEUA) ZERVAS, NICHOLAS T MASSACHUSETTS GENERAL HOSPITAL FRUIT STREET BOSTON, MA 02114 Treatment of postsurgical vasoconstriction
R01HL-22582-14 (IMS) HALONEN, MARILYN J UNIVERSITY OF ARIZONA HSC COLLEGE OF MEDICINE TUCSON, AR 85724 Pulmonary and circulatory alterations induced by IgE
P01HL-22619-14 (HLBA) SCHWARTZ, ARNOLD UNIVERSITY OF CINCINNATI 231 BETHESDA AVENUE CINCINNATI, OHIO 45267-0575 Cellular mechanisms of heart failure
P01HL-22619-14 0018 (HLBA) SOLARO, R. JOHN Cellular mechanisms of heart failure The activity and regulation of cardiac myofibrils in heart failure
P01HL-22619-14 0019 (HLBA) ROBBINS, JEFFREY Cellular mechanisms of heart failure Regulation of myosin heavy chain expression
P01HL-22619-14 0020 (HLBA) PAUL, RICHARD Cellular mechanisms of heart failure Mechanisms of calcium control of smooth muscle
P01HL-22619-14 9001 (HLBA) MILLARD, RONALD W Cellular mechanisms of heart failure CORE--Experimental pathological models
P01HL-22619-14 9002 (HLBA) WALLICK, EARL T Cellular mechanisms of

heart failure CORE--Medicinal chemistry and clinical intervention

P01HL-22619-14 9003 (HLBA) JOHNSON, CARL Cellular mechanisms of heart failure CORE--Computer facility

P01HL-22619-14 0001 (HLBA) LANE, LOIS K Cellular mechanisms of heart failure Cell membrane isolation and reconstitution

P01HL-22619-14 0002 (HLBA) COLLINS, JOHN Cellular mechanisms of heart failure Structure of sodium, potassium-adenosine triphosphatase

P01HL-22619-14 0003 (HLBA) SCHWARTZ, ARNOLD Cellular mechanisms of heart failure Modulation of action of cardiac glycosides

P01HL-22619-14 0004 (HLBA) WALLICK, EARL T Cellular mechanisms of heart failure Mechanism of action of Na, K-atpase

P01HL-22619-14 0005 (HLBA) POTTER, JAMES D Cellular mechanisms of heart failure Molecular mechanism of regulation of cardiac muscle contraction

P01HL-22619-14 0006 (HLBA) MANDEL, FREDERIC Cellular mechanisms of heart failure Phosphorylation of contractile proteins in cardiac muscle contraction

P01HL-22619-14 0008 (HLBA) DISALVO, JOSEPH Cellular mechanisms of heart failure Molecular mechanisms and differential contractile responsiveness in VSM

P01HL-22619-14 0009 (HLBA) WANG, TAITZER Cellular mechanisms of heart failure Sarcoplasmic reticulum in cardiac, skeletal and smooth muscle

P01HL-22619-14 0011 (HLBA) JACKSON, RICHARD L Cellular mechanisms of heart failure Lipoproteins and apolipoproteins reaction with lipoprotein lipase

P01HL-22619-14 0013 (HLBA) BROWN, TRUMAN R Cellular mechanisms of heart failure P31-NMR detection of metabolic characteristics of acute myocardial ischemia

P01HL-22619-14 0014 (HLBA) MILLARD, RONALD W Cellular mechanisms of heart failure Membrane lipid alterations in myocardial ischemia & infarction

P01HL-22619-14 0015 (HLBA) SCHWARTZ, ARNOLD Cellular mechanisms of heart failure Mechanisms of organic calcium channel modulators

P01HL-22619-14 0016 (HLBA) LINGREL, JERRY B. Cellular mechanisms of heart failure Na k ATPase genes and their expression

P01HL-22619-14 0017 (HLBA) BRYANT, SHIRLEY Cellular mechanisms of heart failure Mechanisms of calcium channel modulators on skeletal muscle

P01HL-22633-14 (HLBB) PHILLIPS, MICHAEL C THE MEDICAL COLL OF PENN 3300 HENRY AVENUE PHILADELPHIA, PA 19129 Cellular and molecular biology of lipoprotein metabolism

P01HL-22633-14 0001 (HLBB) MARSH, JULIAN B Cellular and molecular biology of lipoprotein metabolism Regulation of the metabolism of plasma lipoproteins

P01HL-22633-14 0002 (HLBB) ROTHBLAT, GEORGE H Cellular and molecular biology of lipoprotein metabolism Cholesterol flux between cells and lipoproteins

P01HL-22633-14 0004 (HLBB) PHILLIPS, MICHAEL C Cellular and molecular biology of lipoprotein metabolism Structure-function relationships in serum lipoproteins

P01HL-22633-14 0006 (HLBB) GLICK, JANE Cellular and molecular biology of lipoprotein metabolism Cellular cholesteryl ester metabolism

P01HL-22633-14 0007 (HLBB) ROSS, A. CATHERINE Cellular and molecular biology of lipoprotein metabolism Retinol metabolism in liver and mammary gland

P01HL-22633-14 9001 (HLBB) ROTHBLAT, GEORGE H Cellular and molecular biology of lipoprotein metabolism Tissue culture core

R01HL-22654-12A1 (HEM) JOSEPHS, ROBERT 920 EAST 58TH ST CHICAGO, IL 60637 Molecular structure of sickle cell fibers

R01HL-22682-14 (PC) TALL, ALAN R COLUMBIA UNIVERSITY 630 WEST 168TH STREET NEW YORK, NY 10032 Structure and function of high density lipoproteins

R37HL-22828-14 (CVA) DOBSON, JAMES G, JR UNIVERSITY OF MASSACHUSETTS 55 LAKE AVENUE NORTH WORCESTER, MA 01655 Adenosine and catecholamine interaction in the heart

R01HL-22996-14 (PC) KRESS, LAWRENCE F ROSWELL PARK MEMORIAL INSTITUT 666 ELM STREET BUFFALO, N Y 14263 Venom proteases--Action on plasma protease inhibitors

R01HL-23016-13 (SAT) ESKIN, SUZANNE G UNIV OF TEXAS HLTH SCIS CTR 6431 FARNIN HOUSTON, TX 77030 Effects of flow and pressure on cultured endothelial cells

R01HL-23081-11 (ECS) JOSE, PEDRO A GEORGETOWN UNIVERSITY HOSPITAL 3800 RESERVOIR ROAD, NW WASHINGTON, D.C. 20007 Ontogeny of renal dopamine receptors

R01HL-23217-12 (RAP) RORIE, DUANE K MAYO FOUNDATION 200 FIRST STREET SOUTHWEST ROCHESTER, MINN 55905 Pulmonary artery neuroeffector junctions

R01HL-23306-13 (PHY) HOSEY, M MARLENE NORTHWESTEN UNIV MED SCHOOL 303 E CHICAGO AVENUE CHICAGO, IL 60611 Membrane phosphorylation in the developing myocardium

R01HL-23312-14 (ECS) OVERBECK, HENRY W WEST VIRGINIA UNIVERSITY HEALTH SCIENCES CTR NORTH MORGANTOWN, W VA 26506 Hemodynamics and vasoactivity in hypertension

R01HL-23315-13 (CVB) SANTIAGO, TEODORO V CMDNJ RUTGERS MEDICAL SCHOOL P O BOX 101 PISCATAWAY, NJ 08854 Respiratory consequences of opiates

R01HL-23502-12 (ECS) HALL, JOHN E UNIV OF MISSISSIPPI MED. CTR. 2500 N STATE STREET JACKSON, MISS 39216 Hormonal control of renal function

P50HL-23584-13 (SRC) MOSER, KENNETH M UNIV OF CA, SAN DIEGO 225 DICKINSON STREET SAN DIEGO, CALIF 92103 Pulmonary SCOR--Adult respiratory failure

P50HL-23584-13 0001 (SRC) COCHRANE, CHARLES G Pulmonary SCOR--Adult respiratory failure Biochemical mechanisms in pulmonary inflammation

P50HL-23584-13 0007 (SRC) SPRAGG, ROGER G Pulmonary SCOR--Adult respiratory failure Clinical models of the adult respiratory distress syndrome

P50HL-23584-13 0008 (SRC) MERRITT, T ALLEN Pulmonary SCOR--Adult respiratory failure Effects of inflammation on surfactant treatment of ARDS

P50HL-23584-13 9001 (SRC) SPRAGG, ROGER G Pulmonary SCOR--Adult respiratory failure Core--Clinical

P50HL-23584-13 9002 (SRC) COCHRANE, CHARLES G Pulmonary SCOR--Adult respiratory failure Core--Biochemistry

P50HL-23584-13 9003 (SRC) BLOOR, COLIN M Pulmonary SCOR--Adult respiratory failure Core--Pathology

R01HL-23597-10 (CVA) ASHRAF, MUHAMMAD UNIV OF CINCINNATI MED CTR 231 BETHESDA AVE CINCINNATI, OH 45267 Myocardial ischemic injury--Modification by drug therapy

R01HL-23603-14 (PTHA) WIENER, JOSEPH WAYNE STATE UNIVERSITY 540 EAST CANFIELD DETROIT, MICH 48201 Pathogenesis of hypertensive cardiovascular disease

R01HL-23615-14 (CTY) HARTSHORNE, DAVID J UNIVERSITY OF ARIZONA TUCSON, ARIZ 85721 Biochemistry of contractile proteins

R01HL-23629-12 (SRC) CARLETON, RICHARD A MEMORIAL HOSPITAL/RHODE ISLAND 111 BREWSTER ST PAWTUCKET, R I 02860 Pawtucket heart health program

R01HL-23632-12 (PHRA) SCHIMERLIK, MICHAEL I OREGON STATE UNIVERSITY WENIGER 535 CORVALLIS, OR 97331-6503 Characterization of heart atrial muscarinic receptor

R01HL-23714-12 (HEM) KAPLAN, ALLEN P SUNY AT STONY BROOK HEALTH SCIENCES CTR, T16 STONY BROOK, NY 11794 Initiation of coagulation and fibrinolysis in man

R01HL-23727-13 (SRC) BLACKBURN, HENRY W UNIVERSITY OF MINNESOTA 611 BEACON STREET S E MINNEAPOLIS, MN 55455 Community surveillance of cardiovascular disease

R01HL-23728-12 (SB) HOCHMUTH, ROBERT M DUKE UNIVERSITY AND MATERIALS SCIENCE DURHAM, NC 27706 Dissipation in red cells and red cell membrane

R01HL-23787-13 (BBCB) HUESTIS, WRAY H STANFORD UNIVERSITY DEPARTMENT OF CHEMISTRY STANFORD, CALIF 94305 Cell-vesicle interactions

R01HL-24020-10A2 (SB) SEFTON, MICHAEL V UNIVERSITY OF TORONTO TORONTO ONTARIO, CANADA M5S 1A Surface modified materials - blood interaction

R01HL-24046-12 (SB) COOPER, STUART L UNIVERSITY OF WISCONSIN MADISON, WI 53706 In-vivo evaluation of surface-induced thrombogenesis

R37HL-24061-13 (GMA) MOSBACH, ERWIN H BETH ISRAEL MEDICAL CTR FIRST AVE AT 16TH ST NEW YORK, NY 10003 Role of intestinal bacteria in steroid metabolism

R01HL-24066-13 (HEM) PIZZO, SALVATORE V DUKE UNIVERSITY MEDICAL CTR BOX 3712 DURHAM, NC 27710 Cell receptors in coagulation and atherogenesis

P01HL-24075-13 (HLBA) CLEMENTS, JOHN A UNIVERSITY OF CALIFORNIA 1327 MOFFITT HOSPITAL SAN FRANCISCO, CALIF 94143 Control and disorders of pulmonary alveolar stability

P01HL-24075-13 0001 (HLBA) GOERKE, JON Control and disorders of pulmonary alveolar stability Biophysical properties of pulmonary surfactant

P01HL-24075-13 0003 (HLBA) WILLIAMS, MARY C Control and disorders of pulmonary alveolar stability Structural studies of lung cells and their secretions

P01HL-24075-13 0004 (HLBA) DOBBS, LELAND G Control and disorders of pulmonary alveolar stability Metaboism and functions of alvedlar type II cells

P01HL-24075-13 0005 (HLBA) BALLARD, PHILIP L Control and disorders of pulmonary alveolar stability Regulation of surfactant synthesis and secretion in fetal lung

P01HL-24075-13 0006 (HLBA) CLEMENTS, JOHN A Control and disorders of pulmonary alveolar stability Control of lung surfactant turnover

P01HL-24075-13 0007 (HLBA) HAWFOOD, SAMUEL Control and disorders of pulmonary alveolar stability Structure and function of pulmonary surfactant proteins

P01HL-24075-13 9001 (HLBA) MC DONALD, DONALD M Control and disorders of pulmonary alveolar stability Core--Microscopy

P01HL-24075-13 9002 (HLBA) CLEMENTS, JOHN A Control and disorders of pulmonary alveolar stability Core--Art and photographic services

P01HL-24075-13 9003 (HLBA) CLEMENTS, JOHN A Control and disorders of pulmonary alveolar stability Core--Electronics facility

R01HL-24103-13 (CVB) CABOT, JOHN B S U N Y AT STONY BROOK NEUROBIOL & BEHAVIOR DEPTS STONY BROOK, N Y 11794-5230 Neural mechanisms of central cardiovascular control

R01HL-24111-13 (CVB) FINK, GREGORY D MICHIGAN STATE UNIVERSITY EAST LANSING, MI 48824-1317 Neural control of fluid homeostasis in hypertension

P01HL-24136-13 (HLBA) NADEL, JAY A UNIVERSITY OF CALIFORNIA, S F CARDIOVAS RES INST, BOX 0130 SAN FRANCISCO, CA 94143 Interaction of airway cells in health and disease

P01HL-24136-13 9001 (HLBA) MC DONALD, DONALD M Interaction of airway cells in health and disease CORE--Microscopy laboratory

P01HL-24136-13 9002 (HLBA) BRISCOE, M Interaction of airway cells in health and disease CORE--Illustration services

P01HL-24136-13 9003 (HLBA) RUTKIN, B Interaction of airway cells in health and disease CORE--Electronic facility

P01HL-24136-13 0001 (HLBA) BASBAUM, CAROL B Interaction of airway cells in health and disease Airway submucosal glands and intramural ganglia

P01HL-24136-13 0006 (HLBA) GOLD, WARREN M Interaction of airway cells in health and disease Regulation of biological expression of mast cells

P01HL-24136-13 0007 (HLBA) NADEL, JAY A Interaction of airway cells in health and disease Role of mast cell proteases in airway function

P01HL-24136-13 0008 (HLBA) BOUSHEY, HOMER A Interaction of airway cells in health and disease Bronchial hyperreactivity

P01HL-24136-13 0011 (HLBA) NADEL, JAY A Interaction of airway cells in health and disease Airway inflammation and smooth muscle

P01HL-24136-13 0012 (HLBA) MC DONALD, DONALD M Interaction of airway cells in health and disease Sensory nerves in airways inflammation

P01HL-24136-13 0013 (HLBA) NADEL, JAY A Interaction of airway cells in health and disease 15-Lipoxygenase in airway function

P01HL-24163-13 (SRC) HLASTALA, MICHAEL P UNIVERSITY OF WASHINGTON MAIL STOP RM-12 SEATTLE, WA 98195 Mechanisms of heterogeneity in the lung

PROJECT NO., ORGANIZATIONAL UNIT., INVESTIGATOR, ADDRESS, TITLE

P01HL-24163-13 0002 (SRC) BUTLER, JOHN Mechanisms of heterogeneity in the lung Vascular responses to pulmonary blood flow restriction
P01HL-24163-13 0007 (SRC) HLASTALA, MICHAEL P Mechanisms of heterogeneity in the lung Solubility/diffusion dependent ventilation heterogeneity
P01HL-24163-13 0012 (SRC) ALBERT, RICHARD K Mechanisms of heterogeneity in the lung Effects of prone position on regional ventilation and perfusion
P01HL-24163-13 0013 (SRC) ROBERTSON, H THOMAS Mechanisms of heterogeneity in the lung Regional determinants of lung blood and gas flows
P01HL-24163-13 0014 (SRC) LUCHTEL, DANIEL L Mechanisms of heterogeneity in the lung Corner vessel anatomy an function
P01HL-24163-13 9004 (SRC) ROBERTSON, H THOMAS Mechanisms of heterogeneity in the lung Analysis core
P01HL-24163-13 9005 (SRC) GRAHAM, MICHAEL M Mechanisms of heterogeneity in the lung Imaging core
R37HL-24232-13 (ECS) SPARKS, HARVEY V MICHIGAN STATE UNIVERSITY DEPT OF PHYSIOLOGY EAST LANSING, MICH 48824-1101 Dynamic control of coronary blood flow
R01HL-24264-13 (SSS) RILEY, DAVID J UMNDJ-ROBERT W JOHNSON MED SCH 675 HOES LANE RM C-B04/MED SCH PISCATAWAY, NJ 08854-5635 Cells and extracellular matrix in pulmonary hypertension
R01HL-24314-12 (CVB) WATSON, PHILIP D UNIVERSITY OF SOUTH CAROLINA SCHOOL OF MEDICINE COLUMBIA, SC 29208 Transcapillary water movement in skeletal muscle
R01HL-24347-11 (ECS) SAPRU, HREDAY N UMDNJ-NEW JERSEY MEDICAL SCHOO 185 SOUTH ORANGE AVENUE NEWARK, NJ 07103-2757 Cardiovascular actions of putative transmitters
R01HL-24349-13 (RAP) LINEHAN, JOHN H MARQUETTE UNIVERSITY 1515 W WISCONSIN AVENUE MILWAUKEE, WI 53233 Lung metabolism of vasoactive hormones
R01HL-24354-12 (PHRA) DANGMAN, KENNETH H COLUMBIA UNIVERSITY DEPT/PHARMACOLOGY NEW YORK, NY 10032 Drug effects on impulse initiation in the heart
R01HL-24382-13 (HEM) COHEN, CARL M ST ELIZABETH'S HOSPITAL 736 CAMBRIDGE ST BOSTON, MA 02135 Phosphorylation red cell membrane skeletal proteins
R01HL-24385-13 (HEM) BENZ, EDWARD J, JR 333 CEDAR STREET-WWW 403 NEW HAVEN, CT 06510-8056 Gene expression in normal & thalassemic red cell
R01HL-24415-13 (CTY) ENGEL, JAMES D NORTHWESTERN UNIVERSITY 2153 SHERIDAN ROAD EVANSTON, IL 60208 Expression of developmentally related avian genes
R37HL-24525-13 (NSS) HO, CHIEN CARNEGIE MELLON UNIVERSITY 4400 FIFTH AVENUE PITTSBURGH, PA 15213 Biophysical studies of hemoglobins and erythrocytes
R01HL-24526-13 (PB) CAPALDI, RODERICK A UNIVERSITY OF OREGON EUGENE, OREG 97403 Studies of ATP synthase
R01HL-24530-12 (HEM) LE BRETON, GUY C UNIVERSITY OF ILLINOIS 835 S WOLCOTT CHICAGO, IL 60612 Direct antagonism of the TXA2 blood platelet receptor
R01HL-24571-13 (RAP) PARKER, JAMES C UNIV OF SO ALABAMA/COLL OF MED 307 UNIVERSITY BLVD MOBILE, AL 36688 Fluid pressure and excluded volumes in lung
R01HL-24585-10A1 (ECS) ALLEN, JULIUS C BAYLOR COLLEGE OF MEDICINE ONE BAYLOR PLAZA HOUSTON, TX 77030 Pharmacologic basis of smooth muscle heterogeneity
R01HL-24606-13 (SB) JONES, JANICE L VA MEDICAL CENTER 50 IRVING ST, NW WASHINGTON, DC 20422 Defibrillator waveshape optimization
R01HL-24736-12 (NTN) RUDEL, LAWRENCE L WAKE FOREST UNIVERSITY 300 S HAWTHORNE RD WINSTON-SALEM, NC 27103 Nutrition and HDL metabolism in primate atherosclerosis
R01HL-24799-13 (ORTH) STERN, MICHAEL P UNIV OF TEXAS HLTH SCI CTR 7703 FLOYD CURL DRIVE SAN ANTONIO, TX 78284-7873 Diabetes and cardiovascular risk in Mexican Americans
R01HL-24855-11S1 (SSS) WILLIAMS, ROGER R UNIV OF UTAH RESEARCH PARK 410 CHIPETA WAY, ROOM 161 SALT LAKE CITY, UT 84108 Genetic and environmental determinants of hypertension
R01HL-24873-12 (MET) BENSADOUN, ANDRE CORNELL UNIVERSITY 321 SAVAGE HALL ITHACA, N Y 14853 Radioimmunoassay for human lipoprotein lipase
R01HL-24880-12 (CVB) CHURCHILL, PAUL C WAYNE STATE UNIV SCHOOL OF MED 540 EAST CANFIELD DETROIT, MICH 48201 Control of renin secretion
R01HL-24916-11 (SB) GARSON, ARTHUR, JR TEXAS CHILDREN'S HOSPITAL 6621 FANNIN HOUSTON, TX 77030 Model of dysrhythmias after congenital heart surgery
R01HL-24935-11 (CBY) BORG, THOMAS K UNIV OF SOUTH CAROLINA COLUMBIA, SC 29208 Characterization of the extracellular matrix of heart
R37HL-24962-12 (CVB) MARK, ALLYN L UNIVERSITY OF IOWA HOSPITALS CARDIOVASCULAR DIVISION IOWA CITY, IOWA 52242 Modulation of baroreceptor reflexes
R01HL-25015-10 (PTHA) KREUTZER, DONALD L UNIV OF CONNECTICUT HLTH CTR 263 FARMINGTON AVENUE FARMINGTON, CONN 06032 Response of pulmonary endothelium to injury
R01HL-25022-12A1 (END) DILLMANN, WOLFGANG H UCSD MEDICAL CENTER 225 DICKINSON STREET SAN DIEGO, CA 92103 Thyroid hormone action in the heart
R01HL-25055-10 (CVB) PACKER, MILTON MOUNT SINAI SCHOOL OF MEDICINE ONE GUSTAVE L LEVY PLACE NEW YORK, N Y 10029 Determinants of vasodilator response in heart failure
R01HL-25106-10 (RAD) WARD, WILLIAM F NORTHWESTERN UNIVERSITY 303 EAST CHICAGO AVENUE CHICAGO, IL 60611 Response of the pulmonary endothelium to injury
R01HL-25182-11A1 (TOX) LIMBIRD, LEE E VANDERBILT UNIVERSITY 1161 21ST AVENUE SOUTH NASHVILLE, TN 37232-6600 Basis for Na+ modulation of alpha2-receptor function
R01HL-25239-10 (SB) HILTNER, P ANNE CASE WESTERN RESERVE UNIVERSIT 2040 ADELBERT RD CLEVELAND, OH 44106 Long term biodegradation of elastomeric biomaterials

PROJECT NO., ORGANIZATIONAL UNIT., INVESTIGATOR, ADDRESS, TITLE

R01HL-25258-12 (TOX) HUXTABLE, RYAN J UNIVERSITY OF ARIZONA ARIZONA HLTH SCIENCES CENTER TUCSON, AZ 85724 Pyrolizidines and the lung-liver axis
R01HL-25316-12A1 (ECS) WONG, PATRICK Y-K NEW YORK MEDICAL COLLEGE VALHALLA, NY 10595 Eicosanoids blood vessels and hypertension
R37HL-25394-13 (ECS) MC GIFF, JOHN C NEW YORK MEDICAL COLLEGE VALHALLA, N Y 10595 Prostaglandins--Kinin, angiotensin interaction
R01HL-25404-10 (PTHA) HEBERT, LEE A OHIO STATE UNIVERSITY 1654 UPHAM DRIVE/RM N210 COLUMBUS, OH 43210-1228 The immune complex-mediated glomerulopathies
R01HL-25408-13 (PBC) LARGMAN, COREY VETERANS ADMIN MEDICAL CENTER 150 MUIR ROAD MARTINEZ, CALIF 94553 Panceatic elastase--structural control of activty
R37HL-25449-16 (CVB) LOEWY, ARTHUR D WASHINGTON UNIV SCH OF MED 660 SOUTH EUCLID AVENUE ST LOUIS , MO 63110 CNS autonomic pathways--central cardiovascular control
R01HL-25455-11A2 (HEM) SCHICK, PAUL K JEFFERSON MEDICAL COLLEGE 1015 WALNUT STREET PHILADELPHIA, PA 19107-5099 The structure and function of platelet membranes
R01HL-25478-09A2 (IMB) HERSCOWITZ, HERBERT B GEORGETOWN UNIVERSITY 3900 RESERVOIR ROAD, N W WASHINGTON, D C 20007 Regulation of lung immunopathology by macrophages
R01HL-25523-12 (SRC) LUEPKER, RUSSELL V UNIVERSITY OF MINNESOTA 611 BEACON STREET SE MINNEAPOLIS, MN 55455 Minnesota heart health program
R37HL-25552-13 (HEM) BEUTLER, ERNEST SCRIPPS CLINIC & RES FOUNDATIO 10666 NORTH TORREY PINES ROAD LA JOLLA, CALIF 92037 Formation and survival of red blood cells
R01HL-25575-11 (ECS) LEFER, ALLAN M 1020 LOCUST STREET PHILADELPHIA, PA 19107-6799 Thromboxanne and PAF analogs in ischemia-shock
P01HL-25596-12 (SRC) ROHEIM, PAUL S LOUISIANA STATE UNIV MED CTR 1542 TULANE AVENUE, RM. 638 NEW ORLEANS, LA 70112 Apolipoprotein metabolism--Regulation and function
P01HL-25596-12 0001 (SRC) HORNICK, CONRAD A Apolipoprotein metabolism--Regulation and function Endosomal lipoprotein metabolism
P01HL-25596-12 0002 (SRC) WONG, LAURENCE Apolipoprotein metabolism--Regulation and function Biogenesis of lipoproteins
P01HL-25596-12 0004 (SRC) LEFEVRE, MICHAEL Apolipoprotein metabolism--Regulation and function Interstitial fluid lipoprotein metabolism
P01HL-25596-12 0005 (SRC) ROHEIM, PAUL S Apolipoprotein metabolism--Regulation and function Human interstitial fluid metabolism
P01HL-25596-12 9002 (SRC) THOMPSON, JAMES J Apolipoprotein metabolism--Regulation and function Core--Immunochemistry and tissue culture
P01HL-25596-12 9003 (SRC) ROHEIM, PAUL S Apolipoprotein metabolism--Regulation and function Core--Developmental and lymph collection
R37HL-25629-12 (EDC) FERENCZ, CHARLOTTE UNIVERSITY OF MARYLAND 660 WEST REDWOOD ST BALTIMORE, MD 21201 Environmental risk factors in congenital heart disease
R01HL-25634-12 (MCHA) STILL, WILLIAM C, JR COLUMBIA UNIVERSITY BOX 663, HAVEMEYER HALL NEW YORK, NY 10027 Synthesis of cardiovascular polyether antibiotics
R01HL-25635-12 (MCHA) STORK, GILBERT COLUMBIA UNIVERSITY CHEMISTRY DEPT, BOX 666 NEW YORK, NY 10027 Syntheses of the hypotensive germine alkaloids
R01HL-25658-11 (ALY) HUGLI, TONY E RES INST OF SCRIPPS CLINIC 10666 N TORREY PINES ROAD LA JOLLA, CA 92037 Humoral factors in inflammation
R01HL-25661-10 (HEM) WALSH, PETER N TEMPLE UNIVERSITY SCH OF MED 3400 NORTH BROAD STREET PHILADELPHIA, PA 19140 Platelet interaction with cogulation factors IX & X
R01HL-25670-10 (HEM) SHORE, JOSEPH D HENRY FORD HOSPITAL 2799 W GRAND BOULEVARD DETROIT, MICH 48202 Molecular mechanisms of blood coagulation activation
R01HL-25675-12 (PHRA) LEDERER, WILLIAM J UNIVERSITY OF MARYLAND 660 WEST REDWOOD STREET BALTIMORE, MD 21201 Sodium-calcium exchange in heart muscle
R01HL-25767-12 (BEM) MATTHEWS, KAREN A WESTERN PSYCH INST & CLINIC 3811 O'HARA STREET PITTSBURGH, PA 15213 Antecedents of the type a behavior pattern
R01HL-25776-10 (PTHA) POLGAR, PETER R BOSTON UNIVERSITY 80 E CONCORD STREET BOSTON, MASS 02118 Regulation of prostaglandin synthesis by lung cells
R01HL-25779-12 (ECS) KAISER, LANA MICHIGAN STATE UNIVERSITY EAST LANSING, MICH 48824-1101 Mechanism of exercise hyperemia
R37HL-25785-13 (BIO) MURPHY, ROBERT C NATIONAL JEWISH CENTER 1400 JACKSON STREET DENVER, CO 80206-1997 Leukotrienes and slow reacting substance of anaphylaxis
P01HL-25816-11 (HLBA) STAUB, NORMAN C UNIVERSITY OF CALIFORNIA CARDIOVASCULAR RES INST.1327-M SAN FRANCISCO, CA 94143-0130 Pathophysiology of lung water and solute exchange
P01HL-25816-11 0002 (HLBA) MATTHAY, MICHAEL Pathophysiology of lung water and solute exchange Mechanisms of alveolar clearance
P01HL-25816-11 0003 (HLBA) STAUB, NORMAN C Pathophysiology of lung water and solute exchange Anatomy and physiology of caudal mediastinal lymph node
P01HL-25816-11 0004 (HLBA) BLAND, RICHARD D Pathophysiology of lung water and solute exchange Fluid filtration and microvascular permeability
P01HL-25816-11 0005 (HLBA) SIMON, ROGER P Pathophysiology of lung water and solute exchange Neurogenic pulmonary edema
P01HL-25816-11 0016 (HLBA) STAUB, NORMAN C Pathophysiology of lung water and solute exchange Pathophysiology of vascular injury
P01HL-25816-11 0017 (HLBA) LAI-FOOK, STEPHEN J Pathophysiology of lung water and solute exchange Mechanics of lung interstitium in lung fluid balance
P01HL-25816-11 0018 (HLBA) GOLDSTEIN, IRA M Pathophysiology of lung water and solute exchange In Vitro studies of pulmonary intravascular macrophages

PROJECT NO., ORGANIZATIONAL UNIT., INVESTIGATOR, ADDRESS, TITLE

P01HL-25816-11 9003 (HLBA) SCHULTZ, ELIZABETH Pathophysiology of lung water and solute exchange CORE--Technical services
P01HL-25816-11 9004 (HLBA) BRISCO, M H Pathophysiology of lung water and solute exchange CORE--Art and photography
P01HL-25816-11 9005 (HLBA) HUDSON, J Pathophysiology of lung water and solute exchange CORE--Electronics
R01HL-25820-10 (TOX) PRYOR, WILLIAM A LOUISIANA STATE UNIVERSITY BIODYNAMICS INSTITUTE BATON ROUGE, LA 70803 Tobacco smoke and automobile exhaust toxicology
R01HL-25822-12 (RAP) SCHNEEBERGER, EVELINE E MASSACHUSETTS GENERAL HOSPITAL FRUIT STREET BOSTON, MA 02114 Permeability of the lung to water soluble solutes
R01HL-25824-12 (CVB) BOHLEN, HAROLD G INDIANA UNIV. SCH. OF MEDICINE 635 BARNHILL DRIVE INDIANAPOLIS, IN 46202-5120 Microvascular characteristics of diabetes mellitus
P01HL-25830-11A1 (HLBA) CHERNIACK, NEIL S UNIVERSITY HOSP OF CLEVELAND 2074 ABINGTON ROAD CLEVELAND, OH 44106 Control of respiratory skeletal and smooth muscle
P01HL-25830-11A1 0001 (HLBA) CHERNIACK, NEIL S Control of respiratory skeletal and smooth muscle Central excitatory and depressive cardiorespiratory actions of hypoxia
P01HL-25830-11A1 0003 (HLBA) RICHARD, J MARTIN Control of respiratory skeletal and smooth muscle Neurochemical mechanisms that regulate airway function
P01HL-25830-11A1 0006 (HLBA) DEAL, E CHANDLER Control of respiratory skeletal and smooth muscle CNS effects on the airway smooth muscle
P01HL-25830-11A1 0007 (HLBA) BRUCE, EUGENE N Control of respiratory skeletal and smooth muscle Dynamics of respiratory neuromuscular control mechanisms
P01HL-25830-11A1 0008 (HLBA) MARTIN, PAUL J Control of respiratory skeletal and smooth muscle Cardiorespiratory interaction at the VMS
P01HL-25830-11A1 0009 (HLBA) STROHL, KINGMAN Control of respiratory skeletal and smooth muscle Mechanical function of the upper airway
P01HL-25830-11A1 0012 (HLBA) CHIEL, HILLEL J Control of respiratory skeletal and smooth muscle Neural network control of quasi-rhythmic behavior
P01HL-25830-11A1 0013 (HLBA) WHITTINGHAM, TIM S Control of respiratory skeletal and smooth muscle Cellular mechanisms of neuronal dysfunction
P01HL-25830-11A1 0014 (HLBA) KATZ, DAVID M Control of respiratory skeletal and smooth muscle Neural substrates in hypoxic excitation of breathing
P01HL-25830-11A1 0015 (HLBA) SUPINSKI, GERALD Control of respiratory skeletal and smooth muscle Phrenic afferent reflexes and diaphragm function
P01HL-25830-11A1 9005 (HLBA) KATZ, DAVID M Control of respiratory skeletal and smooth muscle CORE--Neuroanatomy and cellular neurochemistry
P01HL-25830-11A1 9006 (HLBA) ERNSBERGER, PAUL Control of respiratory skeletal and smooth muscle CORE--Molecular pharmacology
P01HL-25847-12 (HLBA) HOFFMAN, JULIEN I UNIV OF CALIF, SAN FRANCISCO 1315 MOFFITT HOSPITAL SAN FRANCISCO, CALIF 94143 Myocardial ischemia
P01HL-25847-12 0003 (HLBA) HOFFMAN, JULIEN I Myocardial ischemia Myocardial blood flow
P01HL-25847-12 0005 (HLBA) KARLINER, JOEL S Myocardial ischemia Receptor and biochemical regulation in ischemia and hypoxia
P01HL-25847-12 0006 (HLBA) COLERIDGE, JOHN C Myocardial ischemia Afferent reflex of cardiac nerve stimulated by myocardial ischemia
P01HL-25847-12 0007 (HLBA) MASSIE, BARRIE Myocardial ischemia Myocardial metabolic studies in ventricular hypertrophy
P01HL-25847-12 0008 (HLBA) BOTRINICK, ELIAS H Myocardial ischemia Myocardial ischemia, sympathetic innervation and electrical stability
P01HL-25847-12 0009 (HLBA) BRASCH, ROBERT C Myocardial ischemia Perfusion/blood volume contrast agents for MR imaging
P01HL-25847-12 9001 (HLBA) PAYNE, BRUCE D Myocardial ischemia Core--Radionuclide (microsphere) laboratory
P01HL-25847-12 9004 (HLBA) KARLINER, JOEL S Myocardial ischemia CORE--Biochemistry laboratory
R01HL-25848-12 (MCHA) DANISHEFSKY, SAMUEL J YALE UNIVERSITY 225 PROSPECT STREET NEW HAVEN, CT 06511-8118 New synthetic reactions for active principles
R01HL-25854-12 (MCHA) OVERMAN, LARRY E UNIVERSITY OF CALIFORNIA IRVINE, CA 92717 Synthesis of new cardiotonic and myotonic agents
R01HL-25861-12 (PHY) MOSS, RICHARD L REGENTS UNIVERSITY 470 NORTH CHARTER STREET MADISON, WIS 53706 Mechanical properties of Ca-activated heart muscle
R01HL-25869-10 (CVA) GLANTZ, STANTON A UNIVERSITY OF CALIFORNIA 505 PARNASSUS AVENUE SAN FRANCISCO, CALIF 94143 Cardiac mechanics
R01HL-25877-10 (CVB) BEALER, STEVEN L UNIV OF TENNESSEE, MEMPHIS 894 UNION AVE MEMPHIS, TENN 38163 Central control of sodium and cardiovascular homeostasis
R01HL-25934-11 (BMT) SUSLICK, KENNETH S UNIVERSITY OF ILLINOIS 505 S MATHEWS AVENUE URBANA, IL 61801 Synthetic analogues of heme proteins
R01HL-25942-09 (BBCB) TULINSKY, ALEXANDER MICHIGAN STATE UNIVERSITY EAST LANSING, MI 48824-1322 Crystallographic structures of kringles and gla-domains
R01HL-25951-11 (SB) RATNER, BUDDY D UNIVERSITY OF WASHINGTON, BF-1 SEATTLE, WA 98195 Surface and bulk structure of polyetherurethanes
R01HL-25973-11 (PTHA) MAJNO, GUIDO UNIV OF MASSACHUSETTS MED SCH 55 LAKE AVE NORTH WORCESTER, MA 01605 Pathophysiology of arterial stenosis
R37HL-26043-11A1 (PHY) STULL, JAMES T UNIVERSITY OF TEXAS 5323 HARRY HINES BLVD DALLAS, TX 75235-9040 Biochemical mechanisms of smooth muscle contraction
R01HL-26057-11 (CVA) KRANIAS, EVANGELIA G UNIV OF CINCINNATI COLL OF MED 231 BETHESDA AVENUE CINCINNATI, OH 45267-0575 Phosphorylation as a regulatory mechanism in heart
R01HL-26090-09 (SB) WEINBAUM, SHELDON CITY COLLEGE OF CUNY CONVENT AVE AT 138TH ST NEW YORK, NY 10031 Blood flow effects on tissue heat transfer

PROJECT NO., ORGANIZATIONAL UNIT., INVESTIGATOR, ADDRESS, TITLE

R01HL-26091-10 (RAP) ST JOHN, WALTER M DARTMOUTH MEDICAL SCHOOL HANOVER, NH 03756 Mechanisms and sites of ventilatory neurogenesis
R01HL-26148-12 (PBC) TRAVIS, JAMES UNIVERSITY OF GEORGIA DEPARTMENT OF BIOCHEMISTRY ATHENS, GA 30602 Proteolytic enzymes and inhibitors in lung desease
R01HL-26176-08 (RAP) RICHARDSON, CHARLES A UNIVERSITY OF CALIFORNIA 1386 HEALTH SCIENCES EAST SAN FRANCISCO, CA 94143 Brain stem respiratory pattern generation
R01HL-26205-11 (ECS) BELLER, GEORGE A UNIV OF VIRGINIA HLTH SCIS CTR BOX 158 CHARLOTTESVILLE, VA 22908 Assessment of myocardial perfusion & viability
R01HL-26257-11 (PTHA) O'FLAHERTY, JOSEPH T BOWMAN GRAY SCHOOL OF MED DEPT OF MEDICINE/300 S. HAWTHO WINSTON-SALEM, N C 27103 Arachidonate metabolites and neutrophil function
R37HL-26284-12 (NSS) STEWART, JOHN M UNIVERSITY OF COLORADO PO BOX B126 DENVER, CO 80262 Kinin system inhibitors
P50HL-26309-11 (SRC) ROBERTS, HAROLD R UNIV OF NC AT CHAPEL HILL DEPARTMENT OF MEDICINE CHAPEL HILL, N C 27599 SCOR in thrombosis
P50HL-26309-11 0008 (SRC) GREENBERG, CHARLES S SCOR in thrombosis Vascular transglutaminases and thrombosis
P50HL-26309-11 9001 (SRC) DEHMER, GREGORY J SCOR in thrombosis Core--Clinical
P50HL-26309-11 9002 (SRC) GRIGGS, THOMAS R SCOR in thrombosis Core--Animal
P50HL-26309-11 0002 (SRC) GRIGGS, THOMAS R SCOR in thrombosis Studies on the endothelium in relation to atherosclerosis
P50HL-26309-11 0003 (SRC) CLEMMONS, DAVID R SCOR in thrombosis Role of insulin-like growth factor binding proteins in muscle cell
P50HL-26309-11 0004 (SRC) WHITE, GILBERT C SCOR in thrombosis Intracellular messengers in platelet activation
P50HL-26309-11 0007 (SRC) DITTMAN, WILLIAM A SCOR in thrombosis Molecular biology of coagulation and endothelium
R01HL-26320-11 (ECS) COFFMAN, JAY D UNIVERSITY HOSPITAL 88 EAST NEWTON STREET BOSTON, MA 02118 Digital blood flow and vascular tone
P01HL-26335-11A1 (HLBB) SMALL, DONALD M BOSTON UNIV. SCHOOL OF MEDICIN 80 EAST CONCORD STREET BOSTON, MA 02118 Lipid physical chemistry in biology and pathology
P01HL-26335-11A1 0001 (HLBB) SHIPLEY, G GRAHAM Lipid physical chemistry in biology and pathology Structure and interactions of complex polar lipids
P01HL-26335-11A1 0002 (HLBB) SMALL, DONALD M Lipid physical chemistry in biology and pathology Physical chemistry of lipoprotein model systems
P01HL-26335-11A1 0003 (HLBB) ATKINSON, DAVID Lipid physical chemistry in biology and pathology Lipoprotein structure and molecular interactions
P01HL-26335-11A1 0007 (HLBB) HAMILTON, JAMES A Lipid physical chemistry in biology and pathology Interaction of polar lipids with membranes and proteins
P01HL-26335-11A1 9001 (HLBB) ATKINSON, DAVID Lipid physical chemistry in biology and pathology Core--physical equipment facilities
P01HL-26335-11A1 9002 (HLBB) TERCYAK, ANNA Lipid physical chemistry in biology and pathology Core--chemical and biochemical techniques
R01HL-26371-10 (CVB) NAVAR, L GABRIEL TULANE UNIVERSITY SCH OF MED 1430 TULANE AVENUE NEW ORLEANS, LA 70112 Renal functional derangements in hypertension
R01HL-26405-11 (PTHA) SCHWARTZ, STEPHEN M UNIVERSITY OF WASHINGTON PATHOLOGY DEPARTMENT SJ-60 SEATTLE, WA 98195 Endothelial injury in small vessels
R01HL-26441-11A1 (CLIN) GRANGER, DANIEL N LSU MEDICAL CENTER 1501 KINGS HIGHWAY, PO BOX 339 SHREVEPORT, LA 71130-3932 Transcapillary fluid exchange
R01HL-26499-10 (GMA) MECHAM, ROBERT P JEWISH HOSPITAL OF ST LOUIS 216 SOUTH KINGSHIGHWAY ST LOUIS, MO 63110 Extracellular matrix influences on elastogenesis
R01HL-26502-11 (MET) SIMONI, ROBERT D STANFORD UNIVERSITY STANFORD, CA 94305-5020 Cholesterol metabolism in compactin resistant cells
R01HL-26640-10 (SAT) FOKER, JOHN E UNIVERSITY HOSPITAL & CLINICS 420 DELAWARE ST S E MINNEAPOLIS, MN 55455 Adenosine metabolism in cardiac surgery
R01HL-26647-11 (RAP) FUNG, YUAN-CHENG B UNIVERSITY OF CALIFORNIA LA JOLLA, CA 92093-0411 Continuum mechanics in pulmonary physiology
R01HL-26710-10 (RAP) FISHER, ARON B UNIVERSITY OF PENNSYLVANIA 37TH & HAMITON WALK PHILADELPHIA, PA 19104 Choline and lung surfactant metabolism
R01HL-26807-11 (CVB) BELL, DONALD R ALBANY MED COLLEGE 47 NEW SCOTLAND AVENUE ALBANY, N Y 12208 Capillary and interstitial fluid and solute exchange
R01HL-26818-11 (HEM) WYKLE, ROBERT L WAKE FOREST UNIVERSITY 300 SOUTH HAWTHORNE ROAD WINSTON-SALEM, N C 27103 Metabolism of platelet activating factor
R01HL-26831-11 (PTHA) SWAIN, JUDITH L UNIVERSITY OF PENNSYLVANIA 37TH & HAMILTON WALK PHILADELPHIA, PA 19104 Control of capillary growth in the myocardium
R01HL-26858-10 (PC) MENDICINO, JOSEPH F UNIVERSITY OF GEORGIA 626 GRADUATE STUDIES RES CTR ATHENS, GA 30602 Regulation of glycoprotein biosynthesis in lung
R01HL-26862-10 (CVA) GOULD, K LANCE UNIVERSITY OF TEXAS MEDICAL SC 6431 FANNIN HOUSTON, TX 77030 Coronary flow reserve--Detection of CAD by PET
R37HL-26863-10 (RAP) HOPPIN, FREDERIC G, JR MEMORIAL HOSPITAL 111 BREWSTER STREET PAWTUCKET, R I 02860 Mechanisms of lung recoil
R37HL-26873-11 (NSS) DOOLITTLE, RUSSELL F UNIV OF CALIFORNIA SAN DIEGO LA JOLLA, CALIF 92093 Structural studies on fibrinogen and fibrin
P01HL-26890-09 (SSS) SCHWARTZ, COLIN J UNIVERSITY OF TEXAS 7703 FLOYD CURL DRIVE SAN ANTONIO, TX 78284-7750 Smooth muscle cell-derived chemotactic factor in atherogenesis
P01HL-26890-09 9002 (SSS) SPRAGUE, EUGENE A Smooth muscle cell-derived chemotactic factor in atherogenesis Core--Cell culture
P01HL-26890-09 0002 (SSS) NEREM, ROBERT M Smooth muscle

PROJECT NO., ORGANIZATIONAL UNIT., INVESTIGATOR, ADDRESS, TITLE

cell-derived chemotactic factor in atherogenesis Biological responses of endothelium and sheer stress

P01HL-26890-09 0003 (SSS) KELLEY, JIM L Smooth muscle cell-derived chemotactic factor in atherogenesis Expression of acetyl LDL receptor in mononuclear phagocytes

P01HL-26890-09 0004 (SSS) VALENTE, ANTHONY J Smooth muscle cell-derived chemotactic factor in atherogenesis smooth muscle cell-derived chemotacticfactor in atherogenesis

P01HL-26890-09 0006 (SSS) ELBEIN, ALAN D Smooth muscle cell-derived chemotactic factor in atherogenesis Role of N-linked oligosaccharides in receptor function & LDL metabolism

P01HL-26890-09 9001 (SSS) SCHWARTZ, COLIN Smooth muscle cell-derived chemotactic factor in atherogenesis Core--Pathology, electron microscopy and morphometry

P01HL-26890-09 9003 (SSS) SUENRAM, C ALAN Smooth muscle cell-derived chemotactic factor in atherogenesis Core--Biochemistsry

R01HL-26922-11 (PTHA) KAPLAN, JERRY UNIVERSITY OF UTAH 50 NORTH MEDICAL DRIVE SALT LAKE CITY, UTAH 84132 Receptor mediated endocytosis in alveolar macrophages

R01HL-26927-11 (ECS) CAIN, STEPHEN M UNIVERSITY OF ALABAMA UAB STATION BIRMINGHAM, AL 35294 Regional oxygen supply and demand during hypoxia

R01HL-26973-11 (CTY) BRYAN, JOSEPH BAYLOR COLLEGE OF MEDICINE ONE BAYLOR PLAZA HOUSTON, TX 77030 In vitro studies on calcium sensitive actin assembly

R01HL-27007-09 (HEM) LIAN, ERIC C UNIVERSITY OF MIAMI SCH OF MED P O BOX 016960 (R7) MIAMI, FLA 33101 Platelet agglutination in thrombotic microangiopathy

R01HL-27014-09 (HEM) GEAR, ADRIAN R UNIVERSITY OF VIRGINIA CHARLOTTESVILLE, VA 22908 Early events in platelet function

R37HL-27016-11 (SAT) MALIK, ASRAR B ALBANY MEDICAL COLLEGE 47 NEW SCOTLAND AVENUE ALBANY, NY 12208 Neurogenic mechanisms in pulmonary edema

R01HL-27026-11 (CVA) TEN EICK, ROBERT E NORTHWESTERN UNIVERSITY 320 EAST SUPERIOR ST CHICAGO, IL 60611 Heart disease and membrane ionic channel function

R01HL-27038-10 (PHRA) VASSALLE, MARIO STATE UNIVERSITY OF NEW YORK 450 CLARKSON AVENUE BROOKLYN, N Y 11203 Mechanism of overdrive excitation guinea pigs, dogs, sheep

R01HL-27059-11 (HEM) LUBIN, BERTRAM H CHILDREN'S HOSPITAL OAKLAND 747 52ND ST. OAKLAND, CALIF 94609 Significance of membrane phospholipid asymmetry

R01HL-27068-08 (IMS) SCHREIBER, ALAN D UNIV OF PENNSYLVANIA 3451 WALNUT STREET PHILADELPHIA, PA 19104 Pulmonary alveolar macrophage function in man

R01HL-27073-09 (HEM) WALZ, DANIEL A WAYNE STATE UNIVERSITY 540 E CANFIELD DETROIT, MI 48201 Content and assemblage of platelet granule proteins

R01HL-27105-11 (CVA) LIEBERMAN, MELVYN DUKE UNIVERSITY MEDICAL CENTER BOX 3709 DURHAM, N C 27710 Interactive regulation of ion transport in heart

R01HL-27208-09 (SSS) YONAS, HOWARD UNIVERSITY OF PITTSBURGH 230 LOTHROP ST PITTSBURGH, PA 15213 Stable xenon activation of CBF--Impact on XE/CT CBF

R37HL-27215-11 (NSS) PALEK, JIRI ST ELIZABETH'S HOSPITAL 736 CAMBRIDGE STREET BOSTON, MA 02135 Membrane skeleton in abnormal red cells

R37HL-27234-11 (NSS) RAPAPORT, SAMUEL I UNIV OF CALIFORNIA, SAN DIEGO 225 DICKINSON STREET (H811K) SAN DIEGO, CA 92103 Relationships between coagulation and thrombosis

R01HL-27255-11 (ECS) GOMEZ-SANCHEZ, CELSO E UNIVERSITY OF SOUTH FLORIDA 13000 BRUCE DOWNS BLVD/VAH 111 TAMPA, FL 33612 Role of mineralocorticoids in hypertension

R01HL-27274-10 (RAP) SNAPPER, JAMES R VANDERBILT UNIVERSITY B-1308, MEDICAL CENTER NORTH NASHVILLE, TN 37232 Mechanisms of airway responses to endotoxemia

R01HL-27300-10 (RAP) COHEN, MORTON I ALBERT EINSTEIN COL OF MED 1300 MORRIS PARK AVE BRONX, NY 10461 Neural genesis of respiratory rhythm

R37HL-27333-12 (CTY) HARMONY, JUDITH A UNIVERSITY OF CINCINNATI 231 BETHESDA AVENUE CINCINNATI, OH 45267-0575 Cell behavior--Role of membrane bound lipoproteins

R01HL-27334-12 (CLIN) PHILLIPS, M IAN UNIVERSITY OF FLORIDA BOX J-274 JHMHC GAINESVILLE, FL 32610-0274 Central angiotensin in fluid balance and hypertension

R01HL-27336-10A1 (CVA) ROVETTO, MICHAEL J UNIVERSITY OF MISSOURI COLUMBIA, MO 65212 Myocardial function and metabolism following ischemia

R01HL-27339-09 (ECS) MUSTAFA, S JAMAL EAST CAROLINA UNIVERSITY SCH OF MED GREENVILLE, NC 27858 Mechanisms of coronary flow regulation by adenosine

P60HL-27341-10 (SRC) GOTTO, ANTONIO M, JR BAYLOR COLLEGE OF MEDICINE 6565 FANNIN STREET HOUSTON, TX 77030 National research and demonstration center--Arteriosclerosis

P60HL-27341-10 0009 (SRC) CHAN, LAWRENCE C National research and demonstration center--Arteriosclerosis Molecular biology of apo B

P60HL-27341-10 9001 (SRC) KNAPP, ROGER D National research and demonstration center--Arteriosclerosis Core--Instrumentation and computation

P60HL-27341-10 9002 (SRC) MORRISETT, JOEL D National research and demonstration center--Arteriosclerosis Core--Lipoprotein isolation and analytical services unit

P60HL-27341-10 0001 (SRC) BRADLEY, WILLIAM A National research and demonstration center--Arteriosclerosis Interaction of E, B-containing lipoproteins with GLA-protein

P60HL-27341-10 0002 (SRC) SPARROW, JAMES T National research and demonstration center--Arteriosclerosis Synthesis and biochemical properties of peptide fragments of apolipoproteins

P60HL-27341-10 0003 (SRC) POWNALL, HENRY J National research and demonstration center--Arteriosclerosis Thermodynamics of lipoprotein structure and function

P60HL-27341-10 0005 (SRC) MORRISETT, JOEL D National research and demonstration center--Arteriosclerosis Cholesteryl ester dynamics and metabolism in lipoproteins

P60HL-27341-10 0006 (SRC) PATSCH, JOSEF R National research and demonstration center--Arteriosclerosis Metabolic relationship among different high density lipoproteins

P60HL-27341-10 0007 (SRC) SMITH, LOUIS C National research and demonstration center--Arteriosclerosis Cholesterol transfer among arterial cells

P60HL-27341-10 0008 (SRC) GIANTURCO, SANDRA H National research and demonstration center--Arteriosclerosis Hypertriglyceridemic vldl/abnormal cellular metabolism

P60HL-27341-10 9003 (SRC) BRADLEY, WILLIAM A National research and demonstration center--Arteriosclerosis Core--Radioimmunoassay

P60HL-27341-10 9004 (SRC) YANG, CHAO-YUH National research and demonstration center--Arteriosclerosis Core--Protein sequencing and amino acid analysis

R01HL-27346-13 (HEM) WEISS, HARVEY J ROOSEVELT HOSPITAL 428 WEST 59TH STREET NEW YORK, N Y 10019 Platelet reactivity and disorders of platelet function

P50HL-27353-10 (SRC) MASON, ROBERT J NATIONAL JEWISH CENTER 1400 JACKSON STREET DENVER, CO 80206-1997 SCOR--Occupational and immunological lung diseases

P50HL-27353-10 0004 (SRC) MASON, ROBERT J SCOR--Occupational and immunological lung diseases Type II cells and interstitial lung disease

P50HL-27353-10 0007 (SRC) KING, TALMADGE E SCOR--Occupational and immunological lung diseases Idiopathic pulmonary fibrosis--Pathogenesis and staging

P50HL-27353-10 0008 (SRC) HENSON, PETER SCOR--Occupational and immunological lung diseases Resolution and progression of pulmonary inflammation

P50HL-27353-10 0010 (SRC) DOHERTY, DENNIS SCOR--Occupational and immunological lung diseases Fibroblasts and the fibrotic lung

P50HL-27353-10 9001 (SRC) WALDRON, JAMES SCOR--Occupational and immunological lung diseases CORE--Morphology

R01HL-27354-11 (TOX) GIRI, SHRI N UNIVERSITY OF CALIFORNIA DAVIS, CA 95616 Evalutaion of antifibrotic agents in pulmonary fibrosis

P50HL-27356-10 (SRC) TOOLEY, WILLIAM H UNIVERSITY OF CALIFORNIA UNIVERSITY BUILDING # 503 SAN FRANCISCO, CA 94143 SCOR--Respiratory disorders of neonates and children

P50HL-27356-10 0001 (SRC) KITTERMAN, JOSEPH A SCOR--Respiratory disorders of neonates and children Control of surfactant, tracheal fluid and breathing movements in fetal lamb

P50HL-27356-10 0003 (SRC) CLYMAN, RONALD I SCOR--Respiratory disorders of neonates and children Respiratory distress therapy and patency of ductus arteriosus in premature lambs

P50HL-27356-10 0004 (SRC) PHIBBS, RODERIC H SCOR--Respiratory disorders of neonates and children Prevent neonatal respiratory distress by instilling artificial surfactant

P50HL-27356-10 0005 (SRC) TOOLEY, WILLIAM H SCOR--Respiratory disorders of neonates and children CNS and respiratory development in infants treated with EXOSURF

P50HL-27356-10 0006 (SRC) MCILROY, MALCOLM B SCOR--Respiratory disorders of neonates and children EXOSURF effect on non-invasive measurements of cardiopulmonary function

R01HL-27368-11 (PBC) VANAMAN, THOMAS C UNIVERSITY OF KENTUCKY 101 SANDERS-BROWN BUILDING LEXINGTON, KY 40536-0230 Peptide inhibitors of proteases in disease

P01HL-27385-11 (HLBA) DEHAAN, ROBERT L EMORY UNIVERSITY ATLANTA, GA 30322 Regulation of heart cell function by membrane components

P01HL-27385-11 0002 (HLBA) DEFELICE, LOUIS J Regulation of heart cell function by membrane components Analysis of voltage gated K current in cardiac cell membrane

P01HL-27385-11 0004 (HLBA) HARTZELL, H CRISS Regulation of heart cell function by membrane components Regulation of ion channels in heart

P01HL-27385-11 0008 (HLBA) DEHAAN, ROBERT L Regulation of heart cell function by membrane components Development of ionic currents and beat rate in the heart

P01HL-27385-11 0009 (HLBA) DEHAAN, ROBERT L Regulation of heart cell function by membrane components Insulin action on heart cell electrical properties

P01HL-27385-11 0010 (HLBA) GARGUS, JOHN J Regulation of heart cell function by membrane components Expression, isolation & characterization of the cardiac inward rectifier protein

P01HL-27385-11 0011 (HLBA) JOYNER, RONALD W Regulation of heart cell function by membrane components Geometrical determinants of an ectopic focus

P01HL-27385-11 9001 (HLBA) DEHAAN, ROBERT L Regulation of heart cell function by membrane components CORE-Tissue culture

P01HL-27385-11 9002 (HLBA) DEFELICE, LOUIS J Regulation of heart cell function by membrane components CORE--Computer and electronics

R01HL-27416-10 (CVA) REIMER, KEITH A DUKE UNIVERSITY MEDICAL CENTER BOX 3712 DURHAM, NC 27710 Myocardial ischemia and reperfusion

P01HL-27430-10 (SRC) GETTES, LEONARD S UNIVERSITY OF NORTH CAROLINA 349 BURNETT-WOMAK, CB #7075 CHAPEL HILL, N C 27599-7075 Mechanisms of sudden cardiac death

P01HL-27430-10 0002 (SRC) GETTES, LEONARD S Mechanisms of sudden cardiac death Effects of ischemia and drugs on conduction

P01HL-27430-10 0005 (SRC) BOYD, LILLIE Mechanisms of sudden cardiac death Myocardial inhomogeneity

P01HL-27430-10 0008 (SRC) BUCHANAN, JACK W Mechanisms of sudden cardiac death Effects of coupling on propagation in ventricular muscle

P01HL-27430-10 9001 (SRC) GETTES, LEONARD S Mechanisms of sudden cardiac death Animal/electrode--Core

P01HL-27430-10 9003 (SRC) JOHNSON, TIMOTHY A Mechanisms of sudden cardiac death Compter/biostatistics - Core

P01HL-27430-10 9004 (SRC) HSIAO, HENRY SHIH-HAN Mechanisms of sudden cardiac death Electronics--Core

P01HL-27430-10 0001 (SRC) MEISSNER, GERHARD Mechanisms of sudden cardiac death Mechanism of sarcoplasmic reticulum calcium release in heart

R01HL-27470-09 (PHRA) SUTKO, JOHN L UNIVERSITY OF NEVADA HOWARD

BUILDING RENO, NV 89557 Pharmacology of ryanodine and the SR Ca channel
R01HL-27472-08 (RNM) MALLOY, CRAIG UNIV OF TEXAS HEALTH SCIS CTR 5323 HARRY HINES BOULEVARD DALLAS, TX 75235-9071 Global and regional cardiac metabolism: NMR studies
R01HL-27504-09 (RAP) PROPPE, DUANE W UNIV OF TEXAS HLTH SCI CTR SAN ANTONIO, TX 78284 Control of the circulation during thermal stress
R01HL-27520-07 (CVB) KUNA, SAMUEL T UNIV OF TEXAS MEDICAL BRANCH PULMONARY DIVISION ROUTE E-61 GALVESTON, TX 77550 Motor control of the upper airway during respiration
R01HL-27555-10 (RNM) WIELAND, DONALD M UNIVERSITY OF MICHIGAN ANN ARBOR, MI 48109-0028 Heart imaging agents--Structural mechanistic study
R01HL-27595-10 (CVA) RANDALL, WALTER C LOYOLA UNIVERSITY OF CHICAGO 2160 SOUTH FIRST AVENUE MAYWOOD, ILL 60153 Selective innervation of SA and AV nodal regions of the
R01HL-27652-07 (CVB) LIPSIUS, STEPHEN L LOYOLA UNIVERSITY MEDICAL CENT 2160 SOUTH FIRST AVENUE MAYWOOD, IL 60153 Electrophysiology of right artial subsidiary pacemakers
R01HL-27669-11 (RAP) BROWN, JAMES K VA MED CNTR RESP. CARE SEC. 4150 CLEMENT STREET, 111D SAN FRANCISCO, CA 94121 Airway smooth muscle--Regulation of responsiveness
R01HL-27737-09A2 (CVB) GOMEZ-SANCHEZ, CELSO E UNIVERSITY OF SOUTH FLORIDA 13000 BRUCE B DOWNS BLVD/VAH 1 TAMPA, FL 33612 Role of endothelin in experimental hypertension
R37HL-27752-09 (HEM) ZUCKER, MARJORIE B NEW YORK UNIVERSITY 550 FIRST AVENUE NEW YORK, N Y 10016 A new function for platelet factor 4
R01HL-27763-08A1 (ECS) LEE, TONY J SOUTHERN ILLINOIS UNIVERSITY PO BOX 19230 SPRINGFIELD, IL 62794-9230 Cerebral vessel innervation in hypertension
R01HL-27781-11 (ECS) KREULEN, DAVID L UNIVERSITY OF ARIZONA HSC, DEPT. OF PHARMACOLOGY TUCSON, AZ 85724 Ganglionic control of mesenteric blood vessels
R01HL-27799-11 (PTHA) O'FLAHERTY, JOSEPH T BOWMAN GRAY SCHOOL OF MED 300 SOUTH HAWTHORNE ROAD WINSTON-SALEM, N C 27103 Glycerolipids, their derivatives, and neutrophils
R01HL-27821-10 (CVA) PHILIPSON, KENNETH D UNIV OF CALIF, LOS ANGELES 10833 LE CONTE AVENUE LOS ANGELES, CALIF 90024 Interaction of ions with cardiac sarcolemma
R01HL-27838-09 (ECS) SEN, SUBHA CLEVELAND CLINIC FDN 9500 EUCLID AVE CLEVELAND, OH 44195 Reversal of myocardial hypertrophy in hypertension
P01HL-27867-10 (SRC) INESI, GIUSEPPE UNIVERSITY OF MARYLAND 660 W REDWOOD STREET BALTIMORE, MD 21201 Calcium ion control in cardiac function
P01HL-27867-10 0002 (SRC) INESI, GIUSEPPE Calcium ion control in cardiac function Calcium transport in the sarcoplasmic reticulum membrane
P01HL-27867-10 0007 (SRC) FAMBROUGH, DOUGLAS M Calcium ion control in cardiac function Cell and molecular biology of the calcium pump
P01HL-27867-10 0008 (SRC) SCHENEIDER,MARTIN F Calcium ion control in cardiac function Electrophysiology
P01HL-27867-10 9001 (SRC) WADE, JAMES B. Calcium ion control in cardiac function Core-electron microscopy
R01HL-27993-07A2 (HEM) KIRBY, EDWARD P TEMPLE UNIVERSITY 3420 N BROAD STREET PHILADELPHIA, PA 19140 Von Willebrand factor and platelet-mediated hemostasis
R01HL-27995-07 (HEM) PEDERSEN, LEE G UNIVERSITY OF NORTH CAROLINA VENABLE HALL 045A CHAPEL HILL, N C 27514 Studies of Ca(II)/Mg(II) binding in coagulation systems
R01HL-27999-08 (RAP) KINASEWITZ, GARY T UNIV OF OKLAHOMA HLTH SCIS CTR P O BOX 26901, ROOM 3 SP-400 OKLAHOMA CITY, OK 73190 Dynamics of pleural fluid exchange
P01HL-28001-10 (HLBA) ALPERT, NORMAN R UNIVERSITY OF VERMONT COLLEGE OF MEDICINE BURLINGTON, VT 05405 Subcellular adaptation in myocardial hypertrophy
P01HL-28001-10 0008 (HLBA) WARSHAW, DAVID M Subcellular adaptation in myocardial hypertrophy Smooth muscle crossbridge interactions--A motility assay
P01HL-28001-10 0009 (HLBA) HAEBERIE, JOE R Subcellular adaptation in myocardial hypertrophy Caldesmon and regulation of smooth muscle contraction
P01HL-28001-10 0010 (HLBA) PERIASAMY, MUTHU Subcellular adaptation in myocardial hypertrophy Control of gene expression in heart muscle
P01HL-28001-10 9001 (HLBA) GOULETTE, ROBERT P Subcellular adaptation in myocardial hypertrophy CORE--Computer
P01HL-28001-10 9002 (HLBA) HAMRELL, BURT B Subcellular adaptation in myocardial hypertrophy CORE--Animals
P01HL-28001-10 9003 (HLBA) KORNECKI, ELIZABETH H Subcellular adaptation in myocardial hypertrophy CORE--Monoclonal antibodies
P01HL-28001-10 0001 (HLBA) ALPERT, NORMAN R Subcellular adaptation in myocardial hypertrophy Energetics of cardiac hypertrophy
P01HL-28001-10 0006 (HLBA) LEWINTER, MARTIN Subcellular adaptation in myocardial hypertrophy Energetics of the isolated left ventricle
R01HL-28015-10 (HEM) MATSUEDA, GARY R PRINCETON UNIVERSITY PRINCETON, N J 08544-1014 Thrombus detection using fibrin-specific antibodies
R01HL-28018-24 (HEM) BOOKCHIN, ROBERT M ALBERT EINSTEIN COLLEGE OF MED 1300 MORRIS PARK AVE RM 913U BRONX, N Y 10461 Studies of sickling mechanisms and red cell membranes
R01HL-28024-10 (PTHA) WEISS, STEPHEN J SIMPSON MEMORIAL INSTITUTE 102 OBSERVATORY STREET ANN ARBOR, MI 48109-0010 Mechanisms of neutrophil-dependent vascular damage
R01HL-28028-10 (GMA) DOVER, GEORGE J JOHNS HOPKINS UNIVERSITY 720 RUTLAND AVENUE BALTIMORE, MD 21205 Mechanisms controlling fetal cellular hemoglobin content
R01HL-28066-11 (RAP) NATTIE, EUGENE E DARTMOUTH MEDICAL SCHOOL HANOVER, NH 03756 CSF and the central chemical control of breathing
R01HL-28102-10 (MEDB) FERRONE, FRANK A DREXEL UNIVERSITY 32ND & CHESTNUT STREETS PHILADELPHIA, PA 19104 Photolysis studies of sickle hemoglobin polymerization
R01HL-28138-10 (CVA) ROGERS, TERRY B UNIV OF MARYLAND AT BALTIMORE 660 WEST REDWOOD STREET BALTIMORE, MD 21201 Biochemical studies of slow ca channels in heart cells
R01HL-28143-10 (PHRA) BROWN, JOAN H UNIVERSITY OF CALIFORNIA LA JOLLA, CA 92093 Phospholipid signalling mechanisms in cardiomyocytes
R01HL-28149-09 (HEM) TUSZYNSKI, GEORGE P MED COLL OF PENNSYLVANIA 3300 HENRY AVENUE PHILADELPHIA, PA 19129 Role of thrombospondin in hemostatis and cell adhesion
R01HL-28165-09 (RAP) NIELSON, DENNIS W UNIVERSITY OF UTAH SALT LAKE CITY, UT 84132 The alveolar subphase in living lungs
R01HL-28167-10 (BNP) MAY, SHELDON W GEORGIA INST OF TECHNOLOGY SCHOOL OF CHEMISTRY ATLANTA, GA 30332 Novel antihypertensives--rational design and evaluation
R01HL-28176-08 (PC) DEMPSEY, MARY E UNIV OF MINNESOTA 4-225 MILLARD HALL MINNEAPOLIS, MN 55455 Structure and role of sterol carrier protein
R01HL-28183-10 (HEM) PEERSCHKE, ELLINOR I B SUNY AT STONY BROOK STONY BROOK, NY 11794 Platelet interactions with fibrinogen
R01HL-28193-07 (HED) KATYAL, SIKANDAR L UNIVERSITY OF PITTSBURGH 776 SCAIFE HALL PITTSBURGH, PA 15261 Pathophysiology of pulmonary surfactant
R37HL-28207-10 (HEM) SCHREIBER, ALAN D HOSPITAL OF THE UNIV OF PA 3400 SPRUCE ST PHILADELPHIA, PA 19104 The human platelet in immunohematologic disease
R01HL-28220-10 (VR) FRIEDMAN, HARVEY M UNIVERSITY OF PENNSYLVANIA 534 JOHNSON PAVILION/6073 PHILADELPHIA, PA 19104-6073 Virus and immune injury to vessel wall cells
R01HL-28235-10 (HEM) GINSBERG, MARK H SCRIPPS CLINIC & RES FDN 10666 N TORREY PINES ROAD LA JOLLA, CA 92037 Plasma fibronectin and platelet function
R01HL-28266-09 (EDC) KULLER, LEWIS H UNIVERSITY OF PITTSBURGH 130 DESOTO STREET PITTSBURGH, PA 15261 Epidemiology of cardiovascular risk factors in women
R01HL-28274-09 (RAP) DOUGLAS, JAMES S JOHN B PIERCE FDN LAB, INC 290 CONGRESS AVENUE NEW HAVEN, CT 06519 Airway pharmacology during ontogenesis
R01HL-28292-09 (CLTR) ALDERMAN, EDWIN L STANFORD UNIV SCHOOL OF MED 300 PASTEUR DRIVE STANFORD, CA 94305-5246 Risk factor intervention in coronary disease
R01HL-28373-10 (PTHA) MADRI, JOSEPH A YALE UNIVERSITY SCH OF MEDICIN PO BOX 3333 NEW HAVEN, CT 06510 The pathology of endothelial neovascularization
P60HL-28381-09 (SRC) PIOMELLI, SERGIO COLUMBIA UNIVERSITY 630 WEST 168TH STREET NEW YORK, N Y 10032 Comprehensive sickle cell disease center
P60HL-28381-09 0001 (SRC) BANK, ARTHUR Comprehensive sickle cell disease center Antenatal diagnosis of sickle cell anemia
P60HL-28381-09 0003 (SRC) SMITH, JEANNE A Comprehensive sickle cell disease center Educational program for sickle cell anemia and allied disorders
P60HL-28381-09 0007 (SRC) FAIRCHILD, BEATRICE M Comprehensive sickle cell disease center Sickle cell hemoglobin interaction and aggregation
P60HL-28381-09 0008 (SRC) PIOMELLI, SERGIO Comprehensive sickle cell disease center Iron metabolism (deficiency and excess) in sickle cell diseases
P60HL-28381-09 0009 (SRC) BIERMAN, FREDRICK Z. Comprehensive sickle cell disease center Evaluation of cardiovascular status in sickle cell syndromes
P60HL-28381-09 0011 (SRC) BANK, ARTHUR Comprehensive sickle cell disease center Transfer and expression of human beta globin genes
P60HL-28381-09 0012 (SRC) COSTANTINI, FRANK Comprehensive sickle cell disease center Transgenic mice containing human hemoglobin
P60HL-28381-09 0013 (SRC) DEVIVO, DARRYL C. Comprehensive sickle cell disease center Cerebrovascular involvement in sickle cell disease
P60HL-28381-09 9002 (SRC) PIOMELLI, SERGIO Comprehensive sickle cell disease center Data management and laboratory core
P60HL-28381-09 0005 (SRC) LIPOWSKY, HERBERT H Comprehensive sickle cell disease center Microvascular function in sickle cell disease
P60HL-28381-09 0006 (SRC) USAMI, SHUNICHI Comprehensive sickle cell disease center Rheology in sickle cell disease
P60HL-28391-09 (SRC) ROSSE, WENDELL F DUKE UNIVERSITY MEDICAL CENTER PO BOX 3934 DURHAM, NC 27710 Comprehensive sickle cell disease center
P60HL-28391-09 0001 (SRC) KINNEY, THOMAS R Comprehensive sickle cell disease center Comprehensive sickle disease clinics
P60HL-28391-09 0002 (SRC) DRAYER, BURTON P Comprehensive sickle cell disease center Cerebral glucose metabolism in sickle cell disease
P60HL-28391-09 0003 (SRC) ARMSTRONG, BRENDA E Comprehensive sickle cell disease center Cardiopulmonary function in sickle cell anemia during exercise and rest
P60HL-28391-09 0004 (SRC) KAUFMAN, RUSSELL E Comprehensive sickle cell disease center Genetic determinants affecting sickle cell disease
P60HL-28391-09 0006 (SRC) HOCHMUTH, ROBERT M Comprehensive sickle cell disease center Material properties of sickle cell membrane
P60HL-28391-09 0007 (SRC) MC MANUS, THOMAS J Comprehensive sickle cell disease center Ion transport and cell volume regulation in sickle cell disease
P60HL-28391-09 0008 (SRC) ROBINSON, GLADYS Comprehensive sickle cell disease center Triad sickle cell foundation and community education
P60HL-28391-09 0009 (SRC) MC ALLISTER, MARY E Comprehensive sickle cell disease center Operation sickle cell
P60HL-28391-09 0010 (SRC) KAUFMAN, RUSSELL E Comprehensive sickle cell disease center Diagnostic and screening laboratory
P60HL-28391-09 0011 (SRC) WILLIAMS, ANITA Comprehensive sickle cell disease center Education program
P60HL-28391-09 0012 (SRC) ABRAMS, MARY Comprehensive sickle cell disease center Counseling program
R01HL-28393-10 (CVB) MOORE, E NEIL UNIVERSITY OF PENNSYLVANIA 3800 SPRUCE STREET PHILADELPHIA, PA 19104 The role of infarct distribution in arrhythmogenesis
R01HL-28399-08 (NTN) ILLINGWORTH, D ROGER OREGON HLTH SCIS UNIV 3181 SW SAM JACKSON PARK RD PORTLAND, OREG 97201 Nutritional and

PROJECT NO., ORGANIZATIONAL UNIT., INVESTIGATOR, ADDRESS, TITLE

metabolic studies in abetalipoproteinemia
R01HL-28429-10 (CVB) IDEKER, RAYMOND E DUKE UNIVERSITY MEDICAL CENTER BOX 3140 DURHAM, NC 27710 Computer assisted mapping of ventricular fibrillation
R01HL-28438-11 (SSS) HERMAN, GABOR T MEDICAL IMAGE PROCESSING GROUP 418 SERVICE DRIVE PHILADELPHIA, PA 19104-6021 Longitudinal changes in craniofacial onlay bone grafts
R37HL-28440-10 (NLS) GREENBERG, MICHAEL J UNIVERSITY OF FLORIDA 9505 OCEAN SHORE BLVD ST AUGUSTINE, FL 32086-8623 Pharmacology and distribution of a cardioexcitatory neuropeptides
R01HL-28448-11 (CTY) LANGE, YVONNE RUSH-PRESBYTERIAN-ST LUKES 1653 W CONGRESS PARKWAY CHICAGO, IL 60612-3864 The disposition and movement of cholesterol in cells
R01HL-28452-09 (RAD) SHUNG, K KIRK PENNSYLVANIA STATE UNIVERSITY 231 HALLOWELL BLDG UNIVERSITY PARK, PA 16802 Ultrasonic scattering by biological tissues
R01HL-28467-10 (NTN) THOMPSON, PAUL D MIRIAM HOSPITAL 164 SUMMIT AVENUE PROVIDENCE, R I 02906 Lipoproteins in active men--Role of exercise and diet
R01HL-28474-10 (BIO) MURAD, FERID ABBOTT LABORATORIES ABBOTT PARK, IL 60064 ABBOTT PARK, IL 60064 Cyclic nucleotide metabolism in lung tissues
P01HL-28481-09 (HLBB) SCHUMAKER, VERNE N UNIVERSITY OF CALIFORNIA 405 HILGARD AVENUE LOS ANGELES, CALIF 90024 Molecular genetic approaches in atherosclerosis research
P01HL-28481-09 0006 (HLBB) SPARKES, ROBERT S Molecular genetic approaches in atherosclerosis research Genetic factors in atherosclerosis
P01HL-28481-09 0007 (HLBB) SCHOTZ, MICHAEL C Molecular genetic approaches in atherosclerosis research Hepatic lipase--Genetics and expression
P01HL-28481-09 9002 (HLBB) SHIVELY, JOHN E Molecular genetic approaches in atherosclerosis research Core--Protein chemistry and immunochemistry
P01HL-28481-09 9004 (HLBB) PUPPIONE, DONALD L Molecular genetic approaches in atherosclerosis research Core--Lipoprotein analysis and preparation
P01HL-28481-09 9005 (HLBB) LUSIS, ALDONS J Molecular genetic approaches in atherosclerosis research Core--Molecular biology laboratory
P01HL-28481-09 9006 (HLBB) ROTTER, JEROME I Molecular genetic approaches in atherosclerosis research Core--Genetic epidemiology
P01HL-28481-09 0001 (HLBB) SCHUMAKER, VERNE N Molecular genetic approaches in atherosclerosis research Genetic polymorphism of apo-B
P01HL-28481-09 0002 (HLBB) SCHOTZ, MICHAEL C Molecular genetic approaches in atherosclerosis research Lipoprotein lipase--Structure function and regulation
P01HL-28481-09 0003 (HLBB) LUSIS, ALDONS J Molecular genetic approaches in atherosclerosis research Genetic control of lipid metabolism--Mouse model
R01HL-28521-09 (PB) GILBERT, HIRAM F BAYLOR COLLEGE OF MEDICINE ONE BAYLOR PLAZA HOUSTON, TX 77030 Redox regulation of HMG-Coa reductase
R01HL-28539-10 (CVA) LANGER, GLENN A UNIVERSITY OF CALIFORNIA MACDONALD RESEARCH LAB LOS ANGELES, CA 90024 Role of the sarcolemma in myocardial contractile control
P01HL-28542-10 (HLBA) HONG, SUK E S U N Y AT BUFFALO 124 SHERMAN HALL BUFFALO, N Y 14214 Environment and oxygenation
P01HL-28542-10 0001 (HLBA) PENDERGAST, DAVID R Environment and oxygenation Effect of water temperature and exercise in man
P01HL-28542-10 0002 (HLBA) KRASNEY, JOHN A Environment and oxygenation Control of the peripheral circulation
P01HL-28542-10 0003 (HLBA) REEVES, ROBERT B Environment and oxygenation kinetics of respiratory gas exchange with whole blood
P01HL-28542-10 0004 (HLBA) HOGAN, PERRY M Environment and oxygenation Hyperbaric, electrical and mechanical phenomena in cardiac muscle
P01HL-28542-10 0005 (HLBA) HONG, SUK KI Environment and oxygenation Effect of pressure and hyperoxia on epithelial transport
P01HL-28542-10 0006 (HLBA) PAGANELLI, CHARLES V Environment and oxygenation Effect of ambient pressure on gas phase diffusion processes
P01HL-28542-10 9001 (HLBA) HOGAN, PERRY M Environment and oxygenation CORE--Technical
R01HL-28556-09 (PHY) JONES, LARRY R KRANNERT INST OF CARDIOLOGY 1001 WEST 10TH ST INDIANAPOLIS, IN 46202-2859 Subspecialization of cardiac sarcoplasmic reticulum
R01HL-28560-09 (HEM) MORROW, JON S YALE UNIVERSITY 310 CEDAR ST B140 NEW HAVEN, CT 06510 Membrane skeletal control in hemolytic disorders
R01HL-28573-09 (BIO) LINGREL, JERRY B UNIV OF CINCINNATI MED CTR 231 BETHESDA AVE CINCINNATI, OH 45267-0524 Characterization of Na,K-ATPase and it's genes
R01HL-28607-10 (RAP) CURRY, FITZ-ROY E UNIVERSITY OF CALIFORNIA DAVIS, CA 95616-8671 Water and solute transport across capillary endothelium
R01HL-28623-10 (RAP) WHITSETT, JEFFREY A UNIV OF CINCINNATI COLL OF MED 231 BETHESDA AVENUE CINCINNATI, OH 45267-0541 Regulation of surfactant release in type II lung cell
R01HL-28669-10 (SOH) RUSSELL, JAMES A STATE UNIVERSITY AT BUFFALO 3435 MAIN ST, 166 ACHESON HALL BUFFALO, NY 14214 Pulmonary pathophysiology of organic dusts
R37HL-28674-10 (CBY) GUNN, ROBERT B EMORY UNIVERSITY SCHOOL OF MED ATLANTA, GA 30322 Molecular mechanisms of anion transport
R01HL-28690-09 (SB) EBERHART, ROBERT C UNIV OF TEXAS HLTH SCIENCE CTR 5323 HARRY HINES BOULEVARD DALLAS, TX 75235 Analysis of blood trauma from microporous oxygenators
R01HL-28715-10 (EDC) NEATON, JAMES D UNIVERSITY OF MINNESOTA 2221 UNIVERSITY AVE/SE MINNEAPOLIS, MN 55414 Mortality surveillance of MRFIT screenees
R01HL-28737-09 (RAP) PHAN, SEM HIN THE UNIVERSITY OF MICHIGAN 1301 CATHERINE ROAD ANN ARBOR, MI 48109 Mechanism of pulmonary fibrosis

PROJECT NO., ORGANIZATIONAL UNIT., INVESTIGATOR, ADDRESS, TITLE

R01HL-28749-11 (HEM) LAWLER, JOHN W BRIGHAM AND WOMEN'S HOSPITAL 75 FRANCIS STREET/THORN 3 BOSTON, MA 02115 Functional characterization of platelet thrombospondin
R01HL-28785-10 (ECS) GUYENET, PATRICE G UNIVERSITY OF VIRGINIA DEPT OF PHARMACOLOGY CHARLOTTESVILLE, VA 22908 Organization of central sympathetic system
R01HL-28791-10 (CVB) FRANK, JOY S UCLA SCHOOL OF MEDICINE 10833 LE CONTE AVENUE LOS ANGELES, CA 90024-1760 Ultrastructure of the myocardial sarcolemma
R01HL-28833-11 (IMS) HUBER, SALLY A UNIVERSITY OF VERMONT BURLINGTON, VT 05405 Autoimmunity and coxsackieviral myocarditis
R01HL-28907-10 (SRC) MELLINS, ROBERT B COLUMBIA UNIVERSITY 630 WEST 168TH STREET NEW YORK, N Y 10032 Health education for high risk urban asthmatic children
R37HL-28935-23 (HEM) JACOB, HARRY S UNIV OF MINNESOTA HARVARD ST AT EAST RIVER RD MINNEAPOLIS, MN 55455 Abnormal blood cell membranes in disease
R01HL-28940-09 (PHRA) BROOKER, GARY GEORGETOWN UNIVERSITY 3900 RESERVOIR RD N W WASHINGTON, D C 20007 Metabolic and hormonal control of cardiac contraction
R37HL-28947-12 (NSS) PHILLIPS, DAVID R COR THERAPEUTICS, INC 256 EAST GRAND AVENUE SOUTH SAN FRANCISCO, CA 94080 Platelet membrane proteins in aggregation
P01HL-28958-09 (HLBA) ROSEN, MICHAEL R COLUMBIA UNIVERSITY 630 WEST 168TH STREET NEW YORK, N Y 10032 Developmental approach to cardiac rhythm and arrhythmias
P01HL-28958-09 0001 (HLBA) ROSEN, MICHAEL R Developmental approach to cardiac rhythm and arrhythmias Developmental cellular electrophysiology and pharmacology
P01HL-28958-09 0002 (HLBA) COHEN, IRA S Developmental approach to cardiac rhythm and arrhythmias Membrane currents in neonatal Purkinje fibers
P01HL-28958-09 0003 (HLBA) BILEZIKIAN, JOHN P Developmental approach to cardiac rhythm and arrhythmias Action of adrenergic receptors in cultured myogenic cells
P01HL-28958-09 0004 (HLBA) ROBINSON, RICHARD B Developmental approach to cardiac rhythm and arrhythmias Neural and hormonal interactions with cardiac cell in culture
P01HL-28958-09 0005 (HLBA) ROSEN, MICHAEL R Developmental approach to cardiac rhythm and arrhythmias Developmental changes in cardiac electrophysiology and pharmacology
P01HL-28958-09 9001 (HLBA) ROBINSON, RICHARD B Developmental approach to cardiac rhythm and arrhythmias Core--Tissue culture
P01HL-28958-09 9002 (HLBA) LEGATO, MARIANNE J Developmental approach to cardiac rhythm and arrhythmias Core--Ultrastructure
P01HL-28972-10 (SRC) MC GILL, HENRY C, JR SOUTHWEST FND FOR BIOMED RES P O BOX 28147 SAN ANTONIO, TX 78228-0147 Diet, stress, and genotype in primate atherosclerosis
P01HL-28972-10 0001 (SRC) KUSHWAHA, RAMPRATAP S Diet, stress, and genotype in primate atherosclerosis Metabolic basis of dyslipoproteinemias in pedigreed baboons
P01HL-28972-10 0003 (SRC) VANDEBERG, JOHN L Diet, stress, and genotype in primate atherosclerosis Genetic variants of apolipoprotein and LDL receptor
P01HL-28972-10 0004 (SRC) MACCLUER, JEAN W Diet, stress, and genotype in primate atherosclerosis Pedigree analysis of lipoprotein phenotypes
P01HL-28972-10 0007 (SRC) MCGILL JR, HENRY C Diet, stress, and genotype in primate atherosclerosis Lipoproteins and blood pressure in atherogenesis
P01HL-28972-10 0008 (SRC) LANFORD, ROBERT E. Diet, stress, and genotype in primate atherosclerosis Lipoprotein metabolism in hepatocyte cell lines
P01HL-28972-10 0009 (SRC) KAMMERER, CANDACE Diet, stress, and genotype in primate atherosclerosis Genetic markers and linkage analysis
P01HL-28972-10 9001 (SRC) MOTT, GLEN E Diet, stress, and genotype in primate atherosclerosis Core--Lipid and lipoprotein biochemistry
P01HL-28972-10 9003 (SRC) CAREY, KENNETH D Diet, stress, and genotype in primate atherosclerosis Core--Veterinary services
P01HL-28972-10 9004 (SRC) MCMAHAN, C ALEX Diet, stress, and genotype in primate atherosclerosis Core--Biometry
P01HL-28972-10 9005 (SRC) SHARP, R MARK Diet, stress, and genotype in primate atherosclerosis Core--Monoclonal antibodies
P01HL-28972-10 9006 (SRC) GETZ, GODFREY S. Diet, stress, and genotype in primate atherosclerosis Core--Molecular biology
P01HL-28982-10 (HLBB) CARRETERO, OSCAR A HENRY FORD HOSPITAL 2799 WEST GRAND BLVD DETROIT, MI 48202 Vasoactive hormones in blood pressure regulation
P01HL-28982-10 9003 (HLBB) TILLEY, BARBARA C. Vasoactive hormones in blood pressure regulation Biostatistical core
P01HL-28982-10 0001 (HLBB) CARRETERO, OSCAR A Vasoactive hormones in blood pressure regulation Kinins in the regulation of blood pressuare
P01HL-28982-10 0002 (HLBB) FEJES-TOTH, GEZA Vasoactive hormones in blood pressure regulation The kallikrein-kinin system in the isolated-perfused kidney
P01HL-28982-10 0003 (HLBB) BEIERWALTES, WILLIAM H Vasoactive hormones in blood pressure regulation Renal eicosanoids, the endothelium and renin release
P01HL-28982-10 0005 (HLBB) SCICLI, A GUILLERMO Vasoactive hormones in blood pressure regulation Kallicrein in neuroendocrine regulation of blood pressure
P01HL-28982-10 0007 (HLBB) ROLLINS VAN, MIKE Vasoactive hormones in blood pressure regulation Cardiovascular effects of novel metabolites
P01HL-28982-10 0008 (HLBB) SCICLI, GUILLOZMO A. Vasoactive hormones in blood pressure regulation Vascular wall kallikren in the regulation of vascular tone.
P01HL-28982-10 0009 (HLBB) CARRETERO, OSCAR A. Vasoactive hormones in blood pressure regulation Intrarenal control of renin release
P01HL-28982-10 9001 (HLBB) SCICLI, A GUILLERMO Vasoactive hormones in blood pressure regulation Biochemistry--Core
P01HL-28982-10 9002 (HLBB) SMITH, STUART W Vasoactive hormones in blood pressure regulation Radioimmunoassay--Core

PROJECT NO., ORGANIZATIONAL UNIT., INVESTIGATOR, ADDRESS, TITLE

R01HL-28995-09 (CVA) CORR, PETER B WASHINGTON UNIVERSITY 660 SOUTH EUCLID AVENUE ST LOUIS, MO 63110 Adrenergic factors and arrhythmogenic metabolites

P01HL-29019-10 (HLBB) NEMERSON, YALE R MOUNT SINAI SCHOOL OF MEDICINE 1 GUSTAVE L LEVY PLACE NEW YORK, N Y 10029 Tissue factor in blood coagulation

P01HL-29019-10 0001 (HLBB) NEMERSON, YALE R Tissue factor in blood coagulation Kinetics of tissue factor pathway

P01HL-29019-10 0002 (HLBB) ZUR, MARGALIT Tissue factor in blood coagulation Structural analysis of domains involved in tissue factor effects

P01HL-29019-10 0003 (HLBB) BACH, RONALD R Tissue factor in blood coagulation Biological regulation of tissue factor-initiated coagulation

P01HL-29019-10 0004 (HLBB) KONIGSBERG, WILLIAM H Tissue factor in blood coagulation Molecular biology of tissue factor

P01HL-29019-10 9001 (HLBB) GUHA, ARABINDA Tissue factor in blood coagulation Protein purification core

R01HL-29034-08 (HEM) BROEKMAN, M JOHAN N Y VA MEDICAL CENTER 408 FIRST AVENUE NEW YORK, N Y 10010 Lipid metabolism in stimulated human platelets

R01HL-29037-10 (HEM) BURSTEIN, SAMUEL A UNIV OF OKLAHOMA HLTH SCIS CTR P O BOX 26901 OKLAHOMA CITY, OK 73190 Studies of megakaryocytopoiesis

R01HL-29068-10 (RAP) DAUBENSPECK, JOHN A DARTMOUTH MEDICAL SCHOOL HANOVER, NH 03756 Reflex regulation of the human breathing pattern

R01HL-29077-10 (SAT) LEVITSKY, SIDNEY NEW ENGLAND DEACONESS HOSPITAL 110 FRANCIS ST BOSTON, MA 02215 Myocardial protection -- Reperfusion injury amelioration

R01HL-29095-10 (SB) FRY, DONALD L OHIO STATE UNIVERSITY 400 WEST 12TH AVE-2025 WISEMAN COLUMBUS, OHIO 43210-1214 Transmural transport in blood vessels

R01HL-29113-11 (CBY) YIN, HELEN L UNIV OF TEXAS SW MEDICAL CTR 5323 HARRY HINES BLVD DALLAS, TX 75235-9040 structure-function analysis of cytoplasmic gelsolin

R01HL-29229-08 (MET) OSTLUND, RICHARD E, JR WASHINGTON UNIV SCHOOL OF MED 660 SOUTH EUCLID ST LOUIS, MO 63110 Lipoprotein receptors in health and disease

R01HL-29232-06A3 (CVA) JONES, CARL E TEXAS COLL OF OSTEOPATHIC MED 3500 CAMP BOWIE BLVD FORT WORTH, TX 76107-2690 Anti-infarction effects in the denervated heart

R01HL-29246-11 (PTHA) SHELLITO, JUDD ERNEST LSU MEDICAL CENTER 1542 TULANE AVENUE NEW ORLEANS, LA 70112 Alveolar macrophage function during immunosuppression

R37HL-29252-10 (MET) GRUNDY, SCOTT M UT SOUTHWESTERN MED. CTR. DALL 5323 HARRY HINES BOULEVARD DALLAS, TX 75235 Causes & management of primary hypercholesterolemia

R01HL-29282-09 (HEM) SCHICK, BARBARA P CARDEZA FDN FOR HEMATOLOGIC RE 1015 WALNUT STREET PHILADELPHIA, PA 19107 Megakaryocyte & platelet proteoglycans

R01HL-29293-10 (PTHA) MC CALL, CHARLES E BOWMAN GRAY SCHOOL OF MEDICINE MEDICAL CENTER BLVD WINSTON-SALEM, NC 27157-1042 Pathogenic mechanisms producing lung injury

R01HL-29305-09 (HEM) BARKER, JANE E JACKSON LABORATORY 600 MAIN STREET BAR HARBOR, ME 04609-0800 Hemolytic anemias--Models

R01HL-29325-08 (SB) TILSON, MARTIN D ST. LUKE'S -ROOSEVELT HOSPITAL 428 WEST 59TH ST NEW YORK, NY 10019 Inhibition of proteolysis in aortic aneurysm disease

R01HL-29351-07 (CVA) MARINO, THOMAS A TEMPLE UNIVERSITY SCH OF MED 3400 NORTH BROAD STREET PHILADELPHIA, PA 19140 Quantitative morphology of cardiac hypertrophy

R01HL-29364-08 (GMB) NISHIMURA, HIROKO UNIVERSITY OF TENNESSEE 894 UNION AVENUE MEMPHIS, TN 38163 Urinary concentrating mechanism--Unique avian models

R01HL-29379-09 (VR) SHAEFFER, JOSEPH R CENTER FOR BLOOD RESEARCH 800 HUNTINGTON AVENUE BOSTON, MASS 02115 Proteolysis in human erythroid cells

R01HL-29396-06 (RAP) ADAMS, JAMES M UNIVERSITY OF VIRGINIA SCH OF ENGR & APPLIED SCIENCE CHARLOTTESVILLE, VA 22903-244 Carbon dioxide transport and chemosensitivity

R01HL-29397-09 (CVB) CHAO, JULIE MEDICAL UNIV OF SOUTH CAROLINA 171 ASHLEY AVENUE CHARLESTON, SC 29425 Regulation and function of renal kallikrein

R01HL-29409-10 (BBCB) LLINAS, MIGUEL CARNEGIE-MELLON UNIVERSITY 4400 FIFTH AVENUE PITTSBURGH, PA 15213-3890 NMR studies of plasminogen structure and dynamics

R01HL-29436-09 (SB) RANKIN, J SCOTT UNIVERSITY OF CALIFORNIA 3RD AVENUE AND PARNASSUS SAN FRANCISCO, CA 94143 Basic and clinical studies of cardiac function

R01HL-29439-10 (CVA) JALIFE, JOSE SUNY HEALTH SCIENCE CENTER 750 EAST ADAMS STREET SYRACUSE, N Y 13210 Control of heart rate and AV conduction

R01HL-29473-11 (PHY) WIER, WITHROW G UNIVERSITY OF MARYLAND 660 WEST BALTIMORE STREET BALTIMORE, MD 21201 Ca2+ in heart--Entry, release, & ca2+-induced release

R01HL-29492-09 (PBC) KEFALIDES, NICHOLAS A CONNECTIVE TISSUE RES INST 3624 MARKET STREET PHILADELPHIA, PA 19104 Matrix synthesis by blood vessel cells

R01HL-29499-10 (CVB) SHLAFER, MARSHAL THE UNIVERSITY OF MICHIGAN M6322 MEDICAL SCIENCE I ANN ARBOR, MICH 48109 Heart ischemic damage--Modulating oxygen metabolites

R01HL-29512-11 (HEM) MCDONAGH, JAN BETH ISRAEL HOSPITAL 330 BROOKLINE AVE BOSTON, MA 02215 Biology of factor XIII

R37HL-29515-12 (PBC) YOSHIDA, AKIRA BECHMAN INST OF CITY OF HOPE 1450 EAST DUARTE ROAD DUARTE, CA 91010 Molecular pathology of genetic disorders in man

R01HL-29543-10 (IMB) TOEWS, GALEN B UNIVERSITY OF MICHIGAN 3916 TAUBMAN CTR, BOX 0360 ANN ARBOR, MI 48109 Immunoregulatory role of human alveolar macrophages

R01HL-29578-10 (BBCB) URRY, DAN W 1670 UNIVERSITY BLVD BIRMINGHAM, AL 35294-0019 Molecular structure, function and pathology of elastin

PROJECT NO., ORGANIZATIONAL UNIT., INVESTIGATOR, ADDRESS, TITLE

P01HL-29582-09 (HLBB) HOFF, HENRY F CLEVELAND CLINIC FDN 9500 EUCLID AVENUE CLEVELAND, OHIO 44195 Lipoprotein and cell-derived factors in atherogenesis

P01HL-29582-09 0001 (HLBB) CHISOLM, GUY M Lipoprotein and cell-derived factors in atherogenesis Toxicity of oxidized LDL in vitro and in vivo

P01HL-29582-09 0003 (HLBB) HOFF, HENRY F Lipoprotein and cell-derived factors in atherogenesis Aorta-extracted LDL--Composition and function

P01HL-29582-09 0004 (HLBB) DICORLETO, PAUL E Lipoprotein and cell-derived factors in atherogenesis Smooth muscle cell proliferation in atherogenesis

P01HL-29582-09 0005 (HLBB) EHRHART, ALLEN Lipoprotein and cell-derived factors in atherogenesis Regulation of collagen synthesis in atherosclerosis

P01HL-29582-09 0006 (HLBB) HAMILTON,THOMAS A Lipoprotein and cell-derived factors in atherogenesis Macrophage inflammatory responses in atherogenesis

P01HL-29582-09 0007 (HLBB) MORTON, RICHARD E Lipoprotein and cell-derived factors in atherogenesis Plasma lipid transfer protein--regulation and function

P01HL-29582-09 9001 (HLBB) DICORLETO, PAUL E Lipoprotein and cell-derived factors in atherogenesis Core--Tissue culture

P01HL-29582-09 9002 (HLBB) HOFF, HENRY F Lipoprotein and cell-derived factors in atherogenesis Core--Morphology

P01HL-29582-09 9003 (HLBB) MORTON, RICHARD E Lipoprotein and cell-derived factors in atherogenesis Core--Lipoproteins

P01HL-29583-09 (HLBB) ALPER, CHESTER A CENTER FOR BLOOD RESEARCH, INC 800 HUNTINGTON AVENUE BOSTON, MASS 02115 Improved blood service care for cytopenic patients

P01HL-29583-09 0001 (HLBB) KENNEY, DIANNE M Improved blood service care for cytopenic patients Platelet function--microtubules and structural proteins

P01HL-29583-09 0002 (HLBB) ANTONIADES, HARRY N Improved blood service care for cytopenic patients Physiological functions of platelet derived factors

P01HL-29583-09 0004 (HLBB) YUNIS, EDMOND J Improved blood service care for cytopenic patients Molecular typing of class I and class II HLA alloantigens

P01HL-29583-09 0005 (HLBB) AWDEH, ZUHEIR L. Improved blood service care for cytopenic patients Genetic determinants of mixed lymphocyte reaction

P01HL-29583-09 0006 (HLBB) ALPER, CHESTER A. Improved blood service care for cytopenic patients Genetic markers of extended haplotypes

P01HL-29583-09 9004 (HLBB) AWDEH, ZUHEIR Improved blood service care for cytopenic patients CORE--MHC markers and cell culture

P01HL-29586-09 (HLBB) MOSHER, DEANE F, JR 2550 MEDICAL SCIENCES CENTER 1300 UNIVERSITY AVENUE MADISON, WI 53706 Synthesis and function of coagulation proteins

P01HL-29586-09 0001 (HLBB) ALBRECHT, RALPH M Synthesis and function of coagulation proteins Platelet structure/function relationships

P01HL-29586-09 0002 (HLBB) MOSHER, DEANE F Synthesis and function of coagulation proteins Localization and function of thrombospondin and vitronectin

P01HL-29586-09 0003 (HLBB) FOLTS, JOHN D Synthesis and function of coagulation proteins Arterial thrombosis

P01HL-29586-09 0004 (HLBB) SUTTIE, JOHN W Synthesis and function of coagulation proteins Coagulopoietin--Vitamin K-dependent clotting factors

P01HL-29587-09 (HLBB) COWLEY, ALLEN W, JR MEDICAL COLLEGE OF WISCONSIN 8701 WATERTOWN PLANK ROAD MILWAUKEE, WI 53226 Blood pressure--Determinants and controllers

P01HL-29587-09 0007 (HLBB) BARBER, BILLY J Blood pressure--Determinants and controllers Extracellular matrix changes in hypertension

P01HL-29587-09 0008 (HLBB) HARDER, DAVID R Blood pressure--Determinants and controllers Cellular mechanism of myogenic autoregulation in renal arteries

P01HL-29587-09 0009 (HLBB) LIARD, JEAN-FRANCOIS Blood pressure--Determinants and controllers Vasopressin, renin-angiotensin-aldosterone and AF peptide systems

P01HL-29587-09 0010 (HLBB) LOMBARD, JULIAN H Blood pressure--Determinants and controllers Mechanisms of vascular oxygen sensitivity

P01HL-29587-09 9001 (HLBB) BARBER, BILLY J Blood pressure--Determinants and controllers CORE--Computer services

P01HL-29587-09 9002 (HLBB) COWLEY, ALLEN W Blood pressure--Determinants and controllers CORE--Biochemical and analytical laboratory

P01HL-29587-09 9003 (HLBB) BARBER, BILLY J Blood pressure--Determinants and controllers CORE--Electronic and machine instrumentation shop

P01HL-29587-09 9004 (HLBB) COWLEY, ALLEN W Blood pressure--Determinants and controllers CORE--Animal monitoring facility

P01HL-29587-09 0001 (HLBB) COWLEY, ALLEN W Blood pressure--Determinants and controllers Mechanisms of salt-sensitive hypertension

P01HL-29587-09 0003 (HLBB) ROMAN, RICHARD J Blood pressure--Determinants and controllers Relationships between arterial pressure and natriuresis

P01HL-29587-09 0005 (HLBB) OSBORN, JEFFREY L Blood pressure--Determinants and controllers Neural regulation of renal function and arterial pressure

P01HL-29587-09 0006 (HLBB) STEKIEL, WILLIAM J Blood pressure--Determinants and controllers Electrical and mechanical properties of blood vessels in hypertension

R01HL-29589-09 (SB) MILLER, D CRAIG STANFORD UNIV MEDICAL CENTER STANFORD, CA 94305 Ventricular dynamics from surgically inserted markers

P01HL-29594-09 (SRC) SENIOR, ROBERT M JEWISH HOSPITAL OF ST LOUIS 216 SOUTH KINGSHIGHWAY BLVD ST LOUIS, MO 63110 Mechanisms in the remodeling of lung structure

PROJECT NO., ORGANIZATIONAL UNIT., INVESTIGATOR, ADDRESS, TITLE

P01HL-29594-09 0001 (SRC) MC DONALD, JOHN A Mechanisms in the remodeling of lung structure Fibronectin's role in cell & matrix interactions in lung
P01HL-29594-09 0002 (SRC) CROUCH, EDMOND C Mechanisms in the remodeling of lung structure Pneumocyte-derived collagenous proteins
P01HL-29594-09 0004 (SRC) SENIOR, ROBERT M Mechanisms in the remodeling of lung structure Degrading of lung connective tissue--Mechanisms and consequences
P01HL-29594-09 0005 (SRC) MECHAM, ROBERT P Mechanisms in the remodeling of lung structure Connective tissue remodelling
P01HL-29594-09 0006 (SRC) WELGUS, HOWARD G Mechanisms in the remodeling of lung structure Lung collagen turnover by inflammatory cells
P01HL-29594-09 9001 (SRC) MC DONALD, JOHN A Mechanisms in the remodeling of lung structure Immunology--Core
P01HL-29594-09 9002 (SRC) CROUCH, EDMUND C Mechanisms in the remodeling of lung structure Morphology--core
R01HL-29604-10 (HEM) HUISMAN, TITUS H MEDICAL COLLEGE OF GEORGIA DEPT OF CELL & MOLECULAR BIO. AUGUSTA, GA 30912 Inhomogeneity of hemoglobin types
R01HL-29618-10 (ECS) BLAIR, ROBERT W UNIVERSITY OF OKLAHOMA DPT OF PHYSIOLOGY & BIOPHYSICS OKLAHOMA CITY, OK 73190 Cardiac and other inputs onto reticulospinal neurons
R01HL-29623-09 (HEM) ZENG, YI-TAO SHANGHAI CHILDREN'S HOSPITAL 380 KANG DING ROAD SHANGHAI, CHINA The molecular basis of hemoglobin abnormalities in China
R01HL-29680-09 (PTHA) GUYTON, JOHN R METHODIST HOSPITAL A-601 6565 FANNIN ST HOUSTON, TX 77030 Lipid-rich regions in atherosclerosis
P01HL-29714-29 (HLBB) GANONG, WILLIAM F UNIVERSITY OF CALIFORNIA SAN FRANCISCO, CA 94143-0444 Neural and humoral control of endocrine function
P01HL-29714-29 0004 (HLBB) GANONG, WILLIAM F Neural and humoral control of endocrine function Brain regulation of renin and angiotensin
P01HL-29714-29 0006 (HLBB) REID, IAN A Neural and humoral control of endocrine function Interactions between vasopresin, the kidneys, and brain
P01HL-29714-29 0007 (HLBB) DESCHEPPER, CHRISTIAN F Neural and humoral control of endocrine function Brain renin-angiotensin system
P01HL-29714-29 0008 (HLBB) STEELE, MARIANNE K Neural and humoral control of endocrine function Relationship of brain angiotensin to LH/PRL secretion
P01HL-29714-29 0009 (HLBB) GARDNER, DAVID G Neural and humoral control of endocrine function Regulation of gene for atrial natriuretic peptide in CNS
P01HL-29714-29 9002 (HLBB) REID, IAN A Neural and humoral control of endocrine function Laboratory service core
R01HL-29761-09 (CVA) PROTHERO, JOHN W UNIV OF WASHINGTON SM 20 SEATTLE, WA 98195 Cardiac myofiber morphogenesis
R01HL-29807-10 (HEM) ESMON, CHARLES T OKLAHOMA MED RES FOUNDATION 825 NORTHEAST THIRTEENTH ST OKLAHOMA CITY, OK 73104 Roles of protease and EGF domains in coagulation proteins
R01HL-29842-07 (RAP) MC BRIDE, JOHN T UNIVERSITY OF ROCHESTER 601 ELMWOOD AVENUE, BOX 667 ROCHESTER, NY 14642 Mechanisms of postpneumonectomy airway growth
R01HL-29847-09 (ECS) DETH, RICHARD C NORTHEASTERN UNIVERSITY 360 HUNTINGTON AVENUE BOSTON, MASS 02115 Protein kinase control of arterial alpha receptors
R01HL-29851-09 (PHY) WELSH, MICHAEL J UNIVERSITY OF IOWA COLL OF MED 500 EMRB IOWA CITY, IA 52242 Pathophysiology of respiratory tract fluid production
R37HL-29891-09 (RAP) MASON, ROBERT J NAT JEWISH CTR FOR IMM & RES 1400 JACKSON STREET DENVER, CO 80206 Functions of pulmonary alveolar type II cells in vitro
R01HL-29957-09 (SRC) SECKER-WALKER, ROGER H UNIVERSITY OF VERMONT 235 ROWELL BUILDING BURLINGTON, VT 05405 Smoking cessation during obstetric care
R01HL-30026-09 (RAP) RITCHIE, BRENDA B J B PIERCE FOUNDATION LAB, INC 290 CONGRESS AVENUE NEW HAVEN, CT 06519 Sites of respiratory muscle fatigue
R01HL-30035-07A1 (OBM) BROWN, WALTER E AMERICAN DENTAL ASSOC HLTH FDN 211 EAST CHICAGO AVENUE CHICAGO, IL 60611 Calcification in the cardiovascular system
R01HL-30038-09 (TOX) JOLLOW, DAVID J MED UNIV OF SOUTH CAROLINA DEPT OF PHARMACOLOGY CHARLESTON, S C 29425 Studies of hemolytic anemia
R01HL-30046-10 (PHRA) BUCCAFUSCO, JERRY J MEDICAL COLLEGE OF GEORGIA AUGUSTA, GA 30912-2300 Mechanism of centrally-acting antihypertensive drugs
R37HL-30050-10 (PB) MASTERS, BETTIE S UNIVERSITY OF TEXAS HLTH SCI C 7703 FLOYD CURL DR SAN ANTONIO, TX 78284-7760 Microsomal electron transport in liver and heart
R01HL-30061-09 (PBC) FOSTER, JUDITH A BOSTON UNIVERSITY 80 E CONCORD ST BOSTON, MA 02118 Elastic fiber structure, fibrogenesis and disease
R01HL-30065-07 (SB) SEGEL, LEIGH D UNIVERSITY OF CALIFORNIA DIV OF CARDIOVASCULAR MEDICINE DAVIS, CA 95616 Isolated heart perfusion with perfluorochemical emulsion
R01HL-30077-09A1 (PHY) BERS, DONALD M UNIVERSITY OF CALIFORNIA RIVERSIDE, CA 92521-0121 Ionic control of cardiac muscle contraction
P01HL-30086-09 (HLBB) ALBERS, JOHN J HARBORVIEW MEDICAL CENTER 325 NINTH AVENUE SEATTLE, WASH 98104 Human lipoprotein pathophysiology program project
P01HL-30086-09 0001 (HLBB) BRUNZELL, JOHN D Human lipoprotein pathophysiology program project Mechanisms of genetic hypertriglyceridemias
P01HL-30086-09 0002 (HLBB) MOTULSKY, ARNO G Human lipoprotein pathophysiology program project Genetics of familial combined hyperlipidemia
P01HL-30086-09 0003 (HLBB) ALBERS, JOHN J Human lipoprotein pathophysiology program project Lcat and lipid transfer proteins
P01HL-30086-09 0005 (HLBB) CHEUNG, MARIAN C Human lipoprotein pathophysiology program project Characterization, metabolism and function of HDL
P01HL-30086-09 0006 (HLBB) CHAIT, ALAN Human lipoprotein pathophysiology program project Role of macrophages in lipoprotein metabolism
P01HL-30086-09 0008 (HLBB) BROWN, B GREG Human lipoprotein pathophysiology program project Lipoprotein alterations and atherosclerosis progression
P01HL-30086-09 9001 (HLBB) ALBERS, JOHN A Human lipoprotein pathophysiology program project Core--Immunoassay and hybridoma
P01HL-30086-09 9002 (HLBB) WARNICK, G RUSSELL Human lipoprotein pathophysiology program project Core--Lipids and lipoproteins laboratory
P01HL-30086-09 9004 (HLBB) FOSTER, DAVID M Human lipoprotein pathophysiology program project Core--Biomathematics and biostatistics
P01HL-30086-09 9005 (HLBB) MOTULSKY, ARNO G Human lipoprotein pathophysiology program project Core--Genetic patient registry of the familial hyperlipidemias
P01HL-30121-08 (HLBB) GOLDWASSER, EUGENE UNIVERSITY OF CHICAGO 920 E 58TH ST ROOM 661 CHICAGO, ILL 60637 The biology of sickle cell disease
P01HL-30121-08 0001 (HLBB) JOSEPHS, ROBERT The biology of sickle cell disease Molecular basis of sickle hemoglobin assembly
P01HL-30121-08 0004 (HLBB) GOLDWASSER, EUGENE The biology of sickle cell disease Expression of the erythropoietin and globin genes
P01HL-30121-08 0005 (HLBB) GROSS, MARTIN The biology of sickle cell disease Post-transcriptional regulation of hemoglobin synthesis
P01HL-30121-08 0006 (HLBB) GARAVITO, MICHAEL R The biology of sickle cell disease Enzymes of the prostaglandin cascade
P01HL-30121-08 0007 (HLBB) PALFREY, CLIVE H The biology of sickle cell disease Protein kinase C and membrane substrate
P01HL-30121-08 9001 (HLBB) JOSEPHS, ROBERT The biology of sickle cell disease Core--Electron microscopy
R01HL-30143-10 (PHRA) HUME, JOSEPH R UNIVERSITY OF NEVADA SCH OF ME RENO, NV 89557-0046 Pharmacology and regulation of channels and carriers in the heart
R01HL-30160-08 (HEM) HEBBEL, ROBERT P UNIVERSITY OF MINNESOTA 420 DELAWARE STREET, S E MINNEAPOLIS, MINN 55455 Erythrocyte membrane abnormalities in sickle disease
R01HL-30195-09 (RAP) SPANNHAKE, ERNST W JOHNS HOPKINS UNIVERSITY 615 NORTH WOLFE STREET BALTIMORE, MD 21205 Arachidonate metabolites in the sensitized lung
R01HL-30200-07 (HEM) STRICKLAND, DUDLEY K AMERICAN RED CROSS 15601 CRABBS BRANCH WAY ROCKVILLE, MD 20855 Regulatory events in fibrinolysis and coagulation
R01HL-30260-10 (ECS) BUSIJA, DAVID W WAKE FOREST UNIVERSITY 300 S HAWTHORNE RD WINSTON-SALEM, NC 27103 Effects of prostaglandins on cerebral blood flow
R01HL-30270-08 (HEM) ROSSE, WENDELL F DUKE UNIVERSITY DURHAM, N C 27710 Platelet studies in thrombocytopenia
R01HL-30315-09 (PHY) KAPLAN, JACK H UNIVERSITY OF PENNSYLVANIA DEPT OF PHYSIOLOGY PHILADELPHIA, PA 19104 Physiology of active sodium transport in red blood cells
R01HL-30339-10 (CVB) PETTINGER, WILLIAM A CREIGHTON UNIVERSITY CALIFORNIA AT 24TH STREET OMAHA, NEBR 68178 Sodium, hypertension, and renal alpha2-receptors
R37HL-30340-09 (HEM) ESMON, CHARLES T OKLAHOMA MED RES FOUNDATION 825 NORTHEAST THIRTEENTH ST OKLAHOMA CITY, OK 73104 The functions of protein C
R01HL-30391-08 (PHRA) OLSSON, RAY A USF COLLEGE OF MEDICINE 12901 BRUCE B DOWNS BLVD BOX 1 TAMPA, FL 33612 Cardiac adenosine receptors
R01HL-30400-08 (HEM) FITZGERALD, GARRET A VANDERBILT UNIV. MED. CTR 532 MEDICAL RESEARCH BLDG. NASHVILLE, TENN 37232 Pharmacology of platelet vascular interactions
R01HL-30428-08 (EDC) TURNER, STEPHEN T MAYO FOUNDATION 200 FIRST STREET SOUTHWEST ROCHESTER, MN 55905 Red cell sodium transport--Genetics and hypertension
R55HL-30443-09 (HEM) COMP, PHILIP C UNIV OF OKLAHOMA HLTH SCI CTR P O BOX 26901 OKLAHOMA CITY, OK 73190 Protein S and myocardial infarction
R01HL-30450-10 (RAP) SAID, SAMI I UNIV OF ILLINOIS AT CHICAGO 1940 WEST TAYLOR (M/C 789) CHICAGO, IL 60612 VIP and other novel peptides in lung
R01HL-30478-07 (PHRA) BARRY, WILLIAM H UNIVERSITY OF UTAH 50 NORTH MEDICAL DRIVE SALT LAKE CITY, UTAH 84132 Ischemic injury--Effects of ca channel blocking drugs
R01HL-30480-08 (HEM) WOODS, VIRGIL L, JR UNIV OF CALIFORNIA, SAN DIEGO 225 DICKINSON STREET SAN DIEGO, CA 92103 Structure and function of platelet GPIIB/IIIa
R01HL-30496-07 (ECS) TULENKO, THOMAS N MEDICAL COLL OF PENNSYLVANIA 3300 HENRY AVENUE PHILADELPHIA, PA 19129 Altered vascular smooth muscle in hypercholesterolemia
R01HL-30506-10 (ECS) THAMES, MARC DAVID UNIVERSITY HOSP OF CLEVELAND 2074 ABINGTON ROAD CLEVELAND, OH 44106 Cardiac receptors with vagal c-fiber afferents
P50HL-30542-08 (SRC) HUDSON, LEONARD D HARBORVIEW MEDICAL CENTER 325 NINTH AVE, ZA-62 SEATTLE, WASH 98104 Scor--adult respiratory failure
P50HL-30542-08 0001 (SRC) HENDERSON, WILLIAM R Scor--adult respiratory failure Lipoxygenase products of arachidonic acid in ARDS
P50HL-30542-08 0002 (SRC) HARLAN, JOHN M Scor--adult respiratory failure Mediators of sepsis
P50HL-30542-08 0003 (SRC) BISHOP, MICHAEL J Scor--adult respiratory failure Ischemia and reperfusion as a cause of lung injury
P50HL-30542-08 0004 (SRC) BUTLER, JOHN Scor--adult respiratory failure The bronchial blood flow response to ARDS
P50HL-30542-08 0006 (SRC) HUDSON, LEONARD D Scor--adult respiratory failure Infection and inflammation and the natural history outcome of ARDS
P50HL-30542-08 0007 (SRC) CLARK, JOAN Scor--adult respiratory failure Regulation of collagen in acute lung injury
P50HL-30542-08 0008 (SRC) MARTIN, THOMAS Scor--adult respiratory

failure Neutrophil function in ARDS
P50HL-30542-08 9001 (SRC) CHI, EMIL Y Scor--adult respiratory failure Core--morphology
P50HL-30542-08 9002 (SRC) HUDSON, LEONARD D Scor--adult respiratory failure Core--Clinical and data management
R01HL-30552-07 (CVA) HUNTER, WILLIAM C JOHN HOPKINS SCH OF MEDICINE 720 RUTLAND AVENUE BALTIMORE, MD 21205 From cardiac muscle to ventricle
P01HL-30557-08 (HLBA) HOFFMAN, BRIAN F COLUMBIA UNIVERSITY 630 WEST 168TH STREET NEW YORK, N Y 10032 Cardiac arrhythmias--Mechanisms, diagnosis and treatment
P01HL-30557-08 0010 (HLBA) WIT, ANDREW L. Cardiac arrhythmias--Mechanisms, diagnosis and treatment Reentrant mechanisms in myocardial infarction
P01HL-30557-08 0011 (HLBA) DILLON, STEPHEN M. Cardiac arrhythmias--Mechanisms, diagnosis and treatment Optical studies of fibrillation and defibrillation
P01HL-30557-08 0001 (HLBA) SIEGELBAUM, STEVEN A Cardiac arrhythmias--Mechanisms, diagnosis and treatment Patch clamp studies on single ion channels
P01HL-30557-08 0004 (HLBA) HOFFMAN, BRIAN F Cardiac arrhythmias--Mechanisms, diagnosis and treatment Cellular electrophysiology and pharmacology
P01HL-30557-08 0006 (HLBA) HOFFMAN, BRIAN F Cardiac arrhythmias--Mechanisms, diagnosis and treatment Reentrant atrial arrhythmias
P01HL-30557-08 0007 (HLBA) WIT, ANDREW L Cardiac arrhythmias--Mechanisms, diagnosis and treatment Antiarrhythmic drugs on reentrant circuits
P01HL-30557-08 0009 (HLBA) BOYDEN, PENELOPE Cardiac arrhythmias--Mechanisms, diagnosis and treatment Activation sequences during antiarhythmic drug action
P01HL-30557-08 9001 (HLBA) ROSS, SAMUEL M Cardiac arrhythmias--Mechanisms, diagnosis and treatment CORE--Electronics and machine shops
P01HL-30557-08 9002 (HLBA) FENOGLIO, JOHN J Cardiac arrhythmias--Mechanisms, diagnosis and treatment CORE--Structure and ultrastructure
P01HL-30557-08 9003 (HLBA) ROBINSON, RICHARD B Cardiac arrhythmias--Mechanisms, diagnosis and treatment Cell culture and disaggregation
R01HL-30561-08 (SRC) WEINBERGER, MYRON INDIANA UNIVERSITY MEDICAL CTR 541 CLINICAL DRIVE, ROOM 477 INDIANAPOLIS, IN 46223 Dietary sodium restriction in general medical practice
P01HL-30568-09 (HLBB) FOGELMAN, ALAN M UNIV OF CALIF, LOS ANGELES 10833 LE CONTE AVENUE LOS ANGELES, CALIF 90024 Lipid and lipoprotein metabolism in atherosclerosis
P01HL-30568-09 0001 (HLBB) HABERLAND, MARGARET E Lipid and lipoprotein metabolism in atherosclerosis Monocyte-macrophage receptor functions in atherosclerosis
P01HL-30568-09 0002 (HLBB) FOGELMAN, ALAN M Lipid and lipoprotein metabolism in atherosclerosis Cholesteryl ester accumulation in macrophages
P01HL-30568-09 0005 (HLBB) EDWARDS, PETER A Lipid and lipoprotein metabolism in atherosclerosis Regulation of cholesterol metabolism
P01HL-30568-09 0006 (HLBB) BERLINER, JUDITH Lipid and lipoprotein metabolism in atherosclerosis Atherogenesis--Lipoprotein-monocytes-endothelial cells
P01HL-30568-09 0007 (HLBB) FOGELMAN, ALAN M Lipid and lipoprotein metabolism in atherosclerosis An in vitro approach to artery wall metabolism
P01HL-30568-09 0008 (HLBB) FRANK, JOY S Lipid and lipoprotein metabolism in atherosclerosis Ultrastructure of the artery wall
P01HL-30568-09 0009 (HLBB) LUSIS, ALDONS J Lipid and lipoprotein metabolism in atherosclerosis Regulation of cholesterol synthesis--Genetic approach
P01HL-30568-09 9001 (HLBB) HABERLAND, MARGARET Lipid and lipoprotein metabolism in atherosclerosis CORE--Essential laboratory services
P01HL-30568-09 9002 (HLBB) LUSIS, ALDONS J Lipid and lipoprotein metabolism in atherosclerosis Core--Molecular biology laboratory
R01HL-30570-10 (SSS) BURTON, KAREN P UNIV OF TEXAS MED CTR. 5323 HARRY HINES BLVD DALLAS, TX 75235 Ischemia induced alterations in myocardial membranes
P50HL-30572-08 (SRC) HYERS, THOMAS M ST LOUIS UNIV SCH OF MEDICINE 1402 S GRAND BLVD ST LOUIS, MISSOURI 63104 SCOR--Adult respiratory failure
P50HL-30572-08 0003 (SRC) LONIGRO, ANDREW J SCOR--Adult respiratory failure Participation of humoral agents in pathogenesis of ARDS
P50HL-30572-08 0004 (SRC) WEBSTER, ROBERT O SCOR--Adult respiratory failure Complement, PMN and platelets in acute pulmonary injury
P50HL-30572-08 0005 (SRC) BAJAJ, S PAUL SCOR--Adult respiratory failure Role of coagulation in acute lung injury
P50HL-30572-08 0006 (SRC) LAGUNOFF, DAVID SCOR--Adult respiratory failure Endothelial cell reactivity--Lipid mediators contraction
P50HL-30572-08 9001 (SRC) LONIGRO, ANDREW J SCOR--Adult respiratory failure Core--Biochemistry
P50HL-30572-08 9002 (SRC) HYERS, THOMAS M SCOR--Adult respiratory failure Core--Clinical
P50HL-30572-08 9003 (SRC) LAGUNOFF, WILLIAM J SCOR--Adult respiratory failure Core--Tissue culture
R01HL-30604-08 (BEM) FREEDMAN, ROBERT R LAFAYETTE CLINIC 951 E LAFAYETTE DETROIT, MI 48207 Behavioral treatment of Raynaud's phenomenon
R01HL-30605-07 (SSP) PICKERING, THOMAS G NEW YORK HOSP-CORNELL MED COLL 525 EAST 68TH STREET NEW YORK, N Y 10021 Ambulatory blood pressure and behavior
P01HL-30616-09 (HLBB) MARDER, VICTOR J UNIVERSITY OF ROCHESTER 601 ELMWOOD AVENUE ROCHESTER, N Y 14642 Basic and clinical studies of coagulation proteins
P01HL-30616-09 0001 (HLBB) FRANCES, CHARLES W Basic and clinical studies of coagulation proteins Fibrinogen structure, function and physiology
P01HL-30616-09 0002 (HLBB) SCHERAGA, HAROLD A Basic and clinical studies of coagulation proteins Thermodynamics of clotting factor interactions
P01HL-30616-09 0004 (HLBB) MARDER, VICTOR J Basic and clinical studies of coagulation proteins Thrombi and fibrinolysis
P01HL-30616-09 0007 (HLBB) SIMPSON, PATRICIA J. Basic and clinical studies of coagulation proteins Tissue-specific control of fibrinogen gamma chain expression
P01HL-30616-09 0008 (HLBB) FRANCIS, CHARLES W. Basic and clinical studies of coagulation proteins Thrombosis prevention--Warfarin vs. leg compression
P01HL-30616-09 9001 (HLBB) WAGNER, DENISA D Basic and clinical studies of coagulation proteins Core--Tissue culture /hybridoma
P01HL-30616-09 9003 (HLBB) FRANCIS, CHARLES W. Basic and clinical studies of coagulation proteins Core--Clinical support services
R01HL-30639-08 (PHRA) NATHANSON, NEIL M UNIV OF WASHINGTON SEATTLE, WA 98195 Regulation of muscarinic cholinergic receptors in heart
R37HL-30647-09 (SSS) HAWIGER, JACK J DEPARTMENT OF MICROBIOLOGY VANDERBILT MEDICAL CENTER NORT NASHVILLE, TN 37232-2363 Pathobiology of thromboembolic disorders
R01HL-30648-09 (HEM) HAWIGER, JACK J VANDERBILT UNIVERSITY VANDERBILT MEDICAL CTR. NORTH NASHVILLE, TN 37232-2363 endothelial injury and cytoprotection
R01HL-30652-08 (ALY) SLAVIN, RAYMOND G ST LOUIS UNIVERSITY 1402 SOUTH GRAND BLVD ST LOUIS, MO 63104 Pathogenesis of allergic aspergillosis
R01HL-30657-09 (HEM) FOX, JOAN E GLADSTONE FOUNDATION LABS 2550 23RD ST; P O BOX 40608 SAN FRANCISCO, CA 94140-0608 Role of contractile proteins in platelet function
R01HL-30663-07 (ECS) PROCTOR, KENNETH G UNIVERSITY OF TENNESSEE 894 UNION AVENUE MEMPHIS, TN 38163 Regulation of peripheral circulation
R01HL-30696-09 (CVA) GERDES, ANTHONY M UNIVERSITY OF SOUTH FLORIDA 12901 BRUCE B. DOWNS BLVD. TAMPA, FLORIDA 33612 Cellular remodeling in cardiac hypertrophy
R01HL-30710-09 (EVR) KAUFMAN, MARC P UNIVERSITY OF CALIFORNIA DIV OF CARDIOVASCULAR MEDICINE DAVIS, CA 95616 Metabolite effects on group 111 and IV muscle afferents
R01HL-30712-09 (HEM) BOCK, SUSAN C TEMPLE UNIVERSITY 3400 N BROAD STREET PHILADELPHIA, PA 19140 Molecular genetics of protease inhibitor deficiencies
R01HL-30722-08 (PHRA) FREED, CURT R UNIV OF COLORADO HLTH SCIS CTR 4200 EAST NINTH AVENUE DENVER, COLO 80262 Catecholamines and serotonin in blood pressure control
R01HL-30724-10 (PHRA) WASSERSTROM, JOHN A NORTHWESTERN UNIVERSITY 310 EAST SUPERIOR STREET CHICAGO, IL 60611 Drug effects on the Ca2 transients and contraction in heart
R37HL-30793-08 (NSS) KULLER, LEWIS H UNIVERSITY OF PITTSBURGH 130 DESOTO STREET PITTSBURGH, PA 15261 Epidemiology of decline in heart disease mortality
R01HL-30842-09 (NTN) KAYDEN, HERBERT J NEW YORK UNIV MEDICAL CTR 550 FIRST AVENUE NEW YORK, NY 10016 metabolic role of vit.E--Clinical & cellular studies
R01HL-30847-09 (MEDB) SCHULZ, HORST H CITY COLLEGE OF CUNY CONVENT AVENUE AT 138TH STREET NEW YORK, N Y 10031 Metabolism of unsaturated and hydroxy fatty acids
R01HL-30897-09 (MET) WEINBERG, RICHARD B BOWMAN GRAY SCHOOL OF MEDICINE MEDICAL CENTER BLVD WINSTON-SALEM, NC 27157 Structure and lipid binding of human apolipoprotein A-IV
R01HL-30914-08 (MET) POWNALL, HENRY J BAYLOR COLLEGE OF MEDICINE 6535 FANNIN STREET HOUSTON, TX 77030 Enzymic reactions of model plasma lipoproteins
R01HL-30923-09 (RAP) WRIGHT, JO R UNIVERSITY OF CALIFORNIA CARDIOVASCULAR RES INSTITUTE SAN FRANCISCO, CA 94143-0130 Alveolar factors in uptake of lung surfactant
R01HL-30926-07A1 (PB) ROUSLIN, WILLIAM UNIV OF CINCINNATI COLL OF MED 231 BETHESDA AVENUE CINCINNATI, OH 45267-0575 Mitochondrial functional changes in ischemic myocardium
R01HL-30946-08 (SB) CLOWES, ALEXANDER W UNIVERSITY OF WASHINGTON SCHOOL OF MEDICINE SEATTLE, WASH 98195 Mechanisms of arterial graft failure
R01HL-30954-07 (HEM) WEISEL, JOHN W UNIVERSITY OF PENNSYLVANIA DEPARTMENT OF ANATOMY PHILADELPHIA, PA 19104-6058 Structural studies of blood clotting proteins
R01HL-31008-08 (CBY) BURT, JANIS M UNIVERSITY OF ARIZONA DEPT OF PHYSIOLOGY TUSCON, AZ 85724 Myocardial conduction & gap junction permeability
R01HL-31010-09 (EDC) SCHIEKEN, RICHARD M VIRGINIA COMMONWEALTH UNIV BOX 26 MCV STATION RICHMOND, VA 23298 Longitudinal twin study - cohort study of blood pressure
R01HL-31012-08 (HEM) FOWLKES, DANA M UNIVERSITY OF NORTH CAROLINA CB 7525 CHAPEL HILL, NC 27599 The regulation of fibrinogen biosynthesis
R01HL-31021-07 (PTHA) GODLESKI, JOHN J HARVARD UNIVERSITY 665 HUNTINGTON AVENUE BOSTON, MA 02115 Inhaled particle retention in normal and diseased lungs
R37HL-31029-09 (NSS) BRAIN, JOSEPH D HARVARD SCH OF PUBLIC HLTH 665 HUNTINGTON AVENUE BOSTON, MA 02115 Magnetic particles to assess macrophage behavior
R01HL-31048-08 (HEM) LORD, SUSAN T UNIVERSITY OF NORTH CAROLINA CB# 7525 CHAPEL HILL, NC 27599 A genetic approach to the fibrinogen-fibrin conversion
R01HL-31069-08 (ECS) WOLIN, MICHAEL S NEW YORK MEDICAL COLLEGE VALHALLA, NY 10595 Pulmonary vasodilation and guanylate cyclase regulation
R01HL-31070-09 (RAP) MARON, MICHAEL B NORTHEASTERN OHIO UNIVERSITIES 4209 STATE ROUTE 44 ROOTSTOWN, OH 44272 Mechanisms of neurogenic pulmonary edema
R37HL-31102-09 (HEM) DEUEL, THOMAS F JEWISH HOSPITAL 216 S KINGSHIGHWAY ST LOUIS, MO 63110 Platelets and cell growth--Role PDGF
R01HL-31107-08 (BIO) MUMBY, MARC C UNIV OF TEX SW MED CTR AT DALL 5323 HARRY HINES BOULEVARD DALLAS, TX 75235-9016 Immunological analysis of cardiac protein phosphatases

PROJECT NO., ORGANIZATIONAL UNIT., INVESTIGATOR, ADDRESS, TITLE

R01HL-31117-08 (CVB) MORGAN, JAMES P BETH ISRAEL HOSPITAL 330 BROOKLINE AVENUE BOSTON, MA 02215 Pathophysiology of cardiac hypertrophy
R01HL-31159-15 (BBCA) SHARMA, VIJAY S UNIVERSITY OF CALIFORNIA 9500 GILMAN DRIVE LA JOLLA, CA 92093-0652 Mechanism of reactions of hemoglobin with ligands
R01HL-31172-07 (PBC) BRUCE, MARGARET C CASE WESTERN RESERVE UNIV 2101 ADELBERT RD CLEVELAND, OH 44106 Role of proteolysis in the pathogenesis of BPD
R01HL-31175-08 (HED) ROONEY, SEAMUS A YALE UNIV SCH OF MEDICINE 333 CEDAR ST/P O BOX 3333 NEW HAVEN, CT 06510 Control of lung surfactant secretion in the newborn
R01HL-31183-08 (ECS) VANHOUTTE, PAUL M BAYLOR COLLEGE OF MEDICINE ONE BAYLOR PLAZA HOUSTON, TX 77030 Endothelium, smooth muscle and vascular heterogeneity
R01HL-31184-07 (BEM) SHAPIRO, DAVID UNIVERSITY OF CALIFORNIA 405 HILGARD AVE LOS ANGELES, CA 90024-1406 Behavioral regulation of postural hypotension
R01HL-31189-04A3 (BEM) BLANCHARD, EDWARD B CTR/STRESS & ANXIETY DISORDERS 1535 WESTERN AVENUE ALBANY, NY 12203 Biobehavioral mechanisms in treatment of hypertension
R01HL-31193-06 (HEM) THOMPSON, ARTHUR R PUGET SOUND BLOOD CENTER TERRY AND MADISON SEATTLE, WA 98104 Intrinsic system clotting--Structure and function
R01HL-31194-07 (MET) ORAM, JOHN F UNIVERSITY OF WASHINGTON MAIL STOP RG-26 SEATTLE, WA 98195 Characterization of the HDL receptor in arterial cells
R01HL-31195-07 (PC) BRECHER, PETER I BOSTON UNIVERSITY SCH OF MED 80 E CONCORD STREET BOSTON, MA 02118 Long chain acyl CoA interactions in the heart
R01HL-31197-08 (PTHA) MATALON, SADIS UNIVERSITY OF ALABAMA 619 SOUTH 19TH STREET BIRMINGHAM, AL 35233 Pathophysiology of sublethal oxygen in injured lungs
R01HL-31210-08 (MET) KUNITAKE, STEVEN T UNIVERSITY OF CALIFORNIA 1327 MOFFITT HOSPITAL SAN FRANCISCO, CA 94143 HDL subspecies--Characterization and intestinal origin
R01HL-31216-07A1 (RNM) CUTILLO, ANTONIO G UNIVERSITY OF UTAH HLTH SCI CT 50 NORTH MEDICAL DRIVE SALT LAKE CITY, UT 84132 NMR quantitation of lung edema
R01HL-31237-07 (PTHA) KUNKEL, STEVEN L UNIVERSITY OF MICHIGAN 1301 CATHERINE RD ANN ARBOR, MI 48109-0602 Monokine gene expression/regulation in lung injury
R01HL-31245-08 (TOX) REDDY, CHINTHAMANI C PENNSYLVANIA STATE UNIVERSITY 226 FENSKE LABORATORY UNIVERSITY PARK, PA 16802 Vitamin E, selenium, oxidant stress and pulmonary arachidonic cascade
R01HL-31248-07 (RAP) JACKSON, ANDREW C BOSTON UNIVERSITY 110 COMMINGTON ST BOSTON, MA 02215 Lung parameters from respiratory impedance measurements
R01HL-31249-08 (CVB) TORMEY, JOHN M UNIVERSITY OF CALIFORNIA 405 HILGARD AVENUE LOS ANGELES, CALIF 90024 Quantitative localization of electrolytes in heart
R01HL-31299-06 (PHY) BRINK, PETER R STATE UNIVERSITY OF NEW YORK STONY BROOK, N Y 11794 Model of the intercalated disc of myocardium
R01HL-31305-08 (SRC) GULLION, DAVID S UNIV. OF CALIF., SAN FRAN. SAN FRANCISCO, CALIF 94143 Optimal treatment of hypercholesterolemia--a CME model
R01HL-31311-08 (HEM) LYNCH, DENNIS C DANA-FARBER CANCER INSTITUTE 44 BINNEY STREET BOSTON, MA 02115 Biosynthesis of Von Willebrand factor
R01HL-31315-07 (PBC) SPIRO, MARY J JOSLIN DIABETES CENTER ONE JOSLIN PLACE BOSTON, MASS 02215 Myocardial glycoproteins in normal and diabetic states
R01HL-31338-08 (SSS) WAITE, B MOSELEY BOWMAN GRAY SCH OF MEDICINE 300 SOUTH HAWTHORNE ROAD WINSTON-SALEM, N C 27103 Macrophage eicosanoid and phospholipid metabolism
R37HL-31393-08 (CVA) WIT, ANDREW L COLUMBIA UNIVERSITY 630 WEST 168TH STREET NEW YORK, N Y 10032 Ventricular arrhythmias and infarction
R01HL-31397-08 (EDC) KEIL, JULIAN E MED UNIV OF SOUTH CAROLINA 171 ASHLEY AVENUE CHARLESTON, SC 29425 Predictors of coronary disease in blacks
R01HL-31406-08A1 (HEM) CARSON, STEVEN D UNIV OF NEBRASKA MED CENTER 600 S 42ND STREET OMAHA, NE 68198-3135 Functional studies of tissue factor
R01HL-31422-08 (TOX) CATRAVAS, JOHN D MEDICAL COLLEGE OF GEORGIA AUGUSTA, GA 30912-2300 Toxicology and pharmacology of lung endothelial enzymes
R01HL-31429-07 (TOX) FOSTER, WILLIAM M SUNY AT STONY BROOK HSC T-17, RM 040 STONY BROOK, NY 11794 Ozone effect on respiratory tract mucus and permeability
R01HL-31461-08 (BBCB) PERUTZ, MAX F UNIVERISTY OF MEDICAL SCHOOL HILLS ROAD CAMBRIDGE CB2 2QH, ENGLAND Studies on hemoglobin and other proteins
R01HL-31467-07 (RAP) GRUNSTEIN, MICHAEL M CHILDREN'S HOSP OF PHIL THE JOSEPH STROKES JR. RES INS PHILADELPHIA, PA 19104 Maturation of non-specific airway reactivity
R01HL-31469-09 (SAT) HANSON, STEPHEN R EMORY UNIVERSITY ATLANTA, GA 30322 Evaluation of small vessel prostheses
R01HL-31472-05 (SRC) GREENE, H LEON HARBORVIEW MEDICAL CENTER 325 9TH AVE SEATTLE, WA 98104 Randomized amiodarone therapy for survivors of VF
R01HL-31481-06 (SRC) BAILEY, WILLIAM C UNIVERSITY OF ALABAMA UAB STATION BIRMINGHAM, AL 35294 Strategies for promoting adult asthma self-management
R01HL-31497-08 (MET) KWITEROVICH, PETER O, JR JOHNS HOPKINS HOSPITAL 600 N WOLFE ST, CMSC 604 BALTIMORE, MD 21205 Hyperapob and coronary heart disease
R01HL-31515-08 (CVB) BERECEK, KATHLEEN H UNIVERSITY OF ALABAMA UAB STATION BIRMINGHAM, AL 35294 Brain angiotensin II in the pathogenesis of hypertension
R01HL-31524-08 (HEM) WAUGH, RICHARD E UNIVERSITY OF ROCHESTER DEPT OF BIOPHYSICS ROCHESTER, N Y 14642 Mechanochemistry of membranes and other cell components

PROJECT NO., ORGANIZATIONAL UNIT., INVESTIGATOR, ADDRESS, TITLE

R01HL-31533-08 (BEM) LIGHT, KATHLEEN C UNIVERSITY OF NORTH CAROLINA CB #7175 CHAPEL HILL, NC 27599 Blood pressure control--Racial and psychosocial influences
R01HL-31536-08 (CVA) URTHALER, FERDINAND UAB, 538 ZEIGLER BLDG. UNIVERSITY STATION BIRMINGHAM, ALA 35294 Differential control of sinus node and AV junction
R01HL-31543-07 (ECS) HIGHSMITH, ROBERT F UNIVERSITY OF CINCINNATI COLLEGE OF MEDICINE CINCINNATI, OH 45267-0576 The endothelial cell in coronary vasospasm and thrombosis
R01HL-31560-09 (PTHA) RANNELS, D EUGENE, JR Extracellular matrix and type II lung cell metabolism
R01HL-31579-10 (HEM) NARLA, MOHANDAS LAWRENCE BERKELEY LABORATORY 1 CYCLOTRON RD BERKELEY, CA 94720 Rheological and adherence properties of sickle cells
R01HL-31588-07 (HEM) MC INTIRE, LARRY V RICE UNIVERSITY P O BOX 1892 HOSTON, TX 77251 Rheological studies of sickle cell disease
R01HL-31598-08 (HEM) JACKSON, CARL W ST JUDE CHILDREN'S RESEARCH HO 332 N LAUDERDALE, PO BOX 318 MEMPHIS, TN 38101 New approaches to the study of megakaryocytopoiesis
R01HL-31601-08 (BIO) HOSEY, M MARLENE NORTHWESTERN UNIV MED SCH 303 E. CHICAGO AVE CHICAGO, IL 60611 Inhibitory & stimulatory receptors in the developing heart animals
R01HL-31607-09 (CLIN) COHEN, RICHARD A UNIVERSITY HOSPITAL 88 E NEWTON ST BOSTON, MA 02118 Cholesterol, LDL, and coronary endothelial cell function
R37HL-31610-09 (NSS) BAINTON, DOROTHY F UNIVERSITY OF CALIFORNIA SAN FRANCISCO, CA 94143-0506 Immunocytochemistry of megakaryocytes and platelets
R01HL-31698-08 (HEM) SWANK, RICHARD T ROSWELL PARK MEMORIAL INST ELM & CARLTON ST BUFFALO, N Y 14263 Megakaryocyte-platelet granules in storage pool disease
R01HL-31701-09 (CVA) WEBER, KARL T UNIV. OF MISSOURI-COLUMBIA ONE HOSPITAL DRIVE COLUMBIA, MO 65212 Collagen and the hypertrophied heart
R01HL-31704-08 (ECS) MORGAN, KATHLEEN G BETH ISRAEL HOSPITAL 330 BROOKLINE AVENUE BOSTON, MASS 02215 Regulation of contraction of blood vessels
R01HL-31753-07 (HEM) BELL, THOMAS G ANIMAL HEALTH DIAGNOSTIC LAB PO BOX 30076 LANSING, MI 48909-7576 Fibrinogen receptors in hereditary thrombopathia
R01HL-31768-07 (EDC) KAUFMAN, DAVID W DRUG EPIDEMIOLOGY UNIT 1371 BEACON STREET BROOKLINE, MA 02146 Drug etiology of aplastic anemia and related dyscrasias
R01HL-31782-08 (HEM) SINGER, JACK W VA MEDICAL CENTER 1660 SO COLUMBIAN WAY SEATTLE, WA 98108 Studies of the in vitro hematopoietic microenvironment
R01HL-31809-09 (ALY) GOETZL, EDWARD J UNIVERSITY OF CA MEDICAL CTR SAN FRANCISCO, CA 94143-0724 Leukotriene modulation of leukocyte function
R01HL-31823-08 (HEM) ABKOWITZ, JANIS L UNIV OF WASHINGTON DIV OF HEMATOLOGY SEATTLE, WA 98195 Feline leukemia virus-induced hematologic disease
R01HL-31854-07 (BIO) SLAKEY, LINDA L UNIVERSITY OF MASSACHUSETTS AMHERST, MASS 01003 Pericellular nucleotide metabolism and vascular response
R01HL-31922-08 (BIO) JAKSCHIK, BARBARA A WASHINGTON UNIVERSITY 660 SOUTH EUCLID AVENUE ST LOUIS, MO 63110 Cardiovascular role of leukotrienes in anaphylaxis
R01HL-31932-06A1 (HEM) PIZZO, SALVATORE V DUKE UNIVERSITY MEDICAL CTR BOX 3712 DURHAM, N C 27710 Fibrinolysis in vitro and in vivo
R01HL-31933-08 (CVB) BAYLIS, CHRISTINE WEST VIRGINIA UNIVERSITY 3048 BASIC SCIENCE BUILDING MORGANTOWN, WV 26506 Glomerular function in pregnancy in health and disease
R01HL-31940-08 (RAP) SOUHRADA, MAGDALENA JOHN B PIERCE FDN LAB, INC 290 CONGRESS AVENUE NEW HAVEN, CT 06519 Alteration of airway smooth muscle in disease
R01HL-31942-09 (CVA) SPERELAKIS, NICHOLAS UNIVERSITY OF CINCINNATI 231 BETHESDA AVE CINCINNATI, OH 45267-0576 Electrophysiology of developing heart cells
P01HL-31950-08 (HLBB) GRIFFIN, JOHN H SCRIPPS CLINIC & RESEARCH FDN 10666 N TORREY PINES ROAD LA JOLLA, CALIF 92037 Thrombus formation and dissolution
P01HL-31950-08 0005 (HLBB) ZIMMERMAN, THEODORE S Thrombus formation and dissolution Factor VIII procoagulation protein
P01HL-31950-08 0001 (HLBB) HANSON, STEPHEN R Thrombus formation and dissolution Platelet interaction with adhesive glycoproteins
P01HL-31950-08 0002 (HLBB) HARKER, LAURENCE A Thrombus formation and dissolution Antithrombotic therapy in experimental thrombosis
P01HL-31950-08 0004 (HLBB) RUGGERI, ZAVERIO M Thrombus formation and dissolution Platelet interactions with von Willebrand factor and fibrinogen
P01HL-31950-08 0006 (HLBB) LOSKUTOFF, DAVID J Thrombus formation and dissolution Cofactor for type-1 plasminogen activator
P01HL-31950-08 0007 (HLBB) GINSBERG, MARK H Thrombus formation and dissolution Ligand induced binding sites in platelet
P01HL-31950-08 0008 (HLBB) GRIFFIN, JOHN H Thrombus formation and dissolution Inhibition of activated protein C
P01HL-31950-08 9001 (HLBB) HANSON, STEPHEN R Thrombus formation and dissolution CORE--Animal unit
P01HL-31950-08 9002 (HLBB) ZIMMERMAN, THEODORE S Thrombus formation and dissolution CORE--Hybridoma unit
P01HL-31950-08 9003 (HLBB) HOUGHTEN, RICHARD A Thrombus formation and dissolution Peptide synthesis lab--core
P01HL-31962-08 (HLBA) POLLACK, GERALD H UNIVERSITY OF WASHINGTON SEATTLE, WA 98195 Mechanism of contraction in cardiac muscle
P01HL-31962-08 0001 (HLBA) POLLACK, GERALD H Mechanism of contraction in cardiac muscle Ultrastructural dynamics and implications for contraction
P01HL-31962-08 0002 (HLBA) HUNTSMAN, LEE L Mechanism of contraction in cardiac muscle Mechanical activation in striated muscle
P01HL-31962-08 0003 (HLBA) JOHNSON, DALE E Mechanism of contraction in cardiac muscle Myocardial subcellular calcium distribution

PROJECT NO., ORGANIZATIONAL UNIT., INVESTIGATOR, ADDRESS, TITLE

P01HL-31962-08 0004 (HLBA) GORDON, ALBERT M Mechanism of contraction in cardiac muscle Fluorescent probe study of calcium activation
P01HL-31962-08 0005 (HLBA) GORDON, ALBERT M Mechanism of contraction in cardiac muscle Calcium regulation of striated muscle
P01HL-31962-08 0006 (HLBA) KUSHMERICK, MARTIN J Mechanism of contraction in cardiac muscle Chemomechanics--ATPase product and peptide inhibition
P01HL-31962-08 9001 (HLBA) HUNTSMAN, LEE L Mechanism of contraction in cardiac muscle CORE--Computer programming
P01HL-31962-08 9002 (HLBA) JOHNSON, DALE E Mechanism of contraction in cardiac muscle CORE--Electron microscopy
P01HL-31962-08 9003 (HLBA) POLLACK, GERALD H Mechanism of contraction in cardiac muscle Core--Instrumentation
P01HL-31962-08 9004 (HLBA) GORDON, ALBERT M Mechanism of contraction in cardiac muscle CORE--Skinned fiber solutions
P01HL-31963-08 (HLBA) WARD, PETER A 1301 CATHERINE ROAD ANN ARBOR, MI 48109-0602 Inflammatory cells and lung injury
P01HL-31963-08 0001 (HLBA) WARD, PETER A Inflammatory cells and lung injury Immune complex-induced acute lung injury
P01HL-31963-08 0002 (HLBA) KUNKEL, STEVEN L Inflammatory cells and lung injury Granulomatous lung inflammation
P01HL-31963-08 0003 (HLBA) BOXER, LAURENCE A Inflammatory cells and lung injury Neutrophil activation in acute pulmonary disease
P01HL-31963-08 0004 (HLBA) PHAN, SEM H Inflammatory cells and lung injury Macrophage function in lung injury and fibrosis
P01HL-31963-08 0005 (HLBA) WARD, PETER A Inflammatory cells and lung injury Adenine nucleotide--leukocyte activation and O2 radical formation
P01HL-31963-08 0006 (HLBA) KILLEN, PAUL Inflammatory cells and lung injury Molecular biology of injury to alveolar wall cells
P01HL-31963-08 9001 (HLBA) KUNKEL, STEVEN L Inflammatory cells and lung injury Core--Immunology and molecular biology
P01HL-31963-08 9002 (HLBA) JOHNSON, KENT J Inflammatory cells and lung injury Core--Morphology
R01HL-31979-08 (CVA) GREEN, JERRY F UNIVERSITY OF CALIFORNIA DAVIS, CALIF 95616 Regulatory reflexes from isolated pulmonary vasculature
R01HL-31987-07 (ECS) PETERSON, THOMAS V TEXAS A & M UNIVERSITY COLLEGE OF MEDICINE COLLEGE STATION, TEXAS 77843 Neurohumoral controling of blood volume
P01HL-31992-08 (HLBA) CRAPO, JAMES D DUKE UNIVERSITY MEDICAL CENTER PO BOX 3177 DURHAM, NC 27710 Acute lung injury and repair
P01HL-31992-08 0002 (HLBA) CRAPO, JAMES D Acute lung injury and repair Immunocytochemical localization of superoxide dismutases
P01HL-31992-08 0004 (HLBA) THET, LYN A Acute lung injury and repair Mechanisms of repair of hyperoxic lung injury
P01HL-31992-08 0005 (HLBA) FRACICA, PHILIP J Acute lung injury and repair Protection from oxygen toxicity with antioxidant enzyme therapy
P01HL-31992-08 0006 (HLBA) PIANTADOSI, CLAUDE A Acute lung injury and repair: Oxygen delivery, tissue oxygenation and energy metabolism in sepsis
P01HL-31992-08 0007 (HLBA) YOUNG, STEPHEN L Acute lung injury and repair Surfactant treatment of diffuse lung injury
P01HL-31992-08 0008 (HLBA) HO, YE-SHIH Acute lung injury and repair Superoxide dismutase gene regulation in lung injury
P01HL-31992-08 9001 (HLBA) PRATT, PHILIP C Acute lung injury and repair CORE--Pathology
P01HL-31992-08 9002 (HLBA) WOLFE, WALTER G Acute lung injury and repair CORE--Primate studies
R01HL-32021-06 (SRC) DAVIS, SALLY M PHD UNIVERSITY OF NEW MEXICO 2701 FRONTIER N E ALBUQUERQUE, N MEX 87131 Checkerboard cardiovascular curriculum
R01HL-32026-08 (PBC) MAWHINNEY, THOMAS P UNIVERSITY OF MISSOURI 322A CHEMISTRY BLDG COLUMBIA, MO 65211 Tracheobronchial glycoprotein structure
R01HL-32032-08 (MGN) KARATHANASIS, SOTIRIOS K CHILDREN'S HOSPITAL CORP 300 LONGWOOD AVE BOSTON, MA 02115 Apolipoprotein gene expression & premature atheroscleros
R01HL-32043-07A1 (CVA) GALLAGHER, KIM P UNIVERISTY OF MICHIGAN B560 MSRB II BOX 0686 ANN ARBOR, MI 48109 Regional function in ischemic and infarcted myocardium
R01HL-32050-07 (SSP) LOVALLO, WILLIAM R VA MEDICAL CENTER 921 NE 13TH STREET OKLAHOMA CITY, OK 73104 Caffeine influences on exercise and psychological stress
R01HL-32070-07 (HEM) WALLIN, REIDAR BOWMAN GRAY SCH OF MED 300 S HAWTHORNE RD WINSTON-SALEM, N C 27103 Vitamin K dependent proteins in liver & isolated cells
R01HL-32087-07 (MGN) PAIGEN, BEVERLY J THE JACKSON LABORATORY 600 MAIN STREET BAR HARBOR, ME 04609-0800 Genetic factors in murine atherosclerosis
R01HL-32093-08 (CVA) CLUSIN, WILLIAM T STANFORD UNIVERSITY 300 PASTEUR DR, FALK CVRC STANFORD CA 94305-5246 Ionic mechanisms in the acutely ischemic heart
R01HL-32129-08 (CVB) CAREY, ROBERT M UNIV OF VIRGINIA BOX 395 CHARLOTTESVILLE, VA 22908 Control of renal function by intrarenal angiotensin
R01HL-32131-06 (SAT) ARZBAECHER, ROBERT C PRITZKER INST OF MED ENGR ILLINOIS INSTITUTE OF TECH CHICAGO, IL 60616 Closed-loop implantable antiarrhythmic drug infusion
R01HL-32132-06 (SB) REICHERT, WILLIAM M DUKE UNIVERSITY DURHAM, NC 27706 Protein adsorption by polymer waveguide optics
R01HL-32145-06 (CTY) COOKE, ROGER A UNIVERSITY OF CALIFORNIA 841 HEALTH SCIENCES WEST SAN FRANCISCO, CA 94143 Modulators of muscle cross-bridge function
R01HL-32154-09 (RAP) PITT, BRUCE R UNIVERSITY OF PITTSBURGH E1352 BIOMEDICAL SCIENCE TOWER PITTSBURGH, PA 15261 Pulmonary microcirculation during postnatal development
R01HL-32185-07 (SRC) FARQUHAR, JOHN W CTR FOR RES IN DIS PREV 1000 WELCH RD PALO ALTO, CA 94304-1885 Teenage CVD risk reduction--A dissemination model
R01HL-32188-08 (HED) YOUNG, STEPHEN L DUKE UNIVERSITY MED CENTER BOX 3177 DURHAM, NC 27710 Fetal lung biochemistry and 3-dimensional microanatomy

PROJECT NO., ORGANIZATIONAL UNIT., INVESTIGATOR, ADDRESS, TITLE

R01HL-32200-06 (HEM) RAND, JACOB H MOUNT SINAI SCHOOL OF MEDICINE ONE GUSTAVE L LEVY PLACE NEW YORK, N Y 10029 Subendothelial binding of Von Willebrand factor
R01HL-32205-04A3 (NEUA) TALMAN, WILLIAM T UNIV OF IOWA COLL OF MED IOWA CITY, IA 52242 Neurotransmitters and central control of blood pressure
R01HL-32210-08 (PTHA) SILVERSTEIN, SAMUEL C COLUMBIA UNIVERSITY 630 WEST 168TH STREET NEW YORK, NY 10032 Interaction of endothelial cells and leukocytes
R01HL-32214-08 (PB) BALL, WILLIAM J, JR UNIVERSITY OF CINCINNATI 231 BETHESDA AVENUE CINCINNATI, OH 45267-0575 Immunological studies of the digitalis receptor
R01HL-32257-09 (SAT) COX, JAMES L WASHINGTON UNIVERSITY ONE BARNES HOSPITAL PLAZA ST LOUIS, MO 63110 Surgical treatment of cardiac arrhythmias
R01HL-32257-09 0003 (SAT) COX, JAMES L Surgical treatment of cardiac arrhythmias Operative electrophysiologic monitoring system
R01HL-32257-09 0004 (SAT) COX, JAMES L Surgical treatment of cardiac arrhythmias Atrial flutter and atrial fibrillation
R01HL-32257-09 0005 (SAT) COX, JAMES L Surgical treatment of cardiac arrhythmias Electrophysiologic mapping of ventricular tachyarrhythmias
R01HL-32259-10 (HEM) ORKIN, STUART H CHILDREN'S HOSPITAL 300 LONGWOOD AVENUE BOSTON, MA 02115 Molecular analysis of normal and thalassemic DNA
P01HL-32262-10 (HLBB) NATHAN, DAVID G CHILDREN'S HOSPITAL CORPORATIO 300 LONGWOOD AVENUE BOSTON, MA 02115 The developmental biology of human erythropoiesis
P01HL-32262-10 0003 (HLBB) LUX, SAMUEL E The developmental biology of human erythropoiesis Structure and function of erythrocyte membrane skeleton
P01HL-32262-10 0006 (HLBB) NATHAN, DAVID G The developmental biology of human erythropoiesis GM-CSF receptor gene expression regulation during hematopoietic differentiation
P01HL-32262-10 0007 (HLBB) LODISH, HARVEY F The developmental biology of human erythropoiesis Studies on the erythropoietin receptor
P01HL-32262-10 0008 (HLBB) ZON, LEONARD I The developmental biology of human erythropoiesis Extracytoplasmic region of the erythropoietin receptor and disease states
P01HL-32262-10 0009 (HLBB) ORKIN, STUART H The developmental biology of human erythropoiesis Homologous recomination--Genetic dissection of erythroid cell development
P01HL-32262-10 0002 (HLBB) ORKIN, STUART H The developmental biology of human erythropoiesis Retroviral transfer and expression of DHFR and ADA genes
R01HL-32270-06 (ECS) SONGU-MIZE, EMEL UNIVERSITY OF TENNESSEE 874 UNION AVENUE MEMPHIS, TN 38163 Vascular Na pump activity and hypertension
R01HL-32272-07 (PTHA) PROUD, DAVID THE GOOD SAMARITAN HOSP 5601 LOCH RAVEN BLVD BALTIMORE, MD 21239 Kinins as mediators of human reactions
R01HL-32279-07 (HEM) KUNICKI, THOMAS J BLOOD CTR OF SOUTHEASTERN WISC 1701 WEST WISCONSIN AVENUE MILWAUKEE, WI 53233 Molecular basis of platelet function
P50HL-32295-07 (SRC) SKORTON, DAVID UNIVERSITY OF IOWA IOWA CITY, IOWA 52242 Specialized center of research--Coronary and vascular diseases
P50HL-32295-07 0001 (SRC) DELLSPERGER, KEVIN C Specialized center of research--Coronary and vascular diseases Abnormalities in coronary microcirculation--Myocardial ischemia
P50HL-32295-07 0002 (SRC) KERBER, RICHARD E Specialized center of research--Coronary and vascular diseases Echocardiography--Arterial morphology & remodeling--Atherosclerosis
P50HL-32295-07 0004 (SRC) MARTINS, JAMES B Specialized center of research--Coronary and vascular diseases Autonomic control of ventricular electrophysiology in ischemia
P50HL-32295-07 0007 (SRC) BRODY, MICHAEL J Specialized center of research--Coronary and vascular diseases Central control of the coronary circulation
P50HL-32295-07 0008 (SRC) SKORTON, DAVID J Specialized center of research--Coronary and vascular diseases Coronary circulation studies with cine computed tomography
P50HL-32295-07 0010 (SRC) WINNIFORD, MICHAEL D Specialized center of research--Coronary and vascular diseases Coronary flow reserve and myocardial ischemia
P50HL-32295-07 0011 (SRC) SKORTON, DAVID J Specialized center of research--Coronary and vascular diseases Ultrasound and NMR characterization of cardiac tissue
P50HL-32295-07 0012 (SRC) GEBHART, GERALD F Specialized center of research--Coronary and vascular diseases Mechanisms of cardiac pain
P50HL-32295-07 9002 (SRC) SKORTON, DAVID J Specialized center of research--Coronary and vascular diseases Core--Computer image processing
P50HL-32295-07 9003 (SRC) TOMANEK, ROBERT J Specialized center of research--Coronary and vascular diseases Core--Anatomy and pathology
P50HL-32295-07 9004 (SRC) BURNS, TRUDY L. Specialized center of research--Coronary and vascular diseases Core--Biostatistics unit
R01HL-32318-06A1 (BEM) NIAURA, RAYMOND S MIRIAM HOSPITAL 164 SUMMIT AVENUE PROVIDENCE, RI 02906 Nicotine dependence and smoking relapse
R01HL-32348-08 (CBY) MACIAG, THOMAS AMERICAN RED CROSS 15601 CRABBS BRANCH WAY ROCKVILLE, MD 20855 Endothelial cell growth--Prevention of thrombosis in vivo
R01HL-32383-08 (ECS) BEVAN, JOHN A UNIVERSITY OF VERMONT BURLINGTON, VT 05405 Cerebral arterial tone and reactivity
P01HL-32427-06 (SRC) COHN, JAY N UNIVERSITY OF MINNESOTA BOX 508 UMHC MINNEAPOLIS, MN 55455 Myocardial and vascular factors in heart failure
P01HL-32427-06 0001 (SRC) UGURBIL, KAMIL Myocardial and vascular factors in heart failure NMR studies of the myocardium in situ
P01HL-32427-06 0004 (SRC) BACHE, ROBERT J Myocardial and vascular factors in heart failure Post-ischemic myocardial and coronary vascular function

PROJECT NO., ORGANIZATIONAL UNIT., INVESTIGATOR, ADDRESS, TITLE

P01HL-32427-06 0005 (SRC) COHN, JAY N Myocardial and vascular factors in heart failure Experimental heart failure
P01HL-32427-06 0007 (SRC) COHN, JAY N Myocardial and vascular factors in heart failure Vasoconstrictor mechanisms in heart failure
P01HL-32427-06 9001 (SRC) RECTOR, THOMAS H Myocardial and vascular factors in heart failure Biostatistics core
P01HL-32427-06 9002 (SRC) COHN, JAY N Myocardial and vascular factors in heart failure Biochemistry core
P01HL-32427-06 9003 (SRC) BACCHE, ROBERT Myocardial and vascular factors in heart failure Microsphere core
R01HL-32435-08 (NTN) BRESLOW, JAN L ROCKEFELLER UNIVERSITY 1230 YORK AVENUE NEW YORK, N Y 10021-6399 Human dietary cholesterol tolerance
R01HL-32459-07 (CBY) KRIEGER, MONTY MASS INSTITUTE OF TECHNOLOGY 77 MASSACHUSETTS AVE CAMBRIDGE, MASS 02139 Immunological analysis of LDL receptor defective cells
R01HL-32469-09 (ECS) JACKSON, WILLIAM FREDERICK WESTERN MICHIGAN UNIVERSITY 5020 MCCRACKEN HALL KALAMAZOO, MI 49008 Control of microvascular function by oxygen
R01HL-32482-08 (PTHA) PIETRA, GIUSEPPE G UNIV OF PENNSYLVANIA/HOSP 3400 SPRUCE STREET PHILADELPHIA, PA 19104 Charge permselectivity of pulmonary endothelium
R01HL-32495-07 (RAP) LEFF, ALAN R UNIVERSITY OF CHICAGO 5841 SOUTH MARYLAND AVENUE CHICAGO, ILL 60637 Autonomic regulation of respiratory muscle and secretion
R01HL-32583-08 (CVA) COVELL, JAMES W UNIVERSITY OF CALIFORNIA LA JOLLA, CA 92093-0613 Transmural deformation
R01HL-32595-06 (BBCB) GETTINS, PETER VANDERBILT UNIVERSITY 607 LIGHT HALL NASHVILLE, TN 37232 Structural studies on heparin-binding proteins
R01HL-32607-07 (PHY) KAMM, KRISTINE E UNIV OF TX SOUTHWESTERN MED CT 5323 HARRY HINES BOULEVARD DALLAS, TX 75235 Regulation of contractility in smooth muscle
R01HL-32609-08 (MET) ONTKO, JOSEPH A LSU MEDICAL CENTER 1100 FLORIDA AVE NEW ORLEANS, LA 70119 Mechanisms of cellular lipid droplet mobilization
R01HL-32636-06 (RNM) STRAUSS, HARRY W MASSACHUSETTS GENERAL HOSPITAL 32 FRUIT ST/NUCLEAR MED DIV BOSTON, MASS 02114 Heart imaging with single photon agents
R55HL-32646-07A1 (RAP) SCHUMACKER, PAUL T UNIVERSITY OF CHICAGO 5841 S MARYLAND AVE BOX 83 CHICAGO, IL 60637 Mechanisms for a dependence of O2 uptake on delivery
R01HL-32650-07 (RAP) SNYDER, JEANNE M UNIVERSITY OF IOWA IOWA CITY, IA 52242 Lung alveolar epithelial cell differentiation
R01HL-32656-06A2 (HEM) CHURCH, FRANK C UNIVERSITY OF NORTH CAROLINA CB#7015-435 BURNETT WOMACK BLD CHAPEL HILL, N C 27599-7015 Heparin cofactor II in tissue injury and wound repair
R01HL-32670-07 (CVB) BLOOR, COLIN M UNIVERSITY OF CALIFORNIA LA JOLLA, CA 92093-0023 Determinants of coronary collateral development
R01HL-32688-07 (PHRA) ARONSON, RONALD S ALBERT EINSTEIN COLL. OF MED. 1300 MORRIS PARK AVENUE BRONX, NEW YORK 10461 Effects of cadioactive agents on cardiac myocytes
R01HL-32690-07 (PBC) LAST, JEROLD A CALIFORNIA PRIMATE RES CENTER UNIVERSITY OF CALIFORNIA DAVIS, CA 95616 Lung collagen crosslinking--biosynthesis and maturation
R01HL-32694-07 (CVA) RODEN, DAN M VANDERBILT UNIVERSITY SCHOOL OF MEDICINE NASHVILLE, TENN 37232 Role of prolonged repolarization in cardiac arrhythmias
R01HL-32708-08 (PHRA) GRANT, AUGUSTUS O DUKE UNIVERSITY MEDICAL SCHOOL BOX 3504 DURHAM, NC 27710 Pharmacology of unitary conductances in cardiac muscle
R01HL-32711-07 (PB) FLEISCHER, SIDNEY VANDERBILT UNIVERSITY BOX 1820 STATION B NASHVILLE, TN 37235 Modulation of Ca++ fluxes in heart and smooth muscle
R01HL-32717-08 (CVA) HARRISON, DAVID G EMORY UNIVERSITY 1634 CLIFTON,RD ATLANTA, GEORGIA 30322 Factors that regulate coronary collateral resistance
R37HL-32723-08 (RAP) FANBURG, BARRY L NEW ENGLAND MED CTR 750 WASHINGTON ST, NEMC #257 BOSTON, MA 02111 Effect of injury on function of pulmonary endothelium
R01HL-32726-07 (RAP) OLSON, NEIL C DVM PHD NORTH CAROLINA STATE UNIV 4700 HILLSBOROUGH STREET RALEIGH, N C 27606 Lipoxygenase products in acute respiratory failure
R01HL-32738-06 (BEM) MCCUBBIN, JAMES A UNIVERSITY OF KENTUCKY COLLEGE OF MED OFFICE BLDG LEXINGTON, KY 40536-0086 Endogenous opiates, stress and risk for hypertension
R01HL-32752-07 (HEM) JOHNSON, CHRISTOPHER M MAYO FOUNDATION 200 FIRST STREET S W ROCHESTER, MN 55905 Regional variations in cardiac and vascular cells
R01HL-32788-06 (CVA) CHILIAN, WILLIAM M TEXAS A&M UNIVERSITY COLLEGE STATION, TX 77843 Microcirculatory dynamics in the coronary circulation
R01HL-32793-08 (BNP) ABRAHAM, DONALD J VIRGINIA COMMONWEALTH UNIV BOX 540 MCV STATION RICHMOND, VA 23298-0540 Design and development of potential antisicking agents
R01HL-32800-05 (CVA) FRANKLIN, DEAN UNIVERSITY OF MISSOURI COLUMBIA, MO 65211 Coronary collateral dynamics
R01HL-32802-07 (ALY) CENTER, DAVID M BOSTON UNIVERSITY SCHOOL OF ME 80 EAST CONCORD STREET BOSTON, MA 02118 Histamine-induced accumulation of T cells in the lung
R01HL-32815-07 (RNM) SCHUSTER, DANIEL P WASHINGTON UNIV SCH OF MED 660 S EUCLID AVE, BOX 8052 ST LOUIS, MO 63110 Lung perfusion by positron emission tomography
R01HL-32816-06 (SB) OLSEN, DON B UNIVERSITY OF UTAH INST FOR BIOMEDICAL ENGR SALT LAKE CITY, UTAH 84112 100 ml stroke volume elliptical TAH in 50 kg recipients
R01HL-32821-08 (EDC) GOLDBERG, ROBERT J UNIVERSITY OF MASS MED CENTER 55 LAKE AVENUE NORTH WORCESTER, MA 01655 Diet modification and blood pressure in young people
R01HL-32824-08 (RAP) DENEKE, SUSAN M UNIVERSITY OF TEXAS SW MED CTR 7703 FLOYD CURL DRIVE SAN ANTONIO, TX 78284 Regulation of glutathione in the lung
R01HL-32847-08 (SRC) POMREHN, PAUL UNIVERSITY OF IOWA DIV OF PEDIATRICS CARDIOLOGY IOWA CITY, IA 52242 Community program to prevent adolescent cigarette smoking
R01HL-32853-06 (HEM) MILLER, JONATHAN L ST UNIV OF NEW YORK HLTH SCI C 750 EAST ADAMS STREET SYRACUSE, NY 13210 Regulation of platelet GPIB/IX receptor complex
R01HL-32854-08 (HEM) GOLAN, DAVID E HARVARD MEDICAL SCHOOL 250 LONGWOOD AVENUE BOSTON, MA 02115 Membrane dynamics in normal and abnormal red blood cells
R01HL-32868-08 (PC) REYLAND, MARY SUNY HLTH SCIS CTR DEPT PHARMACOLOGICAL SCIS STONY BROOK, NY 11794-8651 Atherosclerosis and peripheral apoprotein E synthesis
R01HL-32894-06 (HED) SNYDER, GREGORY K UNIVERSITY OF COLORADO CAMPUS BOX 334 BOULDER, CO 80309-0334 The effects of activity & hypoxia on capillary growth
R01HL-32898-08 (PTHA) WILLIAMS, LEWIS T UNIVERSITY OF CALIFORNIA U-426, 3RD & PARNASSUS AVES SAN FRANCISCO, CA 94143-0724 Vascular receptors for platelet-derived growth factor
R01HL-32908-07 (HEM) ADACHI, KAZUHIKO CHILDREN'S HOSPITAL 34TH STREET AND CIVIC CTR BLVD PHILADELPHIA, PA 19104 Mechanism of polymerization of hb S
R01HL-32911-06 (PHRA) WARLTIER, DAVID C MEDICAL COLLEGE OF WISCONSIN 8701 WATERTOWN PLANK ROAD MILWAUKEE, WI 53226 Pharmacology of ischemic myocardium
R01HL-32921-08 (MEP) MATHEW, OOMMEN P EAST CAROLINA UNIVERSITY SCHOOL OF MEDICINE GREENVILLE, NC 27858 Control of breathing--Influences of upper airway origin
R01HL-32934-07 (BBCA) JOHNSON, ARTHUR E UNIVERSITY OF OKLAHOMA 620 PARRINGTON OVAL NORMAN, OK 73019 Membrane-bound procoagulant and anticoagulant complexes
R01HL-32971-07 (PC) MORRISETT, JOEL D BAYLOR COLLEGE OF MEDICINE 6535 FANNIN STREET HOUSTON, TX 77030 Structure and function of human lipoprotein(a)
R37HL-32985-08 (ECS) BEVAN, JOHN A UNIVERSITY OF VERMONT GIVEN BLDG BURLINGTON, VT 05405 Resistance arteries and their innervation
R01HL-32987-06 (HEM) AUERBACH, ARLEEN D ROCKEFELLER UNIVERSITY 1230 YORK AVENUE NEW YORK, NY 10021-6399 Fanconi anemia--heterogeneity and carrier detection
R01HL-32994-08 (PHRA) STARMER, C FRANK DUKE UNIV MED CTR P O BOX 3181 DURHAM, NC 27710 Models of drug binding to cardiac sodium channels
P01HL-33009-07 (HLBA) FREDBERG, JEFFREY J HARVARD SCHOOL OF PUBLIC HEALT 665 HUNTINGTON AVENUE BOSTON, MA 02115 Physical determinants of lung function and dysfunction
P01HL-33009-07 0001 (HLBA) BUTLER, JAMES P Physical determinants of lung function and dysfunction Parenchymal mechanics
P01HL-33009-07 0003 (HLBA) DRAZEN, JEFFERY M Physical determinants of lung function and dysfunction Amplification of airway responses by liquid lining layers
P01HL-33009-07 0004 (HLBA) FREDBERG, JEFFREY J Physical determinants of lung function and dysfunction Oscillation mechanics of the lung
P01HL-33009-07 0006 (HLBA) LORING, STEPHEN H Physical determinants of lung function and dysfunction Chest wall mechanics
P01HL-33009-07 0007 (HLBA) KAMM, ROGER D Physical determinants of lung function and dysfunction Airway closure and liquid film dynamics
P01HL-33009-07 0008 (HLBA) KAMM, ROGER D Physical determinants of lung function and dysfunction Indices of lung function and dysfunction
P01HL-33009-07 9001 (HLBA) LEHR, JOHN L Physical determinants of lung function and dysfunction CORE--Instrumentation
P01HL-33014-07 (HLBB) ROSENBERG, ROBERT D MASSACHUSETTS INST OF TECH 77 MASSACHUSETTS AVENUE CAMBRIDGE, MA 02139 Thrombosis and atherosclerosis
P01HL-33014-07 0001 (HLBB) ROSENBERG, ROBERT D Thrombosis and atherosclerosis Regulation of anticoagulant mechanisms of blood vessel wall
P01HL-33014-07 0002 (HLBB) MC DONAGH, JAN Thrombosis and atherosclerosis Molecular interactions of fibrin and fibrinogen
P01HL-33014-07 0003 (HLBB) SALZMAN, EDWIN W Thrombosis and atherosclerosis Intracellular regulation of platelet functions--role of calcium
P01HL-33014-07 0005 (HLBB) HANDIN, ROBERT I Thrombosis and atherosclerosis Molecular basis of platelet adhesion
P01HL-33014-07 0006 (HLBB) SLAYTER, HENRY S Thrombosis and atherosclerosis Characterization of platelet thrombospondin
P01HL-33014-07 0007 (HLBB) FRIEDMAN, PAUL A Thrombosis and atherosclerosis Biochemistry and pharmacology of coumarin anticoagulants
P01HL-33014-07 0009 (HLBB) LYNCH, DENNIS C Thrombosis and atherosclerosis Transcriptional regulation of vWF gene
P01HL-33014-07 0010 (HLBB) OLSEN, BJORN R Thrombosis and atherosclerosis Non-Fibrillar collagen in subendothelial matrix
P01HL-33014-07 0011 (HLBB) :BAUER, KENNETH A Thrombosis and atherosclerosis Clinical studies--Detection of the prethrombotic state
P01HL-33014-07 9001 (HLBB) SLAYTER, HENRY S Thrombosis and atherosclerosis Electron microscopy--core
R01HL-33022-09 (PTHA) AUSPRUNK, DIANNA H CHILDREN'S HOSPITAL 300 LONGWOOD AVENUE BOSTON, MA 02115 Structure and development of regenerating capillaries
P01HL-33026-07 (HLBA) KATZ, ARNOLD M UNIVERSITY OF CONNECTICUT 263 FARMINGTON AVENUE FARMINGTON, CONN 06032 Cardiovascular membrane structure and function
P01HL-33026-07 0001 (HLBA) KATZ, ARNOLD M Cardiovascular membrane structure and function Calcium release from sarcoplasmic reticulum
P01HL-33026-07 0002 (HLBA) WATRAS, JAMES M Cardiovascular membrane structure and function Inositol trisphosphate-gated calcium channel in smooth muscle
P01HL-33026-07 0003 (HLBA) HERBETTE, LEO G Cardiovascular membrane structure and function Structural basis for durg-membrane interaction mechanism
P01HL-33026-07 0006 (HLBA) KIM, DO HAN Cardiovascular membrane structure and function Calcium release channel of the sarcoplasmic reticulum
P01HL-33026-07 0007 (HLBA) EHRLICH, BARBARA E Cardiovascular membrane structure and function Regulation of ion channels in planar

bilayar

R01HL-33041-07 (SSS) LONG, WILLIAM J MASSACHUSETTS INST OF TECHNOLO 545 TECHNOLOGY SQUARE CAMBRIDGE, MA 02139 **Artificial intelligence and cardiovascular reasoning**

R01HL-33070-08 (PTHA) SOROKIN, SERGEI P BOSTON UNIVERSITY SCH OF MED 80 EAST CONCORD ST BOSTON, MA 02118 **Macrophage development in intact and cultured fetal lung**

R01HL-33091-07 (ARR) SARASON, IRWIN G UNIVERSITY OF WASHINGTON NI - 25 SEATTLE, WA 98195 AIDS and blood donor recruitment

R01HL-33095-06 (SB) GRABOWSKI, ERIC F CORNELL UNIVERSITY MED COLLEGE 1300 YORK AVE NEW YORK, N Y 10021 **Platelet-endothelial cell interactions**

R01HL-33100-07 (SB) ECKSTEIN, EUGENE C UNIVERSITY OF MIAMI PO BOX 248494 CORAL GABLES, FL 33124-0621 **Flow-induced near-wall excess of platelets**

R01HL-33107-08 (ECS) VATNER, STEPHEN F N ENG REG PRIMATE RES CENTER 1 PINE HILL DRIVE SOUTHBORO, MASS 01772 **Cardiovascular control in normal and disease states**

R01HL-33142-08 (PTHA) CHOPRA, DHARAM P WAYNE STATE UNIVERSITY 2727 SECOND AVENUE #402 DETROIT, MI 48201 **Regulation of normal human airway epithelial cultures**

R01HL-33177-07 (RNM) SCHELBERT, HEINRICH R UNIVERSITY OF CALIFORNIA 405 HILGARD AVENUE LOS ANGELES, CA 90024-1721 **Positron tomography in ischemic heart disease**

R01HL-33233-07 (SRC) KISTLER, J PHILIP MASSACHUSETTS GENERAL HOSPITAL BURNHAM 802, NEUROLOGY SERVICE BOSTON, MASS 02114 **NIH-Boston area anticoagulation trial for atrial fibrillation**

R01HL-33237-07 (IMS) GRAZIANO, FRANK M UNIVERSITY OF WISCONSIN 600 HIGHLAND AVE. MADISON, WI 53792 **IGg1 and igE receptor mechanisms in guinea pig lung**

R01HL-33254-07 (HEM) SHEN, BETTY W ARGONNE NATIONAL LABORATORY 9700 SOUTH CASS AVE ARGONNE, ILLINOIS 60439 **Red cell membrane skeleton--Ultrastructure and function**

R01HL-33259-07 (RAP) SHEPPARD, DEAN SAN FRANCISCO GENERAL HOSPITAL 22ND AND POTRERO STREETS SAN FRANCISCO, CALIF 94110 **Role of inflammation in induced airway hyperreactivity**

R01HL-33266-08 (CVB) BARMAN, SUSAN M MICHIGAN STATE UNIVERSITY EAST LANSING, MI 48824-1317 **Blood pressure control by forebrain and brainstem neurons**

R01HL-33269-05 (CLTR) ROGERS, ROBERT M UNIVERSITY OF PITTSBURGH 3550 TERRACE STREET PITTSBURGH, PA 15261 **Emphysema--Physiologic effects of nutritional support**

R01HL-33274-06 (CVB) CHANG, H K UNIV OF SOUTHERN CALIFORNIA UNIVERSITY PARK LOS ANGELES, CA 90089-1451 **Flow dynamics and resistances in the upper airways**

R01HL-33277-06 (PBC) SHUMAN, MARC A UNIVERSITY OF CALIFORNIA 3RD AVE AND PARNASSUS SAN FRANCISCO, CA 94143 **Biosynthesis of genetics and glycoproteins IIB and IIIA**

U01HL-33292-07 (SRC) DETRE, KATHERINE M UNIVERSITY OF PITTSBURGH 130 DESOTO STREET PITTSBURGH, PA 15261 **Follow-up study of NHLBI PICA registry patients**

R01HL-33324-07 (ECS) HILL, MICHAEL TEXAS A&M UNIVERSITY DEPT OF MEDICAL PHYSIOLOGY COLLEGE STATION, TEX 77843 **Microvascular control and its role in hypertension**

R01HL-33332-06 (RNM) ARENSON, RONALD L UNIVERSITY OF PENNSYLAVANIA HO 3400 SPRUCE STREET PHILADELPHIA, PA 19104 **Clinical evaluation of an image distribution system**

R01HL-33333-06 (PHY) SHEU, SHEY-SHING UNIVERSITY OF ROCHESTER DEPT OF PHARMACOLOGY ROCHESTER, NY 14642 **Myocardial Ca2+ Transport and metabolism**

R01HL-33343-07 (ECS) RUDY, YORAM CASE WESTERN RESERVE UNIV DEPT OF BIOMEDICAL ENGINEERING CLEVELAND, OH 44106 **Inverse and forward problems in electrocardiography**

R01HL-33360-04A2 (ECS) BECKER, LEWIS C JOHNS HOPKINS HOSPITAL 600 N WOLFE ST, HALSTED 500 BALTIMORE, MD 21205 **Dysfunction of post-ischemic myocardium**

R01HL-33372-05 (EI) STEIN-STREILEIN, JOAN E UNIVERSITY OF MIAMI SCH OF MED P O BOX 016960 MIAMI, FL 33101 **Natural killer cells in the lung**

R01HL-33387-06S1 (EDC) STAMLER, JEREMIAH NORTHWESTERN UNIVERSITY 680 N LAKE SHORE DR CHICAGO, IL 60611-4402 **Intersalt: Intnt'l study of Na, K, & blood pressure**

R01HL-33389-06 (PHRA) SHEN, DANNY D UNIVERSITY OF WASHINGTON SCHOOL OF PHARMACY SEATTLE, WASH 98195 **Metabolism of propranolol in uremic rat liver**

R01HL-33391-08 (VR) BRACIALE, THOMAS J UNIVERSITY OF VIRGINIA CHARLOTTESVILLE, VA 22908 **T cell function in pulmonary viral infection and immunity**

R01HL-33407-08 (EDC) LANDIS, J RICHARD MILTON HERSHEY MED CTR/PENN ST POST OFFICE BOX 850 HERSHEY, PA 17033 **Cardiovascular risk factors in US adolescents & adults**

R01HL-33441-07 (PTHA) CASTLEMAN, WILLIAM L UNIV OF WISCONSIN-MADISON 2015 LINDEN DRIVE WEST MADISON, WISCONSIN 53706 **Viral induced alterations in postnatal pulmonary growth**

R01HL-33514-06 (RNM) BIANCO, JESUS A UNIV OF WISCONSIN MEDICAL SCH 600 HIGHLAND AVENUE MADISON, WI 53792 **Autoradiography of cardiac ischemia**

R01HL-33534-05 (SSS) STEWART, JOHN M UNIVERSITY OF COLORADO PO BOX B126 DENVER, CO 80262 **Substance P in cardiovascular regulation**

R01HL-33540-07 (PTHA) SHASBY, DOUGLAS M UNIVERSITY OF IOWA IOWA CITY, IA 52242 **Mechanisms of inflammatory edems**

R01HL-33550-06 (PTHA) ROSEN, GERALD M UNIVERSITY OF MARYLAND 20 N PINE STREET BALTIMORE, MD 21201 **Toxic oxygen species mediated acute lung injury**

R01HL-33565-07 (HEM) TAUBER, ALFRED I BOSTON UNIV SCHOOL OF MEDICINE 801 ALBANY ST BOSTON, MA 02118 **Production of toxic oxygen species in acute lung injury**

R01HL-33567-08 (BPO) VERRIER, RICHARD L GEORGETOWN UNIVERSITY 37TH AND O STREETS, N.W. WASHINGTON, D.C. 20057 **Coronary constriction and behaviorally induced arrhythmia**

R01HL-33572-07 (HEM) TELEN, MARILYN J DUKE UNIVERSITY POST OFFICE BOX 3387 DURHAM, N C 27710 **Erythrocyte blood group antigens regulated by In(Lu)**

R01HL-33577-07 (CLTR) KRAUSS, RONALD M THE REGENTS OF THE UNIV OF C.A UNIVERSITY OF CALIFORNIA BERKELEY, CALIFORNIA 94720 **Plasma lipoproteins in coronary artery disease**

R01HL-33579-07 (CVA) WALSH, RICHARD A UNIVERSITY OF CINCINNATI 231 BETHESDA AVE. (ML 542) **Hypertension and hypertrophy in the non-human primate**

R01HL-33593-07 (CVA) SPEAR, JOSEPH F UNIVERSITY OF PENNSYLVANIA 3800 SPRUCE STREET PHILADELPHIA, PA 19143 **Electrophysiology of conduction in infarcted myocardium**

R01HL-33600-07 (BBCB) UGURBIL, KAMIL GRAY FRESHWATER BIOLOGICAL INS 4-225 MILLARD HALL MINNEAPOLIS, MN 55455 **NMR studies of myocardial metabolism**

R01HL-33610-06 (ECS) RAIZADA, MOHAN K UNIVERSITY OF FLORIDA BOX J-274, JHMHC GAINESVILLE, FL 32610 **Brain angiotensin in hypertensive neurons in culture**

R01HL-33616-08 (CVB) DECKER, ROBERT S NORTHWESTERN UNIVERSITY 303 E CHICAGO AVENUE CHICAGO, IL 60611 **Protein turnover in cultured adult cardiac myocytes**

R01HL-33621-07 (CVA) YIN, FRANK CHI-PONG JOHNS HOPKINS UNIVERSITY 538 CARNEGIE BLDG BALTIMORE, MD 21205 **Mechanical properties of myocardium and pericardium**

R01HL-33629-07 (HEM) BUCCI, ENRICO UNIVERSITY OF MARYLAND 660 WEST REDWOOD STREET BALTIMORE, MD 21201 **Hemoglobin based oxygen carriers**

R01HL-33637-07 (CVA) SMITH, WILLIAM M DUKE UNIVERSITY MEDICAL CENTER BOX 3140 DURHAM, N C 27710 **Signal acquisition and analysis in cardiac mapping**

R01HL-33652-08 (CVA) HAWORTH, ROBERT A UNIVERSITY OF WISCONSIN 600 HIGHLAND AVENUE MADISON, WI 53792 **Ca and the pathophysiology of the adult heart cell**

R55HL-33692-07 (CVA) FLOWERS, NANCY C MEDICAL COLLEGE OF GEORGIA 1120 15TH STREET AUGUSTA, GA 30912-3105 **Recording and analysis of low-level cardiac signals**

R01HL-33699-07 (BIO) BAENZIGER, NANCY L WASHINGTON UNIVERSITY 660 SOUTH ECULID AVENUE ST LOUIS, MO 63110 **Histamine metabolism in human pulmonary vascular cells**

R01HL-33709-06 (PTHA) STEIN-STREILEIN, JOAN E UNIV OF MIAMI SCH OF MEDICINE PO BOX 016960 MIAMI, FL 33101 **Pulmonary interstitial disease induced by haptens**

R01HL-33711-09 (CBY) CHEN, WEN-TIEN GEORGETOWN UNIV SCH OF MED 3900 RESERVOIR ROAD, N W WASHINGTON, D C 20007 **Membrane-matrix interactions and lung cell function**

P50HL-33713-06 (SRC) GRAHAM, ROBERT M CLEVELAND CLINIC FOUNDATION RESEARCH INSTITUTE CLEVELAND, OH 44195 **Specialized center of research in hypertension**

P50HL-33713-06 9006 (SRC) FOUAD-TARAZI, FEDNAT **Specialized center of research in hypertension Core--Clinical core**

P50HL-33713-06 0007 (SRC) NOVICK, ANDREW C **Specialized center of research in hypertension Atherosclerotic renal artery disease--Implications for renal function**

P50HL-33713-06 0012 (SRC) HUSAIN, AHSAN **Specialized center of research in hypertension A novel cardiac angiotensin-II forming pathway in the heart**

P50HL-33713-06 0013 (SRC) GRAHAM, ROBERT M **Specialized center of research in hypertension Cardiac GTP-binding proteins and stimulus-secretion coupling**

P50HL-33713-06 0014 (SRC) BOND, MEREDITH **Specialized center of research in hypertension Calcium regulation of cardiac contractility in hypertensive hypertrophy**

P50HL-33713-06 0015 (SRC) BRAVO, EMMANUEL L **Specialized center of research in hypertension Mechanisms of salt sensitivity and salt resistance in human hypertension**

P50HL-33713-06 9002 (SRC) SCHLUCHTER, MARK D **Specialized center of research in hypertension Core--Biostatistics and computing**

P50HL-33713-06 9005 (SRC) MISONO, KUNIO **Specialized center of research in hypertension Core--Protein chemistry**

R01HL-33714-08 (MGN) BRESLOW, JAN L ROCKEFELLER UNIVERSITY 1230 YORK AVENUE NEW YORK, N Y 10021-6399 **In vitro study of lipoproteins in vascular disease**

R01HL-33715-05 (SSS) HORAN, LEO G VET ADM MED CTR CARD SECT (111A) AUGUSTA, GA 30910 **Ventricular intramural effects on surface potential**

R01HL-33721-08 (HEM) MONTGOMERY, ROBERT R BLOOD CENTER OF SE WISCONSIN 1701 WEST WISCONSIN AVENUE MILWAUKEE, WI 53233 **Von Willebrand proteins & and their cellular relationships**

R01HL-33722-06A1 (CVA) BOINEAU, JOHN P WASHINGTON UNIVERSITY 660 S EUCLID AVE, BOX 8109 ST LOUIS, MO 63110 **Atrial pacemaker complex-Atrial flutter and fibrillation**

R10HL-33728-07 (SRC) MILLER, EDWARD J UNIVERSITY OF ALABAMA UAB STATION BIRMINGHAM, AL 35294 **Pathobiological determinants of atherosclerosis in youth**

R01HL-33730-09A1 (CVA) NADAL-GINARD, BERNARDO CHILDREN'S HOSPITAL 300 LONGWOOD AVENUE BOSTON, MA 02115 **Molecular mechanisms of cardiac ontogeny and hypertrophy**

R10HL-33740-07 (SRC) WISSLER, ROBERT W UNIVERSITY OF CHICAGO 5841 SOUTH MARYLAND AVENUE CHICAGO, ILL 60637 **Pathobiological determinants of atherosclerosis in youth**

R01HL-33741-08 (HEM) PROCHOWNIK, EDWARD V UNIV OF MICHIGAN/PED HEMA ONCO 1150 W MEDICAL CENTER DRIVE ANN ARBOR, MI 48109-0684 **Human ATIII genes and coagulopathyo of atIII deficiency**

R01HL-33742-08 (PTHA) STEMERMAN, MICHAEL B NEW YORK MEDICAL COLLEGE VOSBURGH PAVILION 302 VALHALLA, NY 10595 **Mechanism of hemostatic and vascular interactions**

R10HL-33746-07 (SRC) STRONG, JACK P LOUISIANA STATE UNIV MED CTR 1901 PERDIDO ST NEW OLREANS, LA 70112-1393 **Pathobiological determinants of atherosclerosis in youth**

R37HL-33756-08 (HED) MARKWALD, ROGER R MEDICAL COLLEGE OF WISCONSIN 8701 WATERTOWN PLANK ROAD MILWAUKEE, WI 53226 **Mucopolysaccharide metabolism in cardiac anomalies**

R10HL-33758-07 (SRC) ROBERTSON, ABEL L UNIVERSITY OF ILLINOIS PO BOX 6998 CHICAGO, IL 60680 **Pathobiological determinants of atherosclerosis in youth**

R10HL-33760-07 (SRC) CORNHILL, J FREDRICK OHIO STATE UNIV

MEDICAL CENTER 376 W 10TH AVENUE COLUMBUS, OH 43210-1240 Pathobiological determinants of atherosclerosis in youth

R01HL-33768-08 (SSS) NICHOLSON-WELLER, ANNE BETH ISRAEL HOSPITAL 330 BROOKLINE AVENUE BOSTON, MA 02215 Membrane protein deficiency of PNH erythrocytes

R01HL-33769-08 (ECS) HASSID, AVIV I UNIVERSITY OF TENNESSEE 894 UNION AVENUE MEMPHIS, TN 38163 Atriopeptin-evoked calcium and lipid metabolism

P50HL-33774-06 (SRC) SURGENOR, DOUGLAS M CENTER FOR BLOOD RESEARCH 800 HUNTINGTON AVENUE BOSTON, MA 02115 Specialized center of research in transfusion medicine

P50HL-33774-06 0001 (SRC) ESSEX, MYRON Specialized center of research in transfusion medicine Markers for human immunodeficiency virus

P50HL-33774-06 0004 (SRC) SURGENOR, DOUGLAS M Specialized center of research in transfusion medicine Epidemiologic studies of blood use in the United States

P50HL-33774-06 0005 (SRC) GROOPMAN, JEROME E Specialized center of research in transfusion medicine Tropism of HIV for blood cells

P50HL-33774-06 0006 (SRC) LEE, TUN-HOU Specialized center of research in transfusion medicine Markers for human T-cell leukemia virus infection

R01HL-33782-05 (RAP) TIPTON, CHARLES M UNIVERSITY OF ARIZONA EXER/SPORT SCIS: GITTINGS BLDG TUCSON, AZ 85721 Exercise and animals models of hypertension

R01HL-33783-06 (RAP) DONNELLY, DAVID F YALE UNIVERSITY SCHOOL OF MED 333 CEDAR ST - DEPT/PEDIATRICS NEW HAVEN, CT 06510 Modulation of breathing by upper airway chemoreceptors

R01HL-33791-08 (RAP) MCFADDEN, E R, JR UNIVERSITY HOSPITALS 2074 ABINGTON RD CLEVELAND, OH 44106 Pathophysiology of exercise induced asthma

R01HL-33793-05 (HEM) VERCELLOTTI, GREGORY M UNIVERSITY OF MINNESOTA HARVARD ST @ E RIVER RD MINNEAPOLIS, MN 55455 Neutrophil/endothelial cell communication

R01HL-33797-06 (CVA) SCHULTZ, HAROLD UNIVERSITY OF NEBRASKA MEDICAL 600 S 42ND STREET OMAHA, NE 68108-4575 C fiber baroreceptors--Afferent & reflex properties

P50HL-33811-06 (SRC) GRUMET, FRANK C STANFORD UNIV BLOOD CENTER 800 WELCH RD PALO ALTO, CA 94304 Specialized center of research in transfusion medicine

P50HL-33811-06 9001 (SRC) FOUNG, STEVEN K H Specialized center of research in transfusion medicine Core--Human monoclonal antibodies

P50HL-33811-06 9003 (SRC) ENGLEMAN, EDGAR G Specialized center of research in transfusion medicine Core--Cell sorter facility

P50HL-33811-06 0002 (SRC) MOCARSKI, EDWARD S Specialized center of research in transfusion medicine Cytomegalovirus--Risk, detection and immunomodulation

P50HL-33811-06 0003 (SRC) ENGLEMAN, EDGAR G Specialized center of research in transfusion medicine Human immunodeficiency virus type I

P50HL-33811-06 0004 (SRC) ROBINSON, WILLIAM S Specialized center of research in transfusion medicine Hepatitis B

P50HL-33811-06 0006 (SRC) GRUMET, F CARL Specialized center of research in transfusion medicine Tolerance

P50HL-33811-06 0007 (SRC) FOUNG, STEVEN Specialized center of research in transfusion medicine Immunology of a new human retrovirus

R01HL-33831-07 (RAP) MILLHORN, DAVID E UNIVERSITY NORTH CAROLINA MEDICAL SCIENCES RESEARCH BLDG CHAPEL HILL, NC 27599 Regulation of respiration--Central mechanisms

R37HL-33833-07 (ECS) HARDER, DAVID R MEDICAL COLLEGE OF WISCONSIN 8701 WATERTOWN PLANK ROAD MILWAUKEE, WI 53226 Cellular control mechanisms of cerebrovascular tone

R01HL-33841-07 (HEM) REDMAN, COLVIN M NEW YORK BLOOD CENTER 310 EAST 67TH STREET NEW YORK, NY 10021 Kell blood group proteins in normal and McLeod red cells

R01HL-33849-07 (SB) ANDERSON, JAMES M INSTITUTE OF PATHOLOGY 2085 ADELBERT ROAD CLEVELAND, OHIO 44106 Biomedical polymers--cell activation and interleukin 1

R01HL-33878-07 (SSS) ROSE, NOEL R JOHNS HOPKINS UNIVERSITY 615 NORTH WOLFE STREET BALTIMORE, MD 21205 Post infectious autoimmunity

R01HL-33881-07 (MET) REAVEN, EVE P V A MEDICAL CENTER 3801 MIRANDA AVE PALO ALTO, CA 94304 How do cells process high density lipoproteins?

R01HL-33884-07 (CTY) CURTIS, PETER J WISTAR INSTITUTE 36TH & SPRUCE STREETS PHILDELPHIA, PA 19104 Genetics of human erythrocyte alpha-spectrin

R01HL-33891-06 (RAP) SCHERER, PETER W UNIVERSITY OF PENNSYLVANIA 220 SOUTH 33RD STREET PHILADELPHIA, PA 19104 Flow visualization of jet ventilation in neonatal airways

R01HL-33914-05 (BBCB) POWNALL, HENRY J BAYLOR COLLEGE OF MEDICINE 6565 FANNIN HOUSTON, TEX 77030 Lipid-protein interactions

R01HL-33921-07 (PHRA) HOUSER, STEVEN R TEMPLE UNIVERSITY SCH OF MED 3420 N BROAD STREET PHILADELPHIA, PA 19140 Ca ++ homeostasis in isolated hypertrophied heart cells

R01HL-33935-07 (ECS) WAGNER, ROGER C UNIVERSITY OF DELAWARE 112 WOLF HALL NEWARK, DEL 19716 Capillary transport in capillaries rete mirabile

R01HL-33940-07 (MGN) GOODMAN, MORRIS WAYNE STATE UNIVERSITY 540 E CANFIELD DETROIT, MI 48201 Fetal globin genes--Evolution of ontogenetic programs

R01HL-33942-07 (MBY) CRABTREE, GERALD R STANFORD UNIVERSITY STANFORD, CA 94305 HNF-1 and developmental control of fibrinogen production

R01HL-33952-08 (MGN) ZANNIS, VASSILIS I BOSTON UNIVERSITY MED CTR 80 E CONCORD ST, R420 BOSTON, MA 02118 Apolipoprotein variation and human disease

R01HL-33960-05 (BEM) KOSTIS, JOHN B UNIV OF MED & DENT OF NEW JERS ONE ROBERT WOOD JOHNSON PLACE NEW BRUNSWICK, NJ 08903-0019 CN9 effects of antihypertensive therapies

R01HL-33965-05 (CLTR) KING, SPENCER B EMORY UNIVERSITY HOSPITAL 1364 CLIFTON ROAD, N.E. ATLANTA, GEORGIA 30322 Comparison of PTCA and CABG in coronary disorders

R01HL-33991-07 (HEM) AGRE, PETER C THE JOHNS HOPKINS HOSPITAL 600 N WOLFE STREET BALTIMORE, MD 21205 Red cell membrane protein defects in hemolytic anemias

R01HL-34005-06A2 (PTHA) MACARAK, EDWARD J CONNECTIVE TISSUE RES INST 3624 MARKET STREET PHILADELPHIA, PA 19104 Effect of mechanical forces on vascular cells

R01HL-34009-05A3 (PTHA) ROUNDS, SHARON I S PROVIDENCE VA MEDICAL CENTER DAVIS PARK PROVIDENCE, RI 02908 Modulation of PMN adherence by endothelial cells

R01HL-34012-08 (MEDB) SACHDEV, GOVERDHAN P UNIV OF OKLAHOMA HLTH SCI CTR 1110 N STONEWALL OKLAHOMA CITY, OK 73190 Biochemistry of cystic fibrosis mucous secretions

R01HL-34014-05A2 (CVA) GEE, MARLYS H THOMAS JEFFERSON UNIVERSITY 1020 LOCUST STREET PHILADELPHIA, PA 19107 Mechanisms of acute vascular injury

R01HL-34034-05 (BPO) TURKKAN, JAYLAN S JOHNS HOPKINS UNIVERSITY 720 RUTLAND AVENUE BALTIMORE, MD 21205 Antihypertensive drugs--Biobehavioral effects

R01HL-34035-04A3 (BNP) POWERS, JAMES C GEORGIA INST OF TECHNOLOGY ATLANTA, GA 30332 Synthetic antithrombotic agents

R01HL-34036-07 (CVB) CHAPNICK, BARRY M ST LOUIS UNIVERSITY 1402 SOUTH GRAND BOULEVARD ST LOUIS, MO 63104 Peripheral vascular control mechanisms

R01HL-34059-07 (HED) LEFFLER, CHARLES W UNIVERSITY OF TENNESSEE 894 UNION AVE MEMPHIS, TN 38163 Studies of the control of neonatal circulation

R01HL-34062-06 (BMT) HERSHKO, CHAIM HEBREW UNIV HADASSAH MEDICAL C PO BOX 1172 JERUSALEM, ISRAEL 91010 Cultured cardiac myocytes--model of iron overload

R01HL-34071-06 (CLTR) MASON, JAY W UNIV OF UTAH SCHOOL OF MED 50 NORTH MEDICAL DRIVE SALT LAKE CITY, UT 84132 Comparison of electrophysiologic study to ECG monitoring

R01HL-34111-07 (PTHA) VIA, DAVID P BAYLOR COLLEGE OF MEDICINE 6565 FANNINN HOUSTON, TX 77030 Macrophage receptor for modified lipoproteins

R01HL-34127-07 (BIO) PRESCOTT, STEPHEN M UNIVERSITY OF UTAH 235 NORA ECCLES HARRISON BLVD SALT LAKE CITY, UTAH 84112 Regulation of lipid autocoids in cardiovascular cells

R01HL-34143-06 (RAP) DI MARCO, ANTHONY F 3395 SCRANTON ROAD CLEVELAND, OH 44109 Activation and function of intercostal muscles

R01HL-34151-07 (RAP) KRAMER, GEORGE C UNIVERSITY OF TEXAS GALVESTON, TX 77550 Bronchial circulation and lung fluid balance

R01HL-34161-05 (PHY) NERBONNE, JEANNE M WASHINGTON UNIVERSITY 660 SOUTH EUCLID AVENUE ST LOUIS, MO 63110 Ion channel regulation and modulation in cardiac muscle

R01HL-34172-05 (CVA) GWIRTZ, PATRICIA A PHD TEXAS COLLEGE OF OSTEOPATHIC M 3500 CAMP BOWIE BLVD FORT WORTH, TX 76107-2690 Adrenergic limitation of coronary flow during exercise

R01HL-34174-07 (EDC) PAFFENBARGER, RALPH S, JR STANFORD UNIVERSITY HLTH RES & POLICY BUILDING STANFORD, CA 94305 Life-style and chronic disease in college alumni

R01HL-34193-07 (BNP) GRUNEWALD, GARY L UNIVERSITY OF KANSAS DPT OF MEDICINAL CHEMISTRY LAWRENCE, KS 66045 Design of inhibitors of epinephrine biosynthesis

R01HL-34199-06 (RNM) LEPPO, JEFFREY A UNIV OF MASSACHUSETTS MED CTR 55 LAKE AVENUE NORTH WORCESTER, MA 01655 Effect of flow and metabolic changes on cardiac isotopes

R01HL-34208-07 (RAP) MEYRICK, BARBARA O VANDERBILT UNIVERSITY SCH OF M 21ST AVENUE & GARLAND STREET NASHVILLE, TN 37232-2650 Cellular mechanisms of pulmonary endothelial injury

R01HL-34215-17 (TOX) LEVI, ROBERTO CORNELL UNIVERSITY MED COLLEGE 1300 YORK AVENUE NEW YORK, NY 10021 Cardiac dysfunctions caused by histamine release

R01HL-34221-06 (CVB) SANTOS-BUCH, CHARLES A CORNELL UNIVERSITY MED COLLEGE 1300 YORK AVE NEW YORK, NY 10021 Induction and suppression of experimental cardiomyopathy

R01HL-34228-09 (RAP) MURLAS, CHRISTOPHER G RUSH-PRESBYTERIAN 1653 W. CONGRESS PARKWAY CHICAGO, IL 60612 Airway smooth muscle in bronchial hyperreactivity

R44HL-34242-02A5 (HUD) DENNISON, KATHRYN F DINE SYSTEMS, INC 5 BLUEBIRD LANE AMHERST, NY 14228 Dine weight management program in a worksite setting

R01HL-34276-07 (HEM) ROBBINS, KENNETH C VA LAKESIDE MEDICAL CENTER 333 E HURON STREET CHICAGO, IL 60611 Plasminogen--Activation and structure

R01HL-34280-07 (ECS) ALLEN, JULIUS C BAYLOR COLLEGE OF MEDICINE ONE BAYLOR PLAZA HOUSTON, TX 77030 Sodium in vsm protein production

R01HL-34286-05 (NTN) MEDEIROS, DENIS M OHIO STATE UNIVERSITY 265 CAMPBELL HALL COLUMBUS, OH 43210-1295 Cardiac characteristics in copper deficiency

R01HL-34288-06A1 (CVA) BURGESS, MARY JO UNIVERSITY OF UTAH NORA ECCLES HARRISON BLDG SALT LAKE CITY, UT 84112 Effects of activation order on repolarization

P01HL-34300-07 (HLBB) MC GIFF, JOHN C NEW YORK MEDICAL COLLEGE VALHALLA, N Y 10595 Hormonal regulation of blood pressure

P01HL-34300-07 0001 (HLBB) MCGIFF, JOHN C Hormonal regulation of blood pressure Cytochrome P450 arachidonate metabolites and hypertension

P01HL-34300-07 0002 (HLBB) NASJLETTI, ALBERTO Hormonal regulation of blood pressure Interaction of glucocorticoids and renal eicosanoids

P01HL-34300-07 0003 (HLBB) QUILLEY, JOHN Hormonal regulation of blood pressure Vascular cytochrome P450 related arachidonic acid products

P01HL-34300-07 0005 (HLBB) SCHWARTZMAN, MICHAL Hormonal regulation of blood pressure Arachidonate omega/omega-1 hydroxylation in hypertension

P01HL-34300-07 9002 (HLBB) WONG, PATRICK Y-K Hormonal regulation of blood pressure CORE--Gas chromatography/mass spectrometry

P01HL-34300-07 9003 (HLBB) HASSID, AVIV Hormonal regulation of blood pressure CORE--Tissue culture

P01HL-34303-07 (HLBA) MURPHY, ROBERT C NATL JEWISH CTR IMM & RES 1400 JACKSON STREET DENVER, CO 80206-1997 Ether lipids, eicosanoids and lung cell pathophysiology

P01HL-34303-07 0001 (HLBA) MURPHY, ROBERT C Ether lipids, eicosanoids and lung cell pathophysiology The PAF cycle

P01HL-34303-07 0003 (HLBA) LESLIE, CHRISTINA C Ether lipids, eicosanoids and lung cell pathophysiology Properties of an arachidonoyl-specific PLA2
P01HL-34303-07 0004 (HLBA) HENSON, PETER M Ether lipids, eicosanoids and lung cell pathophysiology Secretion and uptake of lipid mediators
P01HL-34303-07 0006 (HLBA) MURPHY, ROBERT C Ether lipids, eicosanoids and lung cell pathophysiology Translocation and transcellular biosynthesis
P01HL-34303-07 0007 (HLBA) FITZPATRICK, FRANK A Ether lipids, eicosanoids and lung cell pathophysiology Suicide inactivation of LTA4 hydrolase and thromboxane synthase
P01HL-34303-07 0008 (HLBA) WORTHEN, G SCOTT Ether lipids, eicosanoids and lung cell pathophysiology Neutrophil regulation of acute inflammatory response--lipid mediators
P01HL-34303-07 9003 (HLBA) LESLIE, CHRISTINA C Ether lipids, eicosanoids and lung cell pathophysiology CORE--Cell culture
P01HL-34303-07 9004 (HLBA) HENSON, PETER M Ether lipids, eicosanoids and lung cell pathophysiology CORE--Morphology
R01HL-34318-06 (HED) BADER, DAVID M CORNELL UNIV MEDICAL COLLEGE 1300 YORK AVENUE NEW YORK, NY 10021 Determination and diversification of cardiac myoblasts
P01HL-34322-06 (HLBA) BOUCHER, RICHARD C U OF NC AT CHAPEL HILL CB#7020 724 BURNETT-WOMACK BLD CHAPEL HILL, N C 27599-7020 Pulmonary epithelia in health and disease
P01HL-34322-06 0003 (HLBA) STUTTS, M JACKSON Pulmonary epithelia in health and disease Nucleotide binding in chloride channel regulation
P01HL-34322-06 0005 (HLBA) BOUCHER, RICHARD C Pulmonary epithelia in health and disease Pattern and control of airway epithelial ion transport
P01HL-34322-06 0006 (HLBA) KNOWLES, MICHAEL R Pulmonary epithelia in health and disease Respiratory epithelial function in vivo
P01HL-34322-06 0007 (HLBA) HARDEN, T KENDALL Pulmonary epithelia in health and disease Epithelial cell P2 purinerginic receptors
P01HL-34322-06 0008 (HLBA) VAN SCOTT, MICHAEL R Pulmonary epithelia in health and disease Secretory and ion transport functions of airway surface epithelial goblet cells
P01HL-34322-06 9001 (HLBA) HSIAO, HENRY S Pulmonary epithelia in health and disease CORE--Bioengineering
P01HL-34322-06 9002 (HLBA) YANKASKAS, JAMES R Pulmonary epithelia in health and disease CORE--Tissue culture
P01HL-34322-06 9004 (HLBA) DAVIS, C WILLIAM Pulmonary epithelia in health and disease CORE--Imaging
R01HL-34327-07 (BM) NAUSEEF, WILLIAM M UNIVERSITY OF IOWA HOSP/CLINIC DEPARTMENT OF MEDICINE IOWA CITY, IOWA 52242 Monoclonal antibodies for analysis of neutrophil activation
R01HL-34328-07 (MET) SAMAREL, ALLEN M LOYOLA UNIVERSITY MED CTR 2160 S FIRST AVENUE MAYWOOD, IL 60153 Developmental alterations in cardiac protein turnover
R01HL-34346-06 (BNP) RANDO, ROBERT R HARVARD MEDICAL SCHOOL 25 SHATTUCK STREET BOSTON, MA 02115 Medicinal chemistry of novel antithrombotic drugs
R01HL-34360-04A1 (SB) DAS, DIPAK K UNIV OF CONNECTICUT HLTH CTR 263 FARMINGTON AVENUE FARMINGTON, CT 06032-9984 Phospholipid degradation in reperfusion injury
R01HL-34363-07 (HEM) MC EVER, RODGER P UNIVERSITY OF OKLAHOMA P.O. BOX 26901 OKLAHOMA CITY, OK 73190 Properties of a platelet granule membrane protein
R01HL-34408-21 (HEM) WASI, PRAWASE FACULTY OF MED SIRIRAJ HOSPITA DIVISION OF HEMATOLOGY BANGKOK, THAILAND 10700 Thalassemias, hemoglobinopathies and related problems
R01HL-34462-07 (HEM) BROZE, GEORGE J JEWISH HOSPITAL 216 SOUTH KINGSHIGHWAY ST LOUIS, MO 63110 Human tissue factor and its plasma inhibitor
R01HL-34477-05 (CVB) BOYDEN, PENELOPE A COLUMBIA UNIVERSITY 630 WEST 168TH STREET NEW YORK, N Y 10032 Infarcted hearts--Arrhythmogenic Purkinje cells
R01HL-34552-06 (PTHA) JONES, ROSEMARY C MASSACHUSETTS GENERAL HOSP FRUIT STREET BOSTON, MA 02114 Oxygen toxicity and pulmonary vascular injury
R01HL-34555-07 (CVB) SECOMB, TIMOTHY W UNIVERSITY OF ARIZONA DEPARTMENT OF PHYSIOLOGY TUCSON, ARIZ 85724 Microvascular blood rheology and red blood cell mechanics
R01HL-34557-04 (BBCB) SHERRY, A DEAN UNIVERSITY OF TEXAS AT DALLAS P O BOX 830688 RICHARDSON, TX 75083-0688 Intermediary metabolism in the heart by NMR
R37HL-34575-07 (HEM) MANN, KENNETH G UNIVERSITY OF VERMONT COLLEGE OF MEDICINE BURLINGTON, VT 05405 Primary structure of prothrombin
R01HL-34579-07 (SB) MENTZER, ROBERT M, JR UNIVERSITY OF WISCONSIN 600 HIGHLAND AVENUE MADISON, WI 53792 Adenosine and pyruvate protection during heart surgery
R01HL-34593-05 (CLTR) SACKS, FRANK M CHANNING LABORATORY 180 LONGWOOD AVENUE BOSTON, MA 02115 Polyunsaturates and KC1 to control mild hypertension
R01HL-34594-07 (EDC) HENNEKENS, CHARLES H BRIGHAM AND WOMEN'S HOSPITAL 55 POND AVENUE BROOKLINE, MA 02146 Risk factors for myocardial infarction in women
R01HL-34595-07 (CLTR) HENNEKENS, CHARLES H BRIGHAM & WOMEN'S HOSPITAL 55 POND AVENUE BROOKLINE, MA 02146 A randomized trial of aspirin and mortality in US MDs
P50HL-34616-07 (SRC) AVERY, MARY E BRIGHAM AND WOMEN'S HOSPITAL 75 FRANCIS STREET BOSTON, MA 02115 SCOR--Respiratory disorders of neonates and children
P50HL-34616-07 0001 (SRC) TORDAY, JOHN S SCOR--Respiratory disorders of neonates and children Molecular regulation of cell-cell interactions in developing lung
P50HL-34616-07 0003 (SRC) AVERY, MARY ELLEN SCOR--Respiratory disorders of neonates and children Surfactant replacement therapy in infants with RDS
P50HL-34616-07 0004 (SRC) FREDBERG, JEFFREY J SCOR--Respiratory disorders of neonates and children Interaction of mechanisms, structure and regional transport in HFV
P50HL-34616-07 0005 (SRC) STARK, ANN R SCOR--Respiratory disorders of neonates and children Respiratory muscles in control of infant breathing
P50HL-34616-07 0007 (SRC) WOHL, MARY ELLEN B SCOR--Respiratory disorders of neonates and children Prematurity, respiratory distress syndrome and bronchopulmonary dysplasia
P50HL-34616-07 9001 (SRC) WARE, JAMES SCOR--Respiratory disorders of neonates and children Core--Statistics
R01HL-34625-08 (HEM) STERN, DAVID M COLUMBIA UNIVERSITY 630 WEST 168 STREET NEW YORK, N. Y. 10032 Functions of endothelial cell factor IX binding protein
R01HL-34636-08 (PTHA) LIBBY, PETER BRIGHAM & WOMEN'S HOSPITAL 75 FRANCIS ST BOSTON, MA 02115 Control of growth of vascular wall cells
R01HL-34645-07 (EDC) WEISS, SCOTT T CHANNING LABORATORY 180 LONGWOOD AVENUE BOSTON, MA 02115 The epidemiology of airways responsiveness
R01HL-34646-07 (PHRA) LINCOLN, THOMAS M UNIVERSITY OF SOUTH ALABAMA COLLEGE OF MEDICINE-MSB 3130 MOBILE, AL 36688 Biochemical actions of cyclic GMP in smooth muscle
R01HL-34659-06S1 (SRC) SINAIKO, ALAN R UNIVERSITY OF MINNESOTA 420 DELAWARE STREET, S E MINNEAPOLIS, MINN 55455 Sodium-potassium blood pressure trial in children
R01HL-34664-07 (PHRA) MATLIB, MOHAMMED A UNIVERSITY OF CINCINNATI 231 BETHESDA AVENUE CINCINNATI, OHIO 45267-0575 Sodium-calcium exchange in vascular smooth muscle
R01HL-34674-07 (TOX) BASSETT, DAVID J JOHNS HOPKINS UNIVERSITY 615 NORTH WOLFE STREET BALTIMORE, MD 21205 Early effects of oxygen on lung metabolic function
R01HL-34691-05A1 (CVA) BUDA, ANDREW J TULANE UNIVERSITY SCHOOL OF ME SECTION OF CARDIOLOGY NEW ORLEANS, LA 70112 Mechanisms of neutrophil-dependent myocardial damage
R01HL-34698-06 (EDC) DANIELS, STEPHEN R CHILDREN'S HOSP MEDICAL CENTER ELLAND AND BETHESDA AVENUE CINCINNATI, OH 45229 End-organ pathology in childhood essential hypertension
R01HL-34708-06 (SAT) BOSNJAK, ZELJKO J MEDICAL COLLEGE OF WISCONSIN MFRC- ANESTHESIOLOGY-A1000 MILWAUKEE, WI 53226 Interaction between anesthetics and calcium antagonists
R01HL-34727-07 (PTHA) DICORLETO, PAUL E CLEVELAND CLINIC FDN 9500 EUCLID AVENUE CLEVELAND, OH 44195 Monocyte-endothelial cell interactions in atherogenesis
R01HL-34732-07 (SRC) KAPLAN, ROBERT M UNIVERSITY OF CALIFORNIA LA JOLLA, CA 92093 Randomized trial of rehabilitation in COPD
R01HL-34737-07 (BBCB) BETH, ALBERT H VANDERBILT UNIV MEDICAL SCHOOL 627 LIGHT HALL NASHVILLE, TN 37232 EPR studies of membrane proteins
R01HL-34740-05 (SRC) JEFFERY, ROBERT W UNIVERSITY OF MINNESOTA 515 DELAWARE STREET, SE MINNEAPOLIS, MN 55455 Worksite health incentives program
R01HL-34744-04 (SRC) MASON, JAY W UNIV OF UTAH MEDICAL CENTER 50 NORTH MEDICAL DRIVE SALT LAKE CITY, UT 84132 Immunosuppressive therapy for biopsy-proven myocarditis
R01HL-34767-06 (SRC) GRIMM, RICHARD H JR UNIV OF MINNESOTA 611 BEACON ST, SE MINNEAPOLIS, MN 55455 Treatment of mild hypertension study
R01HL-34768-07 (RAP) BRODY, JEROME S BOSTON UNIVERSITY SCH OF MED 80 EAST CONCORD STREET BOSTON, MA 02118 Differentiation markers of alveolar epithelial cells
R01HL-34778-08 (SB) STEPHENSON, LARRY W WAYNE STATE UNIVERSITY 3990 JOHN R DETROIT, MI 48201 Cardiac assist devices energized by skeletal muscle
R01HL-34779-04A1 (CVA) FERGUSON, DONALD G UNIVERSITY OF CINCINNATI CINCINNATI, OH 45267-0576 Cardiac sarcoplasmic reticulum--Ultrastructure and immunocytochemistry
R01HL-34780-07 (SB) ABBOTT, WILLIAM M MASSACHUSETTS GEN HOSP ACC 358 15 PARKMAN STREET BOSTON, MA 02114 Substrate properties and human endothelial growth
R01HL-34786-07 (TMP) RYAN, ROBERT O UNIVERSITY OF ALBERTA 328 HERITAGE MED. CTR. EDMONTON ALBERTA CANADA T6G 2S Lipoprotein metabolism in insects
R37HL-34787-07 (HEM) HANDIN, ROBERT I BRIGHAM'S & WOMEN'S HOSP. 75 FRANCIS STREET BOSTON, MA 02115 Role of PF-4 in detecting and promoting thrombosis
R01HL-34788-08 (SSS) FLOROS, JOANNA PENNSYLVANIA STATE UNIVERSITY PO BOX 850 HERSHEY, PA 17033 Surfactant proteins and respiratory distress syndrome
R01HL-34813-05A1 (PTHA) SHANLEY, JOHN D UNIVERSITY OF CONNECTICUT 555 WILLARD AVENUE NEWINGTON, CT 06111 Cytomegalovirus pneumonitis: the role of TNF A and B
R01HL-34817-07 (RAP) SIECK, GARY C MAYO FOUNDATION 200 FIRST ST SOUTHWEST ROCHESTER, MN 55905 Respiratory muscles during development
R01HL-34839-06A1 (PC) GROSS, RICHARD W WASHINGTON UNIVERSITY 660 S EUCLID AVE, BOX 8020 ST LOUIS, MO 63110 Modulation of myocardial plasmalogen catabolism
R01HL-34873-08 (PHY) CLAPHAM, DAVID E MAYO FOUNDATION 200 FIRST STREET SOUTHWEST ROCHESTER, MN 55905 Intracellular regulation of cardiac K+ channels
R01HL-34919-06 (HED) LAWSON, EDWARD E UNIVERSITY OF NORTH CAROLINA 509 CLINICAL SCIS BLDG. CHAPEL HILL, N C 27599 Neural mechanisms of apnea
R01HL-35013-07 (ECS) GIMBRONE, MICHAEL A, JR BRIGHAM AND WOMEN'S HOSPITAL 75 FRANCIS STREET BOSTON, MA 02115 Cultured blood vessel cells--Pathophysiology
R01HL-35027-06A2 (CVA) DOWNEY, H FRED TEXAS COLL OF OSTEOPATHIC MED 3500 CAMP BOWIE BLVD FORT WORTH, TX 76109-2690 Regional non-ischemic myocardial hypoxia
R01HL-35034-08 (PHY) BEAN, BRUCE P HARVARD MEDICAL SCHOOL 25 SHATTUCK STREET BOSTON, MA 02115 Neurotransmitter control of ionic channels
R01HL-35047-03 (CVB) LAZZARA, RALPH OU HEALTH SCIENCES CENTER P O BOX 26901 OKLAHOMA CITY, OK 73190 After depolarizations and arrhythmia generation
R01HL-35068-04 (EDC) ISSARAGRISIL, SURAPOL MAHIDOL UNIVERSITY SIRIRAJ HOSPITAL BANGKOK,THAILAND 10700 Aplastic anemia epidemiology--Incidence and case-control

PROJECT NO., ORGANIZATIONAL UNIT., INVESTIGATOR, ADDRESS, TITLE

R01HL-35079-06 (RNM) GLICKSON, JERRY D JOHNS HOPKINS UNIVERSITY 600 NORTH WOLFE STREET BALTIMORE, MD 21205 Screening for anthracycline cardiotoxicity by NMR
R01HL-35090-07 (HEM) FULCHER, CAROL A SCRIPPS CLINIC & RESEARCH FDN 10666 N TORREY PINES ROAD LA JOLLA, CALIF 92037 Immunochemistry of factor VIII inhibitors
R01HL-35124-06 (HEM) KAO, KUO-JANG UNIVERSITY OF FLORIDA BOX J-275 GAINESVILLE, FL 32610 Biochemical relationship of platelet and plasma HLA
R01HL-35134-06 (TOX) STILES, GARY L DUKE UNIV MED CTR BOX 3444 DURHAM, NC 27710 Pharmacology of cardiac A1 adenosine receptors
R01HL-35136-06 (SSS) COELHO, ANTHONY M, JR SOUTHWEST FDN FOR BIOMEDICAL R PO BOX 28147 SAN ANTONIO, TX 78284 Exercise, stress and blood pressure regulation
R01HL-35137-06 (NLS) SAWCHENKO, PAUL E SALK INST FOR BIOLOGICAL STUDI PO BOX 85800 SAN DIEGO, CA 92138 Pathways integrating stress and cardiovascular responses
R01HL-35194-05 (CVA) LIANG, CHANG-SENG UNIVERSITY OF ROCHESTER 601 ELMWOOD AVE, BOX 679 ROCHESTER, NY 14642 Opiate receptor inhibition in congestive heart failure
R01HL-35202-05 (CLIN) WESTFALL, THOMAS C ST LOUIS UNIVERSITY 1402 S GRAND BLVD ST LOUIS, MO 63104 Neuropeptide Y and catecholamines in hypertension
R01HL-35204-06 (CVA) ABILDSKOV, J A UNIVERSITY OF UTAH NORA ECCLES HARRISON CVRTI SALT LAKE CITY, UT 84112 Physiologic studies of ECG potential distributions
R01HL-35246-06 (HEM) KISIEL, WALTER UNIVERSITY OF NEW MEXICO DEPARTMENT OF PATHOLOGY ALBUQUERQUE, NM 87131 Human factor VII and tissue factor
R01HL-35252-06 (CVB) DZAU, VICTOR J STANFORD UNIVERSITY 300 PASTEUR DR STANFORD, CA 94305-5246 Endothelial cell renin angiotensin interaction in vascular disease
R01HL-35255-04 (HEM) LONG, MICHAEL W UNIVERSITY OF MICHIGAN M7510A MSRB I, BOX 0684 ANN ARBOR, MI 48109 Extracellular matrix in hematopoietic microenvironment
R01HL-35272-07 (CVB) BELARDINELLI, LUIZ UNIVERSITY OF FLORIDA BOX J-277 JHMHC GAINESVILLE, FL 32610 Cellular mechanism of adenosine's cardiac actions
R01HL-35276-05 (PTHA) KUNKEL, STEVEN L UNIVERSITY OF MICHIGAN 1301 CATHERINE RD ANN ARBOR, MI 48109-0602 Monocyte/macrophage signals in lung granuloma
R01HL-35280-06 (BM) CUNNINGHAM, MADELEINE W UNIVERSITY OF OKLAHOMA PO BOX 26901 OKLAHOMA CITY, OK 73104 Myosin--A link between streptococcal and heart
R01HL-35297-06 (PBC) CURTISS, LINDA K SCRIPPS CLINIC AND RES FDN 10666 NORTH TORREY PINES ROAD LA JOLLA, CALIF 92037 Immunobiology of apolipoprotein E
R01HL-35309-06 (CVA) LE WINTER, MARTIN M MEDICAL CENTER HOSP OF VERMONT CARDIOLOGY UNIT BURLINGTON, VT 05401 Aspect of diastolic function in the heart
R01HL-35323-06 (ECS) INAGAMI, TADASHI VANDERBILT UNIV SCH OF MED 21ST AVE AT GARLAND AVENUE NASHVILLE, TN 37232 Intracellular renin-angiotensin and blood pressure control
R01HL-35334-04 (SRC) ORENSTEIN, DAVID M CHILDREN'S HOSP OF PITTSBURGH 3705 FIFTH AVE AT DESOTO ST PITTSBURGH, PA 15213 Long-term exercise intervention in cystic fibrosis
R01HL-35380-06 (ECS) KNAPP, HOWARD R UNIV OF IOWA COLLEGE OF MEDICI C31-P, GH IOWA CITY, IA 52242 The pharmacology of omega-3 fatty acids
R01HL-35389-06 (RAP) LUCAS, CAROL L UNIVERSITY OF NORTH CAROLINA CAMPUS BOX 7065 CHAPEL HILL, NC 27599-7065 Determinants of pulmonary artery blood velocity profile
R01HL-35420-06 (RAP) BANZETT, ROBERT B HARVARD SCHOOL OF PUBLIC HLTH 665 HUNTINGTON AVENUE BOSTON, MA 02115 Mechanisms of aerodynamic valving in avian lungs
R01HL-35422-06 (PHRA) ADAMS, DAVID J UNIVERSITY OF MIAMI PO BOX 016189 MIAMI, FL 33101 Ionic basis of excitability in intrinsic cardiac neurons
R01HL-35433-03 (PHRA) QUIST, EUGENE E TEXAS COLL OF OSTEOPATHIC MED 3500 CAMP BOWIE BLVD FORT WORTH, TX 76107 Regulation of cardiac function by muscarinic agonists
R01HL-35434-05 (EDC) GOLDBERG, ROBERT J UNIV OF MASSACHUSETTS MED SCH 55 LAKE AVENUE NORTH WORCESTER, MA 01655 Recent trends in coronary disease--Community-based study
R01HL-35435-06 (CVB) BOVEE, KENNETH C UNIVERSITY OF PENNSYLVANIA 3850 SPRUCE STREET PHILADELPHIA, PA 19104-6010 Physiology of genetically hypertensive model
R01HL-35440-06 (RAP) WOOD, LAWRENCE MD PHD THE UNIV OF CHICAGO DEP/MED 5841 S. MARYLAND AVE BOX 83 CHICAGO, IL 60637 Alternative modes of mechanical ventilation
R01HL-35464-06 (EDC) WILLETT, WALTER C HARVARD SCHOOL OF PUBLIC HLTH 677 HUNTINGTON AVENUE BOSTON, MA 02115 Dietary etiologies of heart disease and cancer
R01HL-35495-05 (BIO) SNYDER, FRED L OAK RIDGE ASSOC UNIVERSITIES P O BOX 117 OAK RIDGE, TN 37831-0117 An antihypertensive class of neutral lipids in kidney
R01HL-35518-06 (HED) SOIFER, SCOTT J UNIVERSITY OF CALIFORNIA 505 PARNASSUS, M-646 SAN FRANCISCO, CA 94143 Abnormal fetal lung circulation--Vasoactive mediators
R01HL-35522-06 (CVB) STIER, CHARLES T, JR NEW YORK MEDICAL COLLEGE VALHALLA, NY 10595 Prevention of stroke and kidney dysfunction by ACE inhibition
R01HL-35528-05 (EDC) HAWKINS, MORTON C UNIV OF TEX HLTH SCI CTR, HOU P.O. BOX 20036/SCHOOL OF PUB H HOUSTON, TX 77225-0186 Extended analysis of the HDFP--Benefits and risks
R01HL-35549-06 (SB) TARBELL, JOHN M PENNSYLVAINA STATE UNIVERSITY 155 FENSKE LABORATORY UNIVERSITY PARK, PA 16802 Wall shear stress in the cardiovascular system
R01HL-35553-05 (HEM) SCHMAIER, ALVIN H TEMPLE UNIVERSITY SCH OF MED 3400 NORTH BROAD STREET PHILADELPHIA, PA 19140 Platelet high molecular weight kininogen
R01HL-35554-06 (SAT) ARZBAECHER, ROBERT C PRITZKER INST OF MED ENGR ILLINOIS INSTITUTE OF TECH CHICAGO, IL 60616 Algorithms for arrhythmia identification
R01HL-35559-06 (MBY) TOWNES, TIM M UNIVERSITY OF ALABAMA DEPT OF BIOCHEMISTRY BIRMINGHAM, AL 35294 Human globin gene expression during development
R01HL-35561-07 (CVA) ORDAHL, CHARLES P UNIVERSITY OF CALIFORNIA 513 PARNASSUS, BOX 0452 SAN FRANCISCO, CA 94143 Molecular study of cardiogenesis
R01HL-35570-07 (PTHA) HERMAN, IRA M TUFTS UNIVERSITY SCHOOL OF MED 136 HARRISON AVE. BOSTON, MA 02111 Microvascular pericytes--Control of cerebral blood flow
R01HL-35576-06 (CTY) MAHDAVI, VIJAK CHILDREN'S HOSPITAL CORPORATIO 300 LONGWOOD AVENUE BOSTON, MA 02115 Cellular & molecular mechanisms of cardiac hypertrophy
R01HL-35610-07A1 (ECS) DZAU, VICTOR J STANFORD UNIVERSITY 300 PASTEUR DR, FALK CVRC STANFORD, CA 94305 Renin gene expression in cardiovascular regulation
R01HL-35617-07 (NEUA) HARIK, SAMI I DEPARTMENT OF NEUROLOGY UNIV HOSPITALS OF CLEVELAND CLEVELAND, OH 44106 Cellular biology of brain microvessels
R01HL-35627-08 (PTHA) MACIAG, THOMAS AMERICAN RED CROSS 15601 CRABBS BRANCH WAY ROCKVILLE, MD 20855 The pathology of human endothelial cell phenotypes
R01HL-35635-04 (PTHA) WU, REEN UNIVERSITY OF CALIFORNIA DAVIS, CA 95616 Mucous cell differentiation in airway epithelium
R01HL-35639-08 (CVA) WILLIAMS, ROBERT S UNIV OF TEXAS SW MED CTR, DALL 5323 HARRY HINES BLVD DURHAM, N C 27710 Exercise and mitochondrial biogenesis
R01HL-35640-06A1 (PTHA) GANZ, TOMAS UNIVERSITY OF CALIFORNIA CTR FOR HEALTH SCIENCES LOS ANGELES, CA 90024-1406 The role of cationic peptides in the lung
R01HL-35653-07 (EDC) ELLISON, ROBERT C BOSTON UNIVERSITY MEDICAL CTR 80 EAST CONCORD STREET BOSTON, MA 02118 Food and exercise habits in Framingham study descendents
R55HL-35664-06A1 (CVB) CANESSA, MITZY L BRIGHAM & WOMEN'S HOSPITAL 221 LONGWOOD AVE BOSTON, MA 02115 Hypertension and Na-K-Cl cotransport and Na/H exchange
R01HL-35687-05 (RAP) BOYLE, JOHN T RAINBOW BABIES/CHILDRENS HOSP 2074 ABINGTON ROAD RM 706 CLEVELAND, OH 44106 Esophageal function mediated by the respiratory system
R01HL-35689-05 (TOX) KEHRER, JAMES P UNIVERSITY OF TEXAS DEPARTMENT OF PHARMACOLOGY AUSTIN, TEX 78712-1074 Lung toxic interactions involving therapeutic drugs
R01HL-35706-06A1 (CVB) BAXTER, JOHN D UNIVERSITY OF CALIFORNIA 3RD AND PARNASSUS AVE, BOX 051 SAN FRANCISCO, CA 94143-0516 Molecular biology of renin and its gene
R01HL-35711-07 (PTHA) GRUETTER, CARL A MARSHALL UNIVERSITY 1542 SPRING VALLEY DRIVE HUNTINGTON, W VA 25704-2901 Role of endothelium in pulmonary vasoreactivity rrrrrrr
R01HL-35716-07 (PTHA) COLLINS, TUCKER BRIGHAM AND WOMEN'S HOSPITAL VASCULAR RESEARCH DIV BOSTON, MA 02115 Endothelial gene expression control of PDGF production
R01HL-35718-06 (RAP) LEFF, ALAN R UNIVERSITY OF CHICAGO 5841 SOUTH MARYLAND AVENUE CHICAGO, IL 60637 Morphological correlates of airway contraction
R01HL-35724-07 (PTHA) WEKSLER, BABETTE B CORNELL UNIVERSITY MED COLLEGE 1300 YORK AVENUE NEW YORK, N Y 10021 Age effects on arterial cell function in atherosclerosis
R01HL-35726-04A2 (PHY) HITCHCOCK-DEGREGORI, SARAH E UMDNJ-R W JOHNSON MED SCH 675 HOES LANE PISCATAWAY, N J 08854-5635 Site directed mutagenesis of tropomyosin
R01HL-35739-04A2 (PTHA) GERRITSEN, MARY E NEW YORK MEDICAL COLLEGE VALHALLA, NY 10595 Glucocorticoids and microvessel endothelium
R01HL-35753-07 (CVB) GARDNER, DAVID G UNIVERSITY OF CALIFORNIA 3RD & PARNASSUS AVE, 671-HSE SAN FRANCISCO, CA 94143 Expression and regulation of atrial natriuretic factor
R01HL-35762-05A1 (CBY) BURGESS, WILSON H AMERICAN RED CROSS 15601 CRABBS BRANCH WAY ROCKVILLE, MD 20855 Structural basis for vascular homeostasis in vitro
R01HL-35774-06 (HEM) LEVITT, LEE J STANFORD UNIVERSITY SCH OF MED DIV OF HEMATOLOGY - ROOM S161 STANFORD, CA 94305 Immunoregulation of erythropoiesis
R01HL-35781-07 (CVA) MARSH, JAMES D BRIGHAM AND WOMENS HOSPITAL 75 FRANCIS ST BOSTON, MA 02115 Regulation of the cardiac calcium channel
R01HL-35788-07 (BEM) ALPERT, BRUCE S DIVISION OF CARDIOLOGY 848 ADAMS AVENUE MEMPHIS, TN 38103 Familial hypertension & biracial CV reactivity in youth
R01HL-35792-07 (CVB) GROSS, KENNETH W ROSWELL PARK MEMORIAL INST 666 ELM STREET BUFFALO, NY 14263 Renin transgenics for studies of smooth muscle ontogeny
R01HL-35795-06 (EDC) PRATT, JOHN H INDIANA UNIV MEDICAL CENTER 541 CLINICAL DRIVE INDIANAPOLIS, IN 46202-5111 Blood pressure control in juveniles--Longitudinal study
R01HL-35807-05 (RAP) YAMAGUCHI, HIROSHI UNIV OF MASSACHUSETTS 55 LAKE AVE NORTH WORCESTER, MA 01655 Control of calcium in airway smooth muscle cells
R01HL-35808-06 (GMB) DE LANEROLLE, PRIMAL UNIVERSITY OF ILLINOIS P O BOX 6998 CHICAGO, ILL 60680 Myosin and the regulation of smooth muscles
R01HL-35817-06 (RAP) BLOOMQUIST, EUNICE I TUFTS UNIVERSITY 136 HARRISON AVENUE BOSTON, MA 02111 Leukotriene-Substance P interactions in the airways
R01HL-35828-06 (BIO) MC INTYRE, THOMAS M UNIVERSITY OF UTAH NORA ECCLES CURTI, BLDG 500 SALT LAKE CITY, UTAH 84112 Metabolism of platelet-activating factor
R37HL-35842-06 (NSS) RUDOLPH, ABRAHAM M UNIVERSITY OF CALIFORNIA 1403 HLTH SCI EST TOWER BOX 05 SAN FRANCISCO, CA 94143 Circulatory and metabolic adjustments at birth
R01HL-35849-06 (PC) RASMUSSEN, HOWARD MD PHD YALE UNIVERSITY PO BOX 3333 NEW HAVEN, CT 06510 Protein kinase C and smooth muscle contraction
R01HL-35864-06 (HEM) GROSS, RICHARD W WASHINGTON UNIVERSITY 660 SOUTH EUCLID AVENUE ST LOUIS, MO 63110 Initiation of platelet

eicosanoid and paf synthesis
R01HL-35877-06 (EDC) PYERITZ, REED E JOHNS HOPKINS HOSPITAL 600 N WOLFE STREET BALTIMORE, MD 21205 Congenital heart disease--Modeling and genetic analysis
R01HL-35908-05 (PTHA) BLOCK, EDWARD R VA MEDICAL CTR GAINESVILLE, FL 32608-1197 Lung endothelial cell lipids and tolerance to hyperoxia
R01HL-35909-05 (ECS) JACKSON, EDWIN K UNIVERSITY OF PITTSBURGH CENTER FOR CLINICAL PHARMACOLO PITTSBURGH, PA 15261 Defective modulation of neurotransmission
R01HL-35911-06 (ECS) BRAYDEN, JOSEPH E UNIVERSITY OF VERMONT DEPT OF PHARMACOLOGY BURLINGTON, VT 05405 Neural and endothelial regulators of cerebrovascular tone
R01HL-35914-05 (RAP) JOHNSON, ROBERT L, JR UNIVERSITY OF TEXAS SW MED CTR 5323 HARRY HINES BLVD DALLAS, TX 75235-9034 Regional mechanics of the diaphragm
R01HL-35924-04A2 (ECS) ZIEGLER, MICHAEL G UCSD MEDICAL CENTER 225 DICKINSON STREET SAN DIEGO, CA 92103 Sympathetic nervous system abnormalities of hypertension
R01HL-35935-07 (ECS) ROSENBLUM, WILLIAM I MEDICAL COLLEGE OF VIRGINIA BOX 17, MCV STATION RICHMOND, VA 23298-0017 Brain microcirculation and endothelial injury
R01HL-36000-07 (MET) GINSBERG, HENRY N COLUMBIA UNIV COLL OF P&S 630 WEST 168TH STREET NEW YORK, N Y 10032 Regulation of apoprotein-B metabolism in humans
R01HL-36002-07 (EDC) SPEIZER, FRANK E CHANNING LABORATORY 180 LONGWOOD AVENUE BOSTON, MA 02115 Early risk predictors for chronic pulmonary disease
R01HL-36003-07 (PTHA) POBER, JORDAN S BOYER CTR FOR MOLEC MEDICINE 295 CONGRESS AVE PO BOX 9812 NEW HAVEN, CT 06536 Proteins of the endothelial cell surface
R01HL-36005-08 (SSP) DIMSDALE, JOEL E UNIVERSITY OF CALIFORNIA M-003 LA JOLLA, CA 92093-0203 Stress physiology, dietary salt, and hypertension
R01HL-36014-07 (PHRA) GALPER, JONAS B BRIGHAM AND WOMEN'S HOSPITAL 75 FRANCIS STREET BOSTON, MA 02115 Muscarinic receptors in cultured heart cells
R01HL-36015-07A1 (SB) HAKIM, RAYMOND M VANDERBILT UNIV MED CENTER NASHVILLE, TN 37232-2373 Biocompatibility of hemodialysis membranes
R01HL-36024-07 (RAP) BHATTACHARYA, JAHAR ST LUKES-ROOSEVELT HOSP CENTER 428 WEST 59TH STREET NEW YORK, NY 10019 Micropuncture studies of lung, water and solute exchange
P01HL-36028-07 (SRC) GIMBRONE, MICHAEL A, JR BRIGHAM AND WOMEN'S HOSPITAL 75 FRANCIS STREET BOSTON, MA 02115 Pathophysiology of the endothelium
P01HL-36028-07 9004 (SRC) DEWEY, C FORBES Pathophysiology of the endothelium Core--Image analysis and computer support
P01HL-36028-07 0001 (SRC) GIMBRONE, MICHAEL A Pathophysiology of the endothelium Endothelial-dependent mechanisms of leukocyte adhesion
P01HL-36028-07 0003 (SRC) COTRAN, RAMZI S Pathophysiology of the endothelium Endothelial cell activation in vivo--mechanisms and consequences
P01HL-36028-07 0005 (SRC) DAVIES, PETER F Pathophysiology of the endothelium Focal and regional responses of endothelium to disturbed flow in vitro
P01HL-36028-07 0007 (SRC) POBER, JORDAN S Pathophysiology of the endothelium Immunologic interactions between endothelium and lymphocytes
P01HL-36028-07 0008 (SRC) SCHAFER, ANDREW I Pathophysiology of the endothelium Vascular endothelial arachidonic acid metabolism
P01HL-36028-07 0009 (SRC) BEVILACQUA, MICHAEL P Pathophysiology of the endothelium Molecular cloning and characterization of endothelia-leukocyte adhesion molecules
P01HL-36028-07 0010 (SRC) COLLINS, TUCKER Pathophysiology of the endothelium Structure and regulation of endothelial PDGF
P01HL-36028-07 9001 (SRC) COTRAN, RAMZI S Pathophysiology of the endothelium Core--Morphology
P01HL-36028-07 9002 (SRC) GIMBRONE, MICHAEL A Pathophysiology of the endothelium Core--Cell culture
P01HL-36028-07 9003 (SRC) SERHAN, CHARLES N Pathophysiology of the endothelium Core--biochemistry
R01HL-36033-07 (RAP) WAGNER, WILTZ W, JR INDIANA UNIVERSITY SCH OF MED 635 BARNHILL DRIVE INDIANAPOLIS, IN 46202-5120 Pulmonary microcirculatory hemodynamics
R01HL-36045-08 (HEM) SCHAFER, ANDREW I HOUSTON VETERANS ADMINSTRATION 2002 HOLCOMBE BLVD HOUSTON, TX 77211 Regulation of platelet-endothelial interactions
R01HL-36046-04 (ORTH) URBANIAK, JAMES R DUKE UNIVERSITY DURHAM, NC 27710 Blood no reflow after microsurgical reconstruction
R01HL-36049-07 (CBY) DAVIES, PETER F UNIVERSITY OF CHICAGO 5841 S MARYLAND AVE CHICAGO, IL 60637 Endothelium in relation to atherogenesis
R01HL-36055-06 (PC) WEAVER, TIMOTHY E UNIV OF CINCINNATI MED CTR DEPARTMENT OF PEDIATRICS CINCINNATI, OH 45267-0541 Proteolytic processing of surfactant hydrophobic protein
P01HL-36059-06 (SRC) KIRBY, MARGARET L MEDICAL COLLEGE OF GEORGIA 1459 LANEY-WALKER BLVD AUGUSTA, GA 30912-2000 Development of the heart--Role of neural crest
P01HL-36059-06 0001 (SRC) KIRBY, MARGARET L Development of the heart--Role of neural crest Characterization and modification of cardiac neural crest
P01HL-36059-06 0002 (SRC) ROSENQUIST, THOMAS H Development of the heart--Role of neural crest Regulation and function of the outflow septation complex
P01HL-36059-06 0003 (SRC) LEATHERBURY, LINDA Development of the heart--Role of neural crest Hemodynamics of heart development
P01HL-36059-06 0005 (SRC) CREAZZO, TONY L Development of the heart--Role of neural crest Membrane ionic currents in developing heart
P01HL-36059-06 0007 (SRC) MULROY, MICHAEL J Development of the heart--Role of neural crest Neural interactions of neural crest--Developmental basis of long QT syndrome
P01HL-36059-06 0008 (SRC) GODT, ROBERT E Development of the heart--Role of neural crest Developmental changes in control of myocardial contraction
P01HL-36059-06 9001 (SRC) KIRBY, MARGARET L Development of the heart--Role of neural crest Core-Microsurgery
R01HL-36061-07 (HEM) SIMS, PETER J OKLAHOMA MEDICAL RESEARCH FDN 825 NORTHEAST THIRTEENTH ST OKLAHOMA CITY, OK 73104 Function of a C5b-9 inhibitor and vascular cells
R01HL-36069-06 (ECS) KORTHUIS, RONALD J LOUISIANA STATE UNIV MED CTR P O BOX 33932 SHREVEPORT, LA 71130 Transcapillary fluid exchange in skeletal muscle
R01HL-36079-05 (SAT) PARKER, JANET L UNIVERSITY OF MISSOURI DALTON RESEARCH CENTER COLUMBIA, MO 65211 Mycocardial dysfunction and Ca++ fluxes in shock
P01HL-36080-06 (HLBA) BISHOP, VERNON S UNIV OF TEXAS HLTH SCI CTR 7703 FLOYD CURL DRIVE SAN ANTONIO, TX 78284-7764 Sympathetic nervous system and blood pressure regulation
P01HL-36080-06 0001 (HLBA) BISHOP, VERNON S Sympathetic nervous system and blood pressure regulation Neurogenic hypertension in sub-human primate
P01HL-36080-06 0002 (HLBA) HAYWOOD, JOSEPH R Sympathetic nervous system and blood pressure regulation Sympathetic nervous system in sodium dependent hypertension
P01HL-36080-06 0006 (HLBA) SHADE, ROBERT E Sympathetic nervous system and blood pressure regulation Neurogenic hypertension in the subhuman primate
P01HL-36080-06 0007 (HLBA) BISHOP, VERNON S Sympathetic nervous system and blood pressure regulation Area postrema modulation of the arterial baroreflex
P01HL-36080-06 0008 (HLBA) MIFFLIN, STEVEN W Sympathetic nervous system and blood pressure regulation Somatic afferent inputs to the nucleus tractus solitarius
P01HL-36080-06 0009 (HLBA) JOHNSON, JOHN M Sympathetic nervous system and blood pressure regulation Sympathetic regulation of skin blood flow
P01HL-36080-06 0010 (HLBA) DAMON, DEBORAH H Sympathetic nervous system and blood pressure regulation Interactions of SHR-derived endothelium and vascular smooth muscle
P01HL-36080-06 9001 (HLBA) SHADE, ROBERT E Sympathetic nervous system and blood pressure regulation Core--Biochemistry assay
R01HL-36081-05 (CVB) ERDOS, ERVIN G UNIV OF ILLINOIS AT CHICAGO 835 SOUTH WOLCOTT AVE CHICAGO, IL 60612 Renal enzymes that regulate blood pressure
R01HL-36082-05 (RAP) ERDOS, ERVIN G UNIV OF ILLINOIS AT CHICAGO 835 S. WOLCOTT AVE CHICAGO, IL 60612 Metabolism of peptides by human lung enzyme
R01HL-36088-05 (ECS) LAUGHLIN, MAURICE H UNIVERSITY OF MISSOURI W117 VET MEDICAL BUILDING COLUMBIA, MO 65211 Training--Muscle blood flow and capillary dynamics
R37HL-36095-05 (RNM) STRANDNESS, DONALD E, JR UNIVERSITY OF WASHINGTON 1959 PACIFIC AVE NE SEATTLE, WA 98195 Direct, noninvasive study of venous flow and thrombosis
R01HL-36096-04A1 (PHRA) CLARKSON, CRAIG W TULANE UNIVERSITY 1430 TULANE AVE NEW ORLEANS, LA 70112 Action of antiarrhythmic drugs on cardiac INa
R01HL-36099-05 (HEM) HOYER, LEON W AMERICAN RED CROSS 15601 CRABBS BRANCH WAY ROCKVILLE, MD 20855 Studies of antibodies to antihemophilic factors
P01HL-36110-07 (HLBA) AUSTEN, K FRANK SEELEY G MUDD BUILDING 250 LONGWOOD AVENUE, RM 604 BOSTON, MA 02115 Chemical mediators of acute pulmonary disorders
P01HL-36110-07 0001 (HLBA) MC FADDEN, E REGIS Chemical mediators of acute pulmonary disorders Chemical mediators and human airway disease
P01HL-36110-07 0002 (HLBA) DRAZEN, JEFFREY M Chemical mediators of acute pulmonary disorders Functional implications of altering pulmonary mast cells
P01HL-36110-07 0003 (HLBA) AUSTEN, K FRANK Chemical mediators of acute pulmonary disorders Immortalization of mast cells by coculture of progenitor cells
P01HL-36110-07 0004 (HLBA) SERAFIN, WILLIAM E Chemical mediators of acute pulmonary disorders: Cell and molecular biology of murine mast cells of differing phenotype
P01HL-36110-07 0005 (HLBA) STEVENS, RICHARD Chemical mediators of acute pulmonary disorders Bilateral in vitro interactions between murine mast cells and fibroblasts
P01HL-36110-07 0006 (HLBA) SOBERMAN, ROY J Chemical mediators of acute pulmonary disorders Molecular mechanisms of leukotriene generation and catabolism in asthma
P01HL-36110-07 0007 (HLBA) OWEN, WILLIAM F Chemical mediators of acute pulmonary disorders Cytokine-like activity that mediates post-mitotic phenotypic changes
P01HL-36110-07 0008 (HLBA) DRAZEN, JEFFREY M Chemical mediators of acute pulmonary disorders Differential response to the cysteinyl leukotrienes
P01HL-36110-07 0009 (HLBA) WEIDNER, NOEL Chemical mediators of acute pulmonary disorders Characterization of mast cells in lung tissue
P01HL-36110-07 0010 (HLBA) INGRAM, ROLAND H Chemical mediators of acute pulmonary disorders: Inflammation, airway responsiveness and volume history in asthmatics
R55HL-36114-04A3 (PC) NEURATH, HANS UNIVERSITY OF WASHINGTON SEATTLE, WA 98195 Mast cell proteases -- Specificity and regulation
R01HL-36115-06 (CVB) LAINE, GLEN A UNIV OF TEXAS HLTH SCIENCE CTR 6431 FANNIN, MSB 5:020 HOUSTON, TX 77030 Basic determinants of lymph flow in edema
R01HL-36124-06 (TOX) MARTIN, WILLIAM J II WISHARD MEMORIAL HOSPITAL 1001 WEST 10TH STREET, OPW 425 INDIANAPOLIS, IN 46202-2879 Amiodarone pulmonary toxicity
R01HL-36126-05 (RAP) KRASNEY, JOHN A SUNY 124 SHERMAN HALL BUFFALO, NY 14214 Cerebral blood flow, ventilation, and chronic hypoxia
R01HL-36135-04 (BIO) KANG, DAVID S RUSH-PRESBYTERIAN ST LUKE'S CT 1753 W CONGRESS PKWY CHICAGO, IL 60612 Studies of homocysteinemia
R01HL-36139-06 (CVA) CHIEN, KENNETH R MD PHD UNIVERSITY OF

PROJECT NO., ORGANIZATIONAL UNIT., INVESTIGATOR, ADDRESS, TITLE

CALIFORNIA LA JOLLA, CA 92093 Adrenergic regulation of neonatal myocardial cell growth

R37HL-36141-07 (PHRA) SMITH, THOMAS W BRIGHAM AND WOMEN'S HOSPITAL 75 FRANCIS STREET BOSTON, MA 02115 Digitalis--Mechanism and reversal studies

R01HL-36158-05 (SSS) SIMON, TOBY L UNIVERSITY OF NEW MEXICO DEPT OF PATHOLOGY ALBUQUERQUE, N M 87131 Blood donations in the elderly

R01HL-36162-07 (PTHA) GERARD, NORMA P PHD BETH ISRAEL HOSPITAL 330 BROOKLINE AVENUE BOSTON, MA 02215 Immunopharmacology of complement anaphylatoxins in lung

R01HL-36171-04 (SRC) BEST, J ALLAN UNIVERSITY OF WATERLOO CANADA N2L 3G1 Providers for smoking prevention programs

R01HL-36185-06 (CVB) SHROFF, SANJEEV G UNIVERSITY OF CHICAGO 5841 SOUTH MARYLAND AVE CHICAGO, IL 60637 Ventricular mechano-energetics and myocardial remodeling

R01HL-36235-06 (BNP) GELB, MICHAEL H UNIVERSITY OF WASHINGTON SEATTLE, WA 98195 Studies in enzymology using inhibitors

R01HL-36240-06 (PB) ALTSCHULD, RUTH A OHIO STATE UNIVERSITY 5171 GRAVES HALL, 333 W 10TH A COLUMBUS, OH 43210 Cardiac myocytes and the cellular response to ischemia

R01HL-36245-06 (ECS) HEESCH, CHERYL M OHIO STATE UNIVERSITY 4114 GRAVES HALL/333 W. 10TH A COLUMBUS, OHIO 43210-1239 Neural control of the circulation in pregnancy

R01HL-36260-05 (HEM) BELL, WILLIAM R JOHNS HOPKINS UNIVERSITY 600 N WOLFE ST/1036 BLALOCK BL BALTIMORE, MD 21205 Structure-function studies of fibrinogen

R01HL-36271-05 (PB) SWEADNER, KATHLEEN J MASSACHUSETTS GENERAL HOSPITAL FRUIT STREET BOSTON, MA 02114-2696 Isozymes of the Na, K-ATPase--Monoclonal antibody probes

R01HL-36274-06 (CVB) ABENDSCHEIN, DANA R WASHINGTON UNIV SCH OF MED 660 SOUTH EUCLID AVENUE ST LOUIS, MO 63130 Isoforms of creatine kinase after myocrdial infarction

R01HL-36279-06 (CVB) ROMAN, RICHARD J MEDICAL COLLEGE OF WISCONSIN 8701 WATERTOWN PLANK ROAD MILWAUKEE, WI 53226 Vasa recta hemodynamics in genetic hypertension

R01HL-36301-06 (HED) ROSENBERG, ADAM ARTHUR UNIV COLORADO HLTH SCIS CTR 4200 EAST 9TH AVE DENVER, CO 80262 Mechanisms of perinatal cerebral blood flow regulation

R01HL-36308-06 (SB) EDMUNDS, L HENRY, JR HOSPITAL OF UNIV OF PENNSYLVAN 3400 SPRUCE ST, 4 SILVERSTEIN PHILADELPHIA, PA 19104 Extracorporeal perfusion for acute myocardial infarction

R01HL-36310-06 (BEM) MARMOT, MICHAEL G UNIVERSITY COLLEGE LONDON 66-72 GOWER ST, COMM MED LONDON, ENGLAND WC1E 6EA Social and occupational influences on health and illness

R55HL-36365-07 (HEM) BAJAJ, S PAUL ST LOUIS UNIVERSITY MED CTR 3635 VISTA AVE/PO BOX 15250 ST LOUIS, MO 63110-0250 Biochemistry of normal and abnormal variants of factor IX

R01HL-36371-06 (NTN) BURK, RAYMOND F, JR VANDERBILT UNIVERSITY C-2104 MCN NASHVILLE, TN 37232 Myocardial oxidant injury--Keshan disease as a model

R01HL-36372-05 (SAT) AUCHINCLOSS, HUGH, JR MASSACHUSETTS GENERAL HOSPITAL BOSTON, MA 02114 Mechanisms and control of xenograft rejection

R01HL-36378-06A2 (ECS) AMMONS, WILLIAM S THOMAS JEFFERSON UNIVERSITY 1020 LOCUST STREET PHILADELPHIA, PA 19107 Renal input to spinoreticular and spinothalamic neurons

R01HL-36392-05 (EDC) SACKS, FRANK M CHANNING LABORATORY 180 LONGWOOD AVENUE BOSTON, MA 02115 A controlled trial to reverse coronary atherosclerosis

R01HL-36404-06 (TOX) OLSON, JACK W UNIVERSITY OF KENTUCKY ROSE STREET LEXINGTON, KY 40536-0082 Polyamines and monocrotaline pneumotoxicity

P01HL-36444-11 (HLBB) STORB, RAINER F FRED HUTCHINSON CANCER RES CTR 1124 COLUMBIA STREET SEATTLE, WA 98104 Aplastic anemia center

P01HL-36444-11 0001 (HLBB) APPELBAUM, FREDERICK R Aplastic anemia center Marrow transplantation for myelodysplasia

P01HL-36444-11 0002 (HLBB) DONEY, KRISTINE C Aplastic anemia center Treatment of aplastic anemia with supportive care

P01HL-36444-11 0003 (HLBB) STORB, RAINER F Aplastic anemia center Transplantation of marrow from HLA-identical family members

P01HL-36444-11 0006 (HLBB) TOROK-STORB, BEVERLY J Aplastic anemia center In vitro studies on cellular interaction

P01HL-36444-11 0007 (HLBB) HANSEN, JOHN A Aplastic anemia center Horse anti-human globulin and anti-human T-cell antibodies

P01HL-36444-11 0008 (HLBB) MEYERS, JOEL D Aplastic anemia center Infectious diseases

P01HL-36444-11 0009 (HLBB) ANASETTI, CLAUDIO Aplastic anemia center Unrelated and HLA-mismatched related donor transplants

P01HL-36444-11 0010 (HLBB) MILLER, ARTHUR Aplastic anemia center Retroviral system for gene therapy in bone marrow

P01HL-36444-11 0011 (HLBB) SULLIVAN, KEITH Aplastic anemia center Outpatient department and long-term follow-up program

P01HL-36444-11 0012 (HLBB) BEAN, MICHAEL Aplastic anemia center Transfusion-induced sensitization to bone marrow transplants

P01HL-36444-11 9001 (HLBB) SALE, GEORGE E Aplastic anemia center CORE--Pathology

P01HL-36444-11 9008 (HLBB) PEPE, MARGARET S Aplastic anemia center CORE--Information management and statistical support

R01HL-36450-06A1 (CVA) STARLING, MARK R VA MEDICAL CENTER 2215 FULLER ROAD ANN ARBOR, MI 48105 Clinical application of end-systolic P-V relations

R37HL-36461-06 (NSS) BRESLOW, JAN L ROCKEFELLER UNIVERSITY 1230 YORK AVENUE NEW YORK, N Y 10021-6399 Apolipoprotein B molecular biology and genetic variation

R01HL-36472-04 (RNM) SAHN, DAVID J UNIV OF CALIFORNIA/SAN DIEGO LA JOLLA, CA 92093-0026 Phased arrays for multiplane esophageal echos in infants

R37HL-36473-06 (CVB) ERDOS, ERVIN G UNIVERSITY OF ILLINOIS 835 SOUTH WOLCOTT AVE CHICAGO, IL 60612 Vasoactive peptides which stimulate smooth muscles

R01HL-36474-06A1 (EDC) SPEIZER, FRANK E CHANNING LABORATORY 180 LONGWOOD AVENUE BOSTON, MA 02115 Effect of maternal smoking on neonatal lung function

R55HL-36526-07 (PTHA) HOOVER, RICHARD L VANDERBILT UNIVERSITY 21ST GARLAND AVE NASHVILLE, TN 37232 Leukocyte endothelial adhesion in inflammation

R01HL-36527-08 (ECS) LONGHURST, JOHN C MD PHD UNIVERSITY OF CALIFORNIA DAVIS, CA 95616 Mechanisms of visceral and somatic reflexes

R01HL-36530-07 (RAP) ROSENTHAL, FRANK S PURDUE UNIVERSITY CIVIL ENGINEERING BLDG WEST LAFAYETTE, IN 47907 Aerosol determination of pulmonary dimensions

R01HL-36531-05A2 (RAP) LAUGHLIN, MAURICE H UNIVERSITY OF MISSOURI COLUMBIA, MO 65211 Exercise--Coronary reserve, coronary heart disease

P50HL-36536-05 (SRC) COALSON, JACQUELINE SOUTHWEST FDN FOR BIOMED RES PO BOX 28147 SAN ANTONIO, TX 78228-0147 SCOR--Respiratory disorders in neonates and children

P50HL-36536-05 0004 (SRC) DELEMOS, ROBERT A SCOR--Respiratory disorders in neonates and children Lung development following severe lung injury in premature baboons

P50HL-36536-05 9001 (SRC) CAREY, K D SCOR--Respiratory disorders in neonates and children CORE--Animal models

P50HL-36536-05 9002 (SRC) COALSON, J J SCOR--Respiratory disorders in neonates and children CORE--Pathology

P50HL-36536-05 9003 (SRC) NULL, DONALD M JR SCOR--Respiratory disorders in neonates and children CORE--Clinical

P50HL-36536-05 0001 (SRC) DELEMOS, ROBERT A SCOR--Respiratory disorders in neonates and children High frequency ventilation and hyaline membrane disease

P50HL-36536-05 0002 (SRC) KING, RICHARD J SCOR--Respiratory disorders in neonates and children Metabolism of platelet activating factor by fibroblasts in premature baboons

P50HL-36536-05 0003 (SRC) ROBERTS, ROBERT J SCOR--Respiratory disorders in neonates and children Pharmacologic manipulation in the prevention of pulmonary injury

P50HL-36543-05 (SRC) NOTTER, ROBERT H UNIV OF ROCHESTER 601 ELMWOOD AVENUE ROCHESTER, NY 14642 SCOR--Respiratory disorders of neonates and children

P50HL-36543-05 0001 (SRC) FINKELSTEIN, JACOB SCOR--Respiratory disorders of neonates and children Isolation and study of fetal lung cells

P50HL-36543-05 0002 (SRC) MANISCALCO, WILLIAM M SCOR--Respiratory disorders of neonates and children Surfactant lipid synthesis in development lung

P50HL-36543-05 0003 (SRC) FINKELSTEIN, JACOB N SCOR--Respiratory disorders of neonates and children Synthesis-Secretion coupling in type II pneumocytes

P50HL-36543-05 0004 (SRC) NOTTER, ROBERT H SCOR--Respiratory disorders of neonates and children Biophysical and physiologic studies of lung surfactant

P50HL-36543-05 0005 (SRC) PHELPS, DALE L SCOR--Respiratory disorders of neonates and children Therapeutic interventions for bronchopulmonary dysplasia

P50HL-36543-05 0006 (SRC) KENDIG, JAMES SCOR--Respiratory disorders of neonates and children Surfactant replacement therapy for RDS

R01HL-36546-06 (BBCA) HERZFELD, JUDITH BRANDEIS UNIVERSITY WALTHAM, MA 02254-9110 Phase behavior of reversibly polymerizing systems

P01HL-36552-07 (HLBA) DIANA, JOHN N UNIVERSITY OF KENTUCKY COOPER & ALUMNI DRIVES LEXINGTON, KY 40536 Physiology and pathophysiology of the microcirculation

P01HL-36552-07 0001 (HLBA) DIANA, JOHN N Physiology and pathophysiology of the microcirculation Physiloical regulation of capillary permeability

P01HL-36552-07 0007 (HLBA) LAI-FOOK, STEPHEN J Physiology and pathophysiology of the microcirculation Pulmonary interstitial mechanics--Regulation of liquid and solute exchange

P01HL-36552-07 0008 (HLBA) HENNIG, BERNHARD Physiology and pathophysiology of the microcirculation Lipid-Mediated endothelial injury

P01HL-36552-07 0009 (HLBA) ANDERSON, JAMES W Physiology and pathophysiology of the microcirculation Diabetes, diet, glycemia, and microcirculation

P01HL-36552-07 0010 (HLBA) BRUCKNER, GEZA G Physiology and pathophysiology of the microcirculation Fats, microcirculation and platelet-endothelial cell interaction

P01HL-36552-07 0011 (HLBA) RICHARDSON, DANIEL Physiology and pathophysiology of the microcirculation Regulation of regional and capillary blood flow in skin

P01HL-36552-07 0012 (HLBA) DOWELL, RUSSELL Physiology and pathophysiology of the microcirculation Neovascularization in heart development and adaptation

P01HL-36552-07 9001 (HLBA) KLITZMAN, BRUCE M Physiology and pathophysiology of the microcirculation CORE--Electron microscopy

P01HL-36552-07 9002 (HLBA) TURBEK, JOHN Physiology and pathophysiology of the microcirculation CORE--Biostatistics

P01HL-36573-06 (HLBA) ASKARI, AMIR MEDICAL COLLEGE OF OHIO 3000 ARLINGTON AVENUE TOLEDO, OH 43614 Control mechanisms of cardiac proteins and enzymes

P01HL-36573-06 0001 (HLBA) ASKARI, AMIR Control mechanisms of cardiac proteins and enzymes Mechanism and regulation of NaK-ATPase

P01HL-36573-06 0002 (HLBA) GARLID, KEITH D Control mechanisms of cardiac proteins and enzymes Mechanisms of ion transport in heart mitochondria

P01HL-36573-06 0003 (HLBA) BEAVIS, ANDREW D Control mechanisms of cardiac proteins and enzymes Potassium ion uniporter in cardiac mitochondria

P01HL-36573-06 0004 (HLBA) SCHLENDER, KEITH K Control mechanisms of cardiac proteins and enzymes Characterization of cardiac protein phosphatases

P01HL-36573-06 0006 (HLBA) MELLGREN, RONALD L Control mechanisms of cardiac proteins and enzymes Function of a cardiac calcium-dependent protease system

P01HL-36573-06 0008 (HLBA) MERCER, ROBERT W Control mechanisms of cardiac proteins and enzymes Characterization of Nak-ATPase structure and function

P01HL-36573-06 0009 (HLBA) TRUMBLY, ROBERT J Control mechanisms of cardiac proteins and enzymes Molecular genetics of yeast NaH antiporters

P01HL-36573-06 9001 (HLBA) REIMANN, ERWIN M Control mechanisms of cardiac proteins and enzymes CORE--Preparative

P01HL-36573-06 9002 (HLBA) LANE, RICHARD D Control mechanisms of cardiac proteins and enzymes CORE--Antibody facility

P01HL-36577-06 (HLBA) LARSEN, GARY NAT JEWISH CNTR FOR IMM & RES 1400 JACKSON STREET DENVER, CO 80206-1997 Inflammation airways reactivity and asthma

P01HL-36577-06 0001 (HLBA) LARSEN, GARY L Inflammation airways reactivity and asthma Antigen-induced changes in airways function

P01HL-36577-06 0006 (HLBA) CERNIACK, REUBEN M Inflammation airways reactivity and asthma Airways inflammation and asthma in man

P01HL-36577-06 0008 (HLBA) MARTIN, RICHARD Inflammation airways reactivity and asthma Nocturnal asthma and airways inflammation

P01HL-36577-06 0009 (HLBA) ROSENWASSER, LANNY Inflammation airways reactivity and asthma Immune and inflammatory reactions in human allergic asthma

P01HL-36577-06 0010 (HLBA) LEUNG, DONALD Inflammation airways reactivity and asthma Mechanisms of steroid resistant asthma

P01HL-36577-06 0011 (HLBA) GELFAND, ERWIN W Inflammation airways reactivity and asthma Humoral and cell-mediated immunity indevelopment of bronchial hyperresponsiveness

P01HL-36577-06 0012 (HLBA) IRVIN, CHARLES G Inflammation airways reactivity and asthma Physiologic effects of granulocytes on airway function

P01HL-36577-06 9001 (HLBA) CLARK, RICHARD A Inflammation airways reactivity and asthma Morphology core

P01HL-36577-06 9003 (HLBA) CHERNIACK, REUBEN M Inflammation airways reactivity and asthma CORE--Clinical

P01HL-36588-06 (HLBA) SCHNEIDERMAN, NEIL UNIVERSITY OF MIAMI P O BOX 248185 CORAL GABLES, FL 33124 Psychophysiology of cardiovascular reactivity

P01HL-36588-06 0001 (HLBA) SCHNEIDERMAN, NEIL Psychophysiology of cardiovascular reactivity Psychophysiology and hypertension in black and white Americans

P01HL-36588-06 0003 (HLBA) SKYLER, JAY S Psychophysiology of cardiovascular reactivity Insulin sensitivity, blood pressure, and glucose tolerance

P01HL-36588-06 0004 (HLBA) MC CABE, PHILIP M Psychophysiology of cardiovascular reactivity CNS mediation of sympathetic reactivity

P01HL-36588-06 0005 (HLBA) IRONSON, GAIL Psychophysiology of cardiovascular reactivity Race, sodium, insulin and cardiovascular reactivity

P01HL-36588-06 0006 (HLBA) NAGEL, JOACHIM H Psychophysiology of cardiovascular reactivity Validity assessment of impedance cardiography

P01HL-36588-06 9002 (HLBA) GERACE, TERENCE A Psychophysiology of cardiovascular reactivity Core--Computation and statistics

P01HL-36588-06 9004 (HLBA) KUMAR, MAHENDRA Psychophysiology of cardiovascular reactivity Core--Biochemistry

P01HL-36588-06 9006 (HLBA) NAGEL, JOACHIM H Psychophysiology of cardiovascular reactivity CORE--Biomedical engineering

R01HL-36591-06 (HEM) DORSHKIND, KENNETH A UNIVERSITY OF CALIFORNIA DIV OF BIOMEDICAL SCIENCES RIVERSIDE, CA 92521-0121 Basic studies of CSF effects on hemopoiesis

R01HL-36597-06 (PTHA) LAI-FOOK, STEPHEN J WENNER-GREN LABORATORY ROSE STREET LEXINGTON, KY 40506-0070 Pleural liquid exchange and lung mechanics

R01HL-36611-06 (BM) SCHLIEVERT, PATRICK M UNIVERSITY OF MINNESOTA BOX 196 420 DELEWARE ST SE MINNEAPOLIS, MN 55455 Cardiotoxicity of streptococcal pyrogenic exotoxin

R01HL-36634-05 (CVB) BURNETT, JOHN C, JR MAYO FOUNDATION 200 FIRST STREET SOUTHWEST ROCHESTER, MN 55905 Intrarenal regulation of sodium excretion

R01HL-36635-06 (ECS) GABEL, JOSEPH UNIV OF TEXAS HLTH SCI CTR 6431 FANNIN/MSB 5.020 HOUSTON, TX 77030 Fluid exchange in edematous lungs

R01HL-36670-06 (CVB) NASJLETTI, ALBERTO NEW YORK MEDICAL COLLEGE VALHALLA, NY 10595 Role of pressor prostanoids in hypertension

R01HL-36699-05 (MET) BANERJEE, DEBENDRANATH NEW YORK BLOOD CENTER 310 EAST 67TH STREET NEW YORK, N Y 10021 Regulation of HDL synthesis and secretion

R01HL-36708-05 (PTHA) ELIAS, JACK A YALE UNIVERSITY 333 CEDAR STREET NEW HAVEN, CT 06510 Modulators of pulmonary inflammation and fibrosis

R01HL-36709-06 (MET) CHANG, TA-YUAN DARTMOUTH MEDICAL SCHOOL HANOVER, NH 03756 Cell mutants defective in cholesterol ester formation

R01HL-36715-05 (SRC) TOY, PEARL T SAN FRANCISCO GENERAL HOSPITAL 1001 POTRERO AVENUE SAN FRANCISCO, CALIF 94110 A model autologous predeposit blood donation program

R01HL-36729-06 (CVA) WEISS, JAMES N UNIVERSITY OF CALIFORNIA 405 HILGARD AVENUE LOS ANGELES, CA 90024-1406 Cardiac function during impaired metabolism

R01HL-36734-05 (SRC) DEBUSK, ROBERT F STANFORD UNIVERSITY 780 WELCH ROAD PALO ALTO, CA 94304 Occupational work evaluation soon after coronary surgery

R01HL-36735-05 (EDC) KAPOOR, WISHWA N UNIVERISTY OF PITTSBURGH 190 LOTHROP ST, ROOM 100 PITTSBURGH, PA 15261 Identifying high risk patients with syncope

R01HL-36744-05 (EDC) MANGANO, DENNIS T VETERANS ADMIN MEDICAL CENTER 4150 CLEMENT STREET SAN FRANCISCO, CA 94121 Predictors of perioperative cardiac morbidity

R01HL-36745-05 (PTHA) RHOADES, RODNEY A INDIANA UNIVERSITY SCH OF MED 635 BARNHILL DR INDIANAPOLIS, IN 46202-5120 Pathophysiology of lung vascular permeability

R01HL-36763-05 (RAP) KERN, DAVID F EAST TENNESSEE STATE UNIV BOX 19780A JOHNSON CITY, TN 37614-0002 Effect of charge on lung permeability

PROJECT NO., ORGANIZATIONAL UNIT., INVESTIGATOR, ADDRESS, TITLE

R01HL-36765-05 (RAP) TRAYSTMAN, RICHARD J JOHNS HOPKINS HOSPITAL 600 NORTH WOLFE ST BALTIMORE, MD 21205 Collateral mechanics: Effect of age & lung dysfunction

R01HL-36771-05 (RAP) MARKOV, ANGEL UNIV OF MISSISSIPPI MEDICAL CT 2500 NORTH STATE STREET JACKSON, MI 39216 Treatment of ARDS with fructose diphosphate

R01HL-36780-05 (RAP) MITCHELL, GORDON S UNIV OF WISCONSIN 2015 LINDEN DR WEST MADISON, WI 53706 Interactions in ventilatory control during exercise

R01HL-36781-06 (RAP) SCHNEEBERGER, EVELINE E MASSACHUSSETTS GENERAL HOSPITA FRUIT STREET BOSTON, MA 02114 Immune functions of accessory cells in the lung

R01HL-36783-05 (PHY) GADSBY, DAVID C ROCKEFELLER UNIVERSITY 1230 YORK AVENUE NEW YORK, NY 10021 Na/K pump current in isolated heart cells

R01HL-36802-05 (CVB) RAMWELL, PETER W GEORGETOWN UNIVERSITY 3900 RESERVOIR RD N W WASHINGTON, D C 20007 Sex/hormonal regulation of pulmonary artery reactivity

R29HL-36811-05 (SB) BURNS, GREGORY L UNIVERSITY OF UTAH DUMKE 535 SALT LAKE CITY, UTAH 84112 Immune-response changes with blood pump use in calves

R37HL-36820-05 (EDC) STERN, MICHAEL P UNIV OF TEXAS SCIENCE CTR 7703 FLOYD CURL DRIVE SAN ANTONIO, TX 78284-7873 Incidence of diabetes and CVD in Mexican Americans

R01HL-36829-04A1 (SAT) HALES, CHARLES A MASSACHUSETTS GENERAL HOSPITAL BULFINCH ONE BOSTON, MA 02114 Pulmonary edema from synthetic smoke inhalation

R01HL-36838-05A1 (PHRA) HALUSHKA, PERRY V MEDICAL UNIV OF SOUTH CAROLINA 171 ASHLEY AVENUE CHARLESTON, SC 29425 Thromboxane A2 receptors in health and disease

R01HL-36840-06 (ECS) KUNZE, DIANA L BAYLOR COLLEGE OF MEDICINE ONE BAYLOR PLAZA HOUSTON, TX 77030 Physiology and pharmacology of cardiovascular neurons

R01HL-36879-05 (EDC) MICHELS, VIRGINIA V MAYO FOUNDATION 200 FIRST STREET SOUTHWEST ROCHESTER, MN 55905 Idiopathic dilated cardiomyopathy

R01HL-36892-05 (CVA) BISHOP, SANFORD P UNIV OF ALABAMA UAB STATION BIRMINGHAM, AL 35294 Pathology of regional ischemia in cardiac hypertrophy

R01HL-36894-05 (PTHA) HENRY, PHILIP D BAYLOR COLLEGE OF MEDICINE ONE BALYOR PLAZA, SUITE 513E HOUSTON, TX 77030 Autofluorescence of atherosclerotic human arteries

R01HL-36898-05 (SB) CALLOW, ALLAN D WASHINGTON UNIVERSITY 4960 AUDUBON AVE ST LOUIS, MO 63110 Cellular mechanisms of vascular graft failure

R01HL-36907-05 (ECS) GORDON, FRANK J EMORY UNIVERSITY SCHOOL OF MED ATLANTA, GA 30322 Neuropharmacology of the baroreceptor reflex

R01HL-36930-06 (PHY) BROWN, ARTHUR M MD PHD BAYLOR COLLEGE OF MEDICINE ONE BAYLOR PLAZA HOUSTON, TX 77030 Membrane currents in cardiac muscle

R01HL-36946-05 (HEM) SIMS, PETER J OKLAHOMA MEDICAL RESEARCH FDN 825 NORTHEAST 13TH ST OKLAHOMA CITY, OK 73104 Effect of C5b-9 proteins on blood platelet membranes

R01HL-36957-06 (PHY) MARBAN, EDUARDO MD PHD JOHNS HOPKINS UNIVERSITY 725 N WOLFE ST BALTIMORE, MD 21205 Regulation of cardic Ca and Na channel gatings

R01HL-36974-05 (CVA) LEDERER, WILLIAM J UNIV. OF MARYLAND AT BALTIMORE 660 WEST REDWOOD STREET BALTIMORE, MD 21201 Cellular origins of cardiac arrhythmias

R01HL-36977-05 (ECS) BARRETT, PAULA Q UNIVERSITY OF VIRGINIA BOX 448 JORDON HALL 5-50 CHARLOTTESVILLE, VA 22908 Atrial natriuretic peptide and aldosterone secretion

R01HL-36982-05 (RAP) ADLER, KENNETH B NORTH CAROLINA STATE UNIV. 4700 HILLSBOROUGH STREET RALEIGH, NC 27606 Mechanism of oxidant-induced respiratory mucin secretion

R01HL-37001-06 (HEM) SMITHIES, OLIVER UNIVERSITY OF NORTH CAROLINA CB 7525 CHAPEL HILL, NC 27599-7525 Targeted correction of faulty beta-globin genes

R01HL-37005-06 (CVA) SLINKER, BRYAN K UNIVERSITY OF VERMONT CARDIOLOGY--MCCLURE 1 MFU BURLINGTON, VT 05405 Dynamic determinants of left ventricular function

R01HL-37015-04 (CVB) MC GUFFEE, LINDA J UNIVERSITY OF NEW MEXICO DEPT OF PHARMACOLOGY ALBUQUERQUE, N M 87131 Cell to matrix coupling in smooth muscle

R55HL-37023-04 (MBY) ALLAN, MAGGI COLUMBIA UNIV HEALTH SCIENCES 630 WEST 168TH STREET NEW YORK, NY 10032 Sequences controlling human globin gene expression

R01HL-37028-07 (PHRA) HAMILTON, SUSAN L BAYLOR COLLEGE OF MEDICINE ONE BAYLOR PLAZA HOUSTON, TX 77030 Dihdropyridine binding sites and calcium channels

P01HL-37044-06 (HLBA) BROWN, ARTHUR M BAYLOR COLLEGE OF MEDICINE ONE BAYLOR PLAZA HOUSTON, TX 77030 Structure and function of cardiovascular ion channels

P01HL-37044-06 0007 (HLBA) BIRNBOWNER, LUTZ Structure and function of cardiovascular ion channels Primary structure of calcium channels

P01HL-37044-06 0001 (HLBA) BROWN, ARTHUR M Structure and function of cardiovascular ion channels Structure function correlation of the calcium channel

P01HL-37044-06 0008 (HLBA) HAMILTON, SUSAN L Structure and function of cardiovascular ion channels Structure of dihydropyridine binding protein from skeletal muscle

P01HL-37044-06 0009 (HLBA) JOHO, ROLF H Structure and function of cardiovascular ion channels Cloning, expression and mapping of heart potassium channels

P01HL-37044-06 0010 (HLBA) STEFANI, ENRICO Structure and function of cardiovascular ion channels Ionic channels in coronary smooth muscle

P01HL-37044-06 9003 (HLBA) SAKAR, HEMANTA K Structure and function of cardiovascular ion channels CORE--Molecular biology

P01HL-37044-06 9004 (HLBA) PEDERSEN, STEEN E Structure and function of cardiovascular ion channels CORE--Biochemistry, oocyte expression and tissue culture

R01HL-37063-06 (PC) TAYLOR, JOHN M GLADSTONE FDN LABORATORIES P O BOX 40608 SAN FRANCISCO, CA 94140-0608 Regulation of

apolipoprotein synthesis
R37HL-37090-06 (NSS) TRAVIS, JAMES UNIVERSITY OF GEORGIA ATHENS, GA 30602 Alpha-1-proteinase inhibitor deficiency and emphysema
P50HL-37117-05 (SRC) MC FADDEN, EDWARD R, JR UNIVERSITY HOSPITALS 2074 ABINGTON ROAD CLEVELAND, OHIO 44106 SCOR-Chronic diseases of the airways
P50HL-37117-05 0001 (SRC) MCFADDEN, EDWARD R, JR SCOR-Chronic diseases of the airways Factors determining airway responsiveness
P50HL-37117-05 0002 (SRC) CHERNIACK, NEIL S SCOR-Chronic diseases of the airways Obstructive disease – Control of respiration and effects on ventilation
P50HL-37117-05 0003 (SRC) STROHL, KINGMAN P SCOR-Chronic diseases of the airways Nasal function and airway reactivity
P50HL-37117-05 0004 (SRC) LAMM, MICHAEL E SCOR-Chronic diseases of the airways Secretory immunity against respiratory pathogens via the gut
P50HL-37117-05 0005 (SRC) KAZURA, JAMES W SCOR-Chronic diseases of the airways Inflammatory cells in obstructive airway disease
P50HL-37117-05 9001 (SRC) DUNN, MICHAEL J SCOR-Chronic diseases of the airways Eicosanoid laboratory--Core
R01HL-37118-07 (HEM) PERRINE, SUSAN P CHILDREN'S HOSP OAKLAND 747-52ND STREET OAKLAND, CA 94609 Biology of the fetal globin switch
P50HL-37119-05 (SRC) PERMUTT, SOLBERT FRANCIS SCOTT KEY MEDICAL CTR 4940 EASTERN AVENUE BALTIMORE, MD 21224 SCOR--Chronic diseases of the airways
P50HL-37119-05 0001 (SRC) NACLERIO, ROBERT M SCOR--Chronic diseases of the airways The response of the nasal mucosa to hyperventilation with cold, dry air
P50HL-37119-05 0002 (SRC) HIRSHMAN, CAROL A SCOR--Chronic diseases of the airways Responses of the lung periphery to dry air and antigen
P50HL-37119-05 0003 (SRC) PERMUTT, SOLBERT SCOR--Chronic diseases of the airways Mediators of immediate hypersensitivity & asthma cellular pathophysiology
P50HL-37119-05 0004 (SRC) PLAUT, MARSHALL SCOR--Chronic diseases of the airways Human basophil activation by IgE dependent factors
P50HL-37119-05 9001 (SRC) LICHTENSTEIN, LAWRENCE M SCOR--Chronic diseases of the airways Core--Mediator/cell laboratory
P50HL-37121-05 (SRC) HUNNINGHAKE, GARY W UNIVERSITY OF IOWA COLLEGE OF MEDICINE IOWA CITY, IA 52242 SCOR--Occupational and immunologic lung diseases
P50HL-37121-05 0001 (SRC) HUNNINGHAKE, GARY W SCOR--Occupational and immunologic lung diseases Bronchoalveolar lavage and interstitial lung disease
P50HL-37121-05 0002 (SRC) HUNNINGHAKE, GARY W SCOR--Occupational and immunologic lung diseases Local immune response at sites of disease in sarcoidosis
P50HL-37121-05 0003 (SRC) FICK, ROBERT SCOR--Occupational and immunologic lung diseases Transport of immunoglobulin proteins in the lung
P50HL-37121-05 0004 (SRC) MERCHANT, JAMES SCOR--Occupational and immunologic lung diseases Epidemiology and pulmonary responses to organic dust exposure
P50HL-37121-05 0005 (SRC) RICHERSON, HAL B. SCOR--Occupational and immunologic lung diseases Specific cellular mechanisms in hypersensitivity pneumonitis
P50HL-37121-05 9001 (SRC) BURMEISTER, LEON SCOR--Occupational and immunologic lung diseases CORE--Biometry
R01HL-37124-06 (CVA) HESS, PETER HARVARD MEDICAL SCHOOL 25 SHATTUCK STREET BOSTON, MA 02115 Calcium channels in the cardiovascular systems
R37HL-37127-07 (PHY) SZABO, GABOR UNIVERSITY OF VIRGINIA BOX 449 JORDON HALL CHARLOTTESVILLE, VA 22908 Regulatory mechanisms of K+ channel function in heart
R01HL-37128-06 (PTHA) BROWN, JERRY L UNIV OF COLORADO HLTH SCI CTR 4200 E 9TH AVENUE DENVER, CO 80262 Alpha-1-proteinase inhibitor deficiency and emphysema
R01HL-37130-06 (PTHA) JOHNSON, EDWARD M MT SINAI SCHOOL OF MEDICINE ONE GUSTLAVE L LEVY PLACE NEW YORK, NY 10029 Alpha-1-antitrypsin deficiency and emphysema
R44HL-37168-02A6 (SSS) TAMARI, YEHUDA CIRCULATORY TECHNOLOGY, INC 21 SINGWORTH STREET OYSTER BAY, NY 11771-3703 A self regulating pump chamber for the roller pump
R01HL-37195-07 (GMA) DAVIS, ROGER A UNIV. OF COLORADO HEALTH SCIEN 4200 E 9TH AVE DENVER, CO 80262 Regulation of bile acid synthesis and 7-alpha-hydroxylase
R01HL-37196-05 (CVA) COOPER, GEORGE, IV UNIVERSITY OF SOUTH CAROLINA 171 ASHLEY AVE CHARLESTON, SC 29425 Load regulation of adult mammalian myocardium
R01HL-37217-03 (PHY) ROGART, RICHARD B UNIVERSITY OF CHICAGO 5841 SOUTH MARYLAND, BOX 249 CHICAGO, ILL 60637 Molecular characterization of cardiac Na+ channels
R37HL-37250-05 (HEM) DETWILER, THOMAS C SUNY HEALTH SCIENCE CENTER BOX 8 BROOKLYN, NY 11203 Structure and function of thrombospondin
R01HL-37251-05 (MET) ATTIE, ALAN D UNIV OF WISCONSIN-MADISON 420 HENRY MALL MADISON, WI 53706 Apolipoprotein-b mutations and low density lipoprotein
R01HL-37254-03 (RAP) MAROM, ZVI M MOUNT SINAI SCHOOL OF MEDICINE PULMONARY DIV ANNEBERG 24-30 NEW YORK, N Y 10029 Mucus secretagogue--Novel peptide in bronchitis
R01HL-37260-05 (PTHA) LEUNG, DONALD Y NATIONAL JEWISH CENTER 1400 JACKSON STREET DENVER, CO 80206 Pathogenesis and etiology of Kawasaki syndrome
R01HL-37289-04 (CVA) HAGEMAN, GILBERT R UNIVERSITY OF ALABAMA UAB STATION BIRMINGHAM, AL 35294 Autonomic cardiac activity during ischemia
R01HL-37318-04A1 (HED) FARBER, JAY P UNIVERSITY OF OKLAHOMA 940 S L YOUNG BLVD OKLAHOMA CITY, OK 73190 Maturation of respiratory neuronal discharge
R01HL-37374-05 (CVB) LOMBARD, JULIAN H MEDICAL COLLEGE OF WISCONSIN 8701 WATERTOWN PLANK MILWAUKEE, WI 53226 Mechanism of vascular oxygen response in hypertension
R01HL-37379-05 (RAP) SMITH, PHILIP L JOHNS HOPKINS CTR/ASTHMA & ALL 301 BAYVIEW BLVD/FSK MED CTR BALTIMORE, MD 21224 Neuromechanical regulation of airflow in upper airways
R01HL-37387-04A1 (RAP) TERJUNG, RONALD L SUNY HEALTH SCI CTR AT SYRACUS 750 EAST ADAMS ST SYRACUSE, NY 13210 Exercise training and peripheral arterial insufficiency
R01HL-37388-05 (TOX) NOTTER, ROBERT H MD PHD UNIV OF ROCHESTER SCH OF MED ROCHESTER, NEW YORK 14642 Fundamental characterization of neonatal oxygen toxicity
R01HL-37396-05 (CVA) ANTZELEVITCH, CHARLES MASONIC MED RES LABORATORY 2150 BLEECKER ST UTICA, N Y 13504 Electrophysiology of cardiac arrhythmias
R01HL-37404-05 (CVA) VATNER, DOROTHY E MASSACHUSETTS GENERAL HOSPITAL FRUIT ST - JACKSON 14 BOSTON, MA 02114 Autonomic receptor function in LV hypertrophy and failure
P01HL-37412-04 (HLBA) SONNENBLICK, EDMUND H ALBERT EINSTEIN COLL OF MED 1300 MORRIS PARK AVENUE BRONX, N Y 10461 Mechanisms of myocardial dysfunction and failure
P01HL-37412-04 0001 (HLBA) SONNENBLICK, EDMUND H Mechanisms of myocardial dysfunction and failure Structure/function in reactive hypertrophy after myocardial infarction
P01HL-37412-04 0002 (HLBA) ARONSON, RONALD S Mechanisms of myocardial dysfunction and failure Cellular basis of electrical alteration in cardiac hypertrophy & failure
P01HL-37412-04 0003 (HLBA) KRUEGER, JOHN W Mechanisms of myocardial dysfunction and failure Relaxation-diastolic coupling in cardiac muscle dysfunction
P01HL-37412-04 0004 (HLBA) FACTOR, STEPHEN M Mechanisms of myocardial dysfunction and failure Intrinsic connective tissuein hypertrophied & failing myocardium
P01HL-37412-04 0005 (HLBA) ENG, CALVIN Mechanisms of myocardial dysfunction and failure Vascular considerations in cardiomyopathy
P01HL-37412-04 0006 (HLBA) WELLS, JAMES W Mechanisms of myocardial dysfunction and failure Sarcolemmal receptors and the pathogenesis of cardiomyopathy
P01HL-37412-04 0007 (HLBA) LIEW, C C Mechanisms of myocardial dysfunction and failure Pathogenesis of myocardiol hypertrophy & failure--Molecular biological approach
P01HL-37412-04 0008 (HLBA) LEINWAND, LESLIE A Mechanisms of myocardial dysfunction and failure Molecular genetic analysis of myosin heavy chain expression
P01HL-37412-04 0009 (HLBA) YELLIN, EDWARD Mechanisms of myocardial dysfunction and failure Diastolic function in the intact hypertrophied heart
P01HL-37412-04 9001 (HLBA) SCHEUER, JAMES Mechanisms of myocardial dysfunction and failure Core--Biochemistry
P01HL-37412-04 9002 (HLBA) FACTOR, STEPHEN M Mechanisms of myocardial dysfunction and failure Core--Pathology
P01HL-37412-04 9003 (HLBA) FEIN, FREDERICK Mechanisms of myocardial dysfunction and failure Core--Animal models
R01HL-37413-06 (ECS) LA BELLE, EDWARD F, JR GRADUATE HOSPITAL ONE GRADUATE PLAZA PHILADELPHIA, PA 19146 Inositol lipid stimulation of aortal contraction
R01HL-37419-05 (HEM) PONCZ, MORTIMER CHILDREN'S HOSP OF PHILADELPHI 34TH STREET AND CIVIC CTR BLVD PHILADELPHIA, PA 19104 Studies of platelet factor 4 and beta-thromboglobulin
R37HL-37422-05 (HEM) FEINSTEIN, MAURICE B UNIV OF CONNECTICUT HLTH CTR 263 FARMINGTON AVENUE FARMINGTON, CT 06032 Antibodies to ip3-receptor/channel in human platelets
R01HL-37438-05 (PTHA) BOYD, CHARLES D UMDNJ-RUTGERS MEDICAL SCHOOL ACADEMIC HLTH SCI CTR, CN-19 NEW BRUNSWICK, N J 08903 The role of the extracellular matrix in atherogenesis
R01HL-37451-05 (HED) BROWN, GAIL P SUNY AT BUFFALO 3435 MAIN STREET BUFFALO, NY 14214 Angiotensin prostanoids & hemodynamics during pregnancy
R01HL-37457-05 (HEM) REDMAN, COLVIN M NEW YORK BLOOD CENTER 310 EAST 67TH STREET NEW YORK, NY 10021 Human fibrinogen--Mechanisms of assembly
P01HL-37462-05 (HLBB) PALEK, JIRI ST ELIZABETH'S HOSPITAL 736 CAMBRIDGE STREET BOSTON, MA 02135 Membrane skeleton of normal and abnormal red cells
P01HL-37462-05 0001 (HLBB) PALEK, JIRI Membrane skeleton of normal and abnormal red cells Structural characterization on mutant skeletal proteins
P01HL-37462-05 0002 (HLBB) PRCHAL, JOSEF T Membrane skeleton of normal and abnormal red cells Characterization of spectrin genes in disease
P01HL-37462-05 0003 (HLBB) LIU, SHIH-CHUN D Membrane skeleton of normal and abnormal red cells Skeletal ultrastructure and composition
P01HL-37462-05 0004 (HLBB) COHEN, CARL M Membrane skeleton of normal and abnormal red cells Band 4.2 protein of normal and abnormal erythrocytes
R37HL-37464-05 (BEM) JULIUS, STEVO UNIV OF MICHIGAN MED CTR 3918 TAUBMAN CENTER ANN ARBOR, MI 48109-0356 Neurocontrol, behavior and hypertension in a population
R01HL-37479-04A2 (PHY) JENNINGS, MICHAEL L UNIVERSITY OF TEXAS MED BRANCH 301 UNIVERSITY BOULEVARD GALVESTON, TX 77550 Erythrocyte potassium transport and volume regulation
R37HL-37498-05 (RAP) COBURN, RONALD F UNIVERSITY OF PENNSYLVANIA B400 RICHARDS BLDG PHILADELPHIA, PA 19104-6085 Airway smooth muscle in health and disease
R01HL-37499-05 (SAT) MILLER, D CRAIG STANFORD UNIVERSITY MED CTR CARDIOVASCULAR RESEARCH CENTER STANFORD, CA 94305 Cardiovascular surgical studies of omega-3 fatty acids
R01HL-37500-05 (PTHA) DE COURSEY, THOMAS E RUSH PRESBYTERIAN ST LUKE'S 1653 WEST CONGRESS PARKWAY CHICAGO, IL 60612 Pulmonary type II epithelial cells--Role of ion channel
R01HL-37504-05 (SRC) WARWICK, WARREN J UNIVERSITY OF MINNESOTA 420 DELAWARE ST, S E MINNEAPOLIS, MN 55455 Health benefits of psycho-social interventions in cystic fibrosis
R01HL-37510-04 (PTHA) LIAU, GENE JEROME HOLLAND LAB 15601 CRABBS BRANCH WAY ROCKVILLE, MD 20855 Vessel wall injury and repair
R55HL-37515-04A1 (HEM) JOINER, CLINTON H UNIVERSITY OF CINCINNATI

231 BETHESDA AVE CINCINNATI, OH 45267-0541 Cation fluxes activated by deoxygenation of sickle cells

R01HL-37528-06 (HEM) HEBBEL, ROBERT P UNIVERSITY OF MINNESOTA HARVARD ST-E RIVER RD-BOX 480 MINNEAPOLIS, MN 55455 Oxidation and deformation in sickle RBC dehydration

R01HL-37556-06A1 (RAP) FORMAN, HENRY J CHILDRENS HOSPITAL 4650 SUNSET BLVD, BOX 83 LOS ANGELES, CA 90027 Effect of oxidant stress on alveolar macrophage function

R01HL-37569-05 (HEM) MULLIGAN, RICHARD C WHITEHEAD INST FOR BIOMED RES NINE CAMBRIDGE CENTER CAMBRIDGE, MA 02142 Gene transfer/expression in murine/human stem cells

R01HL-37570-05A2 (HEM) MORGAN, WILLIAM T UNIVERSITY OF MISSOURI 5100 ROCKHILL RD/SCH BS LF SCI KANSAS CITY, MO 64110 Role of histidine-rich glycoprotein in hemostasis

R01HL-37591-06 (ALY) COLTEN, HARVEY R WASHINGTON UNIVERSITY 400 SOUTH KINGSHIGHWAY BLVD ST LOUIS, MO 63110 Lung cell metabolism in vitro

R01HL-37592-05 (BIO) TROXLER, ROBERT F BOSTON UNIVERSITY 80 EAST CONCORD STREET BOSTON, MA 02118 Human heart fatty acid binding proteins

R01HL-37596-03 (RAP) DAVENPORT, PAUL W UNIVERSITY OF FLORIDA BOX J-144, JHMHC GAINESVILLE, FLA 32610 Respiratory afferent projections to the cerebral cortex

R01HL-37597-05 (CLTR) OBERMAN, ALBERT UNIV OF ALABAMA IN BIRMINGHAM UNIVERSITY STATION -721 MTB BIRMINGHAM, AL 35294 Training level vs cardiac adaptations in patients w/CHD

R01HL-37610-05 (SB) SALZMAN, EDWIN W BETH ISRAEL HOSPITAL 330 BROOKLINE AVENUE BOSTON, MA 02215 Thromboresistant materials

R01HL-37615-05 (PTHA) HOIDAL, JOHN R UNIVERSITY OF UTAH 1400 EAST 200 SOUTH SALT LAKE CITY, UT 84112 Pulmonary emphysema--Role of PMN leukocytes proteinase

R01HL-37640-05 (SRC) MC DOWELL, ELIZABETH M UNIVERSITY OF MARYLAND 10 S PINE STREET BALTIMORE, MD 21201 Development and differentiation of airway epithelium

R01HL-37641-06 (HED) HOFFMAN, STANLEY R MEDICAL UNIV OF SOUTH CAROLINA 171 ASHLEY AVE CHARLESTON, SC 29425 Cell-cell and matrix adhesion in cardiac morphogenesis

R01HL-37653-05 (HEM) EDGELL, CORA-JEAN S UNIVERSITY OF NORTH CAROLINA CHAPEL HILL, NC 27599 Transcriptional regulation of endothelial cell functions

R01HL-37675-06A1 (CVA) BADER, DAVID M CORNELL UNIV MEDICAL COLLEGE 1300 YORK AVENUE NEW YORK, NY 10021 Regulation of cardiac myocyte differentiation

R01HL-37680-06 (RAP) SIECK, GARY C MAYO FOUNDATION 200 FIRST STREET SOUTHWEST ROCHESTER, MN 55905 Diaphragm fatigue

R01HL-37694-04A1 (CVB) LINAS, STUART L DENVER GENERAL HOSPITAL 777 BANNOCK STREET, BOX 4000 DENVER, CO 80204-4507 Angiotensin receptors in renal tubular epithelial cells

R01HL-37716-07 (NLS) BROWN, MARVIN R UCSD MEDICAL CENTER 225 DICKINSON STREET SAN DIEGO, CA 92103 Somatostatin-28 control of vasopressin and epinephrine

R01HL-37722-04A1 (ECS) WYSS, J MICHAEL UNIVERSITY OF ALABAMA UAB STATION, BOX 302 BIRMINGHAM, AL 35294 Neural mechanism of nacl sensitive hypertension

R25HL-37736-05 (MR) BOWIE, WALTER C TUSKEGEE UNIVERSITY TUSKEGEE, AL 36088 Junior research investigator enhancement program

R01HL-37770-06 (HEM) IDELL, STEVEN UNIV OF TEXAS HLTH CTR P O BOX 2003 TYLER, TX 75710 Molecular biology and physiology of human factor VII

R01HL-37784-06 (PBC) PERLMUTTER, DAVID H WASHINGTON UNIVERSITY 660 SOUTH EUCLID AVE/BOX 8116 ST LOUIS, MO 63110 Local expression of alpha-1-antitrypsin in emphysema

R01HL-37833-05 (SRC) SEGREST, JERE P U OF ALABAMA AT BIRMINGHAM 1808 7TH AVENUE SOUTH BIRMINGHAM, AL 35294 Postprandial changes in plasma lipoprotein subspecies

U01HL-37849-06 (SRC) APPLEGATE, WILLIAM B UNIV OF TENNESSEE, MEMPHIS 800 MADISON AVENUE MEMPHIS, TN 38163 Clinical centers for trials of hypertension prevention

U01HL-37852-06 (SRC) HENNEKENS, CHARLES H BRIGHAM & WOMEN'S HOSPITAL 55 POND AVE BROOKLINE, MA 02146 Coordinationg center-Trials of hypertension prevention

U01HL-37853-06 (SRC) KULLER, LEWIS H UNIVERSITY OF PITTSBURGH 130 DESOTO STREET PITTSBURGH, PA 15261 Clinical center for trials of hypertension prevention

U01HL-37854-06 (SRC) KIRCHNER, KENT A UNIV OF MISSISSIPPI MED CTR 2500 NORTH STATE STREET JACKSON, MS 39216 Trials of hypertension prevention

R44HL-37879-03 (SSS) WHALEN, ROBERT L WHALEN BIOMEDICAL, INC 5 HOWLAND STREET CAMBRIDGE, MA 02138 A simple, reliable, electronic pneumatic pump actuator

U01HL-37884-06 (SRC) LASSER, NORMAN L MARTLAND BUILDING, GB20 65 BERGEN STREET NEWARK, NEW JERSEY 07107 Prevention of hypertension

U01HL-37899-06 (SRC) HOLLIS, JACK F KAISER FOUNDATION HOSPITALS 4610 S E BELMONT STREET PORTLAND, OR 97215 Clinical center for trials of hypertension prevention

U01HL-37904-06 (SRC) BOLT, ROBERT J UNIV OF CALIFORNIA SCHOOL OF M DAVIS, CA 95616 Clinical centers for trials of hypertension prevention

U01HL-37906-06 (SRC) COHEN, JEROME D ST LOUIS UNIVERSITY 3525 CAROLINE AVENUE ST LOUIS, MO 63104 Clinical centers for trials of hypertension prevention

U01HL-37907-06 (SRC) OBERMAN, ALBERT UNIV OF ALABAMA AT BIRMINGHAM UNIVERSITY STATION 609 MEB BIRMINGHAM, AL 35294 Clinical center for trials of hypertension prevention

U01HL-37924-06 (SRC) WHELTON, PAUL K THE JOHNS HOPKINS UNIVERSITY 615 NORTH WOLFE STREET BALTIMORE, MD 21205 Clinical centers for trials of hypertension prevention

R01HL-37940-05 (SRC) ILLINGWORTH, D ROGER OREGON HEALTH SCIENCES UNIV. 3181 SW SAM JACKSON PARK ROAD PORTLAND, OR 97201 Dietary lipids--Effects on lipid-lipoprotein metabolism

R37HL-37941-06 (RAP) FELDMAN, JACK L UNIVERSITY OF CALIFORNIA 405 HILGARD AVE LOS ANGELES, CA 90024 Respiratory pattern generation

R55HL-37942-06 (PHRA) LINDEN, JOEL M UNIV OF VIRGINIA HLTH SCIS CTR BOX 158 CHARLOTTESVILLE, VA 22908 Purification and characterization of adenosine receptors

R01HL-37945-19 (HEM) MC MILLAN, ROBERT RES INST OF SCRIPPS CLINIC 10666 NORTH TORREY PINES ROAD LA JOLLA, CA 92037 Pathogenesis of the immune thrombocytopenias

U01HL-37947-05 (SRC) VAN HORN, LINDA V NORTHWESTERN UNIV MED SCH 303 EAST CHICAGO AVENUE CHICAGO, IL 60611 Dietary intervention in children with elevated IDL-C

U01HL-37948-05 (SRC) BARTON, BRUCE MD MEDICAL RESEARCH INSTITUTE 600 WYNDHURST AVENUE BALTIMORE, MD 21210 Diet intervention in children with high LDL--COord ctr

U01HL-37954-05 (SRC) STEVENS, VICTOR KAISER FOUNDATION HOSPITALS 4610 S.E. BELMONT STREET PORTLAND, OREG 97215 Clinical center--diet intervention in high LDL children

R01HL-37956-07 (ECS) MORELAND, ROBERT S GRADUATE HOSPITAL 415 SOUTH 19TH STREET PHILADELPHIA, PA 19146 Phosphorylation, calcium and smooth muscle contraction

U01HL-37962-05 (SRC) LAUER, RONALD M UNIV OF IOWA HOSPITALS & CLINI IOWA CITY, IA 52242 Dietary management of elevated LDL-C in Iowa children

U01HL-37966-05 (SRC) LASSER, NORMAN L NEW JERSEY MEDICAL SCHOOL 65 BERGEN STREET NEWARK, NJ 07107 Diet intervention in children with high LDL

U01HL-37975-05 (SRC) KWITEROVICH, PETER O, JR JOHNS HOPKINS HOSPITAL 600 NORTH WOLFE STREET BALTIMORE, MD 21205 Dietary intervention in children with high LDL levels

R01HL-37981-02 (CVB) CAMPBELL, WILLIAM B UNIV OF TEXAS SW MEDICAL CENTE 5323 HARRY HINES BOULEVARD DALLAS, TX 75235-9041 Eicosanoids, vascular tone and blood pressure

R01HL-37983-05 (SRC) DACEY, RALPH G, JR WASHINGTON UNIVERSITY 660 SOUTH EUCLID AVENUE ST LOUIS, MO 63110 Age and hypertension changes in cerebral arterioles

R01HL-38034-05 (CVA) DOWNING, S EVANS YALE UNIVERSITY SCH OF MED 310 CEDAR ST NEW HAVEN, CT 06510 Ischemia and hypoxia in the neonatal heart

R01HL-38041-05 (CVA) TEN EICK, ROBERT E NORTHWESTERN UNIV MED SCHOOL 303 EAST CHICAGO AVE CHICAGO, IL 60611 Modulation of AV conduction--Basic mechanisms

R01HL-38048-05 (BNP) GROUTAS, WILLIAM C WICHITA STATE UNIVERSITY WICHITA, KANS 67208 Inhibitors of proteolytic enzymes

R01HL-38049-04A2 (NTN) SPADY, DAVID K UNIV OF TEXAS SW MED CENTER 5323 HARRY HINES BLVD DALLAS, TX 75235-8887 Effect of fish oil on lipoprotein metabolism

P01HL-38070-05 (HLBA) VATNER, STEPHEN F NEW ENGLAND REG PRIMATE RES CT 1 PINE HILL DRIVE, BOX 9102 SOUTHBOROUGH, MA 01772 Myocardial hypertrophy and heart failure

P01HL-38070-05 0001 (HLBA) VATNER, STEPHEN F Myocardial hypertrophy and heart failure Myocardial function and perfusion in LV hypertrophy and failure

P01HL-38070-05 0002 (HLBA) HOMCY, CHARLES J Myocardial hypertrophy and heart failure Molecular basis for altered receptor-cyclase coupling in heart failure

P01HL-38070-05 0003 (HLBA) GRAHAM, ROBERT M Myocardial hypertrophy and heart failure Atrial natriuretic factor in myocardial hypertrophy and failure

P01HL-38070-05 0004 (HLBA) MIRSKY, ISRAEL Myocardial hypertrophy and heart failure Systolic myocardial stiffness--Myocardial contractility

P01HL-38070-05 9001 (HLBA) HUNT, RONALD D Myocardial hypertrophy and heart failure Animal facilities and care

P01HL-38070-05 9002 (HLBA) VATNER, STEPHEN F Myocardial hypertrophy and heart failure Electronics - Core

P01HL-38070-05 9003 (HLBA) VATNER, DOROTHY E Myocardial hypertrophy and heart failure Biochemistry - Core

R01HL-38078-04 (SB) MAGOVERN, GEORGE J ALLEGHENY-SINGER RESEARCH INST 320 EAST NORTH AVENUE PITTSBURGH, PA 15212 Paced conditioned muscular flaps for cardiac assistance

P01HL-38079-05 (HLBA) WEGLICKI, WILLIAM B GEORGE WASHINGTON UNIV MED CTR 2300 EYE ST NW WASHINGTON, DC 20037 Molecular mechanisms of cardiovascular injury

P01HL-38079-05 0001 (HLBA) WEGLICKI, WILLIAM B Molecular mechanisms of cardiovascular injury Mechanisms of free radical myocardial injury

P01HL-38079-05 0002 (HLBA) WEGLICKI, WILLIAM B Molecular mechanisms of cardiovascular injury Dietary magnesium, cardiomyopathy and arrhythmia

P01HL-38079-05 0003 (HLBA) VARGHESE, P J Molecular mechanisms of cardiovascular injury Arrhythmias

P01HL-38079-05 0004 (HLBA) BAILEY, J M Molecular mechanisms of cardiovascular injury Prostaglandins and thromboxanes in vascular injury

P01HL-38079-05 9001 (HLBA) CASSIDY, M M Molecular mechanisms of cardiovascular injury CORE--Morphology/Immunology

R01HL-38083-04 (SRC) CLARK, NOREEN M UNIVERSITY OF MICHIGAN 1420 WASHINGTON HEIGHTS ANN ARBOR, MI 48109-2029 Enhancing self-management by elderly cardiac patients

R29HL-38095-04 (RAP) UNDEM, BRADLEY J JOHNS HOPKINS ASTHMA AND 301 BAYVIEW BLVD. BALTIMORE, MD 21224 The interactions between mast cells & nerves in airways

R29HL-38096-04 (HEM) GREEN, GLORIA A USC SCHOOL OF MEDICINE 2011 ZONAL AVE LOS ANGELES, CA 90033 The transformation of sickle erythrocytes

R29HL-38104-05 (CVB) DAVIS, MICHAEL J TEXAS A&M UNIVERSITY COLLEGE OF MEDICINE COLLEGE STATION, TEX 77843 Microvascular control of capillary hydrostatic pressure

R29HL-38105-04 (CVA) DAE, MICHAEL W UNIVERSITY OF CALIFORNIA 505 PARNASSUS AVE SAN FRANCISCO, CA 94143-0420 Noninvasive assessment of cardiac adrenergic innervation

R29HL-38107-04 (RAP) HUBMAYR, ROLF D MAYO FOUNDATION 200 FIRST STREET SOUTHWEST ROCHESTER, MN 55905 Respiratory pump failure--applied physiology

U01HL-38110-06 (SRC) ROBSON, ALAN CHILDREN'S HOSPITAL 200 HENRY CLAY AVE NEW ORLEANS, LA 70118 Diet intervention in children with high LDL--Clinics

R29HL-38113-05 (CBY) TRYBUS, KATHLEEN M BRANDEIS UNIVERSITY PO

BOX 9110 WALTHAM, MA 02254 Vascular smooth muscle myosin--Conformation and activity

R01HL-38118-04A2 (SB) LEVY, ROBERT J UNIVERSITY OF MICHIGAN R-5080 KRESGE II ANN ARBOR, MI 48109-0576 Cardiovascular calcification -- Pathophysiology

R01HL-38126-05 (ECS) WESTFALL, DAVID P UNIV OF NEVADA SCH OF MED HOWARD MEDICAL SCIENCES BLDG RENO, NV 89557 Role of ATP in vascular neuroeffector processes

R01HL-38132-05 (CVA) ANVERSA, PIERO NEW YORK MEDICAL COLLEGE VALHALLA, N Y 10595 Myocardial response to infarction

R29HL-38135-04 (ECS) PEULER, JACOB D WAYNE STATE UNIVERSITY DETROIT, MI 48202 Autonomic neural effects of dietary calcium

R29HL-38137-05 (CVA) PARDINI, BENET J VETERANS ADMIN MED CTR 10W20 IOWA CITY, IA 52240 Vagal innervation of the heart

R29HL-38138-05 (HEM) MICHELSON, ALAN D UNIV OF MASSACHUSETTS MED SCH 55 LAKE AVENUE NORTH WORCESTER, MA 01655 Human blood platelet glycoprotein Ib

R01HL-38149-05 (EDC) PALTA, MARI 420 NORTH CHARTER STREET MADISON, WISCONSIN 53706 Risk factors in bronchopulmonary dysplasia

P01HL-38156-05 (HLBA) AGNEW, WILLIAM YALE UNIVERSITY SCH OF MEDICIN P O BOX 3333 NEW HAVEN, CT 06510 Molecular biophysics and biochemistry of ion channels

P01HL-38156-05 0001 (HLBA) TSIEN, RICHARD W Molecular biophysics and biochemistry of ion channels Calcium channels in sympathetic neurons and smooth muscle cells

P01HL-38156-05 0002 (HLBA) SELINFREUND, RICHARD H Molecular biophysics and biochemistry of ion channels Prolonged excitability changes in smooth muscle and neurons

P01HL-38156-05 0003 (HLBA) MOCZYDLOWSKI, EDWARD Molecular biophysics and biochemistry of ion channels Molecular pharmacology of potassium channel toxins

P01HL-38156-05 0004 (HLBA) CLAUDIO, T Molecular biophysics and biochemistry of ion channels Functional correlates of mutations in the nicotinic AChR

P01HL-38156-05 0005 (HLBA) AGNEW, WILLIAM S Molecular biophysics and biochemistry of ion channels Molecular biology and biophysics of voltage-sensitive sodium channel

P01HL-38156-05 9001 (HLBA) KACZMAREK, L K Molecular biophysics and biochemistry of ion channels CORE--Digital fluorescence imaging

P01HL-38156-05 9002 (HLBA) AGNEW, WILLIAM S Molecular biophysics and biochemistry of ion channels CORE--Biochemistry and molecular biology

P01HL-38156-05 9003 (HLBA) CLAUDIO, T Molecular biophysics and biochemistry of ion channels CORE--Tissue culture

R01HL-38165-05 (HEM) ANTONARAKIS, STYLIANOS E JOHNS HOPKINS HOSPITAL 600 N WOLFE ST/CMSC 1003 BALTIMORE, MD 21205 Molecular genetics of hemophilia A

R01HL-38170-05 (REN) LUCKY, ANNE W UNIV OF CINCINNATI 231 BETHESDA AVENUE CINCINNATI, OHIO 45267 Sex steroids, obesity and lipids in adolescent females

R29HL-38171-05 (HEM) JENNINGS, LISA K UNIVERSITY OF TENNESSEE 956 COURT AVE MEMPHIS, TN 38163 Glycoproteins IIb and IIIa in platelets and neutrophils

R29HL-38172-04 (HED) WATANABE, MICHIKO CASE WESTERN RES. UNIVERSITY 2109 ADELBERT ROAD CLEVELAND, OH 44106-4901 Cell adhesion and cardiogenesis

R29HL-38176-05 (CVA) LEVINE, ROBERT A MASSACHUSETTS GENERAL HOSPITAL FRUIT STREET BOSTON, MASS 02114 The mechanism of ventricular outflow obstruction in IHSS

R01HL-38180-05 (GMA) DAVIDSON, NICHOLAS O UNIVERSITY OF CHICAGO 5841 S MARYLAND AVE, BOX 400 CHICAGO, IL 60637 Enterohepatic lipid flux and apoprotein biosynthesis

R01HL-38185-04 (CVA) CARABELLO, BLASE A MEDICAL UNIVERSITY OF S C 171 ASHLEY AVE CHARLESTON, S C 29425-2111 Contractility in experimental volume overload

R01HL-38189-04 (HLBA) GROSSMAN, WILLIAM BETH ISRAEL HOSPITAL 330 BROOKLINE AVENUE BOSTON, MA 02215 Diastolic relaxation in ischemia, hypertrophy and failure

P01HL-38189-04 0001 (HLBA) APSTEIN, CARL Diastolic relaxation in ischemia, hypertrophy and failure Demand and supply ischemia in isolated perfused hearts

P01HL-38189-04 0002 (HLBA) LORELL, BEVERLY Diastolic relaxation in ischemia, hypertrophy and failure Myocardial relaxation in the hypertrophied heart

P01HL-38189-04 0003 (HLBA) INGWALL, JOANNE S Diastolic relaxation in ischemia, hypertrophy and failure Diastolic dysfunction in hypertrophied hypoxic myocardium--NMR studies

P01HL-38189-04 9001 (HLBA) INGWALL, JOANNE S Diastolic relaxation in ischemia, hypertrophy and failure CORE--Metabolism

P01HL-38189-04 9002 (HLBA) SHOEN, FREDERICK Diastolic relaxation in ischemia, hypertrophy and failure CORE--Morphology

R01HL-38190-05 (BBCB) POWELL, GARY L CLEMSON UNIVERSITY CLEMSON, SC 29634-1903 Function of cardiolipin phase polymorphism

R01HL-38193-03 (HUD) SINGER, LYNN T RAINBOW BABIES & CHLDRNS HOSP 2101 ADELBERT ROAD, RM 373 CLEVELAND, OH 44106 Developmental sequelae of severe chronic lung disorders

R01HL-38194-04 (CLTR) FURBERG, CURT D WAKE FOREST UNIVERSITY 300 SOUTH HAWTHORNE ROAD WINSTON SALEM, NC 27103 Trial of lovastatin and warfarin in atherosclerosis

R01HL-38199-04 (HEM) FAY, PHILIP J UNIVERSITY OF ROCHESTER 601 ELMWOOD AVENUE ROCHESTER, N Y 14642 Structure and regulation of human factor VIII

R29HL-38206-06 (ECS) GRIENDLING, KATHY K EMORY UNIVERSITY PO BOX LL ATLANTA, GA 30322 Diacylglycerol signaling in vascular smooth muscle

R01HL-38208-05 (SSS) BUONASSISI, VINCENZO W ALTON JONES CELL SCIENCE CEN OLD BARN ROAD LAKE PLACID, N Y 12946 Properties and interaction of proteoglycans

R29HL-38210-05 (CVA) GUARNIERI, THOMAS JOHNS HOPKINS HOSPITAL 530 CARNEGIE/600 N WOLFE ST BALTIMORE, MD 21205 Intracellular sodium/calcium during reperfusion states

R01HL-38212-05 (BNP) BURTON, JAMES A UNIVERSITY HOSPITAL 75 EAST NEWTON STREET BOSTON, MASS 02118 Specific kallikrein inhibitors for cardiovascular study

R37HL-38216-05 (HEM) FURIE, BRUCE NEW ENGLAND MEDICAL CTR HOSPS 750 WASHINGTON STREET, BOX 832 BOSTON, MA 02111 Biosynthesis of blood clotting proteins

R29HL-38223-04 (NTN) HAMM, MICHAEL W COOK COLLEGE, RUTGERS UNIV P O BOX 23 NEW BRUNSWICK, N J 08903 Altered dietary lipid and beta--adrenergic system in heart

R01HL-38228-03 (CBY) HAYNES, DUNCAN H UNIVERSITY OF MIAMI PO BOX 016189 MIAMI, FL 33101 Calcium movements in platlet activation

R01HL-38231-04 (CVB) OSOL, GEORGE UNIVERSITY OF VERMONT COLLEGE OF MEDICINE BURLINGTON, VT 05405 Cerebral artery reactivity in hypertension

R29HL-38232-05 (HEM) DEGEN, SANDRA J CHILDRENS HOSP RES FDN ELLAN & BETHESDA AVE CINNCINNATI, OH 45229-2899 Human blood coagulation and vitamin K

R01HL-38243-05 (RAP) OLSON, LYNNE E OHIO STATE UNIVERSITY 1900 COFFEY RD, 309 SISSON HAL COLUMBUS, OH 43210-1092 Mediastinal effects on pulmonary function

R01HL-38245-03 (HEM) GREENBERG, CHARLES S DUKE UNIVERSITY MEDICAL CENTER BOX 3934 DURHAM, N C 27710 Role of factor XIII binding to the hemostatic plug

R29HL-38248-05 (HEM) LEVEN, ROBERT M RUSH-PRESBY-ST LUKE'S MED CTR 1653 W CONGRESS PKWY CHICAGO, IL 60612 Cell biology of megakaryocytopoiesis

R01HL-38260-03 (EDC) SHEA, STEVEN J COLUMBIA UNIVERSITY HEALTH SCIS - 630 W 168TH ST NEW YORK, NY 10032 Epidemiology of hypertensive emergency

R29HL-38272-04 (HEM) MILES, LINDSEY A SCRIPPS CLINIC AND RESEARCH FD 10666 NORTH TORREY PINES ROAD LA JOLLA, CA 92037 Regulation of fibrinolysis by cell surfaces

R01HL-38285-05 (HED) KOEHLER, RAYMOND C THE JOHNS HOPKINS HOSPITAL 1408 BLALOCK BALTIMORE, MD 21205 Fetal circulatory response to cerebral compression

R01HL-38288-05 (RAP) FLOROS, JOANNA PENNSYLVANIA STATE UNIVERSITY P.O. BOX 850 HERSHEY, PA 17033 Control of surfactant protein in lung development

R01HL-38291-04 (SAT) MURRAY, PAUL A JOHNS HOPKINS HOSPITAL 600 NORTH WOLFE STREET BALTIMORE, MD 21205 Anesthesia modulates neurohumoral pulmonary vasoactivity

R01HL-38292-05 (HEM) PLOW, EDWARD F SCRIPPS CLINIC & RES FNDN 10666 NORTH TORREY PINES ROAD LA JOLLA, CALIF 92037 Platelet gpiib/iiia: a member of the cytoadhesin family

R29HL-38294-05 (CVB) FORMAN, MERVYN B VANDERBILT UNIVERSITY 21ST & GARLAND AVE NASHVILLE, TN 37232 Role of perfluorochemical on myocardial ischemia (dogs)

R29HL-38296-05 (HED) VEILLE, JEAN-CLAUDE L BOWMAN GRAY SCHOOL OF MEDICINE 300 S HAWTHORNE RD WINSTON-SALEM, NC 27103 Cardiovascular changes in growth retarded fetuses

R29HL-38303-04 (HED) MAUTONE, ALAN J NEW JERSEY MEDICAL SCHOOL 185 SOUTH ORANGE AVENUE NEWARK, N J 07103-2714 Biophysics of surfactant during lung development

R01HL-38306-03 (SB) LEONARD, EDWARD F COLUMBIA UNIVERSITY 351 ENGINEERING TERRACE NEW YORK, NY 10027 UV flow photoreactors for blood and blood components

R29HL-38310-04 (RAP) GOODMAN, BARBARA E UNIVERSITY OF SOUTH DAKOTA VERMILLION, SD 57069 Specialized transport properties of alveolar epithelium

R29HL-38312-03 (HEM) FEINMARK, STEVEN J COLUMBIA UNIVERSITY 630 WEST 168TH STREET NEW YORK, NY 10032 Leukotrienes and leukocyte/vascular cell interactions

R29HL-38316-04 (CVB) BRUNNER, MARTHA J MSTF BLDG. RM. 400 BALTIMORE, MARYLAND 21201 Carotid baroreflex control in normo- and hypertension

R29HL-38324-05 (PB) ZWEIER, JAY L THE JOHNS HOPKINS HOSPITAL 600 NORTH WOLFE STREET BALTIMORE, MARYLAND 21205 Measurement of free radical generation in the heart

R29HL-38329-05 (MET) GARBER, DAVID W UNIV OF ALABAMA AT BIRMINGHAM 1808 7TH AVE. BIRMINGHAM, AL 35294 VLDL metabolism in experimental diabetes

R29HL-38333-04 (RNM) DUNCAN, JAMES S YALE UNIV SCHOOL OF MEDICINE 333 CEDAR STREET NEW HAVEN, CT 06510 Multimodality cardiac image understanding

R29HL-38337-06 (HEM) KRISHNASWAMY, SRIRAM EMORY UNIVERSITY ATLANTA, GA 30322 The prothrombinase complex--Stopped-flow kinetics

R01HL-38339-05 (SRC) SEILHEIMER, DAN K 2201 W. HOLCOMBE, # 310 HOUSTON, TEXAS 77030 Study of effectiveness of health education for cystic fibrosis

R29HL-38345-05 (CVA) KAUL, SANJIV UNIVERSITY OF VIRGINIA DIV OF CARDIOLOGY, BOX 158 CHARLOTTESVILLE, VA 22908 Echocardiographic assessment of myocardial perfusion and function

R29HL-38349-04 (CVB) EBERT, THOMAS J MEDICAL COLLEGE OF WISCONSIN 8701 WATERTOWN PLANK ROAD MILWAUKEE, WI 53226 Effect of atrial natriuretic factor

R29HL-38353-05 (SB) YANG, VICTOR C UNIVERSITY OF MICHIGAN ANN ARBOR, MI 48109-1065 An immobilized protamine system for removing heparin

R01HL-38354-04A1 (SSS) LINDSTROM, DANIEL P VANDERBILT UNIVERSITY HOSPITAL MEDICAL CENTER NORTH S-4311 NASHVILLE, TN 37232-2370 Computer-based respiratory support consultant

R29HL-38355-05 (PHY) PERIASAMY, MUTHU UNIV OF VERMONT/COLL OF MED BURLINGTON, VT 05405 Molecular analysis of smooth muscle contractile proteins

R29HL-38358-05 (RAP) BROWN, LOU ANN S EMORY UNIVERSITY 2040 RIDGEWOOD DR N E ATLANTA, GA 30322 Regulation of surfactant secretion by type II cells

R01HL-38361-05 (HEM) FUNG, LESLIE W LOYOLA UNIVERSITY OF CHICAGO 6525 NORTH SHERIDAN ROAD CHICAGO, IL 60626 Molecular studies of membrane rigidity in sickle cell

R29HL-38366-04 (PHRA) VENKATESH, NAGAMMAL VA WADSWORTH MEDICAL CENTER WILSHIRE/SAWTELLE BLVDS LOS ANGELES, CA 90073 Electrophysiologic effects of T3 inhibition in the heart

R29HL-38384-05 (CVA) CONNELLY, CAROLYN M BOSTON UNIV SCH OF MED 80 E. CONCORD STREET, R-215 BOSTON, MA 02118 Effect of reperfusion on post-mi aneurysm formation

PROJECT NO., ORGANIZATIONAL UNIT., INVESTIGATOR, ADDRESS, TITLE

R01HL-38386-04 (CVA) FRAME, LAWRENCE H UNIVERSITY OF PENNSYLVANIA 3400 SPRUCE ST/943 GATES BLDG PHILADELPHIA, PA 19104 Mechanisms of antiarrhythmic action in reentrant rhythms
R01HL-38401-13 (CTY) SCHWARTZ, ROBERT J BAYLOR COLLEGE OF MEDICINE ONE BAYLOR PLAZA HOUSTON, TX 77030 Differentiation of actin in myogenesis
R29HL-38405-06 (HEM) PARISE, LESLIE V UNIVERSITY OF NORTH CAROLINA CAMPUS BOX 7365 CHAPEL HILL, NC 27599-7365 Ligand binding domains on platelet glycoprotein IIb-IIIa
R29HL-38406-04 (HEM) HALENDA, STEPHEN P UNIVERSITY OF MISSOURI M-519 MEDICAL SCIENCES BLDG COLUMBIA, MO 65212 Role of c-kinase in platelet arachidonate release
R01HL-38408-02A1 (CVA) WALDO, ALBERT L UNIVERSITY HOSPITALS/CLEVELAND 2074 ABINGTON RD CLEVELAND, OH 44106 Studies of atrial flutter in a model
R01HL-38409-05 (RNM) VAN LYSEL, MICHAEL S UNIVERSITY OF WISCONSIN 600 HIGHLAND AVE, H6/339 MADISON, WI 53792 Quantitative ventriculography using dual-energy DSA
R29HL-38414-05 (BEM) ISTVAN, JOSEPH A OREGON HLTH SCIENCES UNIV 3181 SW SAM JACKSON PARK RD PORTLAND, OR 97201 Smoking cessation and weight gain
R01HL-38429-05 (EDC) LABARTHE, DARWIN R UNIVERSITY OF TEXAS HLTH SCI C 1200 HERMAN PRESSLER HOUSTON, TX 77225 Survival after MI in a biethnic Texas community
R01HL-38438-04 (PTHA) RAJ, J USHA HARBOR-UCLA MEDICAL CENTER 1000 W CARSON ST TORRANCE, CA 90509 Studies of the lung microcirculation in the newborn
R29HL-38442-06 (PTHA) HASKELL, JOYCE F UNIV OF ALABAMA AT BIRMINGHAM UAB STATION BIRMINGHAM, AL 35294 Insulin-like growth factor receptors in vascular tissue
R01HL-38449-04 (CBY) SPRAY, DAVID C ALBERT EINSTEIN COLLEGE OF MED 1410 PELHAM PARKWAY SOUTH BRONX, N Y 10461 Cardiac gap junctions--Control of expression and function
R01HL-38454-04 (CLTR) WEAVER, W DOUGLAS UNIVERSITY OF WASHINGTON 1959 NORTHEAST PACIFIC SEATTLE, WA 98195 Prehospital systemic thrombolytic trial--MITI
R01HL-38456-06 (HEM) MC DONALD, MELISENDA J UNIVERSITY OF LOWELL ONE UNIVERSITY AVENUE LOWELL, MA 01854 Subunit assembly of normal and variant hemoglobins
R01HL-38460-06 (SRC) MANN, KENNETH G UNIVERSITY OF VERMONT COLLEGE OF MEDICINE BURLINGTON, VT 05405 Components of coagulation-fibrinolytic system in TIMI II
R01HL-38479-05 (SAT) ALEXANDER, J WESLEY UNIVERSITY OF CINCINNATI 231 BETHESDA AVENUE CINCINNATI, OH 45267-0558 Augmentation of the transfusion effect
R29HL-38485-04 (EVR) SHERIDAN, JOHN F OHIO STATE UNIVERSITY 305 WEST 12TH AVE. COLUMBUS, OH 43210 CMI regulation and reinfection--Role of contalympholine
R01HL-38488-06 (CVA) BERMAN, MICHAEL R JOHNS HOPKINS UNIVERSITY 600 NORTH WOLFE STREET BALTIMORE, MD 21205 Altered force kinetics in normal and stressed hearts
U01HL-38493-05 (SRC) MOCK, MICHAEL B MAYO FOUNDATION 200 FIRST STREET SOUTHWEST ROCHESTER, MN 55905 Bypass angioplasty revascularization investigation clinical units
R01HL-38495-04A1 (RAP) GILLESPIE, MARK N UNIVERSITY OF KENTUCKY ROSE STREET LEXINGTON, KY 40536-0082 Hypoxic pulmonary hypertension and polyamines
R01HL-38499-05 (ECS) GRANGER, JOEY P UNIV OF MISSISSIPPI MED CTE 2500 NORTH STATE STREET JACKSON, MS 39216-4505 Abnormal pressure natriuresis in hypertension
R01HL-38503-10 (SOH) YU, C P SUNY AT BUFFALO 314 JARVIS HALL AMHERST, NY 14260 Aerosol deposition in the human respiratory system
U01HL-38504-05 (SRC) CHAITMAN, BERNARD R ST LOUIS UNIVERSITY HOSPITAL 3635 VISTA AVENUE AT GRAND BLV ST. LOUIS, MO 63110-0250 Bypass angioplasty revascularization investigation
U01HL-38509-05 (SRC) BOURASSA, MARTIAL G MONTREAL HEART INSTITUTE 5000 BELANGER ST EAST MONTREAL, QUEBEC H1T, CANADA Bypass angioplasty revascularization investigation
U01HL-38512-05 (SRC) ROGERS, WILLIAM J UAB MEDICAL CENTER 330 LHR BUILDING BIRMINGHAM, AL 35294 Bypass angioplasty revascularization investigation
U01HL-38514-05 (SRC) BAIM, DONALD S BETH ISRAEL HOSPITAL 330 BROOKLINE AVE, L-453 BOSTON, MA 02215 Bypass angioplasty revascularization investigation
U01HL-38515-05 (SRC) COWLEY, MICHAEL J VIRGINIA COMMONWEALTH UNIV BOX 59, MCV STATION RICHMOND, VA 23298 Bypass angioplasty revascularization investigation
U01HL-38516-05 (SRC) CALIFF, ROBERT M DUKE UNIVERSITY MED CENTER BOX 31123, ERWIN RD DURHAM, NC 27710 Bypass angioplasty revascularization investigation
U01HL-38518-05 (SRC) WHITLOW, PATRICK CLEVELAND CLINIC FOUNDATION 9500 EUCLID AVENUE CLEVELAND, OHIO 44106 Bypass angioplasty revascularization investigation
R29HL-38521-05 (HEM) KURANTSIN-MILLS, JOSEPH GEORGE WASHINGTON UNIVERSITY 2300 EYE STREET, N W RM 456 WASHINGTON, D C 20037 Microvascular flow and vaso-occlusion of sickle cells
U01HL-38524-05 (SRC) HERMAN, MICHAEL V WESTCHESTER COUNTY MED CTR DIVISION OF CARDIOLOGY VALHALLA, NY 10595 Bypass angioplasty revascularization investigation
U01HL-38525-05 (SRC) FAXON, DAVID P THE UNIVERSITY HOSPITAL 88 E. NEWTON STREET BOSTON, MA 02118 Bypass angioplasty revascularization investigation
U01HL-38529-05 (SRC) TOPOL, ERIC J UNIV HOSPITAL, DEPT. OF MED. 1500 E MEDICAL CENTER DRIVE ANN ARBOR, MI 48109-0022 Bypass angioplasty revascularization investigation
U01HL-38532-05 (SRC) WILLIAMS, DAVID O RHODE ISLAND HOSPITAL 593 EDDY STREET PROVIDENCE, RI 02903 Bypass angioplasty revascularization investigation
R29HL-38535-04 (ECS) DIZ, DEBRA I CLEVELAND CLINIC FOUNDATION 9500 EUCLID AVENUE CLEVELAND, OH 44106 Angiotensin II binding sites and function in the medulla
R01HL-38537-06 (ECS) HERMSMEYER, R KENT PROVIDENCE MEDICAL CENTER. 4805 N E GLISAN PORTLAND, OREGON 97213 Membrane electrical properties of vascular muscle
U01HL-38556-05 (SRC) WEINER, BONNIE UNIV OF MASSACHUSETTES MED SCH 55 LAKE AVENUE, NORTH WORCESTER, MA 01655 Bypass angioplasty revascularization investigation
R44HL-38564-03 (SSS) GRABOWY, RICHARD S MIRCOWAVE MEDICAL SYSTEMS, INC 9 GOLDSMITH STREET/PO BOX 188 LITTLETON, MA 01460-0188 Microwave device for blood warming & temperature control
R37HL-38578-07 (RAP) CRANDALL, EDWARD D UNIV. OF SOUTHERN CALIFORNIA 2025 ZONAL AVENUE LOS ANGELES, CA 90033 Lung epithelial transport properties and alveolar edema
R44HL-38588-03 (SSS) DECAMILLA, JOHN J SCIENTIFIC ASSOCIATES, INC 1349 SOUTH AVENUE ROCHESTER, N Y 14620 Multiarrhythmia ambulatory ECG database design
R29HL-38605-05 (SSS) FIELD, LOREN J INDIANA UNIVERSITY 1001 WEST 10TH ST INDIANAPOLIS, IN 46202-2859 Hypertension and anf expression in transgenic mice
U01HL-38610-05 (SRC) DETRE, KATHERINE M UNIVERSITY OF PITTSBURGH 130 DESOTA STREET PITTSBURGH, PA 15261 Bypass angioplasty revascularization investigation--Data center
R01HL-38621-06A1 (RAP) CRANDALL, EDWARD D USC MEDICAL CTR. 2025 ZONAL AVE LOS ANGELES, CA 90033 Alveolar pneumocyte pH -- Regulatory mechanisms/effects
R01HL-38622-06 (HEM) RITTENHOUSE, SUSAN E UNIVERSITY OF VERMONT GIVEN BUILDING BURLINGTON, VT 05405 Human platelet activation and phospholipid metabolism
R01HL-38630-06 (BPO) CONTRERAS, ROBERT J FLORIDA STATE UNIVERSITY R-54 . Behavioral aspects of salt intake and hypertension
P60HL-38632-04 (SRC) OHENE-FREMPONG, KWAKU CHILDREN'S HOSPITAL 34TH STREET AND CIVIC CENTER PHILADELPHIA, PA 19104 Comprehensive sickle cell center
P60HL-38632-04 0001 (SRC) SCHWARTZ, ELIAS Comprehensive sickle cell center Control of fetal hemoglobin synthesis
P60HL-38632-04 0002 (SRC) SURREY, SAUL Comprehensive sickle cell center Studies on Hb S using recombinant DNA engineered hemoglobins
P60HL-38632-04 0003 (SRC) REIVICH, MARTIN Comprehensive sickle cell center Central nervous system studies in sickle cell disease
P60HL-38632-04 0004 (SRC) COHEN, ALAN Comprehensive sickle cell center Prevention and treatment of excess iron accumulation in sickle cell disease
P60HL-38632-04 0005 (SRC) SCHWARTZ, WILLIAM Comprehensive sickle cell center Training of medical students and physicians regarding sickle cell disease
P60HL-38632-04 0006 (SRC) OHENE-FREMPONG, KWAKU Comprehensive sickle cell center Organized educational program for sickle cell patients and families
P60HL-38632-04 0007 (SRC) BUTLER, REGINA Comprehensive sickle cell center Nursing education in sickle cell anemia disease
P60HL-38632-04 0008 (SRC) FITHIAN, JANET Comprehensive sickle cell center Program to improve educational outcome for sickle cell disease students
P60HL-38632-04 0009 (SRC) SCHWARTZ, ELIAS Comprehensive sickle cell center National bulletin board for sickle cell disease
P60HL-38632-04 0010 (SRC) OHENE-FREMPONG, KWAKU Comprehensive sickle cell center Selective testing of newborns for sickle cell disease
P60HL-38632-04 9001 (SRC) OHENE-FREMPONG, KWAKU Comprehensive sickle cell center Hemoglobin laboratory and diagnostic facility--Core
P60HL-38632-04 9002 (SRC) OHENE-FREMPONG, KWAKU Comprehensive sickle cell center Clinical research unit core--Children's Hospital of Philadelphia
P60HL-38632-04 9003 (SRC) BALLAS, SAMIR Comprehensive sickle cell center Clinical research unit CORE--Jefferson University Hospital
P60HL-38632-04 9004 (SRC) GAY, ROY Comprehensive sickle cell center Clinical research unit at Presbyterian--University of Pennsylvania Medical Clinic
P60HL-38639-04 (SRC) MANKAD, VIPUL N UNIVERSITY OF SOUTH ALABAMA 2451 FILLINGIM STREET MOBILE, ALA 36617 Comprehensive sickle cell center
P60HL-38639-04 0003 (SRC) LONGENECKER, GESINA Comprehensive sickle cell center Red cell, platelet, and endothelial interaction--Arachidonic acid analogs in SCD
P60HL-38639-04 0004 (SRC) SINDEL, LAWRENCE Comprehensive sickle cell center Importance of decrease O2 radical formation in neutrophils in sickle cell disease
P60HL-38639-04 0005 (SRC) MANKAD, VIPUL N Comprehensive sickle cell center Magnetic resonance images of bone marrow in sickle cell disease
P60HL-38639-04 0006 (SRC) CHUA-LIM, CHRISTINA Comprehensive sickle cell center Evaluation of sickle cell children for school readiness
P60HL-38639-04 0001 (SRC) MOORE, R BLAINE Comprehensive sickle cell center Role of cysteine oxidation in formation of irreversible sickle cells
P60HL-38639-04 0002 (SRC) MOORE, R BLAINE Comprehensive sickle cell center Calpromotin--Role in dehydration of sickle cell erythrocytes
P60HL-38639-04 0007 (SRC) MANKAD, VIPUL N Comprehensive sickle cell center Education of health professions in sickle cell disease
P60HL-38639-04 0008 (SRC) YANG, YIH-MING Comprehensive sickle cell center Neonatal screening and conseling program for sickle cell anemia
P60HL-38639-04 0009 (SRC) PETERSON, ROSE Comprehensive sickle cell center Sickle cell disease--Education, screening, and counseling
P60HL-38639-04 0010 (SRC) LIU, PAUL Comprehensive sickle cell center Laboratory core for sickle cell disease
U01HL-38642-05 (SRC) ALDERMAN, EDWIN L STANFORD UNIV SCHOOL OF MED 300 PASTEUR DRIVE STANFORD, CA 94305-5246 Bypass angioplasty revascularization investigation--Radiographic lab
R01HL-38644-06 (HEM) KURACHI, KOTOKU UNIVERSITY OF MICHIGAN ANN ARBOR, MI 48109-0618 Molecular genetics of factor ix and other blood proteins
R29HL-38650-05 (PB) WILLIAMS, DAVID E OREGON STATE UNIVERSITY WIEGAND HALL CORVALLIS, OR 97331-6602 Novel fad-containing monooxygenase in lung
P60HL-38655-04 (SRC) NAGEL, RONALD L MONTEFIORE MEDICAL CENTER 111 E 210TH STREET BRONX, NY 10467 Comprehensive sickle cell center
P60HL-38655-04 0001 (SRC) SHERWOOD, JUDITH Comprehensive sickle

PROJECT NO., ORGANIZATIONAL UNIT., INVESTIGATOR, ADDRESS, TITLE

cell center Erythropoietin levels in sickle cell anemia and related hemoglobinopathies
P60HL-38655-04 0002 (SRC) ROTH, EUGENE F Comprehensive sickle cell center Sickle cell disease and oxidative stress
P60HL-38655-04 0003 (SRC) ALTER, BLANCHE P Comprehensive sickle cell center Humoral regulation of erythropoiesis and hemoglobin synthesis
P60HL-38655-04 0004 (SRC) SCHWARTZ, ROBERT Comprehensive sickle cell center Erythrocyte membrane skeletal protein dysfunction and sickle cell disease
P60HL-38655-04 0005 (SRC) ACHARYA, SEETHARAMA A Comprehensive sickle cell center Protein engineering of quinary structure of hemoglobin
P60HL-38655-04 0006 (SRC) SKOULTCHI, ARTHUR Comprehensive sickle cell center Developmental regulation of human beta-like globin genes
P60HL-38655-04 0007 (SRC) BENJAMIN, LENNETTE J Comprehensive sickle cell center Membrane active antisickling agents
P60HL-38655-04 0008 (SRC) BENJAMIN, LENNETTE J Comprehensive sickle cell center Acute and chronic pain
P60HL-38655-04 0009 (SRC) FABRY, MARY E Comprehensive sickle cell center Magnetic resonance imging of sickle cell disease
P60HL-38655-04 0010 (SRC) CHAPAR, GEORGE N Comprehensive sickle cell center Sickle cell disease--Neuropsychological studies
P60HL-38655-04 0011 (SRC) BILLETT, HENNY H Comprehensive sickle cell center Novel calmodulin-regulated transglutaminase in normal, sickled red blood cells
P60HL-38655-04 0012 (SRC) FABRY, MARY E Comprehensive sickle cell center Haplotype-defined SS disease and SC-s/beta-o thalassemia combinations
P60HL-38655-04 0013 (SRC) WILKINSON, WILLIAM H Comprehensive sickle cell center Education research--Sensitization of ER, outpatient and inpatient personnel
P60HL-38655-04 9001 (SRC) NAGEL, RONALD L Comprehensive sickle cell center CORE--laboratory
P60HL-38655-04 9002 (SRC) GILBERT, HARRIET S Comprehensive sickle cell center Core--Data management
P60HL-38655-04 9003 (SRC) BENJAMIN, LENNETTE J Comprehensive sickle cell center Core--Research clinical outpatient facilities
R01HL-38658-04 (RAP) KIM, KWANG-JIN LAC-USC MEDICAL CENTER 2025 ZONAL AVENUE LOS ANGELES, CA 90033 Macromolecular transport across lung alveolar epithelium
R01HL-38668-04 (SAT) SILL, JOHN C MAYO FOUNDATION 200 FIRST ST SW ROCHESTER, MN 55905 Inhalational anesthetics and coronary vasomotion
R29HL-38675-05 (RAP) CASTELLINI, MICHAEL A UNIVERSITY OF ALASKA FAIRBANKS, AK 99775-1080 Sleep apnea in seals--Metabolic implications
R01HL-38680-03 (GMA) QUINN, JOHN A UNIVERSITY OF PENNSYLVANIA 220 S 33RD STREET PHILADELPHIA, PA 19104 Physiologic mechanisms of permeation through human skin
R29HL-38683-04 (PTHA) BOWDEN, RALEIGH A FRED HUTCHINSON CANCER RES CTR 1124 COLUMBIA ST SEATTLE, WA 98104 Cytotoxicity in the lung after marrow transplant /human
R01HL-38690-05 (CVB) ZUCKER, IRVING H UNIV OF NEBRASKA MED CTR 600 SOUTH 42ND ST. OMAHA, NE 68198-4575 Cardiac and arterial baroreflexes in heart failure
R29HL-38694-02 (CTY) STRAUCH, ARTHUR R OHIO STATE UNIVERSITY 333 WEST 10TH AVENUE COLUMBUS, OH 43210-1239 Molecular anatomy of actin assemblies in BC3H1 cells
R01HL-38698-02 (RNM) HAACKE, E M CASE WESTERN RESERVE UNIV 2078 ABINGTON ROAD CLEVELAND, OH 44106 MRI of the central cardiovascular system
R01HL-38701-05 (RAP) VAN LUNTEREN, ERIK UNIVERSITY HOSPITAL OF CLEVELA 2074 ABINGTON RD CLEVELAND, OH 44106-4389 Neural control respiratory muscles during expiration
R01HL-38702-04 (EDC) MOSS, ARTHUR J UNIVERSITY OF ROCHESTER MEDICAL CENTER/BOX 653 ROCHESTER, NY 14642 Multicenter study of silent myocardial ischemia
R37HL-38712-05 (BEM) MATTHEWS, KAREN A WESTERN PSYCHIATRIC INST & CLI 3811 O'HARA STREET PITTSBURGH, PA 15213 CHD risk, behavioral stress and reproductive hormones
R01HL-38731-05 (CVB) COHEN, RICHARD A UNIVERSITY HOSPITAL 88 EAST NEWTON STREET BOSTON, MA 02118 Diabetic vascular endothelium and adrenergic nerves
P01HL-38736-05 (HLBA) BASSINGTHWAIGHTE, JAMES B UNIVERSITY OF WASHINGTON CTR FOR BIOENGINEERING, WD-12 SEATTLE, WA 98195 Imaging regional cardiopulmonary metabolism and flows
P01HL-38736-05 0001 (HLBA) BASSINGTHWAIGHTE, JAMES B Imaging regional cardiopulmonary metabolism and flows Myocardial flow heterogeneity
P01HL-38736-05 0002 (HLBA) ROBERTSON, H THOMAS Imaging regional cardiopulmonary metabolism and flows Pulmonary blood and gas flow
P01HL-38736-05 0003 (HLBA) CALDWELL, JAMES H Imaging regional cardiopulmonary metabolism and flows Spect myocardial viability following reperfusion
P01HL-38736-05 9001 (HLBA) KROHN, KENNETH Imaging regional cardiopulmonary metabolism and flows Nuclear imaging--Core
P01HL-38736-05 9002 (HLBA) KING, RICHARD B Imaging regional cardiopulmonary metabolism and flows Mathematical analysis--Core
P01HL-38736-05 9003 (HLBA) MODELL, HAROLD Imaging regional cardiopulmonary metabolism and flows Animal physiology--Core
P60HL-38737-04 (SRC) TURNER, ERNEST A MEHARRY MEDICAL COLLEGE 1005 D B TODD JR BLVD NASHVILLE, TN 37208 Comprehensive sickle cell center
P60HL-38737-04 0001 (SRC) OHI, SEIGO Comprehensive sickle cell center Recombinant human parvoviruses for gene therapy of hemoglobinopathies
P60HL-38737-04 0002 (SRC) WILSON, DONELLA Comprehensive sickle cell center Isolation and characterization of glycophorin
P60HL-38737-04 0003 (SRC) PROGRAIS, LAWRENCE Comprehensive sickle cell center Complement activation in sickle cell anemia
P60HL-38737-04 0004 (SRC) SIMS, GRETHA Comprehensive sickle cell center Hearing loss and sickle cell anemia

PROJECT NO., ORGANIZATIONAL UNIT., INVESTIGATOR, ADDRESS, TITLE

P60HL-38737-04 0005 (SRC) MCCLELLAN, LINDA Comprehensive sickle cell center Hemolobinopathies in Southeast Asians
P60HL-38737-04 9001 (SRC) TURNER, ERNEST A Comprehensive sickle cell center Laboratory core
R29HL-38741-04 (CVB) BERNSTEIN, DANIEL STANFORD UNIVERSITY HSE-1403 STANFORD, CALIF 94305 Myocardial beta-receptor regulation in chronic hypoxemia /lambs
R01HL-38744-05 (RAP) TSAO, FRANCIS H UNIVERSITY OF WISCONSIN 202 SOUTH PARK ST, 7E MADISON, WI 53715 Characterization of lung phospholipid transfer proteins
R01HL-38750-04 (HED) FUNKHOUSER, JANE D UNIVERSITY OF SOUTH ALABAMA 307 UNIVERSITY BOULEVARD MOBILE, AL 36688 Surfactant recycling by type II epithelial cells
R29HL-38760-06 (EDC) AUSTIN, MELISSA A UNIVERSITY OF WASHINGTON DEPT OF EPIDEMIOLOGY SEATTLE, WA 98195 Genetics of LDL subclasses in hypercholesterolemia
R01HL-38763-04 (EDC) WILLIAMS, PAUL T LAWRENCE BERKELEY LABORATORY 1 CYCLOTRON ROAD BERKELEY, CA 94720 Lipoprotein subfractions & CHD during 25 yr follow-up
R29HL-38764-05 (HED) RICE, WARD R UC COLLEGE OF MEDICINE 231 BETHESDA AVE CINCINNATI, OH 45267-0541 Purinoceptor control of surfactant secretion
R29HL-38767-05 (ECS) EIKENBURG, DOUGLAS C UNIVERSITY OF HOUSTON HOUSTON, TX 77204-5515 Plasma catecholamines and prejunctional adrenoceptors
R29HL-38774-05 (CVB) DESCHEPPER, CHRISTIAN F UNIVERSITY OF CALIFORNIA 3RD AND PARNASSUS SAN FRANCISCO, CA 94143-0444 Angiotensin II in endocrine organs
R01HL-38776-05 (SSS) SMITH, JACK W, JR OHIO STATE UNIVERSITY 376 W 10TH AVENUE COLUMBUS, OH 43210 Problem-solving and man-machine systems for decision support and education
R29HL-38779-06 (HEM) BOCK, PAUL E VANDERBILT UNIVERSITY C-3321 MEDICAL CENTER NORTH NASHVILLE, TN 37232-2561 Factor Va interactions regulating prothrombin activation
R01HL-38780-03 (EDC) SELWYN, ANDREW P BRIGHAM & WOMEN'S HOSPITAL 75 FRANCIS STREET BOSTON, MA 02115 Prognostic importance of myocardial ischemia out of hosp
R01HL-38783-05 (ECS) FABER, JAMES E UNIVERSITY OF NORTH CAROLINA CB #7545 CHAPEL HILL, NC 27599-7545 Neural and humoral regulation of the microcirculation
R01HL-38786-06 (ECS) SVED, ALAN F UNIVERSITY OF PITTSBURGH 446 CRAWFORD HALL PITTSBURGH, PA 15260 Brainstem GABA neurons in experimental hypertension
R01HL-38794-05 (HEM) SPEICHER, DAVID W THE WISTAR INSTITUTE 36TH AND SPRUCE STREET PHILADELPHIA, PA 19104 Membrane proteins of normal and abnormal human red cells
R01HL-38819-05 (RAP) BALDWIN, KENNETH M UNIVERSITY OF CALIFORNIA CHENEY HALL/RM D340 MED SCI I IRVINE, CA 92717 Exercise induced regulation of cardiac myosin expression
R29HL-38820-05 (HEM) WARE, JOE A HARVARD MEDICAL SCHOOL 330 BROOKLINE AVENUE BOSTON, MA 02215 Abnormalities of platelet calcium in disease
R01HL-38833-04 (PHRA) ODYA, CHARLES E INDIANA UNIVERSITY SCH OF MED MYERS HALL ROOM 306 BLOOMINGTON, IN 47405 Bradykinin receptor studies--immunological approches
R29HL-38834-05 (PHY) TOBACMAN, LARRY S UNIVERSITY OF IOWA HOSPITALS IOWA CITY, IA 52242 Cardiac contractile protein cooperativity
R01HL-38844-05 (SRC) BERENSON, GERALD S LOUISIANA STATE UNIV MED CTR 1542 TULANE AVENUE NEW ORLEANS, LA 70112 National research and demonstration center--Arteriosclerosis
R01HL-38844-05 0001 (SRC) BERENSON, GERALD S National research and demonstration center--Arteriosclerosis Early natural history of atherosclerosis and hypertension
R01HL-38844-05 0014 (SRC) RADHAKRISHNAMURTHY, B National research and demonstration center--Arteriosclerosis Biochemistry of atherosclerotic lesions
R01HL-38844-05 0015 (SRC) CROFT, JANET B National research and demonstration center--Arteriosclerosis Post high school study
R01HL-38844-05 0016 (SRC) ELSTON, ROBERT C National research and demonstration center--Arteriosclerosis Genetics study
R01HL-38844-05 0017 (SRC) HUNTER, SAUNDRA M National research and demonstration center--Arteriosclerosis Biobehavioral study of cardiovascular risk factors in children
R01HL-38844-05 0018 (SRC) NEWMAN, WILLIAM P National research and demonstration center--Arteriosclerosis Collaborative pediatric pathology risk factor program
R01HL-38844-05 0019 (SRC) BERENSON, GERALD S National research and demonstration center--Arteriosclerosis Cardiovascular health promotion and risk reduction in school-aged children
R01HL-38844-05 9001 (SRC) WEBBER, LARRY S National research and demonstration center--Arteriosclerosis Core--Planning and analysis service
R01HL-38844-05 9002 (SRC) SRINIVASAN, SATHANUR R National research and demonstration center--Arteriosclerosis Core--Lipid and clinical laboratory
R01HL-38844-05 9003 (SRC) FRANK, GAIL C National research and demonstration center--Arteriosclerosis Core--Nutrition
R29HL-38853-05 (PHRA) SHREEVE, STEPHEN M UNIVERSITY OF VERMONT B-318 GIVEN BUILDING BURLINGTON, VT 05405 Classification of vascular smooth muscle alpha-receptors
R01HL-38854-05 (PTHA) OWENS, GARY K UNIV OF VIRGINIA BOX 449, HLTH SCIS CTR CHARLOTTESVILLE, VA 22908 Growth and differentiation of vascular smooth muscle
R29HL-38855-05 (CTY) CASELLA, JAMES F THE JOHNS HOPKINS HOSPITAL 600 NORTH WOLFE STREET BALTIMORE, MD 21205 Actin-capping protein interactions in muscle
R01HL-38859-05 (HED) WHITSETT, JEFFREY A CHILDREN'S HOSPITAL MED CTR ELLAND & BETHESDA AVES CINCINNATI, OH 45229-2899 Perinatal expression of surfactant protein gene
R01HL-38868-05 (BIO) BILLADELLO, JOSEPH J WASHINGTON UNIVERSITY 660 SOUTH EUCLID AVENUE ST LOUIS, MO 63110 Regulation of expression of creatine kinase gene family

PROJECT NO., ORGANIZATIONAL UNIT., INVESTIGATOR, ADDRESS, TITLE

R01HL-38876-01A3 (HED) NELSON, SHARON H UNIVERSITY OF TEXAS GALVESTON, TX 77550-2778 Vascular adaptations in pregnancy

R29HL-38878-03 (EDC) MOSKOWITZ, WILLIAM B VIRGINIA COMMONWEALTH UNIV P O BOX 543, MCV STATION RICHMOND, VA 23298 Childhood passive smoking--Cohort study of cardiac risk

R01HL-38884-05 (PC) ASSOIAN, RICHARD K COLUMBIA UNIVERSITY 630 WEST 168TH STREET NEW YORK, NY 10032 Expression of tgf-beta in monocytes and macrophages

R37HL-38885-05 (CVB) GETTES, LEONARD S UNIV. OF N.C., CHAPEL HILL 349 BURNETT-WOMACK CB#7075 CHAPEL HILL, N C 27599-7075 Ischemia and drug effects on ventricular conduction

R01HL-38899-05 (BIO) LONG, GEORGE L UNIVERSITY OF VERMONT GIVEN BUILDING BURLINGTON, VT 05405 Structure and molecular biology of the protein S gene

R29HL-38901-05 (ECS) FARACI, FRANK M UNIV OF IOWA COLL OF MEDICINE IOWA CITY, IA 52242-1009 Regulation of circulation to brain stem

R29HL-38902-05 (HED) STILES, ALAN D UNIVERSITY OF NORTH CAROLINA 509 BURNETT-WOMACK BLDG 229-H CHAPEL HILL, NC 27514 Cellular mechanisms of lung development

R01HL-38904-03 (RNM) MAHONY, CHERYL UNIV OF KENTUCKY ROSE STREET/WENNER-GREN RES LA LEXINGTON. KY 40506-0070 Etiology of spontaneous contrast

R29HL-38906-04 (RNM) BURSTEIN, DEBORAH BETH ISRAEL HOSPITAL 330 BROOKLINE AVE BOSTON, MA 02215 Cardiac NMR H, Na, & K spectroscopy & imaging

R29HL-38909-04 (CVA) BARRINGTON, PEGGY L NORTHWESTERN UNIVERSITY 303 EAST CHICAGO AVENUE CHICAGO, IL 60611 Calcium and free radical injury in cardiocytes

R29HL-38910-03 (HEM) SALEH, MANSOOR N UNIV OF ALABAMA AT BIRMINGHAM UNIVERSITY STATION BIRMINGHAM, ALA 35294 Fc-receptor mediated cell-cell interaction in ITP

R29HL-38916-03 (RAP) PEREZ FONTAN, J J YALE UNIV SCHOOL OF MEDICINE 333 CEDAR STREET, P O BOX 3333 NEW HAVEN, CT 06510 Mechanical interdependence in the developing lung

R29HL-38917-05 (CVA) ROZANSKI, GEORGE J UNIVERSITY OF NEBRASKA 600 SOUTH 42ND ST OMAHA, NEBRASKA NE 68198 Models of ectopic atrial automaticity

R55HL-38918-05A1 (PHY) REMBOLD, CHRISTOPHER M UNIV OF VIRGINIA HLTH SCI CTR PO BOX 146 CHARLOTTESVILLE, VA 22908 Ca2+, Ca2+ sensitivity, and smooth muscle contraction

R01HL-38924-05 (RAP) EVANS, JOHN N UNIVERSITY OF VERMONT BURLINGTON, VT 05045 Mechanics of pulmonary vascular smooth muscle

R01HL-38927-03 (CVA) JANUARY, CRAIG T UNIVERSITY OF CHICAGO 5841 S MARYLAND AVENUE,#322 CHICAGO, IL 60637 Early after depolarizations--Mechanisms and role of calcium

R01HL-38933-06 (SB) TURITTO, VINCENT T MEMPHIS STATE UNIVERSITY MEMPHIS, TN 38152 Thrombosis on biomaterials--Role of vascular components

R01HL-38940-06 (ECS) SURPRENANT, ANNMARIE OREGON HEALTH SCIENCES UNIVER 3181 SW SAM JACKSON PARK ROAD PORTLAND, OR 97201 Functional innervation of small resistance vessels

R01HL-38941-04 (SRC) DAVIS, KATHRYN A UNIVERSITY OF WASHINGTON 1107 NE 45TH STREET, RM 530 SEATTLE, WA 98105 Coronary artery surgery study (CASS) coordinating

R29HL-38942-05 (RAP) MALVIN, GARY M LOVELACE MEDICAL FOUNDATION 2425 RIDGECREST DR SE ALBUQUERQUE, N M 87108 Microvascular dimensions & gas exchange

R29HL-38944-05 (HED) SANFORD, GARY L MOREHOUSE SCHOOL OF MEDICINE 720 WESTVIEW DRIVE, S W ATLANTA, GA 30310-1495 Metabolism and function of galaptin in lung development

R29HL-38947-05 (RAP) BORSON, D B UNIVERSITY OF CALIFORNIA 505 PARNASSUS AVE SAN FRANCISCO, CALIF 94143 Role of enkephalinase in regulating airways

R29HL-38950-03 (BEM) SHERWOOD, ANDREW UNIV OF NC AT CHAPEL HILL CHAPEL HILL, NC 27599 Stress factors in blood pressure regulation

R29HL-38956-06 (NTN) WILLIAMS, KEVIN J MEDICAL COLLEGE OF PENN. 3300 HENRY AVENUE PHILADELPHIA, PA 19129 Metabolism of a synthetic anti-atherogenic lipoprotein

R01HL-38959-04A1 (RAP) GISOLFI, CARL V UNIVERSITY OF IOWA BOWEN SCIENCES BUILDING IOWA CITY, IA 52242 Mechanism of circulatory insufficiency in heat stroke

R01HL-38964-04 (SSS) CLARKSON, THOMAS B WAKE FOREST UNIVERSITY 300 S HAWTHORNE ROAD WINSTON-SALEM, N C 27103 Randomized trial of estrogen-atherosclerosis regression

R01HL-38973-06 (HEM) STAFFORD, DARREL W UNIV OF NORTH CAROLINA CB 3280 WILSON HALL CHAPEL HILL, NC 27599-3280 Mutagenesis & function of human factor IX in blood clotting

R01HL-38976-04 (PHRA) STEINBERG, SUSAN F COLUMBIA UNIVERSITY 630 WEST 168 STREET NEW YORK, N Y 10032 Alpha 1-adrenergic catecholamine actions in the heart

R29HL-38986-04 (RAP) PRABHAKAR, NANDURI R UNIVERSITY HOSPITALS CLEVELAND 2074 ABINGTON RD CLEVELAND, OHIO 44106 Tachykinins & arterial chemoreceptor excitation

R29HL-38990-05 (PTHA) SKRINSKA, VICTOR A UNIV. OF WISCONSIN-MILWAUKEE PO BOX 413 MILWAUKEE, WI 53201 Mechanisms of suppressing atherosclerosis

R01HL-39006-04 (CVB) HARRISON, DAVID G EMORY UNIVERSITY P O BOX DRAWER LL ATLANTA, GA 30322 Regulation of vascular function by the endothelium

R01HL-39023-04 (HED) BUCK, CLAYTON A WISTAR INSTITUTE 36TH & SPRUCE STREET PHILADELPHIA, PA 19104 Vascular development in the early embryo

R29HL-39025-06 (MET) GEISBUHLER, TIMOTHY P UNIVERSITY OF MISSOURI MA415 MEDICAL SCIENCES COLUMBIA, MO 65212 Metabolism of guanosine in ischemic myocardium

R01HL-39032-06 (SRC) WYLIE-ROSETT, JUDITH ALBERT EINSTEIN COLLEGE OF MED 1300 MORRIS PARK AVENUE BRONX, N Y 10461 Dietary intervention--Evaluation of technology

R01HL-39035-04 (RNM) PATZ, SAMUEL BRIGHAM & WOMEN'S HOSPITAL 75 FRANCIS STREET BOSTON, MA 02115 Magnetic resonance imaging of slow fluid flow

R01HL-39037-06 (HEM) DIXIT, VISHVA M UNIVERSITY OF MICHIGAN 1301 CATHERINE STREET ANN ARBOR, MI 48109-0602 Structure and regulation of human platelet thrombospondin

R29HL-39039-05 (CVA) CREAZZO, TONY L MEDICAL COLLEGE OF GEORGIA DEPARTMENT OF ANATOMY AUGUSTA, GA 30912 Heart muscle ionic currents--Cholinergic mechanisms

R01HL-39040-05 (HEM) PAINTER, RICHARD G UNIV OF TEXAS HLTH CTR P O BOX 2003 TYLER, TX 75710 Molecular interactions of blood coagulation factor X

R29HL-39045-06 (RAP) TOWNSLEY, MARY I UNIVERSITY OF SOUTH ALABAMA MOBILE, AL 36688 Lung capillary permeability with high vascular pressures

R29HL-39048-05 (HED) TUCKER, DIANE C UNIVERSITY OF ALABAMA 201 CAMPBELL HALL UAB STATION BIRMINGHAM, AL 35294-1170 Neural controls of cardiac growth and intrinsic rate

R29HL-39050-05 (CVA) LAMPING, KATHRYN G UNIVERSITY OF IOWA IOWA CITY, IA 52242 Effect of humoral agents on coronary microvasculature

R29HL-39052-05 (EDC) MORRIS, CYNTHIA D OREGON HEALTH SCIENCES UNIV 3181 S W SAM JACKSON PARK RD PORTLAND, OR 97201 Reproduction and survival post cardiac malformation repair

R01HL-39070-05 (CVA) HAUSCHKA, STEPHEN D UNIVERSITY OF WASHINGTON SEATTLE, WA 98195 Creatine kinase control elements and cardiac determination

R01HL-39081-05 (SB) PARK, KINAM PURDUE UNIVERSITY WEST LAFAYETTE, IN 47907 Platelet behavior at polymer blood interfaces

R01HL-39085-05 (HEM) GELEHRTER, THOMAS D UNIVERSITY OF MICHIGAN MED SCH 1500 E MEDICAL CENTER DR ANN ARBOR, MI 48109-0618 Regulation of fibrinolysis in human endothelial cells

R01HL-39086-03 (PC) RABEN, DANIEL M JOHNS HOPKINS UNIVERSITY 725 N WOLFE ST BALTIMORE, MD 21205 Mitogen-stimulated diacylglycerol metabolism

R29HL-39091-05 (CVA) GWATHMEY, JUDITH K BETH ISRAEL HOSPITAL 330 BROOKLINE AVENUE BOSTON, MA 02215 Pathophysiology of cardiomyopathy

R29HL-39102-05 (EDC) BUSH, TRUDY L JOHNS HOPKINS UNIVERSITY 615 NORTH WOLFE STREET BALTIMORE, MD 21205 Epidemiology of cardiovascular diseases in the elderly

R01HL-39103-05A1 (END) RAFF, HERSHEL ST LUKE'S MEDICAL CENTER 2900 WEST OKLAHOMA AVENUE MILWAUKEE, WI 53215 Vasopressin-CRF-ACTH interactions in the conscious state

R01HL-39105-02 (ECS) DORMER, KENNETH J UNIV OF OKLAHOMA HEALTH SCI CT P O BOX 26901 OKLAHOMA CITY, OK 73190 Vasomotor center control of cardiovascular function

R01HL-39107-05 (EDC) SING, CHARLES F UNIV OF MICHIGAN MEDICAL SCIENCE II M4708 ANN ARBOR, MI 48109-0618 Genetic epidemiology of coronary heart disease

R01HL-39116-05 (PC) WELLS, MICHAEL A UNIVERSITY OF ARIZONA TUCSON, AZ 85721 Lipoprotein metabolism in an insect model system

R29HL-39124-05 (BEM) GIL, KAREN M DUKE UNIVERSITY MEDICAL CENTER BOX 3926 DURHAM, NC 27710 Sickle cell disease: analysis of pain coping strategies

R01HL-39137-05 (HEM) GINSBURG, DAVID UNIV OF MICH MED CENTER 1150 W MEDICAL CAMPUS DRIVE ANN ARBOR, MI 48109 Human plasminogen activator-inhibitor (PAI-1) gene

R01HL-39138-04A1 (RAP) ROBOTHAM, JAMES JOHNS HOPKINS HOSPITAL 600 N WOLFE ST BALTIMORE, MD 21205 Transient analysis of cardiorespiratory interactions

R01HL-39141-04 (CTY) SCHNEIDER, MICHAEL D BAYLOR COLLEGE OF MEDICINE 6535 FANNIN STREET - MS F-905 HOUSTON, TX 77030 Control of cardiac growth by cellular oncogenes

R01HL-39144-03 (EDC) POSNER, BARBARA M BOSTON UNIV. SCHOOL PUB HEALTH 80 EAST CONCORD STREET BOSTON, MA 02118 Nutritional determinants of cardiovascular disease

R29HL-39147-05 (PTHA) JACKSON, ROBERT M UNIV OF ALABAMA, BIRMINGHAM ROOM 323, LYONS HARRISON BLDG BIRMINGHAM, ALABAMA 35294 Basic mechanisms of re-expansion pulmonary edema

R01HL-39154-05 (MEP) FREGLY, MELVIN J UNIV OF FLORIDA COLL OF MED BOX J274 GAINESVILLE, FL 32610 Physiologic responses to chronic cold exposure

R01HL-39155-01A3 (RAP) HARRIS, THOMAS R VANDERBILT UNIVERSITY BOX 1724, STATION B NASHVILLE, TN 37235 Optical probes of lung vascular endothelial function

P01HL-39157-05 (HLBA) HODSON, WILLIAM A UNIVERSITY OF WASHINGTON MAIL STOP RD-20 SEATTLE, WA 98195 Pathophysiology of respiratory disorders of the newborn

P01HL-39157-05 0001 (HLBA) HODSON, WILLIAM A Pathophysiology of respiratory disorders of the newborn Lung injury and repair in hyalin membrane disease

P01HL-39157-05 0002 (HLBA) WILSON, CHRISTOPHER B Pathophysiology of respiratory disorders of the newborn Host defenses in neonatal lung

P01HL-39157-05 0003 (HLBA) TROUG, WILLIAM E Pathophysiology of respiratory disorders of the newborn Regulation of gas exchance in neonatal lung injury

P01HL-39157-05 0004 (HLBA) WOODRUM, DAVID E Pathophysiology of respiratory disorders of the newborn Respiration muscles in neonatal respiratory failure

P01HL-39157-05 9001 (HLBA) STANDART, THOMAS A Pathophysiology of respiratory disorders of the newborn Core--Research resources

R01HL-39171-05 (SRC) KAUFMAN, LEON UNIV CA, SAN FRANCISCO 400 GRANDVIEW DRIVE SAN FRANCISCO, CALIF 94080 MRI of human coronary arteries

R29HL-39175-05 (CVA) FREEDMAN, ROGER A UNIV OF UTAH MED CTR 50 NORTH MEDICAL DRIVE SALT LAKE CITY, UT 84132 Body surface localization of qrs late poatentials

R55HL-39185-04A2 (CVA) WHITE, CARL W UNIVERSITY OF MINNESOTA BOX 508 UMHC MINNEAPOLIS, MN 55455 Neural control of the coronary circulation in humans

R01HL-39208-05 (RNM) OSBAKKEN, MARY D UNIVERSITY OF PENNSYLVANIA 37TH AND HAMILTON WALK PHILDELPHIA, PA 19104 31P MRS study of heart energetics during volume loading

R29HL-39226-05 (ECS) ELLSWORTH, MARY L ST LOUIS UNIVERSITY 1402 S GRAND BOULEVARD ST LOUIS, MO 63104 Oxygen affinity and oxygen transport in striated muscle

R01HL-39238-06 (SRC) SCHICK, PAUL K THOMAS JEFFERSON UNIVERSITY

PROJECT NO., ORGANIZATIONAL UNIT., INVESTIGATOR, ADDRESS, TITLE

1015 WALNUT STREET PHILADELPHIA, PA 19104 Effects of polyunsaturated fatty acids on megakaryocytes
R01HL-39239-05 (SRC) BENSADOUN, ANDRE CORNELL UNIVERSITY 321 SAVAGE HALL ITHACA, N Y 14853 Effects of omega-3 fatty acids on lipid transport
R01HL-39262-05 (SRC) BROWN, ARTHUR M BAYLOR COLLEGE OF MEDICINE ONE BAYLOR PLAZA HOUSTON, TX 77030 Molecular biology of cardiac ion channels
R01HL-39263-05 (SRC) LEVENSON, ROBERT YALE UNIVERSITY 333 CEDAR STREET, P.O. BX 3333 NEW HAVEN, CT 06510 Cardiac NA,K-ATPASE genes--Structure & function
R01HL-39265-05 (SRC) CAMPBELL, KEVIN P UNIVERSITY OF IOWA RM 6-530 BOWEN SCIENCE BLDG IOWA CITY, IA 52242 Ca2+ release channel from cardiac sarcoplasmic reticulum
R01HL-39267-05 (SRC) RUIZ-OPAZO, NELSON BOSTON UNIVERSITY MED CTR 80 EAST CONCORD STREET BOSTON, MA 02118 Analysis of 3 cardiac na,k- tpase alpha- subunit isoforms
R01HL-39286-06 (CVB) LIPOWSKY, HERVERT H PENNSYLVANIA STATE UNIVERSITY HALLOWELL BUILDING UNIVERSITY PARK, PA 16802 Rheological determinants of microvascular function
R01HL-39291-03 (SSS) COHEN, RICHARD J MASSACHUSETTS INSTITUTE 77 MASS AVE/RM E25-330D CAMBRIDGE, MA 02139 Beat-to-beat variability in hemodynamic parameters
R01HL-39295-05 (SRC) FARLEY, ROBERT A DEPT. OF PHYS & BIO 1333 SAN PABLO STREET LOS ANGLES, CA 90033 Structure, function, and regulation of cardiac Na,K-aTPAse
R01HL-39297-05 (SRC) MACOVSKI, ALBERT STANFORD UNIVERSITY DURAND BLDG ROOM 109 STANFORD, CA 94305 Projection angiography using magnetic resonance
R01HL-39299-05 (SRC) GUR, DAVID UNIVERSITY OF PITTSBURGH RC508 SCAIFE HALL PITTSBURGH, PA 15261 Minimally invasive techniques for detection and quantification
R01HL-39300-04 (PHY) ISMAIL-BEIGI, GARAMARZ COLUMBIA UNIVERSITY 630 WEST 168TH STREET NEW YORK CITY, N Y 10032 Physiological control of myocardial na,k-pump expression
R01HL-39303-05 (SRC) ALPERT, NORMAN R UNIVERSITY OF VERMONT COLLEGE OF MEDICINE BURLINGTON, VT 05405 Molecular and functional analysis of heart SR regulation
R01HL-39308-05 (SRC) SPECTOR, ARTHUR A UNIVERSITY OF IOWA BOWEN SCIENCE BUILDING IOWA CITY, IOWA 52242 Fish oil fatty acids and arterial smooth muscle cells
R01HL-39312-05 (SRC) POWNALL, HENRY J BAYLOR COLLEGE OF MEDICINE 6565 FANNIN ST HOUSTON, TX 77030 Dietary effects on lipoprotein metabolism
R01HL-39326-05 (MET) SCHAEFER, ERNST J TUFTS UNIVERSITY 711 WASHINGTON STREET BOSTON, MA 02111 Effects of dietary fats on lipoprotein metabolism
R01HL-39332-04 (BEM) KLESGES, ROBERT C MEMPHIS STATE UNIVERSITY CTR / APPLIED PSYCHOL RESEARCH MEMPHIS, TN 38152 Weight gain and smoking relapse--A biobehavioral approach
R44HL-39342-04 (SSS) KEYES, MELVIN H ANATRACE INC 1280 DUSSEL DRIVE MAUMEE, OH 43537 Glycated hemoglobin by automated affinity chromatography
R29HL-39352-04 (PC) KOMAROMY, MICHAEL C PALO ALTO MEDICAL FOUNDATION 860 BRYANT STREET PALO ALTO, CA 94301 Structure and function studies on hepatic lipase
R01HL-39369-06 (SRC) HALLS, LINDA M SUNY AT BUFFALO 317 HOCHSTETTER HALL BUFFALO, N Y 14260 Molecular genetic analysis of cardiac channels
R01HL-39371-05 (SRC) KANTOR, HOWARD L MASSACHUSETTS GENERAL HOSPITAL FRUIT STREET BOSTON, MASS 02114 Techniques for detection of lesions in coronary arteries
R01HL-39383-05 (SRC) BUNAG, RUBEN D UNIV OF KANSAS MEDICAL CENTER 39TH STREET & RAINBOW BLVD KANSAS CITY, KS 66103 Fat rats and hypertension
R01HL-39385-04 (NTN) NICOLOSI, ROBERT J UNIVERSITY OF LOWELL ONE UNIVERSITY AVENUE LOWELL, MA 01854 Dietary fat/cholesterol on low density lipoprotein
R01HL-39387-05 (SRC) ROCKHOLD, ROBIN W UNIVERSITY OF MISSISSIPPI 2500 NORTH STATE STREET JACKSON, MS 38216-4505 Hypothalamic opiates in obesity-accelerated hypertension
R01HL-39390-05 (SRC) BROWNIE, ALEXANDER C STATE UNIV OF NY AT BUFFALO 102 CARY HALL BUFFALO, N Y 14214 Adrenocortical hormones in obesity-related hypertension
R01HL-39399-05 (SRC) HALL, JOHN E UNIV OF MISSISSIPPI MED. CTR. 2500 N STATE STREET JACKSON, MISS 39216 Blood pressure & renal function in hyperinsulinemia
R29HL-39406-05 (RAP) FREED, ARTHUR N JOHNS HOPKINS UNIVERSITY 615 N WOLFE ST BALTIMORE, MD 21205 Airflow-induced responses in the canine lung periphery
R01HL-39419-02 (CVA) BARKA, TIBOR MOUNT SINAI SCHOOL OF MEDICINE ONE GUSTAVE L LEVY PLACE NEW YORK, NY 10029 Proto-oncogenes in cardiac tissues
R01HL-39423-05 (RAP) VANHOUTTE, PAUL M BAYLOR COLLEGE OF MEDICINE ONE BAYLOR PLAZA HOUSTON, TEXAS 77030 Epithelium and bronchial reactivity
R29HL-39435-04 (RAP) BROWER, ROY G JOHNS HOPKINS HOSPITAL BRADY 416 BALTIMORE, MD 21205 Pulmonary circulation--Flow, volume, and filtration
R29HL-39437-05 (SB) KU, DAVID N GEORGIA INSTITUTE OF TECHN ATLANTA, GA 30332-0405 Human atherosclerosis--Role of pulsatile flow
R37HL-39438-04 (HEM) JAMIESON, GRAHAM A AMERICAN RED CROSS 15601 CRABBS BRANCH WAY ROCKVILLE, MD 20855 Characterization & isolation of platelet ADP receptors
R01HL-39455-03 (SB) ZYDNEY, ANDREW L UNIVERSITY OF DELAWARE 227 COLBURN LAB. NEWARK, DE 19716 Selective filtration of plasma proteins
R29HL-39458-04 (PHRA) BAI, STEPHEN A NORTH CAROLINA STATE UNIV 4700 HILLSBOROUGH STREET RALEIGH, N C 27606 Calcium channel blockers: kinetics, action & metabolism
R01HL-39469-05 (SRC) MOSSMAN, BROOKE T UNIVERSITY OF VERMONT DEPT. OF PATHOLOGY BURLINGTON, VT 05405 Molecular biology of lung antioxidant enzyme

PROJECT NO., ORGANIZATIONAL UNIT., INVESTIGATOR, ADDRESS, TITLE

R01HL-39585-05 (SRC) HO, YE-SHIH DUKE UNIV MEDICAL CENTER BOX 3177 DURHAM, N C 27710 Superoxide dismutes gene regulation in lung injury
R01HL-39588-03S1 (NEUA) OBRIST, WALTER D UNIVERSITY OF PITTSBURGH 9402 PRESBYTERIAN-UNIV HOSP PITTSBURGH, PA 15213 CBF and neurological function in heart transplant patients
R01HL-39593-05 (SRC) NICK, HARRY S UNIV OF FLORIDA BOX 100245 JHMHC GAINESVILLE, FL 32610 Molecular biology of the superoxide dismutases
R01HL-39594-05 (SRC) KAVANAGH, TERRANCE J UNIVERSITY OF WASHINGTON CARE MEDICINE SEATTLE, WA 98195 Altered lung glutathione induced by insertion mutagenesis
R29HL-39595-04 (MET) IVERIUS, PER-HENRIK VA MEDICAL CENTER 500 FOOTHILL BLVD SALT LAKE CITY, UT 84148 Effects of sex steroids of adipocyte lipoprotein lipase
R01HL-39614-01A3 (SSS) WILSON, PHILLIP D UNIVERSITY OF MARYLAND 660 W REDWOOD STREET BALTIMORE, MD 21201 Model-free time curves for longitudinal data analysis
R29HL-39619-05 (ECS) OSBORN, JOHN W, JR UNIVERSITY OF MINNESOTA 1988 FITCH AVENUE ST PAUL, MN 55108 Arterial pressure in paraplegia--Role of spinal system
R29HL-39622-04 (SAT) CAMBRIA, RICHARD P MASSACHUSETTS GENERAL HOSPITAL 15 PARKMAN STREET-ACC 358 BOSTON, MA 02114 Vascular cell interactions and intimal hyperplasia
R01HL-39631-05 (SRC) SHAFFER, JACQUELIN B N Y STATE DEPT OF HEALTH ALBANY, N Y 12201 Regulation of lung catalase and SOD gene expression
R29HL-39633-04 (EDC) JOHNSON, JEFFREY V THE JOHNS HOPKINS UNIVERSITY 624 NORTH BROADWAY BALTIMORE, MD 21205 Work organization & cardiovascular disease
R29HL-39661-02 (HEM) HARRISON, ROBERT L UNIVERSITY OF TEXAS MED BRANCH 301 UNIVERSITY BOULEVARD GALVESTON, TX 77550-2774 Synthesis and processing of factor VIII/Von Willebrand factor
R29HL-39665-05 (HEM) LIEBMAN, HOWARD A UNIV OF SOUTHERN CALIFORNIA 1975 ZONAL AVENUE LOS ANGELES, CA 90033 Metal ions in the function of factor IX
R01HL-39670-04 (SB) JACKMAN, WARREN M UNIV OF OKLAHOMA HLTH SCI CTR PO BOX 26901 OKLAHOMA CITY, OK 73190 Catheter ablation of ventricular myocardium
R01HL-39672-04 (PTHA) SITRIN, ROBERT G UNIVERSITY OF MICHIGAN 3916 TAUBMAN CENTER, BOX 0360 ANN ARBOR, MI 48109-0360 Plasminogen activator in inflammatory lung diseases
R29HL-39680-04 (ECS) SKALAK, THOMAS C UNIVERSITY OF VIRGINIA THORNTON HALL CHARLOTTESVILLE, VA 22901 Microvascular network in growth and hypertension
R01HL-39681-05 (EDC) SIGUEL, EDWARD N EDUARDO SIGUEL POST OFFICE BOX 5 BROOKLINE, MA 02146 Patterns of fatty acids in Framingham offspring
R01HL-39682-04 (TOX) PHALEN, ROBERT F UNIVERSITY OF CALIFORNIA IRVINE, CA 92717 Age and body size factors in inhaled particle deposition
R29HL-39683-04 (SAT) SITZMANN, JAMES V JOHNS HOPKINS HOSPITAL 665 BLALOCK BL, 601 N BROADWAY BALTIMORE, MD 21205 Splanchnic hemodynamics in portal hypertension
R01HL-39684-04 (MEDB) RYAN, JAMES W UNIVERSITY OF MIAMI P O BOX 016960 MIAMI, FL 33101 Pulmonary aminopeptidase P
R01HL-39689-03 (NTN) JENKINS, DAVID J UNIVERSITY OF TORONTO FACULTY OF MEDICINE TORONTO, CANADA M5S 1A8 Soluble and insoluble fiber diets in hyperlipidemia
R01HL-39691-04 (CVB) WOLF, MATTHEW B UNIVERSITY OF SOUTH CAROLINA DEPT OF PHYSIOLOGY COLUMBIA, SC 29208 Transcapillary macromolecule movement in skeletal muscle
R01HL-39693-03 (HEM) GINSBURG, DAVID UNIV OF MICH MED CENTER 1150 W MEDICAL CENTER DRIVE ANN ARBOR, MI 48109 Molecular genetic studies of von willebrand factor
R01HL-39698-04 (CVB) ZIMMERMAN, BEN G UNIVERSITY OF MINNESOTA 435 DELAWARE STREET, SE MINNEAPOLIS, MN 55455 Functional analysis of vascular angiotensin II
R01HL-39701-04 (PTHA) HAJJAR, DAVID P CORNELL UNIVERSITY MED COLLEGE 1300 YORK AVENUE NEW YORK, N Y 10021 Eicosanoid regulation of arterial cholesterol metabolism
R29HL-39702-04 (HEM) AIKEN, MARTHA L UNIVERSITY OF TEXAS HEALTH CTR PO BOX 2003 TYLER, TX 75710 Identification of TSP receptors on human cells
R01HL-39703-04 (PC) TABAS, IRA A COLUMBIA UNIVERSITY 630 WEST 168TH STREET NEW YORK 10032 ACAT reactivity in macrophages
R29HL-39706-04 (ECS) JOHNS, ROGER A UNIVERSITY OF VIRGINIA CHARLOTTESVILLE, VA 22908 Oxygen tension and endothelium-dependent vasodilation
P01HL-39707-02 (SRC) JALIFE, JOSE SUNY HEALTH SCIENCE CENTER 750 EAST ADAMS STREET SYRACUSE, N Y 13210 Intercellular communication and impulse propagation
P01HL-39707-02 0003 (SRC) MICHAELS, DONALD C Intercellular communication and impulse propagation Mathematical models of propagation in cardiac cells
P01HL-39707-02 0004 (SRC) VEENSTRA, RICHARD D Intercellular communication and impulse propagation Pharmacologic regulation of gap junction channels
P01HL-39707-02 0005 (SRC) VALLANO, MARY LOU Intercellular communication and impulse propagation Structure, function, regulation of gap junction proteins
P01HL-39707-02 9001 (SRC) MICHAELS, DONALD C Intercellular communication and impulse propagation Core--Computer and electronics
P01HL-39707-02 9002 (SRC) LEMANSKI, LARRY F Intercellular communication and impulse propagation Core--Molecular biology and immunology
P01HL-39707-02 0001 (SRC) JALIFE, JOSE Intercellular communication and impulse propagation Nonlinear dynamics of propagation in cardiac tissue
P01HL-39707-02 0002 (SRC) DELMAR, MARIO Intercellular communication and impulse propagation Intercellular coupling and propagation in cardiac tissue
R29HL-39712-03 (RAP) CLIFFORD, PHILIP S VA MEDICAL CENTER 5000

W NATIONAL AVE MILWAUKEE, WI 53295 Respiratory control during exercise
R29HL-39714-04 (SB) HUBBELL, JEFFREY A UNIVERSITY OF TEXAS DEPT OF CHEMICAL ENGINEERING AUSTIN, TX 78712 Mural thrombosis on natural and artificial surfaces
R29HL-39719-03 (CVB) FELDMAN, ARTHUR M JOHNS HOPKINS UNIVERSITY 720 RUTLAND AVE BALTIMORE, MD 21205 Regulation of g proteins in heart failure
R29HL-39723-04 (PHRA) NG, YUK-CHOW PENNSYLVANIA STATE UNIVERSITY P O BOX 850 HERSHEY, PA 17033 Two isoforms of NA,K-ATPase in the heart
R29HL-39727-04 (CTY) WINKLES, JEFFREY A AMERICAN RED CROSS 15601 CRABBS BRANCH WAY ROCKVILLE, MD 20855 Vascular smooth muscle cell proliferation
R29HL-39752-04 (CVA) STEENBERGEN, CHARLES DUKE UNIVERSITY POST OFFICE BOX 3712 DURHAM, N C 27710 Role of elevated Ca2+ in myocardial ischemic injury
R37HL-39753-04 (HEM) ROSENBERG, ROBERT D MASSACHUSETTS INSTIT OF TECH 77 MASSACHUSETTS AVENUE CAMBRIDGE, MA 02139 Regulation of blood platelet production
R01HL-39757-05 (ECS) THIBONNIER, MARC CASE WESTERN RESERVE UNIV CLEVELAND, OH 44106 Vasopressin receptors and hypertension
R01HL-39759-03 (NTN) ALLEN, KENNETH G COLORADO ST UNIV CONGRESSIONAL DISTRICT #4 FT COLLINS, CO 80523 Dietary copper, lipid hydroperoxide & PG synthesis
R01HL-39762-03 (HEM) SOMMER, STEVE S MAYO FOUNDATION 200 FIRST STREET SOUTHWEST ROCHESTER, MN 55905 Delineation of causative mutations in hemophilia B
R01HL-39770-04 (SRC) FORTMANN, STEPHEN P STANFORD UNIVERSITY CTR. FOR RES. IN DISEASE PREV. STANFORD, CALIF 94305 A population-based study of cessation in heavy smokers
R29HL-39773-04 (ALY) ZURAW, BRUCE L SCRIPPS CLINIC 10666 NORTH TORREY PINES RD LA JOLLA, CA 92037 Regulation of C1 inhibitor synthesis and catabolism
R01HL-39775-04 (RAP) FISHMAN, ALFRED P UNIVERSITY OF PENNA HOSPITAL 3600 SPRUCE STREET PHILADELPHIA, PA 19104-4283 Neural control of ventilation and arousal
R01HL-39776-04 (SAT) BOSNJAK, ZELJKO J MEDICAL COLLEGE OF WISCONSIN 8701 W WATERTOWN PLANK RD MILWAUKEE, WI 53226 Cellular effects of anesthetics in the heart
R01HL-39789-04 (BPO) SHIVELY, CAROL A BOWMAN GRAY SCHOOL OF MEDICINE 300 S HAWTHORNE ROAD WINSTON-SALEM, NC 27103 Social status and atherosclerosis in females
R01HL-39792-04 (RAD) GULLBERG, GRANT T UNIVERSITY OF UTAH MEDICAL IMAGING RESEARCH LAB SALT LAKE CITY, UT 84132 Improved heart imaging using spect
R01HL-39794-03 (CVA) FEINSTEIN, STEVEN B UNIVERSITY OF CHICAGO 5841 S MARYLAND AVE/BOX 44 CHICAGO, IL 60637 Quantitation of perfusion in ischemic heart disease
R01HL-39795-03 (SAT) BURT, JANIS M UNIVERSITY OF ARIZONA DEPT OF PHYSIOLOGY TUCSON, AZ 85724 Microcirculatory injury during myocardial preservation
R01HL-39811-03 (RAP) MCCOOL, FRANKLIN D MEMORIAL HOSPITAL - RHODE ISLA 111 BREWSTER STREET PAWTUCKET, RI 02860 Inspiratory pump--Pressure-flow-volume performance
R29HL-39818-04 (RAP) MACK, GARY W JOHNS B PIERCE FOUNDATION LAB 290 CONGRESS AVENUE NEW HAVEN, CONNECTICUT 06519 Interaction of cardiovascular reflexes in exercise
R01HL-39827-04 (RAP) DRAZEN, JEFFREY M BETH ISRAEL HOSPITAL 330 BROOKLINE AVENUE BOSTON, MA 02215 Peptidase regulation of substance P bronchoconstriction
R01HL-39829-04 (HED) LOUGH, JOHN W, JR MEDICAL COLLEGE OF WISCONSIN 8701 W WATERTOWN PLANK ROAD MILWAUKEE, WI 53226 Induction of early embryonic heart development
R01HL-39831-04 (ECS) VAN BREEMEN, CORNELIUS UNIVERSITY OF MIAMI P O BOX 016189 MIAMI, FL 33101 Calcium and excitation-contraction coupling in endothelium
R01HL-39833-05 (SRC) BITTERMAN, PETER B UNIVERSITY OF MINNESOTA HOSPTL 420 DELSWARE STREET SE MINNEAPOLIS, MN 55455 Mesenchymal cell subpopulations in acute lung fibrosis
R29HL-39834-04 (HEM) WINKELMANN, JOHN C UNIVERSITY OF MINNESOTA HARVARD ST AT E RIVER ROAD MINNEAPOLIS, M N 55455 Molecular genetics of human red blood cell spectrin
R01HL-39841-05 (SRC) GUYENET, PATRICE G UNIVERSITY OF VIRGINIA 1300 JEFFERSON PARK AVENUE CHARLOTTESVILLE, VA 22908 The neuronal basis for cardiorespiratory integration
R29HL-39846-04 (PHRA) PRESSLEY, THOMAS A UNIVERSITY OF TEXAS P O BOX 20708 HOUSTON, TEXAS 77225 Molecular basis of cardiac glycoside affinity
U01HL-39852-05 (SRC) PERRY, CHERYL L UNIVERSITY OF MINNESOTA 515 DELAWARE STREET SE MINNEAPOLIS, MN 55455 Promoting cardiovascular health with children
R01HL-39854-05 (SRC) RAGHU, GANESH UNIVERSITY OF WASHINGTON SEATTLE, WA 98195 Fibroblast heterogeneity in normal and fibrotic lungs
R29HL-39856-03 (SB) BEISSINGER, RICHARD L ILLINOIS INST OF TECHNOLOGY 3300 SOUTH FEDERAL STREET CHICAGO, IL 60616 Augmented protein transport in sheared suspensions
R29HL-39858-04 (RAP) HUTCHISON, ALASTAIR MB UNIVERSITY OF FLORIDA BOX J-296 JHMHC GAINESVILLE, FLA 32610 Function and control of the larynx in the neonate
R29HL-39869-04 (PBC) DEAK, SUSAN B UMDNJ-ROBERT WOOD JOHNSON MED ONE ROBERT WOOD JOHNSON, PLACE NEW BRUNSWICK, NJ 08903 A new elastin-related protein in elastic tissue
U01HL-39870-05 (SRC) NADER, PHILIP R UNIVERSITY OF CALIFORNIA LA JOLLA, CA 92093-0927 Child and adolescent trial for cardiovascular health
R29HL-39871-04 (EDC) TYRRELL, KIM SUTTON UNIVERSITY OF PITTSBURGH 130 DESOTO STREET PITTSBURGH, PA 15261 Epidemiology of carotid disease in elderly adults
R29HL-39872-04 (SB) PAE, WALTER E, JR PENNSYLVANIA STATE UNIVERSITY P O BOX 850 HERSHEY, PA 17033 Assist pumping in myocardial infarction and shock
R01HL-39875-04 (HEM) HARRISON, MICHAEL R UNIV OF CALIFORNIA 513 PARNASSUS AVE 585 HSE SAN FRANCISCO, CA 94143-0570 Transplantation of fetal hematopoietic stem cells
R29HL-39888-04 (HEM) OLSON, STEVEN T HENRY FORD HOSPITAL 2799 W GRAND BOULEVARD DETROIT, MI 48202 Molecular basis of blood coagulation regulation
R01HL-39890-04 (PTHA) VANDEBERG, JOHN L SOUTHWEST FDN FOR BIOMED RES WEST LOOP 410 MILITARY DR SAN ANTONIO, TX 78228-0147 G6PD marker for monotypism in baboon atherosclerosis
R01HL-39894-05 (SRC) MC DONALD, JOHN A MAYO FOUNDATION 200 FIRST STREET SW ROCHESTER, MN 55905 Growth factors and the fibroproliferative lung diseases
R01HL-39902-03 (CVA) ANVERSA, PIERO NEW YORK MEDICAL COLLEGE BASIC SCIENCES BLDG VALHALLA, N Y 10595 Aging of the heart
R29HL-39903-04 (SB) SOBEL, MICHAEL MEDICAL COLLEGE OF VIRGINIA P O BOX 108, MCV STATION RICHMOND, VA 23298 Platelet-heparin interactions in cardiovascular surgery
U01HL-39906-05 (SRC) WEBBER, LARRY S LOUISIANA STATE UNIV MED CTR 1542 TULANE AVENUE NEW ORLEANS, LA 70112 Child and adolescent trial for cardiovascular health
R01HL-39913-04 (SRC) HIXSON, JAMES E SW FDN FOR BIOMEDICAL RESEARCH P O BOX 28147 SAN ANTONIO, TX 78228-0147 Pathobiological determinants of atherosclerosis in youth
R01HL-39916-06 (SRC) BENEDICT, CLAUDE R UNIVERSITY OF TEXAS 6431 FANNIN, MSB 6.039 HOUSTON, TEXAS 77030 Mechanisms of occlusion in a stenosed coronary artery
R01HL-39924-05 (SRC) HADDAD, GABRIEL G YALE UNIVERSITY/PEDIATRICS 333 CEDAR ST NEW HAVEN, CT 06510 Postnatal maturation and modulation of respiratory neurons
R01HL-39925-05 (SRC) PHAN, SEM HIN THE UNIVERSITY OF MICHIGAN 1500 E MEDICAL CENTER DRIVE ANN ARBOR, MI 48109 Fibroblasthet pregeneity in pulmonary fibrosis
R01HL-39926-04 (PTHA) POLVERINI, PETER J NORTHWESTERN UNIVERSITY 303 EAST CHICAGO AVENUE CHICAGO, IL 60611 Regulation of macrophage angiogenic activity
U01HL-39927-05 (SRC) PARCEL, GUY S UNIV OF TEXAS HLTH SCI CTR P O BOX 20186 HOUSTON, TX 77225 Texas children's activity trial of CV health--Study center
R01HL-39934-04 (MET) WILLIAMSON, JOSEPH R WASHINGTON UNIVERSITY 660 S EUCLID AVENUE ST LOUIS, MO 63110 Pathogenetic mechanisms in diabetic vascular disease
R01HL-39939-04 (PTHA) THRALL, ROGER S UNIV OF CONNECTICUT HLTH CTR 263 FARMINGTON AVE FARMINGTON, CONN 06032 Bleomycin-induced lung fibrosis--Fibroblast heterogeneity
R01HL-39943-05 (SRC) PAINTER, RICHARD G UNIV OF TEXAS HEALTH SCIENCES P O BOX 2003 TYLER, TX 75710 Fibroblast heterogeneity in pulmonary fibrosis
R01HL-39947-04 (HEM) ROTH, GERALD J VETERANS ADMIN MEDICAL CTR 1660 S COLUMBIAN WAY SEATTLE, WA 98108 Molecular cloning of human platelet glycoprotein Ib
R01HL-39949-05 (SRC) PENNEY, DAVID P UNIVERSITY OF ROCHESTER 601 ELMWOOD AVE, BOX 704 ROCHESTER, NY 14642 Fibroblast involvement in developing pulmonary fibrosis
R01HL-39952-04 (CVA) NEWMAN, JOHN H VANDERBILT UNIVERSITY B-1308 MEDICAL CENTER NORTH NASHVILLE, TENN 37232 Physiological mechanisms of oxygen toxicity
R01HL-39966-04 (RAP) SEALS, DOUGLAS R UNIVERSITY OF ARIZONA 228B MCKALE CENTER TUCSON, AZ 85721 Regulation of sympathetic nerve activity during exercise
R01HL-39968-04A1 (PTHA) JONES, DEAN P EMORY UNIVERSITY ATLANTA, GA 30322 Glutathione protection against hyperoxic injury in lung
R01HL-40029-05 (SRC) MYATT, LESLIE UNIVERSITY OF CINCINNATI 231 BETHESDA AVENUE CINCINNATI, OH 45267-0526 Regulation of placental vascular reactivity in PIH
R01HL-40041-05 (SRC) MORTON, MARK J OREGON HEALTH SCIENCES UNIV L4 3181 SW SAM JACKSON PARK ROAD PORTLAND, OREG 97201-3098 Cardiac response to estrogen and hypertension
R29HL-40047-04 (SB) MARCHANT, ROGER E CASE WESTERN RESERVE UNIV 2085 ADELBERT ROAD CLEVELAND, OH 44106 New biomedical interface materials
R29HL-40056-04 (HEM) FITZGERALD, DESMOND J SCHOOL OF MEDICINE VANDERBILT UNIVERSITY NASHVILLE, TENNESSEE 37232 Coronary thrombolysis and platelet activation
P01HL-40069-04 (HLBA) RAMWELL, PETER W GEORGETOWN UNIVERSITY 3900 RESERVOIR RD N W WASHINGTON, D C 20007 Sex steroids & coronary vascular disease
P01HL-40069-04 0001 (HLBA) FOEGH, MARIE L. Sex steroids & coronary vascular disease Gonadol steroids and transplant atherosclerosis
P01HL-40069-04 0002 (HLBA) FOEGH, MARIE L. Sex steroids & coronary vascular disease Thromboxone in ischemic heart disease
P01HL-40069-04 0003 (HLBA) RAMWELL, PETER W. Sex steroids & coronary vascular disease Vascular reactivity of the internal mammamy artery
P01HL-40069-04 9001 (HLBA) MYERS, ADAM K. Sex steroids & coronary vascular disease Animal--Core
R01HL-40070-04 (CVB) JOHNSON, ROBERT L, JR U T SOUTHWESTERN MEDICAL CENTE 5323 HARRY HINES BLVD DALLAS, TX 75235-9034 Limitations to exercise after pneumonectomy
R01HL-40072-04 (SRC) DAVIS, BARRY R UNIV OF TEXAS HLTH SCI CTR 1200 HERMAN PRESSLER ST HOUSTON, TX 77030 Continuation of trial of antihypertensive interventions & mgme.
R01HL-40076-03 (SRC) FRIEDMAN, ROBERT H UNIVERSITY HOSPITAL 720 HARRISON AVENUE BOSTON, MASS 02118 BP control in the elderly--Eval of phone-linked computer system
R01HL-40078-04 (PTHA) HOLTZMAN, MICHAEL J WASHINGTON UNIV MEDICAL SCHOOL 660 S. EUCLID BOX 8052 ST LOUIS, MO 63110 Lung epithelial mechanisms for mediator release
R01HL-40079-04 (PBC) BENDITT, EARL P UNIVERSITY OF WASHINGTON PATHOLOGY DEPARTMENT, SJ-60 SEATTLE, WASH 98195 Saa lipoprotein family--Function and role in amyloidodis
R01HL-40092-04 (SB) PILKINGTON, THEO C DUKE UNIVERSITY 136 ENGINEERING BUILDING DURHAM, N C 27706 Optimizing defibrillation systems--Models and experiment

PROJECT NO., ORGANIZATIONAL UNIT., INVESTIGATOR, ADDRESS, TITLE

R01HL-40098-02 (RNM) SELZER, ROBERT H JET PROPULSION LABORATORY 4800 OAK GROVE DRIVE PASADENA, CA 91109-8099 Assessment of carotid atherosclerosis with 3d ultrasound

R01HL-40102-05 (SRC) DIMSDALE, JOEL E UNIV OF CALIF, SAN DIEGO DEPT OF PSYCHIATRY, M-003 LA JOLLA, CA 92093 Converting enzyme inhibition and cardiovascular reactivity

R01HL-40113-05 (SRC) GRUENSTEIN, ERIC I THE UNIVERSITY OF CINCINNATI 231 BETHESDA AVE CINCINNATI, OH 45267-0522 Fibroblast heterogeneity in adult lung

R01HL-40123-03 (BCE) GRIFFING, GEORGE T UNIVERSITY HOSPITAL 88 EAST NEWTON STREET BOSTON, MA 02118 19-NOR-deoxycoticosterone in hypertension

R01HL-40134-05 (SRC) SZILAGYI, JULIANNA E UNIVERSITY OF HOUSTON-UNIV PK 4800 CALHOUN HOUSTON, TEXAS 77004 Sodium and neuropeptides in stress induced hypertension

R01HL-40137-03 (CVB) OSBORN, JEFFREY L MEDICAL COLLEGE OF WISCONSIN 8701 WATERTOWN PLANK ROAD MILWAUKEE, WI 53226 Sodium intake and neural control of arterial pressure

R01HL-40138-05 (SRC) TURKKAN, JAYLAN S JOHNS HOPKINS UNIV SCH OF MED 720 RUTLAND AVENUE BALTIMORE, MD 21205 Chronic stress and sodium effects on hypertension

R01HL-40152-05 (SRC) SEALEY, JEAN E CARDIOVASCULAR CENTER, CUMC 525 EAST 68TH STREET NEW YORK, NY 10021 Renin & prorenin in pregnancy

U01HL-40154-05 (SRC) PAUERSTEIN, CARL J U OF TEXAS HLTH SCI CTR 7703 FLOYD CURL DRIVE SAN ANTONIO, TEX 78284 Clinical center--Postmenopausal estrogen/progestin inaterventions

R01HL-40162-05 (SRC) WOO, SAVIO BAYLOR COLLEGE OF MEDICINE ONE BAYLOR PLAZA HOUSTON, TX 77030 Somatic gene therapy for alpha-1-antitrypsin deficiency

R01HL-40178-05 (SRC) GUGGINO, WILLIAM B JOHNS HOPKINS UNIV. 725 NORTH WOLFE ST BALTIMORE, MD 21205-2196 Ion channels in fetal and adult trachea

R01HL-40184-05 (SRC) VAN BREEMEN, CORNELIUS UNIV OF MIAMI SCH OF MEDICINE PO BOX 016189 MIAMI, FLA 33101 Ion channels and airway smooth muscle activation

U01HL-40185-05 (SRC) LA ROSA, JOHN C GEORGE WASHINGTON UNIV MED CTR 901 23RD ST N.W. SUITE 2500N WASHINGTON, D C 20037 Clinical center--Postmenopausal estrogen-progestin intervention

R01HL-40186-05 (SRC) CARROLL, DANA UNIVERSITY OF UTAH SCH OF MED SALT LAKE CITY, UTAH 84132 Expression of epithelial chloride channels in frog oocytes

U01HL-40195-05 (SRC) SCHROTT, HELMUT G UNIVERSITY OF IOWA 2800 STEINDLER BLDG IOWA CITY, IOWA 52242 Clinical center--Postmenopausal estrogen/progestin intervention

R01HL-40203-05 (SRC) BROWN, JERRY L UNIV OF COLORADO HLTH SCI CTR 4200 E 9TH AVENUE DENVER, CO 80262 Alpha-1-protease inhibitor deficiency--Vector for gene therapy

U01HL-40205-05 (SRC) WOOD, PETER D STANFORD UNIVERSITY 730 WELCH RD, SUITE B PALO ALTO, CALIF 94304 Clinical center--Postmenopausal estrogen-progestin intervention

U01HL-40207-05 (SRC) BARRETT-CONNOR, ELIZABETH L UNIV. OF CALIFORNIA, SAN DIEGO COMMUNITY & FAMILY MED, M-0628 LA JOLLA, CA 92093 Clinical center--Postmenopausal estrogen progestin intervention

R01HL-40222-05 (SRC) DI BONA, GERALD F UNIVERSITY OF IOWA DEPT OF INTERNAL MEDICINE IOWA CITY, IOWA 52242 Stress, sodium and blood pressure regulation

U01HL-40231-05 (SRC) BUSH, TRUDY L JOHNS HOPKINS UNIVERSITY 615 NORTH WOLFE STREET BALTIMORE, MD 21205 Clinical center--Postmenopausal estrogen-progestin intervention

U01HL-40232-05 (SRC) WELLS, H BRADLEY BOWMAN GRAY SCHOOL OF MEDICINE MEDICAL CENTER BOULEVARD WINSTON-SALEM, NC 27157-1063 Coordinating center--Postmenopausal estrogen-progestin intervention

R44HL-40256-03 (SSS) SWETTE, LARRY GINER, INC 14 SPRING STREET WALTHAM, MA 02254-9147 Electrochemical generator for in-home oxygen therapy

R01HL-40270-05 (SRC) KALIA, MADHU THOMAS JEFFERSON UNIVERSITY 1020 LOCUST STREET PHILADELPHIA, PA 19107 Respiratory neurons--Neurochemical interrelationships

U01HL-40273-05 (SRC) JUDD, HOWARD L UCLA SCHOOL OF MEDICINE 10833 LE CONTE AVE,22-177,CHS LOS ANGELES, CA 90024-1740 Clinical center--Postmenopausal estrogen-progestin intervention

R44HL-40280-03 (SSS) CLAPPER, DAVID L BIO-METRIC SYSTEMS, INC 9924 WEST 74TH STREET EDEN PRAIRIE, MN 55344 In vivo testing of an improved vascular prosthesis

R01HL-40295-05 (RAP) KELSEN, STEVEN G TEMPLE UNIV HEALTH SCIENCE CTR BROAD & ONTARIO STREETS PHILADELPHIA, PA 19140 Respiratory muscle function in health and disease

R01HL-40296-04 (SAT) KRAMER, GEORGE C UNIV OF TEXAS MED BRANCH GALVESTON, TX 77550-2778 Physiological mechanisms of hypertonic resuscitation

R01HL-40302-04 (RNM) MILLER, JAMES G WASHINGTON UNIVERSITY SKINNER AND LINDELL BOULEVARDS ST LOUIS, MO 63130 Compensating for anisotropy in myocardial ultrasound

R29HL-40305-04 (SB) SUMPIO, BAUER E YALE UNIVERSITY P.O. BOX 3333 NEW HAVEN, CT 06510 Effect of mechanical stress on vascular cells in culture

R01HL-40306-02 (RAP) MOORE, RUSSELL L MILTON S HERSHEY MEDICAL CTR P O BOX 850 HERSHEY, PA 17033 Exercise training and the myocardium -- Cellular adaptations

R01HL-40319-05 (ECS) JACKSON, EDWIN K UNIVERSITY OF PITTSBURGH 623 SCAIFE HALL PITTSBURGH, PA 15261 Physiological role of All-induced adenosine release

R29HL-40320-04 (SB) SCHOLZ, PETER M UMDNJ ONE ROBERT WOOD JOHNSON PLACE NEW BRUNSWICK, NJ 08903 Subendocardial O2 supply and demand in aortic stenosis

R01HL-40327-04 (CVA) SANTAMORE, WILLIAM P PRESBYTERIAN MEDICAL CENTER 39TH AND MARKET STREETS PHILADELPHIA, PA 19104 Right ventricular function

R01HL-40328-04 (HEM) WALKER, FREDERICK J AMER RED CROSS BLOOD SERVICES 209 FARMINGTON AVENUE FARMINGTON, CT 06032 Anticoagulant properties of activated protein C

R29HL-40333-04 (CVA) ANDERSON, KELLEY P UNIVERSITY OF UTAH MEDICAL CTR 50 NORTH MEDICAL DRIVE SALT LAKE CITY, UTAH 84132 Ventricular tachyarrhythmia in left ventricular hypertrophy

PROJECT NO., ORGANIZATIONAL UNIT., INVESTIGATOR, ADDRESS, TITLE

R01HL-40336-03 (RAP) MCCRIMMON, DONALD R NORTHWESTERN UNIVERSITY 303 E. CHICAGO AVE. CHICAGO, IL 60611 Pulmonary afferent processing in ventilatory control

R01HL-40348-04 (BIO) PAUL, SUDHIR UNIVERSITY OF NEBRASKA 600 S 42ND ST. OMAHA, NE 68198-6810 Characterization of the VIP receptor in the lung

R29HL-40349-04 (PTHA) MOSELEY, POPE L UNIVERSITY OF IOWA HOSPITALS IOWA CITY, IOWA 52242 Mechanisms of bleomycin lung disease

R29HL-40352-04 (PTHA) FOX, PAUL LOUIS CLEVELAND CLINIC FOUNDATION 9500 EUCLID AVENUE CLEVELAND, OH 44195 Marine lipids and endothelial cells in atherosclerosis

R29HL-40354-03 (BBCB) KORETSKY, ALAN PAUL CARNEGIE MELLON UNIVERSITY 4400 FIFTH AVE PITTSBURGH, PA 15213 The mechanism of respiratory control in heart

R01HL-40361-03 (SAT) MURRAY, PAUL A JOHNS HOPKINS HOSPITAL 600 NORTH WOLFE STREET BALTIMORE, MD 21205 Mechanisms of vascular regulation in transplanted lung

R01HL-40362-05 (RAP) LAI-FOOK, STEPHEN J UNIVERSITY OF KENTUCKY LEXINGTON, KY 40506-0070 Pulmonary interstitial mechanics

R01HL-40367-04 (PTHA) VAN SCOTT, MICHAEL R EAST CAROLINA UNIVERSITY BRODY BLDG 6N98 GREENVILLE, NC 27858-4354 Pulmonary nonciliated bronchiolar epithelial cells

P01HL-40369-03 (HLBA) FRAZIER, DONALD T UNIVERSITY OF KENTUCKY DEPT PHYSIOLOGY/COLLEGE OF MED LEXINGTON, KY 40536-00840 Respiratory afferents and the control of breathing

P01HL-40369-03 0001 (HLBA) FRAZIER, DONALD T Respiratory afferents and the control of breathing Autogenic reflexes of the diaphram

P01HL-40369-03 0002 (HLBA) REVELETTE, W ROBERT Respiratory afferents and the control of breathing Respiratory related evoked potentials

P01HL-40369-03 0003 (HLBA) LEE, LU-YUAN Respiratory afferents and the control of breathing Reflexogenic effects of cigarette smoke on breathing

P01HL-40369-03 0004 (HLBA) SPECK, DEXTER F Respiratory afferents and the control of breathing Role of brainstem nuclei in the inhibition of inspiration

P01HL-40369-03 0005 (HLBA) DEKIN, MICHAEL S Respiratory afferents and the control of breathing Neuropharmacological organization of the dorsal respiratory group

P01HL-40369-03 0006 (HLBA) LAI, YIH-LOONG Respiratory afferents and the control of breathing New nervous systems in bronchial hypersensitivity

P01HL-40369-03 9001 (HLBA) FRAZIER, DONALD T Respiratory afferents and the control of breathing Technical core

P01HL-40387-04 (HLBB) BENNETT, JOEL S UNIVERSITY OF PENNSYLVANIA 3400 SPRUCE STREET PHILADELPHIA, PA 19104 Regulation of platelet and endothelial cell function

P01HL-40387-04 0001 (HLBB) BENNETT, JOEL S Regulation of platelet and endothelial cell function Platelet membranes and glycoprotein complex

P01HL-40387-04 0002 (HLBB) PONCZ, MORTIMER Regulation of platelet and endothelial cell function Molecular biology of glcoproteins complex

P01HL-40387-04 0003 (HLBB) SHATTIL, SANFORD J Regulation of platelet and endothelial cell function Mechanisms of signal transduction in platelets

P01HL-40387-04 0004 (HLBB) BRASS, LAWRENCE F Regulation of platelet and endothelial cell function Subcellular mechanisms of platelet function

P01HL-40387-04 0005 (HLBB) CINES, DOUGLAS Regulation of platelet and endothelial cell function Immune vascular injury and thrombosis

P01HL-40387-04 0006 (HLBB) SCHREIBER, ALAN D Regulation of platelet and endothelial cell function Biology of platelet fc(gamma) receptors

P01HL-40387-04 9001 (HLBB) HOXIE, JAMES A Regulation of platelet and endothelial cell function Cell culture and hybridoma--core

P01HL-40387-04 9002 (HLBB) SURREY, SAUL Regulation of platelet and endothelial cell function Nucleic acid--protein core facility

R01HL-40392-03 (EDC) PRITCHETT, EDWARD L DUKE UNIVERSITY MEDICAL CENTER BOX 3477 DURHAM, N C 27710 Epidemiology of symptomatic arrhythmias

R29HL-40395-04 (CVA) JOHNSTON, WILLIAM E BOWMAN GRAY SCHOOL OF MEDICINE 300 SOUTH HAWTHORNE ROAD WINSTON-SALEM, NC 27103 Determinants of right ventricular infarction

R29HL-40396-03 (CVA) ECHT, DEBRA S VANDERBILT UNIVERSITY SCH MED 1161 21ST AVENUE SOUTH NASHVILLE, TN 37232 Modulation of ventricular defibrillation by drugs

R01HL-40397-04 (EDC) STAMLER, JEREMIAH NORTHWESTERN UNIV MED SCH 680 N. LAKE SHORE DR. #1102 CHICAGO, IL 60611 5-Yr followup, Gubbio study -- LCT, BP, other variables

R01HL-40399-04A1 (CVA) KEEF, KATHLEEN D UNIVERSITY OF NEVADA ANDERSON BUILDING #115 RENO, NV 89557 Electromechanical coupling in the coronary artery

R01HL-40404-04 (NTN) DECKELBAUM, RICHARD J COLUMBIA UNIVERSITY 630 WEST 168TH ST NEW YORK, NY 10032 Metabolism of intravenous lipid emulsions

R01HL-40411-04 (HEM) LOSCALZO, JOSEPH BRIGHAM AND WOMEN'S HOSPITAL 75 FRANCIS STREET BOSTON, MA 02115 Platelets, platelet aggregates & plasminogen activation

R01HL-40417-02 (CBY) MILLIS, ALBERT J STATE UNIVERSITY OF NEW YORK 1400 WASHINGTON AVE ALBANY, NY 12222 Smooth muscle cell differentiation in vitro

R29HL-40422-04 (CVA) TUNG, LESLIE THE JOHNS HOPKINS UNIVERSITY 720 RUTLAND AVE BALTIMORE, MD 21205 Contractility of isolated hearts cells

R55HL-40423-04 (EDC) D'AGOSTINO, RALPH B BOSTON UNIVERSITY 111 CUMMINGTON ST BOSTON, MA 02215 Decline in cardiovascular mortality -- Framingham 1950-199

R01HL-40424-03 (CVA) TERRACIO, LOUIS UNIVERSITY OF SOUTH CAROLINA SCHOOL OF MEDICINE COLUMBIA, S C 29208 Cardiac hypertrophy--Role of the extracellular matrix

R01HL-40435-02 (HEM) LEVIN, EUGENE G SCRIPPS CLINIC & RES FDN 10666 N TORREY PINES ROAD LA JOLLA, CA 92037 Tissue plasminogen activator from the human endothelium

PROJECT NO., ORGANIZATIONAL UNIT., INVESTIGATOR, ADDRESS, TITLE

R01HL-40445-04 (MET) WATSON, JOHN A UNIV OF CALIF, SAN FRANCISCO 3RD AND PARNASSUS AVENUES SAN FRANCISCO, CA 94143 Sterol dependent regulation of mevalonate synthesis
P01HL-40453-04 (HLBB) WALDER, JOSEPH A UNIVERSITY OF IOWA IOWA CITY, IA 52242 Hemoglobin structure/function & blood substitute design
R01HL-40458-03 (PTHA) FREEMAN, BRUCE A UNIV OF ALABAMA AT BIRM. UNIVERSITY STATION BIRMINGHAM, AL 35294 Reactive oxygen metabolism by the alveolar epithelium
R01HL-40466-04 (BEM) SHAPIRO, DAVID UNIVERSITY OF CALIFORNIA 405 HILGARD AVE LOS ANGELES, CA 90024-1406 Stress & blood pressure – lab & natural settings
R29HL-40467-03 (HEM) CHURCH, WILLIAM R UNIVERSITY OF VERMONT DEPT OF BIOCHEMISTRY BURLINGTON, VT 05405 Definition of functional sites on coagulation Factor X
R01HL-40473-04 (HED) HEYMANN, MICHAEL A UNIV. OF CALIFORNIA 1403-HEALTH SCI EAST SAN FRANCISCO, CA 94143 Perinatal pulmonary circulation–Vasoactive mediators
R29HL-40474-04 (ECS) RUSCH, NANCY J MEDICAL COLLEGE OF WISCONSIN 8701 WATERTOWN PLANK ROAD MILWAUKEE, WI 53226 Vascular muscle calcium currents in hypertension
R29HL-40480-04 (ECS) KAHN, ANDREW M UNIV/TX HLTH SCI CTR HOUSTON MEDICAL SCHOOL PO BOX 20708 HOUSTON, TX 77225 Na influx pathways in VSM sarcolemmal vesicles
R29HL-40483-04 (CVA) FRANZ, MICHAEL R GEORGETOWN UNIVERSITY 3900 RESERVOIR ROAD, NW WASHINGTON, DC 20007 Repolarization mapping of the heart
R01HL-40488-04 (RAP) HOFMAN, WENDELL F MEDICAL COLLEGE OF GEORGIA AUGUSTA. GA 30912 Serotonin and eicosanoid interaction in lung vasomotion
R29HL-40489-04 (EDC) CAULEY, JANE A UNIVERSITY PITTSBURGH 130 DESOTO STREET PITTSBURGH, PA 15260 Epidemiology of apo- and lipo-proteins in elderly women
R01HL-40506-04 (HEM) SANTORO, SAMUEL A WASHINGTON UNIVERSITY 660 S EUCLID AVENUE ST LOUIS, MO 63130 Molecular basis of blood platelet adhesion to collagen
R01HL-40521-04 (PTHA) BASTACKY, SAMUEL J UNIVERSITY OF CALIFORNIA LAWRENCE BERKELEY LABORATORY BERKELEY, CA 94720 The alveolar lining layer in the lung
R29HL-40526-03 (PTHA) WARREN, JEFFERY SCOTT UNIVERSITY OF MICHIGAN 1301 CATHERINE ROAD ANN ARBOR, MI 48109-0602 Monocyte-macrophage cytokines in immune complex lung injury
R01HL-40537-01A3 (RAP) WOOD, STEPHEN C LOVELACE MEDICAL FOUNDATION 2425 RIDGECREST DRIVE/SE ALBUQUERQUE, NM 87108 Mechanism and importance of hypoxia-induced hypothermia
U01HL-40548-03 (CLTR) LEAF, ALEXANDER MASS. GENERAL HOSPITAL 32 FRUIT STREET BOSTON, MA 02114 Do fish oils prevent restenosis post-coronary angioplast
R01HL-40553-01A4 (CVB) BAERTSCHI, ALEX J UNIVERSITY OF VIRGINIA JORDAN HALL BOX 449 CHARLOTTESVILLE, VA 22908 Neural control of ANF in pulmonary hypertension
R01HL-40554-04 (RAP) HASELTON, FREDERICK R VANDERBILT UNIVERSITY BOX 1631 STATION B NASHVILLE, TN 37235 Modulation of lung endothelial permeability by autacoids
R01HL-40561-03 (CVB) ANVERSA, PIERO NEW YORK MEDICAL COLLEGE VOSBURGH PAVILLION VALHALLA, NY 10595 Post-infarction dilated cardiomyopathy
R01HL-40563-03 (HED) FUNDERBURG, FIONA M MEDICAL COLLEGE OF WISCONSIN 8701 WATERTOWN PLANK RD MILWAUKEE, WI 53226 Mesenchymal cell migration during cardiac morphogenesis
R01HL-40566-04 (RNM) BLAUFOX, MORTON D YESHIVA UNIVERSITY 1300 MORRIS PARK AVENUE BRONX, N Y 10461 Nuclear medicine procedures in hypertension
R01HL-40567-04 (RNM) PICKERING, THOMAS G NEW YORK HOSP-CORNELL MED COLL 525 EAST 68TH STREET NEW YORK, N Y 10021 Nuclear medicine procedures in hypertension
R15HL-40568-01A3 (BBCB) SNOW, JULIAN W PHILADELPHIA COLL OF PHARM & S 43RD STREET & WOODLAND AVENUE PHILADELPHIA, PA 19104 Cholesteryl ester fluidity in atherosclerosis research
R01HL-40572-02 (ECS) SPERELAKIS, NICHOLAS UNIVERSITY OF CINCINNATI COLLEGE OF MEDICINE CINCINNATI, OH Regulation of ion channels in vascular smooth muscle
R29HL-40573-03 (HEM) SHIH, DANIEL T B OREGON HEALTH SCIENCES UNIV 3181 S W SAM JACKSON PARK ROAD PORTLAND, OR 97201 Site-directed mutagenetic study of hemoglobin function
R29HL-40576-03 (HEM) MILLER, BARBARA A MILTON S HERSHEY MEDICAL CTR P O BOX 850 HERSHEY, PA 17033 Mechanism of action of hematopoietic growth factors
R01HL-40583-02 (PHRA) GREEN, RICHARD D UNIVERSITY OF ILLINOIS 835 SOUTH WOLCOTT AVENUE CHICAGO, IL 60612 Characterization of cardiac adenosine receptors
R01HL-40584-04 (BEM) SHAPIRO, DAVID UNIVERSITY OF CALIFORNMIA 405 HILGARD AVE LOS ANGELES, CA 90024-1406 Evaluation of drug and behavioral control of hypertension
R29HL-40586-05 (PHRA) KIM, DONGHEE UNIVERSITY OF HEALTH SCIENCES 3333 GREEN BAY ROAD NORTH CHICAGO, IL 60064 Ph and myocardial contractility
R29HL-40587-04 (EDC) COULTAS, DAVID B UNIVERSITY OF NEW MEXICO 2211 LOMAS, NE ALBUQUERQUE, NM 87131 The epidemiology of interstitial lung disease
R29HL-40603-03 (CBY) RETTENMIER, CARL W CHILDRENS HOSPITAL OF LA 4650 SUNSET BLVD BOX 103 LOS ANGELES, CA 90027 The CSF-1 growth factor
R29HL-40608-03 (PHRA) BENNETT, PAUL B VANDERBILT UNIVERSITY SCHOOL OF MEDICINE NASHVILLE, TN 37232 Antiarrhythmic drugs–Single channel blocking mechanisms
R01HL-40609-04 (SB) PLONSEY, ROBERT DUKE UNIVERSITY 136 ENGINEERING SCHOOL DURHAM, NC 27706 Model study of electromagnetic cardiac activation
R29HL-40613-04 (EDC) BOERWINKLE, ERIC UNIVERSITY OF TEXAS POST OFFICE BOX 20334 HOUSTON, TX 77225 Epidemiology of genetic factors in lipid metabolism
R29HL-40615-02 (HEM) MOON, DUDLEY G ALBANY MEDICAL COLLEGE 47 NEW SCOTLAND AVE ALBANY, NY 12208 Adhesive glycoproteins in platelet-leukocyte contacts

PROJECT NO., ORGANIZATIONAL UNIT., INVESTIGATOR, ADDRESS, TITLE

R01HL-40619-04 (EDC) ROSNER, BERNARD A CHANNING LABORATORY 180 LONGWOOD AVENUE BOSTON, MA 02115 Analysis of longitudinal cardiopulmonary data
R29HL-40624-04 (ECS) NAVRAN, STEPHEN S BAYLOR COLLEGE OF MEDICINE ONE BAYLOR PLAZA HOUSTON, TX 77030 Alpha adrenergic regulation of the vascular na pump
R29HL-40628-04 (EDC) PSATY, BRUCE M UNIVERSITY OF WASHINGTON 325 NINTH AVENUE, ZA-60 SEATTLE, WA 98104 Postmenopausal progestins and the risk of coronary disease
R29HL-40637-04 (MET) RAINWATER, DAVID L S W FOUNDATION FOR BIOMED RES P O BOX 28147 SAN ANTONIO, TX 78284-0147 Lp(a) phenotype atherosclerosis in the baboon
R29HL-40659-04 (CVB) KOHTZ, DONALD S CUNY MOUNT SINAI SCHOOL OF MED 1 GUSTAVE L LEVY PLACE NEW YORK, NY 10029 Growth and differentiation of cardioblasts
R29HL-40667-05 (CVA) KADISH, ALAN H NORTHWESTERN UNIVERSITY 215 E. CHICAGO AVENUE, STE 711 CHICAGO, IL 60611 Vector mapping of myocardial activation
R29HL-40679-04 (CVB) MAGID, NORMAN M CORNELL UNIV MEDICAL COLLEGE 1300 YORK AVENUE NEW YORK, N. Y. 10021 Regulation of cardiac mass in aortic regurgitation
R01HL-40685-03 (SRC) SECKER-WALKER, ROGER H UNIV OF VERMONT-HLTH PROMO RES 235 ROWELL BUILDING BURLINGTON, VT 05405 Community coalitions to help women quit smoking
R01HL-40695-03 (CVB) KEHRER, JAMES P UNIVERSITY OF TEXAS DEPARTMENT OF PHARMACOLOGY AUSTIN, TX 78712-1074 Toxicity of cardiac hypoxia and reoxygenation
R29HL-40696-04 (SB) FRANGOS, JOHN A PENNSYLVANIA STATE UNIVERSITY 149 FENSKE BLDG. UNIVERSITY PARK, PA 16802 Shear stress activation of endothelial membrane function
R29HL-40702-03 (CVA) ANDERSON, PETER G UNIV OF ALABAMA AT BIRMINGHAM VOLKER HALL G-023, UNIV STN BIRMINGHAM, AL 35294 Ischemic and reperfusion injury in cardiac hypertrophy
R01HL-40711-03 (CVB) KOZLOVSKIS, PATRICIA L UNIVERSITY OF MIAMI PO BOX 016960/MED, CARDIO R-94 MIAMI, FL 33101 Regional biochemical changes in healed MI
R29HL-40718-01A3 (ECS) ZUKOWSKA - GROJEC, ZOFIA GEORGETOWN UNIVERSITY 3900 RESERVOIR ROAD NW WASHINGTON, DC 20007 Gender and neuropeptide Y–Adrenergic interactions
R01HL-40722-13 (HEM) ZANJANI, ESMAIL D UNIVERSITY OF NEVADA, RENO DEPT. OF INTERNAL MEDICINE RENO, NEVADA 89557 Regulation of fetal and adult erythropoiesis
R44HL-40740-03 (SSS) TAKEUCHI, ESTHER S WILSON GREATBATCH LTD 10000 WEHRLE DRIVE CLARENCE, NY 14031 Rechargeable lithium battery/ventricular assist systems
R44HL-40752-03 (SSS) CLARK, JUSTIN S MEDICAL PHYSICS, INC 401 12TH AVENUE SALT LAKE CITY, UT 84103 Pressure enhanced oximetry & combined pressure monitor
R44HL-40772-03 (SSS) WINGET, RODNER R BIOMARINE TECHNOLOGIES, INC. PO BOX 20159 SEATTLE, WA 98102 Eicosapentaenoic acid–Algae culture technology
R44HL-40775-03 (SSS) BARLOW, CLYDE H BARLOW SCIENTIFIC, INC. 6307 TAMOSHAN DR NW OLYMPIA, WA 98502 Digital imaging for skin graft viability
P50HL-40784-03 (SRC) REPINE, JOHN E WEBB-WARING LUNG INSTITUTE BOX C322, 4200 E NINTH AVE DENVER, COLO 80262 SCOR in adult respiratory failure
P50HL-40784-03 0001 (SRC) REPINE, JOHN E SCOR in adult respiratory failure Neutrophil and oxygen metabolite mediated lung endothelial injury
P50HL-40784-03 0002 (SRC) WORTHEN, G SCOTT SCOR in adult respiratory failure Neutrophil localization to pulmonary capillaries in ARDS
P50HL-40784-03 0003 (SRC) LINAS, STUART L SCOR in adult respiratory failure Acute renal failure in ARDS
P50HL-40784-03 0004 (SRC) PARSONS, POLLY SCOR in adult respiratory failure The pathogenesis of ARDS
P50HL-40784-03 9003 (SRC) PARSONS, POLLY SCOR in adult respiratory failure CORE–Clinical
R29HL-40796-04 (HEM) WIEDMER, THERESE OKLAHOMA MEDICAL RESEARCH FDN 825 NORTHEAST THIRTEENTH ST OKLAHOMA CITY, OK 73104 Platelet procoagulant activity & C3/C5-activation
R01HL-40800-03 (CVA) GILMOUR, ROBERT F JR CORNELL UNIVERSITY VETERINARY RESEARCH TOWER ITHACA, NY 14853-6401 Phase resetting of circus movement reentry
R29HL-40801-04 (HEM) TAIT, JONATHAN F SEATTLE, WA 98195 SB-10 Characterization of placental anticoagulant protein
R01HL-40802-04 (HED) BLAND, RICHARD D UNIVERSITY OF UTAH 50 NORTH MEDICAL DRIVE SALT LAKE CITY, UT 84132 Perinatal pulmonary microcirculation & lung fluid
R01HL-40819-02 (PTHA) FALCONE, DOMENICK J CORNELL MEDICAL COLLEGE 1300 YORK AVENUE NEW YORK, NY 10021 Modified-LDL regulates macrophage plasminogen activation
R01HL-40822-04 (MET) CHANG, TA-YUAN DARTMOUTH MEDICAL SCHOOL HANOVER, N H 03756 Regulatory cell mutants in cholesterol biosynthesis
R29HL-40832-04 (MET) HARRIS, WILLIAM S UNIVERSITY OF KANSAS MED CTR 39TH AND RAINBOW BLVD KANSAS CITY, KS 66103 Fish oils & lipoprotein metabolism
R01HL-40837-03 (SSS) DWORKIN, BARRY R PENNSYLVANIA STATE UNIVERSITY P O BOX 850 HERSHEY, PA 17033 Control of vascular tone by contingents CNS stimulation
R01HL-40844-02 (EDC) KAHN, HENRY S EMORY UNIVERSITY 1599 CLIFTON RD NE ATLANTA, GA 30329 IHD incidence & indices of body-fat distribution
R01HL-40848-04 (EDC) ECKFELDT, JOHN H UNIV OF MINNESOTA HOSP & CLIN BOX 198 420 DELAWARE ST S E MINNEAPOLIS, MN 55455 Epidemiology of plasma fatty acids and atherosclerosis
R01HL-40858-03 (HEM) JAMIESON, GRAHAM A AMERICAN RED CROSS 15601 CRABBS BRANCH WAY ROCKVILLE, MD 20855 Role of platelet GPIV as an adhesion receptor

PROJECT NO., ORGANIZATIONAL UNIT., INVESTIGATOR, ADDRESS, TITLE

R01HL-40860-04 (HEM) THIAGARAJAN, PERUMAL HARBORVIEW MEDICAL CTR 325 9TH AVENUE SEATTLE, WA 98104 Platelet-fibrinogen interactions
R01HL-40865-04 (RNM) EIGLER, NEAL L CEDARS-SINAI MEDICAL CENTER 8700 BEVERLY BLVD. LOS ANGELES, CA 90048 Digital angiographic analysis of myocardial perfusion
R29HL-40871-03 (PTHA) WEWERS, MARK D OHIO STATE UNIVERSITY HOSPITAL 1654 UPHAM DRIVE COLUMBUS, OH 43210 Regulation of macrophage interleukin-1 beta production
R01HL-40872-03 (HED) CHAUDHURI, GAUTAM UNIV OF CALIFORNIA SCHOOL OF M 10833 LECONTE AVENUE LOS ANGELES, CA 90024 EDRF and prostacyclin in human umbilical vessels
R01HL-40875-04 (HEM) SCHAPIRA, MARC M VANDERBILT UNIVERSITY 21ST & GARLAND NASHVILLE, TN 37232 Pathophysiology of the blood coagulation-kinin system
R29HL-40878-04 (NEUA) VAN WYLEN, DAVID G S U N Y OF N Y, CLIN CTR BLDG 462 GRIDER ST BUFFALO, N Y 14215 The role of adenosine in cerebral blood flow regulation
R01HL-40880-05 (CVA) RUSSELL, BRENDA R MD PHD UNIV OF ILLINOIS AT CHICAGO BOX 6998 CHICAGO, IL 60680 Subcellular mRNA distribution in cardiac myocytes
R01HL-40881-03 (RAP) LYDIC, RALPH PENNSYLVANIA STATE UNIVERSITY P O BOX 850 HERSHEY, PA 17033 Cholinergic mechanisms of breathing during sleep
R29HL-40889-03 (SB) OURIEL, KENNETH UNIVERSITY OF ROCHESTER 601 ELMWOOD AVE/SURGERY DPT ROCHESTER, NY 14642 Venous thrombosis -- Blood-intimal interactions
R01HL-40892-04 (CVB) FORMAN, MERVYN B VANDERBILT UNIVERSITY NASHVILLE, TN 37232-2170 Role of adenosine in myocardial reperfusion injury
R01HL-40894-02 (RAP) RHOADES, RODNEY A INDIANA UNIV SCHOOL OF MED 635 BARNHILL DRIVE INDIANAPOLIS, IN 46202-5120 Hypoxia-induced changes in the pulmonary arterial muscle
R01HL-40899-03 (HED) ROSS, MICHAEL G HARBOR-UCLA MEDICAL CENTER 1124 WEST CARSON STREET TORRANCE, CA 90502 Maternal dehydration--Fetal and amniotic fluid homeostasis
R01HL-40901-04 (HEM) BALDASSARE, JOSEPH J ST LOUIS UNIV MED CENTER 3635 VISTA AVE AT GRAND BLVD ST LOUIS, MO 63110-0250 Characterization soluble phospholipase C from platelets
R01HL-40910-04 (RAP) KAUFMAN, MARC P UNIVERSITY OF CA DAVIS MED CTR 4301 X STREET SACRAMENTO, CA 95817 Control of airway caliber during exercise
R01HL-40914-02 (HED) WILKES, BARRY M NORTH SHORE UNIVERSITY HOSP 300 COMMUNITY DRIVE MANHASSET, NY 11030 Vascular thromboxane receptors in human placenta
R01HL-40916-02 (EDC) BIXLER, EDWARD O PENNSYLVANIA STATE UNIVERSITY PO BOX 850 HERSHEY, PA 17033 Sleep apnea: age effects on prevalence & natural history
R01HL-40921-04 (HEM) LOLLAR, JOHN S EMORY UNIVERSITY DRAWER AR Structure/function of F-VIII-Willebrand factor complex
R01HL-40922-02 (PHRA) IGNARRO, LOUIS J UNIVERSITY OF CALIFORNIA 23 278 CHS LOS ANGELES, CA 90024-1735 Pharmacodynamics of endothelium-derived nitric oxide
R01HL-40926-04 (HEM) NEWMAN, PETER J BLOOD CTR OF SOUTHEASTERN WISC 1701 WEST WISCONSIN AVENUE MILWAUKEE, WI 53233 Molecular biology and function of PECAM-1
R01HL-40929-04 (MET) COOK, GEORGE A UNIVERSITY OF TENNESSEE 874 UNION AVENUE MEMPHIS, TENN 38163 Regulation of hepatic fatty acid oxidation
R01HL-40930-02 (EDC) KRIPKE, DANIEL F UNIV OF CALIFORNIA SAN DIEGO LA JOLLA, CA 92093 Age-related prevalence of sleep respiratory disturbances
R01HL-40944-03 (TOX) WILSON, BARBARA D ALBERT EINSTEIN MEDICAL CTR 5501 OLD YORK RD PHILADELPHIA, PA 91941-3098 Pathogenesis of amiodarone-induced pulmonary toxicity
R29HL-40945-03 (TOX) BASCOM, REBECCA UNIV OF MARYLAND MSTF-800/10 S PINE ST BALTIMORE, MD 21201 Respiratory sensitivity to environmental tobacco smoke
R29HL-40953-04 (CVA) BARSOTTI, ROBERT J BOCKUS RESEARCH INST. ONE GRADUATE PLAZA PHILDELPHIA, PA 19146 Mechanism of cardiac muscle contraction
R01HL-40959-04 (RAP) SMITH, JEFFREY C UCLA, DEPT OF KINESIOLOGY SLICHTER HALL/405 HILGARD AVE LOS ANGELES, CA 90024-1568 In vitro studies of the neural control of breathing
P01HL-40962-04 (HLBB) MANUCK, STEPHEN B UNIVERSITY OF PITTSBURGH 626 OLD ENGINEERING HALL PITTSBURGH, PA 15260 Biobehavioral studies of cardiovascular disease
P01HL-40962-04 0001 (HLBB) KAPLAN, JAY R Biobehavioral studies of cardiovascular disease Atherosclerosis, exercise, reactivity and behavior
P01HL-40962-04 0002 (HLBB) MANUCK, STEPHEN B Biobehavioral studies of cardiovascular disease Hypertension risk, reactivity and behavior
P01HL-40962-04 0003 (HLBB) JACOB, ROLF G Biobehavioral studies of cardiovascular disease Ambulatory measurement, reactivity and behavior
P01HL-40962-04 0004 (HLBB) MANUCK, STEPHEN Biobehavioral studies of cardiovascular disease Antihypertensive drug effects on behvior and reactivity
P01HL-40962-04 9001 (HLBB) JENNINGS, J RICHARD Biobehavioral studies of cardiovascular disease Core--Instrumentation
P01HL-40962-04 9002 (HLBB) JACOB, ROLF G Biobehavioral studies of cardiovascular disease CORE--Statistics
R29HL-40963-03 (ECS) BENOIT, JOSEPH N LOUISIANA STATE UNIV MED CTR SHREVEPORT, LA 71130-3932 Physiology of the mesenteric lymphatic pump
R29HL-40967-04 (RNM) KRAFT, KENNETH A VIRGINA COMMONWEALTH UNI BOX 72 MCV STATION RICHMOND, VA 23298-0072 Quantitation of vascular flow patterns using NMR imaging
R01HL-40986-02 (RAP) KING, RICHARD J UNIVERSITY OF TEXAS 7703 FLOYD CURL DRIVE SAN ANTONIO, TX 78284-7756 Epithelial-mesenchymal interactions among lung cells
R01HL-40987-03 (RAP) MORRIS, RANDAL E UNIVERSITY OF CINCINNATI 231 BETHESDA AVE/DEPT CELL BIO CINCINNATI, OH 45267-0521 Endocytic uptake of surfactant in the developing lung
R01HL-40990-04 (PC) WALSH, KENNETH A UNIVERSITY OF WASHINGTON DEPT. OF BIOCHEMISTRY, SJ-70 SEATLE, WA 98195 Structural organization of von Willebrand factor

PROJECT NO., ORGANIZATIONAL UNIT., INVESTIGATOR, ADDRESS, TITLE

R01HL-40992-04 (ECS) SINGER, HAROLD A GEISINGER CLINIC NORTH ACADEMY AVE DANVILLE, PA 17822 Protein kinase C activation in arterial smooth muscle
R01HL-40998-04 (ECS) WITTENBERG, BEATRICE A ALBERT EINSTEIN COLL OF MED 1300 MORRIS PARK AVE BRONX, NY 10461 Carrier-mediated O2 transport in isolated heart cells
R01HL-41002-04 (HEM) WAGNER, DENISA D NEW ENGLAND MEDICAL CENTER 750 WASHINGTON ST, BOX 832 BOSTON, MA 02111 Von Willerbrand factor processing & role in hemostasis
R29HL-41008-04 (RAP) SICA, ANTHONY L SCHNEIDER CHILDRENS HOSPITAL L 270-05 76TH AVE. NEW HYDE PARK, NY 11042 Postnatal development of respiratory activities in pigs
R01HL-41009-04 (RAP) SOLWAY, JULIAN UNIVERSITY OF CHICAGO 5841 SOUTH MARYLAND AVENUE CHICAGO, IL 60637 Mechanisms of airflow obstruction
R29HL-41012-04 (HED) ABMAN, STEVEN H UNIV OF COLORADO HLTH SCIS CTR 4200 E NINTH AVENUE DENVER, CO 80262 Mechanisms of abnormal perinatal vasoreactivity
R01HL-41016-03 (EDC) MULLER, JAMES E NEW ENGLAND DEACONESS HOSPITAL 185 PILGRIM ROAD BOSTON, MA 02215 Determinants of the onset of myocardial infarction
R29HL-41026-04 (CVB) SEGAL, STEVEN S THE PENNSYLVANIA STATE UNIV. 119 NOLL LABORATORY UNIVERSITY PARK, PA 16802 functional hyperemia;
R29HL-41028-04 (CVB) BENJAMIN, BRUCE A DUKE UNIVERSITY P O BOX 3709 DURHAM, N C 27710 Atrial natriuretic factor in the conscious monkey
R29HL-41031-04 (PHRA) SHIBATA, ERWIN F UNIVERSITY OF IOWA 5-610 BOWEN SCIENCE BUILDING IOWA CITY, IA 52242 Transmitter modulation of repolarization in heart
R29HL-41033-02 (PHRA) STUREK, MICHAEL S UNIVERSITY OF MISSOURI DALTON RESEARCH CENTER COLUMBIA, MO 65211 Pharmacology of coronary artery calcium channels
R01HL-41035-02 (SSS) SUAREZ, BRIAN K WASHINGTON UNIVERSITY 660 SOUTH EUCLID AVE BOX 8134 ST LOUIS, MO 63110 A linkage study of long qt syndrome in an amish kindred
R01HL-41038-04 (PBC) BALIAN, GARY UNIVERSITY OF VIRGINIA DEPT OF ORTHOPAEDICS, BOX 374 CHARLOTTESVILLE, VA 22908 Small collagen in hemopoietic cell stroma
R29HL-41039-04 (EDC) VOLLMER, WILLIAM M CAISER FOUNDATION HOSPITALS 4610 S. E. BELMONT ST PORTLAND, OR 97215 The clinical epidemiology of asthma in an HMO
R29HL-41040-04 (PTHA) PARKS, WILLIAM C WASHINGTON UNIVERSITY 216 S. KINGSHIGHWAY BLVD. ST. LOUIS, MO 63110 Characterization of tropoelastin isoforms
R01HL-41046-03 (RNM) GREENLEAF, JAMES F MAYO FOUNDATION 200 FIRST STREET SOUTHWEST ROCHESTER, MN 55902 Multidimensional heart imaging with ultrasound
R01HL-41047-03 (RNM) SCHWAIGER, MARKUS UNIVERSITY OF MICHIGAN 1500 EAST MEDICAL CENTER DRIVE ANN ARBOR, MI 48109-0028 PET in acute myocardial infarction
R29HL-41071-03 (PTHA) FISHER, RORY A UNIVERSITY OF IOWA COLL OF MED IOWA CITY, IA 52242 Platelet activating factor and thromboxanes in liver
R01HL-41074-04 (NTN) KRAMSCH, DIETER M UNIVERSITY OF SOUTHERN CA HMR 804 2011 ZONAL AVENUE LOS ANGELES, CA 90033 Vascular/metabolic effects of repeat weight loss/regain
R01HL-41075-04 (PTHA) ROVAINEN, CARL M WASHINGTON UNIVERSITY 660 S EUCLID AVE, BOX 8228 ST LOUIS, MO 63110 Models for brain angiogenesis
R29HL-41084-04 (PHY) KOTLIKOFF, MICHAEL I UNIVERSITY OF PENNSYLVANIA 3800 SPRUCE STREET PHILADELPHIA, PA 19104-6046 Ion channels in airway smooth muscle
R01HL-41086-02 (SRC) CONNELLY, DONALD P UNIVERSITY OF MINNESOTA BOX 511 UMHC/420 DELEWARE ST S MINNEAPOLIS, MN 55455 Effect of an expert system on platelet transfusion
R01HL-41087-04 (SB) SMITH, PETER K DUKE UNIVERSITY MEDICAL CENTER BOX 3442 DURHAM, NC 27710 Atrioventricular interactions related to cardiac surgery
R01HL-41088-04 (PHRA) VAGHY, PAL L UNIVERSITY OF CINCINNATI 231 BETHESDA AVENUE CINCINNATI, OHIO 45267-0575 Receptors for calcium channel inhibitors
R01HL-41097-03 (SRC) LEVENKRON, JEFFREY C UNIVERSITY OF ROCHESTER 300 CRITTENDEN BLVD ROCHESTER, NY 14642 Evaluating clinical skills in preventive cardiology
R01HL-41103-04 (SRC) REIDY, MICHAEL A UNIVERSITY OF WASHINGTON SEATTLE, WA 98195 Smooth muscle cell proliferation in vascular grafts
R01HL-41104-05 (SRC) RAMIREZ, FRANCESCO MT SINAI SCHOOL OF MEDICINE ONE GUSTAVE L LEVY PLACE NEW YORK, N Y 10029 Control of collagen gene expression in lung fibrosis
R01HL-41119-01A1 (ECS) ANDRESEN, MICHAEL C UNIV OF TEXAS MED BRANCH 301 UNIVERSITY BLVD GALVESTON, TX 77550-2774 Transmission across first synapse of the baroreflex
R01HL-41129-03 (RAP) ROSELLI, ROBERT J VANDERBILT UNIVERSITY BOX 36, STATION B NASHVILLE, TN 37235 An optical measure of lung vascular filtration
R29HL-41130-04 (CVA) HUMPHREY, JAY D UNIVERSITY OF MARYLAND BALTIMORE COUNTY CAMPUS BALTIMORE, MD 21228 Regional mechanical properties of passive heart tissue
R29HL-41132-04 (RAP) ALLEN, JULIAN L ST CHRISTOPHER'S HOSPITAL 5TH ST & LEHIGH AVE PHILADELPHIA, PA 19133 Thoracoabdominal asynchrony in infant airway obstruction
R01HL-41135-04 (SRC) RUDEL, LAWRENCE L BOWMAN GRAY SCH OF MED MEDICAL CENTER BLVD WINSTON-SALEM, NC 27517 Dietary cholesterol effects on lipoprotein metabolism
R29HL-41155-04 (RAD) RUBIN, DAVID B RUSH-PRESBYTERIAN-ST. LUKE'S 1725 W HARRISON, #350 CHICAGO, IL 60612 Endothelial cell cycle antioxidants and radiation
R01HL-41156-03 (CVB) RAMSAY, DAVID J UNIVERSITY OF CALIFORNIA MEDICAL SCI BLDG, BOX 0400 SAN FRANCISCO, CA 94143 Inhibitory left atrial influences on the baroreflex

U01HL-41166-02 (SRC) LABARTHE, DARWIN R UNIV OF TEXAS HEATLH SCI CENTE PO BOX 20186 HOUSTON, TX 77225 Pediatric epidemiology of CVD risk factors--US/Japan

R29HL-41169-03 (RAP) MANAKER, SCOTT HOSPITAL OF THE UNIV OF PENN 3600 SPRUCE STREET PHILADELPHIA, PA 19104-4283 Neurochemical integration of respiration in the NTS

R01HL-41175-04 (SRC) SCHWARTZ, COLIN J UNIVERSITY OF TEXAS 7703 FLOYD CURL DRIVE SAN ANTONIO, TEX 78284 Vascular healing--Cell biology and rheologic factors

R01HL-41178-03 (SB) GRAHAM, LINDA M VA MEDICAL CENTER 10701 EAST BOULEVARD CLEVELAND, OH 44106 Role of endothelium in graft intimal hyperplasia

R01HL-41180-05 (SRC) BROCK, TOMMY A UNIV OF ALABAMA AT BIRMINGHAM UAB STATION BIRMINGHAM, AL 35294 Receptor signaling in polyploid vascular smooth muscle

R01HL-41187-04 (SRC) KARINO, TAKESHI MCGILL UNIVERSITY MED CLINIC 1650 CEDAR AVENUE MONTREAL, QUEBEC, CANADA Rheologic and geometric factors in vascular homeostasis

R01HL-41188-04 (SRC) SCHEID, CHERYL R UNIV OF MASSACHUSETTS MED SCH 55 LAKE AVE NORTH WORCESTER, MA 01655 Changes in ion transport in hypertension--Role of pH

R01HL-41196-04 (SRC) SAGE, E HELENE UNIVERSITY OF WASHINGTON SCHOOL OF MEDICINE SEATTLE, WA 98195 Regulation of collagen gene expression in lung fibrosis

R01HL-41199-04 (SRC) PATSCH, WOLFGANG P BAYLOR COLLEGE OF MEDICINE 6565 FANNIN, MAIL STATION A601 HOUSTON, TEX 77030 Cholesterol-rich diet and plasma lipid transport

R01HL-41200-04 (SRC) SACHDEV, GOVERDHAN P UNIVERSITY OF OKLAHOMA 1110 N. STONEWALL, BX 26901 OKLAHOMA CITY, OKLA 73190 Biochemical & molecular biological studies of airway mucins

R01HL-41206-04 (SRC) SCARPA, ANTONIO CWRU SCHOOL OF MEDICINE 2119 ABINGTON ROAD CLEVELAND, OH 44106 Channel regulation in normal/hypertensive smooth muscle

R01HL-41210-04 (SRC) IVES, HARLAN E UNIVERSITY OF CALIFORNIA 1065 HEALTH SCIENCES E TOWER SAN FRANCISCO, CALIF 94143 G proteins, ion transport, and growth of vascular cells

R01HL-41212-03 (SRC) MILLER, ARTHUR D FRED HUTCHINSON CANCER RES CTR 1124 COLUMBIA STREET SEATTLE, WASH 98104-1124 Hemophilia treatment by clotting factor gene transfer

R01HL-41213-02 (PTHA) EVANS, JOHN N UNIVERSITY OF VERMONT BURLINGTON, VT 05045 Molecular signals in pulmonary hypertension

R01HL-41214-04 (SRC) JIMENEZ, SERGIO A THOMAS JEFFERSON UNIVERSITY 1020 LOCUST STREET PHILADELPHIA, PA 19107 Lung fibrosis--Mechanisms of collagen gene expression

R01HL-41216-05 (SRC) ELIAS, JACK A YALE UNIVERSITY 333 CEDAR STREET NEW HAVEN, CT 06510 Mechanisms of cytokine regulation of fibroblast collagen

R01HL-41221-04 (SRC) HOROWITZ, BERNARD NEW YORK BLOOD CENTER 310 EAST 67TH STREET NEW YORK, N Y 10021 Inactivation of HIV and other transfusion-transmitted viruses in blood

R01HL-41222-04 (SRC) LYNCH, DENNIS C DANA-FARBER CANCER INSTITUTE 44 BINNEY STREET BOSTON, MA 02115 Development of a synthetic von Willebrand factor

R01HL-41224-04 (SRC) FIELDING, CHRISTOPHER J UNIVERSITY OF CALIFORNIA 505 PARNASSUS AVENUE SAN FRANCISCO, CA 94143-0130 Dietary cholesterol effects on plasma lipoproteins

R01HL-41225-04 (SRC) FRY, DONALD L OHIO STATE UNIVERSITY 400 WEST 12TH AVE-2025 WISEMAN COLUMBUS, OHIO 43210 Vascular healing--Cell and rheologic factors

R01HL-41250-04 (SRC) GROSS, RICHARD W WASHINGTON UNIV SCHOOL OF MED 660 SOUTH EUCLID AVENUE ST LOUIS, MO 63110 Lipid mediators of signal transduction in smooth muscle

R01HL-41256-04 (SRC) KUSHWAHA, RAMPRATAP S SOUTHWEST FDN FOR BIOM RES P O BOX 28147 SAN ANTONIO, TX 78228-0147 Effects of dietary cholesterol on lipoprotein metabolism

R01HL-41264-04 (SRC) DE CROMBRUGGHE, BENOIT U. OF TEXAS SYSTEM CANCER CTR. 1515 HOLCOMBE HOUSTON, TEXAS 77030 Control of type I & III collagen genes in lung fibrosis

R01HL-41267-04 (SRC) ZARINS, CHRISTOPHER K UNIVERSITY OF CHICAGO 5841 SOUTH MARYLAND CHICAGO, IL 60637 Biomechanical factors in anastomotic intimal hyperplasia

R01HL-41272-04 (SRC) GREISLER, HOWARD P LOYOLA UNIVERSITY 2160 SOUTH FIRST AVENUE MAYWOOD, IL 60141 Growth factor mediation of healing of vascular grafts

R01HL-41277-04 (SRC) GERARD, CRAIG J CHILDREN'S HOSPITAL CORPORATIO 300 LONGWOOD AVENUE BOSTON, MA 02115 Structure & regulation of human lung mucus glucoprotein

R01HL-41281-02 (SAT) COOPER, JOEL D WASHINGTON UNIVERSITY 660 S EUCLID AVE ST LOUIS, MO 63110 Lung preservation for transplantation

R29HL-41287-04 (RNM) PEARLMAN, JUSTIN D MASSACHUSETTS GENERAL HOSPITAL CARDIAC UNIT-BULLFINCH 4 BOSTON, MA 02114 Atheroma detection using nuclear magnetic resonance

R01HL-41290-03 (RAP) MARTIN, WADE H 4566 SCOTT AVENUE BOX 8046 ST LOUIS, MO 63110 Skeletal muscle adrenergic receptor pathophysiology

R01HL-41295-02 (CVB) TUCK, MICHAEL L VA MEDICAL CENTER 16111 PLUMMER STREET SEPULVEDA, CA 91343 Lipoxygenase pathway and vascular effect of ang II

R01HL-41303-04 (PHRA) CLAPHAM, DAVID E MAYO FOUNDATION 200 FIRST STREET SOUTHWEST ROCHESTER, MN 55905 G protein coupling of muscarinic receptors

R01HL-41307-03 (PHRA) BRUNTON, LAURENCE L UNIV OF CALIFORNIA, SAN DIEGO LA JOLLA, CALIF 92093 Cyclic AMP metabolism in cardiac myocytes

R01HL-41312-04 (PTHA) ROSE, RICHARD M NEW ENGLAND DEACONESS HOSPITAL 185 PILGRIM ROAD BOSTON, MA 02215 The role of macrophage CSFS in respiratory biology

R01HL-41313-04 (CVB) THRASHER, TERRY N UNIVERSITY OF CALIFORNIA PARNASSUS AVENUE SAN FRANCISCO, CA 94143 Neural and humoral mechanisms during hypovolemia

R01HL-41315-04 (PHRA) HOFFMAN, BRIAN B VA HOSPITAL 3801 MIRANDA AVE PALO ALTO, CA 94304 Desensitization of alpha-1 adrenergic receptor responses

R01HL-41320-04 (PBC) FISHER, JAMES H UNIV OF COLORADO HLTH SCI CTR 4200 EAST NINTH AVE, BOX C272 DENVER, CO 80262 Regulation of the pulmonary surfactant protein genes

R01HL-41323-04 (SRC) CARLSON, DON M UNIVERSITY OF CALIFORNIA DAVIS, CA 95616 Tracheal mucins-Molecular biology and structure analysis

R01HL-41330-03 (SRC) WING, RENA R WESTERN PSY INST & CLINIC 3811 O'HARA STREET PITTSBURGH, PA 15213 Dietary intervention methods for clinical trials

R01HL-41332-03 (SRC) JEFFERY, ROBERT W UNIVERSITY OF MINNESOTA 515 DELAWARE STREET, SE MINNEAPOLIS, MN 55455 Dietary intervention methods for clinical trials

R01HL-41341-03 (HEM) MEISELMAN, HERBERT J USC SCHOOL OF MEDICINE 2025 ZONAL AVENUE LOS ANGELES, CA 90033 Hemorheology in sickle cell anemia and related disorders

R01HL-41347-04 (ECS) PEARCE, WILLIAM J WHITE MEMORIAL MEDICAL CTR 1720 BROOKLYN AVENUE LOS ANGELES, CA 90033 Mechanisms of hypoxic cerebral vasodilatation in newborns

R55HL-41357-04 (NTN) HARKER, LAURENCE ARDELL EMORY UNIVERSITY DRAWER AR ATLANTA, GA 30322 Dietary omega 3 fatty acids--Thrombosis/vascular healing

R01HL-41358-03 (SAT) ASHRAF, MUHAMMAD UNIV OF CINCINNATI MED CTR 231 BETHESDA AVE CINCINNATI, OH 45267 O2 radicals-mediated cardiac injury during Ca++ paradox

R29HL-41366-01A2 (PTHA) DORINSKY, PAUL M OHIO STATE UNIVERSITY 1654 UPHAM DRIVE COLUMBUS, OH 43210 Pathogenesis of nonpulmonary organ failure in ARDS

R01HL-41370-04 (BPN) SIEGEL, JEROME M UNIVERSITY OF CALIFORNIA 405 HILGARD AVE LOS ANGELES, CALIF 90024 Location and control of medullary neurons mediating atonia

R01HL-41371-04 (RAP) HENDRICKS, JOAN C VETERINARY HOSPITAL 3850 SPRUCE STREET PHILADELPHIA, PA 19104 Neural inhibition and rem sleep disordered breathing

R29HL-41372-04 (CVB) TRUSKEY, GEORGE A DUKE UNIVERSITY DURHAM, NC 27706 Hemodynamics and LDL permeability in the arterial wall

R01HL-41373-04 (SRC) SMITH, BARBARA D BOSTON UNIVERSITY 80 EAST CONCORD STREET K-725 BOSTON, MASS 02118 Lung fibrosis--Mechanisms of collagen gene expression

R29HL-41378-05 (PTHA) SCHELLING, MARGARET E WASHINGTON STATE UNIVERSITY PULLMAN, WA 99164-4234 Receptor mediation of coronary angiogenesis

R29HL-41382-04 (HEM) RYBICKI, ANNE C MONTEFIORE HOSPITAL MED CENTER 210TH ST & BAINBRIDGE AVE/MOSE BRONX, NY 10467 Studies on human erythrocyte protein 4.2

R01HL-41384-03 (SRC) KNATTERUD, GENELL L MARYLAND MED RES INSTITUTE 600 WYNDHURST AVENUE BALTIMORE, MD 21210 Thrombolysis in myocardial infarction (TIMI) II follow-up

R01HL-41387-02 (RAP) MORIN, FREDERICK C, III CHILDREN'S HOSPITAL 219 BRYANT STREET BUFFALO, NY 14222 Development of sustained pulmonary hypertension at birth

R01HL-41408-04 (PTHA) ROSSEN, ROGER D BAYLOR COLLEGE OF MEDICINE 1 BAYLOR PLAZA HOUSTON, TEX 77030 Complement and leukocytes in myocardial infarction (human, dogs)

R01HL-41411-07 (BBCB) WANG, CHIH-LUEH A BOSTON BIOMEDICAL RES INST 20 STANIFORD STREET BOSTON, MASS 02114 Comparative study on troponin-C and calmodulin

R44HL-41423-02 (SSS) ALLEN, MICHAEL P CHEMTRAK 484 OAKMEAD PARKWAY SUNNYVALE, CA 94086 Non-instrumented quantitative cholesterol test

R44HL-41426-02 (SSS) TAMARI, YEHUDA CIRCULATORY TECHNOLOGY, INC 21 SINGWORTH STREET OYSTER BAY, NY 11771-3703 A self inflating pressure infusion cuff

R44HL-41433-03 (SSS) SOULE, HOWARD R CORVAS, INC 3030 SCIENCE PARK ROAD SAN DIEGO, CA 92121 Immunoassay for thrombosis and thrombolytic therapy

R01HL-41445-04 (SRC) WASSERTHEIL-SMOLLER, SYLVIA ALBERT EINSTEIN COLLEGE OF MED 1300 MORRIS PARK AVENUE BRONX, N Y 10461 Effect of dietary modification on blood pressure control

R44HL-41457-03 (ARR) STEWART, ALEXANDRIA A ONCOGENE SCIENCE, INC 350 COMMUNITY DRIVE MANHASSET, NY 11030 Platelet derived growth factor-receptor kinase inhibitors for atherosclerosis

R29HL-41470-04 (MET) RAPP, JOSEPH H VA MEDICAL CENTER SURGER, 112, 4150 CLEMENT ST SAN FRANCISCO, CA 94121 Lipoprotein isolation from surgical speciments and plasma

R29HL-41474-04 (CVA) SEIDMAN, CHRISTINE BRIGHAM & WOMEN'S HOSPITAL CARDIOVAS DIV 75 FRANCIS ST BOSTON, MA 02115 Development of stable cardiac cell lines

P01HL-41484-03 (SRC) ROSENBERG, ROBERT D MASSACHUSETTS INSTIT OF TECH 77 MASSACHUSETTS AVENUE CAMBRIDGE, MA 02139 Programs of excellence in molecular biology

P01HL-41484-03 0002 (SRC) LODISH, HARVEY Programs of excellence in molecular biology Glucose transporters in cardiac, smooth muscle & endothelial cells

P01HL-41484-03 0003 (SRC) KRIEGER, MONTY Programs of excellence in molecular biology analysis of the scavenger cell acetyl-LDL receptor

P01HL-41484-03 0004 (SRC) RULEY, EARL Programs of excellence in molecular biology Oncogene-induced lipogenesis in smooth muscle cells

P01HL-41484-03 0005 (SRC) JAENISH, RUDOLF Programs of excellence in molecular biology collagen type I mutations in transgenic mice

P01HL-41484-03 0001 (SRC) ROSENBERG, ROBERT Programs of excellence in molecular biology Molecular biology of endothelial cell heparan sulfate proteoglycans

P01HL-41484-03 0006 (SRC) HYNES, RICHARD Programs of excellence in molecular biology Study of the fibronectin function

P01HL-41484-03 0007 (SRC) HOUSMAN, DAVID Programs of excellence in molecular biology Genes responsible for predisposition to darciovascular disease

P01HL-41484-03 0008 (SRC) MULLIGAN, RICHARD Programs of excellence in molecular biology Genetic therapy of familial hypocholesterolemia

R01HL-41495-04 (SRC) CHEITLIN, MELVIN D SAN FRANCISCO GENERAL HOSPITAL 1001 POTRERO AVENUE SAN FRANCISCO, CA 94110 Aids-associated heart disease--Incidence and etiology

P01HL-41496-03 (SRC) LINGREL, JERRY B UNIVERSITY OF CINCINNATI

PROJECT NO., ORGANIZATIONAL UNIT., INVESTIGATOR, ADDRESS, TITLE

DEPT/MICROBIO/MOLECULAR GENETI CINCINNATI, OHIO 45267 Programs of excellence in molecular biology
P01HL-41496-03 0001 (SRC) LINGREL, JERRY Programs of excellence in molecular biology Role of Na,K-ATPase in human tissue
P01HL-41496-03 0004 (SRC) WHITSETT, JEFFREY Programs of excellence in molecular biology Molecular analysis of lung surfactant protein
P01HL-41496-03 0005 (SRC) KAO, WINSTON Programs of excellence in molecular biology Expression of prolyl 4-hydroxylase genes
P01HL-41496-03 0006 (SRC) SHULL, GARY Programs of excellence in molecular biology Structure/function and regulation of calcium transporting ATPase
P01HL-41496-03 0007 (SRC) ROBBINS, JEFFREY Programs of excellence in molecular biology Growth and protein expression during cardiac & pulmonary development
P01HL-41496-03 0008 (SRC) LUSE, DONAL S Programs of excellence in molecular biology The molecular basis of lung specific gene expression
P01HL-41496-03 0009 (SRC) POTTER, STEVEN Programs of excellence in molecular biology Gene expession and structure-function using transgenic mice
P01HL-41496-03 0010 (SRC) SCHWARTZ, ARNOLD Programs of excellence in molecular biology Calcium channel modulators and voltage dependent calcium channels
P01HL-41496-03 0011 (SRC) HARMONY, JUDITH Programs of excellence in molecular biology Molecular basis of lipid disorders
P01HL-41496-03 0012 (SRC) DOETSCHMAN, THOMAS Programs of excellence in molecular biology Targeted gene modification in embryonic stem cells
P01HL-41496-03 9001 (SRC) LINGREL, JERRY Programs of excellence in molecular biology Core--DNA laboratory
P01HL-41496-03 9002 (SRC) POTTER, STEVEN Programs of excellence in molecular biology Core--Transgenic mice laboratory
P01HL-41496-03 9003 (SRC) DOETSCHMAN, TOMAS Programs of excellence in molecular biology Core--Cell culture laboratory
R01HL-41507-04 (SRC) HSIA, JUDITH GEORGE WASHINGTON UNIVERSITY 2150 PENNSYLVANIA AVENUE, N W WASHINGTON, D C 20037 HIV associated heart disease
R01HL-41514-04 (SRC) HERSKOWITZ, AHVIE THE JOHNS HOPKINS UNIVERSITY BALTIMORE, MD 21205 AIDS-associated cardiomyopathy
R01HL-41522-03 (PBC) KUEPPERS, FRIEDRICH TEMPLE UNIV HLTH SCIS CENTER 3401 NORTH BROAD ST PHILADELPHIA, PENN 19140 Evaluation of alpha-1-antitrypsin replacement
R01HL-41523-02 (EDC) CARSON, JEFFREY L UMDNJ-R W JOHNSON MEDICAL SCHO 97 PATERSON STREET NEW BRUNSWICK, NJ 08903 Anemia and surgery: indications for transfusion
R29HL-41533-02 (CVB) KHRAIBI, ALI A MAYO FOUNDATION 200 FIRST ST SW ROCHESTER, MN 55905 Renal interstitial hydrostatic pressure in hypertension
R01HL-41536-03 (HED) GITLIN, JONATHAN D WASHINGTON UNIVERSITY 400 S KINGSHIGHWAY BLVD ST LOUIS, MO 63110 Developmental regulation of fetal antioxidant expression
R01HL-41543-02 (PC) BLUMENTHAL, KENNETH M UNIV OF CINCINNATI COLL OF MED 231 BETHESDA AVENUE (ML 524) CINCINNATI, OH 45267-0524 Structure and function of a cardiotonic anemone
P01HL-41544-04 (HLBB) HUISMAN, TITUS H MEDICAL COLLEGE OF GEORGIA DEPT BIOCHEM & MOLECULAR BIO AUGUSTA, GA 30912 Sickle cell anemia and related hemoglobinopathies
P01HL-41544-04 0003 (HLBB) STOMING, TERRANCE Sickle cell anemia and related hemoglobinopathies Molecular defects in beta-thalassemia and non-deletional HPFH
P01HL-41544-04 0004 (HLBB) GARVER, FRED A Sickle cell anemia and related hemoglobinopathies Monoclonal antibodies and immunoassays for hemoglobin
P01HL-41544-04 0001 (HLBB) HUISMAN, TITUS H Sickle cell anemia and related hemoglobinopathies Structure/function/DNA analysis of mutations affecting expression of globin genes
P01HL-41544-04 0002 (HLBB) ADAMS, ROBERT J Sickle cell anemia and related hemoglobinopathies Non-invasive detection of cerebrovascular occulsions in sickle cell disease
P01HL-41544-04 0005 (HLBB) WHITNEY, J BARRY Sickle cell anemia and related hemoglobinopathies Gene therapy of a hemoglobinopathy in an animal model
P01HL-41544-04 9001 (HLBB) HUISMAN, TITUS H Sickle cell anemia and related hemoglobinopathies Core--Laboratory
R29HL-41548-01A3 (PTHA) SZAREK, JOHN L MARSHALL UNIVERSITY SCH OF MED 1542 SPRING VALLEY DRIVE HUNTINGTON, WV 25755-9310 Mechanisms of hyperoxia induced airway hyperreactivity
R01HL-41552-03 (CVA) BIGGER, JOHN T, JR COLUMBIA UNIVERSITY 630 WEST 168TH STREET NEW YORK, N Y 10032 Heart rate variability and sudden cardiac death
R01HL-41553-03 (HEM) BECKERLE, MARY C UNIVERSITY OF UTAH 228 SO. BIOLOGY BLDG. SALT LAKE CITY, UT 84112 Function of talin in platelets
R01HL-41558-03 (CBY) SHULL, GARY E UNIVERSITY OF CINCINNATI 231 BETHESDA AVE CINCINNATI, OHIO 45267 Regulation & function of calcium transporting ATPases
R01HL-41565-03 (PTHA) UNDERHILL, CHARLES B GEORGETOWN UNIVERSITY 3900 RESERVOIR ROAD, N W WASHINGTON, D C 20007 Role of hyaluranote receptors in lung physiology
R01HL-41579-07 (PBC) REMOLD-O'DONNELL, EILEEN CENTER FOR BLOOD RESEARCH 800 HUNTINGTON AVENUE BOSTON, MA 02115 Elastase inhibitor of macrophages and neutrophils
R29HL-41581-04 (BLR) SPACKMAN, KENT A OREGON HLTH SCIENCES UNIVERSIT 3181 S W SAM JACKSON PARK RD PORTLAND, OR 97201 Criteria-based knowledge acquisition tools in medicine
R01HL-41582-01A2 (CVA) CHEUNG, JOSEPH Y PENNSYLVANIA STATE UNIVERSITY PO BOX 850 HERSHEY, PA 17033 Calcium and congestive heart failure
R01HL-41587-03 (RAP) GERARD-STIMLER, NORMA P BETH ISRAEL HOSPITAL 330 BROOKLINE AVENUE BOSTON, MA 02215 Cellular and molecular biology of neurokinins in lung
R01HL-41594-03 (SB) BAUMGARTNER, WILLIAM A JOHNS HOPKINS HOSPITAL 600 N WOLFE ST, BLALOCK 618 BALTIMORE, MD 21205 Metabolic analysis of rejection in heart transplantation

PROJECT NO., ORGANIZATIONAL UNIT., INVESTIGATOR, ADDRESS, TITLE

R29HL-41599-03 (CVA) WARNER, MARGARET ROSE INDIANA UNIVERSITY 1001 WEST 10TH STREET INDIANAPOLIS, IN 46202-5167 Role of neuropeptide y in neural control of the heart
R29HL-41603-03 (CVA) MC CULLOCH, ANDREW D UNIVERSITY OF CA, SAN DIEGO LA JOLLA, CA 92093-0605 Regional mechanics of the intact venticular wall
R01HL-41610-04 (RAP) MASSARO, DONALD J GEORGETOWN UNIVERSITY 3900 RESERVOIR RD NW WASHINGTON, DC 20007 Regulation of the gas exchange surface in the lung
P01HL-41618-03 (SRC) DOUGLAS, JANICE G CASE WESTERN RESERVE UNIV 2074 ABINGTON ROAD CLEVELAND, OH 44106 Vasoactive hormones--Receptors and signaling mechanisms
P01HL-41618-03 0001 (SRC) DOUGLAS, JANICE G Vasoactive hormones--Receptors and signaling mechanisms Signal transduction mechanisms in proximal tubular epithelium
P01HL-41618-03 0002 (SRC) KOOP, DENNIS Vasoactive hormones--Receptors and signaling mechanisms: Proximal tubule epithelial cytochrome P450 isozymes
P01HL-41618-03 0003 (SRC) HOPFER, ULRICH Vasoactive hormones--Receptors and signaling mechanisms Proximal tubular transport mechanisms
P01HL-41618-03 0004 (SRC) THIBONNIER, MARC Vasoactive hormones--Receptors and signaling mechanisms V1-vascular vasopressin receptors of mesangial cell
P01HL-41618-03 9001 (SRC) DOUGLAS, JANICE G Vasoactive hormones--Receptors and signaling mechanisms Core--Cell isolation and tissue culture
P01HL-41618-03 9002 (SRC) SCARPA, ANTONIA Vasoactive hormones--Receptors and signaling mechanisms Core--Analytical instrumentation
R37HL-41619-04 (SAT) HARKER, LAURENCE ARDELL EMORY UNIVERSITY DRAWER AR ATLANTA, GA 30322 Endarterectomy--Prevention of thrombosis and restenosis
R01HL-41624-03 (NTN) DAVIS, ROGER A UNIVERSITY OF COLORADO 4200 EAST 9TH AVENUE B158 DENVER, CO 80262 Molecular mechanisms of VLDL assembly
R01HL-41628-03 (CVA) MADDAHI, JAMSHID CEDARS SINAI MEDICAL CENTER 8700 BEVERLY BLVD LOS ANGELES, CA 90048 Quantitation of myocardial perfusion by Tc-99m-MIBI
P01HL-41633-03 (SRC) MAHLEY, ROBERT W GLADSTONE FOUNDATION LAB P O BOX 40608 SAN FRANCISCO, CA 94140-0608 Lipoprotein structure/function in cholesterol metabolism
P01HL-41633-03 0001 (SRC) RALL, STANLEY C. Lipoprotein structure/function in cholesterol metabolism Mapping the functional domains of apolipoprotein E
P01HL-41633-03 0002 (SRC) WEISGRABER, KARL H. Lipoprotein structure/function in cholesterol metabolism Structural and physical biochemical analysis of Apo E
P01HL-41633-03 0003 (SRC) TAYLOR, JOHN M. Lipoprotein structure/function in cholesterol metabolism Expression of transfected Apo E gene in animals
P01HL-41633-03 0004 (SRC) BOYLES, JANET K. Lipoprotein structure/function in cholesterol metabolism Apo-E cholesterol transport and metabolism
P01HL-41633-03 0005 (SRC) YOUNG, STEVEN G. Lipoprotein structure/function in cholesterol metabolism Analysis of apolipoprotein B polymorphism
P01HL-41633-03 0006 (SRC) LEVY WILSON, BEATRIZ Lipoprotein structure/function in cholesterol metabolism Control of human apolipoprotein B gene expression
P01HL-41633-03 0007 (SRC) MCCARTHY, BRIAN J. Lipoprotein structure/function in cholesterol metabolism Assembly of Apo-B-containibg lipoproteins
P01HL-41633-03 9001 (SRC) INNERARITY, THOMAS L. Lipoprotein structure/function in cholesterol metabolism Core--Tissue Culture
P01HL-41633-03 9002 (SRC) RALL, STANLEY C. Lipoprotein structure/function in cholesterol metabolism Core--Lipoprotein and protein chemistry
P01HL-41633-03 9003 (SRC) MCCARTHY, BRIAN J. Lipoprotein structure/function in cholesterol metabolism Core--Molecular biology
R01HL-41635-03 (BEM) WARD, MARCIA M SRI INTERNATIONAL 333 RAVENSWOOD AVENUE MENLO PARK, CALIF 94025 Stability of ambulatory monitoring in the lab and field
U01HL-41642-04 (SRC) HOWARD, BARBARA V MEDLANTIC RESEARCH FOUNDATION 108 IRVING STREET, NW WASHINGTON, DC 20010 A study of cardiovascular disease in Pima indians
R01HL-41644-02 (RAP) CHANDER, AVINASH INST FOR ENVIRONMENTAL MED 36TH & HAMILTON WALK PHILADELPHIA, PA 19104-6068 Mechanisms of pH regulation of lung surfactant secretion
U01HL-41652-04 (SRC) WELTY, THOMAS K PHS INDIAN HOSPITAL 3200 CANYON LAKE DR RAPID CITY, SD 57702 Cardiovascular disease in Sioux Indians
U01HL-41654-04 (SRC) LEE, ELISA T UNIV OF OKLAHOMA HLTH SCI CTR 801 N.E 13TH ST P O BOX 26901 OKLAHOMA CITY, OK 73190 Cardiovascular disease in American Indians
R29HL-41656-04 (PHY) VANDENBERG, CAROL UNIVERSITY OF CALIFORNIA INST OF ENVIRONMENTAL STRESS SANTA BARBARA, CA 93106 Physiology of cardiac ion channels
R01HL-41657-03 (BEM) MC CANN, BARBARA S UNIV OF WASHINGTON 465 HARBORVIEW HALL/326 9TH AV SEATTLE, WA 98104 Psychological stress, catecholamines & lipid metabolism
R01HL-41661-03 (ECS) HORWITZ, LAWRENCE D UNIVERSITY OF COLORADO 4200 EAST NINTH AVENUE DENVER, COLO 80262 Reperfusion injury to coronary endothelium
R01HL-41663-03 (SB) LEVY, ROBERT J UNIVERSITY OF MICHIGAN R-5080 KRESGE II ANN ARBOR, MI 48109-0576 Myocardial controlled release implants for arrhythmias
R01HL-41776-03 (PB) WHITE, HOWARD D LEWIS HALL-EASTERN VA MED SCHL 700 OLNEY RD NORFOLK, VA 23501 Mechanism of cardiac actomyosin NTP hydrolysis
R29HL-41777-03 (SB) PANTALOS, GEORGE M UNIVERSITY OF UTAH DUMKE BLD., INST FOR BIOMEDICA SALT LAKE CITY, UT 84112 Energetic comparison of ventricular assist techniques

PROJECT NO., ORGANIZATIONAL UNIT., INVESTIGATOR, ADDRESS, TITLE

R29HL-41781-03 (BEM) TREIBER, FRANK A MEDICAL COLLEGE OF GEORGIA 1427 HARPER STREET HG-100 AUGUSTA, GEORGIA 30912-3770 Antecedents of hypertension--Role of race and stress

R01HL-41782-03 (HEM) HUANG, JUNG S ST LOUIS UNIV SCH OF MED 1402 S GRAND BOULEVARD ST LOUIS, MO 63104 PDGF/TGf beta and alpha-2-macroglobulin interactions

R01HL-41786-03 (SRC) NEWBURGER, JANE W CHILDREN'S HOSPITAL CORPORATIO 300 LONGWOOD AVE BOSTON, MA 02115 Infant heart surgery--CNS sequelae of circulatory arrest

R01HL-41788-03 (NEUA) ELLIS, EARL F MEDICAL COLLEGE OF VIRGINIA RICHMOND, VA 23298 Omega-3 fatty acids and the cerebral circulation

R29HL-41790-02 (RAP) FREGOSI, RALPH F UNIVERSITY OF ARIZONA TUCSON, AZ 85721 Reflex regulation of expiratory motor activity

R29HL-41793-04 (HEM) LAM, STEPHEN C T UNIVERSITY OF ILLINOIS 835 S WOLCOTT AVENUE CHICAGO, ILL 60612 A novel RDG-binding membrane protein on blood platelets

R01HL-41796-01A1 (BEM) JULIUS, MARA UNIVERSITY OF MICHIGAN 109 OBSERVATORY ANN ARBOR, MI 48109-2029 Suppressed anger, blood pressure and mortality follow-up

R01HL-41814-03 (RAP) MILLER, MARTHA J RAINBOW BABIES & CHILDRENS HOS 2101 ADELBERT ROAD CLEVELAND, OHIO 44106 Pharyngeal resistance in sleeping premature infants

R29HL-41816-03 (ECS) BUKOSKI, RICHARD D OREGON HEALTH SCIENCES UNIV 3181 S W SAM JACKSON PARK RD PORTLAND, OREG 97201 Calciotropic hormone action on arterial muscle

R01HL-41819-03 (SRC) WILSON, SANDRA R AMERICAN INSTITUTE FOR RES P O BOX 1113 PALO ALTO, CA 94302 "Wee Wheezers"--Asthma management education for parents

R01HL-41830-03 (EDC) SELBY, JOSEPH V MED METHODS RES KAISER PERMAN 3451 PIEDMONT AVENUE OAKLAND, CA 94611 Genetic epidemiology of CHD risk factors in women twins

R01HL-41840-03 (SB) BOERBOOM, LAWRENCE E MILWAUKEE COUNTY MED COMPLEX 8700 W WISCONSIN AVENUE MILWAUKEE, WI 53226 Prevention of vein graft atherosclerosis with fish oil

R29HL-41845-03 (SB) FIELDS, BARRY L UNIVERSITY OF WISCONSIN 600 HIGHLAND AVENUE MADISON, WI 53792 Extended heart preservation with uw solution

R01HL-41854-02 (HED) LWEBUGA-MUKASA, JAMSON S YALE UNIVERSITY P O BOX 3333/333 CEDAR ST NEW HAVEN, CT 06510-8057 Matrix driven pneumocyte differentiation

R01HL-41874-03 (RNM) SIGEL, BERNARD MEDICAL COLLEGE OF PENNSYLVANI 3300 HENRY AVE PHILADELPHIA, PA 19129 Ultrasonic tissue characterization of vascular thrombi

R01HL-41882-03 (ECS) MYERS, JEANNE CAROL UNIVERSITY OF PENNSYLVANIA 37TH AND HAMILTON WALK PHILADELPHIA, PA 19104-6059 Bleomycin modulation of collagen gene expression

R01HL-41883-02 (ECS) BOND, MEREDITH CLEVELAND CLINIC FOUNDATION 9500 EUCLID AVE CLEVELAND, OH 44195-5069 Cellular calcium regulation in myopathic hearts in vitro

R29HL-41886-03 (BEM) STRECHER, VICTOR J UNIV OF N CAROLINA AT CHP HILL 319 ROSENAU HALL, CB #7400 CHAPEL HILL, N C 27514 Improving physicians preventive care activities

R01HL-41888-03 (SB) HARASAKI, HIROAKI CLEVELAND CLINC FOUNDATION 9500 EUCLID AVENUER CLEVELAND, OH 44195 Pathogenesis and prevention of valve calcification

R01HL-41889-03 (SB) MCCARTHY, DENNIS J SOUTHERN RESEARCH INSTITUTE P. O. BOX 55305 BIRMINGHAM, AL 35255 Design of material for removal of blood toxic agents

R01HL-41891-03 (CVB) MUELLER, STEPHEN N CORIELL INST FOR MED RES 401 HADDON AVE CAMDEN, NJ 08103 Endothelial cell monolayer permeability characteristics

R29HL-41894-04 (RAP) MIFFLIN, STEVEN W UNIV OF TEXAS HLTH SCI CTR 7703 FLOYD CURL DRIVE SAN ANTONIO, TX 78284-7764 Chemoreceptor input to non-respiratory cells in NTS

R01HL-41898-03 (BM) LOTTENBERG, RICHARD UNIVERSITY OF FLORIDA BOX J-277 GAINESVILLE, FLA 32610 Characterization of the streptococcal plasmin receptor

R01HL-41899-03 (CVB) GOMEZ, ROBERTO A UNIVERSITY OF VIRGINIA DEPARTMENT OF PEDIATRICS CHARLOTTESVILLE, VA 22908 Regulation of renin synthesis and release in the kidney

R01HL-41904-01A2 (BBCB) HAMILTON, JAMES A BOSTON UNIV SCHOOL OF MED 80 EAST CONCORD STREET BOSTON, MA 02118 NMR studies of weakly polar lipids

R01HL-41910-03 (HEM) RIVIER, JEAN SALK INSTITUTE P.O. BOX 85800 SAN DIEGO, CA 92138 Neuropeptide y analogs as hypotensive agents

R01HL-41914-03 (RNM) LIEDTKE, A JAMES UNIV OF WISCONSIN MED SCH 600 HIGHLAND AVENUE H6/339 MADISON, WIS 53792 Tracer kinetics evaluating positron tomography

R29HL-41916-03 (PC) SORCI-THOMAS, MARY G BOWMAN GRAY SCHL OF MED OF WFU MEDICAL CENTER BOULEVARD WINSTON-SALEM, NC 27157 Atherosclerosis and apolipoprotein a-i regulation

R01HL-41918-03 (SB) MANNION, JOHN D JEFFERSON MEDICAL COLLEGE 1025 WALNUT STREET, SUITE 607 PHILADELPHIA, PA 19107 Skeletal muscle for myocardial assistance

R01HL-41921-02 (CVB) PRIVITERA, PHILIP J MEDICAL UNIV OF SOUTH CAROLINA 171 ASHLEY AVENUE CHARLESTON, SC 29425 Brain kallikrein--Kinin and arterial pressure control

R01HL-41926-03 (CBY) MECHAM, ROBERT P JEWISH HOSPITAL OF ST LOUIS 216 SOUTH KINGSHIGHWAY ST LOUIS, MO 63110 Characterization of the elastin/laminin receptor

R01HL-41928-04 (SRC) GRUENERT, DIETER C CARDIOVASCULAR RESEARCH INST. UNIVERSITY OF CALIFORNIA, BOX SAN FRANCISCO, CA 94143 CF TS transformants--Biochemical and genetic analysis

R01HL-41935-03 (HEM) TAM, JAMES P ROCKFELLER UNIVERSITY 1230 YORK AVENUE NEW YORK, NY 10021-6399 Cysteinyl-rich domain in blood clotting factors

R01HL-41939-04 (SRC) FISHER, ARON B UNIVERSITY OF PENNSYLVANIA 36TH & HAMITON WALK PHILADELPHIA, PA 19104-6068 Ischemia-reperfusion injury to the lung

R01HL-41943-04 (SRC) COOPER, JOEL D WASHINGTON UNIV/SURGERY 660 S EUCLID AVE BOX 8109 ST LOUIS, MO 63110 Ischemia-reperfusion injury after lung transplantation

R01HL-41945-04 (SRC) JACOBBERGER, JAMES W 2119 ABINGTON ROAD CLEVELAND, OH 44106 Immortalizating cystic fibrosis airway epithelial cells

R01HL-41952-04 (SRC) LOYD, JAMES E VANDERBILT UNIVERISTY SCH MED B-1308 MEDICAL CENTER NORTH NASHVILLE, TN 37232 Mechanisms of ischemia/reperfusion lung injury

R29HL-41954-03 (CVB) CASSIS, LISA A UNIVERSITY KENTUCKY ROSE STREET LEXINGTON, KY 40536 Adipose angiotensionogen-angiotensin system

R01HL-41958-03 (PTHA) DOBBS, LELAND G UNIV OF CALIFORNIA, S. F. 1327 MOFFITT HOSPITAL SAN FRANCISCO, CA. 94143-0130 Isolation, markers, culture of human lung type I cells

R01HL-41960-02 (ECS) BRYAN, ROBERT M, JR PENNSYLVANIA STATE UNIVERSITY PO BOX 850 HERSHEY, PA 17033 Blood flow and energy metabolism in the neurohypophysis

R01HL-41961-04 (SRC) TAYLOR, AUBREY E UNIVERSITY OF SOUTH ALABAMA COLLEGE OF MEDICINE, MSB 3024 MOBILE, AL 36688 Pathophysiology of ischemia-reperfusion lung injury

R01HL-41963-03 (HEM) MILETICH, JOSEPH P WASHINGTON UNIV SCHOOL OF MED 660 SOUTH EUCLID AVE ST. LOUIS, MO 63110 Protein C structure/function & risk of thrombosis

R01HL-41964-03 (SRC) VOLLMER, WILLIAM M KAISER FOUNDATION HOSPITALS 4610 S. E. BELMONT ST PORTLAND, OR 97215 Alternative management strategies for asthmatic children

R01HL-41970-04 (SRC) SYLVESTER, J T FRANCIS SCOTT KEY MED CENTER 4940 EASTERN AVENUE BALTIMORE, MD 21224 Ischemia-reperfusion injury in isolated lungs

R01HL-41972-03 (PHY) BREITWIESER, GERDA E JOHNS HOPKINS UNIV SCH OF MED DEPT OF PHYSIOLOGY BALTIMORE, MD 21205 G protein-mediated K+ channel activation in heart

R01HL-41979-05 (SRC) CHOPRA, DHARAM P WAYNE STATE UNIVERSITY 2727 SECOND AVENUE #402 DETROIT, MI 48201 Epithelial cell lines from CF and normal tracheas

R01HL-41983-04 (SRC) YANKASKAS, JAMES R UNIVERSITY OF NORTH CAROLINA DEPT OF MEDICINE, CB 7020 CHAPEL HILL, N C 27599-7020 Immortalized cells for cystic fibrosis research

R01HL-41990-03 (PTHA) LEWIS, JON C BOWMAN GRAY SCHOOL OF MEDICINE WAKE FOREST UNIVERSITY WINSTON-SALEM, N C 27103 Monocyte/macrophage subcellular lipoprotein processing

R29HL-41991-02 (NTN) KASIM, SIDIKA E WAYNE STATE UNIVESITY 4201 ST ANTOINE DETROIT, MI 48201 Mechanism of atherogenic lipid response to omega 3 fish oils

R01HL-41993-02 (EDC) SISCOVICK, DAVID S UNIVERSITY OF WASHINGTON 325 NINTH AVENUE SEATTLE, WA 98104 Polyunsaturated fats and risk of primary cardiac arrest

R01HL-42020-03 (CVA) MADDAHI, JAMSHID CEDARS SINAI MEDICAL CENTER 8700 BEVERLY BLVD. LOS ANGELES, CA 90048 Thrombus imaging by radiolabeled monoclonal antibodies

R01HL-42021-02 (RNM) PETTIGREW, RODERIC I EMORY UNIVERSITY HOSPITAL 1364 CLIFTON ROAD ATLANTA, GA 30322 Quantitative stress cine MRI for ischemic heart disease

R01HL-42030-03 (PTHA) HOLIAN, ANDRIJ UNIVERSITY OF TEXAS MEDICAL SC 6431 FANNIN STREET HOUSTON, TX 77030 Role of intracellular ph in macrophage activation

R29HL-42032-03 (MET) KINNUNEN, PAULA M JEWISH HOSPITAL OF ST LOUIS 216 S. KINGSHIGHWAY ST LOUIS, MISSOURI 63112 Intracellular cholesterol metabolism in atherogenesis

R01HL-42040-03 (PHRA) LINDENMAYER, GEORGE MD PHD MED UNIV OF SOUTH CAROLINA CHARLESTON, SC 29425 Sodium/calcium exchange across cardiac sarcolemma

R01HL-42050-03 (CVA) STERN, MICHAEL D JOHNS HOPKINS UNIV 600 N WOLFE ST BALTIMORE, MD 21205 Excitation-contraction coupling in anoxic myocytes

R01HL-42052-03 (CVA) GARCIA, ERNEST V EMORY UNIVERSITY HOSPITAL 1364 CLIFTON ROAD, N E ATLANTA, GA 30322 Unified approach to quantify & visualize cardiac imagery

R01HL-42057-03 (TOX) ROBERTS, ROBERT J UNIV OF VIRGINIA SCH OF MED BOX 386 CHARLOTTESVILLE, VA 22908 Role of diffusible cytotoxins in O2-induced lung injury

R01HL-42069-04 (SRC) HAMBURGER, ANNE W UNIV OF MARYLAND CANCER CTR BRESSLER RESEARCH BLDG, RM 905 BALTIMORE, MD 21201 Pathobiology of bone marrow suppression in AIDS

R01HL-42074-01A3 (PHY) WHITE, ROY L TEMPLE UNIV. MEDICAL SCHOOL 3420 NORTH BROAD STREET PHILADELPHIA, PA 19140 The effects of ischemia on gap junctions in heart

R01HL-42075-03 (RAP) LUCAS, CAROL L UNIVERSITY OF NORTH CAROLINA 150 MACNIDER HALL-CB#7575 CHAPEL HILL, NC 27599-7575 Cardiopulmonary geometry and blood flow

R01HL-42077-03 (CVB) WEBB, JERRY G MEDICAL UNIV OF SOUTH CAROLINA 171 ASHLEY AVENUEOGY CHARLESTON, SC 29425 Beta receptors & vascular arachidonic acid metabolism

R01HL-42082-03 (PTHA) NEWMAN, WILLIAM P, III LOUISIANA STATE UNIVERSITY 1901 PERDIDO STREET NEW ORLEANS, LA 70112-1393 Atherosclerosis & W-3 fatty acids in Alaskan natives

R01HL-42084-03 (RAP) SOBIN, SIDNEY S MD PHD UNIV OF SOUTHERN CALIFORNIA 1200 N STATE ST LOS ANGELES, CA 90033 Cellular mechanisms in lung vascular response to hypoxia

R01HL-42087-04 (SRC) BYRNES, JOHN J UNIV OF MIAMI SCHOOL OF MED VETS ADMIN MEDICAL CENTER MIAMI, FL 33125 Inhibition of marrow DNA replication by antivirals

R01HL-42090-04 (SRC) PRYSTOWSKY, MICHAEL B UNIVERSITY OF PENNSYLVANIA RM 231 JOHN MORGAN BLDG PHILADELPHIA, PA 19104-6082 Effect of retroviral infection on bone marrow

R01HL-42096-04 (SRC) EMERSON, STEPHEN G MSRB I, ROOM 5510B 1150 W MEDICAL CTR DRIVE ANN ARBOR, MI 48109 Immune mediated hematopoietic suppression and AIDS

R01HL-42103-02 (ARR) ZUCKER-FRANKLIN, DOROTHEA NEW YORK UNIVERSITY MED CENTER 550 FIRST AVENUE NEW YORK, NY 10016 Effect of HIV on hematopoietic and stromal marrow cells

R01HL-42105-04 (SRC) DAVIS, BRIAN R MEDICAL RESEARCH INSTITUTE 2200 WEBSTER STREET SAN FRANCISCO, CA 94115 Bone marrow suppression in ARC/AIDS

R01HL-42107-04 (SRC) GOLDE, DAVID W SLOAN-KETTERING INSTITUTE 1275 YORK AVE NEW YORK, NY 10021 Hematopoietic cell function in AIDS

R01HL-42112-04 (SRC) GROOPMAN, JEROME E NEW ENGLAND DEACONESS

PROJECT NO., ORGANIZATIONAL UNIT., INVESTIGATOR, ADDRESS, TITLE

HOSPITAL 110 FRANCIS STREET, SUITE 4A BOSTON, MA 02215 Bone marrow suppression in AIDS or ARC

R01HL-42115-04 (SRC) CRONKITE, EUGENE P BROOKHAVEN NATIONAL LABORATORY MEDICAL DEPARTMENT UPTON, NY 11973 Early-late toxic effects of AZT on hemo-stem cells

R01HL-42119-03 (PTHA) GORDON, DAVID UNIVERSITY OF WASHINGTON SEATTLE, WA 98195 Proliferation and growth factors in atherosclerosis

R01HL-42120-03 (CVB) CANESSA, MITZY L BRIGHAM & WOMEN'S HOSP, INC 75 FRANCIS STREET BOSTON, MA 02115 Cell ph and calcium ion in normal and hypertensive adrenals

R01HL-42125-04 (SRC) SOMMADOSSI, JEAN-PIERRE C UNIVERSITY OF ALABAMA DEPT OF PHARMACOLOGY BIRMINGHAM, AL 35294 Toxicity of anit-AIDS on the bone marrow

R01HL-42131-03 (RAP) KATZ, DAVID M CASE WESTERN RESERVE UNIV 2119 ABINGTON ROAD CLEVELAND, OH 44106 Regulation of carotid body afferent development

R01HL-42142-04 (SRC) MLADENOVIC, JEANETTE UNIVERSITY OF NEW YORK HLTH SCIENCES CTR, T-17,060 STONY BROOK, NY 11794-8173 Pathogenesis of bone marrow failure in HIV disease

R01HL-42145-03 (CLTR) CHAITMAN, BERNARD R ST LOUIS UNIVERSITY HOSPITAL 3635 VISTA AVENUE AT GRAND BLV ST. LOUIS, MO 63110-0250 Core electrocardiographic laboratory--BARI trial

R01HL-42148-04 (SRC) STEINBERG, HOWARD N BETH ISREAL HOSPITAL 330 BROOKLINE AVENUE BOSTON, MASS 02215 Pathobiology of bone marrow suppression in AIDS

R01HL-42150-03 (CVA) SIMPSON, PAUL C, JR FT MILEY VETERANS ADMINIS HOSP 4150 CLEMENT STREET SAN FRANCISCO, CA 94121 A1-Adrenergic regulation of cardiac gene expression

R01HL-42151-04 (SRC) CLARK, EDWARD B UNIVERSITY OF ROCHESTER SCH OF MEDICINE, BOX 631 ROCHESTER, NY 14642 Function-structure relation in ventricular development

R01HL-42164-04 (SRC) ROSENQUIST, THOMAS H MEDICAL COLLEGE OF GEORGIA DEPARTMENT OF ANATOMY AUGUSTA, GEORGIA 30912-2000 Elastic artery development and congenital heart defects

R01HL-42165-03 (SRC) BUZZARD, I MARILYN UNIVERSITY OF MINNESOTA 2221 UNIVERSITY AVENUE, SE MINNEAPOLIS, MN 55414 Nutrition data system for research and education

R29HL-42168-03 (SB) KINGSLEY, PETER B UMHC, BOX 495 420 DELAWARE STREET SE MINNEAPOLIS, MN 55455 Ischemia & cardioplegia in newborn hearts--NMR studies

R01HL-42172-03 (SSS) GOLDBERGER, ARY L BETH ISRAEL HOSPITAL 330 BROOKLINE AVE BOSTON, MA 02215 Nonlinear and fractal mechanisms of neural control

R44HL-42176-03 (SSS) SHEFER, RUTH E SCIENCE RESEARCH LABORATORY 15 WARD STREET SOMERVILLE, MA 02143 K alpha dual-energy X-ray source for coronary angiography

R44HL-42199-03 (SSS) CURLEY, MICHAEL G THERMAL TECHNOLOGIES, INC 222 3RD ST., SUITE 123 CAMBRIDGE, MA 02142 Continuous oxygen tension--perfusion measurement system

R44HL-42208-03 (SSS) RAMANATHAN, JAYASHREE UNIVERSAL ENERGY SYSTEMS INC 4401 DAYTON-XENIA RD DAYTON, OH 45432 Hypercube workstation for 3D coronary arteriography

R01HL-42209-03 (CVB) SCHIEBINGER, RICK J WAYNE STATE UNIVERSITY 4201 ST ANTOINE DETROIT, MI 48201 Mechanisms regulating atriopeptin secretion

R44HL-42214-02A1 (SSS) HARDS, ROBERT G OXFORD BIOMEDICAL RESEARCH, IN PO BOX 522/1600 HOSNER ROAD OXFORD, MI 48051 Isolation/purification mammalian prostacyclin synthase

P50HL-42215-04 (SRC) STROHL, KINGMAN P UNIV HOSPITALS OF CLEVELAND 2074 ABINGTON ROAD CLEVELAND, OH 44106 SCOR in cardiopulmonary disorders during sleep

P50HL-42215-04 0001 (SRC) STROHL, KINGMAN SCOR in cardiopulmonary disorders during sleep Response to hypoxia and sleep apnea

P50HL-42215-04 0002 (SRC) HUDGEL, DAVID W SCOR in cardiopulmonary disorders during sleep Nasopharyngeal muscle control in obstructive apnea

P50HL-42215-04 0003 (SRC) VAN LUNTEREN, ERIC SCOR in cardiopulmonary disorders during sleep Cardiovascular responsese to repiratory disturbance during sleep

P50HL-42215-04 0004 (SRC) LA MANNA, JOSEPH SCOR in cardiopulmonary disorders during sleep Brain vascular and metabolic adaptations to hypoxemia

P50HL-42215-04 9001 (SRC) HUDGEL, DAVID W SCOR in cardiopulmonary disorders during sleep Core--Human assessment

P50HL-42215-04 9002 (SRC) STROHL, KINGMAN SCOR in cardiopulmonary disorders during sleep Animal models of chronic hypoxia and sleep interruption

R01HL-42218-04 (SRC) ENGELMANN, GARY L LOYOLA UNIVERSITY OF CHICAGO 2160 SOUTH FIRST AVENUE MAYWOOD, IL 60153 Basic biology of cardiac development

R01HL-42220-04 (SRC) VEENSTRA, RICHARD D SUNY HEALTH SCIENCE CTR 750 E ADAMS STREET SYRACUSE, NY 13210 Gap junctions and ionic currents in developing heart

R01HL-42227-04 (SRC) TIDBALL, JAMES G UNIVERSITY OF CALIFORNIA 405 HILGARD AVENUE LOS ANGELES, CA 90024-1406 Cell adhesion in embryonic hearts

R44HL-42232-03 (SSS) JENNY, RICHARD J HAEMATOLOGIC TECHNOLOGIES, INC PINEWOOD PLAZA ESSEX JUNCTION, VT 05452 Selective capture and quantitation of serine proteases

P50HL-42236-04 (SRC) PACK, ALLAN I HOSP OF THE UNIV OF PENN 3600 SPRUCE STREET PHILADELPHIA, PA 19104 SCOR in cardiopulmonary disorders during sleep

P50HL-42236-04 0001 (SRC) MORRISON, ADRIAN R SCOR in cardiopulmonary disorders during sleep Neural basis of repiratory muscles inhibition in REM sleep

P50HL-42236-04 0002 (SRC) DAVIES, RICHARD SCOR in cardiopulmonary disorders during sleep Respiratory neuronal activity during active sleep

P50HL-42236-04 0003 (SRC) HENDRICKS, JOAN C SCOR in cardiopulmonary disorders during sleep Neural inhibition and REM sleep-disorderd breathing

P50HL-42236-04 0004 (SRC) PACK, ALLAN I SCOR in cardiopulmonary disorders during sleep Mechanisms initiation apneas in NREM sleep and REM sleep

P50HL-42236-04 0005 (SRC) DINGES, DAVID F SCOR in cardiopulmonary disorders during sleep Daytime functioning and intermittent cPAP used in OSAS

P50HL-42236-04 9001 (SRC) SILAGE, DENNIS A SCOR in cardiopulmonary disorders during sleep Core--Computer and electronics

P50HL-42236-04 9002 (SRC) KLINE, LEWIS SCOR in cardiopulmonary disorders during sleep Core--Human assessment and data management

P01HL-42242-04 (SRC) DEMPSEY, JEROME A UNIV OF WISCONSIN MEDICAL SCH 504 N WALNUT STREET MADISON, WI 53705 SCOR in cardiopulmonary disorders during sleep

P01HL-42242-04 0002 (SRC) DEMPSEY, JEROME A SCOR in cardiopulmonary disorders during sleep Sleep effects on respiratory regulation

P01HL-42242-04 0001 (SRC) SKATRUD, JAMES B SCOR in cardiopulmonary disorders during sleep sleep effects on repiratory muscle regulation

P01HL-42242-04 0003 (SRC) YOUNG, THERESA B SCOR in cardiopulmonary disorders during sleep Epidemiology of sleep disorders breathing

P01HL-42242-04 0004 (SRC) GOODFRIEND, THEODORE SCOR in cardiopulmonary disorders during sleep Mechanisms of hypertension in sleep-induced disorders breathing

P01HL-42242-04 0005 (SRC) BUSSE, WILLIAM SCOR in cardiopulmonary disorders during sleep Airway biology of nocturnal asthma

P01HL-42242-04 9001 (SRC) DEMPSEY, JEROME SCOR in cardiopulmonary disorders during sleep Core--Sleep studies laboratory

P01HL-42242-04 9002 (SRC) PALTA, MARI SCOR in cardiopulmonary disorders during sleep Core--Biostatistic

P01HL-42242-04 9003 (SRC) DEMPSEY, JEROME A SCOR in cardiopulmonary disorders during sleep Core unit

R01HL-42249-04 (SRC) TERRACIO, LOUIS UNIVERSITY OF SOUTH CAROLINA SCHOOL OF MED/ANATOMY DEPT COLUMBIA, SC 29208 Chemical and physical factors affect heart development

R01HL-42250-04 (CVA) ANDERSON, PAGE A DUKE UNIV MEDICAL CENTER BOX 3218 DURHAM, NC 27710 Developmental correlates--Membrane/contractile protein

R01HL-42254-04 (CVA) KLOPFENSTEIN, HAROLD S THE BOWMAN GRAY SCHOOL OF MED 300 S HAWTHORNE RD WINSTON-SALEM, NC 27103 Hemodynamics of cardiac tamponade

R01HL-42257-09 (SSS) SULLIVAN, JOHN L UNIV OF MASSACHUSETTS DEPT OF PEDIATRICS WORCHESTER, MA 01605 Immunoregulatory defects in hemophilia

R01HL-42258-04 (SRC) WOODS, W THOMAS SOUTHERN ILLINOIS UNIVERSITY P O BOX 19230 SPRINGFIELD, IL 62794-9230 Pacemaker development in embryonic heart

P50HL-42266-02 (SRC) LAUER, RONALD M UNIV OF IOWA HOSP & CLINICS CARDIOVASCULAR CENTER IOWA CITY, IA 52242 SCOR in congenital heart disease

P50HL-42266-02 0001 (SRC) LAUER, RONALD SCOR in congenital heart disease Molecular epidemiology of endocardial cushion defects

P50HL-42266-02 0002 (SRC) SOLURSH, MICHAEL SCOR in congenital heart disease Extracellular interactions in early cardiac morphogenesis

P50HL-42266-02 0003 (SRC) RUNYAN, RAYMOND SCOR in congenital heart disease Atrioventricular canal mesenchyme formation

P50HL-42266-02 0004 (SRC) LIN, JIM J SCOR in congenital heart disease: Molecular basis of contractile protein isoform switches in heart development

P50HL-42266-02 9001 (SRC) BURNS, TRUDY SCOR in congenital heart disease Biostatistics core

P50HL-42267-02 (SRC) ROBERTS, ROBERT BAYLOR COLLEGE 6535 FANNIN, MAIL STATION F905 HOUSTON, TX 77030 SCOR in heart failure

P50HL-42267-02 0001 (SRC) EPSTEIN, HENRY SCOR in heart failure Familial hypertrophic cardiomyopathy--Cellular,genetic alterations

P50HL-42267-02 0002 (SRC) ROBERTS, ROBERT SCOR in heart failure DNA linkage--Gene causing familial hypertrophic cardiomyopathy

P50HL-42267-02 0003 (SRC) JOHO, ROLF SCOR in heart failure Cardiac sodium channels--Cloning & structure/function analysis

P50HL-42267-02 0004 (SRC) SCHWARTZ, ROBERT SCOR in heart failure Alpha-actin gene expression--Cardiac myogenesis & hypertrophy

P50HL-42267-02 0005 (SRC) BOLLI, ROBERTO SCOR in heart failure Acute cardiac failure secondary to postischemic dysfunction

P50HL-42267-02 0006 (SRC) HENRY, PHILIP D SCOR in heart failure: Arteriosclerosis development after transplantation--Immune, nonimmune

P50HL-42267-02 9001 (SRC) ROBERTS, ROBERT SCOR in heart failure Core--Molecular biology

P50HL-42267-02 9002 (SRC) MICHAEL, LLOYD SCOR in heart failure Animal core

P50HL-42267-02 9003 (SRC) PRATT, CRAIG M SCOR in heart failure Clinical core

P50HL-42270-02 (SRC) STRANDNESS, DONALD E, JR UNIVERSITY OF WASHINGTON SEATTLE, WA 98195 SCOR in coronary and vascular diseases

P50HL-42270-02 0005 (SRC) CLOWES, ALEXANDER W SCOR in coronary and vascular diseases Arterial injury and repair--Role of proliferogenic smooth muscle cells

P50HL-42270-02 0006 (SRC) REIDY, MICHAEL A SCOR in coronary and vascular diseases Regrowth of vascular endothelium

P50HL-42270-02 0007 (SRC) BOWEN-POPE, DANIEL F SCOR in coronary and vascular diseases Expression of PDGF by vascular cells

P50HL-42270-02 9001 (SRC) GORDON, DAVID SCOR in coronary and vascular diseases Core--Morphology

P50HL-42270-02 9002 (SRC) NELSON, ALAN C SCOR in coronary and vascular diseases Core--Image analysis

P50HL-42270-02 0001 (SRC) STRANDNESS, DONALD E, JR SCOR in coronary and vascular diseases Clinical characterization of the atherosclerotic lesion

P50HL-42270-02 0002 (SRC) STRANDNESS, DONALD E, JR SCOR in coronary and vascular diseases Ultrasonic characterization of normal and atherosclerotic arterial wall

P50HL-42270-02 0003 (SRC) GORDON, DAVID SCOR in coronary and vascular diseases Proliferation and growth factors in atherosclerosis

R01HL-42282-03 (RAP) COLERIDGE, JOHN C UNIVERSITY OF CALIFORNIA 1327 MOFFITT HOSPITAL SAN FRANCISCO, CA 94143-0130 Lung and airway afferents and their reflex role

R01HL-42283-04 (SSS) DAVIS, BRIAN R MEDICAL RESEARCH INSTITUTE 2200 WEBSTER STREET SAN FRANCISCO, CA 94115 Study of HIV infection in bone marrow stem cells

R01HL-42293-03 (ECS) MORGAN, KATHLEEN G BETH ISRAEL HOSP 330 BROOKLINE AVENUE BOSTON, MA 02215 Contraction of vascular smooth muscle cells

R01HL-42303-03 (SRC) BUTLER, KENNETH C NIMBUS, INC 2890 KILGORE ROAD RANCHO CORDOVA, CA 95670 Research-development of a thermal cardiac assist system

R01HL-42304-03 (SRC) WHITE, MAURICE A STIRLING TECHNOLOGY COMPANY 2952 GEORGE WASHINGTON WAY RICHLAND, WA 99352 Investigation of thermal ventricular assist system, TVAS

R01HL-42305-03 (EDC) STEVENS, JUNE MEDICAL UNIV OF SOUTH CAROLINA 171 ASHLEY AVENUE CHARLESTON, SC 29425 Adiposity and fat patterning in black Americans

R01HL-42311-02 (SRC) BRAUNWALD, EUGENE BRIGHAM AND WOMEN'S HOSPITAL 75 FRANCIS STREET BOSTON, MA 02115 Thrombolysis in myocardial ischemia-clinical application

R01HL-42320-03 (EDC) WING, STEVEN B UNIV. OF NORTH CAROLINA SCHOOL OF PUBLIC HEALTH CHAPEL HILL, NC 27599-7400 Community structure and cardiovascular mortality trends

R01HL-42321-02 (CVB) FOREMAN, ROBERT D UNIVERSITY OF OKLAHOMA PO BOX 26901 OKLAHOMA CITY, OK 73190 Sudden cardiac death: prevention by neural modulation

R01HL-42322-03 (BBCB) HOLDEN, HAZEL M INSTITUTE OF ENZYME RESEARCH 1710 UNIVERSITY AVE MADISON, WI 53705 Structural studies of lipid binding proteins

R37HL-42325-03 (CVA) POTTER, JAMES D UNIVERSITY OF MIAMI 1600 NW 10 AVENUE, PO BOX 0161 MIAMI, FL 33101 Mechanism of cardiac muscle regulation by troponin

R01HL-42330-03 (HED) FUNKHOUSER, JANE D UNIVERSITY OF SOUTH ALABAMA 307 UNIVERSITY BOULEVARD MOBILE, AL 36688 Lung epithelial development--A molecular approach

R01HL-42332-04 (SRC) DAVIDSON, EUGENE A GEORGETOWN UNIVERSITY 3900 RESERVOIR RD, NW/BIOCHEM WASHINGTON, DC 20007 Molecular biology studies on respiratory mucins

R29HL-42333-04 (MET) LEBOEUF, RENEE C UNIVERSITY OF WASHINGTON DIV OF METABOLISM RG-26 SEATTLE, WA 98195 High density lipoproteins and atherosclerosis

R01HL-42353-01A3 (CVB) KLINE, RICHARD P COLUMBIA UNIVERSITY 630 WEST 168TH STREET NEW YORK, NY 10032 Arrhythmogenic ion activity changes in chronic ischemia

R01HL-42354-02 (CVB) QUINN, STEPHEN J BRIGHAM & WOMEN'S HOSPITAL 75 FRANCIS STREET BOSTON, MA 02115 Ionic and steroid responses to vasoactive hormones

R01HL-42357-03 (CVA) BRIDGE, JOHN H B UNIVERSITY OF UTAH BLDG 100, ROOM 207 SALT LAKE CITY, UT 84112 Mechanisms of diastolic relaxation in the heart

R29HL-42358-03 (PHRA) MACHIDA, CURTIS A OREGON REGIONAL PRIMATE RES CT 505 N W 185TH AVE/NEUROSCI DIV BEAVERTON, OR 97006 B-adrenergic receptor activation and expression

R01HL-42362-03 (RAP) KEITH, INGEGERD M UNIVERSITY OF WISCONSIN 2015 LINDEN DRIVE WEST MADISON, WI 53706 Role of regulatory peptides in pulmonary hypertension

R01HL-42364-02 (CVA) LITTLE, WILLIAM C BOWMAN GRAY SCHOOL OF MEDICINE 300 SOUTH HAWTHORNE ROAD WINSTON-SALEM, NC 27103 Left ventricular-arterial coupling

R01HL-42365-02 (CVA) WATSON, PETER A GEISINGER CLINIC NORTH ACADEMY AVE DANVILLE, PA 17822 Cell stretch and cardiac hypertrophy

R01HL-42366-03 (BEM) BRENER, JASPER SUNY AT STONY BROOK STONY BROOK, NY 11794-2500 Cognitive processing of visceral afference

P50HL-42368-04 (SRC) WIDDICOMBE, JONATHAN H UNIVERSITY OF CALIFORNIA CARDIOVASCULAR RESEARCH INST SAN FRANCISCO, CA 94143 Regulation of apical membrane CL channels in airways

P50HL-42368-04 0001 (SRC) WIDDICOMBE, JONATHAN Regulation of apical membrane CL channels in airways Regularory pathways and altered chloride secretion by respiratory epithelium

P50HL-42368-04 0002 (SRC) WINE, JEFFREY Regulation of apical membrane CL channels in airways Pathophysiology of cystic fibrosis--Ion channels

P50HL-42368-04 9002 (SRC) FINKBEINER, WALTER E Regulation of apical membrane CL channels in airways Core--Airway cell culture facility

P50HL-42368-04 0003 (SRC) VERKMAN, ALLAN S Regulation of apical membrane CL channels in airways Purifying chloride channels from secretory epithelia

P50HL-42368-04 9001 (SRC) LEWISTON, NORMAN J Regulation of apical membrane CL channels in airways Core--Clinical/cell acquisition

R01HL-42370-03 (CVB) ZIPES, DOUGLAS P KRANNERT INST OF CARDIOLOGY 1001 WEST 10TH STREET INDIANAPOLIS, IN 46202 Autonomic modulation of ischemic arrhythmias

R01HL-42376-03 (RAP) FANBURG, BARRY L NEW ENGLAND MED CTR 750 WASHINGTON ST, NEMC #257 BOSTON, MA 02111 Regulation of SOD production in lung cells

R29HL-42377-04 (ECS) DIXON, BRADLEY S UNIVERSITY OF IOWA IOWA CITY, IOWA 52242 Activation of protein kinase C in vasular smooth muscle

P50HL-42384-04 (SRC) BOUCHER, RICHARD C U OF N CAROLINA AT CHAPEL HILL CB #7020, 724 BURNETT-WOMACK CHAPEL HILL, NC 27599-7020 Cystic fibrosis research center

P50HL-42384-04 0001 (SRC) BOUCHER, RICHARD C Cystic fibrosis research center Function of transfected genes in human airway epithelium

P50HL-42384-04 0002 (SRC) STUTTS, M JACKSON Cystic fibrosis research center Regulation of Na transport in human airway epithelium

P50HL-42384-04 0003 (SRC) BOAT, THOMAS Cystic fibrosis research center Sulfate metabolism &glycoconjugate sulfation in cystic fibrosis

P50HL-42384-04 9001 (SRC) YANKASKAS, JAMES Cystic fibrosis research center Core--Tissue culture and molecular biology research center

P50HL-42385-04 (SRC) WELSH, MICHAEL J UNIVERSITY OF IOWA CARDIOVASCULAR CENTER IOWA CITY, IA 52242 Cystic fibrosis research center--membrane biology of CF

P50HL-42385-04 0001 (SRC) WELSH, MICHAEL CYSTIC FIBROSIS RESEARCH CENTER--MEMBRANE BIOLOGY OF CF Chloride and sodium channel regulation in airway epithelium

P50HL-42385-04 0002 (SRC) WELSH, MICHAEL CYSTIC FIBROSIS RESEARCH CENTER--MEMBRANE BIOLOGY OF CF Calcium function and metabolism in airway epitheium

P50HL-42385-04 0003 (SRC) STETSON, DAVID CYSTIC FIBROSIS RESEARCH CENTER--MEMBRANE BIOLOGY OF CF Cyclic AMP stimulated apical vesical insertion in airway epithelia

P50HL-42385-04 0004 (SRC) SHASBY, MICHAEL CYSTIC FIBROSIS RESEARCH CENTER--MEMBRANE BIOLOGY OF CF Mechanisms of inflammation and injury in airway epithelia

P50HL-42385-04 9001 (SRC) WELSH, MICHAEL CYSTIC FIBROSIS RESEARCH CENTER--MEMBRANE BIOLOGY OF CF Core--Cell culture

R01HL-42388-03 (CVA) LUX, ROBERT L UNIV OF UTAH BLDG 100, RM 207 SALT LAKE CITY, UT 84112 Cardiac electrophysiologic imaging from potential fields

R01HL-42392-03 (MET) WEINBERGER, JUDAH Z COLUMBIA UNIVERSITY 630 WEST 168TH ST NEW YORK, NY 10032 Cellular metabolism in response to hypercholesterolemia

R29HL-42395-03 (PBC) KOERNER, THEODORE A JR UNIVERSITY OF IOWA MRC 143 PATHOLOGY IOWA CITY, IA 52242 Pathobiochemistry of blood platelet glycosphingolipids

R01HL-42397-02 (SAT) ZAPOL, WARREN M MASSACHUSETTS GENERAL HOSPITAL BOSTON, MA 02114 Heparin-protamine lung vasoconstriction at heart surgery

R01HL-42398-02 (HEM) GERARD, ROBERT D UNIV OF TEXAS SW MED CTR 5323 HARRY HINES BOULEVARD DALLAS, TX 75235-9038 Analysis of plasminogen activator-inhibitor interaction

R01HL-42402-03 (CVB) ADAIR, THOMAS H UNIVERSITY OF MISSISSIPPI 2500 NORTH STATE STREET JACKSON, MS 39216 Microcirculatory adaptations and their control

R01HL-42412-03 (HEM) HENSCHEN, AGNES H UNIVERSITY OF CALIFORNIA DEPT OF MOLEC BIO/BIOCHEMISTRY IRVINE, CA 92717 Fibrinogen variants--Structure and function

R29HL-42416-02 (BNP) LANSBURY, PETER T JR MASSACHUSETTS INST OF TECH 77 MASSACHUSETTS AVE/18-486 CAMBRIDGE, MA 02139 Molecular basis for anticoagulant activity of heparin

R01HL-42419-03 (SRC) BRAUNWALD, EUGENE BRIGHAM AND WOMEN'S HOSPITAL 75 FRANCIS STREET BOSTON, MA 02115 Thrombolysis in myocardial ischemia-Core application

R01HL-42419-03 9001 (SRC) DODGE, HAROLD Thrombolysis in myocardial ischemia-Core application Quantitative angiographic core laboratory

R01HL-42419-03 9002 (SRC) CHAITMAN, BERNARD Thrombolysis in myocardial ischemia-Core application Electrocardiogram/exercise tolerance test core laboratory

R01HL-42419-03 9003 (SRC) STONE, PETER Thrombolysis in myocardial ischemia-Core application Ambulatory ECG monitoring core laboratory

R01HL-42419-03 9004 (SRC) WILLIAMS, DAVID Thrombolysis in myocardial ischemia-Core application Qualitative angiographic core laboratory

R01HL-42419-03 9005 (SRC) ZARET, BARRY L Thrombolysis in myocardial ischemia-Core application Radionuclide (thallium) core laboratory

R01HL-42426-04 (SB) LUPINETTI, FLAVIAN M UNIVERSITY OF MICHIGAN 2120 TAUBMAN CTR BOX 0344 ANN ARBOR, MI 48109 Studies of aortic valve allografts in rats

R01HL-42427-03 (BEM) CARNEY, ROBERT M DEPARTMENT OF PSYCHIATRY 660 S EUCLID AVE ST LOUIS, MO 63110 Depression & coronary heart disease

R01HL-42428-03 (SRC) KNATTERUD, GENELL L MARYLAND MEDICAL RES INST, INC 600 WYNDHURST AVENUE BALTIMORE, MD 21210 Thrombolysis in myocardial ischemia coordinating center

R29HL-42435-03 (RNM) MOLLOI, SABEE UNIVERSITY OF CALIFORNIA DIV. OF PHYSICS & ENGINEERING IRVINE, CA 92717 Quantitative coronary angiography by dual energy DSA

R01HL-42439-02 (SRC) BRITTENHAM, GARY M CLEVELAND METRO GENERAL HOSP 3395 SCRANTON ROAD CLEVELAND, OH 44109 Carbonyl iron supplementation for female blood donors

R01HL-42441-02 (EDC) BURING, JULIE E BRIGHAM & WOMENS HOSP. 55 POND AVE BROOKLINE, MA 02146 Randomized trial of MDS--Study of low CV mortality

P01HL-42443-03 (HLBB) FURIE, BRUCE NEW ENGLAND MEDICAL CENTER 750 WASHINGTON STREET BOSTON, MA 02111 Membrane proteins in blood coagulation

P01HL-42443-03 0001 (HLBB) WALSH, CHRISTOPHER T Membrane proteins in blood coagulation Mechanism of action of the vitamin K-dependent carboxnase

P01HL-42443-03 0002 (HLBB) FURIE, BARBARA Membrane proteins in blood coagulation Structure of the vitamin K-dependent carboxylase

P01HL-42443-03 0003 (HLBB) FURIE, BRUCE Membrane proteins in blood coagulation Assembly of factor IX and factor VIII in membranes

P01HL-42443-03 0004 (HLBB) WAGNER, DENISA D Membrane proteins in blood coagulation Endothelial cell recptors an membrane proteins

P01HL-42443-03 0005 (HLBB) FURIE, BRUCE Membrane proteins in blood coagulation Alpha granule proteins translocated to plasma membranes

P01HL-42443-03 0006 (HLBB) LAWLER, JOHN W Membrane proteins in blood coagulation Adhesive protein receptors on vascular cells

P01HL-42443-03 9001 (HLBB) FURIE, BRUCE Membrane proteins in blood coagulation Analytical--Core

P01HL-42443-03 9002 (HLBB) WAGNER, DENISA D Membrane proteins in blood coagulation Tissue culture--Core

P01HL-42444-02 (HLBA) PIANTADOSI, CLAUDE A DUKE UNIVERSITY MED CTR P O BOX 3315 DURHAM, NC 27710 Toxic and therapeutic effects of hyperbaric oxygen

P01HL-42444-02 0001 (HLBA) PIANTADES, CLAUDE A Toxic and therapeutic effects of hyperbaric oxygen Oxygen and co-cytochrome interactions in vivo

P01HL-42444-02 0002 (HLBA) KENNEDY, THOMAS P Toxic and therapeutic effects of hyperbaric oxygen Iron OH generation and lipid peroxidation during hyperoxia

P01HL-42444-02 0003 (HLBA) WHORTON, A RICHARD Toxic and therapeutic effects of hyperbaric oxygen Regulation of arachidonate metabolism by oxygen

P01HL-42444-02 0004 (HLBA) KLITZMAN, BRUCE M Toxic and therapeutic effects of hyperbaric oxygen Microvascular control of tissue oxygenation

P01HL-42444-02 0005 (HLBA) CYAPO, JAMES D Toxic and therapeutic

PROJECT NO., ORGANIZATIONAL UNIT., INVESTIGATOR, ADDRESS, TITLE

effects of hyperbaric oxygen Sites of oxidants and antioxidants in lung cells
P01HL-42444-02 9001 (HLBA) MERCER, ROBERT R Toxic and therapeutic effects of hyperbaric oxygen CORE--Microscopy
R29HL-42445-02 (RAP) PARISI, RICHARD A UMDNJ-R W JOHNSON MEDICAL SCHO ONE R W JOHNSON PLACE-CN 19 NEW BRUNSWICK, NJ 08903-0019 Determinants of compartmental upper airway resistance
R29HL-42447-02 (CVB) FLEMING, JOHN T UNIVERSITY OF LOUISVILLE LOUISVILLE, KY 40292 Renal glomerular hemodynamics--Neural control mechanism
R01HL-42453-03 (SRC) GOULD, K LANCE UNIVERSITY OF TEXAS MED SCHOOL DIV/CARD-RM 4 258, 6431 FANNIN HOUSTON, TX 77030 Effects of lifestyle changes on coronary heart disease
R29HL-42454-03 (HEM) OROURKE, FLAVIA A UNIVERSITY OF CONNECTICUT 263 FARMINGTON AVE FARMINGTON, CT 06030 Purification and properties of IP3 receptor in platelets
R29HL-42455-02 (ECS) BELL, LEONARD B VA MEDICAL CENTER MILWAUKEE, WI 53295 Baroreflex modulation in conscious hypertensive rabbits
R01HL-42456-02 (EDC) SISCOVICK, DAVID S HARBORVIEW MEDICAL CTR (ZA-60) 325 NINTH AVENUE SEATTLE, WA 98104 Antihypertensive therapy & primary cardiac arrest
R01HL-42457-03 (HEM) LIND, STUART E BRIGHAM AND WOMEN'S HOSPITAL 75 FRANCIS STREET BOSTON, MA 02115 Interaction of actin with plasma proteins and platelets
R01HL-42460-03 (NTN) SCHONFELD, GUSTAV WASHINGTON UNIVERSITY 4566 SCOTT AVE, BOX 8046 ST LOUIS, MO 63110 Metabolism of genetic variants of apolipoprotein B
R01HL-42463-02 (CVB) GRAY, SARAH D UNIVERSITY OF CALIFORNIA DEPT OF HUMAN PHYSIOLOGY DAVIS, CA 95616 Skeletal muscle microvascular perfusion in hypertension
R01HL-42467-02 (EDC) SEIDMAN, CHRISTINE BRIGHAM & WOMEN'S HOSPITAL 75 FRANCIS STREET BOSTON, MA 02115 Genetic analysis of familial hypertrophic cardiomyopathy
R01HL-42470-03 (RAP) REMMERS, JOHN E UNIV OF CALGARY FACULTY OF MED 3330 HOSPITAL DRIVE, N W CALGARY, ALBERTA CNDA T2N 1N4 Obstructive sleep apnea & periodic breathing in sleep
R01HL-42482-03 (RAP) RANNELS, STEPHEN R PENNSYLVANIA STATE UNIVERSITY M S HERSHEY MED CTR/PO BOX 850 HERSHEY, PA 17033 Surfactant protein carboxylation in type II lung cells
R01HL-42483-03 (EDC) ROSENBERG, LYNN BOSTON UNIVERSITY SCH OF MED 1371 BEACON STREET BROOKLINE, MA 02146 Myocardial infarction and current oral contraceptive use
R01HL-42485-03 (SRC) MERMELSTEIN, ROBIN J UNIVERSITY OF ILLINOIS BOX 6998 CHICAGO, IL 60680 Recycling attempters and relapsers in smoking cessation
R01HL-42488-03 (BIO) LUSIS, ALDONS J UNIVERSITY OF CALIFORNIA, L A DEPT/MEDICINE, 405 HILGARD AVE LOS ANGELES, CA 90024 Lipoprotein metabolism genetic control--Mouse model
R01HL-42489-02 (SRC) DOLCE, JEFFREY J UNIVERSITY OF ALABAMA UAB STATION BIRMINGHAM, AL 35294 Medication adherence in COPD--A self regulation study
R01HL-42490-02 (TOX) DAISEY, JOAN M LAWRENCE BERKELEY LABORATORY MAIL STOP 90-3058/1 CYCLOTRON BERKELEY, CA 94720 Environmental tobacco smoke--physico-chemical properties
R01HL-42493-03 (HEM) HAJJAR, KATHERINE A CORNELL UNIVERSITY 1300 YORK AVENUE- ROOM C-606 NEW YORK, N Y 10021 Assembly of the fibrinolytic system on endothelial cells
R01HL-42496-03 (PTHA) FOWLER, STANLEY D UNIVERSITY OF SOUTH CAROLINA DEPARTMENT OF PATHOLOGY COLUMBIA, SC 29208 Hypertension, diabetes accelerated atherosclerosis
R01HL-42498-02 (EDC) LESSIN, LAWRENCE S GEORGE WASHINGTON UNIV MED CTR 2150 PENNSYLVANIA AVENUE N W WASHINGTON, D C 20037 Indices of severity & prognosis for sickle cell disease
R29HL-42506-03 (RNM) SALONER, DAVID A VA MEDICAL CENTER SAN FRANCISCO, CA 94121 Flow velocity quantitation by MRI
R01HL-42507-03 (PTHA) STERN, DAVID M COLUMBIA UNIVERSITY 630 WEST 168 STREET NEW YORK, NY 10032 Modulation of endothelial cell function of hypoxia
R01HL-42512-01A2 (PHRA) PAPPANO, ACHILLES J UNIVERSITY OF CONNECTICUT 263 FARMINGTON AVENUE FARMINGTON, CT 06032 L-Palmitoylcarnitine mechanism(s) on heart ion currents
R01HL-42525-01A3 (ECS) TRACHTE, GEORGE J UNIVERSITY OF MINNESOTA 10 UNIVERSITY DRIVE DULUTH, MN 55812 Atrial natriuretic factor and adrenergic nerves
R01HL-42527-03 (PHRA) PALADE, PHILIP T UNIV OF TEXAS MEDICAL BRANCH PHYSIOLOGY & BIOPHYSICS DEPT GALVESTON, TX 77550 Pharmacology of muscle excitation-contraction coupling
R01HL-42528-02 (ECS) HUXLEY, VIRGINIA H UNIVERSITY OF MISSOURI MA415 MEDICAL SCIENCES COLUMBIA, MO 65212 Regulation of single capillary permeability properties
R01HL-42532-02 (BEM) GLUSMAN, MURRAY NEW YORK STATE PSYCHIATRIC INS 722 WEST 168TH STREET NEW YORK, NY 10032 Silent myocardial ischemia and pain sensitivity
R01HL-42535-01A1 (CVA) BARRY, WILLIAM H UNIV OF UTAH MEDICAL CENTER 50 NORTH MEDICAL DRIVE SALT LAKE CITY, UT 84132 Mechanisms of myocyte injury during cardiac rejection
R01HL-42536-02 (MBY) ENGEL, JAMES D NORTHWESTERN UNIVERSITY 2153 SHERIDAN ROAD EVANSTON, IL 60208 Hematopoietic stem cells
R01HL-42539-03 (ECS) COLUCCI, WILSON S BRIGHAM & WOMEN'S HOSP INC 75 FRANCIS STREET BOSTON, MA 02115 Regulation of vascular alpha-1 adrenergic responses
R01HL-42540-03 (HEM) SILVERSTEIN, ROY L CORNELL UNIVERSITY 1300 YORK AVENUE NEW YORK, NY 10021 Molecular and cell biology of a thrombospondin receptor
P01HL-42550-02 (HLBA) ENTMAN, MARK L BAYLOR COLLEGE OF MEDICINE ONE BAYLOR PLAZA HOUSTON, TX 77030 Role of inflammation in early myocardial ischemia
P01HL-42550-02 0001 (HLBA) ENTMAN, MARK L Role of inflammation in early myocardial ischemia Inflammation in the course of early myocardial ischemia
P01HL-42550-02 0002 (HLBA) ANDERSON, DONALD C Role of inflammation in early myocardial ischemia Neutrophil adherence determinants in myocardial reperfusion injury
P01HL-42550-02 0003 (HLBA) SMITH, C WAYNE Role of inflammation in early myocardial ischemia Endothelial determinants of neutrophil adherence and migration
P01HL-42550-02 9001 (HLBA) HAWKINS, HAROLD K Role of inflammation in early myocardial ischemia Pathology--Core
P01HL-42550-02 9002 (HLBA) MICHAEL, LLOYD Role of inflammation in early myocardial ischemia Quantitation-intervention--Core
R01HL-42554-04 (SRC) ORNISH, DEAN PREVENTIVE MEDICINE RES INST 7 MILLER AVE SAUSALITO, CA 94965 Effects of lifestyle changes on coronary heart disease
R01HL-42555-02 (SAT) MOHAMMAD, SYED F UNIVERSITY OF UTAH SALT LAKE CITY, UT 84112 Thrombogenesis in blood pumping devices
R01HL-42562-03 (CVA) COBB, FREDERICK R DURHAM VETERANS ADM MED CENTER 508 FULTON STREET DURHAM, NC 27705 Heterogeneity of coronary artery vasomotion
R01HL-42583-01A3 (PHRA) GALLANT, SHERYLE J UNIFORMED SERVS UNIV OF HLTH S 4301 JONES BRIDGE ROAD BETHESDA, MD 20814-4799 Stress and responses to phenylpropanolamine and caffeine
R01HL-42584-02 (RAP) ALTIERE, RALPH J UNIVERSITY OF COLORADO CAMPUS BOX 297 BOULDER, CO 80309-0297 Pulmonary vascular muscarinic receptors
R01HL-42585-03 (ECS) HEALY, DENNIS P MOUNT SINAI SCHOOL OF MEDICINE ONE GUSTAVE L LEVY PL BOX 1215 NEW YORK, NY 10029 Regulation of brain angiotensin II in hypertension
R29HL-42606-02 (PTHA) MCCAFFREY, TIMOTHY A CORNELL UNIV MEDICAL COLLEGE 1300 YORK AVE NEW YORK, NY 10021 Aging and atherosclerosis -- Effects of growth inhibitors
R01HL-42607-03 (PTHA) JOHNSON, KENT J UNIV OF MICHIGAN MED SCHOOL 1301 CATHERINE ROAD ANN ARBOR, MI 48109 Oxidant and protease interaction in acute lung injury
R01HL-42609-03 (PTHA) CRAPO, JAMES D DUKE UNIVERSITY PO BOX 3177 DURHAM, NC 27710 Sites of oxidants and antioxidants in lung cells
R29HL-42614-03 (SB) MILLER, VIRGINIA M MAYO FOUNDATION 200 FIRST ST SOUTHWEST ROCHESTER, MN 55905 Modulation of endothelial function in vascular grafts
R29HL-42617-03 (PTHA) ROSENFELD, MICHAEL E UNIV OF CA. SAN DIEGO . LA JOLLA, CA 92093 Heterogeneity of arterial macrophage derived foam cells
R29HL-42622-02 (PTHA) DENHOLM, ELIZABETH M UNION UNIV ALBANY MED COLLEGE 47 NEW SCOTLAND AVE ALBANY, NY 12208 Monocyte chemotactic factors in pulmonary fibrosis
R01HL-42630-03 (MGN) MAEDA, NOBUYO UNIV. OF NC AT CHAPEL HILL CHAPEL HILL, NC 27599 Apolipoprotein genes and atherogenesis in animals
R01HL-42636-03 (ECS) BARRETT, JACK D VA MEDICAL CENTER VASCULAR BIOPHARMACOLOGY LAB SEPULVEDA, CA 91343 Dopaminergic control of tissue renin
R29HL-42637-02 (RAP) BREEN, PETER H UNIVERSITY OF CHICAGO 5841 S MARYLAND AVE CHICAGO, IL 60637 Carbon dioxide kinetics during non-steady state
R29HL-42646-02 (PHY) SIMARD, J MARC UNIVERSITY OF TEXAS MED BRANCH 301 UNIVERSITY BLVD GALVESTON, TX 77550 Ionic channels in cerebrovascular smooth muscle cells
R01HL-42651-03 (PBC) BHAVANANDAN, VEER P PENNSYLVANIA STATE UNIVERSITY HERSHEY, PA 17033 The polymeric structure of mucous glycoproteins
R01HL-42654-02 (SB) ELGEBALY, SALWA A UNIV OF CONNECTICUT HEALTH CTR 263 FARMINGTON AVENUE FARMINGTON, CT 06032-9984 Cardiac derived neutrophil chemotactic factors
R01HL-42660-03 (BEM) ANDERSON, NORMAN B DUKE UNIVERSITY MEDICAL CENTER BOX 3830 DURHAM, NC 27710 Patterns of cardiovascular reactivity in blacks
R01HL-42662-04 (PTHA) CHARO, ISRAEL F GLADSTONE FOUNDATION LAB P.O. BOX 40608 SAN FRANCISCO, CA 94140 Monocyte receptors mediating adhesion to endothelial cells
R01HL-42663-04 (CVB) PRATT, RICHARD E STANFORD UNIVERSITY 300 PASTEUR DRIVE STANFORD, CA 94305 Vascular angiotensin in blood vessel hypertrophy
R29HL-42665-03 (CVB) FORD, DAVID A WASHINGTON UNIV SCH OF MED 660 SOUTH EUCLID AVE. BOX 8020 ST LOUIS, MO 63110 Plasmalogen catabolism during myocardial ischemia
R01HL-42666-02 (CVB) EGHBALI, MAHBOUBEH MICHAEL REESE HOSP/MEDICAL CTR LAKE SHORE DR AT 31ST ST CHICAGO, IL 60616 Collagen gene expression in cardiac hypertrophy
R01HL-42672-04 (RNM) HOFFMAN, ERIC A UNIVERSITY OF PENNSYLVANIA HOS 3400 SPRUCE STREET PHILADELPHIA, PA 19104 Determinants of regional lung expansion and perfusion
R01HL-42674-03 (ARR) HOFFMAN, RONALD INDIANA UNIVERSITY SCH OF MED 541 CLINICAL DRIVE, ROOM 379 INDIANAPOLIS, IN 46223 Mechanism of hematpoietic suppression in HIV-1 infection
R44HL-42731-02 (HEM) CLAPPER, DAVID L BIO-METRIC SYSTEMS, INC 9924 WEST 74TH STREET EDEN PRAIRIE, MN 55344 Covalent surface coating with antithrombotic agents
R01HL-42734-04 (EDC) PEARSON, THOMAS A MARY IMOGENE BASSETT HOSPITAL ONE ATWELL ROAD COOPERSTOWN, NY 13326 Cardiovascular disease in black versus white physicians
R44HL-42738-02 (HUD) FEY, MICHAEL S NEW LIFE HEALTH PRODUCTS CORPS 8 BLACK BIRCH DRIVE RANDOLPH, NJ 07869 Clinical evaluation of an OTC smoking deterrent lozenge
R01HL-42758-03 (CVB) MITCHELL, RICHARD W UNIVERSITY OF CHICAGO BOX 98 5841 S MARYLAND AVE CHICAGO, IL 60637 Neural and pharmacological control of airway smooth muscle
R01HL-42760-03 (CVB) IDEKER, RAYMOND E DUKE UNIVERSITY BOX 3140 DURHAM, NC 27710 Cardiac mapping of ventricular defibrillation
R01HL-42780-02 (SRC) MARTELL, ARTHUR E TEXAS A & M UNIVERSITY COLLEGE STATION, TX 77843 Development and testing of new chelators
R01HL-42798-12 (PBC) BOYD, CHARLES D UMDNJ R W JOHNSON MED SCHOOL ONE ROBERT WOOD JOHNSON PLACE NEW BRUNSWICK, NJ 08903 Structure and organization of basement membranes
U01HL-42799-03 (SRC) SLICHTER, SHERRILL J PUGET SOUND BLOOD CENTER 921 TERRY AVENUE SEATTLE, WA 98104-1256 Prevention of platelet alloimmunization

PROJECT NO., ORGANIZATIONAL UNIT., INVESTIGATOR, ADDRESS, TITLE

R01HL-42800-02 (SRC) HIDER, ROBERT C KINGS COLL LONDON/CHELSEA CAMP MANRESA ROAD LONDON SW3 6LX, ENGLAND Design and clinical assessment of pyridinone chelators

U01HL-42802-03 (SRC) MCCULLOUGH, J JEFFREY UNIV OF MINNESOTA HOSPITAL HARVARD AT E RIVER; BOX 198 UM MINNEAPOLIS, MN 55455 Transfusion trial to prevent platelet alloimmunization

U01HL-42805-03 (SRC) ROSSE, WENDELL F DUKE UNIVERSITY MEDICAL CTR BOX 3934 DURHAM, NC 27710 Transfusion trial to prevent platelet alloimmunizations

U01HL-42810-03 (SRC) BRAINE, HAYDEN G JOHNS HOPKINS UNIVERSITY 600 NORTH WOLFE STREET BALTIMORE, MD 21205 Transfusion trial to prevent platelet allo immunization

U01HL-42811-03 (SRC) KAO, KUO-JANG UNIV OF FLORIDA COLL OF MED BOX J-275 GAINESVILLE, FL 32610 Transfusion trial to prevent platelet alloimmunization

R01HL-42812-03 (SRC) MCGEE, MARIA P BOWMAN GRAY SCHOOL OF MED MEDICAL CTR BLVD WINSTON-SALEM, NC 27103 Cancer-induced coagulation--Monocytes and hyaluronic acid

R01HL-42813-03 (SRC) LELLA, VIJAYA M UNIVERSITY OF CALIFORNIA 225 DICKINSON STREET SAN DIEGO, CA 92103 Thrombosis in malignancy--Role of tissue factor

R01HL-42814-03 (SRC) BRITTENHAM, GARY M METOHEALTH MEDICAL CENTER 3395 SCRANTON ROAD CLEVELAND, OH 44109 Chelation therapy of iron overload with PIH

U01HL-42815-03 (SRC) SCHIFFER, CHARLES A UNIVERSITY OF MARYLAND 22 SOUTH GREENE STREET BALTIMORE, MD 21201 Transfusion trial to prevent platelet alloimmunization

R01HL-42817-03 (SRC) BERGERON, RAYMOND J UNIVERSITY OF FLORIDA BOX J485, JHMHC GAINESVILLE, FL 32610 Development of orally effective iron chelators

R01HL-42822-03 (SRC) TODD, MARY B YALE UNIVERSITY SCH OF MED 333 CEDAR STREET; POB 3333 NEW HAVEN, CT 06510 Tissue factor messenger RNA, antigen, and activity in malignancy

U01HL-42824-03 (SRC) DAVIS, KATHRYN B UNIVERSITY OF WASHINGTON 1107 NE 45TH STREET SEATTLE, WA 98105 Transfusion trial to prevent platelet alloimmunization

U01HL-42832-03 (SRC) MCFARLAND, JANICE G BLOOD CTR/SOUTHEASTERN WISCONS 1701 WEST WISCONSIN AVENUE MILWAUKEE, WI 53233 Transfusion trial to prevent platelet alloimmunization

R01HL-42833-03 (SRC) STERN, DAVID M COLUMBIA UNIVERSITY 630 WEST 168TH STREET NEW YORK, NY 10032 Tumor-induced modulation of endothelial cell function

R01HL-42846-03 (HEM) RUGGERI, ZAVERIO M SCRIPPS CLINIC & RESEARCH FDN 10666 NORTH TORREY PINES ROAD LA JOLLA, CA 92037 Structure and function of platelet membrane glycoproteins

R01HL-42851-01A2 (HED) LEFFLER, CHARLES W UNIVERSITY OF TENNESSEE 894 UNION AVE MEMPHIS, TN 38163 Newborn cerebral hemorrhage and arachidonate metabolites

R01HL-42856-02 (ECS) AVIV, ABRAHAM UMDNJ-NEW JERSEY MED SCHOOL 185 SOUTH ORANGE AVE NEWARK, NJ 07103-2757 Platelet calcium ion homeostasis in essential hypertension

R01HL-42865-03 (MET) KRAEMER, FREDRIC B STANFORD UNIVERSITY SCH OF MED STANFORD, CA 94305 Regulation of LDL receptors in adipocytes

R01HL-42873-03 (CVA) SPITZER, KENNETH W UNIVERSITY OF UTAH BLDG 500 SALT LAKE CITY, UT 841112 Ph regulation in ventricular cells

R29HL-42875-03 (NEUA) MIRRO, ROBERT UNIVERSITY OF TENNESSEE 853 JEFFERSON AVENUE MEMPHIS, TN 38163 Pressure ventilation and neonatal cerebral hemodynamics

R29HL-42883-03 (RAP) FIKE, CANDICE D UNIVERSITY OF UTAH 50 NORTH MEDICAL DRIVE SALT LAKE CITY, UT 84132 Maturational changes in the pulmonary microcirculation

R01HL-42884-02 (RNM) MILLER, TOM R MALLINCKRODT INST OF RADIOLOGY 510 SOUTH KINGSHIGHWAY BOULEVA ST LOUIS, MO 63110 Improved analysis and display of cardiac PET images

R01HL-42886-03 (BBCB) STOOPS, JAMES K UNIVERSITY OF TEXAS HLTH SCI C PO BOX 20708 HHOUSTON, TX 77225 Electron microscopy of human alpha2-macroglobulin

R01HL-42893-02 (HED) ANDERSON, DEBRA F OREGON HLTH SCICS UNIVERSITY 3181 SW SAM JACKSON PARK RD PORTLAND, OREGON 97201 Long-term regulation of fetal blood volume

R29HL-42898-01A2 (CVB) UNTHANK, JOSEPH L INDIANA UNIVERSITY 1001 WEST 10TH STREET INDIANAPOLIS, IN 46202-2879 Vascular adaptation in pathophysiology

R01HL-42908-03 (RAP) KULIK, THOMAS J CHILDRENS HOSPITAL 300 LONGWOOD AVE BOSTON, MA 02115 Stretch as a growth stimulus in vascular smooth muscle

R01HL-42911-03 (RAP) ZWILLICH, CLIFFORD W PENNSYLVANIA STATE UNIVERSITY P O BOX 850 HERSHEY, PA 17033 Sleep influence on the pharynx and ventilatory control

R01HL-42919-03 (HEM) ATWEH, GEORGE F V A MEDICAL CENTER 800 POLY PL BROOKLYN, NY 11209 Normal and aberrant globin gene expression

R01HL-42932-01A1 (EDC) DWYER, JAMES H UNIV. OF SOUTHERN CA 1000 S. FREMONT, SUITE 641 ALHAMBRA, CA 91803 Dietary calcium and prevention of hypertension in Blacks

R29HL-42939-03 (ECS) ARMSTEAD, WILLIAM M UNIVERSITY OF TENNESSEE 894 UNION AVENUE MEMPHIS, TN 38163 Opioids and cerebral hemodynamics

R01HL-42940-03 (SRC) MANN, KENNETH G UNIVERSITY OF VERMONT GIVEN BLDG BURLINGTON, VT 05405 Coagulation and fibrinolysis in TIMI III

R01HL-42943-03 (HEM) LEUNG, LAWRENCE L STANFORD UNIVERSITY STANFORD, CA 94305-5112 Molecular and cellular biology of glycoprotein IIIB

R37HL-42949-03 (HEM) BUNN, H FRANKLIN BRIGHAM AND WOMEN'S HOSP, INC 75 FRANCIS STREET BOSTON, MA 02115 Erythropoietin--Structure function relationships

R01HL-42950-03 (RNM) WICKLINE, SAMUEL A WASHINGTON UNIVERSITY 660 SOUTH EUCLID AVE BOX 8086 ST LOUIS, MO 63110 Physical determinants of intrinsic acoustic properties

R01HL-42958-02 (CVA) REICHEK, NATHANIEL UNIV OF PENNSYLVANIA HOSP 3400 SPRUCE ST PHILADELPHIA, PA 19104 Structure & function of infarcted left ventricle

R29HL-42966-02 (CVA) PIWNICA-WORMS, DAVID R BRIGHAM & WOMEN'S HOSPITAL 75 FRANCIS STREET BOSTON, MA 02115 Uptake mechanisms of Tc perfusion agents in heart cells

PROJECT NO., ORGANIZATIONAL UNIT., INVESTIGATOR, ADDRESS, TITLE

R01HL-42968-03 (HEM) GITSCHIER, JANE M UNIVERSITY OF CALIFORNIA U-426 SAN FRANCISCO, CA 94143-0724 Molecular basis and therapy of hemophilia A

R01HL-42973-02 (EDC) CRIQUI, MICHAEL H UCSD LA JOLLA, CA 92093 The natural history of peripheral arterial disease

R01HL-42975-02 (CVA) GU, JIANG DEBORAH RESEARCH INSTITUTE TRENTON ROAD BROWNS MILLS, NJ 08015-1799 A morphological study of cardiac innervation

R29HL-42977-02 (HEM) LOFTUS, JOSEPH C RESEARCH INST/SCRIPPS CLINIC 10666 N TORREY PINES ROAD LA JOLLA, CA 92037 Structure & function of blood platelet GPIIb-IIIa

R01HL-42987-02 (SRC) JASON, LEONARD A DEPAUL UNIVERSITY 2219 N KENMORE AVE CHICAGO, IL 60614 Worksite incentives for becoming a nonsmoker

R01HL-42992-03 (PTHA) LYNCH, ROBERT E VA MEDICAL CENTER (113) 500 FOOTHILL DRIVE SALT LAKE CITY, UT 84148 Toxicity of O2- and H2O2

R01HL-42993-03 (PTHA) VIJAYAGOPAL, PARAKAT LOUISIANA STATE UNIV MED CTR 1542 TULANE AVE NEW ORLEANS, LA 70112 Arterial wall proteoglycans and foam cell formation

R01HL-42997-02 (RNM) WHITING, JAMES S CEDARS-SINAI MEDICAL CENTER 8700 BEVERLY BOULEVARD LOS ANGELES, CA 90048 Angiographic imaging of coronary lesion morphology

R01HL-43002-03 (PTHA) DANIELE, RONALD P HOSP OF UNIV OF PENNSYLVANIA 3400 SPRUCE STREET PHILADELPHIA, PA 19104 Pulmonary defenses--Role of lung macrophage motility

R01HL-43006-02 (CVB) PELLEG, AMIR HANNEMANN UNIVERSITY BROAD AND VINE PHILADELPHIA, PA 19102-1192 Adenosine--a biological cardioprotective agent

R01HL-43008-02 (CVA) TARR, CHARLES M UNIVERSITY OF KANSAS MED CTR 39TH & RAINBOW BLVD KANSAS CITY, KS 66103-8410 Reactive oxygen species and single cardiac cell function

R01HL-43014-02 (RNM) AXEL, LEON UNIVERSITY OF PENNSYLVANIA 36TH ST & HAMILTON WALK PHILADELPHIA, PA 19104-6086 Development of a new MRI method to study cardiac motion

R01HL-43015-03 (HED) THORNBURG, KENT L OREGON HEALTH SCIENCES UNIV 3181 S W SAM JACKSON PARK ROAD PORTLAND, OR 97201 Diastolic properties of developing myocardium

R29HL-43020-03 (HEM) BRAY, PAUL F JOHN HOPKINS UNIVERSITY 600 N WOLFE STREET BALTIMORE, MD 21205 Cellular consequences of defective IIB and IIIA genes

P01HL-43023-01A2 (HLBA) KALEY, GABOR NEW YORK MEDICAL COLLEGE VALHALLA, NY 10595 Endothelium and vascular function

P01HL-43023-01A2 0001 (HLBA) WONG, PATRICK Y-K Endothelium and vascular function Phospholipase A2, eicosanoids, and vascular interactions

P01HL-43023-01A2 0002 (HLBA) WOLIN, MICHAEL S Endothelium and vascular function Reactive oxygen species and coronary arterial tone

P01HL-43023-01A2 0003 (HLBA) GURTNER, GAIL H Endothelium and vascular function Role of vascular endothelium in acute lung injury

P01HL-43023-01A2 0004 (HLBA) KALEY, GABOR Endothelium and vascular function Endothelial dependence of microcirculatory regulation

P01HL-43023-01A2 0005 (HLBA) HINTZE, THOMAS H Endothelium and vascular function Vascular regulation by flow velocity/endothelium

P01HL-43023-01A2 9001 (HLBA) STEMERMAN, MICHAEL B Endothelium and vascular function CORE--Cell culture

R01HL-43025-01A2 (RNM) RITMAN, ERIK L MAYO FOUNDATION 200 FIRST STREET SOUTHWEST ROCHESTER, MN 55905 Heterogeneity of myocardial perfusion and solute transfer

P01HL-43026-02 (HLBB) CHIEN, SHU THE REG. OF THE UNIV. OF CA LA JOLLA, CA 92093-0934 Biomechanics of blood cells, vessels and microcirculation

P01HL-43026-02 0001 (HLBB) SUNG, LANPING AMY Biomechanics of blood cells, vessels and microcirculation Molecular biology of membrane skeletal proteins

P01HL-43026-02 0002 (HLBB) SKLAR, LARRY A Biomechanics of blood cells, vessels and microcirculation Energetics and amplification of neutrophil adhesion

P01HL-43026-02 0003 (HLBB) SUNG, KUO-LI PAUL Biomechanics of blood cells, vessels and microcirculation Microrheology of blood cells and endothelial cells

P01HL-43026-02 0004 (HLBB) CHIEN, SHU Biomechanics of blood cells, vessels and microcirculation Energy balance in blood cell interactions

P01HL-43026-02 0005 (HLBB) SKALAK, RICHARD Biomechanics of blood cells, vessels and microcirculation Modeling of cellular micromotion and adhesion

P01HL-43026-02 0006 (HLBB) FUNG, YUAN-CHENG Biomechanics of blood cells, vessels and microcirculation Biomechanics of microblood vessels and microcirculation

P01HL-43026-02 0007 (HLBB) SCHMID-SCHONBEIN, GEERT W Biomechanics of blood cells, vessels and microcirculation Leukocyte kinectics in the microcirculation

P01HL-43026-02 9001 (HLBB) HOFFMAN, ROBERT Biomechanics of blood cells, vessels and microcirculation CORE--Cell and tissue culture

P01HL-43026-02 9002 (HLBB) MCCULLOCH, ANDREW Biomechanics of blood cells, vessels and microcirculation CORE--Computer modeling and image processing

P01HL-43026-02 9003 (HLBB) USAMI, SUNICHI Biomechanics of blood cells, vessels and microcirculation CORE--Instrumentation

R01HL-43027-03 (SRC) HILGARTNER, MARGARET W CORNELL MEDICAL COLLEGE 1300 YORK AVENUE NEW YORK, NY 10021 New promise for oral iron chelation

R01HL-43028-03 (BEM) BLUMENTHAL, JAMES A DUKE UNIV MEDICAL CENTER POST OFFICE BOX 3119 DURHAM, N C 27710 Behavioral treatment of transient myocardial ischemia

R29HL-43030-03 (SAT) BAKER, JOHN E MILWAUKEE REGIONAL MED CENTER 8700 WEST WISCONSIN AVENUE MILWAUKEE, WI 53226 Age, reactive oxygen metabolites and myocardial injury

R01HL-43032-03 (HED) PLOPPER, CHARLES G UNIV OF CALIF SCH OF VET MED DAVIS, CA 95616 Regulators of clara cell differentiation in lung

R29HL-43034-03 (MGN) WANG, SUE M UNIVERSITY OF MARYLAND 655

PROJECT NO., ORGANIZATIONAL UNIT., INVESTIGATOR, ADDRESS, TITLE

WEST BALTIMORE STREET BALTIMORE, MD 21201 Regulation of renin gene expression in dahl rats
R01HL-43035-03 (HED) COLLINS, DELWOOD C UNIVERSITY OF KENTUCKY LEXINGTON, KY 40536-0084 Antiangiogenic activity of steroids & steroid conjugates
R01HL-43041-02 (BEM) RACZYNSKI, JAMES M UNIVERSITY OF ALABAMA UAB STATION, 101 MTB BIRMINGHAM, AL 35294 Lipid variability--Influence of stress
R01HL-43048-02 (SRC) LUBIN, BERTRAM H CHILDREN'S HOSPITAL 747 52ND STREET OAKLAND, CA 94609 New approaches to therapy in iron overload states
R29HL-43052-03 (CTY) NAFTILAN, ALLAN J UNIVERSITY OF ALABAMA UAB STATION/1012 ZEIGLER BLDG BIRMINGHAM, AL 35294 Angiotensin II induction of PDGF smooth muscle cells
R29HL-43089-02 (ECS) HESTER, ROBERT L UNIV OF MISSISSIPPI MEDICAL CT 2500 NORTH STATE STREET JACKSON, MS 39216-4505 Venular-arteriolar communication in the microcirculation
R01HL-43091-01A2 (ECS) GOLDMAN, WILLIAM F UNIV OF MARYLAND SCH OF MEDICI 655 WEST BALTIMORE STREET BALTIMORE, MD 21201 Calcium regulation in arterial myocytes
R01HL-43098-03 (CVA) KERBER, RICHARD E UNIVERSITY OF IOWA HOSPITAL IOWA CITY, IA 52242 Arterial morphology and remodeling in atherosclerosis
R01HL-43106-01A2 (HEM) KANE, WILLIAM H DUKE UNIVERSITY MEDICAL CENTER BOX 3656 DURHAM, NC 27710 Molecular biology of human coagulation factor v
R01HL-43111-03 (MET) KELLER, RONALD K USF COLLEGE OF MEDICINE 12901 BRUCE B DOWNS BLVD TAMPA, FL 33612 Regulation of isoprenoid biosynthesis in liver
R01HL-43124-01A2 (CVB) CLAYCOMB, WILLIAM C LOUISIANA STATE UNIV MED CTR 1901 PERDIDO ST NEW ORLEANS, LA 70112 Growth of the heart muscle cell
R01HL-43133-01A2 (CVA) TAEGTMEYER, HEINRICH UNIVERSITY OF TEXAS MEDICAL SC 6431 FANNIN HOUSTON, TX 77030 Kinetics of muscle metabolism by positron tracers
R01HL-43141-02 (PTHA) WINN, ROBERT K HARBORVIEW MEDICAL CENTER 325 NINTH AVENUE SEATTLE, WA 98102 Granulocyte emigration and septic lung injury
R01HL-43146-01A2 (ECS) DURAN, WALTER N NEW JERSEY MEDICAL SCHOOL 185 SOUTH ORANGE AVE NEWARK, NJ 07103-2757 Control of microcirculatory exchange function
R29HL-43148-03 (CVB) LUKAS, ANTON MASONIC MEDICAL RES LABORATORY 2150 BLEECKER ST UTICA, NY 13501-1787 Selective depression of epicardium by ischemia
R01HL-43151-03 (CVB) BOLLI, ROBERTO BAYLOR COLLEGE OF MEDICINE 6535 FANNIN, MAIL STATION F-90 HOUSTON, TX 77030 Role of oxygen radicals in postischemic dysfunction
R01HL-43153-03 (EDC) SAMET, JONATHON UNIV OF NEW MEXICO/CANCER CTR 900 CAMINO DE SALUD, NE ALBUQUERQUE, NM 87131 Idiopathic pulmonary fibrosis: a case control study
R01HL-43154-03 (ECS) BROWN, MARVIN R UNIV OF CALIFORNIA 9500 GILMAN DR LA JOLLA, CA 92093-0934 Cardiovascular biology of neuropeptide Y
R01HL-43155-02 (HEM) FULLER, GERALD M UNIVERSITY OF ALABAMA UAB STATION BIRMINGHAM, AL 35294 Transcriptional regulation of fibrinogen biosynthesis
R01HL-43159-03 (CVA) SIDDIQUI, M SUNY HEALTH SCIENCE CENTER 450 CLARKSON AVENUE, BOX #5 BROOKLYN, NY 11203-2098 Regulatory factors in cardiac adaptation to hemodynamic overload
R01HL-43160-02 (ECS) MYERS, ADAM K GEORGETOWN UNIVERSITY 3900 RESERVOIR RD/NW WASHINGTON, DC 20007 NPY and the platelet-vascular interaction
R01HL-43161-04 (RAP) DICKEY, BURTON F BAYLOR COLLEGE OF MEDICINE ONE BAYLOR PLAZA HOUSTON, TX 77030 Control of surfactant secretion by GTP binding proteins
R01HL-43164-01A2 (NTN) EGAN, BRENT M MEDICAL COLLEGE OF WISCONSIN 8700 W WISCONSIN AVE MILWAUKEE, WI 53226 Hyperinsulinemia and hypertension in overweight men
R01HL-43165-03 (NTN) TALL, ALAN R COLUMBIA UNIVERSITY 630 WEST 168TH STREET NEW YORK, NY 10032 Nutritional effects on transfer protein gene expression
R01HL-43167-02 (CLTR) BERNARD, GORDON R VANDERBILT UNIVERSITY 21ST AVE S AND GARLAND ST NASHVILLE, TN 37232-2650 Cardiopulmonary effects of ibuprofen in human sepsis
R01HL-43170-03 (CVA) INGWALL, JOANNE S THE BRIGHAM & WOMEN'S HOSP. IN 221 LONGWOOD AVENUE BOSTON, MA 02115 Energetics and cation movements in postischemic heart
R01HL-43173-03 (CVA) ATKINS, DIANNE L UNIV OF IOWA HOSPITALS & CLINI IOWA CITY, IA 52242 Ontogenesis of hypertrophic cardiomyopathy
R01HL-43174-03 (PTHA) BAUTCH, VICTORIA L UNIVERSITY OF NORTH CAROLINA CB# 3280 CHAPEL HILL, NC 27599-3280 Molecular control of angiogenesis
R01HL-43178-02 (END) MORRIS, MARIANA WAKE FOREST UNIVERSITY 300 SOUTH HAWTHORNE ROAD WINSTON-SALEM, NC 27103 Baroreceptor/hormonal interactions
R01HL-43183-02 (PHRA) BJORNSSON, THORIR D JEFFERSON MEDICAL COLLEGE 1100 WALNUT STREET PHILADELPHIA, PA 19107 Aspirin's fibrinolytic effect--Acetylation of fibrinogen
R01HL-43194-02 (BBCB) MAYO, KEVIN H TEMPLE UNIVERSITY 13TH & NORRIS STREETS PHILADELPHIA, PA 19122 NMR structures of platelet factor 4 and beta-thromboglobulin
R01HL-43201-01A2 (EDC) PSATY, BRUCE M UNIVERSITY OF WASHINGTON 325 NINTH AVE ZA-60 SEATTLE, WA 98104 Calcium-channel blockers and primary prevention of CHD
R01HL-43202-03 (RAP) RAVEN, PETER B TEXAS COLLEGE OF OSTEOPATHIC M 3500 CAMP BOWIE BLVD FT WORTH, TX 76107 Baroreflexes and orthostatism--A fitness effect
R01HL-43203-03 (MGN) GRAY, MARK R TUFTS UNIV SCHOOL OF MED 136 HARRISON AVENUE BOSTON, MA 02111 Single base differences in the human factor viii gene
R29HL-43213-02 (SAT) HOLMAN, WILLIAM L UNIVERSITY OF ALABAMA 619 SOUTH 19TH STREET BIRMINGHAM, AL 35294 Electrophysiology during post-cardioplegia reperfusion

PROJECT NO., ORGANIZATIONAL UNIT., INVESTIGATOR, ADDRESS, TITLE

R01HL-43215-01A2 (CVA) SCADUTO, RUSSELL C, JR PENNSYLVANIA STATE UNIVERSITY PO BOX 850 HERSHEY, PA 17033 Control of cardiac respiration by calcium
R01HL-43216-03 (BEM) BARSKY, ARTHUR J MASSACHUSETTS GENERAL HOSPITAL FRUIT ST BOSTON, MA 02114 Cardiac arrhythmias and the perception of symptoms
R01HL-43220-01A1 (HEM) CORASH, LAURENCE M UNIVERSITY OF CALIFORNIA SAN FRANCISCO, CA 94143-0100 Photochemical decontamination of platelet concentrates
R55HL-43222-01A1 (RAP) BENITZ, WILLIAM E STANFORD UNIVERSITY 300 PASTEUR DR/RM S-222 STANFORD, CA 94305-5119 Proteoheparan sulfate inhibitor of smooth muscle growth
R01HL-43229-03 (BBCB) TULINSKY, ALEXANDER MICHIGAN STATE UNIVERSITY EAST LANSING, MI 48824-1322 Structures of catalytic domains of blood proteins
R01HL-43230-03 (BBCB) OTVOS, JAMES D NORTH CAROLINA STATE UNIVERSIT PO BOX 7622 RALEIGH, NC 27695 Analysis of plasma lipoproteins by 1H NMR spectroscopy
R37HL-43231-03 (PHRA) SCHWARTZ, ARNOLD UNIVERSITY OF CINCINNATI 231 BETHESDA AVENUE CINCINNATI, OH 45267-0575 Cardiovascular Ca antagonist receptors--Structure-function
R01HL-43232-02 (EDC) KJELSBERG, MARCUS O UNIVERSITY OF MINNESOTA 2221 UNIVERSITY AVENUE, SE MINNEAPOLIS, MN 55414 Mortality follow-up and analysis--MRFIT randomized men
R29HL-43242-03 (ECS) IKEDA, STEPHEN R MEDICAL COLLEGE OF GEORGIA 1459 LANEY-WALKER BLVD AGUSTA, GA 30912-2300 Neuronal calcium current alterations in hypertension
R29HL-43245-03 (CVA) PILATI, CHARLES F NORTHEASTERN OHIO UNIVERSITIES 4209 STATE ROUTE 44 ROOTSTOWN, OH 44272 Left ventricular dysfunction with massive sympathetic activity
R01HL-43252-02 (HEM) VILLANUEVA, GERMAN B NEW YORK MEDICAL COLLEGE VALHALLA, NY 10595 Conformational studies of proteins in contact activation
R01HL-43256-03 (RAP) THET, LYN A UNIVERSITY OF WISCONSIN 750 UNIVERSITY AVENUE Mechanisms of repair of hyperoxic lung injury
R29HL-43275-03 (END) TAKIYYUDDIN, MARWAN A UNIV OF CALIF, SAN DIEGO V-111 H LA JOLLA, CA 92093-0023 Chromogranin a in experimental hypertension
R01HL-43276-03 (CVA) TACCARDI, BRUNO UNIVERSITY OF UTAH BUILDING 500 SALT LAKE CITY, UT 84112 Three-dimensional mapping of cardiac electric fields
R01HL-43277-03 (EDC) DETRANO, ROBERT C RES & EDUCATION INST 1124 WEST CARSON ST TORRANCE, CA 90502 Coronary screening in a high risk subset
R29HL-43278-04 (CVB) SCHNITZER, JAN E UNIV. OF CALIF., SAN DIEGO 9500 GILMAN DRIVE LA JOLLA, CA 92093-0651 Albumin-endothelium interactions in normal and diabetics
R01HL-43285-02 (RAP) SCHRAMM, CRAIG M CHILDREN'S HOSP OF PHILADELPHI 34TH STREET & CIVIC CENTER BLV PHILADELPHIA, PA 19104 Corticosteroid effect on airway beta-adrenergic function
R01HL-43286-02 (RNM) GEFTER, WARREN B HOSP OF THE UNIV OF PENNSYLVAN 3400 SPRUCE STREET PHILADELPHIA, PA 19104 Obstructive sleep apnea--Multi-parametric imaging study
R01HL-43287-02 (RNM) SAHN, DAVID J UCSD SCHOOL OF MEDICINE 225 W. DICKINSON STREET SAN DIEGO, CA 92103-0808K Improved understanding of cardiac flows
R01HL-43302-03 (PTHA) TAUBMAN, MARK B MOUNT SINAI SCHOOL OF MEDICINE 1 GUSTAVE L LEVY PLACE-BOX 111 NEW YORK, NY 10029 Growth-related genes in vascular smooth muscle
R29HL-43304-02 (HED) TOD, MARY L UNIV OF MD AT BALTIMORE 10 S PINE ST BALTIMORE, MD 21201 Development of neonatal pulmonary vascular reactivity
R29HL-43307-03 (CVA) YUE, DAVID Y MD PHD JOHNS HOPKINS UNIVERSITY 720 RUTLAND AVENUE BALTIMORE, MD 21205 Cardiac Ca channels--regulation of slow gating behavior
R01HL-43311-03 (NTN) BRUCKNER, GEZA G UNIVERSITY OF KENTUCKY LEXINGTON, KY 40536-0080 Fats, microcirculation & platelet-endothelial cells
R29HL-43312-03 (RAP) KARP, MARSHA W JOHNS HOPKINS UNIVERSITY 615 NORTH WOLFE STREET BALTIMORE, MD 21205 G protein and age-related changes in airway reactivity
R01HL-43318-03 (SRC) KARNOVSKY, MORRIS J HARVARD MEDICAL SCHOOL 200 LONGWOOD AVENUE BOSTON, MA 02115 Experimental cardiac transplant atherosclerosis
R01HL-43320-16 (HED) ROONEY, SEAMUS A YALE UNIV SCH OF MEDICINE 333 CEDAR ST/P O BOX 3333 NEW HAVEN, CT 06510 Effect of hormones on lung phospholipid biosynthesis
R01HL-43322-03 (SRC) COUGHLIN, SHAUN UNIVERSITY OF CALIFORNIA BOX 0524 SAN FRANCISCO, CA 94143-0524 Cell and molecules mediating graft atherosclerosis
R01HL-43331-01A2 (SAT) BENDER, JEFFREY R YALE UNIVERSITY SCH OF MEDICIN 333 CEDAR STREET, PO BOX 3333 NEW HAVEN, CT 06510 Molecular models of immune mediated vascular injury
R01HL-43339-03 (SRC) PIZZO, SALVATORE V DUKE UNIVERSITY MEDICAL CENTER BOX 3712 DURHAM, NC 27710 Lipoprotein (a), coagulation and fibrinolysis
R01HL-43340-03 (SRC) RUSSELL, PAUL S MASSACHUSETTS GENERAL HOSPITAL 32 FRUIT STREET BOSTON, MA 02114 Cardiac transplant atherosclerosis
R01HL-43344-03 (SRC) SCANU, ANGELO M UNIVERSITY OF CHICAGO 5841 S MARYLAND AVE/BOX 231 CHICAGO, IL 60637 Prothrombotic effects in lipoprotein(a)
R01HL-43364-03 (PTHB) LIBBY, PETER BRIGHAM & WOMEN'S HOSPITAL 75 FRANCIS ST BOSTON, MA 02115 Pathogenesis of transplant-associated arteriosclerosis
R29HL-43365-02 (ECS) FLAVAHAN, NICHOLAS A JOHNS HOPKINS MED INSTITUTIONS 600 NORTH WOLFE STREET BALTIMORE, MD 21205 Endothelium-dependent relaxation--G protein regulation
R01HL-43369-02 (PTHA) HOSENPUD, JEFFREY D OREGON HLTH SCIENCES UNIVERSIT 3181 SW SAM JACKSON PARK ROAD PORTLAND, OR 97201 Recipient immune response to donor-specific endothelium
R01HL-43370-03 (SRC) STRAUCH, ARTHUR R OHIO STATE UNIVERSITY 1654 UPHAM DRIVE COLUMBUS, OH 43210 Coronary phenotypic modulation

after cardiac transplant

R01HL-43373-03 (SRC) BRADLEY, WILLIAM A UNIVERSITY OF ALABAMA UAB STATION BIRMINGHAM, AL 35294 VLDL, atherosclerosis, and thrombosis--mechanistic links

R01HL-43375-03 (SRC) POPP, RAYMOND A OAK RIDGE NATIONAL LABORATORY P O BOX 2009 OAK RIDGE, TN 37831-8077 Mouse mutant hemoglobins that allow HbS to sickle

R29HL-43379-03 (CVA) DEMER, LINDA L UNIVERSITY OF CALIFORNIA 10833 LECONTE AVENUE LOS ANGELES, CA 90024-1679 Mechanical basis for optimal balloon angioplasty

R01HL-43380-03 (CVB) MOCHLY-ROSEN, DARIA D SAN FRANCISCO GENERAL HOSPITAL BUILDING 1 SAN FRANSISCO, CA 94110 Roles of protein kinase C in cardiac myocytes

R01HL-43388-02 (ARR) STEIN-STREILEIN, JOAN E UNIV OF MIAMI SCH OF MED PO BOX 016960/DEPT MED R-47 MIAMI, FL 33101 Mechanisms of defective natural killer (nk) cytotoxicity

R29HL-43392-03 (PTHA) NICOSIA, ROBERTO F MED. COLLEGE OF PENNSYLVANIA 3300 HENRY AVENUE PHILADELPHIA, PA 19129 Function of extracellular matrix in angiogenesis

R01HL-43395-03 (SRC) LEVINE, ROY A CORNELL UNIVERSITY ITHACA, N Y 14853 Regulation of alveolar epithelial cell differentiation

R01HL-43397-03 (SRC) BOTHWELL, MARK A UNIVERSITY OF WASHINGTON SEATTLE, WA 98195 NGF in lung development

R01HL-43399-03 (SRC) NAVRE, MARC E SYNTEX RESEARCH 3401 HILLVIEW AVE; M/S R7-275 PALO ALTO, CA 94304 Growth factor action in developing lung

R01HL-43407-03 (SRC) NIELSEN, HEBER C NEW ENGLAND MEDICAL CENTER HOS BOX 97, 750 WASHINGTON STREET BOSTON, MA 02111 Myc oncogenes in fetal lung growth and maturation

R01HL-43410-03 (SRC) MULLIGAN, EILEEN M TEMPLE UNIV SCH OF MEDICINE 3420 NORTH BROAD STREET PHILADELPHIA, PA 19140 Carotid body cellular Ca++ and PH responses

R01HL-43412-03 (SRC) NURSE, COLIN A MC MASTER UNIVESITY 1280 MAIN STREET WEST HAMILTON, ONTARIO CANADA L8S 4 Chemosensory mechanisms in cultured carotid body cells

R01HL-43413-03 (SRC) LAHIRI, SUKHAMAY UPA SCHOOL OF MEDICINE PHILADELPHIA, PA 19104-6085 O2 sensing and cell biology in the carotid body

R01HL-43416-03 (SRC) POST, MARTIN HOSPITAL FOR SICK CHILDREN 555 UNIVERSITY AVENUE TORONTO, ONTARIO, CANADA M5G 1 Influence of stretch on lung growth and response to injury

R01HL-43418-03 (SRC) DEAN, DOUGLAS C WASHINGTON UNIVERSITY SCH OF M 660 SOUTH EUCLID AVE/BOX 8052 ST LOUIS, MO 63110 Fibronectin and its receptor in lung development

R01HL-43421-03 (ARR) MATTHEWS, JAMES L BAYLOR RESEARCH INST. P.O. BOX 710699 Preventing transmission of diseases (AIDS) via blood

R44HL-43441-02 (HEM) BING, DAVID H CBR LABORATORIES, INC 800 HUNTINGTON AVENUE BOSTON, MA 02115 Simplified frozen blood methodology for autologous blood

R44HL-43444-02 (HUD) AVIS, NANCY E NEW ENGLAND RESEARCH INST, INC 9 GALEN ST WATERTOWN, MA 02172 Instrument to assess quality of life in CVD -phase II

R44HL-43447-02 (HUD) SMITH, MICHAEL G CONSTRUCTIVE SOLUTIONS, INC 5506 MERCEDES AVE DALLAS, TX 75206 Development of an all-cause mortality risk profile

R44HL-43465-02 (SSS) DOMINEY, LAWRENCE A COVALENT ASSOCIATES, INC 52 DRAGON COURT WOBURN, MA 01801 Advanced implantable rechargeable batteries for ventricular assist system

R44HL-43473-02 (SSS) BARLOW, CLYDE H BARLOW SCIENTIFIC, INC 6307 TAMOSHAN DR, NW OLYMPIA, WA 98502 Epicardial oxygen monitor

R44HL-43476-02 (SSS) NICHOLS, MICHAEL F NICHOLS TECHNOLOGIES, INC 3208 LEMONE INDUSTRIAL BOULEVA COLUMBIA, MO 65201 Insulation of implant devices by plasma polymer coatings

R01HL-43506-07A2 (HEM) SCHWARTZ, BRADFORD S UNIVERSITY OF WISCONSIN 1300 UNIVERSITY AVENUE MADISON, WI 53706 Regulation of monocyte fibrinolytic inhibitors

R01HL-43508-03 (SRC) TOWNES, TIM M UNIVERSITY OF ALABAMA UAB STATION BIRMINGHAM, AL 35294 A transgenic mouse model for sickle cell disease

P01HL-43510-03 (HLBA) ROSE, RICHARD M NEW ENGLAND DEACONESS HOSPITAL 185 PILGRIM ROAD BOSTON, MA 02215 HIV-alveolar macrophage interaction

P01HL-43510-03 0001 (HLBA) ESEKOWITZ, R ALAN HIV-alveolar macrophage interaction Mechanisms of HIV entry

P01HL-43510-03 0002 (HLBA) BYRN, RANDAL A HIV-alveolar macrophage interaction Macrophage interaction with other lung cell

P01HL-43510-03 0003 (HLBA) BALTIMORE, DAVID HIV-alveolar macrophage interaction Molecular analysis of HIV infection in macrophages

P01HL-43510-03 0004 (HLBA) REMOLD, HEINZ G HIV-alveolar macrophage interaction Macrophage immune function

P01HL-43510-03 0005 (HLBA) ROSE, RICHARD M HIV-alveolar macrophage interaction Macrophage host defense function

P01HL-43510-03 0006 (HLBA) HAMMER, SCOTT M HIV-alveolar macrophage interaction Control of HIV replication in macrophages

P01HL-43510-03 9001 (HLBA) PINKSTON, PAULA HIV-alveolar macrophage interaction Cell services--Core

P01HL-43510-03 9002 (HLBA) BRAIN, JOSEPH D HIV-alveolar macrophage interaction Histopathology, ultrastructure, and morphology--Core

P01HL-43510-03 9003 (HLBA) FISHMAN, JAY A HIV-alveolar macrophage interaction Pneumocystis carinii growth and isolation--Core

R01HL-43512-02 (ARR) GJERSET, GEORGE F PUGET SOUND BLOOD CENTER/PROGR 921 TERRY AVENUE SEATTLE, WA 98104-1256 A prospective study of HIV infection in hemophiliacs

R29HL-43514-02 (BEM) ANDERSON, ERLING A UNIVERSITY OF IOWA IOWA CITY, IA 52242 Regulation of sympathetic nerve response to stress

R01HL-43521-03 (SRC) KRAMER, FRED R PUBLIC HEALTH RESEARCH INST 455 FIRST AVENUE NEW YORK, NY 10016 Extremely sensitive assays for human retroviruses

R01HL-43523-03 (SRC) KORNBLUTH, RICHARD S V A MEDICAL CENTER 3350 LA JOLLA VILLAGE DRIVE SAN DIEGO, CA 92161 Alveolar macrophages and defense of the lung in AIDS

R01HL-43524-03 (ARR) MARTIN, WILLIAM J INDIANA UNIVERSITY MEDICAL CTR 1001 WEST 10TH STREET INDIANAPOLIS, IN 46202 Mechanisms of pneumocystis carinii pneumonia

R01HL-43528-03 (SRC) WEINBERGER, OFRA COLUMBIA UNIVERSITY 630 WEST 168TH ST NEW YORK, NY 10032 Alveolar macrophages and defense of the lung in AIDS

R01HL-43529-03 (SRC) WEISSMAN, DAVID N 2100 RIDGECREST DRIVE SE ALBUQUERQUE, NM 87108 Alveolar macrophages and defense of the lung in AIDS

R01HL-43532-03 (SRC) MULLIS, KARY B SPECIALTY LABORATORIES, INC 2211 MICHIGAN AVE SANTA MONICA, CA 90404 Mass screening strategy--Detection of human retroviruses

R01HL-43555-03 (SRC) FISHER, EDWIN B, JR WASHINGTON UNIVERSITY #33 S EUCLID, 2ND FLOOR ST LOUIS, MO 63108 Community organ for smoking cessation among Black Americans

R01HL-43557-03 (SRC) EGHBALI, MAHBOUBEH MICHAEL REESE HOSP/MEDICAL CTR LAKE SHORE DR AT 31ST ST CHICAGO, IL 60616 Molecular and cellular biology of cardiac interstitium

R01HL-43560-03 (SRC) MANAK, MARK M BIOTECH RES LABORATORIES, INC 1600 EAST GUDE DRIVE ROCKVILLE, MD 20850 Combined assay for HIV-1 and HTLV-1 using polymerase chain reaction

R01HL-43561-03 (SRC) LEE, TUN-HOU HARVARD SCH OF PUBLIC HLTH 665 HUNTINGTON AVENUE BOSTON, MA 02115 Assays for screening HIV-2 and HLTV-1 antibodies

R01HL-43564-03 (SRC) BASHEY, REZA I THOMAS JEFFERSON UNIVERSITY 1020 LOCUST STREET PHILADELPHIA, PA 19107 Molecular and cellular biology of cardiac interstitium

R01HL-43571-03 (SRC) RICH, ELIZABETH A UNIVERSITY HOSPITALS 2074 ABINGTON ROAD CLEVELAND, OH 44106 Alveolar macrophages and defense of the lung in AIDS

R01HL-43582-03 (SRC) SAMAREL, ALLEN M LOYOLA UNIVERSITY MEDICAL CENT 2160 S FIRST AVENUE MAYWOOD, IL 60153 Procollagen degradation by the cardiac interstitium

R01HL-43583-03 (SRC) KOHTZ, DONALD S MOUNT SINAI SCHOOL OF MED 1 GUSTAVE LEVY PLACE NEW YORK, NY 10029 Cardiac myogenesis--Matrix dependent developmental processes

R01HL-43586-03 (SRC) VISCIDI, RAPHAEL P JOHNS HOPKINS UNIVERSITY 600 N WOLFE ST, CMSC 1109 BALTIMORE, MD 21205 Protein-gene sequence specific retrovirus diagnosis

R01HL-43594-03 (SRC) CANTIN, EDOUARD M CITY OF HOPE NATIONAL MED CTR 1500 EAST DUARTE ROAD DUARTE, CA 91010 Development of universal PCR assay for retroviruses

R01HL-43600-03 (CBY) SOLURSH, MICHAEL UNIVERSITY OF IOWA 436 BB IOWA CITY, IOWA 52242 Cell--ECM interactions in myocardial form and function

R01HL-43602-03 (SRC) POIESZ, BERNARD J SUNY HEALTH SCIENCE CENTER 750 EAST ADAMS STREET SYRACUSE, NY 13210 Development and evaluation of new screening tests for human retroviruses

R01HL-43604-03 (SRC) LEVINE, DAVID M 1830 EAST MONUMENT STREET ROOM 8047 BALTIMORE, MD 21205 Church-based smoking cessation strategies in urban blacks

R01HL-43606-03 (SRC) NEVID, JEFFREY S ST JOHN'S UNIVERSITY DEPARTMENT OF PSYCHOLOGY JAMAICA, NY 11439 Minority specific intervention for Hispanic smokers

R01HL-43608-03 (SRC) GRITZ, ELLEN R UNIVERSITY OF CALIFORNIA 1100 GLENDON AVENUE LOS ANGELES, CA 90024-3511 Targeting adult minority smokers through public schools

R01HL-43609-03 (SRC) LUCIW, PAUL A UNIVERSITY OF CALIFORNIA DAVIS, CA 95616 Alveolar macrophages and defense of the lung in AIDS

R01HL-43611-01A1 (SRC) SCHORLING, JOHN B UNIV OF VIRGINIA HLTH SCI CTR BOX 494 CHARLOTTESVILLE, VA 22908 A trial of smoking cessation programs in black churches

R01HL-43615-03 (SRC) JOHNSON, KAREN M AMERICAN INDIAN HLTH CARE ASSO 245 EAST 6TH STREET ST PAUL, MN 55101 Smoking cessation strategies for minorities

R01HL-43617-03 (SRC) COVELL, JAMES W UNIV. OF CALIFORNIA, SAN DIEGO LA JOLLA, CA 92093-0613 Cardiac interstitium hypertrophy

R01HL-43628-03 (SRC) VOLSKY, DAVID J ST LUKE'S-ROOSEVELT HOSP CTR 432 WEST 58TH STREET NEW YORK, NY 10019 Alveolar macrophages and defense of the lung in AIDS

R01HL-43650-02 (RAP) COHEN, ALLEN B UNIVERSITY OF TEXAS HEALTH CTR P O BOX 2003 TYLER, TX 75710 Peptide mediators of lung injury in ARDS

R01HL-43651-02 (PHY) GUERRIERO, VINCE, JR UNIVERSITY OF ARIZONA TUCSON, AZ 85721 Structure vs function in myosin light chain kinase

R01HL-43654-02 (SRC) KULIK, JAMES A UNIVERSITY OF CALIFORNIA LA JOLLA, CA 92093-0023 Psychological preparation & coronary bypass recovery

R29HL-43656-02 (ECS) SCHOFIELD, GEOFFREY G TULANE UNIV SCHOOL OF MEDICINE 1430 TULANE AVE NEW ORLEANS, LA 70112 Neuronal excitability of SHR

R01HL-43660-02 (MET) HOWARD, BARBARA V MEDLANTIC RESEARCH FOUNDATION 108 IRVING STREET, NW WASHINGTON, DC 20010 Fatty acid alterations and LDL receptor interactions

R01HL-43662-02 (CVB) MARKHAM, BRUCE E MEDICAL COLLEGE OF WISCONSIN 8701 WATERTOWN PLANK ROAD MILWAUKEE, WI 53226 Intracellular pathways that mediate cardiac hypertrophy

R37HL-43671-02 (TOX) LIMBIRD, LEE E VANDERBILT UNIVERSITY SCHOOL OF MEDICINE NASHVILLE, TN 37232-6600 Expression & mutagenesis of cloned alpha2-receptors

R29HL-43689-01A2 (MEDB) WHATLEY, RALPH E UNIVERSITY OF UTAH SALT LAKE CITY, UT 84112 Growth-dependant regulation of lipid autacoid production

R29HL-43696-02 (SAT) BANERJEE, ANIRBAN UNIVERSITY OF COLORADO CAMPUS BOX C-311/4200 E 9TH AV DENVER, CO 80262 Cellular oxidative targets in cardiac reperfusion injury

R01HL-43700-02 (ECS) HASSER, EILEEN M THE UNIV OF MISSOURI-COLUMBIA 310 JESSE HALL COLUMBIA, MO 65211 Area postrema & cardiovascular control in dehydration

R01HL-43704-02 (RAP) KING, RICHARD J UNIVERSITY OF TEXAS 7703 FLOYD CURL DRIVE SAN ANTONIO, TX 78284 Molecular changes in pulmonary surfactant in BPD

R01HL-43707-02 (HEM) HANNUN, YUSUF A DUKE UNIVERSITY MEDICAL CENTER PO BOX 3355 DURHAM, NC 27710 Role and regulation of platelet protein kinase C

PROJECT NO., ORGANIZATIONAL UNIT., INVESTIGATOR, ADDRESS, TITLE

R29HL-43710-02 (CVA) LEE, HON-CHI UNIVERSITY OF IOWA COL OF MED CARDIOVASCULAR DIVISION IOWA CITY, IA 52242 Mechanisms of myocardial calcium ion regulation during ischemia
R29HL-43711-02 (CBY) SPORN, LEE A UNIVERSITY OF ROCHESTER P O BOX 610/601 ELMWOOD AVENUE ROCHESTER, NY 14642 Polarity and fate of vwf secreted from endothelial cells
R29HL-43712-02 (CVA) BERLIN, JOSHUA R GRADUATE HOSPITAL ONE GRADUATE PLAZA PHILADELPHIA, PA 19146 Sarcolemmal calcium transport mechanisms in heart cells
R29HL-43721-01A1 (HEM) D'SOUZA, STANLEY E SCRIPPS CLINIC & RES FDN 10666 NORTH TORREY PINES ROAD LA JOLLA, CA 92037 Structure--Function of platelets and blood cell integrins
R01HL-43722-02 (CVA) WEISS, JAMES L JOHNS HOPKINS HOSPITAL 600 N WOLFE STREET BALTIMORE, MD 21205 Functional consequences of ischemia and reperfusion
R01HL-43731-02 (CVB) ROSEN, MICHAEL R COLUMBIA UNIVERSITY 630 WEST 168TH STREET NEW YORK, NY 10032 Ischemia, neurohumors, arrhythmias and diagnosis
R01HL-43758-01A1 (EDC) GREEN, DAVID ATHEROSCLEROSIS PROGRAM 345 EAST SUPERIOR STREET CHICAGO, IL 60611 Hemostatic coronary risk factors in young adults
R01HL-43762-02 (RAP) BASBAUM, CAROL B UNIVERSITY OF CALIFORNIA 513 PARNASSUS AVENUE SAN FRANCISCO, CA 94143-0452 Analysis of regulation of mucin gene expression
R01HL-43771-02 (SAT) BIRINYI, LOUIS K BRIGHAM & WOMEN'S HOSPITAL 75 FRANCIS STREET BOSTON, MA 02115 Cellular alteration of vascular injury
R01HL-43773-02 (HEM) ALTIERI, DARIO C SCRIPPS CLINIC & RESEARCH FDN 10666 NORTH TORREY PINES ROAD LA JOLLA, CA 92037 Mac 1 dependent regulation of coagulation
R01HL-43781-02 (ARR) CUNNINGHAM-RUNDLES, SUSANNA CORNELL UNIVERSITY MEDICAL COL BOX 268/1300 YORK AVENUE NEW YORK, NY 10021 Effect on immunity by prostaglandin in HIV+ hemophiliacs
R29HL-43787-01A2 (CVA) SPOTNITZ, WILLIAM D UNIVERSITY OF VIRGINIA PO BOX 181 CHARLOTTESVILLE, VA 22908 Intraoperative assessment of myocardial perfusion
R01HL-43793-02 (SAT) KURNICK, JAMES T MASSACHUSETTS GENERAL HOSP 149 THIRTEENTH ST CHARLESTOWN, MA 02129 Cardiac infiltrating T cells in rejection & myocarditis
R01HL-43794-02 (PTHA) GREENSPAN, PHILLIP UNIVERSITY OF SOUTH CAROLINA SCHOOL OF MEDICINE COLUMBIA, SC 29208 Macrophage phospholipid recognition in atherogenesis
R29HL-43796-02 (CVB) BURTON, HAROLD W ST UNIV OF NEW YORK AT BUFFALO 411 KIMBALL HALL BUFFALO, NY 14214 Microvascular studies in regenerated skeletal muscle
R01HL-43812-02 (RNM) MASARYK, THOMAS J CLEVELAND CLINIC FOUNDATION 9500 EUCLID AVENUE CLEVELAND, OHIO 44195 Magnetic resonance flow techniques for cerebrovascular disease
R01HL-43814-02 (PHRA) GARLID, KEITH D MEDICAL COLLEGE OF OHIO PO BOX 10008 TOLEDO, OH 43699-0008 Structure/function of cardiac K+/H+ and NA+/H+ exchanges
R01HL-43815-02 (PBC) CURTISS, LINDA K SCRIPPS CLINIC AND RES FDN 10666 NORTH TORREY PINES ROAD LA JOLLA, CA 92037 Immunochemical structure/function of apolipoprotein A-I
R01HL-43819-01A2 (RAP) HITZIG, BERNARD M MASSACHUSETTS GENERAL HOSPITAL 32 FRUIT STREET BOSTON, MA 02114 Ventilatory and acid-base regulation in hypothermia
P01HL-43821-02 (SRC) WILLIAMS, LEWIS T UNIVERSITY OF CALIFORNIA 505 PARNASSUS, BOX 0724 SAN FRANCISCO, CA 94143 Program of excellence in molecular biology
P01HL-43821-02 0001 (SRC) WILLIAMS, LEWIS T Program of excellence in molecular biology Regulation of angiogenesis by growth factors
P01HL-43821-02 0002 (SRC) MARTIN, GAIL R Program of excellence in molecular biology Function of fibroblast growth factor gene in mammalian embryogenesis
P01HL-43821-02 0003 (SRC) KIRSCHNER, MARC Program of excellence in molecular biology Precursors to the heart, vasculate and blood in the early mesoderm
P01HL-43821-02 0004 (SRC) ORDAHL, CHARLES Program of excellence in molecular biology Molecular analysis of myofibrillar isoprotein switching
P01HL-43821-02 0005 (SRC) FLETTERICK, ROBERT J Program of excellence in molecular biology Structure analysis of proteins involved in cardiovascular function
P01HL-43821-02 0006 (SRC) YAMAMOTO, KEITH R Program of excellence in molecular biology Regulatiion of gene expression in developing lung
P01HL-43821-02 0008 (SRC) O'FARRELL, PATRICK Program of excellence in molecular biology Developmental coordination of cell proliferation
P01HL-43821-02 9002 (SRC) MARTIN, GAIL R Program of excellence in molecular biology Core--Molecular cytology
P01HL-43821-02 9003 (SRC) ESCOBEDO, JAIME A Program of excellence in molecular biology Core--Monoclonal antibody
R01HL-43827-02 (ARR) KRADIN, RICHARD L MASSACHUSETTS GENERAL HOSPITAL 100 BLOSSOM STREET BOSTON, MA 02114 Pulmonary dendritic cells in HIV infection
R01HL-43831-01A2 (PTHA) GILLESPIE, MARK N UNIVERSITY OF KENTUCKY ROSE STREET LEXINGTON, KY 40536-0082 Epidermal growth factor in pulmonary hypertension
R01HL-43842-02 (SB) GILLETTE, PAUL C MEDICAL UNIV OF SOUTH CAROLINA 171 ASHLEY AVENUE CHARLESTON, SC 29425 Arrhythmia treatment by transvenous cardiac cryoablation
R01HL-43851-01A2 (CLTR) HENNEKENS, CHARLES H BRIGHAM & WOMEN'S HOSPITAL 55 POND AVE BROOKLINE, MA 02146 Randomized trial of low dose aspirin in nurses
R29HL-43853-02 (RAP) TANAKA, DAVID T DUKE UNIVERSITY MEDICAL CENTER BOX 3179 DURHAM, NC 27710 Maturation of neurokinin reactivity in rabbit airways
R29HL-43860-02 (RAP) CARLEY, DAVID W UNIV OF ILLINOIS COLL OF MED PO BOX 6998 CHICAGO, IL 60680 Sleep-induced apnea--Role of state of consciousness
R01HL-43865-02 (RAP) FARKAS, GASPAR A MAYO FOUNDATION 200 FIRST STREET SOUTHWEST ROCHESTER, MN 55905 Breathing strategy in the dog
R01HL-43875-02 (CVB) SHEPRO, DAVID BOSTON UNIVERSITY 2 CUMMINGTON STREET BOSTON, MA 02215 Physiological regulation of microvascular permeability
R01HL-43880-02 (SRC) SHANNON, BARBARA M PENNSYLVANIA STATE UNIVERSITY S-125 HENDERSON DEVEL BLDG UNIVERSITY PARK, PA 16802 Evaluation of cholesterol education for at-risk children
R01HL-43883-02 (RAP) HUNNINGHAKE, GARY W UNIV OF IOWA COLLEGE OF MEDICINE IOWA CITY, IA 52242 Isolation of lines of type II cells
R29HL-43884-02 (RNM) BERRIDGE, MARC S CASE WESTERN RESERVE UNIVERSIT 2058 ADELBERT RD CLEVELAND, OH 44106 Beta adrenergic ligands for PET; synthesis & testing
R01HL-43907-02 (CBY) LIEDTKE, CAROLE M CASE WESTERN RESERVE UNIVERSIT 2101 ADELBERT RD CLEVELAND, OH 44106 Modulation of an airway epithelial cotransporter
R29HL-43909-02 (BIO) CLADARAS, CHRISTOS BOSTON UNIVERSITY MEDICAL CTR 80 EAST CONCORD STREET BOSTON, MA 02118 Transcriptional activation of the apolipoprotein B gene
R01HL-43922-01A1 (EDC) RENNARD, STEPHEN I UNIVERSITY OF NEBRASKA MED CTR 42ND AND DEWEY AVENUE OMAHA, NE 68105 Influence of smoking reduction on lung disease factors
R01HL-43923-02 (SRC) SEVERSON, HERBERT H OREGON RESEARCH INSTITUTE 1899 WILLAMETTE EUGENE, OR 97401 Modification of maternal smoking--Pediatric intervention
R01HL-44004-02 (PHY) DOYLE, DONALD D UNIVERSITY OF CHICAGO 5841 SOUTH MARYLAND AVENUE CHICAGO, IL 60637 Cardiac myocyte-specific sodium channel proteins
R01HL-44006-02 (MET) PEFFLEY, DENNIS M CHICAGO MEDICAL SCHOOL 3333 GREEN BAY ROAD NORTH CHICAGO, IL 60064 Regulation of HMG-CoA reductase in mammalian cells
R01HL-44010-02 (ECS) VICTOR, RONALD G U T SOUTHWESTERN MED CTR 5323 HARRY HINES BLVD DALLAS, TX 75235-9034 Neural mechanism of cyclosporine-induced hypertension
R29HL-44012-03 (CVB) BOEGEHOLD, MATTHEW ALAN WEST VIRGINIA UNIVERSITY MORGANTOWN, WEST VIRGINIA 2650 Microvascular alterations in NaCl-induced hypertension
R01HL-44015-02 (PBC) CROUCH, EDMOND C MD PHD JEWISH HOSPITAL OF ST LOUIS 216 S KINGSHIGHWAY ST LOUIS, MO 63110 Structure and function of surfactant protein D
R01HL-44042-02 (HEM) TELEN, MARILYN J DUKE UNIVERSITY POST OFFICE BOX 3387 DURHAM, N C 27710 Phosphatidylinositol-anchored blood group antigens
R01HL-44060-01A1 (HED) WARBURTON, DAVID CHILDRENS HOSPITAL OF LA 4650 SUNSET BLVD BIN 83 LOS ANGELES, CA 90027 Developmental type II pneumocyte protein phosphorylation
R01HL-44065-02 (CVA) MARBAN, EDUARDO JOHNS HOPKINS UNIVERSITY 725 NORTH WOLFE STREET BALTIMORE, MD 21205 Cellular mechanisms of cardiac contractile dysfunction
R01HL-44066-02 (CVB) IDEKER, RAYMOND E DUKE UNIVERSITY PO BOX 3140 DURHAM, NC 27710 Electrical therapy of arrhythmias
R01HL-44069-02 (EDC) BOUGHMAN, JOANN A UNIVERSITY OF MARYLAND 655 W BALTIMORE STREET BALTIMORE, MD 21201 Family study of congenital cardiovascular malformations
R01HL-44071-02 (PTHA) WEISSMAN, DAVID N VAMC ALBUQUERQUE 2100 RIDGECREST DRIVE SE ALBUQUERQUE, NM 87108 Functional immunity of the human lung
R01HL-44081-02 (PTHA) RILEY, DAVID J UNIV OF MED/DENTISTRY OF NJ/R ONE ROBERT WOOD JOHNSON PLACE NEW BRUNSWICK, N J 08903-0019 Familial pulmonary fibrosis
R01HL-44083-02 (CVB) CHAO, JULIE MEDICAL UNIV OF SOUTH CAROLINA 171 ASHLEY AVENUE CHARLESTON, SC 29425 Renal kallikrein-binding protein in hypertension
R01HL-44084-02 (TOX) OLSON, JACK W UNIVERSITY OF KENTUCKY ROSE STREET LEXINGTON, KY 40536-0082 Monocrotaline toxicity and transforming growth factor beta
R01HL-44085-02 (CVB) FANTONE, JOSEPH C UNIVERSITY OF MICHIGAN 1301 CATHERINE ROAD ANN ARBOR, MI 48109-0602 Mechanisms of myocardial ischemia reperfusion injury
R01HL-44092-02 (SB) HALPERIN, HENRY R JOHNS HOPKINS HOSPITAL 600 N WOLFE ST, CARNEGIA 592 BALTIMORE, MD 21205 Mechanical properties of reperfused myocardium
R01HL-44094-02 (CVA) UMEDA, PATRICK K UNIV OF ALABAMA AT BIRMINGHAM UAB STATION BIRMINGHAM, AL 35294 Molecular determinants of gene expression in the heart
R44HL-44095-02 (HEM) HUANG, SHU-ZHEN CHI ASSOCIATES, INC 2000 NORTH 14TH STREET ARLINGTON, VA 22201 Clinical diagnostic kits for inherited blood disorders
R01HL-44097-02 (BEM) LEHRER, PAUL M UMDNJ-ROBERT W JOHNSON MED SCH 671 HOES LANE PISCATAWAY, NJ 08854-5633 Airway reactivity to suggestion and stress in asthma
R01HL-44098-12 (IMS) BUSSE, WILLIAM W UNIVERSITY OF WISCONSIN 600 HIGHLAND AVE, H6/360 MADISON, WI 53792 Mechanisms of virus induced asthma
R01HL-44105-02 (NTN) ALBERS, JOHN J NORTHWEST LIPID RESEARCH CTR 2121 N. 35TH STREET SEATTLE, WA 98103 Apolipoprotein standardization
R01HL-44114-02 (CVA) WALKER, JEFFERY W UNIVERSITY OF WISCONSIN 1300 UNIVERSITY AVE MADISON, WI 53706 Adrenergic regulation of cardiac muscle contraction
R29HL-44116-02 (ECS) KATUSIC, ZVONIMIR S MAYO FOUNDATION 200 FIRST STREET SOUTHWEST ROCHESTER, MN 55905 Endothelium-dependent contractions and cerebral vasospasm
R29HL-44119-02 (PHY) SCHILLING, WILLIAM P BAYLOR COLLEGE OF MEDICINE ONE BAYLOR PLAZA HOUSTON, TX 77030 Calcium signaling in vascular endothelial cells
R29HL-44122-02 (PTHA) WESTCOTT, JAY Y UNIVERSITY OF COLORADO 4200 EAST 9TH AVENUE DENVER, CO 80262 Leukotriene synthesis and inactivation in the lung
R01HL-44125-02 (SSS) CHANCE, BRITTON UNIVERSITY CITY SCIENCE CENTER 3401 MARKET STREET PHILADELPHIA, PA 19104 Optical ranging of HB/MB in tissues
R01HL-44126-02 (BIO) PAUL, SUDHIR UNIV OF NEBRASKA MEDICAL CTR 42ND AND DEWEY AVENUE OMAHA, NE 68105 Catalytic anti-vasoactive intestinal peptide antibodies
R29HL-44128-02 (RAP) BARNAS, GEORGE M UNIVERSITY OF MARYLAND 22

SOUTH GREENE STREET BALTIMORE, MD 21201 Lung and chest wall impedances in health and disease

R01HL-44137-04 (GMB) KUMAR, ASHOK SUNY HEALTH SCIENCE CENTER 450 CLARKSON AVE BOX 5 BROOKLYN, NY 11203 Role of renin-angiotensin system in hypertension

R01HL-44138-02 (SSS) CARSKADON, MARY A E P BRADLEY HOSPITAL 1011 VETERANS MEMORIAL PARKWAY EAST PROVIDENCE, RI 02915 Sleep apnea in children and adolescents

R01HL-44141-03 (SRC) ELMER, PATRICIA PHD UNIVERSITY OF MINNESOTA 611 BEACON STREET SE MINNEAPOLIS, MN 55455 Models for treating high blood cholesterol

R01HL-44146-02 (RAP) MOORE, RUSSELL L PENNSYLVANIA STATE UNIVERSITY P O BOX 850 HERSHEY, PA 17033 Hypertension--Training-induced increase in work capacity

R37HL-44147-03 (CVB) CHIEN, SHU THE REGENTS OF UNIV. OF CALIF UNIVERSITY OF CALIF; SAN DIEGO LA JOLLA, CA 92093 Role of blood cell properties in circulatory regulation

R01HL-44157-03 (SRC) SIMPSON, ROSS J, JR UNIV. OF NORTH CAROLINA-CH DEPARTMENT OF MEDICINE CHAPEL HILL, NC 27599-7460 A cholesterol treatment model for low income patients

R01HL-44160-03 (SRC) CAGGIULA, ARLENE W UNIVERSITY OF PITTSBURGH 130 DESOTO STREET PITTSBURGH, PA 15261 Models for treating high blood cholesterol

R01HL-44173-02 (RAP) PARADISO, ANTHONY M UNIVERSITY OF NORTH CAROLINA CB# 7020 CHAPEL HILL, NC 27599-7020 Control of cellular ph in human nasal epithelium

R01HL-44177-03 (SRC) PEARSON, THOMAS A MARY IMOGENE BASSETT HOSPITAL ONE ATWELL ROAD COOPERSTOWN, NY 13326 Rural lipid resource center--A physician-assist model

R29HL-44181-02 (ECS) BROZOVICH, FRANK V GRADUATE HOSPITAL ONE GRADUATE PLAZA PHILADELPHIA, PA 19146 Regulation of vascular smooth muscle contraction

R01HL-44186-02 (SAT) HARKEN, ALDEN H UNIVERSITY OF COLORADO 4200 EAST NINTH AVE/CAMPUS C-3 DENVER, CO 80262 Cytokine enhancement of post-ischemic cardiac function

R29HL-44188-03 (PHRA) LIANG, BRUCE T UNIVERSITY OF PENNSYLVANIA HOS 3400 SPRUCE STREET PHILADELPHIA, PA 19104 A1 adenosine receptor in cultured heart cells

R29HL-44194-02 (SSS) LIANG, JEROME Z DUKE UNIVERSITY MEDICAL CENTER P O BOX 3949 DURHAM, NC 27710 Bayesian reconstruction for computer tomography

R01HL-44195-02 (RAP) CHEN, YIU-FAI UNIV OF ALABAMA AT BIRMINGHAM 1047 ZEIGLER RESEARCH BLGD BIRMINGHAM, AL 35294 Atrial natriuretic peptide in pulmonary hypertension

R29HL-44196-01A2 (ECS) GARDNER, JEFFREY P UMDNJ-NEW JERSEY MEDICAL SCHOO 185 S ORANGE AVE NEWARK, NJ 07103-2757 Altered Na/H exchange in vascular cells from SHR

R01HL-44199-02 (EDC) KAPLAN, GEORGE A WESTERN CONSORTIUM PUBLIC HEAL 2151 BERKELEY WAY BERKELEY, CA 94704-9980 Mechanisms underlying psychosocial association with IHD

R37HL-44200-03 (BBCB) MORALES, MANUEL F UNIVERSITY OF THE PACIFIC 2155 WEBSTER STREET SAN FRANCISCO, CA 94115 Chemo-mechanical transduction--Heart/skeletal muscle

R01HL-44202-02 (PHRA) MENICK, DONALD R UNIVERSITY OF SOUTH CAROLINA 171 ASHLEY AVE CHARLESTON, SC 29425-2221 Structure function studies of the cardiac SR Ca ++-ATPase

R01HL-44225-03 (HEM) MORRISSEY, JAMES H OKLAHOMA MED RESCH FOUNDATION 825 N E 13TH STREET OKLAHOMA CITY, OK 73104 Initiation of the coagulation cascade by vascular cells

R44HL-44230-02 (SSS) BUSSE, LAWRENCE J TETRAD CORPORATION 12741 EAST CALEY AVENUE ENGLEWOOD, CO 80111 Three-dimensional intravascular imaging with ultrasound

R44HL-44233-02 (SSS) MAY, STERLING R LIFECELL CORPORATION 3606-A RESEARCH FOREST DRIVE THE WOODLANDS, TX 77381 Preservation of low damage allogenic heart valves

R01HL-44253-02 (SOH) SCHUYLER, MARK R ALBUQUERQUE VA MEDICAL CTR 2100 RIDGECREST DRIVE, SE ALBUQUERQUE, NM 87108 Experimental occupational hypersensitivity pneumonitis

R43HL-44260-01A2 (HUD) FREDERIKSEN, LEE W HEALTH INNOVATIONS, INC 12355 SUNRISE VALLEY DRIVE RESTON, VA 22091 Computer-assisted cholesterol reduction program

R29HL-44275-03 (BBCB) BRITIGAN, BRADLEY E UNIVERSITY OF IOWA HOSPITALS IOWA CITY, IA 52242 Monocyte/macrophage free radical biology assessed by EPR

R01HL-44277-01A1 (ECS) DIPETTE, DONALD J UNIVERSITY OF TEXAS MED BRANCH ROOM 4, 156 OJSH, E72 GALVESTON, TX 77550 Calcitonin gene-related peptide in hypertension

R43HL-44279-01A1 (SSS) CLARK, JUSTIN S MEDICAL PHYSICS 401 12TH AVENUE SALT LAKE CITY, UT 84103 Cardiac output--Blood gas anesthesia monitor

R43HL-44280-01A2 (HUD) PASS, THEODORE M PASS DATA SYSTEMS 4 HARTFORD STREET NEWTON, MA 02161 Health promotion in the elderly--Prevention of cardiovascular disorders

R01HL-44281-02 (ARR) ANTONY, VEENA B RICHARD L ROUDEBUSH MEDICAL CT 1481 W 10TH STREET INDIANAPOLIS, IN 46202-2884 Mechanism of action inhaled pentamidine in AIDS

R01HL-44284-02 (SRC) DETRE, KATHERINE M UNIVERSITY OF PITTSBURGH 130 DESOTO STREET PITTSBURGH, PA 15261 PTCA III--Multi-device registry

U01HL-44298-02 (SRC) APPLEGATE, WILLIAM B UNIVERSITY OF TENNESSEE 66 N PAULINE MEMPHIS, TN 38163 HMG CoA reductase inhibitors in the elderly--Pilot study

U01HL-44299-02 (SRC) KNOPP, ROBERT H NORTHWEST LIPID RES CLINIC 326 NINTH AVENUE SEATTLE, WA 98104 HMG COA reductase inhibitors in the elderly--Pilot study

R01HL-44307-03 (HEM) RUNGE, MARSCHALL S EMORY UNIVERSITY POST OFFICE DRAWER LL ATLANTA, GA 30322 Structure determines plasminogen activator function

U01HL-44311-02 (SRC) DAVIS, CLARENCE E COLLABORATIVE STUDIES COOR CTR 137 EAST FRANKLIN STREET/CB 80 CHAPEL HILL, NC 27514 HMG COA reductase inhibitors in the elderly--Pilot study

U01HL-44315-02 (SRC) LA ROSA, JOHN C GEORGE WASHINGTON UNIV MED CTR 2300 I STREET NW, ROSS HALL 71 WASHINGTON, DC 20037 Cholesterol lowering in the elderly--A pilot study

U01HL-44319-02 (SRC) CROUSE, JOHN R BOWMAN GRAY SCHOOL OF MEDICINE MEDICAL CENTER BLVD. WINSTON SALEM, NC 27157 HMG COA reductase inhibitors in the elderly--Pilot study

U01HL-44327-02 (SRC) HUNNINGHAKE, DONALD B UNIVERSITY OF MINNESOTA BOX 192 - UMHC MINNEAPOLIS, MN 55455 HMG COA reductase inhibitors in the elderly--Pilot study

P50HL-44336-01 (SRC) HOYER, LEON W JEROME H HOLLAND LABORATORY 15601 CRABBS BRANCH WAY ROCKVILLE, MD 20855 Specialized centers of research in transfusion medicine

P50HL-44336-01 0002 (SRC) INGHAM, KENNETH Specialized centers of research in transfusion medicine Molecular interactions of fibronectin

P50HL-44336-01 0003 (SRC) BURGESS, WILSON H Specialized centers of research in transfusion medicine Structural basis for regulation of cellular iron

P50HL-44336-01 0004 (SRC) MACIAG, THOMAS Specialized centers of research in transfusion medicine Control and manipulation of murine organoid neovessels In Vivo

P50HL-44336-01 0005 (SRC) JAY, GILBERT Specialized centers of research in transfusion medicine Hepatitis B virus role in inducing malignancy in transgenic mice

P50HL-44336-01 0006 (SRC) HOYER, LEON W Specialized centers of research in transfusion medicine Factor VIII fragments that bind factor VIII inhibitor antibodies

P50HL-44336-01 9001 (SRC) STRICKLAND, DUDLEY Specialized centers of research in transfusion medicine Core--Immunology

P50HL-44336-01 9002 (SRC) INGHAM, KENNETH Specialized centers of research in transfusion medicine Core--Protein and nucleic acid chemistry

P50HL-44336-01 0001 (SRC) STRICKLAND, DUDLEY Specialized centers of research in transfusion medicine Alpha 2-macroglobulin receptor structure and function

R01HL-44341-01A1 (CVB) COGAN, MARTIN G VETERANS ADMIN MEDICAL CENTER 4150 CLEMENT ST SAN FRANCISCO, CA 94121 Angiotensin in proximal tubule reponse to dietary sodium

R01HL-44363-02 (HEM) SHAW, DENISE R UNIVERSITY OF ALABAMA UAB STATION BIRMINGHAM, AL 35294 Characterization of autoantibodies in immune cytopenias

R01HL-44370-01A1 (ECS) ZIMMERMAN, BEN G UNIVERSITY OF MINNESOTA 435 DELAWARE STREET, SE MINNEAPOLIS, MN 55455 Bradykinin vascular influence and ACE inhibition

R01HL-44373-01A1 (HED) WILKES, BARRY M NORTH SHORE UNIVERSITY HOSP 300 COMMUNITY DRIVE MANHASSET, NY 11030 Endothelin in high-risk pregnancies

R01HL-44379-01A2 (PHRA) BAKER, KENNETH M WEIS CENTER FOR RESEARCH NORTH ACADEMY AVENUE DANVILLE, PA 17822 Regulation of cardiac second messengers by angiotensin

R01HL-44389-01A2 (HEM) ASCH, ADAM S CORNELL UNIV MEDICAL COLLEGE 1300 YORK AVE NEW YORK, NY 10021 Structure and function of the TSP - CD36 system

R01HL-44398-02 (CVA) FORD, LINCOLN E UNIVERSITY OF CHICAGO 5841 S MARYLAND AVE, BOX 249 CHICAGO, IL 60637 Inotropic mechanisms of myocardium

R01HL-44408-01A1 (PHRA) SMITH, JEFFREY B UNIVERSITY OF ALABAMA UAB STATION BIRMINGHAM, AL 35294 Sodium-calcium exchange in vascular smooth muscle

R01HL-44413-01A1 (EDC) BUNKER, CLAREANN H UNIVERSITY OF PITTSBURGH 130 DESOTO STREET PITTSBURGH, PA 15261 Epidemic hypertension in Nigerian workers

R01HL-44430-02 (HEM) BENZ, EDWARD J, JR YALE UNIVERSITY 333 CEDAR STREET NEW HAVEN, CT 06510 Expression and function of a novel NA+,K+-ATPase isoform

R29HL-44434-02 (SAT) NEELY, CONSTANCE F UNIVERSITY OF PENNSYLVANIA 7 DULLES/3400 SPRUCE ST PHILADELPHIA, PA 19104 Role of purinergic mechanisms in endotoxic shock lung

R01HL-44436-01A1 (BEM) SCHEIER, MICHAEL F CARNEGIE-MELLON UNIVERSITY 5000 FORBES AVENUE PITTSBURGH, PA 15213 Effects of personality & context on recovery from coronary artery bypass

R29HL-44447-01A1 (HED) REID, DEBORAH L MERITER HOSPITAL/MADISON GENER 202 SOUTH PARK STREET MADISON, WI 53715 Regulation of heart rate variability in hypoxic fetuses

R01HL-44454-02 (PTHA) BARCHOWSKY, AARON DARTMOUTH COLLEGE P O BOX 7 HANOVER, NH 03755 Endothelial cell biology following oxidative stress

R01HL-44455-01A1 (PHRA) NELSON, MARK T UNIVERSITY OF VERMONT BURLINGTON, VT 05405 Regulation of cerebral artery dilation

R01HL-44458-01A1 (NEUA) MAYBERG, MARC R VA MEDICAL CTR 1660 SOUTH COLUMBIAN WAY SEATTLE, WA 98108 Cellular mechanisms of cerebral vasospasm

R01HL-44467-03 (SRC) SALLIS, JAMES F SAN DIEGO STATE UNIVERSITY 5300 CAMPANILE DRIVE SAN DIEGO, CA 92182 Sports, play and active recreation for kids

R01HL-44480-01A1 (MET) GIANTURCO, SANDRA H UNIVERSITY OF ALABAMA 690 DIABETES BLDG BIRMINGHAM, AL 35294 Distinct macrophage receptor for abnormal VLDL

R01HL-44485-01A1 (SB) CURRY, FITZ-ROY E UNIVERSITY OF CALIFORNIA DAVIS, CA 95616 A new approach to endothelial cleft structure

R01HL-44491-01A1 (HEM) WOJCHOWSKI, DON M PENNSYLVANIA STATE UNIVERSITY UNIVERSITY PARK, PA 16802 In vitro studies of erythropoietin action

R01HL-44492-01A1 (SRC) OCKENE, IRA S UNIV OF MASSACHUSETTS MED CTR 55 LAKE AVENUE, NORTH WORCESTER, MA 01655 Physicians role in lowering elevated lipids by diet

R29HL-44495-02 (RAP) GILBERT, ILEEN A UNIVERSITY HOSPS OF CLEVELAND 2074 ABINGTON ROAD CLEVELAND, OH 44106 The bronchial circulation in acute airway obstruction

R29HL-44508-02 (HEM) BARNATHAN, ELLIOT S HOSPITAL OF UNIV OF PENNSYLVAN 3400 SPRUCE ST PHILADELPHIA, PA 19104 Endothelial cell plasminogen activator receptors

R29HL-44511-02 (SB) PASQUE, MICHAEL K WASHINGTON UNIVERSITY 4989 BARNES HOSPITAL PLAZA ST LOUIS, MI 63110 Quantification of myocardial function in 3 dimensions

R01HL-44513-02 (PTHA) MCINTYRE, THOMAS M UNIVERSITY OF UTAH

CVRTI, BUILDING 500 SALT LAKE CITY, UT 84112 Biological activity of oxidized phospholipids

R29HL-44514-01A1 (PHRA) ERNSBERGER, PAUL R CASE WESTERN RESERVE UNIVERSIT 10900 EUCLID AVE; CLEVELAND, OH 44106-7015 Clonidine and the imidazole receptor in hypertension

R01HL-44523-02 (TOX) RASMUSSEN, RONALD E UNIVERSITY OF CALIFORNIA IRVINE, CA 92717 Juvenile ferret lung--Toxicological model for children

R01HL-44525-02 (PTHA) ZIMMERMAN, GUY A UNIVERSITY OF UTAH SALT LAKE CITY, UT 84112 Mechanisms of neutrophil adhesion to endothelium

R15HL-44531-01A1 (ECS) MARTIN, JOHN R KIRKSVILLE COL OSTEOPATHIC MED 800 W JEFFERSON ST KIRKSVILLE, MO 63501 Baroreflex and posterior hypothalamic neuropeptide-y

R01HL-44535-01A1 (SB) LEONARD, EDWARD F COLUMBIA UNIVERSITY 500 W 120TH STREET NEW YORK, NY 10027 Plasma protein reactions in separated flows

R01HL-44538-02 (SB) ANDRADE, JOSEPH D UNIVERSITY OF UTAH 2480 MERRILL ENGINEERING BLDG SALT LAKE CITY, UT 84112 Protein interfacial processes direct observation--SFM, scanning force microscopy

R01HL-44539-04A1 (SB) KIM, SUNG W UNIVERSITY OF UTAH 421 WAKARA WAY, RESEARCH PARK SALT LAKE CITY, UT 84108 Biodegradable polymer as antihypertensive drug carrier

R01HL-44554-02 (NEUA) PETERSON, JOHN W MASSACHUSETTS GENERAL HOSPITAL WARREN BUILDING 465 BOSTON, MA 02114 Complement-induced hemolysis and cerebral vasospasm

R29HL-44555-02 (CVA) HANSEN, DAVID E VANDERBILT UNIVERSITY SCH OF M NASHVILLE, TN 37232-2179 Stretch-induced arrhythmias in isolated ventricle

R15HL-44564-01A1 (PTHA) NAGEL, WALTER O HARTWICK COLLEGE ONEONTA, NY 13820 Molecular probes for studies of monoclonality

R01HL-44571-02 (PTHA) HO, YE-SHIH DUKE UNIV MEDICAL CENTER BOX 3177 DURHAM, NC 27710 Transgenic models for study of lung biology and disease

R01HL-44575-02 (PBC) MURPHY-ULLRICH, JOANNE UNIVERSITY OF ALABAMA UAB STATION BIRMINGHAM, AL 35294 Thrombospondin and tenascin--Cell adhesion regulators

R29HL-44578-02 (CVA) WEBSTER, KEITH A SRI INTERNATIONAL 333 RAVENSWOOD AVENUE MENLO PARK, CA 94025 Cardiocyte responses to hypoxia

R01HL-44583-01A1 (CVA) BERS, DONALD M UNIVERSITY OF CALIFORNIA RIVERSIDE, CA 92521-0121 The action of Ca-channel agonist BAY K 8644 on the SR

R01HL-44586-02 (REB) MANCO-JOHNSON, MARILYN J UNIV/COLORADO HLTH SCI CENTER 4200 EAST NINTH AVENUE DENVER, CO 80262 Ontogeny of the protein C system

R01HL-44589-02 (PHRA) ROBERTSON, DAVID H VANDERBILT UNIVERSITY 1161 21ST AVENUE SOUTH NASHVILLE, TN 37232-2195 Clinical pharmacology of dopamine-beta-hydroxylase

R01HL-44600-01A1 (BEM) PRINEAS, RONALD J UNIV OF MIAMI SCHOOL OF MEDICI P O BOX 016069 (R669) MIAMI, FL 33101 Biobehavior, ethnicity, hormones and blood pressure

R15HL-44602-01A1 (HEM) LACROIX, KAROL A UNIVERSITY OF NEW HAMPSHIRE DURHAM, NH 03824 A study of non-responders following venous occlusion

P01HL-44612-02 (SRC) KUNICKI, THOMAS J BLOOD CTR/SOUTHEASTERN WISCONS 1701 WEST WISCONSIN AVENUE MILWAUKEE, WI 53233 Molecular polymorphism and transfusion medicine

P01HL-44612-02 0001 (SRC) KUNICKI, THOMAS J Molecular polymorphism and transfusion medicine Immunogenicity of human platelet integrins

P01HL-44612-02 0002 (SRC) NEWMAN, PETER J Molecular polymorphism and transfusion medicine Molecular biology of human platelet integrins

P01HL-44612-02 0003 (SRC) ASTER, RICHARD H Molecular polymorphism and transfusion medicine Class I HLA molecules in transfusion medicine

P01HL-44612-02 0004 (SRC) MONTGOMERY, ROBERT R Molecular polymorphism and transfusion medicine Molecular variants of von Willebrand's disease

P01HL-44612-02 0005 (SRC) GORSKI, JACK Molecular polymorphism and transfusion medicine Polymorphism in regulation of HLA class II expression

P01HL-44612-02 0006 (SRC) ECKELS, DAVID D Molecular polymorphism and transfusion medicine Modulation of T-cell alloregulation

P01HL-44612-02 9001 (SRC) MONTGOMERY, ROBERT R Molecular polymorphism and transfusion medicine Cell culture/hybridoma--Core

P01HL-44612-02 9002 (SRC) ECKELS, DAVID D Molecular polymorphism and transfusion medicine Flow cytometry--Core

P01HL-44612-02 9003 (SRC) GORSKI, JACK Molecular polymorphism and transfusion medicine Molecular biology--Core

P01HL-44612-02 9004 (SRC) KUNICKI, THOMAS J Molecular polymorphism and transfusion medicine Protein chemistry--Core

R29HL-44630-02 (PHRA) SHEETS, MICHAEL F NORTHWESTERN UNIVERSITY 310 E SUPERIOR/MORTON 2-694 CHICAGO, IL 60611 Pharmacology of cardiac sodium channel modifiers

R29HL-44640-02 (HEM) HORIUCHI, KAZUMI CHILDRENS HOSP OF PHILADELPHIA 34TH & CIVIC CENTER BOULEVARD PHILADELPHIA, PA 19104 Shape variation and pathophysiology of sickle cells

R01HL-44647-02 (PTHA) NILES, RICHARD M BOSTON UNIVERSITY SCH OF MED 80 E CONCORD STREET BOSTON, MA 02118 Tracheal epithelial cell growth and differentiation

R01HL-44657-01A1 (CVB) TOBIAN, LOUIS UNIVERSITY OF MINNESOTA HOSPIT 420 DELAWARE STREET SE MINNEAPOLIS, MN 55455 How does K reduce and NaCl increase hypertensive injury?

R29HL-44660-02 (PHRA) STIMERS, JOSEPH R UNIVERSITY OF ARKANSAS/MED SCI 4301 WEST MARKHAM ST LITTLE ROCK, AR 72205 Regulation of Na/K pump function

R01HL-44664-01A2 (EDC) TALBOTT, EVELYN O UNIVERSITY OF PITTSBURGH 130 DESOTO STREET PITTSBURGH, PA 15261 Risk of CHD in women with polycystic ovary syndrome

R29HL-44667-02 (RAP) SINOWAY, LAWRENCE I MILTON S HERSHEY MED CENTER P O BOX 850 HERSHEY, PA 17033 Skeletal muscle metaboreflex activity in humans

R01HL-44668-01A1 (BNP) BROUILLETTE, WAYNE J UNIV OF ALABAMA UAB STATION BIRMINGHAM, AL 35294 Rigid carnitine analogs--Carnitine acyltransferase probe

R01HL-44671-01A1 (CVB) MARGOLIUS, HARRY S MED UNIV OF SOUTH CAROLINA 171 ASHLEY AVENUE CHARLESTON, SC 29425 Kinins and epithelial ion transport mechanisms

R01HL-44672-01A1 (EDC) KAMBOH, MOHAMMAD I UNIVERSITY OF PITTSBURGH 130 DESOTO STREET PITTSBURGH, PA 15261 Genetic epidemiology of lipoprotein-lipid levels

R29HL-44675-02 (ECS) MUNCH, PAUL A UNIVERSITY OF CALIFORNIA TB 172 DAVIS, CA 95616 Neural and hormonal modulation of baroreceptors

R29HL-44676-02 (CVB) BHATNAGAR, ARUNI UNIVERSITY OF TEXAS MED BRANCH GALVESTON, TX 77550 Mechanism of free radical induced myocardial injury

R29HL-44678-02 (RAP) MELTON, JOSEPH E UNIV OF MED & DENT OF NEW JERS ONE ROBERT WOOD JOHNSON PLACE NEW BRUNSWICK, NJ 08903-0019 Respiratory control--Determinants of hypoxic gasping

R01HL-44682-01A2 (EDC) FERRELL, ROBERT E UNIVERSITY OF PITTSBURGH 130 DESOTO ST PITTSBURGH, PA 15261 Genetic basis of abdominal aortic aneurysm

R01HL-44689-01A1 (EDC) LANGER, ROBERT D UNIV. OF CALIFORNIA, SAN DIEGO 9500 GILMAN DR LA JOLLA, CA 92093-0607 Predictors of cardiovascular disease in the elderly

R01HL-44695-02 (SB) BERBARI, EDWARD J VA MEDICAL CENTER 921 NE 13TH STREET OKLAHOMA CITY, OK 73104 High resolution electrocardiograms and arrhythmia risk

R01HL-44710-01A1 (MET) HAMILTON, ROBERT L UNIVERSITY OF CALIFORNIA 505 PARNASSUS AVENUE SAN FRANCISCO, CA 94143-0130 Assembly of nascent plasma lipoproteins by hepatocytes

R01HL-44712-01A1 (PTHA) CHAPMAN, HAROLD A BRIGHAM & WOMEN'S HOSPITAL 75 FRANCIS STREET BOSTON, MA 02115 Alveolar macrophage serine proteinases in lung biology

R29HL-44715-02 (CVB) MYERS, TERRY O CUNY MEDICAL SCHOOL CONVENT AVENUE @ 138TH STREET NEW YORK, NY 10031 Microcirculation in diabetes mellitus

R01HL-44719-01A1 (HUD) GOLD, JEFFREY CORNELL UNIVERSITY MEDICAL COL 1300 YORK AVENUE NEW YORK, NY 10021 Peri-operative morbidity and quality of life after CABG

R01HL-44721-01A2 (ECS) BERK, BRADFORD C EMORY UNIVERSITY PO DRAWER LL ATLANTA, GA 30322 Regulation of Na/H exchange in vascular smooth muscle

R29HL-44727-01A2 (PTHA) FRYER, ALLISON D JOHNS HOPKINS UNIVERSITY 615 NORTH WOLFE STREET BALTIMORE, MD 21205 Viral enzymes & neuronal muscarinic receptors in lung

R01HL-44738-02 (EDC) HUNT, STEVEN C UNIVERSITY OF UTAH 410 CHIPETA WAY SALT LAKE CITY, UT 84108 Urinary kallikrein & hypertension--A prospective study

R29HL-44739-02 (BEM) RICH, MICHAEL W JEWISH HOSPITAL 216 S. KINGSHIGHWAY ST. LOUIS, MO 63110 Prevention of early readmission in elderly CHF patients

R01HL-44740-02 (ECS) WHORTON, A RICHARD DUKE UNIVERSITY MEDICAL CENTER BOX 3813 DURHAM, NC 27710 Regulation of vascular endothelin production

R29HL-44746-02 (RAP) GARCIA, JOE G INDIANA UNIVERSITY SCH OF MED 1001 W TENTH STREET INDIANAPOLIS, IN 46202-2879 Regulation of myosin phosphorylation in endothelium

R01HL-44747-03 (SB) LERMAN, BRUCE B CORNELL MEDICAL COLLEGE 525 EAST 68TH ST NEW YORK, NY 10021 Experimental and numerical analyses of defibrillation

R01HL-44761-03 (CVB) HASSID, AVIV UNIVERSITY OF TENNESSEE 894 UNION AVENUE MEMPHIS, TN 38163 Inhibition of vascular and renal cell proliferation

R44HL-44767-02 (SSS) COHEN, MARGO P EXOCELL, INC 3508 MARKET STREET PHILADELPHIA, PA 19104 Monoclonal antibody immunoassays for glycohemoglobin

R43HL-44771-01A1 (SSS) WUCHINICH, DAVID G SONOKINETICS INC 614 RIVER STREET HOBOKEN, NJ 07030 Flexible magnetohydraulic acoustic catheter

R43HL-44794-01A1 (HEM) ALBERT, DAVID E ANATRACE INC 1280 DUSSEL DR MAUMEE, OH 43537 Imidoesters as antisickling agents

R44HL-44802-02 (HEM) STEINKE, JOHN M AVOX SYSTEMS, INC 15315 GREY FOX SAN ANTONIO, TX 78255-1210 Auto-analyzer for five hemoglobin species and bilirubin

R43HL-44811-01A1 (SSS) TOMLINSON, HAROLD W INAIR LIMITED 378-B DELAWARE AVE, BOX 126 DELMAR, NY 12054 DICO calibrator

R43HL-44818-01A2 (SSS) KLEINFELD, ALAN M LIDAK PHARMACEUTICALS 11077 NORTH TORREY PINES RD LA JOLLA, CA 92037 Biochemical method for monitoring free fatty acids

R44HL-44822-02 (SSS) WEST, JAMES B BEND RESEARCH, INC 64550 RESEARCH ROAD BEND, OR 97701-8599 Enzyme reactors for the synthesis of peptide inhibitors

R01HL-44846-02 (ARR) KORNFELD, HARDY BOSTON UNIVERSITY SCHOOL OF ME 80 EAST CONCORD STREET BOSTON, MA 02118 Antimicrobial function HIV-infected alveolar macrophages

R01HL-44847-03 (BEM) MURPHY, JOSEPH K THE MIRIAM HOSPITAL 164 SUMMIT AVENUE PROVIDENCE, RI 02906 Pediatric cardiovascular tone and salt sensitivity

R01HL-44851-01 (ARR) SCADDEN, DAVID T NEW ENGLAND DEACONESS HOSPITAL 185 PILGRIM ROAD BOSTON, MA 02215 Mechanisms of hematopoiesis in AIDS

R29HL-44853-01A1 (HED) VISCARDI, ROSE M UNIVERSITY OF MARYLAND HOSPITA 22 S GREENE STREET BALTIMORE, MD 21201 Role of nutrition in lung development

R01HL-44868-01A1 (CVB) DIETZ, JOHN R UNIVERSITY OF SOUTH FLORIDA 12901 BRUCE B DOWNS BLVD TAMPA, FL 33612 Cardiac peptides in the control of blood volume

R01HL-44878-01A1 (SRC) KNOPP, ROBERT H NORTHWEST LIPID RES CLINIC 326 NINTH AVENUE SEATTLE, WA 98104 Dietary treatment of hyperlipidemia in women vs men

R01HL-44880-02 (CVA) WEISS, JAMES N UNIVERSITY OF CALIFORNIA 405 HILGARD AVENUE LOS ANGELES, CA 90024-1406 Intracellular calcium during impaired cardiac metabolism

R01HL-44881-02 (ECS) FRIEDMAN, JULIUS J INDIANA UNIV SCH OF MEDICINE 635 BARNHILL DRIVE INDIANAPOLIS, IN 46202-5120 Interstitial distribution of collagen and hyaluronic acid

R01HL-44883-02 (CVA) BAKER, KENNETH M WEIS CENTER FOR RESEARCH

NORTH ACADEMY AVE DANVILLE, PA 17822 Regulation of cardiac hypertrophy by angiotensins

R01HL-44889-01A1 (RAP) BRUCE, EUGENE N CASE WESTERN RESERVE UNIVERSIT CLEVELAND, OH 44106 Stochastic factors in irregular and periodic breathing

R01HL-44897-02 (HEM) GREENWALT, TIBOR J UNIVERSITY OF CINCINNATI MED C 3231 BURNET AVE CINCINNATI, OH 45267 Red cell preservation

R01HL-44898-02 (SRC) MULLEN, PATRICIA D UNIV OF TX HLTH SCI CTR PO BOX 20186 HOUSTON, TX 77225 Sustaining womens smoking cessation postpartum

R01HL-44900-01A1 (MGN) RAPACZ, JAN UNIVERSITY OF WISCONSIN R666 ANIMAL SCIENCES BLDG MADISON, WI 53706 Apolipoprotein and DNA variants and lipidemias in pigs

R29HL-44904-02 (EDC) COUGHLIN, STEVEN S GEORGETOWN UNIVERSITY 3750 RESERVOIR RD, NW WASHINGTON, DC 20007 The epidemiology of idiopathic dilated cardiomyopathy

R01HL-44907-01A1 (HEM) COUGHLIN, SHAUN UNIVERSITY OF CALIFORNIA 505 PARNASSUS AVE/BOX 0724 SAN FRANCISCO, CA 94143 Molecular mechanisms of thrombin signalling

R29HL-44914-02 (ECS) HOUSE, STEVEN D SETON HALL UNIVERSITY SOUTH ORANGE, NJ 07079 Microvascular cell dynamics in the inflammatory process

R01HL-44915-01A1 (BEM) DIMSDALE, JOEL E UNIVERSITY OF CALIFORNIA 0603 LA JOLLA, CA 92093 Sleep apnea and hypertension--Role of sympathetic nervous system

R01HL-44916-02 (ARR) GU, JIANG DEBORAH RESEARCH INSTITUTE TRENTON ROAD BROWNS MILLS, NJ 08015-1799 HIV-I proteins and RNA in the heart of AIDS patients

R01HL-44917-02 (HEM) CHRISTIE, DOUGLAS J UNIVERSITY OF MINNESOTA 420 DELEWARE STREET SE MINNEAPOLIS, MN 55455 Immune mediated refractoriness to platelet transfusion

R01HL-44918-01A1 (HEM) BURRIDGE, KEITH W UNIV OF N C AT CHAPEL HILL 226 TAYLOR HALL CHAPEL HILL, NC 27599 Integrin-cytoskeletal interactions in platelets

R01HL-44920-01A1 (PTHA) MC FADDEN, E REGIS, JR UNIV HOSPITALS OF CLEVELAND 2074 ABINGTON RD CLEVELAND, OH 44106 Pathophysiology of airway effects to cold exposure

R01HL-44928-01A1 (HED) KRUG, EDWARD L MEDICAL COLLEGE OF WISCONSIN 8701 WATERTOWN PLANK ROAD MILWAUKEE, WI 53226 Molecular analysis of induction in cardiac morphogenesis

R01HL-44944-01A1 (SAT) JOHNSTON, WILLIAM E BOWMAN GRAY SCHOOL OF MEDICINE 300 SOUTH HAWTHORNE RD WINSTON-SALEM, NC 27103 Surgical cardiopulmonary bypass and cerebral resistance

P01HL-44948-01A1 (HLBA) CATTERALL, WILLIAM A UNIVERSITY OF WASHINGTON SEATTLE, WA 98195 Molecular analysis of signal transduction in the heart

P01HL-44948-01A1 0001 (HLBA) CATTERALL, WILLIAM Molecular analysis of signal transduction in the heart Molecular analysis of sodium channel function in the heart

P01HL-44948-01A1 0002 (HLBA) TEMPEL, BRUCE Molecular analysis of signal transduction in the heart Cardiac potassium channel gene expression

P01HL-44948-01A1 0003 (HLBA) NATHANSON, NEIL M Molecular analysis of signal transduction in the heart Regulation of cardiac m2 mACHR by protein kinases

P01HL-44948-01A1 0004 (HLBA) STORM, DANIEL R Molecular analysis of signal transduction in the heart Cyclic nucleotide metabolism in heart

P01HL-44948-01A1 0005 (HLBA) BEAVO, JOSEPH A Molecular analysis of signal transduction in the heart Molecular analysis of cardiac cGMP-inhibited phosphodiesterase

P01HL-44948-01A1 9001 (HLBA) IDZERDA, REJEAN L Molecular analysis of signal transduction in the heart CORE--DNA

R01HL-44951-01A1 (HED) CHRISTENSEN, ROBERT D UNIVERSITY OF UTAH 50 N MEDICAL DR SALT LAKE CITY, UT 84132 Developmental mechanisms of fetal/neonatal cytopenias

R29HL-44956-02 (HEM) KONKLE, BARBARA A CARDEZA FDN FOR HEMATOLOGIC RE 1015 WALNUT STREET PHILADELPHIA, PA 19107 Plasminogen activator inhibitor-1 gene expression

R29HL-44960-01A1 (SB) WICK, TIMOTHY M GEORGIA INST. OF TECHNOLOGY 778 ATLANTIC DR The mechanism of sickle erythrocyte/endothelial adhesion

R01HL-44964-01A1 (MBY) BERGET, SUSAN M BAYLOR COLLEGE OF MEDICINE ONE BAYLOR PLAZA HOUSTON, TX 77030 Processing of human apolipoprotein-b mRNA

R01HL-44965-02 (SRC) CHEN, MOON S, JR OHIO STATE UNIVERSITY 320 W 10TH AVE COLUMBUS, OH 43210 Lay-led smoking cessation approach for Southeast Asian men

R01HL-44972-02 (SB) REICHERT, WILLIAM M DUKE UNIVERSITY 136 ENGINEERING BUILDING DURHAM, NC 27706 Endothelial cell adhesion to polymers studied by TIRF

R01HL-44977-01A1 (HED) WARBURTON, DAVID UNIV OF SOUTHERN CALIFORNIA CSA #1 FLOOR LOS ANGELES, CA 90033 Autocrine/ paracrine growth factors and lung morphogenesis

R01HL-44984-02 (PTHA) SUNDAY, MARY E BRIGHAM & WOMEN'S HOSPITAL 75 FRANCIS STREET BOSTON, MA 02115 Molecular basis of pulmonary cell differentiation

R01HL-44985-02 (HEM) BENZ, EDWARD J, JR YALE UNIVERSITY SCH OF MED 333 CEDAR STREET NEW HAVEN, CT 06510 Structure-function relationships of protein 4.1 in blood cells

R01HL-44986-02 (SAT) SOUBA, WILEY W UNIVERSITY OF FLORIDA BOX J-286 GAINESVILLE, FL 32610 Lung glutamine metabolism following injury and infection

R01HL-44992-02 (SRC) LANDO, HARRY A UNIVERSITY OF MINNESOTA 611 BEACON STREET SE MINNEAPOLIS, MN 55455 Recycling of chronic smokers to sustained abstinence

R01HL-44998-01A1 (BEM) WILLIAMS, REDFORD B, JR DUKE UNIVERSITY MEDICAL CENTER PO BOX 3926 DURHAM, NC 27710 Hostility and coronary risk--Role of weak vagal function

R01HL-45005-01 (EDC) BLANKENHORN, DAVID H UNIV. OF SOUTHERN CALIFORNIA 2025 ZONAL AVENUE LOS ANGELES, CA 90033 Three vessel risk factor analysis--Completion of CLAS

R01HL-45011-02 (HED) SHANNON, JOHN M NATL JEWISH CTR/IMM & RESP MED 1400 JACKSON STREET DENVER, CO 80206 Surfactant protein regulation in developing lung

R01HL-45018-01A1 (PTHA) IDELL, STEVEN UNIVERSITY OF TEXAS HLTH CTR P O BOX 2003 TYLER, TX 75710 Control of fibrin turnover in pleural disease

R29HL-45024-01A1 (CVA) SPINALE, FRANCIS G MEDICAL UNIV OF SOUTH CAROLINA 171 ASHLEY AVENUE CHARLESTON, SC 29425-2111 Structural remodeling in cardiomyopathy and recovery

R29HL-45027-01A1 (PTHA) SCHWENKE, DAWN C BOWMAN GRAY SCHOOL OF MEDICINE 300 SOUTH HAWTHORNE ROAD WINSTON-SALEM, NC 27103 Retention of lipoprotein by lesion-prone rabbit aorta

R29HL-45038-01A1 (RAP) O'LEARY, DONAL S WAYNE STATE UNIVERSITY 540 EAST CANFIELD DETROIT, MI 48201 Mechanisms of arterial pressure control during exercise

R29HL-45045-01A1 (RAD) JACQUES, STEVEN L UT/MD ANDERSON CANCER CTR 1515 HOLCOMBE BLVD HOUSTON, TX 77030 Dosimetry of laser-tissue interactions

R01HL-45048-02 (SAT) KALYANARAMAN, BALARAMAN MEDICAL COLLEGE OF WISCONSIN 8701 WATERTOWN PLANK ROAD MILWAUKEE, WI 53226 Radical generation during cardiac surgery

R01HL-45050-01A1 (PTHA) HILL, NICHOLAS S RHODE ISLAND HOSPITAL 593 EDDY STREET PROVIDENCE, RI 02903 Atrial natriuretic peptide and the lung

R18HL-45057-01A1 (SRC) KLESGES, ROBERT C MEMPHIS STATE UNIVERSITY MEMPHIS, TN 38152 Pharmacologic intervention for postcessation weight gain

R29HL-45058-02 (HED) PERSSON, ANDERS V JEWISH HOSPITAL 216 S KINGSHIGHWAY ST LOUIS, MO 63110 Role of glycolipids and lectins in surfactant metabolism

R01HL-45063-02 (RAP) GRUNSTEIN, MICHAEL M JOSEPH STOKES JR RESEARCH INST 34TH & CIVIC CTR BLVD PHILADELPHIA, PA 19104 Mediators, airway smooth muscle growth and contractility

R01HL-45069-01A1 (CVB) CHIEN, KENNETH R UNIVERSITY OF CALIFORNIA LA JOLLA, CA 92093 Regulation of ventricular ANF expression

R01HL-45077-01A1 (RNM) TOBIS, JONATHAN M UCI MEDICAL CENTER 101 CITY DRIVE, RT 81 ORANGE, CA 92668 Intravascular ultrasound imaging of atherosclerosis

R01HL-45089-02 (EDC) SPARROW, DAVID W CHANNING LABORATORY 180 LONGWOOD AVENUE BOSTON, MA 02115 Inflammation, autonomic dysfunction and airway disease

R01HL-45090-02 (RNM) BRODY, WILLIAM R JOHNS HOPKINS HOSPITAL MRI BUILDING-143 BALTIMORE, MD 21205 Dynamic 3-D tagged MRI of the cardiac cycle in ischemia

R01HL-45095-01A1 (MET) GOLDBERG, IRA J COLUMBIA UNIVERSITY 630 WEST 168 STREET NEW YORK, NY 10032 Extracellular regulation of lipoprotein lipase activity

R01HL-45098-02 (MET) FREEMAN, MASON MASSACHUSETTS GENERAL HOSPITAL BIGELOW 840 BOSTON, MA 02114 Regulation of scavenger receptors in atherosclerosis

R01HL-45099-05 (SB) EVANS, EVAN A UNIV OF BRITISH COLUMBIA VANCOUVER, B C CANADA V6T 1W5 Biomembrane mechanics, surface affinity and adhesion

R01HL-45107-02 (RAP) NEWMAN, JOHN H VANDERBILT UNIVERSITY B-1308 MEDICAL CENTER NORTH NASHVILLE, TN 37232 Pressure, flow, and filtration in the lung during exercise

R29HL-45115-02 (PTHA) MOLLER, DAVID JOHNS HOPKINS HOSPITAL 600 NORTH WOLFE STREET BALTIMORE, MD 21205 Pulmonary sarcoidosis and T-cell receptor genes

R01HL-45116-02 (CVB) LE WINTER, MARTIN M MEDICAL CENTER HOSP OF VERMONT BURLINGTON, VT 05401 Energetics of the isolated left ventricle

R55HL-45120-01A1 (BBCB) ROBITAILLE, PIERRE-MARIE L OHIO STATE UNIVERSITY HOSPITAL 410 WEST 10TH AVENUE COLUMBUS, OH 43210 NMR studies of congestive heart failure

R29HL-45123-01A1 (HEM) STOECKERT, CHRISTIAN J, JR UNIVERSITY OF PENNSYLVANIA PHILADELPHIA, PA 19104-6058 Transferred globin regulation in human erythroblasts

R01HL-45129-01A1 (SAT) WANG, TINGCHUNG UNIVERSITY OF ROCHESTER 601 ELMWOOD AVENUE ROCHESTER, NY 14642 Freezing storage of heart at high subzero temperatures

R01HL-45132-02 (CVA) STRAUSS, HAROLD C DUKE UNIVERSITY MEDICAL CTR PO BOX 3845 DURHAM, NC 27710 Electrophylologic properties of endothelial cells

R01HL-45135-01A1 (PTHA) MC GOWAN, STEPHEN E UNIV OF IOWA HOSPITALS & CLINI IOWA CITY, IA 52242 Effects of transforming growth factor-beta on elastin

R29HL-45136-02 (PTHA) UHAL, BRUCE D PENNSYLVANIA STATE UNIVERSITY PO BOX 850 HERSHEY, PA 17033 Control of type II pneumocyte proliferation

R01HL-45138-02 (RAP) CUTRONEO, KENNETH R UNIVERSITY OF VERMONT COLLEGE OF MEDICINE BURLINGTON, VT 05405 Modulation of collagen synthesis in lung fibroblasts

R01HL-45139-01A1 (BEM) EWART, CRAIG K JOHNS HOPKINS UNIVERSITY 624 NORTH BROADWAY, ROOM 750 BALTIMORE, MD 21205 School based exercise to lower adolescent blood pressure

R29HL-45141-02 (CVA) HARVEY, ROBERT D CASE WESTERN RESERVE UNIVERSIT 2109 ADELBERT ROAD CLEVELAND, OH 44106 Cardiac chloride current pharmacology and physiology

R01HL-45142-02 (ECS) BROCK, TOMMY A UNIV OF ALABAMA AT BIRMINGHAM 1046 ZEIGLER RESEARCH BLDG BIRMINGHAM, AL 35294 VSM chloride permeability in hypertension

R29HL-45143-01A1 (BBCB) LODDER, ROBERT A UNIVERSITY OF KENTUCKY MED CTR ROSE STREET LEXINGTON, KY 40536-0082 Near-IR spectra of lipoproteins and apolipoproteins

R01HL-45151-02 (RAP) BRIGHAM, KENNETH L VANDERBILT UNIV SCH OF MED 21ST AVENUE AT GARLAND STREET NASHVILLE, TN 37232 Evaluation of gene therapy for acute lung injury

R01HL-45157-01A1 (EDC) FRITZ, GREGORY K RHODE ISLAND HOSPITAL 593 EDDY STREET PROVIDENCE, RI 02903 Epidemiology symptom perception in childhood asthma

R01HL-45159-01A1 (PTHA) SIMMONS, WILLIAM H LOYOLA UNIVERSITY 2160 SOUTH FIRST AVE MAYWOOD, IL 60153 A novel route for bradykinin degradation in lung

R01HL-45161-02 (PHY) WARSHAW, DAVID M UNIVERSITY OF VERMONT GIVEN BUILDING BURLINGTON, VT 05405 Smooth muscle crossbridge interactions--A motility assay

P01HL-45168-01A1 (HLBB) LORAND, LASZLO NORTHWESTERN UNIVERSITY 2153 SHERIDAN RD EVANSTON, IL 60208 Blood cell development and function

P01HL-45168-01A1 0001 (HLBB) DOUGLAS, ENGEL J Blood cell development and function Transformation of hematopoietic progenitor cells

P01HL-45168-01A1 0002 (HLBB) PATEL, VIKRAM P Blood cell development and function Analysis of hematopoietic stem-stromal interactions

P01HL-45168-01A1 0003 (HLBB) PIERCE, SUSAN K Blood cell development and function Antigen-Derived lymphocyte interaction structures

P01HL-45168-01A1 0004 (HLBB) MACDONALD, ROBERT C Blood cell development and function The molecular basis of the mechanical properties of erythrocytes

P01HL-45168-01A1 0005 (HLBB) LORAND, LASZLO Blood cell development and function Function of erythrocyte transglutaminase

P01HL-45168-01A1 9001 (HLBB) PIERCE, SUSAN K Blood cell development and function CORE--Cell production and analysis laboratory

R01HL-45170-01A1 (TOX) HOLM, BRUCE A CHILDREN'S HOSPITAL OF BUFFALO 219 BRYANT STREET BUFFALO, NY 14222 Pulmonary oxygen toxicity--mechanisms and interventions

R01HL-45176-02 (HUD) THULBORN, KEITH R MGH THE GENERAL HOSPITAL CORP FRUIT STREET BOSTON, MA 02114 MRI imaging of hemorrhage

R29HL-45179-01A1 (RAD) LISTERUD, JOHN UNIVERSITY OF PENNSYLVANIA 36TH ST & HAMILTON WALK PHILADELPHIA, PA 19104 Signal loss in magnetic resonance angiography

R01HL-45181-02 (HEM) BRASS, LAWRENCE F HOSP OF THE UNIV OF PENNSYLVAN 3400 SPRUCE STREET PHILADELPHIA, PA 19104-4283 Characterization of a novel G protein in human platelets

R01HL-45182-02 (HEM) CONBOY, JOHN G LAWRENCE BERKELEY LAB 1 CYCLOTRON RD BERKELEY, CA 94720 Red cell band 4.1--Developmental changes in RNA splicing

R29HL-45194-01A1 (HEM) HENRIKSEN, RUTH A EAST CAROLINA UNIVERSITY GREENVILLE, NC 27858-4354 Structure function studies for thrombin and fibrinogen

R01HL-45198-02 (PHRA) BIRNBAUMER, LUTZ BAYLOR COLLEGE OF MEDICINE ONE BAYLOR PLAZA HOUSTON, TX 77030 Receptor coupling mechanisms

R01HL-45206-01A1 (PTHA) SEVANIAN, ALEX UNIV OF SOUTHERN CALIFORNIA 1985 ZONAL AVENUE LOS ANGELES, CA 90033 Endothelial phospholipase a2 in oxidant membrane injury

R01HL-45215-08 (PHY) BLAUSTEIN, MORDECAI P UNIVERSITY OF MARYLAND 655 WEST BALTIMORE STREET BALTIMORE, MD 21201 Calcium and sodium transport in muscle

R29HL-45220-02 (RAP) NAKAMURA, KENNETH T KAPIOLANI MED CTR WOMEN CHILDR 1319 PUNAHOU ST HONOLULU, HI 96826 Ontogeny of airway smooth muscle function

R01HL-45239-02 (RAP) KOTLIKOFF, MICHAEL, IV UNIVERSITY OF PENNSYLVANIA 3800 SPRUCE STREET PHILADELPHIA, PA 19104-6046 Calcium influx in human airway smooth muscle cells

R29HL-45240-02 (PHY) HILGEMANN, DONALD W UT SOUTHWESTERN MEDICAL CENTER 5323 HARRY HINES BOULEVARD DALLAS, TX 75235-9040 Cardiac sodium-calcium exchange regulation and function

R29HL-45241-02 (ECS) MC KENZIE, JAMES C HOWARD UNIVERSITY 520 W ST NW WASHINGTON, DC 20059 Neocortical ANP synthesis in hypertension

R01HL-45243-02 (RNM) THOMAS, STEPHEN R UNIV OF CINCINNATI COLLEGE OF MEDICINE ML 579 CINCINNATI, OH 45267 Pfc blood substitutes for oxygen quantitation in vivo

R29HL-45245-02 (RAP) DICARLO, STEPHEN E NORTHEASTERN OHIO UNIV COLL/ M ST RT 44 ROOTSTOWN, OH 44272 Exercise training and cardiovascular regulation

R29HL-45258-01 (CVA) CHENG, CHE PING BOWMAN GRAY SCHOOL OF MEDICINE 300 S HAWTHORNE RD WINSTON-SALEM, NC 27103 Diastolic filling dynamics of exercise and heart failure

R18HL-45265-02 (SRC) SLICHTER, SHERRILL J PUGET SOUND BLOOD CENTER 921 TERRY AVENUE SEATTLE, WA 98104-1256 Donor participation in transfusion and transplantation

R18HL-45265-02 0001 (SRC) BIER, TRACY Donor participation in transfusion and transplantation Retaining donors and increasing donation frequency

R18HL-45265-02 0002 (SRC) BEATTY, PATRICK Donor participation in transfusion and transplantation Optimization of an unrelated bone marrow donor program

R18HL-45265-02 0003 (SRC) SLICHTER, SHERRILL J Donor participation in transfusion and transplantation Routine blood donation by apheresis technology

R01HL-45267-01A1 (SB) TAYLOR, LLOYD M, JR OREGON HLTH SCIENCES UNIV 3181 SW SAM JACKSON PARK RD PORTLAND, OR 97201-3098 Homocysteine and progression of atherosclerosis

R01HL-45279-02 (SRC) MURPHY, SHIRLEY UNIVERISTY OF NEW MEXICO ALBUQUERQUE, NM 87131 A self-management educational program for hispanic asthmatic children

R29HL-45284-01A1 (PTHA) SKITA, VICTOR UNIV OF CONNECTICUT HLTH CTR 263 FARMINGTON AVE FARMINGTON, CT 06032 Lung surfactant -- x-ray and neutron diffraction study

R01HL-45286-02 (RAP) VOELKER, DENNIS R NAT'L JEWISH IMMUN CTR/RES MED 1400 JACKSON ST DENVER, CO 80206 Pulmonary surfactant dynamics and surfactant protein A

R01HL-45287-02 (BNP) FRYE, LEAH L RENSSELAER POLYTECH INSTITUTE COGSWELL LABORATORY TROY, NY 12180-3590 Dual-action inhibitors of cholesterol biosynthesis

R29HL-45290-01A1 (BEM) EMERY, CHARLES F DUKE UNIVERSITY MEDICAL CENTER BOX 3119 DURHAM, NC 27710 Exercise and cognition in older adults with COPD

R01HL-45293-02 (SRC) FISHER, EDWIN B, JR WASHINGTON UNIVERSITY #33 S EUCLID, 2ND FLOOR ST LOUIS, MO 63108 Development and evaluation of community asthma program

R01HL-45297-02 (SRC) WOOD, PAMELA R UNIV OF TEXAS HLTH SCI CTR 7703 FLOYD CURL DRIVE SAN ANTONIO, TX 78284 An intervention for Hispanic children with asthma

R01HL-45304-02 (SRC) MELLINS, ROBERT B COLUMBIA UNIVERSITY 630 WEST 168TH STREET NEW YORK, NY 10032 A childhood asthma program in NYC health department clinics

R29HL-45306-02 (NTN) MOREL, DIANE W MEDICAL COLLEGE OF PA 3300 HENRY AVENUE PHILADELPHIA, PA 19129 Metabolism of dietary or peroxidation-derived oxysterols

R01HL-45312-02 (SRC) MALVEAUX, FLOYD HOWARD UNIVERSITY COLLEGE OF M 520 W STREET NW WASHINGTON, DC 20059 Community intervention for minority children with asthma

R01HL-45313-02 (CVB) SOFFER, RICHARD L CORNELL UNIV MEDICAL COLLEGE 1300 YORK AVE NEW YORK, NY 10021 Soluble angiotensin receptor structure and regulation

R29HL-45317-02 (CVB) DELAFONTAINE, PATRICE EMORY UNIVERSITY SCH OF MEDICI P O DRAWER LL ATLANTA, GA 30322 Insulin-like growth I action in heart and blood vessels

R01HL-45321-02 (SRC) DLUHY, ROBERT G BRIGHAM AND WOMEN'S HOSPITAL 221 LONGWOOD AVENUE BOSTON, MA 02115 Genetics of non-modulating hypertension

R01HL-45323-02 (SRC) KAMMERER, CANDACE M SOUTHWEST FDN FOR BIOMEDICAL R PO BOX 28147 SAN ANTONIO, TX 78284 Pedigree analysis of hypertension markers in primates

R01HL-45325-02 (SRC) LALOUEL, JEAN-MARC UNIV OF UTAH HLTH SCI CTR SALT LAKE CITY, UT 84132 Selected candidate genes in human hypertension

R01HL-45326-02 (CVB) MUNTZ, KATHRYN H UNIV OF TEXAS SW MEDICAL CTR 5323 HARRY HINES BOULEVARD DALLAS, TX 75235 Localization of adrenergic and NPY receptors in heart

R01HL-45332-02 (CVB) VATNER, DOROTHY E MASSACHUSETTS GENERAL HOSPITAL FRUIT STREET, JACKSON 13 BOSTON, MA 02114 Autonomic receptor function in myocardial ischemia

R01HL-45335-03 (SRC) HEIMARK, RONALD L ICOS CORPORATION 22021 - 20TH AVENUE, SE BOTHELL, WA 98021 The role of V-cadherin in vascular morphogenesis

R01HL-45337-02 (SRC) ROSENQUIST, THOMAS H MEDICAL COLLEGE OF GEORGIA AUGUSTA, GA 30912 Developmental heterogeneity among the great arteries

R01HL-45341-02 (SRC) RAPP, JOHN P MEDICAL COLLEGE OF OHIO PO BOX 10008 TOLEDO, OH 43699 Molecular genetic analysis of blood pressure in the rat

R01HL-45343-02 (SRC) HAJJAR, DAVID P CORNELL UNIVERSITY MED COLLEGE 1300 YORK AVENUE NEW YORK, NY 10021 Viral tropism in vascular aging--Role of the FGF receptor

R01HL-45345-02 (SRC) WALSH, KENNETH CASE WESTERN RESERVE UNIVERSIT 2119 ABINGTON ROAD CLEVELAND, OH 44106 Molecular biology of smooth muscle differentiation

R01HL-45348-02 (SRC) LITTLE, CHARLES D UNIVERSITY OF VIRGINIA BOX 439, HEALTH SCIENCES CTR CHARLOTTESVILLE, VA 22908 The cell biology of vasculogenesis

R01HL-45351-02 (SRC) DIXIT, VISHVA M UNIV OF MICHIGAN MED SCHOOL 1301 CATHERINE RD BOX 0602 ANN ARBOR, MI 48109-0602 Cytokine modulation of endothelial gene expression

R43HL-45354-01A1 (HEM) SHETTIGAR, UDIPI R BIOPROCESS SYSTEMS, INC 1324 MEDICAL PLAZA SALT LAKE CITY, UT 84112 Membrane autotransfusion system

R43HL-45376-01 (SSS) LEDET, EARL G INTRA-SONIX INC 42 THIRD AVENUE BURLINGTON, MA 01803 Real-time imaging array optimized for vascular therapy

R29HL-45377-02 (PHY) EBIHARA, LISA MD PHD COLUMBIA UNIVERSITY 630 W 168TH ST NEW YORK, NY 10032 Physiology of cardiac gap junctions

R01HL-45394-01A1 (MET) LEFF, TODD ROCKEFELLER UNIVERSITY 1230 YORK AVE NEW YORK, NY 10021 Regulation of apolipoprotein CIII

R43HL-45398-01A1 (SSS) EVANS, DALE B COROMED INC 185 JORDAN ROAD TROY, NY 12180-8343 CaM-PDE I inhibitors for cardiovascular therapy

R43HL-45402-01 (SSS) DIAMOND, HOWARD DIAMOND GENERAL DEVELOPMENT CO 3965 RESEARCH PARK DRIVE ANN ARBOR, MI 48108-2296 Tissue transfer viability-- Long term bedside monitoring

R01HL-45422-02 (SRC) ZEHNER, ZENDRA E VIRGINIA COMMONWEALTH UNIV MCV STATION BOX 614 RICHMOND, VA 23298-0614 A negative factor which regulates cardiac development

R01HL-45425-02 (SRC) MAHDAVI, VIJAK CHILDREN'S HOSPITAL CORP. 300 LONGWOOD AVENUE BOSTON, MA 02115 Determinants of cardiac cell lineages

R01HL-45429-02 (SRC) MILLER, JEFFREY B MASSACHUSETTS GENERAL HOSPITAL 149 13TH STREET CHARLESTOWN, MA 02129 Development and diversification of cardiac myocytes

R01HL-45438-02 (SRC) WILLIAMS, GORDON H BRIGHAM AND WOMENS HOSPITAL 221 LONGWOOD AVENUE BOSTON, MA 02115 Alteration of murine expression of renin and ANP

R01HL-45453-03 (SRC) FIELD, LOREN J INDIANA UNIVERSITY 1001 WEST 10TH ST INDIANAPOLIS, IN 46202-2859 Cloning genes that regulate myocardiocyte proliferation

R01HL-45458-02 (SRC) FISCHMAN, DONALD A CORNELL UNIV MEDICAL COLLEGE 1300 YORK AVE NEW YORK, NY 10021 Molecular/cellular biology of cardiomyocyte development

U01HL-45460-02 (SRC) GINSBERG, HENRY N COLUMBIA UNIVERSITY 630 WEST 168TH STREET NEW YORK, NY 10032 Coronary artery disease and postprandial lipoproteins

R01HL-45462-02 (SRC) COLLINS, TUCKER BRIGHAM AND WOMEN'S HOSPITAL 75 FRANCIS STREET BOSTON, MA 02115 Endothelial specific gene expression

R01HL-45466-02 (SRC) BEYER, ERIC C WASHINGTON UNIVERSITY 400 S KINGSHIGHWAY ST LOUIS, MO 63110 Intercellular communication in the developing heart

U01HL-45467-02 (SRC) HEISS, GERARDO UNIVERSITY OF NORTH CAROLINA CB #7400 CHAPEL HILL, NC 27599-7400 Postprandial lipoproteins and atherosclerosis--Core

R01HL-45468-02 (SRC) MULLINS, JOHN UNIV OF HEIDELBERG IM NEUENHEIMER FELD 366 D-6900 HEIDELBERG, FRG Transgenic rats in hypertension--Renin angiotensin system ribozyme inhibition

R01HL-45476-02 (SRC) SCHWARTZ, ROBERT J BAYLOR COLLEGE OF MEDICINE ONE BAYLOR PLAZA HOUSTON, TX 77030 Regulation of embryonic heart development

R29HL-45478-01 (PC) DRISCOLL, DONNA M SOUTHWEST FDN FOR BIOMED RES PO BOX 28147 SAN ANTONIO, TX 78228-0147 Editing of apolipoprotein B mRNA

R01HL-45480-01 (MET) LINGAPPA, VISHWANATH R UNIVERSITY OF CALIFORNIA PARNASSUS AVENUE SAN FRANCISCO, CA 94143 Molecular mechanisms of apolipoprotein B biogenesis
R01HL-45485-01 (SAT) YOGANATHAN, AJIT P GEORGIA INST OF TECHNOLOGY SCHOOL OF CHEMICAL ENGINEERING ATLANTA, GA 30332-0100 Quantitation of valvular regurgitation an in vitro study
P50HL-45486-01 (SRC) COLMAN, ROBERT W TEMPLE UNIVERSITY 3400 N BROAD ST PHILADELPHIA, PA 19140 SCOR in thrombosis
P50HL-45486-01 0001 (SRC) COLMAN, ROBERT W SCOR in thrombosis Structural requirements of kininogen-neutrophil interactions
P50HL-45486-01 0002 (SRC) SCHMAIER, ALVIN SCOR in thrombosis Modulation of production and clearance of C1 inhibitor
P50HL-45486-01 0003 (SRC) WALSH, PETER N SCOR in thrombosis Interaction of platelets with coagulation factors IX and X
P50HL-45486-01 0004 (SRC) BOCK, SUSAN SCOR in thrombosis Arg-serpin target protease specificity
P50HL-45486-01 0005 (SRC) NIEWIAROWSKI, STEFAN SCOR in thrombosis Disintegrins--Antiadhesive peptides from viper venoms
P50HL-45486-01 9001 (SRC) JAMESON, BRADFORD SCOR in thrombosis Core--Protein structure
P50HL-45486-01 9002 (SRC) STEWART, GWENDOLYN J SCOR in thrombosis Core--Research resources
R29HL-45500-02 (PC) BRASIER, ALLAN ROBERT UNIVERSITY OF TEXAS MED BRANCH GALVESTON, TX 77550 Angiotensinogen gene acute phase response element
R01HL-45508-01 (EDC) COOPER, RICHARD S LOYOLA UNIVERSITY OF CHICAGO 2160 S FIRST AVENUE MAYWOOD, IL 60153 Hypertension in blacks--The US, Africa, and the Caribbean
R01HL-45510-01 (HEM) MC EVER, RODGER P UNIVERSITY OF OKLAHOMA PO BOX 26901 OKLAHOMA CITY, OK 73104 Structure and function of gmp-140
R01HL-45513-01A1 (MET) DORY, LADISLAV UNIVERSITY OF TENNESSEE 874 UNION AVENUE MEMPHIS, TN 38163 Regulation of apoE expression in macrophages
R01HL-45516-01 (NTN) CHAN, LAWRENCE C BAYLOR COLLEGE OF MEDICINE ONE BAYLOR PLAZA HOUSTON, TX 77030 Mechanism of apolipoprotein B-48 biogenesis
R55HL-45520-01 (HED) ENGLAND, SANDRA J UMDNJ-ROBERT WOOD JOHNSON MED ONE ROBERT WOOD JOHNSON PLACE NEW BRUNSWICK, NJ 08903-0019 Control of respiratory muscles in the neonate
P01HL-45522-01A1 (SRC) MACCLUER, JEAN W SOUTHWEST FDN FOR BIOMED RES P O BOX 28147 SAN ANTONIO, TX 78228-0147 Genetics of atherosclerosis in Mexican Americans
P01HL-45522-01A1 0001 (SRC) MACCLUER, JEAN W Genetics of atherosclerosis in Mexican Americans Pedigree analysis of lipoprotein phenotypes
P01HL-45522-01A1 0002 (SRC) HIXSON, JAMES E Genetics of atherosclerosis in Mexican Americans Molecular genetics of lipoproteins
P01HL-45522-01A1 0003 (SRC) KAMMERER, CANDACE M Genetics of atherosclerosis in Mexican Americans Genetic analysis using candidate genes
P01HL-45522-01A1 0004 (SRC) VANDEBERG, JOHN L Genetics of atherosclerosis in Mexican Americans Biochemical genetics of lipoproteins
P01HL-45522-01A1 0005 (SRC) RAINWATER, DAVID L Genetics of atherosclerosis in Mexican Americans Genetic effects on apolipoprotein distribution
P01HL-45522-01A1 9001 (SRC) STERN, MICHAEL P Genetics of atherosclerosis in Mexican Americans Core-- Field and clinic operations
P01HL-45522-01A1 9002 (SRC) DYKE, BENNETT Genetics of atherosclerosis in Mexican Americans Core-- Computing and data management
R01HL-45532-02 (SAT) WARNER, DAVID O MAYO FOUNDATION 200 FIRST STREET SOUTHWEST ROCHESTER, MN 55905 Anesthesia and airways
R01HL-45533-01 (RAP) RAFFIN, THOMAS A STANFORD UNIVERSITY STANFORD, CA 94305-5236 Mechanisms of protection against acute lung injury
R01HL-45545-01 (RAP) WILSON, THEODORE A UNIVERSITY OF MINNESOTA 110 UNION STREET, SOUTHEAST MINNEAPOLIS, MN 55455 Respiratory action of the intercostal muscles
R01HL-45548-01 (SRC) GLASGOW, RUSSELL E OREGON RESEARCH INSTITUTE 1899 WILLAMETTE, SUITE 2 EUGENE, OR 97401 Worksite issues in organizational health promotion
R01HL-45554-01 (PHRA) HUANG, WU-HSIUNG MEDICAL COLLEGE OF OHIO 3000 ARLINGTON AVENUE TOLEDO, OH 43614 Cardiac sodium pump--Interactions with oxidants
R01HL-45559-01 (GMA) BENOIT, JOSEPH N LOUISIANA STATE UNIV MED CTR P O BOX 33932 SHREVEPORT, LA 71130-3932 The intestine in chronic portal hypertension
R01HL-45563-01 (PTHA) CYBULSKY, MYRON I BRIGHAM & WOMEN'S HOSPITAL 75 FRANCIS STREET BOSTON, MA 02115 Monocyte-endothelial interactions during atherogenesis
R29HL-45565-01 (CTY) COOPER, THOMAS A BAYLOR COLLEGE OF MEDICINE ONE BAYLOR PLAZA HOUSTON, TX 77030 Troponin T alternative splicing in embryonic heart
R29HL-45571-01 (RAP) SWENSON, ERIK R VETERANS ADMIN MEDICAL CENTER 1660 SOUTH COLUMBIAN WAY SEATTLE, WA 98108 Lung carbonic anhydrase and ventilation perfusion matching
R01HL-45572-01 (MGN) WALLACE, DOUGLAS C EMORY UNIVERSITY 109 WOODRUFF MEMORIAL BLDG ATLANTA, GA 30322 Mitochondrial genes and cardiomyopathy
R29HL-45573-01 (HED) PALIS, JAMES UNIVERSITY OF ROCHESTER 601 ELMWOOD AVE ROCHESTER, NY 14642 Gene expression during mammalian yolk sac hematopoiesis
R01HL-45574-01 (MET) SCHOELLER, DALE A UNIVERSITY OF CHICAGO 5841 SOUTH MARYLAND AVE, BOX 4 CHICAGO, IL 60637 Cholesterol metabolism--New methods for acute studies
R01HL-45578-01 (CVA) GALLAGHER, KIM P UNIVERSITY OF MICHIGAN B560 MSRB II BOX 0686 ANN ARBOR, MI 48109 Myocardial preconditioning
R01HL-45588-01 (RAP) CHRISTENSEN, THOMAS G MALLORY INST OF PATHOLOGY FDN 784 MASSACHUSETTS AVENUE BOSTON, MA 02118 Bronchial epithelial cell kinetics
R01HL-45593-01 (PHRA) BJORNSSON, THORIR D JEFFERSON MEDICAL COLLEGE 1100 WALNUT STREET PHILADELPHIA, PA 19107 Pharmacology of endothelial cell TPA/UPA synthesis
R01HL-45608-01 (CVA) FARRAR, DAVID J MED RES INST OF SAN FRANCISCO 2200 WEBSTER STREET SAN FRANCISCO, CA 94115 Ventricular systolic interactions during heart failure
R01HL-45617-01 (ECS) ROSENBLUM, WILLIAM I MEDICAL COLLEGE OF VIRGINIA BOX 17, MCV STATION RICHMOND, VA 23298-0017 Role of l-arginine in control of brain microcirculation
R01HL-45619-01A1 (PTHA) GUYTON, JOHN R METHODIST HOSPITAL 6565 FANNIN ST HOUSTON, TX 77030 Lipoprotein oxidation and atherosclerosis
R29HL-45621-01A1 (HEM) DONOVAN-PELUSO, MARYANN A UNIVERSITY OF PITTSBURGH 712 SCAIFE HALL PITTSBURGH, PA 15261 Molecular biology of monocyte tissue factor expression
R29HL-45623-01A1 (CVB) HOLSTEIN-RATHLOU, NIELS-HENRIK UNIV OF SOUTHERN CALIFORNIA 1333 SAN PABLO STREET LOS ANGELES, CA 90033 Dynamics of renal blood regulation in WKY and SHR
R01HL-45624-01A1 (CVA) JOSEPHSON, IRA R UNIVERSITY OF CINCINNATI COLLEGE OF MEDICINE CINCINNATI, OH 45267 Cardiac Na and Ca channel gating currents
R01HL-45635-01 (MEDB) DINAUER, MARY C THE CHILDREN'S HOSPITAL 300 LONGWOOD AVENUE BOSTON, MA 02115 Structure/function analysis of phagocyte proteins
R01HL-45636-01 (SB) GRIEPP, RANDALL B MOUNT SINAI SCHOOL OF MEDICINE BOX 1028 NEW YORK, NY 10029 Cerebral function after hypothermic circulatory arrest
R01HL-45638-01 (RAP) MALIK, ASRAR B ALBANY MEDICAL COLLEGE 47 NEW SCOTLAND AVENUE ALBANY, NY 12208 Thrombin induced pulmonary vascular permeability
R01HL-45646-01A1 (CVB) ZAK, RADOVAN UNIV OF CHICAGO 970 EAST 58 ST CHICAGO, IL 60637 Regulation of myosin heavy-chain alpha gene by cAMP
R01HL-45650-01 (RAP) HARD, ROBERT P SUNNY AT BUFFALO BUFFALO, NY 14214 Waveform and coordination of respiratory cilia
R01HL-45659-01 (HEM) HOSKINS, LANSING C VA MEDICAL CENTER 10701 EAST BOULEVARD CLEVELAND, OH 44106 Enzymatic production of universal donor erythrocytes
R29HL-45664-01 (SB) LESH, MICHAEL D UNIVERSITY OF CALIFORNIA 505 PARNASSUS AVE, BOX 0214 SAN FRANCISCO, CA 94143-0214 Reentry in a computer model of heterogenous myocardium
P01HL-45666-01 (SRC) CLARKSON, THOMAS B WAKE FOREST UNIVERSITY MEDICAL CENTER BOULEVARD WINSTON-SALEM, NC 27157-1040 Coronary atherosclerosis in female monkeys
P01HL-45666-01 0001 (SRC) CLARKSON, THOMAS B Coronary atherosclerosis in female monkeys Pre/postmenopausal steroid effects of CAA and osteoporosis
P01HL-45666-01 0002 (SRC) ADAMS, MICHAEL R Coronary atherosclerosis in female monkeys Effects of estrogens and progestins on atherogenesis
P01HL-45666-01 0003 (SRC) KAPLAN, JAY R Coronary atherosclerosis in female monkeys Psychophysiologic mechanisms-Estrogen/progestin effects
P01HL-45666-01 9001 (SRC) ST CLAIR, RICHARD W Coronary atherosclerosis in female monkeys Core--Lipid analytic laboratory
P01HL-45666-01 9002 (SRC) RUDEL, LAWRENCE L Coronary atherosclerosis in female monkeys Core--Lipoprotein analytic laboratory
P01HL-45666-01 9003 (SRC) WILSON, MARK E Coronary atherosclerosis in female monkeys Core--Endocrine Assay
P01HL-45666-01 9004 (SRC) MOYER, CAROLYN F Coronary atherosclerosis in female monkeys Core--Comparative pathology
P01HL-45666-01 9005 (SRC) WAGNER, JANICE D Coronary atherosclerosis in female monkeys Core--Laboratory Animal Medicine
P01HL-45666-01 9006 (SRC) ANTHONY, MARY S Coronary atherosclerosis in female monkeys Core--Animal care/clinical studies
P01HL-45666-01 9007 (SRC) MORGAN, TIMOTHY M Coronary atherosclerosis in female monkeys Core--Biostatistics /Data service
R29HL-45673-01A1 (CVB) BRUNER, CATHY A ALBANY MEDICAL COLLEGE 47 NEW SCOTLAND AVE ALBANY, NY 12208 Physiologic mechanisms in steroid-salt hypertension
R01HL-45674-01A1 (CVB) O'DONNELL, MARTHA E UNIVERSITY OF CALIFORNIA DAVIS, CA 95616 Ion fluxes in endothelial cell volume regulation
R01HL-45679-01 (RAP) KAMM, ROGER D MASSACHUSETTS INST OF TECH 77 MASSACHUSETTS AVENUE CAMBRIDGE, MA 02139 Airway obstruction and liquid layer mobility
R29HL-45683-01A1 (RNM) MC VEIGH, ELLIOT R JOHNS HOPKINS HOSPITAL 600 N WOLFE STREET BALTIMORE, MD 21205 High-resolution MRI of myocardial deformation
R29HL-45684-01A1 (CVA) PIKE, MARTIN M UNIVERSITY OF ALABAMA 1900 UNIVERSITY BLVD BIRMINGHAM, AL 35294 NMR studies of ischemic injury in the perfused heart
R29HL-45687-01 (RAP) INGENITO, EDWARD P BRIGHAM AND WOMEN'S HOSPITAL 75 FRANCIS STREET BOSTON, MA 02115 Determinants of tissue resistance in the guinea pig
U01HL-45692-01A1 (CLTR) CHARACHE, SAMUEL JOHNS HOPKINS HOSPITAL 600 NORTH WOLFE STREET BALTIMORE, MD 21205 Multicenter study of hydroxyurea in sickle cell anemia
R10HL-45693-01 (SRC) MERGNER, WOLFGANG J UNIVERSITY OF MARYLAND 10 S PINE STREET BALTIMORE, MD 21201 Risk factors in early human atherogenesis
R10HL-45694-01 (SRC) CORNHILL, J FREDERICK OHIO STATE UNIV MEDICAL CENTER 1080 CARMACK ROAD COLUMBUS, OH 43210-1240 Risk factors in early human atherogenesis
U01HL-45696-01A1 (CLTR) TERRIN, MICHAEL L MARYLAND MEDICAL RES INST INC 600 WYNDHURST AVE BALTIMORE, MD 21210 Multicenter study of hydroxyurea in sickle cell anemia
U01HL-45700-01A1 (CLTR) BUXTON, ALFRED E UNIVERSITY OF PENNSYLVANIA 3400 SPRUCE STREET PHILADELPHIA, PA 19104-3246 Nonsustained ventricular tachycardia
R01HL-45707-01 (BEM) MC CANN, BARBARA S HARBORVIEW MEDICAL CENTER 325 NINTH AVENUE SEATTLE, WA 98104 Job stress, diet, and plasma lipids
R10HL-45715-01 (SRC) WISSLER, ROBERT W UNIVERSITY OF CHICAGO

PROJECT NO., ORGANIZATIONAL UNIT., INVESTIGATOR, ADDRESS, TITLE

5841 SOUTH MARYLAND AVE/BOX 41 CHICAGO, IL 60637 Risk factors in early human atherogenesis

R10HL-45718-01 (SRC) VIRMANI, RENU VANDERBILT UNIV SCH OF MED 21ST AND GARLAND AVENUE NASHVILLE, TN 37232 Risk factors in early human atherogenesis

R10HL-45719-01 (SRC) MC MAHAN, C ALEX UNIV OF TX HEALTH SCI CTR 7703 FLOYD CURL DR SAN ANTONIO, TX 78284 Risk factors in early human atherogenesis

R10HL-45720-01 (SRC) STRONG, JACK P LOUISIANA STATE UNIVERSITY 1901 PERDIDO ST NEW ORLEANS, LA 70112-1393 Risk factors in early human atherogenesis

U01HL-45726-01A1 (CLTR) LEE, KERRY L DUKE UNIVERSITY MEDICAL CENTER BOX 3363 DURHAM, NC 27710 Data coordinating center for trial of electrophysiologic-guided therapy

R29HL-45731-01A1 (EDC) CASSANO, PATRICIA A CORNELL UNIVERSITY 209 SAVAGE HALL ITHACA, NY 14853 Risk factors for chronic obstructive pulmonary disease

R01HL-45733-01A1 (CLTR) WOOD, PETER D STANFORD UNIVERSITY 730 WELCH ROAD PALO ALTO, CA 94304 Hygienic treatment of low HDL in older women and men

R29HL-45735-01A1 (PTHA) ARCHER, STEPHEN L VA MEDICAL CENTER 1 VETERANS DRIVE MINNEAPOLIS, MN 55417 EDRF in normal and hypertensive pulmonary vasculature

R01HL-45742-02 (CVB) NICHOLS, COLIN G WASHINGTON UNIVERSITY 660 S EUCLID AVENUE ST LOUIS, MO 63110 ATP-sensitive potassium channels in the heart

R01HL-45745-01 (PTHA) MILLER, YORK E VETERANS ADMINISTR MED CTR 1055 CLERMONT ST DENVER, CO 80220 Gastrin releasing peptide receptor analysis in the lung

R01HL-45753-01 (MET) LALOUEL, JEAN-MARC UNIV OF UTAH HLTH SCI CTR SALT LAKE CITY, UT 84132 Lipoprotein lipase deficiency--Genetics and biochemistry

R01HL-45782-01 (RAP) GROSS, NICHOLAS J P O BOX 505 HINES, IL 60141 A serine protease required for metabolism of surfactant

R01HL-45786-02 (SRC) GONIAS, STEVEN L UNIVERSITY OF VIRGINIA BOX 214 CHARLOTTESVILLE, VA 22908 Environmental modulation of fibrinolysis inhibitors

R29HL-45788-01 (PTHA) WYSOLMERSKI, ROBERT B ST LOUIS UNIVERSITY 1402 SOUTH GRAND BOULEVARD ST LOUIS, MO 63104 Endothelial cell retraction and edema of ARDS

R55HL-45789-01A1 (PHRA) WALSH, KENNETH B UNIVERSITY OF SOUTH CAROLINA SCHOOL OF MEDICINE COLUMBIA, SC 29208 Beta-adrenergic activation of a heart chloride channel

R01HL-45791-01 (CVB) WARD, PATRICK E 333 WEST 10TH AVENUE COLUMBUS, OH 43210 Cardiovascular action and metabolism of kinin analogs

R01HL-45794-01 (HEM) BRIDGES, KENNETH R BRIGHAM & WOMEN'S HOSPITAL 75 FRANCIS STREET BOSTON, MA 02115 Modulation of iron metabolism by cytokines

R01HL-45848-01A1 (PTHA) WAGNER, WILLIAM D BOWMAN GRAY SCHOOL OF MEDICINE 300 S HAWTHORNE ROAD WINSTON-SALEM, NC 27103 Smooth muscle cell proliferation and atherosclerosis

R01HL-45851-01 (PBC) YEH, EDWARD T 149 13TH ST/8TH FLOOR CHARLESTOWN, MA 02129 Pathobiology of paroxysmal nocturnal hemoglobinuria

R29HL-45891-01A1 (SB) JOHNSON, PETER C UNIVERSITY OF PITTSBURGH 676 SCAIFE HALL PITTSBURGH, PA 15261 Local antithrombotic agents in microvascular surgery

R29HL-45892-01A1 (BMT) CHANCE, MARK R GEORGETOWN UNIVERSITY 37TH & O STREETS, NW WASHINGTON, DC 20057 Control of reactivity in hemeproteins-- Cryogenic O2 study

R29HL-45895-01 (PTHA) BLOCH, KENNETH D MASSACHUSETTS GENERAL HOSPITAL 15 FRUIT STREET BOSTON, MA 02114 Biosynthesis of endothelin family of vasoactive peptides

R01HL-45897-01 (CVA) WALDMAN, LEWIS K UNIVERSITY OF CALIFORNIA LA JOLLA, CA 92093-0613 Distributed electromechanics of the beating heart

R01HL-45903-01 (CVB) IZUMO, SEIGO BETH ISRAEL HOSPITAL 330 BROOKLINE AVE BOSTON, MA 02215 Molecular studies of the cardiac sodium/calcium exchanger

R01HL-45906-02 (CVA) IWAZUMI, TATSUO ALBERT EINSTEIN COLL OF MEDICI 1300 MORRIS PARK AVENUE BRONX, NY 10461 Mechano-chemical properties of skinned cardiac myocytes

R01HL-45915-01 (TOX) DRECHSLER-PARKS, DEBORAH M UNIVERSITY OF CALIFORNIA SANTA BARBARA, CA 93106 Mechanisms of the responses to ozone exposure in humans

R01HL-45916-01 (PB) LENTZ, BARRY R UNIVERSITY OF NORTH CAROLINA CB#7260 CHAPEL HILL, NC 27599 Membrane biophysics and control of thrombin generation

R01HL-45922-02 (SRC) LUTTY, GERARD A JOHNS HOPKINS HOSPITAL 600 NORTH WOLFE STREET BALTIMORE, MD 21205 Vaso-occlusive processes in sickle cell retinopathy

R01HL-45923-02 (SRC) PARISE, LESLIE V UNIVERSITY OF NORTH CAROLINA CAMPUS BOX 7365 CHAPEL HILL, NC 27599-7365 Sickle cell adhesion to the endothelium

R01HL-45930-02 (SRC) SHORE, JOSEPH D HENRY FORD HOSPITAL 2799 WEST GRAND BOULEVARD DETROIT, MI 48202 Molecular interactions of fibrinolysis

R01HL-45931-02 (SRC) KAUL, DHANANJAYA K ALBERT EINSTEIN COLL OF MEDICI 1300 MORRIS PARK AVENUE BRONX, NY 10461 Sickle cell-endothelial interactions and vasoocclusion

R55HL-45933-01A1 (END) MEDFORD, RUSSELL M EMORY UNIVERSITY 1639 PIERCE DRIVE ATLANTA, GA 30322 Control of NA, K-atpase gene transcription and expression

R01HL-45934-02 (SRC) MILES, LINDSEY A SCRIPPS CLINIC AND RESEARCH FD 10666 NORTH TORREY PINES ROAD LA JOLLA, CA 92037 Plasminogen activator assembly systems on cell surfaces

R01HL-45936-02 (SRC) SOBEL, JOAN H COLUMBIA UNIVERSITY 630 WEST 168TH STREET NEW YORK, NY 10032 Fibrin alpha chain crosslinks as markers of fibrinolysis

R01HL-45940-02 (SRC) FALLER, DOUGLAS V DANA-FARBER CANCER INSTITUTE 44 BINNEY ST RM 1640 BOSTON, MA 02115 Mechanisms of vaso-occlusion in sickle cell anemia

PROJECT NO., ORGANIZATIONAL UNIT., INVESTIGATOR, ADDRESS, TITLE

R01HL-45944-02 (SRC) SAMBROOK, JOSEPH F UNIVERSITY OF TEXAS 5323 HARRY HINES BOULEVARD DALLAS, TX 75235-9038 Novel thrombolytic enzymes

R01HL-45947-02 (SRC) BARNES, PETER J NATIONAL HEART & LUNG INSTITUT DOVENHOUSE STREET LONDON SW3 6LY, UK Inflammatory and steroid modulation of airway B-receptor

R01HL-45954-02 (SRC) SCHLEEF, RAYMOND R SCRIPPS CLINIC & RESEARCH FDN 10666 NORTH TORREY PINES ROAD LA JOLLA, CA 92037 Platelet plasminogen activator inhibitors

R01HL-45955-02 (SRC) JESTY, JOLYON SUNY AT STONY BROOK STONY BROOK, NY 11794 Procoagulant properties of the sickle cell membrane

R55HL-45957-01 (SB) BRIGGS, FRED N VIRGINIA COMMONWEALTH UNIV P O BOX 551, MCV STATION RICHMOND, VA 23298 Gene regulation in cardiac assist skeletal muscle

R01HL-45964-02 (SRC) BENOVIC, JEFFREY L THOMAS JEFFERSON UNIVERSITY 1025 WALNUT STREET PHILADELPHIA, PA 19107 Beta-adrenergic receptor regulation in airway epithelium

R01HL-45967-02 (SRC) LIGGETT, STEPHEN B DUKE UNIVERSITY MEDICAL CTR PO BOX 3821 DURHAM, NC 27710 Molecular properties of b-adrenergic receptors in asthma

R01HL-45969-02 (SRC) STUART, MARIE J ST CHRISTOPHER'S HOSP/CHILDREN 5TH AND LEHIGH AVENUE PHILADELPHIA, PA 19133 Eicosanoids in the complications of sickle cell anemia

R01HL-45974-02 (SRC) HIRSHMAN, CAROL A JOHNS HOPKINS HOSPITAL 600 N WOLFE ST/BLALOCK 1501 BALTIMORE, MD 21205 Beta adrenergic modulation of airway function in asthma

R01HL-45977-01 (BBCB) JOHNSON, MICHAEL E UNIVERSITY OF ILLINOIS PO BOX 6998 (M/C 781) CHICAGO, IL 60680 Structural approaches to antisickling agent design

R01HL-45979-01 (EVR) GAUNTT, CHARLES J UNIV OF TEXAS HEALTH SCI CTR 7703 FLOYD CURL DRIVE SAN ANTONIO, TX 78284-7758 Chronic myocarditis in a coxsackievirus murine model

R29HL-45993-01 (GNM) MC ELLIGOTT, DAVID L THE SALK INSTITUTE PO BOX 85800 SAN DIEGO, CA 92138 Physical mapping of human chromosome 5q31-32

R01HL-45994-02 (HEM) HAWIGER, JACK J VANDERBILT UNIVERSITY VANDERBILT MEDICAL CENTER NORT NASHVILLE, TN 37232-2363 Adhesive proteins platelet receptor regulation

R01HL-45996-01A1 (PBC) KUIVANIEMI, S HELENA JEFFERSON MEDICAL COLLEGE 1020 LOCUST STREET PHILADELPHIA, PA 19107 Molecular biology of aortic aneurysms

R01HL-45998-01 (SSS) WHEELESS, LEON L UNIV OF ROCHESTER/SHC MED DENT 601 ELMWOOD AVENUE BOX 626 ROCHESTER, NY 14642 Quantitative image analysis study of sickle cells

R01HL-46005-01A1 (PHRA) KOREN, GIDEON BRIGHAM & WOMEN'S HOSPITAL 75 FRANCIS STREET BOSTON, MA 02115 Heart and muscle K+ channels -- Structure and function

R01HL-46013-01 (CVA) KLOCKE, ROBERT A SUNYAB-ECMC 462 GRIDER STREET BUFFALO, NY 14215 Kinetics of gas exchange in the pulmonary circulation

R01HL-46017-01 (HEM) FUNK, COLIN D VANDERBILT UNIVERSITY 532 MEDICAL RESEARCH BLDG NASHVILLE, TN 37232-6602 The molecular biology of 12-lipoxygenase

R01HL-46027-01 (CVA) VAN WYLEN, DAVID G SUNY BB201 CLIN CENTER, 462 GRIDER BUFFALO, NY 14215 Cardiac microdialysis, adenosine, and cardiac function

R01HL-46029-02 (PTHB) RYAN, UNA S 4960 AUDUBON AVENUE ST LOUIS, MO 63110 Human pulmonary endothelium--Gene transfer and responses

R29HL-46033-01A1 (CVA) BALSCHI, JAMES A UNIVERSITY OF ALABAMA CMLR BLDG BIRMINGHAM, AL 35294 NMR measurement of Na gradient and energetics--Ischemia

R29HL-46034-01 (CVA) BUTTRICK, PETER M MONTEFIORE MEDICAL CENTER 111 EAST 210TH STREET BRONX, NY 10467 Molecular adaptations in cardiac hypertrophy

R43HL-46035-01 (HEM) JENNY, RICHARD J HAEMATOLOGIC TECHNOLOGIES, INC PINEWOOD PLAZA, PO BOX 1021 ESSEX JUNCTION, VT 05452 Iron clearance by transferrin half-molecules

R43HL-46036-01 (HEM) BROWN, SCOTT M CORVAS INC 3030 SCIENCE PARK ROAD SAN DIEGO, CA 92121 Human recombinant tissue factor prothrombin time reagent

R43HL-46037-01 (HEM) ORTNER, DAVID L D & M COMPUTING INC 1010 32ND AVE SOUTH MOORHEAD, MN 56560 RISC processor for red cell volume distribution analysis

R43HL-46038-01 (HEM) MOORE, ROBERT M ISOLAB INC DRAWER 4350 AKRON, OH 44321 A test to screen for alpha-thalassemia-1 in adults

R43HL-46043-01 (SSS) IVY, JOHN M HAWAII BIOTECHNOLOGY GROUP, IN 99-193 AIEA HEIGHTS DRIVE AIEA, HI 96701 Coffee galactosidase cDNA cloning for blood processing

R43HL-46046-01A1 (SSS) MOORE, LARRY J EASTERN ANALYTICAL, INC 335 PAINT BRANCH DR COLLEGE PARK, MD 20742 A stable isotope method to determine blood volume

R43HL-46049-01A1 (SSS) SODERLAND, CARL CELL SYSTEMS CORP 12815 NE 124TH STREET KIRKLAND, WA 98034 Defined human microvascular endothelial cell system

R43HL-46061-01 (SSS) TORTI, RICHARD P SATCON TECHNOLOGY CORPORATION 12 EMILY STREET CAMBRIDGE, MA 02139 A magnetically guided cardiac catheter

R43HL-46064-01 (SSS) DOELLGAST, GEORGE J ELCATECH, INC 4291 LANTERN DRIVE WINSTON-SALEM, NC 27106 Ultrasensitive immunoassays for clotting factors

R43HL-46071-01 (SSS) GORKIN, LARRY INSTITUTE FOR BEHAVIORAL MED 120 WAYLAND AVENUE PROVIDENCE, R I 02906 CPR for families-- Videotape development

R43HL-46073-01 (SSS) LIBERTI, PAUL A IMMUNICON CORPORATION 1310 MASONS MILL II HUNTINGDON VALLEY, PA 19006 Bioprocessing cells from blood using BR-FF and HGMS

R43HL-46075-01 (SSS) WOLF, JAMES L FOREFRONT ENGINEERING, INC 883 PARFET STREET UNIT 3E LAKEWOOD CO 80215 Pulmonary peak flow monitor and recorder

R43HL-46078-01 (HUD) KRAUSMAN, DAVID T INDIVIDUAL MONITORING SYSTEMS 6310 HARFORD RD BALTIMORE, MD 21214 Physical activity monitoring with feedback

R43HL-46079-01A1 (SSS) SCHLAGER, KENNETH J BIOTRONICS

TECHNOLOGIES, INC 12020 WEST RIPLEY AVENUE WAUWATOSA, WI 53226 A phonoangiographic spectral analyzer for coronary artery stenosis

R43HL-46094-01 (SSS) TAMURA, SUSAN Y CORVAS, INC 3030 SCIENCE PARK RD SAN DIEGO, CA 92121 Novel inhibitors of coagulation proteases

R43HL-46095-01 (SSS) HALE, PAUL D SUNY/MOLTECH CORPORATION STONY BROOK, NY 11794 Advanced biosensors for the measurement of cholesterol

R43HL-46096-01 (SB) MORSE, BRENDA S CRYOLIFE, INC 2211 NEW MARKET PKWY, SUITE 14 MARIETTA, GA 30067 Development of a fibrin sealant delivery method

R43HL-46097-01 (SB) SIOSHANSI, PIRAN SPIRE CORPORATION ONE PATRIOTS PARK BEDFORD, MA 01730-2396 Low friction, bactericidal silver coated catheters

R43HL-46098-01 (SSS) SWEETNAM, PAUL M NOVA PHARMACEUTICAL CORP 6200 FREEPORT CENTRE BALTIMORE, MD 21224-2788 Development of endothelin-1 antagonists

R43HL-46099-01 (SSS) TOMLINSON, JAMES E COR THERAPEUTICS, INC 256 EAST GRAND AVE, SUITE 80 SAN FRANCISCO, CA 94080 Development of an assay for screening PDGF antagonists

R01HL-46100-02 (RAP) FOSTER, JUDITH A BOSTON UNIVERSITY SCH OF MED 80 EAST CONCORD STREET BOSTON, MA 02118 In vitro model for pulmonary emphysema

R03HL-46115-02 (SRC) CARMELLI, DORIT SRI INTERNATIONAL 333 RAVENSWOOD AVENUE MENLO PARK, CA 94025 CVD mortality in the NAS-NRC twin registry

R03HL-46117-02 (SRC) KLESGES, ROBERT C MEMPHIS STATE UNIVERSITY MEMPHIS, TN 38152 Smoking and body weight--Analysis of NHANES II and HHAN

R03HL-46120-01 (SRC) COOPER, RICHARD S LOYOLA UNIVERSITY OF CHICAGO 2160 S FIRST AVENUE MAYWOOD, IL 60153 Heart disease and the black health disadvantage

R03HL-46144-01A1 (SRC) SHEEHAN, FLORENCE H UNIVERSITY OF WASHINGTON 1959 NORTHEAST PACIFIC SEATTLE, WA 98195 Prognosis and ventricular curvature in TIMI trial

R01HL-46152-01 (HEM) GARTNER, THEODORE K MEMPHIS STATE UNIVERSITY MEMPHIS, TN 38152 Peptide mimics of the FG receptor ligand binding sites

R01HL-46154-01 (GEN) AVERY, LEON B UNIV OF TEXAS SOUTHWESTERN MED 5323 HARRY HINES BLVD DALLAS, TX 75235 Genetics of nematode pharyngeal muscle excitability

R13HL-46157-01 (CVA) ROSE, NOEL R JOHNS HOPKINS UNIVERSITY 615 NORTH WOLFE STREET BALTIMORE, MD 21205 Second international symposium on immune mediated heart disease

R03HL-46163-01 (SRC) GLYNN, ROBERT J BRIGHAM AND WOMEN'S HOSPITAL 55 POND AVE BROOKLINE, MA 02146 Compliance in the physicians' health study

R03HL-46168-01A1 (SRC) NESS, ROBERTA UNIVERSITY OF PENNSYLVANIA 420 SERVICE DRIVE PHILADELPHIA, PA 19104-6095 Parity and serum lipids in white and Hispanic women

R29HL-46195-01 (EVR) BECK, MELINDA A UNIV OF NEBRASKA MEDICAL CTR 600 SOUTH 42ND STREET OMAHA, NE 68198-6495 Enterovirus infection & reinfection-- CMI & myocarditis

R29HL-46198-01 (HED) CATLIN, ELIZABETH A MASSACHUSETTS GENERAL HOSPITAL FRUIT STREET BOSTON, MA 02114 Lung development--A new sex-specific role for MIS receptor

R01HL-46206-01 (HEM) SPITALNIK, STEVEN L UNIVERSITY OF PENNSYLVANIA 220 JOHN MORGAN BLDG PHILADELPHIA, PA 19104-6082 Biology of the human glycophorin blood group antigens

R01HL-46208-0? (EDC) CROUSE, JOHN R BOWMAN GRAY SCHOOL OF MEDICINE 30? SOUTH HAWTHORNE ROAD WINSTON-SALEM, N C 27103 Adipose distribution and atherosclerosis

R03HL-46211-01A1 (SRC) DONAHUE, RICHARD P UNIVERSITY OF MIAMI SCH OF MED PO BOX 016069, (R-669) MIAMI, FL 33101 Change in CHD risk factors in young adults

R03HL-46212-01 (SRC) ROSNER, BERNARD A CHANNING LABORATORY 180 LONGWOOD AVENUE BOSTON, MA 02115 Statistical analysis of pediatric task force data base

R01HL-46213-01 (HEM) WALSH, PETER N TEMPLE UNIVERSITY SCH OF MED 3400 NORTH BROAD STREET PHILADELPHIA, PA 19140 Molecular and cellular interactions of factor XI

R55HL-46224-01 (HEM) CHASIS, JOEL A LAWRENCE BERKELEY LABORATORY 1 CYCLOTRON ROAD BERKELEY, CA 94720 Protein 4.1 expression during erythroid differentiation

R01HL-46230-01 (RAP) RODARTE, JOSEPH R 6550 FANNIN HOUSTON, TX 77030 Respiratory system mechanics

R01HL-46260-01 (HSR) DEBUSK, ROBERT F 780 WELCH ROAD PALO ALTO, CA 94304 Hospital-based nurse-managed smoking interventions

R29HL-46280-01 (SAT) VISNER, MARC S UNIVERSITY OF MASSACHUSETTS 55 LAKE AVE NORTH WORCESTER, MA 01655 The mechanism for TNF-induced myocardial dysfunction

R01HL-46281-01 (MET) NICHOLS, ALEXANDER V UNIVERSITY OF CALIFORNIA LAWRENCE BERKELEY LABORATORY BERKELEY, CA 94720 Apolipoprotein-specific HDL and cholesterol transport

R29HL-46283-01 (BEM) SUAREZ, EDWARD C DUKE UNIVERSITY MEDICAL CENTER PO BOX 3926 DURHAM, NC 27710 Hostility and pathogenic mechanisms of CHD in women

R01HL-46286-01 (NEUA) GUGLIELMI, GUIDO UCLA ENDOVASCULAR THERAPY 10833 LE CONTE AVE LOS ANGELES, CA 90024-1721 Endovascular occlusion of aneurysms by electrothrombosis

R29HL-46287-01 (SB) FERGUSON, T BRUCE, JR WASHINGTON UNIVERSITY ST LOUIS, MISSOURI Electrophysiologic monitoring of allograft rejection

R01HL-46292-01 (EDC) MOLL, PATRICIA P UNIVERSITY OF MICHIGAN 109 S OBSERVATORY ST ANN ARBOR, MI 48109 Epidemiology of coronary artery calcification

R01HL-46297-01 (SRC) GARBER, ALAN M NATL BUREAU OF ECONOMIC RESEAR 204 JUNIPERO SERRA BOULEVARD STANFORD, CA 94305 Evaluating strategies to control hypercholesterolemia

R29HL-46311-01 (PTHA) ALBELDA, STEVEN M UNIVERSITY OF PENNSYLVANIA 3600 SPRUCE ST PHILADELPHIA, PA 19104-4283 EndoCAM/PECAM - A novel vascular cell adhesion molecule

R01HL-46312-01 (SRC) GERRITY, ROSS G MEDICAL COLLEGE OF GEORGIA 1120 15TH STREET AUGUSTA, GA 30912 Endothelial cell heterogeneity in early atherosclerosis

R01HL-46315-01 (SRC) WEINSTEIN, MILTON C HARVARD SCH OF PUBLIC HLTH 677 HUNTINGTON AVENUE BOSTON, MA 02115 Population-based modeling of cholesterol lowering in US

R01HL-46320-01 (CVA) SEIDMAN, JONATHAN G HARVARD MEDICAL SCHOOL 25 SHATTUCK STREET BOSTON, MA 02115 Molecular cause of familial hypertrophic cardiomyopathy

R01HL-46338-01 (PTHA) STONE, PHILLIP J BOSTON UNIV SCHOOL OF MEDICINE 80 EAST CONCORD STREET BOSTON, MA 02118 Urinary markers of elastin degradation in emphysema

R29HL-46344-01 (CVA) ALEXANDER, JOE, JR VANDERBILT UNIVERSITY NASHVILLE, TN 37235 Pulmonary venous admittance--Role in left heart failure

R29HL-46348-01 (ECS) RAO, RAYASAM H MONTEFIORE UNIVERSITY HOSPITAL 3459 FIFTH AVE PITTSBURGH, PA 15213 Spontaneous hypertension and insulin resistance

R29HL-46356-01 (ECS) SCHINI, VALERIE B BAYLOR COLLEGE OF MEDICINE ONE BAYLOR PLAZA HOUSTON, TX 77030 Arginine-nitric oxide pathway and vascular responsiveness

R55HL-46367-01 (CVA) TABER, LARRY A UNIVERSITY OF ROCHESTER ROCHESTER, NY 14627 Ventricular mechanics in the developing embryonic heart

R01HL-46368-01 (RAP) LEFF, ALAN R UNIVERSITY OF CHICAGO 5801 SOUTH ELLIS AVENUE CHICAGO, IL 60637 Mechanisms of airway hyperresponsiveness

R01HL-46373-01 (CVB) WILLIAMS, GORDON H BRIGHAM AND WOMENS HOSPITAL 221 LONGWOOD AVENUE BOSTON, MA 02115 Effect of Na and K intake on aldosterone in hypertension

R01HL-46380-02 (EDC) REDLINE, SUSAN UNIV HOSPITALS OF CLEVELAND 2074 ABINGTON ROAD CLEVELAND, OH 44106 Familial aggregation of obstructive sleep apnea

R29HL-46401-01 (CVA) KEATING, MARK T UNIVERSITY OF UTAH MED CTR 50 NORTH MEDICAL DRIVE SALT LAKE CITY, UT 84132 The long QT syndrome--A genetic approach

P01HL-46403-01 (HLBB) HAJJAR, DAVID P CORNELL UNIVERSITY MED COLLEGE 1300 YORK AVENUE NEW YORK, NY 10021 Vascular cell signaling and metabolism in atherogenesis

P01HL-46403-01 0001 (HLBB) MARCUS, AARON J Vascular cell signaling and metabolism in atherogenesis Vascular and cellular controls in atherosclerosis

P01HL-46403-01 0002 (HLBB) GROSS, STEVEN S Vascular cell signaling and metabolism in atherogenesis EDRF-synthesis--Mechanisms and role in atherosclerosis

P01HL-46403-01 0003 (HLBB) SILVERSTEIN, ROY L Vascular cell signaling and metabolism in atherogenesis: Molecular mechanisms of cell-cell interactions in atherosclerosis

P01HL-46403-01 0004 (HLBB) HAJJAR, KATHERINE A Vascular cell signaling and metabolism in atherogenesis Molecular control mechanisms in cell surface fibrinolysis

P01HL-46403-01 0005 (HLBB) FALCONE, DOMENICK J Vascular cell signaling and metabolism in atherogenesis Modified-LDL, foam cells and vascular remodeling

P01HL-46403-01 0006 (HLBB) MCCAFFREY, TIMOTHY A Vascular cell signaling and metabolism in atherogenesis Novel inhibitors of intimal hyperplasia

P01HL-46403-01 0007 (HLBB) HAJJAR, DAVID P Vascular cell signaling and metabolism in atherogenesis Endothelial cell modulation of arterial cholesterol trafficking

P01HL-46403-01 9001 (HLBB) HAJJAR, DAVID P Vascular cell signaling and metabolism in atherogenesis CORE--Tissue culture

R15HL-46405-01 (HEM) STRANEVA, JOHN E STATE UNIVERSITY OF NEW YORK PO BOX 2000 CORTLAND, NY 13045 Significance of polyploidization in megakaryocytopoiesis

R01HL-46407-01 (PTHA) BECKMAN, JOSEPH S UNIVERSITY OF ALABAMA UNIVERSITY STATION BIRMINGHAM, AL 35294 Role of nitric oxide in superoxide-mediated pathology

R01HL-46409-01 (PTHA) ADAMS, MICHAEL R BOWMAN GRAY SCHOOL OF MEDICINE 300 S HAWTHORNE ROAD WINSTON-SALEM, NC 27103 Oral contraception and atherosclerosis in female monkeys

R15HL-46428-01 (RAP) SMITS, ALLAN W UNIVERSITY OF TEXAS PO BOX 19145 ARLINGTON, TX 76019 Mechanisms of fluid balance in lower vertebrate lungs

R01HL-46440-01 (PTHA) CAMPBELL, EDWARD J UNIVERSITY OF UTAH 50 NORTH MEDICAL DR SALT LAKE CITY, UT 84132 Cell-surface proteinases in pulmonary inflammation

R15HL-46444-01 (SB) SCHOEPHOERSTER, RICHARD T FLORIDA INTERNATIONAL UNIVERSI UNIVERSITY PARK CAMPUS MIAMI, FL 33199 Influence of flow dynamics on thrombogenesis

R01HL-46448-02 (BEM) SULS, JERRY M UNIVERSITY OF IOWA IOWA CITY, IA 52242 Coronary-prone behavior and life stress

R01HL-46461-02 (CVB) JANICKI, JOSEPH S THE CURATORS OF THE UNIV.OF MO OFFICE OF SPONSORED PROG ADMIN COLUMBIA, MO 65211 Role of myocardial collagen in volume overload ventricle

R15HL-46475-01 (HEM) JAKUBOWSKI, HENRY V SAINT JOHN'S UNIVERSITY COLLEGEVILLE, MN 56321 Structural analysis of thrombin specificity sites

R15HL-46476-01 (PBC) ROSS, CHRISTOPHER R KANSAS STATE UNIVERSITY 232 VETERINARY MEDICAL SCIENCE MANHATTAN, KS 66506 Molecular characterization of a bFGF-binding proteoglycan

R15HL-46504-01 (NLS) ROWE, BRIAN P EAST TENNESSEE STATE UNIVERSIT QUILLEN COLLEGE OF MEDICINE JOHNSON CITY, TN 37614-0002 Angiotensin receptor subtypes in the rat brain

R43HL-46507-01 (SSS) GOODRICH, RAYMOND P 171 N WILSON PASADENA, CA 91106 Inactivation of blood-borne viruses

R15HL-46511-01 (CVA) CLAYDON, FRANK J MEMPHIS STATE UNIVERSITY MEMPHIS, TN 38152 Intracavitary mapping--Models and experiments

R01HL-46514-02 (PTHB) CALLOW, ALLAN D WASHINGTON UNIV SCH OF MED 4960 AUDUBON AVE BOX 8109 ST LOUIS, MO 63110 A prototype gene therapy delivery system

R01HL-46524-01 (SRC) ADAMSON, JOHN W THE NEW YORK BLOOD CENTER 310 EAST 67TH STREET NEW YORK, N Y 10021 Proliferation and differentiation of isolated stem cells

R01HL-46528-01 (SRC) WILLIAMS, DAVID A CHILDREN'S HOSPITAL 300

PROJECT NO., ORGANIZATIONAL UNIT., INVESTIGATOR, ADDRESS, TITLE

LONGWOOD AVENUE BOSTON, MA 02115 Role of adhesion in stem cell survival and engraftment
R01HL-46532-01 (SRC) SACHS, DAVID H MASSACHUSETTS GENERAL HOSPITAL BUILDING 149, 13TH STREET CHARLESTOWN, MA 02129 Bone marrow culture and engraftment in a swine model
R01HL-46533-01 (SRC) SHARKIS, SAUL J THE JOHNS HOPKINS UNVI SCH/MED 600 NORTH WOLFE STREET BALTIMORE, MD 21205 Structure and function of the hematopoietic stem cell
R01HL-46536-01 (SRC) HARRISON, DAVID E THE JACKSON LABORATORY 600 MAIN STREET BAR HARBOR, ME 04609-0800 Primitive hemopoietic stem cells (PHSC) for engraftment
R15HL-46542-01 (ECS) MALLOY, LAURA G BATES COLLEGE CAMPUS AVENUE LEWISTON, ME 04240 Histamine adrenergics and skeletal muscle arteries
R13HL-46543-01 (PTHA) GRUNDY, SCOTT M U T SOUTHWESTERN MEDICAL CTR 5323 HARRY HINES BOULEVARD DALLAS, TX 75235-9052 Support for international symposium on atherosclerosis
R01HL-46546-01 (SRC) MOORE, MALCOLM A SLOAN-KETTERING INSTITUTE 1275 YORK AVENUE NEW YORK, N Y 10021 Stem cell isolation characterization and amplification
R01HL-46548-01 (SRC) HOFFMAN, RONALD INDIANA UNIVERSITY SCH OF MED 975 WEST WALNUT STREET INDIANAPOLIS, IN 46202-5121 In vitro reconstitution of normal hematopoiesis
R01HL-46549-01 (SRC) BROXMEYER, HAL E INDIANA UNIV SCHOOL OF MED 975 W WALNUT STREET INDIANAPOLIS, IN 46202-5121 Human umbilical cord blood stem cells and immunology
R01HL-46555-02 (SRC) FIELD, LOREN J INDIANA UNIVERSITY 1001 WEST 10TH ST INDIANAPOLIS, IN 46202 Physiology of ANF in transgenic mice
R01HL-46556-01 (SRC) ZANJANI, ESMAIL D VETERANS AFFAIRS MEDICAL CTR 1000 LOCUST STREET RENO, NV 89520 In utero bone marrow transplantation
R01HL-46557-01 (SRC) PAPAYANNOPOULOU, THALIA UNIVERSITY OF WASHINGTON SEATTLE, WA 98195 Biological properties and regulation of stem cells
R01HL-46558-01 (ECS) BUSIJA, DAVID W WAKE FOREST UNIVERSITY 300 S HAWTHORNE RD WINSTON-SALEM, NC 27103 Vascular responses during cortical spreading depression
R03HL-46559-01 (SRC) WASSERTHEIL-SMOLLER, SYLVIA ALBERT EINSTEIN COLLEGE OF MED 1300 MORRIS PARK AVENUE BRONX, NY 10461 Dish data analysis study
R29HL-46573-02 (PHRA) MOORMAN, JOSEPH R UNIV OF VIRGINIA HLTH SCI CTR CHARLOTTESVILLE, VA 22908 Approaching arrhythmia therapy through Na channel gating
R43HL-46576-01 (HEM) HALEY, PAUL E HAEMATOLOGIC TECHNOLOGIES, INC PINEWOOD PLAZA-PO BOX 1021 ESSEX JUNCTION, VT 05452 Quantitation of proteases of the fibrinolytic system
R43HL-46578-01 (SSS) GRADY, JOHN K XRE CORPORATION 300 FOSTER ST, BOX 1154 LITTLETON, MA 01460 Rotational angiographic digital imaging
R43HL-46580-01 (SSS) CARR, KENNETH L MICROWAVE MEDICAL SYSTEMS INC 9 GOLDSMITH ST/ PO BOX 24 LITTLETON, MA 01460-0188 Microwave device for myocardial ablation
R43HL-46584-01 (HEM) RIPKA, WILLIAM C CORVAS, INC 3030 SCIENCE PARK ROAD SAN DIEGO, CA 92121 Novel peptide boronic acid inhibitors of coagulation
R43HL-46585-01 (HEM) TAI, MEI-SHENG CREATIVE BIOMOLECULES, INC 35 SOUTH STREET HOPKINTON, MA 01748 Single-chain fv-peptide fusion inhibitor of fibrin clots
R01HL-46598-01 (SRC) ABKOWITZ, JANIS L UNIV OF WASHINGTON DIV OF HEMATOLOGY SEATTLE, WA 98195 The kinetics and behavior of hematopoietic stem cells
R43HL-46602-01 (SSS) BUTLER, KENNETH C NIMBUS, INC 2890 KILGORE ROAD RANCHO CORDOVA, CA 95670 Floating rotor axial flow blood pump
R43HL-46606-01 (SSS) NAG, ABHIJIT LIFECELL CORPORATION 3606-A RESEARCH FOREST DRIVE THE WOODLANDS, TX 77381 Dry preservation of transplantable veins
R43HL-46607-01 (SSS) BROCKBANK, KELVIN G CRYOLIFE, INC 2211 NEW MARKET PKWY MARIETTA, GA 30067 Repopulation of xenograft heart valves with fibroblasts
R43HL-46608-01 (SSS) DILLON, MARK E BIO MED SCIENCES, INC 115 RESEARCH DRIVE BETHLEHEM, PA 18015 Novel vascular prosthetic device
R43HL-46613-01 (SSS) MONTOYA, JEAN P MICHIGAN CRITICAL CARE CONS IN 1610 HARBAL DRIVE ANN ARBOR, MI 48105 Low hemolysis blood pump with integral pressure controls
R43HL-46614-01 (HEM) LEWIS, NEIL J JACOBUS PHARMACEUTICAL CO, INC 37 CLEVELAND LANE, PO BOX 5290 PRINCETON, NJ 08540 New PIH prodrug for chelation therapy of iron overload
R43HL-46618-01 (HEM) LEBKOWSKI, JANE S APPLIED IMMUNE SCIENCES INC 200 CONSTITUTION DRIVE MENLO PARK, CA 94025-1109 Purification of peripheral blood stem cells
R43HL-46621-01 (SSS) PARISH, HARLIE A PO BOX 41777 MEMPHIS, TN 38174 Development of elastase inhibitors to treat emphysema
R43HL-46623-01 (SSS) CASE, CASEY C ONCOGENE SCIENCE INC 350 COMMUNITY DRIVE MANHASSET, NY 11030 Transcriptional inhibition of the scavenger receptor
R43HL-46625-01 (SSS) RICHARDSON, CHARLES P BUNNELL INC 436 LAWNDALE DRIVE SALT LAKE CITY, UT 84115 A servo-controlled ventilator for infants and children
R43HL-46626-01 (SSS) KOPIA, GREGORY A ZYNAXIS CELL SCIENCE, INC 371 PHOENIXVILLE PIKE MALVERN, PA 19355 Zynpeptides as modulators of responses to biomaterials
R43HL-46628-01 (SSS) BURGER, DOUGLAS E ABIOMED, INC 33 CHERRY HILL DRIVE DANVERS, MA 01923 Blood cell typing using optical phase and flow cytometry
R43HL-46629-01 (SSS) GHOSH, SOUMITRA S SIBIA, INC PO BOX 85200 SAN DIEGO, CA 92186-9268 Design of suicide inhibitors for enkephalinase
R01HL-46631-02 (SRC) DZAU, VICTOR J STANFORD UNIVERSITY 300 PASTEUR DR, FALK CVRC STANFORD, CA 94305-5246 Mapping the genes responsible for hypertension in the rats
R43HL-46635-01 (SOH) SMITH, NATHAN L CYTOSIGNET, INC PO BOX 219 NORTH ANDOVER, MA 01845 Assay to rapidly detect endotoxin in whole blood
R43HL-46637-01 (SSS) SIPIN, A J ANATOLE J SIPIN CO, INC 505 EIGHTH AVENUE NEW YORK, NY 10018 Vibratory orbiting blood pump
R01HL-46647-01 (SRC) MARTIN, WILLIAM J, II INDIANA UNIV MED CENTER 1001 WEST 10TH STREET INDIANAPOLIS, IN 46202-2879 Adherence mechanisms of Pneumocystis carinii
R01HL-46651-01 (SRC) CRAWFORD, TIMOTHY B WASHINGTON STATE UNIVERSITY PULLMAN, WA 99164-7040 Mechanisms of equine lentivirus-induced thrombocytopenia
R01HL-46652-01 (SRC) ANDERSON, CLARK L THE OHIO STATE UNIVERSITY 480 W NINTH AVENUE COLUMBUS, OH 43210-1228 Platelet Fc receptor in HIV thrombocytopenia
R01HL-46653-01 (SRC) RICE, WARD R UNIVERSITY OF CINCINNATI CINCINNATI, OHIO 45267-0541 Control of type II cell function by Pneumocystis carinii
R01HL-46659-01 (SRC) PEREIRA, MIERCIO E NEW ENGLAND MEDICAL CTR HOSP 750 WASHINGTON STREET BOSTON, MA 02111 Pathobiology of the pneumocystis carinii lectin
R01HL-46668-01 (SRC) GROOPMAN, JEROME E NEW ENGLAND DEACONESS HOSPITAL 185 PILGRAM RD BOSTON, MA 02215 HIV infection of human megakaryocytes
R55HL-46670-01 (SRC) LEISSINGER, CINDY A TULANE UNIV SCHOOL OF MEDICINE 1430 TULANE AVE NEW ORLEANS, LA 70112 Retrovirus-induced immune platelet abnormalities
R03HL-46674-01 (SRC) WILLIAMS, CHRISTOPHER J INDIANA UNIV SCHOOL OF MEDICIN 975 WEST WALNUT STREET INDIANAPOLIS, IN 46202-5251 Reanalysis of CVD risk factors via likelihood methods
R01HL-46683-01 (ECS) BEIERWALTES, WILLIAM H HENRY FORD HOSPITAL 2799 WEST GRAND BLVD DETROIT, MI 48202 Renin, renal function and the endothelium
R55HL-46689-01 (TOX) RYAN, JAMES W UNIVERSITY OF MIAMI P O BOX 016960 MIAMI, FL 33101 Toxic effects of drugs on lung capillaries
R01HL-46690-01 (RAP) BANZETT, ROBERT B HARVARD SCHOOL OF PUBLIC HLTH 665 HUNTINGTON AVENUE BOSTON, MA 02115 Afferent and CNS mechanisms underlying air hunger
R55HL-46702-01 (PHRA) PEREZ-REYES, EDWARD BAYLOR COLLEGE OF MEDICINE ONE BAYLOR PLAZA HOUSTON, TX 77030 Functional characterization of cardiac calcium channels
P01HL-46703-01 (HLBB) MANN, KENNETH G UNIVERSITY OF VERMONT UNIVERSITY OF VERMONT BURLINGTON, VT 05405 Surface dependent reactions in thrombosis and thrombolysis
P01HL-46703-01 0001 (HLBB) MANN, KENNETH G Surface dependent reactions in thrombosis and thrombolysis The activation of prothrombin
P01HL-46703-01 0002 (HLBB) LONG, GEORGE L Surface dependent reactions in thrombosis and thrombolysis Role of the precursor protein in gamma carboxylation
P01HL-46703-01 0003 (HLBB) NESHEIM, MICHAEL Surface dependent reactions in thrombosis and thrombolysis Binding and reaction kinectics in fibrinolysis
P01HL-46703-01 0004 (HLBB) TRACY, PAULA B Surface dependent reactions in thrombosis and thrombolysis Regulation of human platelet prothrombinase activity
P01HL-46703-01 9001 (HLBB) CHURCH, WILLIAM Surface dependent reactions in thrombosis and thrombolysis CORE--Immunology/assay
R13HL-46708-01 (PC) STEINBERG, DANIEL UNIVERSITY OF CALIFORNIA LA JOLLA, CA 92093 Aspen bile acid/cholesterol/lipoprotein conference
R43HL-46747-01 (SSS) BRUNCK, TERENCE K CORVAS, INC 3030 SCIENCE PARK ROAD SAN DIEGO, CA 92121 Inhibitors of the extrinsic blood coagulation pathway
R01HL-46764-01 (CVA) BAUMGARTEN, CLIVE M VIRGINIA COMMONWEALTH UNIVERSI BOX 551 MCV STATION RICHMOND, VA 23298-0551 Cardiac cell volume regulation in cardioplegia
R01HL-46775-01 (SRC) STRECHER, VICTOR J UNIVERSITY OF NORTH CAROLINA CB #7400 CHAPEL HILL, NC 27599-7400 CVD nutrition modules tailored to low literacy skills
R01HL-46778-01 (SRC) KUMANYIKA, SHIRIKI S PENNSYLVANIA STATE UNIVERSITY UNIVERSITY PARK, PA 16802 Low literacy CVD diet education for blacks
R01HL-46781-01 (SRC) KUSHI, LAWRENCE H UNIVERSITY OF MINNESOTA 420 DELAWARE STR SE MINNEAPOLIS, MN 55455 Evaluation of low literacy CVD nutrition education
R01HL-46782-01 (SRC) FORTMANN, STEPHEN P STANFORD UNIVERSITY 1000 WELCH ROAD PALO ALTO, CA 94304-1885 CVD nutrition education for low literate adults
R01HL-46802-01 (SAT) BACH, FRITZ H UNIV OF MINNESOTA 420 DELAWARE ST SOUTHEAST MINNEAPOLIS, MN 55455 Discordant xenografting
R01HL-46810-01 (SAT) PLATT, JEFFREY L UNIVERSITY OF MINNESOTA 420 DELAWARE STREET, SE MINNEAPOLIS, MN 55455 Heparan sulfate in cellular immunity and graft rejection
R29HL-46813-01 (ECS) KOLLER, AKOS NEW YORK MEDICAL COLLEGE VALHALLA, NY 10595 Endothelial control of arteriolar tone in hypertension
P01HL-46826-01 (HLBA) ROBBINS, JEFFREY UNIV OF CINCINNATI COL OF MED 231 BETHESDA AVENUE CINCINNATI, OH 45267-0575 Cardiogenesis during differentiation and development
P01HL-46826-01 0001 (HLBA) ROBBINS, JEFFREY Cardiogenesis during differentiation and development Functional analysis of alpha-cardiac myosin
P01HL-46826-01 0002 (HLBA) DOETSCHMAN, TOM Cardiogenesis during differentiation and development Basic fibroblast growth factor gene ablation in cardiogenesis
P01HL-46826-01 0003 (HLBA) LESSARD, J L Cardiogenesis during differentiation and development Targeted ablation and alteration of cardiac actin
P01HL-46826-01 0004 (HLBA) WIECZOREK, DAVID Cardiogenesis during differentiation and development Effect of alpha-tropomyosin ablation on cardiogenesis
P01HL-46826-01 9001 (HLBA) DOETSCHMAN, THOMAS Cardiogenesis during differentiation and development CORE--ES cell transgenic facility
P01HL-46826-01 9002 (HLBA) DOETSCHMAN, THOMAS Cardiogenesis during differentiation and development CORE--Comparative pathology
R01HL-46843-01 (HED) CHAUDHURI, GAUTAM UCLA SCHOOL OF MEDICINE 10833 LE CONTE AVE LOS ANGELES, CA 90024-1740 EDNO and uterine blood

flow in pregnancy
R01HL-46849-01 (PTHA) MULLER, WILLIAM A ROCKEFELLER UNIVERSITY 1230 YORK AVE NEW YORK, NY 10021 Two novel vascular adhesion molecules – PECAM and HEC-1
R13HL-46857-01 (MET) DAVIES, PETER F UNIVERSITY OF CHICAGO 5841 S MARYLAND AVE CHICAGO, IL 60637 Gordon research conference on atherosclerosis 1991
R13HL-46864-01 (PBC) KEELEY, FRED W 555 UNIVERSITY AVE TORONTO, ONTARIO M5G 1X8 1991 Gordon Research Conference on elastin
R29HL-46865-01 (HED) MC GUIRE, PAUL G UNIVERSITY OF NEW MEXICO ALBUQUERQUE, NM 87131 Matrix and proteases in heart and vascular development
R01HL-46880-01 (EDC) AUSTIN, MELISSA A UNIVERSITY OF WASHINGTON SEATTLE, WA 98195 Genetic mapping of atherogenic lipoprotein phenotypes
R01HL-46895-01 (RNM) BERGMANN, STEVEN R WASHINGTON UNIVERSITY SCH OF M 660 SOUTH EUCLID AVE ST LOUIS, MO 63110 Optimization of PET estimates of myocardial perfusion
R13HL-46912-01 (SRC) BERGERON, RAYMOND J BOX J-485 JHMHC GAINESVILLE, FL 32610 Iron chelation therapy symposium
R03HL-46923-01 (SRC) HEBERT, PATRICIA R 55 POND AVENUE BROOKLINE, MA 02146 Longitudinal studies of blood pressure in the elderly
R29HL-46929-01 (CVA) POGWIZD, STEVEN M WASHINGTON UNIVERSITY 660 S EUCLID AVE ST LOUIS, MO 63110 Mechanism of arrhythmias in the setting of heart failure
R13HL-46948-01 (SRC) NARLA, MOHANDAS LAWRENCE BERKELEY LABORATORY 1 CYCLOTRON RD BERKELEY, CA 94720 Gordon conference on the red cell
R01HL-46951-01 (RAP) WEISS, JAMES W BETH ISRAEL HOSPITAL 330 BROOKLINE AVE BOSTON, MA 02215 Hemodynamic events in sleep apnea – Causes and consequences
R29HL-46966-01 (PTHA) VERMEULEN, MARY W MASSACHUSETTS GENERAL HOSPITAL 149 13TH STREET CHARLESTOWN, MA 02129 Lung injury and ARDS – LPS effects on TNF regulation
R01HL-46967-01 (MET) MC CONATHY, WALTER J OKLAHOMA MEDICAL RES FDN 825 N E 13TH STREET OKLAHOMA CITY, OK 73104 Interactions of Lp(a) with subendothelial cell matrix
R01HL-46971-01 (PTHA) SNAPPER, JAMES R VANDERBILT UNIVERSITY 21ST AVENUE & GARLAND STREET NASHVILLE, TN 37232-2650 Effects of pulmonary edema on airway responsiveness
R01HL-46973-01 (HEM) MANN, KENNETH G UNIV OF VERMONT GIVEN BLDG BURLINGTON, VT 05405 The activation of prothrombin
R01HL-46974-01 (EDC) SILVERSTEIN, MARC D MAYO FOUNDATION 200 FIRST STREET SOUTHWEST ROCHESTER, MN 55905 Incidence and outcomes of venous thromboembolism
R55HL-46981-01 (HEM) PHILLIPS, MARTIN D METHODIST HOSPITAL 6565 FANNIN HOUSTON, TX 77030 New antithrombotic agents: anionic aromatic polymers
R01HL-46994-01 (ECS) QUERTERMOUS, THOMAS MASSACHUSETTS GENERAL HOSPITAL BOSTON, MA 02114 Regulation of endothelin-1 gene expression
R01HL-47000-01 (HEM) MOSESSON, MICHAEL W SINAI SAMARITAN MED CTR 950 NORTH 12TH STREET MILWAUKEE, WI 53233 Fibrinogen/fibrin structural and functional domains
R29HL-47003-01 (RNM) STONE, CHARLES K UNIVERSITY OF WISCONSIN 600 HIGHLAND AVENUE MADISON, WI 53792 Myocardial perfusion by copper PTSM ligands with PET
R01HL-47011-01 (SB) SHUNG, K KIRK PENNSYLVANIA STATE UNIVERSITY UNIVERSITY PARK, PA 16802 Ultrasonic contrast blood flowmetry
R01HL-47020-01 (HEM) OLSON, JOHN S RICE UNIVERSITY PO BOX 1892 HOUSTON, TX 77251 The design of heme-protein based blood substitutes
R29HL-47022-01 (PTHA) LEW, DUKHEE B UNIVERSITY OF TENNESSEE 956 COURT AVE/COLEMAN BLDG MEMPHIS, TN 38163 Airway myocyte proliferation and lysosomal hydrolase
R01HL-47035-01 (CVB) DELAFONTAINE, PATRICK EMORY UNIVERSITY SCH OF MEDICI P O DRAWER LL ATLANTA, GA 30322 The role of IGF I and its receptor in vascular growth
R01HL-47043-01 (EDC) PETITTI, DIANA B KAISER PERMANENTE 3451 PIEDMONT AVE OAKLAND, CA 94611 Stroke and MI in users of estrogen/progestogen
R13HL-47058-01 (CVB) VANHOUTTE, PAUL M BAYLOR COLLEGE OF MEDICINE ONE BAYLOR PLAZA HOUSTON, TX 77030 FASEB conf on endothelium and cardiovascular function
R01HL-47063-01 (BIO) CHINKERS, MICHAEL OREGON HLTH SCIENCES UNIV 3181 SW SAM JACKSON PARK RD PORTLAND, OR 97201-3098 Regulation of the ANP receptor/guanylyl cyclase
R29HL-47064-01 (BEM) QUITTNER, ALEXANDRA L INDIANA UNIVERSITY BLOOMINGTON, IN 47405 A contextual model of family coping with cystic fibrosis
R01HL-47065-01 (CVA) ROOS, KENNETH P UNIVERSITY OF CALIFORNIA 10833 LECONTE AVENUE LOS ANGELES, CA 90024-1751 Cellular mechanical performance in cardiomyopathies
R01HL-47073-01 (HEM) MARCUS, AARON J NEW YORK VA MEDICAL CENTER 423 EAST 23RD STREET NEW YORK, NY 10010 Cell-cell interactions in thrombosis
R29HL-47074-01 (BEM) MILLS, PAUL J UNIV OF CALIFORNIA SAN DIEGO LA JOLLA, CA 92093-0804 The contribution of adrenergic receptors to reactivity
R01HL-47079-01 (ECS) VASSILEV, PETER M BRIGHAM & WOMEN'S HOSPITAL 221 LONGWOOD AVENUE BOSTON, MA 02115 Modulation of adrenal ion channels in hypertension
R29HL-47080-01 (EDC) PETRI, MICHELLE JOHNS HOPKINS UNIVERSITY 1830 E MONUMENT ST, STE 7500 BALTIMORE, MD 21205 Lupus cohort--Thrombotic events & coronary artery disease
U01HL-47098-01 (SRC) MC KINLAY, SONJA M NEW ENGLAND RES INSTITUTE,INC 9 GALEN STREET WATERTOWN, MA 02172 Coordinating center for children's activity trial of CV health
R01HL-47101-01 (PTHA) THOMPSON, DAVID C UNIVERSITY OF COLORADO CAMPUS BOX 297 BOULDER, CO 80309-0297 Local reflexes in the airways
R01HL-47113-01 (PC) RODWELL, VICTOR W PURDUE UNIVERSITY WEST LAFAYETTE, IN 47907 Structure of the active site of HMG-CoA reductase
R01HL-47119-01 (DDK) FRIEDMANN, THEODORE UNIV. OF CALIFORNIA, SAN DIEGO CNETER FOR MOLEC. GENETICS LA JOLLA, CA 92093-0634 Transduction of airway epithelia by retroviral vectors
R01HL-47120-01 (DDK) SMITH, ALAN E GENZYME CORPORATION ONE MOUNTAIN ROAD FRAMINGHAM, MA 01701 Development of CFTR as a therapeutic protein
R01HL-47121-01 (DDK) OLSEN, JOHN C UNIVERSITY OF NORTH CAROLINA CB #7295 CHAPEL HILL, NC 27599 Retrovirus-mediated gene transfer into airway epithelia
R01HL-47122-01 (DDK) GUGGINO, WILLIAM B JOHNS HOPKINS UNIVERSITY 725 NORTH WOLFE ST BALTIMORE, MD 21205 CFTR regulation of chloride secretion in normal and cystic fibrosis airways
P50HL-47124-01 (SRC) CHOBANIAN, ARAM V BOSTON UNIV SCH OF MED 80 E CONCORD STREET BOSTON, MA 02118 Specialized center of research in hypertension
P50HL-47124-01 0003 (SRC) HARALAMBOS, GAVRAS Specialized center of research in hypertension Vasopressin inhibition
P50HL-47124-01 0005 (SRC) CHOBANIAN, ARAM V Specialized center of research in hypertension Hypertension and atherogenesis
P50HL-47124-01 0006 (SRC) COHEN, RICHARD Specialized center of research in hypertension Hypertension and arterial reactivity
P50HL-47124-01 0007 (SRC) HERRERA, VICTORIA L M Specialized center of research in hypertension Na, K-ATPase and hypertension
P50HL-47124-01 9001 (SRC) HARALAMBOS, GAVRAS Specialized center of research in hypertension Core--Animal facility
P50HL-47124-01 9002 (SRC) ZANNIS, VASSILIS Specialized center of research in hypertension Core--Molecular biology laboratory
R01HL-47125-01 (RAP) KIM, KWANG C UNIVERSITY OF MARYLAND 20 N PINE ST/SCH OF PHARMACY BALTIMORE, MD 21201 Regulation of airway goblet cell mucin release in vitro
R29HL-47126-01 (RAP) JACOBY, DAVID B JOHNS HOPKINS UNIVERSITY 720 RUTLAND AVENUE BALTIMORE, MD 21205 Virus-induced changes in airway epithelial function
R01HL-47138-01 (SRC) WAKELAND, EDWARD K UNIVERSITY OF FLORIDA BOX J-275, JHMHC GAINESVILLE, FL 32610 HLA class II genotyping by DGGE and direct sequencing
R01HL-47141-01 (SRC) YANG, SOO Y SLOAN-KETTERING INST/CANCER RE 1275 YORK AVENUE NEW YORK, NY 10021 Molecular typing and sequencing of HLA class I alleles
R01HL-47145-01 (SRC) STASTNY, PETER UNIV OF TEXAS SW MEDICAL CTR 5323 HARRY HINES BOULEVARD DALLAS, TX 75235 Polymorphic sequences of HLA alleles
R01HL-47149-01 (SRC) BAXTER-LOWE, LEE A BLOOD CTR OF SE WISCONSIN 1701 W WISCONSIN AVENUE MILWAUKEE, WI 53233 Molecular biological techniques for studing HLA antigens
R01HL-47152-01 (ECS) NAFTILAN, ALLAN J UNIVERSITY OF ALABAMA UAB STATION BIRMINGHAM, AL 35294 Early gene induction by angiotensin II
R01HL-47153-01 (SRC) PARHAM, PETER R STANFORD UNIVERSITY STANFORD, CA 94305-5400 Molecular typing of class I HLA alleles
R01HL-47159-01 (SRC) HINDMAN, BRADLEY J UNIV OF IOWA HOSPITALS & CLINI IOWA CITY, IA 52242 Cardiopulmonary bypass--brain function and protection
R01HL-47163-01 (SRC) DREYER, WILLIAM J TEXAS CHILDREN'S HOSPITAL 8080 N STADIUM DRIVE HOUSTON, TX 77054 PMN adherence reactions--Role in cardiopulmonary bypass
R01HL-47170-01 (SRC) ERLICH, HENRY A CETUS CORPORATION 1400 FIFTY-THIRD STREET EMERYVILLE, CA 94608 HLA typing using PCR amplification and immobilized probe
R13HL-47174-01 (SRC) STULL, JAMES T UNIVERSITY OF TEXAS 5323 HARRY HINES BLVD DALLAS, TX 75235-9040 FASEB summer research conference--Smooth muscle
R44HL-47175-02 (SSS) LANGMUIR, MARGARET E COVALENT ASSOCIATES, INC 52 DRAGON COURT WOBURN, MA 01801 Cytosolic Ca2+ ionophores for fluorescence and 19F NMR
R01HL-47179-01 (SRC) COOPER, STUART L UNIVERSITY OF WISCONSIN 1415 JOHNSON DRIVE MADISON, WI 53706 Mechanisms of damage caused by cardiopulmonary bypass
R01HL-47181-01 (SRC) KELLY, ANDREW B EMORY UNIVERSITY ATLANTA, GA 30322 Mechanism of damage caused by extracorporeal circulation
R01HL-47186-01 (SRC) EDMUNDS, L HENRY, JR HOSP OF THE UNIVERSITY OF PENN 3400 SPRUCE ST, 4 SILVERSTEIN PHILADELPHIA, PA 19104 Control of blood activation by synthetic surfaces
R01HL-47191-01 (SRC) CAMERON, DUKE E JOHN HOPKINS HOSPITAL 600 N WOLFE STREET BALTIMORE, MD 21205 Prevention of organ injury during cardiopulmonary bypass
R01HL-47193-01 (SRC) SMITH, BRIAN R YALE UNIVERSITY SCH OF MED 333 CEDAR STREET, PO BOX 3333 NEW HAVEN, CT 06510 Platelet-leukocyte pathobiology in cardiopulmonary bypass
R01HL-47196-01 (ECS) MORRISON, SHAUN F NORTHWESTERN UNIV MEDICAL SCHO 303 E CHICAGO AVENUE CHICAGO, IL 60611 Cardiovascular regulation--spinal sympathetic mechanisms
R03HL-47208-01 (SRC) ADAMS-CAMPBELL, LUCILE L HOWARD UNIVERSITY 2041 GEORGIA AVENUE NW WASHINGTON, DC 20060 Epidemiology of coronary heart disease in blacks
R43HL-47220-01 (SSS) ENDEMANN, GERDA C CALIFORNIA BIOTECHNOLOGY INC 2450 BAYSHORE PARKWAY MOUNTAIN VIEW, CA 94043 Molecular cloning of cDNA encoding oxidized LDL receptor
R43HL-47223-01 (HEM) OBERHARDT, BRUCE J BIOTHERM, INC PO BOX 13417 RES TRIANGLE PARK, NC 27709 Drug challenge assay for use in thrombolytic therapy
R43HL-47225-01 (HEM) DIAMOND, ALAN D BIPHASICS, INC 115 RESEARCH DRIVE BETHLEHEM, PA 18015 Protein C purification using aqueous two-phase systems
R43HL-47230-01 (HEM) TOCE, JOSEPH A RELIABLE CHEMICAL COMPANY 1161 RESEARCH BLVD ST LOUIS, MO 63119 Synthesis and testing of a new class of heparinoids
R13HL-47232-01 (PTHA) FOX, C FRED KEYSTONE CENTER PO BOX 606 KEYSTONE, CO 80435 Conference on molecular mechanisms of vascular diseases
R43HL-47233-01 (SSS) FRASER, ROBERT B NORTHWEST RESEARCH ASSOC, INC 300 120TH AVENUE N E BELLEVUE, WA 98005 A portable respiratory gas analyzer and pneumotachometer
R43HL-47237-01 (SSS) BUNOW, BARRY J CIVILIZED SOFTWARE, INC

PROJECT NO., ORGANIZATIONAL UNIT., INVESTIGATOR, ADDRESS, TITLE

7735 OLD GEORGETOWN ROAD BETHESDA, MD 20814 Ti-PC software for analyzing longitudinal data
R43HL-47238-01 (SSS) SARANGAPANI, S GINER INCORPORATED 14 SPRING STREET WALTHAM, MA 02254-9147 Diamond coated heart valves
R01HL-47250-01 (PTHA) KALYANARAMAN, BALARAMAN MEDICAL COLLEGE OF WISCONSIN 8701 WATERTOWN PLANK ROAD MILWAUKEE, WI 53226 Low density lipoprotein in free radical oxidative damage
R43HL-47255-01 (SSS) SIOSHANSI, PIRAN SPIRE CORPORATION PATRIOTS PARK BEDFORD, MA 01730 Surface metalization of polyurethane--improved pacemaker lead biostability
R43HL-47256-01 (SSS) OSGANIAN, STAVROULA NEW ENGLAND RESEARCH INST INC 9 GALEN STREET WATERTOWN, MA 02172 Inner city childhood asthma--Self management video
R43HL-47257-01 (SSS) MC REA, JAMES C RESEARCH MEDICAL, INC 6864 SOUTH 300 WEST SALT LAKE CITY, UT 84119 A heparin removal device for cardiopulmonary bypass
R43HL-47259-01 (HEM) HANKINS, DAVID W MERRIFIELD LABORATORIES INC 2723-B MERRILEE DR FAIRFAX, VA 22031 "serum erythropoietin bioassay using a new cell line"
R43HL-47260-01 (SSS) RIPKA, WILLIAM C CORVAS INC 3030 SCIENCE PARK ROAD SAN DIEGO, CA 92121 BPTI-mutants as general serine protease inhibitors
R43HL-47268-01 (HEM) SINHA, UMA COR THERAPEUTICS INC 256 E GRAND AVE SUITE 80 SOUTH SAN FRANCISCO, CA 94080 Therapeutic coagulation inhibitor
R01HL-47272-04 (SAT) ANSARI, AFTAB A WINSHIP CANCER CENTER 1327 CLIFTON RD ATLANTA, GA 30322 Expression & function of HLA antigen on cardiac myocytes
R43HL-47273-01 (SSS) STEINKE, JOHN M AVOX SYSTEMS, INC 15315 GREY FOX SAN ANTONIO, TX 78255-1210 Capillary-tube hemoglobinometer-oximeter
R43HL-47277-01 (SSS) SAWATARI, TAKEO SENTEC CORPORATION 2000 OAKLEY PARK RD WALLED LAKE, MI 48390 Fiber optics pressure catheter
R43HL-47278-01 (SSS) YANG, KE S MEDICAL PHYSICS INC 401 12TH AVE SALT LAKE CITY, UT 84103 Pediatric PaCO2, PvO2 and cardiac output home monitor
R43HL-47286-01 (NTN) KYLE, DAVID J MARTEK CORPORATION 6480 DOBBIN ROAD COLUMBIA, MD 21045 Eicosapentaenoic acid from heterotrophic microalgae
R01HL-47300-01 (SRC) ANDERSON, JAMES M INSTITUTE OF PATHOLOGY 2085 ADELBERT ROAD CLEVELAND, OH 44106 Infection mechanism with cardiovascular prostheses
R01HL-47313-01 (SRC) HOOK, MAGNUS UNIVERSITY OF ALABAMA 1918 UNIVERSITY BLVD BIRMINGHAM, AL 35294 S. aureus adhesion to implanted cardiovascular devices
R13HL-47343-01 (LBPA) WAGNER, WILTZ W, JR INDIANA UNIVERSITY SCH OF MED 635 BARNHILL DRIVE INDIANAPOLIS, IN 46202-5120 The pulmonary circulation and gas exchange
R03HL-47388-01 (SRC) IANNOTTI, RONALD J GEORGETOWN UNIV SCHOOL OF MED 3750 RESERVOIR RD, NW WASHINGTON, DC 20007 D C scan--Extended analyses
R03HL-47451-01 (SRC) BRASS, LAWRENCE M YALE UNIVERSITY SCH OF MED 333 CEDAR ST NEW HAVEN, CT 06510 Stroke risk in the NAS-NRC twin registry
R01HL-47453-01 (HED) WIDNESS, JOHN A UNIVERSITY OF IOWA IOWA CITY, IA 52242 Response to anemia during the neonatal period
R03HL-47478-01 (SRC) BLAIR, STEVEN N INSTITUTE FOR AEROBICS RES 12330 PRESTON ROAD DALLAS, TX 75230 Validation of a historical physical activity survey
R43HL-47662-01 (SSS) AMBRUS, CLARA M HEMEX, INC. 143 WINDSOR AVENUE BUFFALO, NY 14209 Immobilized chelator for extracorporeal lead removal
R03HL-47677-01 (SRC) PERRY, H MITCHELL, JR WASHINGTON UNIVERSITY BOX 8048/660 S EUCLID ST LOUIS, MO 63110 15yr follow-up of 5500 black and 5500 other hypertensives
S15HL-47686-01 (NSS) MORGAN, HOWARD E GEISINGER CLINIC NORTH ACADEMY AVE DANVILLE, PA 17822-2601 Small instrumentation grant
S15HL-47687-01 (NSS) HOLBROOK, KAREN A UNIVERSITY OF WASHINGTON A-300 HEALTH SCIENCES BLDG SEATTLE, WA 98195 Small instrumentation grant
S15HL-47688-01 (NSS) LAGUNOFF, DAVID ST LOUIS UNIV MED CTR 1402 SOUTH GRAND BLVD ST LOUIS, MO 63104 Small instrumentation grant
S15HL-47689-01 (NSS) BEHRENS, B LYN LOMA LINDA UNIVERSITY LOMA LINDA, CA 92350 Small instrumentation grant
S15HL-47690-01 (NSS) SCALETTI, JOSEPH V UNIVERSITY OF NEW MEXICO 915 CAMINO DE SALUD, NE ALBUQUERQUE, NM 87131 Small instrumentation grant
S15HL-47691-01 (NSS) COX, ROBERT H BOCKUS RES INST, GRAD HOSP ONE GRADUATE PLAZA PHILADELPHIA, PA 19146 Small instrumentation grant
S15HL-47692-01 (NSS) HUSTON, RICHARD L UNIVERSITY OF ILLINOIS PO BOX 6998 CHICAGO, IL 60680 Small instrumentation grant
S15HL-47693-01 (NSS) MOSBACH, ERWIN H BETH ISRAEL MEDICAL CTR FIRST AVE AT 16TH ST NEW YORK, NY 10003 Small instrumentation grant
S15HL-47694-01 (NSS) MILLER, BARRY ALBERT EINSTEIN MEDICAL CENTER 5501 OLD YORK ROAD PHILADELPHIA, PA 19141 Small instrumentation grant
S15HL-47695-01 (NSS) LUCAS, JOHN J SUNY HEALTH SCIENCE CTR 750 E ADAMS STREET SYRACUSE, NY 13210 Small instrumentation grant
S15HL-47696-01 (NSS) SHERIDAN, JUDSON D UNIV OF MISSOURI 202 JESSE HALL COLUMBIA, MO 65211 Small instrumentation grant
S15HL-47697-01 (NSS) SISKIND, GREGORY W CORNELL UNIV MEDICAL COLLEGE 1300 YORK AVENUE NEW YORK, NY 10021 Small instrumentation grant
S15HL-47698-01 (NSS) SUMMITT, ROBERT L UNIVERSITY OF TENNESSEE 800 MADISON AVENUE MEMPHIS, TN 38163 Small instrumentation grant
S15HL-47699-01 (NSS) TAYLOR, JOHN M GLADSTONE FDN LABORATORIES P O BOX 40608 SAN FRANCISCO, CA 94140-0608 Small instrumentation grant
S15HL-47700-01 (NSS) HOYER, LEON W AMERICAN RED CROSS 15601 CRABBS BRANCH WAY ROCKVILLE, MD 20855 Small instrumentation grant
S15HL-47701-01 (NSS) SCHUBERT, WILLIAM K CHILDREN'S HOSP MED CENTER ELLAND & BETHESDA AVENUES CINCINNATI, OHIO 45229-2899 Small instrumentation grant

PROJECT NO., ORGANIZATIONAL UNIT., INVESTIGATOR, ADDRESS, TITLE

S15HL-47702-01 (NSS) BLAKE, CHARLES A UNIVERSITY OF SOUTH CAROLINA SCHOOL OF MEDICINE COLUMBIA, SC 29208 Small instrumentation grant
S15HL-47703-01 (NSS) COOK, PAUL F TEXAS COLL OF OSTEOPATHIC MED 3500 CAMP BOWIE BOULEVARD FORT WORTH, TX 76107-2690 Small instrumentation grant
S15HL-47704-01 (NSS) BANERJEE, AMIYA K CLEVELAND CLINIC FDN 9500 EUCLID AVE CLEVELAND, OH 44195 Small instrumentation grant
S15HL-47705-01 (NSS) CARSKADON, MARY A E.P. BRADLEY HOSPITAL 1011 VETERANS MEMORIAL PARKWAY EAST PROVIDENCE, RI 02915 Small instrumentation grant
S15HL-47706-01 (NSS) HEDGE, GEORGE A WVU SCHOOL OF MEDICINE 2266 HEALTH SCIENCES SOUTH MORGANTOWN, WV 26506 Small instrumentation grant
S15HL-47707-01 (NSS) ROCKHOLD, ROBIN W UNIVERSITY OF MISSISSIPPI 2500 NORTH STATE STREET JACKSON, MS 38216-4505 Small instrumentation grant
S15HL-47708-01 (NSS) CHOBANIAN, ARAM V BOSTON UNIV SCH OF MEDICINE 80 EAST CONCORD STREET BOSTON, MA 02118 Small instrumentation grant
S15HL-47709-01 (NSS) SHORE, JOSEPH D HENRY FORD HOSPITAL 2799 W GRAND BLVD DETROIT, MI 48202 Small instrumentation grant
S15HL-47710-01 (NSS) HAUG, PETER J LDS HOSPITAL 8TH AVENUE AND C STREET SALT LAKE CITY, UT 84143 Small instrumentation grant
S15HL-47711-01 (NSS) STOUT, FRANK G NEW ENGLAND MEDICAL CTR HOSP 750 WASHINGTON ST, BOX 817 BOSTON, MA 02111 Small instrumentation grant
S15HL-47712-01 (NSS) YANCHICK, VICTOR A UNIVERSITY OF OKLAHOMA PO BOX 26901 OKLAHOMA CITY, OK 73190 Small instrumentation grant
S15HL-47713-01 (NSS) HALLOCK, JAMES A EAST CAROLINA UNIVERSITY GREENVILLE, NC 27858-4354 Small instrumentation grant
S15HL-47714-01 (NSS) CHILIAN, WILLIAM M TEXAS A&M UNIV COLL OF MEDICIN REYNOLDS MED BLDG RM 350 COLLEGE STATION, TX 77843-111 Small instrumentation grant
S15HL-47715-01 (NSS) LAIRSON, PAUL D KAISER FDN RESEARCH INSTITUTE 3505 BROADWAY, SUITE 1112 OAKLAND, CA 94611 Small instrumentation grant
S15HL-47716-01 (NSS) MC DONALD, TED P UNIVERSITY OF TENNESSEE P.O. BOX 1071 KNOXVILLE, TN 37901-1071 Small instrumentation grant
S15HL-47717-01 (NSS) TURNER, ERNEST A MEHARRY MEDICAL COLLEGE 1005 D B TODD JR BLVD NASHVILLE, TN 37208 Small instrumentation grant
S15HL-47718-01 (NSS) SURREY, SAUL CHILDREN'S HOSP PHILADELPHIA 34TH & CIVIC CENTER BLVD PHILADELPHIA, PA 19104 Small instrumentation grant
S15HL-47719-01 (NSS) HASH, JOHN H VANDERBILT UNIVERSITY CCC-3322, MEDICAL CENTER NORTH NASHVILLE, TN 37232-2103 Small instrumentation grant
S15HL-47720-01 (NSS) REED, ROBERTA G MARY IMOGENE BASSETT HOSPITAL ONE ATWELL RD COOPERSTOWN, N Y 13326 Small instrumentation grant
S15HL-47721-01 (NSS) GRAY, WILLIAM R UNIVERSITY OF UTAH 201 S BIOLOGY SALT LAKE CITY, UT 84112 Small instrumentation grant
S15HL-47722-01 (NSS) MATTISON, DONALD R UNIVERSITY OF PITTSBURGH 130 DESOTO STREET PITTSBURGH, PA 15261 Small instrumentation grant
S15HL-47723-01 (NSS) HUBER, PAUL W UNIVERSITY OF NOTRE DAME NOTRE DAME, IN 46556 Small instrumentation grant
S15HL-47724-01 (NSS) JOHNS, MICHAEL E JOHNS HOPKINS UNIVERSITY 720 RUTLAND AVE BALTIMORE, MD 21205 Small instrumentation grant
S15HL-47725-01 (NSS) ATEN, MARILYN J, PHD UNIVERSITY OF ROCHESTER 601 ELMWOOD AVE ROCHESTER, NY 14642 Small instrumentation grant
S15HL-47726-01 (NSS) WARTELL, ROGER M GEORGIA INSTITUTE OF TECHNOLOG ATLANTA, GA 30332 Small instrumentation grant
S15HL-47727-01 (NSS) MOSELEY, JOHN T UNIVERSITY OF OREGON 110 JOHNSON HALL EUGENE, OR 97403-1219 Small instrumentation grant
S15HL-47728-01 (NSS) DEVINE, ELIZABETH C UNIVERSITY OF WISCONSIN PO BOX 413 MILWAUKEE, WI 53201 Small instrumentation grant
S15HL-47729-01 (NSS) OBERST, MARILYN T UNIVERSITY OF WISCONSIN 600 HIGHLAND AVENUE RM K6/342 MADISON, WI 53792 Small instrumentation grant
S15HL-47730-01 (NSS) PRENDERGAST, FRANKLYN G MAYO FOUNDATION 200 FIRST STREET SOUTHWEST ROCHESTER, MN 55905 Small instrumentation grant
S15HL-47731-01 (NSS) CROUCH, EDMOND C JEWISH HOSPITAL OF ST LOUIS 216 S KINGSHIGHWAY ST LOUIS, MO 63110 Small instrumentation grant
S15HL-47732-01 (NSS) WILLIAMS, EVAN F MOREHOUSE SCHOOL OF MEDICINE 720 WESTVIEW DRIVE, SW ATLANTA, GA 30310-1495 Small instrumentation grant
S15HL-47733-01 (NSS) ABRAHAM, WILLIAM M MOUNT SINAI MEDICAL CENTER 4300 ALTON ROAD MIAMI BEACH, FL 33140 Small instrumentation grant
S15HL-47734-01 (NSS) EYSTER, KATHLEEN M UNIVERSITY OF SOUTH DAKOTA 414 EAST CLARK VERMILLION, SD 57069-9986 Small instrumentation grant
S15HL-47735-01 (NSS) TURITTO, VINCENT T MEMPHIS STATE UNIVERSITY MEMPHIS, TN 38152 Small instrumentation grant
S15HL-47736-01 (NSS) HAWKINS, C MORTON UNIV OF TEXAS HEALTH SCI CTR PO BOX 20186 HOUSTON, TX 77225 Small instrumentation grant
S15HL-47737-01 (NSS) BRANDT, EDWARD N, JR UNIVERSITY OF OKLAHOMA PO BOX 26901 OKLAHOMA CITY, OK 73190 Small instrumentation grant
S15HL-47738-01 (NSS) PEACH, MICHAEL J UNIV OF VIRGINIA BOX 325 CHARLOTTESVILLE, VA 22908 Small instrumentation grant
S15HL-47739-01 (NSS) SCHWARZ, RICHARD H SUNY-HEALTH SCIENCE CENTER 450 CLARKSON AVENUE BROOKLYN, N Y 11203 Small instrumentation grant
S15HL-47740-01 (NSS) HOWARD, BARBARA V MEDLANTIC RESEARCH FOUNDATION 108 IRVING STREET, NW WASHINGTON, DC 20010 Small instrumentation grant
S15HL-47741-01 (NSS) MATTHEWS, KATHLEEN S RICE UNIVERSITY PO BOX 1892 HOUSTON, TX 77251 Small instrumentation grant

PROJECT NO., ORGANIZATIONAL UNIT., INVESTIGATOR, ADDRESS, TITLE

S15HL-47742-01 (NSS) **MYERS, ALLEN R** TEMPLE UNIVERSITY SCH OF MED 3400 NORTH BROAD STREET PHILADELPHIA, PA 19140 Small instrumentation grant

S15HL-47743-01 (NSS) **NADEL, ETHAN R** JOHN B PIERCE LABORATORY INC 290 CONGRESS AVE NEW HAVEN, CT 06519 Small instrumentation grant

S15HL-47744-01 (NSS) **ROSEN, FRED S** THE CENTER FOR BLOOD RESEARCH 800 HUNTINGTON AVENUE BOSTON, MA 02115 Small instrumentation grant

S15HL-47745-01 (NSS) **ARZBAECHER, ROBERT** PRITZKER INST OF MED ENGR ILLINOIS INSTITUTE OF TECH CHICAGO, IL 60616 Small instrumentation grant

S15HL-47746-01 (NSS) **WHITE, H STEVE** UNIVERSITY OF UTAH 112 SKAGGS HALL SALT LAKE CITY, UT 84112 Small instrumentation grant

S15HL-47747-01 (NSS) **BIEBER, ALLAN L** ARIZONA STATE UNIVERSITY TEMPE, AZ 85287-1604 Small instrumentation grant

S15HL-47748-01 (NSS) **STEVENS, WALTER** UNIVERSITY OF UTAH 50 NORTH MEDICAL DRIVE SALT LAKE CITY, UT 84132 Small instrumentation grant

S15HL-47749-01 (NSS) **EVARTS, C MC COLLISTER** MILTON S HERSHEY MEDICAL CENTE P O BOX 850 HERSHEY, PA 17033 Small instrumentation grant

S15HL-47750-01 (NSS) **KEFALIDES, NICHOLAS A** UNIVERSITY CITY SCIENCE CENTER 3624 MARKET STREET PHILADELPHIA, PA 19104 Small instrumentation grant

S15HL-47751-01 (NSS) **BISSELL, MINA J** UNIVERSITY OF CALIFORNIA LAWRENCE BERKELEY LAB BERKELEY, CA 94720 Small instrumentation grant

S15HL-47752-01 (NSS) **SANTAMORE, WILLIAM P** PRESBYTERIAN MEDICAL CENTER 39TH & MARKET STREETS PHILADELPHIA, PA 19104 Small instrumentation grant

S15HL-47753-01 (NSS) **SHERIDAN, JOHN F** OHIO STATE UNIVERSITY 305 WEST 12TH AVE. COLUMBUS, OH 43210 Small instrumentation grant

S15HL-47754-01 (NSS) **MAKOWSKI, LEE** BOSTON UNIVERSITY 590 COMMONWEALTH AVE BOSTON, MA 02215 Small instrumentation grant

S15HL-47755-01 (NSS) **WEBER, JAMES L** MARSHFIELD MED RES & EDUC FDN 1000 NORTH OAK AVE MARSHFIELD, WI 54449-5790 Small instrumentation grant

S15HL-47756-01 (NSS) **SHERIDAN, MARY E** OHIO STATE UNIVERSITY 190 N OVAL MALL/208 BRICKER HA COLUMBUS, OH 43210 Small instrumentation grant

S15HL-47757-01 (NSS) **SCHNEIDERMAN, NEIL** UNIVERSITY OF MIAMI P O BOX 248185 CORAL GABLES, FL 33124 Small instrumentation grant

S15HL-47758-01 (NSS) **COGGIN, JOSEPH H, JR** UNIVERSITY OF SOUTH ALABAMA COLLEGE OF MEDICINE MOBILE, AL 36688 Small instrumentation grant

S15HL-47759-01 (NSS) **NESSON, H RICHARD** BRIGHAM & WOMENS HOSPITAL 75 FRANCIS STREET BOSTON, MA 02115 Small instrumentation grant

S15HL-47760-01 (NSS) **WINDRIDGE, GRAHAM C** VIRGINIA COMMONWEALTH UNIV BOX 581, MCV STATION RICHMOND, VA 23298-0581 Small instrumentation grant

S15HL-47761-01 (NSS) **MONDRAGON, ALFONSO** NORTHWESTERN UNIVERSITY 2153 SHERIDAN ROAD EVANSTON, IL 60208 Small instrumentation grant

S15HL-47762-01 (NSS) **HUTTON, JOHN J JR** UNIVERSITY OF CINCINNATI 231 BETHESDA AVE CINCINNATI, OH 45267-0555 Small instrumentation grant

S15HL-47763-01 (NSS) **DICARLO, STEPHEN E** NORTHEASTERN OHIO UNIV COLL/ M 4209 STATE ROUTE 44 ROOTSTOWN, OH 44272 Small instrumentation grant

S15HL-47764-01 (NSS) **MONTGOMERY, ROBERT R** BLOOD CENTER OF SE WISCONSIN 1701 WEST WISCONSIN AVENUE MILWAUKEE, WI 53233 Small instrumentation grant

S15HL-47765-01 (NSS) **OLSON, JACK W** UNIVERSITY OF KENTUCKY ROSE STREET PHARMACY BLDG LEXINGTON, KY 40536-0082 Small instrumentation grant

S15HL-47766-01 (NSS) **HIGHSMITH, STEFAN** UNIVERSITY OF THE PACIFIC 2155 WEBSTER STREET SAN FRANCISCO, CA 94115 Small instrumentation grant

S15HL-47767-01 (NSS) **BARONDES, SAMUEL H** LANGLEY PORTER INST 401 PARNASSUS AVENUE BOX F SAN FRANCISCO, CA 94143-0984 Small instrumentation grant

S15HL-47768-01 (NSS) **ASBURY, ARTHUR K** UNIVERISTY OF PENNSYLVANIA 3600 HAMILTON WALK PHILADELPHIA, PA 19104-6055 Small instrumentation grant

S15HL-47769-01 (NSS) **HOPPIN, FREDERIC G** MEMORIAL HOSPITAL 111 BREWSTER STREET PAWTUCKET, R I 02860 Small instrumentation grant

S15HL-47770-01 (NSS) **CALLERY, PATRICK S** UNIVERSITY OF MARYLAND 20 NORTH PINE STREET BALTIMORE, MD 21201 Small instrumentation grant

S15HL-47771-01 (NSS) **LINDSTEDT, STAN L** NORTHERN ARIZONA UNIVERSITY PO BOX 5640 FLAGSTAFF, AZ 86011 Small instrumentation grant

S15HL-47772-01 (NSS) **PENRY, J KIFFIN** BOWMAN GRAY SCH OF MED 300 SOUTH HAWTHORNE ROAD WINSTON-SALEM, N C 27103 Small instrumentation grant

S15HL-47773-01 (NSS) **ATTIYEH, RICHARD** UNIVERSITY OF CALIFORNIA MAIL CODE 0003 LA JOLLA, CA 92093-0003 Small instrumentation grant

S15HL-47774-01 (NSS) **AYRES, S M** VIRGINIA COMMONWEALTH UNIVERSI BOX 565 MCV STATION RICHMOND, VA 23298-0565 Small instrumentation grant

S15HL-47775-01 (NSS) **LEYASMEYER, EDITH D** UNIVERSITY OF MINNESOTA BOX 197-420 DELAWARE STREET MINNEAPOLIS, MN 55455 Small instrumentation grant

S15HL-47776-01 (NSS) **RICHARDS, RICHARD D** UNIVERSITY OF MARYLAND HOSP 655 W BALTIMORE ST BALTIMORE, MD 21201 Small instrumentation grant

S15HL-47777-01 (NSS) **LERNER, RICHARD A** RESEARCH INST OF SCRIPPS CLINI 10666 NORTH TORREY PINES ROAD LA JOLLA, CA 92037 Small instrumentation grant

S15HL-47778-01 (NSS) **BRUCE, JOHN I** UNIVERSITY OF LOWELL 450 AIKEN ST LOWELL, MASS 01854 Small instrumentation grant

S15HL-47779-01 (NSS) **SNYDERMAN, RALPH** DUKE UNIV MEDICAL CENTER PO BOX 3001 DURHAM, NC 27710 Small instrumentation grant

S15HL-47780-01 (NSS) **KURTH, MARK J** UNIVERSITY OF CALIFORNIA DAVIS, CA 95616 Small instrumentation grant

PROJECT NO., ORGANIZATIONAL UNIT., INVESTIGATOR, ADDRESS, TITLE

S15HL-47781-01 (NSS) **COHEN, JORDAN J** HEALTH SCIENCES CENTER SUNY DEANS OFFICE STONY BROOK, NY 11794-8430 Small instrumentation grant

S15HL-47782-01 (NSS) **JORDAN, ANGEL G** CARNEGIE MELLON UNIVERSITY 5000 FORBES AVENUE PITTSBURGH, PA 15213 Small instrumentation grant

S15HL-47783-01 (NSS) **JOHNSON, DALE E** UNIVERSITY OF WASHINGTON 201 ADMIN BLDG SEATTLE, WA 98195 Small instrumentation grant

S15HL-47784-01 (NSS) **DIAMOND, IVAN** ERNEST GALLO CLINIC & RES CTR BLDG 1 RM 101 SAN FRANCISCO, CA 94110 Small instrumentation grant

S15HL-47785-01 (NSS) **KERN, DAVID F** EAST TENNESSEE STATE UNIV BOX 19780A JOHNSON CITY, TN 37614-0002 Small instrumentation grant

S15HL-47786-01 (NSS) **LEVINE, LOUIS** CITY COLLEGE OF CUNY 138TH ST & CONVENT AVE NEW YORK, N Y 10031 Small instrumentation grant

S15HL-47787-01 (NSS) **GONNELLA, JOSEPH S** JEFFERSON MEDICAL COLLEGE 1025 WALNUT STREET PHILADELPHIA, PA 19107 Small instrumentation grant

S15HL-47788-01 (NSS) **HERMSMEYER, R KENT** CHILES RESEARCH INST 4805 NE GLISAN PORTLAND, OR 97213 Small instrumentation grant

S15HL-47789-01 (NSS) **PANGBURN, MICHAEL K** UNIV OF TEXAS HLTH SCI CENTER TYLER, TX 75710-20003 Small instrumentation grant

R01HL-47838-01 (SRC) **WILCOX, JOSIAH N** EMORY UNIVERSITY ATLANTA, GA 30322 Thrombosis and vascular lesion formation

R01HL-47839-01 (SRC) **BARNATHAN, ELLIOT S** HOSPITAL OF THE UNIV OF PENN 3400 SPRUCE ST PHILADELPHIA, PA 19104 Plasminogen activator regulation during restenosis

R01HL-47840-01 (SRC) **LIBBY, PETER** BRIGHAM & WOMEN'S HOSPITAL 75 FRANCIS ST BOSTON, MA 02115 Restenosis pathobiology--A cascade mechanism

R01HL-47849-01 (SRC) **SAREMBOCK, IAN J** UNIV OF VIRGINIA BOX 158 CHARLOTTESVILLE, VA 22908 Effect of thrombin inhibition by hirudin on angioplasty restenosis

R01HL-47852-01 (SRC) **CHISOLM, GUY M** THE CLEVELAND CLINIC FND 9500 EUCLID AVE CLEVELAND, OH 44195 Interactive roles of oxidants and TGF-beta in restenosis

R01HL-47862-01 (SRC) **WEISSFELD, JOEL L** PITTSBURGH CANCER INSTITUTE 200 MEYRAN AVENUE PITTSBURGH, PA 15213 Cost-effectiveness of high cholesterol case-finding

R01HL-47874-01 (HEM) **HARTWIG, JOHN H** BRIGHAM AND WOMEN'S HOSPITAL 75 FRANCIS STREET BOSTON, MA 02115 Regulation of platelet shape changes

R01HL-47876-01 (SAT) **ESKIN, SUZANNE G** UNIV OF TEXAS HLTH SCI CTR 6431 FANNIN HOUSTON, TX 77030 Transduction of hemodynamic signals into vascular cells

R01HL-47881-01 (SRC) **CAMPESE, VITO M** UNIVERSITY OF SOUTHERN CALIF 2025 ZONAL AVENUE LOS ANGELES, CA 90033 The kidney in hypertensive black men and women

U01HL-47887-01 (SRC) **HOWARD, GEORGE** BOWMAN GRAY SCHOOL OF MEDICINE 300 S HAWTHORNE ROAD WINSTON-SALEM, NC 27103 Insulin, insulin resistance, hyperglycemia and cardiovascular disease

U01HL-47889-01 (SRC) **SELBY, JOSEPH V** KAISER PERMANENTE 3451 PIEDMONT AVENUE OAKLAND, CA 94611 Insulin resistance, hyperglycemia and atherosclerosis

U01HL-47890-01 (SRC) **BERGMAN, RICHARD N** UNIV OF SOUTHERN CALIFORNIA 2025 ZONAL AVE LOS ANGELES, CA 90033 Insulin, insulin resistance, hyperglycemia and cardiovascular disease

U01HL-47892-01 (SRC) **REWERS, MARIAN J** UNIVERSITY OF COLORADO 4200 E NINTH AVE C245 DENVER, CO 80262 Insulin resistance and cardiovascular disease

U01HL-47902-01 (SRC) **SAAD, MOHAMMED F** LAC/USC MEDICAL CENTER 1200 N STATE STREET LOS ANGELES, CA 90033 Insulin, insulin resistance, hyperglycemia and cardiovascular disease

R01HL-47910-01 (SRC) **COOPER, RICHARD S** LOYOLA UNIV MEDICAL CENTER 2160 S FIRST AVENUE MAYWOOD, IL 60153 Cell calcium and hypertension in blacks

R01HL-47923-01 (SRC) **GRIM, CLARENCE E** CHARLES R DREW UNIV OF MEDICIN 1621 E 120TH STREET LOS ANGELES, CA 90059 Salt sensitivity in blacks--Physiologic and genetic studies

R29HL-47926-01 (PTHA) **BARMAN, SCOTT A** MED COLL OF GEORGIA RES INST,I 1120 15TH STREET AUGUSTA, GA 30912-2300 Characterization of vascular tone on lung fluid balance

R01HL-47943-01 (SRC) **MORRIS, R CURTIS, JR** UNIVERSITY OF CALIFORNIA 1202 MOFFITT HOSPITAL SAN FRANCISCO, CA 94143-0126 Dietary potassium as a determinant of Black hypertension

R01HL-48006-01 (SRC) **PHELPS, DAVID S** PENNSYLVANIA STATE UNIVERSITY PO BOX 850/M S HERSHEY MED CTR HERSHEY, PA 17033 Pneumocyte-immune cell interactions in the distal lung

R01HL-48008-01 (HEM) **BOKOCH, GARY M** SCIRPPS RESEARCH INSTITUTE 10666 N TORREY PINES ROAD LA JOLLA, CA 92037 G protein regulation of the neutrophil nadph oxidase

R01HL-48363-01 (BEM) **STONEY, CATHERINE M** THE MIRIAM HOSPITAL 164 SUMMIT AVENUE PROVIDENCE, RI 02906 Effects of behavioral stress on lipids and lipoproteins

R13HL-48384-01 (SRC) **CLAUSEN, JACK L** UCSD MEDICAL CENTER 225 DICKINSON STREET SAN DIEGO, CA 92103 Conference on measurement of lung volumes

R01HL-48406-01 (PTHA) **JOHNSON, ARNOLD** ALBANY MEDICAL COLLEGE 47 NEW SCOTLAND AVE ALBANY, NY 12208 Mechanisms of tumor necrosis factor-induced edema

R01HL-48478-01 (PHRA) **REYNOLDS, ELWOOD E** PARKE-DAVIS PHARMACEUTICAL RES 2800 PLYMOUTH ROAD ANN ARBOR, MI 48105 Endothelin signalling mechanisms in smooth muscle cells

N01HO-09007-02 (**) **ALLDREDGE, ELHAM-EID** Blood resource physicians survey

N01HO-09009-03 (**) **KEARNEY, CHERRI L.** Technical, analytical, and documentation support service

N01HO-89004-08 (**) **KELLY, JOSEPH A.** Strategies for education programs

N01HO-99005-06 (**) **SEACH, JAMES** Information systems branch automated data processing

N01HR-16044-00 (**) **TONASCIA, JAMES A** Clinical coordinating center for cAMP

N01HR-16045-00 (**) **ZEIGER, ROBERT S** Clinical center for Childhood Asthma Management Program

PROJECT NO., ORGANIZATIONAL UNIT., INVESTIGATOR, ADDRESS, TITLE

N01HR-16046-00 (**) MCWILLIAMS, BENNIE C Clinical center for Childhood Asthma Management Program
N01HR-16047-00 (**) LEVISON, HENRY Clinical center for Childhood Asthma Management Program
N01HR-16048-00 (**) SZEFLER, STANLEY J Clinical center for Childhood Asthma Management Program
N01HR-16049-00 (**) WEISS, SCOTT Clinical center for Childhood Asthma Management Program
N01HR-16050-00 (**) SHAPIRO, GAIL G Clinical center for Childwood Asthma Management Program
N01HR-16051-00 (**) STRUNK, ROBERT Clinical center for Chilwood Asthma Management Program
N01HR-16052-00 (**) ADKINSON, N FRANKLIN, JR Clinical center for Childhood Asthma Management Program
N01HR-16053-00 (**) SNIDER, MICHAEL T Artificial lung research and development
N01HR-46002-22 (**) CONNETT, JOHN E Data center for early intervention for chronic obstructive pulmonary disease
N01HR-46013-21 (**) OWENS, GREGORY R. Intervention for chronic obstructive pulmonary disease
N01HR-46014-16 (**) KANNER, RICHARD E. Early intervention for chronic obstructive pulmonary disease
N01HR-46015-16 (**) CONWAY, WILLIAM A. Early intervention for chronic obstructive pulmonary disease
N01HR-46016-17 (**) BUIST, A SONIA Intervention for chronic obstructive pulmonary disease
N01HR-46017-18 (**) ANTHONISEN, NICHOLAS R. Early intervention for chronic obstructive pulmonary disease
N01HR-46018-16 (**) ENRIGHT, PAUL L. Early intervention for chronic obstructive pulmonary disease
N01HR-46019-16 (**) BAILEY, WILLIAM C Intervention for chronic obstructive pulmonary disease
N01HR-46020-16 (**) ALTOSE, MURRAY D. Early intervention for chronic obstructive pulmonary disease
N01HR-46021-18 (**) WISE, ROBERT Early intervention for chronic obstructive pulmonary disease
N01HR-46022-19 (**) TASHKIN, DONALD P. Early intervention/chronic obstructive pulmonary disease
N01HR-76029-04 (**) POOLE, KENNETH W. Pulmonary complications of HTV-III/lav (HIV) infection
N01HR-76030-05 (**) WALLACE, JEANNE M. Pulmonary complications of HTLV-III (HIV) infection
N01HR-76031-04 (**) ROSEN, MARK J. Pulmonary complications of HTLV-III/LAV (HIV) infection
N01HR-76032-05 (**) REICHMAN, LEE B. Pulmonary complications of HTLV-III/LAV (HIV) infection
N01HR-76033-04 (**) KVALE, PAUL Pulmonary complications of HTLV-III/LAV (HIV) infection
N01HR-76034-04 (**) HOPEWELL, PHILIP C. Pulmonary complications of HTLV-III/LAV (HIV) infection
N01HR-76035-05 (**) GLASSROTH, JEFFREY Pulmonary complications of HTLV-III/LAV (HIV) infection
N01HR-86036-06 (**) WILLIAMS, GEORGE W. Registry-congenital deficiency of alpha1-antitrypsin
N01HR-96037-07 (**) SCHLUCHTER, MARK D. Study of pediatric lung and heart complications of HIV
N01HR-96038-06 (**) KAPLAN, SAMUEL L. Pediatric lung and heart complications of HIV infection
N01HR-96040-06 (**) SHEARER, WILLIAM T. Pediatric lung and heart complications of HIV infection
N01HR-96041-06 (**) LIPSCHULTZ, STEPHEN M. Pediatric lung and heart complication of HIV infection
N01HR-96042-06 (**) KATTAN, MEYER L. Pediatric heart and lung complications of HIV infection
N01HR-96043-07 (**) MELLINS, ROBERT B. Pediatric lung and heart complications of HIV infection
R18HS-05626-04 (HCT) MC DONALD, CLEMENT J INDIANA UNIVERSITY SCH OF MED 1001 WEST TENTH STREET INDIANAPOLIS, IN 46202-2859 Assessment of technology use via a computerized ordering
R18HS-05635-05 (HCT) MARK, DANIEL B DUKE UNIV MED CTR P O BOX 3485 DURHAM, N C 27710 Multidimensional technology assessment of PTCA
R01HS-05640-05 (HSR) BARMES, DAVID E WORLD HEALTH ORGANIZATION AVE APPIA 1211 GENEVA 27 SWITZERLAND International collaborative study of oral health outcome
R01HS-05705-02 (HSR) ADELMAN, ALAN M UNIV OF MARYLAND AT BALTIMORE 405 W REDWOOD STREET BALTIMORE, MD 21201 Health care utilization and recurrence of abdominal pain
R18HS-05745-04 (HCT) WENNBERG, JOHN E DARTMOUTH MEDICAL SCHOOL STRASENBURGH HALL HB 7250 HANOVER, N H 03756 Facilitating outcomes research using claims data
R01HS-05760-03 (HSDG) MUELLER, KEITH J UNIV OF NEBRASKA 600 SOUTH 42ND ST OMAHA, NE 68198-4350 Access to medical care among the indigent in Nebraska
R01HS-05787-04 (HSR) KNAUS, WILLIAM A GEORGE WASHINGTON UNIVERSITY 2300 K STREET, N W WASHINGTON, D C 20037 Developing a severity of illness classification system
R01HS-05936-04 (HCT) MOSTELLER, FREDERICK HARVARD SCHOOL OF PUBLIC HLTH 677 HUNTINGTON AVE, ROOM L 7A BOSTON, MASS 02115 Meta-analysis for medicine--Application and methods
R18HS-06028-03 (HCT) EVANS, R SCOTT LDS HOSPITAL 8TH AVENUE & C STREET SALT LAKE CITY, UT 84143 Clinical applications of an expert system
R01HS-06048-02 (HCT) RESTUCCIA, JOSEPH D BOSTON UNIVERSITY 621 COMMONWEALTH AVENUE BOSTON, MA 02215 Inappropriateness and variations in hospital use
R01HS-06060-02 (HCT) PERRIN, JAMES M MASSACHUSETTS GENERAL HOSPITAL FRUIT STREET BOSTON, MA 02114 Regional variation in pediatric hospitalization
R01HS-06062-04 (HSR) MADDEN, CAROLYN W UNIVERSITY OF WASHINGTON SEATTLE, WA 98195 Health insurance for the low income--An evaluation
R01HS-06073-03S1 (HSDG) WARE, JOHN E JR NEW ENGLAND MEDICAL CENTER 750 WASHINGTON STREET BOSTON, MA 02111 Variations in physicians practice style & outcomes

PROJECT NO., ORGANIZATIONAL UNIT., INVESTIGATOR, ADDRESS, TITLE

R01HS-06098-03 (HCT) GANIATS, THEODORE G UNIV OF CALIFORNIA, SAN DIEGO 9500 GILMAN DRIVE LA JOLLA, CALIFORNIA 92093-08 Cost/utility of stroke prevention
R01HS-06121-03 (HSDG) MILLER, BUELL A 260 WESTERN AVENUE SOUTH PORTLAND, ME 04106 The hysterectomy decision--Assessment of outcomes
R01HS-06123-03 (HCT) RICHARDSON, DOUGLAS K CHILDRENS HOSPITAL 300 LONGWOOD AVE BOSTON, MA 02115 Physiologic severity index for neonatal intensive care
R01HS-06125-02 (HCT) MCNUTT, ROBERT A UNIVERSITY OF NORTH CAROLINA 5039 OLD CLINIC BUILDING CHAPEL HILL, NC 27599-7110 Visual cues and physicians judgments in heart disease
R01HS-06138-03 (HCT) DE LISSOVOY, GREGORY JHU SCH OF HYGIENE & PUB HLTH 624 NORTH BROADWAY BALTIMORE, MD 21205 Benefits/costs of the implantable cardiac defibrillator
R01HS-06149-02 (HCT) HAZELKORN, HERBERT M UNIVERSITY OF ILLINOIS PO BOX 6998 CHICAGO, IL 60680 Appropriate dental care under different payment systems
R18HS-06152-02 (HCT) HALLSTROM, ALFRED P UNIVERSITY OF WASHINGTON 1107 NE 45TH SEATTLE, WA 98105 Computer aided dispatching and a trial of CPR methods
R01HS-06156-01A1 (HSR) SILVERS, J B CASE WESTERN RESERVE UNIV 454 SEARS LIBRARY BUILDING CLEVELAND, OH 44106-1712 Variation in inpatient cost & net corporate value by DRG
R01HS-06166-03 (HSR) ROSENBLATT, ROGER A UNIVERSITY OF WASHINGTON RESEARCH SECTION, HQ-30 SEATTLE, WA 98195 Practice variations in prenatal and intrapartum care
R18HS-06167-02 (HSR) BERTAKIS, KLEA D UNIV OF CALIF/DAVIS MED CTR 2221 STOCKTON BLVD SACRAMENTO, CA 95817 A comparison of practice styles and health outcomes
R01HS-06168-03 (HSDG) VON KORFF, MICHAEL R CENTER FOR HEALTH STUDIES 1730 MINOR AVENUE - SUITE 1600 SEATTLE, WA 98101-1448 Medical care and risks of dysfunctional chronic pain
R01HS-06170-03 (HSR) STARFIELD, BARBARA JOHNS HOPKINS UNIVERSITY 624 N. BROADWAY STREET BALTIMORE, MD 21205 Practice variation and outcomes in ambulatory care
R18HS-06173-03 (HCT) MARTIN, DOUGLAS K REGENSTRIEF HEALTH CENTER 1001 WEST TENTH ST INDIANAPOLIS, IN 46202-2859 Elderly outpatients, computerized record, and efficiency
R18HS-06177-02 (HSDG) GUSTAFSON, DAVID H UNIVERSITY OF WISCONSIN SYSTEM 1300 UNIVERSITY AVE MADISON, WI 53706 Impact of computer support on HIV infected
R13HS-06190-03 (HSR) HERSH, ALICE S FDN FOR HLTH SERVICES RESEARCH 1350 CONNECTICUT AVENUE, NW WASHINGTON, DC 20036 National dissemination program--Health services research
R01HS-06208-03 (HSR) SELKER, HARRY P NEW ENGLAND MEDICAL CENTER 750 WASHINGTON STREET/BOX 63 BOSTON, MA 02111 Myocardial infarct thrombolytic therapy outcome predictive instrument
R01HS-06211-03 (HCT) FRIES, JAMES F STANFORD UNIVERSITY 701 WELCH RD PALO ALTO, CA 94304 ATHOS -- AIDS time-oriented health outcome study
R01HS-06214-03 (HSR) MOR, VINCENT BROWN UNIVERSITY BOX G PROVIDENCE, RI 02912 Longitudinal study of AIDS health services use and costs
R01HS-06216-02 (HSR) LUFT, HAROLD S UNIVERSITY OF CALIFORNIA 1388 SUTTER STREET, 11TH FLOOR SAN FRANCISCO, CA 94109 Volume, outcome, market share & admission rates
R01HS-06239-03 (HSDG) EPSTEIN, ARNOLD M HARVARD MEDICAL SCHOOL 25 SHATTUCK STREET BOSTON, MA 02115 Costs, correlates and outcomes for persons with AIDS
R01HS-06250-02 (HSR) MANHEIM, LARRY M HOSPITAL RES & EDUCATIONAL TRU 840 NORTH LAKE SHORE DRIVE CHICAGO, IL 60611 Effects of horizontal consolidation of hospital markets
R01HS-06258-03 (HCT) WEINSTEIN, MILTON C HARVARD SCHOOL OF PUBLIC HEALT 677 HUNTINGTON AVENUE BOSTON, MA 02115 Policy modeling for coronary heart disease
R01HS-06271-03 (HSR) ALLISON-COOKE, SHERRY NAT'L PERINATAL INFO CTR, INC ONE STATE STREET, SUITE 102 PROVIDENCE, RI 02908 Pediatric AIDS--Local responses, service use and cost
R01HS-06274-02 (HSR) POSES, ROY M VIRGINIA COMMONWEALTH UNIVERSI BOX 102 MCV STATION RICHMOND, VA 23298 Predictions and outcomes in congestive heart failure
P01HS-06280-03 (HSDG) STEINBERG, EARL P JOHNS HOPKINS UNIVERSITY 1830 E MONUMENT STREET BALTIMORE, MD 21205 Variations in cataract MGMT -- Patient and economic outcomes
P01HS-06280-03 0001 (HSDG) STEINBERG, EARL P Variations in cataract MGMT -- Patient and economic outcomes Variation in clinical outcome and patient satisfaction
P01HS-06280-03 0002 (HSDG) STEINBERG, EARL P Variations in cataract MGMT -- Patient and economic outcomes Decision analysis and development of models
R01HS-06283-02 (HCT) FRAME, PAUL S TRI-COUNTY FAMILY MEDICINE BOX 112, PARK AVENUE COHOCTON, NY 14826 Controlled trial of a health maintenance tracking system
R18HS-06284-01A1 (HCT) SCHRIGER, DAVID L UNIVERSITY OF CALIFORNIA 924 WESTWOOD BLVD LOS ANGELES, CA 90024-2924 Clinical standards & quality cost of emergency care
R01HS-06288-02 (HCT) SAFRAN, CHARLES HARVARD MEDICAL SCHOOL 350 LONGWOOD AVENUE BOSTON, MA 02115 Knowledge-based records for patients with HIV infections
R18HS-06330-02 (HCT) SHORTLIFFE, EDWARD H STANFORD UNIV MEDICAL CENTER MEDICAL SCHOOL OFFICE BLDG. STANFORD, CA 94305-5479 Computer support for protocol-directed therapy
P01HS-06336-03 (HSDG) WENNBERG, JOHN E DARTMOUTH MEDICAL SCHOOL HANOVER, NH 03756 Assessing therapies for BPH and localized prostate cancer
R01HS-06339-03 (HSR) CRYSTAL, STEPHEN RUTGERS UNIVERSITY 30 COLLEGE AVE NEW BRUNSWICK, NJ 08903 Health care costs and utilization in AIDS home care
P01HS-06341-03 (HSDG) MCNEIL, BARBARA J HARVARD MEDICAL SCHOOL 25 SHATTUCK STREET BOSTON, MA 02115 The consequences of variation in treatment for acute MI
P01HS-06341-03 0001 (HSDG) MCNEIL, BARBARA J The consequences of variation in treatment for acute MI Clinical problems and data

collection

P01HS-06341-03 0002 (HSDG) MCNAIL, BARBARA J The consequences of variation in treatment for acute MI Dissemination and education

R01HS-06343-03 (HSR) UHLMANN, RICHARD F HARBORVIEW MEDICAL CENTER 325 NINTH AVENUE ZA-87 SEATTLE, WA 98104 Measurement of preferences for life-sustaining treatment

P01HS-06344-03 (HSDG) DEYO, RICHARD A UNIVERSITY OF WASHINGTON MAIL STOP: JD-23 SEATTLE, WA 98195 Back pain outcome assessment team

P01HS-06344-03 0001 (HSDG) DEYO, RICHARD A Back pain outcome assessment team Geographic variation and outcome of lumbar spine surgery

P01HS-06344-03 0002 (HSDG) DEYO, RICHARD A Back pain outcome assessment team Non-surgical hospitalization for back pain

P01HS-06344-03 0003 (HSDG) DEYO, RICHARD A Back pain outcome assessment team Technology used to diagnose spinal stenosis

P01HS-06344-03 0004 (HSDG) DEYO, RICHARD A Back pain outcome assessment team Dissemination and recommendations

R01HS-06348-02 (HCT) KULIK, JAMES A UNIV OF CALIF, SAN DIEGO LA JOLLA, CA 92093 Surgical preplanning and patient outcomes

R01HS-06359-03 (HSR) COLOMBOTOS, JOHN COLUMBIA UNIV SCH OF PUB HLTH 600 WEST 168TH STREET NEW YORK, NY 10032 Physicians, nurses and AIDS--a national study

R01HS-06366-02 (HSR) PHELPS, CHARLES E UNIVERSITY OF ROCHESTER HARKNESS HALL ROCHESTER, NY 14627 A study of the causes of medical practice variations

R01HS-06391-01A1 (HCT) DOLAN, JAMES G UNIVERSITY OF ROCHESTER 1425 PORTLAND AVENUE ROCHESTER, NY 14621 The role of endoscopy in upper gastrointestinal bleeding

R01HS-06396-01A1 (HCT) SONNENBERG, FRANK A UMDNJ RWJ MEDICAL SCHOOL 97 PATERSON STREET NEW BRUNSWICK, NJ 08903 A clinical decision aid for genital chlamydia in women

R01HS-06404-02 (HSDG) HANLEY, BARBARA E UNIV OF MARYLAND SCH OF NURSIN 655 WEST LOMBARD STREET BALTIMORE, MD 21201 HIV home health care services--Survey and policy analysis

R01HS-06406-02 (HSR) PROCTOR, ENOLA K WASHINGTON UNIVERSITY ONE BROOKINGS DRIVE ST LOUIS, MO 63130 Adequacy of home care plans for chronically ill elderly

R01HS-06409-02 (HSR) GREEN, LEE A UNIVERSITY OF MICHIGAN 1018 FULLER ROAD ANN ARBOR, MI 48109-0708 Diagnostic uncertainty & variation in use of services

R01HS-06414-02 (HSDG) NEWHOUSE, JOSEPH P HARVARD MEDICAL SCHOOL 25 SHATTUCK STREET BOSTON, MA 02115 Costs in United States and Canadian hospitals

R01HS-06415-01A1 (HCT) RAPKIN, BRUCE D NEW YORK UNIVERSITY 6 WASH PL, RM 276 NEW YORK, NY 10003 Alternative assessments of functional status of AIDS patients

R01HS-06418-01A1 (HCT) CEBUL, RANDALL D METROHEALTH MEDICAL CENTER 3395 SCRANTON RD CLEVELAND, OH 44109 Computer assisted guidelines for admission testing

R01HS-06419-02 (HSDG) ROLPH, JOHN E RAND CORPORATION 1700 MAIN STREET/PO BOX 2138 SANTA MONICA, CA 90407-2138 Targeting negligence-prone physicians

R01HS-06420-02 (HSR) WASSON, JOHN H DARTMOUTH MEDICAL SCHOOL HANOVER, NH 03756 Assessing functional health status in clinical practice

P01HS-06432-02 (HSR) FREUND, DEBORAH A INDIANA UNIVERSITY 801 WEST MICHIGAN STREET INDIANAPOLIS, IN 46202-5152 Assessing and improving outcomes--Total knee replacements

R03HS-06441-02 (NSS) SOLOMON, LIZA JOHNS HOPKINS UNIVERSITY 615 NORTH WOLFE STREET BALTIMORE, MD 21205 Utilization and insurance among HIV positive drug users

R01HS-06443-02 (HSDG) LIPTON, HELENE L UNIV OF CALIF, SAN FRANCISCO 1326 THIRD AVENUE SAN FRANCISCO, CA 94143 Geriatric drug-related hospitalization

R01HS-06448-02 (HSDG) DUFFY, PAM R UNIVERSITY OF ARIZONA 3113 EAST FIRST STREET TUCSON, AZ 85716 Health care workers overcoming fear of HIV contagion

R01HS-06452-02 (HCT) LEE, THOMAS H, JR BRIGHAM & WOMEN'S HOSPITAL 75 FRANCIS STREET BOSTON, MA 02115 Outcomes of management strategies for chest pain

R01HS-06454-02 (HSDG) RAMSEY, PAUL G UNIVERSITY OF WASHINGTON SEATTLE, WA 98195 Primary care of patients with or at-risk for HIV

R01HS-06465-02 (HSR) TURNER, BARBARA J JEFFERSON MEDICAL COLLEGE 1025 WALNUT ST PHILADELPHIA, PA 19107 Consequences of patterns of provider care for AIDS

R01HS-06466-02 (HCT) MEHTA, RAVINDRA L UNIV OF CALIFORNIA, SAN DIEGO 225 DICKINSON STREET, H-781-D SAN DIEGO, CA 92103 CAVHD vs hemodialysis treatment in acute renal failure

R01HS-06468-02 (HCT) KAPOOR, WISHWA N UNIV OF PITTSBURGH 190 LOTHROP ST PITTSBURGH, PA 15261 Assessment of the variation and outcomes of pneumonia

R01HS-06469-02 (HCT) PALMER, R HEATHER HARVARD SCHOOL OF PUBLIC HLTH 677 HUNTINGTON AVENUE BOSTON, MA 02115 Measuring effectiveness of clinical management systems

R18HS-06473-01 (HSR) EISENBERG, MICKEY S KING CO EMERGENCY MEDICAL SERV 110 PREFONATAINE PLACE SOUTH SEATTLE, WA 98104 Outcomes following community interventions for acute MI

R01HS-06475-02 (HCT) BERRY, DONALD A DUKE UNIVERSITY DURHAM, NC 27706 Using historical data and public health decision making

P01HS-06481-02 (HSDG) SCHWARTZ, J SANFORD UNIVERSITY OF PENNSYLVANIA 3641 LOCUST WALK PHILADELPHIA, PA 19104-6218 Outcome assessment/ patients with biliary tract disease

P01HS-06481-02 0001 (HSDG) SCHWARTZ, JS Outcome assessment/ patients with biliary tract disease Review and analysis of the literature

P01HS-06481-02 0002 (HSDG) SCHWARTZ, JS Outcome assessment/ patients with biliary tract disease Clinical outcome and intervention impact

R01HS-06486-02 (HSDG) MC MAHON, LAURENCE F UNIVERSITY OF MICHIGAN 1500 E MEDICAL CENTER DRIVE ANN ARBOR, MI 48109-0376 Evaluation of clinical outcomes in small areas of Michigan

R01HS-06490-02 (HSDG) MELNICK, GLENN A THE RAND CORPORATION 1700 MAIN STREET 90407-2138 Market structure and hospital performance

R01HS-06491-02 (HSR) FRYBACK, DENNIS G UNIVERSITY OF WISCONSIN 1513 UNIVERSITY AVE MADISON, WI 53706 Longitudinal comparison of measures for health outcomes

R01HS-06494-02 (HSDG) BENNETT, CHARLES L DUKE UNIVERSITY 125 OLD CHEMISTRY BUILDING DURHAM, NC 27706 Variations in care of AIDS patients with 1st episode PCP

R01HS-06497-01 (HSR) DIKMEN, SUREYYA S UNIVERSITY OF WASHINGTON SEATTLE, WASH 98195 Head injury outcome

R01HS-06499-02 (HSDG) SLOAN, FRANK A VANDERBILT UNIVERSITY BOX 1503 STATION B NASHVILLE, TN 37235 Birth outcomes satisfaction with care and malpractice

P01HS-06503-02 (HSDG) PRYOR, DAVID B DUKE UNIVERSITY MEDICAL CTR BOX 3531 DURHAM, NC 27710 Outcome assessment program in ischemic heart disease

P01HS-06503-02 0001 (HSDG) PRYOR, DAVID B Outcome assessment program in ischemic heart disease Health care model -- The Duke and Minnesota groups

P01HS-06503-02 0002 (HSDG) PRYOR, DAVID B Outcome assessment program in ischemic heart disease Coronary heart disease -- Literature review

R01HS-06507-02 (NURS) SELBY, MAIJA L UNIVERSITY OF NORTH CAROLINA GREENSBORO, NC 27412-5001 Nursing interventions to improve EPSDT utilization

R01HS-06510-01 (HSDG) ODA, DOROTHY S UNIVERSITY OF CALIFORNIA SAN FRANCISCO , CA 94143-0608 Nursing effectiveness in preventive child health program

R01HS-06512-02 (HCT) IEZZONI, LISA I BETH ISRAEL HOSPITAL 330 BROOKLINE AVENUE BOSTON, MA 02215 Screening quality of care using administrative data

R01HS-06516-02 (HSDG) MARMOT, MICHAEL G UNIVERSITY COLLEGE LONDON 66-72 GOWER STREET LONDON, WC1E 6EA ENGLAND Social factors influencing medical outcome measures

R01HS-06527-01 (HSR) RUTLEDGE, ROBERT UNIVERSITY OF NORTH CAROLINA CB#7490 CHASE HALL CHAPEL HILL, NC 27599 The role of the rural hospital in the trauma care system

R01HS-06539-01 (HSDG) YEDIDIA, MICHAEL J NEW YORK UNIVERSITY 738 TISCH HALL NEW YORK, NY 10003 Determinants of house officers' responses to AIDS

R01HS-06540-01A1 (HSDG) BARRY, MICHAEL J MASSACHUSETTS GENERAL HOSPITAL FRUIT ST/BULFINCH 1 BOSTON, MA 02114 Randomized trial of SDP for patients with benign prostatic hyperplasia

R01HS-06544-01S1 (HSDG) KONRAD, THOMAS R UNIVERSITY OF NORTH CAROLINA CAMPUS BOX 7490/CHASE HALL CHAPEL HILL, NC 27599-7490 The rural HMSA physician retention study

R01HS-06545-01 (HSDG) TAYLOR, THOMAS R UNIVERSITY OF WASHINGTON SEATTLE, WA 98195 Breast cancer screening policy and practice

R01HS-06546-01 (HSR) KAHN, KATHERINE L THE RAND CORPORATION 1700 MAIN ST PO BOX 2138 SANTA MONICA, CA 90406-2138 Refining the measurement of quality of care

R01HS-06554-01A1 (HSR) MILGROM, PETER M UNIVERSITY OF WASHINGTON SEATTLE, WA 98195 Determinants of dental malpractice

R01HS-06567-01 (HSR) RICHARDS, TONI RAND CORPORATION 1700 MAIN ST, PO BOX 2138 SANTA MONICA, CA 90406-2138 Survival and health costs of very low birthweight babies

R01HS-06573-01 (HSDG) GOLDMAN, LEE BRIGHAM AND WOMEN'S HOSPITAL 75 FRANCIS STREET BOSTON, MA 02115 Effectiveness and outcomes of non-cardiac surgery

R01HS-06574-02 (HSDG) NEIGHBOR, WILLIAM E UNIVERSITY OF WASHINGTON SEATTLE, WA 98195 Primary care lipid practice and policy in hypertension

R18HS-06575-01 (HCT) BARNETT, GUY O MASSACHUSETTS GENERAL HOSPITAL 50 STANIFORD ST 5TH FLOOR BOSTON, MA 02114 Computer-based access to guidelines for clinical care

R01HS-06579-02 (HSDG) SIMINOFF, LAURA A WESTERN PSYCHIATRIC INST & CLI 3811 O'HARA ST PITTSBURGH, PA 15213 Organ procurement--Dilemmas of required request

R01HS-06580-01 (HSDG) ROBINSON, JAMES C UNIVERSITY OF CALIFORNIA BERKELEY, CA 94720 Adverse selection and risk rating in insurance markets

R01HS-06589-01A1 (HCT) RETCHIN, SHELDON M PROJECT HOPE CENTER TWO WISCONSIN CIRCLE CHEVY CHASE, MD 20815 Evaluation of practice variations and costs for cancer

R03HS-06627-01S1 (NSS) POERTNER, GRACE C S 620 REBECCA DRIVE ST. CHARLES, MO 63301 Medicaid policy and infant survivability

R03HS-06639-01 (NSS) EPSTEIN, MARK H NATIONAL ASSOC OF HLTH DATA OR 254B NORTH WASHINGTON STREET FALLS CHURCH, VA 22046 Linking health data bases--A blueprint for action

R03HS-06642-01 (NSS) GARDNER, LAURA B SAN JOSE STATE UNIVERSITY ONE WASHINGTON SQUARE SAN JOSE, CA 95192 Hospital and regional factors in C-section rate variations

R13HS-06647-01S1 (NSS) SHORTLIFFE, EDWARD H STANFORD UNIV SCH OF MEDICINE STANFORD, CA 94305-5479 Symposium and short courses on health outcomes research

R01HS-06655-02 (HSR) DANIS, MARION UNIVERSITY OF NORTH CAROLINA 5025A OLD CLINIC BLDG CHAPEL HILL, NC 27599-7110 Making choices and allocating resources near life's end

R01HS-06658-02 (HSDG) HUDSON, JAMES I UNIVERSITY OF MARYLAND 660 W REDWOOD ST BALTIMORE, MD 21201 Analysis/practices--Hip fracture repair and osteoarthritis

R01HS-06660-01 (HSR) CROYLE, ROBERT T UNIVERSITY OF UTAH SALT LAKE CITY , UT 84112 Cognitive errors concerning personal health

R01HS-06664-01A1 (HSDG) CAREY, TIMOTHY S UNIVERSITY OF NORTH CAROLINA CB#7490 CHASE HALL CHAPEL HILL, NC 27599-7490 Low back pain--Outcomes and efficiency of care

R01HS-06665-02 (HSDG) GREENFIELD, SHELDON NEW ENGLAND MEDICAL CENTER 750 WASHINGTON ST/BOX 345 BOSTON, MA 02111 Variations in the management and outcomes of diabetes

R01HS-06669-02 (OBM) BADER, JAMES D UNIVERSITY OF NORTH CAROLINA CHAPEL HILL, NC 27599-7450 Restorative oral health status outcome measure

R01HS-06670-02 (HCT) ATCHISON, KATHRYN A UCLA SCHOOL OF DENTISTRY LOS ANGELES, CA 90024-1668 Evalution of guidelines for prescribing dental X-rays

R03HS-06673-01 (NSS) TSEVAT, JOEL BETH ISRAEL HOSPITAL 330 BROOKLINE AVE BOSTON, MA 02215 Quality of life in HIV and primary care patients

PROJECT NO., ORGANIZATIONAL UNIT., INVESTIGATOR, ADDRESS, TITLE

R03HS-06675-01S1 (NSS) MC DANIEL, MARTHA D DARTMOUTH-HITCHCOCK MED CENTER 2 MAYNARD ST HANOVER, NH 03756 Health-related quality of life in intermittent claudication

R01HS-06680-01 (HSDG) HOLMAN, HALSTED R STANFORD UNIVERSITY 750 WELCH RD SUITE 305 PALO ALTO, CA 94304 Improving chronic disease by self-management education

R01HS-06685-01 (HSDG) OHSFELDT, ROBERT L UNIVERSITY OF ALABAMA UAB STATION, PICKWICK PL 118 BIRMINGHAM, AL 35294 Infant health and state abortion regulation

R01HS-06694-02 (HSDG) TOSTESON, ANNA BRIGHAM AND WOMEN'S HOSPITAL 75 FRANCIS STREET PBB-A2 BOSTON, MA 02115 Cost-effective management of HIV-related illnesses

R01HS-06696-01 (HSR) GELBERG, LILLIAN UNIVERSITY OF CALIFORNIA 10833 LE CONTE AVE LOS ANGELES, CA 90024-1683 Physical health and medical care in a homeless cohort

R18HS-06706-01 (HSRD) RICKETTS, THOMAS C UNIV OF NORTH CAROLINA CB#7490 CHASE HALL CHAPEL HILL, NC 27599-7490 Preparation of a geographical study of rural health

R01HS-06721-01 (HCT) CHAMPION, HOWARD R WASHINGTON HOSPITAL CENTER 110 IRVING STREET, N W WASHINGTON, DC 20010 Research in trauma outcomes using the MTOS database

R01HS-06728-01 (HCT) ROBERTS, MARK S NEW ENGLAND DEACONESS HOSPITAL ONE AUTUMN STREET BOSTON, MA 02215 Methodologic research in simulating complex disease

R01HS-06735-01 (HSR) MORLOCK, LAURA L JOHNS HOPKINS UNIVERSITY 624 NORTH BROADWAY BALTIMORE, MD 21205 Impact of risk management on liability claims experience

R01HS-06740-01 (HSDG) CLARKE, JOHN R MEDICAL COLLEGE OF PENNSYLVANI 3300 HENRY AVE PHILADELPHIA, PA 19129 Testing a decision aid for the management of injuries

R01HS-06742-01 (HCT) IEZZONI, LISA I BETH ISRAEL HOSPITAL 330 BROOKLINE AVENUE BOSTON, MA 02215 Evaluating severity adjustors for patient-outcome studies

R01HS-06752-01 (HSDG) DASHEIFF, RICHARD M UNIVERSITY OF PITTSBURGH 3515 FIFTH AVENUE PITTSBURGH, PA 15213 Comparison of surgery vs drug for epilepsy

R01HS-06754-01 (HSR) DAWSON, NEAL V CASE WESTERN RESERVE UNIVERSIT 3395 SCRANTON RD H331 CLEVELAND, OH 44109 A model of patients' preferences in serious illness

R18HS-06757-01A1 (HSR) GREENE, VERNON L SYRACUSE UNIVERSITY 313 MAXWELL HALL SYRACUSE, NY 13244-1090 Cost effectiveness in community care for the elderly

R01HS-06770-01 (HCT) ALBERTSEN, PETER C UNIV OF CONNECTICUT HLTH CTR 263 FARMINGTON AVENUE FARMINGTON, CT 06032-9984 Prostate cancer--A retrospective survival analyis

R13HS-06772-01 (HSRD) NICKENS, HERBERT W ASSOCIATION OF AMERICAN MED CO ONE DUPONT CIRCLE SUITE 200 WASHINGTON, DC 20036 Minority capacity building in health services research

R01HS-06775-01 (HSDG) SHAPIRO, MARTIN F UNIVERSITY OF CALIFORNIA 405 HILGARD AVENUE LOS ANGELES, CA 90024-1685 Outcomes of symptomatic episodes in HIV infection

R13HS-06776-01 (NSS) GEHSHAN, MICHELE L COUNCIL OF STATE GOVERNMENTS 444 N CAPITOL ST NW #240 WASHINGTON, DC 20001 Southern states malpractice reform dissemination conference

R13HS-06782-01S1 (NSS) WEISS, KEVIN B GEORGE WASHINGTON UNIVERSITY 2150 PENNSYLVANIA AVE NW WASHINGTON, DC 20037 Asthma care effectiveness--A proposed workshop

R01HS-06785-01 (HSDG) BERESFORD, SHIRLEY A UNIVERSITY OF WASHINGTON SEATTLE, WA 98195 Components of prenatal care and low birthweight

R01HS-06786-01 (HSR) HAYDEN, WILLIAM J JR UNIVERSITY OF MISSOURI 650 EAST 25TH STREET KANSAS CITY, MO 64108-2795 A new multicarrier database for dental care evaluation

R01HS-06795-01 (SSP) MOR, VINCENT BROWN UNIVERSITY BOX G PROVIDENCE, RI 02912 Functional change in older adults

R01HS-06798-01 (HSDG) CHONG, LAWRENCE P DOHENY EYE INSTITUTE 1355 SAN PABLO ST LOS ANGELES, CA 90033 Diabetic retinopathy education study II

R01HS-06799-01 (HSDG) CUPPLES, HOWARD P GEORGETOWN UNIVERSITY MED CTR 3800 RESERVOIR RD, NW WASHINGTON, DC 20007 Diabetic retinopathy education study I

R18HS-06801-02 (SRC) FERKETICH, SANDRA L UNIVERSITY OF ARIZONA TUCSON, AZ 85721 Multilevel practice model for rural hispanics

R01HS-06802-01 (HSDG) WELLS, KENNETH RAND CORPORATION 1700 MAIN STREET SANTA MONICA, CA 90406-2138 Variations in the process/outcomes of care/depression

R03HS-06803-01 (NSS) MAGOFFIN, CAROLE J Quality of care/skills and capacity building institute

R13HS-06806-01 (NSS) SECHREST, LEE UNIVERSITY OF ARIZONA UDALL CENTER/PUBLIC POLICY TUCSON, AZ 85721 Conference on research dissemination

R18HS-06813-01 (HSRD) KELLER, ROBERT B MAINE MEDICAL ASSESSMENT FDN 19 FAHEY STREET BELFAST, ME 04915 Outcomes dissemination--The Maine study group model

R01HS-06826-01 (HSR) TAVARES, MARY A FORSYTH DENTAL CENTER 140 THE FENWAY BOSTON, MA 02115 Developing a dental implant patient satisfaction survey

R01HS-06854-01 (HSDG) KILLINGSWORTH, MARK R RUTGERS UNIVERSITY NEW BRUNSWICK, NJ 08903 Labor supply and wages of registered nurses

R01HS-06856-01 (HCT) VICKREY, BARBARA RAND CORPORATION 1700 MAIN STREET, PO BOX 2138 SANTA MONICA, CA 90406-2138 Quality of life and seizures after epilepsy surgery

R01HS-06860-01 (HSDG) ESTES, CARROLL L UNIVERSITY OF CALIFORNIA 201 FILBERT ST SUIT 500 SAN FRANCISCO, CA 94133 Uncertified unlicensed homecare structure & performance

R01HS-06865-01 (HSDG) KJERULFF, KRISTEN H UNIVERSITY OF MARYLAND 660 WEST REDWOOD STREET BALTIMORE, MD 21201 Effectiveness and outcomes of hysterectomy

R01HS-06874-01 (HCT) ZAPKA, JANE M UNIVERSITY OF MASSACHUSETTS 313 ARNOLD HOUSE AMHERST, MA 01003 Validating women's self report of mammogram experience

R13HS-06876-01 (NSS) BULGER, ROGER J ASSOC OF ACADEMIC HEALTH CENTE 1400 16TH STREET NW WASHINGTON, DC 20036 Clinical evaluation in academic health centers

PROJECT NO., ORGANIZATIONAL UNIT., INVESTIGATOR, ADDRESS, TITLE

R13HS-06877-01 (NSS) HANFT, RUTH S INTL SOC/TECH ASSESS/HLTH CARE 600 21ST STREET, NW WASHINGTON, DC 20052 Maternity care--Science, guidelines, medical practice

R13HS-06878-01 (NSS) ROLPH, ELIZABETH S RAND CORPORATION 1700 MAIN STREET SANTA MONICA, CA 90406-2138 Changing health care delivery and liability law

R03HS-06879-01 (NSS) SAMET, JONATHAN M UNIV OF NEW MEXICO SCH OF MED 900 CAMINO DE SALUD, NE ALBUQUERQUE, NM 87131-5306 Regional variation in cancer treatment and mortality

R01HS-06897-01 (HSR) KAPLAN, SHERRIE H NEW ENGLAND MEDICAL CENTER 750 WASHINGTON ST BOX 345 BOSTON, MA 02111 Improving children's health outcomes--Negotiated care

R13HS-06902-01 (NSS) RAZZOOG, MICHAEL E UNIVERSITY OF MICHIGAN 1011 NORTH UNIVERSITY ANN ARBOR, MI 48109-1078 National workshop "Black dentistry in the 21st century"

R13HS-06904-01 (NSS) BECK, JOHN R PORTLAND, OR 97201-3098 Conference support for outcomes research

R03HS-06905-01 (SRC) GRAHAM, GLENN G STATE UNIVERSITY OF NEW YORK PO BOX 6000 BINGHAMPTON, NY 13902-6000 Demand uncertainty, reserve margins and hospital costs

R03HS-06906-01 (SRC) WEST, SUZANNE L UNIVERSITY OF NORTH CAROLINA CHAPEL HILL, NC 27599-7400 Assessing recall accuracy for prescription medications

R03HS-06910-01 (SRC) JONES, BETH A YALE UNIVERSITY 26 HIGH ST NEW HAVEN, CT 06510 Race differences in stage at diagnosis of breast cancer

R18HS-06912-01 (HSDG) SCHNEIDERMAN, LAWRENCE J UNIVERSITY OF CALIFORNIA M-022 LA JOLLA, CA 92093 Advance directives and communication in medical care

R03HS-06914-01 (SRC) PIETTE, JOHN BROWN UNIVERSITY BOX G PROVIDENCE, RI 02912 Staging AIDS prognoses--Extension of the Turner system

R03HS-06916-01 (SRC) LAOURI, MARIANNE RAND CORPORATION 1700 MAIN ST PO BOX 2138 SANTA MONICA, CA 90407-2138 Study of the under-utilization of coronary angiography

R03HS-06920-01 (SRC) SHEKELLE, PAUL G THE RAND CORPORATION 1700 MAIN STREET SANTA MONICA, CA 90407 Chiropractic--Use, cost and effectiveness

R03HS-06923-01 (SRC) MION, LORRAINE C 5634 COLUMBIA ROAD MEDINA, OH 44256 Use of physical restraints for elderly patients

R03HS-06925-01 (SRC) GRABBE, LINDA L GEORGIA STATE UNIVERSITY 304 VICKERS DR ATLANTA, GA 30307 Use of home care services in the last year of life

R03HS-06930-01 (SRC) BARBOSA, GAIL A 557 BLACKSTRAP RETREAT MOUNT PLEASANT, SC 29464 Life stress and preterm birth among urban black women

R03HS-06934-01 (SRC) HIRTH, RICHARD A RICHARD A HIRTH 3718 LOCUST WALK PHILADELPHIA, PA 19104-6297 Nursing home quality--Role of information and nonprofits

R03HS-06944-01 (SRC) HALL, S PAIGE 407 N GREGSON ST APT 3 DURHAM, NC 27701 Intimate relationship abuse perception scale

R03HS-06947-01 (SRC) LAU, LEE MIN UNIVERSITY OF UTAH SALT LAKE CITY, UT 84132 An expert system as a screen for quality of care

R03HS-06948-01 (SRC) LANGA, KENNETH M 1005 EAST 60TH ST APT 127 CHICAGO, IL 60637 Cost-containment and inter-payer differences in treatment

R03HS-06949-01 (SRC) LOWE, JOHN M UNIVERSITY OF ILLINOIS CHICAGO COLLEGE OF ARCHITECTURE CHICAGO, IL 60680 Gravity model analysis of hospital patient flows

R03HS-06950-01 (SRC) MCGOVERN, PATRICIA MARIE RESEARCH & TECHNOLOGY TRAN ADM 420 DELAWARE STREET SE MINNEAPOLIS, MN 55455 Parental leave policies and maternal and infant health

R03HS-06952-01 (SRC) DEVERS, KELLY JEAN NORTHWESTERN UNIVERSITY 1810 CHICAGO AVENUE EVANSTON, IL 60208 Triage of intensive care unit patients

R03HS-06954-01 (SRC) HODNICKI, DONNA R GEORGIA SOUTHERN UNIVERSITY 14 GREENWOOD AVE STATESBORO, GA 30458 Homeless women's experience and needs

R03HS-06961-01 (SRC) POWER, KAREN L BOSTON DEPT HEALTH HOSPITALS 1010 MASSACHUSETTS AVE BOSTON, MA 02118 Boston's case control studies of infant death and VLBW

R03HS-06962-01 (SRC) SCHOLLE, SARAH HUDSON JOHNS HOPKINS UNIV 615 N WOLFE BALTIMORE, MD 21205 Patterns of maternity care--Effects on cost and quality

R03HS-06964-01 (SRC) COMPTON, MARGARET A 81 PAINTER AVE WEST HAVEN, CT 06516 Perception drug preference and pain in drug users

R03HS-06971-01 (SRC) REYNOLDS, NANCY R 110 BRIGHTON RD SPRINGFIELD, OH 45504 Effects of case management on AIDS informal caregivers

R03HS-06978-01 (SRC) PERNEGER, THOMAS JOHNS HOPKINS UNIVERSITY 615 NORTH WOLFE ST, BOX 112 BALTIMORE, MD 21205 Case-control study of end-stage renal disease

R03HS-06980-01 (SRC) MACDONALD, STEVEN C UNIVERSITY OF WASHINGTON SCHOOL OF PUBLIC HEALTH SEATTLE, WA 98195 Quality of mortality data for injury control programs

R03HS-06984-01 (SRC) FINEMAN, NORMAN UNIVERSITY OF CALIFORNIA 1350 7TH AVE CSBS-318 SAN FRANCISCO, CA 94143-0850 Provider perception and management of difficult patients

R03HS-06985-01 (SRC) TRACY, SARAH W UNIVERSITY OF PENNSYLVANIA 215 SOUTH 34TH STREET PHILADELPHIA, PA 19104-6310 The medicalization of alcoholism in America 1870-1919

R13HS-06991-01 (NSS) HUGHES, ALISON M UNIVERSITY OF ARIZONA 3131 W SECOND STREET TUCSON, AZ 85716 Southwest border rural health research conference

R01HS-06992-01 (SRC) COHEN, STUART J AMC CANCER RESEARCH CENTER 1600 PIERCE STREET DENVER, CO 80214 A physician insurer's impact on early cancer detection

R01HS-06999-01 (HSR) HALL, JUDITH A NORTHEASTERN UNIV 360 HUNTINGTON AVE BOSTON, MA 02115 Modeling the health status-satisfaction relationship

R01HS-07018-01 (HCT) NYMAN, JOHN A UNIV OF MINNESOTA SCH OF PUB H BOX 729 UMHC MINNEAPOLIS, MN 55455 Prospective case-adjusted

payments--Profits and access
R01HS-07067-01 (HSDG) LOCALIO, ARTHUR R PENN STATE UNIV/HERSHEY MED CT PO BOX 850 HERSHEY, PA 17033 Clinical decision making on medical adverse events
R01HS-07074-01 (HSR) SATCHER, DAVID MEHARRY MEDICAL COLLEGE 1005 D.B. TODD BOULEVARD NASHVILLE, TN 37208 Minority health services research development
R01HS-07075-01 (HSDG) LYNN, DORCAS J GEORGE WASHINGTON UNIVERSITY 2150 PENNSYLVANIA AVE NW 5TH F WASHINGTON, DC 20037 Advance directives--Effectiveness of mandatory notice
R01HS-07076-01 (HSRD) GEMSON, DONALD COLUMBIA UNIV SCH OF PUBLIC HL 600 WEST 168TH ST NEW YORK, NY 10032 Dissemination of prevention guidelines to Harlem physicians
R01HS-07079-01 (HSRD) HELFRICK, JOHN F UNIVERSITY OF TEXAS 6516 JOHN FREEMAN AVE HOUSTON, TX 77030-3402 Dissemination of professional parameters of care
R18HS-07080-01 (HSRD) EISENBERG, JOHN M UNIVERSITY OF PENNSYLVANIA 3400 SPRUCE STREET PHILADELPHIA, PA 19104-4283 A structured criteria review process for four surgical procedures
R01HS-07084-01 (OBM) ANDERSEN, RONALD M UNIVERSITY OF CALIFORNIA SCHOOL OF PUBLIC HEALTH LOS ANGELES, CA 90024 Determinants of oral health in older persons
R01HS-07085-01 (HSDG) ANDERSON, GERARD F JOHNS HOPKINS UNIVERSITY 615 N WOLFE STREET BALTIMORE, MD 21205 Cataract extraction -- An international comparison
N01HV-08112-03 ( ) WILLIAMS, O DALE** International programs component for the CSCC
N01HV-18114-04 ( ) KNATTERUD, GENELL L** Clinical coordinating center for asymptomatic cardiac ischemia pilot
N01HV-18115-02 ( ) BOURASSA, MARTIAL G.** Clinical unit for asymptomatic cardiac ischemia pilot
N01HV-18116-02 ( ) ROGERS, WILLIAM J.** Clinical unit for asymptomatic cardiac ischemia pilot
N01HV-18117-02 ( ) DAVIES, RICHARD F.** Clinical unit for asymptomatic cardiac ischemia pilot
N01HV-18118-02 ( ) SIGNEY, GOTTLIEB O.** Clinical unit for asymptomatic cardiac ischemia pilot
N01HV-18119-03 ( ) PEPINE, CARL J** Clinical unit for asymptomatic cardiac ischemia pilot
N01HV-18120-03 ( ) COHEN, JEROME D** Clinical unit for asymptomatic cardiac ischemia pilot
N01HV-18121-02 ( ) GOLDSTEIN, SIDNEY** Clinical unit for asymptomatic cardiac ischemia pilot
N01HV-18122-02 ( ) MUELLER, HILTRUD** Clinical unit for asymptomatic cardiac ischemia pilot
N01HV-18123-02 ( ) PRATT, CRAIG M.** Clinical unit for asymptomatic cardiac ischemia pilot
N01HV-18124-02 ( ) SELWYN, ANDREW** Clinical unit for asymptomatic cardiac ischemia pilot
N01HV-18125-02 ( ) DEANFIELD, JOHN E.** Clinical unit for asymptomatic cardiac ischemia pilot
N01HV-53029-26 ( ) CLARKSON, THOMAS B** Nonhuman primate models of atherosclerosis
N01HV-53030-30 ( ) MC GILL, HENRY C. JR.** Nonhuman primate models of atherosclerosis/hypertension
N01HV-78100-08 ( ) DAVIS, KATHRYN B** Balloon valvuloplasty registry
N01HV-78102-06 ( ) BACHORIK, PAUL S** Lipoprotein and apolipoprotein determinations for NHANES
N01HV-88103-05 ( ) BUTLER, KENNETH C** Cardiac biventricular assist and replacement devices
N01HV-88104-04 ( ) KUNG, ROBERT T V** Cardiac biventricular assist and replacement devices
N01HV-88105-04 ( ) ROSENBERG, GERSON** Cardiac biventricular assist and replacement devices
N01HV-88106-04 ( ) OLSEN, DONALD B** Cardiac biventricular assist and replacement devices
N01HV-98107-04 ( ) PORTNER, PEER** Ventricular assist system production, support and evaluation
N01HV-98108-05 ( ) WEBER, STEPHEN J.** Physician attitudes/practices in cholesterol and CHD
K10LM-00092-01 (BLR) CHALMERS, THOMAS C TECHNOLOGY ASSESSMENT GROUP 677 HUNTINGTON AVE/RM L-7A BOSTON, MA 02115 Meta-analysis in biomedical applications
N01LM-03503-01 ( ) BOEHR, DIANE** Cataloging of audiovisual monographs and archival films
N01LM-03505-01 ( ) HAMBURG, CHERYL** Meharry medical college information access project
N01LM-03506-01 ( ) SIERRA, MARTHA-LUCIA** In-house conservation services
N01LM-03508-02 ( ) BLAINE, LOIS** Directory of biotechnology information resources
N01LM-03509-02 ( ) SIMS, FRED** Data entry of CRISP abstracts
N01LM-03510-01 ( ) SULLIVAN, CONSTANCE** Revising cataloging-in-publication records
N01LM-03511-11 ( ) FULTZ, MICHAEL** General software support
N01LM-03512-05 ( ) MISRA, DHARITRI** General software support
N01LM-03513-02 ( ) CHU, ROBERT L** Technical support services
N01LM-03514-06 ( ) BARRICK, DALE** Technical support services
N01LM-03515-05 ( ) TUTTLE, MARK** Support for metathesaurus expansion
N01LM-03516-01 ( ) FITCH, JOHN** Specific integrated circuit
N01LM-03520-01 ( ) PANGE, JENNY** Information support/NLM/toxicology files
R01LM-04174-06 (BLR) KALET, IRA J UNIVERSITY OF WASHINGTON MN111 UNIV HOSPITAL, RC-08 SEATTLE, WASH 98195 A cancer radiotherapy expert system using simulation
R01LM-04298-06 (BLR) SMITH, JACK W, JR OHIO STATE UNIVERSITY 410 W 10TH AVENUE COLUMBUS, OHIO 43210 Computer based pathology consultation submodule
G08LM-04392-06 (SRC) BROERING, NAOMI C GEORGETOWN UNIVERSITY 3900 RESERVOIR ROAD, N W WASHINGTON, D C 20007 Biotechnology and biomedical knowledge network
G08LM-04419-06 (SRC) CLAYTON, PAUL D COLUMBIA U CTR MED INFORMATICS 161 FT WASHINGTON AVE, AP-1310 NEW YORK, NY 10032 Phase III IAIMS implementation at Columbia-Presbyterian
P50LM-04492-07 (BLR) WALTERS, LEROY B GEORGETOWN UNIVERSITY 1437 37TH STREET, NW WASHINGTON, DC 20057 National reference center for bioethics literature
R01LM-04493-07 (BLR) SZOLOVITS, PETER MASSACHUSETTS INST/TECHNOLOGY 545 TECHNOLOGY SQUARE CAMBRIDGE, MA 02139 An artificial intelligence clinical decision making
R01LM-04572-04A1 (BLR) GREENES, ROBERT A BRIGHAM & WOMEN'S HOSPITAL 75 FRANCIS STREET BOSTON, MA 02115 Investigations in knowledge management
R01LM-04583-06 (BLR) ELSTEIN, ARTHUR S UNIVERSITY OF ILLINOIS 808 S WOOD STREET CHICAGO, IL 60612-4325 Expert and novice intensive care decision making
R01LM-04605-05 (SRC) SIEVERT, MARYELLEN UNIV OF MISSOURI 104 STEWART HALL COLUMBIA, MO 65211 Full-text retrieval of medical journal literature
G08LM-04613-05 (BLR) STOUGHTON, W VICKERY DUKE UNIVERSITY MEDICAL CENTER BOX 3900 DURHAM, NC 27710 IAIMS pilot implementation
R01LM-04622-04 (BLR) MILLER, RANDOLPH A UNIV OF PITTSBURGH, SCH OF MED 190 LOTHROP STREET PITTSBURGH, PA 15261 Developing QMR knowledge base into a resource
R29LM-04667-04 (BLR) O'CONNOR, GERALD T DEPARTMENT OF MEDICINE DARTMOUTH-HITCHCOCK MED CTR HANOVER, NH 03756 Epidemiologic systems in cardiovascular decision making
R29LM-04692-05 (BLR) EZQUERRA, NORBERTO F GEORGIA INSTITUTE OF TECHNOLOG CRB 323 ATLANTA, GEORGIA 30332 Knowledge-based system for cardiac image interpretation
R01LM-04696-05 (BLR) HAYNES, ROBERT B MCMASTER UNIVERSITY 1200 MAIN STREET WEST HAMILTON, ONT L8N 3Z5 CANADA Evaluation of online characteristics and clinical use
R29LM-04707-05 (BLR) PERLIN, MARK W CARNEGIE-MELLON UNIV COMPUTER SCI DEPT PITTSBURGH, PA 15213 Contrast--a computer consultant for optimal nmr imging
R29LM-04715-04 (SSS) BERGERON, BRYAN P BRIGHAM & WOMEN'S HOSPITAL 75 FRANCIS STREET BOSTON, MA 02115 Computer simulation in clinical medicine
R01LM-04836-03 (BLR) HERZENBERG, LEONORE STANFORD UNIV MED CENTER STANFORD, CA 94305-5120 FACS-Penguin--An expert workstation for flow cytometry
R01LM-04843-04 (BLR) FRIEDMAN, CHARLES P U. OF N. CAROLINA AT CHAPEL HI CB#7530 OED CHAPEL HILL, NC 27599-7530 Information and cognition in medical education
R01LM-04896-04 (GNM) MERRIAM, JOHN R UNIVERSITY OF CALIFORNIA 405 HILGARD AVENUE LOS ANGELES, CALIF 90024 Cloned DNA by chromosome location
R01LM-04901-03 (SSS) WEINER, DORA B UNIVERSITY OF CALIFORNIA 405 HILGARD AVE LOS ANGELES, CA 90024-1722 Philippe pinel--Clinician of the french revolution
G08LM-04905-04 (BLR) GORRY, G ANTHONY BAYLOR COLLEGE OF MEDICINE ONE BAYLOR PLAZA HOUSTON, TX 77030 Phase III IAIMS at Baylor College of Medicine
G08LM-04915-02 (BLR) PEARSE, WARREN H AMERICAN COLLEGE OF OB/GYN 409 12TH STREET, SW WASHINGTON, DC 20024-2188 ACOG intergrated academic information management system--Model phase
R01LM-04925-03 (BLR) ROSSE, CORNELIUS SCHOOL OF MEDICINE UNIV OF WASHINGTON, SM-20 SEATTLE, WA 98195 Image-based knowledge system in anatomy
R01LM-04958-04 (SRC) MARKLEY, JOHN L UNIVERSITY OF WISCONSIN 420 HENRY MALL MADISON, WIS 53706 Creation & analysis of archival protein NMR database
R01LM-04965-02S1 (SRC) MARR, THOMAS G COLD SPRING HARBOR LABORATORY P O BOX 100 COLD SPRING HARBOR, N Y 11724 Computer representation and reduction of chromosome mapping data
R01LM-04969-04 (BLR) PEARSON, WILLIAM R UNIVERSITY OF VIRGINIA JORDAN HALL, BOX 440 CHARLOTTESVILLE, VA 22908 Comparison of protein sequences and structures
R01LM-04971-04 (BLR) ROBERTS, RICHARD J COLD SPRING HARBOR LABORATORY POST OFFICE BOX 100 COLD SPRING HARBOR, NY 11724 Functional motifs in biological sequences
R01LM-05005-03 (BLR) DANIELS, NORMAN TUFTS UNIVERSITY DEPT OF PHILOSOPHY MEDFORD, MA 02155 Justice & AIDS policy
R01LM-05007-02 (BLR) JAFFE, CONRADE C YALE UNIVERSITY SCH OF MEDICIN 333 CEDAR STREET NEW HAVEN, CT 06510 Indexing of electronic medical image database
G08LM-05012-02 (BLR) EATON, ELIZABETH DIRECTOR, HEALTH SCIENCES LIB SACKLER 6, 136 HARRISION AVE BOSTON, MA 02111 Iaims planning at Tufts University
R01LM-05044-03 (BLR) MILLER, PERRY L YALE UNIV SCH OF MED PO BOX 3333 333 CEDAR ST NEW HAVEN, CT 06510 Parallel computation and molecular genetics
G08LM-05047-04 (BLR) JACKNOWITZ, LINDA WEST VIRGINIA UNIVERSITY MORGANTOWN, WV 26506 Wv consult: a computer-based health information network
G08LM-05050-02 (BLR) FULLER, SHERRILYNNE UNIVERSITY OF WASHINGTON SB-55 SEATTLE, WA 98195 Iaims planning U Washington health sciences center
R01LM-05067-02 (SSS) HORNSTEIN, GAIL A MOUNT HOLYOKE COLLEGE SOUTH HADLEY, MA 01075 Fromm-Reichmann and the treatment of psychosis, 1920-55
R29LM-05074-02S1 (BLR) JAMIESON, PATRICK W UNIVERSITY OF KANSAS MED CTR 39TH AND RAINBOW BLVD KANSAS CITY, KS 66160-7314 Advancing medical explanatory systems
R01LM-05094-03 (BLR) STORMO, GARY D UNIVERSITY OF COLORADO CAMPUS BOX 347/MCD BIOLOGY BOULDER, CO 80309 Automated feature detection for biological sequences
R01LM-05102-03 (BLR) MOULT, JOHN CTR FOR ADV RES BIOTECH/CARB 9600 GUDELSKY DR ROCKVILLE, MD 20850 Comparative modeling of protein structure
R01LM-05104-03 (BLR) BUCHANAN, BRUCE G UNIVERSITY OF PITTSBURGH 206 MINERAL INDUSTRIES BLDG PITTSBURGH, PA 15260 An intelligent biomedical assistant

PROJECT NO., ORGANIZATIONAL UNIT., INVESTIGATOR, ADDRESS, TITLE

G08LM-05105-02 (BLR) BOWDEN, VIRGINIA M UNIVERSITY OF TEXAS 7703 FLOYD CURL DRIVE SAN ANTONIO, TX 78284-7940 FLIS (LIS users group) planning & development
R01LM-05110-03 (BLR) MILLER, WEBB C PENNSYLVANIA STATE UNIVERSITY UNIVERSITY PARK, PA 16802 Algorithms for analyzing biosequence data
R01LM-05118-03 (BLR) WEITH, H LEE DEPARTMENT OF BIOCHEMISTRY PURDUE UNIVERSITY WEST LAFAYETTE, IN 47907 Algorithms for macromolecular structure analysis
R01LM-05125-02 (BLR) BERNER, ETA S UNIVERSITY OF ALABAMA/BIRMINGH 401 COMMUNITY HLTH SVCS BLDG BIRMINGHAM, AL 35294 A method to test diagnostic decision support software
R01LM-05139-02 (SSS) JARCHO, SAUL 11 WEST 69TH STREET NEW YORK, NY 10023 Torti and Frassoni--Manuscript consultations on fever
R01LM-05140-02 (SSS) YOUNG, JAMES H 272 HEATON PARK DRIVE DECATUR, GA 30030 Enforcing the 1906 food and drugs act, 1907-1940
G07LM-05145-01S1 (BLR) HOLST, RUTH COLUMBIA HOSPITAL 2025 EAST NEWPORT AVENUE MILWAUKEE, WI 53211 An end-user search using CD-ROM MEDLINE
G07LM-05146-01S1 (BLR) HORNER, MARCIA E KOOTENAI MEDICAL CENTER 2003 LINCOLN WAY COEUR D'ALENE, ID 83814 Enhanced information access for rural north Idaho
G07LM-05151-02 (BLR) BOTHMER, A JAMES UNIVERSITY OF NEBRASKA MED CTR 42ND & DEWEY AVENUE OMAHA, NE 68105 Omaha consortium
R29LM-05157-02 (BLR) MUSEN, MARK A STANFORD UNIVERSITY MEDICAL CT STANFORD, CA 94305-5479 Custom-tailored tools for protocol-knowledge management
G08LM-05160-02 (BLR) GERSTNER, PATSY CLEVELAND MEDICAL LIBRARY ASSO 11000 EUCLID AVENUE CLEVELAND, OHIO 44106 Machine readable cataloguing medical artifacts
G08LM-05168-02 (BLR) LEMKAU, HENRY L, JR UNIVERSITY OF MIAMI PO BOX 016950 MIAMI, FL 33101 Southeast Florida AIDS information network
R01LM-05175-02 (HSR) ADAY, LU ANN UT HEALTH SCIENCE CTR AT HOUST PO BOX 20186 HOUSTON, TX 77225 Book--Health and health care of vulnerable populations
R01LM-05189-02 (BLR) ABATE, MARIE A WEST VIRGINIA UNIVERSITY 1124-D HEALTH SCIENCES NORTH MORGANTOWN, WV 26506 Pharmacist use of online information services
G08LM-05197-02 (BLR) FRYER, REGINA K YALE UNIVERSITY SCHOOL OF MED 333 CEDAR STREET NEW HAVEN, CT 06510 An integrated approach to medical information services
R01LM-05200-02 (BLR) BARNETT, GUY O MASSACHUSETTS GENERAL HOSPITAL 50 STANIFORD STREET BOSTON, MA 02114 Problem-based knowledge access
G07LM-05201-01A1 (BLR) WRIGHT, BARBARA A FAYETTEVILLE AHEC 1601 OWEN DRIVE FAYETTEVILLE, NC 28304 S. Central health information network information access grant
R01LM-05202-01A1 (BLR) WARNER, HOMER R UNIVERSITY OF UTAH SALT LAKE CITY, UT 84132 Impact of an expert system on the practice of medicine
P41LM-05205-08 (SSS) SMITH, TEMPLE F BOSTON UNIVERSITY 38 CUMMINGTON STREET BOSTON, MA 02215 Molecular biology computer resource and research program
P41LM-05205-08 0001 (SSS) GOLDSTEIN, LARRY Molecular biology computer resource and research program Comparative genome maps
P41LM-05205-08 0002 (SSS) WEBSTER, TERESA Molecular biology computer resource and research program Protein functional pattern descriptor developments
P41LM-05205-08 9001 (SSS) BENSON, DENNIS Molecular biology computer resource and research program Core--Callaborative project on IRX
P41LM-05205-08 9002 (SSS) SMITH, TEMPLE Molecular biology computer resource and research program Core--Development of search tools
P41LM-05205-08 9003 (SSS) DRAKE, NEIL Molecular biology computer resource and research program Core--Assembly of DNA regulatory sites database
P41LM-05205-08 9004 (SSS) SMITH, TEMPLE Molecular biology computer resource and research program Core--Development of integrated software analysis report
P41LM-05205-08 9005 (SSS) WEBSTER, TERESA Molecular biology computer resource and research program Minimum protein functional pattern description extensions
P41LM-05205-08 9006 (SSS) SMITH, RANDALL Molecular biology computer resource and research program Machine learning and parallel computer technology
P41LM-05205-08 9007 (SSS) SCHMELZER, MICHAEL Molecular biology computer resource and research program Alternate and improved secondary structure prediction
P41LM-05205-08 9008 (SSS) SMITH, RANDALL Molecular biology computer resource and research program Proposed enhancements to pattern library and search tool
P41LM-05205-08 9009 (SSS) ZHU, QINGLIN Molecular biology computer resource and research program Viral evolution studies--Core
P41LM-05205-08 9010 (SSS) KLOSE, KATHLEEN Molecular biology computer resource and research program SAM tutorial under teach/advise-Core
P41LM-05205-08 9011 (SSS) GUIGO, RODERIC Molecular biology computer resource and research program Statistical evaluation of pattern libraries--Core
P41LM-05206-08 (SSS) LEDLEY, ROBERT S NATIONAL BIOMEDICAL RES FDN 3900 RESERVOIR ROAD N W WASHINGTON, D C 20007 Protein identification resource
R24LM-05207-07 (BLR) LAWRENCE, CHARLES B BAYLOR COLLEGE OF MEDICINE 1 BAYLOR PLAZA HOUSTON, TX 77030 The molecular biology information resource
P41LM-05208-18S1 (SSS) SHORTLIFFE, EDWARD H STANFORD UNIV MED CTR STANFORD, CA 94305-5479 Medical experimental computer resource
R01LM-05217-01 (BLR) WEBBER, BONNIE L UNIVERSITY OF PENNSYLVANIA 200 S 33RD STREET PHILADELPHIA, PA 19104-6389 Responsive planning for multiple goal satisfaction
G07LM-05238-01A1 (BLR) RODY, NANCY UNIVERSITY OF NEVADA, RENO RENO, NV 89557 Nevada Health Science Information Access Program
G07LM-05245-01 (BLR) AVEN, LAURALEE LUTHERAN HOSPITAL OF INDIANA I 3024 FAIRFIELD AVE FORT WAYNE, IN 46807 NEIHSL--Strengthening the network with basic technology
G08LM-05246-01 (BLR) VAN DEN TOP, JERALDINE J ALASKA HEALTH SCIENCES LIBRARY 3211 PROVIDENCE DRIVE ANCHORAGE, AK 99508 Rural Alaska health information access project
G07LM-05256-01A1 (BLR) NIMS, JUDITH C MASSACHUSETTS EYE-EAR INFIRMAR 243 CHARLES ST BOSTON, MA 02114 Infrastructure for a shared integrated library system
R29LM-05260-01 (BLR) LINCOLN, MICHAEL J UNIVERSITY OF UTAH SALT LAKE CITY, UT 84112 Knowledge engineering tools to improve knowledge bases
G08LM-05261-01 (BLR) ROMOFF, JEFFREY A UNIVERSITY OF PITTSBURGH 190 LOTHROP STREET PITTSBURGH, PA 15261 University of Pittsburgh IAIMS phase II
R29LM-05266-02 (BLR) SONNENBERG, FRANK A UMDNJ RWJ MEDICAL SCHOOL 97 PATERSON STREET NEW BRUNSWICK, NJ 08903 An intelligent decision system for lung disease in AIDS
R29LM-05268-02 (BLR) GIOIA, PETER J 1180 WELCH RD #831 PALO ALTO, CA 94304 A bilingual diagnostic system
G07LM-05275-01 (BLR) KINGSBURY, MILDRED E MARQUETTE GENERAL HOSPITAL, IN 420 WEST MAGNETIC ST MARQUETTE, MI 49855 General Library/Clinic Fax Transmission Project
R29LM-05278-01 (BLR) MAVROVOUNIOTIS, MICHAEL L UNIVERSITY OF MARYLAND A.V. WILLIAMS BUILDING (#115) COLLEGE PARK, MD 20742 Qualitative analysis of metabolic pathways
R01LM-05279-01 (SSS) APPLE, RIMA D 2013 MADISON STREET MADISON, WI 53711 The commercialization of vitamins 1920s to 1980s
R01LM-05281-01 (HSRD) JENISTA, JERRI A UNIVERSITY OF MICHIGAN 1500 E MEDICAL CTR DR ANN ARBOR, MI 48109-0244 Intercountry adoption -- A medical guide
R29LM-05284-01 (BLR) SITTIG, DEAN F YALE UNIVERSITY SCH OF MEDICIN PO BOX 3333, 333 CEDAR STREET NEW HAVEN, CT 06510 Intelligent real-time information synthesis for monitors
G08LM-05286-01 (BLR) LOVE, ERIKA UNIVERSITY OF NEW MEXICO NORTH CAMPUS ALBUQUERQUE, NM 87131 Interactive medical information system in New Mexico medical center
G07LM-05295-01 (BLR) SCOTT, KATHLEEN J DUBOIS REGIONAL MEDICAL CENTER 100 HOSPITAL AVENUE DUBOIS, PA 15801 Dubois computer network
R01LM-05299-01 (BLR) BUCHANAN, BRUCE G INTELLIGENT SYSTEMS LABORATORY PITTSBURGH, PA 15260 Explanation in the clinical setting
R29LM-05307-01 (BLR) HERSH, WILLIAM R OREGON HEALTH SCIENCES UNIV 3181 SW SAM JACKSON PARK ROAD PORTLAND, OR 97201 Saphire--A concept-based approach to information retrieval
R01LM-05310-01 (SSS) GAMBLE, VANESSA N UNIVERSITY OF WISCONSIN 1300 UNIVERSITY AVE MADISON, WI 53706 The black hospital movement 1920-1945
G07LM-05312-01 (BLR) ZALUDEK, SUSAN K JC BLAIR MEMORIAL HOSPITAL WARM SPRINGS AVENUE HUNTINGDON, PA 16652 J.C. Blair Memorial Hospital library computer system
R01LM-05320-01 (SSS) KIPLE, KENNETH F BOWLING GREEN STATE UNIVERSITY BOWLING GREEN, OH 43403 History and culture of human nutrition
R01LM-05323-01 (BLR) HAUG, PETER J LDS HOSPITAL 8TH AVENUE AND C STREET SALT LAKE CITY, UT 84143 Development of a semantic parser for medical text
R01LM-05326-01 (SSS) LEDERER, SUSAN E PENNSYLVANIA STATE UNIVERSITY PO BOX 850 HERSHEY, PA 17033 American medical research & antivivisection 1900-1990
G08LM-05329-01 (BLR) PANKO, WALTER B UNIVERSITY OF MICHIGAN 1414 CATHERINE ROAD ANN ARBOR, MI 48109-0704 IAIMS model development--Phase II
R01LM-05334-01 (SSS) STOWE, STEVEN M INDIANA UNIVERSITY BLOOMINGTON, IN 47402 Doing physic--Southern doctors and their work, 1800-1880
G07LM-05338-01 (BLR) SNODGRASS-PILLA, LYNN SACRED HEART HOSPITAL 1430 DEKALB ST NORRISTOWN, PA 19401 Sacred Heart Hospital library automation project
R01LM-05339-01 (SSS) BAKER, JEFFREY P DUKE UNIVERSITY MEDICAL CENTER BOX 3675 DURHAM, NC 27713 A history of the premature infant nursery in the U.S.
G07LM-05341-01 (BLR) MANGINO, ARLENE D CLARA MAASS MEDICAL CENTER FRANKLIN AVE BELLEVILLE, NJ 07109 CMMC library's business information service
R43LM-05343-01 (SSS) KNOTT, GARY D CIVILIZED SOFTWARE INC 7735 OLD GEORGETOWN RD #410 BETHESDA, MD 20814 Probability and statistics functions for MLAB
R43LM-05349-01 (SSS) ROSS, DONALD R LIFESTYLE ENHANCEMENT SYSTEMS 7670 EAST BROADWAY, SUITE 208 TUCSON, AZ 85710 Computer-based system to determine functional capacity
G07LM-05365-01 (BLR) COLGLAZIER, MERLE L RICHMOND MEMORIAL HOSPITAL 1300 WESTWOOD AVE RICHMOND, VA 23227 Centralized automation for a two-branch hospital library
G07LM-05377-01 (BLR) RANKIN, JOCELYN A MERCER UNIVERSITY MACON, GA 31207 Gain hospital libraries' local automation project
G07LM-05390-01 (BLR) SKOLNIK, DEBORAH C SUBURBAN HOSPITAL 8600 OLD GEORGETOWN RD BETHESDA, MD 20814 Integrated library system project with remote access
G07LM-05391-01 (BLR) BLOWERS, VIRGINIA K NAVAPACHE HOSPITAL 2200 SHOW LOW LAKE ROAD SHOW LOW, AZ 85901 Access to NLM Library information
N01LM-13501-00 ( ) DOWNING, ARTHUR** National Network of Libraries of Medicine
N01LM-13502-02 ( ) CUNNINGHAM, DIANA** National Network of Libraries of Medicine
N01LM-13503-00 ( ) WEISE, FRIEDA O** National Network of Libraries of Medicine
N01LM-13504-00 ( ) WOELFL, NANCY** National Network of Libraries of Medicine
N01LM-13505-00 ( ) LYDERS, RICHARD** National Network of Libraries of Medicine
N01LM-13506-00 ( ) FULLER, SHERRILYNNE** National network of libraries of medicine
N01LM-13507-00 ( ) BUNTING, ALISON** National network of libraries of medicine

PROJECT NUMBER LISTING

PROJECT NO., ORGANIZATIONAL UNIT., INVESTIGATOR, ADDRESS, TITLE

N01LM-13508-00 ( ) ARCARI, RALPH** National network of libraries of medicine
N01LM-13509-00 ( ) PIZZIMENTI, BRUCE** High definition videodisc player/monitor
N01LM-13510-00 ( ) WHITE, JOHN** Chemical abstracts service licenses and royalties
N01LM-13511-00 ( ) SILVERMAN, JAY** Task management and software enhancement of Application Services Branch
N01LM-13512-00 ( ) HELVEY, WILLIAM** Biomonthly update for Grateful Med users, Gratefully Yours
N01LM-13513-00 ( ) PADGETT, DUDLEY** Statistical software and support services
N01LM-13514-00 ( ) MC CORMICK, RICK** Software upgrade for IBM MVS system
N01LM-13515-00 ( ) LINDSEY, THOMAS K** Shelving of general and reference collections
N01LM-13516-00 ( ) GORRY, ANTHONY G** Grateful medr network server
N01LM-13517-00 ( ) TAYLOR, MARY** Keyboarding of Medlars user information and change of address information
N01LM-13518-00 ( ) WELLS, INA G** Processing limited cataloging records prepared by the Library of Congress
N01LM-13519-00 ( ) SULLIVAN, CONSTANCE** Limited cataloging of foreign language monographs
N01LM-13520-00 ( ) SULEIMAN, JOANN D** Limited cataloging of foreign language monographs
N01LM-13521-02 ( )** NLM computer systems maintenance
N01LM-13522-00 ( ) KELLY, EDWARD I** Indexing of biomedical literature
N01LM-13523-00 ( ) KLEINSTEIN, BRUCE** Indexing of biomedical literature
N01LM-13524-00 ( ) KESSLER, S SIM** Indexing of biomedical literature
N01LM-13525-01 ( ) HILL, GENE E** Specialized data entry for GenInfo databases
N01LM-13526-01 ( ) HUFF, STEVEN** Multimodality radiological image processing system
N01LM-13527-02 ( ) CASEY, STEPHEN M** NLM Toxnet system support
N01LM-13528-01 ( ) ORIGONI, REGINA** Hazardous Substances Data Bank
N01LM-13529-00 ( ) HOWARD, PHILLIP** Environmental fate and exposure information
N01LM-13530-01 ( ) REID, DARRELL** Maintenance and enhancement of NCBI and LHNCBC computing
N01LM-13531-00 ( ) WALTERS, LEROY** Support for the Bioethicsline database
N01LM-13532-00 ( ) SILVERMAN, JOHN** Design a relational database software package to track grants awarded by NCHGR
N01LM-13533-00 ( ) STERN, MARVIN** Trademark & copyright legal services for Department of Health & Human Services
N01LM-13534-00 ( ) BROWN, SUSAN** Trademark & copyright legal services for Department of Health & Human Services
N01LM-13535-00 ( ) MILLER, RANDOLPH** Unified medical language system (UMLS) research and development
N01LM-13536-00 ( ) CIMINO, JAMES** Unified medical language system research and development
N01LM-13537-00 ( ) MILLER, PERRY** Unified medical language system research and development support
N01LM-13538-00 ( ) BARNETT, G OCTO** Unified medical language system research and development
N01LM-13539-00 ( ) GREENES, ROBERT G** Unified medical language system (UMLS) research and development
N01LM-13540-00 ( ) KIESEL, BRUCE** Biosis/Toxline component
N01LM-13541-00 ( ) HAHN, ANN** Preservation microfilming--Bibliographic control and volume preparation
N01LM-13542-00 ( ) DELCERVO, DIANE** Preservation microfilming
N01LM-13543-00 ( ) SPITZER, VICTOR** Visible human project
N01LM-13544-00 ( ) PERLMAN, WILLIAM** Technical services system (TESS) software development
N01LM-13545-00 ( ) COATES, VIVIAN** Health services research support
N01LM-13546-00 ( ) RODGERS, DON** CD ROM write once system
N01LM-13547-00 ( ) STEWART, MCDONALD** Inspection of preservation microfilm
N01LM-13548-00 ( ) RUZICKA, GLEN** Rare book conservation
N01LM-13549-00 ( ) RUSSELL, ANN** Rare book conservation and microfilming
N01LM-53523-06 ( ) KOKIKO, ELAINE** NLM education/outreach program to health professionals
N01LM-63505-14 ( ) MILLER, JEAN** Regional medical library services for region 5
N01LM-63521-09 ( ) MAUCHER, PETER** Preservation microfilming
N01LM-63529-15 ( ) TO BE APPOINTED** Equipment upgrade
N01LM-73509-07 ( ) BECKELHEIMER, MEL** 3084 Multi-processor title upgrade
N01LM-83502-24 ( ) CASEY, STEVE** NLM TOXINET system support
N01LM-83507-03 ( ) KLEINSTEIN, BRUCE** Indexing of biomedical literature
N01LM-83508-07 ( ) DAY, MELVIN** Indexing of biomedical literature
N01LM-83509-06 ( ) KESSLER, SHEILA** Indexing of biomedical literature
N01LM-83511-08 ( ) PAGE, NORBERT P** Hazardous substances data bank
N01LM-83517-03 ( ) GOSHORN, JEANNE** BIOSIS/TOXLINE component
N01LM-83525-04 ( ) WELLS, INA G** Limited cataloging of language monographs
N01LM-83527-11 ( ) AMACHER, RICHARD** Support services for the National Library of Medicine
N01LM-83531-03 ( ) LUCIER, RICHARD E** Online reference works (ORW) in medicine

PROJECT NO., ORGANIZATIONAL UNIT., INVESTIGATOR, ADDRESS, TITLE

N01LM-83532-26 ( ) FULTZ, MICHAEL J** General software support
N01LM-84716-16 ( ) HENDERSON, EARL** Technical services for LHNCBC
N01LM-93502-08 ( ) BROOME, PAMELA** DHHS value-added network services
N01LM-93503-11 ( ) SMITH, MARJORIE** DHHS value-added network services
N01LM-93504-05 ( ) CAPALBO, FRANK J** DHHS value-added network services
N01LM-93505-06 ( ) HOFFMAN, GARY** DHHS value-added network services
N01LM-93508-02 ( ) BROWN, CARTER N** Chemical abstracts services registry service
N01LM-93509-05 ( ) COLBERT, MELISSA R** Editing and keyboarding services
N01LM-93510-04 ( )** Technical support for audio & video equipment systems
N01LM-93511-02 ( ) HALKETT, IAN W** Non-colatile high-performance storage unit
N01LM-93512-15 ( ) MARTI, BERNSTEIN** Conference management and related technical and resource support services
N01LM-93513-03 ( ) POPE, ANDREW** Program advisory services
N01LM-93514-10 ( ) DEGRAFFENREID, LINDA** Conference management and related technical and resource support
N01LM-93518-07 ( ) MC CARN, DAVIS B** GRATEFUL MED software development and maintenance support
N01LM-93519-07 ( ) KOSER, UGER** GRATEFUL MED software development and maintenance support
N01LM-93520-05 ( ) MC CARN, DAVIS B** Grateful med software dev/apple macintosh component
N01LM-93521-03 ( ) EDER, WARREN** NLM local area network
N01LM-93523-04 ( ) BERGER, JEANNE** Binding preparation
N01LM-93524-04 ( ) SILVERMAN, JOHN** General software support and documentation of existing computer systems
N01LM-93525-04 ( ) MC CLURE, JOAN** Addition of gene sequence data to MEDLINE records
N01LM-93526-03 ( ) WELLS, EUGENE** Chemical structure search and display system
N01LM-93528-05 ( ) KILDUFF, MICHAEL** Inspection of 35mm microfilm
N01LM-93529-02 ( ) BENJAMIN, TOM** Off site archival microfilm storage
N01LM-93530-06 ( ) FULTZ, MICHAEL** Biotechnology information software support
N01LM-93531-04 ( ) KAELBER, NANCY** A bibliographic teratology/development toxicology data
N01LM-93532-03 ( ) KODAMA, VICKI** Minority enhancement in research grants (MERG) video
N01MH-00003-00 ( ) NATL ACADEMY OF SCIENCES** 2101 CONSTITUTION AVENUE, N W WASHINGTON, D C 20418 Research associate program in neuroscience
K05MH-00004-17 (MHK) DAVIS, MICHAEL CONNECTICUT MENTAL HEALTH CTR 34 PARK ST NEW HAVEN, CT 06508 Neurochemical modulation of acoustic startle reflex
N01MH-00005-00 ( ) SRA TECHNOLOGIES INC** 4700 KING STREET SUITE 300 ALEXANDRIA, VA 22302 Data management center for NIMH molecular genetics project
N01MH-00007-00 ( ) RESEARCH BIOCHEMICALS, INC** ONE STRATHMORE ROAD NATICK, MASSACHUSETTS 01760 Synthesis of chemical compounds
N01MH-00013-00 ( ) UNIV SOUTHERN CALIF HLTH SCIENCES CAMPUS** 1975 ZONAL AVENUE, KAM B-34 LOS ANGELES, CA 90033 Efficacy of peptide T on HIV-positive patients with cognitive disorders
K05MH-00058-16 (MHK) ZIGMOND, MICHAEL J UNIVERSITY OF PITTSBURGH PITTSBURGH, PA 15260 Biochemistry of behavioral recovery after CNS damage
K05MH-00078-16 (MHK) PICKEL, VIRGINIA M CORNELL UNIV MEDICAL COLLEGE 411 EAST 69TH STREET NEW YORK, NY 10021 Central monoaminergic and peptidergic neurons
Z01MH-00086-16 (CNG) GERSHON, E S NIMH Outpatient clinic for genetic and pharmacologic studies of affective disorders
K05MH-00117-15 (MHK) KRIPKE, DANIEL F UNIVERSITY OF CALIFORNIA 9500 GILMAN DRIVE LA JOLLA, CA 92093-0603 Bio-oscillator effects on mental function
K05MH-00129-10 (MHK) MARGOLIS, RICHARD U N Y UNIV MEDICAL CENTER 550 FIRST AVENUE NEW YORK, NY 10016 Complex carbohydrates of nervous tissue
K05MH-00133-14 (MHK) WHITEHEAD, WILLIAM E FRANCIS SCOTT KEY MED CENTER 4940 EASTERN AVENUE BALTIMORE, MD 21224 Role of perception in control of visceral responses
K05MH-00135-14 (MHK) CREWS, DAVID P UNIVERSITY OF TEXAS AT AUSTIN DEPARTMENT OF ZOOLOGY AUSTIN, TX 78712 Psychobiological studies of reproductive behavior
K05MH-00149-10 (MHK) SMITH, GERARD P N Y HOSP-CORNELL MED CENTER 21 BLOOMINGDALE ROAD WHITE PLAINS, NY 10605 Physiological psychology of motivated behavior
Z01MH-00153-14 (CHP) RAPOPORT, J L NIMH Treatment of obsessional children and adolescents with clomipramine
K05MH-00162-16 (MHK) ZIGMOND, RICHARD E CASE WESTERN RESERVE DIV OF GENERAL MEDICAL SCIS CLEVELAND, OH 44106 Environmental influences on synaptic pharmacology
K02MH-00176-10 (MHK) BARON, MIRON N Y STATE PSYCHIATRIC INST 722 W 168TH STREET NEW YORK, N Y 10032 Genetics of affective disorders
K05MH-00177-15 (MHK) SNOWDON, CHARLES T UNIVERSITY OF WISCONSIN 1202 W JOHNSON ST-DPT OF PSYCH MADISON, WIS 53706 Biopsychology of communication and behavior
Z01MH-00178-08 (CHP) RUMSEY, J M NIMH Brain structure and function in developmental neuropsychiatric disorders
K05MH-00179-13 (MHK) ZAIDEL, ERAN UNIVERSITY OF CALIFORNIA 1283 FRANZ HALL LOS ANGELES, CA 90024-1563 Hemispheric specialization of higher functions in humans
Z01MH-00180-09 (BP) RUBINOW, D R NIMH Psychobiology and

PROJECT NO., ORGANIZATIONAL UNIT., INVESTIGATOR, ADDRESS, TITLE

treatment of menstrually-related mood disorders
Z01MH-00181-02 (BP) RUBINOW, D R NIMH Hormonal studies of affective disorders
Z01MH-00182-08 (BP) RUBINOW, D R NIMH Behavioral medicine
K02MH-00188-08 (MHK) GEYER, MARK A UNIV OF CALIF, SAN DIEGO DEPT OF PSY, 0804 LA JOLLA, CA 92093 Limbic monoamines, behavior and psychopathology
K05MH-00192-11A2 (MHK) TORAN-ALLERAND, C DOMINIQUE COLUMBIA UNIVERSITY 630 WEST 168TH STREET NEW YORK, NY 10032 Cellular aspects of sexual differentiation of brain
K05MH-00219-12 (MHK) CIARANELLO, ROLAND D STANFORD UNIVERSITY MEDICAL CT STANFORD, CA 94305 Program in molecular neurobiology & developmental disorders
K05MH-00245-13 (MHK) STUNKARD, ALBERT J UNIVERSITY OF PENNSYLVANIA 133 S 36TH STREET - SUITE 507 PHILADELPHIA, PA 19104-3246 Clinical and experimental study of human obesity
K05MH-00254-12 (MHK) FERNSTROM, JOHN D WESTERN PSYCHIATRIC INST & CLI 3811 O'HARA STREET PITTSBURGH, PA 15213 Biosynthesis of neurotransmitters in the CNS
K05MH-00257-13 (MHK) GOTTMAN, JOHN M UNIVERSITY OF WASHINGTON SEATTLE, WA 98195 The maintenance of close dyadic relationships
K02MH-00269-10 (MHK) WYATT, GAIL E UCLA 760 WESTWOOD PLAZA LOS ANGELES, CA 90024-1759 Effects of women's sexuality--Psychological and sex outcomes
Z01MH-00274-17 (LCS) MARKEY, S P NIMH Methods of ionization in mass spectroscopy
Z01MH-00279-09 (LCS) MARKEY, S P NIMH Pharmacology of neurotoxins
K05MH-00289-12 (SRCM) HOFFER, BARRY J UNIV OF COLORADO HLTH SCIS CTR 4200 E NINTH AVE, BOX C236 DENVER, CO 80262 Physiological and behavioral function of CNS grafts
K05MH-00295-12 (MHK) REYNOLDS, CHARLES F, III WESTERN PSYCHIATRIC INST CLINI 3811 O'HARA ST PITTSBURGH, PA 15213 Electroencephalography,sleep,aging and mental illness
K05MH-00298-12 (MHK) GOLDMAN-RAKIC, PATRICIA S YALE UNIVERSITY 333 CEDAR STREET NEW HAVEN, CT 06510 Organization and development of primate prefrontal cortex
K02MH-00303-10 (MHK) SURWIT, RICHARD S DUKE UNIVERSITY MEDICAL CTR PO BOX 3842 DURHAM, NC 27710 Behavioral control of neuroendocrine function
K05MH-00314-11 (MHK) MAIER, STEVEN F UNIVERSITY OF COLORADO CAMPUS BOX 345 BOULDER, COLO 80309-0345 Stressor controllability--Immunology,physiology,behavior
K05MH-00316-12 (MHK) CREESE, IAN N RUTGERS, THE STATE UNIV OF NJ 195 UNIVERSITY AVENUE NEWARK, NEW JERSEY 07102 Dopamine receptors, antipsychotic drugs & schizophrenia
K05MH-00321-11A1 (MHK) WADE, GEORGE N UNIVERSITY OF MASSACHUSETTS AMHERST, MA 01003 Hormone actions on behaviors
K02MH-00327-10 (MHK) JARRETT, DAVID B WESTERN PSY INSTITUTE & CLINIC 3811 O'HARA STREET PITTSBURGH, PA 15213 Neuroendocrine regulation in depression
K06MH-00332-11 (MHK) CLIFTON, RACHEL K UNIV OF MASSACHUSETTES TOBIN HALL AMHERST, MA 01003 Development of perceptual-motor competence in infants
Z01MH-00332-13 (LCS) AULAKH, C S NIMH Animal models for the study of neuropharmacologic effects
Z01MH-00336-12 (LCS) MURPHY, D L NIMH The phenomenology and treatment of obsessive-compulsive disorder in adults
Z01MH-00337-12 (LCS) MURPHY, D L NIMH Neuropharmacology of neuroendocrine and neurotransmitter regulatory mechanisms
Z01MH-00339-10 (LCS) SUNDERLAND, T NIMH Neuropharmacology of cognition and mood in geriatric neuropsychiatry
K05MH-00340-11 (MHK) STRAUSS, JOHN S YALE SCHOOL OF MEDICINE 34 PARK STREET NEW HAVEN, CT 06519 Processes of improvement in schizophrenia
K02MH-00343-09 (MHK) BERGER, THEODORE W UNIVERSITY OF PITTSBURGH 465 CRAWFORD HALL PITTSBURGH, PA 15260 Limbic cortical bases of associative learning
K05MH-00350-11 (MHK) WILK, SHERWIN MT SINAI SCH OF MED ONE GUSTAVE L LEVY PLACE NEW YORK, N Y 10029 Enzymology of neuropeptide formation and degradation
K05MH-00353-10 (MHK) KAZDIN, ALAN E YALE UNIVERSITY P O BOX 11A YALE STATION NEW HAVEN, CT 06520-7447 Treatment of antisocial behavior in children
K05MH-00358-11 (MHK) LYNCH, GARY S UNIVERSITY OF CALIFORNIA IRVINE, CA 92717 Plasticity of hippocampal synapses
K05MH-00363-07 (MHK) EPSTEIN, SEYMOUR UNIVERSITY OF MASSACHUSETTS AMHERST, MA 01003 Constructive thinking and coping with stress
K05MH-00364-09 (MHK) VAILLANT, GEORGE E DARTMOUTH HITCHCOCK MEDICAL CT ONE MEDICAL CENTER DRIVE HANOVER, NH 0756 Longitudinal studies of psychopathology
K05MH-00367-10 (MHK) HAITH, MARSHALL M UNIVERSITY OF DENVER DENVER, CO 80208 Visual competence in early infancy
K02MH-00371-10 (MHK) LEON, MICHAEL A UNIVERSITY OF CALIFORNIA IRVINE, CA 92717-4550 The psychobiology of mother-young interactions
K02MH-00380-09 (MHK) BRESLAU, NAOMI HENRY FORD HOSPITAL 2799 W GRAND BLVD DETROIT, MI 48202 Child disability and the family
Z01MH-00382-03 (LCS) JACOBOWITZ, D M NIMH Localization and characterization of brain neurochemicals
K02MH-00385-11 (MHK) MC CLELLAND, JAMES L CARNEGIE-MELLON UNIVERSITY 5000 FORBES AVENUE PITTSBURGH, PA 15213 Simulation of mental processes in light of the brain
Z01MH-00388-15 (LCS) JACOBOWITZ, D M NIMH Coexistence of peptides and neurotransmitters
K02MH-00392-10 (MHK) BAUM, MICHAEL J BOSTON UNIVERSITY 5 CUMMINGTON ST BOSTON, MA 02215 Behavioral effects of sex steroids
Z01MH-00396-13 (LCS) JACOBOWITZ, D M NIMH A study of proteins within the CNS by two-dimensional gel electrophoresis
Z01MH-00397-13 (LCS) JACOBOWITZ, D M NIMH Autoimmune aspects of disease
K02MH-00406-10 (MHK) GALLAGHER, MICHELA UNIVERSITY OF NORTH CAROLINA DAVIE HALL 013A CHAPEL HILL, NC 27514 Amygdala neurochemical contribution to learning & memory
K02MH-00416-10 (MHK) GORMAN, JACK M COLUMBIA UNIVERSITY 722 WEST 168TH STREET NEW YORK, N Y 10032 Psychobiology of anxiety disorders
K02MH-00419-09 (MHK) PENNINGTON, BRUCE F UNIV OF COLO HLTH SCIS CTR 4200 EAST 9TH AVE, BOX C259 DENVER, CO 80262 Genotype and phenotype analyses of famili dyslexia
Z01MH-00422-20 (LCB) ZATZ, M NIMH Neuropharmacology of circadian rhythms
K02MH-00423-10 (MHK) BENES, FRANCINE M MCLEAN HOSPITAL 115 MILL STREET BELMONT, MA 02178 Morphometric and immunocytochemical studies of neocortex
Z01MH-00424-16 (LCB) BROWNSTEIN, M J NIMH Biologically active peptides in the brain
K02MH-00427-07 (MHK) YOUNG, ELIZABETH A MENTAL HEALTH RESEARCH INST 205 ZINA PITCHER PLACE ANN ARBOR, MI 48109-0720 Hypothalamo-pituitary adrenal axis in depression
Z01MH-00433-11 (LCS) SAAVEDRA, J M NIMH Role of neuropeptides and biogenic amines in neuroendocrine regulation
Z01MH-00434-10 (LCB) AXELROD, J NIMH Molecular mechanisms of receptor-mediated signal transduction
K05MH-00437-09 (MHK) NICOLL, ROGER A UNIVERSITY OF CALIFORNIA DEPARTMENT OF PHARMACOLOGY SAN FRANCISCO, CALIF 94143 Local nueronal circuits in the CNS
K02MH-00452-05 (MHK) FAZIO, RUSSELL H INDIANA UNIVERSITY BLOOMINGTON, IN 47405 Attitude-behavior processes, stress, and mental health
Z01MH-00471-36 (LPP) MIRSKY, A F NIMH Studies of heredity and environment in schizophrenia
K02MH-00478-07 (MHK) YAHR, PAULINE I UNIVERSITY OF CALIFORNIA IRVINE, CA 92717 Hormonal control of social behavior
Z01MH-00478-01 (LN) MISHKIN, M NIMH Neural mechanisms of stimulus memory and habit formation
K02MH-00484-08 (MHK) RUBLE, DIANE N NEW YORK UNIVERSITY 6 WASHINGTON PLACE NEW YORK, NY 10003 The development of orientations toward peer interaction
Z01MH-00484-31 (LPP) ZAHN, T P NIMH Psychophysiological responsivity and behavior in schizophrenia
Z01MH-00486-19 (LPP) ZAHN, T P NIMH Psychophysiological effects of stimulant drugs in children
Z01MH-00491-15 (LPP) ZAHN, T P NIMH Personality factors and psychophysiological response to changing stimulus input
K01MH-00493-05 (MHK) AVERY, DAVID H HARBORVIEW MEDICAL CENTER 325 NINTH AVE SEATTLE, WA 98104 EEG sleep and temperature rhythm in primary depression
K02MH-00498-08 (MHK) SWANN, WILLIAM B UNIVERSITY OF TEXAS AUSTIN, TX 78712 Self-concept stability and interpersonal processes
K02MH-00499-07 (MHK) MERIKANGAS, KATHLEEN R 40 TEMPLE STREET LOWER LEVEL NEW HAVEN, CT 06510-3223 Genetic epidemiology of psychiatric disorders
Z01MH-00503-11 (LPP) MIRSKY, A F NIMH Human clinical studies of attention disorders
K02MH-00507-08 (MHK) KESSLER, RONALD C UNIVERSITY OF MICHIGAN PO BOX 1248 ANN ARBOR, MI 48106 Stress models for high risk population
Z01MH-00507-09 (LCM) COHEN, R M NIMH Clinical brain imaging
K02MH-00508-08 (MHK) PAULS, DAVID L YALE UNIVERSITY 333 CEDAR ST PO BOX 3333 NEW HAVEN, CT 06510 Genetics of the behavioral disorder Tourette syndrome
Z01MH-00508-09 (LPP) MIRSKY, A F NIMH Neuropsychological evaluation of psychiatric and neurological patients
Z01MH-00509-09 (LPP) MIRSKY, A F NIMH Attention disorders as assessed by event-related brain potentials
K02MH-00510-08 (MHK) FRIEDMAN, DAVID COLUMBIA UNIVERSITY 722 WEST 168 STREET NEW YORK, NY 10032 Cognitive brain potentials--Normal and abnormal
K02MH-00516-06A1 (MHK) HALMI, KATHERINE A NEW YORK HOSP-WESTCHESTER DIV 21 BLOOMINGDALE ROAD WHITE PLAINS, NY 10605 The psychobiology of eating in eating disorders
K02MH-00519-07 (MHK) LEWIS, DAVID A WESTERN PSYCHIATRIC INST & CLN 3811 O'HARA STREET PITTSBURGH, PA 15213 Neural circuitry of primate prefrontal cortex
K02MH-00521-07 (MHK) SIMMONS, JAMES A BROWN UNIVERSITY 89 WATERMAN STREET PROVIDENCE, RI 02912 Mechanisms of perception by sonar
K05MH-00524-08 (MHK) BLASS, ELLIOTT M CORNELL UNIVERSITY ITHACA , NY 14853 Biopsychological development of infant humans and rats
K02MH-00533-07 (MHK) KIESLER, SARA B CARNEGIE-MELLON UNIVERSITY 5000 FORBES AVENUE PITTSBURGH, PA 15213 Social and mental health aspects of new computing technology
K02MH-00534-05 (MHK) POLAND, RUSSELL E HARBOR-U C L A MEDICAL CENTER 1124 WEST CARSON STREET TORRANCE, CA 90502 Neuroendocrine aspects of depressive illness
K02MH-00537-06 (MHK) LIEBERMAN, JEFFREY A HILLSIDE HOSPITAL 75-59 263RD ST GLEN OAKS, NY 11004 Psychobiology of schizophrenia
K02MH-00540-06 (MHK) ZUBENKO, GEORGE S WESTERN PSYCH INST & CLINIC 3811 O'HARA STREET PITTSBURGH, PA 15213 Determinants of clinical variation in primary dementia
K05MH-00567-07 (MHK) ELDER, GLEN H, JR UNIVERSITY OF NORTH CAROLINA CB# 3210 CHAPEL HILL, NC 27599 Mental health and social change--A life course perspective
K02MH-00571-05 (MHK) HALL, WARREN G DUKE UNIVERSITY DURHAM, NC 27706 Developmental psychobiology of motivation
K02MH-00586-07 (MHK) GUR, RAQUEL E UNIVERSITY OF PENNSYLVANIA 205 PIERSOL BLDG PHILADELPHIA, PA 19104 Regional brain activity and psychopathology
K02MH-00590-05 (MHK) STOFF, DAVID M MEDICAL COLL OF PENNSYLVANIA 3200 HENRY AVE PHILADELPHIA, PA 19129 Studies of serotonin in aggression of children
K01MH-00616-05 (MHK) WEISS, MITCHELL G HARVARD MEDICAL SCHOOL 25 SHATTUCK STREET BOSTON, MA 02115 Tropical disease (leprosy) and mental health
K05MH-00619-06 (MHK) MEDNICK, SARNOFF A UNIV OF SOUTHERN

CALIFORNIA UNIVERSITY PARK LOS ANGELES, CA 90089-1111 Schizophrenia in high risk populations

K02MH-00621-05 (MHK) CRNIC, LINDA S UNIV OF COLORADO SCH OF MED 4200 EAST 9TH AVENUE DENVER, CO 80262 A viral model of hyperactivity

K05MH-00625-06 (MHK) ANDREASEN, NANCY C UNIVERSITY OF IOWA 500 NEWTON ROAD IOWA CITY, IOWA 52242 Major psychoses--Phenomenology, behavior, genetics

K01MH-00626-05 (MHK) GANGULI, ROHAN WESTERN PSYCHIATRY INSTITUTE 3811 O'HARA STREET PITTSBURGH, PA 15213 Autoimmune mechanisms in schizophrenia

K11MH-00630-05 (SRCM) ZORUMSKI, CHARLES F WASHINGTON UNIVERSITY 660 S. EUCLID AVE - BOX 8134 ST LOUIS, MO 63110 Excitatory transmitters and seizure related brain

K02MH-00636-06 (MHK) ETGEN, ANNE M ALBERT EINSTEIN COLLEGE OF MED 1300 MORRIS PARK AVENUE BRONX, NY 10461 Neuroendocrine regulation of behavior

K05MH-00643-12 (MHK) REDMOND, DONALD E, JR YALE UNIVERSITY 333 CEDAR ST - P O BOX 3333 NEW HAVEN, CT 06510-8068 Plasticity and function of central catecholaminergic systems

K02MH-00651-05 (MHK) KELLOGG, CAROL K UNIVERSITY OF ROCHESTER COLLEGE OF ARTS & SCIENCES ROCHESTER, NY 14627 Developmental drug exposure--Mechanisms and effects

K02MH-00652-05 (MHK) RUFF, HOLLY A ALBERT EINSTEIN COLL OF MED 1300 MORRIS PARK AVENUE BRONX, NY 10461 Sustained attention in infants and young children

K05MH-00653-06 (MHK) NORGREN, RALPH E MILTON S HERSHEY MEDICAL CENTE P O BOX 850 HERSHEY, PA 17033 Neural systems of taste and ingestive behavior

K01MH-00660-03 (MHK) EMORY, EUGENE K EMORY UNVIERSITY ATLANTA, GEORGIA 30322 Fetal responsivity during labor and behavioral outcome

K02MH-00661-05 (MHK) CARPENTER, PATRICIA A CARNEGIE-MELLON UNIVERSITY 5000 FORBES AVE PITTSBURGH, PA 15213 Eye movements in reading and reasoning

K02MH-00662-05 (MHK) JUST, MARCEL A CARNEGIE-MELLON UNIVERSITY 5000 FORBES AVENUE PITTSBURGH, PA 15213 Cognitive linkage of brain function and eye movements

K05MH-00663-04 (MHK) TACHE, YVETTE F VA WADSWORTH MEDICAL CENTER BLDG 115, RM 203 LOS ANGELES, CA 90073 Brain control of gastric secretion and stress-induced gastric lesions

K01MH-00671-05 (MHK) GREBB, JACK A ROCKEFELLER UNIVERSITY 1230 YORK AVENUE NEW YORK, N Y 10021 Neuronal phosphoproteins in neuropsychiatric disorders

Z01MH-00672-26 (LSES) SCHOOLER, C NIMH Social psychological correlates of occupational position

K11MH-00673-05 (MHK) COHEN, JONATHAN D STANFORD UNIVERSITY SCH OF MED DEPARTMENT OF PSYCHIATRY STANFORD, CA 94305 Contex disturbance in schizophrenia--models and measure

K01MH-00678-05 (MHK) SCHULKIN, JAY J UNIVERSITY OF PENNSYLVANIA PHILADELPHIA, PA 19104 Brain mechanisms of a hormone-induced behavior--Salt appetite

K01MH-00680-04 (MHK) MILLER, ANDREW H MOUNT SINAI MEDICAL CENTER DEPT OF PSYCHIATRY NEW YORK, NY 10029 Neuroendocrine-immune relationships in depression

Z01MH-00680-08 (LSES) LIEBOW, E NIMH Work experiences and the deinstitutionalized mentally ill

K01MH-00681-05 (MHK) TUCKER, M BELINDA UNIVERISTY OF CALIFORNIA CAAS 160 HAINES HALL LOS ANGELES, CA 90024-1545 Black sex ratios and social psychological functioning

K11MH-00682-05 (MHK) KAUFMANN, CHARLES A N Y STATE PSYCHIATRIC INST 722 WEST 168TH STREET NEW YORK, N Y 10032 Molecular neurobiology of schizophrenia

Z01MH-00682-05 (LSES) CAPLAN, L NIMH Environmental determinants of cognitive functioning

Z01MH-00683-04 (LSES) SCHOOLER, C NIMH Study of social and cognitive aspects of schizophrenia

Z01MH-00684-04 (LSES) CAPLAN, L NIMH The representation of semantic categories

K11MH-00686-05 (MHK) SOHMER, BARBARA H JOHNS HOPKINS SCH OF MEDICINE 600 NORTH WOLFE ST BALTIMORE, MD 21205 Delirium--A childhood psychiatric disorder

K01MH-00691-03 (MHK) ZEANAH, CHARLES H WOMEN AND INFANTS' HOSPITAL 101 DUDLEY STREET PROVIDENCE, RI 02905 Intergenerational transmission of attachment

K02MH-00699-05 (MHK) RASENICK, MARK M UNIVERSITY OF ILLINOIS P O BOX 6998 CHICAGO, ILLINOIS 60680 Regulation of neuronal signal transduction

K01MH-00702-05 (MHK) WADDEN, THOMAS A UNIVERSITY OF PENNSYLVANIA 133 S 36TH ST., SUITE 507 PHILADELPHIA, PA 19104-3246 Behavioral treatment of obese children and adults

K02MH-00703-05 (MHK) LEWY, ALFRED J OREGON HEALTH SCIENCES UNIV 3181 S W SAM JACKSON PARK RD PORTLAND, OR 97201 Melatonin and light in sleep and mood disorders

K01MH-00704-05 (MHK) LARSEN, RANDY J UNIVERSITY OF MICHIGAN 580 UNION DRIVE ANN ARBOR, MI 48109-1346 Emotion management and arousal regulation

K01MH-00705-04 (MHK) RAYPORT, STEPHEN G NEW YORK STATE PSYCHIATRIC INS BOX 62, 722 WEST 168TH ST NEW YORK, N Y 10032 Physiology and plasticity of CNS synapses

K02MH-00706-02 (MHK) GOWATY, PATRICIA A CLEMSON UNIVERSITY CLEMSON, SC 29634-1903 Correlates of uncertain parentage in a monogamous bird

K05MH-00707-05 (MHK) ROCK, IRVIN UNIVERSITY OF CALIFORNIA DEPARTMENT OF PSYCHOLOGY BERKELEY, CA 94720 Object and event perception

K11MH-00708-05 (MHK) LESLIE, CATHERINE A UNIV OF VIRGINIA HOSPITALS 6E, BLUE RIDGE HOSPITAL DIV CHARLOTTESVILLE, VA 22901 In vivo pharmacology of dopamine receptor subtypes

K02MH-00709-04 (MHK) DE PAULO, BELLA M UNIVERSITY OF VIRGINIA 102 GILMER HALL CHARLOTTESVILLE, VA 22903-2477 The communication of deception

K02MH-00718-04 (MHK) THELEN, ESTHER INDIANA UNIVERSITY BLOOMINGTON, IN 47405 The development of skills in infants

K01MH-00719-03 (MHK) LEE, JAMES E DUKE UNIVERSITY MEDICAL CENTER P O BOX 3825 DURHAM, N C 27710 Molecular genetic studies of affective disorders

K11MH-00720-04 (MHK) BAUER, MARK S UNIVERSITY OF PENNSYLVANIA 133 SO 36TH ST PHILADELPHIA, PA 19104 Neuropharmacology of the circadian timekeeping system

K02MH-00721-05 (MHK) COHEN, SHELDON A CARNEGIE-MELLON UNIVERSITY PITTSBURGH, PA 15213 Social support, stress, & physical disease

K11MH-00722-05 (MHK) MC CRACKEN, JAMES T HARBOR-UCLA MEDICAL CENTER 1000 W CARSON ST, F-5 TORRANCE, CA 90509 Sleep & hormone regulation in juvenile depression

K01MH-00723-05 (MHK) TUNE, LARRY E JOHNS HOPKINS SCH OF MEDICINE 600 N WOLFE ST BALTIMORE, MD 21205 RSDA training program in PET and schizophrenia research

K11MH-00726-05 (MHK) REISS, ALLAN L JOHNS HOPKINS UNIVERSITY 600 NORTH WOLFE STREET BALTIMORE, MD 21205 Psychopathology and neurobiology of fragile-X syndrome

K11MH-00727-03 (MHK) JAUCH, DIANA A MARYLAND PSYCHIATRIC RES CTR PO BOX 21247 BALTIMORE, MD 21228 PCP and extracellular dopamine in brain

K01MH-00728-04 (MHK) ADLER, LAWRENCE E UNIVERSITY OF COLORADO 4200 EAST NINTH AVENUE DENVER, CO 80262 Catecholamines & sensory gating in schizophrenia

K11MH-00731-04 (MHK) PLISZKA, STEVEN R THE UNIVERSITY OF TEXAS 7703 FLOYD CURL DRIVE SAN ANTONIO, TX 78284-7792 Clinical and neurochemical subtypes of attention deficit disorder

K07MH-00733-04 (LCR) TARIOT, PIERRE N MONROE COMMUNITY HOSPITAL 435 E HENRIETTA ROAD ROCHESTER, NY 14620 Geriatric mental health academic award

K02MH-00735-04 (MHK) CROWE, RAYMOND R UNIV OF IOWA COLL OF MEDICINE 500 NEWTON ROAD IOWA CITY, IOWA 52242 Molecular genetics of panic disorder

K05MH-00743-04 (MHK) CHAPMAN, LOREN J UNIVERSITY OF WISCONSIN 1202 WEST JOHNSON STREET MADISON, WI 53706 Markers of psychosis and psychosis proneness

K01MH-00746-04 (MHK) SHENTON, MARTHA E BROCKTON VA MEDICAL CENTER 940 BELMONT ST BROCKTON, MA 02401 Schizophrenia--Clinical symptoms and brain mechanisms

K11MH-00747-04 (MHK) RUBINSTEIN, JOAN E SUNY AT STONY BROOK HLTH SCIS CENTER, T-10-040 STONY BROOK, N Y 11794-8101 Interaction between second messenger systems

K07MH-00748-04 (LCR) CONWELL, YEATES UNIV OF ROCHESTER MED CTR 300 CRITTENDEN BLVD ROCHESTER, NY 14642 Geriatric mental health academic award

K01MH-00750-04 (MHK) HOLLANDER, ERIC COLUMBIA UNIVERSITY 722 WEST 168TH STREET NEW YORK, NY 10032 Psychobiology of obsessive-compulsive & related disorders

K01MH-00752-04 (MHK) BAXTER, LEWIS R UCLA-NPI 760 WESTWOOD PLAZA LOS ANGELES, CA 90024 P.E.T. in obsessive-compulsive and Tourette's disorder

K02MH-00756-03 (MHK) CRITS-CHRISTOPH, PAUL HOSPITAL OF THE UNIV OF PENN 3400 SPRUCE ST PHILADELPHIA, PA 19104-4283 Research on dynamic psychotherapy

K02MH-00757-03 (MHK) GERHARDT, HOWARD C UNIVERSITY OF MISSOURI 305 JESSE HALL COLUMBIA, MO 65211 Psychobiology and neuroethology of sexual signalling

K07MH-00763-03 (SRCM) SPENCER, ELIZABETH K NEW YORK UNIVERSITY MEDICAL CT 550 FIRST AVENUE NEW YORK, NY 10016 Haloperidol in schizophrenic children

K07MH-00764-03 (SRCM) KILLEEN, MAUREEN R MEDICAL COLLEGE OF GEORGIA 1905 BARNETT SHOALS RD ATHENS, GA 30605 Interdisciplinary research in child psychiatric nursing

K07MH-00766-03 (SRCM) FEINSTEIN, CARL B E P BRADLEY HOSPITAL 1011 VETERANS MEMORIAL PARKWAY EAST PROVIDENCE, RI 02915 Language & developmental disabilities in children

K07MH-00767-03 (SRCM) HUMPHRIES, LAURIE L UNIVERSITY OF KENTUCKY 820 SOUTH LIMESTONE STREET LEXINGTON, KY 40536-0080 Child and adolescent mental health academic award

K07MH-00769-03 (SRCM) SONIS, WILLIAM A PHILADELPHIA CHILD GUIDANCE CL 34TH & CIVIC CENTER BLVD PHILADELPHIA, PA 19104 Mood sleep and seasonality in children and adolescents

K05MH-00778-03 (MHK) MONTAL, S MAURICIO UNIV OF CALIF, SAN DIEGO DEPT OF BIOLOGY/PHYSICS, B-019 LA JOLLA, CA 92093-0319 Molecular anatomy of channel proteins and mental illness

K02MH-00779-01A1 (MHK) MARTIN, JOHN L COLUMBIA UNIVESITY 600 WEST 168TH STREET NEW YORK, NY 10032 Mental health and the AIDS epidemic among gay men

K02MH-00780-03 (MHK) FREYD, JENNIFER J UNIVERSITY OF OREGON DEPARTMENT OF PSYCHOLOGY EUGENE, OR 97403 Integrating theories of mental representation

K07MH-00787-02 (LCR) COLENDA, CHRISTOPHER C III WAKE FOREST UNIVERSITY 300 SOUTH HAWTHORNE RD WINSTON-SALEM, NC 27103 Geriatric mental health academic award

K05MH-00788-03 (MHK) ANDERSON, JOHN R CARNEGIE MELLON UNIVERSITY PITTSBURGH, PA 15213 Rational analysis of learning and cognition

K07MH-00789-03 (MHK) EDELSOHN, GAIL JOHNS HOPKINS SCHOOL OF MED 600 N WOLFE ST BALTIMORE, MD 21205 Epidemiology research training in child psychiatry

K07MH-00791-02 (MHK) CHATOOR, IRENE CHILDREN'S NTL MEDICAL CENTER 111 MICHIGAN AVENUE, NW WASHINGTON, DC 20010 Child and adolescent mental health academic award

K07MH-00792-03 (LCR) HOCH, CAROLYN C WESTERN PSYCHIATRIC INST & CLI 3811 O'HARA STREET PITTSBURGH, PA 15213 Sleep apnea, behavioral assessment & Alzheimer's disease

K07MH-00793-02 (LCR) FINKEL, SANFORD I 259 EAST ERIE, 4TH FLOOR CHICAGO, IL 60611 Geriatric mental health academic award

K05MH-00796-03 (MHK) SHIH, JEAN C UNIV OF SOUTHERN CALIFORNIA SCH/PHARMACY, 1985 ZONAL AVE LOS ANGELES, CA 90033 Molecular studies of monoamine oxidases (MAOs)

Z01MH-00796-05 (LCS) MACLEAN, P D NIMH Cytochemical tracing of thalamic connections with midline frontal cortex

K05MH-00797-03 (MHK) COIE, JOHN D DUKE UNIVERSITY PSYCHOLOGY

PROJECT NO., ORGANIZATIONAL UNIT., INVESTIGATOR, ADDRESS, TITLE

DEPT DURHAM, N C 27706 Prevention research with aggressive, rejected children

Z01MH-00797-05 (LCS) INSEL, T R NIMH Neurobiology of attachment

Z01MH-00798-05 (LCS) STANFIELD, B B NIMH Studies on the development of the cerebral cortex

Z01MH-00799-05 (LCS) STANFIELD, B B NIMH Studies on postnatal neurogenesis

K02MH-00801-03 (MHK) WHITE, JEFFREY D SUNY STONY BROOK DIVISION OF ENDOCRINOLOGY STONY BROOK, NY 11794 Molecular mechanisms regulating NPY synthesis in the CNS

K11MH-00802-03 (MHK) RICHARD, CHARLES W UNIVERSITY OF CALIFORNIA 401 PARNASSUS AVE, BOX GMO-098 SAN FRANCISCO, CA 94143-0984 Molecular genetics of bipolar affective disorder

K01MH-00803-03 (MHK) YONGUE, BRANDON G N Y STATE PSYCHIATRIC INST 722 W 168TH ST/BOX 40 NEW YORK, N Y 10032 Neuroendocrinology of salt appetite and blood pressure

K20MH-00814-02 (SRCM) WALTRIP, ROYCE W, II MARYLAND PSYCHIATRIC RESEARCH P O BOX 21247 BALTIMORE, MD 21228 Neuroimmunology/virology of schizophrenia

K02MH-00815-03 (MHK) ARIEL, MICHAEL UNIVERSITY OF PITTSBURGH 458 CRAWFORD HALL PITTSBURGH, PA 15260 Directionally sensitive input to oculomotor pathways

K07MH-00816-01S1 (LCR) BAKER, F M UNIV OF TEXAS HEALTH SCIENCE C 7703 FLOYD CURL DRIVE SAN ANTONIO, TX 78284-7792 Geriatric mental health academic award

K01MH-00818-02 (MHK) MEADOR-WOODRUFF, JAMES H UNIVERSITY OF MICHIGAN 205 WASHTENAW PLACE ANN ARBOR, MI 48109-0720 Neocortical kappa opioid systems in schizophrenia

K01MH-00820-03 (MHK) KEMENY, MARGARET E UNIVERSITY OF CALIFORNIA 405 HILGARD AVE LOS ANGELES, CA 90024-175919 Psychoneuroimmunology and hiv infection

K07MH-00821-03 (LCR) KELLNER, CHARLES H MEDICAL UNIV OF SOUTH CAROLINA 171 ASHLEY AVENUE CHARLESTON, SC 29425 Neuropsychiatric aspects of depression in the aging

K07MH-00822-02 (MHK) COOK, EDWIN H, JR UNIVERSITY OF CHICAGO 5841 SOUTH MARYLAND AVENUE CHICAGO, IL 60637 Child and adolescent mental health academic award

K07MH-00823-03 (LCR) PLOTKIN, DANIEL A NEUROPSYCHIATRIC INSTITUTE, UC 760 WESTWOOD PLAZA LOS ANGELES, CA 90024-1759 Geriatiric mental health academic award

K07MH-00824-03 (MHK) MALASPINA, DOLORES NY STATE PSYCHIATRIC INST 722 WEST 168TH STREET NEW YORK, NY 10032 Schizophrenia academic award

K07MH-00826-03 (MHK) MUNIR, KERIM CAMBRIDGE HOSPITAL 1493 CAMBRIDGE STREET CAMBRIDGE, MA 02139 NIMH child & adolescent mental health faculty award

K02MH-00827-01A2 (MHK) KOSS, MARY P UNIVERSITY OF ARIZONA 1501 N CAMPBELL AVENUE TUCSON, AZ 85724 Cognitive processing of traumatic sexual victimization

K05MH-00832-03 (SRCM) MC GUIRE, THOMAS G BOSTON UNIVERSITY 270 BAY STATE ROAD BOSTON, MA 02215 Payment systems for mental health care

K02MH-00833-02 (MHK) MANSON, SPERO M UNIV OF COLORADO HLTH SCIS CTR 4200 EAST NINTH AVE, BX C249 DENVER, CO 80262 Managing depression in American Indian primary care

K05MH-00834-03 (SRCM) TESSLER, RICHARD C UNIVERSITY OF MASSACHUSETTS MUNSON HALL AMHERST, MA 01003 Family, mental illness, & homelessness

K02MH-00839-03 (SRCM) DRAKE, ROBERT E TRUSTEES OF DARTMOUTH COLLEGE PO BOX 7 HANOVER, NH 03755 Adamha research scientist development award, level 2

K02MH-00840-02 (MHK) VALENTINO, RITA J HAHNEMANN UNIVERSITY BROAD & VINE PHILADELPHIA, PA 19102 Brainstem CRF function during hemodynamic stress

K02MH-00841-02 (MHK) BARTNESS, TIMOTHY J GEORGIA STATE UNIVERSITY UNIVERSITY PLAZA ATLANTA, GA 30303 CNS melatonin targets and photoperiod-induced obesity

K02MH-00842-03 (SRCM) BOND, GARY R INDIANA UNIVERSITY 1125 EAST 38TH STREET INDIANAPOLIS, IN 46205 Research scientist development award (level II)

K02MH-00843-03 (SRCM) SMITH, G RICHARD UNIV OF ARKANSAS/MED SCIENCE 4301 W MARKHAM, SLOT 554 LITTLE ROCK, AR 72205 Mental health services scientist development award

K20MH-00848-03 (SRCM) DORWART, ROBERT A CENTER FOR SOCIAL POLICY 79 KENNEDY STREET CAMBRIDGE, MA 02139 Economics of mental health care provider behavior

K01MH-00849-03 (SRCM) PESCOSOLIDO, BERNICE A INDIANA UNIVERSITY BALLANTINE HALL 744 BLOOMINGTON, IN 47405 A multi-level network model for mental health services

K02MH-00855-02 (MHK) HART, RONALD P RUTGERS STATE UNIVERSITY 101 WARREN STREET NEWARK, NJ 07102 Tryptophan hydroxylase gene structure and regulation

K20MH-00856-02 (MHK) LOMBROSO, PAUL J YALE UNIVERSITY SCH OF MEDICIN PO BOX 3333, 333 CEDAR STREET NEW HAVEN, CT 06510 Transcripts in normal B ganglia and after neuroleptics

K20MH-00858-01A1 (MHK) PAPP, LASZLO A COLUMBIA UNIVERSITY 722 WEST 168TH STREET NEW YORK, NY 10032 Respiratory psychophysiology of anxiety

K20MH-00859-02 (MHK) SCHWARZKOPF, STEVEN B OHIO STATE UNIVERSITY 473 W TWELFTH AVE/UPHAM HALL COLUMBUS, OH 43210 Sensory gating and animal models in schizophrenia

K20MH-00860-02 (MHK) ROSENTHAL, LEON HENRY FORD HOSPITAL 2921 WEST GRAND BOULEVARD DETROIT, MI 48202 The nature of pathological daytime sleepiness

K20MH-00864-03 (SRCM) HARRIS, EMILY S CHILDREN'S HOSPITAL AT STANFOR 520 SAND HILL ROAD, BOX 17 PALO ALTO, CA 94304 Mental disorders in pediatric care settings

K02MH-00868-02 (MHK) JACOBSON, NEIL S UNIVERSITY OF WASHINGTON SEATTLE, WA 98195 Analysis and treatment of marital problems and depression

K20MH-00869-02 (MHK) MELLON, CHARLES DAVID UNIVERSITY OF UTAH 50 NORTH MEDICAL DRIVE SALT LAKE CITY, UT 84132 Molecular genetics of psychiatric disorders

PROJECT NO., ORGANIZATIONAL UNIT., INVESTIGATOR, ADDRESS, TITLE

K20MH-00870-01A1 (MHK) RISBY, EMILE D EMORY UNIV SCHOOL OF MEDICINE PO BOX AF ATLANTA, GA 30322 Effects of lithium on G-proteins in psychiatric patients

K02MH-00871-02 (MHK) RATCLIFF, ROGER NORTHWESTERN UNIVERSITY 2029 SHERIDAN ROAD EVANSTON, IL 60208 Retrieval processes in memory

K20MH-00873-01A2 (MHK) PAPOLOS, DEMETRI F ALBERT EINSTEIN COLLEGE OF MED 1300 MORRIS PARK AVE BRONX, NY 10461 Molecular basis of lithium action

K02MH-00875-02 (MHK) DAVIDSON, RICHARD J UNIVERSITY OF WISCONSIN 1202 WEST JOHNSON STREET MADISON, WIS 53706 Cerebral asymmetry,emotion and psychopathology

K02MH-00876-02 (MHK) WALKER, ELAINE F EMORY UNIVERSITY ATLANTA, GA 30322 Childhood precursors and clinical outcome in schizophrenia

K21MH-00878-02 (MHK) COCHRAN, SUSAN D CALIFORNIA STATE UNIVERSITY 18111 NORDHOFF STREET NORTHRIDGE, CA 91330 Psychosocial methodology in AIDS risk reduction

K02MH-00880-02 (MHK) BECK, SHERYL G LOYOLA UNIVERSITY OF CHICAGO 2160 SOUTH FIRST AVENUE MAYWOOD, ILLINOIS 60153 Psychotropic drugs and hippocampal serotonin receptors

K20MH-00881-01A1 (MHK) TIEN, ALLEN Y JOHNS HOPKINS UNIVERSITY 624 NORTH BROADWAY BALTIMORE, MD 21205 Schizophrenia– Oculomotor, cognitive, personality aspects

Z01MH-00881-35 (LCM) KAUFMAN, E E NIMH, NIH Intermediary energy metabolism in mammalian brain

K02MH-00882-02 (MHK) REDD, WILLIAM H MEMORIAL HOSPITAL FOR 1275 YORK AVENUE NEW YORK, NY 10021 Analysis of behavioral effect of cancer treatment

Z01MH-00882-24 (LCM) SOKOLOFF, L NIMH, NIH Regional cerebral circulation and metabolism

K21MH-00884-02 (MHK) VIELAND, VERONICA J NY STATE PSYCHIATRIC INSTITUTE BOX 14, 722 WEST 168TH ST NEW YORK, NY 10032 Genetic modeling of child psychopathology

K02MH-00885-02 (MHK) BLAUSTEIN, JEFFREY D UNIVERSITY OF MASSACHUSETTS TOBIN HALL AMHERST, MA 01003 Steroid hormones neuroedocrine function and behavior

Z01MH-00889-12 (LCM) SMITH, C B NIMH A method for the determination of local rates of protein synthesis in brain

K20MH-00891-02 (MHK) SCHWARTZ, CARL E MASS MENTAL HEALTH CENTER 74 FENWOOD ROAD BOSTON, MA 02115 Inhibited infants--Adolescent behavior and psychopathology

K02MH-00892-02 (MHK) HYMAN, STEVEN E MASSACHUSETTS GENERAL HOSPITAL FRUIT STREET BOSTON, MA 02114 Molecular mechanisms of proenkephalin gene expression

K02MH-00897-02 (MHK) BARNES, CAROL A UNIVERSITY OF ARIZONA NORTH BLDG., ROOM 384 TUCSON, AZ 85724 Neural mechanisms of congnitive decline in senescence

K20MH-00898-02 (MHK) FULWILER, CARL E HARVARD UNIVERSITY 16 DIVINITY AVENUE CAMBRIDGE, MA 02138 A genetic approach to vertebrate neural development

K02MH-00899-02 (MHK) FELTEN, SUZANNE Y UNIV OF ROCHESTER 601 ELMWOOD AVE ROCHESTER, NY 14642 Noradrenergic modulation of immune response

K05MH-00900-01 (MHK) HARGREAVES, WILLIAM A UNIVERSITY OF CALIFORNIA SFGH ROOM 7M36 SAN FRANCISCO, CA 94143-0852 Services for the severely mentally ill

K05MH-00902-01 (MHK) ROVEE-COLLIER, CAROLYN RUTGERS UNIVERSITY BUSCH CAMPUS NEW BRUNSWICK, NJ 08903 A conditioning analysis of infant memory

K02MH-00903-01 (MHK) EISENBERG, NANCY ARIZONA STATE UNIVERSITY TEMPE, AZ 85287 Emotional responding – Socialization and social correlates

Z01MH-00903-14 (LCM) DEIBLER, G E NIMH Purification of brain proteinases and identification of their cleavage products

K20MH-00906-01A1 (MHK) WEIHS, KAREN L THE GEORGE WASHINGTON UNIVERSI ROSS HALL RM 613 WASHINGTON, DC 20037 Family coping and breast cancer progression

K07MH-00910-01 (LCR) SULTZER, DAVID L UNIVERSITY OF CALIFORNIA 710 WW PLAZA/RM 1-230 LOS ANGELES, CA 90024-1769 Psychiatric and behavioral disturbances in Alzheimer's disease

K07MH-00912-01 (LCR) GUZE, BARRY H NEUROPSYCHIATRIC INSTITUTE 760 WESTWOOD PLAZA RM 27-384 LOS ANGELES, CA 90024 Early identification of Alzheimer's disease

K07MH-00915-01A1 (LCR) SHERRILL, KIMBERLY A BOWMAN GRAY SCHOOL OF MEDICINE 300 S HAWTHORNE RD WINSTON-SALEM, NC 27103 Geriatric mental health academic award

K21MH-00916-01 (MHK) FREIMER, NELSON B UNIVERSITY OF CALIFORNIA 401 PARNASSUS AVENUE SAN FRANCISCO, CA 94143-0984 Molecular genetics of X-linked bipolar disorder

K20MH-00917-01 (MHK) KING, BRYAN H UCLA NEUROPSYCHIATRIC INSTITUT 760 WESTWOOD PLAZA LOS ANGELES, CA 90024 Serotonergic mechanisms and self-injurious behavior

K02MH-00919-01 (MHK) NEIGHBORS, HAROLD THE UNIVERSITY OF MICHIGAN 1420 WASHINGTON HEIGHTS ANN ARBOR, MI 48109-2029 Social psychiatric epidemiology and African Americans

K05MH-00924-01A1 (MHK) HOWARD, KENNETH I NORTHWESTERN UNIV 2029 SHERIDAN RD EVANSTON, IL 60208 Psychotherapy services delivery

K20MH-00925-01A1 (MHK) KIRKPATRICK, BRIAN MARYLAND PSYCHIATRIC RES CENTE PO BOX 21247 BALTIMORE, MD 21228 The neurobiology of social affiliation

K20MH-00928-01 (MHK) DREVETS, WAYNE C WASHINGTON UNIVERSITY 4940 AUDUBON AVENUE ST LOUIS, MO 63110 PET and the functional neuroanatomy of depression

K20MH-00929-01 (MHK) MC INTOSH, J M UNIVERSITY OF UTAH 2122 SOUTH IDALIA STREET AURORA, CO 80013 Study of NMDA and dopamine receptors using conotoxins

K21MH-00930-01 (MHK) MANGUN, GEORGE R DARTMOUTH MEDICAL SCHOOL PIKE HOUSE HANOVER, NH 03756 Neural mechanisms of selective attention in humans

K20MH-00931-01 (MHK) GELERNTER, JOEL WEST HAVEN VA MEDICAL CENTER WEST HAVEN, CT 06516 Molecular genetic studies of anxiety disorders

Z01MH-00931-18 (LGCB) AKSAMIT, R R NIMH Characteristics and regulation of S-adenosylhomocysteine hydrolase

PROJECT NO., ORGANIZATIONAL UNIT., INVESTIGATOR, ADDRESS, TITLE

Z01MH-00934-19 (LMB) KLEE, W A NIMH The biochemical basis of peptide receptor activity
Z01MH-00935-24 (LBG) MERRIL, C R NIMH Studies of plasmids and small genomes in human cells
K02MH-00939-01 (MHK) GILBERT, DANIEL T UNIVERSITY OF TEXAS AT AUSTIN AUSTIN, TX 78712 Sequential operations in self and other attribution
Z01MH-00941-11 (LBG) MERRIL, C R NIMH Biochemical genetics and metabolic disease
K02MH-00942-01 (MHK) MALENKA, ROBERT C UNIVERSITY OF CALIFORNIA 401 PARNASSUS AVE SAN FRANCISCO, CA 94143-0984 Modulation of synaptic transmission in the hippocampus
Z01MH-00942-10 (LGCB) BACKLUND, P S NIMH Biochemical reactions in mammalian cell chemotaxis
K02MH-00944-01 (MHK) JOHNSON, JON W UNIVERSITY OF PITTSBURGH 446 CRAWFORD HALL PITTSBURGH, PA 15260 Properties and regulation of glutamate receptors
K02MH-00945-01 (MHK) EHRLICH, MICHELLE E NYU MEDICAL CENTER 550 FIRST AVENUE NEW YORK, NY 10016 Transcriptional regulation of DARPP-32 and ARPP-21
K02MH-00946-01 (MHK) GUNNAR, MEGAN R UNIVERSITY OF MINNESOTA 51 EAST RIVER ROAD MINNESAPOLIS, MN 55455 Behavioral and hormonal responses to stress in human infants
K02MH-00951-01 (MHK) COCCARO, EMIL F MEDICAL COLL OF PENNSYLVANIA 3200 HENRY AVENUE PHILADELPHIA, PA 19129 5-HT in aggression-- Biological and treatment correlates in personality disorder
K12MH-00990-01 (SRCM) WELLS, KENNETH B UCLA 760 WESTWOOD PLAZA LOS ANGELES, CA 90024 Faculty training in mental health services research
K12MH-00991-01 (SRCM) MRAZEK, DAVID A NAT'L JEWISH CTR/IMMUNOLOGY 1400 JACKSON STREET DENVER, CO 80206 AACAP physician scientist development award program
Z01MH-01031-23 (LNC) KAUFMAN, S NIMH The conversion of phenylalanine to tyrosine
Z01MH-01032-23 (LNC) KAUFMAN, S NIMH Biosynthesis of catecholamines
Z01MH-01035-22 (LMB) NASH, H A NIMH The process of lysogeny
Z01MH-01037-23 (LMB) NEVILLE, D M NIMH Receptor-mediated transport of proteins and viruses across cell membranes
Z01MH-01038-23 (LNC) KAUFMAN, S NIMH Phenylketonuria & other diseases caused by defects in biopterin-dependent enzymes
Z01MH-01039-23 (LNC) MILSTIEN, S NIMH Pteridine biosynthesis
Z01MH-01040-23 (LNC) KAUFMAN, S NIMH Molecular biology of the pterin-dependent hydroxylases and ancillary enzymes
Z01MH-01090-14 (CNE) HERKENHAM, M NIMH Studies of central nervous system functional anatomy
Z01MH-01092-13 (LNP) WISE, S P NIMH The frontal lobe and the cerebral control of behavior
Z01MH-01098-05 (LNP) STANFIELD, C A NIMH Anatomical analysis of neuronal circuits
R01MH-01206-36 (PYB) ERIKSEN, CHARLES W 603 EAST DANIEL CHAMPAIGN, IL 61820 Attention and visual information processing
R37MH-01293-31 (CEP) EPSTEIN, SEYMOUR UNIVERSITY OF MASSACHUSETTS AMHERST, MASS 01003 Measurement of drive and conflict
Z01MH-01532-13 (BP) HOUGH, C NIMH Regulation of catecholamine receptors
Z01MH-01559-10 (LBG) YANG, H-Y T NIMH Phe-Met-Arg-Phe-NH2 like peptides in CNS--Function and distribution
R37MH-01562-33 (BBP) CAMPBELL, BYRON A PRINCETON UNIVERSITY PRINCETON, NJ 08544-1010 Generalized effects of early traumatic experiences
Z01MH-01850-01 (NS) POTTER, W Z NIMH Clinical pharmacology of antidepressants
Z01MH-01860-01 (NS) MEFFORD, I N NIMH The role of epinephrine in brain
Z01MH-02032-01 (LN) RICHMOND, B J NIMH Neural coding of visual stimuli
Z01MH-02035-01 (LN) UNGERLEIDER, L G NIMH Anatomy of the primate visual system
Z01MH-02036-01 (LN) DESIMONE, R NIMH Neural mechanisms for attention and memory in the extrastriate cortex
Z01MH-02037-01 (LN) PONS, T P NIMH Functional anatomy of the somatosensory cortex of monkeys
Z01MH-02038-01 (LN) BACHEVALIER, J NIMH Ontogenetic development and decline of cognitive memory and habit formation
Z01MH-02039-01 (LN) AIGNER, T G NIMH Pharmacology of cognitive memory and habit formation
Z01MH-02206-07 (CP) OREN, D A NIMH Neurobiology of seasonal affective disorder and light therapy
Z01MH-02216-08 (LCM) PORRINO, L J NIMH Metabolic mapping of the brain during rewarding self-stimulation
Z01MH-02219-08 (LCS) INSEL, T R NIMH Animal models of anxiety
Z01MH-02228-06 (LMB) NASH, H A NIMH Genetic neurobiology drosophila
Z01MH-02231-07 (LDP) NOTTELMANN, E D NIMH Biological-behavioral relations in early adolescence
Z01MH-02237-07 (CNG) DETERA-WADLEIGH, S D NIMH Mapping of psychiatric disease and neurotransmission related genes
Z01MH-02240-07 (CHP) RAPOPORT, J L NIMH Neurobiology of disruptive behavior disorders
Z01MH-02252-07 (NPB) FREED, W J NIMH Behavioral pharmacology and toxicology
Z01MH-02253-07 (NPB) FREED, W J NIMH Brain tissue transplantation
Z01MH-02257-07 (NPB) EGAN, M F NIMH Biochemical and neuroradiologic abnormalities in tardive dyskinesia
Z01MH-02259-07 (NPB) KAROUM, F NIMH Peripheral and central catecholamine turnover in mental illnesses
Z01MH-02262-07 (NPB) JAFFE, M J NIMH Electroretinography in schizophrenia
Z01MH-02263-07 (NPB) KIRCH, D G NIMH Haloperidol pharmacocynamics and clinical response in schizophrenia

PROJECT NO., ORGANIZATIONAL UNIT., INVESTIGATOR, ADDRESS, TITLE

Z01MH-02275-07 (NPB) STEVENS, J R NIMH Search for virus in CSF and post-mortem brain of patients with schizophrenia
Z01MH-02280-07 (NPB) WYATT, R J NIMH Brain tissue transplantation in primates
Z01MH-02282-07 (NPB) KIRCH, D G NIMH Neurovirology and neuroimmunology of schizophrenia
Z01MH-02288-07 (LPP) KETY, S S NIMH Studies on etiological factors in schizophrenia
Z01MH-02294-07 (CP) DUNCAN, W C NIMH Antidepressant pharmacology of the rodent circadian system
Z01MH-02295-06 (LPP) MIRSKY, A F NIMH Genetic factors in response to alcohol
Z01MH-02296-06 (LCM) CHIVEH, C C NIMH Positron tomographic imaging of dopaminergic systems and their turnover
Z01MH-02298-06 (BCG) FUKAMAUCHI, F NIMH Receptor regulation in cultured cerebellum granule cells
Z01MH-02301-06 (LBG) YANY, H-Y T NIMH Functional role of adrenal NPY
Z01MH-02308-06 (LCM) DRISCOLL, B F NIMH Growth and development of dopaminergic neurons
Z01MH-02321-06 (LGCB) CANTONI, G L NIMH DNA methylation and gene expression
Z01MH-02322-01 (NS) MEFFORD, I N NIMH Interactions between the immune system and central catecholamines
Z01MH-02340-06 (NS) GINNS, E I NIMH Studies of Gaucher disease and other neurogenetic disorders toward gene therapy
Z01MH-02341-06 (NS) GINNS, E I NIMH Correction of inherited protein deficiencies by gene therapy
Z01MH-02343-06 (NS) GINNS, E I NIMH Molecular genetics of inherited neurologic and psychiatric disorders
Z01MH-02344-06 (NS) MARTIN, B NIMH Neuropsychiatric disorders--Protein structure-activity studies
Z01MH-02352-05 (CBDB) LIPSKA, B NIMH Prefrontal cortical modulation of subcortical dopamine system
Z01MH-02360-05 (CBDB) COPPOLA, R NIMH Topographic analysis of brain activity
Z01MH-02361-05 (LDP) RADKE-YARROW, M NIMH Multi-method assessment of children's psychosocial development
Z01MH-02365-05 (LDP) PUTNAM, F W NIMH The psychobiological effects of sexual abuse
Z01MH-02366-05 (LDP) PUTNAM, F NIMH The psychophysiology of multiple personality disorders
Z01MH-02367-05 (LDP) PUTNAM, F W NIMH Clinical phenomenology of multiple personality disorder
Z01MH-02368-05 (LDP) PUTNAM, F W NIMH The dissociative experiences scale
Z01MH-02369-05 (LDP) KOCHANSKA, G NIMH Mutual mother-child influences in families with and without affective disorder
Z01MH-02370-05 (LDP) RADKE-YARROW, M NIMH Caregiving patterns in stressed families
Z01MH-02372-05 (LDP) RADKE-YARROW, M NIMH Psychiatric status of children of depressed parents
Z01MH-02373-05 (NPB) EGAN, MICHAEL F NIMH The effects of cocaine on central and peripheral catecholamines
Z01MH-02377-05 (LCS) JACOBOWITZ, D M NIMH A study of adenosine receptors--Isolation and characterization
Z01MH-02381-05 (LDP) RADKE-YARROW, M NIMH Functioning of depressed mothers in and between episodes
Z01MH-02384-05 (LCS) HEYES, M P NIMH Brain quinolinic acid metabolism--Role in neuropathology
Z01MH-02386-05 (LCB) EIDEN, L E NIMH Neuropeptide signalling pathways in neural and endocrine cells
Z01MH-02387-05 (LCB) EIDEN, L E NIMH Mapping of CD4/GP120 and model for AIDS and AIDS dementia complex
Z01MH-02396-05 (LCB) Tasaki, I NIMH Mechanical, thermal, and optical signs of excitation in the nervous system
Z01MH-02399-06 (CBDB) KLEINMAN, J E NIMH Postmortem brain tissue examination in neuropsychiatric disorders
Z01MH-02402-05 (CP) ROSENTHAL, N E NIMH Effects of light in HIV patients
Z01MH-02404-05 (LPP) MIRSKY, A J NIMH Psychophysiological investigations of preattentional and attentional function
Z01MH-02405-04 (CP) DUNCAN, W C NIMH Chemical antidepressant effects on body mass and body composition in hamsters
Z01MH-02408-04 (LDP) FREE, K NIMH Competency in children at risk for psychiatric disorder
Z01MH-02409-04 (LDP) NOTTELMANN, E NIMH Differential development of siblings in shared and nonshared family environments
Z01MH-02410-04 (LDP) NOTTELMANN, E NIMH Observational assessment of parent and child from toddlerhood to late childhood
Z01MH-02411-03 (LDP) NOTTELMANN, E NIMH Sleep disturbances in young children of mothers with an affective disorder
Z01MH-02414-04 (LCM) KAUFMAN, E C NIMH Metabolic interdependence of neurons and glia
Z01MH-02420-04 (NPB) KAROUM, F NIMH Effect of chronic exposure to cocaine on metabolism of catecholamines
Z01MH-02424-04 (CP) WEHR, T A NIMH Biological mechanisms of the antidepressant effects of sleep deprivation
Z01MH-02426-04 (CP) EVERSON, C NIMH Physiology of sleep and sleep loss
Z01MH-02428-04 (NPB) POLTORAK, M NIMH Biological properties of intraventricular grafts
Z01MH-02429-04 (LCS) ROTHMAN, R B NIMH Characterization of CNS opioid receptors and psychotomimetic binding sites
Z01MH-02430-05 (CP) DUNCAN, W C NIMH Effect of antidepressant drug on sensitivity of the circadian pacemaker
Z01MH-02431-04 (LCM) NELSON, T NIMH Carbohydrate transport and metabolism in neurons and glia
Z01MH-02436-04 (CBDB) DANIEL, D G NIMH Combined sinemet and neuroleptic treatment in schizophrenia
Z01MH-02442-03 (LDP) FREE, K NIMH Suicidal thinking in the children of depressed and well parents
Z01MH-02443-03 (LDP) FREE, K NIMH The potential impact of

PROJECT NO., ORGANIZATIONAL UNIT., INVESTIGATOR, ADDRESS, TITLE

psychiatric treatment upon mother-child communication
Z01MH-02444-03 (LDP) KOCHANSKA, G NIMH Temperament and socialization in the development of guilt and conscience
Z01MH-02446-02 (LDP) NOTTELMANN, E D NIMH Postpartum depression and the development of mother-child relations
Z01MH-02447-03 (LDP) ZAHN-WAXLER, C NIMH The early development of proscocial an aggressive behavior
Z01MH-02448-03 (LDP) COLE, P M NIMH, NIH Prediction of conduct problems during transition from preschool to school age
Z01MH-02449-03 (LDP) COLE, P M NIMH Long-term effects of father-daughter incest
Z01MH-02450-03 (NPB) GLOVINSKY, D NIMH Screening brain DNA for HTLV-1 proviral sequences using PCR amplification
Z01MH-02453-03 (NPB) KAROUM, F NIMH Brain dopamine release and metabolism after atypical and typical neuroleptics
Z01MH-02455-03 (NPB) ALEXANDER, R C NIMH Anti-HLA antibodies and chlorpromazine
Z01MH-02456-03 (NPB) ALEXANDER, R C NIMH HLA and schizophrenia
Z01MH-02457-03 (NPB) STEVENS, J R NIMH Neuropathologic studies of post mortem brain of schizophrenic patients
Z01MH-02458-03 (NPB) KHOT, V NIMH Not all that moves is tardive dyskinesia
Z01MH-02459-02 (BP) CLARK, M NIMH Mechanism of action of carbamazepine in the central nervous system of the rat
Z01MH-02460-03 (BP) CLARK, M NIMH Animal models of epilepsy -- Molecular substrates
Z01MH-02461-02 (BP) CLARK, M NIMH Pharmacology of adenosine and peripheral-type benzodiazepine receptors
Z01MH-02462-03 (LGCB) CANTONI, G L NIMH S-adenosylmethionine and affective disorders
Z01MH-02463-03 (CNG) GOLDIN, L R NIMH Mathematical issues in genetic analysis
Z01MH-02465-03 (CNG) GEJMAN, P V NIMH Genetic mapping development
Z01MH-02467-03 (BP) LIN, W-W NIMH Receptors for endothelin and sarafotoxin in neurons
Z01MH-02468-03 (BCG) GAO, X-M NIMH Mechanisms of action of psychoactive drugs
Z01MH-02472-03 (CBDB) CASANOVA, M F NIMH Pathology of schizophrenia
Z01MH-02476-04 (CBDB) BIGELOW, L B NIMH Clozapine vs. Haloperidol in treatment refractory schizophrenia
Z01MH-02478-04 (CBDB) DANIEL, D G NIMH Effect of amphetamine on cerebral blood flow in schizophrenia
Z01MH-02482-03 (LCS) MACLEAN, P D NIMH Comparative cytoarchitecture of the cingulate cortex
Z01MH-02483-03 (NPB) GILAD, G M NIMH Compensatory neuroplasticity in stress and aging
Z01MH-02484-03 (NPB) HITRI, A NIMH Characterization of the 3H-GBR 12935 receptor sites in the frontal cortex
Z01MH-02486-01 (NS) POTTER, W Z NIMH Molecular mechanisms of action of antidepressants
Z01MH-02487-02 (LDP) DEMULDER, E NIMH Attachment relationships and maternal affects in high risk families
Z01MH-02488-02 (LDP) TARULLO, L NIMH Parent-child relationships in late childhood and early adolescence
Z01MH-02489-02 (LDP) KOCHANSKA, G NIMH Determinants of peer competence in children of well and depressed mothers
Z01MH-02490-02 (LDP) MARTINEZ, P NIMH Predictions from early childhood to later psychological functioning
Z01MH-02491-02 (LDP) RADKE-YARROW, M NIMH Development of offspring of affectively ill and well parents
Z01MH-02493-02 (LDP) MARTINEZ, P E NIMH Effects on children of exposure to chronic community violence
Z01MH-02494-02 (CP) WEHR, T A NIMH Regulation of human biology by changes in daylength
Z01MH-02495-02 (LSES) SCHOOLER, C NIMH Memory functioning in normal and neurologically-impaired individuals
Z01MH-02496-02 (LSES) SCHOOLER, C NIMH Age differences in large-scale spatial processing
Z01MH-02497-02 (LCB) GERFEN, C R NIMH Functional organization of the basal ganglia
Z01MH-02498-02 (LCB) YOUNG, W S NIMH Regulation of gene expression in the brain
Z01MH-02499-02 (LDP) ZAHN-WAXLER, C NIMH Development of problem aggression in children
Z01MH-02501-02 (CP) OREN, D A NIMH Novel treatment modalities for SAD
Z01MH-02502-02 (CP) LEIBENLUFT, E NIMH An investigation of primary depressives with secondary alcoholism
Z01MH-02503-02 (CP) LEIBENLUFT, E NIMH A controlled study of the antidepressant efficacy of sleep deprivation
Z01MH-02505-02 (LBG) ZHU, J NIMH Trophic material in neuronal tissue
Z01MH-02506-02 (LBG) ZHU, J NIMH Secretion of FMRF-amide like peptides, endogenous antiopiod peptides
Z01MH-02509-02 (BP) POST, R M NIMH Anticonvulsants in lithium-refractory bipolar patients
Z01MH-02510-02 (BP) POST, R M NIMH Mechanisms of action of the anticonvulsants in the affective disorders
Z01MH-02511-02 (BP) POST, R M NIMH Longitudinal course of affective illness--Implications for underlying mechanisms
Z01MH-02512-02 (BP) POST, R M NIMH Neuropsychological, anatomical, and physiological correlates of mood disorders
Z01MH-02513-02 (BP) POST, R M NIMH Therapeutic and mechanistic effects of sleep deprivation in depression
Z01MH-02514-03 (BP) POST, R M NIMH Carbamazepine and lithium treatment of bipolar illness
Z01MH-02515-02 (BP) UHDE, T W NIMH Clonidine and GRF studies in pathological anxiety and normal controls
Z01MH-02516-02 (BP) UHDE, T W NIMH Psychobiologic correlates and treatment in social phobia
Z01MH-02517-02 (BP) UHDE, T W NIMH The utility of carbamazepine in alprazolam withdrawal
Z01MH-02518-02 (BP) UHDE, T W NIMH Caffeine withdrawal--Physiological, biological, and psychological effects
Z01MH-02519-02 (BP) UHDE, T W NIMH Panic disorders--Comparison with social phobics, depressed and normal volunteers
Z01MH-02520-02 (BP) UHDE, T W NIMH Dose response effects of intravenous caffeine in normal control subjects
Z01MH-02521-02 (BP) UHDE, T W NI NIMH Thyroid function and abnormalities in panic disorders
Z01MH-02522-02 (BP) UHDE, T W NIMH Assessment of family functioning, fear, and panic disorders
Z01MH-02523-02 (BP) ROSEN, J NIMH Second messenger systems in behavioral sensitization and kindling
Z01MH-02524-02 (BP) ROSEN, J NIMH C-fos and peptide mRNA expression in kindling
Z01MH-02525-02 (BP) ROSEN, J NIMH C-fos activation by panicogenic drugs
Z01MH-02526-02 (BP) ROSEN, J NIMH Olfactory bulb and seizures
Z01MH-02527-02 (BP) WEISS, S R NIMH Behavioral sensitization
Z01MH-02528-02 (BP) WEISS, S R NIMH Pharmacological kindling
Z01MH-02529-02 (BP) WEISS, S R NIMH Pharmacological and biochemical studies of amygdala kindling
Z01MH-02530-02 (BP) WEISS, S R NIMH Contingent inefficacy and contingent tolerance
Z01MH-02531-02 (BP) PERT, A NIMH Alterations in brain neurochemistry as assessed with microdialysis procedures
Z01MH-02532-02 (BP) PERT, A NIMH Conditioned determinants of cocaine-induced behavioral sensitization
Z01MH-02533-02 (BP) PERT, A NIMH Central nervous system regulation of immune function
Z01MH-02534-02 (BP) PERT, A NIMH Neurobiological mechanisms underlying cocaine-induced sensitization
Z01MH-02535-02 (BP) PERT, A NIMH Neurobiology of non-competitve NMDA antagonists
Z01MH-02536-02 (LCM) SMITH, C B NIMH Development, involution and plasticity in the central nervous system
Z01MH-02537-02 (BP) RUBINOW, D R NIMH Psychobiology and treatment of peri-menopausal mood disorders
Z01MH-02538-02 (BP) CHUANG, D M NIMH A study of effects of HIV-1 on neurons and lymphocytes
Z01MH-02539-01 (BP) CHUANG, D M NIMH Receptor regulation in neurohybrid cell lines
Z01MH-02540-01 (BP) UHDE, T W NIMH Neurobiology of panic disorder humans and nervous pointer dogs
Z01MH-02541-02 (NPB) DE MEDINACELI, L NIMH Computed determination of gait abnormalities in rats with CNS lesions
Z01MH-02542-02 (NPB) TAYLOR, E H NIMH Relationships between negative symptoms, depression, and social cognition
Z01MH-02543-02 (NPB) HITRI, A NIMH Relevance to schizophrenia of dopamine transporter binding in the frontal cortex
Z01MH-02544-02 (NPB) GLOVINSKY, D NIMH Patient response to resumption of neuroleptic following a drug free interval
Z01MH-02545-02 (NPB) EL-MALLAKH, R S NIMH A symptom checklist for diagnosis of schizoaffective disorder
Z01MH-02546-02 (NPB) EL-MALLAKH, R S NIMH A clinical trial of clonidine in patients with schizoaffective disorder
Z01MH-02547-02 (NPB) EL-MALLAKH, R S NIMH Physical stress and brain function
Z01MH-02548-02 (NPB) EL-MALLAKH, R S NIMH Carbidopa in the treatment of psychotic states
Z01MH-02549-02 (NPB) KULAGA, H NIMH Infection of rabbits with human immunodeficiency virus 1
Z01MH-02552-02 (CBDB) BIGELOW, L B NIMH Pentosan polysulfate as prophylaxis for migraine
Z01MH-02553-02 (CBDB) BIGELOW, L B NIMH Single dose amphetamine effects in schizophrenia
Z01MH-02554-02 (CBDB) DANIEL, D G NIMH Clinical trial of fluvoxamine in the treatment of chronic schizophrenia
Z01MH-02555-02 (CBDB) BIGELOW, L B NIMH Pemoline treatment of deficit symptoms in schizophrenia
Z01MH-02559-01 (LDP) ZAHN-WAXLER, C NIMH Children's views about conflict as a function of gender and maternal depression
Z01MH-02560-01 (LDP) RADKE-YARROW, M NIMH Individual differences in empathic behavior in children
Z01MH-02561-01 (LDP) NOTTELMANN, E NIMH Cohesion in families with affectively ill and well parents
Z01MH-02562-01 (LDP) CHROUSOS, G NIMH HPA axis function in offspring of depressed mothers and normal control mothers
Z01MH-02563-01 (LNC) KAUFMAN, S NIMH Role of tetrahydrobiopterin in nitric oxide synthesis
Z01MH-02564-01 (LNC) MILSTIEN, S NIMH Tetrahydrobiopterin biosynthesis and HIV pathogenesis
Z01MH-02565-01 (LCS) JACOBOWITZ, D M NIMH Calretinin-containing neurons and excitotoxic injury
Z01MH-02566-01 (LSES) LEE, J NIMH Abstraction, aging, and environmental complexity
Z01MH-02567-01 (NPB) EL-MALLAKH, R S NIMH, NIH Corticosteroids, stress and synaptosomal glutamate uptake
Z01MH-02568-01 (NPB) HITRI, A NIMH, NIH Dopamine transport receptor in the frontal cortex of cocaine addicts
Z01MH-02569-01 (LCM) SCHMIDT, K NIMH Kinetic modeling of tissue heterogeneity in metabolism and blood flow studies
Z01MH-02570-01 (LCM) DRISCOLL, B F NIMH Studies on the metabolism of neurons and astroglia in tissue ulture
Z01MH-02571-01 (LBG) POLYMEROPOULOS, M H NIMH Genome mapping
Z01MH-02572-01 (LBG) PAYZA, K NIMH Characterization of receptors for FMRFamide related neuropeptides
Z01MH-02573-01 (CBDB) GOLDBERG, T E NIMH Neuropsychological testing
Z01MH-02574-01 (CBDB) BIGELOW, L B NIMH Chronic amphetamine administration in schizophrenic
Z01MH-02575-01 (CBDB) KOLACHANA, B S NIMH Microdialysis -- In

vivo measurement of neurotransmitters in the monkey brain
Z01MH-02576-01 (CBDB) BERMAN, K F NIMH Positron emission tomography of normal subjects and neuropsychiatric patients
Z01MH-02577-01 (CP) MADDEN, P A NIMH The heritability of seasonal change in mood and behavior
Z01MH-02578-01 (CNG) HOCHGESCHWENDER, U NIMH Molecular genetic analysis of brain development
Z01MH-02579-01 (CNG) BRENNAN, M B NIMH Isolation and functional characterization of yeast cyclophilin genes
Z01MH-02580-01 (CNG) BRENNAN, M B NIMH An integrated transcriptional map of chromosome 21
Z01MH-02581-01 (CHP) RAPOPORT, J L NIMH Childhood onset schizophrenia
Z01MH-02583-01 (CNE) GOLD, P W NIMH Melancholia as a dysregulation of the stress response
Z01MH-02584-01 (CNE) GOLD, P W NIMH Pathophysiology of atypical depression across medical illnesses
Z01MH-02585-01 (CNE) STERNBERG, E M NIMH Role of the CNS in the susceptibility to inflammatory illness
Z01MH-02586-01 (CNE) GOLD, P W NIMH Common pathobiology of eating, obsessional, and affective disorders
Z01MH-02587-01 (CNE) JOSHI, J B NIMH Regulation of neuropeptide gene expression by viral and physiologic modulators
Z01MH-02588-01 (LCS) MARTIN, A NIMH Cognitive dysfunction in dementia and related neuropsychiatric disorders
Z01MH-02590-01 (LCM) KENNEDY, C NIMH Role of nitric oxide in regulation of local cerebral blood flow
Z01MH-02591-01 (LCB) EIDEN, M V NIMH Identification of a human cDNA that suppresses hamster cell tumorigenicity
Z01MH-02592-01 (LCB) EIDEN, M V NIMH Viral and cellular factors governing retroviral infection
Z01MH-02593-01 (LCB) STONE, A L NIMH Modulation of protein and cell membrane function by heparin/heparan sulfate
Z01MH-02594-01 (LCB) COHEN, R NIMH Signalling mechanisms in CNS development
R37MH-04151-32 (BPN) RECHTSCHAFFEN, ALLAN UNIVERSITY OF CHICAGO 5743 SOUTH DREXEL AVENUE CHICAGO, ILL 60637 Psychology and physiology of sleep
R01MH-04849-30 (BPN) DIAMOND, IRVING T DUKE UNIVERSITY DURHAM, N C 27706 Behavioral analysis of sensory neocortex
R01MH-05286-29 (BPN) MC CARTHY, GREGORY YALE UNIVERSITY PO BOX 3333 /333 CEDAR STREET NEW HAVEN, CT 06510 Psychobiology of event related potentials
K05MH-05804-22 (MHK) DEMENT, WILLIAM C STANFORD UNIVERSITY SCH/MEDICI 701 WELCH RD. STE. 2226 STANFORD, CA 94305 Sleep and its disorders
K05MH-06092-15 (MHK) EKMAN, PAUL LANGLEY PORTER PSYCH INST 401 PARNASSUS/BOX HIL SAN FRANCISCO, CA 94143-0984 Communication through nonverbal behavior
K05MH-06318-22 (MHK) ADER, ROBERT UNIVERSITY OF ROCHESTER 300 CRITTENDEN BLVD ROCHESTER, NY 14642 Psychoneuroimmunology
R37MH-06686-29 (SRCM) FREEMAN, WALTER J UNIVERSITY OF CALIFORNIA MOLECULAR AND CELL BIOLOGY BERKELEY, CA 94720 Correlation of EEG and behavior
R01MH-06723-29 (BPN) AREZZO, JOSEPH C ALBERT EINSTEIN COLLEGE OF MED 1300 MORRIS PARK AVENUE BRONX, NEW YORK 10461 Electrophysiologic studies of psychomotor processes
R37MH-07658-28 (DABR) MORSE, WILLIAM H HARVARD MEDICAL SCHOOL 25 SHATTUCK STREET BOSTON, MASS 02115 Drug action on behavior controlled by noxious stimuli
R37MH-08366-29 (BPN) ZEIGLER, HARRIS P HUNTER COLL OF CUNY 695 PARK AVE, DEPT PSYCHOLOGY NEW YORK, N Y 10021 Neural control of behavior
P01MH-08618-27 (SRCM) FRIEDHOFF, ARNOLD J NEW YORK UNIV MEDICAL CNTR 550 FIRST AVENUE NEW YORK, NY 10016 Biological studies of psychotic disorders
P01MH-08618-27 0099 (SRCM) FRIEDHOFF, ARNOLD J Biological studies of psychotic disorders Adaptation of the dopaminergic system to perturbations
P01MH-08618-27 0100 (SRCM) MILLER, JEANNETTE C Biological studies of psychotic disorders Studies on the regulation of adaptive aspects of the dopaminergic system
P01MH-08618-27 0101 (SRCM) ROSENGARTEN, HELEN Biological studies of psychotic disorders Adaptation of functional relationships of D1 and D2 dopamine receptors
P01MH-08618-27 0102 (SRCM) MILLER, JEANNETTE C Biological studies of psychotic disorders Prenatal influences on the development of catecholaminergic system
R37MH-08957-27 (TDA) RICKELS, KARL M UNIVERSITY HOSPITAL 3400 SPRUCE STREET PHILADELPHIA, PA 19104 Early drug evaluation in neurotic outpatients
N01MH-10001-00 ( ) SEMA, INC** 2501 RESEARCH BOULEVARD ROCKVILLE, MD 20850 SIV Rhesus Macaque model for pediatric AIDS
K05MH-10562-15 (SRCM) SEIDEN, LEWIS S 947 EAST 58TH STREET CHICAGO, IL 60637 Brain monoamines, drugs and conditioned behavior
R37MH-11191-26 (BPN) SEIDEN, LEWIS S UNIVERSITY OF CHICAGO 947 E 58TH ST, ABBOTT HALL 109 CHICAGO, ILL 60637 Brain monamines and conditioned behavior
R01MH-12507-26 (PCB) SHAGASS, CHARLES PHILADELPHIA PSYCHIATRIC CTR FORD ROAD & MONUMENT AVENUE PHILADELPHIA, PA 19131 Electrophysiological studies of psychiatric disorder
R37MH-12526-24 (BPN) MC GAUGH, JAMES L UNIVERSITY OF CALIFORNIA IRVINE, CA 92717 Drug effects on learning and memory
R37MH-12717-23 (PYB) SHIFFRIN, RICHARD M INDIANA UNIVERSITY BLOOMINGTON, IN 47405 Information processing, search and retrieval
R01MH-13688-25 (BPN) SCHANBERG, SAUL M DUKE UNIV MED CTR. BOX 3813 DURHAM, N C 27710 Neurotropic drugs, hormones and brain function
R01MH-13923-23 (SRCM) HOBSON, J ALLAN HARVARD MEDICAL SCHOOL 74 FENWOOD RD BOSTON, MA 02115 Neurophysiological mechanisms of sleep cycle control
K05MH-14024-24 (MHK) FRIEDHOFF, ARNOLD J NEW YORK UNIV MEDICAL CNTR 550 FIRST AVENUE NEW YORK, N Y 10016 Chemical factors in abnormal behavior
R01MH-14076-23 (BBP) THIESSEN, DELBERT D UNIVERSITY OF TEXAS MEZES HALL 320 AUSTIN, TX 78712 Pheromone communication and social behavior
R37MH-14092-24 (BPN) ROTH, ROBERT H YALE UNIVERSITY 333 CEDAR STREET NEW HAVEN, CT 06510 Antipsychotic drugs and control of dopaminergic neurons
R37MH-14651-25 (BBP) MARLER, PETER ROBERT UNIVERSITY OF CALIFORNIA DEPT ZOOLOGY DAVIS, CA 95616 Comparative study of vocal learning
R01MH-15413-23 (PCB) SCHILDKRAUT, JOSEPH J MASSACHUSETTS MENTAL HLTH CTR 74 FENWOOD ROAD BOSTON, MA 02115 Psychopharmacology of biogenic amines in depressions
R37MH-15455-21 (BPN) SMITH, GERARD P N Y HOSP-CORNELL MED CENTER 21 BLOOMINGDALE ROAD WHITE PLAINS, N Y 10605 Neurobehavioral analysis of ingestion
R37MH-15872-24 (CEP) KINTSCH, WALTER UNIVERSITY OF COLORADO CAMPUS BOX 345 BOULDER, COLO 80309-0345 Text comprehension and memory
R01MH-15965-18 (PYB) ROSENBLUM, LEONARD A STATE UNIVERSITY OF NEW YORK 450 CLARKSON AVE; BOX 1203 BROOKLYN, NY 11203 Environmental demands and mother-infant relations
R01MH-16360-22 (PYB) NELSON, DOUGLAS L UNIVERSITY OF SOUTH FLORIDA TAMPA, FL 33620 Words and pictures--Coding sensory and meaning features
R01MH-16496-18 (CEP) AARONSON, DORIS R NEW YORK UNIVERSITY 6 WASHINGTON PLACE, RM 860 NEW YORK, NY 10003 Perception and memory for verbal materials
R37MH-16841-24 (SRCM) HARVEY, JOHN A MED COL OF PENN AT EPPI 3200 HENRY AVENUE PHILADELPHIA, PA 19129 Effect of CNS lesions on drug action
R01MH-17691-22 (BPN) JENDEN, DONALD J UNIVERSITY OF CALIFORNIA HEALTH SCIENCES CTR LOS ANGELES, CA 90024-1735 Interaction of drugs with brain acetylcholine
K05MH-17785-15 (MHK) MUSACCHIO, JOSE M NEW YORK UNIVERSITY MED CTR 550 FIRST AVENUE NEW YORK, NY 10016 Neuropeptides receptors
R37MH-17871-22 (BPN) AGHAJANIAN, GEORGE K CONNECTICUT MENTAL HEALTH CTR 34 PARK STREET NEW HAVEN, CT 06508 Psychotogenic drug action on chemically defined neurons
R37MH-18343-21 (BPN) NOTTEBOHM, FERNANDO ROCKEFELLER UNIVERSITY 1230 YORK AVENUE NEW YORK, N Y 10021 Neurogenesis in adult brain
K05MH-18428-25 (MHK) RECHTSCHAFFEN, ALLAN UNIVERSITY OF CHICAGO 5743 SOUTH DREXEL AVENUE CHICAGO, IL 60637 The psychology and physiology of sleep
R37MH-18501-22 (BPN) SNYDER, SOLOMON H JOHNS HOPKINS UNIVERSITY 725 NORTH WOLFE STREET BALTIMORE, MD 21205 Neurochemical actions of psychotropic drugs
R01MH-18579-19 (PCB) KLEIN, RACHEL G CHILDRENS BEHAV DISORDERS CLIN 270-05 76TH AVENUE NEW HYDE PARK, NY 11042 Prospective longitudinal study of hyperactive children
R01MH-19420-21 (BPN) GROSS, CHARLES G PRINCETON UNIVERSITY 1-E-14 GREEN HALL PRINCETON, NJ 08544-1010 Functions of occipito-temporal cortex
R01MH-19506-17 (BPN) MICHAEL, RICHARD P GEORGIA MENTAL HEALTH INST 1256 BRIARCLIFF RD NE ATLANTA, GA 30306 Hormones, the brain & primate behavior
R37MH-19560-20 (EPS) ERLENMEYER-KIMLING, L 722 WEST 168TH STREET NEW YORK, NY 10032 Prospective study of children of schizophrenic parents
R37MH-19604-18A1 (SRCM) SELIGMAN, MARTIN E UNIVERSITY OF PENNSYLVANIA 3815 WALNUT STREET PHILADELPHIA, PA 19104 Prevention of depression by change in explanatory style
K05MH-20342-15 (MHK) LIEBERMAN, MORTON A UNIVERSITY OF CALIFORNIA 1350 7TH AVE, CSBS 237 SAN FRANCISCO, CA 94143 Processes and outcomes of people-changing groups
K06MH-22014-29 (MHK) ERIKSEN, CHARLES W UNIVERSITY OF ILLINOIS 603 E DANIEL STREET CHAMPAIGN, IL 61820 Coding and attentional factors in visual perception
R01MH-22149-17 (PCB) CALLAWAY, ENOCH VETERANS ADMINISTRATION MED CT 4150 CLEMENT STREET (116T) SAN FRANCISCO, CA 94121 The pharmacology of human information processing
K05MH-22536-22 (MHK) PRANGE, ARTHUR J, JR UNIV OF N C AT CHAPEL HILL MEDICAL SCH WING B, CB#7160 CHAPEL HILL, NC 27599 Hormones in cause and treatment of affective disorders
R37MH-22803-18 (SRCM) EMDE, ROBERT N UNIVERSITY OF COLORADO 4200 E NINTH AVE, BOX C268-69 DENVER, CO 80262 Social affective development in infancy
R01MH-23433-18 (BPN) JACOBS, BARRY L PRINCETON UNIVERSITY PROGRAM IN NEUROSCIENCE PRINCETON, N J 08544 Neural substrates of arousal and emotion
U01MH-23864-19 (SRCM) ENDICOTT, JEAN 722 WEST 168TH STREET NEW YORK, N Y 10032 Clinical studies of the NIMH collaborative program on depression
R01MH-24114-14 (SRCM) ANTELMAN, SEYMOUR M W PSYCHIATRIC INST & CLINIC 3811 O'HARA STREET PITTSBURGH, PA 15213 Long-term sensitization after acute stressors
R01MH-24115-15 (PYB) FOWLER, HARRY UNIVERSITY OF PITTSBURGH PITTSBURGH, PA 15260 Signaling and affective functions in conditioning
R37MH-24285-16 (BPN) JOH, TONG H W.M. BURKE MEDICAL RESEARCH 785 MAMARONECK AVENUE WHITE PLAINS, NY 10605 Structural analysis of catecholamine enzyme genes
R37MH-24600-18 (CEP) SQUIRE, LARRY R UNIV OF CALIF, SAN DIEGO LA JOLLA, CA 92093 Memory as affected in injury, disease and ECT
R37MH-24652-17 (SRCM) KUPFER, DAVID J WESTERN PSYCHIATRIC INST & CLI 3811 O'HARA STREET PITTSBURGH, PA 15213 EEG sleep studies in relation to affective illness
K05MH-25082-21 (MHK) FUSTER, JOAQUIN M UNIVERSITY OF CALIFORNIA 760 WESTWOOD PLAZA LOS ANGELES, CA 90024-1759 Cortical processes in perception and memory
R37MH-25140-18 (BPN) STRICKER, EDWARD M UNIVERSITY OF PITTSBURGH 479 CRAWFORD HALL PITTSBURGH, PA 15260 Homeostatic origins of motivation
R37MH-25281-18 (NSS) ROUTTENBERG, ARYEH NORTHWESTERN UNIVERSITY 2021 SHERIDAN ROAD EVANSTON, IL 60208 Memory consolidation

localization

U01MH-25416-18 (SRCM) CORYELL, WILLIAM UNIVERSITY OF IOWA 500 NEWTON ROAD IOWA CITY, IA 52242 NIMH collaborative studies of depression

U01MH-25430-18 (SRCM) RICE, JOHN P WASHINGTON UNIVERSITY 660 S EUCLID AVE BOX 8134 ST LOUIS, MO 63110 Collaborative clinical studies on psychobiology of depression

U01MH-25478-18 (SRCM) KELLER, MARTIN B BROWN UNIVERSITY SCH OF MED BOX G PROVIDENCE, RI 02912 Collaborative clinical studies on psychobiology of depression

R37MH-25594-18 (CEP) HILLYARD, STEVEN A UNIV OF CALIFORNIA SAN DIEGO LA JOLLA, CA 92093-0608 Electrophysiological studies of selective perception

P01MH-25642-18 (SRCM) HENINGER, GEORGE R CONNECTICUT MENTAL HEALTH 34 PARK ST NEW HAVEN, CT 06508 Neurobiological basis of major psychiatric disorders

P01MH-25642-18 0011 (SRCM) AGHAJANIAN, GEORGE K Neurobiological basis of major psychiatric disorders Serotonin, affective disorders and antidepressants

P01MH-25642-18 0013 (SRCM) DAVIS, MICHEAL Neurobiological basis of major psychiatric disorders Amygdala kindling as a model of panic

P01MH-25642-18 0014 (SRCM) DAVIS, MICHAEL Neurobiological basis of major psychiatric disorders Evaluation of quantitative SPECT imaging of the benzodiazepine receptor

P01MH-25642-18 0015 (SRCM) DAVIS, MICHAEL Neurobiological basis of major psychiatric disorders Opiate withdrawal

P01MH-25642-18 0016 (SRCM) DAVIS, MICHAEL Neurobiological basis of major psychiatric disorders Fear-potentiated startle in humans

P01MH-25642-18 0017 (SRCM) DAVIS, MICHAEL Neurobiological basis of major psychiatric disorders Roles of serotonin and norepinephrine in panic

P01MH-25642-18 0018 (SRCM) DAVIS, MICHAEL Neurobiological basis of major psychiatric disorders Brain dopamine and obsessive compulsive disorders

P01MH-25642-18 0019 (SRCM) AGHAJANIAN, GEORGE K Neurobiological basis of major psychiatric disorders Interaction of 5HT receptor sybtypes with NPY and CRF

P01MH-25642-18 0021 (SRCM) DEUTCH, ARIEL Y Neurobiological basis of major psychiatric disorders Atypical and typical antipsychotics and their actions on D2 and 5HT receptors

P01MH-25642-18 0022 (SRCM) DEUTCH, ARIEL Y Neurobiological basis of major psychiatric disorders Acute and chronic antipsychotics on brain c-fos and c-fos protein

P01MH-25642-18 0023 (SRCM) DEUTCH, ARIEL Y Neurobiological basis of major psychiatric disorders Selective D2 antagonists and 5HT2 antagonists with haloperidol on G proteins

P01MH-25642-18 0024 (SRCM) BUNNEY, BENJAMIN S Neurobiological basis of major psychiatric disorders 5HT and D2 receptor antagonists--Electrophysiology and biochemistry of dopamine

P01MH-25642-18 0025 (SRCM) DEUTCH, ARIEL Y Neurobiological basis of major psychiatric disorders Dopamine release and the displacement of D2 ligands by endogenous dopamine

P01MH-25642-18 0026 (SRCM) DEUTCH, ARIEL Y Neurobiological basis of major psychiatric disorders 5HT receptors in MCPP induced exacerbation of psychotic symptoms in Schizophrenia

P01MH-25642-18 9002 (SRCM) PRICE, LAWRENCE H Neurobiological basis of major psychiatric disorders Core--Clinical behavior

P01MH-25642-18 9003 (SRCM) AGHAJANIAN, GEORGE K Neurobiological basis of major psychiatric disorders Core--Electronics

P01MH-25642-18 9004 (SRCM) ROTH, ROBERT H Neurobiological basis of major psychiatric disorders Core--Neuropharmacology

P01MH-25642-18 9005 (SRCM) NESTLER, ERIC J Neurobiological basis of major psychiatric disorders Core--Molecular pharmacology

P01MH-25642-18 9006 (SRCM) INNIS, ROBERT B Neurobiological basis of major psychiatric disorders Core--Radiochemistry-Imaging

R37MH-26149-16 (BPN) HEILIGENBERG, WALTER F UNIVERSITY OF CALIFORNIA 9500 GILMAN DR LA JOLLA, CA 92093-0202 Information processing in laminated neuronal networks

R01MH-26212-18 (BPN) HAWKINS, ROBERT D COLUMBIA UNIVERSITY 722 WEST 168TH STREET NEW YORK, NY 10032 Learning mechanisms in abdominal ganglion of Aplysia

R01MH-26341-16 (PCB) HARROW, MARTIN MICHAEL REESE HOSPITAL & MED C 31ST ST AT LAKE SHORE DRIVE CHICAGO, IL 60616 Schizophrenic cognition -- A longitudinal study

R37MH-26481-16 (BPN) YAHR, PAULINE I UNIVERSITY OF CALIFORNIA DEPT OF PSYCHOBIOLOGY IRVINE, CA 92717 Hormonal control of social behavior

R01MH-27692-17 (BPN) RICHELSON, ELLIOTT MAYO FOUNDATION 200 FIRST STREET SOUTHWEST ROCHESTER, MN 55905 Psychotropic drugs and receptor sensitivity changes

R01MH-28210-14A1 (SRCM) KOEGEL, ROBERT L UNIVERSITY OF CALIFORNIA SANTA BARBARA, CA 93106 Research in autism--Parent intervention

R01MH-28216-16 (SRCM) BOWERS, MALCOLM B, JR CONNECTICUT MENTAL HEALTH CENT 25 PARK STREET NEW HAVEN, CT 06519 Dopamine and chronic antipsychotic drug treatment

R37MH-28274-16 (SRCM) WEISSMAN, MYRNA M RES FDN FOR MENTAL HYGIENE 722 WEST 168TH ST NEW YORK, NY 10032 Genetic studies of depressive disorders

R01MH-28287-15 (EPS) EGELAND, JANICE A N. RESEARCH OFFICE 49 SYLVANIA ROAD HERSHEY, PA 17033 Genetic studies of affective disorders among Amish

R37MH-28355-16 (SRCM) ALBERTS, JEFFREY R DEPT OF PSYCHOLOGY INDIANA UNIVERSITY BLOOMINGTON, IN 47405 Ontogeny of control and organization of behavior

R01MH-28380-13S1 (SRCM) RUBIN, ROBERT T HARBOR-UCLA MEDICAL CENTER 1000 WEST CARSON ST , BLDG F-5 TORRANCE, CA 90509 Hormone rhythms--Metabolic significance in depression

R37MH-28783-15 (BPN) WURTMAN, RICHARD J MASSACHUSETTS INST OF TECH 77 MASSACHUSETTS AVENUE CAMBRIDGE, MA 02139 Psychopharmacological effects of exogenous choline

R37MH-28849-15 (BPN) BUNNEY, BENJAMIN S YALE UNIVERSITY 333 CEDAR ST, P O BOX 3333 NEW HAVEN, CT 06510 Neuroleptic CNS effects--Acute and chronic studies

R01MH-28942-13 (BPN) HELLER, ALFRED UNIVERSITY OF CHICAGO 947 EAST 58TH STREET CHICAGO, ILLINOIS 60637 Drug mechanism in neuronal dopamine organization

R37MH-29094-15 (BPN) FRAZER, ALAN UNIV OF PENN, MED CTR (151E) UNIVERSITY AND WOODLAND AVES PHILADELPHIA, PA 19104 Antidepressants and monoamine receptors and responses

R37MH-29228-15 (BPN) SULSER, FRIDOLIN VANDERBILT UNIVERSITY SCHOOL OF MEDICINE NASHVILLE, TENN 37232 Psychopharmacology--Beta adrenoreceptor regulation in brain

R01MH-29380-15 (PYB) SILVER, RAE BARNARD COLLEGE 3009 BROADWAY NEW YORK, N Y 10027 Factors underlying parental behavior

R01MH-29617-12 (SRCM) JUST, MARCEL A CARNEGIE-MELLON UNIVERSITY 5000 FORBES AVENUE PITTSBURGH, PA 15213 Cognitive capacity and language comprehension

R01MH-29618-13S1 (TDA) FRANK, ELLEN WESTERN PSYCHIATRIC INST & CL 3811 O'HARA STREET PITTSBURGH, PA 15213 Maintenance therapies in recurrent depression

R01MH-29670-14 (BPN) STRICKER, EDWARD M UNIVERSITY OF PITTSBURGH 479 CRAWFORD HALL PITTSBURGH, PA 15260 Adaptive behavior and brain monoamines

R01MH-29775-14 (PYB) SNOWDON, CHARLES T UNIVERSITY OF WISCONSIN 1202 W JOHNSON ST MADISON, WI 53706 Evolution and development of primate speech analogues

U01MH-29957-15 (SRCM) FAWCETT, JAN A RUSH-PRESBYTERIAN ST LUKE'S ME 1653 W CONGRESS PARKWAY CHICAGO, IL 60612 Psychobiology of depression--Clinical collaborative studies

R01MH-30569-14 (SRCM) RODRIGUEZ, ORLANDO FORDHAM UNIVERSITY BRONX, N Y 10458 Spanish speaking mental health R and D center

R01MH-30710-10A1 (EPS) DOHRENWEND, BRUCE P RES FOUND FOR MENTAL HYGIENE 722 WEST 168TH STREET NEW YORK, NY 10032 Social stress social selection and psychiatric disorders

R37MH-30723-14 (TDA) WEINER, RICHARD D DURHAM VA MEDICAL CENTER DURHAM, N C 27705 Long-term effects of electroconvulsive therapy

R37MH-30750-14 (TDAA) HOGARTY, GERARD E WESTERN PSYCH INST & CLINIC 3811 O'HARA STREET PITTSBURGH, PA 15213 Environmental-personal treatment of schizophrenia

P50MH-30854-14 (SRCM) PFEFFERBAUM, ADOLF VETERANS ADMINISTRATION 3801 MIRANDA PALO ALTO, CA 94304 MHCRC to study biological correlates of psychopathology

P50MH-30854-14 0010 (SRCM) ZARCONE, VINCENT P MHCRC to study biological correlates of psychopathology Sleep electrophysiology

P50MH-30854-14 0015 (SRCM) PFEFFERBAUM, ADOLF MHCRC to study biological correlates of psychopathology Neuroimaging

P50MH-30854-14 0016 (SRCM) PFEFFERBAUM, ADOLF MHCRC to study biological correlates of psychopathology Neurochemistry and psychopharmacology

P50MH-30854-14 0017 (SRCM) PFEFFERBAUN, ADOLF MHCRC to study biological correlates of psychopathology Waking psychophysiology

P50MH-30854-14 9001 (SRCM) PFEFFERBAUM, ADOLF MHCRC to study biological correlates of psychopathology Core--Methodology and statistics

P50MH-30906-14 (SRCM) KLEIN, DONALD F RESEARCH FDN FOR MENTAL HYGIEN 722 WEST 168TH STREET NEW YORK, NY 10032 MHCRC-New York State Psychiatric Institute

P50MH-30906-14 9001 (SRCM) ENDICOTT, JEAN MHCRC-New York State Psychiatric Institute Core--Research assessment and training

P50MH-30906-14 9002 (SRCM) ROSS, DONALD C MHCRC-New York State Psychiatric Institute Core--Computer facility

P50MH-30906-14 9005 (SRCM) GORMAN, JACK MHCRC-New York State Psychiatric Institute Core--Biologic studies unit

P50MH-30906-14 9006 (SRCM) ENDICOTT, JEAN MHCRC-New York State Psychiatric Institute Core--Normal controls

P50MH-30906-14 9007 (SRCM) COOPER, THOMAS MHCRC-New York State Psychiatric Institute Core--Analytical psychopharmacology

P50MH-30906-14 9008 (SRCM) GILLIAM, CONRAD MHCRC-New York State Psychiatric Institute Core--Molecular genetics

P50MH-30906-14 9009 (SRCM) LIEBOWITZ, MICHAEL MHCRC-New York State Psychiatric Institute Core--Anxiety diagnosis and recruitment center

P50MH-30906-14 9010 (SRCM) SCHNEIER, FRANK MHCRC-New York State Psychiatric Institute Core--Open treatment center

P50MH-30911-14 (TDA) LIBERMAN, ROBERT P BRENTWOOD VA MEDICAL CENTER 11301 WILSHIRE BLVD LOS ANGELES, CA 90073 Clinical research center for the study of schizophrenia

P50MH-30911-14 0005 (TDA) GOLDSTEIN, MICHAEL J Clinical research center for the study of schizophrenia Coping behavior and schizophrenia

P50MH-30911-14 0007 (TDA) MARDER, STEPHEN R Clinical research center for the study of schizophrenia Predicting optimal neuroleptic therapy for schizophrenic outpatients

P50MH-30911-14 9001 (TDA) WALLACE, CHARLES Clinical research center for the study of schizophrenia CORE--Behavioral assessment and social skills laboratory

P50MH-30911-14 9002 (TDA) GOLDSTEIN, MICHAEL J Clinical research center for the study of schizophrenia CORE--Family assessment and treatment laboratory

P50MH-30911-14 9003 (TDA) NUECHTERLEIN, KEITH H Clinical research center for the study of schizophrenia CORE--Cognition and psychophysiology laboratory

P50MH-30911-14 9004 (TDA) MARDER, STEPHEN R Clinical research center for the study of schizophrenia CORE--Psychopharmacology laboratory

P50MH-30911-14 9005 (TDA) VENTURA, JOSEPH Clinical research center for the study of schizophrenia CORE--Diagnosis and psychopathology laboratory

P50MH-30911-14 9006 (TDA) MINTZ, JAMES Clinical research center for the study of schizophrenia CORE--Data management

P50MH-30911-14 9007 (TDA) NUECHTERLEIN, KEITH H Clinical research center for the study of schizophrenia CORE--Aftercare clinic

P50MH-30911-14 9008 (TDA) LIBERMAN, ROBERT P Clinical research center for the study of schizophrenia CORE--Rehabilitative medicine service--Camarillo-UCLA

P50MH-30911-14 9009 (TDA) FALLOON, IAN Clinical research center for the study of schizophrenia CORE--Diagnostic and psychopathology

P50MH-30911-14 0009 (TDA) NUECHTERLEIN, KEITH H Clinical research center for the study of schizophrenia Developmental processes in schizophrenic relapse
P50MH-30911-14 0012 (TDA) CUMMINGS, JEFFREY L Clinical research center for the study of schizophrenia Measurement and prognostic value of EPS--Effects of neuroleptics
P50MH-30911-14 0013 (TDA) MARSHALL, B D JR Clinical research center for the study of schizophrenia Fenfluramine therapy for treatment-resistant schizophrenics
P50MH-30911-14 0014 (TDA) LIBERMAN, ROBERT P Clinical research center for the study of schizophrenia Psychiatric symptoms and the functional capacity to work
P50MH-30911-14 0015 (TDA) LIBERMAN, ROBERT P Clinical research center for the study of schizophrenia Job finding club for psychiatric patients
P50MH-30911-14 0016 (TDA) KOEGEL, PAUL Clinical research center for the study of schizophrenia Adaptation of the homeless mentally ill
P50MH-30911-14 0017 (TDA) ETH, SPENCER Clinical research center for the study of schizophrenia Behavioral family therapy for veterans with schizophrenia
P50MH-30911-14 0018 (TDA) BUCHSBAUM, MONTE Clinical research center for the study of schizophrenia Brain imaging studies of attention in schizophrenia
P50MH-30911-14 0019 (TDA) NUECHTERLEIN, KEITH H Clinical research center for the study of schizophrenia Attentional vulnerability indicators in familial schizophrenics
P50MH-30911-14 0020 (TDA) GREEN, MICHAEL F Clinical research center for the study of schizophrenia Neurobehavioral and attentional factors in schizophrenia
P50MH-30911-14 0021 (TDA) JACOBS, HARVEY Clinical research center for the study of schizophrenia Head injury family training project
P50MH-30911-14 0022 (TDA) LIBERMAN, ROBERT Clinical research center for the study of schizophrenia Brentwood VA rehabilitation service
P50MH-30911-14 0023 (TDA) BUCHSBAUM, MONTE Clinical research center for the study of schizophrenia Regional brain glucose metabolic rate in schizophrenic relatives
P50MH-30911-14 0024 (TDA) GREEN, MICHAEL F Clinical research center for the study of schizophrenia Early visual processing in schizophrenia
P50MH-30911-14 0025 (TDA) DAWSON, MICHAEL E Clinical research center for the study of schizophrenia Electrodermal dysfunctions and schizophrenia
P50MH-30911-14 0026 (TDA) SATZ, PAUL Clinical research center for the study of schizophrenia Laterality and cognitive subtypes in schizophrenia
P50MH-30911-14 0027 (TDA) HANS, SYDNEY L Clinical research center for the study of schizophrenia Jerusalem infant development study--adolescent follow-up
P50MH-30911-14 0028 (TDA) WYNNE, LYMAN Clinical research center for the study of schizophrenia Finnish adoptive family study of schizophrenia
P50MH-30911-14 0029 (TDA) JACOBS, HARVEY E Clinical research center for the study of schizophrenia Validation of a rehabilitation readiness inventory
P50MH-30911-14 0030 (TDA) MARDER, STEPHEN R Clinical research center for the study of schizophrenia Predicting optimal neuroleptic therapy for schizophrenia
P50MH-30911-14 0031 (TDA) MARDER, STEPHEN R Clinical research center for the study of schizophrenia Management of risk for relapse in schizophrenia
P50MH-30911-14 0032 (TDA) PUTTEN, THEODORE VAN Clinical research center for the study of schizophrenia Dose-Response of neuroleptics in schizophrenia
P50MH-30911-14 0033 (TDA) BARTZOKIS, GEORGE Clinical research center for the study of schizophrenia Magnetic resonance imaging studies of tardive dyskinesia
P50MH-30911-14 0034 (TDA) GOLDSTEIN, MICHAEL J Clinical research center for the study of schizophrenia Coping behavior in schizophrenia
P50MH-30911-14 0035 (TDA) KARNO, MARVIN Clinical research center for the study of schizophrenia Family intervention for Hispanic-American schizophrenics
P50MH-30911-14 0036 (TDA) GOLDSTEIN, MICHAEL J Clinical research center for the study of schizophrenia Lithium and family management of bipolar disorder
P50MH-30914-14 (SRCM) GILLIN, J CHRISTIAN UNIVERSITY OF CALIFORNIA 9500 GILMAN DRIVE LA JOLLA, CA 92093-0603 Psychopharmacological study of psychiatric disorders
P50MH-30914-14 0046 (SRCM) GILLIN, J CHRISTIAN Psychopharmacological study of psychiatric disorders Polygraphic sleep recordings in depression and alcoholism
P50MH-30914-14 0047 (SRCM) KRIPKE, DANIEL F Psychopharmacological study of psychiatric disorders Photoperiodic treatment of depression
P50MH-30914-14 0048 (SRCM) PARRY, BARBARA L Psychopharmacological study of psychiatric disorders Chronobiology of premenstrual depression
P50MH-30914-14 0049 (SRCM) SHIROMANI, PRIYATTAM J Psychopharmacological study of psychiatric disorders Testing three hypotheses for depression in a rodent model of depression
P50MH-30914-14 0050 (SRCM) STAHL, STEPHEN M Psychopharmacological study of psychiatric disorders 5HT receptor dysregulation hypothesis
P50MH-30914-14 0051 (SRCM) GILLIN, J CHRISTIAN Psychopharmacological study of psychiatric disorders The cholinergic/aminergic hypothesis of affective disorders
P50MH-30914-14 0052 (SRCM) GILLIN, J CHRISTIAN Psychopharmacological study of psychiatric disorders Mood and psychobiological changes during acute withdrawal in stimulant abusers
P50MH-30914-14 0053 (SRCM) DUPONT, RENEE M Psychopharmacological study of psychiatric disorders Cognitive, MRI and SPECT abnormalities in major affective disorders
P50MH-30914-14 0054 (SRCM) BUCHSBAUM, MONTE Psychopharmacological study of psychiatric disorders Localized cerebral metabolism during sleep in normals and depressives
P50MH-30914-14 0055 (SRCM) WU, JOSEPH Psychopharmacological study of psychiatric disorders Effects of sleep deprivation on mood and localized cerebral glucose metabolism
P50MH-30914-14 0056 (SRCM) ZISOOK, SIDNEY Psychopharmacological study of psychiatric disorders Depression and spousal bereavement
P50MH-30914-14 0057 (SRCM) IRWIN, MICHAEL Psychopharmacological study of psychiatric disorders Effects of central corticotropin administration on natural killer cytotoxicity
P50MH-30914-14 0058 (SRCM) DARKO, DENIS F Psychopharmacological study of psychiatric disorders Depression, stress, and cellular immune function
P50MH-30914-14 0059 (SRCM) BROWN, SANDRA A Psychopharmacological study of psychiatric disorders Life events in relation to affective disorders and alcohol dependence
P50MH-30914-14 9001 (SRCM) GILLIN, J CHRISTIAN Psychopharmacological study of psychiatric disorders Core--Patient accrual and assessment
P50MH-30914-14 9002 (SRCM) GILLIN, J CHRISTIAN Psychopharmacological study of psychiatric disorders Core--Laboratory component
P50MH-30914-14 9003 (SRCM) GILLIN, J CHRISTIAN Psychopharmacological study of psychiatric disorders Core--Data management
P50MH-30915-15 (TDA) KUPFER, DAVID J WESTERN PSYCHIATRIC INST & CLI 3811 O'HARA STREET PITTSBURGH, PA 15213 Clinical research center study of affective disorders
P50MH-30915-15 0001 (TDA) KUPFER, DAVID J Clinical research center study of affective disorders Clinical psychobiology and regulatory systems
P50MH-30915-15 0002 (TDA) KUPFER, DAVID J Clinical research center study of affective disorders Treatment approaches in affective disorders
P50MH-30915-15 0003 (TDA) KUPFER, DAVID J Clinical research center study of affective disorders Selected comorbid conditions
P50MH-30915-15 9011 (TDA) KAUFMAN, CAROL Clinical research center study of affective disorders Core--Grants development and management
P50MH-30915-15 9015 (TDA) LIDZ, CHARLES W Clinical research center study of affective disorders Core--Informed consent
P50MH-30915-15 9016 (TDA) KUPFER, DAVID J Clinical research center study of affective disorders Core--Laboratory
P50MH-30915-15 9017 (TDA) KUPFER, DAVID J Clinical research center study of affective disorders CORE--Biological rhythms and psychobiology
P50MH-30915-15 9018 (TDA) KAPLAN, BARRY Clinical research center study of affective disorders CORE--Molecular neurobiology and genetics
P50MH-30915-15 9019 (TDA) PEREL, JAMES M Clinical research center study of affective disorders CORE--Clinical psychopharmacology
P50MH-30915-15 9020 (TDA) GREENHOUSE, JOEL B Clinical research center study of affective disorders CORE--Methodology
P50MH-30915-15 9021 (TDA) REYNOLDS, CHARLES F Clinical research center study of affective disorders CORE--Late-life mental disorders
P50MH-30929-15 (SRCM) BOWERS, MALCOLM B, JR YALE UNIVERSITY P O BOX 3333 NEW HAVEN, CONN 06510 Clinical science research center in psychiatry
P50MH-30929-15 0032 (SRCM) BOWERS, MALCOLM B Clinical science research center in psychiatry Affective disorders
P50MH-30929-15 9001 (SRCM) HENINGER, GEORGE R Clinical science research center in psychiatry Core--Clinical psychopharmacology and molecular neurochemistry
P50MH-30929-15 9003 (SRCM) JATLOW, PETER Clinical science research center in psychiatry Core--Laboratory for drugs and drugs metabolites
P50MH-30929-15 9004 (SRCM) YOUNG, J GERALD Clinical science research center in psychiatry Core--Laboratory for developmental neurochemistry
P50MH-30929-15 9005 (SRCM) KIDD, KENNETH K Clinical science research center in psychiatry Core--Genetics and epidemiology unit
P50MH-30929-15 9006 (SRCM) ROTH, ROBERT Clinical science research center in psychiatry Core--Laboratory of neuroanatomy and neuropathology
P50MH-30929-15 9007 (SRCM) QUINLAN, DONALD Clinical science research center in psychiatry Core--Clinical methodology and cohort development and maintenane
P01MH-31050-15 (TDA) STUNKARD, ALBERT J UNIVERSITY OF PENNSYLVANIA 133 S 36TH ST, SUITE 507 PHILADELPHIA, PA 19104-3246 Clinical and experimental study of human obesity
P01MH-31050-15 0001 (TDA) STUNKARD, ALBERT J Clinical and experimental study of human obesity Behavioral treatment of obesity
P01MH-31050-15 0002 (TDA) STUNKARD, ALBERT J Clinical and experimental study of human obesity Non-behavioral treatment of obesity
P01MH-31050-15 0003 (TDA) STUNKARD, ALBERT J Clinical and experimental study of human obesity Gentic studies of obesity
P01MH-31050-15 0004 (TDA) STUNKARD, ALBERT J Clinical and experimental study of human obesity Studies of familial obesity
P01MH-31050-15 0005 (TDA) STUNKARD, ALBERT J Clinical and experimental study of human obesity Nutritional aspects of obesity
R37MH-31067-11 (PCB) CHAPMAN, LOREN J UNIVERSITY OF WISCONSIN 1202 WEST JOHNSON STREET MADISON, WI 53706 Studies of psychosis-prone young adults and psychotics
R01MH-31109-11 (LCR) COWAN, PHILIP A UNIVERSITY OF CALIFORNIA BERKELEY, CA 94720 Couple relationships in family formation
P01MH-31154-14 (TDAC) HOLZMAN, PHILIP S MCLEAN HOSPITAL 115 MILL ST BELMONT, MA 02178 Collaborative biological research in schizophrenia
P01MH-31154-14 0014 (TDAC) GILBERT, JEFFREY M Collaborative biological research in schizophrenia Protein synthesis after prolonged treatment with antipsychotic drugs
P01MH-31154-14 0015 (TDAC) BALDESSARINI, ROSS J Collaborative biological research in schizophrenia Pharmacology of apomorphine induced stereotyped behavior
P01MH-31154-14 0017 (TDAC) BALDESSARINI, ROSS J Collaborative biological research in schizophrenia Stereotyped behavior in goldfish
P01MH-31154-14 0018 (TDAC) BALDESSARINI, ROSS J Collaborative biological research in schizophrenia Actions of neuroleptic drugs on synaptic membranes
P01MH-31154-14 0001 (TDAC) NAUTA, WALLE J Collaborative biological research in schizophrenia Neuroanatomy
P01MH-31154-14 0002 (TDAC) POPE, ALFRED Collaborative biological

PROJECT NO., ORGANIZATIONAL UNIT., INVESTIGATOR, ADDRESS, TITLE

research in schizophrenia General neuropathology
P01MH-31154-14 0005 (TDAC) KETY, SEYMOUR S Collaborative biological research in schizophrenia Nosology, genetic relationships of schizophrenia, affective disorders
P01MH-31154-14 0006 (TDAC) KETY, SEYMOUR S Collaborative biological research in schizophrenia Adopted biological half-siblings
P01MH-31154-14 0007 (TDAC) KETY, SEYMOUR S Collaborative biological research in schizophrenia Continuation and follow-up of adoption studies
P01MH-31154-14 0008 (TDAC) KINNEY, DENNIS Collaborative biological research in schizophrenia Environmental factors in schizophrenia
P01MH-31154-14 0010 (TDAC) MATTHYSSE, STEVEN W Collaborative biological research in schizophrenia Mathematical genetics
P01MH-31154-14 0012 (TDAC) BALDESSARINI, ROSS J Collaborative biological research in schizophrenia Pharmacology of long acting agents affecting dopamine receptors
P01MH-31154-14 0019 (TDAC) BALDESSARINI, ROSS J Collaborative biological research in schizophrenia Transmethylation
P01MH-31154-14 0021 (TDAC) HOLZMAN, PHILIP S Collaborative biological research in schizophrenia Attention as a variable connecting linguistic and cognitive disorders
P01MH-31154-14 0022 (TDAC) LIPINSKI, JOSEPH F Collaborative biological research in schizophrenia Diagnosis and treatment of schizophrenia and other psychotic disorders
P01MH-31154-14 0023 (TDAC) LIPINSKI, JOSEPH F Collaborative biological research in schizophrenia High dose antipsychotic drug treatment
P01MH-31154-14 0024 (TDAC) LIPINSKI, JOSEPH F Collaborative biological research in schizophrenia Effects of gluten on plasma levels of chlorpromazine and clinical state
P01MH-31154-14 0025 (TDAC) LIPINSKI, JOSEPH F Collaborative biological research in schizophrenia Transmethylation in schizophrenia
P50MH-31302-14 (TDA) CLONINGER, C ROBERT WASHINGTON UNIVERSITY 4940 AUDUBON AVE ST LOUIS, MO 63110 Epidemiological genetics and family studies
P50MH-31302-14 0014 (TDA) EARLS, FELTON J Epidemiological genetics and family studies The child assessment unit and registry
P50MH-31302-14 0015 (TDA) HELZER, JOHN E Epidemiological genetics and family studies Adult assessment unit and twin registry
P50MH-31302-14 0016 (TDA) ROO, DABEERU C Epidemiological genetics and family studies Biostatistical consultation facility
P50MH-31302-14 0022 (TDA) ROO, DABEERU C Epidemiological genetics and family studies Genetic study of lipid research center family data
P50MH-31302-14 0023 (TDA) KNESEVICH, JOHN W Epidemiological genetics and family studies A twin-family study of affective disorder
P50MH-31302-14 0024 (TDA) DEVOR, ERIC Epidemiological genetics and family studies Human DNA polymorphism laboratory
P50MH-31302-14 0025 (TDA) TODD, RICHARD Epidemiological genetics and family studies Tissue culture and neurochemistry
R01MH-31340-15 (PCB) HOLZMAN, PHILIP S HARVARD COLLEGE 33 KIRKLAND STREET CAMBRIDGE, MA 02138 Psychomotility and cognitive style in the schizophrenias
R01MH-31862-14 (BPN) BIRD, EDWARD D MC LEAN HOSPITAL 115 MILL STREET BELMONT, MA 02178 Brain tissue resource for neuropsychiatric research
R01MH-32205-11 (CEP) NELSON, THOMAS O UNIVERSITY OF WASHINGTON SEATTLE, WA 98195 Subthreshold memory phenomena
R01MH-32212-12S1 (SRCM) CAMPBELL, MAGDA NEW YORK UNIVERSITY MED CTR 550 FIRST AVENUE NEW YORK, NY 10016 Haloperidol and attentional learning in autistic children
R37MH-32307-13 (PYB) ROVEE-COLLIER, CAROLYN K RUTGERS UNIVERSITY BUSCH CAMPUS NEW BRUNSWICK, NJ 08903 A conditioning analysis of infant memory
R01MH-32309-10 (CVR) KNIGHT, RAYMOND A P O BOX 9110 WALTHAM, MA 02254-9110 Classification of rapists--Implementation & validation
R37MH-32369-13 (TDA) KANE, JOHN M HILLSIDE HOSP/L I JEW MED CTR 75-59 263RD STREET GLEN OAKS, NY 11004 Prospective study of tardive dyskinesia development
R01MH-32457-13 (TDA) OVERALL, JOHN E UNIV OF TEXAS HLTH SCI CTR PO BOX 20708 HOUSTON, TX 77225 Clinical psychopharmacology computer laboratory
R01MH-32588-11 (BSR) MCGUIRE, WILLIAM J YALE UNIVERSITY PSYCH/BOX 11A YALE STATION NEW HAVEN, CT 06520-7447 Content, structure, and functioning of thought systems
R01MH-32675-12 (TDA) COLE, JONATHAN O MCLEAN HOSPITAL 115 MILL ST BELMONT, MA 02178 Course of dyskinesia
P50MH-33127-13 (TDA) PRANGE, ARTHUR J, JR UNIVERSITY OF NORTH CAROLINA CB# 7160 CHAPEL HILL, NC 27599 MHCRC - psychoendocrinology--Children and adults
P50MH-33127-13 0008 (TDA) PEDERSEN, CORT A MHCRC - psychoendocrinology--Children and adults Behavioral pharmacology
P50MH-33127-13 0010 (TDA) GUALTIERI, C THOMAS MHCRC - psychoendocrinology--Children and adults Development neuropsychiatry
P50MH-33127-13 0011 (TDA) EVANS, DWIGHT L MHCRC - psychoendocrinology--Children and adults Affective disorders unit
P50MH-33127-13 0012 (TDA) MAILMAN, RICHARD B MHCRC - psychoendocrinology--Children and adults Biochemical pharmacology
P50MH-33127-13 0013 (TDA) HAGGERTY, JOHN J MHCRC - psychoendocrinology--Children and adults Clinical neuroendocrinology
P50MH-33127-13 0014 (TDA) GOLDEN, ROBERT N MHCRC - psychoendocrinology--Children and adults Psychopharmacology
P50MH-33127-13 9001 (TDA) MASON, GEORGE A MHCRC - psychoendocrinology--Children and adults Core--Endocrine assay laboratory
P50MH-33127-13 9002 (TDA) MCKEE, DAPHNE MHCRC - psychoendocrinology--Children and adults Core--Psychodiagnostic laboratory
P50MH-33127-13 9003 (TDA) RICHARDSON, WILLIAM G MHCRC - psychoendocrinology--Children and adults Core--Information services
P50MH-33127-13 9004 (TDA) BROWNE, JERRY L MHCRC - psychoendocrinology--Children and adults Core--Bioanalytical consortium
P50MH-33127-13 9005 (TDA) QUADE, DANA MHCRC - psychoendocrinology--Children and adults Core--Biostatistics
P50MH-33127-13 0001 (TDA) GARBUTT, JAMES C MHCRC - psychoendocrinology--Children and adults Psychoendocrinology
P50MH-33127-13 0005 (TDA) KIZER, JOHN S MHCRC - psychoendocrinology--Children and adults Neuroendocrine studies
P50MH-33127-13 0007 (TDA) BREESE, GEORGE R MHCRC - psychoendocrinology--Children and adults Neuropharmacology
R01MH-33443-13 (BPN) WECKER, LYNN USF COLLEGE OF MEDICINE 12901 BRUCE B DOWNS BLVD TAMPA, FL 33612-4799 Exogenous choline effects on ACh function in brain
R01MH-33553-13 (PCB) BARLOW, DAVID H STATE UNIV OF NEW YORK ALBANY, NY 12222 Arousal and anxiety in dysfunctional men
R37MH-33688-12 (SRCM) PRINZ, PATRICIA N UNIVERSITY OF WASHINGTON 1959 NE PACIFIC SEATTLE, WA 98195 Biomarkers for early expression of Alzheimers disease
U01MH-33753-09S1 (TDA) IMBER, STANLEY D WESTERN PSYCHIATRIC INST & CLC 3811 O'HARA STREET PITTSBURGH, PA 15213 Treatment of depression: Cooperative data analysis
R01MH-33881-10 (PYB) MILLER, RALPH R SUNY AT BINGHAMTON BINGHAMTON, NY 13901 Extra-acquisition associative determinants of performance
R37MH-33990-12 (PCB) KOVACS, MARIA WESTERN PSYCH, INST, & CLINIC 3811 O'HARA ST PITTSBURGH, PA 15213 Childhood depression-nosologic/developmental aspects
R01MH-34006-12 (BPN) BALDESSARINI, ROSS J MCLEAN HOSPITAL 115 MILL STREET BELMONT, MA 02178 Pharmacology of dopamine receptors in mammalian brain
R01MH-34007-12 (BPN) SANDERS-BUSH, ELAINE VANDERBILT UNIVERSITY SCHOOL OF MEDICINE NASHVILLE, TN 37232-2104 Characterization of central serotonin receptors
R37MH-34176-12 (TDA) BARLOW, DAVID H SUNY AT ALBANY 1400 WASHINGTON AVE ALBANY, NY 12222 Couples treatment of agoraphobia
R37MH-34223-13 (TDA) SHADER, RICHARD I NEW ENGLAND MEDICAL CTR PO BOX 1007 BOSTON, MA 02111 Applications of pharmacokinetics in clinical psychiatry
R37MH-34223-13 0001 (TDA) SHADER, RICHARD I Applications of pharmacokinetics in clinical psychiatry Psychotropic drug disposition and absorption in the elderly
R37MH-34223-13 0002 (TDA) SHADER, RICHARD I Applications of pharmacokinetics in clinical psychiatry Psychotropic drug disposition in abnormal states of nutrition
R37MH-34223-13 0003 (TDA) SHADER, RICHARD I Applications of pharmacokinetics in clinical psychiatry Pharmacokinetic interactions with psychotropic drugs
R37MH-34223-13 0004 (TDA) SHADER, RICHARD I Applications of pharmacokinetics in clinical psychiatry Risks and benefits of hyponotic drug therapy
R01MH-34252-08 (LCR) MILNER, JOEL S NORTHERN ILLINIS UNIVERSITY DEKALB, IL 60115 Description/prediction of intrafamily sexual child abuse
R37MH-34471-10A2 (TDA) POLAND, RUSSELL E HARBOR-U C L A MEDICAL CENTER 1000 WEST CARSON ST., BLDG F5 TORRANCE, CA 90509 Chronoendocrinology of sleep disturbances in depression
R01MH-34486-10 (TDA) LINEHAN, MARSHA M UNIVERSITY OF WASHINGTON SEATTLE, WA 98195 Assessment and treatment of parasuicide patients
R01MH-34728-07 (PCB) CROWE, RAYMOND R UNIV OF IOWA COLLEGE OF MED. 500 NEWTON ROAD IOWA CITY, IA 52242 Linkage study of panic disorder
R01MH-34770-10 (SRCM) HAMILTON, CHARLES TEXAS A&M UNIVERSITY COLLEGE OF MEDICINE COLLEGE STATION, TX 77843-111 Hemispheric specialization
R37MH-35182-08 (LCR) YESAVAGE, JEROME A STANFORD UNIV SCHOOL OF MEDICI 125 PANAMA ST STANFORD, CA 94305-5490 Memory and mental health in aging
R01MH-35202-08A5 (PYB) WRIGHT, ANTHONY A UNIVERSITY OF TEXAS 6420 LAMAR FLEMING AVENUE HOUSTON, TX 77030 Avian and primate learning and memory
R37MH-35219-12 (SRCM) SPEAR, NORMAN E SUNY AT BINGHAMTON P.O. BOX 6000 BINGHAMTON, NY 13902-6000 Stimulus selection and infantile amnesia alleviation
R37MH-35321-09 (BPN) GREENOUGH, WILLIAM T UNIVERSITY OF ILLINOIS 603 EAST DANIEL CHAMPAIGN, IL 61820 Structural substrates of synapse plasticity
R37MH-35408-11 (TDA) KAZDIN, ALAN E YALE UNIVERSITY BOX 11A YALE STATION NEW HAVEN, CT 06520-7447 Social and cognitive treatments for conduct problems
R01MH-35525-09A2 (LCR) MARKMAN, HOWARD J UNIVERSITY OF DENVER 2450 S VINE STREET DENVER, CO 80208 Long term effects of premarital intervention
R01MH-35554-11 (BPN) GALLAGHER, MICHELA UNIV OF N C AT CHAPEL HILL CAMPUS BOX 3270, DAVIE HALL CHAPEL HILL, N C 27599-3270 Amygdala opioid peptides--Role in learning and memory
R37MH-35564-18 (BPN) KUPFERMANN, IRVING RES FDN/MENTAL HYG/NYS PSY INS 722 W 168TH ST NEW YORK, NY 10032 Behavioral and neural analysis of learning in Aplysia
R37MH-35636-10 (TDA) SACKEIM, HAROLD A RESEARCH FDN FOR MENTAL HYGIEN 722 WEST 168TH STREET NEW YORK, NY 10032 Affective and cognitive consequences of ECT
R37MH-35664-12 (BPN) MARTIN, DAVID L NEW YORK STATE DEPT OF HEALTH EMPIRE STATE PLAZA, PO BOX 509 ALBANY, NY 12201-0509 Control of gamma aminobutyric acid synthesis
R37MH-35779-07 (SRCM) KLEIN, RACHEL G N Y ST PSYCHITRIC INSTITUTE 722 WEST 168TH STREET NEW YORK, N Y 10032 Methylphenidate in childhood behavior disorders
R37MH-35856-12 (SRCM) KIHLSTROM, JOHN F UNIVERSITY OF ARIZONA TUCSON, AZ 85721 Personality and cognition in hypnotic phenomena
U01MH-35883-09 (SRCM) SARTORIUS, NORMAN WORLD HEALTH ORGANIZATION AVENUE APPIA SWITZERLAND WHO/ADAMHA joint project on diagnosis and classification
P50MH-35976-10 (SRCM) FRIEDHOFF, ARNOLD J NEW YORK UNIV MEDICAL CNTR 550 FIRST AVENUE NEW YORK, NY 10016 MHCRC for organic, affective and schizophrenic disorders
P50MH-35976-10 9001 (SRCM) ALPERT, MURRY MHCRC for organic,

affective and schizophrenic disorders Core--Psychology and assessment
P50MH-35976-10 9004 (SRCM) GOLDSTEIN, MENEK MHCRC for organic, affective and schizophrenic disorders Biochemistry and molecular neuroscience core
P50MH-35976-10 9005 (SRCM) PEARSON, JOHN MHCRC for organic, affective and schizophrenic disorders Core--Neuropathology
P50MH-35976-10 9006 (SRCM) DIAMOND, FLORENCE MHCRC for organic, affective and schizophrenic disorders Core--Clinical support
P50MH-35976-10 9007 (SRCM) WELKOWITZ, JOAN MHCRC for organic, affective and schizophrenic disorders Core--Statistics and data analysis group
R37MH-35996-10 (TDA) CARPENTER, WILLIAM T, JR MARYLAND PSYCHIATRIC RES CTR PO BOX 21247 BALTIMORE, MD 21228 Outpatient treatment--Targeted vs maintenance medication
R01MH-36044-11 (SRCM) GNEGY, MARGARET E UNIVERSITY OF MICHIGAN M6322 MEDICAL SCIENCE I ANN ARBOR, MI 48109-0626 Chronic neuroleptics calmodulin and DA sensitivity
R01MH-36169-08A2 (TDA) PANDEY, GHANSHYAM N 912 SOUTH WOOD STREET CHICAGO, IL 60612 Monoamine receptor sensitivity and mental illness
P50MH-36224-08S2 (TDAC) COHEN, BRUCE M MAILMAN RESEARCH CENTER 115 MILL STREET BELMONT, MA 02178 MH Clinical Res Ctr for study of psychotic disorders
R01MH-36229-10 (TDA) HENINGER, GEORGE R 34 PARK ST NEW HAVEN, CT 06508 Monoamine receptor sensitivity and antidepressant drugs
R01MH-36230-08 (EPS) BRAVO, MILAGROS UNIV OF PUERTO RICO GPO BOX 5067 SAN JUAN, PR 00936 Psychiatric epidemiology/mental disorders in Puerto Rico
R37MH-36262-10 (BPN) LUCKI, IRWIN 207 PIERSON BLDG 3400 SPRUCE STREET PHILADELPHIA, PA 19104-4283 Serotonin receptor regulation and behavior
R01MH-36295-08 (PCB) BRUDER, GERARD E N Y STATE PSYCH INSTITUTE 722 WEST 168TH STREET NEW YORK, N Y 10032 Behavioral, ERP and RCBF asymmetry in affective disorder
R01MH-36595-08 (CVR) MARGOLIN, GAYLA UNIVERSITY OF SOUTHERN CA UNIVERSITY PARK LOS ANGELES, CA 90089-1061 Marital conflict--Intrapersonal & interpersonal factors
R01MH-36644-07 (BPN) COOK, JAMES M UNIVERSITY OF WISCONSIN P O BOX 413 MILWAUKEE, WIS 53201 Beta-carbolines--Search for valium agonists and antagonists
R37MH-36657-10 (BPN) CASEY, DANIEL E OREGON REG PRIMATE RES CENTER 505 NW 185TH AVE BEAVERTON, OREG 97006 Antipsychotic drug-induced dyskinesias
R37MH-36730-10 (BPN) WEISS, KLAUDIUSZ R MOUNT SINAI SCHOOL OF MEDICINE ONE GUSTAVE L LEVY PLACE NEW YORK, NY 10029 Neural basis of behavioral arousal
R01MH-36800-09 (TDA) BARLOW, DAVID H ST UNIV OF NEW YORK AT ALBANY 1400 WASHINGTON AVENUE ALBANY, N Y 12222 Treatments of anxiety
R01MH-36801-07A1 (PCB) SARGENT, THORNTON, III LAWRENCE BERKELEY LABORATORY 1 CYCLOTRON ROAD BERKELEY, CA 94720 The methyl carbon pathway in psychosis
K05MH-36808-14 (MHK) EMDE, ROBERT N UNIVERSITY OF COLORADO 4200 E NINTH AVE, BOX C268 DENVER, COLO 80262 Emotional signaling in infancy
R01MH-36840-08 (PCB) COURCHESNE, ERIC CHILDREN'S HOSPITAL RES CENTER 8001 FROST STREET SAN DIEGO, CA 92123 Investigaton of cognitive dysfunction in autism
R01MH-37020-07A2 (BPN) SHIH, JEAN C UNIV OF SOUTHERN CALIFORNIA 1985 ZONAL AVENUE LOS ANGELES, CA 90033 Protein(s) involved in neurotransmission
R37MH-37073-09 (NSS) TAMMINGA, CAROL A MARYLAND PSYCHIATRIC RES CTR BOX 21247/INPATIENT UNIT BALTIMORE, MD 21228 GABA agonist therapy in tardive dyskinesia
R01MH-37103-07 (SRCM) KOCSIS, JAMES H 525 EAST 68TH STREET NEW YORK, NY 10021 Diagnosis and treatment of dysthymic disorders
R01MH-37110-08 (TDA) STRAIN, PHILLIP S ALLEGHENY-SINGER RES INSTITUTE 320 EAST NORTH AVENUE PITTSBURGH, PA 15212 Peer-mediated treatment of autistic children
R01MH-37134-09 (BPN) BAILEY, CRAIG H NEW YORK ST PSYCHIATRIC INST 722 WEST 168TH STREET NEW YORK, N Y 10032 Morphological basis of synaptic plasticity
R01MH-37188-08 (EPS) LITTLE, RODERICK J A UNIV OF CALIF, LOS ANGELES 10833 LE CONTE AVENUE LOS ANGELES, CA 90024-1766 Statistical methodology for mental health research
R37MH-37215-09 (BSR) RUBLE, DIANE N NEW YORK UNIVERSITY 6 WASHINGTON PLACE NEW YORK, NY 10003 Social comparison--Developmental and functional analyses
R01MH-37310-08A1 (CVR) SEGAL, STEVEN P INST FOR SCIENTIFIC ANALYSIS 2235 LOMBARD STREET SAN FRANCISCO, CA 94123 Informed service strategy in psychiatric emergency evaluation
R01MH-37373-09 (MHAZ) LAUDENSLAGER, MARK L UNIVERSITY OF COLORADO 700 DELAWARE ST DENVER, CO 80204 Loss and separation--Immune status
R37MH-37535-11 (SRCM) RICCIO, DAVID C KENT STATE UNIVERSITY KENT, OHIO 44242-0001 Modulation of memory
R01MH-37575-09 (BPN) TAMIR, HADASSAH RESEARCH FDN FOR MENTAL HYGIEN 722 WEST 168TH STREET NEW YORK, NY 10032 Serotonin binding protein--Function in synaptic vesicle
R01MH-37578-08 (PCB) KINSBOURNE, MARCEL EUNICE KENNEDY SHRIVER CENTER 200 TRAPELO ROAD WALTHAM, MA 02254 A neuropsychological analysis of ADHD
P01MH-37592-08 (TDA) KLEIN, DONALD F COLUMBIA UNIVERSITY 722 WEST 168TH STREET NEW YORK, NY 10032 Psychobiology/genetics/treatment of anxiety disorders
P01MH-37592-08 0001 (TDA) GORMAN, JACK Psychobiology/genetics/treatment of anxiety disorders Comparison of respiratory challenges in anxiety disorder
P01MH-37592-08 0002 (TDA) GORMAN, JACK Psychobiology/genetics/treatment of anxiety disorders Anxiogenic and ventilatory effects of carbon dioxide
P01MH-37592-08 0003 (TDA) GORMAN, JACK Psychobiology/genetics/treatment of anxiety disorders Mitral valve prolapse in anxiety disorders
P01MH-37592-08 0004 (TDA) FYER, ABBEY Psychobiology/genetics/treatment of anxiety disorders Family study of DSM-III anxiety disorders
P01MH-37592-08 0005 (TDA) KLEIN, RACHEL G Psychobiology/genetics/treatment of anxiety disorders Children at risk for anxiety disorder
P01MH-37592-08 0007 (TDA) FYER, ABBY Psychobiology/genetics/treatment of anxiety disorders DNA polymorphisms in linkage analysis of panic disorders
R01MH-37598-09 (BSR) SWANN, WILLIAM B UNIVERSITY OF TEXAS DEPARTMENT OF PSYCHOLOGY AUSTIN, TX 78712 Interpersonal dynamics of self-concept stability
R01MH-37685-09 (EPS) RICE, JOHN P WASHINGTON UNIVERSITY 660 S EUCLID AVENUE ST LOUIS, MO 63110 The quantitative genetics of clinical psychopathology
R01MH-37705-08 (PCB) NUECHTERLEIN, KEITH H UNIV OF CALIFORNIA, LOS ANGELE 300 UCLA MEDICAL PLAZA, RM 225 LOS ANGELES, CA 90024-6968 Developmental processes in schizophrenic disorders
R37MH-37757-10 (PCB) LANG, PETER J UNIVERSITY OF FLORIDA BOX J-165, JHMHC GAINESVILLE, FL 32610 Fear modification--Imagery, cognition, and control
R01MH-37860-07 (SRCM) LYKKEN, DAVID T UNIVERSITY OF MINNESOTA 75 EAST RIVER ROAD MINNEAPOLIS, MN 55455 The Minnesota twin family registry
R01MH-37869-09 (LCR) REYNOLDS, CHARLES F, III WESTERN PSYCHIATRIC INST CLINI 3811 O'HARA ST PITTSBURGH, PA 15213 EEG sleep, aging and mental illness
R01MH-37892-08 (PYB) TIMBERLAKE, WILLIAM D INDIANA UNIVERSITY BLOOMINGTON, IN 47405 Behavioral organization, constraint, and learning
R01MH-37899-04A2 (PCB) PETTY, FREDERICK DEPT OF VA MEDICAL CENTER 4500 SOUTH LANCASTER ROAD DALLAS, TX 75216 Plasma GABA and mood disorders
R01MH-37911-09 (BSR) FAGOT, BEVERLY I OREGON SOCIAL LEARNING CENTER 207 E 5TH AVE EUGENE, OR 97401 The origins of mental health problems in the family
R01MH-37916-09 (SRCM) PHELPS, MICHAEL E UCLA SCHOOL OF MEDICINE 405 HILGARD AVENUE LOS ANGELES, CA 90024 PET--Biochemical mechanisms of alterations in mood
R01MH-37922-08 (PCB) DAVIDSON, MICHAEL VETERANS ADMIN MEDICAL CENTER 130 W KINGSBRIDGE ROAD BRONX, NY 10468 Toward a rational use of plasma HVA in mental illness
R37MH-37940-10 (CVR) PATTERSON, GERALD R OREGON SOCIAL LEARNING CENTER 207 E 5TH AVENUE, SUITE 202 EUGENE, OR 94701 Understanding and prediction of delinquent behavior
R37MH-37972-09 (BPN) HOPKINS, CARL D CORNELL UNIVERSTIY SEELEY G MUDD HALL ITHACA, N Y 14853 Neuroethology of electric communication
R01MH-38118-05 (TDA) KLORMAN, RAFAEL UNIVERSITY OF ROCHESTER RIVER CAMPUS STATION ROCHESTER, NY 14627 Stimulants and adolescent attention deficit disorder
R01MH-38142-09 (LCR) PETERSEN, ANNE C PENNSYLVANIA STATE UNIVERSITY UNIVERSITY PARK, PA 16802 Developmental study of acolescent mental health
R01MH-38240-08 (BSR) WEISZ, JOHN R UCLA PSYCHOLOGY LOS ANGELES, CA 90024-1563 Child behavior problems in cultural context
R37MH-38256-08 (BPNB) NICOLL, ROGER A UNIVERSITY OF CALIFORNIA 513 PARNASSUS AVE SAN FRANCISCO, CALIF 94143 Norepinephrine effects on local neuronal circuits
R01MH-38273-06 (BPN) PFAFF, DONALD W ROCKEFELLER UNIVERSITY 1230 YORK AVENUE NEW YORK, NY 10021 Reticulospinal and vestibulospinal control of back muscles
P50MH-38280-08 (SRCM) STEIN, RUTH E ALBERT EINSTEIN COLL OF MED 1300 MORRIS PARK AVE BORNX, NY 10461 Preventive intervention research center for child health
P50MH-38280-08 0007 (SRCM) STEIN, RUTH E Preventive intervention research center for child health Neonatal project
P50MH-38280-08 0008 (SRCM) STEIN, RUTH E Preventive intervention research center for child health Childhood project
P50MH-38280-08 0009 (SRCM) STEIN, RUTH E Preventive intervention research center for child health Adolescent project
R01MH-38321-08 (PCB) FREEDMAN, ROBERT UNIV/COLORADO HLTH SCIENCE CTR 4200 EAST NINTH AVENUE DENVER, CO 80262 Electrophysiology of sensory gating in schizophrenia
R01MH-38324-07 (LCR) LARSON, REED W UNIVERSITY OF ILLINOIS 1105 W NEVADA URBANA, IL 61801 Stress in daily life during early adolescence
P50MH-38330-08 (SRCM) PRICE, RICHARD H UNIVERSITY OF MICHIGAN PO BOX 1248 ANN ARBOR, MI 48106-1248 Michigan prevention research center
R01MH-38333-05 (EPS) HERZOG, DAVID B MASSACHUSETTS GENERAL HOSPITAL BOSTON, MA 02114 A longitudinal study of anorexia nervosa and bulimic disorders
R01MH-38355-09 (TDA) WALSH, BERNARD T RESEARCH FDN FOR MENTAL HYGIEN 722 WEST 168TH STREET NEW YORK, NY 10032 Psychological & pharmacological treatment of bulimia
R01MH-38373-07 (LCR) BRAYDEN, ROBERT M VANDERBILT UNIVERSITY 2948 TVC NASHVILLE, TN 37232-5577 Prediction and primary prevention of child maltreatment
R01MH-38399-08A1 (BPN) BERMAN, NANCY E UNIVERSITY OF KANSAS MED CTR 39TH AND RAINBOW BLVD KANSAS CITY, KS 66103-8410 Effects of experience on maturation of brain pathways
R37MH-38546-12 (BPN) GOLDMAN-RAKIC, PATRICIA S YALE UNIVERSITY 333 CEDAR ST NEW HAVEN, CT 06510 Neurobiology of primate frontal lobes
R01MH-38585-07 (BSR) WYER, ROBERT S JR UNIVERSITY OF ILLINOIS CHAMPAIGN, IL 61820 The cognitive processing of social information
R37MH-38623-12 (BPN) DAVIES, PETER ALBERT EINSTEIN COLLEGE OF MED 1300 MORRIS PARK AVENUE BRONX, N Y 10461 Aging and dementia--Cholinergic neuron biochemistry
K05MH-38632-14 (MHK) HOFER, MYRON A COLUMBIA UNIVERSITY 630 WEST 168TH STREET NEW YORK, N Y 10032 Developmental effects of early maternal separation
R37MH-38633-08 (BPNB) HOWARD, BRUCE D UNIVERSITY OF CALIFORNIA SCHOOL OF MEDICINE LOS ANGELES, CA 90024 PC-12 cells and neuronal function

PROJECT NO., ORGANIZATIONAL UNIT., INVESTIGATOR, ADDRESS, TITLE

R37MH-38636-08 (NSS) BELLACK, ALAN S MEDICAL COLL PENNSYLVANIA-EPPI 3200 HENRY AVENUE PHILADELPHIA, PA 19129 Social skills and schizophrenia
R01MH-38637-08 (TDA) AGRAS, W STEWART STANFORD UNIVERSITY STANFORD, CA 94305-5490 Studies of the treatment and psychopathology of bulimia
R01MH-38667-06 (LCR) PRINZ, RONALD J UNIVERSITY OF SOUTH CAROLINA DEPT OF PSYCHOLOGY COLUMBIA, SC 29208 Early intervention for antisocial behavior in children
R01MH-38710-06 (BPN) SCHELLER, RICHARD H STANFORD UNIVERSITY MED CENTER B-155 BECKMAN CENTER STANFORD, CA 94305-5426 Neuropeptides--Gene expression and behavior
P50MH-38725-07 (SRCM) KELLAM, SHEPPARD G JOHNS HOPKINS UNIVERSITY 624 NORTH BROADWAY BALTIMORE, MD 21205 Epidemiologic prevention center for early risk behaviors
R01MH-38726-07A1 (BPN) WALTERS, EDGAR T UNIVERSITY OF TEXAS MED SCH PO BOX 20708 HOUSTON, TX 77225 Associative information processing--Cellular mechanisms
R01MH-38738-08 (PCB) GILLIN, J CHRISTIAN UNIV OF CALIF, SAN DIEGO 9500 GILMAN DRIVE LA JOLLA, CA 92093-0603 A muscarinic hypothesis for affective illness
R01MH-38752-08 (BPN) JOPE, RICHARD S UNIVERSITY OF ALABAMA SPARKS CENTER 910 BIRMINGHAM, AL 35294 Effects of lithium on cholinergic activity
R37MH-38774-07 (BPN) LE DOUX, JOSEPH E, JR NEW YORK UNIVERSITY 6 WASHINGTON PLACE NEW YORK, N Y 10003 Neural pathways underlying emotional conditioning
R01MH-38777-08 (SRCM) CORYELL, WILLIAM H UNIVERSITY OF IOWA 500 NEWTON ROAD IOWA CITY, IOWA 52242 Extended follow-up of nonmanic psychosis
R01MH-38819-06 (BPN) BROSIUS, JURGEN MT SINAI SCHOOL OF MEDICINE ONE GUSTAVE L LEVY PLACE NEW YORK, NY 10029 Developmental/tissue-specific expression of neural genes
R37MH-38820-09 (PCB) PENNINGTON, BRUCE F UNIVERSITY OF DENVER 2460 S. VINE ST DENVER, CO 80208-0198 The linguistic phenotype in familia dyslexia
R37MH-38832-08 (NSS) FAZIO, RUSSELL H INDIANA UNIVERSITY BLOOMINGTON, IN 47405 Cognitive processes in the attitude-behavior relation
R01MH-38880-07 (TDA) LIEBERMAN, JEFFREY A Prediction of relapse in schizophrenia
K05MH-38894-14 (SRCM) OLNEY, JOHN W WASHINGTON UNIV 660 S. EUCLID AVE - BOX 8134 ST LOUIS, MO 63110 CNS ultrastructure--Disease, drugs, and development
R01MH-39077-08 (SRCM) GOLDBERG, LEWIS R OREGON RESEARCH INSTITUTE 1899 WILLAMETTE STREET EUGENE, OREG 97401 Personality traits as semantic categories
R37MH-39085-07 (BPN) SHIH, JEAN C UNIV OF SOUTHERN CALIF 1985 ZONAL AVENUE LOS ANGELES, CALIF 90033-1086 Two types of monoamine oxidase
R01MH-39096-08 (TDA) BARLOW, DAVID H ST UNIV OF NEW YORK AT ALBANY 1400 WASHINGTON AVENUE ALBANY, N Y 12222 The classification of anxiety disorders
R01MH-39140-08 (SRCM) COIE, JOHN D DUKE UNIVERSITY PSYCHOLOGY DEPT DURHAM, N C 27706 Prevention with black preadolescents at social risk
R01MH-39144-06 (BPN) BREESE, GEORGE R UNIVERSITY OF NORTH CAROLINA CB# 7250 CHAPEL HILL, NC 27599-7250 Neurobiology of antidepressant drugs
R37MH-39145-08 (PCB) MILLER, CAROL A UNIV SOUTHERN CALIF SCH OF MED 2011 ZONAL AVENUE LOS ANGELES, CA 90033 Mental illness in Alzheimer's disease of the aged
R01MH-39163-04A3 (BPN) GALLAGHER, JOEL P UNIVERSITY OF TEXAS MED BRANCH GALVESTON, TX 77550-2774 Cellular pharmacology and physiology of septal neurons
R01MH-39172-07 (TDA) BORKOVEC, THOMAS D PENNSYLVANIA STATE UNIVERSITY UNIVERSITY PARK, PA 16802 Desensitization and cognitive therapy in general anxiety
R01MH-39188-04A1 (PCB) EMSLIE, GRAHAM J UNIV OF TEXAS S.W. MEDICAL CNT 5323 HARRY HINES BLVD DALLAS, TX 75235 Childhood depression-biological correlates
R01MH-39230-05 (PYB) BRUSH, F ROBERT PURDUE UNIVERSITY WEST LAFAYETTE, IN 47907 A behavior-genetic analysis of avoidance learning
R37MH-39239-08 (PCB) KIDD, KENNETH K YALE UNIVERSITY SCH OF MED 333 CEDAR STREET NEW HAVEN, CT 06510 Genetic studies of psychiatric disorders
P50MH-39246-07 (SRCM) SANDLER, IRWIN N ARIZONA STATE UNIVERSITY DEPT OF PSYCHOLOGY TEMPE, ARIZONA 85287-1104 Center for the prevention of child and family stress
P50MH-39246-07 0001 (SRCM) SANDLER, IRWIN N Center for the prevention of child and family stress Coping in children of divorce
P50MH-39246-07 0002 (SRCM) WOLCHIK, SHARLENE A Center for the prevention of child and family stress Cihldren of divorce intervention project
P50MH-39246-07 0003 (SRCM) SANDLER, IRWIN N Center for the prevention of child and family stress Selection issues in children of divorce preventive interventions
P50MH-39246-07 0004 (SRCM) ROOSA, MARK W Center for the prevention of child and family stress Children of alcoholics--Selection and family influence study
P50MH-39246-07 0005 (SRCM) ROOSA, MARK W Center for the prevention of child and family stress Children of alcoholics--Intervention study
R01MH-39267-07 (BSR) COLLINS, W ANDREW UNIVERSITY OF MINNESOTA 51 EAST RIVER ROAD MINNEAPOLIS, MN 55455-0345 Development and stress in parent-adolescent interactions
R01MH-39327-09 (BPN) GREENGARD, PAUL ROCKEFELLER UNIVERSITY 1230 YORK AVENUE NEW YORK, NY 10021 Synapsins--Regulators of neurotransmitter release
R01MH-39346-08 (MHAZ) SCHWARTZ, STANLEY A UNIVERSITY OF MICHIGAN 109 OBSERVATORY ANN ARBOR, MI 48109 Psychosocial studies of a cohort at risk for AIDS
R37MH-39349-08 (BSR) MISCHEL, WALTER COLUMBIA UNIVERSITY 406 SCHERMERHORN HALL NEW YORK, NY 10027 Consistency in social behavior

PROJECT NO., ORGANIZATIONAL UNIT., INVESTIGATOR, ADDRESS, TITLE

R37MH-39415-08 (NSS) NEMEROFF, CHARLES B DUKE UNIVERSITY MEDICAL CENTER P O BOX 3859 DURHAM, N C 27710 Neurotensin, an endogenous neuroleptic-like peptide
R37MH-39429-08 (BSR) HIGGINS, EDWARD TORY COLUMBIA UNIVERSITY SCHERMERHORN HALL NEW YORK, N Y 10027 Context-driven processing and its personal consequences
R01MH-39434-06A1 (SRCM) SCHREIBMAN, LAURA E UNIV OF CALIF, SAN DIEGO LA JOLLA, CA 92093 Research in autism--Parent intervention
P01MH-39437-07 (SRCM) CIARANELLO, ROLAND D STANFORD UNIV SCH OF MEDICINE STANFORD UNIVERSITY STANFORD, CA 94305 Molecular neurobiology and developmental disorders
P01MH-39437-07 0003 (SRCM) DEMENT, WILLIAM C Molecular neurobiology and developmental disorders Developmental neurobiology of narcolepsy
P01MH-39437-07 0005 (SRCM) CAVALLI-SFORZA, LUIGI L Molecular neurobiology and developmental disorders Molecular and linkage genetics of infantile autism
P01MH-39437-07 0006 (SRCM) RUBENSTEIN, JOHN L Molecular neurobiology and developmental disorders Developmentally regulated genes of mammalian central nervous system
P01MH-39437-07 0001 (SRCM) WONG, DONA L Molecular neurobiology and developmental disorders Enzyme regulation
P01MH-39437-07 9001 (SRCM) CIARANELLO, ROLAND D Molecular neurobiology and developmental disorders Core facilities
P01MH-39437-07 0002 (SRCM) CIARANELLO, ROLAND D Molecular neurobiology and developmental disorders Regulation of serotonin and beta-adrenergic receptors
R01MH-39449-03A2 (CEP) FAGEN, JEFFREY W ST JOHN'S UNIVERSITY JAMAICA, NY 11439 The interaction of affect and memory in infancy
R01MH-39453-08 (SRCM) CAPALDI, ELIZABETH D UNIVERSITY OF FLORIDA GAINESVILLE, FL 32611 Motivation and learning
R01MH-39531-07 (PCB) GILES, DONNA E WESTERN PSYCH INST & CLINIC 3811 O'HARA STREET PITTSBURGH, PA 15213 Is EEG sleep abnormal in those at risk for depression
R01MH-39557-08 (SRCM) MARTIN, JOHN L COLUMBIA UNIVESITY 600 WEST 168TH STREET NEW YORK, NY 10032 Mental health effects of AIDS on at-risk homosexual men
R01MH-39576-07 (EPS) MURPHY, JANE M MASSACHUSETTS GENERAL HOSPITAL FRUIT ST BOSTON, MA 02114 A longitudinal study in psychiatric epidemiology
R01MH-39588-05 (LCR) SAMEROFF, ARNOLD J E P BRADLEY HOSPITAL 1011 VETERANS MEMORIAL PARKWAY EAST PROVIDENCE, RI 02915 Preventing adolescent social and cognitive disabilities
R37MH-39592-07 (BPN) TAKAHASHI, JOSEPH S NORTHWESTERN UNIVERSITY 2153 SHERIDAN ROAD EVANSTON, IL 60208-3520 Cellular analysis of vertebrate circadian pacemakers
R01MH-39593-07 (PCBB) CARROLL, BERNARD J DUKE UNIVERSITY MEDICAL CENTER BOX 3950 DURHAM, N C 27710 Neuroendocrine regulation in depression
R01MH-39595-07A1 (BPN) RASENICK, MARK M UNIVERSITY OF ILLINOIS 901 SOUTH WOLCOTT AVE M/C 901 CHICAGO, IL 60680 Cytoskeletal interaction with neuronal adenylate cyclase
R01MH-39628-05 (PCB) MILLER, GREGORY A UNIVERSITY OF ILLINOIS 603 EAST DANIEL STREET CHAMPAIGN, IL 61820 Psychophysiological assessment for psychosis prevention
R01MH-39633-05 (CEP) RIPS, LANCE J UNIVERSITY OF CHICAGO 5848 SOUTH UNIVERSITY AVENUE CHICAGO, IL 60637 Conceptions of mental activity
R01MH-39661-08 (TDAB) FISHER, SEYMOUR UNIVERSITY OF TEXAS MED BRANCH 219 ADM ANNEX I, D-41 GALVESTON, TX 77590-2777 Monitoring of psychotropic adverse drug reactions
R01MH-39663-06 (SRCM) WYNNE, LYMAN C UNIV OF ROCHESTER MED CTR 300 CRITTENDEN BLVD ROCHESTER, N Y 14642 Finnish adoptive family study of schizophrenia
R01MH-39665-07 (EPS) GLAZER, WILLIAM M CONNECTICUT MENTAL HEALTH CTR 34 PARK STREET NEW HAVEN, CONN 06519 Epidemiologic studies of tardive dyskinesia
R37MH-39683-08 (SRCM) MC CARLEY, ROBERT W HARVARD MEDICAL SCHOOL 940 BELMONT STREET BROCKTON, MA 02401 The synaptic basis of sleep cycle control
R01MH-39772-06 (CEP) MATHENY, ADAM P, JR UNIVERSITY OF LOUISVILLE LOUISVILLE, KY 40292 School achievement and low-ses children
R01MH-39784-07 (CEP) FREYD, JENNIFER J UNIVERSITY OF OREGON EUGENE, OR 97403 Dynamic information and mental representation
R01MH-39786-06 (PYB) FANSELOW, MICHAEL S UNIVERSITY OF CALIFORNIA LOS ANGELES, CA 90024-1563 A functional approach to aversively motivated behavior
R01MH-39917-07S1 (SRCM) GLICKMAN, STEPHEN E UNIVERSITY OF CALIFORNIA BERKELEY, CA 94720 Patterns of behavioral and hormonal development
R01MH-39936-06 (PCB) FOLSTEIN, SUSAN E JOHNS HOPKINS UNIVERSITY 600 NORTH WOLFE STREET BALTIMORE, MD 21205 Autism--disorders in parents and sibs
R01MH-39940-05 (PYB) DOMJAN, MICHAEL UNIVERSITY OF TEXAS AUSTIN, TX 78712 Learning and reproductive behavior
R01MH-39961-07A1 (BPN) ELLISON, GAYLORD D UNIVERSITY OF CALIFORNIA 405 HILGARD AVE LOS ANGELES, CA 90024 Neuroleptic-induced dyskinesias and dystonias
R01MH-39967-06 (BPN) KILTS, CLINTON D DUKE UNIVERSITY MEDICAL CENTER P O BOX 3833 DURHAM, N C 27710 Meso-amygdaloid dopamine neurons and antipsychotic drugs
R01MH-39976-06A1 (TDA) KOLKO, DAVID J WESTERN PSYCH INSTITUTE & CLIN 3811 O'HARA STREET PITTSBURGH, PA 15213 Child firesetting--A treatment outcome evaluation
U10MH-39992-08 (SRCM) KANE, JOHN M HILLSIDE HOSP/L I JEW MED CTR 75-59 263RD STREET GLEN OAKS, NY 11004 Treatment strategies in schizophrenia
U10MH-39998-08 (SRCM) BELLACK, ALAN S MEDICAL COLL PENNSYLVANIA-EPPI 3200 HENRY AVENUE PHILADELPHIA, PA 19129 Treatment strategies in schizophrenia
U10MH-40007-08 (SRCM) GLICK, IRA D PAYNE WHITNEY CLINIC 525 EAST 68TH STREET NEW YORK, NY 10021 Treatment strategies in schizophrenia
R01MH-40010-07 (BPN) SMITH, GERARD P NEW YORK HOSP CORNELL MED

CTR 21 BLOOMINGDALE RD WHITE PLAINS, NY 10605 Analysis of the satiety effect of cholecystokinin

R01MH-40015-05A1 (LCR) KANE, JOHN M HILLSIDE HOSP/L I JEW MED CTR 75-59 263RD STREET GLEN OAKS, NY 11004 Prospective study of tardive dyskinesia in the elderly

R01MH-40023-07 (TDA) REYNOLDS, CHARLES F, III WESTERN PSYCH INST AND CLINIC 3811 O'HARA STREET PITTSBURGH, PA 15213 Nocturnal penile tumescence in depression

R01MH-40025-03A2 (LCR) SMITH, ELIZABETH M WASHINGTON UNIV-SCH OF MED 660 S EUCLID AVE; BOX 8134 ST LOUIS, MO 63110 Psychosocial consequences of disasters--A longitudinal study

R01MH-40030-07 (CVR) LIDZ, CHARLES W WESTERN PSYCHIATRIC INSTITUTE 3811 O'HARA STREET PITTSBURGH, PA 15213 Conditional prediction and the management of dangerousness

P50MH-40041-08 (TDA) YESAVAGE, JEROME A STANFORD UNIVERSITY SCH OF MED STANFORD, CA 94305-5490 Clinical research center for study of senile dementia

P50MH-40041-08 0001 (TDA) YESAVAGE, JEROME A Clinical research center for study of senile dementia Biochemical correlates of PDD

P50MH-40041-08 0002 (TDA) PFEFFERBAUM, ADOLF Clinical research center for study of senile dementia Electrophysiological correlates of PDD

P50MH-40041-08 0003 (TDA) GUELLEMINAULT, CHRISTIAN Clinical research center for study of senile dementia Sleep component

P50MH-40041-08 0004 (TDA) WINOGRAD, CAROL H Clinical research center for study of senile dementia Medical correlates of PDD

P50MH-40041-08 0005 (TDA) GALLAGHER, DOLORES E Clinical research center for study of senile dementia Caregiver correlates of PDD

P50MH-40041-08 0006 (TDA) ENG, LAWRENCE Clinical research center for study of senile dementia Neurobiology

P50MH-40041-08 0007 (TDA) BILWISE, DONALD Clinical research center for study of senile dementia sundowning and sleep

P50MH-40041-08 9001 (TDA) YESAVAGE, JEROME A Clinical research center for study of senile dementia Identifying correlates of progression of PDD

U10MH-40042-08 (SRCM) HARGREAVES, WILLIAM A SAN FRANCISCO GENERAL HOSP 1001 POTRERO AVE ROOM 7-M-36 SAN FRANCISCO, CA 94110 Treatment strategies in schizophrenia--San Francisco

R01MH-40052-06 (PCB) ROTH, WALTON T VA MEDICAL CENTER 3801 MIRANDA AVE PALO ALTO, CA 94304 Automatic elicitation of cognitive ERP components

R01MH-40053-05 (EPSB) BABIGIAN, HAROUTUN M UNIVERSITY OF ROCHESTER 300 CRITTENDEN BLVD ROCHESTER, NY 14642 Mental health services study--Capitation payments system

R37MH-40058-07 (BSR) HAMILTON, DAVID L UNIVERSITY OF CALIFORNIA SANTA BARBARA, CA 93106 Effects of stereotypes based on illusory correlations

R01MH-40090-05 (BPN) VOLPE, BRUCE T W.M. BURKE MEDICAL RESEARCH 785 MAMARONECK AVENUE WHITE PLAINS, NY 10605 Behavior/histopathology of model cerebral ischemia

R01MH-40106-05 (LCR) BAUM, ANDREW S UNIFORMED SERV UNIVERSITY 4301 JONES BRIDGE ROAD BETHESDA, MD 20814-4799 Chronic stress and mental health outcomes of trauma

R01MH-40121-08 (TDA) LIEBOWITZ, MICHAEL R N Y STATE PSYCHIATRIC INST 722 WEST 168 STREET NEW YORK, N Y 10032 Pharmacotherapy of social phobia

R01MH-40140-05 (TDA) CHARNEY, DENNIS S CLINICAL NEUROSCIENCES RES UNI 34 PARK STREET NEW HAVEN, CT 06510 Etiology and treatment of panic anxiety

R01MH-40151-04S1 (TDA) BUDMAN, SIMON H HARVARD COMMUNITY HEALTH PLAN ONE FENWAY PLACE BOSTON, MA 02215 Instrument development in group therapy

R01MH-40157-07 (BPN) CARLSON, MARY L HARVARD MEDICAL SCHOOL 220 LONGWOOD AVENUE BOSTON, MA 02115 Sensorimotor cortex in prosimian primate

P50MH-40159-08 (TDA) BLAZER, DAN G, II DUKE UNIVERSITY MEDICAL CENTER BOX 3215 DURHAM, N C 27710 CRC/PE for the study of depression

P50MH-40159-08 0001 (TDA) BLAZER, DAN G CRC/PE for the study of depression Social support for depression in late life

P50MH-40159-08 0003 (TDA) WEINER, RICHARD D CRC/PE for the study of depression Non-dominant ECT elderly patients

P50MH-40159-08 0005 (TDA) NEMEROFF, CHARLES CRC/PE for the study of depression Biological markers of major depression

P50MH-40159-08 0007 (TDA) COFFEY, EDWARD CRC/PE for the study of depression Brain MRI

P50MH-40159-08 0008 (TDA) GEORGE, LINDA K CRC/PE for the study of depression Natural history of late life depression

P50MH-40159-08 0009 (TDA) MARSH, GAIL CRC/PE for the study of depression Polysomnography

R01MH-40161-07 (PCB) LEWY, ALFRED J OREGON HEALTH SCIENCES UNIV 3181 S W SAM JACKSON PARK RD PORTLAND, OREGON 97201 Melatonin physiology in health and affective disorders

R37MH-40165-07 (SRCM) MILLER, RICHARD J THE UNIVERSITY OF CHICAGO 947 EAST 58TH STREET CHICAGO, IL 60637 The interaction of drugs with neuronal calcium channels

R01MH-40177-04A2 (TDA) CAMPBELL, MAGDA NEW YORK UNIVERSITY MED CTR 550 FIRST AVE NEW YORK, N Y 10016 Lithium in aggressive children with conduct disorder

R01MH-40196-07 (SRCM) GOLDFRIED, MARVIN R STATE UNIVERSITY OF NEW YORK DEPT OF PSYCHOLOGY STONY BROOK, NY 11794-2500 A taxonomy of psychotherapy feedback principles

R01MH-40210-08 (BPN) MANN, JOSEPH J WESTERN PSYCHIATRIC INSTITUTE 3811 O'HARA STREET PITTSBURGH, PA 15213 Postmortem neurochemical studies in suicide

R01MH-40273-08 (TDA) GELLER, BARBARA WASHINGTON UNIVERSITY 660 SOUTH EUCLID AVE., BOX 813 ST LOUIS, MO 63110 Nortriptyline in childhood depression--Follow-up study

P50MH-40279-05 (SRCM) CARPENTER, WILLIAM T, JR MARYLAND PSYCHIATRIC RES CTR PO BOX 21247 BALTIMORE, MD 21228 CRC--Classification and course of the schizophrenias

P50MH-40279-05 9001 (SRCM) CARPENTER, WILLIAM T CRC--Classification and course of the schizophrenias Assessment core

P50MH-40279-05 9002 (SRCM) O'GRADY, KEVIN CRC--Classification and course of the schizophrenias Data management core

P50MH-40279-05 9003 (SRCM) TAMMINGA, CAROL CRC--Classification and course of the schizophrenias Clinical biochemistry laboratory core

P50MH-40279-05 9004 (SRCM) CARPENTER, WILLIAM T CRC--Classification and course of the schizophrenias Patient and subject recruitment core

R01MH-40303-07A1 (BPN) WEBER, ECKARD UNIV OF CALIF, IRVINE COLLEGE OF MEDICINE IRVINE, CA 92717 Studies on sigma receptors and their ligands

R01MH-40305-07 (EPS) ACHENBACH, THOMAS M UNIVERSITY OF VERMONT 1 SOUTH PROSPECT STREET BURLINGTON, VT 05405 National survey of children and youth: A six-year follow-up

R01MH-40314-06 (EPS) ESTROFF, SUE E UNIVERSITY OF NORTH CAROLINA CB #7240, WING D CHAPEL HILL, NC 27599 Income maintenance dependence and service system use

R01MH-40340-05S1 (PCB) LORANGER, ARMAND W CORNELL MEDICAL CENTER 21 BLOOMINGDALE ROAD WHITE PLAINS, N Y 10605 The personality disorder examination--A clinical trial

R37MH-40342-07 (BPN) PICKEL, VIRGINIA M LABORATORY OF NEUROBIOLOGY 411 EAST 69TH STREET NEW YORK, NEW YORK 10021 Ultrastructure of mesolimbic transmitter interactions

R01MH-40355-05 (PCBB) ROBINSON, ROBERT G UNIVERSITY OF IOWA 500 NEWTON ROAD IOWA CITY, IA 52242 Mood disorders in stroke patients

R01MH-40362-05 (PCB) TUNE, LARRY E JOHNS HOPKINS HOSPITAL 600 N WOLFE ST BALTIMORE, MD 21205 11C-N-methylspiperone PET scans in schizophrenia

R01MH-40363-05 (SRCM) GARRISON, CAROL Z UNIVERSITY OF SOUTH CAROLINA COLUMBIA, SC 29208 Epidemiology of adolescent depression

P50MH-40380-07 (TDA) KATZ, IRA R PHILADELPHIA GERIATRIC CENTER 5301 OLD YORK ROAD PHILADELPHIA, PA 19141 Depression in residential care settings

P50MH-40380-07 0002 (TDA) SIMPSON, GEORGE Depression in residential care settings Depression in the institutional aged--Psychopharmacology

P50MH-40380-07 0006 (TDA) KATZ, IRA Depression in residential care settings Psychopathology and amino acid metabolism

P50MH-40380-07 0007 (TDA) FEINBERG, MICHAEL Depression in residential care settings HPA and immune function in dementia

P50MH-40380-07 0008 (TDA) PRESSMAN, MARK R Depression in residential care settings Environmental and therapeutic effects of light on the elderly

P50MH-40380-07 0009 (TDA) BRODY, ELAINE M Depression in residential care settings Staff role perceptions--Congruence, ambiguity and conflict

P50MH-40380-07 0010 (TDA) PARMELEE, PATRICIA A Depression in residential care settings Personal control--Planning for therapeutic intervention

P50MH-40380-07 0011 (TDA) LUBORSKY, MARK R Depression in residential care settings Personal explanations and experiences of depression

P50MH-40380-07 0012 (TDA) LAWTON, M POWELL Depression in residential care settings Physical health and affective states

P50MH-40381-06 (SRCM) CAINE, ERIC D UNIVERSITY OF ROCHESTER MED CT 300 CRITTENDEN BOULEVARD ROCHESTER, NY 14642 CRC/PE for the study of psychopathology for the elderly

P50MH-40381-06 0005 (SRCM) TARIOT, PIERRE N CRC/PE for the study of psychopathology for the elderly Laboratory of psychopharmacology

P50MH-40381-06 0006 (SRCM) CAINE, ERIC D CRC/PE for the study of psychopathology for the elderly Laboratory of neuropsychology

P50MH-40381-06 0007 (SRCM) CONWELL, YEATES CRC/PE for the study of psychopathology for the elderly Laboratory of suicide studies

P50MH-40381-06 0008 (SRCM) FELTEN, DAVID L CRC/PE for the study of psychopathology for the elderly Laboratory of neuroscience

P50MH-40381-06 9001 (SRCM) SALZMAN, LEONARD CRC/PE for the study of psychopathology for the elderly Data management/Biostatistics core

P50MH-40381-06 9002 (SRCM) BONACI, DAVID A CRC/PE for the study of psychopathology for the elderly Research clinical assessment core

P50MH-40381-06 9003 (SRCM) FELTEN, DAVID L CRC/PE for the study of psychopathology for the elderly Brain acquisition core

P50MH-40381-06 9004 (SRCM) SALZMAN, LEONARD F CRC/PE for the study of psychopathology for the elderly Education and training core

R37MH-40418-07 (NSS) JENNINGS, J RICHARD WESTERN PSYCHIATRIC INST & CLI 3811 O'HARA STREET PITTSBURGH, PA 15213 Cognitive-energetic interactions: Cardiovascular aspects

R37MH-40430-08 (BBP) HOFER, MYRON A RES FDN/MENTAL HYGIENE INC 722 WEST 168TH STREET NEW YORK, N Y 10032 The developmental effects of early maternal separation

R01MH-40459-07 (PYB) STERN, JUDITH M RUTGERS, STATE UNIVERSITY OF N BUSCH CAMPUS NEW BRUNSWICK, NJ 08903 Psychobiology of maternal behavior

R01MH-40487-06 (EPS) BARSKY, ARTHUR J MASSACHUSETTS GENERAL HOSPITAL FRUIT ST BOSTON, MA 02114 Hypochondriasis--Diagnosis, description and medical care

R01MH-40524-06 (SRCM) NEMEROFF, CHARLES B DUKE UNIVERSITY MEDICAL CENTER P O BOX 3859 DURHAM, N C 27710 Neuropeptide/cholinergic function in Alzheimer's disease

R01MH-40537-07 (BPN) MAILMAN, RICHARD B UNIVERSITY OF NORTH CAROLINA CB#7250 BDRC CHAPEL HILL, NC 27599-7250 Novel molecular site for antidopaminergic effects

R01MH-40552-06S1 (TDA) CARTWRIGHT, ROSALIND D RUSH-PRESBY-ST LUKE'S MED CTR 1653 W CONGRESS PARKWAY CHICAGO, IL 60612 Factors in divorce-related depression and its treatment

U10MH-40597-07 (SRCM) NINAN, PHILIP T EMORY UNIVERSITY CLINIC 1365 CLIFTON RD ATLANTA, GA 30322 Treatment strategies in schizophrenia at Grady Memorial Hospital

R01MH-40603-05 (EPS) LEAF, PHILIP J JOHNS HOPKINS UNIVERSITY 624 NORTH BROADWAY BALTIMORE, MD 21205 Epidemiologic catchment area program

R01MH-40631-06 (BPN) GREENOUGH, WILLIAM T BECKMAN INSTITUTE 405 N MATHEWS AVE URBANA, IL 61801 CNS substance of a learned motor task

R37MH-40662-07 (BSR) ROTHBART, MYRON UNIVERSITY OF OREGON EUGENE, OR 97403 Stability and change in sterotypic beliefs

R37MH-40687-07 (CEP) FLAVELL, JOHN H STANFORD UNIVERSITY DEPT OF PSYCHOLOGY, BLDG 420 STANFORD, CALIF 94305-2130 Development of knowledge about mental representations

PROJECT NO., ORGANIZATIONAL UNIT., INVESTIGATOR, ADDRESS, TITLE

R01MH-40694-07 (BPN) O'DONNELL, JAMES M LOUISIANA STATE UNIVERSITY PO BOX 33932 SHREVEPORT, LA 71130-3932 Centrally acting beta adrenergic agonists
R01MH-40695-05 (PCB) MANN, J JOHN WESTERN PSYCHIATRIC INSTITUTE 3811 O'HARA STREET PITTSBURGH, PA 15213 Neurobiological studies of ECT in depression
R37MH-40698-07 (BPN) BRAUTH, STEVEN E UNIVERSITY OF MARYLAND COLLEGE PARK, MD 20742 Neural basis of associative learning
R01MH-40703-05 (PCB) CHAPMAN, ROBERT M UNIVERSITY OF ROCHESTER 274 MELIORA HALL, RIVER CAMPUS ROCHESTER, NY 14627-0270 Electrical brain activity and information processing
R01MH-40705-06 (LCR) LEUCHTER, ANDREW F UNIVERSITY OF CALIFORNIA 760 WESTWOOD PLAZA LOS ANGELES, CA 90024-1769 Mental illness in the elderly--Diagnostic testing
K05MH-40710-22 (MHK) LUBORSKY, LESTER B UNIV OF PENNSYLVANIA-HOSPITAL 3400 SPRUCE STREET PHILADELPHIA, PA 19104 Psychotheraphy outcome and symptom-onset conditions
R01MH-40716-05 (BPN) TEITLER, MILT ALBANY MEDICAL COLLEGE 47 NEW SCOTLAND AVE ALBANY, NY 12208 Regulation of brain serotonin receptors
R01MH-40787-07 (SRCM) GLASER, RONALD OHIO STATE UNIVERSITY 333 WEST 10TH AVE COLUMBUS, OH 43210 Personality, psychological stress, and immunocompetence
R01MH-40799-05 (PCB) MC CARLEY, ROBERT W HARVARD MEDICAL SCHOOL 940 BELMONT ST BROCKTON, MA 02401 Neurophysiological studies of schizophrenia
R01MH-40801-05 (CEP) SHURE, MYRNA B HAHNEMANN UNIVERSITY BROAD AND VINE PHILADELPHIA, PA 19102 Interpersonal problem solving and prevention
R01MH-40814-07 (BSR) COLBY, ANNE RADCLIFFE COLLEGE 10 GARDEN STREET CAMBRIDGE, MA 02138 Longitudinal mental health data archive
R01MH-40817-07 (BPN) KALIVAS, PETER W WASHINGTON STATE UNIVERSITY 205 WEGNER HALL PULLMAN, WA 99164-6520 Regulation of mesolimbic dopamine by endogenous compound
R01MH-40828-06 (PCB) KENDLER, KENNETH S VIRGINIA COMMONWEALTH UNIV BOX 710 MCV STATION RICHMOND, VA 23298-0710 Epidemiology of anxiety and depression
R01MH-40832-06 (BPN) WHITE, FRANCIS J LAFAYETTE CLINIC 951 E LAFAYETTE DETROIT, MI 48207 Nucleus accumbens neurons and schizophrenia
R01MH-40843-04 (LCR) RABINS, PETER V JOHNS HOPKINS UNIV HOSP 600 N WOLFE STREET BALTIMORE, MD 21205 Structural brain changes in late life mental disorders
R01MH-40855-05 (BPN) KALIN, NED H W S MIDDLETON MEMORIAL VA HOSP 2500 OVERLOOK TERRACE MADISON, WI 53705 Role of central CRF in stress-induced behaviors
R01MH-40856-06 (SRCM) ANDREASEN, NANCY C UNIVERSITY OF IOWA 500 NEWTON RD IOWA CITY, IA 52242 Brain imaging in the major psychoses
R01MH-40858-04 (PCB) MINSHEW, NANCY J WESTERN PSYCHIATRIC INST & CLC 3811 O'HARA STREET PITTSBURGH, PA 15213 Psychobiology of autism
R37MH-40860-06 (SRCM) CROW, TERRY J UNIV OF TEXAS HEALTH SCIENCE C PO BOX 20708 HOUSTON, TX 77225 Pharmacology and neural circuit underlying behavior
R01MH-40864-06 (BSR) EGELAND, BYRON R UNIVERSITY OF MINNESOTA 230 INSTITUTE OF CHILD DEV MINNEAPOLIS, MN 55455 Adaptation in a risk sample--Childhood to adolescence
R01MH-40867-06 (PCB) CAMPBELL, SUSAN B UNIVERSITY OF PITTSBURGH 4015 O'HARA STREET PITTSBURGH, PA 15260 Postpartum depression--Risk factor for infants
R01MH-40880-06 (BPN) VOGEL, GERALD W GEORGIA MENTAL HEALTH INST 1256 BRIARCLIFF RD ATLANTA, GA 30306 REM sleep deprivation and depression
P01MH-40899-07 (SRCM) GREENGARD, PAUL ROCKEFELLER UNIVERSITY 1230 YORK AVENUE NEW YORK, NY 10021 Region-specific phosphoproteins in the basal ganglia
P01MH-40899-07 0001 (SRCM) NAIRN, ANGUS C Region-specific phosphoproteins in the basal ganglia Purification of basal ganglia phosphoproteins
P01MH-40899-07 0004 (SRCM) GREENGARD, PAUL Region-specific phosphoproteins in the basal ganglia Phosphoproteins in basal ganglia/limbic regions--Physiology/pharmacology
P01MH-40899-07 0005 (SRCM) GUSTAFSON, ERIC L Region-specific phosphoproteins in the basal ganglia Anatomy of neurotransmitter-phosphoprotein interactions in extended amygdala
P01MH-40899-07 0006 (SRCM) EHRLICH, MICHELLE Region-specific phosphoproteins in the basal ganglia: Molecular biology of basal ganglia-specific phosphoproteins
P01MH-40899-07 9001 (SRCM) TSOU, KANG Region-specific phosphoproteins in the basal ganglia Core--Monoclonal antibodies against basal ganglia phosphoproteins
R01MH-40900-05S1 (BPN) VICARIO, DAVID S ROCKEFELLER UNIVERSITY 1230 YORK AVE NEW YORK, NY 10021-6369 Sensory-motor representation of a learned skill
R37MH-40930-06 (PCB) SMALL, JOYCE G LARUE D CARTER MEMORIAL HOSP 1315 WEST 10TH STREET INDIANAPOLIS, IN 46202-2885 Lithium and carbamazepine in the treatment of mania
R01MH-40935-05 (TDA) MAAS, JAMES W UNIV OF TEXAS HLTH SCIS CENTER 7703 FLOYD CURL DRIVE SAN ANTONIO, TX 78284-7792 Debrisoquin as an agent for study of psychotic states
R37MH-41083-05 (BPN) CAREW, THOMAS J YALE UNIVERSITY P O BOX 11A YALE STATION NEW HAVEN, CT 06520 Cellular mechanisms of operant conditioning in Aplysia
P50MH-41115-05 (TDA) RUSH, AUGUSTUS J UNIV OF TEXAS S W MEDICAL CTR 5323 HARRY HINES BOULEVARD DALLAS, TEX 75235 CRC study of neuropsychobiology in affective disorders
P50MH-41115-05 0019 (TDA) BASCO, MONICA R CRC study of neuropsychobiology in affective disorders Psychiatric assessment core
P50MH-41115-05 0020 (TDA) GUILLON, CHRISTINA M CRC study of neuropsychobiology in affective disorders Data management and statistics core
P50MH-41115-05 0021 (TDA) ROFFWARG, HOWARD P CRC study of neuropsychobiology in affective disorders Sleep study core
P50MH-41115-05 0022 (TDA) JARRETT, ROBIN B CRC study of neuropsychobiology in affective disorders Psychosocial core
P50MH-41115-05 0023 (TDA) ORSULAK, PAUL J CRC study of neuropsychobiology in affective disorders Psychiatric clinical diagnostic core
P50MH-41115-05 0024 (TDA) DEVOUS, MICHAEL D CRC study of neuropsychobiology in affective disorders Brain imaging core
R01MH-41125-03 (SRCM) MASON, JOHN W YALE UNIVERSITY SCH OF MED VA MEDICAL CENTER/116A NEW HAVEN, CT 06516 Multidimensional hormonal assessment of post-traumatic stress disorder
R01MH-41135-05 (BSR) KESSLER, RONALD C UNIVERSITY OF MICHIGAN PO BOX 1248 ANN ARBOR, MI 48106 Sex differences in daily stress and coping
R01MH-41138-06 (PYB) SATINOFF, EVELYN UNIVERSITY OF ILLINOIS 603 EAST DANIEL ST CHAMPAIGN, ILL 61820 Pharmacology of thermoregulation and sleep
R01MH-41170-03 (PYB) MINOR, THOMAS R UNIVERSITY OF CALIFORNIA 405 HILGARD AVENUE LOS ANGELES, CA 90024-1563 Anxiety and helplessness: mechanisms of coping
R01MH-41176-04S1 (PCBB) TORREY, E FULLER 6204 RIDGE DRIVE BETHESDA, MD 20816 Biological markers in discordant monozygotic twins
R01MH-41205-06 (PCB) FARDE, LARS F KAROLINSKA HOSPITAL STOCKHOLM, SWEDEN S-104 01 PET analysis of dopamine-D 2 receptors in schizophrenia
R01MH-41244-05 (LCR) THOMAN, EVELYN B UNIVERSITY OF CONNECTICUT STORRS, CT 06269-4154 Early intervention for prematures and mothers
R01MH-41256-06 (BPN) MC EWEN, BRUCE S ROCKEFELLER UNIVERSITY 1230 YORK AVENUE NEW YORK, N Y 10021 Stress, adrenal steroids and the brain
R01MH-41278-06 (TDA) LEWINSOHN, PETER M OREGON RESEARCH INSTITUTE 1899 WILLAMETTE, SUITE 2 EUGENE, OR 97401 Cognitive behavioral treatment for depressed adolescents
R01MH-41314-04 (SRCM) BIEDERMAN, JOSEPH MASSACHUSETTS GENERAL HOSPITAL 15 PARKMAN ST BOSTON, MA 02114 Prospective high risk study of ADHD and related disorders
R01MH-41327-05 (LCR) ELDER, GLEN H, JR UNIVERSITY OF NORTH CAROLINA 123 W FRANKLIN ST CB# 8120 CHAPEL HILL, N C 27516-3997 Military service in adult development and aging
R37MH-41414-07 (BPN) ETGEN, ANNE M ALBERT EINSTEIN COLLEGE OF MED 1300 MORRIS PARK AVENUE BRONX, N Y 10461 Steroid hormones, the brain and behavior
R01MH-41440-06 (BPN) WANG, REX Y RES FDN OF SUNY AT STONY BROOK STONY BROOK, NY 11794-8101 Regulation of dopamine neurons and schizophrenia
R01MH-41445-06 (BPN) COLES, MICHAEL G UNIVERSITY OF ILLINOIS 603 EAST DANIEL STREET CHAMPAIGN, IL 61820 Cognitive psychophysiology and information processing
R01MH-41446-03 (TDA) SANDMAN, CURT A UNIVERSITY OF CALIFORNIA 101 CITY DR SOUTH ORANGE, CA 92668 Long term treatment of sib with naltrexone
R37MH-41447-06 (PYB) BUNTIN, JOHN D UNIV OF WISCONSIN-MILWAUKEE 3201 N MARYLAND AVENUE MILWAUKEE, WI 53211 Prolactin effects on behavior--Sites and modes of action
R37MH-41474-05 (NSS) GELFAND, DONNA M UNIVERSITY OF UTAH SALT LAKE CITY, UT 84112 Problem prevention in infants of depressed mothers
R37MH-41479-06 (BPN) AMARAL, DAVID G SALK INST/BIOLOGICAL STUDIES P O BOX 85800 SAN DIEGO, CA 92186-5800 Anatomy of the amygdaloid complex
R01MH-41487-05 (BSR) TESSER, ABRAHAM UNIVERSITY OF GEORGIA 111 BARROW HALL, IBR ATHENS, GA 30602 Emotion in marriage--Social reflection & comparisonon
R01MH-41511-06 (CEP) FERNALD, ANNE STANFORD UNIVERSITY DEPARTMENT OF PSYCHOLOGY STANFORD, CA 94305-2130 Affective processes in the development of language
R01MH-41544-04 (BPN) RAFAL, ROBERT D VA MEDICAL CENTER 150 MUIR ROAD MARTINEZ, CA 94553 Neurobiology of preparatory set in mental disorders
R01MH-41551-03 (BPN) MASSERANO, JOSEPH M UNIV OF COLORADO HLTH SCIS CTR 4200 EAST NINTH AVENUE DENVER, CO 80262 Autoreceptor regulation of dopamine release
R01MH-41557-06 (BPN) CHIODO, LOUIS A SINAI RESEARCH INSTITUTE 6767 W OUTER DRIVE DETROIT, MI 48235 Psychopharmacology of DA agonists CNS effect
R01MH-41569-05 (EPS) REINHERZ, HELEN Z SIMMONS COLLEGE 51 COMMONWEALTH AVENUE BOSTON, MA 02116 Transition to adulthood--A community study
R01MH-41577-05 (TDA) BELLACK, ALAN S MEDICAL COLL PENNSYLVANIA-EPPI 3200 HENRY AVENUE PHILADELPHIA, PA 19129 A functional analysis of family therapy in schizophrenia
R37MH-41637-06 (PYB) LOFTUS, GEOFFREY R UNIVERSITY OF WASHINGTON SEATTLE, WA 98195 Encoding processes on complex visual stimuli
R01MH-41638-05 (SRCM) LEAF, PHILIP J YALE UNIVERSITY 350 CONGRESS AVENUE NEW HAVEN, CT 06519 Pediatric provision of mental health services
R01MH-41644-03S1 (PCB) FERNSTROM, MADELYN H WESTERN PSYCHIATRIC INST/CLINI 3811 O'HARA STREET PITTSBURGH, PA 15213 Metabolic aspects of body weight change in depression
R01MH-41649-06 (PYB) GIBBON, JOHN RES FDN FOR MENTAL HYGIENE 722 WEST 168TH STREET NEW YORK, N Y 10032 Theory of animal timing--memory and association
R01MH-41659-07 (MHAZ) COE, CHRISTOPHER L UNIVERSITY OF WISCONSIN 1202 WEST JOHNSON STREET MADISON, WI 53706 Psychological stress and immune responsiveness
P50MH-41684-07 (TDA) MELTZER, HERBERT Y CASE WESTERN RESERVE UNIV 2040 ADELBERT ROAD CLEVELAND, OH 44106 Clinical research center for the study of the major psychoses
P50MH-41684-07 0073 (TDA) VRTUNSKI, P BART Clinical research center for the study of the major psychoses Psychomotor control in schizophenia--Choice reaction
P50MH-41684-07 0074 (TDA) KENNY, JOHN T Clinical research center for the study of the major psychoses Neuropsychological dysfunction in schizophrenia

PROJECT NO., ORGANIZATIONAL UNIT., INVESTIGATOR, ADDRESS, TITLE

P50MH-41684-07 0075 (TDA) SILVERSTEIN, MARSHALL L Clinical research center for the study of the major psychoses Neuropsychological dysfunction in the major psychoses
P50MH-41684-07 0076 (TDA) BRESLAU, NAOMI Clinical research center for the study of the major psychoses Prospective study of anxiety in unipolar depression
P50MH-41684-07 0077 (TDA) DAVID, GLENN Clinical research center for the study of the major psychoses Post-traumatic stress syndrome
P50MH-41684-07 0078 (TDA) KENNY, JOHN T Clinical research center for the study of the major psychoses Positive and negative symptoms in schizophrenia
P50MH-41684-07 0079 (TDA) GILMORE, G C Clinical research center for the study of the major psychoses Visual information processing in schizophenia
P50MH-41684-07 0080 (TDA) AMBROSINI, PAUL J Clinical research center for the study of the major psychoses Child psychopathology--SADS-III reliability
P50MH-41684-07 0081 (TDA) EMERY, OLGA Clinical research center for the study of the major psychoses Cognitive studies of Alzeimer's disease and major depression
P50MH-41684-07 0082 (TDA) HARROW, MARTIN Clinical research center for the study of the major psychoses Prognostic implications of psychopathology
P50MH-41684-07 0083 (TDA) ALLOY, LAUREN B Clinical research center for the study of the major psychoses Depression, meaning and inference
P50MH-41684-07 0084 (TDA) SUDAK, HOWARD Clinical research center for the study of the major psychoses Epidemiologic studies of suicide
P50MH-41684-07 0014 (TDA) MELTZER, HERBERT Y Clinical research center for the study of the major psychoses Effect of apomorphine on plasma HVA and serum PRL and GH
P50MH-41684-07 0031 (TDA) BRESLAU, NAOMI Clinical research center for the study of the major psychoses Clinical assessment and diagnosis
P50MH-41684-07 0032 (TDA) MELTZER, HERBERT Y Clinical research center for the study of the major psychoses Platelet monoamine oxidase
P50MH-41684-07 0033 (TDA) OHMORI, TETSURO Clinical research center for the study of the major psychoses Plasma homovanillac acid levels in schizophrenia
P50MH-41684-07 0034 (TDA) MELTZER, HERBERT Y Clinical research center for the study of the major psychoses Plasma tryptophan and 5-hydroxyindoleascetic acid levels in depression
P50MH-41684-07 0035 (TDA) ARORA, RAMESH Clinical research center for the study of the major psychoses Platelet serotonin uptake and imipramine binding in affective disorders
P50MH-41684-07 0036 (TDA) AMBROSINI, PAUL Clinical research center for the study of the major psychoses Platelet markers of childhood disorders
P50MH-41684-07 0037 (TDA) SUDAK, HOWARD S Clinical research center for the study of the major psychoses Biopsychosocial correlates of suicide
P50MH-41684-07 0038 (TDA) ANDORN, ANNE Clinical research center for the study of the major psychoses Alpha-adrenergic receptors in brains of suicides
P50MH-41684-07 0039 (TDA) HALARIS, ANGELOS Clinical research center for the study of the major psychoses Brain and platelet alpha-2 adrenoreceptors in depression
P50MH-41684-07 0040 (TDA) STOCKMEIER, CRAIG Clinical research center for the study of the major psychoses Noradrenergic receptor binding in brain tissue from suicide victims
P50MH-41684-07 0041 (TDA) STOCKMEIER, CRAIG Clinical research center for the study of the major psychoses Serotonin effect on beta-adrenergic receptor binding and function
P50MH-41684-07 0042 (TDA) STOCKMEIER, CRAIG Clinical research center for the study of the major psychoses ECS and psychotropic drugs on recepter binding & phosphoinositide turnover
P50MH-41684-07 0043 (TDA) STOCKMEIER, CRAIG Clinical research center for the study of the major psychoses Regulation of in vivo binding of methyl spiroperidol to serotonin receptors
P50MH-41684-07 0044 (TDA) STOCKMEIER, CRAIG Clinical research center for the study of the major psychoses Olfactory bulbectomy model of depression
P50MH-41684-07 0045 (TDA) OHMORI, TETSURO Clinical research center for the study of the major psychoses Plasma HIAA and 5-HTP--Indices of central serotonergic activity
P50MH-41684-07 0046 (TDA) MELTZER, HERBERT Y Clinical research center for the study of the major psychoses Serotonergic involvement antidepressant drug action in an animal model
P50MH-41684-07 0047 (TDA) LOWY, MARTIN T Clinical research center for the study of the major psychoses Glycocorticoid receptor regulation in depression
P50MH-41684-07 0048 (TDA) LOWY, MARTIN T Clinical research center for the study of the major psychoses Glucocorticoid metabolism in depression
P50MH-41684-07 0049 (TDA) MELTZER, HERBERT Y Clinical research center for the study of the major psychoses Serotonin in depression, mania, suicide & the action of thymoleptic drugs
P50MH-41684-07 0050 (TDA) NASH, JAY Clinical research center for the study of the major psychoses Effect of MK-212 on hormone secretion in depression
P50MH-41684-07 0051 (TDA) LEE, MYUNG Clinical research center for the study of the major psychoses Effect of insulin-induced hypoglycemia on the secretion of cortisol ACTH and GH
P50MH-41684-07 0052 (TDA) LEE, MYUNG Clinical research center for the study of the major psychoses Buspirone effect on cortisol secretion, ACTH and prolactin in depression
P50MH-41684-07 0053 (TDA) BASTANI, BIJAN Clinical research center for the study of the major psychoses Prolactin response to fenfluramine in depression
P50MH-41684-07 0054 (TDA) LOWY, MARTIN T Clinical research center for the study of the major psychoses Glucocorticoid and MAO activity in mental disorders
P50MH-41684-07 0055 (TDA) MC CORMACK, RICHARD Clinical research center for the study of the major psychoses Biological correlates of pathological gambling

PROJECT NO., ORGANIZATIONAL UNIT., INVESTIGATOR, ADDRESS, TITLE

P50MH-41684-07 0056 (TDA) GUDELSKY, GARY Clinical research center for the study of the major psychoses Neuroendocrine pharmacology of atypical neuroleptics
P50MH-41684-07 0057 (TDA) GUDELSKY, GARY Clinical research center for the study of the major psychoses In vivo measures of 5-HT receptor function
P50MH-41684-07 0058 (TDA) GUDELSKY, GARY Clinical research center for the study of the major psychoses Serotonergic control of ACTH secretion
P50MH-41684-07 0059 (TDA) GUDELSKY, GARY Clinical research center for the study of the major psychoses Modulation of neuroendocrine function by lithium
P50MH-41684-07 0060 (TDA) MELTZER, HERBERT Y Clinical research center for the study of the major psychoses Chlorpromazine/benztropine in treatment-resistant schizophrenia
P50MH-41684-07 0061 (TDA) MELTZER, HERBERT Y Clinical research center for the study of the major psychoses Clozapine in treatment-resistant patients
P50MH-41684-07 0062 (TDA) MELTZER, HERBERT Y Clinical research center for the study of the major psychoses Treatment of tardive dyskinesia in schizophrenic patients receiving haloperidol
P50MH-41684-07 0063 (TDA) MELTZER, HERBERT Y Clinical research center fcr the study of the major psychoses Effect of L-tryptophan and Li vs Li in treatment of mania & schizophrenia
P50MH-41684-07 0064 (TDA) MELTZER, HERBERT Y Clinical research center for the study of the major psychoses Bromocriptine treatment of non-delusional major depression
P50MH-41684-07 0065 (TDA) MELTZER, HERBERT Y Clinical research center for the study of the major psychoses Fluoxeting in the treatment of major depressive disorders
P50MH-41684-07 0066 (TDA) FRIEDMAN, LEE Clinical research center for the study of the major psychoses Positron emission tomography
P50MH-41684-07 0067 (TDA) FRIEDMAN, LEE Clinical research center for the study of the major psychoses Dopamine and serotonin receptors with 3-N-methylspiperone and PET
P50MH-41684-07 0068 (TDA) METZ, JOHN Clinical research center for the study of the major psychoses Positron emission tomography
P50MH-41684-07 0069 (TDA) FRIEDMAN, LEE Clinical research center for the study of the major psychoses Brain morphology in psychiatric disorders using MRT
P50MH-41684-07 0070 (TDA) LUCHINS, DANIEL Clinical research center for the study of the major psychoses Computed tomographic studies in psychosis
P50MH-41684-07 0071 (TDA) ABEL, LARRY Clinical research center for the study of the major psychoses Ocular motor control disorder in psychiatric disease
P50MH-41684-07 0072 (TDA) METZ, JOHN Clinical research center for the study of the major psychoses Evoked potential studies in schizophenia
R01MH-41695-05 (PCB) LONEY, JAN SUNY AT STONY BROOK STONY BROOK, NY 11794-8790 Hyperkinetic boys and their siblings as young adults
R01MH-41704-04 (CEP) MURPHY, GREGORY L 603 EAST DANIEL CHAMPAIGN, ILL 61820 Conceptual structures and processes
P01MH-41712-06 (SRCM) RYAN, NEAL D WESTERN PSYCHIATRIC INST & CLI 3811 O'HARA STREET PITTSBURGH, PA 15213 Psychobiology of depression in children and adolescents
P01MH-41712-06 0001 (SRCM) RYAN, NEAL D Psychobiology of depression in children and adolescents Neurobiological correlates of depression
P01MH-41712-06 0002 (SRCM) BRENT, DAVID A Psychobiology of depression in children and adolescents Biology and family adversity in prepubertal behavior
P01MH-41712-06 0004 (SRCM) DAHL, RONALD E Psychobiology of depression in children and adolescents Physiological maturation of sleep and neuroendocrine regulation
P01MH-41712-06 0005 (SRCM) DAHL, RONALD E Psychobiology of depression in children and adolescents Quantitative EEG sleep analysis
P01MH-41712-06 9001 (SRCM) BRENT, DAVID A Psychobiology of depression in children and adolescents Core--Clinical
P01MH-41712-06 9002 (SRCM) DAHL, RONALD E Psychobiology of depression in children and adolescents Core--Sleep and neuroendocrinology
P01MH-41712-06 9003 (SRCM) IYENGAR, SATISH Psychobiology of depression in children and adolescents Core--Data analytic unit
R01MH-41734-04 (LCR) STANLEY, BARBARA H C U N Y - JOHN JAY COLLEGE 445 W 59TH STREET NEW YORK, NY 10019 Informed consent in aged psychiatric patients
R01MH-41739-04A1 (EPS) KATON, WAYNE J UNIVERSITY OF WASHINGTON 1959 N E PACIFIC STREET SEATTLE, WA 98195 A randomized trial of liaison psychiatry in primary care
R01MH-41761-05 (DAPA) ELLIOTT, DELBERT S INST OF BEHAVIORAL SCIENCE CAMPUS BOX 483 BOULDER, CO 80309 Dynamics of deviant behavior--A national survey
R01MH-41766-05 (LCR) COLLINS, CLARE E MICHIGAN STATE UNIVERSITY A230 LIFE SCIENCES BLDG EAST LANSING, MI 48824-1317 Impact of Alzheimer's disease on family caregivers
R37MH-41770-06 (PYB) CREWS, DAVID P UNIVERSITY OF TEXAS AT AUSTIN DEPT OF ZOOLOGY AUSTIN, TX 78712 Evolution of brain-behavior controlling mechanisms
R01MH-41772-05 (TDA) VOLAVKA, JAN NATHAN S KLINE INSTITUTE OLD ORANGEBURG ROAD ORANGEBURG, NY 10962 Haloperidol blood levels and effects in schizophrenia
R01MH-41778-04A1 (PCB) GORMAN, JACK M RESEARCH FDN FOR MENTAL HYGIEN 722 WEST 168TH STREET NEW YORK, NY 10032 Carbon dioxide challenge of panic disorder
R01MH-41781-06 (LCR) DEAN, ALFRED SAN DIEGO STATE UNIVERSITY SAN DIEGO, CA 92182 Social supports, aging, and psychiatric disturbances
R01MH-41784-05 (BPN) MOSS, ROBERT L UNIV TEX S W MEDICAL CENTER 5323 HARRY HINES BOULEVARD DALLAS, TX 75235-9040 Neuropeptides in the control of reproductive behavior
R01MH-41791-04 (LCR) KOOCHER, GERALD P CHILDREN'S HOSPITAL CORP 300 LONGWOOD AVENUE BOSTON, MA 02115 Preventive mutual support for

PROJECT NO., ORGANIZATIONAL UNIT., INVESTIGATOR, ADDRESS, TITLE

families after child death
R01MH-41800-07 (MHAZ) KELLY, JEFFREY A MEDICAL COLLEGE OF WISCONSIN 8701 WATERTOWN PLANK RD MILWAUKEE, WI 53226 Behavioral training to reduce AIDS at-risk activities
R01MH-41801-06 (BSR) FISKE, SUSAN T UNIVERSITY OF MASSACHUSETTS TOBIN HALL AMHERST, MA 01003 Interdependence and category-based responses
R01MH-41821-03 (TDA) BECKER, ROBERT E SO ILLINOIS UNIV SCHL OF MED P O BOX 19230 SPRINGFIELD, IL 62794-9230 Effects of long-acting anticholinesterase in Alzheimers
R01MH-41841-06 (BSR) WILSON, TIMOTHY D UNIVERSITY OF VIRGINIA GILMER HALL CHARLOTTESVILLE, VA 22903 Self-reflection--Its effects, benefits and drawbacks
R01MH-41842-05 (CEP) DIAMOND, ADELE D UNIVERSITY OF PENNSYLVANIA 3815 WALNUT STREET PHILADELPHIA, PA 19104-6196 Development of cognitive function linked to frontal lobe
R29MH-41865-05 (BPN) FUCHS, JANNON L UNIVERSITY OF NORTH TEXAS PO BOX 5396 NT STATION DENTON, TX 76203 Circadian distribution of SCN neurotransmitter receptors
R01MH-41879-05 (LCRA) EGELAND, BYRON R UNIVERSITY OF MINNESOTA 75 EAST RIVER ROAD MINNEAPOLIS, MN 55455 An evaluation of STEEP--A program for high risk mothers
R01MH-41883-05 (PCB) GANGULI, ROHAN WESTERN PSYCHIATRY INSTITUTE 3811 O'HARA STREET PITTSBURGH, PA 15213 Autoimmune phenomena & psychotic relapse--Schizophrenia
R01MH-41884-04A1 (PCB) THASE, MICHAEL E WESTERN PSYCHIATRIC INST 3811 O'HARA STREET PITTSBURGH, PA 15213 Psychobiological correlates of recovery in depression-II
R01MH-41935-03 (TDA) WENDER, PAUL H UNIVERSITY OF UTAH SALT LAKE CITY, UTAH 84132 Studies of attention deficit disorder
R01MH-41948-04 (EPS) DOREIAN, PATRICK UNIVERSITY OF PITTSBURGH 2G03 FORBES QUADRANGLE PITTSBURGH, PA 15260 Social services delivery under resource constraints
R01MH-41953-05 (EPSA) KENDLER, KENNETH S VIRGINIA COMMONWEALTH UNIV BOX 710 MCV STATION RICHMOND, VA 23298-0710 The genetic epidemiology of schizophrenia in Ireland
P50MH-41960-05S1 (TDAC) KANE, JOHN M HILLSIDE HOSP/L I JEW MED CTR 75-59 263RD STREET GLEN OAKS, NY 11004 CRC for the study of schizophrenia
P50MH-41960-05S1 0001 (TDAC) KANE, JOHN M CRC for the study of schizophrenia Clinical psychopharmacology unit
P50MH-41960-05S1 0002 (TDAC) KINON, BRUCE J CRC for the study of schizophrenia Preclinical neuropharmacology unit
P50MH-41960-05S1 0003 (TDAC) ZITO, JOSEPH CRC for the study of schizophrenia Neuroimaging unit
P50MH-41960-05S1 0004 (TDAC) SCHNEIDER, BRUCE S CRC for the study of schizophrenia Neurobiology
P50MH-41960-05S1 0005 (TDAC) KENDLER, KENNETH CRC for the study of schizophrenia Genetics unit
P50MH-41960-05S1 0006 (TDAC) KANE, JOHN M CRC for the study of schizophrenia Training unit
P50MH-41960-05S1 9001 (TDAC) KANE, JOHN M CRC for the study of schizophrenia Clinical assessment and training core
P50MH-41960-05S1 9002 (TDAC) KANE, JOHN M CRC for the study of schizophrenia Study management unit core
P50MH-41960-05S1 9003 (TDAC) KANE, JOHN M CRC for the study of schizophrenia Biostatistis core
R01MH-41967-05 (LCR) SIEGEL, KAROLYNN MEM HOSP/CANCER/ALLIED DIS 1275 YORK AVE NEW YORK, NY 10021 Parent guidance prevention program for bereaved children
R01MH-41979-05A1 (BPN) ESKIN, ARNOLD UNIVERSITY OF HOUSTON HOUSTON, TX 77204-5500 Basis of regulation and timing of circadian systems
R01MH-41987-04A1 (PYB) SIMANSKY, KENNY J MED COLLEGE OF PA/EPPI 3200 HENRY AVENUE PHILADELPHIA, PA 19129 Actions of peripheral 5-hydroxytryptamine in feeding
R01MH-42023-05 (MHAZ) MARKS, GARY S UNIV OF SOUTHERN CALIFORNIA 1420 SAN PABLO ST LOS ANGELES, CA 90033 Assessment of self-disclosure among patients with AIDS
R01MH-42051-15 (MHAZ) ADER, ROBERT UNIV OF ROCHESTER MED CTR 300 CRITTENDEN BLVD ROCHESTER, NY 14642 Behaviorally conditioned immunosuppression
R01MH-42057-06 (CEP) LARSEN, RANDY J UNIVERSITY OF MICHIGAN 580 UNION DRIVE ANN ARBOR, MI 48109-1346 Affect intensity--Physiological and cognitive mechanisms
R01MH-42064-02 (CEP) HIRST, WILLIAM C NEW SCHOOL FOR SOCIAL RESEARCH 65 FIFTH AVENUE NEW YORK, NY 10003 Amnesics' representation of direct memories
R01MH-42074-04A1 (BPN) WHITE, JEFFREY D SUNY AT STONY BROOK HSC T15-060 STONY BROOK, NY 11794-8154 Neuropeptide biosynthesis and metabolism in the CNS
R37MH-42076-06 (MHAZ) FELTEN, DAVID L UNIV OF ROCHESTER SCH OF MED 601 ELMWOOD AVE ROCHESTER, NY 14642 Sympathetic innervation and immune regulation
R01MH-42088-05 (BPN) NEMEROFF, CHARLES B DUKE UNIVERSITY MEDICAL CENTER P O BOX 3859 DURHAM, N C 27710 The psychobiology of corticotropin-releasing factor
R01MH-42096-05 (LCR) KIECOLT-GLASER, JANICE K OHIO STATE UNIVERSITY 473 WEST 12TH AVENUE COLUMBUS, OH 43210 Caregivers of Alzheimer's disease victims--Stress and mental health
R01MH-42103-04 (LCR) BILLIG, NATHAN GEORGETOWN UNIVERSITY MED CTR 3800 RESERVOIR ROAD, N W WASHINGTON, D C 20007 Mental status changes after surgery in the elderly
R01MH-42122-05 (BSR) PEARLIN, LEONARD I UNIVERSITY OF CALIFORNIA 1350 7TH AVENUE, CSBS 237 SAN FRANCISCO, CA 94143 Sources and mediators of Alzheimer's caregiver stress
R01MH-42129-03 (SRCM) TUCKER, DON M UNIVERSITY OF OREGON EUGENE, OR 97403-1227 Depression and anxiety as neural control processes
R01MH-42131-04 (LCR) GREENBERG, MARK T DEPT OF PSYCHOLOGY UNIVERSITY OF WASHINGTON SEATTLE, WA 98195 The PATHS project--Preventive intervention for children
R37MH-42134-05 (NSS) HELLER, ALFRED UNIVERSITY OF CHICAGO 947 EAST 58TH STREET CHICAGO, IL 60637 Neurotoxicity of psychotropic

PROJECT NO., ORGANIZATIONAL UNIT., INVESTIGATOR, ADDRESS, TITLE

drugs
R01MH-42145-05 (PCB) GOLDEN, ROBERT N UNIV OF N C AT CHAPLE HILL CB#7160, MED SCHOOL WING B CHAPEL HILL, NC 27599-7160 5HT challenge-- Pre/post treatment response in depression
R37MH-42148-05 (NSS) WEISS, BENJAMIN MEDICAL COL OF PENSYLVANIA 3200 HENRY AVE PHILADELPHIA, PA 19120 Behavioral and biochemical correlates of dopamine response
R37MH-42152-05 (NSS) TAYLOR, SHELLEY E UNIVERSITY OF CALIFORNIA 405 HILGARD AVE LOS ANGELES, CA 90024 Adjustment to life-threatening illnesses & treatments
R01MH-42163-04 (LCR) PILLEMER, KARL A CORNELL UNIVERSITY G 43 MARTHA VAN RENSSELAER HAL ITHACA, NEW YORK 14853 Social relations of Alzheimer's caregivers across time
R01MH-42172-02 (CEP) BOROD, JOAN C QUEENS COLLEGE OF C U N Y 65-30 KISSENA BLVD FLUSHING, N Y 11367 Emotional processing in brain-damaged patients
R01MH-42178-06 (SRCM) FOA, EDNA B MEDICAL COLL OF PENNSYLVANIA 3300 HENRY AVENUE PHILADELPHIA, PA 19129 Rape victims--Persistent reactions and their treatment
R01MH-42181-03 (LCR) BARKLEY, RUSSELL A UNIV OF MASSACHUSETTS MED CENT 55 LAKE AVENUE NORTH WORCESTER, MA 01655 Adult outcome of ADHD children--Social/parenting competence
R37MH-42191-05 (SRCM) GUR, RAQUEL E UNIVERSITY OF PENNSYLVANIA 36TH & SPRUCE STREETS PHILADELPHIA, PA 19104 A neurobehavioral study of schizophrenia
R01MH-42206-04 (PCB) WALSH, B TIMOTHY COLUMBIA UNIVERSITY 722 WEST 168TH STREET NEW YORK, NY 10032 Psychobiology of eating behavior in bulimia
R01MH-42216-05 (LCR) FERRIS, STEVEN H NEW YORK MEDICAL CENTER 550 FIRST AVENUE NEW YORK, NY 10016 Alzheimer's disease caregiver well-being--Counseling/institutionalization
R01MH-42217-04A1 (BPN) GRACE, ANTHONY A UNIVERSITY OF PITTSBURGH 464 CRAWFORD HALL PITTSBURGH, PA 15260 In vitro electrophysiology of midbrain dopamine systems
R01MH-42228-05 (PCB) BRAFF, DAVID L UNIV OF CALIF, SAN DIEGO 9500 GILMAN DRIVE LA JOLLA, CALIF 92093-0804 Sensory gating and habituation in schizophrenia
R01MH-42229-03S2A1 (EPS) WELLS, KENNETH B Effects of health care systems on depression
R01MH-42243-04 (SRCM) DEPAULO, J RAYMOND, JR JOHNS HOPKINS HOSPITAL 600 NORTH WOLFE STREET BALTIMORE, MD 21205 Genetic linkage studies in bipolar families
R37MH-42248-05 (LCR) VAILLANT, GEORGE E DARTMOUTH MEDICAL SCHOOL 9 MAYNARD ST HANOVER, NH 03756 Life course, mental health and later development
P01MH-42251-05 (SRCM) WATSON, STANLEY J, JR 205 WASHTENAW PLACE ANN ARBOR, MI 48109-0010 Hypothalmaic and pituitary peptides--Fundamental studies
P01MH-42251-05 0001 (SRCM) AKIL, HUDA Hypothalmaic and pituitary peptides--Fundamental studies Dynorphin and vasopressin, regulation in hypothalamus and pituitary
P01MH-42251-05 0002 (SRCM) AKIL, HUDA Hypothalmaic and pituitary peptides--Fundamental studies Regulation of POMC in hypothalamus and pituitary
P01MH-42251-05 0003 (SRCM) WATSON, STANLEY J Hypothalmaic and pituitary peptides--Fundamental studies ACTH beta-endorphin and related peptides in depression
P01MH-42251-05 0004 (SRCM) WATSON, STANLEY J Hypothalmaic and pituitary peptides--Fundamental studies CRF in affective disease
R01MH-42261-05 (BPN) BENES, FRANCINE M MC LEAN HOSPITAL 115 MILL STREET BELMONT, MA 02178 Quantitative analysis of corticolimbic system in schizophrenic brain
R01MH-42277-06 (MHAZ) PERRY, SAMUEL W PAYNE WHITNEY CLINIC 525 EAST 68TH STREET NEW YORK, NY 10021 Psychoeducational interventions after HTLV-III test
R01MH-42427-06 (CEP) FUNDER, DAVID C UNIVERSITY OF CALIFORNIA RIVERSIDE, CA 92521 Factors affecting the accuracy of personality judgments
P50MH-42459-06 (SRCM) COATES, THOMAS J CTR FOR AIDS PREVENTION STUDIE 74 NEW MONTGOMERY STREET SAN FRANCISCO, CA 94105 Center for AIDS prevention studies
P50MH-42459-06 0005 (SRCM) BOWSER, BENJAMIN Center for AIDS prevention studies AIDS risk in disadvantaged Black adolescents in housing projects
P50MH-42459-06 0006 (SRCM) GERBERT, BARBARA Center for AIDS prevention studies Improving physicians' sexual risk counseling
P50MH-42459-06 0007 (SRCM) CATANIA, JOSEPH Center for AIDS prevention studies Methodological issues in surveys of AIDS-related sexual behaviors
P50MH-42459-06 0008 (SRCM) PETERSON, JOHN L Center for AIDS prevention studies Coping, mental health and HIV risk behavior in Black men
P50MH-42459-06 0009 (SRCM) COATES, THOMAS J Center for AIDS prevention studies Community mobilization for primary and secondary prevention
P50MH-42459-06 0010 (SRCM) CHESNEY, MARGARET A Center for AIDS prevention studies Adherence in clinical trials for HIV disease
P50MH-42459-06 0011 (SRCM) ALLEN, SUSAN Center for AIDS prevention studies Preventing heterosexual transmission of HIV in Rwanda
P50MH-42459-06 9002 (SRCM) FOLKMAN, SUSAN Center for AIDS prevention studies Core--Scientific theory and methods
P50MH-42459-06 9003 (SRCM) LO, BERNARD Center for AIDS prevention studies Core--Ethics
P50MH-42459-06 9004 (SRCM) LEE, PHILIP R Center for AIDS prevention studies Core--Policy
P50MH-42459-06 0002 (SRCM) HEARST, NORMAN Center for AIDS prevention studies Collaborative studies in developing countries
P50MH-42459-06 0004 (SRCM) SIEGEL, DAVID Center for AIDS prevention studies HIV prevention in high risk adolescents
R01MH-42465-06 (CEP) GRAHAM, FRANCES K UNIVERSITY OF DELAWARE NEWARK, DE 19716 Automatic mechanisms for detection & identification
R01MH-42473-06 (SRCM) MANSON, SPERO M UNIV OF COLORADO HLTH SCIS CTR 4200 EAST NINTH AVE, BOX C249 DENVER, CO 80262 American Indian

PROJECT NO., ORGANIZATIONAL UNIT., INVESTIGATOR, ADDRESS, TITLE

and Alaska Native mental health research
R01MH-42473-06 0001 (SRCM) BEALS, JANETTE American Indian and Alaska Native mental health research Psychiatric epidemiologic methods--American Indians/Alaska Natives
R01MH-42473-06 0002 (SRCM) SOMERVELL, PHILIP American Indian and Alaska Native mental health research Management of common mental disorders in American Indian/Alaska Native
R01MH-42473-06 0003 (SRCM) WILSON-DUCLOS, CHRISTINE American Indian and Alaska Native mental health research Detection, management and prevention among incarcinated American Indians
R37MH-42484-04 (SRCM) GOTTMAN, JOHN M UNIVERSITY OF WASHINGTON SEATTLE, WA 98195 Marital discord, parenting & child emotional development
R01MH-42488-01A1 (CVR) O'LEARY, K DANIEL STATE UNIVERSITY OF NEW YORK STONY BROOK, NY 11794-2500 Treatment of spouse abuse
R01MH-42498-05 (CVR) DODGE, KENNETH A VANDERBILT UNIVERSITY BOX 86 PEABODY COLLEGE NASHVILLE, TN 37203 Development of aggressive behavior
R01MH-42499-03 (TDA) POMARA, NUNZIO RES FDN FOR MENTAL HYGIENE INC NATHAN KLINE INST/PSYCH RES ORANGEBURG, N Y 10962 Lorazepam and alprazolam--Performance effects in elderly
R01MH-42522-04 (PCB) YOUNG, ROBERT C NEW YORK HOSP-CORNELL MED CTR 21 BLOOMINGDALE ROAD WHITE PLAINS, N Y 10605 Geriatric mania
R01MH-42529-05 (PCB) LOEBER, ROLF WESTERN PSYCHIATRIC INST & CLN 3811 O'HARA STREET PITTSBURGH, PA 15213 The development of conduct disorder in boys
R01MH-42535-05 (PCB) BARON, MIRON RES FDN FOR MENTAL HYGIENE 722 W 168TH STREET NEW YORK, N Y 10032 Genetic markers in affective disorders
R01MH-42547-02 (LCR) ZEPELIN, HAROLD OAKLAND UNIVERSITY DEPT OF PSYCHOLOGY ROCHESTER, MI 48309-4401 Intensity of sleep over the human life span
R37MH-42556-03 (TDA) GOLDSTEIN, MICHAEL J UNIVERSITY OF CALIFORNIA 1285 FRANZ HALL LOS ANGELES, CA 90024-1563 Lithium and family management of bipolar disorder
R01MH-42575-03 (PCB) DUPONT, RENEE UNIV OF CALIF, SAN DIEGO LA JOLLA, CA 92093-0934 Cognitive and MRI changes in affective disorders
R01MH-42579-03A1 (PCB) HOEHN-SARIC, RUDOLPH JOHNS HOPKINS HOSPITAL 600 N WOLFE STREET BALTIMORE, MD 21205 Somatic symptoms and the psychobiology of anxiety
R01MH-42584-04S1 (MHAZ) MAYS, VICKIE M UNIVERSITY OF CALIFORNIA 405 HILGARD AVENUE LOS ANGELES, CA 90024 AIDS risk reduction among black gay and bisexual men
R01MH-42620-03 (EPS) BENSON, PETER L SEARCH INSTITUTE 122 W FRANKLIN AVE MINNEAPOLIS, MN 55404 Service and mental health needs of adopted adolescents
P01MH-42652-05 (SRCM) AGRANOFF, BERNARD W UNIV OF MICHIGAN 1103 EAST HURON ANN ARBOR, MI 48104-1687 Regulation of phosphoinositide-linked CNS receptors
P01MH-42652-05 0004 (SRCM) UEDA, TETSUFUMI Regulation of phosphoinositide-linked CNS receptors Lipid and protein phosphorylation in presynaptic structures
P01MH-42652-05 9001 (SRCM) AGRANOFF, BERNARD W Regulation of phosphoinositide-linked CNS receptors Core--Phosphoinositide, inositol phosphate and myo-inositol determinations
P01MH-42652-05 0001 (SRCM) FREY, KIRK A Regulation of phosphoinositide-linked CNS receptors Regional regulation of muscarinic receptor subtypes & acetylcholine release
P01MH-42652-05 0002 (SRCM) FISHER, STEPHEN K Regulation of phosphoinositide-linked CNS receptors Regulation of inositide-linked second messenger systems
P01MH-42652-05 0003 (SRCM) HEACOCK, ANNE M Regulation of phosphoinositide-linked CNS receptors Developmental correlates of mAChR-stimulated PPI turnover
R01MH-42669-02 (SRCM) TUCKER, DON M UNIVERSITY OF OREGON EUGENE, OR 97403-1227 Depression and spatial orienting
R01MH-42684-05 (BSR) ZEBROWITZ, LESLIE A BRANDEIS UNIVERSITY PO BOX 9110 WALTHAM, MA 02254-9110 Psychosocial effects of variatons in facial maturity
R01MH-42705-08 (BPN) NICHOLS, DAVID E PURDUE UNIVERSITY WEST LAFAYETTE, IN 47907 Development of potentially selective dopamine agonists
R37MH-42714-05 (BSR) KESSLER, RONALD C UNIVERSITY OF MICHIGAN P O BOX 1248 ANN ARBOR, MICH 48106 Dyadic responses to stress--A study of married couples
R01MH-42715-05 (CEP) LEWICKI, PAWEL UNIVERSITY OF TULSA 600 SO COLLEGE AVE TULSA, OK 74104 Self-perpetuating development of encoding biases
R01MH-42722-05 (LCR) GOTTMAN, JOHN M UNIVERSITY OF WASHINGTON SEATTLE, WA 98195 Emotional communication in distressed marriages
R01MH-42730-05 (TDA) MAVISSAKALIAN, MATIG R OHIO STATE UNIVERSITY 473 WEST TWELFTH AVE COLUMBUS, OH 43210 Antidepressant drugs in treatment of anxiety disorders
R29MH-42762-04 (PCB) DARKO, DENIS F VAMC 3350 LA JOLLA VILLEGE DR SAN DIEGO, CALIF 92161 Depression stress and immune and endocrine function
R01MH-42768-04 (PCB) EASTMAN, CHARMANE I RUSH MEDICAL CTR 1653 W CONGRESS PKWY CHICAGO, IL 60612-3864 Mechanisms of antidepressant effects of bright lights
R01MH-42769-05A1 (PCB) JOSIASSEN, RICHARD C MED COLLEGE OF PENN/EPPI 3200 HENRY AVENUE PHILADELPHIA, PA 19129 Longitudinal ERP studies of schizophrenics and siblings
R01MH-42782-04A1 (PCB) HOOLEY, JILL M HARVARD UNIVERSITY 33 KIRKLAND STREET CAMBRIDGE, MA 02138 Expressed emotion and relapse in schizophrenic patients
R29MH-42795-05 (CVR) WURTELE, SANDY K UNIVERSITY OF COLORADO DEPARTMENT OF PSYCHOLOGY COLORADO SPRINGS, CO 80933 Evaluating sexual abuse prevention programs
R01MH-42800-03 (BPN) WEISZ, DONALD J UNIVERSITY OF PITTSBURGH PITTSBURGH, PA 15260 Physiology of reflex modification
R37MH-42802-25 (BPN) MOORE, KENNETH E MICHIGAN STATE UNIVERSITY EAST LANSING, MI 48824 The role of catecholamines in drug toxicity
R01MH-42803-03 (BPN) BLANCHARD, D CAROLINE UNIVERSITY OF HAWAII 1993 EAST-WEST ROAD HONOLULU, HI 96822 The ethopharmacology of defense and anxiety
R01MH-42805-03 (PCB) KOENIGSBERG, HAROLD W NEW YORK HOSP-CORNELL MED CTR 21 BLOOMINGDALE RD WHITE PLAINS, NY 10605 Sleep arousal and the mechanism of panic anxiety
R01MH-42819-03 (LCR) ALEXOPOULOS, GEORGE S NEW YORK HOSPITAL 21 BLOOMINGDALE ROAD WHITE PLAINS, N Y 10605 Longitudinal study of late life depression
R37MH-42827-03 (PCB) SIEVER, LARRY J MT SINAI SCHOOL OF MEDICINE FIFTH AVENUE & 100TH STREET NEW YORK, NY 10029 Schizotypal person disorder & schizophrenia
R29MH-42831-03 (PCB) PARRY, BARBARA L UCSD MEDICAL CENTER T-004 225 DICKINSON STREET SAN DIEGO, CA 92103 Chronobiology of premenstrual syndrome
R01MH-42834-05 (BPN) MILNER, TERESA A CORNELL UNIV MEDICAL COLLEGE 411 EAST 69TH STREET NEW YORK, NY 10021 Transmitter interactions of septo-hippocampal neurons
R01MH-42840-03S1 (LCR) GRANT, IGOR UNIV OF CALIFORNIA SAN DIEGO 9500 GILMAN DR, 0603 LA JOLLA, CA 92093-0603 Alzheimer caregiver coping--Mental and physical health
R01MH-42843-04 (BSR) MORTIMER, JEYLAN T UNIV OF MINNESOTA 267-19TH AVE SOUTH MINNEAPOLIS, MN 55455 Work experience and adolescent well-being
R01MH-42859-03 (PCB) HALARIS, ANGELOS E METRO HEALTH MEDICAL CENTER 3395 SCRANTON ROAD CLEVELAND, OH 44109 Brain & platelet adrenergic receptors in depression
R01MH-42872-04 (TDA) PITMAN, ROGER K VA RESEARCH SERVICE (151) 228 MAPLE ST MANCHESTER, NH 03103 Psychophysiology of imaginal flooding treatment of PTSD
R01MH-42878-05 (SRCM) SIEGEL, KAROLYNN MEMORIAL HOSP/CANCER/ALLD DIS 1275 YORK AVENUE NEW YORK, N Y 10021 Social support as a resource among gay men with AIDS
R01MH-42884-02 (PCB) TURNER, SAMUEL M WESTERN PSYCHIATRIC INST & CL 3811 O'HARA STREET PITTSBURGH, PA 15213 Children at risk for anxiety disorders
R01MH-42900-05 (SRCM) KELSO, J A 500 N W 20TH ST BOCA RATON, FL 33431 Dynamic patterns in complex biological systems
R01MH-42901-04 (TDA) HOWARD, KENNETH I NORTHWESTERN UNIV MED SCH 446 E ONTARIO - 18TH FL CHICAGO, IL 60611 Long term psychotherapy--Patients, processes and outcome
R37MH-42903-05 (BPN) MORRISON, ADRIAN R, JR UNIVERSITY OF PENNSYLVANIA 3800 SPRUCE/H1/6045-VET MED PHILADELPHIA, PA 19104-6045 Brainstem mechanisms of alerting
R01MH-42908-04 (SRCM) KELLY, JEFFREY A MEDICAL COLLEGE OF WISCONSIN MILWAUKEE, WI 53266 Community intervention to reduce AIDS risk behavior
R01MH-42909-05 (BSR) GORE, SUSAN L CENTER FOR SURVEY RESEARCH 100 ARLINGTON STREET BOSTON, MA 02116 Gender, stress, and coping--Social relational influences
R01MH-42918-05 (MHAZ) KEMENY, MARGARET E UNIV OF CALIF, LOS ANGELES LOS ANGELES, CA 90024 Psychosocial processes as cofactors in AIDS
R01MH-42927-03 (SRCM) SACK, WILLIAM H OREGON HEALTH SCIS UNIVERSITY 3181 SW SAM JACKSON PARK ROAD PORTLAND, OR 97201 Childhood trauma and the cambodian adolescent refugee
R01MH-42929-05 (TDA) KANE, JOHN M HILLSIDE HOSP DIV OF LIJMC 75-59 263RD STREET GLEN OAKS, NY 11004 Treatment of neuroleptic nonresponsive schizophrenia
R01MH-42931-04A1 (TDA) TERMAN, MICHAEL RES FDN FOR MENTAL HYGIENE 722 WEST 168TH STREET NEW YORK, NY 10032 Light therapy for seasonal affective disorder
R01MH-42935-03 (PCB) GARA, MICHAEL A UNIV OF MED & DENT OF N J 671 HOES LANE PISCATAWAY, NJ 08855-1392 Self perception, person perception and depression
R01MH-42940-04 (BSR) MILLER, JOAN G YALE UNIVERSITY BOX 11A YALE STATION NEW HAVEN, CT 06520-7447 Cultural and moral development--A cross-cultural study
R01MH-42955-03A1 (PCB) WU, JOSEPH CHONG-SANG UNIVERSITY OF CALIFORNIA D-402, MEDICAL SCIENCE I IRVINE, CA 92717 PET study of sleep deprivation in affective illness
R01MH-42959-04 (SRCM) LASKA, EUGENE M RES FDN FOR MENTAL HYGIENE INC NATHAN S. KLINE INST PSYCH RES ORANGEBURG, NY 10962 Clinical trial methodology in schizophrenia
R01MH-42968-03 (LCR) KELLAM, SHEPPARD G JOHNS HOPKINS UNIVERSITY 615 NORTH WOLFE STREET BALTIMORE, MD 21205 Periodic outcome of two preventive trials
R29MH-42974-04 (EPS) LENNON, MARY CLARE COLUMBIA UNIVERSITY 600 WEST 168TH STREET NEW YORK, N Y 10032 Gender, work and mental illness--An epidemiological study
R01MH-42988-04 (PCB) KRONFOL, ZIAD A UNIV OF MICHIGAN MEDICAL CTR 1500 E MEDICAL CENTER DRIVE ANN ARBOR, MI 48109-0118 Cellular immunity in depressive illness
R29MH-43017-05 (BPN) STEIN, STUART A UNIV OF TEXAS SW MEDICAL CTR 5323 HARRY HINES BLVD DALLAS, TX 75235 Thyroid hormone control of behavior and gene expression
R01MH-43026-05 (BPN) BANNON, MICHAEL J SINAI HOSPITAL OF DETROIT 6767 W OUTER DRIVE DETROIT, MI 48235 Regulation of brain peptide biosythesis
R01MH-43029-05 (TDA) WILSON, NANCY Z COLORADO DIV OF MENTAL HLTH 3520 WEST OXFORD AVE DENVER, CO 80236 CMI client types and system reforms--an outcome study
R29MH-43031-04 (TDA) THAKER, GUNVANT K MARYLAND PSYCHIATRIC RES CTR MAPLE & LOCUST ST PO BOX 21247 BALTIMORE, MD 21228 Eye movement measurements in schizophrenia
R29MH-43040-05 (BPN) ROSS, CHRISTOPHER A JOHNS HOPKINS UNIV SCH OF MED 725 N WOLFE STREET BALTIMORE, MD 21205 Enkephalin convertase as a probe for opioid systems
R44MH-43072-03 (MHSB) O'HALLORAN, JAMES P NEUROCOMP SYSTEMS, INC 369 SAN MIGUEL, STE 305 NEWPORT BEACH, CA 92660 Integrated EEG add-on module for IBM microcomputers
R44MH-43075-02 (MHSB) GEVINS, ALAN S SAM TECHNOLOGY, INC 51 FEDERAL STREET SAN FRANCISCO, CA 94107 EEG artifact detection
U01MH-43077-05 (SRCM) KLERMAN, GERALD L PAYNE WHITNEY CLINIC 525

PROJECT NO., ORGANIZATIONAL UNIT., INVESTIGATOR, ADDRESS, TITLE

E 68TH ST NEW YORK, NY 10021 NIMH clinical collaborative studies of the psychobiology of depression

R44MH-43083-03 (MHSB) BORENSTEIN, MICHAEL T BIOSTATISTICAL PROGRAMMING ASS POB 3407 NEW HYDE PARK, NY 11040 Micro-computer program for statistical power

R01MH-43084-04S1 (LCR) SEIDMAN, EDWARD NEW YORK UNIVERSITY 6 WASHINGTON PLACE NEW YORK, NY 10003 Pathways to adaptive/maladaptive outcomes in adolescence

R01MH-43097-02 (BSR) CROYLE, ROBERT T UNIVERSITY OF UTAH SALT LAKE CITY, UTAH 84112 Illness cognition and behavior--An experimental approach

R01MH-43101-03 (CVR) JACOBSON, NEIL S UNIVERSITY OF WASHINGTON SEATTLE, WASH 98195 Marital violence--Cognitive and physiological correlates

R01MH-43212-04 (BPN) CROWE, RAYMOND R UNIV OF IOWA COLLEGE OF MEDICI 500 NEWTON ROAD IOWA CITY, IA 52242 Iowa multiplex family study--Molecular genetics

R01MH-43222-03 (LCR) BARNETT, ROSALIND WELLESLEY COLLEGE CENTER FOR RESEARCH ON WOMEN WELLESLEY, MA 02181 Family and work role stress in men

P01MH-43230-04 (SRCM) GOLDSTEIN, MENEK NEW YORK UNIV MEDICAL CENTER 560 FIRST AVENUE, RM H-544 NEW YORK, N Y 10016 Dopamine-neuropeptide coexistence and mental function

R01MH-43240-04 (PCB) HESTON, LEONARD L UNIVERSITY OF MINNESOTA BOX 393 MAYO MEMORIAL BUILDING MINNEAPOLIS, MN 55455 Family studies in dementia

R29MH-43252-04 (PCB) BEIDEL, DEBORAH C WESTERN PSYCHIATRIC INST & CLN 3811 O'HARA STREET PITTSBURGH, PA 15213 Reactivity, cognition & childhood anxiety disorders

R01MH-43253-06 (MHAZ) HEREK, GREGORY M UNIVERSITY OF CALIFORNIA DAVIS, CA 95616 Public knowledge, attitudes, and behavior concerning AIDS

R01MH-43261-04 (PCB) ZUBENKO, GEORGE S WESTERN PSYCH INST AND CLINIC 3811 O'HARA STREET PITTSBURGH, PA 15213 Biological marker for primary dementia in the elderly

R01MH-43265-04 (BSR) BARGH, JOHN A NEW YORK UNIVERSITY 6 WASHINGTON PLACE, ROOM 769 NEW YORK, NY 10003 The preconscious analysis of the social environment

R29MH-43266-04 (LCR) TERI, LINDA UNIVERSITY OF WASHINGTON PSYCHIATRY & BEHAV SCIS-RP-10 SEATTLE, WA 98195 Treatment of depression in Alzheimer's patients

R01MH-43267-04 (LCR) VITALIANO, PETER P UNIVERSITY OF WASHINGTON SEATTLE, WA 98195 Correlates of mental health in Alzheimer spouses

R01MH-43270-04 (BSR) CONGER, RAND D IOWA STATE UNIVERSITY AMES, IOWA 50011 Rural family resilience to economic stress

P50MH-43271-05 (TDA) ANDREASEN, NANCY C UNIV OF IOWA/COLL OF MED 500 NEWTON ROAD IOWA CITY, IA 52242 MH-CRC--neurobiology and phenomenology of major psychoses

P50MH-43271-05 0001 (TDA) CORYELL, WILLIAM MH-CRC--neurobiology and phenomenology of major psychoses Diagnosis and phenomenology studies

P50MH-43271-05 0002 (TDA) ANDREASEN, NANCY C MH-CRC--neurobiology and phenomenology of major psychoses Brain imaging studies

P50MH-43271-05 0003 (TDA) CROWE, RAYMOND MH-CRC--neurobiology and phenomenology of major psychoses Genetic studies

P50MH-43271-05 0005 (TDA) PFOHL, BRUCE MH-CRC--neurobiology and phenomenology of major psychoses Epidemiology studies

P50MH-43271-05 0006 (TDA) SHERMAN, ARNOLD MH-CRC--neurobiology and phenomenology of major psychoses Basic neurobiology studies

P50MH-43271-05 0007 (TDA) KATHOL, ROGER MH-CRC--neurobiology and phenomenology of major psychoses Neuropharmacology studies

P50MH-43271-05 9001 (TDA) WOOLSON, ROBERT MH-CRC--neurobiology and phenomenology of major psychoses CORE--Biostatistics

P50MH-43271-05 9002 (TDA) ANDERSEN, NANCY MH-CRC--neurobiology and phenomenology of major psychoses CORE--Assessment and training

R29MH-43285-04 (TDA) WILLIAMS, S LLOYD LEHIGH UNIVERSITY CHANDLER-ULLMANN HALL #17 BETHLEHEM, PA 18015 Procedures and mechanisms of change in agoraphobia

R01MH-43287-03 (CEP) KORNBLUM, SYLVAN MENTAL HLTH RESEARCH INSTITUTE 205 WASHTENAW PLACE ANN ARBOR, MI 48109-0720 Cognitive foundations of stimulus-response compatibility

R29MH-43292-04 (PCB) GREEN, MICHAEL F UNIV OF CALIFORNIA RES CTR CAMARILLO STATE HOSPITAL BOX A CAMARILLO, CA 93011 Early visual processing in schizophrenia

R29MH-43302-04 (BPN) LEONARD, JANET L UNIVERSITY OF OKLAHOMA 730 VAN VLEET OVAL NORMAN, OK 73019 Neuroethological analysis of behavioral control

R01MH-43311-04A1 (LCR) HOPS, HYMAN OREGON RESEARCH INSTITUTE 1899 WILLAMETTE, SUITE 2 EUGENE, OR 97401 Longitudinal predictors of adolescent adjustment

R01MH-43323-04 (TDA) MUNROE-BLUM, HEATHER MCMASTER UNIVERSITY BOX 2000, STATION A HAMILTON, ONT. CAN. LBN 325 RCT--An enriched psychosocial therapy for schizophrenia

R01MH-43324-04 (PCB) GEVINS, ALAN S EEG SYSTEMS LABORATORY 51 FEDERAL STREET, #401 SAN FRANCISCO, CA 94107 Mass action of human neocortex

R01MH-43325-02 (PCB) NURNBERGER, JOHN I, JR INDIANA UNIV SCH OF MEDICINE 791 UNION DRIVE INDIANAPOLIS, IN 46202-4887 Melatonin suppression by light in affective disorder

R01MH-43326-03 (PCB) PEARLSON, GODFREY D JOHNS HOPKINS HOSPITAL 600 NORTH WOLFE STREET BALTIMORE, MD 21205 PET DA receptor, MRI and CT in late onset schizophrenia

R29MH-43352-03 (PCB) STEINBERG, MARLENE YALE UNIVERSITY 333 CEDAR ST NEW HAVEN, CT 06510 Structured clinical interview for DSM-III-R dissociative disorders

R01MH-43353-05 (BPN) GONZALEZ-LIMA, FRANCISCO UNIVERSITY OF TEXAS AUSTIN AUSTIN, TX 78712 Functional mapping of associative learning in brain

R01MH-43361-04A1 (CEP) ROTHBART, MARY K UNIVERSITY OF OREGON EUGENE, OR 97403 Early development of temperamental self-regulation

R01MH-43364-02 (EPS) WALLACE, CHARLES J UNIV OF CALIF, LOS ANGELES BOX A, 1878 LEWIS RD CAMARILLO, CA 93011 Skills training for the severely mentally ill

PROJECT NO., ORGANIZATIONAL UNIT., INVESTIGATOR, ADDRESS, TITLE

R01MH-43366-03 (PCB) BRENT, DAVID A W PSYCHIATRIC INST & CLIN 3811 O'HARA ST PITTSBURGH, PA 15260 Adolescent suicide & suicidal behavior--A family study

R01MH-43370-02 (PCB) BRESSLER, STEVEN L EEG SYSTEMS LABORATORY 51 FEDERAL ST SAN FRANCISCO, CA 94107 Functional topography of primate neocortex

P01MH-43371-04 (LCR) LAWTON, M POWELL PHILADELPHIA GERIATRIC CENTER 5301 OLD YORK ROAD PHILADELPHIA, PA 19141 Caregiving and mental health--A multifaceted approach

P01MH-43371-04 0001 (LCR) BRODY, ELAINE M Caregiving and mental health--A multifaceted approach Marital status, parent care and mental health

P01MH-43371-04 0002 (LCR) PRUCHNO, RACHEL A Caregiving and mental health--A multifaceted approach Caregiving families--Methodological advances

P01MH-43371-04 0003 (LCR) LAWTON, M POWELL Caregiving and mental health--A multifaceted approach Career of caregiving to an imparied parent

P01MH-43371-04 9001 (LCR) LAWTON, M POWELL Caregiving and mental health--A multifaceted approach Research core

R01MH-43373-05 (SRCM) REISS, DAVID GEORGE WASHINGTON UNIVERSITY 2300 EYE STREET, N W WASHINGTON, D C 20037 Non-shared environment in adolescent development

R01MH-43374-03 (BPN) NEFF, NORTON H OHIO STATE UNIV COL OF MED 333 WEST TENTH AVENUE COLUMBUS, OHIO 43210 Aromatic l-amino acid decarboxylase modulation

R29MH-43378-03 (EPS) FULOP, GEORGE MOUNT SINAI MEDICAL CTR ONE G L LEVY PLACE NEW YORK, NY 10029 Geriatric comorbidity--hospital course and cost

R29MH-43379-04 (LCR) BAUMAN, LAURIE J ALBERT EINSTEIN COLLEGE OF MED 1300 MORRIS PARK AVE BRONX, N Y 10461 Prevention research on social support in minority groups

R29MH-43388-04 (TDA) RAUSCH, JEFFREY L UNIV OF CALIFORNIA, SAN DIEGO DEPT OF PSYCHIATRY, 0603 LA JOLLA, CALIF 92093-0603 Platelet LSD binding & 5-HT uptake in depression

R01MH-43390-02S1 (LCR) VALLE, J R SAN DIEGO STATE UNIVERSITY SAN DIEGO, CA 92182 Hispanic elderly cognitive screen validation study

R01MH-43396-04A1 (SRCM) KRISTAN, WILLIAM B, JR UNIVERSITY OF CALIFORNIA LA JOLLA, CA 92093 Neuronal control of interactions among behaviors

R01MH-43398-02 (SRCM) TRONICK, EDWARD Z CHILDREN'S HOSPITAL MEDICAL CT 300 LONGWOOD AVE BOSTON, MA 02115 Preintervention--Depressed mothers and their infants

R01MH-43407-03 (LCR) GALLAGHER-THOMPSON, DOLORES E VA MEDICAL CENTER 3801 MIRANDA AVENUE PALO ALTO, CA 94304 Mh risk factors in caregiving--Assessment and intervention

R29MH-43409-04 (PCB) PRICE, R ARLEN UNIVERSITY OF PENNSYLVANIA CRB-118, 422 CURIE BLVD PHILADELPHIA, PA 19104 Genetic analysis of human obesity

R01MH-43411-05 (MHAZ) RABIN, BRUCE S PRESBYTERIAN UNIVERSITY HOSPIT 5725 CHILDRENS PLACE PITTSBURGH, PA 15218-2582 Characterization of stressor induced immune alteration

R37MH-43417-04 (LCR) REISS, DAVID GEORGE WASHINGTON UNIVERSITY 2300 EYE STREET, N W WASHINGTON, D C 20037 Family influences on chronic illness survival

R01MH-43422-04 (BPN) LEIBOWITZ, SARAH F THE ROCKEFELLER UNIVERSITY 1230 YORK AVE NEW YORK, N Y 10021-6399 Hypothalamic neurotransmitter systems and eating behavior

R29MH-43426-04 (BPN) MADDEN, JOHN, IV STANFORD UNIVERSITY STANFORD, CA 94305 Cerebellar GABAergic processes in classical conditioning

R01MH-43429-04 (BPN) FOWLER, STEPHEN C UNIVERSITY OF MISSISSIPPI UNIVERSITY, MS 38677 Biophysical analysis of neuroleptics' behavioral effects

R29MH-43433-04 (BPN) KAGAN, BRUCE L UNIV OF CALIFORNIA 405 HILGARD AVE LOS ANGELES, CA 90024 Gating and translocation in the diphtheria toxin channel

R01MH-43435-04 (LCR) POON, LEONARD W UNIVERSITY OF GEORGIA 100 CANDLER HALL ATHENS, GA 30602 Adaptation and mental health of the oldest-old

R29MH-43439-03 (PCB) HILE, MATTHEW G MISSOURI INST OF PSYCHIATRY 5400 ARSENAL STREET MS 059 ST LOUIS, MO 63139 Automated expert consultation for maladaptive behaviors

R01MH-43448-03 (PCB) BARDEN, NICHOLAS LAVAL UNIVERSITY HOSPITAL CTR 2705 BOUL LAURIER STE-FOY, QUEBEC G1V 4G2 RFLP linkage of bipolar affective disorders

P50MH-43450-04 (SRCM) MECHANIC, DAVID RUTGERS UNIVERSITY 30 COLLEGE AVENUE NEW BRUNSWICK, NJ 08903 Organization financing care for severely mentally ill

P50MH-43450-04 0008 (SRCM) MECHANIC, DAVID Organization financing care for severely mentally ill Evaluation of New York's new psychiatric rate methodology

P50MH-43450-04 0009 (SRCM) ROSENFIELD, SARAH Organization financing care for severely mentally ill Service effects on patient outcomes

P50MH-43450-04 0010 (SRCM) AVIRAM, URI Organization financing care for severely mentally ill Discharge planning

P50MH-43450-04 0011 (SRCM) AVIRAM, URI Organization financing care for severely mentally ill Assessing New Jersey's new civil commitment law

P50MH-43450-04 0012 (SRCM) MECHANIC, DAVID Organization financing care for severely mentally ill Pilot studies on acute psychiatric inpatient care

P50MH-43450-04 0013 (SRCM) RUBIN, JEFFREY Organization financing care for severely mentally ill Insurance and the use of mental health care

P50MH-43450-04 0014 (SRCM) LIKE, ROBERT Organization financing care for severely mentally ill The provision of primary health care to adults with chronic disabilities

P50MH-43450-04 0015 (SRCM) HORWITZ, ALLAN Organization financing care for severely mentally ill Caretakers of the seriously mentally ill

P50MH-43450-04 0016 (SRCM) GUARNACCIA, PETER Organization financing care for severely mentally ill Interaction of minority family members with the mental health system

P50MH-43450-04 0017 (SRCM) GORMAN, DENNIS Organization financing care for severely mentally ill Family belief systems and expressed emotion in recovery of patients

P50MH-43450-04 0020 (SRCM) GUTTERMAN, ELAINE Organization financing care for severely mentally ill Pilot--Emergency mental health services for youth

P50MH-43450-04 0018 (SRCM) RUBIN, JEFFREY Organization financing care for severely mentally ill Indirect costs of mental illness

P50MH-43450-04 0019 (SRCM) POTTICK, KATHLEEN Organization financing care for severely mentally ill Acute inpatient and aftercare services and adolescent outcomes

P50MH-43450-04 0021 (SRCM) LERMAN, PAUL Organization financing care for severely mentally ill Behavior and mental health problems of youth--Comparison of intitutional systems

P50MH-43450-04 0022 (SRCM) CRYSTAL, STEPHEN Organization financing care for severely mentally ill Research on HIV and mental health

P50MH-43450-04 0023 (SRCM) RUBIN, JEFFREY Organization financing care for severely mentally ill The chronically mentally ill and housing markets

P50MH-43450-04 0024 (SRCM) RUBIN, JEFFREY Organization financing care for severely mentally ill Legal change and mental health care

R01MH-43454-03 (CEP) DAVIDSON, RICHARD J UNIVERSITY OF WISCONSIN 1202 WEST JOHNSON STREET MADISON, WI 53706 Emotional reactivity and anterior brain asymmetry

P50MH-43458-04 (SRCM) MCFARLAND, BENTSON H OREGON HEALTH SCIENCES UNIV 3181 S W SAM JACKSON PARK RD PORTLAND, OR 97201 Center for research on the severely mentally ill

P50MH-43458-04 0003 (SRCM) BLOOM, JOSEPH D Center for research on the severely mentally ill Insanity aquittees--Release decisions and civil commitment comparisons

P50MH-43458-04 0004 (SRCM) LIMANDRI, BARBARA Center for research on the severely mentally ill Pilot--Nurses' prediction of acute violence

P50MH-43458-04 0005 (SRCM) POPE, CLYDE R Center for research on the severely mentally ill Tracking service utilization by persons with severe mental illness

P50MH-43458-04 0006 (SRCM) BIGELOW, DOUGLAS A Center for research on the severely mentally ill Comparison of mental health financing systems in the United States and Canada

P50MH-43458-04 0007 (SRCM) RILEY, CRYSTAL Center for research on the severely mentally ill Evaluating a socialization center for Indochinese mental health recipients

P50MH-43486-03 (SRCM) FERRIS, STEVEN H NEW YORK MEDICAL CENTER 550 FIRST AVENUE NEW YORK, NY 10016 Geriatric psychopharmacology CRC/PE

P50MH-43486-03 0001 (SRCM) FERRIS, S H Geriatric psychopharmacology CRC/PE Captopril treatment of mildly impaired subjects with white matter lesions

P50MH-43486-03 9001 (SRCM) FERRIS, S H Geriatric psychopharmacology CRC/PE Longitudinal MRI study of white matter disease and temporal lobe in AD

P50MH-43486-03 9002 (SRCM) FERRIS, S H Geriatric psychopharmacology CRC/PE Psychometric detectionof very early dementia

P50MH-43486-03 9003 (SRCM) FERRIS, S H Geriatric psychopharmacology CRC/PE Pathophysiology of glucose metabolism in AD

R37MH-43518-04 (PCB) TSUANG, MING T BROCKTON-W ROXBURY VA MED CTR 940 BELMONT STREET BROCKTON, MA 02401 Schizophrenia--Psychopathology and heterogeneity

P50MH-43520-04 (SRCM) EHRHARDT, ANKE A RESEARCH FDN MNTL HYGIENE, INC 722 WEST 168TH STREET NEW YORK, N Y 10032 Natural history and progression of HIV infection

P50MH-43520-04 0001 (SRCM) KLINE, JENNIE Natural history and progression of HIV infection Prenatal HIV infection--Sequelae in children and women

P50MH-43520-04 0002 (SRCM) WALTER, HEATHER J Natural history and progression of HIV infection AIDS prevention for adolescents in school

P50MH-43520-04 0003 (SRCM) ROTHERAN, MARYJANE Natural history and progression of HIV infection AIDS prevention among youth with high risk behaviors

P50MH-43520-04 0004 (SRCM) BECKER, JUDITH V Natural history and progression of HIV infection AIDS prevention for adolescent sex offenders

P50MH-43520-04 0005 (SRCM) GORMAN, JACK M Natural history and progression of HIV infection Natural history and progression of HIV infection

P50MH-43520-04 9001 (SRCM) WILLIAMS, JANET B W Natural history and progression of HIV infection Core--Psychiatric-psychosocial assessment

P50MH-43520-04 9002 (SRCM) MEYER-BAHLBURG, HEINO Natural history and progression of HIV infection Core--Psychosexual assessment

P50MH-43520-04 9003 (SRCM) MAYEUX, RICHARD Natural history and progression of HIV infection Core--Neurology-neuropsychology assessment

P50MH-43520-04 9004 (SRCM) NEU, HAROLD C Natural history and progression of HIV infection Core--Medical diagnosis, lab and treatment assessment

P50MH-43520-04 9005 (SRCM) TAVARES, RAPHAEL Natural history and progression of HIV infection Core--Community health education and prevention

P50MH-43520-04 9006 (SRCM) WEINSTEIN, I BERNARD Natural history and progression of HIV infection Core--Basic science

R29MH-43524-03 (BPN) MULLEN, KEVIN D CLEVELAND METROPOLITAN HOSP 3395 SCRANTON ROAD CLEVELAND, OH 44109 An endogenous benzodiazepine in hepatic encephalopathy

R29MH-43537-06 (SRCM) BRACHA, H STEFAN VA MEDICAL CENTER NEUROPSYCHIATRIC RESEARCH LAB NORTH LITTLE ROCK, AR 72114 Circling as a probe of lateral DA activity in schizophrenia

P50MH-43555-04 (SRCM) GREENLEY, JAMES R UNIVERSITY OF WISCONSIN 1180 OBSERVATORY DRIVE MADISON, WI 53706 Mental health services research center in Wisconsin

R29MH-43586-05 (TDA) HOFFMAN, WILLIAM F OREGON HEALTH SCIENCES UNIV 3181 S W SAM JACKSON PARK RD PORTLAND, OREGON 97201 Drug-induced movement disorders in schizophrenia

R29MH-43612-05 (TDA) WOLKOWITZ, OWEN M UNIVERSITY OF CALIFORNIA 401 PARNASSUS AVENUE, BOX 39F SAN FRANCISCO, CA 94143-0984 Alprazolam neuroleptic treatment in schizophrenia

R29MH-43613-06 (EPS) HAAS, GRETCHEN L WESTERN PSYCHIATRIC INSTITUTE 3811 O'HARA STREET PITTSBURGH, PA 15213 Sex differences in schizophrenia

R29MH-43618-03 (PCB) GOLDMAN, MORRIS B UNIVERSITY OF CHICAGO MED CTR 5841 SOUTH MARYLAND AVE CHICAGO, ILL 60637 Mechanism of abnormal water excretion in schizophrenia

R29MH-43635-06 (TDA) WEIDEN, PETER J ST LUKE'S ROOSEVELT HOSP CTR 428 WEST 59TH ST TOWER 8 NEW YORK, NY 10019 Neuroleptic noncompliance in schizophrenia

R29MH-43640-03 (EPS) BREKKE, JOHN S UNIVERSITY OF SOUTHERN CALIF LOS ANGELES, CA 90089 Long-term community rehabilitation of schizophrenics

R29MH-43650-04 (PCB) OLSON, STEPHEN C OHIO STATE UNIVERSITY 473 WEST 12TH AVENUE COLUMBUS, OH 43212 Brain development in schizophrenics and their siblings

R29MH-43666-03 (PCB) POGUE-GEILE, MICHAEL F UNIVERSITY OF PITTSBURGH 4015 O'HARA STREET PITTSBURGH, PA 15260 Family studies of schizophrenia and neuropsychology

R37MH-43693-04 (TDA) JESTE, DILIP V UNIVERSITY OF CALIFORNIA 3350 LA JOLLA VILLAGE DRIVE LA JOLLA, CA 92093-0603 Late-onset schizophrenia--A neuropsychiatric study

P50MH-43694-04 (SRCM) SCHEFFLER, RICHARD M UNIVERSITY OF CALIF 403 WARREN HALL BERKELEY, CA 94720 Center on financing of care for severely mentally ill

P50MH-43694-04 0013 (SRCM) SEGAL, STEVEN P Center on financing of care for severely mentally ill Innovative service delivery systems for the SMI

P50MH-43694-04 0014 (SRCM) HU, TEH-WEI Center on financing of care for severely mentally ill Alternative financing methods for the SMI

P50MH-43694-04 0015 (SRCM) SNOWDEN, LONNIE R Center on financing of care for severely mentally ill Special populations of SMI persons

P50MH-43694-04 0016 (SRCM) HARGREAVES, WILLIAM A Center on financing of care for severely mentally ill Conceptualization and measurement--Care for SMI persons

P50MH-43703-05 (SRCM) STEINWACHS, DONALD M SMI CENTER 624 NORTH BROADWAY BALTIMORE, MD 21205 Organization and financing of care for the severely mentally ill

R44MH-43712-03 (MHSB) BAXLEY, NORMAN E NORMAN BAXLEY & ASSOCIATES, IN 110 WEST MAIN STREET URBANA, IL 61801 Behavioral treatment of stress in pediatric patients

R29MH-43723-04 (BSR) ENSEL, WALTER M STATE UNIVERSITY OF N Y ALBANY 1400 WASHINGTON AVE ALBANY, N Y 12222 Structure of social support: Effects on mental health

R01MH-43742-04 (PCB) YAO, JEFFREY K VETERANS ADMIN MEDICAL CENTER HIGHLAND DRIVE PITTSBURGH, PA 15206 Membrane phospholipids role in schizophrenia

R29MH-43743-04 (BPN) TEICHER, MARTIN H MCLEAN HOSPITAL 115 MILL STREET BELMONT, MA 02178 Neuropharmacological response to early brain injury

R01MH-43760-03 (LCR) NOLEN-HOEKSEMA, SUSAN KAY STANFORD UNIVERSITY BLDG 420 JORDAN HALL STANFORD, CA 94305 Physical and emotional health in the bereaved

R01MH-43772-03 (PCB) KAPLAN, SANDRA J NORTH SHORE UNIVERSITY HOSP 400 COMMUNITY DRIVE MANHASSET, NY 11030 Psychopathology, suicidal behavior & adolescent abuse

R01MH-43775-04 (PCB) PEARLSON, GODFREY D JOHNS HOPKINS HOSPITAL 600 NORTH WOLFE STREET BALTIMORE, MD 21205 Neuro-imaging & neuropsychologic impairment in psychosis

R01MH-43783-01A3 (EPS) PROVAN, KEITH G UNIVERSITY OF KENTUCKY LEXINGTON, KY 40506-0034 Interorganizational delivery of mental health services

P01MH-43787-03 (SRCM) EPSTEIN, ALAN N UNIVERSITY OF PENNSYLVANIA RM. 326 LEIDY LABS/BIOLOGY PHILADELPHIA, PA 19104-6018 Neurohormonal mechanisms of salt appetite

P01MH-43787-03 0001 (SRCM) WILLIAMSON, JOHN R Neurohormonal mechanisms of salt appetite Second messenger systems for angiotensin II action in brain

P01MH-43787-03 0002 (SRCM) MC EWEN, BRUCE S Neurohormonal mechanisms of salt appetite Brain aldosterone, salt intake and molecular biology of ANG/ALDO synergy

P01MH-43787-03 0003 (SRCM) EPSTEIN, ALAN N Neurohormonal mechanisms of salt appetite Functional neuroanatomy--ANG/ALDO synergy and its suppression by ANF

P01MH-43787-03 0004 (SRCM) NICOLAIDIS, STELIO Neurohormonal mechanisms of salt appetite Microiontophoretic investigations of neurons implicated in salt intake

P01MH-43787-03 0005 (SRCM) NORGREN, RALPH Neurohormonal mechanisms of salt appetite Role of central gustatory system in hormonal control of salt appetite

P01MH-43787-03 9001 (SRCM) EPSTEIN, ALAN N Neurohormonal mechanisms of salt appetite Core--Technology

R01MH-43796-02 (EPS) COYNE, JAMES C UNIV OF MICHIGAN MEDICAL SCH 1018 FULLER STREET ANN ARBOR, MI 48109-0708 Depression in family practice and psychiatric settings

R01MH-43797-03 (BPN) FRIEDBERG, FELIX HOWARD UNIVERSITY MED SCHOOL 520 W STREET, NW WASHINGTON, DC 20059 Structure of the human calmodulin gene--Its expression

R01MH-43802-04 (BSR) THOITS, PEGGY A VANDERBILT UNIVERSITY BOX 1811 STATION B NASHVILLE, TN 37335 Identity-relevant events & psychological distress

R29MH-43809-03 (PCB) MC NALLY, RICHARD J HARVARD UNIVERSITY 33 KIRKLAND STREET CAMBRIDGE, MA 02138 Cognition and panic

R29MH-43821-04 (BPN) MCGONIGLE, PAUL UNIVERSITY OF PENNSYLVANIA PHILADELPHIA, PA 19104-6084 Regulation of serotonin receptors

R01MH-43822-04 (CEP) SEIFER, RONALD E P BRADLEY HOSPITAL 1011 VETERANS MEMORIAL PKWY EAST PROVIDENCE, RI 02915 Assessing infant temperament using aggregate methods

R01MH-43826-01A2 (BSR) BAUMEISTER, ROY F CASE WESTERN RESERVE UNIV CLEVELAND, OH 44106 Repressive responses to self-concept threats

R37MH-43832-03 (TDA) REYNOLDS, CHARLES F, III WESTERN PSYCH INST AND CLINIC 3811 O'HARA STREET PITTSBURGH, PA 15213 Maintenance

PROJECT NO., ORGANIZATIONAL UNIT., INVESTIGATOR, ADDRESS, TITLE

therapies in late-life depression
R29MH-43836-04 (BPN) JOHNSON, CARL H VANDERBILT UNIVERSITY BOX 1812, STATION B NASHVILLE, TN 37235 Input/output analysis of cellular circadian rhythms
R01MH-43843-03 (LCR) LEVY, LEON H UNIV OF MARYLAND/BALTIMORE 5401 WILKENS AVENUE BALTIMORE, MD 21228 Hospice care and the course and outcome of bereavement
R01MH-43845-03 (PCB) LIEBOWITZ, MICHAEL R NY STATE PSYCHIATRIC INST 722 WEST 168 STREET NEW YORK, NY 10032 Psychobiology of obsessive-compulsive disorder
R29MH-43846-03 (PCB) MORROW, LISA A UNIVERSITY OF PITTSBURGH 350 THACKERAY HALL PITTSBURGH, PA. 15260 Neuropsychiatric changes in adults exposed to solvents
R01MH-43851-04 (TDA) SPREAT, SCOTT TEMPLE UNIVERSITY 2900 SOUTHAMPTON RD PHILADELPHIA, PA 19154 Lithium for treatment of aggression in retarded persons
R29MH-43852-04 (BPN) JOYCE, JEFFREY N UNIV OF PENNSYLVANIA SCH OF ME CLINICAL RESEARCH BLDG PHILADELPHIA, PA 19104-6141 Neurotransmitter disorders in schizophrenia
R29MH-43856-04 (LCR) MEYERS, BARNETT S NEW YORK HOSP WESTCHESTER DIV 21 BLOOMINGDALE ROAD WHITE PLAINS, N Y 10605 Geriatric major depression and delusions
R29MH-43857-04 (BSR) FISKE, ALAN P UNIVERSITY OF PENNSYLVANIA 3815 WALNUT ST PHILADELPHIA, PA 19104-6196 Structures of social relations--Ethnographic evidence
R01MH-43866-02 (SRCM) ABRAMSON, LYN Y UNIVERSITY OF WISCONSIN 1202 WEST JOHNSON STREET MADISON, WI 53706 Negative cognition depression--Etiology and course
R29MH-43868-04 (CEP) CHIARELLO, CHRISTINE L SYRACUSE UNIVERSITY 430 HUNTINGTON HALL SYRACUSE, NY 13244-2340 Lateralization of semantic facilitation and inhibition
R01MH-43872-03 (LCR) BAYLES, KATHRYN A UNIVERSITY OF ARIZONA TUCSON, ARIZ 85721 Communication and neuropsychiatric status in dementia
P50MH-43878-03 (TDA) SHAFFER, DAVID NEW YORK PSYCHIATRIC INSTITUTE 722 WEST 168TH STREET NEW YORK, NY 10032 Center to study youth depression, anxiety and suicide
P50MH-43878-03 0001 (TDA) KLEIN, RACHEL Center to study youth depression, anxiety and suicide Clinical core
P50MH-43878-03 0002 (TDA) WEISSMAN, MYMA Center to study youth depression, anxiety and suicide Family genetics core
P50MH-43878-03 0003 (TDA) SHROUT, PATRICK Center to study youth depression, anxiety and suicide Biostatistics and measurement core
P50MH-43878-03 0004 (TDA) SHAFFER, DAVID Center to study youth depression, anxiety and suicide Epidemiological survey of depression, anxiety and suicidal behavior in adolescent
P50MH-43878-03 0005 (TDA) BIRD, HECTOR R Center to study youth depression, anxiety and suicide Comorbidity between anxiety and depression in a community sample
P50MH-43878-03 0006 (TDA) GOULD, MADELYN Center to study youth depression, anxiety and suicide Suicide mortality data from National Center for Health Statistics
P50MH-43878-03 0007 (TDA) GOULD, MADELYN Center to study youth depression, anxiety and suicide Suicide imitation and contagion
P50MH-43878-03 0008 (TDA) FENDRICH, MICHAEL Center to study youth depression, anxiety and suicide Depression and conduct disorders in children
P50MH-43878-03 0009 (TDA) MOREAU, DONNA L Center to study youth depression, anxiety and suicide Follow-up of children and adolescents previously assessed for depression
P50MH-43878-03 0010 (TDA) KANDEL, DENISE Center to study youth depression, anxiety and suicide Consequences of parental depression in adolescence for children's depression
P50MH-43878-03 0014 (TDA) ALLEN, RHIANNON Center to study youth depression, anxiety and suicide Post-traumatic stress disorder symptoms in abused children
P50MH-43878-03 0015 (TDA) SHAFFER, DAVID Center to study youth depression, anxiety and suicide Risk factors for anxiety behaviors and abnormal motor signs
P50MH-43878-03 0016 (TDA) MOREAU, DONNA L Center to study youth depression, anxiety and suicide Panic disorder in children
P50MH-43878-03 0011 (TDA) MOREAU, DONNA Center to study youth depression, anxiety and suicide Prepubertal onset major depression
P50MH-43878-03 0012 (TDA) PIACENTINI, JOHN Center to study youth depression, anxiety and suicide Substance abuse in depressed adolescence
P50MH-43878-03 0013 (TDA) BRUDER, GERALD Center to study youth depression, anxiety and suicide psychophysical studies of anxiety and depressive disorders
P50MH-43878-03 0017 (TDA) COHEN, LEE S Center to study youth depression, anxiety and suicide Behavioral study of high risk adolescent suicide attempters
P50MH-43878-03 0018 (TDA) TRAUTMAN, PAUL Center to study youth depression, anxiety and suicide Prospective follow-up of adolescent suicide attempters
P50MH-43878-03 0019 (TDA) GOULD, MADELYN Center to study youth depression, anxiety and suicide Content and imitative effects of suicide dramatization
P50MH-43878-03 0020 (TDA) FISHER, PRUDENCE Center to study youth depression, anxiety and suicide Suicide mortality among runaway youth
P50MH-43878-03 0021 (TDA) WEISSMAN, MICHAEL Center to study youth depression, anxiety and suicide Assessing risk in children of the epidemiologic catchment area
P50MH-43878-03 0022 (TDA) KLEIN, RACHEL Center to study youth depression, anxiety and suicide Offspring of atypically depressed parents
P50MH-43878-03 0023 (TDA) KLEIN, RACHEL Center to study youth depression, anxiety and suicide Probands with panic, social phobia, and depression
P50MH-43878-03 0024 (TDA) WEISSMAN, MICHAEL Center to study youth depression, anxiety and suicide Offspring of orthodox Jewish pedigree with affective disorder
P50MH-43878-03 0025 (TDA) FREIMER, NELSON Center to study youth depression, anxiety and suicide Thyroid markers for pedigree studies of affective disorders
P50MH-43878-03 0026 (TDA) TERMAN, MICHAEL Center to study youth depression, anxiety and suicide Treatment of child and adolescent seasonal affective disorders
P50MH-43878-03 0027 (TDA) SHAFFER, DAVID Center to study youth depression, anxiety and suicide Pedigree evaluation of families in which there has been a youth suicide
P50MH-43878-03 0028 (TDA) MOREAU, DONNA Center to study youth depression, anxiety and suicide Interpersonal psychotherapy for testing with depressed adolescents
P50MH-43878-03 0029 (TDA) MOREAU, DONNA Center to study youth depression, anxiety and suicide MAO inhibitors in depressed adolescents
P50MH-43878-03 0030 (TDA) KLEIN, RACHEL Center to study youth depression, anxiety and suicide Conduct disorders treatment for depression in teenagers with dual diagnoses
P50MH-43878-03 0031 (TDA) ROTHERMAN, MARY J Center to study youth depression, anxiety and suicide Treatment of panic disorder in adolescents
P50MH-43878-03 0032 (TDA) ROTHERAM, MARY J Center to study youth depression, anxiety and suicide Social phobia in adolescence
P50MH-43878-03 0033 (TDA) HOLLANDER, ERIC Center to study youth depression, anxiety and suicide Obsessive compulsive disorder
P50MH-43878-03 0034 (TDA) KLEIN, RACHEL Center to study youth depression, anxiety and suicide Alprazolam in separation anxiety disorder of childhood and adolescence
P50MH-43878-03 0035 (TDA) TRAUTMAN, PAUL Center to study youth depression, anxiety and suicide Cognitive-behavioral family treatment of adolescent suicide attempters
P50MH-43878-03 0036 (TDA) GREENHILL, LARRY Center to study youth depression, anxiety and suicide Psychopharmacological treatment of suicidal adolescents
P50MH-43878-03 0037 (TDA) SHAFFER, DAVID Center to study youth depression, anxiety and suicide Fluoxetine treatment of outpatient adolescent suicide attempters
P50MH-43878-03 0038 (TDA) SHAFFER, DAVID Center to study youth depression, anxiety and suicide School based adolescent suicide prevention programs
P50MH-43878-03 0039 (TDA) SHAFFER, DAVID Center to study youth depression, anxiety and suicide Teenagers self identified as needing psychiatric help
P50MH-43878-03 0040 (TDA) WHITTLE, BARRY Center to study youth depression, anxiety and suicide Adolescents who call hotlines--are the helped
P50MH-43878-03 0041 (TDA) PIACENTINI, JOHN Center to study youth depression, anxiety and suicide Structured diagnostic instrument for children and adolescents
P50MH-43878-03 0042 (TDA) RAPHAEL, KAREN Center to study youth depression, anxiety and suicide Measurement of life events in childhood
P50MH-43878-03 0043 (TDA) GOULD, MADELYN S Center to study youth depression, anxiety and suicide Multiple informants of depressive and anxiety symptomatology
P50MH-43880-04 (TDA) GUR, RAQUEL E UNIVERSITY OF PENNSYLVANIA 36TH SPRUCE STS 205 PIERSOL BL PHILADELPHIA, PA 19104 Regional brain function in schizophrenia
P50MH-43880-04 9001 (TDA) GUR, REGUEL E Regional brain function in schizophrenia CORE--Patient accrual and assessment
P50MH-43880-04 9002 (TDA) GUR, RUBEN C Regional brain function in schizophrenia CORE--Database management and statistics
P50MH-43880-04 9003 (TDA) GUR, RUBEN C Regional brain function in schizophrenia CORE--Neuropsychology
P50MH-43880-04 9004 (TDA) GUR, RAQUEL E Regional brain function in schizophrenia CORE--Neuroimaging
P50MH-43880-04 9005 (TDA) RESNICK, SUSAN M Regional brain function in schizophrenia CORE--Genetics
P50MH-43880-04 9006 (TDA) WINOKUR, ANDREW Regional brain function in schizophrenia CORE--Neuropharmacology
P50MH-43880-04 9007 (TDA) TROJANOWSKI, JOHN C Regional brain function in schizophrenia CORE--Neuropathology
R01MH-43892-03 (MHAZ) CATANIA, JOSEPH A UNIVERSITY OF CALIFORNIA 74 NEW MONTGOMERY #600 SAN FRANCISCO, CA 94105 AIDS risk in a population based sample of the US
R01MH-43899-04 (LCR) FULKER, DAVID W UNIV OF COLORADO CAMPUS BOX 447 BOULDER, COLO 80309 The Colorado adoption project--Adolescent mental health
R01MH-43904-03 (CEP) ORNSTEIN, PETER A UNIVERSITY OF NORTH CAROLINA DAVIE HALL CB# 3270 CHAPEL HILL, NC 27599-3270 Childrens memory--Implications for testimony
R01MH-43908-02 (TDA) BUDMAN, SIMON H HARVARD COMMUNITY HEALTH PLAN ONE FENWAY PLAZA BOSTON, MA 02215 Personality disorders, group therapy and change
R01MH-43911-03 (MHAZ) COATES, THOMAS J UNIVERSITY OF CALIFORNIA 400 PARNASSUS AVENUE SAN FRANCISCO, CA 94143-0320 AIDS risk reduction among black gay men
R29MH-43930-01A3 (BSR) BAUMGARDNER, ANN HUDSON MICHIGAN STATE UNIVERSITY PSYCHOLOGY RESEARCH BUILDING EAST LANSING, MI 48824-1117 Strategic self-presentation and the self-concept
R29MH-43931-01A2 (PCB) MIKLOWITZ, DAVID J UNIVERSITY OF COLORADO CAMPUS BOX 345 BOULDER, CO 80309-0345 Family factors and outcome in bipolar disorder
R01MH-43947-04 (SRCM) ZIGMOND, MICHAEL J UNIVERSITY OF PITTSBURGH 570 CRAWFORD HALL PITTSBURGH, PA 15260 Stress & monoamines--Neurophysiology and neurochemistry
R01MH-43948-03 (BSR) HELSON, RAVENNA M UNIVERSITY OF CALIFORNIA 2150 KITTREDGE ST M 2C BERKELEY, CA 94720 Long/term influences on mental health of women in their 50s
R01MH-43959-04 (BSR) ULEMAN, JAMES S NEW YORK UNIVERSITY 6 WASHINGTON PLACE, RM 753 NEW YORK, N Y 10003 Intentional and automatic processes in trait inferences
R01MH-43960-01A3 (PCB) LESSER, IRA M HARBOR-UCLA MEDICAL SCHOOL 1000 WEST CARSON STREET TORRANCE, CA 90509 Brain lesions and

PROJECT NO., ORGANIZATIONAL UNIT., INVESTIGATOR, ADDRESS, TITLE

cognition in late-onset depression

R01MH-43965-04 (PCB) DE LEON, MONY J NEW YORK UNIVERSITY MED CTR 550 FIRST AVENUE NEW YORK, NY 10016 **Clinical correlates of longitudinal PET changes in Alzheimer disease**

R01MH-43974-02 (CEP) DIENSTBIER, RICHARD A UNIVERSITY OF NEBRASKA LINCOLN, NE 68588-0308 **Neuroendocrine effects from aerobic training in humans**

R01MH-43975-04 (CEP) LANG, PETER J UNIVERSITY OF FLORIDA BOX J-165, JHMHC GAINESVILLE, FL 32610 **The startle probe in the study of emotion**

R01MH-43977-02 (PCB) GORMAN, JACK M NEW YORK STATE PSYCH INSTI 722 W 168 ST NEW YORK, NY 10032 **Cardiac denervation and psychophysiological reactivity**

R01MH-43979-03 (PCB) BARON, MIRON RES FDN FOR MENTAL HYGIENE 722 W 168TH STREET NEW YORK, N Y 10032 **Genetic linkage studies in affective disorders**

R29MH-43985-04 (BPN) ANDRADE, RODRIGO ST. LOUIS UNIVERSITY MED CTR 1402 SOUTH GRAND BOULEVARD ST. LOUIS, MO 63104 **Mechanisms and regulation of 5-HT receptors in the CNS**

R01MH-43986-03 (BPN) KALIN, NED H CLINICAL SCIENCES CENTER 600 HIGHLAND AVENUE MADISON, WI 53792 **Prenatal stress--HPA function and behavior in offspring**

R44MH-44010-02A1 (MHSB) RUEHLMAN, LINDA S CONSULTANTS IN BEHAV RESEARCH 2818 NORTH YUCCA STREET CHANDLER, AZ 85224 **Development of the multidimensional health profile**

P01MH-44043-04 (SRCM) JOH, TONG H CORNELL UNIV MEDICAL COLLEGE BURKE MEDICAL RESEARCH INST. WHITE PLAINS, NY 10605 **Molecular biology of catecholamine enzymes**

P01MH-44043-04 0001 (SRCM) JOH, TONG H Molecular biology of catecholamine enzymes Catecholamine enzyme gene expression--Neuronal degeneration & regeneration

P01MH-44043-04 0002 (SRCM) BAKER, HARRIET D Molecular biology of catecholamine enzymes: Olfactory afferent regulation--Catecholamine enzyme gene expression

P01MH-44043-04 0003 (SRCM) GIBSON, GARY Molecular biology of catecholamine enzymes: Signal transduction systems--Catecholamine enzyme gene expression regulation

P01MH-44043-04 0004 (SRCM) PARK, DONG H Molecular biology of catecholamine enzymes Molecular characterization of tryptophan hydroxylase expression

P01MH-44043-04 9001 (SRCM) PARK, DONG H Molecular biology of catecholamine enzymes Biochemistry /histology core

R01MH-44045-03 (MHAZ) FOLKMAN, SUSAN UCSF PREVENTION SCIENCES CTR 74 NEW MONTGOMERY ST SAN FRANCISCO, CA 94105 **Effects of bereavement in partners of persons with AIDS**

R01MH-44049-03 (SRCM) RACHLIN, HOWARD S U N Y AT STONY BROOK DEPT OF PSYCHOLOGY STONY BROOK, N Y 11794 **Operant analysis of delay & probability in choice**

R29MH-44052-04 (BPN) STEINMETZ, JOSEPH E INDIANA UNIVERSITY BLOOMINGTON, IN 47405 **The interpositus nucleus & classical nictitating membrane conditioning**

R01MH-44062-04 (PCB) CHAPMAN, LOREN J UNIVERSITY OF WISCONSIN 1202 WEST JOHNSON STREET MADISON, WI 53706 **Cognitive markers of the predisposition to schizophrenia**

R37MH-44063-03 (PCB) JACOBSON, NEIL S UNIVERSITY OF WASHINGTON CENTER FOR CLINICAL RESEARCH SEATTLE, WA 98195 **Component analysis of cognitive therapy for depression**

R01MH-44069-03 (BSR) MILLER, DALE T PRINCETON UNIVERSITY DEPT OF PSYCHOLOGY PRINCETON, NJ 08544 **Bias in perception of interpersonal similarity**

R01MH-44078-03 (LCR) FINCHAM, FRANCIS D UNIVERSITY OF ILLINOIS 603 EAST DANIEL ST CHAMPAIGN, IL 61820 **Attribution processes and marital dysfunction**

R01MH-44090-03 (SRCM) THOMPSON, CHARLES P KANSAS STATE UNIVERSITY BLUEMONT HALL MANHATTAN, KS 66506 **The study of an exceptional memory**

R29MH-44100-03 (PYB) EDWARDS, CHARLES A EDINBORO UNIV OF PENNSYLVANIA DEPT OF PSYCH & COUNSELING EDINBORO, PA 16444 **Relational responding in avians**

R01MH-44115-03 (PCB) BARON, MIRON N Y STATE PSYCHIATRIC INST 722 W 168TH STREET NEW YORK, N Y 10032 **Gene markers in schizophrenia & other psychoses**

R01MH-44116-03 (PCB) NEALE, JOHN M SUNY AT STONY BROOK DEPARTMENT OF PSYCHOLOGY STONY BROOK, NY 11794 **Flat affect in schizophrenia**

R01MH-44119-04 (TDA) HEIMBERG, RICHARD G SUNY AT ALBANY 1400 WASHINGTON AVENUE ALBANY, N Y 12222 **Pharmacotherapy of social phobia**

R01MH-44122-03 (TDA) AMAN, MICHAEL G THE OHIO STATE UNIVERSITY 1581 DODD DRIVE COLUMBUS, OH 43210-1296 **Fenfluramine and methylphenidate in mental retardation**

R01MH-44131-04 (BPN) BOCCIA, MARIA L UNIV OF COLORADO HLTH SCIS CTR 4200 EAST 9TH AVE DENVER, CO 80262 **Dominance status and immunity--A non-human primate model**

R01MH-44132-03 (BPN) BITTMAN, ERIC L UNIVERSITY OF MASSACHUSETTS DEPARTMENT OF ZOOLOGY AMHERST, MA 01003 **Opiates and the biopsychology of photoperiodism**

R01MH-44142-04 (SRCM) KELLER, STEVEN E UMDNJ - NEW JERSEY MED SCHOOL 185 SOUTH ORANGE AVE NEWARK, NJ 07103-2714 **The psychoimmunology of adolescents at risk for AIDS**

R01MH-44149-04 (SRCM) KELLY, JEFFREY A MEDICAL COLLEGE OF WISCONSIN 8701 WATERTOWN PLANK ROAD MILWAUKEE, WI 53226 **Evaluation of counseling methods following HIV testing**

R37MH-44151-03 (PCB) LEWINE, RICHARD R J EMORY UNIVERSITY 1701 UPPERGATE DRIVE 4TH FLOOR ATLANTA, GA 30322 **Schizophrenia heterogeneity and brain sex differences**

R29MH-44160-04 (BPN) HYMAN, STEVEN E MASSACHUSETTS GENERAL HOSPITAL E BLDG 149, 13TH ST CHARLESTOWN, MA 02129 **Regulation of proenkephalin gene expression**

R01MH-44175-03 (PCB) FYER, ABBY J RES FDN FOR MENTAL HYGIENE 722 WEST 168TH STREET NEW YORK, N Y 10032 **A family study of obsessive compulsive disorder**

R29MH-44176-03 (TDA) DEVANAND, DAVANGERE P COLUMBIA UNIVERSITY 722 WEST 168TH STREET NEW YORK, N Y 10032 **Haloperidol treatment in Alzheimer's disease**

R29MH-44177-03 (PCB) MCBRIDE, P ANNE PAYNE WHITNEY CLINIC 525 EAST 68TH STREET NEW YORK, NY 10021 **Serotonergic function in autistic disorder**

P50MH-44188-03 (SRCM) BUNNEY, WILLIAM E UNIVERSITY OF CALIFORNIA COLLEGE OF MEDICINE IRVINE, CA 92717 **Neurobiological brain abnormalities in schizophrenia**

P50MH-44188-03 0001 (SRCM) MEDNICK, SARNOFF Neurobiological brain abnormalities in schizophrenia Brain abnormalities in schizophrenia

P50MH-44188-03 0002 (SRCM) COTMAN, CARL Neurobiological brain abnormalities in schizophrenia The role of excitatory amino acids in schizophrenia

P50MH-44188-03 0003 (SRCM) BUCHSBAUM, MONTE S Neurobiological brain abnormalities in schizophrenia The PET-PCP patient study

P50MH-44188-03 0004 (SRCM) BUCHSBAUM, MONTE S Neurobiological brain abnormalities in schizophrenia PET PCP-NMDA ligand development

P50MH-44188-03 0005 (SRCM) MARSHALL, JOHN F Neurobiological brain abnormalities in schizophrenia The role D1 and D2 receptors in schizophrenia

P50MH-44188-03 0006 (SRCM) CONTRERAS, PATRICIA C Neurobiological brain abnormalities in schizophrenia Endogenous PCP like ligands in schizophrenia

P50MH-44188-03 9001 (SRCM) MEDNICK, SARNOFF Neurobiological brain abnormalities in schizophrenia Core--Brain repository

P50MH-44188-03 9002 (SRCM) JAMES, EDWARD Neurobiological brain abnormalities in schizophrenia Core--Histopathochemistry

P50MH-44188-03 9003 (SRCM) BUNNEY, WILLIAM E Neurobiological brain abnormalities in schizophrenia Clinical core

P50MH-44188-03 9004 (SRCM) BUCHSBAUM, MONTE Neurobiological brain abnormalities in schizophrenia PET core

R01MH-44190-03 (TDA) STEKETEE, GAIL S BOSTON UNIVERSITY 264 BAY STATE ROAD BOSTON, MA 02215 **Expressed emotion in anxiety disorders**

P01MH-44193-03 (SRCM) DINGES, DAVID F INSTITUTE OF PENNSYLVANIA HOSP 111 NORTH 49TH STREET PHILADELPHIA, PA 19139 **Psychobiology of hypnosis in stress, pain and sleep**

P01MH-44193-03 0001 (SRCM) DINGES, DAVID F. Psychobiology of hypnosis in stress, pain and sleep Hypnosis effect on emotional, behavioral, immunologic functions in life stress

P01MH-44193-03 0002 (SRCM) ORNE, MARTIN T. Psychobiology of hypnosis in stress, pain and sleep Use of hypnosis to control acute pain in children with sickle cell disease

P01MH-44193-03 0003 (SRCM) ORNE, MARTIN T Psychobiology of hypnosis in stress, pain and sleep Use of hypnosis to control acute pain in adults with sickle cell disease

P01MH-44193-03 0004 (SRCM) ORNE, MARTIN T Psychobiology of hypnosis in stress, pain and sleep Hypnosis effect on pain, sleep, immune function in fibromyalgia syndrome

P01MH-44193-03 0005 (SRCM) DINGES, DAVID F. Psychobiology of hypnosis in stress, pain and sleep Effects of sleep and sleep loss on immune function

P01MH-44193-03 9001 (SRCM) ORNE, MARTIN T Psychobiology of hypnosis in stress, pain and sleep Core--Hypnosis assessment

P01MH-44193-03 9002 (SRCM) DINGES, DAVID F. Psychobiology of hypnosis in stress, pain and sleep Core--Sleep assessment

P01MH-44193-03 9003 (SRCM) KELLER, STEVEN E. Psychobiology of hypnosis in stress, pain and sleep Core--Immune assessement

P01MH-44193-03 9004 (SRCM) WHITEHOUSE, WAYNE G. Psychobiology of hypnosis in stress, pain and sleep Core--Data analysis

R01MH-44194-03 (TDA) POMARA, NUNZIO RES FDN FOR MENTAL HYGIENE INC NATHAN KLINE INST/PSYCH RES ORANGEBURG, N Y 10962 **Nortriptyline effects on elderly depressed**

R01MH-44200-04 (SRCM) KAMIL, ALAN C UNIVERSITY OF MASSACHUSETTS MIDDLESEX HOUSE AMHERST, MA 01003 **Mechanisms of spatial memory**

R01MH-44206-03 (CEP) BUSS, DAVID M UNIVERSITY OF MICHIGAN INSTITUTE FOR SOCIAL RESEARCH ANN ARBOR, MI 48106-1248 **Personality and the evocation of anger and upset**

P01MH-44210-03 (SRCM) WHYBROW, PETER C UNIVERSITY OF PENNSYLVANIA 305 BLOCKLEY HALL PHILADELPHIA, PA 19104-6021 **Thyroid axis episodic behavior and affective illness**

P01MH-44210-03 0001 (SRCM) WHYBROW, PETER C Thyroid axis episodic behavior and affective illness Thyroid hormones and affective illness--Clinical studies

P01MH-44210-03 0002 (SRCM) GUR, RUBEN C Thyroid axis episodic behavior and affective illness Thyroid function, affective disturbance and regional cerebral blood flow

P01MH-44210-03 0003 (SRCM) PRICE, R ARLEN Thyroid axis episodic behavior and affective illness Genetic family study of thyroid function in rapid cycling disease

P01MH-44210-03 0004 (SRCM) DRATMAN, MARY Thyroid axis episodic behavior and affective illness Psychopharmacology and thyroid hormone processing in the brain

P01MH-44210-03 9001 (SRCM) KREIDER, MARGARET S Thyroid axis episodic behavior and affective illness Core--Radioimmunoassay and chemical analysis

P01MH-44210-03 9002 (SRCM) MUENZ, LARRY Thyroid axis episodic behavior and affective illness Core--Data management and statistics

P50MH-44211-03 (SRCM) CARPENTER, WILLIAM T, JR MARYLAND PSYCHIATRIC RES CTR P O BOX 21247 BALTIMORE, MD 21228 **Neuroscience center for research in schizophrenia**

P50MH-44211-03 0011 (SRCM) WONG, DEAN F Neuroscience center for research in schizophrenia Human in vivo neurochemistry--Serotonin receptors

P50MH-44211-03 0001 (SRCM) CARON, MARC G Neuroscience center for research in schizophrenia Biochemical status of dopamine receptors after neuroliptic treatment

P50MH-44211-03 0002 (SRCM) CREESE, IAN Neuroscience center for research in schizophrenia Postsynaptic receptor changes after neuroleptic treatment

P50MH-44211-03 0003 (SRCM) UNGERSTEDT, URBAN Neuroscience center for research in schizophrenia Behaviorial and in vivo neurochemical analysis of neuroleptic effects

P50MH-44211-03 0004 (SRCM) SCHWARCZ, ROBERT Neuroscience center for research in schizophrenia Neuroleptic treatment and brain kynurenines

P50MH-44211-03 0005 (SRCM) BLAUSTEIN, MORDECAI P Neuroscience center for research in schizophrenia Purification of a brain PCP receptor

P50MH-44211-03 0006 (SRCM) ALBUQUERQUE, EDSON X Neuroscience center for research in schizophrenia Molecular pharmacology of PCP ion channel mechanisms

P50MH-44211-03 0007 (SRCM) FRENCH, EDWARD D Neuroscience center for research in schizophrenia Neuropharmacology of PCP/Sigma activation of A10 dopamine neurons

P50MH-44211-03 0012 (SRCM) TAMMINGA, CAROL A Neuroscience center for research in schizophrenia Human in vivo neurochemistry--Dual detector scanner

P50MH-44211-03 0008 (SRCM) JAUCH, DIANA Neuroscience center for research in schizophrenia Chronic effects of PCP on excitatory amino acids

P50MH-44211-03 0009 (SRCM) TAMMINGA, CAROL A Neuroscience center for research in schizophrenia Mapping PCP/Sigma pathways using autoradiography

P50MH-44211-03 0010 (SRCM) FROST, JAMES Neuroscience center for research in schizophrenia

P50MH-44211-03 0013 (SRCM) HOLCOMB, HENRY H Neuroscience center for research in schizophrenia Human in vivo nerochemistry--Image reconstruction

P50MH-44211-03 0014 (SRCM) WALTRIP, ROYCE W Neuroscience center for research in schizophrenia Immunology of viral reactivation in schizophrenia

P50MH-44211-03 9001 (SRCM) CARPENTER, WILLIAM T Neuroscience center for research in schizophrenia Core--Cell line repository

P50MH-44211-03 9002 (SRCM) TAMMINGA, CAROL A Neuroscience center for research in schizophrenia Core--Brain collection

P50MH-44212-03 (SRCM) FREEDMAN, ROBERT UNIV OF COL HLTH SCIS CTR 4200 EAST 9TH AVENUE DENVER, COLO 80262 Genetic and neurobiological investigation of schizophrenia

P50MH-44212-03 0001 (SRCM) FREEDMAN, ROBERT Genetic and neurobiological investigation of schizophrenia Neurophysiological abnormalities--Sensory gating phenotypes

P50MH-44212-03 0002 (SRCM) BYERLEY, WILLIAM Genetic and neurobiological investigation of schizophrenia Genetic linkage for sensory gating phenotypes

P50MH-44212-03 0003 (SRCM) ROSE, GREGORY M Genetic and neurobiological investigation of schizophrenia Sensory gating physiology in limbic forebrain

P50MH-44212-03 0004 (SRCM) REITE, MARTIN L Genetic and neurobiological investigation of schizophrenia Auditory P50 waves in temporal lobe--Magnetoencephalography

P50MH-44212-03 0005 (SRCM) FREEDMAN, ROBERT Genetic and neurobiological investigation of schizophrenia Neurobiology sensory gating

R01MH-44233-02 (PCB) DELISI, LYNN E SUNY AT STONY BROOK HEALTH SCIENCE CTR, T-10 STONY BROOK, NY 11794-8101 Brain morphology at the onset of schizophrenia

R01MH-44234-04 (PYB) CHURCH, RUSSELL M BROWN UNIVERSITY 89 WATERMAN ST BOX 1853 PROVIDENCE, RI 02912 Temporal discrimination learning

R01MH-44245-01A4 (PCB) DELISI, LYNN E STATE UNIVERSITY OF NEW YORK HEALTH SCIENCE CTR, T-10 STONY BROOK, NY 11794-8101 The detection of major gene loci for schizophrenia

R01MH-44246-03 (CEP) KROLL, JUDITH F MOUNT HOLYOKE COLLEGE SOUTH HADLEY, MA 01075 Cognitive processes in second language acquisition

R29MH-44258-04 (CVR) CALLAHAN, LISA A RUSSELL SAGE COLLEGE TROY, NY 12180 Comparing programs for monitoring NGRI's

R01MH-44268-02 (BSR) MACKINNON, CAROL E UNIVERSITY OF NORTH CAROLINA GREENSBORO, NC 27412-5001 Mother-son attributions and aggressive interactions

R29MH-44275-04 (BPN) IRWIN, MICHAEL R UNIV OF CALIFORNIA, SAN DIEGO 9500 GILMAN DRIVE LA JOLLA, CA 92093 Depression--Neuropeptides and natural cytotoxicity

R01MH-44276-03 (PCB) SOMMER, STEVE S MAYO FOUNDATION 200 FIRST STREET SOUTHWEST ROCHESTER, MN 55905 Genes of the catecholamine system & schizophrenia

R29MH-44284-03 (BPN) KRUEGER, KARL E GEORGETOWN UNIVERSITY 3900 RESERVOIR ROAD, NW WASHINGTON, DC 20007 Role of brain peripheral-type benzodiazepine receptors

R29MH-44287-04 (EPS) WISNER, KATHERINE L WESTERN PSYCHIATRIC INSTITUTE 3811 O'HARA STREET PITTSBURGH, PA 15213 Puerperal mental illness and maternal/child functioning

R01MH-44292-03 (EPS) OTT, JURG RES FDN MENT HYG @ NYS PSY INS 722 W 168TH ST NEW YORK, NY 10032 Linkage analysis methods in schizophrenia

R01MH-44311-03 (BSR) WRIGHT, JOHN C UNIVERSITY OF KANSAS DEPT OF HUMAN DEVELOPMENT LAWRENCE,KS 66045 Reality of children's TV--Cognitive & emotional effects

R01MH-44315-03 (PCB) WELLER, ELIZABETH B OHIO STATE UNIVERSITY 473 W 12TH AVENUE COLUMBUS, OH 43210 Psychopathology and grief in children after parental death

R01MH-44317-03 (EPS) JOHNSON, DAVID R UNIVERSITY OF NEBRASKA LINCOLN, NE 68588-0430 Economic decline and psychosocial impairment

R01MH-44321-03 (BSR) ROSS, LEE D STANFORD UNIV STANFORD, CA 94305-2130 Construal biases in the mediation of conflict /human/

R01MH-44325-02 (EPS) SCHINNAR, ARIE P UNIVERSITY OF PENNSYLVANIA 3814 WALNUT STREET PHILADELPHIA, PA 19104-6197 Capitation and health services in chronic mental illness

R01MH-44331-04 (SRCM) SUE, STANLEY UNIVERSITY OF CALIFORNIA AT LA 405 HILGARD AVENUE LOS ANGELES, CA 90024-1563 National research center on Asian American mental health

R01MH-44331-04 0001 (SRCM) SUE, STANLEY National research center on Asian American mental health Pilot--Cultural dimensions underlying assessment instruments

R01MH-44331-04 0003 (SRCM) ZANE, NOLAN National research center on Asian American mental health Cognitive match and treatment outcome

P01MH-44337-03 (SRCM) WOODWARD, DONALD J UNIVERSITY OF TEXAS SW MED CTR 5323 HARRY HINES BOULEVARD DALLAS, TX 75235 Behavioral neurophysiology

P01MH-44337-03 0001 (SRCM) CHAPIN, JOHN K Behavioral neurophysiology Modulation of input to sensory-motor cortex

P01MH-44337-03 0002 (SRCM) DEADWYLER, SAMMUAL A Behavioral neurophysiology Multi-neuron recording in hippocampus--Sensory and spatial information processing

P01MH-44337-03 0003 (SRCM) HOFFER, BARRY J Behavioral neurophysiology Chronoamperometric measurements of monoamine release in freely-moving rats

P01MH-44337-03 0004 (SRCM) BE MENT, SPENCER Behavioral neurophysiology Fabrication and use of semiconductor microprobes

P01MH-44337-03 9001 (SRCM) WOODWARD, DONALD J Behavioral neurophysiology Core

R01MH-44340-03 (BSR) HYDE, JANET S UNIVERSITY OF WISCONSIN 209 N BROOKS STREET MADISON, WI 53715 Maternity leave and health--Psychosocial factors

R01MH-44345-03 (MHAZ) MAYS, VICKIE M UNIVERSITY OF CALIFORNIA 405 HILGARD AVENUE LOS ANGELES, CA 90024-1563 HIV immunologic and psychosocial factors in black men

R37MH-44346-04 (BPN) SIGGINS, GEORGE R THE SCRIPPS RESEARCH INSTITUTE 10666 NORTH TORREY PINES ROAD LA JOLLA, CA 92037 Somatostatin and brain function

R01MH-44359-03 (SRCM) REVELEY, ADRIANNE M INSTITUTE OF PSYCHIATRY DE CRESPIGNY PK/DENMARK HILL LONDON SE5 8AF, ENGLAND A twin study of nosology and aetiology in schizophrenia

R44MH-44411-03 (MHSB) ABREU, MARY E NOVA PHARMACEUTICAL CORP 6200 FREEPORT CENTRE BALTIMORE, MD 21224-2788 Development of corticotropin-releasing factor antagonist

R01MH-44449-03 (HUD) CONNELL, JAMES P UNIVERSITY OF ROCHESTER GRAD SCH/EDUCATION/HUMAN DEV ROCHESTER, NY 14627 The development of emotional self-regulation

R01MH-44586-02 (PCB) BRESLAU, NAOMI HENRY FORD HOSPITAL 2799 WEST GRAND BLVD DETROIT, MI 48202 Neuropsychiatric sequelae of low birthweight

R01MH-44600-02 (MHAZ) PEARLIN, LEONARD I UNIVERSITY OF CALIFORNIA 1350 7TH AVE SAN FRANCISCO, CA 94143-0848 Stress and coping among AIDS caregivers

R01MH-44604-02 (LCR) BELSKY, JAY PENNSYLVANIA STATE UNIVERSITY UNIVERSITY PARK, PA 16802 Family stress and conflict--The "terrible twos"

R01MH-44609-03 (BBP) ORIANS, GORDON H UNIVERSITY OF WASHINGTON SEATTLE, WA 98195 Inter-relations of territorial behavior & physiology

R01MH-44618-03 (MHAZ) EVANS, DWIGHT L UNIV OF N C AT CHAPEL HILL CB #7160, MED. SCH WING B CHAPEL HILL, NC 27599 HIV -- Neuropsychiatric and psychoimmune relationships

R01MH-44623-02 (CVR) GRISSO, THOMAS UNIVERSITY OF MASSACHUSETTS 55 LAKE AVE., NORTH WORCESTER, MA 01655 Emergent models of pretrial forensic evaluation systems

R01MH-44626-03 (EPS) SCHOPLER, ERIC UNIV OF N C AT CHAPEL HILL CB# 7180 MEDICAL SCHOOL WING E CHAPEL HILL, N C 27599 Effects of a model treatment approach on autistic adults

R01MH-44638-03 (BPN) MONTAL, S MAURICIO UNIV OF CALIF, SAN DIEGO LA JOLLA, CA 92093-0319 Molecular anatomy of channel proteins and mental illness

R01MH-44640-03 (CEP) RATCLIFF, ROGER NORTHWESTERN UNIVERSITY 1859 SHERIDAN ROAD EVANSTON, IL 60208 Retrieval processes in memory

R01MH-44647-03 (BPN) PAYNE, BERTRAM R BOSTON UNIV SCHOOL OF MED. 80 EAST CONCORD STREET BOSTON, MA 02118 Sparing and loss of function after cerebral cortex lesions

R29MH-44648-04 (EPS) WORLEY, NANCY K MEDICAL UNIV OF SOUTH CAROLINA 171 ASHLEY AVE CHARLESTON, SC 29425 Intensive case management for chronic mentally ill

R01MH-44651-03 (BPN) DUNLAP, JAY C DARTMOUTH MEDICAL SCHOOL DEPT OF BIOCHEMISTRY HANOVER, HEW HAMPSHIRE 03756 Identification and analysis of clock controlled genes

P01MH-44660-04 (SRCM) GLASER, RONALD OHIO STATE UNIVERSITY 333 WEST 10TH AVENUE COLUMBUS, OHIO 43210 Stress--Impact on the immune-endocrine axis and health

P01MH-44660-04 0001 (SRCM) GLASER, RONALD Stress--Impact on the immune-endocrine axis and health Academic stress--impact on immune-endocrine axis

P01MH-44660-04 0002 (SRCM) KIECOLT-GLASER, JANICE K Stress--Impact on the immune-endocrine axis and health Physiological consequences of marital discord

P01MH-44660-04 0003 (SRCM) MALARKEY, WILLIAM B Stress--Impact on the immune-endocrine axis and health impact of stress on endocrine and immunologic function

P01MH-44660-04 0004 (SRCM) WHITACRE, CAROLINE C Stress--Impact on the immune-endocrine axis and health Neuroendocrine effects on autoimmune encephalomyelitis

P01MH-44660-04 9001 (SRCM) PEARL, DENNIS K Stress--Impact on the immune-endocrine axis and health Core--Statistical analysis and data management

R01MH-44662-04 (SRC) MC LOYD, VONNIE C UNIVERSITY OF MICHIGAN 3433 MASON HALL ANN ARBOR, MI 48109 The effects of unemployment on afro-american children

R29MH-44665-02 (LCR) VIVIAN, DINA STATE UNIVERSITY OF NEW YORK STONY BROOK, NY 11794 Emotion/communication in physically abusive couples

R01MH-44672-02 (PCB) PILKONIS, PAUL A WESTERN PSYCHIATRIC INST/CLINI 3811 O'HARA STREET PITTSBURGH, PA 15213 Validity in the diagnosis of personality disorders

R01MH-44683-03 (EPS) TESSLER, RICHARD C UNIVERSITY OF MASSACHUSETTS MUNSON HALL AMHERST, MA 01003 Continuity of care, residency and family burden

R01MH-44688-02 (EPS) ZITO, JULIE M NATHAN S KLINE INST/PSY RESEAR OLD ORANGEBURG ROAD ORANGEBURG, NY 10962 Drug treatment refusal impact on severely mentally ill

R01MH-44689-02 (CEP) VOELLER, KYTJA UNIVERSITY OF FLORIDA BOX J-234, JHMHC GAINESVILLE, FL 32610 Early brain lesions and affective behavior in children

R01MH-44690-02A1 (EPS) STRUENING, ELMER L RES FDN FOR MENT HYGIENE 722 WEST 168TH ST NEW YORK, NY 10032 Measures of impact on caretakers of the mentally ill

R29MH-44691-03 (EPS) DOZIER, MARY TRINITY UNIVERSITY 715 STADIUM DR. SAN ANTONIO, TX 78212 Tailoring treatment for the chronically mentally ill

R29MH-44697-03 (LCR) KLUGER, ALAN NYU MEDICAL CTR/DEPT OF PSYCH 550 FIRST AVE (HN 314) NEW YORK, NY 10016 Motor deficit and white matter lesions in aging and Alzheimer's Disease

R29MH-44699-03 (BPN) LOWY, MARTIN T UNIVERSITY HOSP OF CLEVELAND 2040 ABINGTON ROAD CLEVELAND, OH 44106 Regulation of brain and lymphoid glucocorticoid receptors

R29MH-44701-02 (TDA) TELCH, MICHAEL J UNIV OF TEXAS AT AUSTIN AUSTIN, TX 78712 Psychological treatment for panic disorder with agoraphobia

R01MH-44705-03S2 (EPS) CATON, CAROL L COLUMBIA UNIVERSITY 722 WEST 168TH ST. NEW YORK, NY 10032 Service uses & homelessness in chronic mental illness

R01MH-44711-03 (EPS) BRENT, DAVID A WESTERN PSYCHIATRIC INST & CLI 3811 O'HARA STREET PITTSBURGH, PA 15213 Psychiatric effects of exposure to suicide in youth

R29MH-44713-03 (LCR) TETI, DOUGLAS M UNIVERSITY OF MARYLAND 5401 WILKENS AVENUE BALTIMORE, MD 21228 Security of attachment and infant-sibling relations

R01MH-44716-03 (PCB) KRISHNAN, RANGA R DUKE UNIVERSITY MEDICAL CENTER BOX 3215 DURHAM, NC 27710 Cortisol cognition brain atrophy and depression

R01MH-44729-01A2 (CEP) KLINNERT, MARY D NATIONAL JEWISH CENTER 1400 JACKSON STREET DENVER, CO 80206 Emotional factors in childhood asthma

R01MH-44730-03 (CEP) SMITH, STEVEN M TEXAS A&M UNIV COLLEGE STATION, TX 77843 Inducing and reducing cognitive fixation

R01MH-44734-03 (BPN) HAUN, FORREST A MED COLLEGE OF PENNSYLVANIA PHILADELPHIA, PA 19129 Behavioral effects of specific neurotrophic agents

R29MH-44736-03 (BPN) RAYPORT, STEPHEN G NEW YORK STATE PSYCHIATRIC INS 722 WEST 168TH STREET, BOX #62 NEW YORK, N Y 10032 Mesocorticolimbic dopamine neurons in vitro

R01MH-44742-03 (EPS) SPENCE, M ANNE UNIV OF CALIF, LOS ANGELES 760 WESTWOOD PLAZA/RM 48-228 LOS ANGELES, CALIF 90024-1759 Genetic influences in autism and tuberous sclerosis

R01MH-44746-03 (BBP) RILEY, DONALD A UNIVERSITY OF CALIFORNIA DEPT. OF PSYCHOLOGY BERKELEY, CA 94720 Information in processing and short-term memory

R37MH-44754-03 (BPN) JOHNSTON, DANIEL BAYLOR COLLEGE OF MEDICINE ONE BAYLOR PLAZA HOUSTON, TX 77030 Pharmacology of mossy fiber synaptic plasticity

R01MH-44755-03 (PCB) SAMEROFF, ARNOLD J E P BRADLEY HOSPITAL 1011 VETERANS MEMORIAL PARKWAY EAST PROVIDENCE, RI 02915 Family-child study of affective and anxiety disorders

R01MH-44756-02 (TDA) SPAULDING, WILLIAM D UNIVERSITY OF NEBRASKA LINCOLN, NE 68588-0308 Cognitive therapy in rehabilitation of schizophrenia

R29MH-44762-03 (CVR) CROWNER, MARTHA L MANHATTAN PSYCHIATRIC CENTER DUNLAP 14-A, RESEARCH DEPT. WARD'S ISLAND, NY 10035 Videotape recording of psychiatric inpatient assaults

R01MH-44763-03 (LCR) COX, MARTHA J WESTERN CAROLINA CENTER 300 ENOLA ROAD MORGANTON, NC 28655 Marital & parent-child relations--Effects in the family

R01MH-44778-02 (TDA) MILLER, IVAN W BUTLER HOSPITAL 345 BLACKSTONE BLVD PROVIDENCE, RI 02906 Matched vs mismatched treatment for depression

R01MH-44779-03 (PCB) SACKEIM, HAROLD A NEW YORK STATE PSYCHIATRIC INS 722 WEST 168TH STREET NEW YORK, NY 10032 Neurophysiological correlates of cognitive effort

R29MH-44780-03 (EPS) PESCOSOLIDO, BERNICE A INDIANA UNIVERSITY BLOOMINGTON, IN 47405 A network-episode model for mental health services

R29MH-44781-03 (TDA) SILVERMAN, WENDY K FLORIDA INTERNATIONAL UNIVERSI UNIVERSITY PARK MIAMI, FL 33199 Psychosocial treatment of childhood phobias

R29MH-44787-02 (LCR) MEEKS, SUZANNE UNIVERSITY OF LOUISVILLE LOUISVILLE, KY 40292 Chronically mentally ill aged--MH services and other factors in adjustment

R01MH-44789-01A2 (BPN) SAHLEY, CHRISTIE L PURDUE UNIVERSITY WEST LAFAYETTE, IN 47907 Cellular analysis of learning

R01MH-44791-02 (LCR) COHEN, PATRICIA R RES FOUND FOR MNTL HYGIENE 722 WEST 168TH STREET NEW YORK, NY 10032 Basic models of parenting and temperament

R01MH-44799-03 (BPN) RANDALL, PATRICK K UNIVERSITY OF TEXAS AT AUSTIN INST FOR NEUROLOGICAL SCIS RES AUSTIN, TX 78712-1074 Neuroleptic interaction with dopamine receptor subtypes

R01MH-44801-03 (EPS) BROMET, EVELYN J SUNY, DEPT OF PSYCHIATRY PUTNAM HALL, S CAMPUS, RM 157 STONY BROOK, NY 11794-8790 Epidemiology of newly diagnosed psychotic disorders

R01MH-44809-03 (BPN) COHEN, AVIS H UNIVERSITY OF MARYLAND COLLEGE PARK, MD 20742 Encoding time--A dynamic analysis of behavior

R29MH-44811-02 (BSR) NIEDENTHAL, PAULA M JOHNS HOPKINS UNIVERSITY CHARLES & 34TH STREETS BALTIMORE, MD 21218 Affective bases of person perception

R01MH-44813-03 (BBP) GOTTLIEB, GILBERT UNIV OF NORTH CAROLINA 1000 SPRING GARDEN ST RM 100 GREENBORO, NC 27412-5001 Sensory and perceptual determinants of imprinting

R37MH-44814-03 (PCB) SEDVALL, GORAN KAROLINKSA INSTITUTE P.O. BOX 60500 S-104 01 STOCKHOLM, SWEDEN PET analysis of D1-dopamine receptors in schizophrenia

R01MH-44815-02 (PCB) TOWEY, JAMES PATRICK RESEARCH FDNTN/MENTAL HYGIENE 722 WEST 168TH STREET NEW YORK, NY 10032 Endogenous ERPS in obsessive-compulsive disorder

R01MH-44826-01A2 (EPS) GIBBONS, ROBERT D ILLINOIS ST PSYCHIATRIC INST 1609 WEST TAYLOR STREET CHICAGO, IL 60612 Regression models for longitudinal psychiatric data

R01MH-44828-01A3 (TDA) WING, RENA R WESTERN PSY INST & CLINIC 3811 O'HARA STREET PITTSBURGH, PA 15213 Cognitive behavioral treatment of obese binge eaters

R01MH-44832-02 (PCB) LEVY, ALEJANDRO V BROOKHAVEN NATIONAL LAB UPTON, NY 11973 The spectral signature method for brain pattern analysis

R01MH-44839-03 (EPS) PAULSON, ROBERT I UNIVERSITY OF CINCINNATI CINCINNATI, OHIO 45221 Mental health service networks in RWJ sites

R01MH-44841-02 (TDA) VAN KAMMEN, DANIEL P WESTERN PSYCHIATRIC INST/CLINI 3811 O'HARA STREET PITTSBURG, PA 15213-2593 Norepinephrine and relapse prediction in schizophrenia

R01MH-44842-03 (TDA) HECHTMAN, LILY MONTREAL CHILDREN'S HOSPITAL 2300 TUPPER STREET MONTREAL, QUE H3H1P3, CANADA Methylphenidate & multimodal treatment in ADHD

R01MH-44843-03 (SRCM) LECKMAN, JAMES F YALE UNIVERSITY 155 WHITNEY AVE NEW HAVEN, CT 06520 Neurobiology of Tourette's syndrome and related disorders

R01MH-44844-03 (TDA) SWANSON, JAMES M STATE DEVELOPMENTAL RES INST 2501 HARBOR BLVD COSTA MESA, CA 92626 Withdrawal of neuroleptic drugs in the developmentally disabled

R01MH-44848-03 (TDA) ABIKOFF, HOWARD B LONG ISLAND JEWISH MED CTR NEW HYDE PARK, NY 11042 Methylphenidate and treatment in attention deficit hyperactivity disorders

R01MH-44849-03 (SRCM) DAVIDSON, WILLIAM S II MICHIGAN STATE UNIVERSITY EAST LANSING, MI 48824-1117 Effects of alternative interventions for battered women

P50MH-44866-04 (SRCM) GOLDMAN-RAKIC, PATRICIA S YALE UNIV-SECT OF NEUROBIOLOGY 333 CEDAR STREET NEW HAVEN, CT 06510 Cortical mechanisms in schizophrenia

P50MH-44866-04 0001 (SRCM) GOLDMAN-RAKIC, PATRICIA S Cortical mechanisms in schizophrenia Neuronal mechanisms of cognition in nonhuman primates

P50MH-44866-04 0002 (SRCM) HOLZMAN, PHILIP S Cortical mechanisms in schizophrenia Disorder of eye tracking and working memory

P50MH-44866-04 0003 (SRCM) LERANTH, CSABA Cortical mechanisms in schizophrenia Cytometric and cytochemical correlates in schizophrenia

P50MH-44866-04 0004 (SRCM) INNIS, ROBERT B Cortical mechanisms in schizophrenia Receptor autoradiography & neurochemistry--Schizophrenic & macaque cortex

P50MH-44866-04 0005 (SRCM) BUNNEY, BENJAMIN S Cortical mechanisms in schizophrenia Pharmacology and behavior of primate prefrontal cortex

P50MH-44866-04 0006 (SRCM) GOLDMAN-RAKIC, PATRICIA A Cortical mechanisms in schizophrenia Developmental model of schizophrenia

P50MH-44866-04 9001 (SRCM) GOLDMAN-RAKIC, PATRICIA S Cortical mechanisms in schizophrenia Core--Animals

P50MH-44866-04 9002 (SRCM) BIRD, EDWARD D Cortical mechanisms in schizophrenia Core--Brain tissue resource center

R37MH-44876-03 (SRCM) HOLZMAN, PHILIP S HARVARD COLLEGE 33 KIRKLAND STREET CAMBRIDGE, MA 02138 Linkage analysis in pedigrees at risk for schizophrenia

R03MH-44889-01A2 (MSM) BOROD, JOAN C QUEENS COLLEGE OF C U N Y 65-30 KISSENA BLVD FLUSHING, N Y 11367 Hedonic experience of odors in brain-damaged patients

R01MH-44894-03 (BPN) CHESSELET, MARIE-FRANCOISE S UNIVERSITY OF PENNSYLVANIA 36TH AND HAMILTON WALK PHILADELPHIA, PA 19104 Plasticity of GAD gene expression in the basal ganglia

R01MH-44913-04 (EPS) COOK, JUDITH A THRESHOLDS 561 WEST DIVERSEY PARKWAY CHICAGO, IL 60614 Efficacy of two models of vocational service to the chronically mentally ill

R01MH-44934-03 (LCR) HAUSER, STUART T MASS MENTAL HEALTH CENTER 74 FENWOOD ROAD BOSTON, MA 02115 Adolescent paths to early adult social development

R01MH-44935-02 (LCR) WATERS, EVERETT STATE UNIVERSITY OF NEW YORK SUNY STONY BROOK STONY BROOK, NY 11794-2500 Adult attachment models--Development after marriage?

R01MH-44938-03 (CEP) GLANZER, MURRAY NEW YORK UNIVERSITY 6 WASHINGTON PL NEW YORK, NY 10003 Mirror effect in recognition memory

R44MH-44943-03 (MHSB) GRUEN, WILLIAM AMBULATORY MONITORING, INC 731 SAW MILL RIVER ROAD ARDSLEY, NY 10502 Actillume-- A monitor for activity and light exposure

R44MH-44946-02 (MHSB) O'HALLORAN, JAMES P NEUROCOMP SYSTEMS, INC 366 SAN MIGUEL NEWPORT BEACH, CA 92660 Patient interactive automated dementia battery

R44MH-44952-02 (MHSB) WEINROTT, MARK R NORTHWEST MEDIA, INC P.O. BOX 56 EUGENE, OR 97401 Reducing deviant arousal in juvenile sex offenders

R01MH-44959-03 (MHAZ) MAYEUX, RICHARD P NEUROLOGICAL INSTITUTE 710 WEST 168TH STREET NEW YORK, NY 10032 Behavioral correlates of magnetic resonance imaging in HIV disorders

R29MH-44964-05 (PBC) TRZEPACZ, PAULA T WESTERN PSYCHIATRIC INSTITUTE 3811 O'HARA STREET PITTSBURGH, PA 15213 Behavior and hyperthyroidism--A beta-adrenergic mechanism

R01MH-44970-03 (MHAZ) CRNIC, LINDA S UNIV OF COLORADO SCH OF MED 4200 E. 9TH AVENUE, C233 DENVER, CO 80262 Effects of neonatal HSV-1 infection on brain & behavior

R29MH-44984-03 (LCR) BRUCE, MARTHA L YALE UNIVERSITY 350 CONGRESS AVE/ SUITE 1B NEW HAVEN, CT 06519 Social roles and depression: Variation with age

R01MH-44997-02 (LCR) GAL, REUVEN ISRAELI INST FOR MILITARY STUD 9 HANASSI ST, PO BOX 97 ZIKHRON YA'AKOV 30900, ISRAEL Coping with effects of terrorism by victims and families

R01MH-44999-02 (BSR) AMABILE, TERESA M BRANDEIS UNIVERSITY WALTHAM, MA 02254 Mechanisms of creativity

R01MH-45003-02 (BPN) WILLIAMS, JOHN T OREGON HEALTH SCIENCES UNIV 3181 SW SAM JACKSON PARK RD PORTLAND, OR 97201 Sigma-receptor psychotomimetics--Actions on single neurons

R01MH-45004-02 (PYB) BROWN, MICHAEL F VILLANOVA UNIVERSITY VILLANOVA, PA 19085 Choice criterion effects in spatial memory performance

R37MH-45006-03 (PYB) LEVINE, SEYMOUR STANFORD UNIV SCHOOL OF MED DEPT OF PSY & BEHAVIORAL SCIS STANFORD, CA 94305 Maternal regulation of infant physiology and behavior

R01MH-45015-02 (EPS) MCFARLAND, BENTSON H KAISER FOUNDATION HOSPITALS 4610 S E BELMONT ST PORTLAND, OR 97215 Severely mentally ill HMO members

R01MH-45019-03 (BPN) TODD, RICHARD D WASHINGTON UNIVERSITY 660

PROJECT NO., ORGANIZATIONAL UNIT., INVESTIGATOR, ADDRESS, TITLE

SOUTH EUCLID AVE BOX 8134 ST LOUIS, MO 63110 Molecular cloning of dopamine receptor
R29MH-45020-03 (EPS) DEW, MARY A WESTERN PSYCHIATRIC INSTITUTE 3811 O'HARA STREET PITTSBURGH, PA 15213 Mental health and compliance in cardiac transplantation
R37MH-45027-01A1 (LCR) CICCHETTI, DANTE MT HOPE FAMILY CENTER 187 EDINBURGH STREET ROCHESTER, NY 14608 Preventive intervention for toddlers of depressed mothers
R01MH-45040-01A2 (TDA) GREENBERG, LESLIE S YORK UNIVERSITY 4700 KEELE STREET NORTH YORK, ONTARIO M3J 1P3 Change processes in experiential psychotherapy
R01MH-45043-03 (TDA) JARRETT, ROBIN B UNIV OF TEXAS SW MED CTR AT DA 5323 HARRY HINES BLVD DALLAS TX 75235 Does atypical depression respond to cognitive therapy
R03MH-45044-02 (MSM) BALK, DAVID E KANSAS STATE UNIVERSITY MANHATTAN, KS 66506 Social support for bereaved college students
R01MH-45045-03 (MHAZ) MAIER, STEVEN F UNIVERSITY OF COLORADO CAMPUS BOX 345 BOULDER, COLO 80309-0345 Stress and immunity--Behavioral and physiological mechanisms
R01MH-45048-03 (LCR) GOLDSTEIN, MARION Z ERIE COUNTY MEDICAL CENTER 462 GRIDER ST BUFFALO, NY 14215 Neuropsychological disorders in the elderly undergoing surgery
R01MH-45049-01A2 (BSR) PARK, BERNADETTE M UNIVERSITY OF COLORADO BOULDER, CO 80309-0345 Category representation and perception of variability
R29MH-45050-03 (EPS) SCHOTT, THOMAS UNIVERSITY OF PITTSBURGH PITTSBURGH, PA 15260 Cooperation in systems of services for the mentally ill
R01MH-45051-02 (BPN) YAMAMURA, HENRY I UNIVERSITY OF ARIZONA 1501 N CAMPBELL AVENUE TUCSON, AZ 85724 Psychotropic drugs and muscarinic receptor types
R01MH-45058-02S1 (BSR) MALAMUTH, NEIL M UNIV OF CALIF, LOS ANGELES 405 HILGARD AVE LOS ANGELES, CA 90024-1504 Predicting men's antisocial behavior against women
R29MH-45060-01A2 (CVR) CONVIT, ANTONIO J KIRBY FORENSIC PSYCHIATRY CENT WARD'S ISLAND NEW YORK, NY 10035 Prediction of assault in mentally ill offenders
R29MH-45064-02 (TDA) HINSHAW, STEPHEN P UNIV OF CALIFORNIA AT BERK INSTITUTE OF HUMAN DEVELOPMENT BERKELEY, CA 94720 Peer status, social behavior, and intervention for ADHD
R01MH-45067-04 (LCR) CAMPBELL, SCOTT S NY HOSPITAL-CORNELL MED CTR 21 BLOOMINGDALE ROAD WHITE PLAINS, NY 10605 Bright light treatment of sleep disturbance in elderly
R01MH-45069-02 (SRCM) NORRIS, FRAN H GEORGIA STATE UNIVERSITY UNIVERSITY PLAZA ATLANTA, GA 30303 Social stress and functioning following Hurricane Hugo
R01MH-45070-03 (CVR) MOFFITT, TERRIE E UNIVERSITY OF WISCONSIN 1202 WEST JOHNSON STREET MADISON, WI 53706 Self-report delinquency--A longitudinal study
R01MH-45072-03 (EPS) JERRELL, JEANETTE M SANTA CLARA BUREAU MENTAL HLTH 645 S BASCOM AVENUE SAN JOSE, CA 95128 Cost effectiveness of service for severely mentally ill
R29MH-45073-03 (LCR) VUCHINICH, SAMUEL OREGON STATE UNIVERSITY CORVALLIS, OR 97331 Family alliances in therapy and at home
R01MH-45074-02 (TDA) BREIER, ALAN MARYLAND PSYCHIATRIC RES CTR P O BOX 21247 BALTIMORE, MD 21228 Clozapine treatment of schizophrenia
R01MH-45075-04 (BPN) VERTES, ROBERT P FLORIDA ATLANTIC UNIV BOCA RATON, FL 33431 Brainstem modulation of the hippocampus
R01MH-45083-02 (CVR) WHITE, JACQUELYN W UNIVERSITY OF NORTH CAROLINA 276 EBERHART GREENSBORO, NC 27412 Risk factors in sexual assault among college students
R01MH-45096-03 (BPN) NORDEEN, ERNEST J UNIVERSITY OF ROCHESTER DEPT OF PSYCHOLOGY ROCHESTER, N Y 14627 Neural changes associated with critical learning periods
R01MH-45097-02 (PCB) LEVINSON, DOUGLAS F MED COLLEGE OF PENNSYLVANIA 3200 HENRY AVENUE PHILADELPHIA, PA 19129 Genetic linkage of schizophrenia using RFLP genome map
R37MH-45112-03 (PCB) ASARNOW, ROBERT F UNIV OF CALIFORNIA LOS ANGELES 760 WESTWOOD PLAZA LOS ANGELES, CA 90024-1759 Familial psychiatric disorders & attention in schizophrenia
R29MH-45113-03 (PCB) ERWIN, ROLAND J UNIVERSITY OF PENNSYLVANIA PHILADELPHIA, PA 19104 Electrophysiology and neuroimaging in schizophrenia
R01MH-45118-03 (MHAZ) STIFFMAN, ARLENE R WASHINGTON UNIVERSITY ONE BROOKINGS DRIVE ST LOUIS, MO 63130 Behavior change in young adults at risk for AIDS
R01MH-45122-02 (TDA) LIEBERMAN, JEFFREY A LONG ISLAND JEWISH MEDICAL CTR 75-59 263RD STREET GLEN OAKS, NY 11004 Clozapine treatment of severe tardive dyskinesia
R01MH-45124-03 (BPN) DEUTCH, ARIEL Y YALE UNIV SCHOOL OF MEDICINE 34 PARK STREET, CMHC NEW HAVEN, CT 06508 Dopamine system interaction and schizophrenia
R01MH-45128-01A1 (SRCM) SWIFT, MICHAEL R UNIV OF N C AT CHAPEL HILL CB #7520 CHAPEL HILL, NC 27599-7250 Psychiatric disorders in Wolfram syndrome families
R01MH-45130-03 (PCB) CZEISLER, CHARLES A BRIGHAM AND WOMEN'S HOSPITAL 221 LONGWOOD AVE BOSTON, MASS 02115 Treatment of circadian sleep disorders w/bright light
R01MH-45131-03 (TDA) JESTE, DILIP V UNIV OF CALIF, SAN DIEGO DEPT OF PSYCHIATRY, M-003 LA JOLLA, CA 92093 Risk factor for tardive dyskinesia in older patients
R01MH-45133-03 (TDA) JENIKE, MICHAEL A MASSACHUSETTS GENERAL HOSPITAL FRUIT ST - BULFINCH 3/PSYCH BOSTON, MA 02114 Phenelzine and fluoxentine trial in obsessive compulsive disoders
R29MH-45135-02 (CEP) SCHOOLER, JONATHAN W UNIVERSITY OF PITTSBURGH 3939 O'HARA ST PITTSBURGH, PA 15260 Verbal overshadowing of non-verbal memories
R01MH-45137-03 (PYB) SIEGEL, SHEPARD MCMASTER UNIVERSITY HAMILTON, CANADA L8S 4K1 Mccollough effect--Associative and semantic mechanisms
R01MH-45139-02 (LCR) KEANE, ANNE UNIVERSITY OF PENNSYLVANIA PHILADELPHIA, PA 19104-6096 Bereavement and attributions in fire survivors
R29MH-45142-03 (TDA) LOHR, JAMES B UNIV OF CALIF, SAN DIEGO DEPT OF PSYCHIATRY 0603 LA JOLLA, CA 92093.0603 Tardive dyskinesia: free radical mechanisms and vitamin E
R01MH-45143-02 (PCB) YESAVAGE, JEROME A STANFORD UNIVERSITY SCH OF MED STANFORD, CA 94305-5490 Treatments for insomnia
R29MH-45145-02 (PYB) ABRAMS, RICHARD A WASHINGTON UNIVERSITY ONE BROOKINGS DR ST LOUIS, MO 63130 Mechanisms of spatial localization for aimed movements
P50MH-45156-02 (SRCM) STRICKER, EDWARD M UNIVERSITY OF PITTSBURGH 479 CRAWFORD HALL PITTSBURGH, PA 15260 Behavioral neuroscience and schizophrenia
P50MH-45156-02 0001 (SRCM) BERGER, THEODORE W Behavioral neuroscience and schizophrenia PCP & NMDA receptors contribution to hippocampal formation network
P50MH-45156-02 0002 (SRCM) LEWIS, DAVID A Behavioral neuroscience and schizophrenia Organization of primate prefrontal cortex
P50MH-45156-02 0003 (SRCM) GRACE, ANTHONY A Behavioral neuroscience and schizophrenia Frontal cortical regulation of subcortical dopamine systems
P50MH-45156-02 0004 (SRCM) PETTEGREW, JAY W Behavioral neuroscience and schizophrenia in vivo assessment of neuroanatomy by magnetic resonance imaging (MRI)
P50MH-45156-02 9001 (SRCM) SCHOOLER, NINA R Behavioral neuroscience and schizophrenia Clinical core
R01MH-45157-03 (BEM) REDD, WILLIAM H MEMORIAL HOSPITAL 1275 YORK AVENUE NEW YORK, NY 10021 Classically conditioned immune suppression in humans
R01MH-45161-01 (PYB) CHASE, SHEILA HUNTER COLLEGE OF CUNY 695 PARK AVENUE NEW YORK, NY 10021 Cognitive maps, tracking and continuous repertoires
R01MH-45164-02 (EPS) CHRISTIANSON, JON B INTERSTUDY PO BOX 458 EXCELSIOR, MN 55331 Managing mental health care in HMO
R01MH-45166-03 (PCB) FRIEDMAN, EITAN MED COLL OF PENNSYLVANIA 3200 HENRY AVE PHILADELPHIA, PA 19129 Protein kinase C in mania and in lithium's actions
R29MH-45173-02 (TDA) SHELTON RICHARD, C VANDERBILT CLINIC 22ND AVENUE SOUTH NASHVILLE, TN 37232-5646 Rapid response to antidepressants by sleep deprivation
R01MH-45174-03 (BPN) DIETZSCHOLD, BERNHARD THE WISTAR INSTITUTE 36TH AND SPRUCE STREETS PHILADELPHIA, PA 19104 Study on Borna disease using nucleic acid probes
P50MH-45178-02 (SRCM) CRITS-CHRISTOPH, PAUL HOSPITAL OF THE UNIV OF PENN 3600 SPRUCE ST PHILADELPHIA, PA 19104-4283 Clinical research center for the study of psychotherapy
P50MH-45178-02 0001 (SRCM) BECK, AARON T Clinical research center for the study of psychotherapy Cognitive therapy of generalized anxiety disorder--Pilot study
P50MH-45178-02 0002 (SRCM) CRITS-CHRISTOPH, PAUL Clinical research center for the study of psychotherapy Dynamic therapy for generalized anxiety disorder--Pilot study
P50MH-45178-02 0003 (SRCM) DERUBEIS, ROBERT Clinical research center for the study of psychotherapy Cognitive therapy for chronic depression--Pilot study
P50MH-45178-02 0004 (SRCM) LUBORSKY, LESTER Clinical research center for the study of psychotherapy Supportive, expressive dynamic psychotherapy for chronic depression--Pilot
P50MH-45178-02 0005 (SRCM) FREEMAN, ARTHUR Clinical research center for the study of psychotherapy: Cognitive therapy for avoidant & obsessive compulsive personality disorders
P50MH-45178-02 0006 (SRCM) BARBER, JACQUES Clinical research center for the study of psychotherapy Dynamic therapy for avoidant & obsessive compulsive personality disorders
P50MH-45178-02 0007 (SRCM) SELIGMAN, MARTIN E P Clinical research center for the study of psychotherapy: Chnge in explanatory style & treatment outcome in chronic depression--Pilot
P50MH-45178-02 0008 (SRCM) WRIGHT, FRED D Clinical research center for the study of psychotherapy Cognitive therapy for dependent personality disorders--Pilot
P50MH-45178-02 0009 (SRCM) CRITS-CHRISTOPH, PAUL Clinical research center for the study of psychotherapy Dynamic therapy for dependent personality disorder--Pilot
P50MH-45178-02 0010 (SRCM) SELIGMAN, MARTIN E P Clinical research center for the study of psychotherapy Integration of brief cognitive therapy based training with dynamic psychotherapy
P50MH-45178-02 9001 (SRCM) LUBORSKY, LESTER Clinical research center for the study of psychotherapy Core--Therapeutics and training
P50MH-45178-02 9002 (SRCM) CRITS-CHRISTOPH, PAUL Clinical research center for the study of psychotherapy Core--Clinical assessment accrual
P50MH-45178-02 9003 (SRCM) MUENZ, LARRY Clinical research center for the study of psychotherapy Core--Data management and statistics
R29MH-45180-02 (BPN) NAPIER, TAVYE C LOYOLA UNIV OF CHICAGO 2160 SOUTH FIRST AVENUE MAYWOOD, IL 60153 Neurophysiology of a novel dopaminergic system
R01MH-45181-03 (BPN) WISE, BRADLEY C GEORGETOWN UNIVERSITY MED CTR 3900 RESERVOIR RD, NW WASHINGTON, DC 20007 Characterization of cholinergic neurotrophic factor
R01MH-45186-02 (PCB) VITIELLO, MICHAEL V UNIVERSITY OF WASHINGTON SEATTLE, WA 98195 Aerobic fitness--Sleep and its correlates in the aged
R01MH-45188-02 (LCR) LEWIN, LEWIS M OREGON RESEARCH INSTITUTE 1899 WILLAMETTE, EUGENE, OR 97401 Social predictors of adolescent adjustment
R01MH-45191-02 (BPN) DE CAMILLI, PIETRO YALE UNIVERSITY 333 CEDAR ST PO BOX 3333 NEW HAVEN, CT 06510 Mechanisms of secretion from neurons and endocrine cells
R29MH-45195-03 (PCB) MYLES-WORSLEY, MARINA UNIVERSITY OF UTAH MEDICAL CTR 50 NORTH MEDICAL DR, DEPT/PSY SALT LAKE CITY, UT 84132 A genetic marker study of selective attention in schizophrenia
R01MH-45203-01A1 (PCB) KESHAVAN, MATCHERI S WESTERN PSYCHIATRIC INST/CLIN 3811 O'HARA STREET PITTSBURGH, PA 15213 EEG sleep and heterogeneity in schizophrenia

R01MH-45207-03 (LCR) MCEVOY, CATHY L UNIVERSITY OF SOUTH FLORIDA 13301 N BRUCE B DOWNS BLVD TAMPA, FL 33612 Prior knowledge effects in cognitive aging
R01MH-45208-02 (PCB) HANS, SYDNEY L UNIVERSITY OF CHICAGO HOSPITAL 5841 SO MARYLAND AVE, BOX 411 CHICAGO, IL 60637 Jerusalem infant development study--Adolescent follow-up
P01MH-45212-02 (SRCM) DAVIS, KENNETH L MT SINAI SCHOOL OF MEDICINE ONE GUSTAVE L LEVY PLACE/BX 12 NEW YORK, NY 10029 Cellular and molecular markers in schizophrenia
P01MH-45212-02 9003 (SRCM) SILVERMAN, JEREMY M Cellular and molecular markers in schizophrenia Core--Family study
P01MH-45212-02 0001 (SRCM) MOHS, RICHARD C Cellular and molecular markers in schizophrenia Linkage and segregation analysis
P01MH-45212-02 0002 (SRCM) MORRISON, JOHN H Cellular and molecular markers in schizophrenia Characterization of cortical dopamine target neurons
P01MH-45212-02 0003 (SRCM) BENES, FRANCINE M Cellular and molecular markers in schizophrenia Cortical morphology
P01MH-45212-02 0004 (SRCM) BLUM, MARIANN Cellular and molecular markers in schizophrenia Cloning and expression of gene for tyrosine hydroxylase
P01MH-45212-02 0005 (SRCM) ROBAKIS, NIKOLAOS K Cellular and molecular markers in schizophrenia Cloning, expression of gene for human dopamine D2 receptor
P01MH-45212-02 0006 (SRCM) ROBERTS, JAMES L Cellular and molecular markers in schizophrenia Cloning and expression of gene for rodent dopamine D2 receptor
P01MH-45212-02 0007 (SRCM) LANDAU, EMMANUAL M Cellular and molecular markers in schizophrenia Cloning, expression of dopamine D2 and CKK receptors
P01MH-45212-02 9001 (SRCM) PERL, DANIEL P Cellular and molecular markers in schizophrenia Core--Recruitment, assessment and neuropathology
P01MH-45212-02 9002 (SRCM) ROBERTS, JAMES L Cellular and molecular markers in schizophrenia Core--Molecular biology
R01MH-45216-03 (BPN) PLOTSKY, PAUL M SALK INSTITUTE FOR BIOL STUD P O BOX 85800 SAN DIEGO, CALIF 92138 Dexamethasone resistance--Neuroendocrine mechnisms
R01MH-45218-03 (EPS) KAUFMANN, CAROLINE L WESTERN PSYCHIATRIC INST/CLIN 3811 O'HARA STREET PITTSBURGH, PA 15213 Self help and severe mental illness
R01MH-45223-03 (BPN) WOJCIK, WALTER J GEORGETOWN UNIV MEDICAL CENTER 3900 RESERVOIR RD, NW WASHINGTON, DC 20007 Neuronal muscarinic receptor desensitization
R01MH-45225-01A2 (BPN) GLENNON, RICHARD A VIRGINIA COMMONWEALTH UNIV BOX 581-B MCV STATION RICHMOND, VA 23298-0581 Selective sigma ligands--Design synthesis and evaluation
R29MH-45232-02 (BPN) YOUNG, ELIZABETH A UNIVERSITY OF MICHIGAN 205 ZINA PITCHER PLACE ANN ARBOR, MI 48109-0720 Cortisol feedback in diurnal rhythm of HPA axis
R01MH-45237-04 (SRC) HALSEY, NEAL A JOHNS HOPKINS UNIVERSITY 615 NORTH WOLFE STREET BALTIMORE, MD 21205 HIV in street youth--Epidemiology and prevention
R01MH-45238-04 (SRC) O'LEARY, ANN M RUTGERS UNIVERSITY TILLETT HALL, KILMER CAMPUS NEW BRUNSWICK, NJ 08903 Social cognitive theory and AIDS prevention
R01MH-45242-02 (PCB) HALBREICH, URIEL ERIE COUNTY MEDICAL CENTER 462 GRIDER STREET BUFFALO, NY 14215 Menstrually related changes in cognitive function
R01MH-45244-03 (EPS) COSTELLO, ELIZABETH DUKE UNIV MEDICAL CENTER CHILD/ADOLESCENT PSYCHIATRY DURHAM, NC 27710 HMO and psychiatric child assessments--a follow-up study
R29MH-45245-03S1 (CEP) KANWISHER, NANCY G UNIV OF CALIFORNIA 405 HILGARD AVENUE LOS ANGELES, CA 90024-1563 Visual integration of type and token information
R29MH-45246-04 (BPN) LYTE, MARK MANKATO STATE UNIVERSITY MATH/BOX 34 MANKATO, MN 56001 Social conflict--Immunologic and endocrinologic consequences
R01MH-45252-03 (BPN) DRATMAN, MARY B MEDICAL COLL OF PENNSYLVANIA 3300 HENRY AVENUE PHILADELPHIA, PA 19129 Central iodothyronine kinetics-- Basic studies
R03MH-45253-01A2 (MSM) NORMAN, ANDREW B UNIVERSITY OF CINCINNATI 231 BETHESDA AVE/M L 559 CINCINNATI, OH 45267-0559 Pharmacology of striatal tissue transplants
R37MH-45265-03 (BPN) STONE, ERIC A NEW YORK UNIVERSITY MED CTR 550 FIRST AVE NEW YORK, NY 10016 Regulation of brain noradrenergic neurotransmission
R01MH-45268-03 (PCB) HEWITT, JOHN K MEDICAL COLLEGE OF VIRGINIA RICHMOND, VA 23298-0033 Adolescent behavioral development--Twin study
R01MH-45271-03 (BPN) ZIPSER, DAVID UNIV OF CALIF, SAN DIEGO 9500 GILMAN DRIVE LA JOLLA, CA 92093-0515 Back propagation technique-Modeling cortical computation
R44MH-45278-02A1 (MHSB) LANGMUIR, MARGARET E COVALENT ASSOCIATES, INC 52 DRAGON COURT WOBURN, MA 01801 Lipophilic Li+ ion fluorophores
R29MH-45286-04 (BPN) TEPPER, JAMES M RUTGERS, THE STATE UNIV OF N J 195 UNIVERSITY AVENUE NEWARK, N J 07102 Schizophrenia and afferent control of dopamine neurons
R01MH-45293-03 (LCR) ROVNER, BARRY W THOMAS JEFFERSON UNIVERSITY 1025 WALNUT STREET PHILADELPHIA, PA 19107 A randomized trial of dementia care in nursing homes
P50MH-45294-03 (SRCM) GRANT, IGOR UNIV OF CALIF, SAN DIEGO LA JOLLA, CA 92093 HIV neurobehavioral research center
P50MH-45294-03 0001 (SRCM) BUTLERS, NELSON HIV neurobehavioral research center Memory study
P50MH-45294-03 0002 (SRCM) DUPONT, RENEE HIV neurobehavioral research center SPECT/PET in HIV disease
P50MH-45294-03 0003 (SRCM) POLICH, JOHN M HIV neurobehavioral research center Magnetoencephalography
P50MH-45294-03 0004 (SRCM) PATTERSON, THOMAS HIV neurobehavioral research center Life events
P50MH-45294-03 0005 (SRCM) ZISOOK, SIDNEY HIV neurobehavioral research center Mood disorders--Treatment of HIV associated depression
P50MH-45294-03 0006 (SRCM) JESTE, DILIP V HIV neurobehavioral research center Psychotic symptoms in HIV disease
P50MH-45294-03 0007 (SRCM) WILEY, CLAYTON A HIV neurobehavioral research center Immune responsiveness, HLA phenotype & HIV encephalopathy in AIDS
P50MH-45294-03 9001 (SRCM) MCCUTCHAN, J ALLEN HIV neurobehavioral research center Medical core
P50MH-45294-03 9002 (SRCM) SPECTOR, STEPHEN HIV neurobehavioral research center Virology core
P50MH-45294-03 9003 (SRCM) THAL, LEON HIV neurobehavioral research center Neurology core
P50MH-45294-03 9005 (SRCM) HESSELINK, JOHN HIV neurobehavioral research center Imaging core
P50MH-45294-03 9006 (SRCM) POLICH, JOHN HIV neurobehavioral research center Electrophysiology core
P50MH-45294-03 9007 (SRCM) ATKINSON, J HAMPTON HIV neurobehavioral research center Psychodiagnostic core
P50MH-45294-03 9008 (SRCM) WILEY, CLAYTON HIV neurobehavioral research center Neuropathology core
P50MH-45294-03 9009 (SRCM) OLSHEN, RICHARD HIV neurobehavioral research center Data management/biostatistics core
P50MH-45294-03 9004 (SRCM) HEATON, ROBERT HIV neurobehavioral research center Neuropsychology core
R01MH-45306-03 (MHAZ) SLONIM-NEVO, VERED WASHINGTON UNVIERSITY ONE BROOKINGS DRIVE ST LOUIS, MO 63130 Aids prevention for teenagers in residential centers
R01MH-45311-02 (MHAZ) BECKER, JAMES T WESTERN PSYCHIATRIC INST & CLI 3811 O'HARA STREET PITTSBURGH, PA 15213 HIV-1 related neuropsychological abnormalities
R29MH-45323-02 (LCR) HAIGHT, BARBARA K MED UNIV OF SOUTH CAROLINA 171 ASHLEY AVENUE CHARLESTON, SC 29425-2404 Life review--Prevention of depression and suicidality
R01MH-45324-03 (BPN) STRYER, LUBERT STANFORD UNIVERSITY FAIRCHILD BUILDING D133 STANFORD, CA 94305 Mechanism of calcium spiking in signal transduction
R29MH-45334-03 (BPN) MALENKA, ROBERT C UNIV OF CA/L PORTER PSY INST 401 PARNASSUS AVE/BOX GMO-0984 SAN FRANCISCO, CA 94143 Mechanisms of synaptic plasticity in the hippocampus
R01MH-45341-03 (BPN) RYAN, LAWRENCE J OREGON STATE UNIVERSITY CORVALLIS, OR 97331-5303 Behavioral functions of neostriatal compartments
R01MH-45350-03 (BPN) WILCZYNSKI, WALTER UNIVERSITY OF TEXAS DEPT OF PSYCHOLOGY AUSTIN, TX 78712 Coordinating inputs to forebrain control centers
R01MH-45353-02 (PYB) LEON, MICHAEL A UNIVERSITY OF CALIFORNIA IRVINE, CA 92717 Glucose pathways and early learning
R01MH-45358-01A1 (TDA) GADOW, KENNETH D SUNY AT STONY BROOK SOUTH CAMPUS/PUTNAM HALL STONY BROOK, NY 11794-8790 Methylphenidate treatment of ADHD in children with Tourette syndrome
R01MH-45360-01A1 (CEP) DERRYBERRY, DOUGLAS A OREGON STATE UNIVERSITY CORVALLIS, OR 97331-2132 Components of temperamental reactivity
R29MH-45361-03 (BPN) BAGHDOYAN, HELEN A PENNSYLVANIA STATE UNIVERSITY PO BOX 850 HERSHEY, PA 17033 Cholinergic mechanisms of REM sleep generation
R29MH-45362-03 (BPN) SHEKHAR, ANANTHA INDIANA UNIVERSITY SCH OF MED 534 CLINICAL DR., CG 118 INDIANAPOLIS, IN 46202-5109 Neurobiological substrates of anxiety and panic disorder
R01MH-45364-01A2 (PCB) SCHOENFELD, FRANK B SAN FRANCISCO VA MEDICAL CTR 4150 CLEMENT ST (116C) SAN FRANCISCO, CA 94121 Leukodystrophic states in psychiatric patients
R01MH-45371-01A2 (PYB) LEWIS, MARK H UNIVERSITY OF NORTH CAROLINA CB#7250, RM 305 BSRC CHAPEL HILL, NC 27599-7250 Neurobiology of aggression--Genetics and development
R01MH-45372-03 (BPN) NEVE, KIM A VETERANS ADMINISTRATION MED CT 3710 SW US VETERAN HOSP RD PORTLAND, OR 97207 Desensitization of dopamine D-2 receptors
R01MH-45388-01A2 (CEP) HANSEN, RANALD D OAKLAND UNIVERSITY ROCHESTER, MI 48309-4401 Cognitive-emotive processes--Investigating repression
R01MH-45389-02 (LCR) CAMP, CAMERON J UNIVERSITY OF NEW ORLEANS LAKEFRONT NEW ORLEANS, LA 70148 Mental disorder in SDAT--Prospective memory intervention
R01MH-45390-03 (PCB) DIEHL, SCOTT R VIRGINIA COMMONWEALTH UNIVERSI PO BOX 710, MCV STATION RICHMOND, VA 23298-0710 Linkage studies of schizophrenia in Irish pedigrees
R03MH-45392-02 (MSM) BYSTRITSKY, ALEXANDER UNIV OF CALIF, LOS ANGELES 760 WESTWOOD PLAZA LOS ANGELES, CA 90024-1759 Subjective and physiological changes in panic patients
R01MH-45397-03 (BPN) KLEIN, MARC CLINICAL RES INST OF MONTREAL 110 PINE AVENUE WEST MONTREAL, QUEBEC H2W 1R7 CANAD Cellular mechanisms of learning in aplysia
R01MH-45401-03 (PYB) VANDENBERGH, JOHN G NORTH CAROLINA STATE UNIVERSIT DEPT OF ZOOLOGY RALEIGH, NC 27695-7617 Perinatal factors influencing puberty
R01MH-45402-03 (CEP) HUTTENLOCHER, JANELLEN UNIVERSITY OF CHICAGO 5835 SOUTH KIMBARK AVENUE CHICAGO, IL 60637 Estimating when events occurred
R01MH-45404-02 (TDA) FOA, EDNA B MEDICAL COLL OF PENNSYLVANIA 3300 HENRY AVENUE PHILADELPHIA, PA 19129 Chlorimipramine and behavior therapy in OCD
R01MH-45417-02 (BSR) RUSBULT, CARYL E UNIVERSITY OF NORTH CAROLINA CAMPUS BOX #3270 CHAPEL HILL, NC 27599-3270 A longitudinal study of accommodation processes in marriage
R01MH-45423-03 (BPN) ZARE, RICHARD N STANFORD UNIVERSITY STANFORD, CA 94305 Capillary electrophoresis analysis of single neurons
R01MH-45424-02 (TDA) RYAN, NEAL D WESTERN PSYCHIATRIC INST & CLI 3811 O'HARA STREET PITTSBURGH, PA 15213 Imipramine treatment of school refusal
R01MH-45431-02 (EPS) TAYLOR, CRAIG B STANFORD UNIVERSITY MED CTR STANFORD, CA 94305-5490 A prospective study of panic attacks in adolescents
R01MH-45436-02 (TDA) LIEBOWITZ, MICHAEL R COLUMBIA UNIVERSITY

PROJECT NO., ORGANIZATIONAL UNIT., INVESTIGATOR, ADDRESS, TITLE

630 WEST 168 STREET NEW YORK, NY 10032 Chlorimipramine and behavior therapy for OCD
R01MH-45437-01A2 (LCR) SPELTZ, MATTHEW L UNIVERSITY OF WASHINGTON MAILSTOP ZC-10 SEATTLE, WA 98195 Developmental risk for disruptive behavior disorders
R29MH-45441-02 (EPS) DEGRUY, FRANK V, III USA FAMILY PRACTICE CLINIC 1504 SPRINGHILL AVENUE MOBILE, AL 36604 Somatization in primary care
R29MH-45448-02 (PCB) LENZENWEGER, MARK FRANCIS CORNELL UNIVERSITY ITHACA, NY 14853-4401 Longitudinal study of personality disorders
R29MH-45454-02 (CVR) KRAKOWSKI, MENACHEM I NATHAN KLINE INSTITUTE OLD ORANGEBURG ROAD ORANGEBURG, NY 10962 Inpatient violence trait and state
R29MH-45458-01A1 (PCB) GARBER, JUDY VANDERBILT UNIVERSITY BOX 512 PEABODY COLLEGE NASHVILLE, TN 37203 Development of depression in children and adolescents
R29MH-45465-02 (TDA) JANICAK, PHILIP G ILLINOIS STATE PSYCHIATRIC INS 1601 WEST TAYLOR STREET CHICAGO, IL 60612 Targeted haldol levels, HVA changes and clinical effect
R01MH-45466-01A2 (PCB) JIMERSON, DAVID C BETH ISRAEL HOSPITAL 330 BROOKLINE AVENUE BOSTON, MA 02215 Serotonin function in patients with eating disorders
R01MH-45470-03 (ARR) LEVY, SUSAN R UNIVERSITY OF ILLINOIS PO BOX 6998 CHICAGO, IL 60612 Youth aids prevention project
R01MH-45472-02 (BPN) TEJANI-BUTT, SHANAZ M VA MEDICAL CENTER UNIVERSITY AND WOODLAND AVE PHILADELPHIA, PA 19104 Radioligands for central noradrenergic uptake sites
R01MH-45480-03 (BPN) GABRIEL, STEVEN M BRONX VA MEDICAL CENTER 130 W KINGSBRIDGE ROAD BRONX, NY 10468 Hypothalamic neuropeptides and schizophrenia
R29MH-45481-03 (BPN) DUMAN, RONALD S YALE UNIVERSITY 34 PARK STREET NEW HAVEN, CT 06508 Antidepressants--Signal transduction and gene expression
R01MH-45484-02 (CVR) KLASSEN, DEIDRE GR KANSAS CITY MENT HLTH FDN 2055 HOLMES KANSAS CITY, MO 64108 Assessing the risk of violence in mental patients
R01MH-45486-03 (PCB) GELLER, BARBARA W S HALL PSYCHIATRIC INSTITUTE 4940 AUDUBON AVENUE ST LOUIS, MO 63110 Lithium in pediatric mood disorders
R01MH-45488-03 (PCB) STOCKMEIER, CRAIG A CASE WESTERN RESERVE UNIV 2040 ABINGTON RD CLEVELAND, OH 44106 Serotonin receptors in suicides with psychiatric autopsy
R01MH-45491-01A1 (LCR) ZILL, NICHOLAS CHILD TRENDS, INC 2100 M STREET, NORTWEST WASHINGTON, DC 20037 Marital conflict/disruption--Long-term effects on youth
R29MH-45493-03 (BPN) ZORUMSKI, CHARLES F WASHINGTON UNIVERSITY 660 SOUTH EUCLID AVE - BX 8134 ST LOUIS, MO 63110 Desensitization of non-NMDA glutamate receptors
R01MH-45501-02 (PCB) CLARK, DAVID C RUSH-PRESBYTERIAN-ST LUKE'S CT 1720 WEST POLK STREET CHICAGO, IL 60612 Affective disorder, substance abuse, teen suicide & health care utilization
R37MH-45507-03 (BPN) LEVITT, PAT R MED COLLEGE OF PENNSYLVANIA 3200 HENRY AVENUE PHILADELPHIA, PA 19129 Factors regulating limbic system assembly
R01MH-45522-02 (PCB) REICH, THEODORE WASHINGTON UNIVERSITY 660 S EUCLID AVE, BOX 8134 ST LOUIS, MO 63110 Bipolar genetic linkage--Two large extended pedigrees
R01MH-45527-02 (LCR) BELSKY, JAY PENNSYLVANIA STATE UNIVERSITY UNIVERSITY PARK, PA 16802 Parental representations of attachment
R01MH-45530-03 (BPN) O'MALLEY, KAREN L WASHINGTON UNIVERSITY 660 SOUTH EUCLID AVENUE ST LOUIS, MO 63110 Transcriptional control of neuroendocrine genes
R01MH-45531-02 (BSR) GILOVICH, THOMAS D CORNELL UNIVERSITY URIS HALL ITHACA, NY 14853 Ambiguity resolution & perceptions of social consensus
R01MH-45532-03 (CVR) CAIRNS, ROBERT B UNIVERSITY OF NORTH CAROLINA DAVIE HALL CB#3270 CHAPEL HILL, NC 27514 Antisocial and violent behavior--Longitudinal sequelae
R01MH-45533-03 (BPN) REISINE, TERRY D UNVI OF PENN 36TH ST & HAMILTON WALK PHILADELPHIA, PA 19104 Biochemical properties of somatostatin receptors
R01MH-45534-01A1 (PCB) WELLER, ELIZABETH B OHIO STATE UNIVERSITY 473 W 12TH AVENUE COLUMBUS, OH 43210 Psychopathology & grief in teenagers post-parental death
R01MH-45545-03 (PYB) WEISS, STANLEY J AMERICAN UNIVERSITY 4400 MASSACHUSETTS AVE NW WASHINGTON, D C 20016 Preference and selective associations
R01MH-45547-02 (LCR) TRONICK, EDWARD Z CHILDREN'S HOSPITAL CORP 300 LONGWOOD AVENUE BOSTON, MA 02115 Depressive symptoms and mother-infant interaction
R01MH-45548-03 (CVR) MOFFITT, TERRIE E UNIVERSITY OF WISCONSIN 1202 WEST JOHNSON STREET MADISON, WI 53706 Neuropsychology, behavior disorder & delinquency risk
R01MH-45557-01A1 (BSR) TROPE, YAACOV NEW YORK UNIVERSITY 6 WASHINGTON PLACE NEW YORK, NY 10003 Identification and inference in dispositional judgement
R01MH-45566-02 (BSR) BOGGIANO, ANN K UNIVERSITY OF COLORADO CAMPUS BOX 345 BOULDER, CO 80309-0345 Social situational determinants of helplessness
R37MH-45573-03 (BPN) HABER, SUZANNE UNIV OF ROCHESTER SCHL OF MED 601 ELMWOOD AVE, BOX 603 ROCHESTER, NEW YORK 14642 Continuity of limbic circuit through the basal ganglia
R01MH-45583-02 (CVR) TEPLIN, LINDA A NORTHWESTERN MEMORIAL HOSPITAL 215 E CHICAGO AVE CHICAGO, IL 60611 Mental disorder in an urban jail
R29MH-45584-03 (CEP) PASHLER, HAROLD E UNIV OF CALIFORNIA, SAN DIEGO DEPT OF PSYCHOLOGY LA JOLLA, CA 92093-0109 Perceptual and cognitive components in dual-task interference
R29MH-45585-03 (CEP) WATTENMAKER, WILLIAM D UNIVERSITY OF PITTSBURGH 3939 O'HARA STREET PITTSBURGH, PA 15260 Memory-based concept formation
R01MH-45588-03 (SRCM) PULVER, ANN E JOHNS HOPKINS-SCH OF MED 720 RUTLAND AVE BALTIMORE, MD 21205 Genetic-epidemiologic studies of schizophrenia
R03MH-45591-02 (MSM) DOMAR, ALICE D NEW ENGLAND DEACONESS HOSPITAL 185 PILGRIM ROAD BOSTON, MA 02215-5399 An assessment of depression in infertile women
R03MH-45604-02 (MSM) EMERY, DENNIS G IOWA STATE UNIVERSITY AMES, IA 50011 Response of cultured mollusk neurons to injury
R03MH-45610-02 (MSM) GRANT, STEVEN J UNIVERSITY OF DELAWARE NEWARK, DE 19716 Extracellular activity of brainstem cholinergic neurons
R01MH-45614-03 (NEUC) CIVELLI, OLIVIER OREGON HEALTH SCIENCES UNIV 3181 S W SAM JACKSON PK RD PORTLAND, OR 97201 Cloning and expression of a new neuroreceptor
R03MH-45617-03 (MSM) JACOBS, LUCIA F UNIVERSITY OF UTAH SALT LAKE CITY, UT 84112 Spatial memory and hippocampal anatomy--Natural patterns
R03MH-45640-01A1 (MHAZ) O'BRIEN, CAROLEEN J PORTLAND STATE UNIVERSITY PO BOX 751 PORTLAND, OR 97207-0751 Social relationships of men at risk for AIDS
R01MH-45641-03 (MHAZ) DEWS, PETER B HARVARD MEDICAL SCHOOL 25 SHATTUCK STREET BOSTON, MA 02115 Neurobehavioral effects of simian AIDS
R01MH-45647-03 (MHAZ) SACKS, MICHAEL H NEW YORK HOSPITAL 525 EAST 68TH STREET NEW YORK, NY 10021 HIV risk/prevalence/CNS effects in psychiatric patients
R01MH-45649-03 (MHAZ) BORNSTEIN, ROBERT A OHIO STATE UNIVERSITY 473 W 12TH AVE COLUMBUS, OH 43210 Neurobehavioral deficit and psychopathology in HIV+ men
R01MH-45651-02 (MHAZ) BIGLAN, ANTHONY OREGON RESEARCH INSTITUTE 1899 WILLAMETTE EUGENE, OREG 97401 Social competence and prevention of high risk sexual behavior
R01MH-45652-03 (MHAZ) RABKIN, JUDITH G RES FDN FOR MENTAL HYGIENE 722 WEST 168TH STREET NEW YORK, NY 10032 Imipramine effects on depression and immune status in HIV
R01MH-45654-02 (MHAZ) WITTNER, MURRAY ALBERT EINSTEIN COLL OF MED 1300 MORRIS PARK AVENUE BRONX, NY 10461 Mental and behavioral manifestations in AIDS encephalitis
R01MH-45664-03 (MHAZ) BREITBART, WILLIAM MEMORIAL HOSPITAL 1275 YORK AVENUE NEW YORK, NY 10021 Pharmacological management of AIDS delirium
R01MH-45668-01A2 (MHAZ) JEMMOTT, JOHN B, III PRINCETON UNIVERSITY PRINCETON, NJ 08544-1010 AIDS and adolescents--Risk reduction by behavior intervention
R01MH-45669-02 (MHAZ) HOBFOLL, STEVAN E KENT STATE UNIVERSITY KENT, OH 44242 AIDS prevention among young inner-city women
R01MH-45679-03 (MHAZ) ZWILLING, BRUCE S OHIO STATE UNIVERSITY 484 WEST 12TH AVENUE COLUMBUS, OH 43210-1292 Restraint stress--suppression of IA expression
R01MH-45680-02 (MHAZ) FEIN, GEORGE SAN FRANCISCO VA MEDICAL CENTE 4150 CLEMENT STREET SAN FRANCISCO, CA 94121 In-vivo brain phosphorus metabolism in AIDS dementia
R01MH-45681-03 (MHAZ) MOYNIHAN, JAN A UNIV OF ROCHESTER MED CTR 300 CRITTENDEN BLVD BOX PSYCH ROCHESTER, NY 14642 Stress-induced modulation of immune function
R01MH-45686-01A2 (MHAZ) SACKS, HENRY S MOUNT SINAI MEDICAL CENTER 1 GUSTAVE L LEVY PLACE NEW YORK, NY 10029 Meta-analysis of the AIDS literature
R29MH-45688-03 (MHAZ) SIEBURG, HANS B UNIVERSITY OF CALIFORNIA 9500 GILMAN DR LA JOLLA, CA 92093-0603 Object-oriented simulation of HIV- and CNS/HIV infection
R44MH-45692-03 (SRCM) NEUMEYER, JOHN L RESEARCH BIOCHEMICALS, INC 1 STRATHMORE RD NATICK, MA 01760 Affinity labels for dopamine receptors
R01MH-45696-02 (CEP) SERGENT, JUSTINE MONTREAL NEUROLOGICAL INSTITUT 3801 UNIVERSITY ST MONTREAL, CANADA H3A 2B4 Hemispheric cooperation and specialization
R01MH-45700-01A1 (CVR) HALL, GORDON C KENT STATE UNIVERSITY KENT, OH 44242-0001 Sexual aggression against children--Quadripartite model
R01MH-45714-01A1 (TDA) BARKLEY, RUSSELL A UNIV OF MASSACHUSETTS MED CENT 55 LAKE AVENUE NORTH WORCESTER, MA 01655 Multi-method intervention with aggressive adhd children
R01MH-45719-02 (BSR) NEUBERG, STEVEN L ARIZONA STATE UNIVERSITY TEMPE, AZ 85287 Social goals as moderators of expectancy confirmation
R01MH-45722-01A2 (LCR) HEINICKE, CHRISTOPH M UNIVERSITY OF CALIFORNIA 760 WESTWOOD PLAZA LOS ANGELES, CA 90024-1759 Family status and outcomes of preventive intervention
R01MH-45729-01A1 (PCB) KARSON, CRAIG N VA MEDICAL CENTER 4300 W 7TH ST LITTLE ROCK, AR 72205 Brain stem reticular formation in schizophrenia
R03MH-45731-02 (MSM) HARVER, ANDREW R UNIVERSITY OF NORTH CAROLINA CHARLOTTE, NC 28223 Biobehavioral correlates of added loads in lung disease
R44MH-45735-03 (MHSB) FISCHER, JAMES B CAMBRIDGE NEUROSCIENCE RES, IN ONE KENDALL SQUARE CAMBRIDGE, MA 02139 Ditolyl guanidine analogs as antipsychotic drugs
R01MH-45750-01A1 (EPS) BROADHEAD, WALTER E DUKE UNIV MED CTR BOX 2914 DURHAM, NC 27710 Services outcomes of minor depression in primary care
R01MH-45752-02 (SRCM) STANTON, PATRIC K ALBERT EINSTEIN COLLEGE OF MED 1300 MORRIS PARK AVE BRONX, NY 10461 Cellular mechanism of hippocampal long-term depression
R01MH-45754-03 (MHAZ) LEWIS, MARY ANN UNIV OF CALIF, LOS ANGELES 3-246 FACTOR BUILDING LOS ANGELES, CA 90024-1702 Impact of AIDs on dependent infants of the court
R01MH-45757-01A1 (PCB) KLEIN, DANIEL N SUNY AT STONY BROOK STONY BROOK, NY 11794-2500 Classification of early-onset dysthymia
R01MH-45763-01A1 (EPS) SHROUT, PATRICK E COLUMBIA UNIVERSITY 600 WEST 168TH ST/5TH FLOOR NEW YORK, N Y 10032-3799 Statistical issues in mental health epidemiology
R29MH-45764-02 (CEP) PALMER, CAROLINE M THE OHIO STATE UNIVERSITY 1885 NEIL AVENUE COLUMBUS, OH 43210 Constraints on cognitive theories of performance
R03MH-45767-02 (MSM) BRUMAGHIM, JOAN T UNIVERSITY OF ROCHESTER

PROJECT NO., ORGANIZATIONAL UNIT., INVESTIGATOR, ADDRESS, TITLE

ROCHESTER, NY 14627 P3 latency and response processing effects
R01MH-45779-02 (LCR) OXMAN, THOMAS E DARTMOUTH MEDICAL SCHOOL 9 MAYNARD STREET HANOVER, NH 03756 Age, social support and physical & emotional disability
R01MH-45780-03 (LCR) COHEN, CARL I ST UNIV OF NEW YORK HLTH SCI C 450 CLARKSON AVE, BOX 1203 BROOKLYN, NY 11203 Older homeless women
R01MH-45787-01A1 (PCB) STAHL, STEPHEN M UNIVERSITY OF CALIFORNIA 3350 LA JOLLA VILLAGE DR LA JOLLA, CA 92093-0603 Human 5ht receptor regulation by antidepressants
R29MH-45789-02 (EPS) GUARNACCIA, PETER J RUTGERS UNIVERSITY 30 COLLEGE AVE NEW BRUNSWICK, NJ 08903 Cultural categories and cross-cultural psychiatric research
R03MH-45791-02 (MSM) BADGER, LEE W UNIVERSITY OF ALABAMA PO BOX 870378 TUSCALOOSA, AL 35487-0378 Predictors of psychiatric underdiagnosis
R01MH-45796-01A2 (SRCM) MOORE, LEE E UNIV OF TEXAS MEDICAL BRANCH 301 UNIVERSITY BOULEVARD GALVESTON, TEXAS 77550-2774 Network simulation of a locomotion neural circuit
R29MH-45800-01A1 (PCB) STRAUMAN, TIMOTHY J UNIVERSITY OF WISCONSIN 1202 W JOHNSON ST MADISON, WI 53706 Anxiogenic self-beliefs in generalized anxiety disorder
R01MH-45812-02 (BPN) VAN DE KAR, LOUIS D LOYOLA UNIVERSITY OF CHICAGO 2160 SOUTH FIRST STREET MAYWOOD, IL 60153 Vasopressin as a neuroendocrine marker in depression
R01MH-45815-02 (EPS) SCHULBERG, HERBERT C WESTERN PSYCHIATRIC INST 3811 O'HARA STREET PITTSBURGH, PA 15213 Transferring care specialist to generalist settings
R29MH-45817-02 (BPN) JOHNSON, JON W UNIVERSITY OF PITTSBURGH PITTSBURGH, PA 15260 Properties and regulation of glutamate receptors
R01MH-45827-02 (PCB) FAIRBANK, JOHN A RESEARCH TRIANGLE INSTITUTE 3040 CORNWALLIS ROAD RESEARCH TRIANGLE PARK, NC 277 Toward DSM-IV–PTSD as a diagnostic entity
R01MH-45830-02 (LCR) FURMAN, WYNDOL C UNIV OF DENVER 2155 S. RACE ST DENVER, CO 80208-0198 Implementing classroom-based peer intervention programs
R01MH-45834-01A1 (EPS) WHITAKER, AGNES H RES FOUNDATION MENTAL HYGIENE 722 WEST 168TH STREET NEW YORK, NY 10032 Epidemiology of early CNS injury and behavior problems
R01MH-45836-01A3 (PYB) CARTER, C SUE UNIVERSITY OF MARYLAND COLLEGE PARK, MD 20742 Hormones and social bonding
R01MH-45838-01A1 (PCB) HENDREN, ROBERT L UNIV OF NEW MEXICO SCH OF MED 2400 TUCKER NE ALBUQUERQUE, NM 87131 Neuropsychophysiologic study-severely disturbed children
R01MH-45840-01A1 (LCR) MONTGOMERY, RHONDA J WAYNE STATE UNIVERSITY 71 C EAST FERRY DETROIT, MI 48202 Targeting respite to promote mental health of Alzheimer families
R29MH-45841-02 (EPS) GAYNOR, MARTIN S JOHNS HOPKINS UNIVERSITY 615 NORTH WOLFE STREET BALTIMORE, MD 21205 Public mental health care--incentives and privatization
R03MH-45847-01A2 (MSM) HOLTGRAVES, THOMAS M BALL STATE UNIVERSITY 2000 UNIVERSITY AVENUE MUNCIE, IN 47306-0520 Social cognition and language processing
R01MH-45856-02 (SRCM) STADDON, JOHN E DUKE UNIVERSITY DURHAM, NC 27706 Models for learning memory and inference
R01MH-45862-02 (PYB) REDEI, EVA UNIVERSITY OF PENNSYLVANIA CLINICAL RESEARCH BLDG PHILADELPHIA, PA 19104-6141 Ovarian function, ACTH regulation and the stress response
R01MH-45863-02 (PYB) WASSER, SAMUEL K SMITHSONIAN CONSERVATION RES C NATIONAL ZOOLOGICAL PARK FRONT ROYAL, VA 22630 Noninvasive measures of stress and reproductive steroids
R01MH-45889-02 (BSR) STEELE, CLAUDE M STANFORD UNIVERSITY STANFORD, CA 94305-2130 Protective dis-identification and academic performance
R01MH-45891-01A1 (PYB) ROSENBLATT, JAY S INSTITUTE OF ANIMAL BEHAVIOR 101 WARREN STREET NEWARK, NJ 07102 Psychobiology of maternal behavior
R01MH-45908-02 (PCB) FLANAGAN, STEVEN D BECKMAN RESEARCH INSTITUTE 1450 EAST DUARTE ROAD DUARTE, CA 91010 Dopamine receptor genes--locus for schizophrenia?
R01MH-45916-02 (PCB) HAGERMAN, RANDI J THE CHILDREN'S HOSPITAL 1056 E 19TH AVE DENVER, CO 80218 Neurocoginitive,emotional and phenotype of fragile x females
R01MH-45918-01A1 (LCR) NOELKER, LINDA S BENJAMIN ROSE INSTITUTE 1422 EUCLID AVENUE CLEVELAND, OH 44115-1989 Service use by impaired elderly and informal caregivers
R37MH-45923-02 (BPN) KANDEL, ERIC R COLUMBIA UNIVERSITY CTR OF NEUROBIOLOGY & BEHAVIOR NEW YORK, NY 10032 Molecular biological approach to LTP in the hippocampus
R29MH-45926-02 (BPN) MOTA DE FREITAS, DUARTE E LOYOLA UNIVERSITY OF CHICAGO 6525 N SHERIDAN ROAD CHICAGO, IL 60626 NMR study of lithium interactions in human erythrocytes
R29MH-45931-03 (BPN) FUCHS, BRUCE A VIRGINIA COMMONWEALTH UNIV BOX 613, MCV STATION RICHMOND, VA 23298-0613 Neuroimmunomodulation by the sympathetic nervous system
R01MH-45945-02 (PCB) CARSKADON, MARY A E.P. BRADLEY HOSPITAL 1011 VETERANS MEMORIAL PARKWAY EAST PROVIDENCE, RI 02915 Sleep patterns and waking vulnerabilities in adolescents
R01MH-45951-02 (BPN) YONGUE, BRANDON G N Y STATE PSYCHIATRIC INST 722 W 168TH STREET NEW YORK, N Y 10032 Neurohormonal control of salt appetite and blood pressure
R29MH-45959-01A2 (PCB) CALIGIURI, MICHAEL P UNIV OF CALIF, SAN DIEGO LA JOLLA, CA 92093 Quantitative studies of neuroleptic-induced Parkinsonism
R29MH-45961-01A2 (BPN) BURDETTE, LINDA J GRADUATE HOSPITAL 415 SOUTH 19TH STREET PHILADELPHIA, PA 19146 Role of protein kinase C in synaptic plasticity
R01MH-45962-02 (PCB) POTKIN, STEVEN G UNIVERSITY OF CALIFORNIA 101 CITY DRIVE SOUTH, RT 88 ORANGE, CA 92668 Treatment-resistant schizophrenia--Pet and EEG studies
R01MH-45963-02 (TDA) GORMAN, JACK M HILLSIDE HOSPITAL, PHOBIA CLIN 75-59 263RD STREET GLEN OAKS, NY 11004 Multicenter comparative treatment study of panic disorder
R01MH-45964-02 (TDA) SHEAR, M KATHERINE PAYNE WHITNEY CLINIC 525 E 68TH STREET NEW YORK, N Y 10021 Multi-center comparative treatment study of panic disorder

PROJECT NO., ORGANIZATIONAL UNIT., INVESTIGATOR, ADDRESS, TITLE

R01MH-45965-02 (TDA) BARLOW, DAVID H STATE UNIVERSITY OF NEW YORK 1400 WASHINGTON AVENUE ALBANY, NY 12222 Multi-center comparative treatment study of panic disorder
R01MH-45966-02 (TDA) WOODS, SCOTT W CONNECTICUT MENTAL HEALTH CTR 34 PARK STREET NEW HAVEN, CT 06519 Multi-center comparative treatment study of panic disorder
R01MH-45968-02 (PCB) ZUBENKO, GEORGE S WESTERN PSYCHIATRIC INST 3811 O'HARA STREET PITTSBURGH, PA 15213 Genetics of the pmf locus primary dementia
R01MH-45969-02 (SRCM) SCHWARTZ, ERIC L NYU MEDICAL CENTER 550 FIRST AVENUE NEW YORK, NY 10016 Quantitative modeling of cortical architecture
R01MH-45975-01 (BPN) BISSETTE, GARTH DUKE UNIVERSITY MEDICAL CENTER BOX 3859 DURHAM, NC 27710 TRH in thermoregulation and depression--Basic and clinical
R01MH-45979-01A1 (PYB) ZENTALL, THOMAS R UNIVERSITY OF KENTUCKY LEXINGTON, KY 40506 Anticipation effects in animal memory
R01MH-45988-02 (TDA) GREENBERG, JAN R UNIVERSITY OF WISCONSIN 425 HENRY MALL MADISON, WI 53706 Caregiver burden and services for the mentally ill
R01MH-45994-02 (LCR) MISCHEL, WALTER COLUMBIA UNIVERSITY 406 SCHERMERHORN HALL NEW YORK, NY 10027 Children's self-regulatory competencies in risk prevention
R29MH-45999-02 (EPS) NESTADT, GERALD JOHNS HOPKINS HOSPITAL 600 N WOLFE ST BALTIMORE, MD 21205 Characterization of personality disorders
R01MH-46001-02 (PCB) KAYE, WALTER H WESTERN PSYCHIATRIC INST & CLI 3811 O'HARA STREET PITTSBURGH, PA 15213 Serotonin--Trait related disturbance in anorexia nervosa
R01MH-46003-02 (LCR) HOCK, ELLEN I OHIO STATE UNIVERSITY 1787 NEIL AVENUE COLUMBUS, OH 43210 Determinants and correlates of maternal depression
R01MH-46005-02 (SRCM) SCHLESINGER, HERBERT J NEW SCHOOL FOR SOCIAL RESEARCH 65 FIFTH AVE NEW YORK, N Y 10003 Minorities' use of mental health and medical services
R01MH-46011-02 (EPS) WOOLSON, ROBERT F UNIVERSITY OF IOWA DEPT OF PREVENTIVE MEDICINE IOWA CITY, IA 52242 Psychiatric epidemiology--Longitudinal study methodology
R01MH-46014-02 (EPS) MEDNICK, SARNOFF A UNIV OF SOUTHERN CALIFORNIA UNIVERSITY PARK LOS ANGELES, CA 90089-1111 Obstetrical complications and adult schizophrenia
R29MH-46036-02 (BPN) BRINTON, ROBERTA E UNIV OF SOUTHERN CALIFORNIA 1985 ZONAL AVE LOS ANGELES, CA 90033 Neuromodulation--Biochemical analog of associative event
R29MH-46040-02 (BPN) FOCHTMANN, LAURA J STATE UNIVERSITY OF NEW YORK SCHOOL OF MEDICINE STONY BROOK, NY 11794-8101 Receptors, calcium and mechanisms of ECT
R03MH-46048-01A1 (MSM) BELGRAVE, FAYE Z GEORGE WASHINGTON UNIVERSITY 2125 G STREET WASHINGTON, DC 20052 Social support and outcomes of disabled Black persons
R29MH-46057-02 (LCR) BURTON, LINDA M PENNSYLVANIA STATE UNIVERSITY BEECHER HOUSE UNIVERSITY PARK, PA 16802 Teen pregnancy, socioeconomic context, and family transitions
R18MH-46059-03 (SRCM) RALPH, RUTH O CASE MANAGEMENT RESEARCH PROJ 222 ST. JOHN ST, 18G PORTLAND, ME 04102 Controlled study of two case management models
R18MH-46060-03 (SRCM) MILLER, LARRY D INDIANA DEPT OF MENTAL HEALTH 117 E WASHINGTON ST INDIANAPOLIS, IN 46204-3647 Rural assertive community treatment project
R18MH-46061-02 (SRCM) MEISLER, NEIL DELAWARE DPT OF HLTH & SOC SRV 1901 NORTH DUPONT HIGHWAY NEW CASTLE, DE 19720 Restructuring existing CMHC clinic services--Case management models
R18MH-46062-03 (SRCM) ESSOCK, SUSAN M CONN DEPT OF MENTAL HEALTH 90 WASHINGTON STREET HARTFORD, CT 06106 Experimental analysis of assertive community treatment
R18MH-46065-03 (SRCM) PENNINGTON, MARGARET A CABINET FOR HUMAN RESOURCES 275 EAST MAIN STREET FRANKFORT, KY 40621 Consumer providers in crisis response systems
R18MH-46070-02 (SRCM) FRASER, MARY E UTAH DIVISION OF MENTAL HEALTH 120 NORTH 200 WEST SALT LAKE CITY, UT 84103 Community services demonstration project
R18MH-46072-03 (SRCM) DRAKE, ROBERT E STATE OFFICE PARK SOUTH 105 PLEASANT STREET CONCORD, NH 03301 Assertive case management for dually diagnosed clients
R01MH-46078-03 (SRCM) LANDSVERK, JOHN A SAN DIEGO STATE UNIVERSITY DEPT OF SOCIOLOGY SAN DIEGO, CA 92182 Screening impact on services & costs for foster children
R18MH-46081-03 (SRCM) MOWBRAY, CAROL T WAYNE STATE UNIVERSITY 4756 CASS AVENUE DETROIT, MI 48202 Enhancing vocational opportunities
R18MH-46082-03 (SRCM) DEAN-JOHNSON, BARBARA A PENNSYLVANIA DEPT OF MENTAL HL 1401 N. 7TH STREET HARRISBURG, PA 17102-1422 MH services demonstration grants (csp for adults)
R01MH-46093-02 (SRCM) ACHENBACH, THOMAS M UNIVERSITY OF VERMONT DEGOESBRIAND BUILDING BURLINGTON, VT 05405 Outcomes of clinical referrals for children and youth
R01MH-46095-01A2 (BPN) BLUSZTAJN, JAN K BOSTON UNIVERSITY 85 EAST NEWTON ST,RM M1009 BOSTON, MA 02118 Acetylcholine synthesis and release in cultured cells
R01MH-46096-01A2 (SRCM) TORO, PAUL A STATE UNIVERSITY OF NEW YORK PARK HALL BUFFALO, NY 14260 Paths out of homelessness among the mentally ill
R01MH-46097-02 (SRCM) NEWMAN, SANDRA J JOHNS HOPKINS UNIVERSITY INSTITUTE FOR POLICY STUDIES BALTIMORE, MD 21218 The cost of developing housing for the mentally ill
R01MH-46104-03 (SRCM) ROBERSTON, MARJORIE J MED RES INST OF SAN FRANCISCO 1816 SCENIC AVENUE BERKELEY, CA 94709 Mental illness, service use and homeless careers
R01MH-46106-03 (SRCM) FISCHER, PAMELA J THE JOHN HOPKINS HOSPITAL 600 NORTH WOLFE STREET BALTIMORE, MD 21205 Women & children in continuum of residential stability
R01MH-46111-02S1 (SRCM) TOOMEY, BEVERLY G OHIO STATE UNIVERSITY

1960 KENNY ROAD COLUMBUS, OHIO 43210-1063 Rural homelessness in Ohio--Five-year replication study

R01MH-46116-02 (SRCM) **SHINN, MARYBETH** NEW YORK UNIVERSITY 6 WASHINGTON PLACE NEW YORK, NY 10003 Dynamics of homelessness and mental illness in families

R01MH-46121-03 (SRCM) **BURNAM, M AUDREY** RAND CORPORATION 1700 MAIN STREET SANTA MONICA, CA 90407-2138 Course of homelessness among the seriously mentally ill

R01MH-46122-03 (SRCM) **ATTKISSON, C CLIFFORD** UNIVERSITY OF CALIFORNIA 401 PARNASSUS AVENUE SAN FRANCISCO, CA 94143-0984 Clinical epidemiology in three systems of care for youth

R01MH-46124-03 (SRCM) **GLISSON, CHARLES A** UNIV OF TENNESSEE 308 HENSON HALL KNOXVILLE, TN 37996-3333 Coordinating mental health services to children

R01MH-46130-02 (SRCM) **STRUENING, ELMER L** RES FDN FOR MENT HYGIENE 722 WEST 168TH ST NEW YORK, NY 10032 A follow-up study of homeless adult shelter residents

R01MH-46132-02 (LCR) **SAN AGUSTIN, MUTYA** NORTH CENTRAL BRONX HOSPITAL 3424 KOSSUTH AVENUE BRONX, N Y 10467 Emotional development & cognition in homeless children

R01MH-46134-03 (SRCM) **WISSOW, LAWRENCE S** JOHNS HOPKINS HOSPITAL 600 N WOLFE ST BALTIMORE, MD 21205 Physician interview style & detection of child abuse

R01MH-46136-03 (SRCM) **BICKMAN, LEONARD** VANDERBILT UNIVERSITY HOBBS BLDG, RM 205 NASHVILLE, TN 37203 Assessing treatment effectiveness and family empowerment

R18MH-46140-04 (SRCM) **BLANCH, ANDREA K** NEW YORK ST OFFICE MNTL HLTH 44 HOLLAND AVENUE ALBANY, N Y 12229 Peer specialists as members of intensive case management teams

R01MH-46141-02 (CEP) **PALMER, STEPHEN E** UNIVERSITY OF CALIFORNIA BERKELEY, CA 94720 Frames of reference in visual perception

R18MH-46145-03 (SRCM) **LILLEY, GEORGE WOOD, JR** WEST VIRGINIA DPT OF HEALTH 1900 KANAWHA BLVD., EAST CHARLESTON, WV 25305 Csp community services demonstration project

R18MH-46146-03 (SRCM) **STONEKING, BETH** L.C.S.W SACRAMENTO COUNTY M H 4875 BROADWAY SAXRAMENTO, CA 95820 CSP consumer case management project

R44MH-46152-02 (SRCM) **NEUMEYER, JOHN L** RESEARCH BIOCHEMICALS, INC 1 STRATHMORE ROAD NATICK, MA 01760 Fluorescent probes for brain serotonin receptors

R43MH-46153-01A2 (MHSB) **WILSON, SCOTT B** PERSYST CONSULTING SERVICES, I 139 OLD ORCHARD LANE WAYSIDE, NJ 07712 Expert system detection of EEG sharp and spike waves

R18MH-46160-03 (SRCM) **MORSE, GARY ANDREW** HOMELESS/CASA PROGRAM 910 SOUTH 14TH STREET ST LOUIS, MO 63103 Cost effectiveness of case management for the homeless

R18MH-46162-03 (SRCM) **SOLOMON, PHYLLIS L** HAHNEMANN UNIVERSITY BROAD & VINE, MAIL STOP 403 PHILADELPHIA, PA 19102 Case management for jailed homeless cmi: two models

R19MH-46177-03 (SRCM) **STYC, KATHLEEN** Grants to states - MH data collection systems - Ca

R19MH-46178-03 (SRCM) **ANDERSON, DAN** Montana's uniform integrated mental health data collecti

R19MH-46179-03 (SRCM) **PARSONS, REGIS** Grants to states - mh data collection systems - Sc

R19MH-46180-03 (SRCM) **LOCKETT, WILLIAM** Kansas data collection and decision support system

R19MH-46181-03 (SRCM) **BORYS, SUZANNE** Grants to states--Mental health data collection systems

R19MH-46182-03 (SRCM) **TENNEY, JEFF** Grants to states - MH data collection systems

R19MH-46183-03 (SRCM) **TREMPER, RONALD** Grants to states - MH data collection systems - RI

R19MH-46186-03 (SRCM) **GEERTSEN, DENNIS C** Grants to states - MH data collection systems UT

R19MH-46187-03 (SRCM) **HUTTON, LYNN** Grants to states - MH data collection systems - AK

R19MH-46188-03 (SRCM) **WILSON, NANCY Z** Grants to states--Mental health data collection systems--Colorado

R19MH-46189-03 (SRCM) **CALLAGHAN, JOHN** Grants to states - MH data collection systems New Mexico.

R19MH-46191-03 (SRCM) **AMOS, JIM R** Grants to states - Mental health data collection systems--Idaho

R19MH-46192-03 (SRCM) **DAVIS, STEVEN P** Grants to states-Mental health data collection systems-Oklahoma

R19MH-46193-03 (SRCM) **FERGUSON, JAMES M** Grants to states--Mental health data collection systems-Arizona

R19MH-46194-03 (SRCM) **WATERS, ROBERT M** Grants to states - MH data collection systems - Tn

R19MH-46197-03 (SRCM) **MAEDKE, JAMES M** Grants to states - mh data collection systems illinois

R19MH-46200-03 (SRCM) **ANDERSON, SALLY** Grants to states - Mental health data collection systems--Texas

R19MH-46202-03 (SRCM) **TIPPETT, MAURICE L** Grants to states--Mental health data collection systems

R19MH-46203-03 (SRCM) **PANDIANI, JOHN A** Grants to states--Mental health data collection systems

R19MH-46205-03 (SRCM) **GARDINE, ROBERTA** Grants to states--Mental health data collection systems

R19MH-46206-03 (SRCM) **LOCKE, PATRICK** Grants to states--Mental health data collection systems

R19MH-46207-03 (SRCM) **MILLS, JOY** Grants to states - mh data collections systems - ar

R19MH-46208-03 (SRCM) **PAYNE, EDWARD A** Grants to states - mh data collection systems - MS

R19MH-46210-03 (SRCM) **HORNIK, JOHN A** Grants to states - mh data collection systems - ny

R19MH-46211-03 (SRCM) **WIANT, JOSEPH** Grants to states--Mental health data collection systems--Ohio

R19MH-46213-03 (SRCM) **LENGENFELDER, JAMES T** Grants to states - MH data collection systems - wa

R19MH-46214-03 (SRCM) **FLEMING, MICHAEL** Grants to states - MH data collection systems maine

R19MH-46215-03 (SRCM) **TEAGUE, GREGORY B** Grants to states--Mental health data collection systems--New Hampshire

R01MH-46224-03 (SRCM) **FISHER, JEFFREY D** UNIVERSITY OF CONNECTICUT 406 BABBIDGE ROAD STORRS, CT 06269-1020 General technology for AIDS risk behavior change

R19MH-46225-03 (SRCM) **PURTLE, RONALD** Grants to states--Mental health data collection systems

R19MH-46227-03 (SRCM) **WARD, WILLIAM L** Grants to states--Mental health data collection systems-Georgia

R19MH-46228-03 (SRCM) **FERDINAND, BARBARA** Grants to states - mh data collection systems louisiana

R19MH-46229-03 (SRCM) **CROMPTON, DAVID A** Grants to states - mh data collection systems - ct

R19MH-46230-03 (SRCM) **BEESON, PETER G** Grants to states - MH data collection systems - NE

R19MH-46231-03 (SRCM) **GUDEMAN, HOWARD** Grants to states--Mental health data collection systems--Hawaii

R19MH-46235-03 (SRCM) **KING, ROYCE G** Grants to states-mh data collection systems alabama

R19MH-46246-03 (SRCM) **BROOKS, SARAH R** Grants to states--Mental health data collection systems

R01MH-46250-02 (MHAZ) **PERRY, SAMUEL W** THE NEW YORK HOSPITAL 525 EAST 68TH STREET NEW YORK, NY 10021 Treatments of depression in HIV-infected outpatients

R01MH-46255-02 (SRCM) **PATTERSON, THOMAS** UNIV OF CALIF, SAN DIEGO 9500 GILMAN DRIVE LA JOLLA, CA 92093-0603 Psychosocial moderators of disease progression in AIDS

R01MH-46261-03 (MHAZ) **DUNN, ADRIAN J** LSU MED CTR SCH OF MEDICINE PO BOX 33932 SHREVEPORT, LA 71130-3932 Cytokine effects on the central nervous system

U01MH-46274-03 (SRCM) **DEPAULO, J RAYMOND, JR** JOHNS HOPKINS HOSPITAL 600 NORTH WOLFE STREET BALTIMORE, MD 21205 Diagnostic centers for psychiatric linkage studies

U01MH-46276-03 (SRCM) **CLONINGER, CLAUDE R** WASHINTON UNIV SCH OF MED 660 SOUTH EUCLID AVE; BX 8134 ST LOUIS, MO 63110 Diagnostic center for linkage studies of schizophrenia

U01MH-46280-03 (SRCM) **REICH, THEODORE** WASHINGTON UNIVERSITY 660 S EUCLID AVE/BOX 8134 ST LOUIS, MO 63110 Diagnostic cenetr for linkage studies of bipolar disorder

U01MH-46281-03 (SRCM) **ALBERT, MARILYN S** MASSACHUSETTS GENERAL HOSPITAL FRUIT ST BOSTON, MA 02114 Genetic studies of Alzheimer's disease

U01MH-46282-03 (SRCM) **NURNBERGER, JOHN I, JR** INDIANA UNIV SCH OF MEDICINE 791 UNION DRIVE INDIANAPOLIS, IN 46202-4887 Diagnostic center for linkage studies in bipolar illness

R01MH-46284-04 (MHAZ) **LYSLE, DONALD T** UNIV OF NORTH CAROLINA DAVIE HALL, CB# 3270 CHAPEL HILL, N C 27599-3270 Immune alterations mediated by conditioning

U01MH-46289-03 (SRCM) **KAUFMANN, CHARLES A** NEW YORK STATE PSYCHIATRIC INS 722 WEST 168TH STREET NEW YORK, NY 10032 Diagnostic center for schizophrenia linkage studies

U01MH-46290-03 (SRCM) **FOLSTEIN, MARSHAL F** JOHNS HOPKINS HOSPITAL 600 N WOLFE ST BALTIMORE, MD 21205 Diagnostic centers for psychiatric linkage studies

R19MH-46296-03 (SRCM) **WIEDERANDERS, MARK** Enhancing research capacity in state mental health agencies--California

R19MH-46306-03 (SRCM) **ESSOCK, SUSAN M** Treatment comparisons--Research to enhance state mental health agency capacity

R19MH-46307-03 (SRCM) **HERMAN, SANDRA E** Enhancing research capacity in state mental health agencies

R01MH-46310-01A1 (SRCM) **HOVEN, CHRISTINA W** RES FDN FOR MENTAL HYGIENE 722 W 168TH STREET NEW YORK, NY 10032 Dual disorders and entitlement among the homeless

U01MH-46318-03 (SRCM) **TSUANG, MING T** BROCKTON/WEST ROXBURY VAMC 940 BELMONT STREET BROCKTON, MA 02401 Diagnostic center for linkage studies of schizophrenia

R01MH-46323-03 (SRCM) **ANGOLD, ADRIAN** DUKE UNIVERSITY MEDICAL CTR BOX 3454 DURHAM, NC 27710 Adolescent ADM -- Service use and risks of co-morbidity

R19MH-46324-03 (SRCM) **POKORNY, LOIS J** Enhancing research capacity in state mental health agencies

R01MH-46327-03 (SRCM) **ROSENTHAL, RICHARD N** BETH ISRAEL MEDICAL CENTER FIRST AVENUE AT 16TH STREET NEW YORK, NY 10003 Integrated services for mentally ill chemical abusers

R01MH-46331-03 (SRCM) **JERRELL, JEANETTE M** SANTA CLARA COUNTY BUREAU OF M 645 S BASCOM AVENUE SAN JOSE, CA 95128 Cost-effectiveness of substance abuse treatment of severely mentally ill

K05MH-46335-21 (MHK) **REITE, MARTIN L** UNIV OF COLORADO HLTH SCI CTR BOX C268-68 4200 EAST 9TH AVE DENVER, CO 80262 Models of psychobiological development

R01MH-46335-03 (SRCM) **PENK, WALTER E** UNIVERSITY OF MASSACHUSETTS 55 LAKE AVE NORTH WORCESTER, MA 01655 Treating substance abuse among chronic mental patients

R19MH-46348-03 (SRCM) **ROTH, DEE** Services in systems--Impact on client outcomes

R29MH-46363-04 (SRCM) **CORSE, SARA J** UNIVERSITY OF PENNSYLVANIA 418 SERVICE DRIVE PHILADELPHIA, PA 19104-6021 Substance abuse in the severely mentally ill

R19MH-46365-02 (SRCM) **SHERN, DAVID L** Enhancing research capacity in state mental health agencies

R01MH-46370-02 (EPS) **WELLS, KENNETH** RAND CORPORATION PO BOX 2138/1700 MAIN STREET SANTA MONICA, CA 90406-2138 Impact of comorbid alcoholism in depression

R24MH-46371-02 (SRCM) **SEGAL, STEVEN P** UNIVERSITY OF CALIFORNIA 120 HAVILAND HALL BERKELEY, CA 94720 Center for self-help research

U01MH-46373-03 (SRCM) **GO, RODNEY C** UNIVERSITY OF ALABAMA UAB STATION BIRMINGHAM, AL 35294 Etiologic heterogeneity in familial Alzheimer's disease

R01MH-46376-03 (SRCM) **KESSLER, RONALD C** UNIVERSITY OF MICHIGAN ROOM 5062 ANN ARBOR, MI 48106 Epidemiology--Alchohol, drug abuse, and mental disorders

R19MH-46391-03 (SRCM) **MARQUES, JANICE** Enhancing res capacity in state MH agencies - CA

R24MH-46399-03 (SRCM) POWELL, THOMAS J UNIVERSITY OF MICHIGAN SCHOOL OF SOCIAL WORK ANN ARBOR, MI 48109-1285 The national self-help research center

R03MH-46400-01A1 (MSM) WHITNEY, PAUL M WASHINGTON STATE UNIVERSITY PULLMAN, WA 99164-4820 Spontaneous inference generation in social cognition

R01MH-46410-01A1 (BSR) GIORDANO, PEGGY C BOWLING GREEN STATE UNIVERSITY BOWLING GREEN, OH 43403 Social networks and development in cultural perspective

R01MH-46412-02 (BSR) KRUGLANSKI, ARIE W UNIVERSITY OF MARYLAND COLLEGE PARK, MD 20742-4411 Need for closure on social cognition/interaction

R29MH-46424-02 (LCR) SMALL, GARY W UCLA NEUROPSYCHIATRIC INST 760 WESTWOOD PLAZA LOS ANGELES, CA 90024-1759 Mental illness in aging--Early diagnosis

R01MH-46427-01A1 (BSR) STIPEK, DEBORAH J UNIVERSITY OF CALIFORNIA LOS ANGELES, CA 90024 Children's motivation in different educational contexts

R37MH-46428-02 (SRCM) GERSTEIN, GEORGE L UNIVERSITY OF PENNSYLVANIA 37TH & HAMILTON WALK PHILADELPHIA, PA 19104-6085 NEURAL ASSEMBLIES--Somatic map experiments and models

R03MH-46430-02 (MSM) REID, JAMES D PENNSYLVANIA STATE UNIVERSITY S110 HENDERSON BUILDING UNIVERSITY PARK, PA 16802 Stress, adaptation, and successful aging

R01MH-46433-02 (PCB) DAWSON, MICHAEL E UNIV OF SOUTHERN CALIFORNIA LOS ANGELES, CA 90089-1061 Electrodermal dysfunctions and schizophrenia

R01MH-46435-01A1 (CVR) RAINE, ADRIAN UNIV OF SOUTHERN CALIFORNIA UNIVERSITY PARK LOS ANGELES, CA 90089-1111 Psychophysiology of violent and antisocial behavior

R01MH-46436-02 (PCB) DAVIDSON, MICHAEL MOUNT SINAI SCHOOL OF MEDICINE 1 GUSTAVE LEVY PLACE NEW YORK, NY 10029 Neuropathology of dementia in elderly schizophrenic

R01MH-46439-02 (TDA) LIEBOWITZ, MICHAEL R RESEARCH FDN FOR MENTAL HYGIEN 722 WEST 168TH STREET NEW YORK, NY 10032 Fluoxetine in adolescent obsessive compulsive disorder

R29MH-46442-02 (PYB) NOONAN, LINDA R UNIV OF N C AT CHAPEL HILL BDRC CHAPEL HILL, N C 27599 Maternal regulation of the infant's HPA axis

R01MH-46448-02 (PCB) HALPERIN, JEFFREY M QUEENS COLLEGE OF CUNY 65-30 KISSENA BLVD FLUSHING, NY 11367 Validation of inattentive and aggressive ADHD subtypes

R03MH-46451-01A1 (MSM) FARRELL, JOAN M LARUE CARTER OUTPATIENT CLINIC 1315 WEST 10TH STREET INDIANAPOLIS, IN 46202-2885 Psychoeducation group program for borderline patients

R01MH-46452-01A2 (PCB) GATCHEL, ROBERT J UNIV OF TEXAS SW MEDICAL CENTE 5323 HARRY HINES BLVD DALLAS, TX 75235-9044 DSM III-R diagnosis and low back pain -- Prospective study

R01MH-46453-01A1 (SRCM) JOHNSON, DON H RICE UNIVERSITY P.O. BOX 1892 HOUSTON, TX 77251 Neural fractal activity in auditory spatial localization

R03MH-46455-01A2 (MSM) VONDRA, JOAN T UNIVERSITY OF PITTSBURGH PITTSBURGH, PA 15260 Origins of coping motivation and competence

R01MH-46465-01A1 (TDA) WOLKIN, ADAM NY VA MEDICAL CENTER 408 FIRST AVE NEW YORK, NY 10010 Presynaptic regulation in neuroleptic non-response

R01MH-46475-01A1 (LCR) LESKO, LYNNA M MEMORIAL HOSP/CANCER/ALLIED DI 1275 YORK AVE NEW YORK, NY 10021 Off treatment adaptation of adolescent cancer patients

R01MH-46479-01A1 (PCB) KINNEY, DENNIS K MCLEAN HOSPITAL 115 MILL STREET BELMONT, MA 02178 Bipolar disorder and pre- and perinatal complications

R01MH-46482-01A1 (SRCM) SEJNOWSKI, TERRENCE J SALK INSTITUTE PO BOX 85800 SAN DIEGO, CA 92138 Computational models of hippocampal neurons

R01MH-46485-02 (SRCM) ALBERTS, JEFFREY R INDIANA UNIVERSITY BLOOMINGTON, IN 47405 Sensation and behavior in fetus and newborn

R03MH-46493-01A1 (MSM) MACDONALD, KEVIN B CALIF ST. UNIV-LONG BEACH 1250 BELLFLOWER BLVD LONG BEACH, CA 90840 The effects of ritalin on physical play in adhd children

R01MH-46496-02 (PCB) WALKER, ELAINE F EMORY UNIVERSITY ATLANTA, GA 30322 Neurodevelopmental and socioemotional antecedents of schizophrenia

R01MH-46500-01A1 (TDA) BRENT, DAVID A WESTERN PSYCH INST & CLINIC 3811 O'HARA STREET PITTSBURGH, PA 15213 Depressed adolescent suicide attempters--Clinical trial

R01MH-46501-01A1 (BPN) CHAVKIN, CHARLES UNIVERSITY OF WASHINGTON SEATTLE, WA 98195 Sigma receptors and psychotomimetic drug action

R29MH-46510-02 (PCB) DAHL, RONALD E WESTERN PSYCHIATRIC INST & CLI 3811 O'HARA STREET PITTSBURGH, PA 15213 EEG sleep changes in adolescent depression

R03MH-46511-02 (MHAZ) GATTONE, VINCENT H, II UNIV OF KANSAS MEDICAL CENTER 39TH & RAINBOW BLVD KANSAS CITY, KS 66103 Neural aspects of immune deficiency

R03MH-46512-02 (MSM) THOMPSON, LEE ANNE CASE WESTERN RESERVE UNIV 2040 ADELBERT ROAD CLEVELAND, OH 44106 Temperament and early cognitive processing

R01MH-46516-01A1 (BPN) LE DOUX, JOSEPH E, JR NEW YORK UNIVERSITY 6 WASHINGTON PLACE NEW YORK, NY 10003 Synaptic transmission in fear conditioning circuits

P01MH-46529-02 (SRCM) COYLE, JOSEPH T JOHNS HOPKINS SCH OF MEDICINE 600 NORTH WOLFE STREET BALTIMORE, MD 21205 Gene dosage effects on the developing brain

P01MH-46529-02 0001 (SRCM) GEARHART, JOHN Gene dosage effects on the developing brain Transgenic mice in the study of mouse trisomy 16

P01MH-46529-02 0002 (SRCM) OSTER-GRANITE, MARY LOU Gene dosage effects on the developing brain Amyloid precursor protein expression in aneuploid mice

P01MH-46529-02 0003 (SRCM) HOHMANN, CHRISTINE F Gene dosage effects on the developing brain Ts16 brain tissue development after transplantation into euploid host brain

P01MH-46529-02 0004 (SRCM) COYLE, JOSEPH T Gene dosage effects on the developing brain Neuronal dysgenesis and gene expression in T16 and transgenic mice

P01MH-46529-02 9001 (SRCM) COYLE, JOSEPH T Gene dosage effects on the developing brain Core--Animals, Neurochemistry, behavior

R03MH-46530-01A1 (MSM) SAUTTER, FREDERIC J TULANE UNIVERSITY 1430 TULANE AVE NEW ORLEANS, LA 70112 Negative symptoms--Relationship to family history

R01MH-46531-01A2 (BPN) SCHNEIDER, JAY S HAHNEMANN UNIVERSITY BROAD AND VINE PHILADELPHIA, PA 19102 Neuropsychology of catecholamine deficiencies

R03MH-46532-02 (MSM) CAMPER, SALLY ANN UNIV OF MICHIGAN MED SCHOOL MEDICAL SCIENCE II M4708 ANN ARBOR, MI 48109-0618 Tissue-specific expression of CRH transgenes

R03MH-46535-02 (MSM) DUNN, JUDITH F PENNSYLVANIA STATE UNIV S-120 HENDERSON BLDG UNIVERSITY PARK, PA 16802 Family relationships in early adolescence

R03MH-46546-01A1 (MSM) MAHADIK, SAHEBARAO P RESEARCH FDN FOR MENTAL HYGIEN 722 WEST 168TH ST NEW YORK, NY 10032 Abnormalities in fibroblasts of schizophrenic patients

R01MH-46549-01A1 (BSR) ANTONUCCI, TONI C UNIVERSITY OF MICHIGAN 475 EAST JEFFERSON ANN ARBOR, MI 48109 Social relations and mental health over the life course

R03MH-46551-01A1 (MSM) SCHECHTER, DIANNE E RES FDN FOR MENTAL HYGIENE 722 WEST 168TH STREET NEW YORK, NY 10032 Steroid patterns in relation to female dysphoric moods

R03MH-46564-02 (MSM) GREENBERG, JAN S UNIVERSITY OF WISCONSIN MADISON, WI 53706 Aging parents with a mentally ill adult child at home

R29MH-46567-01A1 (BSR) ACITELLI, LINDA K UNIVERSITY OF MICHIGAN PO BX 1248 RM 5080 ANN ARBOR, MI 48109-1248 Awareness of self, partner and relationship

R01MH-46568-01A1 (CEP) BERG, WILLIAM K UNIVERSITY OF FLORIDA GAINESVILLE, FL 32611 Ontogeny of anticipation in human infants

R03MH-46572-02 (MSM) CASSIDY, JUDE A PENNSYLVANIA STATE UNIVERSITY 416 MOORE BLDG UNIVERSITY PARK, PA 16802 Children's conceptions of loneliness--Age difference

R01MH-46577-01A1 (BPN) SNYDER-KELLER, ABIGAIL M WADSWORTH CENTER IMPIRE STATE PLAZA BOX 509 ALBANY, NY 12201-0509 Development of striatal compartmentalization

R01MH-46584-01 (LCR) AUGUST, GERALD J UNIVERSITY OF MINNESOTA PO BOX 95 MINNEAPOLIS, MN 55455 School-based secondary prevention for ADHD children

R37MH-46586-01A1 (LCR) FIELD, TIFFANY M UNIVERSITY OF MIAMI PO BOX 016820 MIAMI, FL 33101 Preventing depression in infants of depressed mothers

R01MH-46594-01A1 (BPN) WINOKUR, ANDREW UNIVERSITY OF PENNSYLVANIA 422 CURIE BLVD PHILADELPHIA, PA 19104-6141 TRH in CNS--Implications for affective disorders

R03MH-46596-01A1 (MSM) REINHARDT, JOANN P THE LIGHTHOUSE 111 EAST 59TH STREET NEW YORK, NY 10022 Friendship as a resource in age-related vision loss

R01MH-46613-02 (BPN) WESTBROOK, GARY L OREGON HEALTH SCIENCES UNIV 3181 SW SAM JACKSON PARK ROAD PORTLAND, OR 97201 Endogenous regulators of glutamate-activated channels

R01MH-46614-02 (PCB) PETTEGREW, JAY W WESTERN PSYCHIATRIC INST & CLN 3811 O'HARA STREET PITTSBURGH, PA 15213 In vivo 31-P NMR studies in schizophrenics

R01MH-46618-02 (EPS) SNOWDEN, LONNIE R UNIVERSITY OF CALIFORNIA BERKELEY, CA 94720 Ethnic matching and use of mental health services

R01MH-46624-03 (EPS) BURNS, BARBARA J DUKE UNIVERSITY MEDICAL CENTER BOX 3930 DURHAM, NC 27710 Cost effectiveness programs of assertive community treatment

R29MH-46625-02 (TDA) NEWHOUSE, PAUL A UNIVERSTIY OF VERMONT 1 SOUTH PROSPECT STREET BURLINGTON, VT 05401 Nicotinic cholinergic model of dementia

R03MH-46628-02 (MSM) SCHULDBERG, DAVID UNIVERSITY OF MONTANA MISSOULA, MT 59812-1041 Post-college attitude and experience study

R03MH-46629-02 (MSM) SCHROEDER, HAROLD E KENT STATE UNIVERSITY KENT, OH 44242 Implicit models of AIDS for two high risk populations

R01MH-46630-02 (TDA) VRTUNSKI, P BART CLEVELAND VA MEDICAL CENTER BRECKSVILLE, OH 44141 Force control dysfunction in schizophrenia

R03MH-46631-02 (MSM) MANSBACH, ROBERT S MEDICAL COLLEGE OF VIRGINIA BOX 613 MCV STATION RICHMOND, VA 23298-0613 Model of schizophrenia gating deficits--NMDA effects

R03MH-46632-01A1 (MSM) SCHNUR, DAVID B NEW YORK STATE PSYCHIATRIC INS 722 WEST 168TH STREET NEW YORK, NY 10032 Autonomic orienting response in schizophrenia & mania

R03MH-46637-01A2 (MSM) HOOKER, KAREN A SYRACUSE UNIVERSITY 430 HUNTINGTON HALL SYRACUSE, NY 13244-2340 Health of caregivers--The role of personality

R01MH-46643-02 (EPS) RATCLIFF, GRAHAM G WESTERN PSYCHIATRIC INST & CLI 3811 O'HARA STREET PITTSBURGH, PA 15213 Age-associated memory impairment--community-based study

R03MH-46650-01A1 (MSM) HAMERA, EDNA K UNIV OF KANSAS MEDICAL CTR 39TH & RAINBOW BLVD KANSAS CITY, KS 66103 Self-regulation substance use/abuse in schizophrenia

R03MH-46653-01A1 (MSM) HAYCOCK, JOHN W LOUISIANA STATE UNIV MED CTR 1100 FLORIDA AVE NEW ORLEANS, LA 70119 Multiple forms of human tyrosine hydroxylase

R37MH-46660-02 (PYB) HASTINGS, JOHN W HARVARD COLLEGE 16 DIVINITY AVENUE CAMBRIDGE, MA 02138 Photobiological control of a cellular circadian clock

R01MH-46673-02 (TDA) SALLEE, FLOYD R MEDICAL UNIV OF SOUTH CAROLINA 171 ASHLEY AVE CHARLESTON, SC 29425 Pharmacotherapeutics of children with Tourette syndrome

R03MH-46676-02 (MSM) GUST, DEBORAH A YERKES REGIONAL PRIMATE CENTER 2409 TAYLOR ROAD LAWRENCEVILLE, GA 30245 Social relationships and stress

P50MH-46690-02 (SRCM) REID, JOHN B OREGON SOCIAL LEARNING CENTER 207 EAST 5TH AVENUE EUGENE, OR 97401 Oregon prevention research center

P50MH-46690-02 0001 (SRCM) REID, JOHN B Oregon prevention research center Fifth grade prevention trial

PROJECT NO., ORGANIZATIONAL UNIT., INVESTIGATOR, ADDRESS, TITLE

P50MH-46690-02 0002 (SRCM) REID, JOHN B Oregon prevention research center First grade prevention trial
P50MH-46690-02 0003 (SRCM) REID, JOHN B Oregon prevention research center Model development, assessment and analysis
P50MH-46690-02 0004 (SRCM) REID, JOHN B Oregon prevention research center Intervention and assessment pilot projects
P50MH-46690-02 9001 (SRCM) REID, JOHN B Oregon prevention research center Core
R01MH-46692-01A2 (BPN) ORDWAY, GREGORY A CASE WESTERN RESERVE UNIV 3395 SCRANTON RD/PSYCHIATRY CLEVELAND, OH 44109 Noradrenergic system in depression--mRNAs and receptors
R01MH-46698-01A2 (EPS) RANZ, JULES RESEARCH FDN FOR MENTAL HYGIEN 722 WEST 168TH ST NEW YORK, NY 10032 Evaluation of psychoeducation in a supervised residence
R29MH-46700-03 (TDA) WILSON, WILLIAM H DAMMASCH STATE HOSPITAL BOX 38 WILSONVILLE, OR 97070 Pharmacological approach to non-responsive schizophrenia
R03MH-46701-01A1 (MSM) COOK, EDWIN W, III UNIVERSITY OF ALABAMA UNIVERSITY STATION BIRMINGHAM, AL 35294 Development of affective modulation of acoustic startle
R03MH-46711-01A1 (MSM) FLEISCHMANN, AMOS ALBERT EINSTEIN COLLEGE/MEDICI 1300 MORRIS PARK AVENUE BRONX, NY 10461 Sexual dimorphisms in neurotransmission
R01MH-46712-01A1 (EPS) TROCHIM, WILLIAM MK CORNELL UNIVERSITY RM N136C MVR HALL ITHACA, NY 14853-2801 Regression-Discontinuity designs in mental health
U01MH-46717-03 (SRCM) SCHWAB-STONE, MARY YALE CHILD STUDY CENTER 230 S. FRONTAGE ROAD NEW HAVEN, CT 06510-8009 Yale child and adolescent psychiatric epidemiologic study
U01MH-46718-03 (SRCM) BIRD, HECTOR R NEW YORK PSYCHIATRIC INSTITUTE 722 WEST 168TH ST NEW YORK, NY 10032 Methods for child psychiatry epidemiologic surveys
U01MH-46725-03 (SRCM) DULCAN, MINA K EMORY UNIV SCHOOL OF MEDICINE 2032 RIDGEWOOD DRIVE, N.E. ATLANTA, GA 30322 Epidemiology of child & adolescent mental disorders
R01MH-46729-02 (PYB) KALIN, NED H CLINICAL SCIENCES CENTER 600 HIGHLAND AVENUE MADISON, WI 53792 Development and regulation of emotion in primates
U01MH-46732-03 (SRCM) CANINO, GLORISA UNIV OF PUERTO RICO P.O. BOX 365067 SAN JUAN, PR 00936-5067 A methodological study of child assessment in Puerto Rico
R01MH-46742-02 (SRCM) MARDER, EVE E BRANDEIS UNIVERSITY 415 SOUTH STREET WALTHAM, MA 02254 Theory and modeling of oscillatory neural networks
P50MH-46745-02 (SRCM) MANN, J JOHN WESTERN PSYCHIATRIC INST/CLINI 3811 O'HARA ST PITTSBURGH, PA 15213 Suicide clinical research center
P50MH-46745-02 9003 (SRCM) SWEENEY, JOHN A Suicide clinical research center Core--Data management and statistics
P50MH-46745-02 9004 (SRCM) ARANGO, VICTORIA Suicide clinical research center Core--Human neurobiology
P50MH-46745-02 9005 (SRCM) HAAS, GRETCHEN L Suicide clinical research center Core--Clinical evaluation
P50MH-46745-02 0001 (SRCM) MANN, J JOHN Suicide clinical research center Suicidal behavior in DSM-III-R major depression
P50MH-46745-02 0002 (SRCM) HAAS, GRETCHEN L Suicide clinical research center Clinical and psychosocial correlates of suicide in schizophrenia
P50MH-46745-02 0003 (SRCM) SWEENEY, JOHN A Suicide clinical research center psychological studies of suicide in schizophrenia
P50MH-46745-02 0004 (SRCM) MANN, J JOHN Suicide clinical research center Neurobiological studies of suicidal behavior in nonaffective disorders
P50MH-46745-02 9002 (SRCM) MANN, J JOHN Suicide clinical research center Core--Clinical laboratory
R01MH-46747-03 (TDA) MICHELSON, LARRY PENNSYLVANIA STATE UNIVERSITY 417 MOORE BUILDING UNIVERSITY PARK, PA 16802 Cognitive model of panic disorder with agoraphobia
R44MH-46756-02 (SSS) BOYLE, JAMES G ANALYTICA OF BRANFORD INC 29 BUSINESS PARK DRIVE BRANFORD, CT 06405 Electrospray tandem time of flight mass spectrometer
R43MH-46761-01A1 (MHSB) HU, CHIA-LING STANDARD SCIENTIFICS, INC PO BOX 322 CAMBRIDGE, MA 02238 Non-radioactive immunoassays for opioid peptides
R01MH-46777-03 (SRC) MARIN, BARBARA A UNIVERSITY OF CALIFORNIA BOX 0886 SAN FRANCISCO, CALIF 94143 Predictors of condom use in two groups of hispanics
R01MH-46783-02 (LCR) THOMPSON, LARRY W VA MEDICAL CENTER 3801 MIRANDA AVENUE PALO ALTO, CA 94304 Cognitive changes in older diabetics due to treatment
R01MH-46788-02 (MHAZ) COHEN, FRANCES UNIVERSITY OF CALIFORNIA 1350 7TH AVE, CSBS 204 SAN FRANCISCO, CA 94143-0844 Chronic stressors, gender differences, and immunity
R01MH-46789-01A1 (MHAZ) MARIN, BARBARA A UNIVERSITY OF CALIFORNIA BOX 0886 SAN FRANCISCO, CA 94143 Interventions to change HIV risk behaviors in Hispanics
R01MH-46790-02 (MHAZ) WILEY, CLAYTON A UNIV OF CALIF, SAN DIEGO LA JOLLA, CALIF 92093-0612 Role of immune responsiveness in HIV encephalopathy
R01MH-46792-01A2 (MHAZ) ROFFMAN, ROGER A UNIVERSITY OF WASHINGTON 4101 FIFTEENTH AVENUE, N E SEATTLE, WA 98105 Phone counseling in reducing barriers to AIDS prevention
R01MH-46801-01A1 (MHAZ) SHERIDAN, JOHN F OHIO STATE UNIVERSITY 305 WEST 12TH AVE. COLUMBUS, OH 43210 Stress-induced immunosuppression of anti-viral immunity
R01MH-46805-02 (SRCM) CHESNEY, MARGARET A UCSF PREVENTION SCIENCES GROUP 74 NEW MONTGOMERY ST, 600 SAN FRANCISCO, CA 94105 Coping effectiveness training for HIV+ and HIV- men
R01MH-46808-02 (MHAZ) PHELPS, CHRISTOPHER P UNIVERSITY OF SOUTH FLORIDA SCHOOL OF MEDICINE BOX 6 TAMPA, FL 33612 Neuroendocrine control of the thymus gland
R37MH-46815-02 (MHAZ) LYMAN, WILLIAM D ALBERT EINSTEIN COLLEGE OF MED 1300 MORRIS PARK AVENUE BRONX, NY 10461 Neural cell tropism of HIV-1 isolates

PROJECT NO., ORGANIZATIONAL UNIT., INVESTIGATOR, ADDRESS, TITLE

R01MH-46816-02 (MHAZ) KEGELES, SUSAN M UNIVERSITY OF CALIFORNIA 74 NEW MONTGOMERY SAN FRANCISCO, CA 94105 AIDS intervention for young homosexual men
R29MH-46820-02 (PCB) ATKINS, MARC S THE CHILDREN'S HOSPITAL OF PHI 34TH & CIVIC CTR BLVD/SUITE 23 PHILADELPHIA, PA 19104 Subtypes of childhood agressive disorders
R01MH-46823-02 (SRCM) MCNAUGHTON, BRUCE UNIVERSITY OF ARIZONA NORTH BUILDING TUCSON, AZ 85724 Hebb Marr networks, the hippocampus, and spatial memory
R01MH-46828-01 (BSR) TALLMAN, IRVING WASHINGTON STATE UNIVERSITY PULLMAN, WA 99164-4020 Socialization into marital roles
R01MH-46840-01A1 (BSR) SMITH, ELIOT R PURDUE UNIVERSITY WEST LAFAYETTE, IN 47907 Exemplar-based processing in social judgment
R03MH-46841-01 (MSM) GARNIER, PHILIP C UNIVERSITY OF ILLINOIS 603 E DANIEL STREET CHAMPAIGN, IL 61820 Longitudinal investigation of commitment in marriage
R01MH-46851-01A1 (BPN) COOK, JAMES M UNIVERSITY OF WISCONSIN PO BOX 413 MILWAUKEE, WI 53201 Rigid probes--Modeling selective anxiolytics for benzodiazepine receptor
R03MH-46855-02 (MSM) DUFFY, SUSAN A AMHERST COLLEGE AMHERST, MA 01002 Message level influences on word recognition
R01MH-46865-01 (PCB) LORD, CATHERINE UNIVERSITY OF NORTH CAROLINA MEDICAL SCHOOL WING E CHAPEL HILL, NC 27599-7180 Early diagnosis of autism
R03MH-46869-01A1 (MSM) SARTER, MARTIN F OHIO STATE UNIVERSITY 1885 NEIL AVENUE COLUMBUS, OH 43210-1222 Cognitive effects of benzodiazepines-neuronal substrates
R29MH-46885-02 (CEP) SHAFIR, ELDAR B PRINCETON UNIVERSITY GREEN HALL PRINCETON, NJ 08544-1010 Internal conflict in choice and judgment
R01MH-46889-02 (EPS) TUCKMAN, HOWARD P MEMPHIS STATE UNIVERSITY MEMPHIS, TN 38152 Baseline psychiatric hospital profits
R29MH-46894-01A1 (TDA) BIRMAHER, BORIS WESTERN PSYCHIATRIC INST/CLINI 3811 O HARA STREET PITTSBURGH, PA 15213 Amitriptyline vs placebo in adolescent major depression
R03MH-46900-02 (MSM) CONTRADA, RICHARD J RUTGERS STATE UNIVERSITY TILLET HALL NEW BRUNSWICK, NJ 08903 New method for assessing approach and avoidant coping
R01MH-46901-01 (PCB) HALBREICH, URIEL STATE UNIVERSITY OF NEW YORK 462 GRIDER ST (K-ANNEX) BUFFALO, NY 14215 Alpha 2 receptors, luteal depression & gonadal hormones
R03MH-46915-02 (MSM) MC CRACKEN, JAMES T HARBOR-UCLA MEDICAL CENTER 1000 W CARSON ST, F-5 TORRANCE, CA 90509 Developmental aspects of antidepressant responses
R29MH-46925-01A1 (LCR) SHAW, DANIEL S UNIVERSITY OF PITTSBURGH 4015 O'HARA ST PITTSBURGH, PA 15260 Developmental precursors of antisocial behavior
R29MH-46927-02 (CVR) HOLTZWORTH-MUNROE, AMY INDIANA UNIVERSITY BLOOMINGTON, IN 47405 Social skills deficits in martially violent men
R29MH-46940-02 (CVR) AZAR, SANDRA T CLARK UNIVERSITY 950 MAIN STREET WORCESTER, MA 01610 Cognition, childrearing stress and maladaptive parenting
R01MH-46943-02 (BPN) KESSLER, ROBERT M VANDERBILT UNIVERSITY NASHVILLE, TN 37232 D2 receptors in schizophrenia--Optimized PET ligands
R03MH-46944-02 (MSM) KENDLER, KENNETH S VIRGINIA COMMONWEALTH UNIVERSI BOX 710, MCV STATION RICHMOND, VA 23298-0710 Pilot phase of a Swedish twin study of schizophrenia
R29MH-46946-02 (LCR) COONEY, TERESA M UNIVERSITY OF DELAWARE INDIVIDUAL & FAMILY STUDIES NEWARK, DE 19716 Consequences of recent parental divorce for young adults
R01MH-46948-01 (PCB) COCCARO, EMIL F MEDICAL COLL OF PENNSYLVANIA 3200 HENRY AVENUE PHILADELPHIA, PA 19129 Serotonin and impulsive aggression in personality disorder
R03MH-46955-02 (MHAZ) BRODY, DAVID S TEMPLE UNIVERSITY SCH OF MED 3401 N BROAD ST PHILADELPHIA, PA 19140 Reduction of AIDS risk factors and concerns
R01MH-46959-01A1 (CVR) DROSSMAN, DOUGLAS A UNIV OF N C AT CHAPEL HILL CHAPEL HILL, NC 27599-7080 Abuse/psychosocial factors in patients with GI disorders
R01MH-46961-01 (EPS) VOLKMAR, FRED R YALE UNIVERSITY PO BOX 3333 NEW HAVEN, CT 06510 Diagnosing diagnostic criteria--The case of autism
R03MH-46962-02 (MSM) JAVITT, DANIEL C ALBERT EINSTEIN COLLEGE OF MED 1300 MORRIS PARK AVENUE BRONX, N Y 10461 NMDA receptors in processing contingent--Event-related potential
R29MH-46965-01 (CVR) AXSOM, DANNY K VA POLYTECHNIC INST & STATE UN BLACKSBURG, VA 24061-0436 A longitudinal study of adjustment after homicide
R29MH-46967-02 (EPS) FORD, DANIEL E JOHNS HOPKINS HOSPITAL 600 N WOLFE STREET BALTIMORE, MD 21205 Sleep and mental disorders in general medical settings
R03MH-46977-01A1 (MSM) JONES, SUSAN S INDIANA UNIVERSITY BLOOMINGTON, IN 47405 The socialization of smile production in infancy
P01MH-46981-01A1 (SRCM) CANTWELL, DENNIS P UCLA NEUROPSYCHIATRIC INST 760 WESTWOOD PLAZA LOS ANGELES, CA 90024-1759 Family studies of childhood psychiatric disorders
P01MH-46981-01A1 0001 (SRCM) SPENCE, M ANNE Family studies of childhood psychiatric disorders Genetic studies of childhood psychiatric disorders
P01MH-46981-01A1 0002 (SRCM) CANTWELL, DENNIS P Family studies of childhood psychiatric disorders Attention deficit disorder with and without hyperactivity
P01MH-46981-01A1 0003 (SRCM) ASARNOW, JOAN Family studies of childhood psychiatric disorders The study of childhood-onset depressive disorder
P01MH-46981-01A1 0004 (SRCM) ASARNOW, ROBERT Family studies of childhood psychiatric disorders Familial psychiatric disorders and attention in schizophrenia
P01MH-46981-01A1 9001 (SRCM) CANTWELL, DENNIS P Family studies of childhood psychiatric disorders Core--Clinical

PROJECT NO., ORGANIZATIONAL UNIT., INVESTIGATOR, ADDRESS, TITLE

P01MH-46981-01A1 9002 (SRCM) SPENCE, M ANNE Family studies of childhood psychiatric disorders Core--Data base and statistical analysis
R13MH-46982-02 (MHAZ) WAKSMAN, BYRON H NAT'L MULTIPLE SCLEROSIS SOCIE 205 EAST 42ND STREET NEW YORK, NY 10017 Course--pathogenesis of neuroimmunologic diseases
R01MH-46988-01A1 (LCR) ROTH, DAVID L UNIVERSITY OF ALABAMA 201 CAMPBELL HALL BIRMINGHAM, AL 35294 Exercise activity and stress-resistance in older adults
R29MH-46990-01A1 (PCB) NORDAHL, THOMAS E LAWRENCE BERKELEY LAB 1 CYCLOTRON RD BERKELEY, CA 94720 Hippocampal metabolism in schizophrenia
R01MH-46992-01A1 (TDA) RESICK, PATRICIA A UNIVERSITY OF MISSOURI 8001 NATURAL BRIDGE ROAD ST LOUIS, MO 63121 Cognitive processes in PTSD--Etiology and treatment
R03MH-47002-01A1 (MSM) REDDY, RAVINDER D RESEARCH FDN FOR MENTAL HYGIEN 722 WEST 168TH STREET NEW YORK, NY 10032 Indices of oxyradical metabolism in schizophrenia
R03MH-47005-02 (MSM) JUNGINGER, JOHN A LOUISIANA STATE UNIVERSITY 236 AUDUBON HALL BATON ROUGE, LA 70803-5501 Predicting compliance with command hallucinations
R01MH-47010-02 (PYB) CHENG, MEI-FANG RUTGERS UNIVERSITY 101 WARREN STREET NEWARK, N J 07102 Neurobiological study of vocalization
R29MH-47020-02 (TDA) MORIN, CHARLES M VIRGINIA COMMONWEALTH UNIVERSI BOX 268, MCV STATION RICHMOND, VA 23298-0268 Cognitive behavior and pharmacotherapy for late-life insomnia
R03MH-47023-02 (MSM) SLEDGE, WILLIAM H CONNECTICUT MENTAL HLTH CTR 34 PARK ST NEW HAVEN, CT 06519 Language disturbance in schizophrenia
R29MH-47028-02 (BPN) EHRLICH, MICHELLE E NYU MEDICAL CENTER 550 FIRST AVENUE NEW YORK, NY 10016 Transcriptional regulation of caudate phosphoproteins
R01MH-47056-01 (EPS) HARGREAVES, WILLIAM A SAN FRANCISCO GENERAL HOSP 1001 POTRERO AVE SAN FRANCISCO, CA 94110 Cost-effectiveness of six treatments for schizophrenia
R01MH-47059-02 (MHAZ) MONTANO, DANIEL E UNIVERSITY OF WASHINGTON CARE SYSTEMS SM-24 SEATTLE, WA 98195 Determinants of condom use to prevent AIDS
R01MH-47063-01A1 (EPS) HU, TEH-WEI UNIVERSITY OF CALIFORNIA BERKLEY, CA 94720 Costs/outcomes of California mental health capitation experiment
R29MH-47073-01A1 (PCB) COHEN, JONATHAN D WESTERN PSYCHIATRIC INST/CLINI 3811 O HARA STREET PITTSBURGH, PA 15213 Mechanism of context processing in schizophrenia
R01MH-47089-01 (PCB) SACK, ROBERT L OREGON HLTH SCIS UNIVERSITY 3181 SW SAM JACKSON PARK RD PORTLAND, OR 97201-3098 Effect of melatonin on human circadian rhythms
R03MH-47090-01A1 (MSM) PLATT, JANE E NEW YORK UNIVERSITY MEDICAL CT 550 FIRST AVE NEW YORK, NY 10016 Depression and adaptation to repeated stress
R03MH-47091-01 (MSM) VIOLANTI, JOHN M ROCHESTER INSTITUTE OF TECH ONE LOMB MEMORIAL DRIVE-BLDG 6 ROCHESTER, NY 14623-0887 Epidemiology of police suicide
R03MH-47103-02 (MSM) OPP, MARK R UNIVERSITY OF TENNESSEE 894 UNION AVENUE MEMPHIS, TN 38163 Somnogenic muramyl peptides produced by macrophages
R03MH-47104-01 (MSM) WEISS, MITCHELL G HARVARD MEDICAL SCHOOL 25 SHATTUCK STREET BOSTON, MA 02115 Comparative cultural study of psychiatric illness
R03MH-47110-02 (MSM) SUCHMAN, ANTHONY L HIGHLAND HOSPITAL 1000 SOUTH AVENUE ROCHESTER, NY 14620 Conditioned drug effects--Steps towards practical uses
R01MH-47117-01 (PCB) DAWSON, GERALDINE UNIVERSITY OF WASHINGTON SEATTLE, WA 98195 Psychophysiology of depression--Adol mothers/infants
R01MH-47118-01 (TDA) GASTON, LOUISE ALLAN MEMORIAL INST 1025 PINE AVE WEST MONTREAL, CANADA H3A 1A1 Processes predicting outcome of psychotherapy
R01MH-47126-01 (CEP) BUSEMEYER, JEROME R PURDUE UNIVERSITY WEST LAFAYETTE, IN 47907 Learning intervening concepts in multivariate environment
R01MH-47137-02 (BPN) ROSENFELD, MICHAEL G UNIV. OF CALIFORNIA, SAN DIEGO DEPT OF MEDICINE, 0648 LA JOLLA, CA 92093 Brain specific factors in development and disease
R01MH-47144-02 (PCB) FOSTER, NORMAN L UNIVERSITY OF MICHIGAN MED CTR 1500 EAST MEDICAL CENTER DRIVE ANN ARBOR, MI 48109-0316 Neuropharmacologic challenges in dementia
R29MH-47149-02 (BPN) BALABAN, EVAN S HARVARD UNIVERSITY 26 OXFORD STREET CAMBRIDGE, MA 02138 Neural mechanisms for species behavioral difference
R01MH-47150-02 (SRCM) KOPELL, NANCY BOSTON UNIVERSITY 111 CUMMINGTON STREET BOSTON, MA 02215 Mathematical theory of oscillatory neural networks
R29MH-47154-02 (PCB) SUSSER, EZRA RES FNDN FOR MENTAL HYGIENE FOR PSYCHIATRIC RESEARCH ORANGEBURG, NY 10962 International schizophrenia study
R01MH-47162-01 (TDA) SIMPSON, GEORGE M Double-blind clozapine in treatment-resistant schizophrenia
R24MH-47167-02 (SRCM) GOGGIN, JUDITH P UNIV OF TEXAS AT EL PASO EL PASO, TX 79968-0553 ADM research development at the University of Texas at El Paso
R24MH-47167-02 0001 (SRCM) COHN, LAWRENCE ADM research development at the University of Texas at El Paso Perceived susceptibility to harm during adolescence
R24MH-47167-02 0002 (SRCM) DAUDISTEL, HOWARD ADM research development at the University of Texas at El Paso Faculty and minority student stress in higher education
R24MH-47167-02 0003 (SRCM) DEVINE, JAMES ADM research development at the University of Texas at El Paso Event-related potentials in primate visual memory
R24MH-47167-02 0004 (SRCM) GOGGIN, JUDITH ADM research development at the University of Texas at El Paso Event-related potentials as correlates of bilingualism

PROJECT NO., ORGANIZATIONAL UNIT., INVESTIGATOR, ADDRESS, TITLE

R24MH-47167-02 0005 (SRCM) HOSCH, HARMON ADM research development at the University of Texas at El Paso Acculturation and family support as predictors of adherence
R24MH-47167-02 0006 (SRCM) HOWARD, CHERYL ADM research development at the University of Texas at El Paso Sex and ethnic differences in youth risk taking in El Paso
R24MH-47167-02 0007 (SRCM) LUCKER, G WILLIAM ADM research development at the University of Texas at El Paso Evaluation of a pre-trial intervention program for first-time DWI offenders
R24MH-47167-02 0008 (SRCM) MOSS, DONALD ADM research development at the University of Texas at El Paso Experimental therapy for hyperkinetic disorders
R24MH-47167-02 0009 (SRCM) WHITWORTH, RANDOLPH ADM research development at the University of Texas at El Paso Evaluation of Alzheimer's disease in Hispanics
R24MH-47181-02 (SRCM) BARRACO, ROBIN A WAYNE STATE UNIVERSITY 540 E CANFIELD DETROIT, MI 48201 ADM research and career development at Wayne State Univesity
R24MH-47181-02 0004 (SRCM) NORMILE, HOWARD J ADM research and career development at Wayne State Univesity Behavioral examination--Interactions between adenosine & dopamine receptors
R24MH-47181-02 0005 (SRCM) ABBEY, ANTONIA ADM research and career development at Wayne State Univesity Alcohol and acquaintance rape
R24MH-47181-02 0001 (SRCM) YOUNG, ROSALIE ADM research and career development at Wayne State Univesity Black coronary heart disease patients, personal and clinical aspects of health
R24MH-47181-02 0002 (SRCM) SCHOENER, EUGENE P ADM research and career development at Wayne State Univesity The effects of cocaine and buprenorphine on neurons of the nucleus accumbens
R24MH-47181-02 0003 (SRCM) DAVIS, EDWARD ADM research and career development at Wayne State Univesity Teenage violence--An action research and prevention proposal
R24MH-47181-02 0006 (SRCM) HANKIN, JANET R ADM research and career development at Wayne State Univesity Special population studies of depression in gynecology patients
R24MH-47181-02 0007 (SRCM) COMMISSARIS, RANDALL L ADM research and career development at Wayne State Univesity Pharmacological evaluation of an animal model for panic disorder
R01MH-47182-02 (SRCM) JACKSON, JAMES S UNIVERSITY OF MICHIGAN 426 THOMPSON ST ANN ARBOR, MI 48106-1248 Research center for black mental health
R01MH-47184-02 (SRCM) FARMER, J DOYNE LOS ALAMOS NATIONAL LAB P.O. BOX 1663 LOS ALAMOS, NM 87545 Low dimensional chaos, nonlinear maps and nervous system
R24MH-47187-02 (SRCM) HUDGINS, JOHN L HAMPTON UNIVERSITY HAMPTON, VA 23668 Multidisciplinary mental health research program
R24MH-47187-02 0001 (SRCM) HUDGINS, JOHN Multidisciplinary mental health research program Correlates of drug use/abuse--Subjective norms of drug use/abuse tolerance
R24MH-47187-02 0002 (SRCM) DAVIS, BERTHA Multidisciplinary mental health research program African American family resources for coping with stress
R24MH-47187-02 0003 (SRCM) DANIEL, ELNORA Multidisciplinary mental health research program African American family interactions
R24MH-47187-02 0004 (SRCM) SLOAN, PATRICIA Multidisciplinary mental health research program Elderly African American family coping behavior
R24MH-47187-02 0005 (SRCM) FERGUSON, APRIL Multidisciplinary mental health research program Coping, coronary-proneness and Black women in academics
R24MH-47188-02 (SRCM) MUKENGE, IDA R MOREHOUSE COLLEGE 830 WESTVIEW DR, SW ATLANTA, GA 30314 Morehouse faculty development project in ADM research
R24MH-47188-02 0001 (SRCM) BRAITHWAITE, HAROLD Morehouse faculty development project in ADM research Cocaine use among homeless Black males
R24MH-47188-02 0002 (SRCM) CLARK, VANESSA Morehouse faculty development project in ADM research Stress and hypertension among African Americans
R24MH-47188-02 0003 (SRCM) GONZALEZ, FERNANDO Morehouse faculty development project in ADM research Computer models of choice
R24MH-47188-02 0004 (SRCM) ROSENMAN, MARTIN Morehouse faculty development project in ADM research Relationship between depression and environmental neurotoxicants
R24MH-47188-02 0005 (SRCM) WADE, BRUCE Morehouse faculty development project in ADM research Mental health services to Black males
R01MH-47189-02 (BPN) FARIS, PATRICIA L UNIVERSITY OF MINNESOTA 420 DELAWARE ST, SE MINNEAPOLIS, MN 55455 Role of CCK in feeding--Anatomy-aided behavioral studies
R01MH-47193-02 (SRCM) LIN, KEH-MING HARBOR-UCLA MEDICAL CENTER 1000 WEST CARSON STREET TORRANCE, CA 90509 Research center on the psychobiology of ethnicity
R01MH-47193-02 0001 (SRCM) LIN, KEH-MING Research center on the psychobiology of ethnicity Pilot--Ethnicity and differential responses to tricyclic antidepressants
R01MH-47193-02 0002 (SRCM) FU, PAUL Research center on the psychobiology of ethnicity Pilot--Ethnicity, lithium pharmacokinetics, and RBC/plasma lithium ratio
R01MH-47193-02 0003 (SRCM) POLAND, RUSSELL E Research center on the psychobiology of ethnicity Pilot--Ethnicity and biological markers in depression
R01MH-47194-01A1 (CVR) KOSS, MARY P UNIVERSITY OF ARIZONA 1501 N CAMPBELL AVENUE TUCSON, AZ 85724 Cognitive processing of traumatic sexual victimization
R24MH-47199-02 (SRCM) HICKS, LESLIE H HOWARD UNIVERSITY WASHINGTON, DC 20059 Mental health research development support
R24MH-47199-02 0001 (SRCM) SLOAN, LLOYD Mental health research development support Evaluating and evolving culture assimilator technology
R24MH-47199-02 0002 (SRCM) HARRELL, JULES Mental health research development support Coping processes in African American population
P01MH-47200-02 (SRCM) FRANCES, ALLEN AMERICAN PSYCHIATRIC ASSOC 1400 K STREET NW WASHINGTON, DC 20005 DSM-IV field trials program

project
P01MH-47200-02 0005 (SRCM) KELLER, M DSM-IV field trials program project Major depression, dysthymia, depressive personality, minor depression
P01MH-47200-02 0006 (SRCM) FOA, E DSM-IV field trials program project Obsessive-compulsive disorder (OCD)
P01MH-47200-02 0007 (SRCM) KILPATRICK, D DSM-IV field trials program project Post traumatic stress disorder (PTSD)
P01MH-47200-02 0008 (SRCM) ANDREASEN, N DSM-IV field trials program project Schizophrenia
P01MH-47200-02 0009 (SRCM) CLONINGER, R DSM-IV field trials program project Somatization disorder
P01MH-47200-02 0010 (SRCM) HELZER, J DSM-IV field trials program project Substance abuse
P01MH-47200-02 0001 (SRCM) WIDIGER, T DSM-IV field trials program project Antisocial personality disorder (ASPD)
P01MH-47200-02 0002 (SRCM) VOLKMAR, F DSM-IV field trials program project Autism and related pervasive development disorders
P01MH-47200-02 0003 (SRCM) LAHEY, B DSM-IV field trials program project Disruptive behavior disorders
P01MH-47200-02 0004 (SRCM) REYNOLDS, C DSM-IV field trials program project Insomnia
R43MH-47211-01A1 (MHSB) VERNON, D SUE EDGE ENTERPRISES, INC PO BOX 1304 LAWRENCE, KS 66044 Cooperative strategies in the classroom
R43MH-47213-01A1 (MHSB) KARBON, EDWARD W, JR NOVA PHARMACEUTICAL CORP 6200 FREEPORT CENTRE BALTIMORE, MD 21224-2788 Identification of sigma antagonists
R01MH-47225-02 (MHAZ) SCHWARTZ, STANLEY A UNIVERSITY OF MICHIGAN 109 S OBSERVATORY ANN ARBOR, MI 48109-2029 Perinatal HIV infections--Prevention of CNS pathology
R01MH-47226-02 (MHAZ) SPIEGEL, DAVID STANFORD UNIVERSITY JORDAN QUAD/BIRCH STANFORD, CA 94305 Effects of psychological treatment on cancer survival
R03MH-47227-02 (MHAZ) BAILEY, J MICHAEL NORTHWESTERN UNIVERSITY 633 CLARK ST EVANSTON, IL 60208-2710 Twin study of sexual orientation, attitudes and behavior
R03MH-47232-01A1 (MHAZ) CARBALLO-DIEGUEZ, ALEX RES FDN FOR MENTAL HYGIENE, IN 722 WEST 168TH ST, BOX 24 NEW YORK, NY 10032 HIV risk in Latin men who have sex with men
R01MH-47234-01A2 (MHAZ) COHEN, SHELDON A CARNEGIE MELLON UNIVERSITY PITTSBURGH, PA 15213 Social stress and susceptibility to infectious disease
R01MH-47241-02 (MHAZ) GILLMORE, MARY R UNIVERSITY OF WASHINGTON 4101 15TH AVE., NE SEATTLE, WA 98195 Reducing adolescents' risk of AIDS
R01MH-47246-02 (SRC) EBERSTEIN, ISAAC W FLORIDA STATE UNIVERSITY TALLAHASSEE, FL 32306-4063 AIDS--Children's and parents' knowledge and beliefs
R01MH-47250-02 (SRC) TURIEL, ELLIOT UNIVERSITY OF CALIFORNIA BERKELEY, CA 94720 Children's sexual knowledge--Social/biological aspects
R29MH-47251-02 (SRC) SCHONFELD, DAVID J YALE UNIVERSITY SCH OF MEDICIN 333 CEDAR STREET/PO BOX 3333 NEW HAVEN, CT 06510-8064 School-based AIDS education and children's health concepts
R01MH-47252-02 (SRC) IANNOTTI, RONALD J GEORGETOWN UNIV SCHOOL OF MED 3750 RESERVOIR RD, NW WASHINGTON, DC 20007 AIDS--Children's understanding and attitudes
R01MH-47260-01 (PYB) HONIG, WERNER K DALHOUSIE UNIVERSITY HALIFAX, NOVA SCOTIA B3H 4J1 CANADA Discrimitive basis of spatial cognition
R03MH-47263-01 (MSM) EMMONS, ROBERT A UNIVERSITY OF CALIFORNIA DAVIS, CA 95616 Ambivalence re expressing emotion-effects on well-being
R01MH-47277-01A1 (PCB) BRODIE, JONATHAN D NEW YORK UNIV MEDICAL CENTER 550 FIRST AVENUE NEW YORK, NY 10016 PET and schizophrenia -- Cerebral response to neuroleptics
R01MH-47281-01 (MHAZ) TOURTELLOTTE, WALLACE W VAMC WADSWORTH NEUROLOGY SERVICE (W127A) LOS ANGELES, CA 90073 PCR and CSF inflammatory response in HIV neurodisease
R13MH-47289-01 (PYB) WILCZYNSKI, WALTER UNIVERSITY OF TEXAS AUSTIN, TX 78712 Mechanisms of mate choice
R01MH-47292-01A1 (LCR) CAPLAN, ROBERT D GEORGE WASHINGTON UNIVERSITY 2125 G ST, NW RM GG202 WASHINGTON, DC 20052 Social support's antecedents--Prevention and mental health
R01MH-47293-01 (SRCM) DECI, EDWARD L UNIVERSITY OF ROCHESTER ROCHESTER, NY 14627 Motivation in Bulgaria and the US--A study of change
R01MH-47305-01A1 (SRCM) ROSS, MURIEL D NASA-AMES RESEARCH CENTER MAIL STOP 261-2 MOFFETT FIELD, CA 94035 Computational symbolic models of neural network dynamics
R29MH-47307-01 (BPN) SUPPLE, WILLIAM F, JR UNIVERSITY OF VERMONT JOHN DEWEY HALL BURLINGTON, VT 05405 Cerebellar-brainstem circuits and conditioned bradycardia
R01MH-47312-01 (LCR) BASSUK, ELLEN L THE BETTER HOMES FOUNDATION 181 WELLS AVE NEWTON CENTRE, MA 02159 Homeless mothers and children--A population based study
R01MH-47313-01 (PYB) WASSERMAN, EDWARD A UNIVERSITY OF IOWA IOWA CITY, IA 52242 Perceptual bases of visual concepts
R01MH-47317-01 (CEP) KUBOVY, MICHAEL UNIVERSITY OF VIRGINIA 102 GILMER HALL CHARLOTTESVILLE, VA 22903-247 Gestalt detection
R29MH-47330-01A1 (BPN) VOLMAN, SUSAN F OHIO STATE UNIVERSITY 1735 NEIL AVE COLUMBUS, OH 43210 Neural correlates of vocal learning in songbirds
R01MH-47333-01A1 (PCB) KLORMAN, RAFAEL UNIVERSITY OF ROCHESTER RIVER CAMPUS STATION ROCHESTER, NY 14627 Cognitive deficits in attention deficit disorder
R29MH-47343-01 (SRCM) CHURCH, AUSTIN T WASHINGTON STATE UNIVERSITY CLEVELAND HALL PULLMAN, WA 99164-2131 Cross-cultural personality and emotion structure
R01MH-47354-01 (SRCM) BYLUND, DAVID B UNIV OF NEBRASKA MED CTR 42ND ST & DEWEY AVE OMAHA, NE 68105 Regulation of serotonin-1 receptors
R01MH-47355-01 (TDA) LIN, KEH-MING HARBOR-UCLA MEDICAL CENTER 1000 WEST CARSON ST/D-5 ANNEX TORRANCE, CA 90509 Ethnicity and differential responses to benzodiazepines
K05MH-47363-10 (MHK) RUBIN, ROBERT T HARBOR UCLA MEDICAL CENTER 1000 WEST CARSON ST BLDG F5 TORRANCE, CA 90509 Hormone rhythms--Metabolic significance in psychiatry
R03MH-47367-01A1 (MSM) FIESE, BARBARA H SYRACUSE UNIVERSITY 430 HUNTINGTON HALL SYRACUSE, NY 13244-2340 Family stories and rituals--Relation to child mental health
R03MH-47368-01A1 (MSM) MA, POKEY M HARVARD MEDICAL SCHOOL 220 LONGWOOD AVENUE BOSTON, MA 02115 Neural mechanism underlying aggressive behavior
K05MH-47370-17 (MHK) BALDESSARINI, ROSS J MCLEAN HOSPITAL 115 MILL STREET BELMONT, MA 02178 Synaptic transmission in the central nervous system
R03MH-47371-01 (MSM) SCHLESINGER, MARK J HARVARD UNIVERSITY 79 KENNEDY STREET CAMBRIDGE, MA 02138 Incentives and management affecting psychiatric practice
R29MH-47374-01 (PYB) ROBINSON, GENE E UNIVERSITY OF ILLINOIS 505 S GOODWIN AVE/320 MORRILL URBANA, IL 61801 Mechanisms of behavioral plasticity in a model system
R03MH-47377-01 (MSM) BEALS, JANETTE L UNIVERSITY OF COLORADO 4200 E NINTH BOX A080 DENVER, CO 80262 CES-D among American Indians--Psychometric properties
R01MH-47382-02 (SRCM) MARMAR, CHARLES R SAN FRANCISCO VA MEDICAL CTR 4150 CLEMENT STREET SAN FRANCISCO, CA 94121 Rescue worker responses to the I-880 freeway collapse
R01MH-47383-01 (SRCM) BECK, AARON T Risk factors for suicide in psychiatric outpatients
R29MH-47390-01 (PCB) HOZA, BETSY WESTERN PSYCHIATRIC INSTITUTE 3811 O'HARA ST PITTSBURGH, PA 15213 Cognitive motivational factors in adhd children
R24MH-47392-02 (SRCM) STEFANO, GEORGE B SUNY/COLLEGE AT OLD WESTBURY PO BOX 210 OLD WESTBURY, NY 11568-0210 Old Westbury neurosciences research institute
R24MH-47392-02 0001 (SRCM) STEFANO, GEORGE Old Westbury neurosciences research institute Opioid involvement in neuroimmune stress response
R24MH-47392-02 0002 (SRCM) LEUNG, MICHAEL Old Westbury neurosciences research institute Opioid neuropeptides in circulating biological fluids
R24MH-47392-02 0003 (SRCM) MARTINEZ, EDWIN Old Westbury neurosciences research institute Opioid involvement in neuroendocrine regulation
R03MH-47409-01A1 (MSM) LIEDERMAN, JACQUELINE BOSTON UNIVERSITY 64 CUMMINGTON STREET BOSTON, MA 02215 Male prevalence for neurodevelopmental disorders
R01MH-47418-01 (SRCM) MOSS, ROBERT L UNIV TEX S W MEDICAL CENTER 5323 HARRY HINES BOULEVARD DALLAS, TX 75235-9040 LHRH--Membrane and cellular effects on hippocampal neurons
R03MH-47422-02 (MHAZ) DOUGLAS, STEVEN D CHILDREN'S HOSP OF PHILADELPHI 34TH ST & CIVIC CENTER BLVD PHILADELPHIA, PA 19104 Neuropeptides, mononuclear phagocytes & HIV-I infection
R03MH-47428-02 (MSM) MURTHY, LEELAVATTI R MOUNT SINAI SCHOOL OF MEDICINE ONE GUSTAVE L. LEVY PLACE NEW YORK, NY 10029 Phosphorylation of neuronal proteins in ad
R03MH-47440-01 (MSM) GERSON, STANTON L UNIV HOSPITALS OF CLEVELAND DIV OF HEMATOLOGY/ONCOLOGY CLEVELAND, OH 44106 Clozapine induced agranulocytosis in schizophrenia
R01MH-47448-01A1 (CVR) DAVIDSON, JONATHAN R DUKE UNIVERSITY MEDICAL CENTER DUKE SOUTH TRENT DR/BOX 3812 DURHAM, NC 27710 Victims of violence--Family risk for PTSD following rape
R01MH-47451-01A1 (TDA) SHOHAM-SALOMON, VARDA UNIVERSITY OF ARIZONA TUSCON, AZ 85721 Outcome and process analyses of therapeutic paradoxes
R29MH-47457-01A1 (PCB) ROTHSCHILD, ANTHONY J MCLEAN HOSPITAL 115 MILL STREET BELMONT, MA 02178 Cortisol cognition psychosis and outcome in depression
R01MH-47458-01 (CVR) CHAMBERLAIN, PATRICIA OREGON SOCIAL LEARNING CENTER 207E 5TH AVE EUGENE, OR 97401 Mediators of male delinquency--Clinical trial
R03MH-47459-01A1 (MSM) VAN DYCK, CHRISTOPHER H YALE UNIV SCHOOL OF MEDICINE 333 CEDAR STREET NEW HAVEN, CT 06510 Comparison of IMP and HMPAO cerebral SPECT in Alzheimers
R01MH-47460-01A1 (EPS) KUO, WEN UNIVERSITY OF CALIFORNIA NATIONAL RESEARCH CENTER LOS ANGELES, CA 90024-1563 Mental health problems among Chinese Americans
R01MH-47474-01 (CVR) HUESMANN, L ROWELL UNIV OF ILLINOIS AT CHICAGO BOX 4348 CHICAGO, IL 60680 Childhood TV violence viewing and adult aggression
R01MH-47476-01 (SRCM) REITE, MARTIN L UNIV OF COLORADO HLTH SCIS CTR 4200 EAST NINTH AVENUE DENVER, CO 80262 MEG evoked in schizophrenia
R01MH-47487-01 (EPS) SEGAL, STEVEN P 1918 UNIVERSITY AVE BERKELEY, CA 94704 Self-help agency functions/empowerment/member outcomes
R01MH-47501-01 (PYB) PICKARD, GARY E UNIVERSITY OF PENNSYLVANIA 422 CURRIE BLVD PHILADELPHIA, PA 19104-6141 Cross-species transplantation of circadian behavior
R29MH-47503-01 (PCB) DUNN, LAWRENCE A DUKE UNIVERSITY MEDICAL CENTER BOX 3833 DURHAM, NC 27710 Neural substrates of attention deficits in schizophrenia
R01MH-47506-01 (BPN) REED, RANDALL R JOHNS HOPKINS UNIVERSITY 725 N WOLFE ST BALTIMORE, MD 21205 Role of adenylyl cyclase in regulating neural function
R01MH-47508-01A1 (LCR) KILPATRICK, DEAN G MEDICAL UNIV OF SOUTH CAROLINA 171 ASHLEY AVENUE CHARLESTON, SC 29425-0742 The impact of distasters upon adults and aolescents
R29MH-47509-01A1 (BPN) CADET, JEAN L COLUMBIA UNIVERSITY 630 WEST 168TH STREET NEW YORK, NY 10032 Transplantation of modified dopamine cells into brain
R01MH-47510-01A1 (BPN) SUDHOF, THOMAS C UNIV OF TEXAS SOUTHWEST MED CT 5323 HARRY HINES BLVD DALLAS, TX 75235 Structure-function relationship--Inositol 1,4,5-triphosphate receptors

PROJECT NO., ORGANIZATIONAL UNIT., INVESTIGATOR, ADDRESS, TITLE

R03MH-47520-01 (MSM) SALAMONE, JOHN D UNIVERSITY OF CONNECTICUT 406 BABBIDGE RD STORRS, CT 06269-1020 The role of dopamine in appetitive and aversive behavior
R03MH-47524-01 (MSM) COBBETT, PETER J MICHIGAN STATE UNIVERSITY EAST LANSING, MI 48824 Opioid control of the neuroendocrine supraoptic nucleus
R01MH-47538-01 (BPN) DE VRIES, GEERT J UNIVERSITY OF MASSACHUSETTS PROGRAM IN NEUROSCIENCE AMHERST, MA 01003 Neural basis of sexual differentiation of brain function
R01MH-47542-01 (SRCM) MILTON, JOHN G UNIVERSITY OF CHICAGO 5841 S MARYLAND AVE/BX 425 CHICAGO, IL 60637 Complex dynamics and noise in the pupil light reflex
R01MH-47543-01 (CEP) CAMPOS, JOSEPH J UNIVERSITY OF CALIFORNIA BERKELEY, CA 94720 Cross-cultural studies of infant emotional expression
R01MH-47551-02 (SRCM) HARDIN, SALLY B UNIVERSITY OF SOUTH CAROLINA COLUMBIA, SC 29208 Intervention to decrease disaster stress in adolescents
R01MH-47559-01 (EPS) GOULD, MADELYN S NEW YORK STATE PHYS INST 722 WEST 168TH STREET NEW YORK, N Y 10032 Psychological autopsy of cluster suicides in adolescents
R01MH-47563-01 (EPS) BARONDES, SAMUEL H UNIVERSITY OF CALIFORNIA 401 PARNASSUS AVENUE SAN FRANCISCO, CA 94143 Genetics of bipolar disorder
P01MH-47566-01 (SRCM) MC CLELLAND, JAMES L CARNEGIE-MELLON UNIVERSITY 5000 FORBES AVENUE PITTSBURGH, PA 15213 Toward a model of normal and disordered cognition
P01MH-47566-01 0001 (SRCM) MC CLELLAND, JAMES L Toward a model of normal and disordered cognition Basic aspects of normal cognition
P01MH-47566-01 0002 (SRCM) COHEN, JONATHAN D Toward a model of normal and disordered cognition Neuromodulation and the processing of context in schizophrenia
P01MH-47566-01 0003 (SRCM) SEIDENBERG, MARK S Toward a model of normal and disordered cognition Normal and disordered word identification and naming
P01MH-47566-01 9001 (SRCM) MC CLELLAND, JAMES L Toward a model of normal and disordered cognition Core--Computational resource
R01MH-47567-02 (EPS) TEAGUE, GREGORY B TRUSTEES OF DARTMOUTH COLLEGE PO BOX 7 HANOVER, NH 03755 Cost effectiveness of dual diagnosis treatment
R01MH-47572-01 (LCR) FOGEL, BARRY S BROWN UNIVERSITY BOX G-B219 PROVIDENCE, RI 02912 Psychotropic drugs and care outcomes in nursing homes
R01MH-47573-01A1 (PYB) LEVINE, SEYMOUR STANFORD UNIVERSITY SCHOOL OF MEDICINE STANFORD, CA 94305-5095 Long term consequences of postnatal stress
R03MH-47574-01 (MSM) FRIEDMAN, LEE UNIV HOSP OF CLEVELAND 2074 ABINGTON ROAD CLEVELAND, OHIO 44106 Smooth pursuit, saccades, and fixation in schizophrenia
R37MH-47575-01 (CEP) BOWER, GORDON H STANFORD UNIVERSITY STANFORD, CA 94305 Focus in mental models
R03MH-47577-01A1 (MSM) GARNICK, DEBORAH W HARVARD SCHOOL OF PUBLIC HEALT 677 HUNTINGTON AVENUE BOSTON, MA 02115 Private sector initiatives in managed mental health care
R01MH-47597-01 (BCE) STOUDEMIRE, ALAN G EMORY CENTRAL CLINIC 5TH FL 1365 CLIFTON ROAD, NE ATLANTA, GA 30322 Long-term antidepressant use--Affective/cognitive effect
R01MH-47598-01 (BCE) MILLER, LAWRENCE G NEW ENGLAND MEDICAL CENTER 171 HARRISON AVENUE, BOX 1007 BOSTON, MA 02111 Psychotropic drug sensitivity in the elderly
R01MH-47611-01A1 (RNM) KILBOURN, MICHAEL R UNIVER OF MICHIGAN MED CTR B1G412 UNIVERSITY HOSPITAL ANN ARBOR, MI 48109-0028 New PET radiotracers--Monoamine reuptake inhibitors
R43MH-47615-01A1 (MHSB) TANNER, T BRADLEY SYMPOSIA INC 5105 BAYARD STREET PITTSBURGH, PA 15232 Medication--Educating the psychiatric patient
R43MH-47618-01A1 (MHSB) LOCKE, KENNETH W INTERNEURON PHARMACEUTICALS, I 99 HAYDEN AVE, ONE LEDGEMONT C LEXINGTON, MA 02173 Tyrosine potentiation of sympathomimetic-induced anorexia
R18MH-47634-02 (SRCM) TOPRAC, MARCIA G TX DEPT OF MH & MR P O BOX 12668 AUSTIN, TX 78711-2668 Cost-effectiveness of nine residential crisis modalities
R18MH-47638-02 (SRCM) SLEDGE, WILLIAM H CONNECTICUT MENTAL HEALTH CENT 34 PARK ST NEW HAVEN, CT 06519 Respite vs inpatient care--An experimental study
R18MH-47640-01 (SRCM) BLANCH, ANDREA K NEW YORK ST OFFICE MNTL HLTH 44 HOLLAND AVENUE ALBANY, NY 12229 Early intervention in schizophrenia
R18MH-47642-02 (SRCM) MC FARLANE, WILLIAM R RES FOUNDATN FOR MENTAL HYGIEN 722 WEST 168TH STREET NEW YORK, NY 10032 Work in family aided assertive community treatment
R18MH-47644-01A1 (SRCM) HIGGINS, JANE A REGION IV OFFICE 66 CEDAR ST NEWINGTON, CT 06111 Bridge building--Connecting with the community
R01MH-47649-01 (MHAZ) LOVELY, RICHARD H BATTELLE SEATTLE RESEARCH CENT 4000 NORTHEAST 41ST STREET SEATTLE, WA 98105 Social networks of minority youth at risk for AIDS
R18MH-47650-02 (SRCM) DRAKE, ROBERT E DIV OF MENT HLTH & DEVELOPMENT 105 PLEASANT STREET CONCORD, NH 03301 Outcomes and cost-effectiveness of supported employment
R01MH-47656-01A1 (MHAZ) SIEGEL, KAROLYNN MEMORIAL HOSP/CANCER/ALLD DIS 1275 YORK AVENUE NEW YORK, N Y 10021 Living w/ HIV infection--White-Black-Hispanic differences
P01MH-47667-02 (SRCM) LYMAN, WILLIAM D ALBERT EINSTEIN COLLEGE OF MED 1300 MORRIS PARK AVE BRONX, NY 10461 HIV-associated CNS dysfunction in pediatric AIDS
P01MH-47667-02 0001 (SRCM) DAVIES, PETER HIV-associated CNS dysfunction in pediatric AIDS Neuronal abnormalities in pediatric AIDS
P01MH-47667-02 0002 (SRCM) CHIU, FUNG-CHOW A HIV-associated CNS dysfunction in pediatric AIDS Astroglias and neuronal responses to HIV-1
P01MH-47667-02 0003 (SRCM) DICKSON, DENNIS HIV-associated CNS dysfunction in pediatric AIDS Microglia, cytokines and HIV-1 in fetal CNS

PROJECT NO., ORGANIZATIONAL UNIT., INVESTIGATOR, ADDRESS, TITLE

P01MH-47667-02 0004 (SRCM) LYMAN, WILLIAM D HIV-associated CNS dysfunction in pediatric AIDS The effect of HIV-1 on fetal CNS myelination
P01MH-47667-02 0005 (SRCM) BERMAN, JOAN W HIV-associated CNS dysfunction in pediatric AIDS The interaction of HIV-1 with the vascular endothelium
P01MH-47667-02 9001 (SRCM) LYMAN, WILLIAM D HIV-associated CNS dysfunction in pediatric AIDS Core--Laboratory
R01MH-47673-01A1 (MHAZ) SNYDER, MARK UNIVERSITY OF MINNESOTA 75 EAST RIVER ROAD MINNEAPOLIS, MN 55455 Social and psychological aspects of AIDS volunteerism
R01MH-47674-01 (MHAZ) MILLER, ANDREW H MOUNT SINAI SCHOOL OF MEDICINE 1 GUSTAVE L LEVY PLACE-BOX 122 NEW YORK, NY 10029 Adrenal steroid receptors in immune cells and tissues
R01MH-47679-01 (MHAZ) ROSZMAN, THOMAS L LEXINGTON, KY 40536-0084 Psychoneuroimmunology -- Modulation of T-cell function
P50MH-47680-02 (SRCM) BLOOM, FLOYD E SCRIPPS RESEARCH INSTITUTE 10666 NORTH TORREY PINES ROAD LA JOLLA, CA 92037 AIDS dementia--Molecular and cellular mechanisms
P50MH-47680-02 0001 (SRCM) ELDER, JOHN AIDS dementia--Molecular and cellular mechanisms Component #1
P50MH-47680-02 0002 (SRCM) BUCHMEIER, MICHAEL AIDS dementia--Molecular and cellular mechanisms Component #2
P50MH-47680-02 0003 (SRCM) SUTTCLIFFE, GREGOR AIDS dementia--Molecular and cellular mechanisms Component #3
P50MH-47680-02 0004 (SRCM) MILNER, ROBERT AIDS dementia--Molecular and cellular mechanisms Component #4
P50MH-47680-02 0005 (SRCM) WILSON, MICHAEL AIDS dementia--Molecular and cellular mechanisms Component #5
P50MH-47680-02 0006 (SRCM) OLDSTONE, MICHAEL AIDS dementia--Molecular and cellular mechanisms Component #6
P50MH-47680-02 0008 (SRCM) EDGINGTON, THOMAS AIDS dementia--Molecular and cellular mechanisms Component #8
P50MH-47680-02 0009 (SRCM) NARENBERG, MICHAEL AIDS dementia--Molecular and cellular mechanisms Component #9
P50MH-47680-02 0010 (SRCM) SARVENTNICK, NORA AIDS dementia--Molecular and cellular mechanisms Component #10
P50MH-47680-02 0011 (SRCM) GRUOL, DONNA AIDS dementia--Molecular and cellular mechanisms Component #11
P50MH-47680-02 0012 (SRCM) HENRIKSEN, STEVEN AIDS dementia--Molecular and cellular mechanisms Component #12
P50MH-47680-02 0013 (SRCM) SIGGINS, GEORGE AIDS dementia--Molecular and cellular mechanisms Component #13
P50MH-47680-02 0014 (SRCM) FOOTE, STEPHEN AIDS dementia--Molecular and cellular mechanisms Component #14
P50MH-47680-02 0016 (SRCM) KOOB, GEORGE AIDS dementia--Molecular and cellular mechanisms Component #16
P50MH-47680-02 0017 (SRCM) MITLER, MERRILL AIDS dementia--Molecular and cellular mechanisms Component #17
P50MH-47680-02 0018 (SRCM) POLICH, JOHN AIDS dementia--Molecular and cellular mechanisms Component #18
R18MH-47686-02 (SRCM) JOHNSON, BARBARA DEAN PA OFFICE OF MENTAL HEALTH 7TH AND FORSTER STREETS HARRISBURG, PA 17120 Self help employment center for severe mental illness
R43MH-47689-01A1 (MHSB) SOLDZ, STEPHEN M INNOVATIVE TRAINING SYSTEMS IN 24 LORING STREET NEWTON, MA 02159 Brief psychotherapy training in managed care programs
R19MH-47693-02 (SRCM) GUIDERA, SHARON L Nevada MH/MR MHSIP implementation
R19MH-47695-02 (SRCM) SANTONI, TIMOTHY W Improving mental health statistics in Maryland
R19MH-47697-02 (SRCM) ENNIS, JACQUELINE M Achieving integration across community services boards
R19MH-47698-02 (SRCM) PENNINGTON, MARGARET A Kentucky mental health statistics improvment project
R19MH-47699-02 (SRCM) WACHAL, MARILYN Oregons MHSIP impementation project - pilot study
R03MH-47712-01 (MSM) EMORY, EUGENE K EMORY UNVIERSITY ATLANTA, GA 30322 Individual and sex differences in stress reactivity
R01MH-47715-01 (NLS) BARNES, EUGENE M, JR BAYLOR COLLEGE OF MEDICINE ONE BAYLOR PLAZA HOUSTON, TX 77030 Regulation of neuronal receptors
R01MH-47719-01 (CVR) O'TOOLE, RICHARD E KENT STATE UNIVERSITY KENT, OH 44242 Teachers' response to child abuse
R01MH-47720-01A1 (EPS) DESHARNAIS, SUSAN I UNIV OF NORTH CAROLINA 1107 MCGAVRAN GREENBERG BLDG CHAPEL HILL, NC 27599-7400 Hospital closures and medicare multiple ADM patients
R29MH-47746-01 (CEP) HACKLEY, STEVEN A UNIVERSITY OF MISSOURI 210 MCALESTER HALL COLUMBIA, MO 65211 Prestimulus modulation of reflexive/voluntary reactions
R03MH-47751-01 (MSM) STANGER, CATHERINE UNIVERSITY OF VERMONT BURLINGTON, VT 05405 Accelerating longitudinal research on psychopathology
R01MH-47756-02 (ARR) DANNENBERG, ANDREW L THE JOHN HOPKINS UNIVERSITY 624 NORTH BROADWAY, 5TH FLOOR BALTIMORE, MD 21205 Mortality among HIV-positive military service applicants
R03MH-47765-01 (MSM) SIMON, GREGORY E CENTER FOR HEALTH STUDIES-GHC 1730 MINOR AVE SEATTLE, WA 98101-1448 Psychological disorders and somatization in primary care
R01MH-47769-01 (PCB) MENDELSON, WALLACE B STATE UNIVERSITY OF NEW YORK STONY BROOK, NY 11794-8101 Benzodiazepine effects on the perception of sleep
R03MH-47775-02 (MSM) LISSNER, LAUREN REDBERGSVAGEN 6 S-416 65 GOTEBORG, SWEDEN Weight loss, weight gain and chronic disease outcomes
R29MH-47783-01 (MHAZ) BELLINGER, DENISE L UNIVERSITY OF ROCHESTER 601 ELMWOOD AVENUE, BOX 603 ROCHESTER, NY 14642 Psychoneuroimmunonodulation in aging
R01MH-47786-02 (SRCM) HOBERMAN, HARRY M UNIVERSITY OF MINNESOTA 420 DELWARE ST SE BOX 95 UMHC MINNEAPOLIS, MN 55455 Psychiatric disorders among native american adolescents
K05MH-47808-17 (MHK) MELTZER, HERBERT Y CASE WESTERN RESERVE UNIVERSIT 2040 ABINGTON ROAD CLEVELAND, OH 44106 Biological studies of the major psychoses

PROJECT NO., ORGANIZATIONAL UNIT., INVESTIGATOR, ADDRESS, TITLE

R18MH-47814-02 (SRCM) WILSON, NANCY Z COLORADO DIV OF MENTAL HLTH 3520 WEST OXFORD AVE DENVER, CO 80236 Alternative models for delivering rural crisis services
R01MH-47817-02 (SRCM) THOMPSON, JAMES W UNIVERSITY OF MARYLAND 645 WEST REDWOOD STREET BALTIMORE, MD 21201 Mental health services use by schizophrenics
R03MH-47826-01 (SRCM) KAIRISS, EDWARD W YALE UNIVERSITY P O BOX 11A YALE STATION NEW HAVEN, CT 06520-7447 Structure-function relationships in hippocampal circuits
R29MH-47831-01 (TDA) SCHNEIER, FRANKLIN R RESEARCH FDN FOR MENTAL HYGIEN 722 WEST 168TH STREET NEW YORK, NY 10032 Moclobemide in social phobia
R03MH-47834-01 (MSM) SAYERS, STEVEN L MEDICAL COLLEGE OF PA/EPPI 3200 HENRY AVENUE PHILADELPHIA, PA 19129 Marital interaction and depression
R37MH-47840-01 (BPN) DAVIS, MICHAEL CONNECTICUT MENTAL HEALTH CTR 34 PARK ST NEW HAVEN, CT 06508 Anatomy and pharmacology of fear-potentiated startle
R03MH-47849-01 (MSM) MOREAU, DONNA L RES FDN FOR MENTAL HYGIENE INC 722 W 168TH ST NEW YORK, NY 10032 Validation study of panic disorder in children
R29MH-47855-02 (SRCM) MIRANDA, JEANNE UNIVERSITY OF CALIFORNIA SAN FRANCISCO, CA 94143-0852 Depression treatments in disadvantaged medical patients
R29MH-47857-01 (BPN) PITTS, DAVID K WAYNE STATE UNIVERSITY COLLEGEOF PHARMACY & A.H.P. DETROIT, MI 48202 Psychopharmacology of dopamine ontogeny
R29MH-47907-02 (SRCM) SULLIVAN, J GREER RAND PO BOX 2138-1700 MAIN ST SANT MONICA, CA 90407-2138 Use of public sector services by seriously mentally ill
R18MH-47910-02 (SRCM) HARDY, DEVON J ALC, DA & MH PROGRAM OFFICE 1317 WINEWOOD BOULEVARD TALLAHASSEE, FL 36399-0700 Fostering individualized mental health care--A study
R29MH-47920-02 (BSR) JENKINS, JANIS H CASE WESTERN RESERVE UNIVERSIT CLEVELAND, OH 44106 Sociocultural factors & course of chronic mental illness
R18MH-47951-02 (SRCM) LUBRECHT, JODY 1250 IRONWOOD DRIVE COEUR D'ALENE, IDAHO 83814 North Idaho CASSP--A rural system of care model
R18MH-47958-02 (SRCM) FOSTER, MARTHA A GEORGIA STATE UNIVERSITY UNIVERSITY PLAZA ATLANTA, GA 30303 Evaluation of interventions in childhood brain injuries
R03MH-47965-01 (MSM) MADELIAN, VERGINE NEW YORK STATE DEPT OF HEALTH P O BOX 509 ALBANY, NY 12201-0509 Cyclic nucleotide phosphodiesterase in astroglia
R01MH-47994-02 (SRCM) TEPLIN, LINDA A MCGAW MED CTR OF N WESTERN UNI 215 E CHICAGO AVE, SUITE 708 CHICAGO, IL 60611 Codisorders among female jail detainees-- mh trtmt needs
U01MH-48008-02 (SRCM) HARTWELL, TYLER D RESEARCH TRIANGLE INSTITUTE PO BOX 12194 RES TRIANGLE PARK, NC 27709 Multi-site trials of behavioral strategies to prevent HIV
U01MH-48013-02 (SRCM) O'LEARY, ANN M RUTGERS UNIVERSITY TILLETT HALL, KILMER CAMPUS NEW BRUNSWICK, NJ 08903 Comparison of AIDS prevention strategies in high risk inner-city men
R18MH-48018-02 (SRCM) PRINZ, RONALD J UNIVERSITY OF SOUTH CAROLINA COLUMBIA, SC 29208 Preventive interventions for chronic conduct problems
U01MH-48019-02 (SRCM) CELENTANO, DAVID D JOHNS HOPKINS UNIVERSITY 615 NORTH WOLFE STREET BALTIMORE, MD 21205 Trials to promote behavior change to prevent HIV spread
R18MH-48034-02 (SRCM) GUERRA, NANCY G UNIV OF ILLINOIS AT CHICAGO BOX 4348, M/C 285 CHICAGO, IL 60680 Preventing antisocial behavior in high-risk children
R18MH-48036-02 (SRCM) FORD, JANET HAMILTON COUNTY MENTAL HEALTH 222 EAST CENTRAL PARKWAY CINCINNATI, OH 45202 Transitional vs permanent housing for homeless mentally ill
R18MH-48041-03 (SRCM) VALENCIA, ELIECER S PSYCHIATRY SHELTER PROGRAM 622 WEST 168TH STREET NEW YORK, N Y 10032 Critical time intervention for homeless mentally ill men
R18MH-48043-02 (SRCM) COIE, JOHN D DUKE UNIVERSITY PSYCHOLOGY DEPT DURHAM, N C 27706 Multisite prevention of conduct disorder
R01MH-48053-01 (SRCM) BEHAR, LENORE DEPT OF HUMAN RESOURCES 325 SALISBURY STREET RALEIGH, NC 27603 Assessing care for children and youth with severe emotional disorders
R18MH-48059-02 (SRCM) ROTHERAM-BORUS, MARY J RES FOUND FOR MENTAL HYGIENE 722 WEST 168TH STREET NEW YORK, N Y 10032 Specialized family ER program with suicide attempters
R29MH-48066-02 (CEP) METCALFE, JANET A DARTMOUTH COLLEGE HANOVER, NH 03755 Composite holographic associative recognition memory
U01MH-48068-02 (SRCM) STANTON, BONITA F UNIVERSITY OF MARYLAND 700 W LOMBARD STREET BALTIMORE, MD 21201 AIDS risk prevention in youths
R18MH-48070-02 (SRCM) LEHMAN, ANTHONY F UNIV OF MARYLAND AT BALTIMORE 645 W REDWOOD ST BALTIMORE, MD 21201 Baltimore program for the homeless mentally ill
R18MH-48072-02 (SRCM) EVANS, MARY E NY STATE OFFICE OF MENT HEALTH 44 HOLLAND AVENUE ALBANY, NY 12229 Outcomes of 2 intensive service programs for children
R01MH-48073-01 (SRCM) WALKER, DERALD R MENTAL HLTH & DEV DIS SERV DIV 2575 BITTERN STREET NE SALEM , OR 97310 The Oregon Partner's Project--A randomized study
R03MH-48077-01 (MSM) HOWES, PAUL W MT HOPE FAMILY CENTER 187 EDINBURGH ST ROCHESTER, NY 14608 Family interaction identifying maltreating families
R18MH-48080-02 (SRCM) GOLDFINGER, STEPHEN M MASSACHUSETTS MENTAL HLTH CTR 74 FERNWOOD ROAD BOSTON, MA 02115 Apartments vs. evolving consumer households for the homeless mentally ill
R01MH-48081-02 (SRCM) SHANER, ANDREW BRENTWOOD VA MEDICAL CENTER 11301 WILSHIRE BLVD LOS ANGELES, CA 90073 Treatment of schizophrenia and stimulant abuse
R01MH-48085-01A1 (EPS) COSTELLO, ELIZABETH J DUKE UNIVERSITY MEDICAL CTR BOX 3454 DURHAM, NC 27710-3454 Service use for adm comorbidity in rural adolescents

PROJECT NO., ORGANIZATIONAL UNIT., INVESTIGATOR, ADDRESS, TITLE

R18MH-48087-02 (SRCM) CAUCE, ANA MARIE UNIVERSITY OF WASHINGTON SEATTLE, WA 98125 Effectiveness of case managment for homeless adolescents
R18MH-48095-02 (SRCM) HOUGH, RICHARD SAN DIEGO STATE UNIVERSITY 1202 MORENA BLVD., SUITE 100 SAN DIEGO, CA 92110 Client-focused housing support services for the homeless
R18MH-48097-02 (SRCM) RUDD, M DAVID 918 ESTATE DRIVE BELTON, TX 76513 Partial hospitalization of high risk suicidal youth
R03MH-48101-01 (SRCM) KUPERSMIDT, JANIS B UNC- CHAPEL HILL CB#3270, DAVIE HALL CHAPEL HILL, NC 27599-3270 Mental health of children of migrant farmworkers
P50MH-48108-01 (SRCM) TSIEN, RICHARD W STANFORD UNIVERSITY STANFORD, CA 94305-5426 Molecular and cellular signalling in synaptic plasticity
P50MH-48108-01 0005 (SRCM) TSIEN, RICHARD W Molecular and cellular signalling in synaptic plasticity Ca++ signalling, protein kinases and hippocampal LTP
P50MH-48108-01 0006 (SRCM) SCHULMAN, HOWARD Molecular and cellular signalling in synaptic plasticity Ca++-dependent protein phosphorylation in LTP and gene expression
P50MH-48108-01 0007 (SRCM) SMITH, STEPHEN Molecular and cellular signalling in synaptic plasticity Astrocyte signalling and synaptic plasticity
P50MH-48108-01 0008 (SRCM) SHATZ, CARLA J Molecular and cellular signalling in synaptic plasticity Activity-dependent synaptic plasticity in visual system development
P50MH-48108-01 9001 (SRCM) BUCHANON, JO ANN Molecular and cellular signalling in synaptic plasticity Core--Microscopy
P50MH-48108-01 9002 (SRCM) TSIEN, RICHARD W Molecular and cellular signalling in synaptic plasticity Core--Molecular biology and biochemistry
P50MH-48108-01 0001 (SRCM) ALDRICH, RICHARD W Molecular and cellular signalling in synaptic plasticity Molecular mechanisms of potassium channel function
P50MH-48108-01 0002 (SRCM) TSIEN, RICHARD W Molecular and cellular signalling in synaptic plasticity Modulation of neuronal Ca channel by Ca++ and protein kinases
P50MH-48108-01 0003 (SRCM) SCHELLER, RICHARD H Molecular and cellular signalling in synaptic plasticity GTP binding proteins of the presynaptic nerve terminal
P50MH-48108-01 0004 (SRCM) SCHWARZ, THOMAS L Molecular and cellular signalling in synaptic plasticity Genetic dissection of transmitter release
R03MH-48118-01 (MSM) CLARKE, GREGORY N OREGON HLTH SCIENCES UNIV 3181 S W SAM JACKSON PARK ROAD PORTLAND, OR 97201-3098 School based prevention of adolescent depression
P01MH-48125-01 (SRCM) FRAZER, ALAN VETERANS ADMINISTRATION HOSP UNIVERSITY & WOODLAND AVE PHILADELPHIA, PA 19104 Biology of serotonin in brain
P01MH-48125-01 0001 (SRCM) MOLINOFF, PERRY B Biology of serotonin in brain Model systems for the study of serotonin receptors
P01MH-48125-01 0002 (SRCM) CHESSELET, MARIE-FRANCOISE Biology of serotonin in brain Serotonin receptor mRNAs in basal ganglia
P01MH-48125-01 0003 (SRCM) MANNING, DAVID R Biology of serotonin in brain Linkages among G proteins and receptors for serotonin
P01MH-48125-01 0004 (SRCM) FRAZER, ALAN Biology of serotonin in brain Serotonin-1A agonists--Functional and biochemical studies
P01MH-48125-01 0005 (SRCM) LUCKI, IRWIN Biology of serotonin in brain Serotonin release and behavior
P01MH-48125-01 0006 (SRCM) KUNG, HANK F Biology of serotonin in brain Serotonin reuptake inhibitors for SPECT imaging
P01MH-48125-01 9001 (SRCM) PRITCHETT, DOLAN Biology of serotonin in brain Core--Molecular biology
P01MH-48125-01 9002 (SRCM) LUCKI, IRWIN Biology of serotonin in brain Core--Behavior
P01MH-48125-01 9003 (SRCM) KUNG, HANK F Biology of serotonin in brain Core--Radiochemistry
R18MH-48133-02 (SRCM) CLUM, GEORGE A VIRGINIA POLYTECHNIC INSTITUTE BLACKSBURG, VA 24061-0436 Prevention of suicidality in adolescent ideators
R18MH-48136-01A1 (SRCM) HANLEY, JEROME H SC DEPARTMENT OF MENTAL HEALTH PO BOX 485 COLUMBIA, SC 29202 Diffusion of multisystemic family preservation services
R18MH-48139-02 (SRCM) EGGERT, LEONA L UNIVERSITY OF WASHINGTON SEATTLE, WA 98195 Preventing suicide lethality among vulnerable youth
R01MH-48141-02 (SRCM) HARGREAVES, WILLIAM A UNIVERSITY OF CALIFORNIA SAN FRANCISCO GENERAL HOSPITAL SAN FRANCISCO, CA 94143-0852 Services trial methods-- Clozapine cost effectiveness
R01MH-48144-01A1 (EPS) WELLS, KENNETH RAND CORPORATION PO BOX 2138/1700 MAIN STREET SANTA MONICA, CA 90406-2138 Effectiveness of care for depression
R01MH-48157-01 (TDA) PELHAM, WILLIAM E WESTERN PSYCHIATRIC INST & CLI 3811 O'HARA STREET PITTSBURGH, PA 15213 Pharmacology and cognitive motivation in ADHD
R01MH-48161-01 (SRCM) LEVY, WILLIAM B UNIVERSITY OF VIRGINIA HEALTH SCIENCES CENTER CHARLOTTESVILLE, VA 22908 A computational approach for studing the brain
P50MH-48165-02 (SRCM) CONGER, RAND D IOWA STATE UNIVERSITY 107 EAST HALL AMES, IA 50011 Center for family research in rural mental health
P50MH-48165-02 0001 (SRCM) LORENZ, F Center for family research in rural mental health Extensions of the family model to specific populations
P50MH-48165-02 0002 (SRCM) CADORET, R Center for family research in rural mental health Genetic/environmental interactions in risk for disorder
P50MH-48165-02 0003 (SRCM) NAPLES, NANCY Center for family research in rural mental health Ethnographic study of low income rural women
P50MH-48165-02 0004 (SRCM) SIMONS, R Center for family research in rural mental health Economic strain, social support, and rural single-parent families
P50MH-48165-02 0005 (SRCM) GERRARD, MEG Center for family research in rural mental health Risk behaviors in rural adolescents

R01MH-48168-01 (SRCM) SMITH, ROBERT G UNIVERSITY OF PENNSYLVANIA SCHOOL OF MEDICINE PHILADELPHIA, PA 19104-6058 Struct/funct of retinal circuit for scotopic luminance
P50MH-48185-01 (SRCM) HOUK, JAMES C NORTHWESTERN UNIVERSITY 303 E CHICAGO AVE CHICAGO, IL 60611 Neuronal populations and behavior
P50MH-48185-01 0001 (SRCM) GEORGOPOULOS, APOSTOLOS Neuronal populations and behavior Cortical representations of perceptual motor processes
P50MH-48185-01 0002 (SRCM) BARTO, ANDREW G Neuronal populations and behavior Adaptive network models for sensory-motor processes
P50MH-48185-01 0003 (SRCM) HOUK, JAMES C Neuronal populations and behavior Control of limb representations in cerebellum and motor cortex
P50MH-48185-01 0004 (SRCM) HOUK, JAMES C Neuronal populations and behavior Visualization and analysis of in vitro networks
P50MH-48185-01 0005 (SRCM) PETERSON, BARRY W Neuronal populations and behavior Adaptation of eye representations in cerebellum
P50MH-48185-01 9001 (SRCM) HOUK, JAMES C Neuronal populations and behavior Core
R29MH-48192-01 (CVR) PRICE, JOSEPH M SAN DIEGO STATE UNIVERSITY 6363 ALVARADO CT SAN DIEGO, CA 92182 Maltreatment and social maladjustment
P50MH-48197-02 (SRCM) SMITH, G RICHARD UNIV OF ARKANSAS/MED SCIENCE 4301 W MARKHAM, SLOT 554 LITTLE ROCK, AR 72205 Center for rural mental health care research
P50MH-48197-02 0001 (SRCM) KELLEHER, KELLY Center for rural mental health care research Child and adolescent mental health measures
P50MH-48197-02 0002 (SRCM) CUFFEL, BRIAN Center for rural mental health care research Rural schizophrenia registry
P50MH-48197-02 0003 (SRCM) BECK, CORNELIA Center for rural mental health care research Home-based mental health services for rural elderly
R13MH-48199-01 (BPN) RAY, OAKLEY S VANDERBILT UNIVERSITY A & S PSYCHOLOGY BUILDING NASHVILLE, TN 37240 ACNP annual meeting special programs
P50MH-48200-01 (SRCM) JAN, LILY Y UNIV OF CALIF, SAN FRANCISCO PARNASSUS AVENUE SAN FRANCISCO, CA 94143 Analysis of long-term changes in the mammalian brain
P50MH-48200-01 0001 (SRCM) JAN, LILY Y Analysis of long-term changes in the mammalian brain Molecular studies of potassium channels in the hippocampus
P50MH-48200-01 0002 (SRCM) JAN, YUH NUNG Analysis of long-term changes in the mammalian brain Study of genes involved in mammalian neural development
P50MH-48200-01 0003 (SRCM) JULIUS, DAVID J Analysis of long-term changes in the mammalian brain Receptor gene expression in hippocampal neurons
P50MH-48200-01 0004 (SRCM) NICOLL, ROGER A Analysis of long-term changes in the mammalian brain Mechanisms underlying mossy fiber LTP in the hippocampus
P50MH-48200-01 0005 (SRCM) REICHARDT, LOUIS F Analysis of long-term changes in the mammalian brain Tropic factor, integrin, and CAM functions in the CNS
P50MH-48200-01 9001 (SRCM) JAN, LILY Y Analysis of long-term changes in the mammalian brain Core
R29MH-48211-01 (BSR) MCLEOD, JANE D UNIVERSITY OF MINNESOTA 267-19TH AVENUE SOUTH MINNEAPOLIS, MN 55455 Spouse concordance for mental health behavioral outcomes
R18MH-48215-02 (SRCM) SHERN, DAVID L BUREAU OF SURVEY/EVALUA RES 44 HOLLAND AVE ALBANY, NY 12229 Housing mentally ill street people--A rehabilitation approach
R01MH-48216-02 (SRCM) ALLOY, LAUREN B TEMPLE UNIVERSITY WEISS HALL PHILADELPHIA, PA 19122 Negative cognition depression--Etiology and course
R29MH-48228-02 (BPN) JOHNSTON, CRAIG A SCHOOL OF PHARMACY MISSOULA, MT 59812-1075 Neurohypophyseal influence on adenohypophyseal secretion
R18MH-48238-02 (SRCM) BEHAR, LENORE CHILD & FAMILY SERV BRANCH 325 NORTH SALISBURY STREET RALEIGH, NC 27603 A demonstration of infant mental health services
R01MH-48239-01 (SRCM) LILLEY, GEORGE W, JR WEST VIRGINIA DEPT OF HEALTH 1900 KANAWHA BLVD EAST CHARLESTON, WV 25305 CASSP community-level system development
R44MH-48240-02 (SSS) WEINSHANK, RICHARD L NEUROGENETIC CORP 215 COLLEGE ROAD PARAMUS, NJ 07652 Cloning of the dopamine D1 receptor family
R43MH-48241-01 (SRCD) BURRILL, PETER H MERIDIAN INSTRUMENTS INC 2310 SCIENCE PARKWAY OKEMOS, MI 48864 Integrating transient recorder for tof mass spectrometry
R44MH-48243-03 (SRCD) NEUMEYER, JOHN L RESEARCH BIOCHEMICALS, INC 1 STRATHMORE ROAD NATICK, MA 01760 High affinity ligands for the cocaine receptor
R01MH-48248-02 (CVR) TOLAN, PATRICK H 907 S WOLCOTT CHICAGO, IL 60612 Pathways of adolescent anti-social behavior
R01MH-48251-02 (CVR) URQUIZA, ANTHONY J UNIVERSITY OF CALIFORNIA, DAVI 2516 STOCKTON BLVD, MEDICAL CT SACRAMENTO, CA 95817 Prevalence and effects of sex abuse--A multi-ethnic study
R03MH-48252-02 (MSM) JOHNSTON, CRAIG A SCHOOL OF PHARMACY 32 CAMPUS DRIVE MISSOULA, MT 59812-1075 Central oxytocin stimulation of LHRH and LH release
R43MH-48255-01 (MHSB) STORTI, GEORGE M QUANTEX CORPORATION 2 RESEARCH COURT ROCKVILLE, MD 20850 New imaging media for in-vivo and in-vitro autoradiography
R43MH-48261-01 (MHSB) PETERSON, JAMES L SOCIOMETRICS CORPORATION 170 STATE STREET LOS ALTOS, CA 94022 Archive of longitudinal data on children's mental health
R43MH-48270-01A1 (MHSB) GREENBLATT, RICHARD E SOURCE/SIGNAL IMAGING 1935 31TH ST SAN DIEGO, CA 92102 EEG source imaging
R43MH-48273-01 (SSS) DHEANDHANNO, SEKSAN EXTREL CORPORATION 575 EPSILON DR, PO BOX 11512 PITTSBURGH, PA 15238 Microwave induced plasma source for determination
R01MH-48274-01 (CEP) FARAH, MARTHA J CARNEGIE MELLON UNIVERSITY 5000 FORBES AVE PITTSBURGH, PA 15213 The neural bases of spatial representation
R01MH-48290-01 (MHAZ) KOHRMAN, ARTHUR F LA RABIDA CHILDRENS HOSP & RES EAST 65TH STR AT LAKE MICHIGAN CHICAGO, IL 60649 Mental health service needs in children of hiv + parents
R43MH-48296-01S1 (SSS) KLAUSNER, MITCHELL MATTEK CORPORATION 200 HOMER AVENUE ASHLAND, MA 01721 Modified surfaces for chemically defined cell culture
R01MH-48299-01 (MHAZ) CAGGIULA, ANTHONY R UNIVERSITY OF PITTSBURGH 412 LANGLEY HALL PITTSBURGH, PA 15260 Ovarian hormones stress, and immunologic responsiveness
R01MH-48330-01 (CVR) TRICKETT, PENELOPE K UNIV OF SOUTHERN CALIFORNIA LOS ANGELES, CA 90089-1061 Sexual abuse of females--Effects in the pubertal period
R01MH-48358-01 (BPN) MILEDI, RICARDO UNIVERSITY OF CALIFORNIA IRVINE, CA 92717 Studies on a novel class of mammalian GABA receptor
R01MH-48359-01 (PYB) FETTERMAN, J GREGOR INDIANA UNIVERSITY 1125 E 38TH STREET INDIANAPOLIS, IN 46205 Theoretical approaches to temporal control
R03MH-48402-01 (MSM) FOUNTAIN, STEPHEN B KENT STATE UNIVERSITY KENT, OH 44242-0001 Serial-pattern learning in rats
R01MH-48405-01 (PCB) SCHULZ, ROCKWELL I ROCKWELL SCHULZ 230 BRADLEY MEMORIAL MADISON, WI 53706 Management practices and staff burnout in care of SMI
R03MH-48406-01 (MSM) HARDING, CHERYL F HUNTER COLLEGE OF CUNY 695 PARK AVENUE NEW YORK, N Y 10021 Catecholaminergic modulation of behavior
R03MH-48413-01 (MSM) PADEN, CHARLES M MONTANA STATE UNIVERSITY BOZEMAN, MT 59717 Cellular correlates of axonal sprouting
R01MH-48432-01 (SRCM) JOHNSTON, DANIEL BAYLOR COLLEGE OF MEDICINE ONE BAYLOR PLAZA HOUSTON, TX 77030 Cellular information processing in hippocampus
R03MH-48444-01 (MSM) TOHEN, MAURICIO MC LEAN HOSPITAL 115 MILL STREET BELMONT, MA 02178 Predictors of outcome after a first episode of psychosis
R01MH-48456-01 (EPS) HORWITZ, SARAH M 60 COLLEGE ST-PO BOX 3333 NEW HAVEN, CT 06510 The impact of mental health services on foster children
R01MH-48470-01 (SRCM) LERER, BERNARD HADASSAH HOSPITAL PO BOX 12000 JERUSALEM, ISRAEL 91120 ECT--Optimum schedule and antidepressant mechanisms
R01MH-48476-01 (SRCM) BLANCHARD, EDWARD B 1535 WESTERN AVENUE ALBANY, NY 12203 Motor vehicle accidents and post-traumatic stress disorder
R01MH-48492-01 (EPS) HAAS, GRETCHEN L WESTERN PSYCHIATRIC INSTITUTE 3811 O'HARA STREET PITTSBURGH, PA 15213 Suicidal behavior in schizophrenia
R01MH-48494-01 (CEP) NOSOFSKY, ROBERT M INDIANA UNIVERSITY PO BOX 1847 BLOOMINGTON, IN 47405 Perceptual classification, learning and memory
R01MH-48518-01 (BPN) REISINE, TERRY D UNVI OF PENN SCH OF MED 36TH ST & HAMILTON WALK PHILADELPHIA, PA 19104 Functional properties of brain somatostatin receptors
R24MH-48519-01 (SRCM) CHAMBERS, JOHN W, JR FLORIDA A & M UNIVERSITY TALLAHASSEE, FL 32307 Minority institutions research development program
R24MH-48519-01 0001 (SRCM) BALDWIN, JOSEPH A Minority institutions research development program African self-consciousness among Black adolescents
R24MH-48519-01 0002 (SRCM) CHAMBERS JR, JOHN W Minority institutions research development program Cultural factors in the stress of Black college students
R24MH-48519-01 0003 (SRCM) CHAMBERS JR, JOHN W Minority institutions research development program Physiological stress responses in young Black adults
R01MH-48523-01 (EPS) STEADMAN, HENRY J POLICY RESEARCH ASSOCS, INC 262 DELAWARE AVENUE DELMAR, NY 12054 Diverting mentally ill jail detainees
R29MH-48536-01 (SRCM) FROST, WILLIAM UNIVERSITY OF TEXAS MEDICAL SC PO BOX 20708 HOUSTON, TX 77225 Network organization of memory in Tritonia
P30MH-48539-01 (SRCM) GUR, RAQUEL E UNIVERSITY OF PENNSYLVANIA 205 PIERSOL BLDG PHILADELPHIA, PA 19104 Functional brain imaging center to study mental disorders
P30MH-48539-01 0001 (SRCM) GYULAI, LASZLO Functional brain imaging center to study mental disorders Pilot--Brain imaging in patients with bipolar disorder using PET
P30MH-48539-01 0002 (SRCM) SCHWEIZER, EDWARD Functional brain imaging center to study mental disorders Pilot--PET scan evaluations in anxious patients
P30MH-48539-01 9001 (SRCM) KUNG, HANK F Functional brain imaging center to study mental disorders Core--Serotonin ligands for PET imaging
P30MH-48539-01 9002 (SRCM) KARP, JOEL Functional brain imaging center to study mental disorders Core--Image analysis
P30MH-48539-01 9003 (SRCM) GUR, RUBEN C Functional brain imaging center to study mental disorders Core--Neuropsychology
P30MH-48539-01 0003 (SRCM) KUMAR, ANAND Functional brain imaging center to study mental disorders Pilot--Psychosis in the elderly
R29MH-48545-01 (BPN) FREEDMAN, JONATHAN E NORTHEASTERN UNIVERSITY 360 HUNTINGTON AVE BOSTON, MA 02115 Ionic mechanisms of postsynaptic dopamine receptors
R01MH-48590-01 (EPS) FISER, DEBRA H UNIVERSITY OF ARKANSAS MED SCI 4301 WEST MARKHAMRM 512 LITTLE ROCK, AR 72205 Psychosocial morbidity in childhood asthma
R29MH-48593-01 (LCR) REPETTI, RENA L UNIVERSITY OF CALIFORNIA LOS ANGELES, CA 90024-1563 Stress, parent-child relations, and child mental health
R01MH-48603-01 (BPN) MORRISON, JOHN H MT SINAI SCHOOL OF MEDICINE ONE GUSTAVE L LEVY PLACE NEW YORK, N Y 10029 Characterization of cortical target cells for dopamine
R01MH-48609-01 (MHAZ) KLUGER, MATTHEW J UNIVERSITY OF MICHIGAN 1301 EAST CATHERINE ANN ARBOR, MI 48109-0622 Psychosocial stress-induced fever--The roles of cytokines

PROJECT NO., ORGANIZATIONAL UNIT., INVESTIGATOR, ADDRESS, TITLE

R43MH-48610-01 (MHSB) ASHBAUGH, JOHN W HUMAN SERVICES GROUP INC 2336 MASSACHUSETTS AVE CAMBRIDGE, MA 02140 Voice-generated records and reports for mental health case managers
R01MH-48628-01 (MHAZ) GOODKIN, KARL UNIVERSITY OF MIAMI 1425 NW 10TH AVE MIAMI, FL 33136 Impact of a bereavement support group in HIV infection
R01MH-48630-01 (MHAZ) DELAMATER, JOHN D SINAI SAMARITAN MEDICAL CTR. 844 N. 12TH STREET, RM. V 117 MILWAUKEE, WISCONSIN 53201 STD prevention--Behavior change in an at-risk population
R01MH-48638-01 (MHAZ) CATANIA, JOSEPH A UNIV OF CA, SAN FRANCISCO 74 NEW MONTGOMERY SAN FRANCISCO, CA 94105 Longitudinal follow-up of the AMEN cohort
R01MH-48642-01 (MHAZ) CATANIA, JOSEPH A UNIVERSITY OF CALIFORNIA 74 NEW MONTGOMERY SAN FRANCISCO, CA 94105 A longitudinal national AIDS behavioral survey
R29MH-48644-01 (MHAZ) CARLSON, SONIA L UNIV OF KENTUCKY MED CTR 800 ROSE ST LEXINGTON, KY 40536-0084 Psychoneuroimmunology--Modulation of T-cell trafficking
R01MH-48652-01 (MHAZ) GIULIAN, DANA J BAYLOR COLLEGE OF MEDICINE ONE BAYLOR PLAZA HOUSTON, TX 77030 Role of inflammatory cells in AIDS dementia
R01MH-48654-01 (SRCM) WHITSEL, BARRY L UNIVERSITY OF NORTH CAROLINA CHAPEL HILL, NC 27599-7545 Stimulus coding by somatosensory cortex
R01MH-48825-01 (SRCM) REISS, DAVID GEORGE WASHINGTON UNIV MED CTR 2300 EYE STREET NW WASHINGTON, DC 20037 Nonshared environment genes and adolescent mental health
R03MH-48827-01 (MSM) SCANLAN, JAMES M UNIV OF COLORADO HEALTH SCI CT 4200 E NINTH AVE DENVER, CO 80262 Anger expression--Endocrine, lipid and immune effects
R01MH-48848-01 (MHAZ) ST LAWRENCE, JANET S JACKSON STATE UNIV SCH OF LIB 1400 JR LYNCH STREET JACKSON, MS 39217 Behavioral AIDS risk reduction with minority adolescents
R03MH-48887-01 (SRCM) KARAM, ELIE G AMERICAN UNIVERSITY OF BEIRUT 850 THIRD AVE 18TH FLOOR NEW YORK, NY 10022 PTSD and war in Lebanon
R01MH-48948-01 (SRC) CARBONE, KATHRYN M JOHNS HOPKINS MED INSTITUTIONS 600 NORTH WOLFE ST/BLALOCK 111 BALTIMORE, MD 21205 Borna virus alters perinatal behavior development
R01MH-48949-01 (SRC) LICKLITER, ROBERT E VIRGINIA POLYTECHNIC INST & SU BLACKSBURG, VA 24061-0436 Mechanisms of perinatal perceptual organization
R01MH-48950-01 (SRC) LEON, MICHAEL A UNIVERSITY OF CALIFORNIA IRVINE, CA 92717 Neural mechanisms of early learning
R03MH-48951-01 (MSM) MC BURNETT, ROBERT K UNIVERSITY OF CALIFORNIA IRVINE, CA 92717 Central and peripheral actions of amphetamine in ADHD
R03MH-48954-01 (SRCM) LEMPERS, JACQUES D IOWA STATE UNIVERSITY 205 RICHARDS AMES, IOWA 50011 War stress support and well-being in military families
R03MH-48979-01 (SRCM) LEVAV, ITZHAK COLUMBIA UNIVERSITY 100 HAVEN AVE TOWER 3-19H NEW YORK, NY 10032 Israeli reactions to missile attacks during the gulf war
R01MH-48987-01 (CVR) MERCER, DOROTHY L EASTERN KENTUCKY UNIVERSITY LANCASTER AVE RICHMOND, KY 40475-3101 Drunken driving victim impact panels--Victim outcomes
R03MH-48999-01 (SRCM) MARKOW, THERESE A ARIZONA STATE UNIVERSITY TEMPE, ARIZONA 85287-1501 The HAVASU canyon flood
R03MH-49007-01 (SRCM) SOLOMON, ZAHAVA TEL AVIV UNIVERSITY RAMAT AVIV, ISRAEL Psychological sequelae of missile attacks on evacuees
R43MH-49009-01 (SRCM) KRAUSMAN, DAVID T INDIVIDUAL MONITORING SYSTEMS 6310 HARFORD RD BALTIMORE, MD 21214 Ambulatory eye blink monitoring
R01MH-49044-01 (SRCM) TYLER, CHRISTOPHER W SMITH-KETTLEWELL EYE RES INST 2232 WEBSTER STREET SAN FRANCISCO, CA 94115 A generalized aurocorrelation theory for image analysis
R01MH-49047-01 (MHAZ) PAGE, JOHN B UNIVERSITY OF MIAMI 1425 NW 10TH AVE SUITE 302 MAIMI, FL 33136 Haitian women and the risk of HIV infection
R29MH-49050-01 (MHAZ) LORTON, DIANNE GLIATECH INC 23420 COMMERCE PARK RD BEACHWOOD, OH 44122 Psychoneuroimmunology--Innervation and autoimmune disease
U01MH-49055-01 (SRCM) KELLY, JEFFREY A MEDICAL COLLEGE OF WISCONSIN 8701 WATERTOWN PLANK ROAD MILWAUKEE, WI 53226 AIDS/HIV prevention for community chronic mentally ill
U01MH-49058-01 (SRCM) SCHILLING, ROBERT F COLUMBIA SCHOOL OF SOCIAL WORK 622 WEST 113TH STREET NEW YORK, NY 10025 Preventing HIV transmission in work-release participants
U01MH-49059-01 (SRCM) ROTHERAM-BORUS, MARY J RES FOUND FOR MENTAL HYGIENE I 722 WEST 168TH STREET NEW YORK, NY 10032 Secondary prevention with HIV+ youths in SF, LA and NYC
U01MH-49062-01 (SRCM) MAIBACH, EDWARD W EMORY UNIV SCH OF PUB HLTH 1599 CLIFTON RD NE ATLANTA, GA 30329 Small-group social-cognitive approach to HIV prevention
U01MH-49070-01 (SRCM) MAGANA, J RAUL ALTAMED HEALTH SERVICES CORP 5240 E BEVERLY BLVD LOS ANGELES, CA 90022 AIDS education to empower Latino IDU partners
R18MH-49072-01 (SRCM) WALKER, DERALD R MENTAL HLTH & DEV DIS SERV DIV 2575 BITTERN STREET NE SALEM, OR 97310 Family connections project--EPSDT implementation/access
R18MH-49102-01 (SRCM) MOSHER, LOREN R MD DEPT/HEALTH & MENTAL HYGIEN 401 HUNGERFORD DRIVE ROCKVILLE, MD 20850 MD CSP research demonstration project-crisis response
R01MH-49114-01 (SRCM) CIARLO, JAMES A UNIVERSITY OF DENVER UNIVERSITY PARK DENVER, CO 80208 Psychological problems and service use in rural Colorado
R01MH-49116-01 (SRCM) ROST, KATHRYN M UNIV OF AR MEDICAL SCIENCES 4301 W MARKHAM, SLOT 554 LITTLE ROCK, AR 72205 Use of services by rural people with depression
R18MH-49169-01 (SRCM) PENK, WALTER E DEPARTMENT OF MENTAL HEALTH 25 STANIFORD STREET BOSTON, MA 02114 Investigating two vocational rehabilitation models
R18MH-49193-01 (SRCM) GARDINE, ROBERTA DIV OF COMPREHENSIVE PSYCHIATR 1706 EAST ELM P O BOX 687 JEFFERSON CITY, MO 65102 Missouri small systems improvement grant phase four
S15MH-49274-01 (SRCA) KUPFER, DAVID J WESTERN PSYCHIATRIC INST & CLI 3811 O'HARA STREET PITTSBURGH, PA 15213 Small instrumentation grant
S15MH-49275-01 (SRCA) SAPIRSTEIN, VICTOR S RESEARCH FDN FOR MENTAL HYGIEN ORANGEBURG, NY 10962 Small instrumentation grant
S15MH-49276-01 (SRCA) MYLES-WORSLEY, MARINA UNIVERSITY OF UTAH MEDICAL CTR 50 NORTH MEDICAL DR SALT LAKE CITY, UT 84132 Small instrumentation grant
S15MH-49277-01 (SRCA) COOPERMAN, BARRY S UNIVERSITY OF PENNSYLVANIA 106 COLLEGE HALL PHILADELPHIA, PA 19104-6381 Small instrumentation grant
S15MH-49278-01 (SRCA) THOMPSON, BRIAN J UNIVERSITY OF ROCHESTER 200 ADMINISTRATION BUILDING ROCHESTER, NY 14627-0021 Small instrumentation grant
S15MH-49279-01 (SRCA) DELEUSE, BETSEY W THE ROCKEFELLER UNIVERSITY 1230 YORK AVENUE NEW YORK, NY 10021 Small instrumentation grant
S15MH-49280-01 (SRCA) WOLLMAN, HARRY HAHNEMANN UNIVERSITY BROAD AND VINE PHILADELPHIA, PA 19102-1192 Small instrumentation grant
S15MH-49281-01 (SRCA) WILLARD, DEREK H UNIVERSITY OF IOWA IOWA CITY, IA 52242 Small instrumentation grant
S15MH-49282-01 (SRCA) CAMPBELL, BYRON A PRINCETON UNIVERSITY PRINCETON, NJ 08544 Small instrumentation grant
S15MH-49283-01 (SRCA) MOSELEY, JOHN T UNIVERSITY OF OREGON 110 JOHNSON HALL EUGENE, OR 97403 Small instrumentation grant
S15MH-49284-01 (SRCA) FARBER, SAUL J NEW YORK UNIV MEDICAL CTR 550 FIRST AVENUE NEW YORK, NY 10016 Small instrumentation grant
S15MH-49285-01 (SRCA) PINGS, CORNELIUS J UNIV OF SOUTHERN CALIFORNIA UNIVERSITY PARK ADM 152 LOS ANGELES, CA 90089-4019 Small instrumentation grant
S15MH-49286-01 (SRCA) SCHNEIDER, ROBERT F STATE UNIV OF NY AT STONY BROO STONY BROOK, NY 11794-0001 Small instrumentation grant
S15MH-49287-01 (SRCA) LAUMANN, EDWARD O OFFICE OF THE DEAN 1126 E 59TH ST CHICAGO, IL 60637 Small instrumentation grant
S15MH-49288-01 (SRCA) HULLEY, STEPHEN B PREVENTION SCIENCE GROUP 74 NEW MONTGOMERY STREET SAN FRANCISCO, CA 94105 Small instrumentation grant
S15MH-49289-01 (SRCA) DELONG, STEPHEN E STATE UNIVERSITY OF NEW YORK 1400 WASHINGTON AVENUE ALBANY, NY 12222 Small instrumentation grant
S15MH-49290-01 (SRCA) ARGON, JUDITH K DUKE UNIVERSITY DURHAM, NC 27706 Small instrumentation grant
S15MH-49291-01 (SRCA) COHON, JARED L JOHNS HOPKINS UNIVERSITY 34TH & CHARLES STREETS BALTIMORE, MD 21218 Small instrumentation grant
S15MH-49292-01 (SRCA) ISOM, GARY E PURDUE UNIVERSITY WEST LAFAYETTE, IN 47907-1021 Small instrumentation grant
S15MH-49293-01 (SRCA) CHERNIACK, NEIL S CASE WESTERN RESERVE UNIV 10900 EUCLID AVE CLEVELAND, OH 44106-4915 Small instrumentation grant
S15MH-49294-01 (SRCA) PURPURA, DOMINICK P ALBERT EINSTEIN COLL OF MED 1300 MORRIS PARK AVENUE BRONX, N Y 10461 Small instrumentation grant
S15MH-49296-01 (SRCA) MILLER, GREGORY A UNIVERSITY OF ILLINOIS 603 EAST DANIEL STREET CHAMPAIGN, IL 61820 Small instrumentation grant
S15MH-49298-01 (SRCA) ZUCKER, IRVING UNIV OF CALIFORNIA 200 CALIFORNIA HALL BERKELEY, CA 94720 Small instrumentation grant
S15MH-49299-01 (SRCA) PRICE, DONALD R UNIVERSITY OF FLORIDA 219 GRINTER HALL GAINESVILLE, FL 32611 Small instrumentation grant
S15MH-49300-01 (SRCA) RATCLIFF, ROGER NORTHWESTERN UNIV EVANSTON, IL 60208-2710 Small instrumentation grant
S15MH-49301-01 (SRCA) RUDCZYNSKI, ANDREW B RUTGERS, THE STATE UNIV PO BOX 1089 PISCATAWAY, NJ 08855-1089 Small instrumentation grant
S15MH-49302-01 (SRCA) CORNWELL, DAVID G THE OHIO STATE UNIV 370 WEST TENTH AVE COLUMBUS, OH 43210 Small instrumentation grant
R18MH-49303-01 (SRCM) BEVILACQUA, JOSEPH J S C DEPT OF MENTAL HEALTH 2414 BULL STREET COLUMBIA, SC 29201 Rural outreach advocacy and direct services (ROADS)
S15MH-49304-01 (SRCA) OLDHAM, JOHN M RES FDN FOR MENTAL HYGIENE 722 WEST 168TH ST NEW YORK, NY 10032 Small instrumentation grant
S15MH-49305-01 (SRCA) FRANK, JOY S UCLA SCHOOL OF MEDICINE LOS ANGELES, CA 90024-1722 Small instrumentation grant
S15MH-49306-01 (SRCA) SHORE, MILES F MASSACHUSETTS MTL HLTH CENTER 74 FENWOOD RD BOSTON, MA 02115 Small instrumentation grant
S15MH-49307-01 (SRCA) AASLESTAD, HALVOR G YALE UNIVERSITY SCH OF MED 333 CEDAR ST, SHM L209 NEW HAVEN, CT 06510 Small instrumentation grant
S15MH-49308-01 (SRCA) LOW, ROBERT B UNIVERSITY OF VERMONT BURLINGTON, VT 05405 ASIP - University of Vermont
S15MH-49309-01 (SRCA) MELCHIOR, DONALD L UNIV OF MASSACHUSETTS MED SCH 55 LAKE AVENUE NORTH WORCESTER, MA 01655 Small instrumentation grant
S15MH-49310-01 (SRCA) COHEN, JOEL M BRANDEIS UNIVERSITY 415 SOUTH ST, PO BX 9110 WALTHAM, MA 02254-9110 Small instrumentation grant
S15MH-49311-01 (SRCA) ROSS, LEONARD MEDICAL COLLEGE OF PENNSYLVANI 3300 HENRY AVENUE PHILADELPHIA, PA 19129 Small instrumentation grant
S15MH-49312-01 (SRCA) REED, PETER W VANDERBILT UNIVERSITY 411 KIRKLAND HALL NASHVILLE, TN 37240 Small instrumentation grant
S15MH-49313-01 (SRCA) HOPS, HYMAN OREGON RESEARCH INSTITUTE 1899 WILLAMETTE EUGENE, OREG 97401 Small instrumentation grant
S15MH-49314-01 (SRCA) STEERS, C WILLIAM HARBOR UCLA MEDICAL CTR 1124 W CARSON ST TORRANCE, CA 90502-2064 Small instrumentation grant
S15MH-49315-01 (SRCA) SOHN, RICHARD J COLUMBIA UNIVERSITY HLTH SCI 630 W 168TH ST NEW YORK, NY 10032 Small instrumentation grant
S15MH-49316-01 (SRCA) DAVIDSON, RICHARD J UNIVERSITY OF WISCONSIN 1202 WEST JOHNSON STREET MADISON, WI 53706 Small instrumentation grant

S15MH-49317-01 (SRCA) **SWAN, PATRICIA B** IOWA STATE UNIVERSITY AMES, IA 50011 Small instrumentation grant
S15MH-49318-01 (SRCA) **COLEMAN, MARY S** UNIVERSITY OF NORTH CAROLINA CB #4000 CHAPEL HILL, NC 27599-4000 Small instrumentation grant
S15MH-49319-01 (SRCA) **LEON, MICHAEL A** UNIVERSITY OF CALIFORNIA IRVINE, CA 92717 Small instrumentation grant
S15MH-49320-01 (SRCA) **PFEFFERBAUM, ADOLF** VA MEDICAL CENTER 3801 MIRANDA AVE PALO ALTO, CA 94304 ASIP Stanford University
S15MH-49321-01 (SRCA) **FISKE, SUSAN T** UNIVERSITY OF MASSACHUSETTS AMHERST, MA 01003 Small instrumentation grant
R18MH-49325-01 (SRCM) **TOWNSEND, WILMA** OFFICE OF CONSUMER SERV 30 E BROAD ST SUITE 1115 COLUMBUS, OH 43266-0414 Self-directed job search by adult consumers of mental health
R18MH-49327-01 (SRCM) **PENNINGTON, MARGARET** DIV OF MENTAL HEALTH DMHMRS 275 EAST MAIN ST FRANKFORT, KY 40621 Consumer/family leadership in service evaluation/system planning
S15MH-49328-01 (SRCA) **HALLICK, LESLEY M** OREGON HEALTH SCIENCES UNIV 3181 SW SAM JACKSON PARK ROAD PORTLAND, OR 97201-3098 Small instrumentation grant
S15MH-49329-01 (SRCA) **NEWMAN, SARAH** UNIVERSITY OF MICHIGAN ANN ARBOR, MI 48109-1340 Small instrumentation grant
S15MH-49330-01 (SRCA) **KWIRAM, ALVIN L** UNIVERSITY OF WASHINGTON SEATTLE, WA 98195 Small instrumentation grant
S15MH-49331-01 (SRCA) **LI, TING-KAI** INDIANA UNIVERSITY 545 BARNHILL DRIVE INDIANAPOLIS, IN 46202-5124 Small instrumentation grant
S15MH-49332-01 (SRCA) **TEMPEL, ANN** LONG ISLAND JEWISH MEDICAL CTR 75-59 263RD STREET GLEN OAKS, NY 11004 Small instrumentation grant
S15MH-49333-01 (SRCA) **WALKER, GEORGE E** INDIANA UNIVERSITY PO BOX 1847 BLOOMINGTON, IN 47402 Small instrumentation grant
S15MH-49345-01 (SRCA) **HU, TEH-WEI** UNIV OF CALIFORNIA BERKELEY, CA 94720 ASIP - Western Consortium for public health
R18MH-49373-01 (SRCM) **FUJIOKA, GEORGE** HAWAII STATE DEPT OF HEALTH PO BOX 3378 HONOLULU, HAWAII 96801 Consumer and family collaboration project on the islands
R18MH-49374-01 (SRCM) **DINICH, DAVID** PA DEPT OF PUBLIC WELFARE OFC/ 7TH AND FORSTER STREETS HARRISBURG, PA 17102 Education and advocacy for vocational rehabilitation
R18MH-49376-01 (SRCM) **NISENBAUM, JAN** MASS DEPT OF MENTAL HEALTH 25 STANIFORD ST BOSTON, MA 02114 Consumer support and minority family outreach
R18MH-49377-01 (SRCM) **PLUM, THOMAS B** LANSING, MI 48913 Michigan CSP SSSI - Consumer and family support system improvement
R18MH-49378-01 (SRCM) **NEFF-DANIELS, MARIANNE** OLYMPIA, WA 98509 Washington CSP SSSI - Consumer and family support activities
R18MH-49379-01 (SRCM) **BRADFORD, M** 1200 NE 13TH OKLAHOMA CITY, OK 73152 Oklahoma CSP SSSI - Improvement through consumer and family support
R18MH-49380-01 (SRCM) **EDWARDS, DAVID V** 2575 BITTERN ST NE SALEM, OR 97310 Oregon CSP SSSI - Consumer and family support activities
R18MH-49382-01 (SRCM) **WENNER, DENNIS** MNTL HLTH SERVICES DIV 706 CHURCH ST NASHVILLE, TN 37243-0675 Tennessee CSP SSSI - Family and consumer rural support network
P50MH-49454-01 (SRCM) **GOLDMAN, HOWARD H** Center for research, knowledge dissemination & technical assistance on housing
P50MH-49454-01 0001 (SRCM) **GOLDMAN, HOWARD H** Center for research, knowledge dissemination & technical assistance on housing Research on housing for individuals with SPMI
P50MH-49454-01 0002 (SRCM) **GOLDMAN, HOWARD H** Center for research, knowledge dissemination & technical assistance on housing Knowledge dissemination on housing for persons with SPMI
P50MH-49454-01 0003 (SRCM) **GOLDMAN, HOWARD H** Center for research, knowledge dissemination & technical assistance on housing Technical assistance on housing for persons with SPMI
R03MH-49485-01 (SRCM) **FREEDY, JOHN R** MED UNIV OF SOUTH CAROLINA 171 ASHLEY AVE CHARLESTON, SC 29425-0742 Adult psychological functioning after earthquakes
S15MH-49509-01 (SRCA) **GIOLAS, THOMAS G** UNIVERSITY OF CONNECTICUT 438 WHITNEY RD EXTENSION STORRS, CT 06269-1133 Small instrumentation grant
S15MH-49510-01 (SRCA) **BURRIS, JAMES F** GEORGETOWN UNIVERSITY 3900 RESERVOIR RD, NW WASHINGTON, DC 20007 Small instrumentation grant
S15MH-49511-01 (SRCA) **KRZANOWSKI, JOSEPH J** 12901 BRUCE B DOWNS BLVD TAMPA, FL 33612 Small instrumentation grant
S15MH-49512-01 (SRCA) **MC MILLAN, DONALD E** UNIV OF ARKANSAS FOR MED SCI 4301 WEST MARKHAM STREET LITTLE ROCK, AR 72205 Small instrumentation grant
S15MH-49513-01 (SRCA) **NEWBOWER, RONALD S** MASSACHUSETTS GENERAL HOSPITAL FRUIT ST., BAR-3 BOSTON, MA 02114 Small instrumentation grant
S15MH-49514-01 (SRCA) **PETERS, LEONARD K** UNIV OF KENTUCKY 207 ADMINISTRATION BLDG LEXINGTON, KY 40506-0057 Small instrumentation grant
S15MH-49515-01 (SRCA) **BLUSZTAJN, JAN K** 85 EAST NEWTON STREET BOSTON, MA 02118 Small instrumentation grant
S15MH-49516-01 (SRCA) **ADAMS, PERRIE M** UNIVERSITY OF TEXAS 5323 HARRY HINES BLVD DALLAS, TX 75235-9016 Small instrumentation grant
S15MH-49517-01 (SRCA) **YIELDING, K LEMONE** UNIVERSITY OF TEXAS MED BRANCH 301 UNIVERSITY BLVD A33 GALVESTON, TX 77550 Small instrumentation grant
R01MH-49522-01 (EPS) **WEISZ, JOHN R** UCLA PSYCHOLOGY LOS ANGELES, CA 90024-1563 Studying clinic-based child mental health care
R01MH-49523-01 (SRCM) **NEMEROFF, CHARLES B** EMORY UNIVERSITY SCH OF MEDICI PO BOX AF ATLANTA, GA 30322 Pancreatic cancer, depression and immune function
R03MH-49536-01 (MSM) **YEHUDA, RACHEL** MT SINAI SCHOOL OF MEDICINE ONE GUSTAVE L LEVY PLACE NEW YORK, NY 10029 Glucocorticoid receptors and cortisol regulation in PTSD
R03MH-49538-01 (MSM) **NICHOLS, RUTHANN** UNIVERSITY OF MICHIGAN 830 N UNIVERSITY ST ANN ARBOR, MI 48109-1048 Isolation of vertebrate neural cholecystokinin homologs

PROJECT NO., ORGANIZATIONAL UNIT., INVESTIGATOR, ADDRESS, TITLE

R03MH-49541-01 (MSM) **PELLEYMOUNTER, MARY A** AMGEN CENTER 1840 DEHAVILLAND DR THOUSAND OAKS, CA 91320 Controllability and the effects of stress on cognition
R03MH-49552-01 (ARRD) **KENT, THOMAS A** UNIV OF TEXAS MEDICAL BRANCH 301 UNIVERSITY BLVD GALVESTON, TX 77550 Quantitative brain MRI analysis to assess AIDS treatment
R29MH-49553-01 (PCB) **MAYBERG, HELEN S** UNIV OF TEXAS HLTH SCIENCE CTR 7703 FLOYD CURL DRIVE SAN ANTONIO, TX 78284-7883 Fluoxetine effects on mood, cognition and metabolism
N01MH-70017-00 (**) **TECHNICAL RESOURECES, INC.** 3202 MONROE STREET, SUITE 300 ROCKVILLE, MARYLAND 20852 Mental health education campaign
N01MH-70018-00 (**) **THE CIRCLE, INC** 8201 GREENSBORO DRIVE SUITE 600 MCLEAN, VIRGINIA 22102 Workshops and conferences - administrative and logistical support
N01MH-70021-00 (**) **THE CIRCLE, INC** 8201 GREENSBORO DRIVE SUITE 600 MCLEAN, VIRGINIA National plan for schizophrenia research
K05MH-70178-08 (MHK) **HAUSER, STUART T** MASSACHUSETTS MENTAL HLTH CTR 74 FENWOOD ROAD BOSTON, MA 02115 Family contexts of adolescent ego development
K05MH-70183-18 (MHK) **SEGAL, DAVID S** UNIV OF CALIFORNIA, SAN DIEGO PSYCHIATRY DEPARTMENT 0603 LA JOLLA, CALIF 92093-0934 Psychopharmacology of stimulants and opioid peptides
K05MH-70482-18 (MHK) **WILLIAMS, REDFORD B, JR** DUKE UNIVERSITY MEDICAL CENTER PO BOX 3926 DURHAM, NC 27710 Behavioral mechanisms in cardiovascular diseases
N01MH-80010-00 (**) **UNIV ARIZONA** DEPT OF FAMILY & COMMUNITY MED 1501 N CAMPBELL AVENUE TUCSON, AZ 85724 Training for health care providers to address AIDS
N01MH-80011-00 (**) **MICHIGAN STATE UNIV** DEPT OF PSYCHIATRY A222 EAST FEE HALL EAST LANSING, MI 48824 Training for health care providers to address AIDS
N01MH-80012-00 (**) **WAYNE STATE UNIV** 5050 CASS AVENUE DETROIT, MI 48202-3489 Training for health care providers to address AIDS
N01MH-80019-00 (**) **SOCIAL AND SCIENTIFIC SYSTS, I** 7101 WISCONSIN AVENUE SUITE 610 BETHESDA, MD 20814 1989 Sample client survey of outpatient psychiatric programs
N01MH-80023-00 (**) **KENDRICK & COMPANY** 800 -18TH STREET, N W WASHINGTON, D C 20006 Administration of clinical training grant program
N01MH-80024-00 (**) **THE CIRCLE, INC** 8201 GREENSBORO DRIVE SUITE 600 MC LEAN, VA 22102 Conference and technical assistance for mental health education campaign
N01MH-80025-00 (**) **NATIONAL ACADEMY OF SCIENCES** INSTITUTE OF MEDICINE 2101 CONSTITUTION AVE, N W WASHINGTON, D C Child and adolescent mental disorders research
N01MH-80026-00 (**) **EBON RESEARCH SYSTEMS** 820 QUINCY STREET, N W WASHINGTON, D C 20011 Improve mental health program
N01MH-90001-00 (**) **PROSPECT ASSOCIATES, LTD** SUITE 500 1801 ROCKVILLE PIKE ROCKVILLE, MD 20852 Public education campaign on depression
N01MH-90004-00 (**) **NAT'L ASIAN PACIFIC AM FAMILIE** AGAINST SUBSTANCE ABUSE, INC 6303 FRIENDSHIP COURT BETHESDA, MD 20817 Model community-based prevention program
N01MH-90005-00 (**) **NAT'L COALITION OF HISPANIC HL** AND HUMAN SERVICES ORG 1030 - 15TH STREET, NW, SUITE WASHINGTON, D C 20005 Model community-based prevention program
N01MH-90006-00 (**) **NATL PARENTS' RESOURCE INST** THE HURT BLDG, SUITE 210 50 HURT PLAZA ATLANTA, GA 30303 Model community-based prevention program
N01MH-90008-00 (**) **QUEST INTERNATIONAL** 537 JONES ROAD P O BOX 566 GRANVILLE, OHIO 43023 Model community-based prevention program
N01MH-90011-00 (**) **CAMP FIRE, INC** 4601 MADISON AVENUE KANSAS CITY, MO 64112 Model community-based prevention project
K08NR-00001-05 (NRRC) **LEWIS, SHARON L** UNIVERSITY OF NEW MEXICO SCHOOL OF MEDICINE, BRF 323 ALBUQUERQUE, NM 87131 Altered immune responses in chronic dialysis patients
K07NR-00007-05 (SRC) **HEITKEMPER, MARGARET M** UNIVERSITY OF WASHINGTON SCHOOL OF NURSING, SM-28 SEATTLE, WA 98195 Central control of gastrointestinal function
K07NR-00010-05 (NRRC) **BETRUS, PATRICIA A** UNIVERSITY OF WASHINGTON DEPT OF PSYCHOSOCIAL NURSING SEATTLE, WA 98195 NCNR academic award: Stress-related depression
K07NR-00020-02 (NRRC) **SMITH, CAROL E** UNIVERSITY OF KANSAS MED CENTE 39TH & RAINBOW BLVD KANSAS CITY, KS 66103 Adaptation in families with technological care at home
K08NR-00021-03 (NRRC) **DENNIS, KAREN E** UNIVERSITY OF MARYLAND 655 WEST LOMBARD STREET BALTIMORE, MD 21201 Self-directed strategies for weight loss & maintenance
K08NR-00029-02 (NRRC) **HATHAWAY, DONNA K** UNIV OF TENNESSEE, MEMPHIS 800 MADISON AVENUE MEMPHIS, TN 38163 Renal transplant outcomes with low-dose steroid therapy
K07NR-00030-02 (NRRC) **JORDAN, PAMELA L** UNIVERSITY OF WASHINGTON MAILSTOP SC-74 SEATTLE, WA 98195 Expectant/new fathers at risk
K07NR-00032-01A1 (NRRC) **JAY, SUSAN S** UNIV OF COLORADO HEALTH SCI CT 4200 EAST NINTH AVENUE DENVER, CO 80262 Nursing assessment of child pain and mother/child stress
K08NR-00033-01 (NRRC) **SAUNDERS, JUDITH M** CITY OF HOPE NATIONAL MED CENT 1500 EAST DUARTE ROAD DUARTE, CA 91010 Nursing,self-care and HIV disease
K07NR-00038-01 (NRRC) **HALL, LYNNE A** UNIVERSITY OF KENTUCKY HEALTH SCIENCES LEARNING CTR LEXINGTON, KY 40536-0232 Predictors of mental health in postpartum mothers
K07NR-00040-01 (NRRC) **BROOKE, VIRGINIA** WASHINGTON STATE UNIVERSITY W 2917 FT. GEORGE WRIGHT DR SPOKANE, WA 99204 Involuntary admissions in a nursing home
K07NR-00044-01 (NRRC) **ALLEN, JERILYN K** THE JOHN HOPKINS UNIV 600 NORTH WOLFE STREET BALTIMORE, MD 21205 A nursing intervention in women after CABG
R01NR-01007-06A2 (NURS) **WALLSTON, KENNETH A** VANDERBILT UNIVERSITY MED CENT NASHVILLE, TN 37240 Behavioral aspects of rheumatoid arthritis
R01NR-01045-05 (NURS) **SAVEDRA, MARILYN** UNIV OF CALIFORNIA SCH OF

PROJECT NO., ORGANIZATIONAL UNIT., INVESTIGATOR, ADDRESS, TITLE

NURS BOX 0606 SAN FRANCISCO, CA 94143 Children's pain--Measurement of analgesic effectiveness
R55NR-01054-07 (NURS) WOODS, NANCY F UNIVERSITY OF WASHINGTON PARENT CHILD NURSING, SC-74 SEATTLE, WA 98195 Perimenstrual symptoms--Biopsychosocial patterns
R01NR-01075-07 (NURS) WEBSTER-STRATTON, CAROLYN H UNIV OF WASHINGTON SCH OF NURS T412 HLTH SCI BLDG, SC-74 SEATTLE, WA 98195 Comparing parent training models for antisocial children
R01NR-01086-06 (NURS) HOFFMAN, LESLIE A UNIVERSITY OF PITTSBURGH 367 VICTORIA BLDG PITTSBURGH, PA 15261 Nasal cannula and transtracheal delivery of oxygen
R01NR-01089-07 (HUD) MOOD, DARLENE W WAYNE STATE UNIVERSITY CENTER FOR HEALTH RESEARCH DETROIT, MI 48202 Psychosocial interventions in radiation therapy
R01NR-01094-07A1 (NURS) HEITKEMPER, MARGARET M UNIVERSITY OF WASHINGTON SCHOOL OF NURSING SEATTLE, WA 98195 A nursing study of gut function in menstruating women
R01NR-01115-07 (NURS) DOUGHERTY, MOLLY C UNIVERSITY OF FLORIDA GAINESVILLE, FL 32610 Circumvaginal muscle function--Clinical interventions
R01NR-01245-04A2 (NURS) ROTHERT, MARILYN L MICHIGAN STATE UNIVERSITY A-230 LIFE SCIENCES BLDG EAST LANSING, MI 48824-1317 Women's judgments of estrogen replacement therapy
R01NR-01282-04 (NURS) GEDEN, ELIZABETH A UNIV OF MISSOURI-COLUMBIA S329 SCHOOL OF NURSING COLUMBIA, MO 65211 Cognitive strategies on recovery from cesarean delivery
R01NR-01297-06 (NURS) CHANG, BETTY LEE UNIV OF CALIF, LOS ANGELES 405 HILGARD AVENUE LOS ANGELES, CA 90024-1702 Computer-aided research on nursing diagnosis
R01NR-01315-07 (NURS) SCHRAEDER, BARBARA D THOMAS JEFFESON UNIVERSITY 901 WALNUT - G20 PHILADELPHIA, PA 19107 Development, temperament and very low birth weight
R01NR-01323-06 (NURS) PHILLIPS, LINDA R UNIVERSITY OF ARIZONA COLLEGE OF NURSING TUCSON, ARIZ 85721 Cultural and causal factors and the quality of family caregiving
R01NR-01339-06 (NURS) NEELON, VIRGINIA J UNIVERSITY OF NORTH CAROLINA CB# 7460, CARRINGTON HALL CHAPEL HILL, NC 27599 Acute confusion in hospitalized elderly--Patterns-factors
R01NR-01373-05 (NURS) REAME, NANCY E UNIVERSITY OF MICHIGAN 400 N INGALLS ANN ARBOR, MI 48109-0482 Nursing assessment--Menstrual cycle clinical models
P01NR-01413-04 (NURS) CARLSON, CAROLYN E REHABILITATION INST OF CHICAGO 345 EAST SUPERIOR STREET CHICAGO, IL 60611 Prevention of pressure sores after spinal cord injury
R01NR-01428-06 (HUD) LARSON, J UNIVERSITY OF ILLINOIS PO BOX 6998 CHICAGO, IL 60680 Nurse managed inspiratory muscle training in COPD patients
R55NR-01453-05 (NURS) HOLM, KARYN UNIVERSITY OF ILLINOIS PO BOX 6998 CHICAGO, IL 60680 Bone density in black and white mothers and daughters
R01NR-01459-06 (NURS) NORBECK, JANE S UNIVERSITY OF CALIFORNIA SCHOOL OF NURSING - ROOM N319 SAN FRANCISCO, CA 94143-0606 Predictors of pregnancy complication in lower socioeconomic status women
R01NR-01465-04 (HUD) FULLER, BARBARA F UNIV OF COLORADO HEALTH SCIS C 4200 EAST 9TH AVENUE DENVER, CO 80262 Vocal measures of stress-anxiety--Nursing applications
R29NR-01483-04 (NURS) GROBE, SUSAN UNIVERSITY OF TEXAS 1700 RED RIVER AUSTIN, TX 78701 A nursing intervention lexicon & taxonomy
R01NR-01522-02 (NURS) GANONG, LAWRENCE H UNIVERSITY OF MISSOURI S313 COLUMBIA, MO 65211 Effects of family structure stereotypes on nurses
R01NR-01525-06 (NURS) RUDY, ELLEN B UNIVERSITY OF PITTSBURGH 350 VICTORIA BUILDING PITTSBURGH, PA 15261 Endotracheal suctioning in head injured adults
R01NR-01539-04 (NURS) DEVINE, ELIZABETH C UNIV OF WISCONSIN, MILWAUKEE PO BOX 413 MILWAUKEE, WI 53201 Effects of patient education and psychosocial support
R01NR-01549-06 (NURS) TURNER, BARBARA S MADIGAN ARMY MEDICAL CENTER TACOMA, WA 98431-5000 Endotracheal suctioning in newborns
R01NR-01552-05 (NURS) STONE, KATHLEEN S OHIO STATE UNIVERSITY 1585 NEIL AVENUE COLUMBUS, OH 43210-1289 Endotracheal suctioning in acutely ill adults
R01NR-01554-04A1 (NURS) COLLING, JOYCE C OREGON HEALTH SCIENCES UNIV 3181 SW SAM JACKSON PARK ROAD PORTLAND, OR 97201-3098 Continence for care-dependent community elderly
R01NR-01594-05 (NURS) KNAFL, KATHLEEN A UNIV OF ILLINOIS AT CHICAGO 845 SOUTH DAMEN AVENUE CHICAGO, IL 60612 How families define and manage a child's chronic illness
R01NR-01596-04 (NURS) RUDY, ELLEN B UNIVERSITY OF PITTSBURGH 350 VICTORIA BUILDING PITTSBURGH, PA 15261 Menstrual response to running--Nursing implications
R29NR-01620-05 (NURS) KEEFE, MAUREEN R THE CHILDREN'S HOSPITAL 1056 EAST NINETEENTH AVENUE DENVER, CO 80218 The irritable infant syndrome
R01NR-01636-05 (HSR) VENTURA, MARLENE R VA MEDICAL CENTER 3495 BAILEY AVENUE BUFFALO, NY 14215 Reducing hospital costs and improving patient well being
R01NR-01637-06 (NURS) SWANSON, JANICE M SAMUEL MERRITT COL OF NURSING 370 HAWTHORNE AVENUE OAKLAND, CA 94609 Young adults' adaptation to chronic disease
R01NR-01657-04 (NURS) FRANTZ, RITA A UNIVERSITY OF IOWA IOWA CITY, IA 52242 Nursing interventions--Healing decubitus ulcers with TENS
R01NR-01669-03A2 (NURS) METHENY, NORMA A SAINT LOUIS UNIV SCH OF NURSIN 3525 CAROLINE STREET ST LOUIS, MO 63104 Measures to test feeding tube placement
R01NR-01670-04 (NURS) STEMBER, MARILYN L UNIVERSITY OF COLORADO 4200 EAST NINTH AVENUE, C288 DENVER, CO 80262 Infant growth failure & nursing care
R29NR-01678-05 (NURS) CAMPBELL, JACQUELYN C WAYNE STATE UNIVERSITY 5557 CASS AVENUE DETROIT, MI 48202 Women's responses to battering
R01NR-01691-04 (NURS) OLDS, DAVID L UNIV OF ROCHESTER MEDICAL CTR 601 ELMWOOD AVENUE ROCHESTER, NY 14642 Study of nurse home visitation for mothers and children
R01NR-01693-05 (NURS) JALOWIEC, ANNE M LOYOLA UNIVERSITY MEDICAL CENT 2160 SOUTH FIRST AVENUE, 131S MAYWOOD, IL 60153 Predictors of quality of life after cardiac transplant
R29NR-01696-05 (NURS) BRADEN, CARRIE J UNIVERSITY OF ARIZONA ARIZONA HEALTH SCIENCES CENTER TUCSON, AZ 85721 Learned self help response to chronic illness experience
R01NR-01707-04 (NURS) SANDELOWSKI, MARGARETE J UNIVERSITY OF NORTH CAROLINA CB# 7460, CARRINGTON HALL CHAPEL HILL, NC 27599-7460 The transition to parenthood in infertile couples
R01NR-01822-04 (NURS) HAYMAN, LAURA L UNIVERSITY OF PENNSYLVANIA 420 SERVICE DRIVE PHILADELPHIA, PA 19104-6096 Biobehavioral cardiovascular rick factors
R29NR-01830-04 (NURS) CHRISTMAN, NORMA J UNIV OF KENTUCKY COLL OF NURS 539 HLTH SCIENCE LEARNING CENT LEXINGTON, KY 40536-0232 Preparation for radiotherapy--Outcomes and explanations
R01NR-01837-02 (NURS) HARRELL, JOANNE S UNIVERSITY OF NORTH CAROLINA CB# 7460, CARRINGTON HALL CHAPEL HILL, NC 27599 Health promotion in children--Cardiovascular risk factors
R29NR-01839-05 (NURS) BARSEVICK, ANDREA M FOX CHASE CANCER CENTER 7701 BURHOLME AVE PHILADELPHIA, PA 19111 Factors affecting recovery from hip surgery
R01NR-01840-03 (NURS) LOWERY, BARBARA J UNIVERSITY OF PENNSYLVANIA NURSING EDUCATION BLDG PHILADELPHIA, PA 19104-6096 Denial and stress following myocardial infarction
R01NR-01843-04 (NURS) CHAMPION, VICTORIA L INDIANA UNIV SCHOOL OF NURSING 610 BARNHILL DRIVE INDIANAPOLIS, IN 46223 Interventions for breast self-examination in older women
R01NR-01852-02 (NURS) WEINERT, CLARANN MONTANA STATE UNIVERSITY BOZEMAN, MT 59717 Families living with long-term illness--A national study
R01NR-01857-03 (NURS) PEARSON, BETTY D UNIVERSITY OF WISCONSIN SCH OF NURSING, P.O. BOX 413 MILWAUKEE, WI 53201 Urinary incontinence--Prevention and treatment for elders
R01NR-01887-03 (NURS) OAKLEY, DEBORAH J UNIV OF MICH SCH OF NURSING CENTER FOR NURSING RESEARCH ANN ARBOR, MI 48109-0482 Nurse-midwives and physicians--A study of comparisons
R29NR-01894-04 (NURS) DAVIS, DIANE H UNIVERSITY OF NORTH CAROLINA CARRINGTON HALL 214H, CB 7460 CHAPEL HILL, NC 27599 Sleep-wake states in preterms--Relation to outcome at age 3
R29NR-01899-04 (NURS) SWANSON, KRISTEN M UNIVERSITY OF WASHINGTON MAIL STOP: SC-74 SEATTLE, WA 98195 Caring-based nursing intervention for women who miscarry
R01NR-01905-11 (BEM) MORROW, GARY R UNIVERSITY OF ROCHESTER 601 ELMWOOD AVENUE, BOX 704 ROCHESTER, NY 14642 Counseling intervention for chemotherapy side effects
R01NR-01917-04A1 (NURS) WELLS, THELMA J UNIVERSITY OF ROCHESTER 601 ELMWOOD AVE, PO BOX NWH ROCHESTER, NY 14642 Nursing interventions--Exercise for stress incontinence
R01NR-01920-03 (NURS) KILLIEN, MARCIA G UNIVERSITY OF WASHINGTON T416D HEALTH SCIENCE BLDG. SEATTLE, WA 98195 Returning to work--Impact on mothers' postpartum health
R01NR-01922-04 (NURS) BECKSTRAND, JANIS K INDIANA UNIVERSITY 610 BARNHILL DR. INDIANAPOLIS, IN 46223 Predicting the insertion length for gastric gavage tubes
R01NR-01926-01A2 (NURS) MURPHY, SHIRLEY A UNIVERSITY OF WASHINGTON PSYCHOSOCIAL NURSING, SC-76 SEATTLE, WA 98195 Parent bereavement stress and nursing intervention
R01NR-01931-03 (NURS) QUAYHAGEN, MARY P UNIVERSITY OF SAN DIEGO ALCALA PARK SAN DIEGO, CA 92110 Cognitive stimulation training in Alzheimers families
R29NR-01935-04 (NURS) MEIER, PAULA P UNIV OF ILLINOIS COL OF NURS 845 SOUTH DAMEN AVENUE CHICAGO, IL 60612 Nursing management of breast feeding for preterm infants
R01NR-01938-03 (NURS) DUCKETT, LAURA J UNIV OF MINN SCH OF NURSING 308 HARVARD STREET SE MINNEAPOLIS, MN 55455 Breast feeding behaviors--Testing a structural model
R01NR-01939-03 (NURS) CLARKE, BERNARDINE A VIRGINIA COMMONWEALTH UNIVERSI BOX 567, MCV STATION RICHMOND, VA 23298 Nursing role supplementation for adolescent parents
R29NR-01950-02 (NURS) SAMPSELLE, CAROLYN M UNIVERSITY OF MICHIGAN RISK REDUCTION ANN ARBOR, MI 48109-0482 Nursing intervention--Pelvic floor exercise in pregnancy
R55NR-01956-01A3 (NURS) NORR, KATHLEEN F UNIVERSITY OF ILLINOIS PO BOX 6998 CHICAGO, IL 60680 Psychosocial factors & outcomes of teen childbearing
R01NR-01970-01A3 (NURS) COWAN, MARIE J UNIVERSITY OF WASHINGTON OFC OF NURSING RESEARCH, SM-27 SEATTLE, WA 98195 Self-management therapy following sudden cardiac arrest
R29NR-02000-03 (NURS) HELBERG, JUNE L UNIV OF ROCHESTER SCH OF NURS 601 ELMWOOD AVENUE ROCHESTER, NY 14642 Community health nursing services utilization
R01NR-02006-03 (NURS) MAGILVY, JOAN K UNIV OF COLORADO HEALTH SCIS C 4200 EAST NINTH AVE, BOX C-288 DENVER, CO 80262 Rural home care for older adults--Pattern and process
R29NR-02013-03 (NURS) GROSS, DEBORAH A RUSH-PRESBY-ST LUKE'S MED CENT 1653 WEST CONGRESS PARKWAY CHICAGO, IL 60612 Maternal confidence during toddlerhood
R29NR-02019-03 (NURS) NORTHOUSE, LAUREL L WAYNE STATE UNIV, COL OF NURS 5557 CASS AVENUE DETROIT, MI 48202 Psychosocial adjustment to cancer--Couples at risk
R01NR-02030-03 (NURS) KILLION, CHERYL M UNIV OF CALIF SCH OF NURSING 10833 LE CONTE AVENUE LOS ANGELES, CA 90024-1702 The coexistence of pregnancy and homelessness
R01NR-02043-04 (NURS) THOMAS, SUE A LIFE CARE HEALTH FOUNDATION 606 BALTIMORE AVENUE TOWSON, MD 21204 Psychosocial factors in sudden cardiac death
R01NR-02044-02 (NURS) FULLER, BARBARA F UNIV OF COLORADO HEALTH SCIS C 4200 EAST 9TH AVENUE DENVER, CO 80262 A model to improve nursing assessment of infant pain
R01NR-02050-03 (NURS) LUSK, SALLY L UNIV OF MICH SCH OF NURSING 400 NORTH INGALLS ANN ARBOR, MI 48109-0482 Nursing model to prevent

PROJECT NO., ORGANIZATIONAL UNIT., INVESTIGATOR, ADDRESS, TITLE

noise-induced hearing loss

R01NR-02064-03 (NURS) MORRIS, JOHN N HEBREW REHAB CTR AGED 1200 CENTRE STREET BOSTON, MA 02131 Nursing intervention to promote nursing home patient functioning

R01NR-02068-03 (ARR) O'BRIEN, MARY E CATHOLIC UNIV OF AMERICA GOWAN BUILDING/RM 122 WASHINGTON, DC 20064 Coping response in HIV infection--A panel analysis

R29NR-02076-04 (NURS) CENSULLO, MEREDITH V WELLESLEY COLLEGE WELLESLEY, MA 02181 Infant development and mother-infant synchrony

R01NR-02078-03 (NURS) BUHLER-WILKERSON, KAREN A UNIVERSITY OF PENNSYLVANIA 420 SERVICE DRIVE PHILADELPHIA, PA 19104-6096 Sick at home--Public policy, personal consequences

R01NR-02079-02 (NURS) MCCLOSKEY, JOANNE C UNIVERSITY OF IOWA IOWA CITY, IA 52242 Classification of nursing interventions

R01NR-02085-02 (NURS) GENNARO, SUSAN UNIVERSITY OF PENNSYLVANIA 420 SERVICE DRIVE PHILADELPHIA, PA 19104-6096 VLBW infants--Economic and family outcomes

R29NR-02087-02 (NURS) GILLETT, PATRICIA A UNIVERSITY OF UTAH 25 S MEDICAL DR SALT LAKE CITY, UT 84112 Nurse exercise intervention for overweight older women

R01NR-02088-02 (NURS) ARCHBOLD, PATRICIA G OREGON HEALTH SCIENCES UNIV 3181 S W SAM JACKSON PORTLAND, OR 97201 Evaluation of caregiving support program

R01NR-02091-03 (NURS) GORDON, DOROTHY L THE JOHNS HOPKINS UNIVERSITY SCHOOL OF NURSING-HOUCK 324 BALTIMORE, MD 21205 A model for reorganizing nursing resources

R01NR-02092-03 (NURS) TAUNTON, ROMA L UNIVERSITY OF KANSAS 39TH AND RAINBOW BOULEVARD KANSAS CITY, KS 66103 Nurse managers, nurse retention, patient outcomes

R01NR-02093-03 (NURS) MEDOFF-COOPER, BARBARA S UNIV OF PENN SCHOOL OF NURSING 420 GUARDIAN DRIVE PHILADELPHIA, PA 19104-6096 Neonatal sucking as a clinical assessment tool

R01NR-02095-03 (NURS) NAYLOR, MARY D UNIVERSITY OF PENNSYLVANIA 420 SERVICE DRIVE PHILADELPHIA, PA 19104 Comprehensive discharge planning for the elderly

R01NR-02096-02 (NURS) POTEMPA, KATHLEEN UNIV OF ILLINOIS-CHICAGO PO BOX 6998 CHICAGO, IL 60680 Functional benefits of aerobic training after stroke /human/

R01NR-02101-02 (NURS) DENYES, MARY J WAYNE STATE UNIVERSITY 5557 CASS AVENUE DETROIT, MI 48202-3489 Effect of nursing actions to alleviate pain in children

R01NR-02107-02 (NURS) DUNBAR, JACQUELINE M UNIVERSITY OF PITTSBURGH SCHOOL OF NURSING PITTSBURGH, PA 15261 Adherence in rheumatoid arthritis--Nursing interventions

R01NR-02108-01A2 (NURS) CONSTANTINO, ROSE E UNIVERSITY OF PITTSBURGH 3500 VICTORIA STREET PITTSBURGH, PA 15261 Nursing postvention for widows and widowers

R15NR-02114-01A2 (NURS) SCANDRETT-HIBDON, SHARON L UNIVERSITY OF TENNESSEE 606 LAMAR ALEXANDER BLDG MEMPHIS, TN 38163 The endogenous healing process in acute grief

R55NR-02128-01A3 (NURS) FINKELSTEIN, STANLEY M UNIVERSITY OF MINNESOTA 420 DELAWARE STREET, SE MINNEAPOLIS, MN 55455 Early detection--Lung transplant rejection/infection

R01NR-02130-03 (NURS) MORSE, JANICE M 3RD FL, CLINICAL SCIENCES BLDG UNIV. OF ALBERTA, EDMONTON ALBERTA T6G 2G3 CANADA Defining comfort for the improvement of nursing care

R01NR-02131-03 (NURS) CARRIERI-KOHLMAN, VIRGINIA L UNIV OF CALIF, SCH OF NURSING DEPT OF PHYSIOL NURSING N611Y SAN FRANCISCO, CA 94143-0610 Nurse coached practice for relief of dyspnea

R15NR-02144-01A2 (NURS) MACKEY, MARLENE C UNIVERSITY OF SOUTH CAROLINA COLLEGE OF NURSING COLUMBIA, SC 29208 The preterm labor experience: a naturalistic study

U01NR-02153-04 (SRC) VERRAN, JOYCE A UNIVERSITY OF ARIZONA TUCSON, AZ 85721 Differentiated group practice in nursing

U01NR-02156-04 (SRC) INGERSOLL, GAIL L UNIV OF ROCHESTER SCH OF NURS 601 ELMWOOD AVE., BOX HWH ROCHESTER, NY 14642 Enhanced professional practice model for nursing

R01NR-02192-03 (HSR) MARTIN, KAREN S VISITING NURSE ASSOC OF OMAHA 10840 HARNEY CIRCLE OMAHA, NE 68154 A home health agency practice and documentation model

R29NR-02203-03 (SSS) SCHWERTZ, DORIE W UNIV OF ILLINOIS AT CHICAGO 845 SOUTH DAMEN, AVE, CHICAGO, IL 60612 Phosphoinositide metabolism in early myocardial ischemia

R29NR-02204-04 (NURS) KASPER, CHRISTINE E UNIV OF CALIF SCH OF NURSING 10833 LE CONTE AVENUE LOS ANGELES, CA 90024-6918 Atrophy of skeletal muscle--Change in tension development

R44NR-02210-02 (NURS) WILNER, MARY A NEW ENGLAND RESEARCH INSTITUTE 9 GALEN STREET WATERTOWN, MA 02172 Evaluation of nurse aide support groups in nursing homes

R01NR-02215-03 (ARR) HOLZEMER, WILLIAM L UNIVERSITY OF CALIFORNIA BOX 0604 SAN FRANCISCO, CA 94143-0604 Quality of nursing care of people with AIDS

R29NR-02231-01A1 (NURS) FOREMAN, MARQUIS D UNIV OF ILLINOIS AT CHICAGO P.O. BOX 6998 CHICAGO, IL 60680 Confusion__A three wave longitudinal causal model

R01NR-02235-02 (NURS) FARR, LYNNE A UNIV OF NEBRASKA MEDICAL CENTE 600 SOUTH 42ND ST OMAHA, NE 68198-5330 Interventions to accelerate postoperative recovery

R01NR-02241-01A1 (NURS) BECKER, DIANE M JOHNS HOPKINS HOSPITAL 1830 E MONUMENT ST BLDG BALTIMORE, MD 21205-2196 Nursing interventions to reduce coronary risk factors

R29NR-02243-03 (NURS) FREY, MAUREEN A UNIV OF MICHIGAN SCH OF NURS 400 NORTH INGALLS BLDG ANN ARBOR, MI 48109-0482 Nursing perspective--Families, children and chronic illness

R29NR-02247-03 (NURS) LEE, KATHRYN A DEPT OF FAMILY HLTH CARE NURS UNIV OF CALIF, 3RD & PARNASSUS SAN FRANCISCO, CA 94143 Fatigue and sleep patterns in childbearing women

R01NR-02248-01A1 (NURS) DALY, BARBARA CASE WESTERN RESERVE UNIVERSIT 2121 ABINGTON RD CLEVELAND, OH 44106 Special care unit model for long-term critically ill

R01NR-02249-01A2 (NURS) BULL, MARGARET J UNIVERSITY OF MINNESOTA 308 HARVARD STREET SE MINNEAPOLIS, MN 55455 Testing a model for hospital to home transition

PROJECT NO., ORGANIZATIONAL UNIT., INVESTIGATOR, ADDRESS, TITLE

R01NR-02251-01A1 (NURS) LUDINGTON, SUSAN M UNIVERSITY OF CALIFORNIA 10833 LE CONTE AVENUE LOS ANGELES, CA 90024-6919 Skin to skin contact for preterm infants and their mothers

R01NR-02253-03 (NURS) KELLER, MARY L UNIV OF WIS, CLINICAL SCI CTR 600 HIGHLAND AVE, RM K2/326 MADISON, WI 53792 Genital herpes/genital warts--representations & coping

R29NR-02258-03 (NURS) MCCARTHY, DONNA UNIV OF WISC, SCH OF NURSING 600 HIGHLAND AVE, RM K6/324 MADISON, WI 53792 Mechanisms of anorexia with tumor growth

R01NR-02259-02 (NURS) WEINRICH, SALLY P UNIVERSITY OF SOUTH CAROLINA COLUMBIA, SC 29208 Nursing interventions to increase colorectal screening

R01NR-02262-02 (NURS) KELLEHER, CATHERINE P JOHNS HOPKINS ONCOLOGY CTR 600 NORTH WOLFE ST BALTIMORE, MD 21205 Predictors of cancer inpatient length of stay and costs

R29NR-02263-03 (NURS) MCGRATH, MARGARET M UNIVERSITY OF RHODE ISLAND COLLEGE OF NURSING, WHITE HALL KINGSTON, RI 02881-0814 Developmental outcome: 4-yr old children born at risk

R01NR-02280-02 (ARR) AIKEN, LINDA H UNIVERSITY OF PENNSYLVANIA NURSING EDUCATION BLDG PHILADELPHIA, PA 19104-6096 AIDS care--Nurse retention and patient satisfaction

R01NR-02281-03 (ARR) NICKEL, JENNIE T OHIO STATE UNIVERSITY 1585 NEIL AVENUE COLUMBUS, OH 43210 Effects of nurse case managed home care for HIV patients

R01NR-02297-01A1 (NURS) HUMENICK, SHARRON S UNIVERSITY OF WYOMING BOX 3065 UNIVERSITY STATION LARAMIE, WY 82071 Insufficient milk supply--Nursing diagnosis/intervention

P20NR-02300-03 (NRRC) DONALDSON, SUE K UNIV OF MINN SCH OF NURS 308 HARVARD ST., 6-101 UNIT F MINNEAPOLIS, MN 55455 Long term care of the elderly

P50NR-02323-03 (NRRC) WOODS, NANCY F UNIVERSITY OF WASHINGTON SEATTLE, WA 98195 Midlife women's experience of waning fertility

P50NR-02324-03 (NRRC) MCCORKLE, RUTH UNIV OF PENN, SCH OF NURSING ADULT HLTH AND ILLNESS DEPT PHILADELPHIA, PA 19104-6096 Advancing care in serious illness

P20NR-02334-03 (NRRC) DUNBAR-JACOB, JACQUELINE M UNIV OF PITTSBURGH SCH OF NURS 455 VICTORIA BUILDING PITTSBURGH, PA 15261 Center for research in critical care nursing

R01NR-02340-02 (NURS) TULMAN, LORRAINE UNIVERSITY OF PENNSYLVANIA SCHOOL OF NURSING PHILADELPHIA, PA 19104-6086 Functional status during pregnancy and the postpartum

R01NR-02343-01A1 (NURS) MITCHELL, PAMELA H UNIVERSITY OF WASHINGTON SEATTLE, WA 98195 Critical care nursing systems, retention and patient outcomes

R01NR-02348-02 (NURS) PRIDHAM, KAREN F UNIVERSITY OF WISCONSIN 600 HIGHLAND AVENUE MADISON, WI 53792 Correlates of preterm and term infant feeding outcomes

R01NR-02352-01A1 (NURS) BARANOSKI, MADELON V YALE UNIVERSITY SCH OF NURSING PO BOX 9740 NEW HAVEN, CT 06536-0740 Promoting mastery in children after trauma

R01NR-02367-02 (NURS) BECK, CORNELIA M UNIVERSITY OF ARKANSAS 4301 WEST MARKHAM LITTLE ROCK, AR 72205 Improving dressing behavior in impaired elderly

R01NR-02376-03 (NURS) JACOX, ADA K JOHNS HOPKINS UNIVERSITY 600 NORTH WOLFE ST BALTIMORE, MD 21205 Determinants of nursing care costs & patient outcomes

R01NR-02377-02 (NURS) MAY, KATHARYN A VANDERBILT UNIVERSITY 412 GODCHAUX HALL NASHVILLE, TN 37240 Impact of home-managed preterm labor on families

R01NR-02405-01A1 (NURS) BOWERS, BARBARA J UNIVERSITY OF WISCONSIN 600 HIGHLAND AVENUE MADISON, WI 53792 Caregiver perceptions of caring for older adults

R01NR-02410-02 (NURS) MOORE, MARY L BOWMAN GRAY SCHOOL OF MEDICINE WAKE FOREST UNIVERSITY WINSTON-SALEM, NC 27103 Reducing LBW deliveries through intensive nursing interventions.

R01NR-02412-02 (NURS) THERRIEN, BARBARA A UNIVERSITY OF MICHIGAN 400 NORTH INGALLS BUILDING ANN ARBOR, MI 48109-0482 Disorientation--A model for nursing therapy

R01NR-02416-01A1 (NURS) KING, ROSEMARIE B REHABILITATION INST OF CHICAGO 345 EAST SUPERIOR CHICAGO, IL 60611 Adaptation after stroke--Patient and support person

R29NR-02420-02 (NURS) THOMAS, KAREN A UNIVERSITY OF WASHINGTON SEATTLE, WA 98195 Effect of temperature on preterm infant sleep-wake state

R55NR-02429-01A1 (NURS) BURR, ROBERT L UNIV OF WASHINGTON SCH OF NURS MAIL STOP SC-76 SEATTLE, WA 98195 Recovery after myocardial infarction

R01NR-02434-01A1 (NURS) DRACUP, KATHLEEN A UNIVERSITY OF CALIFORNIA 10833 LE CONTE AVE LOS ANGELES, CA 90024-6918 Nursing intervention--Infants at risk for sudden death

R15NR-02435-01A1 (NURS) COATES, CAROLIE J UNIV OF COLORADO HLTH SCI CENT 4200 EAST 9TH AVENUE DENVER, CO 80262 Health and coping--Child witnesses of spouse abuse

R01NR-02443-02 (NURS) YORK, RUTH UNIVERSITY OF PENNSYLVANIA PHILADELPHIA, PA 19104-6096 Maternal factors related to adequacy of prenatal care

R01NR-02444-01 (NURS) ANDERSON, GENE C UNIVERSITY OF FLORIDA BOX J-187, JHMHC GAINESVILLE, FL 32610 Self-regulatory newborn care and extrauterine adaptation

R15NR-02460-01A1 (NURS) GILBERT, DOROTHY A UNIVERSITY OF MASSACHUSETTS ARNOLD HOUSE AMHERST, MA 01003 Relational messages in nurses' listening behavior

R15NR-02482-01A1 (NURS) STEEVES, RICHARD H UNIVERSITY OF VIRGINIA MCLEOD HALL CHARLOTTESVILLE, VA 22903-339 Experiences of rural caregivers of persons with cancer

R01NR-02515-01A2 (NURS) SAUVE, MARY J UNIVERSITY OF CALIFORNIA 3RD & PARNASSUS/N611Y SAN FRANCISCO, CA 94143-0610 Patterns of cognitive recovery in sudden death survivors

R15NR-02518-01A1 (NURS) COWELL, JULIA M UNIVERSITY OF ILLINOIS PO BOX 6998 (M/C 802) CHICAGO, IL 60680 Nursing focus/children's cardiovascular health behaviors

R01NR-02541-01A1 (NURS) JOHNSON, JEAN E UNIV OF ROCHESTER CANCER CENTE 601 ELMWOOD AVENUE, BOX 704 ROCHESTER, NY 14642 Nursing care

PROJECT NO., ORGANIZATIONAL UNIT., INVESTIGATOR, ADDRESS, TITLE

and coping with cancer treatment
R01NR-02557-02 (NURS) MOORE, IDA M UNIVERSITY OF ARIZONA 1401 N MARTIN TUCSON, AZ 85721 CNS tissue damage and cognitive deficits-- A nursing model
R01NR-02561-02 (NURS) WYMAN, JEAN F VIRGINIA COMMONWEALTH UNIV MCV STATION, BOX 567 RICHMOND, VA 23298-0567 Balance assessment intervention in the elderly
R29NR-02563-02 (NURS) MCCUBBIN, MARILYN A UNIVERSITY OF WISCONSIN 600 HIGHLAND AVE MADISON, WI 53792 Children's chronic illness--Parent and family adaptation
R29NR-02568-01A1 (NURS) ALLAN, JANET THE UNIVERSITY OF TEXAS 1700 RED RIVER AUSTIN, TX 78701 Cross-ethnic nursing study of weight management in women
R01NR-02571-02 (NURS) CAMPBELL, JACQUELYN C WAYNE STATE UNIVERSITY 5557 CASS AVE DETROIT, MI 48202 Birth weight and abuse during pregnancy--Cultural influence
R01NR-02575-01A1 (NURS) ROBERTS, BEVERLY L CASE WESTERN RESERVE UNIV 2121 ABINGTON ROAD CLEVELAND, OH 44106 Walking--A nursing intervention
R43NR-02591-01A1 (NURS) HAGGER, JODY A PO BOX 1107 TEMPLE HILLS, MD 20748 Nursing resource and allocation and utilization system
R43NR-02594-01 (NURS) TODD, SELDON P, JR MICRO-MARKETING SYSTEMS, INC PO BOX 3039 GAITHERSBURG, MD 20885-3039 Helpskin--A nursing pressure sore prevention system
R01NR-02618-01 (NURS) JACOBSON, SHAROL F UNIVERSITY OF OKLAHOMA PO BOX 26901 OKLAHOMA CITY, OK 73190 Diabetes representations and signs of Mvskoke Indians
U01NR-02638-02 (AGE) WALLACE, ROBERT B UNIVERSITY OF IOWA 2800 STEINDLER BLDG IOWA CITY, IA 52242 Nursing interventions for falls--A field experiment
R01NR-02642-01 (NURS) MOSSEY, JANA M MEDICAL COLLEGE OF PA/EPPI 3200 HENRY AVENUE PHILADELPHIA, PA 19004 Nurse intervention with depressed medically ill elderly
R43NR-02645-01A1 (NURS) KAUFMAN, STEPHEN B HEALTHTECH SERVICES CORPORATIO 255 REVERE DRIVE NORTHBROOK, IL 60062 Testing of home assisted nursing care device for elderly
R01NR-02662-02 (NURS) WINEMAN, NANCY M UNIVERSITY OF AKRON 209 CARROLL STREET AKRON, OH 44325-3701 Emotional well-being in the disabled--A nursing study
R29NR-02665-02 (NURS) JONES, ELAINE G UNIVERSITY OF ARIZONA TUCSON, AZ 85721 Family functioning--Deaf parents with non-deaf children
R29NR-02673-02 (NURS) LAMONTAGNE, LYNDA L VANDERBILT UNIV SCH OF NURSING 310 GODCHAUX HALL NASHVILLE, TN 34240 Children's preoperative coping and postoperative outcome
R18NR-02678-02 (SRC) AFFONSO, DYANNE D UNIV OF CALIF SCHOOL OF NURSIN BOX 0606 SAN FRANCISCO, CA 94143-0606 Caring for pregnant women--Malama Na wahine hapai
R18NR-02685-02 (SRC) BURTON, DEBORAH OREGON HEALTH DIVISION PO BOX 231 PORTLAND, OR 97207-0231 Rural Oregon minority prenatal case management project
R01NR-02701-01 (NURS) BECKER, PATRICIA T UNIV OF WISCONSIN-MADISON 600 HIGHLAND AVE MADISON, WI 53792 Reducing stress during handling in the NICU
R01NR-02705-01 (NURS) STRICKLAND, ORA L NELL HODGSON WOODRUFF SCH OF EMORY UNIVERSITY ATLANTA, GA 30322 Nursing assessment of PMS--Neurometric indices
R29NR-02713-01 (NURS) GAFFNEY, KATHLEEN F GEORGE MASON UNIVERSITY 4400 UNIVERSITY DRIVE FAIRFAX, VA 22030 Maternal role sufficiency--Predictors and interventions
R15NR-02719-01 (NURS) PHIPPS, SU AN UNIVERSITY OF OKLAHOMA 700 NORTH GREENWOOD TULSA , OK 74106-0700 Couples' infertility--Racial and socioeconomic context
R01NR-02754-02 (ARRF) AIKEN, LINDA UNIVERSITY OF PENNSYLVANIA SCHOOL OF NURSING PHILADELPHIA, PA 19104-6096 A nursing intervention to prevent AIDS in Chile
R15NR-02757-01 (NURS) WALKER, GLENDA C UNIV OF TEXAS HEALTH SCIENCE C 1100 HOLCOMBE BOULEVARD HOUSTON, TX 77030 Applicability/information processing of trauma model
R15NR-02764-01 (NURS) HILL, PAMELA D UNIVERSITY OF ILLINOIS 2525 24TH STREET, SUITE 202 ROCK ISLAND, IL 61201 Breastfeeding mothers of low birthweight infants
R15NR-02768-01 (NURS) EVANS, JANE C WRIGHT STATE UNIVERSITY 3640 COLONEL GLENN HWY DAYTON, OH 45435 Low birth weight infant responses to routine caregiving
R01NR-02795-02 (NURS) SCHNELLE, JOHN F UCLA SCHOOL OF MEDICINE 10833 LECONTE AVENUE LOS ANGELES, CA 90024-1687 Nighttime incontinence care in nursing homes
R03NR-02798-01 (SRC) FERRELL, BETTY R CITY OF HOPE NATIONAL MED CENT 1500 E DUARTE ROAD DUARTE, CA 91010 Ethical issues and clinical decision making in cancer pain
R03NR-02818-01 (SRC) TILDEN, VIRGINIA P OREGON HEALTH SCIS UNIVERSITY 3181 SW SAM JACKSON PARK ROAD PORTLAND, OR 97201-3098 Family decision making for incompetent patients
R03NR-02819-01 (SRC) PINCH, WINIFRED J CREIGHTON UNIVERSITY CALIFORNIA AT 24TH STREET OMAHA, NE 68157 Parents' ethical decision making for high risk infants
R43NR-02824-01 (NURS) MATHERLY, SANDRA C HEALTHTRUST CONSULTING GROUP 1007 MAPLETREE LANE MAHOMET, IL 61953 Nurse on call telephone nursing program
R03NR-02829-01 (SRC) HURLEY, ANN C NORTHEASTERN UNIVERSITY 360 HUNTINGTON AVE, RB BOSTON, MA 02115 Nursing role in the advance directive decision
R03NR-02831-01 (SRC) OMERY, ANNA K UNIVERSITY OF CALIFORNIA 10833 LE CONTE AVENUE LOS ANGELES, CA 90024-6918 Pain--Bioethical, clinical and quality of life judgement
R43NR-02838-01 (NURS) ORZECHOWSKI, BEVERLY J NIAGARA SYSTEMS & SOFTWARE, IN 3960 HARLEM ROAD SNYDER, NY 14226-4706 Home health care intelligent portable (HIP) workstation
R01NR-02855-01 (NURS) CARLSON, JOHN G UNIVERSITY OF HAWAII 2430 CAMPUS RD HONOLULU, HI 96822 PTSD treatment and assessment in nursing and psychology
R01NR-02867-01 (NURS) BROOTEN, DOROTHY A UNIV OF PENN SCH OF NURSING 420 GUARDIAN DRIVE PHILADELPHIA, PA 19104-6096 Nurse home care-high risk pregnant women--Outcome and cost
R01NR-02875-01 (NURS) PRIDHAM, KAREN F UNIVERSITY OF WISCONSIN 600 HIGHLAND AVENUE, ROOM H6/2 MADISON, WI 53792 Caloric density and ad lib feeding for preterm infants
R01NR-02903-01 (ARRF) HANSELL, PHYLLIS S SETON HALL UNIVERSITY SOUTH ORANGE, NJ 07079 Stress and coping in caregivers of AIDS children
R15NR-02929-01 (NURS) BROADWELL-JACKSON, DEBRA CLEMSON UNIVERSITY COLLEGE OF NURSING BLDG, RM 53 CLEMSON, SC 29634-1703 Study of variables affecting ostomy patient outcome
S15NR-02930-01 (NSS) PADILLA, GERALDINE V UNIV OF CALIF., SAN FRANCISCO 10833 LE CONTE AVE SAN FRANCISCO, CA 94143-0962 Small instrumentation grant
S15NR-02931-01 (NSS) FITZPATRICK, JOYCE J CASE WESTERN RESERVE UNIVERSIT 2040 ADELBERT ROAD CLEVELAND, OH 44106 Small instrumentation grant
S15NR-02933-01 (NSS) HOLZEMER, WILLIAM L UNIV OF CALIF., SAN FRANCISCO BOX 0604 SAN FRANCISCO, CA 94143-0604 Small instrumentation grant
S15NR-02934-01 (NSS) STEMBER, MARILYN L UNIV OF COLORADO HLTH SCI CTR 4200 EAST NINTH AVE C288 DENVER, CO 80262 Small instrumentation grant
P20NR-02962-01 (NRRC) PENDER, NOLA J UNIVERSITY OF MICHIGAN 400 NORTH INGALLS ANN ARBOR, MI 48109-0482 Center for child/adolescent health behavior research
P20NR-02962-01 0001 (NRRC) GUTHRIE, BARBARA J Center for child/adolescent health behavior research Antecedents of alcohol use/misuse and health outcomes in adolescents
P20NR-02962-01 0002 (NRRC) NORTON, MARY A Center for child/adolescent health behavior research Antecedents, patterns and health outcomes of exercise among adolescents
P20NR-02962-01 0003 (NRRC) STEIN, KAREN Center for child/adolescent health behavior research Cognition of the self as regulators of adolescent exercise and alcohol use
P20NR-02962-01 0004 (NRRC) PORTER, CORNELIA P Center for child/adolescent health behavior research Antecedents of sexual activity in preadolescent and adolescents
R01NR-02965-01 (NRRC) RYDEN, MURIEL B UNIVERSITY OF MINNESOTA 308 HARVARD ST SE MINNEAPOLIS, MN 55455 Treating aggression through dementia care education
R01NR-02968-01 (NRRC) DOWLING, GLENNA A UNIVERSITY OF CALIFORNIA 3RD & PARNASSUS, N611Y SAN FRANCISCO, CA 94143-0610 Management of sleep-activity disruption in Alzheimer's
P20NR-02979-01 (NRRC) DEWALT, KATHLEEN M UNIVERSITY OF KENTUCKY 127 COLL OF MEDICINE BUILDING LEXINGTON, KY 40536-0086 Research center for health risk reduction in rural youth
P20NR-02979-01 0001 (NRRC) NOLAND, MELODY Research center for health risk reduction in rural youth The initiation and maintenance of tobacco use in rural youth
R01NR-02988-01 (NRRC) BURGIO, LOUIS D UNIVERSITY OF PITTSBURGH 190 LOTHROP ST PITTSBURGH, PA 15213 Use of microcomputers to study behavioral symptoms
R01NR-02998-01 (NRRC) MATTESON, MARY A UNIV OF TEXAS HLTH SCI CTR 7703 FLOYD CURL DRIVE SAN ANTONIO, TX 78284 Management of behaviors associated with dementia
R01NR-03032-01 (NRRC) ERICKSON, HELEN L UNIVERSITY OF TEXAS 1700 RED RIVER AUSTIN, TX 78701-1499 Modeling and role-modeling with Alzheimer's patients
R01NR-03034-01 (NRRC) VAN ORT, SUZANNE R UNIVERSITY OF ARIZONA 1401 N MARTIN TUCSON, AZ 85721 Nursing interventions for preserving mealtime behaviors
P20NR-03039-01 (NRRC) MCGURN, WEALTHA C UNIV OF TEXAS HEALTH SCIS CENT 7703 FLOYD CURL DRIVE SAN ANTONIO, TX 78284-7947 Exploratory research center--Minority adolescents' health
P20NR-03039-01 0001 (NRRC) YOUNG, ELEANOR A Exploratory research center--Minority adolescents' health Body weight, diet, exercise--Modulation in Hispanic teens
P20NR-03039-01 0002 (NRRC) MCGURN, WEALTHA Exploratory research center--Minority adolescents' health Health promoting pregnant adolescents
P20NR-03039-01 0003 (NRRC) SAUNDERS, MICHELE J Exploratory research center--Minority adolescents' health Direct versus simulated oral health instructions
R01NR-03125-01 (SRC) ROWLEY, PETER T UNIV OF ROCHESTER SCHOOL OF ME 601 ELMWOOD AVENUE BOX 641 ROCHESTER, NY 14642 Testing and counseling for cystic fibrosis mutations
R01NS-00021-43 (NEUB) BULLOCK, THEODORE H UNIV OF CALIFORNIA, SAN DIEGO LA JOLLA, CA 92093 Comparative neurophysiology of afferent processing
Z01NS-00200-39 (MNB) FEDIO, P NINDS, NIH Cognitive and emotional profile of neuropsychiatric disorders
R01NS-00294-37 (VISB) COHEN, BERNARD MOUNT SINAI SCH MED OF CUNY ONE EAST 100TH STREET NEW YORK, N Y 10029 The oculomotor system and body postural mechanisms
R01NS-00702-35 (NLS) LARRABEE, MARTIN G JOHNS HOPKINS UNIVERSITY CHARLES AND 34TH STREETS BALTIMORE, MD 21218 Metabolism and function in sympathetic neurons
Z01NS-00813-30 (LNC) ALBERS, R W NINDS, NIH Enzymological aspects of neural function
Z01NS-00815-31 (DMN) PENTCHEV, P G NINDS, NIH Metabolism of complex lipids of nervous tissues
Z01NS-00969-27 (CNSS) GAJDUSEK, D C NINDS, NIH Chronic CNS disease studies--Slow, latent and temperate virus infections
K08NS-00986-06 (NSPA) JENNINGS, MARK T DEPT OF NEUROLOGY 2100 PIERCE AVENUE NASHVILLE, TN 37232 Serologic analysis of pediatric brain tumors
K08NS-01026-05 (NSPB) LIPKIN, WALTER I UNIVERSITY OF CALIFORNIA 375A MED SURGE II IRVINE, CA 92717 Viruses neurotransmitters and neurological diseases
K04NS-01050-05 (NLS) HUANG, LI-YEN M UNIVERSITY OF TEXAS 200 UNIVERSITY BOULEVARD GALVESTON, TEX 77550 Electrical properties of isolated dorsal horn

K04NS-01065-05 (NEUA) RAO, STEPHEN M MEDICAL COLLEGE OF WISCONSIN 1000 N 92ND STREET MILWAUKEE, WI 53226 Neuropsychology of multiple sclerosis
K04NS-01121-05 (BIO) SABBAN, ESTHER L NEW YORK MEDICAL COLLEGE VALHALLA, NY 10595 Catecholamine biosynthetic enzymes
K04NS-01161-05 (NEUB) HAMMER, RONALD P, JR UNIV OF HAWAII SCHOOL OF MED 1960 EAST-WEST ROAD HONOLULU, HI 96822 Brain opiate systems--Structural and functional relation
K08NS-01162-05 (NSPA) GOLDSTEIN, LARRY B BOX 3821, DEPT OF MEDICINE DUKE UNIVERSITY MED CTR DURHAM, N C 27710 Biochemical receptor studies in stroke
K08NS-01163-05 (NSPB) PUCKETT, CARMIE CALIFORNIA INST OF TECHNOLOGY DIVISION OF BIOLOGY 147-75 PASADENA, CA 91125 Expression of the myelin basic protein gene
K08NS-01164-04 (NSPA) CHANGARIS, DAVID G UNIVERSITY OF LOUISVILLE HSC BLD A, ROOM 125 LOUISVILLE, KY 40292 Injured brain & the novel generation of angiotensin
K08NS-01166-05 (NSPB) SPAIN, WILLIAM J UNIVERSITY OF WASHINGTON SEATTLE, WA 98195 Seizure mechanisms in neocortex
K08NS-01168-05 (NSPB) MAREK, KENNETH L YALE UNIVERSITY SCH OF MEDICIN 333 CEDAR STREET NEW HAVEN, CT 06510 On the biosynthesis and regulation of neuropeptide Y
K08NS-01174-05 (NSPB) TRUGMAN, JOEL M UNIVERSITY OF VIRGINIA MED CTR BOX 394 CHARLOTTESVILLE, VA 22908 Pharmacologic and physiologic mechanisms in Parkinsonism
K04NS-01177-05 (NEUB) ROTHMAN, BARRY S SAN FRANCISCO STATE UNIVERSITY 1600 HOLLOWAY AVENUE SAN FRANCISCO, CA 94132 Inactivation of peptide neurotransmitters
K04NS-01184-05 (NLS) SAYRE, LAWRENCE M CASE WESTERN RESERVE UNIVERSIT 2040 ADELBERT ROAD CLEVELAND, OH 44106-7019 Mechanisms of action of small-molecule neurotoxins
K08NS-01191-05 (NSPA) MAYBERG, MARC R VA MED CTR, NEUROSURG SEC 1660 SOUTH COLUMBIAN WAY SEATTLE, WASH 98108 Pathophysiology of blood induced cerebral arteriopathy
K04NS-01196-05 (NEUB) BARRIONUEVO, GERMAN UNIVERSITY OF PITTSBURGH 441 CRAWFORD HALL PITTSBURGH, PA 15260 Neurophysiology of associative long term potentiation
K08NS-01200-05 (NSPB) HARRIS, DAVID A WASH UNIV SCHOOL OF MEDICINE 660 SOUTH EUCLID AVENUE ST LOUIS, MO 63110 Molecular mechanisms of synaptogenesis
K08NS-01202-05 (NSPA) SNIDER, WILLIAM D WASHINGTON UNIVERSITY 660 SOUTH EUCLID AVE ST LOUIS, MO 63110 Trophic interctions of neurons
K08NS-01208-05 (NSPA) ANTHONY, DOUGLAS C DUKE UNIVERSITY MED CENTER BOX 3712 DURHAM, NORTH CAROLINA 22710 Toxic models of neurofibrillary pathology
K08NS-01212-04 (CDR) BUSCH, BETSY NEW ENGLAND MEDICAL CENTER 750 WASHINGTON ST, BOX 334 BOSTON, MA 02111 Longitudinal stability of neurodevelopmental findings
K04NS-01217-04 (NEUB) HULSEBOSCH, CLAIRE E UNIVERSITY OF TEXAS MED BRANCH 200 UNIVERSITY BOULEVARD GALVESTON, TX 77550-2772 Molecular mechanisms of sprouting in the spinal cord
K04NS-01218-05 (BBCA) ANGELIDES, KIMON J BAYLOR COLLEGE OF MEDICINE ONE BAYLOR PLAZA HOUSTON, TEX 77030 Structural/kinetic/cellular mapping--Na+ channel
K08NS-01222-05 (NSPB) FERRIERO, DONNA M SAN FRANCISCO GENERAL HOSP 1001 POTRERO ST SAN FRANCISCO, CA 94110 Development of somatostatin-containing neurons
K08NS-01225-05 (NSPA) KIRSCH, JEFFREY R THE JOHNS HOPKINS UNIV. 600 NORTH WOLFE STREET BALTIMORE, MD 21205 Cerebral ischemia and free oxygen radicals
K08NS-01226-02 (NSPB) AGIUS, MARK A UNIVERSITY OF CALIFORNIA OFFICE OF RESEARCH DAVIS, CA 94616 Immune network in myasthenia
K04NS-01227-05 (BNP) CHAMBERLIN, ARTHUR R UNIVERSITY OF CALIFORNIA DEPT. OF CHEMISTRY IRVINE, CALIF 92717 Synthesis and binding studies of receptors models
K04NS-01228-05 (NLS) BOTTENSTEIN, JANE E UNIVERSITY OF TEXAS MED BRANCH 200 UNIVERSITY BOULEVARD GALVESTON, TEXAS 77550 Proliferation of oligodendrocytes in vitro
K08NS-01230-05 (NSPB) SCHWEITZER, JOHN B UNIVERSITY OF TENNESSEE 800 MADISON AVENUE, RM 568 MEMPHIS, TENNESSEE 38163 Nerve growth factor receptor mediated transport topics
K08NS-01232-05 (NSPB) HOSFORD, DAVID A VA HOSPITAL 508 FULTON STREET DURHAM, N C 27705 Role of entopeduncular nucleus in kindled seizures
K04NS-01233-05 (NLS) WATERHOUSE, BARRY D HAHNEMANN UNIVERSITY BROAD AND VINE STREET PHILADELPHIA, PA 19102-1192 Physiology of CNS biogenic amines and seizure disorders
K08NS-01235-04 (NSPA) LO, WARREN D CHILDREN'S HOSPITAL 700 CHILDRENS DRIVE COLUMBUS, OHIO 43205 Vascular permeability and brain edema in brain abscess
K08NS-01240-05 (NSPA) YANKNER, BRUCE A CHILDREN'S HOSPITAL CORP 300 LONGWOOD AVENUE BOSTON, MA 02115 Gene therapy in the nervous system using retroviruses
K08NS-01241-05 (NSPB) ALBERTS, MARK J DUKE UNIVERSITY MEDICAL CENTER P O BOX 2900 DURHAM, NC 27710 The role of nerve growth factor in Alzheimer's disease
K08NS-01244-05 (NSPB) HAMMOND, DAVID N THE UNIVERSITY OF CHICAGO 5841 S. MARYLAND AVE./BOX 228 CHICAGO, IL 60637 Trophic influences on cholinergic innervation of cortex
Z01NS-01245-25 (MNB) FEDIO, P NINDS, NIH EEG learning correlates using scalp and intracranial depth electrodes
K08NS-01247-05 (NSPB) KALB, ROBERT G YALE MEDICAL SCHOOL 333 CEDAR STREET NEW HAVEN, CT 06510 Molecular effects of early experience on motor neuron
K08NS-01251-04 (NSPA) SHORT, MARION P MASSACHUSETTS GENERAL HOSPITAL BUILDING 149, 13TH STREET CHARLESTOWN, MA 02129 Retroviral gene transfer into primary astrocyte culture
K08NS-01253-04 (NSPA) BERGER, MITCHEL S UNIVERSITY OF WASHINGTON DEPT. OF NEUROLOGICAL SURGERY SEATTLE, WA 98195 Drug resistance and DNA repair in brain tumors
K08NS-01254-04 (NSPB) SPECHT, LINDA A CHILDREN'S HOSP. - ENDERS 13 320 LONGWOOD AVENUE BOSTON, MA 02115 The cellular and myonuclear phenotype of myosin
K08NS-01255-04 (NSPA) DMYTRENKO, GEORGE M UNIV OF MARYLAND SCH OF MED 22 S GREENE STREET BALTIMORE, MD 21201 Basal lamina in regeneration and reinnervation
K04NS-01258-04 (NEUB) TUBLITZ, NATHAN J UNIVERSITY OF OREGON DEPARTMENT OF BIOLOGY EUGENE, OR 97403 Neurobiology of identified peptidergic neurons
K08NS-01261-04 (NSPA) SHY, MICHAEL E DEPARTMENT OF NEUROLOGY 1025 WALNUT ST SUITE 511 PHILADELPHIA, PA 19107 Antibodies to gangliosides GM1 and GD1b--Effect on motor neurons
K08NS-01265-05 (NSPA) RANSOHOFF, RICHARD M CLEVELAND CLINIC FOUNDATION 9500 EUCLID AVENUE CLEVELAND, OH 44195 Molecular basis of interferon action--Relation to multiple sclerosis
K08NS-01266-04 (NSPB) TWYMAN, ROY E NEUROSCIENCE LABORATORY 1103 E HURON ANN ARBOR, MI 48104 Anticonvulsant regulation of GABA chloride channels
K08NS-01272-04 (NSPB) ENGLAND, JOHN D UNIVERSITY OF COLORADO 4200 EAST NINTH AVENUE DENVER, COLORADO 80262 Doxorubicin-induced motor neuron and schwann cell death
K08NS-01276-04 (NSPB) KOROSHETZ, WALTER J MASSACHUSETTS GENERAL HOSPITAL FRUIT STREET BOSTON, MA 02114 The biophysical basis of glutamate and dopamine effects
K04NS-01278-04 (CMS) ZAKON, HAROLD H UNIVERSITY OF TEXAS PATTERSON LABORATORY AUSTIN, TX 78712 Cellular basis of steroid action in excitable cells
K08NS-01279-05 (NSPA) PHILLIPS, PETER C CHILDREN'S HOSP OF PHILADELPHI 34TH AND CIVIC CENTER BLVD PHILADELPHIA, PA 19104 Neurotoxicity of antifolate cancer chemotherapy
K08NS-01281-04 (NSPA) HARSH, GRIFFITH R UNIV OF CALIFORNIA, BOX 0112 DEPT OF NEUROLOGICAL SURGERY SAN FRANCISCO, CA 94143 PDGF in CNS tumors, atherosclerosis, and vasospasm
K08NS-01282-05 (NSPA) NARAYANAN, VINODH CHILDREN'S HOSP OF PITTSBURGH 3705 FIFTH AVE @ DE SOTO ST PITTSBURGH, PA 15213 Myelin P2 protein--study of expression and regulation
Z01NS-01282-28 (CNSS) GAJDUSEK, D C NINDS, NIH Neurobiology--Child development, and disease patterns in primitive culture
K08NS-01284-04 (NSPA) COHEN, JEFFREY A HOSP OF THE UNIV OF PA 3400 SPRUCE STREET PHILADELPHIA, PA 19104 Molecular biology of the beta-adrenergic/reovirus receptor
K08NS-01289-04 (NSPB) VANCE, JEFFREY M DUKE UNIVERSITY MED CENTER P O BOX 2900 DURHAM, NC 27710 Mapping the myotonic dystrophy gene
K04NS-01292-04 (NLS) ROTUNDO, RICHARD L UNIVERSITY OF MIAMI 1600 N W 10TH AVE MIAMI, FL 33101 Transport and sorting of neuronal membrane proteins
K08NS-01300-04 (NSPA) ALBIN, ROGER L NEUROSCIENCE BUILDING 1103 E. HURON ANN ARBOR, MI 48104 Huntington disease and quinolinate: Striatal cell types
K08NS-01307-04 (NSPB) BARAM, TALLIE Z CHILDRENS HOSP OF LOS ANGELES PO BOX 54700 LOS ANGELES, CA 90054-0700 Molecular mechanism of CRH expression
Z01NS-01309-26 (LMCN) FISHMAN, P H NINDS, NIH Biosynthesis and function of glycosphingolipids and other glycoconjugates
K08NS-01310-04 (NSPB) VORNOV, JAMES J THE JOHNS HOPKINS HOSPITAL MEYER 1-130 BALTIMORE, MD 21205 Reversible events preceding neuronal death in vitro
K04NS-01314-04 (NEUB) ZISKIND-CONHAIM, LEA UNIVERSITY OF WISCONSIN 1300 UNIVERSITY AVENUE MADISON, WI 53706 Studies of sensory-motoneuron contacts
K08NS-01315-04 (NSPB) AARONS, RALPH D STANFORD UNIVERSITY SCHOOL OF MEDICINE STANFORD, CA 94305 Role of oncogenes in nerve growth factor's action
K08NS-01316-04 (NSPA) GOLDMAN, STEVEN A CORNELL UNIV MED COLLEGE 1300 YORK AVE NEW YORK, NY 10021 The cellular neurobiology of adult neuronal replacement
K04NS-01318-04 (NEUC) PADEN, CHARLES M MONTANA STATE UNIVERSITY BOZEMAN, MT 59717 Cell sorting & antibodies to neuroendocrine cells
K08NS-01319-04 (NSPA) KITTNER, STEVEN J UNIV OF MARYLAND SCH OF MED 660 WEST REDWOOD STREET BALTIMORE, MD 21201 The epidemiology of stroke in biracial populations
K08NS-01325-04 (NSPA) JOHNSON, KEITH A MASSACHUSETTS GENERAL HOSPITAL FRUIT STREET BOSTON, MA 02114 NMR imaging in diseases of cerebral white matter
K08NS-01328-04 (NSPB) VITEK, JERROLD L EMORY UNIVERSITY 401 WOODRUFF MEMORIAL BUILDING ATLANTA, GA 30322 Role of ventrolateral thalamus in cerebellar tremor
K08NS-01329-03 (NSPA) LATERRA, JOHN J UNIVERSITY OF MICHIGAN 1299 E. ANN ST ANN ARBOR, MI 48109-0570 Adhesion molecules of brain microvessel cells
K08NS-01330-03 (NSPB) NERENBERG, MICHAEL I SCRIPPS CLINIC & RES. FOUND. 10666 N TORREY PINES ROAD LA JOLLA, CA 92037 Transgenic models of viral neuropathy
K08NS-01331-03 (NSPB) MACDONALD, GREGORY P UNIV OF CALIF., SAN FRANCISCO DEPT. OF PEDIATRICS, 1530B HSE SAN FRANCISCO, CA 94143 Models of down syndrome based on genetic homology
K08NS-01335-03 (NSPA) ALTMAN, DENNIS I WASHINGTON UNIV SCH OF MED 400 SOUTH KINGSHIGHWAY ST. LOUIS, MO 63110 PET in cerebrovascular disorders of newborn infants
K08NS-01336-03 (NSPB) SHOFFNER, JOHN M EMORY UNIVERSITY DEPT OF BIOCHEMISTRY ATLANTA, GA 30322 Molecular genetics of maternally transmitted disease
K08NS-01337-03 (NSPB) SCHREIBER, STEVEN S USC SCHOOL OF MEDICINE 2025 ZONAL AVE., MCH 142 LOS ANGELES, CA 90033 Molecular biology of memory
K08NS-01339-03 (NST) GILBERT, MARK PITTSBURGH CANCER INSTITUTE PARKVALE BUILDING PITTSBURGH, PA 15260 Neuronal cytoskeleton in culture models of injury and repair
K04NS-01340-03 (NLS) YEH, HERMES H UNIV OF ROCHESTER SCH OF MED 601 ELMWOOD AVE BOX 603 ROCHESTER, N Y 14642 Morphophysiology of peptides in mammalian CNS
K08NS-01341-03 (NSPB) CHANCE, PHILIP F UNIVERSITY OF UTAH MEDICAL CTR 50 NORTH MEDICAL DRIVE SALT LAKE CITY, UT 84132 Genetic

analysis of Charcot-Marie-Tooth disease
K08NS-01342-03 (NSPB) KIRSCHNER, MARC A OREGON HEALTH SCIENCES UNIV 3181 SW SAM JACKSON PARK ROAD PORTLAND, OR 97201-3098 Regulation of neuropeptide gene expression
K04NS-01344-03 (NEUB) FOREHAND, CYNTHIA J UNIV OF VERMONT COLL OF MED DEPT OF ANATOMY/NEUROBIOLOGY BURLINGTON, VT 05405 Innervation of target-identified sympathetic neurons
K08NS-01351-03 (NSPA) BHAGAVATI, SATYAKAM SUNY HEALTH SCIENCE CENTER 450 CLARKSON AVENUE BROOKLYN, NY 11203 Molecular genetic analysis of myotonic dystrophy
K04NS-01352-03 (NEUC) ROGERS, SHERRY L UNIV OF NEW MEXICO SCH OF MED DEPARTMENT OF ANATOMY ALBUQUERQUE, N M 87131 Laminin and fibronectin
K08NS-01355-03 (NSPA) ROTHSTEIN, JEFFREY D JOHNS HOPKINS UNIVERSITY MEYER 1-130 BALTIMORE, MD 21205 Diazepam binding inhibitor in hepatic encephalopathy
K04NS-01356-04 (NEUB) BREGMAN, BARBARA S GEORGETOWN UNIV SCHOOL OF MED 3900 RESERVOIR ROAD NW WASHINGTON, DC 20007 CNS regeneration in neonatal and adult spinal cord
K08NS-01357-02 (NSPA) MOSTER, MARK L TEMPLE UNIVERSITY HOSPITAL 3401 NORTH BROAD STREET PHILADELPHIA, PA 19140 Cerebral cortical mechanisms for control of saccades
K08NS-01359-03 (NSPB) JOHNS, DONALD R MEYER 6-119 600 N WOLFE ST BALTIMORE, MD 21205 Molecular biologic analysis of mitochondrial myopathies
K08NS-01360-03 (NSPB) COLE, ANDREW J JOHNS HOPKINS UNIV SCH OF MED 725 N WOLFE ST, WBSB 908 BALTIMORE, MD 21205 Transcription factor gene expression following LTP
K08NS-01361-03 (NSPB) LANGAN, THOMAS J SUNY/SCHOOL OF MEDICINE 219 BRYANT ST/NEUROLOGY DEPT BUFFALO, NY 14222 Isoprenoids and cell cycling in developing glial cells
K08NS-01367-03 (NSPB) DARRAS, BASIL THEODORE NEW ENGLAND MED CTR HOSPITALS 750 WSHINGTON ST BOX 393 BOSTON, MA 02111 Molecular studies of sodium channels in skeletal muscle
K08NS-01368-03 (NSPB) MC KEE, ANN C MASSACHUSETTS GENERAL HOSPITAL DEPT OF NEUROPATHOLOGY BOSTON, MA 02114 Cytoskeletal disorganization Alzheimer's disease
K04NS-01369-03 (EVR) PERLMAN, STANLEY UNIVERSITY OF IOWA IOWA CITY, IA 52242 Antibody-modulated demyelination
K08NS-01371-03 (NSPA) GRADY, MICHAEL S UNIV OF WASHINGTON, HARBORVIEW DEPT OF NEUROLOGICAL SURGERY SEATTLE, WA 98104 Can grafts modify host neuron death?
K04NS-01373-03 (NEUB) MOODY, SALLY A UNIVERSITY OF VIRGINIA BOX 439, MEDICAL CENTER CHARLOTTESVILLE, VA 22908 Neuronal lineage determinants in embryos
K04NS-01376-03 (HUD) GERNSBACHER, MORTON A UNIVERSITY OF OREGON DEPARTMENT OF PSYCHOLOGY EUGENE, OR 97403-1227 Cognitive processes & mechanisms in comprehension
K08NS-01380-03 (NSPA) SIEBER, FREDERICK E JOHNS HOPKINS HOSPITAL 600 NORTH WOLFE STREET BALTIMORE, MD 21205 Effects of glucose on cerebral blood flow and metabolism
K08NS-01381-03 (NSPB) FELDMAN, EVA L UNIVERSITY OF MICHIGAN MED CTR 1500 E MEDICAL CENTER DRIVE ANN ARBOR, MI 48109-0316 The role of insulin-like growth factors in the PNS
K04NS-01383-03 (NLS) JOHNSON, DAVID BRIGHAM & WOMEN'S HOSPITAL 75 FRANCIS STREET BOSTON, MA 02115 Regulation of nervous system mast cell activity
K08NS-01384-03 (NSPA) LENZ, FREDERICK A JOHNS HOPKINS HOSPITAL 600 N WOLFE ST BALTIMORE, MD 21205 Studies of the ventrocaudal thalamus in pain
K08NS-01386-03 (NSPB) BENARDO, LARRY STATE UNIVERSITY OF NEW YORK DEPARTMENT OF PHARMACOLOGY BROOKLYN, N. Y. 11203 Cortical development and epilepsy
K08NS-01387-03 (NSPB) LEVEY, ALLAN I JOHNS HOPKINS HOSPITAL 600 NORTH WOLFE ST/MEYER 1-130 BALTIMORE, MD 21205 Localization of muscarinic receptor proteins m1-m5
K08NS-01390-02 (NSPB) KAYE, EDWARD M NEW ENGLAND MEDICAL CENTER HOS 750 WASHINGTON ST, BOX 373 BOSTON, MA 02111 Molecular genetic studies of human gm1 ganglion
K08NS-01395-03 (NSPB) DREYER, EVAN B MASSACHUSETTS EYE/EAR INFIRMAR 9 HAWTHORNE PLACE, 15H BOSTON, MA 02114 Thy-1 receptor and CNS neurite regeneration
K04NS-01396-03 (NLS) EHLERT, FREDERICK J UNIVERSITY OF CALIFORNIA COLLEGE OF MEDICINE IRVINE, CA 92717 Mechanisms of muscarinic receptor cross-talk in brain
K04NS-01401-02 (NEUA) KRUSE, CAROL A UNIV OF COLORADO HLTH SCI CTR BOX C307, 4200 EAST NINTH AVE DENVER, CO 80262 Immunotherapy for primary brain glioma
K08NS-01403-03 (NSPA) SNYDER, EVAN Y HARVARD MEDICAL SCHOOL 25 SHATTUCK STREET BOSTON, MA 02115 Use of retroviral vectors to study neural plasticity
K04NS-01404-03 (NEUC) LEFF, STUART E STANFORD UNIVERSITY SCH OF MED STANFORD, CA 94305-5332 Control of neuroendocrine gene expression
K04NS-01405-03 (CMS) FARAH, MARTHA J CARNEGIE MELLON UNIVERSITY DEPT. OF PSYCHOLOGY PITTSBURGH, PA 15213 Computational neuropsychology of spatial cognition
K08NS-01407-03 (NSPB) SEGAL, MICHAEL M HARVARD MEDICAL SCHOOL 220 LONGWOOD AVENUE BOSTON, MA 02115 Epileptiform activity on hippocampal microcultures
K08NS-01411-02 (NSPB) CHEN, LAN SHU UNIV OF CALIFORNIA, SAN DIEGO DEPT. OF NEUROSCIENCE, M-024 LA JOLLA, CA 92093 Antiepileptic effect of genetically modified fibroblasts
K08NS-01412-02 (NSPA) CRAWFORD, THOMAS O JOHNS HOPKINS UNIVERSITY 600 N WOLFE STREET BALTIMORE, MD 21205 Studies on motor neuron regeneration
K08NS-01419-02 (NSPB) HSIAO, KAREN K UNIVERSITY OF CALIFORNIA BOX 0518, HSE-781 SAN FRANCISCO, CA 94143-0518 Prion protein mutations in inherited prion diseases
K08NS-01421-02 (NSPA) SMITH, CHARLES D DEPARTMENT OF NEUROLOGY 800 ROSE STREET LEXINGTON, KY 40536 Brain reperfusion injury--Energy state and free radicals
K08NS-01423-02 (NSPA) JOHNSON, STEVEN W OREGON HEALTH SCIENCES UNIV 3181 SW SAM JACKSON PARK ROAD PORTLAND, OR 97201 Dopamine effects on identified striatal neurons
K08NS-01424-02 (NSPB) LOWENSTEIN, DANIEL H UNIVERSITY OF CALIFORNIA SFGH 4M62/BOX 0870 SAN FRANCISCO, CA 94143-0870 The CNS stress protein response following seizures
Z01NS-01424-25 (MNB) FEDIO, P NINDS, NIH Behavioral modulation by the limbic system in man
K08NS-01425-02 (NSPA) GIFFARD, RONA G STANFORD UNIVERSITY SCH OF MEDICINE STANFORD, CA 94305-5117 Anesthetics & ischemic neuronal injury in vitro
K04NS-01427-02 (NLS) HORN, JOHN P UNIVERSITY OF PITTSBURGH 3500 TERRACE STREET PITTSBURGH, PA 15261 Development and function of synaptic co-transmission
K08NS-01428-02 (NSPB) PULST, STEFAN M CEDARS-SINAI MEDICAL CENTER 8700 BEVERLY BOULEVARD LOS ANGELES, CA 90048 Neurofibromatosis--A molecular-genetic approach
K08NS-01433-01A1 (NST) CLARK, GARY D LSU MEDICAL CENTER 1542 TULANE AVENUE NEW ORLEANS, LA 70112 Calcium dependent regulation of NMDA currents
K08NS-01438-01A1 (NST) TOMASULO, RICHARD A UNIV OF VIRGINIA SCH OF MEDICI BOX 230 CHARLOTTESVILLE, VA 22908 Plasticity of inhibitory circuits in the dentate gyrus
K08NS-01442-02 (NSPA) GRAFE, MARJORIE R UCSD MEDICAL CENTER 225 DICKINSON STREET SAN DIEGO, CA 92103 Effects of hypoxic/ischemic injury on the neonatal brain
Z01NS-01442-25 (LN) REESE, T S NINDS, NIH Permeability of cellular layers in the vertebrate nervous system
K08NS-01443-02 (NSPB) YAMADA, KELVIN A WASHINGTON UNIVERSITY 400 SOUTH KINGSHIGHWAY ST LOUIS, MO 63110 Glutamate receptor modulation in neurons
K04NS-01445-02 (NLS) WESTLUND, KARIN N UNIVERSITY OF TEXAS MED BRANCH 200 UNIVERSITY BOULEVARD GALVESTON, TX 77550-2772 Inducible alteration of CGRP in primary afferent neurons
K08NS-01449-02 (NSPA) FRIEDMAN, EMILY D UNIVERSITY OF PENNSYLVANIA 3400 SPRUCE STREET PHILADELPHIA, PA 19104 Functional domains of the myelin basic proteins
K08NS-01451-01A1 (NST) SHNEIDMAN, PAUL S UNIVERSITY OF PENNSYLVANIA JOHNSON PAVILION PHILADELPHIA, PA 19104 Regulation of neurofilament gene expression
K08NS-01453-02 (NSPA) NEIL, JEFFREY J WASHINGTON UNIVERSITY 400 S KINGSHIGHWAY ST LOUIS, MO 63110 Magnetic resonance quantification of cerebral perfusion
K08NS-01454-02 (NSPB) HARRISON, MADALINE B UNIVERSITY OF VIRGINIA BOX 394 CHARLOTTESVILLE, VA 22908 Cellular localization of dopamine receptor subtypes
K08NS-01455-02 (NSPB) KINSMAN, STEPHEN L KENNEDY RESEARCH INSTITUTE, IN 707 N. BROADWAY Somatostatin overexpression--Neurobiological consequences
K08NS-01460-02 (NSPB) HERSHKOWITZ, NORMAN GEORGETOWN UNIVERSITY 3800 RESERVOIR RD NW WASHINGTON, DC 20007-297 Electrophysiologic mechanisms--Ischemic neuronal injury
K08NS-01461-02 (NSPA) DARNELL, ROBERT B DEPARTMENT OF NEUROLOGY 1275 YORK AVENUE NEW YORK, NY 10021 Molecular biology of neural plasticity and growth control
K08NS-01464-02 (NSPB) GARBERN, JAMES Y HOSPITAL OF THE UNIV. OF PENN. 3400 SPRUCE STREET PHILADELPHIA, PA 19104 Analysis of function of Hox 1.2 and Hox 1.3
K08NS-01466-01A1 (NST) CAPONE, GEORGE T KENNEDY RESEARCH INSTITUTE 707 N BROADWAY BALTIMORE, MD 21205 Neuropeptide gene expression in cultured cortical neuron
K08NS-01467-02 (NSPA) STRITTMATTER, STEPHEN M MASSACHUSETTS GENERAL HOSPITAL FRUIT STREET BOSTON, MA 02114 Neuronal development in the absence of gap-43
K08NS-01470-01A1 (NST) BREY, ROBIN L UNIV OF TEXAS HEALTH SCIENCE C 7703 FLOYD CURL DRIVE SAN ANTONIO, TX 78284 Autoimmune nervous system disease--B cell repertoire
K08NS-01471-02 (NSPB) MADSEN, JOSEPH R CHILDRENS HOSPITAL 300 LONGWOOD AVENUE BOSTON, MA 02115 Glial cell line molecules affecting neurite growth
K08NS-01472-02 (NSPB) KELLY, KEVIN M UNIVERSITY OF MICHIGAN 1103 E HURON STREET ANN ARBOR, MI 48104-1687 Antiepileptic drug effects on Ca2+ and GABA Cl- currents
K04NS-01473-01 (NEUB) WEEKS, JANIS C UNIVERSITY OF OREGON EUGENE, OR 97403 Metamorphic changes in neuronal form and function
K04NS-01476-01 (NEUB) EISEN, JUDITH S UNIVERSITY OF OREGON EUGENE, OR 97403 Neuronal pathfinding by identified motoneurons
K04NS-01481-02 (NEUB) SIEGLER, MELODY V EMORY UNIVERSITY 1555 PIERCE DRIVE ATLANTA, GA 30322 Lineal origin of neuron groups
K08NS-01482-01 (NST) TRESCHER, WILLIAM H KENNEDY RESEARCH INSTITUTE, IN 707 NORTH BROADWAY BALTIMORE, MD 21205 Excitatory neurotransmitter injury in developing brain
K08NS-01483-01 (NST) BARFIELD, JAMES A EMORY UNIVERSITY 2040 RIDGEWOOD DRIVE, NE ATLANTA, GA 30322 Generation of cell diversity in the cerebral cortex
K08NS-01484-01 (NST) ROSENBAUM, DANIEL M ALBERT EINSTEIN COLL OF MEDICI 1300 MORRIS PARK AVE BRONX, NY 10461 Free radicals and cerebral ischemia
K08NS-01487-01 (NST) GREENAMYRE, JOHN T UNIVERSITY OF ROCHESTER MED CT 601 ELMWOOD AVENUE ROCHESTER, NY 14642 Mechanisms of selective neuronal vulnerability
K08NS-01488-01 (NST) SEGAL, ROSALIND A MIT E25-435 CAMBRIDGE, MA 02139 Differentiation mechanisms in retinal stem cells
K08NS-01489-01 (NST) CLARK, WAYNE M OREGON HEALTH SCIENCES UNIV. 3181 SW SAM JACKSON PARK ROAD PORTLAND, OR 97201 Role of leukocyte adhesion in CNS ischemic injury
K08NS-01492-01 (NST) VISKOCHIL, DAVID H UNIVERSITY OF UTAH 50 N MEDICAL DRIVE; RM 413 MRE SALT LAKE CITY, UT 84132 The molecular genetics of neurofibromatosis type 1
K04NS-01493-01 (NLS) MESSER, WILLIAM S, JR UNIVERSITY OF TOLEDO 2801 W BANCROFT STREET TOLEDO, OH 43606 Multidisciplinary studies of muscarinic receptors
K08NS-01497-01 (NST) DAVAR, GUDARZ MASSACHUSETTS GENERAL HOSPITAL FRUIT STREET BOSTON, MA 02114 NMDA receptor and opioid effects in painful neuropathy

K08NS-01498-01 (NST) **TROMMER, BARBARA L** EVANSTON HOSPITAL 2650 RIDGE AVENUE EVANSTON, IL 60201 Long-term potentiation in developing hippocampus

K08NS-01500-01 (NST) **ROSENFELD, STEVEN S** UNIVERSITY OF ALABAMA UAB STATION BIRMINGHAM, AL 35294 Role of myosins I and II in cell motility

K08NS-01502-01 (NST) **STECKER, MARK M** HOSP OF THE UNIV OF PENNSYLVAN 3400 SPRUCE STREET PHILADELPHIA, PA 19104 Representation of visual space in cerebral cortex

K08NS-01503-01 (NST) **EVANS, MILES S** SOUTHERN ILLINOIS UNIVERSITY P O BOX 19230 SPRINGFIELD, IL 62794-9230 Amino acid neurotransmission in the epilepsy prone

K08NS-01504-01 (NST) **GEORGE, EDWIN B** JOHNS HOPKINS UNIVERSITY 600 NORTH WOLFE STREET BALTIMORE, MD 21205 Axon regeneration and the cytoskeleton

K08NS-01505-01 (NST) **PETTIGREW, LUTHER C** UNIVERSITY OF KENTUCKY 800 ROSE ST LEXINGTON, KY 40536-0084 Eicosanoids mediate effects of PAF in cerebral ischemia

K04NS-01509-01 (NLS) **WAXHAM, MELVIN N** UNIVERSITY OF TEXAS MED SCHOOL 6431 FANNIN ST HOUSTON, TX 77030 CaM-kinase autoregulation and role in synaptic function

K08NS-01510-01 (NST) **NAVIA, BRADFORD A** CHILDREN'S HOSPITAL BOSTON, MA 02115 Cloning the X-linked retinitis pigmentosa genes

K08NS-01514-02 (NSPB) **WOLLACK, JAN B** UNIVERSITY OF MARYLAND HOSPITA GREENE STREET BALTIMORE, MD 21201 Purinergic mechanisms in epilepsy

K08NS-01515-02 (NST) **SACKTOR, TODD C** SUNY HEALTH SCIENCE CTR 450 CLARKSON AVE BOX 29 BROOKLYN, NY 11203 Protein kinase C isozymes in the hippocampus

K08NS-01516-01 (NST) **NYE, JEFFREY S** COLUMBIA UNIVERSITY 630 WEST 168TH STREET NEW YORK, NY 10032 Does lateral inhibition direct neurogenesis?

K08NS-01518-01 (NST) **SHAPIRO, ROBERT E** JOHN HOPKINS HOSPITAL 600 N WOLFE ST BALTIMORE, MD 21205 Ganglioside binding molecules of rat skeletal muscle

K08NS-01523-01 (NST) **HAUN, STEVEN E** CHILDREN'S HOSP RESEARCH FDN 700 CHILDREN'S DRIVE COLUMBUS, OH 43205 Cell culture model of hypoxic-ischemic brain injury

K08NS-01524-01 (NST) **LEBER, STEVEN M** UNIVERSITY OF MICHIGAN 130 EAST CATHERINE STREET ANN ARBOR, MI 48109-0570 Abnormalities of neural migration in optic tectum

K08NS-01525-01 (NST) **RAYMOND, LYNN A** JOHNS HOPKINS HOSPITAL 600 NORTH WOLFE STREET BALTIMORE, MD 21205 Regulation of glutamate receptors by phosphorylation

K08NS-01528-01 (NST) **CHIRIBOGA, CLAUDIA** NEUROLOGICAL INSTITUTE 710 WEST 168TH STREET NEW YORK, NY 10032 In-utero cocaine exposures--Neurodevelopement

K08NS-01530-01 (NST) **VRIESENDORP, FRANCINE J** UNIV OF MARYLAND 22 S GREENE STREET BALTIMORE, MD 21201 Neutral glycolipid antigens in experimental allergic neuritis

K04NS-01531-01 (NEUB) **RIBERA, ANGELES B** UNIV OF COLORADO HLTH SCI CENT 4200 E 9TH AVENUE DENVER, CO 80262 Potassium currents role in the developing nervous system

K08NS-01533-01 (NST) **BURKE, JAMES R** DUKE UNIVERSITY MEDICAL CENTER DUKE BOX 3676 DURHAM, NC 27710 Early genes and kindling development

K04NS-01536-01 (NEUC) **LAFER, EILEEN M** UNIVERSITY OF PITTSBURGH PITTSBURGH, PA 15260 Molecular biology of the synapse

K04NS-01537-01 (REB) **MC DONNELL, SUE M** NEW BOLTON CENTER 382 W STREET ROAD KENNETT SQUARE, PA 19348 Pharmacological manipulation of erection and ejaculation

K08NS-01551-01 (CT) **PRESS, RICHARD D** THE WISTAR INSTITUTE 36TH & SPRUCE STREETS PHILADELPHIA, PA 19104 Structure and function of myb oncogene in neuronal cells

K08NS-01571-01 (NST) **HENSKI, ELIZABETH P** BRIGHAM & WOMEN'S HOSPITAL 221 LONGWOOD AVENUE, LMRC 3 BOSTON, MA 02115 Dystonia and tuberous sclerosis-- Localization on 9q32-34

K08NS-01573-01 (NST) **STALEY, KEVIN J** UNIV OF COLORADO HLTH SCI CENT 4200 EAST 9TH AVE DENVER, CO 80262 Modulation of inhibition in the neonatal hippocampus

Z01NS-01658-24 (MNB) **FEDIO, P** NINDS, NIH Hemispheric development and specialization of intellectual functions

Z01NS-01659-23 (LNP) **LASANSKY, A** NINDS, NIH Synaptic contacts of retinal neurons

Z01NS-01686-23 (LNLC) **BURKE, R E** NINDS, NIH Motor control system in the spinal cord

Z01NS-01687-23 (LNLC) **BAK, M** NINDS, NIH Techniques for making connections with the nervous musculoskeletal systems

Z01NS-01688-23 (LNLC) **SCHMIDT, E M** NINDS, NIH Cortical mechanism of voluntary motor control

Z01NS-01805-23 (LN) **SANOVICH, E** NINDS, NIH Membrane structure of astrocytes

Z01NS-01808-22 (LMCN) **QUARLES, R H** NINDS, NIH Glycoproteins of myelin in development and disease

Z01NS-01881-21 (LN) **REESE, T S** NINDS, NIH Structural basis of synaptic transmission and development

Z01NS-01924-21 (NEB) **ELDRIDGE, R** NINDS, NIH Clinical, genetic, pathophysiologic study of hereditary movement disorders

Z01NS-01927-21 (NEB) **ELDRIDGE, R** NINDS, NIH Clinical, genetic, pathophysiologic study of hereditary nervous system tumors

Z01NS-01983-20 (LVMP) **MAJOR, E O** NINDS, NIH Molecular biology of human virus infections, HIV-1 AND JCV

Z01NS-01995-19 (LENP) **WEBSTER, H F** NINDS, NIH Cellular and molecular studies of myelin formation, breakdown, and regeneration

Z01NS-02019-19 (LNP) **BARKER, J L** NINDS, NIH Physiological properties on developing CNS cells

Z01NS-02034-19 (LVMP) **DUBOIS-DALCQ, M** NINDS, NIH Biology of myelin-forming cells in vitro and in vivo including remyelination

Z01NS-02038-18 (MNB) **DALAKAS, M C** NINDS, NIH Combined clinical, viral, and immunological studies of neuromuscular diseases

Z01NS-02073-18 (MNB) **DICHIRO, G** NINDS, NIH Nuclear magnetic resonance

Z01NS-02079-18 (LNLC) **MARKS, W B** NINDS, NIH Models of neurophysiological systems

Z01NS-02086-18 (LN) **SIMPSON, D L** NINDS, NIH Regeneration specificity in transplanted neural tissue

Z01NS-02115-18 (CNB) **POLINSKY, R J** NINDS, NIH Biochemical indices of adrenergic function in humans

Z01NS-02139-17 (ET) **WALTERS, J R** NINDS, NIH Pharmacology and physiology of the substantia nigra and basal ganglia

Z01NS-02144-17 (LN) **ISHIHARA, S** NINDS, NIH Blood-brain barrier

Z01NS-02151-17 (LMCN) **ALKON, D L** NINDS, NIH Memory storage in neural networks

Z01NS-02160-17 (LNLC) **BURKE, R E** NINDS, NIH Intrinsic properties of motor unit

Z01NS-02162-17 (DMN) **MILLER, S P** NINDS, NIH Synthesis of compounds analogous to glycolipids

Z01NS-02163-17 (DMN) **MILLER, S P** NINDS, NIH Development of analytical methods for the use of research of sphingolipidoses

Z01NS-02167-17 (NEB) **ELDRIDGE, R** NINDS, NIH Genetic epidemiology of MS and other multifactorial neurologic disorders

Z01NS-02202-16 (NI) **MCFARLIN, D E** NINDS, NIH Immunological studies in patients with multiple sclerosis and other CNS diseases

Z01NS-02204-16 (NI) **MCFARLIN, D E** NINDS, NIH Immunologic mechanisms on experimental autoimmune diseases of the nervous system

Z01NS-02205-16 (NI) **MCFARLAND, H F** NINDS, NIH Interactions between the human immune system and antigens in the nervous system

Z01NS-02218-16 (LB) **GILBERT, D L** NINDS, NIH Sources and effects of reactive oxygen intermediates in the brain

Z01NS-02236-14 (MNB) **THEODORE, W** NINDS, NIH Diagnostic and therapeutic reevaluation of patients with intractable epilepsy

Z01NS-02240-15 (NEB) **ROMAN, G C** NINDS, NIH Epidemiology of dementia and other neurodegenerative disorders

Z01NS-02243-15 (NEB) **NELSON, K B** NINDS, NIH Pediatric neuroepidemiology

P01NS-02253-32 (NSPB) **FURSHPAN, EDWIN J** HARVARD MEDICAL SCHOOL 220 LONGWOOD AVENUE BOSTON, MA 02115 Neurophysiological and neurochemical studies

P01NS-02253-32 0002 (NSPB) **FURSHPAN, EDWIN J** Neurophysiological and neurochemical studies Synaptic mechanisms of limbic neurons in culture

P01NS-02253-32 0011 (NSPB) **POTTER, DAVID D** Neurophysiological and neurochemical studies Plasticity in cultured central and peripheral neurons

P01NS-02253-32 0013 (NSPB) **MATTHEW, WILLIAM D** Neurophysiological and neurochemical studies Axon growth-promoting antigens in the hippocampus

P01NS-02253-32 0014 (NSPB) **KRAVITZ, EDWARD A** Neurophysiological and neurochemical studies Steroid hormone actions on vertebrate CNS neurons in culture

P01NS-02253-32 9001 (NSPB) **LAFRATTA, J** Neurophysiological and neurochemical studies Core--Machine and electronic shop

P01NS-02253-32 9003 (NSPB) **KRAVITZ, EDWARD A** Neurophysiological and neurochemical studies Core--Photographic facility

P01NS-02253-32 9004 (NSPB) **FURSHPAN, EDWIN J** Neurophysiological and neurochemical studies Core--EM/histology facility

P01NS-02253-32 0015 (NSPB) **BEAN, BRUCE P** Neurophysiological and neurochemical studies Pharmacology of calcium entry pathways in hippocampal neurons

Z01NS-02254-15 (LNLC) **ZALEWSKI, A A** NINDS, NIH Repair of injured nervous tissue with foreign grafts

Z01NS-02263-15 (ET) **SIBLEY, D R** NINDS, NIH Biochemical and pharmacological studies of dopamine receptors

Z01NS-02265-14 (ET) **CHASE, T N** NINDS, NIH Pharmacology, biochemistry and physiology of central neurotransmitters

Z01NS-02297-15 (NEB) **ROMAN, G C** NINDS, NIH Mortality from neurologic disorders--National and international comparisons

Z01NS-02299-15 (NEB) **ROMAN, G C** NINDS, NIH Reviews of epidemiologic aspects of neurologic disease

Z01NS-02301-15 (NEB) **ROMAN, G C** NINDS, NIH Collaborative studies of less common or less debilitating neurologic disorders

Z01NS-02307-15 (NEB) **ROMAN, G C** NINDS, NIH Educational resources in neurological epidemiology

Z01NS-02315-14 (MNB) **DICHIRO, G** NINDS, NIH Positron emission tomography

Z01NS-02318-15 (MNB) **THEODORE, W** NINDS, NIH Clinical pharmacology of antiepileptic drugs

Z01NS-02324-14 (SB) **MCCARRON, R M** NINDS, NIH Blood-brain barrier--In vitro cerebrovascular endothelial permeability

Z01NS-02330-14 (LNP) **BARKER, J L** NINDS, NIH Cell biological studies of developing CNS cells

Z01NS-02357-13 (SB) **SPATZ, M** NINDS, NIH Cerebral ischemia and monoamines

Z01NS-02366-14 (LMCN) **FISHMAN, P H** NINDS, NIH Regulation of hormone-responsive adenylate cyclase

Z01NS-02370-13 (NEB) **ROMAN, G C** NINDS, NIH Racial and geographic differences in occurrence of neurologic disease

N01NS-02373-03 (**) **LEVINE, STEVEN R** Phase II-B randomized controlled study of tissue plasminogen activator

N01NS-02374-02 (**) **BROTT, THOMAS G** Phase II-B randomized controlled study of tissue plasmininogen activator

N01NS-02375-02 (**) **PRICE, THOMAS R** Phase II-B randomized controlled study of tissue plasminogen activator

N01NS-02376-02 (**) **HALEY, E C, JR** Phase II-B randomized controlled study of tissue plasminogen activator

N01NS-02377-02 (**) **LYDEN, PATRICK D** Phase II-B randomized controlled study of tissue plasminogen activator

N01NS-02378-02 (**) **MACKAY, BRUCE C** Phase II-B randomized controlled study of tissue plasminogen activator

N01NS-02379-03 (**) **HOROWITZ, STEVEN H** Phase II-B study of tissue plasminogen activator for acute ischemic stroke

N01NS-02380-03 (**) **GAINES, KENNETH J** Phase II-B randomized controlled study of tissue plasminogen activator

N01NS-02381-03 (**) **GROTTA, JAMES C** Phase II-B randomized controlled study of tissue plasminogen activator

N01NS-02382-02 (**) **TILLEY, BARBARA C** Phase II-B randomized

PROJECT NO., ORGANIZATIONAL UNIT., INVESTIGATOR, ADDRESS, TITLE

controlled study of tissue plasmininogen activator
N01NS-02383-02 (**) **PINE, JEROME** Cultured neuron probe
N01NS-02384-42 (**) **BROWN, MICHAEL** NINDS technical and resource support contract
N01NS-02385-01 (**) **CONNEALLY, P MICHAEL** National research roster for Huntington's disease patients
N01NS-02386-01 (**) **WEIS, ALEXANDER** Preparation of radiolabeled sphingolipids
N01NS-02387-01 (**) **MAO, JENRI** Large scale automated DNA sequencing of neurotransmitter
N01NS-02388-05 (**) **GREER, WILLIAM E** Study of viral infections of the nervous system
N01NS-02389-02 (**) **VOGL, THOMAS** Computational neuronal modeling
N01NS-02395-01 (**) **MORTIMER, JOHN T** Percutaneous electrodes for functional neuromuscular stimulation
N01NS-02396-01 (**) **WISE, KENSAL D** Micromachined intracortical recording electrode arrays
N01NS-02397-02 (**) **WEINER, HOWARD L** MRI studies in multiple sclerosis
N01NS-02398-03 (**) **BASAK, SUBHASH, C** Structure activity relationships (SAR) for anticonvulsant drug development
N01NS-02399-02 (**) **EDELL, DAVID J** Biomaterials for insulation of implantable electrodes
Z01NS-02453-11 (DMN) **BARTON, N** NINDS, NIH Gaucher's disease--Biochemical and clinical studies
Z01NS-02454-11 (SN) **OLDFIELD, E H** NINDS, NIH Studies of human pituitary tumors
R01NS-02476-32 (NEUB) **NORTON, WILLIAM T** ALBERT EINSTEIN COLLEGE OF MED 1300 MORRIS PARK AVENUE BRONX, N Y 10461 The chemistry of cells and cell portions from the CNS
Z01NS-02483-11 (BFSB) **EMOTO, S E** NINDS, NIH Predictive value of the EEG in febrile seizures
Z01NS-02490-11 (BFSB) **DAMBROSIA, J M** NINDS, NIH Research in statistics
Z01NS-02516-10 (BFSB) **FOULKES, M A** NINDS, NIH Traumatic coma data bank
Z01NS-02528-10 (LVMP) **Hudson, L D** NINDS, NIH Regulation of myelin synthesis
Z01NS-02531-10 (MNB) **DALAKAS, M C** NINDS, NIH Neuromuscular and central nervous system diseases and their experimental models
Z01NS-02549-10 (LENP) **MARTIN, J R** NINDS, NIH Herpesvirus infections and nervous system diseases
Z01NS-02550-10 (LENP) **STONER, G L** NINDS, NIH Biochemical and immunologic mechanisms in virally-induced CNS demyelination
Z01NS-02551-11 (LN) **REESE, T S** NINDS, NIH Structure and function of cytoplasmic transport motors
Z01NS-02598-09 (BFSB) **FOULKES, MARY A** NINDS, NIH Stroke data bank
Z01NS-02603-08 (NI) **BIDDISON, WILLIAM E** NINDS, NIH Molecular mechanisms of lymphoid cell-cell interactions
Z01NS-02606-08 (LB) **STANLEY, E F** NINDS, NIH Calcium channels in vertebrate nerve terminals
Z01NS-02608-08 (LB) **CLAY, J R** NINDS, NIH Comparative aspects of ionic conductances in nerve and heart cell membranes
Z01NS-02609-08 (LB) **IWASA, K** NINDS, NIH Mechanism of egg activation following fertilization
Z01NS-02610-08 (LN) **ANDREWS, S B** NINDS, NIH Elemental and structural organization of neurons and glia
R01NS-02619-32 (NEUB) **WILSON, VICTOR J** ROCKEFELLER UNIVERSITY 1230 YORK AVENUE NEW YORK, N Y 10021 Motor control--Tonic neck and vestibulospinal reflexes
Z01NS-02623-08 (SB) **ISHII, H** NINDS, NIH Cerebral ischemia and edema -- Extracellular biogenic amines
Z01NS-02630-08 (CNB) **POLINSKY, R J** NINDS, NIH Clinical, genetic, and biochemical studies of familial Alzheimer's disease
Z01NS-02631-08 (LNP) **NELSON, R** NINDS, NIH Structure and function in retinal neurons
Z01NS-02652-07 (BFSB) **DAMBROSIA, J M** NINDS, NIH Statistical collaboration and consultation
Z01NS-02657-07 (DMN) **BARTON, N** NINDS, NIH Molecular and genetic studies of Neimann-Pick disease
Z01NS-02664-07 (DMN) **BARTON, N** NINDS, NIH Clinical studies of neurogenetic diseases
Z01NS-02667-08 (MNB) **HALLETT, M** NINDS, NIH Physiological analysis of involuntary movements
Z01NS-02669-07 (MNB) **HALLETT, M** NINDS, NIH Physiological analysis of voluntary movement
Z01NS-02674-07 (SN) **YOULE, R** NINDS, NIH Monoclonal antibody-toxin conjugates for tumor therapy in vivo
Z01NS-02675-07 (OCD) **HALLETT, M** NINDS, NIH Evaluation of neuromuscular diseases
Z01NS-02677-07 (LMB) **BRENNER, M** NINDS, NIH Regulation of gene activity in astrocytes
Z01NS-02689-07 (SB) **SPATZ, M** NINDS, NIH Regulation of endothelin and prostanoid in cerebromicrovascular endothelium
Z01NS-02697-07 (SN) **OLDFIELD, E H** NINDS, NIH Protection of the brain against injury by ionizing radiation with pentobarbital
Z01NS-02698-06 (LNC) **Oderwald, W F** NINDS, NIH Biology of mammalian homeodomain proteins
Z01NS-02699-06 (LENP) **CHAN, K-F** NINDS, NIH Ganglioside roles myelin and neuron function and neurotoxicity
Z01NS-02707-06 (SN) **MERRILL, M J** NINDS, NIH Role of insulin and insulin-like growth factors in glioma cells
Z01NS-02708-06 (SN) **MERRILL, M** NINDS, NIH Vascular permeability factor produced by human glioma cells
Z01NS-02709-06 (90) **EHRENSTEIN, G** NINDS, NIH Secretion of neurotransmitters and hormones
Z01NS-02710-07 (RBMB) **VENTER, J C** NINDS, NIH Molecular biology of neurotransmitter receptors
Z01NS-02711-06 (MNB) **HALLETT, M** NINDS, NIH Utility and physiology of botulinum toxin for involuntary movement disorders
Z01NS-02712-07 (MNB) **HALLETT, M** NINDS, NIH Noninvasive

PROJECT NO., ORGANIZATIONAL UNIT., INVESTIGATOR, ADDRESS, TITLE

stimulation of human central nervous system
Z01NS-02715-06 (NEB) **NELSON, K B** NINDS, NIH Epilepsy neuroepidemiology
Z01NS-02717-06 (CNB) **KOPIN, I J** NINDS, NIH Biochemical evaluation of aminergic function during responses to stress & disease
Z01NS-02718-06 (SB) **WAGNER, H G** NINDS, NIH Cerebral electrical activity associated with ischemia and brain injury
Z01NS-02720-05 (SB) **NOWAK, T S** NINDS, NIH Stress protein induction in brain after ischemia
Z01NS-02723-05 (LNC) **GAINER, H** NINDS, NIH Peptides in the adult and developing vertebrate nervous systems
Z01NS-02724-05 (LNC) **GAINER, H** NINDS, NIH Molecular mechanisms in neuronal structure and function
Z01NS-02725-06 (LNC) **PANT, H C** NINDS, NIH Calcium metabolism and protein phosphorylation in neuronal systems
Z01NS-02729-05 (SN) **PLUNKETT, R J** NINDS, NIH Adrenal medullary autografts in parkinsonian patients
Z01NS-02730-05 (DMN) **KARLSSON, S** NINDS, NIH Retroviral mediated transfer of human globin genes
Z01NS-02731-05 (DMN) **KARLSSON, S** NINDS, NIH Gene therapy of inherited enzyme deficiencies
Z01NS-02732-05 (MNB) **ROGAWSKI, M** NINDS, NIH Pharmacological studies of ion channels in cultured cells
Z01NS-02733-06 (MNB) **ROGAWSKI, M** NINDS, NIH Excitability properties of enzymatically dissociated CNS neurons
Z01NS-02739-05 (SN) **OLDFIELD, E H** NINDS, NIH Clinical and lab investigation of CNS vascular disorders
Z01NS-02742-05 (LVMP) **ARNHEITER, H** NINDS, NIH Mechanisms of viral pathogenesis
Z01NS-02746-06 (NEB) **NELSON, K B** NINDS, NIH Phenobarbital clinical trials in children with febrile seizures
Z01NS-02747-05 (NEB) **NELSON, K B** NINDS, NIH Dental markers of maldevelopment
Z01NS-02748-06 (NEB) **NELSON, K B** NINDS, NIH Dermatoglyphic markers of maldevelopment
Z01NS-02751-06 (SB) **SPATZ, M** NINDS, NIH Cultures of mouse capillary endothelium--Establishment,growth & characterization
Z01NS-02752-06 (CNB) **SCHWARTZ, J P** NINDS, NIH Regulation of synthesis and expression of neurotrophic agents and neuropeptides
Z01NS-02753-03 (LNC) **BATTEY, J** NINDS, NIH Regulation of the prepro GRP gene
Z01NS-02754-05 (RBMB) **VENTOR, J C** NINDS, NIH Megabase DNA sequencing
Z01NS-02757-04 (LNC) **KUSANO, K** NINDS, NIH Analyses of peptide receptors
Z01NS-02760-04 (SN..) **PORRINO, L** NINDS, NIH Metabolic mapping of the brain during rewarding brain stimulation
Z01NS-02761-03 (89N) **PORRINO, L** NINDS, NIH Metabolic mapping of a primate model of Parkinsonism
Z01NS-02762-04 (90.) **PORRINO, L** NINDS, NIH Autoadinographic determination of dopamine receptor distribution in primates
Z01NS-02767-05 (LNP) **SMITH, T G** NINDS, NIH Image processing and analysis of cellular structures
Z01NS-02769-04 (DMN) **O'NEILL, R R** NINDS, NIH Exploration of strategies for the treatment of AIDS
Z01NS-02770-04 (DMN) **BRADY, R O** NINDS, NIH Strategies for the treatment of autoimmune neuropathies
Z01NS-02771-04 (DMN) **KULKARNI, A** NINDS, NIH Modification of growth factor genes by gene targeting
Z01NS-02772-04 (MNB) **ROGAWSKI, M A** NINDS, NIH Development of uncompetitive NMDA antagonists as anticonvulsants
Z01NS-02774-03 (LNC) **BATTEY, J** NINDS, NIH Molecular analysis of mammalian bombesin receptor
Z01NS-02776-03 (SB) **MCCARRON, R M** NINDS, NIH Mechanism of production of experimental allergic encephalomyelitis
Z01NS-02777-03 (SB) **BACIC, F** NINDS, NIH Human cerebromicrovascular endothelium-- Studies in vitro
Z01NS-02778-04 (SN) **SARIS, S** NINDS, NIH Adoptive immunotherapy of brain tumors
Z01NS-02780-04 (SB) **MCCARRON, R M** NINDS, NIH Cerebral vascular endothelial cell-specific monoclonal antibodies
Z01NS-02781-04 (SN) **BANKIEWICZ, K** NINDS, NIH Tissue implantation in Parkinsonian models
Z01NS-02782-03 (DMN) **O'NEILL, R R** NINDS, NIH Preparation of transgenic murine analogs of human metabolic storage disorders
Z01NS-02784-03 (LMCN) **REBOIS, R V** NINDS, NIH Structure and function relationships in cellular signal transduction mechanisms
R01NS-02785-32 (NLS) **SMITH, MARION E** VETERANS ADM SCHOOL OF MED CTR DEPARTMENT OF NEUROLOGY 127A STANFORD, CA 94304 Biosynthesis of lipids in experimental demyelination
Z01NS-02785-03 (DMN) **KARLSSON, S** NINDS, NIH Generation of mice with sickle cell anemia
Z01NS-02786-03 (LMCN) **QUARLES, R H** NINDS, NIH Antibodies to glycoconjugates in neurological diseases
Z01NS-02787-03 (LNLC) **O'DONOVAN, M J** NINDS,NIH Network function in the developing spinal cord of the chick embryo
Z01NS-02788-03 (LNLC) **SMITH, C L** NINDS, NIH Development of primary sensory neurons
Z01NS-02789-03 (LVMP) **DUBOIS-DALCQ, M** NINDS, NIH Neurotropism of human retroviruses
Z01NS-02790-03 (LVMP) **ARNHEITER, H** NINDS, NIH Analysis of insertional mutations in transgenic mice
Z01NS-02791-03 (LVMP) **SCHUBERT, M** NINDS, NIH Replication and pathogenesis of enveloped viruses
Z01NS-02792-03 (MNB) **GRAFMAN, J** NINDS, NIH Neuropsychological investigations of human cognition and mood state
Z01NS-02793-03 (MNB) **GRAFMAN, J** NINDS, NIH Cognitive neuroscience
Z01NS-02794-03 (MNB) **JOHNSON, R** NINDS, NIH Event-related potential studies of normal and abnormal cognitive processing
Z01NS-02795-03 (SB) **BACIC, F** NINDS, NIH Human cerebromicrovascular endothelial receptors
Z01NS-02797-03 (SB) **SPATZ, M** NINDS, NIH Cultures of human

cerebromicrovascular endothelium – Endothelin secretion
Z01NS-02799-03 (LB) IWASA, K NINDS, NIH Electro-mechanical transduction mechanism in outer hair cells
Z01NS-02800-03 (LMB) WESS, J NINDS, NIH Studies on neurotransmitter receptor genes
Z01NS-02801-03 (90) MCCARRON, R M NINDS, NIH Interactions between cerebrovascular endothelial cells and immune lymphocytes
Z01NS-02802-03 (SB) MCCARRON, R M NINDS, NIH Immune mechanisms–Regulation of EC surface antigen expression
Z01NS-02803-02 (LENP) MITCHELL, W J NINDS, NIH Mechanism of latency and pathogenesis of herpes simplex virus in nervous system
Z01NS-02804-02 (LENP) HENKEN, D B NINDS, NIH Nervous system regeneration in a herpesvirus model
Z01NS-02805-02 (LMCN) QUARLES, R H NINDS, NIH Molecular and immunological aspects of myelin abnormalities in neuro-AIDS
Z01NS-02806-02 (RBMB) VENTER, J C NINDS, NIH Human brain cDNA project
Z01NS-02807-02 (LENP) RESSETAR, H G NINDS, NIH JC human polyomavirus infection and tumor induction in neonatal brain
P01NS-02808-30 (NSPB) ENGEL, JEROME JR UNIV OF CALIFORNIA, LOS ANGELE 405 HILGARD AVE. LOS ANGELES, CALIF 90024 A clinical research program for the partial epilepsies
P01NS-02808-30 0002 (NSPB) ISOKAWA-AKESSON, MASAKO A clinical research program for the partial epilepsies In vitro pathophysiology
P01NS-02808-30 0003 (NSPB) WILSON, CHARLES A clinical research program for the partial epilepsies In vivo pathophysiology
P01NS-02808-30 0005 (NSPB) ENGEL, JEROME A clinical research program for the partial epilepsies Functional imaging
P01NS-02808-30 0044 (NSPB) BABB, THOMAS L A clinical research program for the partial epilepsies Microanatomy of human epileptic hippocampal formation
P01NS-02808-30 0045 (NSPB) RAUSCH, H REBECCA A clinical research program for the partial epilepsies Memory studies
P01NS-02808-30 0046 (NSPB) HARPER, RONALD M A clinical research program for the partial epilepsies Cardiorespiratory function
P01NS-02808-30 9001 (NSPB) ENGEL, JEROME A clinical research program for the partial epilepsies Core–Clinical
P01NS-02808-30 9002 (NSPB) FRYSINGER, ROBERT A clinical research program for the partial epilepsies Core–Technical
Z01NS-02808-02 (LENP) KOMOLY, S NINDS, NIH Molecular studies of GF during myelin breakdown and regeneration in the CNS
Z01NS-02810-02 (BFSB) FOULKES, M A NINDS, NIH Statistical coordinating center for collaborative clinical studies
Z01NS-02811-02 (SN) OLDFIELD, E H NINDS, NIH Phase II clinical trial of suramin and hydrocortisone for malignant glioma
Z01NS-02812-02 (SN) BOBO, R H NINDS, NIH Pentobarbital effects on damage of the primate brain by whole brain irradiation
Z01NS-02813-02 (SN) BOBO, R H NINDS, NIH Pharmacokinetics of direct brain infusion
Z01NS-02814-02 (SN) ALI, I U NINDS, NIH Genetic abnormalities in primary glial tumors
Z01NS-02815-02 (SN) ALI, I U NINDS, NIH Molecular genetics of pituitary corticotroph adenomas
Z01NS-02816-02 (DMN) MILLER, S NINDS, NIH Synthesis of inhibitors of N-myristoyltransferase
Z01NS-02817-02 (NI) JACOBSON, S NINDS, NIH Involvement of human retrovirus associated with chronic neurologic disease
Z01NS-02818-02 (LVMP) SCHUBERT, M NINDS, NIH Pseudotypic defective interfering HIV particles as an antiviral therapy for AIDS
Z01NS-02819-02 (NEB) NELSON, K B NINDS, NIH California cerebral palsy registry
Z01NS-02820-02 (LNC) ODENWALD, W F NINDS, NIH Cloning and functional analysis of genes active in neurogenesis
Z01NS-02821-02 (SB) MIES, G NINDS, NIH Dynamics of postischemic calcium accumulation and protein synthesis in brain
Z01NS-02822-02 (SB) SAITO, N NINDS, NIH Glutamate microdialysis during repeated ischemia and cold lesions
Z01NS-02823-02 (SN) YOULE, R J NINDS, NIH Antibody-Toxin conjugates for the treatment of human brain tumors
Z01NS-02824-01 (LNC) WRAY, S NINDS, NIH Ontogeny of the lutinizing hormone releasing hormone system
Z01NS-02825-01 (LMB) MILL, JOHN NINDS, NIH Transcriptional regulation of glutamine synthetase and glutaminase
Z01NS-02826-01 (ET) MOURADIAN, M M NINDS, NIH Molecular regulation of transmitter receptor genes
Z01NS-02827-01 (LENP) ISHAQ, M NINDS, NIH Identification and etiologic role of human polyomavirus in neurologic diseases
Z01NS-02828-01 (LMB) CHIN, HEMIN R NINDS, NIH Molecular basis for functional diversities of voltage-sensitive calcium channels
Z01NS-02829-01 (LMB) NAKATANI, Y NINDS, NIH Molecular analysis of trans-activation mechanisms in man, fly, and yeast
Z01NS-02830-01 (LVMP) VERDIN, E NINDS, NIH Regulation of HIV transcription in vitro and vivo
Z01NS-02831-01 (NI) COWANS, E P NINDS, NIH Regulation of class II major histocompatibility complex genes in the CNS
Z01NS-02832-01 (SB) NITECKA, L NINDS, NIH Immunochemical observations on neurotransmitter changes in cerebral ischemia
Z01NS-02833-01 (SB) KAWAI, K NINDS, NIH Early neuronal changes in global cerebral ischemia
Z01NS-02834-01 (LN) FLUCHER, B E NINDS,NIH Development of excitation-contraction coupling in muscle
Z01NS-02835-02 (LN) RALSTON, E NINDS,NIH Regulation of subcellular organization in excitable cells
Z01NS-02836-02 (LN) ANDREWS, B S NINDS,NIH Structural and elemental analysis of marcomolecular assemblies
Z01NS-02837-01 (RBMB) MCCOMBIE, W R NINDS, NIH Structure and function of neurological genes in Caenorhabditis elegans
Z01NS-02838-01 (NEB) ROMAN, G C NINDS,NIH Retroviral diseases of the nervous system
Z01NS-02839-01 (CNB) GOLDSTEIN, D S NINDS, NIH Sympathoadrenal and catecholaminergic function in health and disease
Z01NS-02840-01 (SN) ALI, I U NINDS, NIH Analysis of Alpha subunits of G proteins

PROJECT NO., ORGANIZATIONAL UNIT., INVESTIGATOR, ADDRESS, TITLE

Z01NS-02841-01 (LN) TERASAKI, M NINDS,NIH Structure and function of the endoplasmic reticulum
Z01NS-02842-01 (LN) BEUSHAUSEN, S A NINDS,NIH Catalytic subunit of molluscan cyclic AMP-dependent protein kinases
R01NS-02957-31 (NEUA) PRESTON, JAMES B S U N Y AT SYRACUSE 750 E ADAMS STREET SYRACUSE, N Y 13210 Suprasegmental influences on spinal motoneurons
P01NS-03346-31 (NSPA) PULSINELLI, WILLIAM CORNELL UNIV MEDICAL COLLEGE 1300 YORK AVENUE NEW YORK, NY 10021 Research center in cerebrovascular disease
P01NS-03346-31 0030 (NSPA) GIBSON, GARY E Research center in cerebrovascular disease Calcium homeostasis in cerebral hypoxia-ischemia
P01NS-03346-31 0041 (NSPA) REIS, DONALD J Research center in cerebrovascular disease Intrinsic neural mechanisms in cerebral infarction
P01NS-03346-31 0042 (NSPA) PULSINELLI, WILLIAM Research center in cerebrovascular disease Cognitive dysfunction in coronary artery bypass surgery
P01NS-03346-31 0043 (NSPA) PLUM, FRED Research center in cerebrovascular disease Anisoylated plasminogen streptokinase activator complex in ischemia
P01NS-03346-31 0044 (NSPA) PULSINELLI, WILLIAM A Research center in cerebrovascular disease Neurotransmitters and ischemic injury to neurons
P01NS-03346-31 0045 (NSPA) PETITO, CAROL K Research center in cerebrovascular disease Cellular responses to cerebral ischemia
P01NS-03346-31 9001 (NSPA) LEVY, DAVID Research center in cerebrovascular disease Core–Clinical
P01NS-03346-31 9002 (NSPA) PETITO, CAROL K Research center in cerebrovascular disease Core–Neuropathology and animal models
R01NS-03437-31 (PHY) MOORE, JOHN W DUKE UNIVERSITY MEDICAL CENTER BOX 3709-H DURHAM, NC 27710 Physiology of excitable membranes
R01NS-03469-30 (BPO) EPSTEIN, ALAN N UNIVERSITY OF PENNSYLVANIA RM 326 LEIDY LABS PHILADELPHIA, PA 19104-6018 Neurological bases of feeding and drinking
R01NS-04270-29 (NEUB) SHOOTER, ERIC M STANFORD UNIV SCH OF MEDICINE STANFORD, CA 94305-5401 Nerve growth factor in neuronal development
R01NS-04761-28 (RAD) GILMORE, SHIRLEY A UNIVERSITY OF ARKANSAS 4301 WEST MARKHAM LITTLE ROCK, ARK 72205 Radiation-induced changes in the neonatal nervous system
R01NS-04834-29 (NEUC) LEDEEN, ROBERT W UNIV OF MEDICINE & DENTISTRY N 185 ORANGE AVENUE NEWARK, N J 07103 Study of nervous system gangliosides and related lipids
R01NS-05096-28 (BIO) SHIH, VIVIAN E MASSACHUSETTS GEN HOSP/NEURO BLDG, 149, 13TH STREET BOSTON, MA 02129-2000 New amino acid disorders in cerebral disease
R01NS-05423-25 (NEUB) LARIMER, JAMES L UNIVERSITY OF TEXAS DEPARTMENT OF ZOOLOGY AUSTIN, TEX 78712 Neural basis of behavior
R01NS-05430-25 (PHRA) ROBINSON, JOSEPH D SUNY HLTH SCI CNTR/SYRACUSE 766 IRVING AVE SYRACUSE, N Y 13210 Neural transport mechanisms
R01NS-05572-27 (PTHA) GONATAS, NICHOLAS K UNIVERSITY OF PENNSYLVANIA 36TH ST & HAMILTON WALK PHILADELPHIA, PA 19104-6079 Cellular aspects of neurological disorders
R01NS-05685-27 (NEUB) KRUGER, LAWRENCE UNIVERSITY OF CALIFORNIA DEPT. OF ANATOMY & CELL BIO LOS ANGELES, CA 90024-1763 Cutaneous morphological correlates of pain
P01NS-05820-26 (NSPA) GINSBERG, MYRON D UNIV MIAMI SCHOOL OF MEDICINE PO BOX 016960 MIAMI, FL 33101 Research center for cerebral vascular disease
P01NS-05820-26 0019 (NSPA) ROSENTHAL, MYRON Research center for cerebral vascular disease Electrophysiology and ion transport in acute focal ischemia
P01NS-05820-26 0020 (NSPA) DIETRICH, W DALTON Research center for cerebral vascular disease Recovery of function following stroke
P01NS-05820-26 0023 (NSPA) SICK, THOMAS J Research center for cerebral vascular disease Early indices of cell damage in the hippocampal slice
P01NS-05820-26 0024 (NSPA) GINSBERG, MYRON D Research center for cerebral vascular disease Treatable mechanisms of brain injury in focal ischemia
P01NS-05820-26 0025 (NSPA) BUSTO, RAUL Research center for cerebral vascular disease Protective effect of cerebral hypothermia in global ischemia
P01NS-05820-26 0026 (NSPA) GLOBUS, MORDECAI Y-T Research center for cerebral vascular disease Glutamatergic mediation of ischemic vulnerability
P01NS-05820-26 9001 (NSPA) GINSBERG, MYRON D Research center for cerebral vascular disease Core–Metabolite analysis and sample preparation
P01NS-05820-26 9002 (NSPA) GINSBERG, MYRON D Research center for cerebral vascular disease Core–Animal physiology, radioisotopic strategies, and morphologic methods
P01NS-05820-26 9003 (NSPA) SMITH, DAVID W Research center for cerebral vascular disease Core–Computing and image-processing
P01NS-05820-26 9004 (NSPA) SCHNEIDERMAN, NEIL Research center for cerebral vascular disease Core–Behavioral correlates of cerebral ischemia
R01NS-06232-27 (NEUB) GRINNELL, ALAN D JERRY LEWIS CENTER UCLA SCHOOL OF MEDICINE LOS ANGELES, CALIF 90024 Formation, function, and plasticity of synapses
P50NS-06233-25 (NSPA) DAVIS, JAMES N DUKE UNIVERSITY MEDICAL CENTER BOX 2900 DURHAM, NC 27710 Duke-V.A. center for cerebrovascular research
P50NS-06233-25 0037 (NSPA) MARCHASE, RICHARD B Duke-V.A. center for cerebrovascular research Intercellular adhesive specificities in central nervous system
P50NS-06233-25 0040 (NSPA) LIN, CHIA-SHENG Duke-V.A. center for cerebrovascular research Functional plasticity in the somatosensory cortex
P50NS-06233-25 0041 (NSPA) HEYMAN, ALBERT Duke-V.A. center for

cerebrovascular research Study of precursors of completed stroke
P50NS-06233-25 0042 (NSPA) DAVIS, JAMES N Duke-V.A. center for cerebrovascular research Catecholamine neuron model for the study of stroke
P50NS-06233-25 0043 (NSPA) WILSON, WILKIE A Duke-V.A. center for cerebrovascular research Cholinergic and adrenergic modulation of mossy fiber synapses
P50NS-06233-25 0044 (NSPA) NADLER, J VICTOR Duke-V.A. center for cerebrovascular research Neuronal responses to destruction of postsynaptic targets
P50NS-06233-25 0045 (NSPA) MC NAMARA, JAMES O Duke-V.A. center for cerebrovascular research Neurobiologic studies of limbic seizures following brain injury
R01NS-06277-26 (NEUB) ENGEL, ANDREW G MAYO FOUNDATION 200 FIRST STREET SOUTHWEST ROCHESTER, MN 55905 Electron microscopy of myopathies
R01NS-06477-26 (NEUA) PRINCE, DAVID A STANFORD UNIVERSITY DEPARTMENT OF NEUROLOGY STANFORD, CA 94305 Cellular mechanisms in epileptogenesis
P50NS-06663-25 (NSPA) WHISNANT, JACK P MAYO FOUNDATION 200 FIRST STREET, SW ROCHESTER, MN 55905 Mayo cerebrovascular clinical research center
P50NS-06663-25 0055 (NSPA) WHISNANT, JACK P Mayo cerebrovascular clinical research center Stroke prevalence & risk w/ hypertension, diabetes, TIA & cardiovascular factors
P50NS-06663-25 0056 (NSPA) WHISNANT, JACK P Mayo cerebrovascular clinical research center Prevalence & survival for first stroke & TIA in Rochester, Minn. 1985-89
P50NS-06663-25 0057 (NSPA) WHISNANT, JACK P Mayo cerebrovascular clinical research center Mitral valve prolapse and its relationship to cerebral infaction and TIA
P50NS-06663-25 0058 (NSPA) WHISNANT, JACK P Mayo cerebrovascular clinical research center Population-based study of valvular heart disease and stroke
P50NS-06663-25 9001 (NSPA) WHISNANT, JACK P Mayo cerebrovascular clinical research center Core-Statistics
R01NS-06701-24 (NLS) BJORKLUND, ANDERS DEPT OF MEDICAL CELL RESEARCH BISKOPSGATAN 5 S-223 62 LUND, SWEDEN Transmitter mechanisms in intracerebral neural implants
P01NS-06833-25 (SRC) RAICHLE, MARCUS E WASHINGTON UNIVERSITY 510 S KINGSHIGHWAY ST LOUIS, MO 63110 Brain and its vasculature
P01NS-06833-25 0026 (SRC) CRYER, PHILIP E Brain and its vasculature Blood brain barrier and vascular reactivity
P01NS-06833-25 0027 (SRC) SNYDER, ABRAHAM Brain and its vasculature Localization constrained dipole moment recovery
P01NS-06833-25 0028 (SRC) GRUBB, ROBERT L Brain and its vasculature Role of cerebral hemodynamics in the pathogenesis of ischemic stroke
P01NS-06833-25 0029 (SRC) POWERS, WILLIAM Brain and its vasculature Role of subcortical motor systems in neurological recovery following stroke
P01NS-06833-25 0030 (SRC) PETERSON, STEVEN E Brain and its vasculature PET activation studies of words and word strings
P01NS-06833-25 9001 (SRC) TEL-POGOSSIAN, MICHEL M Brain and its vasculature Computer and instrumentation core
P01NS-06833-25 9002 (SRC) RAICHLE, MARCUS E Brain and its vasculature Clinical core
P01NS-06833-25 9003 (SRC) WELCH, MICHAEL J Brain and its vasculature Chemistry core
P01NS-06833-25 9004 (SRC) O'VIDEEN, TOM Brain and its vasculature Core--computers and data analysis
R01NS-06985-25 (IMS) SWANBORG, ROBERT H WAYNE STATE UNIV SCH OF MED 540 EAST CANFIELD DETROIT, MI 48201 Encephalitogenic nature of altered brain preparation
R01NS-07016-25 (NEUA) PETERS, ALAN BOSTON UNIVERSITY 80 EAST CONCORD STREET BOSTON, MASS 02118 Structure and organization of the cerebral cortex
R01NS-07065-25 (NLS) KARLIN, ARTHUR COLUMBIA UNIVERSITY 630 WEST 168TH STREET NEW YORK, N Y 10032 Structures of acetylcholine receptors
R01NS-07080-25 (NEUB) MC EWEN, BRUCE S ROCKEFELLER UNIVERSITY 1230 YORK AVENUE NEW YORK, N Y 10021 Gene expression in nervous tissue
P01NS-07226-19A2 (SRC) JOHNS, RICHARD J DEPT OF BIOMED. ENGINEERING 720 RUTLAND AVENUE BALTIMORE, MD 21205 A neurosensory interdisciplinary research program
P01NS-07226-19A2 0001 (SRC) JOHNSON, KENNETH O A neurosensory interdisciplinary research program Spike sorter
P01NS-07226-19A2 0002 (SRC) GEORGOPOULOS, APOSTOLOS P A neurosensory interdisciplinary research program Test apparatus for neurophysiological research
P01NS-07226-19A2 0003 (SRC) COHEN, RICHARD H A neurosensory interdisciplinary research program Pain stimulator
P01NS-07226-19A2 0004 (SRC) DUNCAN, DONALD D A neurosensory interdisciplinary research program Middle ear mechanics
R01NS-07261-25 (NLS) VIERCK, CHARLES J, JR UNIVERSITY OF FLORIDA COLLEGE OF MEDICINE GAINESVILLE, FL 32610 Spinal somesthetic pathways
P01NS-07464-24 (SRC) ORKAND, RICHARD K INST OF NEUROBIOLOGY 201 BLVD DEL VALLE SAN JUAN, P R 00901 Laboratory of neurobiology--Comparative cellular studies
P01NS-07464-24 0051 (SRC) ORKLAND, RICHARD K. Laboratory of neurobiology--Comparative cellular studies Long-term interactions of neurons and glia
P01NS-07464-24 9001 (SRC) MC KENZIE, FAUSTINO Laboratory of neurobiology--Comparative cellular studies Zoology core
P01NS-07464-24 9003 (SRC) ZUAZAGA, CONCHITA Laboratory of neurobiology--Comparative cellular studies External communication core
P01NS-07464-24 9004 (SRC) ORKAND, PAULA Laboratory of neurobiology--Comparative cellular studies Histology core
P01NS-07464-24 0031 (SRC) ZUAZAGA, CONCHITA Laboratory of neurobiology--Comparative cellular studies Modulation of crustacean muscle
P01NS-07464-24 0042 (SRC) SPECHT, SUSAN C Laboratory of neurobiology--Comparative cellular studies Studies of neuronal Na,K-ATPase regulation
P01NS-07464-24 0044 (SRC) LUGO-GARCIA , NIDZA Laboratory of neurobiology--Comparative cellular studies Anatomical basis of color vision in ground squirrels
P01NS-07464-24 0046 (SRC) DEL CASTILLO, JOSE Laboratory of neurobiology--Comparative cellular studies Mechanical and pharmacological properties of the spine ligaments in sea urchins
P01NS-07464-24 0050 (SRC) BLAGBURN, JONATHAN Laboratory of neurobiology--Comparative cellular studies Development of synapses
R01NS-07495-23 (NEUA) ROSENBLUTH, JACK NEW YORK UNIVERSITY MED CENTER 550 FIRST AVENUE NEW YORK, N Y 10016 Comparative cytology of nerve and muscle tissues
P01NS-07512-23 (NSPB) BENNETT, MICHAEL V ALBERT EINSTEIN COLL OF MED 1300 MORRIS PARK AVENUE BRONX, N Y 10461 Neuronal development, interaction, and organization
P01NS-07512-23 0042 (NSPB) SPRAY, DAVID C Neuronal development, interaction, and organization Properties of gap junctions in various tissues
P01NS-07512-23 0043 (NSPB) KESSLER, JOHN A Neuronal development, interaction, and organization Gap junctions in the nervous system
P01NS-07512-23 0047 (NSPB) BENNETT, MICHAEL Neuronal development, interaction, and organization Exogenous expression of gap junction proteins
P01NS-07512-23 0048 (NSPB) SAEZ, JUAN Neuronal development, interaction, and organization Pinealocyte gap junctions
P01NS-07512-23 0049 (NSPB) BARGIELLO, THADDEUS Neuronal development, interaction, and organization Molecular genetics approach to gap junctions
P01NS-07512-23 9001 (NSPB) BENNETT, MICHAEL V Neuronal development, interaction, and organization Core--Cytology
P01NS-07512-23 9002 (NSPB) BENNETT, MICHAEL V Neuronal development, interaction, and organization Core--Neurophysiology
R01NS-07628-24 (NLS) LIEBESKIND, JOHN C UNIVERSITY OF CALIFORNIA 405 HILGARD AVENUE LOS ANGELES, CALIF 90024 Behavioral and electrophysiological studies of pain
R01NS-07685-22 (HAR) POMPEIANO, OTTAVIO DIPART DI FISIO E BIOCHIMICA VIA S ZENO 31 56127 PISA, ITALY Sensory mechanisms and motor control
R01NS-07726-24S1 (NEUB) MASTERTON, R BRUCE FLORIDA STATE UNIVERSITY TALLAHASSEE, FL 32306-1051 Study of sensory cortex
R01NS-07778-24 (NEUB) EDWARDS, JOHN S DEPARTMENT OF ZOOLOGY UNIVERSITY OF WASHINGTON SEATTLE, WASH 98195 Neural development
R01NS-07838-22 (NEUB) SIESJO, BO K LUND UNIVERSITY HOSPITAL LUND, SWEDEN S-221 85 Mechanisms of ischemic cell damage in the brain
R01NS-07907-24 (NEUB) HUNT, CARLTON C WASHINGTON UNIV SCH OF MED DEPARTMENT OF NEUROLOGY ST LOUIS, MO 63110 Muscle receptors
P01NS-07938-22 (SRC) FIDONE, SALVATORE J UNIVERSITY OF UTAH SCHOOL OF M 410 CHIPETA WAY, RESEARCH PARK SALT LAKE CITY, UT 84108 Chemical and ionic mechanisms in sensory transduction
P01NS-07938-22 0019 (SRC) EYZAGUIRRE, CARLOS E Chemical and ionic mechanisms in sensory transduction Communication between carotid body glomus cells--Chemical transmission
P01NS-07938-22 0026 (SRC) BROWN, H MACK Chemical and ionic mechanisms in sensory transduction Phototransduction in invertebrate photoreceptors
P01NS-07938-22 0028 (SRC) LASATER, ERIC Chemical and ionic mechanisms in sensory transduction Neurotransmitter modulation of second messengers in retinal ganglion
P01NS-07938-22 0030 (SRC) FIDONE, SALVATORE J Chemical and ionic mechanisms in sensory transduction Chemical transduction of chemoreceptor stimuli
P01NS-07938-22 0031 (SRC) STENSAAS, LARRY Chemical and ionic mechanisms in sensory transduction Chemical messengers in the carotid body
P01NS-07938-22 0032 (SRC) ENGLISH, KATHLEEN Chemical and ionic mechanisms in sensory transduction Role of putative transmitters in the Merkle cell/neural complex
P01NS-07938-22 9001 (SRC) EYZAGUIRRE, CARLOS E Chemical and ionic mechanisms in sensory transduction Shop core
P01NS-07938-22 9002 (SRC) STENSAAS, LARRY J Chemical and ionic mechanisms in sensory transduction Neuromorphology core
R01NS-07941-21 (BPO) SIEGEL, ALLAN DEPARTMENT OF NEUROSCIENCES 185 S ORANGE AVENUE NEWARK, NJ 07103-2714 Role of the limbic-midbrain system in hypothalamic aggression
P01NS-08075-21 (NSPB) PLEASURE, DAVID E HOSP OF UNIV OF PENNSYLVANIA 3400 SPRUCE STREET PHILADELPHIA, PA 19104 Studies of human neuromuscular diseases
P01NS-08075-21 0013 (NSPB) ROSTAMI, ABDOLMOHAMMAD Studies of human neuromuscular diseases Mechanisms of immunoregulation in experimental allergic neuritis
P01NS-08075-21 0014 (NSPB) FISCHBECK, KENNETH H Studies of human neuromuscular diseases Genes for Charcot-Marie-Tooth disease and X-linked spinal muscular atrophy
P01NS-08075-21 0016 (NSPB) COHEN, JEFFREY A Studies of human neuromuscular diseases Expression and function of the neu gene in Schwann cells
P01NS-08075-21 0004 (NSPB) PLEASURE, DAVID E Studies of human neuromuscular diseases Biology of Schwann cells
P01NS-08075-21 0009 (NSPB) BARCHI, ROBERT L Studies of human neuromuscular diseases Voltage-sensitive skeletal muscle sodium channels
P01NS-08075-21 0017 (NSPB) KAMHOLZ, JOHN Studies of human neuromuscular diseases Myelin specific cDNAs from the peripheral nervous system
R01NS-08108-24 (BPO) KRASNE, FRANKLIN B UNIV OF CALIFORNIA, L. A. 405 HILGARD AVENUE LOS ANGELES, CA 90024-1563 Escape behavior integration and plasticity
R01NS-08174-23 (NEUB) HILLE, BERTIL UNIVERSITY OF WASHINGTON SEATTLE, WA 98195 Molecular properties of ionic permeability in nerve
R01NS-08304-23A1 (PHY) RITCHIE, J MURDOCH YALE UNIVERSITY 155 WHITNEY AVENUE NEW HAVEN, CT 06510 Study of C fibers
R01NS-08384-23 (GMB) GORDON, ALBERT M UNIVERSITY OF WASHINGTON

SEATTLE, WA 98195 Control of contraction in striated muscle
R01NS-08437-23 (NEUB) COHEN, LAWRENCE B YALE UNIVERSITY DEPT OF PHYSIOLOGY NEW HAVEN, CONN 06510 Optical studies of neuron activity and organization
R01NS-08682-22 (MGN) O'BRIEN, JOHN S UNIVERSITY OF CALIFORNIA 9500 GILLMAN DRIVE LA JOLLA, CA 92093-0638 Molecular basis of cerebral degeneration
R01NS-08740-25 (NLS) ADAMS, RALPH N UNIVERSITY OF KANSAS LAWRENCE, KS 66045 Electrochemistry-EPR of biological electron transfer
R55NS-08798-19 (NEUA) KING, JAMES S OHIO STATE UNIVERSITY 333 W 10TH AVE COLUMBUS, OH 43210 Peptides in adult and developing cerebellar circuits
P01NS-08803-20A1 (NSPA) GENNARELLI, THOMAS A HOSP OF UNIV OF PENNSYLVANIA 3400 SPRUCE STREET PHILADELPHIA, PA 19104 Head injury clinical research center
P01NS-08803-20A1 0008 (NSPA) JOYCE, JEFFREY M Head injury clinical research center Receptor changes in non-survivors of human head injury
P01NS-08803-20A1 0009 (NSPA) GENNARELLI, THOMAS A Head injury clinical research center Focal axonal injury in the guinea pig optic nerve
P01NS-08803-20A1 0010 (NSPA) GENNARELLI, THOMAS A Head injury clinical research center Brain axonal injury in the rat
P01NS-08803-20A1 0011 (NSPA) GENNARELLI, THOMAS A Head injury clinical research center Development of a model of diffuse axonal injury
P01NS-08803-20A1 9001 (NSPA) GENNARELLI, THOMAS A Head injury clinical research center Core--Methodology core
R01NS-08817-21 (PTHA) DAS, GOPAL D DEPT OF BIOLOGICAL SCIENCES PURDUE UNIVERSITY WEST LAFAYETTE, IND 47907 Transplantation of neural tissues and neurogenesis
R01NS-08862-22 (NLS) LOWRY, OLIVER H WASHINGTON UNIV MEDICAL SCH 660 SOUTH EUCLID AVENUE ST LOUIS, MO 63110 Metabolism of cells in muscle and nervous system
R01NS-08952-23 (PTHA) RAINE, CEDRIC S ALBERT EINSTEIN COLLEGE OF MED 1300 MORRIS PARK AVENUE BRONX, NY 10461 EM cytopathology of organized CNS and PNS cultures
R01NS-09015-21 (NEUB) GRAFSTEIN, BERNICE DEPARTMENT OF PSYCIOLOGY 1300 YORK AVENUE NEW YORK, NY 10021 Growth of axons in development and regeneration
R01NS-09074-22 (NEUB) BENTLEY, DAVID R UNIVERSITY OF CALIFORNIA 291 LIFE SCIENCE ADDITION BERKELEY, CA 94720 Guidance and steering of neuronal growth cones in vivo
R01NS-09137-21 (NLS) DOUGLAS, WILLIAM W YALE SCHOOL OF MEDICINE POST OFFICE BOX 3333 NEW HAVEN, CT 06510 Stimulus-secretion coupling--Chromaffin and other cells
R01NS-09140-21 (BPO) HATTON, GLENN I MICHIGAN STATE UNIVERSITY EAST LANSING, MI 48824 Internal sensing systems and drinking behavior
R01NS-09196-18 (NLS) RUDOMIN, PEDRO N CENTRO/INVESTIGACION DEL ESTUD APARTADO POSTAL 14-740 MEXICO, DF 07000 Discharge patterns of motoneurons
P50NS-09199-21 (NSPB) HOFFER, BARRY J UNIV OF COLORADO HLTH SCI CTR 4200 E NINTH AVENUE DENVER, COLO 80262 Basal ganglia disorders and neurotransmitter function
P50NS-09199-21 9001 (NSPB) STEVENS, JAMES O Basal ganglia disorders and neurotransmitter function Core--Laboratory animals and immunological investigations
P50NS-09199-21 9002 (NSPB) ZERBE, GARY O Basal ganglia disorders and neurotransmitter function Core--Statistics
P50NS-09199-21 9003 (NSPB) BOYSON, SALLY J Basal ganglia disorders and neurotransmitter function Core--Quantitative autoradiography
P50NS-09199-21 0006 (NSPB) WEINER, NORMAN Basal ganglia disorders and neurotransmitter function Biochemical indices of dopaminergic transmission
P50NS-09199-21 0024 (NSPB) HOFFER, BARRY J Basal ganglia disorders and neurotransmitter function Function of CNS neural grafts
P50NS-09199-21 0032 (NSPB) FINGER, THOMAS E Basal ganglia disorders and neurotransmitter function Specificity and development of dopaminergic intracerebral grafts
P50NS-09199-21 0035 (NSPB) GERHARDT, GREG A Basal ganglia disorders and neurotransmitter function Studies of pre- and postsynaptic dopamine physiology in the basal ganglia
P50NS-09199-21 0036 (NSPB) OLSON, LARS Basal ganglia disorders and neurotransmitter function Chromaffin cell transplants and trophic factors
R01NS-09315-22 (NEUB) SALPETER, MIRIAM M CORNELL UNIVERSITY ITHACA, NY 14853 Functional ultrastructure of the nervous system
R01NS-09322-17 (NEUB) SELVERSTON, ALLEN I UNIV. OF CA, SAN DIEGO 9500 GILMAN DRIVE Mechanisms of central pattern generation in ganglia
R01NS-09343-22 (ORTH) BIZZI, EMILIO MASS. INST. OF TECH. 77 MASSACHUSETTS AVE CAMBRIDGE, MA 02139 Study of eye-head-arm coordination
R01NS-09348-21 (NEUB) MARGOLIS, RENEE K SUNY-HEALTH SCIENCES CENTER 450 CLARKSON AVE BROOKLYN, NY 11203 Studies on nervous tissue glycoconjugates
R01NS-09626-21 (MEDB) LI, YU-TEH TULANE UNIV SCH OF MED 1430 TULANE AVE NEW ORLEANS, LA 70112 Glycosidases as related to sphingolipidoses
R01NS-09658-21 (NLS) SCHUBERT, DAVID R SALK INST FOR BIOL STUDIES P O BOX 85800 SAN DIEGO, CA 92186-5800 Physiology of nerve, glial and muscle cell lines
R01NS-09666-18 (NEUA) WRIGHT, ERNEST M UNIV OF CALIFORNIA/LOS ANGELES LOS ANGELES, CALIF 90024-1751 The secretion of cerebrospinal fluid
R01NS-09678-19 (NEUA) WESTRUM, LESNICK E UNIVERSITY OF WASHINGTON SEATTLE, WA 98195 Fine structure of deafferentation
R01NS-09743-22 (NLS) WILLIS, WILLIAM D, JR MARINE BIOMEDICAL INSTITUTE 200 UNIVERSITY BLVD GALVESTON, TEX 77550 Synaptic connections of spinal cord neurons
R01NS-09818-19 (NLS) SEEDS, NICHOLAS W UNIVERSITY OF COLORADO 4200 EAST NINTH AVENUE DENVER, CO 80262 In vitro biochemical differentiation of nerve cells
R01NS-09871-20 (SAT) KITAHATA, LUKE M YALE UNIVERSITY 333 CEDAR STREET NEW HAVEN, CONN 06510 Surgical anesthesia & pain control--Neuropharmacology
R01NS-09878-21 (NLS) KELLY, REGIS B UNIV OF CALIFORNIA SAN FRANCISCO, CA 94143-0534 Biochemistry of synaptic transmission
R01NS-09904-20 (NEUB) MUGNAINI, ENRICO UNIVERSITY OF CONNECTICUT BOX U-154/DEPT BIOBEH SCI STORRS, CONN 06268 Organization and development of nervous tissue
R01NS-09910-20 (NEUB) WILSON, JOHN E MICHIGAN STATE UNIVERSITY EAST LANSING, MI 48824-1319 Hexokinase and energy metabolism in the brain
R01NS-09923-21 (NEUB) BUNGE, RICHARD P UNIVERSITY OF MIAMI 1600 NW 10TH AVENE R48 MIAMI, FL 33136 Cytological studies of developing and mature neurons
R01NS-09999-16 (SSS) CHASE, MICHAEL H UNIV OF CALIF - L A SCHOOL OF MEDICINE LOS ANGELES, CA 90024-1751 State-Dependent control of somatic relex activity
R01NS-10046-17 (BCE) LIPTON, JAMES M UNIV OF TEXAS SW MED CTR 5323 HARRY HINES BLVD DALLAS, TX 75235-9040 Neuropeptide modulation of fever and host defense
R01NS-10161-18 (NEUB) COGGESHALL, RICHARD E UNIVERSITY OF TEXAS 200 UNIVERSITY BOULEVARD GALVESTON, TX 77550-2772 Development and regeneration of nerves
P50NS-10164-19 (NSPA) YOUNG, WISE NEW YORK UNIVERSITY MED CTR 550 FIRST AVENUE NEW YORK, N Y 10016 Clinical research center for acute spinal cord injuries
P50NS-10164-19 0023 (NSPA) CHESLER, MITCH Clinical research center for acute spinal cord injuries Extracellular ionic and pH regulation
P50NS-10164-19 0024 (NSPA) GRUNER, JOHN A Clinical research center for acute spinal cord injuries Mechanisms of motor and sensory recovery in spinal cord injury
P50NS-10164-19 0025 (NSPA) YOUNG, WISE Clinical research center for acute spinal cord injuries Experimental therapy in injured spinal cords
P50NS-10164-19 0026 (NSPA) SAKATANI, KAORU Clinical research center for acute spinal cord injuries Axonal dysfunction
P50NS-10164-19 9001 (NSPA) DECRESCITO, VINCENT Clinical research center for acute spinal cord injuries Core--Scientific
P50NS-10165-20 (SRC) STOKES, BRADFORT T OHIO STATE UNIVERSITY 410 WEST TENTH AVENUE COLUMBUS, OHIO 43210 Spinal cord injury research center
P50NS-10165-20 0017 (SRC) HORROCKS, LLOYD A Spinal cord injury research center Mechanisms of membrane injury
P50NS-10165-20 0023 (SRC) YATES, ALLAN J Spinal cord injury research center Ganglioside metabolism in traumatized nerve
P50NS-10165-20 0027 (SRC) MARTIN, GEORGE F Spinal cord injury research center Ontogeny and remodeling of spinal systems in the opossum
P50NS-10165-20 0028 (SRC) NOYES, DAVID H Spinal cord injury research center Evaluation of method to produce experimental cord injury
P50NS-10165-20 0029 (SRC) TASSAVA, ROY A Spinal cord injury research center Effect of nerve augmentation on frog limb regeneration
P50NS-10165-20 0025 (SRC) BRESNAHAN, JACQUELINE C Spinal cord injury research center Reorganization of sensory mechanisms after spinal lesions
P50NS-10165-20 0026 (SRC) BEATTIE, MICHAEL S Spinal cord injury research center Plasticity and regeneration in amphibian spinal cord
P50NS-10174-20 (NSPA) COLLINS, WILLIAM F, JR YALE UNIVERSITY MED SCH PO BOX 3333, 333 CEDAR ST NEW HAVEN, CT 06510 A center for acute spinal cord injury
P50NS-10174-20 0014 (NSPA) COHEN, MELVIN J A center for acute spinal cord injury Regeneration of identified neurons in lamprey spinal cord
P50NS-10174-20 0018 (NSPA) VAN DEN POL, ANTHONY A center for acute spinal cord injury Immunocytochemical neurophysin axons in normal and hemisected spinal cord
P50NS-10174-20 0019 (NSPA) SHEPHERD, GORDON M A center for acute spinal cord injury A model of regeneration in the central nervous system
P50NS-10174-20 0024 (NSPA) LA MOTTE, CAROLE C A center for acute spinal cord injury Axonal sprouting following spinal lesions
P50NS-10174-20 0026 (NSPA) GREER, CHARLES A. A center for acute spinal cord injury Reorganization of axonal tracts following transection
R01NS-10207-20 (NLS) BETZ, WILLIAM J UNIV OF COLORADO MED SCHOOL 4200 EAST NINTH AVE DENVER, COLO 80262 Nerve muscle synapse formation
R01NS-10259-21 (NEUC) BLACK, IRA B UNIV OF MEDICINE & DENTISTRY-N 675 HOES LANE PISCATAWAY, NJ 08854 Regulation of neuronal growth and development
R01NS-10294-20 (NLS) RAFTERY, MICHAEL A UNIVERSITY OF MINNESOTA 1479 GORTNER AVENUE MINNEAPOLIS, MN 55104 Studies of the nicotinic acetylcholine receptor
R01NS-10320-19 (NLS) VAN DER KLOOT, WILLIAM G SUNY AT STONY BROOK,, HSC STONY BROOK, NY 11794 Transmitter release by nerve terminals
R01NS-10321-20 (NEUB) PERL, EDWARD R UNIV OF N C AT CHAPEL HILL 54 MED RESEARCH BLDG CB#7545 CHAPEL HILL, NC 27599 Spinal and projection mechanisms related to pain
R01NS-10338-18 (NLS) PILAR, GUILLERMO R UNIVERSITY OF CONNECTICUT 75 NORTH EAGLEVILLE ROAD STORRS, CONN 06269 Ganglionic synaptic transmission
R01NS-10414-19S1 (SSS) MERZENICH, MICHAEL M UNIV OF CALIF/COLEMAN MEM LAB 3RD & PARNASSUS AVENUES SAN FRANCISCO, CA 94143-0732 Functional organization of the central auditory system
R01NS-10546-25 (PC) FROMM, HERBERT J IOWA STATE UNIVERSITY 397 GILMAN HALL AMES, IA 50011 Mechanism and regulation of brain and liver phosphatases
R01NS-10580-16 (NEUB) PRICE, DONALD L JOHNS HOPKINS UNIVERSITY 600 NORTH WOLFE STREET BALTIMORE, MD 21205 Diseases of motor neurons
R01NS-10705-19 (NEUB) ASANUMA, HIROSHI ROCKEFELLER UNIVERSITY 1230 YORK AVE NEW YORK, NY 10021-6399 Cerebral cortical control of movement
R01NS-10783-19 (ORTH) GRIGG, PETER UNIV OF MASSACHUSETTS 55 LAKE

PROJECT NO., ORGANIZATIONAL UNIT., INVESTIGATOR, ADDRESS, TITLE

AVENUE NORTH WORCESTER, MA 01655 Mechanical sensitivity of joint afferent neurons
R01NS-10813-18 (NEUC) HAHN, WILLIAM E UNIV OF COLORADO HLTH SCI CTR 4200 E NINTH AVE DENVER, CO 80262 Genetic expression in the mammalian brain
R01NS-10821-18 (NLS) DE VRIES, GEORGE H BIOCHEM & MOLECULAR BIOPHYSICS BOX 614, MCV STATION RICHMOND, VA 23298 Molecular basis of axolemmal-glial interaction
P50NS-10828-16 (NSPA) MOSKOWITZ, MICHAEL A MASSACHUSETTS GENERAL HOSPITAL 32 FRUIT STREET BOSTON, MA 02114 Interdepartmental stroke center grant
P50NS-10828-16 0025 (NSPA) BONVENTRE, JOSEPH V Interdepartmental stroke center grant Phospholipase A2 activation in ischemic injury
P50NS-10828-16 0026 (NSPA) KOROSHETZ, WALTER J Interdepartmental stroke center grant Physiological basis of excitotoxic ischemic neuronal death
P50NS-10828-16 0027 (NSPA) SWEADNER, KATHLEEN J Interdepartmental stroke center grant Na, K-ATPase isozyme localization & function in CNS
P50NS-10828-16 0028 (NSPA) FINKLESTEIN, SETH Interdepartmental stroke center grant Angiogenic factors in stroke
P50NS-10828-16 0029 (NSPA) ALPERT, NATHANIEL Interdepartmental stroke center grant Measurement of brain pH and oxidative metabolism by PET
P50NS-10828-16 0030 (NSPA) MOSKOWITZ, MICHAEL A Interdepartmental stroke center grant Trigeminal control of the cerebral circulation
P50NS-10828-16 0031 (NSPA) BEAL, M FLINT Interdepartmental stroke center grant Excitotoxins and stroke
P50NS-10828-16 9001 (NSPA) CORREIA, JOHN A Interdepartmental stroke center grant Core--PET laboratory
P50NS-10828-16 9002 (NSPA) MOSKOWITZ, MICHAEL A Interdepartmental stroke center grant Core--Scientific core
R01NS-10861-17 (NLS) PFEIFFER, STEVEN E UNIV OF CONNECTICUT HLTH CTR FARMINGTON, CT 06032 Clonal cell lines of the nervous system
R01NS-10873-19 (BPO) WADE, GEORGE N UNIVERSITY OF MASSACHUSETTS DEPT. OF PSYCHOLOGY AMHERST, MA 01003 Hormones, brain function, and behavior
R01NS-10928-15 (NLS) BUTCHER, LARRY L UNIVERSITY OF CALIFORNIA 405 HILGARD AVENUE LOS ANGELES, CALIF 90024 Acetylcholinesterase and cholinergic neurons in the brain
P50NS-10939-18A1S1 (SRC) REIVICH, MARTIN UNIVERSITY OF PENNSYLVANIA 36TH AND HAMILTON WALK PHILADELPHIA, PA 19104 Cerebral blood flow and metabolism in stroke and shock
P50NS-10939-18A1S1 0028 (SRC) ERECINSKA, MARIA Cerebral blood flow and metabolism in stroke and shock Sodium pump in neuronal ion and neurotransmitter homeostasis
P50NS-10939-18A1S1 0029 (SRC) WILSON, D Cerebral blood flow and metabolism in stroke and shock Microcirculatory failure and lipid peroxides in ischemic reperfusion injury
P50NS-10939-18A1S1 0030 (SRC) GREENBERG, J Cerebral blood flow and metabolism in stroke and shock Factors responsible for tissue damage during focal cerebral ischemia
P50NS-10939-18A1S1 0031 (SRC) SANDOR, P Cerebral blood flow and metabolism in stroke and shock Endorphins in regulation of cerebral and spinal cord blood flow and metabolism
P50NS-10939-18A1S1 0032 (SRC) GROSSMAN, M Cerebral blood flow and metabolism in stroke and shock Cerebral cognitive networks and their alteration in stroke
P50NS-10939-18A1S1 9003 (SRC) ALVES, W Cerebral blood flow and metabolism in stroke and shock Data management and biostatistics core
P50NS-10939-18A1S1 9004 (SRC) WILSON, D Cerebral blood flow and metabolism in stroke and shock Physiologic imaging core
P50NS-11036-18 (SRC) KOPROWSKI, HILARY THE WISTAR INSTITUTE 36TH AND SPRUCE STREETS PHILADELPHIA, PA 19104 Etiology and pathogenesis of multiple sclerosis
P50NS-11036-18 0015 (SRC) MC MORRIS, ARTHUR Etiology and pathogenesis of multiple sclerosis Regulation of myelin associated biochemical properties
P50NS-11036-18 0035 (SRC) FRASER, NIGEL W Etiology and pathogenesis of multiple sclerosis Mechanisms of HSV-1 latency
P50NS-11036-18 0046 (SRC) HEBER-KATZ, ELLEN Etiology and pathogenesis of multiple sclerosis Idiotypic regulation in multiple sclerosis
P50NS-11036-18 0051 (SRC) DE FERRA, FRANCESCA Etiology and pathogenesis of multiple sclerosis Modulating of MBP gene expression
P50NS-11036-18 0052 (SRC) DE FREITAS, ELAINE C Etiology and pathogenesis of multiple sclerosis T-lymphotropic retroviruses in demylinating disease
P50NS-11036-18 9002 (SRC) RORKE, LUCY B Etiology and pathogenesis of multiple sclerosis Studies of MS, neurological disease and non-disease control
P50NS-11036-18 9003 (SRC) KOPROWSKI, HILARY Etiology and pathogenesis of multiple sclerosis Central service core
P01NS-11037-18 (SRC) SILBERBERG, DONALD H UNIV OF PENNSYLVANIA HOSPITAL 3400 SPRUCE STREET PHILADELPHIA, PA 19104 Etiology and pathogenesis of multiple sclerosis
P01NS-11037-18 0054 (SRC) SILBERBERG, DONALD H Etiology and pathogenesis of multiple sclerosis Oligodendrocyte interactions and development
P01NS-11037-18 0055 (SRC) GILDEN, DONALD Etiology and pathogenesis of multiple sclerosis Mechanism of viral latency
P01NS-11037-18 0057 (SRC) KAMHOLZ, JOHN Etiology and pathogenesis of multiple sclerosis Patterns of myelin specific gene expression
P01NS-11037-18 0058 (SRC) BROWN, MARK J. Etiology and pathogenesis of multiple sclerosis Antibody-induced CNS demyelination and remyelination
P01NS-11037-18 0059 (SRC) WEISS, SUSAN Etiology and pathogenesis of multiple sclerosis MHC class I antigens in MHV demyelination
R01NS-11050-19 (NEUB) CSERR, HELEN F BROWN UNIVERSITY PROVIDENCE, RI 02912 Functional studies of brain extracellular fluids
R01NS-11061-13 (NLS) WAYMIRE, JACK C DEPT OF NEUROBIOLOGY & ANATOMY P O BOX 20708 HOUSTON, TX 77025 Regulation of adrenergic metabolism

PROJECT NO., ORGANIZATIONAL UNIT., INVESTIGATOR, ADDRESS, TITLE

P01NS-11066-17 (NSPA) PEROT, PHANOR L, JR DEPARTMENT OF NEUROSURGERY 171 ASHLEY AVENUE CHARLESTON, SC 29425 Fundamental studies in spinal cord injury
P01NS-11066-17 9001 (NSPA) PEROT, PHANOR L Fundamental studies in spinal cord injury Therapeutic core
P01NS-11066-17 0005 (NSPA) VERA, CHRISTIAN L Fundamental studies in spinal cord injury Clinical electrophysiological
P01NS-11066-17 0007 (NSPA) BALENTINE, J DOUGLAS Fundamental studies in spinal cord injury Neuropathology
P01NS-11066-17 0008 (NSPA) HOGAN, EDWARD L Fundamental studies in spinal cord injury Mechanism of axono and myelinolysis
P01NS-11066-17 0012 (NSPA) HSU, CHUNG Y Fundamental studies in spinal cord injury Arachidonic acid metabolism and vascular injury in spinal cord trauma
R01NS-11149-17 (NLS) ARCH, STEPHEN W REED COLLEGE 2303 S E WOODSTOCK BLVD PORTLAND, OR 97202 Regulatory physiology and biochemistry in nerve cells
R01NS-11199-16 (NEUA) RUCHKIN, DANIEL S UNIV OF MARYLAND SCHOOL OF MED DEPT OF PHYSIOLOGY BALTIMORE, MD 21201 The late positive complex and cognitive activity
R01NS-11223-20 (PHY) DE WEER, PAUL J U OF PA, SCHOOL OF MED. B400 RICHARDS BLDG PHILADELPHIA, PA 19104-6085 Modes of operation of the sodium pump
R01NS-11238-17 (NLS) JOLLY, ROBERT D MASSEY UNIV PALMERSTON NORTH, NEW ZEALAND Studies on ceroid-lipofuscinosis
R01NS-11252-18 (NLS) WOLFF, DONALD J UNIV OF MED & DENT NJ 675 HOES LANE PISCATAWAY, NJ 08854 Function of a brain calcium binding protein
P01NS-11255-17 (NSPB) WILLIS, WILLIAM D, JR UNIV OF TEXAS MEDICAL BRANCH 200 UNIVERSITY BLVD GALVESTON, TX 77550-2772 Comparative neurobiology of the spinal cord
P01NS-11255-17 0017 (NSPB) HULSEBOSCH, CLAIRE E. Comparative neurobiology of the spinal cord Molecular mechanisms of sprouting in the spinal cord
P01NS-11255-17 0018 (NSPB) CHUNG, KYUNGSOON Comparative neurobiology of the spinal cord Sacral autonomic circuitry plasticity during development & after transection
P01NS-11255-17 0020 (NSPB) WESTLUND, KARIN N. Comparative neurobiology of the spinal cord Na and glut/asp STT cell innervation-normal and after inflammation
P01NS-11255-17 0024 (NSPB) COGGESHALL, RICHARD E. Comparative neurobiology of the spinal cord Axonal sprouting and its relation to a central pain state
P01NS-11255-17 0025 (NSPB) CARLTON, SUSAN M Comparative neurobiology of the spinal cord Input to spinothalamic tract cells-normal and neuropathic dorsal horn
P01NS-11255-17 0026 (NSPB) HUANG, LI Y M Comparative neurobiology of the spinal cord A study of the mechanisms for chronic pain
P01NS-11255-17 0027 (NSPB) CHUNG, JIN M Comparative neurobiology of the spinal cord Functional classification of somatosensory neurons
P01NS-11255-17 0028 (NSPB) SORKIN, LINDA S Comparative neurobiology of the spinal cord Dorsal horn neurotransmitter release & sensory transmission modulation
P01NS-11255-17 0029 (NSPB) MCADOO, DAVID J Comparative neurobiology of the spinal cord Neurotransmitter release in spinal cord injury
P01NS-11255-17 0030 (NSPB) CHRISTENSEN, BURGESS N Comparative neurobiology of the spinal cord Mechanisms regulating excitatory amino acid stimulation of chick spinal neurons
P01NS-11255-17 9002 (NSPB) MCADOO, DAVID J Comparative neurobiology of the spinal cord Core--Computer facility
P01NS-11255-17 9003 (NSPB) LEONARD, ROBERT Comparative neurobiology of the spinal cord Core--Electronics shop
P01NS-11255-17 9004 (NSPB) WESTLUND, KARIN N Comparative neurobiology of the spinal cord Core--Light microscope facility
P01NS-11255-17 9005 (NSPB) CARLTON, SUSAN M Comparative neurobiology of the spinal cord Core-Electron microscope facility
R01NS-11272-18 (HAR) BOORD, ROBERT L UNIVERSITY OF DELAWARE SCH OF LIFE & HEALTH SCIENCES NEWARK, DELAWARE 19716 Lateral line pathways
R01NS-11323-18 (IMS) LINDSTROM, JON M UNIVERSITY OF PENNSYLVANIA 422 CURIE BLVD PHILADELPHIA, PA 19104-6142 Studies using purified acetylcholine
R01NS-11425-17A1 (NEUC) WOLF, MERRILL K UNIV OF MASSACHUSETTS MED CTR 55 LAKE AVENUE NORTH WORCESTER, MA 01655 Hypomyelinated mutant and double mutant mice
R01NS-11487-17 (PTHA) STITT, JOHN T THE JOHN B PIERCE LAB 290 CONGRESS AVE NEW HAVEN, CT 06519 Temperature regulation: action of pyrogens
P50NS-11535-17 (NSPB) KELLAWAY, PETER BAYLOR COLLEGE OF MEDICINE ONE BAYLOR PLAZA HOUSTON, TX 77030 Epilepsy research center
P50NS-11535-17 0020 (NSPB) BARNES, EUGENE M Epilepsy research center Maturation of ion channel complexes in neurons
P50NS-11535-17 9001 (NSPB) KELLAWAY, PETER A Epilepsy research center Antiepileptic drug laboratory core
P50NS-11535-17 0002 (NSPB) FROST, JAMES D Epilepsy research center Predicting response to medical treatment in temporal lobe epilepsy
P50NS-11535-17 0012 (NSPB) JOHNSTON, DANIEL Epilepsy research center Membrane and synaptic mechanisms in epileptogenesis
P50NS-11535-17 0013 (NSPB) PLISKHER, GORDON A Epilepsy research center Regulation of calcium and calcium-dependent potassium transport
P50NS-11535-17 0017 (NSPB) KELLAWAY, PETER A Epilepsy research center Time modulation of epileptic activity in the brain
P50NS-11535-17 0018 (NSPB) HRACHOVY, RICHARD A Epilepsy research center Pathophysiology and treatment of infantile spasms
P50NS-11535-17 0019 (NSPB) KELLAWAY, PETER A Epilepsy research center Pathophysiological studies in neonatal seizures
R01NS-11549-18 (NEUC) HEINEMANN, STEPHEN F SALK INSTITUTE/BIOL STUDIES P O BOX 85800 SAN DIEGO, CA 92186-5800 Synapse formation in cloned cell lines
R01NS-11613-16 (SSS) HINES, MICHAEL L DUKE UNIV MED CTR BOX 3209 DURHAM, N C 27710 Computer methods for physiological problems
R01NS-11615-19 (NEUB) MORELL, PIERRE UNIV OF NC AT CHAPEL HILL BDRC, CB#7250 CHAPEL HILL, N C 27599 Assembly and maintenance of the myelin sheath

R01NS-11632-17 (NLS) ENG, LAWRENCE F STANFORD UNIV SCHOOL OF MED. DEPARTMENT OF PATHOLOGY STANFORD, CALIF 94305 Cytoskeletal proteins in astrocytic gliosis
R01NS-11756-17 (NEUB) LESTER, HENRY A CALIFORNIA INSTITUTE 1201 EAST CALIFORNIA BOULEVARD PASADENA, CALIF 91125 Chemical synapses, biophysical studies
P01NS-11766-17A1 (NSPB) ROWLAND, LEWIS P COLUMBIA-PRESBYTERIAN MED CTR 710 WEST 168TH STREET NEW YORK, NY 10032 Clinical research center for neuromuscular disease
P01NS-11766-17A1 0023 (NSPB) DIMAURO, SALVATORE Clinical research center for neuromuscular disease Muscle disease biochemistry
P01NS-11766-17A1 0032 (NSPB) BONILLA, EDUARDO Clinical research center for neuromuscular disease Muscle morphology
P01NS-11766-17A1 0035 (NSPB) LATOV, NORMAN Clinical research center for neuromuscular disease Anti-GM1 antibodies in neuropathy and motor neuron disease
P01NS-11766-17A1 0036 (NSPB) MIRANDA, ARMAND Clinical research center for neuromuscular disease Muscle tissue culture
P01NS-11766-17A1 0037 (NSPB) SCHON, ERIC A Clinical research center for neuromuscular disease Deletions of mitochondrial DNA in neuromuscular disease
R01NS-11788-18 (GEN) KANKEL, DOUGLAS R YALE UNIVERSITY BOX 1504A YALE STATION NEW HAVEN, CT 06520 Nervous system development and synapse formation
R01NS-11822-14 (NLS) CHANG, YUNG-FENG UNIVERSITY OF MARYLAND 666 W BALTIMORE STREET BALTIMORE, MD 21201-1586 Metabolism and neurochemistry of lysine in the brain
R01NS-11853-17 (NEUB) YU, ROBERT K VIRGINIA COMMONWEALTH UNIVERSI BOX 614, MCV STATION RICHMOND, VA 23298-0614 Sphingoglycolipids of normal and pathological brains
R01NS-11862-14 (NEUB) GARDNER, ESTHER P NEW YORK UNIVERSITY MED CENTER 550 FIRST AVENUE NEW YORK, NY 10016 Neural mechanisms of cutaneous spatial integration
R01NS-11892-17 (NEUB) CONTRERAS, ROBERT J FLORIDA STATE UNIVERSITY TALLAHASSEE, FL 32306-1051 Sensory innervation of female pelvic organs
P50NS-11920-17 (NSPA) BORNSTEIN, MURRAY B ALBERT EINSTEIN COLL OF MED 1300 MORRIS PARK AVENUE BRONX, NY 10461 Pathogenesis and treatment of multiple sclerosis
P50NS-11920-17 0006 (NSPA) RAINE, CEDRIC S Pathogenesis and treatment of multiple sclerosis Ultrastructural analysis of autoimmune demyelination in vitro
P50NS-11920-17 0017 (NSPA) BORNSTEIN, MURRAY B Pathogenesis and treatment of multiple sclerosis The role of cytokines in myelin pathology
P50NS-11920-17 0018 (NSPA) TRAUGOTT, UTE Pathogenesis and treatment of multiple sclerosis Immunocytochemical and functional analysis of lesion development in EAE
P50NS-11920-17 0019 (NSPA) BROSNAN, CELIA F Pathogenesis and treatment of multiple sclerosis Cytokine involvement in inflammation in the CNS
P50NS-11920-17 0020 (NSPA) SHAFIT-ZAGARDO, BRIDGET Pathogenesis and treatment of multiple sclerosis Reactive gliosis in inflammatory demyelinating diseases
P50NS-11920-17 9001 (NSPA) BORNSTEIN, MURRAY B Pathogenesis and treatment of multiple sclerosis Core
R01NS-11946-18 (PHY) RUSSELL, JOHN M UNIVERSITY OF TEXAS GALVESTON, TEX 77550 Chloride transport in nerve and muscle
R01NS-12005-17A1 (NEUB) CAVINESS, VERNE S, JR MASSACHUSETTS GENERAL HOSPITAL FRUIT STREET BOSTON, MA 02114 Cortical development
R01NS-12061-13 (NEUB) BROWN, PAUL B DEPARTMENT OF PHYSIOLOGY HEALTH SCIENCES CENTER MORGANTOWN, W VA 26505 Morphology & somatotopy in the dorsal horn
R01NS-12103-15 (NEUB) MC ILWAIN, DAVID L UNC AT CHAPEL HILL 174 MEDICAL RES WING CB#7545 CHAPEL HILL, NC 27599 Bulk isolation of large spinal neurons
R01NS-12108-17 (MCHA) KISHI, YOSHITO HARVARD UNIVERSITY 12 OXFORD STREET CAMBRIDGE, MASS 02138 Synthetic studies on complex natural products
R01NS-12127-17 (EVR) NARAYAN, OPENDRA JOHNS HOPKINS UNIV SCH OF MED 720 RUTLAND AVENUE BALTIMORE, MD 21205 Pathogenesis of visna, a slow demyelinating disease
P50NS-12151-17 (NSPB) PRINCE, DAVID A STANFORD UNIVERSITY RM C-338, STANFORD MEDICAL CTR STANFORD, CA 94305 Epilepsy research program
P50NS-12151-17 0001 (NSPB) PRINCE, DAVID A Epilepsy research program Regulation of neuronal excitability and epileptogenesis
P50NS-12151-17 0015 (NSPB) MODY, ISTVAN Epilepsy research program Changes in neuronal excitability during kindling-induced epilepsy
P50NS-12151-17 0016 (NSPB) MADISON, V DANIEL Epilepsy research program Regulation of neuronal excitability by norepinephrine
P50NS-12151-17 0017 (NSPB) KRIEGSTEIN, ARNOLD R Epilepsy research program Development of excitatory synaptic transmission in cortex
P50NS-12151-17 9001 (NSPB) PRINCE, DAVID A Epilepsy research program Core-Histology
R01NS-12207-17 (NLS) BARRETT, JOHN N DEPT OF PHYSIOLOGY/BIOPHYSICS UNIV OF MIAMI SCH OF MED MIAMI, FLA 33101 CNS cholinergic and dopaminergic neurons--Tropic control
N01NS-12300-00 ( ) ROBBLEE, LOIS S** Studies on the electrochemistry of stimulating electrode
N01NS-12301-02 ( )** Logistical and research support services
N01NS-12308-00 ( ) HUMPHREY, DONALD R** Cortical control of neural prosthetic devices
N43NS-12309-00 ( ) LIN, CHARLES** Inorganic polymer coatings for neural prostheses
N43NS-12310-00 ( ) NUWAYSER, E S** Suppositories for rapid anti-epileptic delivery of diazepam
N43NS-12311-00 ( ) COGAN, STUART F** Thin-film hermetic coatings
R01NS-12311-17 (NEUB) HARTMAN, BOYD K UNIVERSITY OF MINNESOTA BOX 392 MAYO MEMORIAL BUILDING MINNEAPOLIS, MN 55455 Noradrenergic system in brain--anatomy and function

PROJECT NO., ORGANIZATIONAL UNIT., INVESTIGATOR, ADDRESS, TITLE

N43NS-12312-00 ( ) NICHOLS, MICHAEL F** Hermetic encapsulation of wires and cables
N43NS-12313-00 ( ) SIOSHANSI, PIRAN** IBAD hermetic seals -- Iridium coatings for neural stimulating electrodes
N01NS-12314-00 ( ) NAJAFI, KHALIL** Inductively powered microstimulator
N01NS-12315-00 ( ) CLANCEY, ROBERT** Clinical research center for neonatal seizures
N01NS-12316-00 ( ) MIZRAHI, ELI** Clinical research center for neonatal seizures
N01NS-12317-00 ( ) SANDS, STEPHEN F** Channel brain mapping system
N01NS-12318-00 ( ) KUNITZ, SELMA** Clinical cerebrovascular research data management
R01NS-12327-17 (NEUB) RITCHIE, J MURDOCH YALE UNIV/PHARMACOLOGY P.O. BOX 3333 NEW HAVEN, CT 06510 Demyelinating disease-biophysics of nerve dysfunction
R01NS-12333-17 (NEUA) STEWARD, OSWALD UNIV. OF VIRGINIA SCH. OF MED. DEPARTMENT OF NEUROSCIENCE CHARLOTTESVILLE, VA 22908 Post-lesion plasticity of neuronal circuitry
R01NS-12337-17 (BPO) BASTIAN, JOSEPH A, JR UNIVERSITY OF OKLAHOMA RICHARDS HALL, ROOM 116 NORMAN, OKLAHOMA 73019 Sensory processing in cerebellum
R01NS-12344-17 (END) MACRIDES, FOTEOS WORCESTER FDN/EXPER BIOL, INC 222 MAPLE AVENUE SHREWSBURY, MA 01545 Olfactory and neuroendocrine functions
R01NS-12389-17 (SSS) OVERMAN, LARRY E UNIVERSITY OF CALIFORNIA IRVINE, CA 92717 Synthesis of active neurological agents
R01NS-12404-17 (NEUB) BARRETT, ELLEN F UNIV OF MIAMI SCH OF MEDICINE P O BOX 016430 MIAMI, FL 33101 Electrophysiology of myelinated axons
P50NS-12428-17 (NSPA) OLDSTONE, MICHAEL B SCRIPPS CLINIC AND RES FNDN 10666 N TORREY PINES ROAD LA JOLLA, CALIF 92037 Demyelinating (MS) and degenerative (ALS) CNS diseases
P50NS-12428-17 0011 (NSPA) HOGLE, JAMES Demyelinating (MS) and degenerative (ALS) CNS diseases Theiler's murine encephalomyelitis virus
P50NS-12428-17 9001 (NSPA) OLDSTONE, MICHAEL B Demyelinating (MS) and degenerative (ALS) CNS diseases Core--Tissue culture
P50NS-12428-17 0001 (NSPA) OLDSTONE, MICHAEL B Demyelinating (MS) and degenerative (ALS) CNS diseases Immunopathology--Virus diseases
P50NS-12428-17 0005 (NSPA) BUCHMEIER, MICHAEL J Demyelinating (MS) and degenerative (ALS) CNS diseases Molecular biology of acute demyelination
P50NS-12428-17 0008 (NSPA) LAMPERT, PETER W Demyelinating (MS) and degenerative (ALS) CNS diseases Pathogenesis of demyelination in virally infected mice
P50NS-12428-17 0009 (NSPA) WHITTON, LINDSAY Demyelinating (MS) and degenerative (ALS) CNS diseases LCM virus infection in the natural host
P50NS-12428-17 0010 (NSPA) NERENBERG, MICHAEL Demyelinating (MS) and degenerative (ALS) CNS diseases MHC antigen expression in CNS disease
R01NS-12440-16 (NLS) RUSTIONI, ALDO CELL BIOLOGY AND ANATOMY 108 TAYLOR CB# 7090 CHAPEL HILL, NC 27599 Neurotransmitters in DRGs and somesthesic paths
R01NS-12467-16 (NLS) PUSZKIN, SAUL MT SINAI SCHOOL OF MEDICINE 5TH AVE & 100 ST/PATHOLOGY NEW YORK, NY 140029 Synaptosomes, vesicle subtypes and structural proteins
R01NS-12542-17 (NEUB) FETZ, EBERHARD E UNIV OF WASHINGTON, SJ-40 DEPT PHYSIOLOGY & BIOPHYSICS SEATTLE, WA 98195 Neural control of muscle activity
R01NS-12547-16 (PHY) ARMSTRONG, CLAY M UNIVERSITY OF PENNSYLVANIA B-701 RICHARDS BLDG PHILA., PA 19104-6085 Permeability mechanisms in excitable membranes
P01NS-12587-16 (NSPA) YOUNG, HAROLD F VIRGINIA COMMONWEALTH UNIV NEUROSURG / BOX 631, MCV STN RICHMOND, VA 23298-0678 Head injury clinical and laboratory research center
P01NS-12587-16 0001 (NSPA) WARD, JOHN D. Head injury clinical and laboratory research center Improving outcome in severe head injury--A clinical trial
P01NS-12587-16 0005 (NSPA) POVLISHOCK, JOHN T Head injury clinical and laboratory research center Neural and vascular change with trauma and subarachnoid hemorrhage
P01NS-12587-16 0008 (NSPA) ELLIS, EARL F Head injury clinical and laboratory research center Arachidonic acid cascade in experimental brain injury
P01NS-12587-16 0009 (NSPA) PATTERSON, JOHN L Head injury clinical and laboratory research center Brain energetics in experimental head injury
P01NS-12587-16 0011 (NSPA) MARMAROU, ANTHONY Head injury clinical and laboratory research center Mechanical brain injury--physiology and therapy
P01NS-12587-16 0012 (NSPA) HAYES, RONALD L Head injury clinical and laboratory research center Brain glucose utilization in experimental head injury
P01NS-12587-16 0013 (NSPA) MARMAROU, ANTHONY Head injury clinical and laboratory research center Dynamics of intracranial pressure in head injury
P01NS-12587-16 0014 (NSPA) SGRO, JOSEPH A. Head injury clinical and laboratory research center Assessment of afferent & efferent neuropathways in severe head injury
P01NS-12587-16 0015 (NSPA) HAYES, RONALD L. Head injury clinical and laboratory research center Neuropharmacological studies of experimental concussion
P01NS-12587-16 0016 (NSPA) JENKINS, LAWRENCE Head injury clinical and laboratory research center Receptor mediated post-traumatic sensitivity to ischemia
P01NS-12587-16 0017 (NSPA) LYETH, BRUCE Head injury clinical and laboratory research center Role of opioids in traumatic brain injury
P01NS-12587-16 0018 (NSPA) HAMM, ROBERT J. Head injury clinical and laboratory research center Role of age & cholinergic system on brain injury
P01NS-12587-16 0019 (NSPA) POVLISHOCK, JOHN T. Head injury clinical

PROJECT NO., ORGANIZATIONAL UNIT., INVESTIGATOR, ADDRESS, TITLE

and laboratory research center Blood-brain barrier alteration following traumatic brain injury
P01NS-12587-16 0020 (NSPA) ELLIS, EARL E. Head injury clinical and laboratory research center Biochemical mechanisms of brain injury---Fatty acids & free radicals
P01NS-12587-16 9003 (NSPA) CHOI, SUNG C Head injury clinical and laboratory research center Head injury biostatistics core
P01NS-12587-16 9004 (NSPA) WARD, JOHN D Head injury clinical and laboratory research center Core--Human and intensive care and outcome core
P01NS-12587-16 9006 (NSPA) LUTZ, HARRY A. Head injury clinical and laboratory research center Core--Computing center
P01NS-12587-16 9007 (NSPA) LYETH, BRUCE Head injury clinical and laboratory research center Core--Rat surgery / behavioral core
R01NS-12601-16 (NEUC) BERG, DARWIN K DEPT OF BIOLOGY, B-022 UNIV OF CALIF - SAN DIEGO LA JOLLA, CA 92093 Neuronal development and synapse formation in vitro
R01NS-12636-17 (NEUA) FIDONE, SALVATORE J UNIV OF UTAH SCHOOL OF MED 410 CHIPETA WAY, RES PARK SALT LAKE CITY, UT 84108 Chemical transmission in sensory receptors
R01NS-12651-16 (NLS) ZIGMOND, RICHARD E CASE WESTERN RESERVE SCH OF ME 2119 ABINGTON ROAD CLEVELAND, OH 44106 Experience and the neurochemistry of the synapse
R01NS-12674-16 (PTHA) MANUELIDIS, ELIAS E YALE UNIVERSITY SCHOOL OF MED 333 CEDAR ST, PO BOX 3333 NEW HAVEN, CT 06510 Experimental Creutzfeldt-Jakob disease
R01NS-12745-15 (ET) GROOTHUIS, DENNIS R EVANSTON HOSP NEUROLOGY DIV 2650 RIDGE AVENUE EVANSTON, ILL 60201 Permeability and blood flow in brain tumors
R01NS-12777-16 (NEUB) THACH, WILLIAM T, JR WASHINGTON UNIVERSITY 724 SOUTH EUCLID AVENUE ST LOUIS, MO 63110 Neural control of trained movement
R01NS-12782-13 (NLS) SILINSKY, EUGENE M NORTHWESTERN UNIVERSITY 303 EAST CHICAGO AVENUE CHICAGO, IL 60611 Adenosine derivatives and cholinergic nerve endings
R01NS-12818-38 (NEUB) STENT, GUNTHER S UNIVERSITY OF CALIFORNIA MOLECULAR & CELL BIOLOGY BERKELEY, CA 94720 Behavior and development of a simple nervous system
R01NS-12867-16 (NEUA) GOTTLIEB, DAVID I WASHINGTON UNIVERSITY 660 SOUTH EUCLID AVENUE ST LOUIS, MO 63110 Molecular basis of cell recognition in development
R01NS-12890-13 (NLS) CAMMER, WENDY ALBERT EINSTEIN COLLEGE OF MED 1300 MORRIS PARK AVENUE BRONX, NY 10461 Myelin-related enzymes in CNS cells and membranes
R01NS-12961-17 (PHY) STEVENS, CHARLES F SALK INSTITUTE P O BOX 85800 SAN DIEGO, CA 92037 Basic neuro mechanisms
R01NS-12969-16 (NEUB) GERSHON, MICHAEL D DEPT OF ANATOMY AND CELL BIOLO 630 WEST 168TH STREET NEW YORK, NY 10032 Neural control of gastrointestinal activity
R01NS-13011-16 (PTHA) DAL CANTO, MAURO C NORTHWESTERN UNIV MED SCHOOL 303 EAST CHICAGO AVENUE CHICAGO, IL 60611 Ultrastructural and immunopathological studies
R01NS-13031-15 (NEUB) EBNER, FORD F DEPT OF NEUROBIOLOGY BOX G PROVIDENCE, R I 02912 Innervation of transplanted cerebral cortex
R01NS-13034-17 (PTHA) BIGNAMI, AMICO VETERANS ADMIN MEDICAL CENTER 1400 VFW PARKWAY WEST ROXBURY, MASS 02132 Brain specific protein (GFA protein) in astrocytes
R01NS-13050-16 (BBCB) MC NAMEE, MARK G UNIVERSITY OF CALIFORNIA DEPT OF BIOCHEMISTRY & BIOPHYS DAVIS, CA 95616 Dynamic interactions of the acetylcholine receptor
R01NS-13079-16 (NEUC) TRUMAN, JAMES W UNIVERSITY OF WASHINGTON DEPARTMENT OF ZOOLOGY SEATTLE, WA 98195 Hormone action on the CNS
R01NS-13108-15 (SAT) KENDIG, JOAN J STANFORD UNIV SCHOOL OF MED DEPARTMENT OF ANESTHESIA STANFORD, CALIF 94305 Excitable cell function at hyperbaric pressure
R01NS-13143-14 (NLS) BENJAMINS, JOYCE A WAYNE STATE UNIVERSITY 540 E CANFIELD DETROIT, MICH 48201 Myelination: Assembly of lipids and proteins
R01NS-13230-15 (BPO) CASTRO, ANTHONY J DEPARTMENT OF ANATOMY 2160 SOUTH FIRST AVENUE MAYWOOD, IL 60153 Fetal cortical transplants in the repair of brain damage
R01NS-13243-13 (BCE) BEN-JONATHAN, NIRA INDIANA UNIV. SCH. OF MEDICINE 635 BARNHILL DRIVE INDIANAPOLIS, IN 46202-5120 Control of prolactin secretion by catecholamines
R01NS-13335-13 (NLS) LA MOTTE, CAROLE C YALE UNIVERSITY, SURGERY 333 CEDAR STREET NEW HAVEN, CONN 06510 Distribution of pain and temperature afferents
R01NS-13447-10A1 (NLS) ROBERTS, WILLIAM J R S DOW NEUROLOGICAL SCIS INST 1120 NW 20TH AVENUE PORTLAND, OR 97209 Sympathetic efferent modulation of pain
R01NS-13515-13 (NEUA) WASTERLAIN, CLAUDE G VA MEDICAL CENTER 16111 PLUMMER STREET SEPULVEDA, CA 91343 Brain development in experimental epilepsy
R01NS-13521-16 (NEUB) HALL, ZACH W UNIV. OF CAL., SAN FRANCISCO PARNASSUS AVE SAN FRANCISCO, CALIF 94143 Postsynaptic proteins at the neuromuscular junction
R01NS-13546-16 (NEUB) PATRICK, JAMES W BAYLOR COLLEGE OF MEDICINE ONE BAYLOR PLAZA HOUSTON, TX 77030 Trophic interaction of nerve and muscle
R01NS-13559-17A1 (NEUB) KISHIMOTO, YASUO CENTER FOR MOLECULAR GENETICS SCHOOL OF MEDICINE LA JOLLA, CA 92093 Sphingolipid metabolism and brain development
R01NS-13560-15 (CBY) WILSON, LESLIE DEPT. OF BIOLOGICAL SCIENCES UNIVERSITY OF CALIFORNIA SANTA BARBARA, CALIF 93106 Drug interactions with brain microtubule proteins
R01NS-13584-15 (NEUA) COYLE, JOSEPH T MCLEAN HOSPITAL 115 MILL STREET BELMONT, MA 02178-9106 Huntington's chorea model--Striatal lesion by kainate
R01NS-13600-14 (NEUB) SMITH, DEAN O UNIVERSITY OF WISCONSIN 1300 UNIVERSITY AVENUE MADISON, WI 53706 Mechanisms of synaptic transmission failure
R01NS-13649-15 (NEUB) LEES, MARJORIE B EUNICE KENNEDY SHRIVER CENTER 200 TRAPELO ROAD WALTHAM, MA 02254 Relationship between brain proteins and lipids
P01NS-13742-15 (NSPB) LLINAS, RODOLFO R NEW YORK UNIV MEDICAL CENTER 550 FIRST AVENUE NEW YORK, NY 10016 Neurobiology of cerebellar-brainstem system
P01NS-13742-15 0001 (NSPB) NICHOLSON, CHARLES Neurobiology of cerebellar-brainstem system Mossy fiber--Parallel fiber relay in cerebellum
P01NS-13742-15 0003 (NSPB) HILLMAN, DEAN E Neurobiology of cerebellar-brainstem system Neuronal form--Shape and structure
P01NS-13742-15 0006 (NSPB) LLINAS, RODOLFO R Neurobiology of cerebellar-brainstem system Neurobiology of cerebellar circuit--Relation to motor control
P01NS-13742-15 0011 (NSPB) SIMPSON, JOHN I Neurobiology of cerebellar-brainstem system Visual-vestibular interaction in eye movement control
P01NS-13742-15 0014 (NSPB) BAKER, ROBERT Neurobiology of cerebellar-brainstem system Development of eye movement coordination
P01NS-13742-15 9001 (NSPB) LLINAS, RODOLFO R Neurobiology of cerebellar-brainstem system Core--Instrumentation, techniques and data mangement
R01NS-13748-16 (BPO) ROSE, JAMES D UNIVERSITY OF WYOMING BOX 3415 UNIVERSITY STATION LARAMIE, WY 82071 Electrophysiology of the sensory system
R01NS-13799-11 (NLS) WIGGINS, RICHARD CALVIN WEST VIRGINIA UNIVERSITY HEALTH SCIENCES CTR, 4052 HSN MORGANTOWN, WV 26506 Starvation-vulnerable brain subcellular membranes
K06NS-13838-30 (NCR) WOODBURY, DIXON M UNIV OF UTAH SCH OF MED 410 CHIPETA WAY, #167 SALT LAKE CITY, UTAH 84108 Pharmacology and cellular biochemistry of the CNS
R01NS-13876-14 (NLS) MARGOLIS, RICHARD U N Y UNIV MEDICAL CENTER 550 FIRST AVENUE NEW YORK, N Y 10016 Complex carbohydrates of nervous tissue
R01NS-13980-14 (NLS) GOULD, ROBERT M N Y S INST FOR BASIC RES IN MR 1050 FOREST HILL ROAD STATEN ISLAND, N Y 10314 Complex lipid metabolism in the axon
P01NS-14069-14 (SRC) PRUSINER, STANLEY B UC SAN FRANCISCO NEUROLOGY RM HSE 781 SAN FRANCISCO, CA 94143-0518 Multiple sclerosis and viral infections of the CNS
P01NS-14069-14 0008 (SRC) HOOD, LEROY E Multiple sclerosis and viral infections of the CNS The structure and expression of myelin protein genes
P01NS-14069-14 0009 (SRC) CARLSON, GEORGE A Multiple sclerosis and viral infections of the CNS Genetics of scrapie prions and murine hosts
P01NS-14069-14 0010 (SRC) PRUSINER, STANLEY B Multiple sclerosis and viral infections of the CNS Molecular genetics of PrP in transgenic and chimeric mice
P01NS-14069-14 0011 (SRC) MYERS, RICHARD M Multiple sclerosis and viral infections of the CNS PrP mRNAs
P01NS-14069-14 0012 (SRC) DEARMOND, STEPHEN J Multiple sclerosis and viral infections of the CNS Molecular pathology of prion disease and human PrP genes
R01NS-14090-11 (NLS) BIBER, MARGARET C MEDICAL COLLEGE OF VIRGINIA BOX 551, MCV STATION RICHMOND, VA 23298-0551 Sound stress, steroids, CRF, and 5-HT neuronal function
R01NS-14096-14 (NEUB) STELZNER, DENNIS J SUNY HEALTH SCI CTR AT SYRACUS 750 EAST ADAMS STREET SYRACUSE, NY 13210 Factors in CNS regeneration
R01NS-14138-12 (PHY) BEGENISICH, TED B UNIV OF ROCHESTER SCHOOL OF ME 601 ELMWOOD AVENUE, BOX 642 ROCHESTER, NY 14642 Chemical and molecular properties of ion channel proteins
R01NS-14143-15 (TOX) NARAHASHI, TOSHIO NORTHWESTERN UNIV MED SCHOOL 303 EAST CHICAGO AVENUE CHICAGO, ILL 60611 Mode of action of insecticides--Electrophysiological
R01NS-14144-15 (NLS) NARAHASHI, TOSHIO NORTHWESTERN UNIVERSITY MED SC 303 E CHICAGO AVENUE CHICAGO, IL 60611-3008 Cellular neurophysiological study of drug action
R01NS-14162-14 (PTHA) POWELL, HENRY C UNIVERSITY OF CALIFORNIA LA JOLLA, CA 92093-0612 Pathogenesis of toxic and metabolic neuropathies
P01NS-14304-13 (NSPB) DYCK, PETER J MAYO FOUNDATION 200 FIRST STREET SOUTHWEST ROCHESTER, MN 55905 Mayo peripheral neuropathy clinical research center
P01NS-14304-13 0009 (NSPB) SCHMID, HAROLD H. O. Mayo peripheral neuropathy clinical research center Structure, turnover, & function of membrane phospholipids in neuropathies
P01NS-14304-13 0031 (NSPB) LOW, PHILLIP A Mayo peripheral neuropathy clinical research center Ischemic conduction failure/development of neuropathy in diabetics
P01NS-14304-13 0036 (NSPB) DYCK, PETER J. Mayo peripheral neuropathy clinical research center Neuropathy among diabetics in Rochester, Mn
P01NS-14304-13 0037 (NSPB) DYCK, PETER J Mayo peripheral neuropathy clinical research center Pathologic abnormalities of sural nerves in diabetic neuropathies
P01NS-14304-13 0038 (NSPB) PODUSLO, J.F. Mayo peripheral neuropathy clinical research center Blood nerve barrier alterations in neuropathies
P01NS-14304-13 0039 (NSPB) WINDEBANK, ANTHONY Mayo peripheral neuropathy clinical research center Mechanism of axonal regeneration in response to nerve injury
R01NS-14325-13 (NEUA) ROSENTHAL, MYRON UNIVERSITY OF MIAMI P O BOX 016960/1501 NW 9 AVE MIAMI, FL 33101 Cerebral ischemia, viability and oxidative metabolism
R01NS-14332-11 (NEUB) RUBINSTEIN, NEAL A UNIVERSITY OF PENNSYLVANIA SCHOOL OF MEDICINE PHILADELPHIA, PA 19104 Control of myosin types in individual muscle fibers
R01NS-14426-11 (PTHA) GHETTI, BERNARDINO INDIANA UNIVERSITY 635 BARNHILL DRIVE INDIANAPOLIS, IN 46202-5120 Selective neuronal loss and its sequelae--a model
R01NS-14428-14 (NEUB) KALIL, KATHERINE UNIVERSITY OF WISCONSIN 1300 UNIVERSITY AVENUE MADISON, WI 53706 Developmental studies on the motor system
R01NS-14447-13 (CMS) CAMPBELL, JAMES N JOHNS HOPKINS HOSPITAL

600 N WOLFE STREET BALTIMORE, MD 21205 Neurophysiological and psychophysical studies of pain

R01NS-14497-13 (BPO) RANCK, JAMES B, JR SUNY, HEALTH SCI CNTR/BROOKLYN 450 CLARKSON AVE BOX 31 BROOKLYN, NY 11203 Electrophysiology of limbic neurons

R01NS-14506-15 (NEUB) MC MAHAN, UEL J STANFORD UNIV SCH OF MED SHERMAN FAIRCHILD SCI BLDG STANFORD, CA 94305-5401 Structure and function of regenerating synapses

R01NS-14509-14 (NEUB) GAMBETTI, PIERLUIGI CASE WESTERN RESERVE UNIV 2085 ADELBERT ROAD CLEVELAND, OHIO 44106 Studies in synaptosomes and axons

R01NS-14519-12A1 (PHY) THOMPSON, STUART H STANFORD UNIVERSITY HOPKINS MARINE STATION PACIFIC GROVE, CA 93950 Calcium and current responses to agonists

R01NS-14521-14 (TOX) ROSENBERG, PHILIP UNIVERSITY OF CONNECTICUT SCH OF PHARM, BOX U-92 STORRS, CONN 06268 Properties of chemically modified phospholipase A2

P50NS-14543-14 (SRC) CHAN, PAK HOO UNIVERSITY OF CALIFORNIA SAN FRANCISCO, CA 94143-0114 Brain edema clinical research center

P50NS-14543-14 0001 (SRC) CHAN, PAK Brain edema clinical research center Molecular mechanism and metabolic basis of cellular (cytotoxic) edema

P50NS-14543-14 0014 (SRC) SIMON, ROGER P Brain edema clinical research center Cell excitation in cerebral ischemia

P50NS-14543-14 0015 (SRC) NOBLE, LINDA J Brain edema clinical research center Blood brain barrier dysfunction after hypoxic traumatic head injury

P50NS-14543-14 0016 (SRC) SHARP, FRANK R Brain edema clinical research center Heat shock responses in cerebral ischemia

P50NS-14543-14 9001 (SRC) CHAN, PAK H Brain edema clinical research center Core--Cell culture

R01NS-14565-13 (NLS) AXELROD, DANIEL UNIVERSITY OF MICHIGAN 2200 BONISTEEL BLVD ANN ARBOR, MICH 48109 Receptor clustering on developing muscle cells

R01NS-14609-13 (PHY) CAHALAN, MICHAEL D UNIVERSITY OF CALIFORNIA IRVINE, CA 92717 Molecular mechanisms of ion channels in cell membranes

R01NS-14610-12 (BPO) SIEGEL, JEROME M UCLA MEDICAL CENTER LOS ANGELES, CA 90024-1406 Pontine unit activity in narcoleptics

R01NS-14624-13 (CMS) LA MOTTE, ROBERT H YALE UNIVERSITY 155 WHITNEY AVE NEW HAVEN, CT 06520 Neurophysiology of pain adaptation and hyperalgesia

R01NS-14627-14 (NLS) BASBAUM, ALLAN I UNIVERSITY OF CALIFORNIA SAN FRANCISCO, CA 94143-0452 Brainstem control of pain transmission

R01NS-14644-10A3 (NEUB) BOULANT, JACK A OHIO STATE UNIVERSITY 333 W 10TH AVE COLUMBUS, OH 43210 The neural control of temperature regulation

R01NS-14705-11 (NEUA) GOSHGARIAN, HARRY G WAYNE STATE UNIVERSITY 540 EAST CANFIELD AVE DETROIT, MI 48201 Functional plasticity in the spinal cord

R01NS-14718-12 (NEUB) ELLISMAN, MARK H UNIVERSITY OF CALIFORNIA UNIV OF CALIFORNIA, SAN DIEGO LA JOLLA, CA 92093-0608 Dynamics of membrane organization at node of Ranvier

R01NS-14784-14 (NLS) GRIFFIN, JOHN W JOHNS HOPKINS HOSPITAL 600 N WOLFE STREET BALTIMORE, MD 21205 Axonal transport in models of neurofilamentous pathology

P50NS-14834-13 (NSPB) FERRENDELLI, JAMES A WASHINGTON UNIVERSITY 660 SOUTH EUCLID AVENUE ST LOUIS, MO 63110 Basic mechanisms of seizures

P50NS-14834-13 0009 (NSPB) COVEY, DOUGLAS F Basic mechanisms of seizures Chemistry of convulsants and anticonvulsants

P50NS-14834-13 0010 (NSPB) FERRENDELLI, JAMES A Basic mechanisms of seizures Neuropharmacology of convulsants and anticonvulsants

P50NS-14834-13 0011 (NSPB) ROTHMAN, STEVEN Basic mechanisms of seizures Cellular mechanisms of inhibitory transmission

P50NS-14834-13 0012 (NSPB) MILLER, JOHN W Basic mechanisms of seizures Neural systems involved in seizure regulation

R01NS-14837-10A1 (HAR) SELZER, MICHAEL E DEPARTMENT OF NEUROLOGY 3400 SPRUCE STREET PHILADELPHIA, PA 19104 Regeneration in the spinal cord--Role of neurofilament

R01NS-14841-14 (NEUB) RAKIC, PASKO T YALE UNIVERSITY PO BOX 3333 NEW HAVEN, CT 06510 Neurogenetic processes in the fetal brain

R01NS-14857-13 (RAP) BERGER, ALBERT J UNIV OF WASHINGTON SJ-40 SEATTLE, WA 98195 Respiratory system integration by the brain stem

P01NS-14867-13 (SRC) REIVICH, MARTIN UNIVERSITY OF PENNSYLVANIA 36TH AND HAMILTON WALK PHILADELPHIA, PA 19104-6063 Local cerebral glucose metabolism in man

P01NS-14867-13 0005 (SRC) GREENBERG, JOEL Local cerebral glucose metabolism in man Local CBF and LCMRO2 with 15O equilibrium imaging and PET

P01NS-14867-13 0006 (SRC) GUR, RUBEN C Local cerebral glucose metabolism in man Cerebral metabolism and blood flow in epilepsy

P01NS-14867-13 0008 (SRC) BOSLEY, T Local cerebral glucose metabolism in man Positron emission tomographic studies of the human visual cortex

P01NS-14867-13 0009 (SRC) REIVICH, MARTIN Local cerebral glucose metabolism in man PET studies of acute cerebral infarction

P01NS-14867-13 9001 (SRC) MUEHLLEHNER, G Local cerebral glucose metabolism in man Instrumentation core facility

P01NS-14867-13 9002 (SRC) ROBINSON, GERRY Local cerebral glucose metabolism in man Cyclotron core facility

R01NS-14871-13 (NLS) FROEHNER, STANLEY C DARTMOUTH MEDICAL SCHOOL HANOVER, NH 03756 Assembly of the neuromuscular postsynaptic membrane

P01NS-14899-13 (SRC) PERL, EDWARD R UNIV OF N C AT CHAPEL HILL CB #7545 MACNIDER CHAPEL HILL, N C 27599 Recovery and regeneration after spinal neuron injury

P01NS-14899-13 0001 (SRC) FAREL, PAUL B Recovery and regeneration after spinal neuron injury Recovery from spinal cord transection

P01NS-14899-13 0005 (SRC) MENDELL, LORNE Recovery and regeneration after spinal neuron injury Plasticity of cutaneous connections in the spinal cord

P01NS-14899-13 0006 (SRC) BULLITT, ELIZABETH Recovery and regeneration after spinal neuron injury Function recovery/neural reorganization--Anterolateral cordotomy

P01NS-14899-13 0008 (SRC) VIERCK, CHARLES Recovery and regeneration after spinal neuron injury Plasticity of cutaneous connections in the spinal cord

P01NS-14899-13 0010 (SRC) MARSHALL, LAWRENCE Recovery and regeneration after spinal neuron injury Consequences of incorrect innervation of postsynaptic neurons

P01NS-14899-13 0011 (SRC) MENDELL, LORNE M Recovery and regeneration after spinal neuron injury Spared root model for study of recovery from neuronal injury

P01NS-14899-13 0012 (SRC) PERL, EDWARD R Recovery and regeneration after spinal neuron injury Mechanism for pain of causalgia/reflex sympathetic dystrophies

P01NS-14899-13 0013 (SRC) WILLARD, ALAN Recovery and regeneration after spinal neuron injury Effects of spinal cord or spinal nerve injury on peripheral nervous system

P01NS-14899-13 9005 (SRC) PERL, EDWARD R Recovery and regeneration after spinal neuron injury Core

R01NS-14900-13 (NEUB) LASEK, RAYMOND J DIV OF GENERAL MEDICAL SCIS 2119 ABINGTON ROAD CLEVELAND, OHIO 44106 Axonal regeneration in spinal cord

K06NS-14938-30 (NCR) DEL CASTILLO, JOSE LAB OF NEUROBIOLOGY 201 BLVD DE VALLE SAN JUAN, P R 00901 Physiology and pharmacology of excitation

R01NS-14944-12 (NEUA) VAN HOESEN, GARY W UNIVERSITY OF IOWA DEPARTMENT OF ANATOMY IOWA CITY, IA 52242 Mesocortical anatomy and plasticity

R01NS-15013-13 (NEUB) OH, TAE HWAN DEPARTMENT OF ANATOMY 655 W. BALTIMORE ST. ANATOMY BALTIMORE, MD 21201 Nerve-muscle interaction and neurotrophic agents

R01NS-15017-12A1 (NEUA) ANDERSON, MARJORIE E UNIVERSITY OF WASHINGTON SEATTLE, WA 98195 Analysis of basal ganglia output

R01NS-15018-12 (ORTH) SOECHTING, JOHN F UNIVERSITY OF MINNESOTA 6-255 MILLARD HALL MINNEAPOLIS, MINN 55455 Organization and control of movements

R01NS-15037-10A1 (NLS) MC CLUER, ROBERT H EUNICE KENNEDY SHRIVER CENTER 200 TRAPELO ROAD WALTHAM, MA 02254 Hormone induced effects on glycolipid metabolism

R01NS-15047-12 (NLS) PARSONS, STANLEY M UNIVERSITY OF CALIFORNIA SANTA BARBARA, CA 93106 Transport enzymes in synaptic vesicles

R01NS-15076-13 (NEUB) SHELANSKI, MICHAEL L COLUMBIA UNIV/COLL PHYS/SURG 630 WEST 168TH STREET NEW YORK, NY 10032 Pathology and biology of the neuronal fibrous proteins

R01NS-15078-12 (NSPA) BRACKEN, MICHAEL B YALE UNIVERSITY 60 COLLEGE STREET NEW HAVEN, CT 06510 National acute spinal cord injury study III

P01NS-15080-12 (SRC) WAGNER, HENRY N, JR DEPT OF RADIOLOGY/RADIOLO. SCI 615 N WOLFE STREET BALTIMORE, MD 21205-2179 Neuroreceptor binding in man

P01NS-15080-12 0008 (SRC) ROBINSON, ROBERT G Neuroreceptor binding in man Neuroreceptor and metabolic changes in persons with mood disorders

P01NS-15080-12 0010 (SRC) FROST, J JAMES Neuroreceptor binding in man Benzodiazepine receptor quantification in epilepsy

P01NS-15080-12 0011 (SRC) FROST, J JAMES Neuroreceptor binding in man Opiate receptor quantification in Alzheimer's disease

P01NS-15080-12 0012 (SRC) WONG, DEAN F Neuroreceptor binding in man Dopamine receptors in Tourette's syndrome

P01NS-15080-12 9003 (SRC) DANNALS, ROBERT F Neuroreceptor binding in man Core--chemistry

P01NS-15080-12 9004 (SRC) LINKS, JONATHAN M Neuroreceptor binding in man Core--physics, instrumentation, and image processing

P01NS-15080-12 9005 (SRC) KUHAR, MICHAEL J Neuroreceptor binding in man Core--biology

P01NS-15080-12 9006 (SRC) LOATS, HARRY L Neuroreceptor binding in man Core--model development, validation, and implementation

P01NS-15080-12 9007 (SRC) BRANDT, JASON Neuroreceptor binding in man Core--neuropsychology

P01NS-15080-12 9008 (SRC) KIMBALL, ALLYN W Neuroreceptor binding in man Core--biostatistics

R01NS-15109-13 (NEUA) GASH, DON M UNIV OF ROCHESTER, ANATOMY 601 ELMWOOD AVE ROCHESTER, N Y 14642 Neural transplants--Growth, reinnervation in the brain

R01NS-15114-13 (PHY) ZUCKER, ROBERT S UNIVER. OF CAL. AT BERKELEY MOLECULAR & CELL BIOLOGY BERKELEY, CALIF 94720 Regulation of synaptic transmission

R01NS-15182-13 (NEUB) LIEM, RONALD K COLUMBIA UNIVERSITY 630 WEST 168 STREET NEW YORK, N Y 10032 Biochemistry of the neuronal cytoskeleton

R01NS-15184-12 (SRC) DEMENT, WILLIAM C STANFORD UNIVERSITY STANFORD, CA 94305 An indispensable resource for the study of narcolepsy

R01NS-15190-12 (NEUC) CARSON, JOHN H UNIVERSITY OF CONNECTICUT HEALTH CENTER FARMINGTON, CT 06032 Myelin protein polymorphism and membrane biogenesis

R01NS-15199-11 (NLS) MOLLIVER, MARK E JOHNS HOPKINS UNIVERSITY 725 NORTH WOLFE STREET BALTIMORE, MD 21205 Organization of serotonergic projections to forebrain

R01NS-15264-13 (BPO) BLOCK, GENE D UNIVERSITY OF VIRGINIA DEPARTMENT OF BIOLOGY CHARLOTTESVILLE, VA 22903 Neural basis of circadian organization

R01NS-15293-11A1 (NLS) SEALOCK, ROBERT UNIVERSITY OF NORTH CAROLINA CB# 7545 CHAPEL HILL, NC 27599-7545 Mechanisms of acetylcholine receptor localization

R01NS-15295-12 (SRC) ABRAMSON, NORMAN S UNIVERSITY OF PITTSBURGH 3434 FIFTH AVENUE, 2ND FLOOR PITTSBURGH, PA 15260 Brain resuscitation clinical trial III

R01NS-15317-12 (NLS) SCHWARTZKROIN, PHILIP A UNIVERSITY OF WASHINGTON SEATTLE, WA 98195 Development and epileptogenesis of a CNS synapse

R01NS-15319-12 (PB) BURKE, MORRIS CASE WESTERN RESERVE UNIV

PROJECT NO., ORGANIZATIONAL UNIT., INVESTIGATOR, ADDRESS, TITLE

2080 ADELBERT ROAD CLEVELAND, OH 44106 Molecular mechanism of muscle contraction
R01NS-15321-12 (NLS) FALLON, JAMES H UNIV OF CALIFORNIA IRVINE, CA 92717 Forebrain and peptide control of neuroendocrine systems
R01NS-15335-12 (NEUB) FABER, DONALD S STATE UNIVERSITY OF NEW YORK 313 CARY HALL BUFFALO, N Y 14214 Vertebrate neuronal interactions and electrogenesis
R01NS-15338-14 (NLS) SKOFF, ROBERT P WAYNE STATE UNIVERSITY 540 E CANFIELD DETROIT, MI 48201 The study of normal and abnormal gliogenesis
R01NS-15339-12A1 (NLS) TICKU, MAHARAJ K UNIV OF TEXAS HLTH SCI CTR 7703 FLOYD CURL DRIVE SAN ANTONIO, TX 78284-7764 Molecular mechanisms of drugs on GABA postsynaptic events
P01NS-15350-13 (NSPB) DENBURG, JEFFREY L DEPARTMENT OF BIOLOGY UNIVERSITY OF IOWA IOWA CITY, IOWA 52242 Generation of neuronal form and function
P01NS-15350-13 0006 (NSPB) WU, CHUN-FANG Generation of neuronal form and function Development of neural function and form in Drosophila
P01NS-15350-13 0007 (NSPB) STAY, BARBARA A Generation of neuronal form and function Brain regulation of corpora allata during development
P01NS-15350-13 0010 (NSPB) DENBURG, JEFFREY L Generation of neuronal form and function Molecular determinants of the development of the nervous system
P01NS-15350-13 0011 (NSPB) KOLLROS, JERRY J Generation of neuronal form and function Control of cell number in the amphibian central nervous system
P01NS-15350-13 0012 (NSPB) O'DONOVAN, MICHAEL J Generation of neuronal form and function Development of sensorimotor synaptic connections
P01NS-15350-13 9002 (NSPB) DENBURG, JEFFREY L Generation of neuronal form and function Core--Histology and transmission electron microscopy
P01NS-15350-13 9003 (NSPB) DENBURG, JEFFREY L Generation of neuronal form and function Core--Hybridoma facilities
R01NS-15380-16 (SSS) WOLF, ALFRED P DEPARTMENT OF CHEMISTRY BROOKHAVEN NATIONAL LABORATORY UPTON, N Y 11973 Radiotracer R & D in nuclear medicine and neuroscience
R01NS-15390-12 (GEN) GANETZKY, BARRY S UNIVERSITY OF WISCONSIN GENETICS BUILDING MADISON, WIS 53706 Neurogenetics of behavior mutants
R01NS-15408-13 (NLS) DE VRIES, GEORGE H MEDICAL COLLEGE OF VIRGINIA 1101 E MARSHALL ST RICHMOND, VA 23298-0614 Axolemmal and myelin-induced Schwann cell proliferation
R01NS-15417-11 (NEUB) DE LONG, MAHLON R EMORY UNIVERSITY 1639 PIERCE DR. ATLANTA, GA 30322 Motor functions of the basal ganglia
R01NS-15426-12 (VISA) SONG, PILL-SOON DEPARTMENT OF CHEMISTRY LINCOLN, NE 68588-0304 Aneural photosensory transduction in Stentor coeruleus
R01NS-15429-13A1 (NEUB) HATTEN, MARY E COLUMBIA UNIVERSITY 630 W 168TH STREET NEW YORK, N Y 10032 Molecular mechanisms of granule cell migration
R01NS-15462-12 (IMS) RICHMAN, DAVID P UNIVERSITY OF CHICAGO 5841 S MARYLAND/BOX 425 CHICAGO, IL 60637 Anti-idiotypic antibodies in myasthenia
R01NS-15488-13 (NEUB) LEVY, WILLIAM B UNIV OF VIRGINIA SCH OF MED BOX 420, DEPT OF NEUROSURG CHARLOTTESVILLE, VA 22908 Synapses as information processing-memory elements
R01NS-15513-11 (NEUB) PUMPLIN, DAVID W UNIV OF MARYLAND AT BALTIMORE 655 W BALTIMORE ST BALTIMORE, MD 21201 Ultrastructure of acetylcholine receptor clusters
R01NS-15547-12 (NEUB) GERSHON, MICHAEL D COLUMBIA UNIVERSITY 630 WEST 168TH STREET NEW YORK, N Y 10032 Microenvironment in enteric neuron development
R01NS-15571-13 (NEUB) MURPHEY, RODNEY K UNIVERSITY OF MASSACHUSETTS MORRILL HALL AMHERST, MA 01003 Origins of neuronal specificity
R01NS-15581-11S1 (ALY) ERLANGER, BERNARD F COLUMBIA UNIVERSITY 630 W 168TH STREET NEW YORK, NY 10032 Immunochemical studies on ligands of the acetylcholine receptor
R01NS-15584-11 (SSS) BRENNER, JOHN F NEW ENGLAND MEDICAL CENTER HOS 750 WASHINGTON STREET, NEMC 85 BOSTON, MA 02111 A computer model of motor unit reorganization
R01NS-15589-13 (NEUA) RANSOM, BRUCE R YALE UNIVERSITY SCH OF MED PO BOX 3333 NEW HAVEN, CT 06510 Studies on neurons and glia in vitro
R01NS-15590-13 (NEUA) YOUNG, WISE NEW YORK UNIV MEDICAL CENTER DEPARTMENT OF NEUROSURGERY NEW YORK, N Y 10016 Neurophysiology of spinal cord injury
R01NS-15630-12 (NEUA) PENN, RICHARD D RUSH-PRES-ST LUKE'S MED CTR 1653 WEST CONGRESS PARKWAY CHICAGO, IL 60612 Studies of spasticity in brain-injured patients
P01NS-15638-13 (SRC) WOLF, ALFRED P ASSOC UNIVERSITIES, INC BROOKHAVEN NATIONAL LABORATORY UPTON, NY 11973 Positron emitters and PETT in metabolism and neurology
P01NS-15638-13 0001 (SRC) FOWLER, JOANNA S Positron emitters and PETT in metabolism and neurology Radionuclides and labeled tracers
P01NS-15638-13 0002 (SRC) SIMON, ERIC J Positron emitters and PETT in metabolism and neurology Study of opiate receptors in brain
P01NS-15638-13 0010 (SRC) HIESIGER, EMILE M Positron emitters and PETT in metabolism and neurology PETT studies in cerebral malignancy
P01NS-15638-13 0011 (SRC) VOLKOW, NORA D Positron emitters and PETT in metabolism and neurology Substance abuse
P01NS-15638-13 0012 (SRC) BRODIE, JONATHAN D Positron emitters and PETT in metabolism and neurology Schizophrenia
P01NS-15638-13 0013 (SRC) DELEON, MONY J Positron emitters and PETT in metabolism and neurology Energy metabolism in Alzheimer's disease
P01NS-15638-13 9001 (SRC) WOLF, ALFRED P Positron emitters and PETT in metabolism and neurology Core facilities--Brookhaven national laboratory
P01NS-15638-13 9002 (SRC) BRODIE, JONATHAN D Positron emitters and PETT in metabolism and neurology Core facilities--New York university
P01NS-15638-13 9003 (SRC) HENN, FRITZ A Positron emitters and PETT in metabolism and neurology Core facilities--Stoney brook
P01NS-15654-13 (SRC) PHELPS, MICHAEL E UNIVERSITY OF CALIFORNIA LAB OF NUCLEAR MEDICINE LOS ANGELES, CA 90024 Neuroscience research with PET
P01NS-15654-13 0004 (SRC) PHELPS, MICHAEL E Neuroscience research with PET Huntington's disease--Model inherited neurodegenerative process
P01NS-15654-13 0006 (SRC) MAZZIOTTA, JOHN C Neuroscience research with PET Three dimensional structure-function relationships of the human brain
P01NS-15654-13 0007 (SRC) CHUGANI, HARRY T Neuroscience research with PET Metabolic maturation of the brain
P01NS-15654-13 0008 (SRC) CHUGANI, DIANE Neuroscience research with PET Dopamine-mediated receptor endocytosis--Brain D-2 receptors
P01NS-15654-13 0009 (SRC) BARRIO, JORGE R Neuroscience research with PET Pre- and postsynaptic dopaminergic probes
P01NS-15654-13 0010 (SRC) ACKERMAN, ROBERT A Neuroscience research with PET Axoplasmic transport of glucose
P01NS-15654-13 9001 (SRC) PHELPS, MICHAEL E Neuroscience research with PET Core-Nuclear medicine
P50NS-15655-12 (SRC) KUHL, DAVID E DEPT. OF INTERNAL MEDICINE NUCLEAR MED, 1500 E MED CTR DR ANN ARBOR, MI 48109 PET study of biochemistry and metabolism of the CNS
P50NS-15655-12 0003 (SRC) GILMAN, SID PET study of biochemistry and metabolism of the CNS PET studies in disorders of motor function
P50NS-15655-12 0005 (SRC) YOUNG, ANNE B PET study of biochemistry and metabolism of the CNS Pet-scan investigation of Huntington's disease
P50NS-15655-12 0008 (SRC) JUNCK, LARRY PET study of biochemistry and metabolism of the CNS PET studies of malignant brain tumors
P50NS-15655-12 0009 (SRC) KILBOURN, MICHAEL R PET study of biochemistry and metabolism of the CNS New radiotracers for neurological PET
P50NS-15655-12 0010 (SRC) AGRANOFF, BERNARD PET study of biochemistry and metabolism of the CNS Amino acid uptake
P50NS-15655-12 9002 (SRC) KILBOURN, MICHAEL R PET study of biochemistry and metabolism of the CNS Core--Cyclotron
P50NS-15655-12 9005 (SRC) KILBOURN, MICHAEL A. PET study of biochemistry and metabolism of the CNS Core--Chemistry
P50NS-15655-12 9006 (SRC) HUTCHINS, GARY D. PET study of biochemistry and metabolism of the CNS Core--Tomography and quantitation
P50NS-15655-12 9007 (SRC) KOEPPE, ROBERT E. PET study of biochemistry and metabolism of the CNS Core--Data analysis
P50NS-15655-12 0011 (SRC) FREY, KIRK A PET study of biochemistry and metabolism of the CNS PET markers for muscarinic cholinergic synapses
P50NS-15655-12 0012 (SRC) SACKELLARES, J CHRIS PET study of biochemistry and metabolism of the CNS PET studies in partial epilepsy
R01NS-15662-12 (NEUC) SHIN, MOON L UNIVERSITY OF MARYLAND 10 S PINE STREET BALTIMORE, MD 21201 Mechanism of demyelination in multiple sclerosis
R01NS-15669-11 (NEUB) RIBAK, CHARLES E UNIV OF CALIFORNIA, IRVINE COLLEGE OF MEDICINE IRVINE, CA 92717 Chemical neuroanatomy of experimental models of epilepsy
R01NS-15692-13 (BNP) BORCHARDT, RONALD T THE UNIVERSITY OF KANSAS 3006 MALOTT HALL LAWRENCE, KS 66045 Mechanism of action of neurocytotoxins
R01NS-15703-13 (PB) SILVERMAN, RICHARD B NORTHWESTERN UNIVERSITY 2145 SHERIDAN RD EVANSTON, IL 60208-3113 New inactivators of GABA transaminase
R01NS-15722-14 (NLS) SCHLAEPFER, WILLIAM W UNIVERSITY OF PENNSYLVANIA 36TH & HAMILTON WALK PHILADELPHIA, PA 19104-6079 Neurofilaments--Degradation turnover and role in disease
R01NS-15747-12 (PC) HAJRA, AMIYA K THE UNIVERSITY OF MICHIGAN 1103 E HURON ANN ARBOR, MI 48109 Glycerolipid metabolism in microbodies
R01NS-15751-12 (PHY) CATTERALL, WILLIAM A UNIVERSITY OF WASHINGTON DEPT OF PHARMACOLOGY SJ-30 SEATTLE, WA 98195 Voltage-sensitive sodium channels in brain
R01NS-15841-13 (BMT) WIGHTMAN, R MARK UNIVERSITY OF NORTH CAROLINA G B 6290, VENABLE HALL CHAPEL HILL, NC 27599-3290 Electroanalysis of modulated monoamine release
R01NS-15879-12 (PHY) LEVINSON, SIMON R UNIV OF COLORADO SCH OF MED 4200 EAST NINTH AVE DENVER, CO 80262 Mechanisms of the voltage-dependent sodium channel
R01NS-15888-12 (CMS) LA MOTTE, ROBERT H YALE UNIV SCHOOL OF MEDICINE 333 CEDAR STREET NEW HAVEN, CT 06510 Neurophysiology of cutaneous perception of texture
R01NS-15911-23 (NLS) MOORE, KENNETH E DEPT. OF PHARM. AND TOXICOLOGY B440 LIFE SCIENCES BUILDING EAST LANSING, MI 48824 Catecholamines as central nervous transmitters
R01NS-15913-11 (NEUB) MUNSON, JOHN B UNIV FLORIDA/COLL OF MED DEPT OF NEUROSCIENCE GAINSVILLE, FL 32610 Recovery of spinal cord function following injury
R01NS-15918-12 (NLS) SPITZER, NICHOLAS C CTR FOR MOLEC GENETICS, B-022 UNIV OF CALIFORNIA, SAN DIEGO LA JOLLA, CA 92093-0322 The development of neurons
R01NS-15927-12 (NEUC) KELLY, REGIS B UNIVERSITY OF CALIFORNIA HORMONE RESEARCH INSTITUTE SAN FRANCISCO, CALIF 94143 Antibodies to synaptic vesicles
R01NS-15963-11 (NEUC) JAN, LILY K UNIV OF CALIF, SAN FRANCISCO PARNASSUS AVENUE SAN FRANCISCO, CA 94143 Genetic studies of the synapse
P01NS-16033-11 (NSPB) HALL, ZACH W UNIV OF CALIFORNIA PARNASSUS AVENUE SAN FRANCISCO, CA 94143 Synaptic excitation of retinal ganglion cells
P01NS-16033-11 0002 (NSPB) HALL, ZACH W Synaptic excitation of retinal ganglion cells Basal lamina at the neuromuscular junction
P01NS-16033-11 0005 (NSPB) KELLY, REGIS B Synaptic excitation of retinal ganglion cells Antibodies to synaptic vesicles
P01NS-16033-11 0007 (NSPB) BASBAUM, ALLAN I Synaptic excitation of retinal ganglion cells Acth, B endorphin and enkephalin circuitry
P01NS-16033-11 0008 (NSPB) JAN, LILY K Synaptic excitation of retinal ganglion cells Peptidergic innervation in developing autonomic

ganglia
P01NS-16033-11 0010 (NSPB) MAYERI, EARL Synaptic excitation of retinal ganglion cells Localization of neuropeptides and receptors in Aplysia
P01NS-16033-11 0011 (NSPB) REICHARDT, LOUIS F Synaptic excitation of retinal ganglion cells Development of synaptic antigens in cholinergic neurons
P01NS-16033-11 9001 (NSPB) HALL, ZACH W Synaptic excitation of retinal ganglion cells Electron microscopy core
R01NS-16036-14 (NEUC) GREENE, LLOYD A COLUMBIA UNIVERSITY 630 WEST 168TH STREET NEW YORK, N Y 10032 Neurochemical studies on cultured neurons
R01NS-16058-11 (NEUB) BURROWS, MALCOLM UNIVERSITY OF CAMBRIDGE DOWNING STREET CAMBRIDGE, ENGLAND CB2 3EJ Integrative function of local interneurones
R01NS-16064-12 (NLS) NADLER, J VICTOR DUKE UNIV MED CTR BOX 3813 DURHAM, N C 27710 Excitatory amino acid transmitters in CNS
R01NS-16067-10 (NEUB) SCOTT, SHERYL A STATE UNIVERSITY OF NEW YORK STONY BROOK, NY 11794 Development of sensory innervation patterns
R01NS-16102-11 (NEUA) SCHWARCZ, ROBERT MARYLAND PSYCHIATRIC RES CTR P O BOX 21247 BALTIMORE, MD 21228 Quinolinic acid and seizure disorders
R01NS-16106-13 (NLS) BLAUSTEIN, MORDECAI P UNIVERSITY OF MARYLAND 655 WEST BALTIMORE ST BALTIMORE, MD 21201 Calcium homeostasis in neurons and glia
R01NS-16115-10A2 (NEUB) MAXWELL, GERALD D UNIV OF CONNECTICUT HLTH CNTR 263 FARMINGTON AVE FARMINGTON, CT 06030 Developmental influences on neural crest cells
R01NS-16181-12 (NLS) LEDEEN, ROBERT W NMDNJ-NEW JERSEY MED SCH 185 SOUTH ORANGE AVENUE NEWARK, N J 07103-2714 Study of myelin enzymes and receptors and their relation to the axon
R01NS-16204-13 (GEN) HALL, LINDA M SUNY AT BUFFALO 321 HOCHSTETTER HALL BUFFALO, NEW YORK 14260 Genetic analysis of sodium channels
R01NS-16264-12 (NEUB) RUSTIONI, ALDO UNIV OF N C AT CHAPEL HILL TAYLOR HALL CB# 7090 CHAPEL HILL, N C 27599 Descending control of somatosensory input
R01NS-16285-11 (PHY) BLAUSTEIN, MORDECAI MD UNIV OF MARYLAND SCH OF MED 660 WEST REDWOOD STREET BALTIMORE, MD 21201 Biochemistry of excitable membranes
R01NS-16295-11 (PHY) ROSS, WILLIAM N NEW YORK MEDICAL COLLEGE VALHALLA, NY 10595 Optical analysis of the regional properties of neurons
R01NS-16304-11A1 (NEUB) MOORE, ROBERT Y WESTERN PSYCHIATRIC INSTITUTE 3811 O'HARA STREET PITTSBURGH, PA 15213 Central mechanisms of circadian rhythm regulation
P50NS-16308-12A1 (SRC) GUMNIT, ROBERT J EPILEPSY CLINICAL RESEARCH PRO 5775 WAYZATA BLVD MINNEAPOLIS, MN 55416 Epilepsy clinical research program
P50NS-16308-12A1 0008 (SRC) KURLAND, LEONARD T Epilepsy clinical research program Epidemiology of epilepsy
P50NS-16308-12A1 0009 (SRC) ANDERSON, V ELVING Epilepsy clinical research program Genetic epidemiology of epilepsy
P50NS-16308-12A1 0014 (SRC) LEPPIK, ILO E Epilepsy clinical research program Genetics of antiepileptic drug metabolism and the sudden death syndrome
P50NS-16308-12A1 0017 (SRC) ORR, HARRY T Epilepsy clinical research program Gene mapping in epilepsy
P50NS-16308-12A1 9001 (SRC) GUMMIT, ROBERT J Epilepsy clinical research program Core--Research core
P01NS-16332-09A2 (SRC) PRICE, THOMAS R UNIV OF MARYLAND HOSPITAL 22 S GREENE STREET BALTIMORE, MD 21201 Clinical stroke research center
P01NS-16332-09A2 0001 (SRC) KITTNER, STEVEN J Clinical stroke research center Stroke prevention in young women
P01NS-16332-09A2 0002 (SRC) SLONE, MICHAEL A Clinical stroke research center Case control study of drug use/abuse in stroke
P01NS-16332-09A2 0003 (SRC) PRICE, THOMAS R Clinical stroke research center Prediction of ischemic stroke progression
P01NS-16333-11S1 (NSPA) EDGERTON, V REGGIE UNIVERSITY OF CALIFORNIA 405 HILGARD AVE LOS ANGELES, CA 90024-1406 Neuromuscular plasticity--Recovery after spinalization
P01NS-16333-11S1 0003 (NSPA) ROY, ROLAND R Neuromuscular plasticity--Recovery after spinalization Plasticity of muscular system in response to spinalization and activity
P01NS-16333-11S1 0008 (NSPA) GREGOR, ROBERT J Neuromuscular plasticity--Recovery after spinalization Neural control of normal and spinal cats
P01NS-16333-11S1 0009 (NSPA) EDGERTON, V REGGIE Neuromuscular plasticity--Recovery after spinalization Motorneuron-muscle fiber connectivity and interdependence
P01NS-16333-11S1 9001 (NSPA) EDGERTON, V REGGIE Neuromuscular plasticity--Recovery after spinalization Core--Neuromuscular plasticity
R01NS-16349-12 (NEUB) VARON, SILVIO S DEPARTMENT OF BIOLOGY UNIV OF CALIF, SAN DIEGO LA JOLLA, CALIF 92093 Neuronotrophic factors in development and regeneration
P01NS-16367-12 (NSPB) GUSELLA, JAMES F MASSACHUSETTS GENERAL HOSPITAL FRUIT STREET BOSTON, MA 02114 Huntington's disease center without walls
P01NS-16367-12 0005 (NSPB) BEAL, M FLINT Huntington's disease center without walls Neurochemistry of Huntington's disease
P01NS-16367-12 0007 (NSPB) DIFIGLIA, MARIAN Huntington's disease center without walls Mechanisms of degeneration and regeneration in Huntington's disease
P01NS-16367-12 0012 (NSPB) GUSELLA, JAMES F Huntington's disease center without walls Isolation and characterization of the Huntington disease gene
P01NS-16367-12 0014 (NSPB) MYERS, RICHARD Huntington's disease center without walls Genetic and neurobiological studies of Huntington disease
P01NS-16367-12 0016 (NSPB) ISACSON, OLE Huntington's disease center without walls Primate Model of Huntington Disease
P01NS-16367-12 9002 (NSPB) BIRD, EDWARD Huntington's disease center without walls Core--Neuropathology
P01NS-16375-11 (SRC) FOLSTEIN, SUSAN E JOHNS HOPKINS UNIVERSITY 600 NORTH WOLFE STREET BALTIMORE, MD 21205 Research program without walls for Huntingtons disease
P01NS-16375-11 0003 (SRC) ZEE, DAVID S Research program without walls for Huntingtons disease Ocular motor function in Huntington's disease
P01NS-16375-11 0009 (SRC) COYLE, JOSEPH T Research program without walls for Huntingtons disease Mechanisms of selective neuronal vulnerability
P01NS-16375-11 0012 (SRC) BRANDT, JASON Research program without walls for Huntingtons disease Cognitive & functional correlates of fronto-striatal degeneration in HD
P01NS-16375-11 0013 (SRC) ROSS, CHRISTOPHER Research program without walls for Huntingtons disease Significance of extrastriatal pathology in HD
P01NS-16375-11 0014 (SRC) HURKO, OREST Research program without walls for Huntingtons disease Mitochondrial function in HD
P01NS-16375-11 9001 (SRC) FOLSTEIN, SUSAN E Research program without walls for Huntingtons disease Clinical core
P01NS-16375-11 9002 (SRC) HEDREEN, JOHN Research program without walls for Huntingtons disease Core--Neuropathology
P01NS-16375-11 9003 (SRC) FOLSTEIN, SUSAN E Research program without walls for Huntingtons disease Stastical core
R01NS-16389-11 (NEUA) HAWKINS, RICHARD A UHS/CHICAGO MEDICAL SCHOOL 3333 GREEN BAY ROAD NORTH CHICAGO, IL 60064 Regional brain metabolism in hepatic coma
R01NS-16433-12 (CMS) LIGHT, ALAN R DEPARTMENT OF PHYSIOLOGY AT CHAPEL HILL CHAPEL HILL, NC 27599-7545 Descending modulation of spinal substantia gelatinosa
R01NS-16446-11 (NEUA) KAAS, JON H VANDERBILT UNIVERSITY DEPARTMENT OF PSYCHOLOGY NASHVILLE, TENN 37240 Functional organization of the somatosensory system
R01NS-16447-10 (NLS) MC CLUER, ROBERT H EUNICE KENNEDY SHRIVER CENTER 200 TRAPELO ROAD WALTHAM, MA 02254 Micro-HPLC and LC/MS methods for neural systems
R01NS-16483-10 (NLS) DUNLAP, KATHLEEN L TUFTS UNIVERSITY 136 HARRISON AVE BOSTON, MASS 02111 Presynaptic receptors on embryonic sensory neurons
R01NS-16487-11 (NEUB) CUNNINGHAM, TIMOTHY J MEDICAL COLL OF PENNSYLVANIA 3200 HENRY AVENUE PHILADELPHIA, PA 19129 Survival and death of neurons
R01NS-16490-11 (NEUB) MAYERI, EARL UNIVERSITY OF CALIFORNIA PARNASSUS AVENUE SAN FRANCISCO, CA 94143 Roles of peptides in neural function
R01NS-16524-11 (PHY) SPRAY, DAVID C ALBERT EINSTEIN COLLEGE OF MED 1300 MORRIS PARK AVE BRONX, N Y 10461 Biophysics of gap junction channels
R01NS-16541-12 (NLS) YAKSH, TONY L UNIV. OF CALIFORNIA, SAN DIEGO MAIL CODE T-001 LA JOLLA, CA 92093 Pain evoked release of amines and enkephalins in CNS
R01NS-16556-12 (NEUB) MURRAY, MARION MED COLL OF PENNSYLVANIA 3200 HENRY AVENUE PHILADELPHIA, PA 19129 Generation and regeneration of axons
R01NS-16577-12 (NLS) ROSENBERRY, TERRONE L CASE WESTERN RESERVE UNIV 2119 ABINGTON ROAD CLEVELAND, OHIO 44106 Structural distinctions among acetylcholinesterases
R01NS-16605-10 (NLS) MARTIN, ARNOLD R COLLEGE OF PHARMACY UNIVERSITY OF ARIZONA TUCSON, AZ 75721 Characterization of central serotonergic receptors
R01NS-16629-10 (NEUB) GOLDBERGER, MICHAEL E DEPT OF ANATOMY 3300 HENRY AVENUE PHILADELPHIA, PA 19129 Axonal sprouting and functional recovery in the CNS
R01NS-16648-12 (EDC) PAULS, DAVID L YALE UNIVERSITY 333 CEDAR STREET NEW HAVEN, CT 06510 Genetics of Tourette and obsessive compulsive disorder
K06NS-16677-29 (NCR) HEYMAN, ALBERT DUKE UNIV MEDICAL CENTER BOX 3203 DURHAM, N C 27710 Circulatory changes in cerebrovascular disease
R01NS-16683-10 (NEUA) DUDEK, FRANCIS E U. C. L. A. NPI 58-258 760 WESTWOOD PLAZA LOS ANGELES, CA 90024-1759 Local interactions between hippocampal neurons
R01NS-16686-13 (NEUA) SWANSON, LARRY W UNIV OF SOUTHERN CALIFORNIA UNIVERSITY PARK CAMPUS LOS ANGELES, CA 90089-2520 Connections of the limbic system and hypothalumus
R01NS-16694-09 (RAD) KIMLER, BRUCE F UNIVERSITY OF KANSAS MED CTR 39TH AND RAINBOW BLVD KANSAS CITY, KS 66103-8410 Toxicity of x-irradiation to developing neurons
R01NS-16721-09 (NEUB) FINCH, DAVID M UNIVERSITY OF CALIFORNIA 405 HILGARD AVE LOS ANGELES, CA 90024-1406 Synaptic organization of retrohippocampal pathways
R01NS-16792-10 (NEUB) CRILL, WAYNE E UNIVERSITY OF WASHINGTON PHYSIOL & BIOPHYSICS SJ-40 SEATTLE, WASH 98195 Membrane properties of neocortical neurons
R01NS-16824-11 (PHY) SALZBERG, BRIAN M DEPT OF PHYSIOLOGY A-201 RICHARDS BUILDING PHILADELPHIA, PA 19104-6085 Multiple site optical recording of membrane potential
R01NS-16832-11 (HAR) WINER, JEFFERY A UNIVERSITY OF CALIFORNIA DIVISION OF NEUROBIOLOGY BERKELEY, CALIF 94720 Structure of primary auditory cortex
R01NS-16841-11 (NEUB) PANDYA, DEEPAK N E N R / VA MEDICAL CENTER 200 SPRINGS ROAD BEDFORD, MA 01730 Organization of the cerebral cortex in primates
R01NS-16871-11 (NEUC) PLAITAKIS, ANDREAS MOUNT SINAI SCHOOL OF MEDICINE FIFTH AVE & 100TH ST NEW YORK, NY 10029 Glutamic dehydrogenase in neurologic disorders
R01NS-16886-11 (PTHA) JONES, MARGARET Z MICHIGAN STATE UNIVERSITY 622 EAST FEE HALL EAST LANSING, MICH 48824 Pathogenesis of oligosaccharide disorder
R01NS-16942-11 (NEUB) HATTON, GLENN I MICHIGAN STATE UNIV EAST LANSING, MI 48824-1117 Neural control of magnocellular neuroendocrine

PROJECT NO., ORGANIZATIONAL UNIT., INVESTIGATOR, ADDRESS, TITLE

cells
R01NS-16945-11 (NEUB) LEES, MARJORIE B EUNICE KENNEDY SHRIVER CENTER 200 TRAPELO ROAD WALTHAM, MA 02254 Brain white matter proteolipid--Immunological studies
R01NS-16951-11 (NEUB) MASON, CAROL A COLUMBIA UNIV COLL PHYS & SURG 630 W 168 ST/DEPT PATHOLOGY NEW YORK, N Y 10032 Axon-target interactions in developing cerebellum
R01NS-16980-12 (NEUB) AMARAL, DAVID G SALK INST/BIOLOGICAL STUDIES PO BOX 85800 SAN DIEGO, CA 92138 Studies of neuronal specificity in the hippocampus
R01NS-16996-12 (NEUB) MENDELL, LORNE M S U N Y AT STONY BROOK STONY BROOK, NY 11794-5230 Mechanisms of plasticity in neuronal connections
P50NS-16998-11 (NSPA) FIELDS, BERNARD N HARVARD MEDICAL SCHOOL 200 LONGWOOD AVENUE BOSTON, MA 02115 Molecular basis of viral injury to nervous system
P50NS-16998-11 0001 (NSPA) FIELDS, BERNARD N Molecular basis of viral injury to nervous system Genetics of neurovirulence
P50NS-16998-11 0005 (NSPA) CEPLO, CONSTANCE Molecular basis of viral injury to nervous system Expression of reovirus proteins in retrovirus vectors
P50NS-16998-11 0006 (NSPA) GREENE, MARK Molecular basis of viral injury to nervous system Growth-related functions of the reovirus neuronal receptor
P50NS-16998-11 9001 (NSPA) DICHTER, MARC Molecular basis of viral injury to nervous system Core tissue culture facility
R01NS-17095-09A1 (NEUA) FOX, STEVEN E STATE UNIVERSITY OF NEW YORK 450 CLARKSON AVE, BOX 31 BROOKLYN, NY 11203 Synaptic sources of hippocampal theta rhythm
P01NS-17111-11 (NSPB) OJEMANN, GEORGE A UNIVERSITY OF WASHINGTON DEPT OF SURG/RI-20 SEATTLE, WA 98195 Center for clinical research in epilepsy
P01NS-17111-11 0009 (NSPB) LEVY, RENE H Center for clinical research in epilepsy Determinants of the formation of toxic metabolites of valproic acid
P01NS-17111-11 0011 (NSPB) TEMKIN, NANCY R Center for clinical research in epilepsy Statistical methods for antiepileptic drug studies
P01NS-17111-11 0013 (NSPB) WILENSKY, ALAN Center for clinical research in epilepsy Statistical methods in evaluation of new antiepileptic drugs
P01NS-17111-11 0014 (NSPB) FRIEL, PATRICK Center for clinical research in epilepsy Anticonvulsant concentration-response relationships during surgery
P01NS-17111-11 0015 (NSPB) WILKUS, ROBERT Center for clinical research in epilepsy Characteristics and correlates of psychogenic seizures
P01NS-17111-11 0016 (NSPB) FRASER, ROBERT Center for clinical research in epilepsy Intensive intervention in epilepsy rehabilitation
P01NS-17111-11 9002 (NSPB) TEMKIN, NANCY R Center for clinical research in epilepsy Core--Biostatistics unit
P01NS-17111-11 9003 (NSPB) KALK, DOUGLAS F Center for clinical research in epilepsy Core--Computer data processing laboratory
R01NS-17112-11 (NEUA) BANKER, GARY A UNIVERSITY OF VIRGINIA BOX 230 HEALTH SCIENCES CENTER CHARLOTTESVILLE, VA 22908 The development of hippocampal neurons in culture
R01NS-17117-10 (NEUA) SNEAD, ORLANDO C, III CHILDREN'S HOSPITAL 4650 SUNSET BOULEVARD, #82 LOS ANGELES, CA 90027 Gamma hydroxybutyric acid - mechanism of action
R01NS-17125-10 (NLS) GOLDMAN, JAMES E COLUMBIA UNIVERSITY 630 WEST 168TH STREET NEW YORK, N Y 10032 Cellular and biochemical studies of CNS glia
R01NS-17131-10 (NEUB) CRUTCHER, KEITH A UNIVERSITY OF CINCINNATI 231 BETHESDA AVENUE CINCINNATI, OH 45267-0515 Axonal growth in the mature CNS
R01NS-17139-11 (PBC) CULP, LLOYD A DEPT MOLEC BIOLOGY/MICROBIOLOG CLEVELAND, OH 44106 Adhesion mechanisms of neural tumor cells
R01NS-17269-10 (NLS) ASWAD, DANA W DEPARTMENT OF PSYCHOBIOLOGY IRVINE, CALIF 92717 Protein carboxyl methylation in brain
R01NS-17282-11 (NLS) BLOCH, ROBERT J UNIVERSITY OF MARYLAND 660 W REDWOOD ST BALTIMORE, MD 21201 Macromolecules involved in synapse formation
R01NS-17323-10 (NEUB) HARRIS-WARRICK, RONALD M NEUROBIOLOGY AND BEHAVIOR 123 DAY HALL ITHACA, N Y 14853 Neurotransmitters, neuromodulators, and motor systems
R01NS-17360-11 (NLS) NICKLAS, WILLIAM J UNIV OF MED & DENTISTRY OF N J 675 HOES LANE PISCATAWAY, N J 08854-5635 Glutamate, excitotoxins and neuronal-glial interactions
R01NS-17366-11 (CMS) ARAM, DOROTHY M RAINBOW BABIES & CHILDR'S HOSP 2101 ADELBERT ROAD CLEVELAND, OHIO 44106 Linguistic sequelae of unilateral lesions
R01NS-17392-11 (NLS) WILK, SHERWIN MT SINAI SCH OF MED ONE GUSTAVE L LEVY PLACE NEW YORK, N Y 10029 Brain endopeptidases and neuropeptide metabolism
R01NS-17411-10 (BPO) RITZMANN, ROY E CASE WESTERN RESERVE UNIVERSIT 10900 EUCLID AVE CLEVELAND, OH 44106-7080 Control of patterned motor activity
R01NS-17413-11 (NEUB) GEORGOPOULOS, APOSTOLOS P VA MEDCAL CENTER ONE VETERANS DRIVE MINNESPOLIS, MN 55417 Neurophysiology of cognitive processes in motor behavior
R01NS-17423-10 (NEUC) ROSZMAN, THOMAS L UNIVERSITY OF KENTUCKY 800 ROSE STREET LEXINGTON, KY 40536-0084 Neuroimmunomodulation
R01NS-17468-09 (NEUB) ROSENSTEIN, JEFFREY M SCHOOL OF MEDICINE 2300 EYE STREET, N. W. Neural transplant: interactions with developing brain
R01NS-17479-08 (REB) SAR, MADHABANANDA UNIVERSITY OF NORTH CAROLINA CB#7090 CHAPEL HILL, NC 27599-7090 Hormone and neurotransmitter relationships in the brain
P01NS-17489-10 (NSPB) PETERSON, BARRY W DEPT. OF PHYSIOLOGY 303 E CHICAGO AVENUE CHICAGO, IL 60611 Mechanisms for neural control
P01NS-17489-10 0004 (NSPB) PETERSON, BARRY W Mechanisms for neural control Neural control of head movement

PROJECT NO., ORGANIZATIONAL UNIT., INVESTIGATOR, ADDRESS, TITLE

P01NS-17489-10 0005 (NSPB) BAKER, JAMES F Mechanisms for neural control Role of vestibulocerebellum in vestibulo-ocular reflex plasticity
P01NS-17489-10 0009 (NSPB) MCCRIMMON, DONALD Mechanisms for neural control Pharmacology of the afferent control of respiratory motor output
P01NS-17489-10 0010 (NSPB) MCKENNA, KEVIN E Mechanisms for neural control Brainstem control of spinal sexual reflexes
P01NS-17489-10 0011 (NSPB) RYMER, W ZEV Mechanisms for neural control Neural substrates for goal directed behavior in spinalized frog
P01NS-17489-10 0012 (NSPB) SLATER, N TRAVERSE Mechanisms for neural control Synaptic plasticity in the cerebellum
P01NS-17489-10 0013 (NSPB) HOCKBERGER, PHILIP Mechanisms for neural control Analysis of Purkinje cell pacemaker activity in vitro
P01NS-17489-10 0014 (NSPB) HOUK, JAMES C Mechanisms for neural control Motor programs in red nucleus and cerebellum
P01NS-17489-10 9001 (NSPB) PETERSON, BARRY W Mechanisms for neural control Core--Computer
P01NS-17489-10 9002 (NSPB) BAKER, JAMES F Mechanisms for neural control Core--Instrumentation
P01NS-17489-10 9003 (NSPB) MC KENNA, KEVIN Mechanisms for neural control Core--Histology
P01NS-17493-08 (SRC) COULL, BRUCE M OREG HLTH SCIS UNIVERSITY 3181 S W SAM JACKSON PK ROAD PORTLAND, OR 97201 Mechanism of injury and repair in ischemic stroke
P01NS-17493-08 0009 (SRC) COULL, BRUCE M Mechanism of injury and repair in ischemic stroke Longitudinal study of hyperviscosity in recurrent stroke
P01NS-17493-08 0010 (SRC) MCCALL, ANTHONY L Mechanism of injury and repair in ischemic stroke Dexamethasone and stroke--Effects on brain transport and metabolism
P01NS-17493-08 0011 (SRC) ECKENSTEIN, FELIX Mechanism of injury and repair in ischemic stroke The role of fibroblast growth factors in stroke
P01NS-17493-08 0012 (SRC) SEIL, FREDRICK Mechanism of injury and repair in ischemic stroke Role of neuronal activity in reorganization after injury
P01NS-17493-08 9001 (SRC) DOWNES, HALL Mechanism of injury and repair in ischemic stroke Core--Animal Core
R01NS-17510-10 (PHY) GILLY, WILLIAM F STANFORD UNIVERSITY PACIFIC GROVE, CALIF 93950 Electrical properties of triads/diads in striated muscle
R01NS-17574-10 (NLS) CHIAPPINELLI, VINCENT A ST LOUIS UNIVERSITY 1402 SOUTH GRAND BLVD ST LOUIS, MO 63104 Functional properties of neuronal nicotinic receptors
R01NS-17577-10 (NEUB) DAVIDOFF, ROBERT A UNIVERSITY OF MIAMI SCH OF MED P.O. BOX 16960 MIAMI, FL 33101 Modulation of motoneuron output in the spinal cord
R01NS-17620-10 (PHY) BAYLOR, STEPHEN M UNIV OF PENNSYLVANIA MED CENTE PHILADELPHIA, PA 19104-6085 Excitation-contraction coupling in striated muscle
R01NS-17660-11 (NLS) KENNEDY, MARY B CALIFORNIA INST OF TECHNOLOGY 1201 E CALIFORNIA BLVD PASADENA, CA 91125 Brain calcium and calmodulin-dependent protein kinase
R01NS-17661-10 (NEUA) WAINER, BRUCE H THE UNIVERSITY OF CHICAGO 947 EAST 58TH STREET CHICAGO, IL 60637 Central cholinergic neurons--Synaptic organization
R01NS-17662-10 (ORTH) ZAJAC, FELIX E, III STANFORD UNIVERSITY MECHANICAL ENGR DEPT STANFORD, CA 94305-4125 Intermuscular coordination of movement
R01NS-17678-11 (NEUB) ALEXANDER, GARRETT E EMORY UNIVERSITY WMB, 6TH FLOOR, PO DRAWER V ATLANTA, GA 30322 Motor and complex functions of basal ganglia and cortex
R01NS-17681-09 (NLS) BLACK, MARK M TEMPLE UNIV SCHOOL OF MEDICINE 3420 N BROAD ST, DEPT/ANATOMY PHILADELPHIA, PA 19140 Transformation of the cytoskeleton during neurite growth
R01NS-17702-08 (NEUB) SEYBOLD, VIRGINIA S UNIVERSITY OF MINNESOTA 321 CHURCH ST, SE MINNEAPOLIS, MINN 55455 Peptidergic neurons in the spinal cord
R01NS-17708-10 (NLS) DE BLAS, ANGEL L UNIVERSITY OF MISSOURI 5100 ROCKHILL ROAD KANSAS CITY, MO 64110-2499 Monoclonal antibodies to GABA-benzodiazepine receptors
R01NS-17731-11 (NLS) WOOD, JOHN G EMORY UNIV SCHOOL OF MEDICINE ATLANTA, GA 30322 Location and function of carbohydrates in the brain
R01NS-17742-09 (TOX) DASGUPTA, BIBHUTI R UNIV OF WISCONSIN-MADISON 1925 WILLOW DR MADISON, WI 53706 Botulinum neurotoxin--Structure and structure-function
R01NS-17743-11 (NEUB) HEIMER, LENNART UNIV OF VIRGINIA HLTH SCI CTR BOX 430 CHARLOTTESVILLE, VA 22908 Basal forebrain organization
P50NS-17750-10 (SRC) KURLAND, LEONARD T MAYO FOUNDATION 200 FIRST STREET, S W ROCHESTER, MINN 55905 Rochester neuroepidemiology program project
P50NS-17750-10 0001 (SRC) KURLAND, LEONARD T Rochester neuroepidemiology program project Mental retardation--Descriptive and case-control study
P50NS-17750-10 0002 (SRC) LUCAS, ALEXANDER R Rochester neuroepidemiology program project Anorexia nervosa--Descriptive, follow-up and case-control studies
P50NS-17750-10 0018 (SRC) LAWS, EDWARD R Rochester neuroepidemiology program project Brain tumors
P50NS-17750-10 0023 (SRC) LITCHY, WILLIAM J Rochester neuroepidemiology program project Epidemiology of cervical radiculopathy
P50NS-17750-10 9001 (SRC) KURLAND, LEONARD T Rochester neuroepidemiology program project Core unit
R01NS-17760-11 (NEUA) HOFF, JULIAN T DEPARTMENT OF SURGERY UNIV OF MICHIGAN HOSPITALS ANN ARBOR, MICH 48109-0338 Intracranial pressure gradients and ischemic edema
P01NS-17763-10 (NSPB) WOOLSEY, THOMAS A WASH. UNIV./SCHOOL OF MED. 660 SOUTH EUCLID AVENUE ST LOUIS, MO 63110 Studies of neuronal structure as related to function
P01NS-17763-10 0003 (NSPB) MILLER, ROBERT F Studies of neuronal

structure as related to function Functional anatomy of retinal neurons

P01NS-17763-10 0004 (NSPB) WOOLSEY, THOMAS A Studies of neuronal structure as related to function Axon target cell interactions in the developing brain

P01NS-17763-10 0008 (NSPB) WOOLSEY, THOMAS A Studies of neuronal structure as related to function Modular functional organization of barrel cortex

P01NS-17763-10 0009 (NSPB) O'LEARY, DENNIS D M Studies of neuronal structure as related to function Transplant studies of the somatosensory cortex

P01NS-17763-10 0011 (NSPB) HIGHSTEIN, STEPHEN M Studies of neuronal structure as related to function Morphology of pre-ocular and vestibular cells

P01NS-17763-10 0012 (NSPB) HUNT, CARLTON C Studies of neuronal structure as related to function Sensory and motor innervation of muscles

P01NS-17763-10 0013 (NSPB) SNIDER, WILLIAM Studies of neuronal structure as related to function Tropic influences of neuronal morphometry

P01NS-17763-10 9002 (NSPB) WOOLSEY, THOMAS A Studies of neuronal structure as related to function Core--Computer systems for processing neuroanatomical data

P01NS-17771-10 (SRC) MC NAMARA, JAMES O VA HOSPITAL 508 FULTON STREET DURHAM, NC 27705 Limbic epilepsy: a neurobiologic approach

P01NS-17771-10 0001 (SRC) MC NAMARA, JAMES O Limbic epilepsy: a neurobiologic approach NMDA receptors and intracellular signalling in kindling model

P01NS-17771-10 0002 (SRC) SOMJEN, GEORGE G Limbic epilepsy: a neurobiologic approach Microphysiology of hippocampal seizures

P01NS-17771-10 0003 (SRC) DINGLEDINE, RAYMOND J Limbic epilepsy: a neurobiologic approach Regulation of excitability in hippocampal neurons

P01NS-17771-10 0004 (SRC) WILSON, WILKIE A Limbic epilepsy: a neurobiologic approach In vitro epileptogenesis and seizure expression

P01NS-17771-10 0005 (SRC) NADLER, J VICTOR Limbic epilepsy: a neurobiologic approach Eliptogenesis and neuonal cell death in limbic epilepsy

P01NS-17771-10 9001 (SRC) MC NAMARA, JAMES O Limbic epilepsy: a neurobiologic approach Core facilities

P01NS-17778-10 (SRC) GAZZANIGA, MICHAEL S DARTMOUTH MEDICAL SCHOOL PIKE HOUSE HANOVER, NH 03756 Program in cognitive neuroscience

P01NS-17778-10 0009 (SRC) HUGHES, HOWARD C Program in cognitive neuroscience Brain mechanism of overt and covert orienting

P01NS-17778-10 0010 (SRC) KOSSLYN, STEPHEN M Program in cognitive neuroscience Lateralization of imagery processing

P01NS-17778-10 9001 (SRC) GAZZANIGA, MICHAEL S Program in cognitive neuroscience Core

P01NS-17778-10 0004 (SRC) TRAMO, MARK JUDE Program in cognitive neuroscience Cortical networks in auditory pattern perception

P01NS-17778-10 0007 (SRC) HILLYARD, STEVEN A Program in cognitive neuroscience Event-related potentials and cognition

P01NS-17778-10 0008 (SRC) FENDRICH, ROBERT Program in cognitive neuroscience Hemispheric processing of visual spatial and pattern formation

R01NS-17813-10 (NEUB) MARDER, EVE E DEPARTMENT OF BIOLOGY 415 SOUTH ST/DEPT BIOLOGY WALTHAM, MASS 02254 Neurotransmitter modulation of neuronal circuits

R01NS-17904-10 (IMS) PENN, AUDREY S COLUMBIA UNIV HLTH SCI 620 WEST 168TH ST/RM 4-420 NEW YORK, NY 10032 Initiation of autoimmunity in myasthenia gravis

R01NS-17907-08 (BNP) MILLER, DUANE D OHIO STATE UNIVERSITY 500 WEST 12TH AVENUE COLUMBUS, OH 43210 Non-nitrogen and nitrogen containing dopamine drugs

R01NS-17910-10 (PHY) LEVITAN, IRWIN B BRANDEIS UNIVERSITY 415 SOUTH ST WALTHAM, MA 02254 Regulation of ion channels in nerve cells

R01NS-17928-10 (CBY) AGNEW, WILLIAM S YALE UNIVERSITY SCH OF MEDICIN 333 CEDAR STREET NEW HAVEN, CT 06510-8026 Voltage-regulated Na channel--Sturcture and mechanisms

R01NS-17950-10 (EDC) WOLF, PHILIP A BOSTON UNIVERSITY MEDICAL CTR 80 EAST CONCORD STREET, B-608 BOSTON, MS 02118 Precursors of stroke incidence and prognosis

R01NS-17963-10 (NEUC) KIMMEL, CHARLES B UNIVERSITY OF OREGON EUGENE, OR 97403 Development of characterized neurons

R01NS-18005-09 (BIO) BASU, SUBHASH C UNIVERSITY OF NOTRE DAME COLLEGE OF SCIENCE NOTRE DAME, IN 46556 Glycolipid metabolism in normal and pathological tissues

R01NS-18013-10 (PHY) BARCHI, ROBERT L UNIV OF PENNSYLVANIA HOSPITAL 3400 SPRUCE STREET PHILADELPHIA, PA 19104 Studies of purified sodium channels from sarcolemma

R01NS-18027-10 (HAR) KUWADA, SHIGEYUKI UNIVERSITY OF CONNETICUT DEPARTMENT OF ANATOMY FARMINGTON, CT 06032 Inferior colliculus neurons: physiology and anatomy

R01NS-18028-10 (NEUA) BISHOP, GEORGIA A OHIO STATE UNIVERSITY 333 WEST 10TH AVE COLUMBUS, OH 43210 Neuromodulators in cerebellar circuitry

R01NS-18029-10 (SAT) TANAGHO, EMIL A UNIVERSITY OF CALIFORNIA 533 PARNASSUS AVE SAN FRANCISCO, CA 94143-0738 Bladder evacuation by direct sacral root stimulation

R01NS-18047-10 (PTHA) KOENIG, HAROLD VA LAKESIDE MEDICAL CENTER 333 E HURON ST CHICAGO, IL 60611 Molecular pathology of blood-brain barrier breakdown

R01NS-18089-09 (NEUB) ROTTER, ANDREJ OHIO STATE UNIVERSITY 333 W. 10TH AVENUE COLUMBUS, OH 43210 Neurochemical correlates of cerebellar development

R01NS-18105-10A2 (NEUA) GRUNDKE-IQBAL, INGE N Y STATE INST FOR BASIC RES DEPARTMENT OF NEUROCHEMISTRY STATEN ISLAND, NY 10314 Neurofibrillary pathology in aging

R01NS-18112-10 (HED) SCHOENWOLF, GARY C UNIV. OF UTAH, COL OF MED SALT LAKE CITY, UTAH 84132 Research on neurulation

R01NS-18114-11 (TMP) GRANGER, NOELLE A UNIV. OF N. C. AT CHAPEL HILL 111 TAYLOR HALL CHAPEL HILL, NC 27599 Neuroendocrine regulation of endocrine glands

R01NS-18122-09A2 (NLS) WONG-RILEY, MARGARET T MEDICAL COLLEGE OF WISCONSIN 8701 WATERTOWN PLANK ROAD MILWAUKEE, WI 53226 Functionally related enzymatic changes in CNS

R01NS-18145-09 (NEUB) HABLITZ, JOHN J UNIVERSITY OF ALABAMA UAB STATION BIRMINGHAM, AL 35294 Ionic mechanism of excitatory amino acids

P01NS-18146-10 (NSPB) WEINER, LESLIE P UNIV OF SOUTHERN CALIFORNIA 2025 ZONAL AVENUE LOS ANGELES, CA 90033 Demyelinating disease--Viral and immune function

P01NS-18146-10 0002 (NSPB) STOHLMAN, STEPHEN A Demyelinating disease--Viral and immune function Role of CD8+ T cells in prevention of viral-induced demyelination

P01NS-18146-10 0004 (NSPB) DEANS, ROBERT J Demyelinating disease--Viral and immune function RNA/protein interactions regulating coronavirus assembly

P01NS-18146-10 0005 (NSPB) WEINER, LESLIE B Demyelinating disease--Viral and immune function Neurobiology of infected glial cells

P01NS-18146-10 0006 (NSPB) LAI, MICHAEL M C Demyelinating disease--Viral and immune function Molecular mechanisms of coronavirus neuropathogenicity

P01NS-18146-10 0007 (NSPB) WILLIAMSON, JO SIEW-PING Demyelinating disease--Viral and immune function CD4+ T cells and their role in JHMV-induced demyelination

P01NS-18146-10 0008 (NSPB) MCMILLAN, MINNIE Demyelinating disease--Viral and immune function Molecular characterization of JHMV-specific TCR-MHC complexes

P01NS-18146-10 9001 (NSPB) WEINER, LESLIE P Demyelinating disease--Viral and immune function Core--Core facility

R01NS-18170-08 (NEUB) BRIMIJOIN, WILLIAM S MAYO FOUNDATION 200 FIRST ST, S W ROCHESTER, MN 55905 Axonal transport in peripheral nerve disease

R01NS-18201-07 (NEUA) SLOVITER, ROBERT S HELEN HAYES HOSPITAL ROUTE 9W WEST HAVERSTRAW, NY 10993 Epileptic neuronal activity and hippocampal damage

R01NS-18205-11 (PHY) BREHM, PAUL S U N Y AT STONY BROOK DEPT. NEUROBIOLOGY & BEHAVIOR STONY BROOK, NY 11794 Regulation of acetylcholine receptors on muscle

R01NS-18218-09 (NEUC) HALEGOUA, SIMON STATE UNIV OF NEW YORK STONY BROOK, NY 11794-5230 Molecular mechanisms of neuronal differentiation

R01NS-18235-10 (IMS) STEINMAN, LAWRENCE STANFORD UNIVERSITY DEPT OF NEUROLOGY, C338 STANFORD, CA 94305-5235 In vivo treatment of EAE with anti-IA antibodies

R01NS-18254-08A1 (BNP) SMITH, AMOS B, III UNIVERSITY OF PENNSYLVANIA 133 SOUTH 36TH STREET PHILADELPHIA, PA 19104 Synthesis of novel tremorgenic agents

R01NS-18291-10 (BPN) HOREL, JAMES A SUNY HEALTH SCIENCE CENTER 750 EAST ADAMS STREET SYRACUSE, NY 13210 Neuroanatomy of memory

R01NS-18309-10 (NLS) SWANN, JOHN W CTR FOR LAB AND RESEARCH N Y STATE DEPT. OF HEALTH ALBANY, N Y 12201 Immature hippocampus--Epileptogenic properties

R01NS-18338-10 (NEUA) EBNER, TIMOTHY J UNIVERSITY OF MINNESOTA 420 DELAWARE STREET SE MINNEAPOLIS, MN 55455 Role of the cerebellum in visually guided arm movements

R01NS-18366-10 (NEUC) GOODMAN, COREY S UNIVERSITY OF CALIFORNIA BERKELEY, CA 94720 Cell determination & interactions of embryonic neurons

R01NS-18381-11 (NEUB) HERRUP, KARL EUNICE KENNEDY SHRIVER CENTER 200 TRAPELO ROAD WALTHAM, MA 02254 Cerebellar Purkinje cell development

R01NS-18400-10 (PHY) BORON, WALTER F YALE UNIV SCHOOL OF MEDICINE 333 CEDAR STREET NEW HAVEN, CT 06510 Mechanism of intracellular pH regulation in neurons

R01NS-18413-08 (NEUC) CHELMICKA-SCHORR, EWA UNIVERSITY OF CHICAGO 5841 SOUTH MARYLAND AVENUE CHICAGO, IL 60637 The sympathetic nervous system and immune responses

R01NS-18414-10 (NLS) COYLE, JOSEPH T MCLEAN HOSPITAL 115 MILL STREET BELMONT, MA 02178-9106 Cortical cholinergic lesion/model for Alzheimer dementia

R01NS-18427-10 (PTHA) BAUDRY, MICHEL UNIV OF SOUTHERN CALIFORNIA HNB 311 LOS ANGELES, CA 90089-2520 Mechanisms of growth and degeneration in adult CNS

R01NS-18458-12 (NLS) FISCHBACH, GERALD D HARVARD MEDICAL SCHOOL 220 LONGWOOD AVENUE BOSTON, MA 02115 Synapse formation in cell culture

R01NS-18479-10 (NLS) MOLINOFF, PERRY B UNIVERSITY OF PENNSYLVANIA DEPARTMENT OF PHARMACOLOGY PHILADELPHIA, PA 19104-6084 Regulation of catecholamine receptors

R01NS-18492-09 (PHY) KACZMAREK, LEONARD K YALE UNIVERSITY 333 CEDAR ST P O BOX 3333 NEW HAVEN, CT 06510 Biochemical control of excitability in neurons

R01NS-18500-09 (PHY) WU, CHUN-FANG UNIVERSITY OF IOWA IOWA CITY, IA 52242 Physiology of Drosophila excitable membrane and synapse

R01NS-18509-09 (RNM) KUNG, HANK F DEPT OF RADIOLOGY 3400 SPRUCE STREET PHILADELPHIA, PA 19104 New brain perfusion imaging agents

R01NS-18591-10 (NLS) MOLINOFF, PERRY B UNIVERSITY OF PENNSYLVANIA DEPT. OF PHARMACOLOGY PHILADELPHIA, PA 19104-6084 Neurotransmitter receptors in the basal ganglia

R01NS-18596-09 (EVR) GRIFFIN, DIANE E JOHNS HOPKINS UNIVERSITY 600 NORTH WOLFE STREET BALTIMORE, MD 21205 Acute alphaviral encephalitis

R01NS-18607-09 (NEUB) KIM, YONG I UNIVERSITY OF VIRGINIA DEPT. NEUROLOGY BOX 394 CHARLOTTESVILLE, VA 22908 Calcium channel dysfunction in Lambert-Eaton Syndrome

R01NS-18616-10 (NLS) LEE, VIRGINIA M UNIVERSITY OF PENNSYLVANIA DPT OF PATHOLOGY & LAB MEDICIN PHILADELPHIA, PA 19104 Regulation of neurofilament phosphorylation & expression

R01NS-18626-08 (NEUA) PIEKUT, DIANE T UNIVERSITY OF ROCHESTER 601 ELMWOOD AVENUE ROCHESTER, NY 14642 Paraventricular nucleus--Afferent synaptology

R01NS-18639-07A2 (NEUB) FREED, CURT R UNIVERSITY OF COLORADO 4200 E NINTH AVE, C-237 DENVER, CO 80262 Neuronal grafts and conditioned behavior

R01NS-18660-07A2 (NLS) OSWALD, ROBERT E CORNELL UNIVERSITY ITHACA, N Y 14853-6401 Noncompetitive blockers of the acetylcholine receptor

R01NS-18667-08 (NLS) BEINFELD, MARGERY C ST LOUIS UNIVERSITY 1402 SOUTH GRAND BOULEVARD ST LOUIS, MO 63104 Striatal CCK--Anatomy, release, and biosynthesis

R01NS-18670-08 (NEUA) SOMJEN, GEORGE G DEPARTMENT OF CELL BIOLOGY RESEARCH DR, RM 314, MS1A DURHAM, N C 27710 Hypoxia of brain tissue slices

R01NS-18710-10 (NLS) DUN, NAE J MEDICAL COLLEGE OF OHIO 3000 ARLINGTON AVE TOLEDO, OH 43699-0008 Activity of preganglionic neurons in vitro

R01NS-18715-08 (SAT) MYERS, ROBERT R UNIVERSITY OF CALIFORNIA 9500 GILMAN DRIVE LA JOLLA, CA 92093-9125 Pathogenesis and treatment of nerve block injuries

R01NS-18741-09 (NEUA) HALGREN, ERIC UNIV OF CALIFORNIA 405 HILGARD AVE LOS ANGELES, CA 90024-1406 Neural basis of endogenous potentials in humans

R01NS-18773-10 (NEUB) NORDLANDER, RUTH H PROF. OF ORAL BIOLOGY 305 WEST 12TH AVE COLUMBUS, OH 43210-1241 Pathway formation in the developing spinal cord

R01NS-18787-09 (CMS) JOHNSON, KENNETH O JOHNS HOPKINS SCHOOL OF MED 725 N WOLFE ST BALTIMORE, MD 21205 Cortical processing of tactual spatial information

R01NS-18788-10 (NLS) OXFORD, GERRY S UNIV OF N C AT CHAPEL HILL CAMPUS BOX 7545 CHAPEL HILL, N C 27599 Ionic mechanisms related to secretion in pituitary cells

R01NS-18804-08 (NEUB) WALKLEY, STEVEN U ROSE F KENNEDY CENTER 1410 PELHAM PARKWAY SOUTH BRONX, NY 10461 Pathobiology of neuronal storage disease

R01NS-18856-11 (PHY) IKEDA, KAZUO BECKMAN REEARCH INSTITUTE 1450 EAST DUARTE ROAD DUARTE, CALIF 91010 Physiology of synapse

P01NS-18858-09A2 (NSPB) VAUGHN, JAMES E BECKMAN RES INST OF CITY OF HO 1450 E DUARTE ROAD DUARTE, CA 91010 Neurodevelopment and neurological diseases

P01NS-18858-09A2 0011 (NSPB) SALVATERRA, PAUL E Neurodevelopment and neurological diseases Molecular logic of neuronal development

P01NS-18858-09A2 0015 (NSPB) IVERSON, LINDA E Neurodevelopment and neurological diseases Genetic regulation of developing ion channels

P01NS-18858-09A2 0016 (NSPB) VAUGHN, JAMES E Neurodevelopment and neurological diseases Epigenetic influences on neuronal development

P01NS-18858-09A2 9001 (NSPB) VAUGHN, JAMES E. Neurodevelopment and neurological diseases Core--Collaborative morphological techniques

R01NS-18883-09 (NEUB) SKOFF, ROBERT P WAYNE STATE UNIVERSITY 540 E CANFIELD DETROIT, MI 48201 A unique system to study myelination

R01NS-18895-09 (NLS) SCHWARTZKROIN, PHILIP A UNIVERSITY OF WASHINGTON DEPT OF NEURO SURG RI-20 SEATTLE, WA 98195 Local interactions among hippocampal neurons

R01NS-18954-08 (NEUB) WITELSON, SANDRA F MCMASTER UNIVERSITY 1200 MAIN ST WEST HAMILTON, ONTARIO CANADA L8N 3 Neuroanatomical asymmetry and psychological characteristics

R01NS-19013-09 (NEUC) BRINTON, MARGO A GEORGIA STATE UNIVERSITY UNIVERSITY PLAZA ATLANTA, GA 30303 LDV-induced genetically restricted CNS disease

R01NS-19063-08 (BPO) ZOLA-MORGAN, STUART M UNIVERSITY OF CALIFORNIA 9500 GILMAN DRIVE LA JOLLA, CA 92093-0603 The neurology of memory

R01NS-19065-08 (NLS) FLYNN, DONNA D UNIVERSITY OF MIAMI PO BOX 016189 MIAMI, FL 33101 Immunological studies of receptor subtypes

R01NS-19090-09 (NEUC) REICHARDT, LOUIS F UNIVERSITY OF CALIFORNIA THIRD AND PARNASS, ROOM 426 SAN FRANCISCO, CA 94143 Studies on neurite outgrowth

R01NS-19133-04A2 (BPO) KRALY, F SCOTT COLGATE UNIVERSITY HAMILTON, NY 13346 Neuroendocrine control of drinking elicited by eating

R01NS-19194-10 (PHY) ABERCROMBIE, RONALD F DEPARTMENT OF PHYSIOLOGY EMORY UNIV SCH OF MED ATLANTA, GA 30322 Interactions between H+1 and Ca2+ in myxicola axon

R01NS-19195-09 (NEUB) SANES, JOSHUA R WASHINGTON UNIV SCH OF MED DEPT OF ANATOMY/NEUROBIOLOGY ST LOUIS, MO 63110 Extracellular matrix and neuromuscular development

R01NS-19235-07 (NEUA) MARMAROU, ANTHONY MEDICAL COLLEGE OF VIRGINIA BOX 508 RICHMOND, VA 23298 Biomechanics of brain edema and intracranial pressure

R01NS-19245-08 (VISB) FINLAY, BARBARA L CORNELL UNIVERSITY ITHACA, NY 14853-7601 Neuron death in central nervous system development

R01NS-19259-09 (NEUB) BREGMAN, BARBARA S GEORGETOWN UNIV SCHOOL OF MED 3900 RESERVOIR ROAD NW WASHINGTON, DC 20007 CNS regeneration in neonatals and adults

R01NS-19304-08 (PHY) GILL, DONALD L UNIV. OF MARYLAND SCH. OF MED. 660 W. REDWOOD STREET BALTIMORE, MARYLAND 21201 Calcium regulatory mechanisms in neural cells

R01NS-19316-09 (NEUB) KONTOS, HERMES A MEDICAL COLLEGE OF VIRGINIA BOX 281, MCV STATION RICHMOND, VA 23298-0001 Cerebral microcirculation in experimental brain injury

R01NS-19328-07 (PHY) KOESTER, JOHN D RESEARCH FDN FOR MENTAL HYGIEN 722 WEST 168TH STREET NEW YORK, NY 10032 Cellular neuronal control of behavior

R01NS-19331-08 (NEUA) RYMER, WILLIAM Z REHABILITATION INST OF CHICAGO 345 EAST SUPERIOR ST., RM 1406 CHICAGO, IL 60611 Spasticity mechanisms and quantification

R01NS-19342-07 (BPO) CRAWFORD, MORRIS L UNIV OF TEXAS HEALTH SCI CNTR 6420 LAMAR FLEMING AVENUE HOUSTON, TX 77030 Color and luminance processing in cortex

R01NS-19353-10 (BBCA) WAGGONER, ALAN S CARNEGIE-MELLON UNIVERSITY 4440 FIFTH AVENUE PITTSBURGH, PA 15213 Optical probes of cell structure and dynamics

R01NS-19441-08 (NLS) SUMNERS, COLIN UNIVERSITY OF FLORIDA BOX J274 GAINESVILLE, FL 32610-0274 Catecholamine/angiotensin II interactions in the brain

R55NS-19482-09 (NEUC) SALVATERRA, PAUL M BECKMAN RESEARCH INSTITUTE 1450 E DUARTE RD DUARTE, CA 91010 Genetic studies of choline acetyltransferase

R01NS-19486-09 (CMS) PUBOLS, BENJAMIN H, JR RS DOW NEUROLOGICAL SCI INST 1120 N W 20TH AVENUE PORTLAND, OR 97209 Neural pathways involved in tactile discrimination

R01NS-19492-08 (NLS) KIMELBERG, HAROLD K ALBANY MEDICAL COLLEGE 47 NEW SCOTLAND AVENUE ALBANY, NY 12208 Uptake and receptors for monoamines in astrocytes

R01NS-19509-08A2 (NLS) YEZIERSKI, ROBERT P UNIV OF MIAMI SCH OF MED 1600 N W 10TH AVENUE MIAMI, FL 33136 The spinomesencephalic tract--Anatomy and physiology

R01NS-19522-09 (NLS) COHEN, JONATHAN B DEPT. OF ANATOMY/NEUROBIOLOGY 660 SOUTH EUCLID AVENUE ST LOUIS, MO 63110 Permeability control by acetylcholine receptor

R01NS-19546-09 (NEUC) LEVINSON, ARNOLD I UNIVERSITY OF PENNSYLVANIA 515 JOHNSON PAVILION PHILADELPHIA, PA 19104-6057 Thymic B cell activation in myasthenia gravis

R01NS-19550-05 (NEUA) JENKINS, LARRY W MEDICAL COLLEGE OF VIRGINIA PO BOX 693, MCV STATION RICHMOND, VA 23298-0693 Head trauma and secondary insults

R01NS-19569-09 (PHY) SIEGELBAUM, STEVEN A COLUMBIA UNIVERSITY DEPARTMENT OF PHARMACOLOGY NEW YORK, NY 10032 Ion channel modulation in control of synaptic effication

R01NS-19576-08 (BCE) CARON, MARC G DUKE UNIV MED CTR PO BOX 3287 RESEARCH DR DURHAM, NC 27710 Dopamine receptors--Characterization and endocrine regulation

P01NS-19608-09 (NSPA) ZIGMOND, MICHAEL J UNIVERSITY OF PITTSBURGH PITTSBURGH, PA 15260 Neurobiology of the intact and damaged basal ganglia

P01NS-19608-09 0002 (NSPA) ZIGMOND, MICHAEL J Neurobiology of the intact and damaged basal ganglia Neurochemistry of recovery from loss of dopamine neurons

P01NS-19608-09 0004 (NSPA) KAPLAN, BARRY Neurobiology of the intact and damaged basal ganglia Cell-specific regulation of tyrosine hydroxylase gene expression

P01NS-19608-09 0006 (NSPA) ABERCROMBIE, ELIZABETH D Neurobiology of the intact and damaged basal ganglia Neurochemistry of therapeutics in Parkinson's disease

P01NS-19608-09 0007 (NSPA) GRACE, ANTHONY A Neurobiology of the intact and damaged basal ganglia Physiology of dopamine regulation in the basal ganglia

P01NS-19608-09 0008 (NSPA) BERGER, THEODORE W Neurobiology of the intact and damaged basal ganglia Electrophysiological analysis of striatal neurons

P01NS-19608-09 0009 (NSPA) WOODWARD, DONALD J Neurobiology of the intact and damaged basal ganglia Neostriatal activity and dopamine

P01NS-19608-09 0010 (NSPA) GLORIOSO, JOSEPH C Neurobiology of the intact and damaged basal ganglia HSV mediated tyrosine hydroxylase gene transfer into CNS

P01NS-19608-09 9002 (NSPA) LEWIS, DAVID A Neurobiology of the intact and damaged basal ganglia Core-Histological Services

P01NS-19608-09 9003 (NSPA) SVED, ALAN F Neurobiology of the intact and damaged basal ganglia Core--Animal and surgery services

P01NS-19608-09 9004 (NSPA) ZIGMOND, MICHAEL J Neurobiology of the intact and damaged basal ganglia Core--Neurochemistry services

P01NS-19608-09 9005 (NSPA) PAGANO, ROBERT R Neurobiology of the intact and damaged basal ganglia Core--Statistical services

P01NS-19611-08 (NSPB) SPENCER, PETER S OREGON HLTH SCIS UNIVERSITY 3181 SW SAM JACKSON PARK ROAD PORTLAND, OR 97201-3098 Toxic probes of neurodegenerative diseases

P01NS-19611-08 0002 (NSPB) GOLD, BRUCE G Toxic probes of neurodegenerative diseases Mechanisms of axonal degeneration in toxic states

P01NS-19611-08 0004 (NSPB) KISBY, GLENN E Toxic probes of neurodegenerative diseases Chemical triggers of motor-system disease

P01NS-19611-08 0005 (NSPB) ALLEN, CHARLES N Toxic probes of neurodegenerative diseases Excitotoxic mechanisms of neuronal degeneration

P01NS-19611-08 9001 (NSPB) SPENCER, PETER S Toxic probes of neurodegenerative diseases Core--Technical services facility

P01NS-19613-07 (SRC) GILMAN, SID UNIVERSITY OF MICHIGAN 1500 E MEDICAL CENTER DRIVE ANN ARBOR, MI 48109-0316 Amino acid and peptide transmitters in the motor system

P01NS-19613-07 0001 (SRC) GILMAN, SID Amino acid and peptide transmitters in the motor system Lesions of basal ganglia amino acidergic pathways -- Neuron unit studies

P01NS-19613-07 0002 (SRC) YOUNG, ANNE B Amino acid and peptide transmitters in the motor system Basal ganglia neurotransmitters and receptors

P01NS-19613-07 0003 (SRC) MACDONALD, ROBERT L Amino acid and peptide transmitters in the motor system amino acid receptor channels -- Kinetic studies

P01NS-19613-07 0005 (SRC) GROSS, ROBERT A Amino acid and peptide transmitters in the motor system Peptidergic regulation of calcium channels

P01NS-19613-07 9001 (SRC) PENNEY, JOHN B Amino acid and peptide transmitters in the motor system Core--Histology, autoradiography

P01NS-19613-07 9002 (SRC) MCDONALD, ROBERT L Amino acid and peptide transmitters in the motor system Computer core

R01NS-19620-09 (NEUA) REINER, ANTON J UNIVERSITY OF TENNESSEE 875 MONROE AVENUE MEMPHIS, TN 38163 Basal ganglia--Anatomical and functional organization

P01NS-19632-09 (SRC) DAMASIO, ANTONIO R THE UNIVERSITY OF IOWA IOWA CITY, IOWA 52242 Anatomical substrates of complex behavior

P01NS-19632-09 0003 (SRC) TRANEL, DANIEL Anatomical substrates of complex behavior Facial recognition in humans

P01NS-19632-09 0004 (SRC) DAMASIO, ANTONIO R Anatomical substrates of complex behavior Anatomical basis of memory

P01NS-19632-09 0005 (SRC) FROMKIN, VICTORIA Anatomical substrates of complex behavior Anatomical basis of language

P01NS-19632-09 0008 (SRC) DAMASIO, ANTONIO R Anatomical substrates of complex behavior Anatomical basis of disorders of executive function

PROJECT NO., ORGANIZATIONAL UNIT., INVESTIGATOR, ADDRESS, TITLE

P01NS-19632-09 0001 (SRC) RIZZO, MATTHEW Anatomical substrates of complex behavior Anatomical basis of vision

P01NS-19632-09 0009 (SRC) VAN HOESEN, GARY W Anatomical substrates of complex behavior Experimental neuroanatomy of systems related to cognition

P01NS-19632-09 9001 (SRC) DAMASIO, HANNA C Anatomical substrates of complex behavior Core

R01NS-19640-09 (NEUB) LANDMESSER, LYNN T UNIVERSITY OF CONNECTICUT 75 N. FAGLEVILLE RD./RM.416 STORRS, CONN 06268 Developmental and trophic neural interactions

R01NS-19643-08 (NEUA) WINN, H RICHARD UNIVERSITY OF WASHINGTON RI-20 SEATTLE, WA 98195 Valproate for prophylaxis of post-traumatic seizures

R01NS-19716-07 (SSS) RAPP, PAUL E MEDICAL COLL OF PENNSYLVANIA 3300 HENRY AVENUE PHILADELPHIA, PA 19129 Focal epilepsy and deterministic chaos

R01NS-19733-08 (NEUB) MCDONALD, ALEXANDER J UNIVERSITY OF SOUTH CAROLINA COLUMBIA, SC 29208 Neuronal organization of the basolateral amygdala

R01NS-19779-08 (EI) RICHMAN, DAVID P UNIVERSITY OF CALIFORNIA 2315 STOCKTON BLVD SACRAMENTO, CA 95817 Pathogenic mechanisms in Myasthenia gravis

R01NS-19794-09 (NEUA) WIKSWO, JOHN P, JR VANDERBILT UNIVERSITY BOX 1807, STATION B NASHVILLE, TN 37235 Magnetic measurements of peripheral nerve function III

R01NS-19814-07A1 (RAP) LINDSEY, BRUCE G UNIVERSITY OF SOUTH FLORIDA 12901 BRUCE B DOWNS BLVD, BOX TAMPA, FL 33612 Brainstem respiratory neuron interactions

R01NS-19839-09 (NEUB) DAIL, WILLIAM G DEPARTMENT OF ANATOMY UNIV OF NEW MEXICO MED SCH ALBUQUERQUE, N MEX 87131 Innervation of penile erectile tissue

R01NS-19855-08 (NEUA) COURCHESNE, ERIC CHILDREN'S HOSPITAL RES CENTER 8001 FROST STREET SAN DIEGO, CA 92123 Autism--MR investigation of neuroanatomical abnormalities

R01NS-19864-09 (ORTH) SMITH, JUDITH L UNIVERSITY OF CALIFORNIA 405 HILGARD AVE LOS ANGELES, CA 90024-1568 Control of stereotypic limb movement

R01NS-19865-09 (NEUA) HABERLY, LEWIS B MEDICAL SCIENCES CENTER 1300 UNIVERSITY AVENUE MADISON, WI 53706 Analysis of inhibitory processes in piriform cortex

R01NS-19889-04 (NLS) FROMM, GERHARD H UNIVERSTY OF PITTSBURGH 322 SCAIFE HALL PITTSBURGH, PA 15261 Neuropharmacology of the trigeminal nucleus

R01NS-19895-09 (NEUB) BYRNE, JOHN H UNIV OF TEXAS MED SCHOOL P O BOX 20708 HOUSTON, TEX 77225 Analysis of the neural control of behavior

R01NS-19904-09 (NEUC) DAVIS, RONALD L BAYLOR COLLEGE OF MEDICINE ONE BAYLOR PLAZA HOUSTON, TX 77030 Neurobiologically important genes II

R01NS-19910-10 (NLS) MERLIE, JOHN P WASHINGTON UNIVERSITY MED SCH 660 SOUTH EUCLID AVENUE ST LOUIS, MO 63110 Molecular mechanisms in neuromuscular development

R01NS-19912-09 (CMS) GEBHART, GERALD F UNIVERSITY OF IOWA IOWA CITY, IA 52242 Mechanisms and modulation of visceral pain

R01NS-19923-09 (NLS) BUNGE, RICHARD P UNIV. OF MIAMI, SCH. OF MED. 1600 NW 10TH AVENUE R48 MAIMI, FL 33136 Control of Schwann cell growth

R01NS-19943-06 (NEUC) BARBARESE, ELISA UNIVERSITY OF CONNECTICUT HEALTH CENTER FARMINGTON, CT 06032 Oligodendrocyte ontogeny and differentiation

R01NS-19949-09 (NEUB) KELLEY, DARCY B COLUMBIA UNIVERSITY 911 FAIRCHILD BUILDING NEW YORK, NY 10027 Androgen regulation of neuromuscular function

R01NS-19950-09 (NEUB) SIMONS, DANIEL J UNIVERSITY OF PITTSBURGH 3550 TERRACE ST PITTSBURGH, PA 15261 Neuronal integration in the neocortex

R01NS-19972-08 (NLS) HRUBY, VICTOR J UNIVERSITY OF ARIZONA DEPARTMENT OF CHEMISTRY TUCSON, ARIZONA 85721 Receptor specific enkephalin analogues

R01NS-19988-08 (NLS) ROTHMAN, STEVEN M WASHINGTON UNIVERSITY 400 S KINGSHIGHWAY ST LOUIS, MO 63110 Physiology of amino acids in vitro

R01NS-19999-08S1 (MGN) ROSES, ALLEN D DUKE UNIVERSITY MEDICAL CENTER PO BOX 2900 DURHAM, NC 27710 Heterozygote diagnosis in myotonic muscular dystrophy

R01NS-20013-08 (NEUB) KESSLER, JOHN A ALBERT EINSTEIN COLLEGE OF MED 1300 MORRIS PARK AVENUE BRONX, NY 10461 Mechanisms governing neuronal development

P01NS-20020-08 (SRC) TRAYSTMAN, RICHARD J JOHNS HOPKINS HOSPITAL 600 NORTH WOLFE ST BALTIMORE, MD 21205 Mechanisms of regulation of cerebral blood flow

P01NS-20020-08 0002 (SRC) JONES, M DOUGLAS Mechanisms of regulation of cerebral blood flow Regulation of cerebral blood flow in fetus and neonate

P01NS-20020-08 0003 (SRC) ROGERS, MARK C Mechanisms of regulation of cerebral blood flow Cerebral blood flow and metabolism in cardiopulmonary resuscitation

P01NS-20020-08 0004 (SRC) WILSON, DAVID A Mechanisms of regulation of cerebral blood flow Regulation of hypophyseal blood flow

P01NS-20020-08 0001 (SRC) TRAYSTMAN, RICHARD J Mechanisms of regulation of cerebral blood flow Focal cerebral circulation and oxygenfree radicals

P01NS-20020-08 0005 (SRC) KOEHLER, RAYMOND C Mechanisms of regulation of cerebral blood flow Complete and incomplete cerebral ischemia

P01NS-20020-08 0006 (SRC) TRAYSTMAN, RICHARD J Mechanisms of regulation of cerebral blood flow Cerebrovascular and metabolism alterations during hyperammonemia

P01NS-20020-08 9001 (SRC) KOEHLER, RAYMOND C Mechanisms of regulation of cerebral blood flow Core--Radiolabeled microscpheres

P01NS-20020-08 9002 (SRC) JACOBUS, WILLIAM E Mechanisms of regulation of cerebral blood flow Core--Spectroscopy

P01NS-20020-08 9003 (SRC) MCPHERSON, ROBERT W Mechanisms of regulation of cerebral blood flow Core--Electrophysiology

P50NS-20022-08 (NSPA) JOHNSON, KENNETH P UNIVERSITY OF MARYLAND 660 WEST REDWOOD STREET BALTIMORE, MD 21201 ALS and MS clinical center grant

P50NS-20022-08 0001 (NSPA) BISWALL, NILAMBAR ALS and MS clinical center grant Non-lytic effects of viruses on neuroblastoma cells in vitro

P50NS-20022-08 0002 (NSPA) COLE, GERALD A ALS and MS clinical center grant Virus-induced T cell-mediated CNS inflammation

P50NS-20022-08 0003 (NSPA) CARRIGAN, DONALD R ALS and MS clinical center grant Molecular pathogenesis of measles infection of the CNS

P50NS-20022-08 0004 (NSPA) SHIN, MOON L ALS and MS clinical center grant Complement-mediated demyelination in multiple sclerosis

P50NS-20022-08 0005 (NSPA) KOSKI, CAROL L ALS and MS clinical center grant Mechanism of peripheral nerve demyelination

P50NS-20023-08 (SRC) BIGNER, DARRELL D DUKE UNIVERSITY MEDICAL CENTER P.O. BOX 3156 DURHAM, NC 27710 SRC on malignant human gliomas and medulloblastomas

P50NS-20023-08 0002 (SRC) WIKSTRAND, CAROL J SRC on malignant human gliomas and medulloblastomas Specific monoclonal antibodies against glioma and medulloblastoma

P50NS-20023-08 0006 (SRC) BIGNER, DARELL D SRC on malignant human gliomas and medulloblastomas Increased delivery of monoclonal antibody radioimmunoatherapy

P50NS-20023-08 0008 (SRC) BIGNER, SANDRA H SRC on malignant human gliomas and medulloblastomas Cytogenetics and molelcular genetics of childhood brain tumors

P50NS-20023-08 0010 (SRC) SCHOLD, S CLIFFORD SRC on malignant human gliomas and medulloblastomas Multimodality clinical therapy trials with brain tumor patients

P50NS-20023-08 0013 (SRC) PIZZO, SALVATORE V SRC on malignant human gliomas and medulloblastomas protein biochemistry

P50NS-20023-08 0014 (SRC) SVENNERHOLM, LARS SRC on malignant human gliomas and medulloblastomas Ganglioside and glycoside structure

P50NS-20023-08 0015 (SRC) HUMPHREY, PETER A SRC on malignant human gliomas and medulloblastomas Epidermal growth facor receptor and growth control

P50NS-20023-08 0016 (SRC) ZALUTSKY, MICHAEL R SRC on malignant human gliomas and medulloblastomas Development of radiolabeled monoclonal antibodies for radioimmunotherapy

P50NS-20023-08 0017 (SRC) COAKHAM, HUGH B SRC on malignant human gliomas and medulloblastomas Intrathecal therapy of neoplastic meningitis with monoclonal antibody

P50NS-20023-08 0018 (SRC) FRIEDMAN, HENRY S SRC on malignant human gliomas and medulloblastomas Bifunctional alkylator therapy of medulloblastoma and childhood glioma

R13NS-20032-09 (NSPB) RASMINSKY, MICHAEL MONTREAL GENERAL HOSPITAL MONTREAL, QUEBEC, H3G 1A4 CANADA The neurobiology of disease teaching workshops

R01NS-20036-07A2 (BNP) JOHNSON, RODNEY L UNIVERSITY OF MINNESOTA 308 HARVARD ST, SE MINNEAPOLIS, MN 55455 Pro-leu-gly-NH2 and DOPAmine receptor modulation study

R01NS-20040-08A1 (NEUB) TOLBERT, LESLIE P UNIVERSITY OF ARIZONA TUCSON, AZ 85721 Ultrastructural development of antennal center

R01NS-20052-08 (BPO) DOTY, ROBERT W UNIV OF ROCHESTER MEDICAL CTR 601 ELMWOOD AVENUE ROCHESTER, N Y 14642 Hemispheric distribution of visual memory

R01NS-20055-08A1 (NEUA) WILSON, DORIS B UNIVERSITY OF CALIFORNIA LA JOLLA, CA 92093-0604 Normal and abnormal development of the neural tube

R01NS-20147-08 (NLS) COLMAN, DAVID R COLUMBIA UNIVERSITY DEPT. OF ANATOMY & CELL BIOLOG NEW YORK, NY 10032 Biosynthesis and assembly of myelin membrane proteins

R01NS-20149-08 (NEUB) WHITE, EDWARD L BEN GURION UNIV OF THE NEGEV P O BOX 653 BEER SHEVA, ISRAEL Synaptic connectivity in cerebral cortex

R01NS-20178-07A1 (NEUC) SKENE, J PATE DUKE UNIVERSITY BOX 3209 DUKE UNIV MEDICAL CTR DURHAM, NC 27710 Genes of growth-associated proteins in CNS regeneration

R01NS-20181-07A2 (NLS) ROFFLER-TARLOV, SUZANNE K TUFTS UNIVERSITY 136 HARRISON AVENUE BOSTON, MA 02111 Studies of inherited dopamine loss

R01NS-20187-08 (CMS) ZAIDEL, ERAN UNIVERSITY OF CALIFORNIA 1283 FRANZ HALL LOS ANGELES, CA 90024-1563 Hemispheric specialization and interaction in humans

R01NS-20193-08 (NEUA) POVLISHOCK, JOHN T DEPARTMENT OF ANATOMY 1101 E MARSHALL STREET RICHMOND, VA 23298-0709 Neural change following traumatic brain injury

R01NS-20212-08 (NLS) MC CARTHY, KENNY D UNIV OF N. C. AT CHAPEL HILL CB#7356 FAC LAB OFF BLDG CHAPEL HILL, N C 27599 Analysis of receptors present in astrocytes

R01NS-20227-08 (NEUB) TOLBERT, DANIEL L ST LOUIS UNIV SCHOOL OF MEDICI 1402 S GRAND BLVD ST LOUIS, MO 63104 Developmental shaping of cerebellar afferent topography

R01NS-20233-06 (NLS) SCHMIDT, JAKOB S U N Y AT STONY BROOK STONY BROOK, N Y 11794 Regulation of muscle acetylcholine receptor

R01NS-20246-08 (BPO) GARCIA-RILL, EDGAR E UNIV OF ARKANSAS MED SCIENCES 4301 WEST MARKHAM ST LITTLE ROCK, ARK 72205 Central modulation of locomotor rhythms

R01NS-20253-06 (NEUA) MOSHE, SOLOMON L ALBERT EINSTEIN COLL OF MED 1300 MORRIS PARK AVE BRONX, NY 10461 Age related seizure suppression

R01NS-20254-04 (NEUB) LOVELL, KATHRYN L MICHIGAN STATE UNIVERSITY A622 EAST FEE HALL EAST LANSING, MI 48824 Pathogenesis of myelin deficits in betya-mannosidosis

R01NS-20270-08 (NEUA) CHRISTAKOS, SYLVIA UNIV OF MED & DENT OF NEW JERS 185 SOUTH ORANGE AVENUE NEWARK, NJ 07103 Molecular and cellular basis of epileptogenesis

R01NS-20285-07 (NEUB) MESULAM, MAREK-MARSEL BETH ISRAEL HOSP 330 BROOKLINE AVENUE BOSTON, MASS 02215 Central cholinergic pathways

R01NS-20311-08 (NEUB) DORSA, DANIEL M VETERANS ADM MEDICAL CENTER 1660 S COLUMBIAN WAY SEATTLE, WA 98108 Regulation and ontogeny of brain vasopressin systems

PROJECT NO., ORGANIZATIONAL UNIT., INVESTIGATOR, ADDRESS, TITLE

R01NS-20331-09 (BPO) MCNAUGHTON, BRUCE L UNIVERSITY OF ARIZONA TUCSON, ARIZONA 85721 Neural basis of internal representation of place

R01NS-20335-07A2 (REN) GIBSON, MARIE J MOUNT SINAI SCHOOL OF MEDICINE 1 GUSTAVE LEVY PLACE, BOX 1055 NEW YORK, NY 10029 GnRH deficiency--Correction by preoptic area grafts

R01NS-20336-08A1 (NEUB) MACAGNO, EDUARDO R COLUMBIA UNIVERSITY DEPT OF BIOLOGICAL SCIENCES NEW YORK, N Y 10027 Segmental differentiation in the nervous system

R01NS-20356-08 (MGN) TOBIN, ALLAN J UNIV OF CALIFORNIA 405 HILGARD AVENUE LOS ANGELES, CA 90024 Gene regulation in cerebellum development

R01NS-20357-06 (BBCB) HEAD, JAMES F BOSTON UNIVERSITY SCH OF MED 80 EAST CONCORD STREET BOSTON, MA 02118 Calcium-binding proteins from optic lobes

R01NS-20364-08 (NEUB) LICHTMAN, JEFF W WASHINGTON UNIV SCHOOL OF MED 660 SOUTH EUCLID AVENUE ST LOUIS, MO 63110 Competition between axons at the neuromuscular junction

R01NS-20402-09 (NEUB) OPPENHEIM, RONALD W WAKE FOREST UNIVERSITY 300 SOUTH HAWTHORNE ROAD WINSTON-SALEM, NC 27103 Study of neuronal death & survival

P50NS-20471-08 (NSPB) PRICE, DONALD L JOHNS HOPKINS UNIVERSITY 600 NORTH WOLFE STREET BALTIMORE, MD 21205 The forebrain cholinergic system in health and disease

P50NS-20471-08 0001 (NSPB) DELONG, MAHLON R The forebrain cholinergic system in health and disease The cholinergic system in normal brain

P50NS-20471-08 0002 (NSPB) PRICE, DONALD L The forebrain cholinergic system in health and disease The cholinergic system in the neocortex

P50NS-20471-08 0003 (NSPB) DELONG, MAHLON R The forebrain cholinergic system in health and disease Selective lesions of the Ch system--Behavior

P50NS-20471-08 0004 (NSPB) PRICE, DONALD L The forebrain cholinergic system in health and disease Selective lesions of the Ch system by ibotenic acid

P50NS-20471-08 0005 (NSPB) CORK, LINDA C The forebrain cholinergic system in health and disease The Ch system in aged non-human primates--Cognition

P50NS-20471-08 0006 (NSPB) PRICE, DONALD L The forebrain cholinergic system in health and disease The Ch system in aged non-human primates--Neuroanatomy

R13NS-20478-09 (NSPB) HALVORSON, HARLYN O MARINE BIOLOGICAL LABORATORY WOODS HOLE, MA 02543 Summer neurobiology course

P01NS-20482-08 (SRC) SCHWARTZKROIN, PHILIP A UNIVERSITY OF WASHINGTON SEATTLE, WA 98195 Epilepsy research--studies of chronic epileptic foci

P01NS-20482-08 0009 (SRC) OJEMANN, GEORGE A Epilepsy research--studies of chronic epileptic foci Activity of single units in the epileptic focus

P01NS-20482-08 0012 (SRC) CRILL, WAYNE E. Epilepsy research--studies of chronic epileptic foci Electrophysiology of membrane properties in cortex

P01NS-20482-08 0013 (SRC) CATTERAL, WILLIAM A Epilepsy research--studies of chronic epileptic foci Molecular properties of dihydropyridine-calcium channels

P01NS-20482-08 0015 (SRC) SCHWARTZKROIN, PHILIP A Epilepsy research--studies of chronic epileptic foci Chronic model of eleptogenesis

P01NS-20482-08 9001 (SRC) WARD, ARTHUR A Epilepsy research--studies of chronic epileptic foci Biomedical core

P01NS-20482-08 0010 (SRC) STAHL, WILLIAM L Epilepsy research--studies of chronic epileptic foci The structure & function of Na, K-ATPase in epileptic cortex

P01NS-20482-08 0011 (SRC) FRANCK, J.E. Epilepsy research--studies of chronic epileptic foci Intracellular studies of neurons from chronic epileptic cortex

R01NS-20483-08A1 (NEUC) BARNSTABLE, COLIN J YALE UNIVERSITY 330 CEDAR ST, PO BOX 3333 NEW HAVEN, CT 06510 Molecular analysis of neural cell development

P50NS-20489-07 (SRC) RAPIN, ISABELLE ALBERT EINSTEIN COLL OF MED 1300 MORRIS PARK AVENUE BRONX, NY 10461 Nosology--Higher cerebral function disorders in children

P50NS-20489-07 0001 (SRC) RAPIN, ISABELLE Nosology--Higher cerebral function disorders in children Longitudinal study

P50NS-20489-07 0003 (SRC) KURTZBERG, DIANE Nosology--Higher cerebral function disorders in children Electrophysiologic validation study

P50NS-20489-07 0004 (SRC) CAVINESS, VERNE S Nosology--Higher cerebral function disorders in children Neuroanatomic validation study

P50NS-20489-07 9002 (SRC) MORRIS, ROBIN Nosology--Higher cerebral function disorders in children Core--Methodology

P50NS-20489-07 9003 (SRC) RAPIN, ISABELLE Nosology--Higher cerebral function disorders in children Core--Language and play

R01NS-20498-08 (BIO) STORM, DANIEL R UNIVERSITY OF WASHINGTON DEPT OF PHARMACOLOGY SJ-30 SEATTLE, WA 98195 Purification and characterization of adenylate cyclase

R01NS-20500-07 (NEUA) ZAGON, IAN S PENNSYLVANIA STATE UNIVERSITY P O BOX 850 HERSHEY, PENNSYLVANIA 17033 Brain development and endogenous opioid systems

R01NS-20536-08 (SSS) SCHULTZ, ALBERT B DEPT OF MECHANICAL ENGNG UNIVERSITY OF MICHIGAN ANN ARBOR, MICH 48109 Biomechanics of the human spine

R01NS-20544-08 (ORTH) ENOKA, ROGER M ARIZONA HEALTH SCIENCE CTR TUCSON, AZ 85724 Effects of limb immobilization on motor control

R01NS-20545-06 (NEUB) ENGLISH, ARTHUR W EMORY UNIVERSITY ATLANTA, GA 30322 Motor unit specificity and developmental shaping

R01NS-20551-07A2 (NEUB) PODUSLO, JOSEPH F MAYO FOUNDATION 200 FIRST STREET SOUTHWEST ROCHESTER, MN 55905 Regulation of myelination

R01NS-20561-08 (BPN) RITTER, ROBERT C WASHINGTON STATE UNIVERSITY COLLEGE OF VETERINARY MEDICINE PULLMAN, WA 99164-6520 Neural substrates of peptide-induced satiety

R01NS-20576-08 (NEUA) GALE, KAREN N GEORGETOWN UNIVERSITY 3900 RESERVOIR ROAD, N W WASHINGTON, D C 20007 Gaba-mediated anticonvulsant actions and basal ganglia

PROJECT NO., ORGANIZATIONAL UNIT., INVESTIGATOR, ADDRESS, TITLE

R01NS-20581-08 (NEUB) SCHOLD, STANLEY C, JR DUKE UNIVERSITY P O BOX 3963 DURHAM, N C 27710 Drug sensitivity & resistance in human gliomas

R55NS-20585-07 (RAP) MILLER, ALAN D ROCKEFELLER UNIVERSITY 1230 YORK AVENUE NEW YORK, NY 10021-6399 Neurophysiological studies of vomiting

R01NS-20591-08A1 (NEUB) HERRUP, KARL EUNICE KENNEDY SHRIVER CENTER 200 TRAPELO ROAD WALTHAM, MA 02254 neuron-target interactions

R01NS-20607-09 (NEUB) MULLER, KENNETH J UNIVERSITY OF MIAMI PO BX 016430 MIAMI, FL 33101 Regeneration of particular synapses

R01NS-20618-08 (RNM) MOODY, DIXON M BOWMAN GRAY SCHOOL OF MEDICINE 300 S HAWTHORNE ROAD WINSTON-SALEM, N C 27103 Brain vasculature in leukoaraiosis and cardiac surgery

R01NS-20629-08 (NEUB) NEWMAN, SARAH W DEPT OF ANATOMY & CELL BIOLOGY UNIV OF MICHIGAN ANN ARBOR, MI 48109 Testosterone influence on vomeronasal neuron morphology

R01NS-20637-07 (NEUA) DUFF, THOMAS A UNIVERSITY OF WISCONSIN 600 HIGHLAND AVE. MADISON, WI 53792 Mechanism and therapy of cerebrovascular spasm

R01NS-20643-07 (NLS) BEHBEHANI, MICHAEL M UNIVERSITY OF CINCINNATI COLLEGE OF MEDICINE CINCINNATI, OH 45267-0553 Role of neuropeptides in the pain inhibitory system

R01NS-20660-07 (NLS) GUNION, MARK W VET AFFAIRS MED CENTER 16111 PLUMMER STREET SEPULVEDA, CA 91343 Brain peptides--Central control of glucose homeostasis

R01NS-20680-08 (HAR) PARKINS, CHARLES W DEPT. OF OTOLARYNGOLOGY 2020 GRAVIER ST, SUITE A NEW ORLEANS, LA 70112-2234 Stimulus coding for scala tympani cochlear prostheses

R01NS-20683-04A1 (PHRA) ATCHISON, WILLIAM D MICHIGAN STATE UNIVERSITY EAST LANSING, MI 48824 Chemical models of presynaptic neuromuscular diseases

R01NS-20686-06 (BPO) KUBIE, JOHN L HEALTH SCIENCE CTR AT BROOKLYN S U N Y, 450 CLARKSON AVENUE BROOKLYN, NEW YORK 11203 Spatial firing properties of hippocampal neurons

R01NS-20702-09 (NEUB) KITAI, STEPHEN T DEPT OF ANATOMY AND NEUROBIOLO 875 MONROE AVENUE MEMPHIS, TN 38163 Experimental studies of sensory pathways

R01NS-20728-07 (NLS) MILNER, ROBERT J SCRIPPS RESEARCH INSTITUTE 10666 N TORREY PINES RD LA JOLLA, CA 92037 Characterization of myelin associated glycoprotein

R01NS-20752-06 (NEUB) ZUKIN, RUTH S ALBERT EINSTEIN COLLEGE OF MED 1300 MORRIS PARK AVENUE BRONX, N Y 10461 Characterization of neuroblastoma NMDA receptors

R13NS-20758-07 (NSPA) REINGOLD, STEPHEN C NAT MULTIPLE SCLEROSIS SOCIETY 205 EAST 42ND ST NEW YORK CITY, NY 10017-5706 Multidisciplinary workshops on multiple sclerosis

R01NS-20762-06 (NEUB) NEMETH, PATTI M WASHINGTON UNIVERSITY 660 S. EUCLID AVE., BX 8111 ST. LOUIS, MO 63110 Biochemistry and physiology of single motor units

R01NS-20771-07A1 (BPO) KESNER, RAYMOND P UNIVERSITY OF UTAH SALT LAKE CITY, UT 84112 Prefrontal cortex and temporal information processing

R01NS-20778-08 (NEUC) KESSLER, JOHN A ALBERT EINSTEIN COLLEGE OF MED 1300 MORRIS PARK AVENUE BRONX, NY 10461 Regulation of neurotransmitter metabolism

R01NS-20794-07 (BPO) AMINI-SERESHKI, LATIFEH UNIV OF PENNSYLVANIA 420 GUARDIAN DR PHILADELPHIA, PA 19104 Extrahypothalamic thermoregulation in sleep and waking

R01NS-20805-07 (BPO) MAHUT, HELEN NORTHEASTERN UNIVERSITY 360 HUNTINGTON AVENUE BOSTON, MA 02115 Study of spared learning in amnesic monkeys

R01NS-20806-08 (NEUA) SUTHERLING, WILLIAM W UNIVERSITY OF CALIFORNIA 710 WESTWOOD PLAZA LOS ANGELES, CA 90024-1769 Magnetoencephalography in epilepsy

R01NS-20820-10A1 (SSS) SIDMAN, RICHARD L CHILDREN'S HOSPITAL 320 LONGWOOD AVE BOSTON, MA 02115 Neurological mutants--Genetic and phenotypic study

R01NS-20824-09 (BBCB) KIRSCHNER, DANIEL A CHILDREN'S HOSPITAL 300 LONGWOOD AVENUE BOSTON, MA 02115 Myelin membrane structure--Stability and pathology

R01NS-20832-09A1 (NEUB) HAMILL, ROBERT W UNIVERSITY OF ROCHESTER BOX 603, 601 ELMWOOD AVENUE ROCHESTER, N Y 14642 Glucocorticoids and brain development

R01NS-20855-09 (ORTH) NICHOLS, T RICHARD EMORY UNIVERSITY DEPARTMENT OF PHYSIOLOGY ATLANTA, GA 30322 Spinal mechanisms regulating muscle and limb mechanics

R01NS-20856-07 (NEUA) STEINDLER, DENNIS A UNIVERSITY OF TENNESSEE 875 MONROE AVENUE MEMPHIS, TN 38163 Brainstem projections to cerebrum and cerebellum

R01NS-20904-11 (VR) NATHANSON, NEAL UNIV OF PENNSYLVANIA SCHOOL OF MEDICINE PHILADELPHIA, PA 19104-6076 Bunyavirus encephalitis: Genetic approach

R01NS-20916-09 (NEUC) PATTERSON, PAUL H DIV OF BIOLOGY, 216-76 CALIFORNIA INSTITUTE OF TECH PASADENA, CA 91125 Environmental determination of transmitter functions

R01NS-20961-05 (BPO) UNDERWOOD, HERBERT A, JR NORTH CAROLINA STATE UNIVERSIT RALEIGH, NC 27695-7617 Physiology of circadian systems in Japanese quail

R01NS-20973-07 (NEUA) ELBLE, RODGER J SOUTHERN ILLINOIS UNIVERSITY P.O. BOX 19230 SPRINGFIELD, IL 62794-9230 Neuromuscular control in action tremor

R01NS-20989-08 (NEUA) FISHER, MARK J UNIV OF SOUTHERN CALIF MED SCH 2025 ZONAL AVE LOS ANGELES, CA 90033 Hemorheological factors in cerebral ischemia

R01NS-20991-06 (NLS) HELKE, CINDA J UNIFORMED SERVICES UNIVERSITY 4301 JONES BRIDGE ROAD BETHESDA, MD 20814-4799 Neurotransmitters and visceral sensory neurons

R01NS-21015-07 (NEUB) HOUK, JAMES C NORTHWESTERN UNIVERSITY 303 E. CHICAGO AVE/PHYSIOLOGY CHICAGO, IL 60611 Sensorimotor functions of the inferior olive

R01NS-21023-07 (NEUB) COPE, TIMOTHY C HAHNEMANN UNIV/DEPT PHYSIO/BIO MAIL STOP 409/BROAD & VINE PHILADELPHIA, PA 19102 Function and modifiability of single motoneuron pools

PROJECT NO., ORGANIZATIONAL UNIT., INVESTIGATOR, ADDRESS, TITLE

R01NS-21027-06S1 (HAR) CLARK, GRAEME M DEPT OF OTOLARYNGOLOGY UNIV OF MELBOURNE PARKVILLE, VICTORIA, AUS 3052 Improved cochlear implants: psychophysics and engineering

R01NS-21045-08 (NEUA) PARK, TAE S WASHINGTON UNIVERSITY 660 SOUTH EUCLID AVE BOX 8057 ST LOUIS, MO 63110 Adenosine and cerebral blood flow in hypoglycemic neonatal

R01NS-21046-08 (SSS) STRUMWASSER, FELIX MARINE BIOLOGICAL LABORATORY WATER STREET WOODS HOLE, MA 02543 Neuroendocrine pacers, peptides, receptors, antibodies

R01NS-21047-06 (CMS) MC CLOSKEY, MICHAEL E JOHNS HOPKINS UNIVERSITY 34TH & CHARLES STREETS BALTIMORE, MD 21218 Cognitive processes in dyscalculia

R01NS-21057-07 (NLS) LESKAWA, KENNETH C UNIVERSITY OF LOUISVILLE SCHOOL OF MEDICINE LOUISVILLE, KY 40292 Glycosphingolipids during myogenesis in vitro

R01NS-21062-08 (NLS) NUTT, JOHN G OREGON HEALTH SCIENCES UNIV 3181 S W SAM JACKSON PARK ROAD PORTLAND, OR 97201-3098 Levodopa pharmacokinetics and pharmacodynamics

R01NS-21065-07A2 (NLS) HORN, JOHN P UNIVERSITY OF PITTSBURGH 3500 TERRACE STREET PITTSBURGH, PA 15261 Physiology of muscarinic synapses in sympathetic ganglia

R01NS-21072-07 (NEUC) CHAO, MOSES VICTOR CORNELL UNIVERSITY MED COLLEGE 1300 YORK AVENUE NEW YORK, N Y 10021 Molecular biology of the nerve growth factor receptor

R01NS-21076-08 (NEUA) WINN, H RICHARD HARBORVIEW MEDICAL CTR 325 9TH AVENUE SEATTLE, WA 98104 Regulation of cerebral blood flow by adenosine

R01NS-21097-07 (NLS) HATTEN, MARY E COLUMBIA UNIVERSITY 630 WEST 168TH STREET NEW YORK, NY 10032 Influence of neurons on astroglial differentiation

R01NS-21105-07 (CMS) WALL, JOHN T, JR MEDICAL COLLEGE OF OHIO P.O. BOX 10008 TOLEDO, OHIO 43699-0008 Central effects of somatosensory system injury

R01NS-21108-06 (NEUC) CARLSON, BRUCE M UNIV OF MICHIGAN MED SCH 5779 MEDICAL SCIENCES II BLDG ANN ARBOR, MICH 48109 Role of the neuroepithelial basal lamina in neurulation

R01NS-21122-06 (NEUB) BLIGHT, ANDREW R PURDUE UNIVERSITY WEST LAFAYETTE, IN 47907 Demyelination in spinal cord trauma

R01NS-21132-07 (NEUB) WESTERFIELD, MONTE UNIVERSITY OF OREGON EUGENE, OR 97403 Development of motoneuronal connectivity

R01NS-21135-06 (NEUA) KNIGHT, ROBERT T VA MEDICAL CENTER 150 MUIR RD, NEUROLOGY SVC 127 MARTINEZ, CA 94553 Attention, orientation and human prefrontal cortex

R01NS-21142-04A2 (NLS) FRANKFURTER, ANTHONY DEPARTMENT OF BIOLOGY CHARLOTTESVILLE, VA 22901 Characterization of brain microtubules

R01NS-21143-06 (NEUB) POPPELE, RICHARD E UNIVERSITY OF MINNESOTA 435 DELAWARE STREET, S E MINNEAPOLIS, MINN 55455 Neurophysiological study of dorsal spinocerebellar tract

R01NS-21165-07 (BPO) PICKARD, GARY E UNIVERSITY OF PENNSYLVANIA 422 CURIE BLVD. Neural basis of circadian rhythms

R01NS-21182-07 (NEUB) SAWCHENKO, PAUL E SALK INST FOR BIOL STUDIES P O BOX 85800 SAN DIEGO, CA 92186-5800 Neuropeptide co-expression in the hypothalamus

R01NS-21198-08 (NEUC) LEVINE, JOEL M SUNY AT STONY BROOK STONY BROOK, N Y 11794-5230 Cell surface molecules of the developing nervous system

R01NS-21219-06 (NLS) SHAIN, WILLIAM G NEW YORK STATE DEPT OF HEALTH EMPIRE STATE PLAZA, BOX 509 ALBANY, NY 12201-0509 Receptor mediated release from glia

R01NS-21220-08 (NLS) MICEVYCH, PAUL E UNIVERSITY OF CALIFORNIA 405 HILGARD AVENUE LOS ANGELES, CA 90024 Differences in CCK release and function

R01NS-21223-07 (NEUB) KRIEGSTEIN, ARNOLD R STANFORD UNIVERSITY MED CTR DEPARTMENT OF NEUROLOGY STANFORD, CA 94305 Development of inhibitory function in turtle cortex

R01NS-21229-07A1 (NLS) DANI, JOHN A BAYLOR MEDICAL COLLEGE ONE BAYLOR PLAZA HOUSTON, TX 77030 Structure and function of excitatory synaptic channels

R01NS-21234-07 (NLS) KLEIN, WILLIAM L NORTHWESTERN UNIVERSITY EVANSTON, ILLINOIS 60201 Molecular characterization of muscarinic ACh receptors

R01NS-21238-07 (BPO) PECK, CAROL UNIVERSITY OF MISSOURI 8001 NATURAL BRIDGE ROAD ST LOUIS, MO 63121 Visual rearrangement and neural plasticity

R01NS-21246-08 (HEM) ZAGON, IAN S PENNSYLVANIA STATE UNIVERSITY P O BOX 850 HERSHEY, PENNSYLVANIA 17033 Spectrin-like protein in developing brain

R01NS-21255-07 (NLS) CHOW, SIEN-YAO UNIVERSITY OF UTAH 410 CHIPETA WAY ROOM 167 SALT LAKE CITY, UT 84108 Thyroid hormone, epilepsy, and CNS maturation

R01NS-21256-05 (NLS) SALAND, LINDA C UNIVERSITY OF NEW MEXICO ALBUQUERQUE, NM 87131 Regulation of pituitary opiate peptide secretion

R01NS-21266-08 (CMS) CHUNG, JIN MO UNIV OF TEXAS MED BRANCH 200 UNIVERSITY BLVD GALVESTON, TX 77550-2772 Peripheral and central mechanisms of nociception

R01NS-21278-07 (NLS) MILETIC, VJEKOSLAV UNIVERSITY OF WISCONSIN DEPT. OF COMPARATIVE BIOSCIENC MADISON, WI 53706 Role of serotonin in trigeminal and spinal analgesia

R55NS-21281-07 (NLS) FAINGOLD, CARL L SOUTHERN ILLINOIS UNIVERSITY PO BOX 19230 SPRINGFIELD, IL 62794-9230 Neurotransmitter mechanisms in epilepsy

R01NS-21289-08 (NLS) CARROLL, PAUL T TEXAS TECH UNIVERSITY HEALTH SCIENCES CENTER LUBBOCK, TX 79430 Vesicular synthesis and release of acetylcholine

R01NS-21306-04A2 (NLS) SPETH, ROBERT C WASHINGTON STATE UNIVERSITY PULLMAN, WA 99164-6520 Brain angiotensin receptor function control and anatomy

R01NS-21309-05 (NEUB) NORNES, HOWARD O DEPT OF ANATOMY AND NEUROBIOLO COLORADO STATE UNIVERSITY FORT COLLINS, CO 80523 CNS transplants in adults spinal cord

R01NS-21323-06 (NLS) JOSEPH, SHIRLEY A UNIVERSITY OF ROCHESTER 601 ELMWOOD AVENUE, BOX 609 ROCHESTER, N Y 14642 Neural connectivity/intrinsic organization in brain stem

R01NS-21325-08 (NLS) MINNEMAN, KENNETH P EMORY UNIV SCHOOL OF MED ATLANTA, GA 30322 Alpha-adrenergic receptor binding and function in rat brain

R01NS-21328-08 (MGN) WALLACE, DOUGLAS C EMORY UNIVERSITY 1639 PIERCE DR ATLANTA, GA 30322 Mitochondrial inborn errors of metabolism

R01NS-21334-08 (BIO) QUINN, DANIEL M UNIVERSITY OF IOWA IOWA CITY, IA 52242 Acetylcholinesterase-catalyzed hydrolysis of anilides

R01NS-21356-06 (NEUA) BROWN, LUCY L ALBERT EINSTEIN COLLEGE OF MED 1300 MORRIS PARK AVENUE BRONX, N Y 10461 Functional neuroanatomy of a movement disorder

R01NS-21377-08 (NEUB) JONES, EDWARD G UNIVERSITY OF CALIFORNIA IRVINE, CA 92717 Activity dependent plasticity of primate somatosensory cortex

R01NS-21418-08 (BPO) LIDSKY, THEODORE I INST FOR BASIC RESEARCH 1050 FOREST HILL ROAD STATEN ISLAND, N Y 10314 Biopsychology of basal ganglia-reticular interactions

R01NS-21419-08 (NLS) JAHR, CRAIG E OREGON HEALTH SCIENCES UNIV 3181 SAM JACKSON PARK ROAD PORTLAND, OR 97201 Electrophysiological analysis of neurotransmission

R01NS-21423-08 (VR) HAASE, ASHLEY T UNIVERSITY OF MINNESOTA 420 DELAWARE STREET S E MINNEAPOLIS, MN 55455 The molecular pathogenesis of the slow infection Visna

P50NS-21442-07 (NSPA) ROOS, RAYMOND P UNIVERSITY OF CHICAGO 5841 SO MARYLAND AVE CHICAGO, ILL 60637 Motor neuron disease--A program project

P50NS-21442-07 0003 (NSPA) ROOS, RAYMOND Motor neuron disease--A program project Theiler's virus neurotropism and neurovirulence

P50NS-21442-07 0004 (NSPA) SIDDIQUE, TEEPU Motor neuron disease--A program project DNA RFLP linkage analysis in familial ALS

P50NS-21442-07 0005 (NSPA) GURNEY, MARK E Motor neuron disease--A program project In vivo effects of neuroleukin and its antagonists

P50NS-21442-07 0006 (NSPA) STEFANSSON, KARI Motor neuron disease--A program project Two polypeptides in regenerating nervous tissue

P01NS-21445-07 (NSPA) FIELDS, HOWARD L UNIVERSITY OF CALIFORNIA BOX 0114 SAN FRANCISCO, CA 94143 Mechanisms of pain and analgesia

P01NS-21445-07 0001 (NSPA) BASBAUM, ALLAN I Mechanisms of pain and analgesia Neurochemistry of pain modulation

P01NS-21445-07 0002 (NSPA) FIELDS, HOWARD L Mechanisms of pain and analgesia Brainstem circuitry of pain modulation

P01NS-21445-07 0004 (NSPA) RALSTON, HENRY J Mechanisms of pain and analgesia Thalamic afferents underlying nociception

P01NS-21445-07 9001 (NSPA) RALSTON, HENRY J Mechanisms of pain and analgesia Core--Electron microscopy

R01NS-21455-07 (NLS) SAUBERMANN, ALBERT J STATE UNIVERSITY OF NEW YORK STONY BROOK, NY 11794-8480 Neuron-glia interaction--Ion/element and H20 homeostasis

R01NS-21458-07 (NEUA) HAYES, RONALD LAWRENCE UNIVERSITY OF TEXAS HLTH SCI C 6431 FANNIN HOUSTON, TX 77030 Neurophysiological studies of experimental concussion

R01NS-21460-06 (NEUB) GUTH, LLOYD THE COLLEGE OF WILLIAM AND MAR WILLIAMSBURG, VA. 23185 Models of spinal cord injury for drug evaluation

R01NS-21466-07 (NEUC) HASHIM, GEORGE A ST LUKE'S-ROOSEVELT HOSPITAL AMSTERDAM AVE AT 114TH STREET NEW YORK, N Y 10025 Control of EAE by synthetic peptides

P01NS-21469-07 (NSPB) DUVOISIN, ROGER C UMDNJ-ROBERT WOOD JOHNSON MEDICAL SCHOOL NEW BRUNSWICK, N J 08903 Neurodegenerative disorders of the basal ganglia

P01NS-21469-07 0001 (NSPB) HEIKKILA, RICHARD E Neurodegenerative disorders of the basal ganglia Neural degeneration induced by tetrahydropyridine analogs

P01NS-21469-07 0006 (NSPB) MPTP, MITOLCHONDRIA AND AGING Neurodegenerative disorders of the basal ganglia

P01NS-21469-07 0007 (NSPB) GELLER, HERBERT M Neurodegenerative disorders of the basal ganglia Intracerebral implants of cell lines

R01NS-21496-07 (VR) AHMED, RAFI UNIVERSITY OF CALIFORNIA DEPT OF MICROBIOL/IMMUNOLOGY LOS ANGELES, CALIF 90024 Viral persistence: genetic & immunological studies /mice/

R01NS-21501-07 (PHY) SIGWORTH, FREDERICK J YALE UNIVERSITY SCHOOL OF MED 333 CEDAR ST/DEPT PHYSIOLOGY NEW HAVEN, CONN 06510 Fluctuations in ionic current through membrane channels

R01NS-21512-05 (MBY) SUEOKA, NOBORU UNIVERSITY OF COLORADO CAMPUS BOX 347 BOULDER, CO 80309-0347 Neuronal-glial differentiation

R01NS-21550-08 (NLS) GREENGARD, PAUL ROCKEFELLER UNIVERISTY 1230 YORK AVENUE NEW YORK, N Y 20021-6399 Metabolic basis of neural function

R01NS-21558-07 (NEUA) MOSKOWITZ, MICHAEL A MASSACHUSETTS GENERAL HOSPITAL FRUIT ST BOSTON, MA 02114 Trigeminal nerve--Control of the brain vasculature

R01NS-21571-07 (NLS) OBLINGER, MONICA M 3333 GREEN BAY ROAD UNIV HLTH SCI/CHICAGO MED SCH NORTH CHICAGO, ILL 60064 Slow axonal transport in CNS development

R01NS-21579-08 (NLS) BURDEN, STEVEN J MASSACHUSETTS INST OF TECH 77 MASSACHUSETTS AVE CAMBRIDGE, MA 02139 Subsynaptic proteins at nerve-muscle synapses

R01NS-21580-08 (VR) HAASE, ASHLEY T UNIVERSITY OF MINNESOTA 420 DELAWARE STREET S E MINNEAPOLIS, MN 55455 Viral genes in the central nervous system

R01NS-21624-07 (NLS) AUGUSTINE, GEORGE J DUKE UNIVERSITY BOX 3209 DURHAM, N C 27710 Role of calcium ions in presynaptic function

R01NS-21629-07 (NEUB) GRUMET, MARTIN H NEW YORK UNIV. MED. CTR. 550 FIRST AVENUE NEW YORK, NEW YORK 10016 Molecular mechanisms of neuron-glia adhesion

R01NS-21647-06 (NLS) LEVINE, JON D UNIVERSITY OF CALIFORNIA 3RD & PARNASSUS (BOX 0724) SAN FRANCISCO, CA 94143 Neural mechanisms of pain and hyperalgesia

R01NS-21671-07 (NLS) LOTHMAN, ERIC W UNIV OF VIRGINIA MEDICAL CTR BOX 394 CHARLOTTESVILLE, VA 22908 Antiepileptic screening with recurrent focal seizures

R01NS-21700-08 (NEUB) TENNEKOON, GIHAN I UNIVERSITY OF MICHIGAN 171 ZINA PITCHER PLACE ANN ARBOR, MI 48109-0570 Studies on schwann cell axon interaction in vitro

PROJECT NO., ORGANIZATIONAL UNIT., INVESTIGATOR, ADDRESS, TITLE

R01NS-21708-07 (HUD) PRICHARD, JAMES W YALE MEDICAL SCHOOL 333 CEDAR STREET NEW HAVEN, CT 06510 NMR studies of human cerebral metabolism in vivo
R01NS-21710-07 (NEUC) PAYAN, DONALD G UNIV. OF CALIFORNIA - S. F. 533 PARNASSUS, U-426 SAN FRANCISCO, CA 94143-0724 Modulation of lymphocyte function by substance P
R01NS-21713-07 (NEUA) THALMANN, ROBERT H BAYLOR COLLEGE OF MEDICINE ONE BAYLOR PLAZA HOUSTON, TX 77030 The regulation of a slow inhibitory synaptic event
R01NS-21714-07 (PHY) CLAUDIO, TONI YALE UNIV SCHOOL OF MEDICINE P O BOX 3333 NEW HAVEN, CT 06510 Molecular and cellular physiology of cloned ach receptors
R01NS-21718-06 (SRC) LONG, DONLIN M JOHNS HOPKINS HOSPITAL 600 NORTH WOLFE STREET BALTIMORE, MD 21205 Low back pain and sciatica -- Factors for success of therapy
R01NS-21724-07 (CMS) OJEMANN, GEORGE A UNIVERSITY OF WASHINGTON SEATTLE, WA 98195 Electrocorticographic changes with human higher function
R01NS-21725-06 (NEUB) JACOB, MICHELE H WORCESTER FDN EXP BIOLOGY 222 MAPLE AVENUE SHREWSBURY, MA 01545 Regulation of neuronal synaptic components
R01NS-21749-07 (NLS) TAGHERT, PAUL H WASHINGTON UNIVERSITY 660 S EUCLID AVE ST LOUIS, MO 63110 Developmental regulation of neuropeptide expression
R01NS-21752-07 (NLS) NICKLAS, WILLIAM J UNIV OF MED & DENISTRY OF N J ROBERT WOOD JOHNSON MED SCH PISCATAWAY, NJ 08854-5635 Neural degeneration induced by tetrahydropyridine analogs
R01NS-21758-07 (PHY) BARTSCHAT, DIETER K EASTERN VIRGINIA MED SCHOOL DEPARTMENT PHYSIOLOGY NORFOLK, VA 23501 Potassium channels in presynaptic nerve terminals
R01NS-21767-07 (NLS) RUBIN, LEE L HLTH SCIENCES COLUMBIA UNIV 630 WEST 168TH STREET NEW YORK, N Y 10031 Molecular components of acetylcholine receptor clusters
R01NS-21777-07 (NLS) GRUOL, DONNA L SCRIPPS CLINIC AND RES FDN 10666 NORTH TORREY PINES RD LA JOLLA, CALIF 92037 Ion channel in mature and developing CNS neurons
R01NS-21778-07 (NEUB) FRIESEN, WOLFGANG O UNIVERSITY OF VIRGINIA GILMER HALL CHARLOTTESVILLE, VA 22903 Neuronal regulation of behavior
R01NS-21834-07 (NLS) CHOW, SIEN-YAO UNIVERSITY OF UTAH 410 CHIPETA WAY ROOM 167 SALT LAKE CITY, UT 84108 Anticonvulsant & tolerance mechanisms of acetazolamide
R01NS-21848-06 (NEUB) FABER, DONALD S STATE UNIVERSITY OF NEW YORK 313 CARY HALL BUFFALO, N Y 14214 Postsynaptic factors affecting synaptic efficacy in vivo
R01NS-21860-06 (NLS) KESSLER, MARKUS UNIVERSITY OF CALIFORNIA IRVINE, CA 92717-3800 Regulation of brain glutamate receptors
R01NS-21868-06 (NLS) VANAMAN, THOMAS C UNIV OF KENTUCKY MEDICAL CTR 800 ROSE ST LEXINGTON, KY 40536-0084 Role of brain specific proteins in nerve function
R01NS-21878-06 (NEUB) SPERRY, DAVID G UNIVERSITY OF DELAWARE SCH OF LIFE & HLTH SCIENCES NEWARK, DE 19716 Control of neuron population size
R01NS-21889-06 (HUD) LEVIN, HARVEY S UNIV OF TEXAS MED BRANCH 301 UNIVERSITY BOULEVARD GALVESTON, TX 77550 Neurobehavioral outcome of head injury in children
R01NS-21896-05 (NLS) LENTZ, THOMAS L YALE UNIVERSITY SCH OF MED 333 CEDAR STREET P.O. BOX 333 NEW HAVEN, CT 06510 Functional domains on the acetylcholine receptor
P01NS-21908-06A1 (NSPB) DELGADO-ESCUETA, ANTONIO V WEST LOS ANGELES VA MEDICAL CT SAWTELLE & WILSHIRE BLVDS. WEST LOS ANGELES, CA 90073 California CEP--Basic mechanisms of human epilepsies
P01NS-21908-06A1 0006 (NSPB) HOUSER, CAROLYN R California CEP--Basic mechanisms of human epilepsies Neurochemical anatomy of partial epilepsies
P01NS-21908-06A1 0010 (NSPB) TOURTELLOTTE, WALLACE W California CEP--Basic mechanisms of human epilepsies HSV-1 detection in partial epilepsies by PCR
P01NS-21908-06A1 0011 (NSPB) DELGADO-ESCUETA, ANTONIO V California CEP--Basic mechanisms of human epilepsies Genetics of juvenile myoclonic, absence, and grand mal epilepsies
P01NS-21908-06A1 9001 (NSPB) DELGADO-ESCUETA, ANTONIO V California CEP--Basic mechanisms of human epilepsies Core--Computer laboratory
P01NS-21908-06A1 9002 (NSPB) NAGY, AGNES K California CEP--Basic mechanisms of human epilepsies Core--Basic research in partial and generalized epilepsies
P01NS-21908-06A1 9003 (NSPB) TOURTELLOTTE, WALLACE W California CEP--Basic mechanisms of human epilepsies Core--Human neurospecimen bank for epilepsy
R01NS-21913-16 (PTHA) LIPTON, HOWARD L UNIV OF COLORADO HLTH SCIS 4200 EAST NINTH AVENUE DENVER, CO 80262 Theiler's virus induced demyelinating disease in mice
R01NS-21921-09 (NEUC) BREAKFIELD, XANDRA O MASSACHUSETTS GENERAL HOSPITAL CHARLESTOWN, MA 02129 Biochemical and genetic analysis of monoamine oxidase
R01NS-21925-07 (NEUC) CAREY, DAVID J WEIS CENTER FOR RESEARCH NORTH ACADEMY AVENUE DANVILLE, PA 17822 Biosynthesis of Schwann cell extracellular matrix
R01NS-21937-08 (NEUC) KRAUSE, JAMES E WASHINGTON UNIVERSITY 660 S. EUCLID AVE. ST LOUIS, MO 63110 Substance P biosynthesis and axonal transport in the CNS
R01NS-21958-08 (NEUA) BLOEDEL, JAMES R BARROW NEUROLOGICAL INSTITUTE 350 W THOMAS ROAD PHOENIX, AZ 85013 Patterns of integration along cerebellar afferent system
R01NS-21970-06 (HED) PINTAR, JOHN E COLUMBIA UNIVERSITY 630 WEST 168TH STREET NEW YORK, N Y 10032 Molecular studies of growth factors during development
R01NS-21981-06 (NEUB) SKINNER, ROBERT D UNIV OF ARKANSAS MEDICAL SCIS 4301 W MARKHAM ST LITTLE ROCK, AR 72205-7199 Neurological substrates of induced locomotion
R01NS-21990-08 (NEUC) STALLCUP, WILLIAM B LA JOLA CANCER RESEARCH FDN 10901 NORTH TORREY PINES ROAD LA JOLLA, CA 92037 Surface antigens of neural cells
R01NS-21991-08 (NLS) MC KAY, RONALD D MASSACHUSETTS INSTITUTE OF TEC CAMBRIDGE, MA 02139 Molecular analysis of the nervous system
R01NS-21997-07 (PTHA) SCHMALE, MICHAEL C 4600 RICKENBACKER CAUSEWAY MIAMI, FL 33149 Damselfish neurofibromatosis as a model for human NF
R01NS-22010-07 (NLS) ALGER, BRADLEY E UNIV OF MD AT BALTIMORE BALTIMORE, MD 21201 Electrophysiological effects of phorbol esters in CNS
R01NS-22012-06 (NEUB) BURTON, HAROLD WASHINGTON UNIV SCH OF MED 660 SOUTH EUCLID AVENUE ST LOUIS, MO 63110 Somatosensory cortex interactions
R01NS-22022-06A1 (NEUA) WEINSTEIN, PHILIP R UNIVERSITY OF CALIFORNIA 3RD & PARNASSUS SAN FRANCISCO, CA 94143-0112 NMR metabolic studies of brain ischemia and reperfusion
R01NS-22031-07 (NEUA) WEXLER, NANCY S HEREDITARY DISEASE FOUNDATION 1427 7TH STREET SANTA MONICA, CA 90401 Huntington's disease in Venezuela and other studies
R01NS-22039-08 (PTHA) FRANTZ, CHRISTOPHER N UNIVERSITY OF MARYLAND HOSPITA 22 SOUTH GREENE STREET BALTIMORE, MD 21201 Antibodies to investigate and treat neuroblastoma
R01NS-22061-07 (NLS) ROLE, LORNA W COLUMBIA UNIVERSITY 630 WEST 168TH STREET NEW YORK, NY 10032 Modulation and regulation of neuronal ACh receptors
R01NS-22069-07 (NEUC) WEINREICH, DANIEL UNIV MARYLAND SCHOOL OF MED 660 W REDWOOD STREET BALTIMORE, MD 21201 Chemoreception and signal processing in vagal afferents
R01NS-22071-07 (NLS) OLSEN, RICHARD W UNIVERSITY OF CALIFORNIA 23-278 LOS ANGELES, CA 90024-1735 GABA/benzodiazepine/barbiturate receptors in epilepsy
R01NS-22077-06 (NEUA) LAMANNA, JOSEPH C UNIVERISTY HOSPITALS 2074 ABINGTON ROAD CLEVELAND, OH 44106 Recovery from stroke--Metabolic and vascular factors
R01NS-22093-06 (NEUB) EISENMAN, LEONARD M THOMAS JEFFERSON UNIVERSITY 1020 LOCUST STREET PHILADELPHIA, PA 19107 Afferent organization in neurologically mutants
R01NS-22099-06 (MET) GRIGGS, ROBERT C UNIVERSITY OF ROCHESTER 601 ELMWOOD AVENUE, BOX 673 ROCHESTER, N Y 14642 Muscle protein synthesis in neuromuscular disease
R01NS-22103-05 (NEUC) HAMILL, ROBERT W UNIVERSITY OF ROCHESTER 601 ELMWOOD AVE ROCHESTER, NY 14642 Hormonal regulation of neuronal ontogeny
R01NS-22108-06 (RAD) WABER, DEBORAH P CHILDREN'S HOSPITAL 300 LONGWOOD AVENUE BOSTON, MA 02115 Consequences of CNS prophylaxis in children with all
R01NS-22111-06 (NLS) SUTCLIFFE, J GREGOR SCRIPPS CLINIC & RES FDN 10666 NORTH TORREY PINES RD LA JOLLA, CA 92037 Molecular description of the cortex and hippocampus
R01NS-22116-08 (NLS) FARB, DAVID H BOSTON UNIVERSITY 80 E CONCORD ST BOSTON, MA 02118 Pharmacology of the GABA receptor
R01NS-22128-06 (NEUA) RAO, STEPHEN M MEDICAL COLLEGE OF WISCONSIN 1000 NORTH 92ND STREET MILWAUKEE, WI 53226 Neuropsychology of multiple sclerosis
R01NS-22145-04 (EVR) KNOBLER, ROBERT L JEFFERSON MEDICAL COLLEGE 1025 WALNUT STREET PHILADELPHIA, PA 19107 Genetic, viral & immune studies of demyelination
R01NS-22150-05 (NLS) AMBRON, RICHARD T COLUMBIA UNIVERSITY 630 WEST 168TH STREET NEW YORK, NY 10032 Sorting and transport of specific neuronal glycoproteins
R01NS-22153-08 (TOX) SIMPSON, LANCE L THOMAS JEFFERSON UNIVERSITY 1025 WALNUT STREET PHILADELPHIA, PA 19107 Pharmacological studies on clostridial toxins
R01NS-22155-06 (NEUB) GILLETTE, MARTHA U UNIVERSITY OF ILLINOIS 505 S GOODWIN AVE URBANA, IL 61801 Physiological substrates of a circadian oscillator
R01NS-22157-06 (NEUB) BECKER, JILL B NEUROSCIENCE LABORATORY BLDG 1103 E HURON ST ANN ARBOR, MI 48104-1687 Brain tissue transplantation--Neurochemical studies
R01NS-22168-06 (BPO) MORIN, LAWRENCE P SUNY HEALTH SCIENCES CTR T-10 STONY BROOK, NY 11794-8101 Behavior, biological rhythms, and brain
R01NS-22188-06 (EDC) ALTER, MILTON DEPARTMENT OF NEUROLOGY 3300 HENRY AVENUE PHILADELPHIA, PA 19129 Recurrent stroke--Risk factors, control and interaction
R01NS-22189-07 (BPO) WOLPAW, JONATHAN R NEW YORK STATE DEPT OF HEALTH EMPIRE STATE PLAZA ALBANY, NY 12201 Adaptive plasticity in the spinal stretch reflex
R01NS-22200-06 (NLS) WHITE, H STEVE UNIVERSITY OF UTAH 421 WAKARA WAY SALT LAKE CITY, UT 84108 Effects of anticonvulsants on glial ion transport
R01NS-22201-07 (CMS) CARAMAZZA, ALFONSO DEPARTMENT OF COGNITIVE SCIENC THE JOHNS HOPKINS UNIVERSITY BALTIMORE, MD 21218 Cognitive-linguistic mechanisms in writing disorders
R01NS-22213-05 (NEUA) MCCALL, ANTHONY L DEPT OF MEDICINE 3710 SW VETERANS HOSPITAL ROAD PORTLAND, OR 97207 Brain transport and metabolism in hypoglycemia and diabetes
R01NS-22224-07 (MGN) GUSELLA, JAMES F MASSACHUSETTS GENERAL HOSPITAL 32 FRUIT STREET BOSTON, MA 02114 DNA marker linkage studies of the phakomatoses
R01NS-22230-05 (NEUA) PANASCI, LAWRENCE C SIR MORTIMER B DAVIS-JEWISH GE 3755 COTE ST CATHERINE ROAD MONTREAL, QUEBEC, CANDA H3T 1E Mechanism of increased cytotoxicity of sarcnu in gliomas
R01NS-22244-06 (CMS) HEILIGENBERG, WALTER F UNIVERSITY OF CALIF,SAN DIEGO LA JOLLA, CA 92093 Neuronal structure and function in a sensory processor
R01NS-22254-07 (NEUA) LUST, WESLEY D CASE WESTERN RESERVE UNIV LAB OF EXPER NEUROL SURGERY CLEVELAND, OHIO 44106 Biochemistry of delayed neuronal death after ischemia
R01NS-22256-07 (NLS) TOBIN, ALLAN J UNIV OF CALIFORNIA 405 HILGARD AVENUE LOS ANGELES, CA 90024 GAD and GABA-r--Candidate genes for epilepsy
R55NS-22274-06A1 (BPO) FITTS, DOUGLAS A UNIVERSITY OF WASHINGTON SEATTLE, WA 98195 CNS and salt appetite
R01NS-22281-07 (NEUB) NOWYCKY, MARTHA C MEDICAL COLL OF PENNSYLVANIA 3200 HENRY AVENUE PHILADELPHIA, PA 19129 Modulation and

PROJECT NO., ORGANIZATIONAL UNIT., INVESTIGATOR, ADDRESS, TITLE

regulation of neuronal calcium channels
R01NS-22283-05 (CMS) HAND, PETER J UNIVERSITY OF PENNSYLVANIA 3800 SPRUCE STREET PHILADELPHIA, PA 19104-6045 Sensory reorganization--Metabolic, behavioral alteration
R01NS-22317-08 (NEUB) JONES, EDWARD G UNIVERSITY OF CALIFORNIA CALIFORNIA COLLEGE OF MEDICINE IRVINE, CA 92717 Thalamic mechanisms in somesthesis
N44NS-22319-00 ( ) CORBETT, SCOTT S** Miniature, flexible cable for in-vivo application
P50NS-22343-06A1 (SRC) BATES, ELIZABETH UNIVERSITY OF CALIFORNIA LA JOLLA, CA 92093 Center for the study of the neurological basis of language
P50NS-22343-06A1 0001 (SRC) JERNIGAN, TERRY L Center for the study of the neurological basis of language Brain structure--Early focal lesions,language impairment, Williams/Down syndrome
P50NS-22343-06A1 0003 (SRC) STILES-DAVIS, JOAN Center for the study of the neurological basis of language Behavioral studies of children with focal brain injury
P50NS-22343-06A1 0004 (SRC) BELLUGI, URSULA Center for the study of the neurological basis of language Developmental profile of Williams syndrome
P50NS-22343-06A1 0005 (SRC) WULFECK, BEVERLY Center for the study of the neurological basis of language Neurobiological studies of specific language impairment
P50NS-22343-06A1 0006 (SRC) NYHAN, WILLIAM L Center for the study of the neurological basis of language Neurobehavioral studies of children with inborn errors of metabolism
P50NS-22343-06A1 0007 (SRC) NEVILLE, HELEN Center for the study of the neurological basis of language Electophysiological studies of brain development
P50NS-22343-06A1 9001 (SRC) BATES, ELIZABETH Center for the study of the neurological basis of language Core--statistical
P50NS-22343-06A1 9002 (SRC) TRAUNER, DORIS A Center for the study of the neurological basis of language Core--Diagnostic medical/behavior
R01NS-22344-06 (TMP) SCHARRER, BERTA V ALBERT EINSTEIN COLL OF MED 1300 MORRIS PARK AVENUE BRONX, NY 10461 Immunocytochemical study of invertebrate nervous system
P01NS-22347-06 (NSPB) BLOOM, FLOYD E SCRIPPS CLINIC & RESEARCH FDN 10666 NORTH TORREY PINES ROAD LA JOLLA, CA 92037 Molecular characterization of neuronal specificity
P01NS-22347-06 0005 (NSPB) SUTCLIFFE, J GREGOR Molecular characterization of neuronal specificity Recombinant DNA
P01NS-22347-06 0006 (NSPB) MILNER, ROBERT Molecular characterization of neuronal specificity Properties of proteins expressed in a brain region-specific manner
P01NS-22347-06 0007 (NSPB) BUCHMEIER, MICHAEL J Molecular characterization of neuronal specificity Viral induced CNS diseases
P01NS-22347-06 0008 (NSPB) PETERSON, PER A Molecular characterization of neuronal specificity Substance K receptor cDNA
P01NS-22347-06 0009 (NSPB) BLOOM, FLOYD E Molecular characterization of neuronal specificity Identification of cell specific mRNAs
P01NS-22347-06 9002 (NSPB) BUCHMEIER, MICHAEL J Molecular characterization of neuronal specificity Core--Immunology
R01NS-22352-07 (NEUA) LOW, PHILLIP A MAYO FOUNDATION 200 FIRST STREET SOUTHWEST ROCHESTER, MN 55905 Nerve blood flow in normal and ischemic peripheral nerve
R01NS-22356-07 (NLS) STEINBACH, JOSEPH H WASHINGTON UNIV SCHOOL OF MED 660 SOUTH EUCLID AVE, BOX 8054 ST LOUIS, MO 63110 Acetylcholine receptor function
R01NS-22367-07 (NEUB) CARLSON, STEVEN S PHYSIOLOGY & BIOPHYSICS DEPT UNIVERSITY OF WASHINGTON SEATTLE, WA 98195 Extracellular matrix nerve terminal anchorage proteins
R01NS-22373-07 (NEUA) HABLITZ, JOHN J UNIV OF ALABAMA AT BIRMINGHAM UNIVERSITY STATION BIRMINGHAM, AL 35294 Ionic alterations accompanying neocortical epilepsy
R01NS-22376-07 (BIO) NEUFELD, ELIZABETH F UNIVERSITY OF CALIFORNIA LOS ANGELES, CA 90024-1737 Molecular studies of beta-hexosaminidase in genetic disease
R01NS-22402-07 (NEUB) GARNER, JUDY A UNIV OF SOUTHERN CALIFORNIA 1333 SAN PABLO STREET LOS ANGELES, CA 90033 Molecular organization of neuron terminals
R01NS-22404-06 (HUD) MADISON, ROGER DUKE UNIVERSITY BOX 3807 DURHAM, NC 27710 Nerve guide; neurosurgical alternative for nerve repair
R01NS-22416-05 (BEM) AUSTIN, JOAN K INDIANA UNIVERSITY 610 BARNHILL DRIVE INDIANAPOLIS, IN 46202 Childhood epilepsy--Factors affecting adaptation
R01NS-22422-04A2 (NEUC) HEINRICH, GERHARD UNIVERSITY HOSPITAL 88 EAST NEWTON STREET BOSTON, MA 02118 Nerve growth factor--Biosynthesis and physiology
R01NS-22452-07 (NEUC) KELLY, PAUL T UNIVERSITY OF TEXAS PO BOX 20708 HOUSTON, TX 77225 Molecular basis of synapse formation
R01NS-22454-06 (NEUB) HAMM, THOMAS M ST JOSEPHS HOSP & MED CENTER 350 W THOMAS RD PHOENIX, AZ 85013 Analysis of the recurrent Renshaw circuit
R01NS-22457-03 (NLS) MIYAMOTO, MICHAEL D EAST TENNESSEE STATE UNIVERSIT PO BOX 19810A JOHNSON CITY, TN 37614-0002 Subcellular neurobiology of transmitter release
R01NS-22472-06 (NLS) LORING, RALPH HARROP NORTHEASTERN UNIVERSITY 360 HUNTINGTON AVE BOSTON, MA 02115 Characterization of neuronal nicotinic receptors
R01NS-22475-06 (NEUC) MESSING, ALBEE UNIVERSITY OF WISCONSIN MADISO 2015 LINDEN DRIVE WEST MADISON, WI 53706-1102 Neuropathology in transgenic mice
R01NS-22490-06 (ORTH) PETERSON, BARRY W NORTHWESTERN UNIVERSITY 633 CLARK ST CHICAGO, IL 60208 Systems analysis of human head stabilization
R01NS-22511-06 (NEUA) HABER, SUZANNE UNIV OF ROCHESTER 601 ELMWOOD AVE, BOX 603 ROCHESTER, NY 14642 The basal ganglia--Chemical and functional circuitry
R01NS-22517-06 (NEUB) DONOGHUE, JOHN P BROWN UNIVERSITY BOX 1953, CTR FOR NEURAL SCI PROVIDENCE, RI 02912 Motor cortex reorganization
R01NS-22518-07 (NEUC) MANDEL, GAIL RESEACH FOUNDATION OF SUNY STONY BROOK, NY 11794-5230 Regulation of the sodium channel in excitable cells
R01NS-22526-06 (NLS) PAPKA, RAYMOND E UNIV OF OKLAHOMA HLTH SCI CTR P O BOX 26901 OKLAHOMA CITY, OK 73190 Female reproductive organs and their innervation
R01NS-22543-09 (BPO) STEIN, BARRY E VIRGINIA COMMONWEALTH UNIVERSI BOX 551/MCV STATION RICHMOND, VA 23298 Result of modality convergence in the brain
R01NS-22571-04A1 (NEUB) LUST, WESLEY D UNIV HOSPITALS OF CLEVELAND 2074 ABINGTON ROAD CLEVELAND, OH 44106 Focal stroke--Metabolism and pH using neutral red
R01NS-22576-06 (NLS) SINGH, INDERJIT MEDICAL UNIV OF SOUTH CAROLINA 171 ASHLEY AVE CHARLESTON, SC 29425 Peroxisomal oxidation in X-linked adrenoleukodystrophy
R01NS-22577-07 (PHY) CAMPBELL, DONALD T OREGON STATE UNIVERSITY MARK O HATFIELD MARINE SCI CTR NEWPORT, OREG 97365-5296 Molecular basis of membrane excitability
R01NS-22589-05 (NLS) MELLER, EMANUEL NEW YORK UNIVERSITY MED CTR 550 FIRST AVENUE NEW YORK, N Y 10016 Dopamine receptor subtypes and function
R01NS-22603-07 (NEUB) GINSBERG, MYRON D UNIV MIAMI SCHOOL OF MEDICINE PO BOX 016960 MIAMI, FL 33101 Vulnerability to brain ischemia--Role of neural activity
R01NS-22611-07 (SRC) TOOLE, JAMES F BOWMAN GRAY SCHOOL OF MEDICINE 300 S HAWTHORNE ROAD WINSTON-SALEM, N C 27103 Stroke prevention--Medical/surgical carotid stenosis study
R01NS-22614-06 (NEUA) LANDIS, DENNIS M CWRU SCHOOL OF MEDICINE DEPT OF NEUROLOGY CLEVELAND, OH 44106 Structure and function of astrocytes
R01NS-22621-06 (NEUB) EATON, ROBERT C UNIVERSITY OF COLORADO CAMPUS BOX 334/BIOLOGY DEPT BOULDER, CO 80309-0334 A cellular model for brain stem control of movement
R01NS-22625-06A1 (PHY) CATTERALL, WILLIAM A UNIVERSITY OF WASHINGTON SEATTLE, WA 98195 Molecular properties of voltage-sensitive calcium channels
R01NS-22626-07 (NEUA) GAZZANIGA, MICHAEL S DARTMOUTH MEDICAL SCHOOL HANOVER, NH 03756 Neurologic and cognitive analysis of callosotomy patients
R01NS-22628-06 (NLS) FRESCHI, JOSEPH E EMORY UNIVERSITY SCH OF MED PO DRAWER V, WMB SUITE 6000 ATLANTA, GA 30322 The muscarinic acetylcholine synaptic potential
R01NS-22637-06 (NEUB) GERSHON, MICHAEL D COLUMBIA UNIVERSITY 630 WEST 168TH STREET NEW YORK, N Y 10032 Serotonin receptors--Characterization and ontogeny
R01NS-22663-05 (NLS) PITTMAN, RANDALL N DEPARTMENT OF PHARMACOLOGY 133 SOUTH 36TH ST, SUITE 300 PHILADELPHIA, PA 19104-6084 Neuronal molecules relevant to neurite outgrowth
R01NS-22671-05 (NLS) CONNOR, JAMES R PENNSYLVANIA STATE UNIVERSITY MILTON S. HERSHEY MEDICAL CTR HERSHEY, PA 17033 Iron proteins and oligodendrocytic function
R01NS-22672-04 (NEUA) JOBE, PHILLIP C UNIVERSITY OF ILLINOIS BOX 1649 PEORIA, IL 61656 Noradrenergic seizure regulation
R01NS-22675-07 (BIO) CHIKARAISHI, DONA M TUFTS UNIVERSITY 136 HARRISON AVENUE BOSTON, MA 02111 Molecular basis of tyrosine hydroxylase regulation
R01NS-22677-04A2 (BEM) CLEELAND, CHARLES S DEPARTMENT OF NEUROLOGY 610 WALNUT ST MADISON, WI 53705 Laboratory studies of pain control methods
R55NS-22688-07 (NLS) SAYRE, LAWRENCE M CASE WESTERN RESERVE UNIVERSIT 10900 EUCLID AVE CLEVELAND, OH 44106-7078 Mechanisms of neurotoxic action and metabolic activation
R01NS-22695-06 (NLS) SHAW, GERARD PJ UNIVERSITY OF FLORIDA BOX 100244, JHMHC GAINESVILLE, FL 32601-0244 Neurofilament modifications--Extent and significance
R55NS-22697-07 (NEUC) ANGELETTI, RUTH H ALBERT EINSTEIN COLLEGE OF MED 1300 MORRIS PARK AVENUE BRONX, NY 10461 Chromogranin and the neuroendocrine system
R01NS-22698-06 (NLS) MARSHALL, JOHN F UNIVERSITY OF CALIFORNIA IRVINE, CA 92717 Striatal organization and dopamine receptor localization
R01NS-22703-04 (HUD) CUFFIN, BENJAMIN N MASSACHUSETTS INST TECHNOLOGY 77 MASSACHUSETTS AVENUE CAMBRIDGE, MA 02139 Effects of the skull and head shape on EEG's and MEG's
R01NS-22716-05 (NEUC) BLATTEIS, CLARK M UNIVERSITY OF TENNESSEE 894 UNION AVENUE MEMPHIS, TN 38163 Central monoamines in acute-phase reaction
R01NS-22764-08 (PHY) POO, MU-MING COLUMBIA UNIVERSITY NEW YORK, NY 10027 Nerve growth, transmitter release, and synaptogenesis
P01NS-22786-07 (NSPA) PRUSINER, STANLEY B UNIVERSITY OF CALIFORNIA SAN FRANCISCO, CA 94143-0518 Transmissible and genetic neurodegenerative diseases
P01NS-22786-07 0001 (NSPA) CARLSON, GEORGE A Transmissible and genetic neurodegenerative diseases Congenic mice and scrapie isolates
P01NS-22786-07 0002 (NSPA) WEISSMANN, CHARLES Transmissible and genetic neurodegenerative diseases Ablation of PrP genes in mice and search for a scrapie-specific nucleic acid
P01NS-22786-07 0003 (NSPA) RIESNER, DETLEV Transmissible and genetic neurodegenerative diseases Search for a scrapie-specific nucleic acid and characterization of PrP mRNAs
P01NS-22786-07 0004 (NSPA) HOOD, LEROY Transmissible and genetic neurodegenerative diseases Characterization and sequencing of prion proteins
P01NS-22786-07 0005 (NSPA) PRUSINER, STANLEY B Transmissible and genetic neurodegenerative diseases Molecular genetics and cell biology of prion diseases
P01NS-22786-07 9001 (NSPA) PRUSINER, STANLEY B Transmissible and genetic neurodegenerative diseases Core--Animal core
P01NS-22786-07 9002 (NSPA) PRUSINER, STANLEY B Transmissible and genetic neurodegenerative diseases Core--Scientific core
P01NS-22807-07 (SRC) RAKIC, PASKO T YALE UNIV SCH OF MED 333 CEDAR STREET NEW HAVEN, CT 06510 Developmental neurobiology of the

neocortex

P01NS-22807-07 0001 (SRC) RAKIC, PASKO T Developmental neurobiology of the neocortex Molecular mechanisms of neuronal migration

P01NS-22807-07 0002 (SRC) HOCKFIELD, SUSAN Developmental neurobiology of the neocortex Regulation of cell phenotype in the developing neocortex

P01NS-22807-07 0003 (SRC) SCHWARTZ, MICHAEL Developmental neurobiology of the neocortex Transmitter and axonal development

P01NS-22807-07 0004 (SRC) LIDOW, MICHAEL Developmental neurobiology of the neocortex Ontogeny of major neurotransmitter receptors in the cerebral cortex

P01NS-22807-07 0005 (SRC) MCCORMICK, DAVID A Developmental neurobiology of the neocortex Development and modulation of synaptic plasticity in the neocortex

P01NS-22807-07 9001 (SRC) RAKIC, PASKO T Developmental neurobiology of the neocortex Core

R01NS-22835-06 (ECS) SAPER, CLIFFORD B UNIV OF CHICAGO 947 E 58TH ST/DEPT PHARM/PHYSI CHICAGO, IL 60637 Central cardiac pathways

P01NS-22849-06 (NSPA) GRIFFIN, JOHN W JOHNS HOPKINS UNIVERSITY 600 N WOLFE ST / MEYER 6-113 BALTIMORE, MD 21205 Pathogenesis of peripheral nerve disease

P01NS-22849-06 0003 (NSPA) TRAPP, BRUCE D Pathogenesis of peripheral nerve disease Molecular mechanisms of Schwann cell myelination

P01NS-22849-06 0006 (NSPA) HOFFMAN, PAUL N Pathogenesis of peripheral nerve disease The axotomy response

P01NS-22849-06 0007 (NSPA) CLEVELAND, DON W Pathogenesis of peripheral nerve disease Functional roles of the NF-H neurofilament protein

P01NS-22849-06 0008 (NSPA) GRIFFIN, JOHN W Pathogenesis of peripheral nerve disease Human nerve pathology & cell interactions in peripheral nerve disease

P01NS-22849-06 9001 (NSPA) GRIFFIN, JOHN W Pathogenesis of peripheral nerve disease Core--Scientific core

R01NS-22897-06 (NEUB) MARIN-PADILLA, MIGUEL DARTMOUTH MEDICAL SCHOOL HANOVER, NH 03756 Normal and abnormal neurogenesis of the human cerebellum

R01NS-22899-06 (RNM) MATHIS, CHESTER A THE REGENTS OF THE UNIV. CA. DEPT. OF RES. MED. & RAD. BIO. BERKELEY, CA 94720 Serotonin uptake inhibitor ligands for PET studies

R01NS-22933-05 (NEUB) HEFTI, FRANZ F UNIV OF SOUTHERN CALIFORNIA 3715 MCCLINTOCK AVE LOS ANGELES, CA 90089-0191 Pharmacology of NGF for forebrain cholinergic neurons

R01NS-22941-04A1 (NLS) MCNAMEE, MARK G UNIVERSITY OF CALIFORNIA DAVIS, CA 95616 Chemical modifications of the acetylcholine receptor

R01NS-22961-06 (NLS) MAGGIO, JOHN HARVARD MEDICAL SCHOOL 240 LONGWOOD AVENUE BOSTON, MA 02115 Tachykinins and tachykinin receptors

R01NS-22966-06 (NLS) RANDICH, ALAN UNIV OF ALABAMA AT BIRMINGHAM UAB STATION BIRMINGHAM, AL 35294 Cardiovascular/pain--Regulatory system interactions

R01NS-22974-06 (BPO) WILLOWS, A O DENNIS UNIVERSITY OF WASHINGTON DEPT OF ZOOLOGY SEATTLE, WA 98195 Neurosensory mechanisms of orientation to geomagnetism

R01NS-22979-07 (PHY) RAKOWSKI, ROBERT F UNIV HLTH SCI/CHICAGO MED SCH 3333 GREEN BAY RD N CHICAGO, IL 60064 Voltage-clamp studies of sodium pump current and flux

R01NS-23002-06 (NEUA) BAZAN, NICOLAS G LSU EYE CENTER 2020 GRAVIER STREET NEW ORLEANS, LA 70112 Role of phospholipids and arachidonic acid in epilepsy

R01NS-23006-06 (NLS) LUTHIN, GARY R HAHNEMANN UNIVERSITY BROAD & VINE MAIL STOP 409 PHILADELPHIA, PA 19102 Muscarinic receptor coupling mechanisms

R01NS-23017-06 (TOX) COHEN, GERALD MOUNT SINAI SCHOOL OF MEDICINE 1 GUSTAVE L LEVY PL BOX 1137 NEW YORK, N Y 10029 H202 and oxy-radical stress in catecholamine neurons

R01NS-23021-06 (NEUC) CEPKO, CONSTANCE L HARVARD MEDICAL SCHOOL 25 SHATTUCK STREET BOSTON, MA 02115 Lineage analysis of the CNS

R01NS-23022-06 (NLS) CAMPAGNONI, ANTHONY T NEUROPSYCHIATRIC INSTITUTE 760 WESTWOOD PLAZA LOS ANGELES, CALIF 90024-1406 Synthesis and assembly of basic proteins in myelin

R01NS-23028-06 (RAP) RUSSELL, DAVID F UNIVERSITY OF MISSOURI-ST. LOU 8001 NATURAL BRIDGE ROAD ST. LOUIS, MO 63121-4499 Neural control of respiration

R01NS-23036-06 (NLS) LUMPKIN, MICHAEL D DEPT OF PHYSIOLOGY/BIOPHYSICS GEORGETOWN UNIV SCH OF MED WASHINGTON, DC 20007 Self regulation of hypothalamic GRF and somatostatin

R01NS-23039-05 (VR) CLEMENTS, JANICE E JOHNS HOPKINS UNIVERSITY 720 RUTLAND AVE BALTIMORE, MD 21205 Regulating gene expression of neurotropic lentivirus

R01NS-23055-06 (NEUA) KADEKARO, MASSAKO UNIV OF TEXAS MEDICAL BRANCH 301 UNIVERSITY BLVD GALVESTON, TX 77550 Neural regulation of thirst

R01NS-23058-06 (NEUB) MC MANAMAN, JAMES BAYLOR COLL OF MEDICINE ONE BAYLOR PLAZA HOUSTON, TX 77030 Action of muscle trophic factors on spinal motor neuron

R01NS-23061-06 (NLS) HUANG, LI-YEN M UNIVERSITY OF TEXAS 200 UNIVERSITY BLVD GALVESTON, TX 77550 Electrical properties of isolated dorsal horn project neurons

R01NS-23071-06 (NEUA) BRADY, ROBERT J NEW YORK STATE DEPT OF HEALTH WADSWORTH CTR FOR LABS & RES ALBANY, N Y 12201 The role of ex amino acid receptors in epileptogenesis

R01NS-23074-06 (NEUB) FINCH, DAVID M BRAIN RESEARCH INSTITUTE 405 HILGARD AVE LOS ANGELES, CA 90024-1406 Synaptic organization of basal forebrain projections

R01NS-23077-07 (NEUA) MASUKAWA, LEONA M GRADUATE HOSPITAL 415 SOUTH 19TH STREET PHILADELPHIA, PA 19146 Cellular mechanisms of epilepsy

R01NS-23079-06 (NEUB) ARIANO, MARJORIE A UNIV OF VERMONT COLLEGE OF MED BURLINGTON, VT 05405 DoPAmine receptor localization in rat striatum

R01NS-23084-07 (NLS) SCHWEITZER, ERIK S UNIVERSITY OF CALIFORNIA 10833 LE CONTE AVENUE LOS ANGELES, CA 90024-1763 Mechanisms of peptide secretion in PC-12 cells

R01NS-23094-07 (NEUB) BANKER, GARY A UNIVERSITY OF VIRGINIA BOX 230 HLTH SCIS CTR CHARLOTTESVILLE, VA 22908 Dendritic transport

R01NS-23102-05A1 (NLS) YU, ROBERT K VIRGINIA COMMONWEALTH UNIV BOX 614, MCV STATION RICHMOND, VA 23298-0614 Biochemical study of myelination and demyelination

R01NS-23113-06 (NLS) GIULIAN, DANA J BAYLOR COLLEGE OF MEDICINE ONE BAYLOR PLAZA HOUSTON, TX 77030 Interleukin-1 in brain development and injury

R01NS-23124-05 (NEUB) DUNCAN, IAN D UNIVERSITY OF WISCONSIN 2015 LINDEN DRIVE WEST MADISON, WI 53706 Dysmelination in the x-linked myelin mutants

R01NS-23132-07 (IMS) WEINER, HOWARD L BRIGHAM AND WOMEN'S HOSPITAL 75 FRANCIS STREET BOSTON, MASS 02115 Study of immunoregulatory T cells in multiple sclerosis

R01NS-23140-06 (NLS) FARB, DAVID H BOSTON UNIVERSITY 80 EAST CONCORD STREET BOSTON, MA 02118 Regulation and turnover of the benzodiazepine receptor

R01NS-23158-06 (NEUB) MOODY, SALLY A UNIVERSITY OF VIRGINIA DEPT. ANATOMY AND CELL BIOLOGY CHARLOTTESVILLE, VA 22908 Neuronal lineage determinants

R01NS-23160-06 (NEUA) DE LONG, MAHLON R EMORY UNIVERSITY 601 WMB, DRAWER V ATLANTA, GA 30322 Sensorimotor integration in neostriatum

R01NS-23162-06 (EVR) FUJINAMI, ROBERT S UNIVERSITY OF UTAH MEDICAL CENTER SALT LAKE CITY, UTAH 84132 Molecular mimicry and virus induced autoimmunity

R01NS-23208-06 (NEUB) WEEKS, JANIS C UNIVERSITY OF OREGON INSTITUTE OF NEUROSCIENCE EUGENE, OR 97403 Developmental changes in neuronal form and function

R01NS-23209-06 (HAR) MC COLLUM, GIN GOOD SAMARITAN HOSP & MED CTR 1120 NORTHWEST 20TH AVENUE PORTLAND, OR 97209 Neural calculation in sensorimotor control

R01NS-23218-05A1 (NEUA) OLSON, JAMES E COX HEART INSTITUTE 3525 SOUTHERN BLVD KETTERING, OH 45429 Mechanisms of cytotoxic brain edema

R01NS-23221-05 (NEUC) VANDENBARK, ARTHUR A VA MEDICAL CENTER 3710 SW US VETERANS HOSPITAL R PORTLAND, OR 97201 Genetic basis of T cell response to myelin basic protein

R01NS-23240-07 (NEUB) WHITAKER, JOHN N UNIV OF ALABAMA AT BIRMINGHAM UAB STATION BIRMINGHAM, AL 35294 Myelin basic protein peptides in body fluids

R01NS-23241-07 (CTY) FAMBROUGH, DOUGLAS M JOHNS HOPKINS UNIVERSITY 34TH & CHARLES STREETS BALIMORE, MD 21218 Biophysics of gap junction channels

R01NS-23244-06 (NEUA) WATSON, BRANT D UNIVERSITY OF MIAMI PO BOX 016960 MIAMI, FL 33101 Brain recovery in reversible thrombotic stroke

R55NS-23262-04A1 (NLS) WEISS, GERALD K UNIVERSITY OF NEW MEXICO SCHOOL OF MEDICINE ALUQUERQUE, NM 87131 Neuroendocrine regulation of seizure development

R01NS-23266-05 (NEUB) WELLS, JOSEPH UNIVERSITY OF VERMONT BURLINGTON, VT 05405 Does recovery continue after neural transplants die

R01NS-23273-06 (NLS) MCCAMAN, MARILYN W BECKMAN RESEARCH INSTITUTE NEUROSCIENCES DUARTE, CA 91010 Presynaptic mechanisms in sympathetic ganglia

R01NS-23284-06 (PHY) MILEDI, RICARDO DEPARTMENT OF PSYCHOBIOLOGY UNIVERSITY OF CALIFORNIA IRVINE, CALIF 92717 Serotonin receptors and chloride channels

R01NS-23294-07 (PHY) ALDRICH, RICHARD W STANFORD UNIVERSITY SCH OF MED 173 BECKMAN CENTER STANFORD, CA 94305-5426 Gating of ion channels in excitable cells

R01NS-23307-04A2 (NLS) FLOYD, ROBERT A OKLAHOMA MEDICAL RESEARCH FDN 825 NE 13TH STREET OKLAHOMA CITY, OK 73104 Mechanisms of oxidative damage in brain

R01NS-23317-07 (NLS) KAPCALA, LEONARD P UNIV OF MARYLAND SCH OF MED 655 W BALTIMORE ST BALTIMORE, MD 21201 Regulation of secretion of POMC peptides in brain

R01NS-23320-07 (NEUB) BRADY, SCOTT T DEPT OF CELL BIOL. & NEUROSCI. MEDICAL CENTER AT DALLAS DALLAS, TX 75235-9039 Properties of axonal tubulin related to neuronal growth

R01NS-23321-06 (DABR) GALLAGER, DOROTHY W YALE UNIVERSITY 34 PARK STREET NEW HAVEN, CT 06508 Tolerance to benzodiazepines and GABAergic subsensitivity

R01NS-23322-06 (NEUC) CAMPAGNONI, ANTHONY T NEUROPSYCHIATRIC INSTITUTE 760 WESTWOOD PLAZA 48-241 LOS ANGELES, CA 90024-1759 Structural organization of myelin protein genes

R01NS-23324-06A1 (NEUB) NOBLE, LINDA J SAN FRANCISCO GEN HOSP 1001 POTRERO AVE RM 4M39 SAN FRANCISCO, CA 94110 Spinal cord injury--Alterations in barrier permeability

R01NS-23325-07 (TOX) LOWNDES, HERBERT E RUTGERS UNIV/BUSCH CAMPUS COLLEGE OF PHARMACY PISCATAWAY, NJ 08854 Spinal cord correlates of peripheral neuropathies

P50NS-23327-07 (NSPA) WU, KENNETH K UNIVERSITY OF TEXAS PO BOX 20036 HOUSTON, TEXAS 77225 Prostaglandins in cerebrovascular thrombosis

P50NS-23327-07 0004 (NSPA) HELLUMS, JESSE D Prostaglandins in cerebrovascular thrombosis Platelet reactions in controlled shear fields

P50NS-23327-07 0005 (NSPA) HALL, ELIZABETH R Prostaglandins in cerebrovascular thrombosis Biosynthesis of thromboxane A2

P50NS-23327-07 0006 (NSPA) GIULIAN, DANA Prostaglandins in cerebrovascular thrombosis Arachidonate metabolism in nervous system cells

P50NS-23327-07 0007 (NSPA) WU, KENNETH K Prostaglandins in cerebrovascular thrombosis Regulation of eicosanoid synthesis

P50NS-23327-07 0008 (NSPA) MC INTIRE, LARRY V Prostaglandins in cerebrovascular thrombosis Mechanical stresses on arachidonic acid metabolism

P50NS-23327-07 0009 (NSPA) WU, KENNETH K Prostaglandins in cerebrovascular thrombosis PGI2 and serumbinding proteins/platelet receptors

P50NS-23327-07 9001 (NSPA) WU, KENNETH K Prostaglandins in cerebrovascular thrombosis Core--Analytical core

R01NS-23343-07 (NEUC) BOTHWELL, MARK A UNIVERSITY OF WASHINGTON SEATTLE, WA 98195 Nerve growth factor

PROJECT NO., ORGANIZATIONAL UNIT., INVESTIGATOR, ADDRESS, TITLE

R01NS-23345-06 (NLS) SHEETZ, MICHAEL P DUKE UNIV MED CENTER BOX 3011 DURHAM, NC 27710 Molecular basis of organelle movement in axons
R01NS-23346-07 (PHY) SCHNEIDER, MARTIN F UNIVERSITY OF MARYLAND 660 W REDWOOD ST BALTIMORE, MD 21201 Excitation-contraction coupling in cut muscle fibers
R01NS-23347-18 (NEUB) RALSTON, HENRY J, III UNIVERSITY OF CALIFORNIA 513 PARNASSUS AVENUE SAN FRANCISCO, CALIF 94143 Synaptic organization in spinal cord and thalamus
P01NS-23349-06 (NSPA) MILLER, STEPHEN D NORTHWESTERN UNIVERSITY 303 E CHICAGO AVE CHICAGO, IL 60611 CNS damage from Theiler's virus persistence--MS model
P01NS-23349-06 0001 (NSPA) MILLER, STEPHEN CNS damage from Theiler's virus persistence--MS model T-cell immunity in TMEV-induced demyelination
P01NS-23349-06 0005 (NSPA) MELVOLD, ROGER W CNS damage from Theiler's virus persistence--MS model Immunogenetics of susceptibility to TMEV-induced demyelination
P01NS-23349-06 0006 (NSPA) LUO, MING CNS damage from Theiler's virus persistence--MS model Crystallographic analysis of the 3-D structure of TMEV
P01NS-23349-06 0007 (NSPA) LIPTON, HOWARD L CNS damage from Theiler's virus persistence--MS model Mutations and deletions of TMEV surface residues
P01NS-23349-06 0008 (NSPA) RUNDELL, MARY K CNS damage from Theiler's virus persistence--MS model Expression of individual TMEV proteins
P01NS-23349-06 9001 (NSPA) DAL CANTO, MAURO CNS damage from Theiler's virus persistence--MS model Core--Neuropathology
R01NS-23350-07 (NEUA) DE LORENZO, ROBERT J VIRGINIA COMMONWEALTH UNIV MCV STATION 599 RICHMOND, VA 23298 Protein phosphorylation, epilepsy, & anticonvulsants
R01NS-23354-05A2 (PBC) KADOWAKI, HIROKO FRAMINGHAM MEDICAL BUILDING 475 FRANKLIN ST FRAMINGHAM, MA 01701 Regulation of neuronal glycosphingolipid biosynthesis
R01NS-23355-06 (NLS) SEYFRIED, THOMAS N DEPT OF BIOLOGY BOSTON COLLEGE CHESTNUT HILL, MA 02167 Neurochemical studies in genetic models of epilepsy
R01NS-23360-04 (PHY) ROGART, RICHARD B UNIVERSITY OF CHICAGO 5841 SOUTH MARYLAND, BOX 249 CHICAGO, IL 60637 Na+ channels in normal & abnormal nerve membrane
R01NS-23368-07 (NEUC) ROGERS, SHERRY L UNIV OF NEW MEXICO SCH OF MED DEPARTMENT OF ANATOMY ALBUQUERQUE, N M 87131 Laminin and fibronectin in peripheral nerve development
R01NS-23375-06 (PHY) CHIU, SHING Y UNIVERSITY OF WISCONSIN 1300 UNIVERSITY AVENUE MADISON, WI 53706 Ionic channels in mammalian myelinated nerves
R01NS-23384-05 (SSS) LEE, CHUAN-PU WAYNE STATE UNIV SCH OF MED SCOTT HALL/540 E CANFIELD ST DETROIT, MI 48201 Neurological hereditary degenerative diseases
P01NS-23393-06 (NSPA) WELCH, KENNETH M HENRY FORD HOSPITAL 2799 WEST GRANT BLVD. DETROIT, MI 48202 Center for stroke research
P01NS-23393-06 0001 (NSPA) EWING, JAMES R Center for stroke research NMR indicator dilution technique in CBF
P01NS-23393-06 0002 (NSPA) CHOPP, MICHAEL Center for stroke research In vivo spectroscopy in experimental ischemia
P01NS-23393-06 0003 (NSPA) WELCH, KENNETH Center for stroke research In vivo spectroscopy in clinical stroke
P01NS-23393-06 0004 (NSPA) BROWN, GREGORY Center for stroke research In vivo spectroscopy of vascular and degenerative dementia
P01NS-23393-06 9001 (NSPA) SMITH, MICHAEL B Center for stroke research Core--NMR spectroscopy
P01NS-23393-06 9002 (NSPA) HERSHON, DAVE Center for stroke research Core--Functional imaging-image analysis
P01NS-23393-06 9003 (NSPA) EWING, JAMES R Center for stroke research Core--Cerebral blood flow methods
P01NS-23393-06 9004 (NSPA) BROWN, GREGORY G Center for stroke research Core--Neuropsychology
P01NS-23393-06 9005 (NSPA) EWING, JAMES R Center for stroke research Core--Data management and statistics
R01NS-23410-06 (NEUC) COLLINS, FRANCIS S UNIVERSITY OF MICHIGAN 4708 MEDICAL SCIENCE II, BOX 0 ANN ARBOR, MI 48109-0618 Linkage studies in neurofibromatosis
R01NS-23421-06 (PCB) EASTMAN, CHARMANE I RUSH MEDICAL CENTER 1653 W CONGRESS PKWY CHICAGO, IL 60612-3864 Shifting human circadian rhythms with bright light
R01NS-23426-05 (HUD) CHASE, MICHAEL H UNIV OF CALIF, LOS ANGELES 405 HILGARD AVE LOS ANGELES, CA 90024-1406 Motoneurons during sleep
R01NS-23430-01A4 (NLS) STRAUSS, WILLIAM L UNIVERSITY OF MIAMI PO BOX 016189 MIAMI, FL 33101 Cloning of the gene for choline acetyltransferase
R01NS-23444-05 (IMS) OFFNER, HALINA VA MEDICAL CENTER 3710 SW US VETERANS HOSPITAL R PORTLAND, OR 97201 Clonotypic regulation of encephalitogenic T lymphocytes
R01NS-23446-05 (VR) HAASE, ASHLEY T UNIVERSITY OF MINNESOTA MAYO BOX 196, 420 DELAWARE SE MINNEAPOLIS, MN 55455 Activation of genes in the aging brain and in scrapie
R01NS-23466-04A1 (NEUB) BETZ, WILLIAM J UNIV OF COLORADO MED SCHOOL 4200 E NINTH AVE DENVER, CO 80262 Nerve-muscle synapse elimination during development
R01NS-23476-06 (NEUB) ANDERSON, DAVID J CALIFORNIA INST OF TECHNOLOGY 1201 EAST CALIFORNIA BOULEVARD PASADENA, CA 91125 Mechanisms of neural crest development and plasticity
R01NS-23502-06 (NEUB) SMITH, PETER G UNIVERSITY OF KANSAS MED CTR 39TH AND RAINBOW BLVD KANSAS CITY, KS 66103-8410 Sympathetic neuroplasticity
R01NS-23510-06 (NEUC) WHITE, KALPANA P BRANDEIS UNIVERSITY 415 SOUTH STREET: DEPT/BIOLOGY WALTHAM, MA 02254 Molecular genetics of biogenic amine neurons
R01NS-23512-05 (NLS) JACKSON, MEYER B 470 NORTH CHARTER STREET MADISON, WI 53706 Gating mechanisms of chemically activated channels
R01NS-23541-05 (NLS) WASZCZAK, BARBARA LEE NORTHEASTERN UNIVERSITY 360 HUNTINGTON AVENUE BOSTON, MA 02115 Dopamine effects on substantia nigra neurons

PROJECT NO., ORGANIZATIONAL UNIT., INVESTIGATOR, ADDRESS, TITLE

R01NS-23558-05 (NEUA) GEVINS, ALAN S EEG SYSTEMS LABORATORY 51 FEDERAL ST., SUITE 401 SAN FRANCISCO, CA 94107 Multiple source localization from EEGS and MEGS
R01NS-23560-04S1 (NLS) HOFFMAN, WILLIAM STANFORD UNIVERSITY STANFORD, CA 94305-5235 Characterization of serotonin receptor subtypes
R01NS-23561-04A1 (IMS) WHITACRE, CAROLINE C OHIO STATE UNIVERSITY 333 WEST TENTH AVENUE COLUMBUS, OHIO 43210 Oral tolerance in allergic encephalomyelitis
R01NS-23569-06 (NEUB) LLOYD, PHILIP E UNIVERSITY OF CHICAGO 947 EAST 58TH ST CHICAGO, IL 60637 Modulatory neuropeptides in aplysia
R01NS-23583-07 (NLS) PENG, HSIAO-MING B UNC, AT CHAPEL HILL DEPT OF CELL BIOLOGY & ANATOMY CHAPEL HILL, NC 27599 Development of synapse
R01NS-23618-05 (NLS) MELLER, EMANUEL NEW YORK UNIVERSITY MED CTR 550 FIRST AVENUE NEW YORK, NY 10016 Receptor reserve at brain neurotransmitter receptors
R01NS-23641-06 (NEUA) LANDIS, DENNIS M CASE WESTERN RESERVE 2119 ABINGTON ROAD CLEVELAND, OH 44106 Structure and function at synapses
R01NS-23678-07 (NEUB) LANDIS, STORY C CASE WESTERN RESERVE UNIV DEPARTMENT OF PHARMACOLOGY CLEVELAND, OHIO 44106 Studies of synapse formation
R01NS-23682-06 (NEUA) HEROS, ROBERTO C UNIVERSITY OF MINNESOTA 420 DELAWARE STREET SE MINNEAPOLIS, MN 55455 Isovolemic hemodilution incerebral ischemia
R01NS-23684-11 (NEUB) KELLEY, DARCY B COLUMBIA UNIVERSITY DEPT OF BIOLOGICAL SCIENCES NEW YORK, N Y 10027 Neural substrates for reproductive behavior
P01NS-23705-04A1 (NSPB) NORTON, WILLIAM T ALBERT EINSTEIN COLL OF MEDICI 1300 MORRIS PARK AVENUE BRONX, NY 10461 Neurobiology of development
P01NS-23705-04A1 0002 (NSPB) CAMMER, WENDY Neurobiology of development Glial cell enzymes--Normal and abnormal development
P01NS-23705-04A1 0004 (NSPB) NORTON, WILLIAM T Neurobiology of development Function of glial precursor cells during development
P01NS-23705-04A1 0005 (NSPB) CHIU, FUNG-CHOW ALEX Neurobiology of development Molecular biology and expression of a 66kD neurofilament protein
P01NS-23705-04A1 0006 (NSPB) AQUINO, DENNIS A Neurobiology of development The heat stress response during disease and development
P01NS-23705-04A1 9001 (NSPB) NORTON, WILLIAM T Neurobiology of development Core--Histology facilities
R01NS-23719-06 (NEUC) DRACHMAN, DANIEL B JOHNS HOPKINS UNIV SCH OF MED 600 NORTH WOLFE STREET BALTIMORE, MD 21205 Nerve-muscle interactions in development and disease
P50NS-23724-06 (SRC) DEMENT, WILLIAM C STANFORD UNIV SCHOOL OF MEDICI BUILDING TD, RM 114 STANFORD, CA 94305 Center for narcolepsy and related disorders
P50NS-23724-06 0001 (SRC) MCDEVITT, HUGH O Center for narcolepsy and related disorders Immunogenetics and neuroimmunology
P50NS-23724-06 0003 (SRC) DEMENT, WILLIAM C Center for narcolepsy and related disorders Neurotransmitter mechanisms in canine narcolepsy
P50NS-23724-06 0005 (SRC) SIEGEL, JEROME Center for narcolepsy and related disorders Neurophysiology of canine narcolepsy
P50NS-23724-06 0008 (SRC) DEMENT, WILLIAM C Center for narcolepsy and related disorders Pharmacology of narcolepsy
P50NS-23724-06 0009 (SRC) DEMENT, WILLIAM C Center for narcolepsy and related disorders Receptor mechanisms in narcolepsy
P50NS-23724-06 0010 (SRC) HELLER, H CRAIG Center for narcolepsy and related disorders Thermoregulation in canine narcolepsy
P50NS-23724-06 0011 (SRC) GRUMET, CARL Center for narcolepsy and related disorders Linkage markers in narcolepsy
P50NS-23724-06 0012 (SRC) GUILLEMINAULT, CHRISTIAN Center for narcolepsy and related disorders Human twin studies
P50NS-23724-06 9001 (SRC) DEMENT, WILLIAM C Center for narcolepsy and related disorders Core--Clinical and laboratory data base
R01NS-23725-07 (NEUB) KOERBER, H RICHARD UNIVERSITY OF PITTSBURGH 3550 TERRACE STREET PITTSBURGH, PA 15261 Peripheral nerve regeneration and dorsal horn somatotopy
R01NS-23740-06 (MGN) KUNKEL, LOUIS M CHILDREN'S HOSPITAL CORPORATIO 300 LONGWOOD AVENUE BOSTON, MA 02115 Dystrophin and related proteins in neuromuscular disease
R01NS-23750-05 (NLS) KIMELBERG, HAROLD K ALBANY MEDICAL COLLEGE 47 NEW SCOTLAND AVENUE ALBANY, NY 12208 Volume regulation and membrane transport in astrocytes
R01NS-23753-06 (NEUB) KIDOKORO, YOSHIAKI UNIVERSITY OF CALIFORNIA LOS ANGELES, CA 90024-1751 Muscle differentiation and synaptic interaction
R01NS-23780-05 (NEUB) HOLT, CHRISTINE UNIV OF CALIF., SAN DIEGO 9500 GILMAN DRIVE LA JOLLA, CA 92093-0934 Axonal pathfinding in the embryonic brain
R01NS-23783-06 (NEUB) COULTER, JOE D DEPARTMENT OF ANATOMY 1-470 BSB IOWA CITY, IA 52242 Synaptic specificity in the spinal cord
R01NS-23805-06 (NEUB) ZAHM, DANIEL S ST LOUIS UNIVERSITY SCH OF MED 1402 SOUTH GRAND BLVD ST LOUIS, MO 63104 Convergent vs. parallel striatal dopaminergic afferents
R01NS-23807-06 (NLS) CARPENTER, DAVID O HEALTH RESEARCH, INC. WADSWORTH LABORATORIES ALBANY, NY 12201 Mechanisms of excitatory amino acid actions and toxicity
R01NS-23808-05 (NEUB) ZISKIND-CONHAIM, LEA UNIVERSITY OF WISCONSIN 1300 UNIVERSITY AVENUE MADISON, WI 53706 Development of sensory - motoneuron contacts
R01NS-23814-05 (NEUA) ZIVIN, JUSTIN A UNIVERSITY OF CALIFORNIA SCHOOL OF MEDICINE LA JOLLA, CA 92093 Experimental embolic stroke
R01NS-23831-06 (NLS) FISHER, STEPHEN K UNIVERSITY OF MICHIGAN 1103 EAST HURON STREET ANN ARBOR, MI 48104-1687 Muscarinic receptor coupling to inositides in CNS
R01NS-23840-05 (NLS) CHIU, FUNG-CHOW A ALBERT EINSTEIN COLLEGE OF MED 1300 MORRIS PARK AVENUE BRONX, NY 10461 Neurofilaments--Biochemistry and assembly
R01NS-23858-05 (NLS) SILVERMAN, ANN-JUDITH N Y STATE PSYCHIATRIC INST 722 WEST 168TH STREET NEW YORK, N Y 10032 Modification of hypothalamic neurons by behavioral stress

PROJECT NO., ORGANIZATIONAL UNIT., INVESTIGATOR, ADDRESS, TITLE

R01NS-23868-06 (NLS) BRADY, SCOTT T UNIV OF TEXAS SW MEDICAL CTR 5323 HARRY HINES BOULEVARD DALLAS, TX 75235 Molecular mechanisms of axonal transport

R01NS-23870-04A1 (NEUA) BETZ, A LORRIS DEPT. OF PED., SURG., NEUROLOG ANN ARBOR, MI 48109-0718 Blood to brain sodium transport

R01NS-23877-06 (NEUC) BROWN, ARTHUR M BAYLOR COLLEGE OF MEDICINE ONE BAYLOR PLAZA HOUSTON, TX 77030 Ionic movements across nerve cell body membranes

R01NS-23883-06 (PTHA) CIMENT, GARY S OREGON HEALTH SCIS UNIVERSITY 3181 S W SAM JACKSON PARK ROAD PORTLAND, OR 97201-3098 Neurofibromatosis--A model system using phorbol esters

R01NS-23885-06 (NEUC) WHITE, MICHAEL M UNIVERSITY OF PENNSYLVANIA PHILADELPHIA, PA 19104-6084 Structural aspects of ion channel function and assembly

R01NS-23896-06 (NLS) LEMKE, GREG E SALK INST FOR BIOLOGICAL STUDI PO BOX 85800 SAN DIEGO, CA 92186-5800 Myelination genes--Structure, function & regulation

R01NS-23915-06 (NEUB) EISEN, JUDITH S UNIVERSITY OF OREGON EUGENE, OR 97403 Neuronal pathfinding by identified motoneurons

R01NS-23916-06 (NEUB) YIP, JOSEPH W UNIV OF PITTSBURGH SCHOOL OF M 3550 TERRACE STREET PITTSBURGH, PA 15261 Specificity of synapse formation

R01NS-23918-04 (NEUA) FREED, CURT R UNIVERSITY OF COLORADO 4200 E NINTH AVE, C-237 DENVER, CO 80262 Brain transplant treatment for Parkinsonians

R01NS-23919-05 (NEUC) CONTI-TRONCONI, BIANCA M UNIVERSITY OF MINNESOTA 1479 GORTNER AVENUE ST PAUL, MN 55108 Autoimmunity to acetylcholine receptor

R01NS-23941-06 (NLS) ARMSTRONG, WILLIAM E UNIVERSITY OF TENNESSEE 875 MONROE AVENUE MEMPHIS, TN 38163 Electrophysiological correlates of vasopressin release

R01NS-23959-06 (BPO) BERRIDGE, KENT C UNIVERSITY OF MICHIGAN 1103 E HURON STREET ANN ARBOR, MI 48104-1687 Sensorimotor integration

R01NS-23960-04 (NEUA) HUTTENLOCHER, PETER R UNIVERSITY OF CHICAGO 5841 S MARYLAND AVE HOSP BOX 2 CHICAGO, IL 60637 Postnatal plasticity and recovery from brain damage

R01NS-23964-06 (BPO) SCHALLERT, TIMOTHY J UNIVERSITY OF TEXAS AUSTIN, TX 78712 Diazepam effects on recovery of function

R01NS-23970-06 (NLS) MANTYH, PATRICK W VA MEDICAL CENTER DEPT. OF PSYCHIATRY MINNEAPOLIS, MN 55417 Peripheral nociceptors in inflammation

R01NS-23975-04A2 (NLS) MURRIN, LEONARD C DEPT. OF PHARMACOLOGY 600 42ND STREET Development of nigrostriatal neuronal systems

R01NS-23978-06 (NLS) PARSONS, RODNEY L UNIVERSITY OF VERMONT GIVEN BLDG BURLINGTON, VT 05405 Transmitter interaction in a cardiac ganglion

R01NS-23979-04A1 (NEUA) GROTTA, JAMES C UNIVERSITY OF TEXAS MEDICAL SC 6431 FANNIN HOUSTON, TX 77030 Calcium blocker and related therapy for cerebral ischemia

R01NS-24014-05 (NLS) JULIANO, SHARON L UNIFORMED SERV UNIV OF HLTH SC 4301 JONES BRIDGE ROAD BETHESDA, MD 20784-4799 Structural correlates of cortical information processing

P01NS-24032-06 (NSPA) REDMOND, DONALD E, JR YALE UNIVERSTIY 333 CEDAR STREET NEW HAVEN, CT 06510-8068 Neural grafts in a model of Parkinson's disease

P01NS-24032-06 0003 (NSPA) REDMOND, DONALD E Neural grafts in a model of Parkinson's disease Behavioral/functional assessment of MPTP effects and neural grafting

P01NS-24032-06 0005 (NSPA) COLLIER, TIMOTHY Neural grafts in a model of Parkinson's disease Transplantation methods

P01NS-24032-06 9001 (NSPA) REDMOND, DONALD E Neural grafts in a model of Parkinson's disease Primate breeding, MPTP treatment and transplant facility core

P01NS-24032-06 0001 (NSPA) SLADEK, JOHN R Neural grafts in a model of Parkinson's disease Morphological evaluation of MPTP treatment and neural grafting

P01NS-24032-06 0002 (NSPA) ROTH, ROBERT H Neural grafts in a model of Parkinson's disease Biochemical and pharmacological assessment of MPTP & neural grafting

R01NS-24042-06 (NEUB) GIBSON, ALAN R ST JOSEPH'S HOSPITAL & MED CTR 350 WEST THOMAS ROAD PHOENIX, ARIZ 85013 Movement control by a cerebellar circuit

R01NS-24054-06 (NEUC) MOBLEY, WILLIAM C UNIVERSITY OF CALIFORNIA SAN FRANCISCO, CA 94143-0114 Nerve growth factor--Tropic effects on CNS neurons

R01NS-24058-05 (ORTH) ASHTON-MILLER, JAMES A UNIVERSITY OF MICHIGAN 3208 G. G. BROWN LAB ANN ARBOR, MI 48109-2125 Control of trunk equilibrium in sitting individuals

R29NS-24066-05 (MGN) GROSSMAN, MARK H ST CHRISTOPHERS HOSPITAL 3601 A STREET PHILADELPHIA, PA 19134 Catechol-o-methyltransferase--Biochemistry and genetics

R01NS-24067-07 (PHY) TSIEN, RICHARD W STANFORD UNIVERSITY B105 BECKMAN CENTER STANFORD, CA 94305-5426 Neuronal functions of multiple types of calcium channel

R01NS-24072-07 (NEUB) CALABRESE, RONALD L EMORY UNIVERSITY 1510 CLIFTON RD ATLANTA, GA 30322 Neuromodulatory influences on motor systems

R01NS-24078-04 (PHY) KULLBERG, RICHARD W UNIVERSITY OF ALASKA 3211 PROVIDENCE DRIVE ANCHORAGE, AK 99508 Development of nicotinic acetylcholine receptor function

R01NS-24109-05 (ECS) DUCKROW, ROBERT B THE MILTON S. HERSHEY MED. CNT P.O. BOX 850 HERSHEY, PA 17033 Cerebral blood flow during hyperglycemia

R01NS-24125-04A2 (HUD) HOLMES, LEWIS B MASSACHUSETTS GENERAL HOSPITAL 32 FRUIT STREET BOSTON, MA 02114 Maternal epilepsy--Effects on the brain and other organs

R01NS-24148-06 (NLS) HARLAN, RICHARD E TULANE UNIVERSITY 1430 TULANE AVENUE NEW ORLEANS, LA 70112 Immunoreactive prolactin in brain

R01NS-24172-06 (NEUC) LEDEEN, ROBERT W UNIVERSITY OF MED & DENT OF NJ 185 SOUTH ORANGE AVENUE NEWARK, N J 07103-2714 Neutral glycosphingolipids of the developing nervous systems

R01NS-24180-05 (NEUC) RODRIGUEZ, MOSES MAYO FOUNDATION 200 FIRST STREET SOUTHWEST ROCHESTER, MN 55905 Immune promotion of remyelination

R01NS-24188-04A2 (NEUA) ILINSKY, IGOR UNIVERSITY OF IOWA IOWA CITY, IA 52242 Synaptic organization of the motor thalamus

R01NS-24204-04 (NLS) IACOVITTI, LORRAINE M HAHNEMANN UNIVERSITY BROAD AND VINE PHILADELPHIA, PA 19102-1192 Studies on muscle-derived differentiation factor

R01NS-24205-05 (NLS) NICOLL, ROGER A DEPT. OF PHARMACOLOGY SAN FRANCISCO, CA 94143 Central serotonin receptors--Ionic and molecular mechanisms

R01NS-24207-07 (NLS) SARGENT, PETER B UNIVERSITY OF CALIFORNIA SAN FRANCISCO, CA 94143-0512 Neuronal nicotinic acetylcholine receptors

R29NS-24217-05 (BPO) RINGO, JAMES L UNIVERSITY OF ROCHESTER 601 ELMWOOD AVE, BOX 642 ROCHESTER, NY 14642 Reversible split-brain by commissural conduction block

R01NS-24224-05 (SRC) SHERMAN, DAVID G UNIV OF TEXAS HLTH SCI CENTER 7703 FLOYD CURL DRIVE SAN ANTONIO, TX 78284 Stroke prevention in atrial fibrillation

R01NS-24226-05 (NEUB) DUN, NAE J 3000 ARLINGTON AVENUE P.O. BOX 10008 TOLEDO, OHIO 43699-0008 Transmission modes and their mediators in motoneurons

R01NS-24233-05 (NLS) HAYDON, PHILIP G DEPARTMENT OF ZOOLOGY 339 SCIENCE II AMES, IA 50011 The regulation of synaptogenesis

R01NS-24236-05A2 (MGN) CARLOCK, LEON R WAYNE STATE UNIVERSITY 3216 SCOTT HALL DETROIT, MI 48201 Methods for cloning the Huntingtons disease gene

R01NS-24247-04A1 (IMS) HAFLER, DAVID A BRIGHAM & WOMEN'S HOSPITAL 75 FRANCIS STREET BOSTON, MA 02115 T cell receptor recognition of myelin basic protein in multiple sclerosis

R01NS-24268-05A1 (BPO) STANLEY, BILLY G UNIVERSITY OF CALIFORNIA RIVERSIDE, CA 92521 Mechanisms of neuropeptide Y-induced eating and obesity

R01NS-24275-05 (PB) FREEMAN, BRUCE A DEPT OF ANESTHESIOLOGY UNIV OF ALABAMA AT BIRMINGHAM BIRMINGHAM, AL 35294 Cerebrovascular injury from oxygen radicals

R01NS-24278-05 (NEUC) KURLAN, ROGER M UNIVERSITY ROCHESTER MED CTR 601 ELMWOOD AVE BOX 673 ROCHESER, N Y 14642 Linkage analysis of Tourette syndrome--Clinical aspects

P01NS-24279-06 (NSPB) BREAKEFIELD, XANDRA O MASSACHUSETTS GENERAL HOSPITAL 13TH STREET CHARLESTOWN, MA 02129 Molecular genetics of inherited neurologic diseases

P01NS-24279-06 0007 (NSPB) DANIEL, PETER Molecular genetics of inherited neurologic diseases Pathogenesis of neuronal ceroid lipofuscinosis

P01NS-24279-06 9004 (NSPB) HAINES, JONATHAN Molecular genetics of inherited neurologic diseases Core--Tissue culture and linkage analysis

P01NS-24279-06 9005 (NSPB) FILIPEK, PAULINE Molecular genetics of inherited neurologic diseases Core--Morphometric neuroimaging

P01NS-24279-06 0001 (NSPB) GUSELLA, JAMES F Molecular genetics of inherited neurologic diseases Identification of the neurofibromatosis gene

P01NS-24279-06 0005 (NSPB) BREAKFIELD, XANDRA O Molecular genetics of inherited neurologic diseases Genetic modification of the nervous system

P01NS-24279-06 0006 (NSPB) MARTUZA, ROBERT Molecular genetics of inherited neurologic diseases Genetic alteration of nervous system tumors

R01NS-24287-04A2 (HED) RODIER, PATRICIA M UNIVERSITY OF ROCHESTER 601 ELMWOOD AVENUE ROCHESTER, NY 14642 Developmental toxicology of neuroendocrine systems

R01NS-24288-05 (NEUB) BARRIONUEVO, GERMAN UNIVERSITY OF PITTSBURGH 446 CRAWFORD HALL PITTSBURGH, PA 15260 Neurophysiology of associative long term potentiation

R01NS-24289-06 (NLS) SUZUKI, KUNIHIKO UNIV OF NC AT CHAPEL HILL BRAIN & DEVELOPMENT RES. CTR. CHAPEL HILL, NC 27599 Chemical pathology of neurological disorders

R29NS-24291-07 (NLS) GUPTA, MADHU UNIVERSITY OF LOUISVILLE HEALTH SCIENCES CENTER LOUISVILLE, KY 40292 MPTP induced model of Parkinson's disease

R01NS-24292-04A2 (BPO) SILVER, RAE BARNARD COLLEGE 3009 BROADWAY NEW YORK, NY 10027 Coupling mechanisms of the biological clock

P01NS-24304-05 (NSPB) RICHMAN, DAVID P UNIVERSITY OF CHICAGO 5841 S MARYLAND AVE, BOX 425 CHICAGO, ILLINOIS 60637 Structure/function analysis of acetylcholine receptor epitopes

P01NS-24304-05 0001 (NSPB) FAIRCLOUGH, ROBERT Structure/function analysis of acetylcholine receptor epitopes Monoclonal antibodies--Probes of acetylcholine receptor function

P01NS-24304-05 0002 (NSPB) MARTINEZ-CARRION, MARINO Structure/function analysis of acetylcholine receptor epitopes Acetylcholine receptor epitopes involved in ion flux

P01NS-24304-05 0003 (NSPB) NELSON, DEBORAH J Structure/function analysis of acetylcholine receptor epitopes Patch clamp analysis of acetylcholine receptor

P01NS-24304-05 0004 (NSPB) RICHMAN, DAVID P Structure/function analysis of acetylcholine receptor epitopes In vivo effects of antibodies blocking AChR function ion

P01NS-24304-05 0005 (NSPB) KEZDY, FERENC Structure/function analysis of acetylcholine receptor epitopes Mapping of epitopes on the primary structure of AChR

P01NS-24304-05 0006 (NSPB) FAIRCLOUGH, ROBERT Structure/function analysis of acetylcholine receptor epitopes Mapping of epitopes on the tertiary structure of AChR

P01NS-24304-05 9001 (NSPB) RICHMAN, DAVID P Structure/function analysis of acetylcholine receptor epitopes Core--Scientific

R01NS-24314-05 (HUD) NUNEZ, PAUL L TULANE UNIVERSITY UPTOWN CAMPUS - ST CHARLES AVE NEW ORLEANS, LA 70118 New methods to improve spatial resolution of EEG

R01NS-24327-05 (PTHA) ISHII, DOUGLAS N COLORADO STATE UNIVERSITY FORT COLLINS, CO 80523 Pathogenesis of diabetic neuropathy

R01NS-24328-05 (NEUB) STRICK, PETER L SUNY HLTH SCI CNTR AT SYRACUSE 750 EAST ADAMS STREET SYRACUSE, N Y 13210 Premotor areas in the frontal lobe

PROJECT NUMBER LISTING

PROJECT NO., ORGANIZATIONAL UNIT., INVESTIGATOR, ADDRESS, TITLE

R01NS-24340-03 (NEUA) BAKAY, ROY A E EMORY CLINIC 1327 CLIFTON RD, NE, 3 SOUTH ATLANTA, GA 30322 CNS grafting for Parkinsonism
R01NS-24362-05 (NLS) WILLARD, ALAN L UNIV OF N.C. AT CHAPEL HILL CB #7545 CHAPEL HILL, NC 27599-7545 Studies of myenteric neural transmission in cell culture
R01NS-24373-06 (NEUC) FRANK, ERIC UNIVERSITY OF PITTSBURGH 3550 TERRACE STREET PITTSBURGH, PA 15261 Development and regeneration of sensory-motor synapses
R01NS-24377-05 (NEUB) BURSZTAJN, SHERRY MC LEAN HOSPITAL 115 MILL STREET BELMONT, MA 02178 Role of coated vesicles in synapse formation
R01NS-24380-05 (NEUC) NEET, KENNETH E UHS/CHICAGO MEDICAL SCHOOL NORTH CHICAGO, IL 60064 Structure and function of nerve growth factor
R01NS-24401-05 (EVR) PERLMAN, STANLEY UNIVERSITY OF IOWA IOWA CITY, IA 52242 Pathogenesis of antibody-modulated mhv demyelination
R01NS-24405-04A1 (NEUC) JUNGALWALA, FIROZE B EUNICE KENNEDY SHRIVER CENTER 200 TRAPELO ROAD WALTHAM, MA 02254 Neurobiology of sulfated glucuronyl glycoconjugates
R01NS-24417-06 (NLS) MARGIOTTA, JOSEPH F MOUNT SINAI SCHOOL OF MEDICINE 1 GUSTAVE L LEVY PL, BOX 1218 NEW YORK, NY 10029 Neuronal acetylcholine receptor mechanisms
R01NS-24418-06 (NLS) HUGANIR, RICHARD L JOHNS HOPKINS SCHOOL OF MED 725 N WOLFE STREET BALTIMORE, MD 21205 Tyrosine phosphorylation of the acetylcholine receptor
R01NS-24423-06 (NEUB) STERNBERGER, LUDWIG A UNIV OF MARYLAND SCH OF MED 22 SOUTH GREEN STREET BALTIMORE, MD 21201 Monoclonal antibody probes for neurofilament processing
R01NS-24427-05 (CMS) ROBBINS, JOANNE WM S MIDDLETON MEM VA HOSPITAL 2500 OVERLOOK TERRACE MADISON, WI 53705 Swallowing and speech after stroke
R01NS-24444-06 (GMB) BEAM, KURT G, JR COLORADO STATE UNIVERSITY FORT COLLINS, CO 80523 Regulation of membrane excitability
R01NS-24448-05 (NLS) MC NAMARA, JAMES O DUKE UNIV MED CTR DUKE BOX 3676 DURHAM, NC 27710 The kindling model of epilepsy
R01NS-24453-06 (NEUC) SUZUKI, KINUKO UNIV OF NC AT CHAPEL HILL CB#7525, 409 BRINKHOUS BUL BLG CHAPEL HILL, NC 27599-7525 Experimental pathology of developing nervous system
R01NS-24456-05 (SRC) BARNETT, HENRY J JOHN P ROBARTS RES INST PO BOX 5015 / 100 PERTH DR LONDON ONTARIO, CANADA N6A 5K8 North American carotid endarterectomy trial
R01NS-24467-05 (PHY) NOWAK, LINDA M CORNELL UNIVERSITY ITHACA, NY 14853-6401 Characterization of glutamate receptors and ion channel
R01NS-24471-06 (NLS) JONES, STEPHEN W CASE WESTERN RESERVE UNIV 2119 ABINGTON ROAD CLEVELAND, OH 44106 Neurotransmitters & ion channels in autonomic ganglia
R01NS-24472-05 (TOX) ADAMS, MICHAEL E UNIVERSITY OF CALIFORNIA RIVERSIDE, CA 92521 Novel synaptic antagonists from spider venoms
R01NS-24489-05A1 (NEUA) GASKIN, FELICIA UNIV OF VIRGINIA SCH OF MED 6 EAST BLUE RIDGE HOSPITAL CHARLOTTESVILLE, VA 22901 Neurofibrous proteins in normal and aging brain
R44NS-24505-03 (BPO) BUCHANAN, D SCOTT BIOMAGNETIC TECHNOLOGIES, INC 9727 PACIFIC HEIGHTS BLVD SAN DIEGO, CA 92121 Source localization software for magnetoencephalography
R01NS-24517-06 (SAT) TODD, MICHAEL M DEPT OF ANESTHESIA UNIVERSITY OF IOWA IOWA CITY, IA 52242 Cerebral effects of fluid resuscitation
R01NS-24519-06 (NEUA) WONG, ROBERT K SUNY HLTH SCS CNTR-BROOKLYN 450 CLARKSON AVE Studies on mammalian nerve cells
R01NS-24520-06 (BBCB) FREIRE, ERNESTO I THE JOHNS HOPKINS UNIVERSITY 34TH AND CHARLES STREETS BALTIMORE, MD 21218 Structure and function of glycolipid receptors
R01NS-24530-06 (GMA) ROGERS, RICHARD C OHIO STATE UNIVERSITY 333 WEST 10TH AVENUE COLUMBUS, OH 43210 Gastrointestinal function--central control
R01NS-24538-06 (RNM) KUNG, HANK F UNIVERSITY OF PENNSYLVANIA 36TH ST & HAMILTON WALK PHILADELPHIA, PA 19104 New CNS dopamine receptor imaging agents
R01NS-24542-06 (NEUB) SCHWARTZ, WILLIAM J UNIV OF MASSACHUSETTS MED SCH 55 LAKE AVENUE NORTH WORCESTER, MA 01655 Suprachiasmatic nuclei-neurobiology of a circadian clock
R01NS-24545-03S1 (TOX) DASGUPTA, BIBHUTI R UNIVERSITY OF WISCONSIN 1925 WILLOW DR MADISON, WI 53706 Botulinum neurotoxin: mechanism of toxicity
R01NS-24553-05 (BIO) HOOK, VIVIAN Y H UNIF SERVICES UNIV OF HLTH SCI 4301 JONES BRIDGE ROAD BETHESDA, MD 20814-4799 Process enzymes for enkephalin and substance P precursors
R01NS-24560-05 (NEUA) KARTEN, HARVEY J UNIVERSITY OF CALIFORNIA DEPT OF NEUROSCIENCES, 0608 LA JOLLA, CA 92093-0608 Dvr--Visual pathways and the origins of neocortex
R29NS-24566-05 (NLS) PETERSON, STEVEN L TEXAS A&M UNIVERSITY COLLEGE STATION, TX 77843 Glycine potentiation of anticonvulsant drugs
P01NS-24575-04 (NSPB) ARNASON, BARRY G W UNIVERSITY OF CHICAGO 5841 S MARYLAND AVENUE CHICAGO, IL 60637 Multiple sclerosis--A program project
P01NS-24575-04 0001 (NSPB) ARNASON, BARRY G W Multiple sclerosis--A program project Suppressor cell function in multiple sclerosis
P01NS-24575-04 0002 (NSPB) SZUCHET, SARA Multiple sclerosis--A program project The role of sulfated macromolecules in CNS myelination
P01NS-24575-04 0003 (NSPB) STEFANSSON, KARI Multiple sclerosis--A program project OMgp--A protein in myelin and myelin-forming cells
P01NS-24575-04 0004 (NSPB) ROOS, RAYMOND P Multiple sclerosis--A program project Theiler's virus demyelinating disease
P01NS-24575-04 0006 (NSPB) NELSON, DEBORAH J Multiple sclerosis--A program project Modulation of ion channel activity in multiple sclerosis
P01NS-24575-04 9001 (NSPB) ARNASON, BARRY G W Multiple sclerosis--A program project Core--Scientific core
R29NS-24577-06 (NLS) SCHWARTZ, ROCHELLE D DUKE UNIV MED CTR BOX 3813/NANALINE DUKE BLDG DURHAM, N C 27710 Regulation of the GABA receptor-Chloride ion channel
R01NS-24591-06 (BPO) KELSO, STEPHEN R UNIVERSITY OF ILLINOIS P.O. BOX 4348, MAIL CODE 066 CHICAGO, IL 60680 Possible neurophysiological substrate for rapid learning
R29NS-24594-04 (NLS) STRASSMAN, ANDREW M NEUROLOGY SERVICE MASS GEN HOSPITAL BOSTON, MA 02114 Activity of visceral and nociceptive trigeminal neurons
R29NS-24596-04 (NEUA) FISHER, ROBIN S UNIVERSIYT OF CALIFORNIA 760 WESTWOOD PLAZA LOS ANGELES, CA 90024-1759 Development of synaptic connections in basal ganglia
R01NS-24602-03 (NEUB) KENNEDY, PHILIP R GEORGIA TECH RESEARCH CORP 400 10TH ST NW ATLANTA, GA 30332-0200 Structure and connections of red nucleus
R01NS-24605-06 (NEUA) YOUNG, RICHARD S YALE UNIVERSITY SCHOOL OF MED 333 CEDAR ST, P O BOX 3333 NEW HAVEN, CT 06510-8064 Brain damage due to neonatal seizure
R29NS-24616-05 (PHRA) FLEISHER, DAVID UNIVERSITY OF MICHIGAN 428 CHURCH ST ANN ARBOR, MI 48109-1065 Interactions affecting phenytoin intestinal absorption
R01NS-24620-06 (NEUA) ROSMAN, NORMAN P NEW ENGLAND MED CTR HOSPITALS 750 WASHINGTON STREET/BOX 330 BOSTON, MA 02111 Seizures--Prevention with intermittent oral diazepam
P01NS-24621-05 (SRC) HEISTAD, DONALD D UNIVERSITY OF IOWA E325-1 GH IOWA CITY, IA 52242 Cerebral blood vessels
P01NS-24621-05 0001 (SRC) HART, MICHAEL Cerebral blood vessels Studies of the blood-brain barrier in vitro
P01NS-24621-05 0002 (SRC) MAYHAN, WILLIAM G. Cerebral blood vessels Leukotrienes and blood-brain barrier--Bloodflow regulation in choroid plexus
P01NS-24621-05 0003 (SRC) TALMAN, WILLIAM T Cerebral blood vessels Central neuroregulation of cerebral blood flow
P01NS-24621-05 0004 (SRC) HEISTAD, DONALD D Cerebral blood vessels Neurohumoral regulation of cerebral blood vessels
P01NS-24621-05 0005 (SRC) BAUMBACH, GARY L. Cerebral blood vessels Cerebral circulation in chronic hypertension--Vascular mechanics
P01NS-24621-05 0006 (SRC) MOORE, STEVEN A. Cerebral blood vessels Fatty acid metabolism and transport at the blood-brain barrier
P01NS-24621-05 0007 (SRC) HEISTAD, DONALD D. Cerebral blood vessels Cerebral circulation in chronic hypertension --Vascular hypertrophy
P01NS-24621-05 9001 (SRC) WOOLSON, ROBERT F. Cerebral blood vessels Biostatistics--core
P01NS-24621-05 9002 (SRC) HART, MICHAEL N Cerebral blood vessels Morphology--core
P01NS-24621-05 9003 (SRC) BRODY, MICHAEL J Cerebral blood vessels Hypertensive animal core
R29NS-24622-05 (RNM) RICHARDS, TODD L UNIVERSITY OF WASHINGTON SCHOOL OF MEDICINE SEATTLE, WA 98195 NMR spectroscopy of demyelination in the brain
R01NS-24636-04A1 (NEUC) WEIGENT, DOUGLAS A UNIV OF ALABAMA AT BIRMINGHAM UAB STATION BIRMINGHAM, AL 35294 Growth hormone and the immune system
R01NS-24641-03 (NEUA) FARWELL, JACQUELINE R CHILDREN'S ORTHOPEDIC HOSP 4800 SAND POINT WAY, NE SEATTLE, WA 98105 Febrile seizure patients at eight years of age
R29NS-24645-04 (NLS) GEE, KELVIN W UNIVERSITY OF SOUTHERN CALIF 1985 ZONAL AVENUE LOS ANGELES, CALIF 90033 Characterization of a novel benzodiazepine binding site
R29NS-24656-05 (NEUB) HOLSTEIN, GAY R MOUNT SINAI SCHOOL OF MEDICINE 5TH AVE. & 100TH ST., BOX 1140 NEW YORK, NY 10029 Growth and aging--Anatomy of substantia nigra
R29NS-24661-05 (NLS) EARNEST, DAVID J UNIVERSITY OF ROCHESTER 601 ELMWOOD AVE ROCHESTER, NY 14642 Neural control of suprachiasmatic function
R29NS-24662-06 (NEUB) KIRK, MARK DOUGLAS UNIVERSITY OF MISSOURI LEFEVRE HALL, RM 103 COLUMBIA, MO 65211 Behavioral roles of peptides--Physiology and biophysics
R01NS-24669-04A1 (HAR) NORTHCUTT, RICHARD G UNIVERSITY OF CALIFORNIA LA JOLLA, CA 92093 Lateral line system--Anatomy and development
R01NS-24672-06 (NEUB) PFENNINGER, KARL H UNIV OF COLORADO HLTH SCI CTR 4200 EAST NINTH AVENUE, B-111 DENVER, CO 80262 Molecular control of CNS growth and regeneration
R01NS-24676-05 (NEUC) PFENNINGER, KARL H UNIV OF COLORADO HLTH SCI CTR 4200 EAST NINTH AVENUE, B-111 DENVER, CO 80262 Surface events during axonal growth
R01NS-24679-05 (NEUB) JOHNSON, EUGENE M, JR WASHINGTON UNIV / PHARMACOL 660 SOUTH EUCLID ST LOUIS, MO 63110 NGF receptors on Schwann cells
R01NS-24682-06 (NEUA) WONG, ROBERT K SUNY HLTH SCI CTR AT BROOKLYN 450 CLARKSON AVE BROOKLYN, NY 11203 Membrane properties of cortical neurons
R01NS-24683-06 (NEUB) KATER, STANLEY B COLORADO STATE UNIVERSITY COLL VET MED & BIOM SCI FORT COLLINS, CO 80523 Properties of identified neuronal growth cones
R29NS-24688-06 (EVR) MOKHTARIAN, FOROOZAN MAIMONIDES MEDICAL CENTER 4802 TENTH AVENUE BROOKLYN, N Y 11219 Virus-induced autoimmune mediated encephalomyelitis
R29NS-24694-05 (NEUC) MC CORMICK, DANIEL J MAYO FOUNDATION 200 FIRST STREET S W ROCHESTER, MINNESOTA 55905 Synthesis of human autoantigens of myasthenia gravis
R01NS-24698-04 (NLS) ASTON-JONES, GARY S HAHNEMANN UNIVERSITY BROAD & VINE PHILADELPHIA, PA 19102-1192 Afferent control of locus coeruleus
R29NS-24705-04 (NLS) VALLANO, MARY L HSC AT SYRACUSE 766 IRVING AVE SYRACUSE, N Y 13210 Calmodulin dependent kinase and synaptic function
P01NS-24707-05 (NSPA) GOLDBERGER, MICHAEL E MEDICAL COLLEGE OF PENNSYLVANI 3200 HENRY AVE PHILADELPHIA, PA 19129 Recovery of function after spinal cord damage
P01NS-24707-05 0001 (NSPA) MURPHY, E HAZEL Recovery of function after spinal cord damage Regeneration in axotomized motor neurons
P01NS-24707-05 0002 (NSPA) MURRAY, MARION Recovery of function after spinal cord damage Modification of protein synthesis in axotomized neurons
P01NS-24707-05 0003 (NSPA) MURRAY, MARION Recovery of function after

spinal cord damage Consequences of lumbosacral deafferentiation in the spinal cord
P01NS-24707-05 0004 (NSPA) GOLDBERGER, MICHAEL Recovery of function after spinal cord damage Physiological and anatomical recovery in Clarke's nucleus
P01NS-24707-05 0006 (NSPA) PINTER, MARTIN Recovery of function after spinal cord damage Regulation of spinal motoneurons
P01NS-24707-05 0007 (NSPA) TESSLER, ALAN R Recovery of function after spinal cord damage Neural transplantation into spinal cord
P01NS-24707-05 9001 (NSPA) LEVITT, PAT Recovery of function after spinal cord damage Core--Morphology
P01NS-24707-05 9002 (NSPA) TESSLER, ALAN Recovery of function after spinal cord damage Core--Surgical and cell culture
R01NS-24711-05 (PHY) NAKAJIMA, SHIGEHIRO UNIVERSITY OF ILLINOIS/CHICAGO 835 SO WOLCOTT AVENUE CHICAGO, IL 60612 Cellular biophysics of brain neurons in culture
R01NS-24719-05 (NEUA) LOWRY, OLIVER H WASHINGTON UNIVERSITY 660 SOUTH EUCLID AVENUE ST LOUIS, MO 63110 Measurement of rapid change in regional brain metabolism
R29NS-24720-04 (NEUB) BENDHEIM, PAUL E NYS INSTITUTE/BASIC RESEARCH 1050 FOREST HILL ROAD STATEN ISLAND, N Y 10314 Conversion of a normal protein to the scrapie protein
R29NS-24725-05 (NEUC) FISCHER, ITZHAK MEDICAL COLL OF PENNSYLVANIA 3300 HENRY AVENUE PHILADELPHIA, PA 19129 Regulation of MAP2 in brain
R29NS-24738-04 (NEUC) EDELMAN, ARTHUR M S U N Y AT BUFFALO 102 FARBER HALL BUFFALO, NY 14214 Myosin phosphorylation in the nervous system
R01NS-24742-05 (NEUB) FELDMAN, JACK L UNIVERSITY OF CALIFORNIA 405 HILGARD AVE DEPT/KINESIO LOS ANGELES, CA 90024 Transmission of respiratory drive to phrenic motoneurons
R29NS-24747-05 (NEUC) ISACKSON, PAUL J UNIVERSITY OF CALIFORNIA 364 MED SURGE II IRVINE, CA 92717 Structure of biologically active nerve growth factor
R01NS-24751-05 (NEUA) WIKSWO, JOHN P, JR VANDERBILT UNIVERSITY BOX 1807, STATION B NASHVILLE, TN 37235 Action currents & skeletal muscle electrophysiology II
R29NS-24752-05 (NEUB) WILKINSON, ROBERT S WASHINGTON UNIVERSITY 660 S EUCLID AVE, BOX 8228 ST LOUIS, MO 63110 Determinants of synaptic strength in muscle
R01NS-24760-05 (NEUB) BARBAS, HELEN BOSTON UNIVERSITY 635 COMMONWEALTH AVE BOSTON, MA 02215 Anatomy of limbic prefrontal cortex
R01NS-24766-05 (CMS) OCHOA, JOSE L GOOD SAMARITAN HOSP & MED CTR 1040 NORTHWEST 22ND STREET PORTLAND, OR 97210 Pain and hyperalgesia--Microneurography in patients
R01NS-24778-05 (SRC) SHOULSON, IRA UNIVERSITY OF ROCHESTER BOX 649, ELMWOOD AVE ROCHESTER, N Y 14642 Deprenyl/tocopherol antioxidative therapy of Parkinson's
R29NS-24781-06 (BPO) SCHNEIDER, LINDA H NEW YORK HOSP, CORNELL MED CTR 21 BLOOMINGDALE ROAD WHITE PLAINS, NY 10605 Brain DOPAmine sites stimulated by sucrose sham feeding
R01NS-24782-04 (NEUA) LEE, KEVIN SCOTT UNIVERSITY OF VIRGINIA CHARLOTTESVILLE, VA 22908 Brain DOPAmine sites stimulated by sucrose sham feeding
R01NS-24785-05 (PHY) SALKOFF, LAWRENCE B WASHINGTON UNIVERSITY 660 SOUTH EUCLID AVE ST LOUIS, MO 63110 Voltage gated ion channels; structure & expression
R29NS-24794-04 (BPO) MECK, WARREN H COLUMBIA UNIVERSITY SCHERMERHORN HALL NEW YORK, NEW YORK 10027 Brain mechanisms, timing and temporal memory
R01NS-24805-04A1 (NLS) HERRERA, ALBERT A UNIV OF SOUTHERN CALIFORNIA LOS ANGELES, CA 90089-2520 Remodeling and elimination of synapses
R01NS-24806-05 (SRC) KASSELL, NEAL F UNIV OF VIRGINIA/SCH OF MED BOX 212 CHARLOTTESVILLE, VA 22908 Randomized study of nicardipine in subarachnoid hemorrhage/human
R29NS-24813-05 (NLS) MC KAY, DENNIS B OHIO STATE UNIVERSITY 500 W 12TH AVENUE COLUMBUS, OH 43210 Receptor regulation of adrenal catecholamine secretion
R29NS-24814-05 (NLS) YAMAMOTO, BRYAN KEN CASE WESTERN RESERVE UNIVERSIT 2040 ABINGTON CLEVELAND, OH 44106 Striatal subregion systems and locomotion
R29NS-24821-05 (NLS) LANIER, STEPHEN M MEDICAL UNIV OF SOUTH CAROLINA 171 ASHLEY AVENUE CHARLESTON, SC 29425 Structural analysis of the alpha2-adrenergic receptor
R01NS-24823-05 (BEM) DODRILL, CARL B HARBORVIEW MEDICAL CENTER 325 NINTH AVENUE SEATTLE, WA 98104 Long-term effects of resection surgery for epilepsy
R01NS-24826-04 (NLS) SEYFRIED, THOMAS N BOSTON COLLEGE 140 COMMONWEALTH AVENUE CHESTNUT HILL, MA 02167 Ganglioside studies in mutant mouse embryo
R01NS-24830-05 (NLS) YEH, HERMES H UNIV OF ROCHESTER MED CTR 601 ELMWOOD AVE BOX 603 ROCHESTER, N Y 14642 Studies of CNS peptides in cell culture
R29NS-24833-05 (SAT) KALICHMAN, MICHAEL W VA MEDICAL CENTER, V-151 3350 LA JOLLA VILLAGE DRIVE SAN DIEGO, CA 92161 Local anesthetic neurotoxicity in the spinal cord
R01NS-24834-04 (PTHA) GULATI, ADARSH K MEDICAL COLLEGE OF GEORGIA AUGUSTA, GA 30912-2000 Immunogenicity of nerve allografts and nerve repair
R01NS-24848-05 (NEUB) KUWADA, JOHN Y UNIVERSITY OF MICHIGAN 300 NORTH INGALLS ANN ARBOR, MI 48109-2007 Growth cone guidance in the spinal cord
R29NS-24853-06 (NEUB) BRUCE, JOCELYN B UNIVERSITY OF MIAMI 1600 NW 10TH AVENUE MIAMI, FL 33101 Methotrexate effects on astrocytes
R29NS-24862-05 (BPO) NORDEEN, KATHY W UNIVERSITY OF ROCHESTER DEPT. OF PSYCHOLOGY ROCHESTER, NY 14627 Neural development in relation to vocal behavior
R01NS-24869-06 (NEUA) NORTHCUTT, RICHARD G UNIVERSITY OF CA SAN DIEGO DEPT OF NEUROSCIENCES A-001 LA JOLLA, CA 92093 Evolution of the telencephalon
R01NS-24876-05 (NEUB) HELKE, CINDA J UNIFORMED SERVICES UNIVERSITY 4301 JONES BRIDGE ROAD BETHESDA, MD 20814-4799 Ventral medullary transmitters & cardiovascular control
R01NS-24878-06 (NLS) LAMPSON, LOIS A BRIGHAM AND WOMENS HOSPITAL 75 FRANCIS STREET BOSTON, MA 02115 Polymorphic neuronal surface proteins
R01NS-24879-05 (BPO) FLYNN, FRANCIS W UNIVERSITY OF WYOMING BOX 3415 UNIVERSITY STATION LARAMIE, WY 82071 Caudal brainstem control of energy homeostasis
R01NS-24880-06 (NLS) JESSELL, THOMAS M COLUMBIA UNIVERSITY 722 WEST 168TH STREET NEW YORK, NY 10032 Neurotransmitter function in spinal sensory transmission
R01NS-24883-05 (NLS) BENNETT, GUDRUN S UNIVERSITY OF FLORIDA GAINESVILLE, FL 32610 Neurofilament metabolism in embryoninc and mature neurons
R01NS-24890-06 (NLS) FLOOR, ERIK UNIVERSITY OF KANSAS LAWRENCE, KS 66045-2106 Biochemistry of synaptic vesicles from mammalian brain
R01NS-24896-06 (RNM) KUHL, DAVID E UNIVERSITY HOSPITAL 1500 E MEDICAL CENTER DRIVE ANN ARBOR, MI 48109 Emission computed tomography of local cerebral functions
R01NS-24926-06 (SSS) ARBIB, MICHAEL A UNIV OF SOUTHERN CALIFORNIA UNIVERSITY PARK LOS ANGELES, CA 90089-2520 Visuomotor coordination--Neural networks and schemas
R01NS-24927-05 (NEUA) DICHTER, MARC A UNIV OF PENNSYLVANIA HOSPITAL 3400 SPRUCE ST PHILADELPHIA, PA 19104 Molecular regulation of postsynaptic GABA responses
R01NS-24930-05 (HAR) SCHOR, ROBERT H THE EYE AND EAR INSTITUTE 203 LOTHROP STREET PITTSBURGH, PA 15213 Processing of information by the vestibulospinal system
R01NS-24932-05 (NLS) ABELL, CREED W UNIVERSITY OF TEXAS AUSTIN, TX 78712 Biochemical and molecular properties of MAO A and B
R01NS-24933-03 (NLS) HARRIS, ROBERT B VIRGINIA COMMONWEALTH UNIV BOX 614 MCV STATION RICHMOND, VA 23298-0614 Processing hypothalamic peptide hormones
R55NS-24954-04A1 (NEUC) KROLICK, KEITH A UNIV OF TEXAS HLTH SCI CTR 7703 FLOYD CURL DRIVE SAN ANTONIO, TX 78284 Neuromuscular immunopathology in EAMG -- Helper T-cell
R01NS-24960-05 (NEUA) YORK, DONALD H UNIVERSITY OF MISSOURI COLUMBIA, MO 65212 Cerebral activity associated with movement
R01NS-24969-05 (BIO) SIEGEL, FRANK L UNIVERSITY OF WISCONSIN 655 WAISMAN CENTER MADISON, WISCONSIN 53706 Enzymatic N-methylation of calmodulin
R01NS-24971-03 (NLS) BECKSTEAD, ROBERT M MEDICAL UNIV OF SOUTH CAROLINA 171 ASHLEY AVENUE CHARLESTON, SC 29425 Functional mechanisms of the corpus striatum
R29NS-24991-05 (NEUA) KUKULKA, CARL G UNIVERSITY OF IOWA 2600 STEINDLER BUILDING IOWA CITY, IOWA 52242 Studies of cutaneous afferent effects
R01NS-24995-02 (CMS) CLARK, FRANCIS J UNIVERSITY OF NEBRASKA MED CTR 600 SOUTH 42ND SSTREET OMAHA, NE 68198-4370 Neural mechanisms of position sense
R29NS-25007-05 (NEUC) MAYER, CECILIA C UNIVERSITY OF CALIFORNIA 3RD AND PARNASSUS SAN FRANCISCO, CA 94143-0128 Molecular and biologic analyses of HIV from the brain
R29NS-25020-05 (NEUA) SUTULA, THOMAS P UNIVERSITY OF WISCONSIN 600 HIGHLAND AVE MADISON, WI 53792 Lesion-induced synaptic reorganization & epilepsy
R01NS-25037-05 (PC) GLEMBOTSKI, CHRISTOPHER C DEPARTMENT OF BIOLOGY 5300 CAMPANILE DRIVE SAN DIEGO, CA 92182 Biochemistry of atrial natriuretic peptide
R29NS-25041-05 (CMS) LEGATT, ALAN D MONTEFIORE MEDICAL CENTER 111 EAST 210TH STREET BRONX, N Y 10467 Spatio-temporal analysis of evoked potentials
R29NS-25042-06 (NEUC) HOSKINS, SALLY G CITY OF COLLEGE OF CUNY COVENT AVENUE AT 138TH STREET NEW YORK, N Y 10031 Directed axon growth--Hormonal control and gene expression
R01NS-25044-05 (NEUB) PLEASURE, DAVID E CHILDREN'S HOSPITAL 3400 CIVIC CENTER BLVD PHILADELPHIA, PA 19104 Oligodendroglial proliferation and differentiation
R01NS-25054-04A1 (NLS) SAGEN, JACQUELINE UNIVERSITY OF ILLINOIS 808 SOUTH WOOD STREET CHICAGO, IL 60612 Pain reduction by grafts of chromaffin cell derivatives
R01NS-25074-05 (NEUB) DONOGHUE, JOHN P BROWN UNIVERSITY BOX 1953, CTR FOR NEURAL SCI PROVIDENCE, RI 02912 Static and dynamic organization
R01NS-25077-05 (ORTH) STUART, DOUGLAS G ARIZONA HEALTH SCIS CTR COLLEGE OF MEDICINE TUCSON, AZ 85724 Fatigue of segmental motor mechanisms
R29NS-25078-05 (NLS) HOGAN, PATRICK G HARVARD MEDICAL SCHOOL 25 SHATTUCK STREET BOSTON, MASS 02115 Physiological actions of bradykinin on sensory
R01NS-25079-05 (BPO) STELLAR, ELIOT UNIVERSITY OF PENNSYLVANIA PHILADELPHIA, PA 19104-6058 CNS CCK in appetitive and consummatory food motivation
R29NS-25087-05 (NLS) HWANG, BANG H DEPARTMENT OF ANATOMY MEDICAL SCI BUILDING 258 INDIANAPOLIS, IN 46202-5120 Role of gabaergic neurons in autonomic nuclei
R01NS-25095-05 (NEUA) MARTIN, GEORGE F OHIO STATE UNIV/ANATOMY DEPT 4072 GRAVES HALL/333 W 10TH AV COLUMBUS, OH 43210 Developmental plasticity of descending spinal pathways
R01NS-25100-03 (NEUA) WEISS, HARVEY R UMDNJ-ROBERT W JOHNSON MED SCH 675 HOES LANE PISCATAWAY, NJ 08854-5635 Cerebral capillary perfusion during 02 lack
R29NS-25102-05 (NEUC) DANILOFF, JOANNE K LOUISIANA STATE UNIVERSITY SOUTH STADIUM DRIVE BATON ROUGE, LA 70803 Contributions of cell adhesion to nerve regeneration
R01NS-25129-05 (NEUC) LACY, ELIZABETH H SLOAN-KETTERING INSTITUTE 1275 YORK AVENUE NEW YORK, N Y 10021 The role of T4 in the neurotropism of the AIDS virus
R29NS-25134-05 (NLS) HAYCOCK, JOHN W LOUISIANA STATE UNIV MED CTR 1100 FLORIDA AVE NEW ORLEANS, LA 70119 Cellular regulation of tyrosine hydroxylase
R29NS-25139-05 (NEUA) CASSELL, MARTIN D UNIVERSITY OF IOWA DEPT OF ANATOMY IOWA CITY, IA 52242 Afferents and endogenous peptides in the amygdala

PROJECT NO., ORGANIZATIONAL UNIT., INVESTIGATOR, ADDRESS, TITLE

R29NS-25149-05 (CMS) POIZNER, HOWARD RUTGERS, THE STATE UNIVERSITY 195 UNIVERSITY AVENUE NEWARK, N J 07102 The neural basis of motor behavior
R01NS-25150-03 (NEUB) NORDEN, JEANETTE J VANDERBILT UNIVERSITY NASHVILLE, TN 37232 Growth-associated protein gap-43 & synaptic plasticity
R29NS-25151-05 (NLS) BOYD, NORMAN D UNIVERSITY OF MASSACHUSETTS 55 LAKE AVE NORTH WORCESTER, MASS 01655 Regulation of neural acetylcholine receptors
R29NS-25153-05 (NEUC) GOLDMAN, DANIEL J 205 ZINA PITCHER PLACE ANN ARBOR, MI 48109-0720 Regulation of acetylcholine receptor expression
R29NS-25155-04 (NLS) FRANCK, JO ANN E UNIVERSITY OF WASH RI-20 DEPT OF NEUROLOGICAL SURGERY SEATTLE, WA 98195 Hippocampal damage as a cause of epilepsy
R01NS-25161-04A1 (NEUB) GOLDBERG, DANIEL J COLUMBIA UNIVERSITY 630 WEST 168TH STREET NEW YORK, NY 10032 Video-enhanced microscopy of living growth cones
R01NS-25168-04A1 (NLS) GELLER, HERBERT M UNIV MED/DENTISTRY OF NEW JERS 675 HOES LANE PISCATAWAY, NJ 08854 Development of hypothalamic neurons in vitro
R01NS-25178-05 (ARR) WILEY, CLAYTON A UNIVERSITY OF CALIFORNIA LA JOLLA, CA 92093-0612 Molecular neuropathology of AIDS encephalitis
R01NS-25183-05 (NEUB) HANDSFIELD, H HUNTER HARBORVIEW MEDICAL CENTER 325 NINTH AVENUE SEATTLE, WASH 98104 Neuropsychological aspects of stage II/III HIV infection
R29NS-25186-05 (NEUB) BELARDETTI, FRANCESCO UNIV OF TEXAS SW MEDICAL CENTE 5323 HARRY HINES BLVD DALLAS, TX 75235-9041 Second messengers of presynaptic inhibition
R01NS-25187-04A1 (IMS) LATOV, NORMAN COLUMBIA UNIVERSITY 630 W 168TH ST NEW YORK, NY 10032 Pathogenesis of anti-MAG antibodies in neuropathy
R01NS-25191-02 (SSS) BLUM, JACOB J DUKE UNIVERSITY MEDICAL CENTER PO BOX 3709-3 DURHAM, NC 27710 Studies of slow axonal transport and neuropathy
R29NS-25194-05 (NEUC) RANSCHT, BARBEL LA JOLLA CANCER RESRCH FDN 10901 N TORREY PINES ROAD LA JOLLA, CA 92037 Neuronal glycoproteins associated with the cytoskeleton
R29NS-25206-06 (NEUB) POWERS, RANDALL K UNIVERSITY OF WASHINGTON SEATTLE, WA 98195 Reflex action of muscle contraction
R29NS-25212-06 (NLS) SHIROMANI, PRIYATTAM J BROCKTON VA MEDICAL CENTER 940 BELMONT ST BROCKTON, MA 02115 Brainstem cholinergic neuronatomy and neurophysiology
R29NS-25215-05 (NLS) MAC DERMOTT, AMY B COLUMBIA UNIVERSITY 630 W 168TH ST NEW YORK, NY 10032 Reg of Ca-2+ following activation of NMDA receptor
R01NS-25216-05 (VISB) MOWER, GEORGE D UNIVERSITY OF LOUISVILLE HEALTH SCIENCES CENTER LOUISVILLE, KY 40292 Environmental control of cortical plasticity
R29NS-25217-04 (NEUB) RIBERA, ANGELES B UNIV OF COLORADO SCH OF MEDICI 4200 E. 9TH AVE DENVER, COLORADO 80262 Development of neuromodulation in sensory neurons
R01NS-25223-05 (NEUC) FELTEN, SUZANNE Y UNIV OF ROCHESTER 601 ELMWOOD AVE ROCHESTER, NY 14642 Targets of NE terminals in secondary lymphoid organs
R01NS-25243-10 (HUD) SIGMAN, MARIAN D UNIVERSITY OF CALIFORNIA 760 WESTWOOD PLAZA LOS ANGELES, CA 90024-1759 Object concepts in autistic children
R29NS-25250-05 (NEUB) DROGE, MICHAEL H TEXAS WOMEN'S UNIVERSITY PO BOX 23971 DENTON, TX 76204 Pattern generation in spinal explants
R29NS-25264-05 (NEUC) COVAULT, JONATHAN M UNIVERSITY OF CONNECTICUT 75 NORTH EAGLEVILLE RD STORRS, CT 06269-3042 Nerve-muscle interactions--Role and regulation of N-CAM
R01NS-25275-05 (NEUA) KOEHLER, RAYMOND C DEPT OF ANES/CRIT CARE MED JOHNS HOPKINS HOSPITAL BALTIMORE, MD 21205 Cerebrovascular alterations during hyperammonemia
R55NS-25289-04A1 (NEUB) EBBESSON, SVEN O E UNIVERSITY OF ALASKA 200 O'NEILL BLDG FAIRBANKS, AK 99775-1080 Neuronal plasticity and thyroid hormone
R01NS-25296-04 (NLS) ALBUQUERQUE, EDSON X UNIVERSITY OF MARYLAND 655 W BALTIMORE ST BALTIMORE, MD 21201 Anatoxin and its analogs as neurotransmitters
R01NS-25304-05 (NEUC) MACKLIN, WENDY B MENTAL RETARD RESEARCH CENTER 760 WESTWOOD PLAZA LOS ANGELES, CA 90024-1579 Myelin protein gene expression in dysmyelinating mutants
R29NS-25308-04 (EVR) RUBENSTEIN, RICHARD NYS INST FOR BASIC RESEARCH 1050 FOREST HILL ROAD STATEN ISLAND, NY 10314 Scrapie agent replication in an in vitro neuronal model
R01NS-25340-05 (NEUB) HOLLYDAY, MARGARET BRYN MAWR COLLEGE BRYN MAWR, PA 19010-2899 Development of specific neuronal connections
R01NS-25350-04 (NLS) FISHER, MARILYN UNIVERSITY OF VIRGINIA BOX 439 HLTH SCI CTR CHARLOTTESVILLE, VA 22908 Neuronal induction of a glial enzyme
R29NS-25354-05 (NLS) CHERNAUSEK, STEVEN D CHILDREN'S HOSPITAL RES FDN ELLAND & BETHESDA AVE CINCINNATI, OH 45229-2899 Somatomedins and brain development
R01NS-25355-03 (NLS) HOF, LISELOTTE B ALBANY MEDICAL COLLEGE DEPT OF BIOCHEMISTRY ALBANY, N Y 12208 Gangliosides in myelin deficient mutant
R01NS-25366-04 (PHY) LEVITAN, IRWIN B BRANDEIS UNIVERSITY 415 SOUTH STREET WALTHAM, MASS 02254 Regulation of synaptic specificity
R01NS-25369-04 (NEUA) TRONCOSO, JUAN C JOHNS HOPKINS UNIVERSITY 600 NORTH WOLFE STREET BALTIMORE, MD 21205 Filamentous pathology in neurodegenerative disorders
R01NS-25372-04 (NEUB) CHAN, PAK HOO UNIVERSITY OF CALIFORNIA SCHOOL OF MEDICINE SAN FRANCISCO, CALIF 94143 Mechanisms of oxidative injury in vasogenic brain edema
R01NS-25374-04 (NEUA) SUNDT, THORALF M JR MAYO FOUNDATION 200 FIRST STREET SOUTHWEST ROCHESTER, MN 55905 Effect of Ca antagonists on focal ischemia & seizures
R01NS-25378-06A1 (SSS) KRUEGER, JAMES M UNIVERSITY OF TENNESSEE 894 UNION AVENUE MEMPHIS, TN 38163 Interleukin-1 -- Promoter of slow wave sleep

PROJECT NO., ORGANIZATIONAL UNIT., INVESTIGATOR, ADDRESS, TITLE

R01NS-25382-04 (PB) PARKER, WILLIAM D, JR UNIV OF COLORADO/HLTH SCI CTR 4200 E 9TH AVEN C233 DENVER, CO 80262 Neurologic disease and the electron transport chain
R29NS-25387-04 (NEUC) BASTIANI, MICHAEL J UNIVERSITY OF UTAH 201 BIOLOGY BLDG SALT LAKE CITY, UT 84112 Growth cone guidance--Interactions and surface molecules
R01NS-25508-04 (SSS) CHEN, IRVIN S UNIV OF CALIF., LOS ANGELES 405 HILGARD AVE LOS ANGELES CALIF 90024 Molecular virological studies of AIDS CNS disorders
R29NS-25512-04 (NEUB) RYER, HELENA I V A MEDICAL CENTER 800 IRVING AVENUE SYRACUSE, N Y 13210 Dermal cholinergic receptors and Alzheimers disease
R01NS-25513-03 (CMS) ZAKON, HAROLD H UNIVERSITY OF TEXAS PAT 319 AUSTIN, TX 78712 Cellular basis for steroid action in an excitable cell
R01NS-25529-04 (NEUA) GRAYBIEL, ANN M DEPT BRAIN AND COGNITIVE SCI 25 CARLETON STREET CAMBRIDGE, MA 02139 Studies on the extrapyramidal system
R01NS-25537-03 (NLS) GORDON, ADRIENNE S SAN FRANCISCO GENERAL HOSPITAL BUILDING 1, ROOM 101 SAN FRANCISCO, CA 94110 Second messenger effects at nicotinic synapses
R01NS-25545-03S1 (NEUA) HSU, CHUNG Y BAYLOR COLLEGE OF MEDICINE HOUSTON, TX 77030 Therapeutic trials in a stroke model
R01NS-25547-04A1 (NEUB) FYFFE, ROBERT E UNIVERSITY OF NORTH CAROLINA MED SCIENCE RES BLDG CB 7545 CHAPEL HILL, NC 27599 Mechanisms of Renshaw cell mediated recurrent inhibition
P01NS-25554-01A2S1 (SRC) PARDRIDGE, WILLIAM M UCLA SCHOOL OF MEDICINE LOS ANGELES, CA 90024-1682 Biology of the blood-brain barrier
P01NS-25554-01A2S1 0001 (SRC) PARDRIDGE, WILLIAM M Biology of the blood-brain barrier Isolation of brain capillary-specific proteins
P01NS-25554-01A2S1 0002 (SRC) CANCILLA, PASQUALE A Biology of the blood-brain barrier Regeneration and interactions of brain epithelium
P01NS-25554-01A2S1 0003 (SRC) CORNFORD, EAIN M Biology of the blood-brain barrier Modulations of blood-brain barrier nutrient transport
P01NS-25554-01A2S1 0004 (SRC) BLACK, KEITH L Biology of the blood-brain barrier Leukotrienes and the blood-brain barrier
P01NS-25554-01A2S1 9001 (SRC) PARDRIDGE, WILLIAM M Biology of the blood-brain barrier Biochemistry core
P01NS-25554-01A2S1 9002 (SRC) CANCILLA, PASQUALE A Biology of the blood-brain barrier Morphology and tissue culture core
R29NS-25563-05 (RNM) STROTHER, STEPHEN C VETERANS ADMINISTRATION MED CT ONE VETERANS DRIVE MINNEAPOLIS, MN 55417 Optimizing PETT measurements / biological image patterns
P01NS-25569-04 (NSPB) BERGER, JOSEPH R UNIV OF MIAMI 1501 N W 9TH AVENUE MIAMI, FL 33136 Neurologic complications of HIV
P01NS-25569-04 0004 (NSPB) KUMAR, MAHENDRA Neurologic complications of HIV Brain reactive antibodies--Marker for AIDS dementia
P01NS-25569-04 9001 (NSPB) BERGER, JOSEPH Neurologic complications of HIV Core--Epidemiology, biosatistics, data management and analysis
P01NS-25569-04 0001 (NSPB) BERGER, JOSEPH Neurologic complications of HIV Longitudinal study of neurological complications of HIV
P01NS-25569-04 0002 (NSPB) PARKS, WADE Neurologic complications of HIV AIDS retrovirus infection of the CNS
P01NS-25569-04 0003 (NSPB) DIX, RICHARD Neurologic complications of HIV Role of CMV in HIV - related neurological disease
R29NS-25572-03 (NEUB) WALROND, JOHN P COLORADO STATE UNIVERSITY FT COLLINS, CO 80523 Structure & function of neurotransmitter release sites
R29NS-25588-04 (NEUA) KOWALL, NEIL W MASSACHUSETTS GENERAL HOSPITAL FRUIT STREET BOSTON, MA 02114 Histochemical studies of Huntington's disease brain
R01NS-25597-04 (NEUA) MILLER, ROBERT H CASE WESTERN RESERVE UNIV 2119 ABINGTON ROAD CLEVELAND, OHIO 44106 Role of astrocyte diversity in CNS axonal growth
R01NS-25598-04 (NLS) WEINREICH, DANIEL UNIVERSITY OF MARYLAND 655 WEST BALTIMORE BALTIMORE, MD 21201 Immunoregulation of autonomic synaptic neurotransmission
R01NS-25605-04 (NEUA) LOTHMAN, ERIC W UNIV OF VIRGINIA HLTH SCI CTR PO BOX 394 CHARLOTTESVILLE, VA 22908 Extracellular ion homeostasis in epilepsy
R29NS-25608-04 (NEUB) SHIN, CHEOLSU VA HOSPITAL 508 FULTON STREET DURHAM, N C 27705 Regulation of limbic excitability
R01NS-25616-04A1 (NLS) CRAIG, ARTHUR D BARROW NEUROLOGICAL INSTITUTE 350 WEST THOMAS RD PHOENIX, AZ 85013 Organization of the lamina I STT projection
R29NS-25621-05 (NEUC) TULLY, TIM COLD SPRING HARBOR LABORATORY P.O. BOX 100 COLD SPRING HARBOR, NY 11724 Neural substrates of learning and memory
R01NS-25624-03 (NEUB) PACHTER, BRUCE R NEW YORK UNIVERSITY 400 EAST 34TH ST NEW YORK, NY 10016 Effects of long-term use of partially denervated muscle
R29NS-25625-04 (IMS) ROHOWSKY-KOCHAN, CHRISTINE M UNIV OF MEDICINE & DENTISTRY 185 SOUTH ORANGE AVENUE NEWARK, NJ 07103 Anti-idiotypic autoimmunity in multiple sclerosis
R01NS-25629-04 (NEUA) SHOUSE, MARGARET N UNIVERSITY OF CALIFORNIA 10833 LECONTE AVENUE LOS ANGELES, CA 90024-1763 Diencephalic mechanisms of sleep-related seizures
P01NS-25630-03 (SRC) DE LORENZO, ROBERT J VIRGINIA COMMONWEALTH UNIV MCV STATION 599 RICHMOND, VA 23298 Medical College of Virginia epilepsy research center
P01NS-25630-03 0001 (SRC) DELORENZO, ROBERT J Medical College of Virginia epilepsy research center Status epilepaticus--A clinical study
P01NS-25630-03 0002 (SRC) SGRO, JOSEPH Medical College of Virginia epilepsy research center Mortality of status epilepticus
P01NS-25630-03 0003 (SRC) KONTOS, HERMES Medical College of Virginia epilepsy research center Microvascular changes and oxygen radicals in seizures
P01NS-25630-03 0004 (SRC) COREY, LINDA Medical College of Virginia epilepsy research center A genetic study of seizures in twins
P01NS-25630-03 9001 (SRC) KO, DAIJIN Medical College of Virginia

PROJECT NO., ORGANIZATIONAL UNIT., INVESTIGATOR, ADDRESS, TITLE

epilepsy research center Core--Data management and biostatistics
P01NS-25630-03 9002 (SRC) SGRO, JOSEPH Medical College of Virginia epilepsy research center Core--Clinical research
P01NS-25630-03 9003 (SRC) CALABRESE, VINCENT Medical College of Virginia epilepsy research center Core--Laboratory
R01NS-25631-04 (NEUC) WASMUTH, JOHN J UNIVERSITY OF CALIFORNIA IRVINE, CA 92717 Isolation of the Huntington's disease gene
R29NS-25635-04 (NEUA) DIMLICH, RUTH V UNIVERSITY OF CINCINNATI 231 BETHESDA AVENUE CINCINNATI, OHIO 45267 Mechanisms and treatment of cerebral ischemia
R01NS-25637-04 (NEUC) GIULIAN, DANA J BAYLOR COLLEGE OF MEDICINE ONE BAYLOR PLAZA HOUSTON, TX 77030 Study of mononuclear phagocytes within the CNS
R29NS-25644-05 (NLS) MATSUMOTO, STEVEN G OREGON HEALTH SCIENCES UNIV 611 SW CAMPUS DRIVE PORTLAND, OR 97201 Sympathetic transmitter mechanisms in visceral control
R01NS-25655-04 (NEUA) KORDOWER, JEFFREY H RUSH-PRESBYTERIAN-ST LUKES 1653 WEST CONGRESS PARKWAY CHICAGO, IL 60612 Lesions and implants of cholinergic neurons
R01NS-25656-04 (RNM) WIELAND, DONALD M UNIVERSITY OF MICHIGAN ANN ARBOR, MI 48109-0028 Radioiodinated tracers for mapping brain neurons
R29NS-25658-04 (NEUB) HONDA, CHRISTOPHER N UNIVERSITY OF MINNESOTA 321 CHURCH STREET S E MINNEAPOLIS, MN 55455 Non-lemniscal integration in ventrobasal thalamus
R01NS-25669-02 (NLS) HACKETT, JOHN T UNIVERSITY OF VIRGINIA CHARLOTTESVILLE, VA 22908 Molecular mechanisms of quantal synaptic transmission
R01NS-25678-04 (MET) PITAS, ROBERT E GLADSTONE FOUNDATION LABS PO BOX 40608 SAN FRANCISCO, CA 94140-0608 Apolipoprotein E in cholesterol transport and metabolism
R01NS-25699-03 (RNM) HARRIS, JOHN JR UNIVERSITY OF TEXAS DEPT RADIOLIOGY 6431 FANNIN HOUSTON, TX 77030 Magnetic resonance imaging of acute spinal cord trauma
P01NS-25701-05 (NSPB) PRICE, RICHARD W UNIVERSITY OF MINNESOTA 420 S E DELAWARE STREET MINNEAPOLIS, MN 55455 AIDS dementia complex
P01NS-25701-05 0001 (NSPB) PRICE, RICHARD W. AIDS dementia complex AIDS dementia complex in symptomatic patients & AIDS patients at very high risk
P01NS-25701-05 0002 (NSPB) SIDTIS, JOHN T. AIDS dementia complex AIDS dementia complex in HIV-seropositive gay men
P01NS-25701-05 0003 (NSPB) CLEARY, PAUL D. AIDS dementia complex AIDS dementia complex in HIV seropositive blood donors
P01NS-25701-05 0004 (NSPB) ROTTENBERG, DAVID A. AIDS dementia complex Study of AIDS dementia complex using PET
P01NS-25701-05 0005 (NSPB) PRICE, RICHARD W. AIDS dementia complex Viral pathogenesis of AIDS dementia complex
P01NS-25701-05 9001 (NSPB) SIDTIS, JOHN J. AIDS dementia complex Neuropsychology core
P01NS-25701-05 9002 (NSPB) FLONENBERG, NEAL AIDS dementia complex Neurovirology core
P01NS-25701-05 9003 (NSPB) THALER, HOWARD TZYI AIDS dementia complex Biostatistical core
R01NS-25704-04 (PHY) CATTERALL, WILLIAM A UNIVERSITY OF WASHINGTON DEPT. OF PHARMACOLOGY SJ-30 SEATTLE, WASH 98195 Cell biology of the neuronal sodium channel
R01NS-25713-04 (HAR) SILVER, JERRY CASE WESTERN RESERVE UNIVERSIT 2040 ADELBERT ROAD CLEVELAND, OH 44106 Factors affecting regeneration thru the glial scar
R29NS-25729-04 (CMS) SCHWARK, HARRIS D UNIVERSITY OF NORTH TEXAS P.O BOX 5218 DENTON, TX 76203 Intrinsic functional organization of SI cortex
R01NS-25742-04 (NEUC) CLAYTON, DAVID FORREST UNIVERSITY OF ILLINOIS 505 S. GOODWIN URBANA, IL 61801 Differential gene expression in the brain
R01NS-25743-04 (NLS) EL-FAKAHANY, ESAM E UNIVERSITY OF MINNESOTA MED SC BOX 392 MAYO MEMORIAL BLDG MINNEAPOLIS, MN 55455 Modulation of muscarinic responses by inositol lipids
R01NS-25767-03 (NLS) NISHI, RAE OREGON HEALTH SCIENCES UNIV 3181 SW SAM JACKSON PARK ROAD PORTLAND, OR 97201-3098 Mechanisms of trophic molecules in neuronal development
R01NS-25771-04 (NEUB) SCHNEIDER, STEPHEN P UNIV OF NORTH CAROLINA CB #7545, MACNIDER CHAPEL HILL, NC 27599. Mechanisms of local synaptic transmission in dorsal horn
R01NS-25782-04 (PHY) HUME, RICHARD I UNIVERSITY OF MICHIGAN ANN ARBOR, MI 48109 Analysis of the excitatory action of ATP
R01NS-25783-04 (NEUA) KITA, HITOSHI UNIVERSITY OF TENNESSEE 875 MONROE AVE MEMPHIS, TN 38163 Physiology & anatomy of extrapyramidal system
R01NS-25784-04 (NEUB) VAUGHN, JAMES E BECKMAN RES INST OF CITY OF HO 1450 E DUARTE ROAD DUARTE, CA 91010-0269 Spinal cord development
R29NS-25785-05 (NLS) MASH, DEBORAH C UNIVERSITY OF MIAMI 1600 NW 10 AVENUE MIAMI, FL 33136 Cholinergic receptor architectonics in age & Alzheimer's
R01NS-25787-04A1 (NEUB) WAINER, BRUCE H THE UNIVERSITY OF CHICAGO 947 EAST 58TH STREET CHICAGO, IL 60637 Neural trophic interactions of the basal forebrain
R01NS-25788-04 (NEUB) ABRAMS, THOMAS W UNIVERSITY OF PENNSYLVANIA 37 & HAMILTON AVE, UNIV OF PA PHILADELPHIA, PA 19104 Associative synaptic plasticity
R29NS-25789-04 (NEUB) COHAN, CHRISTOPHER S SUNY AT BUFFALO FARBER HALL BUFFALO, NEW YORK 14214 Regulation of neurite outgrowth and connectivity
R01NS-25795-03 (PBC) BOGENMANN, EMIL CHILDREN'S HOSPITAL 4650 SUNSET BLVD, BOX 54 LOS ANGELES, CA 90027 Regulation of neuroblastoma differentiation in culture
R55NS-25796-03A2 (NEUB) KUCERA, JAN BOSTON UNIVERSITY 80 EAST CONCORD STREET BOSTON, MA 02118 Developmental origin of the muscle spindle
R01NS-25797-04 (NLS) BUCKMAN, TRENT D UNIV OF CALIFORNIA 405 HILGARD AVE LOS ANGELES, CA 90024-1406 Functions of glutathione peroxidase in the brain

PROJECT NO., ORGANIZATIONAL UNIT., INVESTIGATOR, ADDRESS, TITLE

R01NS-25801-04 (HUD) COULTER, DAVID L BOSTON CITY HOSPITAL 818 HARRISON AVENUE BOSTON, MA 02118 Controlled study of infant HIV Encephalopathy
R01NS-25824-02 (NLS) WATERS, ROBERT S ANATOMY & NEUROBIOLOGY DPT 875 MONROE AVENUE MEMPHIS, TN 38163 Mechanisms underlying immediate cortical reorganization
R01NS-25867-04 (NLS) SIGLER, PAUL B YALE UNIVERSITY P O BOX 6666 NEW HAVEN, CT 06511 Phospholipasic neurotoxins: structure and function
R29NS-25874-04 (NEUB) HUERTA, MICHAEL F UNIVERSITY OF CONNECTICUT FARMINGTON, CT. 06030 Organization of motor cortex
R01NS-25877-06 (VR) CHIU, WAH BAYLOR COLLEGE OF MEDICINE ONE BAYLOR PLAZA HOUSTON, TX 77030 Structure-Function analysis of enveloped viruses
R01NS-25879-04 (VR) THOMPSON, RICHARD L UNIVERSITY OF CINCINNATI 231 BETHESDA AVENUE (M.L. 524) CINCINNATI, OHIO 45267-0524 Functional and molecular analysis of HSV tissue tropisms
R01NS-25882-04 (NEUC) COWAN, NICHOLAS J NEW YORK UNIVERSITY MED CTR 550 FIRST AVENUE NEW YORK, N Y 10016 SV40 T antigen-induced cell type specific tumors
R01NS-25884-04 (NEUA) HRACHOVY, RICHARD A BAYLOR COLLEGE OF MEDICINE ONE BAYLOR PLAZA HOUSTON, TX 77030 Effect of high-dose ACTH on infantile spasms
R01NS-25907-03 (CMS) EBNER, FORD F BROWN UNIVERSITY BOX G-M301 PROVIDENCE, R I 02912 Receptive fields of layer IV (barrel field) neurons
R01NS-25913-04 (NLS) MCCABE, JOSEPH T UNIFORMED SERVICES UNIVERSITY 4301 JONES BRIDGE ROAD BETHESDA, MD 20814-4799 MRNA & peptide synthesis of vasopressin and oxytocin
R29NS-25914-04 (NEUC) JACKSON, F ROB WORCESTER FDN FOR EXPER BIOL 222 MAPLE AVENUE SHREWSBURY, MA 01545 GABAergic neurotransmitter systems
P01NS-25915-04A1 (NSPB) KRAVITZ, EDWARD A HARVARD MEDICAL SCHOOL 220 LONGWOOD AVE BOSTON, MA 02115 Amines, peptides, and aspects of behavior
P01NS-25915-04A1 0001 (NSPB) KRAVITZ, EDWARD A Amines, peptides, and aspects of behavior Developmental and hormonal modulation of synapses
P01NS-25915-04A1 0002 (NSPB) HARRIS-WARRICK, RONALD M Amines, peptides, and aspects of behavior Multi-transmitter modulatory neurons in the stomatogastric system
P01NS-25915-04A1 0003 (NSPB) KRAVITZ, EDWARD A Amines, peptides, and aspects of behavior The roles of identified serotonin and octapamine neurons
P01NS-25915-04A1 0004 (NSPB) GOY, MICHAEL F Amines, peptides, and aspects of behavior Biochemical and physiological studies of cGMP metabolism
P01NS-25915-04A1 0005 (NSPB) BELTZ, BARBARA S Amines, peptides, and aspects of behavior Development of amine neurons and their targets
P01NS-25915-04A1 0006 (NSPB) POTTER, HUNTINGTON Amines, peptides, and aspects of behavior Molecular genetic studies relating to lobster neurohormonal substances
P01NS-25915-04A1 0007 (NSPB) ATEMA, JELLE Amines, peptides, and aspects of behavior Chemical signals regulating social behavior
P01NS-25915-04A1 9001 (NSPB) BELTZ, BARBARA S Amines, peptides, and aspects of behavior Core--Lobster rearing facility
P01NS-25915-04A1 9002 (NSPB) GOY, MICHAEL F Amines, peptides, and aspects of behavior Core--Marine biological laboratory
P01NS-25915-04A1 9003 (NSPB) KRAVITZ, EDWARD A Amines, peptides, and aspects of behavior Core--Photography
P01NS-25915-04A1 9004 (NSPB) POTTER, HUNTINGTON Amines, peptides, and aspects of behavior Core--Shop
P01NS-25916-04 (SRC) SELVERSTON, ALLEN I UNIVERSITY OF CALIFORNIA LA JOLLA, CA 92093 Molecular & biophysical aspects of neuronal signalling
P01NS-25916-04 0001 (SRC) SELVERSTON, ALLEN Molecular & biophysical aspects of neuronal signalling Cellular mechanisms of neuromodulation
P01NS-25916-04 0002 (SRC) BERG, DARWIN Molecular & biophysical aspects of neuronal signalling Neural nicotinic receptors--Expression and regulation
P01NS-25916-04 0003 (SRC) HARRIS, WILLIAM A Molecular & biophysical aspects of neuronal signalling Molecular neurogenesis
P01NS-25916-04 0004 (SRC) KRISTAN, WILLIAM B Molecular & biophysical aspects of neuronal signalling Mechanisms of target-induced neuronal differentiation
P01NS-25916-04 0005 (SRC) SPITZER, NICHOLAS Molecular & biophysical aspects of neuronal signalling Mechanisms of maturation and modulation of ion channels
P01NS-25916-04 0006 (SRC) ZUKER, CHARLES S Molecular & biophysical aspects of neuronal signalling Cellular and molecular basis of sensory signal transduction
P01NS-25916-04 9001 (SRC) HARRIS, W A Molecular & biophysical aspects of neuronal signalling Core--Microscopy
P01NS-25916-04 9002 (SRC) KRISTAN, W Molecular & biophysical aspects of neuronal signalling Core--Computer
P01NS-25916-04 9003 (SRC) ZUCKER, CHARLES Molecular & biophysical aspects of neuronal signalling Core--Molecular biology
P01NS-25916-04 9004 (SRC) BERG, DARWIN Molecular & biophysical aspects of neuronal signalling Core--Monoclonal antibody facility
P01NS-25916-04 9005 (SRC) SPITZER, NICHOLAS Molecular & biophysical aspects of neuronal signalling Core--Electronics and machine shop
R01NS-25921-04 (RNM) HACKNEY, DAVID HOSPITAL OF THE UNIV. OF PA 3400 SPRUCE STREET PHILADELPHIA, PA 19104 Magnetic resonance imaging of spinal cord injury
R01NS-25928-03 (NLS) SUMIKAWA, KATUMI UNIVERSITY OF CALIFORNIA IRVINE, CA 92717-4550 Assembly of a multi-subunit acetylcholine receptor
R01NS-25946-04 (NEUA) WEIR, BRYCE K UNIVERSITY OF ALBERTA WC MACKENZIE HEALTH SCI CTR EDMONTON, CANADA T6G 2B7 Pathophysiology of chronic cerebral vasospasm
R13NS-25952-04 (NSPA) REYES, EDWARD UNIV OF NEW MEXICO SCHOOL OF M ALBUQUERQUE, NM 87131 Conference program for young minority scientists
R01NS-25963-04 (NEUA) BULLOCK, THEODORE H UNIVERSITY OF

CALIFORNIA 9500 GILMAN DR LA JOLLA, CA 92093-0201 Non standard models for study of cognitive ERPS

R01NS-25983-04 (NLS) CONNORS, BARRY W BROWN UNIVERSITY SECTION OF NEUROBIOLOGY, BOX G PROVIDENCE, RI 02912 Cellular physiology of neuronal circuits in neocortex

R01NS-25986-03 (NLS) GEE, KELVIN W UNIV OF SOUTHERN CALIFORNIA 1985 ZONAL AVENUE LOS ANGELES, CA 90033 Steroids, the estrus cycle, and brain excitability

R01NS-25987-04 (NLS) PHELPS, CAROL J TULANE UNIVERSITY MEDICAL CENT 1430 TULANE AVE NEW ORLEANS, LA 70112 Hypophysiotropic neuron differentiation--target feedback

R01NS-25996-04A1 (GMA) SURPRENANT, ANNMARIE OREGON HEALTH SCIENCES UNIVER 3181 SW SAM JACKSON PARK ROAD PORTLAND, OR 97201 Intestinal ion transport -- Submucous neurons

R29NS-25999-06 (NLS) SIMMONS, MARK A MARSHALL UNIVERSITY HUNTINGTON, WV 25755-9310 Mechanisms of synaptic modulation in sympathetic neurons

R01NS-26001-04 (NEUC) SALZER, JAMES L NEW YORK UNIVERSITY MEDICAL CT 550 FIRST AVE NEW YORK, NY 10016 Molecules mediating the cell interactions of myelination

R01NS-26004-04 (NEUA) FENSTERMACHER, JOSEPH D S U N Y - AT STONY BROOK STONY BROOK, N Y 11794 Variations in flow dynamics in cerebral capillary beds

R01NS-26034-04 (NEUA) KISH, STEPHEN J UNIVERSITY OF TORONTO 250 COLLEGE STREET TORONTO, ONTARIO, CANADA M5T 1 Neurobehavior neurochemistry and neuropathology of OPCA

R29NS-26045-04 (NEUC) RUWE, WILLIAM D UNIV OF ARKAMSAS FOR MED SCI 4301 WEST MARKHAM, SLOT 505 LITTLE ROCK, AR 72205 Neuropeptidergic mediation of the acute phase reaction

R29NS-26055-03 (NEUC) SMALHEISER, NEIL R UNIVERSITY OF CHICAGO 5841 S. MARYLAND AV., HO BX413 CHICAGO, ILL 60637 Molecular/cellular action of cranin in neural cells

R29NS-26063-04 (NLS) SIVAM, SUBBIAH P INDIANA UNIVERSITY 3400 BROADWAY GARY, IN 46408 Dopamine and enkephalin/tachykinin dynamic in basal ganglia

R01NS-26064-04 (NEUC) POSNER, JEROME B MEMORIAL HOSP FOR CANCER...... 1275 YORK AVENUE NEW YORK, NY 10021 Studies of neurological paraneoplastic syndromes

R01NS-26068-03 (NEUB) LERANTH, CSABA YALE UNIVERSITY PO BOX 3333 NEW HAVEN, CT 06510 Synaptology of the septo-hippocampal cholinergic system

R01NS-26081-05 (NLS) KAPATOS, GREGORY WAYNE STATE UNIVERSITY 656 WEST KIRBY DETROIT, MI 48202 Tetrahydrobiopterin biosynthesis by dopamine neurons

R01NS-26084-04 (NEUC) ARTAVANIS-TSAKONAS, SPYRIDON YALE UNIVERSITY P O BOX 6666 NEW HAVEN, CT 06511-8112 The cell biology of a protein in Drosophila neurogenesis

R01NS-26086-04 (NLS) WAXHAM, MELVIN NEAL UNIVERSITY OF TEXAS P O BOX 20708 HOUSTON, TX 77225 Structure & function of calmodulin-dependent kinase 2

R01NS-26087-03 (NEUB) COLE, GREGORY J MED UNIV OF SOUTH CAROLINA 171 ASHLEY AVENUE CHARLESTON, SC 29425 Characterization of HSPGs in neural development

R29NS-26091-04 (NLS) MEIRI, KARINA F SUNY HLTH SCI CTR AT SYRACUSE 750, EAST ADAMS STREET SYRACUSE, NY 13210 Signal transduction in the neuronal growth cone

R01NS-26093-01A2S1 (EDC) LEVITON, ALAN CHILDREN'S HOSPITAL 300 LONGWOOD AVENUE BOSTON, MA 02115 Congenital microcephaly

R01NS-26106-03 (NEUB) FARLEY, JOSEPH INDIANA UNIVERSITY P.O. BOX 1847 BLOOMINGTON, IN 47402 Cellular analysis of learning

R01NS-26113-04 (NLS) PUSZKIN, SAUL MOUNT SINAI SCH OF MED FIFTH AVENUE & 100TH STREET NEW YORK, N Y 10029 Brain membrane turnover processes

R29NS-26115-05 (NEUC) MILLER, DAVID M DUKE UNIVERSITY 353 SANDS BLDG. DURHAM, NC 27710 Molecular genetics of neural specificity

R29NS-26116-04 (NLS) HENTALL, IAN D UNIVERSITY OF ILLINOIS 1601 PARKVIEW AVENUE ROCKFORD, IL 61107-1897 Role of individual brainstem neurons in pain inhibition

R01NS-26119-04 (NLS) MC MORRIS, F ARTHUR WISTAR INSTITUTE 36TH & SPRUCE STREETS PHILADELPHIA, PA 19104 Oligodendrocyte gene expression in immortalized clones

R29NS-26125-05 (NEUB) MORRISON, RICHARD STEVEN R.S. DOW NEUROLOGICAL SCI. INS 1120 N W 20TH AVENUE PORTLAND, OR 97209 Fibroblast growth factor--Interactions with CNS neurons

R01NS-26126-03 (NEUC) SCHENGRUND, CARA L MILTON S HERSHEY MEDICAL CENTE P O BOX 850 HERSHEY, PA 17033 Mechanism of neurite formation

R01NS-26127-03 (PHY) RAMON, FIDEL CTR. INVESTIGACION Y ST. AVANZ APDO. POSTAL 14-740 MEXICO, D.F. 07000 Physiological control of intercellular coupling

R01NS-26137-04 (ECS) BEREITER, DAVID A RHODE ISLAND UNIVERSITY 593 EDDY STREET PROVIDENCE, RI 02903 Trigeminal control of adrenal autonomic function

R29NS-26142-03 (NEUB) SILVERSTEIN, FAYE S UNIVERSITY OF MICHIGAN R6028 KRESGE II BLDG., ANN ARBOR, MI 48109-0570 Role of glutamate in perinatal brain injury

R29NS-26143-04 (NLS) MC CORMICK, DAVID A YALE UNIVERSITY 333 CEDAR STREET NEW HAVEN, CT 06510 Ach & NE modulation of cortical & thalamic neurons

R01NS-26146-03 (NEUB) MUFSON, ELLIOTT J INST FOR BIOGERONTOLOGY RES 13220 N 105TH AVE, PO BOX 1278 SUN CITY, AZ 85372 Cortical somatostatinergic systems

R01NS-26150-04 (NEUB) BRIDGMAN, PAUL C WASHINGTON UNIVERSITY 660 S EUCLID AVENUE ST LOUIS, MO 63110 Nerve growth cone locomotion

R01NS-26151-04 (EDC) SHINNAR, SHLOMO MONTEFIORE MEDICAL CENTER 111 E 210TH STREET BRONX, N Y 10467 Prognosis of children with a first unprovoked seizure

R01NS-26157-03 (NEUB) MC KENNA, KEVIN E NORTHWESTERN MEDICAL SCHOOL 303 E CHICAGO AVE CHICAGO, IL 60611-3008 Spinal organization of sexual function

R29NS-26159-04 (NEUB) AEBISCHER, PATRICK BROWN UNIVERSITY BOX G PROVIDENCE, RI 02912 Nerve regeneration through synthetic guidance channels

PROJECT NO., ORGANIZATIONAL UNIT., INVESTIGATOR, ADDRESS, TITLE

R01NS-26160-03 (BBCA) MORRIS, MICHAEL D DEPT. OF CHEMISTRY 930 NORTH UNIVERSITY AVENUE ANN ARBOR, MI 48109 Surface enhanced Raman spectroscopy of neurotransmitters

R01NS-26168-04 (NLS) PARSONS, STANLEY M UNIVERSITY OF CALIFORNIA NEUROSCIENCE RES INST SANTA BARBARA, CA 93106 The brain acetylcholine storage system

R29NS-26175-04 (NEUC) FUKADA, KEIKO SUNY HLTH SCI CTR AT BROOKLYN 450 CLARKSON AVENUE BROOKLYN, NY 11203 Mechanism of action of a neuronal differentiation factor

R01NS-26178-03 (NEUA) SPERLING, MICHAEL R COMPREHENSIVE EPILEPSY CENTER 1 GRADUATE PLAZA PHILADELPHIA, PA 19146 Subcortical metabolic alterations in epilepsy

R01NS-26179-04 (NEUA) TATEMICHI, THOMAS K BOX 107 710 WEST 168TH STREET NEW YORK, N Y 10032 Mechanisms & syndromes of dementia related to stroke

R01NS-26185-04 (ORTH) LAW, PETER K CELL THERAPY RES. FDN. 1770 MORIAH WOODS BLVD STE 18 MEMPHIS, TN 38177 Histoincompatible myoblast injection against dystrophy

R29NS-26189-04 (NLS) FOX, AARON P UNIVERSITY OF CHICAGO 947 EAST 58TH STREET CHICAGO, IL 60637 Hippocampal calcium channels--Pharmacology and function

R44NS-26204-03 (BPO) CHANEY, RICHARD A ALACRON, INC. 84 OLD FARM ROAD NORTH CHAPPAQUA, NY 10514 An event detecting video/EEG monitoring system

R29NS-26222-05 (CMS) FULLER, MARC S UNIV. OF UTAH MEDICAL CTR. 50 NORTH MEDICAL DRIVE SALT LAKE CITY, UT 84132 Dynamic analysis of joint mechanoreceptor neurons

R01NS-26224-03 (MBY) MILBRANDT, JEFFREY D WASHINGTON UNIV SCH OF MED 660 SOUTH EUCLID AVE. ST. LOUIS, MO 63110 Molecular basis of nerve growth factor-regulated gene expression

R01NS-26229-03 (CMS) TUCKETT, ROBERT P UNIVERSITY OF UTAH 410 CHIPETA WAY, RESEARCH PARK SALT LAKE CITY, UT 84108 Sensitization of itch signaling neural pathways

R01NS-26237-04 (SSS) MYERS, RICHARD M UNIVERSITY OF CALIFORNIA 513 PARNASSUS AVE SAN FRANCISCO, CA 94143 Molecular genetics of Huntington disease

R29NS-26242-05 (NLS) FILBIN, MARIE T HUNTER COLLEGE 695 PARK AVENUE NEW YORK, NY 10021 Myelin Po protein--Expression/sorting and adhesion

R29NS-26247-02 (CMS) VAN ORDEN, GUY C PSYCHOLOGY-100443 TEMPE, AZ 85287-1104 Spelling-sound-regularity & stroke-induced dyslexia

R29NS-26251-04 (NEUB) MC GINNIS, MICHAEL E PURDUE UNIV SCHOOL OF VET MED CENTER FOR PARALYSIS RESEARCH WEST LAFAYETTE, IN 47907 Enhanced peripheral nerve regeneration by DC stimulation

R29NS-26272-04 (BPO) ROBERTS, MICHAEL H CLARKSON UNIVERSITY DEPT OF BIOLOGY POTSDAM, N Y 13676 Central neural processing of circadian information

R01NS-26280-03 (NLS) ATASSI, M ZOUHAIR BAYLOR COLLEGE OF MEDICINE DEPARTMENT OF BIOCHEMISTRY HOUSTON, TX 77030 Molecular recognition of acetylcholine receptor

R01NS-26283-03 (NLS) MARGOLIS, RICHARD U NEW YORK UNIVERSITY MED CENTER 550 FIRST AVENUE NEW YORK, N Y 10016 Neuronal cell-surface glycoconjugates

R29NS-26285-04 (HAR) SMITH, PHILIP HAROLD MED SCIENCES CTR-51H BARDEEN 1300 UNIV AVE DEPT OF NEUROPHY MADISON, WI 53706 Analysis of synaptic interaction in inferior colliculus

R01NS-26288-03 (NEUB) MACKEL, ROBERT G ROCKEFELLER UNIVERSITY 1230 YORK AVENUE NEW YORK, NY 10021 Spinal input to motor thalamus

R01NS-26301-03 (NEUA) MEYER, FREDRIC B MAYO FOUNDATION 200 FIRST STREET SOUTHWEST ROCHESTER, MN 55905 Nimodipine as an add-on therapy for intractable epilepsy

R01NS-26310-04 (BM) KIM, KWANG S CHILDRENS HOSP OF LOS ANGELES 4650 SUNSET BLVD LOS ANGELES, CA 90027 Pathogenesis and treatment of neonatal meningitis

R29NS-26312-04 (PTHA) VINTERS, HARRY V UNIVERSITY OF CALIFORNIA 650 CIRCLE DRIVE SOUTH LOS ANGELES, CA 90024 Characterization of cerebral amyloid angiopathic peptide

R01NS-26321-02 (SRC) JACOBS, LAWRENCE D MILLARD FILLMORE HOSPITALS 3 GATES CIRCLE BUFFALO, NY 14209 IM recombinant beta interferon as treatment for MS

R01NS-26333-04 (NEUC) SCHUBART, ULRICH K ALBERT EINSTEIN COLLEGE 1300 MORRIS PARK AVENUE BRONX, NY 10461 Role of P19 in neuronal development

R29NS-26343-03 (END) DE VITO, WILLIAM J UNIVERSITY OF MASSACHUSETTS 55 LAKE AVENUE, NORTH WORCESTER, MA 01605 Immunoreactive brain prolactin

R01NS-26348-03 (NEUA) KENNEDY, WILLIAM R UNIVERSITY OF MINNESOTA BOX 187,HARVARD ST AT E RIVER MINNEAPOLIS, MN 55455 Diabetic neuropathy treated by pancreas transplantation

R55NS-26361-04 (NEUA) MOSKOWITZ, MICHAEL A MASSACHUSETTS GENERAL HOSPITAL FRUIT STREET BOSTON, MA 02114 Trigeminal vasomotor effects on the cerebral circulation

R01NS-26362-03 (NLS) ROBBINS, RICHARD J YALE UNIVERSITY P O BOX 3333 NEW HAVEN, CT 06510 Biology of somatostatin interneurons in the brain

R01NS-26363-03 (NLS) RAJA, SRINIVASA N JOHNS HOPKINS HOSPITAL 600 N. WOLFE ST MEYER 8-134 BALTIMORE, MD 21205 Injury-induced pain--Chemical modulation of nociceptors

R01NS-26375-03 (NEUB) SCHWARTZ, ANDREW B ST JOSEPH'S HOSP & MED CTR 350 W THOMAS RD PHOENIX, AZ 85013 Motor cortical contribution to skilled arm movement

R01NS-26380-04 (NEUB) HOULE, JOHN D UNIVERSITY OF ARKANSAS 4301 WEST MARKHAM ST LITTLE ROCK, AR 72205-7199 Axonal growth in the chronically injured spinal cord

R01NS-26390-03 (BPO) HENDLEY, EDITH D UNIVERSITY OF VERMONT COLLEGE OF MEDICINE BURLINGTON, VT 05405 Brain peptide and amine transmitters in new strains

R29NS-26400-04 (CMS) COSLETT, HARRY B TEMPLE UNIVERSITY HOSPITAL 3401 NORTH BROAD STREET PHILADELPHIA, PA 19140 Attentional processes in disorders of visual perception

R01NS-26402-04 (BPO) EICHENBAUM, HOWARD B UNIVERSITY OF NORTH CAROLINA CB 3270, DAVIE HALL CHAPEL HILL, N C 27599 Behavioral and place correlates of hippocampal neurons

PROJECT NO., ORGANIZATIONAL UNIT., INVESTIGATOR, ADDRESS, TITLE

R01NS-26412-03 (GEN) DOWSE, HAROLD B UNIVERSITY OF MAINE ORONO, MAINE 04469 Genetics of circadian and ultradian oscillators
R01NS-26415-03 (NLS) CUELLO, A CLAUDIO MCGILL UNIVERSITY 3655 DRUMMOND STREET MONTREAL, QUEBEC, CANADA H3G 1 Direct approach to synaptic organization of nociception
R01NS-26416-04 (PHY) BEAM, KURT G, JR COLORADO STATE UNIVERSITY DEPT OF PHYSIOLOGY & BIOPHYSIC FORT COLLINS, COLO 80523 Ontogeny of neuronal ion channels
R29NS-26419-04 (NEUA) BEHAR, KEVIN L YALE UNIVERSITY 260 WHITNEY AVENUE NEW HAVEN, CT 06511 Cerebral intracellular calcium in vivo
R01NS-26429-03 (BPO) TOTH, LINDA A UNIVERSITY OF TENNESSEE 956 COURT, P O BOX 17 MEMPHIS, TN 38163 Sleep patterns during infectious disease
R29NS-26432-04 (PHY) LEONARD, JOHN P UNIVERSITY OF ILLINOIS AT CHIC PO BOX 4348, MAIL CODE 066 CHICAGO, ILLINOIS 60680 Ca channels, molecular studies
R01NS-26449-03 (NLS) FIELDS, JEREMY Z VETERANS ADMINISTRATION HOSP MEDICAL RESEARCH SERVICE 151 HINES, IL 60141 Permanent dopamine hypersensitivity--A unique model
R01NS-26450-04 (EDC) STEWART, WALTER F JOHNS HOPKINS UNIVERSITY 615 N WOLFE STREET BALTIMORE, MD 21205 Follow-up study of neurological risks in amateur boxers
R29NS-26454-04 (MGN) FARRER, LINDSAY A BOSTON UNIVERSITY 720 HARRISON AVE., SUITE 1105 BOSTON, MA 02118 Genetic studies of Wilson's disease
P01NS-26473-04 (NSPB) KITAI, STEPHEN T DEPT. OF ANATOMY & NEUROBIOLOGY 875 MONROE AVENUE MEMPHIS, TN 38163 Morphology and function of the basal ganglia
P01NS-26473-04 0001 (NSPB) KITAI, STEPHEN T Morphology and function of the basal ganglia Development and physiological studies of striatal neurons
P01NS-26473-04 0002 (NSPB) KITA, HITOSHI Morphology and function of the basal ganglia Functions of neuroactive substances in neostriatum
P01NS-26473-04 0003 (NSPB) NELSON, RANDALL J Morphology and function of the basal ganglia Single-unit activity in the basal ganglia
P01NS-26473-04 0004 (NSPB) WILSON, CHARLES J Morphology and function of the basal ganglia Restoration of functional connections by neostriatal brain grafts
R01NS-26479-01A2 (NEUB) HEXUM, TERRY D UNIVERSITY OF NEBRASKA 600 SOUTH 42ND STREET OMAHA, NE 68198-6260 Neuropeptide Y modulation of adrenomedullary secretion
R01NS-26488-02 (NEUB) OHARA, PETER T UNIVERSITY OF CALIFORNIA 513 PARNASSUS AVE SAN FRANCISCO, CA 94143-0452 Study of local circuit neurons of the thalamus
R29NS-26489-01A3 (NEUA) KUMAR, KUSUM MICHIGAN STATE UNIVERSITY EAST LANSING, MI 48824 RNA in postischemic brain
R29NS-26494-04 (NLS) WESTBROOK, GARY L OREGON HEALTH SCIENCES UNIV 3181 SW SAM JACKSON PARK ROAD PORTLAND, OR 97201 Excitatory synaptic mechanisms in the CNS
R29NS-26496-04 (NEUB) HARRINGTON, MARY E CLARK SCIENCE CENTER SMITH COLLEGE NORTHAMPTON, MA 01063 The neural basis of biological rhythms
R01NS-26505-03 (NEUB) CALDWELL, JOHN H UNIV OF COLORADO HLTH SCIS CTR 4200 EAST NINTH AVENUE/B-111 DENVER, CO 80262 Ion channels in muscle
R29NS-26511-04 (NLS) EHLERT, FREDERICK J UNIVERSITY OF CALIFORNIA COLLEGE OF MEDICINE IRVINE, CA 92717 Muscarinic receptor coupling mechanisms in the brain
R01NS-26519-03A2 (NEUC) CHANG, SUSANNAH UNIVERSITY OF PENNSYLVANIA 137 ANATOMY-CHEMISTRY BUILDING PHILADELPHIA, PA 19104-6058 Molecular characterization of a chick neural protein
R29NS-26523-04 (NEUA) BLACK, KEITH L UCLA SCHOOL OF MEDICINE 10833 LE CONTE AVENUE LOS ANGELES, CA 90024-1749 Leukotriene modulation of the blood barrier in tumors
R01NS-26526-04 (BPO) RINGO, JAMES L UNIV OF ROCHESTER MEDICAL CTR 601 ELMWOOD AVE ROCHESTER, N Y 14642 Temporal lobe single unit activity & memory
R01NS-26529-03 (RNM) BOOKSTEIN, FRED L UNIVERSITY OF MICHIGAN 300 NORTH INGALLS BUILDING ANN ARBOR, MI 48109 Deformations and the anatomy of functional images
R01NS-26536-05 (NLS) GOODMAN, STEVEN R UNIVERSITY OF SOUTH ALABAMA 2042 MEDICAL SCIENCE BUILDING MOBILE, ALA 36688 Structure, location,and function of brain amelin
R29NS-26539-04 (NEUB) FETCHO, JOSEPH R SUNY AT STONY BROOK LIFE SCIENCES BLDG ROM 564 STONY BROOK, NY 11794-5230 Central control of motoneurons in a vertebrate
R01NS-26540-04 (NLS) WATKINS, JEFFREY C UNIVERSITY WALK SCHOOL OF MEDICAL SCIENCES BRISTOL, UK BS8 1TD Characterization of excitatory amino acid transmitters
R01NS-26543-04 (PTHA) MILLER, STEPHEN D NORTHWESTERN UNIVERSITY CHICAGO, IL 60611 Immunoregulation and pathology of chronic-relapsing EAE
R44NS-26548-03 (SSS) LOATS, HARRY L LOATS ASSOCIATES, INC 1004 LITTLESTOWN PIKE WESTMINSTER, MD 21157 Brain imaging quantitation techniques
R44NS-26549-03 (SSS) MUEHLLEHNER, GERD UGM MEDICAL SYSTEMS, INC. 3401 MARKET ST., SUITE 222 PHILADELPHIA, PA 19104 Single crystal cylindrical positron tomograph
R01NS-26553-03 (CMS) GORDON, BARRY NEUROLOGY DEPARTMENT MEYER 2-222 600 N WOLFE ST BALTIMORE, MD 21205 Language organization studied by cortical stimulation
R44NS-26571-03 (PSF) HAYES, DONALD J MICROFAB TECHNOLOGIES, INC. 1104 SUMMIT AVE PLANO, TX 75074 Ink-jet system for microchemical stimulation of tissue
R01NS-26595-04 (ALCB) BREESE, GEORGE R UNIV OF NORTH CAROLINA AT C H BIOL SCI RES CTR CB 7250 CHAPEL HILL, NC 27599 Repeated ethanol withdrawal and seizures
R01NS-26598-04 (PTHA) ESKIN, THOMAS A UNIVERSITY OF ROCHESTER 601 ELMWOOD AVENUE ROCHESTER, N Y 14642 Morphometric correlates of encephalopathy in AIDS
R01NS-26606-03 (NLS) WESTHEAD, EDWARD W UNIVERSITY OF MASSACHUSETTS AMHERST, MA 01003 Modulation of secretion in chromaffin cells

PROJECT NO., ORGANIZATIONAL UNIT., INVESTIGATOR, ADDRESS, TITLE

R01NS-26610-01A3 (NEUA) ADLER, SHELDON MONTEFIORE HOSPITAL 3459 FIFTH AVENUE PITTSBURGH, PA 15213 Effect of hyponatremia on brain pH function morphology
R01NS-26612-04 (HUD) EMERSON, RONALD G NEUROLOGICAL INSTITUTE 710 WEST 168TH STREET NEW YORK, NY 10032 Evoked potentials in congenital HIV infection
R01NS-26620-07 (NEUC) MANESS, PATRICIA F UNIV OF NORTH CAROLINA AT CH #CB7260 CHAPEL HILL, NC 27599 expression of c-src in developing nervous system
R29NS-26621-03 (NLS) DEJESUS, ONOFRE T 1530 MEDICAL SCIENCES 1300 UNIVERSITY AVENUE MADISON, WI 53706 Non-catecholic L-dopa analogs
P01NS-26630-03 (SRC) PERICAK-VANCE, MARGARET A DUKE UNIVERSITY MEDICAL CENTER BOX 2900 DURHAM, NC 27710 Center for genetic studies in neurological disorders
P01NS-26630-03 0005 (SRC) MIHOVILOVIC, MIRTA Center for genetic studies in neurological disorders Use of DNA probe for cholinergic and non-cholinergic MG antigen
P01NS-26630-03 9001 (SRC) PERICAK-VANCE, MARGARET A. Center for genetic studies in neurological disorders Core--Family data, DNA banking
R01NS-26632-03 (NLS) POWLEY, TERRY L PURDUE UNIVERSITY DEPT OF PSYCHOLOGICAL SCI WEST LAFAYETTE, IN 47907 Neural organization of vagal alimentary reflexes
R01NS-26638-02 (NEUB) AMBRON, RICHARD T COLUMBIA UNIVERSITY DEPT. OF ANATOMY & CELL BIOLOG NEW YORK, NY 10032 Growth cone surface proteins that mediate target contact
R01NS-26641-03 (NEUC) CHUNG, SU YUN UNIFORMED SERV UNIV OF HLTH SC 4301 JONES BRIDGE ROAD BETHESDA, MD 20814-4799 Expression of homeobox-containing genes in spinal cord
P01NS-26643-04 (SRC) JOHNSON, RICHARD T JOHN HOPKINS UNIVERSITY 600 N WOLFE ST, MEYER BLDG BALTIMORE, MD 21205 Research centers for AIDS dementia and other retroviral neurological disorders
P01NS-26643-04 0001 (SRC) CORNBLATH, D Research centers for AIDS dementia and other retroviral neurological disorders Neurologic manifestations of HIV infection
P01NS-26643-04 0002 (SRC) JOHNSON, R T Research centers for AIDS dementia and other retroviral neurological disorders Cellular neuropathology of HIV infection
P01NS-26643-04 0003 (SRC) GRIFFIN, D E Research centers for AIDS dementia and other retroviral neurological disorders Immunological aspects of nervous system infection with HIV
P01NS-26643-04 0004 (SRC) CLEMENS,J E Research centers for AIDS dementia and other retroviral neurological disorders Role of HIV LTR and TAT gene in CNS and PNS pathogenesis
P01NS-26643-04 0005 (SRC) MOENCH, M D Research centers for AIDS dementia and other retroviral neurological disorders Feline lentivirus induced neurological disease
P01NS-26643-04 9001 (SRC) MCARTHUR, J Research centers for AIDS dementia and other retroviral neurological disorders Core -- Clinical studies
P01NS-26643-04 9002 (SRC) PRICE, D L Research centers for AIDS dementia and other retroviral neurological disorders Core -- Neuropathology
R01NS-26645-03 (NEUA) DESMOND, NANCY L UNIVERSITY OF VIRGINIA NEUROSURGERY BOX 420 CHARLOTTESVILLE, VA 22908 The anatomy of activity-dependent synaptic modification
R01NS-26650-03 (NLS) HAYDON, PHILIP G DEPT OF ZOOLOGY AMES, IA 50011 Calcium channels & G-proteins in synaptic transmission
R01NS-26651-02 (PHY) LANDOWNE, DAVID PO BOX 016430 MIAMI, FL 33101 Molecular motion in nerve sodium channels
R01NS-26656-03 (NEUC) FAHN, STANLEY COLUMBIA UNIVERSITY 630 WEST 168TH ST NEW YORK, NY 10032 Linkage studies & molecular genetics of dystonia
R01NS-26657-03 (RNM) LEAR, JAMES LOUIS DEPT OF RADIOLOGY 4200 E 9TH AVE, NUC MED A034 DENVER, CO 80262 Autoradiographic imaging of cerebral functions
R01NS-26658-03 (HAR) JULIANO, SHARON L UNIFORM SERVICES UNIV/HLTH SCI 4301 JONES BRIDGE ROAD BETHESDA, MD 20814-4799 Immunocytochemistry of vestibular nuclei
R29NS-26660-03 (PHY) ROSENBERG, ROBERT L DEPARTMENT OF PHARMACOLOGY CB #7365, FACULTY LAB OFF BLDG CHAPEL HILL, N.C. 27599-7365 Reconstitution of neuronal calcium channels
R01NS-26661-03 (PHY) RUFF, ROBERT CLEVELAND VA MEDICAL CENTER 10701 EAST BOULEVARD CLEVELAND, OH 44106 Sodium channel gating in models of myotonia
R01NS-26662-03 (BNP) AYLING, JUNE E UNIVERSITY OF SOUTH ALABAMA COLLEGE OF MEDICINE - MSB 3130 MOBILE, AL 36688 Tetrahydropterin treatment for neurological disorders
P01NS-26665-04 (SRC) COLE, GERALD A UNIVERSITY OF MD AT BALTIMORE 655 WEST BALTIMORE STREET BALTIMORE, MD 21201 Comprehensive AIDS research center
P01NS-26665-04 0001 (SRC) JOHNSON, J Comprehensive AIDS research center Perinatal transmission of HIV--Role of antibody
P01NS-26665-04 0002 (SRC) COLE, GERALD Comprehensive AIDS research center Maternal T-cell response to HIV and perinatal infection
P01NS-26665-04 0003 (SRC) LEWIS, GEORGE Comprehensive AIDS research center Novel anti-HIV antibody constructs for immunotherapy
P01NS-26665-04 0004 (SRC) AURELIAN, LAURE Comprehensive AIDS research center Herpesvirus-HIV interactions in cells of neural origin
P01NS-26665-04 0005 (SRC) GRATZ, EDWARD Comprehensive AIDS research center AIDS dementia in children
P01NS-26665-04 9001 (SRC) JOHNSON, JOHN Comprehensive AIDS research center Clinical core
P01NS-26680-04A1 (SRC) HALL, COLIN D UNIV OF NC AT CHAPEL HILL 751 BURNETT WOMACK BLDG CHAPEL HILL, NC 27599 Proposal for an AIDS dementia center
P01NS-26680-04A1 0001 (SRC) HALL, COLIN D Proposal for an AIDS dementia center Adult subject evaluation
P01NS-26680-04A1 0002 (SRC) WHITT, J KENNETH Proposal for an AIDS dementia center Pediatric hemophiliac subject evaluation
P01NS-26680-04A1 0004 (SRC) MESSENHEIMER, JOHN A Proposal for an AIDS dementia center Clinical neurophysiological evaluation

P01NS-26680-04A1 0005 (SRC) HALL, COLIN D Proposal for an AIDS dementia center Neuroradiological evaluation
P01NS-26680-04A1 9001 (SRC) HALL, COLIN D Proposal for an AIDS dementia center Core--Research core
R01NS-26681-04 (EVR) JOHNSTON, ROBERT E UNIVERSITY OF NORTH CAROLINA CB# 7290 804 FLOB CHAPEL HILL, NC 27599 In vitro construction of attenuated VEE virus mutants
R01NS-26722-03 (CMS) CHAPIN, JOHN K HAHNEMANN UNIVERSITY BROAD & VINE PHILADELPHIA, PA 19102-1192 Modulation of somatosensory transmission during movement
R01NS-26723-03 (NLS) SIMERLY, RICHARD B OREGON REGIONAL PRIMATE RES CT 505 NW 185TH AVE BEAVERTON, OR 97006 Peptide expression in hypothalamic & limbic circuitry
R01NS-26729-03 (NLS) GOLDIN, ALAN L UNIVERSITY OF CALIFORNIA IRVINE, CA 92717-4025 Molecular basis of sodium channel diversity
R01NS-26732-02 (EDC) DAVANIPOUR, ZOREH LOMA LINDA UNIVERSITY SCHOOL OF MEDICINE LOMA LINDA, CA 92350 Epidemiologic study of Creutzfeldt-Jakob disease
R01NS-26733-02 (CBY) ANGELIDES, KIMON J BAYLOR COLLEGE OF MEDICINE ONE BAYLOR PLAZA HOUSTON, TX 77030 Molecular cytology of intermediate filaments in nerve
R01NS-26739-03 (NLS) ELLISMAN, MARK H UNIV. OF CALIF., SAN DIEGO 500 GILMAN DRIVE Packaging & axonal transport of three macromolecules
R01NS-26742-03 (NEUB) MULLONEY, BRIAN UNIVERSITY OF CALIFORNIA 2320 STORER HALL DAVIS, CA 95616 Synaptic variability -- Developmental and structural sources
R01NS-26746-03 (NLS) BOWEN, WAYNE D BROWN UNIVERSITY DIV. OF BIO. & MED. BOX G PROVIDENCE, R I 02912 Role of sigma receptors in movement disorders
R01NS-26748-03 (NLS) GALL, CHRISTINE M UNIVERSITY OF CALIFORNIA IRVINE, CA 92717 Physiological regulation of neuropeptide expression
R01NS-26750-03 (VISB) MEYER, RONALD L UNIVERSITY OF CALIFORNIA IRVINE, CA 92717-2300 Retinal explants from the adult mouse
R01NS-26760-03 (NEUC) BAYLEY, HAGAN P WORCESTER FDN FOR EXP BIOLOGY 222 MAPLE AVENUE SHREWSBURY, MA 01545 cAMP-dependent protein kinases in neuronal modulation
R01NS-26761-03 (NEUB) LOUGHLIN, SANDRA E UNIVERSITY OF CALIFORNIA IRVINE, CA 92717 Growth factors in intrastriatal transplants
R01NS-26766-03 (NLS) CHALAZONITIS, ALCMENE COLUMBIA UNIVERSITY P&S 630 WEST 168TH STREET NEW YORK, NY 10032 NGF modulation of sensory neuron action potentials
R01NS-26773-03 (NEUC) SOBEL, RAYMOND A MASSACHUSETTS GENERAL HOSPITAL 100 BLOSSOM STREET BOSTON, MASS 02114 Mechanisms of cellular immune reactions in the CNS
R01NS-26777-04 (VISB) HANKIN, MARK H MEDICAL COLLEGE OF OHIO P O BOX 10008 TOLEDO, OH 43699-0008 Surface and target influenced optic axon outgrowth
R01NS-26782-03 (NEUC) MOSKOWITZ, MICHAEL A MASSACHUSETTS GENERAL HOSPITAL WELLMAN 423, 50 BLOSSOM STREET BOSTON, MA 02114 Opioid peptide gene expression in nucleus caudalis
R29NS-26783-03 (NEUA) LYDEN, PATRICK D UCSD SCHOOL OF MEDICINE DEPT. OF NEUROSCIENCES, -0624 LA JOLLA, CA 92093 Multifocal cerebral ischemia
R01NS-26784-03 (NEUA) GLOBUS, MORDECAI UNIVERSITY OF MIAMI P O BOX 016960 MIAMI, FL 33101 Neurotransmitter release--Role in ischemic neuronal injury
R29NS-26788-03 (RNM) MOERLEIN, STEPHEN M WASHINGTON UNIV SCHOOL OF MED 510 SOUTH KINGSHIGHWAY ST LOUIS, MO 63100 Ligands for cerebral dopaminergic studies by PET and SPECT
R01NS-26793-03 (NEUA) SCHER, MARK S MAGEE WOMENS HOSPITAL 300 HALKET STREET PITTSBURGH, PA 15213 Computer analyses of EEG sleep in preterm neonates
R01NS-26795-02 (EDC) ACTON, RONALD T UNIVERSITY OF ALABAMA PO BOX 201 VOLKER HALL BIRMINGHAM, AL 35294 Genetic epidemiology of narcolepsy
R01NS-26799-03 (NEUC) HAUSER, STEPHEN L MASSACHUSETTS GENERAL HOSPITAL FRUIT STREET BOSTON, MA 02114 Gene linkage study of multiple sclerosis sibling pairs
R01NS-26801-03 (EDC) ASARNOW, ROBERT F UNIV OF CALIFORNIA LOS ANGELES DEPT OF PSYCHIATRY LOS ANGELES, CA 90024-1759 Neurobehavioral sequelae of child mild brain injury
R29NS-26804-03 (NLS) SCHIAVONE, MARC T CLEVELAND CLINIC FOUNDATION 9500 EUCLID AVE;ONE CLINIC CTR CLEVELAND, OH 44195 Angiotensin effects in hypothalamus and adrenal medulla
R01NS-26805-02 (HUD) GLASS, PENNY CHILDREN'S HOSP NAT'L MED CTR 111 MICHIGAN AVE, NW WASHINGTON, DC 20010 Neurobehavioral outcome of ECMO neonates at age 5
R29NS-26806-04 (NEUB) BAIZER, LAWRENCE GOOD SAMARITAN HOSP & MED CNTR PORTLAND, OR 97210 Growth-associated protein-43 in neuronal development
R01NS-26818-03 (NEUA) MC INTOSH, TRACY K UNIVERSITY OF CONNECTICUT 263 FARMINGTON AVE FARMINGTON, CT 06030-1110 Role of magnesium in the pathophysiology of brain injury
R01NS-26819-03 (NEUB) KATER, STANLEY B DEPT OF ANATOMY & NEUROBIOLOGY COLL OF VET MED & BIOMED SCIEN FORT COLLINS, CO 80523 Architecture of hippocampal pyramidal neurons
R29NS-26821-01A3 (NLS) AGUILA, M CECILIA UNIV OF TEXAS SW MEDICAL CENTE 5323 HARRY HINES BLVD DALLAS, TX 75235 Mechanisms of hypothalamic release of SRIF and GRF
R01NS-26823-03 (IMS) TSE, HARLEY Y WAYNE STATE UNIV SCHOOL OF MED 540 E CANFIELD AVENUE DETROIT, MI 48201 Genetic variants as tracers of T cell functions in eae
R01NS-26830-03 (NEUA) ROSENBERG, PAUL A CHILDREN'S HOSP CORPORATION 300 LONGWOOD AVENUE BOSTON, MA 02115 Mechanisms of adenosine accumulation in cerebral cortex
R29NS-26836-03 (NLS) BURKE, ROBERT E COLUMBIA UNIVERSITY BOX 67/710 WEST 168TH STREET NEW YORK, NY 10032 The effect of perinatal asphyxia on striatum
R01NS-26838-02 (NLS) GILLETTE, RHANOR UNIVERSITY OF ILLINOIS 524 BURRILL HALL/407 S GOODWIN URBANA, IL 61801 Interacting second messengers in neuron function

PROJECT NO., ORGANIZATIONAL UNIT., INVESTIGATOR, ADDRESS, TITLE

R01NS-26840-03 (NEUB) BINDER, MARC D UNIVERSITY OF WASHINGTON DEPT OF PHYSIOLOGY & BIOPHYSIC SEATTLE, WASH 98195 Analysis of effective synaptic currents in motoneurons
R01NS-26844-01A4 (NLS) MILLER, SHELDON L WISTAR INSTITUTE 36TH & SPRUCE STREETS PHILADELPHIA, PA 19104 In vivo effect of decreased myelin cerebroside
R01NS-26846-03 (NEUB) SCHNAPP, BRUCE J HARVARD MEDICAL SCHOOL 25 SHATTUCK ST BOSTON, MA 02115 The molecular basis of axonal transport
R01NS-26850-03 (NLS) MILETIC, VJEKOSLAV UNIV OF WISCONSIN-MADISON 2015 LINDEN DRIVE WEST MADISON, WIS 53706 Medial thalamic mechanisms of nociception
R01NS-26851-03 (NLS) ZAHNISER, NANCY R UNIV OF COLORADO HLTH SCIS CTR 4200 EAST NINTH AVE DENVER, CO 80262 Release-modulating D-2 dopamine receptors in striatum
R01NS-26853-01A2 (NEUB) ROBERTSON, J DAVID DUKE UNIVERSITY MEDICAL CENTER BOX 3209 DURHAM, NC 27710 Brain function
R01NS-26854-03 (MGN) GERHARD, DANIELA S WASHINGTON UNIV SCH OF MED 660 SOUTH EUCLID BOX 8232 ST LOUIS, MO 63110 Search for the affective disorders gene on chromosome 11
R01NS-26855-03 (BPO) MAIR, ROBERT G UNIVERSITY OF NEW HAMPSHIRE PSYCHOLOGY DEPARTMENT DURHAM, N H 03824 Neurobiological mechanisms of diencephalic amnesia
R01NS-26862-02 (PBC) LANDER, ARTHUR D MASSACHUSETTS INST OF TECH 77 MASSACHUSETTS AVENUE CAMBRIDGE, MA 02139 Analysis of proteoglycans involved in brain development
R29NS-26865-04 (NEUA) APPLEGATE, CRAIG D UNIVERSITY OF ROCHESTER MED CT 601 ELMWOOD AVENUE ROCHESTER, N Y 14642 Seizure susceptibility--neurogenetic analysis
R01NS-26871-02 (CMS) LEVINE, SUSAN C UNIVERSITY OF CHICAGO 5848 S UNIVERSITY AVENUE CHICAGO, IL 60637 Neuro-cognitive effects of early unilateral brain damage
R01NS-26879-03 (NEUB) CONNOR, ELIZABETH A UNIVERSITY OF MASSACHUSETTS MORRILL SCIENCE CENTER AMHERST, MA 01003 Remodelling of the endplate region in denervated muscle
R29NS-26880-03 (NLS) DEVI, LAKSHMI A NEW YORK UNIVERSITY MEDICAL CT 550 FIRST AVE NEW YORK, NY 10016 Enzymes involved in dynorphin biosynthesis
R01NS-26882-03 (PTHA) GONATAS, NICHOLAS K UNIVERSITY OF PENNSYLVANIA RM 447A JOHNSON PAVILION PHILADELPHIA, PA 19104-6079 The normal & pathologic Golgi apparatus of neurons
R01NS-26884-03 (NEUB) UEDA, TETSUFUMI MENTAL HEALTH RESEARCH INST 205 WASHTENAW PLACE ANN ARBOR, MI 48109-0720 Synaptic vesicle with glutamate uptake system
R29NS-26885-03 (NEUC) RANDALL, WILLIAM R UNIV OF MD SCHOOL OF MEDICINE 655 W. BALTIMORE STREET BALTIMORE, MD 21201 Neural regulation of cholinergic proteins
R01NS-26887-03 (NEUB) WHITTEMORE, SCOTT R UNIVERSITY OF MIAMI 1600 N W 10TH AVE, R48 MIAMI, FL 33136 Novel cells lines for spinal cord transplantation
R29NS-26892-03 (NEUC) HERBERT, JOSEPH COLUMBIA UNIVERSITY DEPT. OF NEUROLOGY BB 3-328 NEW YORK, N Y 10032 Biosynthetic activity of the choroid plexus
R01NS-26899-03 (SSS) LEBOVITZ, ROBERT M UNIV TEXAS SW MEDICAL CENTER 5323 HARRY HINES BLVD DALLAS, TX 75235-9040 Potassium-mediated ionic coupling in CNS--Computer model
R01NS-26907-04 (SSS) CHOI, DENNIS W WASHINGTON UNIV. MED. SCHOOL 660 S. EUCLID AVE. Pharmacologic reduction of hypoxic neuronal injury
R01NS-26908-01A2 (BPO) DEMETER, STEVEN UNIVERSITY OF ROCHESTER MED CT BOX 605 ROCHESTER, NY 14642 Hippocampal commissure function and anatomy
R01NS-26912-03 (NEUA) PHILLIS, JOHN W WAYNE STATE UNIVERSITY 540 E CANFIELD DETROIT, MI 48201 Manipulation of adenosine metabolism & control of stroke
R29NS-26915-03 (NLS) HOCKBERGER, PHILIP E NORTHWESTERN UNIVERSITY DEPT OF PHYSIOLOGY CHICAGO, ILLINOIS 60611 Cyclic nucleotide actions in cultured rat purkinje cells
R01NS-26920-03 (NEUC) NATHANSON, NEIL M DEPT. OF PHARMACOLOGY, SJ-30 UNIVERSITY OF WASHINGTON SEATTLE, WA 98195 Molecular analysis of neural G-protein action
R01NS-26933-03 (NEUA) BROTT, THOMAS G UNIV OF CINCINNATI MEDICAL CTR 231 BETHESDA AVE CINCINNTI, OHIO 45267-0525 Ultra-early evaluation of intracerebral hemorrhage
R01NS-26934-04 (NLS) WOLFE, BARRY B GEORGETOWN UNIVERSITY SCH MED 3900 RESERVOIR ROAD N W WASHINGTON, D C 20007 Molecular properties of muscarinic cholinergic receptors
R01NS-26943-02 (NLS) STOLLBERG, JES BEKESY LAB OF NEUROBIOLOGY 1993 EAST-WEST ROAD HONOLULU, HI 96822 Mechanisms of acetylcholine receptor clustering
R01NS-26945-03 (NEUA) DEL ZOPPO, GREGORY J BASIC AND CLINICAL RESEARCH 10666 NORTH TORREY PINES ROAD LA JOLLA, CA 92037 Microvascular occlusions--acute focal cerebral ischemia
R01NS-26946-02 (HUD) PAINTER, MICHAEL J MAGEE-WOMENS HOSPITAL FORBES AVE & HALKET STREET PITTSBURGH, PA 15213 Efficacy and metabolism of anticonvulsants in neonates
R44NS-26976-03 (NLS) ROSE, TIMOTHY L EIC LABORATORIES, INC 111 DOWNEY STREET NORWOOD, MA 02062 Novel microelectrodes for neural stimulation
R44NS-26978-03 (SSS) KATOOT, MOHAMMAD W NANOPTICS INC 1810 NW 6TH STREET GAINESVILLE, FL 32609 Proton microprobe for trace element analysis of tissue
P50NS-26985-03 (SRC) CERMAK, LAIRD S BOSTON VA MEDICAL 150 S HUNTINGTON AVE BOSTON, MA 02130 Brain-injury memory disorders research center
P50NS-26985-03 0001 (SRC) VERFAELLIE, MIEKE H Brain-injury memory disorders research center Theoretical issues in amnesia
P50NS-26985-03 0002 (SRC) GABRIELI, JOHN D. E. Brain-injury memory disorders research center Clinical case studies
P50NS-26985-03 0003 (SRC) ESLINGER, PAUL J. Brain-injury memory disorders research center Neuroimaging studies in amnesia
P01NS-26991-02 (NSPB) WEINER, LESLIE P UNIV OF SOUTHERN CALIFORNIA 2025 ZONAL AVENUE LOS ANGELES, CA 90033 AIDS-encephalopathy multidisciplinary program

PROJECT NO., ORGANIZATIONAL UNIT., INVESTIGATOR, ADDRESS, TITLE

P01NS-26991-02 0001 (NSPB) PARKMAN, ROBERTSON AIDS-encephalopathy multidisciplinary program Role of T-lymphocytes in the development of AIDS dementia
P01NS-26991-02 0002 (NSPB) DEANS, ROBERT J AIDS-encephalopathy multidisciplinary program Molecular basis for HIV-1 gene control
P01NS-26991-02 0003 (NSPB) TAHARA, STANLEY M AIDS-encephalopathy multidisciplinary program Control of protein biosynthesis in HIV-1 infected CNS cells
P01NS-26991-02 0004 (NSPB) MCMILLAN, MINNIE AIDS-encephalopathy multidisciplinary program Design of novel HLA proteins for use as HIV vaccines
P01NS-26991-02 0005 (NSPB) KOHN, DONALD B AIDS-encephalopathy multidisciplinary program Retroviral vectors producing antisense RNA block CNS HIV infection
P01NS-26991-02 9001 (NSPB) HINTON, DAVID AIDS-encephalopathy multidisciplinary program Neuropathology core
P01NS-26991-02 9002 (NSPB) MCMILLAN, MINNIE AIDS-encephalopathy multidisciplinary program Microchemical core laboratory
R01NS-26994-04 (NEUC) YU, ROBERT K VIRGINIA COMMONWEALTH UNIVERSI BOX 614, MCV STATION RICHMOND, VA 23298-0614 The role of glycolipids in experimental neuropathy
R29NS-26995-04 (NEUB) MAWE, GARY M UNIVERSITY OF VERMONT COLLEGE OF MEDICINE BURLINGTON, VT 05405 Neural control of the gallbladder
R29NS-27011-03 (NLS) CHESLER, MITCHELL NYU MEDICAL CENTER 550 FIRST AVE/NEUROSURG LABS NEW YORK, NY 10016 Intracellular pH homeostasis in glia
R29NS-27013-03 (NEUB) DRYER, STUART E FLORIDA STATE UNIVERSITY TALLAHASSEE, FL 32306 Properties of sodium-activated potassium channels
R01NS-27016-03 (NLS) LEWIS, CAROL A STATE UNIVERSITY OF NEW YORK 313 CARY HALL BUFFALO, NY 14214 Transmitter-gated conductions in brain neurons
R01NS-27019-03 (NEUB) SAWCHUK, RONALD J UNIVERSITY OF MINNESOTA 308 HARVARD ST, SE MINNEAPOLIS, MN 55455 Enhancing brain uptake of AZT by transport inhibition
R01NS-27027-03 (NEUA) WILSON, DAVID F UNIVERSITY OF PENNSYLVANIA DEPT BIOCHEMISTRY/RM 426 CHEM PHILADELPHIA, PA 19104 Biology of neuroblastoma
R01NS-27036-03 (CTY) CLEVELAND, DON W JOHNS HOPKINS UNIVERSITY 725 N WOLFE STREET BALTIMORE, MD 21205 Neuronal filament synthesis, assembly, and function
R01NS-27037-03 (NLS) SODERLING, THOMAS R OREGON HLTH SCI UNIVERSITY 3181 SAM JACKSON PARK ROAD PORTLAND, OR 97201-3098 Ca2+/calmodulin-kinase II--brain substrates
R29NS-27038-03 (NEUB) PORTER, LINDA L UNIVERSITY OF HLTH SCIENCES DEPT OF ANATOMY BETHESDA, MD 20814 Sensory integration in somatosensory-motor cortex
R29NS-27039-03 (BBCA) PHILIPS, LAURA A CORNELL UNIVERSITY ITHACA, NY 14853 Catecholamine neurotransmitters--The role of the molecular environment
R01NS-27042-02 (NEUC) LUPSKI, JAMES R BAYLOR COLLEGE OF MEDICINE ONE BAYLOR PLAZA HOUSTON, TX 77030 CMT peripheral neuropathy--I linkage analysis
R01NS-27047-01A2 (NEUB) VARON, SILVIO S UNIVERSITY OF CALIFORNIA LA JOLLA, CA 92093 Nerve growth factor action on adult CNS neurons in vivo
R01NS-27050-01A2 (HAR) BOYLE, RICHARD D OREGON HEALTH SCI UNIVERSITY 3181 SW SAM JACKSON PARK ROAD PORTLAND, OR 97201 Structure and function of vestibulocollic neurons
R01NS-27054-03 (NEUA) BREGMAN, BARBARA S GEORGETOWN UNIVERSITY 3900 RESERVOIR ROAD NW WASHINGTON, DC 20007 Recovery of function after spinal cord injury
R01NS-27056-03 (NLS) BRIDGES, RICHARD J UNIVERSITY OF CALIFORNIA BIO SCI II IRVINE, CA 92717 Excitotoxicity--The role of non-NMDA receptors
R01NS-27058-03 (NEUA) BUZSAKI, GYORGY RUTGERS, STATE UNIV OF NJ 195 UNIVERSITY AVE NEWARK, NJ 07102 Suppression of epileptic activity by brain grafts
R01NS-27073-02 (NEUB) HOLLENBECK, PETER J HARVARD MEDICAL SCHOOL 220 LONGWOOD AVENUE BOSTON, MA 02115 Control of neuronal organelle transport
R01NS-27081-03 (NLS) DE LANEROLLE, NIHAL C YALE UNIVERSITY 333 CEDAR ST, PO BOX 3333 NEW HAVEN, CT 06510 Characterization & development of a seizure focus
R01NS-27096-03 (NLS) OUIMET, CHARLES C FLORIDA STATE UNIVERSITY TALLAHASSE, FL 32306-1051 Chemical neuroanatomy of dopaminoceptive neurons
R29NS-27102-03 (IMS) FRIEDMAN, JACQUELINE ELISE NEW YORK UNIVERSITY MEDICAL CT 550 FIRST AVENUE NEW YORK, NY 10012 Autoimmune & genetic antigesn in multiple sclerosis
R01NS-27103-02 (MGN) DE LA CHAPELLE, ALBERT UNIVERSITY OF HELSINKI HAARTMANINKATU 3 00290 HELSINKI, FINLAND Mapping of the genes for 2 recessive disorders
R01NS-27107-03 (NLS) SCHWARTZMAN, ROBERT JAY JEFFERSON MEDICAL COLLEGE DEPT OF NEUROLOGY PHILADELPHIA, PA 19107 Mechanism of treatment complications in Parkinsons
R01NS-27113-02 (NEUB) DODD, JANE COLUMBIA UNIVERSITY 630 WEST 168TH STREET NEW YORK, NY 10032 Axon guidance in the spinal cord
R01NS-27116-03 (SRC) MENT, LAURA R YALE UNIVERSITY 333 CEDAR ST, PO BOX 3333 NEW HAVEN, CT 06510 Randomized indomethacin GMH/IVH prevention trial
R01NS-27119-02 (NEUA) GALABURDA, ALBERT M BETH ISRAEL HOSPITAL 330 BROOKLINE AVENUE BOSTON, MA 02215 Mechanisms of neuroanatomical asymmetry
R29NS-27122-03 (NEUB) METCALFE, WALTER K UNIVERSITY OF OREGON EUGENE, OR 97403 Lateral line development
R01NS-27127-02 (NEUA) DIETRICH, W DALTON UNIV OF MIAMI SCH OF MED PO BOX 016960 MIAMI, FL 33101 The importance of the blood-brain barrier in stroke
R01NS-27130-03 (BPO) BROWN, THOMAS H YALE UNIVERSITY PO BOX 11A, YALE STATION NEW HAVEN, CT 06520-7447 Amygdaloid long-term potentiation & Pavlovian conditioning
R29NS-27142-02 (NEUB) ROBERTS, WILLIAM M UNIVERSITY OF OREGON EUGENE, OR 97403 Ion channel distribution and mobility
R01NS-27144-03 (NLS) FABER, DONALD S STATE UNIVERSITY OF NEW YORK 313 CARY HALL BUFFALO, NY 14214 Effects of membrane fatty acids on neuronal ion channels
R01NS-27150-02 (NLS) BERRY, ROBERT W NORTHWESTERN UNIVERSITY 303 EAST CHICAGO AVE CHICAGO. IL 60208-1110 Regulatory mechanisms in peptidergic neurons
R01NS-27170-02 (NLS) BOYSON, SALLY J UNIV OF COLORADO HLTH SCI CTR 4200 EAST 9TH AVE, BOX B-183 DENVER, CO 80262 Neurotransmitters regulating cerebrospinal fluid formation
R01NS-27171-03 (NLS) BLOCH, ROBERT J UNIV OF MARYLAND AT BALTIMORE 660 WEST REDWOOD STREET BALTIMORE, MD 21201 Assembly of a postsynaptic membrane
R01NS-27173-03 (NLS) HAMMERSCHLAG, RICHARD BECKMAN RESEARCH INSTITUTE 1450 EAST DUARTE ROAD DUARTE, CA 91010 Fast axonal transport and neuronal activity
R01NS-27177-04 (NLS) TSIEN, ROGER Y REGENTS OF THE UNIV. OF CALIF. LA JOLLA, CA 92093 Dynamics of ionic messengers in neurons
R29NS-27180-02 (NEUB) FOEHRING, ROBERT C UNIV OF TENNESSEE COLL OF MED 875 MONROE AVE MEMPHIS, TN 38163 Neuromodulation and development in neocortex
R01NS-27185-03 (NEUA) MOSS, JONATHAN UNIVERSITY OF CHICAGO 5841 S MARYLAND AVE, BOX 428 CHICAGO, IL 60637 Cerebrovascular reactivity: modulation by hormones
R01NS-27193-03 (ORTH) LOEB, GERALD E QUEEN'S UNIVERSITY ABRAMSKY HALL KINGSTON, ONT,CANADA K7L3N6 Musculoskeletal dynamics and motor control of the cat hindlimb
R01NS-27197-03 (DABR) ROMAGNANO, MARYANN A MONROE COMMUNITY HOSPITAL 435 EAST HENRIETTA RD ROCHESTER, N Y 14620 Sympathetic opioid interactions--Funtional neuroanatomy
R01NS-27206-03 (NEUC) TEMPEL, BRUCE L VETERANS ADMIN MEDICAL CENTER 1660 SOUTH COLUMBIAN WAY SEATTLE, WA 98108 Expression and structure of a brain K+ channel
R01NS-27209-02 (NEUB) HERRERA, ALBERT A UNIV OF SOUTHERN CALIFORNIA LOS ANGELES, CA 90089-0371 Hormonal regulation of nerve-muscle plasticity
R01NS-27210-03 (NEUB) EBNER, TIMOTHY J UNIVERSITY OF MINNESOTA 420 DELAWARE ST, SE MINNEAPOLIS, MN 55455 Imaging spatial aspects of cerebellar activity
R29NS-27213-04 (NLS) MILLER, KENNETH EUGENE UNIVER OF OKLAHOMA/HSC PO BOX 26901 OKLAHOMA CITY, OK 63190 Excitatory amino acid synpatic circuitry in spinal sensory pathways
R01NS-27214-03 (NEUA) ELLIS, EARL F MEDICAL COLLEGE OF VIRGINIA PHARMACOLOGY & TOXICOLOGY DPT RICHMOND, VA 23298-0613 Biochemical mechanisms of brain injury
R01NS-27215-03 (SSS) COHEN, DAVID MASSACHUSETTS INST OF TECH 77 MASSACHUSETTS AVE NW-14 RM CAMBRIDGE, MA 02139 A focal transcutaneous stimulator as a neurosurgical aid
R01NS-27218-03 (NEUC) GODFREY, EARL W MEDICAL COLLEGE OF WISCONSIN 8701 WATERTOWN PLANK ROAD MILWAUKEE, WI 53226 ECM molecules in neuromuscular junction development
R01NS-27219-02 (NEUC) CRUZ, LOURDES J UNIVERSITY OF UTAH SALT LAKE CITY, UT 84112 Novel neuroactive peptides from Conus
R01NS-27226-02 (NEUA) YOUNG, WISE NEW YORK UNIV MEDICAL CENTER 550 FIRST AVE NEW YORK, N Y 10016 Ionic basis of ischemic cerebral edema
R01NS-27227-03 (NEUB) BRACKENBURY, ROBERT W UNIVERSITY OF CINCINNATI 231 BETHSDA AVENUE, ML #521 CINCINNATI, OHIO 45267-0521 Schwann cell-axon interactions during development
R01NS-27229-03 (NEUA) ANDERSON, PAUL M UNIVERSITY OF MINNESOTA 1100 WASHINGTON AVE. SOUTH, #2 MINNEAPOLIS, MN 55415-1226 Modulation of glucose transporters in brain
R01NS-27243-02 (CMS) MARSCHARK, MARC E UNIV OF NORTH CAROLINA RES SER GREENSBORO, NC 27412-5013 Cognitive abilities following closed-head brain injury
R01NS-27250-03 (EDC) KRUEGER, JAMES M UNIVERSITY OF TENNESSEE 894 UNION AVENUE MEMPHIS, TN 38163 Sleep regulation: involvement of GRF-like peptides
R29NS-27259-03 (NLS) SILVA, WALTER I UNIVERSIDAD CENTRAL DEL CARIBE CALL BOX 60-327 BAYAMON, PUERTO RICO 00621-603 Neuropeptides & their receptors in brain coated vesicles
R01NS-27287-04 (BPO) OLSON, CARL ROGER GEORGE MASON UNIVERSITY 4400 UNIVERSITY DRIVE FAIRFAX, VA 22030-4444 Sensorimotor integration in cingulate cortex
R01NS-27292-01A2 (NEUA) STEINBERG, GARY K STANFORD UNIV SCHOOL OF MED 300 PASTEUR DRIVE STANFORD, CA 94305-5327 Nmda antagonists in the treatment of stroke
R29NS-27296-02 (BPO) BAYLIS, GORDON C UNIV OF CALIF/SAN DIEGO LA JOLLA, CA 92093-0109 Role of the medial temporal lobe in memory
R01NS-27306-02 (EDC) LEVITON, ALAN CHILDREN'S HOSPITAL 300 LONGWOOD AVENUE BOSTON, MA 02115 The epidemiology of neonatal white matter disorders
R01NS-27310-03 (NEUA) TUREEN, JAY H SAN FRANCISCO GENERAL HOSPITAL 1001 POTRERO AVE SAN FRANCISCO, CA 94110 Cerebral blood flow and metabolism in meningitis
R29NS-27311-03 (NLS) BONHAUS, DOUGLAS W VA HOSPITAL 508 FULTON ST., BLDG. 16, RM25 DURHAM, NC 27705 Biochemical analysis of the NMDA receptor ion channel
R01NS-27314-03 (NEUB) BLANKENSHIP, JAMES E UNIV OF TEXAS MED BRANCH 200 UNIVERSITY BLVD GALVESTON, TX 77550 Neural control of swimming
R01NS-27319-03 (NEUC) FIEKERS, JEROME F UNIV OF VERMONT COLLEGE OF MED ANATOMY/NEUROBIO, GIVEN MED BURLINGTON, VT 05405 Autonomic neurons--Modulation by peptides and mast cells
R01NS-27320-03 (NLS) COTMAN, CARL W UNIVERSITY OF CALIFORNIA STEINHAUS HALL, ROOM 249 IRVINE, CA 92717 Plasticity in the developing limbic system
R29NS-27322-03 (NEUC) SIKELA, JAMES M UNIV OF COLORADO HLTH SCI CTR 4200 E 9TH AVE/BX C-236 DENVER, CO 80262 Molecular biology of brain protein phosphorylation
R01NS-27325-01A2 (NEUA) SOLOMON, ROBERT A NEUROLOGICAL INSTITUTE 710 WEST 168TH STREET NEW YORK, NY 10032 Cerebral blood flow after subarachnoid hemorrhage

R29NS-27336-03 (NEUC) POPKO, BRIAN J UNIV. OF NORTH CAROLINA AT CH 320 BIO SCIS RESEARCH CTR CHAPEL HILL, NC 27599 Molecular biology of central nervous system myelination

R01NS-27337-03 (NEUB) LISMAN, JOHN E BRANDEIS UNIVERSITY 415 SOUTH STREET WALTHAM, MA 02254 Mechanism of long-term potentiation

R29NS-27338-04 (SSS) DANDEKAR, SATYA UNIVERSITY OF CALIFORNIA 4301 X ST SACRAMENTO, CA 95817 Human immunodeficiency virus and neuropathogeneses

R01NS-27341-02 (NLS) SUMIKAWA, KATUMI UNIVERSITY OF CALIFORNIA IRVINE, CA 92717 Desensitization of neurotransmitter receptors

R01NS-27346-03 (SSS) CHANCE, BRITTON UNIVERSITY CITY SCIENCE CENTER 3401 MARKET ST, ROOM 320 PHILADELPHIA, PA 19104 Time resolved spectroscopy of hemoglobin in brain

R01NS-27353-03 (PC) RODEN, LENNART UNIVERSITY OF ALABAMA P O BOX 500/UNIVERSITY STATION BIRMINGHAM, AL 35294 Biosynthesis of complex carbohydrates in brain

R29NS-27356-03 (NEUC) CLEGG, DENNIS O UNIVERSITY OF CALIFORNIA NEUROSCIENCE RESEARCH INSTITUT SANTA BARBARA, CA 93106 Role of a laminin receptor in neuromuscular development

R01NS-27365-03 (NLS) LANGSTON, J WILLIAM INSTITUTE FOR MEDICAL RESEARCH 2444 MOORPARK AVE, SUITE 316 SAN JOSE, CA 95128 MPTP: Metabolic activation & mechanisms of cell death

R01NS-27371-03 (SSS) HORCH, KENNETH W UNIVERSITY OF UTAH 2480 MEB SALT LAKE CITY, UT 84112 Information extraction from peripheral nerves

R44NS-27381-03 (PSF) MCBURNEY, ROBERT N CAMBRIDGE NEUROSCIENCE RES INC ONE KENDALL SQUARE, BLDG 700 CAMBRIDGE, MA 02139 Substituted guanidines as neuroprotective drugs

R44NS-27392-02 (BPO) GEVINS, ALAN S SAM TECHNOLOGY, INC 51 FEDERAL STREET SAN FRANCISCO, CA 94107 Neurostation--Neurofunctional research workstation

R44NS-27394-02 (BPO) WIGGINS, HARVEY W SPECTRUM SCIENTIFIC 6500 GREENVILLE AVENUE #480 DALLAS, TX 75206 Spike detector for multichannel neuronal acquisition

R43NS-27396-01A3 (SSS) ZANAKIS, MICHAEL F AMERICAN BIOINTERFACE CORP COOPER STATION,PO BOX 1017 NEW YORK, NY 10276 Electrical stimulation of the damaged optic nerve

P01NS-27405-03 (SRC) NATHANSON, NEAL UNIVERSITY OF PENNSYLVANIA PHILADELPHIA, PA 19104-6076 Molecular and cellular biology of HIV encephalopathy

P01NS-27405-03 0001 (SRC) GONZALEZ-SCARANO, F. Molecular and cellular biology of HIV encephalopathy HIV infection of cultured neural cells

P01NS-27405-03 0002 (SRC) WIGDAHL, BRIAN Molecular and cellular biology of HIV encephalopathy HIV mediated damage and CD4 in cultured human fetal neural tissues

P01NS-27405-03 0003 (SRC) NATHANSON, NEAL Molecular and cellular biology of HIV encephalopathy The role of monocytes in HIV encephalopathy

P01NS-27405-03 0004 (SRC) BUCHHALTER, JEFFREY R. Molecular and cellular biology of HIV encephalopathy Mechanisms for HIV neurotoxicity

R01NS-27409-03 (CBY) TURNER, DAVID C STATE UNIVERSITY OF NEW YORK 750 E ADAMS STREET SYRACUSE, NY 13210 Mechanism of PC12 cell adhesion to collagen and laminin

R01NS-27414-02 (ARR) GRIFFIN, WILMA S UNIVERSITY OF ARKANSAS 4301 WEST MARKHAM STREET LITTLE ROCK, AR 72205 Gene expression in brain cells in AIDS

R01NS-27416-03 (ARR) PETITO, CAROL K CORNELL UNIVERSITY MED COLLEGE 1300 YORK AVENUE NEW YORK, NY 10021 Brain and spinal cord disease in HIV infection

R01NS-27417-03 (ARR) WILEY, CLAYTON A UNIV OF CA, SAN DIEGO DEPT. OF PATHOLOGY, M-012 LA JOLLA, CA 92093-0612 Retroviral infection of the nervous system

R01NS-27418-03 (NEUC) CARDEN, MARTIN J UNIVERSITY OF KENT/CANTERBURY BIOLOGICAL LABORATORY KENT CT2 7NJ, UNITED KINGDOM Neurofilament structure/function--Molecular approach

R01NS-27448-02 (NEUC) SAGAR, STEPHEN M SAN FRANCISCO VA MEDICAL CENTE 4150 CLEMENT STREET SAN FRANCISCO, CA 94121 Third messengers in the central nervous system

R01NS-27452-03 (NEUC) DINGLEDINE, RAYMOND J UNIVERSITY OF NORTH CAROLINA CB#7365 FACULTY LAB OFFICE BLD CHAPEL HILL, NC 27599 Molecular studies of the NMDA-glycine receptor

R01NS-27456-03 (CMS) RISO, RONALD R CLEVELAND METRO GENERAL HOSPIT 3395 SCRANTON ROAD CLEVELAND, OH 44109 Natural skin sensors for neuromotor prostheses control

R01NS-27461-03 (PTHA) MOORE, G WAYNE VANCOUVER GENERAL HOSPITAL 855 WEST 12TH AVENUE VANCOUVER, BC, CANADA V5Z 1M9 Pathology and immunocytology of the oligodendrocyte

R01NS-27463-03 (HUD) GRAZIANI, LEONARD J JEFFERSON MEDICAL COLLEGE 1025 WALNUT STREET PHILADELPHIA, PA 19107 Neurologic studies in infants requiring ECMO

R01NS-27484-03 (ORTH) FLANDERS, MARTHA UNIVERSITY OF MINNESOTA 435 DELAWARE STREET SOUTHEAST MINNEAPOLIS, MN 55455 Patterns of muscle activity in natural arm movement

R01NS-27488-02 (NEUA) LEWIS, DARRELL V, JR DUKE UNIVERSITY MED CTR PO BOX 3430 DURHAM, NC 27710 GABAB mediated disinhibition in the dentate gyrus

P01NS-27500-01A2 (NSPA) PROUGH, DONALD S BOWMAN GRAY SCHOOL OF MEDICINE 300 SOUTH HAWTHORNE ROAD WINSTON-SALEM, NC 27103 Cardiac surgery and cerebrovascular complications

P01NS-27500-01A2 0001 (NSPA) ROGERS, ANNE T Cardiac surgery and cerebrovascular complications Blood glucose and neurologic outcome

P01NS-27500-01A2 0002 (NSPA) MILLS, STEPHEN A Cardiac surgery and cerebrovascular complications Cardiac valve surgery and nimodipine neuroprotection

P01NS-27500-01A2 0003 (NSPA) MOODY, DIXON M Cardiac surgery and cerebrovascular complications Brain microemboli during cardiopulmonary bypass

P01NS-27500-01A2 9001 (NSPA) STUMP, DAVID A Cardiac surgery and cerebrovascular complications Core--Neurophysiologic monitoring

P01NS-27500-01A2 9002 (NSPA) TROOST, B TODD Cardiac surgery and cerebrovascular complications Core--Neurologic and neurobehavioral assessment

P01NS-27500-01A2 9003 (NSPA) FURBERG, CURT D Cardiac surgery and cerebrovascular complications Core--Biostatistics

R29NS-27501-03 (NEUC) O'DOWD, DIANE K UNIV OF CALIF., IRVINE IRVINE, CA 92717 Study of ion channels

R01NS-27504-03 (NLS) FROEHNER, STANLEY C DARTMOUTH COLLEGE HANOVER, NH 03756 Molecular studies of voltage-activated calcium channels

P01NS-27511-03 (NSPA) REIER, PAUL J UNIV OF FLORIDA COLLEGE OF MED PO BOX J-265, JHMHC GAINESVILLE, FL 32610 Spinal cord injury and repair

P01NS-27511-03 0001 (NSPA) REIER, PAUL J Spinal cord injury and repair Transplantation and spinal cord repair

P01NS-27511-03 0002 (NSPA) MUNSON, JOHN B Spinal cord injury and repair Spinal cord dysfunction and repair: Physiology and behavior

P01NS-27511-03 0003 (NSPA) VIERCK, CHARLES J JR Spinal cord injury and repair Functional recovery following spinal cord injury and repair

P01NS-27511-03 0004 (NSPA) RITZ, LOUIS A Spinal cord injury and repair Organization of the sacrocaudal spinal cord

P01NS-27511-03 0005 (NSPA) JOHNSON, RICHARD D Spinal cord injury and repair Spinal cord injury and sexual dysfunction

P01NS-27511-03 9001 (NSPA) REIER, PAUL J Spinal cord injury and repair Centralized services core

R01NS-27513-01A2 (IMS) SRIRAM, SUBRAMANIAM UNIVERSITY OF VERMONT BURLINGTON, VT 05405 Analysis of in vivo HPRT mutant T cells in multiple sclerosis

R01NS-27514-03 (NEUC) FINK, J STEPHEN MASSACHUSETTS GENERAL HOSPITAL 149 13TH STREET CHARLESTOWN, MA 02129 Regulation of VIP gene expression in neural cells

R01NS-27517-03 (EDC) SACCO, RALPH L SCHOOL OF MEDICINE 710 WEST 168TH STREET NEW YORK, NY 10032 Epidemiologic study of stroke outcome in three ethnic groups

R01NS-27528-02 (NLS) MODY, ISTVAN STANFORD UNIVERSITY MED CENTER 300 PASTEUR DRIVE STANFORD, CA 94305 Neuronal calcium homeostasis and long-term potentiation

R01NS-27536-01A2 (NEUC) BUCKLEY, KATHLEEN M HARVARD MEDICAL SCHOOL 220 LONGWOOD AVE BOSTON, MA 02115 Expression of synaptic vesicle proteins

R29NS-27538-03 (NLS) JOHNSON, GAIL V UNIV OF ALA AT BIRMINGHAM SPARKS CENTER, RM. 911 BIRMINGHAM, AL 35294 Phosphorylation & function of heat-stable MAPs in brain

R01NS-27539-03 (NLS) MILLER, RICHARD J UNIVERSITY OF CHICAGO 947 EAST 58TH ST CHICAGO, IL 60637 Electrophysiology of phopholipid metabolites in CNS

R01NS-27541-03 (NEUB) SCHACHER, SAMUEL M RES FDN FOR MENTAL HYGIENE 722 WEST 168TH STREET NEW YORK, NY 10032 Strategies for synapse specificity

R01NS-27543-02 (NLS) PASTUSZKO, ANNA UNIVERSITY OF PENNSYLVANIA SCHOOL OF MEDICINE PHILADELPHIA, PA 19104 Biological role of neurocatin--A novel brain peptide

R01NS-27544-02 (NEUA) BECKER, DONALD P UCLA MEDICAL CENTER 10833 LECONTE AVENUE LOS ANGELES, CA 90024 Ionic fluxes and neuronal dysfunction in brain injury

R29NS-27546-03 (NEUC) HARBOUR, DEBORAH V UNIV OF TEXAS MEDICAL BRANCH GALVESTON, TX 77550 An in vitro neuroendocrine T cell line production of TSH

R01NS-27550-03 (NEUC) CRAVISO, GALE L UNIVERSITY OF NEVADA HOWARD MEDICAL SCIENCES BLDG RENO, NV 89557 Molecular mechanism of adrenergic plasticity

R01NS-27556-03 (NEUC) BURNS, JAMES B UNIV OF UTAH SCH OF MED 50 NORTH MEDICAL DR/3R210 SALT LAKE CITY, UT 84132 T cell immune response to myelin in multiple sclerosis

R01NS-27563-03 (NEUB) SMITH, MARTIN A UNIV OF CALIFORNIA IRVINE, CA 92717 Structural and functional analysis of agrin proteins

R01NS-27580-03 (BIO) DEWJI, NAZNEEN N UNIVERSITY OF CALIFORNIA 9500 GILMAN DRIVE LA JOLLA, CA 92093 Studies on Alzheimer's disease amyloid precursor protein

R01NS-27583-03 (BMT) BLACKBURN, NINIAN J OREGON GRADUATE INSTITUTE 19600 NW VON NEUMANN DR BEAVERTON, OR 97006-1999 Chemistry and spectroscopy of dopamine-b-hydroxylase

R29NS-27586-03 (NEUB) WIRSIG-WIECHMANN, CELESTE R WAKE FOREST UNIVERSITY 300 SOUTH HAWTHORNE ROAD WINSTON-SALEM, N C 27103 Terminal nerve--Ontogeny, circuitry, and function

R29NS-27587-04 (NEUB) BRUNDEN, KURT R GLIATECH INC. 23420 COMMERCE PARK ROAD BEACHWOOD, OH 44122 Axonal regulation of myelin protein synthesis

R01NS-27600-02 (BNP) CHAMBERLIN, ARTHUR R DEPARTMENT OF CHEMISTRY IRVINE, CA 92717 Receptor-specific excitatory amino acid analogues

R01NS-27601-03 (NEUA) JOHANSON, CONRAD E RHODE ISLAND HOSPITAL 593 EDDY STREET PROVIDENCE, RI 02902 Development of choroid plexus-transport systems

R01NS-27603-02 (NLS) VALLANO, MARY L STATE UNIV OF NEW YORK 766 IRVING AVENUE SYRACUSE, NY 13210 Developmental expression of CaM kinase II isoforms

P01NS-27613-01A2 (NSPB) GHETTI, BERNARDINO INDIANA UNIVERSITY 635 BARNHILL DRIVE INDIANAPOLIS, IN 46202-5120 Neurobiology of the weaver mutant mouse

P01NS-27613-01A2 0001 (NSPB) GHETTI, BERNARDINO Neurobiology of the weaver mutant mouse Genetic strain effects and dopamine cell loss in weaver mutant

P01NS-27613-01A2 0002 (NSPB) BAYER, SHIRLEY A Neurobiology of the weaver mutant mouse Developmental analysis of neuron loss in weaver mice

P01NS-27613-01A2 0003 (NSPB) SIMON, JAY R Neurobiology of the weaver mutant mouse Functional neurochemistry in the weaver mutant mouse

P01NS-27613-01A2 0004 (NSPB) HODES, MARION E Neurobiology of the weaver mutant mouse Identification and characterization of the weaver gene

P01NS-27613-01A2 9001 (NSPB) GHETTI, BERNARDINO Neurobiology of the weaver mutant mouse Core-Biostatistics

P01NS-27613-01A2 9002 (NSPB) GHETTI, BERNARDINO Neurobiology of the weaver mutant mouse Core--Scientific core

PROJECT NO., ORGANIZATIONAL UNIT., INVESTIGATOR, ADDRESS, TITLE

R01NS-27615-03 (VISB) MASON, CAROL A COLUMBIA UNIVERSITY 630 WEST 168TH STREET NEW YORK, NY 10032 Growth & guidance of retinal axons

P01NS-27616-02S1 (NSPA) GROSSMAN, ROBERT G BAYLOR COLLEGE OF MEDICINE ONE BAYLOR PLAZA HOUSTON, TX 77030 Treatment of physiological disturbances in head injury

P01NS-27616-02S1 0001 (NSPA) GROSSMAN, ROBERT G Treatment of physiological disturbances in head injury Treatment of the hypermetabolic response to CNS injury

P01NS-27616-02S1 0002 (NSPA) ROBERTSON, CLAUDIA S Treatment of physiological disturbances in head injury Monitoring adequacy of cerebral blood flow in head injury

P01NS-27616-02S1 0003 (NSPA) NARAYAN, RAJ K Treatment of physiological disturbances in head injury Monitoring intracranial compliance by ICP waveform analysis

P01NS-27616-02S1 0004 (NSPA) ROBERTSON, CLAUDIA Treatment of physiological disturbances in head injury Reduction in CNS injury by modification of ischemic energy metabolism

P01NS-27616-02S1 9001 (NSPA) ROBERTSON, CLAUDIA S Treatment of physiological disturbances in head injury Clinical monitoring core

P01NS-27616-02S1 9002 (NSPA) GOODMAN, J CLAY Treatment of physiological disturbances in head injury Laboratory core

R01NS-27634-03 (NEUB) TOSNEY, KATHRYN W UNIVERSITY OF MICHIGAN DEPARTMENT OF BIOLOGY ANN ARBOR, MICH 48109 Guidance of motoneuron growth cones

R01NS-27639-02 (NLS) DE LANDER, GARY E COLLEGE OF PHARMACY CORVALLIS, OR 97331-3507 Neuromodulation of nociception by spinal adenosine

R29NS-27641-03 (NEUA) SELMAN, WARREN R CASE WESTERN RESERVE UNIVERSIT 2074 ABINGTON ROAD CLEVELAND, OH 44106 Reversible focal cerebral ischemia

R01NS-27643-03 (NEUB) HUNT, CARLTON C WASHINGTON UNIVERSITY 660 SOUTH EUCLID AVE, BOX 8111 ST LOUIS, MO 63110 Motor unit organization

R01NS-27644-01A2 (BPO) BAERTSCHI, ALEX J UNIVERSITY OF VIRGINIA JORDAN HALL BOX 449 CHARLOTTESVILLE, VA 22908 Neural signalling of salt intake

R01NS-27645-03 (GMA) KIRCHGESSNER, ANNETTE L COLUMBIA UNIV COLLEGE OF P & S 630 WEST 168TH STREET NEW YORK, NY 10032 Enteric innervation and its pancreatic projections

R01NS-27653-03 (NLS) SWEADNER, KATHLEEN J MASSACHUSETTS GENERAL HOSPITAL FRUIT STREET BOSTON, MA 02114 Na,K-ATPase isozyme localization and function in CNS

R29NS-27668-03 (BPO) BORSZCZ, GEORGE S DARTMOUTH COLLEGE DEPT. OF PSYCHOLOGY HANOVER, NH 03755 Comparison of spinal and supraspinal pain thresholds

R01NS-27672-01A1S1 (NLS) COOPER, JACK R YALE UNIVERSITY P.O. BOX 3333, 333 CEDAR STREE NEW HAVEN, CT 06510 Presynaptic modulation

R01NS-27678-02 (NEUB) JHAVERI, SONAL MASSACHUSETTS INST OF TECHNOLO CAMBRIDGE, MA 02139 Regenerative processes in trigeminal ganglia

R01NS-27679-03 (NLS) PETRUSZ, PETER UNIVERSITY OF NORTH CAROLINA 108 TAYLOR HALL CB# 7090 CHAPEL HILL, NC 27599 Endogenous ligands for glutamate receptors in brain

P50NS-27680-03 (NSPB) GREENE, LLOYD A COLUMBIA UNIVERSITY 630 WEST 168TH STREET NEW YORK, N Y 10032 Mechanism of neuronal degeneration and survival

P50NS-27680-03 0002 (NSPB) LEIM, RONALD Mechanism of neuronal degeneration and survival Effect of intermediate filament content on neuronal survival & function

P50NS-27680-03 0003 (NSPB) COLEMAN, DAVID Mechanism of neuronal degeneration and survival Mediators of glial/axonal interactions

P50NS-27680-03 0001 (NSPB) GREENE, LLOYD Mechanism of neuronal degeneration and survival Neurotropic-factor regulation protein phosphorylation in neuronal survival

P50NS-27680-03 0004 (NSPB) SHELANSKI, MICHAEL Mechanism of neuronal degeneration and survival Alterations in non-neuronal cells in Alzheimer's disease

R01NS-27684-03 (NEUC) FORTE, MICHAEL A OREGON HEALTH SCIENCE UNIV 3181 SW SAM JACKSON PARK RD PORTLAND, OR 97201-3098 G proteins in the CNS

R01NS-27685-02 (NLS) DELFS, JOHN R BETH ISRAEL HOSPITAL 330 BROOKLINE AVENUE BOSTON, MA 02215 Excitotoxin effects on spinal cord in vitro

R01NS-27686-03 (NEUA) SCHIEBER, MARC H WASHINGTON UNIV SCH OF MED 660 S EUCLID AVENUE/BOX 8111 ST LOUIS, MO 63110 Cortical activity during individuated movements

R01NS-27687-02 (NEUB) KNUDSEN, ERIC I CONTRACT AND GRANTS ASSOCIATE DEPT OF NEUROBIOLOGY Neural control of saccadic head movement

R01NS-27694-03 (NEUB) JAEGER, CHRISTINE B PURDUE UNIVERSITY CENTER FOR PARALYSIS RESEARCH WEST LAFAYETTE, IN 47907 Encapsulated dopaminergic tumor cells as brain implants

R29NS-27698-02 (NEUB) MANDLER, RAUL N UNIV OF NEW MEXICO SCH OF MED ALBUQUERQUE, NM 87131 Spinal cord cell excitability in the Wobbler

R01NS-27699-03 (MGN) ZOGHBI, HUDA Y BAYLOR COLLEGE OF MEDICINE ONE BAYLOR PLAZA HOUSTON, TX 77030 Molecular studies of HLA-linked spinocerebellar ataxia

R01NS-27710-03 (NEUC) DEMENT, WILLIAM C STANFORD UNIVERSITY SCHOOL OF MEDICINE STANFORD, CA 94305 Neuropharmacology of narcolepsy

R01NS-27713-01A1S1 (NEUA) YOUNG, WILLIAM L NEUROANESTHESIA DIVISION 161 PORT WASHINGTON AVENUE NEW YORK, NY 10032 Hemodynamics of cerebral arteriovenous malformations

R29NS-27715-01A2 (CMS) WHYTE, JOHN MOSS REHABILITATION HOSPITAL 1200 WEST TABOR ROAD PHILADELPHIA, PA 19141 Attention deficits in traumatic brain injury

R29NS-27728-03 (EDC) BERG, ANNE T YALE UNIV SCHOOL OF MEDICINE 333 CEDAR STREET NEW HAVEN, CT 06510-8064 Risk factors for first and recurrent febrile convulsions

R29NS-27730-02 (SSS) BENCA, RUTH M UNIVERSITY OF CHICAGO 5841 S MARYLAND AVE CHICAGO, IL 60637 Genetic and immunologic analysis of sleep

R01NS-27745-03 (NEUA) SKINNER, JAMES E BAYLOR COLLEGE OF MEDICINE ONE BAYLOR PLAZA HOUSTON, TX 77030 Low-dimensional chaos in neocortex

R01NS-27751-03 (NLS) JEFTINIJA, SRDIJA IOWA STATE UNIVERSITY AMES, IA 50011 An in vitro model to study pain transmission

R01NS-27757-02 (PTHA) NEUWELT, EDWARD A OREGON HEALTH SCIENCES UNIV 3181 S W SAM JACKSON PARK ROAD PORTLAND, OR 97201 Pathogenesis & gene therapy in gm2-gangliosidosis

R01NS-27759-03 (NLS) FOX, KEVIN BROWN UNIVERSITY PO BOX G-M PROVIDENCE, RI 02912 The role of NMDA receptors in cortical plasticity

R29NS-27761-03 (NEUA) WORRINGHAM, CHARLES J UNIVERSITY OF MICHIGAN 401 WASHTENAW AVENUE ANN ARBOR, MI 48109-2214 Motor learning in Parkinson's disease and OPCA

R29NS-27771-03 (NLS) FINK, DAVID J VA MEDICAL CENTER 2215 FULLER ROAD ANN ARBOR, MI 48105 Pathogenesis of diabetic neuropathy

R01NS-27773-04 (NEUB) POMEROY, SCOTT CHILDREN'S HOSPITAL 300 LONGWOOD AVENUE BOSTON, MA 02115 The role of glial cells in synaptic remodeling

R01NS-27776-03 (CMS) MOUNTCASTLE, VERNON B JOHNS HOPKINS UNIVERSITY 725 NORTH WOLFE STREET BALTIMORE, MD 21205 Cerebral cortical mechanisms in somesthesis

R29NS-27784-03 (NLS) FROSTHOLM, ADRIENNE M OHIO STATE UNIVERSITY 1645 NEIL AVE COLUMBUS, OH 43210 Expression of granule cell GABA receptors in the developing cerebral cortex

R44NS-27789-02 (SSS) HARTIG, PAUL R NEUROGENETIC CORPORATION 215 COLLEGE ROAD PARAMUS, NJ 07652 Cloning of the serotonin 5-HT1b and 5-HT1d receptors

R44NS-27793-03 (BPO) LOH, IH-HOUNG ADV SURFACE TECHNOLOGY, INC 76 TREBLE COVE RD N BILLERICA, MA 01862 Novel bioelectrode for neuroscience applications

R44NS-27797-02 (SSS) HARTIG, PAUL R NEUROGENETIC CORPORATION 215 COLLEGE ROAD PARAMUS, NJ 07652 Assay system for cloned G1-coupled receptors

R29NS-27812-03 (ARR) BREDESEN, DALE E UNIVERSITY OF CALIFORNIA 710 WESTWOOD PLAZA LOS ANGELES, CA 90024-1769 Molecular effects of specific HIV proteins on the CNS

R01NS-27814-02 (ARR) GRUENSTEIN, ERIC I UNIVERSITY OF CINCINNATI 231 BETHESDA AVENUE CINCINNATI, OH 45267-0524 Responses of human astrocytes to GP120, VIP and anti-CD4

R01NS-27827-02 (NLS) DEBIASI, SILVIA VIA CELORIA 26 MILANO, ITALY 20133 Neuromediators in ascending somatosensory pathways

R01NS-27832-03 (NEUC) VILLA-KOMAROFF, LYDIA CHILDREN'S HOSPITAL LAB OF BIOCHEMICAL GENETICS BOSTON, MA 02115 IGF-II in fetal and mature nervous system and muscle

R01NS-27833-03 (NEUC) DEGENNARO, LOUIS J UNIV OF MASSACHUSETTS MED SCH 55 LAKE AVE N/DEPT NEUROLOGY WORCESTER, MA 01655 Regulation of synapsin gene expression in vitro

R01NS-27847-02 (NEUC) WOOD, JOHN G EMORY UNIV SCHOOL OF MEDICINE ATLANTA, GA 30322 Tyrosine phosphorylation in brain

R01NS-27849-03 (NLS) FADEN, ALAN I GEORGETOWN UNIVERSITY 3900 RESERVOIR RD N W WASHINGTON, D C 20007 Exitotoxins, bioenergetics & traumatic brain injury

R01NS-27859-02 (NLS) LEWIN, ANITA H RESEARCH TRIANGLE INSTITUTE P O BOX 12194 RES TRIANGLE PK, NC 27709-219 Investigation of the NMDA-PCP-glycine pharmacophore

R01NS-27863-02 (NEUA) ADAMS, HAROLD P, JR UNIVERSITY OF IOWA DIV OF CEREBROVASCULAR DISEASE IOWA CITY, IA 52242 Randomized trial of ORG 10172 in acute ischemic stroke

R01NS-27864-02 (NLS) SAGAR, STEPHEN M VETERANS MEDICAL CENTER 4150 CLEMENT STREET SAN FRANCISCO, CA 94121 Functional mapping of neuroendocrine systems

R01NS-27866-02 (NLS) WIERASZKO, ANDRZEJ COLLEGE OF STATEN ISLAND/CUNY 120 STUYVESANT PL. R. 7-422 STATEN ISLAND, NY 10301 The role of ATP in neurotransmission

R01NS-27867-01A2 (NEUA) MCLAUGHLIN, JOHN F CHILDREN'S HOSP & MEDICAL CENT 4800 SAND POINT WAY NE SEATTLE, WA 98105 Selective dorsal rhizotomy– effects in cerebral palsy

R01NS-27880-02 (EDC) LONGSTRETH, W T, JR HARBORVIEW MEDICAL CENTER 325 NINTH AVENUE SEATTLE , WA 98104-2499 Risk factors for amyotrophic lateral sclerosis

R55NS-27881-01A2 (NEUB) LEONARD, CHRISTOPHER S NEW YORK UNIVERSITY 6 WASHINGTON PLACE NEW YORK, NY 10003 Synaptic modulation of mesopontine cholinergic neurons

R01NS-27883-02 (HUD) PRICHARD, JAMES W YALE MEDICAL SCHOOL 333 CEDAR STREET NEW HAVEN, CT 06510 Cerebral metabolic studies by 1h-13c NMR in vivo

R01NS-27889-01A3 (NLS) YUDKOFF, MARC CHILDREN'S HOSPITAL 34TH & CIVIC CENTER BLVD PHILADELPHIA, PA 19104 Brain glutamate metabolism--GC-MS studies

R01NS-27892-02 (HUD) LEWITT, PETER A SINAI HOSPITAL OF DETROIT 6767 WEST OUTER DRIVE DETROIT, MI 48235 Parkinsons disease pathophysiology--CSF markers

R01NS-27894-01A1 (CMS) BROWNELL, HIRAM H BOSTON COLLEGE CHESTNUT HILL, MA 02167 Theory of mind deficits in adult stroke patients

R01NS-27900-02 (NEUA) SIMPSON, GREGORY V ALBERT EINSTEIN COLL OF MEDICI 1410 PELHAM PARKWAY SOUTH BRONX, NY 10461 Dynamics and cerebral sources of attentional processes

R01NS-27902-03 (NEUA) LAMB, MARVIN EAST BAY INST. FOR RES. & EDUC 150 MUIR ROAD MARTINEZ, CA 94553 Effects of brain damage on attention

R29NS-27903-02 (NLS) JONES, LESLIE S UNIV OF SOUTH CAROLINA SCHOOL OF MEDICINE COLUMBIA, SC 29208 Neuronal plasticity in in vitro epileptogenesis

R29NS-27910-02 (NLS) CARLTON, SUSAN M UNIVERSITY OF TEXAS MED BRANCH 200 UNIVERSITY BLVD GALVESTON, TX 77550-2772 Spinal cord plasticity in peripheral neuropathy

R01NS-27914-01A2 (NEUB) MOORE, STEVEN A UNIVERSITY OF IOWA IOWA CITY, IA 52242 Eicosanoid metabolism at the blood-brain barrier

R29NS-27924-01A2 (SSS) TUHRIM, STANLEY MT SINAI SCHOOL OF MEDICINE 1 GUSTAVE L LEVY PL, BOX 1137 NEW YORK, NY 10029 An automated database-expert system for acute stroke

R01NS-27941-02 (EDC) GREENBERG, DAVID A MT SINAI MEDICAL CENTER 1 GUSTAVE LEVY PLACE, BOX 1230 NEW YORK, NY 10029 Resolving

heterogeneity in epilepsy with genetic markers
R01NS-27951-01A1 (NEUB) SATTERLIE, RICHARD A ARIZONA STATE UNIVERSITY TEMPE, AZ 85287-1501 Peripheral modulation of swimming speed
R29NS-27958-02 (CMS) VAN DOREN, CLAYTON L CLEVELAND METRO GENERAL HOSPIT 3395 SCRANTON ROAD CLEVELAND, OH 44106 Kinesthetic perception in the hand & arm
R01NS-27960-02 (NEUA) WOOLSON, ROBERT F UNIVERSITY OF IOWA IOWA CITY, IA 52242 Data management center--Trial of ORG 10172 in stroke
R01NS-27961-02 (NLS) LEONG, KAM W JOHNS HOPKINS UNIVERSITY 148 NEW ENG BLDG BALTIMORE, MD 21218 Polymeric controlled release for neurological applications
R01NS-27963-02 (NEUC) BURDEN, STEVEN J MASSACHUSETTS INST OF TECH 77 MASSACHUSETTS AVENUE CAMBRIDGE, MA 02139 Regulating AChR gene expression by electrical activity
R01NS-27966-01A2 (RNM) PICKENS, DAVID R VANDERBILT UNIVERSITY NASHVILLE, TN 37232-2675 Quantitative brain perfusion measurements with MRI
R01NS-27968-02 (NLS) PITLER, THOMAS A UNIVERSITY OF MARYLAND 655 WEST BALTIMORE STREET BALTIMORE, MD 21201 Electrophysiology study of muscarinic actions in CNS
R29NS-27971-02 (EDC) DURKIN, MAUREEN S COLUMBIA UNIVERSITY 630 WEST 168TH STREET NEW YORK, NEW YORK 10032 Epidemiology of neurodevelopmental disability
R01NS-27972-02 (GMA) BARBER, WILLIAM D UNIVERSITY OF ARIZONA 1501 N CAMPBELL TUCSON, AZ 85724 Regulation of proximal gastrointestinal tract
R29NS-27974-02 (BPO) NUDO, RANDOLPH J UNIV OF TEXAS HEALTH SCIENCE C P O BOX 20036 HOUSTON, TX 77225 Use-dependent alterations of motor cortex
R01NS-27975-02 (NLS) SLADEK, CELIA D UNIVERSITY OF HEALTH SCIENCES DEPT. OF PHYSIOLOGY NORTH CHICAGO, IL 60064 Regulation of vasopressin mRNA
R01NS-27983-02 (NLS) MISLER, STANLEY THE JEWISH HOSP OF ST LOUIS 216 SOUTH KINGSHIGHWAY BLVD ST LOUIS, MO 63110 Ion channels in volume regulation by neuroblastoma cells
R01NS-27984-01A2 (NEUA) HOLMES, GREGORY L CHILDREN'S HOSPITAL 300 LONGWOOD AVENUE BOSTON, MA 02115 Long term effect of seizures on the developing brain
R01NS-27989-02 (NLS) ROBBINS, RICHARD J YALE UNIVERSITY P O BOX 3333 NEW HAVEN, CT 06510 Na,K-atpase & neuronal excitotoxicity in epilepsy
R29NS-27996-02 (CMS) WARREN, SUSAN UNIV OF MISSISSIPPI MED CTR 2500 NORTH STATE STREET JACKSON, MS 39216-4505 Tactile integration in primate ventral posterior nucleus
R01NS-28000-02 (NEUA) DEMPSEY, ROBERT J UNIV OF KENTUCKY MEDICAL CTR 800 ROSE STREET LEXINGTON, KY 40536 Ornithine decarboxylase and ischemic brain edema
R29NS-28012-02 (NLS) PRELL, GEORGE D MOUNT SINAI SCHOOL OF MEDICINE 1 GUSTAVE L LEVY PL, BOX 1215 NEW YORK, NY 10029 Imidazoleacetic acid, a GABA agonist, in brain
R01NS-28016-02 (NLS) WILLIAMS, FRANK G UNIVERSITY OF MINNESOTA 1988 FITCH AVENUE ST PAUL, MN 55108 Effects of chronic pain on brainstem neurochemistry
R01NS-28019-02 (NLS) CHRONWALL, BIBIE M UNIV OF MISSOURI-KANSAS CITY 5100 ROCKHILL RD KANSAS CITY, MO 64110-2499 Co-transmitter regulation of melanotrope biosynthesis
R01NS-28027-03 (NLS) FOWLER, JOHN C TEXAS TECH UNIV HEALTH SCI CTR LUBBOCK, TX 79430 Adenosine and neuronal activity/survival during hypoxia
R01NS-28033-06 (BPN) BATSHAW, MARK L JOSEPH STOKES JR RESERCH INST 34TH AND CIVIC CENTER BLVD PHILADELPHIA, PA 19104 Neurotransmitters, appetite, & inborn errors of metabolism
P01NS-28059-01A1 (NSPA) BUNGE, RICHARD P UNIV OF MIAMI 1600 N W 10TH AVE R 48 MIAMI, FL 33136 Study of cellular therapy in chronic spinal cord injury
P01NS-28059-01A1 0001 (NSPA) KLOSE, K JOHN Study of cellular therapy in chronic spinal cord injury Clinical assessment of spinal cord injury
P01NS-28059-01A1 0002 (NSPA) QUENCER, ROBERT M Study of cellular therapy in chronic spinal cord injury Imaging and pathology of spinal cord injury
P01NS-28059-01A1 0003 (NSPA) CALANCIE, BLAIR Study of cellular therapy in chronic spinal cord injury Clinical neurophysiology of spinal cord injury
P01NS-28059-01A1 0004 (NSPA) WOOD, PATRICK Study of cellular therapy in chronic spinal cord injury Culture studies for cellular dynamics in cord injury
P01NS-28059-01A1 0005 (NSPA) KIM, JONG HWAN Study of cellular therapy in chronic spinal cord injury Assessment of motor pathways in spinal cord injury
P01NS-28059-01A1 0006 (NSPA) YEZIERSKI, ROBERT P Study of cellular therapy in chronic spinal cord injury Somatosensory functions after spinal cord injury
P01NS-28059-01A1 9001 (NSPA) BUNGE, MARY BARLETT Study of cellular therapy in chronic spinal cord injury Core--Histology and electron microscopy
P01NS-28059-01A1 9002 (NSPA) HOLETS, VICKY R Study of cellular therapy in chronic spinal cord injury Core--Animal care and behavioral testing
P01NS-28059-01A1 9003 (NSPA) BEAN, JUDY A Study of cellular therapy in chronic spinal cord injury Core--Statistics
R01NS-28061-02 (NEUB) NOWAKOWSKI, RICHARD S UMDNJ-R W JOHNSON MEDICAL SCHO 675 HOES LANE PISCATAWAY, NJ 08854-5635 Cell proliferation in developing hippocampal region
R01NS-28062-02 (PHY) FORSAYETH, JOHN UNIVERSITY OF CALIFORNIA PARNASSUS AVENUE SAN FRANCISCO, CA 94143 Synaptic assembly in non-muscle cells
R01NS-28064-01A2 (NLS) WESTLUND, KARIN N UNIVERSITY OF TEXAS MED BRANCH 200 UNIVERSITY BLVD GALVESTON, TX 77550-2772 Inducible alteration of CGRP in primary afferent neurons
R01NS-28069-02 (NEUC) HARBOUR, DEBORAH V UNIV OF TEXAS MEDICAL BRANCH GALVESTON, TX 77550 Characterization of hypothalamic-lymphoid-thyroid axis
R01NS-28072-02 (NEUB) ANGELIDES, KIMON J BAYLOR COLLEGE OF MEDICINE ONE BAYLOR PLAZA HOUSTON, TX 77030 Organization of the axon membrane
R01NS-28073-02 (NEUA) BERTRAM, EDWARD H UNIVERSITY OF VIRGINIA BOX 394 CHARLOTTESVILLE, VA 22908 Ontogeny of limbic seizures
R01NS-28076-02 (NEUB) RYMER, WILLIAM Z NORTHWESTERN UNIVERSITY 303 E CHICAGO AVENUE CHICAGO, IL 60611 Physiological effects of incomplete spinal cord injury
R01NS-28081-02 (NEUB) GOLDBERGER, MICHAEL E MEDICAL COLL OF PENNSYLVANIA 3200 HENRY AVENUE PHILADELPHIA, PA 19129 Behavioral and anatomical studies of spinal cord damage
R01NS-28114-02 (NLS) BAUMGOLD, JESSE GEORGE WASHINGTON UNIVERSITY 2300 I STREET, NW WASHINGTON, DC 20037 Specificity of receptor-mediated phosphoinositide turnover
P01NS-28121-01A1S1 (NSPA) ZIVIN, JUSTIN A UNIVERSITY OF CALIFORNIA LA JOLLA, CA 92093 Experimental intervention in models of CNS injury
P01NS-28121-01A1S1 0004 (NSPA) SAITOH, TSUNAO Experimental intervention in models of CNS injury Molecular changes in neurodegeneration
P01NS-28121-01A1S1 0005 (NSPA) WALICKE, PATRICIA A Experimental intervention in models of CNS injury Fibroblast growth factor in CNS trauma and ischemia
P01NS-28121-01A1S1 0001 (NSPA) ZIVIN, JUSTIN A Experimental intervention in models of CNS injury Effects of CNS ischemia on protein phosphorylation
P01NS-28121-01A1S1 0002 (NSPA) GAGE, FRED H Experimental intervention in models of CNS injury Functional and anatomical analysis of regeneration in the CNS
P01NS-28121-01A1S1 0003 (NSPA) BUZSAKI, GYORGY Experimental intervention in models of CNS injury Trauma-induced epilepsy
R29NS-28126-02 (NEUC) CRAFT, CHERYL M VA MEDICAL CENTER 4500 S LANCASTER RD DALLAS, TX 75216 Molecular analysis of retinal/pineal melatonin synthesis
R29NS-28129-03 (NEUB) BIZZOZERO, OSCAR ANGEL UNIVERSITY OF NEW MEXICO BIOCHEMISTRY ALBUQUERQUE, NM 87131 Fatty acid acylation of myelin PO glycoprotein
P01NS-28130-02 (NSPA) GILLIS, RICHARD A GEORGETOWN UNIVERSITY 3900 RESERVOIR ROAD, NW WASHINGTON, DC 20007 Excitatory amino acids--Role in central nervous system disorders
P01NS-28130-02 0001 (NSPA) GUIDOTTI, ALESSANDRO Excitatory amino acids--Role in central nervous system disorders Excitatory amino acids and neurotoxicity
P01NS-28130-02 0002 (NSPA) WRATHALL, JEAN Excitatory amino acids--Role in central nervous system disorders Excitatory amino acids in traumatic spinal cord injury
P01NS-28130-02 0003 (NSPA) VICINI, STEFANO Excitatory amino acids--Role in central nervous system disorders Excitatory synapse modification and cognitive disorders
P01NS-28130-02 0004 (NSPA) GALE, KAREN N Excitatory amino acids--Role in central nervous system disorders Excitatory amino acids and focally evoked convulsions
P01NS-28130-02 0005 (NSPA) GILLIS, RICHARD A Excitatory amino acids--Role in central nervous system disorders Excitatory amino acids and cardiorespiratory function
P01NS-28130-02 0006 (NSPA) NEALE, JOSEPH H Excitatory amino acids--Role in central nervous system disorders Glutamatergic neurons and N-acetylaspartylglutamate
P01NS-28130-02 9001 (NSPA) WROBLEWSKI, JARDA Excitatory amino acids--Role in central nervous system disorders Analytical core
P01NS-28130-02 9002 (NSPA) WRATHALL, JEAN Excitatory amino acids--Role in central nervous system disorders Morphology core
R29NS-28135-02 (NEUC) IVERSON, LINDA E BECKMAN RESEARCH INSTITUTE 1450 EAST DUARTE ROAD DUARTE, CA 91010 Molecular neurogenetics of drosphila potassium channels
R01NS-28140-02 (NEUB) SLOVITER, ROBERT S HELEN HAYES HOSPITAL ROUTE 9W WEST HAVERSTRAW, NY 10993 Hippocampal neuron vulnerability after adrenalectomy
R01NS-28154-02 (NEUB) ROBINSON, KENNETH R PURDUE UNIVERSITY WEST LAFAYETTE, IN 47907 Response of neurons to electrical fields
R29NS-28158-02 (NLS) TANG, CHA-MIN GRADUATE HOSPITAL 1 GRADUATE PLAZA PHILADELPHIA, PA 19146 Properties and roles of glutamate channels in the CNS
R01NS-28165-01A2 (SAT) STORELLA, ROBERT J HAHNEMANN UNIVERSITY BROAD AND VINE STREETS PHILADELPHIA, PA 19103 Pre- and postjunctional actions of cholinergics
R01NS-28167-02 (NEUB) SHARP, FRANK RAY SAN FRANCISCO VA MEDICAL CTR 4150 CLEMENT STREET SAN FRANCISCO, CA 94121 Markers of CNS injury
R01NS-28172-02 (NEUC) KROLICK, KEITH A UNIV OF TEXAS HLTH SCI CTR 7703 FLOYD CURL DRIVE SAN ANTONIO, TX 78284 Characterization of disease-causing antibodies in EAMG
R01NS-28175-02 (NEUB) LEHMAN, MICHAEL N UNIVERSITY OF CINCINNATI 231 BETHESDA AVE, ML 521 CINCINNATI, OH 45267-0521 Neurotransplantation of the suprachiasmatic nucleus
R01NS-28176-01A2 (NEUB) GOTTLIEB, GERALD L RUSH-PRESBYTERIAN-ST LUKES MED 1653 WEST CONGRESS PARKWAY CHICAGO, IL 60612 Experimental study on a theory for voluntary movement
R01NS-28182-02 (NEUC) ZINN, KAI G CALIFORNIA INST OF TECHNOLOGY 1201 E CALIFORNIA BLVD PASADENA, CA 91125 Molecular genetics of axon guidance in the drosophila EM
R29NS-28190-02 (NLS) YU, LEI INDIANA UNIVERSITY SCHOOL OF M 975 WEST WALNUT STREET INDIANAPOLIS, IN 46202-5251 Molecular dissection of the mouse serotonin 1c receptor
R01NS-28199-01A2 (NEUB) FREDMAN, STEVEN M MEHARRY MEDICAL COLLEGE 1005 D B TODD BLVD NASHVILLE, TN 37208 Cellular mechanisms of synaptic plasticity
R01NS-28200-02 (ECS) RUGGIERO, DAVID A CORNELL UNIVERSITY MED COLLEGE 411 EAST 69TH STREET NEW YORK, NY 10021 Somatosympathetic reflexes--Neuroanatomical substrates
R01NS-28202-02 (NEUB) BLAIR, SETH S UNIVERSITY OF WISCONSIN 250 N MILLS STREET MADISON, WI 53706 Study of axon guidance
R29NS-28206-02 (BCE) COBBETT, PETER J MICHIGAN STATE UNIVERSITY EAST LANSING, MI 48824 Amino acid and peptidergic control of

PROJECT NO., ORGANIZATIONAL UNIT., INVESTIGATOR, ADDRESS, TITLE

supraoptic neurons
R01NS-28208-02 (NLS) JOHNSTON, MICHAEL V KENNEDY INSTITUTE 707 NORTH BROADWAY BALTIMORE, MD 21205 Neurotransmitter injury mechanisms in developing brain
R01NS-28220-01A2 (NEUA) DIKSIC, MIRKO MONTREAL NEUROLOGICAL INSTITUT 3801 UNIVERSITY STREET MONTREAL, QUEBEC CANADA H3A 2 Pharmacokinetics and metabolism of gliomas
R01NS-28225-03 (NEUA) SIREN, ANA-LEENA UNIFORMED SVCS UNIV OF HLTH SC 4301 JONES BRIDGE ROAD BETHESDA, MD 20814-4799 Stroke risk factors and macrophage-endothelium interplay
R29NS-28227-02 (NLS) DURING, MATTHEW J YALE UNIVERSITY 333 CEDAR STREET NEW HAVEN, CT 06510 In vivo neurochemistry of epilepsy
R01NS-28236-02 (NEUA) SCHWARCZ, ROBERT MARYLAND PSYCHIATRIC RES CTR P O BOX 21247 BALTIMORE, MD 21228 Neurotoxic amino acid mechanism in vivo and in vitro
R01NS-28238-02 (NEUB) JONES, KATHRYN J THE UNIV OF ILLINOIS AT CHICAG 1919 W. TAYLOR (M/C 898) CHICAGO, ILLINOIS 60612 Steroid hormones and neuronal regeneration
R44NS-28256-02 (BPO) DOCTROW, SUSAN R ALKERMES, INC 26 LANDSDOWNE STREET CAMBRIDGE, MA 02139-4234 Development of an in vitro blood-brain barrier
R44NS-28265-02 (SSS) RIKER, ROBERT J CORITECHS, INC 655 ORANGE STREET NEW HAVEN, CT 06511-3861 Computer assisted stereotaxic neurosurgical system
R44NS-28275-02 (BPO) LUBRANO, GLENN J UNIVERSAL SENSORS, INC 5258 VETERANS BLVD, SUITE D METAIRIE, LA 70006 Microelectrodes for the determination of neuroregulators
R44NS-28279-02 (SSS) LESIECKI, MICHAEL CANDELA LASER CORPORATION 530 BOSTON POST ROAD WAYLAND, MA 01778 Selective killing of pain neurons by laser photolysis
R43NS-28280-01A1 (BPO) DELGADO, RAFAEL E INTELLIGENT HEARING SYSTEMS 1125 NE 125 STREET NORTH MIAMI, FL 33161 A neural network based seizure detection system
R01NS-28308-03 (VISA) REH, THOMAS A UNIVERSITY OF WASHINGTON SEATTLE, WA 98195 Regulation of neuronal proliferation and differentiation
R01NS-28316-01A1 (GMA) FURNESS, JOHN B UNIVERSITY OF MELBOURNE PARKVILLE, VIC 3052 AUSTRALIA Gastrointestinal nerve circuits in colonic control
P01NS-28323-02 (SRC) KATER, STANLEY B COLORADO STATE UNIVERSITY COLL VET MED & BIOM SCI FORT COLLINS, CO 80523 The determinants of neuronal form
P01NS-28323-02 0001 (SRC) BAMBURG, JAMES R The determinants of neuronal form Actin filament dynamics in growing nerves
P01NS-28323-02 0002 (SRC) KATER, STANLEY The determinants of neuronal form Role of substrate molecules in neuronal pathfinding
P01NS-28323-02 0003 (SRC) ISHII, DOUGLAS N The determinants of neuronal form Role of IGF-I in synaptogenesis and nerve regeneration
P01NS-28323-02 0004 (SRC) BEAM, KURT G The determinants of neuronal form Developmental roles of calcium channels
P01NS-28323-02 9001 (SRC) MYKLES, DON L The determinants of neuronal form Core--Electron microscopy
P01NS-28323-02 9002 (SRC) KATER, STANLEY B The determinants of neuronal form Core--Optical
R01NS-28329-02 (NLS) ERECINSKA, MARIA UNIVERSITY OF PENNSYLVANIA 37TH & HAMILTON WALK PHILADELPHIA, PA 19104-6084 Na pump in neuronal ion and transmitter homeostasis
R01NS-28330-01A1 (NEUA) BUTTER, CHARLES M THE UNIVERSITY OF MICHIGAN 1103 EAST HURON STREET ANN ARBOR, MI 48109 Unilateral spatial neglect following stroke
R01NS-28338-02 (NEUB) BAMBURG, JAMES R COLORADO STATE UNIVERSITY FORT COLLINS, CO 80523 Actin filament dynamics in growing nerves
R29NS-28357-02 (ARR) ZINK, M CHRISTINE JOHNS HOPKINS UNIVERSITY 720 RUTLAND AVENUE BALTIMORE, MD 21205 Neurovirulent visna virus--model for AIDS encephalopathy
R29NS-28369-03 (NEUB) BUCHANAN, JAMES T MARQUETTE UNIVERSITY 530 N. 15TH STREET MILWAUKEE, WI 53233 The role of spinal interneurons in locomotion
R55NS-28374-01A1 (RNM) JACK, CLIFFORD R MAYO FOUNDATION 200 FIRST STREET SW ROCHESTER, MN 55905 Magnetic resonance volume studies -- Temporal lobe epilepsy
R29NS-28377-02 (PHY) CORBETT, ADRIAN M WRIGHT STATE UNIV SCH OF MEDIC PO BOX 927 DAYTON, OH 45401-0927 Sodium channel subtypes
R01NS-28380-02 (VISB) LUSKIN, MARLA B EMORY UNIVERSITY SCH OF MEDICI ATLANTA, GA 30322 Mechanisms of assembly of the visual cortex
R01NS-28384-01A1 (NEUC) BREAKEFIELD, XANDRA O MASSACHUSETTS GENERAL HOSPITAL 13TH STREET CHARLESTOWN, MA 02129 Identification of the human dystonia gene
R01NS-28388-03 (NEUA) GODDARD-FINEGOLD, JAN BAYLOR COLLEGE OF MEDICINE ONE BAYLOR PLAZA HOUSTON, TX 77030 Prevention of hyperemia & hemorrhage in newborn brain
R01NS-28389-03 (BPN) COOPER, DERMOT M UNIV OF COLORADO HLTH SCIS CTR 4200 EAST 9TH AVE DENVER, CO 80262 Dopamine D2-receptor mediated signal transduction
R29NS-28405-02 (NLS) CONN, PETER J EMORY UNIVERSITY SCH OF MED ATLANTA, GA 30322 Cellular mechanisms of kindling-induced epileptogenesis
R01NS-28406-02 (NEUB) NEVE, RACHAEL L UNIVERSITY OF CALIFORNIA IRVINE, CA 92717 Neuronal function of the alzheimer amyloid precursor
R01NS-28407-02 (PHY) JOHO, ROLF H BAYLOR COLLEGE OF MEDICINE ONE BAYLOR PLAZA HOUSTON, TX 77030 Characteristics of potassium channel genes
R01NS-28416-01A1 (SRCM) UEMURA, ETSURO IOWA STATE UNIVERSITY 1044 VETERINARY MEDICINE AMES, IOWA 50011 Mathematical approach to modeling dendritic growth
R01NS-28421-02 (BPO) BREEDLOVE, S MARC UNIVERSITY OF CALIFORNIA BERKELEY, CA 94720 Hormonal effects on behavior & spinal cord morphology
R01NS-28433-02 (NEUB) WEI, JEN Y UNIV. OF CALIF., L. A. 405 HILGARD AVENUE LOS ANGELES, CA 90024 Mechanisms of neurogenic inflammatory response
R01NS-28443-02 (NEUB) COHEN, LAWRENCE B YALE UNIVERSITY SCHOOL OF MED 333 CEDAR STREET NEW HAVEN, CT 06510 Optical recording of

PROJECT NO., ORGANIZATIONAL UNIT., INVESTIGATOR, ADDRESS, TITLE

synaptic potential integration
R01NS-28447-02 (NLS) GRANT, GREGORY A WASHINGTON UNIV SCHOOL OF MED 660 SOUTH EUCLID AVE, BX 8094 ST LOUIS, MO 63110 Development of neuronal nicotinic receptor probes
R01NS-28462-01A1 (NEUB) ESKIN, ARNOLD UNIVERSITY OF HOUSTON HOUSTON, TX 77204-5500 Function of proteins and their modifications in learning
R01NS-28471-02 (PC) KOBILKA, BRIAN K STANFORD UNIVERSITY B105 BECKMAN CENTER STANFORD, CA 94305-5426 Biochemical analysis of adrenergic beta-2 receptor structure
R01NS-28472-02 (NEUC) HOLMGREN, ROBERT A NORTHWESTERN UNIVERSITY 2153 SHERIDAN RD EVANSTON, IL 60208 Cell fate specification in the nervous system
R01NS-28477-01A1 (NEUB) HOFFMAN, GLORIA E UNIVERSITY OF PITTSBURGH 3550 TERRACE STREET PITTSBURGH, PA 15261 Immunoreactive fos maps functional hypothalamic anatomy
R29NS-28478-02 (NEUB) ALVAREZ-BUYLLA, ARTURO ROCKEFFELLER UNIVERSITY 1230 YORK AVE NEW YORK, NY 10021 The origin of new neurons in the adult brain
R29NS-28480-01A1 (NEUA) RICE, MARGARET E NEW YORK UNIVERSITY MEDICAL CT 550 FIRST AVENUE NEW YORK, NY 10016 Dynamics of ascorbate regulation in brain
R01NS-28484-02 (PHY) BYERLY, WILLIAM L UNIV OF SOUTHERN CALIFORNIA LOS ANGELES, CA 90089-0371 Intracellular control of neuronal calcium current
R01NS-28492-01A1 (SRC) WIEBERS, DAVID O MAYO FOUNDATION 200 FIRST STREET SOUTHWEST ROCHESTER, MN 55905 Unruptured intracranial aneurysms neurologic outcome
P01NS-28495-02 (SRC) HILDEBRAND, JOHN G UNIVERSITY OF ARIZONA TUCSON, AZ 85721 Neural development--intercellular and humoral control
P01NS-28495-02 0001 (SRC) HILDEBRAND, JOHN G Neural development--intercellular and humoral control Developmental influences on cultured olfactory neurons
P01NS-28495-02 0002 (SRC) LEVINE, RICHARD B Neural development--intercellular and humoral control Hormonal influences on insect motor neurons developing in cell culture
P01NS-28495-02 0003 (SRC) TOLBERT, LESLIE P Neural development--intercellular and humoral control Hormonal control of olfactory lobe development
P01NS-28495-02 9001 (SRC) TOLBERT, LESLIE P Neural development--intercellular and humoral control Core-Electron and light microscopy
P01NS-28495-02 9002 (SRC) LEVINE, RICHARD B Neural development--intercellular and humoral control Core--Tissue culture
R29NS-28496-02 (NEUC) MINTH, CAROLYN A WRIGHT STATE UNIV SCH OF MED DAYTON, OH 45435 Regulation of neuropeptide Y gene expression
R15NS-28502-01A1 (ORTH) WALL, JAMES C UNIVERSITY OF SOUTH ALABAMA MOBILE, AL 36688 A sway platform to assess and treat stroke patients
R01NS-28504-01A1 (PHY) ADELMAN, JOHN P OREGON HLTH SCIENCES UNIVERSIT 3181 SW SAM JACKSON PARK RD PORTLAND, OR 97201-3098 Structure and function of mammalian potassium channels
R01NS-28510-03 (ARR) WHALEN, L RAY COLORADO STATE UNIVERSITY FORT COLLINS, CO 80523 Feline neurotropic retroviruses
R01NS-28512-01A1 (NLS) BECK, SHERYL G LOYOLA UNIVERSITY CHICAGO 2160 SOUTH FIRST AVE MAYWOOD, IL 60153 Adrenalcorticoid effects on hippocampal neural activity
R01NS-28518-01A1 (NEUA) HALSEY, JAMES H, JR UNIVERSITY OF ALABAMA UAB STATION BIRMINGHAM, AL 35294 Reperfusion and ischemic brain necrosis
R01NS-28525-02 (CMS) LOGEMANN, JERILYN A COMMUNICATION SCI & DISORDERS 2299 SHERIDAN RD EVANSTON, IL 60208-3540 Pathophysiology oropharyngeal swallow after stroke
R01NS-28549-01A1 (NEUC) DAWSON, GLYN UNIVERSITY OF CHICAGO 5841 S MARYLAND AVE CHICAGO, IL 60637 Lipase and cathepsin abnormalities in Batten disease
R01NS-28556-02 (OBM) TALAMO, BARBARA R TUFTS UNIVERSITY 136 HARRISON AVENUE BOSTON, MA 02111 Plasticity--neuronal modulation/postsynaptic sensitivity
R01NS-28562-02 (PB) HACKNEY, DAVID D CARNEGIE-MELLON UNIVERSITY 4400 FIFTH AVENUE PITTSBURGH, PA 15213 Mechanism of kinesin ATPase
R01NS-28565-02 (BPO) SIMMONS, ANDREA M BROWN UNIVERISTY BOX 1853 PROVIDENCE, RI 02912 Neuroethology of vocal communication
R29NS-28566-02 (NEUB) STEERS, WILLIAM D UNIVERSITY OF VIRGINIA BOX 422 CHARLOTTESVILLE, VA 22908 Trophic effects of obstruction on bladder innervation
R29NS-28568-02 (NLS) VICKROY, THOMAS W UNIVERSITY OF FLORIDA J HILLIS MILLER HEALTH CENTER GAINESVILLE, FL 32610-0144 Autoreceptor regulation of CNS cholinergic neurons
R29NS-28571-02 (CMS) CAMPBELL, MICHAEL J MT SINAI SCHOOL OF MEDICINE ONE GUSTAVE L LEVY PLACE NEW YORK, NY 10029 Neuronal organization specific to language areas
R29NS-28580-01A1 (NLS) RUTECKI, PAUL A BAYLOR COLLEGE OF MEDICINE ONE BAYLOR PLAZA HOUSTON, TX 77030 Synaptic mechanisms of epileptiform synchronization
R01NS-28587-01A1 (NEUB) SMITH, STEPHEN J STANFORD UNIVERSITY STANFORD, CA 94305-5426 Cellular physiology of cortical development
R01NS-28595-02 (NEUA) PRICE, DONALD D MEDICAL COLLEGE OF VIRGINIA BOX 516 MCV STATION RICHMOND, VA 23298-0516 Neural mechanisms of analgesia in humans
R29NS-28598-02 (HUD) LENZ, FREDERICK ARTHUR JOHNS HOPKINS HOSPITAL 600 N WOLFE STREET BALTIMORE, MD 21205 Studies of the ventrocaudal thalamus in human pain
R29NS-28599-02 (NEUC) CARBONE, KATHRYN M JOHNS HOPKINS MED INSTITUTIONS 720 RUTLAND AVENUE BALTIMORE, MD 21205 Persistence of disease virus in astrocytes
R29NS-28602-01A1 (SB) GALLOWAY, ROBERT L, JR VANDERBILT UNIVERSITY 1161 21ST AVENUE SOUTH NASHVILLE, TN 37232 Interactive image-guided surgery
R01NS-28603-03 (NEUB) JELLIES, JOHN A UNIV OF ALABAMA UAB STATION BIRMINGHAM, AL 35294-0019 Navigation and guidance of an identified growth cone array

R29NS-28617-02 (CMS) MELARA, ROBERT D PURDUE UNIVERSITY WEST LAFAYETTE, IN 47907 Perceptual processing of multidimensional stimuli
R43NS-28627-01A1 (BPO) OCHS, BURT D ABIOMED, INC 33 CHERRY HILL DRIVE DANVERS, MA 01923 Miniature implantable transcutaneous optical data link
R01NS-28630-01A1 (ARRG) SIMPSON, DAVID M MOUNT SINAI HOSPITAL BOX 1052 NEW YORK, NY 10029 Neuromuscular disorders in HIV infection and role of AZT
R01NS-28631-02 (ARR) OLNESS, KAREN N RAINBOW BABIES & CHILDRENS HOS 2074 ABINGTON RD CLEVELAND, OH 44106 Neurodevelopmental status in HIV+ Ugandan infants
R43NS-28633-01A2 (BPO) JOHNSON, MICHAEL T EMPI INC 1275 GREY FOX RD ST PAUL, MN 55112 Computerized method for quantifying movement disorders
R01NS-28642-02 (HUD) NICHOLSON, CHARLES NEW YORK UNIVERSITY MEDICAL CT 550 FIRST AVENUE NEW YORK, NY 10016 Diffusion of substances through the brain
R01NS-28646-01A1 (NLS) TANELIAN, DARRELL L STANFORD UNIVERSITY SCHOOL OF MEDICINE STANFORD, CA 94305-5123 Sensory transduction in normal and injured nerves
R29NS-28650-01A1 (NLS) MALOUF, ALFRED T UNIVERSITY OF WASHINGTON SEATTLE, WA 98195 GabaB control excitability -- Circuitry and mechanisms
R01NS-28651-02 (NEUC) CITRI, YOAV WEIZMANN INST OF SCIENCE PO BOX 26 REHOVOT 76100, ISRAEL BETA--A brain-specific transcription activator
R01NS-28652-01A1 (NEUC) CAUDY, MICHAEL A CORNELL UNIVERSITY MED COLLEGE 1300 YORK AVE NEW YORK, NY 10021 HLH gene function in fly neuronal cell determination
R01NS-28660-01A1 (NEUC) HERSCHMAN, HARVEY R UCLA SCHOOL OF MEDICINE 10833 LE CONTE AVE LOS ANGELES, CA 90024-1737 Neurotrophic factor and neuronal primary response genes
R01NS-28662-01A1 (NEUC) SARID, JACOB BRIGHAM & WOMEN'S HOSPITAL 75 FRANCIS STREET BOSTON, MA 02115 Transcriptional regulation of the GFAP gene
R01NS-28665-02 (NEUA) POIZNER, HOWARD RUTGERS, THE STATE UNIV OF NJ 195 UNIVERSITY AVENUE NEWARK, N J 07102 Apraxia: neural representations of learned movement
R01NS-28668-02 (NEUB) HENDERSON, LESLIE P DARTMOUTH MEDICAL SCHOOL HANOVER, NH 03756 Regulation of acetylcholine receptor function
R01NS-28695-02 (NLS) FORSCHER, PAUL YALE UNIVERSITY PO BOX 6666 NEW HAVEN, CT 06511 Regulation and mechanochemistry of neuronal motility
R01NS-28698-01A1 (NEUB) TEYLER, TIMOTHY J NE OHIO UNIVERSITIES COLLEGE OF MEDICINE ROOTSTOWN, OH 44272-0095 Role of extracellular K+ and Ca2+ channels in long term potentiation(LTP)
R29NS-28699-02 (NEUC) SNOW, PETER M STATE UNIVERSITY OF NEW YORK ALBANY, NY 12222 Biochemistry of adhesion molecules mediating axon guidance
R01NS-28700-02 (NEUA) POWERS, WILLIAM J DEPARTMENT OF NEUROLOGY 216 S KINGSHIGHWAY BLVD ST LOUIS, MO 63178 Measurement of cerebral metabolism with 1-c-11-glucose
R01NS-28704-02 (NEUC) WOLINSKY, EVE J NYU MEDICAL CENTER 550 FIRST AVENUE NEW YORK, NY 10016 Genetic control of neurodegeneration
R55NS-28706-01A1 (NEUA) GROSS, CORDELL E UNIVERSITY OF VERMONT 1 SOUTH PROSPECT STREET BURLINGTON, VT 05401 Delayed reperfusion with t-pa in a stroke model
R01NS-28709-02 (NEUC) HEINEMANN, STEPHEN F SALK INSTITUTE/BIOLOGICAL STUD PO BOX 85800 SAN DIEGO, CA 92138 Cloning the glutamate receptor gene family
R01NS-28710-02 (NEUC) KENNEDY, MARY B CALIFORNIA INST OF TECHNOLOGY 1201 E CALIFORNIA BLVD PASADENA, CA 91125 Molecular structure of CNS postsynaptic densities
R01NS-28712-01A1 (NEUA) WYLER, ALLEN R UNIVERSITY OF TENNESSEE 956 COURT AVENUE MEMPHIS, TN 38163 Anterior temporal lobectomy: comparison of two surgical methods
R01NS-28721-02 (PTHA) REINER, ANTON J UNIV OF TENNESSEE 875 MONROE AVENUE MEMPHIS, TN 38163 Pathogenetic mechanisms of Huntington's disease
R01NS-28726-01A1 (NEUB) HUTTENLOCHER, PETER R UNIVERSITY OF CHICAGO 5841 S MARYLAND AVE HOSP BOX 2 CHICAGO, IL 60637 Synaptic development in human cerebral cortex
R01NS-28730-01A1 (BCE) HOFFMAN, GLORIA E UNIV OF PITTSBURGH SCH OF MED 3500 TERRACE STREET PITTSBURGH, PA 15261 C-Fos induction maps activation of LHRH neurons
R29NS-28735-01A1 (NEUC) BERNARDS, ANDRE MGH CANCER CENTER 13TH STREET, BLDG 149, 7TH FLO CHARLESTOWN, MA 02129 Studies on the neuronal and lymphoid itk protein kinase
R01NS-28743-02 (NEUC) JOHNSON, WAYNE A UNIVERSITY OF IOWA BOWEN SCIENCE BLDG, 6-430 IOWA CITY, IA 52242 The role of POU-factors in neuronal development
R01NS-28744-02 (NLS) LANDRETH, GARY E CASE WESTERN RESERVE UNIVERSIT 2116 ABINGTON RD CLEVELAND, OH 44106 Nerve growth factor regulated gene expression
R01NS-28747-02 (CMS) OCHOA, JOSE L GOOD SAMARITAN HOSP. & MED. CT 1040 NORTHWEST 22ND STREET PORTLAND, OR 97210 Painful small caliber fiber neuropathy in aging humans
R01NS-28752-02 (IMS) KIM, BYUNG S NORTHWESTERN UNIVERSITY 303 E CHICAGO AVENUE CHICAGO, IL 60611 Epitopes involved in TMEV-induced demyelination
R01NS-28754-05 (ARR) EPSTEIN, LEON G UNIVERSITY OF ROCHESTER MED CT 601 ELMWOOD AVE, BOX 631 ROCHESTER, NY 14642 The role of HTLV-III in AIDS encephalopathy
R29NS-28758-02 (RNM) BICE, ALDEN N UNIVERSITY OF WASHINGTON SEATTLE, WA 98195 Finite spatial resolution effects on CNS PET
R01NS-28759-01S1 (IMS) STEINMAN, LAWRENCE STANFORD UNIVERSITY MED CTR 300 PASTEUR DRIVE STANFORD, CA 94305-5235 Peptide mediated immunotherapy for autoimmune disease
R01NS-28765-02 (NLS) VULLIET, PHILIP R UNIVERSITY OF CALIFORNIA DAVIS, CA 95616 Phosphorylation of the cytoskeleton in neuronal growth
R29NS-28767-01A1 (PHY) MAUE, ROBERT A DARTMOUTH MEDICAL SCHOOL HANOVER, NH 03756 Regulation of sodium channel expression
R01NS-28772-02 (NLS) OLSEN, RICHARD W UCLA SCHOOL OF MEDICINE LOS ANGELES, CA 90024-1735 Gaba-A receptor structure and function
R01NS-28781-02 (NEUA) WOOLSEY, THOMAS A NEUROSURGERY DEPARTMENT 660 SOUTH EUCLID AVENUE ST LOUIS, MO 63110 Imaging brain blood vessels during cortical activity
R01NS-28784-01A1 (ORTH) WOLF, STEVEN L EMORY UNIVERSITY 1441 CLIFTON ROAD, NE ATLANTA, GA 30032 Down-training spinal streach reflexes
R01NS-28785-03 (NEUB) BAAS, PETER W UNIVERSITY OF WISCONSIN 1300 UNIVERSITY AVENUE MADISON, WI 53706 Microtubule dynamics and axon growth
R29NS-28790-02 (HUD) NOVOTNY, EDWARD J YALE UNIV SCHOOL OF MEDICINE 333 CEDAR STREET/P O BOX 3333 NEW HAVEN, CT 06514 In vivo 1h/13c nmr studies of neonatal seizures
R01NS-28792-02 (NLS) CASTAGNOLI, NEAL, JR VIRGINIA POLYTECHNIC INSTITUTE COLLEGE OF ARTS AND SCIENCES BLACKSBURG, VA 24061-0212 Metabolism and neurotoxicity studies on MPTP analogs
R29NS-28797-02 (CMS) DOWMAN, ROBERT CLARKSON UNIVERSITY 156 SCIENCE CENTER POTSDAM, NY 13699 Evoked potential studies of pain
R01NS-28805-02 (ECS) FELDMAN, JACK L UNIVERSITY OF CALIFORNIA 405 HILGARD AVENUE LOS ANGELES, CA 90024-1568 Descending control of sympathetic preganglionic neurons
R01NS-28807-01A1 (NEUC) LETOURNEAU, PAUL C UNIVERSITY OF MINNESOTA 321 CHURCH ST,SE/4-135 JACKSON MINNEAPOLIS, MN 55455 Neuronal proteoglycans and adhesion to fibronectin
R29NS-28811-01A1 (NLS) SENOGLES, SUSAN E UNIVERSITY OF TENNESSEE 858 MADISON AVENUE MEMPHIS, TN 38163 Signal transduction of the D2 dopamine receptor subtypes
R01NS-28813-01A1 (NEUA) SAYKIN, ANDREW J UNIVERSITY OF PENNSYLVANIA PHILADELPHIA, PA 19104 Neurobehavioral outcome of temporal lobectomy
R01NS-28815-02 (NEUB) DUNLAP, KATHLEEN TUFTS UNIVERSITY 136 HARRISON AVENUE BOSTON, MA 02111 Mechanisms of neurosecretion
R29NS-28824-01A1 (NLS) MADL, JAMES E COLORADO STATE UNIVERSITY FORT COLLINS, CO 80523 Amino acid release and hypoxic neuronal damage
R01NS-28828-02 (MBY) SCHON, ERIC A COLUMBIA UNIVERSITY 630 WEST 168TH STREET NEW YORK, NY 10032 Deletions of mitochondrial DNA in neuromuscular disease
R01NS-28829-02 (NEUC) GREENBERG, MICHAEL E HARVARD MEDICAL SCHOOL 200 LONGWOOD AVENUE BOSTON, MA 02115 Electrical stimulation of immediate genes
R01NS-28840-02 (NEUC) RATNER, NANCY UNIVERSITY OF CINCINNATI 231 BETHESDA AVENUE CINCINNATI, OH 45267-0521 Mitogenic activities in neurofibromatosis
R01NS-28846-02 (NLS) MARSHALL, JOHN F UNIVERSITY OF CALIFORNIA IRVINE, CA 92717 Mesotelencephalic injury and regional dopamine uptake
R01NS-28847-02 (NLS) IWAMOTO, EDGAR T UNIVERSITY OF KENTUCKY MS-305 CHANDLER MEDICAL CENTER LEXINGTON, KY 40536 Cholinergic mechanisms of analgesia
R01NS-28850-01A1 (NLS) STEHOUWER, DONALD J UNIVERSITY OF FLORIDA GAINESVILLE, FL 32611 Development of locomotor behaviors
R01NS-28852-02 (HUD) ROSS, DOUGLAS T UNIVERSITY OF PENNSYLVANIA 36TH & HAMILTON WALK PHILADELPHIA, PA 19104-6070 Excitotoxic mechanisms in post traumatic neuronal death
R01NS-28856-02 (NEUB) HAUN, FORREST A MEDICAL COLLEGE OF PENNSYLVANI 3200 HENRY AVENUE PHILADELPHIA, PA 19129 Formation of specific patterns of innervation in the CNS
R29NS-28857-02 (NEUB) JOHANSEN, JORGEN IOWA STATE UNIVERSITY AMES, IA 50011 Molecular analysis of axon fascicle specific glycoproteins
R01NS-28858-01 (NEUB) HUMPHREY, DONALD R EMORY UNIVERSITY ATLANTA, GA 30322 Functions of multiple arm-hand areas of motor cortex
R01NS-28867-01A1 (RNM) MATHIS, CHESTER A UNIVERSITY OF CALIFORNIA 1 CYCLOTRON ROAD BERKELEY, CA 94720 18F-Labeled benzamides for dopamine-D2 studies using PET
R01NS-28869-02 (NEUB) SABBAN, ESTHER L NEW YORK MEDICAL COLLEGE VALHALLA, NY 10595 Molecular biology of norepinephrine biosynthesis
R29NS-28871-02 (NLS) STRINGER, JANET UNIVERSITY OF VIRGINIA MED CTR CHARLOTTESVILLE, VA 22908 Mechanisms of seizure control in limbic circuits
R01NS-28876-02 (NEUB) LA MOTTE, CAROLE C YALE UNIVERSITY SCHOOL OF MED PO BOX 3333, 333 CEDAR ST NEW HAVEN, CT 06510 Deafferentation-induced alterations in spinal systems
R01NS-28877-02 (NEUC) GILLIAM, THOMAS COLUMBIA UNIVERSITY 722 W 168TH ST, BOX 58 NEW YORK, NY 10032 Spinal muscular atrophy--Gene mapping and characterization
R29NS-28879-02 (NLS) PEDERSEN, STEEN E BAYLOR COLLEGE OF MEDICINE ONE BAYLOR PLAZA HOUSTON, TX 77030 Structure of the nicotinic acetylcholine receptor
R01NS-28888-02 (NEUB) RHOADES, ROBERT W MEDICAL COLLEGE OF OHIO PO BOX 10008 TOLEDO, OH 43699-0008 Trigeminal primary afferent development
R29NS-28889-02 (NLS) SURMEIER, DALTON J THE UNIVERSITY OF TENNESSEE 875 MONROE AVENUE MEMPHIS, TN 38163 Muscarinic and dopaminergic control of striatal neurons
R29NS-28894-02 (NLS) LEWIS, DEBORAH L MEDICAL COLLEGE OF GEORGIA AUGUSTA, GA 30912-2300 NGF or V-src differentiated PC12 cells--Ca2+ currents
R01NS-28896-01A1 (NEUB) GIBBS, ROBERT B ROCKEFELLER UNIVERSITY 1230 YORK AVE, BOX 275 NEW YORK, NY 10021 Gonadal steroid effects on NGF and NGF reception in brain
R01NS-28901-01A1 (NEUB) TRUSSELL, LAURENCE O UNIVERSITY OF WISCONSIN 1300 UNIVERSITY AVENUE MADISON, WI 53706 Regulation of synaptic amino acid receptors
R01NS-28905-02 (NEUA) KRUSE, CAROL A UNIV OF COLORADO HLTH SCI CTR BOX C307, 4200 EAST NINTH AVE DENVER, CO 80262 Immunotherapy for primary brain glioma
R01NS-28931-05 (NLS) PAPPAS, GEORGE D UNIV OF ILLINOIS AT CHICAGO 808 SOUTH WOOD STREET CHICAGO, IL 60680 Nociception & EM of chromaffin cell transplants in CNS

PROJECT NO., ORGANIZATIONAL UNIT., INVESTIGATOR, ADDRESS, TITLE

R01NS-28932-02 (NEUC) CUNNINGHAM, BRUCE A ROCKEFELLER UNIVERSITY 1230 YORK AVENUE NEW YORK, N Y 10021 Cell adhesion molecules in the nervous system
R01NS-28937-01A1 (NLS) COHEN, GERALD MOUNT SINAI SCHOOL OF MEDICINE ONE GUSTAVE L LEVY PLACE NEW YORK, NY 10029 Biology of glutathione peroxidase in dopamine neurons
R43NS-28954-01A1 (SSS) ESTES, KERRY S PHARMATEC, INC P O BOX 730 ALACHUA, FL 32615 A parenteral formulation for carbamazepine
R01NS-28965-01A1 (NLS) NEVE, RACHAEL L UNIVERSITY OF CALIFORNIA IRVINE, CA 92717 Molecular biology of Alzheimer disease neurodegeneration
R29NS-28966-01 (NLS) MONAGHAN, DANIEL T UNIV OF NEBRASKA MED CTR 42ND & DEWEY AVE OMAHA, NE 68105-1065 Heterogeneity of NMDA receptors in brain
R01NS-28989-02 (ARR) WIRANOWSKA, MARZENNA USF COLLEGE OF MEDICINE 12901 NORTH BRUCE B DOWNS BLVD TAMPA, FL 33612 Interferon, the blood-brain-barrier and glioma
R01NS-28994-14 (ORTH) KING, ALBERT I WAYNE STATE UNIVERSITY 818 WEST HANCOCK DETROIT, MI 48202 Structural and mechanical properties of the spine
R01NS-28995-02 (NEUA) HSU, CHUNG Y BAYLOR COLLEGE OF MEDICINE ONE BAYLOR PLAZA HOUSTON, TX 77030 Vasogenic brain edema in ischemic stroke
R01NS-28997-01 (NEUC) SUZUKI, KUNIHIKO UNIV OF NC AT CHAPEL HILL CB# 7250 BDRC CHAPEL HILL, NC 27599-7250 Tay-Sachs and related genetic neurological disorders
R01NS-29001-01 (NLS) MATTSON, MARK P UNIVERSITY OF KENTUCKY LEXINGTON, KY 40536-0230 Integration of cellular signals and neuroarchitecture
R01NS-29007-01A1 (NEUB) JAY, DANIEL G HARVARD UNIVERSITY 16 DIVINITY AVENUE CAMBRIDGE, MA 02138 Laser inactivation of proteins in neurodevelopment
R13NS-29022-01A1 (NSPA) MC CALL, ANTHONY L PORTLAND VA MEDICAL CENTER 3710 SW US VETERANS HOSP ROAD PORTLAND, OR 97207 Symposium on the central nervous system and diabetes
R01NS-29025-01A1 (NEUB) MACPHERSON, JANE M R S DOW NEUROLOGICAL SCI INST 1120 N W 20TH AVENUE PORTLAND, OR 97209 Neural control of posture and stance
R01NS-29029-01A1 (RNM) GROSSMAN, ROBERT I UNIVERSITY OF PENNSYLVANIA 308 MEDICAL EDUCATION BLDG PHILADELPHIA, PA 19104 Quantitative imaging/spectroscopy in multiple sclerosis
R01NS-29031-01A1 (NEUB) KOSIK, KENNETH S BRIGHAM & WOMEN'S HOSPITAL DEPT. OF MEDICINE BOSTON, MA 02115 Neuronal polarity -- Disruption in aging & Alzheimer's disease
R29NS-29038-01A1 (NEUC) MC GILLIS, JOSEPH P UNIV OF KENTUCKY RES FND MS 415 LEXINGTON, KY 40536-0084 Immunoregulation by corticotropin-releasing hormone
R01NS-29043-01A1 (NEUB) MC CLELLAN, ANDREW D UNIV OF MISSOURI - COLUMBIA COLUMBIA, MO 65211 Functional regeneration of locomotor command neurons
R29NS-29046-01 (EVR) WILCOX, CHRISTINE L UNIV OF COLORADO SCH/MEDICINE 4200 EAST NINTH AVE DENVER, CO 80262 HSV latency in neurons
R01NS-29051-06 (NEUC) LAFER, EILEEN M UNIVERSITY OF PITTSBURGH 502 LANGLEY HALL PITTSBURGH, PA 15260 Elucidation of the biological role of Z-DNA in E.coli
R01NS-29056-01 (NEUC) LAZZARINI, ROBERT A MOUNT SINAI SCHOOL OF MEDICINE 1 GUSTAVE L LEVY PL, BOX 1128A NEW YORK, NY 10029 Molecular genetic approaches to myelin assembly
R01NS-29059-01A1 (NEUA) PETERSEN, RONALD C MAYO FOUNDATION 200 FIRST ST SOUTHWEST ROCHESTER, MN 55905 Alzheimer's disease and normal aging--Magnetic Resonance volume measures
R01NS-29071-01 (NLS) ROLE, LORNA W COLUMBIA UNIVERSITY 630 WEST 168TH STREET NEW YORK, NY 10032 Expression of neuronal nicotinic acetylcholine receptor
R01NS-29093-01A1 (IMS) INFANTE, ANTHONY J UNIV OF TEXAS HLTH SCI CENTER 7703 FLOYD CURL DRIVE SAN ANTONIO, TX 78284-7810 Peptide strategy for prevention of autoimmune myasthenia
R29NS-29095-01 (IMS) TUOHY, VINCENT K THE CLEVELAND CLINIC FOUNDATIO 9500 EUCLID AVENUE CLEVELAND, OHIO 44195 Immunoregulation of PLP-induced encephalomyelitis
R01NS-29099-01A1 (SRC) KRIVIT, WILLIAM UNIVERSITY OF MINNESOTA BOX 391, 516 DELAWARE STREET, MINNEAPOLIS, MN 55455 Control study of value of BMT for storage diseases
R01NS-29101-01A1 (CMS) CAPLAN, DAVID N MASSACHUSETTS GENERAL HOSPITAL FRUIT STREET BOSTON, MA 02114 Psycholinguistic survey of language impairments
R01NS-29123-01A1 (NEUC) DENERIS, EVAN S CASE WESTERN RESERVE UNIV 2109 ADELBERT RD CLEVELAND, OH 44106 Regulation of neuronal nicotinic acetylcholine receptor gene expression
R01NS-29133-01A1 (EVR) WELSH, C JANE TEXAS A&M UNIVERSITY COLLEGE STATION, TX 77843 Endothelial cells in virus-induced demyelinating disease
R01NS-29161-01 (NLS) LIN, CHIA-SHENG HAHNEMANN UNIVERSITY BROAD AND VINE PHILADELPHIA, PA 19102 The role of GABA inputs from zona incerta to cortex
R01NS-29169-01 (NEUB) SANES, JOSHUA R WASHINGTON UNIV SCH OF MED 660 SOUTH EUCLID AVE ST LOUIS, MO 63110 Lineage migration and phenotypic choice in chick brain
R01NS-29172-01 (NEUC) MERLIE, JOHN P WASHINGTON UNIVERSITY MED SCH 660 SOUTH EUCLID AVENUE ST LOUIS, MO 63110 Transgenic analysis of synaptic protein function
R01NS-29173-01A1 (NLS) DUNWIDDIE, THOMAS V UNIV OF COLORADO HLTH SCI CTR 4200 E 9TH AVENUE DENVER, CO 80262 Adenosine and modulation of synaptic transmission
R29NS-29178-01A1 (NEUB) ISACSON, OLE MCLEAN HOSPITAL 115 MILL STREET BELMONT, MA 02178 Excitotoxic cortex lesions--Degeneration and remodeling
R55NS-29186-01 (NEUC) LEMKE, GREG E SALK INST FOR BIOLOGICAL STUDI PO BOX 85800 SAN DIEGO, CA 92138 Transcriptional controls in glial development
R01NS-29187-01 (NEUB) PURVES, DALE DUKE UNIVERSITY BOX 3209 MEDICAL CENTER DURHAM, NC 27710 Construction of brain circuitry in mouse monkey and man
R01NS-29194-01 (NEUB) LAURENT, GILLES J CALIFORNIA INSTITUTE OF TECH PASADENA, CA 91125 Intrinsic and network properties of local interneurons
R01NS-29203-01 (PTHA) BOYSON, SALLY J UNIV OF COLORADO HLTH SCI CTR 4200 EAST 9TH AVE, BOX B-183 DENVER, CO 80262 Complex I in Parkinsons disease
R01NS-29204-01A1 (NEUB) RUBEN, PETER C 1993 EAST WEST RD HONOLULU, HI 96822 Slow inactivation of sodium channels
R55NS-29215-01A1 (NLS) VAN ELDIK, LINDA J VANDERBILT UNIVERSITY NASHVILLE, TN 37232-6600 Cell biology of a neurotrophic protein from glial cells
R01NS-29218-01 (NEUB) SHIPLEY, MICHAEL T UNIVERSITY OF CINCINNATI 231 BETHESDA AVENUE CINCINNATI, OH 45267-0521 Neuron-glial interactions development & regeneration
R01NS-29220-01 (NEUC) DE VELLIS, JEAN UNIVERSITY OF CALIFORNIA 760 WESTWOOD PLAZA LOS ANGELES, CA 90024-1759 Early response gene expression in glial cell development
R01NS-29224-01 (NLS) LIEM, RONALD K COLUMBIA UNIVERSITY HEALTH SCI 630 WEST 168TH STREET NEW YORK, NY 10032 Functional studies of intermediate filaments in glia
R01NS-29226-01A1 (NLS) MURPHY, SEAN P UNIVERSITY OF IOWA IOWA CITY, IA 52242 Astrocyte-derived vasorelaxant factors
R01NS-29227-01 (NLS) ALVAREZ-LEEFMANS, FRANCISCO J UNIV OF TEXAS MEDICAL BRANCH 301 UNIVERSITY BOULEVARD GALVESTON, TX 77550-2774 Cell volume regulation and maintenance in neurons
R01NS-29230-01 (NEUA) CHESSELET, MARIE-FRANCOISE S UNIVERSITY OF PENNSYLVANIA 36 AND HAMILTON WALK PHILADELPHIA, PA 19104 Cortical control of striatal gene expression
R01NS-29231-01 (NEUA) HOUSER, CAROLYN R UNIV OF CALIFORNIA, LOS ANGELE 405 HILGARD AVE LOS ANGELES, CA 90024-1406 Neurochemical anatomy of epilepsy
R01NS-29234-01 (NEUC) GRIFFIN, DIANE E JOHNS HOPKINS UNIVERSITY MEYER 6-181 BALTIMORE, MD 21205 Inflammation in alphavirus encephalitis
R55NS-29255-01 (NEUB) SCHWARTZ, JAMES H RESEARCH FOUNDATION/MNTL HYGIE 722 WEST 168TH STREET NEW YORK, NY 10032 Protein kinases -- Molecular roles in producing behavior
R01NS-29261-01 (NEUB) KUROSKY, ALEXANDER UNIV OF TEXAS MEDICAL BRANCH GALVESTON, TX 77550 A prohormone processing model in aplysia
R01NS-29265-01 (NEUA) SHINNICK-GALLAGHER, PATRICIA UNIVERSITY OF TEXAS MED BRANCH 301 UNIVERSITY BLVD, J-31 GALVESTON, TX 77550 CRF in the amygdala and--Electrophysiology and pharmacology
R01NS-29267-01 (SRC) YOUNG, HAROLD F VIRGINIA COMMONWEALTH UNIV DIV/NEUROLOGICAL SURGERY RICHMOND, VA 23298-0678 Improving outcome in severe head injury--PEG-SOD trial
R01NS-29276-01A1 (NEUB) GIESLER, GLENN J, JR UNIVERSITY OF MINNESOTA 321 CHURCH ST SE MINNEAPOLIS, MN 55455 Pelvic information and spinohypothalamic tract neurons
R55NS-29277-01A1 (NEUB) VOGEL, MICHAEL W MARYLAND PSYCHIATRIC RES CENTE PO BOX 21247 BALTIMORE, MD 21228 Role of synaptic activity in cerebellar development
R01NS-29278-01 (NLS) UEDA, TETSUFUMI UNIVERSITY OF MICHIGAN 205 ZINA PITCHER PLACE ANN ARBOR, MI 48109-0720 Mechanism of amino acid neurotransmitter release
R29NS-29283-01 (PTHA) TRIARHOU, LAZAROS C INDIANA UNIV SCHOOL OF MEDICIN 635 BARNHILL DRIVE INDIANAPOLIS, IN 46202-5120 Dopamine neuron grafts in genetic extrapyramidal disease
R29NS-29286-01 (CMS) SLOWIACZEK, LOUISA M STATE UNIVERSITY OF NEW YORK ALBANY, NY 12222 Phonological, orthographic and prosodic cues
R43NS-29298-01 (SSS) ALOSACHIE, IYAD J SPECIALTY LABORATORIES INC 2211 MICHIGAN AVENUE SANTA MONICA, CA 90404-3900 Specific immunoassay for the beta-2 adrenergic receptor
R43NS-29300-01 (SSS) RAMACHANDRAN, JANAKIRAMAN NEUREX CORPORATION 3760 HAVEN AVENUE MENLO PARK, CA 94025 Isolation of neuronal voltage sensitive calcium channels
R43NS-29301-01A1 (BPO) ELLIOTT, WILLIAM C FRONTIER TECHNOLOGY INC 530 E MONTECITO STREET SANTA BARBARA, CA 93103 Resettable-pressure hydrocephalic shunt w/remote readout
R43NS-29311-02 (BPO) WESTENSKOW, DWAYNE R ROCKY MOUNTAIN RESEARCH, INC 2715 EAST 3300 SOUTH SALT LAKE CITY, UT 84109 A neuromuscular blockade monitor using piezoelectric motion sensor
R43NS-29316-01 (SSS) SONES, WILLIAM MEDICAL MEASUREMENTS INC 53 MAIN STREET HACKENSACK, NJ 07601 Non-invasive intracranial pressure measurement in the newborn
R43NS-29317-01 (SB) STOLLER, HAROLD M 100 VIA FLORENCE NEWPORT BEACH, CA 92663 Sol-gel coating for protection of implant devices
R01NS-29320-01 (ARRG) ZIEGLER, RICHARD J UNIVERSITY OF MINNESOTA 10 UNIVERSITY DRIVE DULUTH, MN 55812 HIV gp120 effects on neurotransmission
R01NS-29331-01 (NEUA) WELSH, FRANK A UNIVERSITY OF PENNSYLVANIA 36TH & HAMILTON WALK PHILADELPHIA, PA 19104-6070 Cerebral ischemia and expression of stress genes
P01NS-29343-01 (NSPB) COHEN, JONATHAN WASHINGTON UNIVERSITY 724 SOUTH EUCLID AVENUE ST LOUIS, MO 63110 Long-term changes with neurotransmitter receptors
P01NS-29343-01 0001 (NSPB) BRIDGMAN, PAUL C Long-term changes with neurotransmitter receptors Role of 43K & associated proteins in ACh receptor clustering
P01NS-29343-01 0002 (NSPB) COHEN, JONATHAN B Long-term changes with neurotransmitter receptors Interactions between acetylcholine receptors & cytoskeleton
P01NS-29343-01 0003 (NSPB) DAW, NIGEL W Long-term changes with neurotransmitter receptors Long-term changes associated with NMDA receptors in the visual cortex
P01NS-29343-01 0004 (NSPB) KRAUSE, JAMES E Long-term changes with neurotransmitter receptors Substance P receptor reponses and desensitization mechanisms
P01NS-29343-01 0005 (NSPB) LICHTMAN, JEFF W Long-term changes with neurotransmitter receptors Monitoring changes in ACh receptors in living animals

P01NS-29343-01 0006 (NSPB) O'MALLEY, KAREN L Long-term changes with neurotransmitter receptors Effects and interactions of dopamine D2 receptors on second messenger systems

P01NS-29343-01 9001 (NSPB) BRIDGMAN, PAUL Long-term changes with neurotransmitter receptors Core--Electron microscopy

P01NS-29343-01 9002 (NSPB) LICHTMAN, JEFF W Long-term changes with neurotransmitter receptors Core--Image processing

P01NS-29343-01 9003 (NSPB) COHEN, JONATHAN Long-term changes with neurotransmitter receptors Core--Protein chemistry

R13NS-29346-01 (NSPB) FRIEDHOFF, ARNOLD J TOURETTE SYNDROME ASSOC INC 42-40 BELL BOULEVARD BAYSIDE, NY 11361 Second international scientific symposium on Tourette syndrome

R13NS-29348-01 (NSPA) GLOBUS, MORDECAI Y UNIVERSITY OF MIAMI PO BOX 016960 MIAMI, FL 33101 Symposium on role of neurotransmitters in brain injury

R01NS-29352-01A1 (IMS) WEINER, HOWARD L BRIGHAM AND WOMEN'S HOSPITAL 75 FRANCIS STREET BOSTON, MA 02115 Oral tolerance to myelin antigens in EAE

R29NS-29356-01 (NLS) MILES, KATHRYN SUNY HEALTH SCIENCES CENTER 450 CLARKSON AVE BROOKLYN, NY 11203 Regulation of acetylcholine receptor phosphorylation

R01NS-29362-01 (RNM) MARECI, THOMAS H UNIVERSITY OF FLORIDA J HILLIS MILLER HLTH CENTER GAINESVILLE, FL 32610 MRI of fetal neural grafts in injured spinal cords

R29NS-29363-01 (CMS) ALLOWAY, KEVIN D MILTON S HERSHEY MEDICAL CENTE P O BOX 850 HERSHEY, PA 17033 Somatosensory thalamocortical interactions

R01NS-29365-01 (NLS) AIZENMAN, ELIAS UNIVERSITY OF PITTSBURGH 3500 TERRACE ST PITTSBURGH, PA 15261 Redox modulation of NMDA receptors

R01NS-29367-01 (NEUC) HARTENSTEIN, VOLKER UNIVERSITY OF CALIFORNIA 405 HILGARD AVENUE LOS ANGELES, CA 90024 Analysis of Drosophila sensory neuron development

R29NS-29378-02 (NURS) ROGERS, ANN E UNIVERSITY OF MICHIGAN 400 N INGALLS BUILDING ANN ARBOR, MI 48109-0482 A nursing study of excessive sleepiness in narcolepsy

R01NS-29384-01 (NEUB) MAJZOUB, JOSEPH A CHILDREN'S HOSPITAL 300 LONGWOOD AVENUE BOSTON, MA 02115 Circadian regulation of vasopressin gene expression

R01NS-29390-01 (NEUC) FRASER, NIGEL W WISTAR INSTITUTE 36TH AND SPRUCE STREETS PHILADELPHIA, PA 19104 Gene transfer to and expression in neurons in vivo

R01NS-29400-01 (NEUC) OLSCHOWKA, JOHN A UNIV OF ROCHESTER MEDICAL CTR 601 ELMWOOD AVENUE ROCHESTER, NY 14642 Interaction of interleukin 1 with CRF neurons

R01NS-29403-01 (NEUA) ZORNOW, MARK H UNIVERSITY OF CALIFORNIA LA JOLLA, CA 92093 Neurotransmitters and brain injury

R01NS-29412-01A1 (NEUA) MUIZELAAR, J PAUL VIRGINIA COMMONWEALTH UNIV BOX 631, MCV STATION RICHMOND, VA 23298-0631 Ischemia and cerebral blood volume in human head injury

R01NS-29414-02 (SSS) REGGIA, JAMES A UNIVERSITY OF MARYLAND AV WILLIAMS BUILDING COLLEGE PARK, MD 20742 Computational models of cortical map reorganization

R01NS-29416-01 (NEUC) VANCE, JEFFERY M DUKE UNIVERSITY MED CENTER P O BOX 2900 DURHAM, NC 27710 Charcot-Marie-Tooth disease--Localization of types 1a and 2

R29NS-29420-01A1 (BPO) MARSON, LESLEY NORTHWESTERN UNIVERSITY MEDICAL SCHOOL CHICAGO, IL 60611-3008 Integration of CNS mechanisms of sexual reflexes

R01NS-29421-01 (NLS) ASWAD, DANA W UNIVERSITY OF CALIFORNIA IRVINE, CA 92717 Formation of isoaspartate in peptides and proteins

R01NS-29425-01 (NEUC) LIPKIN, WALTER I UNIVERSITY OF CALIFORNIA 148 MED SURGE I IRVINE, CA 92717 Molecular analyis of a neurotropic agent, borna virus

R29NS-29434-01 (RNM) NISHIMURA, DWIGHT G STANFORD UNIVERSITY DURAND BLDG STANFORD, CA 94305 Improved cerebrovascular magnetic resonance angiography

R01NS-29436-01 (NEUB) NUSBAUM, MICHAEL P UNIVERSITY OF ALABAMA UAB STATION BIRMINGHAM, AL 35294 Presynaptic control of neural network modulation

R01NS-29438-01 (NEUB) WESTON, JAMES A UNIVERSITY OF OREGON EUGENE, OR 97403 Fate of avian neural crest-derived neurogenic precursors

R01NS-29441-01 (NLS) HORROCKS, LLOYD A OHIO STATE UNIVERSITY 1645 NEIL AVENUE COLUMBUS, OH 43210 Mechanisms of lipase activation in Alzheimer's disease

R29NS-29458-02 (NLS) FELDMAN, PETER D LSU MEDICAL CENTER 1901 PERDIDO ST NEW ORLEANS, LA 70112-1393 Medullary raphe influences on the solitary tract nucleus

R01NS-29459-01A1 (NLS) DONG, WILLIE K UNIVERSITY OF WASHINGTON SCHOOL OF MEDICINE SEATTLE, WA 98195 Trigeminal mechanisms of nociception in parietal cortex

R01NS-29463-01 (NEUA) CHOPP, MICHAEL HENRY FORD HOSPITAL 2799 W GRAND BLVD DETROIT, MI 48202 Investigation of chronic post ischemic brain alkalosis

R01NS-29467-01 (BPO) SUTHERS, RODERICK A INDIANA UNIVERSITY BLOOMINGTON, IN 47405 Motor control in production and development of birdsong

R01NS-29469-01 (NEUA) POVLISHOCK, JOHN T VIRGINIA COMMONWEALTH UNIVERSI 1101 EAST MARSHALL STREET RICHMOND, VA 23298-0709 The role of microvascular change in brain injury

R01NS-29470-01 (NEUB) LEMOS, JOSE R WORCESTER FDN FOR EXP BIO 222 MAPLE AVENUE SHREWSBURY, MA 01545 Depolarization secretion coupling in nerve terminals

R01NS-29471-01 (NEUB) MC CARTHY, KEN D UNIVERSITY OF NORTH CAROLINA CHAPEL HILL, NC 27599-7365 Calcium in myelin producing cells

R01NS-29473-01A1 (PHRA) KIRSCH, GLENN E BAYLOR COLLEGE OF MEDICINE ONE BAYLOR PLAZA HOUSTON, TX 77030 Toxin and drug sites in cloned brain K+ channels

R01NS-29481-01 (NLS) LANGLAIS, PHILIP J SAN DIEGO STATE UNIVERSITY 5300 CAMPANILE DR SAN DIEGO, CA 92182 Excitotoxic basis of brain damage in thiamine deficiency

R01NS-29482-01 (NEUB) TURNER, DENNIS A DUKE UNIVERSITY BOX 3807 DURHAM, NC 27706 Synaptic integration and lesioning of pre-labeled grafts

PROJECT NO., ORGANIZATIONAL UNIT., INVESTIGATOR, ADDRESS, TITLE

R01NS-29504-01 (NEUA) HAAS, RICHARD H UCSD MEDICAL CENTER H-815-B 225 DICKINSON ST SAN DIEGO, CA 92103 Electron transport complexes in Parkinson's disease

R15NS-29505-01 (NLS) KOSTRZEWA, RICHARD M EAST TENNESSEE STATE UNIVERSIT P O BOX 24460A JOHNSON CITY, TN 37614 Pharmacologic study on models of tardive dyskinesia

R15NS-29509-01 (NEUB) BRODFUEHRER, PETER D BRYN MAWR COLLEGE BRYN MAWR, PA 19010-2899 Inhibitory regulation in the leech swimming

R01NS-29514-01A1 (NLS) FRIEDMAN, EITAN MEDICAL COLLEGE OF PENNSYLVANI 3200 HENRY AVNEUE PHILADELPHIA, PA 19129 Dopamine-linked phosphoinositide metabolism in brain

R15NS-29520-01 (NEUB) LINDGREN, CLARK A ALLEGHENY COLLEGE MEADVILLE, PA 16335 Presynaptic mechanisms of neurotransmitter release

R01NS-29525-01 (CTY) HOFFMAN, ERIC P UNIV OF PITTSBURG SCH OF MED AND BIOCHEMISTRY PITTSBURGH, PA 15261 Improved diagnosis of the muscular dystrophies

R01NS-29536-01 (ARR) PERDUE, MARY H MCMASTER UNIVERSITY 1200 MAIN STREET WEST HAMILTON, ONTARIO L8N 3Z5 CANA Effects of conditioning on mucosal immunophysiology

R01NS-29540-01 (NEUA) PAPANICOLAOU, ANDREW C UNIV OF TEXAS MEDICAL BRANCH 301 UNIVERSITY BOULEVARD GALVESTON, TX 77550 Characterization of the P3 source using MEG, EEG and MRI

R01NS-29549-01 (NEUA) PECKHAM, PAUL H CASE WESTERN RESERVE UNIV 2040 ADELBERT ROAD CLEVELAND, OHIO 44106 Multichannel implantable system for neural control

R15NS-29555-01 (NEUB) WATSON, WINSOR H, III UNIVERSITY OF NEW HAMPSHIRE DURHAM, NH 03824 Neuronal basis of swallowing behavior

R01NS-29561-01 (CMS) NEVILLE, HELEN J SALK INSTITUTE P O BOX 85800 SAN DIEGO, CA 92138 Neurobiology of language acquisition

R15NS-29566-01 (CMS) FISH, STEPHEN E MARSHALL UNIVERSITY 1542 SPRING VALLEY DR HUNTINGTON, WV 25755-9350 Evolution of neurosensory mechanisms

R55NS-29567-01 (NLS) KAJANDER, KEITH C UNIVERSITY OF MINNESOTA 515 DELAWARE ST SE MINNEAPOLIS, MN 55455 Evaluation of an experimental model of neuropathic pain

R15NS-29570-01 (NLS) ONO, JOYCE K CALIFORNIA STATE UNIVERSITY FULLERTON, CA 92634 Expression of neurotransmitter receptors

R01NS-29573-01A1 (NLS) WINOKUR, ANDREW UNIV OF PENNSYLVANIA 422 CURRIE BLVD PHILADELPHIA, PA 19104-6141 TRH in limbic system--Regulation and function

R55NS-29574-01 (BPO) HOPKINS, WILLIAM D EMORY UNIVERSITY YERKES REG PRIMATE RESEARCH CT ATLANTA, GA 30322 Laterality and cognition in nonhumans

R55NS-29582-01 (NEUC) BOTHWELL, MARK A UNIVERSITY OF WASHINGTON SEATTLE, WA 98195 Fibroblast growth factors in neural development

R43NS-29598-01 (BPO) YANG, XIAOWEI MULTICHANNEL CONCEPTS INC 13904 GREY COLT DRIVE GAITHERSBURG, MD 20878 Development of an automated neural spike discriminator

R43NS-29601-01 (BPO) BURBAUM, BEVERLY W ALKERMES, INC 26 LANDSDOWNE STREET CAMBRIDGE, MA 02139 Delivery of nerve growth factor to the brain

R01NS-29603-01 (ARRC) AKSAMIT, ALLEN J MAYO FOUNDATION 200 FIRST ST SOUTHWEST ROCHESTER, MN 55905 JC virus DNA in spinal fluid of PML-AIDS patients

R01NS-29611-01 (ARRC) MORROW, JON S YALE UNIVERSITY 310 CEDAR STREET NEW HAVEN, CT 06510 Mechanism of neuronal skeletal injury in AIDS dementia

R01NS-29613-01 (HAR) MOREST, D KENT UNIV OF CONNECTICUT HLTH CENTE 263 FARMINGTON AVE FARMINGTON, CT 06032 Inner ear and central auditory development

R13NS-29614-01 (NSPA) SEIL, FREDRICK J VA MEDICAL CENTER PORTLAND, OR 97201 International symposium on neural regeneration

R13NS-29616-01 (NSPB) ZIGMOND, RICHARD E CASE WESTERN RESERVE UNIVERSIT 2119 ABINGTON RD CLEVELAND, OH 44106 1991 Gordon Research Conference on Neural Plasticity

R01NS-29621-01 (SSS) SISKEN, BETTY F UNIVERSITY OF KENTUCKY LEXINGTON, KY 40506 Electromagnetic field stimulation of nerve regeneration

R29NS-29623-01 (NEUC) FFRENCH-CONSTANT, RICHARD H UNIVERSITY OF WISCONSIN 1630 LINDEN AVE MADISON, WI 53706 Cloning an insensitive GABA receptor in D. melanogaster

R13NS-29625-01 (NSPA) POVLISHOCK, JOHN T DEPARTMENT OF ANATOMY VIRGINIA COMMONWEALTH UNIV RICHMOND, VIRGINIA 23298-0709 Neurotrauma symposium--Strategies for neural protection

R01NS-29627-01 (SRC) GAINES, KENNETH J UNIVERSITY OF TENNESSEE 956 COURT AVE MEMPHIS, TN 38163 Southeastern consortium on racial differences in strokes

R01NS-29633-01 (PHY) THORNHILL, WILLIAM B MOUNT SINAI SCHOOL OF MEDICINE ONE GUSTAVE L LEVY PLACE NEW YORK, NY 10029 Biochemistry and cell biology of potassium channels

R01NS-29646-01 (NEUB) BRIMIJOIN, WILLIAM S MAYO FOUNDATION 200 FIRST ST, S W ROCHESTER, MN 55905 Autoimmunity to neural acetylcholinesterase

R55NS-29648-01 (NEUC) GARD, ANTHONY L UNIVERSITY OF SOUTH ALABAMA 2058 MED SCIENCES BLDG MOBILE, AL 36688 Trophic determinants of oligodendrocyte development

R01NS-29662-01 (NEUC) HIROMI, YASUSHI PRINCETON UNIVERSITY PRINCETON, NJ 08544-1014 Control of cell fates during neurogenesis

R01NS-29664-01 (NLS) MOCCHETTI, ITALO GEORGETOWN UNIVERSITY 3900 RESERVOIR RD, NW WASHINGTON, DC 20007 Pharmacological regulation of NGF biosynthesis

R29NS-29668-01 (NEUA) ILYAS, AMJAD A UMDNJ-NEW JERSEY MED SCHOOL 185 SOUTH ORANGE AVENUE NEWARK, NEW JERSEY 07103 Role of acidic glycolipids in experimental neuropathy

R01NS-29673-01 (NLS) WALLACE, BRUCE G UNIV OF COLORADO SCHOOL OF MED 4200 EAST NINTH AVE DENVER, CO 80262 Mechanisms of synapse formation

R01NS-29679-01 (NEUC) CHIKARAISHI, DONA M TUFTS UNIVERSITY 136 HARRISON AVENUE BOSTON, MA 02111 Catecholaminergic cell lines from transgenic mice

R01NS-29682-01 (NEUC) FURNEAUX, HENRY M SLOAN-KETTERING INSTITUTE 1275 YORK AVENUE NEW YORK, NY 10021 Molecular biology of antibody associated neurologic paraneoplastic syndromes

R01NS-29683-01 (NEUA) LUCAS, JEN H UNIVERSITY OF NORTH TEXAS DEPT. OF BIOLOGY DENTON, TX 76203 In vitro studies of acute phase CNS trauma interventions

R13NS-29690-01 (NSPB) OPITZ, JOHN M SHODAIR CHILDREN'S HOSPITAL P O BOX 5539, 840 HELENA AVE HELENA, MT 59604 International workshop on genetic pathology

R01NS-29693-01 (PHY) YELLEN, GARY I JOHNS HOPKINS UNIVERSITY 725 N WOLFE STREET BALTIMORE, MD 21205 Molecular physiology of potassium channels

R29NS-29695-01 (IMS) SUN, DEMING ST JUDE CHILDRENS RES HOSPITAL 332 NO LAUDERDALE MEMPHIS, TN 38105 Immunopathogenic studies on autoimmune encephalomyelitis

R01NS-29697-01 (PTHA) JAECKLE, KURT A UNIV OF UTAH HEALTH SCIENCES C 50 NORTH MEDICAL DRIVE SALT LAKE CITY, UT 84132 Paraneoplastic autoimmune neurotoxicity

R01NS-29709-01 (NEUB) NOEBELS, JEFFREY L BAYLOR COLLEGE OF MEDICINE ONE BAYLOR PLAZA HOUSTON, TX 77030 Plasticity in developing epileptic brain

R55NS-29710-01 (NEUC) TENNEKOON, GIHAN I UNIVERSITY OF MICHIGAN KRESGE II R6060 ANN ARBOR, MI 48109-0570 Studies on the regulation of myelin P2 gene

P01NS-29719-01 (NSPB) WHITAKER, JOHN N UNIV OF ALABAMA AT BIRMINGHAM UAB STATION BIRMINGHAM, AL 35294 Molecular immunopathogenesis of demyelinating disease

P01NS-29719-01 0001 (NSPB) BENVENISTE, ETTY N Molecular immunopathogenesis of demyelinating disease Regulation of IL-6 gene expression in astrocytes

P01NS-29719-01 0002 (NSPB) BARNUM, SCOTT R Molecular immunopathogenesis of demyelinating disease Production and regulation of complement by astrocytes

P01NS-29719-01 0003 (NSPB) WHITAKER, JOHN N Molecular immunopathogenesis of demyelinating disease Idiotypes and anti-idiotypes related to myelin basic protein

P01NS-29719-01 0004 (NSPB) BLALOCK, J EDWIN Molecular immunopathogenesis of demyelinating disease Molecular studies of myelin basic protein and the immunologic network

R01NS-29728-01A1 (NEUB) WATTS, ALAN G UNIV OF SOUTHERN CALIFORNIA UNIVERSITY PARK CAMPUS LOS ANGELES, CA 90089-2520 Neuropeptides and their physiological control

R29NS-29740-01 (NLS) MORTON, DAVID B UNIVERSITY OF ARIZONA 611 GOULD-SIMPSON SCIENCE BLDG TUCSON, AZ 85721 Steroid regulation of peptide sensitivity in the CNS

R01NS-29747-01 (NEUB) GUTHRIE, PETER B COLORADO STATE UNIVERSITY FORT COLLINS, CO 80523 Cytoplasmic calcium signalling transients

R01NS-29762-01 (EDC) TUHRIM, STANLEY MT SINAI SCHOOL OF MEDICINE 1 GUSTAVE L LEVY PL, BOX 1137 NEW YORK, NY 10029 MRFASS-Minorities Risk Factors And Stroke Study

R55NS-29771-01 (NEUB) MOLINARI, HELEN H ALBANY MEDICAL COLLEGE 47 NEW SCOTLAND AVENUE ALBANY, NY 12208 Dorsal column nuclei projections to the inferior olive

R01NS-29785-01 (NEUC) HUNTER, DALE D TUFTS UNIVERSITY 136 HARRISON AVENUE BOSTON, MA 02111 The role of extracellular matrix in neural development

R01NS-29793-01 (NEUC) DE LA MONTE, SUZANNE M MOLECULAR NEUROPATHOLOGY LAB 149 13TH STREET CHARLESTOWN, MA 02129 Study of Alzheimer's disease neuronal thread protein

R29NS-29804-01 (PHY) LEVITAN, EDWIN S UNIVERSITY OF PITTSBURGH PITTSBURGH, PA 15261 Regulation of pituitary ion channels

R55NS-29806-01 (NEUB) MARRION, NEIL V STATE UNIVERSITY OF NEW YORK STONY BROOK, NY 11794 Mechanisms of m-channel modulation

R55NS-29818-01 (NEUB) TRAPP, BRUCE D JOHNS HOPKINS UNIV SCH OF MED 600 N WOLFE STREET BALTIMORE, MD 21205 Cellular mechanisms of oligodendrocyte myelination

R01NS-29821-01 (MGN) ST GEORGE-HYSLOP, PETER H UNIVERSITY OF TORONTO MEDICAL SCIENCES BUILDING TORONTO, ONTARIO, M5S 1A8 Alzheimer disease--A novel strategy

R01NS-29822-01 (PTHA) GHETTI, BERNARDINO INDIANA UNIVERSITY 635 BARNHILL DRIVE INDIANAPOLIS, IN 46202-5120 Biology of hereditary PrP amyloidosis with tangles

R13NS-29824-01 (NSPB) GRODZICKER, TERRI I COLD SPRING HARBOR LABORATORY PO BOX 100 COLD SPRING HARBOR, NY 11724 Molecular neurobiology of Drosphila conference

R01NS-29826-01 (NEUC) WHITE, KALPANA P BRANDEIS UNIVERSITY BASSINE 235 WALTHAM, MA 02254 Drosophila neural homolog of amyloid protein precursor

R55NS-29843-01 (NEUB) KIRN, JOHN R ROCKEFELLER UNIVERSITY RR2, BOX 38B, TYRREL ROAD MILLBROOK, NY 12545 Neurogenesis and cell death in adult telencephalon

R29NS-29844-01 (NLS) MELLER, STEPHEN T UNIVERSITY OF IOWA BOWEN SCIENCE BUILDING IOWA CITY, IA 52242 Mechanisms of visceral pain--Heart, lungs and esophagus

R29NS-29847-01 (CMS) JACOBS, GWEN A UNIVERSITY OF CALIFORNIA BOX 6 LIFE SCIENCE ADDITION BERKELEY, CA 94720 Function and plasticity in a mapped sensory system

R01NS-29856-01 (PTHA) KULJIS, RODRIGO O UNIVERSITY OF IOWA IOWA CITY, IA 52242-1053 Chemoarchitecture of the cerebral cortex in dementia

R01NS-29857-01 (HUD) ROSS, JUDITH L MEDICAL COLLEGE OF PENNSYLVANI 3300 HENRY AVENUE PHILADELPHIA, PA 19129 Estrogen effects on cognition in Turner syndrome

R55NS-29871-01 (NLS) GRAY, RICHARD A BAYLOR COLLEGE OF MEDICINE ONE BAYLOR PLAZA, S-603 HOUSTON, TX 77030 Modulation of CA++ entry in hippocampal neurons

R01NS-29875-01 (NEUB) STEWARD, OSWALD UNIVERSITY OF VIRGINIA BOX 230 HEALTH SCIENCES CENTER CHARLOTTESVILLE, VA 22908 Regulation of astroglial gene expression

R01NS-29879-01 (CMS) WEINBERG, RICHARD J UNIVERSITY OF NORTH CAROLINA CHAPEL HILL, NC 27599 Cortical columns and transmitters

R01NS-29881-01 (NLS) PALLOTTA, BARRY S UNIVERSITY OF NORTH CAROLINA CB# 7365, FAC LAB OFFICE BLDG CHAPEL HILL, NC 27599-7365 Activation and desensitization of NMDA receptors

R29NS-29893-01 (MGN) CHATKUPT, SANSNEE UMDNJ-NEW JERSEY MEDICAL SCHOO 185 SOUTH ORANGE AVENUE NEWARK, NJ 07103-2714 Mapping susceptibility gene loci for neural defects

R43NS-29906-01 (SSS) KARBON, EDWARD W, JR NOVA PHARMACEUTICAL CORP 6200 FREEPORT CENTRE BALTIMORE, MD 21224 Characterization of kainate and AMPA receptor antagonist

R43NS-29907-01 (SSS) KNAPP, ANDREW G CAMBRIDGE NEUROSCIENCE RES, IN ONE KENDALL SQUARE CAMBRIDGE, MA 02139 Neuroprotective antagonists of kainate neurotoxicity

R43NS-29908-01 (BPO) MARANGOS, PAUL J NEUROTHERAPEUTIC CORP. SUITE H SAN DIEGO, CA 92121 Novel neuroprotective agents

R43NS-29914-01 (BPO) WUJEK, JEROME R GLIATECH INC 23420 COMMERCE PARK RD BEACHWOOD, OH 44122 An artificial nerve graft for peripheral nerve repair

R43NS-29918-01 (SSS) FRIEDMAN, KAREN LEE AXONIX INCORPORATED 136 SHORE DRIVE BURR RIDGE, IL 60521 Stroke rehabilitation device

R01NS-29919-01 (ARRG) MILLER, BRUCE L UCLA-HARBOR MEDICAL CENTER 1000 W CARSON STREET TORRANCE, CA 90509 Analysis of brain masses in AIDS using NMR spectroscopy

R01NS-29926-01 (HUD) GERNSBACHER, MORTON A UNIVERSITY OF OREGON EUGENE, OR 97403-1227 Language comprehension as structure building

R55NS-29951-01A1 (NLS) ABRAMSON, STEWART N UNIVERSITY OF PITTSBURGH PITTSBURGH, PA 15261 Structure and pharmacology of cholinergic proteins

R29NS-29955-01 (PTHA) HUMPHREY, PETER A DUKE UNIVERSITY MEDICAL CENTER BOX 3156 DURHAM, NC 27710 Deletion mutant EGF receptors in malignant human gliomas

R29NS-29970-01 (NLS) LOOSE, MICHAEL D OBERLIN COLLEGE OBERLIN, OH 44074 The LHRH pulse generator--Electrical effects of LHRH

R01NS-29971-01 (NEUC) TRUMAN, JAMES W UNIVERSITY OF WASHINGTON SEATTLE, WA 98195 Steroid receptors and CNS development

R13NS-29978-01 (NSPA) WELCH, KENNETH M HENRY FORD HOSPITAL 2799 W GRAND BLVD DETROIT, MI 48202 18th Princeton conference on cerebrovascular disease

R29NS-30000-01 (NLS) WILLIAMS, KEITH UNIV OF PENNSYLVANIA 163 JOHN MORGAN BLDG PHILADELPHIA, PA 19104-6084 Regulation of the NMDA receptor by polyamines

R29NS-30012-01 (NEUA) WILLIAMSON, ANNE 333 CEDAR STREET NEW HAVEN, CT 06510 Electrophysiology of dentate gyrus

R01NS-30025-01 (PTHA) GEORGE, DONNA L UNIV OF PENNSYLVANIA 475 CLINICAL RES BLDG PHILADELPHIA, PA 19104-6145 Etiology and pathobiology of meningiomas

R01NS-30029-14 (NEUA) RITTER, WALTER P ALBERT EINSTEIN COLLEGE OF MED 1410 PELHAM PWY SOUTH BRONX, N Y 10461 Electrophysiological correlates of cognitive processes

R01NS-30054-01 (NEUC) TAMANOI, FUYUHIKO UNIVERSITY OF CHICAGO 920 EAST 58TH STREET CHICAGO, IL 60637 Characterization of neurofibromatosis type I gene product

R01NS-30091-01 (NEUA) GHOSH, SANTIBRATA NORTHWESTERN UNIVERSITY 303 E CHICAGO AVE CHICAGO, IL 60611 Control of calcium flux in cerebral ischemia and aging

R01NS-30108-01 (PHRA) SLATTERY, JOHN T UNIVERSITY OF WASHINGTON MAIL STOP BG-20 SEATTLE, WA 98195 Mechanism of carbamazepine induced teratogenicity

S15NS-30110-01 (NSS) FAN, HUNG Y UNIV OF CALIFORNIA, IRVINE STEINHAUS HALL IRVINE, CA 92717 Small instrumentation grant

S15NS-30111-01 (NSS) STANDAERT, FRANK G MEDICAL COLLEGE OF OHIO PO BOX 10008 TOLEDO, OH 43699 Small instrumentation grant

S15NS-30112-01 (NSS) ABELL, CREED W UNIVERSITY OF TEXAS COLLEGE OF PHARMACY AUSTIN, TX 78712 Small instrumentation grant

S15NS-30113-01 (NSS) MC CLUER, ROBERT H EUNICE KENNEDY SHRIVER CENTER 200 TRAPELO ROAD WALTHAM, MA 02254 Small instrumentation grant

S15NS-30114-01 (NSS) RASH, JOHN E COLORADO STATE UNIVERSITY FORT COLLINS, CO 80523 Small instrumentation grant

S15NS-30115-01 (NSS) SPITZER, JOHN J LSU MEDICAL CENTER 1100 FLORIDA AVE NEW ORLEANS, LA 70119 Small instrumentation grant

S15NS-30116-01 (NSS) FREEDMAN, DANIEL X UNIVERSITY OF CALIFORNIA 760 WESTWOOD PLAZA LOS ANGELES, CA 90024-1759 Small instrumentation grant

S15NS-30117-01 (NSS) BAUMSTARK, ALFONS L GEORGIA STATE UNIVERSITY ATLANTA, GA 30303 Small instrumentation grant

S15NS-30118-01 (NSS) LOWERY, BARBARA J UNIVERSITY OF PENNSYLVANIA NURSING EDUCATION BLDG PHILADELPHIA, PA 19104-6096 Small instrumentation grant

S15NS-30119-01 (NSS) KENDALL, JOHN W OREGON HEALTH SCIENCES UNIV 3181 SW SAM JACKSON PARK RD PORTLAND, OR 97201-3098 Small instrumentation grant

S15NS-30120-01 (NSS) BUCHANAN, JAMES T MARQUETTE UNIVERSITY 530 NORTH 15TH STREET MILWAUKEE, WI 53233-2274 Small instrumentation grant

S15NS-30121-01 (NSS) MESSER, WILLIAM S, JR UNIVERSITY OF TOLEDO 2801 W BANCROFT STREET TOLEDO, OH 43606 Small instrumentation grant

S15NS-30122-01 (NSS) KELSO, J A FLORIDA ATLANTIC UNIVERSITY 500 NW 20TH STREET PO BOX 3019 BOCA RATON, FL 33431 Small instrumentation grant

S15NS-30123-01 (NSS) JESTEADT, WALT BOYS TOWN NATIONAL RES HOSP 555 NORTH 30TH STREET OMAHA, NE 68131 Small instrumentation grant

S15NS-30124-01 (NSS) BEAUCHAMP, GARY K MONELL CHEMICAL SENSES CENTER 3500 MARKET STREET PHILADELPHIA, PA 19104 Small instrumentation grant

S15NS-30125-01 (NSS) REVOILE, SALLY G GALLAUDET UNIVERSITY 800 FLORIDA AVENUE, NE WASHINGTON, DC 20002 Small instrumentation grant

S15NS-30126-01 (NSS) REDBURN, DIANNA A UNIV OF TEXAS MEDICAL SCHOOL 6431 FANNIN ST PO BOX 20708 HOUSTON, TX 77225 Small instrumentation grant

S15NS-30127-01 (NSS) SETLOW, RICHARD B BROOKHAVEN NATIONAL LABORATORY UPTON, NY 11973 Small instrumentation grant

S15NS-30128-01 (NSS) WESTHEAD, EDWARD W UNIVERSITY OF MASSACHUSETTS 435 MORRILL NORTH AMHERST, MA 01003 Small instrumentation grant

S15NS-30129-01 (NSS) BARNES, CHARLES D WASHINGTON STATE

UNIVERSITY 205 WEGNER HALL PULLMAN, WA 99164-6520 Small instrumentation grant

S15NS-30130-01 (NSS) DAVIDSON, NORMAN R CALIFORNIA INSTITUTE OF TECH 1201 E CALIFORNIA BLVD PASADENA, CA 91125 Small instrumentation grant

S15NS-30131-01 (NSS) GEOFFRION, CHARLES A UNIVERSITY OF ARIZONA TUCSON, AZ 85721 Small instrumentation grant

S15NS-30132-01 (NSS) BLIGHT, ANDREW R PURDUE UNIVERSITY SCH/VET MED CENTER FOR PARALYSIS RESEARCH WEST LAFAYETTE, IN 47907 Small instrumentation grant

S15NS-30133-01 (NSS) STEIN, DONALD G GRADUATE SCHOOL-NEWARK 360 MARTIN LUTHER KING JR BLVD NEWARK, NJ 07102 Small instrumentation grant

S15NS-30134-01 (NSS) PINGS, CORNELIUS J UNIV OF SOUTHERN CALIFORNIA UNIVERSITY PARK ADM 101 LOS ANGELES, CA 90089-4019 Small instrumentation grant

R01NS-30140-01 (SSS) SHIROMANI, PRIYATTAM J VA MEDICAL CENTER 940 BELMONT STREET BROCKTON, MA 02401 Brainstem cholinergic mechanisms in narcolepsy

R13NS-30146-01 (SRC) LAMARRE, YVES UNIVERSITE DE MONTREAL C. P. 6128 SUCCURSALE A MONTREAL, QUEBEC, CANADA H3C 3 Enhancement and inhibition of axonal growth

R01NS-30148-01 (SRC) DICE, JAMES F, JR TUFTS UNIV 136 HARRISON AVE BOSTON, MA 02111 Lysosomal ATP synthase subunit 9 in Batten disease

R01NS-30152-01 (SRC) BREUNING, MARTIN H LEIDEN UNIVERSITY WASSENAARSEWEG 72 AL LEIDEN, NETHERLANDS 2333 Search for the Batten disease gene on chromosome 16

R01NS-30153-01 (SRC) BRONSON, RODERICK T THE JACKSON LABORATORY 600 MAIN ST BAR HARBOR, ME 04609-0800 Models of neuronal ceroid lipofuscinosis

R01NS-30155-01 (SRC) KATZ, MARTIN L UNIVERSITY OF MISSOURI SCHOOL OF MEDICINE COLUMBIA, MO 65212 Protein methylation in hereditary ceroid-lipofuscinosis

R01NS-30161-01 (SRC) DUNN, WILLIAM A, JR UNIVERSITY OF FLORIDA PO BOX J-235 JHMHC GAINESVILLE, FL 32610 Autophagy in glia and neurons

R29NS-30194-01 (HAR) NEW, JOHN G LOYOLA UNIVERSITY 6525 NORTH SHERIDAN RD CHICAGO, IL 60626 Central electrosensory processing

R01NS-30219-01 (NLS) ALGER, BRADLEY E UNIV OF MD AT BALTIMORE 655 W BALTIMORE ST BALTIMORE, MD 21201 Regulation of inhibition in the hippocampus

R01NS-30243-01 (NLS) GARDNER, PAUL D DARTMOUTH MEDICAL SCHOOL DARTMOUTH MEDICAL SCHOOL HANOVER, NH 03756 Molecular analysis of neuronal ACh receptor expression

R01NS-30248-01 (NEUA) SPRINGER, JOE E HAHNEMANN UNIVERSITY BROAD AND VINE PHILADELPHIA, PA 19102 Neuronal plasticity in amyotrophic lateral sclerosis spinal cord neurons

R29NS-30255-01 (NEUC) PERRONE-BIZZOZERO, NORA I UNIVERSITY OF NEW MEXICO 915 STANFORD NE ALBUQUERQUE, NM 87131 Mechanisms of control of the GAP-43 gene

R29NS-30256-01 (PYB) IVRY, RICHARD UNIVERSITY OF CALIFORNIA TOLMAN HALL BERKELEY, CA 94720 Psychological and neural mechanisms of timing

S15NS-30289-01 (NSS) FERSTL, SONDRA M TEXAS WOMEN'S UNIVERSITY PO BOX 22939 DENTON, TX 76204-0939 Small instrumentation grant

P50NS-30291-01 (SRC) GINSBERG, MYRON D UNIV MIAMI SCHOOL OF MEDICINE PO BOX 016960 MIAMI, FL 33101 Neurotrauma clinical research center

P50NS-30291-01 0004 (SRC) STERNAU, LINDA L Neurotrauma clinical research center Human brain temperature following head injury

P50NS-30291-01 9001 (SRC) STITT, FRANK W Neurotrauma clinical research center Core--Clinical epidemiology and biostatistics

P50NS-30291-01 0001 (SRC) GLOBUS, MORDECAI Y T Neurotrauma clinical research center Hippocampal synaptic function following percussive head injury

P50NS-30291-01 0002 (SRC) DIETRICH, W DALTON Neurotrauma clinical research center Importance of brain temperature in traumatic brain injury

P50NS-30291-01 0003 (SRC) NORENBERG, MICHAEL D Neurotrauma clinical research center Astrocyte swelling in acute CNS trauma--Role of Calcium and protein kinases

P20NS-30295-01 (SRC) RYMER, WILLIAM Z 345 E SUPERIOR CHICAGO, IL 60611 Pharmacological interventions in spinal cord injury

P20NS-30295-01 0001 (SRC) RYMER, WILLIAM Z Pharmacological interventions in spinal cord injury Incomplete spinal cord injury reflex disturbance--Drug intervention

P20NS-30295-01 0002 (SRC) MORRISON, SHAUN Pharmacological interventions in spinal cord injury Inhibition of spinal sympathetic reflexes

P20NS-30295-01 0003 (SRC) MCKENNA, KEVIN E Pharmacological interventions in spinal cord injury Drug treatment of infertility following spinal cord injury

P20NS-30295-01 0004 (SRC) ISAAC, LAWRENCE Pharmacological interventions in spinal cord injury Drugs limiting excitotoxicity

P20NS-30295-01 9001 (SRC) RYMER, WILLIAM Z Pharmacological interventions in spinal cord injury Training core

P20NS-30303-01 (SRC) KIMELBERG, HAROLD K ALBANY MEDICAL COLLEGE 47 NEW SCOTLAND AVENUE ALBANY, NY 12208 Neural injury and blood flow alteration after CNS trauma

P20NS-30303-01 0001 (SRC) KIMELBERG, HAROLD K Neural injury and blood flow alteration after CNS trauma Release of excitotoxin and vasoactive agent from astrocytes

P20NS-30303-01 0002 (SRC) FEUSTEL, PAUL J Neural injury and blood flow alteration after CNS trauma Mechanism of injury and ATI protection

P20NS-30303-01 0003 (SRC) FORTUNE, JOHN B Neural injury and blood flow alteration after CNS trauma Brain oxygenation by continuous jugular venous oximetry

P20NS-30303-01 9001 (SRC) STRATTON, HAROLD H Neural injury and blood flow alteration after CNS trauma Core -- Database and statistics

P20NS-30309-01 (SRC) RANSOHOFF, JOSEPH NEW YORK UNIVERSITY MED CTR 550 FIRST AVE NEW YORK, N Y 10016 Head injury--Basic mechanisms/neurobehavioral outcome

P20NS-30309-01 0001 (SRC) CHESLER, MITCHELL Head injury--Basic mechanisms/neurobehavioral outcome Role of ions in secondary brain injury

P20NS-30309-01 0002 (SRC) LEE, MATTHEW Head injury--Basic mechanisms/neurobehavioral outcome Outpatient brain injury rehabilitation

P20NS-30309-01 9001 (SRC) KAY, THOMAS Head injury--Basic mechanisms/neurobehavioral outcome Core--Epidemiology and biostatistics

P20NS-30318-01 (SRC) MARION, DONALD W PRESBYTERIAN-UNIVERSITY HOSPIT 230 LOTHROP STREET PITTSBURGH, PA 15213 Hypothermia and traumatic brain injury

P20NS-30318-01 0001 (SRC) MARION, DONALD W Hypothermia and traumatic brain injury Moderate hypotermia for severe head injury

P20NS-30318-01 0002 (SRC) OBRIST, WALTER D Hypothermia and traumatic brain injury Time course for cerebral vascular and metabolic changes after head injury

P20NS-30318-01 0003 (SRC) PALMER, ALAN M Hypothermia and traumatic brain injury NMDA receptor in head injury -- Hypothermia

P20NS-30318-01 0004 (SRC) DEKOSKY, STEVEN T Hypothermia and traumatic brain injury Cytokines and neurotrophic responses in head injuries

P20NS-30318-01 0005 (SRC) MARION, DONALD W Hypothermia and traumatic brain injury Treatment of blunt head injury with hypothermia and high dose steroids

P20NS-30318-01 0006 (SRC) SAFAR, PETER Hypothermia and traumatic brain injury Resuscitative hypothermia in a dog epidural compression model of head injury

P20NS-30318-01 9001 (SRC) SCLABASSI, ROBERT J Hypothermia and traumatic brain injury Core -- Data acquisition and biostatistics analysis

P20NS-30318-01 9002 (SRC) DARBY, JOSEPH M Hypothermia and traumatic brain injury Core -- Critical care/outcome

P20NS-30322-01 (SRC) ROCKSWOLD, GAYLAN L HENNEPIN COUNTY MEDICAL CENTER 701 PARK AVENUE SOUTH MINNEAPOLIS, MN 55415 Evaluation of hyperbaric oxygen in head injury

P20NS-30322-01 0001 (SRC) BERGMAN, THOMAS A Evaluation of hyperbaric oxygen in head injury Hyperbaric oxygen therapy in head injury--Optimal dosing schedule

P20NS-30322-01 0002 (SRC) BIROS, MICHELLE H Evaluation of hyperbaric oxygen in head injury 21-aminosteroid U74006F & hyperbaric oxygen effect after head trauma

P20NS-30322-01 0003 (SRC) ROCKSWOLD, GAYLAN L Evaluation of hyperbaric oxygen in head injury: Hyperbaric oxygen therapy & 21-aminosteroid U74006F effect in brain injury

P20NS-30322-01 9001 (SRC) BIROS, MICHELLE H Evaluation of hyperbaric oxygen in head injury Core--Facility

P20NS-30322-01 9002 (SRC) PHELEY, ALFRED Evaluation of hyperbaric oxygen in head injury Core--Epidemiology and biostatistics

P20NS-30324-01 (SRC) SHACKFORD, STEVEN R UNIVERSITY OF VERMONT FLETCHER HOUSE 301, MCHV BURLINGTON, VT 05401 Pathogenesis of secondary brain injury

P20NS-30324-01 0001 (SRC) SHACKFORD, STEVEN R Pathogenesis of secondary brain injury Pial arteriolar response to injury and hemorrhage

P20NS-30324-01 0002 (SRC) SHATOS, MARIE Pathogenesis of secondary brain injury Cerebrovascular endothelial cell dysfunction--Role of trauma

P20NS-30324-01 0003 (SRC) PENAR, PAUL L Pathogenesis of secondary brain injury A computerized mathematical model of the intracranial compartment

P20NS-30324-01 0004 (SRC) GROSS, CORDELL E Pathogenesis of secondary brain injury The role of activated neutrophils in secondary brain injury

P20NS-30324-01 0005 (SRC) SHACKFORD, STEVEN R Pathogenesis of secondary brain injury Intravenous fluid tonicity, intracranial hypertension and brain injury

P20NS-30324-01 9001 (SRC) SHACKFORD, STEVEN R Pathogenesis of secondary brain injury Core--Computations

P20NS-30324-01 9002 (SRC) GROSS, CORDELL E Pathogenesis of secondary brain injury Core--Animal surgery and maintenance

R01NS-30337-01 (SRC) CHOI, DENNIS W WASHINGTON UNIV MED SCHOOL 660 S EUCLID AVE BOX 8111 ST LOUIS, MO 63110 Glutamate neurotoxicity in cortical cell culture

R01NS-30354-01 (SRC) SIEGFRIED, JOHN B PENNSYLVANIA COLL OF OPTOMETRY 1200 WEST GODFREY AVENUE PHILADELPHIA, PA 19141-3399 Visual deficits in Alzheimer's disease

R01NS-30361-01 (SRC) KISILEVSKY, ROBERT QUEEN'S UNIVERSITY KINGSTON, ONTARIO CANADA K7L 3 Beta-amyloid precursor protein:extracellular matrix component binding therapy

R01NS-30371-01 (SRC) MORENS, DAVID M UNIVERSITY OF HAWAII 1960 EAST-WEST RD HONOLULU, HI 96822 Smoking and dietary antecedents of Parkinson's disease

R01NS-30374-01 (SRC) COOK, WILLIAM J UNIVERSITY OF ALABAMA 268 BHS, THT 79 UAB STATION BIRMINGHAM, AL 35294 Structural studies of ubiquitin-mediated proteolysis

R01NS-30384-01 (SRC) COLVIN, ROBERT A OHIO UNIVERSITY ATHENS, OH 45701-2979 Na/Ca exchange, brain aging, and Alzheimer's disease

R01NS-30386-01 (BPN) JACKSON, F ROB WORCESTER FDN FOR EXPER BIO 222 MAPLE AVENUE SHREWSBURY, MA 01545 Molecular and cellular studies of neural clocks

R01NS-30400-01 (SRC) COOPER, MALCOLM UNIVERISTY OF CHICAGO 5841 S MARYLAND AVE CHICAGO, IL 60637 Localization of cerebral dysfunction in dementia (AD)

R01NS-30420-01 (SRC) STEVENS, JACK G UNIVERSITY OF CALIFORNIA 405 HILGARD AVE LOS ANGELES, CA 90024-1747 Latent herpes vectors for neurodegenerative disorders

R01NS-30426-01 (SRC) MC NEILL, THOMAS H UNIV OF SOUTHERN CALIFORNIA LOS ANGELES, CA 90089-0191 Modulation of neuronal plasticity in the hippocampus

R01NS-30428-01 (SRC) TANZI, RUDOLPH E MASS GENERAL HOSPITAL 13TH ST BLDG 149 CHARLESTOWN, MA 02129 Amyloid beta protein precursor

defects in Alzheimer's
R01NS-30451-01 (SRC) TRAPP, BRUCE D JOHNS HOPKINS UNIV SCH OF MED 600 N WOLFE STREET BALTIMORE, MD 21205 The amyloid precursor protein and amyloid accumulation
R01NS-30454-01 (SRC) LEVEY, ALLAN I JOHNS HOPKINS UNIVERSITY 600 N WOLFE ST BALTIMORE, MD 21205 Muscarinic receptor proteins in Alzheimer's disease
R01NS-30455-01 (SRC) FRANGIONE, BLAS NEW YORK UNIVERSITY MEDICAL CT 550 FIRST AVE, TH 427 NEW YORK, NY 10016 Biochemistry of Lewy bodies and gelsolin amyloid
R01NS-30457-01 (SRC) GRAMMAS, PAULA UNIVERSITY OF OKLAHOMA PO BOX 26901 OKLAHOMA CITY, OK 73190 Cerebrovascular signal pathways in aging and Alzheimer's
R01NS-30715-04 (NEUC) KAPLAN, BARRY B WESTERN PSYCHIATRIC INST & CLI 3811 O'HARA STREET PITTSBURGH, PA 15213 Studies on axonal mRNA and polyribosomes
R29NS-30759-01 (NEUB) LARSON-PRIOR, LINDA J UNIVERSITY OF CHICAGO 1025 E 5TH STREET ROOM 107 CHICAGO, IL 60637 Slow synaptic trasmission in the cerebellum
R01NS-30767-04 (NLS) LOCKARD, JOAN S UNIVERSITY OF WASHINGTON SEATTLE, WA 98195 Carbamazepine in pregnancy
R01NS-30771-04 (MGN) GORSKI, JEROME L UNIVERSITY OF MICHIGAN BOX 0688/3570 MSRB II ANN ARBOR, MI 48109-0688 Analysis & cloning of a development skin locus
N01NS-72312-02 (**) FAUGHT, R EDWARD Felbamate concentration response trial (CRT)
N01NS-72313-01 (**) DREIFUSS, FRITZ E Rectal administration of diazepam for acute repetitive seizures
N01NS-72318-02 (**) PELLOCK, JOHN M Felbamate concentration response trial (CRT)
N01NS-72321-01 (**) MATSUO, FUMISUKE Rectal administration of diazepam for acute repetitive seizures
N01NS-72326-02 (**) WRIGHT, FRANCIS S Evaluation of flunarizine in the treatment of partial seizures
N01NS-72328-03 (**) TREIMAN, DAVID M Felbamate concentration response trial (CRT)
N01NS-72330-01 (**) YERBY, MARK S Felbamate concentration response trial
N01NS-72333-01 (**) LAXER, KENNETH D Felbamate concentration response trial
N01NS-72337-02 (**) LEPPIK, ILO E Felbamate concentration response trial (CTR)
N01NS-72398-10 (**) GRIFFITH, PAMELA J Cerebrovascular clinic research data analysis
N01NS-82306-02 (**) PRIVITERA, MICHAEL D Remacemide inpatient seizure evaluation trial
N01NS-82316-04 (**) OSHENOFF, MORRILL, R Toxicology of anticonvulsant drugs
N01NS-92325-04 (**) LAKE, WILLIAM H Biomedical research data management support
N01NS-92326-03 (**) AGNEW, WILLIAM F Development and evaluation of safe methods
N01NS-92327-03 (**) SCHULMAN, JOSEPH H Microstimulator for functional neuromuscular stimulator
N01NS-92328-05 (**) SWINYARD, EWART, A Early evaluation of anticonvulsant drugs
N01NS-92355-02 (**) NEUMAN, MICHAEL R Prosthetic sensory transducers
N01NS-92356-03 (**) CRAGO, PATRICK E Neuromuscular stimulation for restoration of hand grasp
N01NS-92358-04 (**) FURBISH, SCOTT F Preparation and delivery of homogeneous ceramidetrihexosidase
N01NS-92359-03 (**) WISE, KENSALL D Stimulating electrodes base on thin film technology
N01NS-92360-02 (**) FURBISH, F S Preparation and delivery of sphinomyelinase from human placenta
N01NS-92365-04 (**) FURBISH, F SCOTT Preparation and delivery of homogeneous glucocerebrosidase
N01NS-92366-03 (**) ROPPOLO, JAMES R Microstimulation of the sacral spinal cord
N01NS-92367-02 (**) MALLORY, BRENDA Microstimulation of the sacral spinal cord
N01OD-02108-04 (**) NOZICKA, GEORGE J Database development and analytical support for Office of the Director
N01OD-02135-04 (**) MAUST, ANN P Evaluation of needs, barriers and perceptions of training
N01OD-12100-00 (**) FRIEDMAN, DAVID Survey services for the federal health R&D and case surveys
N01OD-12105-00 (**) BELL, JAMES Federal demonstration project and authority within NIH and its research community
N01OD-12109-00 (**) WU, HO-I Technical and support services to the NIH for SBIR program
N01OD-62107-27 (**) KINNEY, ROLAND W Research associates program in biotechnology
N01OD-72108-07 (**) JOLLY, PAUL Acquisition of computerized data
N01OD-92111-11 (**) MULLINS, DON J Technical support services--Research, devel. in tech. assessment and transfer
N01OD-92119-06 (**) WEISS, ROBIN Assessment of the NIH AIDS research program
K01OH-00060-04 (SOH) MURLAS, CHRISTOPHER G RUS/PRESBYTER-ST LUKE'S MED 1653 W CONGRESS PARKWAY CHICAGO, IL 60612 Pharmacomechanical hyperresponsiveness in airway injury
K01OH-00073-03 (SOH) BERNSTEIN, DAVID I UNIVERSITY OF CINCINNATI MED C 231 BETHESDA AVE. CINCINNATI, OHIO 45267-0563 Immunopathogenesis of occupational disease due to reactive chemicals
K01OH-00076-03 (SOH) BRANDT-RAUF, PAUL W COLUMBIA UNIVERSITY SCH OF PH 60 HAVEN AVENUE/B-1 LEVEL NEW YORK, NY 10032 New method for occupational cancer surveillance
K01OH-00077-03 (SOH) ZELLERS, EDWARD T U OF MICHIGAN SCH OF PUBL HLTH 109 SOUTH OBSERVATORY ANN ARBOR, MI 48109-2029 Microsensor array for identification of organic vapors
K01OH-00078-03 (SOH) CONROY, LORRAINE M UNIVERSITY OF ILLINOIS EOHS(M/C 922),BOX 6998 CHICAGO, IL 60680 Field study of local exhaust ventilation performance
K01OH-00079-02 (SOH) BLANC, PAUL D UNIV. OF CALIF. AT SF ENVIRONMENTAL MED SAN FRANCISCO, CA 94143-0924 Effects of zinc oxide welding fume inhalation
K01OH-00081-02 (SOH) LEVY, GERALD N UNIVERSITY OF MICHIGAN 6322 MEDICAL SCIENCE I BLDG ANN ARBOR, MI 48109-0626 Leukocyte DNA adducts after carcinogen exposure
K01OH-00085-02 (SOH) OESTENSTAD, RIEDAR K U. OF ALABAMA @ BIRMINGHAM UAB STATION BIRMINGHAM, AL 35294 Factors affecting respirator leak sites and shapes
K01OH-00087-02 (SOH) BREYSSE, PATRICK N JOHNS HOPKINS UNIVERSITY 615 NORTH WOLFE STREET BALTIMORE, MD 21205 Adsorption of vapor mixtures onto activated carbon
K01OH-00090-02 (SOH) WILDER, DAVID G UNIVERSITY OF VERMONT GIVEN BLDG BURLINGTON, VT 05405 Unexpected trunk loading following seated vibration
K01OH-00093-02 (SOH) SCHWARTZ, DAVID A UNIVERSITY OF IOWA PULMONARY DISEASE DIVISION IOWA CITY, IA 52242 Asbestos-induced pleural fibrosis & lung restriction
K01OH-00098-02 (SOH) GERR, FREDRIC E EMORY UNIVERSITY 1599 CLIFTON ROAD, NE ATLANTA, GA 30329 Quantitative assessment of carpal tunnel syndrome
K01OH-00103-01 (SOH) TODD, LORI A UNIVERSITY OF NORTH CAROLINA CB #7400 CHAPEL HILL, NC 27599-7400 Optical remote sensing and computed tomography
K01OH-00106-01 (SOH) SPIEGELMAN, DONNA TUFTS UNIVERSITY 136 HARRISON AVE BOSTON, MA 02111 Measurement errors in occupational epidemiology
K01OH-00107-01 (SOH) RADWIN, ROBERT G UNIV OF WISCONSIN-MADISON 1513 UNIVERSITY AVE MADISON, WI 53706 Characterization of posture, force and repetitive motion
K01OH-00108-01 (SOH) KOSNETT, MICHAEL J UNIVERSITY OF CALIFORNIA, SF SFGH BLDG 30 5TH FLOOR SAN FRANCISCO, CA 94110 Vascular effects of chelation in lead exposed workers
K01OH-00110-01 (SOH) KELSEY, KARL T HARVARD SCHOOL OF PUBLIC HLTH 665 HUNTINGTON AVENUE BOSTON, MA 02115 Susceptibility to genetic damage from butadiene
R01OH-00823-11A2 (SOH) ABOU-DONIA, MOHAMED B DUKE UNIVERSITY BOX 3813 DURHAM, N C 27710 Occupational neuropathies due to industrial chemicals
R01OH-01122-09 (SOH) KAUFFMAN, CHARLES W UNIVERSITY OF MICHIGAN ANN ARBOR, MI 48109-2140 Explosion hazards related to grain and feed dusts
R01OH-01152-10A2 (SOH) HENDERSON, DONALD SUNY AT BUFFALO BUFFALO, NY 14214 The effects of impulse noise on the auditory system
R01OH-01301-08 (SOH) WILLEKE, KLAUS UNIVERSITY OF CINCINNATI 3223 EDEN AVENUE CINCINNATI, OH 45267-0056 New methods for quantitative respirator fit testing
R01OH-02067-08 (SOH) SWANSON, G MARIE MICHIGAN STATE UNIV EAST LANSING, MI 48824 Occupational cancer surveillance--New approaches
R01OH-02128-07 (HAR) CLARK, WILLIAM W CENTRAL INST FOR THE DEAF 818 SOUTH EUCLID ST LOUIS, MO 63110 Function correlates of cochlear injury
R01OH-02148-07 (SSS) CLEARY, STEPHEN F MEDICAL COLLEGE OF VIRGINIA BOX 551, MCV STATION RICHMOND, VA 23298 Effects of 27MHz radiation on somatic and germ cells
R01OH-02149-06 (SOH) ANSARI, GHULAM A S UNIVERSITY OF TEXAS MED BRANCH GALVESTON, TX 77550-2774 Plasma proteins--Markers of chemical exposure
R01OH-02221-04 (TOX) RAPPAPORT, STEPHEN M UNIVERSITY OF NORTH CAROLINA CB#7400 - CAMPUS CHAPEL HILL, NC 27599-7400 Dose/response for styrene exposures
R01OH-02277-02 (SOH) WARSHAWSKY, DAVID UNIVERSITY OF CINCINNATI 3223 EDEN AVENUE CINCINNATI, OH 45267-0056 Influence of particulates on occupational lung disease
R01OH-02317-07 (SOH) HAMERNIK, ROGER P S U N Y - AUDITORY RES LAB 107 BEAUMONT HALL PLATTSBURGH, NY 12901 Hearing hazard associated with industrial noise exposure
R01OH-02391-03 (SOH) ASAL, NABIH R UNIVERSITY OF OKLAHOMA P O BOX 26901 OKLAHOMA CITY, OKLA 73190 Hydrocarbon exposure & chronic renal disease
R01OH-02421-02A2 (SOH) CHRISTIANI, DAVID C HARVARD SCHOOL OF PUBLIC HLTH 665 HUNTINGTON AVENUE BOSTON, MA 02115 Lung disease in Chinese textile workers
R01OH-02571-04 (SOH) SCHONFELD, IRVIN THE CITY COLLEGE OF CUNY CONVENT AVENUE AT 138TH ST NEW YORK, NEW YORK 10031 Stress in one occupational group--Teachers
R01OH-02598-02 (SOH) MITCHELL, ALLEN A BOSTON UNIVERSITY 1371 BEACON ST BROOKLINE, MA 02146 Occupational exposures and birth defects
R01OH-02611-03 (SOH) BAGLEY, SUSAN T MICHIGAN TECHNOLOGICAL UNIV. 1400 TOWNSEND DR HOUGHTON, MI 49931 Relative health risks of diesel emission control systems
R01OH-02622-03 (SOH) SANTELLA, REGINA M COLUMBIA UNIVERSITY 650 WEST 168TH STREET NEW YORK, NY 10032 Biological monitoring for exposure to coal tar
R01OH-02647-01S2 (SOH) HEMSTREET, GEORGE P, III UNIVERSITY OF OKLAHOMA DEPT OF UROLOGY, PO BOX 26901 OKLAHOMA CITY, OK 73190 Biologic monitoring/risk assessment in an exposed cohort
R01OH-02663-03 (BMT) ZELLERS, EDWARD T UNIVERSITY OF MICHIGAN 109 S. OBSERVATORY ANN ARBOR, MI 48109-2029 Selective real-time detection of olefin gases and vapors
R01OH-02710-02 (SOH) FLYNN, MICHAEL R UNIVERSITY OF NORTH CAROLINA CB 7400 ROSENAU CHAPEL HILL, NC 27599-7400 Computer simulation of push-pull systems
R01OH-02717-02 (SOH) LANDRIGAN, PHILIP J MOUNT SINAI SCHOOL OF MEDICINE ONE GUSTAVE L LEVY PLACE NEW YORK, NY 10029 The health hazards of child labor
R01OH-02719-02 (SOH) ECHEVERRIA, DIANA BATTELLE MEMORIAL INSTITUTE 4000 NE 41ST STREET SEATTLE, WA 98105 Central nervous system effects of PCE exposure in humans
R01OH-02730-02 (SOH) MATANOSKI, GENEVIEVE M JOHNS HOPKINS UNIVERSITY 615 NORTH WOLFE STREET BALTIMORE, MD 21205 Case control

study of cancer in synthetic rubber worker
R01OH-02741-02 (SOH) PUNNETT, LAURA UNIVERSITY OF LOWELL ONE UNVIVERSITY AVENUE LOWELL, MA 01854 Case-control study of sawmill injuries in Maine
R01OH-02761-02 (SOH) ROBINS, THOMAS G UNIVERSITY OF MICHIGAN 1420 WASHINGTON HEIGHTS ANN ARBOR, MI 48109-2029 Coal dust particle size & respiratory disease
R03OH-02765-02 (SOH) MORGENSTERN, HAL UCLA SCHOOL OF PUBLIC HEALTH 405 HILGARD AVENUE LOS ANGELES, CA 90024 Occupational epidemiology of carpal tunnel syndrome
R01OH-02767-01A1 (EDC) WHITE, ROBERTA F BOSTON UNIV SCH OF MED 80 E CONCORD ST P801A BOSTON, MA 02118 Validity of computerized tests in occupational settings
R01OH-02772-02 (SOH) SODERHOLM, SIDNEY C UNIVERSITY OF ROCHESTER 601 ELMWOOD AVE, BOX EHSC ROCHESTER, NY 14642 Detecting lung overload by magnetometry
R43OH-02780-01A1 (SOH) JOHNSON, SAMUEL V FULL CIRCLE SYSTEMS 32 CHERRY TREE RD LOUDONVILLE, NY 12211 Full circle ergonomic auxiliary tool handle
R01OH-02792-01 (CPA) GIESE, ROGER W NORTHEASTERN UNIVERSITY 360 HUNTINGTON AVENUE BOSTON, MA 02115 Measurement of alkenyl/epoxy DNA adducts by GC-MS
R01OH-02794-01A1 (TOX) BHATTACHARYA, AMIT UNIVERSITY OF CINCINNATI 3223 EDEN AVE CINCINNATI, OH 45267-0056 Role of postural stability in industrial falls
R13OH-02795-01 (SOH) COHEN, BEVERLY S NEW YORK UNIVERSITY LONGMEADOW ROAD TUXEDO, NY 10987 International symposium on air sampling instrument performance
R01OH-02804-01 (SOH) WADDEN, RICHARD A UNIVERSITY OF ILLINOIS PO BOX 6998 CHICAGO, IL 60680 Emission factor development for workplace sources
R01OH-02820-01 (SSS) KRIEBEL, DAVID UNIVERSITY OF LOWELL ONE UNIVERSITY AVE LOWELL, MA 01854 Improved magnetic field exposure assessment
R03OH-02856-01 (SOH) FRANK, ROBERT JOHNS HOPKINS UNIVERSITY 615 NORTH WOLFE STREET BALTIMORE, MD 21205 A laboratory model of sick building syndrome
R01OH-02857-01 (SOH) SELIM, MUSTAFA I UNIVERSITY OF IOWA 137 AMRF OAKDALE CAMPUS IOWA CITY, IA 52242 Assessment of occupational exposure to aflatoxin
R01OH-02858-01 (SOH) FLYNN, MICHAEL R UNIVERSITY OF NORTH CAROLINA CB 7400 ROSENAU CHAPEL HILL, NC 27599-7400 Computational methods in industrial ventilation
R01OH-02872-01 (SOH) KRAUS, JESS F UNIVERSITY OF CALIFORNIA 10833 LE CONTE AVENUE LOS ANGELES, CA 90024-1772 Workplace assault-related injuries -- Incidence & risk
R03OH-02880-01 (SOH) KRISHNAN, SURESH P UNIV OF CINCINNATI 3223 EDEN AVE CINCINNATI, OH 45267-0056 Molecular dosimetry for carcinogens
R01OH-02885-01 (SOH) HATCH, MAUREEN C COLUMBIA UNIVERSITY 600 WEST 168TH STREET NEW YORK, NY 10032 Menstrual function and physical and mental job stress
R01OH-02904-01 (HAR) KRYTER, KARL D SAN DIEGO STATE UNIVERSITY 5300 CAMPANILE DR SAN DIEGO, CA 92182 Prediction of NIPTS, hearing impairment and handicap
R43OH-02906-01 (SOH) DRUY, MARK A FOSTER MILLER INC 350 SECOND AVE WALTHAM, MA 02154-1196 Personal benzene vapor detection device
R43OH-02907-01 (SOH) MARCUS, BETH A EXOS, INC 8 BLANCHARD RD BURLINGTON, MA 01803 Prevention of cumulative trauma disorders
R43OH-02913-01 (SOH) HYATT, DAVID E ADA TECHNOLOGIES, INC. 304 INVERNESS WAY SOUTH ENGLEWOOD, CO 80112 Development of a continuous isocyanates monitor
R03OH-02932-01 (SOH) DRUES, MICHAEL E IOWA STATE UNIVERSITY 1146 VETERINARY MEDICINE AMES, IA 50011 Transcranial Doppler as a screening procedure for exposures to toxicants
R03OH-02938-01 (SOH) BROSSEAU, LISA M UNIVERSITY OF MINNESOTA 420 DELAWARE ST SE, BOX 197 UM MINNEAPOLIS, MN 55455 Aerosol penetration behavior of respirator valves
U76PE-00032-08 (STC) WANSLEY, RICHARD A COLLEGE OF OSTEOPATHIC MEDICIN 1111 WEST 17TH STREET TULSA, OKLAHOMA 74107 Oklahoma regional area health education center program
U76PE-00035-08 (STC) FRANCIS, RUPERT A MEHARRY MEDICAL COLLEGE 1005 D.B. TODD BLVD., BOX 74-A NASHVILLE, TN 37208 Area health education center program
U76PE-00036-08 (STC) NICHOLS, ANDREW W UNIVERSITY OF ARIZONA 2501 EAST ELM STREET TUCSON, AZ 85716 Area Health Education Center Program
U76PE-00038-08 (STC) MCNEAL, MERYL MOREHOUSE SCHOOL OF MEDICINE 720 WESTVIEW DRIVE ATLANTA, GEORGIA 30310 Area health education center program
U76PE-00202-07 (STC) SWIGART, RICHARD H UNIVERSITY OF LOUISVILLE LOUISVILLE, KY 40292 Area health education center program
U76PE-00209-07 (STC) NAPOLITANO, LEONARD M UNIVERSITY OF NEW MEXICO 915 STANFORD, N.E. ALBUQUERQUE, NM 87131 Area Health Care Center program
U76PE-00211-07 (STC) ZUCKER, STEVEN B SOUTHEASTERN COLL OF OSTEO MED 1750 N E 168TH STREET NORTH MIAMI BEACH, FL 33162 Area health education center program
U76PE-00212-07 (STC) VAN CITTERS, ROBERT L UNIVERSITY OF WASHINGTON 1325 4TH AVENUE, SUITE 2000 SEATTLE, WA 98101 Area Health Education Center program
U76PE-00215-06 (STC) DAUGHERTY, ROBERT M, JR UNIVERSITY OF NEVADA SCHOOL OF MEDICINE RENO, N V 89557 Area health education center cooperative agreement
U76PE-00219-06 (STC) FOURNIER, ARTHUR M UNIVERSITY OF MIAMI P.O. BOX 016960-R103 MIAMI, FL 33101 Area health education center program
U76PE-00221-06 (STC) CRANFORD, CHARLES O UNIVERSITY OF ARKANSAS 4301 WEST MARKHAM LITTLE ROCK, AR 72205 Area health education center cooperative agreement
U76PE-00222-04 (STC) PLAUCHE, WARREN C LOUISIANA STATE UNIVERSITY 1542 TULANE AVENUE NEW ORLEANS, LOUISIANA 70112 Area health education center program
U76PE-00225-04 (STC) HEAD, JANET A KIRKSVILLE COLLEGE OF OSTEO ME 800 W JEFFERSON KIRKSVILLE, MO 63501 Area health education center
U76PE-00228-02 (STC) SUMAYA, CIRO V UNIV. OF TEXAS HSC @ SAN ANTON 7703 FLOYD CURL DRIVE SAN ANTONIO, TX 78284-7790 Lower Rio Grande/South Texas AHEC
U76PE-00229-02 (STC) REINSCHMIDT, JULIAN OREGON HEALTH SCIENCES UNIV 3181 SW SAM JACKSON PARK ROAD PORTLAND, OREGON 97201 Oregon area health education centers program
U76PE-00231-01 (STC) SCHWARTZ, FREDERIC N CHICAGO OSTEOPATHIC HEALTH SYS 5200 SOUTH ELLIS CHICAGO, ILLINOIS 60615 Area health education center
U76PE-00233-01 (STC) HARRIS, JAMES O UNIVERSITY OF FLORIDA BOX J-215, JHMHC GAINESVILLE, FL 32610 Area health education center program
U76PE-00234-01 (STC) GESSERT, CHARLES E MEDICAL COLLEGE OF WISCONSIN 8701 WATERTOWN PLANK ROAD MILWAUKEE, WISCONSIN 53226 Area health education center
U76PE-00235-01 (STC) ANDRAKO, JOHN VIRGINIA COMMONWEALTH UNIVERSI 1010 E MARSHALL STREET RICHMOND, VIRGINIA 23298 Area health education center
U76PE-00236-01 (STC) DOANE, DAVID G EAST TENNESSEE STATE UNIVERSIT BOX 21,130A JOHNSON CITY, TN 37614-0002 Area health education center
U76PE-00238-01 (NSS) BRYAN, GEORGE T UNIVERSITY OF TEXAS MED BRANCH 301 UNIVERSITY BOULEVARD GALVESTON, TX 77550 Area health education center program
U76PE-00425-02 (STC) HUDSON, JAMES I UNIVERSITY OF MARYLAND 655 W BALTIMORE STREET BALTIMORE, MD 21201 Rural training initiatives in adolescent health
U76PE-00426-02 (STC) NOTTINGHAM, LAMONT D WEST VIRGINIA UNIVERSITY 3110 MACCORKLE AVENUE, SE CHARLESTON, W VA 25304 A quality assurance and risk management training program--West Virginia
U76PE-00429-02 (STC) MORROW, LEWIS B MEDICAL COLLEGE OF OHIO P O BOX 10008 TOLEDO, OH 43699 AHEC special initiative
U76PE-00430-02 (STC) MORROW, LEWIS B MEDICAL COLLEGE OF OHIO P O BOX 10008 TOLEDO, OH 43699 AHEC special initiative - Heath care quality
U76PE-00433-02 (STC) MORROW, LEWIS B MEDICAL COLLEGE OF OHIO P O BOX 10008 TOLEDO, OH 43699 Area health education center special initiatives--Medical College of Ohio
U76PE-00434-02 (STC) WILLIAMS, HIBBARD E UNIVERSITY OF CALIFORNIA 5110 EAST CLINTON WAY, SUITE 1 FRESNO, CA 93727-2098 AHEC special initiative - DREW
U76PE-00437-02 (STC) WILLIAMS, HIBBARD E UNIVERSITY OF CALIFORNIA 5110 EAST CLINTON WAY, SUITE 1 FRESNO, CA 93727-2098 AHEC special initiative - Univ of Calif, Davis
U76PE-00438-02 (STC) WILLIAMS, HIBBARD E UNIVERSITY OF CALIFORNIA 5110 EAST CLINTON WAY, SUITE 1 FRESNO, CA 95616 AHEC special initiative - Stanford
U76PE-00441-02 (STC) HUPPERT, MICHAEL E UNIVERSITY OF MASSACHUSETTS 55 LAKE AVENUE NORTH WORCESTER, MA 01655 AHEC initiative risk management training
U76PE-00442-02 (STC) HUPPERT, MICHAEL E UNIV OF MASSACHUSETTS MED CENT 55 LAKE AVENUE NORTH WORCESTER, MA 01655 Merrimack Valley Area Health Education Center special initiatives
U76PE-00443-02 (STC) CLEGHORN, G DEAN MEDICAL UNIV OF SOUTH CAROLINA 171 ASHLEY AVENUE CHARLESTON, S C 29425 AHEC special initiative - Migrant health education
U76PE-00445-02 (STC) NICHOLS, ANDREW W ARIZONA AREA HLTH EDUC CTR 3131 E. SECOND STREET TUCSON, AZ 85716 SEAHEC initiatives
U76PE-00447-02 (STC) FRANCIS, RUPERT A MEHARRY MEDICAL COLLEGE 1005 D B TODD, JR BLVD NASHVILLE, TN 37208 AHEC special initiative
U76PE-00449-02 (STC) WANSLEY, RICHARD A OKLAHOMA STATE UNIVERSITY 1111 WEST 17TH STREET TULSA, OKLA 74107 AHEC special initiative -
U76PE-00456-02 (STC) CALL, RICHARD L UNIVERSITY OF COLORADO 4200 EAST NINTH AVENUE DENVER, COLO 80262 Quality assurance training for rural care facilities
U76PE-00462-01 (STC) MORROW, LEWIS MEDICAL COLLEGE OF OHIO P. O. BOX 10008 TOLEDO, OHIO 43699-0008 Area health education center special initiatives
U76PE-00467-01 (STC) ZUCKER, STEVEN B SOUTHEASTERN COLL OF OSTEO MED 1750 N.E. 168TH STREET NORTH MIAMI BEACH, FLA 33162 AHEC special initiatives
U76PE-00468-01 (STC) HUPPERT, MICHAEL E UNIV OF MASSACHUSETTS MED CENT 55 LAKE AVENUE NORTH WORCESTER, MA 01655 AHEC special initiatives
U76PE-00469-01 (STC) HUPPERT, MICHAEL E UNIV OF MASSACHUSETTS MED CENT 55 LAKE AVENUE NORTH WORCESTER, MA 01655 AHEC special initiatives
U76PE-00474-01 (STC) WEAVER, SHIRLEY A UNIVERSITY OF NEW ENGLAND HILLS BEACH ROAD BIDDEFORD, MAINE 04005 Ahec special initiatives
U76PE-00475-01 (STC) HUDSON, JAMES I UNIVERSITY OF MARYLAND 655 W. BALTIMORE STREET BALTIMORE, MD 21201 AHEC special initiatives
U76PE-00482-01 (STC) NICHOLS, ANDREW W UNIVERSITY OF ARIZONA 2501 E. ELM STREET TUCSON, AZ 85716 AHEC special initiatives
U76PE-00486-01 (STC) JOHNSON, JEFFREY A EASTERN VIRGINIA MEDICAL SCHOO P. O. BOX 1980 NORFOLK, VA 23501 AHEC special initiatives
U76PE-00491-01 (STC) WILLIAMS, HIBBARD E UNIVERSITY OF CALIFORNIA, DAVI 5110 EAST CLINTON WAY, SUITE 1 FRESNO, CA 93727-2098 AHEC special initiatives
R43PS-00001-01 (HUD) HILLABRANT, WALTER J SUPPORT SERVICES INC 8609 SECOND AVE STE 506 SILVER SPRING, MD 20910 HIV/AIDS educational materials for native American youth
N01RG-12113-00 (**) BELL, JAMES Electronic grant application development project eval
Z01RR-00001-21 (VR) HANSEN, C T NCRR, NIH Animal model development
M01RR-00030-30 (CLR) SNYDERMAN, RALPH J DUKE UNIVERSITY MEDICAL CENTER P O BOX 3001 DURHAM, NC 27710 General clinical research center
M01RR-00030-30 0496 (CLR) EARL, NANCY L General clinical research

PROJECT NO., ORGANIZATIONAL UNIT., INVESTIGATOR, ADDRESS, TITLE

center Efficacy of tacrine in Alzheimer's disease and dementia of the Alzheimers's type
M01RR-00030-30 0497 (CLR) FEINGLOS, MARK N General clinical research center: Liquid glyburide in predicting true secondary failures in type II diabetes
M01RR-00030-30 0498 (CLR) FEINGLOS, MARK S General clinical research center Electroseizure therapy and glucose tolerance in depression
M01RR-00030-30 0499 (CLR) ANDERSON, NORMAN B General clinical research center Dietary sodium, race, and cardiovascular response to stress
M01RR-00030-30 0265 (CLR) CHEN, YUAN T. General clinical research center Glycogen storage disease--Biochemical diagnosis, progression and therapy
M01RR-00030-30 0266 (CLR) DREZNER, MARC K General clinical research center Hereditary osteomalacia
M01RR-00030-30 0295 (CLR) BELL, DIANNE Y General clinical research center Bronchoalveolar lavage in interstitial lung disease
M01RR-00030-30 0297 (CLR) PRITCHETT, EDWARD L General clinical research center Mechanism and behavior of symptomatic tachycardia
M01RR-00030-30 0352 (CLR) ROE, CHARLES R General clinical research center L-Carnitine in amino acid and fat metabolism
M01RR-00030-30 0353 (CLR) POLISSON, RICHARD P General clinical research center Early undifferentiated connective tissue disease
M01RR-00030-30 0367 (CLR) OLSEN, ELISE A General clinical research center Recombinant leukocyte alpha interferon for cutaneous T-cell lymphoma
M01RR-00030-30 0370 (CLR) ROCKWELL, KENNETH General clinical research center Vasopressin response to hypertonic saline in anorectics and bulimics
M01RR-00030-30 0376 (CLR) COBB, FREDERICK R General clinical research center Exercise training in left ventricular dysfunction
M01RR-00030-30 0384 (CLR) MEYERS, WILLIAM C General clinical research center Biliary secretion in biliary fistula and liver transplant
M01RR-00030-30 0388 (CLR) SVETKEY, LAURA P General clinical research center Diagnosis and treatment of renovascular hypertension
M01RR-00030-30 0393 (CLR) DURACK, DAVID General clinical research center Placebo controlled trial of AZT in AIDS & AIDS related complex
M01RR-00030-30 0500 (CLR) SCHOLD, STANLEY C General clinical research center Intrathecal monoclonal antibody fragment Mel-14 F(ab')2 for leptomeningeal tumor
M01RR-00030-30 0501 (CLR) PISETSKY, DAVID S General clinical research center Imunomodulatory effects of ANSAID and MRI scans in rheumatoid arthritis
M01RR-00030-30 0502 (CLR) FEINGLOS, MARK N General clinical research center Determining the effects of combined therapy in insulin-requiring diabetes
M01RR-00030-30 0503 (CLR) GOODWIN, SHEILA D General clinical research center TMP/SMX pharmacokinetic/pharmacodynamics in AIDS and normal volunteers
M01RR-00030-30 0504 (CLR) SURWIT, RICHARD S General clinical research center Response to neuroendocrine stress/risk for non-insulin dependent diabetes
M01RR-00030-30 0505 (CLR) COHEN, HARVEY J General clinical research center Influence of aging on polymorphic and non-polymorphic drug metabolism
M01RR-00030-30 0506 (CLR) STEEGE, JOHN F General clinical research center Psychometric predictors of response in premenstrual syndrome
M01RR-00030-30 0406 (CLR) DUNN, FREDERICK L. General clinical research center Multicenter study of lovastatin in moderate hypercholesterolemia
M01RR-00030-30 0407 (CLR) ROSES, ALLEN S. General clinical research center Alzheimer's disease research center
M01RR-00030-30 0412 (CLR) SURWIT, RICHARD S General clinical research center Behavioral treatment of diabetes mellitus
M01RR-00030-30 0415 (CLR) GRANT, JOHN P. General clinical research center: Organ function and body composition during home total parenteral nutrition
M01RR-00030-30 0436 (CLR) SVETKEY, LAURA P. General clinical research center Potassium and high blood pressure-Mechanism of action
M01RR-00030-30 0440 (CLR) BARTLETT, JOHN A General clinical research center Interleukin-2 augmentation of anti HIV immune responses
M01RR-00030-30 0441 (CLR) BUCKLEY, EDWARD G General clinical research center Multicenter trial of corticosteroid therapy in optic neuritis
M01RR-00030-30 0445 (CLR) SVETKEY, LAURA P General clinical research center Renal insufficiency hypertension--ACE inhibitor vs conventional therapy
M01RR-00030-30 0507 (CLR) BUCKLEY, CHARLES E General clinical research center Allergic reactions allegedly due to aspartame
M01RR-00030-30 0508 (CLR) BUCKLEY, REBECCA H General clinical research center Phase II trial of recombinant interleukin-2 in combined immunodeficiency
M01RR-00030-30 0509 (CLR) POLISSON, RICHARD P General clinical research center Toxicity and efficacy of rIFN-Gamma in progressive systemic sclerosis
M01RR-00030-30 0510 (CLR) POLISSON, RICHARD P General clinical research center Toxicity and efficacy of rIFN-gamma in progressive systemic sclerosis
M01RR-00030-30 0446 (CLR) TYOR, MALCOLM P General clinical research center Lovastatin in hypercholesterolemia and gallstones
M01RR-00030-30 0447 (CLR) COFFMAN, THOMAS M. General clinical research center Thromboxane synthetase inhibition of cyclosporine nephrotoxicity
M01RR-00030-30 0448 (CLR) COFFEY, CHARLES E General clinical research center Electroconvulsive therapy effects on brain function and structure
M01RR-00030-30 0450 (CLR) BLUMENTHAL, JAMES A General clinical research center Exercise and hypertension
M01RR-00030-30 0452 (CLR) ST. CLAIR, EUGENE W. General clinical research center Myocardial dysfunction in systemic lupus erythematosus

PROJECT NO., ORGANIZATIONAL UNIT., INVESTIGATOR, ADDRESS, TITLE

M01RR-00030-30 0456 (CLR) HACKEL, ANDREA J General clinical research center Autonomic cardiovascular responses in the elderly with syncope
M01RR-00030-30 0458 (CLR) SANDERS, DONALD B. General clinical research center 3,4-diaminopyridine in myasthenia gravis & Lambert-eaton Myasthenic syndrome
M01RR-00030-30 0462 (CLR) BUCKLEY, REBECCA H General clinical research center Genetically determined immunodeficiencies--Analyses of defects/therapies
M01RR-00030-30 0463 (CLR) ROSES, ALLEN D General clinical research center Genetic linkage studies in neurological disorders
M01RR-00030-30 0464 (CLR) ANDERSON, NORMAN B General clinical research center Age, race and patterns of cardiovascular/neuroendocrine stress reactivity
M01RR-00030-30 0467 (CLR) ANDERSON, NORMAN B General clinical research center Dietary sodium, race and cardiovascular responses in hypertension
M01RR-00030-30 0469 (CLR) SCHEINMAN, JON I General clinical research center Loss of kidney function in sickle cell disease
M01RR-00030-30 0472 (CLR) LYLES, KENNETH W General clinical research center Prevention of steroid-induced bone loss in chronic pulmonary disease
M01RR-00030-30 0473 (CLR) DUNN, FREDERICK L General clinical research center Implantable insulin infusion pump for type I diabetes mellitus
M01RR-00030-30 0474 (CLR) DENNIS, VINCENT W General clinical research center Effect of diet on progressive renal disease
M01RR-00030-30 0475 (CLR) LIDDLE, ROGER A General clinical research center Cholecystokinin--Secretion regulation and physiologic action
M01RR-00030-30 0476 (CLR) SURWIT, RICHARD S General clinical research center Endogenous beta endorphin in diabetes mellitus--Type I and type II
M01RR-00030-30 0477 (CLR) SIEGEL, WILLIAM C General clinical research center Coronary disease and hemostatic/fibrinolytic risk factors
M01RR-00030-30 0478 (CLR) PETERS, WILLIAM P General clinical research center Reduction of myelosuppression by CSFs in metastatic melanoma therapy
M01RR-00030-30 0480 (CLR) SVETKEY, LAURA P General clinical research center Effect of captopril on progressive type I diabetic renal disease
M01RR-00030-30 0482 (CLR) HUNT, CHRISTINE M General clinical research center Drug metabolism in the elderly
M01RR-00030-30 0484 (CLR) SULLIVAN, MARTIN J General clinical research center 31-P-NMR assessment of skeletal muscle in normals and heart failure
M01RR-00030-30 0485 (CLR) BLUMENTHAL, JAMES A General clinical research center Behavioral treatment of transient myocardial ischemia
M01RR-00030-30 0486 (CLR) SCHIFF, RICHARD I General clinical research center Intravenous gamma globulin in patients with IgG subclass of antibody deficiency
M01RR-00030-30 0487 (CLR) SCHIFF, RICHARD I General clinical research center Evaluation of Intraglobin-R-F in humoral immunodeficiency
M01RR-00030-30 0488 (CLR) FEINGLOS, MARK N General clinical research center Tolrestat in diabetic neuropathy--Double-blind, placebo-controlled study
M01RR-00030-30 0489 (CLR) SCHIFF, RICHARD I General clinical research center Comparing 10% intravenous immunoglobulin without maltose with Gamimune
M01RR-00030-30 0490 (CLR) SCHIFF, RICHARD I General clinical research center Evaluation of liquid venoglobulin in humoral immunodeficiency
M01RR-00030-30 0491 (CLR) BARTLETT, JOHN A General clinical research center Single dose IV soluble T4 in HIV infection--Safety & pharmacokinetics
M01RR-00030-30 0493 (CLR) DUNN, FREDERICK L General clinical research center Multicenter study of lovastatin in moderate hypercholesteremia
M01RR-00030-30 0494 (CLR) WILFERT, CATHERINE M General clinical research center Recombinant CD4 in children with human immunodeficiency virus infection
M01RR-00030-30 0495 (CLR) BUCKLEY, REBECCA H General clinical research center Food hypersensitivity in the pathogenesis of atopic disorders
M01RR-00030-30 0511 (CLR) PHILLIPS, GEORGE JR General clinical research center Rheothrix multiple dose safety in sickle cell disease patients not in crisis
M01RR-00030-30 0512 (CLR) OLSEN, ELISE A General clinical research center Topical methotrexate/azone in psoriasis vulgaris
M01RR-00030-30 0513 (CLR) WASKIN, HETTY A General clinical research center Comparative bioavailability of dideoxyinosine
M01RR-00032-31 (CLR) PITTMAN, JAMES A, JR UNIV OF ALABAMA AT BIRMINGHAM 301 MEDICAL EDUCATION BUILDING BIRMINGHAM, AL 35294 General clinical research center
M01RR-00032-31 0268 (CLR) ROGERS, WILLIAM J. General clinical research center Intravenous torasemide and furosemide in patients with congestive heart failure
M01RR-00032-31 0272 (CLR) TOLBERT, LELLAND General clinical research center One carbon metabolism abnormalities
M01RR-00032-31 0277 (CLR) WHITLEY, RICHARD J General clinical research center Efficacy of antiviral agents for the treatment of severe herpesvirus infections
M01RR-00032-31 0278 (CLR) STAGNO, SERGIO B General clinical research center Natural history of congenitally and natally acquired CMV infections
M01RR-00032-31 0280 (CLR) WEINSIER, General clinical research center Diet-induced thermogenesis in obese postmenopausal patients
M01RR-00032-31 0282 (CLR) JULIAN, BRUCE A General clinical research center Systemic and secretory IgA immune response nephropathy
M01RR-00032-31 0283 (CLR) MORAWETZ, RICHARD B General clinical research center Comparison of AZQ with BCNU in patients with primary anaplastic brain tumors

M01RR-00032-31 0285 (CLR) MORAWETZ, RICHARD B General clinical research center Intravenous melphalin in the treatment of patients with anaplastic gliomas
M01RR-00032-31 0286 (CLR) MORAWETZ, RICHARD B General clinical research center Active immunotherapy of anaplastic glioma patients using U-251 MG cell line
M01RR-00032-31 0287 (CLR) MORAWETZ, RICHARD B General clinical research center Use of intra-arterial cis-platin in the treatment of anaplastic gliomas
M01RR-00032-31 0290 (CLR) CURTIS, JOHN J General clinical research center Mechanisms of cyclosporine induced renal hypertension
M01RR-00032-31 0291 (CLR) MORAWETZ, RICHARD B General clinical research center Intracarotid cis-platin for adults with untreated cerebral anaplastic glioma
M01RR-00032-31 0292 (CLR) WHITELY, RICHARD J General clinical research center Vaccination for JEE, VEE, and yellow fever
M01RR-00032-31 0293 (CLR) KENNEDY, JOHN I General clinical research center Role of eicosanoid by alveolar macrophages in asthma
M01RR-00032-31 0296 (CLR) DISMUKES, WILLIAM E General clinical research center Fluconazole for acute crypotococcal meningitis after amphotericin B
M01RR-00032-31 0298 (CLR) PLUMB, VANCE J General clinical research center Oral deprafenone in patients with ventricular ectopy
M01RR-00032-31 0299 (CLR) AZZIZ, RICARDO General clinical research center Adrenal steroidogenesis in euandrogenic and hyperandrogenic obesity
M01RR-00032-31 0300 (CLR) ROGERS, WILLIAM J General clinical research center By-Pass angioplasty revascularization investigation
M01RR-00032-31 0301 (CLR) ROGERS, WILLIAM J General clinical research center Nisoldipine in stable exertional angina with concommitant beta blocker therapy
M01RR-00032-31 0302 (CLR) MORAWETZ, RICHARD B General clinical research center Cranial radiation and intravenous mitomycin C in anaplastic brain gliomas
M01RR-00032-31 0303 (CLR) WHITELY, RICHARD J General clinical research center Oral acyclovir treatment of localized herpes zoster in patients with AIDS/ARC
M01RR-00032-31 0305 (CLR) SAAG, MICHAEL S General clinical research center Trimetrexate w/leucovorin ca rescue vs trimethoprim/sulfamethoxazole
M01RR-00032-31 0309 (CLR) HIRSCHOWITZ, BASIL I General clinical research center Patients with massive gastric acid hypersecretion
M01RR-00032-31 0310 (CLR) WHITLEY, RICHARD J General clinical research center Localized herpes zoster in normal host--Acyclovir vs placebo
M01RR-00032-31 0311 (CLR) DISMUKES, WILLIAM E General clinical research center Increasing doses of itraconazole for blastomycosis,histoplasmosis,sporotrichosis
M01RR-00032-31 0312 (CLR) DIASIO, ROBERT B General clinical research center Examination of the metabolism of 5-fluorouracil
M01RR-00032-31 0313 (CLR) ROGERS, WILLIAM J General clinical research center Left ventricular dysfunction
M01RR-00032-31 0314 (CLR) WHITLEY, RICHARD J General clinical research center Safety and efficacy of DHPG in CMV/AIDS patients using IV infusion pump
M01RR-00032-31 0315 (CLR) DIASIO, ROBERT B General clinical research center Biochemical pharmacologic studies of anticancer and antiviral drugs
M01RR-00032-31 0316 (CLR) DISMUKES, WILLIAM E General clinical research center Amphotericin B and ketoconozole to suppress disseminated histoplasmosis
M01RR-00032-31 0317 (CLR) SAAG, MICHAEL S General clinical research center Maintenance fluconazole and amphotericin B for crypto meningitis in AIDS
M01RR-00032-31 0318 (CLR) WHITLEY, RICHARD J General clinical research center Oral acyclovir treatment localized herpes zoster in immunocompromised patients
M01RR-00032-31 0025 (CLR) COOPER, MAX D General clinical research center Biological definition of host defense in man
M01RR-00032-31 0319 (CLR) WHITLEY, RICHARD J General clinical research center High dose acyclovir for the treatment of herpes simplex encephalitis
M01RR-00032-31 0320 (CLR) LOBUGLIO, ALBERT F General clinical research center Phase I 131-1 Lym-1 patients with diffuse aggressive lymphomas
M01RR-00032-31 0321 (CLR) COOPER, J ALLEN D, JR General clinical research center Bronchoalveolar lavage in normal volunteers
M01RR-00032-31 0323 (CLR) GIANTURCO, SANDRA H General clinical research center Cellular basis for atherosclerosis in hypertriglyceridemia
M01RR-00032-31 0325 (CLR) MORAWETZ, RICHARD B General clinical research center CCNU vs CCNU plus alpha-interferon in anaplastic gliomas
M01RR-00032-31 0326 (CLR) MORAWETZ, RICHARD B General clinical research center Radiotherapy mitomycin C, BCNU and 6-MP for adults with anaplastic glioma
M01RR-00032-31 0329 (CLR) OLSON, A KENNETH General clinical research center High carbohydrate-low fat vs high fat-low carbohydrate diets on energy
M01RR-00032-31 0330 (CLR) DUNLAP, NANCY E General clinical research center T-cell alveolar macrophage interactions required for mycobacterial infection
M01RR-00032-31 0332 (CLR) LASKOW, DAVID A General clinical research center Mechanisms of cyclosporin nephrotoxicity
M01RR-00032-31 0333 (CLR) KENNEDY, JOHN IRA, JR General clinical research center Dietary fish oil and alveolar macrophage production of cytokine
M01RR-00032-31 0335 (CLR) PLUMB, VANCE J General clinical research center Effects of sematilide hydrochloride in patients with ventricular ectopy
M01RR-00032-31 0337 (CLR) WHITLEY, RICHARD J General clinical research center Dideoxyinosine administered to children with AIDS or cytomegalovirus infections

PROJECT NO., ORGANIZATIONAL UNIT., INVESTIGATOR, ADDRESS, TITLE

M01RR-00032-31 0338 (CLR) WHITLEY, RICHARD J General clinical research center Suppressive therapy with oral acyclovir for recurrent skin vesicles
M01RR-00032-31 0339 (CLR) WHITLEY, RICHARD J General clinical research center Ganciclovir for symptomatic congenital cytomegalovirus infections
M01RR-00032-31 0341 (CLR) DISMUKES, WILLIAM E General clinical research center Itraconazole suppression of relapse disseminated histoplasmosis in AIDS patients
M01RR-00032-31 0342 (CLR) HALSEY, JAMES H, JR General clinical research center Dosage study of IV MK-801 in patients with stable cerebral infarctions
M01RR-00032-31 0345 (CLR) TILDEN, SAMUEL J General clinical research center Caloric and protein dyshomeostasis in cystic fibrosis
M01RR-00032-31 0347 (CLR) DIASIO, ROBERT B General clinical research center Continuous IV infusion of FUDR in patients with metastatic carcinoma
M01RR-00032-31 0348 (CLR) BARBER, W HENRY General clinical research center Donor specific bone marrow transfusion to evaluate L-R tolerance
M01RR-00032-31 0349 (CLR) DISMUKES, WILLIAM E General clinical research center Fluconazole in non-acute histoplasmosis, blastomycosis and sporotrichosis
M01RR-00032-31 0351 (CLR) WHITLEY, RICHARD J General clinical research center IV ganciclovir therapy for peripheral CMV retinitis in AIDS patients
M01RR-00032-31 0352 (CLR) SAAG, MICHAEL S General clinical research center Pharmacokinetic study of single 600mg oral dose of SCH39304
M01RR-00032-31 0353 (CLR) WHITLEY, RICHARD J General clinical research center Oral FIAC in AIDS patients with cytomegalovirus infection--Dose range
M01RR-00032-31 0354 (CLR) WHITLEY, RICHARD J General clinical research center Doses of anti-CMV monoclonal antibody for CMV viremia/viruria in AIDS patients
M01RR-00032-31 0355 (CLR) ALARCON, RENATO D General clinical research center Red blood cell/plasma lithium ratio and clinical outcome
M01RR-00032-31 0356 (CLR) COOPER, MAX D General clinical research center Biological definition of host defense in man
M01RR-00032-31 0357 (CLR) DISMUKES, WILLIAM E General clinical research center Localized herpes zoster in normal host--Oral acyclovir vs placebo
M01RR-00032-31 0358 (CLR) DISMUKES, WILLIAM E General clinical research center Intraconazole in different doses in blastomycosis and histoplasmosis
M01RR-00032-31 0359 (CLR) SEQUEST, JERE P General clinical research center Postprandial changes in plasma lipoprotein
M01RR-00032-31 0360 (CLR) DISMUKES, WILLIAM E General clinical research center Fluconazole vs amphotericin B as treatment of acute crypto meningitis
M01RR-00032-31 0361 (CLR) DISMUKES, WILLIAM E General clinical research center Fluconazole vs amphotericin B maintenance/prevention of crypto in AIDS
M01RR-00032-31 0362 (CLR) DISMUKES, WILLIAM E General clinical research center A515U (acyclovir) treatment of varicella zoster in immunocompromised
M01RR-00032-31 0189 (CLR) HARRELL, LINDY General clinical research center Physostigmine in Alzheimer's disease
M01RR-00032-31 0363 (CLR) WHITLEY, RICHARD J General clinical research center Condyloma acuminatum with interferon and cryotherapy--Placebo controlled
M01RR-00032-31 0364 (CLR) SALEH, MANSOOR N General clinical research center: Murine monoclonal antibody 14G2a in melanoma and small lung cell carcinoma
M01RR-00032-31 0365 (CLR) DISMUKES, WILLIAM E General clinical research center Cilofungen in candida esophagitis--Dose ranging study
M01RR-00032-31 0366 (CLR) DISMUKES, WILLIAM General clinical research center IV ganciclover (DHPG) for peripheral CMV retinitis in patients with AIDS
M01RR-00032-31 0367 (CLR) DISMUKES, WILLIAM General clinical research center High dose acyclovir vs vidarabine therapy for neonatal herpes simplex
M01RR-00032-31 0368 (CLR) DISMUKES, WILLIAM General clinical research center Traconazole suppresion of relapse of disseminated histoplasmosis in AIDS
M01RR-00032-31 0369 (CLR) DISMUKES, WILLIAM E General clinical research center Itraconazole in aspergillus species infections
M01RR-00032-31 0370 (CLR) MEREDITH, RUBY F General clinical research center IV 131-I labeled chimeric IgG4 B72.3 MCA in advanced colorectal cancer
M01RR-00032-31 0371 (CLR) CARR, MARK S General clinical research center SCH 39304 therapy for acute cryptococcal meningitis in HIV infections
M01RR-00032-31 0372 (CLR) CURTIS, JOHN J General clinical research center Effects of cyclosporine on the renin angiotensin system
M01RR-00032-31 0373 (CLR) SAAG, MICHAEL S General clinical research center: SCH 39304 vs ketoconazole for oropharyngeal candidiasis in HIV and patient
M01RR-00032-31 0374 (CLR) PARTRIDGE, EDWARD E General clinical research center Cisplatin/Cytoxan vs cisplatin/taxol in women with ovarian cancer
M01RR-00032-31 0375 (CLR) KOOPMAN, WILLIAM J General clinical research center Chimeric anti-CD4 in rheumatoid arthritis
M01RR-00032-31 0376 (CLR) CURTIS, JOHN J General clinical research center IV corlopam on renal function in transplant patients treated with cyclosporin
M01RR-00032-31 0377 (CLR) WEINSIER, ROLAND L General clinical research center MJ-7068 for AIDS and ARC patients with fat malabsorption
M01RR-00032-31 0378 (CLR) RICHTER, JOEL E General clinical research center Erythromycin in gastroesophageal reflux and peristaltic parameters
M01RR-00032-31 0379 (CLR) SAAG, MICHAEL S General clinical research

PROJECT NO., ORGANIZATIONAL UNIT., INVESTIGATOR, ADDRESS, TITLE

center SQ 32,756 on pharmacokinetics and safety of zidovudine
M01RR-00032-31 0380 (CLR) SEGREST, JERE P General clinical research center HDL-elevating drugs for use in coronary artery disorders regresion
M01RR-00032-31 0381 (CLR) BELL, EMMY K General clinical research center Effect of captopril on hydro-osmotic action of vasopressin
M01RR-00032-31 0382 (CLR) OH, MYUNG-HI KIM General clinical research center Oral contraceptives on serum lipid levels in adolescent females
M01RR-00032-31 0383 (CLR) OH, MYUNG-HI KIM General clinical research center Azithromycin in the treatment of chlamydial urethritis/cervicitis
M01RR-00032-31 0384 (CLR) HINE, R JEAN General clinical research center Assessment of preneoplastic lesions in respiratory epithelia smokers
M01RR-00032-31 0385 (CLR) CRAIN, MARILYN J General clinical research center Pediatric HIV/AIDS health care demonstration project
M01RR-00032-31 0214 (CLR) BAILEY, WILLIAM C General clinical research center Chronic obstructive pulmonary disease--Early intervention
M01RR-00032-31 0216 (CLR) DISMUKES, WILLIAM E General clinical research center M-C study of efficacy and safety of fluconazole for systemic fungal disease
M01RR-00032-31 0225 (CLR) ROGERS, WILLIAM J General clinical research center Thrombolysis in myocardial infarction (TIMI) phase II
M01RR-00032-31 0229 (CLR) WHITAKER, JOHN N General clinical research center Myelin basic protein peptides in body fluids in multiple sclerosis
M01RR-00032-31 0230 (CLR) WHITLEY, R J General clinical research center Kinetics and metabolism of DHPG in AIDS patients
M01RR-00032-31 0233 (CLR) CURTIS, JOHN J General clinical research center Mechanisms of post renal transplantation hypertension
M01RR-00032-31 0250 (CLR) JULIAN, BRUCE A. General clinical research center Change of renal bone disease after living-related kidney transplant
M01RR-00032-31 0254 (CLR) FINE, JO D. General clinical research center National epidermolysis bullosa registry/clinical center
M01RR-00032-31 0259 (CLR) DISMUKES, WILLIAM E. General clinical research center Nystatin therapy for possible hypersensitivity to candida albicans
M01RR-00032-31 0260 (CLR) ROGERS, WILLIAM J. General clinical research center Cardiac arrhythmia suppression trial
M01RR-00032-31 0263 (CLR) LOBUGLIO, ALBERT F. General clinical research center IV 131I labeled chimeric IgG4 B72.3 in advanced colorectal carcinoma
M01RR-00034-31 (CLR) TZAGOURNIS, MANUEL OHIO STATE UNIVERSITY RES FDN 370 WEST NINTH AVENUE COLUMBUS, OH 43210 General clinical research center
M01RR-00034-31 0412 (CLR) MENDELL, JERRY General clinical research center Immunosuppressive therapy in motor neuron disorders
M01RR-00034-31 0413 (CLR) BOSSETTI, BRENDA M General clinical research center Insulin-like growth factor in NIDDM following an energy restricted diet
M01RR-00034-31 0414 (CLR) FOLEY, MICHAEL R General clinical research center Prolonged oral terbutaline therapy and glucose tolerance in pregnancy
M01RR-00034-31 0415 (CLR) IAMS, JAY D General clinical research center Methylmalonic acidemia and pregnancy--A case study
M01RR-00034-31 0416 (CLR) LAMB, DAVID General clinical research center Insulin effects on growth in children with cystic fibrosis
M01RR-00034-31 0417 (CLR) ZIPF, WILLIAM B General clinical research center Sulfonylurea effects on metabolism and growth an cystic fibrosis
M01RR-00034-31 0418 (CLR) ZIPF, WILLIAM B General clinical research center Pancreatic polypeptide administration in Prader-Willi syndrome
M01RR-00034-31 0419 (CLR) LIMA, JOHN J General clinical research center Ancillary effects of acute propanolol exposure
M01RR-00034-31 0420 (CLR) TESI, RAYMOND J General clinical research center Chronic cyclosporine nephrotoxicity
M01RR-00034-31 0421 (CLR) HEBERT, LEE A General clinical research center Cyclosporine in the treatment of adult nephrotic syndrome
M01RR-00034-31 0422 (CLR) HEBERT, LEE A General clinical research center Modification of diet in renal disease
M01RR-00034-31 0423 (CLR) HARTMAN, JUDITH General clinical research center: Comparison of estimated protein intake calculated from nitrogen appearance
M01RR-00034-31 0424 (CLR) WRIGHT, J GORDON General clinical research center Iloprost in treatment of peripheral arterial disease and ischemic ulcers
M01RR-00034-31 0425 (CLR) WRIGHT, J GORDON General clinical research center Effect of amino acid load on renal function and nutritional status
M01RR-00034-31 0426 (CLR) FASS, ROBERT J General clinical research center Phase II study comparing 2,3-dideoxyinosine and zidovudine
M01RR-00034-31 0153 (CLR) CALDWELL, JAMES H General clinical research center Immunoglobulin E in eosinophilic gastroenteritis
M01RR-00034-31 0201 (CLR) CATALAND, SAMUEL General clinical research center Control of metabolic diabetic parameters by portable insulin pump
M01RR-00034-31 0263 (CLR) O'DORSIO, THOMAS General clinical research center Neuroendocrine tumors of the gastroenteropancreatic axis
M01RR-00034-31 0282 (CLR) HERBERT, LEE A General clinical research center Plasmapheresis in severe lupus glomerulonephritis
M01RR-00034-31 0289 (CLR) MENDELL, JERRY General clinical research center Controlled trial of prednisone vs placebo in Duchenne dystrophy
M01RR-00034-31 0294 (CLR) BINKLEY, PHILIP F. General clinical research center Impedance in congestive heart failure
M01RR-00034-31 0427 (CLR) WEWERS, MARY E General clinical research center Cigarette smoking, opoid peptides, and dysphoric states among smokers
M01RR-00034-31 0299 (CLR) MARLARKEY, WILLIAM B General clinical research center Prolactin dopamine relationships in hyperprolactinemia

PROJECT NO., ORGANIZATIONAL UNIT., INVESTIGATOR, ADDRESS, TITLE

M01RR-00034-31 0304 (CLR) OSEI, KWAME General clinical research center Efficacy of somatostatin analogue in type I diabetes
M01RR-00034-31 0334 (CLR) MAZZAFERRI, ERNEST L General clinical research center Thyroid carcinoma--Factors affecting recurrence and survival
M01RR-00034-31 0341 (CLR) FASS, ROBERT General clinical research center Natural history of HIV seropositive cohorts
M01RR-00034-31 0342 (CLR) PAULSON, GEORGE General clinical research center Psychoneurological assessment in demented patient cohorts
M01RR-00034-31 0343 (CLR) PAULSON, GEORGE General clinical research center Deprenyl and tocopherol antioxidative therapy of Parkinsonism
M01RR-00034-31 0301 (CLR) OSEI, KWAME General clinical research center Endocrine evaluation of pancreatic transplant
M01RR-00034-31 0347 (CLR) SHARMA, HARI General clinical research center Ohio State University hospitals autopsy study
M01RR-00034-31 0360 (CLR) MALARKEY, WILLIAM B General clinical research center Stress--Impact on the immune-endocrine axis and health
M01RR-00034-31 0361 (CLR) MAZZAFERRI, ERNEST L General clinical research center Calcitonin gene related peptide--Volume manipulation
M01RR-00034-31 0365 (CLR) DRAKE, MILES E General clinical research center Evaluation of flunarizine in the treatment of partial seizure
M01RR-00034-31 0368 (CLR) KIEN, C LAWRENCE General clinical research center Carbohydrate energy absorption in young adults and premature infants
M01RR-00034-31 0375 (CLR) NAHMAN, N STANLEY General clinical research center: Cimetidine-creatinine clearance test to predict glomerular filtration rate
M01RR-00034-31 0382 (CLR) OSEI, KWAME General clinical research center Metabolic/Energy assessment in non-diabetic relatives of black diabetics
M01RR-00034-31 0383 (CLR) MALARKEY, WILLIAM B General clinical research center Multicenter study to determine efficacy of sandostatin in acromegaly
M01RR-00034-31 0390 (CLR) MENDELL, JERRY R General clinical research center Randomized trial of azathioprine and prednisone in Duchenne dystrophy
M01RR-00034-31 0391 (CLR) MENDELL, JERRY R General clinical research center Late complications of Duchenne dystrophy
M01RR-00034-31 0392 (CLR) WEWERS, MARY ELLEN General clinical research center Nicotine, neuroregulators, and dysphoric states among smokers
M01RR-00034-31 0393 (CLR) MATKOVIC, VELMIR General clinical research center Effect of gallium nitrate on bone turnover indices and calcium balance
M01RR-00034-31 0395 (CLR) MACKICHAN, JANIS J General clinical research center Verapamil isomer dynamics/kinetics following racemate intake
M01RR-00034-31 0397 (CLR) KIECOLT-GLASER, JANICE General clinical research center Physiological consequences of marital discord
M01RR-00034-31 0399 (CLR) SCHAAL, STEPHEN F General clinical research center Autonomic response to passive upright tilt in mitral valve prolapse
M01RR-00034-31 0400 (CLR) SCHROEDER, KATHRYN L General clinical research center Lead, ALA-D levels, peripheral cardiovascular flow in smokeless tobacco users
M01RR-00034-31 0401 (CLR) COTTRELL, DARYL General clinical research center Intermittent glyburide and glipizide therapy in type II diabetics
M01RR-00034-31 0402 (CLR) COTTRELL, DARYL General clinical research center Hepatic autoregulation in glucose metabolism
M01RR-00034-31 0403 (CLR) MATKOVIC, VELIMIR General clinical research center Vitamin D-resistant rickets--Phosphate diabetes
M01RR-00034-31 0404 (CLR) FASS, ROBERT J General clinical research center Safety and efficacy of zidovudine in treatment of patients with early ARC
M01RR-00034-31 0405 (CLR) FASS, ROBERT J General clinical research center Safety and efficacy of zidovudine in asymptomatic HIV infected individuals
M01RR-00034-31 0406 (CLR) FASS, ROBERT J General clinical research center Safety and efficacy of zidovudine in asymptomatic HIV infected individuals
M01RR-00034-31 0407 (CLR) FASS, ROBERT J General clinical research center Trimethoprim-Sulfamethoxazole versus pentamidine for PCP prophylaxis
M01RR-00034-31 0408 (CLR) FASS, ROBERT J General clinical research center Randomized trial of anti-pneumocystis agents in advanced HIV infection
M01RR-00034-31 0409 (CLR) FASS, ROBERT J General clinical research center Phase II study of zidovudine and alpha-2A interferon in Kaposi's sarcoma
M01RR-00034-31 0410 (CLR) FASS, ROBERT J General clinical research center Comparisin of 2,3-dideoxyinosine and zidovudine in HIV infection
M01RR-00034-31 0411 (CLR) FASS, ROBERT J General clinical research center Efficacy study of 2,3-dideoxyinosine in zidovudine-intolerant patients
K01RR-00035-05 (AR) WOLFE, JOHN H UNIVERSITY OF PENNSYLVANIA 3451 WALNUT STREET PHILADELPHIA, PA 19104 Laboratory animal studies in gene therapy
M01RR-00035-31 (CLR) JOHNS, MICHAEL E JOHNS HOPKINS UNIVERSITY 720 RUTLAND AVENUE BALTIMORE, MD 21205 General clinical research center
M01RR-00035-31 0321 (CLR) BECKER, LEWIS C General clinical research center Positive exercise thallium test in asymptomatic siblings with CHD
M01RR-00035-31 0323 (CLR) CHARACHE, SAMUEL General clinical research center Treatment of sickle cell anemia with hydroxyurea
M01RR-00035-31 0324 (CLR) FISCHMAN, MARIAN W General clinical research center Cocaine effects in humans--Physiology and behavior
M01RR-00035-31 0350 (CLR) MOSER, HUGH General clinical research center Diet therapy of adrenoleukodystrophy
M01RR-00035-31 0353 (CLR) SAUDEK, CHRISTOPHER General clinical research center Programmable implantable medication system (PIMS) in

diabetes
M01RR-00035-31 0355 (CLR) ELMAN, MICHAEL L General clinical research center Thrombolysis in central vein occlusion study
M01RR-00035-31 0359 (CLR) MOSES, HAMILTON General clinical research center Deprenyl and tocopherol antioxidative therapy of Parkinsonism
M01RR-00035-31 0368 (CLR) LIETMAN, PAUL S General clinical research center High dose intravenous dexrean sulfate in HIV infected individuals
M01RR-00035-31 0386 (CLR) LIETMAN, PAUL S General clinical research center High dose I.V. dextran sulfate in HIV infected individuals
M01RR-00035-31 0387 (CLR) LIETMAN, PAUL S General clinical research center Pharmacokinetic effect of probenecid on AZT in HIV
M01RR-00035-31 0388 (CLR) MCKUSICH, VICTOR A General clinical research center Studies in clinical genetics
M01RR-00035-31 0389 (CLR) MOSER, HUGO W General clinical research center Glycerol trierucate in treatment of adrenoleukodystrophy
M01RR-00035-31 0390 (CLR) PETRI, MICHELLE A General clinical research center Pulmonary hypertension in lupus--Intervention/channel blockers
M01RR-00035-31 0392 (CLR) SZABA, GEORGE P General clinical research center Shockwave lithotripsy (ESWL) of gallstones
M01RR-00035-31 0394 (CLR) TUNE, LARRY E General clinical research center PET scan in Alzheimer's disease
M01RR-00035-31 0395 (CLR) DOBS, ADRIAN S General clinical research center Hypothalamic-Pituitary-Adrenal axis in alcoholics
M01RR-00035-31 0396 (CLR) DONEHOWER, ROSS C General clinical research center 7U85 Mesylate intravenous administration daily for five days
M01RR-00035-31 0397 (CLR) DONEHOWER, ROSS C General clinical research center Bioavailability of piritrexim isethionate in advanced cancer patients
M01RR-00035-31 0398 (CLR) DONEHOWER, ROSS C General clinical research center Dose proportionality study of piritrexim isethionate in cancer patients
M01RR-00035-31 0399 (CLR) DRACHMAN, DANIEL B General clinical research center Amyotrophic lateral sclerosis--Immunosuppression with cyclophosphamide
M01RR-00035-31 0400 (CLR) FLEXNER, CHARLES W General clinical research center 3'Deoxy-3'-fluorothymidine (FLT)--A new anti-HIV nucleoside
M01RR-00035-31 0401 (CLR) FOLSTEIN, SUSAN E General clinical research center Therapeutics of idebenone in Huntington's disease
M01RR-00035-31 0402 (CLR) GUARNIERI, THOMAS General clinical research center Oral sematilide HCl for paroxysmal atrial fibrillation
M01RR-00035-31 0403 (CLR) HOCHBERG, MARK C General clinical research center Tryptophan metabolism in eosinophilia-myalgia syndrome
M01RR-00035-31 0404 (CLR) JABS, DOUGLAS A General clinical research center CMV retinitis trial--Foscarnet ganciclovir component
M01RR-00035-31 0405 (CLR) KALLOO, ANTHONY N General clinical research center Intragastric pH in rebleeding gastric and duodenal ulcers
M01RR-00035-31 0406 (CLR) KORNHAUSER, DAVID D General clinical research center Increasing pH upon the bioavailability of oral foscarnet
M01RR-00035-31 0407 (CLR) LADENSON, PAUL W General clinical research center Myocardial 31 phosphate NMR in heart failure in hyperthyroidism
M01RR-00035-31 0408 (CLR) LADENSON, PAUL W General clinical research center Clinical and molecular studies of cardiomyopathy in hyperthyroidism
M01RR-00035-31 0409 (CLR) LADENSON, PAUL W General clinical research center Tiratricol suppression therapy in well-differentiated thyroid cancer
M01RR-00035-31 0410 (CLR) LESSER, RONALD P General clinical research center Felbamate as adjuvant therapy in surgical evaluation of seizures
M01RR-00035-31 0413 (CLR) PETTY, BRENT G General clinical research center Sensitization and photoallergic potential of niclosamide
M01RR-00035-31 0414 (CLR) PETTY, BRENT G General clinical research center Zidovudine with probenecid--Safety and tolerance
M01RR-00035-31 0415 (CLR) PETTY, BRENT G General clinical research center Ceftriaxone--Effect of food with absorption enhancer systems
M01RR-00035-31 0416 (CLR) RAVICH, WILLIAM J General clinical research center Investigation of patients with cyclic vomiting
M01RR-00035-31 0417 (CLR) DONEHOWER, ROSS C General clinical research center Hexamethylene biscacetamide in myelodysplastic syndromes
M01RR-00035-31 0418 (CLR) SCHULTHEIS, LESTER W General clinical research center Blood volume and neuroendocrine adaptation to zero gravity
M01RR-00035-31 0419 (CLR) TUNE, LARRY E General clinical research center PET scan in schizophrenia
M01RR-00035-31 0420 (CLR) WEIKEL, CYNTHIA S General clinical research center Spiramycin in AIDS-related crytospordial diarrhea
M01RR-00035-31 0370 (CLR) PEARLSON, GODFREY D General clinical research center Cocaine PET effects on brain metabolism and dopamine D2 receptors
M01RR-00035-31 0371 (CLR) LIETMAN, PAUL S General clinical research center Safety oral doses of sustained-released pyridostimine
M01RR-00035-31 0373 (CLR) PETTY, BRENT G General clinical research center Pharmacokinetics, safety and tolerance of WR 6026 hydrochloride
M01RR-00035-31 0381 (CLR) CHARACHE, SAMUEL General clinical research center Erythropoeitin/hydroxyurea in sickle cell anemia
M01RR-00035-31 0382 (CLR) FISHER, ROBERT S General clinical research center Thalamic stimulation for epilepsy
M01RR-00035-31 0384 (CLR) HANLEY, DANIEL F General clinical research center ANF and ADH in subarachnoid hemorrhage with hyponatremia
M01RR-00036-31 (CLR) PECK, WILLIAM A WASHINGTON UNIVERSITY MED SCH 660 SOUTH EUCLID AVENUE ST. LOUIS, MISSOURI 63110 General clinical research center
M01RR-00036-31 0429 (CLR) AVIOLI, LOUIS V General clinical research center Metabolic bone disease
M01RR-00036-31 1039 (CLR) PETERS, MARION General clinical research center Ursodeoxycholic acid treatment of primary biliary cirrhosis
M01RR-00036-31 1040 (CLR) POLMAR, STEPHEN S General clinical research center Multicenter clinical study of allergic reaction due aspartame
M01RR-00036-31 1041 (CLR) POWDERLY, WILLIAM General clinical research center Prophylaxis of cytomegalovirus infection in organ transplantation
M01RR-00036-31 1042 (CLR) POWDERLY, WILLIAM General clinical research center Anti-Pneumocystis drugs for prevention of pneumocystis pneumonia in HIV infection
M01RR-00036-31 1043 (CLR) ROTHSTEIN, MARCOS General clinical research center Short-Term pharmacological glucagon suppression in chronic renal failure
M01RR-00036-31 1044 (CLR) SCHONFELD, GUSTAV General clinical research center Short-Term exercise training on VLDL and LDL characteristics
M01RR-00036-31 1045 (CLR) TROTTER, JOHN L General clinical research center Dehydration modification of MRI scanning in multiple sclerosis
M01RR-00036-31 1046 (CLR) HAAGENSON, DARROW General clinical research center GCDPP-15 as a risk indiator for breast cancer
M01RR-00036-31 1047 (CLR) HEATH-MONNIGS, ELLEN General clinical research center IGF binding proteins cause IGF-1 resistance in a short person
M01RR-00036-31 1048 (CLR) PERLMAN, JEFFREY General clinical research center Followup of the high risk newborn
M01RR-00036-31 1049 (CLR) ROTHBAUM, ROBERT J General clinical research center Intravascular thrombosis children with central venous catheters
M01RR-00036-31 0469 (CLR) TROTTER, JOHN L General clinical research center Efficacy and safety of cyclosporin A in patients with chronic progressive M.S
M01RR-00036-31 0503 (CLR) CRYER, PHILIP E General clinical research center Diabetes registry--Research and education facility
M01RR-00036-31 0550 (CLR) CRYER, PHILIP E General clinical research center Pathophysiology and management of pituitary tumors
M01RR-00036-31 0599 (CLR) BRUNT, MICHAEL General clinical research center Human medullary thyroid carcinoma
M01RR-00036-31 0607 (CLR) HALVERSON, JOHN D. General clinical research center Post-operative sequelae in morbidly obese patients
M01RR-00036-31 0611 (CLR) ROTHSTEIN, MARCOS General clinical research center Renal acidification in patients with recurrent nephrolithiasis
M01RR-00036-31 0613 (CLR) SANTIAGO, JULIO V General clinical research center Diabetes control and complications trial
M01RR-00036-31 0641 (CLR) GELB, LAWRENCE General clinical research center Long term suppression of herpes with acyclovir
M01RR-00036-31 0650 (CLR) SCHARP, DAVID General clinical research center Clinical islet transplantation in diabetes mellitus
M01RR-00036-31 0661 (CLR) HOLLOSZY, JOHN General clinical research center Exercise glucose tolerance and insulin resistance in older subjects
M01RR-00036-31 0673 (CLR) HOLLOSZY, JOHN O. General clinical research center Adaptations to exercise in the elderly
M01RR-00036-31 0675 (CLR) OSTLUND, RICHARD General clinical research center Physiological adaptation to exercise in the elderly
M01RR-00036-31 0998 (CLR) RUBIN, EUGENE H General clinical research center Geropsychiatry unit data base
M01RR-00036-31 1000 (CLR) WHYTE, MICHAEL M General clinical research center Calcitriol for Vitamin D resistant rickets
M01RR-00036-31 1003 (CLR) BIER, DENNIS General clinical research center Abnormal growth study
M01RR-00036-31 1005 (CLR) CRYER, PHILIP E General clinical research center Treatment of hypoglycemia in insulin dependent diabetes mellitus
M01RR-00036-31 1007 (CLR) CRYER, PHILIP E General clinical research center Beta-adrenergic blockade during euglycemic and stepped hypoglycemic clamps
M01RR-00036-31 1008 (CLR) CRYER, PHILIP E General clinical research center CNS adaptation to antecent hyperglycemia
M01RR-00036-31 1009 (CLR) CRYER, PHILIP E General clinical research center Impact of dissipation of insulin and recurrent hypoglycemia on counterregulation
M01RR-00036-31 1010 (CLR) GELB, LAWRENCE General clinical research center Alternating dideoxycytidine and zidovudine to reduce AZT toxicity
M01RR-00036-31 1011 (CLR) HAIRE-JOSHU, DEBRA General clinical research center Reducing cardiovascular risk--Smoking cessation and diabetes
M01RR-00036-31 1013 (CLR) MCGILL, JANET General clinical research center Insulin delivery occlusions in continuous subcutaneous insulin infusion
M01RR-00036-31 1014 (CLR) MCGILL, JANET General clinical research center Energy metabolism during anesthesia
M01RR-00036-31 1015 (CLR) MCGILL, JANET General clinical research center Multicenter clinical trial converting enzyme inhibition in diabetic nephropathy
M01RR-00036-31 1016 (CLR) MCGILL, JANET General clinical research center Effect of captopril on microalbuminia/insulin dependent diabetes mellitus
M01RR-00036-31 1017 (CLR) NELSON, PATRICIA General clinical research center Safety study of inhaled ICI 200, 880 in obstructive lung disease
M01RR-00036-31 1018 (CLR) PACIFICI, ROBERTO General clinical research center Interleukin-1 in the pathogenesis of human osteoporosis
M01RR-00036-31 1019 (CLR) POWDERLY, WILLIAM General clinical research center Prevention of pneumocystis pneumonia in advanced HIV infection
M01RR-00036-31 1020 (CLR) POWDERLY, WILLIAM General clinical research center Secondary prophylaxis of pneumocystis pneumonia in AIDS
M01RR-00036-31 1022 (CLR) POWDERLY, WILLIAM General clinical

PROJECT NO., ORGANIZATIONAL UNIT., INVESTIGATOR, ADDRESS, TITLE

research center Trial of foscarnet in AIDS patients with CMV retinitis
M01RR-00036-31 1023 (CLR) RAICHLE, MARCUS General clinical research center Function of brain microvessels in diabetes mellitus
M01RR-00036-31 1025 (CLR) SCHONFELD, GUSTAV General clinical research center Effects of exercise on chylomicron and chylomicron remnant metabolism
M01RR-00036-31 1026 (CLR) SCHONFELD, GUSTAV General clinical research center Metabolism of genetic variants of apolipotrotein b
M01RR-00036-31 1027 (CLR) SOPER, NATHANIEL General clinical research center Laparoscopic cholecystectomy
M01RR-00036-31 1029 (CLR) WELLS, SAMUEL A General clinical research center Clinical/Genetic studies in multiple endocrine neoplasia types I,IIa & IIb
M01RR-00036-31 1030 (CLR) WOJTA, DANIEL General clinical research center Very low calorie diet and exercise in obese type II diabetics
M01RR-00036-31 1031 (CLR) KARL, LESLIE General clinical research center Systemic lupus erythematosus database
M01RR-00036-31 1032 (CLR) BESSEY, PALMER G General clinical research center Effects of insulin on the acute hormonal response to injury
M01RR-00036-31 1033 (CLR) CRAFT, SUZANNE General clinical research center Glucose and memory in mild senile dementia of the Alzheimer type
M01RR-00036-31 1034 (CLR) YER, PHILIP E General clinical research center: Adrenergic mechanisms in metabolic pathophysiology--Effect of hypoglycemia
M01RR-00036-31 1035 (CLR) CRYER, PHILIP General clinical research center Effects of position on hypoglycemic unawareness
M01RR-00036-31 1036 (CLR) PERMUTT, M ALAN General clinical research center Evaluation of human leukocyte function in poorly controlled diabetic patients
M01RR-00036-31 1037 (CLR) KUPPER, THOMAS S General clinical research center Regulation of hematopoiesis by cutaneous ultraviolet B light exposure
M01RR-00036-31 1038 (CLR) MARTIN, WADE General clinical research center Physiologic determinants of exercise capacity in hyperthyroidism
M01RR-00036-31 0702 (CLR) MORRIS, JOHN C. General clinical research center Efficacy of tetrahydroaminoacridine in Alzheimer's disease
M01RR-00036-31 0708 (CLR) PERLMUTTER, JOEL General clinical research center Deprenyl and tocopherol antioxidant therapy of Parkinsonism
M01RR-00036-31 0713 (CLR) STATEN, MYRLENE A. General clinical research center Metabolic effects of exercise in older patients
M01RR-00036-31 0716 (CLR) BIER, DENNIS General clinical research center Anabolic effect of growth hormone and exercise in young and elderly males
M01RR-00036-31 0964 (CLR) SOPER, NATHANIEL General clinical research center Ileal pouch adaptation following colectomy ileal pouch-anal anastomosis
M01RR-00036-31 0966 (CLR) CLIFFORD, DAVID B General clinical research center Psychometric and neurologic evaluation in immunodeficiency virus infection
M01RR-00036-31 0968 (CLR) GELB, LAWRENCE General clinical research center Safety and efficacy of zidovudine for asymptomatic HIV individuals
M01RR-00036-31 0970 (CLR) MORRIS, JOHN C General clinical research center Falls in the elderly--Clinical and physiologic factors
M01RR-00036-31 0972 (CLR) PERLMUTT, M ALAN General clinical research center Control of insulin biosynthesis
M01RR-00036-31 0977 (CLR) ROTHSTEIN, MARCOS General clinical research center Glucagon on progression of renal failure
M01RR-00036-31 0981 (CLR) WASSERMAN, TODD General clinical research center Hypoxic sensitizer SR-2508 and radiation in head and neck carcinoma
M01RR-00036-31 0984 (CLR) BECKER, JAMES M General clinical research center Ileal pouch adaptation and dysfunction following colectomy
M01RR-00036-31 0987 (CLR) GRAY, DIANA L General clinical research center Prenatal sonographic diagnosis of urinary tract anomalies
M01RR-00036-31 0988 (CLR) GRAY, DIANA L General clinical research center Gestational age dependent parameter
M01RR-00036-31 0989 (CLR) GRAY, DIANA L General clinical research center Washington University fetal growth curves
M01RR-00036-31 0991 (CLR) KARL, IRENE General clinical research center Muscle glucose and protein metabolism in peritoneal sepsis
M01RR-00036-31 0993 (CLR) KRAYBILL, WILLIAM General clinical research center Complications of venous access in patients with cancer
M01RR-00036-31 0995 (CLR) PERMUTT, M ALAN General clinical research center Glucose transporter-like clones in a human islet cDNA library
M01RR-00036-31 0997 (CLR) ROTWEIN, PETER General clinical research center Insulin-like growth factor II in leiomyosarcoma associated hypoglycemia
K01RR-00037-06 (SRC) PINSON, DAVID M UNIV OF KANSAS CANCER CENTER 39TH & RAINBOW, BUILDING 48 KANSAS CITY, KS 66103 Macrophage immunobiology and pulmonary inflamation
M01RR-00037-31 (CLR) FIALKOW, PHILIP J UNIVERSITY OF WASHINGTON SEATTLE, WASH 98195 General clinical research center
M01RR-00037-31 0453 (CLR) WORTHINGTON, BONNIE S General clinical research center Comparison of iron status between users of red meat and fish
M01RR-00037-31 0457 (CLR) ENSINCK, JOHN W General clinical research center Sulfonylureas on glucose and lipid metabolism in patients with type II diabetes
M01RR-00037-31 0458 (CLR) TENOVER, JOYCE S General clinical research center Effects of low doses of MK-906 in patients with benign prostatic hyperplasia
M01RR-00037-31 0284 (CLR) KNOPP, ROBERT H General clinical research center Metabolism effects of insulin vs caloric restriction in gestational diabetes
M01RR-00037-31 0290 (CLR) PRINZ, PATRICIA N General clinical research center Sleep and waking in Alzheimer's disease
M01RR-00037-31 0297 (CLR) BRUNZELL, JOHN D General clinical research center Mechanisms for hypertriglyceridemia in humans

PROJECT NO., ORGANIZATIONAL UNIT., INVESTIGATOR, ADDRESS, TITLE

M01RR-00037-31 0310 (CLR) OCHS, HANS D General clinical research center Developmental and genetic defects of immunity
M01RR-00037-31 0321 (CLR) FUJIMOTO, WILFRED Y General clinical research center Japanese-American community diabetes study
M01RR-00037-31 0336 (CLR) BROWN, B GREGORY General clinical research center Atherosclerosis progression
M01RR-00037-31 0347 (CLR) LIPKIN, EDWARD W General clinical research center Bone disease and mineral loss in parenteral nutrition
M01RR-00037-31 0390 (CLR) EASTERLING, THOMAS R General clinical research center Hypertension in pregnancy
M01RR-00037-31 0411 (CLR) ESCHBACH, JOSEPH W General clinical research center Recombinant erythropoietin use in end stage renal disease
M01RR-00037-31 0423 (CLR) DALE, DAVID C. General clinical research center Treatment of cyclic neutropenia with granulocyte colony stimulating factor
M01RR-00037-31 0427 (CLR) ENSINCK, JOHN W. General clinical research center Somatostatin-28 as regulator of hormonal secretion
M01RR-00037-31 0428 (CLR) FARWELL, JACQUELINE R. General clinical research center Ontogeny of epoxide hydrolases
M01RR-00037-31 0431 (CLR) LARSON, ERIC B. General clinical research center Alzheimer's disease patient registry
M01RR-00037-31 0433 (CLR) OCHS, HANS D. General clinical research center Identification of carrier females in X-linked immunodeficiency syndrome
M01RR-00037-31 0435 (CLR) PALMER, JERRY P. General clinical research center Diabetes control and complications trial
M01RR-00037-31 0436 (CLR) PALMER, JERRY P. General clinical research center Insulin secretion in families of patients with insulin dependent diabetes
M01RR-00037-31 0437 (CLR) PORTE, DANIEL General clinical research center Effects of glucose and insulin on insulin secretion and sensitivity
M01RR-00037-31 0448 (CLR) SOULES, MICHAEL R General clinical research center Effect of premature luteolysis on ovarian function
M01RR-00037-31 0450 (CLR) OCHS, HANS D General clinical research center Idiopathic inflammatory bowel disease--Treatment with immunoglobulin infusions
M01RR-00037-31 0462 (CLR) VITALIANO, PETER P General clinical research center Correlates of mental health in DAT spouses
M01RR-00037-31 0507 (CLR) SMITH, ARNOLD L General clinical research center Mechanisms of increased metabolic clearance of acetominophen in CF patients
M01RR-00037-31 0508 (CLR) TARTAGLIONE, TERESA A General clinical research center Zidovudine and dapsone interaction study in patients with advanced HIV infection
M01RR-00037-31 0464 (CLR) SMITH, CRAIG H General clinical research center Optic neuritis treatment trial
M01RR-00037-31 0465 (CLR) AVERY, DAVID H General clinical research center Temperature regulation in the 24-hour body clock of depressed patients
M01RR-00037-31 0467 (CLR) SMITH, ARNOLD L General clinical research center Renal elimination of aerosolized quinine
M01RR-00037-31 0470 (CLR) MOORE, DONALD E General clinical research center Gestodene and ethinyl estradiol, triphasic oral contraceptive study
M01RR-00037-31 0471 (CLR) FARWELL, JACQUELINE R General clinical research center An open add-on trial of stiripentol in children with uncontrolled seizures
M01RR-00037-31 0472 (CLR) BREMNER, WILLIAM J General clinical research center Sex steroid modulation of anterior pituitary function in men
M01RR-00037-31 0473 (CLR) OCHS, HANS D General clinical research center Recombinant human interferon-gamma in chronic granulomatous disease patients
M01RR-00037-31 0478 (CLR) EASTERLING, THOMAS R General clinical research center Hypertension in pregnancy
M01RR-00037-31 0479 (CLR) SYBERT, VIRGINIA P General clinical research center National registry for epidermolysis bullosa
M01RR-00037-31 0481 (CLR) ABKOWITZ, JANIS L General clinical research center Marrow aspiration from normal volunteers and patients with hematology disorders
M01RR-00037-31 0483 (CLR) SCHWARTZ, ROBERT S General clinical research center Sympathetic nervous system function in ISH of the elderly
M01RR-00037-31 0486 (CLR) BREMNER, WILLIAM J General clinical research center Effects of sex steroid withdrawal and selective replacement in healthy men
M01RR-00037-31 0487 (CLR) DALE, DAVID C General clinical research center Treatment of severe chronic neutropenia with recombinant human granulocyte
M01RR-00037-31 0488 (CLR) TENOVER, JOYCE A General clinical research center Androgen action in aging men--testosterone replacement
M01RR-00037-31 0490 (CLR) OCHS, HANS D General clinical research center Replacement therapy with a liquid IVIG in primary immune deficiency patients
M01RR-00037-31 0491 (CLR) DALE, DAVID C General clinical research center Effects of aging on bone marrow neutrophil reserves
M01RR-00037-31 0493 (CLR) CHAIT, ALAN General clinical research center Effects of doxazosin on lipoprotein metabolism in hypertensive patients
M01RR-00037-31 0494 (CLR) SMITH, ARNOLD L General clinical research center Mechanisms of increased metabolic clearance of sulfamethoxazole of CF patients
M01RR-00037-31 0495 (CLR) TARTAGLIONE, TERESA A General clinical research center Zidovudine and dapsone interaction study in patients with advanced HIV infection
M01RR-00037-31 0496 (CLR) SOULES, MICHAEL R General clinical research center Different clinical methods for the diagnosis of luteal phase deficiency
M01RR-00037-31 0498 (CLR) WILENSKY, ALAN J General clinical research center Potential interaction between valproic acid and lorazepam

PROJECT NO., ORGANIZATIONAL UNIT., INVESTIGATOR, ADDRESS, TITLE

M01RR-00037-31 0499 (CLR) COLLIER, ANN C General clinical research center Phase I--safety and pharmacokinetics of recombinant human CD4 immunoglobulin G
M01RR-00037-31 0500 (CLR) FUJIMOTO, WILFRED Y General clinical research center Insulin receptors and associated gangliosides
M01RR-00037-31 0501 (CLR) D'ALESSIO, DAVID A General clinical research center S-28 and GLP-1 as entero-insular regulators in healthy and diabetic men
M01RR-00037-31 0502 (CLR) MOORE, DONALD E General clinical research center Gestodene and ethinyl estradiol, monophasic oral contraceptive study
M01RR-00037-31 0504 (CLR) HORN, JOHN R General clinical research center Effects of nitroglycerin on hepatic blood flow
M01RR-00037-31 0505 (CLR) SLICHTER, SHERRILL J General clinical research center Administration of IV to patients with autoimmune thrombocytopenic purpura
M01RR-00037-31 0506 (CLR) SMITH, ARNOLD L General clinical research center Liver blood flow measurement in CF and non-CF subjects
M01RR-00037-31 0509 (CLR) FARWELL, JACQUELINE General clinical research center Trial of a slow-release form of tegretol
M01RR-00037-31 0510 (CLR) BENEDETTI, THOMAS J General clinical research center Maternal and fetal hemodynamic effects of acute blood loss in pregnancy
M01RR-00037-31 0511 (CLR) PALMER, JERRY P General clinical research center Phase 1 studt to determine the safety of xomazyme-H65 in type 1 diabetes mellitus
M01RR-00037-31 0512 (CLR) BREMNER, WILLIAM J General clinical research center GnRH antagonist as a potential male contraceptive agent in men
M01RR-00037-31 0513 (CLR) SMITH, ARNOLD L General clinical research center Bioavailability of enteric-coated dicloxacillin vs crystalline dicloxacillin
M01RR-00037-31 0514 (CLR) KNOPP, ROBERT H General clinical research center Effects of XU62-320 upon lipoprotein metabolism in hyperlipemic diabetics
M01RR-00037-31 0515 (CLR) TARTAGLIONE, TERESA General clinical research center Evaluation of pharmacokinetics and safety of concurrent AZT and DDI
M01RR-00037-31 0516 (CLR) FUJIMOTO, WILFRED Y General clinical research center Hepatic and renal drug clearance of S and R warfarin in cystic fibrosis
M01RR-00037-31 0517 (CLR) WATKINS, SANDRA L General clinical research center Intraperitoneal somatotropin to improve short stature in peritoneal dialysis
M01RR-00037-31 0518 (CLR) HENDERSON, WILLIAM R General clinical research center Omega fatty acid supplementation in cystic fibrosis
M01RR-00037-31 0519 (CLR) SOULES, MICHAEL R General clinical research center Hormone patterns during the midcycle in LH surge
M01RR-00037-31 0520 (CLR) SCOTT, C RONALD General clinical research center Comparison of serum lipid levels in families with one child on restricted diet
M01RR-00037-31 0521 (CLR) AITKEN, MOIRA General clinical research center Safety and systemic absorption of aerosolized rhDNase in cystic fibrosis
M01RR-00037-31 0522 (CLR) SOULES, MICHAEL R General clinical research center Hormonal response to fasting in normal women
M01RR-00037-31 0523 (CLR) WALKER, EDWARD A General clinical research center LH pulsatility patterns in women with depression and chronic stress
M01RR-00037-31 0524 (CLR) VITIELLO, MICHAEL V General clinical research center Fitness--Sleep and its correlates in the aged
M01RR-00037-31 0525 (CLR) PALMER, JERRY P General clinical research center Prevention of insulin dependent diabetes mellitus by azathioprine
M01RR-00037-31 0526 (CLR) FUJIMOTO, WILFRED Y General clinical research center Regulation of fat metabolism, insulin secretion, and insulin action
K01RR-00039-05 (AR) LACKNER, ANDREW A NEW MEXICO STATE UNIVERSITY NEW MEXICO REG PRIMATE LAB HOLLOMAN, AFB, NM 88330-1027 Comparative neuropathogenesis of SAIDS retroviruses
M01RR-00039-31 (CLR) HOUPT, JEFFREY L EMORY UNIVERSITY 1440 CLIFTON ROAD, N.E. ATLANTA, GA 30322 General clinical research center
M01RR-00039-31 0274 (CLR) ELSAS, LOUIS J General clinical research center Inborn errors in metabolism
M01RR-00039-31 0292 (CLR) HENDERSON, JOHN M General clinical research center Comparative evaluation of hepatic function tests--Urea synthesis
M01RR-00039-31 0317 (CLR) ELSAS, LOUIS J General clinical research center Blood phenylalanine in the performance of older PKU children
M01RR-00039-31 0437 (CLR) HASSOLD, JERRY J General clinical research center RFLP's of the insulin receptor gene in insulin resistant disorders
M01RR-00039-31 0439 (CLR) HARKER, LAWRENCE General clinical research center Studies of platelet production and destruction
M01RR-00039-31 0440 (CLR) HALL, W DALLAS General clinical research center Angiotensin converting enzyme inhibition & urinary kallikrein relation
M01RR-00039-31 0441 (CLR) HORD, ALLEN H General clinical research center Efficacy of Magna-Bloc therapy in chronic mechanical low back pain
M01RR-00039-31 0442 (CLR) ELSAS, LOUIS J General clinical research center Metabolic response to growth hormone--Patients with inherited insulin receptor D
M01RR-00039-31 0443 (CLR) CULLER, FLOYD L General clinical research center Carbohydrate intolerance in cystic fibrosis
M01RR-00039-31 0444 (CLR) HUG, CARL C General clinical research center Transdermal iontophoretic delivery of sulfentanil in normal volunteers
M01RR-00039-31 0445 (CLR) HALL, W DALLAS General clinical research center Nifedipine versus hydrochlorothiazide in hypertensive Blacks
M01RR-00039-31 0446 (CLR) GEBHART, SUZANNE General clinical research center Effect of pancreatic transplantation on insulin/glucose homeostasis

PROJECT NO., ORGANIZATIONAL UNIT., INVESTIGATOR, ADDRESS, TITLE

M01RR-00039-31 0447 (CLR) GEBHART, SUZANNE S General clinical research center Assessment of insulin sensitivity in diabetics by modification
M01RR-00039-31 0448 (CLR) MITCH, WILLIAM E General clinical research center Mechanism of adaptation to dietary manipulation in uremia
M01RR-00039-31 0321 (CLR) PARKS, JOHN General clinical research center Growth hormone gene structure and the bioinactive growth hormone syndrome
M01RR-00039-31 0381 (CLR) HENDERSON, JOHN MICHAEL General clinical research center Orthotopic liver transplant--Hepatic function and hemodynamics
M01RR-00039-31 0382 (CLR) WATTS, NELSON B General clinical research center Adrenal medullary transplantation to CNS--Effect on hypothalamic-pituitary
M01RR-00039-31 0384 (CLR) KING, SPENCER B General clinical research center PTCA and CABG therapy in multi-vessel disease
M01RR-00039-31 0387 (CLR) BONKOVSKY, HERBERT L General clinical research center Vitamin B6 and homocysteine in atherosclerotic heart disease
M01RR-00039-31 0392 (CLR) LONGINI, IRA M General clinical research center Analysis of infectious disease data
M01RR-00039-31 0393 (CLR) KUTNER, NANCY General clinical research center End stage renal disease
M01RR-00039-31 0394 (CLR) BROGAN, DONNA R General clinical research center Career paths of male and female medical students
M01RR-00039-31 0398 (CLR) HABER, MICHAEL J General clinical research center Methods of analysis of categorical data
M01RR-00039-31 0399 (CLR) GOODMAN, SHERRYL H General clinical research center Effects of maternal depression on child development
M01RR-00039-31 0400 (CLR) BROGAN, DONNA R General clinical research center Prevalence and incidence of end stage renal disease
M01RR-00039-31 0404 (CLR) HENDERSON, JOHN MICHEAL General clinical research center Prosp. long. effects of surgical portal decompression in shunt procedure
M01RR-00039-31 0411 (CLR) PHILLIPS, LAWRENCE S General clinical research center Nutritional regulation of somatomedins and somatomedin inhibitors
M01RR-00039-31 0412 (CLR) DIGIROLAMO, MARIO General clinical research center Obesity, lactate overproduction and insulin
M01RR-00039-31 0416 (CLR) BONKOVSKY, HERBERT L. General clinical research center Gammaglobulin for the treatment of primary biliary cirrhosis
M01RR-00039-31 0417 (CLR) ELSAS, LOUISE J. General clinical research center Clinical and molecular studies of B-chain ketoacid dehydrogenase
M01RR-00039-31 0419 (CLR) PHILLIPS, LAWRENCE S. General clinical research center Characteristics which predict good response to glipizide in NIDDM
M01RR-00039-31 0420 (CLR) RIETHER, A. M. General clinical research center Quality of life changes and psychiatric outcome after liver transplant
M01RR-00039-31 0421 (CLR) GOODWIN, CAROL E. General clinical research center Self-care practices of patients with diabetes mellitus
M01RR-00039-31 0422 (CLR) WHELCHEL, JOHN D General clinical research center Survival analysis of renal transplantation
M01RR-00039-31 0423 (CLR) MANCE, ROSALIND M. General clinical research center Medication decision study in schizophrenic outpatients
M01RR-00039-31 0425 (CLR) HOPKINS, LINTON General clinical research center Diagnosis and treatment of mitochondrial disease
M01RR-00039-31 0426 (CLR) BONKOVSKY, HERBERT L General clinical research center Studies in heme metabolism
M01RR-00039-31 0427 (CLR) GEBHART, SUZANNE General clinical research center Very low calorie diet effecton insulin secretion and insulin resistance
M01RR-00039-31 0428 (CLR) DIGIROLAMO, MARIO General clinical research center High-fat diet effect on lactate generation /insulin resistance in obesity
M01RR-00039-31 0429 (CLR) WINTON, ELLIOT F General clinical research center Recombinant human granulocyte colony stimulating factor in severe neutropenia
M01RR-00039-31 0430 (CLR) HENDERSON, JOHN MICHAEL General clinical research center Pharmacokinetic anal--Indocyanine green elimination in normal/ cirrhotic patients
M01RR-00039-31 0431 (CLR) SANDS, JEFF General clinical research center Renal concentrating ability of patients lacking RBC urea transporter
M01RR-00039-31 0432 (CLR) GORDON, DAVID S General clinical research center IVIG in prophylaxis of infect in patients with CLL or MM & recurrent infect
M01RR-00039-31 0433 (CLR) ELSAS, LOUIS J General clinical research center Emery-Dreifuss muscular dystrophy--Pathophysiology and cloning the gene
M01RR-00039-31 0434 (CLR) RISBY, EMILE General clinical research center IV administration of alprazolam on psychiatric patients and normal controls
M01RR-00039-31 0435 (CLR) HENDERSON, JOHN MICHAEL General clinical research center Pharmacologic responses in cirrhossis
M01RR-00039-31 0436 (CLR) HASSOLD, JERRY General clinical research center Non-disjunction in trisomy 21
M01RR-00039-31 0368 (CLR) MOLL, GEORGE W, JR General clinical research center Lupron treatment of progressive precocious puberty
M01RR-00039-31 0371 (CLR) PARKS, JOHN S. General clinical research center Safety and efficacy of rhGH in untreated patients with GH deficiency
M01RR-00039-31 0375 (CLR) BONKOVSKY, HERBERT L General clinical research center Assessment of antipyrine metabolism and liver disease
M01RR-00039-31 0377 (CLR) BONKOVSKY, HERBERT L General clinical research center Eval. manag. and longitudinal follow-up of metabolic bone disease
M01RR-00039-31 0378 (CLR) BONKOVSKY, HERBERT L General clinical research center Diagnosis, evaluation and management of iron overload
M01RR-00039-31 0380 (CLR) GORDON, DAVID S General clinical research

center I V G-globulin treatment of rheumatoid arthritis and systemic lupus
K01RR-00040-04 (AR) BRIELAND, JOAN K UNIT FOR LAB ANIMAL MEDICINE ANIMAL RES FACILITY BOX 0614 ANN ARBOR, MI 48109 Pulmonary macrophage metalloproteinases and TIMP
M01RR-00040-31 (CLR) KELLEY, WILLIAM N UNIV OF PENNSYLVANIA 3400 SPRUCE ST PHILADELPHIA, PA 19104-6055 General clinical research center
M01RR-00040-31 0082 (CLR) SCHUMACHER, H RALPH General clinical research center Pathogenesis of articular lesions in systemic rheumatic diseases
M01RR-00040-31 0129 (CLR) SNYDER, PETER J General clinical research center Control of FSH and LH secretion
M01RR-00040-31 0210 (CLR) SNYDER, PETER J General clinical research center Effect of HCG and HMG on spermatogenesis
M01RR-00040-31 0415 (CLR) ENGELMAN, KARL General clinical research center Sensory effects on human plasma glucose insulin levels
M01RR-00040-31 0416 (CLR) SPEIGEL, THERESA A General clinical research center Diurnal cycles in lipid metabolism in lean and obese humans
M01RR-00040-31 0417 (CLR) BAUER, MARK M General clinical research center Entrainment of circadian rhythms in bipolar & seasonal affective disorder
M01RR-00040-31 0418 (CLR) ALAVI, ABASS General clinical research center Evaluation of (123I)TISCH--New D-1 dopamine receptor imaging agent
M01RR-00040-31 0260 (CLR) GUR, RAQUEL E General clinical research center Regional brain function in schizophrenia
M01RR-00040-31 0359 (CLR) DINGES, DAVID F General clinical research center Treatment of obstructive sleep apnea with nasal CPAP
M01RR-00040-31 0272 (CLR) SNYDER, PETER J General clinical research center Effect of Nal-Glu LHRH on gonadotroph adenoma secretion
M01RR-00040-31 0283 (CLR) KUSHNER, MICHAEL J General clinical research center Cerebral blood flow and aging and dementia
M01RR-00040-31 0286 (CLR) PACK, ALLEN General clinical research center Sleep apnea in the elderly
M01RR-00040-31 0297 (CLR) GOLDFARB, STANLEY General clinical research center Effect of captopril on progressive type I diabetic renal disease
M01RR-00040-31 0306 (CLR) OUYANG, ANN General clinical research center Neurohumoral control of small intestinal motility
M01RR-00040-31 0309 (CLR) SNYDER, PETER J General clinical research center Treatment of male hypogonadism with transdermal testosterone
M01RR-00040-31 0312 (CLR) AMSTERDAM, JAY D General clinical research center Psychoneuroendocrine evaluation of affective illness
M01RR-00040-31 0318 (CLR) GRUNWALD, JUAN General clinical research center Diabetic metabolic control and retinal blood flow
M01RR-00040-31 0360 (CLR) PACK, ALLAN I General clinical research center Role of sleep disruption in development of apnea
M01RR-00040-31 0366 (CLR) ATTIE, MAURICE F General clinical research center Genetic study of osteoporosis
M01RR-00040-31 0367 (CLR) SONDHEIMER, STEVEN J General clinical research center Oral progesterone sedation study
M01RR-00040-31 0371 (CLR) LAZARUS, GERALD S General clinical research center Phase I and II study of piritrexim capsules in psoriasis
M01RR-00040-31 0372 (CLR) ENGELMAN, KARL General clinical research center Chemotherapy in malignant pheochromocytoma
M01RR-00040-31 0373 (CLR) SHAW, LESLIE M General clinical research center Cyclosporine pharmacokinetics in heart transplant patients
M01RR-00040-31 0375 (CLR) O'BRIEN, CHRISTOPHER B General clinical research center Ursodeoxycholic acid treatment of chronic active hepatitis
M01RR-00040-31 0378 (CLR) ENGELMAN, KARL General clinical research center Effects of antihypertensive medication on taste and diet
M01RR-00040-31 0379 (CLR) GUERRY, DUPONT General clinical research center PhaseI/II study of murine monoclonal antibodies
M01RR-00040-31 0383 (CLR) GUR, RAQUEL E General clinical research center Tourette syndrome in discordant monzygotic twins
M01RR-00040-31 0385 (CLR) GOLDFARB, STANLEY General clinical research center Omnipaque cooperative study
M01RR-00040-31 0387 (CLR) SCHWARTZ, STANLEY S General clinical research center Esophageal and gastric motor abnormalities in diabetes mellitus
M01RR-00040-31 0388 (CLR) DINGES, DAVID F General clinical research center Effects of continuous and alternate night CPAP on sleep, breathing
M01RR-00040-31 0389 (CLR) ROTHSTEIN, ROBIN D General clinical research center Effect of food composition and calories on the electrical activity of stomach
M01RR-00040-31 0390 (CLR) ENGELMAN, KARL General clinical research center Cephalic phase insulin response in humans
M01RR-00040-31 0391 (CLR) SNYDER, PETER J General clinical research center Effect of sandostatin in treating acromegaly
M01RR-00040-31 0394 (CLR) KAPLAN, FREDERICK S General clinical research center Renal osteodystrophy in patients on dialysis
M01RR-00040-31 0397 (CLR) GOLDFARB, STANLEY General clinical research center Pharmacokinetics of single oral dose of ketoprofen
M01RR-00040-31 0400 (CLR) SEWITCH, DEBORAH E General clinical research center Effects of sertraline on sleep in outpatients with major depression
M01RR-00040-31 0402 (CLR) FREEMAN, ELLEN W General clinical research center ACTH and stress response
M01RR-00040-31 0404 (CLR) BAUER, MARK S General clinical research center Thyroid function in rapid cycling bipolar disorder--Genetic/family study
M01RR-00040-31 0405 (CLR) WINOKUR, ANDREW General clinical research center Sertraline-thyroid function study
M01RR-00040-31 0406 (CLR) HURTIG, HOWARD I General clinical research center In vivo imaging of dopamine receptors in Parkinson's disease
M01RR-00040-31 0407 (CLR) REIVICH, MARTIN General clinical research center Hemodynamic and metabolic alteration in patients at risk for ischemic stroke
M01RR-00040-31 0408 (CLR) MATTES, RICHARD D General clinical research center Physiologic responses to cannabinoids
M01RR-00040-31 0409 (CLR) WASSERSTEIN, ALAN G General clinical research center Dietary protein in idiopathic hypercalciuria
M01RR-00040-31 0410 (CLR) KELLEY, MARK A General clinical research center Prospective investigation of pulmonary embolism diagnosis
M01RR-00040-31 0411 (CLR) ROSTAMI, A M General clinical research center Extracorporeal photopheresis in chronic progressive multiple sclerosis
M01RR-00040-31 0412 (CLR) GROSSMAN, MURRAY General clinical research center Physiologic basis for neurolinguistic impairments
M01RR-00040-31 0413 (CLR) PACK, ALLAN General clinical research center Effect of REM deprovation on ventilation changes in REMS
M01RR-00040-31 0414 (CLR) BOYCE, ERIC G General clinical research center Interaction between methotrexate and naproxen in rheumatoid arthritis patients
M01RR-00040-31 0325 (CLR) SCHWARTZ, STANLEY General clinical research center Diabetes control and complications trial
M01RR-00040-31 0335 (CLR) GENNARELLI, THOMAS A General clinical research center Longitudinal studies of acute and chronic head injured patients
M01RR-00040-31 0336 (CLR) HURTIG, HOWARD L General clinical research center Deprenyl and tocopherol antioxidative therapy of Parkinsonism
M01RR-00040-31 0340 (CLR) KLINE, LEWIS R General clinical research center Progressive exercise vs sleep arterial oxygen desaturation
M01RR-00040-31 0341 (CLR) LOTKE, PAUL A General clinical research center Deep venous thrombosis /Foley catheter in total hip and knee replacement
M01RR-00040-31 0344 (CLR) O'BRIEN, CHRISTOPHER B General clinical research center IFN alone and following prednisone withdrawal in chronic hepatitis B
M01RR-00040-31 0351 (CLR) BAUER, MARK S General clinical research center Thyroid function in rapid cycling bipolar affective disorder
M01RR-00042-31 (CLR) BOLE, GILES G, JR UNIVERSITY OF MICHIGAN 1301 CATHERINE ST. ANN ARBOR, MI 48109-0624 General clinical research center
M01RR-00042-31 0667 (CLR) KIM, SUN KEE General clinical research center Secretory protein synthesis during aging
M01RR-00042-31 0668 (CLR) BROWN, S General clinical research center Actin-binding proteins in yeast
M01RR-00042-31 0669 (CLR) NEIDHARDT, FREDERICK C General clinical research center Regulation of bacterial metabolism
M01RR-00042-31 0670 (CLR) ENSMINGER, WILLIAM D General clinical research center Polymorphism of paraoxonase and variants of human serum
M01RR-00042-31 0671 (CLR) BARKAN, ARIEL General clinical research center Generation of pulsatile growth hormone secretion
M01RR-00042-31 0672 (CLR) THOMPSON, CRAIG B General clinical research center Gene conversion in myc-induced bursal lymphoma
M01RR-00042-31 0673 (CLR) LLOYD, RICARDO V General clinical research center Regulation of pituitary hyperplasia and neoplasia
M01RR-00042-31 0674 (CLR) HOLOSHITZ, JOSEPH General clinical research center T cell clones from rheumatoid arthritic synovial fluid
M01RR-00042-31 0675 (CLR) FUKUNAGA, NINA General clinical research center Molecular cDNA cloning of X-ray induced/repressed genes and proteins
M01RR-00042-31 0676 (CLR) KOOMEY, J MICHAEL General clinical research center Gonococcal pili--Studies of structure and function
M01RR-00042-31 0677 (CLR) EERNISSE, DOUGLAS J General clinical research center Phylogenetic analysis of Mollusca
M01RR-00042-31 0678 (CLR) BRIGGS, JOSEPHINE P General clinical research center Molecular biological approaches to study the renin angiotensin system
M01RR-00042-31 0679 (CLR) NEUBIG, RICHARD General clinical research center Alpha(2) adrenergic receptor-G protein interaction
M01RR-00042-31 0680 (CLR) CAMPBELL, ALAN D General clinical research center Role of hemonectin in hematopoiesis
M01RR-00042-31 0681 (CLR) KELCH, ROBERT P General clinical research center Nursing assessment of the menstrual cycle--Clinical models
M01RR-00042-31 0005 (CLR) STARKMAN, MONICA N General clinical research center Depression, peptides and steroids in Cushing's syndrome
M01RR-00042-31 0635 (CLR) GANTZ, IRA General clinical research center Computer-assisted analysis of gastric parietal cell receptors
M01RR-00042-31 0636 (CLR) ENSMINGER, WILLIAM D General clinical research center Efficacy and side effects of naprosyn on rheumatoid arthritis
M01RR-00042-31 0637 (CLR) ENSMINGER, WILLIAM D General clinical research center Efficacy & side effects of naprosyn in osteoarthritis treatment
M01RR-00042-31 0638 (CLR) BARTLETT, ROBERT H General clinical research center Metabolic effects of dopamine infusion in healthy human subjects
M01RR-00042-31 0639 (CLR) DRESSMAN, JENNIFER B General clinical research center Achlorhydria effect on upper gastrointestinal physiology in the elderly
M01RR-00042-31 0640 (CLR) NASR, SAMYA General clinical research center Vitamin E in cystic fibrosis--Deficiency, fat soluble & water miscible
M01RR-00042-31 0641 (CLR) KOENIG, RONALD J General clinical research center Molecular basis of thyroid hormone resistance
M01RR-00042-31 0642 (CLR) SACKELLARES, J CHRIS General clinical research center Felbamate as adjunctive therapy in subjects undergoing surgical evaluation
M01RR-00042-31 0643 (CLR) ROBERTSON, JOHN M General clinical research center Combined continuous infusional 5-fluorouracil, flurodeoxyuridine/radiation
M01RR-00042-31 0644 (CLR) BARNETT, JEFFREY L General clinical research center Exercise effects on colonic motility--Dynamic scintigraphic study
M01RR-00042-31 0645 (CLR) SACKELLARES, C JAMES General clinical

research center Long-term felbamate therapy in pediatric epilepsy
M01RR-00042-31 0646 (CLR) DRESSMAN, JENNIFER B General clinical research center pH related changes in dipyridamole absorption in the elderly
M01RR-00042-31 0647 (CLR) BRENNER, DEAN E General clinical research center Pharmacogenetic reductive metabolism
M01RR-00042-31 0648 (CLR) BLESKE, BARRY E General clinical research center Immediate & sustained release verapamil on propranolol pharmacokinetics
M01RR-00042-31 0649 (CLR) ENSMINGER, WILLIAM D General clinical research center Dose seeking study--Hepatic arterial fluorouracil with leucovorin
M01RR-00042-31 0650 (CLR) DIXIT, VISHVA MITRA General clinical research center TNF modulation of endothelial cell gene expression
M01RR-00042-31 0651 (CLR) SCHEIMAN, JAMES M General clinical research center Does omeprazole prevent aspirin induced gastroduodenal damage?
M01RR-00042-31 0652 (CLR) DRESSMAN, JENNIFER B General clinical research center Tolerance to methocel K in healthy subjects
M01RR-00042-31 0653 (CLR) HENLEY, KEITH General clinical research center IV prostaglandin E1 effect on rejection following hepatic transplant
M01RR-00042-31 0654 (CLR) POMERLEAU, OVIDE F General clinical research center Noninvasive delivery of specified doses of nicotine
M01RR-00042-31 0655 (CLR) BEEKMAAN, ROBERT H General clinical research center: Hemodynamic response to upright exercise following heart transplant
M01RR-00042-31 0656 (CLR) HASLER, WILLIAM General clinical research center Somatostatin analog octreotide effect on the dumping syndrome
M01RR-00042-31 0657 (CLR) WAHL, RICHARD L General clinical research center Pilot study--FDG PET in genitourinary tumor staging
M01RR-00042-31 0658 (CLR) MUENZER, JOSEPH General clinical research center Biopterin deficiency treatment with tetrahydrobiopterin
M01RR-00042-31 0659 (CLR) TRABER, PETER G General clinical research center Computer-assisted analysis of succrase-isomaltase gene
M01RR-00042-31 0660 (CLR) THIELE, DENNIS J General clinical research center Copper homeostasis in yeast
M01RR-00042-31 0661 (CLR) WEISS, BERNARD General clinical research center Uracil incorporation into DNA--Superoxide response regulon
M01RR-00042-31 0662 (CLR) PAYNE, ANITA H General clinical research center Genetic and hormonal regulation of steroid biosynthetic enzymes
M01RR-00042-31 0663 (CLR) LARGENT, BRIAN LEE General clinical research center Molecular analysis of neurogenesis in olfactory neurons
M01RR-00042-31 0664 (CLR) IMPERIALE, MICHAEL J General clinical research center Post-transcriptional regulation of viral gene expression
M01RR-00042-31 0665 (CLR) FEINBERG, ANDREW P General clinical research center Molecular basis of neoplastic histopathology
M01RR-00042-31 0666 (CLR) CAMPER, SALLY General clinical research center Developmental genetics of pituitary glaaand
M01RR-00042-31 0102 (CLR) HOPWOOD, NANCY J General clinical research center Growth hormone secretion in children and adolescents
M01RR-00042-31 0601 (CLR) DICK, MACDONALD General clinical research center Identification of ventricular arrhythmias in children with heart disease
M01RR-00042-31 0602 (CLR) WAHL, RICHARD General clinical research center Study of the significance of delayed biliary drainage at ERCP
M01RR-00042-31 0603 (CLR) CHAUNCEY, JAMES BROWN General clinical research center Parallel comparison of OXIVENT inhalation aerosol and B1-B2 agonist
M01RR-00042-31 0604 (CLR) MCINTOSH, NANCY A General clinical research center Intervention to reduce passive smoking in children with asthma
M01RR-00042-31 0606 (CLR) SCHWAIGER, MARKUS General clinical research center Localization of pheochromocytoma with positron emission tomography
M01RR-00042-31 0607 (CLR) BARKAN, ARIEL L General clinical research center Safety and efficacy of sandostatin for treatment of acromegaly
M01RR-00042-31 0608 (CLR) FOSTER, NORMAN L General clinical research center Neuropharmacologic challenges in dementia
M01RR-00042-31 0610 (CLR) SISSON, JAMES C General clinical research center Studies of patients in families with multiple endocrine neoplasia
M01RR-00042-31 0611 (CLR) SCHTEINGART, DAVID E General clinical research center Taste related behaviors and metabolic status in man
M01RR-00042-31 0612 (CLR) BARNETT, JEFFREY L General clinical research center Myoelectric & motor effect of dopamine on rectosigmoid colon
M01RR-00042-31 0613 (CLR) CORAN, ARNOLD G General clinical research center Total body water and extracellular fluid changes in infants
M01RR-00042-31 0614 (CLR) BARNETT, JEFF General clinical research center Plasma glucose as a modulator of gastrointestinal motility
M01RR-00042-31 0615 (CLR) ENSMINGER, WILLIAM D General clinical research center Intra-arterial radiosensitization with BUdR and 5-fluorouracil therapy
M01RR-00042-31 0616 (CLR) BARKAN, ARIEL L General clinical research center Long-acting somatostatin analog treatment--Bone mineral density effect
M01RR-00042-31 0617 (CLR) GREENBERG, HARRY S General clinical research center Intra-arterial chemotherapy with BCNU during hyperventilation
M01RR-00042-31 0618 (CLR) MESSANA, JOSEPH M General clinical research center Renal studies during cyclosporine double blind placebo clinical trial
M01RR-00042-31 0619 (CLR) ENSMINGER, WILLIAM D General clinical research center Combination chemo-radiation for liver/porta hepatis involved cancer
M01RR-00042-31 0620 (CLR) CORAN, ARNOLD G General clinical research center Dermatoglyphic patterns in children with congenital anomalies & chronic disorders
M01RR-00042-31 0621 (CLR) BREWER, GEORGE J General clinical research center Initial therapy of Wilson's disease with ammonium tetrathiomolybdate
M01RR-00042-31 0622 (CLR) AISEN, ALEX General clinical research center Glycogen storage disease hyperuricemia--Inorganic phosphate therapy
M01RR-00042-31 0623 (CLR) SACKELLARES, J CHRIS General clinical research center Pharmacophysiologic study of temporal lobe benzodiazepine responses
M01RR-00042-31 0624 (CLR) HOPWOOD, NANCY J General clinical research center Hypoglycemia in infants and young children--Diagnosis and natural history
M01RR-00042-31 0625 (CLR) CHENEVERT, THOMAS L General clinical research center MRI evaluation of children with dermatomyositis
M01RR-00042-31 0626 (CLR) BROMBERG, MARK B General clinical research center L-Threonine and branched chain amino acids in ALS
M01RR-00042-31 0627 (CLR) ALESSI, NORMAN E General clinical research center Time-integrated measurement of saliva cortisol in healthy controls
M01RR-00042-31 0628 (CLR) ELTA, GRACE H General clinical research center Campylobacter phylori treatment effect on non-ulcer dyspepsia
M01RR-00042-31 0629 (CLR) SAMPSELLE, CAROLYN M General clinical research center Standardization and validation of the urine stop test
M01RR-00042-31 0630 (CLR) NICKLAS, JOHN M General clinical research center Serum potassium/magnesium hourly variability in congestive heart failure patients
M01RR-00042-31 0631 (CLR) HOPWOOD, NANCY J General clinical research center Growth hormone neurosecretion assessment in children with poor growth
M01RR-00042-31 0632 (CLR) ELLIS, CHARLES N General clinical research center Multiple dose pharmacokinetics of acetretin (Ro 10-1670) and Ro 13-7652
M01RR-00042-31 0633 (CLR) MODELL, JACK G General clinical research center Intravenous haloperidol pretreatment effect on craving in alcoholics
M01RR-00042-31 0634 (CLR) FOX, DAVID A General clinical research center Safety and efficacy of XomaZyme-H65 in rheumatoid arthritis
M01RR-00042-31 0169 (CLR) THOENE, JESSEE G General clinical research center Aminothiol therapy in nephropathic cystinosis
M01RR-00042-31 0553 (CLR) JENISTA, JERI ANN General clinical research center Growth standards for malnourished children adopted early
M01RR-00042-31 0557 (CLR) FLOYD, JOHN C General clinical research center Metformin alone or in combination with a second generation sulfonylurea
M01RR-00042-31 0560 (CLR) HERMAN, WILLIAM H General clinical research center Screening and intervention for microalbuminuria in diabetes
M01RR-00042-31 0561 (CLR) NICKLAS, JOHN M General clinical research center Effects of flosquinan on exercise tolerance in congestive heart failure patients
M01RR-00042-31 0562 (CLR) WOLF, GREGORY T General clinical research center Phase II interleukin-2 & roferon A in head & neck squamous cell carcinoma
M01RR-00042-31 0565 (CLR) ALESSI, NORMAN E General clinical research center Urinary urgency in response to TRH--Imipramine action mechanism & effect
M01RR-00042-31 0566 (CLR) BEEKMAN, ROBERT H General clinical research center MR evaluation of the central pulmonary arteries in children/obstructive lesions
M01RR-00042-31 0569 (CLR) CHANG, ALFRED E General clinical research center Evaluation of iododeoxyuridine (IUdR) infusion and radiation therapy
M01RR-00042-31 0570 (CLR) ROCCHINI, ALBERT P General clinical research center Insulin and blood pressure sensitivity to sodium
M01RR-00042-31 0571 (CLR) CODY, ROBERT L General clinical research center Bone density in patients undergoing adjuvant treatment for breast cancer
M01RR-00042-31 0572 (CLR) CHANG, ALFRED E General clinical research center Interleukin-2 & interferon-alpha in advanced colorectal cancer therapy
M01RR-00042-31 0573 (CLR) RICHARDSON, BRUCE General clinical research center Treatment of rheumatoid arthritis with cytosine arabinoside
M01RR-00042-31 0574 (CLR) ENSMINGER, WILLIAM D General clinical research center Stimulation of ATP synthesis with beta-hydroxybutyrate and inorganic phosphate
M01RR-00042-31 0576 (CLR) ALDRICH, MICHAEL S General clinical research center Effect of transtracheal oxygen therapy in sleep apnea
M01RR-00042-31 0578 (CLR) ECKHAUSER, FREDERICK E General clinical research center Effects of calcitonin gene-related peptide on mesenteric blood flow
M01RR-00042-31 0580 (CLR) ENSMINGER, WILLIAM D General clinical research center Diagnosis and management of neuroendocrine tumors
M01RR-00042-31 0582 (CLR) STARLING, MARK R General clinical research center Mechanics and energetics of myocardial dysfunction
M01RR-00042-31 0583 (CLR) WHITE, NEIL H General clinical research center Subcutaneous insulin resistance as a cause of recurrent ketoacidosis
M01RR-00042-31 0585 (CLR) HAINES, RICHARD General clinical research center HLA studies in schizophrenics with narcolepsy
M01RR-00042-31 0586 (CLR) HALTER, JEFFREY B General clinical research center Diabetes care for older adults
M01RR-00042-31 0588 (CLR) HOWELL, JOEL D General clinical research center Assessment of early medical technology use
M01RR-00042-31 0589 (CLR) SCHWAIGER, MARKUS General clinical research center F-18 deoxyglucose metabolic imaging of the heart in the diabetic population
M01RR-00042-31 0590 (CLR) O'CONNOR, BRIAN K General clinical research center Long-term effectiveness of balloon valvuloplasty in children
M01RR-00042-31 0591 (CLR) LAING, TIMOTHY J General clinical research center Biochemical efficacy of CP-66,248-2 vs naproxen in rheumatoid arthritis patients
M01RR-00042-31 0592 (CLR) MCCUNE, W JOSEPH General clinical

PROJECT NO., ORGANIZATIONAL UNIT., INVESTIGATOR, ADDRESS, TITLE

research center Pilot prospective study comparing MRI and PET in lupus patients with dementia

M01RR-00042-31 0593 (CLR) MESSANA, JOSEPH M General clinical research center Amino acids in peritoneal dialysate--Osmotic agent and nutritional supplement

M01RR-00042-31 0594 (CLR) HASKETT, ROGER F General clinical research center Pathophysiology of corticosteroid dysregulation in depression

M01RR-00042-31 0595 (CLR) KADISH, ALAN H General clinical research center Electrophysiologic testing in patients with nonsustained ventricular tachycardia

M01RR-00042-31 0597 (CLR) FIG, LORRAINE General clinical research center The effects of treatment of acromegaly on cardiac function

M01RR-00042-31 0598 (CLR) TANDON, RAJIV General clinical research center: Cholinergic mechanism in schizophrenia--Sleep electroencephalographic study

M01RR-00042-31 0599 (CLR) CODY, ROBERT L General clinical research center PET imaging of breast cancer and its response to treatment

M01RR-00042-31 0600 (CLR) SACKELLARES, J CHRIS General clinical research center Evaluation of felbamate in subjects with Lennox-Gastaut syndrome

M01RR-00042-31 0226 (CLR) BREWER, GEORGE J General clinical research center Treatment of Wilson's disease with zinc

M01RR-00042-31 0485 (CLR) SEDMAN, AILEEN General clinical research center Growth failure in children with renal disease

M01RR-00042-31 0488 (CLR) STARLING, MARK R General clinical research center Clinical application of end-systolic P-V relations

M01RR-00042-31 0489 (CLR) THOENE, JESS G General clinical research center Study and treatment of inborn errors of metabolism

M01RR-00042-31 0494 (CLR) AKIL, HUDA General clinical research center Glucocorticoid fast feedback regulation in depression

M01RR-00042-31 0495 (CLR) WHITE, NEIL H General clinical research center Diagnosis/natural history of hypoglycemia in infants and children

M01RR-00042-31 0502 (CLR) HALTER, JEFFREY B General clinical research center Neural regulation of metabolism

M01RR-00042-31 0506 (CLR) ENSMINGER, WILLIAM D General clinical research center Heptic arterial yttrium 90 microsphere therapy for liver neoplasia

M01RR-00042-31 0507 (CLR) OWYANG, CHUNG General clinical research center Secretin and gastrointestinal motility in man

M01RR-00042-31 0508 (CLR) LAWRENCE, THEODORE S General clinical research center Combination chemo-radiation/liver transplantation therapy for malignancy

M01RR-00042-31 0509 (CLR) MCCUNE, JOSEPH General clinical research center Monthly IV cyclophasphamide in severe systemic lupus erythematosus

M01RR-00042-31 0510 (CLR) ECKHAUSER, FREDERIC E General clinical research center ESWL for patients with common bile duct and gallbladder stones

M01RR-00042-31 0511 (CLR) KAMINSKI, MARK S General clinical research center Radiolabeled monoclonal pan B-cell antibody MB1

M01RR-00042-31 0512 (CLR) SACKELLARES, J CHRIS General clinical research center Evaluation of flunarizine in the treatment of partial seizures

M01RR-00042-31 0235 (CLR) KELCH, ROBERT P General clinical research center Maturation of pituitary response to GnRH in children

M01RR-00042-31 0250 (CLR) OWYANG, CHUNG General clinical research center Feedback regulation of pancreatic enzyme system

M01RR-00042-31 0287 (CLR) WATSON, STANLEY J General clinical research center Pro-opiocortin regulation in biological depression

M01RR-00042-31 0288 (CLR) HALTER, JEFFREY B General clinical research center Aging and autonomic nervous system function in aging

M01RR-00042-31 0289 (CLR) SUPIANO, MARK A General clinical research center Sympathetic function in elderly human hypertension/effects of enalapril

M01RR-00042-31 0302 (CLR) BEITINS, INESE Z General clinical research center Heterogeneity of gonadotropins in serum and urine

M01RR-00042-31 0314 (CLR) BOXER, LAURENCE A General clinical research center Mechanisms of granulocyte activation

M01RR-00042-31 0337 (CLR) SISSON, JAMES C General clinical research center Radiopharmaceutical treatment of malignant pheochromocytoma

M01RR-00042-31 0343 (CLR) GRUNHAUS, LEON General clinical research center Comorbidity of major depression and panic disorder--Clinical-biological

M01RR-00042-31 0400 (CLR) MARSHALL, JOHN C General clinical research center Gonadotropin secretion--Role of pulsatile GNRH & gonadal steroid

M01RR-00042-31 0402 (CLR) GREKIN, ROGER J General clinical research center Atrial function of hypertension

M01RR-00042-31 0404 (CLR) HOPWOOD, NANCY J General clinical research center Suppression of gonadotropin secretion with GNRH analog

M01RR-00042-31 0408 (CLR) SCHTEINGART, DAVID E General clinical research center CRH stimulation of ACTH & beta-endorphin secretion in obesity

M01RR-00042-31 0418 (CLR) ENSMINGER, WILLIAM D General clinical research center Pharmacokinetic/phase I-5-bromodeoxyuridine (BUDR)/ via hepatic artery

M01RR-00042-31 0431 (CLR) ROCCHINI, ALBERT P General clinical research center Mechanism of obesity hypertension in adolescents

M01RR-00042-31 0453 (CLR) DRESSMAN, JENNIFER General clinical research center Gastrointestinal pH in the elderly

M01RR-00042-31 0459 (CLR) BEEKMAN, ROBERT H General clinical research center Effects of nifedipine in children with bronchopulmonary dysplasia

M01RR-00042-31 0465 (CLR) GOSNELL, BLAKE A General clinical research center Endogenous opiates, taste and food preference in rats and humans

M01RR-00042-31 0469 (CLR) FOSTER, CAROL M General clinical research center Influence of gonadal steroids on growth hormone bioactivity

M01RR-00042-31 0470 (CLR) HUTCHINSON, RAYMOND J General clinical research center Children's cancer study group protocols

M01RR-00042-31 0473 (CLR) KILENY, PAUL R General clinical research center Cochlear prosthesis--Subject selection and rehabilitation

PROJECT NO., ORGANIZATIONAL UNIT., INVESTIGATOR, ADDRESS, TITLE

M01RR-00042-31 0476 (CLR) MOLER, FRANK W General clinical research center Continuous nebulization of terbutaline for severe childhood asthma

M01RR-00042-31 0481 (CLR) PENNEY, JOHN B General clinical research center Deprenyl and tocopherol antioxidant therapy of Parkinsonism

M01RR-00042-31 0523 (CLR) ABELSON, JAMES C General clinical research center Hypothalamic-pituitary-adrenal function in patients with panic disorder

M01RR-00042-31 0525 (CLR) TROBE, JONATHAN DANIEL General clinical research center Optic neuritis treatment trial

M01RR-00042-31 0527 (CLR) STARKMAN, M N General clinical research center Regional sympathetic activity in anxiety disorders

M01RR-00042-31 0530 (CLR) MESSINA, LOUIS M General clinical research center Iloprost study in patients with severe peripheral atherosclero

M01RR-00042-31 0532 (CLR) NICKLAS, JOHN M General clinical research center SOLVD substudy on sudden death in CHF patients

M01RR-00042-31 0533 (CLR) NICKLAS, JOHN M General clinical research center Chronic efficacy and safety of pimobendan in patients with class III-IV CHF

M01RR-00042-31 0534 (CLR) NICKLAS, JOHN M General clinical research center SOLVD substudy on neurohormone mechanisms in CHF

M01RR-00042-31 0537 (CLR) MOLER, FRANK W General clinical research center ATP degradation product in body fluids of pediatric intensive care patients

M01RR-00042-31 0538 (CLR) ELLIS, CHARLES N General clinical research center Effects of cyclosporine A in the treatment of severe psoriasis

M01RR-00042-31 0539 (CLR) COLLINS, FRANCIS S General clinical research center Computer analysis of human genome using the Wisconsin package

M01RR-00042-31 0540 (CLR) BOXER, LAURENCE A General clinical research center Recombinant human interferon-gamma in chronic granulomatous disease patients

M01RR-00042-31 0541 (CLR) BOXER, LAWRENCE A General clinical research center Recombinant human granulocyte colony stimulating factor

M01RR-00042-31 0542 (CLR) LEE, DOH-YEEL General clinical research center Absorption, turnover, and biochemical studies of zinc in man

M01RR-00042-31 0543 (CLR) BARKAN, ARIEL L General clinical research center Physiopathology of pulsatile GH secretion in humans

M01RR-00042-31 0545 (CLR) FIG, LORRAINE General clinical research center Diagnosis and antibody-directed therapy of breast cancer

M01RR-00042-31 0546 (CLR) GREENE, DOUGLAS A General clinical research center Diabetes control and complications trial

M01RR-00042-31 0549 (CLR) MCCUNE, W JOSEPH General clinical research center The use of methotrexate in steroid-dependent asthma

M01RR-00042-31 0550 (CLR) ABELSON, JAMES L General clinical research center Adrenergic variables--State markers for panic disorder?

M01RR-00042-31 0552 (CLR) CHANG, ALFRED E General clinical research center Adoptive cellular therapy of cancer with vaccine-primed lymphocytes

M01RR-00043-31 (CLR) RYAN, STEPHEN J UNIV OF SOUTHERN CALIFORNIA 2025 ZONAL AVENUE LOS ANGELES, CA 90033 General clinical research center

M01RR-00043-31 0377 (CLR) SPENCER, CAROLE A General clinical research center Sensitivity and specificity of serum TSH test in thyroid screening

M01RR-00043-31 0378 (CLR) SPENCER, CAROLE A General clinical research center Nonthyroidal markers vs TSH and thyroglobulin in thyroid suppression

M01RR-00043-31 0381 (CLR) YELLIN, ALBERT E General clinical research center Efficacy of iloprost in healing ischemic ulcers

M01RR-00043-31 0388 (CLR) HSUEH, WILLA A General clinical research center Use of captopril in diabetic, hypertensive patients

M01RR-00043-31 0394 (CLR) CAMPESE, VITO M. General clinical research center Calcium metabolism in essential hypertension

M01RR-00043-31 0397 (CLR) VALENZUELA, JORGE E. General clinical research center Characteristics of pancreatic secretion in chronic alcoholics

M01RR-00043-31 0407 (CLR) BUCHANAN, THOMAS A. General clinical research center Twins at risk for type II diabetes

M01RR-00043-31 0409 (CLR) HORWITZ, DAVID General clinical research center Therafectin in previously treated rheumatoid arthritis patients

M01RR-00043-31 0411 (CLR) NADLER, JERRY L. General clinical research center Prostaglandin dopamine interaction in man

M01RR-00043-31 0414 (CLR) LOPRESTI, JONATHAN S. General clinical research center Alterations in T4 disposal pathways in low T3 states

M01RR-00043-31 0420 (CLR) HESELTINE, PETER N. General clinical research center Efficacy of peptide T for neuropsychiatric complications of AIDS

M01RR-00043-31 0424 (CLR) BHANDARI, ANIL General clinical research center Electrophysiologic evaluation of parenteral magnesium sulfate

M01RR-00043-31 0435 (CLR) HORTON, RICHARD General clinical research center Interferon alpha-2a-prostaglandin interactions

M01RR-00043-31 0436 (CLR) LOPRESTI, JONATHAN S General clinical research center Unique alterations of thyroid function in AIDS

M01RR-00043-31 0439 (CLR) LEEDOM, JOHN M General clinical research center Maintenance therapy for prevention of CMV retinitis in AIDS patients

M01RR-00043-31 0440 (CLR) GRAY, DAVID S General clinical research center Effects of weight loss in obese NIDDM

M01RR-00043-31 0442 (CLR) SINGER, FREDERICK R General clinical research center Intravenous APD in severe Paget's disease of bone

M01RR-00043-31 0449 (CLR) MUGGIA, FRANCO M General clinical research center Phase I clinical trial of VS103 in advanced malignancies

M01RR-00043-31 0450 (CLR) CAMPESE, VITO M General clinical research center Autonomic nervous function in uremia

M01RR-00043-31 0452 (CLR) SPENCER, CAROLE A General clinical research center Hypophysectomy for metastatic thyroid carcinoma

PROJECT NO., ORGANIZATIONAL UNIT., INVESTIGATOR, ADDRESS, TITLE

M01RR-00043-31 0453 (CLR) CARMEL, RALPH General clinical research center Subtle disturbances of cobalamin status
M01RR-00043-31 0454 (CLR) LOPRESTI, JONATHAN S General clinical research center TFTs as predictors of outcome in critically ill patients
M01RR-00043-31 0455 (CLR) DOOLEY, CORNELIUS General clinical research center Development of standardized test for measurement of GI transit
M01RR-00043-31 0458 (CLR) SHOUPE, DONNA General clinical research center Interaction of CRF, insulin and beta endorphins in normal women and PCS
M01RR-00043-31 0459 (CLR) LOBO, ROGERIO A General clinical research center Is a generic form of premarin identical?
M01RR-00043-31 0460 (CLR) RUDE, ROBERT K General clinical research center Efficacy of MK-217 in treatment of hypercalcemia of malignancy
M01RR-00043-31 0461 (CLR) GRUNBERG, STEVEN M General clinical research center: LY264618 (dideasatetrahydrofolate, DDATHF) phase I study
M01RR-00043-31 0462 (CLR) HU, EDDIE General clinical research center 131 LYM1-1 therapy for B-cell malignancies
M01RR-00043-31 0463 (CLR) BRAY, GEORGE A General clinical research center Fatty distribution of metabolism
M01RR-00043-31 0465 (CLR) CAMPESE, VITO M General clinical research center Effect of nefedipine in hypertension
M01RR-00043-31 0466 (CLR) CAUSEY, DENNIS M General clinical research center Foscarnet for HIV infection in patients receiving long-term ZDV therapy
M01RR-00043-31 0467 (CLR) VALENZUELA, JORGE E General clinical research center Pancreatic protein turnover in normal and alcoholic subjects
M01RR-00043-31 0084 (CLR) SINGER, FREDERICK R General clinical research center Pharmacological effects of salmon and human calcitonin
M01RR-00043-31 0468 (CLR) SHAW, SYLVIA General clinical research center Double-blind placebo parallel trial in type II diabetes mellitus
M01RR-00043-31 0470 (CLR) HESELTINE, PETER N General clinical research center Phase I--AS-101 in combination with zidovudine in AIDS/ARC patients
M01RR-00043-31 0471 (CLR) BUCHANAN, THOMAS A General clinical research center Insulin in class 1A gestational diabetes--Effect on fetal development
M01RR-00043-31 0472 (CLR) BUCHANAN, THOMAS A General clinical research center Blood pressure regulation and insulin in obesity and diabetes mellitus
M01RR-00043-31 0474 (CLR) KAPTEIN, ELAINE M General clinical research center Risks of renal biopsy due to altered coagulation in renal diseases
M01RR-00043-31 0476 (CLR) DEQUATTRO, VINCENT General clinical research center Efficacy of relaxation therapy in patients with primary hypertension
M01RR-00043-31 0094 (CLR) RUDE, ROBERT K General clinical research center Experimental human magnesium deficiency
M01RR-00043-31 0158 (CLR) HORTON, RICHARD General clinical research center Rare states of endocrine dysfunction
M01RR-00043-31 0278 (CLR) HSUEH, WILLA A General clinical research center Renin activation in diabetes mellitus
M01RR-00043-31 0281 (CLR) LOPRESTI, JONATHAN S. General clinical research center Thyroid needle biopsy--Its diagnostic usefulness in thyroid cancer
M01RR-00043-31 0287 (CLR) NADLER, JERRY L General clinical research center Interaction of smoking and renal prostaglandins
M01RR-00043-31 0301 (CLR) CHANDRARATNA, P A N General clinical research center Doppler ultrasound assessment of mitral valve flow in atrial systole
M01RR-00043-31 0305 (CLR) ELKAYAM, URI General clinical research center Hemodynamics of constant rate IV infusion of nitroglycerin
M01RR-00043-31 0315 (CLR) HORWITZ, DAVID General clinical research center Extended study of therafectin safety and efficacy
M01RR-00043-31 0333 (CLR) NADLER, JERRY L General clinical research center Calcium and channel blocker influence on renin and renal prostaglandins
M01RR-00043-31 0351 (CLR) COHEN, HARTLEY General clinical research center Effect and efficacy of the gastric bubble in treating obesity
M01RR-00043-31 0354 (CLR) BRAY, GEORGE A. General clinical research center Body composition with weight change
M01RR-00043-31 0357 (CLR) KAPTEIN, ELAINE M General clinical research center Thyroid hormone kinetics in kidney disease
M01RR-00043-31 0367 (CLR) MASSRY, SHAUL G General clinical research center Diet on rate of progression of renal failure
M01RR-00043-31 0369 (CLR) KAWANISHI, DAVID T General clinical research center Balloon catheter dilation of stenotic heart valve--valvuloplasty
M01RR-00043-31 0373 (CLR) RUDE, ROBERT K General clinical research center Prevalence and treatment of Mg++ deficiency in essential hypertension
M01RR-00043-31 0477 (CLR) DEQUATTRO, VINCENT General clinical research center Pharmacological effects on pressor surge in patients with primary hypertension
M01RR-00043-31 0478 (CLR) REYNOLDS, TELFER B General clinical research center Sclerotherapy and portalsystemic shunt for hemorrhage in cirrhosis
M01RR-00043-31 0479 (CLR) BUCHANAN, THOMAS A General clinical research center Insulin sensitivity in gestational diabetes mellitus
M01RR-00043-31 0480 (CLR) RUDE, ROBERT K General clinical research center Efficacy 24-hr i.v. didronel therapy in hypercalcemia of malignancy
M01RR-00043-31 0481 (CLR) HSUEH, WILLA A General clinical research center Captopril therapy in hypertensive diabetics
M01RR-00043-31 0482 (CLR) GRUNBERG, STEVEN M General clinical research center Urinary excretion of CGP23339A in treatment of malignant hypercalcemia
M01RR-00043-31 0483 (CLR) HSUEH, WILLA A General clinical research center Enalkiren--A new intravenous renin inhibitor

PROJECT NO., ORGANIZATIONAL UNIT., INVESTIGATOR, ADDRESS, TITLE

M01RR-00043-31 0484 (CLR) HORTON, RICHARD General clinical research center Prostaglandin-renin and the diabetic state
M01RR-00043-31 0485 (CLR) SATTLER, FRED R General clinical research center Dapsone pharmacokinetics
M01RR-00043-31 0486 (CLR) BUCHANAN, THOMAS A General clinical research center Antihypertensive therapy and insulin sensitivity in hypertension
M01RR-00043-31 0487 (CLR) SATTLER, FRED R General clinical research center Effect of acetaminophen on the pharmacokinetics of i.v. zidovudine
M01RR-00043-31 0488 (CLR) DOUVAS, ANGELINE General clinical research center Molecular mechanisms in scleroderma--The role of Scl 70/TOPO I
M01RR-00043-31 0489 (CLR) HSUEH, WILLA A General clinical research center Fosinopril vs verapamil on BP and protein excretion in type II diabetes
M01RR-00043-31 0490 (CLR) LOBO, ROGERIO A General clinical research center Sex steroid hormone and insulin action in pre- and postmenopausal women
M01RR-00043-31 0491 (CLR) ELKAYAM, URI General clinical research center The disposition of atenolol during pregnancy
M01RR-00043-31 0492 (CLR) SHOUPE, DONNA General clinical research center Effect of naltrexone on glucose tolerance in obese women and those with PCOS
M01RR-00043-31 0493 (CLR) KOVACS, ANDREA General clinical research center Pediatric pulmonary complications of vertically transmitted HIV infection
M01RR-00043-31 0494 (CLR) KOVACS, ANDREA General clinical research center Pediatric/maternal HIV associated dementia and role of Herpes virus
M01RR-00043-31 0495 (CLR) KOVACS, ANDREA General clinical research center High vs low dose zidovudine administered to children with HIV infection
M01RR-00043-31 0496 (CLR) KOVACS, ANDREA General clinical research center Double-blind study of gamma globulin in children with HIV on zidovudine
M01RR-00044-31 (CLR) LICHTMAN, MARSHALL A UNIVERSITY OF ROCHESTER 601 ELMWOOD AVENUE ROCHESTER, NY 14642 General clinical research center
M01RR-00044-31 0226 (CLR) FORBES, GILBERT B General clinical research center Body composition in obesity
M01RR-00044-31 0229 (CLR) GRIGGS, ROBERT C General clinical research center Metabolic studies in neuromuscular disease
M01RR-00044-31 0248 (CLR) UTELL, MARK J General clinical research center Sulfate aerosols on exposure of ozone on human lung function
M01RR-00044-31 0272 (CLR) BROWN, MARILYN General clinical research center Selenium deficiency and treatment with selenium
M01RR-00044-31 0300 (CLR) FORBES, GILBERT B. General clinical research center Lean body mass in pregnant women
M01RR-00044-31 0302 (CLR) FORBES, GILBERT B. General clinical research center Twins study--Inheritance of lean body mass in man
M01RR-00044-31 0376 (CLR) UTELL, MARK J General clinical research center Air pollution on breathing assessed by lung lavage in healthy humans
M01RR-00044-31 0377 (CLR) RUBIN, PHILIP General clinical research center Hypoxic cell sensitizer with radiation therapy in squamous cell carcinoma
M01RR-00044-31 0378 (CLR) MOTTLEY, JACK G General clinical research center Ultrasonic tissue characterization of myocardium and skeletal muscle
M01RR-00044-31 0379 (CLR) ABERNATHY, ALEXIS D General clinical research center Parenteral history of hypertension and recovery rate after stress
M01RR-00044-31 0380 (CLR) GOLDSTEIN, BRAHAM General clinical research center Autonomic function by heart rate power spectral analysis--Anorexia/bulimia
M01RR-00044-31 0381 (CLR) KEEFER, MICHAEL C General clinical research center DdI & zidovudine comparison in AIDS or ARC patients on long term zidovudine
M01RR-00044-31 0382 (CLR) SCHWARTZ, ROBERT H General clinical research center Food challenge with cow's milk protein hydrolysate in allergic children
M01RR-00044-31 0383 (CLR) FITZPATRICK, PATRICIA G General clinical research center Survival study of oral milrinone in severe heart failure patients
M01RR-00044-31 0384 (CLR) POWELL, KEITH R General clinical research center Cefpirome safety, tolerance & pharmacokinetics in infants & children
M01RR-00044-31 0385 (CLR) MCCUNE, CRAIG S General clinical research center Renal carcinoma and melanoma treatment with vaccines & interleukin-2
M01RR-00044-31 0386 (CLR) LIANG, CHANG-SENG General clinical research center Fosinopril, hydrochlorothiazide & placebo in mild to moderate hypertension
M01RR-00044-31 0387 (CLR) JOZEFOWICZ, RALPH F General clinical research center Effect of age on muscle protein synthesis
M01RR-00044-31 0388 (CLR) HARPER, KRISTINE D General clinical research center Bone metabolism, morphometry & mineral content in adolescents
M01RR-00044-31 0389 (CLR) KIEBURTZ, KARL D General clinical research center Open trial of ddI in patients with AIDS dementia complex
M01RR-00044-31 0390 (CLR) KURLAN, ROGER M General clinical research center RO 19-6327 safety, tolerance & influence on clinical status--Parkinsonism
M01RR-00044-31 0305 (CLR) HOOD, WILLIAM B. General clinical research center Left ventricular dysfunction (SOLVD)--Prevention and treatment
M01RR-00044-31 0306 (CLR) KURLAN, ROGER M. General clinical research center Intraduodenal infusion of levodopa in Parkinson's
M01RR-00044-31 0307 (CLR) KURLAN, ROGER M. General clinical research center Sinemet CR & standard sinemet 25/100 in advanced Parkinson's disease

PROJECT NO., ORGANIZATIONAL UNIT., INVESTIGATOR, ADDRESS, TITLE

M01RR-00044-31 0310 (CLR) LIANG, CHANG-SENG General clinical research center Enalapril and furosemide in patients with congestive heart failure
M01RR-00044-31 0321 (CLR) SAX, HARRY C General clinical research center Body composition & nutrition in spinal cord injury
M01RR-00044-31 0322 (CLR) KURLAN, ROGER M General clinical research center Deprenyl & tocopherol antioxidative therapy in Parkinsonism
M01RR-00044-31 0331 (CLR) FORBES, GILBERT General clinical research center Metabolic response to increased food intake
M01RR-00044-31 0343 (CLR) GIANG, DANIEL General clinical research center Lupus encephalopathy--Clinical and laboratory features
M01RR-00044-31 0346 (CLR) TARIOT, PIERRE N General clinical research center Arecoline in patients with Alzheimers disease and controls
M01RR-00044-31 0351 (CLR) ABERNETHY, ALEXIS D General clinical research center Hypertension and mental arithmetic
M01RR-00044-31 0353 (CLR) ASHRAF, MARY H General clinical research center Iron nutrition in elderly females with chronic health disorders
M01RR-00044-31 0354 (CLR) OURIEL, KENNETH General clinical research center Iloprost in patients with severe atherosclerotic peripheral artery disease
M01RR-00044-31 0355 (CLR) LIANG, CHANG-SENY General clinical research center Fosinopril sodium in patients with moderately severe congestive heart failure
M01RR-00044-31 0356 (CLR) KURLAN, ROGER M General clinical research center Drug holiday in Parkinson's disease--A controlled pilot study
M01RR-00044-31 0357 (CLR) AMATRUDA, JOHN M General clinical research center Metabolic rate and protein turnover in obesity
M01RR-00044-31 0358 (CLR) KEEFER, MICHAEL C General clinical research center Comparison of ddI and zidovudine in patients with AIDS or ARC
M01RR-00044-31 0360 (CLR) UTELL, MARK J General clinical research center Effects of sulfuric acid aerosols on pulmonary defense mechanism in man
M01RR-00044-31 0361 (CLR) GRIGGS, ROBERT C General clinical research center Effect of dehydroepiandrosterone on energy and protein metabolism
M01RR-00044-31 0362 (CLR) MARROW, GARY R General clinical research center Biobehavioral mechanisms of chemotherapy nausea and vomiting
M01RR-00044-31 0363 (CLR) LIANG, CHANG-SENG General clinical research center Hemodynamic activity following acute administration of RGW-2938 in CHF
M01RR-00044-31 0364 (CLR) BROWN, JEAN K General clinical research center Pre-cancer factor & consequence associated with nutrition in lung cancer
M01RR-00044-31 0365 (CLR) ASSELIN, BARBARA General clinical research center Pharmacologic effect of L-asparaginase
M01RR-00044-31 0366 (CLR) DOLIN, RAPHAEL General clinical research center Drugs trials for primary prevention of serious infection in AIDS
M01RR-00044-31 0367 (CLR) BETTS, ROBERT F General clinical research center Foscarnet trial in serious herpes infections with immunodeficiencies
M01RR-00044-31 0368 (CLR) DOLIN, RAPHAEL General clinical research center IV foscarnet in AIDS patients with sight threating CMV retinitis
M01RR-00044-31 0369 (CLR) SCHWARTZ, RONALD G General clinical research center Effect of nadolol on metabolic rate
M01RR-00044-31 0370 (CLR) GRIGGS, ROBERT C General clinical research center Potassium regulation in neuromuscular disease
M01RR-00044-31 0371 (CLR) FORBES, GILBERT B General clinical research center Nutritional recovery in patients with anorexia nervosa
M01RR-00044-31 0372 (CLR) HALL, CAROLINE B General clinical research center Community surveillance of infectious disease in Monroe County
M01RR-00044-31 0373 (CLR) ABERNATHY, ALEXIS D General clinical research center Evaluation of anger management training
M01RR-00044-31 0375 (CLR) LAFORCE, E MARC General clinical research center Effect of influenza vaccine on rates of pneumococcal bacteremia
K01RR-00045-04 (AR) HOWARD, JOGAYLE SMITHSONIAN INSTITUTION NATIONAL ZOOLOGICAL PARK WASHINGTON DC 20008 Fertility and enhanced reproduction
M01RR-00046-31 (SRC) BONDURANT, STUART UNIVERSITY OF NORTH CAROLINA CB #7600 CHAPEL HILL, NC 27514 General clinical research center
M01RR-00046-31 0427 (SRC) PATTERSON, HERBERT J General clinical research center A phase II/III study of oral milrinone
M01RR-00046-31 0428 (SRC) ROBERTS, HAROLD R General clinical research center Activated recombinant factor VII in acute joint bleeds in hemophiliacs
M01RR-00046-31 0429 (SRC) COLLIER, ALBERT C General clinical research center Exposure to sidestream tobacco smoke
M01RR-00046-31 0432 (SRC) PETERSON, GARY General clinical research center Oxytocin/TRH/LHRH infusion study in normal and depressed subjects
M01RR-00046-31 0437 (SRC) BERNARD, STEPHEN A General clinical research center Interferon and fluorouracil in refractory cancer
M01RR-00046-31 0438 (SRC) VAN DER HORST, CHARLES General clinical research center AZT alone vs AZT and acyclovir in AIDS
M01RR-00046-31 0439 (SRC) POWERS, STEPHEN K General clinical research center ImuVert therapy in recurrent or refractory brain tumors
M01RR-00046-31 0440 (SRC) MCMILLAN, CAMPBELL W General clinical research center Monoclonal factor IX in hemophilia B
M01RR-00046-31 0442 (SRC) VAN DER HORST, CHARLES General clinical research center Three regimes compared for prevention of P. carinii in AIDS
M01RR-00046-31 0444 (SRC) VAN DER HORST, CHARLES General clinical research center Ribavarin in the treatment of AIDS and advanced AIDS-related illness
M01RR-00046-31 0446 (SRC) ADAMS, KIRKWOOD F General clinical research center Ventricular arrhythmia variation in dilated cardiomyopathy
M01RR-00046-31 0448 (SRC) FINN, WILLIAM F General clinical research center CMV immune globulin in renal transplant patients
M01RR-00046-31 0449 (SRC) MESSENHEIMER, JOHN A General clinical research center Lamotrigine in patients with partial seizures
M01RR-00046-31 0451 (SRC) GWYNNE, JOHN T General clinical research center Effects of probucol on hypercholesterolemia
M01RR-00046-31 0452 (SRC) PATTERSON, HERBERT J General clinical research center Oral milrinone in combination drug therapy for congestive heart failure
M01RR-00046-31 0454 (SRC) HEIZER, WILLIAM D General clinical research center Human model for diarrhea induced by tube feeding
M01RR-00046-31 0455 (SRC) GRAY, KENNETH T General clinical research center Treatment of osteoporosis with intranasal calcitonin
M01RR-00046-31 0456 (SRC) VAN WYK, JUDSON J General clinical research center Monitoring of steroid replacement in adrenal hyperplasia
M01RR-00046-31 0457 (SRC) ORRINGER, EUGENE P General clinical research center Hydroxyurea in patients with homozygous beta-thalassemia
M01RR-00046-31 0458 (SRC) VAN DER HORST, CHARLES General clinical research center Foscarnet in AIDS patients with CMV retinitis
M01RR-00046-31 0461 (SRC) VAN DER HORST, CHARLES General clinical research center Dideoxyinosine (ddI) vs AZT therapy in AIDS and ARC
M01RR-00046-31 0462 (SRC) VAN DER HORST, CHARLES General clinical research center Dideoxyinosine vs AZT in AIDS or ARC with long term AZT therapy
M01RR-00046-31 0463 (SRC) MESSENHEIMER, JOHN A General clinical research center Efficacy and safety of felbamate in partial seizures
M01RR-00046-31 0464 (SRC) STABLER, BRIAN General clinical research center Psychosocial assessment in adults with childhood growth hormone deficiency
M01RR-00046-31 0465 (SRC) ORRINGER, EUGENE General clinical research center Permeability of RBC in hemolytic anemias
M01RR-00046-31 0466 (SRC) POWERS, STEPHEN General clinical research center Diaziquone plus carmustine in primary aplastic brain tumors
M01RR-00046-31 0467 (SRC) VAN DER HORST, CHARLES General clinical research center Suppressive vs. acute acyclovir for recurrent Herpes infections
M01RR-00046-31 0468 (SRC) POWERS, STEPHEN General clinical research center Melphalan in the treatment of primary anaplastic brain tumors
M01RR-00046-31 0469 (SRC) ADAMS, KIRKWOOD General clinical research center Influence of calcium on the anti-ischemic effects of nifedipine
M01RR-00046-31 0470 (SRC) EVANS, DWIGHT General clinical research center Coping in health and illness project
M01RR-00046-31 0471 (SRC) VAN DER HORST, CHARLES General clinical research center Randomized trial for moderately severe Pneumocystic carini in AIDS patients
M01RR-00046-31 0472 (SRC) KNOWLES, MICHAEL General clinical research center Effects of amiloride on exercise-induced asthma
M01RR-00046-31 0232 (SRC) KNOWLES, MICHAEL R General clinical research center Chronic amiloride aerosol therapy in cystic fibrosis
M01RR-00046-31 0327 (SRC) POWERS, STEPHEN K General clinical research center Interferon administration to patients with malignant gliomas
M01RR-00046-31 0330 (SRC) POWERS, STEPHEN K General clinical research center New agents & techniques for therapy of recurrent brain tumor
M01RR-00046-31 0331 (SRC) POWERS, STEPHEN K General clinical research center Comparison of intraarterial & intravenous BCNU with & without 5 FU
M01RR-00046-31 0339 (SRC) UNDERWOOD, LOUISE E General clinical research center RhGH therapy of growth hormone deficiency
M01RR-00046-31 0342 (SRC) MAIXNER, WILLIAM General clinical research center Somatosensory and cardiovascular responses to oro-facial pain
M01RR-00046-31 0347 (SRC) JAIN, AVANINDRA General clinical research center Restenosis after percutaneous coronary angioplasty
M01RR-00046-31 0358 (SRC) ORRINGER, EUGENE P General clinical research center Treatment of sickle cell anemia with hydroxyurea
M01RR-00046-31 0363 (SRC) MCMILLAN, CAMPBELL W General clinical research center Recombinant factor VIII kinetic in hemophilia
M01RR-00046-31 0371 (SRC) GWYNNE, JOHN T General clinical research center Registry of hyperlipidemic patients
M01RR-00046-31 0373 (SRC) HAGGERTY, JOHN J General clinical research center Marginal hypothyroidism and autoimmune thyroiditis in normal subjects
M01RR-00046-31 0375 (SRC) HAGGERTY, JOHN J General clinical research center Trial of gepirone in depressed patients
M01RR-00046-31 0383 (SRC) STABLER, BRIAN General clinical research center Psychological effects of growth hormone therapy
M01RR-00046-31 0386 (SRC) ADAMS, KIRKWOOD F General clinical research center Exercise, arrhythmias and neurohumoral factors in heart failure
M01RR-00046-31 0389 (SRC) ADAMS, KIRKWOOD F General clinical research center Comparative efficacy of milrinone, digoxin and captopril in heart failure
M01RR-00046-31 0391 (SRC) EVANS, DWIGHT L General clinical research center Neuroendocrine and neuroimmune correlates of depression
M01RR-00046-31 0394 (SRC) DROSSMAN, DOUGLAS A General clinical research center Effect of buspirone and placebo on the irritable bowel syndrome
M01RR-00046-31 0395 (SRC) MESSENHEIMER, JOHN A General clinical research center Continuation study of lamotrigine in patients with partial seizures
M01RR-00046-31 0397 (SRC) VAN DER HORST, CHARLES General clinical research center Safety and efficacy of AZT for asymptommatic HIV positive subjects
M01RR-00046-31 0400 (SRC) ADAMS, KIRKWOOD F General clinical research center Trial of torasemide vs. furosemide in heart failure
M01RR-00046-31 0401 (SRC) WHITT, J KENNETH General clinical research center Infant nonorganic failure to thrive--Neuroendocrine correlates
M01RR-00046-31 0404 (SRC) FINN, WILLIAM F General clinical research

center Pharmacokinetics of cyclosporin in renal transplantion
M01RR-00046-31 0406 (SRC) SANDLER, ROBERT S General clinical research center Case control study of colon adenomas
M01RR-00046-31 0407 (SRC) MESSENHEIMER, JOHN A General clinical research center Dose-response evaluation of lamotrigine for partial seizures
M01RR-00046-31 0409 (SRC) POWERS, STEPHEN K General clinical research center Treatment of anaplastic gliomas with cisplatin and radiotherapy
M01RR-00046-31 0411 (SRC) KLEIN, KENNETH B General clinical research center Pain perception with irritable bowel syndrome and low back pain
M01RR-00046-31 0415 (SRC) KATZ, VERN L General clinical research center Immersion in pregnancy
M01RR-00046-31 0416 (SRC) WHITT, J KENNETH General clinical research center Central nervous system effects of HIV in children with hemophilia
M01RR-00046-31 0418 (SRC) VAN DER HORST, CHARLES M General clinical research center AZT treatment of HIV infection in hemophilia patients
M01RR-00046-31 0419 (SRC) GRAY, T KENNEY General clinical research center Bone density and risk factor survey
M01RR-00046-31 0422 (SRC) HALL, COLIN D General clinical research center AIDS dementia study
M01RR-00046-31 0423 (SRC) WOELFEL, ALAN K General clinical research center The substrate for ventricular tachycardia
M01RR-00046-31 0424 (SRC) FALK, RONALD J General clinical research center Kidney function in sickle cell disease
M01RR-00046-31 0248 (SRC) CLEMMONS, DAVID R General clinical research center Pituitary-adrenal suppressibility
M01RR-00046-31 0505 (SRC) GWINNE, JOHN General clinical research center Pravastatin lovastatin and cholesterolemia in patients with hypercholesterolemia
M01RR-00046-31 0506 (SRC) COHN, SUSAN General clinical research center Demography of HIV-antibody positive patients in North Carolina
M01RR-00046-31 0507 (SRC) ROBERTS, HAROLD General clinical research center Dosage levels of RFVIIA in joint muscle and mucocutaneous hemorrhages
M01RR-00046-31 0508 (SRC) FINE, JO-DAVID General clinical research center National epidermolysis bullosa registry, Southern Clinical Site
M01RR-00046-31 0509 (SRC) POWERS, STEPHEN General clinical research center Phonoangiology as a noninvasive method to detect cerebral vascular anomalies
M01RR-00046-31 0510 (SRC) MAIXNER, WILLIAM General clinical research center Effects of baroreceptor stimulation on pain perceptionva barorec
M01RR-00046-31 0511 (SRC) DOTTERS, DEBORAH General clinical research center A phase III randomized study of cyclophosphamide and cisplating vs taxol
M01RR-00046-31 0512 (SRC) CLEMMONS, DAVID General clinical research center Anabolic effects of IGF-1 and GH in volunteers made catabolic by diet restriction
M01RR-00046-31 0513 (SRC) HALL, COLIN General clinical research center Alpha-interferon to treat HIV+ patients who develop PML
M01RR-00046-31 0514 (SRC) JONES, THOMAS General clinical research center Low dose of alcohol on cognitive and psychomotor function in the elderly
M01RR-00046-31 0515 (SRC) UNDERWOOD, LOUIS General clinical research center Insulin like growth factor-I on growth in Laron dwarfism
M01RR-00046-31 0516 (SRC) JANOWSKY, DAVID General clinical research center Physostigmine as a psychodiagnostic tool
M01RR-00046-31 0517 (SRC) BUSBY, MARJORIE General clinical research center Phytochemical compliance markers in designer food
M01RR-00046-31 0518 (SRC) BUSBY, MARJORIE General clinical research center Development of phytochemical markers in designer foods-long term
M01RR-00046-31 0519 (SRC) ORRINGER, EUGENE General clinical research center Hydroxyurea in recurrent leg ulcers in patients with sickle cell
M01RR-00046-31 0520 (SRC) ORRINGER, EUGENE General clinical research center Sickle cell adhesion to the endothelium
M01RR-00046-31 0521 (SRC) HAGGERTY, JOHN General clinical research center Safety of oral fluparoxan in patients with depressive disorders
M01RR-00046-31 0522 (SRC) GODLEY, PAUL General clinical research center LCRC 8801 – The role of lipids in the etiology of prostate cancer
M01RR-00046-31 0523 (SRC) HAK, LAWRENCE General clinical research center Oral Torsemide in patients with ascites due to cirrhosis
M01RR-00046-31 0524 (SRC) TANCER, MANUEL General clinical research center Bupropion treatment in social phobia
M01RR-00046-31 0525 (SRC) KNOWLES, MICHAEL General clinical research center Association of CFTR allele and the development of non-CF airways disease
M01RR-00046-31 0526 (SRC) CLEMMONS, DAVID General clinical research center Clinical usefulness of the radioimmunoassay of IGFBP-1 in diabetes
M01RR-00046-31 0527 (SRC) VAN DER HOST, CHARLES General clinical research center Phase II ganciclovir/GM-CSF in CMV retinitis in AIDS patients
M01RR-00046-31 0528 (SRC) CLEMMONS, DAVID General clinical research center IGF binding proteins as predictors of growth response to GH Hypopit. dwarfs
M01RR-00046-31 0529 (SRC) CLEMMONS, DAVID General clinical research center IGF-I & IGFBPS in predicting response of low birth Wt. newborns to refeeding
M01RR-00046-31 0530 (SRC) CLEMMONS, DAVID General clinical research center Changes in plasma IFG-I, IFGBPS in during dietary restriction
M01RR-00046-31 0531 (SRC) TANCER, MANUEL General clinical research center Efficacy of XANAS-SR tablets vs placebo in panic disorders
M01RR-00046-31 0532 (SRC) THORP, JOHN General clinical research center Perineal muscle function study
M01RR-00046-31 0300 (SRC) GOLDEN, ROBERT N. General clinical research center Chlorimipramine actions on neurohormones in normal subjects/human
M01RR-00046-31 0473 (SRC) MOORE, DAVID General clinical research center Study of untreated stage of epithelial ovarian adenocarcinoma
M01RR-00046-31 0474 (SRC) HAK, LAWRENCE General clinical research center Effect of food and administration on ranitidine bio-availability
M01RR-00046-31 0475 (SRC) KATZ, VERN General clinical research center Cathecolamines and pregnancy
M01RR-00046-31 0476 (SRC) MESSENHEIMER, JOHN General clinical research center Long term felbamate therapy in adult with epilepsy
M01RR-00046-31 0477 (SRC) VAN DER HORST, CHARLES General clinical research center AZT pharmacokinetics in patients with HIV and renal insufficiency
M01RR-00046-31 0478 (SRC) DROSSMAN, DOUGLAS General clinical research center Abuse/psychosocial factors in patients with GI disorders
M01RR-00046-31 0479 (SRC) ORRINGER, EUGENE General clinical research center Hydroxyurea on RBC volume and ion content in myeloproliferative disease
M01RR-00046-31 0480 (SRC) BROUWER, KIM General clinical research center Acetaminophen & piroxicam in the management of osteoarthritis of the hand
M01RR-00046-31 0481 (SRC) HAK, LAWRENCE General clinical research center AZT on the availability, protein binding and clearance of phenytoin
M01RR-00046-31 0482 (SRC) VAN DER HORST, CHARLES General clinical research center Efficacy of 2', 3-dideoxynosine administered twice daily to zidovudine
M01RR-00046-31 0483 (SRC) ADAMS, KIRKWOOD General clinical research center Effect of withdrawal of benazepril on exercise
M01RR-00046-31 0484 (SRC) MELIN, SUSAN General clinical research center Tamoxifen on calcium metabolism, bone turnover, and lipid metabolism
M01RR-00046-31 0485 (SRC) MESSENHEIMER, JOHN General clinical research center Long term evaluation of felbamate in subjects with epilepsy
M01RR-00046-31 0486 (SRC) ORRINGER, EUGENE General clinical research center Efficacy of hydroxyurea as a prophylactic therapy for sickle cell
M01RR-00046-31 0487 (SRC) MCSHERRY, SUSAN General clinical research center Topical alpha 2 adrenergic agonist on intestinal bladder reservoir
M01RR-00046-31 0488 (SRC) TANCER, MANUEL General clinical research center Central monoamine receptor function in social phobia
M01RR-00046-31 0489 (SRC) DUKES, GEORGE General clinical research center Ondansetron in patients with various degrees of hepatic insufficiency
M01RR-00046-31 0490 (SRC) COHN, SUSAN General clinical research center Incidence and prevalence of Burdetella pertussis in patients with HIV
M01RR-00046-31 0491 (SRC) SUETA, CARLA General clinical research center Magnesium supplementation on ventricular arrhythmia in dilated cardiomyopathy
M01RR-00046-31 0492 (SRC) UNDERWOOD, LOUIS General clinical research center Treatment of central precocious puberty with LHRH analogs
M01RR-00046-31 0493 (SRC) MANASCO, PENELOPE General clinical research center Serum inhibin and LH, FSH, and sex steroid during puberty
M01RR-00046-31 0494 (SRC) VAN DER HORST, CHARLES General clinical research center Fluconazole vs Clotrimazole troches to prevent fungal infections in HIV
M01RR-00046-31 0495 (SRC) VAN DER HORST, CHARLES General clinical research center SCH 39304 for acute cryptococcal maningitis in HIV-infected patients
M01RR-00046-31 0496 (SRC) VAN DER HORST, CHARLES General clinical research center Antiviral potential of combined AZT and DDT in hemophilia and HIV
M01RR-00046-31 0497 (SRC) ADAMS, KIRKWOOD General clinical research center Multicenter study of digoxin withdrawal on exercise tolerance
M01RR-00046-31 0498 (SRC) HAK, LAWRENCE General clinical research center Labetalol & quinidine on debrisoquine isozyme of liver function oxidase
M01RR-00046-31 0499 (SRC) ORRINGER, EUGENE General clinical research center 12C79 intravenous infusion to sickle cell patients not in crisis
M01RR-00046-31 0500 (SRC) HENDERSON, RICHARD General clinical research center Bone mineral loss following hip fracture
M01RR-00046-31 0501 (SRC) CHESCHEIR, NANCY General clinical research center Safety and pharmacokinetic profile of recombinant human relaxin
M01RR-00046-31 0502 (SRC) BUSBY, MARJORIE General clinical research center Dietary factors in chronic renal failure – Poor Blacks in North Carolina
M01RR-00046-31 0503 (SRC) GRAY, KENNEY General clinical research center: Cyclic oral therapy with risedronate in patients receiving glucocorticoids
M01RR-00046-31 0504 (SRC) LIM, WILMA General clinical research center High vs low dose of zidovudine administered to HIV children
M01RR-00046-31 0304 (SRC) KNOWLES, MICHEAL R. General clinical research center Toxicity of chronic amiloride aerosol administration
M01RR-00046-31 0306 (SRC) MESSENHEIMER, JOHN A. General clinical research center Lamotrigine in intractable partial epileptic seizures
M01RR-00046-31 0312 (SRC) UDRY, J R General clinical research center Pubertal & social factors in adolescent sexuality
M01RR-00046-31 0313 (SRC) UNDERWOOD, LOUIS E. General clinical research center Biosynthetic GH therapy of growth hormone deficiency
M01RR-00046-31 0317 (SRC) VAN WYK, JUDSON J General clinical research center Growth hormone in pituitary disorders
M01RR-00046-31 0318 (SRC) POWERS, STEPHEN K General clinical research center BCNU, procarbazine and radiotherapy in treatment of anaplastic gliomas
M01RR-00046-31 0319 (SRC) POWERS, STEPHEN K General clinical

research center Brain tumor immunotherapy-radiotherapy and BCNU +/- levamisole
M01RR-00046-31 0321 (SRC) POWERS, STEPHEN K General clinical research center Active immunotherapy for patients with anaplastic glioma
M01RR-00046-31 0322 (SRC) LIGHT, KATHLEEN C General clinical research center Renal and cardiovascular effects of psychological stress
M01RR-00046-31 0324 (SRC) POWERS, STEPHEN K General clinical research center Brain tumor therapy--Surgery, radiotherapy and chemotherapy
M01RR-00046-31 0325 (SRC) POWERS, STEPHEN K General clinical research center Treatment of solitary metastases to the brain
M01RR-00046-31 0326 (SRC) KNOWLES, MICHAEL R General clinical research center Measurement of airway transepithelial potential in cystic fibrosis
M01RR-00047-31 0394 (SRC) REIDENBERG, MARCUS M General clinical research center Clinical pharmacology of gossypol and hypokalemia
M01RR-00047-31 0464 (SRC) LOWRY, STEPHEN General clinical research center Effects of growth hormone in healthy males receiving hypocaloric TPN
M01RR-00047-31 0465 (SRC) STENZEL, KURT General clinical research center Anti-tumor properties of hemin -- A pilot study
M01RR-00047-31 0466 (SRC) SCHLUSSEL, YVETTE General clinical research center Cyclical stress and cardiovascular risk
M01RR-00047-31 0467 (SRC) BRILLON, DAVID General clinical research center Role of hyperinsulinemia on effects of hypercortisolemia
M01RR-00047-31 0468 (SRC) NEW, MARIA General clinical research center Hypo and hyperadrenal states
M01RR-00047-31 0469 (SRC) AUGUST, PHYLLIS General clinical research center Calcium metabolism and the renin system in hypertensive pregnancy
M01RR-00047-31 0470 (SRC) AUGUST, PHYLLIS General clinical research center Calcium and the renin-angiotensin system in hypertensive pregnancy
M01RR-00047-31 0471 (SRC) JAMES, GARY General clinical research center Ecological studies of blood pressure variation in women
M01RR-00047-31 0472 (SRC) RUBIN, MICHAEL General clinical research center Plasmapheresis in Stiff Man Syndrome
M01RR-00047-31 0473 (SRC) MESSINA, ANTHONY General clinical research center Effect of nitrous oxide in myocardial contractility
M01RR-00047-31 0474 (SRC) STATEN, MYRLENE General clinical research center Metabolic effects of exercise in obese older people
M01RR-00047-31 0475 (SRC) DEVEREUX, RICHARD General clinical research center Effects of infective endocarditis in mitral valve prolapse
M01RR-00047-31 0476 (SRC) KOCSIS, JAMES General clinical research center Diagnosis and treatment of dysthymic disorder
M01RR-00047-31 0477 (SRC) MARIN, DEBORAH General clinical research center Epidemiology and co-morbidity of dysthymic disorder
M01RR-00047-31 0478 (SRC) KAPLAN, ELLEN General clinical research center Pulmonary function and bone marrow transplantation
M01RR-00047-31 0479 (SRC) MURRAY, HENRY General clinical research center Uncontrolled clinical trial of long-term safety of AZT
M01RR-00047-31 0396 (SRC) WEKSLER, MARC E General clinical research center Immunological studies in aging
M01RR-00047-31 0399 (SRC) PICKERING, THOMAS G General clinical research center Endocrine profiling and blood pressure regulation
M01RR-00047-31 0411 (SRC) MATTHEWS, DWIGHT General clinical research center Protein metabolism using different routes of amino and keto acid administration
M01RR-00047-31 0419 (SRC) CEDARBAUM, JESSE M General clinical research center Factors affecting pharmacokinetics of levodopa
M01RR-00047-31 0420 (SRC) LOWRY, STEPHEN F General clinical research center Effect of gut rest on the peripheral and splanchnic amino acid metabolism
M01RR-00047-31 0421 (SRC) IMPERATO, JULIANNE General clinical research center Steroid metabolism 5 alpha-reductase deficiency
M01RR-00047-31 0423 (SRC) BUSSEL, JAMES B General clinical research center Monoclonal antibody 3G8 to treat severe idiopathic thrombocytopenic purpura
M01RR-00047-31 0424 (SRC) ERGUN, GULCHIN A General clinical research center Salivary prostaglandin abnormalities in patients with gastrointestinal reflux
M01RR-00047-31 0426 (SRC) PECKER, MARK S General clinical research center Endocrine profiling and blood pressure regulation
M01RR-00047-31 0427 (SRC) NATHAN, CARL F General clinical research center Safety & efficacy of recombinant interferon-gamma in lepromatous leprosy
M01RR-00047-31 0429 (SRC) HALMI, KATHERINE General clinical research center Insulin kinetics in the eating disorders
M01RR-00047-31 0431 (SRC) STENZEL, KURT H General clinical research center Adoptive immunotherapy for metastatic renal cancer
M01RR-00047-31 0434 (SRC) MANN, J JOHN General clinical research center Monoamine receptor function in depressive disorders
M01RR-00047-31 0437 (SRC) SOAVE, ROSEMARY General clinical research center Intravenous spiramycin for cryptosporidial diarrhea in AIDS patients
M01RR-00047-31 0439 (SRC) MURRAY, HENRY W General clinical research center Treatment of interleukin 2 to activate AIDS monocytes
M01RR-00047-31 0443 (SRC) LOWRY, STEPHEN E General clinical research center Metabolic and immunologic responses in man to endotoxin
M01RR-00047-31 0445 (SRC) FRIEDMAN, RICHARD General clinical research center Clonidine challenge test in psychiatric illness
M01RR-00047-31 0446 (SRC) STENZEL, KURT H General clinical research center Adoptive immunotherapy for metastatic cancer
M01RR-00047-31 0447 (SRC) PICKERING, THOMAS G General clinical research center Blood pressure regulation before and after renal angioplasty
M01RR-00047-31 0449 (SRC) ROBERTS, RICHARD B General clinical research center Tolerance, virology and immunology in high risk patients for AIDS
M01RR-00047-31 0451 (SRC) MURRAY, HENRY W General clinical research center Safety and pharmacokinetic study of 2',3'-dideoxy-2',3'-didehydrothymidine
M01RR-00047-31 0454 (SRC) LOWRY, STEPHEN F General clinical research center Influence of route of feeding on specific response to counter regulation
M01RR-00047-31 0455 (SRC) DEVEREUX, RICHARD B General clinical research center Determination of left ventricular mass by 2-dimensional echocardiography
M01RR-00047-31 0456 (SRC) CAMPBELL, ROBERT General clinical research center Metabolism of free fatty acids-- Effect of glycerol infusion
M01RR-00047-31 0457 (SRC) MURRAY, HENRY General clinical research center Comparative bioavailability of orally-administered ddI
M01RR-00047-31 0458 (SRC) MURRAY, HENRY General clinical research center Uncontrolled clinical trial of long-term safety of AZT
M01RR-00047-31 0459 (SRC) JACOBSON, IRA General clinical research center Roferon--Six months treatment of non-A, non-B hepatitis
M01RR-00047-31 0460 (SRC) BLUMENFELD, JON General clinical research center Interleukin 2 therapy for essential hypertension
M01RR-00047-31 0461 (SRC) SQUIRES, KATHLEEN General clinical research center Pharmacokinetic and tolerance of 28-day regimens of oral ganciclovir
M01RR-00047-31 0462 (SRC) HALMI, KATHERINE General clinical research center Bone mineral content of anorexia and bulimia nervosa patients
M01RR-00047-31 0463 (SRC) LAMBROZA, ARNON General clinical research center Polymyositis/dermatomyositis and mixed connective tissue disease
M01RR-00047-31 (SRC) MICHELS, ROBERT CORNELL UNIV MED COLL 1300 YORK AVE NEW YORK, NY 10021 General clinical research center
M01RR-00047-31 0274 (SRC) PICKERING, THOMAS G General clinical research center Blood pressure before and after renal angioplasty
M01RR-00047-31 0304 (SRC) SOAVE, R General clinical research center Intravenous Spriamycin for cryptosporidiosis in AIDS patients
M01RR-00047-31 0328 (SRC) CAMPBELL, ROBERT General clinical research center Diabetes control and complications trial
M01RR-00048-30 (CLR) BEATY, HARRY N NORTHWESTERN UNIV, MED SCHOOL 303 EAST CHICAGO AVENUE CHICAGO, IL 60611 General clinical research center
M01RR-00048-30 0166 (CLR) BENSON, AL B General clinical research center Continuous infusion 5-Fluorouracil and IV 5-Iodo-2'Deoxyuridine
M01RR-00048-30 0167 (CLR) CRAIG, ROBERT M General clinical research center Malabsorption in patients with AIDS
M01RR-00048-30 0168 (CLR) ROBERTSON, GARY L General clinical research center Genetic basis of familial neurogenic diabetes insipidus
M01RR-00048-30 0169 (CLR) ROBERTSON, GARY L General clinical research center Circadian rhythm of vasopressin and its regulation
M01RR-00048-30 0170 (CLR) GARCIA, PATRICIA General clinical research center Perinatal transmission of HIV-1 in a 22-week gestation
M01RR-00048-30 0171 (CLR) MOLITCH, MARK E General clinical research center Effect of selegiline on prolactin response to L-dopa
M01RR-00048-30 0172 (CLR) ROSEN, STEVEN T General clinical research center DAB486 IL2 used in patients with selected IL2R expressing malignancies
M01RR-00048-30 0101 (CLR) ATKISON, ARTHUR J General clinical research center Long term NAPA therapy
M01RR-00048-30 0119 (CLR) AMBRE, JOHN J. General clinical research center Cocaine kinetics in man
M01RR-00048-30 0143 (CLR) CRAIG, ROBERT M General clinical research center Pharmacokinetics of D-xylose in pts. with malabsorption and AIDS
M01RR-00048-30 0144 (CLR) KAZER, RALPH R General clinical research center Pulsatile administration of gonadotropin releasing hormone GnRH
M01RR-00048-30 0145 (CLR) SMITH, LEWIS J General clinical research center Leukotriene D4-induced bronchoconstriction
M01RR-00048-30 0150 (CLR) MOLITCH, MARK E General clinical research center Effect of Nal-Glu GnRH on gonadotrop cell adenoma secretion
M01RR-00048-30 0151 (CLR) ROSEN, STEVEN T General clinical research center IV CYT-103-90Y in refractory B72.3 reactive carcinoma
M01RR-00048-30 0153 (CLR) MOLITCH, MARK E General clinical research center Safety and efficacy of sandostatin in treating acromegaly
M01RR-00048-30 0156 (CLR) SMITH, LEWIS J General clinical research center Bioactive mediators in asthma
M01RR-00048-30 0159 (CLR) METZGER, BOYD General clinical research center Diabetes in pregnancy
M01RR-00048-30 0161 (CLR) KAZER, RALPH R General clinical research center Altered IGF-1 activity in native Japanese woman
M01RR-00048-30 0162 (CLR) KAZER, RALPH R General clinical research center Polycystic ovary syndrome changes after GnRH agonist ovarian suppression
M01RR-00048-30 0163 (CLR) MOLITCH, MARK E General clinical research center Effect of Verapamil on PRL response to TRH and L-Dopa
M01RR-00048-30 0164 (CLR) ATKINSON, ARTHUR J General clinical research center Postural change in cramping dialysis patients
M01RR-00048-30 0165 (CLR) HENDELY, DALE E General clinical research center Studies of the ocular complications of AIDS
M01RR-00051-30 (CLR) KRUGMAN, RICHARD D UNIV OF COLORADO HLTH SCI CTR 4200 EAST NINTH AVENUE DENVER, CO 80262 General clinical research center
M01RR-00051-30 0330 (CLR) EVERSON, GREGORY T. General clinical research center Estrogen effects on biliary lipid metabolism in in cholesterol synthesis
M01RR-00051-30 0413 (CLR) GABOW, PATRICIA A General clinical research center Natural history of polycystic kidney disease
M01RR-00051-30 0441 (CLR) ECKEL, ROBERT H General clinical research center Hormonal control of adipose tissue lipoprotein lipase
M01RR-00051-30 0460 (CLR) GLODE, L MICHAEL General clinical research center Safety, efficacy and endocrinology of leuprolide
M01RR-00051-30 0471 (CLR) ECKEL, ROBERT General clinical research center Influence of hostility on hormones, cholesterol and immunity
M01RR-00051-30 0476 (CLR) GROVES, BERTRON M General clinical

research center Primary pulmonary hypertension

M01RR-00051-30 0515 (CLR) EVERSON, GREGORY T General clinical research center Liver function in polycystic disease

M01RR-00051-30 0525 (CLR) NORRIS, DAVID A General clinical research center Multidisciplinary study of mycosis fungoides

M01RR-00051-30 0557 (CLR) NIES, ALAN S General clinical research center Changes in norepinephrine clearance with aging

M01RR-00051-30 0605 (CLR) ROBINSON, WILLIAM A General clinical research center Vitamin E in the prevention of recurrence of stage I/II malignant melanoma

M01RR-00051-30 0612 (CLR) BUNN, PAUL A General clinical research center Imaging and treatment of cancers with monoclonal antibodies KC4

M01RR-00051-30 0615 (CLR) BYYNY, RICHARD L. General clinical research center Role of declining renal function and sodium intake in hypertension

M01RR-00051-30 0632 (CLR) RIDGWAY, E C General clinical research center Regulation of glycoprotein pituitary hormones in pituitary tumor patients

M01RR-00051-30 0655 (CLR) FREEDMAN, ROBERT General clinical research center Clinical studies in psychosis-familial transmission of schizophrenia

M01RR-00051-30 0660 (CLR) ROBINSON, W A General clinical research center Efficacy of human recombinant alpha 2 interferon in CML patients

M01RR-00051-30 0666 (CLR) RIDGWAY, E CHES General clinical research center Hormonal regulation of plasma glucose

M01RR-00051-30 0677 (CLR) ECHEL, ROBERT H General clinical research center Metabolic regulation of plasma lipoprotein lipase in man

M01RR-00051-30 0678 (CLR) ECKEL, ROBERT H General clinical research center Diabetes mellitus in the San Luis Valley

M01RR-00051-30 0681 (CLR) ROBINSON, WILLIAM A General clinical research center Effect of dose/length wellferon treatment in hairy cell leukemia patients

M01RR-00051-30 0682 (CLR) BUNN, PAUL A General clinical research center Efficacy of recombinant gamma interferon in patients with T-cell lymphoma

M01RR-00051-30 0689 (CLR) RECTOR, WILLIAM G General clinical research center Determinants of sodium retention in cirrhosis

M01RR-00051-30 0690 (CLR) CHAPMAN, ARLENE B General clinical research center Pathogenetic factors in the hypertension of polycystic disease

M01RR-00051-30 0692 (CLR) ROBINSON, WILLIAM A General clinical research center Recombinant human interferon alpha 2 A in high risk, resected melanoma patients

M01RR-00051-30 0695 (CLR) RIDGEWAY, ELI CHESTER General clinical research center Use of a new dopamine agonist (CV 205-502) in hyperprolactinemia

M01RR-00051-30 0698 (CLR) ADLER, LAWRENCE E General clinical research center Dextroamphetamine on sensory gating in auditory evoked potentials

M01RR-00051-30 0707 (CLR) ECKEL, ROBERT H General clinical research center Regional adipose tissue metabolism after liposuction

M01RR-00051-30 0708 (CLR) ROBINSON, WILLIAM A General clinical research center Recombinant human alpha and gamma interferon in untreated CML patients

M01RR-00051-30 0683 (CLR) CHAPMAN, ARLENE B General clinical research center Intracranial aneurysms in polycystic disease

M01RR-00051-30 0686 (CLR) COLLIER, DAVID HARRIS General clinical research center Double blind study of ketotifen in the treatment of systemic sclerosis

M01RR-00051-30 0687 (CLR) ECKEL, ROBERT H General clinical research center Medium chain triglycerides and glucose and lipid metabolism

M01RR-00051-30 0688 (CLR) ROBINSON, WILLIAM A General clinical research center Malignant melanoma with murine monoclonal antibody

M01RR-00051-30 0711 (CLR) ECKEL, ROBERT H General clinical research center HMG coenzyme A reductase inhibition with XU62-320

M01RR-00051-30 0759 (CLR) SUSSMAN, KARL General clinical research center Tolrestat in the prevention of retinopathy in NIDDM patients

M01RR-00051-30 0760 (CLR) ABRAHAM, WILLIAM General clinical research center Hemodynamic and hormonal changes of early normal human pregnancy

M01RR-00051-30 0761 (CLR) CLAMAN, HENRY General clinical research center Antipaternal antibodies in pregnancy

M01RR-00051-30 0762 (CLR) LINDENFELD, JO A General clinical research center Oral verapamil doses on the disposition of thiophylline

M01RR-00051-30 0763 (CLR) ROBINSON, WILLIAM A General clinical research center Gemcibatine in melanoma

M01RR-00051-30 0764 (CLR) BRAUN, THOMAS General clinical research center Interleukin-2 in patients with advanced renal cell carcinoma

M01RR-00051-30 0765 (CLR) ADLER, LAWRENCE General clinical research center Nicotine on sensory gating of auditory evoked potentials in man

M01RR-00051-30 0766 (CLR) BOYSON, SALLY General clinical research center Mitochondrial enzymes in movement disorders

M01RR-00051-30 0767 (CLR) ECKEL, ROBERT H General clinical research center Tissue specific regulation of lipoprotein lipase by isoproterenol

M01RR-00051-30 0768 (CLR) ECKEL, ROBERT H General clinical research center Dose response of ATLPL to IV isoproterenol in normal weight and obesity

M01RR-00051-30 0769 (CLR) TEITELBAUM, ISSAC General clinical research center Fluconazole in renal failure

M01RR-00051-30 0770 (CLR) NIES, ALAN S General clinical research center Effect of theophylline cardiac response to adrenoreceptor stimulation

M01RR-00051-30 0771 (CLR) SCHOOLEY, ROBERT T General clinical research center Comparison of 2',3' dideoxyinosine and zidovudine in HIV infected

M01RR-00051-30 0713 (CLR) ADLER, LAWRENCE E General clinical research center Catecholaminergic drugs on sensory gating of auditory evoked potentials

M01RR-00051-30 0714 (CLR) ROBINSON, WILLIAM A General clinical research center Recombinant human granulocyte CSF in severe chronic

PROJECT NO., ORGANIZATIONAL UNIT., INVESTIGATOR, ADDRESS, TITLE

neutropenia patients

M01RR-00051-30 0716 (CLR) ROBINSON, WILLIAM A General clinical research center Piritrexim capsules in combination with dicarbazine in advanced melanoma

M01RR-00051-30 0726 (CLR) GERBER, JOHN G General clinical research center Effect of age on B-adrenergic mediated lipolysis in vivo

M01RR-00051-30 0727 (CLR) BYYNY, RICHARD L General clinical research center Insulin resistance and intracellular calcium in essential hypertension

M01RR-00051-30 0728 (CLR) ROBINSON, WILLIAM A General clinical research center Melatonin and malignant melanoma

M01RR-00051-30 0729 (CLR) BUNN, PAUL A General clinical research center Radiolabeled monoclonal antibody to image and treat breast cancer

M01RR-00051-30 0730 (CLR) EVERSON, GREGORY General clinical research center Effects of psyllium mucilloid

M01RR-00051-30 0740 (CLR) ROBINSON, WILLIAM A General clinical research center A phase III double blind adjuvant trial vaccinia oncolysate in melanoma

M01RR-00051-30 0743 (CLR) ROBINSON, WILLIAM A General clinical research center Disrupted allogenic human melanoma vaccine and interleukin II therapy

M01RR-00051-30 0744 (CLR) REITE, MARTIN General clinical research center Pilot study of the effect of interferon on nocturnal sleep

M01RR-00051-30 0745 (CLR) NIES, ALAN S General clinical research center The effect of age on the regulation of adrenergic receptors in man

M01RR-00051-30 0746 (CLR) NIES, ALAN S General clinical research center Effect of age on alpha-adrenergic receptor response in platelets

M01RR-00051-30 0747 (CLR) GLODE, MICHAEL General clinical research center Nafarelin acetate in men with D2 prostatic carcinoma--Comparison with DES

M01RR-00051-30 0749 (CLR) SCHOOLEY, ROBERT T General clinical research center Safety and efficacy of ZDV for asymptomatic HIV infected individuals

M01RR-00051-30 0750 (CLR) NIES, ALAN S General clinical research center Age related changes in stereoselective disposition of propranolol

M01RR-00051-30 0751 (CLR) GOFF, JOHN General clinical research center Sandostatin for dumping syndrome

M01RR-00051-30 0752 (CLR) ECKEL, ROBERT H General clinical research center Effect of MCT dietary substitute on glucose/lipid metabolism in Type II DM

M01RR-00051-30 0753 (CLR) BERL, THOMAS General clinical research center ACE inhibition in diabetic nephropathy

M01RR-00051-30 0754 (CLR) CHAPMAN, ARLENE B General clinical research center Creatine clearance amino acid infusion and oral trimethoprim

M01RR-00051-30 0755 (CLR) EVERSON, GREGORY T General clinical research center Effects of sodium retention in cirrhosis

M01RR-00051-30 0756 (CLR) SUSSMAN, KARL General clinical research center Tolrestat in diabetic retinopathy in insulin dependent diabetics

M01RR-00051-30 0772 (CLR) SCHHOLEY, ROBERT T General clinical research center 2',3'dideoxyinosine and zidovudine with HIV infected patients

M01RR-00051-30 0773 (CLR) SCHOOLEY, ROBERT T General clinical research center 2',3'dideoxyinosine orally to zidovudine intolerant HIV infected patients

M01RR-00051-30 0774 (CLR) NIES, ALAN S General clinical research center Angiotensin converting enzyme inhibitors and prostacyclin synthesis

M01RR-00051-30 0775 (CLR) BUNN, PAUL A General clinical research center A study of radiolabeled breast-directed monoclonal antibodies

M01RR-00051-30 0757 (CLR) SUSSMAN, KARL General clinical research center Tolrestat in diabetic retinopathy in non-insulin dependent diabetics

M01RR-00051-30 0758 (CLR) SUSSMAN, KARL General clinical research center Tolrestat in prevention of diabetic retinopathy in insulin dependent patients

K01RR-00052-03 (AR) DANNEMAN, PEGGY J UNIV OF MICHIGAN MEDICAL SCHOO 018 ANIMAL RESEARCH FACILITY ANN ARBOR, MI 48109-0614 Evoked potentials to study pain and endogenous opiods

M01RR-00052-30 (CLR) JOHNS, MICHAEL E JOHNS HOPKINS UNIV SCH OF MED 720 RUTLAND AVE BALTIMORE, MD 21205-2196 General clinical research center

M01RR-00052-30 0227 (CLR) EGGLESTON, PEYTON A General clinical research center Airway response to airborne animal allergen

M01RR-00052-30 0230 (CLR) KWITEROVICH, PETER O General clinical research center Study of the plasma exchange on hypercholesterolemia

M01RR-00052-30 0231 (CLR) MODLIN, JOHN General clinical research center Outcome of aseptic meningitis I

M01RR-00052-30 0232 (CLR) MOSER, HUGO General clinical research center Glycerol trierucate (GTE) therapy of adrenoleukodystrophy

M01RR-00052-30 0234 (CLR) MODLIN, JOHN F General clinical research center Gammaglobulin in HIV infected children receiving zidovudine

M01RR-00052-30 0235 (CLR) LEDERMAN, HOWARD General clinical research center Gamma interferon in patients with chronic granulomatous disease

M01RR-00052-30 0236 (CLR) FIVUSH, BARBARA General clinical research center Therapy to improve growth velocity of children with chronic renal failure

M01RR-00052-30 0087 (CLR) BRUSILOW, SAUL W General clinical research center Treatment of urea cycle enzymopathies

M01RR-00052-30 0099 (CLR) VALLE, DAVID L General clinical research center Ornithine metabolism in gyrate atrophy patients and heterozygotes

M01RR-00052-30 0149 (CLR) PLOTNICK, LESLIE P General clinical research center Production and integrated concentration of various hormones

M01RR-00052-30 0193 (CLR) PLOTNICK, L. General clinical research center Randomized protropin study with previously treatment patients

PROJECT NO., ORGANIZATIONAL UNIT., INVESTIGATOR, ADDRESS, TITLE

M01RR-00052-30 0194 (CLR) PLOTNICK, L General clinical research center Protropin and rhGH increased doses in previously treated patients
M01RR-00052-30 0198 (CLR) SAMPSON, H General clinical research center Role of food hypersensitivity in atopic dermatitis
M01RR-00052-30 0206 (CLR) PLOTNICK, LESLIE P General clinical research center Somatropin (rhGH) adm. to pts. with growth hormone deficiency
M01RR-00052-30 0208 (CLR) WINGARD, JOHN General clinical research center Late toxicities following bone marrow transplantation
M01RR-00052-30 0210 (CLR) CHISOLM, JULIAN General clinical research center Safety and efficacy of DMSA for lead poisoning
M01RR-00052-30 0213 (CLR) EGGLESTON, PEYTON A General clinical research center Immunotherapy of childhood asthma methacholine inhalation challenge
M01RR-00052-30 0217 (CLR) MODLIN, JOHN General clinical research center AZT in children with symptomatic HIV infection
M01RR-00052-30 0218 (CLR) BERKOVITZ, GARY D General clinical research center Studies in Rett syndrome
M01RR-00052-30 0219 (CLR) PLOTNICK, LESLIE P General clinical research center Humatrope and low dose estrogen in Turner Syndrome
M01RR-00052-30 0237 (CLR) DE ANGELIS, CATHERINE General clinical research center Urinary cotidine in asthmatic children exposed to tobacco smoke
M01RR-00052-30 0238 (CLR) FRANCOMANO, CLAIR A General clinical research center Morbidity and mortality in achondroplasia
M01RR-00052-30 0239 (CLR) EGGLESTON, PEYTON A General clinical research center Modification of the allergic response to Cat exposure
M01RR-00052-30 0240 (CLR) PLOTNICK, LESLIE P General clinical research center Somatropin (rhGH) and estrogens in Turner syndrome
M01RR-00052-30 0241 (CLR) PLOTNICK, LESLIE P General clinical research center GH treatment in children with idiopathic short stature and growth retardation
M01RR-00052-30 0242 (CLR) PERMAN, JAY A General clinical research center Nutrient absorption in infants and children with short gut syndrome
M01RR-00052-30 0243 (CLR) FRANCOMANO, CLAIR A General clinical research center Studies in clinical genetics
M01RR-00052-30 0244 (CLR) PLOTNICK, LESLIE P General clinical research center Safety and efficacy of GRF 1-29 in growth hormone deficient children
M01RR-00054-30 (CLR) RYAN, RICHARD M TUFTS UNIVERSITY 171 HARRISON AVENUE BOSTON, MASS 02111 General clinical research center
M01RR-00054-30 0420 (CLR) ATKINS, MICHAEL General clinical research center IL-4 bolus in advanced metastatic cancers
M01RR-00054-30 0421 (CLR) KONSTAM, MARVIN A General clinical research center UK-79,300 renal hemodynamics, renal function, congestive heart failure
M01RR-00054-30 0422 (CLR) LINZER, MARK General clinical research center Defining impaired autonomic cardiovascular responses in syncope
M01RR-00054-30 0423 (CLR) ATKINS, MICHAEL General clinical research center IL-4 in metastatic melanoma
M01RR-00054-30 0424 (CLR) FAWAZ, KARIM General clinical research center Interferon alfa-2a in chronic non-A, non-B hepatitis
M01RR-00054-30 0425 (CLR) WAZER, DAVID General clinical research center BPA distribution in melanoma, glioblastoma, breast carcinoma
M01RR-00054-30 0426 (CLR) ATKINS, MICHAEL General clinical research center IL-4 in metastatic renal cell carcinoma
M01RR-00054-30 0427 (CLR) GREENBLATT, DAVID General clinical research center Kinetics and dynamics of diphenhydramine
M01RR-00054-30 0429 (CLR) KAPLAN, MARSHALL M General clinical research center Primary biliary cirrhosis -- Treatment with colchicine
M01RR-00054-30 0430 (CLR) CAPLAN, LOUIS General clinical research center Correlation electrophysiological and biopsy findings in polyneuropathy
M01RR-00054-30 0431 (CLR) CAPLAN, LOUIS General clinical research center Amyotrophic lateral sclerosis data study
M01RR-00054-30 0432 (CLR) MUNSAT, THEODORE L General clinical research center Myoblast transfer in Duchenne muscular dystrophy
M01RR-00054-30 0433 (CLR) GORBACH, SHERWOOD L General clinical research center Diet, estrogens, and breast cancer
M01RR-00054-30 0448 (CLR) LICHTENSTEIN, ALICE General clinical research center Effect of lovastatin on lipoprotein metabolism
M01RR-00054-30 0466 (CLR) FURIE, BRUCE General clinical research center Random trial native prothrom RIA vs PIT oral anticoagulation therapy
M01RR-00054-30 0467 (CLR) GANS, BRUCE General clinical research center Assessment of motor performance and function in children and adults
M01RR-00054-30 0468 (CLR) PANDIAN, NATESA General clinical research center Retrospective echocardiographic evaluation of prosthetic valves
M01RR-00054-30 0469 (CLR) REINHOLD, RANDOLPH B General clinical research center Nutritional correlates of obesity
M01RR-00054-30 0471 (CLR) MUNSAT, THEODORE L General clinical research center Myoblast transfer
M01RR-00054-30 0475 (CLR) MUNSAT, THEODORE L General clinical research center Genetic linkage studies of Werdnig-Hoffman disease
M01RR-00054-30 0476 (CLR) PAUKER, STEVEN General clinical research center Echocardiography in aortic insufficiency
M01RR-00054-30 0184 (CLR) REICHLIN, SEYMOUR General clinical research center Medullary carcinoma of the thyroid gland
M01RR-00054-30 0382 (CLR) ARORA, SANJEEV General clinical research center Methotrexate in ulcerative colitis
M01RR-00054-30 0384 (CLR) MUNSAT, THEODORE L General clinical research center Dextromethorphan therapy in ALS
M01RR-00054-30 0385 (CLR) GANS, BRUCE General clinical research center Pediatric trauma information management system
M01RR-00054-30 0386 (CLR) GANS, BRUCE General clinical research center Pediatric trauma registry to assess rehabilitative outcome
M01RR-00054-30 0387 (CLR) GANS, BRUCE General clinical research center Analysis of rehospitalization in severe musculo-skeletal/neuromuscular disorders
M01RR-00054-30 0388 (CLR) GANS, BRUCE General clinical research center Feasibility of model system of medical care management
M01RR-00054-30 0389 (CLR) GANS, BRUCE General clinical research center Validation of Wexler adult intelligence scale
M01RR-00054-30 0390 (CLR) GANS, BRUCE General clinical research center Psychosocial/function abilities in adult myotonic muscular dystrophy
M01RR-00054-30 0395 (CLR) KONSTAM, MARVIN General clinical research center Heart failure database
M01RR-00054-30 0397 (CLR) SNYDMAN, DAVID General clinical research center OKT3 in liver transplant
M01RR-00054-30 0398 (CLR) MUNSAT, THEODORE L General clinical research center TRH in ALS – Natural history file
M01RR-00054-30 0399 (CLR) BINKIEWICZ, ANNA General clinical research center Pathophysiology of growth retardation in failure to thrive
M01RR-00054-30 0400 (CLR) KURTIN, PAUL General clinical research center Body composition metabolic rate chronic renal failure
M01RR-00054-30 0401 (CLR) LEVEY, ANDREW S General clinical research center Modificaion of diet in renal disease
M01RR-00054-30 0402 (CLR) KAPLAN, MARSHALL M General clinical research center Cytomegalovirus immune globin in liver transplant recipients
M01RR-00054-30 0403 (CLR) GORBACH, SHERWOOD L General clinical research center Lactobacillus supplement on fecal bacteria, enzyme activity, sterols
M01RR-00054-30 0404 (CLR) VINTON, NANCY E General clinical research center Methionine metabolism in healthy adults, and pts with ovarian adenocarcinoma
M01RR-00054-30 0405 (CLR) COTTEIRO, RICHARD A General clinical research center Renal function in systemic lupus erythematosus
M01RR-00054-30 0406 (CLR) SCHWENN, MOLLY General clinical research center Pediatric IL-2 in solid tumors
M01RR-00054-30 0407 (CLR) KAPLAN, MARSHALL M General clinical research center Clearance of oral methotrexate from serum
M01RR-00054-30 0408 (CLR) ATKINS, MICHAEL B General clinical research center IL-2 bolus vs IL-2 with alpha interferon in renal cell carcinoma
M01RR-00054-30 0409 (CLR) CUMMINGS, TIMOTHY General clinical research center Weight maintenance after weight loss
M01RR-00054-30 0410 (CLR) SCHAEFER, ERNST J General clinical research center Effect of lovastatin in lipoprotein metabolism
M01RR-00054-30 0411 (CLR) ATKINS, MICHAEL B General clinical research center Alternating IL-2 and Cisplatin in metastatic melanoma
M01RR-00054-30 0412 (CLR) ATKINS, MICHAEL B General clinical research center Il-2 vs Il-2 w/alpha interferon in metastatic melanoma
M01RR-00054-30 0413 (CLR) GRAND, RICHARD J General clinical research center rHGH in children with inflammatory bowel disease and short stature
M01RR-00054-30 0414 (CLR) REIGHLIN, SEYMOUR General clinical research center Sandostatin and pirenzepine alone, in combination in type 1 diabetics
M01RR-00054-30 0415 (CLR) SKOLNIK, PAUL R General clinical research center Concurrent zidovudine and 2'3' dideoxyinosine patients with HIV
M01RR-00054-30 0416 (CLR) BALL, HARRISON G General clinical research center Cyclophosphamide/cisplatin vs taxol/cisplatin in ovarian carcinoma
M01RR-00054-30 0417 (CLR) BALL, HARISON G General clinical research center Taxol in advanced cervical carcinoma
M01RR-00054-30 0418 (CLR) DAWSON-HUGHES, BESS General clinical research center Effects of calcium, estrogen, exercise on bone health, lipid profile
M01RR-00054-30 0419 (CLR) SCHAEFER, ERNST J General clinical research center Lopid-serum triglycerides, chylomicron metabolism-hypertriglyceridemia
M01RR-00054-30 0252 (CLR) KAPLAN, MARSHALL M General clinical research center Clinical trials of colchicine vs placebo in biliary cirrhosis
M01RR-00054-30 0326 (CLR) MUNSAT, THEODORE L General clinical research center TRH in ALS--Double blind placebo controlled constant infusion pump
M01RR-00054-30 0337 (CLR) KAPLAN, MARSHALL General clinical research center Methotrexate in primary sclerosing cholangitis
M01RR-00054-30 0341 (CLR) SNYDMAN, DAVID R General clinical research center Kidney transplant associated cytomegalovirus prevention
M01RR-00054-30 0363 (CLR) KAPLAN, MARSHALL General clinical research center Oral methotrexate vs colchicine in biliary cirrhosis
M01RR-00054-30 0364 (CLR) ATKINS, MICHAEL A General clinical research center High dose IL-2 and cisplatin in metastatic melanoma
M01RR-00054-30 0365 (CLR) HEROS, DEBORAH General clinical research center Imuvert in recurrent/refractory malignant brain tumors
M01RR-00054-30 0366 (CLR) BALL, HARRISON General clinical research center Taxol in patients with advanced pelvic malignancies
M01RR-00054-30 0374 (CLR) GREENBLATT, DAVID General clinical research center Infusion rate of intravenous midazolam
M01RR-00054-30 0375 (CLR) KAPLAN, MARSHALL M General clinical research center Hepatic iron stores
M01RR-00054-30 0377 (CLR) ATKINS, MICHAEL General clinical research center Interleukin-2/roferon-A/LAK cells in renal cell carcinoma
M01RR-00054-30 0378 (CLR) ATKINS, MICHAEL B General clinical research center High dose, IV bolus interleukin-2/interferon-alpha 2b
M01RR-00054-30 0379 (CLR) KAPLAN, GARY General clinical research center Pharmacokinetic, pharmacodynamic caffeine in healthy volunteers
M01RR-00054-30 0380 (CLR) MUNSAT, THEODORE L General clinical research center Interleukin-2/roferon-A outpatient treatment renal cell carcinoma
M01RR-00054-30 0381 (CLR) KEMP, ALAN General clinical research center Methotrexate in Crohn's disease
K01RR-00055-03 (AR) REIMANN, KEITH A NEW ENGLAND RGNL PRIMATE RES C ONE PINE HILL DRIVE SOUTHBOROUGH, MA 01772 Hematopoiesis in retrovirus infected simians
M01RR-00055-30 (CLR) HELLMAN, SAMUEL UNIVERSITY OF CHICAGO 5841 S MARYLAND AVENUE CHICAGO, IL 60637 General clinical research center

PROJECT NO., ORGANIZATIONAL UNIT., INVESTIGATOR, ADDRESS, TITLE

M01RR-00055-30 0520 (CLR) REFETOFF, SAMUEL General clinical research center Pts. with Cushing's disease & non-ACTH secreting pituitary tumors

M01RR-00055-30 0524 (CLR) ROSENFIELD, ROBERT L General clinical research center Glucocorticoid effects on CRH test

M01RR-00055-30 0525 (CLR) JASPAN, JONATHAN B General clinical research center Combined kidney & pancreas transplantation in uremic diabetic pts.

M01RR-00055-30 0533 (CLR) DE WIT, HARRIET General clinical research center Food restriction on responses to marijuana & nicotine

M01RR-00055-30 0535 (CLR) SAMUELS, BRIAN L General clinical research center Combination vinblastine & drug resistance-modulating drug cyclosporine

M01RR-00055-30 0536 (CLR) VAN CAUTER, EVE General clinical research center Role of sleep and circadian rhythmicity in glucose regulation

M01RR-00055-30 0537 (CLR) ROIZAN, NANCY J General clinical research center Obesity in Down Syndrome--Energy expenditure, activity and calories

M01RR-00055-30 0541 (CLR) SCANU, ANGELO M General clinical research center HDL and lipoprotein metabolism--A study of hypolipoproteinemia

M01RR-00055-30 0542 (CLR) EHRMANN, DAVID General clinical research center Treatment of hirsutism with flutamide

M01RR-00055-30 0543 (CLR) JASPAN, JONATHAN B General clinical research center Relationship of obesity, hyperinsulinemia & LH to polycystic ovary syndrome

M01RR-00055-30 0544 (CLR) REFETOFF, SAMUEL General clinical research center Significance of abnormal thyroid function tests in elderly patients

M01RR-00055-30 0545 (CLR) DE WIT, HARRIET General clinical research center Determinants of drug preference in humans

M01RR-00055-30 0546 (CLR) DE WIT, HARRIET General clinical research center Drug preloads and drug choice

M01RR-00055-30 0547 (CLR) POLONSKY, KENNETH S General clinical research center Insulin secretion & clearance in normals & pts. with insulin resistance

M01RR-00055-30 0548 (CLR) ROIZEN, MICHAEL F General clinical research center Safety & pharmacokinetics of methylnaltrexone in healthy volunteers

M01RR-00055-30 0549 (CLR) POLONSKY, KENNETH S General clinical research center Postprandial lipoprotein metabolism--Obesity, diabetes, and low HDL subjects

M01RR-00055-30 0550 (CLR) ROBERTSON, GARY L General clinical research center Genetic disorders of vasopressin function

M01RR-00055-30 0563 (CLR) KUSHNER, ROBERT General clinical research center Dietary carbohydrate and aerobic exercise on weight reduction

M01RR-00055-30 0564 (CLR) GOLDMAN, MORRIS B General clinical research center Relationship of psychiatric illness to abnormal water excretion

M01RR-00055-30 0565 (CLR) GOLDMAN, MORRIS B General clinical research center Water drinking and water excretion/polydipsic hyponatremic psychiatric pts.

M01RR-00055-30 0566 (CLR) SCHOELLER, DALE A General clinical research center Stable isotope methods in the investigation of human obesity

M01RR-00055-30 0567 (CLR) BARNES, RANDALL B General clinical research center Gonadotropin-releasing hormone agonist test in evaluation of oligomenorrhea

M01RR-00055-30 0568 (CLR) GOLDMAN, MORRIS B General clinical research center Oropharyngeal regulation of water balance in schizophrenia

M01RR-00055-30 0569 (CLR) RICHARDS, JON M General clinical research center Phase I-B trial of intravenous anti-CD3 monoclonal antibody

M01RR-00055-30 0570 (CLR) JASPAN, JONATHAN B General clinical research center Pancreas transplantation on target organ disease in diabetes

M01RR-00055-30 0571 (CLR) LASHNER, BRET General clinical research center Magnesium dicycline chelate bioavailability in Crohn's disease

M01RR-00055-30 0572 (CLR) VAN CAUTER, EVE General clinical research center Phase-shifting effects of light and activity on the human circadian clock

M01RR-00055-30 0573 (CLR) CHAIT, LARRY D General clinical research center Marijuana -- Repeated smoking in humans

M01RR-00055-30 0574 (CLR) LOY, GARY L General clinical research center Human maternal and fetal protein degradation in the fasting state

M01RR-00055-30 0575 (CLR) CARA, JOSE F General clinical research center Recovery from GnRH agonist (nafarelin) suppressive therapy

M01RR-00055-30 0576 (CLR) CHELMICKASCHORR, EVA General clinical research center Treatment of multiple sclerosis with terbutaline

M01RR-00055-30 0577 (CLR) HEROLD, KEVAN C General clinical research center Insulin secretion in early insulin-dependent diabetes mellitus

M01RR-00055-30 0407 (CLR) REFETOFF, SAMUEL General clinical research center Definition of state of resistance to thyroid hormone

M01RR-00055-30 0578 (CLR) SCHOELLER, DALE A General clinical research center De novo lipogenesis in obese and nonobese individuals

M01RR-00055-30 0579 (CLR) ROBERTSON, GARY L General clinical research center: Circadian rhythms, thermoregulation & osmoregulation in Shapiro's syndrome

M01RR-00055-30 0580 (CLR) SOMMERFELD, EBERHARD S General clinical research center L-carnitine on fatty acid oxidation & organic acid excretion

M01RR-00055-30 0581 (CLR) KUSHNER, ROBERT General clinical research center Body water estimation by TOBEC & BIA in abnormal fluid balance

M01RR-00055-30 0410 (CLR) POLONSKY, KENNETH S General clinical research center Threshold of adverse effects of hypoglycemia on cerebral function

M01RR-00055-30 0421 (CLR) SCHILSKY, RICHARD L General clinical research center Clinical & pharmacological studies of IP chemotherapy

M01RR-00055-30 0446 (CLR) ROSENFIELD, ROBERT L. General clinical research center GnRH agonist stimulation diagnostic

M01RR-00055-30 0463 (CLR) ROBERTSON, GARY L. General clinical research center Thirst and vasopressin function in diabetes insipidus

M01RR-00055-30 0478 (CLR) ROOS, RAYMOND P General clinical research center Nerve and muscle interactions in amyotropic lateral sclerosis

PROJECT NO., ORGANIZATIONAL UNIT., INVESTIGATOR, ADDRESS, TITLE

M01RR-00055-30 0491 (CLR) ROSENFIELD, ROBERT L. General clinical research center Corticotropin release hormone test vs ACTH and ITT in patients w/adrenal failure

M01RR-00055-30 0498 (CLR) FAVUS, MURRAY J. General clinical research center Characterization of bone and mineral metabolism in Prader-Willi syndrome

M01RR-00055-30 0507 (CLR) BARRON, WILLIAM M. General clinical research center Sensitivity of 50gm oral GTT for diagnosis of gestational diabetes

M01RR-00056-30 (CLR) BERNIER, GEORGE M JR UNIVERSITY OF PITTSBURGH SCHOOL OF MEDICINE PITTSBURGH, PA 15261 **General clinical** research center

M01RR-00056-30 0358 (CLR) KWOH, KENT General clinical research center Xomazyme-H65 in treatment of rheumatoid arthritis

M01RR-00056-30 0359 (CLR) GERICH, JOHN General clinical research center Euglycemic clamp versus hyperglycemic clamp

M01RR-00056-30 0360 (CLR) URETSKY, BARRY General clinical research center Relationship of vasopressin to ANP release in man

M01RR-00056-30 0361 (CLR) HO, MONTO General clinical research center Tolerance and pharmacokinetics of interleukin-2 and zidovudin in AIDS

M01RR-00056-30 0362 (CLR) KIRKWOOD, JOHN General clinical research center Phase 1b clinical evaluation of biological response modifiers/cancer

M01RR-00056-30 0363 (CLR) MEDSGER, THOMAS General clinical research center Progressive systemic sclerosis (scleroderma) and related disorders

M01RR-00056-30 0364 (CLR) MANDARINO, LAWRENCE General clinical research center pathogenesis of skeletal muscle insulin resistance obesity and diabetes

M01RR-00056-30 0365 (CLR) BERGA, SARAH General clinical research center LH and alpha subunit secretion by estrogen in hypogonadal women

M01RR-00056-30 0366 (CLR) KELLEY, DAVID General clinical research center Free fatty acids on insulin stimulated glucose metabolism

M01RR-00056-30 0367 (CLR) KELLEY, DAVID General clinical research center Pathogenesis of skeletal muscle in NIDDM during euglycemia

M01RR-00056-30 0368 (CLR) KELLY, DAVID General clinical research center Ability of insulin and glienclamide therapy to normalize

M01RR-00056-30 0369 (CLR) KORYTOKOWSKI, MARY General clinical research center Assessment of beta-adrenergic sensitivity in diabetic patients

M01RR-00056-30 0370 (CLR) STANKO, RONALD General clinical research center Pyrubate and dihydroxyacetone on blood glucose concentration

M01RR-00056-30 0371 (CLR) STANKO, RONALD General clinical research center Plasma glucose, gluconeogenesis and futile cycling in diabetics

M01RR-00056-30 0372 (CLR) BERGA, SARAH General clinical research center Dopaminergic blockade in women with functional hypothalamic amenorrhea

M01RR-00056-30 0373 (CLR) GERICH, JOHN General clinical research center Oral glucose disposition in NIDDM

M01RR-00056-30 0374 (CLR) VAZQUEZ, JORGE General clinical research center Whole body rate of lipolysis and gluconeogenesis from glycerol

M01RR-00056-30 0375 (CLR) VAGNUCCI, ANTHONY General clinical research center Endocrine and immunologic circadian rythm in AIDS

M01RR-00056-30 0376 (CLR) HOFFMAN, LESLIE General clinical research center Use of concealed and traditional delivery of oxygen

M01RR-00056-30 0377 (CLR) TRZEPACZ, PAULA General clinical research center Behavior and hyperthyroidism--A beta-adrenergic mechanism

M01RR-00056-30 0378 (CLR) GUZICK, DAVID General clinical research center Weight loss on menstrual physiology obese, hyperandrogenic women

M01RR-00056-30 0379 (CLR) ROGERS, ROBERT General clinical research center Long term enternal nutrition in chronic obstructive

M01RR-00056-30 0380 (CLR) HO, MONTO General clinical research center Interaction of acetaminophen (Tylenol) and azidothymidine

M01RR-00056-30 0041 (CLR) ROBINSON, ALAN G General clinical research center Pre and post operative study of patients with pituitary tumor

M01RR-00056-30 0152 (CLR) ROBINSON, ALAN G General clinical research center Physiology of human neurophysins secretion

M01RR-00056-30 0216 (CLR) VAGNUCCI, ANTHONY H General clinical research center Sodium metabolism in hypertensive disease

M01RR-00056-30 0227 (CLR) DRASH, ALLAN L General clinical research center Diabetes control and complication trial

M01RR-00056-30 0264 (CLR) JARET, DAVID General clinical research center Effect on vasopressin stimulation of pituitary function

M01RR-00056-30 0282 (CLR) ROGERS, ROBERT M General clinical research center Emphysema--physiologic effects of nutritional support

M01RR-00056-30 0285 (CLR) STANKO, RONALD T General clinical research center Pyruvate and dihydroxyacetone on respiratory muscle endurance capacity

M01RR-00056-30 0290 (CLR) WING, RENA R General clinical research center Combining behavior modification and very low calorie diet"NIDDM"

M01RR-00056-30 0297 (CLR) GERICH, JOHN E General clinical research center Blood draws from normal volunteers

M01RR-00056-30 0298 (CLR) GERICH, JOHN E General clinical research center Pathogenesis of impaired glucose tolerance

M01RR-00056-30 0312 (CLR) STANKO, RONALD T General clinical research center Hypocaloric dietary therapy of obesity with pyru. & D.oxyacet

M01RR-00056-30 0320 (CLR) GERICH, JOHN E General clinical research center Glucose counterregulation in normal man

M01RR-00056-30 0325 (CLR) STANKO, RONALD T General clinical research center Pyruvate on serum lipoprotein concentration

M01RR-00056-30 0327 (CLR) GERICH, JOHN E General clinical research center quantification of the effects of insulin and glycogenolysis

M01RR-00056-30 0329 (CLR) HO, MONTO General clinical research center Interaction beween acetaminophen and zidovudine

M01RR-00056-30 0330 (CLR) VAZQUEZ, JORGE General clinical research center Protein sparing properties of glutamine during starvation

M01RR-00056-30 0331 (CLR) JEGASOTHY, BRIAN V General clinical

PROJECT NO., ORGANIZATIONAL UNIT., INVESTIGATOR, ADDRESS, TITLE

research center Extracorporeal photopheresis in progressive systemic scleroderma
M01RR-00056-30 0340 (CLR) GERICH, JOHN E General clinical research center Glycerol as a gluconeogenic substrate in NIDDM
M01RR-00056-30 0343 (CLR) WINTERS, STEPHEN J General clinical research center Pulsatile gonadotropin secretion in anovulatory women
M01RR-00056-30 0344 (CLR) GERICH, JOHN E General clinical research center Gluconeogenesis determined by the "alcohol" approach in NIDDM patients
M01RR-00056-30 0346 (CLR) GERICH, JOHN E General clinical research center Ability of insulin and sulfonylutes therapy to normalize glucose NIDDM
M01RR-00056-30 0348 (CLR) JEGASOTHY, BRIAN V General clinical research center Extracorporeal chemophotopheresis for treatment of graft vs host
M01RR-00056-30 0352 (CLR) AMICO, JANET A General clinical research center Pattern of the release of oxytocin in women and men
M01RR-00056-30 0354 (CLR) GERICH, JOHN E General clinical research center Metformin on gluconeogenesis, lactate, and free fatty acid in DIDDM
M01RR-00056-30 0355 (CLR) GUARE, JOHN General clinical research center Obese women with and without type 2 diabetes
M01RR-00056-30 0356 (CLR) GERICH, JOHN General clinical research center Regulation of hepatic glucose output by gluconeogenic substrate, III
M01RR-00056-30 0357 (CLR) CONSOLI, AGOSTINO General clinical research center Regulation of hepatic glucose output by gluconeogenic substrate,I
M01RR-00058-30 (CLR) COOPER, RICHARD A MEDICAL COLLEGE OF WISCONSIN 8701 WATERTOWN PLANK ROAD MILWAUKEE, WI 53226 General clinical research center
M01RR-00058-30 0207 (CLR) LEMANN, JACOB General clinical research center Clinical trial of plasmapheresis in severe lupus nephritis
M01RR-00058-30 0209 (CLR) LEMANN, JACOB JR. General clinical research center Evaluation of donors of kidney for transplantation
M01RR-00058-30 0211 (CLR) LEMANN, JACOB General clinical research center Effect of captopril on progressive type I diabetic kidney disease
M01RR-00058-30 0217 (CLR) DUCK, STEPHEN C. General clinical research center Wisconsin incidence cohort registry of type I diabetes mellitus
M01RR-00058-30 0218 (CLR) BRESHAN, DAVID B. General clinical research center SPECI/IMP brain imaging and neurophysiological assessment in schizophrenia
M01RR-00058-30 0219 (CLR) EGAN, BRENT M. General clinical research center Studies in overweight young men,insulin and salt-sensitive hypertensia
M01RR-00058-30 0220 (CLR) LEMANN, JACOB JR. General clinical research center Potassium effect for reduction of urinary Ca excretion in patients
M01RR-00058-30 0222 (CLR) SCHECTMAN, GORDON General clinical research center Effect of salt on insulin and glucose response in humans
M01RR-00058-30 0223 (CLR) KOCH, TIMOTHY R. General clinical research center Evaluation of cisapride in patients with chronic idiopathic constipation
M01RR-00058-30 0225 (CLR) LEMANN, JACOB General clinical research center Mechanisms of hypercalcuria of phosphate deprivation in man
M01RR-00058-30 0229 (CLR) RAO, STEPHEN General clinical research center Effects of physostigmine on memory loss in multiple sclerosis
M01RR-00058-30 0237 (CLR) HUANG, L General clinical research center Thyroid hormone treat. of rapid cycling bipolar & cyclothymic disorders
M01RR-00058-30 0238 (CLR) HARSCH, HAROLD General clinical research center Identification of Alzheimer's with SPECT and EEG
M01RR-00058-30 0239 (CLR) SARNA, SUSHIL K General clinical research center Measurement of G.I. transit and its relationship to motor activity
M01RR-00058-30 0240 (CLR) CONDON, ROBERT E General clinical research center Human colonic myoelectric activity
M01RR-00058-30 0241 (CLR) EGAN, BRENT M General clinical research center Importance of volume expansion in salt-sensitive hypertension
M01RR-00058-30 0244 (CLR) SCHMALZ, M General clinical research center Effect of somatostatin on the pain of chronic pancreatitis
M01RR-00058-30 0246 (CLR) EGAN, BRENT M General clinical research center Hypertension, hyperinsulinemia and coronary heart disease risk
M01RR-00058-30 0247 (CLR) RUSSELL, THOMAS General clinical research center Laser Doppler assessment in necrobiosis lipoidica diabeticorum
M01RR-00058-30 0248 (CLR) KISSEBAH, AHMED H General clinical research center Molecular & environmental factors of familial combined hyperlipidemia
M01RR-00058-30 0249 (CLR) LEMANN, JACOB General clinical research center Potassium deprivation on urinary calcium & phosphate excretion
M01RR-00058-30 0250 (CLR) JOHNSON, CHRISTOPHER General clinical research center Pancreatic transplant on diabetic enteropathy
M01RR-00058-30 0251 (CLR) SONNENBERG, GABRIELE General clinical research center Pulsatile and circhoral insulin secretion patterns
M01RR-00058-30 0252 (CLR) SCHECTMAN, GORDON General clinical research center Effects of interferon beta on LDL metbolism
M01RR-00058-30 0253 (CLR) ANDERSON, THOMAS General clinical research center Effects of photodynamic cytolysis in chronic lymphocytic leukemia
M01RR-00058-30 0254 (CLR) KISSEBAH, AHMED General clinical research center Effects of weight reduction on body composition and metabolic profile
M01RR-00058-30 0255 (CLR) SONNENBERG, GABRIELE General clinical research center Measurement of C-peptide and insulin kinetic coefficients in man
M01RR-00058-30 0256 (CLR) KISSEBAH, AHMED General clinical research center Relationship of gastric emptying to the hyper-insulinemia of obesity
M01RR-00058-30 0257 (CLR) WERLIN, STEVE General clinical research center Metabolic effects of discontinuation of parenteral nutrition in children

PROJECT NO., ORGANIZATIONAL UNIT., INVESTIGATOR, ADDRESS, TITLE

M01RR-00058-30 0258 (CLR) HOFFMAN, RAYMOND General clinical research center Blood lipid changes with differential alcohol consumption
M01RR-00058-30 0259 (CLR) EGAN, BRENT General clinical research center Effects of dietary fish oil supplementation on BP and vas.reactivity
M01RR-00058-30 0260 (CLR) EGAN, BRENT General clinical research center Hemodynamic effects of lisinopril vs. diltiazen in hypertensive patients
M01RR-00058-30 0010 (CLR) FINK, JORDAN N General clinical research center Hypersensitivity pneumonitis
M01RR-00058-30 0261 (CLR) EBERT, THOMAS General clinical research center Effects of long term infusion of atrial natiuretic factor in human
M01RR-00058-30 0262 (CLR) KINDWALL, ERIC General clinical research center Hyperbaric oxygen and thrombolysis in myocardial infarction
M01RR-00058-30 0263 (CLR) QUEBBEMAN, EDWARD J General clinical research center Acute initiation and discontinuation of TPN on glucose
M01RR-00058-30 0264 (CLR) RUDMAN, DANIEL General clinical research center Clinical trial of growth hormone in post poliomyelitis
M01RR-00058-30 0265 (CLR) SCHECTMAN, GORDON General clinical research center Kinetic heterogeneity of the lipoprotein respose to fish oil
M01RR-00058-30 0266 (CLR) BORDEN, ERNEST General clinical research center Repetitive dose safety trial of an immunomodiator in cancer patients
M01RR-00058-30 0267 (CLR) EGAN, BRENT General clinical research center Angiotension converting enzyme inhibition on insulin dynamics
M01RR-00058-30 0047 (CLR) WILSON, STUART D General clinical research center Dietary habits and pathophysiology in total gastrectomy
M01RR-00058-30 0069 (CLR) DODDS, WYLIE J General clinical research center Esophageal motor function in health and disease
M01RR-00058-30 0072 (CLR) CERLETTY, JAMES M General clinical research center Thyroid cancer screening projects
M01RR-00058-30 0082 (CLR) SOERGEL, KONRAD H General clinical research center Pathophysiology of diarrhea
M01RR-00058-30 0132 (CLR) WILSON, STUART D General clinical research center Multiple endocrine adenopathy type I
M01RR-00058-30 0164 (CLR) LEMANN, JACOB General clinical research center Dietary intervention in patients with progressive chronic renal failure
M01RR-00058-30 0189 (CLR) SCHECTMAN, GORDAN O General clinical research center Effect of fish oil supplement in non-insulin dependent diabetes
M01RR-00059-30 (CLR) CLIFTON, JAMES UNIV OF IOWA HOSPITALS IOWA CITY, IA 52242 General clinical research center
M01RR-00059-30 0724 (CLR) SCHLECHTE, JANET General clinical research center Use of somatostatin in treatment of acromegaly after unsucc.surgery
M01RR-00059-30 0725 (CLR) HOFFMAN, ROBERT General clinical research center Effects of growth hormone and gonadal steroids on insulin resistance
M01RR-00059-30 0726 (CLR) AHRENS, RICHARD General clinical research center Effect of inhaled nedocromil on airways response to inhaled albuterol
M01RR-00059-30 0727 (CLR) SCHNEIDER, ROBERT General clinical research center Cardiovascular reactivity in the laboratory and the field
M01RR-00059-30 0728 (CLR) TONNER, DENISE General clinical research center Bone mineral in children and adolescents
M01RR-00059-30 0729 (CLR) HANSEN, JAMES General clinical research center Hormone secretion in a women with pituitary tumor and cystic ovarian dis.
M01RR-00059-30 0730 (CLR) LABRECQUE, DOUGLAS General clinical research center Dirithromycin--Pharmacokinetics in impaired hepatic function
M01RR-00059-30 0731 (CLR) COOK, JENNIFER General clinical research center Growth hormone and gonadotropin release in childen with prec.puberty
M01RR-00059-30 0732 (CLR) HOFFMAN, ROBERT General clinical research center Effect of short term weight loss on insulin sensitivity in child.obesity
M01RR-00059-30 0733 (CLR) AHRENS, RICHARD General clinical research center Effects of nedocromil on airways response to inhaled albuterol
M01RR-00059-30 0735 (CLR) PERRY, PAUL J General clinical research center Psychiatric symptoms associated with anabolic steroid abuse
M01RR-00059-30 0736 (CLR) TSALIKIAN, EVA General clinical research center Corticotropin releasing-factor--A versatile diagnostic study
M01RR-00059-30 0737 (CLR) ANDREWS, WILLIAM General clinical research center Tumorogenesis and cellular metabolism in null cell pituitary adenomas
M01RR-00059-30 0738 (CLR) SOFFER, EDY General clinical research center The effects of graded exercise on esophageal pH and motility
M01RR-00059-30 0739 (CLR) REBOUCHE, CHARLES J General clinical research center Effects of dietary macronutrients on efficiency of carnitine reabsorption
M01RR-00059-30 0740 (CLR) FIELD, ELIZABETH General clinical research center Trial of alpha-interferon in hyper-IL-4, IL-5, syndrome
M01RR-00059-30 0741 (CLR) HOFFMAN, ROBERT P General clinical research center Hypoglycemia and sympathetic nerve activity in insulin dependent diabetes
M01RR-00059-30 0742 (CLR) SEGAR, JEFFREY General clinical research center Changes in water compartments and prostaglandins with/diuretic therapy
M01RR-00059-30 0743 (CLR) LIM, VICTORIA General clinical research center Dianeal in malnourished ambulatory peritoneal dialysis (CAPD) patients
M01RR-00059-30 0744 (CLR) TONNER, DENISE R General clinical research center Growth hormone in adults with acquired growth hormone deficiency

PROJECT NO., ORGANIZATIONAL UNIT., INVESTIGATOR, ADDRESS, TITLE

M01RR-00059-30 0745 (CLR) FIELD, ELIZABETH General clinical research center Chlorambucil as therapeutic modality in scleroderma
M01RR-00059-30 0746 (CLR) LOENING-BAUCKE, VERA General clinical research center Children with chronic constipation and encopresis
M01RR-00059-30 0747 (CLR) LAUER, RONALD General clinical research center Sodium sensitivity and blood pressure response in childhood
M01RR-00059-30 0748 (CLR) CLAMON, GERALD General clinical research center Randomized trial of somatostatin vs. morphine in patients with severe cancer pain
M01RR-00059-30 0749 (CLR) FELD, RONALD General clinical research center Factors influencing measurement of iron binding capacity
M01RR-00059-30 0750 (CLR) BURNS, C P General clinical research center Diagnosis and evaluation of acute undifferentiated leukemia
M01RR-00059-30 0751 (CLR) FROM, ROBERT P General clinical research center Blinded study of nalbuphine for morphine induced side effects
M01RR-00059-30 0752 (CLR) GLEED, KENT General clinical research center Long term follow-up of patients with ventricular tachycardia
M01RR-00059-30 0235 (CLR) SCHLECHTE, JANET A. General clinical research center Endocrine function and cytology in pituitary tumors
M01RR-00059-30 0691 (CLR) WOODHEAD, JEROLD C General clinical research center Iron absorption by preadolescent males and females
M01RR-00059-30 0692 (CLR) LOMBARD, KENNETH General clinical research center Iron retention in the preterm infant
M01RR-00059-30 0693 (CLR) MURRAY, PETER M General clinical research center The natural history of Scheuerman's disease
M01RR-00059-30 0694 (CLR) GUPTA, SALIL K General clinical research center Genetic variations in EGF and its receptor in infants with neonatal lung disease
M01RR-00059-30 0695 (CLR) REA, ROBERT F General clinical research center Effects of procainamide on sympathetic activity
M01RR-00059-30 0696 (CLR) LIM, VICTORIA General clinical research center Protein metabolism in uremia--The catabolic effects of hemodialysis
M01RR-00059-30 0697 (CLR) WEISMANN, DOUGLAS N General clinical research center Nephrocalcinosis--A complication of bronchopulmonary dysplasia
M01RR-00059-30 0698 (CLR) AHRENS, RICHARD C General clinical research center Effects of inhaled fluticasone proprionate versus placebo in adult asthmatics
M01RR-00059-30 0700 (CLR) ANDERSON, ERLING A General clinical research center Central neural control of sympathetic nerve responses to stress
M01RR-00059-30 0701 (CLR) MARK, ALLYN L General clinical research center Effects of mineralocorticoids on arterial baroreflex control
M01RR-00059-30 0702 (CLR) MARK, ALLYN L General clinical research center Sympathetic nerve responses to alcohol
M01RR-00059-30 0703 (CLR) AHRENS, RICHARD C General clinical research center: Effects of oral azelastine on airway responsiveness to histamine
M01RR-00059-30 0704 (CLR) COOK, BRIAN L General clinical research center Amiloride and hydrochlorithiazide in treatment of lithium-induced polyuria
M01RR-00059-30 0705 (CLR) MARK, ALLYN L General clinical research center Insulin and sympathetic activity in human hypertension
M01RR-00059-30 0706 (CLR) CHEMTOB, SYLVAIN General clinical research center Furosemide and metolazone versus furosemide alone in bronchopulmonary dysplasia
M01RR-00059-30 0707 (CLR) WEINBERGER, MILES M General clinical research center Bioavailability of oral theophylline preparations
M01RR-00059-30 0708 (CLR) HAYREH, SOHAN General clinical research center Glaucomatous optic nerve damage - determining factors
M01RR-00059-30 0709 (CLR) STROTTMANN, PAUL General clinical research center Methotrexate in rheumatoid arthritis
M01RR-00059-30 0710 (CLR) SIVITZ, WILLIAM General clinical research center Diabetes control and complications trial, phase III
M01RR-00059-30 0711 (CLR) WEISS, ROBERT General clinical research center Cardiac size and function with fast CT
M01RR-00059-30 0712 (CLR) HAJDUCZOK, ZINA General clinical research center Ventricular hypertrophy in man
M01RR-00059-30 0713 (CLR) STROTTMAN, PAUL General clinical research center CGS-10-787B versus naproxen in patients with rheumatoid arthritis
M01RR-00059-30 0714 (CLR) KLING, PAMELA General clinical research center Effects of penicillin on bleeding times in the premature infant
M01RR-00059-30 0715 (CLR) THOMPSON, STANLEY General clinical research center Optic neuritis treatment trial
M01RR-00059-30 0716 (CLR) BELL, EDWARD General clinical research center Energy balance and growth with lung disease
M01RR-00059-30 0717 (CLR) LINDGREN, SCOTT General clinical research center Behavioral and cognitive effects of sugar and aspartame in children
M01RR-00059-30 0718 (CLR) LOMBARD, KENNETH General clinical research center Mineral supplementation in preterm infants with bronchopulmonary dysplasia
M01RR-00059-30 0719 (CLR) SOFFER, EDY General clinical research center Effect of meal composition, caloric value and sham feeding on bowel activity
M01RR-00059-30 0720 (CLR) PHILLIPS, BRENDA General clinical research center Effect of anti-resorptive therapy on glucocorticoid induced bone loss
M01RR-00059-30 0721 (CLR) BILLER, JOSE General clinical research center Prevalence and severity of coronary artery disease
M01RR-00059-30 0722 (CLR) MARK, ALLYN General clinical research center Effects of anxiolytic therapy on neural outflow and mental stress
M01RR-00059-30 0723 (CLR) SCHWARTZ, DAVID General clinical research center Interstitial fibrosis in rubber workers
M01RR-00059-30 0301 (CLR) MARK, ALLYN L General clinical research center Modulation of baroreceptor reflexes
M01RR-00059-30 0580 (CLR) MARK, ALLYN L General clinical research center Modulation of baroreceptor reflexes
M01RR-00059-30 0593 (CLR) BURNS, C. P. General clinical research center Effects on leukemia cells due to modification of membrane lipids
M01RR-00059-30 0598 (CLR) FROM, ROBERT P General clinical research center Intubation of the frame for shock wave lithotropsy
M01RR-00059-30 0603 (CLR) HUBEL, KENNETH A General clinical research center Mediated ion transport
M01RR-00059-30 0606 (CLR) TRIGG, MICHAEL E. General clinical research center Mismatched bone marrow transplants
M01RR-00059-30 0613 (CLR) MCGUINNESS, GAIL A. General clinical research center Dexamethasone to prevent bronchopulmonary dysplasia
M01RR-00059-30 0625 (CLR) AHRENS, RICHARD C General clinical research center: Comparison of beta-2 agonists using bronchial provocation with histamine
M01RR-00059-30 0626 (CLR) ZIEGLER, EKHARD E General clinical research center Human milk in preterm infants--Effect of supplementation
M01RR-00059-30 0628 (CLR) REBOUCHE, CHARLES J General clinical research center carnitine biosynthesis and metabolism in mammals
M01RR-00059-30 0629 (CLR) RODNITZKY, ROBERT L General clinical research center Deprenyl and tocopherol antioxidative therapy of Parkinsonism
M01RR-00059-30 0634 (CLR) KIENZLE, MICHAEL G General clinical research center Neurohumoral modulation of ventricular arrhythmias in CHF
M01RR-00059-30 0636 (CLR) ZEITLER, RODNEY R General clinical research center Erythromycin in treatment of non-streptococcal pharyngitis
M01RR-00059-30 0644 (CLR) ZIEGLER, EKHARD E General clinical research center Vitamin D and mineral absorption in premature infants
M01RR-00059-30 0647 (CLR) ZIEGLER, EKHARD E General clinical research center Absorption of zinc by preterm infants
M01RR-00059-30 0648 (CLR) LAUER, RONALD M General clinical research center Dietary intervention study in children
M01RR-00059-30 0651 (CLR) HUNSICKER, LAWRENCE G General clinical research center Effects of captopril on progressive type I diabetic renal disease
M01RR-00059-30 0652 (CLR) LABRECQUE, DOUGLAS R General clinical research center Evaluation of trimethylaminuria
M01RR-00059-30 0655 (CLR) RIGGS, CHARLES E General clinical research center Recombinant tumor necrosis factor and adriamycin in cancer patients
M01RR-00059-30 0659 (CLR) FLANIGAN, MICHAEL J General clinical research center Contrast-induced acute renal failure
M01RR-00059-30 0660 (CLR) NAIDES, STANLEY J General clinical research center Human parvovirus infection and its sequelae in Iowa and Illinois
M01RR-00059-30 0663 (CLR) SMITH, IAN M General clinical research center Geriatric clinic database
M01RR-00059-30 0666 (CLR) GINGRICH, ROGER D General clinical research center Differences in survival after adult bone marrow transplant
M01RR-00059-30 0670 (CLR) FELD, RONALD D General clinical research center Accuracy of measuring urinary and CSF protein
M01RR-00059-30 0673 (CLR) MOCK, DONALD A General clinical research center Growth retardation in fructose intolerance
M01RR-00059-30 0674 (CLR) TSALIKIAN, EVA General clinical research center Integrated growth hormone levels in short children
M01RR-00059-30 0675 (CLR) RICHERSON, HAL B General clinical research center Immunotherapy of ragweed-induced asthma
M01RR-00059-30 0679 (CLR) KUMMER, MARK A General clinical research center Nutrition in cystic fibrosis--Study of dietary regimens by metabolic balance
M01RR-00059-30 0683 (CLR) SCHROTT, HELMUT G General clinical research center Postmenopausal estrogen/progestin intervention (PEPI) trial
M01RR-00059-30 0684 (CLR) DEGOWIN, RICHARD L General clinical research center Studies of the anemia of chronic disorders and malignancy
M01RR-00059-30 0687 (CLR) HUNSICKER, LAWRENCE G General clinical research center Modification of diet in renal disease (MDRD) study (Phase III)
M01RR-00059-30 0688 (CLR) KISKER, THOMAS C General clinical research center Safety and efficacy of recombinant DNA factor VIII in hemophilia A patients
M01RR-00059-30 0689 (CLR) FITZ, ANNETTE E General clinical research center Study of extended relaease felodipine in isolated systolic hypertension
M01RR-00059-30 0331 (CLR) HUNSICKER, LAWRENCE G General clinical research center Plasmapheresis in severe lupus nephritis
M01RR-00059-30 0332 (CLR) LABRECQUE, DOUGLAS R General clinical research center Etiology of inherited intrahepatic cholestasis
M01RR-00059-30 0333 (CLR) RICHERSON, HAL B General clinical research center Immunologic mechanisms in atopic disease
M01RR-00059-30 0356 (CLR) CORYELL, WILLIAM H General clinical research center Hypothalamic disturbances in depressive states
M01RR-00059-30 0395 (CLR) SCHLECHTE, JANET A General clinical research center Natural history of prolactin secreting tumors
M01RR-00059-30 0403 (CLR) BELL, EDWARD F General clinical research center Energy expenditure of young infants determined by calorimetry
M01RR-00059-30 0410 (CLR) SCHLECHTE, JANET A General clinical research center Glucocorticoid resistance in depressives
M01RR-00059-30 0447 (CLR) DAMASIO, ANTONIO R General clinical research center Anatomical and behavioral studies of complex visual disturbances
M01RR-00059-30 0458 (CLR) DUSDIEKER, LOIS B General clinical research center Once a day antibiotic dosing in children with ear infections
M01RR-00059-30 0462 (CLR) LAWTON, WILLIAM J General clinical research center Sodium sensitivity and blood pressure response
M01RR-00059-30 0498 (CLR) GANTZ, BRUCE J General clinical research center Iowa cochlear implant project
M01RR-00059-30 0504 (CLR) KATHOL, ROGER G General clinical research center Mechanisms of ACTH regulation
M01RR-00059-30 0511 (CLR) LIM, VICTORIA S General clinical research

PROJECT NO., ORGANIZATIONAL UNIT., INVESTIGATOR, ADDRESS, TITLE

center Leucine & alanine turnover in chronic renal failure
M01RR-00059-30 0513 (CLR) LOENING-BAUCKE, VERA A General clinical research center Ileum as neorectum after ulcerative colitis surgery
M01RR-00059-30 0525 (CLR) SCHLECHTE, JANET A General clinical research center Hyperprolactinemia and osteopenia
M01RR-00059-30 0545 (CLR) FIELD, ELIZABETH E General clinical research center Methotrexate, auranofin, or their combination in treatment of arthritis
M01RR-00059-30 0546 (CLR) DUSDIEKER, LOIS B General clinical research center Maternal calorie restriction on breast milk production
M01RR-00059-30 0551 (CLR) KATHOL, ROGER G General clinical research center Corticotropin releasing hormone in major depression
M01RR-00059-30 0552 (CLR) MARTINS, JAMES B General clinical research center Electrophysiologic testing in patients with tachycardia and coronary disease
M01RR-00059-30 0553 (CLR) WORSTER, DALE E General clinical research center Charcoal adsorbents--pharmacokinetics
M01RR-00059-30 0562 (CLR) ABBOUD, FRANCOIS M General clinical research center Circulation in humans--Effects of hypoxia
M01RR-00059-30 0579 (CLR) HUNNINGHAKE, GARY W General clinical research center Occupational and immunologic lung diseases
K01RR-00061-02 (AR) WIMSATT, JEFFREY H CORNELL UNIVERSITY 820 VETERINARY RESEARCH TOWER ITHACA NY 14853-6401 Local regulation of myometrial activity
K01RR-00064-02 (AR) HAWK, C TERRANCE UNIVERSITY OF ALABAMA ZEIGLER BUILDING ROOM 618 BIRMINGHAM AL 35294 Regulation of Na+ reabsorption in rat collecting duct
M01RR-00064-27 (CLR) STEVENS, WALTER UNIV OF UTAH MED CTR 50 NORTH MEDICAL DRIVE SALT LAKE CITY, UTAH 84132 General clinical research center
M01RR-00064-27 0347 (CLR) GREGORY, MARTIN C General clinical research center Taste sensitivity and thirst during perindopril therapy in hypertension
M01RR-00064-27 0348 (CLR) HOPKINS, PAUL N General clinical research center Genetics of diet and drug effects in familial hypercholesterolemia
M01RR-00064-27 0352 (CLR) WARD, JOHN H General clinical research center Genetic analysis of breast cancer
M01RR-00064-27 0353 (CLR) DAYTON, MERRIL T General clinical research center Ileal pouch adaptation and dysfunction
M01RR-00064-27 0354 (CLR) JAECKLE, KURT A General clinical research center Phase I-II clinical trial of imuvert in recurrent malignant astrocytomas
M01RR-00064-27 0355 (CLR) MEYER, LAURENCE J General clinical research center Transplantation of human nevi to nude mice
M01RR-00064-27 0357 (CLR) ZONE, JOHN J General clinical research center Dermatitis herpetiformis--Study of immunoreactants in the skin
M01RR-00064-27 0358 (CLR) SAMLOWSKI, WOLFRAM General clinical research center High dose IL-2 and LAK cells in metastatic or unresectable melanoma-R
M01RR-00064-27 0359 (CLR) SAMLOWSKI, WOLFRAM General clinical research center High dose IL-2 and LAK cells in metastatic or unresectable melanoma-N
M01RR-00064-27 0360 (CLR) SAMLOWSKI, WOLFRAM General clinical research center High dose IL-2 and LAK cells in metastatic renal cell carcinoma-R
M01RR-00064-27 0361 (CLR) SAMLOWSKI, WOLFRAM General clinical research center High dose IL-2 and LAK cells in metastatic renal cell carcinoma-NR
M01RR-00064-27 0362 (CLR) SAMLOWSKI, WOLFRAM General clinical research center Lymphokine activated killer (LAK) cell localization into cancers
M01RR-00064-27 0363 (CLR) SAMLOWSKI, WOLFRAM General clinical research center IL 2 and/or LAK cells in Hodgkin's disease or non-Hodgkin's lymphoma
M01RR-00064-27 0365 (CLR) MCGEE, ZELL A General clinical research center Tumor necrosis factor assays and effect of Neisseria infection on TNF
M01RR-00064-27 0367 (CLR) MOYER-MILEUR, LAURIE General clinical research center Growth in infants with BPD following discontinuation of supplementary oxygen
M01RR-00064-27 0369 (CLR) DE LIA, JULIAN E General clinical research center Neodymium YAG laser therapy for monochorionic twin pregnancy
M01RR-00064-27 0370 (CLR) HOIDAL, JOHN R General clinical research center Pathogenesis of vascular leak syndrome associated with LAK-IL2 therapy
M01RR-00064-27 0371 (CLR) ELBEIN, STEVEN C General clinical research center Characterization of the genetics of NIDDM with early age of onset
M01RR-00064-27 0372 (CLR) SMITH, JOSEPH A General clinical research center Prostate ultrasound study
M01RR-00064-27 0374 (CLR) WALKER, KAY B General clinical research center Comparison of four pancreatic enzyme products in cystic fibrosis
M01RR-00064-27 0376 (CLR) SAMLOWSKI, WOLFRAM General clinical research center Intrameningeal IL-2 for meningeal carcinomatosis
M01RR-00064-27 0377 (CLR) MEIKLE, A WAYNE General clinical research center Modulation of the human immune response with DHEA and glucocorticoids
M01RR-00064-27 0379 (CLR) RALLISON, MARVIN L General clinical research center Growth hormone releasing factor in growth hormone deficient children
M01RR-00064-27 0380 (CLR) EDWARD, CORWIN General clinical research center Hereditary hemochromatosis
M01RR-00064-27 0381 (CLR) MASON, JAY General clinical research center Immunosuppresive therapy for biopsy-proven myocarditis
M01RR-00064-27 0382 (CLR) SAMLOWSKI, WOLFRAM General clinical research center Il-2 and/or LAK cells in non-small cell lung cancer
M01RR-00064-27 0383 (CLR) STREISAND, JAMES General clinical research center Oral and transmucosal fentanyl citrate dissolved OTFC in volunteers
M01RR-00064-27 0384 (CLR) MEIKLE, WAYNE General clinical research center Familial factors in benign prostatic hyperplasia and size
M01RR-00064-27 0385 (CLR) CANNON, GRANT General clinical research center A monoclonal antibody treatment of rhematoid arthritis
M01RR-00064-27 0386 (CLR) MYLES-WORSLEY, MARINA General clinical research center Genetic influences on normal attentional development
M01RR-00064-27 0387 (CLR) RENLUND, DALE General clinical research center RS-61443 for treatment of cardiac allograft recipients
M01RR-00064-27 0388 (CLR) MCWHORTER, WILLIAM General clinical research center Prostate cancer and premalignant lesions in high-risk families
M01RR-00064-27 0016 (CLR) RALLISON, MARVIN L General clinical research center Effects of human growth hormone on hypopituitary dwarfism
M01RR-00064-27 0059 (CLR) WILSON, DANA E General clinical research center Physiology of lipoprotein removal in man
M01RR-00064-27 0389 (CLR) BRISTLOW, MICHAEL General clinical research center Carvedilol in patients with idiopathic dilated cardiomyopathy
M01RR-00064-27 0390 (CLR) CHAN, GARY General clinical research center Effect of dietary calcium on growth & bone mineral status in girls
M01RR-00064-27 0391 (CLR) ZONE, JOHN General clinical research center Pathogenesis of dermatitis herpetiformis
M01RR-00064-27 0392 (CLR) BRISTOW, MICHAEL General clinical research center Chronic administration of OPC-8212 in heart failure
M01RR-00064-27 0137 (CLR) BURT, RANDALL General clinical research center Colorectal polyposis and carcinoma in family groups
M01RR-00064-27 0155 (CLR) KUSHNER, JAMES P General clinical research center Disorders of porphyrin metabolism
M01RR-00064-27 0167 (CLR) MEIKLE, A WAYNE General clinical research center Simplified tests for diagnosis of Cushing's syndrome
M01RR-00064-27 0190 (CLR) KUSHNER, JAMES P General clinical research center Studies of hereditary hemochromatosis
M01RR-00064-27 0263 (CLR) CLEGG, DANIEL O General clinical research center Liver biopsy study after high methotrexate dosage in rheumatoid arthritis
M01RR-00064-27 0270 (CLR) KANNER, RICHARD E General clinical research center Early intervention for chronic obstructive pulmonary disease
M01RR-00064-27 0279 (CLR) BRISTOW, MICHAEL R General clinical research center Monitoring heart transplant patients with refractory rejection
M01RR-00064-27 0280 (CLR) BRISTOW, MICHAEL R General clinical research center Bucindolol in congestive heart failure
M01RR-00064-27 0285 (CLR) GREGORY, MARTIN C General clinical research center Hereditary nephritis
M01RR-00064-27 0293 (CLR) MASON, JAY W General clinical research center Comparison of electrophysiologic study to ECG monitoring
M01RR-00064-27 0294 (CLR) MCMURRAY, MARTHA P General clinical research center Bone mineral content in phenylketouria
M01RR-00064-27 0298 (CLR) CAREY, JOHN C General clinical research center Genetic epidemiology of cancer in Utah
M01RR-00064-27 0300 (CLR) WILLIAMS, ROGER General clinical research center Non-modulation and red cell sodium transport in essential hypertension
M01RR-00064-27 0308 (CLR) CLEGG, DANIEL O General clinical research center Methotrexate,auranofin,or both, in rheumatoid arthritis
M01RR-00064-27 0309 (CLR) ELBEIN, STEVEN C General clinical research center Genetics of non-insulin dependent diabetes mellitus
M01RR-00064-27 0311 (CLR) HEILBRUN, PETER General clinical research center Data base analysis of neurosurgical patients
M01RR-00064-27 0312 (CLR) HOBBS, PATRICIA J General clinical research center Energy expenditure in patients with cystic fibrosis
M01RR-00064-27 0313 (CLR) INVERIUS, PER-HENRIK General clinical research center Regulation of lipoprotein lipase (LPL)
M01RR-00064-27 0314 (CLR) JAECKLE, KURT A General clinical research center Immune modifier in primary malignant brain tumors
M01RR-00064-27 0319 (CLR) KUSHNER, JAMES P General clinical research center Intraperitoneal administration of anticancer drugs in hypotonic solution
M01RR-00064-27 0322 (CLR) ODELL, WILLIAM D General clinical research center Determination of pulsation characteristics of HCG
M01RR-00064-27 0323 (CLR) PACE, NATHAN L General clinical research center Analysis of anesthetic variables in cardiopulmonary bypass
M01RR-00064-27 0324 (CLR) RALLISON, MARVIN L General clinical research center Treatment of precocious puberty (and CAH) with an LHRH analog
M01RR-00064-27 0326 (CLR) ROTHSTEIN, GERALD General clinical research center Hematopoiesis in aging man
M01RR-00064-27 0327 (CLR) SPRUANCE, SPOTSWOOD General clinical research center Herpes simplex labialis experimentally induced by ultraviolet light
M01RR-00064-27 0329 (CLR) VODA, ANN General clinical research center Intergenerational analysis of menstrual and reproductive events
M01RR-00064-27 0331 (CLR) BRISTOW, MICHAEL R General clinical research center Adrenergic mechanisms in heart failure
M01RR-00064-27 0334 (CLR) NELSON, DON H General clinical research center Effect of corticosteroids on human leukocytes and red blood cells
M01RR-00064-27 0343 (CLR) MCMURRAY, MARTHA P General clinical research center Effect of elemental diet on disease activity in dermatitis herpetiformis
M01RR-00064-27 0344 (CLR) MYLES-WORSLEY, MARINA General clinical research center Genetic influences on normal attentional development
M01RR-00064-27 0346 (CLR) GREGORY, MARTIN C General clinical research center Taste sensitivity & thirst during perindopril therapy in hypertension
M01RR-00065-29 (CLR) AYRES, STEPHEN M VIRGINIA COMMONWEALTH UNIV P O BOX 155 MCV STATION RICHMOND, VA 23298-0155 General clinical research center
M01RR-00065-29 0049 (CLR) DOWNS, ROBERT General clinical research center Pituitary function after vision trans-sphenoidal hypophyseal surgery

M01RR-00065-29 0084 (CLR) HESS, MICHAEL General clinical research center Heart transplantation
M01RR-00065-29 0153 (CLR) CHAN, JAMES C.M. General clinical research center Growth failure with renal disease in children
M01RR-00065-29 0225 (CLR) DOWNS, ROBERT General clinical research center Cushings disease after transphenoidal surgery & recurrence detection
M01RR-00065-29 0228 (CLR) RIZZO, WILLIAM B General clinical research center Fatty acid metabolism in adrenoleukodystrophy--Euric acid therapy
M01RR-00065-29 0269 (CLR) NESTLER, JOHN E General clinical research center Insulin as an effector of steroidogenesis in women
M01RR-00065-29 0278 (CLR) CHAN, JAMES C. M. General clinical research center X-linked hypophosphatemia
M01RR-00065-29 0281 (CLR) WATLINGTON, CHARLES O General clinical research center Glucocorticoids and hypertension
M01RR-00065-29 0285 (CLR) BLACKARD, WILLIAM G General clinical research center Glucose homeostasis
M01RR-00065-29 0330 (CLR) GEHR, TODD General clinical research center Insulin absorption during peritoneal dialysis
M01RR-00065-29 0331 (CLR) WELLY, DEVIN General clinical research center Serum insulin, glucose levels on phase II glycosylation reactions
M01RR-00065-29 0332 (CLR) RIZZO, WILLIAM R General clinical research center Fatty alcohol metabolism in Sjogren-Larsson syndrome
M01RR-00065-29 0334 (CLR) BLACKARD, WILLIAM G General clinical research center Insulin--An effector of steroidogenesis in females
M01RR-00065-29 0335 (CLR) BANKS, W L General clinical research center Effects of nutrition on cell cycle kinetics
M01RR-00065-29 0286 (CLR) COWLEY, MICHAEL J General clinical research center Prevention of restenosis following coronary angioplasty
M01RR-00065-29 0288 (CLR) GUTCHER, GARY General clinical research center Retinol (vitamin A) status and metabolism in premature infants
M01RR-00065-29 0289 (CLR) WONG, EDWARD S General clinical research center Blood/body fluid exposure incidence in health care workers
M01RR-00065-29 0292 (CLR) BLACKARD, WILLIAM G General clinical research center Insulin as an effector of steroidogenesis in human female
M01RR-00065-29 0295 (CLR) STEINGOLD, KENNETH A General clinical research center: Intramuscular & intravenous administration of human menopausal gonadotropins
M01RR-00065-29 0300 (CLR) SICA, DOMENIC A. General clinical research center Enalapril vs placebo on renal insufficiency on diabetic nephropathy
M01RR-00065-29 0305 (CLR) KAPLOWITZ, PAUL B. General clinical research center Spont.growth hormone secret.in diagnosis of growth hormone deficiency
M01RR-00065-29 0310 (CLR) KOPLOWITZ, LISA General clinical research center Effic. and safety of relovir in asymptomatic patients infected with HIV
M01RR-00065-29 0311 (CLR) SCHMEDTJ, JOHN General clinical research center Hemodynamic consequence of cardiovascular deconditioning
M01RR-00065-29 0312 (CLR) BLACKARD, WILLIAM C. General clinical research center Free fatty acids/glycolysis in tissues with reduced oxidative capacity
M01RR-00065-29 0314 (CLR) BLACKARD, WILLIAM G General clinical research center Assessment of omental fat sensitivity to glucose and insulin in man
M01RR-00065-29 0317 (CLR) GUTCHER, GARY General clinical research center Infasurf (calf lung surfactant extract) in premature human infants
M01RR-00065-29 0320 (CLR) MAKDAD, BONNIE General clinical research center Early bilirubin toxicity using BAERs and unbound bilirubin indices
M01RR-00065-29 0322 (CLR) WOLF, BARRY General clinical research center Biotinidase deficient children
M01RR-00065-29 0336 (CLR) CATTAU, EDWARD General clinical research center Sphincter of Oddi dysfunction
M01RR-00065-29 0337 (CLR) RIZZO, WILLIAM B General clinical research center Erucic acid therapy/presymptomatic adrenoleukodystrophy
M01RR-00065-29 0338 (CLR) CLORE, JOHN N General clinical research center Control mechanism of hepatic glucose output
M01RR-00065-29 0340 (CLR) DOWNS, ROBERT General clinical research center Effects of glucocorticoids on bone formation
M01RR-00065-29 0341 (CLR) BLACKARD, WILLIAM General clinical research center effect of hyperinsulinemia in cerebral vascular permeability
M01RR-00065-29 0342 (CLR) SICA, DOMENIC General clinical research center Evaluation of protein loading on GFR in the transplanted kidney
M01RR-00065-29 0343 (CLR) PELLOCK, JOHN General clinical research center Flunarizine in the treatment of partial seizures
M01RR-00065-29 0344 (CLR) MONTRELLA, MARY General clinical research center Glucocorticoid regulation of renal sodium excretion
M01RR-00065-29 0345 (CLR) CULPEPPER, MICHAEL General clinical research center Extra-renal potassium disposition in person on hemodialysis
M01RR-00065-29 0346 (CLR) SCHNOLL, SIDNEY General clinical research center Withdrawl and fetal stress and development
M01RR-00065-29 0347 (CLR) SCHNOLL, SIDNEY General clinical research center Cocaine withdrawal on fetal stress, development and immune function
M01RR-00065-29 0348 (CLR) KAPLOWITZ, LISA General clinical research center Exploration of T lymphocyte expandability
M01RR-00065-29 0349 (CLR) KLINGER, ROCHELLE General clinical research center Family hist.of suicide and prolactin responses to fenfluramine stimu.
M01RR-00065-29 0350 (CLR) MCKENNY, JAMES General clinical research center Dose response characteristics of TA-3090 tablets
M01RR-00065-29 0351 (CLR) ROBERTS, NEAL General clinical research center Assessment of osteoblast function and glucocorticoid excess
M01RR-00065-29 0352 (CLR) PANDURANGI, ANAND General clinical research center Immunolog. studies biologic heterogen. of Schizophrenic disorders
M01RR-00065-29 0353 (CLR) CLORE, JOHN General clinical research center Renal and skeletal resistance to parathyroid hormone
M01RR-00065-29 0354 (CLR) CULPEPPER, MICHAEL General clinical research center 131I distribution and elimination in hemodialysis
M01RR-00065-29 0355 (CLR) MYER, EDWIN General clinical research center Endogenous opiods on apnea/sudden infant
M01RR-00065-29 0356 (CLR) STEINGOLD, KENNETH General clinical research center Recurrent abortion- Evaluation of immunotherapy
M01RR-00065-29 0357 (CLR) RIZZO, WILLIAM General clinical research center Intravenous immune-globulin therapy for adrenoleukodystrophy
M01RR-00065-29 0358 (CLR) NESTLER, JOHN General clinical research center Exam. of the genetics of multiple endocrine neoplasia type 11A
M01RR-00065-29 0359 (CLR) GEHR, LYNNE General clinical research center The effect of mannitol on the kidney during cardiopulmonary by-pass
M01RR-00065-29 0360 (CLR) CLORE, JOHN General clinical research center Control of hepatic glucose output (HGO) in normal, obese and diabetic man
M01RR-00065-29 0361 (CLR) MCCLANAHAN, MARK General clinical research center Effect of hyperinsulinemia on vascular permeability
M01RR-00065-29 0362 (CLR) REINES, DAVID General clinical research center The effect of minimum trauma on stress mediators
M01RR-00065-29 0363 (CLR) SESSLER, CURTIS General clinical research center Comparasion of an anticholin. and a nethylzan. broncodilator in COPD
M01RR-00065-29 0323 (CLR) GODSCHALK, MICHAEL General clinical research center Role of dopamine in idiopathic edema
M01RR-00065-29 0364 (CLR) DOWNS, ROBERT General clinical research center Age-related changes in vitamin D recepter function
M01RR-00065-29 0365 (CLR) HANNA, JAMES General clinical research center Urinary anion gap
M01RR-00065-29 0366 (CLR) HANNA, JAMES General clinical research center Peritoneal equilibration on children
M01RR-00065-29 0367 (CLR) KING, ANNE General clinical research center Renal functional reserve following renal transplantation
M01RR-00065-29 0368 (CLR) DOWNS, ROBERT General clinical research center Predicators of the clinical behavior of silent pituitary adenomas
M01RR-00065-29 0369 (CLR) DOWNS, ROBERT General clinical research center Effects of bromocrip. on hypothal.-pituitary regulation of prolactin
M01RR-00065-29 0370 (CLR) BLACKARD, WILLIAM General clinical research center The evaluation of patients with glucocorticosteroid excess
M01RR-00065-29 0371 (CLR) GORE, DENNIS General clinical research center Variations in isolation limb protein kinetics with age
M01RR-00065-29 0372 (CLR) PELLOCK, JOHN General clinical research center Chronic epilepsy-Neuro, behavioral, pharmacokin. and envir. factors
M01RR-00065-29 0373 (CLR) HESS, MICHAEL General clinical research center Effects of denerv.,reject., and immunosup.,on cardiac transpl.recipients
M01RR-00065-29 0374 (CLR) STEWART, LAURAINE General clinical research center Same day admission vs overnight on anxiety level on surgery patients
M01RR-00065-29 0375 (CLR) RIZZO, WILLIAM General clinical research center Bile acid therapy for Zellweger syndrome
M01RR-00065-29 0376 (CLR) MOHANTY, PRAMOD General clinical research center Effect of denervation,rejection & immuno. on lung trans.recipiant
M01RR-00065-29 0325 (CLR) GRANT, STEPHAN General clinical research center Deoxycytidine administered alone and with Ara-C
M01RR-00065-29 0326 (CLR) GEHR, TODD General clinical research center Acute effects of triamterene on kidney function
M01RR-00065-29 0329 (CLR) KAPLOWITZ, LISA General clinical research center Multicenter-blind trial to evaluate retrovir and zovirax
M01RR-00069-29 (CLR) KRUGMAN, RICHARD D UNIV OF COLORADO HLTH SCI CTR 4200 EAST NINTH AVENUE DENVER, CO 80262 General clinical research center
M01RR-00069-29 0296 (CLR) GOTLIN, RONALD W General clinical research center Methionyl hGH use in alleviating growth retardation in Turners's syndrome
M01RR-00069-29 0299 (CLR) SOKOL, RONALD J General clinical research center Vit.E deficiency in chronic cholestasis and other malabsorption syndromes
M01RR-00069-29 0301 (CLR) GABOW, PATRICIA General clinical research center Natural history of autosomal dominant polycys. kidney disease in children
M01RR-00069-29 0303 (CLR) HAYWARD, ANTHONY R General clinical research center Congen. specific immunity defect in newborns with herpesvirus infection
M01RR-00069-29 0321 (CLR) O'BRIEN, DONOUGH General clinical research center Cyclosporine A in newly diagnosed insulin dependent diabetes mellitus
M01RR-00069-29 0327 (CLR) MANCO-JOHNSON, MARILYN General clinical research center Congenital thrombotic disease in pediatrics
M01RR-00069-29 0328 (CLR) KLINGENSMITH, GEORGEANNA General clinical research center Long term growth hormone releasing hormone effects on pituit. function
M01RR-00069-29 0348 (CLR) SOKOL, RONALD J General clinical research center Children with chronic diarrhea
M01RR-00069-29 0349 (CLR) CHASE, PETER H General clinical research center Identification of patients with prediabetes
M01RR-00069-29 0364 (CLR) GROOTHUIS, JESSIE R General clinical research center RSV infected children with bronchopul. dysplasia--Ribavirin therapy
M01RR-00069-29 0369 (CLR) ABSHIRE, THOMAS General clinical research center Cord blood diagnosis of coagulopathies in high-risk newborns
M01RR-00069-29 0371 (CLR) AMBRUSO, DANIEL R General clinical research center Functional and biochemical defects of neutrophils from newborn infants

PROJECT NO., ORGANIZATIONAL UNIT., INVESTIGATOR, ADDRESS, TITLE

M01RR-00069-29 0373 (CLR) CHASE, PETER General clinical research center Intervention to prevent or ameliorate type I diabetes
M01RR-00069-29 0378 (CLR) GROOTHIUS, JESSIE R General clinical research center Influenza vaccine in high risk children under 3 years of age
M01RR-00069-29 0382 (CLR) MANCHESTER, D General clinical research center Benzo(a)pyrene-DNA adduct formation in human pregnancy
M01RR-00069-29 0383 (CLR) MRAZEK, DAVID A General clinical research center Asthma risk project--Viral culture
M01RR-00069-29 0386 (CLR) PARKER, W DAVIS General clinical research center Platelet mitochondrial metabolism in degenerative neurologic disease
M01RR-00069-29 0389 (CLR) BATTAGLIA, F C General clinical research center Leucine disposal rate, oxidation rate, synthesis rate in newborns
M01RR-00069-29 0390 (CLR) BUTLER-SIMON, NANCY General clinical research center Develop. and psychosoc. complications in children with biliary atresia
M01RR-00069-29 0394 (CLR) ABMAN, STEVEN General clinical research center Newborn screening--Infectious disease aspects of cystic fibrosis
M01RR-00069-29 0395 (CLR) LUM, GARY General clinical research center Diet protein growth GFR in infants with renal failure
M01RR-00069-29 0396 (CLR) LEVIN, MYRON General clinical research center Placebo for the prophylaxis of influenza A in high risk children
M01RR-00069-29 0400 (CLR) KAEMPF, JOSEPH General clinical research center Antenatal phenobarbital for prevention of intracerebral hemorrhage
M01RR-00069-29 0405 (CLR) JONES, JAMES F General clinical research center Epstein-Barr virus
M01RR-00069-29 0408 (CLR) ZIND, BARBARA General clinical research center Platelet associated antibodies and prolonged bleeding time
M01RR-00069-29 0411 (CLR) GROOTHIUS, JESSIE R General clinical research center Intravenous immune globulin for respiratory syncytial virus in high risks
M01RR-00069-29 0413 (CLR) RIDGEWAY, LISA General clinical research center Prospective diagnosis of sinusitis by CT-scan and MRI
M01RR-00069-29 0414 (CLR) SCHROTER, GERHARD General clinical research center Biliary atresia and infantile cholestatic liver disease
M01RR-00069-29 0025 (CLR) ROBINSON, ARTHUR General clinical research center Follow-up of neonates with sex chromosomal abnormalities
M01RR-00069-29 0415 (CLR) CAMP, BONNIE General clinical research center Attentional problems--Continuous performance testing/drug excretion
M01RR-00069-29 0416 (CLR) BERMAN, STEPHEN General clinical research center Cefaclor and steroid therapy of chronic serious otitis media in children
M01RR-00069-29 0417 (CLR) GOTLIN, RONALD W General clinical research center Urinary free cortisol and its metabolites
M01RR-00069-29 0419 (CLR) HATHAWAY, WILLIAM E General clinical research center Experimental therapy of homozygous protein C deficiency
M01RR-00069-29 0129 (CLR) HAMBIDGE, K MICHAEL General clinical research center Zinc absorption in very low birth weight preterm infants
M01RR-00069-29 0455 (CLR) HAY, WILLIAM W JR General clinical research center Glucose production, utilization & insulin sensitivity in SGA newborns
M01RR-00069-29 0456 (CLR) BERMAN, STEPHEN General clinical research center: Age variability & human observer reliability in respiratory rate determinations
M01RR-00069-29 0457 (CLR) SEO, KYUNG General clinical research center Selected cytokines in blood, amniotic fluid and cord blood of pregnant women
M01RR-00069-29 0458 (CLR) KARRER, FREDERICK M General clinical research center TPGS-vitamin E use to improve cyclosporine absorption
M01RR-00069-29 0459 (CLR) BALDERSTON, SCOTT M General clinical research center Hypertrophic cardiomyopathy & disproportionate septal hypertrophy in newborn
M01RR-00069-29 0460 (CLR) MECKSTROTH, DIANE General clinical research center Baby developmental follow-up network project in Colorado
M01RR-00069-29 0461 (CLR) MANCO-JOHNSON, MARILYN General clinical research center Heparin metabolism in newborn
M01RR-00069-29 0462 (CLR) HAMBIDGE, MICHAEL General clinical research center Longitudinal study of zinc nutrition in pregnancy
M01RR-00069-29 0463 (CLR) SILLIMAN, CHRISTOPHER General clinical research center Chronic transfusion and therapy for refractory anemias
M01RR-00069-29 0464 (CLR) WIGGINS, JAMES General clinical research center Treatment of Kawasaki syndrome (KS) with intravenous gammaglobulin
M01RR-00069-29 0465 (CLR) MANCO-JOHNSON, MARILYN General clinical research center Experimental therapy of homozygous protein C deficiency
M01RR-00069-29 0466 (CLR) SPENDALE, STEVEN General clinical research center Leucine disposal rate oxidation rate, synthetic rate in newborns
M01RR-00069-29 0467 (CLR) SOKOL, RONALD General clinical research center Interferon
M01RR-00069-29 0468 (CLR) HORGAN, GERARD General clinical research center Doppler evaluation/portal vein calibre/flow/biliary atresia
M01RR-00069-29 0469 (CLR) HAMBRIDGE, MICHAEL General clinical research center Effects of food on plasma,whole erythrocyte and erythrocyte membrane zinc
M01RR-00069-29 0470 (CLR) MERENSTEIN, GERALD General clinical research center Correlation/perinatal events/neonatal morbidity: A scoring system.
M01RR-00069-29 0471 (CLR) MANCO-JOHNSON, MARILYN General clinical research center Structure and function of fetal protein C (PC)
M01RR-00069-29 0472 (CLR) KARRER, FREDERICK General clinical research center Assessment of endoscopic elastic band variceal ligation

PROJECT NO., ORGANIZATIONAL UNIT., INVESTIGATOR, ADDRESS, TITLE

M01RR-00069-29 0473 (CLR) MANCO-JOHNSON, MARILYN General clinical research center Measurement coagulation enzyme-inhibitor complex/neonates/diabetes/renal dis.
M01RR-00069-29 0474 (CLR) SILVER, ROBERT General clinical research center Selected cytokines in blood, amniotic fluid and cord blood of pregnant women
M01RR-00069-29 0475 (CLR) SOKOL, RONALD General clinical research center Use of TPGS-vitamin E to improve cyclosporine absorption
M01RR-00069-29 0476 (CLR) MERENSTEIN, GERALD General clinical research center hypertrophic cardiomyopathy and septal hypertrophy in newborns
M01RR-00069-29 0477 (CLR) THOMAS-DOBERSEN, DEBORAH General clinical research center Weight management program for adolescent with type 1 diabetes
M01RR-00069-29 0478 (CLR) HAYWARD, ANTHONY General clinical research center V beta family usage in the development of memory T cells in man
M01RR-00069-29 0479 (CLR) SOKOL, RONALD General clinical research center Colchicine therapy in childhood cirrhosis
M01RR-00069-29 0480 (CLR) CHASE, PETER General clinical research center Enhanced nicotinamide regimen/type 1 diabetes mellitus, a modification
M01RR-00069-29 0481 (CLR) KREBS, NANCY General clinical research center Zinc homeostasis in very low birth weight infants
M01RR-00069-29 0482 (CLR) NARKEWICS, MICHAEL General clinical research center Ursodeoxycholic acid therapy in chronic childhood cholestasis
M01RR-00069-29 0483 (CLR) MANCO-JOHNSON, MARILYN General clinical research center Pilot study-detection early CNS manifestations-HIV positive w/hemophilia
M01RR-00069-29 0484 (CLR) HAGERMAN, RANDI General clinical research center Seizures and EEG abnormalties in fragile X syndrome
M01RR-00069-29 0485 (CLR) GOODMAN, STEPHEN General clinical research center Primary lactic acidosis clinical/biochemical/defects pyruvate/resp.met.
M01RR-00069-29 0486 (CLR) HAGERMAN, RANDI General clinical research center Neurocognitive, emotional and physical phenotypes of fragile X females
M01RR-00069-29 0160 (CLR) AMBRUSO, DANIEL R General clinical research center Humoral and cellular mechanism of idiopathic neutropenia
M01RR-00069-29 0420 (CLR) HAYWARD, ANTHONY R General clinical research center Specific immunity development in human newborns
M01RR-00069-29 0421 (CLR) HAMBIDGE, MICHAEL K General clinical research center Zinc 70 absorption during pregnancy and lactation
M01RR-00069-29 0422 (CLR) BLOCH, CLIFFORD A General clinical research center Insulin sensitivity in children with precocious puberty
M01RR-00069-29 0423 (CLR) CAMP, BONNIE General clinical research center Stress in adolescents
M01RR-00069-29 0424 (CLR) BERMAN, STEPHEN General clinical research center Recurrent otitis media--Epidemiology, pathogenesis, medical management
M01RR-00069-29 0425 (CLR) COHEN, MARK General clinical research center Cyclosporine A in steroid-dependent or resistant nephrotic syndrome
M01RR-00069-29 0426 (CLR) HAMMAN, R F General clinical research center Ethnic differences--Insulin-dependent diabetes mellitus
M01RR-00069-29 0427 (CLR) LEE, PHILIP D General clinical research center Growth hormone treatment for familial hypophosphatemia rickets
M01RR-00069-29 0428 (CLR) LILLY, JOHN R General clinical research center Biliary atresia--Doppler evaluation, portal vein calibre, blood flow
M01RR-00069-29 0429 (CLR) ENGLISH, JAMIE L General clinical research center Kinetic studies of zinc stable isotopes
M01RR-00069-29 0432 (CLR) CAMP, BONNIE General clinical research center Neglectful mothers' perceptions of their babies
M01RR-00069-29 0433 (CLR) SCHOONMAKER, J N General clinical research center Antiprotease activity within fetal membranes
M01RR-00069-29 0434 (CLR) CARTER, BRIAN S General clinical research center Correlation of perinatal events with neonatal morbidity--A scoring system
M01RR-00069-29 0435 (CLR) THUREEN, PATTI J General clinical research center Infectious causes of pulmonary deteriorations--Neonatal intensive care
M01RR-00069-29 0436 (CLR) GREFFE, BRIAN General clinical research center Structure and function of fetal protein C
M01RR-00069-29 0438 (CLR) LEVIN, MYRON J General clinical research center Acyclovir treatment of chickenpox in adolescents
M01RR-00069-29 0439 (CLR) MARLAN, RICHARD General clinical research center Modulation of tissue factor and protein C components
M01RR-00069-29 0440 (CLR) MANCO-JOHNSON, MARILYN J General clinical research center DDAVP treatment of cardiopulmonary bypass-related bleeding
M01RR-00069-29 0441 (CLR) CHASE, PETER H General clinical research center Sugar-cereal on blood glucose levels following breakfast in diabetes
M01RR-00069-29 0442 (CLR) GREENE, CAROL General clinical research center Participation in the national maternal PKU collaborative study
M01RR-00069-29 0443 (CLR) GROOTHUIS, JESSIE R General clinical research center ribavirin treatment of influenza infection in children
M01RR-00069-29 0444 (CLR) GLODE, MARY P General clinical research center blood studies of family members of children with Kawasaki syndrome
M01RR-00069-29 0445 (CLR) SELTZER, WILLIAM K General clinical research center Hereditary persistence of fetal hemoglobin
M01RR-00069-29 0446 (CLR) HAMBIDGE, K MICHAEL General clinical research center Behavioral effects of zinc deficiency in infants and toddlers
M01RR-00069-29 0447 (CLR) KARRER, FREDERICK M General clinical research center Assessment of endoscopic elastic band variceal

ligation
M01RR-00069-29 0448 (CLR) BLOCH, CLIFFORD A General clinical research center Insulin sensitivity in boys with delayed puberty--Testosterone/growth hormone eff
M01RR-00069-29 0449 (CLR) BERMAN, STEPHEN General clinical research center Sickle cell trait and chronic altitude exposure
M01RR-00069-29 0450 (CLR) MANCO-JOHNSON, MARILYN E General clinical research center Whole blood prothrombin time in normal & coumadin-treated neonates
M01RR-00069-29 0451 (CLR) ACCURSO, FRANK J General clinical research center Energy expenditure in infants with cystic fibrosis
M01RR-00069-29 0452 (CLR) PARIS, DIANE General clinical research center Urine drug screen of 600 antenatal patients at University Hospital
M01RR-00069-29 0453 (CLR) ACCURSO, FRANK J General clinical research center: Cystic fibrosis--Steroid therapy on pulmonary function and airways reactivity
M01RR-00069-29 0454 (CLR) ROSENBERG, ADAM A General clinical research center Changes in Exosurf pediatric A-a gradient improvement with RDS
M01RR-00069-29 0164 (CLR) AMBRUSO, R DANIEL General clinical research center Chronic transfusion and therapy for refractory anemias (sickle cell)
M01RR-00069-29 0487 (CLR) JELLEY, DAVID General clinical research center Parental nutrition with high-dose intravenous insulin therapy
M01RR-00069-29 0177 (CLR) GREENE, CAROL General clinical research center Hyperphenylalaninemia and phenylketonuria
M01RR-00069-29 0178 (CLR) GREENE, CAROL General clinical research center Biochemical investigations into disorders of intermediary metabolism
M01RR-00069-29 0189 (CLR) HATHAWAY, WILLIAM E General clinical research center Heparin metabolism in the newborn
M01RR-00069-29 0198 (CLR) WALRAVENS, PHILIP A General clinical research center Zinc supplementation of infants and toddlers
M01RR-00069-29 0206 (CLR) CHASE, H PETER General clinical research center Juvenile diabetes mellitus--Control and complications
M01RR-00069-29 0218 (CLR) CAMP, BONNIE W General clinical research center Mothers clinic study--Developmental studies on vocalization
M01RR-00069-29 0488 (CLR) CAMP, BONNIE General clinical research center Beta-blockers in aggressive and hyperactive children
M01RR-00069-29 0489 (CLR) MANCO-JOHNSON, MARILYN General clinical research center Neonatal at - 111 deficiency
M01RR-00069-29 0490 (CLR) GROOTHIUS, JESSIE General clinical research center Delivery of the vertex very low birth wt. infants: vag. vs. c. sec. delivery
M01RR-00069-29 0491 (CLR) SILLIMAN, CHRISTOPHER General clinical research center Measurement of neutrophil-associated immunoglobulins in neonates
M01RR-00069-29 0492 (CLR) HALE, KATHY General clinical research center Temperature measurement using mercury and electronic in neonates
M01RR-00069-29 0493 (CLR) FORD, DOUGLAS General clinical research center Somatropin (rhGH) to improve short stature assoc. w/chronic renal in suff.
M01RR-00069-29 0494 (CLR) ROSENBERG, ADAM General clinical research center SCOR: Persistent pulmonary hypertention of the newborn
M01RR-00069-29 0233 (CLR) KLINGENSMITH, GEORGEANNA General clinical research center Somatomedin in growth response in hypopit. children treated with hGH
M01RR-00069-29 0248 (CLR) LILLY, JOHN R General clinical research center Endoscopic sclerosis of esophageal varices
M01RR-00069-29 0259 (CLR) GLODE, MARY P General clinical research center Treatment of Kawasaki syndrome with intravenous gamma globulin
M01RR-00069-29 0263 (CLR) PARKER, DAVIS General clinical research center Biochemical neurological degenerative diseases
M01RR-00069-29 0264 (CLR) HAMBIDGE, K MICHAEL General clinical research center Maternal zinc status during lactation growth of the breast fed infant
M01RR-00069-29 0267 (CLR) HAY, WILLIAM General clinical research center Non-invasive oximetry in monitoring of critically ill children
M01RR-00069-29 0285 (CLR) LILLY, JOHN R General clinical research center Splenic embolization--Hypersplenism and portal hypertension
M01RR-00069-29 0292 (CLR) ACCURSO, FRANK J General clinical research center Cystic fibrosis newborn screening--Longitudinal evaluation
M01RR-00070-29 (CLR) KORN, DAVID STANFORD UNIVERSITY STANFORD, CA 94305 General clinical research center
M01RR-00070-29 0153 (CLR) COULSTON, ANN General clinical research center Lipemia--Carbohydrate and lipid metabolism
M01RR-00070-29 0162 (CLR) MYERS, BRYAN D General clinical research center Assessment of diabetic glomerular injury
M01RR-00070-29 0191 (CLR) MYERS, BRYAN D General clinical research center Mechanisms of proteinuria--Role of hemodynamic factors
M01RR-00070-29 0192 (CLR) REAVEN, GERALD M General clinical research center Insulin resistance of type II diabetes mellitus
M01RR-00070-29 0211 (CLR) MERIGAN, THOMAS C General clinical research center Prophylactic ganciclovir in heart transplants with CMV
M01RR-00070-29 0212 (CLR) MYERS, BRYAN D General clinical research center Treatment of lupus nephritis with total lymphoid irradiation
M01RR-00070-29 0214 (CLR) MYERS, BRYAN D General clinical research center Pathophysiology of AIDS glomerulopathy
M01RR-00070-29 0219 (CLR) HOFFMAN, BRIAN General clinical research center Does insulin resistance exist in patients with hypertension
M01RR-00070-29 0223 (CLR) GUILLEMINAULT, CHRISTIAN General clinical research center Polygraphic monitoring of sleep apneic disorders
M01RR-00070-29 0225 (CLR) BLASCKE, TERRANCE General clinical research center Aging and metabolic responses of skeletal muscle
M01RR-00070-29 0226 (CLR) MERIGAN, THOMAS C General clinical research center Dose trial of SC-48334 in patients with AIDS and advanced ARC
M01RR-00070-29 0227 (CLR) TORTI, FRANK M General clinical research center Chemoimmunotherapy with vinblastine and IL-2 with renal cell carcinoma
M01RR-00070-29 0228 (CLR) STARNES, H FLETCHER General clinical research center Tolerance of 5 day dosing of IL-1B in lung cancer or melanoma
M01RR-00070-29 0229 (CLR) CARLSON, ROBERT General clinical research center Phase I-II trial of etoposide
M01RR-00070-29 0230 (CLR) MERIGAN, THOMAS C General clinical research center Safety & pharm. of recombinant CD4 immunoglobulin with AIDS & ARC
M01RR-00070-29 0231 (CLR) MERIGAN, THOMAS C General clinical research center Dose trial of recombinant soluble T4 in patients with AIDS and ARC
M01RR-00070-29 0232 (CLR) BAUER, EUGENE General clinical research center National epidermolysis bullosa registry
M01RR-00070-29 0233 (CLR) BLASCHKE, TERRENCE F General clinical research center Food effect on pharmacokinetics of videx chewable tablet in HIV patients
M01RR-00070-29 0234 (CLR) ADLER, JOHN R General clinical research center Combined immunotherapy--Crynebacterium parvum/IL-2 for globlastoma multiforme
M01RR-00070-29 0235 (CLR) MERIGAN, THAOMS C General clinical research center Zidovudine and polyethylene glycolated IL-2 in HIV infected individuals
M01RR-00071-28A1 (CLR) KASE, NATHAN G MT SINAI SCHOOL OF MEDICINE ONE GUSTAVE L LEVY PLACE NEW YORK, NY 10029 General clinical research center
M01RR-00071-28A1 0218 (CLR) COBIN, RHODA General clinical research center Anterior pituitary function in patients with acute/chronic illness
M01RR-00071-28A1 0219 (CLR) SACKS, HENRY General clinical research center Safety and efficacy of ZVD for asymptomatic HIV infected individuals
M01RR-00071-28A1 0220 (CLR) SACKS, HENRY General clinical research center Safety/efficicy of ZDV in therapy of patients with early ARC
M01RR-00071-28A1 0221 (CLR) SACKS, HENRY General clinical research center Foscarnet salvage therapy for AIDS patients with sight threatening CMV retinitis
M01RR-00071-28A1 0222 (CLR) SACKS, HENRY General clinical research center Potential of low dose therapy with ZDV and interferon alpha 2a
M01RR-00071-28A1 0223 (CLR) SACKS, HENRY General clinical research center Anti-pneumocystis agents plus ZDV for prevention of serious infections
M01RR-00071-28A1 0224 (CLR) SACKS, HENRY General clinical research center Comparison of 2',3'-DDI given oraly 2/day to patients with AIDS or ARC
M01RR-00071-28A1 0225 (CLR) SACKS, HENRY General clinical research center Phase II study comparing 2'3'-DDI and zivoduine therapy in pts with AIDS or ARC
M01RR-00071-28A1 0226 (CLR) SACKS, HENRY General clinical research center Efficacy of 2'3' DDI given orally 2/day to patients with AIDS or ARC
M01RR-00071-28A1 0227 (CLR) COHEN, MARC General clinical research center Antithrombotic therapy in acute coronary syndrome
M01RR-00071-28A1 0228 (CLR) HALPERIN, JEFFREY General clinical research center Neurobiology/neuropsychology dissociation of subtypes-hyperactivity
M01RR-00071-28A1 0229 (CLR) GREENBERG, DAVID General clinical research center Resolving heterogeneity in epilepsy using genetic markers
M01RR-00071-28A1 0230 (CLR) KATTAN, MEYER General clinical research center Pediatric pulmonary and cardiovascular complications of HIV infection
M01RR-00071-28A1 0231 (CLR) FRIEDMAN, ALAN H General clinical research center Studies on the ocular complication of AIDS
M01RR-00071-28A1 0232 (CLR) HALPERIN, JEFFREY General clinical research center Validation of inattentive and agressive ADHD subtypes
M01RR-00071-28A1 0233 (CLR) CUNNINGHAM-R, CHARLOTTE General clinical research center Phase II trial of recombinant PEG IL-2 in pts with combined immunodeficiency
M01RR-00071-28A1 0234 (CLR) ROMAN, SHEILA General clinical research center Post partum thyroid dysfunction in diabetic pregnancies
M01RR-00071-28A1 0235 (CLR) KAUFMANN, HORACIO General clinical research center Orthostatic hypotension in patients with autonomic failure--Vasopressin
M01RR-00071-28A1 0236 (CLR) GRABOWSKI, GREGORY A General clinical research center Ceredase treatment of Gaucher disease
M01RR-00071-28A1 0237 (CLR) TRESTMAN, ROBERT General clinical research center Acute experimental stress and immnue function in chronic fatigue syndrome pts
M01RR-00071-28A1 0238 (CLR) CUTTNER, JANET General clinical research center Fludarabine phosphate in patients with refractory chronic lymphocytic leukemia
M01RR-00071-28A1 0239 (CLR) ROMAN, SHEILA General clinical research center Investigation of interleukin 2 defect and other immune markers
M01RR-00071-28A1 0240 (CLR) HASSETT, JOSEPH General clinical research center Placebo controlled study of low dose oral interferon alfa-n3 in ARC patients
M01RR-00071-28A1 0241 (CLR) LIPTON, JEFFREY M General clinical research center Complications and treatment of iron overload in transfused patients
M01RR-00071-28A1 0242 (CLR) LAWLOR, BRIAN General clinical research center L-deprenyl in management of behavioral complications in Alzheimer's disease
M01RR-00071-28A1 0243 (CLR) MILLER, MYRON General clinical research center Metoclopramine stimulation test for the diagonosis of Alzheimer's
M01RR-00071-28A1 0244 (CLR) HASSETT, JOSEPH General clinical research center Dose ranging study of alferon LDO interferon alfa-n3 in HIV positive subjects
M01RR-00071-28A1 0128 (CLR) DUNAIF, ANDREA General clinical research center Insulin and androgen action
M01RR-00071-28A1 0141 (CLR) MEIER, DIANE General clinical research center Influence of race and age on bone homeostasis
M01RR-00071-28A1 0144 (CLR) DAVIS, KENNETH General clinical

PROJECT NO., ORGANIZATIONAL UNIT., INVESTIGATOR, ADDRESS, TITLE

research center Toward a rational use of plasma HVA in mental illness
M01RR-00071-28A1 0148 (CLR) DAVIS, KENNETH General clinical research center Alzheimers disease research center
M01RR-00071-28A1 0152 (CLR) LARSON, SIGNE General clinical research center Growth hormone secretory pattern in short children
M01RR-00071-28A1 0171 (CLR) DESNICK, ROBERT J General clinical research center Phenotype heterogenity, treatment and prevention of genetic diseases
M01RR-00071-28A1 0172 (CLR) PACKER, MIHON General clinical research center Determinants of vasodilator response in heart failure
M01RR-00071-28A1 0173 (CLR) SIEVER, LARRY T General clinical research center Biological correlates of mood disorders
M01RR-00071-28A1 0177 (CLR) SACKS, HENRY General clinical research center PCP in AIDS--Trimetrexae with leacovorin Ca rescue vs trimethoprim/sulfamethox
M01RR-00071-28A1 0179 (CLR) SACKS, HENRY General clinical research center Fluconqzole and amphotaercin B in AIDS patients with crytococcal meningitis
M01RR-00071-28A1 0180 (CLR) SACKS, HENRY General clinical research center Placebo controlled trial to evaluate ZDV in treatment of HIV in hemophilic pts
M01RR-00071-28A1 0183 (CLR) SHIAVI, RAUL General clinical research center Diabetes mellitus and male sexual behavior
M01RR-00071-28A1 0184 (CLR) MILLER, MYRON General clinical research center Influence of age on basal/exercise stimulated atrial natriuretic hormone
M01RR-00071-28A1 0185 (CLR) PLAITAKIS, ANDREAS General clinical research center Controlled trial of branched chain mino acids in ALS
M01RR-00071-28A1 0186 (CLR) ALEDORT, LOUIS M General clinical research center IVIG in treatment of autoimmune & alloimmune antibodies to coagulation factors
M01RR-00071-28A1 0193 (CLR) SIEVER, LARRY General clinical research center Biological correlates of personality disorder
M01RR-00071-28A1 0194 (CLR) YAHR, MELVIN P General clinical research center L-threo-dops in treatment of Parkinsonism & autonumic dystropy
M01RR-00071-28A1 0196 (CLR) PLAITAKIS, ANDREAS General clinical research center Glutamic dehydrogenase in neurologic disorders
M01RR-00071-28A1 0198 (CLR) MAROM, ZVI General clinical research center Mucus secretagogue--A novel peptide in bronchitis
M01RR-00071-28A1 0201 (CLR) SACKS, HENRY General clinical research center Gamma globulin and AZT in children with HIV infection
M01RR-00071-28A1 0202 (CLR) ALEDORT, LOUIS M General clinical research center Safety & clinical efficacy of recombinant DNA derived factor VIII
M01RR-00071-28A1 0203 (CLR) SCHACTER, NEIL E General clinical research center Deflazacort vs prednisone in the treatment of asthma & asthmatic bronchitis
M01RR-00071-28A1 0205 (CLR) ARKIN, STEVEN General clinical research center Evaluation of growth & development in children with hemophilia
M01RR-00071-28A1 0206 (CLR) ALEDORT, LOUIS M General clinical research center Recovery and half-life studies of factor VII, VIII and IX
M01RR-00071-28A1 0207 (CLR) HASSETT, JOSEPH General clinical research center Inhaled pentamidine for pneumocystis pneumonia prophylaxis
M01RR-00071-28A1 0209 (CLR) THYS-JACOBS, SUSAN General clinical research center Bone mineral content in women with premenstrual syndrome
M01RR-00071-28A1 0210 (CLR) LELEIKO, NEAL S General clinical research center Energy cost of chronic illness
M01RR-00071-28A1 0211 (CLR) KAUFMANN, HORACIO General clinical research center Orthostatic hypotension in patients with Parkinsonism--Role of vasopressin
M01RR-00071-28A1 0212 (CLR) PHILLIPS, ROBERT General clinical research center Hemodynamic and hormonal influences in hypotensive heart disease
M01RR-00071-28A1 0214 (CLR) DAVIDSON, MICHAEL General clinical research center PHVA concentration in schizophrenic patients during change of state
M01RR-00071-28A1 0215 (CLR) LANDRIGAN, PHILLIP J General clinical research center Renal, neurologicc, and reproductive effects--Environmental lead exposure
M01RR-00071-28A1 0216 (CLR) DENSNICK, ROBERT J General clinical research center Enzyme and gene therapy in genetic disease
M01RR-00071-28A1 0217 (CLR) GRABOWSKI, GEORGE A General clinical research center Studies of Gaucher disease--A prototype lipidosis
M01RR-00071-28A1 0139 (CLR) DAVIS, KENNETH L General clinical research center Cholinergic treatment of memory deficits in the aged
Z01RR-00071-07 (VR) CROWELL, J S NCRR, NIH Development of genetic profiles for inbred laboratory rodents
K01RR-00072-01 (AR) WAGNER, JANICE D BOWMAN GRAY SCH OF MEDICINE 300 S HAWTHORNE ROAD WINSTON-SALEM, NC 27103 Effects of estrogens and progestins on atherogenesis
M01RR-00073-29 (CLR) BRYAN, GEORGE T UNIV OF TEXAS MEDICAL BRANCH 301 UNIVERSITY BLVD GALVESTON, TX 77550 General clinical research center
M01RR-00073-29 0089 (CLR) KUNA, SAMUEL T General clinical research center Respiratory disturbances during sleep
M01RR-00073-29 0107 (CLR) KEENAN, BRUCE S General clinical research center Effect of therapy in adrenal steroid production in adrenal hyperplasia
M01RR-00073-29 0147 (CLR) HOLLAND, O BRYAN General clinical research center Aldosterone suppression in hypertensive patients
M01RR-00073-29 0173 (CLR) EMORY, LEE E General clinical research center Medroxyprogesterone acetate treatment of adult male sex offenders
M01RR-00073-29 0197 (CLR) STUART, CHARLES A General clinical research center Insulin resistance, polycystic ovarian disease and acanthosis nigricans
M01RR-00073-29 0207 (CLR) KEENAN, BRUCE General clinical research center Pineal function in childhood and adolescence
M01RR-00073-29 0212 (CLR) ISENBERG, J NEVIN General clinical

PROJECT NO., ORGANIZATIONAL UNIT., INVESTIGATOR, ADDRESS, TITLE

research center Vitamin E liver disease
M01RR-00073-29 0216 (CLR) WOLFE, ROBERT R General clinical research center Dietary protein in protein kinetics
M01RR-00073-29 0102 (CLR) GARDNER, FRANK H General clinical research center Etiocholanolone hematopoietic agents in refractory anemia
M01RR-00073-29 0219 (CLR) RICHARDS, GAIL E General clinical research center Neurotransmitter regulation of growth hormone secretion
M01RR-00073-29 0303 (CLR) STUART, CHARLES A General clinical research center Phosphoenolpyruvate cycle activity in man
M01RR-00073-29 0304 (CLR) HERNDON, DAVID N General clinical research center Peripheral amino acid and substrate turnover in human volunteers
M01RR-00073-29 0306 (CLR) TOWNSEND, RAYMOND R General clinical research center Triglyceride and fatty acid cycling in obese hypertensive man
M01RR-00073-29 0307 (CLR) SOLOWAY, ROGER D General clinical research center Ivermectin biliary excretion study
M01RR-00073-29 0308 (CLR) BOYARS, MICHAEL C General clinical research center Ipratropium and albuterol therapy of chronic obstructive lung disease
M01RR-00073-29 0309 (CLR) GRANT, ANDREW J General clinical research center Cooperative study of immunotherapy in adult asthmatics
M01RR-00073-29 0221 (CLR) WOLFE, ROBERT R General clinical research center Substrate cycling in energy metabolism
M01RR-00073-29 0228 (CLR) JAHOOR, FAROOK General clinical research center Gluconeogenic precursor supply in regulation of glucose and urea
M01RR-00073-29 0231 (CLR) KUNA, SAMUEL General clinical research center Control of laryngeal muscles during wakefulness and sleep
M01RR-00073-29 0242 (CLR) WOLFE, ROBERT General clinical research center Dichloroacetate effect on anaerobic threshold in normal subjects
M01RR-00073-29 0258 (CLR) KLEIN, SAM General clinical research center Lipid metabolism in patients with cancer
M01RR-00073-29 0260 (CLR) KEENAN, BRUCE S. General clinical research center Dihydrotestosterone heptanoate treatment of gynecomastia
M01RR-00073-29 0261 (CLR) KEENAN, BRUCE S. General clinical research center Pubertal and prepubertal gynecomastia
M01RR-00073-29 0263 (CLR) NAGAMANI, MANUBAI General clinical research center Ovarian steroids in menopausal women with endometrial cancer
M01RR-00073-29 0265 (CLR) ANDERSON, KARL E. General clinical research center Histrelin in acute porphyria
M01RR-00073-29 0267 (CLR) THOMPSON, JAMES C. General clinical research center Zollinger-Ellison syndrome and duodonal ulcer disease
M01RR-00073-29 0275 (CLR) WASSEF, ADEL A. General clinical research center Glucocorticoid receptor and post-receptor events in major depression
M01RR-00073-29 0278 (CLR) ISENBERG, J. NEVIN General clinical research center Prone reflux sling evaluation as treatment for gastroesophageal reflux
M01RR-00073-29 0280 (CLR) KLEIN, SAMUEL General clinical research center Metabolic abnormalities in patients with cancer cachexia
M01RR-00073-29 0281 (CLR) ANDERSON, KARL E. General clinical research center Erythropoietin for hemodylasis associated porphyria
M01RR-00073-29 0282 (CLR) ANDERSON, KARL E General clinical research center Nutritional factors in porphyria
M01RR-00073-29 0283 (CLR) POLLARD, RICHARD B General clinical research center AZT levels in patients receiving betaseron
M01RR-00073-29 0285 (CLR) POWELL, GERALDINE K. General clinical research center Neonatal obstructive jaundice
M01RR-00073-29 0292 (CLR) ISENBERG, J NEVIN General clinical research center Hepatic excretory function in biliary atresia
M01RR-00073-29 0293 (CLR) THOMPSON, JAMES C General clinical research center Human gallbladder function correlated with gastrointestinal hormone release
M01RR-00073-29 0294 (CLR) CLOYD, MILES W General clinical research center Immunological and virological studies of patients with HIV infections and AIDS
M01RR-00073-29 0295 (CLR) KLEIN, SAMUEL General clinical research center Enteral feeding in patients with short bowel syndrome
M01RR-00073-29 0296 (CLR) TYRING, STEPHEN K General clinical research center Mechanisms of interferon action against human papillomaviruses
M01RR-00073-29 0300 (CLR) KEENAN, BRUCE S General clinical research center Somatostatin role in growth and growth hormone secretion regulation
M01RR-00073-29 0301 (CLR) TYRING, STEPHEN K General clinical research center Oral acyclovir in immunocompromised patients with herpes zoster
M01RR-00073-29 0310 (CLR) KUNA, SAMUEL T General clinical research center Neural factors in pathogenesis and treatment of obstructive sleep apnea
M01RR-00073-29 0311 (CLR) MEYER, WALTER J General clinical research center Decreased mononuclear leukocyte TSH responsiveness in major depression
M01RR-00073-29 0312 (CLR) SANDSTEAD, HAROLD H General clinical research center Iron and zinc nutriture and neuropsychological function in young women
M01RR-00073-29 0313 (CLR) WOLFE, ROBERT R General clinical research center Exercise training and weight reduction effect on fatty acid metabolism
M01RR-00073-29 0314 (CLR) TOWNSEND, RAYMOND R General clinical research center Angiotensin II role in insulin resistance of essential hypertension
M01RR-00073-29 0315 (CLR) ISENBERG, J NEVIN General clinical research center Carbohydrate absorption in infants with chronic watery diarrhea
M01RR-00073-29 0316 (CLR) ISENBERG, J NEVIN General clinical research center Energy expenditure and substrate cycling in cystic

fibrosis

M01RR-00073-29 0317 (CLR) PONDER, SPEPHEN W General clinical research center Preservation of residual pancreatic beta cell function in diabetic children

M01RR-00073-29 0318 (CLR) HIBBERT, JACQULINE General clinical research center Relationship between total and resting energy expenditure in obesity

M01RR-00073-29 0319 (CLR) SIM, TOMMY C General clinical research center Topical corticosteroids effect on recovery of HRF in allergic rhinitis

M01RR-00073-29 0320 (CLR) KLEIN, SAMUEL General clinical research center Protein metabolism in stress conditions

M01RR-00073-29 0321 (CLR) URBAN, RANDALL J General clinical research center Sex steroid regulation of gonadotropin secretion in aging men

M01RR-00073-29 0322 (CLR) CHONMAITREE, TASNEE General clinical research center Comparison of cell cultures for rapid isolation of enteroviruses

M01RR-00073-29 0323 (CLR) POLLARD, RICHARD B General clinical research center Phase I/II trial of SDZ MSL-109 in patients with AIDS and CMV viremia/viruria

M01RR-00073-29 0324 (CLR) MCCLURE, SUZANNE General clinical research center Phase I study of CP-74,639 in patients with non-hematologic malignancies

M01RR-00073-29 0325 (CLR) POLLARD, RICHARD B General clinical research center Safety, tolerance, and pharmacokinetics of TNF and Cisplatin in resistant tumors

M01RR-00073-29 0326 (CLR) TYRING, STEPHEN K General clinical research center Famciclocir (oral 42810) in treatment of uncomplicated herpes zoster

M01RR-00073-29 0327 (CLR) TYRING, STEPHEN K General clinical research center Intralesional interferon alpha treatment or recurrent genital herpes

K01RR-00075-01 (AR) DAVISON-FAIRBURN, BILLIE B DELTA REG PRIMATE RES CTR 18703 THREE RIVERS ROAD COVINGTON, LA 70433 Model development for maternal-fetal transmission of HIV

Z01RR-00077-07 (VR) SCHMIDT, P M NCRR, NIH Development of an embryo cryopreservation program in laboratory animals

M01RR-00079-29 (CLR) MARTIN, JOSEPH B UNIVERSITY OF CALIFORNIA 3RD & PARNASSUS AVENUES SAN FRANCISCO, CA 94143-0126 General clinical research center

M01RR-00079-29 0377 (CLR) WINTROUB, BRUCE U General clinical research center Extracorporeal photopheresis in treatment of progressive systemic scleroderma

M01RR-00079-29 0382 (CLR) FROST, PHILIP H General clinical research center Measures of reverse cholesterol transport in pts. w/hi blood cholesterol

M01RR-00079-29 0383 (CLR) KANE, JOHN P General clinical research center Effect of complementary drug regimen on coronary arteriosclerosis

M01RR-00079-29 0384 (CLR) O'CONNOR, MICHEAL D L General clinical research center Densitization of pancreatic beta cell to stimulation of insulin secretion

M01RR-00079-29 0385 (CLR) SEBASTIAN, ANTHONY General clinical research center Effect of dietary K+ to Na ratio on renal Cl-handling

M01RR-00079-29 0309 (CLR) PORTALE, ANTHONY A General clinical research center Determinants of vitamin D synthesis and degradation

M01RR-00079-29 0342 (CLR) FROST, PHILIP H General clinical research center Lipoprotein lipase and hepatic lipase

M01RR-00079-29 0343 (CLR) HALLORAN, BERNARD P General clinical research center Aging and vitamin D metabolism and dietary phosphorous

M01RR-00079-29 0356 (CLR) SEBASTIAN, ANTHONY General clinical research center HCO3- salts and calcium metabolism in post menopausal women

M01RR-00079-29 0361 (CLR) SCHWARTZ, JANICE B General clinical research center The effects of aging on calcium blockers kinetics/dynamics

M01RR-00079-29 0387 (CLR) FROST, PHILIP H General clinical research center Dietary cholesterol effects on plasma lipoproteins

M01RR-00079-29 0389 (CLR) SEBASTIAN, ANTHONY General clinical research center Diet potassium & blood pressure "salt-sensitivity" in blacks and whites

M01RR-00079-29 0390 (CLR) SEBASTIAN, ANTHONY General clinical research center Physiological charater of acidification dysfunction in renal acidosis

M01RR-00079-29 0391 (CLR) BIKLE, DANDIEL D General clinical research center Estrogens, vitamin D, and calcium in postmenopausal patients

M01RR-00079-29 0392 (CLR) CONTE, JOHN E General clinical research center Random double blind study of inhaled 300 mg/month pentamidine for pneumocustis

M01RR-00079-29 0393 (CLR) SEBASTIAN, ANTHONY General clinical research center Diet potassium supplementation in patients with essential hypertension

M01RR-00079-29 0394 (CLR) KARAM, JOHN General clinical research center Tachyphylaxis effect on secondary failure to sulfonylurea in patient with NIDDM

M01RR-00079-29 0395 (CLR) JAFFE, ROBERT General clinical research center GnRH antagonist (RS-26306) and serum LH/FSH levels in post menopausal women

M01RR-00079-29 0396 (CLR) JAFFE, ROBERT General clinical research center Phase I open label, crossover study safety/pharmacokinetic profile of rhR1x

M01RR-00079-29 0397 (CLR) O'CONNOR, MICHAEL D L General clinical research center Capillary insulin transport rate and insulin resistance in obese/diabetic pts

M01RR-00079-29 0398 (CLR) STOTTS, NANCY A General clinical research center Study of effect of activity-inactivity on subcutaneous perfusion and healing

M01RR-00079-29 0399 (CLR) WARA, DIANE W General clinical research center AIDS--High risk study

M01RR-00079-29 0400 (CLR) LAVIN, THOMAS General clinical research center Radioligand binding to thyroid hormone receptors

PROJECT NO., ORGANIZATIONAL UNIT., INVESTIGATOR, ADDRESS, TITLE

M01RR-00079-29 0401 (CLR) GLANTZ, STANTON A General clinical research center Quantification of motion artifacts in the left ventricle

M01RR-00079-29 0402 (CLR) NORMAN, MARK General clinical research center Evaluation of thyroid hormone analogues

M01RR-00079-29 0403 (CLR) GLANTZ, STANTON A General clinical research center Determinants of left ventricular filling in acute ischemia

M01RR-00079-29 0404 (CLR) CHATTERJEE, KANU General clinical research center Hemodynamic response to orovasodilator flosequinan in severe heart failure

M01RR-00080-29 (CLR) CHERNIACK, NEIL S CASE WESTERN RESERVE UNIVERSIT SCH OF MED/10900 EUCLID CLEVELAND, OHIO 44106-4915 General clinical research center

M01RR-00080-29 0338 (CLR) RICH, ELIZABETH A General clinical research center Regulation of immune homeostasis in the lung

M01RR-00080-29 0340 (CLR) ARAFAH, BAHA M General clinical research center Adrenal/vascular response to angiotension II and catecholamines

M01RR-00080-29 0353 (CLR) MCFADDEN, E REGIS General clinical research center Immunoligic and non-immunologic stimuli on airway inflammation in asthmatics

M01RR-00080-29 0354 (CLR) BRITTENHAM, GARY M General clinical research center Chelation therapy for iron overload using pyridoxal isonicotinoyl hydrazone

M01RR-00080-29 0357 (CLR) MELTZER, HERBERT Y General clinical research center Effect of buspirone on hormonal respones in psychiatric illness

M01RR-00080-29 0197 (CLR) DAHMS, WILLIAM T General clinical research center Diabetes control and complications trial

M01RR-00080-29 0260 (CLR) BICKERS, DAVID R General clinical research center Human cutaneous porphyria

M01RR-00080-29 0306 (CLR) MELTZER, HERBERT Y General clinical research center Depression--a biological and clinical assessment

M01RR-00080-29 0307 (CLR) MELTZER, HERBERT Y General clinical research center MK-212 on serum cortisol, prolactin and growth hormone

M01RR-00080-29 0315 (CLR) KONSTAN, MICHAEL W General clinical research center Ibuprofen in cystic fibrosis

M01RR-00080-29 0327 (CLR) MCFADDEN, E R General clinical research center Pathogenesis of exercise induced asthma--The late asthmatic response

M01RR-00080-29 0328 (CLR) MELTZER, HERBERT Y. General clinical research center Clonidine and apomorphine on serum growth hormone in psychiatric patients

M01RR-00080-29 0331 (CLR) MELTZER, HEBERT Y. General clinical research center 5-hydroxytryptophan--Pituitary hormone and cortisol secretion

M01RR-00080-29 0337 (CLR) ARAFAH, BAHA M General clinical research center Dynamics of growth hormone secretion in pituitary gland dysfuntion

M01RR-00080-29 0359 (CLR) SORENSEN, RICARDO U General clinical research center Polyethylene glycol modified bovine adenosine deaminase treatment

M01RR-00080-29 0438 (CLR) KALHAN, SATISH C General clinical research center Leucine metabolism in pregnancy and newborn

M01RR-00080-29 0439 (CLR) CZINN, STEVEN J General clinical research center Non-invasive detection of Campylobacter pylori

M01RR-00080-29 0440 (CLR) SUPER, DENNIS M General clinical research center Gestational diabetes mellitus--Early detection and management

M01RR-00080-29 0441 (CLR) LAZARUS, HILLARD M General clinical research center Peripheral blood leukapheresis for use during intensive therapy for malignancy

M01RR-00080-29 0442 (CLR) CAREY, JOHN T General clinical research center AIDS study--Oral 2',3'-dideoxyinosine for AZT intolerant AIDS/ARC patients

M01RR-00080-29 0443 (CLR) LEDERMAN, MICHAEL M General clinical research center ACTG AIDS study--2'3'dideoxyinosine & AZT for AIDS/ARC patients on AZT therapy

M01RR-00080-29 0444 (CLR) GIBAS, ALEXANDRA General clinical research center Evaluation of the safety and efficacy of 1, 3, and 6 million units of Roferon-A

M01RR-00080-29 0445 (CLR) MIRALDI, FLORO D General clinical research center Safety and biochemical activity of MK-217

M01RR-00080-29 0446 (CLR) RESNICK, MARTIN I General clinical research center Phase II dose finding placebo controlled study of 4 dose levels of YM617

M01RR-00080-29 0447 (CLR) BERGER, MELVIN General clinical research center Congenital immunodefficiency syndromes

M01RR-00080-29 0448 (CLR) MELTZER, HERBERT Y General clinical research center Biological and clinical assessment of depression

M01RR-00080-29 0449 (CLR) MELTZER, HERBERT Y General clinical research center Apomorphine on serum growth hormone in psychiatric pts and normal volunteers

M01RR-00080-29 0450 (CLR) BASTANI, BIJAN General clinical research center Sodium valproate on serum growth hormone and prolactin in psychiatric patients

M01RR-00080-29 0451 (CLR) MCFADDEN, E REGIS JR General clinical research center Steroid metabolism in asthma

M01RR-00080-29 0452 (CLR) MELTZER, HERBERT Y General clinical research center Neuroendocrine and biogenic amine response to fenfluramine or placebo

M01RR-00080-29 0453 (CLR) LEDERMAN, MICHAEL M General clinical research center Dideoxycytidine (ddC) vs zidovudine (ZDV) in patients with AIDS or advanced ARC

M01RR-00080-29 0366 (CLR) WALDO, ALBERT L General clinical research center Cardiac arrhythmia suppression trial

M01RR-00080-29 0373 (CLR) ARAFAH, BAHA M General clinical research center Human prolactin secretion in various endocrine disorders

M01RR-00080-29 0374 (CLR) STROHL, KINGMAN P General clinical research center Biochemical markers of hypoxemia

M01RR-00080-29 0381 (CLR) KAMMER, GARY M General clinical research center Human T lymphocyte function in SLE and control populations

M01RR-00080-29 0384 (CLR) KONSTAN, MICHAEL W General clinical research center Clinical trial of Ibuprofen in patients with cystic fibrosis

M01RR-00080-29 0385 (CLR) CRUM, EDWARD D General clinical research center High-dose Il2 and lymphokine activated killer cells for metastatic melanoma

M01RR-00080-29 0454 (CLR) NEBELING, LINDA C General clinical research center Diet induced ketosis--Nutrition and tumor metabolism in pediatric oncology pts

M01RR-00080-29 0455 (CLR) LEDERMAN, MICHAEL M General clinical research center Intravenous spiramycin for cryptosporidial diarrhea in AIDS patients

M01RR-00080-29 0456 (CLR) HOPPEL, CHARLES L General clinical research center Pharmacokinetics of L-carnitine in patients with end stage renal disease

M01RR-00080-29 0457 (CLR) CRUM, EDWARD D General clinical research center Treatment of unresectable non-small cell carcinoma on the lung with IL2

M01RR-00080-29 0558 (CLR) MCFADDEN, E REGIS JR General clinical research center Nocturnal asthma

M01RR-00080-29 0559 (CLR) ASSEL, BARBARA General clinical research center Glucose metabolism in pregnancy--Effect of gestational diabetes

M01RR-00080-29 0560 (CLR) ARAFAH, BAHA M General clinical research center Pulsatile GH/prolactin secretion in normals and patients with pituitary adenomas

M01RR-00080-29 0661 (CLR) JOHNSTON, VICKI General clinical research center Investigation on hypoglycemia in newborn babies

M01RR-00080-29 0662 (CLR) MELTZER, HERBERT Y General clinical research center Ipsapirone on plasma cortisol, prolactin, and GH responses in psychosis

M01RR-00080-29 0663 (CLR) MEHANDRU, PERM General clinical research center Glucose utilization in low birth weight newborns during parenteral nutrition

M01RR-00080-29 0664 (CLR) BATTISTA, MICHAEL General clinical research center Parenteral nutrition and protein metabolism in preterm infant

M01RR-00080-29 0392 (CLR) STERN, ROBERT C General clinical research center Long term parenteral nutrition/intravenous fat emulsion in CF patients

M01RR-00080-29 0394 (CLR) LEDERMAN, MICHAEL M General clinical research center Trial of a single dosing schedule of zidovudine in early AIDS related complex

M01RR-00080-29 0395 (CLR) LEDERMAN, MICHAEL M General clinical research center Zidovudine for asymptomatic HIV infected individuals

M01RR-00080-29 0402 (CLR) GONZALEZ, FRANK General clinical research center Adrenal response to chronic ovarian suppression in polycystic ovarian disease

M01RR-00080-29 0403 (CLR) MCFADDEN, E REGIS JR General clinical research center Esophageal reflux and asthma

M01RR-00080-29 0405 (CLR) LEDERMAN, MICHAEL M General clinical research center Clindamycin and primaquine for mild-moderate pneumonia in AIDS patients

M01RR-00080-29 0407 (CLR) MELTZER, HERBERT Y General clinical research center Effect of cimetidine on prolactin secretion

M01RR-00080-29 0412 (CLR) MUNGER, MARK General clinical research center Multiple dose quinapril HCl on regional blood flow and cardiac function

M01RR-00080-29 0414 (CLR) GREEN, JEFFREY A General clinical research center Cerebral blood flow and metabolism in normals treated orally with fleroxacin

M01RR-00080-29 0417 (CLR) WEBER, FREDERICK L General clinical research center Portal blood flow as measured by Doppler ultrasound in cirrhotic patients

M01RR-00080-29 0422 (CLR) DIMARCO, ANTHONY F General clinical research center Spinal cord stimulation for artificial respiration in humans

M01RR-00080-29 0423 (CLR) CRUM, EDWARD D General clinical research center Metastatic or unresectable renal cell carcinoma with high dose Il-2

M01RR-00080-29 0424 (CLR) RUDY, ELLEN B General clinical research center Menstrual response to running--Nursing implications

M01RR-00080-29 0425 (CLR) MELTZER, HERBERT Y General clinical research center Neuroendocrine and biogenic amine response to fenfluramine or placebo

M01RR-00080-29 0426 (CLR) HOMES, TERRYL L General clinical research center Reasons why patients participate in clinical research

M01RR-00080-29 0427 (CLR) MCFADDEN, E REGIS General clinical research center Oral theophylline and aerosol beclomethasone dipropionate therapy of asthma

M01RR-00080-29 0431 (CLR) TOLTZIS, PHILLIP H General clinical research center Intravenous gamma globulin in children with symptomatic HIV receiving zidovudine

M01RR-00080-29 0434 (CLR) RICH, ELIZABETH A General clinical research center Alveolar macrophages and AIDS

M01RR-00080-29 0435 (CLR) CAREY, JOHN T General clinical research center AIDS study--Anti-PCP agents and zidovudine in advanced HIV infections

M01RR-00080-29 0437 (CLR) ELLNER, JERROLD General clinical research center Tuberculosis in the elderly--Aging on immune system

M01RR-00081-29 (CLR) SCHULMAN, IRVING STANFORD UNIVERSITY DEPT OF PEDIATRICS STANFORD, CALIF 94305 General clinical research center

M01RR-00081-29 0002 (CLR) ARIAGNO, RONALD L General clinical research center Assisted ventilation in treatment of respiratory failure

M01RR-00081-29 0078 (CLR) PROBER, C General clinical research center Perinatal HIV, antiviral therapy

M01RR-00081-29 0087 (CLR) ARIAGNO, RONALD L General clinical research center Follow-up studies of infants weighing 1500 gm or less at birth

M01RR-00081-29 0100 (CLR) BLAU, HELEN M General clinical research center Developmental regulation of human muscle proteins

M01RR-00081-29 0121 (CLR) ARIANGO, RONALD L. General clinical research center Evaluation of antiviral Rx for RSV infections, mortality, morbidity

M01RR-00081-29 0124 (CLR) SUNSHINE, PHILIP General clinical research center Effects of Exosurf prophylaxis protocol

M01RR-00081-29 0135 (CLR) COHEN, SHEILA General clinical research center Fentanyl/sufentanil/bupivacaine for infusion epidural analgesia

M01RR-00081-29 0138 (CLR) BENITZ, WILLIAM E General clinical research center Cellular and biochemical components of lung injury

M01RR-00081-29 0139 (CLR) ARIAGNO, RONALD L General clinical research center Modulation of circadian rhythmicity in preterm infants

M01RR-00081-29 0140 (CLR) LANE, ALFRED T General clinical research center Therapy for the premature infant skin

M01RR-00081-29 0141 (CLR) STARNES, VAUGHN A General clinical research center Clinical heart, heart-lung, and heart transplantation in neonates

M01RR-00081-29 0142 (CLR) DENNERY, PHYLLIS A General clinical research center Infant heme catabolism and carbon monoxide detection

M01RR-00081-29 0143 (CLR) RHINE, WILLIAM D General clinical research center Umbilical arterial catheter placement

M01RR-00081-29 0144 (CLR) VAN MEURS, KRISA General clinical research center Long term follow-up of infant and children treated with ECMO

M01RR-00081-29 0145 (CLR) STEVENSON, DAVID K General clinical research center Effects of Exosurf rescue

M01RR-00081-29 0146 (CLR) ARIAGNO, RONALD L General clinical research center Assisted ventilation in infants with RDS

M01RR-00081-29 0147 (CLR) STEVENSON, DAVID General clinical research center Safety of Exosurf pediatric--A 2 year trial

M01RR-00081-29 0098 (CLR) KORNER, ANNELIESE F General clinical research center Longitudinal neurobehavioral assessment procedure for preterm infants

M01RR-00082-29 (CLR) NEIMS, ALLEN H J. HILLIS MILLER HEALTH CENTER BOX J-215 J H MILLER HEALTH CT GAINESVILLE, FL 32610 General clinical research center

M01RR-00082-29 0402 (CLR) JOHNSON, SUZANNE B General clinical research center Psychological correlates of diabetes onset in high-risk individuals

M01RR-00082-29 0405 (CLR) RILEY, WILLIAM J General clinical research center Natural history of Addison's disease

M01RR-00082-29 0445 (CLR) FISHER, WALDO R General clinical research center Coordinate control of apolipoprotein metabolism

M01RR-00082-29 0448 (CLR) WILCOX, CHRISTOPHER General clinical research center Salt retention after bumetanide diuresis--Volume depletion /retention

M01RR-00082-29 0449 (CLR) ROSENBLOOM, ARLAN General clinical research center Humatrope in the treatment of short stature due to Turner syndrome

M01RR-00082-29 0450 (CLR) GRANT MARIA General clinical research center Hormonal modulation of fibrinolysis in diabetes mellitus

M01RR-00082-29 0453 (CLR) BLAND, KIRBY General clinical research center Regional limb infusion with cisplatinum for invasive melanoma of extremities

M01RR-00082-29 0455 (CLR) KEDAR, AMOS General clinical research center Endocrine function in young patients undergoing bone marrow transplantation

M01RR-00082-29 0456 (CLR) TOSKES, PHILIP General clinical research center Development of a better pancreatic extract preparation

M01RR-00082-29 0461 (CLR) HENDELES, LESLIE G General clinical research center Anti-inflammatory effects of theophylline compared with cromolyn

M01RR-00082-29 0463 (CLR) SILVERSTEIN, JANET H General clinical research center Immunological intervention in newly-diagnosed IDDM

M01RR-00082-29 0464 (CLR) MERIMEE, THOMAS J General clinical research center Short stature and delayed puberty in patients with sickle-Thalassemia

M01RR-00082-29 0465 (CLR) WILCOX, CHRISTOPHER S General clinical research center Adrenal, renal, and blood pressure response to salt intake and angiotensis II

M01RR-00082-29 0466 (CLR) MACLAREN, NOEL K General clinical research center Islet cell autoantibodies in pre-diabetics

M01RR-00082-29 0467 (CLR) STACPOOLE, PETER W General clinical research center Treatment of hyperlipidemia with fish oils

M01RR-00082-29 0468 (CLR) STACOOOLE, PETER W General clinical research center Effects of omega-3 fatty acids on carbohydrate and lipid metabolism in DM

M01RR-00082-29 0469 (CLR) THOMAS, WILLIAM C JR General clinical research center Investigation of patients with metabolic bone disease

M01RR-00082-29 0470 (CLR) ROSENBLOOM, ARLAN L General clinical research center Treatment of precocious sexual maturation with Lupron

M01RR-00082-29 0471 (CLR) FISHER, WALDO R General clinical research center Kinetics of albumin in humans

M01RR-00082-29 0472 (CLR) STACPOOLE, PETER W General clinical research center Treatment of lactic acidosis with dichloroacetate

M01RR-00082-29 0473 (CLR) NEU, JOSEF General clinical research center Dichloroacetate in neonates with severe lactic acidosis

M01RR-00082-29 0474 (CLR) DEMCHAK, PAUL A General clinical research center Phase II study of outpatient interferon A and interleukin 2 for renal cancer

M01RR-00082-29 0475 (CLR) KAUWELL, GAIL P A General clinical research center Effect of folate supplementation on zinc nutriture

M01RR-00082-29 0476 (CLR) PFAFF, WILLIAM W General clinical research center Transplantation of pancreatic islet

M01RR-00082-29 0477 (CLR) SILVERSTEIN, JANET H General clinical research center Prevention of insulin dependent diabetes mellitus by azathioprine

M01RR-00082-29 0478 (CLR) DERENDOFF, HARTMUT General clinical research center Codeine disposition in sickle cell disease

M01RR-00082-29 0479 (CLR) LIMACHER, MARIAN C General clinical research center Controlled study of simvastatin in patient with hypercholesterolemia

M01RR-00082-29 0480 (CLR) CERDA, JAMES J General clinical research center Effect of citrus pectin products on hypercholesterolemia

M01RR-00082-29 0481 (CLR) TOSKES, PHILLIP P General clinical research center Study of Sandostatin in the treatment of chronic pancreatitis

M01RR-00082-29 0277 (CLR) SILVERSTEIN, SUZANNE General clinical research center Compliance and control in childhood diabetes
M01RR-00082-29 0279 (CLR) ROSENBLOOM, ARLAN L General clinical research center Efficacy and safety of met-HGH
M01RR-00082-29 0280 (CLR) GUY, JOHN R General clinical research center Optic neuritis treatment trial cooperating clinic
M01RR-00082-29 0281 (CLR) STACPOOLE, PETER W General clinical research center Nutritional control of intermediatary metabolism
M01RR-00082-29 0282 (CLR) SAMO, JILL General clinical research center Effects of psychological stress on metabolic control
M01RR-00082-29 0285 (CLR) OBLON, DAVID J General clinical research center Cis-platinum plus WR-2721 vs. cis-platinum alone for metastic melanoma
M01RR-00082-29 0286 (CLR) PEPINE, CARL J General clinical research center Studies of left ventricular dysfunction
M01RR-00082-29 0288 (CLR) LOPEZ, LARRY M General clinical research center Evaluation of calcium blocker--Beta blocker reaction
M01RR-00082-29 0289 (CLR) YEE, GARY C General clinical research center Fat and bile salts on oral absorption of cycloesporine in renal transplant pts.
M01RR-00082-29 0290 (CLR) FERRELL, ROBERT S General clinical research center Effects of growth hormone on children with renal insufficiency
M01RR-00082-29 0291 (CLR) HILL, JAMES R General clinical research center Omnipaque 350 and renografin in adult patients undergoing angiocardiography
M01RR-00082-29 0292 (CLR) OBLON, DAVID J General clinical research center Intravenous zacopride in the prevention of cisplatin-induced emesis
M01RR-00082-29 0293 (CLR) OBLON, DAVID J General clinical research center Intravenous BRL 43694A in prevention of cisplatin-induced nausea and emesis
M01RR-00082-29 0294 (CLR) NEU, JOSEF General clinical research center Enteral nutriton in high risk, low birthweight infant
M01RR-00082-29 0296 (CLR) DAVIS, GARY L General clinical research center Interferon alpha 2b for therapy of chronic non-A, non-B, and C hepatitis
M01RR-00082-29 0319 (CLR) THOMAS, WILLIAM C General clinical research center The causes of renal calculi
M01RR-00082-29 0338 (CLR) SHERWOOD, MARK General clinical research center 5-fluorouracil (5-FU) and glaucoma filtering surgery
M01RR-00083-29 (SRC) MARTIN, JOSEPH B UNIVERSITY OF CALIFORNIA 3RD & PARNASSUS AVENUES SAN FRANCISCO, CA 94143 **General clinical research center**
M01RR-00083-29 0234 (SRC) HELLERSTEIN, MARC General clinical research center Growth hormone treatment of HIV associated catabolism
M01RR-00083-29 0040 (SRC) BIGLIERI, EDWARD G General clinical research center Regulation and disorders of mineralocorticoid production
M01RR-00083-29 0100 (SRC) BENOWITZ, NEAL L General clinical research center Dihydroergotamine treatment for orthostatic hypotension
M01RR-00083-29 0235 (SRC) GARDNER, CHRISTOPHER General clinical research center Food intake of new immigrant families in Mission District of San Francisco
M01RR-00083-29 0236 (SRC) GOOSBY, ERIC General clinical research center Phase III study of megestrol acetate in AIDS with anorexia/cachexia
M01RR-00083-29 0115 (SRC) BERSOT, THOMAS P General clinical research center Plasmapheresis for disorders of lipid metabolism
M01RR-00083-29 0138 (SRC) BENOWITZ, NEAL L General clinical research center Stable isotope studies of nicotine and cotinine metabolism
M01RR-00083-29 0154 (SRC) BENOWITZ, NEAL L General clinical research center Substances in blood pressure dysregulation syndrome
M01RR-00083-29 0161 (SRC) KRETCHMER, NORMAN General clinical research center Impact of obesity on maternal profile and body composition of neonate
M01RR-00083-29 0162 (SRC) BIGLIERI, EDWARD G. General clinical research center Syndrome of primary aldosteronism
M01RR-00083-29 0164 (SRC) SCHAMBELAN, MORRIS General clinical research center Pysiology of the renal tubule in tubular disorders
M01RR-00083-29 0178 (SRC) SCHAMBELAN, MORRIS General clinical research center Enalapril vs low protein diet in nephrotic patients
M01RR-00083-29 0189 (SRC) JACOBSON, MARK General clinical research center Foscarnet treatment of serious CMV retinitis infections in pts with AIDS
M01RR-00083-29 0193 (SRC) SEBASTIAN, ANTHONY General clinical research center Mineralocorticoid, electrolyte and acid-base metabolism in chronic renal disease
M01RR-00083-29 0194 (SRC) BIGLIERI, EDWARD G General clinical research center Pituitary CNS function in AIDS and normal subjects
M01RR-00083-29 0201 (SRC) HELLERSTEIN, MARC General clinical research center Use of stable isotopic probes of intercellular pathways with whole body clamp
M01RR-00083-29 0204 (SRC) BERSOF, THOMAS P General clinical research center Phlebotomy & plasmapheresis of normal pts. & Addisonians for plasma pool
M01RR-00083-29 0206 (SRC) KAHN, JAMES General clinical research center Study of CDA in patients with AIDS associated non-Hodgkins lymphoma
M01RR-00083-29 0212 (SRC) BENOWITZ, NEAL L General clinical research center Diagnosis of liver disease by analysis of caffeine metabolism
M01RR-00083-29 0213 (SRC) HELLERSTEIN, MARC General clinical research center Metabolic pathways, monokines, and wasting in HIV infection
M01RR-00083-29 0215 (SRC) BENOWTIZ, NEAL L General clinical research center Kinetics and dynamics of caffeine
M01RR-00083-29 0216 (SRC) BENOWITZ, NEAL General clinical research center Bioavailability of transdermal nicotine
M01RR-00083-29 0217 (SRC) ABRAMS, DONALD General clinical research center High dose megesterole acetate vs. placebo in HIV infection
M01RR-00083-29 0237 (SRC) BENOWITZ, NEAL General clinical research center Pharmacokinetics of subcutaneous nicotine
M01RR-00083-29 0238 (SRC) ABRAMS, DONALD General clinical research center ACTG110--Phase I study of weekly Vp16 for AIDS associated Kaposi's sarcoma
M01RR-00083-29 0239 (SRC) LEE, BELLE L General clinical research center N-acetylator phenotype in patients with AIDS
M01RR-00083-29 0240 (SRC) BENOWITZ, NEAL General clinical research center Comparison of nicotine metabolism in four ethnic groups
M01RR-00083-29 0241 (SRC) BIGLIERI, EDWARD G General clinical research center Effect of licorice on blood pressure, sodium and potassium balance and adrenals
M01RR-00083-29 0242 (SRC) KAHN, JAMES O General clinical research center Study of recombinant human CD4 immunoglobin G in HIV associated purpura
M01RR-00083-29 0218 (SRC) BIGLIERE, EDWARD G General clinical research center Dapsone, trimethroprim, zidovudine (AZT) drug interaction study
M01RR-00083-29 0219 (SRC) BENOWITZ, NEAL T General clinical research center Study of transdermal nicotine
M01RR-00083-29 0220 (SRC) KAHN, JAMES General clinical research center Study of recombinant human rCD4 immunoglobin administered IM in AIDS/ARC pts
M01RR-00083-29 0221 (SRC) KAHN, JAMES O General clinical research center Repeat dose open label study of GLQ223 administered IV in patients with HIV
M01RR-00083-29 0223 (SRC) BIGLIERI, EDWARD G General clinical research center Adrenocortical function in acute and recovery phase of myocardial infarction
M01RR-00083-29 0224 (SRC) BECKER, CHARLES E General clinical research center Hydroxocobalamin/sodium thiosulfate cyanide antidote kit
M01RR-00083-29 0225 (SRC) CELLO, JOHN P General clinical research center EFficacy/safety of sandostatin in treatment of immunodeficiency-related diarrhea
M01RR-00083-29 0226 (SRC) BENOWITZ, NEAL L General clinical research center Characterization of hepatic function by studies of caffeine metabolism
M01RR-00083-29 0227 (SRC) JACOBSON, MARK General clinical research center Phase 1 pharmacokinetic and tolerance study of 28-day oral ganicolovir
M01RR-00083-29 0228 (SRC) HELLERSTEIN, MARC General clinical research center Membrane lipids, cytokines, nutrition, and HIV infection
M01RR-00083-29 0229 (SRC) BOYER, THOMAS D General clinical research center Phrophylactic antibiotics in prevention of spontaneous bacterial peritonitis
M01RR-00083-29 0230 (SRC) BIGLIERRI, EDWARD G General clinical research center Effect of metaclopramide on adrenal steroids in normals and low sodium diets
M01RR-00083-29 0231 (SRC) BECKER, CHARLES E General clinical research center Kinetic study of hydroxycobalimin in smokers
M01RR-00083-29 0233 (SRC) BENOWITZ, NEAL General clinical research center Comparison of effects of cigarette smoking and transdermal nicotine
M01RR-00084-29 (CLR) DONALDSON, WILLIAM F CHILDREN'S HOSP OF PGH 3705 FIFTH AVE @ DESOTO ST PITTSBURGH, PA 15213 **General clinical research center**
M01RR-00084-29 0230 (CLR) BLATT, STEVEN D General clinical research center Short term oral antibiotic therapy in treatment of bacterial conjunctivitis
M01RR-00084-29 0234 (CLR) GREEN, MICHAEL General clinical research center Impact of aerosolized ribaviran vs placebo in acute RSV
M01RR-00084-29 0235 (CLR) FINGOLD, DAVID N General clinical research center Enhancement of GH secretion and periodicity with short-term fasting
M01RR-00084-29 0237 (CLR) ARSLANIAN, SILVA General clinical research center GRF-44 treatment of growth hormone deficient children
M01RR-00084-29 0238 (CLR) KAYE, WALTER H General clinical research center Measurement of CSF in Prader-Willi patients
M01RR-00084-29 0239 (CLR) CHAKRAVARTI, ARAVINDA General clinical research center Genetic analysis of Hirschsprung disease
M01RR-00084-29 0240 (CLR) BECKER, DOROTHY J General clinical research center Control and complications of IDDM--Effect on cognitive function
M01RR-00084-29 0241 (CLR) FINEGOLD, DAVID N General clinical research center Studies of children with abnormalities in carnitine metabolism
M01RR-00084-29 0242 (CLR) ORENSTEIN, SUSAN R General clinical research center Pathophysiology of infant gastroesophageal reflux
M01RR-00084-29 0243 (CLR) CASSELBRANT, MARGARETHA General clinical research center Efficacy of medical and surgical therapies for otitis media--Otorrhea
M01RR-00084-29 0003 (CLR) BECKER, DOROTHY J General clinical research center Hypoglycemia in childhood
M01RR-00084-29 0055 (CLR) BECKER, DOROTHY J General clinical research center Nutritional, lipid and hormonal abnormalities in psychosocial dwarfism
M01RR-00084-29 0096 (CLR) FOLEY, THOMAS P. General clinical research center Endocrine and metabolic factors in physical growth
M01RR-00084-29 0099 (CLR) FIREMAN, PHILIP A General clinical research center Humoral and cellular mediated immunity
M01RR-00084-29 0158 (CLR) LEE, PETER A General clinical research center Pathophysiology of sexual differentiation
M01RR-00084-29 0176 (CLR) FOLEY, THOMAS P General clinical research center Growth hormone therapy in children with short stature
M01RR-00084-29 0177 (CLR) FOLEY, THOMAS P General clinical research center Hormonal control of calcium and phosphorus metabolism
M01RR-00084-29 0178 (CLR) FOLEY, THOMAS P General clinical research center Pathologic alterations of thyroid function
M01RR-00084-29 0180 (CLR) DRASH, ALAN General clinical research center Etiology and epidemiology of IDDM
M01RR-00084-29 0190 (CLR) ORENSTEIN, SUSAN General clinical

PROJECT NO., ORGANIZATIONAL UNIT., INVESTIGATOR, ADDRESS, TITLE

research center Pediatric gastroesophageal reflux
M01RR-00084-29 0196 (CLR) DRASH, ALLAN L. General clinical research center Intensive insulin therapy in the pediatric population
M01RR-00084-29 0197 (CLR) FIREMAN, PHILIP General clinical research center Inflammatory mediators in acute bronchiolitis and asthma in children
M01RR-00084-29 0199 (CLR) BECKER, DOROTHY J General clinical research center Physical training, insulin sensitivity, and glycemic control in IDDM
M01RR-00084-29 0203 (CLR) BECKER, DOROTHY J General clinical research center Abnormalities of gonadal/pubertal development using LHRH analog
M01RR-00084-29 0214 (CLR) BECKER, DOROTHY J General clinical research center Nutritional status in growth, puberty and pancreatic function
M01RR-00084-29 0215 (CLR) ULATMANN, MICHELLE C General clinical research center Salt and water balance in children with nocturnal enuresis
M01RR-00084-29 0217 (CLR) HOFKOSH, DENA General clinical research center Outcome of survivors of extracorporeal membrane oxygenation
M01RR-00084-29 0219 (CLR) GREEN, MICHEAL General clinical research center Vancomycin resistant gram positive cocci--liver transplant
M01RR-00084-29 0221 (CLR) ORENSTEIN, DAVID M General clinical research center Long-term exercise intervention in cystic fibrosis
M01RR-00084-29 0222 (CLR) HOFKOSH, DENA General clinical research center Exercise-induced bronchial hyperresponsiveness in school children
M01RR-00084-29 0228 (CLR) ARSLANIAN, SILVA General clinical research center Pathogenesis of glucose intolerance in cystic fibrosis (CF) patients
M01RR-00084-29 0229 (CLR) ALBRIGHT, LELAND General clinical research center Intrathecal baclofen for spasticity in cerebral palsy
M01RR-00084-29 0244 (CLR) PARADISE, JACK L General clinical research center Child development in relation to early otitis media
M01RR-00084-29 0245 (CLR) BLATT, JULIE General clinical research center Long term cardiac effects of Doxorubicin and mediastial radiation
M01RR-00084-29 0246 (CLR) BAGNATO, STEPHEN J General clinical research center Neurodevelopmental patterns, behavior, and parenting in CF and IDDM children
M01RR-00084-29 0247 (CLR) COHEN, BERNARD A General clinical research center Urticaria pigmentosa
M01RR-00084-29 0248 (CLR) HICKEY, ROBERT W General clinical research center Treatment of bronchiolitis with albuterol delivered my metered dose
M01RR-00084-29 0249 (CLR) BERGMAN, IRA General clinical research center Investigation of vestibulsr disturbance in graduates of NICU with hearing loss
M01RR-00084-29 0250 (CLR) HOBERMAN, ALEJANDRO General clinical research center Prevalence of urinary tract infection
M01RR-00084-29 0251 (CLR) MCWILLIAMS, BETTY J General clinical research center Physical growth among cleft palate children
M01RR-00084-29 0252 (CLR) FIREMAN, PHILLIP General clinical research center Heredity and allergy
M01RR-00084-29 0253 (CLR) HOBERMAN, ALEJANDRO General clinical research center Design and evaluation of educational intervention to enhance otoscopic skills
M01RR-00084-29 0254 (CLR) GREEN, MICHAEL General clinical research center Follow-up of primary liver transplant recipients under FK506
Z01RR-00086-02 (VR) WEYANT, R S NCRR, NIH Characterization of feline pneumonia outbreak associated with group EF4 bacteria
Z01RR-00087-02 (VR) BARNARD, D NCRR, NIH Serum cholesterol and triglyceride values of the N.I.H. WHHL rabbit colony
M01RR-00088-28 (CLR) MARK, ROGER G MASSACHUSETTS INST OF TECHNOLO 77 MASSACHUSETTS AVENUE, 3-240 CAMBRIDGE, MA 02139 Clinical research center
M01RR-00088-28 0036 (CLR) CORKIN, SUZANNE H Clinical research center Behavioral effects of brain lesions in man
M01RR-00088-28 0154 (CLR) DIETZ, WILLIAM H. Clinical research center Body composition and energy expenditure in cerebral palsy
M01RR-00088-28 0177 (CLR) DIETZ, WILLIAM H Clinical research center Optimal dietary therapy for obese adolescents
M01RR-00088-28 0224 (CLR) WURTMAN, RICHARD J. Clinical research center Aspartame and behavior
M01RR-00088-28 0237 (CLR) YOUNG, VERNON R Clinical research center Leucine and valine kinetic interaction
M01RR-00088-28 0240 (CLR) WURTMAN, RICHARD J. Clinical research center CDP-choline administration to nondemented elderly subjects
M01RR-00088-28 0242 (CLR) CORKIN, SUZANNE H. Clinical research center Theoretical analysis of learning in age related disease
M01RR-00088-28 0250 (CLR) DIETZ, WILLIAM H. Clinical research center Body composition and metabolic rate in children, adolescents and adults
M01RR-00088-28 0246 (CLR) CORKIN, SUZANNE Clinical research center Sensory system in Alzheimer's disease
M01RR-00088-28 0251 (CLR) HOERR, ROBERT A. Clinical research center Phenylalanine and tyrosine kinetics in burn trauma--Studies in normal subjects
M01RR-00088-28 0256 (CLR) CABELLERO, BENJAMIN Clinical research center Phenylalanine metabolism in humans
M01RR-00088-28 0257 (CLR) YOUNG, VERNON R Clinical research center Regulation of energy metabolism in the aged
M01RR-00088-28 0258 (CLR) YOUNG, VERNON R Clinical research center Arginine metabolism in young human adults--Acute changes of arginine intake
M01RR-00088-28 0259 (CLR) WURTMAN, RICHARD Clinical research center Psoralen induced melatonin secretion
M01RR-00088-28 0261 (CLR) COHEN, RICHARD Clinical research center Dynamic evaluation of respiratory and baroreflex control of heart rate
M01RR-00088-28 0262 (CLR) WURTMAN, RICHARD L Clinical research center Effect of D-fenfluramine & fluoxetine on weight loss & macronutrient choice
M01RR-00088-28 0263 (CLR) YOUNG, VERNON R Clinical research center Evaluation of FAO/WHO/UNU requirements for indispensable amino acids
M01RR-00088-28 0264 (CLR) WURTMAN, JUDITH Clinical research center Tryptophan & fenfluramine's influence on uncontrolled carbohydrate intake
M01RR-00088-28 0265 (CLR) DIETZ, WILLIAM Clinical research center Energy expenditure in obese and non-obese adolescents
M01RR-00088-28 0266 (CLR) WURTMAN, JUDITH Clinical research center Nutrient choice pattern and behavioral effects of foods
M01RR-00088-28 0267 (CLR) WURTMAN, JUDITH Clinical research center Seasonal affective disorder and carbohydrate craving
M01RR-00088-28 0268 (CLR) WURTMAN, RICHARD Clinical research center Melatonin, sleep and aging
M01RR-00088-28 0269 (CLR) WURTMAN, RICHARD Clinical research center Effects of insulin and amino acid metabolism in obesity
M01RR-00088-28 0270 (CLR) YOUNG, VERNON Clinical research center Bioavailability of meal-derived amino acids
M01RR-00088-28 0271 (CLR) DIETZ, WILLIAM Clinical research center Prospective study of adolescent obesity
M01RR-00088-28 0272 (CLR) LIEBERMAN, HARRIS Clinical research center Circadian locomotor and temperature rhythms in Alzheimer's disease
M01RR-00088-28 0273 (CLR) WURTMAN, JUDITH Clinical research center Effects of D-fenfluramine and fluoxetine on tobacco withdrawal symptoms
M01RR-00088-28 0274 (CLR) CORKIN, SUZANNE Clinical research center Dissociating two visual systems in Alzheimer's disease
M01RR-00088-28 0275 (CLR) CABALLERO, BENJAMIN Clinical research center Energy metabolism in cystic fibrosis
M01RR-00088-28 0276 (CLR) CABALLERO, BENJAMIN Clinical research center Effect of meal composition on dyskinesia in Parkinson's patients receiving L-DOPA
M01RR-00088-28 0277 (CLR) CABALLERO, BENJAMIN Clinical research center Effect of tyrosine on metabolism, sympathetic activity and mood in anorexia
M01RR-00088-28 0278 (CLR) YOUNG, VERNON Clinical research center Evaluation of sequence of changes induced by low-protein diet
M01RR-00088-28 0279 (CLR) YOUNG, VERNON Clinical research center Dispensable amino acids and amino acid kinetics
M01RR-00088-28 0280 (CLR) YOUNG, VERNON Clinical research center Albumin synthesis in man
M01RR-00088-28 0281 (CLR) WURTMAN, RICHARD Clinical research center Effects of light on human nocturnal mood and performance
M01RR-00088-28 0282 (CLR) YOUNG, VERNON Clinical research center Proline intake and proline-leucine kinetics
M01RR-00088-28 0283 (CLR) YOUNG, VERNON Clinical research center Indispensable amino acid requirements in adults
M01RR-00088-28 0284 (CLR) FUKAGAWA, NAOMI Clinical research center Metabolic effects of dietary fructose
Z01RR-00088-02 (VR) SCHIEWE, M C NCRR, NIH Experimental reconstitution of embryonic trophectoderm and inner cell mass
Z01RR-00089-02 (VR) WASSER, S K NCRR, NIH Excreted steroids in primate feces
Z01RR-00090-02 (VR) BARNARD, D NCRR, NIH Characterization of the WHHL rabbit lipoprotein phenotypes
Z01RR-00091-01 (VR) BAYNE, K NCRR, NIH The reduction of abnormal behavior in individually housed Rheesus monkeys
Z01RR-00092-01 (VR) BAYNE, K NCRR, NIH Monitoring an enrichment program--A pilot evaluation
Z01RR-00093-01 (VR) BAYNE, K NCRR, NIH Social housing ameliorates behavioral pathology in Cebus apella
Z01RR-00094-01 (VR) BAYNE, K NCRR, NIH NIH nonhuman primate intramural management plan
M01RR-00095-31 (CLR) HASH, JOHN H VANDERBILT UNIVERSITY CCC-3322 MEDICAL CENTER NORTH NASHVILLE, TENNESSEE 37232 General clinical research center
M01RR-00095-31 0298 (CLR) LAWSON, WILLIAM General clinical research center Disturbed water balance in schizophrenia
M01RR-00095-31 0299 (CLR) BRANCH, ROBERT A. General clinical research center Bioavailability and pharmacokinetics of enoximone in hepatic disease
M01RR-00095-31 0305 (CLR) ROBERTSON, ROSE General clinical research center Dopa as an endogenous neurohormone
M01RR-00095-31 0001 (CLR) ORTH, DAVID N General clinical research center Normal and abnormal hypothalamic-pituitary-adrenal function
M01RR-00095-31 0109 (CLR) EDWARDS, KATHRYN General clinical research center New bacterial and viral candidate vaccine
M01RR-00095-31 0159 (CLR) OATES, JOHN A General clinical research center Endocrine functions of neoplastic and hyperplastic cells
M01RR-00095-31 0166 (CLR) PAVLOU, SPYROS General clinical research center Clinical pharmacology of LHRH antagonists
M01RR-00095-31 0187 (CLR) FITZGERALD, GARRET General clinical research center Biology and inheritance of primary pulmonary hypertension
M01RR-00095-31 0210 (CLR) LORENZ, RODNEY A General clinical research center Diabetes control and complications trial
M01RR-00095-31 0218 (CLR) KRANTZ, SANFORD B General clinical research center Study of pure red cell aplasia and other refractory anemias
M01RR-00095-31 0219 (CLR) EDWARDS, KATHRYN General clinical research center Evaluation of rotavirus vaccines
M01RR-00095-31 0230 (CLR) NADEAU, JOHN H. General clinical research center Medical versus operative management of renovascular hypertension
M01RR-00095-31 0231 (CLR) BRANCH, ROBERT A General clinical research center Pharmacogenetics of mephenytoin metabolism and its implications
M01RR-00095-31 0232 (CLR) BIAGGIONI, ITALO General clinical research center Autonomic dysfuntion--Taxonomy and therapy
M01RR-00095-31 0235 (CLR) WOOD, ALASTAIR JJ General clinical research center Age & hypertension on the response to beta receptor agonists & antagonists
M01RR-00095-31 0237 (CLR) ABUMRAD, NAJI N General clinical research center Branched chain amino acid metabolism

PROJECT NO., ORGANIZATIONAL UNIT., INVESTIGATOR, ADDRESS, TITLE

M01RR-00095-31 0238 (CLR) ABUMRAD, NAJI N General clinical research center Interaction of insulin, glucose and amino acid in muscle metabolism

M01RR-00095-31 0266 (CLR) FITZGERALD, GARRET General clinical research center Antigen induced mediator release in human lung

M01RR-00095-31 0273 (CLR) KRANTZ, SANFORD B. General clinical research center Phase II study safety efficacy multiple dosage recombinant erythropoietin in RA

M01RR-00095-31 0278 (CLR) ABUMRAD, NAJI N. General clinical research center Peptide release during post-vagotomy dumping--A somatostatin analog

M01RR-00095-31 0279 (CLR) HILL, JAMES O. General clinical research center Effects of dietary fatty acid composition on energy balance and blood pressure

M01RR-00095-31 0280 (CLR) HILL, JAMES General clinical research center Characterization of lipid metabolism in obese non-diabetics

M01RR-00095-31 0283 (CLR) FITZGERALD, GARRET General clinical research center Aspirin pharmacokinetics--Slow-release formulation

M01RR-00095-31 0284 (CLR) ALLEN, GEORGE General clinical research center Parkinson's disease

M01RR-00095-31 0288 (CLR) FENICHEL, GERALD General clinical research center Prednisone in Duchenne muscular dystrophy

M01RR-00095-31 0291 (CLR) EDWARDS, KATHRYN General clinical research center Respiratory vaccine evaluation

M01RR-00095-31 0292 (CLR) RODEN, DAN M. General clinical research center Cardiac arrhythmia pilot study

M01RR-00095-31 0294 (CLR) ROBERTSON, ROSE MARIE General clinical research center Dietary calcium and sodium manipulation in essential hypertension

M01RR-00095-31 0297 (CLR) GRAHAM, BARNEY S. General clinical research center Phase I safety and immunogenicity trial of HIV-1 AIDS vaccine

M01RR-00095-31 0306 (CLR) HILL, JAMES O. General clinical research center Body composition and respiratory quotient of short children

M01RR-00095-31 0354 (CLR) LORENZ, RODNEY General clinical research center Growth hormone secretory function in constitutionally short children

M01RR-00095-31 0355 (CLR) LIPMAN, JONATHAN General clinical research center Evaluation of deep brain stimulation for pain in humans

M01RR-00095-31 0356 (CLR) WOOD, ALASTAIR General clinical research center Factors effecting drug dispensation in humans

M01RR-00095-31 0357 (CLR) ROBERTSON, ROSE General clinical research center Caffeine and the baroreceptor

M01RR-00095-31 0311 (CLR) WOOD, ALASTAIR J.J. General clinical research center Enzyme induction inhibits metabolic pathways

M01RR-00095-31 0313 (CLR) RODEN, DAN M. General clinical research center Quinidine-encainide interaction in patients with arrhythmia

M01RR-00095-31 0314 (CLR) RODEN, DAN M. General clinical research center Sematilide hydrochloride pharmacodynamics in ventricular ectopy

M01RR-00095-31 0316 (CLR) LORENZ, RODNEY A. General clinical research center Growth hormone secretion in mothers of growth hormone deficient children

M01RR-00095-31 0318 (CLR) ABUMRAD, NAJI General clinical research center Effects of diet composition on energy expenditure and substrate oxidation

M01RR-00095-31 0319 (CLR) BRANCH, ROBERT A. General clinical research center Mercury vapor poisoning

M01RR-00095-31 0321 (CLR) HANDE, KENNETH General clinical research center Infusion metoclopramide in volunteers and as an antiemetic in cancer patients

M01RR-00095-31 0324 (CLR) LIPMAN, JONATHAN General clinical research center Heat beam dolorimetry assessment of pain

M01RR-00095-31 0326 (CLR) LOOSEN, PETER T General clinical research center Neuroendocrinology of alcoholism

M01RR-00095-31 0328 (CLR) RICHARDS, WILLIAM O General clinical research center Pathophysiology of gastrointestinal motility disorder

M01RR-00095-31 0329 (CLR) GREENE, HARRY L General clinical research center Glycogen storage disease--Renal changes with glycogen storage disease

M01RR-00095-31 0331 (CLR) EDWARDS, KATHRYN M General clinical research center Natural course of pertussis antibody response

M01RR-00095-31 0332 (CLR) OLSEN, NANCY General clinical research center Daily variability of rheumatoid factor synthesis

M01RR-00095-31 0334 (CLR) LEFKOWITZ, LEWIS General clinical research center Multicenter controlled study of safety & efficacy of concurrent zidovudine

M01RR-00095-31 0335 (CLR) RODEN, DAN M General clinical research center Evaluation of acute and chronic effects of antiarrhythmic therapy in man

M01RR-00095-31 0336 (CLR) GRAHAM, BARNEY S General clinical research center Recombinant vaccinia virus expressing the envelope glycoprotein of HIV

M01RR-00095-31 0337 (CLR) WOOD, ALASTAIR J General clinical research center The effect of drugs on balance in the elderly

M01RR-00095-31 0340 (CLR) PHILLIPS, JOHN A General clinical research center Determination of optimal treatment of N5,N10 methylene tetrahydrofolate

M01RR-00095-31 0342 (CLR) STEIN, RICHARD S General clinical research center Recombinant human erythropoietin in myelodysplasia and multiple myeloma

M01RR-00095-31 0344 (CLR) HILL, JAMES O General clinical research center Effect of diet composition on energy expenditure and substrate oxidation

M01RR-00095-31 0346 (CLR) BRANCH, ROBERT A General clinical research center Caffeine in diazoxide induced renin release in beta-blocked normal subjects

M01RR-00095-31 0347 (CLR) OLSEN, NANCY General clinical research center Phase II study to determine the safety and efficacy of xomazyne

M01RR-00095-31 0348 (CLR) HOLLISTER, ALAN S General clinical research center Infusion of atrial natriuretic factor and sympathetic nervous system

M01RR-00095-31 0349 (CLR) BRANCH, ROBERT A General clinical research center Mechanism of angiotensin II modulation in essential hypertension

M01RR-00095-31 0350 (CLR) CARLSON, MICHAEL General clinical research center Plasma glucose concentration in regulation of lipid and carbohydrate metabolism

M01RR-00095-31 0351 (CLR) RODEN, DAN M General clinical research center Modulation of sodium channel block by ACE inhibition in man

M01RR-00095-31 0352 (CLR) GREENE, HARRY General clinical research center Studies in glycogen storage disease

M01RR-00095-31 0353 (CLR) DEBOLD, ROWAN General clinical research center Effects of synthetic ovine corticotropin releasing factor

M01RR-00095-31 0358 (CLR) BRANCH, ROBERT General clinical research center Disposition of hexobarbital

M01RR-00095-31 0359 (CLR) MARTIN, PETER General clinical research center Genetic mechanism of alcoholic organic brain disease

M01RR-00095-31 0360 (CLR) CARLSON, MICHAEL General clinical research center Changes in substrate flux and thermogenesis with intensive insulin therapy

M01RR-00095-31 0361 (CLR) BRANCH, ROBERT General clinical research center Effect of phenylpropanolamine on the pharmacokinetics of caffeine

M01RR-00095-31 0362 (CLR) FITZGERALD, GARRET General clinical research center Human pharmacology of thrombin inhibition

M01RR-00095-31 0363 (CLR) EDWARDS, KATHRYN General clinical research center Ganciclovir treatment for symptomatic congenital infections

M01RR-00095-31 0364 (CLR) EDWARDS, KATHRYN General clinical research center Prostaglandin metabolites and endogenous pyrogens in patients with PFASP

M01RR-00095-31 0365 (CLR) FITZGERALD, GARRET General clinical research center Controlled release of aspirin in bradykinin stimulated prostacyclin production

M01RR-00095-31 0366 (CLR) PAVLOU, SPYROS General clinical research center Clinical pharmacology of RS-26306 GnRH antagonist

M01RR-00095-31 0367 (CLR) PHILLIPS, JOHN General clinical research center Dopamine beta hydroxylase and blood pressure regulation

M01RR-00095-31 0368 (CLR) GERACIOTI, THOMAS General clinical research center Neurohormonal response in CSF to feeding patients with eating disorders

M01RR-00095-31 0369 (CLR) HILL, JAMES General clinical research center Influence of previous diet on substrate oxidation during and after exercise

M01RR-00095-31 0370 (CLR) PAVLOU, SPYROS General clinical research center Pulsatile vs continuous infusion of LH signal for testicular steroideogenosis

M01RR-00095-31 0371 (CLR) HILL, JAMES General clinical research center Effects of physical fitness on the ability to oxide excess dietary fat

M01RR-00095-31 0372 (CLR) FORMAN, MERVYN General clinical research center Effect of intravenous adenosine on tissue plasminogen activator in human

M01RR-00095-31 0373 (CLR) CAMPBELL, PETER General clinical research center Role of lipolysis in human obesity and fasting

M01RR-00095-31 0374 (CLR) KNAPP, HOWARD General clinical research center Dietary fish oil and correlates of human colon cancer

M01RR-00095-31 0375 (CLR) WOOD, ALASTAIR General clinical research center Cardiovascular effects of timolol eye drops in poor & extensive metabolizers

M01RR-00095-31 0376 (CLR) HILL, JAMES General clinical research center Validation of the doubly labelled water method in older adults

M01RR-00095-31 0377 (CLR) DAVIS, STEPHEN General clinical research center Brain insulin levels and the counterregulatory response

M01RR-00095-31 0378 (CLR) GRUBER, WILLIAM General clinical research center Evaluation of live attenuated influenza administration by nose drops or spray

M01RR-00095-31 0379 (CLR) ANTHONY, LOWELL General clinical research center Phase I study of octreotide in the management of neuroendocrine tumors

Z01RR-00095-01 (VR) NICHOLS, D K NCRR, NIH Pathogenesis of ophidian paramyxovirus infection in brown tree snakes

M01RR-00096-30A1 (CLR) FARBER, SAUL J NEW YORK UNIV MEDICAL CTR 550 FIRST AVENUE NEW YORK, NY 10016 General clinical research center

M01RR-00096-30A1 0320 (CLR) GOLOMB, FREDERICK General clinical research center Recombinant gamma interferon for malignant melanomas

M01RR-00096-30A1 0321 (CLR) HOCHSTER, HOWARD General clinical research center Adriamycin and ADR-529 for advanced solid tumors

M01RR-00096-30A1 0322 (CLR) SPEYER, JAMES General clinical research center FAC vs FAC and ADR-529 in the treatment of disseminated breast cancer

M01RR-00096-30A1 0323 (CLR) CHACHOUA, ABRAHAM General clinical research center Recombinant human interleukin 1 in refractory carcinoma patients

M01RR-00096-30A1 0324 (CLR) GOLOMB, FREDERICK General clinical research center Adjuvant chemotherapy and endocrine therapy for node negative breast cancer

M01RR-00096-30A1 0325 (CLR) GOLOMB, FREDERICK General clinical research center Cis-platin/etoposide and bleomycin/ifosfamide in testicular cancer

M01RR-00096-30A1 0109 (CLR) HOLLANDER, CHARLES S General clinical research center Assessment of corticotropin releasing factor in Cushing's syndrome

M01RR-00096-30A1 0175 (CLR) HOLLANDER, CHARLES General clinical research center Diagnosis of Cushing's disease and Cushing's syndrome

M01RR-00096-30A1 0176 (CLR) HOLLANDER, CHARLES General clinical research center Prognostic indicators in determination of pheochromocytoma

M01RR-00096-30A1 0181 (CLR) HOLLANDER, CHARLES General clinical research center Incidence of partial central diabetes insipidus

M01RR-00096-30A1 0185 (CLR) KLEINBERG, DAVID General clinical research center New approaches to the early diagnosis of recurrence of acromegaly

M01RR-00096-30A1 0186 (CLR) KLEINBERG, DAVID General clinical research center Treatment of hyperprolactinemia with CV 205-502

PROJECT NO., ORGANIZATIONAL UNIT., INVESTIGATOR, ADDRESS, TITLE

M01RR-00096-30A1 0189 (CLR) RAPOPORT, DAVID General clinical research center Obstructive sleep apnea syndrome--Neuroendocrinology and ventilation
M01RR-00096-30A1 0201 (CLR) COOPER, JAY General clinical research center Cisplatin and radiation therapy for post-op patients with head/neck cancer
M01RR-00096-30A1 0209 (CLR) DAVID, RAPHAEL General clinical research center Prognostic indicators of gonadotropin deficiency
M01RR-00096-30A1 0222 (CLR) VALENTINE, FRED T General clinical research center Combination of AZT and DHPG for patients with AIDS and cytomegalovirus infection
M01RR-00096-30A1 0126 (CLR) VALENTINE, FREDERICK T General clinical research center Effects of lymphokines on metastatic malignant melanoma
M01RR-00096-30A1 0168 (CLR) DAVID, RAPHAEL General clinical research center Treatment of precocious puberty with leuprolide acetate
M01RR-00096-30A1 0169 (CLR) FRIEDMAN-KIEN, ALVIN General clinical research center AZT therapy for patients with AIDS associated Kaposi's sarcoma
M01RR-00096-30A1 0229 (CLR) SKLAR, CHARLES General clinical research center High-dose cranial irradiation on growth hormone and prolactin in children
M01RR-00096-30A1 0286 (CLR) COOPER, JAY S General clinical research center Hyperfractionated radiation therapy and BCNU for supratentorial malignant glioma
M01RR-00096-30A1 0287 (CLR) HOLLANDER, CHARLES S General clinical research center Corticotropin releasing factor and suppression of human immune function
M01RR-00096-30A1 0288 (CLR) SPEYER, JAMES General clinical research center Phase I study of doxorubicin and ICRF-187 plus GM-CSF
M01RR-00096-30A1 0289 (CLR) KRASINSKI, KEITH General clinical research center Natural history of HIV infection in infants of addicted mothers
M01RR-00096-30A1 0290 (CLR) HOCHSTER, HOWARD General clinical research center Phase I trial of adriamycin with ADR-529 in malignant cancer
M01RR-00096-30A1 0291 (CLR) BLUM, RONALD General clinical research center Leucovorin and 5-FU after resection in Dukes' B,C or colon cancer
M01RR-00096-30A1 0292 (CLR) BLUM, RONALD General clinical research center PAC plus radiotherapy in treatment of limited unresectable invasive thymoma
M01RR-00096-30A1 0294 (CLR) DIETERICH, DOUGLAS General clinical research center Phase III study of ganciclovir and rGM-GSF for AIDS related CMV retinitis
M01RR-00096-30A1 0296 (CLR) RAPOPORT, DAVID General clinical research center Buspirone in the treatment of obstructive sleep apnea
M01RR-00096-30A1 0297 (CLR) VALENTINE, FRED T General clinical research center Efficacy of ddI for AIDS or ARC patients intolerant to ZDV
M01RR-00096-30A1 0298 (CLR) VALENTINE, FRED General clinical research center Comparison of 2', 3'(ddI) and zidovudine for patients with AIDS or ARC
M01RR-00096-30A1 0299 (CLR) BLUM, RONALD General clinical research center 5-FU and rINF-2 alpha in patients with advanced colorectal cancer
M01RR-00096-30A1 0300 (CLR) KLEINBERG, DAVID General clinical research center Safety and efficacy of chronic sandostatin for acromegalic patients
M01RR-00096-30A1 0301 (CLR) HOLLANDER, CHARLES General clinical research center Altered sleep, endocrine and immune physiology in asymptomatic HIV infection
M01RR-00096-30A1 0302 (CLR) VALENTINE, FRED General clinical research center ddI and ZVD therapy for AIDS or ARC patients on long-term ZVD treatment
M01RR-00096-30A1 0303 (CLR) VALENTINE, FRED General clinical research center Immediate vs delayed foscarnet therapy for CMV retinitis in AIDS patients
M01RR-00096-30A1 0304 (CLR) VALENTINE, FRED General clinical research center Foscarnet salvage for immediately sight-threatening CMV retinitis
M01RR-00096-30A1 0305 (CLR) VALENTINE, FRED General clinical research center Zidovudine and recombinant alpha-2a interferon for Kaposi's sarcoma in AIDS
M01RR-00096-30A1 0306 (CLR) BORKOWSKY, WILLIAM General clinical research center High vs low dose zidovudine administered to children with HIV infection
M01RR-00096-30A1 0307 (CLR) ROM, WILLIAM General clinical research center Role of alveolar macrophage growth factors in asbestosis
M01RR-00096-30A1 0308 (CLR) SAMUELS, HERBERT General clinical research center Analysis of thyroid hormone receptors in thyroid hormone resistance
M01RR-00096-30A1 0309 (CLR) VALENTINE, FRED General clinical research center Intravenous spiramycin in AIDS patients with cryptosporidial diarrhea
M01RR-00096-30A1 0310 (CLR) VALENTINE, FRED General clinical research center Active immunization with recombinant gp160 HIV-1 antigen
M01RR-00096-30A1 0311 (CLR) BORKOWSKY, WILLIAM General clinical research center IND for retrovir brand zidovudine for children with HIV disease
M01RR-00096-30A1 0312 (CLR) WALSH, CHRISTINA General clinical research center CGS-16949A vs megestrol acetate in post-menopausal women with breast cancer
M01RR-00096-30A1 0313 (CLR) BLUM, RONALD General clinical research center 5-FU bolus or infusion and cis-platinum in colorectal adenocarcinoma
M01RR-00096-30A1 0314 (CLR) FRIEDBERG, DOROTHY General clinical research center CMV retinitis trial-- Foscarnet ganciclovir component
M01RR-00096-30A1 0315 (CLR) HOLLANDER, CHARLES General clinical research center Desmopressin acetate vs vasopressin tannate treatment of diabetes insipidus

PROJECT NO., ORGANIZATIONAL UNIT., INVESTIGATOR, ADDRESS, TITLE

M01RR-00096-30A1 0316 (CLR) SNYDERMAN, SELMA General clinical research center Dichloroacetate therapy of congenital lacticacidosis
M01RR-00096-30A1 0317 (CLR) DAVID, RAPHAEL General clinical research center GHRF 1-29 for idiopathic prepubertal growth hormone deficient children
M01RR-00096-30A1 0318 (CLR) WERNZ, JAMES General clinical research center 10-ethyl-10-deaza-aminopterin and chemotherapy for non-small cell lung cancer
M01RR-00096-30A1 0319 (CLR) NEWMAN, CONNIE General clinical research center Sandostatin for prolactinomas not responding to bromocriptine therapy
M01RR-00096-30A1 0231 (CLR) VALENTINE, FRED T General clinical research center AZT therapy for patients with early AIDS-related complex
M01RR-00096-30A1 0232 (CLR) VALENTINE, FRED T General clinical research center AZT treatment for HIV-positive asymptomatic patients
M01RR-00096-30A1 0233 (CLR) SEIDLIN, MINDELL General clinical research center Heterosexual transmission of HIV to partners of drug abusers
M01RR-00096-30A1 0239 (CLR) KRASINSKI, KEITH General clinical research center Intravenous gammaglobulin therapy in treatment of HIV-infected children
M01RR-00096-30A1 0241 (CLR) VALENTINE, FRED T General clinical research center Bactrim vs fansidar vs pentamidine aerosol for PCP in AIDS
M01RR-00096-30A1 0242 (CLR) VALENTINE, FRED T General clinical research center Phase I trial of ribavirin for AIDS and advanced ARC
M01RR-00096-30A1 0257 (CLR) KUPERSMITH, MARK General clinical research center Oral vs intravenous corticosteroids in toxicity of optic neuritis
M01RR-00096-30A1 0258 (CLR) BLUM, RONALD General clinical research center Intravenous amonafide for patients with solid tumors refractory to therapy
M01RR-00096-30A1 0260 (CLR) TSAI, JIR General clinical research center Sleep restriction therapy in middle-aged and elderly insomniacs
M01RR-00096-30A1 0261 (CLR) BLUM, RONALD General clinical research center Efficacy of AZT/betaseron vs placebo in treatment of AIDS and ARC patients
M01RR-00096-30A1 0263 (CLR) BORKOWSKY, WILLIAM General clinical research center Oral Retrovir in treatment of children with symptomatic HIV infection
M01RR-00096-30A1 0264 (CLR) VALENTINE, FRED General clinical research center 2',3' dideoxyinosine for treatment of AIDS/ARC
M01RR-00096-30A1 0268 (CLR) SNYDERMAN, SELMA General clinical research center Diagnosis of hyperphenylalaninemic heterozygote states in PKU
M01RR-00096-30A1 0269 (CLR) RUTKOWSKI, MONICA General clinical research center High dose deferoxamine chelation therapy for thalassemia major patients
M01RR-00096-30A1 0270 (CLR) SNYDERMAN, SELMA General clinical research center Biochemically controlled therapy of inherited metabolic abnormalities
M01RR-00096-30A1 0272 (CLR) GOLOMB, FREDERICK General clinical research center Phase III chemotherapy of advanced soft tissue sarcomas
M01RR-00096-30A1 0275 (CLR) VALENTINE, FRED General clinical research center Fluconazole vs amphotericin B in treatment of cryptococcal meningitis in AIDS
M01RR-00096-30A1 0276 (CLR) KLEINBERG, DAVID General clinical research center Placebo vs sandostatin in normalizing or reducing growth hormone in acromegaly
M01RR-00096-30A1 0280 (CLR) VALENTINE, FRED T General clinical research center Intravenous ganciclovir therapy for peripheral CMV retinitis in AIDS
M01RR-00096-30A1 0282 (CLR) BORKOWSKY, WILLIAM General clinical research center Placebo vs IV gammaglobulin for children with mild to symptomatic HIV
M01RR-00096-30A1 0284 (CLR) WALSH, CHRISTINA General clinical research center Evaluation of CGP 19835A lipid infusion for treating malignant melanoma
M01RR-00096-30A1 0285 (CLR) BLUM, RONALD General clinical research center Clinical trial of recombinant yeast GM-CSF as modulator of monocyte/macrophage
M01RR-00102-28 (CLR) BRESLOW, JAN THE ROCKEFELLER UNIVERSITY 1230 YORK AVENUE NEW YORK, N Y 10021 General clinical research center
M01RR-00102-28 0004 (CLR) HIRSCH, JULES General clinical research center Energy homeostasis in human obesity
M01RR-00102-28 0148 (CLR) KREEK, MARY J General clinical research center Methadone action and neuroendocrine function
M01RR-00102-28 0149 (CLR) KREEK, MARY L General clinical research center Ethanol metabolism, pharmacokinetics, mood and neuroendocrine status
M01RR-00102-28 0152 (CLR) SHACHTER, NEIL General clinical research center Genetic basis of hypertriglyceridemia
M01RR-00102-28 0155 (CLR) ZABRISKIE, JOHN B. General clinical research center Biological studies of bacterial arthritis model
M01RR-00102-28 0157 (CLR) GRAVISH, DOV General clinical research center Role of lipoprotein in atherosclerosis
M01RR-00102-28 0158 (CLR) HIRSCH, JULES General clinical research center Metabolism of human adipose tissue
M01RR-00102-28 0159 (CLR) HIRSCH, JULES General clinical research center Composition of human adipose tissue
M01RR-00102-28 0160 (CLR) GALBRAITH, RICHARD General clinical research center Experimental dermatology
M01RR-00102-28 0161 (CLR) KREEK, MARY JEANNE General clinical research center Estradiol metabolism in addictive disease and in chronic liver disease
M01RR-00102-28 0162 (CLR) KREEK, MARY JEANNE General clinical research center Cocaine dependency-- Neuroendocrine function and effects of treatment
M01RR-00102-28 0005 (CLR) KAPPAS, ATTALLAH General clinical research center Hereditary and acquired porphyrias
M01RR-00102-28 0032 (CLR) CARTER, D MARTIN General clinical

research center Wound healing in individuals of different age and genetic background

M01RR-00102-28 0033 (CLR) CARTER, D MARTIN General clinical research center Evaluation of patients with refractory, undiagnosed or unusual dermatoses

M01RR-00102-28 0035 (CLR) CARTER, D. MARTIN General clinical research center Analysis of genetic heterogeneity in Fanconi anemia

M01RR-00102-28 0042 (CLR) ZABRISKIE, JOHN B General clinical research center Immunological probes in multiple sclerosis

M01RR-00102-28 0050 (CLR) KREEK, MARY J General clinical research center Studies of methadone interactions with other drugs of use and abuse

M01RR-00102-28 0053 (CLR) KREEK, MARY J General clinical research center Long term follow-up studies of patients during chronic treatment of addiction

M01RR-00102-28 0054 (CLR) KREEK, MARY J General clinical research center Methadone disposition in maintenance patients with and without liver disease

M01RR-00102-28 0055 (CLR) KREEK, MARY J General clinical research center Role of opioids in gastrointestinal motility

M01RR-00102-28 0061 (CLR) BENJAMIN, LENNETTE General clinical research center Sickle cell disease

M01RR-00102-28 0064 (CLR) JONES, ROBERT L General clinical research center Iron metabolism and thrombosis

M01RR-00102-28 0091 (CLR) BRINTON, ELIOT A General clinical research center Regulation of HDL levels by genetic and environmental factors

M01RR-00102-28 0092 (CLR) GAVISH, DOV General clinical research center Apolipoprotein B metabolism in premature coronary heart disease

M01RR-00102-28 0095 (CLR) CARTER, D MARTIN General clinical research center Psoriasis

M01RR-00102-28 0096 (CLR) CARTER, D MARTIN General clinical research center Treatment and prevention of blisters in dystropic epidermolysis bullosa

M01RR-00102-28 0100 (CLR) VLASSARA, HELEN General clinical research center Monocyte receptors for AGE-protein in diabetes and aging

M01RR-00102-28 0119 (CLR) KAPPAS, ATTALLAH General clinical research center Hepatic function

M01RR-00102-28 0120 (CLR) JONES, ROBERT L General clinical research center Diabetes mellitus and thrombosis

M01RR-00102-28 0121 (CLR) KREEK, MARY JEANNE General clinical research center Neuroendocrine effects of exogenous and endogenous opioids and ethanol

M01RR-00102-28 0139 (CLR) REEVES, WESTLEY H. General clinical research center Mechanisms of autoantibody production in systemic lupus erythematosus

M01RR-00102-28 0143 (CLR) ZABRISKIE, JOHN B. General clinical research center Studies of streptococcal sequel

M01RR-00102-28 0144 (CLR) BRINTON, ELLIOT A General clinical research center Postprandial lipoprotein metabolism

M01RR-00102-28 0145 (CLR) COBB, MARGARET A General clinical research center Effects of dietary fat on lipoprotein and apolipoprotein levels

M01RR-00102-28 0147 (CLR) COHN, ZANVIL A General clinical research center The basic immunology of AIDS

M01RR-00109-28 (CLR) LUGINBUHL, WILLIAM H UNIVERSITY OF VERMONT GIVEN BUILDING BURLINGTON, VT 05405 General clinical research center

M01RR-00109-28 0318 (CLR) CATALANO, PATRICK M. General clinical research center Morphometric measurements in neonates of normal and gestational diabetic women

M01RR-00109-28 0320 (CLR) BOVILLE, EDWIN G General clinical research center In vivo effect of warfarin on vitamin K dependent coagulation proteins

M01RR-00109-28 0325 (CLR) TRACY, PAULA B General clinical research center Prothrombin activation on blood monocuclear cells

M01RR-00109-28 0327 (CLR) POEHLMAN, ERIC General clinical research center Physical activity--Effects on energy metabolism in aging men and women

M01RR-00109-28 0330 (CLR) NAIR, K STREE General clinical research center Plasma amino acids & glucagon response to insulin induced hypoglycemia

M01RR-00109-28 0331 (CLR) SRIRAM, SUBRAMANIAM General clinical research center High dose cytoxan in patients with chronic progressive multiple sclerosis

M01RR-00109-28 0333 (CLR) NAKAJIMA, STEVEN T General clinical research center Modulating role of body composition on reproductive hormones

M01RR-00109-28 0334 (CLR) NAIR, K SREE General clinical research center In vivo regulation of protein turnover by hormones and substances

M01RR-00109-28 0335 (CLR) NEWHOUSE, PAUL General clinical research center The mecamylamine model of dementia

M01RR-00109-28 0336 (CLR) NAKAJIMA, STEVEN T General clinical research center The modulatory roles of exercise on reproductive hormones

M01RR-00109-28 0337 (CLR) CALLES, JORGE General clinical research center Glucagon,substrate cycles,energy used in obesity and type II diabetes

M01RR-00109-28 0338 (CLR) POEHLMAN, ERIC General clinical research center Rates of aging in healthy males and females

M01RR-00109-28 0339 (CLR) TONINO, RICHARD P General clinical research center Potassium supplementation in blood pressure & glucose tolerence in NIDDM

M01RR-00109-28 0340 (CLR) ROBBINS, DAVID C General clinical research center Measurement of apolipoprotein B synthesis and clearance using stable isotope

M01RR-00109-28 0341 (CLR) PLANTE, DENNIS A General clinical research center Subcutaneous RD heparin vs. oral warfarin to prevent DVT in ortho patients

M01RR-00109-28 0344 (CLR) NAKAJIMA, STEVEN General clinical research center Roles of body composition on reproductive hormones with frequent blood sampling

M01RR-00109-28 0106 (CLR) GIBSON, MARK General clinical research center Sequential histology and serum progesterone in luteal phase defect

M01RR-00109-28 0231 (CLR) GRANT, BARBARA W General clinical research center Human megakaryopoiesis

M01RR-00109-28 0345 (CLR) JOHNSON, ROBERT E General clinical research center Follow-up of ACL repair with Macintosh augmentation grafting

M01RR-00109-28 0347 (CLR) HAGSTROM, NATE General clinical research center Respiratory sinus arrhythmia in term and pre-term infants

M01RR-00109-28 0348 (CLR) JOHNSON, ROBERT J General clinical research center Reconstruction of acutely ruptured anterior cruciate ligament

M01RR-00109-28 0349 (CLR) BOVILLE, EDWIN General clinical research center Purification of des-carboxy vitamin K dependent protein from warfarinized blood

M01RR-00109-28 0350 (CLR) POEHLMAN, ERIC General clinical research center Role of age, fitness level and SNS activity on resting metabolic rate

M01RR-00109-28 0351 (CLR) BRADLEY, WALTER General clinical research center Treatment of muscle pain with nitrendipine

M01RR-00109-28 0352 (CLR) BRADLEY, WALTER General clinical research center L-Threonine and branched chain amino acids in amyotrophic lateral sclerosis

M01RR-00109-28 0353 (CLR) HIGGINS, STEPHEN General clinical research center Sedative-stimulant combinations-- Effects on human learning

M01RR-00109-28 0354 (CLR) CALLES, JORGE General clinical research center Synergistic interaction of glucose & epinephrine on metabolism in obesity and DM

M01RR-00109-28 0355 (CLR) DEVLIN, JOHN General clinical research center Effects of dietary supplements with triose compounds in noninsulin dependent DM

M01RR-00109-28 0356 (CLR) DANFORTH, ELLIOT General clinical research center Energy intake, expenditure and balance

M01RR-00109-28 0357 (CLR) BRADLEY, WALTER General clinical research center Quantitation of the effects of exercise in neuromuscular disease

M01RR-00109-28 0358 (CLR) NAIR, K SREE General clinical research center Effect of plasma amino acids on the lipolytic action of catabolic hormones

M01RR-00109-28 0359 (CLR) ADES, PHILIP General clinical research center Effect of ischemia in exercise enhanced blood flow in coronary patients

M01RR-00109-28 0360 (CLR) CALLES, JORGE General clinical research center Substrate cycles in altered nutritional states

M01RR-00109-28 0361 (CLR) DEVLIN, JOHN General clinical research center Effects of exercise on protein metabolism in diabetes

M01RR-00109-28 0234 (CLR) CATALANO, PATRICK M General clinical research center Carbohydrate metabolism in gestational diabetes

M01RR-00109-28 0362 (CLR) NAKAJIMA, STEVEN General clinical research center Diagnosis of luteal phase deficiency-- Evaluation of potential diagnostic tests

M01RR-00109-28 0363 (CLR) CALLES, JORGE General clinical research center MK-6 and warfarin interaction study

M01RR-00109-28 0364 (CLR) GLUM, DIETER General clinical research center Pneumococcal vaccine study

M01RR-00109-28 0365 (CLR) BRODSKY, IRWIN General clinical research center Ketoacid effects on amino acid metabolism in insulin dependent diabetes mellitus

M01RR-00109-28 0366 (CLR) FISCHER, ROBIN General clinical research center Time interval defined for ovulation

M01RR-00109-28 0367 (CLR) BOVILLE, EDWIN General clinical research center Pharmacokinetics and effects of vitamin K in women of child bearing age

M01RR-00109-28 0368 (CLR) DANFORTH, ELLIOT General clinical research center Effect of Ro18-0647 on weight loss in patients with moderate upper body obesity

M01RR-00109-28 0369 (CLR) DANFORTH, ELLIOT General clinical research center Effect of Ro18-0647 on weight loss in patients with severe upper body obesity

M01RR-00109-28 0370 (CLR) NAIR, K SREE General clinical research center Beta-3 agonist effect on energy expenditure & carbohydrate,fat,protein metabolism

M01RR-00109-28 0371 (CLR) FOSTER, ROGER General clinical research center Parathyroidectomy review

M01RR-00109-28 0372 (CLR) SMITH, RICHARD General clinical research center Effects of head position on postoperative complications after tracheal intubation

M01RR-00109-28 0250 (CLR) COLLETTI, RICHARD General clinical research center Cancer, nutrition, and somatomedin-C

M01RR-00109-28 0278 (CLR) HIGGINS, STEPHEN General clinical research center Stimulant-alcohol interactions in humans

M01RR-00109-28 0285 (CLR) NAKAJIMA, STEVEN T General clinical research center The secretory pattern of progesterone in early pregnancy

M01RR-00109-28 0286 (CLR) NAKAJIMA, STEVEN T General clinical research center Metabolic clearance rate of progesterone during graded activity

M01RR-00109-28 0287 (CLR) NAKAJIMA, STEVEN T General clinical research center The single-dose pharmacokinetics of human menopausal gonadotropins

M01RR-00109-28 0297 (CLR) RITTENHOUSE, SUSAN E. General clinical research center Phosphoinositide metabolism and platelet secretion

M01RR-00109-28 0298 (CLR) BRADLEY, WALTER G. General clinical research center Flunarizine for chronic neurodegenerations

M01RR-00109-28 0299 (CLR) BOVILLE, EDWIN G General clinical research center Maturation of neonatal vitamin K dependent hemostasis

M01RR-00109-28 0300 (CLR) TONINO, RICHARD P General clinical research center Exercise effects on sodium-potassium parameters of red blood cells

M01RR-00109-28 0301 (CLR) GIBSON, MARK General clinical research center Physiology of luteal phase defect

M01RR-00109-28 0303 (CLR) BEEKEN, WARREN L. General clinical

PROJECT NO., ORGANIZATIONAL UNIT., INVESTIGATOR, ADDRESS, TITLE

research center Controlled trial of 4-ASA in ulcerative colitis
M01RR-00109-28 0305 (CLR) LUCEY, JEROLD F. General clinical research center Randomized trial on IV immunoglobin to prevent neonatal infection
M01RR-00109-28 0308 (CLR) LEITENBERG, HAROLD General clinical research center Resting metabolic rate in bulimia nervosa
M01RR-00109-28 0310 (CLR) GIBSON, MARK General clinical research center Effect of progesterone on luteinizing hormone secretion
M01RR-00109-28 0311 (CLR) DEATON, JEFFERY L. General clinical research center Effect of spironolactone on hypothalmic pituitary axis
M01RR-00109-28 0314 (CLR) DEVLIN, JOHN T. General clinical research center Dietary protein restriction effect on protein/fuel metabolism in type 1 DM
M01RR-00109-28 0315 (CLR) ADES, PHILLIP A. General clinical research center Magnitude and mechanisms of exercise conditioning in older coronary patients
M01RR-00109-28 0316 (CLR) JARRELL, MAUREEN A General clinical research center Pharmacokinetics of vaginal absorption of 5-fluorouracil
M01RR-00125-28 (CLR) DONALDSON, ROBERT YALE UNIVERSITY P O BOX 3333 NEW HAVEN, CONN 06510 General clinical research center
M01RR-00125-28 0766 (CLR) FRYBURG, DAVID General clinical research center Hormonal regulation of skeletal muscle protein metabolism in humans
M01RR-00125-28 0767 (CLR) INSOGNA, KARL General clinical research center Renal hypophosphatemia
M01RR-00125-28 0768 (CLR) MALAWISTA, STEPHEN General clinical research center Phase III clinical study of the UVAR photopheresis system
M01RR-00125-28 0769 (CLR) RIDDLE, MARK General clinical research center Comparative NMR clinical studies
M01RR-00125-28 0770 (CLR) MILSTONE, LEONARD General clinical research center Effect of retinoids on calcium metabolism and bone mineralization
M01RR-00125-28 0771 (CLR) RIDDLE, MARK General clinical research center Assessment of regional blood flow in healthy subjects
M01RR-00125-28 0772 (CLR) RODIN, JUDITH General clinical research center Metabolic consequences of weight cycling
M01RR-00125-28 0773 (CLR) SHERWIN, ROBERT General clinical research center Hormonal response to hypoglycemia-- Effect of diabetes
M01RR-00125-28 0774 (CLR) TAMBORLANE, WILLIAM General clinical research center Effects of puberty on glucose kinetics
M01RR-00125-28 0775 (CLR) WHITE, ROBERT General clinical research center Pullback atherectomy catheter for treatment of stenoses or occlusion of the leg
M01RR-00125-28 0448 (CLR) TAMBORLANE, WILLIAM V General clinical research center Juvenile diabetes treatment with insulin infusion pump
M01RR-00125-28 0571 (CLR) BARRETT, EUGENE General clinical research center Regulation of skeletal muscle protein metabolism in man
M01RR-00125-28 0575 (CLR) HENDLER, ROSA General clinical research center Catecholamine in obesity during fasting , refeeding with low calorie diet
M01RR-00125-28 0592 (CLR) TAMBORLANE, WILLIAM General clinical research center Diabetes control and complication trial
M01RR-00125-28 0631 (CLR) COMITE, FLORENCE General clinical research center Treatment of endometriosis with nafarelin
M01RR-00125-28 0651 (CLR) MERRILL, WILLIAM W General clinical research center Epithelial surface proteins--Markers of cancer risk
M01RR-00125-28 0656 (CLR) ROBBINS, RICHARD General clinical research center Etiology of acromegaly
M01RR-00125-28 0663 (CLR) TAMBORLANE, WILLIAM V General clinical research center Effects of hospitalization on diabetes management
M01RR-00125-28 0678 (CLR) DIAMOND, MICHAEL General clinical research center Counterregulatory hormonal response to hypoglycemia in diabetic pregnancies
M01RR-00125-28 0679 (CLR) DIAMOND, MICHAEL General clinical research center Glucose homeostasis evaluation
M01RR-00125-28 0685 (CLR) KOSTEN, THOMAS R General clinical research center Cocaine challenge during maintenance pharmacotherapy
M01RR-00125-28 0689 (CLR) MATTSON, RICHARD H General clinical research center Gamma vinyl GABA (vigabatrin) in the treatment of epilepsy
M01RR-00125-28 0690 (CLR) MATTSON, RICHARD H General clinical research center Efficacy and safety of gabapentin in treatment of partial seizures
M01RR-00125-28 0695 (CLR) PRICE, LAWRENCE H General clinical research center Effects of low tryptophan diet on serotonergic function
M01RR-00125-28 0696 (CLR) REUBEN, ADRIAN General clinical research center Biliary tract imaging and stenosis of the sphincter of Oddi
M01RR-00125-28 0697 (CLR) RIDDLE, MARK General clinical research center Fluoxetine treatment of Tourette's syndrome
M01RR-00125-28 0708 (CLR) CHAPPELL, PHILLIP B General clinical research center Spiradolin mesylate in the treatment of Tourette syndrome and related disorders
M01RR-00125-28 0709 (CLR) COMITE, FLORENCE General clinical research center Reversible hypothalamic-pituitary-gonadal suppression using GnRH analog
M01RR-00125-28 0718 (CLR) DIAMOND, MICHAEL P General clinical research center Assessment of counterregulatory hormone response in women
M01RR-00125-28 0720 (CLR) ELEFTERIADES, J A General clinical research center Remote stimulation by radiofrequency transmission
M01RR-00125-28 0722 (CLR) INSOGNA, KARL General clinical research center Intravenous aminohydroxypropylidene bisphosphonate for Paget's disease
M01RR-00125-28 0723 (CLR) LECKMAN, JAMES F General clinical research center Neurobiology of Tourette's syndrome and related disorders
M01RR-00125-28 0724 (CLR) MALAWISTA, STEVEN E General clinical research center Rheumatoid arthritis and photophoresis
M01RR-00125-28 0729 (CLR) SHERWIN, ROBERT S General clinical research center Role of contrainsulin hormones in diabetes

PROJECT NO., ORGANIZATIONAL UNIT., INVESTIGATOR, ADDRESS, TITLE

M01RR-00125-28 0731 (CLR) SHULMAN, GERALD I General clinical research center Carbon 13 NMR studies of liver and muscle glycogen turnover in man
M01RR-00125-28 0732 (CLR) SHULMAN, GERALD I General clinical research center Noninvasive studies of hepatic carbohydrate metabolism using glycoconjugates
M01RR-00125-28 0733 (CLR) BROADUS, ARTHUR E General clinical research center Evaluation of human calcium metabolism
M01RR-00125-28 0734 (CLR) BIA, MARGARET J General clinical research center Investigation of the pathogenesis of hyperkalemia
M01RR-00125-28 0735 (CLR) BLACK, HENRY R General clinical research center Multicenter evaluation of the study and efficacy of once-daily isradipine
M01RR-00125-28 0736 (CLR) BOYER, JAMES L General clinical research center Controlled trial of ursodeoxycholic acid in primary biliary cirrhosis
M01RR-00125-28 0738 (CLR) DUBROW, ROBERT General clinical research center Serum gastrin and colorectal neoplasms
M01RR-00125-28 0740 (CLR) HENDLER, ROSA G General clinical research center Glimepiride (HOE 490) in patients with non-insulin dependent diabetes
M01RR-00125-28 0741 (CLR) INSOGNA, KARL L General clinical research center APD for treatment of Paget's disease
M01RR-00125-28 0743 (CLR) SCHEYER, RICHARD D General clinical research center Gabapentin safety and efficacy for epilepsy
M01RR-00125-28 0744 (CLR) PEREZ, MARITZA I General clinical research center Photophoresis in scleroderma
M01RR-00125-28 0747 (CLR) RANKIN, JOHN A General clinical research center Alveolar macrophage and airways mediators in asthma
M01RR-00125-28 0748 (CLR) RIDDLE, MARK A General clinical research center Cerebral blood flow using TC-99m HM-PAO in adults with Tourette's Syndrome
M01RR-00125-28 0749 (CLR) SHERWIN, ROBERT S General clinical research center Glucose threshold for cerebral dysfunction during hypoglycemia in diabetes
M01RR-00125-28 0754 (CLR) WHITE, ROBERT I General clinical research center Biliary lithotripsy
M01RR-00125-28 0755 (CLR) SHULMAN, GERALD I General clinical research center Safety and efficacy of CP-72, 467 Type II (NIDDM) diabetic patients
M01RR-00125-28 0756 (CLR) BATSFORD, WILLIAM General clinical research center Extended release indecainide for ventricular arrhythmias
M01RR-00125-28 0757 (CLR) AHERN, JOANN General clinical research center Twenty four hour ambulatory blood pressure monitoring in children with IDDM
M01RR-00125-28 0758 (CLR) BARRETT, EUGENE General clinical research center Lovastatin vs gemfibrozil to lower lipids in glipizide treated type II diabetes
M01RR-00125-28 0759 (CLR) BERKMAN, LISA General clinical research center MacArthur network on sucessful aging phase II-- Response to challenge
M01RR-00125-28 0760 (CLR) BINDER, HENRY General clinical research center Diagnosis and treatment of diarrhea
M01RR-00125-28 0761 (CLR) BOULWARE, SUSAN General clinical research center Metabolic effects of IGF-1
M01RR-00125-28 0762 (CLR) BUZAID, ANTONIO General clinical research center Cyclosporin A and vinblastine in refractory malignancies
M01RR-00125-28 0763 (CLR) BUZAID, ANTONIO General clinical research center Cisplatin, decarbazine and tamozifen treatment for neoplasms
M01RR-00125-28 0764 (CLR) DIAMOND, MICHAEL General clinical research center Glucose metabolism in women
M01RR-00125-28 0710 (CLR) COOPER, DENNIS General clinical research center Phase I pilot of weekly carboplatin and methotrexate in cancer patients
M01RR-00125-28 0711 (CLR) COOPER, DENNIS General clinical research center Phase I pilot of carmustine used with thymidine in cancer patients
M01RR-00125-28 0765 (CLR) DIAMOND, MICHAEL General clinical research center Low dose insulin administration as a supplement to ovulation induction
P40RR-00130-28 (AR) STRANDBERG, JOHN D JOHNS HOPKINS UNIV SCHOOL OF M 720 RUTLAND AVENUE BALTIMORE, MD 21205 Animal resources support for biomedical research
P40RR-00130-28 0112 (AR) BUNTON, TRACIE Animal resources support for biomedical research Aspects of copper metabolism in fish
P40RR-00130-28 0113 (AR) ZINK, CHRISTINE Animal resources support for biomedical research Visna virus in sheep
P40RR-00130-28 0114 (AR) CORK, LINDA Animal resources support for biomedical research Genetic linkage in the dog
P40RR-00130-28 0115 (AR) STRANDBERG, J Animal resources support for biomedical research Brahamella catarrhalis--An upper respiratory pathogen
P51RR-00163-32 (AR) KOHLER, PETER O OREGON REGIONAL PRIMATE RES CT 505 NORTHWEST 185TH AVENUE BEAVERTON OR 97006 Support for regional primate research center
P51RR-00163-32 0008 (AR) BETHEA, CYNTHIA L Support for regional primate research center Reproductive biology and behavior
P51RR-00163-32 0009 (AR) BRENNER, R M Support for regional primate research center Reproductive biology and behavior
P51RR-00163-32 0010 (AR) CRITCHLOW, B VAUGHN Support for regional primate research center Reproductive biology and behavior
P51RR-00163-32 0011 (AR) EATON, GRAY G Support for regional primate research center Reproductive biology and behavior
P51RR-00163-32 0013 (AR) HOSKINS, DALE D Support for regional primate research center Reproductive biology and behavior
P51RR-00163-32 0014 (AR) NOVY, MILES J Support for regional primate research center Reproductive biology and behavior
P51RR-00163-32 0015 (AR) PHOENIX, C N Support for regional primate research center Reproductive biology and behavior
P51RR-00163-32 0016 (AR) RESKO, JOHN A Support for regional primate research center Reproductive biology and behavior
P51RR-00163-32 0017 (AR) SPIES, HAROLD G Support for regional

primate research center Reproductive biology and behavior
P51RR-00163-32 0027 (AR) FAHRENBACH, WOLF H Support for regional primate research center Division of Neurosciences
P51RR-00163-32 0028 (AR) MACHIDA, CURTIS Support for regional primate research center Division of neurosciences
P51RR-00163-32 0029 (AR) OJEDA, SERGIO Support for regional primate research center Division of neurosciences
P51RR-00163-32 0034 (AR) STOUFFER, RICHARD L Support for regional primate research center Division of reproductive biology and behavior
P51RR-00163-32 0035 (AR) WOLF, DONALD P Support for regional primate research center Division of reproductive biology and behavior
P51RR-00163-32 0036 (AR) MALINOW, RENE Support for regional primate research center Division of primate medicine
P51RR-00163-32 0037 (AR) HOWARD, CHARLES F Support for regional primate research center Division of primate medicine
P51RR-00163-32 0038 (AR) MALLEY, A Support for regional primate research center Division of primate medicine
P51RR-00163-32 0039 (AR) AXTHELM, MICHAEL K Support for regional primate research center Division of primate medicine--SAIDS
P51RR-00163-32 9001 (AR) TOYOOKA, ARTHUR Support for regional primate research center Core--Physical plant
P51RR-00163-32 9002 (AR) MCNULTY, WILBUR P Support for regional primate research center Core--Primate medicine
P51RR-00163-32 9003 (AR) AXTHELM, MICHAEL Support for regional primate research center Core--Pathology
P51RR-00163-32 9004 (AR) OLSON, LEONARD Support for regional primate research center Core--Animal science and primate breeding
P51RR-00163-32 9005 (AR) OLSON, LEONARD Support for regional primate research center Core--Aging set-aside colony
P51RR-00163-32 9006 (AR) AXTHELM, MICHAEL Support for regional primate research center Core--Surgery
P51RR-00163-32 9007 (AR) COFFIN, ROBERT W Support for regional primate research center Core--Data processing
P51RR-00163-32 9009 (AR) FAHRENBACH, W H Support for regional primate research center Core--Electron microscopy
P51RR-00163-32 9010 (AR) MCDONALD, ISABEL Support for regional primate research center Core--Research library
P51RR-00163-32 9011 (AR) ITO, JOEL Support for regional primate research center Core--Medical illustration
P51RR-00163-32 9012 (AR) HESS, DAVID Support for regional primate research center Core--Radioimmunoassay laboratory
P51RR-00163-32 9014 (AR) KOHLER, PETER O Support for regional primate research center Core--Health and safety
P51RR-00163-32 9015 (AR) GLIESSMAN, PERRY M Support for regional primate research center Core--Bioengineering
P51RR-00163-32 9016 (AR) SHIIGI, S M Support for regional primate research center Core--Flow cytometry laboratory
P51RR-00163-32 9017 (AR) STOUFFER, RICHARD L Support for regional primate research center Core--In vitro fertilization laboratory
P51RR-00163-32 0030 (AR) SANETO, RUSSELL Support for regional primate research center Division of neurosciences
P51RR-00163-32 0031 (AR) URBANSKI, HENRYK Support for regional primate research center Division of neurosciences
P51RR-00163-32 0032 (AR) MASLAR, ILA Support for regional primate research center Division of reproductive biology and behavior
P51RR-00163-32 0033 (AR) MELNER, MICHAEL H Support for regional primate research center Division of reproductive biology and behavior
P51RR-00164-30 (AR) VANSELOW, NEAL A TULANE UNIVERSITY 1430 TULANE AVENUE NEW ORLEANS, LA 70112 Support for regional primate research center
P51RR-00164-30 0006 (AR) GORMUS, ROBERT J Support for regional primate research center Experimental leprosy vaccine study
P51RR-00164-30 0011 (AR) BASKIN, GARY B Support for regional primate research center Pathology of SIV-D infection
P51RR-00164-30 0012 (AR) BLANCHARD, JAMES LEE Support for regional primate research center Pilot study--Antemortem diagnosis of amyloidosis
P51RR-00164-30 0013 (AR) SOIKE, KENNETH F Support for regional primate research center Myocardiatis resulting from encephalomyocarditis virus infection
P51RR-00164-30 0014 (AR) SOIKE, KENNETH F Support for regional primate research center Flow cytometry in the analysis of intracellular viral antigens
P51RR-00164-30 0015 (AR) GORMUS, ROBERT J Support for regional primate research center Peripheral nerve function in primary neuritic leprosy
P51RR-00164-30 0016 (AR) GORMUS, ROBERT J Support for regional primate research center Development of model for experimental leprosy
P51RR-00164-30 0020 (AR) RANGAN, S R S Support for regional primate research center Protection against SIV-induced diseases with monoclonal antibodies
P51RR-00164-30 0021 (AR) CLARKE, MARGARET RUTH Support for regional primate research center Rhesus monkey breeding colony for SAIDS research
P51RR-00164-30 0022 (AR) LOWRIE, ROBERT C Support for regional primate research center Animal model for Wuchereria bancrofti infection
P51RR-00164-30 0023 (AR) LOWRIE, ROBERT C Support for regional primate research center Effect of concomitant filarial infections in mosquitoes
P51RR-00164-30 0024 (AR) LANNERS, H NORBET Support for regional primate research center Cultivation of plasmodium vivax from infected blood
P51RR-00164-30 0025 (AR) LANNERS, H NORBET Support for regional primate research center The spleen in concomitant filarial and malaria infections
P51RR-00164-30 0026 (AR) LANNERS, H NORBERT Support for regional primate research center Immunosuppression in monkeys infected with Plasmodium inui
P51RR-00164-30 0027 (AR) RANGAN, S R S Support for regional primate research center Interactions of SIV, EBV and CMV in experimental AIDS
P51RR-00164-30 0028 (AR) DIDIER, PETER J Support for regional primate research center Endothelial susceptibility and response to SIV infection
P51RR-00164-30 0029 (AR) BLANCHARD, JAMES LEE Support for regional primate research center Pathophysiology of gastroinatestinal disease in SAIDS
P51RR-00164-30 0030 (AR) CLARK, MARGARET RUTH Support for regional primate research center Effects of rearing on behavior and susceptibility to SIV infection
P51RR-00164-30 0031 (AR) ROBERTS, JAMES A Support for regional primate research center Host-parasite interaction in pyelonephritis
P51RR-00164-30 0032 (AR) ROBERTS, JAMES A Support for regional primate research center Induced benign prostatic hyperplasia
P51RR-00164-30 0033 (AR) ROBERTS, JAMES A Support for regional primate research center Pathophysiology of prostatitis
P51RR-00164-30 0034 (AR) ROBERTS, JAMES A Support for regional primate research center Bladder function
P51RR-00164-30 0035 (AR) BRIZZEE, KENNETH R Support for regional primate research center Neuroanatomy of the urinary tract
P51RR-00164-30 0036 (AR) ROBERTS, JAMES A Support for regional primate research center Infertility due to bacterial adherence
P51RR-00164-30 0037 (AR) HARRISON, RICHARD M Support for regional primate research center Insemination with cryopreserved sperm
P51RR-00164-30 9001 (AR) WATKINS, ROBERT A Support for regional primate research center Core--Science information
P51RR-00164-30 9002 (AR) WATKINS, ROBERT A Support for regional primate research center Core--Medical illustrations
P51RR-00164-30 9003 (AR) MENDOW, LOUIS Support for regional primate research center Core--Physical plant
P51RR-00164-30 9004 (AR) WATKINS, ROBERT A Support for regional primate research center Core--Glassware and laundry
P51RR-00164-30 9005 (AR) WOLF, ROBERT H Support for regional primate research center Core--Veterinary sciences department
P51RR-00164-30 9006 (AR) WOLF, ROBERT H Support for regional primate research center Core--Center breeding
P51RR-00164-30 9008 (AR) CABIRAC, HEWITT B Support for regional primate research center Core--Surgery
P51RR-00164-30 9009 (AR) BASKIN, GARY B Support for regional primate research center Core--Pathology unit
P51RR-00164-30 9010 (AR) BASKIN, GARY B Support for regional primate research center Core--Clinical laboratory
P51RR-00164-30 9011 (AR) MEINERS, NORWOOD Support for regional primate research center Core--Electron microscopy
P51RR-00164-30 9013 (AR) BLANCHARD, JAMES LEE Support for regional primate research center Core--Parasitology service laboratory
P51RR-00164-30 9014 (AR) CLARKE, MARGARET RUTH Support for regional primate research center Core--Breeding colony for SIV research
P51RR-00164-30 9015 (AR) GERONE, PETER J Support for regional primate research center Core--Building improvement and modernization
P51RR-00164-30 0017 (AR) GORMUS, ROBERT J Support for regional primate research center Antibody responses to 65KD antigen of Mycobacterium leprae
P51RR-00164-30 0018 (AR) RANGAN, S R S Support for regional primate research center Pilot study--Epstein-Barr virus related lymphoproliferative diseases
P51RR-00164-30 0019 (AR) MURPHEY-CORB, MICHAEL Support for regional primate research center Neonatal development on maternal-fetal transmission of SIV-D
P51RR-00165-31 (AR) HATCHER, CHARLES R EMORY UNIVERSITY ATLANTA, GA 30322 Support of Yerkes Regional Primate Research Center
P51RR-00165-31 0197 (AR) SOMMADOSSI, JEAN-PIERRE Support of Yerkes Regional Primate Research Center Study of SIV-infected rhesus monkeys to evaluate novel anti-HIV drug combinations
P51RR-00165-31 0198 (AR) MCCLURE, HAROLD M Support of Yerkes Regional Primate Research Center Development of experimental HIV-2 infection in macaques as a model for human AIDS
P51RR-00165-31 0199 (AR) VILLINGER, FRANCOIS Support of Yerkes Regional Primate Research Center Polymerase chain reaction (PCR) for the diagnosis of retrovirus infections
P51RR-00165-31 0200 (AR) ANDERSON, DANIEL C Support of Yerkes Regional Primate Research Center Pathogenesis, immunology, & pathology of natural SIV infection
P51RR-00165-31 0201 (AR) JOHNSON, PHILIP Support of Yerkes Regional Primate Research Center Clone and sequence SIV viruses from Sykes monkeys and stumptail macaques
P51RR-00165-31 0202 (AR) MCCLURE, HAROLD M Support of Yerkes Regional Primate Research Center Pathogenesis & pathogenicity of newly isolated SIV's from rhesus & pigtail macaca
P51RR-00165-31 0203 (AR) MCCLURE, HAROLD M Support of Yerkes Regional Primate Research Center Determination of the appropriateness of cynomolgus monkeys for SIV animal model
P51RR-00165-31 0204 (AR) ANSARI, AFTAB A Support of Yerkes Regional Primate Research Center Role of cytokines in disease susceptibility, pig-tailed macaque vs sooty mangabey
P51RR-00165-31 0205 (AR) ANSARI, AFTAB A Support of Yerkes Regional Primate Research Center Role of TNF-a in lethal disease of pig-tailed macaques infected with SIVsmmPBj
P51RR-00165-31 0154 (AR) BARD, KIM A Support of Yerkes Regional Primate Research Center Developmental research on mother-reared chimpanzees
P51RR-00165-31 0162 (AR) MANN, DAVID R Support of Yerkes Regional Primate Research Center Nonhuman primate models for osteoporosis
P51RR-00165-31 0163 (AR) MANN, DAVID R Support of Yerkes Regional Primate Research Center Neonatal testosterone and primate sexual development
P51RR-00165-31 0164 (AR) MARTIN, DAVID E Support of Yerkes Regional Primate Research Center Reproductive function in paraplegic humans
P51RR-00165-31 0169 (AR) SMITH, EUCLID O Support of Yerkes Regional Primate Research Center Coevolution of male & female reproductive tactics in free-ranging baboons, Kenya
P51RR-00165-31 0206 (AR) ANSARI, AFTAB A Support of Yerkes Regional Primate Research Center Role of virus strain, host genetic or

PROJECT NO., ORGANIZATIONAL UNIT., INVESTIGATOR, ADDRESS, TITLE

immunologic makeup in SIV infection
P51RR-00165-31 0207 (AR) ANSARI, AFTAB A Support of Yerkes Regional Primate Research Center SIV proteins or sequences that induce proliferative & cytotoxic response
P51RR-00165-31 0208 (AR) ANSARI, AFTAB A Support of Yerkes Regional Primate Research Center Mechanism of mangabey CD8+ T cells to mediate suppression of SIVsmm replication
P51RR-00165-31 0209 (AR) GORDON, THOMAS P Support of Yerkes Regional Primate Research Center Retrovirus-free mangabey, rhesus macaque, and pig-tailed macaque breeding colony
P51RR-00165-31 0210 (AR) MCCLURE, HAROLD M Support of Yerkes Regional Primate Research Center Surveillance of retrovirus infection at Yerkes Center
P51RR-00165-31 9002 (AR) MCCLURE, HAROLD M. Support of Yerkes Regional Primate Research Center Core--Diagnostic pathology
P51RR-00165-31 9003 (AR) WILSON, MARK E. Support of Yerkes Regional Primate Research Center Core--Radioimmunoassay laboratory
P51RR-00165-31 9005 (AR) SWENSON, BRENT Support of Yerkes Regional Primate Research Center Core--Veterinary medicine
P51RR-00165-31 9006 (AR) PRALINSKY, KAREN Support of Yerkes Regional Primate Research Center Primate care and housing core, great ape wing--Main station
P51RR-00165-31 9007 (AR) PRALINSKY, KAREN Support of Yerkes Regional Primate Research Center Core--Small primate wing
P51RR-00165-31 9008 (AR) CHIKAZAWA, DENNIS Support of Yerkes Regional Primate Research Center Core--Field station for primate care
P51RR-00165-31 9009 (AR) ELSE, JAMES Support of Yerkes Regional Primate Research Center Core--Primate breeding
P51RR-00165-31 9012 (AR) JOHNS, NELLIE O Support of Yerkes Regional Primate Research Center Core--Library
P51RR-00165-31 9013 (AR) KIERNAN, FRANK H. Support of Yerkes Regional Primate Research Center Core--Photography
P51RR-00165-31 9014 (AR) SMITH, MICHAEL Support of Yerkes Regional Primate Research Center Core--General shop
P51RR-00165-31 9015 (AR) PHIPPS, TIMOTHY Support of Yerkes Regional Primate Research Center Core--Bioelectronics and instrumentation shop
P51RR-00165-31 9019 (AR) BUDDINGTON, ROGER W Support of Yerkes Regional Primate Research Center Core--Computer services
P51RR-00165-31 9020 (AR) APKARIAN, ROBERT Support of Yerkes Regional Primate Research Center Core--Scanning electron microscopy
P51RR-00165-31 0170 (AR) MORRIS, R D Support of Yerkes Regional Primate Research Center Neuropsychological foundations project
P51RR-00165-31 0171 (AR) VAUCLAIR, J Support of Yerkes Regional Primate Research Center Task & social influences on the expression of primate laterality
P51RR-00165-31 0172 (AR) BERNTSON, GARY G Support of Yerkes Regional Primate Research Center Numerical competence and reasoning in the chimpanzee
P51RR-00165-31 0173 (AR) DE WAAL, FRANS B M Support of Yerkes Regional Primate Research Center Relation between space and aggression in rhesus macaques
P51RR-00165-31 0174 (AR) GOUZOULES, HAROLD T Support of Yerkes Regional Primate Research Center Comparative studies of primate vocal communication
P51RR-00165-31 0175 (AR) GUST, DEBORAH A Support of Yerkes Regional Primate Research Center Social relationships and stress
P51RR-00165-31 0176 (AR) TIGGES, JOHANNES W Support of Yerkes Regional Primate Research Center Study of the aging rhesus monkey
P51RR-00165-31 0177 (AR) TIGGES, MARGARETE H Support of Yerkes Regional Primate Research Center Visual information processing
P51RR-00165-31 0178 (AR) KENNEDY, PHILIP R Support of Yerkes Regional Primate Research Center Neural prosthetics
P51RR-00165-31 0179 (AR) LAMBERT, SCOTT R Support of Yerkes Regional Primate Research Center Correction of monocular aphakia in monkeys with intraocular lenses
P51RR-00165-31 0180 (AR) STONE, RICHARD A Support of Yerkes Regional Primate Research Center Neurochemical mechanism of ocular growth and refractive errors
P51RR-00165-31 0181 (AR) MCCLURE, HAROLD M Support of Yerkes Regional Primate Research Center Paratuberculosis in macaque monkeys
P51RR-00165-31 0182 (AR) MCCLURE, HAROLD M Support of Yerkes Regional Primate Research Center Arthritis, amyloidosis, and yersiniosis in macaque monkeys
P51RR-00165-31 0183 (AR) KLUMPP, SHERRY A Support of Yerkes Regional Primate Research Center Determination of the pathogenicity of group 2 aerotolerant campylobacter
P51RR-00165-31 0184 (AR) NADLER, RONALD D Support of Yerkes Regional Primate Research Center The basis of nonreproductive mating in chimpanzees
P51RR-00165-31 0185 (AR) NADLER, RONALD Support of Yerkes Regional Primate Research Center Mother-infant relations and lactational amenorrhea in gorillas
P51RR-00165-31 0186 (AR) COLLINS, DELWOOD C Support of Yerkes Regional Primate Research Center Control of reproduction in primates
P51RR-00165-31 0187 (AR) YOUNG, LEONA G Support of Yerkes Regional Primate Research Center Components of the sperm cell surface
P51RR-00165-31 0188 (AR) EBERHARD, MARK L Support of Yerkes Regional Primate Research Center Parasitological response of chimpanzees and mangabeys exposed to O. volvulus
P51RR-00165-31 0189 (AR) LAMMIE, PATRICK Support of Yerkes Regional Primate Research Center Studies of the immunologic characteristics of Bancroftian filariasis
P51RR-00165-31 0190 (AR) OFFENBACHER, STEVEN Support of Yerkes Regional Primate Research Center Studies of gingivitis and periodontitis in the rhesus monkey model
P51RR-00165-31 0191 (AR) WARING, GEORGE O Support of Yerkes Regional Primate Research Center Refractive corneal surgery research
P51RR-00165-31 0192 (AR) KEYSERLING, HARRY L Support of Yerkes Regional Primate Research Center Ontogeny of immune responses to vaccines
P51RR-00165-31 0193 (AR) HARKER, LAURENCE A Support of Yerkes Regional Primate Research Center Studies of thrombus formation, vascular injury, and platelet kinetics
P51RR-00165-31 0194 (AR) HANSON, STEPHEN R Support of Yerkes Regional Primate Research Center Thrombosis, thromboembolism, vascular grafts, and hemostasis in the baboon model
P51RR-00165-31 0195 (AR) ANSARI, AFTAB A Support of Yerkes Regional Primate Research Center Develop assays to measure cytokines in nonhuman primates
P51RR-00165-31 0196 (AR) ANSARI, AFTAB A Support of Yerkes Regional Primate Research Center Association of NK, LAK, MLR, and CTL function with age
P51RR-00165-31 0052 (AR) GOULD, KENNETH Support of Yerkes Regional Primate Research Center Reproductive biology of primates
P51RR-00165-31 0055 (AR) MAPLE, TERRY Support of Yerkes Regional Primate Research Center Atlanta Zoo affiliation
P51RR-00165-31 0067 (AR) BYRD, LARRY D Support of Yerkes Regional Primate Research Center Recall and recognition in aged Rhesus monkeys
P51RR-00165-31 0069 (AR) GORDON, THOMAS P Support of Yerkes Regional Primate Research Center Factors influencing primate reproduction
P51RR-00165-31 0077 (AR) NADLER, RONALD D Support of Yerkes Regional Primate Research Center Reproductive behavior and physiology of the gibbon
P51RR-00165-31 0079 (AR) RUMBAUGH, DUANE M Support of Yerkes Regional Primate Research Center Cognitive studies project
P51RR-00165-31 0084 (AR) TOMASELLO, W MICHAEL Support of Yerkes Regional Primate Research Center Investigation of chimpanzee gestural communication and tool use
P51RR-00165-31 0087 (AR) WALLEN, KIM Support of Yerkes Regional Primate Research Center Steroid binding, estrogen availability, and female behavior
P51RR-00165-31 0090 (AR) BAKAY, ROY A E Support of Yerkes Regional Primate Research Center Plasticity of the neocortex and the development of epilepsy
P51RR-00165-31 0091 (AR) BOOTHE, RONALD G Support of Yerkes Regional Primate Research Center Studies of strabismus and aphakic amblyopia
P51RR-00165-31 0093 (AR) HERNDON, JAMES G Support of Yerkes Regional Primate Research Center Mating seasonality in the male rhesus monkey
P51RR-00165-31 0095 (AR) IUVONE, PAUL MICHAEL Support of Yerkes Regional Primate Research Center Pharmacological manipulation of eye growth and myopia in primates
P51RR-00165-31 0105 (AR) ANDERSON, DANIEL C Support of Yerkes Regional Primate Research Center Amyloidosis in nonhuman primates
P51RR-00165-31 0107 (AR) ANSARI, AFTAB A Support of Yerkes Regional Primate Research Center Studies of phylogeny & ontogeny of immunosurveillance immune system in primates
P51RR-00165-31 0108 (AR) COLLINS, WILLIAM E Support of Yerkes Regional Primate Research Center Induction of Plasmodium infections for malaria vaccine studies
P51RR-00165-31 0111 (AR) ISAHAKIA, MOHAMED Support of Yerkes Regional Primate Research Center Seroprevalence & virus isolation of SIV in feral East African nonhuman primates
P51RR-00165-31 0117 (AR) GREENE, BRUCE M Support of Yerkes Regional Primate Research Center Characterization & cloning of protective antigens of O. volvulus
P51RR-00165-31 0121 (AR) MALIZIA, ANTHONY Support of Yerkes Regional Primate Research Center Subureteric injection of polytef for treatment of urinary incontinence
P51RR-00165-31 0123 (AR) MCCAREY, BERNARD E Support of Yerkes Regional Primate Research Center Refractive keratoplasty
P51RR-00165-31 0124 (AR) MCCLURE, HAROLD M Support of Yerkes Regional Primate Research Center Evaluation of the long-term effects of irradiation in rhesus monkeys
P51RR-00165-31 0127 (AR) MCCLURE, HAROLD M Support of Yerkes Regional Primate Research Center Natural SIVsmm and STLV-1 infection in a breeding colony of sooty mangabeys
P51RR-00165-31 0129 (AR) JOHNSON, PHILIP Support of Yerkes Regional Primate Research Center Characterization of SIVsmmPBj, an acutely lethal strain of SIV
P51RR-00165-31 0131 (AR) MCCLURE, HAROLD M Support of Yerkes Regional Primate Research Center Prevalence of yersinia species in wild rodent population
P51RR-00165-31 0132 (AR) MCCLURE, HAROLD M Support of Yerkes Regional Primate Research Center Prophylactic effects of AZT in SIVsmm-infected pig-tailed macaques
P51RR-00165-31 0133 (AR) MCCLURE, HAROLD M Support of Yerkes Regional Primate Research Center Study of macaques infected w/ SIVsmm to see if they develop an AIDS-like disease
P51RR-00165-31 0134 (AR) MCCLURE, HAROLD M Support of Yerkes Regional Primate Research Center Chimpanzees as models for human AIDS
P51RR-00165-31 0135 (AR) METZGAR, RICHARD S Support of Yerkes Regional Primate Research Center Tumor immunology program
P51RR-00165-31 0138 (AR) PATTERSON, C ANNE Support of Yerkes Regional Primate Research Center Radiotelemetry of fetal physiologic parameters in unrestrained primates
P51RR-00165-31 0141 (AR) SEIGLER, HILLIARD F Support of Yerkes Regional Primate Research Center Evaluation of the immunogenicity of selected human melanoma TAA in the chimpanzee
P51RR-00165-31 0143 (AR) WARING, GEORGE O Support of Yerkes Regional Primate Research Center Laser corneal keratomileusis--Histopathology of wound healing
P51RR-00165-31 0144 (AR) WINTON, ELIOTT F Support of Yerkes Regional Primate Research Center Prechemotherapy marrow priming w/ recombinant colony stimulating factor
P51RR-00165-31 0152 (AR) BARD, KIM A Support of Yerkes Regional Primate Research Center Developmental research on nursery-reared chimpanzees
P51RR-00166-30 0085 (SRC) FEIGL, ERIC O. Regional primate reserach center Autonomic control of coronary circulation
P51RR-00166-30 (SRC) LEIN, JOHN N UNIV OF WASHINGTON SC-61 SEATTLE, WA 98195 Regional primate reserach center
P51RR-00166-30 0016 (SRC) ROSE, LYNN M. Regional primate reserach

PROJECT NO., ORGANIZATIONAL UNIT., INVESTIGATOR, ADDRESS, TITLE

center Role of T-cell subsets in the pathogenesis of EAE
P51RR-00166-30 0038 (SRC) FETZ, EBERHARD E Regional primate reserach center Cortical control of forelimb motor units
P51RR-00166-30 0040 (SRC) GLOMSET, JOHN A Regional primate reserach center Omega-3 fatty acids in membrane function
P51RR-00166-30 0052 (SRC) BOWDEN, DOUGLAS M. Regional primate reserach center Macaca fascicularis brain atlas
P51RR-00166-30 0086 (SRC) GALLATIN, W. MICHAEL Regional primate reserach center Lymphocyte homing in normal and SAINS affected primates
P51RR-00166-30 0053 (SRC) BOWDEN, DOUGLAS M. Regional primate reserach center Biomarkers of aging and resource development
P51RR-00166-30 0054 (SRC) CLARK, EDWARD A. Regional primate reserach center Regulation of T-cell activation in SIV-infected lymphocytes
P51RR-00166-30 0055 (SRC) CLARK, EDWARD A. Regional primate reserach center Characterization of B cell differentiation markers
P51RR-00166-30 0056 (SRC) DE VITO, JUNE L. Regional primate reserach center Brain development in Macaca nemestrina
P51RR-00166-30 0057 (SRC) FETZ, EBERHARD E. Regional primate reserach center Neural responses during active and possive limb movement
P51RR-00166-30 0058 (SRC) FETZ, EBERHARD E. Regional primate reserach center Cross-correlation analysis of cortical cells
P51RR-00166-30 0059 (SRC) FUCHS, ALBERT F. Regional primate reserach center Role of mesencephalon in saccade generation and control
P51RR-00166-30 0060 (SRC) FUCHS, ALBERT F Regional primate reserach center Role of the pontine pause units in saccade generation and control
P51RR-00166-30 0061 (SRC) FUCHS, ALBERT F. Regional primate reserach center Afferents to the burst generator for saccadic eye movements
P51RR-00166-30 0062 (SRC) FUCHS, ALBERT F. Regional primate reserach center Role of rostral medulla in voluntary and reflex eye movements
P51RR-00166-30 0063 (SRC) FUCHS, ALBERT F. Regional primate reserach center Role of the accessory optic system in the optokinetic response
P51RR-00166-30 0064 (SRC) FUCHS, ALBERT F. Regional primate reserach center Role of vestibular nuclei in the VOR and voluntary eye movements
P51RR-00166-30 0065 (SRC) FUCHS, ALBERT F. Regional primate reserach center Flocculus and VOR plasticity
P51RR-00166-30 0066 (SRC) GLOMSET, JOHN A. Regional primate reserach center Piacylglycerol kinase
P51RR-00166-30 0067 (SRC) KATZE, MICHAEL G. Regional primate reserach center Regulation of viral gene expression and the molecular level
P51RR-00166-30 0068 (SRC) SACKETT, GENE P. Regional primate reserach center Effects of weaning on lymphocytes and behavior
P51RR-00166-30 0069 (SRC) SACKETT, GENE P. Regional primate reserach center Normal fetal development in pigtailed macaques
P51RR-00166-30 0070 (SRC) SACKETT, GENE P. Regional primate reserach center Computerized touch screen for study of information processing
P51RR-00166-30 0071 (SRC) SACKETT, GENE P. Regional primate reserach center Amino acid defiency and rat embryo teratogenicity
P51RR-00166-30 0072 (SRC) SACKETT, GENE P. Regional primate reserach center Growth and development of low-birth-weight Pigtailed Macaques
P51RR-00166-30 0073 (SRC) SMITH, ORVILLE A. Regional primate reserach center Telemetry of cardiovascular responses during social behavior
P51RR-00166-30 0074 (SRC) SMITH, ORVILLE A. Regional primate reserach center Central autonomic pathways
P51RR-00166-30 0075 (SRC) ANDERSON, MARJORIE E. Regional primate reserach center Basal ganglia and cerebellar information at the thalmus
P51RR-00166-30 0076 (SRC) ANDERSON, MARJORIE E. Regional primate reserach center Basal ganglia output
P51RR-00166-30 0087 (SRC) GERMAN, DWIGHT C. Regional primate reserach center Chromaffin transplants in a model of Parkinsonism
P51RR-00166-30 0088 (SRC) GOODNER, CHARLES J. Regional primate reserach center Regulation of hormone concentration
P51RR-00166-30 0089 (SRC) GUNDERSON, VIRGINIA M. Regional primate reserach center Modeling mental retardation : Early cognitive processess
P51RR-00166-30 0090 (SRC) HENDRICKSON, ANITA Regional primate reserach center Central connections of the retina
P51RR-00166-30 0091 (SRC) HLASTALA, MICHAEL Regional primate reserach center Infant reoiration in sleep
P51RR-00166-30 0092 (SRC) HODSON, ALAN W. Regional primate reserach center Lung injury and repair in hyaline membrane disease
P51RR-00166-30 0093 (SRC) HOFFMAN, ALAN S. Regional primate reserach center Endothelialization of gas discharge treated Daron vascular grafts
P51RR-00166-30 0094 (SRC) KAKAR, FAIZ Regional primate reserach center Carnitine as a biochemical marker of fat intake
P51RR-00166-30 0095 (SRC) KAUSHANSKY, KENNETH Regional primate reserach center Role of colony-stimulating factors in hematopoiesis
P51RR-00166-30 0096 (SRC) KIORPES, LYNNE Regional primate reserach center Hyperactivity development in infant monkeys
P51RR-00166-30 0097 (SRC) KIORPES, LYNNE Regional primate reserach center Quantitative studies of the central visual system
P51RR-00166-30 0098 (SRC) KOERKER, DONNA J. Regional primate reserach center Development of a diabetic primate
P51RR-00166-30 0099 (SRC) KOERKER, DONNA J. Regional primate reserach center Somatostatin-related malabsorption
P51RR-00166-30 0100 (SRC) KOERKER, DONNA J. Regional primate reserach center Islet cell isolation
P51RR-00166-30 0101 (SRC) KUHL, PATRICIA K. Regional primate reserach center Perception of speech sounds

PROJECT NO., ORGANIZATIONAL UNIT., INVESTIGATOR, ADDRESS, TITLE

P51RR-00166-30 0102 (SRC) LIPKIN, EDWARD W. Regional primate reserach center Calcium balance in parenteral nutrition
P51RR-00166-30 0103 (SRC) LYNN, ANNE M. Regional primate reserach center Narcotics and respiratory function in newborn primates
P51RR-00166-30 0104 (SRC) MOTTET, N. KARLE Regional primate reserach center Brain uptake of inorganic mercury
P51RR-00166-30 0077 (SRC) ANDREWS, ROBERT G. Regional primate reserach center Isolated progenitor cell subpopulations
P51RR-00166-30 0078 (SRC) BURBACHER, THOMAS M. Regional primate reserach center Selenium effects of methylmercury metabolism
P51RR-00166-30 0079 (SRC) BURBACHER, THOMAS M. Regional primate reserach center Primate development effects of methylmercury
P51RR-00166-30 0080 (SRC) CLARREN, STERLING K. Regional primate reserach center Temporal factors in alcohol teratogenesis
P51RR-00166-30 0081 (SRC) CLOWES, ALEXANDER W. Regional primate reserach center Mechanism of graft healing
P51RR-00166-30 0082 (SRC) DAGER, S. R. Regional primate reserach center Calibration of fiber-optic probe for gas analysis during lactate infusion
P51RR-00166-30 0083 (SRC) DUBACH, MARK F. Regional primate reserach center Neuron transplant therapy--A model of Parkinsonism
P51RR-00166-30 0084 (SRC) ENSINCK, JOHN W. Regional primate reserach center Differential effect of somatostatin 14 and 28 on postprandial metab.
P51RR-00166-30 0105 (SRC) PAGE, ROY C. Regional primate reserach center Humoral immunity and periodics in a primate model
P51RR-00166-30 0182 (SRC) WILLIAMS, DARRELL D. Regional primate reserach center Cage/ room manipulable devices
P51RR-00166-30 0183 (SRC) CLARK, EDWARD A. Regional primate reserach center Generation and characterization of MnLa antisera
P51RR-00166-30 0184 (SRC) CLARK, EDWARD A. Regional primate reserach center Screening mnla antisera against immunocyte panel
P51RR-00166-30 0185 (SRC) CLARK, EDWARD A. Regional primate reserach center Breeding for genetic markers
P51RR-00166-30 0186 (SRC) CLARK, EDWARD A. Regional primate reserach center Genetic typing of offspring
P51RR-00166-30 0187 (SRC) SMITH, ORVILLE A Regional primate reserach center International program
P51RR-00166-30 9012 (SRC) SPELMAN, FRANCIS A Regional primate reserach center Bioengineering service core
P51RR-00166-30 9013 (SRC) SPELMAN, FRANCIS A Regional primate reserach center Computer services core
P51RR-00166-30 9014 (SRC) MORTON, WILLIAM P Regional primate reserach center Core--seattle colony
P51RR-00166-30 9015 (SRC) MORTON, WILLIAM R Regional primate reserach center Core--Infant primate research laboratory
P51RR-00166-30 9016 (SRC) MORTON, WILLIAM B Regional primate reserach center Core--tissue program
P51RR-00166-30 9017 (SRC) WILLIAMS, DARRELL D Regional primate reserach center Core--primate field station
P51RR-00166-30 9018 (SRC) TSAI, CHE-CHUNG Regional primate reserach center Pathology services core
P51RR-00166-30 9019 (SRC) DE VITO, JUNE L Regional primate reserach center Core--biostructure technology laboratory
P51RR-00166-30 9020 (SRC) CLARK, EDWARD Regional primate reserach center Core--immunologic typing laboratory
P51RR-00166-30 9021 (SRC) CAMINITI, BENELLA Regional primate reserach center Core--primate information center
P51RR-00166-30 9023 (SRC) BOWDEN, DOUGLAS M. Regional primate reserach center Core -- Set-aside aging colony
P51RR-00166-30 9024 (SRC) BOWDEN, DOUGLAS M. Regional primate reserach center Core -- Aging/reserve colony
P51RR-00166-30 9025 (SRC) ROSS, RUSSELL Regional primate reserach center Tissue culture core
P51RR-00166-30 0106 (SRC) PAPAYANNOPOULOU, THALIA Regional primate reserach center Mechanism of reactivation of HbF in the adult
P51RR-00166-30 0150 (SRC) RATHBUN, WILLIAM B. Regional primate reserach center Comparative aspects of glutathione metabolism in lenses
P51RR-00166-30 0151 (SRC) STEINER, ROBERT A. Regional primate reserach center Sex and age differences in LHRIE activity
P51RR-00166-30 0152 (SRC) CLARK, EDWARD A. Regional primate reserach center Immunopotency of a vaccinia - LAVenv recombinant virus
P51RR-00166-30 0153 (SRC) MORTON, WILLIAM R. Regional primate reserach center SAIDS - D vaccine: Trial number 1
P51RR-00166-30 0154 (SRC) MORTON, WILLIAM R. Regional primate reserach center Immunogenicity of a SAIDS - D/WA recombibant vaccinia virus vaccine
P51RR-00166-30 0155 (SRC) MORTON, WILLIAM R. Regional primate reserach center Spontaneous SAIDS - P viremic or rf animals
P51RR-00166-30 0156 (SRC) MORTON, WILLIAM R. Regional primate reserach center Immunogenicity of recombinant vaccinia virus
P51RR-00166-30 0157 (SRC) MORTON, WILLIAM R. Regional primate reserach center SIV transmission study no. 1
P51RR-00166-30 0158 (SRC) MORTON, WILLIAM R. Regional primate reserach center Posage and route in SIV transmission
P51RR-00166-30 0159 (SRC) MORTON, WILLIAM R. Regional primate reserach center Transmission of SIV/Mne CL 8 to macaques and baboons
P51RR-00166-30 0160 (SRC) THOULESS, MARGARET Regional primate reserach center Natural transmission of SAIDS - D in infants raised apart from mothers
P51RR-00166-30 0161 (SRC) TSAI, CHE-CHUNG Regional primate reserach center Primate model of SAIDS - D retrovirus for testing antiviral agents
P51RR-00166-30 0162 (SRC) TSAI, CHE-CHUNG Regional primate reserach center Screening for antiretro viral conduct animals
P51RR-00166-30 0163 (SRC) TSAI, CHE-CHUNG Regional primate reserach center Pharmacokinetics studies of antiretioviral agents
P51RR-00166-30 0164 (SRC) TSAI, CHE-CHUNG Regional primate reserach center Epidemiology of SAIDS - D virus infections
P51RR-00166-30 0165 (SRC) TSAI, CHE-CHUNG Regional primate reserach center Natural transmission SAIDS - D in harem groups
P51RR-00166-30 0166 (SRC) BIELITZKI, JOSEPH T. Regional primate

PROJECT NO., ORGANIZATIONAL UNIT., INVESTIGATOR, ADDRESS, TITLE

reserach center Adenovirus - Associated diarrhea
P51RR-00166-30 0167 (SRC) BLAKLEY, GERALD A. Regional primate reserach center Hematology reference values
P51RR-00166-30 0168 (SRC) BOWDEN, DOUGLAS M. Regional primate reserach center Environmental enrichment studies
P51RR-00166-30 0169 (SRC) BOWDEN, DOUGLAS M. Regional primate reserach center Space exercise and social needs of laboratory macaques
P51RR-00166-30 0170 (SRC) LOHR, CHARLES Regional primate reserach center Evaluation of flouride polishing in dental prophylaxis regimen
P51RR-00166-30 0171 (SRC) MORTON, WILLIAM R. Regional primate reserach center Recombinant vaccinia virus expressing envelopes glycoproteins
P51RR-00166-30 0172 (SRC) MORTON, WILLIAM R. Regional primate reserach center Fetal ultrasound
P51RR-00166-30 0173 (SRC) MORTON, WILLIAM R. Regional primate reserach center Diffuse idiopathic skeletal hyperostosis
P51RR-00166-30 0174 (SRC) MORTON, WILLIAM R. Regional primate reserach center Alternative infant milk formulas
P51RR-00166-30 0175 (SRC) MORTON, WILLIAM R. Regional primate reserach center Animal model of campylobacter pyloridis
P51RR-00166-30 0176 (SRC) RUPPENTHAL, GERALD C. Regional primate reserach center Genetic anomalies
P51RR-00166-30 0177 (SRC) RUPPENTHAL, GERALD C. Regional primate reserach center Effects of visual barriers on behavior in connected cages
P51RR-00166-30 0178 (SRC) RUPPENTHAL, GERALD C. Regional primate reserach center Effects of paired rearing on behavior development
P51RR-00166-30 0179 (SRC) SACKETT, GENE P. Regional primate reserach center Rprc computer data statistical studies
P51RR-00166-30 0180 (SRC) TSAI, CHE - CHUNG Regional primate reserach center Causes of morbidity and mortality
P51RR-00166-30 0181 (SRC) WILLIAMS, DARRELL D. Regional primate reserach center Enhanced foraging activity
P51RR-00166-30 0107 (SRC) PATTON, DOROTHY L. Regional primate reserach center Neonatal conjunctivitis
P51RR-00166-30 0118 (SRC) ROSS, RUSSELL Regional primate reserach center Studies of hypercholesterolemia
P51RR-00166-30 0119 (SRC) SMITH, ARNOLD L. Regional primate reserach center Virulence of piliated Hacmophilus influence
P51RR-00166-30 0120 (SRC) STEINER, ROBERT A. Regional primate reserach center Regulation of GnRH mRNA
P51RR-00166-30 0121 (SRC) STEINER, ROBERT A. Regional primate reserach center Biological effects of recombinant activin in males
P51RR-00166-30 0122 (SRC) UNADKAT, JASHVANT D. Regional primate reserach center Zidovudin-acetaminophen interactions
P51RR-00166-30 0123 (SRC) UNADKAT, JASHVANT D. Regional primate reserach center Fetal zidovudine (azidothymidine) kinetics
P51RR-00166-30 0124 (SRC) WEIGLE, D. SCOTT Regional primate reserach center Pulsatile vs. continuous insulin delivery in diabetes therapy
P51RR-00166-30 0125 (SRC) WEIGLE, D. SCOTT Regional primate reserach center Nutritional preconditioning of adipose tissue for mRNA preperation
P51RR-00166-30 0126 (SRC) WOODS, STEPHEN C. Regional primate reserach center CSF hormones, pancreatic endocrine function and feeding behavior
P51RR-00166-30 0127 (SRC) MILLS, RICHARD P. Regional primate reserach center Primate glaucoma
P51RR-00166-30 0128 (SRC) NEWELL-MORRIS, LAURA L. Regional primate reserach center Bone and lactation
P51RR-00166-30 0129 (SRC) SPELMAN, FRANCIS A. Regional primate reserach center Effects of immediat electrical stimulation on early development
P51RR-00166-30 0130 (SRC) SPELMAN, FRANCIS A. Regional primate reserach center Effects of delayed electrical stimulation on anatomical development
P51RR-00166-30 0131 (SRC) SPELMAN, FRANCIS A. Regional primate reserach center Peripheral auditory damage and auditory pathways
P51RR-00166-30 0132 (SRC) SPELMAN, FRANCIS A. Regional primate reserach center Measurement of the electrical properties of the inner ear
P51RR-00166-30 0133 (SRC) SPELMAN, FRANCIS A. Regional primate reserach center Effects of high current density
P51RR-00166-30 0134 (SRC) ALBERT, RICHARD K. Regional primate reserach center Flow characteristics of open vessles in gene 1 lungs
P51RR-00166-30 0135 (SRC) BENDITT, EARL P. Regional primate reserach center Tissue proteins related to alzheimer-amyloid-protein precursor
P51RR-00166-30 0136 (SRC) BETHEA, CYNTHIA L. Regional primate reserach center Effect of estrogens and progestins on prolactin production
P51RR-00166-30 0137 (SRC) CHAO, LEE Regional primate reserach center Evolution of kallikrein-like genes
P51RR-00166-30 0138 (SRC) DACEY, DENNIS M. Regional primate reserach center Studies of interneurons in the retina maintained in vitro
P51RR-00166-30 0139 (SRC) HAGEMAN, GREGORY S. Regional primate reserach center Retina: Substructure of cone photoreceptors
P51RR-00166-30 0140 (SRC) HENDRICKSON, ANITA Regional primate reserach center Development of retina
P51RR-00166-30 0141 (SRC) HENDRICKSON, ANITA Regional primate reserach center GABA ergic neurons in the visual cortex
P51RR-00166-30 0142 (SRC) HERR, JOHN C. Regional primate reserach center Molecular biology of sperma togenesis/identification of a model
P51RR-00166-30 0143 (SRC) JOHNSTON, J. O'NEAL Regional primate reserach center Characterization of steroidogenic enzymes
P51RR-00166-30 0144 (SRC) KEMPPAINEN, B.W. Regional primate reserach center Percutaneous penetration of low molecular weight toxins
P51RR-00166-30 0145 (SRC) MARSTAD, ANDREW T. Regional primate reserach center Use of experimental monkeys to evaluate dental implants
P51RR-00166-30 0146 (SRC) MARSHAK, DAVID Regional primate reserach center Peptidergic neurons of the retina and uvea
P51RR-00166-30 0147 (SRC) MARZETTA, CAROL A. Regional primate reserach center Tissue distribution of lipid transfer protein mRNA
P51RR-00166-30 0148 (SRC) PATTON, DOROTHY L. Regional primate reserach center Tissue culture studies of susceptibility to chlamydia
P51RR-00166-30 0149 (SRC) PROTHERO, JOHN W. Regional primate reserach center Fiber pathways in the heart
P51RR-00166-30 0108 (SRC) PATTON, DOROTHY L. Regional primate reserach center Chlamydial salpingitis
P51RR-00166-30 0109 (SRC) PATTON, DOROTHY L. Regional primate reserach center Trachoma pocket model
P51RR-00166-30 0110 (SRC) PATTON, DOROTHY L. Regional primate reserach center Experimental pelvic inflammatory disease
P51RR-00166-30 0111 (SRC) PHILLIPS, NONA K. Regional primate reserach center Infant model of antiepileptic drug exposure
P51RR-00166-30 0112 (SRC) PHILLIPS, NONA K. Regional primate reserach center Effects of prenatal valproate
P51RR-00166-30 0113 (SRC) RICE, CHARLES L. Regional primate reserach center Leukocytes in ischemic-reperfusion injury and multiple organ failure
P51RR-00166-30 0114 (SRC) RICE, CHARLES L. Regional primate reserach center Model of adult respiratory distress syndrome
P51RR-00166-30 0115 (SRC) RICHARDS, TODD L. Regional primate reserach center Proton NMR spectroscopy of demyelination in the brain
P51RR-00166-30 0117 (SRC) ROSE, LYNN M. Regional primate reserach center Anti-CD4 therapy of EAE
P51RR-00167-31 (AR) WILEY, JOHN W UNIV OF WISCONSIN-MADISON ROOM 333 BASCOM HALL MADISON, WI 53706 Wisconsin regional primate research center
P51RR-00167-31 0049 (AR) GOLOS, THADDEUS Wisconsin regional primate research center Hormone action and gene expression
P51RR-00167-31 0050 (AR) MATTERI, ROBERT Wisconsin regional primate research center Reproductive endocrinology--Pituitary function
P51RR-00167-31 9002 (AR) BRIDSON, WILLIAM E. Wisconsin regional primate research center Core--Assay laboratories
P51RR-00167-31 9003 (AR) HOUSER, WALLACE D Wisconsin regional primate research center Core--Animal resources
P51RR-00167-31 0029 (AR) CLAUDE, PHILIPPA Wisconsin regional primate research center Cellular response to trophic factors and hormones
P51RR-00167-31 0030 (AR) DEWAAL, FRANS Wisconsin regional primate research center Behavior of group-living primates
P51RR-00167-31 0031 (AR) DIERSCHKE, DONALD Wisconsin regional primate research center Endocrinology of ovaries and pituitary
P51RR-00167-31 0032 (AR) GARTLAN, STEVE Wisconsin regional primate research center Field ecology and behavior
P51RR-00167-31 0034 (AR) GOY, ROBERT Wisconsin regional primate research center Behavioral endocrinology
P51RR-00167-31 0035 (AR) KEMNITZ, JOSEPH Wisconsin regional primate research center Behavioral and physiological regulation of energy balance
P51RR-00167-31 0037 (AR) SHOLL, SAMUEL Wisconsin regional primate research center Biochemical endocrinology
P51RR-00167-31 0038 (AR) TERASAWA, EI Wisconsin regional primate research center Reproductive neuroendocrinology
P51RR-00167-31 0039 (AR) UNO, HIDEO Wisconsin regional primate research center Comparative pathobiology
P51RR-00167-31 0041 (AR) COE, CHRIS Wisconsin regional primate research center Behavioral endocrinology--Adrenal-immune reactions
P51RR-00167-31 0046 (AR) SCHULTZ, KEVIN T. Wisconsin regional primate research center Virology/microbiology
P51RR-00167-31 0048 (AR) BAVISTER, BARRY D Wisconsin regional primate research center Fertilization and embryonic development
P51RR-00167-31 9008 (AR) UNO, HIDEO Wisconsin regional primate research center Core--Pathology service unit
P51RR-00167-31 9009 (AR) PAPE, RICHARD Wisconsin regional primate research center Core--General shop
P51RR-00167-31 9010 (AR) DODSWORTH, ROBERT Wisconsin regional primate research center Core--Graphic arts
P51RR-00167-31 9011 (AR) DUBOIS, PAUL Wisconsin regional primate research center Core--Data management and instrumentation
P51RR-00167-31 9012 (AR) JACOBSEN, LAWRENCE Wisconsin regional primate research center Core--Library services
P51RR-00168-30 (AR) TOSTESON, DANIEL C NE REGIONAL PRIMATE CENTER ONE PINE HILL DRIVE SOUTHBORO, MA 01772 Primate research center
P51RR-00168-30 0132 (AR) WETTSTEIN, JOSEPH G Primate research center Behavioral effects of the triazolobenzodiazepine alprozolam
P51RR-00168-30 0133 (AR) FUJII, A M Primate research center Pressure dysfunction during atrial pacing in ventricular hypertrophy
P51RR-00168-30 0134 (AR) YOUNG, M A Primate research center Parasympathetic coronary vasoconstriction by nicotine
P51RR-00168-30 0135 (AR) KNIGHT, D R Primate research center Sympathetic activation induces asynchronous contractions in denervation
P51RR-00168-30 0136 (AR) SHEN, Y Primate research center Coronary artery occlusion with selective cardiac denervation
P51RR-00168-30 0137 (AR) GELPI, R J Primate research center Sympathetic augmentation of cardiac function in developing hypertension
P51RR-00168-30 0138 (AR) MORITA, H Primate research center Opiate receptor-mediated renal nerve activity during hemorrhage
P51RR-00168-30 0139 (AR) VATNER, S F Primate research center Reduced subendocardial myocardial perfusion in congestive heart failure
P51RR-00168-30 0140 (AR) KING, N W Primate research center Immune sensitization to epithelial cell components in colitis
P51RR-00168-30 0141 (AR) KING, N W Primate research center Comparative pathology of natural & experimental SIV infection
P51RR-00168-30 0142 (AR) RINGLER, D J Primate research center Infection of alveolar macrophages by SIV
P51RR-00168-30 0143 (AR) RINGLER, D J Primate research center Cellular localization of SIV in lymphoid tissues
P51RR-00168-30 0144 (AR) MA, N S F Primate research center Owl

monkey gene map
P51RR-00168-30 0145 (AR) MA, N S F Primate research center
Homologue of human chromosome 12 in the owl monkey
P51RR-00168-30 0146 (AR) MA, N S F Primate research center
Chromosomal assignment of owl monkey ETS1 and THY1 gene loci
P51RR-00168-30 0147 (AR) MA, N S F Primate research center
Molecular evidence of Y-autosomal translocation in owl monkeys
P51RR-00168-30 0148 (AR) COLLINS, W E Primate research center
Infection of Aotus with Plasmodium falciparum, P vival & P malariae
P51RR-00168-30 0149 (AR) REIMANN, K A Primate research center
Immune response to immunotoxins
P51RR-00168-30 0150 (AR) WATANABE, M Primate research center
Effect of soluable CD4 in rhesus infected with SIV
P51RR-00168-30 0151 (AR) TSUBOTA, H Primate research center
Cytotoxic T lymphocyte inhibits AIDS virus replication in lymphocytes
P51RR-00168-30 0152 (AR) WATKINS, D I Primate research center A primate species with limited MHC class 1 polymorphism
P51RR-00168-30 0153 (AR) DANIEL, M D Primate research center
Specific-virus-free macaque breeding colony
P51RR-00168-30 0154 (AR) DANIEL, M D Primate research center
Persistent infection of macaque monkeys with SIV
P51RR-00168-30 0155 (AR) DESROSIERS, RONALD C Primate research center Molecular genetics of the NEF gene of SIV and HIV-2
P51RR-00168-30 0156 (AR) DESROSIERS, RONALD C Primate research center Significance of premature stop codons in ENV of SIV
P51RR-00168-30 0157 (AR) DANIEL, M D Primate research center
Isolation of SIV from African Green Monkeys and pathogenicity studies
P51RR-00168-30 0158 (AR) YEN, L Primate research center Molecular genetics of SIV from rhesus macaques
P51RR-00168-30 0159 (AR) YEN, L Primate research center Molecular genetics of SIV from african green monkeys
P51RR-00168-30 0160 (AR) DANIEL, M D Primate research center
Vaccine study against SIV
P51RR-00168-30 0161 (AR) PARK, I W Primate research center
Deletional anaylsis of the intragenic region of SIV
P51RR-00168-30 0162 (AR) DESROSIERS, RONALD C Primate research center Molecular genetics of SIV from Sooty Mangabey monkeys
P51RR-00168-30 0163 (AR) YEN, L Primate research center
Transcriptional analysis of SIVmac long terminal repeats
P51RR-00168-30 0088 (AR) MORSE, WILLIAM H Primate research center
Behavioral effects of opioid antagonists
P51RR-00168-30 0164 (AR) DESROSIERS, RONALD C Primate research center Prevalence of antibodies to SIV in wild baboons
P51RR-00168-30 0165 (AR) DESROSIERS, RONALD C Primate research center Dihydrofolate reductase gene conservation among herpesviruses
P51RR-00168-30 0166 (AR) Y-T TUNG, F Primate research center
Construction of SIV packaging cell line
P51RR-00168-30 0167 (AR) AUSMAN, L M Primate research center
Nutritional influences on colon cancer in the tamarin
P51RR-00168-30 0168 (AR) HUNT, R D Primate research center
Specific pathogen free macaque breeding & research program
P51RR-00168-30 0169 (AR) LEE-PARRITZ, D E Primate research center
Gastrointestinal manifestations of experimental SIV infection
P51RR-00168-30 0170 (AR) ROLLAND, R M Primate research center
Coagulopathy in the common marmoset
P51RR-00168-30 0171 (AR) PETTO, A J Primate research center
Maternal hyperphenylalaninemia demostration project
P51RR-00168-30 0172 (AR) NOVAK, M A Primate research center
Psychological well-being of captive primates
P51RR-00168-30 0173 (AR) PETTO, A J Primate research center
Environmental enrichment studies
P51RR-00168-30 0174 (AR) NOVAK, M A Primate research center
Comparative behavior of captive macaques
P51RR-00168-30 0175 (AR) GODFREY, L R Primate research center
Ecoclinal variation in nonhuman primates
P51RR-00168-30 0176 (AR) PETTO, A J Primate research center
Captive primate colony record standardization
P51RR-00168-30 0177 (AR) KING, NORVAL W Primate research center
Life histories & reproductive scheduling in the order of primates
P51RR-00168-30 0178 (AR) BIGGERS, J D Primate research center
Culture media for preimplantation development
P51RR-00168-30 9004 (AR) BELINGER, LYNDA Primate research center
Core--Central supply operating room and pharmacy
P51RR-00168-30 9005 (AR) KING, NORVAL W Primate research center
Core--Education and training
P51RR-00168-30 9006 (AR) CURRAN, JAMES Primate research center
Core--Engineering and maintenance
P51RR-00168-30 9007 (AR) SEHGAL, PRABHAT K Primate research center
Core--Primate medicine
P51RR-00168-30 9008 (AR) SEHGAL, PRABHAT K Primate research center
Core--Primate nursery
P51RR-00168-30 9010 (AR) PETTO, ANDREW J Primate research center
Core--Primatology
P51RR-00168-30 9011 (AR) TOSTES TON, DANIEL C Primate research center Core--Service resources
P51RR-00168-30 9012 (AR) SEHAGAL, PRABBAT K Primate research center Core--Primate surgery and perinatology
P51RR-00168-30 9013 (AR) AUSMAN, LYNNE M Primate research center
Core--Primate nutrition
P51RR-00168-30 9014 (AR) TOSTESTON, DANIEL C Primate research center Core--Building modernization
P51RR-00168-30 9015 (AR) KING, NORVAL W Primate research center
Core--Diagnostic pathology & clinical pathology
P51RR-00168-30 0091 (AR) VATNER, STEPHEN F Primate research center
Myocardial function and blood flow with ischemia and reperfusion
P51RR-00168-30 0100 (AR) KING, NORVAL W Primate research center
Natural history of chronic colitis and colonic carcinoma
P51RR-00168-30 0109 (AR) DANIEL, M D Primate research center
Diagnostic microbiology
P51RR-00168-30 0111 (AR) DESROSIERS, RONALD C Primate research center Molecular basis for herpesvirus saimiri oncogenicity
P51RR-00168-30 0114 (AR) PETTO, ANDREW J Primate research center
Population estimation and projection

P51RR-00168-30 0116 (AR) BERGMAN, JACK Primate research center
Dissimilar behavioral effects of selective dopamine D1 & D2 agonists
P51RR-00168-30 0117 (AR) BERGMAN, JACK Primate research center
Non-histaminic mechanisms in stimulant effects of histamine antagonists
P51RR-00168-30 0118 (AR) BERGMAN, JACK Primate research center
Self-admin. of cocaine & other inhibitors of monoamine transport
P51RR-00168-30 0119 (AR) MORSE, WILLIAM H Primate research center
Behavioral physiology & pharmacology
P51RR-00168-30 0120 (AR) MADRAS, B K Primate research center
Fluorescent & biotin probes for D1 & 2 dopamine receptors
P51RR-00168-30 0121 (AR) MADRAS, B K Primate research center High affinity ligands for cocaine recognition sites
P51RR-00168-30 0122 (AR) MADRAS, B K Primate research center Novel high affinity compounds for cocaine recognition sites
P51RR-00168-30 0123 (AR) MADRAS, B K Primate research center D1 dopamine receptors in frontal cortex
P51RR-00168-30 0124 (AR) SPEALMAN, R D Primate research center
Cocaine-like interoceptive effects of dopamine transport inhibitors
P51RR-00168-30 0125 (AR) SPEALMAN, R D Primate research center
Psychomotor-stimulant effects of cocaine & related drugs
P51RR-00168-30 0126 (AR) SPEALMAN, R D Primate research center
Attenuation of behavioral effects of cocaine & amphetamine by NECA
P51RR-00168-30 0127 (AR) SPEALMAN, R D Primate research center
Psychomotor stimulant effects of 3-isobutyl-1-methylxanthine
P51RR-00168-30 0128 (AR) WETTSTEIN, JOSEPH G Primate research center Behavioral effects of the non-benzodiazepine anxiolytic buspirone
P51RR-00168-30 0129 (AR) WETTSTEIN, JOSEPH G Primate research center Behavioral effects of the B-carboline FG 7142
P51RR-00168-30 0130 (AR) WETTSTEIN, JOSEPH G Primate research center Distinctive behavioral effects of the pyrazoloquinoline CGS 8216
P51RR-00168-30 0131 (AR) WETTSTEIN, JOSEPH G Primate research center GABA-related drugs modulate the behavioral effects of lorazepam
P51RR-00169-30 (AR) MURPHY, FREDERICK A UNIVERSITY OF CALIFORNIA, DAVI DAVIS, CA 95616-8542 California primate research center
P51RR-00169-30 0125 (AR) SHIDELER, SUSAN E California primate research center Fecal metabolites of adrenal and ovarian steroids
P51RR-00169-30 0126 (AR) STYNE, DENNIS M California primate research center Developmental aspects of oxytocin in the cerebrospinal fluid
P51RR-00169-30 0127 (AR) STYNE, DENNIS M California primate research center Growth factors in development
P51RR-00169-30 0128 (AR) TARANTAL, ALICE F California primate research center Dose-finding and teratology study of a quinolone antibiotic
P51RR-00169-30 0129 (AR) WILEY, LYNN M California primate research center Chimeric mice and the relationship to Duchenne muscular dystrophy
P51RR-00169-30 0130 (AR) WILEY, LYNN M California primate research center Detection of reproductive hazards of ICE by embryo chimera assay
P51RR-00169-30 0131 (AR) WILEY, LYNN M California primate research center Morphogenesis in preimplation embryo
P51RR-00169-30 0132 (AR) BUCKPITT, ALAN R California primate research center Bioavailability and pharmacokinetics of physostigmine
P51RR-00169-30 0133 (AR) BUCKPITT, ALAN R California primate research center Pharmacokinetics of chloroquine and desipramine
P51RR-00169-30 0134 (AR) CHEVNG, ANTHONY T California primate research center Intravital microscopy--Design and application
P51RR-00169-30 0135 (AR) CHEUNG, ANTHONY W California primate research center Ontogeny of neutrophil function
P51RR-00169-30 0136 (AR) CONRAD, PATRICIA A California primate research center Piagnosis of Cryptosporidium and Giardia in non-human primates
P51RR-00169-30 0137 (AR) CORNELIUS, CHARLES E California primate research center Fasting hyperbilirubinemia in Bolivan squirrel monkeys
P51RR-00169-30 0138 (AR) CORNELIUS, CHARLES E California primate research center Procollagen peptide type 3 serum levels
P51RR-00169-30 0139 (AR) DOYLE, LAURIE G California primate research center Normal vaginal bacterial flora for Rhesus macaques
P51RR-00169-30 0140 (AR) FULLER, CHARLES A California primate research center Circadian rhythms and thermoregulation in the space enviroment
P51RR-00169-30 0141 (AR) FULLER, CHARLES A California primate research center Circadian rhythms
P51RR-00169-30 0142 (AR) FULLER, CHARLES A California primate research center Neural organization of the suprachiasmatic nucleus
P51RR-00169-30 0143 (AR) FULLER, CHARLES A California primate research center Sleep-wake cycles
P51RR-00169-30 0144 (AR) FULLER, CHARLES A California primate research center Thermal balance
P51RR-00169-30 0145 (AR) FULLER, CHARLES A California primate research center Thermoregulation in space environment
P51RR-00169-30 0146 (AR) GEORGE, JEANNE W California primate research center Effect of repeated phlebotomics on iron status
P51RR-00169-30 0147 (AR) GEORGE, JEANNE W California primate research center Electrolyte abnormalities associated with diarrhea
P51RR-00169-30 0148 (AR) GYERMEK, LAZSLO California primate research center Evaluation of non-depolarizing neuromuscular blocking agents
P51RR-00169-30 0149 (AR) HART, BENJAMIN L California primate research center Influence of a stressor on female Rhesus
P51RR-00169-30 0150 (AR) HENDRICKX, ANDREW G California primate research center Environmental enrichment for laboratory primates
P51RR-00169-30 0151 (AR) HIGGINS, ROBERT California primate research center Human brain tumor xenograft model
P51RR-00169-30 0152 (AR) MARKOVITS, JUDIT M California primate research center Survey of Compylobacter sp. infection and gastritis in macaques
P51RR-00169-30 0153 (AR) ROBERTS, JEFFREY A California primate

research center Behavioral evaluation of a primate toy
P51RR-00169-30 0154 (AR) ROBERTS, JEFFREY A California primate research center Epidemiology of herpes B virus in macaques
P51RR-00169-30 0155 (AR) SCHMUCKER, DOUGLAS L California primate research center Does age/sex compromise hepatic microsomal monooxygenases?
P51RR-00169-30 0156 (AR) SCHMUCKER, DOUGLAS L California primate research center Does aging compromise the gastrointestinal mucosal immune response?
P51RR-00169-30 0060 (AR) HENDRICKX, ANDREW G California primate research center Teratology and pharmacokinetics of diphenylhydantoin
P51RR-00169-30 9005 (AR) LOJEWSKI, FRANK California primate research center Core--Central supply and services
P51RR-00169-30 9006 (AR) WILSON, DENNIS E California primate research center Core--Electron microscopy facility
P51RR-00169-30 9007 (AR) HENRICKSON, ROY V California primate research center Core--Clinical and pathological laboratories
P51RR-00169-30 9010 (AR) HENDRICKSON, ROY V California primate research center Core--Primate medicine
P51RR-00169-30 9011 (AR) HENRICKSON, ROY V California primate research center Core--NIA set-aside colony
P51RR-00169-30 9018 (AR) HENRICKSON, ROY V California primate research center Core--Quality assurance for good laboratory practices
P51RR-00169-30 9019 (AR) PRAHALADA, SRINIVASA California primate research center Core--Primate pathology
P51RR-00169-30 9020 (AR) RHODE, EDWARD A California primate research center Core--Facilities improvement
P51RR-00169-30 9021 (AR) HENDRICKX, ANDREW G California primate research center Core NICHD colony
P51RR-00169-30 0067 (AR) GERSHWIN, M ERIC California primate research center Zinc deficiency and teratogenesis
P51RR-00169-30 0157 (AR) SEYFARTH, ROBERT California primate research center Vocal development in Japanese and Rhesus macaques
P51RR-00169-30 0158 (AR) SILK, JOAN B California primate research center Competition, affiliation and cooperation in social relationship
P51RR-00169-30 0159 (AR) SILK, JOAN B California primate research center Variations in lifetime reproductive performance
P51RR-00169-30 0160 (AR) SMITH, DAVID G California primate research center Genetic management of macaques by DNA RFLP analysis
P51RR-00169-30 0161 (AR) SMITH, DAVID G California primate research center Genetic variation in genus Macaca
P51RR-00169-30 0162 (AR) STEVENSON, DAVID K California primate research center Infant heme catabolism and carbonmonoxide detection
P51RR-00169-30 0163 (AR) HYDE, DALLAS M California primate research center Neutrophil trafficking in ozone-exposed monkeys
P51RR-00169-30 0164 (AR) REISER, KAREN M California primate research center Age-associated changes in collagen
P51RR-00169-30 0165 (AR) REISER, KAREN M California primate research center Collagen crosslink biomarkers of aging
P51RR-00169-30 0166 (AR) REISER, KAREN M California primate research center Lung collagen in silicosis
P51RR-00169-30 0167 (AR) WITSCH, HANSPETER R California primate research center Air pollutants and neuroendocrine lung cancer
P51RR-00169-30 0168 (AR) WITSCHI, HANSPETER R California primate research center Modulation of lung tumor development
P51RR-00169-30 0169 (AR) WU, REEN California primate research center Ozone toxicity and heat shock protein synthesis
P51RR-00169-30 0170 (AR) WU, REEN California primate research center Regulation of mucin synthesis and secretion
P51RR-00169-30 0171 (AR) CHANG, ROBERT S California primate research center Evaluation of HIV inhibitors from medicinal herbs
P51RR-00169-30 0172 (AR) LACKNER, ANDREW A California primate research center Comparative neuropathogenesis of SAIDS retroviruses
P51RR-00169-30 0173 (AR) LOWENSTINE, LINDA J California primate research center Isolation & characterization of simian retroviruses from Talapoin monkey
P51RR-00169-30 0174 (AR) LOWENSTEIN, LINDA J California primate research center Oral aspects of simian AIDS
P51RR-00169-30 0175 (AR) MAC KENZIE, MALCOLM R California primate research center Prevention of simian AIDS by passive protection
P51RR-00169-30 0176 (AR) MAC KENZIE, MALCOLM R California primate research center IgM response to infection with SIV
P51RR-00169-30 0177 (AR) MARX, PRESTON A California primate research center Characterization of HIV-related viruses in African monkeys in Liberia
P51RR-00169-30 0178 (AR) MARX, PRESTON A California primate research center Heterosexual transmission of AIDS--A simian model
P51RR-00169-30 0179 (AR) MARX, PRESTON A California primate research center Pathogenesis of SIV in Asian and African monkey
P51RR-00169-30 0180 (AR) MARX, PRESTON A California primate research center Simian retroviruses in human and non-human primates
P51RR-00169-30 0181 (AR) PEDERSON, NIELS C California primate research center Acquisition of multiple genetic variants of HIV by one individual
P51RR-00169-30 0182 (AR) PEDERSON, NIELS C California primate research center Systemic approach to retrovirus vaccination
P51RR-00169-30 0183 (AR) LUCIW, PAUL California primate research center Development of type D retroviral vectors for gene transfer into rhesus monkeys
P51RR-00169-30 0184 (AR) LACKNER, ANDREW California primate research center Mechanisms of SIV pathogenesis in vivo
P51RR-00169-30 0185 (AR) DANDEKAR, SATYA California primate research center Cytokines in the pathogenesis of GI dysfunction in SIV-infected macaques
P51RR-00169-30 0186 (AR) PENDERSEN, NEILS California primate research center Production of recombinants between pathogenic and nonpathogenic clones of SIVmac
P51RR-00169-30 9003 (AR) RODDAN, PAULINE California primate research center Reference services--Core
P51RR-00169-30 9004 (AR) ROTHGARN, ERIC California primate research center Core--Data services
P51RR-00169-30 0080 (AR) RODMAN, PETER S California primate research center Genetics and social behavior of Macaques
P51RR-00169-30 0093 (AR) GOLUB, MARI S California primate research center Evaluation of Rhesus treated with relaxin
P51RR-00169-30 0094 (AR) GOLUB, MARI S California primate research center Obstetric analgesia and infant outcome
P51RR-00169-30 0095 (AR) MASON, WILLIAM A California primate research center Conflict in social ontogeny--A life span view
P51RR-00169-30 0096 (AR) MENDOZA, SALLY P California primate research center Sociophysiology of reproduction in squirrel monkeys
P51RR-00169-30 0088 (AR) MASON, WILLIAM A California primate research center Social organization of South American monkeys
P51RR-00169-30 0089 (AR) MASON, WILLIAM A California primate research center Psychosocial development
P51RR-00169-30 0097 (AR) GARDNER, MURRAY B California primate research center Comparison of adjunants for HIV and SIV vaccines
P51RR-00169-30 0098 (AR) GARDNER, MURRAY B California primate research center HIV post exposure study
P51RR-00169-30 0099 (AR) GARDNER, MURRAY B California primate research center Non-human primate model of HIV-2 infection
P51RR-00169-30 0100 (AR) GARDNER, MURRAY B California primate research center Primate model to assess HIV-1 vaccines
P51RR-00169-30 0101 (AR) JENNINGS, MYRA B California primate research center Infectivity of SIV/SMM in macaques--A model of pediatric AIDS
P51RR-00169-30 0102 (AR) LERCHE, NICHOLAS W California primate research center Control and pathogenesis of simian AIDS
P51RR-00169-30 0103 (AR) LERCHE, NICHOLAS W California primate research center Natural history of simian AIDS
P51RR-00169-30 0104 (AR) MC GRAW, THOMAS P California primate research center Cellular immunity studies
P51RR-00169-30 0105 (AR) MC GRAW, THOMAS P California primate research center Natural history and immunobiology of SIV infected MMU
P51RR-00169-30 0106 (AR) MC GRAW, THOMAS P California primate research center AIDS 2 study 88-097
P51RR-00169-30 0107 (AR) BROWN, CHERRIE A California primate research center Cellular immunology of ovarian pathology
P51RR-00169-30 0108 (AR) CHALUPA, LEO M California primate research center Ontogeny and plasticity of cortical projection neurons
P51RR-00169-30 0109 (AR) CHANG, JEFFREY R California primate research center Ovarian and sperm function
P51RR-00169-30 0110 (AR) CHANG, JEFFREY R California primate research center Ovarian cyst treatment by medial and surgical castration
P51RR-00169-30 0111 (AR) ENDERS, ALLEN G California primate research center Mechanisms of implantation of the blastocyst
P51RR-00169-30 0112 (AR) GERSHWIN, ERIC M California primate research center Immunization with mitochondrial autoantigens
P51RR-00169-30 0113 (AR) HENDRICKX, ANDREW G California primate research center Effect of antiprogestin RU486 on early pregnancy
P51RR-00169-30 0114 (AR) HENDRICKX, ANDREW G California primate research center Cell proliferation in embryos
P51RR-00169-30 0115 (AR) HENDRICKX, ANDREW G California primate research center Comparative toxicity of interferon
P51RR-00169-30 0116 (AR) HENDRICKX, ANDREW G California primate research center Concentration of metabolite
P51RR-00169-30 0117 (AR) HENDRICKX, ANDREW G California primate research center Teratology study of an antibiotic
P51RR-00169-30 0118 (AR) HENDRICKX, ANDREW G California primate research center Teratology study of a pharmacological compound
P51RR-00169-30 0119 (AR) HENDRICKX, ANDREW G California primate research center Toxicological, teratogenic and reproductive effects of selenium
P51RR-00169-30 0120 (AR) LASLEY, BILL L California primate research center Primate testing facility
P51RR-00169-30 0121 (AR) OVERSTREET, JAMES W California primate research center Role of male accessory glands
P51RR-00169-30 0122 (AR) OVERSTREET, JAMES W California primate research center Sperm location in female reproductive tract
P51RR-00169-30 0123 (AR) OVERSTREET, JAMES W California primate research center Sperm transport in female cynomolgus monkeys
P51RR-00169-30 0124 (AR) READ, LEANNA C California primate research center Effect of epidermal growth factor upon the developing monkey
M01RR-00188-27 0311 (CLR) KLISH, WILLIAM J General clinical research center Adipose tissue mass and sex hormone levels in females 16-22 years old
M01RR-00188-27 (CLR) FEIGIN, RALPH D BAYLOR COLLEGE OF MEDICINE ONE BAYLOR PLAZA HOUSTON, TX 77030 General clinical research center
M01RR-00188-27 0089 (CLR) BEAUDET, ARTHUR L General clinical research center Dietary therapy and vitamin response in metabolic errors inborn
M01RR-00188-27 0136 (CLR) RICCARDI, VINCENT M General clinical research center Natural history of neurofibromatosis
M01RR-00188-27 0188 (CLR) LIN, TSU-HUIBECCA T General clinical research center Humatrope and low dose estrogen in Turner Syndrome
M01RR-00188-27 0189 (CLR) KIRKLAND, JOHN L General clinical research center Treatment of pubertal disorders with nafarelin acetate
M01RR-00188-27 0231 (CLR) LIN, TSU General clinical research center Somatropin therapy in hypopituitary children
M01RR-00188-27 0244 (CLR) GARSON, ARTHUR General clinical research center Ethmozine for control of supraventricular tachycardia
M01RR-00188-27 0246 (CLR) GLASSER, LOREN General clinical research center Use of prednisone in patients with cystic fibrosis
M01RR-00188-27 0260 (CLR) LIN, TSU General clinical research center Humatrope in hypopituitary children-- Dose frequency study
M01RR-00188-27 0264 (CLR) WILLIAMSON, DANIEL General clinical research center Relationship of hearing loss in infants to maternal CMV immune status
M01RR-00188-27 0314 (CLR) DEMMLER, GAIL J General clinical research center Live-attenuated varicella vaccine in children with leukemia in remission
M01RR-00188-27 0317 (CLR) ERICKSON, CHRISTOPHER General clinical research center Propafenone HCl for control of refractory arrhythmias in children

PROJECT NO., ORGANIZATIONAL UNIT., INVESTIGATOR, ADDRESS, TITLE

M01RR-00188-27 0319 (CLR) SCHWARTZ, PATRICIA L General clinical research center Self management of asthma in children
M01RR-00188-27 0320 (CLR) BEAUDET, ARTHUR General clinical research center Delineation of patterns of inheritance
M01RR-00188-27 0321 (CLR) SHEARER, WILLIAM T General clinical research center Evaluation of IVIG and zidovudine in children with symptomatic HIV infection
M01RR-00188-27 0324 (CLR) GABBAY, KENNETH H General clinical research center AIDS in infants and children-- Endocrine and wasting aspects
M01RR-00188-27 0325 (CLR) SHULMAN, ROBERT J General clinical research center Effect of parental nutrition on body composition
M01RR-00188-27 0326 (CLR) IIKIW, ROMA General clinical research center Sotalol HCl for control of arrhythmias in children and adolescents
M01RR-00188-27 0327 (CLR) MOTIL, KATHLEEN General clinical research center Body composition using bioelectrical impedance analysis method
M01RR-00188-27 0328 (CLR) BAKER, CAROL S General clinical research center Safety and pharmacokinetics of dideoxyinosine in children with AIDS
M01RR-00188-27 0329 (CLR) WHITE, CATHY General clinical research center Normal values for bone mineral density in 15-21 year old white females
M01RR-00188-27 0330 (CLR) HACHEY, DAVID General clinical research center Sources of human milk fat
M01RR-00188-27 0331 (CLR) MOAK, JEFFREY General clinical research center Physiologic pacing to improve long term cardiac function
M01RR-00188-27 0332 (CLR) SHULMAN, ROBERT General clinical research center Ultraviolet light therapy to maintain vitamin D sufficiency
M01RR-00188-27 0333 (CLR) MATSON, DAVID General clinical research center Antigenic variation of human rotaviruses
M01RR-00188-27 0334 (CLR) SHERMAN, LORI General clinical research center Insulin resistance in patients with precocious puberty
M01RR-00188-27 0335 (CLR) KLISH, WILLIAM General clinical research center Body composition in paraplegics estimated by TOBEC
M01RR-00188-27 0336 (CLR) SHEARER, WILLIAM General clinical research center Pediatric heart and lung complications of HIV infection
M01RR-00188-27 0337 (CLR) DEMMLER, GAIL General clinical research center Evaluation of ganciclovir in symptomatic congenital CMV infections
M01RR-00188-27 0338 (CLR) SCHANLER, RICHARD General clinical research center Feeding strategies for low birth weight infants
M01RR-00188-27 0339 (CLR) SHEARER, WILLIAM General clinical research center Safety and pharmacokinetics of recombinant CD4 IgG in HIV-1
M01RR-00188-27 0340 (CLR) FERRY, GEORGE General clinical research center Clinical course and management of hepatic transplantation
M01RR-00188-27 0341 (CLR) SHEARER, WILLIAM General clinical research center Use of ddI in zidovudine intolerant patients with AIDS
M01RR-00188-27 0342 (CLR) SHEARER, WILLIAM General clinical research center Safety and tolerance of high versus low dose zidovudine in children
M01RR-00188-27 0274 (CLR) GLAZE, DANIEL General clinical research center Rett syndrome-- Clinical neurophysiology
M01RR-00188-27 0275 (CLR) HERGENROEDER, ALBERT General clinical research center Body composition in ballet dancers
M01RR-00188-27 0280 (CLR) PERCY, ALAN General clinical research center Rett syndrome-- Clinical assessment
M01RR-00188-27 0281 (CLR) PERRY, JAMES General clinical research center Flecainide acetate for control of cardiac tachyarrhythmias
M01RR-00188-27 0286 (CLR) SHEARER, WILLIAM T General clinical research center IVIG treatment of children with symptomatic HIV infection
M01RR-00188-27 0293 (CLR) KIRKLAND, REBECCA T General clinical research center Effect of human growth hormone in children with Turner's syndrome
M01RR-00188-27 0301 (CLR) MOTIL, KATHLEEN L General clinical research center Body composition in lactating and nonlactating women
M01RR-00188-27 0302 (CLR) LIN, TSU-HUI General clinical research center Protropin and naltrexone in children with Prader-Willi syndrome
M01RR-00188-27 0303 (CLR) LIN, TSU-HUI General clinical research center Somatropin administered to patients with growth hormone deficiency
M01RR-00188-27 0306 (CLR) SCHWARTZ, PATRICIA L General clinical research center Self, family environment and discomfort associated with HIV symptomatic children
M01RR-00188-27 0307 (CLR) KLISH, WILLIAM J General clinical research center Determination of body composition by TOBEC
M01RR-00188-27 0308 (CLR) KIRKLAND, JOHN L General clinical research center Trial of protropin for growth hormone deficiency
M01RR-00188-27 0310 (CLR) KIRKLAND, JOHN L General clinical research center Somatropin in increased doses to sustain catch-up growth
P40RR-00200-28 (AR) RINGLER, DANIEL H UNIVERSITY OF MICHIGAN 018 ANIMAL RES FAC/BOX 0614 ANN ARBOR, MI 48109-0614 A university resource in laboratory animal medicine
M01RR-00211-27 (CLR) SUMMITT, ROBERT L 62 SOUTH DUNLAP MEMPHIS, TN 38163 General clinical research center
M01RR-00211-27 0329 (CLR) ALPERT, BRUCE S General clinical research center Renal mechanisms underlying the circadian rhythm of blood pressure
M01RR-00211-27 0330 (CLR) LING, FRANK W General clinical research center Effect of diet/mood in buspirone treated as compared to placebo treated patients
M01RR-00211-27 0331 (CLR) WILIMAS, JUDITH A General clinical research center Outpatient therapy of selected febrile patients with sickle cell disease
M01RR-00211-27 0111 (CLR) SULLIVAN, JAY M General clinical research center Effects of dietary sodium in man
M01RR-00211-27 0203 (CLR) KITABCHI, ABBAS E General clinical research center Diabetes complications and control trials
M01RR-00211-27 0229 (CLR) WYATT, ROBERT J General clinical research center Macroscopic hematuria disease activity in IgA nephropathy
M01RR-00211-27 0237 (CLR) KITABCHI, ABBAS General clinical research center Insulin resistance in noninsulin dependent diabetes mellitus
M01RR-00211-27 0246 (CLR) ALPERT, BRUCE S General clinical research center Familial hypertension and biracial cardiovascular reactivity in youth
M01RR-00211-27 0332 (CLR) BURGHEN, GEORGE A General clinical research center Psychosocial intervention for youths with insulin-dependent diabetes
M01RR-00211-27 0247 (CLR) HERROD, HENRY G General clinical research center Cyclosporine treatment of inflammatory bowel disease in children
M01RR-00211-27 0251 (CLR) ALPERT, BRUCE S General clinical research center Cardiovascular dynamics in Marfan syndrome
M01RR-00211-27 0254 (CLR) ACCHIARDO, SERGIO S General clinical research center Oral fenoldopam(82526) in renal insufficiency diabetes
M01RR-00211-27 0272 (CLR) SCHRIOCK, ELDON D General clinical research center Insulin-dehydroepiandrosterone counter-regulations
M01RR-00211-27 0276 (CLR) HUGHES, THOMAS A General clinical research center Contribution genetic diabetic control abnormalities lipoprotein NIDDM
M01RR-00211-27 0281 (CLR) HACKMAN, BELA B General clinical research center Captopril for ventricular enlargement after myocardial infart
M01RR-00211-27 0289 (CLR) BURSTEIN, STEVEN General clinical research center Growth hormone/children/acute lymphoblastic leukemia
M01RR-00211-27 0291 (CLR) SULLIVAN JAY M General clinical research center Mechanisms of hypertension after cardiac transplantation
M01RR-00211-27 0292 (CLR) FISHER, JOSEPH N General clinical research center Insulin pump vs conventional insulin therapy for glycemic control
M01RR-00211-27 0294 (CLR) BERTORINI, TULIO General clinical research center Combined diltiazem and dantrolene in Duchenne Muscular Dystrophy
M01RR-00211-27 0297 (CLR) CARDOSA, SERGIO S General clinical research center Vasomotor response to cold and posture in subjects with IDDM
M01RR-00211-27 0301 (CLR) GABER, AHMED General clinical research center Pancreas transplantation--Monitoring of graft function
M01RR-00211-27 0305 (CLR) BERTORININ, JULIO E General clinical research center Growth hormone pathogenesis DMD--Growth hormone secretion somatostatin analog
M01RR-00211-27 0306 (CLR) BURGHEN, GEORGE A General clinical research center Immun./endocrine assess. of children new onset type I & II diabetes
M01RR-00211-27 0307 (CLR) ROBERSTON, JAMES General clinical research center Brain tumor cooperative group protocol 87-01 phase III--Malignant glioma
M01RR-00211-27 0308 (CLR) FISHER, JOSEPH N General clinical research center Role of aldosterone in diabetic hyperchloremic acidosis and ketoacidosis
M01RR-00211-27 0309 (CLR) SULLIVAN, JAY M General clinical research center University of Tennessee adult congenital heart disease study
M01RR-00211-27 0310 (CLR) BROWN, CANDACE S General clinical research center Imipramine in the treatment of attention-deficit disorder
M01RR-00211-27 0311 (CLR) KITABCHI, ABBAS E General clinical research center Screening protocol women with hyperandrogenism
M01RR-00211-27 0312 (CLR) HUGHES, THOMAS A General clinical research center Postprandial lipoprotein composition metabolism cardiovascular disease
M01RR-00211-27 0314 (CLR) SKOLL, M AMANDA General clinical research center Establishment normal glucose tolerance at 24 to 28 weeks of pregnancy
M01RR-00211-27 0316 (CLR) ALPERT, BRUCE S General clinical research center Behaviorally induced sns arousal and sodium regulation
M01RR-00211-27 0318 (CLR) ABELL, THOMAS A General clinical research center Evaluation of cisapride (R51,619) treatment of diabetic gastroparesis
M01RR-00211-27 0319 (CLR) ABELL, THOMAS L General clinical research center Cisapride (R51,619) treatment of idiopathic gastroparesis
M01RR-00211-27 0320 (CLR) HATCH, FRED E General clinical research center Renal function in chronic renal failure predialysis patients r-HuEPO
M01RR-00211-27 0321 (CLR) ABELL, THOMAS General clinical research center Evaluation of cisapride in long term patients with symptoms of gastroparesis
M01RR-00211-27 0322 (CLR) ABELL, THOMAS L General clinical research center Cisapride compassionate treat of patients C gastrointestinal motor dysfunction
M01RR-00211-27 0324 (CLR) HUGHES, THOMAS A General clinical research center Beef and human ultralente insulin with NPH in patients with Type I diabetes
M01RR-00211-27 0325 (CLR) HATCH, FRED E General clinical research center Blood pressure in sickle cell anemia--Response to angiotensin II
M01RR-00211-27 0326 (CLR) GOLDEN, GERALD S General clinical research center Myoblast transfer therapy for muscular dystrophy
M01RR-00211-27 0327 (CLR) MAUER, ALVIN M General clinical research center Pharmacokinetics of megestrol acetate in patients with advanced breast cancer
M01RR-00211-27 0328 (CLR) KITABCHI, ABBAS E General clinical research center Insulin and DHEA interaction in polycystic ovarian disease
M01RR-00211-27 0333 (CLR) ALPERT, BRUCE S General clinical research center Effects of sodium reduction on cardiovascular reactivity in black children
M01RR-00211-27 0334 (CLR) BALDREE, LOU A General clinical research center Metabiolic determinants of bone density in adolescent females
M01RR-00211-27 0335 (CLR) BURSTEIN, STEPHEN General clinical research center Growth hormone deficiency/adult height/survivors childhood ALL
M01RR-00211-27 0336 (CLR) CASSON, PETER R General clinical research center Bioavailability of micronized and unmicronized oral DHEA

PROJECT NO., ORGANIZATIONAL UNIT., INVESTIGATOR, ADDRESS, TITLE

M01RR-00211-27 0337 (CLR) SULLIVAN, JAY M General clinical research center Caffeine's effect on vasodilatory capacity and pressor response
M01RR-00211-27 0338 (CLR) BITTLE, JOYCE B General clinical research center Relationship of dietary habits to glycemic control in Type I Diabetes Mellitus
M01RR-00211-27 0339 (CLR) BERTORINI, TULIO E General clinical research center Natural history of Duchenne Muscular Dystrophy
M01RR-00240-27 (CLR) SCHWARTZ, ELIAS CHILDREN'S HOSPITAL PHILA 34TH & CIVIC CENTER BOULEVARD PHILADELPHIA, PA 19104 General clinical research center
M01RR-00240-27 0096 (CLR) BAKER, LESTER General clinical research center Glycogen storage disease
M01RR-00240-27 0199 (CLR) BAKER, LESTER General clinical research center Diabetes control and complications trial
M01RR-00240-27 0202 (CLR) STANLEY, CHARLES A General clinical research center Mechanisms of primary and secondary carnitine deficiency
M01RR-00240-27 0204 (CLR) MOSHANG, THOMAS General clinical research center Treatment of precocious puberty with buserelin (HOE 766)
M01RR-00240-27 0214 (CLR) CORTNER, JEAN A General clinical research center Studies in familial combined hyperlipidemia
M01RR-00240-27 0243 (CLR) PEREIRA, GILBERTO R. General clinical research center Developmental changes and lipid clearance during fat infusions in premies
M01RR-00240-27 0274 (CLR) SPITZER, ALAN R. General clinical research center High frequency jet ventilation in newborns with lung disease
M01RR-00240-27 0279 (CLR) YUDKOFF, MARC General clinical research center Isotope studies of N2 metabolism in premature infants
M01RR-00240-27 0289 (CLR) MOSHANG, THOMAS General clinical research center Growth hormone treatment of partial GH deficiency
M01RR-00240-27 0290 (CLR) MOSHANG, THOMAS General clinical research center Growth hormone treatment in Turner syndrome
M01RR-00240-27 0292 (CLR) PEREIRA, GILBERTA R. General clinical research center Vitamin A in very low birthweight infants receiving total parental nutrition
M01RR-00240-27 0307 (CLR) CORTNER, JEAN A General clinical research center Apolipoprotein synthesis rates disorders lipoprotein metabolism
M01RR-00240-27 0308 (CLR) STANLEY, CHARLES A General clinical research center Somatostatin therapy in hyperinsulinism
M01RR-00240-27 0309 (CLR) LANGE, BEVERLY General clinical research center Monoclonal antibody for recurrent malignant brain tumors
M01RR-00240-27 0310 (CLR) STALLINGS, VIRGINIA General clinical research center Nutritional assessment of children with cerebral palsy
M01RR-00240-27 0319 (CLR) CLANCY, ROBERT C General clinical research center Cranial ultrasound /EEG for neurologic outcome in premature IVH infants
M01RR-00240-27 0322 (CLR) PLOTKIN, SHIRLEY General clinical research center Studies of new vaccines
M01RR-00240-27 0323 (CLR) HARRIS, MARY C General clinical research center Value of sepsis screen in human infants with nosocomial infection
M01RR-00240-27 0326 (CLR) BAUMGART, STEPHEN General clinical research center Lipid/CHO ratio, relief pulmonary CO2 excretion load in premature BPD
M01RR-00240-27 0329 (CLR) MOSHANG, THOMAS JR General clinical research center Growth hormone function and treatment in oncology survivors with growth failure
M01RR-00240-27 0330 (CLR) KAPLAN, PAIGE General clinical research center Body composition, energy expenditure/growth children with maple syrup urine dis.
M01RR-00240-27 0332 (CLR) HARRIS, MARY C General clinical research center Tumor necrosis factor and interleukin-1 levels in septic pediatric patients
M01RR-00240-27 0334 (CLR) STANLEY, CHARLES A General clinical research center Humatrope and low dose estrogen in Turner's syndrome
M01RR-00240-27 0336 (CLR) STANLEY, CHARLES General clinical research center Somatotropin in hypopituitary children
M01RR-00240-27 0337 (CLR) AUGUST, CHARLES S General clinical research center Assessment of safety and efficacy of GM-CSF in children
M01RR-00240-27 0338 (CLR) BROUSSARD, DELMA General clinical research center Study of stomach/small bowel motility in children feeding disorders
M01RR-00240-27 0340 (CLR) HARRIS, MARY C General clinical research center Virulence factors of coagulase negative staphylococci
M01RR-00240-27 0341 (CLR) BAUMGART, STEPHEN General clinical research center Sodium administration versus sodium restriction in the premature infant
M01RR-00240-27 0342 (CLR) BAKER, LESTER General clinical research center Study of endocrine function following neonatal seizures
M01RR-00240-27 0343 (CLR) STALLINGS, VIRGINIA A General clinical research center Body composition, energy expenditure and growth in children with cystic fibrosis
M01RR-00240-27 0344 (CLR) SCHWARTZ, ELIAS General clinical research center Branch-chain amino acid-free hyperalimentation therapy for patients with MSUD
M01RR-00240-27 0345 (CLR) BAKER, LESTER General clinical research center Renal studies in Type I glycogen storage disease
M01RR-00240-27 0346 (CLR) RUTSTEIN, RICHARD M General clinical research center Test of immuthiol as an immune enhancer for treatment of pediatric HIV
M01RR-00240-27 0347 (CLR) MOSHANG, THOMAS General clinical research center Metabolic assessment of thyroid function in congenital hypothyroidism
M01RR-00240-27 0348 (CLR) HARRIS, MARY C General clinical research center Urea plasma associated chronic lung disease in infants
M01RR-00240-27 0349 (CLR) BAUMGART, STEPHEN General clinical research center Metabolic effects anesthesia surface cooling neonates undergoing cardiac surgery
M01RR-00240-27 0350 (CLR) DANZIGER, ROGER General clinical research center Multicentered phase I-II trial of PEG-IL2 in T cell immunodeficiencies

PROJECT NO., ORGANIZATIONAL UNIT., INVESTIGATOR, ADDRESS, TITLE

M01RR-00240-27 0351 (CLR) STARR, STUART E General clinical research center Evaluation of ganciclovir for treatment of symptomatic congenital CMV
P41RR-00292-24S2 (SSS) BOTHNER-BY, AKSEL A CARNEGIE MELLON UNIVERSITY 4400 FIFTH AVENUE PITTSBURGH, PA 15213 NMR facility for biomedical studies
P40RR-00301-26 (AR) SCARPELLI, DANTE G NORTHWESTERN UNIVERSITY 303 EAST CHICAGO AVENUE CHICAGO, IL 60611 Registry of comparative pathology
P41RR-00317-25 (SSS) BIEMANN, KLAUS MASSACHUSETTS INST OF TECHNOLO 77 MASSACHUSETTS AVENUE CAMBRIDGE, MA 02139 Mass spectrometry facility for biomedical research
P41RR-00317-25 0001 (SSS) RAYHUL, RAY Mass spectrometry facility for biomedical research Characterization of Vitamin D sterol-binding domains
P41RR-00317-25 0002 (SSS) ROSSIGNOL, P Mass spectrometry facility for biomedical research Peptidoglycan-degrading enzymes of mosquito salivary glands
P41RR-00317-25 0003 (SSS) HARGROVE, JAMES Mass spectrometry facility for biomedical research Tyrosine aminotransferase
P41RR-00317-25 0004 (SSS) KOSIK, KENNETH Mass spectrometry facility for biomedical research Phosphorylation of protein tau and alzheimer's disease
P41RR-00317-25 0005 (SSS) DAVISON, A Mass spectrometry facility for biomedical research Chemistry of technetium related to nuclear medicine
P41RR-00317-25 0006 (SSS) WARREN, L Mass spectrometry facility for biomedical research Biochemistry of surface membranes
P41RR-00317-25 0007 (SSS) HOLZ, G Mass spectrometry facility for biomedical research Lipids and leishmania and trypanosomes
P41RR-00317-25 0008 (SSS) LIPPARD, STEPHEN Mass spectrometry facility for biomedical research Mechanism of action of cis-diamminedichloroplatinum
P41RR-00317-25 9001 (SSS) BIEMANN, KLAUS Mass spectrometry facility for biomedical research Core--Mass spectrometry
M01RR-00318-25 (CLR) SCHWARZ, RICHARD H SUNY-HEALTH SCIENCE CENTER 450 CLARKSON AVENUE BROOKLYN, N Y 11203 General clinical research center
M01RR-00318-25 0184 (CLR) BANERJI, MARY ANN General clinical research center Pathogenesis and treatment of Type II Diabetes Mellitus
M01RR-00318-25 0213 (CLR) DELANO, BARBARA General clinical research center Renal mass and endocrine function of the kidney
M01RR-00318-25 0214 (CLR) LANDESMAN, SHELDON H General clinical research center Perinatal transmission of HIV in pregnant women and their offspring
M01RR-00318-25 0215 (CLR) CHAIKEN, ROCHELLE L General clinical research center Diabetic nephropathy in type II diabetes
M01RR-00318-25 0216 (CLR) CHAIKEN, ROCHELLE L General clinical research center Angiotensin converting enzyme inhibition in diabetic nephropathy
M01RR-00318-25 0218 (CLR) BANERJI, MARY ANN General clinical research center Low dose sulfonylurea therapy of impaired glucose tolerance
M01RR-00318-25 0219 (CLR) LEBOVITZ, HAROLD E General clinical research center Role of growth hormone in protein mediated increases in GFR
M01RR-00318-25 0222 (CLR) HAMMERSCHLAG, MARGARET R. General clinical research center Interaction of chlamydia trachomatis and human alveolar macrophages
M01RR-00318-25 0182 (CLR) JAFFE, BERNARD M General clinical research center Provocative diagnosis of carcinoid syndrome
M01RR-00318-25 0225 (CLR) BAILEY, TIMOTHY S. General clinical research center Endocrinology abnormalities in sickle cell disease
M01RR-00318-25 0226 (CLR) DELANO, BARBARA General clinical research center Efficacy of enalapril on the course of human renal disease
M01RR-00318-25 0227 (CLR) COHN, KENNETH General clinical research center Localization of monoclonal antibodies in colon-rectal cancer
M01RR-00318-25 0230 (CLR) MARKELL, MARIANA S General clinical research center Probucol and nicotinic acid for hypercholesterolemia in renal transplant
M01RR-00318-25 0231 (CLR) BROWN, CLINTON D General clinical research center Aminoguanidine treatment of chronic complications of diabetes mellitus
M01RR-00318-25 0232 (CLR) CHAIKEN, ROCHELLE General clinical research center Erythromycin and gastrointestinal motility in patients with diabetes mellitus
M01RR-00334-25 (CLR) KENDALL, JOHN W, JR OREGON HEALTH SCIENCES UNIV. 3181 SW SAM JACKSON PARK RD. PORTLAND, OR 97201-3098 General clinical research center
M01RR-00334-25 0048 (CLR) PIROFSKY, BERNARD General clinical research center Intravenous immune globulin in 10% maltose, pH 4.25 therapy
M01RR-00334-25 0161 (CLR) NUTT, JOHN G General clinical research center On-off phenomenon in Parkinsonism--Importance of plasma L-DOPA
M01RR-00334-25 0169 (CLR) ILLINGWORTH, D ROGER General clinical research center Mevinolin therapy of hypercholesterolemia
M01RR-00334-25 0171 (CLR) COOK, DAVID M General clinical research center Cortisol therapy
M01RR-00334-25 0253 (CLR) CONNOR, WILLIAM E General clinical research center Hypertriglyceridemia and phased high carbohydrate diet
M01RR-00334-25 0256 (CLR) CONNOR, WILLIAM E General clinical research center Interaction of fish oils and saturated fatty acids on lipid metabolism
M01RR-00334-25 0257 (CLR) CONNOR, WILLIAM E General clinical research center Mechanism of hypocholesterolemic effects of monosaturated fatty acids
M01RR-00334-25 0260 (CLR) CONNOR, WILLIAM E General clinical research center Effects of dietary cholesterol and saturated fat on LDL receptor activity
M01RR-00334-25 0261 (CLR) CONNOR, WILLIAM E General clinical research center Effects of lovastatin and omega-3 fatty acids in hypercholesterolemia

M01RR-00334-25 0262 (CLR) CONNOR, WILLIAM E General clinical research center Combined therapy of hypercholesterolemia with colestipol and fish oil
M01RR-00334-25 0263 (CLR) CONNER, WILLIAM E General clinical research center Inhibition of carbohydrate induced hypertriglyceridemia with omega-3 fatty acids
M01RR-00334-25 0264 (CLR) PORTER, JOHN M General clinical research center Natural history of Raynaud's syndrome
M01RR-00334-25 0266 (CLR) CONNOR, WILLIAM E General clinical research center Effects of dietary carbohydrate on lipid and glucose metabolism in diabetes
M01RR-00334-25 0269 (CLR) TAYLOR, LLOYD M General clinical research center Homocysteine in cerebral and peripheral vascular disease
M01RR-00334-25 0270 (CLR) PORER, JOHN M General clinical research center Multicenter trial of iloprost for ischemic ulcers
M01RR-00334-25 0271 (CLR) COOK, DAVID M General clinical research center Evaluation of abnormal hypothalamic-pituitary-adrenal axis
M01RR-00334-25 0272 (CLR) COOK, DAVID M General clinical research center Effect of fish oil on lipid metabolism in lipodystrophic diabetes mellitus
M01RR-00334-25 0273 (CLR) COOK, DAVID General clinical research center Cortisol infusion test for separating ectopic & pituitary excess ACTH secretion
M01RR-00334-25 0274 (CLR) LEWY, ALFRED J General clinical research center Effect of advancing dusk and delaying dawn on melatonin production
M01RR-00334-25 0275 (CLR) SAMPLES, JOHN General clinical research center Changes in serum and urine melatonin associated with intraocular pressure
M01RR-00334-25 0276 (CLR) RIDDLE, MATTHEW General clinical research center Intermediate-acting insulin at bedtime vs before breakfast type II diabetes
M01RR-00334-25 0277 (CLR) SACK, ROBERT L General clinical research center Sleep promoting properties of melatonin in circadian rhythm disturbances
M01RR-00334-25 0278 (CLR) SACK, ROBERT General clinical research center Placebo controlled trial of lithium for insomnia in free-running blind people
M01RR-00334-25 0279 (CLR) LEWY, ALFRED J General clinical research center Phase shifting effects of melatonin administration
M01RR-00334-25 0280 (CLR) COULL, BRUCE General clinical research center Mechanisms of injury and repair in ischemic stroke
M01RR-00334-25 0282 (CLR) COOK, DAVID M General clinical research center Effect of chronic alcohol use on the hypothalamic-pituitary-adrenal axis
M01RR-00334-25 0283 (CLR) PIROFSKY, BERNARD General clinical research center Safety of rapid administration of sandoglobulin
M01RR-00334-25 0188 (CLR) PORTER, JOHN M General clinical research center Diagnosis, pathophysiology and clinical course of Raynaud's syndrome
M01RR-00334-25 0212 (CLR) ILLINGWORTH, D ROGER General clinical research center A multicenter study of mevinolin vs cholestyramine in hypercholesterolemia
M01RR-00334-25 0214 (CLR) LEWY, ALFRED J General clinical research center Seasonal rhythms in melatonin production and light sensitivity
M01RR-00334-25 0284 (CLR) TAYLOR, LLOYD General clinical research center Multicenter trial of iloprost for patients with Raynaud's phenomenon
M01RR-00334-25 0224 (CLR) ILLINGWORTH D. ROGER General clinical research center A dose response study of MK-733 in primary hypercholesterolemia
M01RR-00334-25 0285 (CLR) SACK, ROBERT General clinical research center Study of circadian rhythms in shift workers
M01RR-00334-25 0286 (CLR) PORTER, JOHN M General clinical research center Treatment of deep vein thrombosis with urokinase, streptokinase and heparin
M01RR-00334-25 0287 (CLR) CONNOR, WILLIAM General clinical research center Vitamin E absorption in humans
M01RR-00334-25 0288 (CLR) YOUNG, ERIC General clinical research center Regulation of parathyroid hormone and vitamin D in essential hypertension
M01RR-00334-25 0289 (CLR) HANIFIN, JOHN General clinical research center Multiple dose pharmakinetics of acitretin in psoriasis patients
M01RR-00334-25 0290 (CLR) GANCHER, STEPHEN T General clinical research center Control of tolerance to chronic apomorphine stimulation in Parkinson's disease
M01RR-00334-25 0291 (CLR) ORWOLL, ERIC General clinical research center Effect of vitamin D on insulin secretion in type II diabetes mellitus
M01RR-00334-25 0292 (CLR) LEWY, ALFRED J General clinical research center Identification of free-running rhythms in totally blind people
M01RR-00334-25 0231 (CLR) WOLTERING, EUGENE A. General clinical research center Neuroendocrine tumors of gastroenteropancreatic axis
M01RR-00334-25 0293 (CLR) PORTER, JOHN M General clinical research center Efficacy of TA-3090 in the treatment of patients with intermittent claudication
M01RR-00334-25 0295 (CLR) ILLINGWORTH, D ROGER General clinical research center Lovastatin vs niacin in patients with primary hypercholesterolemia
M01RR-00334-25 0296 (CLR) PORTER, JOHN General clinical research center L-carnitine treatment for exercise limiting lower limb claudication
M01RR-00334-25 0297 (CLR) ILLINGWORTH, D ROGER General clinical research center Cholesterol reduction with LDL apheresis in hypercholesterolemia
M01RR-00334-25 0298 (CLR) ILLINGWORTH, D ROGER General clinical research center Lipid metabolism and therapy for hypercholesterolemia
M01RR-00334-25 0299 (CLR) LEWY, ALFRED J General clinical research center Melatonin production in narcolpsy
M01RR-00334-25 0300 (CLR) CONNOR, WILLIAM General clinical research center Absorption of ethyl-ester and triglyceride concentrate of omega-3 fatty acids
M01RR-00334-25 0301 (CLR) CONNOR, WILLIAM E General clinical research center Threshold to ceiling effects of cholesterol on lipoprotein and LDL turnover
M01RR-00334-25 0302 (CLR) PORTER, JOHN M General clinical research center Compassionate use of intravenous iloprost
M01RR-00334-25 0303 (CLR) LEWY, ALFRED J General clinical research center Melatonin production and the sleep/wake cycle in Alzheimer's disease
M01RR-00334-25 0304 (CLR) STRIEGEL, JANE E General clinical research center Somatotropin and the short stature associaed with chronic renal insufficiency
M01RR-00334-25 0305 (CLR) FIREMAN, MARIAN General clinical research center Melatonin physiology of major depression
M01RR-00334-25 0306 (CLR) PORTER, JOHN M General clinical research center Asymptomatic carotid atherosclerosis study
M01RR-00334-25 0307 (CLR) ORWOLL, ERIC General clinical research center Effects of testosterone on mineral metabolism in normal men
M01RR-00334-25 0308 (CLR) PIROFSKY, BERNARD General clinical research center Clinical and lab safety data of 10%IGIV with that of 5%IGIV
M01RR-00334-25 0309 (CLR) PIROFSKY, BERNARD General clinical research center Safety of gammagard IGIV givin at increased rates and concentrations
M01RR-00334-25 0310 (CLR) NUTT, JOHN G General clinical research center Effects of amoxicillin on the response to levodopa
M01RR-00334-25 0311 (CLR) ILLINGWORTH, D ROGER General clinical research center Trial of lovastatin in boys with heterozygous familial hypercholesterolemia
M01RR-00334-25 0312 (CLR) RIDDLE, MATTHEW C General clinical research center Safety of combined insulin and sulfonylurea therapy for Type II diabetes
M01RR-00334-25 0313 (CLR) GANCHER, STEPHEN T General clinical research center Study of SINEMET CR 25/100 in Parkinsonian patients without prior therapy
M01RR-00334-25 0314 (CLR) LOVELESS, MARK O General clinical research center Ampligen in patients with chronic fatigue syndrome and associated encephalopathy
M01RR-00334-25 0315 (CLR) RIDDLE, MATTHEW C General clinical research center Steroid diabetes--Metabolic patterns and basis for treatment
M01RR-00334-25 0233 (CLR) ILLINGWORTH, D ROGER General clinical research center Lipid metabolism in abetalipoproteinemia
M01RR-00334-25 0234 (CLR) BENNETT, WILLIAM M General clinical research center Antibiotic levels of cyst fluid in adult polycystic kidney disease
M01RR-00334-25 0236 (CLR) CONNOR, WILLIAM E General clinical research center Dietary fish oil therapy in hyperlipidemic diabetic subjects
M01RR-00334-25 0237 (CLR) ILLINGWORTH, D ROGER General clinical research center A multicenter trial of Mevinolin in patients with primary hypercholesterolemia
M01RR-00334-25 0242 (CLR) WOLTERING, EUGENE General clinical research center Peptide release during post-vagotomy dumping--Effects of sandostatin
M01RR-00334-25 0244 (CLR) ILLINGWORTH, ROGER General clinical research center MK733 and lovastatin in heterozygous familial hypercholesterolemia
M01RR-00334-25 0247 (CLR) LAFRANCHI, STEPHEN General clinical research center Growth failure due to lack of adequate endogenous growth hormone production
M01RR-00334-25 0250 (CLR) GANCHER, STEPHEN T General clinical research center Deprenyl and tocopheral antioxidative therapy in Parkinsonism
M01RR-00349-25 (CLR) MYERS, ALLEN TEMPLE UNIVERSITY 3400 N BROAD STREET PHILADELPHIA, PA 19140 General clinical research center
M01RR-00349-25 0192 (CLR) GREENSTEIN, JEFFREY I General clinical research center Lymphocytapheresis for study of cellular immune regulation in multiple sclerosis
M01RR-00349-25 0194 (CLR) HOELDTKE, ROBERT D General clinical research center Treatment of postprandial hypotension
M01RR-00349-25 0197 (CLR) KRISHNA,GOPAL General clinical research center Effect of hypokalemia on urinary sodium excretion
M01RR-00349-25 0206 (CLR) HOELDTKE, ROBERT D. General clinical research center Pathophysiology of autonomic neuropathy--Somatostatin deficiency
M01RR-00349-25 0208 (CLR) BODEN, GUENTHER General clinical research center Amino acids effects on CHO and FAT oxidations and on insulin resistance
M01RR-00349-25 0209 (CLR) BODEN, GUENHER General clinical research center Anti-insulin receptor antibodies in diabetes
M01RR-00349-25 0228 (CLR) KRISHNA, GOPAL General clinical research center Effect of acidosis on cardiac function
M01RR-00349-25 0229 (CLR) GEWIRTZ, ALAN M General clinical research center Regulation of human megakaryocytopoiesis
M01RR-00349-25 0230 (CLR) COSLETT, H BRANCH General clinical research center Patterns of cognitive deficit in Alzheimer's disease
M01RR-00349-25 0232 (CLR) BAGASRA, OMAR General clinical research center Ethanol infusion on susceptibility of peripheral blood mononuclear cells
M01RR-00349-25 0233 (CLR) GREENSTEIN, JEFFREY General clinical research center Cellular immune regulation in multiple sclerosis
M01RR-00349-25 0234 (CLR) GREENSTEIN, JEFFREY General clinical research center Phase I study to evaluate the safety and efficacy of IFN-B ser
M01RR-00349-25 0235 (CLR) GREENSTEIN, JEFFREY General clinical research center Phase III study to evaluate the safety and efficacy of Betaseron
M01RR-00349-25 0236 (CLR) BODEN, GUENTHER General clinical research center Effect of ethanol on insulin dependent diabetes mellitus
M01RR-00349-25 0237 (CLR) DWORKIN, GERALD E General clinical research center The relationship of physical recreational activity and leisure lifestyle
M01RR-00349-25 0238 (CLR) BODEN, GUENTHER General clinical research center Evaluation of the 72 hour fast in the diagnosis of insulinoma

PROJECT NO., ORGANIZATIONAL UNIT., INVESTIGATOR, ADDRESS, TITLE

M01RR-00349-25 0239 (CLR) BODEN, GUENTHER General clinical research center The neuroendocrine response to open vs laparoscopic cholecystectomy
M01RR-00349-25 0240 (CLR) MANON-ESPAILLAT, RAMON General clinical research center Efficacy of vagal nerve stimuli in treatment of intractable partial seizures
M01RR-00349-25 0241 (CLR) COMEROTA, ANTHONY J General clinical research center N.A. multicenter symptomatic carotid endarterectomy trial
M01RR-00349-25 0223 (CLR) RAO, A KONETI General clinical research center Vasopressin in bleeding disorders due to platelet function defects
M01RR-00349-25 0226 (CLR) HOELDTKE, ROBERT D General clinical research center Characterization of the hypoglycemia unawareness syndrome of diabetes
M01RR-00349-25 0227 (CLR) KRISHNA, GOPAL General clinical research center Potassium depletion in mineralocorticoid-induced sodium retention
M01RR-00350-25 (CLR) BUTLER, WILLIAM T BAYLOR COLLEGE OF MEDICINE ONE BAYLOR PLAZA HOUSTON, TX 77030 General clinical research center
M01RR-00350-25 0462 (CLR) GRAHAM, DAVID Y General clinical research center Use of colonization factor antigen to prevent enterotoxigenic E. coli
M01RR-00350-25 0463 (CLR) PRATT, CRAIG M General clinical research center Sotalol/quinidine in treatment of patients with ventricular ectopic beats
M01RR-00350-25 0464 (CLR) PRATT, CRAIG M General clinical research center Clinical studies of left ventricular dysfunction
M01RR-00350-25 0465 (CLR) GARBER, ALAN J General clinical research center Impact of glipizide therapy on blood glucose and lipid control
M01RR-00350-25 0466 (CLR) BRESSLER, ROBERT B General clinical research center The pathogenesis and pathophysiology of mastocytosis
M01RR-00350-25 0467 (CLR) BOYD, AUBREY E General clinical research center Genetic aspects of multiple endocrine neoplasia, type I
M01RR-00350-25 0246 (CLR) LAWRENCE, E CLINTON General clinical research center Asbestos effects on human alveolar macrophage functions
M01RR-00350-25 0249 (CLR) PRATT, CRAIG M General clinical research center Ethmozine in non-life threatening ventricular arrhythmias
M01RR-00350-25 0322 (CLR) GRAHAM, DAVID Y General clinical research center Comparison of H2-receptor antagonist on 24 hour intragastric pH
M01RR-00350-25 0323 (CLR) LIONBERGER, DAVID A General clinical research center Radiation synovectomy using dysprosium macroaggregates
M01RR-00350-25 0335 (CLR) JANKOVIC, JOSEPH General clinical research center Deprenyl and tocopheryol antioxidative therapy of Parkinsonism
M01RR-00350-25 0336 (CLR) PRATT, CRAIG M General clinical research center Cardiac arrhythmia suppression trial
M01RR-00350-25 0355 (CLR) RAIZNER, ALBERT E General clinical research center Follow up on coronary angioplasties
M01RR-00350-25 0357 (CLR) YOUNG, JAMES B General clinical research center Fluctuation of ventricular function using echocardiography
M01RR-00350-25 0358 (CLR) ZOGHBI, WILLIAM A General clinical research center Myocardial function with echocardiography
M01RR-00350-25 0360 (CLR) CHEIRIF, JORGE General clinical research center Plasma atrial natriuretic factor levels in CHF
M01RR-00350-25 0361 (CLR) GOTTO, ANTONIO M General clinical research center Mevinolin vs. cholestyramine data
M01RR-00350-25 0363 (CLR) ONEIL, GARY General clinical research center Nafazatrom on lipoxygenase activation in open-chest
M01RR-00350-25 0364 (CLR) DEBAKEY, MICHEAL E General clinical research center Heart and heart-lung transplants
M01RR-00350-25 0368 (CLR) PACIFICO, ANTONIO General clinical research center Clinical predictor of tachycardia response to drugs
M01RR-00350-25 0369 (CLR) VERANI, MARIO S General clinical research center Myocardial salvage by coronary reperfusion
M01RR-00350-25 0370 (CLR) SEIGEL, CHARLES General clinical research center Adaption of vascular smooth muscle to pressure
M01RR-00350-25 0372 (CLR) MCBRIDE, MOLLY General clinical research center Variability in bacterial population of normal skin
M01RR-00350-25 0384 (CLR) GIANNINI, EDWARD General clinical research center Ibuprofen in treatment of JRA--A double blind aspirin controlled study
M01RR-00350-25 0468 (CLR) BUTTE, NANCY General clinical research center Energy expenditure/sleep organization of breast fed/formula fed infants
M01RR-00350-25 0389 (CLR) DELCLOS, GEORGE General clinical research center Office evaluation of the asbestos-exposed subjects
M01RR-00350-25 0390 (CLR) NOON, GEORGE General clinical research center Total artificial heart -- Control group patients
M01RR-00350-25 0391 (CLR) KAROUNOS, DENNIS General clinical research center Antibodies in autoimmune endocrine disease and diabetes
M01RR-00350-25 0401 (CLR) GREENBERG, STEPHEN B General clinical research center Retrovir in patients infected with HIV who are asymptomatic
M01RR-00350-25 0403 (CLR) MCCRARY, JOHN A General clinical research center Optic neuritis treatment trial
M01RR-00350-25 0405 (CLR) LAWRENCE, CLINTON E General clinical research center Monitoring rejection with soluble interleukin-2
M01RR-00350-25 0469 (CLR) ADROGUE, HORACIO General clinical research center Diuretic activity of Adotts in a double blind parallel study in man
M01RR-00350-25 0407 (CLR) LAWRENCE, CLINTON E General clinical research center Interleukin-2 receptors in sarcoidosis
M01RR-00350-25 0410 (CLR) GAGEL, ROBERT General clinical research center Genetic aspects of multiple endocrine neoplasia, type 2A
M01RR-00350-25 0414 (CLR) GRAHAM, DAVID Y General clinical research center Synthetic rate of human plasma apolipoproteins
M01RR-00350-25 0417 (CLR) POOL, JAMES L General clinical research center Pharmacokinetics of terazosin and verapamil in treatment of hypertension

PROJECT NO., ORGANIZATIONAL UNIT., INVESTIGATOR, ADDRESS, TITLE

M01RR-00350-25 0418 (CLR) ELKIND-HIRSCH, KAREN General clinical research center Hyperandrogen states and insulin resistance
M01RR-00350-25 0419 (CLR) GRAHAM, DAVID General clinical research center In vivo measurement of hepatic mixed function oxidase
M01RR-00350-25 0420 (CLR) GRAHAM, DAVID Y General clinical research center Changes in aminopyrine metabolism in patients in the Houston area
M01RR-00350-25 0470 (CLR) POWNALL, HENRY General clinical research center Interaction of dietary alcohol and fat
M01RR-00350-25 0471 (CLR) GAGEL, ROBERT General clinical research center A cyclic treatment for postmenopausal osteroporosis
M01RR-00350-25 0472 (CLR) PRATT, CRAIG M General clinical research center Amiodarone in patients with potentially lethal ventricular arrhythmia
M01RR-00350-25 0473 (CLR) MORRISETT, JOEL D General clinical research center Stable isotope studies of synthesis of human lipoprotein (A)
M01RR-00350-25 0474 (CLR) GOTTO, ANTONIO General clinical research center Lipoproteins and clearance of dietary fat before and after gemfibrozil
M01RR-00350-25 0475 (CLR) CHAPPEL, CYNTHIA General clinical research center Generic and brand-name verapamil and its metabolites in elderly and young
M01RR-00350-25 0476 (CLR) GLENNON, TERRENCE General clinical research center Pravastatin and lovastatin on eccentric exercise-induced changes/muscle
M01RR-00350-25 0477 (CLR) PATEL, VASISHTA General clinical research center Time modulation of epileptiform discharges to physiological rhythms
M01RR-00350-25 0478 (CLR) BOYD, AUBREY E General clinical research center Chronic sandostatin treatment in acromegalic patients
M01RR-00350-25 0479 (CLR) LEWIS, RICHARD General clinical research center Studies of the ocular complications of AIDS--CMV retinitis trial
M01RR-00350-25 0480 (CLR) GRAHAM, DAVID Y General clinical research center Treatment of intractable hiccup with the GABA analogue baclofen
M01RR-00350-25 0481 (CLR) GOTTO, ANTONIO General clinical research center Comparison of extended-released lovastatin to conventional lovastatin
M01RR-00350-25 0482 (CLR) CHUONG, C JAMES General clinical research center Effects of naloxone on luteinizing hormone secretion in PMS
M01RR-00350-25 0483 (CLR) FOREYT, JOHN General clinical research center Glucose and insulin responses to liquid breakfast and carbohydrate meals
M01RR-00350-25 0484 (CLR) KLEIN, PETER General clinical research center Biosynthetically 13C-labeled triglyceride in lipid oxidation studies
M01RR-00350-25 0422 (CLR) RAIZNER, ALBERT E General clinical research center Therapeutic modalities in acute myocardial infarction
M01RR-00350-25 0427 (CLR) PRATT, CRAIG M General clinical research center Antiarrhythmic and hemodynamic effect of cibenzoline
M01RR-00350-25 0429 (CLR) GRAHAM, DAVID Y General clinical research center Production of Norwalk virus in human volunteers
M01RR-00350-25 0433 (CLR) BOYD, AUBREY E General clinical research center Natural history of idiopathic hyperprolactinemia
M01RR-00350-25 0435 (CLR) PATSCH, WOLFANG General clinical research center Cholesterol-rich diet and plasma lipid transport
M01RR-00350-25 0437 (CLR) BOYD, AUBREY E General clinical research center CRH stimulation test in evaluation of patients with Cushing's syndrome
M01RR-00350-25 0438 (CLR) HERD, J ALAN General clinical research center Post coronary artery bypass graft study
M01RR-00350-25 0440 (CLR) POINDEXTER, ALFRED N General clinical research center: Effect of norethindrone microspheres on pituitary gonadotropin pulsatility
M01RR-00350-25 0444 (CLR) CARTER, BARRY L General clinical research center Pharmacokinetic evaluation of generic brand-name verapamil
M01RR-00350-25 0446 (CLR) BOYD, AUBREY E General clinical research center Sandostatin for reduction of growth hormone levels in acromegaly
M01RR-00350-25 0447 (CLR) GRAHAM, DAVID Y General clinical research center Effect of C pylori on bombesin-stimulated plasma gastrin concentration
M01RR-00350-25 0449 (CLR) TAYLOR, ADDISON A General clinical research center Renin inhibitor on cardiovascular hemodynamics in hypertension
M01RR-00350-25 0450 (CLR) TAYLOR, ADDISON A General clinical research center Concurrent administration of CGS 12970 and enalapril for hypertension
M01RR-00350-25 0451 (CLR) ELKIND-HIRSCH, KAREN General clinical research center Nonclassical 21 hydroxylase deficiency--Genotype and phenotype in women
M01RR-00350-25 0454 (CLR) KEITEL, WENDY General clinical research center Evaluation of vaccines for the prevention of typhoid fever
M01RR-00350-25 0457 (CLR) SCHWARTZ, PATRICIA General clinical research center Evaluation of American Lung Association package for school children
M01RR-00350-25 0458 (CLR) HABIB, JUBRAN B General clinical research center Blood pressure reduction with nifedipine on cardiac mass and function
M01RR-00350-25 0459 (CLR) OZCAN, GURHAN General clinical research center Vascularized nerve grafts to repair facial nerve defects
M01RR-00350-25 0460 (CLR) KEITEL, WENDY A General clinical research center Ascending doses of Lederle's poliovirus vaccine vs inactivated PV vaccine
P40RR-00393-24 (AR) JACOBY, ROBERT O YALE UNIVERSITY 333 CEDAR STREET; P.O. BOX 333 NEW HAVEN, CT 06510 Resource for study of laboratory animal diseases
P40RR-00393-24 0002 (AR) BRANDSMA, JANET L Resource for study of laboratory animal diseases A rabbit model of human papillomatosis
P40RR-00393-24 0003 (AR) JACOBY, ROBERT O Resource for study of laboratory animal diseases Studies of Herpesvirus simiae (B virus) infection in monkeys and mice

PROJECT NUMBER LISTING

PROJECT NO., ORGANIZATIONAL UNIT., INVESTIGATOR, ADDRESS, TITLE

P40RR-00393-24 0004 (AR) SMITH, ABIGAIL L Resource for study of laboratory animal diseases Activation of latent Pneumocystis carinii infection in mice with SCID
P40RR-00393-24 0005 (AR) BROWNSTEIN, DAVID G Resource for study of laboratory animal diseases Virus excretion in mice infected with Theiler's mouse encephalomyelitis
P40RR-00393-24 0006 (AR) BROWNSTEIN, DAVID G Resource for study of laboratory animal diseases Molecular pathogenisis of minute virus of mice (MVM) infection
P40RR-00393-24 0007 (AR) GAERTNER, DIANE J Resource for study of laboratory animal diseases Antigenic characterization of rat coronaviruses (RCVs)
P40RR-00393-24 0008 (AR) BRANDSMA, ABIGAIL L Resource for study of laboratory animal diseases Genomic probes for detection of murine viruses
P40RR-00393-24 0009 (AR) WEIR, ELEANOR C Resource for study of laboratory animal diseases Elimination of viral infection in mice by embryo transplantation
M01RR-00400-23 0280 (CLR) ZEHRER, JACINTA L General clinical research center Quality of life following pancreas transplant
M01RR-00400-23 (CLR) CAVERT, H MEAD UNIVERSITY OF MINNESOTA BOX 504 UMHC MINNEAPOLI, MN 55455 General clinical research center
M01RR-00400-23 0075 (CLR) BARBOSA, JOSE J General clinical research center Endocrine and immunological studies of kindreds with diabetes
M01RR-00400-23 0091 (CLR) BLUMENTHAL, MALCOLM N General clinical research center Genetic mapping of Ir gene to ragweed antigen
M01RR-00400-23 0097 (CLR) SUTHERLAND, DAVID E General clinical research center Pancreas transplantation into diabetic patients
M01RR-00400-23 0126 (CLR) BARBOSA, JOSE J General clinical research center Effect of plasma glucose control on renal vascular disease
M01RR-00400-23 0185 (CLR) BANTLE, JOHN P General clinical research center Diabetes control and complications trial
M01RR-00400-23 0286 (CLR) HERTZ, MARSHALL I General clinical research center Bronchoalveolar lavage in the immunocompromised host
M01RR-00400-23 0287 (CLR) BALFOUR, HENRY H General clinical research center The effect of H2 antagonists on the pharmacokinetics of zidovudine
M01RR-00400-23 0288 (CLR) FISH, ALFRED General clinical research center Abnormalities of the ureter--Linkage to the HLA gene region
M01RR-00400-23 0289 (CLR) BANTLE, JOHN P General clinical research center Influence of the anatomic site of insulin injection on subsequent plasma glucose
M01RR-00400-23 0290 (CLR) HATSUKAMI, DOROTHY General clinical research center Smoked cocaine use in humans
M01RR-00400-23 0291 (CLR) ROBERTSON, R PAUL General clinical research center Iron metabolism in diabetes mellitus
M01RR-00400-23 0292 (CLR) BANTLE, JOHN P General clinical research center Effects of two different dietary regimens on glucose and lipid metabolism
M01RR-00400-23 0293 (CLR) MILLER, WESLEY J General clinical research center Molecular biology of tissue macrophages in CML
M01RR-00400-23 0294 (CLR) BARBOSA, JOSE J General clinical research center Natural history of genetics of diabetic nephropathy
M01RR-00400-23 0295 (CLR) OPPENHEIMER, JACK H General clinical research center Evaluation for the presence of a reactive tumor in 21-hydroxylase deficiency
M01RR-00400-23 0296 (CLR) WINKELMANN, JOHN General clinical research center Fibrinogen RFLPs in Japanese and Caucasians
M01RR-00400-23 0206 (CLR) ROBERTSON, R PAUL General clinical research center Pancreas transplantation--Pancreatic function in recipients and donors
M01RR-00400-23 0209 (CLR) MAUER, S MICHAEL General clinical research center Structural-functional relationships in diabetic nephropathy
M01RR-00400-23 0211 (CLR) BANTLE, JOHN P General clinical research center Metabolic effects of chronic dietary fructose/sucrose consumption
M01RR-00400-23 0220 (CLR) BARBOSA, JOSE J General clinical research center Randomized trail of nicotinamide to prevent progressive beta cell destruction
M01RR-00400-23 0229 (CLR) NATH, CARL General clinical research center Rate and determinants of progression in diabetes and other nephropathies
M01RR-00400-23 0230 (CLR) HUNNINGHAKE, DONALD General clinical research center Adherence related behavior in a clinical trial
M01RR-00400-23 0232 (CLR) NEVINS, THOMAS General clinical research center Prognostic determinants of chronic uremia in early life
M01RR-00400-23 0233 (CLR) MANN, HENRY General clinical research center Pharmacokinetics in critically ill patients
M01RR-00400-23 0239 (CLR) SUTHERLAND, DAVID General clinical research center International pancreas transplant registry
M01RR-00400-23 0243 (CLR) HUNNINGHAKE, DONALD General clinical research center Use of soluble fibers to lower serum cholestrol
M01RR-00400-23 0244 (CLR) ESTRIN, JORGE A General clinical research center Intraoperative hemodynamic studies
M01RR-00400-23 0245 (CLR) HERTZ, MARSHALL General clinical research center Cytomegalovirus-induced acute lung injury
M01RR-00400-23 0246 (CLR) MANSKE, CONNIE L General clinical research center Cardiovascular risk factors in diabetic renal transplant
M01RR-00400-23 0255 (CLR) ROBERTSON, PAUL R General clinical research center Pancreatic islet function in cystic fibrosis
M01RR-00400-23 0257 (CLR) KUBO, SPENCER H General clinical research center Vasoconstrictor mechanism in heart failure using an isolated forearm model
M01RR-00400-23 0261 (CLR) HOSTETTER, THOMAS General clinical research center Effect of protein intake on renal function in chronic rejection
M01RR-00400-23 0264 (CLR) BITTERMAN, PETER General clinical research center Acute lung injury study
M01RR-00400-23 0269 (CLR) HOSTETTER, MARGARET K General clinical research center International adoptees
M01RR-00400-23 0271 (CLR) HUNNINGHAKE, DONALD B General clinical research center Post coronary bypass graft studies--An NIH multicenter trial
M01RR-00400-23 0273 (CLR) COLON, EDWARD A General clinical research center Allergy and affective disorders
M01RR-00400-23 0274 (CLR) MELLER, WILLIAM General clinical research center Arginine vasopressin challenge test in major depression
M01RR-00400-23 0275 (CLR) MAUER, S MICHEAL General clinical research center Corr. of AGT act. and outcome of kd. tx. in type I hyperoxaluria
M01RR-00400-23 0276 (CLR) MATAS, ARTHUR J General clinical research center Immunosuppression induced renal lesions in long term kidney tx. patients
M01RR-00400-23 0277 (CLR) MAUER, MICHAEL S General clinical research center Natural history of diabetic nephropathy in young insulin dependent diabetics
M01RR-00400-23 0278 (CLR) BALFOUR, HENRY General clinical research center A trial to evaluate IVIG in children with symptomatic HIV infection
M01RR-00400-23 0279 (CLR) KNOPMAN, DAVID General clinical research center Implicit learning in drug-induced amnesia
P40RR-00419-24 (AR) SHEPP, BRYAN E BROWN UNIVERSITY 89 WATERMAN STREET PROVIDENCE, RI 02912 Support for laboratory primate newsletter
M01RR-00425-22S3 (CLR) SWANSON, WILLIAM H HARBOR-UCLA MEDICAL CENTER 1124 WEST CARSON STREET TORRANCE, CA 90502-2064 General clinical research center
M01RR-00425-22S3 0237 (CLR) CHLEBOWSKI, ROWAN T General clinical research center Hydrazine sulfate in cancer cachexia
M01RR-00425-22S3 0247 (CLR) HEBER, DAVID General clinical research center Superactive GNRH treatment of prostatic adenocarcinoma
M01RR-00425-22S3 0299 (CLR) CASABURI, RICHARD General clinical research center Coupling of external to cellular respiration during exercise
M01RR-00425-22S3 0304 (CLR) SWERDLOFF, RONALD S General clinical research center Use of GnRH in the treatment of prostatic carcinoma
M01RR-00425-22S3 0305 (CLR) POLAND, RUSSELL E General clinical research center Chronoendocrinology of sleep disturbances in depression
M01RR-00425-22S3 0312 (CLR) BRASEL, JO ANNE General clinical research center Therapy with growth hormone analog and oxandrolone in Turner's syndrome
M01RR-00425-22S3 0389 (CLR) SWERDLOFF, RONALD S General clinical research center Systemic tolerance and safety of the transdermal therapeutic system
M01RR-00425-22S3 0390 (CLR) TAYEK, JOHN A General clinical research center Insulin mediated effects on protein metabolism in cancer patients
M01RR-00425-22S3 0391 (CLR) OSEAS, RONALD S General clinical research center Children's cancer study group--High dose cytoxan study
M01RR-00425-22S3 0392 (CLR) MASON, GREGORY General clinical research center Whole lung lavage for treatment of pneumoconiosis
M01RR-00425-22S3 0396 (CLR) KOPPLE, JOEL D General clinical research center Taurine nutrition in patients undergoing long term TPN
M01RR-00425-22S3 0400 (CLR) KANDEEL, FOUAD General clinical research center Opioids and hormonal metabolic abnormalities in polycystic ovarian disease
M01RR-00425-22S3 0401 (CLR) BRASEL, JO ANNE General clinical research center Somatotropin therapy in growth hormone deficient children
M01RR-00425-22S3 0403 (CLR) IPP, ELI General clinical research center Physiological characteristics of response to glipizide in NIDDM
M01RR-00425-22S3 0406 (CLR) BRUBAKER, DAVID General clinical research center Function of elevated plasma fibronectin in pre-eclampsia
M01RR-00425-22S3 0408 (CLR) SNAPE, WILLIAM A General clinical research center Determination of simultaneous colonic motility and transit
M01RR-00425-22S3 0409 (CLR) KANDEEL, FOUAD General clinical research center Treatment of unruptured ectopic pregnancy with methotrexate
M01RR-00425-22S3 0410 (CLR) KOPPLE, JOEL D General clinical research center Energy metabolism in uremia
M01RR-00425-22S3 0411 (CLR) BRASEL, JO ANNE General clinical research center Growth hormone and cancer cachexia
M01RR-00425-22S3 0412 (CLR) MCCRACKEN, JAMES T General clinical research center Sleep and hormone regulation in juvenile depression
M01RR-00425-22S3 0414 (CLR) ADLER, SHARON General clinical research center ACE inhibitors and diabetic nephropathy
M01RR-00425-22S3 0415 (CLR) SIEGER, LANCE General clinical research center Decreased growth velocity/children with pediatric malignancies
M01RR-00425-22S3 0416 (CLR) BHASIN, SHALENDER General clinical research center Metabolic effects of testosterone in man
M01RR-00425-22S3 0418 (CLR) MASON, GREGORY R General clinical research center Aerosolized pentamidine/oral TMP-SX in pneumocytosis in AIDS
M01RR-00425-22S3 0419 (CLR) CHLEBOWSKI, ROWAN T General clinical research center Nutrition, gastrointestinal dysfunction and AIDS
M01RR-00425-22S3 0322 (CLR) RIMOIN, DAVID L General clinical research center Genetics and pathogenesis of birth defects
M01RR-00425-22S3 0325 (CLR) CHLEBOWSKI, ROWAN T General clinical research center Glucose metabolism and hydrazine in cancer cachexia
M01RR-00425-22S3 0327 (CLR) SWERDLOFF, RONALD S General clinical research center Phase I and phase II clinical studies with LHRH antagonist
M01RR-00425-22S3 0345 (CLR) PADBURY, JAMES F General clinical research center Catecholamine response in preterm infants at time of birth
M01RR-00425-22S3 0353 (CLR) IPP, ELI General clinical research center Insulin infusion test as diagnostic tool in investigation of hypoglycemia
M01RR-00425-22S3 0357 (CLR) BRASEL, JO ANNE General clinical research center Buserelin therapy of precocious puberty
M01RR-00425-22S3 0367 (CLR) HEINER, DOUGLAS C General clinical

PROJECT NO., ORGANIZATIONAL UNIT., INVESTIGATOR, ADDRESS, TITLE

research center Immunoglobulin levels associated with premature membrane rupture
M01RR-00425-22S3 0371 (CLR) HYMAN, PAUL E General clinical research center Cisapride in treatment of children with GI motility disorders
M01RR-00425-22S3 0376 (CLR) IPP, ELI General clinical research center Glucagon-stimulated C-peptide secretion--Effect of hyperglycemia
M01RR-00425-22S3 0380 (CLR) KANDEEL, FOUAD R General clinical research center Dexamethasone effect on pituitary release of pro-OLMC peptides
M01RR-00425-22S3 0382 (CLR) KOPPLE, JOEL D General clinical research center Dietary protein and phosphorus and renal insufficiency
M01RR-00425-22S3 0384 (CLR) KOPPLE, JOEL D General clinical research center Enalapril and microalbuminuria in diabetes mellitus
M01RR-00425-22S3 0420 (CLR) HYMAN, PAUL E General clinical research center Cisapride effect in children with pseudo-obstruction
M01RR-00425-22S3 0437 (CLR) HYMAN, PAUL E General clinical research center GI hormones in children with chronic pseudoobstruction
M01RR-00425-22S3 0440 (CLR) SIEGER, LANCE General clinical research center Serum and cerebrospinal fluid alphafetoprotein levels in newborns
M01RR-00425-22S3 0441 (CLR) HENSON, LINDSEY C General clinical research center Energy expenditure in obesity
M01RR-00425-22S3 0442 (CLR) IPP, ELI General clinical research center Type II diabetes mellitus
M01RR-00425-22S3 0443 (CLR) BERMAN, NANCY General clinical research center GCRC biostatistical support
M01RR-00425-22S3 0446 (CLR) BUTLER, JOHN General clinical research center Factors contributing to improvement of malignant biliary obstruction
M01RR-00425-22S3 0447 (CLR) PELIKAN, PETER General clinical research center Early noninvasive testing in predicting high grade stenoses
M01RR-00425-22S3 0448 (CLR) MCCRACKEN, JAMES T General clinical research center Hormone rhythms--Metabolic significance in depression
M01RR-00425-22S3 0449 (CLR) LIN, KEH-MING General clinical research center Psychopharmacological issues in the treatment of asian patients
M01RR-00425-22S3 0450 (CLR) IPP, ELI General clinical research center Central control of glucose homeostasis
M01RR-00425-22S3 0451 (CLR) CHLEBOWSKI, ROWAN T General clinical research center Low fat diet in stage II breast cancer
M01RR-00425-22S3 0452 (CLR) SWERDLOFF, RONALD S General clinical research center Hyperendorphinism and pathophysiology of polycystic ovarian disease
M01RR-00425-22S3 0453 (CLR) KANDEEL, FOUAD General clinical research center Objective measures and GI morbidity reduction
M01RR-00425-22S3 0454 (CLR) BRASEL, JO ANNE General clinical research center Blood and urine growth factor levels in patients with various disease states
M01RR-00425-22S3 0455 (CLR) IPP, ELI General clinical research center Physiological characterization of NIDDM
M01RR-00425-22S3 0456 (CLR) BECK, KEITH C General clinical research center Trimetrexate vs trimethoprim/sulfamethoxazole for pneumocytis pneumonia
M01RR-00425-22S3 0458 (CLR) KLETZKY, OSCAR A General clinical research center Opioids in amenorrhea
M01RR-00425-22S3 0459 (CLR) BHASIN, SHALENDAR General clinical research center Bioavailability of testosterone from a microcapsule in hypogonadal men
M01RR-00425-22S3 0460 (CLR) SNAPE, WILLIAM J General clinical research center MK329 antagonism of meal induced colonic motility
M01RR-00425-22S3 0461 (CLR) KOPPLE, JOEL D General clinical research center Use of dianeal in continuous ambulatory dialysis patients
M01RR-00425-22S3 0462 (CLR) KOPPLE, JOEL D General clinical research center Anabolic effects of growth hormone in chronic renal failure
M01RR-00425-22S3 0463 (CLR) HYMAN, PAUL E General clinical research center Long term evaluation of R51619 in pseudoobstruction
M01RR-00425-22S3 0464 (CLR) ISENBERG, SHERWIN J General clinical research center Povidone-iodine for neonatal ophthalmic prophylaxis
M01RR-00425-22S3 0465 (CLR) ROSS, MICHAEL G General clinical research center Urinary TXA2 and PGI2 in pre-eclampsia
M01RR-00425-22S3 0466 (CLR) BRASEL, JO ANNE General clinical research center Growth factors and hormones in fetal and infant growth
M01RR-00425-22S3 0467 (CLR) PADBURY, JAMES F General clinical research center Naloxone and neonatal adaptation in the human
M01RR-00425-22S3 0468 (CLR) ANTHONY, BASCOM F General clinical research center Group B streptococci and host defense
M01RR-00425-22S3 0422 (CLR) IPP, ELI General clinical research center Insulin-secreting tumors--Improved diagnostic approaches
M01RR-00425-22S3 0423 (CLR) HEINER, DOUGLAS C General clinical research center Multicenter safety study of a new IV immunoglobulin preparation
M01RR-00425-22S3 0424 (CLR) ISENBERG, SHERWIN J General clinical research center Transconjunctival oxygen monitoring in the newborn
M01RR-00425-22S3 0425 (CLR) FISHER, DELBERT A General clinical research center Urinary vasopressin in healthy and sick newborn infants
M01RR-00425-22S3 0426 (CLR) LEAKE, ROSEMARY D General clinical research center Estrogen-stimulated oxytocin-vasotocin material in human plasma
M01RR-00425-22S3 0429 (CLR) PADBURY, JAMES F General clinical research center Physiologic basis for inotropic support in the newborn
M01RR-00425-22S3 0430 (CLR) HEINER, DOUGLAS C General clinical research center Immunoglobulins and antibodies in neonatal necrotizing enterocolitis
M01RR-00425-22S3 0431 (CLR) HEINER, DOUGLAS C General clinical research center Immunoglobulin class and subclass levels in bronchopulmonary dysplasia
M01RR-00425-22S3 0432 (CLR) PADBURY, JAMES F General clinical research center TRH and the prevention of neonatal respiratory distress syndrome

PROJECT NO., ORGANIZATIONAL UNIT., INVESTIGATOR, ADDRESS, TITLE

M01RR-00425-22S3 0433 (CLR) WEICHSEL, MORTON A General clinical research center Serum growth factor in the newborn human
M01RR-00425-22S3 0434 (CLR) LONKY, NEAL M General clinical research center Serum alpha-1-antitrypsin activity and preterm premature membrane rupture
M01RR-00425-22S3 0436 (CLR) IKEGAMI, MACHIKO General clinical research center Multiple doses of surfactant TA in treatment of neonatal RDS
P40RR-00463-23 (AR) LINDSEY, J RUSSELL UNIVERSITY OF ALABAMA SCHOOLS OF MED & DENTISTRY BIRMINGHAM, AL 35294 Laboratory animal resource for biomedical research
P40RR-00463-23 0005 (AR) WOOD, PHILIP A Laboratory animal resource for biomedical research Molecular genetic monitoring of inbred strains of mice
P40RR-00463-23 0001 (AR) SCHOEB, TRENTON R Laboratory animal resource for biomedical research Virulence and diagnosis of cilia-associated respiratory bacillus
P40RR-00463-23 0002 (AR) DAVIDSON, MAUREEN K Laboratory animal resource for biomedical research Derivation of a mycoplasma-free F344 rat stock
P40RR-00463-23 0003 (AR) STEPHENSEN, CHARLES R Laboratory animal resource for biomedical research Detection of coronaviruses by nucleic acid hybridization assay
P40RR-00463-23 0004 (AR) CASEBOLT, DONALD B Laboratory animal resource for biomedical research A reproducible model of Reye's Syndrome
P40RR-00469-23 (AR) LANG, C MAX MILTON S HERSHEY MEDICAL CTR PO BOX 850 HERSHEY PA 17033 Laboratory animal diagnostic resource
P40RR-00471-22 (AR) WAGNER, JOSEPH E UNIVERSITY OF MISSOURI COLLEGE OF VETERINARY MEDICINE COLUMBIA, MO 65211 Research animal diagnostic and investigative laboratory
P41RR-00480-23 (SSS) WATSON, JACK T MICHIGAN STATE UNIVERSITY EAST LANSING, MICH 48824 NIH/MSU mass spectrometry facility
P41RR-00480-23 9001 (SSS) WATSON, JACK T NIH/MSU mass spectrometry facility Core research--Developments in time-array detection
P41RR-00480-23 9002 (SSS) WATSON,JACK T NIH/MSU mass spectrometry facility Core research--Ion-molecule interactions
P41RR-00480-23 9003 (SSS) WATSON, JACK T NIH/MSU mass spectrometry facility Core research--Biochemical metabolic profiling
M01RR-00533-23 (CLR) SANDSON, JOHN I BOSTON UNIVERSITY SCH OF MED 80 EAST CONCORD STREET BOSTON, MA 02118 General clinical research center
M01RR-00533-23 0142 (CLR) SKINNER, MARTHA General clinical research center Human amyloidosis
M01RR-00533-23 0180 (CLR) ZEISEL, STEVEN H General clinical research center Choline deficiency in humans
M01RR-00533-23 0187 (CLR) HOLICK, MICHAEL F. General clinical research center 1,25 Dihydroxyvitamin D3 in patients with psoriasis
M01RR-00533-23 0189 (CLR) FALK, RODNEY General clinical research center Ventricular thrombi in dilated cardiomyopathy
M01RR-00533-23 0197 (CLR) LIEBMAN, HOWARD General clinical research center Phase I-II study of dideoxyinosine in the treatment of HIV disease
M01RR-00533-23 0200 (CLR) MELBY, JAMES General clinical research center Hypothalamic-pituitary-adrenal function in AIDS
M01RR-00533-23 0201 (CLR) MIROCHNICK, MARK General clinical research center Intravenous AZT in infants with HIV
M01RR-00533-23 0202 (CLR) PELTON, STEPHEN General clinical research center Gamma globulin in children with symptomatic HIV
M01RR-00533-23 0203 (CLR) FALK, RODNEY General clinical research center Exercise echocardiography in patients with rheumatic valvular disease
M01RR-00533-23 0204 (CLR) CHIPKIN, STUART R General clinical research center Lopid in patients with noninsulin dependent diabetes mellitus
M01RR-00533-23 0205 (CLR) CRAVEN, DONALD General clinical research center AZT in patients with HIV infection and hepatic disease
M01RR-00533-23 0206 (CLR) CHIPKIN, STUART R General clinical research center Cardiovascular disease in diabetics with autonomic neuropathy
M01RR-00533-23 0207 (CLR) ZEISEL, STEVEN H General clinical research center Oligosaccharides as non-nutritive sweetners
M01RR-00533-23 0208 (CLR) PHILLIPS, TANIA General clinical research center Treatment of epidermal allografts in the treatment of leg ulcers
M01RR-00533-23 0209 (CLR) HOLICK, MICHAEL F General clinical research center Osteoporotic bone disease-- Treatment with PTH and vitamin D
M01RR-00533-23 0210 (CLR) BERNARD, DAVID B General clinical research center Dianeal with 1.1% amino acids in malnourished CAPD patients
M01RR-00533-23 0211 (CLR) HOLICK, MICHAEL F General clinical research center Whole body calcium using Norland XR 26 densitometer
M01RR-00533-23 0212 (CLR) HOLICK, MICHAEL F General clinical research center Effects of calcitriol therapy in renal function
M01RR-00533-23 0213 (CLR) HOLICK, MICHAEL F General clinical research center Stable isotope measure dietary fiber, vitamin D and calcium
P41RR-00570-21 (SSS) SCHATTEN, GERALD P UNIVERSITY OF WISCONSIN 1675 OBSERVATORY DRIVE MADISON WI 53706 Integrated microscopy resource for biomedical research
P41RR-00570-21 0001 (SSS) SCHATTEN, G Integrated microscopy resource for biomedical research 3-D analysis of fertilization and development over time
P41RR-00570-21 0003 (SSS) BORISY, GARY Integrated microscopy resource for biomedical research Cytoskeletal dynamics
P41RR-00570-21 0004 (SSS) SEPSENWOL, SOL Integrated microscopy resource for biomedical research Dynamics of the amoeboid sperm motility of the nematode, Ascaris
P41RR-00570-21 0005 (SSS) LONGO, FRANK Integrated microscopy resource for biomedical research Sperm-egg fusion--Structural-electrical correlations
P41RR-00570-21 0006 (SSS) ALBRECHT, RALPH Integrated microscopy

resource for biomedical research Correlative video, HVEM, & LVSEM-Membrane receptor movement
P41RR-00570-21 0007 (SSS) BORISY, GARY Integrated microscopy resource for biomedical research Dynamics of microfilaments and microtubules in fibroblast
P41RR-00570-21 0008 (SSS) HAGGIS, GEOFFREY Integrated microscopy resource for biomedical research Freeze-fracture for high resolution scanning EM
P41RR-00570-21 0009 (SSS) RIS, HANS Integrated microscopy resource for biomedical research Structure of the nuclear envelope pore complex
P41RR-00570-21 0010 (SSS) SCHATTEN, GERALD Integrated microscopy resource for biomedical research Use of LVSEM to detect carbohydrate moieties and lectin binding
P41RR-00570-21 0011 (SSS) GERHART, JOHN Integrated microscopy resource for biomedical research Microtubule mediated cortical rotation in Xenopus egg
P41RR-00570-21 0012 (SSS) SCHWEITZER, ERIK Integrated microscopy resource for biomedical research Localization of vesicle markers in PC12 cells
P41RR-00570-21 0013 (SSS) OLIVER, CONNIE Integrated microscopy resource for biomedical research Antibody labelling of rat leukemia cells
P41RR-00570-21 0014 (SSS) PETERS, DONNA Integrated microscopy resource for biomedical research Alignment and assembly of fibronectin and collagen
P41RR-00570-21 0015 (SSS) MARTIN, THOMAS Integrated microscopy resource for biomedical research Second messenger regulation of secretion
P41RR-00570-21 0016 (SSS) GREASER, MARION Integrated microscopy resource for biomedical research Structure and function of titin in muscle
P41RR-00570-21 0017 (SSS) FLORMAN, HARVEY Integrated microscopy resource for biomedical research Regulation of intracellular calcium and pH
P41RR-00570-21 9001 (SSS) SCHATTEN, G Integrated microscopy resource for biomedical research Low voltage scanning electron microscopy
P41RR-00570-21 9002 (SSS) SCHATTEN, G Integrated microscopy resource for biomedical research Confocal and video microscopy
P41RR-00570-21 9003 (SSS) SCHATTEN, GERALD Integrated microscopy resource for biomedical research Integrated microscopy
M01RR-00585-20 (CLR) PRENDERGAST, FRANKLYN G MAYO FOUNDATION 200 FIRST STREET SOUTHWEST ROCHESTER, MN 55905 General clinical research center
M01RR-00585-20 0456 (CLR) HOLMES, D R General clinical research center Randomized trial of controlled surgery vs mechanical
M01RR-00585-20 0457 (CLR) DIMAGNO, E P General clinical research center Pancreatitis and pancreatic cancer--A cohort study
M01RR-00585-20 0459 (CLR) RIGGS, B L General clinical research center Circadian rhythms of electrolytes and minerals in osteoporosis
M01RR-00585-20 0460 (CLR) VASSALLO, M General clinical research center GI transit in CUC and IBS patients with diarrhea
M01RR-00585-20 0461 (CLR) CAMILLERI, M General clinical research center Regional colonic transit in patients with severe idiopathic constipation
M01RR-00585-20 0462 (CLR) BERSETH, C General clinical research center Intestinal motility in pre-term and term infants in fasted and fed states
M01RR-00585-20 0463 (CLR) VELOSA, J A General clinical research center Lovastatin renal transplant study
M01RR-00585-20 0464 (CLR) FIELD, C S General clinical research center Estraderm TTS combination estradiol to control menopause/postmenopause symptoms
M01RR-00585-20 0465 (CLR) JENSEN, M D General clinical research center FFA metabolism in different kinds of human obesity--Forearm lypolysis
M01RR-00585-20 0466 (CLR) MCCANNAL, C A General clinical research center Circadian pattern and effect of timolol on aqueous humor flow
M01RR-00585-20 0468 (CLR) STEADMAN, C J General clinical research center Control of muscle tone in the human colon
M01RR-00585-20 0469 (CLR) MIEDEMA, B W General clinical research center GI motility after Roux-Y gastrojejunostomy
M01RR-00585-20 0470 (CLR) EBELING, P General clinical research center Effects of growth hormone on nocturnal bone formation in young women
M01RR-00585-20 0471 (CLR) HAYMOND, M W General clinical research center Effects of insulin withdrawal on protein synthesis in diabetics
M01RR-00585-20 0472 (CLR) MISER, J S General clinical research center Osteosarcoma
M01RR-00585-20 0473 (CLR) KROM, R A General clinical research center Liver transplantation database
M01RR-00585-20 0476 (CLR) PHILLIPS, S F General clinical research center Gastrointestinal enzymes
M01RR-00585-20 0478 (CLR) KENNEDY, F P General clinical research center Glycemia response in diet controlled diabetics using ensure
M01RR-00585-20 0479 (CLR) HAYES, D L General clinical research center Survival and ventricular enlargement effect of captopril
M01RR-00585-20 0481 (CLR) MISER, J S General clinical research center Phase I study of piritrexim capsule in pediatric patients with cancer
M01RR-00585-20 0482 (CLR) ZACHARIAH, P K General clinical research center Zestril vs. verapamil in the treatment of hypertension
M01RR-00585-20 0483 (CLR) RODEHEFFER, R J General clinical research center Randomized, phase III--Milrinone in patients with severe heart failure
M01RR-00585-20 0487 (CLR) RIGGS, B L General clinical research center Defects of structural genes for collagen in osteoporosis
M01RR-00585-20 0488 (CLR) LOW, P A General clinical research center Mathematical modeling and analysis of neurophysiology data
M01RR-00585-20 0490 (CLR) KOTTKE, BRUCE A General clinical research center Plasma apolipoprotein levels in patients--Nuclear cardiologic techniques
M01RR-00585-20 0492 (CLR) KOTTKE, BRUCE A General clinical research center Comparison of immunoreactivity of different antibodies to apolipoprotein A-1
M01RR-00585-20 0493 (CLR) TEXTOR, S C General clinical research center Cyclosporine induced hypertension in patients undergoing liver transplantation
M01RR-00585-20 0494 (CLR) LINDOR, K D General clinical research center Randomized trial evaluating URSO in treatment of primary sclerosing cholangitis
M01RR-00585-20 0495 (CLR) KOTTKE, BRUCE A General clinical research center Effects of an exercise program on plasma lipid and apolipoprotein levels
M01RR-00585-20 0496 (CLR) CHESEBRO, J H General clinical research center Congestive heart failure data file
M01RR-00585-20 0497 (CLR) CAMERON, G STRONG General clinical research center Continuing care program for hypertension
M01RR-00585-20 0498 (CLR) KALTHOFF, L General clinical research center Course of alcoholic / non-alcoholic chronic pancreatitis
M01RR-00585-20 0115 (CLR) RIZZA, R A General clinical research center Gastric inhibitory polypeptide (GIP) in health and disease
M01RR-00585-20 0416 (CLR) SHEPARD, J W General clinical research center Dynamic behavior of the upper airway awake and asleep
M01RR-00585-20 0417 (CLR) SCHWARTZ, G General clinical research center Safety and efficiency of spirapril
M01RR-00585-20 0418 (CLR) SCHIRGER, ALEXANDER General clinical research center Management of patients with orthostatic hypotension with midodrine
M01RR-00585-20 0420 (CLR) CZAJA, A General clinical research center Chronic active liver disease
M01RR-00585-20 0421 (CLR) CZAJA, A General clinical research center Fat soluble vitamins in primary sclerosing cholangitis
M01RR-00585-20 0422 (CLR) RIGGS, B L General clinical research center 1,25 dihydroxyvitamin D receptors in elderly women
M01RR-00585-20 0423 (CLR) RIGGS, B L General clinical research center Epidemiology of age-related bone loss and fractures
M01RR-00585-20 0426 (CLR) REED, C E General clinical research center Allergy immunotherapy for ragweed asthma
M01RR-00585-20 0428 (CLR) MUENTER, M D General clinical research center Deprenyl for Parkinson's disease
M01RR-00585-20 0429 (CLR) LUTHRA, H S General clinical research center Study of rifampin in rheumatoid arthritis
M01RR-00585-20 0430 (CLR) BOWLES, C A General clinical research center Cyclosporine-- Rheumatoid arthritis study
M01RR-00585-20 0431 (CLR) LARUSSO, N F General clinical research center Orthotopic liver transplantation for primary biliary cirrhosis and cholangitis
M01RR-00585-20 0432 (CLR) GLEICH, G J General clinical research center MBP and human pregnancy
M01RR-00585-20 0433 (CLR) PERRY, R E General clinical research center Obstetric injury to the anal sphincter
M01RR-00585-20 0434 (CLR) MILLINER, D General clinical research center Compassionate use of cysteamine in nephropathic cystenosis
M01RR-00585-20 0436 (CLR) ZACHARIAH, P K General clinical research center UK79300 effects on BP/urine output of patients with mild/moderate hypertension
M01RR-00585-20 0437 (CLR) LINDOR, KEITH D General clinical research center T-lymphocyte activation in PBC and PSC--Effects of cyclosporin on T-lymphocytes
M01RR-00585-20 0438 (CLR) FIELD, C S General clinical research center Estraderm low dose efficacy in treatment of postmenopausal symptoms
M01RR-00585-20 0440 (CLR) HURT, R D General clinical research center Inpatient treatment program for patients with severe nicotine dependence
M01RR-00585-20 0441 (CLR) CAMILLERI, M General clinical research center Effect of artificial, nondigestible nonabsorbable fat on human GI transit
M01RR-00585-20 0442 (CLR) AHLSKOG, J ERIC General clinical research center Adrenal brain transplantation
M01RR-00585-20 0443 (CLR) GROSS, J B General clinical research center Assessment of liver function by one-sample salivary antipyrine
M01RR-00585-20 0444 (CLR) KENNEDY, F P General clinical research center Assessment of insulin receptor binding to monocytes and erythrocytes
M01RR-00585-20 0445 (CLR) HAYMOND, M W General clinical research center In vivo estimates of the recursor pool for leucine oxidation
M01RR-00585-20 0446 (CLR) TALLEY, N J General clinical research center Gastritis and non-ulcer dyspepsia--Peptobismol
M01RR-00585-20 0176 (CLR) JENSEN, MICHAEL D General clinical research center Control of free fatty acid, leucine, and glucose metabolism in obesity
M01RR-00585-20 0179 (CLR) LARUSSO, NICHOLAS F General clinical research center Evaluation of D-penicillamine in primary sclerosing cholangitis
M01RR-00585-20 0209 (CLR) HEATH, HUNTER General clinical research center Bioassay of parathyroid hormone and RIA of calcitonin in hypercalcemia
M01RR-00585-20 0447 (CLR) MISER, JAMES S General clinical research center Ifosfamide vs VP-16 in cancer chemotherapy
M01RR-00585-20 0448 (CLR) MUENTER, M D General clinical research center Pergolide in treatment of Parkinson's disease
M01RR-00585-20 0449 (CLR) RICHARDSON, R L General clinical research center Phase II evaluation of suramin in advanced prostate carcinoma
M01RR-00585-20 0450 (CLR) BARATZ, K General clinical research center Effect of cold ambient temperature upon corneal thickness
M01RR-00585-20 0453 (CLR) RIGGS, B L General clinical research center True calcium absorption measured by dual stable isotope technique
M01RR-00585-20 0454 (CLR) AHLSKOG, J E General clinical research center Naxagolide in treated Parkinson's disease
M01RR-00585-20 0455 (CLR) AHLSKOG, J E General clinical research center Naxagolide in untreated Parkinson's disease
M01RR-00585-20 0212 (CLR) RIGGS, B LAWRENCE General clinical research center Fluoride and calcium balance treatment for

osteoporosis

M01RR-00585-20 0349 (CLR) FIREK, A J General clinical research center Studies of cell calcium metabolism in cultured human skin fibroblasts

M01RR-00585-20 0352 (CLR) CHESEBRO, JAMES H General clinical research center Stroke prevention in atrial fibrillation study

M01RR-00585-20 0358 (CLR) TALLEY, N J General clinical research center Effect of 5HT3 antagonist, GR-C 507/75, on small bowel transit

M01RR-00585-20 0361 (CLR) CORTESE, D.A. General clinical research center Severe hypoxia associated with liver disease

M01RR-00585-20 0365 (CLR) PEMBERTON, JOHN H. General clinical research center Rectal axial force probe

M01RR-00585-20 0367 (CLR) CHESEBRO, J.H. General clinical research center Vasoreactivity of minimal coronary artery disease--Mevinolin therapy

M01RR-00585-20 0368 (CLR) CHESEBRO, J. H. General clinical research center Vasoreactivity of CA after percutaneous transluminal coronary angioplasty

M01RR-00585-20 0370 (CLR) GROSS, J. B. General clinical research center Quantitation of liver function in chronic liver disease

M01RR-00585-20 0371 (CLR) JENSEN, MICHAEL D General clinical research center Regulation of free fatty acid metabolism in normal and diabetic man

M01RR-00585-20 0372 (CLR) EASTELL, RICHARD M. General clinical research center Photon absorptiometry of the ultradistal radius

M01RR-00585-20 0373 (CLR) HAYMOND, MOREY W General clinical research center Futile cycling--hyperinsulinemia, hyperglycemia, and diabetes mellitus

M01RR-00585-20 0377 (CLR) KELLY, KEITH A. General clinical research center Regulation of anal motility

M01RR-00585-20 0378 (CLR) DIMAGNO, E.P. General clinical research center Effect of bile on pancreatic enzyme survival during small bowel transit

M01RR-00585-20 0383 (CLR) RIGGS, B. L. General clinical research center Comparative rates of bone loss, bone formation, Ca absorption

M01RR-00585-20 0385 (CLR) RIGGS, B L General clinical research center Calcium absorption and aging and intestinal responsiveness

M01RR-00585-20 0387 (CLR) SINAKI, M General clinical research center Aging, osteopenia and paraspinal muscle strengthening

M01RR-00585-20 0393 (CLR) PHILLIPS, S F General clinical research center Effect of 5HT3, GR-C507/75, on irritable bowel syndrome

M01RR-00585-20 0394 (CLR) HEATH, HUNTER General clinical research center Calcium ingestion study

M01RR-00585-20 0396 (CLR) BOERWINKLE, E A General clinical research center Sodium transport--Genetics and hypertension

M01RR-00585-20 0397 (CLR) MOCK, M B General clinical research center Bypass angioplasty revascularization investigation

M01RR-00585-20 0398 (CLR) RIZZA, R A General clinical research center Characterization of GI motility in patients with diabetes

M01RR-00585-20 0399 (CLR) GLEICH, G J General clinical research center Eosinophils in human disease

M01RR-00585-20 0400 (CLR) HAYMOND, MOREY W General clinical research center Effects of human growth hormone on leucine and protein metabolism in humans

M01RR-00585-20 0401 (CLR) RIZZA, R A General clinical research center Postprandial metabolism in NIDDM--Hepatic glucose cycling

M01RR-00585-20 0402 (CLR) CAMILLERI, M General clinical research center Autonomic, baseline and reflex gut motility and hormone response

M01RR-00585-20 0403 (CLR) CHESEBRO, J H General clinical research center TIMI II-- Thrombolysis in myocardial infarction--Plasminogen activator

M01RR-00585-20 0406 (CLR) RIZZA, R A General clinical research center Effect of meal composition on treatment of hypoglycemia

M01RR-00585-20 0408 (CLR) CAMILLERI, M General clinical research center Treatment of patients with chronic intestinal pseudo-obstruction

M01RR-00585-20 0409 (CLR) RIGGS, B L General clinical research center Pilot study--Measuring osteonectin in plasma

M01RR-00585-20 0411 (CLR) CHAO, E Y General clinical research center Effect of exercise on peak bone mass in young adult women

M01RR-00585-20 0412 (CLR) CAMILLERI, M General clinical research center Effects of eating and proximal colonic distension/tone

M01RR-00585-20 0415 (CLR) KELLY, K A General clinical research center Early physiology and function ileal "J" and "W" pouch-anal anastomosis

M01RR-00585-20 0215 (CLR) THISTLE, JOHNSON L General clinical research center Gallbladder emptying kinetics in gallstone patients--Non surgical treatments

M01RR-00585-20 0499 (CLR) CZAJA, A J General clinical research center Ascites study

M01RR-00585-20 0500 (CLR) AHLQUIST, DAVID General clinical research center Endoscopic laser therapy in colo-rectal and other GI neoplasms

M01RR-00585-20 0502 (CLR) CZAJA, A General clinical research center Oral pulse prednisone in treatment of HBsAG-negative CAH in relapse

M01RR-00585-20 0503 (CLR) PHILLIPS, S F General clinical research center Tracking system for hazardous chemicals

M01RR-00585-20 0505 (CLR) RIGGS, B L General clinical research center Vitamin D kinetics

M01RR-00585-20 0506 (CLR) MISER, J S General clinical research center Ewings sarcoma

M01RR-00585-20 0507 (CLR) O'KEEFE, S J General clinical research center Gut function and the short bowel syndrome

M01RR-00585-20 0508 (CLR) HAYMOND, M W General clinical research center NG infusion of glucose and corn starch in children with GSD Type 1

M01RR-00585-20 0509 (CLR) RIGGS, B L General clinical research center Bone disease of primary biliary cirrhosis

M01RR-00585-20 0511 (CLR) KELLY, K A General clinical research center Ileal absorption, motility and transit after ileal pouch-anal anastomosis

M01RR-00585-20 0512 (CLR) RIZZA, R A General clinical research center Validation and application of nonsteady-state equations

M01RR-00585-20 0513 (CLR) KENNEDY, F P General clinical research center Safety and effectiveness of metformin in control of obese Type II diabetes

M01RR-00585-20 0514 (CLR) EASTELL, RICHARD M General clinical research center Effect of puberty on circadian pattern of bone turnover

M01RR-00585-20 0515 (CLR) CHESEBRO, J H General clinical research center In vivo endothelial injury and dependent vasomotion

M01RR-00585-20 0516 (CLR) JENSEN, MICHAEL D General clinical research center Measure of fatty acid kinetics in premenopausal women during follicular

M01RR-00585-20 0517 (CLR) JENSEN, MICHAEL D General clinical research center Prospective eval. of body composition changes in cancer patients

M01RR-00585-20 0518 (CLR) JENSEN, MICHAEL D General clinical research center The effect of estrogen on lipolysis in humans

M01RR-00585-20 0519 (CLR) DIMAGNO, EUGENE P General clinical research center Comparison between C-terminal octapeptide of CCK and CCK on pancreatic secretion

M01RR-00585-20 0520 (CLR) DEGROEN, P General clinical research center Role of cholesterol on cyclosporin A induced immunosuppression toxicity

M01RR-00585-20 0521 (CLR) JENSEN, MICHAEL D General clinical research center Compartmentalization of CO2 in man

M01RR-00585-20 0522 (CLR) HOMAN, M General clinical research center Assessment of insulin action in NIDDM using variable insulin infusion

M01RR-00585-20 0523 (CLR) BURRITT, M F General clinical research center Skeletal responsiveness to endogenous PTH with short-term calcium

M01RR-00585-20 0524 (CLR) JENSEN, MICHAEL D General clinical research center Comparison of dual energy X-ray absorptiometry, Body K+, and body composition

M01RR-00585-20 0525 (CLR) KOTTKE, BRUCE A General clinical research center Effects of apoprotein E on postprandial lipemia

M01RR-00585-20 0526 (CLR) HOLMES, D R General clinical research center In vivo endothelial injury and dependent vasomotion--acetylcholine

M01RR-00585-20 0527 (CLR) SMITH, C D General clinical research center Effects of vertical Roux-en-Y gastric bypass on gastic acid secretion

M01RR-00585-20 0528 (CLR) FIREK, A F General clinical research center Familial benign hypercalcemia database

M01RR-00585-20 0529 (CLR) RIZZA, ROBERT A General clinical research center Treatment of abnormal insulin kinetics and insulin resistance

M01RR-00585-20 0530 (CLR) ARGUETA, R General clinical research center Trial of oral pamidronate vs placebo in postmenopausal osteoporosis

M01RR-00585-20 0531 (CLR) FITZPATRICK, L A General clinical research center Chronic effects of calcium antagonists on anterior pituitary and gonadal hormones

M01RR-00585-20 0532 (CLR) BURRITT, M General clinical research center Intestinal resistance to endogenous 1,25-dihydroxyvitamin D3 with aging

M01RR-00585-20 0533 (CLR) TORRES, V E General clinical research center Hypertension development in autosomal dominant polycystic kidney disease

M01RR-00585-20 0256 (CLR) SERVICE, F JOHN General clinical research center Diabetes control and complications trial

M01RR-00585-20 0534 (CLR) HOLMES, D R General clinical research center Arterial injury, thrombosis and cellular proliferation

M01RR-00585-20 0535 (CLR) HEATH, HUNTER General clinical research center Genetic linkage mapping of familial benign hypercalcemia

M01RR-00585-20 0536 (CLR) CHESEBRO, JAMES H General clinical research center Antithrombotic therapy in acute coronary syndromes

M01RR-00585-20 0537 (CLR) SING, C F General clinical research center Renal hemodynamic non-modulation and blood pressure

M01RR-00585-20 0538 (CLR) SCHWARTZ, G L General clinical research center Genetics of the ambulatory blood pressure profile

M01RR-00585-20 0539 (CLR) JOYNER, M J General clinical research center Perfusion of active muscles-- Metabolites and nerves

M01RR-00585-20 0540 (CLR) CHESEBRO, JAMES H General clinical research center TIMI II-- Thrombolysis in myocardial infarct with plasminogen activator

M01RR-00585-20 0541 (CLR) PHILLIPS, S F General clinical research center Ambulatory recording of distal colon, rectal and anal canal motor activity

M01RR-00585-20 0542 (CLR) RODEHAFFER, R J General clinical research center Study of oral milrinone in addition to digoxin and other therapies in CHF

M01RR-00585-20 0543 (CLR) CORTESE, D A General clinical research center Severe hypoxemia associated liver disease-- Therapeutic effects of somatostatin

M01RR-00585-20 0544 (CLR) MCEVOY, K M General clinical research center Use of 3,4 diaminopyridine in patients with Lambert-Eaton myasthenic syndrome

M01RR-00585-20 0545 (CLR) LOEB, D S General clinical research center Association of Campylobacter pylori infection with gastroduodenal injury

M01RR-00585-20 0547 (CLR) BURCH, P A General clinical research center Phase I-- Hycamptine given by continuous IV infusion 24hrs every 3 weeks

M01RR-00585-20 0548 (CLR) ALLISON, T General clinical research center Cardiovascular response to hot tub immersion in ischemic heart disease patients

M01RR-00585-20 0549 (CLR) PEMBERTON, J H General clinical research center Effect of allopurinal in patients with pouch ileitis

M01RR-00585-20 0550 (CLR) CAMILLERI, M General clinical research center Seronoergic control of muscle tone and motility of the human colon

M01RR-00585-20 0551 (CLR) KIM, C H General clinical research center Relation between lower esophageal spincter pressure, transit, and symptoms

M01RR-00585-20 0552 (CLR) PEMBERTON, JOHN H General clinical

research center Adaption of an electronic barostat to the study of rectal muscular tone
M01RR-00585-20 0553 (CLR) MILES, J M General clinical research center Substrate regulation of free fatty acid, leucine and glucose metabolism
M01RR-00585-20 0554 (CLR) MIEDEMA, B W General clinical research center Effect of ileal perfusion on morphology, absorption and motility
M01RR-00585-20 0555 (CLR) PEMBERTON, J H General clinical research center Assessment of anorectal physiology following ileal pouch/anal anastomosis
M01RR-00585-20 0556 (CLR) CHESEBRO, JAMES H General clinical research center Single-blind placebo controlled ascending dose study to evaluate hirudin
M01RR-00585-20 0557 (CLR) PHILLIPS, S F General clinical research center Mechanisms of ileocolonic bolus transfers in man
M01RR-00585-20 0558 (CLR) CAMILLERI, M General clinical research center Primary bile acid malabsorption-- Documentation and studies of diarrhea
M01RR-00585-20 0559 (CLR) LIN, S General clinical research center Technical and clinical assessment of narcolepsy
M01RR-00585-20 0560 (CLR) HUNT, L W General clinical research center Bronchoscopy and bronchoalveolar lavage pre/post antigen challenge
M01RR-00585-20 0561 (CLR) MIEDEMA, B W General clinical research center Myoelectric recording and electric pacing of the human stomach
M01RR-00585-20 0562 (CLR) RIZZA, R A General clinical research center Bibliography management
M01RR-00585-20 0563 (CLR) RIGGS, B L General clinical research center Treatment of osteoporosis with estraderm open label extension
M01RR-00585-20 0564 (CLR) KHANDERIA, B K General clinical research center Evaluation of the safety/efficacy of Zofenopril Calcium given BID
M01RR-00585-20 0565 (CLR) NISHIMURA, R A General clinical research center Coronary angiography in patients with left main coronary artery disease
M01RR-00585-20 0566 (CLR) SZURSZEWSKI, J H General clinical research center Laboratory statistics
M01RR-00585-20 0258 (CLR) YUNGINGER, JOHN W General clinical research center Mechanisms underlying insect sting sensitivity
M01RR-00585-20 0567 (CLR) HAYMOND, M W General clinical research center Effects of pancreas and kidney transplant on insulin action
M01RR-00585-20 0266 (CLR) CHESEBRO, JAMES H General clinical research center Effect of oral milrinone and digoxin therapy on left ventricular function
M01RR-00585-20 0291 (CLR) HODGSON, S F General clinical research center Osteodystrophy of primary biliary cirrhosis
M01RR-00585-20 0295 (CLR) FLEMING, C R General clinical research center Metabolic and hepatic effect of L-carnitine administration
M01RR-00585-20 0309 (CLR) RAKELA, J General clinical research center Long-term administration of interferon in chronic active hepatitis B
M01RR-00585-20 0314 (CLR) RIGGS, B LAWRENCE General clinical research center Treatment of osteoporosis with estraderm
M01RR-00585-20 0339 (CLR) ZIMMERMAN, DONALD General clinical research center Buserelin treatment in patients with true precocious puberty
M01RR-00585-20 0344 (CLR) RIZZA, ROBERT A General clinical research center Standardization of radioimmuno and radioenzymatic assays
M01RR-00585-20 0348 (CLR) WINDEBANK, A. S. General clinical research center Use of 3,4-diaminopyridine in myasthenic syndrome
P41RR-00592-22 (SSS) MCINTOSH, J RICHARD UNIVERSITY OF COLORADO CAMPUS BOX 347 BOULDER, CO 80309-0347 High voltage electron microscopy of cells and tissues
P41RR-00592-22 0006 (SSS) WILSON, CHARLES High voltage electron microscopy of cells and tissues Improvements in specimens for 3-D reconstruction
P41RR-00592-22 0007 (SSS) WILSON, CHARLES High voltage electron microscopy of cells and tissues Selective staining of whole neurons and their reconstruction
P41RR-00592-22 0008 (SSS) ELLISON, MARK High voltage electron microscopy of cells and tissues In Situ hybridization with nucleic acid probes
P41RR-00592-22 0009 (SSS) KINNAMON, JOHN C High voltage electron microscopy of cells and tissues Correlating structure with function in vertebrate taste buds
P41RR-00592-22 0010 (SSS) FINGER, THOMAS E High voltage electron microscopy of cells and tissues Selective staining of long distance neuron connections
P41RR-00592-22 0011 (SSS) MCDONALD, KENT L High voltage electron microscopy of cells and tissues Cryofixation of biological materials for fine structural study
P41RR-00592-22 0012 (SSS) MCDONALD, KENT L High voltage electron microscopy of cells and tissues Cryofixation and HVEM immunocytochemistry
P41RR-00592-22 0013 (SSS) MCDONALD, KENT L High voltage electron microscopy of cells and tissues Cryo HVEM of frozen-hydrated materials
P41RR-00592-22 0014 (SSS) MCINTOSH, J RICHARD High voltage electron microscopy of cells and tissues 3-D reconstruction from images of serial sections
P41RR-00592-22 0015 (SSS) MASTRONARDE, DAVID High voltage electron microscopy of cells and tissues Tomographic reconstruction
P41RR-00592-22 0016 (SSS) MCINTOSH, J RICHARD High voltage electron microscopy of cells and tissues Stereo modeling
P41RR-00592-22 0017 (SSS) O'TOOLE, E High voltage electron microscopy of cells and tissues BEAM DAMAGES
P41RR-00592-22 0018 (SSS) O'TOOLE, EILEEN High voltage electron microscopy of cells and tissues Improvements in graphic display
P41RR-00592-22 0019 (SSS) KINNAMON, J C High voltage electron microscopy of cells and tissues Graphic displays of 3-D reconstruction on personal computers
P41RR-00592-22 0020 (SSS) CONNALLY, PAUL High voltage electron microscopy of cells and tissues Graphic display of solid models
P41RR-00592-22 0021 (SSS) MASTRONARDE, DAVID N High voltage electron microscopy of cells and tissues Quantitative analysis in 3-D models
P41RR-00592-22 0022 (SSS) MCINTOSH, J RICHARD High voltage electron microscopy of cells and tissues Equipment for improvements in image processing
P41RR-00592-22 0023 (SSS) YOUNG, STEVE High voltage electron microscopy of cells and tissues Improvements in computer graphics for model display
P41RR-00592-22 0024 (SSS) SCOTT, MATTHEW High voltage electron microscopy of cells and tissues Structural analysis of homeotic mutants in Drosophila
P41RR-00592-22 0025 (SSS) WOOD, W B High voltage electron microscopy of cells and tissues Structural analysis of development mutants in Caenhabdoritis elegans
P41RR-00592-22 0026 (SSS) FULLER, MARGARET High voltage electron microscopy of cells and tissues Analysis of mitotic and meiotic mutants in Drosophila
P41RR-00592-22 0027 (SSS) DUTCHER, SUSAN K High voltage electron microscopy of cells and tissues Structural analysis of basal body and flagellar mutants in Chlamydomonas
P41RR-00592-22 0028 (SSS) BURNSIDE, BETH High voltage electron microscopy of cells and tissues Morphometric analysis of cell elongation in retinal cone cells
P41RR-00592-22 0029 (SSS) BEGG, DAVID High voltage electron microscopy of cells and tissues Sea urchin embryo cytoskeleton
P41RR-00592-22 0030 (SSS) AGARD, DAVID High voltage electron microscopy of cells and tissues 3-D Reconstruction of chromatin by HVEM and axial tomography
P41RR-00592-22 0031 (SSS) KITA, HITOSHI High voltage electron microscopy of cells and tissues HVEM studies of reciprocal striato-nigral connection
P41RR-00592-22 0032 (SSS) GREER, CHARLES G High voltage electron microscopy of cells and tissues Geometric analyses of selectively stained neurons utilizing HVEM
P41RR-00592-22 0033 (SSS) YOUNG, STEVE J High voltage electron microscopy of cells and tissues HVEM sections in Alzheimer's disease
P41RR-00592-22 0034 (SSS) TURNER, RAYMOND High voltage electron microscopy of cells and tissues Distribution of voltage-dependent sodium channels
P41RR-00592-22 0035 (SSS) KELLEY, DARCY High voltage electron microscopy of cells and tissues Sexually dimorphic laryngeal neuromuscular system in Xenopus laevis
M01RR-00633-19 (CLR) PAK, CHARLES Y C UNIV OF TX HLTH SCIENCE CTR 5323 HARRY HINES BLVD DALLAS, TEXAS 75235-9030 **General clinical** research center
M01RR-00633-19 0342 (CLR) UAUY, RICARDO General clinical research center LDL apheresis--Treatment of homozygous familial hypercholesterolemia
M01RR-00633-19 0345 (CLR) PAK, CHARLES Y General clinical research center Prevention of renal stone formation in space flight
M01RR-00633-19 0347 (CLR) SAKHAEE, KHASHAYAR General clinical research center Further elucidation of the cause of hypocitraturia
M01RR-00633-19 0348 (CLR) SAKHAEE, KHASHAYER General clinical research center Pathogenic role of physical exercise in renal stone formation
M01RR-00633-19 0349 (CLR) UAUY, RICARDO General clinical research center Omega-3 fatty acids--Brain visual development in low birthweight infants
M01RR-00633-19 0352 (CLR) BRESLAU, NEIL A General clinical research center Inhibition of 1,25-dihydroxyvitamin D synthesis by ketoconazole
M01RR-00633-19 0358 (CLR) GRUNDY, SCOTT M General clinical research center High carbohydrate diets and glucose metabolism in NIDDM
M01RR-00633-19 0363 (CLR) TYSON, JON E General clinical research center Intravenous immunoglobulin to prevent neonatal infection
M01RR-00633-19 0364 (CLR) ANDREWS, WALTER General clinical research center Renal effects of cyclosporine-A in pediatric liver transplant
M01RR-00633-19 0365 (CLR) UAUY, RICARDO General clinical research center Arginine aztreonam--Glucose homeostasis & metabolic tolerance in LBW
M01RR-00633-19 0366 (CLR) MCCRACKEN, GEORGE H General clinical research center Dexamethasone & cefotaxime--Bacterial meninigitis in infants & children
M01RR-00633-19 0367 (CLR) PAK, CHARLES YC General clinical research center Potassium citrate in nephrolithiasis--Bioavailability
M01RR-00633-19 0368 (CLR) GRUNDY, SCOTT M General clinical research center Causes and management of primary hypercholesteremia
M01RR-00633-19 0371 (CLR) WEINER, MYRON F General clinical research center Cortisol secretion in Alzheimer's disease progression
M01RR-00633-19 0373 (CLR) SAKHAEE, KHASAYAR General clinical research center Impaired alkali absorption following potassium citrate with food
M01RR-00633-19 0375 (CLR) HSIA, CONNIE CW General clinical research center Respiratory muscle limitation to exercise post-pneumonectomy
M01RR-00633-19 0103 (CLR) RASKIN, PHILIP General clinical research center Glucagon secretion in well-controlled diabetes mellitus
M01RR-00633-19 0150 (CLR) SNYDER, WILLIAM General clinical research center Studies in hyperparathyroidism
M01RR-00633-19 0186 (CLR) PAK, CHARLES Y C General clinical research center Ambulatory evaluation of nephrolithiasis
M01RR-00633-19 0200 (CLR) BRESLAU, NEIL A General clinical research center Classification and further characterization of hypoparathyroidism
M01RR-00633-19 0238 (CLR) PAK, CHARLES Y General clinical research center Osteoporosis treatment with intermittent slow-release Na fluoride
M01RR-00633-19 0240 (CLR) PAK, CHARLES Y General clinical research center Long-term management of nephrolithiasis--Clinical response and hazards
M01RR-00633-19 0254 (CLR) RASKIN, PHILIP General clinical research center Diabetes control and complications trial (DCCT)
M01RR-00633-19 0259 (CLR) BRESLAU, NEIL A General clinical research center Hypoparathyroidism--Factors affecting 1,25-(OH)2 D synthesis

PROJECT NO., ORGANIZATIONAL UNIT., INVESTIGATOR, ADDRESS, TITLE

M01RR-00633-19 0262 (CLR) TOTO, ROBERT D General clinical research center Causal role of blood pressure in renal failure
M01RR-00633-19 0270 (CLR) ZELLER, KATHLEEN General clinical research center Effects of protein restriction on diabetic renal disease
M01RR-00633-19 0279 (CLR) SAKHAEE, KHASHAYER General clinical research center Combined sodium fluoride 1,25-(OH)2 vitamin D therapy in osteoporosis
M01RR-00633-19 0281 (CLR) PAK, CHARLES Y General clinical research center Prevention of bone loss in early postmenopausal women with calcium
M01RR-00633-19 0284 (CLR) RASKIN, PHILIP General clinical research center Glipizide in non-insulin dependent diabetes
M01RR-00633-19 0285 (CLR) TINDALL, RICHARD S General clinical research center Multicenter double blind trial of cyclosporine in myasthenia gravis
M01RR-00633-19 0376 (CLR) COMBES, BURTON General clinical research center Ursodeoxycholic acid (UDCA) in primary biliary cirrhosis
M01RR-00633-19 0377 (CLR) SAKHAEE, KHASHAYER General clinical research center Gouty diathesis and hyperuricosuric calcium nephrolithiasis
M01RR-00633-19 0378 (CLR) TINTNER, RON General clinical research center Alzheimer's disease and multi-infarct dimentia
M01RR-00633-19 0379 (CLR) PAK, CHARLES Y C General clinical research center Potassium-magnesium citrate in thiazide treated nephrolithiasis
M01RR-00633-19 0380 (CLR) GARG, ABHIMANYU General clinical research center Skeletal muscle morphology and exercise response in lipodystrophy
M01RR-00633-19 0381 (CLR) PHILLIPS, J THEODORE General clinical research center Multi-center study of cyclosporine in steroid-dependent myasthenia
M01RR-00633-19 0382 (CLR) GRUNDY, SCOTT M General clinical research center Pravastatin in hyperlipidemic primary nephrotic syndrome
M01RR-00633-19 0383 (CLR) TOTO, ROBERT D General clinical research center Lovastatin and hypercholesterolemia in nephrotic syndrome
M01RR-00633-19 0385 (CLR) CARR, BRUCE R General clinical research center GnRH analogs and oral contraceptives in hirsutism
M01RR-00633-19 0386 (CLR) GRUNDY, SCOTT M General clinical research center Energy restriction and weight loss in noninsulin dependent diabetes
M01RR-00633-19 0387 (CLR) PAK, CHARLES Y C General clinical research center Low intestinal absorption of citrate as a cause of hypocitraturia
M01RR-00633-19 0388 (CLR) GRUNDY, SCOTT M General clinical research center Causes of reduced high density lipoproteins
M01RR-00633-19 0389 (CLR) BRESLAU, NEIL A General clinical research center Leuprolide treatment--A model of estrogen deficiency
M01RR-00633-19 0391 (CLR) ANDREWS, WALTER S General clinical research center Neuropsychological function in children before & after liver transplant
M01RR-00633-19 0392 (CLR) SULLIVAN, TIMOTHY General clinical research center Methotrexate in moderate to severe asthmatic children
M01RR-00633-19 0393 (CLR) PAK, CHARLES Y General clinical research center Randomized slow release sodium fluoride & calcium citrate postmenopause
M01RR-00633-19 0305 (CLR) PAK, CHARLES Y C General clinical research center Calcium bioavailability of Ca salts in peri and postmenopausal women
M01RR-00633-19 0306 (CLR) RASKIN, PHILIP General clinical research center Aldose reductase inhibitors and blood vessel complications in diabetes
M01RR-00633-19 0310 (CLR) FOSTER, DANIEL W General clinical research center A program to prevent type I diabetes
M01RR-00633-19 0314 (CLR) GRUNDY, SCOTT M General clinical research center Pathogenic mechanisms of hypertriglyceridemia
M01RR-00633-19 0316 (CLR) LEWIS, STEPHEN F General clinical research center Muscle metabolism and circulatory control in exercise
M01RR-00633-19 0317 (CLR) PAK, CHARLES Y C General clinical research center Ambulatory evaluation of osteoporosis
M01RR-00633-19 0319 (CLR) RASKIN, PHILIP General clinical research center Omega-3 polyunsaturated fatty acids in diabetes mellitus
M01RR-00633-19 0320 (CLR) SAKHAEE, KHASHAYAR General clinical research center Hydrochlorothiazide & 1,25-(OH)2 vitamin D in postmenopausal osteoporosis
M01RR-00633-19 0321 (CLR) SAKHAEE, KHASHAYAR General clinical research center Calcium citrate and propensity for crystallization of Ca salts
M01RR-00633-19 0325 (CLR) ADAMS, BEVERLEY General clinical research center Nephrolithiasis--Computer enhanced classification and diagnosis
M01RR-00633-19 0330 (CLR) PAK, CHARLES General clinical research center Integrated assessment of calcium metabolism
M01RR-00633-19 0332 (CLR) PAK, CHARLES General clinical research center Oral sodium load on calcium metabolism and stone formation
M01RR-00633-19 0333 (CLR) WEISSLER, JONATHAN General clinical research center Human alveolar macrophages and pulmonary immune responses
M01RR-00633-19 0334 (CLR) PAK, CHARLES General clinical research center Treatment of osteoporosis with intermittent slow-release Na fluoride
M01RR-00633-19 0336 (CLR) WEINER, MYRON R General clinical research center Cortisol stress response in Alzheimers disease and normal aging
M01RR-00633-19 0340 (CLR) PAK, CHARLES Y General clinical research center Steroid induced osteoporosis--Slow fluoride, 25-OHD & calcium citrate
M01RR-00633-19 0341 (CLR) TINDALL, RICHARD S General clinical research center Double blind clinical trial of cyclosporine in myasthenia gravis
M01RR-00633-19 0394 (CLR) PAK, CHARLES Y C General clinical research center Inhibition of hip fractures by adjunctive 25-OHD therapy
M01RR-00633-19 0395 (CLR) PAK, CHARLES Y C General clinical research center Inhibition of hip fracture by an adjunctive estrogen therapy
M01RR-00633-19 0396 (CLR) GRUNDY, SCOTT M General clinical research center Various methods of intervention and low HDL-cholesterol levels
M01RR-00633-19 0397 (CLR) DENKE, MARGO A General clinical research center Diet responsiveness in hypercholesteremic women
M01RR-00633-19 0398 (CLR) GRUNDY, SCOTT M General clinical research center Role of beef in the American diet
M01RR-00633-19 0399 (CLR) PAK, CHARLES Y C General clinical research center Chlorthalidone in absorptive hypercalciuria
M01RR-00633-19 0400 (CLR) LIPSKY, PETER E General clinical research center XomaZyme-H65 treatment of systemic lupus erythematosus
M01RR-00633-19 0401 (CLR) CUSH, JOHN J General clinical research center Xomazyme-H65 treatment of rheumatoid arthritis
M01RR-00633-19 0402 (CLR) GRUNDY, SCOTT M General clinical research center Glucose aand lipid metabolism in glipizide treated NIDDM patients
M01RR-00633-19 0403 (CLR) NIGHTINGALE, STEPHEN D General clinical research center Rifabutin and zidovudine in symptomatic HIV-positive patients
M01RR-00633-19 0404 (CLR) TINTNER, RON General clinical research center Effect of physostigmine and clonidine in Alzheimer's disease
M01RR-00633-19 0405 (CLR) HOBBS, HELEN H General clinical research center Molecular basis of cholesterol metabolism and selected genetic diseases
M01RR-00633-19 0406 (CLR) LUSKEY, KENNETH L General clinical research center Amylin expresion at normal and diabetic states
M01RR-00633-19 0407 (CLR) GRUNDY, SCOTT M General clinical research center Heterogeneity of plasma HDL responses to exercise training
M01RR-00633-19 0408 (CLR) GRUNDY, SCOTT M General clinical research center Causes of high LDL and HDL in postmenopausal women
M01RR-00633-19 0409 (CLR) WABNER, CINDY General clinical research center Biomedical relevance of citrus fruit juice
M01RR-00633-19 0410 (CLR) ANTICH, PETER P General clinical research center Ultrasound measurement of bone mechanical property in vivo
M01RR-00633-19 0411 (CLR) JIALAL, ISHWARLAL General clinical research center Superoxide production & oxidative modification of LDL in diabetes
M01RR-00633-19 0412 (CLR) JIALAL, ISHWARLAL General clinical research center Physiologic antioxidant agents & oxidative modification of LDL
M01RR-00633-19 0413 (CLR) DENKE, MARGO A General clinical research center Absorbability of dietary behenic acid
M01RR-00633-19 0414 (CLR) RAMIREZ, LUIS C General clinical research center Evening meal contribution to fasting hyperglycemia in NIDDM
M01RR-00633-19 0415 (CLR) GRUNDY, SCOTT M General clinical research center Low-dose lovastatin treatment of postmenopausal hypercholesterolemia
M01RR-00633-19 0416 (CLR) RAM, C VENKATA General clinical research center Amlodipine & enalapril--Effects on insulin sensitivity in hypertension
M01RR-00633-19 0417 (CLR) COMBES, BURTON General clinical research center Alfa interferon treatment of chronic non-A, non-B hepatitis
M01RR-00633-19 0418 (CLR) SQUIRES, ROBERT General clinical research center Bile salt kinetics in presumed congenital bile salt malabsorption
M01RR-00633-19 0419 (CLR) GEPPERT, THOMAS D General clinical research center Xomazyme-CD5 plus in systemic sclerosis
M01RR-00633-19 0420 (CLR) HOM, JAMES General clinical research center Neuropsychological functioning in population at risk for Alzheimer's
M01RR-00633-19 0421 (CLR) ANDREWS, WALTER S General clinical research center Bioavailability of a new cyclosporine formulation
M01RR-00633-19 0422 (CLR) YUNIS, KHALID A General clinical research center Enteral formula energy composition--Bronchopulmonary dysplasia infants
M01RR-00633-19 0423 (CLR) ALEXANDER, STEVEN R General clinical research center Growth hormone therapy--Height deficit children with chronic renal insufficiency
M01RR-00645-20 (CLR) TAPLEY, DONALD F COLUMBIA UNIVERSITY 630 WEST 168TH STREET NEW YORK, N Y 10032 General clinical research center
M01RR-00645-20 0141 (CLR) BILEZIKIAN, JOHN P General clinical research center Hyperparathyroidism
M01RR-00645-20 0143 (CLR) CANFIELD, ROBERT E General clinical research center Natural history of Paget's disease
M01RR-00645-20 0285 (CLR) SHANE, ELIZABETH J General clinical research center Metabolic bone disease
M01RR-00645-20 0291 (CLR) DRUSIN, R General clinical research center Adaptation in cardiac transplantation
M01RR-00645-20 0294 (CLR) GINSBERG, HENRY N General clinical research center Regulation of APOB metabolism in humans
M01RR-00645-20 0299 (CLR) MAYEUX, RICHARD P General clinical research center Dementia of the Alzheimer type--Oral physistigmine
M01RR-00645-20 0300 (CLR) MAYEUX, RICHARD P General clinical research center Behavioral/biochemical correlates in diseases of aging
M01RR-00645-20 0308 (CLR) REIFFEL, JAMES A General clinical research center Electrophysiologic testing vs electrocardiographic monitoring
M01RR-00645-20 0309 (CLR) ROWLAND, LEWIS P General clinical research center Clinical research in neuromuscular disease
M01RR-00645-20 0326 (CLR) FAHN, STANLEY General clinical research center Dystonia clinical research database
M01RR-00645-20 0328 (CLR) FAHN, STANLEY General clinical research center Analysis of the progression of dystonia in children
M01RR-00645-20 0344 (CLR) MOHR, JAY P General clinical research center MINCDS stroke data bank project
M01RR-00645-20 0347 (CLR) REIFFEL, JAMES A General clinical research center D-Sotalol for the control of supraventricular tachyarrhythmias
M01RR-00645-20 0351 (CLR) SIRIS, ELIZABETH General clinical research center Bone densitometry
M01RR-00645-20 0357 (CLR) BRIN, MITCHELL General clinical research center Parkinson's disease DATATOP multicenter trial

M01RR-00645-20 0362 (CLR) DECKELBAUM, RICHARD General clinical research center Children's cardiovascular health program
M01RR-00645-20 0372 (CLR) GIARDINA, ELSA General clinical research center Mexiletine-quinidine combination for symptomatic arrythmias
M01RR-00645-20 0376 (CLR) HEMBREE, WYLIE General clinical research center Student health service data analysis
M01RR-00645-20 0378 (CLR) LANGE, DALE J General clinical research center Efficacy of cyclosporine in ALS
M01RR-00645-20 0379 (CLR) LEIGHTON, J General clinical research center Predictors of lipid and lipoprotein response to diet intervention
M01RR-00645-20 0383 (CLR) MAYEUX, RICHARD General clinical research center Depression in Parkinson's disease
M01RR-00645-20 0388 (CLR) NEUGUT, A General clinical research center Coincidence of cancers and elevated risk following treatment
M01RR-00645-20 0395 (CLR) SIRIS, ETHEL General clinical research center Compassionate approval for treatment of patients using APD
M01RR-00645-20 0397 (CLR) GOLAND, ROBIN S General clinical research center Corticotropin releasing factor during pregnancy
M01RR-00645-20 0403 (CLR) HEIRD, W General clinical research center Induction & maintenance of oral feeding in infants with dysphagia
M01RR-00645-20 0408 (CLR) BARST, R General clinical research center Long-term prostacyclin in pulmonary hypertension
M01RR-00645-20 0409 (CLR) HEIRD, W C General clinical research center Sodium and phosphorus intakes required for optimal protein
M01RR-00645-20 0410 (CLR) HEIRD, W C General clinical research center Comparison of LBW infant formulas
M01RR-00645-20 0001 (CLR) KRONENBERG, F General clinical research center Hot flashes survey
M01RR-00645-20 0411 (CLR) MORISHIMA, A General clinical research center Evaluation of growth and development in short children
M01RR-00645-20 0414 (CLR) SILVERBERG, S J General clinical research center Phosphate administration in human subjects
M01RR-00645-20 0415 (CLR) BARST, R J General clinical research center Evaluation of prostacyclin and therapy in pulmonary hypertension
M01RR-00645-20 0422 (CLR) SIRIS, E General clinical research center Oral calcium in Paget's disease of bone
M01RR-00645-20 0424 (CLR) CANNON, P General clinical research center Clinical investigation of RS43285 as antianginal agent
M01RR-00645-20 0425 (CLR) MAYEUX, R General clinical research center Acetyl-carnitine as a treatment for Alzheimer's disease
M01RR-00645-20 0420 (CLR) BIGGER, J T General clinical research center Multicenter study of silent myocardial ischemia
M01RR-00645-20 0426 (CLR) GIARDINA, E General clinical research center Ethmozin twice daily vs. thrice daily
M01RR-00645-20 0427 (CLR) BIGGER, J T General clinical research center Effect of Tilt on heart rate variability
M01RR-00645-20 0430 (CLR) SIRIS, E General clinical research center Dosing study of APD in Paget's disease of bone
M01RR-00645-20 0431 (CLR) TATEMICHI, T General clinical research center Mechanisms and syndromes of dementia related to stroke
M01RR-00645-20 0433 (CLR) DEVIVO, D General clinical research center Duchenne muscular dystrophy clinical trial group
M01RR-00645-20 0434 (CLR) KOPELMAN, R General clinical research center Steroidal therapy and renal function in systemic lupus erythryma
M01RR-00645-20 0435 (CLR) KRONENBERG, F General clinical research center Thermoregulation during menopausal hot flashes
M01RR-00645-20 0438 (CLR) DEMPSTER, D General clinical research center SCOR grant in osteoporosis
M01RR-00645-20 0441 (CLR) GRIECO, M General clinical research center St. Luke's/Roosevelt AIDS treatment evaluation unit
M01RR-00645-20 0445 (CLR) COZINE, K General clinical research center Morbidity in outpatients following various anesthesia regimens
M01RR-00645-20 0447 (CLR) KELLER, A General clinical research center Cardiac glutathione redox cycle in reperfusion injury
M01RR-00645-20 0449 (CLR) CONWILL, C General clinical research center Falls and hip fractures in the elderly
M01RR-00645-20 0452 (CLR) BIGGER, J THOM General clinical research center Cardiac arrhythmia suppression trial
M01RR-00645-20 0455 (CLR) PANTUCK, EUGENE General clinical research center Effects of amino acid intake on oxidative biotransformation of antipyrine
M01RR-00645-20 0456 (CLR) FAHN, STANLEY General clinical research center Milacemide for movement disorders
M01RR-00645-20 0457 (CLR) FAHN, STANLEY General clinical research center Fusaric acid for treatment of movement disorders
M01RR-00645-20 0459 (CLR) PI-SUNYER, F XAVIER General clinical research center Glyburide in insulin dependent diabetes
M01RR-00645-20 0464 (CLR) MAYEUX, RICHARD General clinical research center North Manhattan aging project
M01RR-00645-20 0465 (CLR) MAYEUX, RICHARD General clinical research center Prevalence & incidence of dementia and depression in Parkinson's
M01RR-00645-20 0466 (CLR) MAYEUX, RICHARD General clinical research center Tacrine and lecithin in Alzheimer's disease
M01RR-00645-20 0467 (CLR) MAYEUX, RICHARD General clinical research center Predictors of severity in Alzheimer's disease
M01RR-00645-20 0469 (CLR) PITT, JANE General clinical research center AIDS clinical treatment group 051
M01RR-00645-20 0470 (CLR) EISENBERG, DALE General clinical research center Prevalence & incidence of swizure disorders in births/Upstate NY 1935-present
M01RR-00645-20 0471 (CLR) COURVAL, J General clinical research center Distribution and risk factors associated with malarial outbreaks
M01RR-00645-20 0472 (CLR) CHUTER, T A General clinical research center Respiratory patterns after cholecystectomy--Effects of posture and CO2
M01RR-00645-20 0476 (CLR) HATCH, MAUREEN General clinical research center Status of children born to families exposed to radiation in Three Mile Island
M01RR-00645-20 0482 (CLR) JACOBS, JERRY General clinical research center Gammagard immune globulin IV (human) in treatment systemic JRA
M01RR-00645-20 0478 (CLR) SETTON, L General clinical research center Structural parameters of intravertebral discs
M01RR-00645-20 0479 (CLR) ANISFELD, ELIZABETH General clinical research center Effects of different interventions on premature infants
M01RR-00645-20 0481 (CLR) GRAZIANO, JOSEPH General clinical research center DMSA metabolism in children
M01RR-00645-20 0483 (CLR) WARDLAW, SHARON General clinical research center Effect of opioid antagonism in pts. with hyperprolactinemia
M01RR-00645-20 0484 (CLR) FAHN, STANLEY General clinical research center Pharmacology of muscle movement disorder
M01RR-00645-20 0485 (CLR) GINSBERG, HENRY N General clinical research center Diet effects on lipoprotein metabolism and platelet function
M01RR-00645-20 0486 (CLR) PITT, JANE General clinical research center Intravenous gamma globulin in children with HIV infection
M01RR-00645-20 0487 (CLR) BARST, ROBYN General clinical research center Long term prostacyclin in pulmonary hypertension
M01RR-00645-20 0488 (CLR) BROWN, MARY General clinical research center Cancer screening in presbyterian hospital outpatient clinic
M01RR-00645-20 0489 (CLR) MAYEUX, RICHARD General clinical research center Control release physostigmine in Alzheimer's disease
M01RR-00645-20 0490 (CLR) ROSE, ERIC General clinical research center Preventon of rejection of allogenic cardic transplants photopheresis
M01RR-00645-20 0491 (CLR) PRANZATELLI, MICHAEL General clinical research center Efficacy and safety of 5 HTP in pediatric myoclonic disorder
M01RR-00645-20 0492 (CLR) KELSEY, JENNIFER General clinical research center Epidemiology of bone mass in young adults-peak bone mass study
M01RR-00645-20 0493 (CLR) GLUSMAN, MURRAY General clinical research center Silent myocardial ischemia and pain study
M01RR-00645-20 0494 (CLR) SIRIS, ETHEL General clinical research center Effect of tamoxifen on bone mass in post-menopausal women 5yr study
M01RR-00645-20 0495 (CLR) GIARDINA, ELSA G General clinical research center Benazepril, a new angiotensin-converting enzyme inhibitor
M01RR-00645-20 0496 (CLR) WALSH, B TIMOTHY General clinical research center Bone density in women with prior anorexia nervosa
M01RR-00645-20 0497 (CLR) SHANE, ELIZABETH General clinical research center Bone disease after cardiac transplantation
M01RR-00645-20 0498 (CLR) STEINBERG, JONATHAN S General clinical research center Efficacy and safty of sotalol vs. placebo
M01RR-00645-20 0499 (CLR) GINSBERG, HENRY N General clinical research center Association between postprandial lipemia and coronary artery disease
M01RR-00645-20 0500 (CLR) DE VIVO, DARRYL C General clinical research center Duchenne muscular dystrophy clinical trials research project
M01RR-00645-20 0501 (CLR) MAYEUX, RICHARD General clinical research center Celluar ionic calcium levels as diagnostic markers in Alzheimer's dis.
M01RR-00645-20 0502 (CLR) COROMILAS, JAMES General clinical research center Effects of digoxin withdrawal in patients with chronic CHF in NSR
M01RR-00645-20 0503 (CLR) DOBKIN, JAY F General clinical research center A phase II pilot study of BG962 plus AZT in HIV-1 positive patients
M01RR-00645-20 0504 (CLR) SIRIS, ETHEL General clinical research center Phase II study of risedronate (NE 58095) in Paget's disease
M01RR-00645-20 0505 (CLR) FAHN, STANLEY General clinical research center Tissue resource facility
M01RR-00645-20 0506 (CLR) MOW, V C General clinical research center Biomechanics of normal bovine and human meniscus
M01RR-00645-20 0507 (CLR) GRUFT, J General clinical research center Predictors of physical recovery in head injured patients
M01RR-00645-20 0508 (CLR) CORRELL, J General clinical research center Survival after alateral carotid artery resection
M01RR-00645-20 0509 (CLR) MARDER, KAREN General clinical research center The influence of pregnancy on prog. of neuro sign in women with AIDS
M01RR-00645-20 0510 (CLR) GREEN, PETER M General clinical research center Early gastric cancer prognostic factors
M01RR-00722-19 (CLR) JOHNS, MICHAEL E JOHNS HOPKINS UNIVERSITY 720 RUTLAND AVENUE BALTIMORE, MD 21205 General clinical research center
M01RR-00722-19 0041 (CLR) BAYLIN, STEPHEN B General clinical research center Biology of medullary thyroid carcinoma and related endocrine neoplasms
M01RR-00722-19 0068 (CLR) PETRI, MICHELLE General clinical research center Factors associated with pregnancy loss in systemic lupus
M01RR-00722-19 0100 (CLR) GRIFFITH, LAWRENCE S C General clinical research center Evaluation and management of recurring ventricular tachycardia/fibrillation
M01RR-00722-19 0104 (CLR) VANMETRE, THOMAS E General clinical research center Controlled study of immunotherapy with cat extract for cat asthma
M01RR-00722-19 0150 (CLR) CHAISSON, RICHARD E General clinical research center Longitudinal studies of AIDS
M01RR-00722-19 0152 (CLR) PYERITZ, REED E General clinical research center Investigations of heritable disorders of connective tissue
M01RR-00722-19 0158 (CLR) CHARACHE, SAMUEL General clinical research center Multicenter study of hydroxyurea in sickle cell anemia
M01RR-00722-19 0161 (CLR) PEARLSON, GODFREY General clinical research center Cerebral imaging in HIV and allied conditions
M01RR-00722-19 0163 (CLR) LEVINE, MICHAEL A. General clinical research center Clinical hormone resistance due to deficient adenylyl cyclase
M01RR-00722-19 0164 (CLR) MOSES, HAMILTON General clinical research

center Deprenyl and tocopherol antioxidative therapy of Parkinsonism (DATATOP)
M01RR-00722-19 0175 (CLR) WHELTON, PAUL K. General clinical research center Ambulatory blood pressure monitoring study
M01RR-00722-19 0048 (CLR) WALSER, MACKENZIE General clinical research center Ketoacid therapy of renal failure
M01RR-00722-19 0184 (CLR) FOLSTEIN, SUSAN E General clinical research center Experimental therapeutic trial of Vitamin E in Huntington's disease
M01RR-00722-19 0233 (CLR) PETTY, BRENT G General clinical research center Contact sensitization and contact photoallergic potential of niclosamide
M01RR-00722-19 0235 (CLR) SAAH, ALFRED J General clinical research center Multicenter AIDS cohort study--Baltimore site
M01RR-00722-19 0236 (CLR) SABA, GEORGE P III General clinical research center Biliary lithotripsy with adjuvant ursodeoxy-cholic acid chemolysis
M01RR-00722-19 0237 (CLR) TRAYSTMAN, RICHARD J General clinical research center Collateral mechanics--Effects of age and lung dysfunction
M01RR-00722-19 0239 (CLR) WHELTON, PAUL K General clinical research center Blood pressure effects of potassium supplementation
M01RR-00722-19 0240 (CLR) WHELTON, PAUL K General clinical research center Black-white differences in hypertensive end-stage renal disease
M01RR-00722-19 0241 (CLR) WHELTON, PAUL K General clinical research center Cardiovascular reactivity studies
M01RR-00722-19 0242 (CLR) ANSARI, AFTAB A General clinical research center T-cell studies on rye grass allergic patients
M01RR-00722-19 0243 (CLR) DOBS, ADRIAN S General clinical research center Hypothalamic-pituitary-adrenal axis in alcoholics
M01RR-00722-19 0244 (CLR) FLEXNER, CHARLES W General clinical research center Phase I pharmacokinetic evaluation of 3'deoxy-3'-fluorothymidine (FLT)
M01RR-00722-19 0245 (CLR) FRANCOMANO, CLAIR A General clinical research center Genetic epidemiology of schizophrenia
M01RR-00722-19 0246 (CLR) FRIED, LINDA P General clinical research center Physiologic components of postural stability and fall risk in elderly
M01RR-00722-19 0247 (CLR) JABS, DOUGLAS A General clinical research center CMV retinitis trial--Foscarnet/ganciclovir component
M01RR-00722-19 0248 (CLR) JOFFE, ALAIN General clinical research center Relation between social support, depression, stress and teen mother's drug use
M01RR-00722-19 0249 (CLR) KORNHAUSER, DAVID D General clinical research center Effect of increasing pH upon bioavailability of orally-administered foscarnet
M01RR-00722-19 0250 (CLR) LADENSON, PAUL W General clinical research center Tiratricol suppression therapy for well-differentiated thyroid carcinoma
M01RR-00722-19 0251 (CLR) LAUBE, BETH L General clinical research center Pentamidine aerosol distribution within the lungs of HIV positive patients
M01RR-00722-19 0252 (CLR) LAUBE, BETH L General clinical research center Assessment of aerosolized insulin delivered to the lungs to treat diabetes
M01RR-00722-19 0253 (CLR) MOLLER, DAVID R General clinical research center Immune pathogenesis of granulomatous lung disease
M01RR-00722-19 0254 (CLR) PETTY, BRENT G General clinical research center Safety tolerance effect food pharmacokinetics ceftriaxone w/absorption enhancer
M01RR-00722-19 0255 (CLR) REPKE, JOHN T General clinical research center Relationship between histocompatibility antigens and preeclampsia
M01RR-00722-19 0256 (CLR) WEIKEL, CYNTHIA S General clinical research center Single-blind efficacy evaluation spiramycin in AIDS w/cryptosporidial diarrhea
M01RR-00722-19 0257 (CLR) WHELTON, PAUL K General clinical research center Urine collection as proxy for dietary electrolyte intake
M01RR-00722-19 0258 (CLR) WHELTON, PAUL K General clinical research center Influence of sodium and potassium on blood pressure reactivity
M01RR-00722-19 0259 (CLR) WHELTON, PAUL K General clinical research center End-stage renal disease (ESRD) studies
M01RR-00722-19 0260 (CLR) WILDER, LORA B General clinical research center Effect of fasting status on estimation of LDL-cholesterol in a screening setting
M01RR-00722-19 0261 (CLR) CAMPBELL, JAMES General clinical research center Psychophysical evaluation of the analgesic efficacy of NE-21610 in normal males
M01RR-00722-19 0186 (CLR) NELSON, KENRAD General clinical research center Risk of transmission of HIV by transfusion in cardiac surgery patients
M01RR-00722-19 0192 (CLR) ALEXANDER, ELAINE L General clinical research center Genes and autoantibodies in immunopathogenesis of Sjogren's, SS/LE overlap
M01RR-00722-19 0193 (CLR) BARTLET, JOHN G General clinical research center AIDS clinical treatment unit--Protocol 03
M01RR-00722-19 0194 (CLR) BARTLET, JOHN GO General clinical research center AIDS clinical treatment unit--Protocol 04
M01RR-00722-19 0195 (CLR) BARTLET, JOHN G General clinical research center AIDS clinical treatment unit--Protocol 05
M01RR-00722-19 0196 (CLR) BARTLET, JOHN G General clinical research center AIDS clinical treatment unit--Protocol 06
M01RR-00722-19 0197 (CLR) CHARACHE, SAMUEL General clinical research center Combined erythropoitin/hydroxyurea therapy for sickle cell anemia
M01RR-00722-19 0198 (CLR) DOBS, ADRIAN S General clinical research center Testicular injury with amiodarone use
M01RR-00722-19 0203 (CLR) FORD, DANIEL E General clinical research center Profile of prevention knowledge in general medical patients
M01RR-00722-19 0204 (CLR) GEORGOPOULOS, ANGELIKI General clinical research center Atherogenicity of diabetic postprandial TGRLP lipoproteins
M01RR-00722-19 0205 (CLR) GIARDIELLO, FRANK M General clinical research center HLA typing in collagenous/lymphatic colitis
M01RR-00722-19 0206 (CLR) GRAHAM, NEIL M H General clinical research center Serum copper and zinc levels and progression of HIV-1 infection
M01RR-00722-19 0208 (CLR) HELLMAN, DAVID B General clinical research center Investigation of rheumatoid cachexia
M01RR-00722-19 0211 (CLR) HERSKOWITZ, AHVIE General clinical research center HIV-associated cardiomyopathy
M01RR-00722-19 0222 (CLR) PETTY, BRENT G General clinical research center Safety, tolerance, pharmacokinetics and pharmacodynamics of pyridostigmine
M01RR-00722-19 0226 (CLR) MCARTHUR, JUSTIN C General clinical research center Natural history of HIV-1 infection--neurological and neuropsychological studies
M01RR-00722-19 0227 (CLR) MCLEAN, ROBERT H General clinical research center Class III MHC genes in neonatal SLE
M01RR-00722-19 0228 (CLR) MOSER, HUGO W General clinical research center Evaluation of patients suspected of leukodystrophies
M01RR-00722-19 0229 (CLR) MOSER, HUGO W General clinical research center An open study of cronassial in ALD/AMN
M01RR-00722-19 0230 (CLR) MOSER, HUGO W General clinical research center Therapy of adrenoleukodystrophy
M01RR-00722-19 0231 (CLR) MOSER, HUGO W General clinical research center Immunological studies of adrenoleukodystrophy
M01RR-00750-19 (CLR) MERRITT, DORIS H INDIANA UNIV SCHOOL OF MED 302 FESLER HALL INDIANAPOLIS, IN 46202-5114 General clinical research center
M01RR-00750-19 0052 (CLR) BENSON, MERRILL D General clinical research center Presentation and prognosis of human amyloidosis
M01RR-00750-19 0106 (CLR) WEINBERGER, MYRON H General clinical research center Mechanisms of sodium sensitivity of blood pressure
M01RR-00750-19 0159 (CLR) EINHORN, LAWRENCE H General clinical research center Cisplatin and bleomycin and vp16 dosage in testicular cancer
M01RR-00750-19 0198 (CLR) CHRISTIAN, JOE C General clinical research center Studies of bone mass in twins
M01RR-00750-19 0201 (CLR) MILLER, J Z General clinical research center Calcium and bone mass: A co-twin control study
M01RR-00750-19 0183 (CLR) BONSETT, CHARLES A General clinical research center Adenylosuccinic acid in Duchenne muscular dystrophy
M01RR-00750-19 0213 (CLR) EINHORN,LAWRENCE H. General clinical research center Ifosfamide and mesna in testicular cancer or ovarian germ cell tumor
M01RR-00750-19 0218 (CLR) JOHNSTON, CONRAD C. General clinical research center Sex steroids in age-related bone loss
M01RR-00750-19 0225 (CLR) NURNBERGER, JOHN JR. General clinical research center Neurochemical control of melatonin in bipolars and propranolol effects
M01RR-00750-19 0226 (CLR) PEACOCK, MUNRO General clinical research center Effect of 3 consecutive doses of humatrope on calcium and bone metabolism
M01RR-00750-19 0307 (CLR) DENNE, SCOTT C General clinical research center Protein metabolism in the newborn during feeding and fasting
M01RR-00750-19 0308 (CLR) DENNE, SCOTT C General clinical research center Nonprotein substrate and amino acid infusion on protein metabolism in the newborn
M01RR-00750-19 0227 (CLR) PEACOCK, MUNRO General clinical research center Effect of 3 different doses of humatrope on calcium and bone metabolism
M01RR-00750-19 0273 (CLR) WEINBERGER, MYRON H General clinical research center Blood pressure response to high and low sodium diet
M01RR-00750-19 0274 (CLR) BLACK, JOHN R General clinical research center Foscarnet salvage therapy for AIDS patients with CMV retinitis
M01RR-00750-19 0276 (CLR) BRATER, D CRAIG General clinical research center Dose response study of torsemide in chronic renal insufficiency
M01RR-00750-19 0277 (CLR) BRADLEY, JOHN D General clinical research center Intravenous SAMe prior to oral SAMe therapy in pts w/osteoporosis of the knee
M01RR-00750-19 0278 (CLR) WHEAT, L JOSEPH General clinical research center Itraconozole for suppression of relapse of disseminated histoplasmosis in AIDS
M01RR-00750-19 0279 (CLR) BARON, ALAIN D General clinical research center Mechanisms of hemodynamically induced glucose uptake
M01RR-00750-19 0280 (CLR) PEACOCK, MUNRO General clinical research center Interleukin in bone disease
M01RR-00750-19 0281 (CLR) PEACOCK, MUNRO General clinical research center Tartrate resistant acid phosphatase in bone disease
M01RR-00750-19 0282 (CLR) JACKSON, JOSEPH E General clinical research center Determination of variance & co-variances of blood lipid fraction & body weight
M01RR-00750-19 0284 (CLR) EINHORN, LAWRENCE H General clinical research center VP-16 & cisplatin vs ifosfamide chemotherapy for small cell lung cancer
M01RR-00750-19 0285 (CLR) CHRISTIAN, JOE C General clinical research center Huntington disease--A neurological marker of aging
M01RR-00750-19 0286 (CLR) BARON, ALAIN D General clinical research center Role of hemodynamics in in vivo insulin resistance
M01RR-00750-19 0287 (CLR) GARVEY, TIMOTHY General clinical research center Genetics of the glucose transporter in insulin resistace
M01RR-00750-19 0288 (CLR) FIFE, KENNETH H General clinical research center Randomized trial of anti-pneumocystis agents in patients with AIDS
M01RR-00750-19 0289 (CLR) WHEAT, JOSEPH General clinical research center Patient evaluation for potential AIDS clinical trial participants
M01RR-00750-19 0290 (CLR) FIFE, KENNETH H General clinical research center Study of dideoxyinosine in zidovudine intolerant patients with AIDS
M01RR-00750-19 0291 (CLR) FIFE, KENNETH H General clinical research center Comparison of ddI and zidovudine in therapy of patients with AIDS
M01RR-00750-19 0292 (CLR) PRATT, HOWARD General clinical research center Racial and genetic differences in aldosterone production

PROJECT NO., ORGANIZATIONAL UNIT., INVESTIGATOR, ADDRESS, TITLE

M01RR-00750-19 0293 (CLR) REX, DOUGLAS K General clinical research center Effects of oral vs buccal piroxicam on the gastric mucosa
M01RR-00750-19 0294 (CLR) BRATER, D CRAIG General clinical research center Comparative bioavailability of videx as a solution or chewable tablet
M01RR-00750-19 0295 (CLR) BRATER, D CRAIG General clinical research center Pharmacokinetic study of 2',3' dideoxyinosine and ketoconazole in AIDS
M01RR-00750-19 0230 (CLR) STEGNER, JANE General clinical research center Glycemic and insulin response to cooked and raw food normal
M01RR-00750-19 0239 (CLR) BRATER, D CRAIG General clinical research center Clinical pharmacology of nonsteroidal anti-antiinflammatory drugs in elderly pts.
M01RR-00750-19 0296 (CLR) BECKER, GARY General clinical research center Palmaz balloon expandable intraluminal stent for renal artery stenosis
M01RR-00750-19 0297 (CLR) GARVEY, TIMOTHY General clinical research center Role of glucose transporters in diabetes mellitus
M01RR-00750-19 0298 (CLR) WHEAT, JOSEPH General clinical research center Itraconzole for primary treatment of disseminated histoplasmosis in AIDS
M01RR-00750-19 0299 (CLR) SUTTON, GREGORY P General clinical research center Cyclophoshamide and cisplatin vs taxol and cisplatin in ovarian carcinoma
M01RR-00750-19 0300 (CLR) SAWADA, STEPHEN General clinical research center Effect of GP-110 on changes in left ventricular regional wall motion
M01RR-00750-19 0301 (CLR) WHEAT, JOSEPH General clinical research center Sch 39304 as therapy for acute cryptococcal meningitis in HIV patients
M01RR-00750-19 0302 (CLR) EINHORN, LAWRENCE H General clinical research center Double platinum regimen in patients with refractory malignancy
M01RR-00750-19 0303 (CLR) BRATER, CRAIG General clinical research center Absolute bioavailability of ibuprofen enantiomers in normal volunteers
M01RR-00750-19 0304 (CLR) DENNE, SCOTT C General clinical research center Leucine metabolism in normal and premature newborns
M01RR-00750-19 0305 (CLR) DENNE, SCOTT C General clinical research center Effect of nonprotein substrate on glucose and protein metabolism in newborns
M01RR-00750-19 0306 (CLR) DENNE, SCOTT C General clinical research center Energy requirements & intake in cyanotic congenital heart disease
M01RR-00750-19 0240 (CLR) BRADLEY, JOHN D General clinical research center Acetaminophen and ibuprofen in treating osteoarthritis of the hip and knee
M01RR-00750-19 0244 (CLR) CHRISTIAN, JOE C General clinical research center Twin and family studies of the acute effects of alcohol
M01RR-00750-19 0246 (CLR) VOELKER, JAMES R General clinical research center Diuretic synergy bet. furosemide & captopriol in mild congestive heart failure
M01RR-00750-19 0247 (CLR) HAWES, ROBERT H General clinical research center Dissolution of gallstone using methyl tertiary butyl ether
M01RR-00750-19 0248 (CLR) JOHNSTON, C CONRAD JR General clinical research center Nasal calcitonin--Prophylaxis of primary osteoporosis in postmenopausal women
M01RR-00750-19 0249 (CLR) ZIPES, DOUGLAS P General clinical research center Pharmacodynamics & pharmacokinetics of CK-1752A in patients w/ventricular ectopy
M01RR-00750-19 0250 (CLR) NURNBERGER, JOHN I, JR General clinical research center Melatonin suppression by light in effective disorder
M01RR-00750-19 0251 (CLR) PEACOCK, MUNRO General clinical research center Effect of menopause on calcium absorption & relationship to bone density
M01RR-00750-19 0252 (CLR) CHRISTIAN, JOE General clinical research center Inheritance in calcium absorption and its relationship to bone density
M01RR-00750-19 0253 (CLR) SIEMERS, ERIC General clinical research center Assessment of dopaminergic turnover in patients with Parkinson's disease
M01RR-00750-19 0255 (CLR) BLACK, JOHN R General clinical research center Safety/efficacy of clindamycin & primaquine in AIDS patients with pneumonia
M01RR-00750-19 0257 (CLR) MANOLAGA, STAVROS General clinical research center Efficacy/efficacy of salmon calcitonin nasal spray in treatment of osteoporosis
M01RR-00750-19 0258 (CLR) BLACK, JOHN R General clinical research center Trimetrexate/leucovorin vs trimethoprim/sulfamethoxazol in AIDS pts. w/pneumonia
M01RR-00750-19 0259 (CLR) BRATER, D CRAIG General clinical research center Stereoselective disposition of ibuprofen enantiomers: effects on renal function
M01RR-00750-19 0261 (CLR) EINHORN, LAWRENCE General clinical research center Phase II study of advanced germ cell neoplasms, 5-azacytidine
M01RR-00750-19 0262 (CLR) LUFT, FREDERICH C General clinical research center Urinary albumin excretion rate in patients with hypertension
M01RR-00750-19 0263 (CLR) STEHMAN, FREDERICK B General clinical research center Phase II trial of taxol in patients with advanced cervical carcinoma
M01RR-00750-19 0264 (CLR) RUDY, DAVID W General clinical research center Bumetanide infusion of chronic renal failure
M01RR-00750-19 0267 (CLR) FIFE, KENNETH H General clinical research center Safety and efficacy of zidovudine for asyptomatic HIV infected individuals
M01RR-00750-19 0268 (CLR) FIFE, KENNETH H General clinical research center Safety and efficacy of zidovudine in treatment of patients with early ARC
M01RR-00750-19 0270 (CLR) CRABB, DAVID W General clinical research center Correlation of ADH and ALDH genotypes with alcohol flush reaction
M01RR-00750-19 0271 (CLR) COPLEY, J BRIAN General clinical research center Effect of captopril on progressive type I diabetic renal disease
M01RR-00750-19 0272 (CLR) FINEBERA, S EDWIN General clinical research center Metabolic control in adolescents with type I diabetes
M01RR-00827-17 (CLR) BURROW, GERARD N UNIVERSITY OF CALIFORNIA 225 DICKINSON STREET SAN DIEGO, CA 92103-8203 General clinical research center
M01RR-00827-17 0369 (CLR) CLAUSEN, JACK L General clinical research center Investigation of synthetic media in blood gas analyzers
M01RR-00827-17 0370 (CLR) CLAUSEN, JACK L General clinical research center Evaluation of rehabilitation vs education for COPD patients
M01RR-00827-17 0372 (CLR) OLEFSKY, JERROLD M General clinical research center Insulin kinetics in normal, obese and NIDDM patients
M01RR-00827-17 0375 (CLR) JONES, KENNETH LEE General clinical research center Hypothalamic and pituitary function in disorders of hormone release
M01RR-00827-17 0377 (CLR) HENRY, ROBERT R General clinical research center Comparative studies of intracellular glucose metabolism
M01RR-00827-17 0378 (CLR) HENRY, ROBERT R General clinical research center Effect of aging on glucose metabolism
M01RR-00827-17 0380 (CLR) DIMSDALE, JOEL E General clinical research center Converting enzyme inhibition and cardiovascular reactivity
M01RR-00827-17 0381 (CLR) HENRY, ROBERT R General clinical research center Effect of weight reduction on insulin on obesity and diabetes
M01RR-00827-17 0384 (CLR) WEISMAN, MICHAEL H General clinical research center CP-66,248-2 and naparoxen in patients with rheumatoid arthritis
M01RR-00827-17 0016 (CLR) NYHAN, WILLIAM L General clinical research center Amino acid interrelationships in metabolic disease--inborn errors
M01RR-00827-17 0045 (CLR) NYHAN, WILLIAM L General clinical research center Lactic acidemia and its clinical counterparts
M01RR-00827-17 0134 (CLR) SCHNEIDER, JERRY A General clinical research center Use of aminothiols in cystinosis
M01RR-00827-17 0180 (CLR) YEN, SAMUEL S General clinical research center Biological rhythms of reproductive hormones and neurotransmitters
M01RR-00827-17 0235 (CLR) NYHAN, WILLIAM L General clinical research center Disorders of fat metabolism
M01RR-00827-17 0256 (CLR) CRIQUI, MICHAEL H General clinical research center Cardiovascular risk factor assessment for medical students
M01RR-00827-17 0258 (CLR) SCHNEIDER, JERRY A General clinical research center Metabolic defect in cystinosis and Fanconi syndrome
M01RR-00827-17 0276 (CLR) JONES, KENNETH L General clinical research center Methionyl human growth hormone for treatment of GH deficiency
M01RR-00827-17 0278 (CLR) JONES, KENNETH L General clinical research center Effect of nafarelin acetate in precocious puberty
M01RR-00827-17 0283 (CLR) KOLTERMAN, ORVILLE G General clinical research center Diabetes control and complications trial
M01RR-00827-17 0385 (CLR) YEN, SAMUEL General clinical research center Treatment of pelvic endometriosis with RU486
M01RR-00827-17 0387 (CLR) PARRY, BARBARA General clinical research center Chronobiology of PMS, postpartum and seasonal depression
M01RR-00827-17 0388 (CLR) MORTOLA, JOSEPH F General clinical research center Psychoneuroendocrine alterations in eating disorders
M01RR-00827-17 0389 (CLR) GREEN, MARK R General clinical research center Phase I/II trial of recombinant GM-CSF in extensive SCLC
M01RR-00827-17 0390 (CLR) KOLTERMAN, ORVILLE G General clinical research center Skeletal GS and PDH activities in IDDM and controls--Exercise training
M01RR-00827-17 0394 (CLR) WEISMAN, MICHAEL H General clinical research center Aminobenzoate potassium and placebo in progressive systemic sclerosis
M01RR-00827-17 0395 (CLR) YU, ALICE L General clinical research center Murine IgG2a anti-GD2 monoclonal antibody in advanced neuroblastoma
M01RR-00827-17 0397 (CLR) KRIPKE, DANIEL F General clinical research center Light effects on the menstrual cycle
M01RR-00827-17 0399 (CLR) SPECTOR, STEPHEN A General clinical research center IV gamma globulin and AZT in children with symptomatic HIV
M01RR-00827-17 0403 (CLR) YEN, SAMUEL General clinical research center Treatment of uterine leiomyoma with RU486
M01RR-00827-17 0405 (CLR) KOLTERMAN, ORVILLE G General clinical research center Low carbohydrae/high fat diet and performance during exercise
M01RR-00827-17 0406 (CLR) NYHAN, WILLIAM L General clinical research center Investigation of inborn errors of metabolism using carbon 13
M01RR-00827-17 0408 (CLR) FELICE, MARIANNE E General clinical research center Psychosocial aspects of teenage pregnancy
M01RR-00827-17 0411 (CLR) MANNINO, FRANK L General clinical research center Analysis of 1987 neonatal intensive care unit data
M01RR-00827-17 0412 (CLR) KNOWLTON, KIRK U General clinical research center Lymphocyte subsets in heart failure/correlation with catecholamines
M01RR-00827-17 0414 (CLR) JASKI, BRIAN General clinical research center Right ventricular restrictive/constrictive physiology and transplant
M01RR-00827-17 0416 (CLR) COEN, RONALD W General clinical research center Brainstem auditory evoked response thresholds following gentamicin
M01RR-00827-17 0417 (CLR) BEJAR, RAUL F General clinical research center White matter necrosis in premature twins
M01RR-00827-17 0420 (CLR) FELICE, MARIANNE E General clinical research center San Diego sibling abstinence promotion project
M01RR-00827-17 0421 (CLR) FELICE, MARIANNE E General clinical research center Breast feeding practices in primiparous women

PROJECT NO., ORGANIZATIONAL UNIT., INVESTIGATOR, ADDRESS, TITLE

M01RR-00827-17 0422 (CLR) DIMSDALE, JOEL E General clinical research center Evaluation of psychiatric consultation data
M01RR-00827-17 0293 (CLR) MOSER, KENNETH M General clinical research center Chronic thrombotic pulmonary artery occlusion--Evaluation/followup
M01RR-00827-17 0299 (CLR) OLEFSKY, JERROLD M General clinical research center Evaluation of unusual forms of insulin resistance
M01RR-00827-17 0316 (CLR) WEISMAN, MICHAEL H General clinical research center Methotrexate, auranofin in treatment of rheumatoid arthritis
M01RR-00827-17 0318 (CLR) WEISMAN, MICHAEL H General clinical research center Study of ribavirin in rheumatoid arthritis
M01RR-00827-17 0319 (CLR) WITZTUM, JOSEPH L General clinical research center Evaluation of patients with hyperlipidemia
M01RR-00827-17 0321 (CLR) WITZTUM, JOSEPH L General clinical research center Mevinolin vs. probucol study-open extension
M01RR-00827-17 0323 (CLR) YEN, SAMUEL S General clinical research center Pulsatile GnRH treatment of male hypogonadism & ovulation induction
M01RR-00827-17 0324 (CLR) YEN, SAMUEL S General clinical research center GnRH antagonist therapeutic applications
M01RR-00827-17 0327 (CLR) YEN, SAMUEL S General clinical research center Effect of antiprogesterone RU486 and Nal-Glu agonist in luteal phase
M01RR-00827-17 0425 (CLR) WEISMAN, MICHAEL H General clinical research center BGP links in rheumatoid arthritis--Treatment with flurbiprofen
M01RR-00827-17 0426 (CLR) YEN, SAMUEL S General clinical research center Hormonal dynamics during folliculogenesis
M01RR-00827-17 0337 (CLR) MC CUTCHAN, J ALLEN General clinical research center Epidemiology of AIDS
M01RR-00827-17 0341 (CLR) DIMSDALE, JOEL E General clinical research center Stress physiology, dietary salt and hypertension ·
M01RR-00827-17 0346 (CLR) CRIQUI, MICHAEL H General clinical research center Cardiovascular risk assessment and modification
M01RR-00827-17 0350 (CLR) SPECTOR, STEPHEN B General clinical research center CMV vaccine controlled trial
M01RR-00827-17 0356 (CLR) THAL, LEON J General clinical research center Deprenyl-tocopherol antioxidative therapy of Parkinsonism
M01RR-00827-17 0359 (CLR) YEN, SAMUEL S General clinical research center Administration of hypothalamic hormone releasing factors
M01RR-00827-17 0361 (CLR) WEISMAN, MICHAEL H General clinical research center Ridaura and myochrysine in rheumatoid arthritis
M01RR-00827-17 0363 (CLR) JONES, KENNETH L General clinical research center Growth hormone and estrogen in Turner's syndrome
M01RR-00827-17 0364 (CLR) NICOD, PASCAL H General clinical research center Autonomic and cardiac function in diabetes
M01RR-00827-17 0366 (CLR) NYHAN, WILLIAM L General clinical research center Lesch-Nyhan syndrome and related disorders of purine metabolism
M01RR-00827-17 0427 (CLR) HOWELL, STEPHEN B General clinical research center Phase I trial of intraperitoneal etoposide and dibyridamole
M01RR-00827-17 0502 (CLR) YEN, SAMUEL S General clinical research center Relationship of ovarian steroid pattern and IL secretion pattern
M01RR-00827-17 0503 (CLR) JONES, KENNETH L General clinical research center Cortticosterone methyl oxidase deficiency
M01RR-00827-17 0504 (CLR) PARKER, BARBARA A General clinical research center Evaluation of anti-cross reactive idiotype monoclonal antibody
M01RR-00827-17 0505 (CLR) ZIEGLER, MICHAEL G General clinical research center Sympathetic nerves and fosinopril
M01RR-00827-17 0506 (CLR) MATTREY, ROBERT F General clinical research center Detection threshold for arterial flow using contrast sonography
M01RR-00827-17 0507 (CLR) GREEN, MARK R General clinical research center CHOPE and recombinant G-CSF in diffuse lymphomas
M01RR-00827-17 0508 (CLR) SPECTOR, STEPHEN A General clinical research center DHPG for treatment of congenital CMV
M01RR-00827-17 0509 (CLR) BARON, ALAIN D General clinical research center In vivo kinetics of glucose uptake in insulin resistant states
M01RR-00827-17 0429 (CLR) BASUK, PAUL M General clinical research center Efficacy & safety of sandostatin in immunodeficiency related diarrhea
M01RR-00827-17 0470 (CLR) HENRY, ROBERT R General clinical research center Effect of glycemic control on defects in glucose metabolism
M01RR-00827-17 0471 (CLR) MCCLAY, EDWARD F General clinical research center IP carboplatin and etoposide with systemic Gm-CSF
M01RR-00827-17 0472 (CLR) YEN, SAMUEL S General clinical research center Fluoxetine as serotonergic mechanism in PMS and effect on melatonin
M01RR-00827-17 0473 (CLR) SPECTOR, STEPHEN A General clinical research center Pharmacokinetic/tolerance study of 28 day regimen of oral ganciclovir
M01RR-00827-17 0474 (CLR) SPECTOR, STEPHEN A General clinical research center Safety and tolerance of high vs low dose ZDV in HIV children
M01RR-00827-17 0475 (CLR) OLEFSKY, JERROLD M General clinical research center Safety and efficacy of oral BM 13.0907 in type II diabetes
M01RR-00827-17 0476 (CLR) YEN, SAMUEL S General clinical research center Effect of exogenous melatonin in reproduction and circadian rhythm
M01RR-00827-17 0477 (CLR) YEN, SAMUEL S General clinical research center Pathophysiology of hyperandrogenism in adolescent girls
M01RR-00827-17 0478 (CLR) WEISMAN, MICHAEL H General clinical research center Sandimmune vs methotrexate in rheumatoid arthritis
M01RR-00827-17 0430 (CLR) JAGGER, PAUL I General clinical research center Perindopril tert-butylamine administered to patients with hypertension
M01RR-00827-17 0431 (CLR) MORTOLA, JOSEPH F General clinical research center Pulsatile naloxone infusion in hypothalamic amenorrhea and normals
M01RR-00827-17 0436 (CLR) YEN, SAMUEL S General clinical research center Bioavailability of sublingual testosterone tablets
M01RR-00827-17 0437 (CLR) YEN, SAMUEL S General clinical research center Effect of exogenous DHEA on body composition
M01RR-00827-17 0439 (CLR) OLEFSKY, JERROLD M General clinical research center Cellular mechanisms of insulin resistance
M01RR-00827-17 0440 (CLR) WEISMAN, MICHAEL H General clinical research center Deflazacort and prednisone in chronic dependent rheumatoid arthritis
M01RR-00827-17 0441 (CLR) HOWELL, STEPHEN B General clinical research center IP carboplatin and etoposide with splanchnic vaso-constriction
M01RR-00827-17 0443 (CLR) KOLTERMAN, ORVILLE G General clinical research center Psychosocial issues affecting metabolic control in diabetic subjects
M01RR-00827-17 0444 (CLR) WITZTUM, JOSEPH L General clinical research center Dose response study of probucol as an antioxidant
M01RR-00827-17 0446 (CLR) SHEA, THOMAS C General clinical research center High-dose carboplatin with recombinant human GM-CSF
M01RR-00827-17 0447 (CLR) KOLTERMAN, ORVILLE G General clinical research center Four different doses of HOE-843 in subjects with diabetes mellitus
M01RR-00827-17 0448 (CLR) SPECTOR, STEPHEN A General clinical research center Foscarnet in AIDS patients with CMV retinitis
M01RR-00827-17 0449 (CLR) YU, ALICE L General clinical research center Human-mouse anti-GD2 monoclonal antibody for advanced neuroblastoma
M01RR-00827-17 0450 (CLR) RICHMAN, DOUGLAS D General clinical research center Rising dose tolerability of N-butyl deoxynojirimicin in AIDS and ARC
M01RR-00827-17 0452 (CLR) RICHMAN, DOUGLAS D General clinical research center ddC administered with ZDV in patients with AIDS and advanced ARC
M01RR-00827-17 0453 (CLR) BARRETT-CONNOR, ELIZABETH General clinical research center Postmenopausal estrogen progestin intervention
M01RR-00827-17 0456 (CLR) MOORE, THOMAS R General clinical research center Association between hypertension and insulin levels in pregnancy
M01RR-00827-17 0457 (CLR) TRAUNER, DORIS A General clinical research center Neurological basis of learning and language disorders in children
M01RR-00827-17 0458 (CLR) RAMSDELL, JOE W General clinical research center Energy requirement in Alzheimer's patients
M01RR-00827-17 0459 (CLR) WEISMAN, MICHAEL H General clinical research center Xomazyme H65 treatment in rheumatoid arthritis
M01RR-00827-17 0460 (CLR) ZIEGLER, MICHAEL G General clinical research center Epinephrine pharmacokinetics
M01RR-00827-17 0461 (CLR) DEFTOS, LEONARD J General clinical research center Peptide hormones in mineral and skeletal metabolism
M01RR-00827-17 0462 (CLR) JONES, KENNETH L General clinical research center Biochemical predictors of fetal alcohol syndrome
M01RR-00827-17 0463 (CLR) HOFMANN, ALAN F General clinical research center Metabolism of bile acids in man
M01RR-00827-17 0464 (CLR) SHABETAI, RALPH General clinical research center Changes of extent of artery disease/reactivity in lowered cholesterol
M01RR-00827-17 0465 (CLR) MCCLAY, EDWARD F General clinical research center Immunization to autologous tumor cells by interleukin 2
M01RR-00827-17 0466 (CLR) KOLTERMAN, ORVILLE G General clinical research center Dose response study of HOE 490 in NIDDM
M01RR-00827-17 0467 (CLR) DUPONT, RENEE M General clinical research center Cognitive and MRI changes in affective disorder
M01RR-00827-17 0468 (CLR) WEISMAN, MICHAEL H General clinical research center 2CDA infusion therapy in rheumatoid arthritis
M01RR-00827-17 0469 (CLR) KOLTERMAN, ORVILLE G General clinical research center Comparison of glipizide and insulin vs insulin injection in diabetes
M01RR-00827-17 0479 (CLR) KRIPKE, DANIEL F General clinical research center Sleep physiology in normal, neuropsychiatric and medical patients
M01RR-00827-17 0480 (CLR) OLEFSKY, JERROLD M General clinical research center Hyperinsulinemia in pathogenesis of polycystic ovary disease
M01RR-00827-17 0481 (CLR) BROIDE, DAVID H General clinical research center Cytokines in asthmatic airway
M01RR-00827-17 0482 (CLR) DARKO, DENIS F General clinical research center Depression, stress, and immunity
M01RR-00827-17 0483 (CLR) OLEFSKY, JERROLD M General clinical research center Cellular mechanisms of insulin resistance in pregnant women at term
M01RR-00827-17 0484 (CLR) IRWIN, MICHAEL R General clinical research center Sleep activity, plasma catecholamines and immune function
M01RR-00827-17 0485 (CLR) WITZTUM, JOSEPH L General clinical research center Effect of polyunsaturated fatty acids on LDL oxidation
M01RR-00827-17 0486 (CLR) STAHL, STEPHEN M General clinical research center Serotonin receptor subtypes in fenfluramine neuroendocrine challenge
M01RR-00827-17 0487 (CLR) JACOBSEN, STEPHEN J General clinical research center Genetic basis of facio-scapulohmoral muscular dystrophy
M01RR-00827-17 0488 (CLR) BARSHOP, BRUCE A General clinical research center AICA riboside therapy of Lesch-Nyhan disease
M01RR-00827-17 0489 (CLR) WITZTUM, JOSEPH L General clinical research center Effects of beta-carotene and vitamin E on LDL oxidation
M01RR-00827-17 0490 (CLR) KRIPKE, DANIEL F General clinical research center Chronobiology of postpartum depression
M01RR-00827-17 0491 (CLR) RAUSCH, JEFFREY L General clinical research center Markers of antidepressant response to treatment

PROJECT NO., ORGANIZATIONAL UNIT., INVESTIGATOR, ADDRESS, TITLE

M01RR-00827-17 0492 (CLR) SPECTOR, STEPHEN A General clinical research center ddC in treatment of children with HIV unable to receive zidovudine
M01RR-00827-17 0493 (CLR) KOLTERMAN, ORVILLE G General clinical research center Evaluation of safety and efficacy of CP-72,467 in type II diabetes
M01RR-00827-17 0494 (CLR) YEN, SAMUEL S General clinical research center Role of atenolol in modifying secretion of melatonin
M01RR-00827-17 0495 (CLR) WEISMAN, MICHAEL H General clinical research center RS-61443 in rheumatoid arthritis
M01RR-00827-17 0496 (CLR) WEISMAN, MICHAEL H General clinical research center Misoprostol in rheumatoid arthritis
M01RR-00827-17 0497 (CLR) KORNFELD, STEPHEN B General clinical research center Anti-transferrin receptor monoclonal antibody in malignancy
M01RR-00827-17 0498 (CLR) WITZTUM, JOSEPH L General clinical research center Efficacy of lonicin as lipid lowering drug
M01RR-00827-17 0499 (CLR) KELSOE, JOHN R General clinical research center Genetic linkage studies of affective disorder
M01RR-00827-17 0500 (CLR) HOWELL, STEPHEN B General clinical research center Study of intracavitary human recombinant tumor necrosis factor
M01RR-00827-17 0501 (CLR) YEN, SAMUEL S General clinical research center Effect of DHEA replacement in aging women and men
M01RR-00833-17 0198 (CLR) CHAN, EDWARD K General clinical research center Autoantigens in rheumatic disease
M01RR-00833-17 (CLR) BEUTLER, ERNEST SCRIPPS RESEARCH INSTITUTE 10666 NORTH TORREY PINES ROAD LA JOLLA, CALIF 92037 General clinical research center
M01RR-00833-17 0004 (CLR) CARSON, DENNIS General clinical research center 2-Cda for severe rheumatoid arthritis
M01RR-00833-17 0006 (CLR) KLINE, LAWRENCE General clinical research center KS1/4-methotrexate for non-small cell lung cancer
M01RR-00833-17 0080 (CLR) STEVENSON, DONALD B General clinical research center Analgesic challenges in aspirin-sensitive asthmatic patients
M01RR-00833-17 0081 (CLR) BEUTLER, ERNEST General clinical research center Normal blood collection for biomedical research
M01RR-00833-17 0082 (CLR) ZURAW, BRUCE L General clinical research center Complement and Hageman factor system in angioedema
M01RR-00833-17 0089 (CLR) BEUTLER, ERNEST General clinical research center Phase II trial of 2-chlorodeoxyadenosine in hematologic diseases
M01RR-00833-17 0103 (CLR) VAUGHAN, JOHN H General clinical research center Epstein-Barr virus in autoimmune disease
M01RR-00833-17 0109 (CLR) MITLER, MERRILL M General clinical research center Narcolepsy and other sleep disorders
M01RR-00833-17 0120 (CLR) CURD, JOHN G General clinical research center Studies in vasculitis
M01RR-00833-17 0130 (CLR) CHRISTIANSON, SANDRA General clinical research center Kallikrein and kinin in asthmatic disease
M01RR-00833-17 0132 (CLR) EHLERS, CINDY General clinical research center EEG and ERP markers in neuropsychiatric disorders
M01RR-00833-17 0138 (CLR) POCKROS, PAUL General clinical research center Treatment of malignant ascites with oral diuretics
M01RR-00833-17 0147 (CLR) RUBIN, ROBERT L General clinical research center Anti-histone antibodies in drug-induced lupus
M01RR-00833-17 0151 (CLR) STEVENSON, DONALD D General clinical research center Efficacy study of CI-949 arginine in patients with allergic asthma
M01RR-00833-17 0152 (CLR) HENCH, KAHLER P General clinical research center Sleep physiology and neurochemical changes in patients with fibromyalgia
M01RR-00833-17 0156 (CLR) BEUTLER, ERNEST General clinical research center Studies in Gaucher disease
M01RR-00833-17 0157 (CLR) CHISARI, FRANCIS V General clinical research center Immunobiology & pathogenesis of Hepatitis B virus
M01RR-00833-17 0158 (CLR) MITLER, MERRILL General clinical research center Ethanol and respiration during sleep
M01RR-00833-17 0160 (CLR) FOX, ROBERT L General clinical research center Epstein-Barr virus DNA in patients with Sjogren's syndrome
M01RR-00833-17 0161 (CLR) EHLERS, CINDY L General clinical research center Response to ethanol in Asian Americans
M01RR-00833-17 0162 (CLR) MATHISON, DAVID A General clinical research center Allergic & respiratory disease--Basidiomycetes & fungi imperfection
M01RR-00833-17 0163 (CLR) RUGGERI, ZAVERIO M General clinical research center Molecular defects in Benard-Soulier syndrome and von Willebrand disease
M01RR-00833-17 0164 (CLR) CURNUTT, JOHN T General clinical research center Regulation of superoxide production in human neutrophils
M01RR-00833-17 0199 (CLR) NEMEROW, GLEN R General clinical research center EBV receptor studies
M01RR-00833-17 0166 (CLR) BABIOR, BERNARD M General clinical research center Oxidase-related 48K phosphoprotein of human neutrophils
M01RR-00833-17 0167 (CLR) SIMON, RONALD A General clinical research center Urticaria, angioedema and anaphylaxis provoked by food additives
M01RR-00833-17 0168 (CLR) BEUTLER, ERNEST General clinical research center Formation and survival of red blood cells
M01RR-00833-17 0169 (CLR) TAN, ENG M General clinical research center Studies in interstitial cystitis
M01RR-00833-17 0170 (CLR) SIPE, JACK C General clinical research center 2-Chlorodeoxyadenosine (2-CdA) for progressive multiple sclerosis
M01RR-00833-17 0171 (CLR) LERNER, RICHARD A General clinical research center Expressing human antibody genes in bacteria
M01RR-00833-17 0172 (CLR) SILVERMAN, GREGG J General clinical research center Human humoral antibody response to bacterial polysaccharides
M01RR-00833-17 0173 (CLR) BEUTLER, ERNEST General clinical research center Enzyme replacement therapy in Gaucher disease

PROJECT NO., ORGANIZATIONAL UNIT., INVESTIGATOR, ADDRESS, TITLE

M01RR-00833-17 0174 (CLR) DEL ZOPPO, GREGORY J General clinical research center Platelet glycoprotein phenotypes related to platelet function in hematopoiesis
M01RR-00833-17 0200 (CLR) FEY, GEORG H General clinical research center Molecular genetics of inflammatory mediators
M01RR-00833-17 0175 (CLR) BEUTLER, ERNEST General clinical research center Chlorodeoxyadenosine (2-Cda) in treatment of solid tumors
M01RR-00833-17 0176 (CLR) POCKROS, PAUL J General clinical research center Roferon in non-A, non-B hepatitis
M01RR-00833-17 0177 (CLR) ANGELL, WILLIAM W General clinical research center Valve survival, replacement, complication rates, bypass alternatives/CV surgery
M01RR-00833-17 0178 (CLR) BERNSTEIN, EUGENE F General clinical research center Vascular surgery registry
M01RR-00833-17 0179 (CLR) COLWELL, CLIFFORD W General clinical research center Total hip arthroplasty--Evaluation of new prostheses
M01RR-00833-17 0180 (CLR) COLWELL, CLIFFORD W General clinical research center Knee replacement and TENS therapy
M01RR-00833-17 0181 (CLR) LOSKUTOFF, DAVID J General clinical research center Endothelial cell-mediated fibrinolysis
M01RR-00833-17 0182 (CLR) COLWELL, CLIFFORD W General clinical research center Patient controlled analgesia (PCA) in joint replacement
M01RR-00833-17 0183 (CLR) ROBB, JAMES A General clinical research center Solid tumor pathology
M01RR-00833-17 0184 (CLR) ROBERTS, ALAN H General clinical research center Counseling intervention and anxiety disorders
M01RR-00833-17 0185 (CLR) GRIMSHAW, CHARLES E General clinical research center Enzyme kinetics of aldose reductase
M01RR-00833-17 0186 (CLR) MCLACHLAN, ALAN General clinical research center Hepatitis B virus
M01RR-00833-17 0187 (CLR) MCLACHLAN, ALAN General clinical research center Phosphofructokinase--Gene and variants
M01RR-00833-17 0188 (CLR) JOHNSON, ERIC F General clinical research center Cytochrome p450 studies
M01RR-00833-17 0189 (CLR) YU, JOHN General clinical research center Growth factors affecting erythropoiesis
M01RR-00833-17 0190 (CLR) FARBER, LEN H General clinical research center Gene and gene products affecting myelin sheath formation and degradation
M01RR-00833-17 0191 (CLR) MILNER, ROBERT J General clinical research center Genetic sequencing and structure prediction
M01RR-00833-17 0192 (CLR) KIPPS, THOMAS J General clinical research center Immunoglobulin and gene expression
M01RR-00833-17 0193 (CLR) NOBURI, TSUTOMU General clinical research center Human liposomal protein
M01RR-00833-17 0194 (CLR) CHEN, POJEN C General clinical research center Human immunoglobulin gene studies
M01RR-00833-17 0195 (CLR) ROUDIER, JEAN General clinical research center Genetics sequence homology studies
M01RR-00833-17 0196 (CLR) GREENGARD, JUDITH S General clinical research center Protein C deficiency
M01RR-00833-17 0197 (CLR) HOCH, JAMES A General clinical research center Models of genetic differentiation
M01RR-00833-17 0201 (CLR) KLINMAN, NORMAN R General clinical research center Immune response development
M01RR-00833-17 0202 (CLR) WIDERA, GEORG General clinical research center Function and mechanism of MHC2 genes
M01RR-00833-17 0203 (CLR) GINSBERG, MARK H General clinical research center Molecular genetics in cardiovascular disease
M01RR-00833-17 0204 (CLR) TEIRSTEIN, PAUL A General clinical research center Invasive cardiology
M01RR-00833-17 0205 (CLR) COLWELL, CLIFFORD W General clinical research center Quality of well-being and joint replacement
M01RR-00833-17 0206 (CLR) WONG, CHI-HUEY General clinical research center Enzymatic structure and protein synthesis
M01RR-00833-17 0207 (CLR) EDGINGTON, THOMAS S General clinical research center Tissue factor and homeostasis
M01RR-00833-17 0208 (CLR) MATHISON, JOHN C General clinical research center Genetic study of macrophage production
M01RR-00833-17 0209 (CLR) TOBIAS, PETER S General clinical research center Genetics of the endotoxemic phenomenon
M01RR-00833-17 0210 (CLR) TACK, BRIAN F General clinical research center Genetics of the immunologic response
M01RR-00833-17 0211 (CLR) YE, RICHARD D General clinical research center Genetics of the inflammataory response cascade
M01RR-00833-17 0212 (CLR) PHILLIPS, TOM General clinical research center Genetic characterization of an HIV model
M01RR-00833-17 0213 (CLR) MAYFIELD, STEPHEN P General clinical research center Protein synthesis control
M01RR-00833-17 0214 (CLR) SULLIVAN, KEVIN General clinical research center Genetic studies of nuclear division
M01RR-00833-17 0215 (CLR) SUTCLIFFE, J GREGOR General clinical research center Structure of the neuronal cell
M01RR-00833-17 0216 (CLR) GRIFFIN, JOHN H General clinical research center Human protein C inhibitor
M01RR-00833-17 0217 (CLR) LEE, PAULINE General clinical research center Synthesis and transport of human growth factor
M01RR-00833-17 0218 (CLR) LIU, FU-TONG General clinical research center Molecular genetics of IgE binders
M01RR-00833-17 0219 (CLR) TAN, ENG M General clinical research center Autoimmunity and scleroderma
M01RR-00833-17 0220 (CLR) YAGI, TAKAO General clinical research center Protein structure/function and the respiratory chain
M01RR-00833-17 9001 (CLR) GINSBERG, MARK General clinical research center Core--mRNA/DNA tissue bank
M01RR-00847-18 (CLR) CAREY, ROBERT M UNIVERSITY OF VIRGINIA BOX 410 SCH OF MED CHARLOTTESVILLE, VA 22908 General clinical research center
M01RR-00847-18 0006 (CLR) DAVIS, JOHN S General clinical research center Pathogenic mechanisms in systemic lupus erythematous
M01RR-00847-18 0056 (CLR) ATUK, NUZHET O General clinical research center Catecholamine and metabolism in pheochromocytoma

M01RR-00847-18 0091 (CLR) THORNER, MICHAEL O General clinical research center Use of bromocriptine in acromegaly
M01RR-00847-18 0167 (CLR) BLIZZARD, ROBERT M General clinical research center LH-RH to study the pubertal process
M01RR-00847-18 0214 (CLR) PLATTS-MILLS, THOMAS A General clinical research center Prolonged avoidance environment factors in patients with asthma
M01RR-00847-18 0218 (CLR) SURATT, PAUL M General clinical research center Tissue composition of upper airway in obstructive sleep apnea
M01RR-00847-18 0229 (CLR) THORNER, MICHAEL O General clinical research center hpGRF test to define GH reserve in children with GH deficiency
M01RR-00847-18 0580 (CLR) EVANS, WILLIAM S General clinical research center Thyrotropin and prolactin secretory dynamics in post-menopausal females
M01RR-00847-18 0581 (CLR) EVANS, WILLIAM S General clinical research center Prolactin secretory dynamics in post-menopausal females--Exogenous estrogen
M01RR-00847-18 0582 (CLR) VELDHUIS, JOHANNES General clinical research center Feedback actions of cortisol on ACTH release
M01RR-00847-18 0583 (CLR) WILSON, WILLIAM G General clinical research center ACTH-cortisol secretion and sleep changes in depression
M01RR-00847-18 0584 (CLR) PLATTS-MILLS, THOMAS A General clinical research center UVA/Wilmington emergency room asthma study
M01RR-00847-18 0427 (CLR) BLIZZARD, ROBERT M General clinical research center Effect of graded doses of androgens on growth hormone in peripubertal males
M01RR-00847-18 0232 (CLR) THORNER, MICHAEL O General clinical research center Combined hypothalamic hormone test of anterior pituitary function
M01RR-00847-18 0233 (CLR) THORNER, MICHAEL O General clinical research center Does hpGRF-40 therapy stimulate linear growth in GH deficiency
M01RR-00847-18 0242 (CLR) VELDHUIS, JOHANNE D General clinical research center Pulsatile gonadotropin secretion by endogenous opiates
M01RR-00847-18 0272 (CLR) ROGOL, ALAN D General clinical research center Reproductive system function in endurance training women
M01RR-00847-18 0304 (CLR) EVANS, WILLIAM S General clinical research center Pulsatile gonadotropin release in patients with insulin dependent diabetes
M01RR-00847-18 0306 (CLR) MC CALLUM, RICHARD W General clinical research center Clinical evaluation of cisapride
M01RR-00847-18 0321 (CLR) THORNER, MICHAEL O General clinical research center Twenty four-hour growth hormone profile in acromegaly
M01RR-00847-18 0334 (CLR) VELDHUIS, JOHANNES D General clinical research center Flutamide-tamoxifen follow-up study
M01RR-00847-18 0338 (CLR) BLIZZARD, ROBERT M General clinical research center Safety and efficacy of rhGH in untreated growth hormone deficiency patients
M01RR-00847-18 0347 (CLR) CLARKE, WILLIAM L General clinical research center Blood glucose--Perception, stress, function
M01RR-00847-18 0356 (CLR) EVANS, WILLIAM S General clinical research center Characterization of pulatile gonadotropin release--Polycystic ovary
M01RR-00847-18 0362 (CLR) ROGOL, ALAN General clinical research center Hormonal changes, growth skeletal maturation in adolescent short boys
M01RR-00847-18 0364 (CLR) ROGOL, ALAN D General clinical research center Effect of beta blockade on endogenous and human pancreatic GH release
M01RR-00847-18 0367 (CLR) ROGOL, ALAN D General clinical research center GH pulsatility and integrated concentration of GH in growth disorders
M01RR-00847-18 0369 (CLR) THORNER, M O General clinical research center Bromocriptine in hyperprolactinemia
M01RR-00847-18 0381 (CLR) BENNETT, JAMES P General clinical research center Deprenyl and tocopherol antioxidative therapy of Parkinson's disease
M01RR-00847-18 0382 (CLR) BENNETT, JAMES P General clinical research center Use of IV L-DOPA and progabide for advanced Parkinson's disease
M01RR-00847-18 0385 (CLR) BLIZZARD, ROBERT M General clinical research center Safety and efficacy of rhGH alone and with estradiol in patients
M01RR-00847-18 0387 (CLR) BOLTON, WARREN K General clinical research center Diabetic kidney study--Enalapril in type II diabetics with hypertension
M01RR-00847-18 0389 (CLR) CAREY, ROBERT M General clinical research center Effects of sodium balance on SKF82526-J induced natriuresis
M01RR-00847-18 0390 (CLR) DREIFUSS, FRITZ E General clinical research center Double blind study--Gabapentin add-on therapy in seizures
M01RR-00847-18 0392 (CLR) EVANS, WILLIAM S General clinical research center Deconvolution of LH, FSH and prolactin in normal cycling women
M01RR-00847-18 0393 (CLR) GUTGESELL, MARGARET General clinical research center Cardiovascular fitness in first-year residents
M01RR-00847-18 0402 (CLR) MC CALLUM, RICHARD W General clinical research center Gastroesophageal reflux--Does it occur during sleep?
M01RR-00847-18 0403 (CLR) MC CALLUM, RICHARD W General clinical research center Effect and safety of cisapride in treatment of GI motility disorder
M01RR-00847-18 0404 (CLR) ROGOL, ALAN D General clinical research center Variability of 24-hour growth hormone secretion in normal men
M01RR-00847-18 0405 (CLR) ROGOL, ALAN D General clinical research center Variability in growth hormone and gonadotropin secretion in women
M01RR-00847-18 0414 (CLR) VELDHUIS, JOHANNES D General clinical research center Regulation of pulsatile FSH secretion by continuous steroid infusions
M01RR-00847-18 0416 (CLR) VELDHUIS, JOHANNES D General clinical research center Steroidal regulation of FSH secretion in young and older men
M01RR-00847-18 0422 (CLR) ASPLIN, CHRISTOPHER M General clinical research center Pulsatile activity of the pancreatic B-cell
M01RR-00847-18 0424 (CLR) BLIZZARD, ROBERT M General clinical research center Methionyl HGH in subjects with GH failure associated with GH deficiency
M01RR-00847-18 0426 (CLR) BLIZZARD, ROBERT M General clinical research center Efficacy and safety of rhGH children with idiopathic short stature
M01RR-00847-18 0428 (CLR) BLIZZARD, ROBERT M General clinical research center Use of depot leuprolide in precocious puberty
M01RR-00847-18 0548 (CLR) ROGOL, ALAN D General clinical research center Growthy and sexual maturation in childhood diabetes mellitus
M01RR-00847-18 0549 (CLR) DAVIS, JOHN S General clinical research center Follow-up study on a homozygous C3 deficient patient
M01RR-00847-18 0550 (CLR) DREIFUSS, FRITZ E General clinical research center Efficacy of gabapentin in monotherapy in childhood absence epilepsy
M01RR-00847-18 0551 (CLR) EVANS, WILLIAM S General clinical research center Use of exogenously administered GRH in women with luteal phase defect
M01RR-00847-18 0552 (CLR) BLIZZARD, ROBERT M General clinical research center Effect of phase of menstrual cycle of GH pulsatility and on resp. to CAP WSE014
M01RR-00847-18 0553 (CLR) HANKS, JOHN B General clinical research center Glucoregulatory influences in transplantation
M01RR-00847-18 0554 (CLR) HARTMAN, MARK L General clinical research center Effect of continuous glucagon infusion on 24h growth hormone secretory profile
M01RR-00847-18 0555 (CLR) THORNER, MICHAEL O General clinical research center Effect of changes in insulin concentrations on pulsatile growth hormone secretion
M01RR-00847-18 0556 (CLR) KELLY, THADDEUS E General clinical research center Abetalipoproteinemia; dietary management
M01RR-00847-18 0429 (CLR) BLIZZARD, ROBERT M General clinical research center GH pulsatility in children with precocious puberty treated with leuprolide
M01RR-00847-18 0433 (CLR) DREIFUSS, FRITZ E General clinical research center Progabide in partial seizures
M01RR-00847-18 0435 (CLR) EVANS, WILLIAM S General clinical research center Pulsatile gonadotropin release and exogenous gonadotropin releasing hormone
M01RR-00847-18 0437 (CLR) EVANS, WILLIAM S General clinical research center Pulsatile therapy with GnRH in men for hypogonadotropic hypogonadism
M01RR-00847-18 0445 (CLR) MCCALLUM, RICHARD W General clinical research center Compare fed and fasted gastric and small bowel motility in normal subjects
M01RR-00847-18 0446 (CLR) PLATTS-MILLS, THOMAS A General clinical research center Trichophyton sensitized and trichophyton infected patients in asthma etiology
M01RR-00847-18 0447 (CLR) ROGOL, ALAN D General clinical research center Bone mineral content and reproductive hormones in women
M01RR-00847-18 0450 (CLR) THORNER, MICHAEL O General clinical research center Clinical and hormonal effect of GRF--Subcutaneous dose
M01RR-00847-18 0451 (CLR) THORNER, MICHAEL O General clinical research center Growth hormone secretion during sleep in fasting men
M01RR-00847-18 0452 (CLR) THORNER, MICHAEL O General clinical research center Glucose tolerance test for growth hormone secretion in normal subjects
M01RR-00847-18 0453 (CLR) VANCE, MARY LEE General clinical research center Efficacy of CV 205-502 in patients with hyperprolactinemia
M01RR-00847-18 0455 (CLR) VELDHUIS, JOHANNES D General clinical research center Recovery of pulsatile gonadotropin secretion postpartum
M01RR-00847-18 0459 (CLR) VELDHUIS, JOHANNES D General clinical research center Suppressive action of glucocorticoids on male hypothalamo-pituitary-gonad axis
M01RR-00847-18 0461 (CLR) VELDHUIS, JOHANNES D General clinical research center Differential release of carbohydrate-enriched bioactive luteinizing hormone
M01RR-00847-18 0463 (CLR) ATKIN, JOAN F General clinical research center Chromosomes abnormalities--Demographic correlates
M01RR-00847-18 0464 (CLR) CAREY, ROBERT M General clinical research center Dopamine-1 receptors mediate renal function through renal tubular mechanism
M01RR-00847-18 0466 (CLR) EVANS, WILLIAM S General clinical research center Pulsatile gonadotropin release in normal women--Effect of clomiphene
M01RR-00847-18 0468 (CLR) HARTMAN, MARK L General clinical research center In vitro studies of metabolic regulation of growth hormone secretion
M01RR-00847-18 0476 (CLR) THORNER, MICHAEL O General clinical research center Effect of 2-day fast on 24-hr GH secretory profile and urinary GH excretion
M01RR-00847-18 0557 (CLR) EVANS, WILLIAM S General clinical research center Mode of pulsatile LH release during progesterone stimulated LH surge
M01RR-00847-18 0558 (CLR) MCCALLUM, RICHARD W General clinical research center Prospective evaluation of patients with severe constipation
M01RR-00847-18 0559 (CLR) EVANS, WILLIAM S General clinical research center Single-blind trial using leuprolide acetate to treat gastroparesis
M01RR-00847-18 0560 (CLR) MCCALLUM, RICHARD W General clinical research center Randomized trial using erythromycin to treat gastroparesis
M01RR-00847-18 0561 (CLR) MCCALLUM, RICHARD W General clinical research center Effects of food on GI transit of two different sizes of hydrogel beads
M01RR-00847-18 0562 (CLR) PLATTS-MILLS, THOMAS A General clinical research center House dust mite antigen on skin of patients with atopic dermatitis

M01RR-00847-18 0563 (CLR) BLIZZARD, ROBERT M General clinical research center Pulsatility of gonadotropin secretion in patients with adrenal hyperplasia
M01RR-00847-18 0564 (CLR) EVANS, WILLIAM S General clinical research center Opiate receptor blockade and gonadotropin secretin in peri-pubertal males
M01RR-00847-18 0565 (CLR) ROGOL, ALAN D General clinical research center Growth hormone release--Cholinergic vs opiate stimulation
M01RR-00847-18 0566 (CLR) ROGOL, ALAN D General clinical research center GH secretory dynamics in preterm and small for gestation infants
M01RR-00847-18 0567 (CLR) THORNER, MICHAEL O General clinical research center Efficacy of somatostatin analog--Hypersecretory endocrine tumors
M01RR-00847-18 0568 (CLR) EVANS, WILLIAM S General clinical research center Characterization of pulsatile GH secretion in acromegalics
M01RR-00847-18 0569 (CLR) THORNER, MICHAEL O General clinical research center Changes in IGF-1 concentrations on pulsatile GH secretion
M01RR-00847-18 0570 (CLR) HARTMAN, MARK L General clinical research center Investigation of clinical and hormonal effects of oral GHRP
M01RR-00847-18 0571 (CLR) THORNER, MICHAEL O General clinical research center Validation of a frequent sampling technique using double-lumen catheter
M01RR-00847-18 0572 (CLR) HARTMAN, MARK L General clinical research center GH response to IV administration of GHRP and GHRH in GH deficient men
M01RR-00847-18 0573 (CLR) THORNER, MICHAEL O General clinical research center Dose response relationships of synthetic human GH in men
M01RR-00847-18 0574 (CLR) VANCE, MARY L General clinical research center Subcutaneous synthetic GH dose response study in normal man
M01RR-00847-18 0575 (CLR) VANCE, MARY L General clinical research center GH suppression--Effect on proliferative diabetic retinopathy
M01RR-00847-18 0576 (CLR) THORNER, MICHAEL O General clinical research center Interaction of GHRH and GHRP on stimulation of GH in normal man
M01RR-00847-18 0577 (CLR) ROGOL, ALAN D General clinical research center GHRH antagonist pulsatile secretory LH, FSH, prolactin in postmenopausal women
M01RR-00847-18 0578 (CLR) EVANS, WILLIAM S General clinical research center Mechanisms of estradiol-induced GNRH self-priming of LH release
M01RR-00847-18 0579 (CLR) BOLTON, WARREN K General clinical research center Dynamics of endogenous gonadotropin secretion in renal failure
M01RR-00847-18 0479 (CLR) VELDHUIS, JOHANNES D General clinical research center Assessment of false negative errors using cluster pulse analysis
M01RR-00847-18 0482 (CLR) ASPLIN, CHRISTOPHER M General clinical research center Short-term normoglycemia in insulin-dependent diabetes--Hormones secretion
M01RR-00847-18 0483 (CLR) ASPLIN, CHRISTOPHER M General clinical research center Deconvolution of LH, FSH, and PRL in hypogonadal women
M01RR-00847-18 0484 (CLR) ASPLIN, CHRISTOPHER M General clinical research center Impaired glucose tolerance--Glipizide and development of Type II diabetes
M01RR-00847-18 0485 (CLR) EVANS, WILLIAM S General clinical research center One-minute sampling for insulin pulsatility
M01RR-00847-18 0488 (CLR) CLARKE, WILLIAM C General clinical research center Blood glucose awareness training--Enhancement and extension
M01RR-00847-18 0499 (CLR) MCCALLUM, RICHARD W General clinical research center Domperidone--Compassionate clearance
M01RR-00847-18 0502 (CLR) PAULSEN, ELSA P General clinical research center Hyperreninism as etiologic in Type I diabetic nephropathy
M01RR-00847-18 0489 (CLR) DAMMANN, JOHN F General clinical research center Therapy of continuing left ventricle hypertrophy and hyperkinesia
M01RR-00847-18 0491 (CLR) DREIFUSS, FRITZ E General clinical research center Multicenter evaluation of felbamate in subjects with Lennox-Gastaut
M01RR-00847-18 0504 (CLR) ROGOL, ALAN D General clinical research center Effects of gonadal steroid hormones on beta-endorphin and cortisol
M01RR-00847-18 0505 (CLR) ROGOL, ALAN D General clinical research center Alterations in hypopituitarism axes for gonadotropins--Women endurance training
M01RR-00847-18 0506 (CLR) SIRAGY, HELMY General clinical research center Rhythmic and pulsatile release of aldosterone
M01RR-00847-18 0510 (CLR) SUTPHEN, JAMES L General clinical research center Celiac disease as cause of short stature in asymptomatic children
M01RR-00847-18 0513 (CLR) THORNER, MICHAEL O General clinical research center Effect of five day fast on 24-hour secretory profile of GH secretion in humans
M01RR-00847-18 0515 (CLR) THORNER, MICHAEL O General clinical research center Dose response relationship of infusions of GHRP on GH secretion in men
M01RR-00847-18 0516 (CLR) THORNER, MICHAEL O General clinical research center Five-day fast and 24-hour GH secretory profile--GH response to GHRP in obesity
M01RR-00847-18 0494 (CLR) HANKS, JOHN B General clinical research center Enteric and endocrine glucoregulatory influence in pancreas allotransplantation
M01RR-00847-18 0496 (CLR) HARTMAN, MARK L General clinical research center Effect of bariatric surgery on 24-hour growth hormone secretory profile
M01RR-00847-18 0498 (CLR) LIPPERT, MARGUERITE C General clinical research center Safety and efficacy of MK-906 in patients with benign prostatic hypertrophy
M01RR-00847-18 0517 (CLR) THORNER, MICHAEL O General clinical research center Refeeding fasted subjects and 24-hour GH secretory profile--GH response to GHRP
M01RR-00847-18 0518 (CLR) THORNER, MICHAEL O General clinical research center Twenty-four hour profiles of GH secretion--GH response to GHRP in acromegaly
M01RR-00847-18 0519 (CLR) THORNER, MICHAEL O General clinical research center Oral and transdermal estrogen replacement and growth hormone secretion in women
M01RR-00847-18 0522 (CLR) VANCE, MARY L General clinical research center Physiologic GH replacement--Protein, lipid and carbohydrate metabolism
M01RR-00847-18 0524 (CLR) VANCE, MARY L General clinical research center Sandostatin in the treatment of acromegaly
M01RR-00847-18 0525 (CLR) VANCE, MARY L General clinical research center Safety and efficacy of chronic sandostatin treatment in acromegalic patients
M01RR-00847-18 0526 (CLR) VANCE, MARY L General clinical research center Growth hormone secretion in burn injury
M01RR-00847-18 0527 (CLR) VELDHUIS, JOHANNES D General clinical research center Effects of IV diltiazem, IV calcium, and oral diltiazem on pituitary tumors
M01RR-00847-18 0528 (CLR) VELDHUIS, JOHANNES D General clinical research center Effect of fasting on 24-hour LH and cortisol secretion in normal subjects
M01RR-00847-18 0529 (CLR) VELDHUIS, JOHANNES D General clinical research center Primary hypothyroidism--Secretion and metabolism of anterior pituitary hormone
M01RR-00847-18 0530 (CLR) VELDHUIS, JOHANNES D General clinical research center Influence of altered cholinergic tone on the hyposomatotropism of obesity
M01RR-00847-18 0531 (CLR) VIEWEG, VICTOR R General clinical research center Regulation of plasma sodium in water intoxication
M01RR-00847-18 0532 (CLR) WILSON, WILLIAM G General clinical research center Betaine in the treatment of homocystinuria
M01RR-00847-18 0535 (CLR) DREIFUSS, FRITZ E General clinical research center Evaluation of lamotrigine as add-on therapy in patients with partial seizures
M01RR-00847-18 0538 (CLR) VELDHUIS, JOHANNES D General clinical research center Metabolic clearance of pure FSH in man
M01RR-00847-18 0539 (CLR) ASPLIN, CHRISTOPHER M General clinical research center Effect of gemfibrozil on triglyceride levels in patients with type II diabetes
M01RR-00847-18 0540 (CLR) ATUK, NUZHET O General clinical research center Peripheral norepinephrine store in pheochromocytoma
M01RR-00847-18 0541 (CLR) AYERS, CARLOS R General clinical research center Renal hormones in renovascular hypertension
M01RR-00847-18 0543 (CLR) CANTERBURY, RANDOLPH J General clinical research center Effects of blood alcohol on driving simulation performance
M01RR-00847-18 0544 (CLR) CAREY, ROBERT M General clinical research center HCG and progesterone on apparent pregnancy-related Cushing's syndrome
M01RR-00847-18 0545 (CLR) CAREY, ROBERT M General clinical research center Effects of intravenous WY 47,663 in patients with essential hypertension
M01RR-00847-18 0546 (CLR) CAREY, ROBERT M General clinical research center Proximal renal tubular dopamine-1 stimulation in essential hypertension
M01RR-00847-18 0547 (CLR) BLIZZARD, ROBERT M General clinical research center Islet cell antibodies and autoimmunity
P41RR-00862-18 (SSS) CHAIT, BRIAN T ROCKEFELLER UNIVERSITY 1230 YORK AVENUE NEW YORK, NY 10021 A mass spectrometric biotechnology resource
P41RR-00862-18 0002 (SSS) MERRIFIELD, R A mass spectrometric biotechnology resource Peptide synthesis
P41RR-00862-18 0003 (SSS) KAISER, E A mass spectrometric biotechnology resource Protein engineering
P41RR-00862-18 0004 (SSS) LLOYD, K A mass spectrometric biotechnology resource Human tumor glycolipids
P41RR-00862-18 0005 (SSS) TOMASZ, A A mass spectrometric biotechnology resource Bacterial cell wall glycopeptides
P41RR-00862-18 0006 (SSS) BRESLOW, J A mass spectrometric biotechnology resource Mutant apolipoprotein and atherosclerosis susceptibility
P41RR-00862-18 0007 (SSS) NAIRN, A A mass spectrometric biotechnology resource Protein phosphorylation in the nervous system
P41RR-00862-18 9001 (SSS) CHAIT, BRIAN A mass spectrometric biotechnology resource Mass spectrometry--Core
M01RR-00865-18 (CLR) SHINE, KENNETH I UNIVERSITY OF CALIFORNIA 405 HILGARD AVENUE LOS ANGELES, CALIF 90024 General clinical research center
M01RR-00865-18 0334 (CLR) GEFFNER, MITCHELL E General clinical research center Safety, efficacy of protropin given to patients with growth hormone deficiency
M01RR-00865-18 0337 (CLR) CLEMENTS, PHILIP J General clinical research center Cyclosporin (CSA) in treatment of systemic sclerosis
M01RR-00865-18 0338 (CLR) BRYSON, YVONNE J General clinical research center Double-blind, placebo controlled trial to evaluate IV Ig in children with HIV
M01RR-00865-18 0340 (CLR) DEKERNION, JEAN General clinical research center: Recombinant human rIL-2 & Roferon R-A in patients with renal cell carcinoma
M01RR-00865-18 0345 (CLR) HUI, KA KIT General clinical research center Steady-state pharmacokinetics of pravastatin in patients with renal impairment
M01RR-00865-18 0346 (CLR) HEBER, DAVID General clinical research center: Palm oil vs soybean oil vs coconut oil on cholesterol and lipid metabolism
M01RR-00865-18 0347 (CLR) HARDY, W DAVID General clinical research center Phase II study of ganciclovir and GM-CSF therapy in AIDS patients
M01RR-00865-18 0348 (CLR) RAPKIN, ANDREA General clinical research center Opioid tonus in premenstrual syndrome

PROJECT NO., ORGANIZATIONAL UNIT., INVESTIGATOR, ADDRESS, TITLE

M01RR-00865-18 0349 (CLR) HARDY, W DAVID General clinical research center Phase I open label study to evaluate pharmacokinetics and safety of AzdU
M01RR-00865-18 0350 (CLR) BARRIERE, STEVEN L General clinical research center Pharmacokinetic disposition of ampicillin/subacillin in serum and blister fluid
M01RR-00865-18 0351 (CLR) BRYSON, YVONNE J General clinical research center Phase I trial to evaluate zidovudine in HIV-1 infected pregnant women & offspring
M01RR-00865-18 0352 (CLR) SAXON, ANDREW General clinical research center Venoglobulin R-S--Safety & efficacy in subjects with primary immune deficiencies
M01RR-00865-18 0353 (CLR) SAXON, ANDREW General clinical research center Study to evaluate allergic reactions allegedly due to aspartame consumption
M01RR-00865-18 0354 (CLR) HEBER, DAVID General clinical research center Acute effects of carbohydrate load on circulation catecholamines, insulin
M01RR-00865-18 0355 (CLR) SHIELDS, DONALD General clinical research center Evaluation of felbamate in subjects with Lennox-Gastaut syndrome
M01RR-00865-18 0356 (CLR) BARRIERE, STEVE L General clinical research center Comparison of serum & blister fluid activity in IV drug cefepime, ceftazidime
M01RR-00865-18 0357 (CLR) SALUSKY, ISIDRO B General clinical research center Calcitriol therapy on dialyzed children
M01RR-00865-18 0358 (CLR) BELLDEGRUN, ARIE General clinical research center Metastatic renal cell carcinoma treatment using TIL, IL-2, and roferon
M01RR-00865-18 0359 (CLR) HOWARD, JUDD L General clinical research center Postmenopausal estrogen/progestin interventions trial
M01RR-00865-18 0360 (CLR) GEFFNER, MITCHELL E General clinical research center Biosynthetic growth hormone on attention and information processing
M01RR-00865-18 0361 (CLR) IPPOLITI, ANDREW General clinical research center Xomazyme for the treatment of Crohn's disease
M01RR-00865-18 0362 (CLR) SARNA, GREGORY P General clinical research center Phase II study of immther in patients w/ advanced colorectal carcinoma
M01RR-00865-18 0363 (CLR) TREIMAN, DAVID M General clinical research center Evaluation of ADD94507 in treatment of partial seizures
M01RR-00865-18 0048 (CLR) SPARKES, ROBERT S General clinical research center Tay-Sachs disease prevention program
M01RR-00865-18 0117 (CLR) CHAMPLIN, RICHARD E General clinical research center Bone marrow cryopreservation & autologous bone marrow transplantation--Lymphoma
M01RR-00865-18 0128 (CLR) LIPPE, BARBARA M General clinical research center Neurosecretory abnormalities of growth hormone secretion
M01RR-00865-18 0364 (CLR) SHIELDS, DONALD W General clinical research center Open label, follow-on long term felbamate therapy in epilepsy
M01RR-00865-18 0365 (CLR) MCKAY, JUDITH General clinical research center Pharmacokinetic disposition of cefmetazole/ rapid intravenous infusion
M01RR-00865-18 0366 (CLR) MCKAY, JUDITH General clinical research center Effect of hypnosis & relaxation on patient controlled analgesia
M01RR-00865-18 0367 (CLR) CHAUDHURI, GAUTAM General clinical research center Role of arginine & endothelium derived nitric oxide in preeclampsia
M01RR-00865-18 0368 (CLR) LINDSAY, KAREN L General clinical research center Interferon alfa-2b as therapy for chronic non-A, non-B hepatitis & hepatitis C
M01RR-00865-18 0184 (CLR) FOGELMAN, ALAN M General clinical research center Lipid and lipoprotein metabolism in atherosclerosis
M01RR-00865-18 0223 (CLR) MAZZIOTTA, JOHN C General clinical research center Cerebral metabolism in Huntington's disease
M01RR-00865-18 0224 (CLR) TASHKIN, DONALD P General clinical research center Pulmonary effects of habitual heavy marijuana use--Bronchoscopic procedures
M01RR-00865-18 0232 (CLR) GEFFNER, MITCHELL E General clinical research center Growth hormone and oxandrolone on growth in Turner's syndrome
M01RR-00865-18 0272 (CLR) CLEMENTS, PHILIP J General clinical research center Mononuclear cell products from immunocompetent lung cells in scleroderma
M01RR-00865-18 0273 (CLR) CHAMPLIN, RICHARD E General clinical research center Bone marrow transplantation
M01RR-00865-18 0291 (CLR) GORMLEY, GLENN J General clinical research center Regulation of hypothalamic-pituitary-adrenal axis in anorexia nervosa & bulimia
M01RR-00865-18 0292 (CLR) GEFFNER, MITCHELL E General clinical research center Methionine-free human growth hormone alone and in combination with estradiol
M01RR-00865-18 0293 (CLR) GEFFNER, MITCHELL E General clinical research center Somatotropin treatment of growth retardation of children with short stature
M01RR-00865-18 0294 (CLR) BAXTER, LEWIS R General clinical research center Central nervous system metabolism in cerebrospinal fluid and blood
M01RR-00865-18 0318 (CLR) GOLDENHERSH, MARGARET J General clinical research center Corticosteroid bone density study
M01RR-00865-18 0322 (CLR) FINE, RICHARD N General clinical research center Pubertal development in children with chronic renal failure
M01RR-00865-18 0323 (CLR) SARNA, GREGORY P General clinical research center Intralymphatic vs. intravenous interleukin-2 in patients with cancer
M01RR-00865-18 0329 (CLR) CHAMPLIN, RICHARD E General clinical research center Trial of intravenous immunoglobulin in bone marrow transplant recipients
M01RR-00865-18 0333 (CLR) TREIMAN, DAVID M General clinical research center Evaluation of flunarizine in treatment of partial seizures

PROJECT NO., ORGANIZATIONAL UNIT., INVESTIGATOR, ADDRESS, TITLE

P41RR-00886-16 (SSS) FOX, MARYE A UNIVERSITY OF TEXAS CTR FOR FAST KINETICS RES AUSTIN, TX 78712 Center for fast kinetics research
P41RR-00886-16 0001 (SSS) FOX, MARYE Center for fast kinetics research Photo-induced electron transfer
P41RR-00886-16 0002 (SSS) FOX, MARYE Center for fast kinetics research Kinetic involvement of semiquinones in bioreductive alkylation
P41RR-00886-16 0004 (SSS) ATHERTON, STEPHEN Center for fast kinetics research Electron transfer in micelle bound complexes
P41RR-00886-16 0005 (SSS) RODGERS, MICHAEL Center for fast kinetics research Electron transfer in microheterogeneous media
P41RR-00886-16 0006 (SSS) HUBIG, STEPHEN Center for fast kinetics research Chemical actinometry of dye lasers above 650 nanometers
P41RR-00886-16 0007 (SSS) HUBIG, STEPHEN Center for fast kinetics research Photoinduced charge separation in an electron donor-acceptor
P41RR-00886-16 0008 (SSS) DILLON, JAMES Center for fast kinetics research Photophysics of the glucoside of 3-hydroxy kynurenine
P41RR-00886-16 9001 (SSS) POWERS, EDWARD L Center for fast kinetics research Core research and development
P41RR-00886-16 0003 (SSS) ATHERTON, STEPHEN Center for fast kinetics research Quenching of ethidium bromide-DNA fluorescence
P40RR-00890-16 (AR) PAKES, STEVEN P UNIVERSITY OF TEXAS 5323 HARRY HINES BLVD DALLAS, TX 75235 Animal resources diagnostic and investigative laboratory
P40RR-00890-16 0007 (AR) LAI, WAYNE Animal resources diagnostic and investigative laboratory The role of NK cells in mycoplasmosis
P40RR-00890-16 0008 (AR) GERRITY, LAURETTA Animal resources diagnostic and investigative laboratory In utero transmission of E.cuniculi in rabbits
P40RR-00890-16 0009 (AR) LU, Y Animal resources diagnostic and investigative laboratory Development of pasteurella multocida vaccine
P40RR-00890-16 0010 (AR) CLUBB, FRED Animal resources diagnostic and investigative laboratory Elucidation of the Watanabe heritable hyperlipidemic
P40RR-00890-16 0011 (AR) LU, Y Animal resources diagnostic and investigative laboratory Polymerase chain reaction
P40RR-00919-17 (AR) CLARKSON, THOMAS B WAKE FOREST UNIVERSITY 300 SOUTH HAWTHORNE ROAD WINSTON SALEM, NC 27103 A diagnostic/investigational resource
P40RR-00919-17 0006 (AR) ADAMS, MICHAEL R A diagnostic/investigational resource Malaria, filariasis and circulating immune complexes in Cynomolgus macaques
P40RR-00919-17 0013 (AR) LEWS, JON A diagnostic/investigational resource An animal model of thrombasthenia
P40RR-00919-17 9001 (AR) JEROME, CHRISTOPHER P A diagnostic/investigational resource Core diagnostic laboratory
P41RR-00954-15 (SSS) BIER, DENNIS M WASHINGTON UNIV MEDICAL SCH 660 S EUCLID AVENUE, BOX 8127 ST. LOUIS, MO 63110 A resource for biomedical mass spectrometry
P41RR-00954-15 0021 (SSS) FOMON, SAMUEL J A resource for biomedical mass spectrometry Amino acid requirements of infants
P41RR-00954-15 9011 (SSS) YARASHESKI, K E A resource for biomedical mass spectrometry Core research--Protein anabolic effects of weight training in the elderly
P41RR-00954-15 9012 (SSS) GERICH, JOHN E A resource for biomedical mass spectrometry Core research--Regulation of gluconeogenesis in normal and diabetic man
P41RR-00954-15 9013 (SSS) SCHONFELD, GUSTAV A resource for biomedical mass spectrometry Core research--Exercise, weight loss and lipoproteins
P41RR-00954-15 9014 (SSS) OSTLUND, RICHARD E A resource for biomedical mass spectrometry Core research--13C-cholesterol metabolism in man
P41RR-00954-15 0022 (SSS) FJELD, CARLA R A resource for biomedical mass spectrometry Energy expenditure and protein metabolism in children with cystic fibrosis
P41RR-00954-15 0023 (SSS) AVOGARO, ANGELO A resource for biomedical mass spectrometry Insulin secretion and sensitivity responses to epinephrine in type II diabetes
P41RR-00954-15 0024 (SSS) CONSOLI, AGOSTINO A resource for biomedical mass spectrometry Regulation of hepatic glucose output in diabetic and non-diabetic humans
P41RR-00954-15 0025 (SSS) THOMPSON, LINDA F A resource for biomedical mass spectrometry Phosphatidylinositol (PI)-linked membrane proteins
P41RR-00954-15 0026 (SSS) KAO, KENNETH R A resource for biomedical mass spectrometry Measurement of inositol phosphate metabolites in early amphibian embryos
P41RR-00954-15 0027 (SSS) TAYLOR, JOHN-STEPHEN A A resource for biomedical mass spectrometry DNA photoproduct structure-activity relationships
P41RR-00954-15 0028 (SSS) TAYLOR, JOHN-STEPHEN A A resource for biomedical mass spectrometry Construction of model peptides and poteins for the study of protein assembly
P41RR-00954-15 0029 (SSS) TAYLOR, JOHN-STEPHEN A A resource for biomedical mass spectrometry Nucleic acid-targeted reagents, probes and drugs
P41RR-00954-15 0030 (SSS) GRANT, GREGORY A A resource for biomedical mass spectrometry Development of neuronal nicotinic receptor probes
P41RR-00954-15 0031 (SSS) FORD, DAVID A A resource for biomedical mass spectrometry Plasmalogen metabolism during myocardial ischemia and signal transduction
P41RR-00954-15 0032 (SSS) FRIEDEN, CARL A resource for biomedical mass spectrometry Studies of the folding of dihydrofolate reductase using short peptides
P41RR-00954-15 9006 (SSS) SHERMAN, WILLIAM R A resource for biomedical mass spectrometry Core research--Development of a general method for the analysis of IPs
P41RR-00954-15 9009 (SSS) BIER, DENNIS M A resource for biomedical mass spectrometry Core research--Growth, insulin sensitivity, protein and energy metabolism

P41RR-00954-15 9010 (SSS) CORR, PETER B A resource for biomedical mass spectrometry Core research--Mass determinations of inositol phosphates

R01RR-00959-16 (AR) CASSELL, GAIL H UNIV OF ALABAMA AT BIRMINGHAM UNIVERSITY STATION BIRMINGHAM, AL 35294 Control of murine respiratory mycoplasmosis

P41RR-00995-16 (SSS) NEURINGER, LEO J FRANCIS BITTER NATL MAGNET LAB 170 ALBANY STREET CAMBRIDGE, MA 02139 Comprehensive NMR center for biomedical research

P41RR-00995-16 0001 (SSS) CHENG, HONG Comprehensive NMR center for biomedical research Regional NMR multinuclear studies of ocular tissues

P41RR-00995-16 0002 (SSS) HOLTZMAN, DAVID Comprehensive NMR center for biomedical research Cellular energy metabolism in mature and developing brain

P41RR-00995-16 0003 (SSS) NEURINGER, LEO Comprehensive NMR center for biomedical research Prediction of tumor reponse to radiation treatment

P41RR-00995-16 9001 (SSS) NEURINGER, LEO Comprehensive NMR center for biomedical research NMR--Core

M01RR-00997-16 (CLR) NAPOLITANO, LEONARD M UNIVERSITY OF NEW MEXICO 915 STANFORD DR, NE ALBUQUERQUE, NM 87131 General clinical research center

M01RR-00997-16 0085 (CLR) EATON, R P General clinical research center C-peptide responsiveness to glucose manipulation in hypoglycemia

M01RR-00997-16 0135 (CLR) APPENZELLER, OTTO General clinical research center Doppler studies in endurance trained athletes

M01RR-00997-16 0150 (CLR) EATON, ROBERT P General clinical research center Aldose reductase inhibitor effects on stiff hand syndrome in diabetics

M01RR-00997-16 0179 (CLR) RIEDESEL, MARVIN General clinical research center Overhydration with oral glycerol solutions

M01RR-00997-16 0184 (CLR) SCHADE, DAVID S General clinical research center Glucose homeostasis in type I and brittle diabetes

M01RR-00997-16 0217 (CLR) CRIST, DOUGLAS M General clinical research center Exercise and growth hormone effect during aging

M01RR-00997-16 0218 (CLR) EATON, ROBERT P General clinical research center Short-term implant--Insulin delivery system

M01RR-00997-16 0221 (CLR) GARRY, PHILIP General clinical research center Prospective study of nutrition in the elderly

M01RR-00997-16 0223 (CLR) LISANSKY, EDGAR J General clinical research center Hypothalamic-pituitary-adrenal dysfunction in depressive illness

M01RR-00997-16 0235 (CLR) STRASSMAN, RICK General clinical research center Melatonin dynamics, suppressive effects of light in SAD

M01RR-00997-16 0248 (CLR) APPENZELLER, OTTO General clinical research center Vasa and nervi nervorum in neuropathies

M01RR-00997-16 0252 (CLR) BRANN, BENJAMIN S. General clinical research center Neonatal cerebral ventricular volume by ultrasound

M01RR-00997-16 0262 (CLR) SCHADE, DAVID S. General clinical research center Diabetes control and complications trial

M01RR-00997-16 0264 (CLR) SMITH, KENNETH General clinical research center Intravenous gammaglobulin for idiopathic thrombocytopenic purpura

M01RR-00997-16 0410 (CLR) SCHADE, DAVID S General clinical research center The role of free fatty acids in hypertriglyceridemia

M01RR-00997-16 0411 (CLR) DAVIS, ROBIN General clinical research center Phenotyping of P45011E1

M01RR-00997-16 0412 (CLR) CHATTERJEE, MOLLY S General clinical research center Treatment of acute pelvic inflammatory disease w/intravenous trospectomycin

M01RR-00997-16 0283 (CLR) HARFORD, ANTONIA M General clinical research center Renal autocoids, transplant rejection and cyclosporine

M01RR-00997-16 0288 (CLR) OSBORN, LARRY A General clinical research center Monitoring and electrocardiographic changes in hypothyroidism

M01RR-00997-16 0297 (CLR) SIMON, TOBY L General clinical research center Blood donations in the elderly

M01RR-00997-16 0300 (CLR) STRASSMAN, RICK General clinical research center Behavioral and neuroendocrine effects of bright light suppression

M01RR-00997-16 0309 (CLR) EATON, ROBERT P General clinical research center Induction of polyol pathway enzymes in diabetes mellitus

M01RR-00997-16 0312 (CLR) SIMON, TOBY L General clinical research center Immune sequelae of transfusion and donation

M01RR-00997-16 0313 (CLR) MURPHY, SHIRLEY General clinical research center Cromolyn sodium in prevention of bronchopulmonary dysplasia

M01RR-00997-16 0413 (CLR) RIEDESEL, MARVIN L General clinical research center Glycerol solution as a countermeasure to orthostatic intolerance during bedrest

M01RR-00997-16 0324 (CLR) EATON, ROBERT P General clinical research center Study of diabetic neuropathy

M01RR-00997-16 0327 (CLR) MAWHORTER, LINDA General clinical research center Diagnosis of disseminated candidiasis in immunocompromised

M01RR-00997-16 0330 (CLR) NEIDHART, JAMES A General clinical research center Safety and efficacy of GM-CSF in resistant malignancies

M01RR-00997-16 0334 (CLR) BRANN, BEN S General clinical research center Evaluation of central venous catheter complications in newborn

M01RR-00997-16 0337 (CLR) HARFORD, ANTONIA General clinical research center Renal transplantation in the native American

M01RR-00997-16 0338 (CLR) BRUNO, ASKIEL General clinical research center Stroke registry

M01RR-00997-16 0340 (CLR) EATON, ROBERT P General clinical research center Insulin kinetic behavior in obese man

M01RR-00997-16 0341 (CLR) SCOTT, SUSAN General clinical research center Human epidermal growth factor in the perinatal period

M01RR-00997-16 0342 (CLR) JOHNSON, JOHN D General clinical research center Somatotropin in therapy of short stature due to growth hormone deficiency

M01RR-00997-16 0345 (CLR) LOWE, JANE General clinical research center Individualized behavioral & environmental care for the VLBW preterm infant

M01RR-00997-16 0346 (CLR) MCWILLIAMS, BENNIE General clinical research center Comparison of sustained release albuterol and theophylline by methacholine chal.

M01RR-00997-16 0347 (CLR) ALVERSON, DALE C General clinical research center: Safety and efficacy of nebulized albuterol in ventilated premature infants

M01RR-00997-16 0349 (CLR) HASHIMOTO, FRED General clinical research center The effect of pentoxifyllineon xylose malabsorption at high altitude

M01RR-00997-16 0350 (CLR) ZAGER, PHILIP G General clinical research center Aldose reductase activity modulates renal hemodynamics in patients with diabetes

M01RR-00997-16 0351 (CLR) WEISSMAN, DAVID N General clinical research center Functional immunity of the human lung

M01RR-00997-16 0352 (CLR) KOSTER, FREDERICK T General clinical research center Pathophysiology of distal sensory peripheral neuropathy (DSPN) of AIDS

M01RR-00997-16 0353 (CLR) PALMER, ROBERT General clinical research center Predictive value of stool hemoccult for colorectal neoplasia

M01RR-00997-16 0354 (CLR) CURET, LUIS B General clinical research center Prophylactic insulin treatment of patients with gestational diabetes

M01RR-00997-16 0355 (CLR) SIMON, TOBY L General clinical research center In vivo red cell viability following storage of leukopoor red cell CLX bags

M01RR-00997-16 0357 (CLR) SIMON, TOBY L General clinical research center As-5 optisol red cell preservative solution

M01RR-00997-16 0360 (CLR) SIMON, TOBY L General clinical research center Study of techniques for red cell survival

M01RR-00997-16 0361 (CLR) EATON, ROBERT P General clinical research center Aldose reductase--Its role in etiology & treatment of diabetic neuropathy

M01RR-00997-16 0365 (CLR) RIEDESEL, MARVIN L General clinical research center Orthostatic tolerance after head-out immersion (HOI)

M01RR-00997-16 0366 (CLR) BOYLE, PATRICK General clinical research center The effect of oral hypoglycemic agents on the dawn phenomenon

M01RR-00997-16 0367 (CLR) ZAGER, PHILIP General clinical research center Safety of tolerance of magnevist injection in subjects with renal insufficiency

M01RR-00997-16 0368 (CLR) UHLENHUTH, EBERHARD H General clinical research center Pharmacokinetics and pharmacodynamics of alprazolam

M01RR-00997-16 0369 (CLR) CARLSON, KAREN L General clinical research center Maternal self-concept, depression, and social support

M01RR-00997-16 0371 (CLR) SMITH, KENNETH J General clinical research center Safety, half-life recovery of antihemophilic factor, human VIII

M01RR-00997-16 0373 (CLR) BOYLE, PATRICK J General clinical research center Declining insulin requirements during sleep in insulin dependent diabetes

M01RR-00997-16 0374 (CLR) LINDEMAN, ROBERT D General clinical research center Comparison of renal clearances of ascorbic acid in males and females

M01RR-00997-16 0375 (CLR) AGNELUS, PAMELA A General clinical research center Transition to nipple feedings after oral-motor tune-ups in preterm infants

M01RR-00997-16 0376 (CLR) KATZ, ROBERT W General clinical research center Pharmacokinetics of long term continuous fentanyl infusions in critically ill

M01RR-00997-16 0414 (CLR) GREENBERG, ROBERT E General clinical research center Defective & compensating regulatory loops in Bartter's syndrome

M01RR-00997-16 0377 (CLR) MCWILLIAMS, BENNIE General clinical research center Administration of an aerosolized beta adrenergic on bronchial hyperreactivity

M01RR-00997-16 0378 (CLR) BOYLE, PATRICK J General clinical research center Intravenous use of somatostatin analogue

M01RR-00997-16 0379 (CLR) EATON, R PHILIP General clinical research center Non-invasive glucose monitoring with infrared spectroscopy

M01RR-00997-16 0380 (CLR) AGARWAL, VIJAY P General clinical research center Treatment of diversion colitis with short-chain fatty acid irrigation

M01RR-00997-16 0382 (CLR) UHLENHUTH, EBERHARD H General clinical research center Single dose & withdrawal pharmacokinetics & pharmacodynamics of alprazolam

M01RR-00997-16 0383 (CLR) ZAGER, PHILIP G General clinical research center Evaluation of renal prostaglandin activity in patients renal insufficiency

M01RR-00997-16 0384 (CLR) CRAWLEY, ELIZABETH General clinical research center Back-transport of infants--Effects on feedings and oxygenation

M01RR-00997-16 0385 (CLR) SCHADE, DAVID S General clinical research center Catecholamine regulation of ketogenesis

M01RR-00997-16 0386 (CLR) SIMON, TOBY L General clinical research center Therapeutic plasmapheresis

M01RR-00997-16 0387 (CLR) SMITH, KENNETH J General clinical research center Intravenous gammaglobulin in idiopathic thrombocytopenic purpura

M01RR-00997-16 0388 (CLR) SIMON, TOBY L General clinical research center Karmi blood bags

M01RR-00997-16 0389 (CLR) HENDREN, ROBERT L General clinical research center Nutritional deficiencies in children with psychiatric disorders

M01RR-00997-16 0390 (CLR) BENZIGER, JACQUELINE P General clinical research center Effect of age and blood donation on red cell function & viability

M01RR-00997-16 0391 (CLR) MERTZ, GREGORY J General clinical research center Effect of ultraviolet-B radiation on HIV expression in human skin

M01RR-00997-16 0392 (CLR) WEISSMAN, DAVID N General clinical research center Alveolar macrophages and lung immune function in AIDS

M01RR-00997-16 0393 (CLR) STRASSMAN, RICK General clinical research center Human psychopharmacology & neuroendocrinology N,

PROJECT NO., ORGANIZATIONAL UNIT., INVESTIGATOR, ADDRESS, TITLE

N-dimethyltryptamine
M01RR-00997-16 0394 (CLR) RIEDESEL, MARVIN L General clinical research center Extension of glycerol-induced hyperhydration to 48 hours
M01RR-00997-16 0395 (CLR) SIMON, TOBY L General clinical research center Red blood cell survival after infusion by an electromechanical inf. dev.
M01RR-00997-16 0396 (CLR) FELDMAN, BRUCE H General clinical research center Multicomponent nicotine withdrawal program with salivary cotinine level
M01RR-00997-16 0397 (CLR) BOYLE, PATRICK J General clinical research center Brain glucose utilization
M01RR-00997-16 0398 (CLR) SCOTT, SUSAN M General clinical research center Epidermal growth factor & glucocorticoids treatment of bronchopulmonary dysplaia
M01RR-00997-16 0399 (CLR) KELLY, H WILLIAM General clinical research center Effect of cimitidine & ranitidine on theophylline's metabolic clearance
M01RR-00997-16 0400 (CLR) ROSE, SUSAN General clinical research center Factors regulating the nocturnal TSH surge test as a probe for hypothyroidism
M01RR-00997-16 0401 (CLR) ROSE, SUSAN R General clinical research center Clinical trial of LHRHA in pubertal patients with short stature
M01RR-00997-16 0402 (CLR) SIMON, TOBY L General clinical research center In vivo red cell viability following storage in leukotrap III filter systems
M01RR-00997-16 0403 (CLR) SIMON, TOBY L General clinical research center Survival of filtered red cell concentrates after 35 days of storage
M01RR-00997-16 0404 (CLR) ALVERSON, DALE C General clinical research center Surfactant therapy in preterm infants
M01RR-00997-16 0415 (CLR) FRIEDMAN, KENNETH D General clinical research center RBC viability following gamma irradiation and storage in nutricel
M01RR-00997-16 0405 (CLR) DORIN, RICHARD I General clinical research center Application of phosphorous nuclear magnetic resonance spect. of thyroid hormone
M01RR-00997-16 0406 (CLR) KATZ, ROBERT General clinical research center Physiologic approach to the use of blood products following cardiac surgery
M01RR-00997-16 0407 (CLR) SIMON, TOBY L General clinical research center Evaluation of platelets after holding whole blood for 8 hours or 6 hours
M01RR-00997-16 0408 (CLR) CHATTERJEE, MOLLY S General clinical research center Efficacy of atenolol in mild pregnancy induced hypertension
M01RR-00997-16 0409 (CLR) FORMAN, WALTER B General clinical research center Pharmacokinetics of a transdermal delivery system in healthy elderly
M01RR-00997-16 0416 (CLR) SKLAR, LARRY A General clinical research center Molecular mechanisms of human granulocyte activation
M01RR-00997-16 0417 (CLR) BOYLE, PATRICK J General clinical research center Intravenous use of somatostatin analogue, octreotide, for hypoglycemia
M01RR-00997-16 0418 (CLR) FRIEDMAN, KENNETH D General clinical research center Serum potassium changes following transfusion of gamma irradiated packed RBC
M01RR-00997-16 0419 (CLR) MONTER, PAUL General clinical research center Effects of hyperhydration with glycerol on endurance exercise
P41RR-01008-16 (SSS) HYDE, JAMES S MEDICAL COLLEGE OF WISCONSIN 8701 WATERTOWN PLANK RD MILWAUKEE, WI 53226 National biomedical ESR center
P41RR-01008-16 9001 (SSS) HYDE, JAMES S National biomedical ESR center A new look at source modulation
P41RR-01008-16 9002 (SSS) HYDE, JAMES S National biomedical ESR center Frequency swept ELDOR with a loop-gap resonator
P41RR-01008-16 9003 (SSS) HYDE, JAMES S National biomedical ESR center Sensitivity improvement with field effect transistor amplifiers
P41RR-01008-16 9004 (SSS) HYDE, JAMES S National biomedical ESR center Development of a microwave bindge
P41RR-01008-16 9005 (SSS) HYDE, JAMES S National biomedical ESR center New multifrequency spectrometer station
P41RR-01008-16 9006 (SSS) HYDE, JAMES S National biomedical ESR center Microstrip x-band bridge design
P40RR-01024-15 (AR) HANLON, ROGER T UNIV OF TX/200 UNIV BLVD LEAGUE HALL, CAMPUS RTE H 63 GALVESTON, TX 77550-2772 Capture, maintenance, and culture of loliginid squids
M01RR-01032-16 (CLR) RABKIN, MITCHELL T BETH ISRAEL HOSPITAL 330 BROOKLINE AVENUE BOSTON, MA 02215 General clinical research center
M01RR-01032-16 0260 (CLR) ABELMAN, WALTER H General clinical research center Immunosuppressive therapy for biopsy-proven myocarditis
M01RR-01032-16 0331 (CLR) LIPSITZ, LEWIS General clinical research center Syncope and blood pressure homeostasis in the elderly
M01RR-01032-16 0360 (CLR) PALLOTTA, JOHANNA A General clinical research center Methods for diagnosis, localization, and treatment of parathyroid lesions
M01RR-01032-16 0362 (CLR) MINAKER, KENNETH L General clinical research center Thirst and water balance in aging
M01RR-01032-16 0368 (CLR) LANDSBERG, LEWIS General clinical research center Diagnostic tests in pheochromocytoma
M01RR-01032-16 0391 (CLR) MOSES, ALAN C. General clinical research center Biological effect and clinical efficacy of octreotide
M01RR-01032-16 0400 (CLR) FUKAGAWA, NAOMI K General clinical research center Changes in insulin-mediated nutrient utilization during feeding & fasting
M01RR-01032-16 0401 (CLR) GREENSPAN, SUSAN L General clinical research center Hypothalamic-pituitary-adrenal axis during stress and aging
M01RR-01032-16 0405 (CLR) WARREN, SANFORD E General clinical research center Metoprolol in dilated cardiomyopathy
M01RR-01032-16 0407 (CLR) LANDSBERG, LEWIS General clinical research center Sympathetic nervous system in obesity and hypertension--Role of insulin
M01RR-01032-16 0410 (CLR) WEINTRAUB, SANDRA General clinical research center Oral physostigmine and lecithin in treatment of memory disorders
M01RR-01032-16 0411 (CLR) ROSA, ROBERT M General clinical research center Insulin and biogenic amines in cardiovascular disease
M01RR-01032-16 0415 (CLR) SPARK, RICHARD F General clinical research center LY163502 vs placebo in sexual dysfunction
M01RR-01032-16 0468 (CLR) ELAHI, DARIUSH General clinical research center Potentiation of insulin release by GLP and GIP during hyperglycemia
M01RR-01032-16 0427 (CLR) LANDSBERG, LEWIS General clinical research center Ephedrine, caffeine, and aspirin in the treatment of obesity
M01RR-01032-16 0430 (CLR) MINAKER, KENNETH General clinical research center Effect of age on secretion and end-organ response to ANF
M01RR-01032-16 0431 (CLR) MINAKER, KENNETH General clinical research center Relationship of the glucose dependency of GIP & its insulinotropic effect
M01RR-01032-16 0433 (CLR) CLARK, BARBARA General clinical research center Hormonal responses following pancreas transplantation in man
M01RR-01032-16 0437 (CLR) BERMAN, AARON General clinical research center Percutaneous balloon valvuloplasty of critical aortic stenosis
M01RR-01032-16 0438 (CLR) FUKAGAWA, NAOMI K General clinical research center Renal and thermogenic responses to nutrient intake in aging man
M01RR-01032-16 0439 (CLR) FUKAGAWA, NAOMI K General clinical research center Dietary regulation of renal amines in diabetes mellitus
M01RR-01032-16 0441 (CLR) GREENSPAN, SUSAN L General clinical research center Hip fracture risk prediction by quantitative digital radiography
M01RR-01032-16 0442 (CLR) ROSENBERG, ROBERT General clinical research center Antithrombin III concentrate in antithrombin III deficiency
M01RR-01032-16 0443 (CLR) BAUER, KENNETH General clinical research center Recombinant factor VIIa in subjects with hereditary factor VII deficiency
M01RR-01032-16 0445 (CLR) CRUMPACKER, CLYDE S General clinical research center Foscarnet for CMV retinitis in AIDS patients
M01RR-01032-16 0446 (CLR) HEATH-CHIOZZI, MARGO General clinical research center Ganciclovir and GM-CSF for CMV retinitis
M01RR-01032-16 0447 (CLR) MESULAM, MAREK-MARSEL General clinical research center Efficacy of THA in Alzheimer's disease
M01RR-01032-16 0448 (CLR) FREEMAN, ROY General clinical research center Treatment of neurogenic orthostatic hypotension with DL-DOPS
M01RR-01032-16 0449 (CLR) SCHOMER, DONALD General clinical research center Evaluation of flunarizine in the treatment of partial seizures
M01RR-01032-16 0450 (CLR) JIMERSON, DAVID General clinical research center Serotonin function in patients w/ eating disorders & in healthy controls
M01RR-01032-16 0451 (CLR) BROWN, ROBERT General clinical research center Physiology of potassium regulation in man
M01RR-01032-16 0453 (CLR) STROM, TERRY B General clinical research center Fish oil inhibition of cyclosporine nephrotoxicity
M01RR-01032-16 0454 (CLR) EPSTEIN, FRANKLIN H General clinical research center Pharmacodynamics of glycine
M01RR-01032-16 0455 (CLR) CLARK, BARBARA General clinical research center Effect of ANP on potassium homeostasis
M01RR-01032-16 0456 (CLR) CLARK, BARBARA General clinical research center Effect of aging on urinary prostaglandin levels
M01RR-01032-16 0457 (CLR) PASTERNAK, RICHARD General clinical research center Reversal of human coronary atherosclerosis
M01RR-01032-16 0458 (CLR) PASTERNAK, RICHARD C General clinical research center Dose response between fatty acids given as Promega compared with tuna
M01RR-01032-16 0459 (CLR) PASTERNAK, RICHARD General clinical research center Cholesterol and recurrent events (CARE)
M01RR-01032-16 0460 (CLR) PASTERNAK, RICHARD General clinical research center The effect of heparin on serum lipids
M01RR-01032-16 0461 (CLR) SPARK, RICHARD General clinical research center CB-154 (bromergocryptine) in hyperprolactinemic states
M01RR-01032-16 0462 (CLR) FLIER, JEFFERY General clinical research center Studies of human adipose tissue metabolism
M01RR-01032-16 0463 (CLR) LANDSBERG, LEWIS General clinical research center Sympathetic nervous system function in short-term modified fasting
M01RR-01032-16 0464 (CLR) FLIER, JEFFERY General clinical research center Structure of the insulin receptor gene and relationship to insulin action
M01RR-01032-16 0465 (CLR) MINAKER, KENNETH L General clinical research center ANF--Index of volume status in the elderly
M01RR-01032-16 0466 (CLR) LIPSITZ, LEWIS General clinical research center Postprandial hypotension in the elderly
M01RR-01032-16 0467 (CLR) FUKAGAWA, NAOMI K General clinical research center Metabolic effects of dietary fructose
M01RR-01032-16 0469 (CLR) BAUER, KENNETH A General clinical research center Prophylactive & theraputic administration of antithrombin-III concentrate
M01RR-01032-16 0470 (CLR) BAUER, KENNETH A General clinical research center Admin. of activated protein C to pts w/ hereditary protein C deficiency
M01RR-01032-16 0471 (CLR) MORTOLA, JOSEPH General clinical research center Elucidation of the association of ovarian steriods and symptoms of PMS
M01RR-01032-16 0472 (CLR) DRAZEN, JEFFREY M General clinical research center Pulmonary response to inhalation of leukotriene aerosol--Normals and Asthmatics
M01RR-01032-16 0473 (CLR) CLARK, BARBARA A General clinical research center Age, renal & vascular response to atrial natriuretic factor--Dopamine/PGE2
M01RR-01032-16 0474 (CLR) STEINMAN, THEODORE I General clinical

research center Renal function in chronic renal failure predialysis pts receiving r-HuEPO

M01RR-01032-16 0475 (CLR) CLARK, BARBARA General clinical research center Controlled study of a patient w/ suspected nephrogenic diabetes insipidis

M01RR-01032-16 0476 (CLR) CLARK, BARBARA General clinical research center Prostaglandin E2 production--Influence of age, dietary & pharm. intervent.

M01RR-01032-16 0477 (CLR) CLARK, BARBARA General clinical research center Extrarenal potassium homeostasis and O2 consumption during acute exercise

M01RR-01032-16 0478 (CLR) CLARK, BARBARA General clinical research center Phlebotomy for normal standard control

M01RR-01032-16 0479 (CLR) TRENTHAM, DAVID General clinical research center Treatment of rheumatoid arthritis DAB486IL-2

P40RR-01046-16 (AR) FOX, JAMES G MASSACHUSETTS INSTITUTE OF TEC 37 VASSAR ST, 45-104 CAMBRIDGE, MA 02139 Diagnostic and investigative laboratory

P40RR-01046-16 0001 (AR) FOX, JAMES Diagnostic and investigative laboratory Role of gastric bacteria in gastroduodenal disease

P40RR-01046-16 0002 (AR) FOX, JAMES Diagnostic and investigative laboratory Campylobacter species and proliferative bowel disease

P40RR-01046-16 0003 (AR) FOX, JAMES Diagnostic and investigative laboratory Study of the biology and diseases of ferrets

P40RR-01046-16 0004 (AR) MURPHY, JAMES Diagnostic and investigative laboratory Development of a mouse model for Lyme disease

M01RR-01066-14 (CLR) POTTS, JOHN T, JR MASSACHUSETTS GENERAL HOSPITAL FRUIT STREET BOSTON, MA 02114 General clinical research center

M01RR-01066-14 0059 (CLR) NATHAN, DAVID M General clinical research center GRF determination for the diabetes control and complications trial

M01RR-01066-14 0065 (CLR) AXELROD, LLOYD General clinical research center Omega 3 fatty acids in diabetes

M01RR-01066-14 0066 (CLR) GROWDON, JOHN H General clinical research center L-threonine administration in patients with multiple sclerosis

M01RR-01066-14 0012 (CLR) NEER, ROBERT M General clinical research center Rx of postmenopausal osteoporosis w/ hPTH 1-34 & calcitriol or calcium

M01RR-01066-14 0015 (CLR) WHITCOMB, RANDALL General clinical research center Role of gonadotropin pulsations reversal in hypogonadotropic hypogonadism

M01RR-01066-14 0021 (CLR) COGGINS, CECIL General clinical research center Dietary modification of progressive renal disease

M01RR-01066-14 0022 (CLR) BOEPPLE, PAUL A General clinical research center LRF analogue to delay puberty in precocious sexual development

M01RR-01066-14 0024 (CLR) CROWLEY, WILLIAM F General clinical research center Pulsatile release of gonadotropins in normal and clinical conditions

M01RR-01066-14 0026 (CLR) HALL, JANET E General clinical research center Clinical pharmacology of LHRH antagonists in the female

M01RR-01066-14 0027 (CLR) CROWLEY, WILLIAM General clinical research center Role of gonadal steroids in control of gonadotropin secretion in males

M01RR-01066-14 0035 (CLR) KLIBANSKI, ANNE General clinical research center Consequences of functional hypogonadism in hyperprolactinemic women

M01RR-01066-14 0039 (CLR) NEER, ROBERT M General clinical research center Studies of normal and abnormal parathyroid function

M01RR-01066-14 0040 (CLR) NATHAN, DAVID M General clinical research center Diabetes control and complications trial

M01RR-01066-14 0044 (CLR) NEER, ROBERT M General clinical research center Therapy of idiopathic osteoporosis

M01RR-01066-14 0068 (CLR) FAVA, MAURIZIO General clinical research center Oral s-adenosyl-l-methionine in major depression

M01RR-01066-14 0071 (CLR) KLIBANSKI, ANNE General clinical research center Regulation of non-functioning pituitary adenomas by somatostatin analog

M01RR-01066-14 0050 (CLR) BOEPPLE, PAUL A General clinical research center Growth hormone deficiency--Treatment with LHRH analogue

M01RR-01066-14 0053 (CLR) DIENSTAG, JULES L General clinical research center Interferon Alfa-2b alone & after prednisone withdrawal for hepatitis B

M01RR-01066-14 0056 (CLR) GROWDON, JOHN H General clinical research center Deprenyl and tocopherol antioxidative therapy of Parkinsonism

M01RR-01066-14 0076 (CLR) SIMON, LEE General clinical research center Recombinant human interferon gamma for progressive systemic sclerosis

M01RR-01066-14 0109 (CLR) FAVA, MAURIZIO General clinical research center Major depression biological/psychological predictors of response/relapse

M01RR-01066-14 0110 (CLR) BOEPPLE, PAUL A General clinical research center Somatomedin-C modulation of growth hormone secretory dynamics

M01RR-01066-14 0111 (CLR) CROWLEY, WILLIAM F General clinical research center Frequent blood sampling in postmenopausal women

M01RR-01066-14 0112 (CLR) SLOVIK, DAVID M General clinical research center Salmon calcitonin in treatment of glucocorticoid induced osteoporosis

M01RR-01066-14 0080 (CLR) GROWDON, JOHN H General clinical research center Safety and efficacy of Idazoxan in Parkinson's disease

M01RR-01066-14 0081 (CLR) ROSS, DOUGLAS S General clinical research center L-thyroxine therapy in subclinical hypothyroidism--Effect on bone density

M01RR-01066-14 0083 (CLR) NATHAN, DAVID M General clinical research center Measurement of glucagon-like peptide (GLPI (7-37))

M01RR-01066-14 0084 (CLR) ROSS, DOUGLAS S General clinical research center Monitoring suppression of the pituitary-thyroid axis with L-thyroxine

M01RR-01066-14 0085 (CLR) NATHAN, DAVID M General clinical research center Insulin infusion in Type I diabetics using Infusaid model 1000 pump

M01RR-01066-14 0086 (CLR) KLIBANSKI, ANNE General clinical research center Sandostatin normalization/reduction of growth hormone in acromegaly

PROJECT NO., ORGANIZATIONAL UNIT., INVESTIGATOR, ADDRESS, TITLE

M01RR-01066-14 0087 (CLR) COUGHLIN, JOHN General clinical research center Safety/efficacy of chronic sandostatin treatment in acromegalic patients

M01RR-01066-14 0089 (CLR) DOPPELT, SAMUEL H General clinical research center Clinical/biochemical effects of infusions of Ceredase glucocerebrosidase

M01RR-01066-14 0090 (CLR) SCHOOLEY, ROBERT General clinical research center Dose-ranging tolerance trial of SC-48334 in patients with AIDS and ARC

M01RR-01066-14 0091 (CLR) NEER, ROBERT M General clinical research center Human parathyroid hormone 1-34 administration in young/old patients

M01RR-01066-14 0092 (CLR) NEER, ROBERT M General clinical research center Effects of PTH injections administered in young/old patients

M01RR-01066-14 0093 (CLR) BOEPPLE, PAUL A General clinical research center Growth hormone secretory reserve using a growth hormone-releasing agent

M01RR-01066-14 0094 (CLR) BOEPPLE, PAUL A General clinical research center Pubertal changes in sleep physiology

M01RR-01066-14 0095 (CLR) JENIKE, MICHAEL General clinical research center D-amphetamine, methylphenidate & placebo in obsessive-compulsive disorder

M01RR-01066-14 0096 (CLR) NUSSBAUM, SAMUEL General clinical research center Aminohydroxybutylidene bisphosphonate in patients w/ metastic bone disease

M01RR-01066-14 0097 (CLR) DIENSTAG, JULES L General clinical research center Interferon alpha-2b as therapy for chronic NANB and hepatitis C

M01RR-01066-14 0099 (CLR) CROWLEY, WILLIAM F General clinical research center Baselines in reproductive disorders

M01RR-01066-14 0100 (CLR) CROWLEY, WILLIAM F General clinical research center Frequent blood sampling throughout the menstrual cycle in normal women

M01RR-01066-14 0101 (CLR) CROWLEY, WILLIAM F General clinical research center Neuroendocrine modulation of GnRH secretion during sleep

M01RR-01066-14 0102 (CLR) CROWLEY, WILLIAM F General clinical research center Pulsatile GnRH in anovulatory infertility

M01RR-01066-14 0103 (CLR) CROWLEY, WILLIAM F General clinical research center Control of the onset of puberty

M01RR-01066-14 0104 (CLR) NEER, ROBERT M General clinical research center Intranasal calcitonin in primary osteoporosis in post-menopausal women

M01RR-01066-14 0105 (CLR) NATHAN, DAVID M General clinical research center Insulinotropic actions of glucagon-like peptide-I (7-37) in diabetes

M01RR-01066-14 0106 (CLR) CROWLEY, WILLIAM F General clinical research center Sex steroid adminstration in normal women to induce gonadotropin surges

M01RR-01066-14 0107 (CLR) GROWDON, JOHN H General clinical research center Idazoxan in progressive supranuclear palsy

M01RR-01066-14 0108 (CLR) ISRAEL, ESTER J General clinical research center Formula therapy on disease activity and growth in Crohn's

M01RR-01070-15 (CLR) FISCHINGER, PETER J MEDICAL UNIV OF SOUTH CAROLINA 171 ASHLEY AVE CHARLESTON, SC 29425 General clinical research center

M01RR-01070-15 0076 (CLR) COLWELL, JOHN A General clinical research center Diabetes complications and control trial

M01RR-01070-15 0100 (CLR) LEROY, EDWARD C General clinical research center Mechanics of alveolitis in connective tissue disease

M01RR-01070-15 0131 (CLR) BELL, NORMAN H General clinical research center Calcium absorption

M01RR-01070-15 0132 (CLR) WALLE, THOMAS General clinical research center Sex steroid hormones--Effects on drug clearance in man

M01RR-01070-15 0137 (CLR) MIDDAUGH, SUSAN J General clinical research center Chronic pain rehabilitation--Evaluation of treatment efficacy

M01RR-01070-15 0139 (CLR) BELL, NORMAN H General clinical research center Bone and mineral metabolism in blacks and whites

M01RR-01070-15 0140 (CLR) KABALEH, M BASHAR General clinical research center Photopheresis in scleroderma

M01RR-01070-15 0141 (CLR) BELL, NORMAN H General clinical research center Treatment of osteoporosis with diclofenac sodium

M01RR-01070-15 0145 (CLR) CONRADI, EDWARD C General clinical research center Diltiazem ER dose response in patients with mild to moderate hypertension

M01RR-01070-15 0147 (CLR) SILVER, RICHARD M General clinical research center Tryptophan-related connective tissue disease

M01RR-01070-15 0148 (CLR) BALLENGER, JAMES C General clinical research center Biological studies of psychiatric patients and normal controls

M01RR-01070-15 0149 (CLR) LYDIARD, R BRUCE General clinical research center Sleep deprivation in patients with mood and anxiety disorders

M01RR-01070-15 0150 (CLR) PRIEST, DAVID G General clinical research center Reduced folate metabolites of leucovorin in humans

M01RR-01070-15 0151 (CLR) HUTCHISON, FLORENCE N General clinical research center Dietary protein in peritoneal dialysis

P41RR-01081-14 (SSS) LANGRIDGE, ROBERT UNIVERSITY OF CALIFORNIA BOX 0446 SAN FRANCISCO, CA 94143 Special research resource for biomolecular graphics

P41RR-01081-14 0004 (SSS) KUNTZ, IRWIN D Special research resource for biomolecular graphics Macromolecular structure and surfaces

P41RR-01081-14 0015 (SSS) LANGRIDGE, ROBERT Special research resource for biomolecular graphics Rigid body energetic docking procedure--Program development

P41RR-01081-14 0016 (SSS) LANGRIDGE, ROBERT Special research resource for biomolecular graphics Picture system software for molecular modeling

P41RR-01081-14 0017 (SSS) LANGRIDGE, ROBERT Special research resource for biomolecular graphics Artificial intelligence

P41RR-01081-14 0018 (SSS) LANGRIDGE, ROBERT Special research

PROJECT NO., ORGANIZATIONAL UNIT., INVESTIGATOR, ADDRESS, TITLE

resource for biomolecular graphics FRODO--Electron density fitting procedure
P41RR-01081-14 0019 (SSS) LANGRIDGE, ROBERT Special research resource for biomolecular graphics Work stations and networking for dissemination of computer graphics to users
P41RR-01081-14 9001 (SSS) LANGRIDGE, ROBERT Special research resource for biomolecular graphics Core research development--Mirage
P41RR-01081-14 9002 (SSS) LANGRIDGE, ROBERT Special research resource for biomolecular graphics Core research development--Molecular mechanics
P41RR-01081-14 9003 (SSS) LANGRIDGE, ROBERT Special research resource for biomolecular graphics Core research development--Sequence analysis
P41RR-01081-14 9004 (SSS) LANGRIDGE, ROBERT Special research resource for biomolecular graphics Core research development--Drug design
P41RR-01081-14 9005 (SSS) LANGRIDGE, ROBERT Special research resource for biomolecular graphics Core research development--Protein folding
P41RR-01081-14 9006 (SSS) LANGRIDGE, ROBERT Special research resource for biomolecular graphics Core research development--Hardware development
P41RR-01135-14 (SSS) KRETSINGER, ROBERT H UNIVERSITY OF VIRGINIA GILMER HALL 58 CHARLOTTESVILLE VA 22901 Operation, development of an area X-ray diffractometer
P40RR-01180-14 (AR) HAYRE, MICHAEL THE ROCKEFELLER UNIVERSITY 1230 YORK AVENUE, BOX 2 NEW YORK, NY 10021 Diagnostic clinical and research laboratory program
P40RR-01180-14 0001 (AR) MORSE, STEPHEN S Diagnostic clinical and research laboratory program Developing DNA probes for diagnosis using mouse thymic virus as a model system
P40RR-01180-14 0002 (AR) CIOFFE, CHRISTINE J Diagnostic clinical and research laboratory program Rabbit model of bacterial meningitis and cerebrospinal fluid collection methods
P40RR-01180-14 0003 (AR) REINARD, GREGORY R Diagnostic clinical and research laboratory program Protease mutants of Sendai virus
P40RR-01180-14 0004 (AR) GOLDBERG, ALLAN R Diagnostic clinical and research laboratory program Animal models of viroid-like pathogen induced disease
P40RR-01180-14 0005 (AR) STARK, DENNIS M Diagnostic clinical and research laboratory program Diagnostic clinical program
P40RR-01183-14 (AR) DAVISSON, MURIEL T JACKSON LABORATORY 600 MAIN STREET BAR HARBOR, ME 04609-0800 A mouse mutant gene resource
P41RR-01192-12 (SSS) BERNS, MICHAEL W UNIVERSITY OF CALIFORNIA 1002 HEALTH SCIENCES RD, EAST IRVINE, CA 92715 A laser microbeam biotechnology resource
P40RR-01203-13 (SRC) VAN HOOSIER, GERALD L, JR UNIVERSITY OF WASHINGTON DIV OF ANIMAL MEDICINE SB-42 SEATTLE, WASH 98195 Animal diagnostic and investigative laboratory
P41RR-01209-12 (SSS) HODGSON, KEITH O STANFORD UNIVERSITY STANFORD SYNCHROTRON RAD LAB STANFORD, CA 94305 A synchrotron radiation biotechnology resource
P41RR-01209-12 0026 (SSS) DONIACH, S A synchrotron radiation biotechnology resource Solution x-ray scattering from immunoglobulins
P41RR-01209-12 0027 (SSS) BALDWIN, R A synchrotron radiation biotechnology resource Kinetic intermediates on the pathway of protein folding
P41RR-01209-12 0028 (SSS) GILLIS, N A synchrotron radiation biotechnology resource Anomalous dispersion scattering studies of metal clusters
P41RR-01209-12 9001 (SSS) HODGSON, KEITH A synchrotron radiation biotechnology resource X-ray crystallography-Core
P41RR-01209-12 9002 (SSS) HODGSON, K A synchrotron radiation biotechnology resource Core--X-ray absorption spectroscopy
P41RR-01209-12 9003 (SSS) HODGSON, K A synchrotron radiation biotechnology resource CORE--Small angle scattering and diffraction
P41RR-01209-12 0001 (SSS) HODGSON, KEITH O A synchrotron radiation biotechnology resource X-ray absorption spectroscopy
P41RR-01209-12 0002 (SSS) PHIZACKERLEY, PAUL R A synchrotron radiation biotechnology resource X-ray crystallographic studies using synchrotron radiation
P41RR-01209-12 0004 (SSS) BOXER, STEVEN G A synchrotron radiation biotechnology resource Fluorescence lifetime studies
P41RR-01209-12 0005 (SSS) DONIACH, SEBASTIAN A synchrotron radiation biotechnology resource Small angle scattering facility
P41RR-01209-12 0006 (SSS) MATHEWS, F A synchrotron radiation biotechnology resource Crystal structure analsis of amicyanin from P. denitrificans
P41RR-01209-12 0007 (SSS) HATADA, M A synchrotron radiation biotechnology resource Crystallographic structure of IL-2:IL-2 receptor
P41RR-01209-12 0008 (SSS) FREEMAN, H A synchrotron radiation biotechnology resource Structural studies of Cu and Fe containing proteins
P41RR-01209-12 0009 (SSS) BELLAMY, H A synchrotron radiation biotechnology resource Structural studies on two diheme cytochromes
P41RR-01209-12 0010 (SSS) NESTOR, J A synchrotron radiation biotechnology resource Crystallographic structural studies of proteins
P41RR-01209-12 0011 (SSS) HAJDU, J A synchrotron radiation biotechnology resource White beam laue diffraction experiments on glycogen phosphorylase
P41RR-01209-12 0012 (SSS) EDWARDS, S A synchrotron radiation biotechnology resource White beam laue experiments on cytochrome c peroxidase
P41RR-01209-12 0013 (SSS) HEDMAN, B A synchrotron radiation biotechnology resource Studies of A. Vinelandii nitrogenase and its FeMoco
P41RR-01209-12 0014 (SSS) FRANK, P A synchrotron radiation biotechnology resource Sulfur and vanadium in the blood cells of tunicates
P41RR-01209-12 0016 (SSS) SOLOMON, E A synchrotron radiation biotechnology resource X-ray absorption edge studies
P41RR-01209-12 0019 (SSS) SOLOMON, E A synchrotron radiation biotechnology resource Electronic and structural studies of Cu active sites
P41RR-01209-12 0020 (SSS) NATOLI, C A synchrotron radiation biotechnology resource New theoretical approaches to the interpretation of X-ray absorption
P41RR-01209-12 0021 (SSS) GRAY, H A synchrotron radiation biotechnology resource Time-resolved XAS study using a dispersive EXAFS spectrometer
P41RR-01209-12 0022 (SSS) WAKATSUKI, S A synchrotron radiation biotechnology resource Time-resolved X-ray diffraction of bacteriorhodopsin
P41RR-01209-12 0023 (SSS) WAKATSUKI, S A synchrotron radiation biotechnology resource Cation binding study of bacteriorhodopsin
P41RR-01209-12 0024 (SSS) WAKATSUKI, S A synchrotron radiation biotechnology resource Blue membranes
P41RR-01209-12 0025 (SSS) WAKATSUKI, S A synchrotron radiation biotechnology resource X-ray diffraction studies of helix linking regions of bacteriorhodopsin
P41RR-01219-10 (SSS) RIEDER, CONLY L NEW YORK STATE DEPT OF HEALTH EMPIRE STATE PLAZA ALBANY, NY 12201-0509 Biological microscopy and image reconstruction resource
P41RR-01219-10 0001 (SSS) MINNEAR, FRED Biological microscopy and image reconstruction resource Cytoskeleton and cell shape changes of cultured endothelium
P41RR-01219-10 0002 (SSS) SACHS, FREDERICK Biological microscopy and image reconstruction resource HVEM of membrane patches
P41RR-01219-10 0003 (SSS) CASSIMERIS, LYNNE Biological microscopy and image reconstruction resource 3D ultrastructural reconstruction of microtubules
P41RR-01219-10 0004 (SSS) WOODCOCK, C Biological microscopy and image reconstruction resource 3D structure of negatively stained chromatin fibers
P41RR-01219-10 0005 (SSS) FLEISCHER, S Biological microscopy and image reconstruction resource Molecular mechanism of excitation-contraction coupling
P41RR-01219-10 0006 (SSS) SHAIN, W Biological microscopy and image reconstruction resource Biochemical and morphological correlations in astroglial cells
P41RR-01219-10 0007 (SSS) SWANN, J Biological microscopy and image reconstruction resource Correlative physiology and morphology of neurons
P41RR-01219-10 9001 (SSS) RIEDER, CONLY Biological microscopy and image reconstruction resource Ultrastructural reconstruction of cryofixed cells
P41RR-01219-10 9002 (SSS) TURNER, JAMES Biological microscopy and image reconstruction resource Development of confocal light microscopy
P41RR-01219-10 9003 (SSS) TURNER, JAMES Biological microscopy and image reconstruction resource High voltage electron microscope development
P41RR-01219-10 9004 (SSS) FRANK, JOACHIM Biological microscopy and image reconstruction resource Quantitative 3D imaging
P41RR-01237-09 (SSS) WEMMER, DAVID E UNIVERSITY OF CALIFORNIA LAWRENCE BERKELEY LABORATORY BERKELEY, CA 94720 National tritium labeling facility
P41RR-01237-09 0005 (SSS) RAPOPORT, HENRY National tritium labeling facility Synthesis of semisynthetic proteins
P41RR-01237-09 0006 (SSS) RAPOPORT, HENRY National tritium labeling facility Catalytic antibodies
P41RR-01237-09 0007 (SSS) RAPOPORT, HENRY National tritium labeling facility Synthesis and NMR studies of DNA oligomers
P41RR-01237-09 9004 (SSS) RAPAPORT, HENRY National tritium labeling facility Core-NMR
P40RR-01240-12 (AR) BOWDEN, DOUGLAS M UNIVERSITY OF WASHINGTON SJ-50 SEATTLE, WA 98195 Primate supply information clearinghouse
P41RR-01243-10 (SSS) BASSINGTHWAIGHTE, JAMES B UNIVERSITY OF WASHINGTON CENTER FOR BIOENGINEERING WD- SEATTLE, WA 98195 Simulation resource in mass transport and exchange
P41RR-01243-10 0001 (SSS) BASSINGTHWAIGHTE, J Simulation resource in mass transport and exchange Models of non-Kroghian form
P41RR-01243-10 0002 (SSS) LITTLE, STEPHEN E Simulation resource in mass transport and exchange Models for metabolized substrates and hormones--Fatty acid metabolism
P41RR-01243-10 0003 (SSS) KING, RICHARD B Simulation resource in mass transport and exchange Simulation interface development
P41RR-01243-10 0004 (SSS) GOLDSTEIN, ALLEN Simulation resource in mass transport and exchange Optimization for fitting models to data--Core research
P41RR-01243-10 0005 (SSS) BASSINGTHWAIGHTE, JAMES B Simulation resource in mass transport and exchange Core research--Dissemination projects and mechanisms
P41RR-01243-10 0007 (SSS) FINLAYSON, BRUCE Simulation resource in mass transport and exchange Numerical methods for problems with moving fronts
P41RR-01243-10 0008 (SSS) BASSINGTHWAIGHTE, JAMES B Simulation resource in mass transport and exchange Multiple indicator dilution with positron emission tomography
P41RR-01243-10 0010 (SSS) KING, RICHARD B Simulation resource in mass transport and exchange Models incorporating flow heterogeneity
P41RR-01243-10 0012 (SSS) LIGHTFOOT, EDWIN N Simulation resource in mass transport and exchange Modeling of intermediary metabolism in intact cells
P41RR-01243-10 0015 (SSS) GORESKY, C A Simulation resource in mass transport and exchange Oxygen transport from red blood cells to mitochondria
P41RR-01243-10 0019 (SSS) RKING, R Simulation resource in mass transport and exchange Linear reaction sequences in blood-tissue exchange units
P41RR-01243-10 0020 (SSS) WONG, A Simulation resource in mass transport and exchange Modeling of ionic regulation in myocardial excitation-contraction coupling
P41RR-01243-10 0021 (SSS) BASSINGTHWAIGHTE, J Simulation resource in mass transport and exchange Endothelium albumin receptor and fatty acid transport

P41RR-01243-10 0022 (SSS) CHAN, J Simulation resource in mass transport and exchange Evaluation of compartmental versus distributed models
P41RR-01243-10 0023 (SSS) BASSINGTHWAIGHTE, J Simulation resource in mass transport and exchange Models with saturable transporters
P41RR-01243-10 0024 (SSS) BASSINGTHWAIGHTE, J Simulation resource in mass transport and exchange Models of non-Kroghian form
P41RR-01243-10 0025 (SSS) BASSINGTHWAIGHTE, J Simulation resource in mass transport and exchange Heterogeneity of regional capillary permeability
P41RR-01243-10 0026 (SSS) YAMASHIRO, S Simulation resource in mass transport and exchange Fractal vascular networks and flow distributions
P41RR-01243-10 0027 (SSS) KING, R Simulation resource in mass transport and exchange Simple whole body recirculation model
P41RR-01243-10 0028 (SSS) STAPLETON, D Simulation resource in mass transport and exchange Flow distributions in cardiomyopathic hamster hearts
P41RR-01243-10 0029 (SSS) BASSINGTHWAIGHTE, J Simulation resource in mass transport and exchange Transport via capillary clefts and matrix filled pores
P41RR-01243-10 9003 (SSS) KROHN, K Simulation resource in mass transport and exchange Metabolic imaging of cancer
P41RR-01243-10 9005 (SSS) KING, R Simulation resource in mass transport and exchange Imaging regional cardiopulmonary metabolism and flows--Core
P40RR-01254-11 (AR) ABEE, CHRISTIAN R UNIVERSITY OF SOUTH ALABAMA COLLEGE OF MEDICINE, 241 CSAB MOBILE, AL 36688 A squirrel monkey breeding and research resource
P40RR-01254-11 0002 (AR) VITULLI, WILLIAM F A squirrel monkey breeding and research resource Behavior
P40RR-01262-10 (HED) MOBRAATEN, LARRY E THE JACKSON LABORATORY 600 MAIN STREET BAR HARBOR, ME 04609-0800 Cryopreservation of murine germplasm
M01RR-01271-10 (CLR) MARTIN, JOSEPH B UNIVERSITY OF CALIFORNIA 224 MEDICAL SCIENCES BUILDING SAN FRANCISCO, CALIF 94143 General clinical research center
M01RR-01271-10 0012 (CLR) KAPLAN, SELNA L General clinical research center Evaluation of gonadotropin secretion in children
M01RR-01271-10 0040 (CLR) KAPLAN, SELNA L General clinical research center Evaluation of hypothalmic pituitary function in children
M01RR-01271-10 0044 (CLR) KAPLAN, SELNA L General clinical research center TSH secretion in children
M01RR-01271-10 0050 (CLR) KAPLAN, SELNA L General clinical research center Growth retardation with bioinactive GH or abnormal GH metabolism
M01RR-01271-10 0062 (CLR) PACKMAN, SEYMOUR General clinical research center Clinical investigation of patients with inborn errors of metabolism
M01RR-01271-10 0064 (CLR) KOGAN, BARRY A General clinical research center Cryptorchidism--Etiology and infertility
M01RR-01271-10 0065 (CLR) COWAN, MORTON J General clinical research center Maturation of bone marrow stem cells pre- and post-transplantation
M01RR-01271-10 0099 (CLR) HOLLIDAY, MALCOLM A. General clinical research center Comparison of iothalamate clearance with 99mTc-DTPA renography
M01RR-01271-10 0101 (CLR) KAPLAN, SELNA L General clinical research center Efficacy and safety of lupron depot
M01RR-01271-10 0103 (CLR) WARA, DIANE W General clinical research center Zidovudine compared to zidovudine plus intravenous gamma globulin
M01RR-01271-10 0104 (CLR) WARA, DIANE W General clinical research center Phase I study of recombinant CD4
M01RR-01271-10 0105 (CLR) EPSTEIN, LOIS B General clinical research center Phenotype and function of Down's syndrome peripheral blood leukocytes
M01RR-01271-10 0107 (CLR) KAPLAN, SELNA L General clinical research center ACTH stimulation in assessment of abnormalities of adrenal function
M01RR-01271-10 0109 (CLR) KAPLAN, SELNA L General clinical research center Use of synthetic hpGRF-44 in children with growth disorders
M01RR-01271-10 0110 (CLR) HEYMAN, MELVIN B General clinical research center Prevalence of celiac disease in children with short stature
M01RR-01271-10 0111 (CLR) MATTHAY, KATHERINE K General clinical research center 131-I-labeled MIBG for treatment of advanced neuroblastoma
M01RR-01271-10 0112 (CLR) OTT, MARY JANE General clinical research center Improving self-concept of precocious puberty children
M01RR-01271-10 0113 (CLR) HOLLIDAY, MALCOLM A General clinical research center Comparing inulin with iothalamate clearance for measuring kidney function
M01RR-01271-10 0114 (CLR) WARA, DIANE W General clinical research center Zidovudine treatment of children infected with HIV with mild to moderate symptoms
M01RR-01271-10 0115 (CLR) KAPLAN, SELNA L General clinical research center Endocrine dysfunction after bone marrow transplantation
M01RR-01271-10 0116 (CLR) HOLLIDAY, MALCOLM A General clinical research center Use of mannitol to initiate and sustain an osmotic diuresis
M01RR-01271-10 0117 (CLR) KOGAN, BARRY A General clinical research center Oral and intravesical ditropan in children with hyperreflexic bladder
M01RR-01271-10 0118 (CLR) WARA, DIANE W General clinical research center ddC in treatment of children with symptomatic HIV infection
M01RR-01271-10 0070 (CLR) HEYMAN, MELVIN B General clinical research center TPGS vitamin E therapy during chronic cholestasis
M01RR-01271-10 0079 (CLR) WARA, DIANE W General clinical research center Immunologic evaluation
M01RR-01271-10 0081 (CLR) KAPLAN, SELNA L General clinical research center Use of intranasal LRF-agonist for treatment of precocious puberty
M01RR-01271-10 0086 (CLR) WARA, DIANE W General clinical research center Immune function & neurologic development--Infants at risk to develop AIDS
M01RR-01271-10 0093 (CLR) KAPLAN, SELNA L. General clinical research center Use of leuprolide acetate for treatment of precocious puberty
P41RR-01296-08 (SSS) RATNER, BUDDY D UNIVERSITY OF WASHINGTON DEPT OF CHEMICAL ENGINEERING SEATTLE WA 98195 A surface analysis facility for biomedical problems
P41RR-01296-08 9005 (SSS) RATNER, BUDDY D A surface analysis facility for biomedical problems Core research--SIMS studies of biomedical polymers
P41RR-01296-08 9006 (SSS) RATNER, BUDDY D A surface analysis facility for biomedical problems Core research--Protein conformation at interfaces
P41RR-01296-08 0001 (SSS) SPECTOR, M A surface analysis facility for biomedical problems Articular cartilage replacement prosthesis
P41RR-01296-08 0002 (SSS) FEUERSTEIN, I A surface analysis facility for biomedical problems Platelet interaction with biomedical polymers
P41RR-01296-08 0003 (SSS) BARBUCCI,R A surface analysis facility for biomedical problems Heparin-binding polyurethane materials
P41RR-01296-08 0004 (SSS) CHINN, J A A surface analysis facility for biomedical problems Blood interaction studies with polyurethanes
P41RR-01296-08 0005 (SSS) LEONARD E F A surface analysis facility for biomedical problems Timeline of thrombogenesis
P41RR-01296-08 0006 (SSS) CHILKOTI, A A surface analysis facility for biomedical problems Cell culture surfaces
P41RR-01296-08 0007 (SSS) COOPER, S L A surface analysis facility for biomedical problems Surfce structure of a polyurethane ionomer
P41RR-01296-08 0008 (SSS) CRANIN, A N A surface analysis facility for biomedical problems Surface texture and success of dental implants
P41RR-01296-08 0009 (SSS) KIM, S W A surface analysis facility for biomedical problems Surface structure of novel block copolymers
P41RR-01296-08 0010 (SSS) HOFFMAN, A S A surface analysis facility for biomedical problems Surface immobilized polyethylene oxide
P41RR-01296-08 0011 (SSS) HOFFMAN, A S A surface analysis facility for biomedical problems Plasma-treated vascular grafts
P41RR-01296-08 9001 (SSS) RATNER, BUDDY D A surface analysis facility for biomedical problems Core research--Low temperature surface analysis studies
P41RR-01296-08 9002 (SSS) RATNER, BUDDY D A surface analysis facility for biomedical problems Core research--Proteins at surfaces studies by ESCA
P41RR-01296-08 9003 (SSS) RATNER, BUDDY D A surface analysis facility for biomedical problems Core research--Surface analysis studies of metallic implant corrosion
P41RR-01296-08 9004 (SSS) RATNER, BUDDY D A surface analysis facility for biomedical problems Core research--Polyurethane surface
P41RR-01315-10 (SSS) CRAM, L SCOTT LOS ALAMOS NATIONAL LAB LS-1, MAIL STOP M888 LOS ALAMOS, NM 87545 National flow cytometry and sorting research resource
P41RR-01315-10 0001 (SSS) KRAEMER, PAUL M National flow cytometry and sorting research resource Karyotype instability in tumorigenesis
P41RR-01315-10 0020 (SSS) WALDREN, CHARLES National flow cytometry and sorting research resource Reduction of background mutants by flow sorting
P41RR-01315-10 0021 (SSS) CRAM, L SCOTT National flow cytometry and sorting research resource Chromosome analysis and sorting
P41RR-01315-10 0026 (SSS) TOMASI, THOMAS National flow cytometry and sorting research resource Proliferation and differentiation of mononuclear phagocytes
P41RR-01315-10 0028 (SSS) LEHNERT, BRUCE National flow cytometry and sorting research resource Mechanisms of pulmonary damage
P41RR-01315-10 0032 (SSS) D'ANNA, JOE National flow cytometry and sorting research resource H1 content and chromatin structure in early S phase blockage
P41RR-01315-10 0033 (SSS) BACA, OSWALD National flow cytometry and sorting research resource Rickettsial infection and the host cell cycle
P41RR-01315-10 0037 (SSS) ANDERSON, ROBERT National flow cytometry and sorting research resource Effects of low level radiation on the immune response
P41RR-01315-10 0040 (SSS) DARZYNKIEWICA, Z National flow cytometry and sorting research resource Biochemical & molecular markers of the cell cycle in normal and neoplastic cells
P41RR-01315-10 0041 (SSS) FREYER, JAMES P National flow cytometry and sorting research resource Regulation of proliferation and viability in multicellular tumor spheroids
P41RR-01315-10 0042 (SSS) MURPHY, ROBERT J National flow cytometry and sorting research resource Optimization of flow cytometric analysis of ligand processing
P41RR-01315-10 0043 (SSS) HAMKALO, BARBARA National flow cytometry and sorting research resource Analysis of the human inactive X chromosome
P41RR-01315-10 0044 (SSS) GELINAS, RICHARD National flow cytometry and sorting research resource A random partial cosmid library of chromosome 17 DNA from flow sorted material
P41RR-01315-10 0045 (SSS) OLIVER, JANET M National flow cytometry and sorting research resource Membrane dynamics and cellular response in basophils
P41RR-01315-10 0046 (SSS) STEWART, CARLETON C National flow cytometry and sorting research resource Effect of radiation on the host defense to cancer
P41RR-01315-10 0047 (SSS) WILLIAM, CHERYL L National flow cytometry and sorting research resource Gene expression during myelomonocytic development
P41RR-01315-10 0048 (SSS) VAN EPPS, DENNIS E National flow cytometry and sorting research resource Phagocytic cell - Regulation, dysfunction and disease
P41RR-01315-10 0049 (SSS) GRIFFITH, JEFFREY K National flow cytometry and sorting research resource Structure and evolution of mammalian sex chromosomes
P41RR-01315-10 9001 (SSS) BARTHOLDI, MARTY F National flow

PROJECT NO., ORGANIZATIONAL UNIT., INVESTIGATOR, ADDRESS, TITLE

cytometry and sorting research resource Core - Chromosome analysis and sorting
P41RR-01315-10 9002 (SSS) STEINKAMP, JOHN A National flow cytometry and sorting research resource Multiwavelength sorting and analysis
P41RR-01315-10 9003 (SSS) MARTIN, JOHN C National flow cytometry and sorting research resource High speed cell and chromosome sorter
P41RR-01315-10 9006 (SSS) MARTIN, JOHN C National flow cytometry and sorting research resource Single stained cells or chromosomes
P41RR-01315-10 9009 (SSS) JETT, JAMES H National flow cytometry and sorting research resource Flow cytometric data collection and analysis
P41RR-01315-10 9010 (SSS) STEWART, CARLETON National flow cytometry and sorting research resource Core - Cell biology programs
P40RR-01333-12 (AR) ABT, DONALD A LABORATORY FOR MARINE ANIMAL H MARINE BIOLOGICAL LABORATORY WOODS HOLE, MA 02543 Laboratory for marine animal health
M01RR-01346-10 (CLR) YOUNG, JAMES J UNIVERSITY OF TEXAS HEALTH 7703 FLOYD CURL DR SAN ANTONIO, TX 78284 General clinical research center
M01RR-01346-10 0187 (CLR) DEFRONZO, RALPH A General clinical research center Insulin and hyperamino-acidemia in forearm protein synthesis
M01RR-01346-10 0188 (CLR) GRAYBILL, JOHN RICHARD General clinical research center Effect of ampho B lipid complex in patients with coccidioidomycosis
M01RR-01346-10 0189 (CLR) HARPER, KAREN J General clinical research center Diltiazem plasma conc vs pharmacologic effect in chronic atrial fibrill.
M01RR-01346-10 0190 (CLR) LAM, Y W FRANCIS General clinical research center Pharmacogenic differences in drug metabolizing capacity of man
M01RR-01346-10 0191 (CLR) RODRIGUEZ, GLADYS General clinical research center Phase I-II trial of hydroxyurea in treatment of squamous carcinoma
M01RR-01346-10 0192 (CLR) SAMUELS, MARY H General clinical research center Pulsatile secretion of parathyroid hormone in osteoporosis
M01RR-01346-10 0193 (CLR) SHEPHERD, ALEX M General clinical research center Use of AII antagonist DUP 753 in patients with mild to mod. hypertension
M01RR-01346-10 0194 (CLR) VON HOFF, DANIEL D General clinical research center Evaluation of BMY-25801 in patients receiving high-dose cisplatin
M01RR-01346-10 0195 (CLR) VON HOFF, DANIEL D General clinical research center Phase I study of ilmofosine administered every 28 days
M01RR-01346-10 0196 (CLR) VON HOFF, DANIEL D General clinical research center Phase I trial of U73,975
M01RR-01346-10 0197 (CLR) VON HOFF, DANIEL D General clinical research center Phase I trial of topotecan admin. as a continuous infusion for 5 days
M01RR-01346-10 0198 (CLR) VON HOFF, DANIEL D General clinical research center Phase I trial of tetraplatin
M01RR-01346-10 0199 (CLR) WEINER, MARC General clinical research center Study of AZT vs DDI in patients with AIDS
M01RR-01346-10 0200 (CLR) WEISS, GEOFFREY R General clinical research center Phase I trial of 14C piritrexim
M01RR-01346-10 0201 (CLR) WEISS, GEOFFREY R General clinical research center Study of IL-1B, etoposide, & carboplatin in patients w/ metastatic cancer
M01RR-01346-10 0044 (CLR) DUNN, JAMES F General clinical research center The value of provocative testing to uncover multiple endocrine neoplasms
M01RR-01346-10 0124 (CLR) BROWN, THOMAS General clinical research center Phase I trial of taxol as a six hour infusion
M01RR-01346-10 0125 (CLR) DARLAND, CELIA General clinical research center Glucose response to foods in the Mexican-American diet
M01RR-01346-10 0049 (CLR) GRAYBILL, JOHN RICHARD General clinical research center Itraconazole therapy of fungal infections
M01RR-01346-10 0119 (CLR) BROWN, THOMAS General clinical research center LY188011--Phase I, IV every 2 weeks
M01RR-01346-10 0135 (CLR) BEER, WILLIAM General clinical research center Gastrointestinal tolerance and carbohydrate absorption of polydextrose
M01RR-01346-10 0140 (CLR) ERESHEFSKY, LARRY General clinical research center Study of current vs. proposed formulations of taractan in psychotics
M01RR-01346-10 0146 (CLR) TUTTLE, KATHERINE General clinical research center Pathophysiology of glomerular hyperfiltration in diabetes
M01RR-01346-10 0149 (CLR) PUGH, JACQUELINE General clinical research center Metformin with a second generation sulfonylurea in NIDDM
M01RR-01346-10 0151 (CLR) BROWN, THOMAS General clinical research center A phase I trial of liposomal doxorubicin
M01RR-01346-10 0152 (CLR) BROWN, THOMAS General clinical research center Phase I study of BMY-28175 by daily x5 schedule
M01RR-01346-10 0153 (CLR) DEFRONZO, RALPH A General clinical research center Combined sulfonylurea/insulin therapy for non-insulin dependent D.M.
M01RR-01346-10 0154 (CLR) DEFRONZO, RALPH A General clinical research center Insulin effects on glucose transporters of human peripheral tissue
M01RR-01346-10 0155 (CLR) DEFRONZO, RALPH A General clinical research center Leucine metabolism normal, diabetic, obese and uremic man
M01RR-01346-10 0156 (CLR) DEFRONZO, RALPH A General clinical research center Carbohydrate intolerance in diabetes, obesity, uremia, and hypertension
M01RR-01346-10 0157 (CLR) DEFRONZO, RALPH A General clinical research center Quantitative role of glycolysis in insulin-mediated glucose disposal
M01RR-01346-10 0158 (CLR) DEFRONZO, RALPH A General clinical research center Fenoldopam in patients with chronic renal insufficiency
M01RR-01346-10 0159 (CLR) GRAYBILL, JOHN RICHARD General clinical research center SCH-39304 treatment of oropharyngeal candidiasis in patients with AIDS
M01RR-01346-10 0161 (CLR) HOYUMPA, ANASTACIO General clinical research center Venlafaxine pharmacokinetics in patients with liver disease
M01RR-01346-10 0163 (CLR) LIFSCHITZ, MEYER D General clinical research center Dietary modification of the course of progressive renal disease
M01RR-01346-10 0164 (CLR) MUNDY, GREGORY R General clinical research center Phase II study of NE-58095 in patients with hypercalcemia
M01RR-01346-10 0165 (CLR) NEW, PAMELA Z General clinical research center Phase II of crisnatol mesylate in progressive glioma
M01RR-01346-10 0166 (CLR) SAMUELS, MARY General clinical research center Pulsatile pituitary glycoprotein secretion in aging and illness
M01RR-01346-10 0169 (CLR) SHEPHERD, ALEX M General clinical research center Effects of TA 3090 in patients with hypertension
M01RR-01346-10 0175 (CLR) RAVDIN, PETER General clinical research center Phase I trial of hepsulfam administered as a single dose every 21 days
M01RR-01346-10 0176 (CLR) VON HOFF, DANIEL D General clinical research center Phase I trial of hycamptamine (SK&F 104864)
M01RR-01346-10 0178 (CLR) BROWN, THOMAS General clinical research center A phase I/II trial of recombinant human tumor necrosis factor
M01RR-01346-10 0179 (CLR) BROWN, THOMAS General clinical research center Admin of brequinar sodium in combination w/ cisplatin in cancer patients
M01RR-01346-10 0180 (CLR) BROWN, THOMAS General clinical research center Phase I eval. of IV acivicin in adult patients w/ solid tumors
M01RR-01346-10 0181 (CLR) DEFRONZO, RALPH A General clinical research center Study of effect of blood pressure with captopril or nifedipine on NIDDM
M01RR-01346-10 0182 (CLR) DEFRONZO, RALPH A General clinical research center Glucose metabolism after mixed meal ingestion in diabetics and normals
M01RR-01346-10 0183 (CLR) DEFRONZO, RALPH A General clinical research center Effect of elevated plasma free fatty acid levels on gluconeogenesis
M01RR-01346-10 0184 (CLR) DEFRONZO, RALPH A General clinical research center Effect of etomoxir on glucose and lipid metabolism in diabetics
M01RR-01346-10 0185 (CLR) DEFRONZO, RALPH A General clinical research center Leucine, alpha-ketoisocaproic acid, and insulin in protein synthesis
M01RR-01346-10 0186 (CLR) DEFRONZO, RALPH A General clinical research center Quantitation of hepatic glycogen synthesis in man
P41RR-01348-10 (SSS) HOCHSTRASSER, ROBIN M UNIVERSITY OF PENNSYLVANIA 231 S. 34TH ST. PHILADELPHIA, PA 19104-6323 Ultrafast optical processes laboratory
P41RR-01348-10 0001 (SSS) BLASIE, J KENT Ultrafast optical processes laboratory Time-resolved studies of calcium ATPase in sarcoplasmic reticulum
P41RR-01348-10 0002 (SSS) DUTTON, P LESLIE Ultrafast optical processes laboratory Electric field dependency of charge separation in photosynthesis
P41RR-01348-10 0003 (SSS) EATON, WILLIAM A Ultrafast optical processes laboratory Dynamics of conformational changes in hemoglobin
P41RR-01348-10 0004 (SSS) ENGLANDER, S WALTER Ultrafast optical processes laboratory Internal protein dynamics by luminescence quenching
P41RR-01348-10 0005 (SSS) PONZY, LU Ultrafast optical processes laboratory Interaction between gene regulatory proteins and DNA
P41RR-01348-10 0006 (SSS) SMITH, AMOS B Ultrafast optical processes laboratory Photochemistry and photophysics of s-tetrazine and derivatives
P41RR-01348-10 0007 (SSS) SPIRO, THOMAS G Ultrafast optical processes laboratory Picosecond Raman studies of myoglobin photodissociation
P41RR-01348-10 0008 (SSS) VANDERKOOI, JANE M Ultrafast optical processes laboratory Site-selection spectroscopy of chromophores
P41RR-01348-10 0009 (SSS) CHANCE, BRITTON Ultrafast optical processes laboratory Time-resolved structure in laser-activated biochemical reactions
P41RR-01348-10 9001 (SSS) HOCHSTRASSER, ROBIN M Ultrafast optical processes laboratory Ultrafast fluorescence and Raman spectroscopy--Core
P41RR-01348-10 9002 (SSS) TOPP, MICHAEL R Ultrafast optical processes laboratory Energy transfer and relaxation--Core
P41RR-01348-10 9003 (SSS) HOLTOM, G R Ultrafast optical processes laboratory Time correlated single photon counting--core
P40RR-01375-10 (AR) WOLFLE, THOMAS L NATIONAL ACADEMY OF SCIENCES 2101 CONSTITUTION AVENUE NW WASHINGTON DC 20418 Support of NRC Institute of Laboratory Animal Resources
P41RR-01380-10 (SSS) THOMAS, LEWIS J, JR BIOMEDICAL COMPUTER LAB 700 SOUTH EUCLID ST LOUIS, MO 63110 A resource for biomedical computing
P41RR-01380-10 0001 (SSS) TER-POGOSSIAN, MICHEL M A resource for biomedical computing Collaborative research on PETT
P41RR-01380-10 0004 (SSS) HART, WILLIAM M A resource for biomedical computing Collaborative research on microangiography of optic nerve and retina
P41RR-01380-10 0006 (SSS) OLSON, MAYNARD V A resource for biomedical computing Collaborative research on physical mapping of DNA
P41RR-01380-10 0008 (SSS) THOMAS, LEWIS J A resource for biomedical computing Collaborative research on ischemic heart disease
P41RR-01380-10 0009 (SSS) RAICHLE, MARCUS E A resource for biomedical computing Collaborative research on pharmacology, blood flow and metabolism in brain
P41RR-01380-10 0010 (SSS) THOMAS, LEWIS J A resource for biomedical computing Service activities
P41RR-01380-10 9001 (SSS) THOMAS, LEWIS J A resource for biomedical computing Core research--Image-source modeling--Physiological modeling
P41RR-01380-10 9002 (SSS) TOGA, ARTHUR N A resource for biomedical

computing Core research--Image orientation, registration, and distortion correction
P41RR-01380-10 9003 (SSS) SNYDER, DONALD L A resource for biomedical computing Core research--Algorithm development for emission tomography
P41RR-01380-10 9004 (SSS) MILLER, MICHAEL I A resource for biomedical computing Core research--Algorithms for electronmicroscopy autoradiography
P41RR-01380-10 9005 (SSS) BLAINE, G JAMES A resource for biomedical computing Core research--A distributed facility for image analysis
P41RR-01380-10 0002 (SSS) WONG, JOHN W A resource for biomedical computing Collaborative research on radiation treatment
P41RR-01395-10 (SSS) JAFFE, LIONEL F MARINE BIOLOGICAL LABORATORY WOODS HOLE, MA 02543 National vibrating probe facility
P41RR-01395-10 0001 (SSS) ARMSTRONG, DAVID L National vibrating probe facility Collaborative research--Ca++ in Ascidians
P41RR-01395-10 0012 (SSS) CORKEY, BARBARA E National vibrating probe facility Collaborative research--Oscillations in rat pancreatic islets
P41RR-01395-10 0013 (SSS) KATER, STANLEY National vibrating probe facility Collaborative research--The role of Ca++ in neuronal growth cones
P41RR-01395-10 0014 (SSS) POO, MU-MINGY National vibrating probe facility Collab research--Ca gradients and electrical currents at developing synapses
P41RR-01395-10 0015 (SSS) RIPPS, HARRIS National vibrating probe facility Collaborative research--Ca fluxes across the plasma membrane of photoreceptors
P41RR-01395-10 0016 (SSS) STRUMWASSER, FELIX National vibrating probe facility Collaborative research--Circadian rhythms in intracellular calcium patterns
P41RR-01395-10 0017 (SSS) FLUCK, RICHARD A National vibrating probe facility Collaborative research--Ooplasmic segregation and cytokinesis in Medaka fish eggs
P41RR-01395-10 0018 (SSS) DURHAM, JOHN National vibrating probe facility Collaborative research--Ionic and electrical fluxes across the urinary bladder
P41RR-01395-10 9003 (SSS) JAFFE, LIONEL F National vibrating probe facility Core research--Vibrating ion selective electrode
P41RR-01395-10 9004 (SSS) JAFFE, LIONEL F National vibrating probe facility Core research--Aerial probe
P41RR-01395-10 9005 (SSS) JAFFE, LIONEL F National vibrating probe facility Core research--Vibrating oxygen electrode
P41RR-01614-10 (SSS) BURLINGAME, ALMA L UNIVERSITY OF CALIFORNIA SCH OF PHARMACY/3RD & PARNASSU SAN FRANCISCO, CA 94143-0446 Bio-organic biomedical mass spectrometry resource
P41RR-01614-10 0010 (SSS) TRIMBLE, ROBERT B Bio-organic biomedical mass spectrometry resource Structural elucidation of N-linked oligosaccharides
P41RR-01614-10 0011 (SSS) FISHER, SUSAN Bio-organic biomedical mass spectrometry resource Carbohydrate structure of salivary glycoproteins
P41RR-01614-10 0012 (SSS) TJIAN, ROBERT Bio-organic biomedical mass spectrometry resource Large tumor antigen (Tag) of simian virus 40
P41RR-01614-10 0013 (SSS) KENYON, GEORGE L Bio-organic biomedical mass spectrometry resource Development and synthesis of peptidal inhibitors of tyrosine kinase
P41RR-01614-10 0014 (SSS) GRIFFISS, MCLEOD Bio-organic biomedical mass spectrometry resource Structure of the lipooligosaccharides of Neisseria and Haemophilus
P41RR-01614-10 9001 (SSS) BURLINGAME, ALMA L Bio-organic biomedical mass spectrometry resource Core--Mass spectrometry resource--technology R and D
P41RR-01614-10 0001 (SSS) STROUD, ROBERT Bio-organic biomedical mass spectrometry resource Membrane structure and topography
P41RR-01614-10 0002 (SSS) BURLINGAME, A L Bio-organic biomedical mass spectrometry resource Posttranslationally modified proteins
P41RR-01614-10 0003 (SSS) CRAIK, CHARLES S Bio-organic biomedical mass spectrometry resource Structure-function of recombinant proteins
P41RR-01614-10 0004 (SSS) PRUSINER, STANLEY Bio-organic biomedical mass spectrometry resource Structure of the scrapie prion protein
P41RR-01614-10 0005 (SSS) KLINMAN, JUDITH P Bio-organic biomedical mass spectrometry resource Characterization of the active site of bovine plasma amine oxidase
P41RR-01614-10 0006 (SSS) BASS, NATHAN M Bio-organic biomedical mass spectrometry resource Primary structure of vertebrate fatty acid binding protein
P41RR-01614-10 0007 (SSS) LEFFLER, H Bio-organic biomedical mass spectrometry resource Structural studies on mammalian soluble lectins
P41RR-01614-10 0008 (SSS) SHACKLETON, CEDRIC H L Bio-organic biomedical mass spectrometry resource Electrospray MS, LSIMS, and MS/MS for variant hemoglobins
P41RR-01614-10 0009 (SSS) GIBSON, BRADFORD W Bio-organic biomedical mass spectrometry resource The structure, biosynthesis and activities of amphibian peptides
P41RR-01632-09 (SSS) GATEWOOD, LAEL C UNIVERSITY OF MINNESOTA 420 DELAWARE STREET SE MINNEAPOLIS, MN 55455 Simulation resource for stochastic population models
P41RR-01632-09 0025 (SSS) ALTMANN, MICHAEL Simulation resource for stochastic population models HIV studies
P41RR-01632-09 0027 (SSS) KOTTKE, THOMAS Simulation resource for stochastic population models Treatment of coronary disease
P41RR-01632-09 0028 (SSS) MCGUE, MATTHEW Simulation resource for stochastic population models Schizophrenia model
P41RR-01632-09 0029 (SSS) SELLER, THOMAS A Simulation resource for stochastic population models Lung cancer model
P41RR-01632-09 0030 (SSS) RICH, STEPHEN S Simulation resource for stochastic population models Dopamine beta hydroxylase model
P41RR-01632-09 0031 (SSS) RICH, STEPHEN S Simulation resource for stochastic population models Insulin-dependent diabetes model
P41RR-01632-09 9003 (SSS) ALTMANN, MICHAEL Simulation resource for stochastic population models Core research--Monte Carlo simulation tools, SUMMERS
P41RR-01632-09 9006 (SSS) PETERSON, DENTON R Simulation resource for stochastic population models Core research--Epidemics of infectious disease models, VESPERS
P41RR-01632-09 9007 (SSS) GATEWOOD, LAEL C Simulation resource for stochastic population models Core research--Chronic disease simulation--General CRISPERS model development
P41RR-01632-09 9008 (SSS) ALTMANN, MICHAEL Simulation resource for stochastic population models Core research--Genetic disease simulation--GRASPERS Development in SUMMERS
P41RR-01632-09 9009 (SSS) ACKERMAN, EUGENE Simulation resource for stochastic population models Core research--Monte Carolo sensitivity analyses--SENSEN enhancements
P41RR-01632-09 9010 (SSS) ALTMANN, MICHAEL Simulation resource for stochastic population models Core research--Infectious disease simulation--Social newtowrk measures
P41RR-01632-09 9011 (SSS) ALTMANN, MICHAEL Simulation resource for stochastic population models Core research--Monte Carlo simulation--Mating theory and dynamic group models
P41RR-01632-09 9012 (SSS) ALTMANN, MICHAEL Simulation resource for stochastic population models Core research--Monte Carlo sensitivity analyses--Control shell development
P41RR-01632-09 9013 (SSS) GATEWOOD, LAEL C Simulation resource for stochastic population models Core research--Chronic desease simulation--Examination of cardiac risk functions
P41RR-01632-09 9014 (SSS) ALTMANN, MICHAEL Simulation resource for stochastic population models Core research--Simulation program interfaces--DEMOnstration program development
P41RR-01632-09 9015 (SSS) ACKERMAN, EUGENE Simulation resource for stochastic population models Core research--Simulation program interfaces--Error messages
P41RR-01632-09 9016 (SSS) BOULANGER, BRUNO Simulation resource for stochastic population models Core research--Chronic disease simulation--population generation
P41RR-01632-09 9017 (SSS) DAVIDSON, GESTUR Simulation resource for stochastic population models Core research--Infectious disease simulation--HIV/AIDS treatment cost model
P41RR-01632-09 9018 (SSS) GATEWOOD, LAEL C Simulation resource for stochastic population models Core research--Development of an expert system (CRISPERT) for CHD interventions
P41RR-01632-09 9019 (SSS) KOTTKE, THOMAS E Simulation resource for stochastic population models Core research--Chronic disease simulation--CRISPERS health care model development
P41RR-01632-09 9020 (SSS) PETERSON, DENTON R Simulation resource for stochastic population models Core research--Infectious disease simulation--ADDERS specialization from SUMMERS
P41RR-01632-09 9021 (SSS) RICH, STEPHEN S Simulation resource for stochastic population models Core research--Genetic disease simulation--SNAPPERS stabilization
P41RR-01632-09 9022 (SSS) RICH, STEPHEN S Simulation resource for stochastic population models Core research--Population simulation--ELDERS development in SUMMERS
P41RR-01632-09 9023 (SSS) SCHINDLER, JAY Simulation resource for stochastic population models Core research--Simulation program interfaces--Hypersummers development
P41RR-01632-09 9024 (SSS) TSAI, WEI TEK Simulation resource for stochastic population models Core research--SUMMERS--Object abstraction for procedurally structured software
P41RR-01633-10 (SSS) BLASIE, J KENT UNIVERSITY CITY SCIENCE CENTER 3401 MARKET STREET SUITE 320 PHILADELPHIA, PA 19104 Biostructures PRT--Synchrotron X-ray structural studies
P41RR-01633-10 0003 (SSS) ORME-JOHNSON, WILLIAM Biostructures PRT--Synchrotron X-ray structural studies EXAFS studies of nickel, iron, and molybdenum proteins
P41RR-01633-10 0004 (SSS) BLASIE, J KENT Biostructures PRT--Synchrotron X-ray structural studies Time-resolved and resonance X-ray diffraction
P41RR-01633-10 0005 (SSS) GRUNER, SOL M Biostructures PRT--Synchrotron X-ray structural studies Structure and function of biological lipids
P41RR-01633-10 0008 (SSS) BUNKER, GRANT Biostructures PRT--Synchrotron X-ray structural studies Studies on ribonucleotide reductase and hemerythrin
P41RR-01633-10 0009 (SSS) CHANCE, BRITTON Biostructures PRT--Synchrotron X-ray structural studies Trapped intermediates of hemoproteins and their reactions with ligands
P41RR-01633-10 0010 (SSS) PENNER, J Biostructures PRT--Synchrotron X-ray structural studies Polarized X-ray absorption spectroscopy
P41RR-01633-10 0011 (SSS) HERBETTE, LEO Biostructures PRT--Synchrotron X-ray structural studies Ligand receptor binding mechanisms
P41RR-01633-10 0012 (SSS) MAKOWSKI, L Biostructures PRT--Synchrotron X-ray structural studies Structural studies of macromolecular assemblies
P41RR-01633-10 9001 (SSS) ROSENBAUM, GEROLD Biostructures PRT--Synchrotron X-ray structural studies Core research--Operation and development of beam line X9-A
P41RR-01633-10 9002 (SSS) CHANCE, BRITTON Biostructures PRT--Synchrotron X-ray structural studies Core research--Sample stability and rapid flow
P41RR-01633-10 9003 (SSS) KALID, SYED Biostructures PRT--Synchrotron X-ray structural studies Core research--Detector development
P41RR-01633-10 9004 (SSS) CHANCE, BRITTON Biostructures PRT--Synchrotron X-ray structural studies Core research--Beam noise evaluation/compensation
P41RR-01633-10 9005 (SSS) BUNKER, GRANT Biostructures PRT--Synchrotron X-ray structural studies Core research--Computer/data analysis
P41RR-01633-10 9006 (SSS) BLASIE, J KENT Biostructures PRT--Synchrotron X-ray structural studies Core research--Resonance X-ray diffraction in the energy dispersive mode
P41RR-01638-07 (SSS) TRETIAK, OLEH J DREXEL UNIVERSITY 32ND AND CHESTNUT STREETS PHILADELPHIA, PA 19104 Autoradiographic image

processing center
P41RR-01638-07 0024 (SSS) MCEACHRON, D L Autoradiographic image processing center Quantitative receptor autoradiography
P41RR-01638-07 0025 (SSS) TRETIAK, OLEH J Autoradiographic image processing center Quantitative microradiography
P41RR-01638-07 0026 (SSS) MCEACHRON, D L Autoradiographic image processing center Spatio-temporal data correlation for hypothalamic neuroreceptors
P41RR-01638-07 9001 (SSS) TRETIAK, OLEH J Autoradiographic image processing center Core research--Within-region information detection from autocardiograms
P41RR-01638-07 9002 (SSS) EILBERT, JAMES L Autoradiographic image processing center Core research--Computer parcellation of brain structures
P41RR-01638-07 9005 (SSS) TRETIAK, OLEH J Autoradiographic image processing center Core research--Section thickness and quenching
P41RR-01644-09 (SSS) XUONG, NGUYEN-HUU UNIV OF CALIF - SAN DIEGO 9500 GILMAN DRIVE LA JOLLA, CA 92093-0319 Resources for protein crystallography
P41RR-01646-09 (SSS) BILDERBACK, DONALD H CORNELL UNIVERSITY 207 BIOTECHNOLOGY BUILDING ITHACA NY 14853-2703 A macromolecular diffraction resource--MacCHESS
P41RR-01646-09 0006 (SSS) ROSSMANN, MICHAEL A macromolecular diffraction resource--MacCHESS structure determination of some spherical viruses
P41RR-01646-09 0007 (SSS) JOHNSON, JACK A macromolecular diffraction resource--MacCHESS Structural studies of plant and insect viruses
P41RR-01646-09 0008 (SSS) BURNETT A macromolecular diffraction resource--MacCHESS Structural studies of adenovirus
P41RR-01646-09 9002 (SSS) MOFFAT, JOHN K A macromolecular diffraction resource--MacCHESS Core research--Storage phosphors
P41RR-01646-09 9003 (SSS) MOFFAT, JOHN K A macromolecular diffraction resource--MacCHESS Core research--CHESS east
P41RR-01646-09 9004 (SSS) MOFFAT, JOHN K A macromolecular diffraction resource--MacCHESS Core research--Optics
P41RR-01646-09 9005 (SSS) MOFFAT, JOHN K A macromolecular diffraction resource--MacCHESS Core research--Shock freezing and cryostats
P41RR-01646-09 9006 (SSS) MOFFAT, JOHN K A macromolecular diffraction resource--MacCHESS Core research--New methods of phase determination
P41RR-01646-09 0009 (SSS) HARRISON, STEVE A macromolecular diffraction resource--MacCHESS Virus crystallography
P41RR-01646-09 0010 (SSS) HOGLE, JAMES A macromolecular diffraction resource--MacCHESS Virus structure and biological function
P41RR-01646-09 0011 (SSS) STUBBS, GERALD A macromolecular diffraction resource--MacCHESS Fiber diffraction--Viruses, microtubules and filaments
P41RR-01646-09 9001 (SSS) MOFFAT, JOHN K A macromolecular diffraction resource--MacCHESS Core research--Laue diffraction techniques
R24RR-01695-07 (SSS) KUNTZ, IRWIN D JR UNIVERSITY OF CALIFORNIA 926 MEDICAL SCIENCES BLDG SAN FRANCISCO CA 94143-0446 Molecular structure in solution--Feasibility study
P41RR-01777-08 (SSS) WALL, JOSEPH S BROOKHAVEN NATIONAL LABORATORY UPTON, NY 11973 Mass measurement of single molecules with the STEM
P41RR-01777-08 0001 (SSS) WALL, JOSEPH S Mass measurement of single molecules with the STEM Theoretical studies
P41RR-01777-08 9001 (SSS) WALL, JOSEPH Mass measurement of single molecules with the STEM Core research development-speciment preparation
P41RR-01777-08 9002 (SSS) WALL, JOSEPH Mass measurement of single molecules with the STEM Core research development--instrumentation
P41RR-01777-08 9003 (SSS) WALL, JOSEPH Mass measurement of single molecules with the STEM Core research development--heavy atom cluster labels
P41RR-01777-08 9004 (SSS) WALL, JOSEPH Mass measurement of single molecules with the STEM Core research development--image analysis
P41RR-01777-08 9005 (SSS) WALL, JOSEPH Mass measurement of single molecules with the STEM Core research development--energy loss spectroscopy
P41RR-01811-06A1 (SSS) SWARTZ, HAROLD M UNIVERSITY OF ILLINOIS 506 SOUTH MATHEWS AVENUE URBANA, IL 61801 Electron spin resonance center at the University of Illinois
P41RR-01811-06A1 9002 (SSS) BELFORD, R LINN Electron spin resonance center at the University of Illinois Core research-- W-band (VHF) electron paramagnetic resonance spectrometer
P41RR-01811-06A1 9004 (SSS) SWARTZ, HAROLD M Electron spin resonance center at the University of Illinois Core research-- L-band spectrometer for in vivo EPR
P41RR-01811-06A1 9008 (SSS) CLARKSON, ROBERT B Electron spin resonance center at the University of Illinois Core research-- S-band ESE, ENDOR, and computational service
P41RR-01811-06A1 9009 (SSS) NILGES, MARK J Electron spin resonance center at the University of Illinois Core research-- ESR imaging at 9GHz
P41RR-01861-07 (SSS) MARMARELIS, VASILIS Z UNIV OF SOUTHERN CALIFORNIA UNIVERSITY PARK LOS ANGELES, CA 90089-1451 Biomedical simulation resource
P41RR-01861-07 9004 (SSS) MARMARELIS, VASILIS Z Biomedical simulation resource Core--Modeling of nonlinear and/or nonstationary biomedical systems
P41RR-01861-07 9010 (SSS) KHOO, MICHAEL Biomedical simulation resource Practical identification of feedback structures in physiological reflex
P41RR-01861-07 9011 (SSS) O'LEARY, DENNIS Biomedical simulation resource Modeling of vestibulo-ocular reflex
P41RR-01861-07 0001 (SSS) CITRON, MARK Biomedical simulation resource Modeling of spatio-temporal dynamics in the vertebrate retina
P41RR-01861-07 0002 (SSS) GRUNDFEST, WARREN Biomedical simulation resource Modeling of laser-tissue interaction during laser angioplasty
P41RR-01861-07 0003 (SSS) MARKHAM, CHARLES Biomedical simulation resource Quantitative analysis of motor dysfunction in Parkinson's
P41RR-01861-07 0004 (SSS) MARSH, DONALD Biomedical simulation resource Modeling of renal autoregulation dynamics
P41RR-01861-07 0005 (SSS) NAKA, KEN Biomedical simulation resource Modeling of light-adaptation dynamics in the retina
P41RR-01861-07 0006 (SSS) RODMAN, JOHN Biomedical simulation resource Pharmacokinetics and pharmacodynamics of anticancer drugs
P41RR-01861-07 0007 (SSS) SINGH, MANBIR Biomedical simulation resource Pharmacokinetic studies using nuclear medicine
P41RR-01861-07 0008 (SSS) SELZER, ROBERT Biomedical simulation resource Simulation of coronary stenosis hemodynamics
P41RR-01861-07 0009 (SSS) GARFINKEL, DAVID Biomedical simulation resource Development and automation of pharmacokinetic modeling
P41RR-01861-07 0010 (SSS) TALLMAN, RICHARD Biomedical simulation resource Open and closed-loop dynamics of arterial and intrapulmonary CO2 receptors
P41RR-01861-07 0011 (SSS) RICE, DALE Biomedical simulation resource Clinical applications of vestibulo-ocular reflex models
P41RR-01861-07 0012 (SSS) YAMASHIRO, S Biomedical simulation resource Nonlinear dynamics of pulmonary regulation
P41RR-01861-07 9002 (SSS) D'ARGENIO, DAVID Z Biomedical simulation resource Core--Analysis of sparse data systems
R01RR-02022-07 (REB) TARDIF, SUZETTE D OAK RIDGE ASSOCIATED UNIVS P.O. BOX 117 OAK RIDGE, TN 37830 Determinants of reproductive competence in tamarins
P41RR-02024-08 (SSS) LIU, CHUNG-CHIUN CASE WESTERN RESERVE UNIVERSIT 10900 EUCLID AVENUE CLEVELAND, OH 44106-7200 Resource for biomedical sensor technology
P41RR-02024-08 9001 (SSS) W_LIU, CHUNG-CHIUN Resource for biomedical sensor technology Core research -- Electrochemical sensors
P41RR-02024-08 9002 (SSS) KO, WEN H Resource for biomedical sensor technology Core research--Gas sensors for health care
P41RR-02024-08 9003 (SSS) FUNG, Resource for biomedical sensor technology Core research--Chemical microsensors
P41RR-02024-08 9004 (SSS) FUNG, Resource for biomedical sensor technology Core research--On-chip reference electrode
P41RR-02024-08 9005 (SSS) LIU, CHUNG-CHIUM Resource for biomedical sensor technology Core research--Silicon capacitive transducers for physiologic control
P41RR-02024-08 9006 (SSS) LIU, CHUNG-CHIUN Resource for biomedical sensor technology Core research--Thermal sensors for tissue perfusion
P41RR-02024-08 9007 (SSS) PROHASKA, OTTO Resource for biomedical sensor technology Core research--Miniaturized chamber-type sensors
R01RR-02039-08 (AR) BARTHOLD, STEPHEN W YALE UNIVERSITY 333 CEDAR STREET, P.O. BOX 333 NEW HAVEN, CT 06510 Pathogenesis of mouse hepatitis virus in laboratory mice
R24RR-02063-08 (AR) BROWNSTEIN, DAVID G YALE UNIVERSITY SCH OF MEDICIN 333 CEDAR STREET, P.O. BOX 333 NEW HAVEN, CT 06510 Responses of inbred mice to ectromelia virus
R01RR-02165-07 (SSS) ALLINGER, NORMAN L UNIVERSITY OF GEORGIA DEPARTMENT OF CHEMISTRY ATHENS GA 30602 Molecular mechanics development
P41RR-02170-08 (SSS) BROOKS, FREDERICK P, JR UNIVERSITY NORTH CAROLINA SITTERSON HALL CHAPEL HILL, NC 27599-3175 Interactive graphics for molecular studies
M01RR-02172-09 (CLR) NATHAN, DAVID G CHILDREN'S HOSPITAL CORPORATIO 300 LONGWOOD AVENUE BOSTON, MA 02115 General clinical research center
M01RR-02172-09 0190 (CLR) EZEKOWITZ, ALAN General clinical research center Treatment of benign vascular neoplasms with alpha interferon
M01RR-02172-09 0191 (CLR) MCINTOSH, KENNETH General clinical research center Comparison of normal and low-dose oral ZVD/AZT in children with HIV infection
M01RR-02172-09 0192 (CLR) MCINTOSH, KENNETH General clinical research center Women and infants' transmissions study (WITS)
M01RR-02172-09 0193 (CLR) ROSENBLUM, NORMAN D General clinical research center Intermittent intravenous cyclophosphamide in lupus glomerulonephritis
M01RR-02172-09 0194 (CLR) SPECHT, LINDA General clinical research center Neuromuscular disease/DNA analysis
M01RR-02172-09 0035 (CLR) GEHA, RAIF S General clinical research center Studies on antibody deficiency syndromes
M01RR-02172-09 0080 (CLR) WOLSDORF, JOSEPH General clinical research center Continuous glucose feeding in patients with glycogenosis
M01RR-02172-09 0140 (CLR) CROWLEY, WILLIAM General clinical research center Use of LHRH to study the pubertal process
M01RR-02172-09 0160 (CLR) NEWBURGER, JANE General clinical research center Treatment of Kawasaki disease with intravenous gammaglobulin
M01RR-02172-09 0165 (CLR) MCINTOSH, KENNETH General clinical research center Study of the natural history of symptomatic HTLV III/LAV infection
M01RR-02172-09 0173 (CLR) MCINTOSH, KENNETH General clinical research center Eval. of oral retrovir in treatment of children with symptomatic HIV infection
M01RR-02172-09 0175 (CLR) AOTIGLER, JOHN F General clinical research center Control of the onset of puberty
M01RR-02172-09 0178 (CLR) GUINAN, EVA General clinical research center Recombinant human granulocyte macrophage colony
M01RR-02172-09 0180 (CLR) GEHA, RAIF S General clinical research center Evaluation of allergic reactions allegedly due to aspartame consumption
M01RR-02172-09 0181 (CLR) HARMON, WILLIAM General clinical research center Growth in children with chronic renal failure
M01RR-02172-09 0183 (CLR) KELLER, RICHARD General clinical research center B cell rest to prevent B cell destruction in anti-islet antibody positive
M01RR-02172-09 0186 (CLR) MCINTOSH, KENNETH General clinical research center Trial to evaluate IV gamma globulin in children w/HIV, receiving AZT
M01RR-02172-09 0187 (CLR) JABS, KATHY General clinical research center Effects of erythropoietin treatment on children pts.

undergoing hemodialysis
M01RR-02172-09 0188 (CLR) NEWBURGER, JANE General clinical research center Infant heart surgery--CNS sequalae of circulatory arrest
M01RR-02172-09 0189 (CLR) LEVY, HARVEY L General clinical research center Emergency approval to evaluate J. M. for ethylmalonic aciduria
P41RR-02176-05 (SSS) FOSTER, DAVID M UNIVERSITY OF WASHINGTON SEATTLE WA 98195 Resource facility for kinetic analysis
P41RR-02176-05 0002 (SSS) CHEUNG, MARIAN Resource facility for kinetic analysis Metabolism of HDL subpopulations
P41RR-02176-05 0003 (SSS) ORAM, JOHN F Resource facility for kinetic analysis The role of HDL in reverse cholesterol transport
P41RR-02176-05 0005 (SSS) HETENYI, GEZA Resource facility for kinetic analysis Kinetics of intermediary metabolism
P41RR-02176-05 0006 (SSS) HENKIN, ROBERT I Resource facility for kinetic analysis Zinc metabolism in humans
P41RR-02176-05 0007 (SSS) FEIGL, ERIC O Resource facility for kinetic analysis Dynamics of carbon dioxide in the coronary circulation
P41RR-02176-05 0010 (SSS) KOOPMAN, JAMES S Resource facility for kinetic analysis Modeling the transmission of HIV
P41RR-02176-05 9001 (SSS) JACQUEZ, JOHN Resource facility for kinetic analysis Core research--Modeling theory
P41RR-02176-05 9002 (SSS) FOSTER, DAVID Resource facility for kinetic analysis Core research--Design and development of new SAAM
P41RR-02176-05 9003 (SSS) FOSTER, DAVID Resource facility for kinetic analysis Core research--Metabolism of the Apo-B containing particles
P41RR-02188-07 (SSS) GARRELS, JAMES I COLD SPRING HARBOR LABORATORY P.O. BOX 100, GRACE BUILDING COLD SPRING HARBOR, NY 11724 A resource for analysis of two-dimensional protein gels
R01RR-02229-08 (AR) DYKE, BENNETT SOUTHWEST FDN FOR BIOMED RES PO BOX 28147 SAN ANTONIO, TX 78228-0147 Genetics and inbreeding in nonhuman primates
P41RR-02230-06S1 (SSS) KULIKOWSKI, CASIMIR RUTGERS THE STATE UNIVERSITY HILL CENTER BUSCH CAMPUS NEW BRUNSWICK NJ 08903 Research resource on computers in biomedicine
P41RR-02230-06S1 0017 (SSS) KULIKOWSKI, CASIMIR Research resource on computers in biomedicine Expert system design tools/technology transfer
P41RR-02230-06S1 0018 (SSS) KULIKOWSKI, CASIMIR Research resource on computers in biomedicine Empirical analysis/learning/verification in expert systems
P41RR-02230-06S1 0019 (SSS) KULIKOWSKI, CASIMIR Research resource on computers in biomedicine Treatment planning
P41RR-02230-06S1 0020 (SSS) KULIKOWSKI, CASIMIR Research resource on computers in biomedicine Time-dependent analysis in expert system
P41RR-02230-06S1 0021 (SSS) KULIKOWSKI, CASIMIR Research resource on computers in biomedicine Expert control of complex software
P41RR-02230-06S1 0022 (SSS) KULIKOWSKI, CASIMIR Research resource on computers in biomedicine Expertise aquisition and theory formation
P41RR-02230-06S1 0023 (SSS) KULIKOWSKI, CASIMIR Research resource on computers in biomedicine Expert systems in laboratory medicine
P41RR-02230-06S1 0024 (SSS) KULIKOWSKI, CASIMIR Research resource on computers in biomedicine Expert systems in rheumatology
P41RR-02230-06S1 0025 (SSS) KULIKOWSKI, CASIMIR Research resource on computers in biomedicine Expert systems on ophthalmology
P41RR-02230-06S1 0026 (SSS) KULIKOWSKI, CASIMIR Research resource on computers in biomedicine Expert consultation models for other medical domains
P41RR-02231-08 (SSS) FEE, JAMES A LOS ALAMOS NATIONAL LAB INC-4, MS-C345 LOS ALAMOS, NM 87545 A national stable isotope resource at Los Alamos
P41RR-02231-08 9001 (SSS) FEE, JAMES A A national stable isotope resource at Los Alamos Core research--synthesis of labelled l-alpha-amino acids
P41RR-02231-08 9002 (SSS) FEE, JAMES A A national stable isotope resource at Los Alamos Core research--Synthesis of labelled nucleic acids
P41RR-02231-08 9003 (SSS) FEE, JAMES A A national stable isotope resource at Los Alamos Core research--Synthons
P41RR-02250-06 (SSS) CHIU, WAH BAYLOR COLLEGE OF MEDICINE ONE BAYLOR PLAZA HOUSTON TX 77030 3-D electron microscopy of macromolecules
P41RR-02250-06 0001 (SSS) STUBBS, G 3-D electron microscopy of macromolecules Helical plant viruses
P41RR-02250-06 0002 (SSS) RIXON, F 3-D electron microscopy of macromolecules Herpes virus
P41RR-02250-06 0003 (SSS) MATSUDAIRA, P 3-D electron microscopy of macromolecules Actin bundle
P41RR-02250-06 0004 (SSS) ROBINSON, J 3-D electron microscopy of macromolecules Two-dimensional periodic arrays of neurotoxin
P41RR-02250-06 0005 (SSS) DORSET, D 3-D electron microscopy of macromolecules Organic and phospholipid crystals
P41RR-02250-06 0006 (SSS) PHILLIPS, G 3-D electron microscopy of macromolecules Tropomyosin crystal
P41RR-02250-06 0007 (SSS) ESSER, A 3-D electron microscopy of macromolecules Membrane attack complex of complement
P41RR-02250-06 0008 (SSS) DEATHERAGE, J 3-D electron microscopy of macromolecules Z disk from insect flight muscle
P41RR-02250-06 0009 (SSS) GOLDSTEIN, M 3-D electron microscopy of macromolecules Role of the Z band in the vertebrate sarcomere
P41RR-02250-06 0010 (SSS) HEATH, J 3-D electron microscopy of macromolecules Cytoskeleton of motile cells
P41RR-02250-06 0011 (SSS) HAWKINS, H 3-D electron microscopy of macromolecules Polymorphonuclear leukocytes
P41RR-02250-06 0012 (SSS) MCDOWALL, A 3-D electron microscopy of macromolecules Cryo-sectioning of biological specimens
P41RR-02250-06 9001 (SSS) CHIU, WAH 3-D electron microscopy of macromolecules Core--Crotoxin complex crystal
P41RR-02250-06 9002 (SSS) CHIU, WAH 3-D electron microscopy of macromolecules Core--Gp32 crystal
P41RR-02250-06 9003 (SSS) CHIU, WAH 3-D electron microscopy of macromolecules Core--Acrosomal process (actin bundles) from limulus sperm
P41RR-02250-06 9004 (SSS) CHIU, WAH 3-D electron microscopy of macromolecules Core--Herpes virus
P41RR-02278-06A1 (SSS) MARECI, THOMAS H UNIVERSITY OF FLORIDA J. HILLIS MILLER HEALTH CENTER GAINESVILLE, FL 32610 NMR imaging and spectroscopy in vivo resource
P41RR-02278-06A1 0004 (SSS) SCOTT, KATHERINE N NMR imaging and spectroscopy in vivo resource Clinical spectroscopy-- Application to osteosarcomas
P41RR-02278-06A1 0005 (SSS) SCOTT, KATHERINE N NMR imaging and spectroscopy in vivo resource NMR spectroscopy of human osteosarcoma implanted in nude mice
P41RR-02278-06A1 0010 (SSS) REIER, PAUL J NMR imaging and spectroscopy in vivo resource MRI of fetal neural tissue transplants in injured spinal cords
P41RR-02278-06A1 0011 (SSS) GUILLETTE, LOUIS J NMR imaging and spectroscopy in vivo resource NMR imaging and spectroscopy of embryonic development
P41RR-02278-06A1 0012 (SSS) GUY, JOHN NMR imaging and spectroscopy in vivo resource Gadolinium-DTPA enhanced MRI in experimental optic neuritis
P41RR-02278-06A1 9001 (SSS) FITZSIMMONS, JEFFREY R NMR imaging and spectroscopy in vivo resource Core Research-- Radio frequency coil development
P41RR-02278-06A1 9002 (SSS) MARECI, THOMAS H NMR imaging and spectroscopy in vivo resource Core Research-- Methods of imaging and localized spectroscopy
P41RR-02278-06A1 9003 (SSS) ANDREW, E RAYMOND NMR imaging and spectroscopy in vivo resource Core Research-- Magnetic field gradients for imaging and localized spectroscopy
P41RR-02300-05S1 (SSS) JARDETZKY, OLEG STANFORD UNIVERSITY STANFORD, CA 94305-5055 Biomedical NMR resource
P41RR-02301-07 (SSS) MARKLEY, JOHN L UNIVERSITY OF WISCONSIN 420 HENRY MALL MADISON, WI 53706 National biomedical NMR resource at Madison
P41RR-02301-07 0003 (SSS) MARKLEY, JOHN National biomedical NMR resource at Madison The flavin binding site of flavodoxin from Anabaena 7120
P41RR-02301-07 0004 (SSS) ZOLNAI, ZSOLT National biomedical NMR resource at Madison Protein NMR database
P41RR-02301-07 0005 (SSS) MARKLEY, JOHN National biomedical NMR resource at Madison Structure-function relationships in Staphyloccal nuclease
P41RR-02301-07 0006 (SSS) WESTLER, WILLIAM National biomedical NMR resource at Madison Solution structure and dynamics of avian ovumucoid third domains
P41RR-02301-07 0007 (SSS) DARBA, PRASHANTH National biomedical NMR resource at Madison Molecular interactions governing the redox potential of 2Fe-2S ferredoxin
P41RR-02301-07 0009 (SSS) DARBA, PRASHANTH National biomedical NMR resource at Madison Cooperative international development of NMR approaches
P41RR-02301-07 9001 (SSS) MARKLEY, JOHN National biomedical NMR resource at Madison Core--Instrumentation development
P41RR-02301-07 9002 (SSS) MARKLEY, JOHN National biomedical NMR resource at Madison Core--NMR methods for the study of biopolymers
P41RR-02301-07 9003 (SSS) MARKLEY, JOHN National biomedical NMR resource at Madison Core--Development of physiological NMR methods
P41RR-02301-07 9004 (SSS) MARKLEY, JOHN National biomedical NMR resource at Madison Core--Software development
P41RR-02305-08 (SSS) LEIGH, JOHN S UNIVERSITY OF PENNSYLVANIA D501 RICHARDS BUILDING PHILADELPHIA PA 19104-6089 A regional resource for NMR in vivo spectroscopy
P41RR-02305-08 0016 (SSS) EVANS, AUDREY A regional resource for NMR in vivo spectroscopy P31 MRS of neuroblastoma and other solid tomors in childhood
P41RR-02305-08 0017 (SSS) INGWALL, JOANNE A regional resource for NMR in vivo spectroscopy Velocity of creatine kinase reaction in cardiac muscle
P41RR-02305-08 0018 (SSS) POSNER, JOEL A regional resource for NMR in vivo spectroscopy Aging and the mechanics of response to exercise
P41RR-02305-08 0019 (SSS) WILSON, JOHN A regional resource for NMR in vivo spectroscopy Treatment of muscular fatigue in heart failure
P41RR-02305-08 0020 (SSS) GYULAI, LASZLO A regional resource for NMR in vivo spectroscopy LI NMR spectroscopy
P41RR-02305-08 0021 (SSS) YOUNKIN, DONALD A regional resource for NMR in vivo spectroscopy Measurement of cerebral lactate
P41RR-02305-08 9001 (SSS) BOLINGER, LIZANN A regional resource for NMR in vivo spectroscopy Metabolic imaging and spatial localization
P41RR-02305-08 9002 (SSS) SHINNAR, MEIR A regional resource for NMR in vivo spectroscopy R.F. pulse development
P41RR-02305-08 9003 (SSS) SUBRAMANIAN, V A regional resource for NMR in vivo spectroscopy Polarization transfer and spectral editing
P41RR-02305-08 9004 (SSS) CHANCE, BRITTON A regional resource for NMR in vivo spectroscopy Time resolved spectroscopy
P41RR-02305-08 9005 (SSS) SHINNAR, MEIR A regional resource for NMR in vivo spectroscopy Imaging of hemoglobin saturation
P41RR-02305-08 9006 (SSS) SHINNAR, MEIR A regional resource for NMR in vivo spectroscopy In-vivo electrolyte NMR--Multiple quantum
P41RR-02305-08 9007 (SSS) WANG, ZHIYUE A regional resource for NMR in vivo spectroscopy In-vivo NMR of potassium and chloride
P41RR-02305-08 9008 (SSS) PRAMMER, MANFRED A regional resource for NMR in vivo spectroscopy Digital NMR spectrometer
P41RR-02305-08 9009 (SSS) HERMAN, GABOR A regional resource for NMR in vivo spectroscopy Iterative data refinement
P41RR-02305-08 9010 (SSS) LEIGH, JOHN A regional resource for NMR in vivo spectroscopy Microscopic imaging and gradient design
P41RR-02483-05S1 (SSS) PEACHEY, LEE D UNIVERSITY OF PENNSYLVANIA PHILADELPHIA, PA 19104-6018 Mid-Atlantic regional IVEM and image analysis resource
P40RR-02512-07 (AR) PATTERSON, DONALD F UNIVERSITY OF PENNSYLVANIA 3800 SPRUCE STREET PHILADELPHIA, PA 19104-6044 Referral center--Animal models of human genetic disease

PROJECT NO., ORGANIZATIONAL UNIT., INVESTIGATOR, ADDRESS, TITLE

M01RR-02558-07 (CLR) RIBBLE, JOHN C UNIVERSITY OF TEXAS MED SCHOOL 6431 FANNIN STREET HOUSTON, TEXAS 77030 General clinical research center
M01RR-02558-07 0046 (CLR) REVEILLE, JOHN D General clinical research center Molecular genetic aspects of psoriasis and psoriatic arthritis
M01RR-02558-07 0047 (CLR) PICKERING, LARRY K General clinical research center Phase I study of ddI administered to infants and children with AIDS
M01RR-02558-07 0011 (CLR) SCHNEIDER, VICTOR S General clinical research center Prevention of disuse osteoporosis and fluoride therapy
M01RR-02558-07 0024 (CLR) BUTLER, IAN J General clinical research center Neurochemical markers in CSF in neurodegenerative disorders
M01RR-02558-07 0027 (CLR) SELLIN, JOSEPH H General clinical research center Glucose malabsorption and rapid intestinal transit in chronic diarrhea
M01RR-02558-07 0029 (CLR) HOLIAN, ANDRIJ General clinical research center Bronchoalveolar lavage and analysis of cell function in normal controls
M01RR-02558-07 0041 (CLR) GILDENBERG, PHILIP General clinical research center Treatment of Parkinson's disease by autotransplantation of adrenal tissue
M01RR-02558-07 0043 (CLR) JOHNSON, PHILIP C General clinical research center Host susceptibility to Norwalk virus
M01RR-02558-07 0048 (CLR) HOOTS, W KEITH General clinical research center Hemophilia growth and development study
M01RR-02558-07 0049 (CLR) GLEASON, WALLACE A General clinical research center Tryptophan ethyl ester therapy for Hartnup disease
M01RR-02558-07 0050 (CLR) SELLIN, JOSEPH H General clinical research center Role of milk in the prevention of aspirin induced gastric erosions
M01RR-02558-07 0051 (CLR) PORTMAN, RONALD J General clinical research center Prevention of cisplatin nephrotoxicity by the use of L-thyroxine
M01RR-02558-07 0052 (CLR) LEWIS, RICHARD M General clinical research center Renal allograft function in patients with long term cyclosporin A therapy
M01RR-02558-07 0053 (CLR) KAHAN, BARRY D General clinical research center Enisoprost vs placebo on reversal of chronic & stable renal insufficiency
M01RR-02558-07 0054 (CLR) KAHAN, BARRY D General clinical research center Enisoprost, placebo and cyclosporine in renal transplant recipients
M01RR-02558-07 0055 (CLR) LOWLEY, SUSAN General clinical research center Circadian airway function of nocturnal asthmatics on exercise performance
M01RR-02558-07 0057 (CLR) SMOLENSKY, MICHAEL H General clinical research center Circadian rhythmicity in pharmacological effects of diphenhydramine
M01RR-02558-07 0058 (CLR) HOOTS, W KEITH General clinical research center Recombinant DNA factor VIII in hemophilia A patients
M01RR-02558-07 0059 (CLR) SMYTHE, CHEVES MCC General clinical research center Misdiagnosis of left ventricular failure in the very old
M01RR-02558-07 0060 (CLR) PICKERING, LARRY K General clinical research center IV immunoglobulin as treatment in children with AIDS receiving AZT
M01RR-02558-07 0061 (CLR) DOYLE, MARILYN G General clinical research center Comparison of ddI and AZT in patients with AIDS
M01RR-02558-07 0062 (CLR) DOYLE, MARILYN G General clinical research center ddI administered twice daily to AZT intolerant patients with AIDS
M01RR-02558-07 0063 (CLR) DOYLE, MARILYN G General clinical research center High versus low dosage AZT in symtomatic HIV infected children
M01RR-02558-07 0064 (CLR) GATELEY, ANN General clinical research center Bone density and gonadal function in male long distance runners
M01RR-02558-07 0065 (CLR) SCHNEIDER, VICTOR S General clinical research center Prevention of disuse osteoporosis from bed rest--Effect of naproxen
M01RR-02558-07 0066 (CLR) NORTHRUP, HOPE General clinical research center Tuberous sclerosis--Clinical and genetic studies
M01RR-02558-07 0067 (CLR) WHELESS, JAMES General clinical research center Gabapentin in monotherapy in naive childhood absence epilepsy
M01RR-02558-07 0068 (CLR) CONLEY, SUSAN B General clinical research center Recombinant growth hormone and chronic renal insufficiency
M01RR-02558-07 0069 (CLR) LEMIRE, JACQUES M General clinical research center Cyclosporine pharmacokinetics in pediatric renal transplant recipients
M01RR-02558-07 0070 (CLR) CONLAN, MAUREEN G General clinical research center Effects of omega-3 fatty acids on hemostasis in normal human subjects
M01RR-02558-07 0071 (CLR) BULL, JOAN M C General clinical research center Metabolic imaging by PET of thermochemotherapy response
P41RR-02583-07 (SSS) PEISACH, JACK ALBERT EINSTEIN COLL OF MED 1300 MORRIS PARK AVENUE BRONX NY 10461 Biotechnology resource in pulsed EPR spectroscopy
P41RR-02583-07 0001 (SSS) AISEN, PHILIP Biotechnology resource in pulsed EPR spectroscopy Fe(111) complexes of transferrin
P41RR-02583-07 0002 (SSS) AISEN, PHILIP Biotechnology resource in pulsed EPR spectroscopy Uteroferrin
P41RR-02583-07 0008 (SSS) BENKOVIC, STEPHEN Biotechnology resource in pulsed EPR spectroscopy Phenylalanine hydroxylase
P41RR-02583-07 0012 (SSS) PALMER, GRAHAM Biotechnology resource in pulsed EPR spectroscopy Eseem characteristics of Bis-histidine & histidine-lysine heme
P41RR-02583-07 0013 (SSS) QUE, LAWRENCE Biotechnology resource in pulsed EPR spectroscopy Isopenicillin N synthase
P41RR-02583-07 0014 (SSS) SCHOLES, CHARLES Biotechnology resource in pulsed EPR spectroscopy Endonuclease III
P41RR-02583-07 0009 (SSS) CAMMACK, RICHARD Biotechnology resource in pulsed EPR spectroscopy Hydrogenase and Fe-S proteins
P41RR-02583-07 0010 (SSS) DOOLEY, DAVID Biotechnology resource in pulsed EPR spectroscopy The copper site in amine oxidases
P41RR-02583-07 0011 (SSS) MCMILLIN, DAVID Biotechnology resource in pulsed EPR spectroscopy Type 2 sites in copper oxidases
P41RR-02583-07 0015 (SSS) STUBBE, JOANN Biotechnology resource in pulsed EPR spectroscopy Tyrosyl radical dependent ribonucleotide reductase
P41RR-02583-07 9001 (SSS) PEISACH, JACK Biotechnology resource in pulsed EPR spectroscopy Development of spin-echo capability
P41RR-02583-07 9003 (SSS) PEISACH, JACK Biotechnology resource in pulsed EPR spectroscopy Low spin heme proteins and model compounds
P41RR-02583-07 9004 (SSS) PEISACH, JACK Biotechnology resource in pulsed EPR spectroscopy Single crystal protein studies
P41RR-02583-07 9005 (SSS) PEISACH, JACK Biotechnology resource in pulsed EPR spectroscopy Manganese 17o interactions
P41RR-02594-06 (SSS) FELD, MICHAEL S MASSACHUSETTS INST OF TECH 77 MASSACHUSETTS AVENUE CAMBRIDGE, MA 02139 A biotechnology resource center for research in lasers and medicine
P41RR-02594-06 0001 (SSS) JACQUES, S A biotechnology resource center for research in lasers and medicine Radiative transport theory for spectroscopy in turbid tissue
P41RR-02594-06 0002 (SSS) JACGUES, S A biotechnology resource center for research in lasers and medicine Time-resolved measurements of reflectance and transmittance
P41RR-02594-06 0003 (SSS) OSEROFF, A A biotechnology resource center for research in lasers and medicine Fluorescent dyes--Tumor detection and diagnosis
P41RR-02594-06 0004 (SSS) COTHERN, R A biotechnology resource center for research in lasers and medicine In vivo laser-induced autofluorescence spectroscopy
P41RR-02594-06 0005 (SSS) COTHERN, R A biotechnology resource center for research in lasers and medicine Laser-induced autofluorescence microspectroscopy of ceroid deposits
P41RR-02594-06 0006 (SSS) FITZMAURICE, M A biotechnology resource center for research in lasers and medicine Spectral diagnosis of neoplasia in human urinary bladder and colon tissue
P41RR-02594-06 0007 (SSS) GAN, L A biotechnology resource center for research in lasers and medicine Fluorescence methods for molecular dosimetry of carcinogens
P41RR-02594-06 0008 (SSS) MOCKEL, M A biotechnology resource center for research in lasers and medicine Microscope laser light scattering spectroscopy of bile secretion
P41RR-02594-06 0009 (SSS) KRAMER, J A biotechnology resource center for research in lasers and medicine Development on in vivo spectral imaging device for atherosclerosis
P41RR-02594-06 9001 (SSS) FELD, MICHAEL S A biotechnology resource center for research in lasers and medicine Microscopic laser light scattering of biological cells and structures
P41RR-02594-06 9002 (SSS) FELD, MICHAEL S A biotechnology resource center for research in lasers and medicine Spectral diagnostics for medical research studies--Core research
P41RR-02594-06 9003 (SSS) FELD, MICHAEL S A biotechnology resource center for research in lasers and medicine Visible/IR laser ablation of tissue--Core research
M01RR-02602-07 (CLR) WILSON, EMERY A UNIVERSITY OF KENTUCKY 800 ROSE STREET LEXINGTON, KY 40536-0084 General clinical research center
M01RR-02602-07 0004 (CLR) HUMPHRIES, LAURIE L General clinical research center Zinc and eating disorders
M01RR-02602-07 0030 (CLR) GRINES, CINDY L General clinical research center Trial comparing full dose tPA to concomitant tPA and streptokinase MI
M01RR-02602-07 0035 (CLR) YOUNG, A BRYON General clinical research center Zinc supplementation in cognitive rehabilitation of severe brain injury
M01RR-02602-07 0037 (CLR) KNAPP, CHARLES F General clinical research center Smokeless tobacco and blood pressure
M01RR-02602-07 0038 (CLR) GUTHRIE, GORDON P General clinical research center Effect of converting enzyme inhibition upon proximal nephron function
M01RR-02602-07 0045 (CLR) MCCLAIN, C J General clinical research center Protein therapy with anabolic steroids in alcoholic hepatitis
M01RR-02602-07 0046 (CLR) BLOUIN, ROBERT A General clinical research center Age and propranolol enantiomeric kinetics and dynamics
M01RR-02602-07 0047 (CLR) MCCLAIN, CRAIG J General clinical research center Alcoholic hepatitis--The role of cytokines
M01RR-02602-07 0048 (CLR) CHANDLER, MARY H H General clinical research center Terbutaline and the effects of age on beta-2 adrenoceptor sensitivity
M01RR-02602-07 0039 (CLR) GUTHRIE, GORDON P General clinical research center Ambulatory blood pressure monitoring in systolic hypertensive pts. & ctl.
M01RR-02602-07 0041 (CLR) CLIFTON, G DENNIS General clinical research center Differential sensitivity of sinus node & ventricular myocardium to timolol
M01RR-02602-07 0042 (CLR) GUTHRIE, GORDON P General clinical research center Pituitary adrenal axis in a patient with Addison's disease and pregnancy
M01RR-02602-07 0043 (CLR) GUTHRIE, GORDON P General clinical research center Verapamil treatment of primary aldosteronism
M01RR-02602-07 0044 (CLR) YOUNG, A BYRON General clinical research center Asymptomatic carotid artery plaque study (ACAPS)
M01RR-02602-07 0049 (CLR) THOMPSON, JOHN S General clinical research center Monoclonal antibody therapy for kidney transplant rejection
M01RR-02602-07 0050 (CLR) SHEDLOFSKY, STEVEN I General clinical research center Effects of cytokines on hepatic drug metabolism
M01RR-02602-07 0051 (CLR) MCCUBBIN, JAMES A General clinical research center Endogenous opiates, stress and risk of hypertension
M01RR-02602-07 0052 (CLR) NEEFE, JOHN R General clinical research center Phase II study of infusion of recombinant IL-2, renal cell carcinoma
M01RR-02602-07 0053 (CLR) MARSANO, LUIS S General clinical research center Arginine benzoate for treatment of portal systemic encephalopathy

M01RR-02602-07 0054 (CLR) BLONDER, LEE X General clinical research center Disorders of emotion in brain-impaired subjects

M01RR-02602-07 0055 (CLR) KASARSKIS, EDWARD General clinical research center Pilot Study--Branched chain amino acids and enteral nutrition in ALS

M01RR-02602-07 0056 (CLR) SLEVIN, JOHN T General clinical research center Effect of IV infusion of calcium, phenytoin and verapamil on tremors

M01RR-02635-07 (CLR) NESSON, H RICHARD BRIGHAM & WOMEN'S HOSPITAL 75 FRANCIS STREET BOSTON, MA 02115 General clinical research center

M01RR-02635-07 0235 (CLR) DLUHY, ROBERT G General clinical research center Efficacy of Sandoz CV205-502 in prolactinoma

M01RR-02635-07 0237 (CLR) SLEDGE, CLEMENT B General clinical research center Development of radiation synovectomy in rheumatoid arthritis

M01RR-02635-07 0238 (CLR) WILLIAMS, GORDON H General clinical research center Renal hemodynamic response to captopril

M01RR-02635-07 0239 (CLR) ANTIN, JOSEPH General clinical research center Allogeneic BMT for Hodgkin's disease and non-Hodgkin's lymphoma

M01RR-02635-07 0242 (CLR) ANTIN, JOSEPH General clinical research center Ex vivo treatment with ST1 immunotoxin for prevention of GvHD

M01RR-02635-07 0243 (CLR) BROWN, EDWARD M General clinical research center Age-related bone loss and its response to therapy

M01RR-02635-07 0244 (CLR) WILLIAMS, GORDON H General clinical research center Renal sodium handling during acute volume expansion

M01RR-02635-07 0245 (CLR) STONE, PETER H General clinical research center Effect of nadolol on the morning increase in myocardial ischemia

M01RR-02635-07 0247 (CLR) MOORE, THOMAS J General clinical research center PTH potentiation of AII induced aldosterone secretion

M01RR-02635-07 0248 (CLR) BROWN, EDWARD M General clinical research center Nasal calcitonin in the prevention of osteoporosis

M01RR-02635-07 0250 (CLR) EBERLEIN, TIMOTHY J General clinical research center The effect of IL-2 and tumor-infiltrating lymphocytes

M01RR-02635-07 0251 (CLR) COOK, SANDRA General clinical research center Disordered sodium regulation and hypertensive complications of pregnancy

M01RR-02635-07 0253 (CLR) WEINER, HOWARD L General clinical research center Treatment of multiple sclerosis by oral tolerization to myelin antigen

M01RR-02635-07 0254 (CLR) DLUHY, ROBERT G General clinical research center Sandoz CV205-502 vs. bromocriptine in microprolactinoma

M01RR-02635-07 0256 (CLR) GOLDHABER, SAMUEL Z General clinical research center Utility of pneumatic compression in chronic venous insufficiency

M01RR-02635-07 0257 (CLR) HIRSCH, ALAN T General clinical research center Neurohormonal, vascular, and renal effects of SCH34826 in pts. w/ CHF

M01RR-02635-07 0261 (CLR) BARSS, VANESSA General clinical research center PGE2 pessary for cervical ripening for labor induction

M01RR-02635-07 0262 (CLR) BUNN, H F General clinical research center Treatment of sickle cell anemia with erythropoietin

M01RR-02635-07 0263 (CLR) CZEISLER, CHARLES A General clinical research center Disrupted sleep in the elderly--Circadian etiology

M01RR-02635-07 0264 (CLR) CZEISLER, CHARLES A General clinical research center Development of a clinical method for determining the circadian phase

M01RR-02635-07 0267 (CLR) MOORE, THOMAS J General clinical research center Renin inhibitor A64662--Vascular and hormonal effects

M01RR-02635-07 0268 (CLR) HIRSCH, ALAN T General clinical research center Effects of sodium on baroreflex function in man

M01RR-02635-07 0269 (CLR) KOPPLEMAN, MICHELLE General clinical research center Effect of diet on urinary hydroxyproline and serum Gla protein

M01RR-02635-07 0270 (CLR) EISENBARTH, GEORGE General clinical research center Therapy with H65 ricin A chain conjugate in Type I diabetes

M01RR-02635-07 0271 (CLR) WILMORE, DOUGLAS W General clinical research center Metabolic effects of endotoxin

M01RR-02635-07 0272 (CLR) WILMORE, DOUGLAS W General clinical research center Body compositional studies in healthy volunteers

M01RR-02635-07 0273 (CLR) BARBIERI, ROBERT General clinical research center Acute alcohol ingestion and effects on the half-life of estrogen

M01RR-02635-07 0274 (CLR) GOLDHABER, SAMUEL Z General clinical research center Urokinase to treat deep vein thrombosis

M01RR-02635-07 0275 (CLR) WALDMAN, STEPHANIE General clinical research center Nalmefene reversal of systemic effects of intrathecal morphine

M01RR-02635-07 0276 (CLR) BARBIERI, ROBERT L General clinical research center Endocrine changes in women with PMS following mCPP challenge

M01RR-02635-07 0277 (CLR) BROWN, EDWARD M General clinical research center Hormone replacement therapy for osteoporosis

M01RR-02635-07 0278 (CLR) BECKER, JAMES M General clinical research center Assessment of ileal pouch function and dysfunction

M01RR-02635-07 0138 (CLR) BARIBIERI, ROBERT General clinical research center Radiometric analysis of estrogen metabolism among oarswomen

M01RR-02635-07 0141 (CLR) BRENNER, BARRY M General clinical research center Enalapril and the progression of renal disease

M01RR-02635-07 0142 (CLR) BROWN, EDWARD M General clinical research center Normal and abnormal parathyroid function

M01RR-02635-07 0150 (CLR) CZEISLER, CHARLES General clinical research center Mechanisms underlying resetting of the circadian oscillator

M01RR-02635-07 0171 (CLR) WEINER, HOWARD L General clinical research center Northeastern cooperative multiple sclerosis treatment group II

M01RR-02635-07 0177 (CLR) WILMORE, DOUGLAS W General clinical research center Effect of human growth hormone on nitrogen balance in catabolism

M01RR-02635-07 0184 (CLR) MOORE, THOMAS J General clinical research center Identifying salt-sensitive hypertension

M01RR-02635-07 0190 (CLR) SWARTZ, STEPHEN L General clinical research center Captopril vs diuretic vs placebo on AII induced platelet aggregation

M01RR-02635-07 0191 (CLR) RABINOWE, STEVEN General clinical research center Evaluation of sympatho-adrenal medullary function in diabetes

M01RR-02635-07 0194 (CLR) ANTIN, JOSEPH General clinical research center Autologous BMT with ex vivo purging with 4-HC for patients with ANLL

M01RR-02635-07 0195 (CLR) WALSH, BRIAN W General clinical research center Postmenopausal estrogens and apolipoprotein B metabolism

M01RR-02635-07 0198 (CLR) SACKS, FRANK General clinical research center Reversal of coronary atherosclerosis by diet/drug therapy (H.A.R.P.)

M01RR-02635-07 0279 (CLR) HOLLENBERG, NORMAN K General clinical research center The effect of benazepril in salt-sensitive hypertension

M01RR-02635-07 0280 (CLR) BITTL, JOHN General clinical research center Coronary laser angioplasty

M01RR-02635-07 0281 (CLR) MULLER, JAMES General clinical research center Comparison of betaxolol & atenolol on response to mental & phys. stress

M01RR-02635-07 0282 (CLR) MULLER, JAMES General clinical research center Comparison of the effects of metoprolol and propranolol on coagulability

M01RR-02635-07 0283 (CLR) STONE, PETER H General clinical research center Mental stress and the provocation of myocardial ischemia

M01RR-02635-07 0284 (CLR) WILLIAMS, GORDON H General clinical research center Digitalis-like factors in renal failure

M01RR-02635-07 0285 (CLR) YEH, JOHN General clinical research center Hypothalamic-pituitary-adrenal function in smokers

M01RR-02635-07 0286 (CLR) HU, HOWARD General clinical research center The metabolic fate of lead burden during lactation

M01RR-02635-07 0287 (CLR) SIMONSON, DONALD C General clinical research center Cytosolic calcium, insulin-resistance and non-modulation

M01RR-02635-07 0288 (CLR) SIMONSON, DONALD C General clinical research center Mechanism of metabolic changes during intensive insulin therapy

M01RR-02635-07 0289 (CLR) WILLIAMS, WINFRED W JR General clinical research center Renal function in predialysis patients receiving rHuEPO

M01RR-02635-07 0290 (CLR) CZEISLER, CHARLES A General clinical research center Early awakening in healthy vs. depressed elderly--Circadian evaluation

M01RR-02635-07 0206 (CLR) PFEFFER, MARC General clinical research center Survival and ventricular enlargement (SAVE)--Effects of captopril

M01RR-02635-07 0216 (CLR) WILMORE, DOUGLAS W General clinical research center Effects of methionine-free growth hormone treatment on nitrogen retention

M01RR-02635-07 0291 (CLR) MENDELSOHN, MICHAEL E General clinical research center Simvastatin vs. lovastatin in patients with hypercholesterolemia

M01RR-02635-07 0292 (CLR) PFEFFER, MARC A General clinical research center Cholesterol and recurrent events (CARE)

M01RR-02635-07 0293 (CLR) CZEISLER, CHARLES A General clinical research center Comparison of pravastatin and lovastatin

M01RR-02635-07 0294 (CLR) ANTIN, JOSEPH General clinical research center ST1-RTA immunotoxin for unrelated donor bone marrow transplants

M01RR-02635-07 0295 (CLR) CZEISLER, CHARLES A General clinical research center Circadian rhythms of blind persons

M01RR-02635-07 0296 (CLR) GRAVES, STEVEN General clinical research center Effect of dietary sodium on pregnancy induced hypertension

M01RR-02635-07 0297 (CLR) BROWN, EDWARD M General clinical research center Calcium homeostasis in lactating and nonlactating women

M01RR-02635-07 0223 (CLR) MULLER, JAMES E General clinical research center Effect of nadolol on the circadian variability of platelet aggregation

M01RR-02635-07 0228 (CLR) KNAPP, ROBERT General clinical research center Radio-immunotherapy of ovarian cancer

M01RR-02635-07 0229 (CLR) HU, HOWARD General clinical research center Lead, blood pressure, and renal function in two study populations

M01RR-02635-07 0232 (CLR) KELLEY, VICKI General clinical research center Fish oil inhibition of cyclosporine nephrotoxicity

M01RR-02635-07 0233 (CLR) SPEIZER, FRANK General clinical research center Early risk predictors for chronic pulmonary disease

M01RR-02719-06 (CLR) JOHNS, MICHAEL E JOHNS HOPKINS UNIVERSITY 720 RUTLAND AVE BALTIMORE, MD 21205 General clinical research center

M01RR-02719-06 0124 (CLR) BUSBY, M. JANETTE General clinical research center Aerobic capacity and metabolic function in seniors

M01RR-02719-06 0126 (CLR) HARMAN, S MITCHELL General clinical research center Effects of age on regulation of hypothalmic-pituitary-adrenal axis in men

M01RR-02719-06 0127 (CLR) ENGELHARDT, SUSAN General clinical research center Obesity, conditioning, age, and sertraline effects on metabolism

M01RR-02719-06 0128 (CLR) RICAURTE, GEORGE A General clinical research center MDMA neurotoxicity in humans--Occurrence and consequences

M01RR-02719-06 0129 (CLR) CRITCHFIELD, THOMAS General clinical research center Diazepam and buspirone in light and social drinkers

M01RR-02719-06 0130 (CLR) BENNETT, RICHARD G General clinical research center Immunogenicity, safety, and tolerability of hepatitis B vaccine

M01RR-02719-06 0131 (CLR) ORIANI, JULIA General clinical research center Physical activity, obesity, age related difference in flavor perception

M01RR-02719-06 0132 (CLR) BLEECKER, MARGIT General clinical research center Relationship of neurobehavioral aging with risk

PROJECT NO., ORGANIZATIONAL UNIT., INVESTIGATOR, ADDRESS, TITLE

factors
M01RR-02719-06 0133 (CLR) STEWART, KERRY J General clinical research center Effects of propranolol & diltiazem on exercise training in hypertensive patients
M01RR-02719-06 0135 (CLR) WHITEHEAD, WILLIAM E General clinical research center Nalmefene glucuronide in the treatment of consitpation-predominate IBS
M01RR-02719-06 0136 (CLR) SPECTOR, DAVID A General clinical research center Effect of dietary phosphate restriction on the renal hemodynamic response
M01RR-02719-06 0137 (CLR) BUSBY, MARY J General clinical research center Dyslipoproteinemia in silent myocardial ischemia
M01RR-02719-06 0138 (CLR) CHEW, PAUL H General clinical research center Effects of pacing on diurnal cardiac function in patients
M01RR-02719-06 0139 (CLR) WHITEHEAD, WILLIAM E General clinical research center Low dose erythromycin and gastrointestinal motility
M01RR-02719-06 0140 (CLR) WHITEHEAD, WILLIAM E General clinical research center Gastrointestinal motility and transit in anorexia and bulimia
M01RR-02719-06 0141 (CLR) HARMAN, S MITCHELL General clinical research center Hormone replacement therapy in a geriatric population--Clinical side effects
M01RR-02719-06 0142 (CLR) CHEW, PAUL H General clinical research center Effects of two pacer rates on affect states in patients with demand atrial pacing
M01RR-02719-06 0143 (CLR) GOLDBERG, ANDREW P General clinical research center Effect of acute and chronic exercise on glucose and lipid metabolism
M01RR-02719-06 0144 (CLR) HARMAN, S MITCHELL General clinical research center Effects of constant subcutaneous GHRH administration, two different doses
M01RR-02719-06 0145 (CLR) COON, PATRICIA J General clinical research center Metabolic and hemodynamic consequences of hyperinsulimenia
M01RR-02719-06 0146 (CLR) COON, PATRICIA J General clinical research center Aging, obesity, physical exercise, and endocrine metabolic function
M01RR-02719-06 0003 (CLR) LUI, MARK D General clinical research center Immediate hypersensitivity and obstructive airways disease
M01RR-02719-06 0007 (CLR) GOLDBERG, ANDREW P. General clinical research center Physical activity, cardiac and metabolic function in old men
M01RR-02719-06 0009 (CLR) CHESKIN, LAWRENCE J General clinical research center Psychophysiology of irritable bowel syndrome
M01RR-02719-06 0011 (CLR) SHAPIRO, JAY R General clinical research center Johns Hopkins academic teaching nursing home award
M01RR-02719-06 0013 (CLR) LIEBSON, IRA A General clinical research center Sedative sensitivity in children of alcoholics
M01RR-02719-06 0016 (CLR) BOLLA, KAREN General clinical research center Neurological effects of environmental aluminum exposure
M01RR-02719-06 0018 (CLR) ZACKARY, JIM B General clinical research center Enalapril vs hydrochlorthiazide and diabetic nephropathy
M01RR-02719-06 0021 (CLR) WHITEHEAD, WILLIAM E General clinical research center Eval. of cisapride for treatment of gastrointestinal motor dysfunction
M01RR-02719-06 0023 (CLR) LIEBSON, IRA A General clinical research center Naloxone precipitated morphine withdrawal on post-addicts and normals
M01RR-02719-06 0115 (CLR) COON, PATRICIA J General clinical research center Glucose and lipid metabolism in obese aged men
M01RR-02719-06 0116 (CLR) KAWAS, CLAUDIA H. General clinical research center Effects of THA in patients with Alzheimer's disease
M01RR-02719-06 0121 (CLR) DENNIS, KAREN E General clinical research center Self-directed strategies for weight loss and maintenance
P41RR-02722-05 (SSS) LEWIS, JON C BOWMAN GRAY SCHOOL OF MEDICINE MEDICAL CENTER BLVD WINSTON-SALEM, NC 27157 Intermediate voltage electron microscopy in medicine
S03RR-03000-11 (NSS) BENNETT, L LEE, JR SOUTHERN RESEARCH INSTITUTE POST OFFICE BOX 55305 BIRMINGHAM, ALA 35255 Minority high school student research apprentice program
S03RR-03001-11 (NSS) HICKEY, TERRY L UNIV OF ALABAMA/UAB STATION 102 MORTIMER JORDAN HALL BIRMINGHAM, AL 35294 Minority high school student research apprentice program
S03RR-03002-11 (NSS) HICKEY, TERRY L UNIV OF ALABAMA/UAB STATION 102 MORTIMER JORDAN HALL BIRMINGHAM, AL 35294 Minority high school student research apprentice program
S03RR-03003-11 (NSS) COGGIN, JOSEPH H UNIVERSITY OF SOUTH ALABAMA MEDICAL SCIENCES BLDG, RM 1005 MOBILE, ALABAMA 36688 Minority high school student research apprentice program
S03RR-03004-10 (NSS) WITTE, MARLYS H UNIVERSITY OF ARIZONA 1501 N CAMPBELL AVENUE TUCSON, AZ 85724 Minority high school student research apprentice program
S03RR-03005-04 (NSS) MARR, ALLEN G UNIVERSITY OF CALIFORNIA 275 MRAK HALL DAVIS, CA 95616 Minority high school student research apprentice program
S03RR-03006-04 (NSS) HANSEN, ROBERT J UNIVERSITY OF CALIFORNIA SCHOOL OF VETERINARY MEDICINE DAVIS, CA 95616 Minority high school student research apprentice program
S03RR-03009-11 (NSS) RUSSELL, PERCY J UNIV OF CALIFORNIA, SAN DIEGO BASIC SCIENCE BUILDING LA JOLLA, CALIF 92093 Minority high school student research apprentice program
S03RR-03010-09 (NSS) GILULA, NORTON B SCRIPPS CLINIC & RES FDN 10666 N TORREY PINES RD LA JOLLA, CA 92037 Minority high school student research apprentice program
S03RR-03011-08 (NSS) BRINTON, ROBERTA E UNIV OF SOUTHERN CALIFORNIA 1985 ZONAL AVENUE LOS ANGELES, CALIF 90033 Minority high school student research apprentice program
S03RR-03012-10 (NSS) YAMAMOTO, JOE UCLA NEUROPSYCHIATRIC INST 760 WESTWOOD PLAZA LOS ANGELES, CALIF 90024 Minority high school student research apprentice program
S03RR-03015-11 (NSS) LUBIN, BERTRAM H CHILDRENS HOSPITAL 747-52ND STREET OAKLAND, CALIF 94609 Minority high school student research apprentice program

PROJECT NO., ORGANIZATIONAL UNIT., INVESTIGATOR, ADDRESS, TITLE

S03RR-03017-07 (NSS) RAMSAY, DAVID J UNIVERSITY OF CALIFORNIA 100 MEDICAL CTR WAY SAN FRANCISCO, CA 94143 Minority high school student research apprentice program
S03RR-03018-11 (NSS) FU, PAUL C HARBOR-UCLA MEDICAL CENTER 1000 W CARSON STREET TORRANCE, CALIF 90509 Minority high school student research apprentice program
S03RR-03019-11 (NSS) DUBIN, MARK J UNIVERSITY OF COLORADO CAMPUS BOX B-19 BOULDER, CO 80309-0019 Minority high school student research apprentice program
G12RR-03020-07 (SRC) HUMPHRIES, FREDERICK S FLORIDA A & M UNIVERSITY COR/M KING BLVD & GAMBLE ST TALLAHASSEE, FLA 32307 Pharmaceutical research center
G12RR-03020-07 0001 (SRC) SOLIMAN, KARAM F Pharmaceutical research center Research fellowship
G12RR-03020-07 0002 (SRC) LEE, HENRY J Pharmaceutical research center Research center for drug design and development
G12RR-03020-07 0003 (SRC) BLYDEN, GERSHWIN T Pharmaceutical research center Clinical pharmacology research unit
G12RR-03020-07 9001 (SRC) HICKS, PAULINE Pharmaceutical research center Library support
G12RR-03020-07 9002 (SRC) SOLIMAN, MAGDI R Pharmaceutical research center Animal facility improvement
S03RR-03021-11 (NSS) MILLER, CHARLES W COLORADO STATE UNIVERSITY DEPARTMENT OF PHYSIOLOGY FORT COLLINS, COLO 80523 Minority high school student research apprentice program
S03RR-03022-09 (NSS) MILLER, CHARLES W DEPT OF PHYSIOLOGY COLORADO STATE UNIVERSITY FT COLLINS, CO 80523 Minority high school student research apprentice program
S03RR-03023-10 (NSS) SANFORD, KEAT M UNIVERSITY OF CONNECTICUT FARMINGTON, CONN 06032 Minority high school student research apprentice program
S03RR-03024-11 (NSS) GIFFORD, ROBERT H YALE UNIV, SCH OF MED 367 CEDAR STREET NEW HAVEN, CT 06510 Minority high school student research apprentice program
S03RR-03025-10 (NSS) DOEG, KENNETH A UNIV OF CONNECTICUT 75 N EAGLEVILLE ROAD STORRS, CT 06269-3125 Minority high school student research apprentice program
G12RR-03026-05S1 (SRC) WILLIAMS, HENRY S CHARLES R DREW POSTGRAD MED SC 1621 EAST 120TH ST, MP #27 LOS ANGELES, CA 90059 Charles R Drew institutional research
S03RR-03026-11 (NSS) WILLIAMS, JOY P GEORGETOWN UNIV #14 BUTLER BDG 3900 RESERVOIR RD NW WASHINGTON, D C 20007 Minority high school student research apprentice program
S03RR-03027-10 (NSS) ASHE, WARREN K HOWARD UNIVERSITY 520 W STREET, N W WASHINGTON, D C 20059 Minority high school student research apprentice program
S03RR-03029-09 (NSS) ABBOTT, ELIZABETH F UNIVERSITY OF FLORIDA 452 LITTLE HALL DSSSP GAINESVILLE, FLA 32611 Minority high school student research apprentice program
S03RR-03031-11 (NSS) WILLIAMS, MARVIN T 12901 BRUCE B DOWNS BLVD UNIV S FLORIDA MDC BOX 7 TAMPA, FL 33612-4799 Minority high school student research apprentice program
G12RR-03032-07 (SRC) SATCHER, DAVID MEHARRY MEDICAL COLLEGE 1005 TODD BOULEVARD NASHVILLE, TN 37208 Research infrastructure for scientific excellence
G12RR-03032-07 0001 (SRC) TOWNSWL, JAMES G Research infrastructure for scientific excellence Neuroscience component
G12RR-03032-07 0002 (SRC) EVANS, STANLEY L Research infrastructure for scientific excellence Synthesis of non-nucleosidic antiviral agents
G12RR-03032-07 0003 (SRC) HATCHER, FRANK Research infrastructure for scientific excellence pilot--Congenital/perinatal HIV infection--Immune system development effect
G12RR-03032-07 0004 (SRC) OHI, SEIGO Research infrastructure for scientific excellence Pilot--Recombinant adeno-associated virus for AIDS gene therapy
G12RR-03032-07 9001 (SRC) DOLCE, PETER J Research infrastructure for scientific excellence Research support services core
S03RR-03032-11 (NSS) MORIARTY, C MICHAEL UNIVERSITY OF GEORGIA BOYD GRADUATE STUDIES RSCH CTR ATHENS, GA 30602 Minority high school student research apprentice program
G12RR-03033-06 (SRC) HEFNER, JAMES A TENNESSEE STATE UNIVERSITY 3500 JOHN A MERRIT BLVD NASHVILLE, TN 37209-1561 The center of bio-behavioral research on health
G12RR-03034-06 (SRC) GOODMAN, JAMES A MOREHOUSE SCHOOL OF MEDICINE 720 WESTVIEW DRIVE SW ATLANTA, GA 30310-1495 Enhancement of capacity for biomedical research
S03RR-03034-11 (NSS) THURMOND, VERA B MEDICAL COLLEGE OF GEORGIA DEPT OF MEDICINE AA-153 AUGUSTA, GA 30912-1900 Minority high school student research apprentice program
G12RR-03035-06 (SRC) MARCIAL-ROJAS, RAUL UNIVERSIDAD CENTRAL DEL CARIBE CALL BOX 60-327 BAYAMON, PR 00621-6032 Medical research center--Universidad Central Del Caribe
S03RR-03035-11 (NSS) DIRKSEN, THOMAS R MEDICAL COLLEGE OF GEORGIA SCHOOL OF DENTISTRY AUGUSTA, GA 30912 Minority high school student research apprentice program
S03RR-03036-11 (NSS) GREENWOOD, FREDERICK C UNIVERSITY OF HAWAII 1993 EAST WEST ROAD HONOLULU, HAWAII 96822 Minority high school student research apprentice program
G12RR-03037-07 (SRC) LECLERC, PAUL HUNTER COLLEGE 695 PARK AVENUE NEW YORK, NY 10021 A research center for study of gene structure and function
G12RR-03037-07 0001 (SRC) FRANK, RICHARD A research center for study of gene structure and function Drug design and synthesis--Anti-AIDS, anti-HIV, opportunistic infections
G12RR-03037-07 0002 (SRC) DOTTIN, ROBERT A research center for study of gene structure and function Reversible protein phosphorylation in the induction of HIV-1
G12RR-03037-07 0003 (SRC) LECLERC, PAUL A research center for study of gene structure and function RCMI Workshop
G12RR-03037-07 9001 (SRC) BOBIN, STEPHEN A research center for study of gene structure and function Core--Sequence and synthesis
G12RR-03037-07 9002 (SRC) LECLERC, PAUL A research center for study

of gene structure and function Biopreparation core
G12RR-03037-07 9003 (SRC) KRAKOW, JOSEPH A research center for study of gene structure and function Cell culture core
G12RR-03037-07 9004 (SRC) COHEN, WILLIAM A research center for study of gene structure and function Core--Electron microscopy and cytology
G12RR-03037-07 9005 (SRC) LECLERC, PAUL A research center for study of gene structure and function Core--AIDS infrastructure
S03RR-03037-10 (NSS) BOND, ISABEL E UNIVERSITY OF IDAHO UPWARD BOUND PROGRAM MOSCOW, IDAHO 83843 Minority high school student research apprentice program
S03RR-03038-09 (NSS) SCHUG, KENNETH R ILLINOIS INSTITUTE OF TECH DEPARTMENT OF CHEMISTRY CHICAGO, ILL 60616 Minority high school student research apprentice program
S03RR-03040-10 (NSS) WALLACE, WILLIAM D UNIV OF ILLINOIS 1853 WEST POLK STREET, RM 151 CHICAGO, ILL 60612 Minority high school student research apprentice program
S03RR-03041-11 (NSS) BOWEN, RAFAEL L AMERICAN DENTAL ASSN HLTH FDN 211 EAST CHICAGO AVENUE CHICAGO, ILL 60611 Minority high school student research apprentice program
S03RR-03042-10 (NSS) JOHNSON, MICHAEL E UNIVERSITY OF ILLINOIS 833 SOUTH WOOD STREET CHICAGO, ILL 60612 Minority high school student research apprentice program
S03RR-03043-10 (NSS) KRESHECK, GORDON C NORTHERN ILLINOIS UNIVERSITY DEPARTMENT OF CHEMISTRY DEKALB, ILL 60115 Minority high school student research apprentice program
S03RR-03044-09 (NSS) GOLDBERGER, GERALD N NORTHWESTERN UNIVERSITY 633 CLARK STREET EVANSTON, ILL 60208-1111 Minority high school student research apprentice program
G12RR-03045-06 (SRC) LEWIS, HENRY III TEXAS SOUTHERN UNIVIERSITY 3100 CLEBURNE STREET HOUSTON, TX 77004 Ethnic diseases--Pharmacokinetic and basic studies
S03RR-03045-05 (NSS) GROOTHUIS, DENNIS R EVANSTON HOSPITAL BURCH 200/2650 RIDGE EVANSTON, ILL 60201 Minority high school student research apprentice program
S03RR-03046-07 (NSS) HELPER, LLOYD C UNIVERSITY OF ILLINOIS 2001 S LINCOLN AVE URBANA, IL 61801 Minority high school student research apprentice program
S03RR-03047-11 (NSS) FRIEDMAN, STANLEY UNIVERSITY OF ILLINOIS 505 S GOODWIN URBANA, IL 61801 Minority high school student research apprentice program
G12RR-03048-07 (SRC) EPPS, CHARLES H HOWARD UNIVERSITY 520 W STREET, NW WASHINGTON, DC 20059 Howard University RCMI interdisciplinary program
S03RR-03048-10 (NSS) DUNNING, JEREMY D INDIANA UNIVERSITY IMU 662 BLOOMINGTON, IND 47405 Minority high school student research apprentice program
S03RR-03049-11 (NSS) BORELLI, MARIO UNIVERSITY OF NOTRE DAME COLLEGE OF SCIENCE NOTRE DAME, IND 46556 Minority high school student research apprentice program
G12RR-03050-07 (SRC) SALA, LUIS F PONCE SCHOOL OF MEDICINE UNIVERSITY STREET PONCE PR 00732-7004 Ponce school of medicine research center
G12RR-03050-07 0007 (SRC) YAMAMURA, YASUHIRO Ponce school of medicine research center RCMI AIDS infrastructure program
G12RR-03050-07 9001 (SRC) SALA, LUIS F Ponce school of medicine research center Core--Biomedical research facility
G12RR-03050-07 0001 (SRC) MASS, HOWARD J Ponce school of medicine research center Coronary vasodilation and regional myocardial function
G12RR-03050-07 0002 (SRC) YAMAMURA, YASUHIRO Ponce school of medicine research center PCR diagnosis of perinatal HIV infections--A Puerto Rico study
G12RR-03050-07 0003 (SRC) FRAZER, TERESA Ponce school of medicine research center Glucose turnover in infants with cerebral injury
G12RR-03050-07 0004 (SRC) SOTO, CALIXTO Ponce school of medicine research center Vasectomy effects on the leydig cells
G12RR-03050-07 0005 (SRC) HUPKA, ARTHUR Ponce school of medicine research center Environmental toxicology
G12RR-03050-07 0006 (SRC) MONTEALEGRE, FREDERICO Ponce school of medicine research center Clinical immunology-immunochemistry program
G12RR-03051-06 (SRC) MARINA, MANUEL UNIV PUERTO RICO MED SCI CAMPU GPO BOX 5067 SAN JUAN, PR 00936 Medical sciences campus research development
S03RR-03051-11 (NSS) MORRISON, JAMES D THE UNIVERSITY OF IOWA 201 GILMORE HALL IOWA CITY, IOWA 52242 Minority high school student research apprentice program
S03RR-03052-09 (NSS) WILLIAMS, MELVIN UNIVERSITY OF KANSAS 39TH AND RAINBOW BLVD KANSAS CITY, KS 66103 Minority high school student research apprentice program
S03RR-03053-11 (NSS) DIXON, WALTER R UNIVERSITY OF KANSAS 5044 MALOTT HALL LAWRENCE, KANS 66045 Minority high school student research apprentice program
S03RR-03058-11 (NSS) SHAYE, ROBERT LOUISIANA STATE UNIVERSITY 1100 FLORIDA AVENUE NEW ORLEANS, LA 70119 Minority high school student research apprentice program
G12RR-03059-04 (SRC) FERGUSON, JAMES A TUSKEGEE UNIVERSITY PATTERSON HALL DEAN'S OFFICE TUSKEGEE, AL 36088 Center for biomedical research
S03RR-03059-10 (NSS) LAMY, PETER P UNIVERSITY OF MARYLAND 20 N PINE STREET BALTIMORE, MD 21201 Minority high school student research apprentice program
G12RR-03060-07 (SRC) HARLESTON, BERNARD W CITY COLLEGE OF CUNY 138TH ST & CONVENT AVENUE NEW YORK NY 10031 Cellular/molecular basis of development--Research center
G12RR-03060-07 0001 (SRC) MESHNICK, STEVEN R Cellular/molecular basis of development--Research center Biochemistry and molecular biology of Pneumocystis carinii
G12RR-03060-07 0002 (SRC) COICO, RICHARD Cellular/molecular basis of development--Research center Modulation of CD4 expression by T-lymphocytes
G12RR-03060-07 0003 (SRC) BOTO, WILLIAM Cellular/molecular basis of development--Research center Signal for trans-activation of latent HIV-1 genome in T4 cells

PROJECT NO., ORGANIZATIONAL UNIT., INVESTIGATOR, ADDRESS, TITLE

G12RR-03060-07 0004 (SRC) BALOGH-NAIR, VALERIA Cellular/molecular basis of development--Research center Bioorganic studies
S03RR-03060-09 (NSS) GOLDBERG, ALAN M THE JOHNS HOPKINS UNIV 615 N WOLFE STREET BALTIMORE, MARYLAND 21205 Minority high school student research apprentice program
G12RR-03061-06 (SRC) SIMONE, ALBERT J UNIVERSITY OF HAWAII 2540 MAILE WAY HONOLULU HI 96822 Selective excellence in health-related research
S03RR-03061-09 (NSS) HARRELL, ROBERT L, JR UNIVERSITY OF MARYLAND 660 WEST REDWOOD STREET BALTIMORE, MD 21201 Minority high school student research apprentice program
G12RR-03062-07 (SRCA) JACKSON, JULIUS H CLARK ATLANTA UNIVERSITY JAMES P BRAWLEY DR AT FAIR ST ATLANTA, GA 30314 Clark Atlanta University biomedical science development
G12RR-03062-07 0001 (SRCA) WILLIAMS, ARTHUR L Clark Atlanta University biomedical science development Gene structure, function and regulation
G12RR-03062-07 0002 (SRCA) STEWART, JUARINE Clark Atlanta University biomedical science development Chemical modulation of cellular function
S03RR-03062-11 (NSS) EGETH, HOWARD E THE JOHNS HOPKINS UNIV AMES HALL, CHARLES & 34TH STS BALTIMORE, MARYLAND 21218 Minority high school student research apprentice program
S03RR-03063-10 (NSS) ANDERSON, AMEL UNIVERSITY OF MARYLAND 1224 SYMONS HALL COLLEGE PARK, MD 20742 Minority high school student research apprentice program
S03RR-03066-11 (NSS) LANNER, MICHAEL BETH ISRAEL HOSPITAL 330 BROOKLINE AVENUE BOSTON, MASS 02215 Minority high school student research apprentice program
S03RR-03068-05 (NSS) BAUMAN, RAQUEL TUFTS UNIVERSITY 136 HARRISON AVENUE BOSTON, MA 02111 Minority high school student research apprentice program
S03RR-03069-11 (NSS) BLOUT, ELKAN R HARVARD SCH OF PUBLIC HEALTH 677 HUNTINGTON AVENUE BOSTON, MASS 02115 Minority high school student research apprentice program
S03RR-03073-11 (NSS) PAUL, ARA G UNIVERSITY OF MICHIGAN COLLEGE OF PHARMACY ANN ARBOR, MICH 48109 Minority high school student research apprentice program
S03RR-03074-10 (NSS) KELLY, WILLIAM C UNIVERSITY OF MICHIGAN 4080 ADMINISTRATION BUILDING ANN ARBOR, MICH 48109 Minority high school student research apprentice program
S03RR-03075-10 (NSS) BOLE, GILES G JR UNIVERSITY OF MICHIGAN 1301 CATHERINE RD ANN ARBOR, MICH 48109 Minority high school student research apprentice program
S03RR-03076-10 (NSS) JACOBSON, JED J UNIVERSITY OF MICHIGAN 1011 NORTH UNIVERSITY AVENUE ANN ARBOR, MI 48109 Minority high school student research apprentice program
S03RR-03077-11 (NSS) DUMAS, RHETAUGH G UNIVERSITY OF MICHIGAN SCH NURSING 400 N INGALLS ANN ARBOR, MI 48109-0482 Minority high school student research apprentice program
S03RR-03078-11 (NSS) SHORE, JOSEPH D HENRY FORD HOSPITAL 2799 WEST GRAND BOULEVARD DETROIT, MICH 48202 Minority high school student research apprentice program
S03RR-03079-10 (NSS) BREDECK, HENRY E MICHIGAN STATE UNIVERSITY 238 ADMINISTRATION BUILDING EAST LANSING, MICH 48824 Minority high school student research apprentice program
S03RR-03080-11 (NSS) LOWRIE, PATRICIA M MICHIGAN STATE UNIVERSITY A-128 EAST FEE HALL EAST LANSING, MI 48824-1316 Minority high school student research apprentice program
S03RR-03081-11 (NSS) HENRY, EGBERT W OAKLAND UNIVERSITY ROCHESTER, MI 48309-4401 Minority high school student research apprentice program
S03RR-03082-11 (NSS) HOGENKAMP, HARRY P C UNIV OF MINN, 4-225 MLRDH 435 DELAWARE ST SE MINNEAPOLIS, MN 55455 Minority high school student research apprentice program
S03RR-03083-11 (NSS) SHIER, WAYNE T UNIVERSITY OF MINNESOTA 308 HARVARD STREET S.E. MINNEAPOLIS, MN 55455 Minority high school student research apprentice program
S03RR-03085-10 (NSS) BROWN, DAVID M UNIVERSITY OF MINNESOTA BOX 293 MAYO MINNEAPOLIS, MINN 55455 Minority high school student research apprentice program
S03RR-03086-11 (NSS) MITCHELL, EDITH UNIV OF MISSOURI-COLUMBIA 1 HOSPITAL DRIVE COLUMBIA, MO 65212 Minority high school student research apprentice program
S03RR-03087-07 (NSS) DAVID, JOHN D UNIV OF MISSOURI 105 TUCKER HALL COLUMBIA, MO 65211 Minority high school student research apprentice program
S03RR-03089-10 (NSS) NOLAN, CHARLES S WASHINGTON UNIVERSITY CAMPUS BOX 1089,1 BROOKINGS DR ST LOUIS, MO 63130 Minority high school student research apprentice program
S03RR-03090-11 (NSS) LEE, ROBERT WASHINGTON UNIVERSITY CAMPUS BOX 8023 ST LOUIS, MO 63110 Minority high school student research apprentice program
S03RR-03091-11 (NSS) YOUNG, DAVID M 303 CULBERTSON HALL MONTANA STATE UNIVERSITY BOZEMAN, MT 59717 Minority high school student research apprentice program
S03RR-03093-10 (NSS) WOODIN, TERRY S UNIVERSITY OF NEVADA RENO, NV 89557 Minority high school student research apprentice program
S03RR-03094-11 (NSS) FELDMAN, LAWRENCE A UMDNJ-N J MEDICAL SCHOOL 185 SOUTH ORANGE AVENUE NEWARK, NJ 07103-2714 Minority high school student research apprentice program
S03RR-03095-11 (NSS) STEIN, DONALD G RUTGERS UNIV/RM 401 HILL HALL 360 MARTIN LUTHER KING JR BLVD NEWARK, NJ 07102 Minority high school student research apprentice program
S03RR-03096-10 (NSS) EDELMAN, NORMAN H UMDNJ-ROBERT W J MEDICAL SCH 675 HOES LANE PISCATAWAY, N J 08854-5635 Minority high school student research apprentice program
S03RR-03097-10 (NSS) FRESCO, JACQUES R PRINCETON UNIVERSITY DEPT OF BIOCHEMICAL SCIENCES PRINCETON, N J 08544 Minority high school student research apprentice program
S03RR-03098-09 (NSS) SANCHEZ, RICHARD S UNIVERSITY OF NEW MEXICO UNIV COLLEGE BLDG RM 11 ALBUQUERQUE, NM 87131 Minority high school student research apprentice program

PROJECT NO., ORGANIZATIONAL UNIT., INVESTIGATOR, ADDRESS, TITLE

S03RR-03099-11 (NSS) ATENCIO, ALONZO C UNIV OF NEW MEXICO SCH MED BAS MED SCI BLDG RM 106 ALBUQUERQUE, NM 87131 Minority high school student research apprentice program

S03RR-03100-08 (NSS) KUEHN, GLENN D NEW MEXICO STATE UNIVERSITY BOX 3C LAS CRUCES, N M 88003 Minority high school student research apprentice program

S03RR-03101-11 (NSS) DICKERMAN, HERBERT W WADSWORTH CTR FOR LAB AND RES CORNING TOWER BLDG/EMPIRE S PL ALBANY, NY 12201 Minority high school student research apprentice program

S03RR-03102-10 (NSS) MIRAND, EDWIN A ROSWELL PARK MEMORIAL INST 666 ELM ST BUFFALO, N Y 14263 Minority high school student research apprentice program

S03RR-03103-06 (NSS) DUAX, WILLIAM L MEDICAL FDN OF BUFFALO, INC 73 HIGH STREET BUFFALO, NY 14203-1196 Minority high school student research apprentice program

S03RR-03105-11 (NSS) KELMAN, EUGENIA G CORNELL UNIVERSITY C-117 SCHURMAN HALL ITHACA, NY 14853-6401 Minority high school student research apprentice program

S03RR-03106-09 (NSS) HICKS, MELVIN L RESEARCH FDN / MENTAL HYGIENE 44 HOLLAND AVENUE ALBANY, N Y 12229 Minority high school student research apprentice program

S03RR-03107-10 (NSS) FAHEY, THOMAS J JR MEMORIAL HOSP/CANCER & ALLIED 1275 YORK AVENUE NEW YORK, N Y 10021 Minority high school student research apprentice program

S03RR-03110-04 (NSS) ZIMMERMAN, VEVA NEW YORK UNIVERSITY MEDICAL CT 550 FIRST AVENUE NEW YORK, N Y 10016 Minority high school student research apprentice program

S03RR-03112-11 (NSS) KAPLAN, HAROLD S NEW YORK BLOOD CENTER 310 EAST 67TH STREET NEW YORK, NY 10021 Minority high school student research apprentice program

S03RR-03113-10 (NSS) THOMPSON, ALBERT COLUMBIA UNIVERSITY 630 WEST 168TH STREET, ROOM 34 NEW YORK, N Y 10032 Minority high school student research apprentice program

S03RR-03114-08 (NSS) SHERMAN, LLOYD R MOUNT SINAI SCHOOL OF MEDICINE ONE GUSTAVE LEVY PLACE NEW YORK, N Y 10029 Minority high school student research apprentice program

S03RR-03115-10 (NSS) COHEN, SEYMOUR LONG ISLAND JEWISH MED CTR NEW HYDE PARK, N Y 11042 Minority high school student research apprentice program

S03RR-03119-07 (NSS) FLACK, YREANA-RENEE BROOKHAVEN NATIONAL LABORATORY DIRECTORS OFFICE BLDG 185A UPTON, N Y 11973 Minority high school student research apprentice program

R01RR-03120-06 (SSS) KOETZLE, THOMAS F BROOKHAVEN NATIONAL LABORATORY UPTON, NY 11973 Protein data bank--Data evaluation studies

S03RR-03120-11 (NSS) PHILLIPS, MARION UNIV OF NC/SCHOOL OF MEDICINE 126 MACNIDER BLDG, CB#7000 CHAPEL HILL, NC 27599-7000 Minority high school student research apprentice program

R24RR-03121-05 (AR) MORSE, STEPHEN S THE ROCKEFELLER UNIVERSITY 1230 YORK AVENUE NEW YORK, NY 10021-6399 Mouse thymic virus

S03RR-03121-11 (NSS) METCALF, ZUBIE W EAST CAROLINA UNIVERSITY SCHOOL OF MEDICINE GREENVILLE, NC 27858 Minority high school student research apprentice program

S03RR-03122-11 (NSS) HOWARD, DONALD R NORTH CAROLINA STATE UNIV 4700 HILLSBOROUGH STREET RALEIGH, N C 27606 Minority high school student research apprentice program

R24RR-03123-05 (AR) RUSSELL, ROBERT G UNIVERSITY OF MARYLAND 10 SOUTH PINE ST (MSTF/6-00E) BALTIMORE, MD 21201 Campylobacter immunity in primates

S03RR-03123-11 (NSS) DUNN, CHRISTOPHER S BOWLING GREEN STATE UNIVERSITY 120 MC FALL CENTER BOWLING GREEN, OHIO 43403 Minority high school student research apprentice program

S03RR-03125-11 (NSS) SCHUBERT, WILLIAM K CHILDREN'S HOSPITAL MED CENTER ELLAND AND BETHESDA AVENUES CINCINNATI, OHIO 45229 Minority high school student research apprentice program

R01RR-03126-04 (SSS) BERLINER, LAWRENCE J OHIO STATE UNIVERSITY 120 WEST EIGHTEENTH AVENUE COLUMBUS, OH 43210-1173 Topical in-vivo electron spin resonance

S03RR-03126-05 (NSS) KANESHIRO, EDNA S UNIVERSITY OF CINCINNATI BEECHER HALL CINCINNATI, OH 45221-0627 Minority high school student research apprentice program

S03RR-03127-11 (NSS) PHILLIPS, JAMES L CASE WESTERN RESERVE UNIV 2119 ABINGTON ROAD-RM T-412 CLEVELAND, OHIO 44106 Minority high school student research apprentice program

S03RR-03128-11 (NSS) MORROW, LESTER G OHIO STATE UNIVERSITY 1800 CANNON DRIVE COLUMBUS, OHIO 43210 Minority high school student research apprentice program

S03RR-03129-11 (NSS) MORROW, LESTER G OHIO STATE UNIVERSITY 1800 CANNON DRIVE COLUMBUS, OHIO 43210 Minority high school student research apprentice program

S03RR-03130-11 (NSS) MORROW, LESTER G OHIO STATE UNIVERSITY 1800 CANNON DRIVE COLUMBUS, OHIO 43210 Minority high school student research apprentice program

S03RR-03131-11 (NSS) MORROW, LESTER G OHIO STATE UNIVERSITY 1800 CANNON DRIVE COLUMBUS, OHIO 43210 Minority high school student research apprentice program

S03RR-03132-11 (NSS) REAM, LARRY J WRIGHT STATE UNIVERSITY DAYTON, OH 45435 Minority high school student research apprentice program

S03RR-03133-04 (NSS) BATRA, PREM P WRIGHT STATE UNIVERSITY 3640 COLONEL GLENN HIGHWAY DAYTON, OH 45435 Minority high school student research apprentice program

S03RR-03135-08 (NSS) CAMPBELL, COLIN NORTHEASTERN OHIO UNIVERSITY S R 44 ROOTSTOWN, OH 44272 Minority high school student research apprentice program

S03RR-03136-10 (NSS) RICHARDSON, BARRY L MEDICAL COLLEGE OF OHIO C S 10008 TOLEDO, OH 43699 Minority high school student research apprentice program

S03RR-03138-06 (NSS) WESTERFIELD, MONTE UNIVERSITY OF OREGON HUESTIS HALL EUGENE, OREGON 97403 Minority high school student research apprentice program

S03RR-03140-10 (NSS) KENDALL, JOHN OREGON HLTH SCI UNIVERSITY 3181 SW SAM JACKSN PRK RD L102 PORTLAND, OR 97201-3098 Minority high school student research apprentice program

PROJECT NO., ORGANIZATIONAL UNIT., INVESTIGATOR, ADDRESS, TITLE

S03RR-03141-11 (NSS) MENNELLA, JULIE A MONELL CHEMICAL SENSES CENTER 3500 MARKET STREET PHILADELPHIA, PA 19104 Minority high school student research apprentice program

S03RR-03143-09 (NSS) JARON, DOV DREXEL UNIVERSITY 32ND & CHESTNUT STREETS PHILADELPHIA, PA 19104 Minority high school student research apprentice program

S03RR-03144-09 (NSS) COOPERMAN, BARRY S UNIVERSITY OF PENNSYLVANIA 106 COLLEGE HALL PHILADELPHIA, PA 19104 Minority high school student research apprentice program

S03RR-03145-09 (NSS) KEFALIDES, NICHOLAS A UNIVERSITY OF PENNSYLVANIA SCHOOL OF MEDICINE PHILADELPHIA, PA 19104-6055 Minority high school student research apprentice program

S03RR-03146-05 (NSS) NEWTON, CHARLES D UNIV OF PENNSYLVANIA 3800 SPRUCE STREET PHILADELPHIA, PA 19104-6044 Minority high school student research apprentice program

S03RR-03147-06 (NSS) FONSECA, RAYMOND J UNIVERSITY OF PENNSYLVANIA 4001 SPRUCE STREET PHILADELPHIA, PA 19104 Minority high school student research apprentice program

S03RR-03149-11 (NSS) SURREY, SAUL CHILDREN'S HOSP PHILADELPHIA 34TH & CIVIC CENTER BLVD PHILADELPHIA, PA 19104 Minority high school student research apprentice program

S03RR-03150-08 (NSS) WILLIAMS, MOSES L TEMPLE UNIV SCHOOL OF MEDICINE FSU, RM 305/BOARD & ONTARIO ST PHILADELPHIA, PA 19140 Minority high school student research apprentice program

S03RR-03152-11 (NSS) BLACKLOW, ROBERT S THOMAS JEFFERSON UNIVERSITY 1025 WALNUT STREET, ROOM 105 PHILADELPHIA, PA 19107 Minority high school student research apprentice program

S03RR-03154-10 (NSS) WASHINGTON, NANCY D UNIVERSITY OF PITTSBURGH M-247 SCAIFE HALL PITTSBURGH, PA 15261 Minority high school student research apprentice program

P41RR-03155-06 (SSS) GRATTON, ENRICO UNIVERSITY OF ILLINOIS 1110 WEST GREEN STREET URBANA, IL 61801 Laboratory for fluorescence dynamics

P41RR-03155-06 9001 (SSS) GRATTON, ENRICO Laboratory for fluorescence dynamics Core research--Time-resolved fluorescence microscopy

P41RR-03155-06 9004 (SSS) GRATTON, ENRICO Laboratory for fluorescence dynamics Core research--Near-infrared optical imaging system

P41RR-03155-06 9005 (SSS) GRATTON, ENRICO Laboratory for fluorescence dynamics Core research--Laser heterodyning detection

P41RR-03155-06 0004 (SSS) ROYER, CATHERINE A Laboratory for fluorescence dynamics Automation of hydrostatic high pressure instrumentation used for spectroscopy

P41RR-03155-06 0005 (SSS) BEECHEM, JOSEPH M Laboratory for fluorescence dynamics Continued global analysis software development

S03RR-03157-09 (NSS) WOLFSON, SIDNEY K, JR MONTEFIORE HOSPITAL 3459 FIFTH AVENUE PITTSBURGH, PA 15213 Minority high school student research apprentice program

S03RR-03159-11 (NSS) PETTIGREW, CHENITS JR UNIVERSITY OF PITTSBURGH 2717 CATHEDRAL OF LEARNING PITTSBURGH, PA 15260 Minority high school student research apprentice program

R01RR-03163-06 (AR) HILLIARD, JULIA K SOUTHWEST FDN/BIOMEDICAL RES PO BOX 28147 SAN ANTONIO TX 78228-0147 Enhanced B virus diagnosis/control in primate colonies

S03RR-03163-11 (NSS) HIGGINS, EARL B MED UNIV OF SOUTH CAROLINA 171 ASHLEY AVENUE CHARLESTON, S C 29425 Minority high school student research apprentice program

S03RR-03164-11 (NSS) YOUNG, FRANKLIN A, JR MEDICAL UNIV OF SOUTH CAROLINA 171 ASHLEY AVENUE CHARLESTON, S C 29425 Minority high school student research apprentice program

S03RR-03166-08 (NSS) ADDISON, RANDOLPH THE UNIVERSITY OF TENNESSEE 847 MONROE, 241 FACULTY MEMPHIS, TN 38163 Minority high school student research apprentice program

S03RR-03167-11 (NSS) SIMONE, JOSEPH V ST JUDE CHILDREN'S RES HOSP 322 N LAUDERDALE, P O BOX 318 MEMPHIS, TN 38101 Minority high school student research apprentice program

S03RR-03168-10 (NSS) MALDONADO, FILOMENO G TEXAS A&M UNIVERSITY JOE H REYNOLDS BLDG/#159F COLLEGE STATION, TX 77843-1114 Minority high school student research apprentice program

S03RR-03169-10 (NSS) THOMSON, WILLIAM A BAYLOR COLLEGE OF MEDICINE ONE BAYLOR PLAZA HOUSTON, TX 77030 Minority high school student research apprentice program

S03RR-03170-10 (NSS) AHEARN, MICHAEL J UNIVERSITY OF TEXAS 1515 HOLCOMBE BLVD HOUSTON, TX 77030 Minority high school student research apprentice program

S03RR-03173-10 (NSS) STEVENS, WALTER UNIVERSITY OF UTAH 50 NORTH MEDICAL DRIVE SALT LAKE CITY, UT 84112 Minority high school student research apprentice program

S03RR-03174-07 (NSS) WOODE, MOSES K UNIV OF VIRGINIA SCH OF MED BOX 446 CHARLOTTESVILLE, VA 22908 Minority high school student research apprentice program

S03RR-03176-09 (NSS) MCCOMBS, ROBERT M EASTERN VIRGINIA MED SCH 700 OLNEY RD LEWIS HALL 1146 NORFOLK, VA 23507 Minority high school student research apprentice program

S03RR-03178-10 (NSS) AYRES, STEPHEN M MEDICAL COLLEGE OF VIRGINIA BOX 565, MCV STATION RICHMOND, VA 23298 Minority high school student research apprentice program

S03RR-03179-09 (NSS) CHU, JOSEPH UNIVERSITY OF WASHINGTON SC - 64 SEATTLE, WASHINGTON 98195 Minority high school student research apprentice program

S03RR-03180-08 (NSS) MORTON, THOMAS H UNIVERSITY OF WASHINGTON HEALTH SCIENCES CENTER SC-62 SEATTLE, WASH 98195 Minority high school student research apprentice program

S03RR-03183-10 (NSS) LEMBERGER, AUGUST P UNIVERSITY OF WISCONSIN 425 NORTH CHARTER STREET MADISON, WIS 53706 Minority high school student research apprentice program

S03RR-03184-11 (NSS) LOBECK, CHARLES C UNIVERSITY OF WISCONSIN 1300 UNIVERSITY AVENUE MADISON, WIS 53706 Minority high school student research apprentice program

M01RR-03186-06 (CLR) GETTO, CARL J UNIV OF WISCONSIN 1300 UNIVERSITY AVE MADISON, WI 53706 General clinical research center

M01RR-03186-06 0001 (CLR) BUSSE, WILLIAM W General clinical research center Mechanisms of virus-induced asthma

M01RR-03186-06 0004 (CLR) SONDEL, PAUL M General clinical research center Leukapheresis of healthy blood donors to obtain lymphocytes for studies

M01RR-03186-06 0005 (CLR) FARRELL, PHILIP M General clinical research center Pulmonary benefits of cystic fibrosis neonatal screening

M01RR-03186-06 0009 (CLR) CARBONE, PAUL P General clinical research center Phase I trial of combination gamma interferon and tumor necrosis factor

M01RR-03186-06 0010 (CLR) CARBONE, PAUL P General clinical research center Phase I trial of SR2508 & cyclophosphamide administered by IV injection

M01RR-03186-06 0029 (CLR) ZIMMERMAN, JERRY J General clinical research center Polymorphonuclear surfactant degradation in bronchopulmonary dysplasia

M01RR-03186-06 0030 (CLR) BROOKS, BENJAMIN R General clinical research center Aluminum metabolism in patients with amyotrophic lateral sclerosis

M01RR-03186-06 0031 (CLR) BRESNICK, GEORGE H General clinical research center Topography of rod sensitivity

M01RR-03186-06 0011 (CLR) SHENKER, YORAM General clinical research center Physiologic role of atrial natriuretic peptide in aldosterone regulation

M01RR-03186-06 0018 (CLR) CALHOUN, WILLIAM J General clinical research center The airway biology of nocturnal asthma

M01RR-03186-06 0019 (CLR) ROZENTAL, JACK M General clinical research center Early changes in glioma metabolism after treatment

M01RR-03186-06 0020 (CLR) ROBINS, H IAN General clinical research center Phase I trial of carboplatin w/ whole body hyperthermia in advanced cancer

M01RR-03186-06 0024 (CLR) CARBONE, PAUL P General clinical research center Phase I study of difluromethylornithine (DFMO)--A chemoprotective agent

M01RR-03186-06 0032 (CLR) SMALLEY, RICHARD V General clinical research center Tumor associated antigen augmentation by gamma interferon

M01RR-03186-06 0033 (CLR) SMALLEY, RICHARD V General clinical research center Comparison of BMY25801 to metoclopramide in patients receiving cisplatin

M01RR-03186-06 0034 (CLR) WOLFF, JON A General clinical research center Disorders of fat metabolism

M01RR-03186-06 0036 (CLR) GREGER, JANET L General clinical research center Functional effects of dietary manganese and iron interactions

M01RR-03186-06 0037 (CLR) YOUNG, THERESA B General clinical research center Epidemiology of sleep-disordered breathing in a healthy working population

M01RR-03186-06 0039 (CLR) BUSSE, WILLIAM W General clinical research center Evaluation of the bronchodilating effects of MK-571 in patients w/ asthma

M01RR-03186-06 0040 (CLR) SONDEL, PAUL M General clinical research center Autologous LAK cells & repetitive doses of IL-2 in renal cell cancer pts

M01RR-03186-06 0041 (CLR) CARBONE, PAUL P General clinical research center Phase I study of fluorouracil, leucovorin and dipyridamole admin. by IV

M01RR-03186-06 0043 (CLR) JOHNSON, CURTIS A General clinical research center Multiple administration of intravenous piperacillin/tazobactam

M01RR-03186-06 0045 (CLR) CARNES, MARY L General clinical research center The phenomenology of adrenocorticotropic hormone (ACTH) micropulses

M01RR-03186-06 0046 (CLR) HONG, RICHARD General clinical research center Acquistion of immunity following bone marrow transplant

M01RR-03186-06 0047 (CLR) ZACHMAN, RICHARD D General clinical research center Evaluation of multiple doses of surfactant-TA in treatment of neonatal RDS

M01RR-03186-06 0048 (CLR) ZACHMAN, RICHARD D General clinical research center Retinol status and metabolism in neonatal lung injury with oxygen

M01RR-03186-06 0049 (CLR) SHENKER, YORAM General clinical research center Atrial natriuretic hormone and salt sensitivity in hypertension

M01RR-03186-06 0050 (CLR) SONDEL, PAUL M General clinical research center Phase I/IB trial of anti-CD3 plus IL-2 as immune activation in cancer pts

M01RR-03186-06 0051 (CLR) CARBONE, PAUL P General clinical research center Phase I clinical trial of IV L-buthionine sulfoximine and melphalan

M01RR-03186-06 0052 (CLR) SCHILLER, JOAN H General clinical research center WR2721--Chemo-radioprotector for non-small cell lung cancer treatment

M01RR-03186-06 0053 (CLR) KANNER, ANDRES M General clinical research center Monotherapy comparison of felbamate and valproate in partial seizures

M01RR-03186-06 0054 (CLR) RAO, P SYAMASUNDAR General clinical research center Transcatheter closure of cardiac defects

M01RR-03186-06 0055 (CLR) FLEMING, MICHAEL F General clinical research center The role of phosphatidylethanol (PET) in alcoholism

M01RR-03186-06 0056 (CLR) BORDEN, ERNEST C General clinical research center Comparison of biological response modifiers of IFN in normal subjects

M01RR-03186-06 0065 (CLR) SCHILLER, JOAN H General clinical research center Phase IB trial of alpha interferon and IL-2 in patients w/ advanced cancer

M01RR-03186-06 0066 (CLR) SHENKER, YORAM General clinical research center Hypoxemia and atrial natriuretic factor

M01RR-03186-06 0067 (CLR) JOHNSON, CURTIS A General clinical research center Pharmacokinetics of cefpodoxime in contin. ambulatory peritoneal dialysis

M01RR-03186-06 0068 (CLR) HUTSON, PAUL R General clinical research center Hepatic drug metabolism & phenotype & correlation w/ mitoxantrone metab.

M01RR-03186-06 0057 (CLR) BUSSE, WILLIAM General clinical research center The role of eosinophils on nocturnal asthma

M01RR-03186-06 0058 (CLR) CALHOUN, WILLLIAM J General clinical research center Mediators of hypersensitivity in exercise-induced asthma

M01RR-03186-06 0059 (CLR) SKATRUD, JAMES B General clinical research center Effect of thyroid hormone on ventilatory stability during sleep

M01RR-03186-06 0060 (CLR) SONDEL, PAUL M General clinical research center Phase I/IB trial of anti-GD2 + IL-2, children w/ refractory neuroblastoma

M01RR-03186-06 0061 (CLR) CARBONE, PAUL P General clinical research center Phase I trial of mitoxantrone and GM-CSF in advanced solid maligancies

M01RR-03186-06 0062 (CLR) CARBONE, PAUL P General clinical research center Phase I study of tetraplatin

M01RR-03186-06 0063 (CLR) CARBONE, PAUL P General clinical research center Phase I study of fluorouracil, leucovorin, and levamisole

M01RR-03186-06 0064 (CLR) CARBONE, PAUL P General clinical research center Phase I study of suramin

M01RR-03186-06 0069 (CLR) KANNER, ANDRES M General clinical research center Open label, follow on, long term therapy w/ felbamate in epilepsy subjects

M01RR-03186-06 0070 (CLR) KANNER, ANDRES M General clinical research center Multicenter study of the safety of felbamate in sujects with epilepsy

M01RR-03186-06 0071 (CLR) SCHALCH, DON S General clinical research center Metabolic effects of insulin-like growth factor I on type II diabetes

M01RR-03186-06 0072 (CLR) UPDIKE, STUART J General clinical research center Clinical evaluation of continuous glucose monitor

M01RR-03186-06 0073 (CLR) JARJOUR, NIZAR N General clinical research center Influence of circadian rhythm on occurrence of late phase asthma reaction

M01RR-03186-06 0074 (CLR) PRIDHAM, KAREN F General clinical research center Feeding practices for growing preterm infants

M01RR-03186-06 0075 (CLR) BRUSKEWITZ, REGINALD C General clinical research center Phase II dose finding study of YM617 for benign prostatic hyperplasia

S03RR-03186-08 (NSS) THOMAS, LAUREE MEDICAL COLLEGE OF WISCONSIN 8701 WATERTOWN PLANK ROAD MILWAUKEE, WI 53226 Minority high school student research apprentice program

S03RR-03187-08 (NSS) CARDONA, DOLORES S UNIVERSITY OF WYOMING P O BOX 3808, UNIVERSITY STATI LARAMIE, W Y 82071 Minority high school student research apprentice program

S03RR-03190-10 (NSS) HENDERSON, JAMES H TUSKEGEE UNIVERSITY CARVER RES FOUNDATION TUSKEGEE, ALA 36088 Minority high school student research apprentice program

S03RR-03192-11 (NSS) KEYZER, HENDRIK CALIFORNIA STATE UNIVERSITY 5151 STATE UNIVERSITY DRIVE LOS ANGELES, CALIF 90032 Minority high school student research apprentice program

S03RR-03194-10 (NSS) KONDO, NORMAN S UNIV OF DISTRICT OF COLUMBIA 4200 CONNECTICUT AVE, N W WASHINGTON, D C 20008 Minority high school student research apprentice program

S03RR-03195-10 (NSS) RICHARDSON, THOMAS O BETHUNE-COOKMAN COLLEGE 640 SECOND AVENUE DAYTONA BEACH, FLA 32015 Minority high school research apprentice program

S03RR-03196-10 (NSS) REDDA, KINFE K FLORIDA A&M UNIVERSITY POST OFFICE BOX 367 TALLAHASSEE, FL 32307 Minority high school student research apprentice program

S03RR-03200-09 (NSS) CHRISTIAN, FREDERICK A SOUTHERN UNIVERSITY SOUTHERN BRANCH POST OFFICE BATON ROUGE, LA 70813 Minority high school student research apprentice program

S03RR-03203-11 (NSS) SPANN, CHARLES H JACKSON STATE UNIVERSITY P O BOX 18750 JACKSON, MS 39217 Minority high school student research apprentice program

S03RR-03206-09 (NSS) HELLER, RICHARD F BRONX COMMUNITY COLLEGE WEST 181ST ST & UNIVERSITY AVE BRONX, N Y 10453 Minority high school student research apprentice program

S03RR-03209-10 (NSS) FISHMAN, MYER M CITY COLLEGE OF CUNY CONVENT AVE AT 138TH STREET NEW YORK, N Y 10031 Minority high school student research apprentice program

S03RR-03212-06 (NSS) ATKINSON, WILVERIA B WINSTON-SALEM STATE UNIVERSITY 601 MARTIN LUTHER KING JR DR WINSTON-SALEM, N C 27110 Minority high school student research apprentice program

S03RR-03213-06 (NSS) WILLIAMSON, ALEX N N C A&T STATE UNIVERSITY 1601 E MARKET STREET GREENSBORO, N C 27411-001 Minority high school student research apprentice program

S03RR-03216-08 (NSS) FINLAY, MARY F BENEDICT COLLEGE HARDEN & BLANDING STREETS COLUMBIA, S C 29204 Minority high school student research appreentice program

S03RR-03221-08 (NSS) ALDRIDGE, JAMES W PSYCHOLOGY DEPARTMENT PAN AMERICAN UNIVERSITY EDINBURG, TX 78539 Minority high school student research apprentice program

S03RR-03222-09 (NSS) MOSS, DONALD E UNIV OF TX/DEPT OF PSYCHOLOGY 500 UNIVERSITY AVENUE EL PASO, TX 79968-0553 Minority high school student research apprentice program

S03RR-03225-06 (NSS) LEWIS, HENRY III TEXAS SOUTHERN UNIVIERSITY 3100 CLEBURNE STREET HOUSTON, TX 77004 Minority high school student research apprentice program

S03RR-03226-05 (NSS) HOWE, HENRY A NORFOLK STATE UNIVERSITY 2401 CORPREW AVENUE NORFOLK, VA 23504 Minority high school student research apprentice program

S03RR-03228-09 (NSS) SRINIVASAN, ASOKA TOUGALOO COLLEGE TOUGALOO, MS 39174 Minority high school student research apprentice program

S03RR-03231-10 (NSS) CLEMENDOR, ANTHONY A NEW YORK MEDICAL COLLEGE 1901 FIRST AVENUE - 16A2 NEW YORK, N Y 10029 Minority high school student research apprentice program

S03RR-03232-06 (NSS) AFIFI, ABDELMONEM UNIVERSITY OF CALIFORNIA, LOS 10833 LECONTE AVENUE LOS ANGELES, CA 90024-1406 Minority high school student research apprentice program

S03RR-03233-07 (NSS) HICKEY, TERRY L UNIV OF ALABAMA/UAB STATION 102 MORTIMER JORDAN HALL BIRMINGHAM, AL 35294 Minority high

PROJECT NO., ORGANIZATIONAL UNIT., INVESTIGATOR, ADDRESS, TITLE

school student research apprentice program
S03RR-03234-10 (NSS) RUDCZYNSKI, ANDREW B RUTGERS, THE STATE UNIV OF NJ PO BOX 1089, STE 123, ADM BLDG PISCATAWAY, NJ 08855-1089 Minority high school student research apprentice program
S03RR-03235-10 (NSS) HICKEY, TERRY L UNIV OF ALABAMA/UAB STATION 102 MORTIMER JORDAN HALL BIRMINGHAM, AL 35294 Minority high school student research apprentice program
S03RR-03237-07 (NSS) AUGENLICHT, LEONARD H MONTEFIORE MEDICAL CENTER 111 EAST 210TH STREET BRONX, N Y 10467 Minority high school student research apprentice program
S03RR-03239-09 (NSS) LEVI, DENNIS M UNIVERSITY OF HOUSTON 4800 CALHOUN HOUSTON, TX 77204-2163 Minority high school student research apprentice program
S03RR-03241-08 (NSS) ABBOTT, ELIZABETH F FLORIDA FOUNDATION FOR FUTURE 111 NORMAN HALL GAINESVILLE, FL 32611-2053 Minority high school research apprentice program
S03RR-03243-10 (NSS) RODRIGUEZ, PAUL H UNIVERSITY OF TEXAS DIV OF LIFE SCIENCES SAN ANTONIO, TEX 78285 Minority high school student research apprentice program
S03RR-03244-09 (NSS) WILLIAMS, HIBBARD E UNIVERSITY OF CALIFORNIA SCHOOL OF MEDICINE DAVIS, CA 95616 Minority high school student research apprentice program
S03RR-03247-09 (NSS) BACON, ARTHUR L TALLADEGA COLLEGE 627 WEST BATTLE STREET TALLADEGA, ALA 35160 Minority high school student research apprentice program
S03RR-03249-09 (NSS) THURMAN, WILLIAM G OKLAHOMA MEDICAL RESEARCH FDN 825 N E 13TH STREET OKLAHOMA CITY, OKLA 73104 Minority high school student research apprentice program
S03RR-03250-09 (NSS) CONTI, SAMUEL F UNIVERSITY OF MASSACHUSETTS A217 GRADUATE RESEARCH CENTER AMHERST, MA 01003 Minority high school student research apprentice program
S03RR-03252-08 (NSS) HUSSEY, ROBERT G LOUISIANA STATE UNIVERSITY COLLEGE OF BASIC SCIENCES BATON ROUGE, LA 70803 Minority high school student research apprentice program
S03RR-03253-06 (NSS) KUETTNER, KLAUS E RUSH PRES ST LUKES MEDICAL CTR 1653 WEST CONGRESS PARKWAY CHICAGO, IL 60612-3864 Minority high school student research apprentice program
S03RR-03254-02 (NSS) DALY, DANIEL L FATHER FLANAGAN'S BOYS' HOME BOYS TOWN, NE 68010 Minority high school student research apprentice program
S03RR-03259-08 (NSS) ENOCH, JAY M UNIVERSITY OF CALIFORNIA 350 MINOR HALL BERKELEY, CALIF 94720 Minority high school student research apprentice program
S03RR-03260-09 (NSS) RIFKIND, RICHARD A SLOAN-KETT INST CANCER RES 1275 YORK AVENUE NEW YORK, N Y 10021 Minority high school student research apprentice program
S03RR-03261-05 (NSS) COHEN, JORDAN SUNY AT STONY BROOK L4-18 HEALTH SCIENCE CENTER STONY BROOK, N Y 11794-8430 Minority high school student research apprentice program
S03RR-03262-10 (NSS) ACOSTA, DANIEL, JR UNIVERSITY OF TEXAS AT AUSTIN COLLEGE OF PHARMCY AUSTIN, TEX 78712 Minority high school student research apprentice program
S03RR-03263-02 (NSS) CREWS, DOUGLAS E LOYOLA UNIVERSITY MEDICAL CTR 2160 SOUTH FIRST AVENUE MAYWOOD, IL 60153 Minority high school student research apprentice program
S03RR-03264-08 (NSS) LEVIN, ROBERT M BOSTON CITY HOSPITAL HOB-2, 818 HARRISON AVE BOSTON, MASS 02118 Minority high school student research apprentice program
S03RR-03265-10 (NSS) EGGLETON, GORDON L SOUTHEASTERN OKLA STATE UNIV P O BOX 4059, STA A DURANT, OKLA 74701 Minority high school student research apprentice program
S03RR-03267-10 (NSS) MCNAIR, DAVID UNIVERSITY OF NORTH CAROLINA CB# 7450 BRAUER HALL CHAPEL HILL, NC 27599-7450 Minority high school student research apprentice program
S03RR-03268-10 (NSS) RENNIE, DONALD W VICE PROVOST, RES & GRAD ED SUNY AT BUFF, 548 CAPEN HALL AMHERST, NY 14260 Minority high school student research apprentice program
S03RR-03270-07 (NSS) ESCABI, JOSE R CATHOLIC UNIV OF PUERTO RICO BIOMEDICAL RESEARCH PROGRAM PONCE, PUERTO RICO 00732 Minority high school student research apprentice program
S03RR-03271-08 (NSS) CLARKE, DONALD D FORDHAM UNIVERSITY 441 E. FORDHAM ROAD BRONX, NY 10458 Minority high school student research apprentice program
S03RR-03275-10 (NSS) SMITH, ELSKE V VIRGINIA COMMONWEALTH UNIVERSI BOX 2019 RICHMOND, VA 23284 Minority high school student research apprentice program
S03RR-03276-08 (NSS) TRUJILLO, EUGENE D UNIV OF COLORADO HLTH SCI CTR 4200 E 9TH AVE BOX B176 DENVER, CO 80262 Minority high school student research apprentice program
S03RR-03277-10 (NSS) STITT, JOHN T JOHN B PIERCE FOUNDATION 290 CONGRESS AVENUE NEW HAVEN, CONN 06519 Minority high school student research apprentice program
S03RR-03278-10 (NSS) HOLZEMER, WILLIAM L SCHOOL OF NURSING, BOX 0604 UNIVERSITY OF CALIFORNIA SAN FRANCISCO, CA 94143-0604 Minority high school student research apprentice program
S03RR-03280-05 (NSS) OFOSU, GUSTAV A LIBERAL ARTS COL BOX 626 DELAWARE STATE COLLEGE DOVER, DE 19901 Minority high school student research apprentice program
S03RR-03281-09 (NSS) OLDHAM, JOHN RES FDN FOR MENTAL HYGIENE,INC 722 W 168TH STREET NEW YORK, N Y 10032 Minority high school student research apprentice program
S03RR-03284-10 (NSS) WRIGHT, MAGGIE S S U N Y - AT BUFFALO 140 FARBER HALL BUFFALO, N Y 14214 Minority high school student research apprentice program
S03RR-03286-10 (NSS) BALLARD, BILLY R UNIV OF TEXAS MED BRANCH SUITE G-210, ASHBEL SMITH BLDG GALVESTON, TX 77550-2764 Minority high school student research apprentice program
S03RR-03290-10 (NSS) WYNDER, ERNST L AMERICAN HEALTH FOUNDATION 320 EAST 43RD STREET NEW YORK, N Y 10017 Minority high school student research apprentice program
S03RR-03291-10 (NSS) MASLAR, ILA A OREGON REGIONAL PRIMATE RESEAR 505 N W 185TH AVENUE BEAVERTON, OR 97006 Minority high school student research apprentice program

PROJECT NO., ORGANIZATIONAL UNIT., INVESTIGATOR, ADDRESS, TITLE

S03RR-03293-05 (NSS) DONOW, CAROLYN F SOUTHERN ILLINOIS UNIVERSITY OFFICE OF RESEARCH DEV & ADMIN CARBONDALE, IL 62901-4709 Minority high school student research apprentice program
S03RR-03294-10 (NSS) HEPPNER, GLORIA H MICHIGAN CANCER FOUNDATION 110 EAST WARREN AVENUE DETROIT, MICH 48201 Minority high school student research apprentice program
S03RR-03295-10 (NSS) HERNDON, CAROL D SOUTHERN ILLINOIS UNIVERSITY SCH OF MED, PO BOX 19230 SPRINGFIELD, ILL 62708 Minority high school student research apprentice program
S03RR-03296-09 (NSS) POWELL, A JAMES ALBANY MEDICAL COLLEGE 47 NEW SCOTLAND AVE ALBANY, NY 12208 Minority high school student research apprentice program
S03RR-03297-10 (NSS) DAVIS, DAN J UNIVERSITY OF ARKANSAS DEPARTMENT OF CHEMISTRY FAYETTEVILLE, ARKANSAS 72701 Minority high school student research apprentice program
S03RR-03298-10 (NSS) RUSH, JOHN V THE SALK INST FOR BIOLOG STUD P O BOX 85800 SAN DIEGO, CA 92186-5800 Minority high school student research apprentice program
S03RR-03301-10 (NSS) SPEAR, NORMAN E S U N Y - AT BINGHAMTON DEPT OF BIOLOGICAL SCIENCES BINGHAMTON, N Y 13901 Minority high school student research apprentice program
S03RR-03302-10 (NSS) MUSLOW, IKE LSU MED CTR - SHREVEPORT P O BOX 33932 SHREVEPORT, LA 71130-3932 Minority high school student research apprentice program
S03RR-03304-10 (NSS) LAWRENCE, LEONARD E UNIV OF TEXAS HLTH SCI CTR 7703 FLOYD CURL DRIVE SAN ANTONIO, TEX 78284 Minority high school student research apprentice program
S03RR-03305-09 (NSS) MEDINA, MIGUEL A UNIVERSITY OF TEXAS 7703 FLOYD CURL DRIVE SAN ANTONIO, TEX 78284 Minority high school student research apprentice program
S03RR-03309-10 (NSS) FRAZIER, DONALD T UNIVERSITY OF KENTUCKY COLLEGE OF MEDICINE LEXINGTON, KY 40536-0084 Minority high school student research apprentice program
S03RR-03311-10 (NSS) NIEFORTH, KARL A SCH OF PHARM, UNIV OF CONN U-92, 372 FAIRFIELD ROAD STORRS, CT 06269-2092 Minority high school student research apprentice program
S03RR-03314-02 (NSS) ABBOTT, ELIZABETH F UNIVERSITY OF FLORIDA 111 NORMAN HALL GAINESVILLE, FL 32611-2953 Minority high school student research apprentice program
S03RR-03315-08 (NSS) HINES, DEBORAH H UMASS MEDICAL SCHOOL 55 LAKE AVENUE NORTH WORCESTER, MA 01655 Minority high school student research apprentice program
S03RR-03316-10 (NSS) TIGNOR, GREGORY H YALE UNIVERSITY BOX 3333, 60 COLLEGE STREET NEW HAVEN, CONN 06510 Minority high school student research apprentice program
S03RR-03318-07 (NSS) TREVINO, DANIEL L PENNSYLVANIA STATE UNIVERSITY 113 HENDERSON BUILDING UNIVERSITY PARK, PA 16802 Minority high school student research apprentice program
S03RR-03320-04 (NSS) MOSSMAN, KENNETH L ARIZONA STATE UNIVERSITY ADMINISTRATION BLDG, ROOM 213 TEMPE, AZ 85287-2703 Minority high school student research apprentice program
S03RR-03321-08 (NSS) PLUNKETT, PATRICK F 206 MUGAR BLDG, N E UNIV 360 HUNTINGTON AVE BOSTON, MA 02115 Minority high school student research apprentice program
S03RR-03323-09 (NSS) MYLROIE, AUGUSTA A CHICAGO STATE UNIVERSITY 95TH STREET AT KING DRIVE CHICAGO, ILL 60628 Minority high school student research apprentice program
S03RR-03326-10 (NSS) SCHULTZ, TERRY W UNIVERSITY OF TENNESSEE PO BOX 1071, COL VET MED KNOXVILLE, TN 37901-1071 Minority high school student research apprentice program
S03RR-03329-04 (NSS) COOMBE, ROBERT D UNIVERSITY OF DENVER 2101 E WESLEY AVENUE DENVER, CO 80208 Minority high school student research appreentice program
S03RR-03330-05 (NSS) LEWIS, ROBERT B UNIV OF ARKANSAS FOR MED SCI 4301 W MARKHAM, SLOT #625 LITTLE ROCK, AR 72205 Minority high school student research apprentice program
S03RR-03331-09 (NSS) WHITTEN, CHARLES F WAYNE STATE UNIVERSITY 540 EAST CANFIELD DETROIT, MICH 48201 Minority high school student research apprentice program
S03RR-03332-07 (NSS) STATES, J CHRISTOPHER 2727 2ND AVE, M C H T 4120 WAYNE STATE UNIVERSITY DETROIT, MI 48201 Minority high school student research appreentice program
S03RR-03333-07 (NSS) ADAMS, WALTER C KENT STATE UNIVERSITY 107 ADMINISTRATION BUILDING KENT, OH 44242 Minority high school student research apprentice program
S03RR-03334-10 (NSS) FICKLIN, FRED L INDIANA UNIV SCH OF MED 635 BARNHILL DRIVE INDIANAPOLIS, IND 46202 Minority high school student research apprentice program
S03RR-03335-09 (NSS) LOVETT, PAUL S UNIVERSITY OF MARYLAND BLT CTY BALTIMORE, MARYLAND 21228 Minority high school student research apprentice program
S03RR-03336-08 (NSS) HAYNES, MARGARET L COLUMBIA UNIVERSITY COL OF P&S, 630 W. 168 ST NEW YORK, N Y 10032 Minority high school student research apprentice program
S03RR-03338-09 (NSS) RANKIN, GARY O MARSHALL UNIV SCHOOL OF MED 1542 SPRING VALLEY DRIVE HUNTINGTON, WV 25755 Minority high school student research apprentice program
S03RR-03339-09 (NSS) GARCIA-CASTINEIRAS, SIXTO UNIVERSITY OF PUERTO RICO SCH MED GPO BOX 5067 SAN JUAN, PR 00936 Minority high school student research apprentice program
S03RR-03340-09 (NSS) ARCHBALD, LOUIS F UNIVERSITY OF FLORIDA BOX J-125, JHMHSC GAINESVILLE, FL 32610-0125 Minority high school student research apprentice program
S03RR-03341-06 (NSS) MOOD, DARLENE W WAYNE STATE UNIVERSITY 5557 CASS AVENUE DETROIT, MI 48202-3489 Minority high school student research apprentice program
S03RR-03342-09 (NSS) MCHALE, PHILIP A UNIVERSITY OF OKLAHOMA P O BOX 26901 OKLAHOMA CITY, OKLA 73190 Minority high school student research apprentice program
S03RR-03343-08 (NSS) HOLTEN, DAROLD D UNIV OF CALIFORNIA, RIVERSIDE RIVERSIDE, CALIFORNIA 92521 Minority high school student research apprentice program
S03RR-03344-06 (NSS) FISCHER, ALLAN G NORTH DAKOTA ST UNIV

STEVENS HALL, ROOM 201 FARGO, ND 58105 Minority high school student research apprentice program

S03RR-03345-09 (NSS) SMITH, JOHN R OREGON HEALTH SCIENCES UNIV 611 SW CAMPUS DRIVE PORTLAND, ORE 97201 Minority high school student research apprentice program

S03RR-03347-07 (NSS) PAIGEN, KENNETH JACKSON LABORATORY 600 MAIN STREET BAR HARBOR, ME 04609-0800 Minority high school student research apprentice program

S03RR-03348-09 (NSS) PINON, RAMON R, JR UNIVERSITY OF CALIFORNIA DEPT OF BIOLOGY, B-022 LA JOLLA, CALIF 92093 Minority high school student research apprentice program

S03RR-03349-09 (NSS) GOODMAN, JOEL UNIV OF TEXAS S W MED CTR 5323 HARRY HINES BLVD DALLAS, TEX 75235 Minority high school student research apprentice program

S03RR-03350-09 (NSS) YIELDING, K LEMONE UNIV OF TEXAS MEDICAL BRANCH SUITE 2210 ASHBEL SMITH BLDG GALVESTON, TEXAS 77550-2764 Minority high school student research apprentice program

S03RR-03351-09 (NSS) FAN, HUNG UNIV OF CALIFORNIA, IRVINE IRVINE, CA 92717 Minority high school student research apprentice program

S03RR-03353-08 (NSS) GOLDSTEIN, GARY KENNEDY INSTITUTE, INC. 707 NORTH BROADWAY BALTIMORE, MD 21205 Minority high school student research apprentice program

S03RR-03354-09 (NSS) CHOU, CHING-CHUNG MICHIGAN STATE UNIVERSITY DEPT OF PHYSIOLOGY EAST LANSING, MICH 48824 Minority high school student research apprentice program

S03RR-03355-09 (NSS) SEDANO, HEDDIE O UNIVERSITY OF MINNESOTA 515 DELAWARE ST, SE MINNEAPOLIS, MINN 55455 Minority high school student research apprentice program

S03RR-03356-06 (NSS) BAUER, MARK C NAVAJO COMMUNITY COLLEGE P O BOX 580 SHIPROCK, N MEX 87420 Minority high school student research apprentice program

S03RR-03358-07 (NSS) GOMEZ, MANUEL UNIVERSITY OF PUERTO RICO COL OF NATURAL SCI, FB 304 RIO PIEDRAS, PR 00931 Minority high school student research apprentice program

S03RR-03359-09 (NSS) GISSENDANNER, BEVERLY UNIVERSITY OF ROCHESTER 601 ELMWOOD AVE, BOX 601 ROCHESTER, NEW YORK 14642 Minority high school student research apprentice program

S03RR-03361-09 (NSS) GARDNER, RICK M UNIV OF SOUTHERN COLORADO 2200 BONFORTE BLVD/P160 PUEBLO, COLO 81001 Minority high school student research apprentice program

S03RR-03362-08 (NSS) HURLEY, MARJA M UNIVERSITY OF CONNECTICUT SCHOOL OF DENTAL MEDICINE FARMINGTON, CONN 06032 Minority high school student research apprentice program

S03RR-03363-09 (NSS) OMENN, GILBERT S UNIVERSITY OF WASHINGTON SCH OF PUBLIC HLTH, SC-30 SEATTLE, WASH 98195 Minority high school student research apprentice program

S03RR-03365-06 (NSS) CHANCE, BRITTON UNIVERSITY CITY SCIENCE CTR 3401 MARKET STREET, SUITE 320 PHILADELPHIA, PA 19104 Minority high school student research apprentice program

S03RR-03366-08 (NSS) PENRY, J KIFFIN BOWMAN GRAY SCHOOL OF MED 300 SOUTH HAWTHORNE ROAD WINSTON-SALEM, N C 27103 Minority high school student research apprentice program

S03RR-03368-08 (NSS) PRIEUR, DAVID J WASHINGTON STATE UNIVERSITY COLLEGE OF VETERNARY MED PULLMAN, WASH 99164-7040 Minority high school student research apprentice program

S03RR-03369-08 (NSS) PHIPPS, GRANT T SUNY AT BUFFALO 3435 MAIN ST, 246 FARBER HALL BUFFALO, N Y 14214 Minority high school student research apprentice program

S03RR-03370-08 (NSS) WILMER, LEONARD SOUTHERN UNIV-SHREVEPORT 3050 MARTIN LUTHER KING, JR DR SHREVEPORT, LA 71107 Minority high school student research apprentice program

S03RR-03371-07 (NSS) ABRAHAM, WILLIAM M MOUNT SINAI MEDICAL CENTER 4300 ALTON ROAD MIAMI BEACH, FLA 33140 Minority high school student research apprentice program

S03RR-03372-08 (NSS) WILLINGHAM, WILLIAM M UNIVERSITY OF ARKANSAS BOX 4055 PINE BLUFF, ARK 71601 Minority high school student research apprentice program

S03RR-03373-08 (NSS) REIS, ARTHUR H, JR BRANDEIS UNIVERSITY 415 SOUTH ST, PO BOX 9110 WALTHAM, MASS 02254 Minority high school student research apprentice program

S03RR-03375-06 (NSS) FULLILOVE, ROBERT E COLUMBIA UNIVERSITY 617 W. 168TH STREET NEW YORK, N Y 10032 Minority high school student research apprentice program

S03RR-03376-08 (NSS) TRIGGLE, DAVID J SUNY AT BUFFALO 126 COOKE HALL AMHERST, NY 14260 Minority high school student research apprentice program

S03RR-03377-08 (NSS) HARRIS, BEN G TEXAS COLLEGE/OSTEOPATHIC MED 3500 CAMP BOWIE BLVD FORT WORTH, TX 76107-2690 Minority high school student research apprentice program

S03RR-03379-07 (NSS) CHEN, THOMAS T UNIVERSITY OF TENNESSEE KNOXVILLE, TN 37996-0810 Minority high school student research apprentice program

S03RR-03380-08 (NSS) SCHWEIS, JEAN E POPULATION COUNCIL 1230 YORK AVENUE NEW YORK, N Y 10021 Minority high school student research apprentice program

S03RR-03381-05 (NSS) MASON, THOMAS J FOX CHASE CANCER CENTER 7701 BURHOLME AVENUE PHILADELPHIA, PA 19111 Minority high school student research apprentice program

S03RR-03382-07 (NSS) BEAN, BARRY LEHIGH UNIVERSITY CMBB-BIOLOGY, BLDG A. 111 BETHLEHEM, PA 18015 Minority high school student research apprentice program

S03RR-03383-06 (NSS) BARBEE, EVELYN L UNIV OF WISCONSIN-MADISON SCH NURSING 3600 HIGHLAND AVE MADISON, WI 53792 Minority high school student research apprentice program

S03RR-03384-03 (NSS) HILL, GEORGE C MEHARRY MEDICAL COLLEGE 1005 D B TODD, JR BLVD NASHVILLE, TN 37208 Minority high school student research apprentice program

S03RR-03385-07 (NSS) MOSBACH, ERWIN H BETH ISRAEL MEDICAL CTR FIRST AVENUE AT 16TH ST NEW YORK, N Y 10003 Minority high school student research apprentice program

S03RR-03386-07 (NSS) MALAVE-LOPEZ, JOSE HUMACAO UNIVERSITY COLLEGE CUH STATION HUMACAO, PR 00661 Minority high school student research apprentice program

S03RR-03387-08 (NSS) BELL, PAUL B JR UNIVERSITY OF OKLAHOMA NORMAN, OKLA 73019 Minority high school student research apprentice program

S03RR-03388-08 (NSS) SHADDUCK, JOHN A COLLEGE OF VETERINARY MED TEXAS A&M UNIVERSITY COLLEGE STATION, TX 77843 Minority high school student research apprentice program

S03RR-03389-05 (NSS) LOEW, FRANKLIN M TUFTS UNIVERSITY 200 WESTBORO ROAD NORTH GRAFTON, MA 01536-1895 Minority high school student research apprentice program

S03RR-03390-08 (NSS) THOMPSON, HENRY J AMC CANCER RESEARCH CENTER 1600 PIERCE STREET LAKEWOOD, COLORADO 80214 Minority high school student research apprentice program

S03RR-03391-08 (NSS) PATTERSON, RODNEY S UNIVERSITY OF VERMONT 41 SOUTH PROSPECT STREET BURLINGTON, VERMONT 05405 Minority high school student research apprentice program

S03RR-03392-08 (NSS) PATTERSON, RODNEY S UNIVERSITY OF VERMONT 41 SO PROSPECT STREET BURLINGTON, VT 05405 Minority high school student research apprentice program

S03RR-03393-07 (NSS) KENNY, ALEXANDER D TEXAS TECH UNIVERSITY DEPARTMENT OF PHARMACOLOGY LUBBOCK, TEX 79430 Minority high school student research apprentice program

S03RR-03394-08 (NSS) NEWKIRK, ROBERT F TENNESSEE STATE UNIVERSITY 3500 JOHN A MERRIT BLVD NASHVILLE, TN 37209-1561 Minority high school student research apprentice program

S03RR-03397-08 (NSS) ANDERSON, LEON JR UNIVERSITY OF MISSISSIPPI MED 2500 NORTH STATE STREET JACKSON, MISS 39216-4505 Minority high school student research apprentice program

S03RR-03399-07 (NSS) CHAN, CARCY L EAST LOS ANGELES COLLEGE 1301 BROOKLYN AVENUE MONTEREY PARK, CA 91754 Minority high school student research apprentice program

S03RR-03400-08 (NSS) HICKEY, TERRY L UNIV OF ALABAMA/UAB STATION 102 MORTIMER JORDAN HALL BIRMINGHAM, AL 35294 Minority high school student research apprentice program

S03RR-03401-04 (NSS) SPEIDEL, HAROLD K NORTHERN ARIZONA UNIVERSITY BOX 5640 FLAGSTAFF, ARIZ 86001 Minority high school student research appreentice program

S03RR-03402-08 (NSS) PEACOCK, TOM UMD SCHOOL OF MEDICINE 10 UNIVERSITY DR, RM 112 DULUTH, MINNESOTA 55812 Minority high school student research apprentice program

S03RR-03403-07 (NSS) SINGH, SHIVA P ALABAMA STATE UNIVERSITY 915 SOUTH JACKSON STREET MONTGOMERY, ALA 36195 Minority high school student research apprentice program

S03RR-03404-07 (NSS) BECKER, MARSHALL H UNIVERSITY OF MICHIGAN 109 S. OBSERVATORY ANN ARBOR, MI 48109-2029 Minority high school student research apprentice program

S03RR-03406-07 (NSS) HENOCH, NEIL F LAWRENCE LIVERMORE NATL LAB PO BOX 808, L-716 LIVERMORE, CALIF 94550 Minority high school student research apprentice program

S03RR-03407-07 (NSS) WILLIAMS, RUTH E UNIVERSITY OF WISCONSIN PO BOX 413-CHAPMAN 302 MILWAUKEE, WIS 53201 Minority high school student research apprentice program

S03RR-03408-07 (NSS) RUDDON, RAYMOND UNIV NEBRASKA MEDICAL CTR 600 SOUTH 42ND STREET OMAHA, NE 68198-6805 Minority high school student research apprentice program

S03RR-03410-07 (NSS) FLEISSNER, ERWIN HUNTER COLLEGE 695 PARK AVENUE NEW YORK, N Y 10021 Minority high school student research apprentice program

S03RR-03411-07 (NSS) KNAFL, KATHLEEN A UNIVERSITY OF ILLINOIS 845 S. DAMEN AVE, PO BOX 6998 CHICAGO, ILLINOIS 60612 Minority high school student research apprentice program

S03RR-03412-07 (NSS) SHACKS, SAMUEL J CHARLES R DREW POSTGRAD MED SC 1621 EAST 120TH ST, MP #27 LOS ANGELES, CALIF 90059 Minority high school student research apprentice program

S03RR-03413-07 (NSS) SULLIVAN, WALTER W MOREHOUSE SCHOOL OF MEDICINE 720 WESTVIEW DRIVE, S W ATLANTA, GA 30310 Minority high school student research apprentice program

S03RR-03415-05 (NSS) POPS, MARTIN A UNIVERSITY OF CALIFORNIA 405 HILGARD AVENUE LOS ANGELES, CALIF 90024 Minority high school student research apprentice program

S03RR-03416-07 (NSS) BECK, DAVID P PUBLIC HEALTH RESEARCH INST 455 FIRST AVENUE NEW YORK, N Y 10016 Minority high school student research apprentice program

S03RR-03418-07 (NSS) MC MICHAEL, ROBERT F HAHNEMANN UNIVERSITY MAIL STOP 431, BROAD & VINE ST PHILADELPHIA, PA 19102-1192 Minority high school student research apprentice program

S03RR-03421-06 (NSS) SWARTZ, KARYL B HERBERT H LEHMAN COLLEGE BEDFORD PARK BOULEVARD WEST BRONX, NEW YORK 10468 Minority high school student research apprentice program

S03RR-03424-06 (NSS) YEH, FRANK Y RUST COLLEGE DIV OF SCI AND MATHEMATICS HOLLY SPRINGS, MS 38635 Minority high school student research apprentice program

S03RR-03425-06 (NSS) DAVIS, JOHN A 1420 N SAN PABLO STREET UNIV OF S. CALF, PMB C301 LOS ANGELES, CA 90033 Minority high school student research apprentice program

S03RR-03426-05 (NSS) LIN, KUANG-TZU D MEHARRY MEDICAL COLLEGE 1005 D B TODD BOULEVARD NASHVILLE, TN 37208 Minority high school student research apprentice program

S03RR-03427-05 (NSS) HODGSON, ERNEST NORTH CAROLINA STATE UNIV NCSU BOX 7633 RALEIGH, NC 27695-7633 Minority high school student research apprentice program

S03RR-03430-06 (NSS) VAUGHN, JAMES E BECKMAN RES INST CITY OF HOPE 1450 EAST DUARTE ROAD DUARTE, CA 91010 Minority high school student research apprentice program

S03RR-03433-06 (NSS) LANSKY, SHIRLEY B ILLINOIS CANCER COUNCIL 36 S WABASH, SUITE 700 CHICAGO, IL 60603 Minority high school student research apprentice program

S03RR-03435-05 (NSS) SUMMERS, DENISE O PURDUE UNIVERSITY LYNN HALL WEST LAFAYETTE, IN 47907 Minority high school student research apprentice program

S03RR-03436-06 (NSS) HELM, EDWARD G LSU SCH MED, MED ED BLDG 1901 PERDIDO ST, STE 3101 NEW ORLEANS, LA 70112-1393 Minority high school student research apprentice program

PROJECT NO., ORGANIZATIONAL UNIT., INVESTIGATOR, ADDRESS, TITLE

S03RR-03437-06 (NSS) MC CLUER, ROBERT H EUNICE KENNEDY SHRIVER CTR 200 TRAPELO ROAD WALTHAM, MA 02254 Minority high school student research apprentice program
S03RR-03440-06 (NSS) YANOFF, JAY M UMDNJ-SCH OF OSTEOPATHIC MED 401 S CENTRAL PLAZA STRATFORD, NJ 08084 Minority high school student research apprentice program
S03RR-03441-06 (NSS) LEWIS, LESLIE A RES FDN/YORK COLLEGE, C U N Y 94-20 GUY BREWER BLVD JAMAICA, N Y 11451 Minority high school student research apprentice program
S03RR-03442-06 (NSS) LEGUIRE, LAWRENCE E CHILDREN'S HOSPITAL 700 CHILDREN'S DRIVE COLUMBUS, OH 43205 Minority high school student research apprentice program
S03RR-03443-06 (NSS) FRAME, ANNE D INTER AMERICA UNIV/PUERTO RICO P O BOX 1293 HATO REY, P R 00919 Minority high school student research apprentice program
S03RR-03444-06 (NSS) MARKEL, KARLA J BLOOD CTR S E WISCONSIN, INC 1701 W WISCONSIN AVENUE MILKWAUKEE, WI 53233 Minority high school student research apprentice program
S03RR-03445-05 (NSS) HEDGE, GEORGE A W V U RESEARCH CORPORATION 2266-C HLTH SCI SOUTH MORGANTOWN, WV 26506 Minority high school student research apprentice program
S03RR-03446-05 (NSS) DUNCAN, EDGAR N UNIVERSITY OF PITTSBURGH 130 DESOTO STREET PITTSBURGH, PA 15261 Minority high school student research apprentice program
S03RR-03448-04 (NSS) GIBALDI, MILO SCH OF PHARMACY, SC-69 UNIVERSITY OF WASHINGTON SEATTLE, WA 98195 Minority high school student research apprentice program
S03RR-03449-05 (NSS) HICKEY, TERRY L UNIV OF ALABAMA/UAB STATION 102, MORTIMER JORDAN HALL BIRMINGHAM, AL 35294 Minority high school student research apprentice program
S03RR-03450-05 (NSS) ROBLES, LAURA J CALIFORNIA STATE UNIVERSITY 1000 E VICTORIA STREET CARSON, CA 90747 Minority high school student research apprentice program
S03RR-03451-05 (NSS) MURPHY, CLAIRE L COLLEGE OF SCIENCES SAN DIEGO STATE UNIVERSITY SAN DIEGO, CA 92182-0551 Minority high school student research apprentice program
S03RR-03452-05 (NSS) KATOVICH, MICHAEL J UNIVERISTY OF FLORIDA BOX J-487 JHMHC GAINESVILLE, FLA 32610 Minority high school student research apprentice program
S03RR-03454-05 (NSS) WILEY, ROBERT A UNIVERSITY OF IOWA COL OF PHARM IOWA CITY, IA 52242 Minority high school student research apprentice program
S03RR-03455-05 (NSS) FELLOWS, ROBERT E, JR BOWEN SCIENCE BLD, RM 5-572 THE UNIV OF IOWA IOWA CITY, IA 52242 Minority high school student research apprentice program
S03RR-03456-05 (NSS) SQUIER, CHRISTOPHER A UNIVERSITY OF IOWA COLLEGE OF DENTISTRY IOWA CITY, IA 52242 Minority high school student research apprentice program
S03RR-03457-05 (NSS) MYSLINSKI, NORBERT R UNIV OF MARYLAND DENTAL SCHOOL 666 W. BALTIMORE STREET BALTIMORE, MARYLAND 21201 Minority high school student research apprentice program
S03RR-03459-05 (NSS) BLANE, HOWARD T RESEARCH INST ON ALCOHOLISM 1021 MAIN STREET BUFFALO, N Y 14203 Minority high school student research apprentice program
S03RR-03460-05 (NSS) STREKAS, THOMAS C QUEENS COLLEGE-C U N Y 65-30 KISSENA BLVD FLUSHING, N Y 11367 Minority high school student research apprentice program
S03RR-03461-05 (NSS) PERGOLIZZI, ROBERT G NORTH SHORE UNIVERSITY HOSP 350 COMMUNITY DRIVE MANHASSET, N Y 11030 Minority high school student research apprentice program
S03RR-03462-05 (NSS) WARREN, MICHELLE P ST LUKE'S ROOSEVELT HOSP CTR 428 WEST 59TH STREET NEW YORK, N Y 10019 Minority high school student research apprentice program
S03RR-03463-04 (NSS) PAGAN, ELI F PONCE SCHOOL OF MEDICINE PO BOX 7004, UNIVERSITY STR. PONCE, PR 00732 Minority high school student research apprentice program
S03RR-03464-05 (NSS) GIBSON, WILLIAM A BAYLOR COLLEGE OF DENTISTRY 3302 GASTON AVENUE DALLAS, TX 75246 Minority high school student research apprentice program
S03RR-03465-05 (NSS) JACKSON, HENRY P UNIV OF TEXAS HLTH CTR P O BOX 2003 TYLER, TX 75710 Minority high school student research apprentice program
S03RR-03466-05 (NSS) YUILL, THOMAS M UNIVERSITY OF WISCONSIN 2015 LINDEN DRIVE, WEST MADISON, WI 53706 Minority high school student research apprentice program
S03RR-03467-05 (NSS) BIGGERSTAFF, ROBERT H UNIV OF TEXAS HLTH SCI CTR 7703 FLOYD CURL DRIVE SAN ANTONIO, TX 78284-7764 Minority high school student research apprentice program
S03RR-03468-05 (NSS) FUNKHOUSER, EDWARD A TEXAS A&M UNIVERSITY COLLEGE STATION, TX 77843-2128 Minority high school student research apprentice program
S03RR-03469-04 (NSS) WILLIAMS, CAROLYN VANDERBILT UNIVERSITY PO BOX 6006-B NASHVILLE, TN 37235 Minority high school student research apprentice program
S03RR-03470-03 (NSS) SEAGRAVE, JEANCLARE LOVELACE MEDICAL FOUNDATION 2425 RIDGECREST DR, S E ALBUQUERQUE, NM 87108 Minority high school student research apprentice program
S03RR-03471-04 (NSS) JAY, MICHAEL J UNIVERSITY OF KENTUCKY 907-909 ROSE STREET LEXINGTON, KY 40536-0082 Minority high school student research apprentice program
S03RR-03473-04 (NSS) HASH, JOHN H VANDERBILT UNIV SCH OF MED 21ST AND GARLAND AVENUES NASHVILLE, TN 37232 Minority high school student research apprentice program
S03RR-03474-04 (NSS) FOX, LYNDA M ELEANOR ROOSEVELT INSTITUTE 1899 GAYLORD STREET DENVER, CO 80206 Minority high school student research apprentice program
S03RR-03477-04 (NSS) HANCOCK, ROBERT A LINCOLN UNIVERSITY JEFFERSON CITY, MO 65101 Minority high school student research apprentice program
S03RR-03478-04 (NSS) BROWN, JAMES C UNIVERSITY OF MISSISSIPPI 126 SHOEMAKER HALL UNIVERSITY, MS 38677 Minority high school student research apprentice program
S03RR-03479-04 (NSS) FITZSIMONS, KATHLEEN H THE CLEVELAND CLINIC FND 1 CLINIC CTR, 9500 EUCLID AVE CLEVELAND, OHIO 44195 Minority high school student research apprentice program

PROJECT NO., ORGANIZATIONAL UNIT., INVESTIGATOR, ADDRESS, TITLE

S03RR-03482-02 (NSS) SCHNEIDER, ROBERT F SUNY OFFICE OF RESEARCH SERVIC STONY BROOK, NY 11794 Minority high school student research apprentice program
S03RR-03483-04 (NSS) DILL, JOHN RICHARD MEMPHIS STATE UNIVERSITY ACADEMIC AFFAIRS MEMPHIS, TN 38152 Minority high school student research apprentice program
S03RR-03484-04 (NSS) JACKSON, GEORGE A IOWA STATE UNIVERSITY 301 BEARDSHEAR HALL AMES, IA 50011 Minority high school student research apprentice program
S03RR-03485-03 (NSS) CIMADEVILLA, JOSE M ST MARY'S UNIVERSITY ONE CAMINO SANTA MARIA SAN ANTONIO, TX 78284 Minority high school student research apprentice program
S03RR-03488-04 (NSS) MORROW, LESTER G OHIO STATE UNIVERSITY 1000 LINCOLN TOWER COLUMBUS, OH 43210 Minority high school student research apprentice program
S03RR-03490-04 (NSS) HILL, GERALD L UNIV OF MINN, DULUTH 10 UNIVERSITY DRIVE DULUTH, MN 55812 Minority high school student research apprentice program
S03RR-03493-03 (NSS) SINGH, JARNAIL STILLMAN COLLEGE P O BOX 1430 TUSCALOOSA, AL 35403 Minority high school student research apprentice program
S03RR-03494-03 (NSS) RUDOLPH, FREDERICK B RICE UNIVERSITY P O BOX 1892 HOUSTON, TX 77251 Minority high school student research apprentice program
S03RR-03495-03 (NSS) LINDELL, THOMAS J BIOSCIENCES WEST, RM 308 UNIVERSITY OF ARIZONA TUSCON, ARIZONA 85721 Minority high school student research apprentice program
S03RR-03497-03 (NSS) KALE, PURUSHOTTAM G ALABAMA A & M UNIVERSITY P O BOX 610 NORMAL, AL 35762 Minority high school student research apprentice program
S03RR-03499-03 (NSS) SCOTT, JOHN F UNIVEIRSITY OF HAWAII AT HILO 523 W LANIKAULA ST HILO, HI 96720-4091 Minority high school student research apprentice program
S03RR-03500-03 (NSS) DENNISON, DAVID K UNIV OF TEXAS HLTH SCI CTR 6516 JOHN FREEMAN AVENUE HOUSTON, TX 77030 Minority high school student research apprentice program
S03RR-03501-02 (NSS) CARTER-DAWSON, LOVENIA UNIV OF TEXAS HLTH SCI CTR 6420 LAMAR FLEMING AVE, RM 316 HOUSTON, TX 77030 Minority high school student research apprentice program
S03RR-03502-03 (NSS) EISERLING, FREDERICK A UNIVERSITY OF CALIFORNIA 1312 MURPHY HALL LOS ANGELES, CA 90024 Minority high school student research apprentice program
S03RR-03503-03 (NSS) STEMBER, MARILYN L UNIVERSITY OF COLORADO 4200 EAST 9TH AVENUE DENVER, CO 80262 Minority high school student research apprentice program
S03RR-03504-03 (NSS) HELLMAN, SAMUEL UNIVERSITY OF CHICAGO MED CTR 5841 S MARYLAND AVE, BOX 417 CHICAGO, IL 60637 Minority high school student research apprentice program
S03RR-03505-03 (NSS) CHANCE, KENNETH NEW JERSEY DENTAL SCHOOL 110 BERGEN STREET NEWARK, NJ 07103-2425 Minority high school student research apprentice program
S03RR-03507-03 (NSS) BAUN, MARA M UNIV NEBR MED CTR COL NURSING 42ND AND DEWEY AVENUE OMAHA, NE 68105 Minority high school student research apprentice program
S03RR-03509-03 (NSS) SHORTLIFFE, EDWARD H STANFORD UNIVERSITY MED CTR MSOB X215 STANFORD, CA 94305-5479 Minority high school student research apprentice program
S03RR-03510-03 (NSS) RUBIN, ROBERT W UNIVERSITY OF MIAMI P O BOX 016189 MIAMI, FL 33136 Minority high school student research apprentice program
S03RR-03512-03 (NSS) TALLEY, ROBERT C UNIVERSITY OF SOUTH DAKOTA 2501 WEST 22ND STREET SIOUX FALLS, SD 57117 Minority high school student research apprentice program
S03RR-03513-03 (NSS) VAN ORT, SUZANNE R UNIVERSITY OF ARIZONA COLLEGE OF NURSING, BLDG 203 TUCSON, AZ 85721 Minority high school student research apprentice program
S03RR-03516-03 (NSS) THEDFORD, ROOSEVELT CLARK COLLEGE 240 JAMES P BRAWLEY DRIVE, S W ATLANTA, GA 30314 Minority high school student research apprentice program
S03RR-03517-03 (NSS) HARRIS, LOUIS S VIRGINIA COMMONWEALTH UNIV MCV STATION, BOX 613 RICHMOND, VA 23298 Minority high school student research apprentice program
S03RR-03518-02 (NSS) JONES, STANLEY T THE UNIVERSITY OF ALABAMA BOX 870268 TUSCALOOSA, AL 35487-0268 Minority high school student research apprentice program
S03RR-03520-02 (NSS) STOKES, GERALD V THE GEORGE WASHINGTON UNIVERSI 2300 EYE STREET, N W WASHINGTON, D C 20037 Minority high school student research apprentice program
S03RR-03522-02 (NSS) BAST, ROBERT C DUKE UNIVIERSITY MEDICAL CENTE BOX 3814 DURHAM, N C 27710 Minority high school student research apprentice program
S03RR-03523-02 (NSS) EBERLE, RICHARD W OKLAHOMA STATE UNIVERSITY VET MED BLDG STILLWATER, OK 74078 Minority high school student research apprentice program
S03RR-03524-02 (NSS) DE PEYSTER, ANN SAN DIEGO STATE UNIVERSITY GRADUATE SCHOOL OF PUBLIC HEAL SAN DIEGO, CA 92182 Minority high school student research apprentice program
S03RR-03525-02 (NSS) BARNARD, KATHYRN E UNIVERSITY OF WASHINGTON SEATTLE, WA 98195 Minority high school student research apprentice program
S03RR-03526-02 (NSS) CARLSON, GEORGE A THE MCLAUGHLIN RESEARCH INST 1625 3RD AVENUE GREAT FALLS, MT 59401 Minority high school student research apprentice program
S03RR-03527-02 (NSS) LARSON, ELAINE L JOHNS HOPKINS UNIVERSITY 600 N WOLFE STREET BALTIMORE, MD 21205 Minority high school student research apprentice program
S03RR-03528-02 (NSS) WILLIAMS, DIANE L UNIVERSITY OF CINCINNATI 231 BETHESDA AVE (M L 552) CINCINNATI, OH 45267-0552 Minority high school student research apprentice program
S03RR-03529-02 (NSS) DOBBINS, DOROTHY C EAST TENNESSEE STATE UNIVERSIT P O BOX 19900A JOHNSON CITY, TN 27614 Minority high school

student research apprentice program
S03RR-03530-02 (NSS) REYNOLDS, CHARLES P CHILDRENS HOSPITAL OF L A 4650 SUNSET BLVD LOS ANGELES, CA 90054-0700 Minority high school student research apprentice program
S03RR-03531-02 (NSS) HENDERSON, MAUREEN H FRED HUTCHINSON CANCER RES CTR 1124 COLUMBIA STREET SEATTLE, WA 98104 Minority high school student research apprentice program
S03RR-03532-02 (NSS) STEELE, ANNE C UNIV OF N C - GREENSBORO 214 MOSSMAN BUILDING GREENSBORO, NC 27412 Minority high school student research apprentice program
S03RR-03533-02 (NSS) CHOPRA, BALDEO K JOHNSON C SMITH UNIVERSITY 100 BEATTIES FORD ROAD CHARLOTTE, N C 28216 Minority high school student research apprentice program
S03RR-03535-02 (NSS) LINDEMANN, ROBERT A UNIVERSITYOF CALIFORNIA LOS ANGELES, CA 90024-1668 Minority high school student research apprentice program
S03RR-03536-02 (NSS) GOVINDAN, MELEDATH UNIV OF THE VIRGIN ISLANDS ST THOMAS, U S VI 00802 Minority high school student research apprentice program
S03RR-03537-02 (NSS) PEARSON, THOMAS A THE MARY IMOGENE BASSETT HOSP ONE ATWELL ROAD COOPERSTOWN, N Y 13326-1394 Minority high school student research apprentice program
S03RR-03538-01 (NSS) SHULER, CHARLES F UNIV OF SOUTHERN CALIFORNIA 2250 ALCAZAR ST CSA-103 LOS ANGELES, CA 90033 Minority high school student research apprentice program
S03RR-03539-01 (NSS) HALL, KARYL M CALIF INSTITUTE FOR MED RESEAR SAN JOSE, CA 95128 Minority high school student research apprentice program
S03RR-03540-01 (NSS) LAWELLIN, DAVID W THE CHILDREN'S HOSPITAL 1056 EAST 19TH AVENUE DENVER, CO 80218 Minority high school research apprentice program
S03RR-03541-01 (NSS) O'LEARY, TIMOTHY J ARMED FORCES INST OF PATHOLOGY WASHINGTON, DC 20306-6000 Minority high school student research apprentice program
S03RR-03542-01 (NSS) JORDAN, CHESTER L GRAMBLING STATE UNIVERSITY PO BOX 4211 GRAMBLING, LA 71245 Minority high school student research apprentice program
S03RR-03543-01 (NSS) WASHINGTON, ROBERT O UNIVERSITY OF NEW ORLEANS LAKEFRONT CAMPUS NEW ORLEANS, LA 70148 Minority high school research apprentice program
S03RR-03544-01 (NSS) LENZ, ELIZABETH R UNIV OF MARYLAND AT BALTIMORE 655 W LOMBARD STREET BALTIMORE, MD 21201 Minority high school research apprentice program
S03RR-03545-01 (NSS) PHILLIPS, CONSTANCE L BOSTON UNIVERSITY SCHOOL OF ME 80 E CONCORD ST, S202 BOSTON, MA 02118 Minority high school research apprentice program
S03RR-03546-01 (NSS) SEGRE, GINO V MASSACHUSETTS GENERAL HOSPITAL BAR-3 BOSTON, MA 02114 Minority high school research apprentice program
S03RR-03547-01 (NSS) SHARP, BURT M HENNEPIN COUNTY MEDICAL CENTER 701 PARK AVENUE SOUTH MINNEAPOLIS, MN 55415 Minority high school research apprentice program
S03RR-03548-01 (NSS) GLAROS, ALAN G UNIVERSITY OF MISSOURI 650 EAST 25TH STREET KANSAS CITY, MO 64110 Minority high school research apprentice program
S03RR-03549-01 (NSS) LAGUNOFF, DAVID ST LOUIS UNIVERSITY 1402 SOUTH GRAND BLVD ST LOUIS, MO 63104 Minority high school research apprentice program
S03RR-03551-01 (NSS) CARTER, TIMOTHY H ST JOHN'S UNIVERSITY GRAND CENTRAL & UTOPIA PARKWAY JAMAICA, N Y 11439 Minority high school research apprentice program
S03RR-03552-01 (NSS) GARANT, PHILIAS SUNY AT STONY BROOK 160 ROCKLAND HALL STONY BROOK, N Y 11794-8700 Minority high school research apprentice program
S03RR-03553-01 (NSS) CIACCIO, LEONARD A RES FDN/COLLEGE OF STATEN ISLA 130 STUYVESENT PLACE STATEN ISLAND, N Y 10301 Minority high school student research apprentice program
S03RR-03554-01 (NSS) MORROW, LESTER G OHIO STATE UNIVERSITY 1800 CANNON DRIVE COLUMBUS, OH 43210 Minority high school research apprentice program
S03RR-03555-01 (NSS) MCKEAN, DAVID J MAYO FOUNDATION 200 FIRST STREET SOUTHWEST ROCHESTER, MN 55905 Minority high school research apprentice program
S03RR-03556-01 (NSS) BARMACK, NEAL H GOOD SAMARITAN HOSP & MED CTR 1120 N W 20TH AVENUE PORTLAND, OR 97209 Minority high school student research apprentice program
S03RR-03557-01 (NSS) MENASHE, VICTOR D OREGON HEALTH SCIENCES UNIV PORTLAND, OR 97207-0574 Minority high school student research apprentice program
S03RR-03558-01 (NSS) GIBB, JAMES W UNIVERSITY OF UTAH SKAGGS HALL, ROOM 112 SALT LAKE CITY, UT 84112 Minority high school research apprentice program
S03RR-03559-01 (NSS) WESTENSKOW, DWAYNE UNIVERSITY OF UTAH 50 NORTH MEDICAL DRIVE SALT LAKE CITY, UT 84132 Minority high school research apprentice program
S03RR-03560-01 (NSS) ABBOTT, ELIZABETH F UNIVERSITY OF FLORIDA 111 NORMAN HALL GAINESVILLE, FL 32611-2053 Minority high school research apprentice program
R44RR-03565-03 (SSS) LAMSON, MYLES L MICROMATH, INC. 2469 EAST FORT UNION BOULEVARD SALT LAKE CITY, UT 84121 Chemical equilibrium software development
R01RR-03576-06 (AR) FLESNESS, NATHAN R ISIS 12101 JOHNNY CAKE RIDGE RD APPLE VALLEY MN 55124 Chimpanzee population monitoring and analysis
R01RR-03578-06 (AR) BLOOMSMITH, MOLLIE A UNIVERSITY OF TEXAS MD MD ANDERSON CANCER CTR SCI PAR BASTROP TX 78602 Promoting chimpanzee well-being through applied research
U42RR-03582-05A1 (AR) MARX, PRESTON A NEW MEXICO STATE UNIVERSITY HOLLOMAN AFB, NM 88330-1027 National chimpanzee breeding and research program
U42RR-03583-06 (AR) GREER, WILLIAM E UNIV OF SOUTHERN LOUISIANA 100 AVENUE D NEW IBERIA, LA 70560 Establishment of a chimpanzee breeding and research program
R01RR-03587-06 (AR) GOULD, KENNETH G EMORY UNIVERSITY ATLANTA GA 30322 Artificial breeding of chimpanzees
U42RR-03589-06 (AR) KEELING, MICHALE E UT MD ANDERSON CANCER CENTER ROUTE 2 BOX 151-B1 BASTROP TX 78602 National chimpanzee breeding and research program
U42RR-03591-06 (AR) SWENSON, RICHARD B EMORY UNIVERSITY ATLANTA GA 30322 Chimpanzee breeding and research program
U42RR-03602-06 (AR) FRITZ, JO PRIMATE FOUNDATION OF ARIZONA P.O. BOX 86 TEMPE, AZ 85280 Chimpanzee breeding and research program
P40RR-03624-05 (AR) HAMM, THOMAS E STANFORD UNIVERSITY QUAD 7, BUILDING 330 STANFORD, CA 94305 Animal resources diagnostic and investigative laboratory
P40RR-03624-05 0001 (AR) LUKAS, VICTOR Animal resources diagnostic and investigative laboratory The role of carbacillus as a pathogen in rabbits
P40RR-03624-05 0002 (AR) RUEHL, BILL Animal resources diagnostic and investigative laboratory Pasteurella multocida pili--Characterization and role in pathogenesis
P40RR-03624-05 0003 (AR) BLUM, JOANNE Animal resources diagnostic and investigative laboratory Anesthetics and narcotics in laboratory animals
P40RR-03624-05 0004 (AR) HAMM, THOMAS Animal resources diagnostic and investigative laboratory Physiological effects of somatomedins
P40RR-03624-05 9001 (AR) BLUM, JOANNE Animal resources diagnostic and investigative laboratory Core--Animal health program
P40RR-03624-05 9002 (AR) HAMM, THOMAS E, JR Animal resources diagnostic and investigative laboratory Core--Training and education
P41RR-03631-04 (SSS) HO, CHIEN CARNEGIE MELLON UNIVERSITY 4400 FIFTH AVENUE PITTSBURGH, PA 15213 A multidisciplinary NMR center for biomedical research
P41RR-03631-04 9001 (SSS) LOWE, IRVING J A multidisciplinary NMR center for biomedical research Core research--NMR methodology
P41RR-03631-04 9002 (SSS) KORETSKY, ALAN P A multidisciplinary NMR center for biomedical research Core research--NMR analysis of energy metabolism in the cat brain
P41RR-03631-04 0001 (SSS) MAKOWKA, LEONARD A multidisciplinary NMR center for biomedical research NMR imaging & spectroscopy to predict liver viability for transplantation
P41RR-03631-04 0002 (SSS) VAN THIEL, DAVID H A multidisciplinary NMR center for biomedical research NMR spectroscopy--Portal systemic encephalopathy and brain metabolism
P41RR-03631-04 0003 (SSS) VERBALIS, JOSEPH G A multidisciplinary NMR center for biomedical research Hyponatremia & its correction--Effects on CNS morphology and function
P40RR-03640-05 (SRC) KESSLER, MATTHEW J UNIVERSITY OF PUERTO RICO MEDICAL SCIENCES CAMPUS SABANA SECA, PR 00749 The Caribbean primate research center program
P40RR-03640-05 0004 (SRC) DAWSON, WILLIAM W The Caribbean primate research center program Age-related macular degeneration and other eye diseases of rhesus macaques
P40RR-03640-05 0005 (SRC) HOWARD, CHARLES F The Caribbean primate research center program Non-insulin dependent diabetes mellitus
P40RR-03640-05 0006 (SRC) SCHWARTZ, SUSAN M The Caribbean primate research center program Developmental aspects of growth and metabolism in preobese rhesus macaques
P40RR-03640-05 0007 (SRC) STITZER, SUSAN O The Caribbean primate research center program Spontaneous hypertension in rhesus macaques
P40RR-03640-05 0009 (SRC) PRITZKER, KENNETH P H The Caribbean primate research center program Degenerative arthritis in aging non-human primates
P40RR-03640-05 0012 (SRC) BURR, DAVID B The Caribbean primate research center program Skeletal growth and remodeling in rhesus monkeys
P40RR-03640-05 0013 (SRC) AGUILO, FRANCISCO The Caribbean primate research center program Bone densitometry and biological correlational studies in rhesus monkeys
P40RR-03640-05 0023 (SRC) BERARD, JOHN The Caribbean primate research center program DNA fingerprinting and its application to behavioral biology
P40RR-03640-05 0024 (SRC) BERCOVITCH, FRED B The Caribbean primate research center program Comparative socioendocrinology
P40RR-03640-05 0025 (SRC) MARLER, PETER The Caribbean primate research center program Rhesus monkey vocal repetoire--Acoustics, anatomy, and vocal tract modeling
P40RR-03640-05 0026 (SRC) MARRIOTT, BERNADETTE The Caribbean primate research center program Geophagy in the Cayo Santiago monkeys
P40RR-03640-05 0027 (SRC) MCCULLOCH, CHRISTOPHER A G The Caribbean primate research center program Peridontitis and inflammatory bone loss in aging non-human primates
P40RR-03640-05 0028 (SRC) EYLAR, EDWARD H The Caribbean primate research center program Immunodeficiency in aged rhesus T cells
P40RR-03640-05 0029 (SRC) KRAISELBURD, EDMUNDO The Caribbean primate research center program Development of a cebrus monkey model for the study of human AIDS
P40RR-03640-05 0030 (SRC) HILLYER, GEORGE V The Caribbean primate research center program Development of an experimental vaccine against Schistosoma mansoni
P40RR-03640-05 9001 (SRC) KESSLER, MATTHEW J The Caribbean primate research center program Core--Support and animal care
G12RR-03641-06 (SRC) FERNANDEZ, JUAN R UNIVERSITY OF PUERTO RICO RIO PIEDRAS CAMPUS RIO PIEDRAS, PR 00931 Biomedical research center for the University of Puerto Rico, Rio Piedras
P41RR-03655-05 (SSS) ELSTON, ROBERT C LOUISIANA STATE UNIV MED CTR 1901 PERDIDO ST NEW ORLEANS, LA 70112 Human genetic analysis resource
R44RR-03801-03 (SSS) GOLAB, THOMAS J POTOMAC MEDICAL SYSTEMS, INC PO BOX 4212 SILVER SPRING, MD 20904 True color image workstation for pathology research
P40RR-03820-03S1 (AR) KUZIRIAN, ALAN M MARINE BIOLOGICAL LABORATORY WOODS HOLE, MA 02543 Laboratory culture of hermissenda
R01RR-04026-05 (GNM) OVERTON, G CHRISTIAN UNIVERSITY OF PENNSYLVANIA 422 CURIE BLVD PHILADELPHIA, PA 19104-6145 Knowledge based biological modeling information system

PROJECT NO., ORGANIZATIONAL UNIT., INVESTIGATOR, ADDRESS, TITLE

R24RR-04047-04 (AR) JACOBY, ROBERT O YALE UNIVERSITY 155 WHITNEY AVENUE NEW HAVEN, CT 06520 Parvovirus infection of rats
P41RR-04050-03 (SSS) ELLISMAN, MARK H UNIV OF CALIFORNIA, SAN DIEGO 9500 GILMAN DRIVE LA JOLLA, CA 92093-0608 South-western regional IVEM and image analysis resource
P41RR-04050-03 9001 (SSS) SINGER, S South-western regional IVEM and image analysis resource Development of immunolabeling and enzyme histochemistry-Core
P41RR-04050-03 9002 (SSS) TOKUYASU, K South-western regional IVEM and image analysis resource Semi-thin sections for IVEM--Core
P41RR-04050-03 9003 (SSS) ELLISMAN, M South-western regional IVEM and image analysis resource Subcellular complexes associated with neurons--Core
P41RR-04224-04 (SSS) WEBB, WATT W CORNELL UNIVERSITY 210 CLARK HALL ITHACA NY 14853 Biotechnology resource digital electro-optical imaging
P41RR-04224-04 0003 (SSS) HEPPEL, LEON Biotechnology resource digital electro-optical imaging Intracellular calcium signals in ATP permeabilizable cells
P41RR-04224-04 0004 (SSS) MORRISON, G H Biotechnology resource digital electro-optical imaging Comparative imaging of intracellular calcium in cultures cells
P41RR-04224-04 0005 (SSS) HESS, G P Biotechnology resource digital electro-optical imaging Fluorescent screening for CNS cell sorting for neurotransmitter sensitivity
P41RR-04224-04 0006 (SSS) NUSSENWEIG, VICTOR Biotechnology resource digital electro-optical imaging Decay accelerating factor diffusion on Hela cell surfaces
P41RR-04224-04 0007 (SSS) HESS, G P Biotechnology resource digital electro-optical imaging Expression of acetylcholine receptor in yeast and insertion in cell membrane
P41RR-04224-04 0008 (SSS) CANTOR, CHARLES Biotechnology resource digital electro-optical imaging Nascent collaborations using video imaging analysis
P41RR-04224-04 0009 (SSS) LEWIS, AARON Biotechnology resource digital electro-optical imaging Interaction with near-field optical microscopy development
P41RR-04224-04 0001 (SSS) BAIRD, BARBARA Biotechnology resource digital electro-optical imaging Immunoglobulin E on rat basophilic leukemia cells
P41RR-04224-04 0002 (SSS) MILLARD, P J Biotechnology resource digital electro-optical imaging Intracellular calcium ion changes in RBL cells using video microscopy
P41RR-04224-04 9001 (SSS) WEBB, WATT W Biotechnology resource digital electro-optical imaging Core research--Digital electro-optical imaging
P41RR-04224-04 9002 (SSS) WEBB, WATT W Biotechnology resource digital electro-optical imaging Core research--Digital electro-optical image processing and photometry
P41RR-04224-04 9003 (SSS) WEBB, WATT W Biotechnology resource digital electro-optical imaging Core search--Image analysis technology for cellular dynamics
P41RR-04224-04 9004 (SSS) WEBB, WATT W Biotechnology resource digital electro-optical imaging Core research--Methods of studying receptor molecule dynamics
P41RR-04224-04 9005 (SSS) WEBB, WATT W Biotechnology resource digital electro-optical imaging Core research--Dynamic laser interferometric imaging
P41RR-04224-04 9006 (SSS) WEBB, WATT W Biotechnology resource digital electro-optical imaging Core research--Fast UV laser photolytic activation
P41RR-04224-04 9007 (SSS) WEBB, WATT W Biotechnology resource digital electro-optical imaging Core research--Fast pseudo-confocal microscopy
P41RR-04224-04 9008 (SSS) WEBB, WATT W Biotechnology resource digital electro-optical imaging Core research--Quantitative dynamic imaging confocal microscopy
P41RR-04224-04 9009 (SSS) WEBB, WATT W Biotechnology resource digital electro-optical imaging Core research--Tunneling current microscopy forliving cells
R24RR-04226-04 (AR) HANLON, ROGER T MARINE BIOMEDICAL INSTITUTE 200 UNIVERSITY BLVD GALVESTON, TX 77550 Development of a prepared diet for cephalopods
P40RR-04231-05 (GEN) MORTIMER, ROBERT K UNIV OF CALIFORNIA 102 DONNER LABORATORY BERKELEY, CA 94720 In support of the Yeast Genetic Stock Center
R24RR-04301-04 (AR) STONE, WILLIAM H TRINITY UNIVERSITY 715 STADIUM DRIVE SAN ANTONIO, TX 78212 Genetic laboratory for typing nonhuman primates
P40RR-04326-04 (AR) ALTMAN, NORMAN H UNIVERSITY OF MIAMI P.O. BOX 016960 MIAMI, FL 33101 Animal disease diagnostic & investigative laboratory
P41RR-04328-04 (SSS) FREIRE, ERNESTO I JOHNS HOPKINS UNIVERSITY 34TH AND CHARLES STREETS BALTIMORE, MD 21218 Biocalorimetry center
P41RR-04328-04 0001 (SSS) FREIRE, ERNESTO I Biocalorimetry center Membrane biophysics--Assembly of biological membranes
P41RR-04328-04 0002 (SSS) ROSEMAN, SAUL Biocalorimetry center Thermodynamic studies of bacterial sugar transport system
P41RR-04328-04 0003 (SSS) ACKERS, GARY K Biocalorimetry center Site specific energetics of protein-DNA interactions
P41RR-04328-04 0004 (SSS) EDIDIN, MICHAEL E Biocalorimetry center Calorimetry in immunology and cell biology-ligand binding
P41RR-04328-04 0005 (SSS) LEE, YUAN C Biocalorimetry center Protein-carbohydrate interactions
P41RR-04328-04 0006 (SSS) PABO, CARL Biocalorimetry center Computer aided protein design--DNA binding proteins
P41RR-04328-04 9003 (SSS) PREIRE, ERNESTO I Biocalorimetry center Core research--Development of new methods of calorimetric data analysis
P41RR-04328-04 0007 (SSS) MOUDRIANAKIS, EVANGELOS N Biocalorimetry center Structure of the core histone octamer and the nucleosome
P41RR-04328-04 0008 (SSS) SHORTLE, DAVID Biocalorimetry center Folding and stability of staphylococcal nuclease mutants

P41RR-04328-04 0009 (SSS) BUCCI, ENRICO Biocalorimetry center Conformational studies of membrane bound fumarate-reductase
P41RR-04328-04 9001 (SSS) FREIRE, ERNESTO I Biocalorimetry center Core research--Development of new applications of calorimetric techniques
P41RR-04328-04 9002 (SSS) FREIRE, ERNESTO I Biocalorimetry center Core research--Development of calorimetric instrumentation
R44RR-04384-02A1 (SSS) LOWRANCE, JOHN L PRINCETON SCIENTIFIC INSTRUMEN 7 DEER PARK DRIVE MONMOUTH JUNCTION, NJ 08852 CCD camera system for x-ray diffraction imaging
R24RR-04507-04 (AR) SMITH, ABIGAIL L YALE UNIVERSITY SCH OF MEDICIN 333 CEDAR ST, P.O. BOX 3333 NEW HAVEN CT 06510 Mouse hepatitis virus-associated immune dysfunction
R01RR-04515-04 (AR) BOWDEN, DOUGLAS M UNIVERSITY OF WASHINGTON SJ-50 REGIONAL PRIMATE RESEARCH CTR SEATTLE WA 98195 Space, exercise and social needs of lab macaques
R29RR-04568-03 (AR) RILEY, LELA K UNIVERSITY OF MISSOURI DEPT. OF VETERINARY PATHOLOGY COLUMBIA, MO 65211 Molecular basis of Tyzzer's disease in research animals
R24RR-05056-03 (SSS) DAUSSET, JEAN C E P H 27 RUE JULIETTE DODU 75010 PARIS, FRANCE A kit of probes for markers on the human linkage map
P40RR-05062-03 (AR) HILLIARD, JULIA K SOUTHWEST FDN/BIOMEDICAL RES PO BOX 28147 SAN ANTONIO TX 78228-0147 Herpes B virus diagnostic laboratory--National response
G12RR-05075-04 (SRC) GRACE, MARCELLUS XAVIER UNIVERSITY OF LOUISIANA 7325 PALMETTO STREET NEW ORLEANS, LA 70125 Research center in biomedical research
R44RR-05077-03 (AR) KOTLIAR, ABRAHAM M HORIZON MICRO-ENVIRONMENTS 1081 INDUSTRIAL DRIVE WATKINSVILLE, GA 30677 Polymeric membrane barriers for animal isolation and confinement
R44RR-05079-03 (SSS) PEREL, JULIUS PHRASOR SCIENTIFIC INC 1536 HIGHLAND AVENUE DUARTE CA 91010 New technology for improving high mass ion detection
U42RR-05080-04 (AR) KEELING, MICHALE E UNIVERSITY OF TEXAS ROUTE 2 BOX 151-B1 BASTROP TX 78602 Establishment and maintenance of monkey breeding colony
U42RR-05081-03S1 (AR) KINTNER, BARBARA A MICHIGAN DEPT OF PUBLIC HEALTH 3500 NORTH LOGAN STREET LANSING MI 48909 Specific pathogen-free Rhesus breeding colony
U42RR-05083-04 (AR) TAUB, DAVID M LAB ANIMAL BREEDERS SERVICES I PO BOX 557 YEMASSEE SC 29945 Specific pathogen free Rhesus macaque breeding colony
U42RR-05088-04 (AR) WAGNER, JOSEPH L UNIVERSITY OF MIAMI 1600 NORTHWEST 10TH AVENUE MIAMI FL 33136 Establishment of a new SPF Rhesus monkey breeding center
R24RR-05090-04 (AR) SMITH, DAVID G UNIVERSITY OF CALIFORNIA CALIFORNIA PRIMATE RESEARCH CT DAVIS, CA 95616 Genetic management of macaques by DNA RFLP analysis
U42RR-05091-04 (AR) HUNT, RONALD NEW ENGLAND REGIONAL PRIMATE C ONE PINE HILL DRIVE SOUTHBORO MA 01772 Pathogen-free rhesus monkey breeding & research
R01RR-05092-04 (AR) BLOOMSMITH, MOLLIE A UNIV OF TEXAS MD ANDERSON ROUTE 2 BOX 151-B1 BASTROP TX 78602 Applied research for improving the behavioral management
U42RR-05093-04 (AR) BOYD, DALE D HAZLETON RESEARCH PRODUCTS INC PO BOX 549 ALICE TX 78333 Development of a SPF Rhesus monkey breeding colony
M01RR-05096-02 (CLR) FULGINITI, VINCENT A TULANE UNIVERSITY SCH OF MED 1430 TULANE AVE NEW ORLEANS, LA 70112 General clinical research center-Building renovation
P41RR-05097-04 (SSS) CANDE, W ZACHEUS LAWRENCE BERKELEY LABORATORY 1 CYCLOTRON ROAD/CELL BIOLOGY BERKELEY, CA 94720 A west coast facility for IVEM
P40RR-05236-03 (AR) FRAZIER, JOHN M JOHNS HOPKINS UNIVERSITY 615 NORTH WOLFE STREET BALTIMORE, MD 21205 Core support--Center for alternatives to animal testing
R44RR-05269-02 (REN) COLLAS, PHILLIPPE TSI CORP 57 UNION STREET WORCESTER, MA 01608 Genetically identical rabbits
R01RR-05272-03 (SSS) EISINGER, JOSEF CUNY - MT. SINAI SCH OF MEDICI 1 GUSTAVE L. LEVY PLACE NEW YORK, NY 10029 Spectrofluorometric CCD microscope
R01RR-05276-03 (AR) DE WAAL, FRANS B EMORY UNIVERSITY 954 GATEWOOD ROAD ATLANTA, GA 30322 Relation between space and aggression in rhesus macaques
M01RR-05280-03 (CLR) FOGEL, BERNARD J UNIVERSITY OF MIAMI PO BOX 016960 (R-699) MIAMI, FL 33101 General clinical research center
M01RR-05280-03 0001 (CLR) ALEJANDRO, RODOLFO General clinical research center Transplantation of islets of Langerhans in patients w/ insulin dependent diabetes
M01RR-05280-03 0004 (CLR) BURKE, GEORGE W General clinical research center Serial liver biopsies after liver transplantation
M01RR-05280-03 0007 (CLR) LIAN, ERIC C-Y General clinical research center Thrombotic thrombocytopenic purpura (TTP)
M01RR-05280-03 0015 (CLR) YUNIS, ADEL A General clinical research center Pathogenic mechanisms in chloramphenicol-induced aplastic anemia
M01RR-05280-03 0016 (CLR) SOSENKO, ILENE R S General clinical research center Early admin. of intravenous lipids to very low birth weight infants
M01RR-05280-03 0017 (CLR) DAVIS, JANET L General clinical research center Cytomegalovirus retinitis trial--Foscarnet/ganciclovir
M01RR-05280-03 0018 (CLR) BANDSTRA, EMMALEE S General clinical research center Neurodevelopmental outcome of in utero cocaine exposure
S07RR-05300-30 (NSS) BIRKEDAL-HANSEN, HENNING UNIV OF ALABAMA IN BIRMINGHAM UNIV STA, SCH DENT, SDB 746 BIRMINGHAM, ALA 35294 Biomedical research support
S07RR-05300-30 0200 (NSS) HEAVEN, TIM Biomedical research support RADIOGRAPHIC MEASUREMENT OF ARTIFICIAL CARIES LESIONS
S07RR-05300-30 0201 (NSS) RODU, BRAD Biomedical research support HUMAN PAPILLOMAVIRUS EXPRESSION IN HEAD & NECK CANCER
S07RR-05300-30 0202 (NSS) REDDY, MICHAEL Biomedical research

support PERIODONTAL ACTIVITY MODELING
S07RR-05300-30 0203 (NSS) RAHEMTULLA, BRITTA Biomedical research support SALIVARY THIOCYANATE METABOLISM IN PATIENTS UNDERGOING CHEMOTHERAPY
S07RR-05300-30 0204 (NSS) CHILDERS, NOEL Biomedical research support LIPOSOME S MUTANS DELIVERY SYSTEM FOR IMMUNITY
S07RR-05300-30 0205 (NSS) WALLACE, MARTHA C Biomedical research support EVAL OF EDENTULISM EFFECT ON FREQUENCY OF FEBRILE EPISODES; GERIATRIC PATIENTS
S07RR-05300-30 0206 (NSS) WHITE, KEVIN Biomedical research support AN ALTERNATIVE METHOD FOR ASSESSING IN VIVO DENTURE TOOTH WEAR
S07RR-05300-30 0207 (NSS) RETIEF, HUGO Biomedical research support PYRUVIC ACID GLYCINE; STRENGTH OF DENTIN BOND SYSTEM; DENTIN & ENAMEL
S07RR-05300-30 0208 (NSS) RETIEF, HUGO Biomedical research support TEMP & LOAD CYCLING; MICROLEAKAGE CLASS V DENTIN BOND AGENT & COMPOSITE RESTORAT
S07RR-05300-30 0209 (NSS) CHILDERS, NOEL Biomedical research support DETERMINE SALIVARY RISK FACTORS FOR ORAL COMPLICATIONS; CHILDREN W/ LEUKEMIA
S07RR-05300-30 0210 (NSS) LANTZ, MARILYN Biomedical research support EFFECT OF HEMIN LIMITATION ON FIBRINOGEN BINDING BY B INTERMEDIUS
S07RR-05300-30 0211 (NSS) RAHEMTULLA, FIROZ Biomedical research support BIOSYNTHESIS OF DERMATAN SULFATE PROTEOGLYCANS BY HUMAN GINGIVAL FIBROBLASTS
S07RR-05300-30 0212 (NSS) RAHEMTULLA, BRITTA Biomedical research support MONOCLONAL ANTIBODIES AS STRUCTURAL PROBES FOR PEROXIDASES
S07RR-05300-30 0213 (NSS) THORNTON, JOHN Biomedical research support ORAL HEALTH SURVEY; AGING & ELDERLY MENTALLY RETARDED: PILOT STUDY
S07RR-05300-30 0214 (NSS) DECARLO, ARTHUR Biomedical research support STIMULATION OF HOST CELL COLLAGEN BREAKDOWN BY MICROBIAL FACTOR
S07RR-05301-21 (NSS) HIGHSMITH, STEFAN UNIVERSITY OF THE PACIFIC 2155 WEBSTER STREET SAN FRANCISCO, CA 94115 Biomedical research support grant
S07RR-05301-21 0730 (NSS) HIGSON, HOWARD Biomedical research support grant PURCHASE OF SHARED EQUIPMENT: SS34 FIXED ANGLE ROTOR
S07RR-05301-21 0731 (NSS) COHEN, JOEL Biomedical research support grant COMPUTATION OF ION BINDING TO MEMBRANES
S07RR-05301-21 0732 (NSS) UNKNOWN Biomedical research support grant DIAMOND KNIFE REPAIR
S07RR-05301-21 0733 (NSS) MURPHY, ALEXANDER Biomedical research support grant CALCIUM PUMP PROTEIN OF SARCOPLASMIC RETICULUM MEMBRANES
S07RR-05301-21 0734 (NSS) CAROL COAN Biomedical research support grant SUBSCRIPTION TO "CURRENT CONTENTS" ON DISKETTE
S07RR-05301-21 0735 (NSS) SNOWDOWNE, KEN Biomedical research support grant NOVEL METHOD TO STUDY CA(2+) DEPENDENT EXOCYTOSIS
S07RR-05301-21 0736 (NSS) HIGHSMITH, STEFAN Biomedical research support grant TEMPERATURE DEPENDENCE OF TRYTOPHAN POLARIZATION
S07RR-05303-30 (NSS) CRAWFORD, WILLIAM H UNIV OF SOUTHERN CALIFORNIA UNIVERSITY PARK - MC 0641 LOS ANGELES, CA 90089-0641 Biomedical research support
S07RR-05304-30 (NSS) CHERRICK, HENRY M UNIVERSITY OF CALIFORNIA SCHOOL OF DENTISTRY LOS ANGELES, CALIF 90024 Biomedical research support
S07RR-05304-30 0221 (NSS) SEGHI, ROBERT Biomedical research support IN VIVO & IN VITRO RESPONSE TO BIOCERAMICS
S07RR-05304-30 0222 (NSS) ATCHISON, KATHRYN Biomedical research support EFFICACY OF SELECTED PERIAPICAL RADIOGRAPHS
S07RR-05304-30 0223 (NSS) LINDEMANN, ROBERT Biomedical research support MEASUREMENT OF CHANGES IN LYMPHOCYTE INTRACELLULAR CALCIUM
S07RR-05304-30 0224 (NSS) MANGKORNKARN, CHUTMA Biomedical research support COMPARISON OF CANAL ENLARGEMENT USING MODIFIED & UNMODIFIED TIPPED INSTRUMENTS
S07RR-05304-30 0225 (NSS) HEWLETT, EDMOND Biomedical research support EFFECT OF SMEAR REMOVAL ON GLASS IONOMER BOND STRENGTH
S07RR-05304-30 0226 (NSS) STEINER, JAMES Biomedical research support FLOW CYTOMETRY ANALYSIS OF NORMAL DENTAL PULP TISSUE
S07RR-05304-30 0227 (NSS) GRATT, BARTON Biomedical research support THERMAL ASYMETRICS IN ASYMPTOMATIC SUBJECTS
S07RR-05304-30 0228 (NSS) SHETTY, VIVEK Biomedical research support INTERNAL FIXATION TECHNIQUES FOR MANDIBULAR ANGLE FRACTURES
S07RR-05304-30 0229 (NSS) PARK, NO-HEE Biomedical research support DMBA & HAMSTER CHEEK POUCHES
S07RR-05304-30 0230 (NSS) DIXON, ANDREW Biomedical research support MORPHANALYSIS OF FACE GROWTH AFTER PAPAIN ADMINISTRATION: SEPTOSPHENOIDAL, RATS
S07RR-05304-30 0231 (NSS) BERNARD, GEORGE Biomedical research support RELATIONSHIP OF NEUROACTIVE SUBSTANCES TO CALCIFICATION PROCESS IN BONE
S07RR-05304-30 0232 (NSS) EVERSOLE, L ROY Biomedical research support AMELOBLASTIC EPTHELIUM ODONTOGENESIS ORAL CANCEROUS LESIONS
S07RR-05304-30 0233 (NSS) FRANKER, COLIN Biomedical research support ESTABLISHMENT OF LIBRARY OF MICROBIAL ISOLATED FROM HIV SEROPOSITIVE PATIENTS
S07RR-05304-30 0234 (NSS) GRAFF-RADFORD, STEVE Biomedical research support EFFECTS OF STREPTOMYCIN & LIDOCAINE BLOCK ON TRIGEMINAL NEURALGIA
S07RR-05304-30 0215 (NSS) JUNGE, DOUGLAS Biomedical research support EFFECTS OF EXTERNAL CALCIUM ON A CURRENTS IN APLYSIA NEURONS
S07RR-05304-30 0216 (NSS) KINNI, MARK Biomedical research support STRESS ANALYSIS OF BRANEMARK OSSEO INTEGRATED PROSTHESES
S07RR-05304-30 0217 (NSS) HOARD, RICHARD Biomedical research support CASTING ABILITY OF DICOR & TYPE III GOLD ALLOY
S07RR-05304-30 0218 (NSS) DIXON, ANDREW Biomedical research support LONG TERM EFFECTS OF PAPAIN ON CRANIOFACIAL SKELETON OF RATS
S07RR-05304-30 0219 (NSS) TORBINER, MARK Biomedical research support LOCAL ANESTHESIA TOXICITY
S07RR-05304-30 0220 (NSS) ATCHISON, KATHRYN Biomedical research support ANALYSIS OF ORTHODONTIC RADIOGRAPHS
S07RR-05305-30 (NSS) GREENE, JOHN C UNIV OF CA, SAN FRANCISCO 513 PARNASSUS AVE, S-630 SAN FRANCISCO, CA 94143-0430 New methods for hplc optical resolution and detection
S07RR-05305-30 0718 (NSS) ELLISON, JAMES New methods for hplc optical resolution and detection LONG TERM CLINICAL EVALUATION OF DENTAL RESTORATIVE MATERIALS
S07RR-05305-30 0719 (NSS) STANINEC, MICHAL New methods for hplc optical resolution and detection CORRELATION OF PEEL, TENSILE & SHEAR TESTS FOR ADHESION BETWEEN DENTAL MATERIALS
S07RR-05305-30 0720 (NSS) MARSHALL, SALLY New methods for hplc optical resolution and detection XRAY TOMOGRAPHIC MICROSCOPY OF DENTIN
S07RR-05305-30 0721 (NSS) DAVIS, DENNIS New methods for hplc optical resolution and detection RHEOLOGY & PHYSICS OF SETTING EXPANSION
S07RR-05305-30 0722 (NSS) MARSHALL, GRAYSON New methods for hplc optical resolution and detection MULTIPLE USER EQUIPMENT GRANT
S07RR-05305-30 0723 (NSS) MARSHALL, SALLY New methods for hplc optical resolution and detection MULTIPLE USER EQUIPMENT GRANT
S07RR-05305-30 0724 (NSS) PERROTT, DAVID New methods for hplc optical resolution and detection MULTIPLE USER EQUIPMENT GRANT
S07RR-05305-30 0725 (NSS) PALEFSKY, JOEL New methods for hplc optical resolution and detection MULTIPLE USER EQUIPMENT GRANT
S07RR-05305-30 0726 (NSS) DAMSKY, CAROLYN New methods for hplc optical resolution and detection MULTIPLE USER EQUIPMENT GRANT
S07RR-05305-30 0727 (NSS) RABANUS, JORG-PETER New methods for hplc optical resolution and detection MICROSCOPICAL INVESTIGATION OF CELLULAR COMPONENTS OF KERATINOCYTES
S07RR-05305-30 0728 (NSS) KAO, RICHARD New methods for hplc optical resolution and detection MOLECULAR BASIS FOR CELL RECRUITMENT & COLONIZATION IN BONE HEALING
S07RR-05305-30 0729 (NSS) SARGENT, PETER New methods for hplc optical resolution and detection NEURONAL NICOTINIC ACETYLCHOLINE RECEPTORS
S07RR-05305-30 0730 (NSS) BHATNAGAR, RAJENDRA New methods for hplc optical resolution and detection SYNTHETIC POLYPEPTIDES MIMICKING BIOLOGICAL ACTIVITY OF COLLAGEN
S07RR-05305-30 0731 (NSS) WU, YN-LOW H New methods for hplc optical resolution and detection CORRELATION OF RECURRENT CARIES & MARGINAL GAP PF CAST RESTORATIONS
S07RR-05305-30 0732 (NSS) KHOURY, EMILIO New methods for hplc optical resolution and detection MHC CLASS II ANTIGEN EXPRESSION BY HUMAN GRANULOSA LUTEIN CELLS
S07RR-05305-30 0733 (NSS) DAMSKY, CAROLINE New methods for hplc optical resolution and detection BI INEGRINS IN EARLY MOUSE DEVELOPMENT
S07RR-05305-30 0735 (NSS) MARSHALL, GRAYSON New methods for hplc optical resolution and detection SEM OF SECONDARY CARIES
S07RR-05305-30 0736 (NSS) LACY, ALTON New methods for hplc optical resolution and detection ADAPTION OF RESIN DENTIN BONDING AGENTS TO VITAL & NON VITAL DENTIN
S07RR-05305-30 0737 (NSS) BARKHORDAR, RAHMAT New methods for hplc optical resolution and detection LYMPHATIC METASTASIS OF B16 MELANOMA
S07RR-05305-30 0734 (NSS) HUTTON, JOHN New methods for hplc optical resolution and detection RELATIONSHIP BETWEEN RESTORED & UNRESTORED EDENTULISM & HYPERTENSION
S07RR-05305-30 0738 (NSS) KAPILA, SUNIL New methods for hplc optical resolution and detection EFFECT OF ALTERED OCCLUSAL POSITION OF MANDIBLE ON CRANIOMANDIBULAR GROWTH
S07RR-05305-30 0739 (NSS) KAO, RICHARD New methods for hplc optical resolution and detection ANIMAL MODELS FOR DEGENERATIVE TMJ
S07RR-05305-30 0740 (NSS) DODSON, THOMAS New methods for hplc optical resolution and detection COMPLICATIONS OF DENTAL EXTRACTIONS IN HIV+ PATIENTS
S07RR-05305-30 0741 (NSS) POGREL, M ANTHONY New methods for hplc optical resolution and detection THERMAL EFFECTS OF CARBON DIOXIDE LASER ON DENTIN IN VITRO & DENTAL PULP IN VIVO
S07RR-05305-30 0742 (NSS) HUTTON, JOHN New methods for hplc optical resolution and detection RELATIONSHIP BETWEEN RESTORED & UNRESTORED EDENTULISM & HYPERTENSION
S07RR-05305-30 0743 (NSS) PLESH, OCTAVIA New methods for hplc optical resolution and detection FUNCTIONAL JAW MOVEMENTS REFERENCED TO BORDER MOVEMENTS
S07RR-05305-30 0744 (NSS) WALSH, MARGARET New methods for hplc optical resolution and detection BELIEFS, ATTITUDES, SUBJECTIVE NORMS & INTENTIONS RELATED TO ORAL HYGIENE
S07RR-05308-30 (NSS) GREGORY, RICHARD L EMORY UNIV DENTAL SCH 1462 CLIFTON ROAD, N E ATLANTA, GA 30322 Biomedical research support
S07RR-05308-30 0235 (NSS) WIDMER, CHARLES G Biomedical research support MECHANICAL PROPERTIES OF HUMAN MASSETER MOTOR UNITS
S07RR-05308-30 0236 (NSS) GENCO, CAROLINE Biomedical research support ISOLATION OF HEMIN BINDING PROTEINS FROM PERIODONTAL PORPHYROMONAS GINGIVALIS
S07RR-05308-30 0237 (NSS) KALMAR, JOHN Biomedical research support BAUHINIA PURPUREA LECTIN W/ HUMAN SERUM & SECRETORY GLYCOPROTEINS
S07RR-05308-30 0238 (NSS) GREGORY, RICHARD L Biomedical research support JACALIN EFFECTS ON LYMPHOCYTE FUNCTION
S07RR-05308-30 0239 (NSS) AKIN, DIANNE Biomedical research support LACTOFERRIN & IGA IN HUMAN MAMMARY EPITHELIAL CELLS
S07RR-05308-30 0240 (NSS) ARNOLD, ROLAND R Biomedical research support DENTAL RESEARCH CENTER CORE FACILITIES
S07RR-05308-30 0241 (NSS) VANDYKE, T T Biomedical research support CENTRAL DEIONIZED WATER
S07RR-05311-30 (NSS) GREENER, EVAN H NORTHWESTERN UNIVERSITY 240 E HURON STREET CHICAGO, IL 60611 Biomedical research support grant
S07RR-05311-30 0001 (NSS) GREENER, EVAN Biomedical research support grant RESEARCH TECHNICIAN
S07RR-05311-30 0002 (NSS) VEIS, ARTHUR Biomedical research support grant RESEARCH SEMINAR EXPENSES
S07RR-05311-30 0003 (NSS) VEIS, ARTHUR Biomedical research support grant INSTRUMENTATION REPAIR, UPKEEP, TANK SWITCH & ALARM
S07RR-05311-30 0004 (NSS) STERN, PAULA Biomedical research support grant CALCETTE CALCIUM TITRATOR
S07RR-05311-30 0005 (NSS) CIRINCIONE, ULANA Biomedical research support grant DATA ENTRY OPERATOR

PROJECT NO., ORGANIZATIONAL UNIT., INVESTIGATOR, ADDRESS, TITLE

S07RR-05311-30 0006 (NSS) POLVERINI, PETER Biomedical research support grant INTERIM SUPPORT FOR RESEARCH, SUPPLIES; OMEGA CELL, WASH BOTTLES, ETHER, FLASK
S07RR-05311-30 0007 (NSS) JONES, JONATHAN Biomedical research support grant BIOLOGY OF HEMIDESMOSOME STRUCTURE & FUNCTION: CDNA, KERATINOCYTE
S07RR-05311-30 0008 (NSS) SOLT, DENNIS Biomedical research support grant UNSCHEDULED DNA SYNTH: HAMSTER BUCCAL POUCH EPITHELIUM: CYTOTOXIC RESISTANCE
S07RR-05311-30 0009 (NSS) SHEA, BRIAN Biomedical research support grant SKELETAL GROWTH N GIANT TRANSGENIC MICE: ENDOCRINE
S07RR-05313-30 (NSS) SQUIER, CHRISTOPHER A UNIVERSITY OF IOWA N419 DENTAL SCIENCE BUILDING IOWA CITY, IOWA 52242 Biomedical research support
S07RR-05313-30 0245 (NSS) LOGAN, HENRIETTA L Biomedical research support STRESS IN NATURAL PAIN INHIBITION
S07RR-05313-30 0246 (NSS) CONS, NAHAN C Biomedical research support EVALUATION OF DIA IN BEIJING, CHINA
S07RR-05313-30 0247 (NSS) FULLER, JAMES L Biomedical research support PREDICTIVE FALICITY OF SRI DENTIST PERCEIVER
S07RR-05313-30 0248 (NSS) BOYER, MARCIA Biomedical research support MEASURING DENTAL HYGIENISTS EXPOSURE TO NITROUS OXIDE
S07RR-05313-30 0249 (NSS) BOYER, DAN Biomedical research support DEFORMATION OF TEETH BY COMPOSITE RESTORATION
S07RR-05313-30 0242 (NSS) LEVY, STEVEN Biomedical research support METHOD FOR PROSPECTIVE QUANTIFICATION OF FLUORIDE EXPOSURES IN YOUNG CHILDREN
S07RR-05313-30 0243 (NSS) DRAKE, DAVID Biomedical research support BACTERIAL ADHESION TO TITANIUM IMPLANT SURFACES
S07RR-05313-30 0244 (NSS) DIXON, DONNA L Biomedical research support COVERAGE PORCELAIN LAMINATES IN REMOVABLE PARTIAL DENTURE RETENTION
S07RR-05317-21 (NSS) MORGANSTEIN, WARREN M UNIVERSITY OF MARYLAND 666 WEST BALTIMORE STREET BALTIMORE, MD 21201 Biomedical research support
S07RR-05317-21 0745 (NSS) DESSEM, DEAN A Biomedical research support NEVIAL CONTROL OF MASTICATION
S07RR-05317-21 0746 (NSS) SOMERMAN, MARTHA Biomedical research support ANALYSIS OF PERIODONTAL LIGAMENT CELL ATTACHMENT
S07RR-05317-21 0747 (NSS) ARCHIBALD, DAVID Biomedical research support BECKMAN SW 501 ROTOR PACKAGE
S07RR-05317-21 0748 (NSS) COHEN, ROCHELLE Biomedical research support PROTEIN ASSAY KIT
S07RR-05318-30 (NSS) DONOFF, R BRUCE HARVARD SCH OF DENTAL MEDICINE 188 LONGWOOD AVENUE BOSTON, MASS 02115 Biomedical research support
S07RR-05318-30 0250 (NSS) BISWAS, DEBAJIT K Biomedical research support REGULATION OF PROLACTIN GENE EXPRESSION: SEQUENCING
S07RR-05318-30 0251 (NSS) BISWAS, DEBAJIT K Biomedical research support MOLECULAR BASIS OF CHEMICAL CARCINOGENESIS: PROBES
S07RR-05318-30 0252 (NSS) RABADJIJA, LUKA Biomedical research support H+ & PTH STIMULATED BONE RESORPTION IN TISSUE CULTURE BY H ATPASE INHIBITOR
S07RR-05318-30 0253 (NSS) WONG, DAVID T W Biomedical research support TISSUE EOSINOPHILIA, & EOSINOPHIL DERIVED TGF ALPHA IN CUTANEOUS WOUND HEALING
S07RR-05319-18 (NSS) JOHANSEN, ERLING TUFTS UNIVERSITY ONE KNEELAND STREET BOSTON, MA 02111 Biomedical research support
S07RR-05319-18 0620 (NSS) PAPAS, ATHENA Biomedical research support NUTRITION & ORAL HEALTH IN AN AGING POPULATION
S07RR-05319-18 0621 (NSS) BARATZ, ROBERT Biomedical research support ALLERGIES TO MATERIALS USED IN DENTISTRY
S07RR-05319-18 0622 (NSS) SZABO, GEORGE Biomedical research support EFFECT OF ULTRA VIOLET LIGHT ON MAMMALIAN SKIN
S07RR-05319-18 0623 (NSS) THEOHARIDES, THEOHAR Biomedical research support COMPARATIVE MORPHOLOGY & BIOCHEMISTRY OF ORAL MAST CELL MEDIATOR SECRETION
R01RR-05321-03 (AR) ROSENBLUM, LEONARD A STATE UNIVERSITY OF NY 450 CLARKSON AVENUE BROOKLYN NY 11203 Enhancing the psychological well-being of caged primates
S07RR-05321-30 (NSS) MACHEN, J BERNARD UNIVERSITY OF MICHIGAN 1011 NORTH UNIVERSITY AVENUE ANN ARBOR, MICH 48109 Biomedical research support
S07RR-05321-30 0254 (NSS) BLOEM, THOMAS A Biomedical research support: Correlation of prosthodontic tissue index to histologic samples
S07RR-05321-30 0255 (NSS) JACOBSON, JED J Biomedical research support: cost effectiveness of dental implants: decision analysis
S07RR-05321-30 0256 (NSS) LANG, W PAUL Biomedical research support: effect of education upon dentists utilization of pit & fissure sealants
S07RR-05321-30 0264 (NSS) FITZGERALD, MARK Biomedical research support: immunohistochemical & autoradiographic analysis of odontoblast replacement
S07RR-05321-30 0265 (NSS) BRADLEY, BRUCE E Biomedical research support: comparison of myotoxicity of lidocaine & diphenhydramine
S07RR-05321-30 0266 (NSS) SYED, SALAM Biomedical research support: Olympus binocular microscope used for microbiological studies
S07RR-05321-30 0267 (NSS) REGEZI, JOSEPH Biomedical research support: immunohistochem ID cell antigen; formalin fixed plastic embedded ground sections
S07RR-05321-30 0268 (NSS) CHIEGO, DANIEL J JR Biomedical research support: changes in odontoblast activity & associated nerves
S07RR-05321-30 0257 (NSS) MCPHEE, RICHARD Biomedical research support: evaluation of powdered metal process
S07RR-05321-30 0258 (NSS) AVERY, JAMES K Biomedical research support: effects of Retin on epithelial & mesenchymal interaction
S07RR-05321-30 0259 (NSS) BAGRAMIAN, ROBERT A Biomedical research support: biochemical blood studies in relation to dental disease in Amish
S07RR-05321-30 0260 (NSS) MORE, FREDERICK G Biomedical research support: secondary ion mass spectrometry to assess fluoride content of enamel lesions

PROJECT NO., ORGANIZATIONAL UNIT., INVESTIGATOR, ADDRESS, TITLE

S07RR-05321-30 0261 (NSS) JAARDA, MERLE J Biomedical research support: wound healing at interfacial zone
S07RR-05321-30 0262 (NSS) ALCOFORADO, GILL A Biomedical research support: gingival inflammation in children
S07RR-05321-30 0263 (NSS) KOHN, DAVID H Biomedical research support: micromechanics of dental material interfaces
S07RR-05322-30 (NSS) SCHACHTELE, CHARLES F U OF MINN, 18-104 MOOS TWR 515 DELAWARE STREET MINNEAPOLIS, MN 55455 Biomedical research support
S07RR-05322-30 0269 (NSS) KAJANDER, KEITH C Biomedical research support EVALUATION OF AN EXPERIMENTAL MODEL OF NEUROPATHIC PAIN
S07RR-05322-30 0270 (NSS) MATHUR, AMBIKA Biomedical research support HOST REGULATION OF IGE SYNTHESIS IN MURINE HYBRIDOMAS
S07RR-05322-30 0271 (NSS) QUICK, DONALD C Biomedical research support NERVE TERMINALS IN HUMAN FACIAL MUSCLES
S07RR-05322-30 0272 (NSS) HARGREAVES, KENNETH Biomedical research support PERIPHERAL CRF DURING INFLAMMATION & PAIN
S07RR-05322-30 0273 (NSS) MARTENS, LESLIE V Biomedical research support INFECTION CONTROL & WASTE DISPOSAL IN DENTAL OFFICE STUDY: PREVENTION
S07RR-05322-30 0274 (NSS) FEIGAL, ROBERT J Biomedical research support MECHANISM OF CYTOTOXICITY OF CHLORHEXIDINE PRODUCTS: PREVENTION
S07RR-05322-30 0275 (NSS) CONRY, JOHN P Biomedical research support CLINICAL WEAR OF PIT & FISSURE SEALANTS: PREVENTION
S07RR-05322-30 0276 (NSS) SCHIFFMAN, ERIC L Biomedical research support POSTURAL CHARACTERISTICS OF WOMEN SEEKING HELP IN TMJ & CRANIOFACIAL PAIN CLINIC
S07RR-05322-30 0277 (NSS) MORSTAD, ANDREW T Biomedical research support USE OF ANIMALS TO STUDY MASTICATORY STRESS ON IMPLANTS
S07RR-05322-30 0278 (NSS) BROWNBILL, JOHN Biomedical research support PROFILING ON DENTAL RESTORATIONS: PREVENTION
S07RR-05322-30 0279 (NSS) SCHULTE, JOHN K Biomedical research support CRANIOMANDIBULAR DISORDERS: PAIN & PSYCHOSOCIAL FACTORS
S07RR-05322-30 0280 (NSS) HINRICHS, JAMES E Biomedical research support CONSTRUCTION OF LASER DOPPLER PROBE: PREVENTION
S07RR-05322-30 0281 (NSS) SCHACHTELE, CHARLES Biomedical research support PASSIVE IMMUNIZATION USING BOVINE COLOSTRUM FOR HUMAN SUBJECT RINSES
S07RR-05330-30 (NSS) PHIPPS, GRANT T S U N Y AT BUFFALO 355 SQUIRE HALL BUFFALO, N Y 14214 Biomedical research support
S07RR-05330-30 0010 (NSS) AGUIRRE, ALFREDO Biomedical research support HYBRIDIZATION OF SALIVARY GLANDS
S07RR-05330-30 0011 (NSS) BEDI, GURRINDER S Biomedical research support EPITOPE MAPPING PROTEASE OF CYSTATIN
S07RR-05330-30 0012 (NSS) BOBEK, LIBUSEA A Biomedical research support MUTAGENESIS IN SALIVARY CYSTATINS
S07RR-05330-30 0022 (NSS) HERWEIJER, JANTIEN A Biomedical research support CHARACTERIZATION OF BACTEROIDES ENDODONTALIS
S07RR-05330-30 0023 (NSS) LEVINE, MICHAEL J Biomedical research support MOLECULES DENTAL PLAQUE
S07RR-05330-30 0024 (NSS) MOHL, NORMAN D Biomedical research support TEMPOROMANDIBULAR JOINT
S07RR-05330-30 0025 (NSS) ORTMAN, LANCE F Biomedical research support DENTAL IMPLANT MOBILITY CALIBRATION
S07RR-05330-30 0026 (NSS) PHIPPS, GRANT T Biomedical research support EPIDEMIOLOGICAL STUDIES & EQUIPMENT
S07RR-05330-30 0013 (NSS) CARTER, LAURIE C Biomedical research support BONE IMPLANT INTERFACIAL MORPHOLOGY
S07RR-05330-30 0014 (NSS) CHEN, PRISCILLA B Biomedical research support DEFENSE MECHANISMS TO MICROBES
S07RR-05330-30 0015 (NSS) CHO, MOON II Biomedical research support TRANSFORMING GROWTH FACTOR BY FIBROBLASTS
S07RR-05330-30 0016 (NSS) DENARDIN, ERNESTO G Biomedical research support GENE CLONING FORMERLY PEPTIDE RECEPTOR
S07RR-05330-30 0017 (NSS) DENARDIN, ERNESTO G Biomedical research support LOCALIZED JUVENILE PERIODONTITIS DNA
S07RR-05330-30 0018 (NSS) GENCO, ROBERT J Biomedical research support MICROBIAL ECOLOGY
S07RR-05330-30 0019 (NSS) GENCO, ROBERT J Biomedical research support ORAL MICROBIOLOGY & IMMUNOLOGY
S07RR-05330-30 0020 (NSS) GILLESPIE, MARGARET Biomedical research support LEUKOTOXIC ACTIVITY OF WOLENELLA RECTA
S07RR-05330-30 0021 (NSS) HAGEL-BRADWAY, SUSAN Biomedical research support PHORBOL ESTERS AND PGE 2 BINDING
S07RR-05330-30 0027 (NSS) WILSON, MARK E Biomedical research support CELL ENVELOPE COMPONENT CHARACTERIZATION
S07RR-05331-28 (NSS) FORMICOLA, ALLEN J COLUMBIA UNIVERSITY 630 WEST 168TH STREET NEW YORK, N Y 10032 Biomedical research support
S07RR-05331-28 0737 (NSS) HASSELGREN, GUNNAR Biomedical research support PULP BIOLOGY & ITS EFFECTS ON CLINICAL PRACTICE
S07RR-05331-28 0738 (NSS) GONCHAROFF, PAUL Biomedical research support FIMBRIA GENE OF ACTINOMYCETEMCOMITANS LEUKOTOXIN EXPRESSION IN AA
S07RR-05331-28 0739 (NSS) MCALARNEY, MONA Biomedical research support DIFFERENT TITANIUM OXIDE SURFACES ON COMPLEMENT ADSORPTION
S07RR-05331-28 0740 (NSS) MANDEL, IRWIN D Biomedical research support DIAGNOSTIC USES OF SALIVA IN SALIVARY DYSFUNCTION
S07RR-05331-28 0741 (NSS) KIM, SYNGYCK Biomedical research support NEUROPEPTIDES INVOLVED IN NEUROGENIC INFLAMMATION
S07RR-05331-28 0742 (NSS) BINDER, TERRI A Biomedical research support B LYMPHOCYTE SUBPOPULATIONS IN PERIODONTAL DISEASE
S07RR-05333-30 (NSS) ARNOLD, ROLAND R UNIV OF N C AT CHAPEL HILL 101 DENTAL RES CTR SCH DENT CHAPEL HILL, N C 27599-7455 Biomedical research support
S07RR-05333-30 0864 (NSS) AUKHIL, I Biomedical research support CLONING & EXPRESSION OF ALT SPLICED DOMAINS OF RAT T&F
S07RR-05333-30 0865 (NSS) DAVIS, L N Biomedical research support MRNA TRANSCRIPTS FOR EXTRACELLULAR MATRIX PROTEINS & GROWTH
S07RR-05333-30 0866 (NSS) GODSEY, T Biomedical research support A UNIQUE COLLAGENOUS PROTEIN IN PERIODONTAL LIGAMENT
S07RR-05333-30 0867 (NSS) HERMAN, D J Biomedical research support PRIMARY TOOTH WIDTH, INCISOR LIABILITY, & LEEWAY & NAVAJO

S07RR-05333-30 0868 (NSS) HIRSCH, P F Biomedical research support GLUCOCORTICOIDS & ADRENAL PARATHYROID INTERACTION CALCIUM
S07RR-05333-30 0869 (NSS) LIANOS, K Biomedical research support THE RAMIFICATION OF BITE FORCE & VERTICAL DIMENSION & IMPLANT
S07RR-05333-30 0870 (NSS) MCCRACKEN, M C Biomedical research support MICROHARDNESS OF MATERIALS EXPOSED TO BLEACH
S07RR-05333-30 0871 (NSS) NEUWIRTH, B R Biomedical research support AUTOLOGOUS BLOOD REPLACEMENT FOLLOWING ORTHOGNATHIC
S07RR-05333-30 0872 (NSS) PAPAVASILIOU, Biomedical research support FINITE ELEMENT ANALYSIS OF MICROSTRAIN BONE FRACTURES & IM
S07RR-05333-30 0873 (NSS) RICHARDSON, G Biomedical research support HYPOXIA INDUCED CL (P) IN GENETICALLY SUSCEPTIBLE MICE
S07RR-05333-30 0874 (NSS) RICHTER, M Biomedical research support MOLECULAR CHARACTERIZATION OF PERIODONTAL CELLS
S07RR-05333-30 0875 (NSS) SAUNDERS, C Biomedical research support A STUDY OF CERAMIC ORTHODONTIC BRACKETS AND FRICTION
S07RR-05333-30 0876 (NSS) SIGURDSSON, A Biomedical research support PAIN PERCEPTION IN PATIENTS WITH PULPA PAIN
S07RR-05333-30 0877 (NSS) SIMON, A R Biomedical research support CRANIOFACIAL ANOMALIES: OXAPAZM TERATOGENICITY
S07RR-05333-30 0878 (NSS) WASHINGTON, O Biomedical research support IMMUNOGENICITY OF FIMBRILL FROM B GINGIVATIS 381
S07RR-05333-30 0879 (NSS) FLOOD, P Biomedical research support EPITOPE MAPPING OF FIMBRILLIN
S07RR-05333-30 0880 (NSS) HANKER, J Biomedical research support POSITIVE STAIN FOR GRAM NEGATIVE BACTERIA
S07RR-05336-29 (NSS) BROWN, ARTHUR C OREGON HEALTH SCIENCES UNIV 3181 SW SAM JACKSON PARK RD PORTLAND, OR 97201-3098 Biomedical research support
S07RR-05336-29 0298 (NSS) SMITH, JOHN Biomedical research support MEN: ORUDIS VS VICODIN; RELIEF OF POST OPERATIVE PERIODONTAL DISCOMFORT
S07RR-05336-29 0299 (NSS) EMPEY, MARGE Biomedical research support DENTAL HYGIENISTS ATTITUDES DENTAL CARE FOR PATIENTS W/ PSYCHO SOCIAL DISORDERS
S07RR-05336-29 0300 (NSS) MARSHALL, GORDON Biomedical research support HISTOLOGIC EXAM; PULPAL TISSUE IN TEETH W/ ADVANCE PERIODONTITIS; TOOTH VITALIGY
S07RR-05336-29 0301 (NSS) EIGNER, TONI Biomedical research support DENTAL MANAGEMENT OF OREGON TRANSPLANT PATIENTS
S07RR-05336-29 0302 (NSS) MASON, JILL Biomedical research support RE ENTRY POTENTIAL OF INACTIVE OREGON DENTAL HYGIENISTS
S07RR-05336-29 0303 (NSS) KENT, KARLA Biomedical research support NEUROTRANSMITTER RECEPTORS; INSECT NEUROMUSCULAR JUNCTION; DIFFERENT DVMT STAGES
S07RR-05336-29 0304 (NSS) BULLOCK, WESLEY Biomedical research support DOES IGA ENHANCE OR SUPPRESS PMN KILLING OF CANDIDA ALBICANS
S07RR-05336-29 0305 (NSS) MATSUMOTO, STEVEN Biomedical research support ENVIRONMENTAL FACTORS INFLUENCING NEURONAL DEVELOPMENT OF MAMMALIAN NEURAL CREST
S07RR-05336-29 0306 (NSS) BRONS, JOHN Biomedical research support CEREBELLAR CONTROL OF JAW MOVEMENTS IN RABBITS
S07RR-05336-29 0307 (NSS) LEVIN, MARVIN Biomedical research support GUIDED TISSUE REGENERATION W/ BIOMEDICAL GRAFTS & TITANIUM IMPLANTS
S07RR-05336-29 0308 (NSS) MORGAN, LESLIE Biomedical research support STRENGTHENING TEETH W/ GLASS IONOMER RESTORATIONS
S07RR-05336-29 0309 (NSS) MASON, JILL Biomedical research support OREGON ORAL HEALTH SURVEY
S07RR-05336-29 0310 (NSS) THOMPSON, MARTHA E Biomedical research support ARACHIDONIC METAB & PHOSPHOLIPASE A2 IN PITUITARY HORMONE SECRETION
S07RR-05337-30 (NSS) FONSECA, RAYMOND UNIVERSITY OF PENNSYLVANIA 4001 SPRUCE STREET PHILADELPHIA, PA 19104 Biomedical research support
S07RR-05337-30 0768 (NSS) CUMMING, CHRISTOPHER Biomedical research support ORAL YEAST INFECTIONS IN HIV POSITIVE PATIENTS: MEDIAN RHOMBOID GLOSSITIS
S07RR-05337-30 0769 (NSS) DOTY, RICHARD Biomedical research support SMELL & TASTE SMELL DEFICITS IN NEURO DEGENERATIVE DISORDERS ALZHEIMERS
S07RR-05337-30 0770 (NSS) MANTE, FRANCIS Biomedical research support BASE METAL ALLOYS W/ PRE WETTING AS SOLUTIONS TO TECHNIQUE SENSITIVITY
S07RR-05337-30 0771 (NSS) ROSAN, BURTON Biomedical research support PSEUDOMONAS AERUGINOSA TRANSMISSION AMONG CYSTIC FIBROSIS PATIENTS
S07RR-05337-30 0772 (NSS) SILVERTON, SUSAN Biomedical research support CALCIFIED TISSUE DESTRUCTION BY MONONUCLEAR CELLS: CARBONIC ANHYDRASE
S07RR-05337-30 0773 (NSS) YANKELL, SAMUEL L Biomedical research support MICROBIAL CONTAMINATION OF TOOTHBRUSHES
S07RR-05338-26 (NSS) VIG, PETER S UNIVERSITY OF PITTSBURGH SCH OF DENT MED 346 SALK HALL PITTSBURGH, PA 15261 Biomedical research support
S07RR-05346-30 (NSS) OMNELL, KARL-AKE UNIVERSITY OF WASHINGTON SCHOOL OF DENTISTRY SC-62 SEATTLE, WASH 98195 Biomedical research support
S07RR-05346-30 0321 (NSS) TRUELOVE, EDMOND Biomedical research support MASTICATORY MUSCLE
S07RR-05346-30 0322 (NSS) ANDERSON, LEE C Biomedical research support THREE DIMENSIONAL IMAGE
S07RR-05346-30 0323 (NSS) ROBINOVITCH, MURRAY Biomedical research support SECRETORY GRANULES
S07RR-05346-30 0324 (NSS) MILGROM, PETER Biomedical research support ASSESSMENT BATTERY
S07RR-05346-30 0325 (NSS) DALE, BEVERLY A Biomedical research support PROFILAGGRIN GENE R
S07RR-05346-30 0326 (NSS) MILGROM, PETER Biomedical research support CDRC COGNITIVE THERAPY
S07RR-05346-30 0327 (NSS) WELLS, NORMA Biomedical research support CDRC FISSURE SEALANT
S07RR-05346-30 0311 (NSS) ARTUN, JON Biomedical research support LEFORTE OSTEOTOMY
S07RR-05346-30 0312 (NSS) WESTON, SUE Biomedical research support CHEMICAL DISINFECTANTS

S07RR-05346-30 0313 (NSS) MASSOTH, DONNA Biomedical research support PATIENT ADHERENCE
S07RR-05346-30 0314 (NSS) LAMONT, RICHARD Biomedical research support INTERBACTERIAL INTERACTION
S07RR-05346-30 0315 (NSS) OMNELL, KARL-AKE Biomedical research support DENTISTRY BRSG
S07RR-05346-30 0316 (NSS) MA, TSUN Biomedical research support DENTURE RESIN COLOR
S07RR-05346-30 0317 (NSS) OSWALD, ROBERT Biomedical research support RAT DENTAL PULP
S07RR-05346-30 0318 (NSS) MILLER, RICHARD Biomedical research support MEMBRANE DYNAMICS
S07RR-05346-30 0319 (NSS) OMNELL, KARL-AKE Biomedical research support DENTISTRY BRSG
S07RR-05346-30 0320 (NSS) TRUELOVE, EDMOND Biomedical research support SALIVA PAPILLOMAVIRUS
S07RR-05346-30 0328 (NSS) STIEFEL, DORIS Biomedical research support CDRC: CHEMOTHERAPY FOR DISABLED
S07RR-05349-30 (NSS) PITTMAN, JAMES A, JR UNIV OF ALABAMA IN BIRMINGHAM UNIV STA MED ED BLDG 301A BIRMINGHAM, ALA 35294 Biomedical research support
S07RR-05349-30 0749 (NSS) DAVIS, BARRY J Biomedical research support ELECTROPHYSIOLOGICAL STUDIES OF TASTE RELAY NEURONS
S07RR-05349-30 0750 (NSS) BECKMAN, JOSEPH S Biomedical research support CONSTRUCTION OF A NITRIC OXIDE CHEMILUMINESCENT DETECTOR USING ATOMIC OXYGEN
S07RR-05350-30 (NSS) WILSON, I DODD UNIV OF ARKANSAS FOR MED SCIS 4301 WEST MARKHAM, SLOT 550 LITTLE ROCK, AR 72205 Biomedical research support grant
S07RR-05350-30 0329 (NSS) REIS, ROBERT J Biomedical research support grant PLASMA & CHROMOSOMAL ASSAY OF HOMOLOGOUS RECOMBINATION
S07RR-05350-30 0330 (NSS) ELLIS, EILEEN N Biomedical research support grant EFFECT OF AMINOQUANIDINE ON DIABETIC GLOMERULOPATHY
S07RR-05350-30 0331 (NSS) KOMOROSKI, EVA M Biomedical research support grant ANABOLIC STERIOD USE & CARDIOVASCULAR EFFECTS
S07RR-05350-30 0332 (NSS) KARLSON, KARL H Biomedical research support grant DEVELOPMENTAL CHANGES IN RABBIT AIRWAY SMOOTH MUSCLE PHARMOCOLOGY
S07RR-05350-30 0333 (NSS) ROOP, ROY M Biomedical research support grant CHARACTERIZATION OF RECOMBINANT BRUCELLA
S07RR-05350-30 0334 (NSS) NEWTON, BRUCE W Biomedical research support grant CHARACTERIZATION OF PEPTIDES
S07RR-05350-30 0335 (NSS) HENLE, KURT J Biomedical research support grant TUMOR TARGETED DRUG DELIVERY
S07RR-05350-30 0336 (NSS) FENDRICK, JAMES L Biomedical research support grant INFLUENZA VIRUS INHIBITION OF PROTEIN SYNTHESIS
S07RR-05350-30 0337 (NSS) MENDELSON, BRUCE Biomedical research support grant CHARACTERIZATION OF SENSORY AFFERENT CONNECTIONS IN CLARKES COLUMN
S07RR-05350-30 0338 (NSS) HELM, RICKI M Biomedical research support grant ISOLATION & PURIFICATION OF COCKROACH ALLERGENS
P41RR-05351-03 (SSS) ALBERSHEIM, PETER UNIVERSITY OF GEORGIA 220 RIVERBEND ROAD ATHENS GA 30602 Resource center for biomedical complex carbohydrates
P41RR-05351-03 0001 (SSS) HALBEEK, H RESOURCE CENTER FOR BIOMEDICAL COMPLEX CARBOHYDRATES Structural analysis of complex carbohydrates of animal origin
P41RR-05351-03 0002 (SSS) MEYER, BERND RESOURCE CENTER FOR BIOMEDICAL COMPLEX CARBOHYDRATES Conformation analysis of complex carbohydrates of animal origin
P41RR-05351-03 0003 (SSS) CUMMINGS, RICHARD RESOURCE CENTER FOR BIOMEDICAL COMPLEX CARBOHYDRATES Enzymes--Synthesis and depolymerization of complex carbohydrates
P41RR-05351-03 0004 (SSS) HAHN, RICHARD RESOURCE CENTER FOR BIOMEDICAL COMPLEX CARBOHYDRATES Separation of animal cell-derived oligosaccharides
P41RR-05351-03 9001 (SSS) SCHOTT, DOUBET RESOURCE CENTER FOR BIOMEDICAL COMPLEX CARBOHYDRATES Core--Carbohydrate information
S07RR-05351-30 (NSS) HENRY, WALTER L UNIV OF CALIFORNIA, IRVINE COLL OF MED/MED SURG I RM 118 IRVINE, CALIFORNIA 92717 Biomedical research support grant
S07RR-05351-30 0031 (NSS) BALDWIN, KENNETH M Biomedical research support grant ACTIVITY REGULATION OF MYOSIN EXPRESSION
S07RR-05351-30 0028 (NSS) ODOWD, DIANE K Biomedical research support grant REGULATION OF ELECTRICAL EXCITABILITY IN NERVOUS SYSTEM CELLS: DROSOPHILA
S07RR-05351-30 0029 (NSS) QUILLIGAN, EDWARD J Biomedical research support grant EFFECT OF HYPOXIA ON FETAL SPINAL CORD
S07RR-05351-30 0030 (NSS) ARQUILLA, EDWARD R Biomedical research support grant CROSS SECTION OF EFFECTS OF WEIGHT LOSS ON HEALTH PARAMETERS: NUTRI SYSTEM
S07RR-05352-30 (NSS) BEHRENS, B LYN LOMA LINDA UNIVERSITY SCHOOL OF MEDICINE LOMA LINDA, CALIF 92350 Development and evaluation of a time-resolved microscope
S07RR-05352-30 0743 (NSS) SAKALA, ELMAR Development and evaluation of a time-resolved microscope AMINO ACID PROFILES IN FETUSES OF NORMAL & DIABETIC MOTHERS
S07RR-05352-30 0744 (NSS) NYSTROM, GERALD A Development and evaluation of a time-resolved microscope PULMONARY EFFECTS OF POSTNATALLY ADMINISTERED TERBUTALINE SULFATE IN RABBITS
S07RR-05352-30 0745 (NSS) ANHOLM, JAMES Development and evaluation of a time-resolved microscope CARDIOVASCULAR CHANGES DUE TO EXERCISE HYPERPNEA MAY LIMIT EXERCISE CAPACITY
S07RR-05352-30 0746 (NSS) BULLAS, LEONARD Development and evaluation of a time-resolved microscope NUCLEOTIDE SEQUENCE & STRUCTURE OF ENDS OF PHAGE PSP3 GENOME
S07RR-05352-30 0747 (NSS) FRASER, GARY Development and evaluation of a time-resolved microscope EVALUATION OF HEALTHY VOLUNTEER BIAS IN ADVENTIST HEALTH STUDY
S07RR-05352-30 0748 (NSS) KETTERING, JAMES Development and evaluation of a time-resolved microscope IMMUNE MECHANISMS INVOLVED IN ERADICATION OF H23B TUMORS
S07RR-05352-30 0749 (NSS) LAU, BENJAMIN Development and evaluation

of a time-resolved microscope CELL LINES FOR STUDYING CYTOKINE MEDICATED MACROPHAGE T LYMPHOCYTE INTERACTION

S07RR-05352-30 0750 (NSS) RYU, JUNICHI Development and evaluation of a time-resolved microscope CLONING & SEQUENCING OF HSDKPNB OF KLEBSIELLA PNEUMONIAE

S07RR-05352-30 0751 (NSS) ZUCCARELLI, ANTHONY Development and evaluation of a time-resolved microscope PLASMID DNA MOLECULAR ANALYSIS FROM CLINICAL ISOLATES OF STAPHYLOCOCCUS AUREUS

S07RR-05352-30 0752 (NSS) WILCOX, BRUCE Development and evaluation of a time-resolved microscope MOLECULAR STUDY OF ENDOCRINE INDUCED TUMOR REGRESSION & SUBSEQUENT ESCAPE

S07RR-05352-30 0753 (NSS) CAIN, CHRISTOPHER D Development and evaluation of a time-resolved microscope IN UTERO EXPOSURES TO PULSED MAGNETIC FIELDS ON ORNITHINE DECARBOXYLASE

S07RR-05352-30 0754 (NSS) VALENZUELA, GUILLERM Development and evaluation of a time-resolved microscope INTERRELATIONS BETWEEN CONTROL OF SYSTEMIC & UTERINE CIRCULATIONS

S07RR-05352-30 0755 (NSS) BARTLEY, JAMES A Development and evaluation of a time-resolved microscope GLYCEROL KINASE LOCUS BY USING CDNA LIBRARY CREATED BY SUBTRACTION HYBRIDIZATION

S07RR-05352-30 0756 (NSS) FERRY, LINDA H Development and evaluation of a time-resolved microscope COMPARISON OF COLESTIPOL & PSYLLIUM AS HYLIPIDEMIC AGENTS

S07RR-05352-30 0757 (NSS) CAMACHO, ELBER S Development and evaluation of a time-resolved microscope T LYMPHOCYTES, T CELL B LYMPHOCYTES, IL 2 IN BRONCHOGENIC CARCINOMA

S07RR-05352-30 0758 (NSS) COLBURN, KEITH Development and evaluation of a time-resolved microscope PATHOGENIC ANTINUCLEAR ANTIBODIES IN IDIOPATHIC & DRUG INDUCED LUPUS

S07RR-05352-30 0759 (NSS) FINKELMAN, RICHARD D Development and evaluation of a time-resolved microscope PURIFICATION OF A BONE RESORBING FACTOR RELEASED FROM HUMAN OSTEOBLASTS

S07RR-05352-30 0760 (NSS) HILL, KELVIN A W Development and evaluation of a time-resolved microscope ZINC IN ALANYL TRNA SYNTHETASE STRUCTURE & ACTIVITY

S07RR-05352-30 0761 (NSS) BULLAS, LEONARD R Development and evaluation of a time-resolved microscope SALMONELLA GENES FOR RESTRICTION & MODIFICATION OF DNA

S07RR-05352-30 0762 (NSS) RYU, JUNICHI Development and evaluation of a time-resolved microscope CONSTRUCTION OF A PHYSICAL MAP OF KLEBSIELLA PNEUMONIAE GENOME

S07RR-05352-30 0763 (NSS) FRYE, BARBARA Development and evaluation of a time-resolved microscope STRESS & VIOLENCE IN CAMBODIAN REFUGEE FAMILY: PERCEPTION OF CAMBODIAN WOMEN

S07RR-05352-30 0764 (NSS) JAVOR, GEORGE T Development and evaluation of a time-resolved microscope CELLULAR RESPONSES TO THIOL

S07RR-05352-30 0765 (NSS) NEHLSEN-CANNARELLA, Development and evaluation of a time-resolved microscope MACROPHAGE ASSOCIATED PERCARBOXYLATION A FUNDAMENTAL STEP IN ATHEROGENESIS

S07RR-05352-30 0766 (NSS) STRONG, DONNA D Development and evaluation of a time-resolved microscope CLONING OF HUMAN IGFBP 4 PROMOTER

S07RR-05352-30 0767 (NSS) CHEN, YANG K Development and evaluation of a time-resolved microscope NONINVASIVE MONITORING OF HEPATIC FIBRO GENESIS

S07RR-05353-30 (NSS) KORN, DAVID STANFORD UNIVERSITY MED CTR ROOM M121 STANFORD, CALIF 94305 Biomedical research support

S07RR-05353-30 0375 (NSS) ZIPURSKY, ROBERT Biomedical research support HIGHER ORDER MOTOR FUNCTIONS IN PSYCHIATRIC & NEUROLOGIC DISORDERS

S07RR-05353-30 0339 (NSS) ADLER, JOHN Biomedical research support SPINAL SIMULATION WORKSTATION

S07RR-05353-30 0343 (NSS) CLEARY, MICHAEL Biomedical research support ISOLATION OF HUMAN ONCOGENES BY CHROMOSOME MICRODISSECTION

S07RR-05353-30 0344 (NSS) DONLON, TIMOTHY Biomedical research support DNA LOSS FROM CHROMOSOME 15 TO ASCERTAIN LOSS IN PEDIATRIC SYNDROMES

S07RR-05353-30 0340 (NSS) ALBERS, GREGORY Biomedical research support ORAL DEXTROMETHORPHAN FOR PATIENTS AT RISK FOR BRAIN ISCHEMIA

S07RR-05353-30 0341 (NSS) BERNSTEIN, DANIEL Biomedical research support DEVELOPMENTAL REGULATION OF HYPERTROPHIC RESPONSE IN VENTRICULAR MYOCYTES

S07RR-05353-30 0342 (NSS) CLAYBERGER, CAROL Biomedical research support LYMPHOCYTIC INFILTRATES IN ENDOCARDIAL BIOPSIES

S07RR-05353-30 0345 (NSS) GABA, DAVID Biomedical research support CARDIAC ARREST TEAM USING REALISTIC SIMULATION: COMPUTER SIMULATION

S07RR-05353-30 0346 (NSS) HALDER, KASTURI Biomedical research support LIPID TRANSPORT IN MALARIA INFECTED ERYTHROCYTES

S07RR-05353-30 0347 (NSS) HANCOCK, STEVEN Biomedical research support RADIATION INJURY BY INTERLEUKIN 1 & TUMOR NECROSIS FACTOR: METASTASES

S07RR-05353-30 0348 (NSS) HARRIS, EMILY Biomedical research support MENTAL DISORDERS IN PEDIATRIC SETTINGS

S07RR-05353-30 0349 (NSS) JAFFE, RICHARD Biomedical research support SENSORY MODULATION IN MAMMALIAN SPINAL CORD & DORSAL ROOT GANGLIA

S07RR-05353-30 0350 (NSS) KIM, STUART Biomedical research support GENETIC CONTROL OF CELL FATE IN C ELEGANS: VULVAL DEVELOPMENT, LIN 7

S07RR-05353-30 0351 (NSS) KRASNOW, MARK Biomedical research support CELL SORTING TO STUDY CELL INTERACTIONS DURING DEVELOPMENT: DROSOPHILA

S07RR-05353-30 0352 (NSS) LEFF, STUART Biomedical research support CLONING OF BRAIN SPECIFIC SNRNP PROTEINS: MRNA SPLICING

S07RR-05353-30 0353 (NSS) LEWIS, RICHARD Biomedical research support CALCIUM DEPENDENCE OF GENE EXPRESSION IN SINGLE T LYMPHOCYTES

S07RR-05353-30 0354 (NSS) LIEBER, MICHAEL Biomedical research support MOLECULAR IMMUNOLOGY & NUCLEAR ENZYMES THAT CATALYZE DNA STRUCTURAL CHANGES

S07RR-05353-30 0355 (NSS) LIEBER, MICHAEL Biomedical research support NORMAL & MUTANT LYMPHOID VDJ RECOMBINASE: IMMUNITY & LYMPHOCYTES

S07RR-05353-30 0356 (NSS) LOWE, ANSON Biomedical research support SECRETORY GRANULE MEMBRANE PROTEINS IN EXOCRINE PANCREAS

S07RR-05353-30 0357 (NSS) MADISON, DANIEL Biomedical research support SYNAPTIC LONG TERM POTENTIATION IN HIPPOCAMPUS: ELECTROPHYSIOLOGY

S07RR-05353-30 0358 (NSS) MALDONADO, YVONNE Biomedical research support EPIDEMIOLOGY OF POLIOVIRUS AMONG MEXICAN CHILDREN IMMUNE RESPONSE TO OPV

S07RR-05353-30 0359 (NSS) MALDONADO, YVONNE Biomedical research support EPIDEMIOLOGY OF POLIOVIRUS AMONG MEXICAN CHILDREN & IMMUNE RESPONSE TO OPV

S07RR-05353-30 0360 (NSS) MUSEN, MARK Biomedical research support VISUAL LANGUAGES FOR ENCODING CLINICAL PROTOCOL KNOWLEDGE

S07RR-05353-30 0361 (NSS) NEGRIN, ROBERT Biomedical research support MOLECULAR STRUCTURES INVOLVED IN NATURAL KILLER CELL RECOGNITION OF TARGET CELLS

S07RR-05353-30 0362 (NSS) PARSONNET, JULIE Biomedical research support SOURCES OF BACTERIAL DIARRHEA IN WEANING MAYAN CHILDREN

S07RR-05353-30 0363 (NSS) RUEHL, WILLIAM Biomedical research support BACTERIAL SENSORY TRANSDUCTION SYSTEM

S07RR-05353-30 0364 (NSS) RUEHL, WILLIAM W Biomedical research support BACTERIAL IRON ACQUISITION FROM IRON BINDING PROTEINS

S07RR-05353-30 0365 (NSS) SCHWARZ, THOMAS Biomedical research support ALTERNATIVE RNA SPLICING IN SHAKER LOCUS OF DROSOPHILA P ELEMENT

S07RR-05353-30 0366 (NSS) SEGALL, GEORGE Biomedical research support EXERCISE WHOLE BODY THALLIUM SCINTIGRAPHY IN DIAGNOSIS OF CLAUDICATION

S07RR-05353-30 0367 (NSS) SIEGEL, LAWRENCE Biomedical research support PULMONARY HYPERTENSION & ANESTHETICS ON LUNG VASCULAR IMPEDANCE

S07RR-05353-30 0368 (NSS) SMOLLER, BRUCE Biomedical research support ABNORMAL KERATINIZATION IN EPIDERMOLYSIS BULLOSA SIMPLEX

S07RR-05353-30 0369 (NSS) STADIUS, MICHAEL Biomedical research support MODEL TO STUDY CELLULAR RESPONSE TO ACUTE ARTERIAL INJURY

S07RR-05353-30 0370 (NSS) STEINBERG, GARY Biomedical research support NMDA ANTAGONISTS & CEREBRAL ON BLOOD FLOW: STROKE, GLUTAMATE, ISCHEMIA

S07RR-05353-30 0371 (NSS) STEINER, HANS Biomedical research support ADAPTIVE STYLE AS PREDICTOR OF ACUTE STRESS RESPONSE & AUDITORY PROCESSING

S07RR-05353-30 0372 (NSS) TANELIAN, DARRELL L Biomedical research support SENSORY PHYSIOLOGY OF NOCICEPTIVE AFFERENTS

S07RR-05353-30 0373 (NSS) VALANTINE, HANNAH Biomedical research support EVALUATION OF IMMUNE MEDIATORS OF ACUTE CARDIAC ALLOGRAFT DYSFUNCTION

S07RR-05353-30 0374 (NSS) WILSON, DARRELL Biomedical research support RIA DVMT FOR PLASMA PRORENIN: PREDICTOR OF DIABETIC COMPLICATIONS

S07RR-05354-30 0406 (NSS) MURATA, PAUL Biomedical research support PHYSICIAN ATTITUDE TOWARDS RECEIVING HEPATITIS B VACCINATION

S07RR-05354-30 0407 (NSS) BALOH, ROBERT Biomedical research support VISUAL VESTIBULAR INTERACTION IN NORMAL SUBJECTS & PATIENTS

S07RR-05354-30 0408 (NSS) TOGA, ARTHUR Biomedical research support NEURO IMAGING PRERESOURCE

S07RR-05354-30 0409 (NSS) WALFORD, ROY Biomedical research support MAJOR HISTOCOMPATIBILITY COMPLEX & AGING

S07RR-05354-30 0410 (NSS) BAUM, LINDA G Biomedical research support BIOCHEMICAL BASIS FOR SELECTION OF VIRULENT INFLUENZA STRAINS

S07RR-05354-30 0411 (NSS) WAGER, ELIZABETH Biomedical research support CHLAMYDIA TRACHOMATIS INFECTIONS: VARIABLE RECOGNIZED SURFACE ANTIGENS

S07RR-05354-30 0412 (NSS) SEEGER, ROBERT Biomedical research support TREATMENT OF POOR PROGNOSIS NEUROBLASTOMA W/ INTENSIVE MULTIMODAL

S07RR-05354-30 0413 (NSS) GEORGE, ROBERT Biomedical research support NEUROENDOCRINE EFFECTS OF PHENCYCLIDINE: PCP

S07RR-05354-30 0414 (NSS) GUNDERSEN, CAMERON Biomedical research support CLONING OF PRESYNAPTIC CALCIUM CHANNEL CDNA

S07RR-05354-30 (NSS) FRANK, JOY S UCLA SCHOOL OF MED 10833 LE CONTE AVENUE LOS ANGELES, CA 90024 Biomedical research support

S07RR-05354-30 0376 (NSS) PLAEGER/MARSHALL S Biomedical research support DEFECTIVE CD8 T CELL MEDIATED CONTROL IN AIDS

S07RR-05354-30 0377 (NSS) CLEMENT, LORAN Biomedical research support FUNCTIONS OF HUMAN CYTOTOXIC & SUPPRESSOR T CELL SUBPOPULATIONS

S07RR-05354-30 0378 (NSS) VAN DOP, CORNELIUS Biomedical research support G S PROTEIN DYSFUNCTION IN PSEUDOHYPOPARATHYROIDYSM

S07RR-05354-30 0379 (NSS) SALUSKY, ISIDRO Biomedical research support EFFECT OF ANABOLIC HORMONES ON OSTEOBLAST METABOLISM

S07RR-05354-30 0380 (NSS) MCDOUGALL, S Biomedical research support TRANSFORMING ABILITY HTLV 1 TAX, REX, & ENV PROTEINS IN TRANSGENIC MICE

S07RR-05354-30 0381 (NSS) PHELPS, MICHAEL Biomedical research support BIOCHEMICAL & NEUROCHEMICAL BASIS OF ALZHEIMERS DISEASE

S07RR-05354-30 0382 (NSS) CAMPBELL, JOHN Biomedical research support TERATOLOGICS & GENETICS OF PERINATAL EXPOSURE TO MORPHINE & NALOXONE

S07RR-05354-30 0383 (NSS) MICEVYCH, PAUL Biomedical research support INTERACTION OF SEX STEROIDS W/ DEFINED NEURAL CIRCUITS

S07RR-05354-30 0384 (NSS) GORSKI, ROGER A Biomedical research support MOLECULAR MECHANISMS OF STEROID ACTION ON DEVELOPING BRAIN

S07RR-05354-30 0385 (NSS) MICEVYCH, PAUL Biomedical research support GONADAL STEROID REGULATION OF CCK EXPRESSION IN CNS

S07RR-05354-30 0386 (NSS) COOPER, EDWIN L Biomedical research support IMMUNOSUPPRESSION CAUSED BY ENVIRONMENTAL TOXICITY

S07RR-05354-30 0387 (NSS) SEGUNDO, JOSE Biomedical research support NON LINEAR DYNAMICS OF PERIODIC APERIODIC INHIBITORY SYNAPTIC INFLUENCES

S07RR-05354-30 0388 (NSS) GORSKI, ROGER Biomedical research support MECHANISMS OF STEROID ACTION ON DEVELOPING BRAIN

S07RR-05354-30 0389 (NSS) HOUSER, CAROLYN Biomedical research support NEUROCHEMICAL ANATOMY OF EPILEPSY

S07RR-05354-30 0390 (NSS) TACHE, YVETTE Biomedical research support BRAIN REGULATION OF GI FUNCTION BY NEUROPEPTIDES

S07RR-05354-30 0391 (NSS) BRAMHALL, JOHN Biomedical research

support MECHANISMS OF MEMBRANE PERMEATION
S07RR-05354-30 0392 (NSS) CAMPBELL, DAVID Biomedical research support RNA TRANSCRIPTION IN TRYPANOSOMES
S07RR-05354-30 0393 (NSS) KLOTZ, JOAN Biomedical research support B LYMPHOCYTE ACTIVATION & DEFECTIVE T CELL TOLERANCE IN MURINE LUPUS
S07RR-05354-30 0394 (NSS) LOVETT, MICHAEL Biomedical research support PATHOGENIC MECHANISMS IN LYME BORRELIOSIS
S07RR-05354-30 0395 (NSS) MILLER, JEFFREY Biomedical research support REGULATION, TRANSDUCTION, & CONTROL OF BACTERIAL VIRULENCE GENE EXPRESSION
S07RR-05354-30 0396 (NSS) SOLL, ANDREW Biomedical research support INTERACTION OF PARACRINE MODULATORS OF ACID SECRETION
S07RR-05354-30 0397 (NSS) HEBER, DAVID Biomedical research support DIETARY MODULATION OF BREAST CANCER GROWTH FACTORS
S07RR-05354-30 0398 (NSS) GO, VAY LIANG Biomedical research support ELECTRON MICROSCOPY
S07RR-05354-30 0399 (NSS) NEL, ANDRE E Biomedical research support PROTEIN KINASE C & SECOND MESSENGER DURING T ACTIVATION
S07RR-05354-30 0400 (NSS) FANG, MEIKA A Biomedical research support 2ND MESSENGER EFFECTS OF INTERLEUKINS I & 6: OSTEOGENIC SARCOMA CELL
S07RR-05354-30 0401 (NSS) TSAO, BETTY Biomedical research support RECOMBINANT IMMUNOTOXIN FOR SUPPRESSION OF MURINE LUPUS
S07RR-05354-30 0402 (NSS) DUBINETT, STEVE Biomedical research support SITE SPECIFIC RESPONSES IN ADOPTIVE IMMUNOTHERAPY OF METASTATIC CANCER
S07RR-05354-30 0403 (NSS) VAN HERLE, ANDRE Biomedical research support HYPERPARATHYROIDISM: LITHIUM CONNECTION
S07RR-05354-30 0404 (NSS) EISENHAUER, PATRICIA Biomedical research support INTESTINAL DEFENSES AGAINST PARASITIC PROTOZOANS: AIDS
S07RR-05354-30 0405 (NSS) KORENMAN, STANLEY Biomedical research support IMPACT OF SUCCESS THERAPY OF IMPOTENCE ON COUPLE
S07RR-05354-30 0415 (NSS) FUKUTO, JON Biomedical research support MECHANISM OF NITRIC OXIDE BIOSYNTHESIS
S07RR-05354-30 0416 (NSS) LETINSKY, MICHAEL Biomedical research support EFFECT OF ALCOHOL ON SYNAPSE INFORMATION
S07RR-05354-30 0417 (NSS) LETINSKY, MICHAEL Biomedical research support AGE RELATED CHANGES IN NERVE TERMINAL PLASTICITY
S07RR-05354-30 0418 (NSS) WRIGHT, ERNEST Biomedical research support MOLECULAR BIOLOGY OF NA COTRANSPORT PROTEINS
S07RR-05354-30 0419 (NSS) WHIPP, BRIAN Biomedical research support LUNG GAS EXCHANGE DYNAMICS & PERIPHERAL CHEMORECEPTION IN EXCEPTIONAL DYSPNEA
S07RR-05354-30 0420 (NSS) PAPAZIAN, DIANE Biomedical research support STRUCTURE & FUNCTION OF K CHANNELS
S07RR-05354-30 0421 (NSS) VERGARO, JULIO Biomedical research support CALCIUM INTRACELLULAR STORES IN MUSCLE FIBERS W/ PHOTOLABILE ACTIVATORS
S07RR-05354-30 0422 (NSS) BRADY, ALLAN Biomedical research support CYTOSKELETAL & MECHANICAL PROPERTIES OF CARDIAC MYOCYTES
S07RR-05354-30 0423 (NSS) AHN, SAMUEL Biomedical research support LASER WELDING OF VASCULAR & INTESTINAL ANASTOMOSIS
S07RR-05354-30 0424 (NSS) BELLDEGRUN, ARIE Biomedical research support IMMUNOTHERAPY FOR RENAL CANCER: TUMOR INFILTRATING LYMPHOCYTES
R01RR-05355-03 (AR) EATON, GORDON G OREGON REGIONAL PRIMATE RES CT 505 NW 185TH AVENUE BEAVERTON, OR 97006 Psychological well-being of laboratory-paired primates
S07RR-05355-30 (NSS) MARTIN, JOSEPH B UNIV OF CA SAN FRANCISCO SCH OF MED, DEAN'S OFFICE SAN FRANCISCO, CA 94143-0410 Biomedical research support
S07RR-05355-30 0425 (NSS) ENGEL, JOANNE N Biomedical research support: molecular dissection of life cycle of Chlamydia trachomatis
S07RR-05355-30 0426 (NSS) MOSTOV, KEITH E Biomedical research support: transepithelial transport of immunoglobulins
S07RR-05355-30 0427 (NSS) MORGAN, DAVID O Biomedical research support: molecular control of cell proliferation; protein phosphorylation
S07RR-05355-30 0428 (NSS) MALENKA, ROBERT C Biomedical research support: mechanisms of synaptic plasticity
S07RR-05355-30 0429 (NSS) BAINTON, DOROTHY F Biomedical research support: experimental & clinical studies on leukocytes & platelets
S07RR-05355-30 0430 (NSS) FREIMER, NELSON Biomedical research support: genetics of bipolar disorder; manic depressive disorder
S07RR-05356-30 (NSS) TRANQUADA, ROBERT E UNIV OF SOUTHERN CALIFORNIA 1975 ZONAL AVE, KAM 500 LOS ANGELES, CALIF 90033 Biomedical research support
S07RR-05356-30 0431 (NSS) GREENLEE, DONALD V Biomedical research support CALMODULIN MEDIATION OF PROLACTIN SECRETION FROM GH3 CELLS
S07RR-05356-30 0432 (NSS) GILL, PARKASH Biomedical research support RECEPTOR MEDIATED DRUG DELIVERY; CHEMOTHERAPY OF MYCOBACTERIUM INFECTION
S07RR-05356-30 0433 (NSS) NAIDU, YATHI M Biomedical research support NEUROTROPIC HIV ISOLATED; VARIATION IN FUSION PEPTIDE OF TRANSMEMBRANE PROTEIN
S07RR-05356-30 0435 (NSS) SHIBATA, DARRYL Biomedical research support EBV INFECTION ABD T CELL LYMPHOMAS
S07RR-05356-30 0434 (NSS) SCHNEIDER, LON S Biomedical research support HEART RATE VARIABILITY; ELDERLY MAJOR DEPRESSION & ALZHEIMERS DIS OUTPATIENTS
S07RR-05356-30 0436 (NSS) SNOW, MIKEL Biomedical research support MOLECULAR COMPARISON OF NORMAL & TRANSFORMED HUMAN MYOBLASTS
S07RR-05356-30 0437 (NSS) SYAPIN, PETER Biomedical research support RECEPTOR EXPRESSION IN HUMAN CABAERGIC CELLS
S07RR-05356-30 0438 (NSS) TRANQUADA, ROBERT E Biomedical research support VIVARIA; ANIMAL HOUSING
S07RR-05356-30 0439 (NSS) TRANQUADA, ROBERT Biomedical research support PSA
S07RR-05356-30 0440 (NSS) BAKER, RICHARD Biomedical research support SHARED EQUIPMENT
S07RR-05357-30 (NSS) KRUGMAN, RICHARD D U OF COLORADO HLTH SCI CTR 4200 E 9TH AVE BOX C-290 DENVER, COLORADO 80262 Biomedical research support
S07RR-05357-30 0466 (NSS) RIBERA, ANGELES B Biomedical research support IDENTIFICATION OF VERTEBRATE POTASSIUM CHANNEL GENE FAMILY
S07RR-05357-30 0467 (NSS) TRAWICK, JOHN D Biomedical research support DIFFERENTIAL REGULATION OF NUCLEAR ORFU & COX6 GENES BY MITOCHONDRIAL IN YEAST
S07RR-05357-30 0468 (NSS) LEFF, JONATHON A Biomedical research support MECHANISMS OF PROTECTION AGAINST OXIDANT INDUCED VASCULAR INJURY
S07RR-05357-30 0469 (NSS) DEMPSEY, EDWARD C Biomedical research support PROTEIN KINASE C IN PULMONARY ARTERY SMOOTH MUSCLE CELL OXYGEN SENSING & HYPOXIC
S07RR-05357-30 0470 (NSS) PIERSON, DOROTHY E Biomedical research support TWO INVASINS OF YERSINIA ENTEROCOLITICAL, IN PATHOGENESIS PROCESS
S07RR-05357-30 0441 (NSS) STELZNER, THOMAS J Biomedical research support GLUCOCORTICOID INDUCED MODULATION OF ENDOTHELIAL BARRIER PROPERTIES
S07RR-05357-30 0442 (NSS) BABCOCK, SUSAN K Biomedical research support DEVELOPMENT OF T CELL REPERTOIRE IN CYCLOSPORIN INDUCED AUTOIMMUNITY
S07RR-05357-30 0443 (NSS) BANERJEE, ANIRBAN Biomedical research support HYDROGEN PEROXIDE DURING REPERFUSION IN ISOLATED RABBIT MYOCARDIUM
S07RR-05357-30 0444 (NSS) CRUICKSHANKS, KAREN Biomedical research support EPIDEMIOLOGY OF IDDM: ETHNIC DIFFERENCES IN DQ MARKERS OF GENETIC SUSCEPTIBILITY
S07RR-05357-30 0445 (NSS) BALLARD, ROBERT D Biomedical research support SLEEP & LUNG VOLUME ON AIRFLOW RESISTANCE & BRONCHIAL REACTIVITY IN ASTHMA
S07RR-05357-30 0446 (NSS) FORD, DOUGLAS M Biomedical research support MECHANISM OF LATERED PHOSPHATE TRANSPORT IN X LINKED HYPOPHOSPHATEMIC RICKETS
S07RR-05357-30 0447 (NSS) KLEMP, SUZANNE G Biomedical research support DIABETES FAMILY ASSESSMENT SCALE FOR ADOLESCENTS W/ IDDM
S07RR-05357-30 0448 (NSS) STABLER, SALLY P Biomedical research support ANTIMETABOLIC EFFECTS OF COBALAMIN ANALOGUES IN TISSUE CULTURE
S07RR-05357-30 0449 (NSS) FRANKLIN, WILBUR Biomedical research support PRODUCTION OF MONOCLONAL ANTIBODIES AGAINST FOLATE BINDING PROTEIN
S07RR-05357-30 0450 (NSS) HANLEY, MICHAEL Biomedical research support ENDOTHELIAL CELL ASSOCIATED ANTIPROTEASE
S07RR-05357-30 0451 (NSS) REGENSTEINER, JUDITH Biomedical research support MUSCLE ISCHEMIA ON MUSCLE OF PATIENTS W/ PERIPHERAL ARTERIAL DISEASE
S07RR-05357-30 0452 (NSS) KILPATRICK, DAVID Biomedical research support IDENTIFICATION OF THEILERS VIRUS RECEPTOR
S07RR-05357-30 0453 (NSS) BARBOUR, LINDA Biomedical research support ASSESSMENT OF SUBCLINICAL HEPARIN INDUCED OSTEOPOROSIS IN PREGNANCY
S07RR-05357-30 0454 (NSS) CULLUM, C MUNRO Biomedical research support CEREBRAL LESION LOCALIZATION & PSYCHOLOGICAL SEQUELAE FOLLOWING BRAIN INJURY
S07RR-05357-30 0455 (NSS) OHARA, JUNICHI Biomedical research support MOLECULAR STUDY OF MURINE IL 4 RECEPTOR
S07RR-05357-30 0456 (NSS) SPITZER, VICTOR M Biomedical research support TISSUE IDENTIFICATION BY REMOTE SENSING
S07RR-05357-30 0457 (NSS) GOMEZ, MARK A Biomedical research support INCREASED STRESS, ON BIOCHEMICAL & MORPHOLOGICAL PROPERTIES OF HEALING LIGAMENTS
S07RR-05357-30 0458 (NSS) RODGERS, CHRISTINE M Biomedical research support IONTOPHORESIS I 125 GENTAMICIN INTO OSTEOMYELITIC TIBIA
S07RR-05357-30 0459 (NSS) KURITZKES, DANIEL Biomedical research support FUNCTIONAL DOMAINS OF HTLV ENVELOPE PROTEINS
S07RR-05357-30 0460 (NSS) NARKEWICZ, MICHAEL Biomedical research support LIPOGENESIS & LIPID SECRETION IN TPN HEPATIC STEATOSIS
S07RR-05357-30 0461 (NSS) CURRIE, RICHARD A Biomedical research support PURIFICATION & CHARACTERIZATION OF KAPPA ENCHANCER TRANSCRIPTION FACTOR, NF KE
S07RR-05357-30 0462 (NSS) HOEFFLER, JAMES P Biomedical research support PROTEIN & PROTEIN INTERACTIONS TO CLONE TRANSCRIPTIONAL REGULATORY FACTORS
S07RR-05357-30 0463 (NSS) AQUAYO, SAMUEL M Biomedical research support GRP EXPRESSION IN SCLC H345 USING FLOW CYTOMETRY & GRP MRNA ANTISENSE
S07RR-05357-30 0464 (NSS) CHAPMAN, ARLENE Biomedical research support TOXIC OXYGEN METABOLITES IN DIPHENYLTHIAZOLE INDUCED RENAL CYSTIC DISEASE
S07RR-05357-30 0465 (NSS) ECKHOFF, DONALD G Biomedical research support EFFECTS OF FEMORAL TIBIAL COMPONENT ALIGNMENT IN TOTAL KNEE ARTHROPLASTY
S07RR-05358-30 (NSS) AASLESTAD, HALVOR G YALE UNIVERSITY SCH OF MED 333 CEDAR STREET NEW HAVEN, CONN 06510 Biomedical research support
S07RR-05358-30 0471 (NSS) CHANG, GRACE Biomedical research support SURVEY OF EMERGENCY PHYSICIANS ON MANAGEMENT OF INTOXICATED DRIVERS
S07RR-05358-30 0472 (NSS) COLEMAN, DAVID L Biomedical research support PROINFLAMMATORY INTERACTIONS BETWEEN KERATINOCYTES & MACROPHAGES
S07RR-05358-30 0497 (NSS) FERRO-NOVICK, SUSAN Biomedical research support BET 2 MEMBRANE ATTACHMENT TWO GTPASES REGULATE VESICULAR TRAFFIC IN YEAST
S07RR-05358-30 0498 (NSS) HENRICH, JANET B Biomedical research support ESTROGEN USE & BREAST CANCER IN SCREEN MAMMOGRAPHY PROGRAM
S07RR-05358-30 0499 (NSS) SLEDGE, WILLIAM H Biomedical research support EFFECTS OF SLEEP DEPRIVATION ON MEDICAL INTERNS
S07RR-05358-30 0500 (NSS) ZAHLER, RAPHAEL Biomedical research support LOCALIZATION OF NA, K ATPASE ISOFORMS IN RAT HEART
S07RR-05358-30 0473 (NSS) FRIED, DEBORAH Biomedical research support INTERPERSONAL RELATIONSHIPS & PSYCHOTIC ILLNESS
S07RR-05358-30 0474 (NSS) GORDON, THOMAS R Biomedical research support ELECTROPHYSIOLOGY OF NORMAL & MYELIN DEFICIENT MUTANT RAT OPTIC NERVE
S07RR-05358-30 0475 (NSS) HARDING, MATTHEW W Biomedical research support STRUCTURE & FUNCTION OF IMMUNOSUPPRESSIVE DRUG RECEPTORS, TRANSPLANTATION

PROJECT NO., ORGANIZATIONAL UNIT., INVESTIGATOR, ADDRESS, TITLE

S07RR-05358-30 0476 (NSS) HOLLAND, SCOTT K Biomedical research support DEVELOPMENT OF MICROSCOPIC MAGNETIC RESONANCE IMAGING; NMR
S07RR-05358-30 0477 (NSS) MEYN, M STEPHEN Biomedical research support GENES COMPLEMENT DNA REPAIR DEFECTS ATAXIA TELANGIECTASIA FANCONI ANEMIA
S07RR-05358-30 0478 (NSS) RIMAR, STEPHEN Biomedical research support UPTAKE OF ANGIOTENSIN CONCERTING ENZYME INHIBITORS BY CORONARY CIRCULATION
S07RR-05358-30 0479 (NSS) RINDER, CHRISTINE ST Biomedical research support MABS TO PLATELET SURFACE GLYCOPROTEINS MEASURED ON CARDIOPULMONARY BYPASS
S07RR-05358-30 0480 (NSS) STERN, DAVID F Biomedical research support TYROSINE KINASES IN YEAST
S07RR-05358-30 0481 (NSS) WEST, A BRIAN Biomedical research support MOLECULAR BASIS OF MICROVILLUS INCLUSION DISEASE
S07RR-05358-30 0482 (NSS) ZAHNER, GWENDOLYN Biomedical research support PILOT STUDIES IN CHILD PSYCHIATRIC EPIDEMIOLOGY
S07RR-05358-30 0483 (NSS) BOULWARE, SUSAN D Biomedical research support GROWTH HORMONE IN INSULIN RESISTANCE OF PUBERTY
S07RR-05358-30 0484 (NSS) BRASH, DOUGLAS E Biomedical research support GENOMIC DNA SUBTRACTION OF HETEROZYGOTES
S07RR-05358-30 0485 (NSS) GONDA, DAVID KEITH Biomedical research support SUBSTRATE SELECTION IN UBIQUITIN DEPENDENT PROTEOLYSIS
S07RR-05358-30 0486 (NSS) KAVATHAS, PAULA Biomedical research support HLA IN NEONATAL ALLOIMMUNE THROMBOCYTOPENIA
S07RR-05358-30 0487 (NSS) RINALDO, PIERO Biomedical research support STABLE ISOTOPE DILUTION METHOD FOR INHERITED DISORDERS OF FATTY ACID OXIDATION
S07RR-05358-30 0488 (NSS) WARREN, STEPHEN L Biomedical research support REGULATION OF EPITHELIAL MORPHOGENESIS OF PP60C
S07RR-05358-30 0489 (NSS) ANDREWS, NORMA W Biomedical research support T CRUZI C9 RELATED PROTEIN
S07RR-05358-30 0490 (NSS) COMITE, FLORENCE Biomedical research support ENDOMETRIOSIS & BONE: RELATIONSHIP OF BONE & CYTOKINES
S07RR-05358-30 0491 (NSS) GOLDENRING, JAMES R Biomedical research support CALMODULIN DEPENDENT KINASE II CHOLINERGIC STIMULATED PARIETAL CELL SECRETION
S07RR-05358-30 0492 (NSS) KINDER, BARBARA K Biomedical research support INTRACELLULAR HORMONE DEGRADATION IN PARATHYROID CELL
S07RR-05358-30 0493 (NSS) SOYBEL, DAVID I Biomedical research support BARRIER FUNCTIONS OF GASTRIC SURFACE EPITHELIUM
S07RR-05358-30 0494 (NSS) SPICER, ELEANOR K Biomedical research support T4 REGA PROTEIN: STRUCTURE & FUNCTION STUDIES
S07RR-05358-30 0495 (NSS) AVISON, MALCOLM J Biomedical research support MEASUREMENT OF TISSUE IN VIVO 1H NMR
S07RR-05358-30 0496 (NSS) BERG, ANNE T Biomedical research support INTRACTABLE EPILEPSY: RISK FACTORS & NATURAL HISTORY
S07RR-05359-30 (NSS) LAROSA, JOHN C GEORGE WASHINGTON UNIVERSITY 2300 I ST NW ROSS HALL 514 WASHINGTON, D C 20037 Biomedical research support
S07RR-05359-30 0501 (NSS) ALYONO, DAVID Biomedical research support MAGNESIUM IN ELECTROMECHANICAL DYSFUNCTION IN MYOCARDIAL STUNNING
S07RR-05359-30 0502 (NSS) BASS, BARBARA Biomedical research support EFFECT OF CHEMOSENSITIVE NEURONS ON ESOPHAGEAL BLOOD FLOW
S07RR-05359-30 0503 (NSS) BAUMGOLD, JESSE Biomedical research support MUSCARINIC RECEPTOR MEDIATED INCREASE IN CAMP LEVELS
S07RR-05359-30 0504 (NSS) BOCKMAN, JEFFREY Biomedical research support ANALYSIS OF PRION PROTEIN IN AIDS BRAIN
S07RR-05359-30 0505 (NSS) BOUSCAREL, BERNARD Biomedical research support MECHANISM REGULATING LDL UPTAKE BY UDCA IN ISOLATED HAMSTER HEPATOCYTES
S07RR-05359-30 0506 (NSS) CHANDERBHAN, RONALD Biomedical research support ISCHEMIA & RESUSCITATION W/ O2 OR AIR ON BRAIN LIPIDS
S07RR-05359-30 0507 (NSS) CLAWSON, GARY Biomedical research support MODULATION OF NUCLEOCYTOPLASMIC RNA TRANSPORT BY HIV REV & TAT PROTEIN
S07RR-05359-30 0508 (NSS) COSGROVE, JAMES Biomedical research support NUCLEAR ENVELOPE TRYPTOPHAN BINDING PROTEIN IN BRAIN
S07RR-05359-30 0509 (NSS) HENRIQUES, HORACE Biomedical research support MESANGIAL CLASS II MHC ANTIGEN: DIABETES, NEPHROPATHY
S07RR-05359-30 0510 (NSS) HU, VALERIE Biomedical research support MICROCYSTIN W/ MODEL MEMBRANE: HEPATOXIN, LIPOSOMES
S07RR-05359-30 0511 (NSS) HU, VALERIE Biomedical research support INTERCELLULAR COMMUNICATION IN SENESCENT CELLS: AGING
S07RR-05359-30 0512 (NSS) JOHNSON, KURT Biomedical research support FIBRONECTIN & INTEGRIN IN XENOPUS GASTRULATION: FIBRONECTIN
S07RR-05359-30 0513 (NSS) KIMMEL, PAUL Biomedical research support ZINC MODULATION OF MACROPHAGE 1, 25 VITAMIN D SYNTHESIS: RENAL DISEASE
S07RR-05359-30 0514 (NSS) KUMAR, AJIT Biomedical research support HOST CELL METABOLIC CHANGES THAT REGULATE HIV 1 GROWTH: AIDS, RETROVIRUS
S07RR-05359-30 0515 (NSS) LOON, JOEL Biomedical research support SAMPLING FRAME: SURVEY OF ALZHEIMERS SPECIALTY CARE NURSING HOME
S07RR-05359-30 0516 (NSS) LUNDERGAN, CONOR Biomedical research support PEPTIDE ANALOGOUS OF SOMATOSTATIN: ATHEROSCLEROSIS
S07RR-05359-30 0517 (NSS) ORKIN, BRUCE Biomedical research support NOCTURNAL ANORECTAL MOTILITY & RECTAL MOTOR COMPLEX
S07RR-05359-30 0518 (NSS) PATIERNO, STEVEN Biomedical research support MOLECULAR MUTAGENESIS IN TRANSGENIC MICE: CARCINOGENS
S07RR-05359-30 0519 (NSS) PERRY, DAVID Biomedical research support CEREBRAL ISCHEMIA & HIPPOCAMPAL OPIATE RECEPTORS: STROKE, HEART ATTACK
S07RR-05359-30 0520 (NSS) ROBERTS, INGRAM Biomedical research support LINGUAL GLAND GROWTH & GENE EXPRESSION: TONGUE
S07RR-05359-30 0521 (NSS) WALSH, RAYMOND Biomedical research support GROWTH HORMONE RECEPTORS IN CNS: PROLACTIN
S07RR-05359-30 0522 (NSS) WERLING, LINDA Biomedical research support CATECHOLAMINERGIC FUNCTION IN RAT BRAIN: SCHIZOPHRENIA, ISCHEMIA
S07RR-05359-30 0523 (NSS) WHITE, JON Biomedical research support DIABETIC NEPHROPATHY IN RODENT MODEL OF DIABETES FOLLOWING INSULIN
S07RR-05360-30 (NSS) BURRIS, JAMES F GEORGETOWN UNIVERSITY MED CTR 3900 RESERVOIR ROAD, NW WASHINGTON, D C 20007 Biomedical research support
S07RR-05360-30 0774 (NSS) DONIGER, JAY N Biomedical research support HUMAN PAPILLOMAVIRUS INFECTION & CERVICAL DYSPLASIA IN HIV POSITIVE WOMEN AIDS
S07RR-05360-30 0775 (NSS) IRVING, STEVEN G Biomedical research support COORDINATE REGULATION OF CYTOKINE GENE EXPRESSION INFLAMMATION; IMMUNOLOGY
S07RR-05360-30 0776 (NSS) LAUE, LOUISA Biomedical research support MOLECULAR BASIS OF FAMILIAL MALE PRECOCIOUS PUBERTY
S07RR-05360-30 0777 (NSS) WILLETT, GERALD D Biomedical research support PROTEOGLYCAN ANALYSIS OF HYALURONATE IN OVARIAN SEROUS TUMORS & MESOTHELIUM
S07RR-05360-30 0778 (NSS) ZWIEBEL, JAMES A Biomedical research support MODEL SYSTEM FOR GENE THERAPY: RETROVIRAL MEDIATED GENE TRANSFER; TACZ;
S07RR-05361-30 (NSS) ASHE, WARREN K HOWARD UNIVERSITY 520 W STREET NW WASHINGTON, DC 20059 Xxiind international conference on animal genetics
S07RR-05362-30 (NSS) NEIMS, ALLEN H UNIVERSITY OF FLORIDA BOX J-215 JHMHC GAINESVILLE, FLA 32610 Biomedical research support
S07RR-05362-30 0779 (NSS) MURPHY, JAMES J Biomedical research support BIOENGINEERING & BIOELECTRONICS SUPPORT OF RESEARCH & TEACHING OF NEUROSCIENCE
S07RR-05362-30 0780 (NSS) NEIMS, ALLEN H Biomedical research support POLYAMINE ANALOGS AS INHIBITORS OF MITOCHONDRIAL DNA REPLICATION: CANCER
S07RR-05362-30 0781 (NSS) SIDEN, E Biomedical research support PRODUCTION FROM MICROINJECTED TRANSFORMED EMBRYO
S07RR-05362-30 0782 (NSS) BRAYLAN, R Biomedical research support KINETICS OF BCL MURINA LYMPHOMA IN TUMOR BEARING ORGANS
S07RR-05362-30 0783 (NSS) GUY, J Biomedical research support DEMYELINATION OF EXPERIMENTAL ALLERGIC ENCEPHALOMYELITIS
S07RR-05362-30 0784 (NSS) GUY, J Biomedical research support DEMYELINATION OF EXPERIMENTAL ALLERGIC ENCEPHALOMYELITIS
S07RR-05362-30 0785 (NSS) MERWIN, G Biomedical research support COMPARISON OF MATERIALS USED FOR FACIAL AUGMENTATION
S07RR-05362-30 0786 (NSS) MICKLE, P Biomedical research support LIPID PEROXIDATION & SPINAL CORD ISCHEMIA
S07RR-05362-30 0787 (NSS) RAIZADA, M Biomedical research support INSULIN LIKE GROWTH FACTOR (IGF) RECEPTOR STUDIES ON BRAIN
S07RR-05362-30 0788 (NSS) GARG, L Biomedical research support ABNORMAL MINERALOCORTICOIDS ON RENAL FUNCTION & BLOOD PRESSURE
S07RR-05362-30 0789 (NSS) GEE, A Biomedical research support MAGNETIC PURGING OF T LYMPHOCYTES FROM BONE MARROW
S07RR-05362-30 0790 (NSS) PRESTON, J Biomedical research support ANTI THY 1 MAB PREPARED W/ ALPHA AMANITIN OR RICIN A
S07RR-05362-30 0791 (NSS) GREEN, N Biomedical research support AMINE CARBONHYDRATE BY PRODUCTS OF BROWNING REACTION FOR MUTAGENESIS
S07RR-05362-30 0792 (NSS) YOUNG, M Biomedical research support HUMAN SPERMATOZOA TO NERVE GROWTH FACTOR
S07RR-05362-30 0793 (NSS) GREENBURGH, R Biomedical research support INTERVENTION PROGRAM TO REDUCE PASSIVE SMOKING IN INFANTS
S07RR-05362-30 0794 (NSS) ROMRELL, L Biomedical research support EVALUATION OF EFFECTS OF HAZARDOUS AGENTS ON SPERMATOGENESIS
S07RR-05362-30 0795 (NSS) MICKLE, P Biomedical research support NEURONAL CELL SUSPENSIONS TO PREVENT DENERVATION ATROPHY
S07RR-05362-30 0796 (NSS) KOROLY, M Biomedical research support IGA W/ LOW DENSITY LIPOPROTEIN IN CULTURED HUMAN FIBROBLASTS
S07RR-05362-30 0797 (NSS) JANKOWSKA, J Biomedical research support PHYSIOLOGICAL ROLE OF MUSCLE CARBONIC ANHYDRASE
S07RR-05362-30 0798 (NSS) BARRETT, D Biomedical research support IGG2 SUBCLASS RESTRICTION OF HUMAN POLYSACCHARIDE ANTIBODY RESPONSE
S07RR-05362-30 0799 (NSS) CERRA, D Biomedical research support VERAPAMIL IN TREATMENT OF TARDIVE DYSKINESIA
S07RR-05362-30 0800 (NSS) MAHAN, C Biomedical research support PRENATAL SCREENING ON COST OF SUBSEQUENT NEONATAL CARE
S07RR-05362-30 0801 (NSS) RAIZADA, M Biomedical research support ALPHA ADRENERGIC RECEPTOR DRUG INTERACTIONS IN NEURONAL CULTURES
S07RR-05362-30 0802 (NSS) JERNIGAN, J Biomedical research support ASSESSMENT FOR TUBERCULOSIS IN A NURSING HOME
S07RR-05362-30 0803 (NSS) TYLKOWSKI, C Biomedical research support GAIT PATTERNS IN PATIENTS W/ POST OPERATIVE KNEE RESECTION ARTHRODESIS
S07RR-05362-30 0804 (NSS) ANGELIDES, K Biomedical research support ALPHA PEPTIDE OF SODIUM CHANNEL FROM RAT BRAIN
S07RR-05362-30 0807 (NSS) SANDERS, PAULETTA E Biomedical research support HISTOCHEMISTRY OF UTEROSACRAL LIGAMENT
S07RR-05362-30 0808 (NSS) SANDERS, PAULETTA E Biomedical research support LIGHT MICROSCOPY OF HUMAN TEMPORAL BONES
S07RR-05362-30 0809 (NSS) SANDERS, PAULETTA E Biomedical research support PARAFFIN EMBEDDING OF RAT COCHLEAR FOR IMMUNOCYTOCHEMISTRY COATING OF SLIDES
S07RR-05362-30 0810 (NSS) SANDERS, PAULETTA E Biomedical research support SERIAL SECTIONING OF RAT COCHLEAR FOR PRELIMINARY DATA
S07RR-05362-30 0811 (NSS) SANDERS, PAULETTA E Biomedical research support SPECIAL STAINING OF RAT EAR TISSUES FOR PAS
S07RR-05362-30 0812 (NSS) SANDERS, PAULETTA E Biomedical research support OOGENESIS & OOCYTE GROWTH IN TELEOSTS
S07RR-05362-30 0813 (NSS) PLAYER, DENIFIELD W Biomedical research support POLYMORPHONUCLEAR LEUKOCYTES ON VASCULAR SMOOTH MUSCLE TONE
S07RR-05362-30 0814 (NSS) PLAYER, DENIFIELD W Biomedical research support DOGS W/ CORONARY THROMBOSIS W/ MUTANT OF TISSUE PLASMINOGEN ACTIVATOR
S07RR-05362-30 0815 (NSS) PLAYER, DENIFIELD W Biomedical research support OVARY OF SEAHORSE, HIPPOCAMPUS ERECTUS
S07RR-05362-30 0816 (NSS) PLAYER, DENIFIELD W Biomedical research support ELECTROMICROSCOPY OF HUMAN EAR TISSUE
S07RR-05362-30 0817 (NSS) PLAYER, DENIFIELD W Biomedical research support ELECTROMICROSCOPY OF RAT EAR TISSUES
S07RR-05362-30 0805 (NSS) SANDERS, PAULETTA E Biomedical research support CARBOHYDRATE & UTERUS OF GUINEA PIG & UTERINE TUBE
S07RR-05362-30 0806 (NSS) SANDERS, PAULETTA E Biomedical research support RELAXIN ON CELL TURNOVER IN REPRODUCTIVE ORGANS OF MOUSE
R24RR-05363-01A1 (AR) SCHOEB, TRENTON R UNIV OF ALABAMA AT BIRMINGHAM UAB STATION BIRMINGHAM, AL 35294 CAR bacillus infection in rats and mice

PROJECT NUMBER LISTING

PROJECT NO., ORGANIZATIONAL UNIT., INVESTIGATOR, ADDRESS, TITLE

S07RR-05363-30 (NSS) FOGEL, BERNARD J UNV OF MIAMI, SCH OF MED R-699 P O BOX 016960 MIAMI, FLA 33101 Biomedical research support
S07RR-05363-30 0837 (NSS) WHELAN, WILLIAM J Biomedical research support BIOGENESIS OF GLYCOGEN
S07RR-05363-30 0818 (NSS) ADKINS, REBECCA D Biomedical research support DIFFERENTIATION OF T LYMPHOCYTES IN ADULT & FETAL THYMUS
S07RR-05363-30 0819 (NSS) BANDSTRA, EMMALEE S Biomedical research support CARDIORESPIRATORY FUNCTION IN COCAINE EXPOSED NEONATES
S07RR-05363-30 0820 (NSS) BOURGUIGNON, LILLY Biomedical research support GTP BINDING PROTEINS IN LYMPHOCYTE SIGNAL TRANSDUCTION AFTER HIV GP120 BINDING
S07RR-05363-30 0821 (NSS) BREW, KEITH Biomedical research support ENGINEERING CA2+ SITE IN EGG WHITE LYSOZYME ROLE FOR CALCIUM IN PROTEIN FOLDING
S07RR-05363-30 0822 (NSS) HAMILTON, BRIAN L Biomedical research support MECHANISM OF IMMUNODEFICIENCY IN PERINATALLY ACQUIRED HIV INFECTION
S07RR-05363-30 0823 (NSS) BURKE, GEORGE W Biomedical research support HETEROTOPIC IMPLANT & TRANSPLANT OF LEFT HEPATIC LOBES IN PIGS
S07RR-05363-30 0824 (NSS) BRANDT, NEIL R Biomedical research support ANTIBODIES AGAINST PROTEASE RESISTANT OF SKELETAL MUSCLE JUNCTIONAL FOOT PROTEIN
S07RR-05363-30 0825 (NSS) CALANCIE, BLAIR Biomedical research support MOTOR SYSTEMS MONITORING SPINE SURGERY PREVENTION OF INJURY TO NERVOUS SYSTEM
S07RR-05363-30 0826 (NSS) COUSINS, SCOTT W Biomedical research support NEW DIAGNOSTIC TESTS FOR INTRAOCULAR INFLAMMATION
S07RR-05363-30 0827 (NSS) DICKERSON, IAN Biomedical research support BIOSYNTHESIS OF TRANSFECTED NEUROPEPTIDES
S07RR-05363-30 0828 (NSS) FLYNN, DONNA D Biomedical research support SIGMA RECEPTORS IN HUMAN PLACENTA: REGULATION W/ PRENATAL COCAINE USE
S07RR-05363-30 0829 (NSS) JONAS, MAUREEN M Biomedical research support HEPATITIS C INFECT IN MUNICIPAL OBSTETRICAL POPULATION: PERINATAL TRANSMISSION
S07RR-05363-30 0830 (NSS) LEONARDI, CRAIG L Biomedical research support PAPILLOMAVIRUS E5 PROTEIN IN STIMULATION MITOGENESIS
S07RR-05363-30 0831 (NSS) LITOSCH, IRENE Biomedical research support HORMONE REGULATION OF PHOSPHOINOSITIDE HYDROLYSIS
S07RR-05363-30 0832 (NSS) LOUTZENHISER, RODGER Biomedical research support MODULATION OF MYOGENIC VASOCONSTRICTION OF RENAL AFFERENT ARTERIOLES
S07RR-05363-30 0833 (NSS) PATTON, JOHN T Biomedical research support FUNCTIONAL DOMAINS OF MAJOR INNERSHELL PROTEIN OF ROTAVIRUS
S07RR-05363-30 0834 (NSS) RILEY, RICHARD Biomedical research support FUNCTION OF LAMBDA LIGHT CHAIN RELATED GENES IN B CELL DEVELOPMENT
S07RR-05363-30 0835 (NSS) RUIZ, PHILLIP Biomedical research support THROMBOXANE REGULATION OF ALLOIMMUNITY
S07RR-05363-30 0836 (NSS) TALVENHEIMO, JANE A Biomedical research support REGULATION OF DIHYDROPHYRIDINE RECEPTOR MRNA IN HUMAN NEUROBLASTOMA CELLS
S07RR-05364-30 (NSS) HOUPT, JEFFREY L EMORY UNIVERSITY 1440 CLIFTON RD NE 408 WHSCAB ATLANTA, GA 30322 Biomedical research support
S07RR-05364-30 0524 (NSS) CHURCHWARD, GORDON Biomedical research support CONTROL OF REPLICATION OF BACTERIAL PLASMID PSC101
S07RR-05364-30 0525 (NSS) COLUCCIO, L Biomedical research support CALMODULIN CROSS BRIDGES INTESTINAL MICROVILLI: CYTOSKELETAL MEMBRANE INTERACT
S07RR-05364-30 0526 (NSS) CONN, P JEFFREY Biomedical research support IONIC CONDUCTANCES PYRAMIDAL CELLS PYRIFORM CORTEX & HIPPOCAMPUS
S07RR-05364-30 0527 (NSS) GLASS, DAVID Biomedical research support SUBSTRATES & INHIBITORS OF PROTEIN KINASES
S07RR-05364-30 0528 (NSS) GREEN, ROBERT Biomedical research support PLASTIC CHANGES IN HIPPOCAMPUS PRODUCED BY EPILEPTIC ACTIVITY
S07RR-05364-30 0529 (NSS) HERSEY, STEPHEN Biomedical research support INTRACELLULAR REACTIONS IN GASTRIC MUCOSA
S07RR-05364-30 0530 (NSS) HUNT, PATRICIA A Biomedical research support SEX CHROMOSOMES & FERTILITY
S07RR-05364-30 0531 (NSS) JONES, DEAN Biomedical research support REAL TIME DIGITAL IMAGE ANALYSIS SYSTEM: QUANTITATIVE FLUORESCENCE CELLS
S07RR-05364-30 0532 (NSS) JOSHI, HARISH C Biomedical research support MICROTUBULE PROTEINS DURING NEURONAL MORPHOGENESIS
S07RR-05364-30 0533 (NSS) LING, BRIAN Biomedical research support APICAL SODIUM TRANSPORT IN CELL CULTURE SYSTEM MODELS OF DISTAL NEPHRON
S07RR-05364-30 0534 (NSS) LUSKIN, MARLA B Biomedical research support ANALYSIS OF CELL LINEAGE IN CEREBRAL CORTEX W/ RECOMBINANT RETROVIRUS
S07RR-05364-30 0535 (NSS) MARONI, BRAD Biomedical research support MECHANISMS OF ADAPTION TO DIETARY MANIPULATION IN UREMIA
S07RR-05364-30 0536 (NSS) NANES, MARK S Biomedical research support CYTOKINE ACTIONS, IN ISOLATED OSTEOBLASTS
S07RR-05364-30 0537 (NSS) NEWCOM, SAMUEL Biomedical research support TRANSFORMING GROWTH FACTOR BETA NODULAR SCLEROSING HODGKINS POTENTIAL
S07RR-05364-30 0538 (NSS) OFFERMAN, MARGARET Biomedical research support DE REPRESSION OF BETA INTERFERON EXPRESSION IN TRANSFORMED BALB C 3T3 CELLS
S07RR-05364-30 0539 (NSS) REINES, DANIEL Biomedical research support ISOLATION OF FACTORS RESPONSIBLE FOR NERVOUS SYSTEM RESTRICTED GENE EXPRESSION
S07RR-05364-30 0540 (NSS) SAXE, CHARLES Biomedical research support MOLECULAR ANALYSIS OF DICTYOSTELIUM CAMP RECEPTOR, CAR2
S07RR-05364-30 0541 (NSS) SELVARAJ, PERIASAMY Biomedical research support STRUCTURE & FUNCTION OF CD16 ANTIGEN
S07RR-05364-30 0542 (NSS) SHUSTER, ROBERT C Biomedical research support GLUCOSE TRANSPORTER FIBROBLASTS & INHERITED IMPAIRMENT; INSULIN BINDING
S07RR-05364-30 0543 (NSS) STYBLO, TONCRED Biomedical research support MANIPULATION PROTEIN KINASE C CALCIUM ON MURINE LYMPHOKINE ACTIVATED KILLER CELL

PROJECT NO., ORGANIZATIONAL UNIT., INVESTIGATOR, ADDRESS, TITLE

S07RR-05364-30 0544 (NSS) SWERLICK, ROBERT Biomedical research support CYTOADHESIN INTEGRINS ON HUMAN DERMAL MICROVASCULAR ENDOTHELIAL CELLS
S07RR-05364-30 0545 (NSS) UNGER, ELIZABETH Biomedical research support STROMA IN INVASION OF CANCER
S07RR-05364-30 0546 (NSS) WILKINSON, KEITH Biomedical research support UBIQUITIN DEPENDENT SPECIFICITY & MECHANISMS
S07RR-05364-30 0547 (NSS) WOLF, STEVEN L Biomedical research support FALL & INJURY INTERVENTION TECHNIQUES: PREVENTION, REHAB
S07RR-05364-30 0548 (NSS) WU, GUANG-JER Biomedical research support MECHANISMS & REGULATION OF TRANSCRIPTION INITIATION
S07RR-05364-30 0549 (NSS) ZAIDEN, JAMES R Biomedical research support EFFECTS OF VOLATILE ANESTHETICS ON REPERFUSION ARRHYTHMIAS IN HANFORD PIG
S07RR-05364-30 0550 (NSS) FARLEY, MONICA Biomedical research support BIO SIGNIFICANCE OF PILUS EXPRESSION IN HEMOPHILUS INFLUENZAE BIO GROUP A EGYPT
S07RR-05364-30 0551 (NSS) TIGGES, MARGARETE Biomedical research support MONKEY MODEL FOR INFANTILE APHAKIA AMBLYOPIA TREATMENT
S07RR-05365-30 (NSS) EASTWOOD, GREGORY L MED COL OF GA RES INST 1120 15TH STREET AUGUSTA, GA 30912-0067 General research support
S07RR-05365-30 0073 (NSS) ABNEY, THOMAS A General research support REGULATION OF LEYDIG CELL DEVELOPMENT AND FUNCTION
S07RR-05365-30 0074 (NSS) ASHWORTH, CAROLYN S General research support AIDS EDUCATIONAL INTERVENTION & KNOWLEDGE OF ATTITUDES OF WIC MOTHERS
S07RR-05365-30 0106 (NSS) TAORMINA, MICHAEL General research support CEREBROHEMODYNAMICS & CEREBRAL VASO-REACTIVITY IN SLEEP APNEA; DOPPLER SONOGRAPH
S07RR-05365-30 0075 (NSS) BHALLA, VINOD K General research support DOES HCG BIND TO STEROIDOGENIC CELLS TO ELICIT BIOLOGICAL RESPONSE
S07RR-05365-30 0076 (NSS) BOEDY, ROBERT F General research support ASSES GLOMERULAR FILTRATION ON REPRODUCTIVE FUNCTION IN FEMALE RATS
S07RR-05365-30 0077 (NSS) COSTOFF, ALLEN General research support EFFECT OF MILD HYPERPROLACTINEMIA ON REPRODUCTIVE FUNCTION IN FEMALE RAT
S07RR-05365-30 0078 (NSS) DEFOE, DENNIS M General research support ORGAN CULTURE APPROACHES TO OUTER SEGMENT DISASSEMBLY IN RAT RETINAS
S07RR-05365-30 0079 (NSS) GALE, THOMAS F General research support SKELETAL & SOFT TISSUE CONGENITAL MALFORMATION FROM HYPERGLYCEMIA; HAMSTER FETUS
S07RR-05365-30 0080 (NSS) GEST, THOMAS R General research support MIGRATION PATTERNS OF ENDOTHELIAL CELLS & NEURAL CREST CELLS IN DEVELOPING HEART
S07RR-05365-30 0081 (NSS) GONZALEZ-REDONDO, J General research support BINDING OF TRANS-ACTING FACTORS TO CAC BOX OF HUMAN B GLOBIN GENE
S07RR-05365-30 0082 (NSS) HENDRICH, CHESTER E General research support RIBOSOMAL PROTEINS IN MID TO LATE GESTATION FETUSES OF HYPOTHYROID MOTHERS
S07RR-05365-30 0083 (NSS) HODGE, LON General research support CHARACTERIZE PRENUCLEAR DOMAINS DETECTED BY NEWLY-RAISED MONOCLONAL ANTIBODY
S07RR-05365-30 0084 (NSS) HOWARD, EUGENE F General research support I1-6 RESPONSE ELEMENTS IN THE T-KININOGEN ACUTE PHASE GENE
S07RR-05365-30 0085 (NSS) HUMPHRIES, ARTHUR L General research support INTERPOSITION OF URETER BETWEEN SKIN & VENA CAVA
S07RR-05365-30 0086 (NSS) LANCLOS, KENNETH D General research support CIS-ACTING ELEMENTS EFFECT ON FETAL GLOBIN GENE REGULATION: ERYTHROID CELL ASSAY
S07RR-05365-30 0087 (NSS) LAPP, DAVID F General research support MOLECULAR PROBES FOR TREHALASE ENZYME IN PARASITIC NEMATODES
S07RR-05365-30 0088 (NSS) LAUSE, DAVID B General research support CELL SURFACE MOLECULES IN NK & LAK CELL RECOGNITION OF TUMOR CELL TARGETS
S07RR-05365-30 0089 (NSS) MRUTHINTI, SATYANARA General research support ACETYL SALICYLIC ACID & AMINOQUANIDINE INHIBIT GLYCATION OF LENS PROTEINS
S07RR-05365-30 0090 (NSS) MURRO, ANTHONY M General research support ROLE OF ADENOSINE RECEPTORS OF DEEP PREPIRIFORM CORTEX IN KINDLED SEIZURES
S07RR-05365-30 0091 (NSS) NARAYANAN, THOMAS K General research support EXPRESSION OF G-PROTEINS MRNA IN HYPERTENSION
S07RR-05365-30 0092 (NSS) NOLAN, THOMAS E General research support D-DIMER AS A MARKER FOR PLACENTAL ABRUPTION
S07RR-05365-30 0093 (NSS) OGLE, THOMAS F General research support NUCLEAR ACTION OF PROGESTERONE IN RAT PLACENTA
S07RR-05365-30 0094 (NSS) PENDERGRAST, ROBERT General research support CHLAMYDIA TRACHOMATIS IN ADOLESCENT MALES
S07RR-05365-30 0095 (NSS) PLOUFFE, LEO General research support HOMEO BOX GENES IN CHORION & REPRODUCTIVE SYSTEM TISSUES: HUMAN EMBRYONIC DVMT
S07RR-05365-30 0096 (NSS) PORTERFIELD, SUSAN P General research support NEUROCHEMICAL DISORDERS IN PROGENIES OF HYPOTHYROID RATS
S07RR-05365-30 0097 (NSS) RAO, IRUVANTI M General research support RAT ADRENOCORTICAL CELL LINE DVMT GROWTH REQUIREMENTS & STEROIDOGENIC POTENTIAL
S07RR-05365-30 0098 (NSS) RAVINDRA, RUDRAVAJHA General research support STEROID MODULATION OF GNRH RECEPTOR - G PROTEIN INTERACTION
S07RR-05365-30 0099 (NSS) RISSING, J PETER General research support OSTEOMYELITIC STAPHYLOCOCCUS AUREUS MADE DEFICIENT IN BINDING FOR TYPE I COLLAG
S07RR-05365-30 0100 (NSS) SOCCI, ROBIN R General research support FORSKOLIN & PGE 2 ON (CA.)I & CELL SHAPE: BOVINE; HUMAN; RABBIT CORNEAL ENDOTHEL
S07RR-05365-30 0101 (NSS) STEINSAPIR, JAIME General research support SYNTHESIS & DEGRADATION OF ANDROGEN RECEPTOR EFFECTS OF ANDROGEN & ANTIANDROGENS
S07RR-05365-30 0102 (NSS) WRENN, ROBERT W General research support PROTEIN KINASE C IN PANCREAS: ALTERNATIVE REGULATION
S07RR-05365-30 0103 (NSS) COHEN, LESLIE General research support DIETARY ANTIOXIDANTS AND BLOOD PRESSURE

PROJECT NO., ORGANIZATIONAL UNIT., INVESTIGATOR, ADDRESS, TITLE

S07RR-05365-30 0104 (NSS) LONG, MARGARET General research support HYPOXIAS EFFECT ON SARCOPLASMIC RETICULUM & CONTRACTILE PROTEIN FUNCTION
S07RR-05365-30 0105 (NSS) SHEFFIELD, MATTHEW General research support ULTRASONIC PREDICTION OF COMPLICATIONS OF CNS INFECTIONS OF INFANCY
S07RR-05366-30 (NSS) NAIR, VELAYUDHAN CHICAGO MEDICAL SCHOOL 3333 GREEN BAY ROAD NORTH CHICAGO, ILL 60064 Biomedical research support grant
S07RR-05366-30 0552 (NSS) BAUM, LINDA Biomedical research support grant ANTI P24 IN ANTIBODY DEPENDENT CELL MEDIATED CYTOTOXICITY AGAINST HIV
S07RR-05366-30 0553 (NSS) BERENBAUM, SHERI Biomedical research support grant BEHAVIORAL FOLLOW UP STUDIES OF NEWBORNS W/ CONGENITAL ADRENAL HYPERBLASIA
S07RR-05366-30 0554 (NSS) COHEN, MARTIN Biomedical research support grant EFFORT & MEMORY
S07RR-05366-30 0555 (NSS) FENNEWALD, MICHAEL Biomedical research support grant INHIBITORS OF RECOMBINATION IN IMMUNE SYSTEM; TRANSGENIC MICE ERYTHROID CELLS
S07RR-05366-30 0556 (NSS) GILDEN, JANICE Biomedical research support grant OPIATE SYSTEM IN EXERCISE INDUCED HYPOGLYCEMIA IN TYPE I DIABETES MELLITUS
S07RR-05366-30 0557 (NSS) GILMAN-SACHS, ALICE Biomedical research support grant PREGNANCY LOSSES PREDICTED BY FLOW CYTOMETRY
S07RR-05366-30 0558 (NSS) KING, DONNA Biomedical research support grant DIRECTED EXPRESSION OF HUMAN GROWTH HORMONE
S07RR-05366-30 0559 (NSS) LANE, RICHARD D Biomedical research support grant INDIVIDUAL DIFFERENCES IN LATERALIZED PROCESSING OF FACIAL EMOTION
S07RR-05366-30 0560 (NSS) REICHEL, RONALD Biomedical research support grant TRANSCRIPTION FACTOR E2F; RETINOIC ACID INDUCED DIFFER OF MALIGNANT STEM CELLS
S07RR-05366-30 0561 (NSS) REICHEL, RONALD Biomedical research support grant PURIFICATION OF TRANSCRIPTIONAL ACTIVITIES FROM DIFFERENTIATED CELLS
S07RR-05366-30 0562 (NSS) SARMA, BALA Biomedical research support grant EMOTIONAL DISTURBANCE IN ADOLESCENTS
S07RR-05366-30 0563 (NSS) SWARTZ, CONRAD Biomedical research support grant ALCOHOL ABUSE & HYPOGONADISM
S07RR-05366-30 0564 (NSS) VERTEL, BARBARA Biomedical research support grant PROTEOGLYCAN BIOSYNTHESIS IN MAMMALIAN CHONDROCYTES
S07RR-05366-30 0565 (NSS) WISE, STEPHEN Biomedical research support grant EFFECT OF LONG TERM CHOLINERGIC BLOCKADE ON PARIETAL CELL FUNCTION
S07RR-05367-30 (NSS) HELLMAN, SAMUEL UNIVERSITY OF CHICAGO 5841 SOUTH MARYLAND CHICAGO, IL 60637 Biomedical research support
S07RR-05367-30 0566 (NSS) CHARLESWORTH, BRAIN Biomedical research support CULTURES FOR REARING DROSOPHILA, EMPLOYED IN FUNDAMENTAL GENETICS RES
S07RR-05367-30 0567 (NSS) CRAWFORD, DOUGLAS Biomedical research support EVOLUTION & PHYSIOLOGICAL MECHANISMS BY WHICH ANIMALS ADAPT TO THEIR ENVIRON
S07RR-05367-30 0568 (NSS) JONAS, ALBERT Biomedical research support TRANSPORT ANIMALS TO SURGICAL FACILITY
S07RR-05367-30 0569 (NSS) LIPTON, MARTIN Biomedical research support MEASUREMENT OF TUMOR BLOOD FLOW BY MAGNETIC RESONANCE: ELECTRICAL INJURY
S07RR-05367-30 0570 (NSS) MASELLI, RICARDO Biomedical research support MONOCLONAL ANTI ACETYLCHOLINE RECEPTOR ANTIBODY ON AVIAN END PLATE
S07RR-05367-30 0571 (NSS) SNOOK, SANDRA Biomedical research support IMMUNOHISTOCHEMICAL PHENOTYPING OF CELLS W/ IN DIFFERENT PARTS OF PLACENTA
S07RR-05367-30 0572 (NSS) SCANU, ANGELO Biomedical research support HLTH RELATED RES IN AREA OF LUNG & HEART DISEASES
S07RR-05367-30 0573 (NSS) TONSGARD, JAMES Biomedical research support CYTOCHROME P 450 SYSTEM INVOLVED IN OMEGA OXIDATION OF FATTY ACIDS & DRUGS
S07RR-05368-30 (NSS) ROBINSON, JOHN A LOYOLA UNIVERSITY OF CHICAGO 2160 S FIRST AVE RM 1614 MAYWOOD, ILL 60153 Biomedical research support
S07RR-05368-30 0574 (NSS) ORIGITANO, THOMAS C Biomedical research support PHOTODYNAMIC THERAPY FOR INTRACRANIAL NEOPLASMS
S07RR-05368-30 0575 (NSS) BECKER, ROBERT Biomedical research support MOLECULAR GENETIC ANALYSIS OF RABBIT IMMUNOGLOBULIN VDJ REARRANGEMENT
S07RR-05368-30 0576 (NSS) WITTE, PAMELA L Biomedical research support HETEROGENEITY OF MICROENVIRONMENT FOR B CELL DEVELOPMENT
S07RR-05369-30 (NSS) BOSMAN, H BRUCE UNIVERSITY OF ILLINOIS 1853 W POLK STREET (M/C 784) CHICAGO, IL 60612 Biomedical research support
S07RR-05369-30 0577 (NSS) MOLNAR, JANOS Biomedical research support ISOLATE & CHARACTERIZE FIBRONECTIN RECEPTOR OF MACROPHAGES
S07RR-05369-30 0578 (NSS) LOIZZI, ROBERT F Biomedical research support CHARACTERIZATION OF MAMMARY GLAND MICROTUBULE PROTEINS
S07RR-05369-30 0579 (NSS) FOSSLIEN, EGIL Biomedical research support HORMONAL MODULATION OF APOLIPOPROTEIN E SYNTHESIS
S07RR-05369-30 0580 (NSS) GRUNDBACHER, FRED J Biomedical research support SPECIFICITIES OF LECTINS FROM LOTUS TETRAGONOLOBUS
S07RR-05369-30 0581 (NSS) LAVELLE, DONALD Biomedical research support DNA BINDING PROTEINS & FETAL HOMOGLOBIN REGULATION
S07RR-05369-30 0582 (NSS) PITRAK, DAVID L Biomedical research support ADHERENCE TO PNEUMOCOCCI TO RESPIRATORY EPITHELIUM
S07RR-05369-30 0583 (NSS) ROSENBLUM, BARNETT B Biomedical research support SALARY SUPPORT
S07RR-05369-30 0584 (NSS) LAM, STEPHEN C T Biomedical research support ADHESIVE FUNCTIONS OF PLATELET VITRO NECTIN RECEPTOR
S07RR-05369-30 0585 (NSS) SALAFSKY, BERNARD P Biomedical research support SUB BIOMEDICAL RESEARCH SUPPORT GRANT FOR ROCKFORD CAMPUS
S07RR-05369-30 0586 (NSS) SKIAS, DEMETRIOS Biomedical research support EXPERIMENTAL ALLERGIC ENCEPHALOMYELITIS: IDENTITY OF TARGET CELL

PROJECT NO., ORGANIZATIONAL UNIT., INVESTIGATOR, ADDRESS, TITLE

S07RR-05369-30 0587 (NSS) HOGANSON, GEORGE Biomedical research support REGULATION OF TYROSIANSE IN MURINE MELANOMAS
S07RR-05369-30 0588 (NSS) QUOCK, RAYMOND Biomedical research support OPIOD SUBTYPES & NITROUS OXIDE AN ALGESIA IN MICE
S07RR-05369-30 0589 (NSS) DOUGHTY, CLYDE C Biomedical research support COENZYME BINDING & REGULATION OF LENS ALDOSE REDUCTASE
S07RR-05369-30 0590 (NSS) COHEN, EDWARD Biomedical research support ONCOGENE AMPLIFICATION OF BREAST CANCER CELLS
S07RR-05369-30 0591 (NSS) CHAN, YUN LAI Biomedical research support ADRENERGIC CONTROL RENAL TUBULAR TRANSPORT
S07RR-05369-30 0592 (NSS) CHOCA, JOSE Biomedical research support NEUROTRANSMITTER RECEPTORS WHICH MODULATES NOICEPTION
S07RR-05369-30 0593 (NSS) SALAFSKY, BERNARD P Biomedical research support SUB BIOMEDICAL RESEARCH SUPPORT GRANT FOR ROCKFORD CAMPUS
S07RR-05369-30 0594 (NSS) LASLEY, STEPHEN Biomedical research support LEAD NEUROTOXICITY, CALCIUM & EXCITATORY AMINO ACIDS
S07RR-05369-30 0595 (NSS) KLAMEN, DEBRA Biomedical research support ANXIETY, DEPRESSION & COPING SKILLS DURING RESIDENCY: STRESS
S07RR-05369-30 0596 (NSS) MARCZYNSKI, THAD Biomedical research support ATTENTION SPAN FROM ANXIETY & BENZODIAZEPINE
S07RR-05369-30 0597 (NSS) HALLINE, ALLAN Biomedical research support CHANGES IN N 1 ACETYLSPERMIDINE LEVELS IN PATIENTS W/ COLORING NEOPLASMS
S07RR-05369-30 0598 (NSS) GOLDMAN, ALLEN Biomedical research support MECHANISMS OF DIFFERENTIATION: EMBRYOS
S07RR-05369-30 0599 (NSS) WILSON, LAIRD JR Biomedical research support OXYTOCIN ANTAGONIST & MODULATION OF LABOR
S07RR-05369-30 0600 (NSS) STORTI, ROBERT V Biomedical research support DELETION ANALYSIS OF TROPOMYOSIN GENE EXPRESSION
S07RR-05369-30 0601 (NSS) KENTER, AMY L Biomedical research support CHARACTERIZATION OF HIGHLY EXPRESSED 3 5 EXONUCLEASE IN B LYMPHOCYTES
S07RR-05369-30 0602 (NSS) PEPPERBERG, DAVID Biomedical research support VISUAL PIGMENT & PHOTO RECEPTOR ADAPTION
S07RR-05369-30 0603 (NSS) SPIEGEL, DAVID A Biomedical research support PANIC CONTROL THERAPY DURING ALPRAZOLAM DISCONTINUATION
S07RR-05369-30 0604 (NSS) MOORE, PETER D Biomedical research support MINISATELLITE LOCI & SISTER CHROMATID EXCHANGE
S07RR-05369-30 0605 (NSS) SUBRAMANIAN, KIRANUR Biomedical research support PAPILLOMAVIRUS DNA REPLICATIONS: CIS & TRANS FUNCTIONS
S07RR-05369-30 0606 (NSS) RAYCHAUDHURI, PRADIP Biomedical research support TRANSCRIPTION CONTROL BY NUCLEAR ONCOPROTEIN, EIA
S07RR-05369-30 0607 (NSS) LAHMEYER, HENRY Biomedical research support SUMMER WINTER CHANGES IN PSYCHOPHYSIOLOGY OF SAD
S07RR-05369-30 0608 (NSS) YEUNG, CHO-YAU Biomedical research support MOLECULAR CLONING & CHARACTERIZATION OF ESSENTIAL MAMMALIAN TRANSCRIPTION FACTOR
S07RR-05370-30 (NSS) BEATY, HARRY N NORTHWESTERN UNIV, MED SCHOOL 303 EAST CHICAGO AVENUE CHICAGO, ILL 60611 Biomedical research support
S07RR-05370-30 0610 (NSS) WAN, KEE KWONG Biomedical research support MONOCLONAL ANTIBODIES AGAINST HISTAMINE RECEPTOR
S07RR-05370-30 0611 (NSS) JOHNSON, MARK D Biomedical research support PROTEIN KINASE C MEDIATED PATHWAYS IN CELL TRANSFORMATION
S07RR-05370-30 0612 (NSS) LAPIN, GREGORY D Biomedical research support DETERMINATION OF DRUG DIFFUSION IN BRAIN & BRAIN TUMORS
S07RR-05370-30 0613 (NSS) RADOSEVICH, JAMES A Biomedical research support CLONING OF HUMAN ADENOCARCINOMA ANTIGEN
S07RR-05370-30 0614 (NSS) RIZZO, THOMAS A Biomedical research support FRIENDSHIP DEVELOPMENT ON CHILD PSYCHIATRIC UNIT
S07RR-05370-30 0615 (NSS) TROMMER, BARBARA L Biomedical research support LONG TERM POTENTIATION IN IMMATURE NERVOUS SYSTEM
S07RR-05370-30 0609 (NSS) KAUL, KAREN L Biomedical research support GROWTH FACTORS & ONCOGENES IN BENIGN & MALIGNANT TROPHOBLAST; PROLIFERATION
S07RR-05370-30 0616 (NSS) SHEA, BRIAN T Biomedical research support EFFECT OF GROWTH HORMONE ON CRANIOFACIAL GROWTH & PROPORTIONS
S07RR-05370-30 0617 (NSS) ROWLEY, ANNE H Biomedical research support RAPID DETECTION OF HUMAN CYTOMEGALOVIRUS IN BLOOD OF RENAL TRANSPLANT PATIENTS
S07RR-05370-30 0618 (NSS) PALLER, AMY S Biomedical research support GANGLIOSIDES & EPIDERMAL GROWTH & DIFFERENTIATION
S07RR-05370-30 0619 (NSS) BERRY, ROBERT W Biomedical research support REGULATORY MECHANISMS OF PEPTIDERGIC NEURONS
S07RR-05370-30 0620 (NSS) COHN, SUSAN L Biomedical research support MOLECULAR MECHANISMS OF DIFFERENTIATION IN HUMAN NEUROBLASTOMA
S07RR-05370-30 0621 (NSS) HOSEY, M MARLENE Biomedical research support SUBTYPES OF MUSCARINIC ACETYLCHOLINE RECEPTORS: REGULATION BY PHOSPHORYLATION
S07RR-05370-30 0622 (NSS) MCVARY, KEVIN T Biomedical research support MECHANISMS OF DIABETIC IMPOTENCE
S07RR-05370-30 0623 (NSS) DAWES, LILLIAN G Biomedical research support TOTAL PARENTAL NUTRITION: EFFECTS ON BILIRUBIN & BILE SALT SECRETION
S07RR-05370-30 0624 (NSS) COHEN, ISAAC Biomedical research support PLATELET FIBRIN INTERACTION
S07RR-05370-30 0625 (NSS) ROSENBERG, RICHARD S Biomedical research support INTERNAL DISSOCIATION OF CIRCADIAN RHYTHMS IN HAMSTERS
S07RR-05370-30 0626 (NSS) HERZON, GARRETT Biomedical research support CHRONIC LARYNGEAL PACING FOR BILATERAL VOCAL CORD PARALYSIS
S07RR-05370-30 0627 (NSS) CHANG, SHIH-WEN Biomedical research support TUMOR NECROSIS FACTOR IN ACUTE LUNG INJURY
S07RR-05370-30 0628 (NSS) MCCARTHY, WALTER J Biomedical research support ELASTIN CROSSLINKING IN ABDOMINAL AORTIC ANEURYSMAL DISEASE
S07RR-05371-30 (NSS) DALY, WALTER J INDIANA UNIV SCH OF MEDICINE 1120 SOUTH DRIVE INDIANAPOLIS, IN 46202 Biomedical research support grant
S07RR-05371-30 0641 (NSS) NATARAJAN, VISWANATH Biomedical research support grant REGULATION OF PHOSPHOLIPASE D IN VASCULAR ENDOTHELIUM; SIGNAL TRANSDUCTION
S07RR-05371-30 0642 (NSS) RUBIN, LESLIE R Biomedical research support grant SPERM ASSOCIATED FERTILITY POTENTIAL IN MEN W/ CARCINOMA OF TESTIS
S07RR-05371-30 0643 (NSS) SIEMERS, ERIC R Biomedical research

support grant ASSESSMENT OF DOPAMINERGIC TURNOVER IN PATIENTS W/ PARKINSONS DISEASE

S07RR-05371-30 0629 (NSS) **APRISON, MORRIS H** Biomedical research support grant COMPUTER NEUROMODELLING

S07RR-05371-30 0630 (NSS) **BROWN, DARRON R** Biomedical research support grant HUMAN PAPILLOMAVIRUS E4 PROTEIN IN ATHYMIC MOUSE MODEL & GENITAL LESIONS

S07RR-05371-30 0631 (NSS) **COPLEY, JOHN B** Biomedical research support grant STRESS FRACTURES & OVERUSE INJURIES IN POPULATION OF WEST POINT CADETS

S07RR-05371-30 0632 (NSS) **CORCIA, AYUS** Biomedical research support grant PATCH CLAMP STUDY OF HUMAN NEUTROPHILS

S07RR-05371-30 0633 (NSS) **DANIS, RONALD P** Biomedical research support grant ANALYSIS OF RETINAL VESSELS IN HEALTH & DISEASED; RETINAL ISCHEMIA, PERICYTES

S07RR-05371-30 0634 (NSS) **DIMICCO, JOSEPH A** Biomedical research support grant HYPOTHALMIC NEURONS MEDIATING CARDIOVASCULAR RESPONSE STRESS IN RATS

S07RR-05371-30 0635 (NSS) **DLOUGHY, STEPHEN R** Biomedical research support grant GENETICS OF ATAXIA & PRESENILE DEMENTIA; GERSTMANN STRAUSSLER SHEINKER DISEASE

S07RR-05371-30 0636 (NSS) **GOLDMAN, JEFFREY** Biomedical research support grant ANTISENSE TO UNIQUE T CELL ALL MRNA EFFECT ON GROWTH IN CELL CULTURE

S07RR-05371-30 0637 (NSS) **HECKROTH, JOHN A** Biomedical research support grant MORPHOLOGICAL STUDY OF CEREBELLAR DEVELOPMENT IN NORMAL & LURCHER MUTANT MICE

S07RR-05371-30 0644 (NSS) **SOKOL, PAUL P** Biomedical research support grant MECHANISM OF POLYAMINE TRANSPORT IN KIDNEY; ORGANIC CATION, DRUG TRANSPORT

S07RR-05371-30 0645 (NSS) **SOLEMANI, MANOOCHER** Biomedical research support grant NA+:HCO3 COTRANSPORTER IN MEMBRANE VESICLES OF KIDNEY PROXIMAL TUBULE

S07RR-05371-30 0646 (NSS) **SROUR, EDWARD F** Biomedical research support grant CD3+, CD5 & +T LYMPHOCYTES IN GRAFT VERSUS HOST DISEASE

S07RR-05371-30 0647 (NSS) **WALDMAN, BARBARA C** Biomedical research support grant URIDINE NUCLEOTIDE SUGAR TRANSPORT INTO GOGIL APPARATUS; GLYCOSYLATION

S07RR-05371-30 0648 (NSS) **WEBER, GEORGE** Biomedical research support grant EFFECTS OF ANTIPURINE DRUG, TIAZOFURIN, IN NORMAL & CANCER CELLS

S07RR-05371-30 0638 (NSS) **HELPER, DEBRA J** Biomedical research support grant CONTRACTILE MECHANISMS IN ESOPHAGEAL SMOOTH MUSCLE

S07RR-05371-30 0639 (NSS) **HODES, M E** Biomedical research support grant MOLECULAR BIOLOGY OF GRANULE CELLS IN WEAVER MUTANT MICE

S07RR-05371-30 0640 (NSS) **KESTLER, DANIEL P** Biomedical research support grant B & T CELL CDNA LIBRARIES FROM B CHRONIC LYMPHOCYTIC LEUKEMIA LYMPHOCYTES

S07RR-05372-30 (NSS) **CLIFTON, JAMES A** UNIVERSITY OF IOWA COLLEGE OF MEDICINE IOWA CITY, IOWA 52242 Biomedical research support

S07RR-05372-30 0672 (NSS) **METCALF, AMANDA** Biomedical research support MESENTERIC LYMPHATIC REGENERATION

S07RR-05372-30 0673 (NSS) **BURNS, LINDA** Biomedical research support CMV REGULATION OF MAJOR HISTOCOMPATABILITY COMPLEX ANTIGEN EXPRESSION

S07RR-05372-30 0674 (NSS) **NETTLEMAN, MARY** Biomedical research support RISK FACTORS FOR IN HOSPITAL MORTALITY

S07RR-05372-30 0675 (NSS) **KARDON, RANDY** Biomedical research support OBJECTIVE PUPIL PERIMETRY IN PATIENTS W/ VISUAL LOSS

S07RR-05372-30 0676 (NSS) **GROVER-MCKAY, MALEAH** Biomedical research support MYOCARDIAL ADRENERGIC INNERVATION IN PATIENTS W/ HYPERTROPHIC CARDIOMYOPATHY

S07RR-05372-30 0677 (NSS) **KULJIS, RODRIGO** Biomedical research support LOCAL CIRCUIT CORTICAL NEURONS IN DIFFUSE LEWY BODY DISEASE

S07RR-05372-30 0678 (NSS) **KOERNER, THEODORE** Biomedical research support GLYCOLIPIDS IN PLATELET AGGREGATION

S07RR-05372-30 0679 (NSS) **MATHEWS, KATHERINE** Biomedical research support CHARACTERIZATION OF GENETIC DEFECT LEADING TO BORJESON FORSSMAN LEHMANN SYNDROME

S07RR-05372-30 0680 (NSS) **MCKAY, CHARLES** Biomedical research support 3 D RECONSTRUCT INTRALUMINAL ULTRASOUND OF NORMAL & ATHEROSCLEROTIC ARTERIES

S07RR-05372-30 0681 (NSS) **MOYE-ROWLEY, W SCOTT** Biomedical research support FUNCTION OF YEAST JUNFAMILY OF TRANSCRIPTION FACTORS

S07RR-05372-30 0649 (NSS) **CLINE, HOLLIS** Biomedical research support DVMTL EXPRESSION NMDA RECEPTOR RESPONSE IN CULTURED OPTICAL TECTAL CELL; IMAGING

S07RR-05372-30 0650 (NSS) **GEYER, PAMELA** Biomedical research support REGULATION OF TISSUE SPECIFIC GENE EXPRESSION

S07RR-05372-30 0682 (NSS) **PETERS, CHARLES** Biomedical research support EXTRACELLULAR MATRIX MOLECULES IN ONTOGENY OF HEMATOPOIESIS

S07RR-05372-30 0683 (NSS) **THORNE, PETER** Biomedical research support GUINEA PIG INHALATION MODEL FOR HYPERSENSITIVE PNEUMONITIS; MICROPOLYSPORA

S07RR-05372-30 0684 (NSS) **WEINER, GEORGE** Biomedical research support ANTIBODY AFFINITY & ANTIBODY INDUCED ANTIGENIC MODULATION ON MABS MALIGNANCY

S07RR-05372-30 0685 (NSS) **WINFIELD, HOWARD** Biomedical research support EFFECT OF EXTRACORPOREAL SHOCK WAVES ON ABDOMINAL AORTA & KIDNEY

S07RR-05372-30 0686 (NSS) **SWENSON, CHARLES** Biomedical research support TROPONIN I INTERACTION & CONTROL OF CARDIAC & SKELETAL MUSCLE CONTRACTION

S07RR-05372-30 0687 (NSS) **CRAM, MICHAEL** Biomedical research support MOTILITY CHANGES; BARIUM VIDEO FLUOROSCOPY; PARTIALLY OBSTRUCT OPOSSUM ESOPHAGUS

S07RR-05372-30 0688 (NSS) **GHODSI, ABDI S** Biomedical research support PROSTANOID IN AUTOREG OF CHOROIDAL, RETINAL BLOOD FLOW; NEWBORN PRE/POST ASPHYXI

S07RR-05372-30 0689 (NSS) **HUSTON, BUTCH M** Biomedical research support EPIDEMIOLOGIC TYPING OF CANDIDA ALBICANS TO DETERMINE MODE OF TRANSPORTATION

S07RR-05372-30 0690 (NSS) **LUPERCIO, RAFAEL** Biomedical research support BRAIN SITES IN REFLEX NEURAL CONTROL OF CORONARY CIRCULATION

S07RR-05372-30 0691 (NSS) **MARTINEZ, DANIEL** Biomedical research support GLYCINE IN NTS PARTICIPATE IN CARDIOVASCULAR REGULATION BY ACETYLCHOL RELEASE

S07RR-05372-30 0692 (NSS) **MEINCKE-REZA, JEFF** Biomedical research support ACCURACY OF MOTION ANALYSIS OF CERVICAL SPINE BY BIPLAN RADIOGRAPHIC TECHNIQUES

S07RR-05372-30 0693 (NSS) **MELETIOU, STEVEN D** Biomedical research support OSTEOSARCOMA CELLS & INCREASE IN FREQUENCY OF SURFACE STRAIN STIMULUS IN VITRO

S07RR-05372-30 0694 (NSS) **NYSTROM, ANGELA L** Biomedical research support IN VIVO MUTATION OF CLASS II MHC GENE

S07RR-05372-30 0695 (NSS) **OFFNER, ELSA N** Biomedical research support TNF IN MENINGOCOCCAL INFECTION IN INDIVIDUALS W/ INHERITED COMPLEMENT DEFICIENCY

S07RR-05372-30 0696 (NSS) **PACE, WILLIAM** Biomedical research support ORNITHINE DECARBOXYLASE AS AN INTERMEDIATE ACTIVATION EVENT IN B LYMPHOCYTE

S07RR-05372-30 0697 (NSS) **UPCHURCH, BENNIE R** Biomedical research support EFFECTS OF PYOCHELIN ON NEUTROPHIL MEDIATED KILLING OF PSEUDOMONAS AERUGINOSA

S07RR-05372-30 0698 (NSS) **BRSONAHAN, WILLIAM** Biomedical research support COAGULATION FACTOR LEVELS AFTER DILUTIONAL COAGULOPATHY OF MASSIVE TRANSFUSION

S07RR-05372-30 0699 (NSS) **BURGGRAAFF, BARBARA** Biomedical research support COCHLEAR IMPLANT & CHRONIC ELECT STIM ON DVMT AUDITORY SYSTEM; DEAFENED RABBITS

S07RR-05372-30 0700 (NSS) **GRAEFF, RON** Biomedical research support PURIFY & CHARACTERIZE GP140 IN PMNS & MYELOID HL 60 & PLB 985 CELL LINES

S07RR-05372-30 0701 (NSS) **GROSSMAN, PAUL** Biomedical research support MUCOSAL IMMUNE RESPONSE TO CHOLERA TOXIN EVAL INTRANASAL MURINE MODEL

S07RR-05372-30 0702 (NSS) **HUNTER, TIM** Biomedical research support EFFECTS OF VIP ON PARASYMPATHETIC HEART RATE CONTROL

S07RR-05372-30 0703 (NSS) **PETERSON, K LINNEA** Biomedical research support INFLAMMATORY MEDIATORS ON KERATINOCYTES: ROLE IN PATHOGENESIS OF CHOLESTEATOMA

S07RR-05372-30 0651 (NSS) **HOFFMAN, ROBERT** Biomedical research support HYPOGLYCEMIC & SYMPATHETIC NERVE ACTIVITY IN INSULIN

S07RR-05372-30 0704 (NSS) **THUMASATHIT, SUTHEE** Biomedical research support USE OF ULTRAFAST COMPUTED TOMOGRAPHY IN MEASURING MYOCARDIAL PERFUSION

S07RR-05372-30 0705 (NSS) **WAIGHT, DAVID** Biomedical research support EFFECT OF SILICONE VISCOSITY ON VOCAL CORD OSCILLATING PROPERTIES

S07RR-05372-30 0706 (NSS) **BEVERING, CARL** Biomedical research support CHARACTERIZE HEPATIC RECEPTORS REGULATING HEMODYNAMIC RESPONSE TO THROMBOXANE A2

S07RR-05372-30 0707 (NSS) **CAVANAUGH, CHERYL** Biomedical research support CHROMOSOMAL DNA TYPING OF COAGULASE NEGATIVE STAPHYLOCOCCI

S07RR-05372-30 0708 (NSS) **LUPERCIO, RAFAEL** Biomedical research support BRAIN SITES IN REFLEX NEURAL CONTROL OF CORONARY CIRCULATION

S07RR-05372-30 0709 (NSS) **MARLEY, SUSAN** Biomedical research support RECEIVER OPERATING EVAL PICTURE ARCHIVING & COMM SYSTEM PEDIA RADIOLOGY

S07RR-05372-30 0652 (NSS) **JOHLIN, FREDERICK** Biomedical research support POLYGLUTAMATE SYNTHETASE ROLE IN CELLULAR FOLATE CONCENTRATIONS REGULATION

S07RR-05372-30 0653 (NSS) **JONES, MARY** Biomedical research support IMMUNOLOGY IN L TRYPTOPHAN INDUCE EOSINOPHILIA MYALGIA SYNDROME; MURINE MODEL

S07RR-05372-30 0654 (NSS) **KLEIN, JONATHON** Biomedical research support EFFECT OF ANDROGEN ON EPIDERMAL GROWTH FACTOR RECEPTOR ACTIVITY; FETAL LUNG DVMT

S07RR-05372-30 0655 (NSS) **MALINOW, ROBERTO** Biomedical research support PRE SYNAPTIC & POST SYNAPTIC CONTRIBUTIONS TO SYNAPTIC PLASTICITY; MAMMAL

S07RR-05372-30 0656 (NSS) **OSTMAN, PONTUS** Biomedical research support ANTINOCICEPTIC ACTIVITY & HEMODYNAMIC EFFECTS OF EPIDURALLY ADMIN DEXEMEDOMIDINE

S07RR-05372-30 0657 (NSS) **SPRINCE, NANCY** Biomedical research support SHORT TERM, HI CONC COBALT EXPOSURE ON RESPIRATORY DIS; TUNGSTEN CARBIDE WORKER

S07RR-05372-30 0658 (NSS) **TRAYNELIS, VINCENT** Biomedical research support BRAIN & GLIOMA METABOLISM IN AN EXPERIMENTAL MODEL

S07RR-05372-30 0659 (NSS) **VAN VOOHRIS, BRADLEY** Biomedical research support ARACHIDONIC ACID METABOLITES ON FERTILIZATION & EGG ACTIVATION

S07RR-05372-30 0660 (NSS) **VINCENT, ROBERT** Biomedical research support EPIDURAL ANESTHESIA; MATERNAL & FETAL HEMODYNAMIC RESPONSE TO HEMORRHAGE; EWES

S07RR-05372-30 0661 (NSS) **ZWERLING, CRAIG** Biomedical research support INDUSTRY LOW BACK INJURY RISK FACTORS: PRE EMPLOY SCREEN TO DEFINE HI RISK GROUP

S07RR-05372-30 0662 (NSS) **BISHOP, GAIL** Biomedical research support REGULATION OF CLASS II MEDIATED CELL DIFFERENTIATION

S07RR-05372-30 0663 (NSS) **BISHOP, WARREN** Biomedical research support DISTRIBUTION & FUNCTION OF SMALL BOWEL EFG RECEPTOR

S07RR-05372-30 0664 (NSS) **CHEMTOB, SYLVAN** Biomedical research support MATURATION & MECHANISMS GOVERNING PROSTANOID ACTION ON RETINAL VASCULATURE

S07RR-05372-30 0665 (NSS) **RUSSO, ANDREW** Biomedical research support DEVELOPMENTAL REGULATION OF NEURAL CREST PHENOTYPE

S07RR-05372-30 0666 (NSS) **CHRISTIANSEN, JAMES** Biomedical research support DEVELOPMENTAL MODEL OF IDIOPATHIC LONG QT SYNDROME

S07RR-05372-30 0667 (NSS) **DAWSON, DOUGLAS** Biomedical research support EFFECTS OF RADIATION ON INTEGRATED OSSEOUS IMPLANT

S07RR-05372-30 0668 (NSS) **FRODEL, JOHN** Biomedical research support STRESS SHIELDING IN MANDIBULAR RECONSTRUCTION AFTER ONCOLOGIC OBLITERATION

S07RR-05372-30 0669 (NSS) **KAPELANSKI, DAVID** Biomedical research support HEPARINLESS, PUMPLESS ARTERIO VENOUS ECMO FOR VENTILATORY SUPPORT; CANINE MODEL

S07RR-05372-30 0670 (NSS) **JOHNSON, WAYNE** Biomedical research support DEVELOPMENTAL REGULATION OF CFLA GENE

S07RR-05372-30 0671 (NSS) **KEECH, RONALD** Biomedical research support

ADJUSTABLE SUTURE MODEL FOR SUPERIOR OBLIQUE MUSCLE
S07RR-05373-30 (NSS) PRICE, JAMES G UNIVERSITY OF KANSAS MED CTR 39TH & RAINBOW BLVD KANSAS CITY, KANS 66103 Biomedical research support
S07RR-05373-30 0710 (NSS) ALPER, RICHARD Biomedical research support LOCAL REGULATION OF ADRENAL CORTICOSTERONE SECRETION
S07RR-05373-30 0711 (NSS) BELMONT, JOHN Biomedical research support CHRONOMETRIC CHRONOMETRICS OF AGING MEMORY
S07RR-05373-30 0712 (NSS) CALVET, JAMES Biomedical research support U3SNRNA RRNA INTERACTIONS
S07RR-05373-30 0713 (NSS) COWLEY, BENJAMIN D Biomedical research support GENE EXPRESSION DURING RECOVERY FROM ACUTE RENAL FAILURE
S07RR-05373-30 0714 (NSS) DELISLE, ROBERT C Biomedical research support PANCREATIC ACINAR SECRETION: RECONSTITUTED EXOCYTOSIS
S07RR-05373-30 0715 (NSS) FECHTEL, KIM Biomedical research support MOLECULAR GENETICS OF DROSOPHILA ECTODERMAL DEVELOPMENT
S07RR-05373-30 0716 (NSS) HARRIS, WILLIAM Biomedical research support CHYLOMICRON METABOLISM & FISH OIL
S07RR-05373-30 0717 (NSS) HELMKAMP, G M JR Biomedical research support FUNCTION OF PHOSPHATIDYLINOSITOL TRANSFER PROTEIN
S07RR-05373-30 0718 (NSS) HUBBLE, JEAN Biomedical research support INTERMITTENT & MIXED DOPAMINE AGONIST THERAPY IN PARKINSONIAN ANIMAL MODELS
S07RR-05373-30 0719 (NSS) HURWITZ, ARYEH Biomedical research support OMEPRAZOLE EFFECTS ON COLON CANCER IN RATS
S07RR-05373-30 0720 (NSS) LEE, CHIA Biomedical research support SITE SPECIFIC RECOMBINATION OF STAPHYLOCOCCAL PHAGE
S07RR-05373-30 0721 (NSS) LEVINE, STEVEN Biomedical research support ACETYL COA CARBOXYLASE GENE EXPRESSION DURING MYELINATION GLIOSIS
S07RR-05373-30 0722 (NSS) LUKERT, BARBARA Biomedical research support MATERNAL ASCORBIC ACID INTAKE & FETAL SKELETON
S07RR-05373-30 0723 (NSS) MACGREGOR, RONAL Biomedical research support REGULATORY BIOLOGY OF PARATHYROID
S07RR-05373-30 0724 (NSS) MAGUIRE, HELEN Biomedical research support ADENOSINE & VASOACTIVE AUTOCOIDS IN PLACENTA
S07RR-05373-30 0725 (NSS) NARAYANASWAMY, B Biomedical research support PROTEINS OF HUMAN HERPES VIRUS6
S07RR-05373-30 0726 (NSS) PARMELY, MICHAEL Biomedical research support LYMPHOKINE REGULATION BY PLASMINOGEN ACTIVATOR
S07RR-05373-30 0727 (NSS) PONNAPPAN, USHA Biomedical research support IMMUNOREGULATORY & LIPID INDUCED MODULATION IN AGING AN IN VITRO APPROACH
S07RR-05373-30 0728 (NSS) REED, GREGORY Biomedical research support FORMATION & GENOTOXICITY OF BENZO(A) PYRENE TRIOL SULFONATES: CARCINOGENESIS
S07RR-05373-30 0729 (NSS) SARRAS, SARRAS, JR Biomedical research support BASEMENT MEMBRANE & EPITHELIAL INTERACTIONS DURING DEVELOPMENT
S07RR-05373-30 0730 (NSS) SAVIN, VIRGINIA Biomedical research support MODULATION OF GLOMERULAR ULTRAFILTRATION COEFFICIENT
S07RR-05373-30 0731 (NSS) TASH, JOSEPH S Biomedical research support PROTEIN PHOSPHORYLATION IN SPERM FLAGELLAR MOBILITY
S07RR-05373-30 0732 (NSS) WEATHERSTONE, KATHLE Biomedical research support IMMUNE FUNCTION OF NEONATAL MONOCYTES
S07RR-05374-30 (NSS) WILSON, EMERY A UNIVERSITY OF KENTUCKY MN-140 MED CTR 800 ROSE ST LEXINGTON, KY 40536 Biomedical research support
S07RR-05374-30 0734 (NSS) CHEN, KUEY C Biomedical research support EXPRESSION IN MAMMALIAN CELLS OF FUSION GENE CONTAINING SEQUENCES
S07RR-05374-30 0735 (NSS) VASCONEZ, HENRY Biomedical research support FIBRIN GLUE IN CRANIOFACIAL SURGERY
S07RR-05374-30 0736 (NSS) RANSEEN, JOHN D Biomedical research support PSYCHIATRIC & NEUROLOGIC APPLICATIONS OF TOPOGRAPHIC MAPPING IN DISEASES
S07RR-05374-30 0733 (NSS) BLONDER, LEE X Biomedical research support EMOTIONAL KNOWLEDGE IN BRAIN IMPAIRED SUBJECTS
S07RR-05374-30 0737 (NSS) SADOVE, RICHARD C Biomedical research support THROMBOCYTOSIS ON PATENCY OF MICROVASCULAR ANASTOMOSES IN RAT
S07RR-05374-30 0738 (NSS) ELLIOTT, LUCINDA H Biomedical research support SPECIFIC MOLECULAR ABNORMALITIES IN T CELLS OBTAINED FROM BRAIN TUMOR PATIENTS
S07RR-05374-30 0739 (NSS) ANDRYKOWSKI, MICHAEL Biomedical research support NEUROPSYCHOLOGICAL FUNCTIONING OF ADULT BONE MARROW TRANSPLANT RECIPIENTS
S07RR-05374-30 0740 (NSS) LANSKA, MARY JO Biomedical research support NEONATAL SEIZURES: POPULATION BASED STUDY
S07RR-05374-30 0741 (NSS) LANSKA, DOUGLAS Biomedical research support AMYOTROPHIC LATERAL SCLEROSIS MORTALITY
S07RR-05374-30 0742 (NSS) ZIMMER, STEVEN Biomedical research support SUPPRESSION OF INVASION & METASTASIS IN RAT MODEL
S07RR-05374-30 0743 (NSS) WATSON, ROBERT E Biomedical research support HYPOTHALAMIC ESTROGEN RESPONSIVE OPIOID SYSTEMS: AGE RELATED CHANGES
S07RR-05374-30 0744 (NSS) SISKEN, BETTY Biomedical research support MECHANISMS OF ELECTROMAGNETIC FIELD STIMULATION OF NERVE REGENERATION
S07RR-05374-30 0745 (NSS) PAN, BIN-TAO Biomedical research support MEDIATORS OF RAS PROTEIN ACTION IN XENOPUS OOCYTES & FERTILIZED EGGS
S07RR-05374-30 0746 (NSS) OTT, COBERN Biomedical research support PATHOGENESIS OF GENTAMICIN INDUCED IMPAIRED RENAL CONCENTRATING ABILITY
S07RR-05374-30 0747 (NSS) MCGILLIS, JOSEPH Biomedical research support IMMUNOREGULATION BY CORTICOTROPIN RELEASING HORMONE
S07RR-05374-30 0748 (NSS) DEMBO, JEFFREY B Biomedical research support ADRENOCORTICAL RESPONSE TO DENTAL TREATMENT OF VARYING STRESSES
S07RR-05374-30 0749 (NSS) HAGAN, MICHAEL D Biomedical research support NEURAL NETWORK APPROACH TO PRENATAL RISK SCORING
S07RR-05374-30 0750 (NSS) GROSS, DAVID R Biomedical research support CORONARY VASCULAR RESPONSE IN ATHEROSCLEROTIC PIGS: CHRONIC CIGARETTE SMOKING
S07RR-05374-30 0751 (NSS) FRAZIER, DONALD Biomedical research support UPGRADE OF DEPARTMENTAL WATER PURIFICATION SYSTEM
S07RR-05375-30 (NSS) KMETZ, DONALD R U. OF LOUISVILLE RES FDN, INC. HEALTH SCIENCES CENTER LOUISVILLE, KY 40292 Developing and improving institutional animal resources
S07RR-05375-30 0752 (NSS) COLELLA, RITA Developing and improving institutional animal resources CYSTEINE PROTEINASE & THEIR INHIBITORS
S07RR-05375-30 0753 (NSS) CSUKAS, STEPHEN C Developing and improving institutional animal resources FELINE OCULAR INFLAMMATION & MEDIATOR RELEASE: INTRAVITREAL ENDOTOXIN
S07RR-05375-30 0754 (NSS) GOLPER, THOMAS A Developing and improving institutional animal resources CONVECTION & DIFFUSION DURING DIALYSIS RELATED BLOOD PURIFICATION
S07RR-05375-30 0755 (NSS) GUPTA, MADHU Developing and improving institutional animal resources GANGLIOSIDES IN AN MPTP INDUCED PARKINSONIAN MODEL
S07RR-05375-30 0756 (NSS) HARRIS, E NIGEL Developing and improving institutional animal resources PRODUCTION & CHARACTERIZATION OF MONOCLONAL ANTIPHOSPHOLIPID ANTIBODIES
S07RR-05375-30 0757 (NSS) KLEIN, JON B Developing and improving institutional animal resources AFFINITY MEMBRANE ISOLATION OF N FORMYL PEPTIDE RECEPTOR
S07RR-05375-30 0758 (NSS) SCHURR, AVITAL Developing and improving institutional animal resources STREPTOZOTOCIN INDUCED DIABETES & NEURONAL FUNCTION & HYPOXIA IN HIPPOCAMPAL
S07RR-05376-30 (NSS) DANIELS, ROBERT S LOUISIANA STATE UNIVERSITY 1542 TULANE AVENUE NEW ORLEANS, LA 70112 Biomedical research support
S07RR-05376-30 0036 (NSS) HILTON, CHARLES W Biomedical research support DOES CYCLO (HIS-PRO) DECREASE HEPATIC INSULIN CLEARANCE
S07RR-05376-30 0037 (NSS) PARRYM GARETH J Biomedical research support INFLUENCE OF DIET ON DVMT OF NEUROPATHY IN EXPERIMENTAL DIABETES MELLITUS
S07RR-05376-30 0038 (NSS) HORNBY, PAMELA J Biomedical research support CNS SITE OF ACTION FOR MORPHINE-INDUCED GASTROINTESTINAL FUNC INHIBITION
S07RR-05376-30 0039 (NSS) LAWTON, ANDREW W Biomedical research support INTRAOCULAR PRESSURE EFFECT OF VASOPRESSIN ANTAGONIST & W/ ANTI-GLAUCOMA MED
S07RR-05376-30 0040 (NSS) FISCH, BRUCE J Biomedical research support ELECTROPHYSIOLOGICAL LOCALIZATION OF SEIZURE PROPAGATION IN HUMAN EPILEPSY
S07RR-05376-30 0041 (NSS) DILORETO, DAVID A Biomedical research support POSTERIOR EYELID RECONSTRUCTION WITH POROUS ALLOPLASTIC IMPLANTS
S07RR-05376-30 0042 (NSS) KRATZ, KENNETH E Biomedical research support MUSCARINIC RECEPTOR M3 MRNA EXPRESSION IN RAT CORTEX
S07RR-05376-30 0043 (NSS) PAUL, DENNIS Biomedical research support KAPPA OPIOID RECEPTOR SUBTYPE STIMULATION ON PHOSPHOINOSITIDE HYDROLYSIS
S07RR-05376-30 0031 (NSS) JOHNSTON, KENNETH H Biomedical research support STREPTOKINASE GENE PATHOGENESIS OF POST-STREP GLOMERULONEPHRITIS
S07RR-05376-30 0032 (NSS) BIHAIN, BERNARD E Biomedical research support LIPOLYTIC PRODUCT ON ACTIVITY OF LIPOPROTEIN RECEPTOR DISTINCT FROM LDL-RECEPTOR
S07RR-05376-30 0033 (NSS) CLARK, GARY D Biomedical research support CALCIUM DEPENDENT REGULATION OF N-METHYL-D- ASPARTATE RECEPTORS
S07RR-05376-30 0034 (NSS) BURNS, ALASTAIR H Biomedical research support CARDIOLYTIC ACTIONS OF TUMOR NECROSIS FACTOR
S07RR-05376-30 0035 (NSS) SHEPHERD, RAYMOND E Biomedical research support EXERCISE TRAINING REDUCES SEVERTIY OF ENDOTOXIN-INDUCED CARDIAC DYSFUNCTION
S07RR-05377-30 (NSS) FULGINITI, VINCENT A TULANE SCHOOL OF MEDICINE 1430 TULANE AVENUE NEW ORLEANS, LA 70112 Biomedical research support
S07RR-05377-30 0751 (NSS) BOULWARE, DENNIS Biomedical research support INTRAVENOUS CYCLOPHOSPHAMIDE IN TREATMENT OF LUPUS NEPHRITIS
S07RR-05377-30 0752 (NSS) WRIGHT, JAMES Biomedical research support MALNUTRITION ON INDUCTION OF SYSTEMIC TOLERANCE TO AN ORAL ANTIGEN
S07RR-05377-30 0753 (NSS) JOHNSON, MARY K Biomedical research support VIRULENCE FACTORS IN OCULAR INFECTIONS
S07RR-05377-30 0754 (NSS) THAKUR, VASHU Biomedical research support AMINOGLYCOSIDE NEPHROTOXICITY IN HUMANS
S07RR-05377-30 0755 (NSS) STINE, KIMO Biomedical research support DEVELOPMENT OF TARGET SPECIFIC LYMPHOKINE ACTIVATED KILLER ACTIVITY
S07RR-05377-30 0756 (NSS) BARRIOS, NIOKA Biomedical research support GONADAL PROTECTION W/ KETOCONAZOLE DURING TOTAL BODY IRRADIATION TREATMENT
S07RR-05377-30 0757 (NSS) BIENASZ, STANLEY Biomedical research support PULSE OXIMETRY IN DETERMINING PERIPHERAL TISSUE OXYGENATION IN ACUTE ANEMIA
S07RR-05377-30 0758 (NSS) STORCH, THOMAS Biomedical research support RENAL EXPRESSION OF ENDOTHELIAL CELL GROWTH FACTOR
S07RR-05377-30 0759 (NSS) PICKOFF, ARTHUR Biomedical research support ELECTROPHYSIOLOGIC OF NEONATAL CANINE HEART BY TOXIC PARASYMPATHETIC
S07RR-05377-30 0760 (NSS) WALKER, PATRICK Biomedical research support INTRACELLULAR CATALASE IN LLC PKI RENAL CELL LINE BY CATALASE CDNA TRANSFECTION
S07RR-05377-30 0761 (NSS) HYMEL, L Biomedical research support FUNCTIONAL MODULATION OF PURIFIED MUSCLE CALCIUM CHANNELS
S07RR-05377-30 0762 (NSS) JAHR, JONATHAN Biomedical research support DOES OMEPRAZALE REDUCE GASTRIC VOLUME & ACIDITY
S07RR-05377-30 0763 (NSS) LOCKYER, JEAN Biomedical research support GYLCOGEN PHOSPHORRYLASE GENE
S07RR-05377-30 0764 (NSS) ORTENBERG, JOSEPH Biomedical research support DETERMINANTS OF RENAL MICROVASCULAR DYSFUNCTION IN HYPERTENSION
S07RR-05377-30 0765 (NSS) ALSTER, DAVID K Biomedical research support CHARACTERIZATION OF GROWTH HORMONE RELEASING MECHANISMS
S07RR-05377-30 0766 (NSS) EL-DAHR, SAMIER Biomedical research support ONTOGENY OF RENAL KALLIKREIN KININ SYSTEM
S07RR-05377-30 0767 (NSS) HELLSTROM, WAYNE Biomedical research support CAT MODEL FOR ERECTILE RESPONSE TO DIFFERENT PHARMACOLOGIC AGENTS

S07RR-05377-30 0768 (NSS) KREISMAN, NORMAN Biomedical research support POTASSIUM ION HOMEOSTATIS IN HYPOXIA INDUCED SEIZURES IN NEONATAL HIPPOCAMPUS
S07RR-05377-30 0769 (NSS) STEINBERG, STEVEN Biomedical research support HEMORRHAGE & RESUSCITATION ON INTACT INTESTINAL MICRO CIRCULATION
S07RR-05377-30 0770 (NSS) WHITE, JOHN Biomedical research support ELECTROPHYSIOLOGY & CILIARY FUNCT OF RESPIRATORY EPITHELIAL CELLS: PATCH CLAMP
S07RR-05377-30 0771 (NSS) BEILKE, MARK Biomedical research support IMMUNE ACTIVATION OF PRIMATE NEUROENDOTHELIAL CELLS
S07RR-05377-30 0772 (NSS) BEECHERL, ERNEST Biomedical research support VISCOUS RESISTANCE & SICKLE CELL ANEMIA
S07RR-05377-30 0773 (NSS) JAHR, JONATHAN Biomedical research support MECHANISM OF CARDIOVASCULAR ACTIONS OF DDAVP IN ANESTHETIZED RATS
S07RR-05378-30 (NSS) JOHNS, MICHAEL E JOHNS HOPKINS UNIVERSITY 720 RUTLAND AVENUE BALTIMORE, MD 21205 Biomedical research support
S07RR-05378-30 0997 (NSS) GOODMAN, ARNOLD L Biomedical research support LUTEAL ANGIOGENIC FACTOR: PURIF & PRODUCE ANTI LAF ANTIBODY: FERTILITY & INFERT
S07RR-05378-30 0998 (NSS) GRZANNA, REINHARD Biomedical research support CENTRAL NORADRENERGIC NEURON DEGENERATION AFTER NEUROTOSIN 4 EXPOSURE
S07RR-05378-30 0999 (NSS) JENSEN, ROBERT E Biomedical research support IN VITRO ASSAY FOR PROTEIN SORTING MITOCHONDRIAL INTERMEMBRANE SPACE
S07RR-05378-30 0000 (NSS) LABIB, RAMZY S Biomedical research support CHARACTERIZATION OF PEMPHIGUS FOLIACEUS ANTIGEN
S07RR-05378-30 0001 (NSS) LEDERMAN, HOWARD M Biomedical research support EFFECTS OF TEMPERATURE ON T LYMPHOCYTE: CYTOKINES, INFLAMMATION
S07RR-05378-30 0002 (NSS) LENZ, FREDERICK Biomedical research support PERIPHERAL & CENTRAL NERVOUS SYSTEM MECHANISMS OF PARKINSONIAN SYMPTOMS
S07RR-05378-30 0003 (NSS) MARTIN, LYNN D Biomedical research support ANESTHETIC MODULATION OF PULMONARY VASCULAR ENDOTHELIAL CELL EICOSANOID PRODUC
S07RR-05378-30 0004 (NSS) MAY, STRATFORD Biomedical research support CHARACTERIZE IL 3 GROWTH FACTOR RECEPTOR: HEMATOPOIESIS, SIGNAL TRANSDUCTION
S07RR-05378-30 0005 (NSS) MONTROSE, MARSHALL Biomedical research support C1 TRANSPORT IN HUMAN INTESTINE W/ DISRUPT CF TRANSMEMBRANCE CONDUCT REGUL GENE
S07RR-05378-30 0006 (NSS) NIEDERHUBER, JOHN Biomedical research support HUMAN BLK TYROSINE KINASE GENE IN LYMPHOID & NON LYMPHOID HUMAN TUMORS
S07RR-05378-30 0007 (NSS) NYHAN, DANIEL Biomedical research support PULMONARY VASCULAR CHANGES AFTER CARDIOPULMONARY BYPASS
S07RR-05378-30 0008 (NSS) OUYANG, PAMELA Biomedical research support G PROTEINS IN ACH INDUCED RELEASE OF INTRACELL CA IN SOLATED ENDOTHELIAL CELL
S07RR-05378-30 0009 (NSS) PROUD, DAVID Biomedical research support REGULATION OF MACROPHAGES FUNCTION BY RESPIRATORY EPITHELIAL CELLS
S07RR-05378-30 0010 (NSS) RACUSEN, LORRAINE C Biomedical research support CULTURED RENAL TUBULAR CELLS FROM URINE TO STUDY METABOLIC DISEASE
S07RR-05378-30 0011 (NSS) RAJ, N BABU Biomedical research support MURINE ALPHA INTERFERON GENES: IDENTIFY CIS TRANSACTING ELEMENTS INVOLVED
S07RR-05378-30 0012 (NSS) ROLLS, BARBARA J Biomedical research support SENSORY IMPAIRMENTS ON EATING BEHAVIOR IN ELDERLY: MALNUTRITION, FOOD INTAKE
S07RR-05378-30 0013 (NSS) RONNET, GABRIELE V Biomedical research support MECHANISMS OF OLFACTORY SIGNAL TRANSDUCTION: ADENYLATE CYCLASE
S07RR-05378-30 0014 (NSS) SARAL, REIN Biomedical research support CHEMOTHERAPY INDUCED HEPATIC VENO OCCLUSIVE DISEASE: LIVER METABOLISM
S07RR-05378-30 0015 (NSS) SMITH, HAMILTON O Biomedical research support HAEMOPHILUS INFLUENZAE TRANSFORMATION GENES: DNA SEQUENCING, CYCLIC AMP
S07RR-05378-30 0016 (NSS) TOGIAS, ALKIS G Biomedical research support AGING RELATED CHANGES IN HUMAN NASAL MUCOSA: VASOMOTOR RHINITIS
S07RR-05378-30 0017 (NSS) WILSON, KATHRINE Biomedical research support PROTEINS REQUIRED FOR NUCLEAR ENVELOPE ASSEMBLY: VESICLES, GTP HYDROLYSIS
S07RR-05378-30 0018 (NSS) YEAGER, ANDREW M Biomedical research support HEMATOPOIETIC CELL TRANSPLANT IN MURINE GLOBOID CELL LEUKODYSTROPHY
S07RR-05378-30 0019 (NSS) YIN, FRANK C Biomedical research support MECHANICAL EFFECTS ON CORONARY HEMODYNAMICS
S07RR-05378-30 0986 (NSS) ADAMS, KENNETH G Biomedical research support CHEMICAL MEDIATORS & HUMAN AIRWAY ANAPHYLAXIS: BRONCHIAL ASTHMA, IL 1, IL3
S07RR-05378-30 0987 (NSS) ATLAS, SUSAN J Biomedical research support COCAINE: EFFECTS ON CORPUS LUTEUM STRUCTURE & FUNCTION IN PREGNANT RABBIT
S07RR-05378-30 0988 (NSS) CARBONE, KATHRYN M Biomedical research support IMMUNE TOLERANCE TO BORNA DISEASE VIRUS: VIRUS PERSISTENCE IN NERVOUS SYSTEM
S07RR-05378-30 0989 (NSS) CASERO, ROBERT A Biomedical research support SPERMIDINE & SPERMINE N1 ACETYLTRANSFERASE IN HUMAN LUNG CANCER
S07RR-05378-30 0990 (NSS) CLEMENTS, JANICE Biomedical research support MOLECULAR CHARACTERIZATION OF BORNA DISEASE VIRUS
S07RR-05378-30 0991 (NSS) COLOMBANI, PAUL M Biomedical research support IN VIVO IMMUNOSUPPRESSIVE ACTION OF PROTEIN KINASE
S07RR-05378-30 0992 (NSS) CORK, LINDA C Biomedical research support POSTNATAL DEVELOPMENT OF PRIMATE STRIATUM IN MACACA MULATTA
S07RR-05378-30 0993 (NSS) DUBIN, NORMAN H Biomedical research support GENETIC & PARACRINE REGUL OF UTERINE PROSTAGLANDINS IN RAT PERIPARTUM PERIOD
S07RR-05378-30 0994 (NSS) DUDGEON, DAVID L Biomedical research support MITOGENIC FACTORS IN BOVINE COLOSTRUM ON DVMT OF NEONATAL GUINEA PIG INTESTINE
S07RR-05378-30 0995 (NSS) GEARHART, JOHN P Biomedical research support URETHRAL OBSTRUCTION IN FETAL LAMB
S07RR-05378-30 0996 (NSS) GLICKSON, JERRY D Biomedical research support NMR PREDICTION & DETECTION OF RADIATION RESPONSE: TUMOR, RADIOTHERAPY
S07RR-05379-30 (NSS) RICHARDS, RICHARD D UNIV OF MARYLAND SCHOOL OF MED 655 WEST BALTIMORE STREET BALTIMORE, MD 21201 Biomedical research support
S07RR-05379-30 0759 (NSS) BARCAK, GERARD J Biomedical research support MOLECULAR BIOLOGY OF HAEMOPHILUS INFLUENZAE TRANSFORMATION GENES
S07RR-05379-30 0760 (NSS) WADE, ROBERT Biomedical research support REGULATION OF GENE EXPRESSION IN HEART & SKELETAL MUSCLE TISSUE
S07RR-05379-30 0761 (NSS) GOLDBERG, ANDREW Biomedical research support AEROBIC CAPACITY & METABOLIC FUNCTION IN GERIATRIC PATIENTS
S07RR-05379-30 0762 (NSS) HORNBECK, PETER Biomedical research support LYMPHOCYTES IN DEVELOPMENT OF AUTOIMMUNE DISEASES
S07RR-05379-30 0763 (NSS) KLEINBERG, MICHAEL Biomedical research support PRODUCTION OF SUPEROXIDE BY PHAGOCYTIC LEUKOCYTES
S07RR-05379-30 0764 (NSS) LASH, ROBERT Biomedical research support STRUCTURAL DETERMINANTS OF GLYCOPROTEIN HORMONE ACTION
S07RR-05379-30 0765 (NSS) MELTZER, STEPHEN Biomedical research support TUMOR SUPPRESSOR GENES IN GASTROINTESTINAL MALIGNANCY
S07RR-05379-30 0766 (NSS) ZISKIND, ANDREW Biomedical research support NEW CORONARY INTERVENTIONS
S07RR-05379-30 0767 (NSS) FELDMAN, RICARDO A Biomedical research support MECHANISM OF TRANSFORMATION BY TYROSINE PROTEIN KINASES
S07RR-05379-30 0768 (NSS) SCHULZE, DAN Biomedical research support EXPRESSION OF ANTIBODY GENES
S07RR-05379-30 0769 (NSS) ADASHI, ELI Y Biomedical research support REGULATION OF OVARIAN STEROIDOGENESIS
S07RR-05379-30 0770 (NSS) SHIN, MOON L Biomedical research support ION DEREGULATION & ALTERED GENE EXPRESSION
S07RR-05379-30 0771 (NSS) GUSTAFSON, THOMAS A Biomedical research support MECHANISMS OF INSULIN & IGFI RECEPTOR FUNCTION
S07RR-05379-30 0772 (NSS) KAO, JOSEPH P Biomedical research support FLUORESCENT PROBES OF CELL SIGNALLING
S07RR-05379-30 0773 (NSS) CUKIERMAN, SAMUEL S Biomedical research support GATING CHARACTERISTICS OF NA CHANNELS RECONSTITUTED IN PLANAR BILAYERS
S07RR-05379-30 0774 (NSS) HAMLYN, JOHN M Biomedical research support ISOLATION & REGULATION OF ENDOGENOUS DUABAIN
S07RR-05379-30 0775 (NSS) EDDY, HUBERT A Biomedical research support LASER DOPPLER FLOWIMETRY
S07RR-05380-30 (NSS) ARAM, CHOBANIAN BOSTON UNIV SCH OF MEDICINE 80 EAST CONCORD STREET BOSTON, MASS 02118 Biomedical reserach support
S07RR-05380-30 0891 (NSS) MEERS Biomedical reserach support ROLE OF ANNEXINS IN NEUTROPHIL DEGRANULATION
S07RR-05380-30 0892 (NSS) CHOPKIN Biomedical reserach support EFFECTS OF GLUCOCORTICOIDS ON GLUCOSE TRANSPORT
S07RR-05380-30 0893 (NSS) VAUGHAN Biomedical reserach support SEMINAR PROGRAM
S07RR-05380-30 0894 (NSS) DOBSON Biomedical reserach support GPD ACTIVATION DURING FAT & MUSCLE CELL DIFFERENTIATION
S07RR-05380-30 0895 (NSS) SIMONS Biomedical reserach support FLOW CYTOMETER SHARED FACILITY
S07RR-05380-30 0881 (NSS) SCHNAPP Biomedical reserach support AXONAL TRANSPOSE
S07RR-05380-30 0882 (NSS) ORCKLAND Biomedical reserach support EXTRINSIC CONNECTIONS IN VISUAL CORTEX
S07RR-05380-30 0896 (NSS) AMOS Biomedical reserach support HYPERVARIABLE CO INHERITANCE DNA MARKERS & TUBEROUS SCLEROSIS IN MULTIGENERATION
S07RR-05380-30 0883 (NSS) KOZULIN Biomedical reserach support SCHIZOPHRENIC LANGUAGE
S07RR-05380-30 0897 (NSS) SASSON Biomedical reserach support MUSCLE GENE REGULATION DURING LIMB MORPHOGENESIS
S07RR-05380-30 0898 (NSS) LAMORTE Biomedical reserach support DIETARY FISH OIL ON BILIARY CHOLESTEROL TRANSPORT & GALLSTONE FORMATION
S07RR-05380-30 0899 (NSS) OFFNER Biomedical reserach support MOLECULAR CLONING OF LIVER PLASMA MEMBRANE FATTY ACID BINDING PROTEIN
S07RR-05380-30 0900 (NSS) BLUSZTAJN Biomedical reserach support PHOSPHATIDYLCHOLINE SYNTHESIS
S07RR-05380-30 0901 (NSS) TRUCKMAN Biomedical reserach support REGULATION OF MRNA
S07RR-05380-30 0902 (NSS) PAYNE Biomedical reserach support NEURONAL INTERACTIONS ACROSS THE CORPUS CALLOSUM
S07RR-05380-30 0985 (NSS) AMOS Biomedical reserach support MARKERS & TUBEROUS SCLEROSIS IN MULTIGENERATIONAL KINDREDS
S07RR-05380-30 0884 (NSS) SCHRAGER Biomedical reserach support CADMIUM MODULATION OF TCE AND EDB
S07RR-05380-30 0885 (NSS) TONKISS Biomedical reserach support HIPPOCAMPAL FUNCTION & NUTRITION
S07RR-05380-30 0886 (NSS) WHITE Biomedical reserach support FRAMINGHAM CHILDRENS STUDY
S07RR-05380-30 0887 (NSS) GARRAHLE Biomedical reserach support FRAMINGHAM CHILDRENS STUDY
S07RR-05380-30 0888 (NSS) MARMOR Biomedical reserach support FRAMINGHAM CHILDRENS STUDY
S07RR-05380-30 0889 (NSS) MISTSIALIS Biomedical reserach support MOLECULAR GENETIC
S07RR-05380-30 0890 (NSS) EDWARDS Biomedical reserach support VITAMIN A MULLER CELLS
S07RR-05381-30 (NSS) ADELSTEIN, STANLEY J HARVARD MEDICAL SCHOOL 25 SHATTUCK STREET BOSTON, MASS 02115 Biomedical research support
S07RR-05381-30 0776 (NSS) BEGG, DAVID A Biomedical research support CYTOSKELETON IN FERTILIZATION
S07RR-05381-30 0777 (NSS) BESTOR, TIMOTHY H Biomedical research

PROJECT NO., ORGANIZATIONAL UNIT., INVESTIGATOR, ADDRESS, TITLE

support TARGETED GENE INACTIVATION IN MICE
S07RR-05381-30 0778 (NSS) DOCHEUX, RAMON F Biomedical research support STRUCTURE & FUNCTION OF MAMMALIAN RETINA
S07RR-05381-30 0779 (NSS) HOLLENBECK, PETER J Biomedical research support KINESIN IN ORGANELLE MOVEMENT
S07RR-05381-30 0780 (NSS) KIRCHHAUSEN, TOMAS L Biomedical research support PROTEINS ASSOCIATED W/ COATED VESICLES
S07RR-05381-30 0781 (NSS) MATLIN, KARL S Biomedical research support ONCOGENE TRANSFORMATION OF CELL POLARITY
S07RR-05381-30 0794 (NSS) ROSNER, BERNARD A Biomedical research support EXPERIMENTAL DESIGN ISSUES IN LONGITUDAL FOLLOW UP
S07RR-05381-30 0795 (NSS) SINGER, DANIEL E Biomedical research support CRITICAL APPRAISAL IN MEDICINE
S07RR-05381-30 0782 (NSS) PAUL, DAVID L Biomedical research support GAP JUNCTIONS IN XENOPUS DEVELOPMENT: EMBRYOGENESIS
S07RR-05381-30 0783 (NSS) SUGRUE, STEPHEN P Biomedical research support COLLAGEN RECEPTORS IN EPITHELIAL CELL LINES
S07RR-05381-30 0784 (NSS) SWANSON, JOEL A Biomedical research support ALTERATION OF MACROPHAGE SHAPE & SIZE DURING PHAGOCYTOSIS
S07RR-05381-30 0785 (NSS) BELASCO, JOEL G Biomedical research support MRNA DEGRADATION IN BACTERIAL & MAMMALIAN CELLS: FIBROBLAST
S07RR-05381-30 0786 (NSS) HOCHSCHILD, ANN Biomedical research support INTERACTIONS OF DNA BOUND REGULATORS: GENE REGULATOR
S07RR-05381-30 0787 (NSS) FISCHBACH, RUTH L Biomedical research support HEALTH CARE EDUCATION FOR ELDERLY
S07RR-05381-30 0788 (NSS) GOOD, BYRON J Biomedical research support RELATIONSHIP BETWEEN EMOTION ILLNESS & HEALING
S07RR-05381-30 0789 (NSS) GOOD, MARY-JO Biomedical research support CULTURAL MEANINGS OF ILLNESS EXPERIENCE
S07RR-05381-30 0790 (NSS) HEGGENHOUGEN, KRISTI Biomedical research support MEDICAL ANTHROPOLOGY OF HEALTH IN THIRD WORLD NATIONS
S07RR-05381-30 0791 (NSS) SCHLESINGER, MARK J Biomedical research support NONPROFIT & PROFIT & PUBLIC HEALTH CARE ON QUALITY OF DELIVERY
S07RR-05381-30 0792 (NSS) BURING, JULIE E Biomedical research support COHORT STUDIES FOR TEACHING
S07RR-05381-30 0793 (NSS) HENNEKENS, CHARLES H Biomedical research support RCTS IN CLINICAL EPIDEMIOLOGY
S07RR-05382-30 (NSS) RYAN, RICHARD M, JR TUFTS UNIVERSITY 136 HARRISON AVENUE BOSTON, MASS 02111 Biomedical research support
S07RR-05382-30 0868 (NSS) GRAY, MARK Biomedical research support MOLECULAR BASIS OF POLYCYSTIC OVARIAN SYNDROME (PCO): CHRONIC OVULATION
S07RR-05382-30 0869 (NSS) HERMAN, IRA M Biomedical research support EXTRACELLULAR MATRIX & VASCULAR ENDOTHELIAL CELL ACTION: ANGIOGENESIS TUMOR
S07RR-05382-30 0870 (NSS) KISLIUK, ROY L Biomedical research support SYNERGISTIC GROWTH INHIBITION BY COMBINATION OF ANTIFOLATES: LYMPHOMA CELLS
S07RR-05382-30 0871 (NSS) KREAM, RICHARD M Biomedical research support DYNAMICS OF NEUROPEPTIDE PROCESSING: TACHYKININ SUBSTANCE P(SP) IN CNS TISSUE;
S07RR-05382-30 0872 (NSS) LEVY, STUART B Biomedical research support SURVIVAL & PERSISTENCE TRAITS IN SOIL PSEUDOMENADS: GENES & GENE PRODUCTS
S07RR-05382-30 0873 (NSS) MALAMY, MICHAEL Biomedical research support GENETIC SYSTEMS TO STUDY VIRULENCE IN BACTEROIDES: TRANSPOSON TRANSCONJUGENTS
S07RR-05382-30 0874 (NSS) OFNER, PETER Biomedical research support ANDROGENS IN PROSTATIC & EPIDIDYMAL CULTURE: PROSTATE CANCER
S07RR-05382-30 0875 (NSS) PIWNICA-WORMS, HELEN Biomedical research support P34CDC2 & CELL CYCLE CONTROL: TYROSINE KINASE PHOSPHORYLATION
S07RR-05382-30 0876 (NSS) ROFFLER-TARLOV, SUZA Biomedical research support INHERITED DOPAMINE LOSS: MUTANT WEAVER GENE NIGROSTRIATAL, MIDBRAIN, PARKINSON
S07RR-05382-30 0877 (NSS) SHUSTER, LOUIS Biomedical research support LIVER DAMAGE FROM COCAINE:
S07RR-05382-30 0878 (NSS) THOMPSON, MICHAEL L Biomedical research support OPIOD MECHANISMS IN ANALGESIA OF DEFEAT: MORPHINE
S07RR-05383-30 (NSS) BOLE, GILES G JR UNIVERSITY OF MICHIGAN 1301 CATHERINE ROAD ANN ARBOR, MI 48109-0624 Biomedical research support
S07RR-05383-30 0567 (NSS) RICHARDSON, JAMES K Biomedical research support ROCKER SOLED SHOES & BIOMECHANISMS IN PATIENTS W/ CALF CLAUDICATION
S07RR-05383-30 0568 (NSS) SAMUELSON, LINDA C Biomedical research support MOUSE MUTANTS BY HOMOLOGOUS RECOMBINATION IN EMBRYONIC STEM CELLS
S07RR-05383-30 0569 (NSS) SIEGEL, GEORGE J Biomedical research support NEUROCYTOLOGY OF NA K ATPASE
S07RR-05383-30 0570 (NSS) TANDON, RAJIV Biomedical research support CENTRAL MUSCARINIC MECHANISMS IN SCHIZOPHRENIA: EFFECT OF BIPERIDEN
S07RR-05383-30 0571 (NSS) TENNEKOON, GIHAN I Biomedical research support PERIPHERAL NERVE DAMAGE IN AIDS
S07RR-05383-30 0572 (NSS) WEBER, WENDELL W Biomedical research support ACETYLATION PHARMACOGENETICS: ARYLAMINES & DNA DAMAGE
S07RR-05383-30 0550 (NSS) BARRY, SUSAN R Biomedical research support EFFECTS OF ANTIMALARIAL DRUGS ON IONIC CURRENTS IN PARAMECIA
S07RR-05383-30 0551 (NSS) BITAR, KHALIL N Biomedical research support MYOGENIC CONTROL MECHANISMS IN INTERNAL ANAL SPHINCTER & COLON
S07RR-05383-30 0552 (NSS) COOPER, STEPHEN Biomedical research support PLASMID MAINTENANCE & PLASMID REPLICATION DURING DIVISION CYCLE
S07RR-05383-30 0553 (NSS) ERNST, STEPHEN A Biomedical research support LOCALIZATION OF EPITHELIAL CA CHANNEL
S07RR-05383-30 0554 (NSS) GLOVER, THOMAS W Biomedical research support CLONING GENE FOR MENKES SYNDROME
S07RR-05383-30 0555 (NSS) GORSKI, JEROME L Biomedical research support MOLECULAR GENETICS OF NEUROECTODERMAL DEVELOPMENT
S07RR-05383-30 0556 (NSS) GREENBERG, MIRIAM L Biomedical research support GENETIC CONTROL OF MITOCHONDRIAL MEMBRANE BIOGENESIS
S07RR-05383-30 0557 (NSS) HOLLINGSWORTH, PEGGI Biomedical research support NEURONAL FUNCTION AFTER CHRONIC CHOLINERGIC STIMULATION
S07RR-05383-30 0558 (NSS) HUGHES, BRET A Biomedical research

PROJECT NO., ORGANIZATIONAL UNIT., INVESTIGATOR, ADDRESS, TITLE

support ION CONDUCTANCES IN RETINAL PIGMENT EPITHELIUM
S07RR-05383-30 0559 (NSS) HURD, WILLIAM W Biomedical research support EFFECT OF COCAINE ON CONTRACTILE RESPONSE OF PREGNANT HUMAN UTERUS
S07RR-05383-30 0560 (NSS) JUNI, ELLIOT Biomedical research support PLASMID MODIFICATION IN ACINETOBACTOR
S07RR-05383-30 0561 (NSS) KEYES, P LANDIS Biomedical research support REGULATION OF STERIODOGENESIS BY IGF 1 IN CORPUS LUTEUM
S07RR-05383-30 0562 (NSS) KING, CHERYL A Biomedical research support ADOLESCENT INPATIENTS AT RISK FOR SUICIDE: FAMILY SYSTEM PROTECTIVE FACTORS
S07RR-05383-30 0563 (NSS) KOSTYO, JACK L Biomedical research support ACTIVITIES OF HUMAN GROWTH HORMONE MUTANTS
S07RR-05383-30 0564 (NSS) LANDEFELD, THOMAS D Biomedical research support PITUITARY HORMONE MRNAS DURING PUBERTY IN FEMALE LAMB
S07RR-05383-30 0565 (NSS) LOGSDON, CRAIG D Biomedical research support CKK STIMULATED GROWTH IN NORMAL & CANCEROUS PANCREATIC ACINAR CELLS
S07RR-05383-30 0566 (NSS) NEUBIG, RICHARD R Biomedical research support PEPTIDE MODULATORS OF G PROTEIN FUNCTION
S07RR-05384-30 (NSS) DAMBACH, GEORGE E WAYNE STATE UNIVERSITY 540 E CANFIELD AVE RM 1241 DETROIT, MI 48201 Biomedical research support grant
S07RR-05384-30 0774 (NSS) AKINS, ROBERT Biomedical research support grant GENETICS OF FUNGAL MULTIDRUG RESISTANCE GENES HOMOLOGOUS TO TUMOR RESISTANT GENE
S07RR-05384-30 0775 (NSS) GUNTHER, STEPHEN Biomedical research support grant VASCULAR CELLULAR RESPONSES TO LASER IRRADIATION: VASOCONSTRICTION, PHOTOTHERAPY
S07RR-05384-30 0776 (NSS) KALTENBACH, JAMES Biomedical research support grant EARLY HAIR CELL LOSS ON DEVELOPMENT OF TONOTOPIC ORDER
S07RR-05384-30 0777 (NSS) REINHART, HARALD Biomedical research support grant AEROSOLIZED SULFONAMIDES INHIBITORS TO TREAT PCP: ANIMAL MODEL
S07RR-05384-30 0778 (NSS) KING, STEPHEN Biomedical research support grant CELLULAR DETERMINANTS OF HIV INFECTION: VIRUS PENETRATION
S07RR-05384-30 0779 (NSS) HOLLAND, THOMAS Biomedical research support grant TARGETING OF HSV 1 TO HIV INFECTED CELLS:
S07RR-05385-30 (NSS) BROWN, DAVID M UNIVERSITY OF MINNESOTA 420 DELAWARE ST SE, BOX 293 MINNEAPOLIS, MN 55455 Biomedical research support grant
S07RR-05385-30 0800 (NSS) HONDA, CHRISTOPHER N Biomedical research support grant FUNCTIONAL & MORPHOLOGICAL ANALYSIS OF NOCICEPTIVE NEURONS
S07RR-05385-30 0818 (NSS) SCHERER, STEWART Biomedical research support grant MOBILE DNA IN CANDIDA ALBICANS BIOLOGY & EPIDEMIOLOGY
S07RR-05385-30 0819 (NSS) SCHIFF, LESLIE A Biomedical research support grant STRUCTURE & FUNCTION OF REOVIRUS MAJOR OUTER CAPSID PROTEINS
S07RR-05385-30 0820 (NSS) THAYER, STANLEY A Biomedical research support grant NEURODENERATIVE DISORDER OPIATE MODULATE OF ION CHANNEL: NEURONAL CA REG AIDS
S07RR-05385-30 0801 (NSS) SEYBOLD, VIRGINIA Biomedical research support grant COEXISTENCE OF PEPTIDES IN AXON TERMINALS INVOLVED IN PAIN
S07RR-05385-30 0802 (NSS) FARAS,ANTHONY Biomedical research support grant HUMAN PAPILLOMAVIRUSES & MALIGNANT DISEASE
S07RR-05385-30 0803 (NSS) IADECOLA, CONSTANTIN Biomedical research support grant INTRINSIC NEURAL REGULATION OF THE CEREBRAL CIRCULATION
S07RR-05385-30 0804 (NSS) GOMEZ, CHRISTOPHER M Biomedical research support grant MUTANT ACETYLCHOLINE RECEPTOR AS POTENTIAL CAUSE OF EXCITOTOXIC DAMAGE TO MUSCLE
S07RR-05385-30 0805 (NSS) ROSS, MARGARET E Biomedical research support grant MOLECULAR BIOLOGICAL STUDIES OF NEURONAL MIGRATION IN DEVELOPING BRAIN
S07RR-05385-30 0806 (NSS) ROSS, MARGARET E Biomedical research support grant DETERMINANTS OF CELL FATE IN THE DEVELOPING BRAIN
S07RR-05385-30 0807 (NSS) NUTTER, LOUISE M Biomedical research support grant DRUG RESISTANCE TO ANTI CANCER THERAPY
S07RR-05385-30 0808 (NSS) KLEIN, DAVID J Biomedical research support grant PROTEOGLYCANS SYNTHESIZED BY KIDNEY CELLS IN CULTURE
S07RR-05385-30 0809 (NSS) SUNDARAM, RAMAKRISHN Biomedical research support grant OVARIAN CANCER: EXPERIMENTAL THERAPY
S07RR-05385-30 0810 (NSS) WALSETH, TIMOTHY F Biomedical research support grant NUCLEOTIDE METABOLISM IN HIT CELLS
S07RR-05385-30 0811 (NSS) WALSETH, TIMOTHY F Biomedical research support grant CYCLIC ADP RIBOSE LEVELS IN MAMMALIAN TISSUES
S07RR-05385-30 0812 (NSS) BRANTON, WOODY D Biomedical research support grant CALCIUM CHANNELS IN NERVE CELLS
S07RR-05385-30 0813 (NSS) HOGENKAMP, H P C Biomedical research support grant FORMATION OF CARBON MONOXIDE: CC14 + FREONS 11 12 13 CATALYZED BY CORRINNOIDS
S07RR-05385-30 0814 (NSS) PORTER, MARY E Biomedical research support grant STUDY OF DYNEIN MUTANTS CELL MOTILITY, MOTOR PROTEINS, RESPIRATORY DISEASE
S07RR-05385-30 0815 (NSS) LITZ, CRAIG E Biomedical research support grant GENE METHYLATION IN CHRONIC MYELOGENOUS LEUKEMIA
S07RR-05385-30 0816 (NSS) JENKINS, MARC K Biomedical research support grant EFFECTS OF CYCLOSPORINE A ON T CELL DEVELOPMENT
S07RR-05385-30 0817 (NSS) JEMMERSON, RONALD Biomedical research support grant T CELL TOLERANCE TO TESTICULAR CYTOCHROME
S07RR-05386-30 (NSS) NELSON, NORMAN C UNIVERSITY OF MISSISSIPPI 2500 N STATE STREET JACKSON, MISS 39216-4505 Biomedical research support grant
S07RR-05386-30 0573 (NSS) ARD, MARCH D Biomedical research support grant CELL CELL INTERACTIONS OF ASTROCYTES IN CNS SCARRING
S07RR-05386-30 0574 (NSS) BIGELOW, CAROLYN L Biomedical research support grant HYPERLIPIDEMIA & CELLULAR PRODUCTION OF PROTEOGLYCANS
S07RR-05386-30 0575 (NSS) BLY, JAN E Biomedical research support grant PHYLOGENETICALLY CONSERVED ROLE OF OLEIC ACID IN T CELL REGULATION
S07RR-05386-30 0576 (NSS) BORAL, LEONARD I Biomedical research support grant EFFECT OF CHANGES IN SERUM MG ON PLATELET AGGREGATION

RESPONSE
S07RR-05386-30 0577 (NSS) CHAPMAN, STANLEY W Biomedical research support grant DEVELOPMENT OF ANTISERA AGAINST HUMAN HERPES VIRUS TYPE 6 GLYCOPROTEINS
S07RR-05386-30 0578 (NSS) DEBAUCHE, DAVID M Biomedical research support grant ENHANCED G2 CHROMATID RADIOSENSITIVITY IN DYSKERATOSIS CONGENITA FIBROBLASTS
S07RR-05386-30 0579 (NSS) DICKMAN, J DAVID Biomedical research support grant CONVERGENCE IN VESTIBULAR NEURONS TO BILATERAL STIMULATION
S07RR-05386-30 0580 (NSS) DIDLAKE, RALPH Biomedical research support grant HYPOTHERMIC STORAGE OF HEPATOCYTES
S07RR-05386-30 0581 (NSS) DORMAN, NANCY J Biomedical research support grant MEMBRANE PHOSPHOLIPASE PRODUCTS OF NEUTROPHILS IN PATHOGENESIS OF SEPSIS
S07RR-05386-30 0582 (NSS) DZIELAK, DAVID J Biomedical research support grant MICROPERFUSION VS SIMPLE IMMERSION FOR CARDIAC PRESERVATION
S07RR-05386-30 0583 (NSS) FINLEY, RICHARD W Biomedical research support grant NUCLEOSIDE TRANSPORT PROTEINS IN TRYPANOSOMA CRUZI
S07RR-05386-30 0584 (NSS) HARDY, CHERYL L Biomedical research support grant MOLECULAR MECHANISM OF HEMOPOIETIC PROGENITOR CELL HOMING
S07RR-05386-30 0585 (NSS) HUTCHINS, JAMES B Biomedical research support grant PLATELET DERIVED GROWTH FACTOR IN MAMMALIAN NEURAL DEVELOPMENT
S07RR-05386-30 0586 (NSS) HUTCHINS, JAMES B Biomedical research support grant INTERACTIONS BETWEEN NEURONS & GLIA DURING VISUAL SYSTEM DEVELOPMENT
S07RR-05386-30 0587 (NSS) KELLY, JEFFREY A Biomedical research support grant HIV RISK REDUCTION IN URBAN MINORITY WOMEN
S07RR-05386-30 0588 (NSS) KIRCHNER, KENT A Biomedical research support grant MECHANISMS OF INCREASED LOOP TRANSPORT DURING EUGLYCEMIC INSULIN ANTINATRIURESIS
S07RR-05386-30 0589 (NSS) LUNDRIGAN, MICHAEL D Biomedical research support grant POST TRANSCRIPTIONAL CONTROL OF VITAMIN B12 TRANSPORT IN ESCHERICHIA COLI
S07RR-05386-30 0590 (NSS) LUSHBAUGH, WILLIAM B Biomedical research support grant CHARACTERIZATION OF HEAT SHOCK RESPONSE IN TRICHOMONAS VAGINALIS
S07RR-05386-30 0591 (NSS) MA, TERENCE P Biomedical research support grant ID OF SACCADE RELATED NEURONS IN MACAQUE ZONA INCERTA
S07RR-05386-30 0592 (NSS) MINGUELL, JOSE J Biomedical research support grant INTERACT OF HEMOPOIETIC PROGENITOR CELLS W/ EXTRACELLULAR MATRIX MOLECULES
S07RR-05386-30 0593 (NSS) PENDER, EMILY SMITH Biomedical research support grant INTRAOSSEOUS INFUSION OF EMERGENCY DRUGS & EFFECT ON SUBSEQUENT BONE GROWTH
S07RR-05386-30 0594 (NSS) ROCKHOLD, ROBIN WILL Biomedical research support grant MDA RECEPTORS MEDIATE CNS INDUCED CIRCULATORY INJURY
S07RR-05386-30 0595 (NSS) SINNING, ALLAN R Biomedical research support grant MYOCARDIAL SECRETED PROTEINS IN CARDIAC MESENCHYME DIFFERENTIATION
S07RR-05386-30 0596 (NSS) SULLIVAN, DONNA C Biomedical research support grant INTERACTION BETWEEN HUMAN HERPES VIRUS TYPE 6 & HUMAN T CELL LEUKEMIA VIRUS
S07RR-05386-30 0597 (NSS) WARREN, SUSAN Biomedical research support grant ORGANIZATION OF THALAMOCORTICAL CONNECTIVITY IN ERYTHROCEBUS PATAS
S07RR-05386-30 0598 (NSS) WELLMAN, SUSAN E Biomedical research support grant INTERACTIONS OF HISTONE H1 PEPTIDES & DNA
S07RR-05386-30 0599 (NSS) WOODLEY, CHARLES L Biomedical research support grant 62 KDA PROTEIN ANTIGENICALLY RELATED TO EFF TU: PROTEIN SYNTHESIS
S07RR-05387-30 (NSS) GOLDBERG, HERBERT S UNIVERSITY OF MISSOURI MA 204 MEDICAL SCIENCES BLDG COLUMBIA, MO 65212 Biomedical research support
S07RR-05387-30 0600 (NSS) PROUD, VIRGINIA Biomedical research support LIPID METABOLISM IN FETAL ALCOHOL SYNDROME
S07RR-05387-30 0601 (NSS) RHODES, PHILIP Biomedical research support PHOSPHATIDYLSERINE METABOLISM & BRAIN DEVELOPMENT
S07RR-05387-30 0602 (NSS) PETTERBORG, LARRY Biomedical research support BEHAVIORAL & NEUROCHEMICAL CORRELATES IN AN ANIMAL MODEL OF DEPRESSION
S07RR-05387-30 0603 (NSS) BADDOUR, LARRY Biomedical research support VIRULENCE FACTORS ENDOCARDIAL INFECTIONS CAUSED BY STAPHYLOCOCCUS EPIDERMIDIS
S07RR-05387-30 0604 (NSS) CAMPBELL, BENEDICT Biomedical research support BIOCONVERSION OF SULFIDOPEPTIDE LEUKOTRIENES IN LUNG
S07RR-05387-30 0605 (NSS) PETERSEN, SANDRA Biomedical research support USE OF IN SITU HYBRIDIZATION TO STUDY LHRH NEURONAL ACTIVITY
S07RR-05387-30 0606 (NSS) ZOELLER, THOMAS Biomedical research support DIFFERENTIAL REGULATION OF NEUROENDOCRINE PEPTIDE GENE
S07RR-05387-30 0607 (NSS) ALLEN, SUSAN Biomedical research support ACID PHOSPHATASE BIOMARKER OF OSTEOPOROSIS
S07RR-05387-30 0608 (NSS) FORTE, LEONARD Biomedical research support E COLI ENTEROTOXIN RECEPTORS: STRUCTURE & FUNCTION
S07RR-05387-30 0609 (NSS) DUEKER, DAVID Biomedical research support DIFFUSION CHAMBER CULTURE NEW APPROACH TO OCULAR THERAPY
S07RR-05387-30 0610 (NSS) CAMPBELL, SCOTT Biomedical research support VESSEL PERMEABILITY EXTRACELLULAR MATRIX REMODELING RENOVASCULAR HYPERTENSION
S07RR-05387-30 0611 (NSS) CASH, DEREK Biomedical research support EFFECT OF BENZODIAZEPINE CLASS DRUGS ON FUNCTION GABA RECEPTOR BRAIN
S07RR-05387-30 0612 (NSS) SNYDER, SCOTT Biomedical research support INTERLEUKIN 1 & TNF
S07RR-05388-30 (NSS) STONEMAN, WILLIAM, III ST LOUIS UNIVERSITY MEDICAL CE 1402 S GRAND BOULEVARD ST LOUIS, MO 63104 Biomedical research support
S07RR-05388-30 0613 (NSS) PAYVAR, FARHANG Biomedical research support COORDINATE & CELL SPECIFIC REGULATION OF GENE
S07RR-05388-30 0614 (NSS) ZENSER, TERRY V Biomedical research support BLADDER CANCER: METABOLISM & PREVENTION
S07RR-05388-30 0615 (NSS) WEIDMAN, MARGARET J Biomedical research support BIOCHEMICAL ANALYSIS OF MEMBRANE FUSION DURING
S07RR-05388-30 0616 (NSS) MCDONALD, DOUGLAS J Biomedical research support TUMOR LOCALIZATION & THERAPEUTIC POTENTIAL
S07RR-05388-30 0617 (NSS) COSCIA, CARMINE J Biomedical research support REGULATION OF ALKALOID METABOLISM
S07RR-05388-30 0618 (NSS) KAMINSKI, DONALD L Biomedical research support EICOSANOIDS IN HEPATO BILIARY PHYSIOLOGY
S07RR-05388-30 0619 (NSS) BUNCHMAN, TIMOTHY E Biomedical research support CHARACTERIZATION OF HUMAN GLOMERULAR ENDOTHELIUM
S07RR-05388-30 0620 (NSS) WYSOLMERSKI, ROBERT Biomedical research support MECHANISM OF ENDOTHELIAL CELL RETRACTION IN VITRO
S07RR-05388-30 0621 (NSS) ARMBRECHT, HARVEY J Biomedical research support CHANGES IN VITAMIN D METABOLISM W/ AGE
S07RR-05388-30 0622 (NSS) GREEN, MAURICE Biomedical research support BIOCHEMICAL FUNCTIONS OF ADENOVIRUS ONCOGENES
S07RR-05388-30 0623 (NSS) BACON, BRUCE R Biomedical research support HEPATOTOXICITY IN NEW ANIMAL MODEL OF IRON
S07RR-05388-30 0624 (NSS) ZASSENHAUS, H PETER Biomedical research support RNA PROCESSING IN MITOCHONDRIAL GENE EXPRESSION
S07RR-05388-30 0625 (NSS) BOSE, SUBIR K Biomedical research support MOLECULAR DETERMINANTS OF CHLAMYDIA: HOST INTERACTION
S07RR-05388-30 0626 (NSS) ELLIOTT, WILLIAM H Biomedical research support METABOLISM OF NEUTRAL STEROLS
S07RR-05389-30 (NSS) PECK, WILLIAM A WASHINGTON UNIV SCH OF MED 660 S EUCLID AVE, BOX 8106 ST LOUIS, MO 63110 Biomedical research support
S07RR-05389-30 0630 (NSS) CHENEY, CLARISSA M Biomedical research support GENETIC CONTROL OF MICROTUBULE FUNCTION: TUBULIN MUTATIONS DROSOPHILA
S07RR-05389-30 0631 (NSS) CONNOLLY, JANET M Biomedical research support CD8 INTERACTION IN TRANSGENIC MICE: CYTOTOXIC T LYMPHOCYTES
S07RR-05389-30 0632 (NSS) CRAWFORD, SUSAN Y Biomedical research support INFORMATION TECHNOLOGY RESEARCH:
S07RR-05389-30 0633 (NSS) FONG, CHIN-TO Biomedical research support MAPPING OF NEUROFIBROMATOSIS 1 LOCUS: (NFI) GENOMIC STRUCTURE
S07RR-05389-30 0634 (NSS) FRISCH, STEVEN M Biomedical research support ANTI ONCOGENIC EFFECT OF ADENOVIRUS E1A IN HUMAN TUMOR CELLS: TUMOR SUPPRESSOR
S07RR-05389-30 0635 (NSS) GREENWALD, JAMES E Biomedical research support RENAL ATRIOPEPTIN SYNTHESIS IN PHYSIOLOGY & PATHOPHYSIOLOGY: NEPHROTIC SYNDROME
S07RR-05389-30 0636 (NSS) HARDING, CLIFFORD V Biomedical research support MECHANISMS OF ANTIGEN PROCESSING
S07RR-05389-30 0637 (NSS) HOLTZMAN, MICHAEL J Biomedical research support PLATELET ACTIVATING FACTOR SYNTHESIS BY PULMONARY AIRWAY EPITHELIAL CELL: ASTHMA
S07RR-05389-30 0638 (NSS) KELLY, DANIEL P Biomedical research support REGULATION OF MCAD GENE EXPRESSIONS: FATTY ACID GENETIC DEFECT RETINOIC ACID
S07RR-05389-30 0639 (NSS) KHOURI, ROGER K Biomedical research support FABRICATION OF AUTOGENOUS BONY SPARE PARTS BY OSTEOINDUCTIVE GROWTH FACTORS
S07RR-05389-30 0640 (NSS) LINDAY, BRUCE D Biomedical research support ELECTROPHYSIOLOGY ON CATHETER ABLATION OF VENTRICULAR TACHYCARDIA
S07RR-05389-30 0641 (NSS) LUKASIEWICZ, PETER D Biomedical research support NMDA RECEPTORS ON RETINAL GANGLION CELLS
S07RR-05389-30 0642 (NSS) MERCER, ROBERT W Biomedical research support MOLECULAR CLONING OF NA & K & 2C1 6 TRANSPORTER: RENAL DISEASE
S07RR-05389-30 0643 (NSS) NOVACK, NANCY Biomedical research support DEFECT IN NERVE GROWTH FACTOR RECEPTOR GENE IN HUMAN NEURO BLASTOMA
S07RR-05389-30 0644 (NSS) OLIVO, PAUL D Biomedical research support ORIGIN BINDING PROTEINS OF HERPES VIRUSES
S07RR-05389-30 0645 (NSS) PARDO, JOSE V Biomedical research support ANALYSIS METHODS FOR NEUROPSYCHIATRIC DIAGNOSTIC IMAGING: CT PET CAUDATE
S07RR-05389-30 0646 (NSS) POGWIZD, STEVEN M Biomedical research support ETIOLOGY OF SUDDEN DEATH ASSOCIATED W/ CONGESTIVE HEART FAILURE
S07RR-05389-30 0647 (NSS) POMEROY, SCOTT L Biomedical research support RELATIONSHIP OF GLIAL CELLS TO SYNAPTIC REMODELLING: SYNAPTIC REMODELLING
S07RR-05389-30 0648 (NSS) PONDER, JAY W Biomedical research support: de novo design of beta sheet peptides
S07RR-05389-30 0649 (NSS) ROMAN, JESSE Biomedical research support FIBRONECTIN & FIBRONECTIN RECEPTORS IN LUNG DEVELOPMENT
S07RR-05389-30 0650 (NSS) TYCHSEN, LAWRENCE Biomedical research support NEUROANATOMIC BASIS FOR EYE MOVEMENT CROSS EYED INFANTS: STRABISMIC MACAQUE
S07RR-05389-30 0651 (NSS) VOLLMER, DENNIS G Biomedical research support CULTURED ASTROGLIA TO APPLIED MECHANICAL STRESS: ASTROCYTES GLIAL CELLS
S07RR-05389-30 0627 (NSS) ADLER, STUART R Biomedical research support IMMORTAL REGULATED NEUROENDOCRINE CELL LINE HYPOTHALAMUS
S07RR-05389-30 0628 (NSS) BLUMER, KENDALL J Biomedical research support CELLULAR RESPONSE & DESENSITIZATION BY YEAST G PROTEIN COUPLED RECEPTOR
S07RR-05389-30 0629 (NSS) CAPARON, MICHAEL G Biomedical research support M PROTEIN DEFICIENT STREPTOCOCCUS PYOGENES TO HUMAN CELLS; RHEUMATIC FEVER
S07RR-05390-30 (NSS) O'BRIEN, RICHARD L CREIGHTON UNIV SCH OF MED CALIFORNIA AT 24TH STREET OMAHA, NEBR 68178 Biomedical research support grant
S07RR-05390-30 0652 (NSS) WESTERMAN, GARY H Biomedical research support grant ARGON LASER CURED SEALANT & CARIES LIKE LESION FORMATION: IN VITRO STUDY
S07RR-05390-30 0653 (NSS) ANDERSON, ROBERT J Biomedical research support grant BOVINE PITUITARY TYROSYLPROTEIN SULFOTRANSFERASE
S07RR-05390-30 0661 (NSS) SCHNEIDER, ELIZABETH Biomedical research support grant EPIDEMIOLOGY OF PEDIATRIC TRAUMA: AGE GROUPS & INJURY RATES
S07RR-05390-30 0662 (NSS) BABIN, DONALD R Biomedical research

PROJECT NO., ORGANIZATIONAL UNIT., INVESTIGATOR, ADDRESS, TITLE

support grant TRANSFER OF HEME FROM HEMOGLOBIN TO HEME BINDING PROTEINS OF SERUM
S07RR-05390-30 0663 (NSS) BRUCE, LAURA L Biomedical research support grant EFFECTS OF BRAIN DAMAGE ON MATURATION OF NEURONS
S07RR-05390-30 0654 (NSS) EWASKOW, SANDRA P Biomedical research support grant GASTRIN RECEPTORS ON HUMAN BLOOD EOSINOPHILS
S07RR-05390-30 0655 (NSS) JOEKEL, COREY S Biomedical research support grant EFFECTS OF REGULATORY PEPTIDES ON PANCREATIC GROWTH & DEVELOPMENT
S07RR-05390-30 0656 (NSS) JOSHI, SHARMISHTHA Biomedical research support grant INTERACTION OF NEUROPEPTIDES W/ LYMPHOCYTES & AIRWAY SMOOTH MUSCLE
S07RR-05390-30 0657 (NSS) SPENCER, H TRENT Biomedical research support grant MECHANISM OF HEME BINDING BY SERUM HEMOPEXIN
S07RR-05390-30 0658 (NSS) THOMSON, KENNETH S Biomedical research support grant IN VITRO INVESTIGATION TO IDENTIFY NEW ANTI ENTEROCOCCAL AGENTS
S07RR-05390-30 0659 (NSS) MURPHY, H CLAIRE Biomedical research support grant EFFECT OF SECRETIN ON PEPSIN SECRETION FROM CHIEF CELLS OF DOG
S07RR-05390-30 0660 (NSS) SEVERIN, MATTHEW J Biomedical research support grant STREPTOCOCCAL ISOLATES ANTIBIOTIC RESISTANCE SURVEY
S07RR-05390-30 0664 (NSS) CARUSI, EDWARD A Biomedical research support grant DNA RESTRICTION SITE MAP ON FRAGMENT ANALYSIS OF COMPREHENSIVE PARTIAL DIGESTS
S07RR-05390-30 0665 (NSS) OLSEN, MARGARET A Biomedical research support grant INFECTION OF FETAL HEMATOPOIETIC CELLS BY MURINE CYTOMEGALOVIRUS
S07RR-05390-30 0666 (NSS) WATT, DEAN D Biomedical research support grant ISOLATION OF NEUROTOXINS FROM CENTRUROIDES SCULPTURATUS VENOM
S07RR-05390-30 0667 (NSS) BAUMSTARK, JOHN S Biomedical research support grant IRON METABOLISM & FETAL ALCOHOL SYNDROME
S07RR-05390-30 0668 (NSS) PADGITT, PATRICIA J Biomedical research support grant TOXIC FACTOR(S) OF HELICOBACTER PYLORI
S07RR-05390-30 0669 (NSS) DESTACHE, CHRISTOPHE Biomedical research support grant INTERACTION BETWEEN DILTIAZEM & SINGLE DOSE OF WARFARIN IN NORMAL VOLUNTEERS
S07RR-05390-30 0670 (NSS) LISTER, PHILIP D Biomedical research support grant EFFECT OF CIRRHOSIS ON TRANSFERRIN MEDIATED SERUM INHIBITION OF ESCHERICHIA COLI
S07RR-05390-30 0671 (NSS) ANDERSON, ROBERT J Biomedical research support grant PURIFICATION OF BOVINE ANTERIOR PITUITARY PHENOL SULFOTRANSFERASE
S07RR-05390-30 0672 (NSS) GALE, HENRY H Biomedical research support grant EFFECT OF MUSCLE FLATTENING ON MYOFILAMENT SPACING:
S07RR-05390-30 0673 (NSS) GOPE, MOHAN L Biomedical research support grant MOLECULAR ANALYSIS OF PDGF RECEPTOR GENE IN HUMAN TUMORS: COLORECTAL
S07RR-05390-30 0674 (NSS) GOPE, RAJALAKSHMI Biomedical research support grant RETINOBLASTOMA GENE REGULATION IN HUMAN COLONIC EPITHELIUM: COLORECTAL TUMORS
S07RR-05390-30 0675 (NSS) BECKER, SALLY A Biomedical research support grant MECHANISM OF SUPPRESSION OF LYMPHOCYTES BY CEPHALOSPORINS:
S07RR-05390-30 0676 (NSS) GAMBAL, DAVID Biomedical research support grant ARACHIDONIC ACID METABOLISM IN MOUSE TRISOMY 16 BRAIN CELLS
S07RR-05390-30 0677 (NSS) BRENNEISE, CAROLE V Biomedical research support grant CLINICAL EVALUATION OF PHARMACOLOGIC AGENTS COMMONLY USED BY DENTAL PATIENTS
S07RR-05390-30 0678 (NSS) DUNLEVY, MAUREEN E Biomedical research support grant DETECT ALCOHOL ABUSER IN OBSTETRICS: QUESTIONNAIRE VS SERUM TRANSFERRIN
S07RR-05390-30 0679 (NSS) BECHTOLD, CLIFFORD Biomedical research support grant INFECTION OF MYELOID LEUKEMIA CELLS BY HUMAN CYTOMEGALOVIRUS
S07RR-05390-30 0680 (NSS) QUINN, THOMAS H Biomedical research support grant AVIAN & CHIROPTERAN TENDON LOCKING MODIFICATIONS: TENDONS
S07RR-05390-30 0681 (NSS) NEARY, TIMOTHY J Biomedical research support grant TELENCEPHALIC PALLIUM OF URODELES & ANURANS: EVOLUTION
S07RR-05390-30 0682 (NSS) HEE, TOM T Biomedical research support grant LOWER EXTREMITY STRESS INTERPRETATION OF SIGNAL AVERAGED IN MALES ECG
S07RR-05390-30 0683 (NSS) STOYSICH, ANNE M Biomedical research support grant MEXILETINE & PHARMACOKINETICS OF THEOPHYLLINE IN HEALTHY VOLUNTEERS
S07RR-05390-30 0684 (NSS) BROUGHTON, GEORGE E Biomedical research support grant PREV OF TPN ASSOCIATED CHOLELITHIASIS W/ IV CHENODEOXYCHOLATE IN PRAIRIE DOG
S07RR-05390-30 0685 (NSS) ANDREWS, RICHARD V Biomedical research support grant EXPRESSIONS OF HYPOTHERMIC INSULATION BY DEER MICE
S07RR-05390-30 0686 (NSS) CAVALIERI, STEPHEN J Biomedical research support grant INFLUENCE OF PLASMA EXCHANGE PHERESIS ON PLASMA ELIMINATION OF ANTIBIOTICS
S07RR-05390-30 0687 (NSS) JAREO, PATTI W Biomedical research support grant REGULATION OF HUMAN BLOOD MONOCYTE FUNCTION
S07RR-05390-30 0688 (NSS) LEIN, ELIZABETH A Biomedical research support grant SUBLETHAL CONCENTRATIONS & ANTIBIOTICS THAT ALTER PRODUCTION VIRULENCE FACTORS
S07RR-05391-30 (NSS) WALDMAN, ROBERT H UNIV OF NEBRASKA 600 SOUTH 42ND STREET OMAHA, NE 68198-6545 Biomedical research support
S07RR-05391-30 0930 (NSS) WALDMAN, ROBERT H Biomedical research support NO SUBPROJECTS
S07RR-05392-30 (NSS) WALLACE, ANDREW G DARTMOUTH MEDICAL SCHOOL DEAN'S OFFICE HANOVER, N H 03755 Biomedical research support
S07RR-05392-30 0689 (NSS) BZIK, DAVID J Biomedical research support MALARIA PARASITE AMINOACYL TRNA SYNTHETASE ENZYMES
S07RR-05392-30 0690 (NSS) COMI, RICHARD J Biomedical research support PULSATILE SUBCUTANEOUS INSULIN INFUSION IN TYPE II DIABETES; CLINICAL
S07RR-05392-30 0691 (NSS) DELEO, JOYCE A Biomedical research support SPINAL PATHOLOGIC & BEHAVIORAL CHANGES AFTER PERIPHERAL & CRYOGENIC NERVE LESION

PROJECT NO., ORGANIZATIONAL UNIT., INVESTIGATOR, ADDRESS, TITLE

S07RR-05392-30 0692 (NSS) FRIEDMAN, PETER A Biomedical research support TAMM HORSFALL GLYCOPROTEIN EXPRESSION IN CULTURED RENAL CELLS
S07RR-05392-30 0693 (NSS) GALT, SPENCER W Biomedical research support PLATELET ACTIVATION IN NORMAL & ATHEROSCLEROTIC INDIVIDUALS BY FLOW CYTOMETRY
S07RR-05392-30 0694 (NSS) HENDERSON, LESLIE P Biomedical research support STEROID EFFECTS ON ACETYLCHOLINE RECEPTOR CHANNEL FUNCTION
S07RR-05392-30 0695 (NSS) HOWELL, ALEXANDRA L Biomedical research support REGULATION OF CD14 EXPRESSION IN ACUTE MYELOGENOUS LEUKEMIA CELLS
S07RR-05392-30 0696 (NSS) LEITER, JAMES C Biomedical research support UPPER AIRWAY MECHANICS IN WAKEFULNESS & SLEEP IN MEN W/ OBSTRUCTIVE SLEEP APNEA
S07RR-05392-30 0697 (NSS) MAUE, ROBERT A Biomedical research support GLIAL CELL REGULATION OF NEURONAL SODIUM CHANNEL EXPRESSION; MULTIPLE SCLEROSIS
S07RR-05392-30 0698 (NSS) MCCANN, FRANCES V Biomedical research support ELECTROBIOLOGY OF CULTURED HUMAN MACROPHAGES
S07RR-05392-30 0699 (NSS) NESS, KENNETH Biomedical research support TOXOPLASMA GONDII ANTIGENS: ISOLATION FROM GENOMIC DNA LIBRARY
S07RR-05392-30 0700 (NSS) OLSON, ARDIS L Biomedical research support PARENTS ABILITY TO DETECT RESOLUTION OF OTITIS MEDIA IN YOUNG CHILDREN
S07RR-05392-30 0701 (NSS) PETTENGILL, OLIVE S Biomedical research support HORMONAL CONTROL OF GROWTH OF PANCREATIC CANCER
S07RR-05392-30 0702 (NSS) REUS, WILLIAM F, III Biomedical research support VASCULAR RESISTANCE STUDIES IN FREE TISSUE TRANSFER
S07RR-05392-30 0703 (NSS) RIGBY, WILLIAM FC Biomedical research support REGULATION OF LYMPHOKINE MRNA STABILITY BY VITAMIN D
S07RR-05392-30 0704 (NSS) SCHNEIDER, DONALD L Biomedical research support LYSOSOMAL PROTEINS REQUIRED FOR TARGETING; CDNA CLONING
S07RR-05392-30 0705 (NSS) SORENSON, GEORGE D Biomedical research support MOLECULAR GENETIC STUDIES OF METASTASIS IN LUNG CANCER
S07RR-05392-30 0706 (NSS) SPECK, NANCY A Biomedical research support NUCLEAR FACTORS SPECIFIC FOR MOLONEY LEUKEMIA VIRUS ENHANCER "CORE" SEQUENCE
S07RR-05392-30 0707 (NSS) STANTON, BRUCE A Biomedical research support MOLECULAR BIOLOGY OF RENAL SODIUM CHANNEL
S07RR-05392-30 0708 (NSS) VON REYN, C FORDHAM Biomedical research support INTERNATIONAL EPIDEMIOLOGY OF DISSEMINATED M AVIUM IN AIDS
S07RR-05392-30 0709 (NSS) WIRA, CHARLES R Biomedical research support SEX HORMONE REGULATION OF SC MRNA LEVELS IN FEMALE REPRODUCTIVE TRACT
S07RR-05392-30 0710 (NSS) WITTERS, LEE A Biomedical research support MOLECULAR CLONING OF UNIQUE ISOZYME OF ACETYL COA CARBOXYLASE
S07RR-05393-30 (NSS) WELT, CAROL UNIV OF MED & DENT OF N J 185 S ORANGE AVENUE NEWARK, NJ 07103-2714 Biomedical research support
S07RR-05393-30 0879 (NSS) ALTER, CAROL L Biomedical research support PSYCHOLOGICAL DISTRESS OF INTRAVENOUS DRUG USERS W/ AIDS
S07RR-05393-30 0880 (NSS) ATTANASIO, VIRGINIA Biomedical research support TREATMENT OF DEPRESSION IN STROKE & TRAUMATIC BRAIN INJURY
S07RR-05393-30 0881 (NSS) AVIV, ABRAHAM Biomedical research support PLATELET CA++ HOMEOSTASIS IN ESSENTIAL HYPERTENSION
S07RR-05393-30 0882 (NSS) BANK, BRUCE Biomedical research support CHLORAMBUCIL DNA INTERACTION IN LEUKEMIC CELLS
S07RR-05393-30 0883 (NSS) BIELORY, LEONARD Biomedical research support SULFA INDUCED DRUG REACTIONS IN AIDS
S07RR-05393-30 0884 (NSS) CHATKUPT, SANSNEE Biomedical research support MAPPING SUSCEPTIBILITY GENE LOCI FOR NEURAL TUBE DEFECTS
S07RR-05393-30 0885 (NSS) DAYAL, BISHAMBAR Biomedical research support CHEMICAL SYNTHESIS OF BILE ALCOHOL GLUCURONIDES
S07RR-05393-30 0886 (NSS) DOWLING, PETER C Biomedical research support ENTEROVIRAL SEQUENCES IN MOTOR NEURON DISEASE
S07RR-05393-30 0887 (NSS) DURAN, WALTER N Biomedical research support CONTROL OF MICROCIRCULATORY FUNCTION BY MOLECULAR SIGNALS
S07RR-05393-30 0888 (NSS) FERRARIS, RONALDO Biomedical research support REGULATION OF INTESTINAL NUTRIENT TRANSPORT IN AGED ANIMALS
S07RR-05393-30 0889 (NSS) FITZGERALD-BOCARSLY, Biomedical research support NATURAL KILL OF HSV INFECTED TARGETS: BASIC BIOLOGY
S07RR-05393-30 0890 (NSS) FRANCO, CHARLES D Biomedical research support NEUTROPHILS & EICOSANOIDS IN SKELETAL MUSCLE ISCHEMIA REPERFUSION
S07RR-05393-30 0891 (NSS) GARDNER, JEFFREY Biomedical research support ALTERED NA+ & H+ EXCHANGE IN VASCULAR CELLS FROM SHR
S07RR-05393-30 0892 (NSS) GOLDMAN, EMANUEL Biomedical research support EFFECT OF LOW USAGE CODONS ON GENE EXPRESSION
S07RR-05393-30 0893 (NSS) ILYAS, AMJAD A Biomedical research support GLYCOLIPID INDUCED NEUROPATHY: AN ANIMAL MODEL
S07RR-05393-30 0894 (NSS) INGOGLIA, NICHOLAS A Biomedical research support PROTEIN MODIFICATION IN INTACT & REGENERATING NERVES
S07RR-05393-30 0895 (NSS) LAEMLE, LOIS K Biomedical research support EFFECT OF RETINAL DYSTROPHY ON BRAIN OF RSC RAT
S07RR-05393-30 0896 (NSS) LEUNG, CHRISTOPHER Biomedical research support ANTIBODY INDUCED TERATOGENESIS
S07RR-05393-30 0897 (NSS) LIVINGSTON, DAVID H Biomedical research support BONE MARROW FAILURE FOLLOWING SHOCK & TRAUMA
S07RR-05393-30 0898 (NSS) MATHUR, RAVINDRA L Biomedical research support EVALUATION OF CATARACTOGENIC AGENTS: A MULTIFACTORIAL APPROACH
S07RR-05393-30 0899 (NSS) MILLER, MARILYN Biomedical research support PREVENTION OF PROTEINURIA IN DIABETIC RATS
S07RR-05393-30 0900 (NSS) NEWLON, CAROL S Biomedical research support DNA REPLICATION IN SACCHAROMYCES CEREVISIAE
S07RR-05393-30 0901 (NSS) RHOTEN, WILLIAM B Biomedical research support CELLULAR ASPECTS OF GENE EXPRESSION IN DIABETES
S07RR-05393-30 0902 (NSS) ROSE, MICHAEL D Biomedical research support GROSS ANATOMICAL STUDIES OF LIVING & FOSSIL HIGHER PRIMATES
S07RR-05393-30 0903 (NSS) SHAIKH, MAJID B Biomedical research support FOREBRAIN DOPAMINE MODULATION OF AGGRESSION IN CAT
S07RR-05393-30 0904 (NSS) SHAPIRO, HERMAN Biomedical research support BUTYRIC ACID: ANTICANCER COMPONENT IN BUTTER FAT FRACTION OF MILK
S07RR-05393-30 0905 (NSS) SIPSKI, MARCA L Biomedical research support FUNCTIONAL ELECTRIC STIMULATION IN SPINAL CORD INDUCED

PROJECT NUMBER LISTING

PROJECT NO., ORGANIZATIONAL UNIT., INVESTIGATOR, ADDRESS, TITLE

PATIENTS
S07RR-05393-30 0906 (NSS) SMALL, MICHAEL Biomedical research support GENETIC ANALYSIS OF NEOPLASTIC TRANSFORMATION BY MYC
S07RR-05393-30 0907 (NSS) VASAN, NAGASWAMISRI Biomedical research support ANALYSIS OF GENE EXPRESSION DURING EMBRYONIC CHONDROGENESIS
S07RR-05393-30 0908 (NSS) WILUSZ, JEFFREY Biomedical research support RNA PROTEIN INTERACTIONS IN SV40 MRNA 3 END MATURATION
S07RR-05394-30 (NSS) TARTAGLIA, ANTHONY P ALBANY MEDICAL COLLEGE 47 NEW SCOTLAND AVE MS129/A34 ALBANY, N Y 12208 Biomedical research support
S07RR-05394-30 0711 (NSS) WERBER, ANDREW H Biomedical research support MOLECULAR BIOLOGY OF CEREBRAL VASCULAR RECEPTORS
S07RR-05394-30 0712 (NSS) BOLDT, JEFFREY Biomedical research support MECHANISMS OF SPERM EGG FUSION
S07RR-05394-30 0713 (NSS) WOOD, PATRICIA A Biomedical research support MECHANISMS OF DYNAMIC CONTROL OF ERYTHROPOIESIS
S07RR-05394-30 0722 (NSS) WERBER, ANDREW H Biomedical research support REGULATION OF CEREBRAL CIRCULATION
S07RR-05394-30 0723 (NSS) HORGAN, MICHAEL J Biomedical research support NEUTROPHILS IN MEDIATING ISCHEMIC REPERFUSION LUNG INJURY
S07RR-05394-30 0724 (NSS) TABER, HARRY W Biomedical research support REGULATION OF B SUBTILIS MEN GENE CLUSTER
S07RR-05394-30 0725 (NSS) ASCHNER, JUDITH L Biomedical research support TRANSMEMBRANE SIGNAL; THROMBIN MEDIATED ENDOTHELIAL MONOLAYER PERMEABILITY
S07RR-05394-30 0726 (NSS) WALSH, RAYMOND F Biomedical research support CEREBRAL TISSUE OXYGENATION BLOOD FLOW W FIBEROPTIC CATHETER OXIMETER
S07RR-05394-30 0714 (NSS) COUSINS, JOSEPH P Biomedical research support IN VIVO NMR SPECTROSCOPY OF SEPSIS IN SWINE MYOCARDIUM
S07RR-05394-30 0715 (NSS) FLETCHER, PAUL W Biomedical research support DVMT GENE EXPRESSION OF G PROTEINS & SIGNAL TRANSDUCTION IN SERTOLI CELLS
S07RR-05394-30 0716 (NSS) KASLOVSKY, ROBERT A Biomedical research support NEUTROPHIL FUNCTION IN PEDIATRIC AIDS PATIENTS
S07RR-05394-30 0717 (NSS) MIGLIOZZI, JOSEPH Biomedical research support CORRELATION OF NM23 RNA LEVELS W/ INVASIVE PONTENTIAL OF OVARIAN CARCINOMA
S07RR-05394-30 0718 (NSS) ZINK, BRIAN J Biomedical research support EFFECTS OF ETHANOL ON BRAIN INJURY; PORCINE FLUID PERCUSSION HEAD INJURY MODEL
S07RR-05394-30 0719 (NSS) CHIKKAPPA, G Biomedical research support GRANULOPOIESIS: EFFECTS OF GLUCOCORTICOIDS
S07RR-05394-30 0720 (NSS) RUCKDESCHEL, JOHN C Biomedical research support EASTERN COOPERATIVE ONCOLOGY GROUP
S07RR-05394-30 0721 (NSS) EASTMAN-ONEILL, ALLI Biomedical research support PATHOPHYSIOLOGY OF OXIDATIVELY STRESSED T LYMPHOCYTES; SEVERELY INJURED PATIENT
S07RR-05394-30 0727 (NSS) GOLDFARB, ROY D Biomedical research support REACTIVE OXYGEN RADICALS IN SEPTIC CARDIAC INJURY
S07RR-05395-30 (NSS) PARDES, HERBERT COLUMBIA UNIVERSITY HLTH SCIS 630 WEST 168TH STREET NEW YORK, N Y 10032 Biomedical research support grant
S07RR-05395-30 0821 (NSS) BLANER, WILLIAM S Biomedical research support grant RETINOIC ACID PLASMA TURNOVER & TISSUE SITES OF SYNTHESIS IN THE RAT
S07RR-05395-30 0822 (NSS) CANFIELD, ROBERT E Biomedical research support grant HCG URINARY MOLECULAR FORMS EXPRESSED IN LUNG CANCER: MARKERS
S07RR-05395-30 0823 (NSS) ESPOSITO, DIANE Biomedical research support grant RADIATION INDUCED ONCOGENES VIA A NOVEL CLONING METHOD: VECTORS, DNA SEQ, CDNA
S07RR-05395-30 0824 (NSS) FISCHER, STUART G Biomedical research support grant MACRO RESTRICTION MAPPING HUMAN CHROMOSOME 13
S07RR-05395-30 0825 (NSS) GOLAND, ROBIN S Biomedical research support grant REGULATION OF CORTICOTROPIN RELEASING HORMONE IN PLACENTAL PERFUSION SYSTEM
S07RR-05395-30 0826 (NSS) TABAS, IRA A Biomedical research support grant CHOLESTERYL ESTER ACCUMULATION IN MACROPHAGES ON PROTEIN SYNTHESIS & SECRETION
S07RR-05396-30 (NSS) SISKIND, GREGORY W CORNELL UNIV MED COLLEGE 1300 YORK AVENUE NEW YORK, N Y 10021 Biomedical research support
S07RR-05396-30 0778 (NSS) WHITE, PERRIN C Biomedical research support FICTIONAL ANALYSIS OF PUTATIVE DNA BINDING PROTEINS
S07RR-05396-30 0779 (NSS) GROSS, STEVEN Biomedical research support NITRIC OXIDE IN ENDOTOXIN & CYTOKINE INDUCED HYPERTENSION
S07RR-05396-30 0780 (NSS) INTURRISI, CHARLES E Biomedical research support REGULATION OF OPIOID PEPTIDE BIOSYNTHESIS & RELEASE
S07RR-05396-30 0781 (NSS) RIFKIND, ARLEEN B Biomedical research support ARACHIDONATE PRODUCTS IN DIOXIN & PCB TOXICITY
S07RR-05396-30 0782 (NSS) FRANKMANN, SANDRA P Biomedical research support OROSENSORY & POST INGESTIVE FEED BACK SIGNALS IN SALT APPETITE
S07RR-05396-30 0783 (NSS) MOLINE, MARGARET L Biomedical research support SEROTONIN IN PREMENSTRUAL SYNDROME
S07RR-05396-30 0784 (NSS) LATRENTA, GREGORY Biomedical research support REVERSAL OF CRANIOSYNOSTOSIS IN RABBIT
S07RR-05396-30 0785 (NSS) STAIANO-COICO, LISA Biomedical research support SUPPORT OF FLOW CYTOMETRY CORE FACILITY
S07RR-05396-30 0728 (NSS) KRAMER, JAN L Biomedical research support PLATELETS IN PERIOPERATIVE MYOCARDIAL ISCHEMIA
S07RR-05396-30 0746 (NSS) HEMPSTEAD, BARBARA L Biomedical research support HIGH AFFINITY NERVE GROWTH FACTOR RECEPTOR
S07RR-05396-30 0747 (NSS) IMPERATO-MCGINLEY, J Biomedical research support PROSTATE SIZE HOMOZYGOTES & HETEROZY W/ 5 ALPHA REDUCTASE DEFICIENCY
S07RR-05396-30 0748 (NSS) JAFFE, ERIC A Biomedical research support EXPRESSION CLONING ENDOTHELIAL CELL THROMBIN RECEPTOR
S07RR-05396-30 0749 (NSS) KIRON, RAVI Biomedical research support ANGIOTENSIN II RECEPTORS CLONING
S07RR-05396-30 0750 (NSS) MAGID, NORMAN M Biomedical research support MYOCARDIAL HYPERTROPHY IN AORTIC REGURGITATION
S07RR-05396-30 0751 (NSS) MARCUS, AARON J Biomedical research support LIPID METABOLISM IN STIMULATED HUMAN PLATELETS
S07RR-05396-30 0752 (NSS) MARCUS, AARON J Biomedical research support METABOLISM & FUNCTIONAL W 3 & W 6 FATTY ACIDS
S07RR-05396-30 0753 (NSS) MCCAFFREY, TIMOTHY Biomedical research support AFFINITY PURIFICATION OF HEPARIN
S07RR-05396-30 0754 (NSS) NACHMAN, RALPH L Biomedical research support SPECIALIZED CENTER OF RESEARCH IN THROMBOSIS SUPPLEMENTAL FUNDING
S07RR-05396-30 0755 (NSS) NOY, NOA Biomedical research support MOVEMENT OF RETINOID IN EYE
S07RR-05396-30 0756 (NSS) POSNETT, DAVID N Biomedical research support T CELL RECEPTOR V GENE UTILIZATION
S07RR-05396-30 0757 (NSS) POSNETT, DAVID N Biomedical research support REPLACEMENT OF EXISTING FREEZER
S07RR-05396-30 0758 (NSS) ROTHERMEL, CONSTANCE Biomedical research support BINDING OF CHLAYMYDIA TO HUMAN MACROPHAGES
S07RR-05396-30 0759 (NSS) RUSSO, CARLO Biomedical research support EXPRESSION OF MAJOR HISTOCOMPATIBILITY COMPLEX MOLECULES
S07RR-05396-30 0760 (NSS) SCARATA, SUZANNE Biomedical research support MODIFICATION OF FLUOROMETER
S07RR-05396-30 0761 (NSS) WEKSLER, MARC E Biomedical research support AUTOIMMUNE REACTIONS IN AGING
S07RR-05396-30 0762 (NSS) ZAKIM, DAVID Biomedical research support PHOSPHOLIPID PROTEIN INTERACTIONS FUNCTIONS MEMBRANE BOUND ENZYMES
S07RR-05396-30 0763 (NSS) HACKETT, NEIL R Biomedical research support PHYSICAL MAPPING OF AN ARCHAEBACTERIAL GENOME
S07RR-05396-30 0764 (NSS) ODONNELL, MICHAEL Biomedical research support MOLECULAR MECHANISM OF EPSTEIN BARR VIRUS REPLICATION
S07RR-05396-30 0765 (NSS) NEDERGAARD, MAIKEN Biomedical research support DISTURBANCES OF CALCIUM HOMEOSTASIS IN MECHANISMS OF CELL INJURY
S07RR-05396-30 0766 (NSS) VICTOR, JONATHAN Biomedical research support MACAQUE CORTICAL RESPONDS TO COMPLEX VISUAL TEXTURES
S07RR-05396-30 0767 (NSS) WAHLESTEDT, CLAES Biomedical research support MOLECULAR STUDIES OF NEURO TRANSMITTER & HORMONE RECEPTORS
S07RR-05396-30 0768 (NSS) SINGH, MUKUL Biomedical research support AUTO ANTIBODIES TO GONADOTROPIN RECEPTORS IN PREMATURE GONADAL
S07RR-05396-30 0769 (NSS) FALCONE, DOMENICK Biomedical research support BECKMAN SPECTROPHOMETER
S07RR-05396-30 0770 (NSS) PETITO, CAROL K Biomedical research support EXPRESSION OF ASTRICUTE GFAP HYPERTROPHY & HYPERPLASIA
S07RR-05396-30 0771 (NSS) SANTOS-BUCH, CHARLES Biomedical research support CHAGAS HEART DISEASE IN LATIN AMERICAN IMMIGRANTS IN NEW YORK
S07RR-05396-30 0772 (NSS) ANTONIAN, LIDA Biomedical research support TRANSMEMBRANE SEGMENT III; BINDS SEVERAL NEUROTRANSMITTERS
S07RR-05396-30 0773 (NSS) DENNISON, BARBARA Biomedical research support CLINICAL TRIAL OF PSYLLIUM TO LOWER CHOLESTEROL
S07RR-05396-30 0774 (NSS) DRISCOLL, CATHERINE Biomedical research support SECOND MALIGNANCIES IN RETINOBLASTOMA: ROLE FOR IMPRINTING
S07RR-05396-30 0775 (NSS) MAST, JOELLE Biomedical research support SCREENING INFANT VISION W/ PARAXIAL PHOTOREFRACTION
S07RR-05396-30 0776 (NSS) ROSNER, INGRID Biomedical research support HOME MANAGEMENT OF ASTHMA SELF TESTING OF SERUM THEOPHYLLINE
S07RR-05396-30 0777 (NSS) SPEISER, PHYLLIS W Biomedical research support CHARACTERIZATION OF NEW CLASS III MHC GENE
S07RR-05396-30 0729 (NSS) ANDERSON, MARY E Biomedical research support GLUTATHIONE IN HUMAN LYMPHOCYTE ACTIVATION
S07RR-05396-30 0730 (NSS) BRESLOW, ESTHER Biomedical research support MECHANISM OF NEUROPHYSIN FOLDING
S07RR-05396-30 0731 (NSS) BRESLOW, ESTHER Biomedical research support MODULATOR FOR CIRCULAR DICHROISM SPECTROMETER
S07RR-05396-30 0732 (NSS) COOPER, ARTHUR J L Biomedical research support PATHOGENESIS OF HEPATIC COMA
S07RR-05396-30 0733 (NSS) GRIFFITH, OWEN W Biomedical research support SMALL INSTRUMENTATION PROGRAM
S07RR-05396-30 0734 (NSS) WELLNER, DANIEL Biomedical research support SEQUENCER FACULTY SUPPLY SUPPORT
S07RR-05396-30 0735 (NSS) HAJJAR, DAVID P Biomedical research support VASCULAR CELL SIGNALLING IN ATHEROGENIC PROCESS
S07RR-05396-30 0736 (NSS) BACHVAROVA, ROSEMARY Biomedical research support C KIT IN GERM LINE OF FEMALE MICE
S07RR-05396-30 0737 (NSS) CAUDY, MICHAEL A Biomedical research support HLH PROTEIN FUNCTION IN FLY NEURONAL CELL DETERMINATION
S07RR-05396-30 0738 (NSS) CITI, SANDRA Biomedical research support MOLECULAR ANALYSIS OF CINGULIN
S07RR-05396-30 0739 (NSS) FISCHMAN, DONALD A Biomedical research support SHARED LASER SCANNING CONFOCAL MICROSCOPE
S07RR-05396-30 0740 (NSS) RODRIQUEZ-BOULAN, E Biomedical research support SHARED LASER SCANNING CONFOCAL MICROSCOPE
S07RR-05396-30 0741 (NSS) TRAKTMAN, PAULA Biomedical research support VACCINIA: EXPRESSION & PURIFICATION OF VIRAL & RECOMBINANT PROTEINS
S07RR-05396-30 0742 (NSS) ASCH, ADAM S Biomedical research support PEPTIDE CORE FACILITY CENTRAL SHARED RESOURCES
S07RR-05396-30 0743 (NSS) BOVBJERB, DANA H Biomedical research support EFFECTS OF GROWTH HORMONE & PROLACTIN ON IMMUNE SENESCENCE
S07RR-05396-30 0744 (NSS) CRANDALL, EDWARD D Biomedical research support ELECTRON MICROSCOPY FACILITY SUPPORT
S07RR-05396-30 0745 (NSS) FRANCUS, TOVA Biomedical research support CARDIOVASCULAR DISEASE & ENVIRONMENTAL ANTIGENS
S07RR-05397-30 (NSS) PURPURA, DOMINICK P ALBERT EINSTEIN COLL OF MED 1300 MORRIS PARK AVENUE BRONX, N Y 10461 Biomedical research support grant
S07RR-05397-30 0786 (NSS) PRASAD, VINAYAKA R Biomedical research support grant STRUCTURE FUNCTION STUDIES ON HIV REVERSE TRANSCRIPTASE
S07RR-05397-30 0787 (NSS) EISEN, ANDREW Biomedical research support grant CLONING OF TWO EUKARYOTIC RECOMBINATION PROTEINS
S07RR-05397-30 0788 (NSS) CHRIST, GEORGE J Biomedical research support grant PHARMACOLOGICAL & CELLULAR STUDIES OF VASCULAR SMOOTH MUSCLE
S07RR-05397-30 0789 (NSS) CHARRON, MAUREEN J Biomedical research support grant GENE DISRUPTION OF INSULIN RESPONSIVE GLUCOSE TRANSPORTER

PROJECT NO., ORGANIZATIONAL UNIT., INVESTIGATOR, ADDRESS, TITLE

S07RR-05397-30 0790 (NSS) LEYH, THOMAS S Biomedical research support grant SULFATE ADENYLATION: METABOLIC BIOCHEMISTRY & ENZYMOLOGY
S07RR-05398-30 (NSS) ADLER, KARL P NEW YORK MEDICAL COLLEGE VALHALLA, N Y 10595 Biomedical research support
S07RR-05399-30 (NSS) FARBER, SAUL J NEW YORK UNIV MEDICAL CENTER 550 FIRST AVENUE NEW YORK, N Y 10016 Biomedical research support grant
S07RR-05399-30 0925 (NSS) LEE-HUANG, SYLVIA Biomedical research support grant PURIFY & CLONE ANTI AIDS ACTIVITY OF GLQ 223
S07RR-05399-30 0926 (NSS) WOLINSKY, EVE J Biomedical research support grant MUTANT GENE PRODUCT CAUSING NEURODEGENERATION IN CAENORHABDITIS ELEGANS
S07RR-05399-30 0927 (NSS) DAVITZ, MICHAEL A Biomedical research support grant IMMUNITY IN TRANSGENIC MICE TOLERANT TO CS PROTEIN OF MALARIA PARASITE
S07RR-05399-30 0928 (NSS) LEVY, DAVID Biomedical research support grant PURIFICATION OF INTERFERON RESPONSIVE TRANSCRIPTION FACTORS
S07RR-05399-30 0929 (NSS) GOTTESMAN, SUSAN R S Biomedical research support grant T CELL ACTIVATION
S07RR-05399-30 0930 (NSS) RUBINSON, KALMAN Biomedical research support grant IMMUNOHISTOCHEMICAL STUDY OF DEVELOPING RETINAL NEURONS
S07RR-05399-30 0931 (NSS) SNOW, ELIZABETH T Biomedical research support grant NOVEL ASSAY TO MEASURE GENE SPECIFIC CARCINOGEN INDUCED DNA REPAIR
S07RR-05399-30 0932 (NSS) STEINETZ, BERNARD G Biomedical research support grant EFFECTS OF 17 KETOSTEROIDS ON LIPOPROTEIN CHOLESTEROL METABOLISM
S07RR-05399-30 0933 (NSS) COPP, RICHARD P Biomedical research support grant CYCLIC NUCLEOTIDES & GROWTH HORMONE EXPRESSION
S07RR-05399-30 0934 (NSS) BLOOMFIELD, STEWART Biomedical research support grant AMACRINE CELL FUNCTION IN MAMMALIAN RETINA
S07RR-05399-30 0935 (NSS) JACOBY, JEAN Biomedical research support grant USE OF DILTIAZEM TO WEAKEN EXTRAOCULAR MUSCLE CONTRACTILITY
S07RR-05399-30 0936 (NSS) STONE, SUSAN L Biomedical research support grant NEURAL INTERACTIONS IN RETINAL EYECUP SLICE
S07RR-05399-30 0937 (NSS) JAEGER, JUDITH Biomedical research support grant NEUROPHARMACOLOGY & ELECTROPHYSIOLOGY OF DEPRESSION IN ACUTE SCHIZOPHRENIA
S07RR-05399-30 0938 (NSS) PLATT, JANE E Biomedical research support grant DEPRESSION & ADAPTATION TO REPEATED STRESS
S07RR-05399-30 0939 (NSS) STANLEY, FREDERICK M Biomedical research support grant REGULATION OF PROLACTION GENE EXPRESSION IN CELL CULTURE
S07RR-05399-30 0940 (NSS) ZUCKER-FRANKLIN, DOR Biomedical research support grant ULTRASTRUCTURE OF LEUKOCYTES & PLATELETS
S07RR-05399-30 0941 (NSS) LIM, DONGBIN Biomedical research support grant REVERSE TRANSCRIPTASE PRODUCED BY E COLI B
S07RR-05399-30 0942 (NSS) BOORSTEIN, ROBERT Biomedical research support grant GENOMIC DNA REPAIR OF OXIDATIVELY MODIFIED PYRIMIDINES
S07RR-05399-30 0943 (NSS) WIRGIN, ISAAC I Biomedical research support grant MOLECULAR ANALYSIS OF HEPATOCELLULAR CARCINOMAS IN HUDSON RIVER TOMCOD
S07RR-05399-30 0944 (NSS) IMBRA, RICHARD J Biomedical research support grant ATTEMPT TO IDENTIFY A GENE INVOLVED IN NICKEL RESISTANCE TO MOUSE CELLS
S07RR-05399-30 0945 (NSS) ABRAMSON, STEVEN B Biomedical research support grant NEUTROPHIL MEDIATED VASCULAR INJURY
S07RR-05399-30 0946 (NSS) FLUG, FRANCES Biomedical research support grant SCREENING OF PREGNANT WOMEN FOR NEWBORN THROMBOCYTOPENIA
S07RR-05399-30 0947 (NSS) SPENCER, ELIZABETH K Biomedical research support grant PLASMA HOMOVANILLIC ACID & CLINICAL RESPONSE TO HALOPERIDOL
S07RR-05399-30 0909 (NSS) MOHRAZ, MANIJEH Biomedical research support grant CRYSTALLIZATION & STRUCTURAL INVESTIGATION OF H, ATPASE
S07RR-05399-30 0910 (NSS) KLEIN, HANNAH Biomedical research support grant DNA HELICASES IN SACCHAROMYCES CEREVISIAE THROUGH POLYMERASES CHAIN REACTION
S07RR-05399-30 0911 (NSS) GALINSKI, MARY Biomedical research support grant MOLECULAR BIOLOGY OF MALARIA ANTIGENIC VARIATION
S07RR-05399-30 0912 (NSS) LEVITT, ALEXANDRA Biomedical research support grant CELL FREE CLONING TECHNIQUES TO STUDY CDNAS OF MALARIA BIOLOGY
S07RR-05399-30 0913 (NSS) POLOGE, LAURA Biomedical research support grant TRANSCRIPTIONAL REGULATION OF GENE EXPRESSION IN GAMETOCYTES OF P FALCIPARUM
S07RR-05399-30 0914 (NSS) DIMENT, STEPHANIE Biomedical research support grant ANTIGEN PROCESSING OF PHAGOCYTOSED PARASITE PROTEIN
S07RR-05399-30 0915 (NSS) CATANESE, VERONICA Biomedical research support grant MYOCARDIAL IGF I IN DEVELOPMENT OF LEFT VENTRICULAR HYPERTROPHY
S07RR-05399-30 0916 (NSS) CHACHOUA, ABRAHAM Biomedical research support grant TUMOR REJECTION ANTIGENS (TRA) IN OVARIAN CANCER
S07RR-05399-30 0917 (NSS) PHILLIPS-QUAGLIATA, Biomedical research support grant B CELL RECEPTORS FOR IGA
S07RR-05399-30 0918 (NSS) GOLD, LESLIE Biomedical research support grant INTERACTION OF FIBRONECTIN W/ IMMUNOGLOBULINS
S07RR-05399-30 0919 (NSS) RICE, MARGARET Biomedical research support grant SYNTHESIS OF ASCORBATE IN ANOXIA RESISTANT TURTLE BRAIN
S07RR-05399-30 0920 (NSS) ORLOW, SETH Biomedical research support grant MOLECULAR BASIS OF CHEDIAK HIGASHI SYNDROME
S07RR-05399-30 0921 (NSS) KLEINSCHMIDT, JOCHEN Biomedical research support grant CALCIUM CHANNELS INVOLVED IN PHOTORECEPTOR NEUROTRANSMITTER RELEASE
S07RR-05399-30 0922 (NSS) NAKA, KEN-ICHI Biomedical research support grant RETINAL RECEPTIVE FIELD IN TIME & SPACE
S07RR-05399-30 0923 (NSS) SAKAI, HIROKO Biomedical research support grant SYNAPTIC ORGANIZATION OF VERTEBRATE RETINA
S07RR-05399-30 0924 (NSS) MELLER, EMANUEL Biomedical research support grant D2 DOPAMINE RECEPTOR DENSITY & RESERVE
S07RR-05400-30 (NSS) NAUGHTON, JOHN P SUNY AT BUFFALO 101 FARBER HALL BUFFALO, NEW YORK 14214 Biomedical research support grant
S07RR-05400-30 0040 (NSS) PREZIO, JOSEPH A Biomedical research support grant POSITRON EMISSION TOMOGRAPHY CENTER
S07RR-05400-30 0041 (NSS) SOLONIUK, DONALD S Biomedical research support grant EVAL ELECTROPHYSIOLOGIC FUNCTION
S07RR-05400-30 0042 (NSS) SPENGLER, ROBERT N Biomedical research support grant ADRENERGIC & PROSTAGLANDIN REGULATION OF MACROPHAGE
S07RR-05400-30 0032 (NSS) COHEN, GARY N Biomedical research support grant CHILDRENS RECEPTION TO HEIGHT & ATTRIBUTIONS
S07RR-05400-30 0033 (NSS) ELLIS, AVERY K Biomedical research support grant DETECTION & EVALUATION OF CORONARY REPERFUSION
S07RR-05400-30 0034 (NSS) HRESHCHYSHYN, MYROSL Biomedical research support grant URODYNAMIC EVALUATION & RESEARCH
S07RR-05400-30 0035 (NSS) LOHR, JAMES W Biomedical research support grant MECHANIC OF VOLUME REGULATION IN KIDNEY TUBULES
S07RR-05400-30 0036 (NSS) MURPHY, TIMOTHY F Biomedical research support grant INFECTIOUS DISEASES RESEARCH
S07RR-05400-30 0037 (NSS) NILES, EDWARD G Biomedical research support grant INVESTIG VACCINIA VIRUS MRNA CAPPING ENZYME
S07RR-05400-30 0038 (NSS) PINCUS, STEPHANIE Biomedical research support grant EOSINOPHILS IN CUTANEOUS DISEASE
S07RR-05400-30 0039 (NSS) PLUNKETT, ROBERT J Biomedical research support grant INFLAMMATORY CELL IMPLANT IN PARKINSONIAN RATS
S07RR-05401-30 (NSS) SCHERL, DONALD J STATE UNIVERSITY OF NEW YORK 450 CLARKSON AVE BROOKLYN, N Y 11203 Biomedical research support
S07RR-05401-30 0859 (NSS) CRAIN, JOHN P Biomedical research support MODULATION OF IMMUNE RESPONSE TO BACTERIAL TOXOIDS IN SCHISTOSOMIASIS
S07RR-05401-30 0860 (NSS) GICK, GREGORY Biomedical research support THYROID HORMONE REGULATION OF NA, K PUMP GENE EXPRESSION
S07RR-05401-30 0861 (NSS) NEIMARK, HAROLD Biomedical research support CHROMOSOMAL ORGANIZATION IN MICROPLASMS
S07RR-05401-30 0862 (NSS) SIDDIQI, FASEEB Biomedical research support LECTIN MEDIATED INHIBITION OF CHEMORECEPTION: SCHISTOSOMA MANSONI
S07RR-05401-30 0863 (NSS) WONG, PETER C Biomedical research support ESTABLISHMENT OF EFFECTIVE PROTOCOL FOR GENE THERAPY
S07RR-05402-30 (NSS) LUCAS, JOHN J SUNY HLTH SCI CTR AT SYRACUSE 750 E ADAMS STREET SYRACUSE, N Y 13210 Biomedical research support
S07RR-05402-30 0791 (NSS) APKARIAN, A VANIA Biomedical research support SOMATOSENSORY NEURONAL POPULATION RESPONSES DUE TO ENVIRONMENTAL CONSTRAINTS
S07RR-05402-30 0792 (NSS) HEATH, JOHN M Biomedical research support WITHDRAWING ANTIHYPERTENSIVE MEDICATIONS FROM LONG TERM CARE PATIENTS
S07RR-05402-30 0793 (NSS) MITCHELL, SUSAN J Biomedical research support FUNCTIONAL NEURAL CIRCUITRY OF BASAL GANGLIA
S07RR-05402-30 0794 (NSS) MARGO, GEOFFREY M Biomedical research support LONG TERM PSYCHOLOGICAL EFFECTS OF CHILDHOOD SEXUAL ABUSE
S07RR-05402-30 0795 (NSS) RICHMAN, ROBERT A Biomedical research support GROWTH FACTORS IN ARTHOGENESIS
S07RR-05402-30 0796 (NSS) STEIN, JOSEPH P Biomedical research support RETINOIC ACID REGULATION OF TISSUE TRANSGLUTAMINASE GENE
S07RR-05402-30 0797 (NSS) SURYA, BABU V Biomedical research support IN VITRO MODEL OF INTERSTITIAL CYSTITIS
S07RR-05402-30 0798 (NSS) PETRYSHYN, RAYMOND A Biomedical research support REGULATION OF GROWTH & DIFFERENTIATION BY INTERFERON
S07RR-05402-30 0799 (NSS) KNOX, BARRY E Biomedical research support MOLECULAR BIOLOGY OF RETINAL DEVELOPMENT IN XENOPUS LAEVIS
S07RR-05402-30 0800 (NSS) MASSA, PAUL T Biomedical research support TRANSCRIPTIONAL CONTROL OF CLASS I MHC GENES IN CNS
S07RR-05402-30 0801 (NSS) STRED, SUSAN E Biomedical research support FUNCTION OF GROWTH HORMONE RECEPTOR IN DIABETES MELLITUS
S07RR-05402-30 0802 (NSS) BRAGDON, ANDREW C Biomedical research support ANATOMY & PHYSIOLOGY OF ENTORHINAL HIPPOCAMPAL SEIZURES IN VITRO
S07RR-05403-30 (NSS) ABRAHAM, GEORGE N UNIVERSITY OF ROCHESTER 601 ELMWOOD AVE. BOX 706 ROCHESTER, N Y 14642 Biomedical research support
S07RR-05403-30 0803 (NSS) BLAIR, MARTHA L Biomedical research support ANTIHYPERTENSIVE EFFECT OF INTERLEUKIN 2
S07RR-05403-30 0804 (NSS) BOHN, MARTHA C Biomedical research support GLUCOCORTICOID EFFECTS ON GENE EXPRESSION IN HIPPOCAMPAL NEURONS
S07RR-05403-30 0805 (NSS) BURNE, ROBERT A Biomedical research support MOLECULAR ANALYSIS OF S MUTANS FRUCTANASE
S07RR-05403-30 0806 (NSS) DEWHURST, STEPHEN Biomedical research support CHARACTERIZATION OF SIV LTR AIDS
S07RR-05403-30 0807 (NSS) DIPERSIO, JOHN F Biomedical research support MANIPULATION OF PRE HEMATOPOIETIC STEM CELLS
S07RR-05403-30 0808 (NSS) GOLDSTEIN, BRAHM Biomedical research support CATECHOLAMINE & HEART RATE POWER SPECTRUM
S07RR-05403-30 0812 (NSS) LEE, FRANK Biomedical research support MULTI STAGE MONITORING OF BONE MARROW CYTOTOXICITY & ANTI LEUKEMIA EFFICACY
S07RR-05403-30 0813 (NSS) MCBRIDE, JOHN T Biomedical research support MITOGENS & COMPENSATORY LUNG GROWTH
S07RR-05403-30 0809 (NSS) GREENAMYRE, J T Biomedical research support ROTENONE BINDING AS PROBE OF COMPLEX I
S07RR-05403-30 0810 (NSS) GUNTER, THOMAS Biomedical research support RELATIONSHIP BETWEEN CA2+ PULSES & REGULATION OF ATP PRODUCTION
S07RR-05403-30 0811 (NSS) JONES, JEFFERY Biomedical research support KINETIC & MECHANISTIC STUDIES OF UDP GLUCURONONSYLTRANSFERASE
S07RR-05403-30 0814 (NSS) MCDANIEL, KEITH D Biomedical research support DELUSIONS IN DEMENTIA OF ALZHEIMERS TYPE: ROLE OF FRONTAL DYSFUNCTION
S07RR-05403-30 0815 (NSS) NING, RUOLA Biomedical research support DEVELOPMENT OF THREE DIMENSIONAL ANGIOGRAPHIC IMAGER
S07RR-05403-30 0816 (NSS) OLSCHOWKA, JOHN Biomedical research support INTERLEUKIN 1 EXPRESSION IN RAT BRAIN
S07RR-05403-30 0817 (NSS) ORLOWSKI, CRAIG C Biomedical research support MOLECULAR BASIS OF HORMONAL REGULATION OF IGFBP 2
S07RR-05403-30 0818 (NSS) PERSECHINI, ANTHONY Biomedical research support ACTIVATION OF INOSITOL 1 4 5 TRISPHOSPHATE 3 KINASE BY CALMODULIN
S07RR-05403-30 0819 (NSS) PHIZICKY, ERIC Biomedical research support GENETICS OF TRNA SPLICING IN YEAST

PROJECT NO., ORGANIZATIONAL UNIT., INVESTIGATOR, ADDRESS, TITLE

S07RR-05403-30 0820 (NSS) PILCHER, WEBSTER Biomedical research support HUMAN BRAIN FUNCTIONS IN AWAKE PATIENTS DURING EPILEPSY SURGERY

S07RR-05403-30 0821 (NSS) PRAKASH, LOUISE Biomedical research support MAMMALIAN DNA REPAIR GENES & PROTEINS

S07RR-05403-30 0822 (NSS) RUDDELL, ALANNA Biomedical research support CHARACTERIZE LRT ENHANCER SEQUENCES INVOLVED IN ALV LYMPHOMAGENESIS

S07RR-05403-30 0823 (NSS) RYAN, RITA Biomedical research support POLYPEPTIDE GF & NEONATAL TYPE II ALVEOLAR EPITHELIAL CELL PROLIFERATION

S07RR-05403-30 0824 (NSS) SCHWARZ, KARL Q Biomedical research support ACOUSTIC ASSISTED FILTRATION

S07RR-05403-30 0825 (NSS) SESHI, BEERELLI Biomedical research support HEMATOPOIETIC PROGENITOR CELL BINDING PROTEINS BY CELL BLOTTING

S07RR-05403-30 0826 (NSS) SLADEK, CELIA Biomedical research support REGULATION OF VASOPRESSIN SECRETION

S07RR-05403-30 0827 (NSS) SMITH, HAROLD C Biomedical research support REGULATION OF APOLIPOPROTEIN B MRNA EDITING BY FLANKING RNA SEQUENCES

S07RR-05403-30 0828 (NSS) SPARKS, JANET D Biomedical research support HEPATIC METABOLISM OF MODIFIED NASCENT APOLIPOPROTEIN B

S07RR-05403-30 0829 (NSS) WOOLF, PAUL D Biomedical research support ETHANOL & SNS FUNCTION IN TRAUMATIC BRAIN INJURY

S07RR-05403-30 0830 (NSS) YAGIL, YORAM Biomedical research support CELLULAR MEDIATOR OF ACTION OF ADENOSINE IN INNER MEDULLARY CONNECTING UNIT

S07RR-05404-30 (NSS) PENRY, J KIFFIN BOWMAN GRAY SCH OF MED 300 SOUTH HAWTHORNE ROAD WINSTON-SALEM, N C 27103 Biomedical research support

S07RR-05404-30 0843 (NSS) HEISE, EUGENE R Biomedical research support MAJOR HISTOCOMPATIBILITY COMPLEX MHC; CYNOMOLOGUS MARAQUE; HAPLOTYPES

S07RR-05404-30 0844 (NSS) HENKEL, CRAIG K Biomedical research support STRUCTURAL BASIS FOR AUDITORY PROCESSING LATERAL LEMNISCUS; BIOCYTIN; AVIDIN;

S07RR-05404-30 0845 (NSS) HERRINGTON, DAVID M Biomedical research support DHEA & ATHEROSCLEROSIS CARDIAC TRANSPLANTATION; ACTH; ESTROGENS

S07RR-05404-30 0846 (NSS) HUTSON, SUSAN Biomedical research support BRANCHED CHAIN AMINOTRANSFERASE ISOENZYMES MITOCHONDRIA; CYTOSOL; ENZYMES;

S07RR-05404-30 0831 (NSS) ALFORD, PETER T Biomedical research support PULMONARY DYSFUNCT CHICKEN GROWERS: ENVIRON HLTH; DUST; ASTHMA; CHRONIC BRONCHI

S07RR-05404-30 0832 (NSS) APPLEBAUM-BOWDEN, DE Biomedical research support LIPID TRANSFER ZONE IN HUMAN PLASMA: LIPOPROTEINS; CHOLESTEROL ESTER; HDL

S07RR-05404-30 0833 (NSS) APPLEGATE, ROBERT J Biomedical research support PERICARDIUM ON LEFT VENTRICULAR PERFORMANCE CORONARY ARTERY ISCHEMIA

S07RR-05404-30 0834 (NSS) BENNETT, BARBARA A Biomedical research support COCAINE ON CULTURED MESENCEPHALIC DOPAMINE NEURONS TYROSINE HYDROXYLASE

S07RR-05404-30 0835 (NSS) BIDDULPH, DAVID Biomedical research support PROSTAGLANDINS & CYCLIC AMP; CHONDROGENESIS PGE2; LIMB MESENCHYME;

S07RR-05404-30 0836 (NSS) BLIZZARD, DAVID Biomedical research support HEMODYNAMIC ADAPTATION TO PREGNANCY: RAT BLOOD PRESSURE; HEART RATE; NUTRITION

S07RR-05404-30 0837 (NSS) BREWER, GARY A Biomedical research support REGULATION OF ONCOGENE MESSENGER RNA LEVELS; PROTO ONCOGENE; MYC;

S07RR-05404-30 0847 (NSS) KORITNIK, DONALD R Biomedical research support CONTROL OF STEROID SENSITIVE HEPATIC PROTEINS GENDER DIFF; HEPATIC ANDROGEN

S07RR-05404-30 0848 (NSS) KUCERA, LOUIS S Biomedical research support HIV 1 GLYCOPROTEIN MEMBRANE DISTRIBUTION PLASMA MEMBRANE;

S07RR-05404-30 0849 (NSS) MILLER, LARRY R Biomedical research support C REACTIVE PROTEIN IN ATHEROSCLEROSIS: MACROPHAGE LIPOPROTEINS;

S07RR-05404-30 0850 (NSS) MORYKWAS, MICHAEL J Biomedical research support CULTURED KERATINOCYTES FOR FETAL WOUND HEALING: AUTOGRAFTS; AMNIOTIC FLUID

S07RR-05404-30 0851 (NSS) PERRINO, FRED W Biomedical research support ARACMP INTO DNA POLYMERASE MYLOBLASTS; LYMPHOBLASTS; LEUKEMIA; EXONUCLEOLYTIC

S07RR-05404-30 0852 (NSS) PHILP, ELIZABETH Biomedical research support PROGESTERONE & ESTRADIOL CHANGES IN PMS: HEADACHE; MIGRANE; HORMONE

S07RR-05404-30 0853 (NSS) REGISTER, THOMAS C Biomedical research support ATHEROGENESIS & ARTERIAL HEPARAN SULFATE PROTEOGLYCANS: ATHEROSCLEROSIS

S07RR-05404-30 0854 (NSS) ROSE, JAMES C Biomedical research support ATRIAL NATRIURETIC FACTOR EFFECTS: AVP RENIN SECRETION VASOPRESSIN; SHEEP

S07RR-05404-30 0855 (NSS) RYU, JAI H Biomedical research support PERILYMPHATIC FISTULAS TEMPORAL BONE: CAT; AUDITORY BRAINSTEM

S07RR-05404-30 0856 (NSS) SANTAGO, PETER Biomedical research support MEDICAL IMAGE PROCESSING ANALYSIS MAGNETIC RESONANCE IMAGING; CARDIAC BLOOD FLOW

S07RR-05404-30 0857 (NSS) ST CLAIR, WILLIAM H Biomedical research support CELLULAR TRANSFORMED BY TOBACCO LEAF PROTEASE INHIBIT: CHYMOTRYPSIN INHIBITOR I

S07RR-05404-30 0858 (NSS) SHELNESS, GREGORY S Biomedical research support CANINE SIGNAL PEPTIDASE COMPLEX: TRANSLOCATION; OLIGOMERIC

S07RR-05404-30 0859 (NSS) SMITH, THOMAS L Biomedical research support CV EFFECTS OF COCAINE & CEREBRAL MICROCIRCULATION: TACHYPHYLAXIS; ANGIOGENESIS

S07RR-05404-30 0860 (NSS) SUNDBERG, DAVID K Biomedical research support OXYTOCIN & GENE EXPRESSION BRAIN PEPTIDES: IBOTINIC ACID; OLFACTORY BULBS

PROJECT NO., ORGANIZATIONAL UNIT., INVESTIGATOR, ADDRESS, TITLE

S07RR-05404-30 0861 (NSS) THUREN, TOM Y Biomedical research support HEPATIC LIPASE BY APOLIPOPROTEINS PHOSPHOLIPID; APOLIPOPROTEIN E; HDL

S07RR-05404-30 0862 (NSS) TOWNSEND, ALAN J Biomedical research support GLUTATHIONE S TRANSFERASE EXPRESSION IN CELLULAR DEFENSES AGAINST MUTAGENESIS

S07RR-05404-30 0863 (NSS) TUCKER, RICHARD P Biomedical research support TENASCIN MRNA NEURONAL & NON NEURONAL IN TISSUES: CDNA PROBES

S07RR-05404-30 0864 (NSS) TURNER, JAMES E Biomedical research support PHOTORECEPTOR CELL: RETINAL DYSTROPHY ANIMAL MODEL; AGING; CELL GRAFTING;

S07RR-05404-30 0865 (NSS) WALLEN, C ANNE Biomedical research support HETEROGENEITY OF HEAT CYTOTOXICITY IN TUMOR P Q CELLS: RADIATION MAMMARY TUMORS

S07RR-05404-30 0866 (NSS) ZANOLI, MICHAEL D Biomedical research support PLAQUES OF PSORIASIS: KERATINOCYTE HERNIATION PAPILLAE; NEUTROPHILS

S07RR-05404-30 0838 (NSS) BUTTERWORTH, JOHN F Biomedical research support TONIC & PHASIC ACTIONS OF LOCAL ANESTHETICS IN BRAIN CELLS; LIDOCAINE;

S07RR-05404-30 0839 (NSS) CARLSON, CATHY S Biomedical research support RADIOGRAPH OF STIFLE JOINT IN CYNOMOLGUS MACAQUES; OSTEOARTHRITIS; ARTICULAR

S07RR-05404-30 0840 (NSS) CROUSE, J ROBERT Biomedical research support ADIPOSE DISTRIBUTION & RELATED PARAMETERS: LIPIDS; CHOLESTEROL; DYSLIPIDEMIA

S07RR-05404-30 0841 (NSS) DAWSON, PAUL A Biomedical research support CLONING ILEAL BILE ACID TRANSPORTER: ATHEROSCLEROSIS;

S07RR-05404-30 0842 (NSS) FITZGERALD, DAVID M Biomedical research support ABLATION OF RHYTHM DISTURBANCES: CARDIAC ARRHYTHMIA; TACHYCARDIA;

S07RR-05405-30 (NSS) SNYDERMAN, RALPH DUKE UNIVERSITY MEDICAL CENTER P O BOX 3001 DURHAM, NC 27710 Biomedical research support

S07RR-05405-30 0874 (NSS) LEVENSON, RICHARD Biomedical research support EFFECTS OF INSULIN; ON PHOSPHORYLATION & DEPHOSPHORYLATION OF PROTEINS

S07RR-05405-30 0875 (NSS) SCHMADER, KEN Biomedical research support VIRAL DISEASE LATENCY & AGING

S07RR-05405-30 0867 (NSS) LIEBERMAN, MELVYN Biomedical research support CARDIOTOXICITY OF CHEMOTHERAPEUTIC AGENTS

S07RR-05405-30 0868 (NSS) BALES, CONNIE W Biomedical research support ASSESS DIETARY & BIOCHEMICAL INDICATORS OF ZINC STATUS IN ELDERLY WOMEN

S07RR-05405-30 0869 (NSS) BEARON, LUCILLE Biomedical research support CANCER STUDY DEALING W/ HOW PATIENTS UNDERSTAND THEIR SYMPTOMS

S07RR-05405-30 0870 (NSS) GOLD, DEBORAH T Biomedical research support OSTEOPOROSIS STUDY

S07RR-05405-30 0871 (NSS) HOBBINS, MELODY Biomedical research support PROJECT ON MASTICATORY MUSCLE CONTRACTION ESTABLISHMENT OF DENTAL DATA BASE

S07RR-05405-30 0872 (NSS) JACKSON, THOMAS Biomedical research support RESEARCH PROJECTS ON GREENERY REHABILITATION PATIENTS

S07RR-05405-30 0873 (NSS) KOCHERSBERGER, GARY Biomedical research support EXAMINATION OF DELIVERY OF REHABILITATION IN LONG TERM CARE SETTING

S07RR-05405-30 0876 (NSS) WEINBERGER, MORRIS Biomedical research support STUDY ON CAREGIVERS OF PATIENTS W/ ALZHEIMERS DISEASE

S07RR-05405-30 0877 (NSS) WEINER, DEBRA Biomedical research support RADIOGRAPHIC ARTHRITIS OF LUMBOSACRAL SPINE VS BACK RANGE MOTION

S07RR-05406-30 (NSS) BONDURANT, STUART UNIVERSITY OF NORTH CAROLINA CB#7000, 125 MCNIDER CHAPEL HILL, N C 27599 Biomedical research support

S07RR-05406-30 0878 (NSS) ALKEMINDERS, LOUIS C Biomedical research support PROSTAGLANDIN LEVELS FOLLOWING AN EXPERIMENTAL MUSCLE STRAIN

S07RR-05406-30 0879 (NSS) AZIZKHAN, RICHARD G Biomedical research support IN VIVO CHARACTERIZATION OF GRO GENE IN HUMAN COLONIC TUMORS

S07RR-05406-30 0880 (NSS) BENTLEY, STUART A Biomedical research support HEMATOPOIETIC STROMAL PROTEOGLYCANS

S07RR-05406-30 0905 (NSS) EARP, H SHELTON Biomedical research support CLONING SUBCLONING DNA SEQ OF B CELL TYROSINE KINASE; DEVELOP PROBE FOR ALL

S07RR-05406-30 0906 (NSS) FABER, JAMES E Biomedical research support ALPHA1 ALPHA2 ADRENOCEPTORS W/ CONTRACTILE CALCIUM; MICROVASCULAR SMOOTH MUSCLE

S07RR-05406-30 0907 (NSS) FALK, RONALD J Biomedical research support EFFECTS OF ANCA ON NEUTROPHILS IN PRESENCE OF ENDOTHELIAL CELL MONOLAYERS

S07RR-05406-30 0908 (NSS) GILLIGAN, PETER Biomedical research support MICROBIOLOGIC QUALITY OF DRINKING WATER; INTERVENTIONS IN HIGHLANDS GUATEMALA

S07RR-05406-30 0909 (NSS) KALET, ADINA Biomedical research support DOCTALK: HOW DOCTORS TALK W/ PATIENTS ABOUT RISK

S07RR-05406-30 0910 (NSS) LANNON, CAROLE Biomedical research support EFFECTS OF CHOLESTEROL SCREENING IN CHILDREN

S07RR-05406-30 0911 (NSS) LIU, EDISON Biomedical research support MOLECULAR GENETICS OF LEUKEMIC PROGRESSION: CHARACTERIZATION OF AXL ONCOGENE

S07RR-05406-30 0912 (NSS) MAEDA, NOBUYO Biomedical research support MARKER GENE HOMOLOGOUS RECOMBINAT INTO TRANSGENIC MICE; GENE FUNCT DURING DVMT

S07RR-05406-30 0913 (NSS) PETRUSZ, PETER Biomedical research support IMMUNOCYTOCHEMISTRY ID OF EXCITATORY AMINO ACID RECEPTORS IN VERTEBRATE CNS

S07RR-05406-30 0914 (NSS) PRAZMA, JIRI Biomedical research support LONG TERM NOREPINEPHRINE ADMINISTRATION & COCHLEAR BLOOD FLOW

S07RR-05406-30 0881 (NSS) DYKSTRA, CHRISTINE C Biomedical research support P CARINII PNEUMONIA: IDENTIFICATION OF PENTAMIDINE THERAPEUTIC TARGET

S07RR-05406-30 0882 (NSS) GOY, MICHAEL F Biomedical research support FUNCTIONAL & STRUCTURAL ANALYSIS OF PARTICULATE CYCLASE

S07RR-05406-30 0883 (NSS) HAGGERTY, JOHN J, JR Biomedical research support ACETYLCHOLINESTERASE AUTOIMMUNITY IN PSYCHIATRIC ILLNESS

S07RR-05406-30 0884 (NSS) HOPFER, ROY L Biomedical research support STRAINS OF C ALBICANS ARE ISOLATED BASED ON ADHERENCE TO DIFFERENT

TISSUES

S07RR-05406-30 0885 (NSS) LAI, ERIC H C Biomedical research support DEVELOPMENT OF ARTIFICAL VECTORS AS VEHICLES FOR CLONING LARGE DNA FRAGMENTS

S07RR-05406-30 0886 (NSS) JOHNSTONE, BRIAN Biomedical research support PROTEOGLYCANS FROM HERNIATED HUMAN INTERVERTEBRAL DISKS; MABS

S07RR-05406-30 0887 (NSS) LORD, SUSAN T Biomedical research support ANALYSIS OF CELL BINDING DOMAINS OF HUMAN FIBRINOGEN

S07RR-05406-30 0888 (NSS) MANNING, JAMES E Biomedical research support SELECTIVE HEART & BRAIN PROFUSION W/ PERFLUOROCHEMICAL DURING CARDIAC ARREST

S07RR-05406-30 0889 (NSS) OSAWA, SHOJI Biomedical research support SITE OF G PROTEIN ALPHA SUBUNIT AMINO TERMINUS W/ PROTEIN BETA GAMMA DIMERS

S07RR-05406-30 0890 (NSS) RINEHART, CLIFFORD A Biomedical research support INHIBITION OF NEOPLASTIC TRANSFORMATION BY ANTISENSE MYC OR FOS: ENDOMETRIUM

S07RR-05406-30 0891 (NSS) WEISS, ELLEN R Biomedical research support CONSTRUCTION OF CHIMERIC G PROTEIN SUBUNITS TO DEFINE EFFECTOR INTERACTIONS

S07RR-05406-30 0892 (NSS) WEISSMAN, BERNARD E Biomedical research support RO1 OF ANNEXIN 1 IN CONTROL OF EPIDERMAL DIFFERENTIATION

S07RR-05406-30 0893 (NSS) BOWDRE, JEAN H Biomedical research support GENE AMPLIFICATION & EXPRESSION IN MULTI DRUG RESISTANT PLASMODIUM FALCIPARUM

S07RR-05406-30 0894 (NSS) CURIEL, DAVID T Biomedical research support GENE TRANSFER TO RESPIRATORY EPITHELIUM USING MOLECULAR CONJUGATES: LF

S07RR-05406-30 0895 (NSS) HASSETT, DANIEL J Biomedical research support PSEUDOMONAS AERUGINOSA: ALGINATE PYOCYANIN & OXIDANT STRESS; CF; GENETIC REGULAT

S07RR-05406-30 0896 (NSS) HAYWARD, JAMES N Biomedical research support CENTRAL NEURAL REGULATION OF VASOPRESSIN SECRETION; RAT HYPOTHALAMUS

S07RR-05406-30 0897 (NSS) JOHNSTON, ROBERT E Biomedical research support MOLECULAR GENETICS OF ALPHAVIRUS PATHOGENESIS; VACCINES; MUTAGENESIS

S07RR-05406-30 0898 (NSS) PARISE, LESLIE V Biomedical research support ACTIVATION OF PLATELET GLYCOPROTEIN IIB IIIA

S07RR-05406-30 0899 (NSS) PARISE, LESLIE V Biomedical research support MOLECULAR BASIS OF SICKLE CELL ADHESION TO ENDOLTHELIUM

S07RR-05406-30 0900 (NSS) PRYZWANSKY, KATHERIN Biomedical research support REGULATION OF NEUTROPHIL FUNCTIONS BY CYCLIC GMP: HUMAN

S07RR-05406-30 0901 (NSS) SEALOCK, ROBERT Biomedical research support DYSTROPHIN & DYSTROPHIN ASSOCIATED PROTEINS: DUCHENNE MUSCULAR DYSTROPHY

S07RR-05406-30 0902 (NSS) WEISS, ELLEN R Biomedical research support APPLE COMPUTER & PRINTER

S07RR-05406-30 0903 (NSS) WYRICK, PRISCILLA B Biomedical research support CLONING CHLAMYDIA TRACHOMATIS ADHESIN GENES; STD

S07RR-05406-30 0915 (NSS) PRAZMA, JIRI Biomedical research support AUTONOMIC CONTROL OF COCHLEAR MICROCIRCULATION

S07RR-05406-30 0916 (NSS) HERMAN, BRIAN Biomedical research support AUTOMATED CLINICAL IMAGE CYTOMETRY WOMENS DISEASES

S07RR-05406-30 0904 (NSS) ANGLE, MARCIA Biomedical research support KENYAN HEALTH CARE PROVIDERS ATTITUDES TOWARD HIV INFECTION & AIDS PATIENTS

S07RR-05407-30 (NSS) NORDLIE, ROBERT C UNIVERSITY OF NORTH DAKOTA UNIVERSITY STATION GRAND FORKS, N DAK 58202 Biomedical research support grant

S07RR-05407-30 0043 (NSS) STINNETT, HENRY Biomedical research support grant A & D CONVERSION & ANALYSIS

S07RR-05407-30 0044 (NSS) POLITOFF, ALBERTO L Biomedical research support grant CLINICAL NEUROPHYSIOLOGY OF DOWNS SYNDROME

S07RR-05407-30 0045 (NSS) KERBESHIAN, LYNN Biomedical research support grant ANALYSIS W/ HYPERLEXIA

S07RR-05407-30 0046 (NSS) WONDERLICH, STEVEN Biomedical research support grant BULIMIA & ANXIETY DISORDER

S07RR-05407-30 0047 (NSS) SUMBURERU, DALE Biomedical research support grant NORTH DAKOTA DIABETES REGISTRY

S07RR-05407-30 0048 (NSS) JOSHI, MADHUSUDAN S Biomedical research support grant RAT UTERINE ENDOPEPTIDASE

S07RR-05407-30 0049 (NSS) KNULL, HARVEY Biomedical research support grant INTERACTION OF GLYCOLYTIC ENZYMES

S07RR-05407-30 0050 (NSS) LONG, WILLIAM Biomedical research support grant ISOLATED PROFUSED CANINE STUDIES

S07RR-05407-30 0051 (NSS) ROSS, ELLIOTT Biomedical research support grant RT HEMISPHERE DYSFUNCTION

S07RR-05407-30 0052 (NSS) SUKALSKI, KATHERINE Biomedical research support grant OXIDATIVE MODIFICATION OF MEMBRANE ASSOC PROTEIN

S07RR-05408-30 (NSS) HUTTON, JOHN J, JR UNIVERSITY OF CINCINNATI 231 BETHESDA AVENUE CINCINNATI, OHIO 45267 Biomedical research support

S07RR-05408-30 0917 (NSS) BAKER, VICKI V Biomedical research support CERVICAL CELL DNA OF SMOKING VERSUS NON SMOKING WOMEN: MOLECULAR ALTERATIONS

S07RR-05408-30 0918 (NSS) BHAT, GEETHA Biomedical research support NONINVASIVE DETECTION OF CARDIAC ALLOGRAFT REJECTION: URINARY POLYAMINES CGMS

S07RR-05408-30 0919 (NSS) BLISARD, KAREN S Biomedical research support GLUTAMINERGIC MECHANISMS IN CHEMICAL EPILEPTOGENESIS: FROG

S07RR-05408-30 0920 (NSS) BOISSY, RAYMOND E Biomedical research support GLYCOPROTEIN GENE PRODUCTS PRE GOLGI NETWORK; MELANOCYTE SYSTEM MUTANT MODELS

S07RR-05408-30 0921 (NSS) BURNHAM, CHARLES E Biomedical research support MOLECULAR CLONING OF RAT RENAL NA K C1 COTRANSPORTER

S07RR-05408-30 0922 (NSS) CREWS, JAMES C Biomedical research support RODENT MODEL; INVESTIGATION OF TOURNIQUET PAIN

S07RR-05408-30 0923 (NSS) CROEN, KENNETH D Biomedical research support PROMOTER FOR LATENCY & ASSOCIATED TRANSCRIPTS (LATS) OF HSV 1

S07RR-05408-30 0924 (NSS) CUSHION, MELANIE T Biomedical research support TRANSMISSION OF PNEUMOCYSTIS CARINII INFECTION

S07RR-05408-30 0925 (NSS) DIMLICH, RUTH V W Biomedical research support PYRUVATE DEHYDROGENASE ENZYME COMPLEX ASTROCYTES; BRAIN LACTATE CEREBRAL EDEMA

S07RR-05408-30 0926 (NSS) EVERSON, WILLIAM V Biomedical research support HORMONAL REGULATION OF ANNEXIN EXPRESSION IN HUMAN AMNION

S07RR-05408-30 0927 (NSS) FERGUSON, DONALD G Biomedical research support IMMUNOLOCALIZATION OF TRIADIC JUNCTIONAL PROTEINS

S07RR-05408-30 0928 (NSS) GLASSER, STEPHAN W Biomedical research support TOXIC PHENOTYPE TO DEVELOPING PULMONARY EPITHELIUM; INFANT MORTALITY

S07RR-05408-30 0929 (NSS) HOROWITZ, ZEBULUN D Biomedical research support HORMONAL CONTROL OF DIFFERENTIATION IN HUMAN NEUROBLASTOMA CELLS IN CULTURE

S07RR-05408-30 0930 (NSS) JAMIESON, GORDON A, Biomedical research support TRANSFORMATION ALTERATIONS IN BRADYKININ ACTIVATED EICOSANOID METABOLISM

S07RR-05408-30 0931 (NSS) KHAN, SOHAIB A Biomedical research support ESTROGEN INDUCED CELL PROLIFERATION OF UTERINE TISSUES

S07RR-05408-30 0932 (NSS) MCLAUGHLIN, MARGARET Biomedical research support PREGNANCY INDUCED CHANGES IN VASCULAR WALL PROTEINS

S07RR-05408-30 0933 (NSS) MINNEMA, DANIEL J Biomedical research support CARNOSINE AS NEUROTRANSMITTER IN OLFACTORY BULB

S07RR-05408-30 0934 (NSS) MURPHY, R MAUREEN Biomedical research support DEVELOPMENT OF ALZHEIMERS SPECIFIC MONOCLONAL ANTIBODIES

S07RR-05408-30 0935 (NSS) NORGREN, ROBERT B Biomedical research support MIGRATION OF LHRH CONTAINING NEURONS IN DEVELOPING FROG EMBRYO

S07RR-05408-30 0936 (NSS) PAMUKCU, RIFA Biomedical research support GTP BINDING PROTEINS IN REGULATION OF ENTEROCYTE PROLIFERATION & MATURATION

S07RR-05408-30 0937 (NSS) QUINLAN, JOHN G Biomedical research support INHIBITION OF REGENERATION IN MDX MOUSE MUSCLE

S07RR-05408-30 0938 (NSS) RYMASZEWSKI, ZBIGNIE Biomedical research support TRANSGENIC MICE; SECRETE GROWTH HORMONE DIABETIC RETINOPATHY

S07RR-05408-30 0939 (NSS) SINDEN, RICHARD R Biomedical research support EXISTENCE OF TRIPLE STRANDED H DNA IN VIVO

S07RR-05408-30 0940 (NSS) SLEIGHT, RICHARD G Biomedical research support NEW ASSAYS FOR LIVER PHOSPHOLIPID FLIPPASE ACTIVITY

S07RR-05408-30 0941 (NSS) SMITH, ERIC P Biomedical research support SERTOLI CELL FIBROBLAST GROWTH FACTOR; MALE REPRODUCTIVE SPERMATOGENESIS

S07RR-05408-30 0942 (NSS) STOLZ, RUTH I Biomedical research support ISOACTIN EXPRESSION IN SPONTANEOUSLY HYPERTENSIVE RAT HEART & AORTA

S07RR-05408-30 0943 (NSS) SUSZKIW, JANUSZ B Biomedical research support NEUROBIOLOGY OF SEPTOHIPPOCAMPAL CHOLINERGIC NEURONS IN CELL CULTURE

S07RR-05408-30 0944 (NSS) TALASKA, GLENN Biomedical research support CARCINOGEN DNA ADDUCTS IN EXFOLIATED LUNG CELLS

S07RR-05408-30 0945 (NSS) TRICOLI, JAMES V Biomedical research support MOLECULAR GENETICS & EXPRESSION ZFY GENE IN HUMAN RENAL CELL CARCINOMA

S07RR-05409-30 (NSS) CORNWELL, DAVID G OHIO ST UNIV, 260 MEILING HALL 370 W 10TH AVENUE COLUMBUS, OH 43210 Biomedical research support

S07RR-05409-30 0503 (NSS) CORNWELL, DAVID G Biomedical research support NO RESEARCH SUBPROJECTS

S07RR-05410-30 (NSS) CHERNIACK, NEIL S CASE WESTERN RESERVE UNIV 2109 ADELBERT ROAD CLEVELAND, OH 44106-4901 Biomedical research support

S07RR-05410-30 0946 (NSS) DANISH, ELIZABETH Biomedical research support RHEOLOGIC PROPERTIES OF SICKLE HEMOGLOBIN CELLS

S07RR-05410-30 0947 (NSS) GUDELSKY, GARY Biomedical research support NEUROPHARMACOLOGY OF ATYPICAL ANTIPSYCHOTICS

S07RR-05410-30 0948 (NSS) HARRIS, JOHN Biomedical research support HIGH TECHNETIUM MAGNETOMETRIC EVALUATION OF HUMAN IRON STORES

S07RR-05410-30 0949 (NSS) KERR, DOUGLAS Biomedical research support ENZYME ACTIVITY IN CHILDREN W/ INBORN ERRORS OF CARBOHYDRATE OXIDATION

S07RR-05410-30 0950 (NSS) LARGE, THOMAS Biomedical research support STRUCTURE OF NGF NT4 GENE & EFFECTS ON DEVELOPING NERVOUS SYSTEM

S07RR-05410-30 0954 (NSS) ZIGMOND, RICHARD E Biomedical research support MALLEABILITY OF ADULT NERVOUS SYSTEM & RECOVERY AFTER NEURAL DAMAGE

S07RR-05410-30 0955 (NSS) PAYNE, SUSAN L Biomedical research support GENE REGULATION IN EQUINE INFECTIOUS ANEMIA VIRUS; AIDS

S07RR-05410-30 0956 (NSS) SHOHAM, MENACHAM Biomedical research support CRYSTAL STRUCTURE OF ANTICHOLERA TOXIN IN COMPLEX W/ AN ANTIGENIC PEPTIDE

S07RR-05410-30 0951 (NSS) PIOTROWSKI, JOSEPH Biomedical research support OXYGEN RADICAL INDUCED MEMBRANE DAMAGE IN DEVELOPMENT OF ATHEROSCLEROSIS

S07RR-05410-30 0952 (NSS) ROBBINS, NORMAN Biomedical research support IMMUNOLOCALIZATION OF PROTEINS BY ULTRACRYOMICROTOMY

S07RR-05410-30 0953 (NSS) SALZ, HELEN K Biomedical research support REGULATION OF SEX LETHAL: IDENTIFICATION OF NEW SEX DETERMINATION GENES

S07RR-05411-30 (NSS) BRANDT, EDWARD JR UNIV OF OKLA COLL OF MEDICINE P.O. BOX 26901 OKLAHOMA CITY, OK 73190 Biomedical research support

S07RR-05411-30 0957 (NSS) OGILVIE, ROBERT W Biomedical research support DRUG ASSISTED EXERCISE TRAINING THERAPY & ARTERIAL INSUFFICIENCY

S07RR-05411-30 0958 (NSS) GARRETT, K M Biomedical research support EXPRESSION OF GABA A RECEPTOR SUBUNITS: LOCALIZATION & QUANTITATION

S07RR-05411-30 0959 (NSS) HANSON-PAINTON, O Biomedical research support FUNCTIONAL ANALYSIS OF CALMODULIN GENE PROMOTER

S07RR-05411-30 0960 (NSS) ROLF, L L, JR Biomedical research support ANTIBIOTIC ASSOCIATED ENEROCOLITIS IN GUINEA PIG

S07RR-05411-30 0961 (NSS) SILAVIN, S Biomedical research support REGULATION OF HUMAN PLACENTAL ENDOCRINE FUNCTION BY PROTEIN KINASE C

S07RR-05411-30 0962 (NSS) THOMPSON, A M Biomedical research support OLIVOCOCHLEAR INNERVATION OF COCHLEAR NUCLEUS

S07RR-05411-30 0963 (NSS) STITH, R D Biomedical research support EFFECT OF INTERLEUKIN 6 ON HEPATIC PROTEIN SYNTHESIS

S07RR-05411-30 0964 (NSS) ODONOGHUE, D L Biomedical research support INFLUENCE OF METENCEPHALIC DEVELOPMENT ON CORTICOSPINAL AXON

ELIMINATION
S07RR-05411-30 0965 (NSS) GONZALES, L Biomedical research support PREVENTING CNS ADAPTATIONS TO CHRONIC COCAINE
S07RR-05411-30 0966 (NSS) ROSSAVIK, I K Biomedical research support RESEARCH CONCERNING DIAGNOSTIC ULTRASOUND INVESTIGATIONS
S07RR-05411-30 0967 (NSS) CUNNINGHAM, M W Biomedical research support FLOW CYTOMETRY CORE LABORATORY SUPPORT
S07RR-05412-30 (NSS) KENDALL, JOHN W, JR OREGON HLTH SCI UNIV 3181 SW SAM JACKSON PARK RD PORTLAND, OR 97201-3098 Biomedical research support
S07RR-05412-30 0968 (NSS) OLSEN, GEORGE D Biomedical research support FETAL COCAINE EXPOSURE: EFFECT ON NEONATAL BREATHING
S07RR-05412-30 0969 (NSS) KLEIN, ROBERT F Biomedical research support HORMONAL CONTROL OF OSTEOBLAST
S07RR-05412-30 0970 (NSS) THURMOND, AMY S Biomedical research support OUTPATIENT TRANSCERVICAL TUBAL STERILIZATION
S07RR-05412-30 0971 (NSS) ADELMAN, JOHN P Biomedical research support POTASSIUM CHANNELS & GONADOTROPIN RELEASING HORMONE & MOLECULAR BIOLOGY
S07RR-05412-30 0972 (NSS) MACRAE, SCOTT Biomedical research support EFFECT OF CONTACT LENSES ON CORNEAL ENDOTHELIUM
S07RR-05412-30 0973 (NSS) BARKLIS, ERIC Biomedical research support RETROVIRUS HOST RANGE STUDIES
S07RR-05412-30 0974 (NSS) BAUMANN, THOMAS K Biomedical research support HYPEREXCITABILITY OF SOMATIC PRIMARY EFFERENT NEURONS
S07RR-05412-30 0975 (NSS) PIATT, JOSEPH H, JR Biomedical research support CSF SHUNT INSERTION TECHNIQUES & MATH ANALYSIS OF INTRACRANIAL PRESSURE WAVEFORM
S07RR-05412-30 0976 (NSS) PAYAMI, HAYDEH Biomedical research support GENETIC SUSCEPTIBILITY TO ALZHEIMERS DISEASE
S07RR-05412-30 0977 (NSS) GRAVETT, MICHAEL G Biomedical research support DVMT OF NON HUMAN PRIMATE MODEL RELATION OF MATERNAL GENITAL TRACT INFECTIONS
S07RR-05412-30 0978 (NSS) LEONE, MICHAEL R Biomedical research support PLATELET SEROTONIN CONTENT IN PATIENTS W/ KIDNEY DISEASES & KIDNEY TRANSPLANTS
S07RR-05412-30 0979 (NSS) GANCHER, STEPHEN T Biomedical research support ACTIVITY MONITORS FOR QUANTIFYING ALTERATIONS IN BRAIN FUNCTION
S07RR-05412-30 0980 (NSS) HENNER, WILLIAM D Biomedical research support PRODUCT & TRANSFECT OF RECOMBINANT DNA PLASMIDS INTO MAMMALIAN CELLS; GENE
S07RR-05412-30 0981 (NSS) HOSENPUD, JEFFREY D Biomedical research support RECIPIENT IMMUNE RESPONSE TO DONOR SPECIFIC ENDOTHELIUM
S07RR-05412-30 0982 (NSS) SHANGRAW, ROBERT E Biomedical research support CORI CYCLE REGULATION DURING LIVER TRANSPLANTATION
S07RR-05412-30 0983 (NSS) MOSES, ROBB E Biomedical research support RESEARCH OF DNA MUTAGENESIS & REPAIR
S07RR-05413-30 (NSS) WOLLMAN, HARRY HAHNEMANN UNIV SCH OF MED BROAD AND VINE MS 4444 PHILADELPHIA, PA 19102-1192 Biomedical research support grant
S07RR-05413-30 0984 (NSS) RAIBLE, DONALD Biomedical research support grant MECHANISMS OF HUMAN MAST CELL EOSINOPHIL INTERACTION
S07RR-05413-30 0985 (NSS) REBOLI, ANNETTE C Biomedical research support grant DOT IMMUNOBINDING W/ ASSAY TO IDENTIFY CANDIDIASIS
S07RR-05413-30 0986 (NSS) SLIZOFSKI, WALTER Biomedical research support grant SPECT FUNCTIONAL BRAIN IMAGING ASSESSMENT PROCESSING SYSTEMS SPELLING
S07RR-05413-30 0987 (NSS) YASSIN, RIHAB Biomedical research support grant PROTEIN KINASE C & GUANINE BINDING IN MEDIATING COLONIC EPITHELIAL TROPHIC; GI
S07RR-05413-30 0988 (NSS) BRENT, LAWRENCE H Biomedical research support grant POTASSIUM CHANNELS IN HUMAN B CELL DEVELOPMENT
S07RR-05413-30 0989 (NSS) BUCCELLI, PAMELA Biomedical research support grant IMPACT OF AIDS ON ALLIED HEALTH & NURSING RECRUITMENT
S07RR-05413-30 0990 (NSS) COPE, TIMOTHY Biomedical research support grant NEUROPHYSIOLOGY RESEARCH
S07RR-05413-30 0991 (NSS) BRAMUCCI, MICHAEL Biomedical research support grant BACILLUS SUBTILIS GENES REQUIRED BACTERIOPHAGE ENHANCED SPORULATION
S07RR-05413-30 0992 (NSS) SMITH, SHERYL Biomedical research support grant NEUROANATOMY RESEARCH
S07RR-05414-30 (NSS) GONNELLA, JOSEPH S THOMAS JEFFERSON UNIVERSITY JEFF MED COL, 1025 WALNUT ST PHILADELPHIA, PA 19107 Biomedical research support
S07RR-05414-30 0993 (NSS) BARCHOWSKY, AARON Biomedical research support OXIDANT STIMULATION OF PROTEIN PHOSPHORYLATION IN ENDOTHELIAL CELLS
S07RR-05414-30 0994 (NSS) OVERHAUSER, JOAN M Biomedical research support LOCALIZATION OF GENE CAUSING CORNELIA DE LANG SYNDROME
S07RR-05414-30 0995 (NSS) ZALEWSKI, ANDREW P Biomedical research support VASCULAR WALL INJURY ON CENTRAL COMPONENTS OF FIBRINOLYTIC SYSTEM
S07RR-05414-30 0996 (NSS) MCHUGH, KIRK M Biomedical research support CHARACTERIZATION OF ACTIN GENE EXPRESSION IN CONGENITAL MEGACOLON
S07RR-05414-30 0997 (NSS) PIZZUTILLO, PETER D Biomedical research support HORMONAL & MECHANICAL INDUCTION OF FEMORAL SLIPPED EPIPHYSES IN RATS
S07RR-05414-30 0998 (NSS) SCHWARTING, ROLAND Biomedical research support MUCOSA ASSOCIATED HML 1 LATE ACTIVATION ANTIGEN
S07RR-05414-30 0999 (NSS) CARO, JAIME Biomedical research support ERYTHROPOIETIN BIOGENESIS
S07RR-05415-30 (NSS) KEFALIDES, NICHOLAS A UNIVERSITY OF PENNSYLVANIA SCHOOL OF MED, DEAN'S OFFICE PHILADELPHIA, PA 19104-6055 Facility improvement for smith hall animal facility
S07RR-05415-30 0013 (NSS) LESSEY, BRUCE A Facility improvement for smith hall animal facility PHENOTYPIC EXPRESSION OF HUMAN ENDOMETRIUM IN VITRO
S07RR-05415-30 0014 (NSS) LIANG, BRUCE T Facility improvement for smith hall animal facility HETEROLOGUS REGULATION OF CARDIAC ADENOSINE RECEPTOR
S07RR-05415-30 0015 (NSS) MONROE, JOHN G Facility improvement for smith hall animal facility DEVELOPMENTAL BIOLOGY OF B LYMPHOCYTE ACTIVATION SIGNALLING
S07RR-05415-30 0016 (NSS) NACHMIAS, VIVIAN T Facility improvement for smith hall animal facility ACTIN IN CELL PROCESSES & CELL ELONGATION
S07RR-05415-30 0017 (NSS) RONNER, PETER Facility improvement for smith hall animal facility FLOW CYTOMETRY & ELECTROPHYSIOLOGY OF PANCREATIC A CELLS
S07RR-05415-30 0018 (NSS) ROSS, DOUGLAS T Facility improvement for smith hall animal facility DEGENERATION OF THALAMIC RETICULAR NUCLEUS
S07RR-05415-30 0019 (NSS) SILBERSTEIN, LESLIE Facility improvement for smith hall animal facility MOLECULAR CHARACTERIZATION OF RH BLOOD GROUP ANTIGEN COMPLEX
S07RR-05415-30 0020 (NSS) SPITALNIK, STEVEN L Facility improvement for smith hall animal facility MOLECULAR & CELL BIOLOGY OF HUMAN BLOOD GROUP ANTIGEN
S07RR-05415-30 0021 (NSS) SWEENEY, H LEE Facility improvement for smith hall animal facility FUNCTION OF REGULATORY LIGHT CHAIN OF MYOSIN W/ MUTAGENESIS & RECONSTRUCTION
S07RR-05415-30 0022 (NSS) WEISS, MARISA C Facility improvement for smith hall animal facility MECHANISM OF RADIATION RESISTANCE IN ONCOGENE TRANSFORMED CELL LINE
S07RR-05415-30 0000 (NSS) CANCRO, MICHAEL P Facility improvement for smith hall animal facility USE OF TRANSGENIC MICE IN CELL LINEAGE ANALYSIS OF B LYMPHOCYTES
S07RR-05415-30 0001 (NSS) CHANG, SUSANNAH Facility improvement for smith hall animal facility MOLECULAR CLONING OF CHICK DM ANTIGEN
S07RR-05415-30 0002 (NSS) FEUERSTEIN, NILI Facility improvement for smith hall animal facility MECHANISMS OF INSULIN EFFECT ON PHOSPHOPROTEINS
S07RR-05415-30 0003 (NSS) GOODGAL, SOL H Facility improvement for smith hall animal facility TRANSFORMATION IN HAEMOPHILUS
S07RR-05415-30 0004 (NSS) FEINBERG, RONALD F Facility improvement for smith hall animal facility ONCOFETAL FIBRONECTIN: TROPHOBLAST "GLUE" FOR NORMAL HUMAN IMPLANTATION
S07RR-05415-30 0005 (NSS) GREENBERG, JOEL H Facility improvement for smith hall animal facility LASER DOPPLER BLOOD FLOW MEASUREMENTS IN CENTRAL & PERIPHERAL CNS ISCHEMIA
S07RR-05415-30 0006 (NSS) HASHIMOTO, YASHUHIRO Facility improvement for smith hall animal facility RECOMBINASE REGULATION IN AUTOIMMUNE PRONE MICE
S07RR-05415-30 0007 (NSS) HOFFMAN, ERIC A Facility improvement for smith hall animal facility EKG GATED VENTILATION
S07RR-05415-30 0008 (NSS) JARDINES, LORI Facility improvement for smith hall animal facility USE OF GENETIC ALTERATIONS IN STAGING OF COLORECTAL CANCER
S07RR-05415-30 0009 (NSS) JEFFERIES, LEIGH Facility improvement for smith hall animal facility USE OF ANTI IDIOTYPIC ANTIBODIES AGAINST HUMAN RBC AUTOANTIBODIES
S07RR-05415-30 0010 (NSS) KALLEN, ROLAND G Facility improvement for smith hall animal facility STRUCTURE & MECHANISM OF INSULIN RECEPTOR TYROSINE KINASE
S07RR-05415-30 0011 (NSS) KLEINZELLER, ARNOST Facility improvement for smith hall animal facility CYTOSKELETON IN CELL VOLUME MAINTENANCE
S07RR-05415-30 0012 (NSS) KLIMAN, HARVEY Facility improvement for smith hall animal facility REGULATION OF HUMAN TROPHOBLAST & CHORIOCARCINOMA CELL INVASION
S07RR-05416-30 (NSS) BERNIER, GEORGE M, JR 3550 TERRACE STREET, RM M-240 SCAIFE HALL, UNIV PITTSBURGH PITTSBURGH, PA 15261 Biomedical research support
S07RR-05416-30 0552 (NSS) AIZENMAN, ELIAS Biomedical research support INTERACTION OF ASPARTAME W/ NMDA RECEPTOR IN MAMMALIAN CENTRAL
S07RR-05416-30 0553 (NSS) BOGGS, SALLIE S Biomedical research support ISOLATION & MICROINJECTION OF LYMPHOHEMATOPOIETIC STEM CELLS
S07RR-05416-30 0554 (NSS) BORLE, ANDRE B Biomedical research support RENAL NA, CA & H INTERACTIONS & ENDOCRINE CONTROL
S07RR-05416-30 0555 (NSS) CAIRNS, J SCOTT Biomedical research support GENES REGULATING INTRATHYMIC T LYMPHOCYTE DIFFERENTIATION
S07RR-05416-30 0556 (NSS) CAMPBELL, THOMAS F Biomedical research support RELATIONSHIP BETWEEN BONE LEAD LEVELS & LONG TERM SPEECH & LANGUAGE DEFICITS
S07RR-05416-30 0557 (NSS) DINDZANS, VINCENTS J Biomedical research support HEPATIC ENDOTHELIAL CELL RESPONSE TO MEDIATORS OF INFLAMMATION
S07RR-05416-30 0558 (NSS) DOWLING, JOHN N Biomedical research support CHARACTERIZATION OF A UNIQUE LEGIONELLA KINASE
S07RR-05416-30 0559 (NSS) FABISIAK, JAMES P Biomedical research support CHARACTERIZATION OF GROWTH FACTORS DERIVED FROM RAT LUNG FIBROBLASTS
S07RR-05416-30 0560 (NSS) FURMAN, JOSEPH Biomedical research support VESTIBULAR REHABILITATION THERAPY
S07RR-05416-30 0561 (NSS) HALFTER, WILLI Biomedical research support AXONAL NAVIGATION IN EMBRYONIC RETINA
S07RR-05416-30 0562 (NSS) ILDSTAD, SUZANNE T Biomedical research support MIXED ALLOGENEIC BONE MARROW TRANSPLANTATION
S07RR-05416-30 0563 (NSS) JOHNSON, PETER C Biomedical research support PLATELET DISPOSITION AT BLOOD & MICROVASCULAR INTERFACE
S07RR-05416-30 0564 (NSS) KOCHANEK, PATRICK M Biomedical research support PLATELET ACTIVATING FACTOR RECEPTOR ANTAGONISTS CEREBRAL EDEMA
S07RR-05416-30 0565 (NSS) KOERBER, H RICHARD Biomedical research support STRUCTURE & FUNCTION OF SPINAL DORSAL HORN
S07RR-05416-30 0566 (NSS) KORYTKOWSKI, MARY T Biomedical research support ANTIANDROGEN THERAPY ALTER CARBOHYDRATE METAB IN WOMEN W/ POLYCYSTIC OVARY
S07RR-05416-30 0567 (NSS) LAND, PETER W Biomedical research support ORGANIZATION & PLASTICITY OF CORTICAL GABAERGIC NEURONS
S07RR-05416-30 0568 (NSS) LEWIS, ROBERT M Biomedical research support MOLECULAR BIOLOGY OF NEURONS SPECIFIC PROTEINS
S07RR-05416-30 0569 (NSS) MCCARTHY, SUSAN A Biomedical research support ANALYSIS OF APOPTOTIC CELL DEATH IN INTRATHYMIC T LYMPHOCYTE DEVELOPMENT
S07RR-05416-30 0570 (NSS) MURRAY, SANDRA A Biomedical research support EFFECTS OF CYCLOSPORINE UPON RENAL EPITHELIAL CELL PROLIFERATION

PROJECT NO., ORGANIZATIONAL UNIT., INVESTIGATOR, ADDRESS, TITLE

S07RR-05416-30 0571 (NSS) PLANT, TONY M Biomedical research support RESEARCH IN REPRODUCTIVE PHYSIOLOGY
S07RR-05416-30 0573 (NSS) SAFAR, PETER Biomedical research support CONTROL OF CEREBRAL REPERFUSION AFTER CARDIAC ARREST
S07RR-05416-30 0574 (NSS) SANDO, ISAMU Biomedical research support HISTOPATHOLOGY OF TEMPORAL BONES
S07RR-05416-30 0572 (NSS) REYNOLDS, IAN J Biomedical research support NEUROTRANSMITTER MODULATION OF NMDA RECEPTOR ACTIVITY
S07RR-05416-30 0575 (NSS) SMITH, M SUSAN Biomedical research support CONTROL OF GONADOTROPIN SECRETIONS
S07RR-05416-30 0576 (NSS) YALOWICH, JACK C Biomedical research support MECHANISMS & MODULATIONS OF ETOPOSIDE VP 16 RESISTANCE
S07RR-05417-30 (NSS) MEYERS, ALLEN R TEMPLE UNIVERSITY SCH OF MED 3400 NORTH BROAD STREET PHILADELPHIA, PA 19140 Biomedical research support
S07RR-05417-30 0807 (NSS) NARINS, ROBERT G Biomedical research support EFFECT OF ACIDOSIS ON CARDIAC FUNCTION
S07RR-05417-30 0808 (NSS) PAGE, JIMMY D Biomedical research support STRUCTURAL FUNCTION RELATIONSHIPS OF PREKALLIKREIN
S07RR-05417-30 0809 (NSS) PANITCH, HOWARD Biomedical research support MODULATING EFFECTS OF EPITHELIUM ON IMMATURE AIRWAY
S07RR-05417-30 0810 (NSS) PEARSON, HELEN Biomedical research support PROJECTION PATTERNS OF INDIVIDUAL RETINAL GANGLION CELLS
S07RR-05417-30 0811 (NSS) PURI, RAJINDER N Biomedical research support NOVEL PEPTIDE ANALOGOUS TO INHIBITORY SEQUENCE OF KININOGEN IN THROMBOLYTIC
S07RR-05417-30 0812 (NSS) REDDY, E SHYAM P Biomedical research support MOLECULAR GENETICS OF ETS 2 ONCOGENE
S07RR-05417-30 0813 (NSS) ROA, VEENA Biomedical research support MOLECULAR & FUNCTIONAL DISSECTION OF ELK 1 GENE
S07RR-05417-30 0814 (NSS) SCHULMAN, GERRI Biomedical research support REGULATION OF ALDOSTERONE RECEPTOR FUNCTION
S07RR-05417-30 0815 (NSS) SOM, TAPAN Biomedical research support IDENTIFICATION OF GAP HOMOLOGS IN ASPERGILLUS NIDULANS
S07RR-05417-30 0816 (NSS) WHITE, ROY L Biomedical research support EFFECTS OF ISCHEMIA ON CARDIAC GAP JUNCTIONS
S07RR-05417-30 0780 (NSS) ASH, DAVID E Biomedical research support STRUCTURE & MECHANISM OF AGMATINE UREOHYDROLASE
S07RR-05417-30 0781 (NSS) ASHBY, BARRIE Biomedical research support PROSTAGLANDIN REG OF CYCLIC AMP FORMATION IN ERYTHROLEUKEMIA & LMPH CELLS
S07RR-05417-30 0782 (NSS) BAGASRA, OMAR Biomedical research support POLYMERASE CHAIN REACTION IN SITU
S07RR-05417-30 0783 (NSS) BENOVIC, JEFFREY L Biomedical research support CLONING OF B ADRENERGIC RECEPTOR KINASE RELATED CDNAS
S07RR-05417-30 0784 (NSS) BUDZYNSKI, ANDREI Biomedical research support ANTIBODIES DISCRIMINATING ONE CHAIN & TWO CHAIN TISSUE PLASMINOGEN ACTIVATOR
S07RR-05417-30 0785 (NSS) COOPER, SUZANE C Biomedical research support STRETCH & VASOPRESSORS ON INTERNAL MAMMARY ARTERIES & SAPHENOUS VEIN GRAFTS
S07RR-05417-30 0786 (NSS) DANEO-MOORE, LOLITA Biomedical research support REGULATION OF SURFACE SYNTHESIS IN STREPTOCOCCUS MUTANS
S07RR-05417-30 0787 (NSS) DE LA CADENA, RAUL A Biomedical research support SURFACE BINDING DOMAIN ON HISTIDINE RICH REGION OF HMW KININOGEN
S07RR-05417-30 0788 (NSS) DERIEL, JON K Biomedical research support HUMAN GENOMIC CLONE LIBRARIES W/ 100 KB INSERTS
S07RR-05417-30 0789 (NSS) DRISKA, STEVEN P Biomedical research support CALPONIN IN VASCULAR SMOOTH MUSCLE
S07RR-05417-30 0790 (NSS) FRIELLE, THOMAS Biomedical research support CLONING OF ADDITIONAL B ADRENERGIC RECEPTOR SUBTYPES
S07RR-05417-30 0791 (NSS) HAYS, JAMES H Biomedical research support OMEGA 3 FATTY ACID ON INSULIN RELEASE & PHOSPHOINOSITIDE TURNOVER NEONATAL ISLET
S07RR-05417-30 0792 (NSS) HOOBER, KENNETH Biomedical research support CHARACTERIZATION OF A LIGHT INDUCIBLE GENE
S07RR-05417-30 0793 (NSS) HOOBER, KENNETH Biomedical research support INSTALLATION OF FACILITIES FOR MOLECULAR MODELING & SEQUENCE ANALYSIS
S07RR-05417-30 0794 (NSS) JOHNSON, RUSSELL A Biomedical research support INFECTION & INFLAMMATION IN GLANDINS EFFECT FROM TRACHEOBRONCHIAL EPITHELIA
S07RR-05417-30 0795 (NSS) KAPOOR, SHIV C Biomedical research support MECHANISM OF PROTEIN INDUCED ALTERATION IN RENIN SECRETION
S07RR-05417-30 0796 (NSS) KIRBY, EDWARD P Biomedical research support STRUCTURE FUNCTION RELATIONSHIPS IN HUMAN VON WILLEBRAND FACTOR
S07RR-05417-30 0797 (NSS) KREVSKY, BENJAMIN Biomedical research support DYNAMIC IMAGING OF GASTROINTESTINAL TRACT
S07RR-05417-30 0798 (NSS) KRISHNA, G GOPAL Biomedical research support MECHANISM OF HYPERTENSION INDUCED BY POTASSIUM DEPLETION
S07RR-05417-30 0799 (NSS) LOTLIKAR, PRABHAKAR Biomedical research support MODULATION OF MYCOTOXIN CARCINOGENESIS BY GLUTATHIONE
S07RR-05417-30 0800 (NSS) MANGAN, KENNETH F Biomedical research support INTERLEUKIN 3 (IL 3) FOLLOWING MURINE OR HUMAN BONE MARROW TRANSPLANTATION
S07RR-05417-30 0801 (NSS) MARDINI, ISSAM A Biomedical research support CONTROL OF PROSTAGLANDIN METABOLISM IN AIRWAY EPITHELIUM
S07RR-05417-30 0802 (NSS) MARKS, LLOYD Biomedical research support INTRAVASCULAR STENT FOR MAINTENANCE OF DUCTAL PATENCY IN CONGENITAL HEART DIS
S07RR-05417-30 0803 (NSS) MARTIN, JOHN SAMUEL Biomedical research support LENGTH TENSION & AGONIST RESPONSE OF NEONATAL RABBIT COLON
S07RR-05417-30 0804 (NSS) MERCER, EDWARD Biomedical research support CELLULAR GENES ACTIVATED BY WILD TYPE P53 PROTEIN
S07RR-05417-30 0805 (NSS) MOSS, STUART B Biomedical research support MAMMALIAN SPERMIOGENESIS: HISTONES & DNA REORGANIZATION
S07RR-05417-30 0806 (NSS) MAURER, ERIK Biomedical research support ANTISENSE OLIGONUCLEOTIDES TO ASSESS GLUCOSE TRANSPORTER IN ADIPOCYTES & ISLET
S07RR-05418-30 (NSS) ROSS, LEONARD L MEDICAL COLL OF PENNSYLVANIA 3300 HENRY AVENUE PHILADELPHIA, PA 19129 Biomedical research support
S07RR-05418-30 0023 (NSS) EDLIND, THOMAS D Biomedical research support ANTI RIBOSOMAL RNA OLIGONUCLEOTIDE: EFFECT ON GIARDIA PROTEIN SYNTHESIS
S07RR-05418-30 0024 (NSS) FISHER, EDWARD A Biomedical research support PCR OF APOPROTEIN GENE EXPRESSION TRANSLATIONAL CONTROL APOPROTEINB APOPROTEIN
S07RR-05418-30 0025 (NSS) KATHRYN LEARY Biomedical research support MACROPHAGE DIFFERENTIATION & RESISTANCE TO HSV 1; REPLICATION HUMAN HERPES VIRUS
S07RR-05418-30 0026 (NSS) MCCULLY, KEVIN Biomedical research support CORRELATION BETWEEN MAGNETIC RESONANCE SPECTROSCOPY & MUSCLE BIOCHEMICAL ELDERLY
S07RR-05418-30 0027 (NSS) MORAHAN, PAGE Biomedical research support BEHAVIORAL CONDITIONING OF NK CELLS INTERFERON & ANTIVIRAL RESISTANCE:
S07RR-05418-30 0028 (NSS) MCNAMARA, ROBERT M Biomedical research support PERITONEAL FLUID ADMINISTRATION TO TREAT HEMORRHAGE SHOCK IN PORCINE MODEL
S07RR-05418-30 0029 (NSS) LIPUMA, JOHN J Biomedical research support PURIFICATION & IMMUNOGENICITY OF BACTERIOCIN FOR HAEMOPHILUS INFLUENZAE TYPE B
S07RR-05418-30 0030 (NSS) SAYERS, STEVEN L Biomedical research support DYSFUNCTIONAL STANDARDS & EXPECTANCIES IN MARITALLY DISTRESSED SPOUSES
S07RR-05418-30 0031 (NSS) HAUN, FOREST A Biomedical research support FUNCTIONS OF HABENULA INTERPEDUNCULAR SYSTEM: CNS INJURY TRANSPLANT SLEEP STRESS
S07RR-05418-30 0032 (NSS) MURPHY, E HAZEL Biomedical research support EXPERIMENTAL MODELS OF EPILEPTIC CORTICAL ACTIVITY: NEURAL DEVELOPMENT
S07RR-05418-30 0033 (NSS) MALKOWITZ, DENISE Biomedical research support EFFECTS OF REPETITIVE SEIZURES ON SERUM PROLACTIN LEVELS
S07RR-05418-30 0034 (NSS) TUSZYNSKI, GEORGE Biomedical research support THROMBOSPONDIN IN WOUND HEALING: PLATELETS FIBROBLAST ENDOTHELIAL CELLS
S07RR-05418-30 0035 (NSS) VENDER, ROBERT Biomedical research support HYPOXIA & SMOOTH MUSCLE CELL SODIUM METABOLISM: PULMONARY
S07RR-05419-30 (NSS) BAEZ, ADRIANA UNIVERSITY OF PUERTO RICO G P O BOX 5067 SAN JUAN, P R 00936 Biomedical research support
S07RR-05419-30 0824 (NSS) RODRIGUEZ, JOSE R Biomedical research support VARIOUS ASPECTS OF MYOSIN HEAVY CHAIN GENE EXPRESSION IN NON MUSCLE SYSTEM
S07RR-05419-30 0825 (NSS) TORRES-BAUZA, LUIS Biomedical research support PENICILLINASE PRODUCING NEISSERIA GONORRHOEAE ISOLATES
S07RR-05419-30 0826 (NSS) MICHAIL, ANTOUN D Biomedical research support SIGNIFICANCE OF CELL WALL DEFICIENT MICROORGANISMS IN CANCEROUS STATE
S07RR-05419-30 0827 (NSS) GUZMAN, ANGEL L Biomedical research support EFFECTS OF PLANT EXTRACTS ON BLOOD GLUCOSE LEVELS
S07RR-05419-30 0828 (NSS) PRESTON, ALLAN M Biomedical research support METABOLIC CHANGES DURING GESTATION IN CHEMICALLY DIABETIC RATS
S07RR-05419-30 0817 (NSS) CADILLA, CARMEN Biomedical research support DNA SEQUENCE REQUIREMENTS FOR INSULIN CONTROL OF GENE 33 EXPRESSION
S07RR-05419-30 0818 (NSS) DEMELLO, WALMOR Biomedical research support CAMP DEPENDENT PROTEIN KINASE: JUNCTIONAL COMMUNICATION; HEART
S07RR-05419-30 0819 (NSS) DIAZ, ANA M Biomedical research support PURIFICATION & CHARACTERIZATION OF MABS AGAINST HIV 2 FROM ASCITIC FLUID
S07RR-05419-30 0820 (NSS) GRUBER, KENNETH A Biomedical research support ION TRANSPORT IN CHOROID PLEXUS
S07RR-05419-30 0821 (NSS) JIMENEZ, BRAULIO D Biomedical research support DEVELOPMENT OF DETOXICATION ENZYME ASSAYS IN HUMAN LYMPHOCYTES
S07RR-05419-30 0822 (NSS) NIKOLETSEAS, MICHAEL Biomedical research support ELECTROPHYSIO ANATOMICAL CHARACTERIZE MULTISENSORY CELLS SUPERIOR COLLICULUS
S07RR-05419-30 0823 (NSS) RODRIGUEZ DEL VALLE, Biomedical research support CA PHORBOL ESTERS PROTEIN KINASE C INHIBITORS OF CELL DVMT S SCHENKII
S07RR-05420-30 (NSS) BUSE, MARIA G MEDICAL UNIV OF SOUTH CAROLINA 171 ASHLEY AVENUE CHARLESTON, SC 29425-2501 Biomedical research support
S07RR-05420-30 0036 (NSS) BECKSTEAD, ROBERT M Biomedical research support NEUROTRANSMITTER INFLUENCE ON GENE TRANSCRIPTION RECEPTORS, MRNA PEPTIDES
S07RR-05420-30 0037 (NSS) BLACKBURN, JOHN G Biomedical research support CYCLOSPORINE NEPHROTOXICITY: EARLY EFFECTS CYTOTOXICITY KIDNEY ELECTROPHYSIOLOGY
S07RR-05420-30 0038 (NSS) BROMBERG, JONATHAN Biomedical research support IN VIVO ROLE OF CD2 IN CELLULAR IMMUNITY: MABS TRANSPLANTATION MAB RECEPTOR
S07RR-05420-30 0039 (NSS) GEORGIEV, ALEXANDER Biomedical research support TUMOR GROWTH MODELS: NON PARAMETRIC APPROACH CANCER KERNAL ESTIMATES POPULATION
S07RR-05420-30 0040 (NSS) HADLEY, ROBERT D Biomedical research support NEURITE OUTGROWTH & LAMININ RELATED PROTEIN MOLLUSKS EXTRACELLULAR MATRIX
S07RR-05420-30 0041 (NSS) HAZEN-MARTIN, DEBRA Biomedical research support ULTRACUT E MICROTOME ULTRASTRUCTURE ELECTRON MICROSCOPY
S07RR-05420-30 0042 (NSS) PANDEY, JANARDAN P Biomedical research support IMMUNOGLOBULIN ALLOTYPE LINKED IMMUNE RESPONSE GENES
S07RR-05420-30 0043 (NSS) PRIVITERA, PHILIP J Biomedical research support BRAIN KALLIKREIN KININ & ARTERIAL PRESSURE CONTROL
S07RR-05420-30 0044 (NSS) SMOLKA, ADAM Biomedical research support ASSESSMENT OF ANTIBODY EXPRESSION LIBRARY TECHNOLOGY
S07RR-05420-30 0045 (NSS) STEVENS, JUNE Biomedical research support EPIDEMIOLOGY OF FAT PATTERNING; DIABETES CARDIOVASCULAR DISEASE
S07RR-05420-30 0046 (NSS) TROJANOWSKA, MARIA Biomedical research support MOLECULAR CLONING OF SCLERODERMA SPECIFIC GENES; ONCOGENES
S07RR-05421-27 (NSS) TALLEY, ROBERT C UNIV SOUTH DAKOTA SCH MED 414 E. CLARK STREET VERMILLION, SD 57069-2390 Biomedical research support
S07RR-05421-27 0976 (NSS) TRUJILLO, ANGELINA L Biomedical research

support FAT DIET ON GLOMERULOSCLEROSIS IN TYPE II DIABETES MELLITUS
S07RR-05421-27 0977 (NSS) SCHLENKER, EVELYN H Biomedical research support HYPOTHYROIDISM IN DEV OF ALVEOLAR HYPOVENTILATION & LUNG ARCHITECTURE
S07RR-05422-30 (NSS) FOSTER, HENRY W MEHARRY MEDICAL COLLEGE 1005 D B TODD BOULEVARD NASHVILLE, TENN 37208 Biomedical research support
S07RR-05422-30 0047 (NSS) HINDS, JOSEPH E Biomedical research support MECHANICAL PROPERTIES OF HYPERTROPHIED LEFT VENTRICULAR MUSCLE
S07RR-05423-30 (NSS) SUMMITT, ROBERT L UNIVERSITY OF TENNESSEE 800 MADISON AVENUE MEMPHIS, TENN 38163 Biomedical research support
S07RR-05423-30 0057 (NSS) MARSHALL, STEPHEN Biomedical research support METABOLIC REGULATION OF INSULIN RESISTANCE IN ADIPOCYTES
S07RR-05423-30 0058 (NSS) MAUER, ALVIN M Biomedical research support IN VITRO TRANSFORMATION OF HEMATOPOIETIC STEM CELLS
S07RR-05423-30 0059 (NSS) MIRVIS, DAVID M Biomedical research support ELECTROPHYSIOLOGIC CORRELATES OF MYOCARDIAL ISCHEMIA
S07RR-05423-30 0060 (NSS) NIELL, HARVEY B Biomedical research support ACTIVITY OF TUMOR NECROSIS FACTOR IN BLADDER CANCER
S07RR-05423-30 0061 (NSS) SOSKEL, NORMAN T Biomedical research support ELASTIN RICH EXTRACELLULAR MATRIX
S07RR-05423-30 0062 (NSS) WHITE, RICHARD P Biomedical research support EFFECT OF SATURATED FATTY ACIDS ON VASCULAR TONE
S07RR-05423-30 0048 (NSS) BLATTEIS, CLARK M Biomedical research support CENTRAL MONAMINES & ACUTE PHASE REACTION
S07RR-05423-30 0049 (NSS) CARLSON, GERALD M Biomedical research support NOVEL MAMMALIAN PROTEIN KINASE UTILIZES PHOSPHOENOLPYRUVATE AS PHOSPHORYL DONOR
S07RR-05423-30 0050 (NSS) DONALDSON, DONALD J Biomedical research support CELL SUBSTRATE INTERACTIONS IN EPIDERMAL CELL MIGRATION
S07RR-05423-30 0051 (NSS) HEIMBERG, MURRAY Biomedical research support REGULATORY MECHANISMS IN LIPID METABOLISM
S07RR-05423-30 0052 (NSS) ISRAEL, MERVYN Biomedical research support PREPARATION OF ADRIAMYCIN ANALOGS & DERIVATIVES
S07RR-05423-30 0053 (NSS) KANG, ELLEN S Biomedical research support METABOLIC RISKS DURING INFLUENZA IN DIABETES MELLITUS
S07RR-05423-30 0063 (NSS) KITABCHI, ABBAS E Biomedical research support UV VIS SPECTROPHOTOMETER & CONTROLLING COMPUTER
S07RR-05423-30 0064 (NSS) KITABCHI, ABBAS E Biomedical research support PURCHASE OF BECKMAN TYPE 60 TI FIXED ANGLE MOTOR PART #33146
S07RR-05423-30 0054 (NSS) KATZE, JON R Biomedical research support TRNA QUANINE RIBOSYLTRANSFERASE: ANTISENSE RNA
S07RR-05423-30 0055 (NSS) KRAUS, LORRAINE M Biomedical research support CARBAMOYLATION OF AMINO ACIDS IN UREMIC PATIENTS ON CAPD
S07RR-05423-30 0056 (NSS) MARION, TONY Biomedical research support STRUCTURAL BASIS FOR IMMUNITY TO DNA
S07RR-05424-30 (NSS) HASH, JOHN H VANDERBILT UNIVERSITY CCC-3322 MED CTR N NASHVILLE, TN 37232-2103 Biomedical research support
S07RR-05424-30 0088 (NSS) HUNTER, ELLEN B Biomedical research support IN VIVO MODEL OF HEPATIC OXIDANT STRESS INJURY: ORGAN PRESERVATION
S07RR-05424-30 0089 (NSS) SALHANY, KEVIN E Biomedical research support FUNCTIONAL ANALYSIS OF C FOS PROMOTER
S07RR-05424-30 0090 (NSS) DAWSON, ROBERT C Biomedical research support EXPERIMENTAL ANEURYSM OBLITERATION W/ HEMA & GLUTARALDEHYDE CROSS LINK COLLAGEN
S07RR-05424-30 0091 (NSS) HANSEN, DAVID E Biomedical research support DEVELOPMENT & VALIDATION OF DONOR HEART SUPPORT SYSTEM
S07RR-05424-30 0092 (NSS) WHITSELL, RICHARD R Biomedical research support AN IN SITU ASSAY FOR PHOSPHOGLUCOSE ISOMERASE IN CULTURED CELLS
S07RR-05424-30 0093 (NSS) BROADLEY, CAROLINE Biomedical research support MESANGIAL MATRIX GENE EXPRESSION: OXIDANT INJURY VS PROTECTION BY FATTY ACIDS
S07RR-05424-30 0094 (NSS) SUNDELL, HAKAN W Biomedical research support TRIAL OF SURFACTANT REPLACEMENT FOLLOWING MECONIUM ASPIRATION IN LAMBS
S07RR-05424-30 0095 (NSS) GENTILE, DOUGLAS A Biomedical research support SMALL QUANTITY WATER DISINFECTION W/ IODINE
S07RR-05424-30 0096 (NSS) PICKENS, DAVID R Biomedical research support QUANTITATIVE BRAIN PERFUSION MEASUREMENTS W/ MRI
S07RR-05424-30 0097 (NSS) DEBOLD, ROWAN Biomedical research support MODEL SYSTEM DVMT; TRANSFECTED GENE EXPRESSION; ACTH PRODUCING LUNG TUMOR CELLS
S07RR-05424-30 0098 (NSS) PANDEY, KAILASH N Biomedical research support ATRIAL NATRIURETIC FACTOR RECEPTORS & TRANSMEMBRANE SIGNAL TRANSDUCTION
S07RR-05424-30 0099 (NSS) KHOOR, ANDRAS Biomedical research support LOCALIZATION OF SURFACTANT PROTEIN MRNA IN HUMAN LUNG
S07RR-05424-30 0100 (NSS) JOHNSON, MAHLON D Biomedical research support GROWTH FACTOR REGULATION OF OF ARACHNOID CELL PROLIFERATION
S07RR-05424-30 0101 (NSS) SHELTON, RICHARD C Biomedical research support ACTIVITY MONITORING IN DEPRESSION
S07RR-05424-30 0102 (NSS) MURRAY, JOHN J Biomedical research support LEUKOCYTE REGULATION BY PHOSPHATIDIC ACID PHOSPHOHYDROLASE
S07RR-05424-30 0103 (NSS) ROLLINS-SMITH, LOUIS Biomedical research support DEFINITION OF TADPOLE SPECIFIC LYMPHOCYTE ANTIGENS IN FROGS
S07RR-05424-30 0104 (NSS) PRAKASH, CHANDRA Biomedical research support MYRISTOYL TRANSFERASE INHIBITORS: POTENTIAL ANTI AIDS DRUGS
S07RR-05424-30 0105 (NSS) WRIGHT, SETH W Biomedical research support KETOROLAC FOR SICKLE CELL VASO OCCLUSIVE CRISIS PAIN: PILOT STUDY
S07RR-05424-30 0106 (NSS) BENN, STEVEN I Biomedical research support LYSYL OXIDASE GENE EXPRESSION DURING MOUSE LUNG DEVELOPMENT
S07RR-05424-30 0107 (NSS) SHELLER, JAMES R Biomedical research support PURIFICATION OF HUMAN BRONCHOALVEOLAR LAVAGE CELLS
S07RR-05424-30 0108 (NSS) BECKMAN, JEFFREY K Biomedical research support EFFECT OF U74500A ON LIPID PEROXIDATION & RENAL INJURY
S07RR-05424-30 0109 (NSS) BRASH, ALAN R Biomedical research support MOLECULAR CLONING OF SEA URCHIN EGG LIPOXYGENASES
S07RR-05424-30 0110 (NSS) SNYDERS, DIRK J Biomedical research support DETERMINATIONS OF DRUG BINDING TO ACTIVATED & OPEN CHANNELS
S07RR-05424-30 0111 (NSS) ANTHONY, CATHERINE T Biomedical research support CELL CELL INTERACTIONS IN PROSTATE
S07RR-05424-30 0112 (NSS) WILEY, RONALD G Biomedical research support TYROSINE HYDROXYLASE & C FOS EXPRESSION IN A2 NEURONS
S07RR-05424-30 0065 (NSS) BATEMAN, JAMES Biomedical research support SHARED SCIENTIFIC COMPUTING RESOURCE
S07RR-05424-30 0066 (NSS) MILLER, DUNCAN A Biomedical research support LATENCY & TRANSFORMING GROWTH FACTOR BETA GENE FAMILY
S07RR-05424-30 0113 (NSS) POLK, DAVID B Biomedical research support REGULATION OF ENTEROCYTE HYDROLASE ONTOGENY
S07RR-05424-30 0067 (NSS) WILLIAMS, LESTER F Biomedical research support CALCIUM TRANSPORT BY GALL BLADDER DURING GALLSTONE FORMATION
S07RR-05424-30 0068 (NSS) BENN, STEVEN I Biomedical research support FIBROBLAST HETEROGENEITY IN RAT LUNG DURING POSTNATAL DVMT
S07RR-05424-30 0069 (NSS) ANDERSON, WAYNE F Biomedical research support CRYSTALLIZATION & PRELIMINARY ANALYSIS OF ERYTHROCYTE ANION
S07RR-05424-30 0070 (NSS) CASEY, TERENCE T Biomedical research support PRODUCTION OF POLYCLONAL & MABS TO HUMAN CD4 & CD8; HELA AS IMMUNOGEN
S07RR-05424-30 0071 (NSS) MURRAY, JOHN J Biomedical research support PHOSPHOLIPASE D IN HUMAN POLYMORPHONUCLEAR LEUKOCYTES RECEPTOR STIMULATION
S07RR-05424-30 0072 (NSS) ROGERS, BEVERLY J Biomedical research support MECHANISM OF SPERM CAPACITATION & ACROSOME REACTION
S07RR-05424-30 0073 (NSS) SHAH, DINESH M Biomedical research support MODULATION OF RENIN SECRETION IN CHORIONIC CELL CULTURES
S07RR-05424-30 0074 (NSS) OSTEEN, KEVIN G Biomedical research support CHARACTERIZE ENDOMETRIAL CELLS: TUMOR ASSOCIATED GLYCOPROTEIN EXPRESSION
S07RR-05424-30 0075 (NSS) BUTLER, MERLIN G Biomedical research support CYTOGENETICS & MOLECULAR ANALYSIS OF TGF BETA IN GIANT CELL TUMOR OF BONE
S07RR-05424-30 0076 (NSS) MROCZKOWSKI, BARBARA Biomedical research support EFG PRECURSOR FUNCTIONAL DIVERSITY: EFG ROLE IN CELL TO CELL COMMUNICATION
S07RR-05424-30 0077 (NSS) SCHAPIRA, MARC Biomedical research support ANTITHROMBIN METABOLISM & BIOSYNTHESIS
S07RR-05424-30 0078 (NSS) ELLIS, DARREL L Biomedical research support EXTRACELLULAR MATRIX DEGRADATION REGULATION BY GROWTH FACTORS IN MELANOMA
S07RR-05424-30 0079 (NSS) BASTIAS, MARIA C Biomedical research support HUMAN SPERM W/ FEMALE GENITAL FLUIDS: SPERM MOTION VS IN VITRO FERTILIZATION
S07RR-05424-30 0080 (NSS) CARTWRIGHT, PETER S Biomedical research support EXPRESSION OF TGF BETA RELATED GENES; NORMAL VS DYSPLASTIC CERVICAL EPITHELIA
S07RR-05424-30 0081 (NSS) HALTER, SUSAN A Biomedical research support RAS MUTATIONS IN COLONIC CARCINOMA
S07RR-05424-30 0082 (NSS) OCHS, MARLEEN T Biomedical research support SPEECH CONTEXT EFFECTS; CONGENITALLY & ADVENTITIOUSLY HEARING IMPAIRED SUBJECT
S07RR-05424-30 0083 (NSS) GARCIA, FERNANDO V Biomedical research support ANGIOGENIC FACTOR(S) FROM BARTONELLA BACILLIFORMIS
S07RR-05424-30 0084 (NSS) POWERS, ALVIN C Biomedical research support CHARACTERIZE REGULATION OF PANCREATIC ISLET SPECIFIC GLUCOSE TRANSPORTER
S07RR-05424-30 0085 (NSS) SCHWARTZ, HERBERT S Biomedical research support TRANSFORMING GROWTH FACTOR BETA (TGF BETA) BINDING TO HUMAN OSTEOBLASTS
S07RR-05424-30 0114 (NSS) DODD, DEBRA A Biomedical research support REGULATION OF CARDIAC CA2+ RELEASE CHANNEL
S07RR-05424-30 0086 (NSS) MAYER, STEVEN E Biomedical research support DRUG METABOLISM IN CHOROID PLEXUS
S07RR-05424-30 0087 (NSS) MACIUNAS, ROBERT J Biomedical research support MODULATING MOTILITY OF NORMAL & TRANSFORMED GLIAL CELLS
S07RR-05424-30 0115 (NSS) MCCURLEY, THOMAS L Biomedical research support DETECTION OF T CRUZI IN CHAGASIC CARDIOMYOPATHY BY DNA AMPLIFICATION
S07RR-05424-30 0116 (NSS) KINNEY, MARSHA C Biomedical research support FUNCTIONAL PROPERTIES OF KI 1 (CD30) ANTIGEN IN VITRO
S07RR-05424-30 0117 (NSS) HANKS, STEVEN K Biomedical research support DETECTION & CHARACTERIZATION OF PHORK KINASE
S07RR-05424-30 0118 (NSS) WHEELER, ARTHUR P Biomedical research support AUTOGENIC PROTEIN & ANTIBODY PRODUCTION IN RABBITS
S07RR-05424-30 0119 (NSS) ENNIS, BRUCE W Biomedical research support REGULATION OF BREAST CANCER CELL GROWTH: EFG INDUCED PLC GAMMA ACTIVATION
S07RR-05424-30 0120 (NSS) FAVA, ROY A Biomedical research support TGF & BETA IN INFLAMMATION: RELEASE VIA NEUTROPHIL DEGRANULATION
S07RR-05424-30 0121 (NSS) BRIGGS, ROBERT C Biomedical research support CONSTRUCTION OF HUMAN MYELOID CELL CDNA LIBRARIES
S07RR-05424-30 0122 (NSS) VAN ELDIK, LINDA J Biomedical research support NEUROTROPHIC ACTIVITY OF S100 IN NERVOUS SYSTEM CULTURES
S07RR-05424-30 0123 (NSS) NEWCOMER, MARICA E Biomedical research support XRAY CRYSTALLOGRAPHIC STRUCTURE; RETINOIC ACID BINDING PROTEIN
S07RR-05424-30 0125 (NSS) GREEN, NEIL Biomedical research support INTEGRATION OF PROTEINS INTO ENDOPLASMIC RETICULUM
S07RR-05424-30 0126 (NSS) HASH, JOHN H Biomedical research support SUMMER RESEARCH 12 MEDICAL STUDENTS
S07RR-05425-30 (NSS) RICH, ROBERT R BAYLOR COL MED TEX MED CTR ONE BAYLOR PLAZA, ROOM 186A HOUSTON, TEX 77030 Biomedical research support
S07RR-05425-30 0727 (NSS) BAEHR, WOLFGANG Biomedical research support RETINAL PHOTORECEPTOR CGMP PHOSPHODIESTERASE
S07RR-05425-30 0728 (NSS) BELLEN, HUGO Biomedical research support DROSOPHILA PERIPHERAL NERVOUS SYSTEM
S07RR-05425-30 0729 (NSS) CAGLE, PHILIP T Biomedical research support INFLUENCE OF ESTROGENS ON PULMONARY ADENOCARCINOMA
S07RR-05425-30 0730 (NSS) CHU, ALICE Biomedical research support SLOW TWITCH SKELETAL MUSCLE SARCOPLASMIC RETICULUM
S07RR-05425-30 0731 (NSS) COHEN, STEPHEN Biomedical research support MOLECULAR GENETICS OF LIMB DEVELOPMENT IN DROSOPHILA
S07RR-05425-30 0732 (NSS) COOK, SUSAN W Biomedical research support

PROJECT NO., ORGANIZATIONAL UNIT., INVESTIGATOR, ADDRESS, TITLE

PROTEUS MIRABILIS INFECTIOSN OF URINARY TRACT
S07RR-05425-30 0733 (NSS) COOPER, THOMAS Biomedical research support PRE MRNA CIS ELEMENTS REQUIRED FOR ALTERNATIVE SPLICING
S07RR-05425-30 0734 (NSS) DANI, JOHN Biomedical research support FUNCTION OF PHOSPHORYLATION SITES OF NACHR
S07RR-05425-30 0735 (NSS) ELLEDGE, STEPHEN Biomedical research support CELL CYCLE & DNA DAMAGE REGULATION IN YEAST
S07RR-05425-30 0752 (NSS) MAIER, KATHERINE T Biomedical research support 31P MRS & Q EEG MEASURES IN HYPOGLYCEMIA
S07RR-05425-30 0753 (NSS) MARISCALCO, MARY Biomedical research support NEUTROPHIL ADHERENCE REACTIONS IN ENDOTHELIAL INJURY: PEDIATRICS
S07RR-05425-30 0754 (NSS) MARTIN, CHRISTOPHER Biomedical research support REGULATION OF CEREBRAL CIRCULATION IN NEWBORN
S07RR-05425-30 0755 (NSS) MATSON, DAVID D Biomedical research support MOLECULAR BIOLOGY OF HUMAN CALCIVIRUSES PEDIATRICS
S07RR-05425-30 0756 (NSS) MIMS, MARTHA P Biomedical research support ACTIVITY & SPECIFICITY OF LYSOSOMAL ACID LIPASE
S07RR-05425-30 0757 (NSS) MOISE, ALICIA Biomedical research support EFFECTS OF SHEAR & OXIDANT STRESS ON ENDOTHELIAL CELLS
S07RR-05425-30 0758 (NSS) MOSS, LARRY G Biomedical research support CLONING OF NOVEL INSULIN GENE REGULATORY PROTEIN
S07RR-05425-30 0759 (NSS) NELSON, DAVID Biomedical research support SUBTYPE ANALYSIS OF CHILDHOOD HYPERACTIVITY
S07RR-05425-30 0760 (NSS) OSMANI, STEPHEN A Biomedical research support NIM A GENE IN MITOTIC REGULATION
S07RR-05425-30 0761 (NSS) PATEL, PRAGNA I Biomedical research support REGULATORY ELEMENTS OF HPRT GENE
S07RR-05425-30 0762 (NSS) PEDERSEN, STEEN Biomedical research support STRUCTURE & FUNCTION OF YEAST ALPHA MATING FACTOR RECEPTOR
S07RR-05425-30 0763 (NSS) PELEG, SARA Biomedical research support VITAMIN D RECEPTOR EXPRESSION IN NORMAL & DISEASED CELLS
S07RR-05425-30 0764 (NSS) QUARLESS, SHELLY A Biomedical research support IDENTIFICATION OF GLIAL DEVELOPMENTAL MARKERS
S07RR-05425-30 0765 (NSS) RAJAN, ARUN Biomedical research support REGULATION OF GLUCAGON SECRETION IN ALPHA CELLS
S07RR-05425-30 0766 (NSS) REID, MICHAEL Biomedical research support INTRACELLULAR OXIDANT PRODUCTION BY ISOLATED DIAPHRAGM
S07RR-05425-30 0767 (NSS) SIFERS, RICHARD Biomedical research support PROTEIN DEGRADATION IN SECRETORY PATHWAY
S07RR-05425-30 0768 (NSS) SKINNER, SHERI M Biomedical research support DEVELOPMENT OF PREMATURE MENOPAUSE
S07RR-05425-30 0769 (NSS) SPIERING, ANDREA L Biomedical research support NEGATIVE GROWTH EFFECTOR FROM TRANSFORMED HUMAN CELLS
S07RR-05425-30 0770 (NSS) SWEATT, JOHN Biomedical research support BIOCHEMISTRY OF LTP IN CA3 REGION OF RAT HIPPOCAMPUS
S07RR-05425-30 0771 (NSS) TERHUNE, PENELOPE L Biomedical research support CEREBRAL BLOOD FLOW W/ PROLONGED HYPERTENSION PEDIATRIC
S07RR-05425-30 0736 (NSS) FELTES, TIMOTHY Biomedical research support SODIUM IN CORONARY SMOOTH MUSCLE CELL PROLIFERATION
S07RR-05425-30 0737 (NSS) FRAIRE, ARMANDO E Biomedical research support ASBESTOS INDUCED PLEURAL DYSPLASIA IN RATS
S07RR-05425-30 0738 (NSS) GEORGE, SAMUEL Biomedical research support CHIMERIC CALMODULIN TROPONIN C PROTEINS
S07RR-05425-30 0739 (NSS) GIBBS, RICHARD Biomedical research support MOLECULAR ANALYSIS OF HIV
S07RR-05425-30 0740 (NSS) GRAY, RICHARD Biomedical research support CHARACTERIZATION OF PRESYNAPTIC CALCIUM CHANNELS
S07RR-05425-30 0741 (NSS) GUEVARA, JUAN Biomedical research support ADHESIN RELATED SEQUENCES IN PLASMINOGEN
S07RR-05425-30 0742 (NSS) HAMRA, MARY M Biomedical research support DEVELOPMENTAL ELECTROPHYSIOLOGY & ISCHEMIA
S07RR-05425-30 0743 (NSS) HAVERKAMP, LANNY Biomedical research support ENDOGENOUS ENDONUCLEASES IN NEURONAL CELL DEATH
S07RR-05425-30 0744 (NSS) HERRICK, RICHARD C Biomedical research support TWO DIMENSIONAL IN VIVO NMR SPECTROSCOPY
S07RR-05425-30 0745 (NSS) HIGHLANDER, SARAH Biomedical research support REGULATION OF P HAEMOLYTICA LEUKOTOXIN EXPRESSION
S07RR-05425-30 0772 (NSS) TIMMONS, THERESE Biomedical research support BIOCHEMICAL ANALYSIS OF MAMMALIAN FERTILIZATION
S07RR-05425-30 0773 (NSS) VISWANATH, NAGALAPUR Biomedical research support PROCESSES UNDERLYING FRAGMENTATION OF WORDS BY STUTTERER
S07RR-05425-30 0774 (NSS) WHITE, CATHERINE M Biomedical research support BONE DENSITY NORMAL VALUES 15 21 YEAR OLD FEMALES
S07RR-05425-30 0775 (NSS) WILSON, DEBORAH R Biomedical research support C3 GENE REGULATION DURING ACTIVE PHASE RESPONSE
S07RR-05425-30 0776 (NSS) YOFFE, BORIS Biomedical research support HBV AS CO FACTOR IN DEVELOPMENT OF AIDS
S07RR-05425-30 0746 (NSS) JACKSON, MARIAN Biomedical research support DEVELOPMENTAL REGULATION OF ARGININO SUCCINATE SYNTHETASE
S07RR-05425-30 0747 (NSS) KAROUNOS, DENNIS Biomedical research support IDENTIFICATION OF ISLET CELL ANTIGENS
S07RR-05425-30 0748 (NSS) KOENIG, JOYCE Biomedical research support NEUTROPENIA IN PREGNANCY INDUCED HYPERTENSION
S07RR-05425-30 0749 (NSS) KROLL, MICHAEL Biomedical research support PHOSPHATIDIC ACID IN PLATELET STIMULUS RESPONSE COUPLING
S07RR-05425-30 0750 (NSS) LEIBO, STANLEY P Biomedical research support CRYOPRESERVATION OF MOUSE OVARIAN OOCYTES
S07RR-05425-30 0751 (NSS) LUPSKI, JAMES R Biomedical research support REGULATION OF MACROMOLECULAT SYNTHESIS
S07RR-05426-30 (NSS) NEAVES, WILLIAM B UT SOUTHWESTERN MED CTR DALLAS 5323 HARRY HINES BLVD DALLAS, TEX 75235-9003 Biomedical research support
S07RR-05426-30 0133 (NSS) CRUZ, PONCIANO D Biomedical research support ACIDIFICATION & H+ ATPASE IN LANGERHANS CELLS: EFFECTS OF UVB RADIATION
S07RR-05426-30 0134 (NSS) FLICKER, PAUL L Biomedical research support MRI CHARACTERISTICS OF TRUNK MUSCULATURE: EXERCISE ENHANCED IMAGES T2 MEASURE
S07RR-05426-30 0135 (NSS) GARG, ABHIMANYU Biomedical research support INSULIN RESISTANCE IN PATHOGENESIS OF LOW HDL LEVELS
S07RR-05426-30 0136 (NSS) HATHAWAY, RONALD R Biomedical research support COMPUTER MODELING OF CRANIOFACIAL ANOMALIES

PROJECT NO., ORGANIZATIONAL UNIT., INVESTIGATOR, ADDRESS, TITLE

S07RR-05426-30 0137 (NSS) HOBAR, P CRAIG Biomedical research support FRONTAL BONE ADVANCEMENT: CRITICAL ANALYSIS
S07RR-05426-30 0138 (NSS) KAMINSKA, GRAZYNA M Biomedical research support MECHANISM OF CORNEAL NEOVASCULARIZATION
S07RR-05426-30 0139 (NSS) KOUROSH, SOHRAB Biomedical research support EFFECTS OF LOW ENERGY LASER IN HEALING BURN WOUND & PAIN REDUCTION
S07RR-05426-30 0140 (NSS) KOWATCH, ROBERT A Biomedical research support DIGITAL PERIOD ANALYSIS OF SLEEP OF DEPRESSED CHILDREN
S07RR-05426-30 0141 (NSS) LEVINE, BENJAMIN D Biomedical research support POWER SPECTRAL ANALYSIS OF BEAT BY BEAT CHANGE IN HUMAN CARDIAC STROKE VOLUME
S07RR-05426-30 0142 (NSS) LIN, VICTOR K Biomedical research support MOLECULAR STUDY OF CALDESMON IN OBSTRUCTED BLADDER
S07RR-05426-30 0143 (NSS) MCGUIRE, MICHAEL J Biomedical research support PURIFICATION & CHARACTERIZATION OF HUMAN DIPEPTIDYL PEPTIDASE I
S07RR-05426-30 0144 (NSS) MILEWICH, LEON Biomedical research support SYNTHESIS OF NOVEL TUMOR PREVENTIVE STEROIDS DEVOID OF SEX HORMONE ACTIVITIES
S07RR-05426-30 0145 (NSS) MOE, ORSON W Biomedical research support RENAL NA & H ANTIPORTER MRNA IN CHRONIC METABOLIC ACIDOSIS
S07RR-05426-30 0146 (NSS) O, CHUN-SING Biomedical research support INTRAOPERATIVE TISSUE VIABILITY MONITOR: FLUOROMETER NADH & LACTATE MONITORING
S07RR-05426-30 0147 (NSS) OLIVARI, MARIA-TERES Biomedical research support ASSESS CARDIAC REINNERVATION AFTER ORTHOTOPIC CARDIAC TRANSPLANTATION IN HUMANS
S07RR-05426-30 0148 (NSS) SLEGEL, DUANE E Biomedical research support DEPRESSED OUTPATIENTS EXHIBIT CORE BODY TEMPERATURE ABNORMALITIES AT SLEEP
S07RR-05426-30 0149 (NSS) WANSBROUGH, SCOTT R Biomedical research support NEUROMUSCULAR BLOCKADE RESEARCH COMPUTER
S07RR-05426-30 0150 (NSS) WHITTEN, CHARLES W Biomedical research support AUTOLOGOUS BLOOD TRANSFUSION FOLLOWING CARDIOPULMONARY BYPASS
S07RR-05426-30 0151 (NSS) WILEY, ELIZABETH L Biomedical research support IMMUNOLOGY & LECTIN REACTIVITY OF DERMATOFIBROSARCOMA PROTUBERANS
S07RR-05426-30 0152 (NSS) WOOLLETT, LAURA A Biomedical research support WHY PLASMA CHOLESTEROL CONCENTRATIONS VARY BETWEEN INDIVIDUALS FED SIMILAR DIETS
S07RR-05426-30 0153 (NSS) WORD, RUTH A Biomedical research support CONTRACTILE SYSTEM ELEMENTS OF HUMAN MYOMETRIUM DURING PREGNANCY
S07RR-05426-30 0127 (NSS) ANAND, RAJIV Biomedical research support PROLIFERATION & METASTASES OF HUMAN UVEAL MELANOMA CELLS IN MOUSE MODEL
S07RR-05426-30 0128 (NSS) BANSAL, NAVIN Biomedical research support NMR STUDIES OF HEPATIC METABOLISM IN HUMAN W/ DIABETES
S07RR-05426-30 0129 (NSS) BOGGARAM, VIJAYAKUMA Biomedical research support FACTORS OF HUMAN PULMONARY SURFACTANT PROTEIN A (SP A) GENE
S07RR-05426-30 0130 (NSS) BOWMAN, GARY W Biomedical research support ETOMIDATE HYPOTHERMIA: SUPPRESSION OF CEREBRAL METABOLISM INTRACRANIAL ANEURYSM
S07RR-05426-30 0131 (NSS) BRINK, LELA W Biomedical research support DISTRIBUTION OF CARDIAC OUTPUT TO RESPIRATORY MUSCLES
S07RR-05426-30 0132 (NSS) BURNS, ALTON JAY Biomedical research support IMMUNOLOGIC EFFECTS SILICONE & POLY URETHANE BREAST IMPLANTS SURFACE ANTIGENS
S07RR-05427-30 (NSS) BRYAN, GEORGE T UNIV OF TEXAS MEDICAL BRANCH 301 UNIVERSITY BLVD. GALVESTON, TEX 77550 Biomedical research support grant
S07RR-05427-30 0154 (NSS) CORREIA, MANNING J Biomedical research support grant VESTIBULAR HAIR CELL: MECHANOELECTRIC TRANSDUCER OF LINEAR & ANGULAR HEAD MOTION
S07RR-05427-30 0155 (NSS) JONES, ANNE H Biomedical research support grant SEMIOTIC PERSPECTIVES ON LANGUAGE & VERBAL ART; DECONSTRUCTION & HERMENEUTICS
S07RR-05427-30 0156 (NSS) WALKER, DAVID Biomedical research support grant PATHOGENESIS OF DENGUE HEMORRHAGIC FEVER: DENGUE VIRUS DNA & RNA HYBRIDIZATION
S07RR-05427-30 0157 (NSS) ANSARI, NASEEM H Biomedical research support grant MECHANISM OF SUGAR INDUCED CATARACTOGENESIS: ALLOPURINOL HYPERGLYCEMIA MODEL
S07RR-05427-30 0158 (NSS) BAKOS, MARY-ANN Biomedical research support grant MOLECULAR MAP OF HUMAN SECRETORY IGA: IMMUNOGLOBULIN FAMILY: DOMAINS OF DIGA
S07RR-05427-30 0159 (NSS) QUAST, MICHAEL J Biomedical research support grant MRI OF CEREBRAL ISCHEMIA IN ANIMAL MODELS OF STROKE & CEREBRAL HEMORRHAGE
S07RR-05427-30 0160 (NSS) SCHNELL, VICKI L Biomedical research support grant CARBON DIOXIDE LASER VS MICROELECTROCAUTERY DISTAL FALLOPIAN TUBAL OBSTRUCTION
S07RR-05428-30 (NSS) STEVENS, WALTER UNIV OF UTAH SCH OF MED 50 NORTH MEDICAL DRIVE SALT LAKE CITY, UTAH 84132 Biomedical research support
S07RR-05428-30 0163 (NSS) WILEY, H STEVEN Biomedical research support XENOPUS OOCYTES AS SURROGATE CELLS FOR MOLECULAR ANALYSIS OF RECEPTOR DYNAMICS
S07RR-05428-30 0164 (NSS) WEIS, JOHN H Biomedical research support BIOLOGY PERTAINING TO MURINE COMPLEMENT RECEPTORS
S07RR-05428-30 0165 (NSS) BISHOP, D KEITH Biomedical research support INFLAMMATORY ENDOTHELIA LYMPHOCYTE INTERACTIONS IN VIVO
S07RR-05428-30 0166 (NSS) BOHNSACK, JOHN Biomedical research support HUMAN NEUTROPHIL RECEPTOR FOR LAMININ
S07RR-05428-30 0161 (NSS) FARRUKH, IMAD S Biomedical research support ELUCIDATE MECHANISMS THAT REGULATE CA++ IN PULMONARY VASCULAR SMC & EC
S07RR-05428-30 0167 (NSS) DETHLEFSEN, LYLE A Biomedical research support POLY (ADP RIBOSE) POLYMERASE IN RADIATION INDUCED CYTOTOXICITY: CANCER
S07RR-05428-30 0168 (NSS) EVANS, THOMAS G Biomedical research support DEHYDROEPIANDROSTERONE AS ADJUVANT TO INDUCE CELL MEDIATED IMMUNITY

S07RR-05428-30 0169 (NSS) KEATING, MARK T Biomedical research support MOLECULAR GENETICS OF LONG QT SYNDROME
S07RR-05428-30 0170 (NSS) STURROCK, ANN B Biomedical research support ELUCIDATING BIOCHEMICAL & FUNCTIONAL PROPERTIES OF PR 3
S07RR-05428-30 0171 (NSS) SAMOWITZ, WADE S Biomedical research support P53 GENE EXPRESSION & HUMAN COLON CARCINOGENESIS
S07RR-05428-30 0172 (NSS) GONZALEZ, ALFONSO Biomedical research support GROWTH FACTORS IN HORMONAL CARCINOGENESIS
S07RR-05428-30 0173 (NSS) OLIPHANT, ARNOLD Biomedical research support CONTIGUOUS CLONE MAP FROM ORDERED CLONE LIBRARIES USING BINARY INFORMATION
S07RR-05428-30 0174 (NSS) ROWLEY, ROY Biomedical research support RADIATION INDUCED G2 ARREST IN S POMBE
S07RR-05428-30 0175 (NSS) PETERSEN, MARTA J Biomedical research support UV RADIATION ON COLLAGENASE PROD BY CULTURED HUMAN KERATINOCYTES & FIBROBLASTS
S07RR-05428-30 0176 (NSS) LOGHMAN-ADHAM, MAHMO Biomedical research support NA+ & H+ EXCHANGE IN RENAL PROXIMAL TUBULAR CELLS BY GROWTH HORMONE
S07RR-05428-30 0177 (NSS) JACKSON, W DANIEL Biomedical research support BONE MINERALIZATION IN CYSTIC FIBROSIS: PROSPECTIVE STUDY
S07RR-05428-30 0178 (NSS) FIKE, CANDICE D Biomedical research support MATURATIONAL CHANGES IN PULMONARY MICROCIRCULATION
S07RR-05428-30 0162 (NSS) MCCUSKER, KEVIN T Biomedical research support TOXIN FROM LEGIONELLA PNEUMOPHILA SEROGROUP 1 WHICH BLOCKS PROTEIN SYNTHESIS
S07RR-05428-30 0179 (NSS) HEBDEN, JEREMY G Biomedical research support BREAST IMAGING USING PICOSECOND PULSES OF LIGHT
S07RR-05428-30 0180 (NSS) PEETERS, GEORGE A Biomedical research support ENDOTHELIAL CELL CONTROL OF CORONARY VASCULAR RESISTANCE
S07RR-05428-30 0181 (NSS) RFFY, RODOLPHE Biomedical research support AUTONOMIC MODULATION OF CARDIAC DEFIBRILATION
S07RR-05428-30 0182 (NSS) KIM, BENJAMIN Biomedical research support T CELL RECEPTOR V BETA USAGE IN TUMOR INFILTRATING LYMPHOCYTES
S07RR-05428-30 0183 (NSS) KUEHL, LEROY R Biomedical research support NUCLEAR ACCUMULATION SIGNALS OF NON HISTO CHROMOSOMAL PROTEINS HMG1 & HMG17
S07RR-05428-30 0184 (NSS) YIP, VERA S Biomedical research support METABOLIC CHANGES IN DENTATE GYRUS OF HIPPOCAMPUS AFTER SYMPATHETIC SPROUTING
S07RR-05428-30 0185 (NSS) WEIS, JOHN H Biomedical research support GENE EXPRESSION IN DIFFERENTIATION OF CELLS DERIVED FROM MAMMALIAN BONE MARROW
S07RR-05428-30 0186 (NSS) GRUNWALD, DAVID J Biomedical research support IDENT & CHARACTERIZATION OF GENES THAT CONTRIBUTE TO EMBRYO GENESIS IN ZEBRAFISH
S07RR-05428-30 0187 (NSS) MEYER, LAURENCE J Biomedical research support CHEMOPREVENTION OF MELANOMA STUDIED IN GRAFTED DYSPLASTIC NEVI
S07RR-05428-30 0188 (NSS) WHATLEY, RALPH E Biomedical research support REGULATION OF PRODUCTION OF BIOACTIVE LIPIDS BY ENDOTHELIAL CELLS
S07RR-05428-30 0189 (NSS) RODGERS, GEORGE M Biomedical research support CHARACTERIZATION OF CELL BINDING DOMAIN OF COAGULATION FACTOR V
S07RR-05429-30 (NSS) LUGINBUHL, WILLIAM H UNIVERSITY OF VERMONT E109 HEALTH SCIENCE COMPLEX BURLINGTON, VT 05405 Biomedical research support grant
S07RR-05429-30 0194 (NSS) MASON, ANNE B Biomedical research support grant PIG SERUM TRANSFERRIN VS HUMAN SERUM TRANSFERRIN TO HELA CELLS
S07RR-05429-30 0195 (NSS) MAY, VICTOR Biomedical research support grant EXPRESSION OF NEUROENDOCRINE PEPTIDES
S07RR-05429-30 0196 (NSS) BRAAS, KAREN M Biomedical research support grant PEPTIDYLGLYCINE ALPHA MIDATING MONOXYGENASE (PAM) IN CENTRAL NERVOUS SYSTEM
S07RR-05429-30 0197 (NSS) HAEBERLE, JOSEPH R Biomedical research support grant REGULATION OF SMOOTH MUSCLE CONTRACTION
S07RR-05429-30 0198 (NSS) STOKES, IAN F Biomedical research support grant SKELETAL GROWTH & REMODELING IN SCOLIOSIS
S07RR-05429-30 0199 (NSS) SHREEVE, STEPHEN M Biomedical research support grant MOLECULAR CLONING & EXPRESSION OF CDNA FOR RABBIT CARDIAC X1 ADRENOCEPTOR
S07RR-05429-30 0200 (NSS) HART, BETH A Biomedical research support grant SYNTHESIS & ROLE OF METALLOTHIONEIN IN LUNG
S07RR-05429-30 0201 (NSS) FOREHAND, CYNTHIA J Biomedical research support grant PREGANGLIONIC NEURONS THAT CONTROL VASCULATURE
S07RR-05429-30 0190 (NSS) DURAND, DAVID B Biomedical research support grant MALIGNANT MESOTHELIOMA: GROWTH & DIFFERENTIATION PATHWAYS
S07RR-05429-30 0191 (NSS) HAMRELL, BURT B Biomedical research support grant MOLECULAR BASIS OF MYOFILAMENT ACTIVATION & SHORTENING
S07RR-05429-30 0192 (NSS) OSOL, GEORGE J Biomedical research support grant PREGNANCY & SMOOTH MUSCLE IN ARTERIES; MYOGENIC ADRENERGIC
S07RR-05429-30 0193 (NSS) MAWE, GARY M Biomedical research support grant NEURAL CONTROL OF HUMAN GALLBLADDER
S07RR-05429-30 0202 (NSS) WOODWORTH, ROBERT C Biomedical research support grant IRON DELIVERY VIA BLOOD; STRUCTURAL ROLE OF TRANSFERRIN
S07RR-05429-30 0203 (NSS) ADAMS, BRIAN D Biomedical research support grant STRAIN ACROSS TRIANGULAR FIBROCARTILAGE COMPLEX & TENSILE LOADING
S07RR-05429-30 0204 (NSS) TALLMADGE, JAMES M Biomedical research support grant INDEPENDENT MEASURES OF HYPERACTIVITY & AGGRESSION
S07RR-05429-30 0205 (NSS) SCHAEFFER, WARREN I Biomedical research support grant CYTOPLASM IN TRANSFER OF MALIGNANT PHENOTYPE
S07RR-05429-30 0206 (NSS) HEINTZ, NICHOLAS H Biomedical research support grant REGULATION OF DNA SYNTHESIS IN MAMMALIAN CELLS; DNA REPLICATION
S07RR-05429-30 0207 (NSS) ONEILL, J PATRICK Biomedical research support grant ESTABLISH PHYSICAL MAP OF HUMAN X CHROMOSOME
S07RR-05429-30 0208 (NSS) RENSTROM, PER Biomedical research support grant BIOMECHANICS OF ANKLE LIGAMENT INSTABILITY & RECONSTRUCTION
S07RR-05429-30 0209 (NSS) RIMMER, JEFFREY M Biomedical research support grant LOW MOLECULAR WEIGHT PROTEINS IN PROGRESSIVE RENAL FAILURE
S07RR-05429-30 0210 (NSS) LEAVITT, BRUCE J Biomedical research support grant 2 3 BUTANEDIONE MONOXIME & MYOCARDIAL PRESERVATION; CARDIOPULMONARY
S07RR-05429-30 0211 (NSS) NICHOL, CLAUD E Biomedical research support grant RECONSTRUCTION OF ACUTELY RUPTURED ANTERIOR CRUCIATE LIGAMENT
S07RR-05429-30 0212 (NSS) SRIRAM, S Biomedical research support grant VACCINATION W/ PEPTIDE FRAGMENTS: IA MOLECULE ON IMMUNE RESPONSE MYELIN PROTEIN
S07RR-05430-30 (NSS) AYRES, STEPHEN M VA COMMONWEALTH UNIV MED SCH BOX 565, MCV STATION RICHMOND, VIRGINIA 23298-0568 Biomedical research support
S07RR-05430-30 0213 (NSS) SCHIRCH, LAVERNE G Biomedical research support SITE DIRECTED MUTAGENESIS OF SERINE HYDROXYMETHYL TRANSFERASE
S07RR-05430-30 0214 (NSS) NEWMAN, SAMMYE Biomedical research support ANALYSIS OF REGULATORY FACTORS CONTROLLING MYELIN BASIC PROTEIN GENE EXPRESSION
S07RR-05430-30 0215 (NSS) CHELBOWSKI, JAN F Biomedical research support ALTERATION OF E COLI ALKALINE PHOSPHATASE STRUCTURE BY MUTAGENESIS
S07RR-05430-30 0225 (NSS) PERR, HILARY A Biomedical research support GROWTH FACTORS IN FETAL INTESTINE DEVELOPMENT
S07RR-05430-30 0226 (NSS) SALTER, DAVID R Biomedical research support RABBIT MYCOCARDIUM & T3
S07RR-05430-30 0227 (NSS) SMITH-HARRISON, LEON Biomedical research support REPERFUSION INJURY IN TESTICULAR TORSION
S07RR-05430-30 0228 (NSS) WOOGEN, SCOTT Biomedical research support GUT IMMUNE SYSTEM
S07RR-05430-30 0216 (NSS) MCCOY, KATHLEEN L Biomedical research support ANTIGEN PROCESSING PATHWAYS FOR T CELL ACTIVATION
S07RR-05430-30 0217 (NSS) CHLEBOWSKI, JAN F Biomedical research support ASSEMBLY OF BACTERIAL ALKALINE PHOSPHATASE
S07RR-05430-30 0218 (NSS) CHLEBOWSKI, JAN F Biomedical research support INTRACELLULAR SIGNALLING: REGULATION OF CELLULAR PROCESSES
S07RR-05430-30 0219 (NSS) CARTER, ANTHONY Biomedical research support REGULATION OF EXPRESSION OF G PROTEINS IN HUMANS
S07RR-05430-30 0220 (NSS) HECK, GERARD Biomedical research support TRANSEPITHELIAL ELECTRICAL RESPONSE TO TASTANTS
S07RR-05430-30 0221 (NSS) DAMIANO, RALPH Biomedical research support ELECTROPHYSIOLOGICAL CONSEQUENCES OF SURGICAL ISCHEMIA
S07RR-05430-30 0222 (NSS) GEHR, TODD W D Biomedical research support ACE INHIBITION ON PERITONEAL TRANSPORT
S07RR-05430-30 0223 (NSS) KOCH, WILLIAM Biomedical research support PARVOVIRUS B19
S07RR-05430-30 0224 (NSS) MASSEY, GITA Biomedical research support PROTEIN KINASE C ACTIVATORS
S07RR-05431-30 (NSS) CAREY, ROBERT M UNIVERSITY OF VIRGINIA HLTH SCI CTR BOX 395 CHARLOTTESVILLE, VA 22908 Biomedical research support
S07RR-05431-30 0856 (NSS) COWLEY, MARIANNE Biomedical research support EFFECT OF GAMMA KNIFE RADIOSURGERY IN HUMAN OCULAR MELANOMA IN RABBITS
S07RR-05431-30 0857 (NSS) FERGUSON, JAMES E, I Biomedical research support CDNA FOR CALBINDIN D9K & IDENTIFICATION & LOCALIZATION OF VITAMIN D RECEPTOR I
S07RR-05431-30 0858 (NSS) RULE, GORDON S Biomedical research support STRUCTURE OF PHOSPHOLIPASE A2
S07RR-05431-30 0859 (NSS) VAUGHAN, CHRISTOPHER Biomedical research support SEVERITY OF SPASTIC HYPERTONIA USING A DYNAMIC LOCOMOTIVE APPROACH
S07RR-05431-30 0860 (NSS) KOLP, LISA Biomedical research support MECHANISMS SUBSERVING PREOVULATORY LH SURGE
S07RR-05431-30 0861 (NSS) HINTON, BARRY T Biomedical research support EXPRESSION & REGULATION OF GAMMAGLUTAMYL TRANSPEPTIDASE IN RAT EPIDIDYMIS
S07RR-05431-30 0862 (NSS) ENGEL, DANIEL A Biomedical research support CIS ACTING ELEMENTS IN TRANSCRIPTIONAL REGULATION BY ADENOVIRUS EIA PROTEIN
S07RR-05431-30 0863 (NSS) SAROSIEK, JERZY Biomedical research support EPIDERMAL GROWTH FACTOR MAINTENANCE OF ESOPHAGEAL MUCOSAL BARRIER
S07RR-05431-30 0864 (NSS) BLECK, THOMAS P Biomedical research support IN VITRO ANALYSIS OF ELECTROPHYSIOLOGICAL RESPONSES OF EPILEPTIC BRAIN TISSUE
S07RR-05431-30 0865 (NSS) ROCHE, JAMES K Biomedical research support MAB FOR LOCALIZATION OF THYMIC EPITHELIUM; IMMUNOLOGICALLY MEDIATED DISORDERS
S07RR-05431-30 0866 (NSS) HOLLOWAY, PETER W Biomedical research support MEMBRANE BINDING DOMAIN OF CYTOCHROME B5 IN CATALYSIS
S07RR-05431-30 0867 (NSS) MYERS, BRENT M Biomedical research support ALTERATIONS OF HEPATOCYTE LYSOSOMES IN EXPERIMENTAL COPPER OVERLOAD
S07RR-05431-30 0829 (NSS) RHEUBAN, KAREN S Biomedical research support PARADOXICAL HYPERTENSION FOLLOWING COARCTATION RESECTION
S07RR-05431-30 0830 (NSS) GUTGESELL, MARGARET Biomedical research support CHILDHOOD ACTIVITY & CARDIOVASCULAR HEALTH
S07RR-05431-30 0831 (NSS) FARR, BARRY M Biomedical research support CASE CONTROL STUDY OF PNEUMOCOCCAL VACCINE EFFICACY
S07RR-05431-30 0832 (NSS) LEVINE, PAUL A Biomedical research support ANALYSIS OF SQUAMOUS CELL CARCINOMA USING MONOCLONAL ANTIBODIES
S07RR-05431-30 0833 (NSS) KNIGHT, HERBERT Biomedical research support VALIDATION OF FLUOROSCOPIC MEASUREMENT OF DIAPHRAGM SHORTENING VELOCITY
S07RR-05431-30 0834 (NSS) CONNELLY, JULIA E Biomedical research support TEACHING ETHICS IN MEDICAL OFFICE
S07RR-05431-30 0835 (NSS) BERTRAM, EDWARD Biomedical research support ANATOMY OF EPILEPSY
S07RR-05431-30 0836 (NSS) PHILBRICK, JOHN T Biomedical research support DIAGNOSIS & MEDICATION CLUSTERS: DESCRIBING CLINICAL CONTENT OF AMBULATORY CARE
S07RR-05431-30 0837 (NSS) LYNCH, KEVIN R Biomedical research

support ANTI HUMAN ANGIOTENSINOGEN MONOCLONAL ANTIBODIES
S07RR-05431-30 0838 (NSS) ALLAIRE, JANET H Biomedical research support ASSESSMENT OF NON SPEAKING CHILDREN NOT USING AUGMENTATIVE COMMUNICATION SYSTEMS
S07RR-05431-30 0839 (NSS) RULE, GORDON S Biomedical research support NMR STUDIES OF PROTEIN STRUCTURE
S07RR-05431-30 0840 (NSS) LOGIN, IVAN S Biomedical research support CALCIUM TRANSPORT IN RAT CELLS
S07RR-05431-30 0841 (NSS) SHUPNIK, MARGARET A Biomedical research support CONTROL OF PITUITARY GENE TRANSPORTATION
S07RR-05431-30 0842 (NSS) BOROWITZ, STEPHEN M Biomedical research support ONTOGENY OF INTESTINAL PHOSPHATE TRANSPORT IN RABBIT
S07RR-05431-30 0843 (NSS) HANIGAN, MARIE H Biomedical research support GAMMA GLUTAMYL TRANSPEPTIDASE POSITIVE TUMOR CELLS TO CHEMOTHERAPEUTIC DRUGS
S07RR-05431-30 0844 (NSS) MCDANIEL, NANCY L Biomedical research support MECHANISM OF CYCLIC GMP DEPENDENT VASCULAR SMOOTH MUSCLE RELAXATION
S07RR-05431-30 0845 (NSS) MERWIN, ELIZABETH Biomedical research support NURSING MANPOWER: RELATIONSHIP BETWEEN COST, QUALITY CARE & RN RETENTION
S07RR-05431-30 0846 (NSS) TRIBBLE, CURTIS G Biomedical research support INTERSTITIAL FLUID ADENOSINE & CORONARY BLOOD FLOW
S07RR-05431-30 0847 (NSS) KINTER, MICHAEL Biomedical research support ENDOTHELIAL CELLS, PLATELETS & W 3 FATTY ACIDS
S07RR-05431-30 0848 (NSS) MARSHALL, BARRY J Biomedical research support IN VITRO MODEL OF C PYLORI CYTOTOXICITY USING CULTURED GASTRIC EPITHELIAL CELLS
S07RR-05431-30 0849 (NSS) LAURIE, GORDON W Biomedical research support INDUCTION OF ALVEOLARIZATION BY BASEMENT MEMBRANE EXTRACTS
S07RR-05431-30 0850 (NSS) ESAU, SHARON A Biomedical research support DIAPHRAGM MUSCLE DYSFUNCTION IN CHRONICALLY HYPOXIC ANIMALS
S07RR-05431-30 0851 (NSS) LAWSON, DAN Biomedical research support DOES NITROUS OXIDE CAUSE MYOCARDIAL TISSUE DEPRESSION: ALTER CALCIUM MYOFIBRILS
S07RR-05431-30 0852 (NSS) SCHWARTZ, CHARLES F Biomedical research support MECHANISM OF INSULIN ACTION: PHOSPHORYLATION & DEPHOSPHORYLATION CASCADE
S07RR-05431-30 0853 (NSS) AMERO, SALLY A Biomedical research support HORMONE MEDIATED GENE REGULATION
S07RR-05431-30 0854 (NSS) ANGELLO, DEBRA A Biomedical research support ADENOSINE IN MYOCARDIAL GLUCOSE UPTAKE
S07RR-05431-30 0855 (NSS) THOMAS, TED S Biomedical research support DEVELOPMENTAL POTENTIAL OF INDIVIDUAL MOUSE SPERM
S07RR-05432-30 (NSS) HOLBROOK, KAREN A UNIVERSITY OF WASHINGTON SCHOOL OF MEDICINE SC-64 SEATTLE, WASH 98195 Biomedical research support grant
S07RR-05432-30 0229 (NSS) RASEY, JANET S Biomedical research support grant METHODS OF FUNDING BIOMEDICAL RESEARCH
S07RR-05432-30 0230 (NSS) DIKMEN, SUREYYA S Biomedical research support grant SUBARACHNOID HEMORRHAGE
S07RR-05432-30 0231 (NSS) WILLING, MARCIA C Biomedical research support grant OSTEOGENESIS IMPERFECTA; COLLAGEN; MUTATIONS
S07RR-05432-30 0232 (NSS) VAN HOOSIER, GERALD Biomedical research support grant ANIMAL MEDICINE DEVELOPMENT; TRANSGENIC MOUSE FACILITY
S07RR-05432-30 0248 (NSS) WALSH, KENNETH A Biomedical research support grant ELECTROSPRAY MASS SPECTROMETER
S07RR-05432-30 0233 (NSS) TARR, PHILLIP I Biomedical research support grant CLONING OF ADHESIN OF ENTEROHEMORRAGHIC E COLI
S07RR-05432-30 0234 (NSS) REID, BRAIN J Biomedical research support grant PANCREATIC NEOPLASIA; TRANSGENIC MOUSE MODEL OF PANCREATIC CANCER
S07RR-05432-30 0235 (NSS) SISCOVICK, DAVID S Biomedical research support grant POLYUNSATURATED FATTY ACIDS & RISK OF PRIMARY CARDIAC ARREST
S07RR-05432-30 0236 (NSS) DAGER, STEPHEN R Biomedical research support grant LACTATE INFUSION; PANIC ATTACKS; MRI
S07RR-05432-30 0237 (NSS) GROSSMANN, ANGELIKA Biomedical research support grant IMMUNE FUNCTION DECLINES W/ AGE; MICE
S07RR-05432-30 0238 (NSS) GLENN, MICHAEL G Biomedical research support grant MICROVASCULAR THROMBOSIS; NEW METHOD FOR HEPARIN DELIVERY
S07RR-05432-30 0239 (NSS) CLARKE, WILLIAM R Biomedical research support grant OXYGEN EFFECTS; FETUS; INFANT; TRANSITIONAL CIRCULATION
S07RR-05432-30 0240 (NSS) FLINT, PAUL W Biomedical research support grant A MODEL OF SYNKINESIS FOLLOWING LARYNGEAL; REINNERVATION OF LARYNX
S07RR-05432-30 0241 (NSS) SIDLES, JOHN A Biomedical research support grant FREEZE FIXATION OF MECHANICALLY LOADED COLLAGENOUS TISSUES
S07RR-05432-30 0242 (NSS) EASTERLING, THOMAS R Biomedical research support grant PREVENTION OF PREECLAMPSIA; HYPERTENSION
S07RR-05432-30 0243 (NSS) SANGEORZAN, BRUCE J Biomedical research support grant CONTACT PRESSURE IN HUMAN SUBTALAR JOINT; DEGENERATIVE DISEASES; ARTHRITIS
S07RR-05432-30 0244 (NSS) DIGIACOMO, RONALD F Biomedical research support grant ALTERNATIVES TO USE OF FREUDS ADJUVANT FOR ANTISERA PRODUCTION IN RABBITS
S07RR-05432-30 0245 (NSS) GOODSITT, MITCHELL M Biomedical research support grant PHOTON XRAY; FAT & MINERAL CONTENT OF HUMAN BODY
S07RR-05432-30 0246 (NSS) HAMMOND, WILLIAM P Biomedical research support grant GREY COLLIES; CYCLIC NEUTROPENIA; ANIMAL MODELS
S07RR-05432-30 0247 (NSS) ROSS, RUSSELL Biomedical research support grant D502E REMODEL; CELL SORTING FLOW CYTOMETER
S07RR-05433-30 (NSS) HEDGE, GEORGE A WVU SCHOOL OF MEDICINE 2266 HEALTH SCIENCES SOUTH MORGANTOWN, WV 26506 Biomedical research support
S07RR-05433-30 0249 (NSS) NYLES, CHARON Biomedical research support GENETIC BIOCHEMICAL ANALYSIS SPIROCHETER MOTILITY
S07RR-05433-30 0250 (NSS) FAYNOR, STEVEN Biomedical research support CYCLOSPORINE MEASUREMENT IN BLOOD
S07RR-05433-30 0251 (NSS) MAWHINNEY, MICHAEL Biomedical research support PHOSPHOLIPASE A2 & PKC ACTIVATION ANDROGEN INDUCED MUSCLE PROLIFERATION
S07RR-05433-30 0252 (NSS) OMAR, RAWHI Biomedical research support PATHOGENESIS NEURODEGENERATIVE DISEASE
S07RR-05433-30 0253 (NSS) SHIEMKE, ANDREW Biomedical research support CHARACTERIZATION OF METHAN MONO OXYGENASE
S07RR-05433-30 0254 (NSS) SAYED, ATEF Biomedical research support PROTEOGLYCAN SYNTHESIS & CHROMOSOMAL STUDY EPITHELIAL MALIGNANT CELLS
S07RR-05433-30 0255 (NSS) VRANA, KENT Biomedical research support HORMONE PROFILES NEONATAL SPONTANEOUSLY HYPERTENSIVE RAT
S07RR-05433-30 0256 (NSS) JACKSON, TIMOTHY K Biomedical research support PHOSPHORYLATION APO B ISOLATED RAT HEPATOCYTES
S07RR-05434-30 (NSS) COOPER, RICHARD A MEDICAL COLLEGE OF WISCONSIN 8701 WATERTOWN PLANK ROAD MILWAUKEE, WIS 53226 Biomedical research support
S07RR-05434-30 0817 (NSS) CRONIN, MARY E Biomedical research support REGULATION OF CYTOKINES & VIRUS INFECTION ON MYOBLAST EXPRESSION OF MHC ANTIGENS
S07RR-05434-30 0818 (NSS) CHAKRABURTTY, KALPAN Biomedical research support REGULATION OF RIBOSOMAL REACTION
S07RR-05434-30 0819 (NSS) SIEBER-BLUM, MAYA Biomedical research support CLONING OF REGULATORY SEQUENCES FROM DIFFERENTIATING NEURAL CREST CELLS
S07RR-05434-30 0796 (NSS) WILKISON, DOUGLAS M Biomedical research support ABUSE DRUGS: BEHAVIORAL INTEGRATION
S07RR-05434-30 0797 (NSS) HOGAN, KEVIN T Biomedical research support CYTOTOXIC T LYMPHOCYTE RESPONSE TO REOVIRUS
S07RR-05434-30 0798 (NSS) SEETHARAM, BELLUR Biomedical research support MOLECULAR ASPECT OF COBALAMIN TRANSPORT
S07RR-05434-30 0799 (NSS) HAN, DENNIS P Biomedical research support MODEL OF EARLY CELLULAR EVENTS IN PROLIFERATIVE VITREORETINOPATHY
S07RR-05434-30 0800 (NSS) EGAN, BRENT M Biomedical research support IMPORTANCE OF VOLUME EXPANSION IN SALT SENSITIVE HYPERTENSION
S07RR-05434-30 0801 (NSS) SEETHARAM, SHAKUNTLA Biomedical research support STRUCTURAL STUDIES ON METHYLONYL COENZYME MUTASE
S07RR-05434-30 0802 (NSS) DAHMS, NANCY M Biomedical research support LIGAND BONDING SITE OF CATION DEPENDENT MANNOSE 6 PHOSPHATE RECEPTOR
S07RR-05434-30 0803 (NSS) REDDY, M NARAHARI Biomedical research support STRUCTURAL FUNCTION RELATIONSHIPS OF LIPOPROTEIN LIPASE
S07RR-05434-30 0804 (NSS) GIUDICE, GEORGE J Biomedical research support MOLECULAR FUNCTION DOMAINS OF EPIDERMAL HEMIDESMOSOMES
S07RR-05434-30 0805 (NSS) DEAN-BERNHOFT, CARON Biomedical research support ORGANIZATION & CONTROL OF SYMPATHETIC NERVOUS SYSTEM
S07RR-05434-30 0806 (NSS) FRANK, DARA W Biomedical research support REGULATION OF EXOENZYME SECRETION IN PSEUDOMONAS AERUGINOSA
S07RR-05434-30 0807 (NSS) DEYOE, EDGAR A Biomedical research support SENSORY PROCESSING STREAMS OF EXTRASTRIATE CORTEX OF MACAQUE MONKEY
S07RR-05434-30 0808 (NSS) GRAY, RICHARD W Biomedical research support MOLECULAR MECHANISMS OF MAMMALIAN 25 OH01A HYDROXYLASE
S07RR-05434-30 0809 (NSS) STERNBERG, EDWARD A Biomedical research support RELATIONSHIPS OF TGF BETA, RAS, MYOD1, & MCK ENHANCERS IN MYO & CARDIOGENESIS
S07RR-05434-30 0820 (NSS) HAGER, STEPHEN R Biomedical research support MEASUREMENT OF INSULIN REGULATED GLUCOSE TRANSPORTER LEVEL
S07RR-05434-30 0821 (NSS) COWLES, VERNE E Biomedical research support RELATIONSHIP BETWEEN COLONIC FUNCTION & BLOOD FLOW
S07RR-05434-30 0822 (NSS) NORINS, NAN A Biomedical research support EFFECTS OF INDOMETHACIN ON CEREBRAL ARTERY REGULATORY MECHANISMS
S07RR-05434-30 0823 (NSS) CASHDOLLAR, L WILLIA Biomedical research support MOLECULAR MECHANISMS OF REOVIRUS INDUCED DIABETES
S07RR-05434-30 0810 (NSS) TERRY, L CASS Biomedical research support HYPOTHALAMIC REGULATION OF GROWTH HORMONE RHYTHM
S07RR-05434-30 0811 (NSS) KRUG, EDWARD L Biomedical research support MOLECULAR ANALYSIS OF INDUCTION IN CARDIAC MORPHOGENESIS
S07RR-05434-30 0812 (NSS) HENRICKSON, KELLY J Biomedical research support MOLECULAR EPIDEMIOLOGY OF HUMAN PARAINFLUENZA VIRUS I: PEDIATRICS
S07RR-05434-30 0813 (NSS) KOSTREVA, DAVID R Biomedical research support NEURAL INFLUENCES ON CARDIAC DEVELOPMENT & METABOLISM
S07RR-05434-30 0814 (NSS) SCHAPIRA, RALPH M Biomedical research support SECRETION OF GROWTH FACTOR BY STIMULATED ALVEOLAR MACROPHAGES
S07RR-05434-30 0815 (NSS) WAGNER, DAVID K Biomedical research support IMMUNOTHERAPY OF M INTRACELLULARE IN MURINE RETROVIRUS MODEL
S07RR-05434-30 0816 (NSS) LEE, PIN CHEUNG Biomedical research support ENDOCRINE CONTROL OF PANCREATIC DEVELOPMENT
S07RR-05435-30 (NSS) BROWN, ARNOLD L UNIV OF WISCONSIN MED SCH 1300 UNIVERSITY AVENUE MADISON, WIS 53706 Biomedical research support
S07RR-05435-30 0978 (NSS) CHUANG, TSU-YI Biomedical research support ONCOGENIC POTENTIAL OF PHOTOCHEMOTHERAPY A PILOT STUDY
S07RR-05435-30 0979 (NSS) CORNWELL, MARILYN M Biomedical research support MULTIDRUG RESISTANCE IN HUMAN TUMOR CELLS
S07RR-05435-30 0980 (NSS) RAPOZA, PETER Biomedical research support DRY EYES & SEX HORMONES
S07RR-05435-30 0981 (NSS) ALLEN, DAVID B Biomedical research support INFLUENCE OF HUMAN GROWTH HORMONE ON CHRONIC RENAL INSUFFICIENCY IN RATS
S07RR-05435-30 0982 (NSS) STARK, JAMES M Biomedical research support RESPIRATORY VIRUS INFECTION OF HUMAN AIRWAY EPITHELIAL CELLS
S07RR-05435-30 0983 (NSS) DALESSANDRO, ANTHONY Biomedical research support INTESTINAL TRANSPLANTATION: TECHNIQUES, FUNCTION, & IMMUNOLOGY
S07RR-05435-30 0984 (NSS) KALAYOGLU, MUNCI Biomedical research support FOX TO DOG LIVER XENOGRAFTS
S07RR-05435-30 0985 (NSS) BARANSKI, BRUCE G Biomedical research support MECHANISM OF T CELL MEDIATED BONE MARROW GRAFT REJECTION
S07RR-05435-30 0986 (NSS) LUSTIG, ROBERT H Biomedical research support GAP 43 IN CHANGES IN NEURAL ORGANIZATION & ACTIVATION INDUCED BY ESTROGEN
S07RR-05441-30 (NSS) LASHOF, JOYCE C UNIVERSITY OF CALIFORNIA 19 EARL WARREN HALL BERKELEY, CALIF 94720 Biomedical research support grant
S07RR-05442-29 (NSS) AFIFI, ABDELMONEM UNIVERSITY OF CALIFORNIA 405 HILGARD AVENUE LOS ANGELES, CALIF 90024 Biomedical research

support

S07RR-05442-29 0044 (NSS) QUE HEE, SHANE Biomedical research support CHEMILUMINESCENCE FROM MODEL BIOLOGICAL SYSTEMS

S07RR-05442-29 0045 (NSS) LONGNECKER5, MATTHEW Biomedical research support PROTEASE INHIBITOR CONTENTS OF FOOD

S07RR-05442-29 0046 (NSS) MUSTAFA, MOHAMMED G Biomedical research support PREPARATION OF TRACHEAL EPITHELIAL CELLS

S07RR-05442-29 0047 (NSS) MORISKY, DONALD E Biomedical research support HYPERTENSION CONTROL AMONG MINORITY POPULATIONS

S07RR-05442-29 0048 (NSS) CARLISLE, EDITH M Biomedical research support THYROID & DIETARY SILICON & ALUMINUM ON ZINC CONTENT IN BRAIN: ALZHEIMERS

S07RR-05443-30 (NSS) SINGER, BURTON H YALE UNIVERSITY P O BOX 3333, 60 COLLEGE ST NEW HAVEN, CONN 06510 Biomedical research support

S07RR-05443-30 0987 (NSS) BERWICK, MARIANNE Biomedical research support EDUCATING PARENTS TO LIMIT SUN EXPOSURE OF NEWBORNS:

S07RR-05443-30 0988 (NSS) BICE, THOMAS W Biomedical research support TRANSITIONS AMONG LEVELS OF LONG TERM CARE + DATA SETS

S07RR-05443-30 0989 (NSS) DUBROW, ROBERT Biomedical research support FECAL MARKERS FOR EARLY DETECTION OF COLORECTAL NEOPLASMS: CANCER POLYPS

S07RR-05443-30 0994 (NSS) KATZ, BEN A Biomedical research support ONCOGENICITY OF EPSTEIN BARR VIRUS: SCID MICE, LYMPHOMAS, CELL LINES

S07RR-05443-30 0995 (NSS) PATTON, CURTIS L Biomedical research support METHYLATION MEDIATED DIFFERENTIATION IN TRYPANOSOMES: SLEEPING SICKNESS

S07RR-05443-30 0996 (NSS) BERWICK, MARIANNE Biomedical research support MEASUREMENT OF ULTRAVIOLET RADIATION EXPOSURE & RISK FOR MELANOMA

S07RR-05443-30 0997 (NSS) POWELL, LYNDA H Biomedical research support BEHAVIOR & CATECHOLAMINES: CARDIOVASCULAR DISEASE, STRESS

S07RR-05443-30 0990 (NSS) HORWITZ, SARAH M Biomedical research support FOSTER CARE CHILDREN: HEALTH ISSUES, SERVICES USE & OUTCOMES

S07RR-05443-30 0991 (NSS) SCHYMURA, MARIA J Biomedical research support POWER TO DETECT PERIOD VERSUS COHORT EFFECTS IN AN AGE PERIOD COHORT MODEL

S07RR-05443-30 0992 (NSS) HORWITZ, SARAH M Biomedical research support GROWTH PATTERNS OF FOSTER CHILDREN

S07RR-05443-30 0993 (NSS) SINGER, BURTON H Biomedical research support AMAZON MALARIA ILLNESS REPORTS RELATIVE TO SEROLOGY: STATISTICAL ANALYSIS

S07RR-05444-30 (NSS) HAMRICK, JOSEPH T TULANE UNIVERSITY 1430 TULANE AVENUE NEW ORLEANS, LA 70112 Biomedical research support

S07RR-05444-30 0257 (NSS) BLAKLEY, SALLY Biomedical research support PUBLIC SCREENING FOR ELEVATED CHOLESTEROL IN NEW ORLEANS

S07RR-05444-30 0258 (NSS) HARTLEY, WILLIAM R Biomedical research support ORYZIAS LATIPES: IN VIVO SCREENING BIOASSAY FOR CARCINOGEN POTASSIUM

S07RR-05444-30 0259 (NSS) JAMES, MARK Biomedical research support MAB BASED PEPTIDE ELISA FOR DETECTION OF ANTIGEN IN MALARIOUS PTS

S07RR-05444-30 0260 (NSS) LING, JACK Biomedical research support NEW COMMUNICABLE DISEASES: COMMUNICATION CHALLENGE

S07RR-05444-30 0261 (NSS) MATHER, FRANCES Biomedical research support COMPUTER ENHANCEMENT FOR BIOSTATISTICS & EPIDEMIOLOGY

S07RR-05444-30 0262 (NSS) VALDMANIS, VIVIAN Biomedical research support DATA SETS NECESSARY TO ASSESS HOSPITAL PRODUCTIVITY

S07RR-05444-30 0263 (NSS) WISER, MARK F Biomedical research support PROTEIN KINASES & PHOSPHOPROTEINS OF MALARIA PARASITE

S07RR-05445-30 (NSS) GOLDBERG, ALAN M JOHNS HOPKINS UNIVERSITY 615 NORTH WOLFE STREET BALTIMORE, MD 21205 Biomedical research support

S07RR-05445-30 0868 (NSS) BEIER, JOHN C Biomedical research support MALARIA VECTOR POTENTIAL OF ANOPHELES MOSQUITOES

S07RR-05445-30 0869 (NSS) CABALLERO, BENJAMIN Biomedical research support METABOLIC UNIT FOR STUDY OF ENERGY & PROTEIN METABOLISM IN HUMANS

S07RR-05445-30 0870 (NSS) DANNENBERG, ANDREW L Biomedical research support CIVILIAN APPLICANTS EXCLUDED FROM MILITARY SERVICE DUE TO HIV INFECTION

S07RR-05445-30 0871 (NSS) FRONDOZA, CARMELITA Biomedical research support ISOLATION OF HUMAN GENES CONFERRING RESISTANCE TO CYCLOPHOSPHAMIDE

S07RR-05445-30 0872 (NSS) GURRI GLASS, GREGORY Biomedical research support BAND SHIFTING IN DNA FINGERPRINTING

S07RR-05445-30 0873 (NSS) HARRISON, LEE H Biomedical research support BRAZILIAN PURPURIC FEVER

S07RR-05445-30 0874 (NSS) JOHNSON, MICHAEL P Biomedical research support ROLE PLAYING INTERVENTION FOR AIDS PREVENTION

S07RR-05445-30 0875 (NSS) LAVEIST, THOMAS A Biomedical research support MICHIGAN PRENATAL CARE UTILIZATION STUDY: PATTERNS & DETERMINANTS

S07RR-05445-30 0876 (NSS) LEVIN, DAVID Biomedical research support ENGINEERING OF PROTEIN KINASE C FROM YEAST

S07RR-05445-30 0877 (NSS) SCHWARTZ, DAVID Biomedical research support HAEMOPHILUS INFLUENZAE B IN HIV INFECTED INFANTS & CHILDREN

S07RR-05445-30 0878 (NSS) UPCHURCH, DAWN Biomedical research support EARLY ADOLESCENT CHARACTERISTICS ON ADOLESCENT CHILDBEARING

S07RR-05445-30 0879 (NSS) WASHABAUGH, MICHAEL Biomedical research support MECHANISM OF THIAMIN (VITAMIN B1) TRANSPORT

S07RR-05446-30 (NSS) WARE, JAMES H HARVARD SCH OF PUBLIC HLTH 677 HUNTINGTON AVE BOSTON, MA 02115 Biomedical research support grants

S07RR-05446-30 0270 (NSS) DAVID, JOHN R Biomedical research support grants IMMUNOLOGY OF FOUR TROPICAL PARASITIC DISEASES OF MAN

S07RR-05446-30 0271 (NSS) SAMUELSON, JOHN C Biomedical research support grants EPIDEMIOLOGY OF PARASITE ENTAMOEBA HISTOLYTICA & MECHANISMS OF DRUG RESISTANCE

S07RR-05446-30 0272 (NSS) SHOEMAKER, CHARLES Biomedical research support grants MEMBRANE PROTEINS FROM S MANSONI AS VACCINE CANDIDATES

S07RR-05446-30 0273 (NSS) SHOEMAKER, CHARLES Biomedical research support grants LICENSE KIT TO GENERATE & CHARACTERIZE MABS AGAINST VARIETY OF ANTIGENS

S07RR-05446-30 0274 (NSS) HU, HOWARD Biomedical research support grants LEAD LEVELS: YOUNG ADULTS NEUROBEHAVIOR & SCHOOL PERFORM: POSTPARTUM WOMEN BLOOD

S07RR-05446-30 0275 (NSS) KOBZIK, LESTER Biomedical research support grants DELIVERY OF LIPOSOMES W/ ANTISENSE OLIGONUCLEOTIDES BENEFICIAL IN INJURED LUNGS

S07RR-05446-30 0264 (NSS) BOOTHBY, MARK R Biomedical research support grants CONTROL OF MURINE INTERLEUKIN 2 RECEPTOR P75 B CHAIN GENE; IL 2

S07RR-05446-30 0265 (NSS) NICKOLOFF, JAC A Biomedical research support grants MAMMALIAN MODELS FOR RADIATION INDUCED RECOMBINATION; GENETICS

S07RR-05446-30 0266 (NSS) FREI, BLAZ B Biomedical research support grants OXIDANTS & ANTIOXIDANTS IN PATHOGENESIS OF ATHEROSCLEROSIS

S07RR-05446-30 0267 (NSS) WESSLING-RESNICK, M Biomedical research support grants REGULATION OF RECEPTOR MEDIATED ENDOCYTOSIS

S07RR-05446-30 0268 (NSS) GARDNER, JANE D Biomedical research support grants PROJECTING PEDIATRIC AIDS SERVICE NEEDS

S07RR-05446-30 0269 (NSS) LIEBERMAN, ELLICE S Biomedical research support grants MATERNAL SMOKING CESSATION DURING PREGNANCY & FETAL OUTCOME

S07RR-05446-30 0276 (NSS) MILTON, DONALD K Biomedical research support grants MEASUREMENT OF CELL BOUND & SOLUBLE ENDOTOXIN

S07RR-05446-30 0277 (NSS) PAULAUSKIS, JOSEPH D Biomedical research support grants FACTORS INITIATING TERMINAL DIFFERENTIATION OF MONOCYTES TO ALVEOLAR MACROPHAGES

S07RR-05446-30 0278 (NSS) SHORE, STEPHANIE A Biomedical research support grants ENVIRON POLLUTANTS & INFLAMMATION ON FUNCTION OF AIRWAY EPITHELIAL CELLS IN CULT

S07RR-05446-30 0279 (NSS) WARNER, ANGELEINE E Biomedical research support grants INTRAVASCULAR MACROPHAGE IN ENDOTOXIN INDUCED LUNG INJURY: ANIMAL MODEL OF ARDS

S07RR-05446-30 0280 (NSS) YANAGISAWA, YUKIO Biomedical research support grants INDOOR AIR & VOLATILE ORGANIC COMPOUNDS: HUMAN EXPOSURE TO VOC EMISSION FROM TAP

S07RR-05446-30 0281 (NSS) FARR, SPENCER B Biomedical research support grants CELL RESPONSE TO SUPEROXIDE RADICAL STRESS

S07RR-05446-30 0282 (NSS) OFNER, PETER Biomedical research support grants HORMONAL PROSTATIC CARCINOGENESIS; XENOBIOTIC TOXICANT INDUCED CYTOCHROME P450

S07RR-05446-30 0283 (NSS) SCHLEGEL, ROBERT Biomedical research support grants POST TRANSLATION MODIFICATION: PROTEINS DURING MITOTIC ONSET IN MAMMALIAN CELLS

S07RR-05447-30 (NSS) OSBORN, JUNE E UNIVERSITY OF MICHIGAN 109 S OBSERVATORY ANN ARBOR, MI 48109-2029 Biomedical research support grant

S07RR-05448-30 (NSS) LEYASMEYER, EDITH D UNIVERSITY OF MINNESOTA A302 MAYO 420 DELAWARE ST MINNEAPOLIS, MN 55455 Biomedical research support

S07RR-05448-30 0284 (NSS) SELLERS, THOMAS A Biomedical research support FAMILIAL CORRELATION OF DIETARY INTAKE VARIABLES BETWEEN ADULT MALE SIBLINGS

S07RR-05448-30 0285 (NSS) ELMER, PATRICIA Biomedical research support PREVENTION OF BONE LOSS IN AMENORRHEIC FEMALE ATHLETES

S07RR-05448-30 0286 (NSS) LUEPKER, RUSSELL V Biomedical research support SOCIAL SUPPORT ON WOMENS RECOVERY FROM AN ACUTE MYOCARDIAL INFARCTION

S07RR-05448-30 0287 (NSS) FORSTER, JEAN Biomedical research support VENDING MACHINE RESTRICTIONS MERCHANT EDUC ON TEENAGERS ACCESS TO CIGARETTES

S07RR-05448-30 0288 (NSS) VESLEY, DONALD Biomedical research support TESTING OF HUMIDIFIERS TO DETERMINE RELEASE OF ASBESTOS FIBERS

S07RR-05448-30 0289 (NSS) JACOBS, DAVID R Biomedical research support ALCOHOL USE OTHER LIFESTYLE BEHAVIORS INJURY IN YOUNG ADULTS

S07RR-05448-30 0300 (NSS) BRUST, JANNY D Biomedical research support ICE HOCKEY INJURIES IN CHILDREN

S07RR-05448-30 0301 (NSS) GARRARD, JUDITH Biomedical research support PREDICTION EQUATIONS FOR OUTCOMES OF NURSING HOME ADMISSION

S07RR-05448-30 0302 (NSS) FROBERG, DEBRA Biomedical research support PROCESSING TRACING STUDY OF DISCHARGE DECISION MAKING

S07RR-05448-30 0303 (NSS) SMITH, PHILIP J Biomedical research support NONCOVERAGE BIAS REDUCTION VIA MULTIPLE FRAME ESTIMATION FOR NTL HLTH SURVEYS

S07RR-05448-30 0304 (NSS) OSTWALD, SHARON K Biomedical research support PREDICTORS OF CLIENT MOVEMENT DURING FIRST YEAR AFTER PRE ADMISSION SCREENING

S07RR-05448-30 0305 (NSS) LUEPKER, RUSSELL V Biomedical research support OLDER ADULT NUTRITION INTERVENTION

S07RR-05448-30 0306 (NSS) CHOI, THOMAS Biomedical research support PROSPECTIVE EVALUATION OF CHILDRENS HEALTH PLAN

S07RR-05448-30 0307 (NSS) LEONARD, BARBARA J Biomedical research support SELF CONCEPT & BEHAVIOR IN CHILDREN ADOLESCENTS

S07RR-05448-30 0308 (NSS) PIRIE, PHYLLIS Biomedical research support IDENTIFYING CHILDREN EXPOSED TO COCAINE IN UTERO

S07RR-05448-30 0309 (NSS) POTTER, JOHN D Biomedical research support CALCIUM & COLORECTAL EPITHELIAL CELL PROLIFERATION

S07RR-05448-30 0310 (NSS) FLACK, JOHN M Biomedical research support THIAZIDE DIURETICS ON LDL CHOLESTEROL SUBSPECIES

S07RR-05448-30 0311 (NSS) GRIMM, RICHARD H, JR Biomedical research support POPULATION STUDY OF AMBULATORY BP MONITORING & LEFT VENTRICULAR MASS

S07RR-05448-30 0312 (NSS) ELMER, PATRICIA Biomedical research support FEASIBILITY OF DIETARY INTERVENTION TO INCREASE VEGETABLE & FRUIT INTAKE

S07RR-05448-30 0313 (NSS) GREAVES, IAN Biomedical research support DIOXIN ON TRANSCRIPTION RNA OF GROWTH FACTORS

S07RR-05448-30 0314 (NSS) HIMES, JOHN Biomedical research support NUTRITION ASSESSMENTS OF YOUTH

S07RR-05448-30 0315 (NSS) LOUIS, THOMAS Biomedical research support MULTIPLE RISK FACTOR INTERVENTION FOLLOWUP

S07RR-05448-30 0316 (NSS) JOHNSON, GEORGE O Biomedical research support HIGH RISK ADOLESCENT STUDIES

S07RR-05448-30 0290 (NSS) VESLEY, DONALD Biomedical research support TRANSMISSION OF METHICILLIN RESISTANT STAPHYLOCOCCI IN

PROJECT NO., ORGANIZATIONAL UNIT., INVESTIGATOR, ADDRESS, TITLE

HOSPITAL ENVIRONMENT
S07RR-05448-30 0291 (NSS) KUSHI, LARRY Biomedical research support PRE & POST NATAL HEALTH PRACTICES IN VEGETARIAN NON VEGETARIAN WOMEN
S07RR-05448-30 0292 (NSS) NYMAN, JOHN A Biomedical research support MARKET CONCENTRATION ON NURSING HOME PRICES & COSTS
S07RR-05448-30 0293 (NSS) BROWN, JUDITH A Biomedical research support ADEQUACY OF FOOD FREQUENCY IN DETECTING CHANGE DURING PREGNANCY
S07RR-05448-30 0294 (NSS) PATTERSON, JOAN M Biomedical research support FAMILY FACTORS ASSOC W/ 10 MORBIDITY MORTALITY IN CHILDREN CYSTIC FIBROSIS
S07RR-05448-30 0295 (NSS) GROSS, MYRON Biomedical research support MECHANISMS OF CAROTENOID INDUCED CANCER PREVENTION
S07RR-05448-30 0296 (NSS) ELMER, PATRICIA J Biomedical research support FEASIBILITY OF REDUCTION OF DIETARY SODIUM IN BLACK PARTICIPANTS
S07RR-05448-30 0297 (NSS) RESNICK, MICHAEL D Biomedical research support SUBSTANCE USE AMONG DISABLED CHRONICALLY ILL ADOLESCENTS
S07RR-05448-30 0298 (NSS) SELLERS, THOMAS A Biomedical research support BREAST CANCER FAMILY PEDIGREE UPDATE
S07RR-05448-30 0299 (NSS) LELAND,NANCY L Biomedical research support BIRTH OUTCOMES & HEALTH CARE UTILIZATION AMONG NATIVE AMERICANS IN US
S07RR-05449-30 (NSS) ROSENFIELD, ALLAN COLUMBIA UNIVERSITY 600 WEST 168TH STREET NEW YORK, N Y 10032 Biomedical research support grants
S07RR-05449-30 0317 (NSS) LO, SHAW-HWA Biomedical research support grants IMPROVEMENT OF TARING GOOD ROBBINS ESTIMATOR; SPECIES PROBLEM
S07RR-05449-30 0318 (NSS) ANDREWS, LES Biomedical research support grants ENVIRONMENTAL SYSTEMS DESIGN
S07RR-05449-30 0319 (NSS) JEFFREY, ALLAN Biomedical research support grants CHEMISTRY OF FUSARIN C
S07RR-05449-30 0320 (NSS) PERERA, FREDERICA Biomedical research support grants MOLECULAR EPIDEMIOLOGY & DISEASE
S07RR-05449-30 0321 (NSS) SANTELLA, REGINA Biomedical research support grants IMMUNOLOGIC METHODS DETECTION OF CARCINOGEN ADDUCTS IN HUMANS; CANCER
S07RR-05449-30 0322 (NSS) SEWELL, GRANVILLE Biomedical research support grants INTERNATIONAL ENVIRONMENTAL HEALTH
S07RR-05449-30 0323 (NSS) GAMMON, MARILIE Biomedical research support grants BREAST CANCER; WOMEN EPIDEMIOLOGY
S07RR-05449-30 0324 (NSS) RAUH, VIRGINIA Biomedical research support grants FACTORS IN DEVELOPMENT OF ECONOMICALLY DISADVANTAGED CHILDREN
S07RR-05449-30 0325 (NSS) FREEDMAN, LYNN Biomedical research support grants WOMEN & LAW IN ASIA
S07RR-05449-30 0326 (NSS) WEATHERLY, NORMAN Biomedical research support grants INTERNATIONAL HEALTH EDUCATION MODELING
S07RR-05449-30 0327 (NSS) FINDLEY, SALLY Biomedical research support grants AFRICAN DEMOGRAPHIC HEALTH TRENDS
S07RR-05450-30 (NSS) IBRAHIM, MICHEL UNIVERSITY OF NORTH CAROLINA CB #7400 ROSENAU HALL CHAPEL HILL, NC 27599 Biomedical research support
S07RR-05450-30 0328 (NSS) AITKEN, MICHAEL D Biomedical research support MICROORGANISMS CAPABLE OF DEGRADING CHLORINATED SOLVENTS IN SOIL
S07RR-05450-30 0330 (NSS) STRECHER, VICTOR J Biomedical research support TAILORED MESSAGES FOR CHOLESTEROL SCREENING
S07RR-05450-30 0331 (NSS) ANDERSON, JOHN J B Biomedical research support ESTRADIOL REPLACEMENT ON PARATHYROID HORMONE SECRETION IN OVARIECTOMIZED RAT
S07RR-05450-30 0332 (NSS) BARIC, RALPH S Biomedical research support ENTEROVIRUSES DETECTED BY POLYMERASE CHAIN REACTION
S07RR-05450-30 0329 (NSS) WHITE, ALICE D Biomedical research support ARTERIAL DISTENSIBILITY & ATHEROSCLEROSIS
S07RR-05450-30 0333 (NSS) ROGERS, BONNIE, DR Biomedical research support OCCUPATIONAL HAZARDS OF HEALTH CARE WORKERS
S07RR-05450-30 0334 (NSS) SHY, CARL M Biomedical research support PREVENTION OF LEAD INDUCED COGNITIVE IMPAIRMENT IN ELDERLY
S07RR-05450-30 0335 (NSS) LANDIS, SUZANNE E Biomedical research support RISK BEHAVIOR AMONG PERSONS AWARE OF THEIR HIV ANTIBODY STATUS
S07RR-05450-30 0336 (NSS) SALMON, MARLA Biomedical research support OCCUPATIONAL VIOLENCE: AN ASSESSMENT OF RISK FOR FEMALE NURSES
S07RR-05450-30 0337 (NSS) BALL, LOUISE Biomedical research support INTERACTIONS BETWEEN CELLULAR NUCLEOPHILES & MUTAGENIC CHLORINATION PRODUCT
S07RR-05450-30 0338 (NSS) LOPEZ, LAUREEN Biomedical research support LOWERING CANCER RISK THROUGH DIETARY CHANGE
S07RR-05450-30 0339 (NSS) TYROLER, HERMAN A Biomedical research support DIETARY FIBER & CORONARY HEART DISEASE
S07RR-05450-30 0340 (NSS) MILLER, CASS T Biomedical research support COSOLVENT STRATEGY FOR GROUND WATER QUALITY RESTORATION
S07RR-05450-30 0341 (NSS) MCCANN, MARGARET F Biomedical research support RESPIRATORY DERMATOL & NEURO SYMPTOMS IN OCCUPATIONAL EXPOSURES; COSMETOLOGY
S07RR-05450-30 0342 (NSS) THOMAS, JAMES Biomedical research support MODIFYING SEXUAL BEHAVIOR AMONG HIGH FREQUENCY TRANSMITTERS OF STDS
S07RR-05450-30 0343 (NSS) BAUMAN, KARL E Biomedical research support HOME BASED PARENT DIRECTED INTERVENTION TO PREVENT ADOLESCENT ALCOHOL USE
S07RR-05450-30 0344 (NSS) BROWNE, DOROTHY Biomedical research support STUDIES ON CHILD ABUSE & NEGLECT
S07RR-05450-30 0345 (NSS) SAVITZ, DAVID Biomedical research support RISK FACTORS FOR ADVERSE PREGNANCY OUTCOME
S07RR-05450-30 0346 (NSS) FLYNN, MICHAEL Biomedical research support RETROSPECTIVE EXPOSURE ASSESSMENT FOR ELECTRICAL UTILITY INDUSTRY
S07RR-05450-30 0347 (NSS) SOBSEY, MARK Biomedical research support TOXICOLOGY OF ENVIRONMENTAL AGENTS IN WATER
S07RR-05450-30 0348 (NSS) CRAWFORD-BROWN, DOUG Biomedical research support INFLUENCE OF ENVIRON TOBACCO SMOKE ON PROBABILITY OF RADON EXPOSURE LUNG CANCER
S07RR-05450-30 0349 (NSS) ANDREW, RICHARD N L Biomedical research support ANALYSIS OF POLICY INSTRUMENTS IN AIR POLLUTION CONTROL
S07RR-05450-30 0350 (NSS) HARLOW, SIOBAN Biomedical research support NATURE OF VARIABILITY IN MENSTRUAL CYCLE LENGTH
S07RR-05450-30 0351 (NSS) MILLER, CASS T Biomedical research support SORPTION DESORPTION ABIOTIC TRANSFORM OF LINDANE & DIVRON; SUBSURFACE ENVIRON
S07RR-05451-30 (NSS) MATTISON, DONALD R UN PITT. SCH PUBLIC HEALTH 130 DESOTO STREET PITTSBURGH, PA 15261 Biomedical research support
S07RR-05451-30 0352 (NSS) BUNKER, CLAREANN H Biomedical research support BLOOD PRESSURE & CARDIOVASCULAR RISK FACTORS IN SOKOTO NIGERIA
S07RR-05451-30 0353 (NSS) KULLER, LEWIS H Biomedical research support ABDOMINAL AORTIC ANEURYSM & ATHEROSCLEROSIS
S07RR-05451-30 0354 (NSS) ORCHARD, TREVOR J Biomedical research support EPIDEMIOLOGY OF DIABETIC COMPLICATIONS STUDY
S07RR-05451-30 0355 (NSS) KRISKA, ANDREA M Biomedical research support PHYSICAL ACTIVITY IN NIDDM DEVELOPMENT STUDY
S07RR-05451-30 0356 (NSS) GOLLIN, SUSANNE M Biomedical research support FLUORESCENCE IN SITU HYBRIDIZATION TO NUCLEI & CHROMOSOMES
S07RR-05451-30 0357 (NSS) KAMBOH, MOHAMMAD I Biomedical research support GENETIC TYPING OF LP
S07RR-05451-30 0358 (NSS) CONNER, MARY K Biomedical research support HPLC METHODOLOGY USED TO STUDY TRYPTOPHAN METABOLISM
S07RR-05451-30 0359 (NSS) TOBIN, MICHAEL J Biomedical research support PREPARATION OF 125I LABELED COMPOUNDS FOR MICRODOSIMETRY STUDIES
S07RR-05451-30 0360 (NSS) ANDELMAN, JULIAN B Biomedical research support EXPOSURE TO INDOOR & OUTDOOR AIR POLLUTANTS
S07RR-05453-29 (NSS) GOYAN, JERE E UNIVERSITY OF CALIFORNIA 926 MEDICAL SCIENCES BUILDING SAN FRANCISCO, CALIF 94143 Animal resource program improvement
S07RR-05453-29 0504 (NSS) GOYAN, JERE E Animal resource program improvement NO RESEARCH SUBPROJECTS
S07RR-05454-29 (NSS) TRIGGLE, DAVID J S U N Y AT BUFFALO 126 COOKE HALL BUFFALO, NEW YORK 14260 Biomedical research support
S07RR-05454-29 0124 (NSS) FUNK, COLIN D Biomedical research support CLONING OF HUMAN PLATELET & ERYTHROLEUKEMIA CELL POTASSIUM CHANNELS
S07RR-05454-29 0880 (NSS) HALL, LINDA M Biomedical research support GENETIC ANALYSIS OF ION CHANNELS
S07RR-05454-29 0881 (NSS) HALVORSEN, STANLEY Biomedical research support CILIARY NEUROTROPIC FACTOR ACTION AT RECEPTORS
S07RR-05454-29 0882 (NSS) MURAKAMI, KENTARO Biomedical research support NEW SIGNALING PATHWAY OF PROTEIN KINASE C ACTIVATION
S07RR-05454-29 0883 (NSS) SINGH, SATPAL Biomedical research support POTASSIUM CHANNELS IN DROSOPHILA
S07RR-05454-29 0884 (NSS) FUNG, HO-LEUNG Biomedical research support INSTRUMENTATION SUPPORT
S07RR-05454-29 0885 (NSS) HANGAUER, DAVID Biomedical research support PROTEIN KINASE INHIBITORS: ANTI CANCER ANTI AIDS IMMUNOSUPPRESSANT
S07RR-05454-29 0886 (NSS) HO, MENGFEI Biomedical research support DESIGN & SYNTHESIS OF ALPHA HELIX PEPTIDE STABILIZING STRUCTURES
S07RR-05454-29 0887 (NSS) KALMAN, THOMAS Biomedical research support MATCHING FUNDS FOR LIQUID SCINTILLATION
S07RR-05454-29 0888 (NSS) SOLO, ALAN J Biomedical research support INSTRUMENTATION SUPPORT
S07RR-05454-29 0889 (NSS) TRIGGLE, DAVID J Biomedical research support CENTRAL COMPUTER DATA FACILITIES
S07RR-05456-29 (NSS) CONNORS, KENNETH A UNIVERSITY OF WISCONSIN 425 NORTH CHARTER STREET MADISON, WIS 53706 Biomedical research support
S07RR-05456-29 0361 (NSS) ROYER, CATHERINE A Biomedical research support LASER BASED MULTI FREQ FLUOROMETER FOR MACROMOLECULAR INTERACTIONS
S07RR-05456-29 0362 (NSS) WEILER, MOLLY S Biomedical research support AGE RELATED CHANGES IN NEOSTRIATAL CHOLINERGIC FUNCTION
S07RR-05457-29 (NSS) MURPHY, FREDERICK A UNIVERSITY OF CALIFORNIA 1018 HARING HALL DAVIS, CALIF 95616 Biomedical research support
S07RR-05457-29 0000 (NSS) BOYCE, W M Biomedical research support RECOGNITION OF CYSTEINE PROTEASES FROM MITES
S07RR-05457-29 0001 (NSS) CONRAD, P A Biomedical research support MOLECULAR CHARACTERIZATION OF BABESIA SPP
S07RR-05457-29 0002 (NSS) GARDNER, I A Biomedical research support SARCOPTIC MANGE IN PIGS USING AN ELISA ASSAY
S07RR-05457-29 0003 (NSS) HIGGINS, R J Biomedical research support THERAPY OF BRAIN TUMORS W/ A NOVEL CHLORIN PHOTOSENSITISER
S07RR-05457-29 0004 (NSS) MACLACHLAN, N J Biomedical research support VIRULENCE DETERMINANTS OF BLUETONGUE VIRUS
S07RR-05457-29 0005 (NSS) MOHR, F C Biomedical research support REGULATION OF CYTOPLASMIC CALCIUM OF CULTURED MAST CELLS
S07RR-05457-29 0006 (NSS) MOORE, P F Biomedical research support IMMUNOPATHOGENESIS OF EPIDERMOTROPIC LYMPHOSARCOMA OF DOGS
S07RR-05457-29 0007 (NSS) MURRAY, J D Biomedical research support CHARACTERIZATION OF HUMAN PS2 & BOVINE PSB PROMOTERS
S07RR-05457-29 0008 (NSS) PESSAH, I M Biomedical research support SINGLE ION CHANNEL CURRENTS
S07RR-05457-29 0009 (NSS) TABLIN, F Biomedical research support EQUINE PLATELET SECRETION: MORPHOLOGICAL & BIOCHEMICAL ANALYSIS
S07RR-05457-29 0010 (NSS) VASSEUR, P B Biomedical research support FIXATION METHODS FOR OSTEOCHONDRAL SHELL AUTOGRAFTS
S07RR-05457-29 0011 (NSS) VULLIET, P R Biomedical research support PROTEIN PHOSPHORYLATION DURING VIRAL INFECTION
S07RR-05457-29 0998 (NSS) MOORE, P F Biomedical research support MONOCLONAL ANTIBODIES TO CANINE LEUKOCYTE CELL ADHESION
S07RR-05457-29 0999 (NSS) BALDWIN, D M Biomedical research support HORMONAL REGULATION OF GONADOTROPIN SUBUNIT GENE EXPRESSION
S07RR-05458-29 (NSS) NISWENDER, GORDON D COLORADO STATE UNIVERSITY COLLEGE OF VET MED FORT COLLINS, CO 80523 Biomedical research support
S07RR-05458-29 0824 (NSS) BLEHM, KENNETH D Biomedical research support SIGNIFICANT NOISE SOURCES IN AGRICULTURE & THEIR IMPACT ON HEARING ACUITY

PROJECT NO., ORGANIZATIONAL UNIT., INVESTIGATOR, ADDRESS, TITLE

S07RR-05458-29 0825 (NSS) FOX, MICHAEL H Biomedical research support INTRACELLULAR PH IN CHINESE HAMSTER OVARY CELLS; MODIFY BY HYPERTHERMIA
S07RR-05458-29 0826 (NSS) GASPER, PETER W Biomedical research support AUTOLOGOUS MARROW TRANSPLANT IN CAT: RETROVIRAL & GENE TRANSFER STUDY MODEL DVMT
S07RR-05458-29 0827 (NSS) KATER, STANLEY B Biomedical research support TEMPORAL PERSISTENCE OF EXTRINSIC NEURONAL GROWTH CONE GUIDANCE CUES
S07RR-05458-29 0828 (NSS) LAPPIN, MICHAEL R Biomedical research support FELINE LEUKEMIA VIRUS INDUCED IMMUNOSUPPRESSION ON CATS W/ CHRONIC TOXOPLASMOSIS
S07RR-05458-29 0829 (NSS) LUTTGEN, PATRICIA J Biomedical research support EFFECTS OF ANESTHETIC DEPTH ON HEAR FIELD SOMATOSENSORY EVOKED POTENTIALS
S07RR-05458-29 0830 (NSS) MARTIN, HOWARD D Biomedical research support AVIAN MEDICINE
S07RR-05458-29 0831 (NSS) MCILWRAITH C WAYNE Biomedical research support CORTICOSTEROIDS ON ARTICULAR CARTILAGE; EQUINE JOINTS W/ OSTEOCHONDRAL; EXERCISE
S07RR-05458-29 0832 (NSS) MILLER, CHARLES W Biomedical research support FACTORS RESPONSIBLE FOR FLOW INDUCED MODIFICATION ATHEROSCLEROSIS
S07RR-05458-29 0833 (NSS) OGILVIE, GREGORY K Biomedical research support GLUCOSE CLAMP; ALTERATIONS IN CARBOHYDRATE METABOLISM; DOGS W/ LYMPHOMA
S07RR-05458-29 0834 (NSS) ORME, IAN M Biomedical research support IMMUNOGENIC PROTEINS ASSOC W/ GENERATION OF IMMUNITY TO MYCOBACTERIUM TUBERCULOS
S07RR-05458-29 0835 (NSS) REIF, JOHN S Biomedical research support IONIZING RADIAT & ELECTROMAGNETIC FLDS & CHEM EXPOSUR; CANINE MALIGNANT LYMPHOMA
S07RR-05458-29 0836 (NSS) ROBERTS, STEVEN M Biomedical research support OCULAR HYPOTENSIVE EFFECT OF IV MANNITOL: OPTIMAL DOSAGE & RATE OF ADMIN; DOGS
S07RR-05458-29 0837 (NSS) SCHWARZ, PETER D Biomedical research support OPLA TESTING & MEASUREMENT OF SERUM & URINE CONCENTRATIONS
S07RR-05458-29 0838 (NSS) STALLONES, LORANN Biomedical research support PET LOSS & MENTAL HEALTH
S07RR-05458-29 0839 (NSS) STRAW, RODNEY C Biomedical research support ATHYMIC RAT MODEL FOR BIOASSAY OF DEMINERALIZED BONE MATRIX
S07RR-05458-29 0840 (NSS) THRALL, MARY ANNA Biomedical research support PREVALENCE & EPIDEMIOLOGIC SIGNIFICANCE
S07RR-05458-29 0841 (NSS) TROTTER, GAYLE Biomedical research support INTRA ARTICULAR SODIUM MONOIDACETATE CHEM INJURY TO EQUINE ARTRICULAR CARTILAGE
S07RR-05458-29 0842 (NSS) WAGNER, ANN E Biomedical research support QUANTITATIVE HEMODYNAMIC EVAL SPONTANEOUS GASTRIC DIALATION VOLVULUS
S07RR-05458-29 0843 (NSS) WALROND, JOHN P Biomedical research support PRESYNAPTIC STRUCTURE IN REGULATING NEUROTRANSMITTER RELEASE
S07RR-05458-29 0844 (NSS) WHALEN, LAWRENCE R Biomedical research support ELECTRICAL ACTIVITY & CALCIUM ION CURRENTS ON NEURONAL REGENERATION
S07RR-05458-29 0845 (NSS) WINGFIELD, WAYNE E Biomedical research support END TIDAL CARBON DIOXIDE AS AN INDICATOR OF SUCCESSFUL RESUSCITATION IN CATS
S07RR-05460-29 (NSS) DIPIETRO, JOSEPH A UNIVERSITY OF ILLINOIS 3231 VET MED BASIC SCI BLDG URBANA, IL 61801 Biomedical research support
S07RR-05460-29 0363 (NSS) ABBOTT, LOUISE C Biomedical research support TYROSINE HYDROXYLASE EXPRESSION & SEIZURE ACTIVITY GENETICALLY EPILEPTIC MICE
S07RR-05460-29 0364 (NSS) NURNANE, ROBERT D Biomedical research support PREIMPLANTATION PRENATAL DIAGNOSIS OF MURINE LYSOSOMAL STORAGE DISEASE
S07RR-05460-29 0365 (NSS) WALLIG, MATTHEW A Biomedical research support INDUCTION OF GLUTATHIONE S TRANSFERASE ISOENZYMES BY CYANOHYDROXYBATENE
S07RR-05460-29 0366 (NSS) ZUCKERMANN, FEDERICO Biomedical research support EXPRESSION OF PSEUDORABIES VIRUS GLYCOPROTEINS IN TRANSFECTED CELLS
S07RR-05460-29 0367 (NSS) NICKOLS, SHARON Y Biomedical research support QUALITY OF HUMAN RESOURCES RESEARCH CHILD DEVELOPMENT
S07RR-05460-29 0368 (NSS) MCCORD, JEFFREY D Biomedical research support PURCHASE OF GRADIENT PROGRAMMER
S07RR-05462-29 (NSS) PHEMISTER, ROBERT D CORNELL UNIV, COL OF VET MED C114 SCHURMAN HALL ITHACA, N Y 14853 Biomedical research support
S07RR-05462-29 0890 (NSS) BARR, STEPHEN C Biomedical research support AUTOIMMUNITY IN EXPERIMENTAL CANINE TRYPANOSOMIASIS
S07RR-05462-29 0891 (NSS) COOPER, BARRY J Biomedical research support ISOLATION OF DYSTROPHIN ASSOCIATED GLYCOPROTEINS
S07RR-05462-29 0892 (NSS) COOPER, BARRY J Biomedical research support ESTABLISHMENT OF A FELINE MUSCULAR DYSTROPHY COLONY
S07RR-05462-29 0893 (NSS) MOISE, N SYDNEY Biomedical research support INHERITED VENTRICULAR ECTOPY & SUDDEN CARDIAC DEATH IN GERMAN SHEPHERDS
S07RR-05462-29 0894 (NSS) OSWALD, ROBERT E Biomedical research support EXTRACELLULAR DOMAIN OF NICOTINIC ACETYLCHOLINE RECEPTOR ALPHA SUBUNIT IN YEAST
S07RR-05462-29 0895 (NSS) PARRISH, COLIN R Biomedical research support GENETIC & STRUCTURAL STUDIES OF CANINE & FELINE PARVOVIRUSES
S07RR-05462-29 0896 (NSS) RIIS, RONALD Biomedical research support BREEDING COLONY OF TIBETAN AFFECTED W/ NEURONAL CEROID LIPOFUSCINOSIS
S07RR-05462-29 0897 (NSS) SCHWARK, WAYNE Biomedical research support NEUROPHARMACOLOGICAL STUDY OF FLUOROQUINOLONES
S07RR-05462-29 0898 (NSS) SUTER, MAJA M Biomedical research support ACANTHOLYSIS: CYTOSKELETAL ASSOCIATED INJURY TO STRATIFIED SQUAMOUS EPITHELIUM
S07RR-05462-29 0899 (NSS) SUTER, MAJA M Biomedical research support MAB AGAINST NEOPLASTIC CANINE STRATIFIED SQUAMOUS CELL CARCINOMA
S07RR-05462-29 0900 (NSS) YEN, ANDREW Biomedical research support CONTROL OF CELL DIVISION & DIFFERENTIATION STUDY BY HL 60 VARIANTS

PROJECT NO., ORGANIZATIONAL UNIT., INVESTIGATOR, ADDRESS, TITLE

S07RR-05463-29 (NSS) WRIGHT, RONALD A OHIO STATE UNIVERSITY 1900 COFFEY RD 101 SISSON HALL COLUMBUS, OHIO 43210 Biomedical research support
S07RR-05463-29 0369 (NSS) BLAKESLEE, JAMES Biomedical research support RETROVIRUSES IN AUTOIMMUNE DISEASE: HTLV 2 LEUKEMIA LUPUS
S07RR-05464-29 (NSS) ANDREWS, EDWIN J UNIV OF PENN - VET MED 3800 SPRUCE STREET PHILADELPHIA, PA 19104 Biomedical research support
S07RR-05464-29 0370 (NSS) ATCHISON, MICHAEL Biomedical research support CHARACTERIZATION OF TRANSCRIPTION FACTOR CDNA CLONES
S07RR-05464-29 0371 (NSS) FREEMAN, DAVID Biomedical research support ACTIVE TRANSPORT SITES FOR AMINO ACIDS IN HORSE COLONIC MUCOSA
S07RR-05464-29 0372 (NSS) GOLDSCHMIDT, MICHAEL Biomedical research support CANINE BENIGN FAMILIAL CHRONIC PEMPHIGUS: ANIMAL MODEL OF HAILEY HAILEY DISEASE
S07RR-05464-29 0373 (NSS) HENDRICKS, JOAN Biomedical research support SLEEP DISORDERED BREATHING IN PUPS & ADULT DOGS W/ UPPER AIRWAY OBSTRUCTION
S07RR-05464-29 0374 (NSS) MCDEVITT, DAVID Biomedical research support METHYLATION OF DNA IN DORSAL & VENTRAL IRIS: REGENERATION OF EYE LENS
S07RR-05464-29 0375 (NSS) NIEBAUER, GERT, DR Biomedical research support RELAXIN IN CANINE PERINEAL HERNIA
S07RR-05464-29 0376 (NSS) ORSINI, JAMES Biomedical research support IN VITRO UPTAKE OF RADIOLAB GENTAMICIN BY EQUINE CHONDROCYTES & PHAGOCYTIC CELLS
S07RR-05464-29 0377 (NSS) SCHAD, GERHARD A Biomedical research support DEVELOPMENT OF CANINE MODEL FOR HUMAN STRONGYLOIDEASIS
S07RR-05464-29 0378 (NSS) WATSON, ELAINE Biomedical research support CONCENTRATIONS OF ENDOMETRIAL CYTOPLASMIC RECEPTORS FOR ESTRADIOL & PROGESTERONE
S07RR-05465-29 (NSS) PERRYMAN, LANCE E WASHINGTON STATE UNIVERSITY BUSTAD HALL 110 COL VET MED PULLMAN, WA 99164-7010 Biomedical research support
S07RR-05465-29 0388 (NSS) CRAWFORD, TIM B Biomedical research support PATHOGENICITY & PREVALENCE OF AN NEW BOVINE EHRLICHIA
S07RR-05465-29 0379 (NSS) CAMPBELL, KENNETH B Biomedical research support DYNAMIC HOMOLOGY BETWEEN ISOLATED CARDIAC MUSCLE FIBERS & LEFT VENTRICULAR
S07RR-05465-29 0380 (NSS) SPETH, ROBERT C Biomedical research support DISCRIMINATION OF ANGIOTENSIN II RECEPTOR BRAIN ISOLEUCINE8 ANGIOTENSIN II
S07RR-05465-29 0381 (NSS) MCGUIRE, TRAVIS C Biomedical research support IMMUNE CONTROL OF EQUINE INFECTIOUS ANEMIA LENTIVIRUS
S07RR-05465-29 0382 (NSS) WHITE, SUSAN R Biomedical research support INTERLEUKIN EFFECTS ON BRAINSTEM NEURONS CYTOKINE ILIB
S07RR-05465-29 0383 (NSS) BESSER, THOMAS E Biomedical research support MARFAN SYNDROME IN CATTLE
S07RR-05465-29 0384 (NSS) MENARD, MICHELE Biomedical research support DENSE GRANULE PRECURSOR SYNTHESIS IN NORMAL & CHEDIAK HIGASHI MICE MEGAKARYOCYTE
S07RR-05465-29 0385 (NSS) SYLVESTER, PAUL W Biomedical research support MEMBRANE LIPID MODULATION OF ENDOCRINE INDUCED MITOGENESIS
S07RR-05465-29 0386 (NSS) HARDING, JOSEPH W Biomedical research support ANGIOTENSINS ON NERVE CELLS NEURONS
S07RR-05465-29 0387 (NSS) BRISKI, KAREN P Biomedical research support PROLACTIN HORMONAL FORMS RELEASED BY ANTERIOR PITUITARY GLAND
S07RR-05466-24 (NSS) BERNSTEIN, SOL PROFESSIONAL STAFF ASSOCIATION 1739 GRIFFIN AVENUE LOS ANGELES, CALIF 90031 Biomedical research support
S07RR-05467-23 (NSS) LUBIN, BERTRAM H CHILDREN'S HOSPITAL OAKLAND 747 52ND STREET OAKLAND, CALIFORNIA 94609 Biomedical research support
S07RR-05467-23 0023 (NSS) ABRAHAM, SAMUEL Biomedical research support DIETARY FAT MODULATION OF HEPATIC LIPOGENESIS
S07RR-05468-29 (NSS) KLINENBERG, JAMES R CEDARS-SINAI MEDICAL CENTER 8700 BEVERLY BLVD RM 2211 LOS ANGELES, CALIF 90048 Biomedical research support
S07RR-05468-29 0389 (NSS) SIEBENS, HILARY Biomedical research support DEVELOPMENT OF STROKE OUTCOME MEASURES
S07RR-05468-29 0390 (NSS) SHARIFI, BEHROOZ Biomedical research support TGF ALPHA EXPRESSION BY FOAM CELLS
S07RR-05468-29 0391 (NSS) LINKER-ISARAELI, MAR Biomedical research support CYTOKINE PRODUCTION IN SYSTEMIC LUPUS ERYTHEMATOSUS
S07RR-05468-29 0392 (NSS) SHI, WELGIANG Biomedical research support BIOMEDICAL APPLICATIONS OF NOVEL SOLID STATE LASERS
S07RR-05468-29 0393 (NSS) HERMAN-BONERT, VIVIE Biomedical research support HYPOTHALMIC REGULATION OF GROWTH HORMONE IN SOMATOTROPH TUMOR CELLS
S07RR-05468-29 0394 (NSS) LU, SHELLY Biomedical research support REGULATION OF HEPATIC GLUTATHIONE TURNOVER
S07RR-05468-29 0395 (NSS) CRAMER, DONALD Biomedical research support HEMATOPOIETIC CHIMERAS USING OLIGONUCLEOTIDE PROBE FOR ALPHA FETO GENE
S07RR-05468-29 0396 (NSS) MAGOFFIN, DENNIS Biomedical research support BIOACTIVITY OF FOLLICULAR FLUID IN POLYCYSTIC OVARIES
S07RR-05468-29 0397 (NSS) RAPPAPORT, VALERIE Biomedical research support INTERFERON MEDIATED HLA ANTIGEN: TROPHOBLAST DEVELOPMENT OF CYTROTROPHOBLAST
S07RR-05468-29 0398 (NSS) CHING, WENDELL Biomedical research support IMMUNOGENICITY & FUNCTIONAL EPITOPES OF HTLV I ENVELOPE
S07RR-05468-29 0399 (NSS) CHIA, JOHN Biomedical research support IN VITRO MECHANISM FOR AMB INDUCED TNF PRODUCTION IN VIVO CORRELATION
S07RR-05468-29 0400 (NSS) HOWARD, TODD Biomedical research support INITIAL TRIAL OF ARTIFICIAL LIVER IN ANHEPATIC PORCINE MODEL
S07RR-05468-29 0401 (NSS) MOSS, THOMAS Biomedical research support EWINGS SARCOMA CELLS IN BONE MARROW USING
S07RR-05468-29 0402 (NSS) KARLAN, BETH Biomedical research support REGULATION OF HER 2 NEW ONCOGENE
S07RR-05468-29 0403 (NSS) WANG, CHRISTINA Biomedical research support GROWTH FACTORS REGULATION OF PLASMINOGEN ACTIVATOR BY GRANULOSA CELLS
S07RR-05468-29 0404 (NSS) AMER, HAROLD Biomedical research support CARDIOPULMONARY RESUSCITATION IN ANIMAL MODEL OF PEDIATRIC CARDIAC

ARREST
S07RR-05468-29 0405 (NSS) ISRAELE, VICTOR Biomedical research support QUANTITATION OF HIV 1 IN INFECTED CHILDRENS BLOOD
S07RR-05468-29 0406 (NSS) BROWN, DONALD Biomedical research support VIDEO IMAGE ANALYSIS & MEASUREMENT SYSTEM
S07RR-05468-29 0407 (NSS) FAGAN, DIANA Biomedical research support IMMUNOACTION OF VITAMIN D ON NK CELLS
S07RR-05468-29 0408 (NSS) JORDAN, STANLEY Biomedical research support CYTOKINE M RNA TRANSCRIPTION BY CELLS INFILTRATING LUNG ALLOGRAFTS
S07RR-05468-29 0409 (NSS) KLEEMAN, CHARLES Biomedical research support NEW IN VITRO MINERALIZATION MODEL IN OSTEOSARCOMA CELL LINE
S07RR-05468-29 0410 (NSS) FISCHEL-GHODSIAN Biomedical research support GENOME STRUCTURE AROUND ALPHA GLOBIN: GENOME THERAPY
S07RR-05469-29 (NSS) DUKES, PETER P CHILDREN'S HOSP OF L A PO BOX 54700 LOS ANGELES, CA 90054-0700 Biomedical research support
S07RR-05469-29 0411 (NSS) HALL, FREDERICK L Biomedical research support GROWTH FACTOR SENSITIVE PROTEIN KINASE NGF EGF INSULIN EGF 2
S07RR-05469-29 0412 (NSS) KOH, DONALD B Biomedical research support RETROVIRAL MEDIATED GENE TRANSFER & HUMAN HEMATOPOIETIC CELLS GENE THERAPY GF
S07RR-05469-29 0413 (NSS) NITISS, JOHN L Biomedical research support TOPOISOMERASE TARGETING ANTI TUMOR DRUGS: YEAST MODEL SYSTEM GENE MAPPING, SEQ
S07RR-05471-29 (NSS) COMINGS, DAVID E CITY OF HOPE NAT MED CTR 1500 EAST DUARTE ROAD DUARTE, CALIF 91010 Biomedical research support
S07RR-05471-29 0577 (NSS) KANE, SUSAN Biomedical research support DETECTION & LOCALIZATION OF N METHYLADENOSINE IN CATHEPSIN L MRNA
S07RR-05471-29 0578 (NSS) ZAIA, JOHN Biomedical research support CELL GROWTH & DIFFERENTIATION ON HUMAN CYTOMEGALOVIRUS INFECTION
S07RR-05471-29 0579 (NSS) SMITH, STEVEN S Biomedical research support H30S IN STRUCTURAL STUDIES OF HUMAN DNA METHYLATION SYSTEM
S07RR-05471-29 0580 (NSS) VENKATARAMAN, K Biomedical research support ALVEOLAR MACROPHAGES IN LUNG INJURY AFTER CHRONIC AMIODARONE TREATMENT IN RATS
S07RR-05471-29 0581 (NSS) WILSON, LABRESIA Biomedical research support DEVELOPMENT OF AN INTRAOPERATIVE TUMOR DETECTION SYSTEM
S07RR-05471-29 0582 (NSS) SCANLON, KEVIN Biomedical research support RIBOZYME MEDIATED REVERSAL OF MALIGNANT PHENOTYPE: HUMAN BLADDER CARCINOMA CELL
S07RR-05471-29 0583 (NSS) SCHMIDT, GERHARD Biomedical research support QUALITY OF LIFE ON LONG TERM ALLOGENIC MARROW TRANSPLANT SURVIVORS
S07RR-05471-29 0584 (NSS) SCHMIDT, GERHARD Biomedical research support HLA CLASS II DNA TYPING IN BONE MARROW TRANSPLANTATION
S07RR-05471-29 0585 (NSS) ZAIA, JOHN Biomedical research support ADRENOCORTICAL HORMONES IN HUMANS INFECTED W/ HUMAN IMMUNODEFICIENCY VIR TYPE I
S07RR-05471-29 0586 (NSS) MCLAUGHLIN-TAYLOR, E Biomedical research support MOLECULAR ANALYSIS OF T CELL SPECIFIC CLASS I EPITOPES
S07RR-05471-29 0587 (NSS) CANTIN, EDOUARD Biomedical research support HSV DNA SEQUENCES IN BONE MARROW DERIVED STEM CELLS & BLOOD MONONUCLEAR CELLS
S07RR-05471-29 0588 (NSS) SNYDER, DAVID Biomedical research support DETECTION OF BCR ABL IN PATIENTS W/ LEUKEMIA
S07RR-05471-29 0589 (NSS) MORRIS, ALAN Biomedical research support INSULIN LIKE GROWTH FACTOR I BLOOD CELL BINDING IN CHILD ON GROWTH HORMONE THERA
S07RR-05471-29 0590 (NSS) WEISS, LAWRENCE Biomedical research support CYTOKINE EXPRESSION IN HODGKINS DISEASE
S07RR-05471-29 0591 (NSS) DOROSHOW, JAMES Biomedical research support PURIFICATION OF HUMAN PHOSPHOLIPID HYDROPEROXIDE GLUTATHIONE PEROXIDASE
S07RR-05471-29 0592 (NSS) SARMA, J S M Biomedical research support PIG AS CHRONIC MODEL FOR ELECTROCARDIOGRAPHIC MONITORING OF ANTIARRHYTHMIC THERA
S07RR-05471-29 0593 (NSS) ITO, JAMES Biomedical research support CHLAMYDIA TRACHOMATIC CERVICITIS IN MOUSE
S07RR-05471-29 0594 (NSS) SLOVAK, MARILYN Biomedical research support INTERPHASE CYTOGENETICS USING CHROMOSOME SPECIFIC PROBES
S07RR-05471-29 0595 (NSS) TRAWEEK, S THOMAS Biomedical research support ROLE OF P18, A NOVEL LEUKEMIA ASSOCIATED PROTEIN
S07RR-05471-29 0596 (NSS) SOWERS, LAWRENCE Biomedical research support SYNTHESIS OF CATALYTIC RNA (RIBOZYME) FOR PHYSICAL STUDY
S07RR-05475-26 (NSS) MIRKIN, BERNARD L CHILDREN'S MEMORIAL HOSPITAL 2300 CHILDREN'S PLAZA MC:117 CHICAGO, IL 60614 Biomedical research support grant
S07RR-05475-26 0053 (NSS) DAS, JOHN B Biomedical research support grant BILIARY SLUDGE DURING TOTAL PARENTAL NUTRITION IN INFANT: LBW
S07RR-05475-26 0054 (NSS) MYONES, BARRY L Biomedical research support grant LOCALIZATION OF FUNCTIONAL DOMAINS OF EBV & C3DG RECEPTOR: IMMUNOLOGY
S07RR-05476-29 (NSS) SANDLOW, LESLIE MICHAEL REESE HOSP & MED CTR LAKESHORE DRIVE AT 31ST STREET CHICAGO, ILL 60616 Biomedical research support grant
S07RR-05477-29 (NSS) HENIKOFF, LEO M RUSH-PRESBY-ST LUKES MED CTR 1653 WEST CONGRESS PARKWAY CHICAGO, ILL 60612 Biomedical research support
S07RR-05477-29 0414 (NSS) CHONG, ANITA Biomedical research support LYMPHOKINE ACTIVATED KILLER (LAK) CELLS STIMULATED W/ TUMOR CELLS: CYTOKINE
S07RR-05477-29 0415 (NSS) CARVEY, PAUL Biomedical research support PURIFICATION OF DOPAMINE NEURON TROPHIC FACTOR
S07RR-05477-29 0416 (NSS) KERNS, JAMES Biomedical research support SYNAPTIC PLASTICITY IN SPINAL CORD SPASTICITY
S07RR-05477-29 0417 (NSS) WEESE-MAYER, DEBRA Biomedical research support EFFECT OF IN UTERO COCAINE ON POSTNATAL PHYSIOLOGY
S07RR-05477-29 0418 (NSS) LANG, Z H Biomedical research support AIRWAY EPITHELIAL CELL NEUTRAL ENDOPEPTIDASE AFTER OXIDANT EXPOSURE
S07RR-05477-29 0419 (NSS) ROCKWAY, SUSIE Biomedical research support XANTHAN GUM ON PLASMA LIPID LEVELS & BILE ACIDS IN HYPERLIPIDEMIC RATS
S07RR-05477-29 0421 (NSS) XIAO, FEI Biomedical research support IMMUNOTOLERANCE TO RAT SMALL INTESTINAL ALLOGRAFTS W/ LYMPHOCYTE TRANSFUSIONS
S07RR-05477-29 0422 (NSS) LESSICK, MIRA Biomedical research support MATERNAL INFANT INTERACTION IN COCAINE ABUSING MOTHERS
S07RR-05477-29 0423 (NSS) SCHADE, SYLVIA Biomedical research support HIV 1 NA PROVIRUS IN BRONCHOALVEOLAR LAVAGE FROM HIV 1 POSITIVE PATIENTS
S07RR-05477-29 0424 (NSS) OGSTON, WALTER Biomedical research support SITE SPECIFIC MUTAGENESIS OF WOODCHUCK HEPATITIS VIRUS X GENE
S07RR-05477-29 0425 (NSS) HARRIS, DOROTHY Biomedical research support SEARCH FOR NEW MEMBERS OF PENTRAXIN GENE FAMILY
S07RR-05477-29 0426 (NSS) FORCHETTI, CONCETTA Biomedical research support TETANUS TOXIN INDUCED EPILEPSY & EEG STUDY
S07RR-05477-29 0427 (NSS) ASCHKENASY, JEANNIE Biomedical research support CHILDREN SUICIDE ATTEMPTERS & NON ATTEMPTERS: SUBSEQUENT COMPLIANCE
S07RR-05477-29 0428 (NSS) XIE, DONG-LIN Biomedical research support EFFECT OF FIBRONECTION ON MONOCYTE MEDIATED CARTILAGE DESTRUCTION
S07RR-05477-29 0429 (NSS) AJAYI, OLUADE Biomedical research support ENERGY BALANCE STUDY ON INFANTS W/ BRONCHOPULMONARY DYSPLASIA
S07RR-05477-29 0430 (NSS) SHARON, PINHAS Biomedical research support ANTI NEOVASCULARIZATION ROLE FOR SULFASALAZINE IN CHRONIC INFLAMMATORY DISEASES
S07RR-05477-29 0431 (NSS) MOY, JAMES Biomedical research support MAJOR BASIC PROTEIN (MBP) & NEUTROPHIL ACTIVATION
S07RR-05477-29 0432 (NSS) HUFF, JOHN Biomedical research support MOLECULAR STRUCTURE & FUNCTION STUDIES OF CARTILAGE LINK PROTEIN
S07RR-05477-29 0420 (NSS) SCHUMACHER, BARBARA Biomedical research support PROTEIN FROM SUPERFICIAL ZONE OF ARTICULAR CARTILAGE: MARKERS FOR OSTEOARTHRITIS
S07RR-05479-29 (NSS) RABKIN, MITCHELL T BETH ISRAEL HOSPITAL 330 BROOKLINE AVE BOSTON, MASS 02215 Biomedical research support
S07RR-05479-29 0433 (NSS) WARE, J ANTHONY Biomedical research support HUMAN ENDOTHELIAL CELL THROMBOXANE A2
S07RR-05479-29 0434 (NSS) TENEN, DANIEL Biomedical research support RETINOIC ACID RESPONSIVE GENES IN HUMAN MYCLOID LEUKEMIA CELLS
S07RR-05479-29 0435 (NSS) KOLODNY, GERALD Biomedical research support IN VIVO UPTAKE OF RADIOACTIVITY LABELED CHEMOTHERAPY
S07RR-05479-29 0436 (NSS) JIMERSON, DAVID Biomedical research support PSYCHIATRY SUPPORT FUND
S07RR-05479-29 0437 (NSS) BING, DAVID Biomedical research support CI FUNCTION ANALYZED W/ NATURALLY OCCURING INHIBITORS
S07RR-05479-29 0438 (NSS) TENEN, DANIEL Biomedical research support CHARACTERIZATION OF LEUKOCYTE MYSIN HEAVY CHAIN
S07RR-05479-29 0439 (NSS) CHANGIZ, CHEULA Biomedical research support ACETYLCHOLINESTERASE POSITIVE CORTICAL PYRAMIDAL NEURONS
S07RR-05479-29 0440 (NSS) TENEN, DANIEL Biomedical research support PURCHASE OF LIQUID NITROGEN FREEZER FOR PRESERVATION OF LEUKEMIA CELLS
S07RR-05479-29 0441 (NSS) PHILLIPS, RUSSELL Biomedical research support EFFECT OF CATARACT EXTRACTION & INTRAOCULAR LENS IMPLANTATION ON ELDERLY
S07RR-05479-29 0442 (NSS) TRENTHAM, DAVID Biomedical research support MOLECULAR CHARACTERIZATION OF TWO COLLAGEN BINDING T CELL FRACTURES
S07RR-05479-29 0443 (NSS) NICHOLSON-WELLER, AN Biomedical research support FACTOR J NEW INHIBITOR OF COMPLEMENT
S07RR-05479-29 0444 (NSS) BURSTEIN, DEBORAH Biomedical research support DIFFUSION OF INTRACELLULAR CARDIAC IONS AS MEASURED BY NMR
S07RR-05479-29 0445 (NSS) WEINTRAUB, SANDRA Biomedical research support ATTENTIONAL EYE MOVEMENTS IN NEUROLOGY DIS
S07RR-05479-29 0446 (NSS) TENEN, DANIEL Biomedical research support MOLECULAR ANALYSIS OF ACUTE MYELOMONOLYTEC LEUKEMIA
S07RR-05479-29 0447 (NSS) WARE, ANTHONY Biomedical research support EFFECTS OF COCAINE & CATECHOLAMINES ON BLOOD PLATELETS
S07RR-05479-29 0448 (NSS) REIS, MOSHE Biomedical research support NEW METHOD OF VISUALIZATION OF CNS COMPONENTS BY MRI
S07RR-05483-29 (NSS) GIBBONS, RONALD J FORSYTH DENTAL CENTER 140 THE FENWAY BOSTON, MASS 02115 Biomedical research support
S07RR-05483-29 0505 (NSS) HEIN, JOHN W Biomedical research support NO RESEARCH SUBPROJECTS
S07RR-05484-29 (NSS) COHEN, BRUCE M MCLEAN HOSPITAL 115 MILL STREET BELMONT, MASS 02178-9106 Biomedical research support
S07RR-05484-29 0024 (NSS) WOODS, BRYAN T Biomedical research support SPECTROMYOGRAPHIC DETECTION & QUANTITY OF MIRROR MOVEMENT IN PREADOL BOYS
S07RR-05484-29 0025 (NSS) DOMESICK, VALERIE Biomedical research support CROSS ROADS OF LIMBIC & STRIATAL CIRCUITRY
S07RR-05484-29 0026 (NSS) MALTAS, CAROLYN N Biomedical research support DEPRESSION & MANAGEMENT OF EFFECT IN FAMILIES DURING FAMILY THERAPY
S07RR-05484-29 0027 (NSS) KINNEY, DENNIS K Biomedical research support OBSTETRICAL COMPLICATIONS IN MANIC DEPRESSIVE PATIENTS & THEIR SIBLINGS
S07RR-05484-29 0028 (NSS) BALDESSARINI, ROSS J Biomedical research support PHARMACOLOGY OF DOPAMINE RECEPTORS IN MAMMALIAN BRAIN
S07RR-05484-29 0029 (NSS) NIXON, RALPH A Biomedical research support HUMAN BRAIN PROTEOLYSIS IN AGING & ALZHEIMERS DISEASE
S07RR-05484-29 0030 (NSS) BENOWITZ, LARRY Biomedical research support MOLECULAR STUDIES OF NEURONAL DEVELOPMENT & PLASTICITY
S07RR-05484-29 0031 (NSS) BENOWITZ, LARRY Biomedical research support MOLECULAR BASES OF NEURONAL CONNECTIVITY
S07RR-05484-29 0032 (NSS) TEICHER, MARTIN H Biomedical research support NEUROPHARMACOLOGICAL RESPONSE TO EARLY BRAIN INJURY
S07RR-05484-29 0033 (NSS) VALENTINE, NANCY Biomedical research support PRIMARY NURSING CARE MODEL FOR PSYCHIATRIC PATIENTS
S07RR-05484-29 0034 (NSS) WEISS, ROGER Biomedical research support PREDICTORS OF OUTCOME IN COCAINE DEPENDENCE
S07RR-05484-29 0035 (NSS) KINNEY, DENNIS K Biomedical research support COLLABORATIVE BIOLOGICAL RESEARCH IN SCHIZOPHRENIA NEUROLOGY SECTION
S07RR-05484-29 0036 (NSS) COLE, JONATHAN O Biomedical research support COURSE OF DYSKINESIA
S07RR-05485-29 (NSS) JAKOBIEC, FREDERICK A MASS EYE & EAR

INFIRMARY 243 CHARLES STREET BOSTON, MASS 02114 Biomedical research support grant
S07RR-05486-29 (NSS) NEWBOWER, RONALD S MASSACHUSETTS GENERAL HOSPITAL BARTLETT 3 BOSTON, MASSACHUSETTS 02114 Biomedical research support
S07RR-05486-29 0054 (NSS) BEKKEN, KAAREN E Biomedical research support DISSOCIATION OF MATERNAL SPEECH & GESTURE TO ORALLY TRAINED DEAF CHILDREN
S07RR-05486-29 0055 (NSS) BRINGHURST, F RICHAR Biomedical research support CANCER HYPERCALCEMIA: NEW SECRETED BONE RESORBING FACTOR
S07RR-05486-29 0056 (NSS) HITZIG, BERNARD M Biomedical research support TRAUMATIC EFFECTS OF HYPOXIA, & HYPERTHERMIA IN BRAIN CELLS BY NMR
S07RR-05486-29 0057 (NSS) MURPHY, JANE M Biomedical research support LONGITUDINAL STUDY IN PSYCHIATRIC EPIDEMIOLOGY
S07RR-05486-29 0058 (NSS) SMITH, SUZANNE T Biomedical research support WRITING IN ALZHEIMERS DISEASE
S07RR-05486-29 0059 (NSS) VERMEULEN, MARY W Biomedical research support REGULATION OF TNF & CYTOKINES IN LUNG INJURY
S07RR-05486-29 0060 (NSS) SMITH, JOHN A Biomedical research support MASS SPECTROMETER TO ANALYZE MODIFIED PROTEINS & PEPTIDES
S07RR-05486-29 0061 (NSS) HALES, CHARLES A Biomedical research support PULMONARY EDEMA FROM SYNTHETIC SMOKE INHALATION
S07RR-05486-29 0062 (NSS) CAVINESS, VERNE S Biomedical research support CORTICAL DEVELOPMENT
S07RR-05486-29 0063 (NSS) NAGLER-ANDERSON, CAT Biomedical research support CELL PROD MODEL & DISPERSION IN DVLP MURINE NEOCORTEX AUTOIMMUNITY, STRESS
S07RR-05486-29 0037 (NSS) CHUDLER, ERIC H Biomedical research support C1, C2, C3 SPINAL NEURONS IN CEPHALIC NOCICEPTION
S07RR-05486-29 0038 (NSS) HOOP, BERNARD Biomedical research support GABA & GLUTAMATE IN CENTRAL CONTROL OF BREATHING
S07RR-05486-29 0039 (NSS) HOOVER, HERBERT C, J Biomedical research support TUMOR CHEMOSENSITIVITY ASSAY USING ULTRACLONE ONCOSCREEN
S07RR-05486-29 0040 (NSS) JACOBY, LEE B Biomedical research support CLONAL ANALYSIS OF NERVOUS SYSTEM TUMORS
S07RR-05486-29 0041 (NSS) MACLAUGHLIN, DAVID T Biomedical research support GONADAL MULLERIAN INHIBITING SUBSTANCE IN REPRODUCTION
S07RR-05486-29 0042 (NSS) MOSCICKI, RICHARD A Biomedical research support KUPFFER CELL DEVELOPMENT
S07RR-05486-29 0043 (NSS) MURPHY, JANE M Biomedical research support LONGITUDINAL STUDY IN PSYCHIATRIC EPIDEMIOLOGY
S07RR-05486-29 0044 (NSS) OSGOOD, PATRICIA F Biomedical research support MORPHINE DISPOSITION & METABOLISM IN BURNED CHILD & RAT
S07RR-05486-29 0045 (NSS) RUSSELL, WILLIAM E Biomedical research support GROWTH FACTOR MODULATION OF LIVER GROWTH & REPAIR
S07RR-05486-29 0046 (NSS) WARREN, CHRISTOPHER Biomedical research support EXOGENOUS SUBSTRATES FOR GLYCOPROTEIN BIOSYNTHESIS
S07RR-05486-29 0047 (NSS) PASTERNACK, MARK Biomedical research support PROGRAMMABLE LIQUID NITROGEN CONTROLLED RATE FREEZING SYSTEM
S07RR-05486-29 0048 (NSS) AURON, PHILIP E Biomedical research support ACCESSORY CELL ACTIVATION IN IMMUNE RESPONSE
S07RR-05486-29 0049 (NSS) BERNARDS, RENE Biomedical research support TUMOR PROGRESSION IN NEUROBLASTOMA
S07RR-05486-29 0050 (NSS) HITZIG, BERNARD M Biomedical research support TRAUMATIC EFFECTS OF HYPOXIA & HYPERTHERMIA ON BRAIN CELLS BY NMR
S07RR-05486-29 0051 (NSS) SYSTROM, DAVID M Biomedical research support ANAEROBIC THRESHOLD DURING EXERCISE
S07RR-05486-29 0052 (NSS) WARREN, CHRISTOPHER Biomedical research support BIOCHEMICAL & MOLECULAR STUDIES ON L MANNOSIDOSIS
S07RR-05486-29 0053 (NSS) YEH, EDWARD T H Biomedical research support PATHOBIOLOGY OF PAROXYSMAL NOCTURNAL HEMOGLOBINURIA
S07RR-05487-29 (NSS) COFFMAN, JAY D UNIVERSITY HOSPITAL, INC 88 E NEWTON STREET BOSTON, MASS 02118 Biomedical research support
S07RR-05487-29 0687 (NSS) BUCKLEY, JOHN F Biomedical research support ANTICOAGULANTS & WOUND HEALING
S07RR-05487-29 0688 (NSS) GALLER, JAMINA R Biomedical research support SOMATOMEDIN C & GROWTH FAILURE: PERINATAL BLOOD, RADIOIMMUNOASSAY
S07RR-05487-29 0689 (NSS) SCHEMIN, RICHARD J Biomedical research support OXYGEN RADICAL SCAVENGERS & HEART MECHANICS: SUPEROXIDE DISMUTASE, LIPOPEROXIDAT
S07RR-05487-29 0690 (NSS) FREUND, KAREN M Biomedical research support CHLAMYDIA IN A LOW RISK POPULATION: SCREENING PAP SMEARS
S07RR-05487-29 0691 (NSS) LAZAR, HAROLD L Biomedical research support SUBSTRATE ENHANCEMENT FOR HEART STORAGE: TRANSPLANT, L GLUTAMATE, CATALASE
S07RR-05487-29 0708 (NSS) SCHROY, PAUL C Biomedical research support PROTEIN KINASE C, A: COLON CANCER: GROWTH, HEXAMETHYLENE BISACETAMIDE, NA
S07RR-05487-29 0709 (NSS) ROSS, E EDWARDS Biomedical research support INVITRO STUDIES OF EPITHELIUM: RETINAL PIGMENT & MULLER GLIAL CELLS
S07RR-05487-29 0710 (NSS) COX, L CLARKE Biomedical research support ABR IN NEONATAL HEARING SCREENS
S07RR-05487-29 0711 (NSS) VOSBURGH, EVAN Biomedical research support VON WILLEBRAND FACTOR IN RENAL FAILURE
S07RR-05487-29 0712 (NSS) ROSIELLO, ARTHUR P Biomedical research support EXTRACELLULAR VLSI PLANAR MICROELECTRODE ARRAY
S07RR-05487-29 0713 (NSS) MCKENNEY, PATRICIA Biomedical research support CYCLOSPORIN A & CORON RESTENOSIS: ILIAC ARTERY, ANGIOPLASTY, HYPERCHOLESTEROLEMI
S07RR-05487-29 0714 (NSS) GAVRAS, HARALAMBOS Biomedical research support BRADYKININ, MYOCARDIAL BLOOD FLOW & METABOLISM
S07RR-05487-29 0715 (NSS) HUNTER, NANCY Biomedical research support EMOTIONAL PROCESSING & ALCOHOLISM: HEMISPHERIC FUNCTION & DYSFUNCTION
S07RR-05487-29 0716 (NSS) ROTHSTEIN, THOMAS R Biomedical research support B CELL STIMULATION CYTOCHALASIN: ANTI IMMUNOGLOBIN ANTIBODY, CALCIUM IONOPHORE
S07RR-05487-29 0717 (NSS) BEASLEY, DEBBIE S Biomedical research support INTERLEUKIN 1 & VASC CONTRACTION: CYTOSOLIC FREE CALCIUM, INOSITOL TRIPHOSPHATE

PROJECT NO., ORGANIZATIONAL UNIT., INVESTIGATOR, ADDRESS, TITLE

S07RR-05487-29 0692 (NSS) LAZAR, HAROLD L Biomedical research support SUBSTRATE ENHANCEMENT & OXYGEN RADICAL SCAVENGERS: GLUTAMATE, HEART TRANSPLANT
S07RR-05487-29 0693 (NSS) CHEN, JOHN C Biomedical research support PRENATAL NUTRITION & SEROTONIN RELEASE: HIPPOCAMPUS, 5 H1AA, PLATELETS
S07RR-05487-29 0694 (NSS) WEISE, WOLFGANG J Biomedical research support FISH OIL & MEMBRANOUS NEPHROPATHY
S07RR-05487-29 0695 (NSS) KRIMES, PETER E Biomedical research support POST CHOLECYSTECTOMY DYNAMICS: ULTRASONOGRAPHY, NUCLEAR SCINTIGRAPHY
S07RR-05487-29 0696 (NSS) HEINRICH, GERHARD Biomedical research support NERVE GROWTH FACTOR: GENE EXPRESSION & TRANSCRIPTION
S07RR-05487-29 0697 (NSS) SUSSMAN, ILENE Biomedical research support HYPERGLYCEMIA & DIABETIC COMPLICATIONS: MYOINOSITOL, SORBITOL
S07RR-05487-29 0698 (NSS) SUGAR, ALAN M Biomedical research support ESOPHAGEAL IMMUNITY IN CANADA: BLASTOCONIDIA
S07RR-05487-29 0699 (NSS) ROTHSTEIN, THOMAS L Biomedical research support PROLIFERATIVE SIGNALS FOR LYMPHOCYTES: C MYC, C FOS, C JUN, DNA BINDING PROTEINS
S07RR-05487-29 0700 (NSS) BURNS, RISA B Biomedical research support MEDICAL LITERATURE REPORTING IN LAY PRESS NEWSPAPERS
S07RR-05487-29 0701 (NSS) FENTON, MATTHEW J Biomedical research support REGULATORY PROTEINS & INTERLEUKIN 1: TNF, TRANSCRIPTIONAL PROTEINS
S07RR-05487-29 0702 (NSS) KELLY, CIARAN P Biomedical research support CLOSTRIDIUM DIFFICILE ANTI TOXIN: TOXIN A & B
S07RR-05487-29 0703 (NSS) COFFMAN, JAY D Biomedical research support DIGITAL BLOOD FLOW & SEROTONIN: VASCULAR TONE, PLASMA 5 HT LEVELS
S07RR-05487-29 0704 (NSS) GAND, H DANANA Biomedical research support VASCULAR KALLIKREIN KININ SYSTEM: HYPERTENSION, GOLDBLATT KIDNEY
S07RR-05487-29 0705 (NSS) SAFRAN, HOWARD Biomedical research support DIDEOXYNUCLEOTIDES & REVERSE TRANSCRIPTASE: ADENOSINE DEAMINASE, CALF THYMUS
S07RR-05487-29 0706 (NSS) SUSSMAN, ILENE Biomedical research support VASCULAR METABOLISM IN DIABETES: MYOINOSITOL, HYPERGLYCEMIA, NA+ & K APTASE
S07RR-05487-29 0707 (NSS) FRENDL, GYORGY Biomedical research support TYROSINE KINASES & MONOCYTES: THP 1 MONOCYTE LINE CYTOKINE, MRNA
S07RR-05490-29 (NSS) SHORE, JOSEPH D HENRY FORD HOSPITAL 2799 W GRAND BLVD, RES ADM DETROIT, MICH 48202 Biomedical research support
S07RR-05490-29 0449 (NSS) BLAUM, CAROLYN Biomedical research support CHOLESTEROL LEVELS & ATHEROSCLEROSIS IN ELDERLY
S07RR-05490-29 0450 (NSS) LITTLETON, RAY Biomedical research support DEVELOPMENT OF HYPERTENSION FOLLOWING LITHOTRIPSY
S07RR-05490-29 0451 (NSS) FLYNN, MICHAEL Biomedical research support IN VIVO VERTEBRAL BONE ARCHITECTURE IN OSTEOPOROSIS
S07RR-05491-29 (NSS) KLAHR, SAULO JEWISH HOSPITAL OF ST LOUIS 216 SOUTH KINGSHIGHWAY ST LOUIS, MO 63110 Biomedical research support
S07RR-05491-29 0452 (NSS) AMBRUS, JULIAN L Biomedical research support CLONING OF HUMAN B CELL GROWTH FACTOR (HMW BCFG) & ITS RECEPTOR
S07RR-05491-29 0453 (NSS) BRUNT, L MICHAEL Biomedical research support T CELL IMMUNITY & ANTIGEN PROCESSING W/ LISTERIA MONOCYTOGENES
S07RR-05491-29 0454 (NSS) CIVITELLI, ROBERTO Biomedical research support INTRACELLULAR CA2+ HOMEOSTASIS IN DUCHENNE MUSCULAR DYSTROPHY
S07RR-05491-29 0455 (NSS) CROSSEN, KARL Biomedical research support HEART RATE VARIABILITY INCREASED RISK FOR SUDDEN CARDIAC DEATH
S07RR-05491-29 0456 (NSS) DAVILA-ROMAN, VICTOR Biomedical research support INTRAOPERATIVE ULTRASONIC CHARACTERIZATION OF ASCENDING AORTA
S07RR-05491-29 0457 (NSS) FEDDE, KENTON N Biomedical research support CONSTITUENTS OF MATRIX VESICLES RELEASED FROM HUMAN OSTEOSARCOMA CELLS
S07RR-05491-29 0458 (NSS) GROSSO, LEONARD E Biomedical research support BOVINE ELASTIN RECEPTOR COMPLEX: RECOMBINANT TROPOELASTIN PROTEIN FUSION PROTEIN
S07RR-05491-29 0459 (NSS) KAVOUSSI, LOUIS R Biomedical research support ALLOPLASTIC SUBSTITUTED PORTIONS OF URINARY COLLECTING SYSTEM
S07RR-05491-29 0460 (NSS) MILNER, PETER G Biomedical research support FIBROBLAST GROWTH FACTORS IN SSV TRANSFORMED NRK FIBROBLASTS
S07RR-05491-29 0461 (NSS) PERKINS, SHERRIE Biomedical research support 1 25(OH) 2D INDUCTION OF MACROPHAGE DIFFERENTIATION
S07RR-05491-29 0462 (NSS) PERSSONS, ANDERS Biomedical research support MULTIVALENT SURFACTANT ASSOCIATED LECTINS & MULTIVALENT LIGANDS
S07RR-05491-29 0463 (NSS) ROSS, F PATRICK Biomedical research support VITRONECTIN RECEPTOR IN PROCESS OF BONE RESORPTION
S07RR-05491-29 0464 (NSS) ROVIN, BRAD Biomedical research support ESSENTIAL FATTY ACID DEFICIENCY EFFECT ON GLOMERULONEPHRITIS IN RATS
S07RR-05491-29 0465 (NSS) RUBIN, DEBORAH C Biomedical research support MOLECULAR & CELLULAR BIOLOGIC ASPECTS OF GUT DIFFERENTIATION
S07RR-05491-29 0466 (NSS) SHAPIRO, STEVEN D Biomedical research support MOLECULAR BIOLOGY OF MACROPHAGE DERIVED ELASTASE
S07RR-05491-29 0467 (NSS) WAREING, THOMAS H Biomedical research support RT VENT DYSFUNCTION W/ MECHANICAL LT VENT; GLOBAL MYOCARDIAL ISCHEMIA
S07RR-05495-29 (NSS) LANE, JOSEPH M HOSP FOR SPECIAL SURGERY 535 EAST 70TH STREET NEW YORK, N Y 10021 Biomedical research support
S07RR-05495-29 0468 (NSS) ELKON, KEITH Biomedical research support AUTOIMMUNE DISEASES
S07RR-05495-29 0469 (NSS) CROW, PEGGY Biomedical research support AUTOIMMUNE DISEASES
S07RR-05495-29 0470 (NSS) BOSKEY, ADELE Biomedical research support ULTRASTRUCTURAL BIOCHEMISTRY
S07RR-05495-29 0471 (NSS) KIMBERLY, ROBER Biomedical research support AUTOIMMUNE DISEASES
S07RR-05496-29 (NSS) COHEN, SEYMOUR LONG ISLAND JEWISH MED CTR 400 LAKEVILLE RD NEW HYDE PARK, N Y 11042 Biomedical research support
S07RR-05496-29 0901 (NSS) SCHARF, STEVEN Biomedical research support VENTRICULAR FUNCT ISCHEMIA W/ CHANGES IN INTRATHORACIC PRESSURE

PROJECT NO., ORGANIZATIONAL UNIT., INVESTIGATOR, ADDRESS, TITLE

S07RR-05496-29 0902 (NSS) MANNE, JOSEPH Biomedical research support MACROMOLECULES & SOLUTES IN CALCIUM OXALATE UROLITHIASIS
S07RR-05496-29 0903 (NSS) GORRAY, KENNETH C Biomedical research support ISLET BETA CELL DESTRUCTION & REGENERATION BY NUTRITIONAL FACTORS
S07RR-05496-29 0904 (NSS) TRACHTMAN, HOWARD Biomedical research support RENAL STRUCT & FUNCT OBSTRUCTIVE UROPATHY CHRONIC GLOMERULONEPHRITIS
S07RR-05498-22 (NSS) PEARSON, THOMAS A MARY IMOGENE BASSETT HOSPITAL ATWELL ROAD COOPERSTOWN, N Y 13326 Biomedical research support
S07RR-05498-22 0472 (NSS) RUDNICKI, MARKET Biomedical research support PANCREATIC POLYPEPTIDE FAMILY PEPTIDES IN ACUTE PANCREATITIS
S07RR-05499-29 (NSS) FOREMAN, SPENCER MONTEFIORE MEDICAL CENTER 111 EAST 210TH STREET BRONX, N Y 10467 Biomedical research support
S07RR-05499-29 0506 (NSS) FOREMAN, SPENCER Biomedical research support NO RESEARCH SUBPROJECTS
R03RR-05502-01A3 (BRC) ASHER, SANFORD A UNIVERSITY OF PITTSBURGH 219 PARKMAN AVE PITTSBURGH, PA 15260 Development of a UV resonance Raman microscope
S07RR-05505-18 (NSS) MILLER, BARRY ALBERT EINSTEIN MEDICAL CENTER 5501 OLD YORK ROAD PHILADELPHIA, PA 19141 Biomedical research support
S07RR-05505-18 0473 (NSS) PFENDER, ELLEN Biomedical research support BECKMAN MODEL L8 80 ULTRACENTRIFUGE GENETICS
S07RR-05506-29 (NSS) SURREY, SAUL CHILDRENS HOSP OF PHILADELPHIA 34TH ST AND CIVIC CENTER BLVD PHILADELPHIA, PA 19104 Biomedical research support
S07RR-05506-29 0905 (NSS) ANBAR, RAN D Biomedical research support MATURATION ON CALCIUM MOBILIZATION IN TRACHEAL SMOOTH MUSCLE CELLS
S07RR-05506-29 0906 (NSS) FOREHAND, JOHN R Biomedical research support RESPIRATORY BURST OF ACTIVITY IN HUMAN NEUTROPHIL
S07RR-05506-29 0907 (NSS) HEIDENREICH, RANDALL Biomedical research support RECOMBINANT DNA INVESTIGATION OF GALACTOSEMIA:
S07RR-05506-29 0908 (NSS) HORIUCHI, KAZUMI Biomedical research support DESICKLING OF SICKLED CELLS BY STABILIZED HEMOGLOBIN: ARTIFICIAL BLOOD, IMAGING
S07RR-05506-29 0909 (NSS) MUENKE, MAXIMILIAN Biomedical research support GENETIC STUDIES IN PATIENTS W/ INBORN BRAIN MALFORMATIONS
S07RR-05506-29 0910 (NSS) NISSIM, ITZHAK Biomedical research support NUCLEAR MAGNETIC RESONANCE CORE FACILITY
S07RR-05506-29 0911 (NSS) PRITCHETT, DOLAN B Biomedical research support GABA NEUTROTRANSMITTER RECEPTOR GENE DVMTL CHANGES & DRUG SENSITIVITY; SEIZURE
S07RR-05506-29 0912 (NSS) RAPPAPORT, ERIC F Biomedical research support FC RECEPTORS: DISTRIBUTION & DIFFERENTIAL EXPRESSION
S07RR-05506-29 0913 (NSS) SCHNUR, RHONDA E Biomedical research support MOLECULAR APPROACHES TO IDENTIFYING GENE X LINKED OCULAR ALBINISM: RETINAL
S07RR-05507-29 (NSS) SPERLING, MARK A CHILDRENS HOSP OF PITTSBURGH 3705 FIFTH AVE. AT DESOTO ST. PITTSBURGH, PA 15213 Biomedical research support
S07RR-05507-29 0479 (NSS) KARASIC, RAYMOND B Biomedical research support DOSAGE OF EPINEPHRINE ENDOTRACHEALLY; ANIMAL MODEL OF CARDIOPULMONARY ARREST
S07RR-05507-29 0474 (NSS) CAMPBELL, THOMAS F Biomedical research support EARLY OTITIS MEDIA VS SPEECH LANGUAGE & HEARING STATUS; 5 YEAR OLD TWINS
S07RR-05507-29 0475 (NSS) DEL NIDO, PEDRO J Biomedical research support CALCIUM ACCUMULATION; ISCHEMIC & REPERFUSED HEART; ADULT & IMMATURE RABBIT
S07RR-05507-29 0476 (NSS) FRICKER, FREDERICK J Biomedical research support L CARNITINE THERAPY IN PATIENTS W/ CHRONIC CARDIOMYOPATHY
S07RR-05507-29 0477 (NSS) ISAACSON, GLENN Biomedical research support EXTRALARYNGEAL SUPRAGLOTTIC CLOSURE; CHR ASPIRATION; NEURO IMPAIR; CANINE MODEL
S07RR-05507-29 0478 (NSS) KALEIDA, PHILLIP H Biomedical research support BACTERIAL RESPIRATORY PATHOGENS IN NASOPHARYNX; BREAST VS FORMULA FED INFANTS
S07RR-05507-29 0480 (NSS) KENNEDY, SUSAN Biomedical research support ONCOGENES & ONCOFETAL PROTEIN; HEPATIC CARCINOGENESIS; TYROSINEMIA MODEL
S07RR-05507-29 0481 (NSS) KUSAKAWA, ISOA Biomedical research support GROWTH STIM FACTOR IN PERIBRONCHIAL MUSCLE HYPERPLASIA& AIRWAY OBSTRUCT; CONGENI
S07RR-05507-29 0482 (NSS) NOZZA, ROBERT Biomedical research support PURCHASE OF AN EVOKED ACOUSTIC EMISSIONS INTERFACE SYSTEM W/ COMPUTER SUPPORT
S07RR-05507-29 0483 (NSS) PARADISE, JACK L Biomedical research support TONSIL & ADENOID STUDY
S07RR-05507-29 0484 (NSS) SCHOR, NINA F Biomedical research support GLUTAMINE SYNTHETASE & OXYGEN RADICALS IN CNS HYPOXIC ISCHEMIC DAMAGE; RAT
S07RR-05507-29 0485 (NSS) ZEKOWSKI, STEVEN Biomedical research support MONONUCLEAR CELL HISTAMINE RELEAS FACTOR IN ATOPIC DERMATITIS; HUMAN MAST CELL
S07RR-05510-28 (NSS) DONOSO, LARRY A WILLS EYE HOSPITAL NINTH AND WALNUT STREETS PHILADELPHIA, PA 19107 Biomedical research support
S07RR-05510-28 0055 (NSS) SAVINO, PETER J Biomedical research support OPTIC PUPILOMETRIC STUDIES
S07RR-05510-28 0056 (NSS) LAIBSON, PETER R Biomedical research support VIRUS TYPE IN HERPES SIMPLEX INFECTION
S07RR-05510-28 0057 (NSS) SPAETH, GEORGE L Biomedical research support VIROPTIC TRIAL IN GLAUCOMA
S07RR-05510-28 0058 (NSS) DONOSO, LARRY A Biomedical research support MOLECULAR BIOLOGY
S07RR-05511-29 (NSS) BECKER, FREDERICK F UNIVERSITY OF TEXAS 1515 HOLCOMBE BLVD, MDAH 101 HOUSTON, TEXAS 77030 Biomedical research support grant
S07RR-05511-29 0486 (NSS) IOANNIDES, CONSTANTI Biomedical research support grant TUMOR REACTIVE LYMPHOCYTES IN OVARIAN CARCINOMA
S07RR-05511-29 0487 (NSS) KAGAN, JACOB Biomedical research support grant CHROMOSOMAL TRANSLOCATION IN ACUTE T CELL LEUKEMIA & LYMPHOMA

PROJECT NO., ORGANIZATIONAL UNIT., INVESTIGATOR, ADDRESS, TITLE

S07RR-05511-29 0488 (NSS) RAO, POTU N Biomedical research support grant MPM 2 ANTIGENS IN INITIATION OF MITOSIS
S07RR-05511-29 0489 (NSS) PELLIS, NEAL R Biomedical research support grant MOVEMENT OF LYMPHOCYTES THROUGH INTERCELLULAR MATRIX: AN IN VITRO MODEL
S07RR-05511-29 0490 (NSS) YUEN, PICK-HOONG Biomedical research support grant CLONING OF CDNA ENCODING MOMULV ENHANCER BINDING PROTEIN
S07RR-05511-29 0491 (NSS) ITOH, KYOGO Biomedical research support grant T CELLS IN TUMOR SITES W/ HETEROCONJUGATES OF ANTI CD3 MABS INTERLEUKIN 2
S07RR-05511-29 0492 (NSS) SAYA, HIDEYUKI Biomedical research support grant HUMAN NEU GENE MUTATIONS IN BRAIN TUMORS; ENZYME AMPLIFIED HUMAN GENOMIC DNA
S07RR-05511-29 0505 (NSS) ZWELLING, LEONARD A Biomedical research support grant HUMAN LEUKEMIA RESISTANCE TO TOPOISOMERASE II REACTIVE DNA INTERCALATING AGENTS
S07RR-05511-29 0493 (NSS) PERRY, WILLIAM M Biomedical research support grant MYOD1 RELATED GENES IN MESODERM INDUCTION
S07RR-05511-29 0494 (NSS) ULLRICH, STEPHAN Biomedical research support grant SUPPRESS GVHD BY IMMUNOSUPPRESSIVE FACTOR RELEASED BY UV IRRADIATED KERATINOCYTE
S07RR-05511-29 0495 (NSS) KLEIN, WILLIAM Biomedical research support grant INSERTIONAL MUTATIONS TO STUDY EMBRYOGENESIS IN MOUSE
S07RR-05511-29 0496 (NSS) LIAO, WARREN S Biomedical research support grant TRANSCRIPTIONAL REGULATION OF RAT T1 KININOGEN GENE EXPRESSION BY INTERLEUKIN 6
S07RR-05511-29 0497 (NSS) BOUSFIELD, GEORGE R Biomedical research support grant CARBOHYDRATE CHEMISTRY OF EQUINE GONADOTROPINS
S07RR-05511-29 0498 (NSS) VANDYKE, MICHAEL W Biomedical research support grant HUMAN TRANSCRIPTION FACTOR TF IID
S07RR-05511-29 0499 (NSS) GLISSON, BONNIE S Biomedical research support grant SMALL CELL LUNG CANCER IN NUDE MICE: ORGAN SITE ON BIOLOGY & CHEMOSENSITIVITY
S07RR-05511-29 0500 (NSS) CONTI, CLAUDIO J Biomedical research support grant TUMOR SUPPRESSION MECHANISMS IN CHEMICAL CARCINOGENESIS
S07RR-05511-29 0501 (NSS) WARGOVICH, MICHAEL J Biomedical research support grant FIELD PROLIFERATION DEFECTS IN COLON CANCER
S07RR-05511-29 0502 (NSS) HO, BENG T Biomedical research support grant NEUROPSYCHOPHARMACOLOGIC STUDIES OF LYMPHOKINES
S07RR-05511-29 0503 (NSS) SIVARAMAKRISHNAN, MA Biomedical research support grant REGULATION OF MACROPHAGE FUNCTIONS
S07RR-05511-29 0504 (NSS) SEN, SUBRATA Biomedical research support grant EXTRACHROMOSOMAL STRUCTURES: S PHASE CHROMOSOME CONDENSATION AMPLIFIED IN DNA
S07RR-05513-29 (NSS) COOPER, ALLEN D RES INST PALO ALTO MED FDN 860 BRYANT STREET PALO ALTO, CALIF 94301 Biomedical research support
S07RR-05513-29 0059 (NSS) COURTNEY, KENNETH R Biomedical research support NON COMPETITIVE NMDA ANTAGONISTS
S07RR-05513-29 0060 (NSS) HILL, BRUCE C Biomedical research support CLASS III ANTI ARRHYTHMIC DRUG TOXICITY BY POTASSIUM CHANNEL ACTIVATORS
S07RR-05513-29 0061 (NSS) FREUND, YVONNE R Biomedical research support T GONDII & IMMUNE REACTIVITY IN BRAIN TISSUE:
S07RR-05513-29 0062 (NSS) ELLSWORTH, JEFF L Biomedical research support REGULATION OF HEPATIC LDL RECEPTOR GENE TRANSCRIPTION
S07RR-05514-29 (NSS) LERNER, RICHARD A RES INST OF SCRIPPS CLINIC 10666 NORTH TORREY PINES ROAD LA JOLLA, CALIF 92037 Biomedical research support
S07RR-05514-29 0507 (NSS) BEERS, WILLIAM H Biomedical research support NO RESEARCH SUBPROJECTS
S07RR-05515-28 (NSS) ROSENQUIST, GLENN C CHILDREN'S HOSP NAT'L MED CTR 111 MICHIGAN AVE N W WASHINGTON, D C 20010 Biomedical research support
S07RR-05515-28 0064 (NSS) REVENIS, MARY Biomedical research support DEXAMETHASONE TO PREVENT BRONCHOPULMONARY DYSPLASIA BABIES
P41RR-05517-01A1 (SSS) JANZEN, EDWARD G OKLAHOMA MEDICAL RESEARCH FDN 825 NORTHEAST 13TH STREET OKLAHOMA CITY, OK 73104 Spin trapping free radical in biology and medicine
P41RR-05517-01A1 9001 (SSS) JANZEN, EDWARD G Spin trapping free radical in biology and medicine Core research--Spin trapping free radicals in biology and medicine
S07RR-05518-28 (NSS) RE, RICHARD N ALTON OCHSNER MEDICAL FDN 1516 JEFFERSON HIGHWAY NEW ORLEANS, LA 70121 Biomedical research support
S07RR-05518-28 0506 (NSS) DEININGER, PRESCOTT Biomedical research support TO SEQUENCE PLATELET DERIVED GROWTH FACTOR GENE IN XENOPUS
S07RR-05518-28 0507 (NSS) COOK, JULIA L Biomedical research support TKO 100 MINIFLUOROMETER W/ REPIPETTOR
S07RR-05518-28 0508 (NSS) LARSON, JANET Biomedical research support EPPENDORF MODEL 5415C MICROCENTRIFUGE
S07RR-05518-28 0509 (NSS) DEININGER, PRESCOTT Biomedical research support GENE MACHINE II PROGRAMMABLE THERMAL CONTROLLER PC 4005
S07RR-05519-29 (NSS) MC GILL, HENRY C, JR SOUTHWEST FDN FOR BIOMED RES P O BOX 28147 SAN ANTONIO, TX 78228-0147 Biomedical research support
S07RR-05519-29 0510 (NSS) ATTANASIO, ROBERTA Biomedical research support IDIOTYPE MAPPING OF MONOCLONAL ANTI CD4 ANTIBODIES USING SYNTHETIC PEPTIDES
S07RR-05519-29 0511 (NSS) BLANGERO, JOHN Biomedical research support GENETIC DETERMINANTS OF THYROID HORMONES & THEIR EFFECTS ON LIPOPROTEINS
S07RR-05519-29 0512 (NSS) SUREAU, CAMILLE Biomedical research support HEPATITIS DELTA VIRUS MORPHOGENESIS & INFECTIVITY IN VITRO
S07RR-05519-29 0513 (NSS) DRISCOLL, DONNA Biomedical research support EDITING OF APOLIPOPROTEIN B MRNA
S07RR-05519-29 0514 (NSS) WARREN, RONALD Q Biomedical research support IDIOTYPIC EXPRESSION OF HUMAN ANTIBODIES THAT RECOGNIZE HIV 1 CD4 RECEPTOR
S07RR-05519-29 0515 (NSS) BEAMES, BURTON Biomedical research support FUNCTIONAL ASSAYS FOR HEPATITIS B VIRUS CORE PROTEIN ANALYSIS
S07RR-05519-29 0516 (NSS) TARAPOREWALA, IRACH Biomedical research support SYNTHESIS OF NON NUCLEOSIDE ANTIVIRAL AGENTS: NOVEL IMIDAZOACRIDINE DERIVATIVE

PROJECT NO., ORGANIZATIONAL UNIT., INVESTIGATOR, ADDRESS, TITLE

S07RR-05520-28 (NSS) HUTCHINSON, WILLIAM B PACIFIC NORTHWEST RES FDN 720 BROADWAY SEATTLE, WA 98122 Biomedical research support
S07RR-05520-28 0827 (NSS) BEAN MICHAEL A Biomedical research support IMMUNOLOGIC CONDITIONING DESIGNED TO IMPROVE TRANSPLANT SURVIVAL
S07RR-05520-28 0828 (NSS) GRADY, H SHELTON Biomedical research support CLINICAL & HEMATOLOGIC MANIFESTATION OF FELINE IMMUNODEFICIENCY VIRUS INFECTIONS
S07RR-05521-29 (NSS) LAIRSON, PAUL D KAISER FDN RESEARCH INSTITUTE 3505 BROADWAY, SUITE 1112 OAKLAND, CA 94611 Biomedical research support
S07RR-05521-29 0066 (NSS) LAD, PRAMOD M Biomedical research support G PROTEINS & PEPTIDES FOR ANTIBODY PRODUCTION
S07RR-05521-29 0063 (NSS) VOLLMER, WILLIAM M Biomedical research support EPIDEMIOLOGY & NATURAL HISTORY OF ASTHMA
S07RR-05521-29 0067 (NSS) MARCY, S MICHAEL Biomedical research support SCHEDULES OF EDMONSTON ZAGREL (EZ) MORATEN MEASLES VACCINE TRIALS IN US
S07RR-05521-29 0064 (NSS) VALANIS, BARBARA G Biomedical research support MATERNAL CHILD CARE DELIVERY STUDY
S07RR-05521-29 0065 (NSS) SIDNEY, STEPHEN Biomedical research support ALCOHOL USE, OTHER LIFESTYLE BEHAVIORS & INJURY IN YOUNG ADULTS
S07RR-05522-29 (NSS) SUTHERLAND, ROBERT SRI INTERNATIONAL (LA233) 333 RAVENSWOOD AVENUE MENLO PARK, CA 94025 Biomedical research support
S07RR-05522-29 0065 (NSS) CRANE, HEW Biomedical research support DEVELOPMENT OF IMPROVED OPTICAL DEVICES
S07RR-05522-29 0066 (NSS) GREEN, PHILLIP Biomedical research support DEVELOPMENT OF ADVANCED MEDICAL ULTRASOUND IMAGING INSTRUMENTS
S07RR-05522-29 0067 (NSS) VOLD, BARBARA Biomedical research support TECHNIQUE FOR USE IN AMPLIFICATION CLONING & SEQUENCING OF HUMAN + RNA GENES
S07RR-05522-29 0068 (NSS) FAHNESTOCK, MARGARET Biomedical research support MOUSE SUBMAXILLARY GLAND NGF PROCESSING ENZYMES
S07RR-05522-29 0069 (NSS) SWAN, GARY Biomedical research support CARDIOVASCULAR DISEASE & COGNITIVE DECLINE IN ELDERLY
S07RR-05522-29 0070 (NSS) BOWEN, MARY Biomedical research support ELECTROPHYSIOLOGICAL STUDIES ON RECEPTOR CELLS
S07RR-05522-29 0071 (NSS) DAWSON, MARCIA Biomedical research support RECEPTOR SELECTIVE CANCER CHEMOPREVENTIVE RETINOIDS
S07RR-05526-29 (NSS) JANICKI, BERNARD DANA-FARBER CANCER INSTITUTE 44 BINNEY STREET BOSTON, MASS 02115 Magnetically stabilized bioreactor system
S07RR-05526-29 0068 (NSS) BRADLEY, MARGARET K Magnetically stabilized bioreactor system NON STRUCTURAL PROTEIN NS 1 IN PARVOVIRUS MVM
S07RR-05526-29 0069 (NSS) BOOTHMAN, DAVID A Magnetically stabilized bioreactor system MOLECULAR CLONING OF XRAY INDUCIBLE GENES
S07RR-05526-29 0070 (NSS) CANNISTRA, STEPHEN A Magnetically stabilized bioreactor system HEMATOPOIETIC GROWTH FACTOR RECEPTOR
S07RR-05526-29 0071 (NSS) ABE, MIYAKO Magnetically stabilized bioreactor system DF3 BREAST CARCINOMA ASSOC ANTIGEN: GENE CLONING EXPRESSION
S07RR-05526-29 0072 (NSS) CHEN, LAN BO Magnetically stabilized bioreactor system MOLECULAR CLONING OF TENSIN
S07RR-05526-29 0073 (NSS) CROOP, JAMES M Magnetically stabilized bioreactor system ANALYSIS OF MULTIDRUG RESISTANCE GENES IN DROSOPHILA
S07RR-05526-29 0089 (NSS) GRIFFIN, JAMES D Magnetically stabilized bioreactor system CONTROL GENES IN PROLIFERATION & DIFFERENTIATION OF HUMAN HEMATOPOIETIC CELLS
S07RR-05526-29 0090 (NSS) HEMLER, MARTIN E Magnetically stabilized bioreactor system LINKING MULTIPLE ADHESIVE FUNCTION OF VLA 4 W/ MULTIPLE STRUCTURAL FORMS
S07RR-05526-29 0091 (NSS) OKEEFE, STEPHEN J Magnetically stabilized bioreactor system C MOS PROTO ONCOGENE IN MEIOTIC MATURATION OF MAMMALIAN OOCYTE
S07RR-05526-29 0092 (NSS) SPIES, THOMAS Magnetically stabilized bioreactor system GENE CONTROLLING ASSEMBLY & CELL SURFACE EXPRESSION OF MHC CLASS I MOLECULES
S07RR-05526-29 0093 (NSS) JANICKI, BERNARD W Magnetically stabilized bioreactor system PHOTOMICROSCOPY SYSTEM IN SITU HYBRIDIZATION & IMMUNOHISTOCHEMISTRY
S07RR-05526-29 0094 (NSS) CLAYTON, LINDA K Magnetically stabilized bioreactor system FUNCTIONAL ANALYSIS OF CD3 ZETA & CD3 ISOFORMS
S07RR-05526-29 0095 (NSS) ELICES, MARIANO J Magnetically stabilized bioreactor system INDEPENDENT REGULATION OF MULTIPLE VLA 4 ADHESION FUNCTIONS
S07RR-05526-29 0096 (NSS) HUSAIN, ZAHEED Magnetically stabilized bioreactor system MOLECULAR MECHANISM OF DMBA INDUCED & UV LIGHT PROMOTED MOUSE SKIN MELANOMAS
S07RR-05526-29 0097 (NSS) LICHT, JONATHAN D Magnetically stabilized bioreactor system TRANSCRIPTION REPRESSION BY DROSOPHILA KRUPPEL PROTEIN: IN VITRO TRANSCRIPTION
S07RR-05526-29 0098 (NSS) RIEKER, PATRICIA P Magnetically stabilized bioreactor system SOCIODEMOGRAPHIC TREATMENT & PSYCHOSOCIAL OUTCOMES IN PROSTATE CANCER SURVIVORS
S07RR-05526-29 0099 (NSS) ROLLINS, BARRETT J Magnetically stabilized bioreactor system ALLOTYPE ANALYSIS OF HEAD & NECK SQUAMOUS CELL CARCINOMAS
S07RR-05526-29 0100 (NSS) SHIPP, MARGARET A Magnetically stabilized bioreactor system CD10 NEUTRAL ENDOPEPTIDASE 24 11; NORMAL & NEOPLASTIC BRONCHIAL EPITHELIAL CELL
S07RR-05526-29 0101 (NSS) SMITH, TEMPLE F Magnetically stabilized bioreactor system SOFTWARE FOR AUTOMATIC TO IDENTIFY SEQUENCE FUNCTIONAL PATTERNS
S07RR-05526-29 0102 (NSS) BERGELSON, JEFFREY M Magnetically stabilized bioreactor system CHARACTERIZATION OF ECHOVIRUS TYPE 1 RECEPTOR PROTEIN
S07RR-05526-29 0103 (NSS) TEDDER, THOMAS F Magnetically stabilized bioreactor system REGULATION OF HUMAN LEUKOCYTE RECIRCULATION
S07RR-05526-29 0074 (NSS) FINGEROTH, JOYCE D Magnetically stabilized bioreactor system EXPRESS & CHARACTERIZE HUMAN GR2

S07RR-05526-29 0075 (NSS) REISS, CAROL S Magnetically stabilized bioreactor system FINE SPECIFICITY OF IMMUNE RESPONSE TO VESICULAR STOMATITIS VIRUS GLYCOPROTEIN
S07RR-05526-29 0076 (NSS) RUPRECHT, RUTH M Magnetically stabilized bioreactor system PREVENTION OF RETROVIRAL INFECTION: DNA LEVEL ANALYSIS
S07RR-05526-29 0077 (NSS) WAGNER, JOHN A Magnetically stabilized bioreactor system CHARACTERIZE NGF INDUCIBLE CAMP EXTINGUISHED RETROVIRUS LIKE (NICER) ELEMENT
S07RR-05526-29 0078 (NSS) AMBROSINO, DONNA M Magnetically stabilized bioreactor system T CELL & B CELL RESPONSES TO POLYSACCHARIDES
S07RR-05526-29 0079 (NSS) ARCECI, ROBERT J Magnetically stabilized bioreactor system IN VIVO REVERSAL OF MULTIDRUG RESISTANCE W/ PROGESTERONE
S07RR-05526-29 0080 (NSS) LANGHOFF, ERIC Magnetically stabilized bioreactor system HIV 1 REPLICATION IN PRIMARY DENDRITIC CELLS & MACROPHAGES
S07RR-05526-29 0081 (NSS) PATARCA, ROBERTO Magnetically stabilized bioreactor system MAPPING & CHARACTERIZATION OF ETA 1 ALLELES
S07RR-05526-29 0082 (NSS) ROLLINS, BARRETT J Magnetically stabilized bioreactor system PDGF INDUCIBLE CYTOKINE USING TRANSGENIC MICE ANALYSIS
S07RR-05526-29 0083 (NSS) KEYOMARSI, KHANDAN Magnetically stabilized bioreactor system NORMAL VS TUMOR DERIVED BREAST EPITHELIAL CELLS: INHIBITION OF THYMIDYLATE SYNTH
S07RR-05526-29 0084 (NSS) SELLS, MARY ANN Magnetically stabilized bioreactor system FUNCTIONAL CHARACTERIZATION OF EBV BHRF1 PROTEIN
S07RR-05526-29 0085 (NSS) SPIES, THOMAS Magnetically stabilized bioreactor system NOVEL GENES IN HUMAN MAJOR HISTOCOMPATIBILITY COMPLEX CLASS III REGION
S07RR-05526-29 0086 (NSS) DEAR, KEITH B G Magnetically stabilized bioreactor system BIOSTATISTICAL METHODS TO ANALYZE HEMATOLOGIC RECONSTITUTION
S07RR-05526-29 0087 (NSS) SOIFFER, ROBERT Magnetically stabilized bioreactor system IMMUNE FUNCTION; CONTINUOUS INFUSION RECOMBINANT IL 2; BONE MARROW TRANSPLANT
S07RR-05526-29 0088 (NSS) WEAVER, DAVID T Magnetically stabilized bioreactor system BLOOMS SYNDROME: A DNA LIGASE & IMMUNODEFICIENCY
S07RR-05527-29 (NSS) DELORI, FRANCOIS C EYE RES INST OF RETINA FDN 20 STANIFORD STREET BOSTON, MASS 02114 Biomedical research support
S07RR-05527-29 0517 (NSS) FEKE, GILBERT Biomedical research support HUMAN RETINAL BLOOD FLOW; LASER DOPPLER DIABETES RETINOPATHY
S07RR-05527-29 0518 (NSS) SNODDERLY, MAX D Biomedical research support FOVEAL PIGMENT & ANATOMY: MACULAR PIGMENT VISUAL ACUITY CORTICAL RESPONSE
S07RR-05527-29 0519 (NSS) BARTELS, STEPHEN P Biomedical research support PHARMACOLOGY OF ANTERIOR SEGMENT FLUOROPHOTOMETRY CILIARY BODY
S07RR-05527-29 0520 (NSS) DOREY, C KATHLEEN Biomedical research support LIPOFUSION FLUOROPHOTOMETRY
S07RR-05527-29 0521 (NSS) LEVENE, RICHARD Biomedical research support MAST CELL BIOLOGY MOLECULAR BIOLOGY ALLERGIES
S07RR-05527-29 0522 (NSS) CHAKRABARTI, BIRESWA Biomedical research support BIOCHEMISTRY OF VITREOUS & LENS
S07RR-05527-29 0523 (NSS) STEPP, MARY ANN Biomedical research support MOLECULAR ASPECTS OF WOUND HEALING
S07RR-05528-29 (NSS) PEDERSON, THORU WORCESTER FDN FOR EXP BIO, INC 222 MAPLE AVENUE SHREWSBURY, MASS 01545 Biomedical research support
S07RR-05528-29 0508 (NSS) PEDERSON, THORU Biomedical research support NO RESEARCH SUBPROJECTS
S07RR-05529-29 (NSS) HEPPNER, GLORIA H MICHIGAN CANCER FOUNDATION 110 E WARREN AVENUE DETROIT, MICH 48201 Biomedical research support
S07RR-05529-29 0524 (NSS) HEPPNER, GLORIA H Biomedical research support BREAST CANCER PROGRESSION: MCF 10 GENETICS ONCOGENES TUMORGENECITY
S07RR-05529-29 0525 (NSS) MACOSKA, JILL Biomedical research support GENETICS OF HUMAN PROSTATE CANCER: ONCOGENES GROWTH FACTORS HORMONES RECEPTORS
S07RR-05529-29 0526 (NSS) WEI, WEI-ZEN Biomedical research support IMMUNOMODULATION OF MOUSE MAMMARY NEOPLASTIC PREVENTION VACCINES BREAST CANCER
S07RR-05530-29 (NSS) PRENDERGAST, FRANKLYN G MAYO FOUNDATION 200 FIRST STREET SOUTHWEST ROCHESTER, MINN 55905 Biomedical research support
S07RR-05530-29 0527 (NSS) MAIHLE, NITA J Biomedical research support ONCOGENESIS MEDIATED BY C ERBB, EGF R, EPIDERMAL GROWTH FACTOR RECEPTOR
S07RR-05530-29 0528 (NSS) MCMURRAY, CYNTHIA T Biomedical research support SIGNAL TRANSDUCTION IN NUCLEUS HUMAN ENKEPHALIN GENE
S07RR-05533-29 (NSS) NOVICK, RICHARD P P H RES INST OF CITY OF N Y 455 FIRST AVENUE NEW YORK, N Y 10016 Biomedical research support grant
S07RR-05533-29 0529 (NSS) MINDICH, LEONARD E Biomedical research support grant PACKAGING OF GENOME OF VIRUS IN NEWLY FORMED VIRUS PARTICLES
S07RR-05534-19 (NSS) RIFKIND, RICHARD A SLOAN-KETTERING INST CAN RES 1275 YORK AVENUE NEW YORK, N Y 10021 Biomedical research support
S07RR-05534-19 0530 (NSS) ALBINO, ANTHONY P Biomedical research support ONCOGENES IN PATHOGENESIS OF MELANOMA
S07RR-05534-19 0531 (NSS) TEMPST, PAUL Biomedical research support PEPTIDE ANTIBIOTICS
S07RR-05535-29 (NSS) SCHUBERT, WILLIAM K CHILDREN'S HOSP MED CENTER ELLAND & BETHESDA AVENUES CINCINNATI, OHIO 45229 Biomedical research support
S07RR-05535-29 0532 (NSS) LESSARD, JAMES Biomedical research support CORE MONOCLONAL ANTIBODY FACILITY
S07RR-05535-29 0533 (NSS) MARKOFF, EDITH Biomedical research support MEASUREMENT OF HUMAN PROLACTIN VARIANTS
S07RR-05535-29 0534 (NSS) PIETRYGA, DANIEL Biomedical research

PROJECT NO., ORGANIZATIONAL UNIT., INVESTIGATOR, ADDRESS, TITLE

support RETROVIRUS MEDICATED TRANSFER OF HUMAN MDR 1 CDNA INTO MURINE HEMATOPOIETIC CELL
S07RR-05535-29 0535 (NSS) RIS, M DOUGLAS Biomedical research support ADULT OUTCOMES OF EARLY TREATED PKU PATIENTS
S07RR-05535-29 0536 (NSS) SPECKER, BONNIE Biomedical research support RELATION BETWEEN ACTIVITY & BONE CALCIUM HOMEOSTASIS IN CHRONIC PEDIATRIC DIS
S07RR-05535-29 0537 (NSS) WATSON, DAVID Biomedical research support STABLE ISOTOPES MEASURE 125 (OH)2 D3 CLEARANCE IN CHRONICALLY CHOLESTATIC
S07RR-05535-29 0538 (NSS) ZIMMERMAN, ERNEST Biomedical research support MECHANISM OF COCAINE INDUCED BIRTH DEFECTS INFANT MORTALITY
S07RR-05538-29 (NSS) THURMAN, WILLIAM G OKLAHOMA MEDICAL RESEARCH FDN 825 N E 13TH STREET OKLAHOMA CITY, OKLA 73104 Biomedical research support
S07RR-05538-29 0539 (NSS) CUMMINGS, LESTER R Biomedical research support UPGRADE VAX 8250 COMPUTER SYSTEM TO AN 8350 SYSTEM
S07RR-05538-29 0540 (NSS) DUBOSE, COIT M Biomedical research support 1990 CPSS USERS MEETING; COMPUTER; SOFTWARE; FREE RADICALS;
S07RR-05538-29 0541 (NSS) HAWKINS, LAWRENCE J Biomedical research support REMOVE ETHYLENE OXIDE STERILIZER & INSTAL STEAM STERILIZER
S07RR-05538-29 0542 (NSS) HAWKINS, LAWRENCE J Biomedical research support BIOL SAFETY CABINETS & FUME HOODS; AEROSOL GENERATOR; THERMOANEMETER; RADIOMETER
S07RR-05538-29 0543 (NSS) KING, M MARGARET Biomedical research support WILD MAMMALIAN MONITORING TO ASSESS ENVIRONMENT CONTAMINATION; POPULATION
S07RR-05538-29 0544 (NSS) SCHNEIDER, DANIEL J Biomedical research support HYDRATION IN ESSENTIAL HYPERTENSION URINE
S07RR-05538-29 0545 (NSS) WEBB, CAROL F Biomedical research support REGULATORY PROTEINS IN IMMUNOGLOBULIN GENE TRANSCRIPTION; MOUSE; TOPOISOMERASE
S07RR-05539-29 (NSS) YOUNG, ROBERT C INSTITUTE FOR CANCER RESEARCH 7701 BURHOLME AVENUE PHILADELPHIA, PA 19111 Biomedical research support
S07RR-05539-29 0546 (NSS) SKALKA, ANNA MARIE Biomedical research support SUBCELLULAR LOCALIZ OF ROUS SARCOMA VIRUS INTEGRATION PROTEIN; EUKARYOTIC CELL
S07RR-05539-29 0547 (NSS) MASON, WILLIAM Biomedical research support ANTI VIRAL THERAPY OF CHRONIC HEPADNAVIRUS INFECTIONS; DUCKS
S07RR-05539-29 0548 (NSS) BOSMA, MELVIN J Biomedical research support LYMPHOCYTE DIFFERENTIATION & IMMUNODEFICIENCY; MICE
S07RR-05539-29 0549 (NSS) GLUSKER, JENNY P Biomedical research support ENZYME STRUCTURE & FUNCTION: D XYLOSE ISOMERASE
S07RR-05539-29 0550 (NSS) TAYLOR, JOHN M Biomedical research support ANIMAL VIRUS REPLICATION; SPONGE
S07RR-05540-29 (NSS) KOPROWSKI, HILARY THE WISTAR INSTITUTE 36TH AND SPRUCE STREETS PHILADELPHIA, PA 19104 Biomedical research support
S07RR-05540-29 0551 (NSS) CURTIS, PETER Biomedical research support MOLECULAR TECHNIQUES IN HUMAN CANCER IMMUNOTHERAPY
S07RR-05540-29 0552 (NSS) OTVOS, LASZLO Biomedical research support SYNTHESIS & CONFORMATION OF GLYCOPEPTIDES
S07RR-05540-29 0553 (NSS) REDDY, PREMKUMAR Biomedical research support MOLECULAR MECHANISMS ACTIVATING MYELOID B ONCOGENE
S07RR-05540-29 0555 (NSS) WEINMANN, ROBERTO Biomedical research support ONCOGENE EIA INDUCED TRANSACTIVATION
S07RR-05540-29 0554 (NSS) STAMATO, THOMAS Biomedical research support DELAYED MUTATION & SECTORING IN MAMMALIAN CELLS
S07RR-05540-29 0556 (NSS) TSUJIMOTO, YOSHIHIDE Biomedical research support FUNCTIONS OF BCL 2 PROTEIN
S07RR-05540-29 0557 (NSS) SHOWE, LOUISE C Biomedical research support REGULATION OF BAND 3 GENE IN ERYTHROLEUKEMIC CELL LINES
S07RR-05540-29 0558 (NSS) NISHIKURA, KAZUKO Biomedical research support ROLES OF C ONCOGENES IN CELL GROWTH & DIFFERENTIATION
S07RR-05540-29 0559 (NSS) SOLTER, DAVOR Biomedical research support CELLULAR INTERACTIONS IN MAMMALIAN DEVELOPMENT
S07RR-05540-29 0560 (NSS) ROVERA, GIOVANNI Biomedical research support DETECTION OF MINIMAL RESIDUAL DISEASE IN CHILDHOOD LEUKEMIA
S07RR-05545-29 (NSS) PAIGEN, KENNETH JACKSON LABORATORY 600 MAIN STREET BAR HARBOR, ME 04609-0800 Biomedical research support
S07RR-05545-29 0566 (NSS) STONE, JAMES Biomedical research support IDENTIFICATION OF P21H RAS TARGET BY PEPTIDE CROSSLINKING
S07RR-05545-29 0567 (NSS) SHULTZ, LEONARD Biomedical research support SEMINAR 1990 91
S07RR-05545-29 0568 (NSS) SHULTZ, LEONARD Biomedical research support SEMINAR 1990 91
S07RR-05545-29 0569 (NSS) BARKER, JANE Biomedical research support SPLENIC & IMMUNE COMPONENTS OF SCAT MUTATION
S07RR-05545-29 0570 (NSS) EPPIG, JANAN Biomedical research support CONVERSION OF RESEARCH COMPUTER PROGRAMS PHASE II
S07RR-05545-29 0571 (NSS) SUNDBERG, JOHN Biomedical research support GENETIC MODEL OF HYPERKERATOTIC INFLAMMATORY SKIN DISEASE
S07RR-05545-29 0572 (NSS) WATSON, GORDON Biomedical research support HORMONAL REGULATION OF 8 GLUCURONIDASE GENE EXPRESSION
S07RR-05545-29 0573 (NSS) SIDMAN, CHARLES Biomedical research support EQUITY & FRINGE BENEFIT ADJUSTMENT
S07RR-05545-29 0574 (NSS) EVANS, ROBERT Biomedical research support PROGRAM SUPPLEMENT & PAY EQUITY ADJUSTMENT
S07RR-05545-29 0575 (NSS) BEAMER, WESLEY Biomedical research support INTERIM SUPPORT ANDROGEN INDUCTION OF OVARIAN GRANULOSA CELL TUMORS
S07RR-05545-29 0576 (NSS) BIRKENMEIER, EDWARD Biomedical research support GENOME PROJECT: WHOLE MOUSE DNA ISOLATION
S07RR-05545-29 0577 (NSS) SIDMAN, CHARLES Biomedical research support PAY EQUITY & FRINGE BENEFIT ADJUSTMENTS
S07RR-05546-26 (NSS) HANLON, THOMAS E FRIENDS MEDICAL SCIS RES 22 BLOOMSBURY AVENUE BALTIMORE, MD 21228 Biomedical research support grant
S07RR-05546-26 0578 (NSS) SIMMONS, JAMES Biomedical research support grant NEUROBEHAVIORAL VS PSYCHO THERAPEUTIC TREATMENT
S07RR-05547-23 (NSS) HALVORSON, HARLYN O MARINE BIOLOGICAL LABORATORY WATER STREET WOODS HOLE, MA 02543 Biomedical research support
S07RR-05547-23 0072 (NSS) WHITTAKER, J RICHARD Biomedical research support DEVELOPMENT OF NUCLEIC ACID PROBES FOR ANALYSIS OF GENE EXPRESSION
S07RR-05547-23 0073 (NSS) CHIKARMANE, HEMANT Biomedical research support EVOLUTIONARY DIVERGENCE OF NEREIS GENOME
S07RR-05547-23 0074 (NSS) GLICK, DAVID Biomedical research support CREATION OF CDNA LIBRARY
S07RR-05547-23 0075 (NSS) HAROSI, FERENC Biomedical research support DEVELOPMENT OF A NEW MICROSPECTROPHOTOMETER
S07RR-05547-23 0076 (NSS) WHITTAKER, J RICHARD Biomedical research support CYTOPLASMIC FACTORS IN DEVELOPMENT
S07RR-05547-23 0077 (NSS) MEEDEL, THOMAS H Biomedical research support CLONING ACETYLCHOLINESTERASE GENE
S07RR-05547-23 0078 (NSS) SZUTS, ETE Biomedical research support BIOCHEMISTRY OF RETINOIDS IN AQUEOUS MEDIA
S07RR-05547-23 0079 (NSS) STRUMWASSER, FELIX Biomedical research support PRIMARY AMINO ACID SEQUENCE OF A NEW SECOND MESSENGER
S07RR-05547-23 0080 (NSS) KUZIRIAN, ALAN Biomedical research support NEUROBIOLOGY OF DEVELOPING MOLLUSC
S07RR-05547-23 0081 (NSS) SZUTS, ETE Biomedical research support BIOCHEMISTRY OF SIGNAL TRANSDUCTION IN LOBSTER CHEMORECEPTORS
S07RR-05548-26 (NSS) MC HUGH, WILLIAM D EASTMAN DENTAL CENTER 625 ELMWOOD AVENUE ROCHESTER, N Y 14620 Biomedical research support
S07RR-05548-26 0579 (NSS) ZERO, DOMENICK T Biomedical research support EFFECT OF DIFFERENT PH ON VIABILITY STREPTOCOCCUS MUTANS
S07RR-05548-26 0580 (NSS) TALLENTS, ROSS H Biomedical research support BIOLOGY OF TMJ
S07RR-05548-26 0581 (NSS) FEATHERSTONE, JOHN D Biomedical research support EXTRACTION OF DNA FROM HUMAN MUTANS STREPTOCOCCI ISOLATES
S07RR-05548-26 0582 (NSS) FEATHERSTONE, JOHN D Biomedical research support MOLECULAR BIOLOGY
S07RR-05551-29 (NSS) SWANSON, WILLIAM H LA COUNTY HARBOR-RES ED INST 1124 W CARSON STREET TORRANCE, CA 90509 Biomedical research support
S07RR-05551-29 0944 (NSS) PUENTES, STEPHEN Biomedical research support PURIFICATION OF HUMAN COMPLEMENT COMPONENTS
S07RR-05551-29 0945 (NSS) TAYEK, JOHN Biomedical research support METABOLIC PROCESSES BEHIND CANCER CACHEXIA
S07RR-05551-29 0946 (NSS) RUBIN, ROBERT Biomedical research support 123I IODOPERIDOL AS A DOPAMINE RECEPTOR LIGAND FOR SPECT ANIMAL STUDIES
S07RR-05551-29 0947 (NSS) IPP, ELI Biomedical research support PULSATILE INSULIN SECRETION IN ISOLATED RATS ISLETS OF LANGERHANS
S07RR-05551-29 0948 (NSS) LEE, W PAUL Biomedical research support STABLE ISOTOPE STUDIES OF FUEL TRANSPORT IN INFANTS
S07RR-05551-29 0949 (NSS) MORIN, ROBERT J Biomedical research support REGULATION OF ARTERIAL CHOLESTEROL ESTERIFICATION
S07RR-05551-29 0950 (NSS) REDDY, S NARASIMHA Biomedical research support CORRELATION OF HUMAN COLONIC MOTILITY W/ TRANSIT IN HEALTH DISEASE
S07RR-05551-29 0951 (NSS) RAUM, WILLIAM J Biomedical research support COCAINE & SEXUAL DIFFERENTIATION OF THE BRAIN
S07RR-05551-29 0952 (NSS) HILLYARD, ROBERT Biomedical research support RED & WHITE BLOOD CELLS IN HYPOFUSION REPERFUSION & ENDOTOXIN INDUCE
S07RR-05551-29 0953 (NSS) BHASIN, SHALENDER Biomedical research support DVMT REGULATION OF INHIBIN SUBUNIT MRNA SIZE HETEROGENEITY DURING SEXUAL
S07RR-05551-29 0954 (NSS) MCBRIDE, DUNCAN Biomedical research support ELECTROMAGNETIC FIELD FOCUSING INSTRUMENT IN NEUROSURGERY
S07RR-05551-29 0955 (NSS) RAJAVASHISTH, TRIPAT Biomedical research support GENETIC CONTROL OF CHOLESTEROL HOMEOSTATSIS
S07RR-05551-29 0956 (NSS) KELLER, MARGARET Biomedical research support MODULATION OF IMMUNE RESPONSE BY IMMUNIZATION OF MOTHER
S07RR-05551-29 0957 (NSS) YANG, HENRY Biomedical research support DOXORUBICIN INHIBITION OF C FOS INDUCTION IN CARDIOMYOPATHY
S07RR-05551-29 0958 (NSS) WAN, YU-JUI YVONNE Biomedical research support EXPRESSION OF RETINOIC ACID RECEPTOR MRNAS DURING RAT EMBRYONGENESIS
S07RR-05551-29 0959 (NSS) COOPER, DAN Biomedical research support EXERCISE MODULATION OF GHIGF 1 INTERACTION
S07RR-05551-29 0960 (NSS) RAJ, J USHA Biomedical research support ENDOTHELIN: REGULATION OF PULMONARY MICROCIRCULATION
S07RR-05551-29 0961 (NSS) SUH, BO Biomedical research support ABERRATION OF GROWTH HORMONE SECRETION IN HYPERPROLACTINEMIA
S07RR-05551-29 0962 (NSS) MOHAN, OLGA Biomedical research support MIDAZOLAM & OXYGEN CONSUMPTION & ITS DYNAMICS
S07RR-05551-29 0963 (NSS) FRENCH, WILLIAM Biomedical research support NEW TECHNIQUE FOR IMAGING & REPAIR OF ARTERIAL DISSECTIONS
S07RR-05551-29 0964 (NSS) BEN-DOV, ISSAHAR Biomedical research support HEART LUNG INTERACTION DURING PERIODIC BREATHING IN HEART FAILURE IN EXERCISE
S07RR-05551-29 0965 (NSS) MENDOZA, RICARDO Biomedical research support FACTORS INFLUENCING ANGLO & MEXICAN AMERICAN PARENTS PARTICIPATION IN AMI
S07RR-05551-29 0966 (NSS) BRETAN, PETER Biomedical research support RENAL TRANSPLANT PRESERVATION USING MODIFIED INTRACELLULAR COLD FLUSH SOLUTION
S07RR-05551-29 0967 (NSS) YUAN, FQU-XIAO Biomedical research support STOMACH & COLON SMOOTH MUSCLE CELL CULTURE IN NEWBORN RABBIT
S07RR-05551-29 0968 (NSS) KHALKHALI, IRAJ Biomedical research support KINETICS & METABOLISM OF 99M DESFEROXAMINE
S07RR-05551-29 0969 (NSS) BRASEL, JO ANNE Biomedical research support KREBS CYCLE METABOLISM IN CANCER
S07RR-05564-13 (NSS) JOHNSON, MICHAEL E UNIV OF ILL AT CHICAGO 833 S WOOD ST RM 126 CHICAGO, ILL 60680 Biomedical research support
S07RR-05564-13 0914 (NSS) PEZZUTO, JOHN M Biomedical research support HPLC PHOTO DIODE ARRAY DETECTOR FOR NATURAL PRODUCT SEPARATION
S07RR-05564-13 0915 (NSS) SCHLEMMER, R FRANCIS Biomedical research support PARTIAL ASSISTANCE IN ESTABLISHING A PRIMATE BEHAVIORAL LABORATORY
S07RR-05564-13 0916 (NSS) JOHNSON, MICHAEL E Biomedical research

support TAPE DRIVE REPAIR FOR COLL OF PHARMACY BIOMOLECULAR ANALYSIS FACILITY COMPUTER
S07RR-05566-28 (NSS) ABEL, CARLOS MEDICAL RESEARCH INSTITUTE 2200 WEBSTER STREET SAN FRANCISCO, CALIF 94115 Biomedical research support
S07RR-05566-28 0583 (NSS) COX, KENNETH Biomedical research support INTRAVITAL MICROSCOPIC ANALYSIS OF NAILFOLD CIRCULATION IN DIABETICS
S07RR-05566-28 0584 (NSS) HILL, J DONALD Biomedical research support RIGHT HEART INTERACTION W/ LEFT VENTRICULAR ASSISTANCE
S07RR-05566-28 0585 (NSS) YOUNG, LOWELL S Biomedical research support ALCOHOL & MYCOBACTERIAL INFECTION IN AN AIDS MODEL
S07RR-05569-27 (NSS) LEVIN, ROBERT M BOSTON CITY HOSPITAL 818 HARRISON AVENUE BOSTON, MASS 02118 Biomedical research support
S07RR-05569-27 0107 (NSS) AFDAHL, NEZAM H Biomedical research support MOLECULAR BIOLOGICAL APPROACH TO GALLBLADDER MUCIN STRUCTURE
S07RR-05569-27 0108 (NSS) LIEBMAN, HOWARD Biomedical research support DETERMINANTS OF LENGTH OF STAY FOR AIDS/ARC PATIENTS
S07RR-05569-27 0109 (NSS) MARCUS, SAMUEL N Biomedical research support EICOSANOID & PLATELET-ACTIVAT FACTOR IN CARRAGEENAN-INDUCED COLITIS PATHOGENESIS
S07RR-05569-27 0110 (NSS) STEINBERG, JUDITH L Biomedical research support KNOWLEDGE DEFICITS & BEHAVIORAL RISKS FOR HIV TRANSMISSION IN STD CLINIC PTS
S07RR-05569-27 0111 (NSS) SULIS, CAROL ANN Biomedical research support B LYMPHOCYTE DIFFERENTIATION: INDUCTION BY LIPOPOLYSACCHARIDE
S07RR-05569-27 0112 (NSS) CIMINO, WILLIAM G Biomedical research support COMPUTER-AIDED EVALUATION OF MUSCULAR DEFICITS IN LOW BACK PAIN
S07RR-05569-27 0113 (NSS) MEYERS, ALAN Biomedical research support PUBLIC HOUSING & PEDIATRIC UNDERNUTRITION: PILOT STUDY
S07RR-05569-27 0114 (NSS) MONTECALVO, MARISA Biomedical research support HOST DEFENSE, COURSE, OUTCOME OF HIV+ & - IV DRUG USERS W/ STAPHYLOCOCCUS AUREUS
S07RR-05569-27 0115 (NSS) VINCI, ROBERT Biomedical research support UNSUSPECTED COCAINE EXPOSURE IN A PRE-SCHOOL POPULATION
S07RR-05569-27 0116 (NSS) WITZBURG, ROBERT A Biomedical research support PRELIMINARY EVALUATION OF HOUSE OFFICER SELECTION & PREDICTION OF SUCCESS
S07RR-05569-27 0117 (NSS) MARCUS, SAMUEL N Biomedical research support REACTIVE OXYGEN METABOLITES IN PATHOGENESIS OF CARRAGEENAN INDUCED COLITIS
S07RR-05569-27 0118 (NSS) AFDHAL, NEZAM W Biomedical research support CHOLESTEROL CRYSTAL GROWTH AND GALLSTONE FORMATION
S07RR-05569-27 0119 (NSS) BARBER, THOMAS W Biomedical research support PROSPECTIVE EVALUATION OF MYCOBACTERIAL INFECTION IN PATIENTS WITH AIDS
S07RR-05569-27 0120 (NSS) GOLDSTEIN, RICHARD Biomedical research support HORIZONTAL TRANSFER OF BACTERIAL VIRULENCE FACTOR GENES
S07RR-05569-27 0121 (NSS) GOLENBOCK, DOUGLAS T Biomedical research support LIPID-A/LEUKOCYTE INTERACTIONS
S07RR-05569-27 0122 (NSS) GOURDIN, THEODORE Biomedical research support GALLBLADDER MUCIN IN VESICLE AGGREGATION/FUSION
S07RR-05569-27 0123 (NSS) MCQUILLEN, DANIEL P Biomedical research support CHIMERIC ANTI-IDIOTYPE ANTIBODY VACCINE AGAINST LOS OF N GONORRHOEAE
S07RR-05569-27 0124 (NSS) MIROCHNICK, MARK Biomedical research support CATECHOLAMINE PHYSIOLOGY & INFANT BEHAVIOR IN COCAINE-EXPOSED INFANTS
S07RR-05569-27 0125 (NSS) STEINBACH, SUZANNE F Biomedical research support PSEUDOMONAS AERUGINOSA PILLIN GENE PROBES: TOOL IN MOLEC EPIDEMIOL
S07RR-05569-27 0126 (NSS) ZHANG, YOU-XUN Biomedical research support SUBSPECIE SPECIFIC ANTIGEN BINDING SITE MAB AGAINST CHLAMYDIA TRACHOMATIS; SEQ
S07RR-05570-20 (NSS) RULIN, MARVIN C MAGEE WOMEN'S HOSPITAL FORBES AVE AND HALKET ST PITTSBURGH, PA 15213 Biomedical reserach support
S07RR-05570-20 0846 (NSS) CAMERON, WILLIAM E Biomedical reserach support GENIOGLOSSAL MOTONEURONS
S07RR-05570-20 0847 (NSS) GUZICK, DAVID S Biomedical reserach support INFERTILITY EVALUATION IN FERTILE WOMEN: ASSESSING RISK FACTORS FOR INFERTILITY
S07RR-05570-20 0848 (NSS) SHAKIR, AMAL KANBOUR Biomedical reserach support HUMAN LEUKOCYTE ANTIGEN SHARING AS PREDICTOR OF IVF OUTCOME
S07RR-05571-27 (NSS) PAUL, ARA G UNIVERSITY OF MICHIGAN COLLEGE OF PHARMACY ANN ARBOR, MICH 48109-1065 Biomedical research support
S07RR-05571-27 0333 (NSS) SANDOW, BRUCE A Biomedical research support DEVELOPMENT OF GRANULOSA CELL OOCYTE COCULTURE SYSTEM
S07RR-05571-27 0917 (NSS) PAUL, ARA G Biomedical research support NO SUBPROJECTS
S07RR-05573-13 (NSS) SIMPKINS, JAMES W UNIVERSITY OF FLORIDA BOX J 487, JHMHC GAINESVILLE, FL 32610 Biomedical research support
S07RR-05573-13 0082 (NSS) BRUSHWOOD, DAVID B Biomedical research support DATABASE: PHARMACY LIABILITY CASES FROM COLONIAL TIMES TO PRESENT: ADVERSE DRUG
S07RR-05573-13 0083 (NSS) RANELLI, PAUL L Biomedical research support EVALUATING COMMUNICATION BEHAVIOR OF PHARMACISTS & COMMUNITY BASED ELDERLY
S07RR-05573-13 0084 (NSS) LIPOWSKI, EARLENE E Biomedical research support LINKING AUTOMATED DATABASES FOR LONGITUDINAL MEDICAL OUTCOMES STUDIES
S07RR-05573-13 0085 (NSS) SCHREIER, HANS Biomedical research support TARGETED DRUG DELIVERY SYSTEMS CELL CULTURE STUDIES: LIPOSOMES CD4+
S07RR-05573-13 0086 (NSS) HOCHHAUS, GUENTHER Biomedical research support: mu opioid receptor on single cells
S07RR-05573-13 0087 (NSS) DELAFUENTE, JEFFREY Biomedical research support IMMUNOLOGIC EFFECTS OF COCAINE & RELATED TROPANE ALKALOIDS: DRUG ABUSE
S07RR-05573-13 0088 (NSS) DAWSON, RALPH, JR Biomedical research support RENAL EPITHELIAL CELLS AS BIOLOGICAL DOPAMINE DELIVERY SYSTEM IN PARKINSONS DIS
S07RR-05573-13 0089 (NSS) YEE, GARY C Biomedical research support INFUSION ETOPOSIDE + CYCLOPHOSPHAMIDE IN BONE MARROW TRANSPLANT: CANCER
S07RR-05573-13 0090 (NSS) ENG, HOWARD Biomedical research support UNKNOWN
S07RR-05576-27 (NSS) MORRIS, N RONALD ROBERT WOOD JOHNSON MED SCH 675 HOES LANE PISCATAWAY, N J 08854-5635 Biomedical research support
S07RR-05576-27 0603 (NSS) TARAGIN, MARK Biomedical research support PHYSICIAN & PATIENT FACTORS ASSOCIATED W/ MEDICAL MALPRACTICE
S07RR-05576-27 0604 (NSS) STEVENS, RANDALL M Biomedical research support INTERACTION OF GLUCOCORTICOID RECEPTOR W/ STROMELYSIN PROMOTOR
S07RR-05576-27 0605 (NSS) THOMAS, T J Biomedical research support CONFORMATIONAL DYNAMICS OF DNA IN PRESENCE OF AN ANTITUMOR ANTIBIOTIC
S07RR-05576-27 0606 (NSS) SONNENBERG, FRANK A Biomedical research support DISCRETE FEATURE ANALYSIS OF CHEST RADIOGRAPHS IN AIDS RELATED PULMONARY DIS
S07RR-05576-27 0607 (NSS) MASCARENHAS, MARIA R Biomedical research support INTERACTIONS BETWEEN GASTROESOPHAGEAL REFLUX & SLEEP
S07RR-05576-27 0608 (NSS) WAPNIR, J Biomedical research support DNA CONTENT & ONCOPROTEIN EXPRESSION IN REGIONALLY METASTATIC BREAST CANCER
S07RR-05576-27 0609 (NSS) GOODMAN, R J Biomedical research support CHRONIC INTRACEREBRAL DRUG THEREAPY FOR DOPAMINE DEFICIENCY
S07RR-05576-27 0610 (NSS) DUNN, MICHAEL Biomedical research support BIOLOGICAL FIXATION OF TENDON & LIGAMENT PROSTHESES
S07RR-05576-27 0611 (NSS) TING, WINDSOR Biomedical research support EFFECTS OF DIABETES ON LEFT VENTRICULAR FUNCTION AFTER HYPOTHERMIC ARREST
S07RR-05576-27 0612 (NSS) WARD, STEVEN W Biomedical research support CLONING & SEQ OF DNA SPECIFICALLY ASSOCIATED W/ A NOVEL NUCLEAR STRUCTURE SPERM
S07RR-05576-27 0613 (NSS) LOBEL, PETER Biomedical research support MUTANTS INTRACELL TRAFFICKING OF CATION INDEPENDENT MANNOSE 6 PHOSPHATE& INSULIN
S07RR-05576-27 0614 (NSS) PAN, SUEIHUA Biomedical research support MECHANISM OF IMMUNE CONTROL AGAINST PNEUMOCYSTIC INFECTION
S07RR-05576-27 0586 (NSS) MORRIS, N RONALD Biomedical research support RESERVE TO SUPPLEMENT SALARY OF VIVARIUM DIRECTOR
S07RR-05576-27 0587 (NSS) PENG, ISAAC Biomedical research support DYNAMICS OF ACTIN FILAMENTS OF MYOFIBRIL
S07RR-05576-27 0588 (NSS) DICICCO-BLOOM, EMANU Biomedical research support MECHANISMS OF GOVERNING PROLIFERATION OF BRAIN PRECURSORS
S07RR-05576-27 0589 (NSS) HESS, ARTHUR Biomedical research support PATHOPHYSIOLOGY OF DOPAMINERGIC NEUROTOXICITY INDUCED BY MPTP & METHAMPHETAMINE
S07RR-05576-27 0590 (NSS) REINBERG, DANNY Biomedical research support SEARCHING FOR BIOCHEMICAL APPROACH FOR TRANSPOSITION USING P ELEMENTS
S07RR-05576-27 0591 (NSS) POWERS, SCOTT Biomedical research support ANALYSIS OF ROLE OF RAS IN MEIOSIS
S07RR-05576-27 0592 (NSS) ROTH, MONICA Biomedical research support INTEGRATION OF HUMAN IMMUNODEFICIENCY VIRUS
S07RR-05576-27 0593 (NSS) VALES, LYNNE Biomedical research support ACTIVATION OF GENE EXPRESSION BY ADENOVIRUSEIB PROTEIN
S07RR-05576-27 0594 (NSS) DOUGHERTY, JOSEPH Biomedical research support RETROVIRUS MUTATION RATES
S07RR-05576-27 0595 (NSS) O'REAR, JULIAN Biomedical research support CHARACTER NE OVERLAPPING RECOMBINANT HUMAN CHROMOSOME 6 CLONES IN YEAST VECTOR
S07RR-05576-27 0596 (NSS) O'REAR, JULIAN Biomedical research support DEVELOPMENT OF QUANTITATIVE ASSAY FOR HIV 1 REPLICATION
S07RR-05576-27 0597 (NSS) DORNBURG, RALPH Biomedical research support RETROVIRAL VECTOR SYSTEM TO STUDY HIV INFECTION
S07RR-05576-27 0598 (NSS) LACY, CLIFTON R Biomedical research support HOSTILITY & MENTAL STRESS ON CALIBER OF STENOSED & NON CORONARY ARTERIES
S07RR-05576-27 0599 (NSS) SPERBER, STEVEN Biomedical research support SUSCEPTABILITY OF RESPIRATORY VIRUSES TO NOVEL RECOMBINANT INTERFERONS
S07RR-05576-27 0600 (NSS) RUBIN, ALLEN J Biomedical research support FRONTAL VISUO MOTOR DEFECTS & CENTER VISUAL DYSFUNCT IN HEAD TRAUMA & ALZHEIMERS
S07RR-05576-27 0601 (NSS) DASQUPTA, ARUNANSU Biomedical research support DEVELOPMENT OF ULCERATIVE COLITIS SPECIFIC ANTI IDIOTYPE ANTI BODY
S07RR-05576-27 0602 (NSS) SIGAL, LEONARD H Biomedical research support CROSS REACTIVITY BETWEEN B BURGDORFERI FLAGELLIN & HUMAN AXONAL PROTEIN P64
S07RR-05576-27 0615 (NSS) WINKELMANN, DONALD Biomedical research support MOLECULAR ANALYSIS OF MYOSIN ASSEMBLY
S07RR-05576-27 0616 (NSS) AMENTA, PETER Biomedical research support MODULATION OF HEPATIC REGENERATION BY LAMININ
S07RR-05576-27 0617 (NSS) SONSALLA, PATRICIA K Biomedical research support EFFECTS OF DOPAMINERGIC NEUROTOXINS IN AGING
S07RR-05576-27 0618 (NSS) WEISEL, CLIFFORD Biomedical research support EVALUATION OF EXPOSURE TO CHLORINATION BY PRODUCTS W/ IN MUNICIPAL WATER SYSTEM
S07RR-05576-27 0619 (NSS) THOMAS, THRESIA Biomedical research support DNA CONFORMATIONAL DYNAMICS IN GENE REGULATION BY STERIOD HORMONES
S07RR-05583-27 (NSS) NAPOLITANO, LEONARD M UNIVERSITY OF NEW MEXICO SCHOOL OF MED, NORTH CAMPUS ALBUQUERQUE, N MEX 87131 Biomedical research support
S07RR-05583-27 0634 (NSS) MONEIM, MOHEB Biomedical research support KINEMATICS STUDY WRIST PROXIMAL ROW CARPECTOMY
S07RR-05583-27 0635 (NSS) NACHBAR, JAMES M Biomedical research support 3 D IMAGING ANALYSIS CAPATOILITIES BIOSTRUCTURAL IMAGING TECHNOLOGIES
S07RR-05583-27 0636 (NSS) PLATT, MARK W Biomedical research support BIOSYNTHESIS CAPSULAR POLYSACCHARIDES STREPTOCOCCUS SP
S07RR-05583-27 0620 (NSS) AGAWAL, VIJAY Biomedical research support FATTY ACID CONCENTRATION FECES IN PATIENTS RECEIVING IV OR PO ANTIBIOTICS

S07RR-05583-27 0621 (NSS) BAKER, THOMAS Biomedical research support ANALYSIS DNA REPAIR NEUROSPORA

S07RR-05583-27 0622 (NSS) CROWELL, RICHARD Biomedical research support LUNG MACROPHAGE PHAGOCYTIC DYSFUNCTION DURING HYPEROXIA

S07RR-05583-27 0623 (NSS) CROWLEY, MARK Biomedical research support NEONATAL PULMONARY HYPERTENSION ROLL PROTEIN KINASE C

S07RR-05583-27 0637 (NSS) QUENZER, ROANDL W Biomedical research support EVALUATION 3 TECHNIQUES DIAGNOSE DISSEMINATED CANDIDIASIS IMMUNOCOMPROMISED HOST

S07RR-05583-27 0638 (NSS) REYES, PHILLIP Biomedical research support HUMAN MALARIA DRUG DEVELOPMENT ENZYME INHIBITION

S07RR-05583-27 0639 (NSS) SCHUYLER, MARK Biomedical research support MURINE HYPESENSITIVITY PNEUMONITIS

S07RR-05583-27 0640 (NSS) SCOTT, WALTER J Biomedical research support SUBSTRATE CONTROL ENDOTHELIAL CELL FUNCTION

S07RR-05583-27 0641 (NSS) SMITH, SUZANNE MELEG Biomedical research support ANTIGENS MESANGIOPATHIC GLOMERULONEPHRITIS

S07RR-05583-27 0642 (NSS) STUMP, ROBERT Biomedical research support MEASUREMENT PH IONS SINGLE CELLS

S07RR-05583-27 0643 (NSS) VANDER JAGT, DAVID Biomedical research support POLYOL PATHWAY DIABETIC COMPLICATIONS

S07RR-05583-27 0644 (NSS) WHEELER, COZETTE M Biomedical research support PAPILLOMAVIRUS HOST INTERACTIONSRECEPTOR ATTACHMENT SITES

S07RR-05583-27 0645 (NSS) WILLMAN, CHERYL L Biomedical research support MYELOID LINEAGE TYROSINE KINASES NORMAL NECOPLASTIC HEMATOPOIETIC CELLS

S07RR-05583-27 0646 (NSS) WOODFIN, BEULAH M Biomedical research support INFLUENZA PROTEIN TRANSIT PEPTIDE LIKE SEQUENCE

S07RR-05583-27 0624 (NSS) DAY, PHILLIP Biomedical research support VAPORIZER ISOFLURANE

S07RR-05583-27 0625 (NSS) DECOSTER, THOMAS A Biomedical research support PARAMETERS IMPORTANT BONE SCREW DESIGN ORTHOPEDICS

S07RR-05583-27 0626 (NSS) DORIN, RICHARD I Biomedical research support NMRS IMAGING PITUTIARY CORTICOTROPIN HORMONE RECEPTOR USING PARAMAGENTIC LABEL

S07RR-05583-27 0627 (NSS) DUCLOS, TERRY W Biomedical research support ANALYSIS CRP BINDING SITE NUCLEAR ANTIGENS

S07RR-05583-27 0628 (NSS) FOLLIS, FABRIZIO Biomedical research support AORTIC CROSS CLAMPING SPINAL CORD BLOOD FLOW NEURONAL FUNCTION

S07RR-05583-27 0629 (NSS) FRIEDMAN, KENNETH D Biomedical research support GENETIC DYSFUNCT PROTEIN C & S MOLECULES PATIENTS HEREDITARY THROMBOTIC TENDENCY

S07RR-05583-27 0630 (NSS) GRIFFITH, JEFFREY K Biomedical research support POTENTIATING ANTIBIOTIC ACTIVITY ANTIBIOTIC RESISTANT PATHOGENS

S07RR-05583-27 0631 (NSS) KESTERSON, LEE Biomedical research support EFFECTS ISCHEMIA ELECTROPHYSIOLOGIC RESPONSE RAT BRAIN

S07RR-05583-27 0632 (NSS) KOSTER, FREDERICK T Biomedical research support CHARACTERIZATION ANTIMICROBIAL FACTORS SECRETED NATURAL KILLER CELLS

S07RR-05583-27 0633 (NSS) MANDLER, RAUL L Biomedical research support FLOW CYTOMETRIC STUDIES MEMBRANE EXCITABILITY SPINAL CORD CELL WOBBLER MOUSE

S07RR-05584-27 (NSS) SIMONE, JOSEPH V ST JUDE CHILDRENS RES HOSP 332 N LAUDERDALE, PO BOX 318 MEMPHIS, TENN 38101 Biomedical research support

S07RR-05584-27 0647 (NSS) BRENNER, MALCOLM Biomedical research support GENE TRANSFER TO DETECT MINIMAL RESIDUAL ACTURE MYELOBLASTIC LEUKEMIA

S07RR-05584-27 0648 (NSS) CUTTER, GARY Biomedical research support ANALYSIS OF PILOT EPIDEMIOLOGIC DATABASE

S07RR-05584-27 0649 (NSS) REYNOLDS, ALBERT Biomedical research support SUBSTRATES OF P60SRC PROTEIN TYROSINE KINASE

S07RR-05585-19 (NSS) REICHARD, GEORGE A, JR LANKENAU MEDICAL RESEARCH CNTR 100 LANCASTER AVE W CITY LINE WYNNEWOOD, PA 19096 Biomedical research support grant

S07RR-05586-24 (NSS) RUTLEDGE, CHARLES O PURDUE UNIVERSITY SCH OF PHARM & PHARM SCI WEST LAFAYETTE, IND 47907 Biomedical research support

S07RR-05586-24 0121 (NSS) LOUDON, G MARC Biomedical research support SPECIFIC CLEAVAGE OF PROTEINS

S07RR-05586-24 0122 (NSS) NAIL, STEVEN L Biomedical research support PHYSICAL CHEMISTRY OF FREEZE DRYING

S07RR-05586-24 0123 (NSS) MARCUS, CRAIG B Biomedical research support TURNOVER OF CYTOCHROME P 450 ISOZYMES

S07RR-05586-24 0108 (NSS) HEINSTEIN, PETER Biomedical research support ELICITOR RECEPTOR ISOLATION FROM PLANT CELLS

S07RR-05586-24 0109 (NSS) POST, CAROL B Biomedical research support NMR STRUCTURE DETERMINATION OF PROTEIN LIGAND COMPLEXES

S07RR-05586-24 0110 (NSS) BYRN, STEPHEN R Biomedical research support NMR & MASS SPECTROMETER FOR MEDICINAL CHEMISTRY RESEARCH

S07RR-05586-24 0111 (NSS) PARK, KINAM Biomedical research support GRAFTING OF WATER SOLUBLE POLYMERS TO PROTEIN DRUG DELIVERY SYSTEMS

S07RR-05586-24 0112 (NSS) YIM, GEORGE K Biomedical research support EXCITOTOXINS & CASSAVA INDUCED NEUROTOXICITY

S07RR-05586-24 0113 (NSS) YIM, GEORGE K Biomedical research support SPECTROFLUOROMETER FOR PHARMACOLOGY RESEARCH

S07RR-05586-24 0114 (NSS) ZABIK, JOSEPH E Biomedical research support APPLICATION OF MICRODIALYSIS TO STUDY ETHANOL INGESTION

S07RR-05586-24 0115 (NSS) PIDGEON, CHARLES Biomedical research support IMMOBILIZED ARTIFICIAL MEMBRANES

S07RR-05586-24 0116 (NSS) ISOM, GARY E Biomedical research support INTRANEURONAL PEROXIDE GENERATION & GLUTAMATE EXCITOTOXICITY

S07RR-05586-24 0117 (NSS) MCLAUGHLIN, JERRY L Biomedical research support PLANT GRINDING EQUIPMENT FOR NATURAL PRODUCTS RESEARCH

S07RR-05586-24 0118 (NSS) FLETCHER, H PATRICK Biomedical research support NEUROMODULATORY EFFECTS OF ARTIAL NATRIURETIC PEPTIDE ON PC12 CELLS

S07RR-05586-24 0119 (NSS) MORRE, D JAMES Biomedical research support PLASMA MEMBRANE REDOX ENZYMES AS ANTINEOPLASTIC DRUG TARGETS

S07RR-05586-24 0120 (NSS) CARLSON, GARY P Biomedical research support GASTROINTESTINAL TRACT IN ELIMINATION OF HALOGENATED SOLVENTS

S07RR-05587-20 (NSS) PALEK, JIRI ST ELIZABETH'S HOSPITAL 736 CAMBRIDGE STREET BOSTON, MASS 02135 Biomedical research support

S07RR-05587-20 0650 (NSS) WEIR, LAWRENCE Biomedical research support RESTENOSIS & EXPRESSION OF NON MUSCLE MYOSIN: ATHEROSCLEROSIS, RESTENOSIS

S07RR-05587-20 0651 (NSS) MARANTO, ANTHONY Biomedical research support ENTEROCYTE INSP3 RECEPTOR: BINDING & CHANNEL PROPERTIES: SIGNAL TRANSDUCTION

S07RR-05588-25 (NSS) SUTTON, DWIGHT VIRGINIA MASON RESEARCH CENTER 1000 SENECA STREET SEATTLE, WASH 98101 Biomedical research support

S07RR-05588-25 0652 (NSS) NEPOM, GERALD T Biomedical research support MOLECULAR & GENETIC ORGANISMS AS RELATED TO AUTOIMMUNITY

S07RR-05589-24 (NSS) WINCHESTER, ROBERT J HOSPITAL FOR JOINT DISEASES 301 EAST 17TH STREET NEW YORK, N Y 10003 Biomedical research support grant

S07RR-05591-27 (NSS) KISZKISS, DAVID 185 PILGRIM RD - CRI BLDG 185 PILGRIM ROAD BOSTON, MASS 02215 Biomedical research support

S07RR-05591-27 0653 (NSS) AVRAHAM, HAVA Biomedical research support BIOCHEMICAL & BIOLOGICAL PROPERTIES OF HUMAN RHO P21 PROTEIN

S07RR-05591-27 0654 (NSS) CHERN, YIJUANG E Biomedical research support CHARACTERIZE ERYTHROPOIETIN RECEPTOR USING ANTI PEPTIDE ANTIBODIES

S07RR-05591-27 0655 (NSS) SADRZADEH, S M HOSSE Biomedical research support VARIOUS FACTORS IN PATHOGENESIS OF ALCOHOLIC LIVER DISEASE

S07RR-05591-27 0656 (NSS) SPANGLER, RUDOLPH Biomedical research support ID PATHWAY; TRANSMIT SIGNAL FROM CELL SURFACE ERYTHROPOIETIN RECEPTOR TO NUCLEUS

S07RR-05591-27 0657 (NSS) MEISENHELDER, JANICE Biomedical research support IMPROVING QUALITY OF NURSING CARE & CUTTING UNNECESSARY EXPENSES

S07RR-05591-27 0658 (NSS) TOTH, CAROL A Biomedical research support INTERFERON THERAPY PREVENTION TREAT HEPATIC METASTASES HUMAN COLORECTAL CANCER

S07RR-05591-27 0659 (NSS) WAGNER, HANS E Biomedical research support GROWTH PATTERN OF THYROID CARCINOMAS IN NUDE MICE

S07RR-05591-27 0660 (NSS) JESSUP, J MILBURN Biomedical research support ISOLATION OF GOBLET CELL DIFFERENTIATION FACTOR

S07RR-05591-27 0661 (NSS) BOWERS, JOHN L Biomedical research support NMR ASSESSMENT OF LIVER PRESERVATION SOLUTIONS

S07RR-05591-27 0662 (NSS) FILDERMAN, ANDREW E Biomedical research support C FMS & M CSF IN LUNG CANCER BIOLOGY

S07RR-05591-27 0663 (NSS) KRUSKAL, JONATHAN B Biomedical research support HEPATIC MICROVASCULAR FLOW/ CELL CHANGES; REPERFUSION PHASE OF LIVER TRANSPLANT

S07RR-05591-27 0664 (NSS) METZ, KENNETH R Biomedical research support CARBON 13 NMR INVESTIGATIONS OF TUMOR CELL ADHERENCE & MEMBRANE FLUIDITY

S07RR-05591-27 0665 (NSS) BAILEY, STEVEN C Biomedical research support ASSOCIATED SIGNAL TRANSDUCING ELEMENTS OF ERTHROPOIETIN RECEPTOR

S07RR-05591-27 0666 (NSS) FOX, EBEN S Biomedical research support ETHANOL TOXICITY ON EXPRESSION OF CYTOKINES RAT LIVER KUPFFER CELLS

S07RR-05591-27 0667 (NSS) PALOMBO, JOHN Biomedical research support ENTERAL NUTRIENT MODULATION KUPFFER CELL LIPID & FUNCT EFFECT ON IMMUNE RESPONSE

S07RR-05592-21 (NSS) WING, EDWARD J MONTEFIORE UNIV HOSP 3459 FIFTH AVENUE PITTSBURGH, PA 15213 Biomedical research support

S07RR-05592-21 0124 (NSS) RAO, R HARSHA Biomedical research support MALNUTRITION & DIABETES: INSULIN SECRETION RESISTANCE; STREPTOZOCIN

S07RR-05593-24 (NSS) BARMACK, NEAL H GOOD SAMARITAN HOSP & MED CTR 1015 N W 22ND AVENUE PORTLAND, OREG 97210 Biomedical research support

S07RR-05593-24 0125 (NSS) KAPLAN, MICHAEL W Biomedical research support OPTICAL STUDIES OF PHOTORECTOR FUNCTION

S07RR-05595-27 (NSS) ECKHART, WALTER SALK INSTITUTE POST OFFICE BOX 85800 SAN DIEGO, CALIF 92138 Biomedical research support

S07RR-05595-27 0668 (NSS) CHORY, JOANNE Biomedical research support NUCLEAR & CHLOROPLAST GENE EXPRESSION IN PHOTOSYNTHESIS

S07RR-05595-27 0669 (NSS) MELLON, PAMELA L Biomedical research support IMMORTALIZATION DIFFERENTIATED NEURONS OF HYPOTHALAMUS

S07RR-05595-27 0670 (NSS) MONTMINY, MARC R Biomedical research support CREB IN SOMATOTROPH DEVELOPMENT

S07RR-05595-27 0671 (NSS) RIVIER, CATHERINE Biomedical research support EFFECTS OF ALCOHOL ON INTERLEUKINS

S07RR-05595-27 0672 (NSS) GRAY, CHARLES M Biomedical research support OSCILLATORY NEURONAL INTERACTIONS IN CAT VISUAL CORTEX

S07RR-05595-27 0673 (NSS) SUKUMAR, SARASWATI Biomedical research support CIGARETTE SMOKE NITROSAMINES AS INDUCTOR OF BREAST TUMORS

S07RR-05596-27 (NSS) STUDDERT-KENNEDY, MICHAEL HASKINS LABORATORIES, INC 270 CROWN STREET NEW HAVEN, CT 06511-6695 Biomedical research support

S07RR-05596-27 0126 (NSS) RUBIN, PHILIP E Biomedical research support BIOCOMPUTATION CENTER

S07RR-05596-27 0127 (NSS) WILEY, EDWARD Biomedical research support RESEARCH EQUIPMENT MAINTENANCE & DEVELOPMENT CENTER

S07RR-05596-27 0128 (NSS) NYE, PATRICK W Biomedical research support GUEST INVESTIGATOR PROGRAM

S07RR-05596-27 0129 (NSS) NYE, PATRICK W Biomedical research support DIRECTED RESEARCH IN SPEECH & READING BY GRADUATE STUDENTS

S07RR-05596-27 0130 (NSS) TURVEY, MICHAEL T Biomedical research support SERIAL ORDER IN BI MANUAL MOVEMENT SEQUENCES

S07RR-05596-27 0131 (NSS) REPP, BRUNO H Biomedical research support LECTURES ON SPEECH & READING BY INVITED GUESTS

S07RR-05596-27 0132 (NSS) REPP, BRUNO H Biomedical research support EXPRESSIVE MICROSTRUCTURE OF MUSIC

S07RR-05596-27 0133 (NSS) BRADY, SUSAN Biomedical research support PHONOLOGICAL PRECURSORS TO READING ACQUISITION

S07RR-05596-27 0134 (NSS) FOWLER, ANNE E Biomedical research support LANGUAGE ABILITIES OF CHILDREN & ADULTS W/ DOWNS SYNDROME

S07RR-05596-27 0135 (NSS) ALFONSO, PETER Biomedical research support SPEECH PRODUCTION BY STUTTERERS

S07RR-05598-26 (NSS) STOUT, FRANK G NEW ENGLAND MEDICAL CTR HOSP 750 WASHINGTON ST, BOX 817 BOSTON, MA 02111 Biomedical research

support

S07RR-05599-25 (NSS) GULBRANDSEN, CHRISTIAN L UNIVERSITY OF HAWAII 1960 EAST WEST ROAD T-101 HONOLULU, HAWAII 96822 Biomedical research support

S07RR-05599-25 0509 (NSS) GULBRANDSEN, CHRISTI Biomedical research support NO RESEARCH SUBPROJECTS

S07RR-05604-14 (NSS) HOLZEMER, WILLIAM L UNIVERSITY OF CALIFORNIA SCHOOL OF NURSING, BOX 0604 SAN FRANCISCO, CALIF 94143 Biomedical research support

S07RR-05604-14 0674 (NSS) CHESLA, CATHERINE A Biomedical research support FAMILY RITUALS & COPING W/ SCHIZOPHRENIA FAMILY HEALTH

S07RR-05604-14 0675 (NSS) CLARKE, ADELE E Biomedical research support HISTORICAL SOCIOLOGY OF PAP SMEAR WOMENS HEALTH GYNECOLOGY

S07RR-05604-14 0676 (NSS) DOWLING, GLENNA Biomedical research support PERCEIVED SLEEP PATTERNS IN OLDER WOMEN NURSING AGING WOMENS HEALTH

S07RR-05604-14 0677 (NSS) FAUCETT, JULIA Biomedical research support SPOUSAL RESPONSES TO CHRONIC PAIN NURSING SOCIAL SUPPORT

S07RR-05604-14 0678 (NSS) VIRGENE KAYSER, JONE Biomedical research support BEHAVIORAL CONTEXT OF EATING & NUTRITIONAL SUPPORT AGING NURSING HOMES

S07RR-05604-14 0679 (NSS) LAFFREY, SHIRLEY C Biomedical research support HLTH PROMOTING SELF CARE INTERVENTION COMMUNITY ELDERLY; NURSING AGING PREVENT

S07RR-05604-14 0680 (NSS) NEIDLINGER, SUSAN H Biomedical research support NURSE ENTRAPRENEURSHIP AS EXPERIENCED IN ACUTE CARE SETTINGS NURSING

S07RR-05604-14 0681 (NSS) RANKIN, SALLY Biomedical research support CORONARY HEART DISEASE & RISK FACTOR MANAGEMENT WOMENS HEALTH CARDIOVASCULAR

S07RR-05604-14 0682 (NSS) SISSON, REBECCA Biomedical research support PHYSIOLOGICAL EFFECTS OF AUDITORY STIMULI ON COMATOSE PATIENT BRAIN INJURY

S07RR-05604-14 0683 (NSS) STOTTS, NANCY A Biomedical research support PHYSICAL & PSYCHOSOCIAL IMPACT ON DELAYED HEALING AT HOME NURSING WOUND HEALING

S07RR-05604-14 0684 (NSS) WALLHAGEN, MARGARET Biomedical research support EXPLORATION OF MEANING OF CONTROL TO ELDERLY CAREGIVERS NURSING AGING CAREGIVING

S07RR-05605-13 (NSS) SIPES, I GLENN UNIVERSITY OF ARIZONA 1703 E MABEL COL OF PHARM TUCSON, AZ 85721 Biomedical research support

S07RR-05606-25 (NSS) MICHAELIS, ELIAS K UNIVERSITY OF KANSAS SCH PHARM, MALOTT HALL LAWRENCE, KS 66045 Biomedical research support

S07RR-05606-25 0685 (NSS) GEORG, GUNDA I Biomedical research support SEMISYNTHETIC TAXOL DERIVATIES

S07RR-05606-25 0686 (NSS) GRUENEWALD, GARY L Biomedical research support MAINTAIN REFRIGERATED CENTRIFUGE

S07RR-05606-25 0687 (NSS) HANZLIK, ROBERT P Biomedical research support SCINTILLATION COUNTER

S07RR-05606-25 0688 (NSS) AUBE, JEFFREY Biomedical research support SYNTHESIS OF OPTICALLY ACTIVE TRANS HYDRINDANONES

S07RR-05606-25 0689 (NSS) DIXON, WALTER R Biomedical research support EFFECT OF CHRONIC COCAINE ON NEUROTRANSMITTER SYSTEMS

S07RR-05606-25 0690 (NSS) TESSEL, RICHARD E Biomedical research support ESTABLISHMENT OF DEVELOPMENTAL BEHAVIORAL PHARMACOLOGY LABORATORY

S07RR-05606-25 0691 (NSS) AUDUS, KENNETH L Biomedical research support FLUOROMETER SAMPLE TURRET

S07RR-05606-25 0692 (NSS) BORCHARDT, RONALD T Biomedical research support REDOX CYCLING IN MECHANISM OF ACTION OF 5,7 DIHYDROXYTRYPTAMINE

S07RR-05606-25 0693 (NSS) RILEY, CHRIS M Biomedical research support DIODE ARRAY DETECTION OF DRUGS IN LIQUID CHROMATOGRAPHY

S07RR-05606-25 0694 (NSS) TRAIGER, GEORGE Biomedical research support CHEMICAL INDUCED PULMONARY HYPERTENSION

S07RR-05606-25 0695 (NSS) MICHAELIS, ELIAS K Biomedical research support SHARED LASER PRINTER FOR GRAPHICS DISPLAY & DATA ANALYSIS

S07RR-05606-25 0696 (NSS) HANZLIK, ROBERT P Biomedical research support COMPUTER LITERATURE SEARCH

S07RR-05606-25 0697 (NSS) DOUGHTY, MICHAEL Biomedical research support SYNTHESIS OF NEUROPEPTIDE TYROSINE ANALOGS

S07RR-05607-25 (NSS) CASSADY, JOHN M OHIO STATE UNIVERSITY 500 WEST 12TH AVENUE COLUMBUS, OHIO 43210 Biomedical research support

S07RR-05607-25 0698 (NSS) AU, JESSIE L Biomedical research support PHARMACODYNAMICS OF ANTICANCER AGENTS IN HUMAN TUMORS

S07RR-05607-25 0699 (NSS) BRUEGGEMEIER, ROBERT Biomedical research support BIOCHEMICAL PROBES FOR ACTIVE SITE OF AROMATASE

S07RR-05607-25 0700 (NSS) RAHWAN, RALF Biomedical research support ANTI ULCER ACTIVITY OF CALCIUM ANTAGONISTS

S07RR-05607-25 0701 (NSS) SUPKO, JEFFREY Biomedical research support PRECLINICAL PHARMACOLOGY STUDIES OF ANTITUMOR AGENTS

S07RR-05607-25 0702 (NSS) YOUNG, ANTHONY P Biomedical research support REGULATION OF GENE EXPRESSION DEVELOPING RETINA

S07RR-05610-24 (NSS) LATIES, ALAN M PRESBYTERIAN UNIV/PENNSYLVANIA 51 NORTH 39TH STREET PHILADELPHIA, PA 19104 Biomedical research support

S07RR-05610-24 0932 (NSS) LATIES, ALAN M Biomedical research support NO SUBPROJECTS

S07RR-05611-22 (NSS) LAWTON, M POWELL PHILADELPHIA GERIATRIC CENTER 5301 OLD YORK ROAD PHILADELPHIA, PA 19141 Biomedical research support

S07RR-05611-22 0703 (NSS) WOLDOW, ASHER Biomedical research support RELIABILITY OF MEDICAL DIAGNOSIS

S07RR-05611-22 0704 (NSS) MOSS, MIRIAM Biomedical research support MEANING OF PARENTAL DEATH

S07RR-05611-22 0705 (NSS) SANDS, LAURA Biomedical research support EXERCISE & COGNITIVE FUNCTIONING

S07RR-05611-22 0706 (NSS) WOODRUFF-PAK, DIANA Biomedical research support CLASSICAL CONDITIONING OF EYEBLINK RESPONSE ADULTS DOWNS SYNDROME

S07RR-05611-22 0707 (NSS) WANG, REBECCA Biomedical research support ATRIAL FIBRILLATION & STROKE IN ELDERLY

S07RR-05611-22 0708 (NSS) DEMPSEY, NORAH Biomedical research support OLDER VOLUNTEERS PILOT OF SAMPLING & INTERVIEW

S07RR-05611-22 0709 (NSS) GLICKSMAN, ALLEN Biomedical research support AGING IN AN ETHNIC POPULATION: NATIONAL PERSPECTIVE

S07RR-05611-22 0710 (NSS) GLOSSER, GUILA Biomedical research support GESTURAL COMMUNICATION IN ALZHEIMERS DISEASE

S07RR-05611-22 0711 (NSS) ALBERT, STEVEN Biomedical research support CAREGIVERS ROLE AS CARE ASSESSORS FOR IMPAIRED ELDERS

S07RR-05611-22 0712 (NSS) KLEBAN, MORTON Biomedical research support LONGITUDINAL ANALYSIS OF MORTALITY HEALTH & DEPRESSION

S07RR-05612-19 (NSS) HOPS, HYMAN OREGON RESEARCH INSTITUTE 1899 WILLAMETTE, SUITE 2 EUGENE, OREG 97401 Biomedical research support

S07RR-05612-19 0136 (NSS) LEWINSOHN, PETER M Biomedical research support ADOLESCENT DEPRESSION & BEHAVIORAL TREATMENT

S07RR-05623-25 (NSS) ROBINSON, N EDWARD MICHIGAN STATE UNIVERSITY A-9 VETERINARY CLINICAL CENTER EAST LANSING, MI 48824-1314 Biomedical research support

S07RR-05623-25 0713 (NSS) HERDT, THOMAS H Biomedical research support HEPATIC LOW DENSITY LIPOPROTEIN RECEPTORS DURING INDUCED HYPOCHOLESTEROLEMIA

S07RR-05623-25 0714 (NSS) BAKER, JOHN C Biomedical research support CHARACTERIZATION OF BOVINE RESPIRATORY SYNCYTIAL VIRUS PROTEINS & MRNA

S07RR-05623-25 0715 (NSS) CARON, JOHN P Biomedical research support NEURAL MODULATION OF EQUINE SYNOVIAL JOINT METABOLISM

S07RR-05623-25 0716 (NSS) ATCHISON, WILLIAM D Biomedical research support EFFECTS OF DITHIOBIURET ON NEUROMUSCULAR JUNCTIONS IN CULTURE

S07RR-05623-25 0717 (NSS) YAEGER, MICHAEL J Biomedical research support NERVE GROWTH FACTOR FOR TREATMENT OF NEURAL CREST TUMORS

S07RR-05623-25 0718 (NSS) VELICER, LELAND F Biomedical research support ONCOGENIC HERPES VIRUS PROTEIN KINASE ANALYSIS

S07RR-05623-25 0719 (NSS) GRIMES, SHEILA Biomedical research support COMPETITIVE ADHERENCE OF LACTIC ACID BACTERIA TO INTESTINAL MUCOSA

S07RR-05623-25 0720 (NSS) WALKER, ROBERT Biomedical research support EFFECTS OF PASTEURELLA HAEMOLYTICA LEUKOTOXIN ON BOVINE GRANULOCYTES

S07RR-05623-25 0721 (NSS) BELL, THOMAS G Biomedical research support SIMMENTAL HEREDITARY BLEEDING DISORDER

S07RR-05623-25 0722 (NSS) CARON, JOHN P Biomedical research support EFFECTS OF POLSULFATED GLYCOSAMINOGLYCAN ON OSTEOARTHRITIC CARTILAGE

S07RR-05623-25 0723 (NSS) BOWKER, ROBERT Biomedical research support PEPTIDERGIC MEDIATION OF ARTHRITIS & LAMINITIS DISEASE

S07RR-05623-25 0724 (NSS) TANAKA, DUKE Biomedical research support ORGANOPHOSPHORUS DELAYED NEUROTOXINS IN CENTRAL NERVOUS SYSTEM

S07RR-05623-25 0725 (NSS) SONEA, IOANA M Biomedical research support INNERVATION OF LOWER RESPIRATORY TRACT OF HORSE

S07RR-05623-25 0726 (NSS) SCHILLHORN VAN VEEN, Biomedical research support IMPROVED IMMUNOASSAYS FOR EPERYTHROZOON SUIS

S07RR-05626-25 (NSS) ALPER, CHESTER A CENTER FOR BLOOD RESEARCH, INC 800 HUNTINGTON AVENUE BOSTON, MASS 02115 Biomedical research support

S07RR-05626-25 0668 (NSS) ROSEN, FRED S Biomedical research support CHROMOSOME 6

S07RR-05626-25 0669 (NSS) ALPER, CHESTER A Biomedical research support GENETICS OF HUMAN COMPLEMENT

S07RR-05626-25 0670 (NSS) REMOLD-O'DONNELL, EI Biomedical research support SIALOPHORIN (CD43): STRUCTURE FUNCTION IN WAS

S07RR-05626-25 0671 (NSS) BING, DAVID H Biomedical research support IMMUNE TOLEROGENS

S07RR-05626-25 0672 (NSS) SPRINGER, TIMOTHY A Biomedical research support LYMPHOCYTE ADHESION FACTORS

S07RR-05629-22 (NSS) GROOTHUIS, DENNIS EVANSTON HOSPITAL 2650 RIDGE AVENUE EVANSTON, IL 60201 Biomedical research support

S07RR-05629-22 0137 (NSS) FROELICH, CHRISTOPHE Biomedical research support PROTEASE DIGEST EXTRACELL MATRIX PROTEIN; RHEUM ARTHRITIS; CAPILLARY LYMPH; SEQ

S07RR-05634-24 (NSS) VINCE, ROBERT UNIVERSITY OF MINNESOTA 308 HARVARD ST, S E MINNEAPOLIS, MINN 55455 Biomedical research support

S07RR-05634-24 0510 (NSS) VINCE, ROBERT Biomedical research support NO RESEARCH SUBPROJECTS

S07RR-05635-18 (NSS) GIBALDI, MILO UNIVERSITY OF WASHINGTON SCHOOL OF PHARMACY SC-69 SEATTLE, WASH 98195 Biomedical research support

S07RR-05635-18 0777 (NSS) ADKISON, KIMBERLY Biomedical research support CNS TRANSPORT OF VPA & ITS 2 ENE METABOLITE

S07RR-05635-18 0778 (NSS) AMORE, BENNY Biomedical research support EXPLORATORY BIOMEDICAL RESEARCH

S07RR-05635-18 0781 (NSS) KAVANAGH, RON Biomedical research support MECHANISMS OF DRUG METABOLISM IN CHILDREN W/ CYSTIC FIBROSIS

S07RR-05635-18 0782 (NSS) TITUS, MARK Biomedical research support INHIBITION OF STEROID 5 ALPHA REDUCTASE

S07RR-05635-18 0783 (NSS) ZHANG, KANYIN Biomedical research support STEREOSELECTIVE DISPOSITION OF STIRIPENTOL

S07RR-05635-18 0779 (NSS) DAVIS, MARGARET Biomedical research support METABOLISM OF N METHYLFORMANIDE IN RATS

S07RR-05635-18 0780 (NSS) HURST, SUSAN Biomedical research support EXPLORATORY BIOMEDICAL RESEARCH

S07RR-05641-17 (NSS) WHITTY, ALBERT J SINAI HOSPITAL OF DETROIT 6767 WEST OUTER DRIVE DETROIT, MI 48235 Biomedical research support grant

S07RR-05641-17 0849 (NSS) BANNON, MICHAEL Biomedical research support grant COCAINE BINDING DOPAMINE TRANSPORTER: BRAIN PEPTIDE BIOSYNTHESIS

S07RR-05641-17 0850 (NSS) CHIODO, LOUISE A Biomedical research support grant PSYCHOPHARMACOLOGY OF DOPAMINE AGONIST CNS EFFECTS

S07RR-05644-19 (NSS) LEONE, LOUIS A RHODE ISLAND HOSPITAL 593 EDDY STREET PROVIDENCE, R I 02902 Biomedical research support

S07RR-05648-25 (NSS) TOMASI, THOMAS B, JR ROSWELL PARK CANCER INST ELM & CARLTON STREETS BUFFALO, NY 14263 Biomedical research support

S07RR-05648-25 0918 (NSS) ASCH, BONNIE Biomedical research support VL30 RETROTRANSPOSON RELATED COMPONENT IN HUMAN BREAST CANCERS:

S07RR-05648-25 0919 (NSS) BERNSTEIN, ZALE Biomedical research support FLOW CYTOMETRIC OF BONE MARROW OF PATIENTS W/ HIV ASSOCIATED

PROJECT NO., ORGANIZATIONAL UNIT., INVESTIGATOR, ADDRESS, TITLE

LYMPHOMA:
S07RR-05648-25 0920 (NSS) GROSS, KENNETH W Biomedical research support GENETIC REGULATION OF MURINE RENIN GENES: TRANSGENIC MOUSE
S07RR-05648-25 0921 (NSS) HOHMANN, PHILLIP Biomedical research support PEPTIDE SUBSTRATES FOR PROTEIN KINASES:
S07RR-05648-25 0922 (NSS) HUGHES, ROBERT G, JR Biomedical research support SPECIFIC DETECTION OF INHIBITORS OF HIV PROTEASE: HERPES SIMPLEX
S07RR-05648-25 0923 (NSS) MARKUS, GABOR Biomedical research support TYROSINE PHOSPHORYLATION PATHWAYS: PLASMINOGEN ACTIVATOR EPIDERMAL GROWTH FACTOR
S07RR-05648-25 0924 (NSS) MUNSON, BENJAMIN Biomedical research support PHOTODYNAMIC ACTIVITY OF DNA TARGETED PORPHYRINS:
S07RR-05648-25 0925 (NSS) PAULY, JOHN Biomedical research support HUMAN LAK CELL RECEPTORS ANALYZED USING COLLOIDAL GOLD: INTERLEUKIN 2
S07RR-05648-25 0926 (NSS) PERL, ANDRAS Biomedical research support ENDOGENOUS RETROVIRAL SEQUENCES IN HUMAN CANCER: T CELL LYMPHOTROPIC VIRUS RELAT
S07RR-05648-25 0927 (NSS) SOOD, ASHWANI Biomedical research support MHC CLASS I ANTIGENS IN ANTITUMOR IMMUNITY: INTERLEUKIN 2
S07RR-05648-25 0928 (NSS) SUFRIN, JANICE Biomedical research support S ADENOSYLMETHIONINE (SAM) BIOSYNTHESIS & METABOLISM:
S07RR-05648-25 0929 (NSS) TANIGAKI, NOBUYUKI Biomedical research support STRUCTURE & FUNCTION OF A MEMBRANE GLYCOPROTEIN: LYMPHOID CELL
S07RR-05649-25 (NSS) DICKERMAN, HERBERT NEW YORK STATE DEPT OF HEALTH EMPIRE ST PLAZA TOWER R-1408 ALBANY, N Y 12237 Biomedical research support
S07RR-05649-25 0784 (NSS) PASS, KENNETH Biomedical research support SCREENING OF NEWBORNS FOR 1 ANTITRYPSIN DEFICIENCY
S07RR-05649-25 0785 (NSS) PARSONS, DONALD Biomedical research support REAL TIME STUDY FOR TUMOR CELL INVASION BY LIGHT MICROSCOPY
S07RR-05649-25 0786 (NSS) SEMKOW, THOMAS Biomedical research support RADON EMANATION FROM SOLIDS AT ATOMIC LEVEL
S07RR-05649-25 0787 (NSS) COLEMAN, JAMES Biomedical research support CHARACTERIZE MABS TO ANTIGENS OF BORRELIA BURGDORFERI LYME DISEASE
S07RR-05649-25 0788 (NSS) BOSLER, EDWARD Biomedical research support EVALUATION OF METHODS TO REDUCE TRANSMISSION OF LYME DISEASE
S07RR-05649-25 0789 (NSS) DEMPSTER, D W Biomedical research support EFFECTS OF ESTROGENS ON MONOCYTE STIMULATED BONE RESORPTION
S07RR-05649-25 0790 (NSS) SLOVITER, ROBERT Biomedical research support EFFECTS OF ESTROGENS ON MONOCYTE STIMULATED BONE RESORPTION
S07RR-05649-25 0791 (NSS) CHEN, CHANG-HWEI Biomedical research support THERMOCHEMICAL INVESTIGATIONS OF ACTIVE TRANSPORT IN ESCHERICHIA
S07RR-05649-25 0792 (NSS) FASCO, MICHAEL Biomedical research support WARFARIN METABOLISM ANTIVITAMIN K ACTIVITY
S07RR-05649-25 0793 (NSS) KAMINSKY, LAWRENCE Biomedical research support HEPATIC MICROSOMAL ENZYME METABOLISM OF ANESTHETICS
S07RR-05649-25 0794 (NSS) SHAIN, WILLIAM Biomedical research support ETHANOL STIMULATES TOURINE RELEASE FROM ASTROGLIA
S07RR-05649-25 0795 (NSS) RAMSINGH, ARLENE Biomedical research support MOLECULAR PATHOGENESIS OF COXSACKIEVIRUS B4 INFECTIONS
S07RR-05649-25 0796 (NSS) MAHONEY, MARTIN Biomedical research support RETROSPECTIVE SYPHILIS INFECTION & SUBSEQUENT CANCER INCIDENCE
S07RR-05649-25 0797 (NSS) MEONS, ROBERT Biomedical research support LYME DISEASE IN NYS HOST DISTRIBUTION OF IXODES DAMMINEI
S07RR-05649-25 0798 (NSS) SLOVITER, ROBERT Biomedical research support PHOTOMICROSCOPY IN PROJECTS OF NEUROPATHOLOGY
S07RR-05649-25 0799 (NSS) COCHRAN, GEORGE Biomedical research support SYNTHETIC LIGAMENT ARTHROPLASTY OF SPINE
S07RR-05649-25 0800 (NSS) LINDSAY, ROBERT Biomedical research support DUAL ENERGY XRAY ABSORPTIONMETRY & DUAL PHOTON ABSORPTIONMETRY
S07RR-05650-25 (NSS) OLDHAM, JOHN NEW YORK STATE PSYCH INST 722 WEST 168 STREET NEW YORK, N Y 10032 Biomedical research support
S07RR-05650-25 0091 (NSS) ANTHONY, DONNA T Biomedical research support IMMORTALIZATION OF FETAL RAT DOPAMINERGIC NEURONS
S07RR-05650-25 0092 (NSS) BECKER, JUDITH V Biomedical research support FLUOXETINE TREATMENT FOR COMPULSIVE SEXUAL BEHAVIOR
S07RR-05650-25 0093 (NSS) BRUDER, GERARD Biomedical research support SELECTIVE ATTENTION & BRAIN ERPS IN SCHIZOPHRENIA
S07RR-05650-25 0094 (NSS) BRUNELLI, SUSAN Biomedical research support MINORITY FATHERS: ROLE IN CHILD & FAMILY OUTCOME
S07RR-05650-25 0095 (NSS) COPLAN, JEREMY Biomedical research support BIOLOGICAL CHALLENGES IN RELATIVES
S07RR-05650-25 0096 (NSS) DEVLIN, MICHAEL Biomedical research support FLUOXETINE TREATMENT OF OBESE BINGE EATERS
S07RR-05650-25 0097 (NSS) DOHWENREND, BRUCE Biomedical research support SOCIAL STRESS SOCIAL SELECTION & PSYCHIATRIC DISORDERS
S07RR-05650-25 0098 (NSS) GRAAE, FLEMING Biomedical research support CLONAZEPAN & CHILDHOOD ANXIETY DISORDERS
S07RR-05650-25 0099 (NSS) GREEN, ARTHUR Biomedical research support UNKNOWN
S07RR-05650-25 0100 (NSS) HOLLANDER, ERIC Biomedical research support PSYCHOBIOLOGY OF IMPULSIVE PERSONALITY DISORDERS
S07RR-05650-25 0101 (NSS) JAVITCH, JONATHAN Biomedical research support INTERACTION OF GLUTAMATE & DOPAMINE TRANSMISSION IN PSYCHOSES
S07RR-05650-25 0102 (NSS) KARPIAK, STEPHEN E Biomedical research support REDUCTION OF COCAINE INDUCED FETAL CNS INJURY
S07RR-05650-25 0103 (NSS) KERTZNER, ROBERT Biomedical research support PROLECTIN LEVELS IN SUBJECTS W/ HIV INFECTION
S07RR-05650-25 0104 (NSS) MEYER-BAHLBURG, HEIN Biomedical research support CONGENITAL ADRENAL HYPERPLASIA (CAH) IN ADULTHOOD
S07RR-05650-25 0105 (NSS) MUENZENMAIER, KRISTI Biomedical research support ABUSE EXPERIENCES AMONG CHRONICALLY MENTALLY ILL
S07RR-05650-25 0106 (NSS) MUKHERJEE, SUKDEB Biomedical research support INSULIN RECEPTOR SENSITIVITY IN BRAIN & PERIPHERY
S07RR-05650-25 0107 (NSS) MURPHY, CAROL A Biomedical research support EFFECTS OF CROSS STRAIN FETAL HYPOTHALMIC IMPLANTS
S07RR-05650-25 0108 (NSS) PIACENTINI, JOHN Biomedical research support BEHAVIORAL TREATMENT OF CHILD & ADOLESCENT OBSESSIVE COMPULSIVE DISORDER
S07RR-05650-25 0109 (NSS) POTEGAL, MICHAEL Biomedical research support COCAINE ENHANCEMENT OF DEFENSE
S07RR-05650-25 0110 (NSS) SLOAN, RICHARD Biomedical research support PARASYMPATHETIC ACTIVITY & PANIC DISORDER
S07RR-05650-25 0111 (NSS) TAMIR, HADASSAH Biomedical research support AUTOIMMUNE RESPONSE CONTRIBUTES TO PATHOLOGY OF SOME MENTAL DISORDERS
S07RR-05650-25 0112 (NSS) TRAUTMAN, PAUL Biomedical research support BRIEF FAMILY TREATMENT OF ADOLESCENT SUICIDE ATTEMPTERS
S07RR-05651-24 (NSS) CANCRO, ROBERT RES FDN MENTAL HYGIENE INC NATHAN S KLINE INSTITUTE ORANGEBURG, NY 10962 Biomedical research support
S07RR-05651-24 0140 (NSS) SAITO, MITSUO Biomedical research support METABOLISM OF NADNA IN CENTRAL NERVOUS SYSTEM
S07RR-05651-24 0141 (NSS) DUNLOP, DAVID Biomedical research support FUNCTIONAL ASPECTS OF D ASPATATE METABOLISM
S07RR-05651-24 0142 (NSS) CONVIT, ANTONIO Biomedical research support IS SEVERITY OF CRIME RELATED TO NEUROLOGICAL IMPAIRMENT
S07RR-05651-24 0143 (NSS) SMITH, THOMAS Biomedical research support RENAL FAILURE, DESIPRAMINE & HYDROXYLATED & GLUCURONIDATED METABOLITES
S07RR-05651-24 0144 (NSS) CROWNER, MARTHA Biomedical research support AKATHISIA & VIOLENCE
S07RR-05651-24 0145 (NSS) LEVY, ALEJANDRO Biomedical research support ALGORITHMS & GRAPHICAL PROCEDURE IN PET
S07RR-05651-24 0146 (NSS) SERSHEN, HENRY Biomedical research support ACTION OF DOPAMINE ANTAGONISTS ON COCAINE INDUCED BEHAVIOR
S07RR-05651-24 0147 (NSS) FLYNN, CHERYL Biomedical research support PHOSPHOLIPASES IN NEURAL MEMBRANE DYNAMICS
S07RR-05651-24 0148 (NSS) SAITO, MARIKO Biomedical research support FATTY ACID COMPOSITION ON GANGLIOSIDE EXPRESSION IN NERVOUS SYSTEM
S07RR-05651-24 0138 (NSS) GANDY, SAMUEL Biomedical research support REGULATION OF AMYLOID FORMATION IN ALZHEIMERS DISEASE
S07RR-05651-24 0139 (NSS) LASKA, EUGENE Biomedical research support NEEDS ASSESSMENT UTILIZING SOCIAL AREA ANALYSIS
S07RR-05653-24 (NSS) EISENMAN, JOSEPH S MT SINAI SCH OF MEDICINE ONE GUSTAVE L LEVY PLACE NEW YORK, NY 10029-6574 Biomedical research support
S07RR-05653-24 0801 (NSS) APPLEGATE, DIANNE Biomedical research support ACTIN FACILITATED ASSEMBLY OF SMOOTH MUSCLE MYOSIN FILAMENTS
S07RR-05653-24 0802 (NSS) MCGINNIS, MARILYN Y Biomedical research support EXPRESSION OF SEXUAL BEHAVIOR INDUCED BY STEROID HORMONES
S07RR-05653-24 0803 (NSS) ROSE, J B ALEXANDER Biomedical research support CONFORMATION OF BINDING PROTEINS HUMAN TISSUE FACTOR STEROID BINDING
S07RR-05653-24 0804 (NSS) SCHWARTZ, GERALD Biomedical research support PROTEIN STRUCTURE FUNCTION ANALYSIS OXYTOCIN INSULIN, SYNTHESIS NMR
S07RR-05653-24 0805 (NSS) TSAI, PHILIP H Biomedical research support CONGENITAL BONE MARROW FAILURE PROGENITOR CELLS, INTERLEUKIN 3
S07RR-05654-24 (NSS) YOUNG, JAMES J UNIV OF TEXAS HLTH SCI CTR 7703 FLOYD CURL DRIVE SAN ANTONIO, TEX 78284 Biomedical research support
S07RR-05654-24 0113 (NSS) TAPP, DAVID C Biomedical research support NUTRITION ON PATHOLOGY IN REMNANT KIDNEY
S07RR-05654-24 0114 (NSS) OLIVE, DAVID Biomedical research support CD5+B CELLS IN MENSTRUAL CYCLE: EFFECT OF ESTROGEN & PROGESTERONE
S07RR-05654-24 0115 (NSS) ATHANASIOU, K A Biomedical research support BIODEGRADABLE CARRIERS FOR TREATING ARTICULAR CARTILAGE DEFECTS
S07RR-05654-24 0116 (NSS) FRIEDMAN, DAVID J Biomedical research support CANDIDA ALBICANS: GENETIC SEQUENCES INVOLVED IN PATHOGENICITY
S07RR-05654-24 0117 (NSS) LUM, CALIANN T Biomedical research support IMMUNOMODULATION W/ ANTI MHC MONOCLONAL ANTIBODIES
S07RR-05654-24 0118 (NSS) MCGANITY, P L J Biomedical research support MECHANISMS OF JOINT FUSION
S07RR-05654-24 0119 (NSS) ROSSETTI, L Biomedical research support INSULIN LIKE EFFECT OF LITHIUM: MECHANISM(S) OF ACTION
S07RR-05654-24 0120 (NSS) ZYMAN, PAMELA Biomedical research support MACROMOLECULAR STRUCTURE OF GLIOMAS: ASTROCYTOMAS
S07RR-05654-24 0129 (NSS) KNAPE, KELLY G Biomedical research support ANESTHETIC INDUCTION AGENTS ACROSS PERFUSED HUMAN PLACENTA
S07RR-05654-24 0130 (NSS) LEACH, CHARLES T Biomedical research support AIDS COFACTORS: A QUANTITATIVE & QUALITATIVE STUDY
S07RR-05654-24 0131 (NSS) MILLER, MICHAEL L Biomedical research support T CELL RESPONSE TO ACTIVATION SIGNALS IN JUVENILE RHEUMATOID ARTHRITIS
S07RR-05654-24 0132 (NSS) MAGEE, MITCHELL Biomedical research support T CELL SUBSETS IN MURINE COCCIDIOIDOMYCOSIS
S07RR-05654-24 0133 (NSS) SAMUELS, MARY H Biomedical research support PULSATILE SECRETION OF PARATHYROID HORMONE IN OSTEOPAROSIS
S07RR-05654-24 0134 (NSS) VONLANTHEN, MARYELLE Biomedical research support EFFECT OF AGE ON METABOLIC RATE & PHYSICAL ACTIVITY ON YOUNG RATS
S07RR-05654-24 0121 (NSS) ERIAN, RALPH F Biomedical research support SPONTANEOUS VENTILATION & BLOOD FLOW: MUSCLE RELAXATION ONSET, DEPTH & DURATION
S07RR-05654-24 0122 (NSS) EIDELBERG, EDUARDO Biomedical research support GROWTH FACTORS ACTING UPON SPINAL CORD + UPPER MOTONEURONES
S07RR-05654-24 0123 (NSS) BAROHN, RICHARD J Biomedical research support DISEASE CAUSING POTENTIAL OF ANTIBODIES IN MYASTHENIA GRAVIS
S07RR-05654-24 0124 (NSS) BREY, ROBIN L Biomedical research support NERVOUS SYSTEM DISEASE IN AUTOIMMUNE MICE: ROLE OF MEMBRANE ATTACK COMPLEX
S07RR-05654-24 0125 (NSS) BUNEGIN, LEONID Biomedical research support CSF PRESSURE WAVE PROPAGATION FOLLOWING CLOSED EXPERIMENTAL SPINAL CORD INJURY
S07RR-05654-24 0126 (NSS) FISCHBACH, MICHAEL Biomedical research support NOVEL IMMUNOGLOBULIN GENE REARRANGEMENTS
S07RR-05654-24 0127 (NSS) MCGURN, WEALTHA C Biomedical research support THERAPEUTIC REGIMENS IN HYPERTENSIVES THROUGH META ANALYSES & MATHEMATIC MODELS
S07RR-05654-24 0128 (NSS) GASKILL, HAROLD V, I Biomedical research support PROSTAGLANDIAS & TUMOR BLOOD FLOW
S07RR-05654-24 0135 (NSS) SEIDNER, STEVEN, DR Biomedical research

PROJECT NO., ORGANIZATIONAL UNIT., INVESTIGATOR, ADDRESS, TITLE

support PREMATURITY, MECHANICAL VENTILATION, & SURFACTANT ON LUNG ANTIOXIDANT RESPONSE
S07RR-05654-24 0136 (NSS) MATTESON, MARY A Biomedical research support WANDERING BEHAVIOR IN INSTITUTIONALIZED ALZHEIMERS RESIDENTS
S07RR-05654-24 0137 (NSS) SHAH, DINESH M Biomedical research support PROGESTERONE ON RENIN MRNA IN ENDOMETRIAL STROMAL CELLS
S07RR-05654-24 0138 (NSS) BRACKLEY, MARGARET H Biomedical research support EFFECT OF IN HOME MENTAL HEALTH NURSING SERVICES
S07RR-05654-24 0139 (NSS) HIDALGO, HUMBERTO A Biomedical research support INTERACTIONS BETWEEN ALVEOLAR MACROPHAGES & PNEUMOCYSTIS CARINII
S07RR-05654-24 0140 (NSS) KELLY, SHEILA Biomedical research support CHILD ABUSE RISK FACTORS IN FIRST TIME EXPECTANT PARENTS
S07RR-05654-24 0141 (NSS) SCHWAB, THERESE Biomedical research support ATTITUDES & HEALTH BELIEF AMONG MEXICAN AMERICAN DIABETIC PATIENTS
S07RR-05654-24 0142 (NSS) SLOAN, TOD B Biomedical research support MOTOR EVOKED POTENTIALS IN MONKEY
S07RR-05654-24 0143 (NSS) YU, HING-SING Biomedical research support ABSORBANT DECREASE IN CULTURED BOVINE RETINAL PIGMENT EPITHELIAL CELL
S07RR-05654-24 0144 (NSS) HOEVET, GAIL L Biomedical research support CHILDHOOD CANCER: COPING OF PARENT & CHILD & CORRELATES
S07RR-05654-24 0145 (NSS) BURNS, WILLIAM N Biomedical research support CUMULUS CELL MEIOSIS INHIBITOR RNAS W/ OOCYTE MATURITY FERTILIZATION EMBRYO
S07RR-05654-24 0146 (NSS) KAYE, CELIA I Biomedical research support GENETIC LINKAGE STUDIES OF OCULOAURICULOVERTEBRAL DYSPLASIA
S07RR-05654-24 0147 (NSS) STEVENS, KATHLEEN R Biomedical research support PSYCHOLOGICAL & SOCIOLOGICAL CHARACTERISTICS & HEALTH PRACTICES IN ADOLESCENTS
S07RR-05654-24 0148 (NSS) COHEN, DAVID J Biomedical research support CHRONIC BACTERIAL ENDOCARDITIS & CALCIFICATION OF AORTIC HEART VALVES
S07RR-05654-24 0149 (NSS) JAVORS, MARTIN A Biomedical research support BIOGENETIC ALDEHYDE OF NOREPINEPHRINE
S07RR-05654-24 0150 (NSS) LEVINE, STEPHANIE M Biomedical research support OXYGEN FREE RADICALS FORMATION IN RAT DIAPHRAGM FUNCTION
S07RR-05654-24 0151 (NSS) MELBY, PETER Biomedical research support LEISHMANIA ANTIGENS ON SURFACE OF INFECTED MACROPHAGE
S07RR-05654-24 0152 (NSS) INFANTE, ANTHONY Biomedical research support MAJOR HISTOCOMPATIBILITY COMPLEX RECOGNITION OF ACETYLCHOLINE RECEPTORS IN MICE
S07RR-05654-24 0153 (NSS) DZIDA, FRANKLIN J Biomedical research support BIOMECHANICAL PROPERTIES OF HUMAN ACETABULAR & FEMORAL HEADS CARTILAGE
S07RR-05655-21 (NSS) NEFF, JOHN M CHILDRENS ORTH HOSP & MED CTR P O BOXC-5371 SEATTLE, WASH 98105 Biomedical research support
S07RR-05655-21 0812 (NSS) DELBECCARO, MARK Biomedical research support BLOOD CULTURE BY RED CELL LYSING, DIRECT PLATING
S07RR-05655-21 0813 (NSS) RIDER, LISA G Biomedical research support CERBROSPINAL FLUID EXAMS IN CHILDREN W/ SEIZURES
S07RR-05655-21 0814 (NSS) RIDER, LISA G Biomedical research support CERBROSPINAL FLUID EXAMS IN CHILDREN W/ SEIZURES
S07RR-05655-21 0815 (NSS) TARR, PHILLIP Biomedical research support CYTOXIN PRODUCING E COLI
S07RR-05655-21 0816 (NSS) SWAIN, ROBERT Biomedical research support FETAL LUNG DEVELOP BOMBESIN PEPTIDES IN AMNIOTIC FLUID
S07RR-05655-21 0817 (NSS) VINCENT, JENNIFER Biomedical research support STIMULATION INDUCED TIC DISORDERS
S07RR-05655-21 0818 (NSS) SIEBERT, JOSEPH Biomedical research support CONGENITAL DIAPHRAGMATIC HERNIA
S07RR-05655-21 0819 (NSS) JAFFE, KENNETH M Biomedical research support HEAD INJURY STUDY
S07RR-05655-21 0820 (NSS) ZELIKOVIC, ISRAEL Biomedical research support PROTEIN PHOSPHYRATION IN REGULATION AND DEV OF RENAL AMINO ACID TRANSPORT
S07RR-05655-21 0821 (NSS) RIDER, LISA Biomedical research support AUTOANTIBODY PRODUCTION & CLINICAL CORRELATION IN KS
S07RR-05655-21 0822 (NSS) WRIGHT, JEFFREY Biomedical research support VALIDITY & PATIENT ACCEPTANCE OF COMPUTERIZED SCREENING TESTS
S07RR-05655-21 0823 (NSS) SMITH, MARK SCOTT Biomedical research support COLD PRESSOR RESPONSE IN PEDIATRIC HEADACHE
S07RR-05655-21 0824 (NSS) BURCHETT, SANDRA Biomedical research support PATHOGENESIS OF VERTICAL TRANSMISSIONS OF HIV
S07RR-05655-21 0806 (NSS) MCLAUGHLIN, JOHN Biomedical research support SELECT DORSAL RHIZOTOMY
S07RR-05655-21 0807 (NSS) JARDINE, DAVID Biomedical research support THERMAL EQUILIBRIUM POINT
S07RR-05655-21 0808 (NSS) PATCH, LYNNE Biomedical research support FAT EMULSION CONTAMINATION RATES
S07RR-05655-21 0809 (NSS) KRANE, ELLIOT Biomedical research support CONTINUOUS EPIDURAL SUFENTANIL FOR POSTOPERATIVE PAIN RELIEF
S07RR-05655-21 0810 (NSS) MELLINS, ELIZABETH Biomedical research support MOLECULAR INTERACTIONS INVOLVED IN GENERATION OF AN IMMUNE RESPONSE
S07RR-05655-21 0811 (NSS) SHERRY, DAVID Biomedical research support PHENOXYBENZAMINE & PSYCHOGENIC MUSCULOSKELETAL PAIN SYNDROME
S07RR-05655-21 0825 (NSS) THOMAS, JOHN R Biomedical research support EFFECT OF ALBUMIN & HETASTARCH ON COAGULATION & HEMOSTASIS IN CHILDREN
S07RR-05656-24 (NSS) BIEBER, LORAN L MICHIGAN STATE UNIVERSITY A 101 E FEE HALL EAST LANSING, MICH 48824 Biomedical research support
S07RR-05656-24 0826 (NSS) FRIEDMAN, THOMAS Biomedical research support INTERIM FUNDING FOR RE SUBMISSION OF NIH GRANT; MOLECULAR GENETICS
S07RR-05656-24 0827 (NSS) BIEBER, LORAN Biomedical research support BRIDGING FOR NIH GRANT
S07RR-05656-24 0828 (NSS) SAKAI, SHARLEEN Biomedical research support PURCHASE OF DURST ENLARGER
S07RR-05656-24 0829 (NSS) WILSON, BRUCE Biomedical research support SET UP FUNDS FOR DR BRUCE WILSON
S07RR-05656-24 0830 (NSS) ZAROUKIAN, MICHAEL Biomedical research support T100 AND TRANSMEMBRANE SIGNALLING IN NATURAL KILLER CELLS

PROJECT NO., ORGANIZATIONAL UNIT., INVESTIGATOR, ADDRESS, TITLE

S07RR-05656-24 0831 (NSS) FISHER, MARYE Biomedical research support CONTRACTILE ACTIVITY DURING 31P NMR STUDIES OF VASCULAR SMOOTH MUSCLE METABOLISM
S07RR-05656-24 0832 (NSS) FRENCHICK, GARY Biomedical research support PLATELET AGGREGATION STUDIES
S07RR-05656-24 0833 (NSS) OSUCH, JANET Biomedical research support HORMONE RECEPTORS IN NORMAL HUMAN BREAST TISSUE
S07RR-05656-24 0834 (NSS) ESSELMAN, WALTER Biomedical research support INTERIM BUDGETING SUPPORT
S07RR-05656-24 0835 (NSS) HEISEY, RICHARD Biomedical research support ISOLATION & CULTURE OF CHOROID PLEXUS EPITHELIAL CELLS
S07RR-05656-24 0836 (NSS) HASLAM, SANDRA Biomedical research support DEFRAY UNANTICIPATED INCREASE IN ANIMAL CARE COSTS
S07RR-05656-24 0837 (NSS) ANDERSON, RICHARD Biomedical research support CARBOHYDRATE BINDING PROTEIN 35 IN HUMAN FIBROBLASTS; CELLULAR AGING
S07RR-05656-24 0838 (NSS) BROOKS, KATHY Biomedical research support EVALUATION OF B LYMPHOCYTE HYPERACTIVITY IN MURINE AIDS
S07RR-05656-24 0839 (NSS) RECH, RICHARD Biomedical research support COMPARISON OF OPIOID CENTRAL DEPRESSANTS & ANTI INFLAMMATORY DRUGS
S07RR-05656-24 0840 (NSS) GORMAN, MARK Biomedical research support REGULATION OF ADENOSINE FORMATION IN INTACT DOG HEART
S07RR-05656-24 0841 (NSS) HOLMES, TALMAGE Biomedical research support CANCER DETECTION BY MICHIGAN RESEARCH NETWORK PHYSICIANS
S07RR-05656-24 0843 (NSS) MINOCHA, ANIL Biomedical research support COLONIC MOTILITY IN VIVO & IN VITRO IN NORMAL & EXPERIMENTAL COLITIS
S07RR-05656-24 0842 (NSS) ESSELMAN, WALTER Biomedical research support SUPPORT OF CELL SORTER
S07RR-05656-24 0844 (NSS) RICHARDS, ROBERT Biomedical research support PROSTAGLANDINS IN CHRONIC ULCERATIVE COLITIS
S07RR-05656-24 0845 (NSS) HOGAN, ANDY Biomedical research support EFFECTIVENESS OF CANCER TREATMENT IN MICHIGAN
S07RR-05656-24 0846 (NSS) STYRT, BARBARA Biomedical research support COMPARATIVE EFFECTS OF ALGINATE ON HUMAN & BOVINE GRANULOCYTE DEGRANULATION
S07RR-05656-24 0847 (NSS) CUNNINGHAM, SUSAN Biomedical research support GRIEF ISSUES
S07RR-05656-24 0848 (NSS) MAGEN, JED Biomedical research support EPIDEMIOLOGY OF CHILD PSYCHIATRY PATIENTS
S07RR-05656-24 0849 (NSS) COBBETT, PETER Biomedical research support PURCHASE OF MICROSCOPE
S07RR-05656-24 0850 (NSS) MACKENZIE, CHARLES Biomedical research support BRIDGE FOR DR MARUSHIGE
S07RR-05656-24 0851 (NSS) SAKAI, SHARLEEN Biomedical research support BASAL GANGLIA EFFERENTS OF GRANULAR CORTEX
S07RR-05656-24 0852 (NSS) SWEELEY, CHARLES Biomedical research support CLONING C DNA ENCODING CMP SIALIC ACID: LACTOSYLCERCIDE
S07RR-05656-24 0853 (NSS) WEBBER, MUTKA Biomedical research support IMMORTALIZATION OF HUMAN EPITHELIAL CELLS
S07RR-05656-24 0854 (NSS) GANEY, PATRICIA Biomedical research support KUPFFER CELL FUNCTIONS DURING IRON OVERLOAD; GUINEA PIG
S07RR-05656-24 0855 (NSS) LOVELL, KATHRYN Biomedical research support MICRO ULTRANSONIC CELL DISRUPTION
S07RR-05658-24 (NSS) LEVY, MATTHEW N THE MT. SINAI MEDICAL CENTER ONE MT. SINAI DRIVE CLEVELAND, OHIO 44106 Biomedical research support
S07RR-05658-24 0929 (NSS) LEVY, MATTHEW N Biomedical research support NO SUBPROJECTS
S07RR-05662-18 (NSS) SACKNER, MARVIN A MOUNT SINAI MEDICAL CENTER 4300 ALTON ROAD MIAMI BEACH, FLA 33140 Biomedical research support
S07RR-05662-18 0149 (NSS) BLOCK, RONALD Biomedical research support CHARACTERIZATION OF BIOLOGICAL TISSUE BY NMR
S07RR-05662-18 0150 (NSS) AHMED, TAHIR Biomedical research support HEPARIN IN DEGRANULATION OF STIMULATED RAT PERITONEAL MAST CELLS
S07RR-05662-18 0151 (NSS) RESNICK, LIONEL Biomedical research support POLYMERASE CHAIN REACTION TO ID MYCOBACTERIAL ORGANISMS
S07RR-05662-18 0152 (NSS) BOOTHE, THOMAS E Biomedical research support PREPARATION OF COPPER RADIOISOTOPES FOR NUCLEAR MEDICINE
S07RR-05662-18 0153 (NSS) MELNICK, STEVEN J Biomedical research support AFFECT OF NOLMEFEUE ON ACTIVITY INDEX OF PATIENTS W/ CROHNS DISEASE
S07RR-05662-18 0154 (NSS) ADAMS, JOSE A Biomedical research support THORACOCARDIOGRAPHY IN DETERMINATION OF CARDIAC ARREST
S07RR-05664-24 (NSS) GALLETTI, PIERRE M BROWN UNIVERSITY DIV BIOLOGY & MED BOX G PROVIDENCE, R I 02912 Biomedical research support
S07RR-05664-24 0865 (NSS) KOVALEVSKY, GEORGE Biomedical research support BEHAVIORAL CONSEQUENCES OF SLEEP APNEA IN CHILDREN
S07RR-05664-24 0866 (NSS) LOMBARDI, ANTHONY Biomedical research support OUTCOME EVALUATIONS OF ELDERLY PATIENTS IN ACUTE CARE HOSPITALS
S07RR-05664-24 0867 (NSS) MARCOVICH, ROBERT Biomedical research support SEROTONIN & INTRACELLULAR FREE CALCIUM IN RAT CHOROID PLEXUS CELLS
S07RR-05664-24 0868 (NSS) MARK, YVONNE Biomedical research support EFFECT OF NEWBORN BLOOD PRESSURE ON CEREBRAL OXYGENATION, BLOOD VOLUMES & CNS
S07RR-05664-24 0869 (NSS) MEYER, ALEXANDRA Biomedical research support NEUTROPHIC EFFECT OF CULTURED NEOCORTICAL CEREBELLAR CELLS ON THALAMIC NEURON
S07RR-05664-24 0870 (NSS) NADEAU, LISA Biomedical research support HYPERINSULINEMIA ON SYMPATHETIC NERVOUS SYSTEM VIA ALPHA & BETA BLOCKAGE
S07RR-05664-24 0871 (NSS) NAIDU, SRILATA Biomedical research support FUNCTIONAL HETEROGENEITY OF SIGMA RECEPTORS
S07RR-05664-24 0872 (NSS) PAQUETTE, EDMOND Biomedical research support SELF MANAGEMENT IN CHILDREN W/ INSULIN DEPENDENT DIABETES MELLITUS
S07RR-05664-24 0873 (NSS) RESNICK, STACI Biomedical research support HOME OBSERVATIONS OF MOTHER INFANT INTERACTION
S07RR-05664-24 0874 (NSS) ROSSI, HUMBERTO Biomedical research support IDIOTY & ANTIGEN BINDING PROPERTIES OF POLYCLONAL S JAPONICUM ANTIBODIES

PROJECT NO., ORGANIZATIONAL UNIT., INVESTIGATOR, ADDRESS, TITLE

S07RR-05664-24 0875 (NSS) SRIVASTAVA, RACHANA Biomedical research support NMDA RECEPTOR DEVELOPMENT IN CEREBRAL CORTEX
S07RR-05664-24 0876 (NSS) SWARTZ, SHARON Biomedical research support WING SKELETON OF CHIROPTERA
S07RR-05664-24 0856 (NSS) ALLARD, ELIZABETH Biomedical research support CHARACTERIZE MECHANISMS OF PREFERENTIAL CD8 TCELL PROLIFERATION; VIRAL INFECTION
S07RR-05664-24 0857 (NSS) CANCRO, CAROL Biomedical research support RECOVERY OF GAP CROSS LEARNING IN PREVIOUSLY LESIONED RATS
S07RR-05664-24 0858 (NSS) EVANS, DAVID Biomedical research support NEWBORN CRY ANALYSIS AS INDICATOR OF INFANT DEVELOPMENT PATTERNS
S07RR-05664-24 0859 (NSS) FLANAGAN, KATE Biomedical research support THE ROLE OF ANION TRANSPORTER IN CELL VOLUME REGULATION
S07RR-05664-24 0860 (NSS) FREEDMAN, ELIZABETH Biomedical research support ACCURACY OF SYMPTOM SELF PERCEPTION IN PEDIATRIC ASTHMA
S07RR-05664-24 0861 (NSS) FAUSTO-STERLING, ANN Biomedical research support NEW LOOK AT PLANARIUM DEVELOPMENT
S07RR-05664-24 0862 (NSS) GOSLOW, GEORGE E Biomedical research support NEURAL CONTROL OF FLIGHT
S07RR-05664-24 0863 (NSS) HAWROT, EDWARD Biomedical research support ACETYLCHOLINE RECEPTOR LIGAND BINDING SITE; BINDING DOMAIN PEPTIDE FRAGMENTS
S07RR-05664-24 0864 (NSS) HSU, KATHERINE Biomedical research support EFFECTS OF CHRONIC LIGAND APPLICATION UPON SENSITIVITY OF ACH SYSTEMS
S07RR-05664-24 0877 (NSS) TANG, WAI-HONG WILSO Biomedical research support GLUTAMATE EXCITOTOXITY IN CORTICAL GABAERGIC & GLUTAMINERGIC SYSTEMS IN VITRO
S07RR-05665-24 (NSS) BURROW, GERARD N UNIV OF CA SAN DIEGO SCH OF MEDICINE, -0602 LA JOLLA, CA 92093 Biomedical research support
S07RR-05665-24 0896 (NSS) DOBKE, MAREK K Biomedical research support IMMUNOLOCALIZ TGF & TGF BETA GROWTH FACTORS IN MOSAIC AUTO & ALLOGENE SKIN GRAFT
S07RR-05665-24 0897 (NSS) MEINKOTH, JUDY L Biomedical research support MOLECULAR COMPONENTS OF GROWTH SIGNALLING PATHWAYS IN THYROID CELLS
S07RR-05665-24 0878 (NSS) SPRINGER, WAYNE R Biomedical research support IMMUNOHISTOCHEMICAL LOCALIZATION OF CELL ADHESION MOLECULE
S07RR-05665-24 0879 (NSS) ROTHMAN, ABRAHAM Biomedical research support GROWTH RELATED GENES IN PULMONARY ARTERIAL SMOOTH MUSCLE CELL GROWTH
S07RR-05665-24 0880 (NSS) BRALY, PATRICIA S Biomedical research support STRUCTURE & FUNCTION OF HUMAN RETINOBLASTOMA GENE IN HUMAN OVARIAN CANCER
S07RR-05665-24 0881 (NSS) PENN, NOLAN E Biomedical research support POLICE PERCEPTIONS
S07RR-05665-24 0882 (NSS) SWENSON, MICHAEL R Biomedical research support COMPUTER MODELING OF NERVE ACTION POTENTIAL WAVEFORM DISPERSION
S07RR-05665-24 0883 (NSS) RUSSELL, PERCY J Biomedical research support KINETICS OF CONFORMATIONAL CHANGES OF ADENYLATE KINASE
S07RR-05665-24 0884 (NSS) TRAYNOR-KAPLAN, ALEX Biomedical research support NOVEL PHOSPHOINOSITIDES IN COLONIC EPITHELIA
S07RR-05665-24 0885 (NSS) FRONEK, ZDENKA Biomedical research support IMMUNOGENETIC BASIS OF ASSOCIATION OF IBD & ARTHRITIS
S07RR-05665-24 0886 (NSS) MACKERSIE, ROBERT C Biomedical research support LUNG INFLAMMATION FOLLOWING HEMORRHAGIC SHOCK & TRAUMA
S07RR-05665-24 0887 (NSS) FIRESTEIN, GARY S Biomedical research support CYTOKINES IN CHRONIC INFLAMMATORY ARTHRITIS
S07RR-05665-24 0888 (NSS) MORZYCHA-WROBLEWSKA, Biomedical research support MOLECULAR MECHANISM OF IMMUNOGLOBULIN ISOTYPE SWITCHING
S07RR-05665-24 0889 (NSS) HAAS, MARTIN Biomedical research support ISOLATION OF LYMPHOMA GROWTH FACTOR
S07RR-05665-24 0890 (NSS) SHABETAI, RALPH Biomedical research support COMPUTER TECHNIQUES FOR QUANTITATIVE CORONARY ANGIOGRAPH; ISCHEMIC HEART DISEASE
S07RR-05665-24 0891 (NSS) FEIGAL, DAVID Biomedical research support COMMUNITY PROGRAMS FOR RESEARCH ON AIDS; EPIDEMIOLOGY; STATISTICAL ANALYSIS
S07RR-05665-24 0892 (NSS) RAMSDELL, JOE Biomedical research support EVALUATING HOME ENVIRONMENT OF ALZHEIMERS PATIENT
S07RR-05665-24 0893 (NSS) MACLEOD, CAROL L Biomedical research support ISOLATION OF HUMAN LOV CDNA CLONE
S07RR-05665-24 0894 (NSS) SCHRIER, RACHEL D Biomedical research support T CELL INDUCED EXPRESSION OF HIV IN MACROPHAGES
S07RR-05665-24 0895 (NSS) KELSOE, JOHN R Biomedical research support GENETIC LINKAGE STUDIES OF AFFECTIVE DISORDER IN AMISH
S07RR-05673-22 (NSS) KAHN, C RONALD JOSLIN DIABETES CENTER ONE JOSLIN PLACE BOSTON, MASS 02215 Biomedical research support
S07RR-05674-23 (NSS) BANERJEE, AMIYA K CLEVELAND CLINIC HOSPITAL 9500 EUCLID AVENUE CLEVELAND, OH 44195 Biomedical research support
S07RR-05674-23 0931 (NSS) BANERJEE, AMIYA K Biomedical research support NO SUBPROJECTS
S07RR-05675-23 (NSS) DALEN, JAMES P UNIVERSITY OF ARIZONA 1501 N CAMPBELL AVE TUCSON, AZ 85724 Biomedical research support
S07RR-05675-23 0924 (NSS) WITTEN, MARK L Biomedical research support EFFECTS OF SIDESTREAM CIGARETTE SMOKE EXPOSURE ON LUNG
S07RR-05675-23 0925 (NSS) YOHEM, KARIN H Biomedical research support HUMAN TUMOR CELL INTRACELLULAR CALCIUM LEVELS VS INVASIVE METASTATIC PROPERTIES
S07RR-05675-23 0926 (NSS) BARBEE, ROBERT A Biomedical research support EFFECT OF PREGNANCY ON MATERNAL COCCIDIOIDOMYCOSIS IMMUNE STATUS
S07RR-05675-23 0927 (NSS) BERG, ROBERT A Biomedical research support CONTINUOUS INTRAVENOUS DOBUTAMINE INFUSIONS IN CHILDREN
S07RR-05675-23 0928 (NSS) BERNSTEIN, CAROL Biomedical research support BILE ACIDS, DIETARY FIBER & DNA DAMAGE: CONTROL OF COLON CANCER
S07RR-05675-23 0929 (NSS) BEUCHAT, CAROL A Biomedical research support URINE CONCENTRATING ABILITY OF KIDNEY
S07RR-05675-23 0930 (NSS) CAMPOS-OUTCALT, MD Biomedical research support LACK OF PRENATAL CARE IN METROPOLITAN ARIZONA

PROJECT NO., ORGANIZATIONAL UNIT., INVESTIGATOR, ADDRESS, TITLE

S07RR-05675-23 0931 (NSS) FEINBERG, WILLIAM M Biomedical research support EFFECT OF ORAL NIMODIPINE ON PLATELET FUNCTION
S07RR-05675-23 0932 (NSS) HOYER, PATRICIA Biomedical research support INTRACELLULAR CALCIUM IN REGULATING LUTEAL FUNCTION
S07RR-05675-23 0933 (NSS) KUHL, STEVE A Biomedical research support GENETIC & MOLECULAR CHARACTERIZATION RECA GENE FROM BORDETELLA PERTUSSIS
S07RR-05675-23 0934 (NSS) MOORADIAN, ARSHAG D Biomedical research support EFFECT OF AGING ON TISSUE SPECIFIC GENE EXPRESSION
S07RR-05675-23 0935 (NSS) PHILIPPS, ANTHONY F Biomedical research support METABOLIC & GROWTH EFFECTS OF FETAL INSULIN DEFICIENCY
S07RR-05675-23 0898 (NSS) BEUCHAT, CAROL P Biomedical research support WATER & ION BALANCE IN HUMMINGBIRDS
S07RR-05675-23 0899 (NSS) BURD, GAIL D Biomedical research support DVMT EXPRESSION OF MRNA FOR THYROXINE RECEPTOR; OLFACTORY SYSTEM OF XENOPUS
S07RR-05675-23 0900 (NSS) CANFIELD, LOUISE M Biomedical research support RESEARCH ON B CAROTENE ABSORPTION & METABOLISM
S07RR-05675-23 0901 (NSS) CASSIDY, SUZANNE B Biomedical research support EVALUATION OF SLEEP DISORDERS IN PRADER WILLI SYNDROME
S07RR-05675-23 0902 (NSS) HUTTER, JOHN J Biomedical research support ISOLATION & CHARACTERIZATION OF NEWBORNS PLASMINOGEN
S07RR-05675-23 0903 (NSS) EY, JOHN L Biomedical research support CAUSES OF CHRONIC RECURRENT OTITIS MEDIA IN CHILDHOOD
S07RR-05675-23 0904 (NSS) FENNERTY, BRIAN Biomedical research support CHARACTERIZATION OF PREMALIGNANT LESIONS OF STOMACH
S07RR-05675-23 0905 (NSS) GLASSER, LEWIS Biomedical research support MODEL FOR ID & CHARACTERIZATION OF HUMAN HEMATOPOIETIC PLURIPOTENTIAL STEM CELL
S07RR-05675-23 0906 (NSS) GRAD, RONI Biomedical research support INTERACTIONS AMONG MACROPHAGES, INFLAMMATORY STIMULI & DEVELOPING FETAL LUNG
S07RR-05675-23 0907 (NSS) GREENE, HARRY L Biomedical research support OBSERVATIONAL STUDY OF ATTENDING ROUNDS
S07RR-05675-23 0908 (NSS) GRUENER, RAPHAEL Biomedical research support MEMBRANE LIPIDS IN NEURONAL ION CHANNEL INTERACTIONS W/ GENERAL ANESTHETICS
S07RR-05675-23 0909 (NSS) HIXON, LEE J Biomedical research support ASPIRIN & OLSALAZINE SODIUM TO INHIBIT FORMATION OF COLONIC NEOPLASMS IN RAT
S07RR-05675-23 0910 (NSS) JOHNSON, MARY P Biomedical research support ALCOHOL & NERVOUS SYSTEM: IN VITRO
S07RR-05675-23 0911 (NSS) KOLDOVSKY, OTAKAR Biomedical research support FEEDING RAT MILK SUBSTITUTE TO SUCKLING RATS W/ AUTOMATIC MECHANICAL DEVICE
S07RR-05675-23 0912 (NSS) KOSS, MARY P Biomedical research support COGNITIVE PROCESSING OF TRAUMATIC SEXUAL VICTIMIZATION
S07RR-05675-23 0913 (NSS) LAI, JOSEPHINE Biomedical research support STRUCT DOMAIN DELINEATIONS; LIGAND SPECIFICITY & MUSCARINIC RECEPTORS COUPLING
S07RR-05675-23 0914 (NSS) LARSON, DOUGLAS F Biomedical research support EFFECT OF ISCHEMIC INJURY ON CLASS I & II MHC ANTIGEN EXPRESSION
S07RR-05675-23 0915 (NSS) MCMULLEN, NATANIEL T Biomedical research support AFFERENT REGULATION OF DENDRITIC GROWTH IN AUDITORY NEOCORTEX
S07RR-05675-23 0916 (NSS) PHILIPPS, ANTHONY F Biomedical research support SYNTH INSULIN LINE GROWTH FACTOR 1 & 2; EXTRACTION & PROBING OF IGF SPECIFIC
S07RR-05675-23 0917 (NSS) RANGE, NAOMI E Biomedical research support DVMT ANIMAL MODEL FOR POST MENOPAUSE NEURONAL HYPERTROPHY
S07RR-05675-23 0918 (NSS) RYKOWSKI, MARY C Biomedical research support EUKARYOTIC CHROMOSOME STRUCTURE IN 3 DIMENSIONS
S07RR-05675-23 0919 (NSS) SCHUMACHER, MICHAEL Biomedical research support IMMUNOTHERAPY OF AFRICANIZED BEE STINGS
S07RR-05675-23 0920 (NSS) SELL, ELSA J Biomedical research support COMPLETE PREPARATION OF AUDIOVISUAL TEACHING FOR PARENTS OF NICU INFANTS
S07RR-05675-23 0921 (NSS) SPEER, DONALD P Biomedical research support PREP ALLOGRAFT MATRIX; REPOPULATION W/ AUTOGENOUS ARTICULAR CHRONDROCYTES
S07RR-05675-23 0922 (NSS) ST JOHN, PAUL A Biomedical research support GLYCINE RECEPTORS ON MOTONEURONS DEVELOPING IN VITRO
S07RR-05675-23 0923 (NSS) WILSON, JEAN M Biomedical research support MOLECULAR STRUCTURE OF ENDOSOMES IN DEVELOPING
S07RR-05675-23 0936 (NSS) RAYA, THOMAS E Biomedical research support CAPTOPRIL PRE TREAT HEMODYNAMIC RESPONSIV TO ARTRIAL NATRIERETIC PEPTIDE; RAT
S07RR-05675-23 0937 (NSS) REED, RICHARD Biomedical research support PREDICTORS OF SIGNIFICANT FALLS IN ELDERLY
S07RR-05675-23 0938 (NSS) WHITFIELD, G KERR Biomedical research support PHOSPHORYLATION OF VITAMIN D RECEPTOR
S07RR-05675-23 0939 (NSS) FRENCH, EDARD D Biomedical research support NEUROBIOLOGY OF PHENCYCLIDINE PHARMACOLOGY
S07RR-05675-23 0940 (NSS) AHERN, GEOFFREY L Biomedical research support NON CONSCIOUS AUTONOMIC MEMORY IN ALZHEIMERS DISEASE
S07RR-05675-23 0941 (NSS) HARRIS, DAVID T Biomedical research support COMPARATIVE & EVOLUTIONARY ANALYSIS OF NATURAL KILLER CELL ANTIGEN RECEPTOR
S07RR-05675-23 0942 (NSS) LYNCH, RONALD M Biomedical research support HEXOKINASE & GLUCOKINASE; MODULATING CELL EXCITABILITY; INSULIN SECRETING CELLS
S07RR-05675-23 0943 (NSS) NEUMAYER, LEIGH A Biomedical research support BIOCHEMICAL EFFECTS; MITOGEN STIMULATION; NORMAL & NEOPLASTIC BREAST TISSUE
S07RR-05675-23 0944 (NSS) PIETRANTONI, MARCELL Biomedical research support FREE RADICAL TERATOGENICITY IN PHENYTOIN TREATED MICE
S07RR-05675-23 0945 (NSS) SEFTOR, RICHARD E B Biomedical research support VITRONECTIN RECEPTOR IN HUMAN MELANOMA TUMOR CELL INVASION
S07RR-05675-23 0946 (NSS) BLOOM, JOHN W Biomedical research support CHRONIC BRONCHODILATOR THERAPY ON AIRWAY SMOOTH MUSCLE
S07RR-05675-23 0947 (NSS) PAYNE, CLAIRE M Biomedical research support UBIQUITIN IN PROTEIN DEGRADATION DURING " PROGRAMMED CELL DEATH" IN VITRO

S07RR-05675-23 0948 (NSS) SPIER, CATHERINE Biomedical research support EVALUATION OF BIOLOGIC EFFECTS OF SYSTEMIC TREATMENT
S07RR-05676-15 (NSS) BENNETT, L LEE, JR SOUTHERN RESEARCH INSTITUTE 2000 9TH AVE S PO BOX 55305 BIRMINGHAM, AL 35255-5305 Biomedical research support
S07RR-05676-15 0949 (NSS) SINGH, RAJ K Biomedical research support SELECTIVE ADENOSINE RECEPTOR ANTAGONISTS
S07RR-05676-15 0950 (NSS) DECKARD, LINDSAY A Biomedical research support MICROBIAL DETECTION OF ENVIRONMENTAL CONTAMINANTS
S07RR-05676-15 0951 (NSS) SIMPSON-HERREN, LIND Biomedical research support INTRATUMOR DRUG DISTRIBUTION VS CONCENTRATION TO TUMOR RESPONSE CHEMOTHERAPY
S07RR-05676-15 0952 (NSS) ALLEN, LOIS B Biomedical research support MOUSE MODEL FOR HUMAN CYTOMEGALOVIRUS
S07RR-05676-15 0953 (NSS) BUCKHEIT, ROBERT W J Biomedical research support VIRAL & CELLULAR FACTORS INFLUENCING HIV CYTOPATHOLOGY
S07RR-05676-15 0954 (NSS) SULING, WILLIAM J Biomedical research support MECHANISMS OF INHIBITION OF DNA REPAIR BY NITROSOUREAS; ANTI CANCER AGENT
S07RR-05676-15 0955 (NSS) ROGERS, TINA S Biomedical research support EFFECTS OF NUCLEOSIDE ANALOGS ON PROTEIN KINASE & INOSITOL PHOSPHATES
S07RR-05676-15 0956 (NSS) SANI, BRAHMA P Biomedical research support RETINOID BINDING PROTEINS IN ALCOHOL CONSUMPTION
S07RR-05676-15 0957 (NSS) CHOWDHURY, ANISUZZAM Biomedical research support CARCINOGEN INDUCED NEOPLASTIC TRANSFORMATION OF PROSTATE EPITHELIAL CELLS
S07RR-05676-15 0958 (NSS) WAUD, WILLIAM Biomedical research support DNA TOPOISOMERASE II IN RESISTANCE TO CIS PLATIN; ANTI CANCER DRUG RESISTANCE
S07RR-05676-15 0959 (NSS) VASANTHAKUMAR, GEETH Biomedical research support HYPOXANTHINE PHOSPHORIBOSYL TRANSFERASE; ENZYME TO TREAT TOXOPLASMOSI; AIDS
S07RR-05676-15 0960 (NSS) VASANTHAKUMAR, GEETH Biomedical research support ANTITUMOR AGENTS AS INHIBITORS OF RAS & MYC ONCOGENES
S07RR-05676-15 0961 (NSS) SINGH, RAJ K Biomedical research support REGULATION OF GENE EXPRESSION BY NUCLEAR RETINOID RECEPTORS; ONCOGENES
S07RR-05676-15 0962 (NSS) KLINGER, MARTIN J Biomedical research support POLYCLONAL ANTIBODIES SPECIFIC FOR GLUCOSYL B1 3 FUCOSE
S07RR-05676-15 0963 (NSS) VASANTHAKUMAR, GEETH Biomedical research support MOLECULAR MECHANISMS OF DRUG RESISTANCE IN HUMAN LEUKEMIC CELLS
S07RR-05676-15 0964 (NSS) WILKOFF, LEE J Biomedical research support LIPOSOME MEDIATED DELIVERY OF ANTISENSE OLIGONUCLEOTIDES; KB CELLS CANCER
S07RR-05676-15 0965 (NSS) SCHMID, STEVEN M Biomedical research support INTERFERONS & BCNU & NITROSOUREAS OR CIS PLATINUM; HUMAN MURINE TUMOR CELLS
S07RR-05676-15 0966 (NSS) TEMPLE, CARROLL G Biomedical research support SYNTHESIS OF COVALENT NUCLEOTIDE CO FACTOR ADDUCT
S07RR-05676-15 0967 (NSS) ELLIOTT, ROBERT D Biomedical research support SYNTHESIS OF FOUR CANDIDATE ANTHELMINTIC AGENTS
S07RR-05676-15 0968 (NSS) ANATHAN, SUBRAMANIAM Biomedical research support SYNTHESIS OF CANDIDATE ANTI HIV AGENTS: DIDEOXYNUCLEOTIDES
S07RR-05676-15 0969 (NSS) ANANTHAN, SUBRAMANIA Biomedical research support ANALOGS OF ACYCLOVIR & DHPG; ANTI HERPES AGENTS
S07RR-05676-15 0970 (NSS) COMBER, ROBERT W Biomedical research support POTENTIAL ORAL HYPOGLYCEMIC COMPOUNDS: CARNITINE ANALOGS; DIABETES
S07RR-05677-23 (NSS) KENNEDY, JAMES E UNIV OF CONNECTICUT HLTH CTR 263 FARMINGTON AVE FARMINGTON, CONN 06032 Biomedical research support
S07RR-05677-23 0971 (NSS) HELFAND, STEPHEN Biomedical research support OLFACTION IN DROSOPHILA MELANOGASTER
S07RR-05677-23 0972 (NSS) WENDT, STANLEY Biomedical research support CLINICAL EVALUATION OF HEAT CURED COMPOSITE RESIN INLAY
S07RR-05677-23 0973 (NSS) ALTIERI, JAMES Biomedical research support FIBER REINFORCED COMPOSITE BRIDGES
S07RR-05677-23 0974 (NSS) NIEKRASH, CHRISTINE Biomedical research support NON INVASIVE ASSESSMENT OF PERIODONTAL DISEASE ACTIVITY
S07RR-05677-23 0975 (NSS) LITT, MARK Biomedical research support BEHAVIORIAL ASPECTS WHEN PREPARING FOR ORAL SURGERY
S07RR-05678-23 (NSS) SIGMAN, EUGENE M UNIV OF CONNECTICUT HLTH CTR 263 FARMINGTON AVENUE FARMINGTON, CONN 06032 Biomedical research support
S07RR-05678-23 0155 (NSS) GOLDSCHNEINER, IRVIN Biomedical research support DVMT IMMUNOLOGY COMPETENT LYMPHOCYTES
S07RR-05678-23 0156 (NSS) STRITTMATER, PHILIP Biomedical research support STRUCTURE FUNCTION STUDIES ON MICROSOMAL MEMBRANES
S07RR-05678-23 0157 (NSS) OCONNOR, SEAN Biomedical research support CORTICAL MEASURES OF RABBITS RESPONSE TO COCAINE
S07RR-05678-23 0158 (NSS) NOWAK, MICHAEL Biomedical research support WRIST BIOMECHANICS & 2 D COMPUTER MODELING
S07RR-05678-23 0159 (NSS) PILBEAM, CAROL Biomedical research support INTERACTION OF PTH & ESTROGEN IN OSTEOPOROSIS
S07RR-05678-23 0160 (NSS) DOLINSKY, ZELIG Biomedical research support NEUROENDOCRINE FACTORS IN CONTROL OF ALCOHOLIC BEHAVIOR
S07RR-05678-23 0161 (NSS) KREUTZER, DONALD Biomedical research support RESPONSE OF PULMONARY ENDOTHELIUM TO INJURY
S07RR-05678-23 0162 (NSS) ROTHFIELD, NAOMI Biomedical research support AUTOANTIBODIES IN SCLERODERMA
S07RR-05678-23 0163 (NSS) BARBARESE, ELISE Biomedical research support OLIGODENDROCYTE ONTOGENY & DIFFERENTIATION
S07RR-05678-23 0164 (NSS) HURLEY, MARJA Biomedical research support PATHOGENESIS & PREVENTION OF OSTEOPOROSIS
S07RR-05678-23 0165 (NSS) GRONOWITZ, GLORIA Biomedical research support EXTRACELLULAR MATRIX PROTEINS IN CELL CULTURE
S07RR-05678-23 0166 (NSS) FRESTON, JAMES Biomedical research support OVERVIEW OF MEDICAL THERAPY OF PEPTIC ULCER DISEASE
S07RR-05680-23 (NSS) EVARTS, C MC COLLISTER MILTON S HERSHEY MEDICAL CTR P O BOX 850 HERSHEY, PA 17033 Biomedical research support
S07RR-05680-23 0903 (NSS) LYDIC, RALPH Biomedical research support PONTINE CHOLINERGIC RETICULAR CAUSES CHANGES IN RESPIRATORY: SIDS, ANESTHESIA
S07RR-05680-23 0904 (NSS) HOUTS, PETER S Biomedical research support PSYCHOSOCIAL IMPACT OF CANCER ON PATIENTS AND THEIR FAMILIES
S07RR-05680-23 0905 (NSS) HUFFORD, DAVID J Biomedical research support CULTURE VARIATIONS IN U S HEALING PRACTICES
S07RR-05680-23 0906 (NSS) JONES, MARSHALL B Biomedical research support COMPUTER SUPPORT FOR PERFORMANCE TEST WORK
S07RR-05680-23 0907 (NSS) NORGREN, RALPH Biomedical research support GUSTATORY AND INGESTIVE NEURAL SYSTEMS IN RATS AND MONKEYS
S07RR-05680-23 0908 (NSS) BHAVANANDAN, VEER P Biomedical research support STUDIES ON EPITECTIN AND RELATED GLYCOPROTEINS
S07RR-05680-23 0909 (NSS) JEFFERSON, LEONARD S Biomedical research support HORMONE & NUTRIENT ACTION ON GENE EXPRESSION IN RAT LIVER DIABETES
S07RR-05680-23 0910 (NSS) WOOLLEY, DOUGLAS C Biomedical research support HEALTH CARE GIVEN TO NON SHIFT & SHIFT WORKER BY FAMILY PHYSICIANS
S07RR-05680-23 0911 (NSS) HEITJAN, DANIEL F Biomedical research support IN VIVO TUMOR GROWTH DATA ANALYSIS GOMPERTZIAN & NON LINEAR MODEL
S07RR-05680-23 0912 (NSS) MCGARRITY, THOMAS J Biomedical research support MUCOSAL POLYAMINES FOR EARLY DETECT OF COLORECTAL CANCER & PREMALIGNANT POLYPS
S07RR-05680-23 0913 (NSS) SINOWAY, LAWRENCE C Biomedical research support BLOOD PRESSURE CONTROL: DICHLOROACETATE
S07RR-05680-23 0914 (NSS) SMITH, BRENDA C Biomedical research support NUCLEAR CALCIUM GRADIENTS ON HEPATOCYTE PROLIFERATION
S07RR-05680-23 0915 (NSS) SWEER, LEON S Biomedical research support VENTILATORY AFTER DISCHARGE IN NORMAL MAN DURING SLEEP AND WAKEFULNESS
S07RR-05680-23 0916 (NSS) TENSER, RICHARD B Biomedical research support LATENT HERPES SIMPLEX VIRUS INFECTION OF NON NEURONAL NEURAL CELLS
S07RR-05680-23 0917 (NSS) CHORNEY, MICHAEL Biomedical research support FUNCTIONAL STUDIES ON THE THYMUS LEUKEMIA ANTIGEN
S07RR-05680-23 0918 (NSS) FLYER, DAVID Biomedical research support IMMUNE RECOGNITION OF MURINE LEUKEMIA VIRUSES: HISTOCOMPATIBILITY ANTIGENS
S07RR-05680-23 0919 (NSS) WHITFIELD, CAROL Biomedical research support DEFICIENCY OF SPECTRIN SYNTHESIS IN BRU ES IN LETHAL HEREDITARY SPHEROCYTOSIS
S07RR-05680-23 0920 (NSS) ALLOWAY, KEVIN Biomedical research support THALAMOCORTICAL INTERACTIONS IN SOMATOSENSORY SYSTEM
S07RR-05680-23 0921 (NSS) DODSON, WILLIAM C Biomedical research support IS QUALITY OF SERUM SUPPLEMENTS FOR MOUSE IVF AFFECTED BY MENSTRUAL CYCLE
S07RR-05680-23 0922 (NSS) FRAUENHOFFER, ELIZAB Biomedical research support CHARACTER OF BONE RESORPTION AROUND LOOSENED JOINT PROSTHESES
S07RR-05680-23 0923 (NSS) VESELL, ELLIOT S Biomedical research support PYRAZINOYLGUANIDINE (PZG) ON HYDROCHLOROTHIAZIDE INDUCED RENIN RELEASE
S07RR-05680-23 0924 (NSS) LUCKING, STEVEN E Biomedical research support CEREBRAL BLOOD FLOW IN EXPERIMENTAL MENINGITIS
S07RR-05680-23 0925 (NSS) PALMER, CHARLES Biomedical research support REGULATION OF PERINATAL BRAIN DAMAGE W/ AFTER HYPOXIC ISCHEMIC INJURY
S07RR-05680-23 0926 (NSS) GIFFORD, ROBERT R Biomedical research support CYCLOSPORINE MODULATION OF ARTERIAL SMOOTH MUSCLE CELL: WALL INJURY
S07RR-05684-23 (NSS) WILLIAMS, HIBBARD E UNIVERSITY OF CALIFORNIA SCHOOL OF MEDICINE DAVIS, CALIF 95616 Biomedical research support
S07RR-05684-23 0167 (NSS) GUMERLOCK, PAUL Biomedical research support ANTI SENSE GENE THERAPY FOR CANCER
S07RR-05684-23 0168 (NSS) HALPERN, GEORGES Biomedical research support CLONING ALLERGENS IN PATIENTS W/ MOLD SENSITIVITY
S07RR-05684-23 0170 (NSS) JOAD, JESSE Biomedical research support SIDESTREAM SMOKE EFFECTS ON IMMATURE ADENOSINE AIRWAY RECEPTORS
S07RR-05684-23 0171 (NSS) LEUNG, PATRICK Biomedical research support HEAT SHOCK PROTEINS & TUMOR DIFFERENTIATION
S07RR-05684-23 0172 (NSS) BONHAM, ANN Biomedical research support VASOPRESSIN MODULATION OF AFFERENT PROCESSING IN NUCLEAR TRACTUS SOLITARIUS
S07RR-05684-23 0173 (NSS) PARRISH, MARK Biomedical research support MATURATION OF EXERCISE PRESSOR REFLEX
S07RR-05684-23 0174 (NSS) SHEIKH, AZAD Biomedical research support INTRAOSSEOUS FLUID RESUSCITATION; PEDIATRIC ANIMAL MODEL OF HEMORRHAGIC SHOCK
S07RR-05684-23 0175 (NSS) ROBBINS, DICK Biomedical research support IMPROVED DIAGNOSIS & MONITORING OF PATIENTS W/ TEMPORAL ARTERITIS
S07RR-05684-23 0176 (NSS) CARTER, CAMERON Biomedical research support EFFECTS OF CAFFEINE ON ATTENTION TO THREAT RELATED STIMULI
S07RR-05684-23 0177 (NSS) FLEMING, NEIL Biomedical research support CALCITONIN GENE RELATED PEPTIDE EFFECTS ON PERFUSED RAT HEMI DIAPHRAGM
S07RR-05684-23 0169 (NSS) KELLERMAN, PAUL Biomedical research support MICROFILAMENTS IN ISCHEMIC RENAL CELL INJURY
S07RR-05684-23 0178 (NSS) MAURO, THEODORA Biomedical research support MODULATING MEMBRANE CURRENTS EFFECTS ON KERATINOCYTE GROWTH & DIFFERENTIATION
S07RR-05684-23 0179 (NSS) SMITH, LLOYD Biomedical research support HUMORAL IMMUNITY TO HUMAN PAPILLOMAVIRUS; RECOMBINANT FUSION PROTEINS
S07RR-05686-11 (NSS) ABDEL-MONEM, MAHMOUD M WASHINGTON STATE UNIVERSITY COLLEGE OF PHARMACY PULLMAN, WASH 99164 Biomedical research support grant
S07RR-05686-11 0976 (NSS) WHITE, JOHN R Biomedical research support grant DRUG CONCENTRATION MEASUREMENT BY IMMUNOASSAY
S07RR-05686-11 0977 (NSS) KINDER, DAVID H Biomedical research support grant SYNTHESIS OF GLUTATHIONE S TRANSFERASE INHIBITORS; RESISTANCE IN CANCER CELLS
S07RR-05686-11 0978 (NSS) HU, MING Biomedical research support grant TRANSCELLULAR TRANSPORT MECHANISM OF NUCLEOSIDE LIKE DRUGS; AZT AIDS
S07RR-05686-11 0979 (NSS) SYLVESTER, PAUL W Biomedical research support grant MEMBRANE LIPID MODULATION OF SECOND MESSENGER SIGNAL

PROJECT NO., ORGANIZATIONAL UNIT., INVESTIGATOR, ADDRESS, TITLE

TRANSUCTION; TUMOR THERAPY
S07RR-05686-11 0980 (NSS) KINDER, DAVID H Biomedical research support grant BORO PYRIMIDINE ANTIMETABOLITE ANTICANCER AGENCY; HUMAN CELLS
S07RR-05686-11 0981 (NSS) GARRISON, MARK W Biomedical research support grant IN VITRO PHARMACODYNAMIC MODELING; DETERM BACTERIAL SENSITIVITIES TO ANTIBIOTICS
S07RR-05688-23 (NSS) ADAMSON, JOHN W NEW YORK BLOOD CENTER 310 EAST 67TH STREET NEW YORK, N Y 10021 Biomedical research support
S07RR-05688-23 0597 (NSS) GERD, GRIENINGER Biomedical research support EXTENDED FIBRINOGEN GENE FAMILY
S07RR-05689-23 (NSS) VERRUSIO, A CARL AMERICAN DENTAL ASSC HLTH FDN 211 EAST CHICAGO AVENUE CHICAGO, ILL 60611 Biomedical research support
S07RR-05689-23 0851 (NSS) CHOW, LAWRENCE C Biomedical research support TETRACALCIUM PUTTY FOR RIDGE AUGMENTATION
S07RR-05689-23 0852 (NSS) VARDIMON, A D Biomedical research support MAGNETIC FORCES IN ORTHODONTIC THERAPY
S07RR-05689-23 0853 (NSS) SIEW, CHAKWAN Biomedical research support NADT SERUM HEPATITIS
S07RR-05689-23 0854 (NSS) MEULLER, HERBERT Biomedical research support TEMP & PHASE IN AMALGAM
S07RR-05689-23 0855 (NSS) SIEW, CHAKWAN Biomedical research support GENOTOXICITY OF OXYGEN RADICALS
S07RR-05692-22 (NSS) NADEL, ETHAN R JOHN B PIERCE FOUNDATION, INC 290 CONGRESS AVENUE NEW HAVEN, CONN 06519 Biomedical research support
S07RR-05692-22 0988 (NSS) MOHSENIN, V Biomedical research support ULTRA LOW TEMPERATURE FREEZER TO BE USED BY PULMONARY & CELL BIOLOGY GROUP
S07RR-05692-22 0989 (NSS) RITCHIE, B Biomedical research support CONSTRUCT FARADAY CAGE; FOR ARTIFACT FREE RECORD OF NERVOUS SYSTEM ACTIVITIES
S07RR-05692-22 0990 (NSS) ADAIR, E Biomedical research support ANIMAL CAGING; PRIMATE FACILITY; MICROWAVE & THERMAL RESPONSE STUDIES
S07RR-05692-22 0991 (NSS) MACK, G Biomedical research support FINAPRES BLOOD PRESSURE MONITOR TO RAPIDLY TRACK BLOOD PRESSURE; COMPUTER
S07RR-05692-22 0992 (NSS) DOUGLAS, J Biomedical research support MODEL 3000XI POWER SUPPLY TO SEPARATE PROTEIN: IMMUNOCHEMICAL ANALYSIS
S07RR-05692-22 0982 (NSS) SOUHRADA, M Biomedical research support VIBRATION ISOLATION TABLES; ELIMINATE VERTICAL & HORIZONTAL VIBRATIONS
S07RR-05692-22 0983 (NSS) BERGLUND, L Biomedical research support PAINT SPRAY BOOTH & ASSOCIATED VENTILATION EQUIPMENT FOR MACHINE SHOP
S07RR-05692-22 0984 (NSS) NADEL, E Biomedical research support SUMMER STUDENT; PROJECT ON FACTORS THAT INFLUENCE ALBUMIN SYNTHESIS RATES
S07RR-05692-22 0985 (NSS) DUBOIS, A Biomedical research support COLLEGE STUDENT; ASSIST RESEARCH ON BRAIN BLOOD PRESSURE RESPONSE TO HYPOXIA
S07RR-05692-22 0986 (NSS) NADEL, E Biomedical research support PARTIAL SUPPORT OF RESEARCH STAFF SALARIES NOT FUNDED FORM OTHER SOURCES
S07RR-05692-22 0987 (NSS) NADEL, E Biomedical research support ALTERATIONS & RENOVATIONS OF LABORATORY RESEARCH SPACE
S07RR-05694-22 (NSS) CRITCHLOW, B VAUGHN OREG REGIONAL PRIMATE RES CTR 505 NORTHWEST 185TH AVENUE BEAVERTON, OREG 97006 Biomedical research support
S07RR-05694-22 0856 (NSS) MALINOW, M RENE Biomedical research support DEVELOPMENT OF METHODOLOGY FOR MEASURING HOMOCYSTEINE FOR ATHEROSCLEROSIS
S07RR-05694-22 0857 (NSS) MALLEY, ARTHUR Biomedical research support I J EPITOPE ON BONE MARROW DERIVED MACROPHAGE: ANTIGEN SPECIFIC T SUPPRESSOR
S07RR-05694-22 0858 (NSS) SIMERLY, RICHARD Biomedical research support NEURO PEPTIDE GENE EXPRESSION IN HYPOTHALAMIC & LIMBIC CIRCUITRY
S07RR-05694-22 0859 (NSS) URBANSKI, HERYK Biomedical research support EXCITATORY AMINO ACIDS IN CONTROL OF GONADOTROPIN SECRETION: OVULATION, MONKEY
S07RR-05697-22 (NSS) WINDRIDGE, GRAHAM C VIRGINIA COMMONWEALTH UNIV BOX 581, MCV STATION RICHMOND, VA 23298-0581 Biomedical research support
S07RR-05697-22 0000 (NSS) MONACO, JOHN J Biomedical research support CROSS HYBRIDIZATION, MAPPING HUMAN HOMOLOGUES OF MURINE MHC GENES
S07RR-05697-22 0993 (NSS) LORIA, ROGER M Biomedical research support HOST & VIRUS INTERACTIONS & MOBILIZATION OF IMMUNE RESPONSE BY AED, AET
S07RR-05697-22 0994 (NSS) ROSENKRANTZ, MARK Biomedical research support UPSTREAM REGULATORY SEQ OF CITRATE SYNTHASE GENES CITI & CIT2 IN SACCHAROMYCES
S07RR-05697-22 0995 (NSS) CARTER, WALTER H Biomedical research support EXPERIMENTAL DESIGNS FOR FITTING LOGISTIC MODEL
S07RR-05697-22 0996 (NSS) CARTER, WALTER H Biomedical research support THERAPEUTIC SYNERGISM IN NON PARAMETIC REGRESSION MODELS
S07RR-05697-22 0997 (NSS) EVANS, HERBERT Biomedical research support DEVELOPMENT OF SYNTHETIC ANTICOAGULANT PEPTIDES
S07RR-05697-22 0998 (NSS) NEWMAN, SAMMYE Biomedical research support GENE STRUCTURE & REGULATION OF GENE EXPRESSION IN MAMMALIAN NERVOUS SYSTEM
S07RR-05697-22 0999 (NSS) CARTER, ANTHONY D Biomedical research support MULTIPLE CONTROLS & COORDINATE REGULATION OF G PROTEIN EXPRESSION
S07RR-05700-22 (NSS) STANDAERT, FRANK G MEDICAL COLLEGE OF OHIO VPAA/DEAN'S OFFICE, BOX 10008 TOLEDO, OHIO 43699 Biomedical research support
S07RR-05700-22 0872 (NSS) CRISSMAN, ROBERT S Biomedical research support COMPETITIVE INTERACTIONS BETWEEN TRIGEMINAL PRIMARY AFFERENTS
S07RR-05700-22 0873 (NSS) HAMLETT, WILLIAM C Biomedical research support EFFECTS OF TOXICANTS ON REPRODUCTIVE PROCESSES IN MARINE ORGANISMS

PROJECT NO., ORGANIZATIONAL UNIT., INVESTIGATOR, ADDRESS, TITLE

S07RR-05700-22 0874 (NSS) JACOBUS, WILLIAM E Biomedical research support CARDIAC HEXOKINASE: ALTER LOCALIZ & KINETICS INDUCED BY ISCHEMIA & REPERFUSION
S07RR-05700-22 0875 (NSS) KOECHEL, DANIEL Biomedical research support RENAL NECROSIS INDUCED BY CHEMICALS
S07RR-05700-22 0876 (NSS) LANE, RICHARD D Biomedical research support LOW DENSITY LIPOPROTEIN CHOLESTEROL ON MONOCYTE DVMT
S07RR-05700-22 0877 (NSS) APPERT, HUBERT E Biomedical research support MUTATED FORMS OF GALACTOSYLTRANSFERASE
S07RR-05700-22 0878 (NSS) DOKAS, LINDA Biomedical research support BIOCHEMICAL INTERACTIONS OF ACETYLCHOLINE & SOMATOSTATIN
S07RR-05700-22 0860 (NSS) CRUZ, JULIO C Biomedical research support INSPIRED GAS DISTRIBUTION
S07RR-05700-22 0861 (NSS) APPERT, HUBERT E Biomedical research support GALACTOSYLTRANSFERASE IN E COLI CELLS
S07RR-05700-22 0862 (NSS) MCCORQUODALE, D JAME Biomedical research support ABORTIVE INFECTION GENE OF COLI PLASMID & ITS PRODUCT
S07RR-05700-22 0863 (NSS) SAWICKI, STANLEY Biomedical research support CORONAVIRUS TRANSCRIPTION
S07RR-05700-22 0864 (NSS) CRIST, KEITH A Biomedical research support RAT MAMMARY CARCINOMA IN SITU DVMT OF NEW MODEL SYSTEM
S07RR-05700-22 0865 (NSS) DIETRICK, JOHN A Biomedical research support HYPERBARIC OXYGEN POTENTIATES; TUMORICIDAL EFFECT OF PHOTODYNAMIC THERAPY
S07RR-05700-22 0866 (NSS) SZWAJKUN, KONSTANTYN Biomedical research support LEUKOTRIENES & PROSTAGLANDINS; CONSTRICT OF CORONARY ARTERIES TO THROMBOXANE
S07RR-05700-22 0867 (NSS) TIETZ, ELIZABETH Biomedical research support BENZODIAZEPINE TOLERANCE IN KINDLED RATS
S07RR-05700-22 0868 (NSS) YOU, MING Biomedical research support MUTATION IN MOUSE K RAS GENE W/ OUT PHENOTYPIC SELECTION
S07RR-05700-22 0879 (NSS) FAULMAN, ERVIN L W J Biomedical research support SEQ B ANTIGEN OF GROUP B STREPTOCOCCI
S07RR-05700-22 0880 (NSS) LEHMANN, PAUL Biomedical research support PLASMIN RECEPTORS OF CANDIDA & OTHER FUNGI
S07RR-05700-22 0881 (NSS) TIETZ, ELIZABETH Biomedical research support CHRONIC BENZODIAZEPINE EFFECTS ON GABA RECEPTOR COMPLEX
S07RR-05700-22 0882 (NSS) HEGAZY, MOHAMMED Biomedical research support BIOCHEMICAL & IMMUNOLOGICAL STUDIES ON MITOCHONDRIAL K+ UNIPORTER
S07RR-05700-22 0883 (NSS) BOWMAN, DOUGLAS Biomedical research support HUMAN ORAL CAVITY EPITHELIAL CELLS TRANSFECTED W/ HUMAN PAPILLOMAVIRUS 16 DNA
S07RR-05700-22 0884 (NSS) HORNER, JAMES R Biomedical research support IMPLANTABLE HYBRID BIOARTIFICIAL PANCREAS INSULIN DEPENDENT DIABETES MELLITUS
S07RR-05700-22 0885 (NSS) GODFREY, DONALD A Biomedical research support MICROCHEMISTRY OF COCHLEAR NUCLEUS
S07RR-05700-22 0886 (NSS) JHUNJHUNWALA, JAGADI Biomedical research support URINARY BLADDER GLYCOSAMINOGLYCAN LAYER: IMMUNOHISTOCHEM & FUNCTIONAL STUDIES
S07RR-05700-22 0887 (NSS) MCCORQUODALE, D JAME Biomedical research support MURINE GALACTOSYL TRANSFERASE GENE
S07RR-05700-22 0869 (NSS) BENNETT-CLARKE, CARO Biomedical research support VISUAL CORTICAL DEVELOPMENT & SEROTONIN
S07RR-05700-22 0870 (NSS) BRAND, PAUL H Biomedical research support PRESSURE DIURESIS & ARTERIAL PRESSURE REGULATION IN CONSCIOUS DOG
S07RR-05700-22 0871 (NSS) CHIU, TED Biomedical research support REGULATION OF GABA & BENZODIAZEPINE RECEPTOR COMPLEX
S07RR-05704-20 (NSS) RAYSON, JACK H LOUISIANA STATE UNIVERSITY 1100 FLORIDA AVENUE NEW ORLEANS, LA 70119-2799 Biomedical research support
S07RR-05704-20 0001 (NSS) ROY, GREG Biomedical research support EARLY CAFFEINE DIET; AGED RAT; ORGANIC & INORGANIC PROPERTIES OF SKELETAL SYSTEM
S07RR-05704-20 0002 (NSS) SUTTON, FLETCHER Biomedical research support EFFECTS OF CAFFEINE ON TOOTH MOVEMENT & BONE REMODELING IN WEANED RATS
S07RR-05704-20 0003 (NSS) BALLARD, RICHARD Biomedical research support HISTOLOGICAL EVALUATION OF AURICULAR CARTILAGE FOR TMJ DISC REPLACEMENT
S07RR-05704-20 0004 (NSS) MCMICHAEL, THOMAS Biomedical research support RESORBABLE COLLAGEN MEMBRANES; PROMOTE GUIDED TISSUE REGENERATION
S07RR-05704-20 0005 (NSS) SCHWAB, CATHERINE Biomedical research support SUBSTANCE P & CORTICOTROPIN GENE PEPTIDE; TRIGEMINAL COMPLEX AFTER DEAFFERENT
S07RR-05704-20 0006 (NSS) HANACHI, FARID Biomedical research support ABSOLUTE ANCHORAGE FOR ORTHODONTICS USING BIOINTEGRATED ONLAYED IMPLANTS
S07RR-05704-20 0007 (NSS) WITTRIG, ERIN Biomedical research support RESORBABLE COLLAGEN BARRIERS FOR GUIDED TISSUE REGENERATION IN FURCATION DEFECTS
S07RR-05704-20 0008 (NSS) BLOCK, CARL Biomedical research support YAG LASER; STERILIZE & SURFACE ALTER; PLASMA, HYDROXYLAPATITE & TITANIUM IMPLANT
S07RR-05704-20 0009 (NSS) SCHERRMAN, JAYNE Biomedical research support ND YAG LASER VS FORMOCRESOL IN PERMANENT TOOTH PULPOTOMIES IN DOGS
S07RR-05704-20 0010 (NSS) DAIRE, JOHN Biomedical research support MODIFIED ILIZAROV APPROACH TO LENGTHENING MANDIBLE IN DOGS
S07RR-05704-20 0011 (NSS) BOGGS, WILLIAM Biomedical research support FERRIC SULFATE: EVALUATION OF HEMOSTASIS ON OSSEOUS WOUND HEALING
S07RR-05704-20 0012 (NSS) GUIDRY, MARIJA Biomedical research support HEMIDESMOSOMES BETWEEN CULTURED GINGIVAL EPITHELIUM & GROWN SUBSTRATA
S07RR-05704-20 0013 (NSS) DANIELS, ROBERT Biomedical research support RESORBABLE & NON RESORBABLE HYDROXYLAPATITE IN GRAFTING BONY DEFECTS; IMPLANTS
S07RR-05704-20 0014 (NSS) QUINN, JAMES Biomedical research support TMJ FOSSA ABRASION ARTHROPLASTY IN RABBITS
S07RR-05704-20 0015 (NSS) NAKAMOTO, TETSUO Biomedical research

support SUBMUCOSAL ADMINISTRATION OF CAGGEINE TABLETS ON TOOTH GERM DEVELOPMENT

S07RR-05704-20 0016 (NSS) CAUDILL, RICHARD Biomedical research support HYDROXYLAPATITE COATED & TITANIUM SCREW IMPLANTS IN CANINE MANDIBLES

S07RR-05705-22 (NSS) NORTH, ROBERT J TRUDEAU INSTITUTE, INC PO BOX 59 SARANAC LAKE, N Y 12983 Biomedical research support

S07RR-05705-22 0511 (NSS) NORTH, ROBERT J Biomedical research support NO RESEARCH SUBPROJECTS

S07RR-05710-21 (NSS) SMITH, JAMES P RAND CORPORATION PO BOX 2138 1700 MAIN STREET SANTA MONICA, CA 90406-2138 Biomedical research support

S07RR-05710-21 0017 (NSS) WAITE, LINDA Biomedical research support DIVISION OF HOUSEHOLD LABOR AMONG OLDER COUPLES: IMPLICATIONS FOR CHANGE

S07RR-05710-21 0018 (NSS) SMITH, JAMES P Biomedical research support POST DOCTORAL SUPPORT

S07RR-05710-21 0019 (NSS) STRAUSS, JOHN Biomedical research support DEVELOPMENT RESEARCH; CALORIE CONSUMPTION VS INCOME

S07RR-05710-21 0020 (NSS) LILLARD, LEE Biomedical research support NATL INST AGING DATA SUPPLEMENT

S07RR-05710-21 0021 (NSS) MORRISON, PETER Biomedical research support MORRISON SUPPORT; DEMOGRAPHICS; MINORITIES

S07RR-05710-21 0022 (NSS) HAYS, RONALD Biomedical research support COMPUTING SUPPORT FOR HEALTH RELATED RESEARCH OF MEDICAL OUTCOMES

S07RR-05710-21 0023 (NSS) HAYS, RONALD Biomedical research support COMPUTING SUPPORT FOR HEALTH RELATED RESEARCH OF MEDICAL OUTCOMES

S07RR-05710-21 0024 (NSS) CVITANIC, MARILYN Biomedical research support USE OF MENTAL HEALTH & SOCIAL SUPPORT SERVICES BY PERSONS W/ O AIDS

S07RR-05710-21 0025 (NSS) BUCHANAN, JOAN Biomedical research support QUALITY OF LIFE & FRAIL ELDERLY DVMT CONSENSUS PROTOCOLS FOR WORKSHOP

S07RR-05710-21 0026 (NSS) BENNETT, C L Biomedical research support NYC HOSPITAL MORTALITY DATA; LEARNING EFFECTS OF TREATING AIDS

S07RR-05710-21 0027 (NSS) PALTIEL, A D Biomedical research support AIDS MODELING REPORT: PREDICT MODEL FOR AIDS PREVALENCE

S07RR-05710-21 0028 (NSS) DAVIS, LOIS Biomedical research support ELDERLY DEPRESSED REPORT

S07RR-05710-21 0029 (NSS) SIU, A Biomedical research support MORTALITY & MORBIDITY; PREVENTIVE INTERVENTION

S07RR-05710-21 0030 (NSS) PARK, R E Biomedical research support PHASE I NYC HOSPITAL; PUBLIC VS PRIVATE MORTALITY RATES

S07RR-05710-21 0031 (NSS) WELLS, K E Biomedical research support MENTAL HEALTH & PPO STUDY

S07RR-05711-21 (NSS) GERGELY, JOHN BOSTON BIOMEDICAL RES INST,INC 20 STANIFORD STREET BOSTON, MASS 02114 Biomedical research support

S07RR-05711-21 0032 (NSS) PAULUS, HENRY Biomedical research support METABOLIC REGULATION

S07RR-05711-21 0033 (NSS) VOLLOCH, VLADIMIR Biomedical research support RNA DEPENDENT RNA SYNTHESIS

S07RR-05711-21 0034 (NSS) JOSHI, SAROJ Biomedical research support TOPOGRAPHY OF ATPASE IN MEMBRANE

S07RR-05711-21 0035 (NSS) SANADI, D RAO Biomedical research support CLONING OF FACTOR B

S07RR-05711-21 0036 (NSS) HONG, JEN-SHIANG Biomedical research support CLONING OF ENERGY COUPLING FACTOR

S07RR-05711-21 0037 (NSS) WOHLRAB, HARTMUT Biomedical research support BIOLOGICAL MARKER FOR AGING

S07RR-05711-21 0038 (NSS) GERGELY, JOHN Biomedical research support BIOCHEMISTRY OF MUSCLE CONTRACTION

S07RR-05711-21 0039 (NSS) DAVISON, PETER F Biomedical research support COLLAGEN & PATHOLOGY OF VITREOUS

S07RR-05711-21 0040 (NSS) RASO, VICTOR Biomedical research support MONOCLONAL ANTIBODIES TO AIDS RELATED PEPTIDES

S07RR-05711-21 0041 (NSS) TAI, PHANG C Biomedical research support PROTEIN EXPORT BY ACCESSORY PROTEIN SPECIFIED PATHWAY

S07RR-05711-21 0042 (NSS) BADWEY, JOHN A Biomedical research support PHAGOCYTIC LEUKOCYTES

S07RR-05712-20 (NSS) MELCHIOR, DONALD L UNIVERSITY OF MASSACHUSETTS 55 LAKE AVENUE NORTH WORCESTER, MASS 01655 Biomedical research support

S07RR-05712-20 0075 (NSS) BARKLEY, RUSSEL A Biomedical research support ADOLESCENTS W/ ATTENTION DEFICIT HYPERACTIVITY DISORDER

S07RR-05712-20 0076 (NSS) FAY, FRED Biomedical research support MITOCHONDRIAL FUNCTION IN SINGLE CELLS

S07RR-05712-20 0077 (NSS) ANKLESARIA, PERVIN Biomedical research support HOMING OF MYELOID PROGENITORS; HAEMONECTIN; MARROW STROMAL CELLS

S07RR-05712-20 0078 (NSS) AURIGEMMA, GERARD P Biomedical research support QUANITATION OF LEFT VENTRICULAR MASS BY CARDIAC MAGNETIC RESONANCE IMAGING

S07RR-05712-20 0079 (NSS) BENJAMIN, SHELDON Biomedical research support ACTOMETRY IN EVALUATION OF AKATHISIA

S07RR-05712-20 0080 (NSS) BROWN, ROSALIND S Biomedical research support MATERNAL THYROID BLOCKING IMMUNOGLOBULINS IN CONGENITAL HYPOTHYROIDISM

S07RR-05712-20 0081 (NSS) CARLSON, KRISTIN R Biomedical research support GENETIC CONTROL OF OPIATE SELF ADMINISTRATION: WORK PRELIMINARY

S07RR-05712-20 0082 (NSS) CRAWFORD, DANA R Biomedical research support OXIDANT STRESS TRANSFORMATION OF MOUSE PROMYELOCYTES

S07RR-05712-20 0083 (NSS) DEGIROLAMI, UMBERTO Biomedical research support OPHTHALMIC PATHOLOGY IN AIDS

S07RR-05712-20 0084 (NSS) DUDYCZ, LECH W Biomedical research support GLYCOLS IN SYNTHESIS OF ANTI HIV AGENTS

S07RR-05712-20 0085 (NSS) FEY, EDWARD G Biomedical research support MOLECULAR CHARACTERIZATION OF NUCLEAR STRUCTURAL PROTEIN

S07RR-05712-20 0086 (NSS) HAMILTON, GLENYS A Biomedical research support ADHERENCE IN HYPERTENSION: PILOT STUDY

S07RR-05712-20 0087 (NSS) HEBERT, JAMES R Biomedical research support BIOMARKERS OF NUTRIENT EXPOSURE IN NUTRITIONALLY DIVERSE GROUPS

S07RR-05712-20 0088 (NSS) HUANG, SHOEI K STEPH Biomedical research support MODIFICATION OF ATRIOVENTRICULAR CONDUCTION; RADIOFREQUENCY CATHETER ABLATION

S07RR-05712-20 0089 (NSS) KANE, ROBERT L Biomedical research support ANTIHYPERTENSIVE AGENTS & INTELLECTUAL FUNCT: SEPARATE DRUG FROM PRACTICE EFFECT

S07RR-05712-20 0090 (NSS) KANE, ROBERT L Biomedical research support BIOLOGICAL PARENTS OF ADHD CHILDREN: COGNITIVE IMPAIRMENT RELATIVE TO CONTROL

S07RR-05712-20 0091 (NSS) JENNESS, DUANE D Biomedical research support GENES CONTROLLING STABILITY OF INTEGRAL MEMBRANE PROTEINS

S07RR-05712-20 0092 (NSS) LAVELLE, WILLIAM G Biomedical research support GOLGI EM STUDY OF OLFACTORY TARGET NEURONS IN AGING

S07RR-05712-20 0093 (NSS) JEDERLINIC, PETER J Biomedical research support MUSCLE FUNCTION & DETERMINANTS OF DYSPNEA; INSPIRATORY RESISTIVE BREATHING

S07RR-05712-20 0094 (NSS) COUMAS, JAMES M Biomedical research support USING MR IMAGING FOR EARLY, ACCURATE ASSESSMENT OF SCAPHOID AVASCULAR NECROSIS

S07RR-05712-20 0095 (NSS) ABIGAIL, ADAMS Biomedical research support PHYSICIAN DELIVERED INTERVENTION IN ALCOHOL ABUSE IN PRIMARY CARE POPULATION

S07RR-05712-20 0096 (NSS) OCKENE, IRA S Biomedical research support CARDIOVASCULAR RISK FACTOR CHANGES IN MIGRATORY ECUADORIAN POPULATION

S07RR-05712-20 0097 (NSS) FERRIS, CRAIG F Biomedical research support VASOPRESSIN & FLANK MARKING BEHAVIOR; COMPUTER

S07RR-05712-20 0098 (NSS) TIPPER, DONALD J Biomedical research support CIRCULAR PERMUTATION OF PBR322 BLA GENE

S07RR-05712-20 0099 (NSS) FRAM, ROBERT J Biomedical research support GAMMA GLUTAMYL TRANSPEPTIDASE IN RESISTANCE TO CISPLATIN

S07RR-05712-20 0100 (NSS) WOODLAND, ROBERT T Biomedical research support HEAT SHOCK PROTEINS IN B CELL FUNCTION

S07RR-05712-20 0101 (NSS) KORN, JANE E Biomedical research support REDUCING BURDEN OF FECAL INCONTINENCE

S07RR-05712-20 0102 (NSS) SCHERR, PAUL A Biomedical research support PROSPECTIVE STUDY OF DISORDERED EATING BEHAVIORS; COLLEGE FRESHMAN WOMEN

S07RR-05712-20 0103 (NSS) HIRSCHMAN, JODI E Biomedical research support BIOCHEMICAL STUDIES OF HORMONAL RESPONSE IN SACCHAROMYCES CEREVISIAE

S07RR-05712-20 0104 (NSS) PAPE, LINDA A Biomedical research support FRAME BY FRAME COLOR FLOW DOPPLER ULTRASOUND ANALYSIS OF MITRAL REGURGITATION

S07RR-05712-20 0105 (NSS) AURIGEMMA, GERARD P Biomedical research support LONGITUDINAL STUDY OF LEFT VENTRICULAR HYPERTROPHY IN DOCA HYPERTENSIVE SWINE

S07RR-05712-20 0106 (NSS) CUENOUD, HENRI F Biomedical research support CONTRACTION OF HUMAN CAROTID ENDARTERECTOMY ATHEROSCLEROTIC PLAQUES IN VITRO

S07RR-05712-20 0043 (NSS) ANASTOPOULOS, ARTHUR Biomedical research support PARENT TRAINING FOR CHILDREN W/ ATTENTION DEFICIT HYPERACTIVITY DISORDER

S07RR-05712-20 0107 (NSS) HOLLAND, CHRISTIE A Biomedical research support EFFECTS OF SUBSTANCE P ON HIV INFECTED CELLS

S07RR-05712-20 0108 (NSS) MORRISON, TRUDY G Biomedical research support INHIBITION OF VIRAL INFECTION BY ANTISENSE TRANSCRIPTS

S07RR-05712-20 0109 (NSS) PULLMAN, JAMES M Biomedical research support STRESS PROTEIN EXPRESSION AS MARKER OF CELLULAR DAMAGE

S07RR-05712-20 0110 (NSS) TARBELL, SALLY E Biomedical research support ASSESSMENT OF POSTOPERATIVE PAIN IN YOUNG CHILDREN

S07RR-05712-20 0111 (NSS) VONHOFE, ERIC Biomedical research support BIOLOGY OF SPECIFIC DNA ALKYLATION DAMAGE & REPAIR

S07RR-05712-20 0112 (NSS) WODA, BRUCE A Biomedical research support SUPPRESSOR INDUCER CELLS IN BB & WOR RAT

S07RR-05712-20 0113 (NSS) PARKER, DAVID C Biomedical research support INDUCTION OF T CELL TOLERANCE BY B CELLS

S07RR-05712-20 0114 (NSS) SMITH, EMIL R Biomedical research support NEW ENVIRONMENTAL ESTROGENS

S07RR-05712-20 0115 (NSS) STAVNEZER, JANET M Biomedical research support REGULATION OF ANTIBODY CLASS SWITCH TO IGC

S07RR-05712-20 0116 (NSS) WOLF, MERRILL K Biomedical research support HYPOMYELINEATED MUTANT & DOUBLE MUTANT MICE

S07RR-05712-20 0044 (NSS) ANDERSON, KAREN O Biomedical research support ASSESSMENT OF MARITAL FUNCTIONING IN CHRONIC LOW BACK PAIN PATIENTS

S07RR-05712-20 0045 (NSS) BAKER, RICHARD E Biomedical research support GENETIC ANALYSIS OF FACTOR TAU TRNA GENE INTERACTIONS

S07RR-05712-20 0046 (NSS) BECKER, RICHARD C Biomedical research support DILTIAZEM ON TEMPLATE BLEEDING TIME & BLOOD LOSS; R TPA ADMINISTRATION

S07RR-05712-20 0047 (NSS) BONKOVSKY, HERBERT L Biomedical research support REGULATION OF HEPATIC HEME METABOLISM

S07RR-05712-20 0048 (NSS) BROWN, NEAL C Biomedical research support STRUCTURE & FUNCTION OF DNA POLYMERASE III

S07RR-05712-20 0049 (NSS) CRAWFORD, DANA R Biomedical research support TRANSFORMATION SPECIFIC PROTEIN IN MOUSE MYELOID PROGENITOR CELLS

S07RR-05712-20 0050 (NSS) DINKLAGE, DAVID Biomedical research support NEUROPSYCH FUNCTIONING; ATTENTIONALLY DISORDERED CHILDREN W/&W/OUT HYPERACTIVITY

S07RR-05712-20 0051 (NSS) DUPAUL, GEORGE J Biomedical research support NEUROPSYCH FUNCTIONING; ATTENTIONALLY DISORDERED CHILD W/ & W/OUT HYPERACTIVITY

S07RR-05712-20 0052 (NSS) FRICK, G PETER Biomedical research support SYNTHESIS OF GROWTH HORMONES RECEPTORS IN LIVER, MUSCLE, & ADIPOSE TISSUE

S07RR-05712-20 0053 (NSS) GUEVREMONT, DAVID C Biomedical research support ASSESSMENT OF MOTIVATION DEFICITS IN CHILDREN

S07RR-05712-20 0054 (NSS) HARDY, LARRY W Biomedical research support HETERODIMERIC FORMS OF THYMIDYLATE SYNTHASE

S07RR-05712-20 0055 (NSS) HELLER, LOUIS I Biomedical research support RAPID SEQUENTIAL TEBOROXIME IMAGING & DETECTION OF CORONARY

REPERFUSION
S07RR-05712-20 0056 (NSS) IGNOTZ, RONALD A Biomedical research support MONOCLONAL ANTIBODIES TO TGF B RECEPTOR TYPE I
S07RR-05712-20 0057 (NSS) IORIO, RONALD M Biomedical research support SOLUBLE HN PROTEIN FROM NDV FOR CRYSTALLIZATION TRIALS
S07RR-05712-20 0058 (NSS) JUNG, LAWRENCE Biomedical research support CAMP ON LYMPHOCYTE ACTIVATION
S07RR-05712-20 0059 (NSS) KERSHAW, GLENN R Biomedical research support CAPTOPRIL RENOGRAPHY, RENIN ACTIVITY, RENOVASCULAR HYPERTENSION
S07RR-05712-20 0060 (NSS) KNIGHT, KENDALL L Biomedical research support FUNCTIONAL ORGANIZATION OF REGA & RECBCD ENZYMES
S07RR-05712-20 0061 (NSS) LAHUE, ROBERT S Biomedical research support GENE CONVERSION & DNA MISMATCH CORRECTION IN YEAST
S07RR-05712-20 0062 (NSS) LI, JIAN-MING Biomedical research support VASCULAR PROSTHESIS ENDOTHELIALIZATION; HUMAN UMBILICAL & SAPHENOUS VEIN CELL
S07RR-05712-20 0063 (NSS) LUBER-NAROD, J Biomedical research support CAN SUBSTANCE P STIMULATE TNF SECRETION FROM NEUROGLIA; NEUROIMMUNOLOGY
S07RR-05712-20 0064 (NSS) MARINUS, MARTIN G Biomedical research support MUTATIONS PRODUCED BY DNA POLYMERASE
S07RR-05712-20 0065 (NSS) MISRA, HEMANT K Biomedical research support CHEMISTRY & STABILITY OF 2,3 DIDEOXY SUGARS; ANTI HIV NUCLEOSIDE SYNTHESIS
S07RR-05712-20 0066 (NSS) NGUYEN, QUOC V Biomedical research support SUBCELLULAR PROCESSING OF CLASS II MHC ANTIGEN
S07RR-05712-20 0067 (NSS) PARK, CHUN S Biomedical research support CELL MECHANISMS; STIMULATION OF RENIN SECRETION BY LOOP DIURETICS
S07RR-05712-20 0068 (NSS) PATWARDHAN, NILIMA A Biomedical research support CYTOKINES IN AUTOIMMUNE THYROID DISEASE
S07RR-05712-20 0069 (NSS) ROYER, WILLIAM E, JR Biomedical research support STRUCTURAL BASIS FOR COOPERATIVITY IN CLAM HEMOGLOBINS
S07RR-05712-20 0070 (NSS) SCHEID, CHERYL R Biomedical research support NA & H EXCHANGE IN PULMONARY HYPERTENSION
S07RR-05712-20 0071 (NSS) VISNER, MARC S Biomedical research support CORRECT HYPERCARBIC INTRAMYOCARDIAL ACIDOSIS W/ CO2 GENERATING BUFFER
S07RR-05712-20 0072 (NSS) VOLKERT, MICHAEL R Biomedical research support GENETIC REGULATION OF ESCHERICHIA COLI AIDB GENE
S07RR-05712-20 0073 (NSS) YAMAGUCHI, HIROSHI Biomedical research support REGULATION OF INTRACELLULAR MG 2 IN SMOOTH MUSCLE
S07RR-05712-20 0074 (NSS) YOUNG, MARTIN H Biomedical research support ENCOPRESIS: 1ST AND 2ND ORDER TREATMENT EFFECTS
S07RR-05714-21 (NSS) OMENN, GILBERT S UNIVERSITY OF WASHINGTON SCHOOL OF PUBLIC HEALTH, SC-30 SEATTLE, WASH 98195 Biomedical research support
S07RR-05714-21 0117 (NSS) KUO, CHO-CHOU Biomedical research support CHLAMYDIA PNEUMONIAE; SENSITIVE CELL LINE
S07RR-05714-21 0118 (NSS) ROBERTS, MARILYN C Biomedical research support TETRACYCLINE RESISTANCE; FLORA
S07RR-05714-21 0119 (NSS) RAUSCH, ROBERT L Biomedical research support ALVEOLAR HYDATID DISEASE; ECHINOCOCCUS MULTILOCULARIS; PRAZIQUANTEL
S07RR-05714-21 0120 (NSS) DALING, JANET R Biomedical research support RELATION BETWEEN CONTRACEPTIVE USE & OVARIAN CYSTS
S07RR-05714-21 0138 (NSS) ROBKIN, MAURICE A Biomedical research support PATHWAY ANALYSIS & RISK ASSESSMENT; ENVIRONMENTAL COMPLIANCE & DOSE ASSESSMENT
S07RR-05714-21 0121 (NSS) DALING, JANET R Biomedical research support BREAST CANCER RECURRENCE RATES AFTER LUMP ECTOMY OR MASTECTOMY
S07RR-05714-21 0122 (NSS) DAVIS, SCOTT Biomedical research support RISK FACTOR; CANCER OF LARYNX & CARCINOMA IN ESOPHAGUS; TOBACCO: ALCOHOL: DIET
S07RR-05714-21 0123 (NSS) EMANUEL, IRVIN Biomedical research support INFANT MORTALITY IN BLACK, WHITE & MIXED RACE BABIES
S07RR-05714-21 0124 (NSS) GALE, JAMES L Biomedical research support ANALYSIS OF ADVERSE EVENTS & PERTUSSIS VACCINE; SEIZURE; ENCEPHALITIS
S07RR-05714-21 0125 (NSS) PSATY, BRUCE Biomedical research support POSTMENOPAUSAL PROGESTINS & RISK OF CORONARY DISEASE
S07RR-05714-21 0126 (NSS) SISCOVICK, DAVID Biomedical research support ANTIHYPERTENSIVE THERAPY & PRIMARY CARDIAC ARREST
S07RR-05714-21 0127 (NSS) WHITE, J EMILY Biomedical research support VITAMIN & BETA CAROTENE PROTECTION IN DVMT BLADDER CANCER; SMOKING; COFFEE
S07RR-05714-21 0128 (NSS) KOEPSELL, THOMAS D Biomedical research support RISK FACTORS; MOTOR VEHICLE COLLISIONS RESULTING IN INJURIES IN OLDER DRIVERS
S07RR-05714-21 0129 (NSS) HOARE, GEOFFREY A Biomedical research support ASSESSING SERVICES FOR CHILDREN C & DVMTL DISABILITIES IN CHILD WELFARE SYSTEM
S07RR-05714-21 0130 (NSS) COSTA, LUCIO G Biomedical research support MOLECULAR ASPECTS OF DEVELOPMENTAL NEUROTOXICITY OF ALCOHOL
S07RR-05714-21 0131 (NSS) COVERT, DAVID S Biomedical research support PICOBALANCE QUADRUPOLE CAGE: APPLICATION TO TOXIC, INHALABLE PARTICLES
S07RR-05714-21 0132 (NSS) DANIELL, WILLIAM Biomedical research support DETECTION OF OCCULT HEPATOTOXICITY IN SOLVENT EXPOSED WORKERS
S07RR-05714-21 0133 (NSS) FAUSTMAN, ELAINE Biomedical research support ENVIRONMENTAL CHAMBER FOR WHOLE EMBRYO CULTURE
S07RR-05714-21 0134 (NSS) FAUSTMAN, ELAINE Biomedical research support MODULATION OF MICROTUBULES & MICROTUBULES ASSOCIATED PROTEINS BY CHEMICAL AGENTS
S07RR-05714-21 0135 (NSS) GUFFEY, STEVEN E Biomedical research support SHARP EDGED ORIFICE FOR FLOW MEASUREMENT IN VENTILATION DESIGN
S07RR-05714-21 0136 (NSS) KOENIG, JANE Q Biomedical research support RESPIRATORY EFFECTS OF INHALED HCL
S07RR-05714-21 0137 (NSS) OMIECINSKI, CURTIS J Biomedical research support GENETIC POLYMORPHISM OF CHEMICAL METABOLISM IN PARKINSONS DISEASE
S07RR-05716-20 (NSS) HAUPTMAN, HERBERT A MEDICAL FDN OF BUFFALO, INC 73 HIGH STREET BUFFALO, N Y 14203 Biomedical research support
S07RR-05716-20 0139 (NSS) OSAWA, YOSHIO Biomedical research support RAPID 19 DESMOLASE ASSAY METHOD; OVARIAN 19 NORANDROGEN BIOSYNTHESIS
S07RR-05716-20 0140 (NSS) OSAWA, YOSHIO Biomedical research support PREP OF ANTI AROMATASE MONOCLONAL ANTIBODIES FOR CRYSTALLOGRAPHY
S07RR-05716-20 0141 (NSS) DORSET, DOUGLAS L Biomedical research support STRUCTURAL INTERACTIONS OF CYTOTOXIC OXIDIZED CHOLESTEROLS
S07RR-05716-20 0142 (NSS) GHOSH, DEBASHIS Biomedical research support XRAY DIFFRACTION STUDY OF CHOLESTEROL ESTERASE
S07RR-05716-20 0143 (NSS) VAN ROEY, PATRICK Biomedical research support STRUCTURES OF NON STEROIDAL ESTROGEN AROMATASE INHIBITORS
S07RR-05716-20 0144 (NSS) BLESSING, ROBERT Biomedical research support PILOT STUDIES IN SYNTHESIS & CHARACTERIZATION OF PHOSPHOENOLPYRUVATES
S07RR-05717-21 (NSS) ROBERTS, RICHARD J COLD SPRING HARBOR LABORATORY P O BOX 100 COLD SPRING HARBOR, N Y 11724 Biomedical research support
S07RR-05717-21 0127 (NSS) GREIDER, CAROL Biomedical research support WORKSTATION FOR PHOSPHORIMAGER TAPE DRIVE
S07RR-05717-21 0128 (NSS) MARTIENNSSEN, ROB Biomedical research support MICROTOME
S07RR-05717-21 0129 (NSS) UNK Biomedical research support SCOTTSMAN ICE MAKER
S07RR-05717-21 0130 (NSS) UNK Biomedical research support SCINTILLATION COUNTER
S07RR-05717-21 0131 (NSS) SUNDARESESN, VENEKTE Biomedical research support SONICATOR
S07RR-05717-21 0132 (NSS) BAR-SAGI, DAFNA Biomedical research support MICROINJECTION ACCESSORIES
S07RR-05717-21 0134 (NSS) MA, HONG Biomedical research support MINUS 20 FREEZER
S07RR-05717-21 0135 (NSS) KRAINER, ADRIAN Biomedical research support SLIDE MAKER
S07RR-05717-21 0136 (NSS) MA, HONG Biomedical research support ANIMAL CAGES
S07RR-05717-21 0137 (NSS) MA, HONG Biomedical research support ROLLER DRUM
S07RR-05717-21 0138 (NSS) MATHEWS, MICHAEL Biomedical research support ULTRA SPEC PLUS SPECTROPHOTOMETER
S07RR-05718-16 (NSS) MOOD, DARLENE W WAYNE ST UNIV COL NURSING 5557 CASS AVENUE DETROIT, MI 48202 Biomedical research support grant
S07RR-05718-16 0133 (NSS) UNK Biomedical research support grant FPLC
S07RR-05718-16 0145 (NSS) CARNEY, PATRICIA Biomedical research support grant HUMOR TO REDUCE INCIDENCE OF ANV ASSOCIATED W/ CHEMOTHERAPY
S07RR-05724-20 (NSS) SCHENKEIN, HARVEY A VIRGINIA COMMONWEALTH UNIV PO BOX 566, MCV STATION RICHMOND, VA 23298-0566 Biomedical research support
S07RR-05724-20 0180 (NSS) MCCOY, KATHLEEN L Biomedical research support INTRACELLULAR TRANSPORT PATHWAYS FOR PROCESSING ANTIGENS
S07RR-05724-20 0181 (NSS) NEWMAN, SAMMYE Biomedical research support FACTORS CONTROLLING EXPRESSION OF TRYPTOPHAN OXIDASE
S07RR-05724-20 0182 (NSS) NEWMAN, SAMMYE Biomedical research support EXPRESSION OF MYELIN BASIC PROTEIN ISOFORMS IN CNS & PNS
S07RR-05724-20 0183 (NSS) LORIA, ROGER M Biomedical research support MOBILIZATION OF CUTANEOUS IMMUNITY FOR SYSTEMIC PROTECTION AGAINST INFECTIONS
S07RR-05724-20 0184 (NSS) CHELBOWSKI, JAN F Biomedical research support CHARACTERIZE INTERMEDIATE IN ASSEMBLY OF E COLI ALKALINE PHOSPHATASE
S07RR-05724-20 0185 (NSS) JOLLIE, WILLIAM P Biomedical research support CHRONIC INGESTION OF ETHANOL ON CONTROL MECH FOR PLACENTAL TRANSPORT OF IGG
S07RR-05724-20 0186 (NSS) HARRIS, ROBERT B Biomedical research support ROLE OF CONFORMATION IN KININOGEN PROTEIN INTERACTIONS
S07RR-05724-20 0188 (NSS) STANISWALIS, JOAN Biomedical research support SEMIPARAMETRIC REGRESSION IN LIKELIHOOD BASED MODELS
S07RR-05724-20 0189 (NSS) CARTER, WALTER H Biomedical research support DVMT METHODS FOR ANALYZING DATA FROM CLINICAL TRIALS OF PERIDONTAL DISEASE
S07RR-05724-20 0190 (NSS) ROWLAND, RANDAL Biomedical research support AIDS INFECTION & ACUTE NECROTIZING ULCERATIVE GINGIVITIS
S07RR-05724-20 0191 (NSS) COCHRAN, DAVID Biomedical research support CONTROL OF CONNECTIVE TISSUE GROWTH IN PERIODONTAL DISEASE
S07RR-05724-20 0187 (NSS) SHELTON, KEITH R Biomedical research support ISOLATE CLONED CDNA COGNATE FROM 15 AMINO ACID OF INCLUSION BODY PROTEIN P32/6 3
S07RR-05728-20 (NSS) MC ARTHUR, WILLIAM P UNIV OF FLA, COL OF DENTISTRY BOX J-405, JHMHSC GAINESVILLE, FLA 32610 Biomedical research support
S07RR-05728-20 0192 (NSS) BRINKLEY, L Biomedical research support EFFECTS OF EPIDERMAL GROWTH FACTOR ON NORMAL & ORTHODONTIC TOOTH MOVEMENT; RAT
S07RR-05728-20 0193 (NSS) COFFEY, J Biomedical research support NORMAL HUMAN STEADY STATE BITING FORCE
S07RR-05728-20 0194 (NSS) COOPER, B Biomedical research support PROPERTIES OF HIGH THRESHOLD MECHANORECEPTORS IN ORAL CAVITY; MODEL
S07RR-05728-20 0195 (NSS) COURTS, F Biomedical research support EFFECTS OF ORAL AMOXICILLIN IN THERAPY ON SALIVARY STREPTOCOCCI IN CHILDREN
S07RR-05728-20 0196 (NSS) GILBERT, G Biomedical research support DENTAL SERVICES UTILIZATION AMONG FLORIDAS ELDERLY; PSYCHOSOCIAL ISSUES
S07RR-05728-20 0197 (NSS) HASSELL, T Biomedical research support GINGIVAL PATHOLOGY ELICITED BY CYCLOSPORINE A
S07RR-05728-20 0198 (NSS) NIXON, C Biomedical research support INFLAMMATORY RESPONSE; COMPAR AMALGAM & THREE SILICONE BASED RETROGRADE MATERIAL
S07RR-05728-20 0199 (NSS) PINK, F Biomedical research support TOOTH MORTALITY IN ADULT DENTAL PATIENTS: A PREVALENCE STUDY; CLINICAL
S07RR-05728-20 0200 (NSS) PROGULSKE-FOX, A Biomedical research support SURFACE ANTIGENS OF ORAL BACTEROIDES SPECIES

PROJECT NO., ORGANIZATIONAL UNIT., INVESTIGATOR, ADDRESS, TITLE

S07RR-05728-20 0201 (NSS) WHEELER, T Biomedical research support IMMUNE SYSTEM STUDIES IN TOOTH ROOT RESORPTION
S07RR-05728-20 0202 (NSS) HUMPHREYS-BEHER, M Biomedical research support ANALYSIS OF PAROTID GLAND 4B GALACTOSYLTRANSFERASE
S07RR-05728-20 0203 (NSS) MARIOTTI, A Biomedical research support ESTROGENS & SENILE DESQUAMATIVE GINGIVITIS; FEMALE
S07RR-05728-20 0204 (NSS) BROWN, T A Biomedical research support ANTI S MUTANS IGA: SUBCLASSES & EFFECTS OF IGA PROTEASES
S07RR-05728-20 0205 (NSS) VIERA, L Biomedical research support CLONING OF A MAJOR ANTIGEN OF ACTINOBACILLUS ACTINOMYCETEMCOMITANS
S07RR-05728-20 0206 (NSS) ROGERS, J Biomedical research support EFFECTS OF ORTHODONTIC TOOTH MOVEMENT ON DENTAL PULP
S07RR-05730-20 (NSS) MCCLUER, ROBERT H EUNICE KENNEDY SHRIVER CENTER 200 TRAPELO ROAD WALTHAM, MASS 02254 Biomedical research support
S07RR-05730-20 0512 (NSS) KOLODNY, EDWIN H Biomedical research support NO RESEARCH SUBPROJECTS
S07RR-05731-20 (NSS) SETLOW, RICHARD B BIOLOGY DEPARTMENT BROOKHAVEN NATL LABORATORY UPTON, N Y 11973 Biomedical research support
S07RR-05731-20 0146 (NSS) WOLF, ALFRED P Biomedical research support POSITRON EMITTERS & PET IN METABOLISM & NEUROLOGY
S07RR-05731-20 0147 (NSS) JONES, KEITH Biomedical research support SYNCHROTRON XRAY MICROPROBE FACILITY
S07RR-05736-19 (NSS) COHEN, JORDAN J HEALTH SCIENCES CENTER SUNY AT STONY BROOK STONY BROOK, N Y 11794 Biomedical research support
S07RR-05736-19 0148 (NSS) CLAUSEN, CHRIS Biomedical research support K CHANNELS IN BASOLATERAL MEMBRANE OF MAMMALIAN & AMPHIBIAN EPITHELIAL
S07RR-05736-19 0149 (NSS) WILLIAMSON, DAVID Biomedical research support ISOLATION OF MALE LETHAL GENE FROM DROSOPHILIA SPIROPLASMAS
S07RR-05736-19 0150 (NSS) BARNETT, RICHARD Biomedical research support EFFECT OF ATRIAL NATRIURETIC FACTOR IN RAT GLOMERULI & CULTURED MESANGIAL CELLS
S07RR-05736-19 0151 (NSS) GOREVIC, PETER D Biomedical research support CENTER FOR ANALYSIS & SYNTHESIS OF MACROMOLECULES
S07RR-05736-19 0152 (NSS) MARTIN, DWIGHT W Biomedical research support UNDERSTANDING TRANSDUCTION OF INFORMATION ACROSS BIOLOGICALS MEMBRANES
S07RR-05736-19 0153 (NSS) KIM, CHARLES Biomedical research support APRINOCEID IN EXPERIMENTAL CRYPTOSPORIDIOSIS IN IMMUNOSUPPRESSED ADULT HAMSTERS
S07RR-05736-19 0186 (NSS) KRUPP, LAUREN B Biomedical research support PSYCHOLOGY & IMMUNO CHRONIC FATIGUE SYNDROME & OTHER DISORDER W/ SEVERE FATIGUE
S07RR-05736-19 0154 (NSS) HULL, MAGDALEN Biomedical research support LONG TERM EFFECTS OF EXERCISE ON SPERMATOGENESIS
S07RR-05736-19 0155 (NSS) MANNISI, JOHN A Biomedical research support LATER STRUCTURAL CONSEQUENCES OF INFARCT EXPANSION; MYOCARDIAL INFARCT
S07RR-05736-19 0156 (NSS) FURIE, MARTHA B Biomedical research support MONOKINES ON INTERACTIONS W/ NEUTROPHILS & ENDOTHELIAL CELLS; INFLAMMATION
S07RR-05736-19 0157 (NSS) HITZEMAN, ROBERT Biomedical research support OMEGA 3 FATTY ACIDS IN TREATMENT OF MIGRANE
S07RR-05736-19 0158 (NSS) KAUFMAN, LEE D Biomedical research support IGA IMMUNOGLOBULIN IN PATHOGENESIS OF SERONEGATIVE SPONDYLORTHROPATHICS
S07RR-05736-19 0187 (NSS) CARLSON, HAROLD E Biomedical research support C MYC EXPRESSION IN EXPERIMENTAL RAT PITUITARY TUMORS
S07RR-05736-19 0188 (NSS) GRUBER, MARTIN A Biomedical research support THREE DIMENSIONAL VISUALIZATION OF ADOLESCENT SCOLIOTIC SPINE; ULTRASOUND
S07RR-05736-19 0189 (NSS) PRAISSMAN, MELVIN Biomedical research support DISTRIBUTION & QUANTITATION: HORMONE RECEPTORS IN GASTROINTESTINAL TRACT; HUMAN
S07RR-05736-19 0190 (NSS) PETRIKOVSKY, BORIS Biomedical research support DEVELOPMENT OF SAFE & EFFICIENT FETAL ACOUSTIC STIMULATION TECHNIQUE
S07RR-05736-19 0191 (NSS) FOURMAN, STUART B Biomedical research support TONOGRAPHY VS CONSTANT PRESSURE PERFUSION; RABBIT; GLAUCOMA FILTERING SURGERY
S07RR-05736-19 0192 (NSS) FOURMAN, STUART B Biomedical research support INTRACAMERAL CLEARANCE OF PLASMINOGEN ACTIVATOR AFTER GLAUCOMA FILTERING SURGERY
S07RR-05736-19 0193 (NSS) RUBINSTEIN, JOAN E Biomedical research support LITHIUM EFFECTS ON INOSITOL PHOSPHATES
S07RR-05736-19 0194 (NSS) MEEK, ALLEN G Biomedical research support PHASE II CLINICAL TRIAL; N PILOCARPINE TO REDUCE ORAL COMPLICAT OF RADIOTHERAPHY
S07RR-05736-19 0195 (NSS) MAITRA, SUBIR R Biomedical research support INTRACELLULAR CA MOBILIZATION IN HEPATOCYTES DURING SHOCK;
S07RR-05736-19 0196 (NSS) GOLD, AVRAM Biomedical research support EFFECTS OF ALCOHOL UPON UPPER AIRWAY COLLAPSIBILITY IN SLEEP APNEA PATIENTS
S07RR-05736-19 0197 (NSS) KEW, RICHARD R Biomedical research support REGULATE OF C5A BINDING TO NEUTROPHIL C5A RECEPTOR BY VITAMIN D BINDING PROTEIN
S07RR-05736-19 0198 (NSS) BAHOU, WADIE Biomedical research support MOLECULAR BIOLOGY OF HEMONECTIN; CELLS ENDOTHELIAL CELLS
S07RR-05736-19 0199 (NSS) SOMMER, BARBARA Biomedical research support FOLIC ACID IN TREATMENT OF DEMENTED ELDERLY PATIENTS W/ LOW NORMAL FOLATE LEVELS
S07RR-05736-19 0200 (NSS) SPITZER, ERIC D Biomedical research support CLONE & CHARACTERIZE SEROTYPE SPECIFIC GENES FROM CRYPTOCOCCUS NEOFORMANS
S07RR-05736-19 0201 (NSS) BERELOWITZ, MICHAEL Biomedical research support MOLECULAR CLONING OF SOMATOSTATIN RECEPTOR FROM RAT BRAIN
S07RR-05736-19 0202 (NSS) GELATO, MARIE C Biomedical research support GENE EXPRESSION OF IGFS IN DEVELOPING RAT HIPPOCAMPUS
S07RR-05736-19 0203 (NSS) BENJAMIN, WILLIAM B Biomedical research support PROTEIN KINASE: PURIFICATION OF ENZYME & PHOSPHORYLATION OF MODEL PEPTIDE
S07RR-05736-19 0204 (NSS) EDWARDS, EMMELINE Biomedical research support INBRED LEARNED HELPLESSNESS ON PRESYNAPTIC SEROTONIN MECHANISMS; ANIMAL MODEL
S07RR-05736-19 0205 (NSS) LAKE-BAKAAR, GERONE Biomedical research support CALCIUM CHANNEL BLOCKADE & EXPERIMENTAL PANCREATITIS
S07RR-05736-19 0206 (NSS) MANECKE, GERARD R, J Biomedical research support ANESTHESIA; PORPHYRIN ADMIN; PHOTODYNAMIC & NEUTRON CAPTURE THERAPY
S07RR-05736-19 0207 (NSS) JOHNSON, ROGER A Biomedical research support REGULATION OF ADENYLYL CYCLASE & MULTI DRUG RESISTANCE P GLYCOPROTEIN
S07RR-05736-19 0208 (NSS) HOD, YEACOV Biomedical research support CONTROL OF PEP CARBOXYKINASE GENE EXPRESSION BY CAMP
S07RR-05736-19 0209 (NSS) COYLE, PATRICIA K Biomedical research support MUCOSAL IMMUNITY IN MULTIPLE SCLEROSIS
S07RR-05736-19 0159 (NSS) JUNGER, WILLIAM J Biomedical research support AGE RELATED CHANGES IN CONTENT & ORGANIZATION OF BONE & MINERAL IN CHIMPANZES
S07RR-05736-19 0160 (NSS) FRIEDMAN, RICHARD Biomedical research support BEHAVIORAL CARDIOLOGY: PSYCHOPHYSIOLOGIC INTERACTIONS
S07RR-05736-19 0161 (NSS) MORIN, LAWRENCE Biomedical research support NEUROANATOMICAL REGULATION OF CIRCADIAN RHYTHMS & PHOTOPERIODIC TIME MEASUREMENT
S07RR-05736-19 0162 (NSS) REBECCHI, MARIO Biomedical research support REGULATION & MECHANISM PHOSPHOINOSITIDE SPECIFIC PHOSPHOLIPASE C
S07RR-05736-19 0163 (NSS) VOLKOW, NORA Biomedical research support ALCOHOL INTOXIFICATION IN CEREBRAL BLOOD FLOW AN DDEOXYGLUCOSE TRANSPORT
S07RR-05736-19 0164 (NSS) GOLIGORSKY, MICHAEL Biomedical research support CHARACTERIZATION OF CELLS CULTURES IN HOLLOW FIBER UNITS
S07RR-05736-19 0165 (NSS) POMEROY, JOHN Biomedical research support DVMTL ASPECTS OF PSYCHOSIS IN CHILDHOOD; SCHIZOPHRENIA, DEPRESSION
S07RR-05736-19 0166 (NSS) TYSON, GEORGE Biomedical research support RENOVATION OF FACILITY
S07RR-05736-19 0210 (NSS) EDMUNDS, LELAND N Biomedical research support OSCILLATOR CONTROL OF CELL DIVISION CYCLES; CIRCADIAN RHYTHMS
S07RR-05736-19 0211 (NSS) BADALAMENTE, MARIE A Biomedical research support LEUPEPTIN IN RECOVERY AFTER NERVE REPAIR
S07RR-05736-19 0167 (NSS) TESTA, JACQUELINE Biomedical research support RAS ONCOGENE ON PROTEASE SECRETION & METASTATIC ABILITY OF COLON CARCINOMA
S07RR-05736-19 0168 (NSS) ARBEIT, LAWRENCE Biomedical research support CYCLOSPORINE NEPHROTOXICITY
S07RR-05736-19 0169 (NSS) FRANCIS, ANDREW Biomedical research support LESION INDUCED HYPERACTIVITY: AN ANIMAL MODEL IN NEUROPSYCHIATRY
S07RR-05736-19 0170 (NSS) GRUBER, BARRY Biomedical research support MAST CELL HYPERPLASIA
S07RR-05736-19 0171 (NSS) HEARING, JANET Biomedical research support EPSTEIN BARR VIRUS NUCLEAR ANTIGEN 1 IN REPLICATION OF LATENT VIRAL GENOMES
S07RR-05736-19 0172 (NSS) MORIN, LAWRENCE Biomedical research support BEHAVIOR BIOLOGICAL RHYTHMS & BRAIN
S07RR-05736-19 0173 (NSS) REICH, NANCY Biomedical research support CELLULAR & ONCOGENIC CONTROL OF INTERFERON INDUCED GENES
S07RR-05736-19 0174 (NSS) BITKUN, STEPHAN A Biomedical research support MECHANISM OF ACTION OF BRONCHODILATING EFFECT OF ANESTHETIC KETAMINE
S07RR-05736-19 0175 (NSS) HOFF, ANNE L Biomedical research support LATERALITY & COGNITIVE DYSFUNCTION
S07RR-05736-19 0212 (NSS) JACOBSON, ANN B Biomedical research support ANALYSIS OF STRUCTURE IN RNAS OF RELATED RNA COLIPHAGES ELECTRON MICROSCOPY
S07RR-05736-19 0213 (NSS) ANDERSEN, JANET Biomedical research support MOLECUL BASIS FOR HUMAN UTERINE SMOOTH MUSCLE TUMORS DVMT: LEIOMYOMA, MYOMETRIUM
S07RR-05736-19 0176 (NSS) PATAKI, CAROLY Biomedical research support PSYCHOPHARMACOLOGIC TREATMENT OF ATTENTIONAL & MOOD DISORDERS
S07RR-05736-19 0177 (NSS) GADOW, KENNETH D Biomedical research support METHULPHANIDATE ON ATTENTION DEFICIT DISORDERS IN CHILDREN C & DVMTL DISABILITY
S07RR-05736-19 0178 (NSS) WILSON, THOMAS A Biomedical research support THROMBOXANE IN ONTOGENY OF RENIN & HYPERTENSION
S07RR-05736-19 0179 (NSS) BOCK, JAY L Biomedical research support MAGNESIUM 25 NMR STUDIES OF RED BLOOD CELLS
S07RR-05736-19 0180 (NSS) WANG, REX Y Biomedical research support REGULATION OF DOPAMINES NEURONS & SCHIZOPHRENIA; ANTIPSYCHOTIC DRUGS: SEROTONIN
S07RR-05736-19 0181 (NSS) DULCHAVSKY, SCOTT A Biomedical research support TREATMENT OF SHOCK INDUCED HYPOTHYROIDISM W/ T3
S07RR-05736-19 0182 (NSS) WASHECKA, ROBERT M Biomedical research support ANTIBIOTIC PEPTIDES IN HUMAN UROTHELIUM
S07RR-05736-19 0183 (NSS) CROWELL, JUDITH A Biomedical research support MOTHERS VIEW OF THEIR OWN CHILDHOODS; MOTHER CHILD INTERACTION & CHILD BEHAVIOR
S07RR-05736-19 0184 (NSS) FRENCH, DEBORAH L Biomedical research support IMMUNOGLOBULIN IN GENES: PRODUCE BETTER ANTIBODIES AS RESEARCH & DX THERAPEUT
S07RR-05736-19 0185 (NSS) GALAN, JORGE Biomedical research support MOLECULAR CHARACTERIZATION OF SALMONELLA INVASION OF EPITHELIAL CELLS
S07RR-05737-20 (NSS) HOYER, LEON W JEROME H HOLLAND LAB 15601 CRABBS BRANCH WAY ROCKVILLE, MD 20855 Biomedical research support
S07RR-05737-20 0214 (NSS) HAYES, LEON Biomedical research support GRAPHICS ILLUSTRATOR SERVICES
S07RR-05737-20 0215 (NSS) HAYER, LEON W Biomedical research support CENTRAL ANIMAL FACILITIES TRANSGENIC MOUSE STUDIES
S07RR-05737-20 0216 (NSS) GILBERT, JAY Biomedical research support NEOPLASTIC DISORDERS INDUCED BY HTLV 1; HIV 1 GENES; HEPATITIS B W/ CANCER
S07RR-05738-20 (NSS) FULLERTON, DWIGHT S UNIVERSITY OF UTAH COLLEGE OF PHARMACY SALT LAKE CITY, UTAH 84112 Biomedical research

PROJECT NO., ORGANIZATIONAL UNIT., INVESTIGATOR, ADDRESS, TITLE

support
S07RR-05738-20 0217 (NSS) ROBERTS, JEANETTE C Biomedical research support FACTORS THAT MAY INFLUENCE KIDNEY GLUTATHIONE LEVELS
S07RR-05738-20 0218 (NSS) KANDROTAS, ROBERT J Biomedical research support INDIVIDUALIZED DOSAGE USING NON STEADY STATE HEPARIN CONCENTRATIONS
S07RR-05738-20 0219 (NSS) FOX, JEFFREY L Biomedical research support TOOTH SURFACE TEMPERATURE DURING LASER IRRADIATION
S07RR-05738-20 0220 (NSS) ROBERTS, JEANETTE C Biomedical research support INDUCTIVE EFFECTS OF BUTHIONINE SULFOXIMINE RELATED COMPOUNDS
S07RR-05743-14 (NSS) NIEFORTH, KARL A UNIVERSITY OF CONNECTICUT SCH PHARM 372 FAIRFIELD RD STORRS, CT 06269-2092 Biomedical research support
S07RR-05743-14 0615 (NSS) BOGNER, ROBIN Biomedical research support ULTRAVIOLET LIGHT CURABLE SILICONE TABLET FILM COATING
S07RR-05743-14 0616 (NSS) MANGOLD, JAMES Biomedical research support SULFATION & BIOACTIVATION OF NITROTOLUENE DERIVED METABOLITES
S07RR-05743-14 0617 (NSS) BOGNER, ROBIN Biomedical research support TRANSDERMAL DRUG DELIVERY & IONTOPHORESIS MOLECULAR WEIGHT
S07RR-05743-14 0618 (NSS) KALONIA, DEVENDRA Biomedical research support FACTORS INVOLVED IN AGGREGATION OF INTERLEUKIN 2
S07RR-05743-14 0619 (NSS) MORRIS, JOHN Biomedical research support TOXICOLOGY OF HALOGENATED ALIPHATIC HYDROCARBONS
S07RR-05744-14 (NSS) FENTERS, JAMES D IIT RESEARCH INSTITUTE 10 WEST 35TH STREET CHICAGO, ILL 60616 Biomedical research support
S07RR-05744-14 0139 (NSS) MOON, RICHARD C Biomedical research support NO SUBPROJECTS
S07RR-05744-14 0140 (NSS) MCCORMICK, DAVID L Biomedical research support NO SUBPROJECTS
S07RR-05745-19 (NSS) RIBBLE, JOHN C UNIVERSITY OF TEXAS POST OFFICE BOX 20708 HOUSTON, TEXAS 77225 Biomedical research support
S07RR-05745-19 0238 (NSS) RUDY, DELBERT C Biomedical research support ASSESSMENT OF DETRUSOR CONTRACTILITY IN CHRONIC SPINAL CORD INJURED CAT
S07RR-05745-19 0239 (NSS) TEICHGRAEBER, JOHN F Biomedical research support EXPERIMENTAL CRANIOSYNOSTOSIS
S07RR-05745-19 0240 (NSS) STEPKOWSKI, STANISLA Biomedical research support INTERLEUKIN 2 ANTISENSE OLIGONUCLEOTIDES AS AN IMMUNOSUPRESSIVE DRUG
S07RR-05745-19 0221 (NSS) MARSHAK, DAVID W Biomedical research support PEPTIDERGIC NEURONS OF MACAQUE UVEA
S07RR-05745-19 0222 (NSS) CROW, MICHAEL T Biomedical research support REGULATION OF MYOSIN LIGHT CHAIN ISOFORM EXPRESSION
S07RR-05745-19 0223 (NSS) MOLONY, DONALD A Biomedical research support EFFECTS OF AGRICULTURAL CHEMICALS ON DISTAL NEPHRON ANION TRANSPORT
S07RR-05745-19 0224 (NSS) SANSOM, STEVE Biomedical research support CONTROL OF CL SECRETION BY EPITHELIAL TISSUES
S07RR-05745-19 0225 (NSS) GUNTUPALLI, JAYARAMA Biomedical research support EFFECTS OF MALEIC ACID ON PHOSPHORUS TRANSPORT: ROLE OF DIETARY PHOSPHORUS
S07RR-05745-19 0226 (NSS) SLOPIS, JOHN M Biomedical research support IN VIVO PROTON MRS; ANTICONVULSANT INDUCED CHANGES IN ANIMAL BRAIN
S07RR-05745-19 0227 (NSS) CISNEROS, PAULINE Biomedical research support INFLUENCE OF PATERNAL AGE ON EMBRYO DEVELOPMENT
S07RR-05745-19 0228 (NSS) FRENCK, ROBERT Biomedical research support ABILITY OF MURINE GM CSF TO PROTECT NEONATAL RATS FROM SEPTIC DEATH BY SAUREUS
S07RR-05745-19 0229 (NSS) ELDER, FREDERICK Biomedical research support CHROMOSOMAL FRAGILE SITES IN LYMPHOID CELLS; LAB MOUSE & RAT
S07RR-05745-19 0241 (NSS) MEYER, BRUCE Biomedical research support EICOSANOID REGULATION OF FETAL PLACENTAL BLOOD FLOW
S07RR-05745-19 0242 (NSS) KIMBALL, PAMELA Biomedical research support INTRACELLULAR SIGNALS FOR CELL CYCLE PROGRESSION ARE SENSITIVE TO CYCLOSPORINE
S07RR-05745-19 0243 (NSS) SHYU, ANN-BIN Biomedical research support MOLECULAR MECHANISMS CONTROLLING DECAY OF C FOS PROTO ONCOGENE TRANSCRIPT
S07RR-05745-19 0244 (NSS) FROST, WILLIAM N Biomedical research support SIMULATION OF NEURONAL CIRCUIT IN APLYSIA
S07RR-05745-19 0245 (NSS) GOTTESFELD, ZEHAVA Biomedical research support MODULATION OF CORTICOTROPHIC RELEASING HORMONE MRNA IN RESPONSE TO ESTROGEN
S07RR-05745-19 0246 (NSS) MAUK, MICHAEL DEAN Biomedical research support CEREBELLAR CORTEX MECHANISMS OF MOTOR LEARNING
S07RR-05745-19 0247 (NSS) CLEARY, LEONARD Biomedical research support MORPHOLOGICAL CORRELATES OF SENSITIZATION IN APLYSIA
S07RR-05745-19 0248 (NSS) SCHROEDER, WANDA T Biomedical research support NEW 17Q 11 12 GENE ESA: LINKAGEW TO NF 1 LOCUS & EXPRESSION IN NEUROFIBROMAS
S07RR-05745-19 0249 (NSS) CRANE, JOHN K Biomedical research support POTENTIATION OF TOXICITY OF HEAT STABLE E COLI TOXIN STA BY PROTEIN KINASE C
S07RR-05745-19 0250 (NSS) SANSOM, STEVEN C Biomedical research support REGULATION OF SMOOTH MUSCLE CL CHANNELS BY CA & PROTEIN KINASE C
S07RR-05745-19 0251 (NSS) THANDROYEN, FRANCIS Biomedical research support MECHANISMS OF INTRACELLULAR CALCIUM ELEVATION DURING METABOLIC INHIBITION
S07RR-05745-19 0252 (NSS) ANDERSON, H VERNON Biomedical research support ANGIOTENSIN RECEPTOR BLOCKADE ON INTIMAL PROLIFERATION AFTER ANGIOPLASTY
S07RR-05745-19 0253 (NSS) MUELLER, HOWARD W Biomedical research support ENDOTHELIAL CELL LIPIDS IN THROMBOSIS & HEMOSTASIS
S07RR-05745-19 0254 (NSS) WANG, LEE-HO Biomedical research support ISOLATION & CHARACTERIZATION OF HUMAN GENOMIC PROSTAGLANDIN H SYNTHASE
S07RR-05745-19 0255 (NSS) KATZENSTEIN, PAUL L Biomedical research support MUTATIONS IN COL2A1; TYPE II COLLAGEN; OSTEOARTHRITIS & EPIPHYSEAL DYSPLASIA
S07RR-05745-19 0256 (NSS) OLSEN, MARY L Biomedical research support MOLECULAR GENETICS OF MHC CLASS III REGION GENES IN SYSTEMIC LUPUS ERYTHEMATOSUS

PROJECT NO., ORGANIZATIONAL UNIT., INVESTIGATOR, ADDRESS, TITLE

S07RR-05745-19 0257 (NSS) MCCARTHY, MICHELINE Biomedical research support MOLECULAR MIMICRY & CELL MEDIATED IMMUNE RESPONSE DETERMINANTS; RUBELLA VIRUS
S07RR-05745-19 0230 (NSS) RIVERA, AUDELIO Biomedical research support TOLERANCE & ULTILIZATION OF IV INFUSED AMINO ACIDS; LOW BIRTH WEIGHT INFANTS
S07RR-05745-19 0231 (NSS) POLLACK, PAUL Biomedical research support METABOLISM OF BOMBESIN LIKE PEPTIDES BY GI TRACT; DVLP RATS
S07RR-05745-19 0232 (NSS) STRAHILEVITZ, MIER Biomedical research support DOPAMINE RECEPTOR ANTIBODIES; TREATING SCHIZOPHRENIA: ANIMAL MODEL
S07RR-05745-19 0233 (NSS) BOUTROS, NASHAAT N Biomedical research support AUDITORY EVOKED RESPONSES IN SCHIZOPHRENICS
S07RR-05745-19 0234 (NSS) STANLEY, MELINDA A Biomedical research support TREAT OBSESSIVE COMPULSIVE DISORDER; FLUOXETINE & EXPOSURE & RESPONSE PREVENT
S07RR-05745-19 0235 (NSS) SCHMITZ, JOY M Biomedical research support EXPOSURE TO SMOKING CUES W/ RESPONSE PREVENTION: SOME PARAMETRIC INVESTIGATIONS
S07RR-05745-19 0236 (NSS) PEABODY, CECILIA Biomedical research support PROLACTIN VARIANT IN SEIZURES
S07RR-05745-19 0237 (NSS) PEARSON, DEOBRAH Biomedical research support DVMTL DELAYS & CLINICAL ASSESSMENT; ATTENTION DEFICIT DISORDER W/ HYPERACTIVITY
S07RR-05745-19 0258 (NSS) ANDRES, ROBERT L Biomedical research support IV METHAMPHETAMINES ON UTERINE BLOOD FLOW & FETAL OXYGENATION & HEMODYNAMICS
S07RR-05745-19 0259 (NSS) HSU, PEI-LING Biomedical research support IRAC A NOVEL ANTIGEN ASSOC W/ REED; STERNBERG & INTERDIGITATING CELLS
S07RR-05745-19 0260 (NSS) DOYLE, MARILYN Biomedical research support PENICILLIN RESISTANCE IN HOUSTON DAY CARE
S07RR-05745-19 0261 (NSS) NORTHRUP, HOPE Biomedical research support TUBEROUS SCLEROSIS: CLINICAL & GENETIC STUDIES
S07RR-05745-19 0262 (NSS) CASAT, CHARLES D Biomedical research support HOSPITAL EFFECT; DEXAMETHASONE SUPPRESSION TEST; CHILDREN PSYCHIATRIC DISORDER
S07RR-05745-19 0263 (NSS) RUSTIN, TERRY A Biomedical research support COMPARISON OF CRAVING FOR NICOTINE & COCAINE
S07RR-05745-19 0264 (NSS) ROSEN, WARREN D Biomedical research support SOCIO EMOTIONAL DEVELOPMENT OF PEDIATRIC CANCER SURVIVORS & THEIR SIBLINGS
S07RR-05745-19 0265 (NSS) MUSEMECHE, CATHERINE Biomedical research support EXPERIMENTAL NECROTIZING ENTEROCOLITIS: POLYMORPHONUCLEAR NEUTROPHILS
S07RR-05746-19 (NSS) DAVIS, GLENN J OAK RIDGE ASSOCIATED UNIV P O BOX 117 OAK RIDGE, TN 37831 Biomedical research support
S07RR-05746-19 0888 (NSS) SNYDER, FRED L Biomedical research support PAF & RELATED LIPID MEDIATORS ON PULMONARY SURFACTANT IN LUNG LAVAGE
S07RR-05746-19 0889 (NSS) SNYDER, FRED L Biomedical research support NOVEL MAB AGAINST MAJOR ENZYME IN BIOSYNTHESIS OF PLATELET ACTIVATING FACTOR
S07RR-05749-19 (NSS) EDWARDS, CHARLES UNIV OF S FLA HLTH SCI CTR 12901 BRUCE B DOWNS BLVD TAMPA, FL 33612 Biomedical research support
S07RR-05749-19 0266 (NSS) BALLESTER, OSCAR F Biomedical research support CYTOGENETIC ANALYSIS OF INTERLEUKIN 6 STIMULATED MYELOMA CELLS
S07RR-05749-19 0267 (NSS) BLANCK, GEORGE Biomedical research support STRUCTURE & FUNCTION OF MULTIGENIC HLA CLASS II REGION
S07RR-05749-19 0268 (NSS) CAMERON, DON F Biomedical research support SERTOLI JUNCTIONAL SPECIALIZATIONS IN VITRO
S07RR-05749-19 0269 (NSS) EICHLER, DUANE C Biomedical research support RIBONUCLEASE INVOLVEMENT IN RIBOSOMAL RNA PROCESSING
S07RR-05749-19 0270 (NSS) LINDSEY, BRUCE G Biomedical research support NEURAL MECHANISMS IN CARDIORESPIRATORY CONTROL
S07RR-05749-19 0271 (NSS) MEDVECAKY, PETER G Biomedical research support VIRAL U RNAS IN ONCOGENIC TRANSFORMATION
S07RR-05749-19 0272 (NSS) NAZIAN, STANLEY J Biomedical research support INTERACTIONS OF TESTOSTERONE & FSH DURING MALE PUBERTY
S07RR-05749-19 0273 (NSS) NESS, GENE C Biomedical research support CDNA & ANTISERA TO CHOLESTEROL 7 ALPHA HYDROXYLASE
S07RR-05749-19 0274 (NSS) PRICE, JOEL M Biomedical research support TEMPERATURE SENSITIVE PERISTALSIS IN ISOLATED ESOPHAGUS
S07RR-05749-19 0275 (NSS) SPECTER, STEVEN Biomedical research support COMBINED ANTIVIRAL & IMMUNOSTIMULATION THERAPY OF RETROVIRUS INDUCED MURINE AIDS
S07RR-05749-19 0276 (NSS) ZORN, NANCY E Biomedical research support VITAMIN A, PROTEIN KINASE C & GENETIC TRANSCRIPTION
S07RR-05749-19 0277 (NSS) GOWER, WILLIAM Biomedical research support TRANSFORMATION OF RAT ANTROPYLORIC G CELLS
S07RR-05749-19 0278 (NSS) DIAMOND, FRANK Biomedical research support SERUM GROWTH HORMONE BINDING PROTEIN; NORMAL & GROWTH RETARD 5D CHILDREN
S07RR-05749-19 0279 (NSS) GARIN, EDUARDO H Biomedical research support NEPHROTIC LYMPHOKINES: GLOMERULAR METABOLISM & PERMEABILITY
S07RR-05749-19 0280 (NSS) SHANNON, ROGER Biomedical research support INTERCOSTAL TENDON ORGAN EFFECTS ON BRAIN STEM RESPIRATORY NEURONS
S07RR-05753-19 (NSS) FAHEY, THOMAS J JR MEMORIAL HOSP/CANCER & ALD DIS 1275 YORK AVENUE NEW YORK, N Y 10021 Biomedical research support
S07RR-05753-19 0513 (NSS) DEVITA, VINCENT T Biomedical research support NO RESEARCH SUBPROJECTS
S07RR-05755-18 (NSS) BARONDES, SAMUEL H LANGLEY PORTER PSYCHIATRIC 401 PARNASSUS AVENUE SAN FRANCISCO, CALIF 94143 Biomedical research support
S07RR-05755-18 0207 (NSS) MUNOX, RICARDO Biomedical research support METABOLIC CONTROL IN DEPRESSED DIABETICS
S07RR-05755-18 0208 (NSS) ZEGANS, LEONARD Biomedical research support REACTIVATION OF LATENT HERPES VIRUS IN GUINEA PIG
S07RR-05755-18 0209 (NSS) LIEBERMAN, MORTON Biomedical research support SELF HELP & ELDERLY
S07RR-05755-18 0210 (NSS) SOMMER, BARBARA Biomedical research

PROJECT NO., ORGANIZATIONAL UNIT., INVESTIGATOR, ADDRESS, TITLE

support FOLIC ACID IN TREATMENT OF DEMENTED ELDERLY
S07RR-05755-18 0211 (NSS) YINGLING, CHARLES Biomedical research support ERP & COGNITIVE RESPONSE TO SUBCORTICAL STIMULATION
S07RR-05755-18 0212 (NSS) FORSTER, PETER Biomedical research support ADRENERGIC RECEPTOR CHANGES IN PTS W/ POSTTRAUMATIC STRESS DISORDER
S07RR-05755-18 0213 (NSS) TROLL, LILLIAN Biomedical research support DEATH OF OLD PARENT ON FAMILY
S07RR-05755-18 0214 (NSS) HINTON, LADSON Biomedical research support MAJOR DEPRESSION IN VIETNAMESE REFUGEES
S07RR-05755-18 0215 (NSS) COOPER, DOUGLAS N W Biomedical research support LECTIN FUNCTION: ALTERED MUSCLE GENE EXPRESSION
S07RR-05755-18 0216 (NSS) LEFFLER, HAKON Biomedical research support NEW LECTINS IN BRAIN: SUBCORTICAL STIMULATION
S07RR-05755-18 0221 (NSS) PEEKE, HARMAN V S Biomedical research support NEUROBEHAVIORAL DEVELOPMENT & PRENATAL STIMULANTS
S07RR-05755-18 0222 (NSS) RAPPAPORT, MAURICE Biomedical research support PASSIVE P300 EVOKED POTENTIAL PATTERNS IN BRAIN INJURY
S07RR-05755-18 0223 (NSS) WOLKOWITZ, OWEN Biomedical research support DEHYDROEPIANDROSTERONE IN DEPRESSION & DEMENTIA
S07RR-05755-18 0224 (NSS) JACOBS, MARC Biomedical research support SUBSTANCE ABUSE IN SCHIZOPHRENIA
S07RR-05755-18 0225 (NSS) WOLKOWITZ, OWEN Biomedical research support KETOCONAZOLE TREATMENT OF HYPERCORTISOLEMIC DEPRESSION
S07RR-05755-18 0217 (NSS) MUNOZ, RICARDO Biomedical research support BILINGUAL COMPUTERIZED ASSESSMENT OF DEPRESSION
S07RR-05755-18 0226 (NSS) RAO, KAVITHA Biomedical research support ASIAN SEXUAL ABUSE STUDY
S07RR-05755-18 0218 (NSS) SALAMY, ALAN Biomedical research support CNS DEVELOPMENT IN COCAINE EXPOSED INFANTS
S07RR-05755-18 0219 (NSS) JEMERIN, JOHN M Biomedical research support AUTONOMIC REACTIVITY & INFANT MENTAL HEALTH
S07RR-05755-18 0220 (NSS) OUTENREATH, ROBERT Biomedical research support ENDOGENOUS LECTINS ON DRG GROWTH IN CULTURES
S07RR-05755-18 0227 (NSS) MCNEIL, DALE Biomedical research support CONCEALED WEAPONS IN PSYCHIATRIC EMERGENCY ROOM
S07RR-05755-18 0228 (NSS) WEISS, DANIEL Biomedical research support TRAUMATIC STRESS OCTOBER 17, 1989 EARTHQUAKE
S07RR-05755-18 0229 (NSS) EKMAN, PAUL Biomedical research support EXPRESSIVE BEHAVIOR & ALZHEIMERS DISEASE
S07RR-05755-18 0230 (NSS) LIBERMAN, MORTON Biomedical research support CHANGES IN EMOTIONS OVER ADULT YEARS
S07RR-05755-18 0231 (NSS) FREIMER, NELSON Biomedical research support GENETICS OF BIOPOLAR DISORDER
S07RR-05755-18 0232 (NSS) PETERSON, NEAL Biomedical research support SERINE TRANSPORT & SERINE CONTAINING LIPIDS IN CNS
S07RR-05755-18 0233 (NSS) BINDER, RENEE Biomedical research support IMPACT OF SETTLEMENT OF LITIGATION ON SYMPTOMS OF PTSD
S07RR-05755-18 0234 (NSS) WALLERSTEIN, ROBERT Biomedical research support NEW MEASURES OF CHANGE IN PSYCHOTHERAPY
S07RR-05755-18 0235 (NSS) SIEGEL, BRYNA Biomedical research support CLINICAL SUBTYPES OF AUTISM
S07RR-05755-18 0236 (NSS) CALLAWAY, ENOCH Biomedical research support TREATMENT OF APATHETIC ELDERLY W/ DAMP & PRO
S07RR-05755-18 0237 (NSS) SALAMY, ALAN Biomedical research support COCAINE ON BTT & MYELIN CONTENT IN RAT
S07RR-05755-18 0238 (NSS) BERGER, PAUL Biomedical research support MOLECULAR MECHANISMS: COCAINE & OTHER UPTAKE INHIBITORS
S07RR-05755-18 0239 (NSS) FREIMER, NELSON Biomedical research support MOLECULAR GENETICS OF BIPOLAR DISORDER
S07RR-05755-18 0240 (NSS) MEADE, MICHAEL Biomedical research support INFORMED CONSENT W/ ACUTE PSYCHIATRIC PATIENTS
S07RR-05755-18 0241 (NSS) SHAH, SHANTILAL Biomedical research support PITUITARY ADRENAL IMMUNE AXIS
S07RR-05756-18 (NSS) FREEDMAN, DANIEL X UNIV OF CALIFORNIA, LOS ANGELE 760 WESTWOOD PLAZA LOS ANGELES, CALIF 90024 Biomedical research support
S07RR-05756-18 0291 (NSS) PERINI, CHARLES Biomedical research support PSYCH FACTORS IN HYPERTENSIVES W/ PRESSOR MECHANISMS; CAPTOPRIL VS NITEDITINE
S07RR-05756-18 0292 (NSS) PERINI, CHARLES Biomedical research support PSYCH FACTORS IN HYPERTENSIVES PRESSOR MECHANISMS: CAPTOPRIL VS NITEDITINE
S07RR-05756-18 0281 (NSS) CUNAWAN, SONNY Biomedical research support BIOASSAY MODEL DVMT: ISOLATION OF ENDOGENOUS ANTI IDAL SUBSTANCES
S07RR-05756-18 0282 (NSS) CUZE, BARRY Biomedical research support CHANGES IN CEREBRAL BLOOD FLOW INDUCED BY ECT: EVALUATION BY SPECT IMP
S07RR-05756-18 0283 (NSS) HANDFORTH, ADRIAN Biomedical research support NEW ANIMAL MODEL, DVMT: ACQUIRED EPILEPSY W/ LIMBIC ONSET SEIZURES
S07RR-05756-18 0284 (NSS) HOWLAND, REBEKAH Biomedical research support METHYLPHENIDATE CHALLENGE TEST & URINARY MH LEVELS
S07RR-05756-18 0285 (NSS) MANOS, PATRICIA Biomedical research support ENERGY MAINTENANCE IN DEVELOPING BRAIN: CREATN KINASE IN MYELINOGENESIS
S07RR-05756-18 0293 (NSS) KARNO, MARVIN Biomedical research support ETHNIC DIFFERENCES IN SELECTED MENTAL DISORDERS & SUBSTANCE ABUSE DISORDERS
S07RR-05756-18 0294 (NSS) SZUBA, MARTIN Biomedical research support RAPID DEPRESSION TREATMENT W/ LITHIUM SLEEP DEPRIVATION
S07RR-05756-18 0295 (NSS) BUCHWALD, NATHANIAL Biomedical research support MENTAL RETARDATION RESEARCH CENTER
S07RR-05756-18 0296 (NSS) CAMPAGNONI, ANTHONY Biomedical research support DEVELOPMENTAL BIOLOGY RESEARCH GROUP
S07RR-05756-18 0297 (NSS) FLUHARTY, ARVAN L Biomedical research support METACHROMATIC LEUKODYSTROPHY IN CULTURED CELL SYSTEMS
S07RR-05756-18 0286 (NSS) NICOLINI, HUMBERTO Biomedical research support CHROMOSOME 11 LINKAGE ANALYSIS: ADOLESCENTS W/ BIPOLAR ATTENTIVE DISORDERS
S07RR-05756-18 0287 (NSS) PRICE-WILLIAMS, DOUG Biomedical research support CREATIVE PROCESSESS IN MASTER ARTISTS
S07RR-05756-18 0288 (NSS) LIBERMAN, ROBERT Biomedical research support SCHIZOPHRENIA
S07RR-05756-18 0289 (NSS) BROTHERS, LESLIE Biomedical research support SUB CLINICAL MARKERS IN AUTISM
S07RR-05756-18 0290 (NSS) KARNO, MARVIN Biomedical research support ETHNIC DIFFERENCES IN SELECTED MENTAL DISORDERS & SUBSTANCE ABUSE DISORDERS
S07RR-05756-18 0298 (NSS) LIBERMAN, ROBERT Biomedical research support MHCRC FOR SCHIZOPHRENIC & PSYCHIATRIC REHABILITATION
S07RR-05756-18 0299 (NSS) ANGLIN, DOUGLAS Biomedical research support RESEARCH DVMT AT UCLA DRUG ABUSE RESEARCH GROUP
S07RR-05756-18 0300 (NSS) GUZE, BARRY Biomedical research support CHANGES IN CEREBRAL BLOOD FLOW INDUCED BY ECT: EVAL BY SPECT IMP
S07RR-05756-18 0301 (NSS) CAPLAN, ROCHELLE Biomedical research support NONVERBAL COMMUNICATION; CHILDREN W/ INTRACTABLE SEIZURES
S07RR-05756-18 0302 (NSS) DAVIDSON, ROBIN Biomedical research support ADOLESCENT & YOUNG ADULT SURVIVORS OF BONE MARROW TRANSPLANTATION
S07RR-05756-18 0303 (NSS) SMALLEY, SUSAN Biomedical research support GENETIC RELATIONSHIP OF AUTISM & TUBEROS SCLEROSIS
S07RR-05756-18 0304 (NSS) STUBER, MARGARET Biomedical research support LONG TERM STUDY OF PEDIATRIC BONE MARROW TRANSPLANT
S07RR-05756-18 0305 (NSS) BARTZOKIS, GEORGE Biomedical research support MRI STUDIES OF MEDICATION EFFECTS ON BASAL GANGLIA & MOVEMENT DISORDERS
S07RR-05756-18 0306 (NSS) COOMBS, ROBERT Biomedical research support LIFE SPAN DEVELOPMENT OF MEDICAL MARRIAGE CAREER & PERSONALITY
S07RR-05756-18 0307 (NSS) PENIX, LEROY Biomedical research support CHARACTERIZE BINDING OF FELBAMATE: ANTICONVULSANT & NEUROPROTECTIVE AGENT
S07RR-05756-18 0308 (NSS) WALLIS, ROIANN Biomedical research support EXCITOTOXIC MECHANISMS OF HIPPOCAMPAL INJURY
S07RR-05756-18 0309 (NSS) HANDFORTH, ADRIAN Biomedical research support NEW ANIMAL MODEL DVMT OF ACQUIRED EPILEPSY W/ LIMBIC ONSET SEIZURES
S07RR-05756-18 0310 (NSS) BLUM, DAVID Biomedical research support CHARACTERISTICS OF INTERICTAL SPIKE DISCHARGE
S07RR-05756-18 0311 (NSS) LEUCHTER, ANDREW Biomedical research support ALZHEIMERS DISEASE & MEMORY DISORDER CLINIC
S07RR-05756-18 0312 (NSS) TOGA, ARTHUR Biomedical research support NEUROLOGY MAIN ACCOUNT GENERAL RESOURCES
S07RR-05756-18 0313 (NSS) KARNO, MARVIN Biomedical research support FAMILY INTERVENTION FOR HISPANIC AMERICAN SCHIZOPHRENICS
S07RR-05756-18 0314 (NSS) ANGLIN, DOUGLAS Biomedical research support RESEARCH DEVELOPMENT SUPPORT FOR UCLA DRUG ABUSE RESEARCH GROUP
S07RR-05756-18 0315 (NSS) SPAR, JAMES Biomedical research support INTEGRATED GERIATRIC SERVICES COMPUTER NETWORK
S07RR-05756-18 0316 (NSS) STUBER, MARGARET Biomedical research support DATA ANALYSIS; PSYCHIATRIC IMPACT OF PEDIATRIC BONE MARROW TRANSPLANT
S07RR-05756-18 0317 (NSS) VICKREY, BARBARA Biomedical research support QUALITY OF LIFE & SEIZURES AFTER EPILEPSY SURGERY
S07RR-05756-18 0318 (NSS) LIBERMAN, ROBERT Biomedical research support CRC FOR STUDY OF SCHIZOPHRENIA
S07RR-05756-18 0319 (NSS) SZUBE, MARTIN Biomedical research support PSYCHOBIOLOGY OF ANTIDEPRESSANT PROPERTIES OF PARTIAL SLEEP DEPRIVATION
S07RR-05756-18 0320 (NSS) HANDFORTH, ADRIAN Biomedical research support NEW ANIMAL MODEL DVMT OF ACQUIRED EPILEPSY W/ LIMBIC ONSET SEIZURES
S07RR-05756-18 0321 (NSS) FREEDMAN, DANIEL Biomedical research support DEPARTMENTAL MAIN ACCOUNT; GENERAL RESOURCES
S07RR-05756-18 0322 (NSS) FREEDMAN, DANIEL X Biomedical research support DEPARTMENT ACCOUNT; GENERAL RESOURCES
S07RR-05758-18 (NSS) HEGYVARY, SUE T UNIVERSITY OF WASHINGTON SCHOOL OF NURSING SC-72 SEATTLE, WASH 98195 Biomedical research support
S07RR-05758-18 0242 (NSS) ARMSDEN, GAY Biomedical research support CHILDS PERSPECTIVE ON COPING W/ MOTHERS BREAST CANCER
S07RR-05758-18 0243 (NSS) BROWN, MARIE ANNETTE Biomedical research support HOME BASED CARE OF PERSONS W/ AIDS: NEEDS OF FAMILY CAREGIVERS
S07RR-05758-18 0244 (NSS) CORNMAN, JANE Biomedical research support ADOLESCENT RESPONSE TO CHILDHOOD SEXUAL ABUSE
S07RR-05758-18 0245 (NSS) FLAGLER, SUSAN Biomedical research support FUNCTIONAL ABILITY DURING PREGNANCY
S07RR-05758-18 0246 (NSS) GRAHAM, KATHERINE Biomedical research support QUALITY OF LIFE
S07RR-05758-18 0247 (NSS) HEITKEMPER, MARGARET Biomedical research support GASTROINTESTINAL SYMPTOMS ACROSS MENSTRUAL CYCLE
S07RR-05758-18 0248 (NSS) KANG, REBECCA Biomedical research support CAREGIVERS OF SUBSTANCE EXPOSES INFANTS
S07RR-05758-18 0249 (NSS) KIECKHEFER, GAIL Biomedical research support IMPROVING HEALTH OUTCOMES FOR CHILDREN W/ ASTHMA
S07RR-05758-18 0250 (NSS) LALONDE, BERNADETTE Biomedical research support FAMILIES EXPERIENCING BREAST CANCER: BOOKLET EVALUATION
S07RR-05758-18 0251 (NSS) LEWIS, FRANCES Biomedical research support DEMANDS OF ILLNESS ON LESBIAN COUPLE EXPERIENCING BREAST CANCER
S07RR-05758-18 0252 (NSS) LEWIS, LINDA Biomedical research support PATTERNS IN WOMEN W/ PREMENSTRUAL SYNDROME
S07RR-05758-18 0253 (NSS) LIERMAN, LETHA Biomedical research support BREAST SELF EXAMINATION QUESTIONNAIRE DEVELOPMENT
S07RR-05758-18 0254 (NSS) MARVIN, JANET Biomedical research support PAIN EXPRESSION IN INFANTS: A MULTIDIMENSIONAL STUDY
S07RR-05758-18 0255 (NSS) MONTANO, DANIEL Biomedical research support DETERMINANTS OF CONDOM USE TO PREVENT AIDS
S07RR-05758-18 0256 (NSS) MURPHY, SHIRLEY Biomedical research support ABSTAINERS FROM ALCOHOL
S07RR-05758-18 0257 (NSS) NIELD, MARGARET Biomedical research support EFFECT OF MUSCLE TRAINING IN SUBJECTS W/ CHRONIC OBSTRUCTIVE PULMONARY DISEASE
S07RR-05758-18 0258 (NSS) OLSHANSKY, ELLEN Biomedical research support PREGNANCY AFTER INFERTILITY

PROJECT NO., ORGANIZATIONAL UNIT., INVESTIGATOR, ADDRESS, TITLE

S07RR-05758-18 0259 (NSS) SCHULTZ, PHYLLIS Biomedical research support PUBLIC HEALTH CHARTING SYSTEM
S07RR-05758-18 0260 (NSS) THOMAS, KAREN Biomedical research support TYMPANIC MEMBRANE TEMPERATURE
S07RR-05758-18 0261 (NSS) WAGNILD, GAIL Biomedical research support PSYCHOMETRIC PROPERTIES OF RESILIENCE SCALE
S07RR-05758-18 0262 (NSS) WARD, DEBBIE Biomedical research support ELDER KIN CARE BY LOW INCOME WOMEN
S07RR-05758-18 0263 (NSS) WILKIE, DIANA Biomedical research support PAIN EXPRESSION COACHING
S07RR-05758-18 0264 (NSS) WOODS, NANCY Biomedical research support DIFFERENTIATING PERIMENSTRUAL SYMPTOMS
S07RR-05758-18 0265 (NSS) WOODS, NANCY Biomedical research support ESTROGEN ASSAYS
S07RR-05761-17 (NSS) DAY, ROBERT W FRED HUTCHINSON CANCER RES CTR 1124 COLUMBIA STREET SEATTLE, WASH 98104 Biomedical research support
S07RR-05761-17 0202 (NSS) HANSEN, JOHN Biomedical research support ADULT LEUKEMIA CENTER
S07RR-05761-17 0203 (NSS) HANSEN, JOHN Biomedical research support HUMAN IMMUNOGENETICS PROGRAM HLA LAB
S07RR-05761-17 0204 (NSS) HENDERSON, MAUREEN Biomedical research support CANCER PREVENTION RESEARCH UNIT
S07RR-05761-17 0205 (NSS) HANSEN, JOHN Biomedical research support HTLV I & II LABORATORY
S07RR-05761-17 0206 (NSS) PRENTICE, ROSS Biomedical research support CARET COORDINATING CENTER
S07RR-05761-17 0207 (NSS) DAVIS, SCOTT Biomedical research support HANFORD THYROID DISEASE STUDY
S07RR-05761-17 0208 (NSS) CROWLEY, JOHN Biomedical research support SOUTHWEST ONCOLOGY GROUP STATISTICAL CENTER
S07RR-05765-17 (NSS) MAIZEL, ABBY ROGER WILLIAMS GENERAL HOSP 825 CHALKSTONE AVENUE PROVIDENCE, R I 02908 Biomedical research support
S07RR-05765-17 0209 (NSS) REDLINE, SUSAN Biomedical research support SLEEP RELATED DISORDERS
S07RR-05765-17 0210 (NSS) MAIZEL, ABBY Biomedical research support QUANTITATIVE PROLIFERATION INDEX SOFTWARE FOR CELL ANALYSIS SYSTEM
S07RR-05767-17 (NSS) YOUNG, FRANKLIN A, JR MEDICAL UNIV OF SOUTH CAROLINA COL OF DEN MED, 171 ASHLEY AVE CHARLESTON, S C 29425 Biomedical research support
S07RR-05767-17 0323 (NSS) CANTEY, J ROBERT Biomedical research support MABS TO V CHOLERAE VIRULENCE ANTIGENS
S07RR-05767-17 0324 (NSS) MCDONALD, J KEN Biomedical research support LYSOSOMAL PROTEASES OF SPERMATOZOA: FERTILIZATION
S07RR-05767-17 0325 (NSS) OLSON, JOAN C Biomedical research support PRODUCTION OF PSEUDOMONAS TOXIN VACCINE SYNTHETIC SUBCLONED PRODUCTS
S07RR-05767-17 0326 (NSS) VIRELLA, GABRIEL T Biomedical research support FISH OIL EXTRACTS & HOST DEFENSE MECHANISMS
S07RR-05767-17 0327 (NSS) WALLACE, STEPHEN Biomedical research support TREATMENT OF MANDIBULAR CLASS II FURCATIONS: REGENERATION CONNECTIVE TISSUE
S07RR-05767-17 0328 (NSS) WANG, AN-CHUAN Biomedical research support IMMUNOBIOLOGY OF HUMAN THY 1 ANTIGEN
S07RR-05767-17 0329 (NSS) WARR, GREGORY W Biomedical research support EVOLUTION OF LYMPHOCYTE RECOGNITION
S07RR-05768-12 (NSS) LEAVITT, JOHN C CALIF INST FOR MED RES 2260 CLOVE DRIVE SAN JOSE, CA 95128 Biomedical research support grant
S07RR-05770-13 (NSS) LAMY, PETER P UNIVERSITY OF MARYLAND 20 N PINE STREET BALTIMORE, MD 21201 Biomedical research support
S07RR-05770-13 0930 (NSS) REYNOLDS, KEVIN A Biomedical research support AN ENZYMATIC APPROACH TO UNDERSTANDING MACROLIDE & POLYETHER BIOSYNTHESIS
S07RR-05770-13 0931 (NSS) ROSLER, HEINZ Biomedical research support INVESTIGATION & COMPARISON OF ANTHRAQUINONES W/ ANTIVIRAL ACTIVITIES
S07RR-05770-13 0932 (NSS) SPEEDIE, MARILYN K Biomedical research support EXPRESSION OF HETEROLOGOUS PROTEIN BY STREPTOMYCETES
S07RR-05770-13 0933 (NSS) ECCLES, CHRISTINE U Biomedical research support CALCIUM REGULATION & NEUROTOXICITY; EXCITATORY AMINO ACIDS; NITRIC OXIDE
S07RR-05770-13 0934 (NSS) POU, SOVITZ Biomedical research support RAT BRAIN DAMAGES BY MAGNETIC RESONANCE IMAGING & CONTRAST AGENTS
S07RR-05770-13 0935 (NSS) BUTERBAUGH, GARY G Biomedical research support ENDOGENOUS NEUROPROTECTION & NMDA RECEPTOR
S07RR-05770-13 0936 (NSS) DALE, GRADY, JR Biomedical research support PROGRAM FOR PHARMACUETICAL STUDY OF CHILDREN
S07RR-05770-13 0937 (NSS) FEDDER, DONALD O Biomedical research support COMMUNITY HEALTH WORKER OUTREACH & HEALTH PROMOTION PROGRAM
S07RR-05770-13 0938 (NSS) BHAGAT, HITESH Biomedical research support BIODEGRADABLE MICROSPHERES CONTAINING WATER SOLUBLE PROTEINS
S07RR-05771-15 (NSS) COOKE, WILLIAM J EASTERN VIRGINIA MED SCHOOL 358 MOWBRAY ARCH, P O BOX 1980 NORFOLK, VA 23501 Biomedical research support
S07RR-05771-15 0330 (NSS) BOOZER, CAROL N Biomedical research support FUEL OXIDATION & DIET INDUCED OBESITY
S07RR-05771-15 0331 (NSS) PRATT, MICHAEL F Biomedical research support PHARMACOLOGIC ENHANCEMENT OF SKIN FLAP SURVIVAL
S07RR-05771-15 0332 (NSS) LIUZZI, FRANCIS J Biomedical research support NON NEURONAL ENVIRONMENT REGULATE AXON DIAMETER BY MODULATION
S07RR-05771-15 0334 (NSS) ROSENTHAL, MIRIAM D Biomedical research support NOVEL EFFECTS OF NEUTROPHILS PHOSPHOLIPASES A2
S07RR-05771-15 0335 (NSS) GARCIA, MARTHA C Biomedical research support POLYUNSATURATED FATTY ACIDS & SIGNAL TRANSDUCTION IN VASCULAR ENDOTHELIUM
S07RR-05771-15 0336 (NSS) BERGHORN, KATHIE A Biomedical research support ESTROGEN ON FETAL HYPOTHALMIC PITUITARY FUNCTION DURING GESTATION IN BABOON
S07RR-05772-17 (NSS) MCCORMICK, J JUSTIN MICHIGAN STATE UNIVERSITY B620 W FEE HALL EAST LANSING, MI 48824-1316 Biomedical research support
S07RR-05772-17 0338 (NSS) SPARKS, BARBARA Biomedical research support PREGNANCY INDUCED HYPERTENSION IN RURAL ZIMBABWE
S07RR-05772-17 0339 (NSS) HARDING, SHIRLEY Biomedical research support ELMIRON & URODYNAMICS FOR INTERSTITIAL CYSTITIS
S07RR-05772-17 0337 (NSS) GERHARDT, PHILIPP Biomedical research support DIFFERENTIAL SCANNING CALORIMETER STUDY OF HEAT INACTIVATION OF BACTERIAL SPORES
S07RR-05772-17 0340 (NSS) MAGEN, JED Biomedical research support MAGNETIC IMAGING IN CHILDREN W/ PSYCHOTIC SYMPTOMS
S07RR-05772-17 0341 (NSS) HEIDEMANN, STEVEN Biomedical research support TENSION AS REGULATOR OF AXONAL ELONGATION
S07RR-05772-17 0342 (NSS) FRAKER, PAMELA Biomedical research support DIETARY ZINC: EFFECT IN IMMUNE RESPONSE
S07RR-05772-17 0343 (NSS) MCCORMICK, J JUSTIN Biomedical research support TRANSFORMATION OF DIPLOID HUMAN FIBROBLASTS
S07RR-05772-17 0344 (NSS) KINGRY, MARGARET Biomedical research support CANCER EXPERIENCE INVOLVEMENT ITS EFFECT ON ADOLESCENTS
S07RR-05772-17 0345 (NSS) HENDRIX, SUSAN Biomedical research support MAGNETIC RESONANCE IMAGING IN ENDOMETRIOSIS & ADHESIVE DISEASE
S07RR-05772-17 0346 (NSS) GORMAN, MARK Biomedical research support ADENOSINE FORMATION REGULATION IN INTACT DOG HEART
S07RR-05772-17 0347 (NSS) DILLON, PATRICK Biomedical research support INSULIN DEPENDENCE OF BLOOD FLOW IN BLADDER
S07RR-05772-17 0348 (NSS) KAUFMAN, LARYSSA Biomedical research support SALIVARY MELATONIN: MARKER FOR SEASONAL DEPRESSION
S07RR-05772-17 0349 (NSS) KRON, MICHAEL Biomedical research support ANTIGEN GENE CHARACTERIZATION FROM ONCHOCERCA VOLVU
S07RR-05772-17 0350 (NSS) ESSELMAN, WALTER Biomedical research support FLOW CYTOMETER CELL SORTER SUPPORT
S07RR-05772-17 0351 (NSS) HALLGREN, RICHARD Biomedical research support THREE DIMENSIONAL MOTION MECHANICS NORMAL & PATHOLOGICAL
S07RR-05772-17 0352 (NSS) FALLS, WILLIAM Biomedical research support ANATOMICAL STUDIES OF SENSORY TRIGEMINAL NUCLIDE
S07RR-05772-17 0353 (NSS) BURTON, ZACHARY Biomedical research support TRANSCRIPTION FACTORS THAT BIND RNA POLYMERASE II
S07RR-05772-17 0354 (NSS) FRATKIN, JONATHAN D Biomedical research support PHENOTYPES & GENOTYPES OF METASTATIC FIBROSARCOMAS
S07RR-05772-17 0355 (NSS) HEIDEMANN, STEVEN R Biomedical research support REGULATION OF NEURAL GROWTH BY TENSION
S07RR-05772-17 0356 (NSS) KOESTNER, ADALBERT Biomedical research support NEUROOCOGENESIS BY RESORPTIVE CARCINOGENS
S07RR-05772-17 0357 (NSS) REYNOLDS, HERBERT Biomedical research support LUMBAR MOTION AS FUNCTION OF TORSO ANGLE
S07RR-05772-17 0358 (NSS) HAUT, ROGER Biomedical research support SCAR FORMATION IN RABBIT PETELLAR TENDON
S07RR-05772-17 0359 (NSS) FALLS, WILLIAM Biomedical research support EFFERENT PROJECTIONS FROM SENSORY TRIGEMINAL NUCLEI
S07RR-05772-17 0360 (NSS) BENNETT, JAMES Biomedical research support MEVALONATE LABELLED PROTEINS OF S MANSONI
S07RR-05772-17 0361 (NSS) MCCONNELL, DAVID Biomedical research support RAS GENE EXPRESSION IN MUCOR RACEMOSUS & RETINAL PHOTORECEPTORS
S07RR-05773-17 (NSS) BARKER, KENNETH L TX TECH UNIV HLTH SCI CTR SCHOOL OF MEDICINE LUBBOCK, TEX 79430 Biomedical research support
S07RR-05773-17 0362 (NSS) CHAFFIN, W LAJEAN Biomedical research support SURFACE ANTIGENS & MORPHOGENESIS IN CANDIDA ALBICANS
S07RR-05773-17 0363 (NSS) DENARO, F J Biomedical research support MAPPING OF ANTIOXIDANT ENZYME IN BRAIN
S07RR-05773-17 0364 (NSS) MCMAHON, KATHRYN Biomedical research support ENDOGENOUS ADP RIBOSYLATION PRODUCT OF RAT HEART
S07RR-05773-17 0365 (NSS) NEWPORT, MARY LYNN Biomedical research support BIOMECHANICS OF EXTENSOR TENDON REPAIR OVER DIGIT
S07RR-05773-17 0369 (NSS) RITZI, EARL Biomedical research support UNIQUE BREAST TUMOR MUCIN EPITOPES REGULATION
S07RR-05773-17 0370 (NSS) STOCCO, DOUGLAS Biomedical research support MITOCHONDRIA & LEYDIG CELL STEROIDOGENESIS
S07RR-05773-17 0371 (NSS) TENNER, THOMAS Biomedical research support MECHANISM OF VASCULAR MUSCLE CELL GROWTH IN DIABETES
S07RR-05773-17 0372 (NSS) WEITLAUF, HARRY Biomedical research support EFFECTS OF DECIDUAL ENVIRONMENT ON ANTIGEN PRESENTATION
S07RR-05773-17 0373 (NSS) STRAUS, DAVID Biomedical research support CHARACTERIZATION OF PSEUDOMINAS CEPACIA LIPOPOLYSACCHARIDE
S07RR-05773-17 0366 (NSS) PELLEY, JOHN Biomedical research support REGULATION OF LIPOIC ACID BIOSYNTHESIS
S07RR-05773-17 0367 (NSS) PODUSIO, SHIRLEY Biomedical research support REGULATION OF MYELIN PROTEIN GENE EXPRESSION BY THYROID HORMONE
S07RR-05773-17 0368 (NSS) REIGEL, CHARLES Biomedical research support DEVELOPMENTAL INDUCTION OF AUDIOGENIC SEIZURES IN RATS
S07RR-05773-17 0374 (NSS) TENNER, THOMAS Biomedical research support RABBIT PLATELETS: STUDY OF SIGNAL TRANSDUCTION IN DIABETES
S07RR-05773-17 0375 (NSS) DORIS, PETER A Biomedical research support MOLECULAR BIOLOGY OF BRAIN RENIN ANGIOTENSIN SYSTEM
S07RR-05773-17 0376 (NSS) SRIDHARA, S Biomedical research support APPROACHES TO ISOLATE ECDYSONE RECEPTOR & ITS GENES
S07RR-05773-17 0377 (NSS) PELLEY, JOHN Biomedical research support REGULATION OF LIPOIC ACID BIOSYNTHESIS
S07RR-05773-17 0378 (NSS) RHYNE, CRAIG Biomedical research support HUMAN VISCERAL MACROPHAGE IMMUNOLOGIC FUNCTION
S07RR-05773-17 0379 (NSS) RHYNE, CRAIG Biomedical research support ACCESSORY CELL INTERACTION W/ MITOGEN
S07RR-05773-17 0380 (NSS) CHOKHAVATIA, SITA Biomedical research support AGING ON NEUROMUSCULAR STRUCTURE OF HUMAN COLON
S07RR-05773-17 0381 (NSS) LYNESS, W H Biomedical research support CHRONIC PAIN SYNDROMES & NARCOTIC USE
S07RR-05773-17 0382 (NSS) GUERRERO, MARTIN Biomedical research support COGNITIVE PROCESSING IN BIPOLAR DISORDER
S07RR-05774-17 (NSS) COGGIN, JOSEPH H, JR UNIVERSITY OF SOUTH ALABAMA ROOM 170 CSAB MOBILE, ALABAMA 36688 Biomedical research support
S07RR-05774-17 0383 (NSS) GARD, ANTHONY L Biomedical research support TROPHIC DETERMINANTS OF OLIGODENDROCYTE DEVELOPMENT
S07RR-05774-17 0384 (NSS) FLETCHER, JOHN R Biomedical research support EICOSANOIDS & PLATELET ACTIVATING FACTOR IN PERITONITIS
S07RR-05775-16 (NSS) WYNDER, ERNST L AMERICAN HEALTH FOUNDATION ONE DANA ROAD VALHALLA, NY 10595 Biomedical research support

S07RR-05776-11 (NSS) KNAFL, KATHLEEN A UNIV OF ILL AT CHICAGO 845 S DAMEN AVE COL NUR RM 511 CHICAGO, IL 60612 Biomedical research support grant
S07RR-05776-11 0385 (NSS) BARGE, FRANCES C Biomedical research support grant FOCUS GROUPS FOR HOMELESS WOMEN
S07RR-05776-11 0386 (NSS) BREITMAYER, BONNIE J Biomedical research support grant RISK FACTORS FOR ADOLESCENT SUICIDE: PROCEDURE DEVELOPMENT
S07RR-05776-11 0387 (NSS) COHEN, FELISSA L Biomedical research support grant FOSTER CARE POLICIES FOR CHILDREN W/ HIV INFECTION OR AIDS; NATL SURVEY
S07RR-05776-11 0388 (NSS) COWELL, JULIA M Biomedical research support grant EFFECTS OF VIOLENCE ON ADAPTATION & HEALTH; SE ASIAN REFUGEE CHILDREN
S07RR-05776-11 0389 (NSS) DANCY, BARBARA L Biomedical research support grant AFRICAN AMERICAN WOMEN & AIDS
S07RR-05776-11 0398 (NSS) SCHWERTZ, DORIE W Biomedical research support grant INOTROPIC EFFECT OF PIMOBENDAN IN ALCOHOLIC MYOCARDIUM
S07RR-05776-11 0390 (NSS) DAVIS, JANET H Biomedical research support grant DEVELOPING MASTER TEACHERS FOR INFUSION HOME CARE NURSING
S07RR-05776-11 0391 (NSS) ERVIN, NAOMI E Biomedical research support grant ANALYSIS & ASSESS NURSING CARE QUALITY
S07RR-05776-11 0392 (NSS) GERACE, LAINA M Biomedical research support grant ADULT SIBLING RESPONSE TO CHRONIC MENTAL ILLNESS
S07RR-05776-11 0393 (NSS) GILLIES, DEE A Biomedical research support grant LINKING NURSE LEADERSHIP TO JOB & PATIENT SATISFACTION
S07RR-05776-11 0394 (NSS) HANSON, KATHLEEN S Biomedical research support grant SARAH GREGG: QUIET WORK OF CIVIL WAR NURSE
S07RR-05776-11 0395 (NSS) HILL, PAMELA D Biomedical research support grant BREASTFEEDING MOTHERS OF LOW BIRTH WEIGHT INFANTS
S07RR-05776-11 0396 (NSS) HOLM, KARYN Biomedical research support grant PHYSICAL ACTIVITY PATTERNS & BONE MINERAL DENSITY; WOMEN
S07RR-05776-11 0397 (NSS) LOGAN, BARBARA N Biomedical research support grant HIGH RISK BEHAVIOR REDUCTION AMONG MINORITY TEENS
S07RR-05776-11 0399 (NSS) SHAW, REBECCA J Biomedical research support grant CAREGIVER STRESS & HEALTH PROMOTION
S07RR-05776-11 0400 (NSS) SMITH, EVA D Biomedical research support grant SELF CARE IN BLACK WOMEN W/ BREAST CANCER
S07RR-05776-11 0401 (NSS) THEIS, SAUNDRA L Biomedical research support grant EFFECTS OF RESPITE ON FAMILY CAREGIVERS
S07RR-05776-11 0402 (NSS) WILBUR, JOELLEN Biomedical research support grant MEASURING PHYSICAL ACTIVITY IN MIDLIFE WOMEN
S07RR-05778-16 (NSS) GARANT, PHILIAS R STATE UNIVERSITY OF NEW YORK SCHOOL OF DENTAL MEDICINE STONY BROOK, N Y 11794 Biomedical research support
S07RR-05778-16 0403 (NSS) IACONO, VINCENT J Biomedical research support HPLO: NEW TECHNIQUE FOR PURIFICATION OF SALIVARY PEPTIDES & PROTEINS
S07RR-05778-16 0404 (NSS) SHAKUN, MORTIMER S Biomedical research support MATH MODEL FOR FORCE DISTRIBUTION OF COMPLETELY CONTAINED MANDIBULAR MOTION
S07RR-05778-16 0405 (NSS) RAMAMURTHY, N S Biomedical research support VANADIUM SALT & PETRO CORPUS MARSUPIUM ON HYPERGLYCEMIA & COLLAGEN SYNTHESIS
S07RR-05778-16 0406 (NSS) WOLFF, MARK S Biomedical research support PH: DENTOGINGIVAL PLAQUE AFTER UREA VS FLOW OF GINGIVAL CREVICULAR FLUID
S07RR-05778-16 0407 (NSS) WOLFF, MARK S Biomedical research support PREVENTION OF INFECTION & CROSS INFECTION W/ IN DENTAL LAB
S07RR-05778-16 0408 (NSS) POLLOCK, JERRY J Biomedical research support ULTRA PURE WATER SYSTEM FOR HIGH PRESSURE LIQUID CHROMATOGRAPHY SYSTEM
S07RR-05778-16 0409 (NSS) ULLO, CHARLES A Biomedical research support PHYSICAL PROPERTIES OF SILKWRAP REINFORCED COMPOSITE RESIN
S07RR-05778-16 0410 (NSS) POLLOCK, JERRY J Biomedical research support DENTURE STOMATITIS MODEL TO TEST CANDIDA ALBICAN INDUCED IMMUNOSUPPRESSION: AIDS
S07RR-05778-16 0411 (NSS) GWINNETT, A JOHN Biomedical research support EVALUATION OF ENAMEL SURFACES AFTER DEBONDING CERAMIC BRACKETS
S07RR-05778-16 0412 (NSS) IANZANO, JOHN A Biomedical research support IN VIVO EVALUATION OF PORCELAIN INLAYS LUTED W/ COMPOSITE RESIN
S07RR-05778-16 0413 (NSS) COX, DONALD S Biomedical research support SYNTHESIS OF INTERLEUKIN 2 IN PERIODONTAL DISEASE
S07RR-05780-16 (NSS) SHACKS, SAMUEL J CHARLES R DREW UNIVERISTY 1621 E 120TH ST, MAILPOINT #27 LOS ANGELES, CALIF 90059 Biomedical research support
S07RR-05780-16 0970 (NSS) CASEY, RICHARD Biomedical research support INDUCERS & INHIBITORS OF CORNEAL NEOVASCULARIZATION
S07RR-05780-16 0971 (NSS) ESFANDIARI, ADELPH Biomedical research support PREVALENCE OF ENTERIC PARASITES IN SELECTED COMMUNITY IN LOS ANGELES
S07RR-05780-16 0972 (NSS) GHONEUM, MAMDOOH Biomedical research support EFFECT OF SMOKE ON NATURAL KILLER CELL ACTIVITY OF BLACK AMERICANS
S07RR-05780-16 0973 (NSS) HUMPHREY, MOSS Biomedical research support RESEARCH INFORMATION RESOURCES
S07RR-05780-16 0974 (NSS) KAHN, MIRIAM Biomedical research support PROVIDERS HELPING BEHAVIOR: ATTITUDES TOWARD DISEASE RESPONSE & OBESITY
S07RR-05780-16 0975 (NSS) RAO, RAMACHANDRA Biomedical research support FACULTY SUPPORT AWARD
S07RR-05780-16 0976 (NSS) REGALDO, MICHAEL Biomedical research support SLEEP STATE ORGANIZATION IN COCAINE EXPOSED NEWBORN INFANTS
S07RR-05780-16 0977 (NSS) SHACKS, SAMUEL Biomedical research support RESEARCH RESOURCES
S07RR-05780-16 0978 (NSS) WILLIAMS, ELAINE Biomedical research support COMMUNITY HYPERTENSION INTERVENTION PROGRAM
S07RR-05788-15 (NSS) KOSCH, PHILIP C UNIVERSITY OF FLORIDA BOX J-125, HLTH SCI CTR GAINESVILLE, FL 32610 Biomedical research support
S07RR-05788-15 0890 (NSS) ROTH, LOIS Biomedical research support COCAINE INDUCED HEPATOXICITY
S07RR-05788-15 0894 (NSS) BEALE, BRIAN S Biomedical research support NEODYMIUM YAG LASER WELDING SUTURE REPAIR ON INTESTINAL
S07RR-05788-15 0891 (NSS) DAME, JOHN B Biomedical research support HUMAN TRICHOMONIASIS DIAGNOSTIC TEST BASED ON NUCLEIC ACID HYBRIDIZATION TECH
S07RR-05788-15 0892 (NSS) HARVEY, JOHN W Biomedical research support MUSCLE PHOSPHOFRUCTOKINASE DEFICIENCY
S07RR-05788-15 0893 (NSS) STAMPLEY, ANITA R Biomedical research support EFFECTS OF CORTICOSTEROIDS ON CANINE COLONIC MOTILITY
S07RR-05788-15 0895 (NSS) FORSTER-BLOUIN, SHAR Biomedical research support OVARIOHYSTERECTOMY & CASTRATION ON BASAL THYROXINE
S07RR-05788-15 0896 (NSS) MAXWELL, ANNA K Biomedical research support FUNCTIONAL CELL MARKERS FOR CANINE NATURAL KILLER (NK) USING HUMAN ANTI NK CELL
S07RR-05788-15 0897 (NSS) SMITH, SCOTT D Biomedical research support CORONARY PERFUSION PRESSURE ON MYOCARDIAL OXYGEN CONSUMPTION IN NEONATAL RABBITS
S07RR-05791-15 (NSS) COOK, C EDGAR RESEARCH TRIANGLE INSTITUTE P O BOX 12194 RES TRIANGLE PARK, N C 27709 Biomedical research support
S07RR-05791-15 0514 (NSS) WALL, MONROE E Biomedical research support NO RESEARCH SUBPROJECTS
S07RR-05792-15 (NSS) HOCHSTEIN, PAUL UNIVERSITY OF SO CALIFORNIA 1985 ZONAL AVENUE LOS ANGELES, CALIF 90033 Biomedical research support
S07RR-05792-15 0939 (NSS) ADAMS, JAMES D Biomedical research support OXIDATIVE STRESS IN BRAIN
S07RR-05792-15 0940 (NSS) BRINTON, ROBERTA E Biomedical research support STEROIDS & GENE EXPRESSION
S07RR-05792-15 0941 (NSS) CADENAS, ENRIQUE Biomedical research support QUINONE CHEMISTRY
S07RR-05792-15 0942 (NSS) CHAN, TIMOTHY Biomedical research support PROTEIN KINASE & VANADIUM
S07RR-05792-15 0943 (NSS) GUTIERREZ, MARY Biomedical research support COMPUTER MODELING IN PSYCHOPHARMACY
S07RR-05792-15 0944 (NSS) HURST, AGNETA Biomedical research support PROCAINAMIDE PHARMACOKINETICS
S07RR-05792-15 0945 (NSS) JARESKO, GEORGE Biomedical research support GLUTATHIONE IN HIV PATIENTS
S07RR-05792-15 0946 (NSS) LIEN, ERIC Biomedical research support HYDROXYUREA IN TUMOR CELLS
S07RR-05792-15 0947 (NSS) LOUIE, STANLEY Biomedical research support PHAGOCYTIC POTENTIAL & CEFODIZIME
S07RR-05792-15 0948 (NSS) MITANI, GLADYS Biomedical research support PROSTHETIC HEART VALVES
S07RR-05792-15 0949 (NSS) SHEN, WEI-CHIANG Biomedical research support GROWTH OF LEUKEMIC CELL CULTURES
S07RR-05792-15 0950 (NSS) DUNCAN, ROGER Biomedical research support REGULATION OF PROTEIN PHOSPHORYLATION
S07RR-05794-15 (NSS) GOLDENGERG, KIM WRIGHT STATE UNIV SCH OF MED RM 110A MEDICAL SCIS BLDG DAYTON, OH 45435 Biomedical research support
S07RR-05794-15 0898 (NSS) ANDRAGNA-LAUF, NORMA Biomedical research support CELLULAR HOMEOSTASIS OF VASCULAR ENDOTHELIAL CELL BY HYDROXYUREA
S07RR-05794-15 0899 (NSS) ALTER, GERALD M Biomedical research support CLONING & EXPRESSION OF CYTOPLASMIC MALATE DEHYDROGENASE CDNA
S07RR-05794-15 0900 (NSS) GOTSHALL, ROBERT W Biomedical research support GENDER BASED DIFFERENCES IN CARDIOVASCULAR FUNCTION IN BEDREST
S07RR-05794-15 0901 (NSS) JENNES, LOTHAR Biomedical research support AMINO ACID NEUROTRANSMITTER GLUTAMATE IN CONJUNCTION W/ GNRH
S07RR-05794-15 0902 (NSS) PERRINE, KIMBERLY Biomedical research support RESPIRATORY SYNCYTIAL VIRUS BINDING & FUSION: VACCINIA VIRUS
S07RR-05795-14 (NSS) DIRKSEN, THOMAS R MED COL OF GA RES INST SCH DENT, 1120 15TH ST AUGUSTA, GEORGIA 30912 Biomedical research support
S07RR-05795-14 0414 (NSS) ADAIR, STEVEN M Biomedical research support FORMATI OF CAF2 & EFFECT ON FLUORIDE RELEASE FROM SLOW RELEASE DEVICES IN VITRO
S07RR-05795-14 0415 (NSS) BURDETTE, BRYAN H Biomedical research support USE OF TRIAZOLAM TO REDUCE NOCTURNAL BRUXING
S07RR-05795-14 0416 (NSS) CARTER, DAVID Biomedical research support INTERBRACKET DISTANCE EFFECT ON BENDING & TORSIONAL FORCES; ORTHODONTIC WIRES
S07RR-05795-14 0420 (NSS) LEWIS, JILL Biomedical research support MODULATION OF HERPES VIRUS IMMEDIATE EARLY GENE EXPRESSION
S07RR-05795-14 0421 (NSS) MCCOY, BRUCE Biomedical research support EFFECT OF TOPICALLY APPLIED NNK TO HAMSTER CHEEK POUCH MUCOSA; SMOKELESS TOBACCO
S07RR-05795-14 0422 (NSS) RIVERA, WARREN C Biomedical research support INNERVATION OF LATERAL PTERYGOID MUSCLE IN HUMANS & RHESUS MONKEYS
S07RR-05795-14 0417 (NSS) CAPUTA, LEWIS Biomedical research support REVASCULARIZE: MEMBRANOUS VS ENDOCHONDRIAL BONE GRAFT; RABBIT; MOPHOLOGY TIMING
S07RR-05795-14 0418 (NSS) GERMANE, NICHOLAS Biomedical research support CUSPID RETRACTION SPRING MODIFICATION USING FINITE ELEMENT ANALYSIS
S07RR-05795-14 0419 (NSS) LEFEBVRE, CAROL Biomedical research support EFFECTS OF DENTURE BASE RESINS ON ORAL EPITHELIAL CELLS
S07RR-05796-14 (NSS) PENDER, NOLA J UNIVERSITY OF MICHIGAN 400 NORTH INGALLS ANN ARBOR, MI 48109 Biomedical research support
S07RR-05796-14 0423 (NSS) BOEHM, SUSAN Biomedical research support NURSING INTERVENTION FOR REDUCING CHOLESTEROL DIET
S07RR-05796-14 0424 (NSS) BOOTH, DOROTHY Biomedical research support EXPLORATION OF FALL RISK FACTORS IN PERSONS W/ ALZHEIMERS DISEASE
S07RR-05796-14 0425 (NSS) BOYD, CAROL Biomedical research support MOTHER DAUGHTER IDENTIFICATION: CROSS CULTURAL INVESTIGATION
S07RR-05796-14 0426 (NSS) DAWKINS, CECILIA Biomedical research support PREVENTION OF HIV & AIDS AMONG BLACK FEMALES IN AT RISK GROUPS; SUBSTANCE ABUSE
S07RR-05796-14 0427 (NSS) FREY, MAUREEN Biomedical research support

PROJECT NO., ORGANIZATIONAL UNIT., INVESTIGATOR, ADDRESS, TITLE

FURTHER DEVELOPMENT OF SELF CARE INSTRUMENT FOR YOUTHS W/ IDDM
S07RR-05796-14 0428 (NSS) GUTHRIE, BARBARA Biomedical research support RACE & GENDER MEANINGS ATTACHED TO ADOLESCENTS USE & MISUSE OF ALCOHOL; BLACKS
S07RR-05796-14 0429 (NSS) HAGERTY, BONNIE Biomedical research support EXPLORATION OF CONNECTEDNESS: FOCUS GROUPS; DEPRESSION; SUICIDE
S07RR-05796-14 0430 (NSS) HAGERTY, BONNIE Biomedical research support HUMAN RELATEDNESS: CONCEPTS & MEASUREMENTS; MUTUALITY; ARTICULATION
S07RR-05796-14 0431 (NSS) HOYER, PAULETTE Biomedical research support TEEN PEER SUPPORT GROUP DURING PRENATAL CARE: IMPACT & OUTCOME
S07RR-05796-14 0432 (NSS) LOVELAND-CHERRY, CAR Biomedical research support FAMILY ENVIRONMENT SENSE OF COHERENCE, & HEALTH BEHAVIOR
S07RR-05796-14 0433 (NSS) LYNCH-SAUER, JUDITH Biomedical research support DEVELOPMENT OF CONCEPT OF EXPERIENTIAL HUMAN RELATEDNESS; ETHNOGRAPH
S07RR-05796-14 0434 (NSS) NORTON, MARY ANN Biomedical research support RELATIONSHIP OF PARENTAL LIFE STYLES TO CHILDRENS HEALTH BELIEFS & BEHAVIORS
S07RR-05796-14 0435 (NSS) PIERCE, PENNY Biomedical research support WOMENS PARTICIPATION IN BREAST CANCER TREATMENT DECISION
S07RR-05796-14 0436 (NSS) PIERCE, PENNY Biomedical research support VALIDITY TESTING OF DECISION MAKING MEASURES; BREAST CANCER
S07RR-05796-14 0437 (NSS) PORTER, CORNELIA Biomedical research support CHILDREARING PRACTICES OF UNMARRIED TEEN & YOUNG MOTHERS: URBAN POOR
S07RR-05796-14 0438 (NSS) REDMAN, RICHARD W Biomedical research support DRG SPECIFIC DISCHARGE PLANNING IN ACUTE CARE SETTINGS; CARDIOVASCULAR
S07RR-05796-14 0439 (NSS) ROGERS, ANN Biomedical research support CAN WRIST ACTIGRAPH DISCRIMINATE SLEEP FROM WAKING STATES; NARCOLEPSY
S07RR-05796-14 0440 (NSS) SAMPSELLE, CAROLYN Biomedical research support STANDARDIZATION & VALIDATION OF URINE STOP TEST; EXERCISE; PREGNANCY; WEIGHT
S07RR-05796-14 0441 (NSS) SIMMS, LILLIAN M Biomedical research support CREATING NEW NURSING PRACTICE PATTERNS ACROSS SETTINGS
S07RR-05796-14 0442 (NSS) STEWART, CYNTHIA Biomedical research support TOOL REFINEMENT FOR STUDY OF DISCHARGE PLANNING FROM HOME CARE
S07RR-05799-14 (NSS) BROWN, DONALD D CARNEGIE INST OF WASHINGTON 115 W UNIVERSITY PARKWAY BALTIMORE, MD 21210 Biomedical research support
S07RR-05799-14 0680 (NSS) LEE, SE-JIN Biomedical research support CHANGES IN GENE EXPRESSION DURING ORGANOGENESIS IN MOUSE
S07RR-05799-14 0681 (NSS) KOSHLAND, DOUGLAS Biomedical research support CENTROMERE FUNCTION OF YEAST
S07RR-05799-14 0682 (NSS) PAGANO RICHARD E Biomedical research support INTRACELLULAR TRANSLOCATION & METABOLISM OF LIPIDS
S07RR-05799-14 0683 (NSS) GROSSMAN, ARTHUR Biomedical research support GENETIC & BIOCHEMICAL ANALYSIS OF PHYCOBILISOMES
S07RR-05799-14 0684 (NSS) HOFFMAN, NEIL Biomedical research support STUDIES ON ASSEMBLY OF CA POLYPEPTIDES
S07RR-05799-14 0685 (NSS) GROSSMAN, ARTHUR Biomedical research support RESPONSE OF CYANOBACTERIUM ANACYSTIS NIDULANS TO NUTRIENT DEPRIVATION
S07RR-05799-14 0686 (NSS) BRIGGS, WINSLOW R Biomedical research support TRANSDUCTION OF BLUE LIGHT SIGNALS IN HIGHER PLANTS
S07RR-05801-13 (NSS) OKUNEWICK, JAMES P ALLEGHENY-SINGER RES CORP 320 EAST NORTH AVENUE PITTSBURGH, PA 15212-9986 Biomedical research support grant
S07RR-05801-13 0443 (NSS) TONG, JENNIFER Biomedical research support grant MONITOR IMMUNE REACTIVITIES BY IN SITU HYBRID INTERLEUKIN 2; IMMUNE DISORDERS
S07RR-05801-13 0444 (NSS) COAST, DOUGLAS A Biomedical research support: detecting late potentials during silent ischemia
S07RR-05801-13 0445 (NSS) BURHOLT, DENNIS R Biomedical research support: radiosensitivity of human lung cells
S07RR-05801-13 0446 (NSS) ANDERSON, DONALD D Biomedical research support grant 3 D FINITE ELEMENT ANALYSIS OF DISTAL RADIUS; COMPUTER MODELING
S07RR-05801-13 0447 (NSS) SEKHAR, CHANDRA V Biomedical research support grant ANTIBODY LABELING W/ METALLOMACROCYLES; CANCER THERAPY
S07RR-05801-13 0448 (NSS) PERUMAL, NARAYANAN Biomedical research support grant ACTIVATION OF PRODRUGS BY CATALYTIC ANTIBODIES EXPRESSED IN BACTERIA; CHEMOTHER
S07RR-05803-13 (NSS) RUOSLAHTI, ERKKI I LA JOLLA CANCER RES FDN 10901 NORTH TORREY PINES ROAD LA JOLLA, CALIF 92037 Biomedical research support
S07RR-05803-13 0449 (NSS) PASQUALE, ELENA B Biomedical research support DEVELOPMENTAL BIOLOGY OF PROTEIN TYROSINE KINASE
S07RR-05806-13 (NSS) SALTZMAN, GLENN NORTHEASTERN OHIO UNIV STATE ROUTE #44 ROOTSTOWN, OHIO 44272 Biomedical research support
S07RR-05806-13 0903 (NSS) DELUCIA, ANGELO L Biomedical research support MOLECULAR ANALYSIS OF HUMAN PAPILLOMAVIRUS TYPE 16 DNA CELL INTERACTIONS
S07RR-05806-13 0904 (NSS) CARRILLO, ALBERTO E Biomedical research support REGULATION OF PROLACTIN BIOSYNTHESIS
S07RR-05806-13 0905 (NSS) KRIMMER, EDWARD C Biomedical research support BEHAVIORAL & ETHANOL PREFERENCES OF TWO RAT STRAINS
S07RR-05806-13 0906 (NSS) DONZANTI, BRUCE A Biomedical research support MDMA ANTAGONISTS AS POTENTIAL ANTIPSYCHOTIC DRUGS
S07RR-05806-13 0907 (NSS) FINKELSTEIN, JUDITH Biomedical research support STARVATION EFFECTS OF GROWTH HORMONE IN RNA
S07RR-05806-13 0908 (NSS) HARDWICK, JAMES P Biomedical research support DNA SEQUENCE ANALYSIS OF HUMAN P450IV GENE FAMILY
S07RR-05806-13 0909 (NSS) WENSTRUP, JEFFREY J Biomedical research support INTEGRATIVE MECHANISMS OF ACOUSTIC ORIENTATION
S07RR-05806-13 0910 (NSS) DICARLSO, STEPHEN E Biomedical research support OSMOTICALLY RELEASED VASOPRESSIN REGULATION OF SYMPATHETIC NERVE ACTIVITY
S07RR-05806-13 0911 (NSS) DLUZEN, DEAN E Biomedical research support L DOPA STIMULATED DOPAMINE RELEASE: AGE EFFECTS
S07RR-05807-13 (NSS) WILSON, GRAEME S UNIV OF ALABAMA IN BIRMINGHAM 504 OPTOMETRY BIRMINGHAM, ALA 35294 Biomedical research support
S07RR-05807-13 0463 (NSS) RUTSTEIN, ROBERT P Biomedical research support CHANGES IN RETINAL CORRESPONDENCE & IN MAGNITUDE OF STRABISMUS
S07RR-05807-13 0464 (NSS) RUTSTEIN, ROBERT P Biomedical research support VERTIC DISPARITY CURVES & PRISM ADAPTATION; PATIENTS W/ SUPERIOR OBLIQUE PARESIS
S07RR-05807-13 0465 (NSS) KUYK, THOMAS Biomedical research support FLICKER SENSITIVITY FOLLOWING CATARACT SURGERY
S07RR-05807-13 0466 (NSS) WHIKEHART, DAVID R Biomedical research support FILTERS FOR TURNER FLUOROMETER; PROTEIN & DNA ASSAYS
S07RR-05807-13 0467 (NSS) WHIKEHART, DAVID R Biomedical research support STANDARD MICROCELLS FOR SPECTROPHOTOMETER: BIOCHEMICAL ASSAYS
S07RR-05807-13 0468 (NSS) WILSON, GRAEME S Biomedical research support MISCELLANEOUS GRADUATE STUDENT CHARGES
S07RR-05807-13 0469 (NSS) WILSON, GRAEME S Biomedical research support GRADUATE STUDENT PROJECTS
S07RR-05807-13 0470 (NSS) WILSON, GRAEME S Biomedical research support UV SPECTRORADIOMETER: MEASUREMENT OF UV LIGHT; CALIBRATE
S07RR-05807-13 0471 (NSS) WILSON, GRAEME S Biomedical research support MS RESEARCH PROJECT; CATION & ANION CONCENTRATION IN HUMAN TEARS; [CO2+]
S07RR-05807-13 0451 (NSS) BARTLETT, JIMMY D Biomedical research support ID HIGH STEROID RESPONDERS TO OPTICAL OPHTHALMIC PREDNISONE
S07RR-05807-13 0452 (NSS) CORLISS, DAVID A Biomedical research support OCULOMOTOR TRACKING OF CARRIER BASED PILOTS
S07RR-05807-13 0453 (NSS) FULLARD, RODERICK J Biomedical research support NETWORKING COMPUTER MODULE: CORE
S07RR-05807-13 0454 (NSS) FULLARD, RODERICK J Biomedical research support ZEOS VERTICAL SYS PACKAGE PC COMP & PREP TEAR SPECIFIC PREALBUMIN SUB FRACTION
S07RR-05807-13 0455 (NSS) GAMLIN, PAUL D R Biomedical research support DATA ACQUISITION CARD FOR COMPUTER; MEASURE EYE MOVEMENT IN PRIMATES
S07RR-05807-13 0456 (NSS) GAMLIN, PAUL D R Biomedical research support ELECTRONIC TIMING COMPONENT FOR CONTINUOUS RECORDING INFRARED OPTOMETER
S07RR-05807-13 0457 (NSS) KLEINSTEIN, ROBERT N Biomedical research support CLINICAL TRIALS EQUIPMENT; OPHTHALMOSCOPES; CONDENSING LENSES; TONOMETERS
S07RR-05807-13 0458 (NSS) LOOP, MICHAEL S Biomedical research support CALIBRATION & REPAIR OF RADIOMETER SYSTEM
S07RR-05807-13 0459 (NSS) LOOP, MICHAEL S Biomedical research support PHD RESEARCH PROJECT FOR TENG LENG OOI; BINOCULAR RIVALRY
S07RR-05807-13 0460 (NSS) NORTON, THOMAS T Biomedical research support ELECTRONICS CHART RECORDER SOFTWARE & NEUROTRANSMITTER AGONISTS & ANTAGONISTS
S07RR-05807-13 0461 (NSS) NORTON, THOMAS T Biomedical research support ULTRAVIOLET LIGHT GUN & IMPEDANCE METER
S07RR-05807-13 0462 (NSS) NOWAKOWSKI, RODNEY W Biomedical research support MOLECULAR GENETICS OF HEREDITARY DISORDERS OF VISION;
S07RR-05808-13 (NSS) GOLDSTEIN, GARY W KENNEDY INSTITUTE, INC. 707 NORTH BROADWAY BALTIMORE, MD 21205 Biomedical research support
S07RR-05808-13 0912 (NSS) LATERRA, JOHN J Biomedical research support EFFECTS OF LEAD ON BRAIN CAPILLARY CELL PLASMINOGEN ACTIVATOR
S07RR-05808-13 0913 (NSS) KATES, WENDY G Biomedical research support FOSTER FAMILY CHARACTERISTICS & STABILITY OF PLACEMENT IN FOSTER CARE
S07RR-05808-13 0914 (NSS) TRESCHER, WILLIAM H Biomedical research support EXCITATORY AMINO ACID NEUROTRANSMITTER REGULATION OF BRAIN NERVE GROWTH FACTOR
S07RR-05809-06 (NSS) STEMBER, MARILYN L UNIV OF COLORADO HLTH SCI CTR 4200 EAST NINTH AVENUE DENVER, COLORADO 80262 Biomedical research support grant
S07RR-05809-06 0472 (NSS) MAGILVY, JOAN Biomedical research support grant VETERANS LIVING W/ MS
S07RR-05809-06 0473 (NSS) BARLEY, ZOE A Biomedical research support grant ASSESSING QUALITY OF NURSING PRIMARY STUDIES
S07RR-05809-06 0474 (NSS) FULLER, BARBARA Biomedical research support grant VALIDITY OF ACOUSTIC, SELF REPORT, & CARETAKERS MEASURES OF CHILDRENS PAIN
S07RR-05809-06 0475 (NSS) MARSH, GENE Biomedical research support grant REVELATION READINESS MODEL OF LIFESTYLE CHANGE: PROSPECTIVE VIEW
S07RR-05809-06 0476 (NSS) WEBSTER, DENISE Biomedical research support grant WOMENS SELF CARE RESPONSES TO INTERSTITIAL CYSTITIS: INSTRUMENT DEVELOPMENT
S07RR-05809-06 0477 (NSS) BRENNER, PHYLLIS Biomedical research support grant PROFESSIONAL IDENTITY: INSTRUMENT DEVELOPMENT
S07RR-05809-06 0478 (NSS) WEBSTER, DENISE Biomedical research support grant WOMEN SELF CARE RESPONSE TO INTERSTITIAL CYSTITIS: DAILY INTERVIEW GUIDE
S07RR-05810-13 (NSS) OGDEN, THOMAS E DOHENY EYE INSTITUTE 1355 SAN PABLO STREET LOS ANGELES, CALIF 90033 Biomedical research support
S07RR-05810-13 0020 (NSS) KAY, EUNDUCK P Biomedical research support CORNEAL ENDOTHELIAL MODULATION: MOLECULAR CLONING OF CORNEAL ENDOTHELIUM FACTOR
S07RR-05810-13 0021 (NSS) FELDON, STEVEN E Biomedical research support LACRIMAL GLAND IN PATHOGENESIS OF GRAVES OPHTHALMOPATHY
S07RR-05810-13 0022 (NSS) SUZUKI, SHINTARO Biomedical research support MOLECULAR PROPERTIES & BIOLOGICAL ROLE OF CADHERINS IN NEURAL RETINA
S07RR-05810-13 0023 (NSS) TROUSDALE, MELVIN D Biomedical research support N VITRO STUDY OF ACANTHAMOEBA IN RABBIT CORNEAL BUTTONS
S07RR-05812-12 (NSS) HALLOCK, JAMES A EAST CAROLINA UNIVERSITY SCHOOL OF MEDICINE GREENVILLE, NC 27858 Biomedical research support
S07RR-05812-12 0479 (NSS) ABDULNOUR-NAKHOUL, S Biomedical research support EFFECT OF CATECHOLAMINES ON ION TRANSPORT IN RENAL PROXIMAL CELL
S07RR-05812-12 0480 (NSS) ARMSTRONG, SANDRA K Biomedical research support MOLECULAR MECHANISMS OF IRON ACQUISITION IN BORDETELLA PERTUSSIS
S07RR-05812-12 0481 (NSS) COOK, PAUL P Biomedical research support EFFECTS OF RETINOIC ACID & VITAMIN D3 ON PROTEIN KINASE C

S07RR-05812-12 0482 (NSS) DILTS, ROGER P Biomedical research support ONCOGENE C FOS AS AN INDEX OF CNS DOPAMINE SYSTEM ACTIVITY

S07RR-05812-12 0483 (NSS) FISHER, ROBERT H Biomedical research support PRODUCTION OF POLYCLONAL ANTIBODY AGAINST PD HRF

S07RR-05812-12 0484 (NSS) HUSSAIN, TAHIR Biomedical research support ADENOSINE RECEPTOR & G PROTEINS IN CORONARY ARTERY

S07RR-05812-12 0485 (NSS) KAZMIERCZAK, STEVEN Biomedical research support SERUM CONCENTRATIONS OF XO XDH HYPOXANTHINE AS MARKERS OF CELLULAR INJURY

S07RR-05812-12 0486 (NSS) LANGLEY, RICKY L Biomedical research support RETROSPECTIVE STUDY OF TRACTOR FATALITIES IN NC: 1978 1988

S07RR-05812-12 0487 (NSS) MANNIE, MARK D Biomedical research support FUNCTIONAL DIFFERENCES IN CD4 DEFINE T HELPER CELL SUBSETS

S07RR-05812-12 0488 (NSS) NAKHOUL, NAZIH L Biomedical research support HORMONAL EFFECTS OF PHI REGULATION IN RENAL PROXIMAL CELLS

S07RR-05812-12 0489 (NSS) RAKFAL, SUSAN M Biomedical research support EFFECTS MECHANISMS OF TREATMENT IN MURINE TUMOR MODEL

S07RR-05813-12 (NSS) DAUGHERTY, ROBERT M, JR UNIVERSITY OF NEVADA SCHOOL OF MEDICINE RENO, NEV 89557 Biomedical research support

S07RR-05813-12 0515 (NSS) DAUGHERTY, ROBERT M, Biomedical research support NO RESEARCH SUBPROJECTS

S07RR-05814-12 (NSS) SMITH, ELVIN E TEXAS A&M UNIVERSITY RM 102, MEDICAL SCIENCES BLDG COLLEGE STATION, TEX 77843 Biomedical research support

S07RR-05814-12 0141 (NSS) HILL, MICHAEL A Biomedical research support MODEL OF FUNC CHANGES IN RENAL CORTICAL MICROCIRCULATION IN EARLY EXPERIMENT DM

S07RR-05814-12 0142 (NSS) CUSICK, MICHAEL E Biomedical research support ISOLATION OF YEAST RIBONUCLEOPROTEIN GENES BY OLIGONUCLEOTIDE DIRECTED SELECTION

S07RR-05814-12 0143 (NSS) KUO, LIH Biomedical research support PHARMACOLOGICAL RESPONSES OF ISOLATED SUBENDOCARDIAL & SUBEPICARDIAL ARTERIOLES

S07RR-05814-12 0144 (NSS) LEWIS, RUTH Biomedical research support MACROPHAGE-ASSOCIATED ENDOTHELIAL ALTERATIONS IN INFLAMMATION

S07RR-05814-12 0145 (NSS) TAYLOR, LATHROP Biomedical research support DRUGS THAT FACILITATE CELLULAR MECHANISMS OF MEMORY

S07RR-05814-12 0146 (NSS) THACHER, SCOTT M Biomedical research support FUNCT & SPATIAL ORGANIZ OF BULLOUS PEMPHIGOID IN CULTURED EPIDERMAL CELLS

S07RR-05814-12 0147 (NSS) CUSICK, MICHAEL E Biomedical research support PUTATIVE YEAST RIBONUCLEOPROTEIN GENES ISOLATED BY OLIGONUCLEOTIDE SELECTION

S07RR-05814-12 0148 (NSS) FALCONE, JEFFREY C Biomedical research support MYOGENIC RESPONSE OF SKELETAL MUSCLE ARTERIOLE IN SPONTANEOUSLY HYPERTENSIVE RAT

S07RR-05814-12 0149 (NSS) HILL, MICHAEL A Biomedical research support MICROVASCULAR FUNC IN EARLY EXPERIMENTAL DIABETES: ALTERED ARTERIOLAR REACTIVITY

S07RR-05814-12 0150 (NSS) KUO, LIH Biomedical research support PHYSIO-PHARMACOLOGIC RESPONSES: ISOLATED CORONARY ARTERIOLES IN ATHEROSCLEROSIS

S07RR-05814-12 0151 (NSS) MEININGER, CYNTHIA J Biomedical research support CARDIAC TISSUE CULTURE MODEL USED TO DIRECTLY INVESTIGATE CORONARY ANGIOGENESIS

S07RR-05814-12 0152 (NSS) SAMPSON, H WAYNE Biomedical research support LIPID INVOLVEMENT IN ABNORMAL CARTILAGE MINERALIZATION

S07RR-05814-12 0153 (NSS) TAYLOR, LATHROP Biomedical research support AGE-DEPENDENT CHANGES IN MUSCARINIC PHARMA OF RAT HIPPOCAMPUS & BASAL FOREBRAIN

S07RR-05814-12 0154 (NSS) THOMPSON, DAVID C Biomedical research support FORMATION AND REACTIVITY OF QUINONE METHIDES IN BIOLOGICAL SYSTEMS

S07RR-05815-12 (NSS) FOWLER, STANLEY D UNIVERSITY OF SOUTH CAROLINA SCHOOL OF MEDICINE COLUMBIA, S C 29208 Biomedical research support

S07RR-05815-12 0490 (NSS) ABEL, FRANCIS Biomedical research support DETERMINATION OF LEFT VENTRICULAR WALL STRESSES

S07RR-05815-12 0491 (NSS) BUGGY, JAMES Biomedical research support REGULAT VASOPRESSIN GENE EXPRESSION IN BRAIN BY PROTO ONCOGENE C FOS

S07RR-05815-12 0492 (NSS) DADA, M OLUBUNMI Biomedical research support CHLOROQUINE INDUCED TOXICITY IN REPRODUCTION OF MALE RATS

S07RR-05815-12 0493 (NSS) HUNT, MARGARET Biomedical research support N PROTEIN MUTANTS OF VESICULAR STOMATITIS VIRUS

S07RR-05815-12 0494 (NSS) MURONO, EISUKE Biomedical research support ISOLATION & CHARACTERIZATION OF LEYDIG CELL PRECURSORS IN IMMATURE RAT TESTES

S07RR-05815-12 0495 (NSS) NAGPAL, MADAN Biomedical research support TRANSFORM RAT LEYDIG CELLS BY TRANSFECT W/ EARLY REGION OF SIMIAN VIRUS 40 DNA

S07RR-05816-12 (NSS) NORMAN, ANTHONY W UNIVERSITY OF CALIFORNIA DIVISION OF BIOMEDICAL SCIENCE RIVERSIDE, CALIF 92521 Biomedical research support

S07RR-05816-12 0516 (NSS) NORMAN, ANTHONY W Biomedical research support NO RESEARCH SUBPROJECTS

S07RR-05818-12 (NSS) ABRAMS, DAVID B MIRIAM HOSPITAL 164 SUMMIT AVENUE PROVIDENCE, R I 02906 Biomedical research support

S07RR-05818-12 0155 (NSS) MURPHY, JOSEPH K Biomedical research support CHILDREN'S CARDIOVASCULAR REACTIVITY: A FOUR-YEAR FOLLOW-UP

S07RR-05818-12 0156 (NSS) TERRY, RICHARD B Biomedical research support POST-HEPARIN PLASMA LIPASE ACTIVITY RESPONSE TO IV TRIGLYCERIDE VS ORAL GLUCOSE

S07RR-05818-12 0157 (NSS) KING, THOMAS C Biomedical research support MECHANISMS OF RAGV INDUCED LEUKEMOGENSIS

S07RR-05818-12 0158 (NSS) BAUSSERMAN, LINDA L Biomedical research support FACTORS REGULATING LIPOPROTEIN LIPASE (LPL) ACTIVITY IN MUSCLE CELLS

S07RR-05818-12 0159 (NSS) VANDENBERG, HERMAN H Biomedical research support DNA TRANSFECTION OF VERTEBRATE CELLS

S07RR-05818-12 0160 (NSS) MAHNENSMITH, REX Biomedical research support AMBULATORY BLOOD PRESSURE MEASUREMENT IN ELDERLY HYPERTENSIVES

S07RR-05818-12 0161 (NSS) MAZUR, ERIC M Biomedical research support GENE EXPRESSION IN DEVELOPING MEGAKARYOCYTES

PROJECT NO., ORGANIZATIONAL UNIT., INVESTIGATOR, ADDRESS, TITLE

S07RR-05818-12 0162 (NSS) OLDS, G RICHARD Biomedical research support HUMAN & ANIMAL STUDIES OF S. JAPONICUM SCHISTOSOMIASIS

S07RR-05818-12 0163 (NSS) NIAURA, RAYMOND Biomedical research support HIGH DENSITY LIPOPROTEIN & SMOKING

S07RR-05818-12 0164 (NSS) MARCUS, BESS H Biomedical research support PHYSICAL ACTIVITY & SMOKING CESSATION

S07RR-05822-12 (NSS) MUSLOW, IKE LOUISIANA STATE U MED CTR POST OFFICE BOX 33932 SHREVEPORT, LA 71130-3932 Biomedical research support

S07RR-05822-12 0496 (NSS) PRICE, V HUGH Biomedical research support INTESTINAL ISCHEMIA REPERFUSION INJURY & LIPID ABSORPTION

S07RR-05822-12 0497 (NSS) ZUBER, PETER Biomedical research support CHARACTERIZATION OF GENES REQUIRED FOR SYNTHESIS OF LIPOPEPTIDE ANTIBIOTIC

S07RR-05822-12 0498 (NSS) GROSS, DAVID S Biomedical research support STRUCTURE & REGULATION OF HEAT INDUCIBLE YEAST GENE; TRANSCRIPTION, MUTAGENESIS

S07RR-05822-12 0499 (NSS) SCARBOROUGH, DAVID E Biomedical research support NEUROGLIAL & CYTOKINE REGULATION OF SOMATOSTATIN IN VITRO

S07RR-05822-12 0500 (NSS) AW, TAK YEE Biomedical research support SUCCINATE AS NUTRIENT SOURCE FOR PERINATAL ENERGY NEEDS IN VIVO; RABBIT

S07RR-05822-12 0501 (NSS) CARDELLI, JAMES A Biomedical research support DEVELOPMENTAL REGULATION OF PRESTARVATION RESPONSES GENES

S07RR-05822-12 0502 (NSS) WOLCOTT, R MICHAEL Biomedical research support ALCOHOL & DEVELOPMENT OF NK CELLS

S07RR-05822-12 0503 (NSS) CAMPBELL, G DOUGLAS Biomedical research support INDIRECT IMMUNOFLUORESCENT ASSAY: DETECT LIPID FROM RODENT MODEL OF PNEUMONIA

S07RR-05822-12 0504 (NSS) FUSELER, JOHN W Biomedical research support TERATOGENIC EFFECT OF ALCOHOL ON CARDIAC MYOFIBRIL DVMT

S07RR-05822-12 0505 (NSS) CONRAD, STEVEN A Biomedical research support ORGAN BLOOD FLOW & O2 CONSUMPTION IN TREATED & UNTREATED SEPSIS; DISEASE MODELS

S07RR-05822-12 0506 (NSS) CRISSINGER, KAREN D Biomedical research support MUCOSAL BLOOD FLOW & PO2 IN NUTRIENT ABSORPTION; NEONATAL; PIG; ENTEROCOLITIS

S07RR-05822-12 0507 (NSS) PROUTY, LEONARD A Biomedical research support 30NM DIAMETER LOOPING FIBERS OF HUMAN CHROMOSOMES W/ SEM; MAPPING

S07RR-05823-12 (NSS) KEFALIDES, NICHOLAS A UNIVERSITY CITY SCIENCE CENTER 3624 SCIENCE CENTER, 5TH FLR PHILADELPHIA, PA 19104 Biomedical research support

S07RR-05825-12 (NSS) BEAUCHAMP, GARY K MONELL CHEMICAL SENSES CENTER 3500 MARKET STREET PHILADELPHIA, PA 19104 Biomedical research support

S07RR-05825-12 0508 (NSS) BEAUCHAMP, GARY K Biomedical research support SUCKING & SWALLOWING IN HUMAN NEWBORNS

S07RR-05825-12 0509 (NSS) PELCHAT, MARCIA L Biomedical research support LIFESPAN APPROACH TO FOOD PREFERENCE RESEARCH

S07RR-05825-12 0510 (NSS) TORDOFF, MICHAEL Biomedical research support MINERAL DEPRIVATION & SALT INTAKE

S07RR-05825-12 0511 (NSS) HUQUE, TAUFIQUL Biomedical research support ARACHIDONIC ACID IN TASTE TRANSDUCTION

S07RR-05825-12 0514 (NSS) BRYANT, BRUCE P Biomedical research support NEUROPHYSIOLOGICAL OF TASTE AGONISTS & ANTAGONISTS EVALUATIONS

S07RR-05825-12 0515 (NSS) SINGER, ALAN G Biomedical research support CHEMISTRY OF MAMMALIAN PHEROMONES

S07RR-05825-12 0516 (NSS) TEETER, JOHN H Biomedical research support CHARACTERIZATION OF AMINO ACID TASTE RECEPTORS

S07RR-05825-12 0512 (NSS) KALINOSKI, DARLINE L Biomedical research support CLONING OF INOSITOL 1,4,5 TRIPHOSPHATE RECEPTOR FROM CATFISH OLFACTORY ORGANS

S07RR-05825-12 0513 (NSS) RESTREPO, DIEGO Biomedical research support CHARACTERIZATION OF AN INOSITOL 1,4,5 TRIPHOSPHATE RECEPTOR IN OLFACTORY CILIA

S07RR-05825-12 0517 (NSS) KALINOSKI, DARLINE L Biomedical research support BIOCHEMICAL CHARACTERIZATION OF TASTE & OLFACTORY RECEPTOR PROTEINS

S07RR-05825-12 0518 (NSS) HUQUE, TAUFIQUL Biomedical research support EFFECTS OF LIPIDS ON INOSITOL TRIPHOSPHATE BINDING TO TASTE TISSUE

S07RR-05825-12 0519 (NSS) RESTREPO, DIEGO Biomedical research support INTRACELLULAR CALCIUM REGULATION BY ODOR STIMULI IN ISOLATED OLFACTORY NEURONS

S07RR-05825-12 0520 (NSS) BRAND, JOSEPH G Biomedical research support SODIUM & MONOSODIUM GLUTAMATE STIMULATED ION CHANNELS FROM MOUSE TASTE RECEPTORS

S07RR-05825-12 0521 (NSS) MATTES, RICHARD D Biomedical research support CEPHALIC PHASE INSULIN RESPONSE

S07RR-05828-08 (NSS) BEASLEY, R PALMER UNIV OF TEXAS HLTH SCIE CTR P O BOX 20186 HOUSTON, TX 77225 Biomedical research support grant

S07RR-05828-08 0522 (NSS) HARDY, ROBERT J Biomedical research support grant CRYOTHERAPY TREATMENT OF RETINOPATHY OF PREMATURITY FOLLOW UP

S07RR-05828-08 0523 (NSS) BRADSHAW, BENJAMIN S Biomedical research support grant INFANT MORTALITY AMONG MEXICAN AMERICANS

S07RR-05828-08 0524 (NSS) LABARTHE, DARWIN R Biomedical research support grant SURVIVAL AFTER M I IN BIETHNIC TEXAS COMMUNITY

S07RR-05828-08 0525 (NSS) DAVIS, BARRY R Biomedical research support grant CONTINUATION OF TRIAL OF ANTIHYPERTENSIVE INTERVENTIONS

S07RR-05828-08 0526 (NSS) PARCEL, GUY S Biomedical research support grant INTEGRATING TOBACCO USE PREVENTION PROGRAMS INTO SCHOOLS

S07RR-05828-08 0527 (NSS) MCALISTER, ALFRED L Biomedical research support grant BUENA VIDA SIN FUMAR MEDIA & COMMUNITY DEMONSTRATION: SMOKING

S07RR-05828-08 0528 (NSS) LAIRSON, DAVID R Biomedical research support grant PRIMARY CARE PROBLEM INTERVENTION; ALCOHOLISM

S07RR-05828-08 0529 (NSS) BRADSHAW, BENJAMIN S Biomedical research support grant MAPPING VITAL EVENTS IN AN HISPANIC POPULATION: 1929 1991

S07RR-05828-08 0530 (NSS) HOLGUIN, ALFONSO H Biomedical research support grant TRENDS IN SITE SPECIFIC CANCER MORTALITY; PERSONS OF MEXICAN ORIGIN

PROJECT NO., ORGANIZATIONAL UNIT., INVESTIGATOR, ADDRESS, TITLE

S07RR-05828-08 0531 (NSS) MORANDI, MARIA T Biomedical research support grant METHODS; CHARACTERIZE ACIDIC NITROGEN SULFATE SPECIES OUTDOOR & INDOOR AIR
S07RR-05828-08 0532 (NSS) GRUNBAUM, JO ANNE Biomedical research support grant YOUTH RISK BEHAVIORS; SEXUAL; DRUG & ALCOHOL; TOBACCO; DIET
S07RR-05828-08 0533 (NSS) BASEN-ENGQUIST, KARE Biomedical research support grant TEACHER SURVEY OF AIDS & HIV EDUCATION ACTIVITIES & RELATED FACTORS
S07RR-05828-08 0534 (NSS) CRANE, MARTIN M Biomedical research support grant CLINICAL IMMUNOLOGICAL INDEX FOR PROGRESSION OF HIV INFECTION
S07RR-05828-08 0535 (NSS) MULLEN, PATRICIA D Biomedical research support grant SUSTAINING WOMENS SMOKING CESSATION POSTPARTUM
S07RR-05829-09 (NSS) NAVIA, JUAN M UNIV OF ALABAMA IN BIRMINGHAM 720 S 20TH ST, UAB STATION BIRMINGHAM, ALA 35294 Biomedical research support
S07RR-05829-09 0951 (NSS) PERKINS, LAURA L Biomedical research support AIDS ANCILLARY STUDY: AIDS BEHAVIORS IN YOUNG ADULTS, HIV
S07RR-05829-09 0952 (NSS) JACOBS, ROBERT R Biomedical research support ASSESSMENT OF SYSTEMIC PERCUTANEOUS PENETRATION BY MEASURING DOSE
S07RR-05829-09 0953 (NSS) DILLON, KENNETH H Biomedical research support FLUORESCENT MICROSCOPY OF SUPRAVITALLY STAINED FUNGAL SPORES
S07RR-05829-09 0954 (NSS) DEARDEN, KIRK A Biomedical research support LIFE EXPERIENCES IN TEEN FATHERHOOD
S07RR-05829-09 0955 (NSS) STEPHENSEN, CHARLES Biomedical research support MONOCLONAL ANTIBODY SOLUTION HYBRIDIZATION ASSAY FOR DETECTING CORONAVIRUS
S07RR-05829-09 0956 (NSS) OBIRI, GODWIN U Biomedical research support EVALUATION OF MEMPHIS ST LOUIS ENCEPHALITIS SURVEILLANCE PROGRAM
S07RR-05829-09 0957 (NSS) DASANAYAKE, ANADA P Biomedical research support NUTRITRION & RISK FACTORS FOR MALIGNANT TRANSITION OF ORAL PREMALIG LESION
S07RR-05829-09 0958 (NSS) LAMARTINIERE, CORAL Biomedical research support ALTERED METABOLISMS & CARCINOGENESIS
S07RR-05830-12 (NSS) GOZZO, JAMES J NORTHEASTERN UNIVERSTIY COL PHARM 360 HUNTINGTON AVE BOSTON, MA 02115 Biomedical research support
S07RR-05830-12 0959 (NSS) JONES, G Biomedical research support ANTIBACTERIAL ORGANOPHOSPHORUS COMPOUNDS
S07RR-05830-12 0960 (NSS) WASZCZAK, B Biomedical research support DEVELOPMENT OF A MODEL FOR REGIONAL INACTIVATION OF RAT BRAIN
S07RR-05830-12 0961 (NSS) FISHER, D Biomedical research support ROLE OF GLUTATHIONE
S07RR-05830-12 0962 (NSS) BOISSE, N Biomedical research support PILOT STUDIES OF GABA GATED CHLORIDE FLUX IN BRAIN
S07RR-05830-12 0963 (NSS) JONES, G Biomedical research support NEW 4 HYDROXYCOUMARIN DERIV: ANTIBACTERIAL INHIBITORS OF DNA GYRASE
S07RR-05830-12 0964 (NSS) ARASKIEWICZ, P Biomedical research support QUANTITATION OF PLATELET ASSOCIATED IGC
S07RR-05830-12 0965 (NSS) HANSON, R Biomedical research support NEW INHIBITORS OF DOPAMINE REUPTAKE: POTENTIAL COCAINE ANTAGONISTS
S07RR-05830-12 0966 (NSS) BOISSE, N Biomedical research support STRIATAL GABA RELEASE: PILOT STUDIES
S07RR-05830-12 0967 (NSS) MEHDI, BOROUJERDI Biomedical research support DISPOSITION & TISSUE UPTAKE OF DOXORUBICIN BOLUS ADMIN VS CONT INFUSION
S07RR-05830-12 0968 (NSS) SCHRODER, ED Biomedical research support RELATIONSHIP OF PPGUSRC TYROSINE KINASE ACTIVITY TO TUMOR CELL
S07RR-05830-12 0969 (NSS) GOZZO, J Biomedical research support GAMMA COUNTER REPAIR CONTRACT
S07RR-05830-12 0970 (NSS) BOROUJERDI, M Biomedical research support COMPARATIVE PHARMACOKINETICS OF NOVEL DOXORUBICIN CARRIER SYSTEMS
S07RR-05830-12 0971 (NSS) FISHER, D Biomedical research support ALKYLATION GLUTATHIONE DECOMPOSITION PROD 1, 3 BIS (2 CHLORETHYL) 1 NITROSOUREA
S07RR-05831-12 (NSS) DIAMOND, LOUIS UNIVERSITY OF COLORADO SCH OF PHARMACY BOX 297 BOULDER, COLO 80309 Biomedical research support
S07RR-05831-12 0972 (NSS) ERWIN, V GENE Biomedical research support SYSTEM DEVELOPMENT FOR NEUROTENSIN
S07RR-05831-12 0973 (NSS) ROSS, DAVID Biomedical research support BENZENE INDUCED BONE MARROW TOXICITY
S07RR-05831-12 0974 (NSS) ALTIERE, RALPH Biomedical research support APPARATUS DEVELOPMENT FOR MEASUREMENT OF MOUSE RESPIRATION
S07RR-05831-12 0975 (NSS) GLYNN-BARNHART, ANNE Biomedical research support INVESTIGATIONS OF LYMPHOCYTE PROLIFERATION
S07RR-05831-12 0976 (NSS) STRINGER, KATHLEEN Biomedical research support DEVELOPMENT OF ISOLATED PERFUSED HEART SYSTEM
S07RR-05831-12 0977 (NSS) DEITRICH, RICHARD Biomedical research support DEVELOPMENT OF A MOLECULAR BIOLOGY CORE FACILITY
S07RR-05831-12 0978 (NSS) CATALANO, CARLOS Biomedical research support REPLACEMENT OF DERATED LOW SPEED CENTRIFUGE ROTOR
S07RR-05831-12 0979 (NSS) JOHNSON, KENNETH Biomedical research support COMPUTER UP GRADE & PURCHASE OF PHARMACOKINETIC SOFTWARE
S07RR-05831-12 0980 (NSS) MALKINSON, ALVIN Biomedical research support EQUIPMENT & SYSTEM DEVELOPMENT FOR MOLECULAR BIOLOGY
S07RR-05831-12 0981 (NSS) MALKINSON, ALVIN Biomedical research support BIOLOGY SYSTEMS REPLACEMENT OF DERATED ULTRACENTRIFUGE ROTORS
S07RR-05832-12 (NSS) ENOCH, JAY M UNIVERSITY OF CALIFORNIA 350 MINOR HALL BERKELEY, CALIF 94720 Biomedical research support
S07RR-05832-12 0195 (NSS) FREEMAN, RALPH D Biomedical research support PHYSIOLOGICAL PROPERTIES OF CELLS IN VISUAL CORTEX
S07RR-05832-12 0196 (NSS) KLEIN, STANLEY A Biomedical research support VERNIER ACUITY & CONTRAST DISCRIMINATION OF SIMUSOIDAL GRATINGS IN HUMAN VISION
S07RR-05832-12 0197 (NSS) MILLER, SHELDON S Biomedical research support TRANSPORT PROPERTIES OF HUMAN RETINAL PIGMENT EPITHELIUM
S07RR-05832-12 0198 (NSS) POLSE, KENNETH A Biomedical research support EFFECTS OF LACTATE ON CORNEAL FUNCTION
S07RR-05832-12 0199 (NSS) HAEGERTROM-PORTNOY, Biomedical research support VISION OF ROD MONOCHROMATS
S07RR-05832-12 0200 (NSS) SCHOR, CLIFTON M Biomedical research support NON CONJUGATE ADAPTATION OF VERTICAL EYE MOVEMENTS
S07RR-05832-12 0201 (NSS) VAN SLUYTERS, RICHAR Biomedical research support VISUALIZATION OF CYTOCHROME OXIDASE BLOBS IN CAT PRIMARY VISUAL CORTEX
S07RR-05832-12 0189 (NSS) ADAMS, ANTHONY J Biomedical research support ELECTROPHYSIOLOGICAL STUDIES OF HUMAN COLOR VISION
S07RR-05832-12 0190 (NSS) BAILEY, IAN L Biomedical research support EFFECTS OF SPACING & CONTRAST ON VISUAL ACUITY
S07RR-05832-12 0191 (NSS) BANKS, MARTIN S Biomedical research support OPTIC FLOW, LOCOMOTION CONTROL & DEPTH PRECEPTION
S07RR-05832-12 0192 (NSS) BONANNO, JOSEPH A Biomedical research support BICARBONATE TRANSPORT & PH REGULATION IN CORNEAL ENDOTHELIUM
S07RR-05832-12 0193 (NSS) COHN, THEODORE E Biomedical research support VISUAL EFFECTS OF OCULAR VASCULAR PULSE
S07RR-05832-12 0194 (NSS) ENOCH, JAY M Biomedical research support NEW CALIBRATION TECHNIQUE FOR SCANNING LASER
S07RR-05834-12 (NSS) JESTEADT, WALT BOYS TOWN INSTITUTE 555 N 30TH ST OMAHA, NE 68010 Biomedical research support
S07RR-05834-12 0536 (NSS) HIGGINS, MAUREEN Biomedical research support AERODYNAMIC & ELECTROGLOTTOGRAPHIC INVESTIGATIONS OF NORMAL LARYNGEAL FUNCTION
S07RR-05834-12 0537 (NSS) JESTEADT, WALT Biomedical research support DEVELOPMENT OF LABRATORY FACILITY: FILE SERVER
S07RR-05834-12 0538 (NSS) JESTEADT, WALT Biomedical research support DEVELOPMENT OF LABORATORY FACILITY: NEURAL CODING
S07RR-05834-12 0539 (NSS) KIMBERLING, WILLIAM Biomedical research support LINKAGE OF BRACHIO OTO RENAL SYNDROME
S07RR-05834-12 0540 (NSS) KOPUN, JUDY Biomedical research support UNILATERAL HEARING LOSS; COUPLING METHODS FOR FM SYSTEMS
S07RR-05834-12 0541 (NSS) MORLEY, BARBARA J Biomedical research support DEVELOPMENT OF LABORATORY FACILITY: NEUROCHEMISTRY
S07RR-05834-12 0542 (NSS) NEELY, STEPHEN T Biomedical research support DEVELOPMENT OF LABORATORY FACILITY: COMMUNICATION ENGINEERING
S07RR-05834-12 0543 (NSS) NITTROUER, SUSAN Biomedical research support PHONOLOGICAL SKILLS IN GOOD & POOR READERS
S07RR-05834-12 0544 (NSS) ROBERTS, KENNETH Biomedical research support LANGUAGE COGNITION INTERACTION IN EARLY WORD LEARNING
S07RR-05834-12 0545 (NSS) SCHICK, BRENDA S Biomedical research support DVMT PHONOLOGICAL ORGANIZATION IN AMERICAN SIGN LANGUAGE & SIGNING EXACT ENGLISH
S07RR-05834-12 0546 (NSS) SINEX, DONAL G Biomedical research support DEVELOPMENT OF LABORATORY FACILITY: ANIMAL SURGERY
S07RR-05838-12 (NSS) WISNIEWSKI, HENRY M INST FOR BASIC RES IN DEV 1050 FOREST HILL ROAD STATEN ISLAND, NY 10314 Biomedical research support
S07RR-05838-12 0266 (NSS) KIERAS, FRED J Biomedical research support GLYCOPROTEIN METABOLISM IN CEROID LIPOFUSCINOSIS FIBROBLASTS
S07RR-05838-12 0267 (NSS) QUINN, MICHAEL R Biomedical research support NEUROMODULATION OF RECEPTOR GATED CHLORIDE CHANNELS
S07RR-05838-12 0268 (NSS) PULLARKAT, RAJU K Biomedical research support GLYCOPEPTIDES IN CEROID LIPOFUSCINOSIS
S07RR-05838-12 0269 (NSS) CURRIE, JULIA R Biomedical research support IMMUNOCHEMICAL STUDIES OF ALZHEIMERS DISEASE
S07RR-05838-12 0270 (NSS) COHEN, IRA L Biomedical research support INFANTILE AUTISM & FRAGILE X SYNDROME
S07RR-05838-12 0271 (NSS) LEWKOWICZ, DAVID Biomedical research support DEVELOPMENT OF INTERSENSORY PERCEPTION IN HUMAN INFANTS
S07RR-05838-12 0272 (NSS) STURMAN, JOHN A Biomedical research support DIETARY TAURINE ON FELINE PREGNANCY OUTCOME
S07RR-05838-12 0273 (NSS) SAPIN, ROBERT Biomedical research support DIAGNOSTIC & ASSESSMENT OF DEVELOP DISABILITIES
S07RR-05838-12 0274 (NSS) WEGIEL, JERZY Biomedical research support AGING NERVOUS SYSTEM
S07RR-05839-10 (NSS) REID, JOHN B OREGON SOCIAL LEARNING CENTER 207 E 5TH SUITE 202 EUGENE, OREG 97401 Biomedical research support grant
S07RR-05839-10 0927 (NSS) REID, JOHN Biomedical research support grant COMPUTING EQUIPMENT TO AID BEHAVIORAL RESEARCH
S07RR-05840-13 (NSS) LIEBERMAN, SEYMOUR ST LUKE'S-ROOSEVELT INST 428 W 59TH ST (AJA 118) NEW YORK, NY 10019 Biomedical research support
S07RR-05840-13 0275 (NSS) HASHIM, GEORGE A Biomedical research support REGULATION OF AUTOIMMUNITY AGAINST NEURAL ANTIGEN IN LEWIS RATS
S07RR-05840-13 0276 (NSS) PIERSON, RICHARD N, Biomedical research support BODY COMPOSITION STUDIES IN NORMALS, AIDS & OBESITY
S07RR-05841-12 (NSS) HOLDEN, JOSEPH T BECKMAN RES INST, CITY OF HOPE 1500 E DUARTE ROAD DUARTE, CALIF 91010 Biomedical research support
S07RR-05841-12 0250 (NSS) MILLER, MARCIA Biomedical research support GENETIC ANALYSIS OF NEW MEMBERS OF IMMUNOGLOBULIN GENE SUPERFAMILY
S07RR-05841-12 0221 (NSS) WIMER, RICHARD Biomedical research support ISOLATION & SEQUENCING MITOCHONDRIAL DNA OF MOUSE STRAINS S58 & J & LG & J
S07RR-05841-12 0222 (NSS) DIAMOND, DONALD Biomedical research support GAMMA INTERFERON REGULARITY PROTEINS IN T LYMPHOCYTES BY HTLV I INFECTION
S07RR-05841-12 0223 (NSS) SHIVELY, JOHN Biomedical research support SPECIFIC IMMUNOTHERAPY FOR COLON CANCER
S07RR-05841-12 0224 (NSS) FUJITA-YAMAGUCHI, YO Biomedical research support MONOCLONAL ANTIBODIES AGAINST HUMAN IGF I RECEPTOR
S07RR-05841-12 0225 (NSS) FORREST, GERALD Biomedical research support CHARACTERIZATION OF A HUMAN CARBONYL REDUCTASE GENOMIC CLONE
S07RR-05841-12 0226 (NSS) HANIU, MITSURU Biomedical research support IMMUNOCHEMICAL & FUNCTIONAL ANALYSIS OF LIVER NADPH CYTOCHROME P 450
S07RR-05841-12 0227 (NSS) MAS, MARIA Biomedical research support ACTIVE SITE STUDIES IN PHOSPHOGLYCERATE KINASE
S07RR-05841-12 0228 (NSS) WU, ANNA Biomedical research support ANALYSIS OF HARVEY RAS EXPRESSION
S07RR-05841-12 0229 (NSS) FLANAGAN, STEVEN Biomedical research support RAPID DISCOVERY OF RFLPS AT DEFINED CHROMOSOMAL REGIONS &

GENETIC LOCI
S07RR-05841-12 0230 (NSS) TERMINI, JOHN Biomedical research support
MECHANISTIC STUDY OF A CARBOHYDRATE PROCESSING RIBOZYME
S07RR-05841-12 0231 (NSS) CHEN, SHIUAN Biomedical research support
RAT LIVER NAD (P) H QUINONE ACCEPTOR OXIDOREDUCTASE (DT DIAPHORASE):
S07RR-05841-12 0232 (NSS) MILLER, MARCIA Biomedical research
support MAPPING VARIABILITY WITHIN RECOGNITION DOMAINS OF MAJOR HISTOCOMPATIBILITY
S07RR-05841-12 0233 (NSS) PANDE, HEMA Biomedical research support
STRUCTURE FUNCTION STUDIES ON FIBRONECTIN
S07RR-05841-12 0234 (NSS) ROSSI, JOHN Biomedical research support
ISOLATE 3 SPLICE SITE AG RECOGNIZING FACTOR(S) OF A YEAST SPLICEDSOME
S07RR-05841-12 0235 (NSS) FORREST, GERALD Biomedical research
support CLONING & EXPRESSION OF DAUNORUBICIN REDUCTASE
S07RR-05841-12 0236 (NSS) CHIU, ARLENE Biomedical research support
PURIFICATION & FUNCTION OF S LAMININ, A SYNAPTIC FORM OF LAMININ
S07RR-05841-12 0237 (NSS) FU ITA-YAMAGUCHI, YO Biomedical research
support PURIFICATION OF IGF I, IGF II & INSULIN FROM HUMAN PLACENTA
S07RR-05841-12 0238 (NSS) BARISH, MICHAEL E Biomedical research
support GLUTAMATE INDUCED TOXICITY IN EMBRYONIC NEURONS FROM NORMALS TRISOMY 16 MICE
S07RR-05841-12 0239 (NSS) KLEVECZ, ROBERT R Biomedical research
support LIGHT TO GROW BY: BIOLUMINESCENCE IN MAMMALIAN CELLS
S07RR-05841-12 0240 (NSS) HOLDEN, JOSEPH Biomedical research
support SMALL EQUIPMENT
S07RR-05841-12 0241 (NSS) BAILEY, JEROME M Biomedical research
support CHARACTERIZATION OF PORCINE LIVER NMN ADENYLTRANSFERASE
S07RR-05841-12 0242 (NSS) CHEN, SHIUAN Biomedical research support
REGULATORY MECHANISM OF AROMATASE GENE EXPRESSION IN BREAST TUMORS
S07RR-05841-12 0243 (NSS) FEISTNER, GOTTFRIED Biomedical research
support INHIBITION STUDIES ON NAD (P) H QUINONE REDUCTASE FROM PYRUS COMMUNIS
S07RR-05841-12 0244 (NSS) HEFTA, STANLEY A Biomedical research
support LEUKOCYTE NCA ANTIGENS: STRUCTURE FUNCTION
S07RR-05841-12 0245 (NSS) HOLMQUIST, GERALD P Biomedical research
support MAPPING FREQUENCY & REPAIR RATE OF UV ADDUCTS
S07RR-05841-12 0246 (NSS) FUJITA-YAMAGUCHI, YO Biomedical research
support PRODUCTION OF MONOCLONAL ANTIBODIES AGAINST HUMAN IGF 1 RECEPTOR
S07RR-05841-12 0247 (NSS) BOWERS, CHAUNCEY W Biomedical research
support FACTORS REGULATING NEUROTRANSMITTER RECEPTOR EXPRESSION
S07RR-05841-12 0248 (NSS) FLANAGAN, STEVEN D Biomedical research
support AUTO ADJUSTING EYE TRACKER: NEXT GENERATION
S07RR-05841-12 0249 (NSS) CHIU, ARLENE Biomedical research support
DEVELOPMENT OF SOMATIC MOTOR NEURONS IN RATS
S07RR-05842-12 (NSS) HENSON, PETER M NATIONAL JEWISH HOSP/RSCH CTR 1400 JACKSON STREET DENVER, COLORADO 80206-1997 Biomedical research support
S07RR-05842-12 0277 (NSS) CAMBIER, JOHN Biomedical research support
STRUCTURAL & GENETIC REQUIREMENTS FOR MEMBRANE LG MEDIATED SIGNAL TRANSDUCTION
S07RR-05842-12 0278 (NSS) COOK, JAMES Biomedical research support
CELLULAR IMMUNE RESPONSE TO ADENOVIRUS INFECTION
S07RR-05842-12 0279 (NSS) COTT, GARY Biomedical research support
ION TRANSPORT PROPERTIES & REGULATION IN FETAL PULMONARY EPITHELIAL CELLS
S07RR-05842-12 0280 (NSS) EMRIE, PHILIP Biomedical research support
ALVEOLAR TYPE II CELL LINE
S07RR-05842-12 0281 (NSS) FERGUSON, GARY Biomedical research
support RESPIRATORY MUSCLE FATIGUE & RESPIRATORY FAILURE
S07RR-05842-12 0282 (NSS) KIRKPATRICK, CHARLES Biomedical research
support STRUCTURE OF TRANSFER FACTOR
S07RR-05842-12 0283 (NSS) POTTER, TERRY Biomedical research support
DEVELOPMENT OF TRANSGENIC MICE
S07RR-05842-12 0284 (NSS) STAERZ, UWE Biomedical research support
MACROPHAGES AS ACCESSORY CELLS FOR 1MHC RESTRICTED RESPONSE
S07RR-05842-12 0285 (NSS) KELLER, GORDON Biomedical research
support ALTERATION OF HEMATOPOIETIC STERM CELLS
S07RR-05842-12 0286 (NSS) WENZEL, SALLY Biomedical research support
INFLUENCES OF EICOSANOIDS
S07RR-05842-12 0287 (NSS) WYSOCKI, LARRY Biomedical research
support T CELL INTOLERANCE
S07RR-05842-12 0288 (NSS) WORTHEN, G SCOTT Biomedical research
support ENDOTHELIAL INJURY
S07RR-05842-12 0289 (NSS) NEMAZEE, DAVID Biomedical research
support ONCOGENE ARRANGEMENTS
S07RR-05842-12 0290 (NSS) WHITE, CARL Biomedical research support
ADAPTATION TO PULMONARY OXIDATIVE STRESS
S07RR-05842-12 0291 (NSS) PELOQUIN, CHARLES Biomedical research
support PHARMACOKINETICS OF NEW DRUGS FOR MYCOBACTERIUM AVIUM COMPLEX IN MICE
S07RR-05842-12 0292 (NSS) IKLE, DAVID Biomedical research support
UPGRADE OF MAC II FX PHOTOGRAPHY ILLUSTRATION
S07RR-05842-12 0293 (NSS) DOHERTY, DENNY Biomedical research
support NUCLEAR MAC ACQUISITION STATION
S07RR-05842-12 0294 (NSS) FREED, JOHN Biomedical research support
HPLC SYSTEM FOR MOLECULAR RESOURCE CENTER
S07RR-05843-11 (NSS) KABISCH, WILLIAM T SOUTHERN ILLINOIS UNIVERSITY P O BOX 19230 SPRINGFIELD, IL 62794-9230 Biomedical research support
S07RR-05843-11 0547 (NSS) TEWARI, RAM P Biomedical research support
INTERACTIONS OF HUMAN ENDOTHELIAL CELLS W/ HISTOPLASMA
S07RR-05843-11 0548 (NSS) CASPARY, DONALD M Biomedical research
support CODING IN AUDITORY NEURONS: EFFECTS OF AMINO ACIDS; RAT
S07RR-05843-11 0549 (NSS) DUNAWAY, GEORGE A Biomedical research
support DEVELOPMENTAL CHANGES IN HEART & MUSCLE PFK ISOZYMES
S07RR-05843-11 0550 (NSS) ELBLE, RODGER J Biomedical research
support NEUROMUSCULAR CONTROL IN ACTION TREMOR; WRISTS OF PATIENTS W/ ESSENTIAL TREMOR
S07RR-05843-11 0551 (NSS) CAMPBELL, KATHLEEN C Biomedical research
support OTOTOXICITY ON AUDITORY EVOKED POTENTIALS; PREDICT HEARING LOSS; HUMAN ADULTS
S07RR-05845-11 (NSS) SHIRES, GEORGE M UNIV OF TENN, COL OF VET MED P O BOX 1071 KNOXVILLE, TENN 37901 Biomedical research support
S07RR-05845-11 0557 (NSS) KORENEK, NANCY Biomedical research
support PERIPHERAL BLOOD CONTAMINATION ON EQUINE SYNOVIAL FLUID
S07RR-05845-11 0552 (NSS) DANIEL, GREGORY B Biomedical research
support NUCLEAR SCINTIGRAPHIC TECHNIQUE TO EVAL CARDIAC DISEASE IN DOG
S07RR-05845-11 0553 (NSS) SCHMEITZEL, LYNN Biomedical research
support INTRADERMAL SKIN TEST SERUM IGE CONCENTRAT: HORSES W/ OBSTRUCTIVE PULMONARY DIS
S07RR-05845-11 0554 (NSS) WILKINSON, J ERBY Biomedical research
support TARGETED GENE DISRUPTION IN MOUSE EMBRYONIC STEM CELLS
S07RR-05845-11 0555 (NSS) ANDREWS, FRANK M Biomedical research
support GASTRIC SECRETION STUDIES IN HORSE USING DOUBLE LUMEN TUBE
S07RR-05845-11 0556 (NSS) BLACKFORD, JAMES T Biomedical research
support PHARMACOKINETICS OF CEFTIOFUR IN HORSES
S07RR-05849-11 (NSS) HURLEY, LAURENCE H UNIVERSITY OF TEXAS AT AUSTIN COLLEGE OF PHARMACY AUSTIN, TEX 78712 Biomedical research support
S07RR-05849-11 0251 (NSS) BEALE, JOHN Biomedical research support
STUDIES ON MECHANISM OF MANNURONAN C5 EPIMERASE
S07RR-05849-11 0252 (NSS) BEMBENEK, MIKE Biomedical research
support STUDIES ON TYROSINE KINASE
S07RR-05849-11 0253 (NSS) ERICKSON, CARL Biomedical research
support EFFECT OF LOW DOSAGE ETHANOL ON BRAIN OPIOPEPTIDES
S07RR-05849-11 0254 (NSS) KEHRER, JIM Biomedical research support
MECHANISM OF CYCLOPHOSPHAMIDE INDUCED LUNG INJURY
S07RR-05849-11 0255 (NSS) PAAP, CHRISTOPHER Biomedical research
support GENTAMICIN NEPHROTOXICITY IN AN ISOLATED PERFUSED RAT KIDNEY MODEL
S07RR-05849-11 0256 (NSS) WILCOX, RICH Biomedical research support
PARTIAL ANTAGONISTS AS ANTIPSYCHOTICS
S07RR-05852-11 (NSS) LOEW, FRANKLIN M TUFTS UNIV SCH OF VET MED 200 WESTBORO RD. NO. GRAFTON, MA 01536 Biomedical research support
S07RR-05852-11 0257 (NSS) SPAULDING, GLEN Biomedical research
support SLEEP APNEA IN BULLDOGS
S07RR-05852-11 0258 (NSS) SARKAR, SATYAPRIYA Biomedical research
support ROTATING CYLINDER DEVICE
S07RR-05852-11 0259 (NSS) MOORE, ANTONY Biomedical research support
EXPRESSION OF P GLYCOPROTEIN IN MALIGNANT CANINE LYMPHOME CELLS
S07RR-05852-11 0260 (NSS) BRIDGES, ROBERT Biomedical research
support HORMONE OPIATE BRAIN INTERACTIONS IN PARENTAL BEHAVIOR
S07RR-05852-11 0261 (NSS) TZIPORI, SAUL Biomedical research support
INVESTIGATIONS OF PATHOGENESIS OF CRYPTOSPORIDIAL INFECTION IN MAN
S07RR-05853-11 (NSS) FELEPPA, ERNEST J RIVERSIDE RESEARCH INST 330 WEST 42ND STREET NEW YORK, N Y 10036 Biomedical research support
S07RR-05853-11 0982 (NSS) SOKIL-MELGAR, JOAN Biomedical research
support COMPUTER AIDED ULTRASONIC DIAGNOSIS: IMAGING, PROSTATE, CANCER, 3D, SKIN, BREAST
S07RR-05853-11 0983 (NSS) DRILLER, JACK Biomedical research support
HYPERTHERMIC THERAPEUTIC ULTRASOUND: CAUTERY, BONDING, CANCER, INTRAOPERATIVE
S07RR-05853-11 0984 (NSS) DRILLER, JACK Biomedical research support
BIOEFFECTS OF NON HYPERTHERMIC THERAPEUTIC ULTRASOUND: SONOPHORESIS
S07RR-05854-11 (NSS) SHADDUCK, JOHN A TEXAS A&M UNIVERSITY COLLEGE OF VETERINARY MEDICINE COLLEGE STATION, TEX 77843 Biomedical research support
S07RR-05854-11 0915 (NSS) TIFFANY-CASTIGLIONI, Biomedical research
support INTERACTION OF TRANSFERRIN & HEAVY METALS IN ASTROGLIA
S07RR-05854-11 0916 (NSS) WELSH, JANE C Biomedical research support
REPLICATION OF TWO NEUROTROPIC VIRUSES IN MURINE CEREBRAL ENDOTHELIAL CELLS
S07RR-05854-11 0917 (NSS) CLARK, DONALD R Biomedical research
support CIRCULATORY RESPONSE TO HYPERTONIC SALINE & HYDROXYETHYL STARCH IN HYPOVOLEMIA
S07RR-05854-11 0918 (NSS) SRIVASTAVA, VINOD K Biomedical research
support DIETARY RESTRICTION MECHANISM TO INHIBIT AGE RELATED DECLINE IN DNA REPAIR
S07RR-05854-11 0919 (NSS) ILLANES, OSCAR G Biomedical research
support MORPHOLOGICAL & MORPHOMETRIC STUDY OF SCIATIC NERVE IN MICE W/ LUNG CARCINOMA
S07RR-05854-11 0920 (NSS) STOICA, GEORGE Biomedical research
support INHERITED NEURODEGENERATIVE DISEASE OF CNS OF RAT
S07RR-05854-11 0921 (NSS) RAMOS, KENNETH S Biomedical research
support DINITROTOLUENE INDUCED ATHEROGENESIS
S07RR-05854-11 0922 (NSS) WEEKS, BRAD R Biomedical research support
ID & ELECTROPHORETIC CHARACTERIZATION OF PROTEIN OF SALMONELLA TYPHIMURIOM
S07RR-05854-11 0923 (NSS) JOHNSON, LARRY Biomedical research
support CONTROL OF SERTOLI CELL NUMBER & TESTICULAR SIZE
S07RR-05857-11 (NSS) KOSTENBAUDER, HARRY B UNIVERSITY OF KENTUCKY COL PHARMACY, ROSE ST LEXINGTON, KY 40536-0082 Biomedical research support
S07RR-05857-11 0924 (NSS) CROOKS, PETER A Biomedical research
support DVMT ANTISENSE OLIGODEOXYNUCLEOTIDES W/ POTENTIAL CHEMOTHERAPEUTIC VALUE: RATS
S07RR-05857-11 0925 (NSS) DWOSKIN, LINDA Biomedical research
support NEUROTENSINERGIC MODULATION OF DOPAMINE RELEASE IN CNS
S07RR-05857-11 0926 (NSS) RIGGS, ROBERT Biomedical research support
5 TRIPHOSPHORYLATED ADENINE TRIMERS: EVALUATION OF BINDING TO RNASE L
S07RR-05857-11 0927 (NSS) SOLTIS, EDWARD Biomedical research
support MICRODIALYSIS; ONTOGENIC CHANGES IN C V CONTROL; SALT MODEL OF HYPERTENSION
S07RR-05857-11 0928 (NSS) YOKEL, ROBERT Biomedical research support
MECHANISM OF ALUMINUM PERMEATION THROUGH BLOOD BRAIN BARRIER
S07RR-05859-09 (NSS) LIPTON, DOUGLAS S NDRI 11 BEACH STREET NEW YORK, NY 10013 Biomedical research support
S07RR-05859-09 0929 (NSS) FRIEDMAN, SAMUEL Biomedical research
support COMMUNITY INTERVENTIONS REDUCE AIDS TRANSMISSION AMONG IVDUS & SEXUAL PARTNERS
S07RR-05859-09 0930 (NSS) WEXLER, HARRY Biomedical research support
ARRIVE: AIDS RISK REDUCTION FOR IV DRUG USERS ON PAROLE
S07RR-05860-11 (NSS) BARDIN, CLYDE W POPULATION COUNCIL 1230 YORK AVENUE NEW YORK, N Y 10021 Biomedical research support
S07RR-05860-11 0931 (NSS) MONDER, CARL Biomedical research support

PROJECT NO., ORGANIZATIONAL UNIT., INVESTIGATOR, ADDRESS, TITLE

ALTERNATIVE PATHWAYS OF CORTICOSTEROID SIDE CHAIN METABOLISM
S07RR-05860-11 0932 (NSS) MORRIS, PATRICIA L Biomedical research support GONDOTOXINS & IMMUNOLOGY MODULATORS ON TESTICULAR FUNCTION: IN VITRO: DRUG ABUSE
S07RR-05862-10 (NSS) HOPPIN, FREDERIC G, JR MEMORIAL HOSPITAL OF RI 111 BREWSTER STREET PAWTUCKET, R I 02860 Biomedical research support
S07RR-05862-10 0558 (NSS) HELLER, GARY Biomedical research support BETA ENDORPHINS UPON THRESHOLD FOR EXERCISE INDUCED ANGINA PECTORIS: NALOXONE
S07RR-05862-10 0559 (NSS) BARBOUR, MARILYN Biomedical research support PENTOXIFYLLINE UPON EXERCISE SYMPTOMS IN PTS W/ CORONARY ARTERY DISEASE
S07RR-05862-10 0560 (NSS) DAWICKI, DOLORETTA Biomedical research support HUMAN PLATELET TUBULIN PHOSPHORYLATION: AMP DEPENDENT & TYROSINE PROTEIN KINASE
S07RR-05862-10 0561 (NSS) KERN, DAVID Biomedical research support FIRE EXPOSURE & AIRWAY RESPONSIVENESS IN FIREFIGHTERS: OCCUPATION
S07RR-05862-10 0562 (NSS) LAZARUS, BRUCE Biomedical research support PHYSICAL ACTIVITY OF HOSPITALIZED ELDERLY PTS
S07RR-05862-10 0563 (NSS) UNKNOWN Biomedical research support ANIMAL CAGE WASHER
S07RR-05863-11 (NSS) MC KEEHAN, WALLACE L W ALTON JONES CELL SCIENCE CEN 10 OLD BARN ROAD LAKE PLACID, N Y 12946 Biomedical research support
S07RR-05863-11 0564 (NSS) BUONASSISI, VINCENZO Biomedical research support ENDOTHELIUM & THROMBO RESISTANCE
S07RR-05863-11 0565 (NSS) CRABB, JOHN W Biomedical research support PROTEIN CHEMISTRY: BIOLOGY OF VISUAL CYCLE PROTEINS
S07RR-05863-11 0566 (NSS) HAYASHI, JUN Biomedical research support EARLY T CELL DEVELOPMENT
S07RR-05863-11 0567 (NSS) JAKEN, SUSAN Biomedical research support SIGNAL TRANSDUCTION THROUGH PROTEIN KINASE C
S07RR-05863-11 0568 (NSS) MCKEEHAN, WALLACE L Biomedical research support VASCULAR, PROSTATE & LIVER CELL BIOLOGY
S07RR-05863-11 0569 (NSS) MATSUDA, RYOICHI Biomedical research support DEVELOPMENTAL BIOLOGY OF SKELETAL MUSCLES
S07RR-05863-11 0570 (NSS) SATO, GORDON Biomedical research support SERUM FREE CELL CULTURE; CELLULAR ENDOCRINOLOGY
S07RR-05863-11 0571 (NSS) SATO, J DENRY Biomedical research support MONOCLONAL ANTIBODIES TO GROWTH FACTOR RECEPTORS & GROWTH FACTOR ACTION
S07RR-05863-11 0572 (NSS) SERRERO, GINETTE Biomedical research support HORMONAL CONTROL & GENE EXPRESSION OF ADIPOSE DIFFERENTIATION
S07RR-05863-11 0573 (NSS) STEVENS, JAMES L Biomedical research support BIOLOGY OF TISSUE DAMAGE BY TOXIC CHEMICALS & DAMAGE REPAIR
S07RR-05863-11 0574 (NSS) SUSSMAN, DANIEL Biomedical research support MOLECULAR BIOLOGY OF DEVELOPMENT: EMBRYO
S07RR-05864-10 (NSS) EISENMANN, DALE R UNIVERSITY OF ILLINOIS 801 S PAULINA CHICAGO, ILL 60612 Biomedical research support
S07RR-05864-10 0937 (NSS) WATANABE, KEIKO Biomedical research support PREPUBERTAL PERIODONTICS
S07RR-05864-10 0938 (NSS) GERSON, STANLEY Biomedical research support EFFECT OF ZINC NUTRITION ON INDUCTION OF ORAL CANCER
S07RR-05864-10 0933 (NSS) BAPNA, MAHENDRA Biomedical research support DIAMETRICAL STRESS & FRACTURE TOUGHNESS OF REPAIRED DENTAL AMALGAM
S07RR-05864-10 0934 (NSS) FADAVI, SHAHRBANOO Biomedical research support FREEZE DRIED BONE AS PULP DRESSING IN PULPOTOMIZED TEETH IN MONKEYS
S07RR-05864-10 0935 (NSS) SABET, TAWFIK Biomedical research support INFLAMMATION & PHENYTOIN DEPENDENT GINGIVAL OVERGROWTH
S07RR-05864-10 0936 (NSS) WEBER, DENNIS Biomedical research support ORGAN CULTURE STUDIES OF HUMAN DENTINE
S07RR-05866-08 (NSS) OBERST, MARILYN T UNIVERSITY OF WISCONSIN 600 HIGHLAND AVE, RM K6/342 MADISON, WIS 53792 Biomedical research support grant
S07RR-05866-08 0985 (NSS) BECKER, PATRICIA T Biomedical research support grant REDUCING STRESS DURING HANDLING IN NEONATAL INTENSIVE CARE UNIT
S07RR-05866-08 0986 (NSS) BECKER, PATRICIA T Biomedical research support grant REDUCING STRESS DURING HANDLING IN NEONATAL INTENSIVE CARE UNIT
S07RR-05866-08 0987 (NSS) BOWERS, BARBARA J Biomedical research support grant WORK WORLD OF NURSING ASSISTANT IN LONG TERM CARE
S07RR-05866-08 0988 (NSS) CAMPBELL, EMILY B Biomedical research support grant PATTERNED URGE RESPONSE TO INCONTINENCE RESEARCH
S07RR-05866-08 0989 (NSS) MCCARTHY, DONNA O Biomedical research support grant MECHANISMS OF ANOREXIA W/ TUMOR GROWTH
S07RR-05870-10 (NSS) RANKIN, GARY O MARSHALL UNIVERSITY 542 SPRING VALLEY DRIVE HUNTINGTON, WVA 25755-9310 Biomedical research support
S07RR-05870-10 0990 (NSS) BERK, MITCHELL L Biomedical research support NEUROANATOMICAL SUBSTRATE FOR ROLE OF HISTAMINE WITHIN CNS
S07RR-05870-10 0991 (NSS) FISH, STEPHEN E Biomedical research support DEVELOPMENT OF VISUAL SYSTEM: HAMSTERS, CORPUS CALLOSUM, AXONA, VISION
S07RR-05870-10 0992 (NSS) JACKMAN, SUSAN H Biomedical research support IMMUNE RESPONSE TO SKIN EPIDERMAL ANTIGENS MICE, SPLEEN CELLS, SKIN LESIONS
S07RR-05870-10 0993 (NSS) MCCUMBEE, WILLIAM D Biomedical research support PULSATILE PRESSURE ON CYCLIC AMP LEVELS IN PERFUSED RAT AORTA: HYPERTENSION
S07RR-05870-10 0994 (NSS) MOORE, MICHAEL R Biomedical research support PROGESTINS, ESTROGENS, & ANTIHORMONES ON GROWTH OF BREAST CANCER CELLS
S07RR-05870-10 0995 (NSS) PRIMERANO, DONALD A Biomedical research support MOLECULAR ANALYSIS OF SPORULATION REGULATED GENES OF SACCHAROMYCES CEREVISIAE
S07RR-05870-10 0996 (NSS) REICHENBECHER, VERNO Biomedical research support ISOLATION & CHARACTERIZATION OF A PRECURSOR OF CELLULAR CALCIUM MODULATOR
S07RR-05870-10 0997 (NSS) VALENTOVIC, MONICA A Biomedical research support TOXICITY OF TRICHLOROBENZENE: HEPATOTOXICITY, RATS, NALOGENATED HYDROCARBONS

PROJECT NO., ORGANIZATIONAL UNIT., INVESTIGATOR, ADDRESS, TITLE

S07RR-05871-03 (NSS) ROWITZ, LOUIS UNIVERSITY OF ILLINOIS 2121 WEST TAYLOR STREET CHICAGO, ILL 60612 Biomedical research support
S07RR-05871-03 0577 (NSS) DAVIS, FAITH G Biomedical research support CASE CONTROL STUDY OF UNDERNUTRITION & CERVICAL DYSPLASIA
S07RR-05871-03 0578 (NSS) HERSHOW, RONALD C Biomedical research support CIPROFLOXACIN RESIST IN METHICILLIN RESISTANT STAPHYLOCOCCUS AUREUS IN HOSPITAL
S07RR-05871-03 0579 (NSS) MENSAH, EDWARD K Biomedical research support EFFECTS OF ELDER CARE ON CARE GIVERS INCOME & WORK EFFORTS
S07RR-05871-03 0580 (NSS) PROHASKA, THOMAS R Biomedical research support MALL WALKING EXERCISE PROGRAMS FOR OLDER ADULTS
S07RR-05871-03 0581 (NSS) RYDMAN, ROBERT J Biomedical research support MEDICARE DRGS AS COST REIMBURSEMENT SYSTEM FOR URBAN TRAUMA CARE
S07RR-05871-03 0582 (NSS) SCHEFF, PETER A Biomedical research support US & SOVIET: ENVIRONMENTAL ILLNESS IN CHERNIVTSI,UKRAINIAN SSR; ALOPECIA
S07RR-05872-08 (NSS) BLOEDEL, JAMES R BARROW NEUROLOGICAL INSTITUTE 350 W THOMAS ROAD PHOENIX, AZ 85013 Biomedical research support
S07RR-05872-08 0979 (NSS) BERENS, MICHAEL E Biomedical research support EXTRACELLULAR MATRIX IN GLIOMA CELL GROWTH
S07RR-05872-08 0980 (NSS) CRAIG, ARTHUR D Biomedical research support ORGANIZATION OF SPINAL PROJECTION TO THALAMUS
S07RR-05872-08 0981 (NSS) GIBSON, ALAN R Biomedical research support BALANCE FOR HISTOLOGY ROOM
S07RR-05872-08 0982 (NSS) GIBSON, ALAN R Biomedical research support EQUIPMENT FOR MACHINE SHOP
S07RR-05872-08 0983 (NSS) GIBSON, ALAN R Biomedical research support RECORDING & RESPIRATOR EQUIPMENT FOR ANIMAL RESEARCH
S07RR-05872-08 0984 (NSS) STACHOWIAK, MICHAEL Biomedical research support REGULATION OF TYROSINE HYDROXYLASE SYSTEM
S07RR-05872-08 0985 (NSS) VANKAN, PETER Biomedical research support FUNCTIONAL ROLE OF CEREBELLAR SYSTEMS IN LIMB MOVEMENT
S07RR-05874-10 (NSS) COX, ROBERT H BOCKUS RES INST, GRAD HOSP ONE GRADUATE PLAZA PHILADELPHIA, PA 19146 Biomedical research support
S07RR-05874-10 0583 (NSS) DAVIDOFF, AMY J Biomedical research support CA CURRENT KINETICS IN RABBIT MESENTERIC ARTERIAL SMOOTH MUSCLE CELLS
S07RR-05874-10 0584 (NSS) GU, HONG Biomedical research support NOREPINEPHRINE INCREASES INOSITOL PHOSPHATE LEVELS IN VASCULAR SMOOTH MUSCLE
S07RR-05874-10 0585 (NSS) MARTIN, HUNTER Biomedical research support CARDIAC MUSCLE RELAXATION FROM RIGOR INITIATED BY LASER PHOTOLYSIS OF CAGED ATP
S07RR-05876-09 (NSS) VANDERLAAN, WILLARD P WHITTIER INST FOR DIABETES 9894 GENESEE AVENUE LA JOLLA, CALIF 92037 Biomedical research support
S07RR-05876-09 0586 (NSS) HAYEK, ALBERTO Biomedical research support CLINICAL RESEARCH CULTURE OF HUMAN PANCREATIC ISLETS
S07RR-05876-09 0587 (NSS) SINGER, PAUL A Biomedical research support T CELL RECEPTOR GENES IN AUTOIMMUNE DIABETES: CT
S07RR-05876-09 0588 (NSS) SINYA, Y N Biomedical research support GLYCOSYLATED PROLACTIN IN RODENTS
S07RR-05876-09 0589 (NSS) HARO, LUIS S Biomedical research support RECEPTORS FOR LACTOGENIC HORMONES
S07RR-05876-09 0590 (NSS) LING, NICHOLAS C Biomedical research support NEUROENDOCRINOLOGY OF REPRODUCTION & GROWTH
S07RR-05877-09 (NSS) WILEY, ROBERT A UNIVERSITY OF IOWA COLLEGE OF PHARMACY IOWA CITY, IOWA 52242 Biomedical research support
S07RR-05877-09 0591 (NSS) CASTEEL, DEE A Biomedical research support NEW IMIDAZOLINONE & IMIDOZOLONE NUCLEOSIDES: AIDS ANTITUMOR & VIRAL DRUG
S07RR-05877-09 0592 (NSS) DONOVAN, MAUREEN D Biomedical research support MUCOSAL METABOLISM ON SYSTEMIC BIOAVAILABILITY FROM NASAL CAVITY
S07RR-05877-09 0593 (NSS) WOODWARD, JEAN B Biomedical research support ASSESSMENT OF SOCIAL ISOLATION & SUPPORT ON RATE OF NON COMPLIANCE IN ELDERLY
S07RR-05877-09 0594 (NSS) WURSTER, DALE ERICE Biomedical research support IDENTIFICATION & QUANTIFICATION OF SURFACE FUNCTIONAL GROUPS
S07RR-05877-09 0595 (NSS) GERAETS, DOUGLAS R Biomedical research support EFFECT OF AMIODARONE ON PHENYTOIN DISPOSITION IN CARDIAC PTS
S07RR-05877-09 0596 (NSS) MILAVETZ, GARY Biomedical research support RATE & EXTENT OF ABSORPTION OF TOBRAMYCIN FROM RABBIT RESPIRATORY TRACT
S07RR-05877-09 0597 (NSS) VENG-PEDERSEN, PETER Biomedical research support COMPUTER CTRL OF ALFENTANYL INFUSION FOR INDUCTION & MAINTENANCE OF ANESTHESIA
S07RR-05878-09 (NSS) SILVERMAN, MICHAEL R AGOURON INSTITUTE 505 COAST BLVD SOUTH LA JOLLA, CALIF 92037 Biomedical research support
S07RR-05878-09 0998 (NSS) BILLINGS, PETER Biomedical research support NUCLEAR PROTEINS & AUTOIMMUNITY
S07RR-05879-09 (NSS) HARRIS, BEN G TEXAS COLL OF OSTEOPATHIC MED 3500 CAMP BOWIE BLVD FT WORTH, TEX 76107 Biomedical research support
S07RR-05879-09 0598 (NSS) ALVAREZ-GONZALEZ, RA Biomedical research support PROTEIN MONO ADP RIBOSYLATION IN RAT LIVER NUCLEI
S07RR-05879-09 0599 (NSS) DOWNEY, H FRED Biomedical research support REGULATION OF RIGHT CORONARY BLOOD FLOW
S07RR-05879-09 0600 (NSS) FORSTER, MICHAEL J Biomedical research support NEURONAL TARGETS OF BRAIN REACTIVE ANTIBODIES IN AGING MICE
S07RR-05879-09 0601 (NSS) GRANT, STEPHEN R Biomedical research support BIOCHEMISTRY OF NEUTROPHIL CHEMOTACTIC RECEPTOR
S07RR-05879-09 0602 (NSS) NICHOLSON, WAYNE Biomedical research support REPAIR OF ULTRAVIOLET LIGHT DAMAGE IN BACTERIAL SPORES
S07RR-05879-09 0603 (NSS) ROMEO, TONY Biomedical research support GENETIC REGULATION OF BACTERIAL GLYCOGEN BIOSYNTHESIS
S07RR-05879-09 0604 (NSS) SHAKLEE, PATRICK Biomedical research support NUCLEOTIDE SPECIFICITY OF NATIVE & ALTERED QB REPLICASE
S07RR-05879-09 0605 (NSS) SUNDSTROM, PAULA Biomedical research

PROJECT NO., ORGANIZATIONAL UNIT., INVESTIGATOR, ADDRESS, TITLE

support VIRULENCE GENES OF CANDIDA ALBICANS, AN AIDS OPPORTUNIST
S07RR-05880-09 (NSS) MAHLEY, ROBERT W GLADSTONE FDN LABORATORIES P O BOX 40608 SAN FRANCISCO, CALIF 94140 Biomedical research support
S07RR-05880-09 0618 (NSS) MAHLEY, ROBERT W Biomedical research support NO RESEARCH SUBPROJECTS
S07RR-05882-09 (NSS) MOSIER, DONALD E MEDICAL BIOLOGY INSTITUTE 11077 N TORREY PINES ROAD LA JOLLA, CA 92307 Biomedical research support
S07RR-05882-09 0606 (NSS) GOTTESFELD, JOEL M Biomedical research support ISOLATION OF 5S GENE CHROMATIN
S07RR-05883-07 (NSS) ROGERS, ADRIANNE E MALLORY INST OF PATHOLOGY FDN 784 MASSACHUSETTS AVE BOSTON, MASS 02118 Biomedical research support grant
S07RR-05885-06 (NSS) ROSS, RICHARD F IOWA STATE UNIVERSITY VETERINARY ADMINISTRATION AMES, IOWA 50011 Biomedical research support grant
S07RR-05886-08 (NSS) MOSBACH, ERWIN H BETH ISRAEL MEDICAL CENTER FIRST AVE AT 16TH STREET NEW YORK, N Y 10003 Biomedical research support
S07RR-05886-08 0298 (NSS) MOSBACH, ERWIN H Biomedical research support METABOLISM OF 7B METHYL NOR CHENODEOXYCHOLIC ACID IN HAMSTERS
S07RR-05886-08 0299 (NSS) COHEN, BERTRAM I Biomedical research support SPECIFIC FATTY ACID MODULATE CHOLESTEROL CHOLELITHIASIS
S07RR-05886-08 0300 (NSS) COHEN, BERTRAM I Biomedical research support ASPIRIN & DIET DONT ALTER COURSE OF CHOLESTEROL CHOLELITHIASIS; 2 ANIMAL MODELS
S07RR-05886-08 0301 (NSS) BARR, CHARLES E Biomedical research support HIV REPLICATION IN SALIVA
S07RR-05889-09 (NSS) MONTGOMERY, ROBERT R, JR BLOOD CTR OF SOUTHEAST WIS 1701 WEST WISCONSIN AVE MILWAUKEE, WIS 53233 Biomedical research support
S07RR-05889-09 0519 (NSS) MONTGOMERY, RICHARD Biomedical research support NO RESEARCH SUBPROJECTS
S07RR-05894-09 (NSS) THOMPSON, HENRY J AMC CANCER RES CTR AND HOSP 1600 PIERCE STREET LAKEWOOD, COLO 80214 Biomedical research support
S07RR-05894-09 0607 (NSS) COHEN, STUART J Biomedical research support IMPROVING CANCER PREVENTION & EARLY DETECTION IN PRIMARY CARE SETTINGS
S07RR-05894-09 0608 (NSS) MARCUS, ALFRED C Biomedical research support CANCER CONTROL COMMUNICATIONS PROJECT & PILOT STUDY
S07RR-05895-09 (NSS) YOUNG, ROBERT C FOX CHASE CANCER CENTER 7701 BURHOLME AVE PHILADELPHIA, PA 19111 Biomedical research support
S07RR-05895-09 0609 (NSS) MCGLYNN, KATHERINE A Biomedical research support BIOCHEMICAL EPIDEMIOLOGY OF CANCER
S07RR-05895-09 0610 (NSS) TSICHLIS, PHILIP N Biomedical research support SPONTANEOUS RECURRENT INSERTIONAL MUTAGENSIS OF RETROVIRUS INDUCED NEOPLASMS
S07RR-05895-09 0611 (NSS) KLEIN-SZANTO, ANDRES Biomedical research support INVASIVE & METASTATIC NON SMALL CELL CARCINOMA CELLS EXHIBIT P53 ABNORMALITIES
S07RR-05895-09 0612 (NSS) TESTA, JOSEPH R Biomedical research support SMALL CELL LUNG CANCER: KARYOLOGY & MOLECULAR CORRELATES
S07RR-05895-09 0613 (NSS) TEW, KENNETH D Biomedical research support REGULATION OF GST EXPRESSION
S07RR-05895-09 0614 (NSS) TAYLOR, DOUGLAS D Biomedical research support LABORATORY INVESTIGATIONS
S07RR-05895-09 0615 (NSS) MURPHY-BOESCH, JOSEP Biomedical research support NMR STUDIES OF PHOSPHOLIPID METABOLISM
S07RR-05895-09 0616 (NSS) CLAPPER, MARGIE L Biomedical research support REGULATION OF GST EXPRESSION
S07RR-05895-09 0617 (NSS) LERMAN, CARYN Biomedical research support IMPACT OF BREAST CANCER RISK COUNSELING
S07RR-05895-09 0618 (NSS) ROSVOLD, ELIZABETH Biomedical research support VARIATIONS IN DEBRISOQUINE METABOLISM & LUNG CANCER RISK
S07RR-05896-09 (NSS) FRANKS, RONALD D UNIVERSITY OF MINNESOTA 10 UNIVERSITY DRIVE DULUTH, MINN 55812 Biomedical research support
S07RR-05896-09 0619 (NSS) STAUFFER, EDWARD K Biomedical research support TESTING NEW TECHNIQUE FOR RECORDING FROM GOLGI TENDON ORGANS IN CONTINUITY
S07RR-05896-09 0620 (NSS) PROHASKA, JOSEPH R Biomedical research support COPPER DEFICIENCY & IMMUNE RESPONSE
S07RR-05896-09 0621 (NSS) SALO, WILMAR L Biomedical research support ACQUISITION OF MULTIPURPOSE ELECTROPHORESIS EQUIPMENT
S07RR-05896-09 0622 (NSS) ANDERSON, LARRY D Biomedical research support IMPROVEMENT OF ANIMAL HEALTH SURVEILLANCE & DISEASE CONTROL
S07RR-05896-09 0623 (NSS) WITTMERS, LORENTZ E Biomedical research support COMPUTER NETWORK FOR UMD SCHOOL OF MEDICINE
S07RR-05896-09 0624 (NSS) FITZGERALD, THOMAS J Biomedical research support THERMAL CYCLER FOR POLYMERASE CHAIN REACTIONS
S07RR-05896-09 0625 (NSS) SALO, WILMAR L Biomedical research support DETERMINATION OF PARTIAL SEQUENCES OF 16S TRNA FROM MYCOBACTERIUM TUBERCULOSIS
S07RR-05896-09 0626 (NSS) PROHASKA, JOSEPH R Biomedical research support NUTRITIONAL INTERACTION BETWEEN COPPER & SELENIUM
S07RR-05897-09 (NSS) KALKWARF, KENNETH L UNIV OF TEXAS HEALTH SCI CTR 7703 FLOYD CURL DRIVE SAN ANTONIO, TEX 78284 Biomedical research support
S07RR-05897-09 0266 (NSS) ALDER, MARDEN E Biomedical research support MAGNETIC RESONANCE IMAGING & SPECTROSCOPY OF INDUCED INFLAMMATION IN RABBIT TMJ
S07RR-05897-09 0267 (NSS) DODDS, MICHAEL W Biomedical research support RELATIONSHOP BETWEEN DIABETES, SALIVA & ROOT CARIES IN RATS
S07RR-05897-09 0268 (NSS) MCDAVID, WILLIAM D Biomedical research support MRI & MRS ARTICULAR + PERIARTICULAR INFLAMMATORY TISSUE IN TMJ
S07RR-05897-09 0269 (NSS) NOVAK, MICHAEL J Biomedical research support PMN FUNCTION BY OUTER MEMBRANE COMPONENTS OF BACTERIODES GINGIVATIS
S07RR-05897-09 0270 (NSS) NORLING, BARRY K Biomedical research support PLASMA ENHANCED DEPOSITION OF SILICA FOR IMPROVED RESIN METAL ADHESION
S07RR-05899-10 (NSS) NATHAN, DAVID G CHILDRENS HOSP MEDICAL CTR 300 LONGWOOD AVENUE BOSTON, MASS 02115 Biomedical research support
S07RR-05899-10 0271 (NSS) ADLER, GAIL Biomedical research support ENDOCRINE REGULATIONS CORTICOTROPIN RELEASING HORMONE
S07RR-05899-10 0272 (NSS) MAJZOUB, JOSEPH Biomedical research support PLACENTAL CORTICOTROPIN RELEASING HORMONE
S07RR-05899-10 0273 (NSS) BERDE, CHARLES Biomedical research support MECHANISMS OF ANESTHESIA & ANALGESIA
S07RR-05899-10 0274 (NSS) FLEISHER, GARY Biomedical research support PATHOPHYSIOLOGY OF SEPTIC SHOCK
S07RR-05899-10 0275 (NSS) GERARD, CRAIG Biomedical research support STRUCTURE & REGULATION OF HUMAN LUNG, MUCUS, GLYCOPROTEINS
S07RR-05899-10 0276 (NSS) LIPTON, STUART Biomedical research support THY 1 & NEURITE REGENERATION BY RETINAL GANGLION CELLS
S07RR-05899-10 0277 (NSS) KUNKEL, LOUIS Biomedical research support MOLECULAR GENETICS OF DUCHENNE MUSCULAR DYSTROPHY
S07RR-05900-06 (NSS) MARTINEZ, J RICARDO LOVELACE MEDICAL FOUNDATION 2425 RIDGECREST DRIVE SE ALBUQUERQUE, N MEX 87108 Biomedical research support medical foundation
S07RR-05900-06 0627 (NSS) KUSEWITT, D F Biomedical research support medical foundation CONSTRUCT OF CDNA LIBRARIES OF OPUSSUM ISOLATION OF PHOTOLYASE GENE
S07RR-05900-06 0628 (NSS) SEAGRAVE, J D Biomedical research support medical foundation GUANINE NUCLEOTIDE REGULATORY PROTEINS IN SALIVARY GLAND FUNCTION
S07RR-05900-06 0629 (NSS) SHOPP, G Biomedical research support medical foundation CA RESPONSE IN B CELLS AFTER TREATMENT W/ ANTIVIRAL DRUGS
S07RR-05900-06 0630 (NSS) MALVIN, G Biomedical research support medical foundation HYPOXIA ON TEMPERATURE SELECTION OF PROTOZOAN, PARAMECIUM CAUDATUM
S07RR-05901-07 (NSS) BRADBURN, NORMAN M NATIONAL OPINION RESEARCH CENT 1155 E 60TH STREET CHICAGO, ILL 60637 Biomedical research support research center
S07RR-05901-07 0620 (NSS) BRADBURN, NORMAN Biomedical research support research center NO RESEARCH SUBPROJECTS
S07RR-05902-05 (NSS) MILLER, DOROTHY L INST FOR SCIENTIFIC ANALYSIS 2235 LOMBARD STREET SAN FRANCISCO, CA 94123 Biomedical research support grant
S07RR-05902-05 0621 (NSS) MILLER, DOROTHY L Biomedical research support grant NO RESEARCH SUBPROJECTS
S07RR-05903-08 (NSS) GOLDENBERG, DAVID M CTR FOR MOL MED AND IMMUNOLOGY 1 BRUCE STREET NEWARK, N J 07103 Biomedical research support grant research center
S07RR-05903-08 0278 (NSS) DION, ARNOLD S Biomedical research support grant research center HUMAN MAMMARY EPITHELIAL ANTIGENS
S07RR-05905-08 (NSS) MORROW, GRANT, III CHILDREN'S HOSPITAL 700 CHILDREN'S DRIVE COLUMBUS, OHIO 43205 Biomedical research support
S07RR-05905-08 0631 (NSS) BRONER, CYNTHIA W Biomedical research support DETERMINATION OF OXYGEN DERIVED FREE MATERIALS
S07RR-05905-08 0632 (NSS) CHANG, LONG-SHENG Biomedical research support TRANSGENIC MOUSE FACILITY
S07RR-05906-06 (NSS) FORDTRAN, JOHN S BAYLOR RESEARCH FOUNDATION 3812 ELM ST, PO BOX 710699 DALLAS, TX 75226 Biomedical research support grant
S07RR-05906-06 0635 (NSS) HYLAND, KEITH Biomedical research support grant BIOGENIC AMINE & TETRAHYDROBIOPTERIN METABOLISM IN HPH 1 MOUSE: GENETIC DIS
S07RR-05906-06 0636 (NSS) GIBSON, K MICHAEL Biomedical research support grant REGULATORY INTERRELATIONS OF HMG COA REDUCTASE & MEVALONATE KINASE: INBORN ERROR
S07RR-05906-06 0633 (NSS) BOREJDO, JULIAN Biomedical research support grant MOTION OF MYOSIN ON F ACTIN INDUCED BY MGATP MUSCLE, CONTRACTION
S07RR-05906-06 0634 (NSS) FINE, KENNETH D Biomedical research support grant INTESTINAL ABSORPTION OF MAGNESIUM FROM FOOD & SUPPLEMENTS
S07RR-05907-08 (NSS) SULLIVAN, WALTER W MOREHOUSE SCHOOL OF MEDICINE 720 WESTVIEW DR S W ATLANTA, GA 30310-1495 Biomedical research support
S07RR-05907-08 0637 (NSS) KIRLIN, WARD G Biomedical research support CARCINOGENS & IMMUNE RESPONSE CELL COMPETENCE
S07RR-05907-08 0638 (NSS) SRIDARAN, RAJAGOPALA Biomedical research support GNRH & LUTEAL FUNCTION DURING PREGNANCY
S07RR-05907-08 0639 (NSS) SUNG, FUNG-CHANG Biomedical research support INFANT MORTALITY IN ASIAN AMERICANS
S07RR-05907-08 0640 (NSS) SUNG, FUNG-CHANG Biomedical research support MATERNAL MARITAL STATUS & LOW BIRTH WEIGHT INFANT MORTALITY
S07RR-05907-08 0641 (NSS) WINESKI, LAWRENCE E Biomedical research support AUTOMATIC POLAROID CAMERA SYSTEM IN BIOMEDICAL RESEARCH
S07RR-05908-08 (NSS) PLATT, JEROME J UNIV OF MED & DENT OF N J 401 HADDON AVENUE CAMDEN, NJ 08103-1505 Biomedical research support
S07RR-05908-08 0928 (NSS) UNK Biomedical research support NO SUBPROJECTS
S07RR-05909-08 (NSS) COLAIZZI, JOHN L RUTGERS STATE UNIVERSITY BUSCH CAMPUS/PO BOX 789 PISCATAWAY, NJ 08855-0789 Biomedical research support universities
S07RR-05909-08 0948 (NSS) GARDNER, CAROLE Biomedical research support universities CHARACTERIZATION OF IMMUNE MEDIATOR MEDIATOR PRODUCTION BY LUNG MACROPHAGES
S07RR-05909-08 0949 (NSS) KAUFFMAN, FREDERICK Biomedical research support universities RESEARCH LAB FOR CELLULAR & BIOCHEMICAL TOXICOLOGY
S07RR-05909-08 0950 (NSS) SNYDER, ROBERT Biomedical research support universities ESTABLISHMENT OF BONE MARROW CULTURE LABORATORY
S07RR-05909-08 0951 (NSS) YURKOW, EDWARD J Biomedical research support universities PHOSPHOSERINE DETECTION; SERINE PHOSPOHORYLATION IN RECEPTOR SIGNALING SYSTEMS
S07RR-05909-08 0952 (NSS) ZALESKI, JAN Biomedical research support universities METABOLISM; 1 W DICURBOXYLIC LONG CHAIN FATTY ACIDS; HEART & LIVER
S07RR-05909-08 0953 (NSS) FAN-HAVARD, PATTY Biomedical research support universities TEICOPLANIN IN MORPHINE PRETREATED & PHENOBARBITAL PRETREATED & CONTROL RATS

PROJECT NO., ORGANIZATIONAL UNIT., INVESTIGATOR, ADDRESS, TITLE

S07RR-05909-08 0654 (NSS) SHEPARD, THERESA Biomedical research support universities HEPATIC METABOLISM & ENTEROHEPATIC RECIRCULATION
S07RR-05909-08 0655 (NSS) WEYAND, ERIC Biomedical research support universities CHEM DNA ADDUCTS; CRITICAL TO INITIATION OF CHEM CARCINOGENESIS
S07RR-05910-08 (NSS) LEWIS, HUGH B PURDUE UNIVERSITY SCH VET MED, LYNN HALL WEST LAFAYETTE, IND 47907 Biomedical research
S07RR-05910-08 0642 (NSS) GUO, PEIXUAN Biomedical research ATTENUATED AVIAN INFECTIOUS LARYNGOTRACHEITIS VIRUS VACCINES W/ RECOMBINANT DNA
S07RR-05911-08 (NSS) STEVENS, C EDWARD N C STATE UNIV-VET MED 4700 HILLSBOROUGH STREET RALEIGH, NC 27606 Biomedcial research support
S07RR-05911-08 0643 (NSS) ALMOND, G W Biomedcial research support INTRACEREBROVENTRICULAR & PERFUSION TECHNIQUES TO ASSESS GNRH & LH RELEASE
S07RR-05911-08 0644 (NSS) BREUHAUS, B A Biomedcial research support ACTH HYPERTENSION ALTERATION OF CENTRAL CATECHOLAMINE RELEASE IN CONSCIOUS SHEEP
S07RR-05911-08 0645 (NSS) CULLEN, J M Biomedcial research support AGE RELATED INFECTION SUSCEPTIBILITY W/ DUCK HEPATITIS B VIRUS IN PEKING DUCKS
S07RR-05911-08 0646 (NSS) ROBINETTE, C L Biomedcial research support CHARACTERIZATION & LOCALIZATION OF MRNA FOR PROLACTIN LIKE PROTEIN IN PROSTATE
S07RR-05912-08 (NSS) YUILL, THOMAS M UNIVERSITY OF WISCONSIN 2015 LINDEN DRIVE WEST MADISON, WIS 53706 Biomedical research support
S07RR-05912-08 0652 (NSS) HELLEKANT, GORAN Biomedical research support SWEET TASTE MECHANISM IN PRIMATES: PLANT
S07RR-05912-08 0653 (NSS) KEITH, INGEGERD Biomedical research support GENE EXPRESSION OF PEPTIDE IN RAT LUNG
S07RR-05912-08 0647 (NSS) BJORLING, DALE Biomedical research support K CHANNELS IN NON ADRENERGIC NON CHOLINERGIC INHIBITORY SYSTEM OF AIRWAYS: LUNGS
S07RR-05912-08 0654 (NSS) MACEWEN, E GREGORY Biomedical research support ADRIAMYCIN ACTIVATION OF MONOCYTES: IMMUNE EFFECTOR CELL; CANCER TREATMENT
S07RR-05912-08 0655 (NSS) SPLITTER, GARY Biomedical research support T CELL RECOGNITION OF PICODNAVIRUS: IMMUNE RESPONSE
S07RR-05912-08 0656 (NSS) DUELAND, RUDOLPH Biomedical research support COLLAGENOUS BONE INDUCTIVE FACTORS IN IMPLANTS: BIOMECHANICS
S07RR-05912-08 0657 (NSS) DUNCAN, IAN Biomedical research support NEW MURINE MYELIN MUTANT IN RAT: ATAXIA
S07RR-05912-08 0658 (NSS) BJORLING, DALE Biomedical research support MODIFICATION OF REPERFUSION OF ISCHEMIC BOWEL IN RATS: LAZAROIDS
S07RR-05912-08 0648 (NSS) BJORLING, DALE Biomedical research support ENDOTHELIAL FUNCTION OF GRAFTED VESSELS IN RABBIT
S07RR-05912-08 0649 (NSS) BROWNFIELD, MARK Biomedical research support BRAIN SEROTONIN & VASOPRESSIN & OXYTOCIN REGULATION: SEROTONERGIC STIMULATION
S07RR-05912-08 0650 (NSS) CZUPRYNSKI, CHUCK Biomedical research support CYTOKINES & LISTERIA MONOCYTOGENES INFECTION: HEPATOCYTES; TUMOR NECROSIS
S07RR-05912-08 0651 (NSS) HELFAND, STUART C Biomedical research support LYMPHOID CELL LINE INDICATOR OF INTERLEUKIN 2 ACTIVITY: CANINE, LEUKEMIA
S07RR-05913-08 (NSS) PHILLIPS, LINDA R UNIVERSITY OF ARIZONA COL NURSING, 1401 N MARTIN TUCSON, AZ 85721 Biomedical research support
S07RR-05913-08 0659 (NSS) MAY, KATHLEEN Biomedical research support SOCIAL NETWORK CHARACTERIZATION; HELP SEEKING PATTERNS; MOTHERS OF INFANTS
S07RR-05913-08 0660 (NSS) FERKETICH, SANDRA Biomedical research support EFFECT OF LOW BIRTH WEIGHT INFANT ON FAMILY FUNCTION & MEMBERS HEALTH
S07RR-05913-08 0661 (NSS) LONGMAN, ALICE Biomedical research support BEREAVEMENT EXPERIENCES OF SURVIVORS OF PERSONS W/ AIDS
S07RR-05913-08 0662 (NSS) WOODTLI, ANNE Biomedical research support TEST INSTRUMENT; MEASURE STRESS & URGE INCONTINENCE IN ELDERLY WOMEN
S07RR-05913-08 0663 (NSS) CROSBY, LEANNA Biomedical research support PERIPHERAL BLOOD CYTOKINES VS FATIGUE IN RHEUMATOID ARTHRITIS PATIENTS
S07RR-05913-08 0664 (NSS) BADGER, TERRY Biomedical research support DEPRESSION, SOCIAL SUPPORT, WELL BEING & DAILY FUNCTIONING AMONG OLDER ADULTS
S07RR-05913-08 0665 (NSS) CROSBY, LEANNA Biomedical research support DVMT INSTRUMENT TO MEASURE RHEUMATOID ARTHRITIS DISEASE ACTIVITY
S07RR-05913-08 0666 (NSS) MOORE, IDA K Biomedical research support EARLY & DELAYED TISSUE INJURY FOLLOWING CNS TREATMENT OF CHILDREN; CANCER
S07RR-05915-08 (NSS) GIBSON, WILLIAM A BAYLOR COLLEGE OF DENTISTRY 3302 GASTON AVENUE DALLAS, TEX 75246 Biomedical research support
S07RR-05915-08 0667 (NSS) OKABE, T Biomedical research support MERCURY EVAPORATION FROM ELECTROCHEMICALLY CORRODED AMALGAM
S07RR-05915-08 0668 (NSS) ARCORIA, C J Biomedical research support SEM ANALYSIS OF INTERPORE 200 & HTR IMPLANTS IN RAT ALVEOLAR BONE
S07RR-05915-08 0669 (NSS) BUSCHANG, P H Biomedical research support MANDIBULAR GROWTH OF FRENCH CANADIAN CHILDREN
S07RR-05915-08 0670 (NSS) BLAHUT, P Biomedical research support CLINICAL EVALUATION OF ELECTRIC ORAL HYGIENE DEVICE IN GERIATRIC POPULATION
S07RR-05915-08 0671 (NSS) HUTCHINS, B Biomedical research support FREQUENCY OF C1 DORSAL ROOT GANGLION IN CAT
S07RR-05915-08 0672 (NSS) TAYLOR, S E Biomedical research support CARBACHOL POTENTIA ISOPROTERENOL INDUCE MUCIN SECRETION; RAT SUBMANDIBULAR GLAND
S07RR-05915-08 0673 (NSS) FRAZIER, L W Biomedical research support H2O2 BLEACHING AGENTS & PROSTAGLANDIN PRODUCTION; HAMSTER CHEEK POUCH
S07RR-05915-08 0674 (NSS) BUSCHANG, P H Biomedical research support VERTICAL & HORIZONTAL GROWTH OF ALVEOLAR BONE

PROJECT NO., ORGANIZATIONAL UNIT., INVESTIGATOR, ADDRESS, TITLE

S07RR-05915-08 0675 (NSS) BUSCHANG, P H Biomedical research support TECHNICAL ERRORS OF LOCATING CEPHALOMETRIC LANDMARKS
S07RR-05915-08 0682 (NSS) BABLER, W J Biomedical research support HYPERGRAVITATIONAL INFLUENCES ON MANDIBULAR GROWTH OF MICE
S07RR-05915-08 0683 (NSS) FREDERIKSEN, N L Biomedical research support ATTENUATION CHARACTERISTICS OF BUILDING MATERIALS FOR DIAGNOSTIC XRAYS
S07RR-05915-08 0684 (NSS) ARCORIA, C J Biomedical research support COMPOSITE & ENAMEL BOND STRENGTH USING MULTIPLE LASERS VS ACID ETCHING
S07RR-05915-08 0685 (NSS) KOLSTAD, R Biomedical research support LETHAL RATE CALCULATION OF DRY HEAT STERILIZATION
S07RR-05915-08 0686 (NSS) HINTON, R J Biomedical research support REMOVAL OF ARTICULAR FORCES & RAT CONDYLAR CARTILAGE METABOLISM
S07RR-05915-08 0687 (NSS) SCHNEIDERMAN, E D Biomedical research support CARDIOVASC EFFECTS OF DENTAL ANESTHETICS W/ EPINEPHRINE; HYPERTENSIVE PATIENTS
S07RR-05915-08 0688 (NSS) BLAHUT, P Biomedical research support SUITABILITY OF BUILDING MATERIALS AS RADIOPROTECTIVE BARRIERS
S07RR-05915-08 0689 (NSS) DEWALD, J P Biomedical research support AMALGAM ON CEMENT & CASTING DEGRADATION: IN VITRO STUDY
S07RR-05915-08 0690 (NSS) BABLER, W J Biomedical research support INDUCED PREMATURE SUTURE CLOSURE IN NEWBORN RATS
S07RR-05915-08 0691 (NSS) STUKALIN, R Biomedical research support MORPHOMETRIC & RADIOGRAPHIC ANATOMY OF EDENTULOUS MANDIBLE
S07RR-05915-08 0676 (NSS) BUSCHANG, P H Biomedical research support ESTIMATING & INTERPRETING CONDITIONAL CRANIOFACIAL CENTILES
S07RR-05915-08 0677 (NSS) HENRY, C A Biomedical research support EFFECTS OF HEMIN & OXYGEN ON GROWTH OF PORPHYROMONAS SPECIES
S07RR-05915-08 0678 (NSS) TAYLOR, A N Biomedical research support HUMAN PULP ORGAN DISTRIBUTION OF CALBINDIN D28K; 3 D RECONSTRUCTION
S07RR-05915-08 0679 (NSS) BERRY, C W Biomedical research support ANTIBACTERIAL ACTIVITY OF DENTAL IMPLANT METAL IONS ON BACTEROIDES SPECIES
S07RR-05915-08 0680 (NSS) BOWLES, W H Biomedical research support REACTIVITY OF SALIVARY PROTEINS W/ N ACETYLCYSTEINE: POTENTIAL PLAQUE INHIBITOR
S07RR-05915-08 0681 (NSS) DORRIS, R L Biomedical research support MECHANISM OF N2O BEHAVIORAL EFFECTS
S07RR-05916-08 (NSS) OSDOBY, PHILIP A WASHINGTON UNIVERSITY SCH MED, 4559 SCOTT AVE ST LOUIS, MO 63110 Biomedical research support universities
S07RR-05916-08 0302 (NSS) GERMAN, REBECCA Biomedical research support universities ONTOGENETIC ALLOMETRY OF LIMBS
S07RR-05916-08 0303 (NSS) DIEMER, RICHARD Biomedical research support universities PARTIAL KNOWLEDGE THROUGH RESPONSE DETERMINED SCORING
S07RR-05916-08 0304 (NSS) DESSEM, DEAN Biomedical research support universities CENTRAL MODULATION TMJ PROPRIOCEPTIVE AFFERENTS
S07RR-05916-08 0305 (NSS) COLLIN-OSDOBY, PATRI Biomedical research support universities DEMETHYLATION INDUCED GENE ACTIVATION OF OSTEOCLASTS
S07RR-05916-08 0306 (NSS) DESSEM, DEAN Biomedical research support universities INTERMEDIATE JAW MUSCLE AFFERENTS
S07RR-05916-08 0307 (NSS) LEWIS, MEMORY E Biomedical research support universities GOUANIO LUPILOIDES EFFECT ON PLAQUE FORMATION
S07RR-05917-08 (NSS) GLEDHILL, BARTON L LAWRENCE LIVERMORE NAT' LAB P O BOX 5507 L 452 LIVERMORE, CA 94550 Biomedical research support universities
S07RR-05917-08 0692 (NSS) FELTON, JAMES S Biomedical research support universities ACCELERATOR MASS SPECTROMETRY MEASUREMENT OF CHEMICALS BINDING TO DNA
S07RR-05917-08 0693 (NSS) TURTELTAUB, KENNETH Biomedical research support universities MICE DEPLETED IN 14C
S07RR-05917-08 0694 (NSS) GARCIA, EMILIO Biomedical research support universities CHROMOSOME 19 SPECIFIC YAC CLONING
S07RR-05917-08 0695 (NSS) JENSEN, RON Biomedical research support universities HUMAN SOMATIC CELL ASSAY USING IN VITRO APPROACHES
S07RR-05918-08 (NSS) BISSELL, MINA J UNIVERSITY OF CALIFORNIA LAWRENCE BERKELEY LAB BERKELEY, CALIF 94720 Biomedical research support universities
S07RR-05918-08 0705 (NSS) MCCALL, MARK B Biomedical research support universities EMERGENCY REPAIR OF BIOHAZARD HOOD IN 373 DONNER LAB
S07RR-05918-08 0706 (NSS) HARRIS, G SHYAMALA Biomedical research support universities TRANSCRIPTIONAL REGULATION OF UTERINE 90 KILODALTON HEAT SHOCK PROTEIN
S07RR-05918-08 0707 (NSS) TAYLOR, SCOTT E Biomedical research support universities ISOLATION & CHARACTERIZATION OF SEROTONIN RECEPTORS
S07RR-05918-08 0708 (NSS) JAP, BING K Biomedical research support universities CRYSTALLIZATION OF FIBRONECTIN RECEPTOR
S07RR-05918-08 0709 (NSS) NEWMARK, RICHARD D Biomedical research support universities NONINVASIVE INVESTIGATION OF METAB IN CARDIAC MYOCYTES; TRITIUM NMR SPECT
S07RR-05918-08 0710 (NSS) TAYLOR, SCOTT E Biomedical research support universities OXIDANTS & TAURINE IN CARDIAC ISCHEMIC & REPERFUSION INJURY; RABBIT
S07RR-05918-08 0711 (NSS) FRANKEL, KENNETH A Biomedical research support universities DAMAGE & REPAIR OF IRRADIATED MAMMALIAN BRAIN; RABBIT
S07RR-05918-08 0712 (NSS) MAESTRE, MARCOS F Biomedical research support universities FORCES BETWEEN SINGLE DNA MOLECULES
S07RR-05918-08 0713 (NSS) HOSODA, JUNKO Biomedical research support universities MAPPING OF PROTEIN CONFORMATIONAL CHANGES BY LIMITED PROTEOLYSIS
S07RR-05918-08 0696 (NSS) AFZAL, S M JAVED Biomedical research support universities COMBINED CHEMOTHERAPY & HEAVY ION RADIOTHERAPY; RAT RHABDOMYOSARCOMA TUMOR
S07RR-05918-08 0697 (NSS) COOPER, PRISCILLA K Biomedical research support universities DAMAGE INDUCIBLE DNA REPAIR RESPONSES IN HUMAN CELLS
S07RR-05918-08 0698 (NSS) COOPER, PRISCILLA K Biomedical research support universities REPAIR OF REPLICATION BLOCKING DNA DAMAGE

PROJECT NUMBER LISTING

PROJECT NO., ORGANIZATIONAL UNIT., INVESTIGATOR, ADDRESS, TITLE

S07RR-05918-08 0699 (NSS) GOLD, LOIS S Biomedical research support universities THEORETICAL RESEARCH ON CARCINOGENIC POTENCY DATABASE
S07RR-05918-08 0700 (NSS) DOWNING, KENNETH H Biomedical research support universities TUBULIN STRUCTURE BY ELECTRON CRYSTALLOGRAPHY
S07RR-05918-08 0701 (NSS) HARRIS, SHYAMALA Biomedical research support universities ESTROGENIC REGULATION OF MAMMARY PROGESTERONE RECEPTORS; SEQ
S07RR-05918-08 0702 (NSS) KRONENBERG, AMY Biomedical research support universities RNA POLYMERASE IN REPAIR OF POTENTIALLY MUTAGENIC DAMAGE; HUMAN
S07RR-05918-08 0703 (NSS) LEADON, STEVEN A Biomedical research support universities CLONING OF HUMAN DNA REPAIR GENES
S07RR-05918-08 0704 (NSS) GOTH-GOLDSTEIN, REGI Biomedical research support universities CELL RESPONSES TO ALKYLATION DAMAGE: HUMAN PLASMA LIPOPROTEIN METABOLISM
S07RR-05919-08 (NSS) BRADBURY, E MORTON UNIVERSITY OF CALIFORNIA P O BOX 1663, MS-M881 LOS ALAMOS, NM 87545 Biomedical research support universities
S07RR-05919-08 0714 (NSS) REYNOLDS, RICHARD J Biomedical research support universities INDUCTION & REPAIR OF CLOSELY OPPOSED DIMERS IN MAMMALIAN CELLS; UV
S07RR-05919-08 0715 (NSS) FEE, JAMES A Biomedical research support universities STABLE ISOTOPE ASSISTED BIOCHEMICAL & BIOPHYSICAL STUDIES OF ENZYMES: GENES
S07RR-05920-08 (NSS) DAVIS, THOMAS E NORTHERN CALIF CANCER CENTER 1301 SHOREWAY ROAD, SUITE 425 BELMONT, CA 94002-5030 Biomedical research support research institutes
S07RR-05920-08 0622 (NSS) DAVIS, THOMAS E Biomedical research support research institutes NO RESEARCH SUBPROJECTS
S07RR-05924-07 (NSS) RATTAZZI, MARIO C NORTH SHORE UNIV HOSPITAL 300 COMMUNITY DRIVE MANHASSET, N Y 11030 Biomedical research support grant
S07RR-05924-07 0000 (NSS) CHAWLA, ANUPAMA Biomedical research support grant DIET SUPPLEMENTED W/ N 3 PUFA FISH OIL ON MLP INDUCED ILEAL INFLAMMATION
S07RR-05924-07 0001 (NSS) ENG, ELAINE Biomedical research support grant PSYCHIATRIC DISORDERS & MENSTRUAL CYCLE
S07RR-05924-07 0002 (NSS) KARL, PETER I Biomedical research support grant PROTEIN KINASE C & BILE ACID TRANSPORTERS
S07RR-05924-07 0003 (NSS) POWELL, SAUL Biomedical research support grant TETRAMETHYL PIPERIDINE OXYL RADICAL (TEMPO) ON CARDIAC INJURY
S07RR-05924-07 0004 (NSS) SHALON, LINDA Biomedical research support grant T CELL RECEPTOR REPERTOIRE IN PATIENTS W/ CROHNS DISEASE
S07RR-05924-07 0999 (NSS) CHANG, MING-DER Biomedical research support grant MECHANISM OF MICROBIAL ENDOTOXIN INDUCED T CELL ACTIVATION
S07RR-05927-07 (NSS) SCOTCH, NORMAN A BOSTON UNIVERSITY SCHOOL OF ME 80 EAST CONCORD STREET, A-407 BOSTON, MASS 02118 Biomedical research support grant
S07RR-05927-07 0956 (NSS) KAYNE, HERBERT Biomedical research support grant COMMUNITY ASSESSMENT
S07RR-05927-07 0957 (NSS) WALSH, DIANA Biomedical research support grant JOB STRESS INSTRUMENT DEVELOPMENT
S07RR-05927-07 0958 (NSS) SAGER, ALAN Biomedical research support grant DESIGNING & INITIATING MONITORING OF MASS 1988 HEALTH INSURANCE LAWS
S07RR-05927-07 0959 (NSS) MERRIGAN, DANIEL Biomedical research support grant BEHAVIORAL & EDUCATION NEEDS ASSESSMENT
S07RR-05927-07 0960 (NSS) HOWLAND, JONATHON Biomedical research support grant INCIDENCE OF FALLS PREVALENCE OF FEAR OF FALLING; ELDERLY LIVING IN COMMUNITY
S07RR-05927-07 0961 (NSS) BARRY, ANITA Biomedical research support grant HIV SEROPREVALENCE & SPECTRUM OF ASSOCIATED DISEASE IN URBAN POPULATION
S07RR-05927-07 0962 (NSS) HOWLAND, JONATHON Biomedical research support grant BARRIERS TO BICYCLE HELMET USE AMONG CHILDREN
S07RR-05927-07 0963 (NSS) LEVENSON, SUZETTE Biomedical research support grant PEDESTRIAN INJURIES AMONG ELDERLY
S07RR-05927-07 0966 (NSS) BICKNELL, WILLIAM Biomedical research support grant HLTH STATISTICS & CULTURE OF ERITREAU & EPTHIOPIAN REFUGEE FAMILIES; BOSTON
S07RR-05927-07 0967 (NSS) POSNER, BARBARA Biomedical research support grant CYCLE V FRAMINGHAM NUTRITION STUDIES
S07RR-05927-07 0968 (NSS) CASHMAN, SUZANNE Biomedical research support grant DVMT RELATIVE VALUE SCALE TO MEASURE RES UTILIZATION & COST OF HOME SERVICE
S07RR-05927-07 0964 (NSS) OZONOFF, DAVID Biomedical research support grant PREDICTING RADON TESTING AMONG UNIVERSITY EMPLOYEES
S07RR-05927-07 0965 (NSS) ALDWIN, CAROLYN Biomedical research support grant VULNERABILITY & RESILIENCE IN AN AGING POPULATION
S07RR-05927-07 0969 (NSS) SAGER, ALAN Biomedical research support grant DESIGNING EVALUTION OF MASS NEW HEALTH INSURANCE
S07RR-05927-07 0970 (NSS) ROSENBERG, LYNN Biomedical research support grant HISTOLOGIC CLASSIFICATIONS OF BENIGN OVARIAN NEOPLASMS
S07RR-05927-07 0971 (NSS) PAYNE, SUSAN Biomedical research support grant BETTER ASSESS PEDIATRIC HOSPITAL UTILIZATION UNDER MEDICAID
S07RR-05927-07 0972 (NSS) HOWLAND, JONATHON Biomedical research support grant ID KNOWLEDGE DEFICITS & BEHAVIORAL RISKS; HIV TRANSMISSION; SID CLINIC PATIENTS
S07RR-05928-06 (NSS) WALLACE, WILLIAM R OHIO STATE UNIVERSITY 1159 POSTLE HALL, 305 W 12TH COLUMBUS, OH 43210 Biomedical research support grant
S07RR-05928-06 0308 (NSS) BRADWAY, STEVEN D Biomedical research support grant TRANSGLUTAMINASE IN CANDIDA ALBICANS ADHERENCE
S07RR-05928-06 0309 (NSS) MARUCHA, PHILIP T Biomedical research support grant GENE EXPRESSION IN ACTIVATED PMNS
S07RR-05929-06 (NSS) PETERSON, JERRY A JOHN MUIR CANCER & AGING INST 2055 NORTH BROADWAY WALNUT CREEK, CALIF 94596 Biomedical research support grant
S07RR-05929-06 0279 (NSS) PETERSON, JERRY A Biomedical research support grant PCR DETECTION OF BREAST CELLS IN BONE MARROW
S07RR-05929-06 0280 (NSS) LAROCCA, DAVID Biomedical research support grant EPITOPE EXPRESSION & BREAST MUCIN MRNA

PROJECT NO., ORGANIZATIONAL UNIT., INVESTIGATOR, ADDRESS, TITLE

S07RR-05929-06 0281 (NSS) CERIANI, ROBERTO L Biomedical research support grant MICRODOSIMETERS FOR PRECLINICAL RADIOIMMUNOTHERAPY
S07RR-05930-07 (NSS) PIJOAN, CARLOS UNIVERSITY OF MINNESOTA 1365 GORTNER 460 VET TCH HOS ST PAUL, MINN 55108 Biomedical research support grant
S07RR-05930-07 0716 (NSS) RUTH, GEORGE R Biomedical research support grant CYTOGENETIC CAUSES OF PORCINE HYPOPROLIFICACY: REPRODUCTION
S07RR-05930-07 0717 (NSS) BROWN, DAVID R Biomedical research support grant NEURAL & ENDOCRINE REGULAT OF EPITHELIAL TRANSPORT IN PIG INTESTINE
S07RR-05930-07 0718 (NSS) JOHNSON, KENNETH H Biomedical research support grant DIABETES MELLITUS & ISLET AMYLOID POLYPEPTIDE IN CAT
S07RR-05930-07 0719 (NSS) BEITZ, ALVIN J Biomedical research support grant NEUROTRANSMITTERS INVOLVED IN CONTROL OF PAIN PATHWAY EXCITATION
S07RR-05930-07 0720 (NSS) LOUIS, CHARLES Biomedical research support grant MUTATION RESPONSIBLE FOR PORCINE STRESS SYNDROME
S07RR-05930-07 0721 (NSS) MOLITOR, THOMAS W Biomedical research support grant MOLECULAR BIOLOGY SEMINAR
S07RR-05932-07 (NSS) COHEN, ALLAN Y PACIFIC INST FOR RES & EVAL 7315 WISCONSIN AVE, SUITE 900E BETHESDA, MD 20814 Biomedical research support grant
S07RR-05932-07 0005 (NSS) GRUBE, JOEL Biomedical research support grant DATA ANALYSIS ENHANCEMENT THROUGH MICROCOMPUTERS
S07RR-05933-07 (NSS) PERRY, NATHAN W, JR UNIVERSITY OF FLORIDA BOX J-165, JHMHC GAINESVILLE, FLA 32610 Biomedical research support grant
S07RR-05933-07 0310 (NSS) PERRY, NATHAN W Biomedical research support grant GENERAL PURPOSE RES LAB COMPUTER & LAB WORKSTATIONS & TECHNICAL ASSISTANCE
S07RR-05937-07 (NSS) FINK, GERALD R WHITEHEAD INSTITUTE NINE CAMBRIDGE CENTER CAMBRIDGE, MASS 02142 Biomedical research support grant
S07RR-05937-07 0623 (NSS) FINK, GERALD R Biomedical research support grant NO RESEARCH SUBPROJECTS
S07RR-05938-07 (NSS) BLANE, HOWARD T RESEARCH INST ON ALCOHOLISM 1021 MAIN STREET BUFFALO, N Y 14203 Biomedical research support grant
S07RR-05938-07 0311 (NSS) COLE-HARDING, SHIRLE Biomedical research support grant VASOPRESSIN & GENETIC DIFFERENCES IN ETHANOL TOLERANCE
S07RR-05938-07 0312 (NSS) BLANE, HOWARD T Biomedical research support grant PREVENTING SUBSTANCE MISUSE AMONG MENTALLY RETARDED
S07RR-05938-07 0315 (NSS) WINDLE, MICHAEL Biomedical research support grant ADOLESCENT PERCEPTIONS OF SUBSTANCE RISKS & HEALTH
S07RR-05938-07 0316 (NSS) COLE-HARDING, SHIRLE Biomedical research support grant ISBRA & RSA CONFERENCE ACCOUNT
S07RR-05938-07 0313 (NSS) LAPP, WILLIAM M Biomedical research support grant ACUTE ALCOHOL INTOXICATION & AUTOMATIC OR STRATEGIC COGNITIVE PROCESSES
S07RR-05938-07 0314 (NSS) WELTE, JOHN W Biomedical research support grant DRINKING & DELINQUENCY IN YOUNG MEN
S07RR-05938-07 0317 (NSS) MILLER, BRENDA A Biomedical research support grant ALCOHOL, DRUG USE & SPOUSAL VIOLENCE AMONG PAROLEES
S07RR-05938-07 0318 (NSS) LEONARD, KENNETH E Biomedical research support grant EXPERIMENTAL STUDY OF ALCOHOL & MARITAL AGGRESSION
S07RR-05938-07 0319 (NSS) BLANE, HOWARD T Biomedical research support grant MENTALLY I11 CHEMICAL ABUSER PILOT STUDY
S07RR-05938-07 0320 (NSS) RUEFLI, TERRY Biomedical research support grant AIDS RISK TAKING IN GAY MEN
S07RR-05938-07 0321 (NSS) MILLER, BRENDA Biomedical research support grant IMPACT OF FAMILY VIOLENCE ON WOMENS DRUG USE
S07RR-05938-07 0322 (NSS) TUBMAN, JONATHAN Biomedical research support grant PARENTAL ALCOHOL USE, FAMILY FUNCTIONING
S07RR-05938-07 0323 (NSS) CONNORS, GERARD Biomedical research support grant SECULAR ORGANIZATIONS FOR SOBRIETY SURVEY STUDY
S07RR-05938-07 0324 (NSS) SMYTH, NANCY Biomedical research support grant PRELIMINARY STUDY FOR TREATMENT OUTCOME
S07RR-05938-07 0325 (NSS) BLANE, HOWART T Biomedical research support grant ANALYSIS OF RESEARCH DEVELOPMENT & OUTCOME AT RIA
S07RR-05939-07 (NSS) STUART, KENNETH D SEATTLE BIOMEDICAL RES INST 4 NICKERSON STREET SEATTLE, WASHINGTON 98109 Biomedical research support grant
S07RR-05939-07 0722 (NSS) SMITH, JOHN M Biomedical research support grant RELATIONSHIP BETWEEN 1 CARBON PURINE METABOLISM IN PROCARYOTE E COLI K12
S07RR-05939-07 0723 (NSS) FEAGIN, JEAN E Biomedical research support grant CELL & MOLECULAR BIOLOGY OF PLASMODIUM FALCIPARUM
S07RR-05939-07 0724 (NSS) GOLLAHON, KATHERINE Biomedical research support grant CONTROL OF IMMUNOGLOBIN LIGHT CHAIN
S07RR-05939-07 0725 (NSS) HOWARD, RANDALL F Biomedical research support grant GENE REGULATION IN PLASMODIUM FALCIPARUM
S07RR-05939-07 0726 (NSS) PARSONS, MARILYN Biomedical research support grant CONTROL OF GLYCOSOMAL GENE EXPRESSION
S07RR-05939-07 0727 (NSS) REED, STEVEN G Biomedical research support grant IMMUNOSUPPRESSION IN T CRUZI INFECTIONS
S07RR-05939-07 0728 (NSS) SMITH, JOHN M Biomedical research support grant CONTROL OF PURINE BIOSYNTHESIS GENE EXPRESSION
S07RR-05939-07 0729 (NSS) STUART, KENNETH D Biomedical research support grant GENE EXPRESSION IN PROTOZOAN PARASITES
S07RR-05939-07 0730 (NSS) YAGI, MAYUMI Biomedical research support grant ANALYSES OF NOVEL PROLIFERATION ASSOCIATED ANTIGEN
S07RR-05939-07 0731 (NSS) HOWARD, RANDALL F Biomedical research support grant CELL & MOLECULAR BIOLOGY OF P FALCIPARUM
S07RR-05942-06 (NSS) BAUN, MARA M 600S 42ND STREET OMAHA, NE 68198-5330 Biomedical research support grant
S07RR-05942-06 0006 (NSS) LOBIONDO-WOOD, GERI Biomedical research support grant IMPACT OF A CHILDS TRANSPLANT ON FAMILY FAMILY ADAPTATION
S07RR-05942-06 0007 (NSS) FOXALL, MARTHA Biomedical research support grant FACTORS INFLUENCING LONELINESS IN VISUALLY IMPAIRED ADULTS: VISION
S07RR-05942-06 0008 (NSS) YEAWORTH, ROSALEE Biomedical research

support grant VALIDATION OF ADOLESCENT LIFE CHANGE EVENT QUESTIONNAIRE

S07RR-05942-06 0009 (NSS) JONES, COLETTE Biomedical research support grant EFFECTS OF INFANT CHARACTERISTICS ON PARENTING; AN EXTENSION

S07RR-05942-06 0010 (NSS) BAUN, MARA M Biomedical research support grant EFFECT OF A CAGED BIRD ON ADAPTATION, DEPRESSION & LONELINESS OF OLDER ADULTS

S07RR-05942-06 0011 (NSS) BAUN, MARA M Biomedical research support grant CARDIOVASCULAR RESPONSES TO HYPERINFLATION & O2 INSUFFLATION DURING ETS

S07RR-05944-04 (NSS) ANDERSON, CAROLE A OHIO STATE UNIVERSITY 1585 NEIL AVENUE COLUMBUS, OHIO 43210 Biomedical research support grant

S07RR-05944-04 0975 (NSS) WEWERS, MARY ELLEN Biomedical research support grant NICOTINE, NEUROREGULATORS & DYSPHORIC STATES AMONG SMOKERS

S07RR-05944-04 0976 (NSS) MULLER, MARY E Biomedical research support grant TESTING LINK BETWEEN PRENATAL & POSTNATAL ATTACHMENT

S07RR-05944-04 0977 (NSS) HULL, MARGARET M Biomedical research support grant YOUNG WOMEN & CANCER: ISSUES OF LIFETIME

S07RR-05944-04 0978 (NSS) LOWE, NANCY K Biomedical research support grant PARITY & PROGRESSION OF PAIN DURING LABOR

S07RR-05944-04 0979 (NSS) SMITH, BARBARA A Biomedical research support grant REDUCING CARDIOVASCULAR RISK FACTORS IN AFRICAN AMERICAN CHILDREN

S07RR-05944-04 0973 (NSS) SAWYER, ELSPETH H Biomedical research support grant INSPIRATORY MUSCLE TRAINING: CHILDREN W/ CYSTIC FIBROSIS

S07RR-05944-04 0974 (NSS) STONE, KATHLEEN S Biomedical research support grant ENDOTRACHEAL SUCTIONING IN ACUTELY ILL ADULTS

S07RR-05947-07 (NSS) RUDY, ELLEN B CASE WESTERN RESERVE UNIVERSIT 2040 ADELBERT ROAD CLEVELAND, OHIO 44106 Biomedical research support grant

S07RR-05948-05 (NSS) LOWERY, BARBARA J 420 GUARDIAN DRIVE PHILADELPHIA, PA 19104-6096 Biomedical research support grant

S07RR-05948-05 0326 (NSS) AIKEN, LINDA H Biomedical research support grant NURSE PRACTITIONER CARE HIV

S07RR-05948-05 0327 (NSS) DEATRICK, JANET A Biomedical research support grant CHILDRENS PARTICIPATION IN HEALTH DECISIONS

S07RR-05948-05 0328 (NSS) GREY, MARGARET Biomedical research support grant DEPRESSION, IMMUNE RESPONSE DIABETIC ADOLESCENTS

S07RR-05948-05 0329 (NSS) MEDOFF-COOPER, BARBA Biomedical research support grant DEVELOPMENT OF SUCKING APPARATUS

S07RR-05948-05 0330 (NSS) PEINADO, SANDRA Biomedical research support grant HEALTH EFFECTS OF BEREAVEMENT

S07RR-05948-05 0331 (NSS) SCHODT, CAROLYN Biomedical research support grant SUBSTANCE ABUSE DURING PREGNANCY

S07RR-05948-05 0332 (NSS) GENNARO, SUSAN Biomedical research support grant LOW BIRTH WEIGHT INFANTS: ECONOMIC FAMILY OUTCOMES

S07RR-05948-05 0333 (NSS) BARNSTEINER, JANE Biomedical research support grant CHILDREN SEVERE HEART DEFECTS: FAMILY RESPONSES

S07RR-05948-05 0334 (NSS) MUNRO, BARBARA Biomedical research support grant EXERCISE FOLLOWING CABG SURGERY

S07RR-05948-05 0335 (NSS) LYNAUGH, JOAN E Biomedical research support grant ACCESSION DOCUMENTATION NURSING HISTORY CENTER

S07RR-05948-05 0336 (NSS) LOWERY, BARBARA J Biomedical research support grant SPSS SOFTWARE

S07RR-05949-07 (NSS) BUENING, GERALD M UNIVERSITY OF MISSOURI W203 VETERINARY MED BLDG COLUMBIA, MO 65211 Biomedical research support grant

S07RR-05949-07 0732 (NSS) HALE, CALVIN C Biomedical research support grant MOLECULAR CLONING OF BOVINE CARDIAC ENDOTHELIN 1 BINDING SITE

S07RR-05949-07 0733 (NSS) HOOK, REUEL R Biomedical research support grant RHEUMATOID FACTOR IN RESISTANCE TO PLASMODIUM BERGHEI

S07RR-05949-07 0734 (NSS) RUBIN, LEONA J Biomedical research support grant POSTNATAL NEUROPEPTIDE Y NERVE DVMT IN NORMO & HYPERTENSIVE RAT HEARTS

S07RR-05949-07 0735 (NSS) WELSHONS, WADE V Biomedical research support grant LITHIUM STIMULATED PROLIFERATION & PHOSPHATIDYLINOSITOL METABOLITES

S07RR-05950-07 (NSS) NESSON, H RICHARD BRIGHAM AND WOMEN'S HOSPITAL 75 FRANCIS STREET BOSTON, MASS 02115 Biomedical research support grant

S07RR-05950-07 0008 (NSS) CANESSA, MITZY Biomedical research support grant HYPERTENSION & SMOOTH MUSCLE NA K CL COTRANSPORT & NA & H EXCHANGE

S07RR-05950-07 0009 (NSS) MENTZER, STEVEN Biomedical research support grant ADHESION MOLECULES CONTROLLING LYMPHOCYTE MIGRATION IN LUNG TRANSPLANTATION

S07RR-05950-07 0000 (NSS) PATZ, SAMUEL Biomedical research support grant MEASUREMENT OF DIFFUSION W/ MRI

S07RR-05950-07 0001 (NSS) WALSH, BRIAN Biomedical research support grant EFFECT OF ALCOHOL ON HALF LIFE OF ESTROGEN IN POST MENOPAUSAL WOMEN

S07RR-05950-07 0002 (NSS) LAGE, JANICE Biomedical research support grant NUCLEAR PLOIDY & CELL CYCLE ACTIVITY IN GYNECOLOGIC CANCERS

S07RR-05950-07 0003 (NSS) GLOWACKI, JULIANNE Biomedical research support grant SYNTH & DEGRAN; ISOLATED CHONDROCYTES & BONE CELLS & CONNECTIVE TISSUE CELLS

S07RR-05950-07 0004 (NSS) KIJEWSKI, MARIE Biomedical research support grant MAXIMUM ENTROPY ESTIMATION OF NOISE POWER SPECTRUM OF SPECTIMAGES

S07RR-05950-07 0005 (NSS) NOWAK, ROMANA Biomedical research support grant GROWTH FACTORS IN REGULATION OF GROWTH OF UTERINE LEIOMYOMAS

S07RR-05950-07 0006 (NSS) FLETCHER, JONATHON Biomedical research support grant CYTOGENETIC ANALYSIS OF BONE & SOFT TISSUE TUMORS

S07RR-05950-07 0007 (NSS) GUGINO, LAVERN Biomedical research support grant TRANSCRANIAL MOTOR CORTEX STIMULATION

S07RR-05950-07 0010 (NSS) VASSILEV Biomedical research support grant CHANNEL ACTIVITIES IN ADRENAL GLOMERULOSA CELLS MODIFIED BY ANGIOTENSIN II

S07RR-05950-07 0011 (NSS) WILLIAMS, GORDON Biomedical research support grant EFFECT OF SODIUM & POTASSIUM INTAKE ON ALDOSTERONE SECRETION IN HYPERTENSION

S07RR-05950-07 0012 (NSS) BEIER, DAVID Biomedical research support grant HEMATOPOIETIC DIFFERENTIATION OF EMBRYONIC STEM CELLS

S07RR-05950-07 0980 (NSS) WHITTEMORE, ANTHONY Biomedical research support grant FOAM POLYURETHANE & COLLAGEN VASCULAR PROSTHESIS

S07RR-05950-07 0981 (NSS) MUTTER, GEORGE Biomedical research support grant CELLULAR ONCOGENES IN GERM CELL TUMORS

S07RR-05950-07 0982 (NSS) SUGARBAKER, DAVID Biomedical research support grant ESOPHAGEAL LONGITUDINAL MUSCLE IN SECONDARY PERISTALSIS

S07RR-05950-07 0983 (NSS) KRONAUGE, JAMES Biomedical research support grant APPLICATIONS OF NMR SPECTROSCOPY TO RADIO PHARMACEUTICALS

S07RR-05950-07 0984 (NSS) HOLMAN, B LEONARD Biomedical research support grant EVALUATION OF TC 99M ECD FOR BRAIN IMAGING

S07RR-05950-07 0985 (NSS) TYCKO, BENJAMIN Biomedical research support grant DVMT METHOD: AMPLIFIED & CLONED DNA REARRANGEMENTS IN MALIGNANT SOLID TUMORS

S07RR-05950-07 0986 (NSS) PATZ, SAMUEL Biomedical research support grant MRI OF TISSUE FLOW; SEPARATE STATIC & FLOWING COMPONENTS OF SIGNAL

S07RR-05950-07 0987 (NSS) MIRSKY, ISREAL Biomedical research support grant MATHEMATICAL APPROACH TO CARDIOVASCULAR MECHANICS

S07RR-05950-07 0988 (NSS) REIN, MITCHELL Biomedical research support grant HUMAN REGULATION OF PROLACTIN SECRETION IN VITRO BY HUMAN LEIOMYOMATA

S07RR-05950-07 0989 (NSS) CZOP, JOYCE Biomedical research support grant PHAGOCYTOSIS VIA BETA GLUCAN RECEPTORS

S07RR-05950-07 0990 (NSS) KANDARPA, KRISHNA Biomedical research support grant IN VIVO EVALUATION OF ELECTROMAGNETIC FIELD FOCUSING

S07RR-05950-07 0991 (NSS) BLUMBERG, RICHARD Biomedical research support grant ASSEMBLY & FUNCTION OF T CELL RECEPTOR

S07RR-05950-07 0992 (NSS) NEER, EVA Biomedical research support grant CELL BIOLOGY OF SIGNAL TRANSDUCTION

S07RR-05950-07 0993 (NSS) STEINBROOK, RICHARD Biomedical research support grant PERIPHERAL CHEMORECEPTOR FUNCTION DURING SPINAL ANESTHESIA

S07RR-05950-07 0994 (NSS) BODY, SIMON Biomedical research support grant PNEUMONECTOMY & PREOPERATIVE FLUID ADMINISTRATION

S07RR-05950-07 0995 (NSS) BECKER, JAMES Biomedical research support grant SUBSTANCE P: CANDIDATE NEUROTRANSMITTER OF SPHINCTER OF ODDI

S07RR-05950-07 0996 (NSS) EWENSTEIN, BRUCE Biomedical research support grant PROTEINKINASES IN SECRETION OF VON WILLEBRAND FACTOR; VASCULAR ENDOTHELIUM

S07RR-05950-07 0997 (NSS) BEVILACQUA, MICHAEL Biomedical research support grant MOLECULAR MECHANISMS OF TUMOR CELL ENDOTHELIAL ADHESION

S07RR-05950-07 0998 (NSS) JACK, RICHARD Biomedical research support grant MOLECULAR BIOLOGY OF HUMAN INFLAMMATION

S07RR-05950-07 0999 (NSS) HOLMAN, B LEONARD Biomedical research support grant EVALUATION OF AN I 123 COLLIMATOR FOR ASPECT

S07RR-05951-07 (NSS) SCHIFF, GILBERT M JAMES N GAMBLE INST OF MED RES 2141 AUBURN AVENUE CINCINNATI, OHIO 45219 Biomedical research support grant

S07RR-05951-07 0736 (NSS) WARD, RICHARD L Biomedical research support grant MOLECULAR & CLINICAL STUDIES ON ROTAVIRUS

S07RR-05951-07 0737 (NSS) BJORNSON, ANN B Biomedical research support grant HUMORAL FACTORS OF HOST DEFENSE AGAINST BACTEROIDES

R24RR-05952-02 (SSS) CHANCE, BRITTON UNIVERSITY CITY SCIENCE CENTER 3401 MARKET STREET PHILADELPHIA, PA 19104 Beam noise evaluation/compensation

S07RR-05952-06 (NSS) MCCOWN, DARLENE E UNIVERSITY OF ROCHESTER 601 ELMWOOD AVENUE ROCHESTER, N Y 14642 Biomedical research support grant

S07RR-05952-06 0738 (NSS) GRACE, JEANNE T Biomedical research support grant YOUNG WOMEN BECOMING MOTHERS

S07RR-05952-06 0740 (NSS) KANE, CATHERINE F Biomedical research support grant FAMILY ATTRIBUTION OF SYMPTOMATIC BEHAVIOR

S07RR-05952-06 0741 (NSS) SCHMITT, MADELINE H Biomedical research support grant PSYCHOMETRICS OF "ATTITUDES OF HLTH CARE TEAMS" SCALE & "TEAM ANOIME" SCALE

S07RR-05952-06 0739 (NSS) HOLLEN, PATRICIA J Biomedical research support grant COMPREHENSIVE DECISION MAKING CURRICULUM FOR SECONDARY SCHOOL HLTH EDUCATION

S07RR-05952-06 0742 (NSS) WELLS, THELMA J Biomedical research support grant NURSING INTERVENTIONS EXERCISE FOR STRESS INCONTINENCE: WOMEN

R01RR-05956-02 (SSS) TOGA, ARTHUR W UCLA SCHOOL OF MEDICINE 710 WESTWOOD PLAZA LOS ANGELES CA 90024-1769 A neuro imaging pre-resource

S07RR-05956-06 (NSS) COLTMAN, CHARLES A, JR CANCER THERAPY & RES CTR 4450 MEDICAL DRIVE SAN ANTONIO, TX 78229 Biomedical research support grant

S07RR-05956-06 0743 (NSS) WINDLE, BRADFORD E Biomedical research support grant DE NOVO TELOMERE ADDITION TO DAMAGED MAMMALIAN CHROMOSOMES

S07RR-05956-06 0744 (NSS) WINDLE, JOLENE J Biomedical research support grant SU40T ANTIGEN & RETINOBLASTOMA PROTEIN IN TRANSGENIC MICE

S07RR-05958-06 (NSS) COHEN, ALLEN B UNIV OF TEXAS HLTH SCI CTR P O BOX 2003 TYLER, TEXAS 75710 Biomedical research support grant

S07RR-05958-06 0745 (NSS) ATKINSON, MARK D Biomedical research support grant CHEMICAL PHOSPHORYLATION OF SYNTHETIC PEPTIDES

S07RR-05958-06 0746 (NSS) ZWIEB, CHRISTIAN Biomedical research support grant SIGNAL RECOGNITION PARTICLE 19KDA PROTEIN IN PROTEIN SECRETION

S07RR-05958-06 0747 (NSS) STARCHER, BARRY Biomedical research support grant ELASTIN REPAIR FOLLOWING INJURY

S07RR-05958-06 0748 (NSS) FAIR, DARYL Biomedical research support grant EXTRINSIC PATHWAY ON HUMAN UMBILICAL VEIN ENDOTHELIAL CELLS IN HEMOPHILIA

S07RR-05958-06 0749 (NSS) IDELL, STEVEN Biomedical research support grant FIBRIN TURNOVER IN LUNGS OF PREMATURE BABOONS: RESPIRATORY DISTRESS SYND

P41RR-05959-02 (SSS) JOHNSON, G ALLAN DUKE UNIVERSITY MEDICAL CENTER BOX 3302 DURHAM, NC 27710 An integrated center for in vivo

microscopy
P41RR-05959-02 9001 (SSS) JOHNSON, G An integrated center for in vivo microscopy MR microscopy--Core
P41RR-05959-02 9002 (SSS) MACFALL, J An integrated center for in vivo microscopy MR vascular microscopy and microflow measurement--Core
P41RR-05959-02 9003 (SSS) CHARLES, C An integrated center for in vivo microscopy Chemical shift imaging--Core
P41RR-05959-02 9005 (SSS) FLOYD, C An integrated center for in vivo microscopy Real time videodensitometry--Core
P41RR-05959-02 9006 (SSS) FLOYD, C An integrated center for in vivo microscopy Three-dimensional vascular imaging--Core
P41RR-05959-02 9007 (SSS) HEDLUND, L An integrated center for in vivo microscopy Anesthesia and physiological monitoring--Core
S07RR-05959-06 (NSS) KERN, DAVID F EAST TENNESSEE STATE UNIV BOX 19780A JOHNSON CITY, TN 37614 Biomedical research support grant
S07RR-05959-06 0018 (NSS) SUTTLES, JILL Biomedical research support grant MODEL DEVELOPMENT TO STUDY GENE TRANSFER
S07RR-05959-06 0019 (NSS) RATNASINGHE, DUMINDA Biomedical research support grant MECHANISMS OF GENE EXPRESSION
S07RR-05959-06 0020 (NSS) RODEBUSH, WILLIAM E Biomedical research support grant MECHANISMS OF GENE EXPRESSION
S07RR-05959-06 0021 (NSS) DUFFEE, DOUGLAS Biomedical research support grant OZONE DAMAGE TO HUMAN GENETIC STRUCTURE
S07RR-05959-06 0022 (NSS) RICE, PETER J Biomedical research support grant ANIMAL MODEL FOR ATRIAL TACHYCARDIA
S07RR-05959-06 0023 (NSS) CHEN, XIAOHUAI Biomedical research support grant BRAIN RECEPTORS ACTIVE IN HYPERTENSION DEVELOPMENT
S07RR-05959-06 0024 (NSS) TURNER, BARBARA Biomedical research support grant BRAIN RECEPTOR REGULATION OF GENE EXPRESSION
S07RR-05959-06 0025 (NSS) LOVE, RICHARD Biomedical research support grant MATURATION OF OOCYTES IN VITRO
S07RR-05959-06 0026 (NSS) CHITTUM, HAROLD Biomedical research support grant PROTEIN INTERACTIONS IN BACTERIA
S07RR-05959-06 0027 (NSS) WANG, KENNING Biomedical research support grant REGULATION OF LIVER CELL VOLUME
S07RR-05959-06 0028 (NSS) REAGAN, DAVID R Biomedical research support grant EPIDEMIOLOGIC TYPING OF AN INFECTIOUS BACTERIA
S07RR-05962-05 (NSS) DE VOE, ROBERT D INDIANA UNIVERSITY 800 EAST ATWATER BLOOMINGTON, IN 47405 Biomedical research support grant
S07RR-05962-05 0013 (NSS) BEGLEY, CAROLINE Biomedical research support grant CYTOTOXICITY OF CONTACT LENS PRESERVATIVE
S07RR-05962-05 0014 (NSS) HAFNER, GARY S Biomedical research support grant CYTOSKELETAL ORGANIZATION IN PHOTORECEPTORS IN CRAYFISH
S07RR-05962-05 0015 (NSS) MCCONNAHA, DEBRA L Biomedical research support grant CLINICAL COMPARISON OF CONTRAST SENSITIVITY TESTING IN ELDERLY: OCULAR PATHOLOGY
S07RR-05962-05 0016 (NSS) READING, ROGERS, W Biomedical research support grant TRACKING OF FIXATION DISPARITY: BINOCULAR VISION, VISUAL FUNCTION MEASUREMENT
S07RR-05962-05 0017 (NSS) WILLIAMS, DAVID S Biomedical research support grant CELL BIOLOGY OF PROTEIN KINASE C IN PHOTORECEPTORS: PHOTOTRANSDUCTION
P41RR-05964-02 (SSS) LAUTERBUR, PAUL C UNIVERSITY OF ILLINOIS 1307 WEST PARK STREET URBANA, IL 61801 Biomedical magnetic resonance research & technology
P41RR-05964-02 0003 (SSS) LAUTERBUR, PAUL Biomedical magnetic resonance research & technology Labeled cell transplants project
P41RR-05964-02 0004 (SSS) GREENOUGH, WILLIAM Biomedical magnetic resonance research & technology Environment and brain chemistry
P41RR-05964-02 0005 (SSS) BUDINGER, THOMAS Biomedical magnetic resonance research & technology Brain anatomy and neurology
P41RR-05964-02 0006 (SSS) EMBREY, THOMAS Biomedical magnetic resonance research & technology Amphibian retina
P41RR-05964-02 0007 (SSS) DAWSON, M Biomedical magnetic resonance research & technology Skeletal muscle function and metabolism
P41RR-05964-02 0008 (SSS) WILLIS, JOHN Biomedical magnetic resonance research & technology Red cell metabolism
P41RR-05964-02 0009 (SSS) TRUPIN, S Biomedical magnetic resonance research & technology Normal and diseased female reproductive tissue
S07RR-05964-06 (NSS) PATTERSON, DAVID ELEANOR ROOSEVELT INST/CANCER 1899 GAYLORD STREET DENVER, CO 80206 Biomedical research support grant
S07RR-05964-06 0754 (NSS) PATTERSON, DAVID Biomedical research support grant EXPENSES FOR VISIT BY POSTDOCTORAL CANDIDATE
S07RR-05964-06 0755 (NSS) GARDINER, KATHELEEN Biomedical research support grant EXPENSES FOR VISIT BY POSTDOCTORAL CANDIDATE
S07RR-05964-06 0756 (NSS) SINENSKY, MICHAEL Biomedical research support grant EXPENSES FOR VISIT BY POSTDOCTORAL CANDIDATE
S07RR-05964-06 0757 (NSS) PANINI, SANKHAVARAM Biomedical research support grant EXPENSES FOR VISIT BY POSTDOCTORAL CANDIDATE
S07RR-05964-06 0758 (NSS) PANINI, SANKHAVARAM Biomedical research support grant EXPENSES FOR VISIT BY POSTDOCTORAL CANDIDATE
S07RR-05964-06 0759 (NSS) GARDINER, KATHELEEN Biomedical research support grant EXPENSES FOR SEMINAR SPEAKER
S07RR-05964-06 0760 (NSS) GARDINER, KATHELEEN Biomedical research support grant EXPENSES FOR SEMINAR SPEAKER
S07RR-05964-06 0761 (NSS) GEMMILL, ROBERT Biomedical research support grant EXPENSES FOR VISIT BY DR AVERY SANDBERG
S07RR-05964-06 0762 (NSS) SINENSKY, MICHAEL Biomedical research support grant EXPENSES FOR RECRUITMENT VISIT BY SENIOR FELLOW
S07RR-05964-06 0763 (NSS) SCHECHTER, ISHAIAHU Biomedical research support grant SALARY & BENEFIT SUPPORT FOR NEW FACULTY MEMBER
S07RR-05964-06 0764 (NSS) SCHECHTER, ISHAIAHU Biomedical research support grant RECRUITMENT SUPPORT FOR NEW FACULTY MEMBER
S07RR-05964-06 0765 (NSS) GEMMILL, ROBERT Biomedical research support grant PHYSICAL MAPPING OF CHROMOSOMES 3 & 21
S07RR-05964-06 0766 (NSS) LIAO, MARTHA Biomedical research support grant CONSTRUCT PANEL OF SOMATIC CELL HYBRIDS HUMAN CHROMOSOME 12
S07RR-05964-06 0767 (NSS) GARDINER, KATHELEEN Biomedical research support grant PURCHASE PERKIN ELMER CETUS DNA THERMAL CYCLER MACHINE
S07RR-05967-04 (NSS) SWARBRICK, JAMES UNIVERSITY OF NORTH CAROLINA SCHOOL OF PHARMACY CHAPEL HILL, NC 27599-7360 Biomedical research support
S07RR-05967-04 0291 (NSS) RUBINO, JOSEPH Biomedical research support IMPROVED DEIONIZED WATER SYSTEM
S07RR-05967-04 0289 (NSS) BASTOW, KENNETH Biomedical research support SCREENING FOR DNA TOPOISOMERASE II INHIBITORS
S07RR-05967-04 0290 (NSS) SWARBRICK, JAMES Biomedical research support UPGRADING OF MICROCOMPUTER LABORATORY
S07RR-05968-06 (NSS) BLAYNEY, KEITH D UNIV OF ALABAMA AT BIRMINGHAM SCH HLTH REL PROF WEBB 616B BIRMINGHAM, AL 35294 Biomedical research support grant
S07RR-05968-06 0337 (NSS) PRINCE, CHARLES W Biomedical research support grant BIOCHEMISTRY OF MINERALIZED TISSUE PROTEOGLYCANS; BONE; VIT; IN VIVO
S07RR-05968-06 0338 (NSS) MORGAN, SARAH L Biomedical research support grant NEW ANTIFOLATES; MANAGE AUTO IMMUNE DISEASES; ARTHRITIS; ANIMAL MODEL; VIT
S07RR-05968-06 0339 (NSS) ETO, ISAO Biomedical research support grant MACAPSIN; A NEW ENDOPEPTIDASE MAMMARY GLAND, PROTEIN, CANCER
P41RR-05969-02 (SSS) SCHULTEN, K UNIVERSITY OF ILLINOIS 1110 WEST GREEN STREET URBANA, IL 61801 Parallel computation for molecular dynamics
S07RR-05969-05 (NSS) HILL, RICHARD M OHIO STATE UNIVERSITY 338 WEST TENTH AVENUE COLUMBUS, OH 43210 Biomedical research support grant
S07RR-05970-06 (NSS) ALLEN, DON L UNIV OF TX DENTAL BR PO BOX 20068 HOUSTON, TX 77225 Biomedical research support grant
S07RR-05970-06 0768 (NSS) BATTERSON, WILLIAM W Biomedical research support grant ORAL DISEASE IN HIV INFECTED CHILDREN: AIDS DX
S07RR-05970-06 0769 (NSS) CHAN, JARVIS T Biomedical research support grant IN VITRO SCREENING OF THERAPEUTIC AGENTS TO TREAT DENTIN HYPERSENSITIVITY
S07RR-05970-06 0770 (NSS) COLLARD, STEPHEN M Biomedical research support grant ALVEOLAR MACROPHAGE FUNCTION AFTER IN VITRO EXPOSURE TO COMPOSITE RESIN DUSTS
S07RR-05970-06 0771 (NSS) COLLARD, STEPHEN M Biomedical research support grant VAPOR DEPOSITION OF DIAMOND LIKE CARBON FILMS ON RESTORATIVE CERAMICS
S07RR-05970-06 0772 (NSS) DENNISON, DAVID K Biomedical research support grant MODULATION OF FIBROBLAST PROLIFERATION BY GROWTH FACTORS: ORAL
S07RR-05970-06 0773 (NSS) DONLY, KEVIN J Biomedical research support grant BIOMATERIAL RESTORATIVE MARGINS:IN VITRO DEMINERALIZATION & REMINERALIZATION
S07RR-05970-06 0774 (NSS) DONLY, KEVIN J Biomedical research support grant IN VITRO EXAM OF DEMINERALIZATION INHIBITION OF ENAMEL CARIES
S07RR-05970-06 0775 (NSS) D'SOUZA, RENA N Biomedical research support grant IMMUNOLOCATION OF GLA PROTEINS IN RAT REPARATIVE DENTIN
S07RR-05970-06 0776 (NSS) FARACH-CARSON, MARY Biomedical research support grant MODULATION OF OSTEOBLAST CA CHANNELS BY VITAMIN D3 ANALOGS
S07RR-05970-06 0777 (NSS) FRANCHESCHI, RENNY T Biomedical research support grant EXTRACELLULAR MATRIX REGULATION OF OSTEOBLAST FORMATION
S07RR-05970-06 0778 (NSS) GAO, ZHIRONG Biomedical research support grant SPECIFIC MARKERS FOR ODONTOGENIC & JUNCTIONAL EPITHELIA
S07RR-05970-06 0779 (NSS) GOLDSCHMIDT, MILLICE Biomedical research support grant RAPID NON INSTRUMENT METHOD OF ISOLATION & ID OF ORAL ORGANISM ASSOC W/ ORAL DIS
S07RR-05970-06 0780 (NSS) MILLAR, STEPHEN J Biomedical research support grant ANAEROBIOSIS & PANTHOGENESIS OF ORAL INFECTIONS
S07RR-05970-06 0781 (NSS) SMITH, WILLIS W Biomedical research support grant RELATIONSHIP BETWEEN BRUXISM & PINWORM INFECTION IN CHILDREN
S07RR-05970-06 0782 (NSS) TATE, WILLIAM H Biomedical research support grant MONOCLONAL ANTIBODIES FOR TEMPOROSPATIAL STUDIES OF BONE FORMATION
S07RR-05973-05 (NSS) LENZ, ELIZABETH R UNIVERSITY OF MARYLAND 665 WEST LOMBARD STREET BALTIMORE, MD 21201 Biomedical research support Universities
S07RR-05973-05 0783 (NSS) BALDWIN, BEVERLY Biomedical research support Universities INTERVENTIONS TO DECREASE DISRUPTIVE BEHAVIORS IN NURSING HOME
S07RR-05973-05 0784 (NSS) CUSSON, REGINA Biomedical research support Universities SOCIO EMOTIONAL DEVELOPMENT IN 26 MONTH OLD HIGH RISK INFANTS
S07RR-05973-05 0785 (NSS) PARKER, BARBARA Biomedical research support Universities POTENTIAL FOR CHILD ABUSE IN VIOLENT & NON VIOLENT FAMILIES
S07RR-05973-05 0786 (NSS) MCCRONE, SUSAN Biomedical research support Universities QUALITY OF LIFE: CHRONIC MENTALLY ILL RESIDING W/ A FAMILY MEMBER
S07RR-05973-05 0787 (NSS) GIFT, AUDREY Biomedical research support Universities RESPIRATORY MUSCLE FUNCTION IN PATIENTS W/ POST POLIO SYNDROME
S07RR-05973-05 0788 (NSS) SCHOLER-JAQUISH, ALW Biomedical research support Universities PERCEIVED BARRIERS TO HEALTH CARE IN BALTIMORE HOMELESS
S07RR-05973-05 0789 (NSS) CARSON, VERNA Biomedical research support Universities WELLBEING & HARDINESS IN PERSONS W/ AIDS
S07RR-05974-05 (NSS) SCUTCHFIELD, F DOUGLAS SAN DIEGO STATE UNIV FDN 5178 COLLEGE AVENUE SAN DIEGO, CALIF 92182 Biomedical research support universities
R24RR-05976-01A1 (SSS) OPELLA, STANLEY J UNIVERSITY OF PENNSYLVANIA 231 S 34TH STREET PHILADELPHIA, PA 19104 Protein structure by solid-state NMR spectroscopy
S07RR-05978-04 (NSS) DI STEFANO, ANTHONY F PENNSYLVANIA COLL OF OPTOMETRY 1200 W GODFREY AVENUE PHILADELPHIA, PA 19141 Biomedical research support grant
S07RR-05980-05 (NSS) DIAMOND, IVAN ERNEST GALLO CLINIC & RES CTR S F GEN HOSP, BLDG 1 RM 101 SAN FRANCISCO, CALIF 94110 Biomedical research support
S07RR-05980-05 0292 (NSS) DIAMOND, IVAN Biomedical research support BIOCHEMICAL STUDIES ON SIGNAL TRANSDUCTION IN CELLS & CELL MEMBRANES
S07RR-05981-05 (NSS) SCOTT, ALAN B SMITH-KETTLEWELL EYE RES

PROJECT NO., ORGANIZATIONAL UNIT., INVESTIGATOR, ADDRESS, TITLE

INST 2232 WEBSTER STREET SAN FRANCISCO, CALIF 94115 Biomedical research support foundation
S07RR-05981-05 0793 (NSS) KELLER, EDWARD L Biomedical research support foundation OSCILLOSCOPE USED IN NEUROPHYSIOLOGY PROJECTS
S07RR-05981-05 0794 (NSS) KELLER, EDWARD L Biomedical research support foundation MICROINJECTION OF NEURO SPECIFIC CHEMICALS IN PONTINE NUCLEI IN MONKEY
S07RR-05981-05 0795 (NSS) KELLER, EDWARD L Biomedical research support foundation TORISONAL EYE MOVEMENT MEASUREMENT W/ NEURAL LESIONS IN BRAIN STEM STRUCT
S07RR-05981-05 0796 (NSS) SIMON, HELEN J Biomedical research support foundation DIGITAL SIGNAL PROCESSING SYSTEM FOR HEARING RES
S07RR-05981-05 0797 (NSS) KASAMATSU, TAKUJI Biomedical research support foundation LONG RANGE CONNECTIONS W/ IN CAT VISUAL CORTEX: NON INVASIVE RECORDING
S07RR-05981-05 0798 (NSS) MILLER, JOEL M Biomedical research support foundation EGOCENTRIC LOCALIZATION & SACCADIC PLASTICITY
S07RR-05981-05 0799 (NSS) MILLER, JOEL M Biomedical research support foundation LOCAL & GLOBAL ELECTRONIC MAIL, DATABASE ACCESS
S07RR-05981-05 0800 (NSS) MILLER, JOEL M Biomedical research support foundation OCULOMOTOR DATA COLLECTION & ANALYSIS
S07RR-05981-05 0801 (NSS) MILLER, JOEL M Biomedical research support foundation IBM PC COMPATIBLE SYSTEM IS NEEDED FOR DOCUMENT PROCESSING
S07RR-05981-05 0802 (NSS) MCKEE, SUZANNE P Biomedical research support foundation LASER PRINTER FOR IMPROVING QUALITY & SPEED OF PUBLICATIONS
S07RR-05981-05 0803 (NSS) COGAN, ALEXANDER Biomedical research support foundation STEREOPSIS W/ TEMPORAL EDGES OF OPPOSITE SIGN HUMAN VISION
S07RR-05981-05 0804 (NSS) NORCIA, ANTHONY Biomedical research support foundation STEREOPSIS & BINOCULARITY IN INFANTS & STRABISMUS PATIENTS
S07RR-05981-05 0805 (NSS) NORCIA, ANTHONY Biomedical research support foundation CD ROM FOR RECEIVING INFORMATION DISTRIBUTIONS FROM GOVERNMENT & VENDORS
S07RR-05981-05 0806 (NSS) NORCIA, ANTHONY Biomedical research support foundation SIMPLE CLINICAL TEST OF MOTION PROCESSING IN STRABISMUS
S07RR-05981-05 0807 (NSS) NORCIA, ANTHONY Biomedical research support foundation IMPROVED SIGNAL PROCESSING OF VEP
S07RR-05981-05 0808 (NSS) TYLER, CHRISTOPHER W Biomedical research support foundation ADVANCED IMAGE PROCESSING SYSTEM: GLAUCOMA
S07RR-05981-05 0809 (NSS) KASAMATSU, TAKUJI Biomedical research support foundation NEURAL ORIGIN OF VISUAL EVOKED POTENTIALS
S07RR-05981-05 0810 (NSS) NORCIA, ANTHONY Biomedical research support foundation INFANT EYE SCREENING STUDY ASSESSMENT OF POLAROID BASED PHOTOREFRACTION DEVICE
S07RR-05983-05 (NSS) BEEBE, DAVID C HENRY M JACKSON FDN/ADV/MILT M 4301 JONES BRIDGE ROAD BETHESDA, MD 20814 Biomedical research support
S07RR-05983-05 0354 (NSS) HAY, JOHN I Biomedical research support ORAL CARCINOMA IN KERALA, INDIA
S07RR-05983-05 0355 (NSS) MMERMAN, KATHERINE L Biomedical research support USE OF CAGE QUESTIONS IN ROUTINE MEDICAL INTERVIEW
S07RR-05983-05 0346 (NSS) ADELMAN, MARK R Biomedical research support USE OF CONFOCAL SCANNING MICROSCOPY IN RESEARCH & TEACHING
S07RR-05983-05 0347 (NSS) ADERA, TILAHUN Biomedical research support DEVELOPING A PHARMACOEPIDEMIOLOGIC DATA SYSTEM AT USUHS
S07RR-05983-05 0348 (NSS) BEEBE, DAVID C Biomedical research support PILOT PROJECT
S07RR-05983-05 0349 (NSS) BEELER, TROY J Biomedical research support CA2+ REGULATION BY S CEREVISIAE
S07RR-05983-05 0350 (NSS) CANTILENA, LOUIS R Biomedical research support MONOCLONAL ANTIBODIES TO METALLOTHIONEIN BY IN VITRO IMMUNIZATION
S07RR-05983-05 0356 (NSS) JULIANO, SHARON L Biomedical research support PILOT PROJECT
S07RR-05983-05 0357 (NSS) KROENKE, KURT K Biomedical research support DIZZINESS: PROSPECTIVE STUDY OF PATIENT CHARACTERISTICS & OUTCOME
S07RR-05983-05 0358 (NSS) LYNCH, KATHRYN J Biomedical research support TREATMENT OF MUSCULAR DYSTROPHIC MICE
S07RR-05983-05 0359 (NSS) MILLER, KURT W Biomedical research support ISOLATION OF TETRACYCLINE RESISTANCE PROTEIN OF E COLI
S07RR-05983-05 0360 (NSS) MOUL, JUDD W Biomedical research support RAS ONCOGENE MUTATIONS IN TESTICULAR CANCER
S07RR-05983-05 0351 (NSS) CHANG, ESTHER H Biomedical research support MODULATION OF TUMOR CELL GROWTH & ONCOGENE EXPRESSION
S07RR-05983-05 0352 (NSS) FRITZ, MARC A Biomedical research support ISOLATION & CHARACTERIZATION OF HUMAN LUTEAL CELL SUBPOPULATIONS
S07RR-05983-05 0361 (NSS) RASPA, ROBERT F Biomedical research support EVALUATION OF INTERVENTION TO IMPROVE DIAGNOSTIC ACCURACY
S07RR-05983-05 0362 (NSS) RUNDELL, JAMES R Biomedical research support HIV INFECTION & PERCEPTION OF SOCIAL SUPPORTS
S07RR-05983-05 0363 (NSS) SARVEY, JOHN M Biomedical research support EFFECT OF CHRONIC NICOTINE ON HIPPOCAMPAL LONG TERM POTENTIATION
S07RR-05983-05 0364 (NSS) WHITE, CHRISTOPHER B Biomedical research support ASSESSING MEDICAL PROBLEM SOLVING BY COMPUTER SIMULATION
S07RR-05983-05 0365 (NSS) YANCEY, KIM B Biomedical research support MECHANISMS OF NATURAL RESISTANCE TO MURINE TYPHOID
S07RR-05983-05 0366 (NSS) HOLMES, KATHRYN V Biomedical research support CORONAVIRUS RECEPTOR INTERACTIONS
S07RR-05983-05 0367 (NSS) SHEPLER, THOMAS R Biomedical research support ORTHOPEDIC CURRICULUM IN INTERACTIVE VIDEO MEDIUM
S07RR-05983-05 0353 (NSS) GAUSE, WILLIAM C Biomedical research support EFFECT OF 1PR GENE ON EARLY T CELL MATURATION
S07RR-05987-05 (NSS) MILLER, JAMES D CENTRAL INSTITUTE FOR THE DEAF 818 SOUTH EUCLID AVENUE ST LOUIS, MO 63110 Biomedical research support
S07RR-05987-05 0024 (NSS) HIRSH, IRA J Biomedical research support PERCEPTION OF TIMING OF EVENTS BY EAR & SKIN: DEAFNESS RES

PROJECT NO., ORGANIZATIONAL UNIT., INVESTIGATOR, ADDRESS, TITLE

S07RR-05989-04 (NSS) FRANKL, SPENCER BOSTON UNIV GOLDMAN SCHOOL 100 E NEWTON STREET BOSTON, MA 02118 Biomedical research support grant
S07RR-05989-04 0624 (NSS) FRANKL, SPENCER W Biomedical research support grant NO RESEARCH SUBPROJECTS
U24RR-05991-02 (SRC) HIRSCHEL, MARK D ENDOTRONICS INC 8500 EVERGREEN BOULEVARD COON RAPIDS MN 55433 Production of animal cells and secreted product
S07RR-05992-04 (NSS) OTTO, DAVID A BAPTIST MEDICAL CENTER 701 PRINCETON AVENUE BIRMINGHAM, AL 35211 Biomedical research support grant
S07RR-05992-04 0811 (NSS) BALTZELL, JANET K Biomedical research support grant OMEGA 3 FATTY ACIDS IN DIABETES: FISH OIL, DIABETES, ANIMAL MODEL
S07RR-05992-04 0812 (NSS) MARTIN, A KEITH Biomedical research support grant TWO METHODS TO PREDICT ENERGY EXPENDITURE IN PATIENTS: INTENSIVE CARE NMR
S07RR-05992-04 0813 (NSS) NELSON, KARL M Biomedical research support grant MODEL OF HEPATIC METABOLISM IN SEPSIS: CYTOKINES, KETOGENESIS, GLUCONEOGENESIS
S07RR-05992-04 0814 (NSS) PASCUAL, VIRGINIA H Biomedical research support grant IMMUNE DYSFUNCTION IN SRH CAUSED BY MONONUCLEAR CELL: HYPERTENSION, LYMPHOCYTES
S07RR-05992-04 0815 (NSS) RICHARDS, ERNEST W Biomedical research support grant GLUTAMINE IN PREVENTION OF RADIATION INDUCED ENTEROCOLITIS
S07RR-05992-04 0816 (NSS) STRICKLAND, JAMES H, Biomedical research support grant COMPUTER CONTROLLED VENTILATOR WEANING SYSTEM: CLOSED LOOP, CRITICAL CARE
R01RR-05994-02 (AR) GOULD, KENNETH G EMORY UNIVERSITY ATLANTA, GA 30322 Reproductive parameters of the chimpanzee AIDS model
S07RR-05994-03 (NSS) DABBOUS, MUSTAFA K UNIVERSITY OF TENNESSEE 894 UNION AVENUE MEMPHIS, TN 38163 Biomedical research support
S07RR-05994-03 0297 (NSS) BEHRENTS, ROLF G Biomedical research support: occlusal load duration on dentofacial development
S07RR-05994-03 0298 (NSS) TIPTON, DAVID A Biomedical research support: macrophage & monocyte mediated effects: cyclosporine on gingival fibroblasts
S07RR-05994-03 0293 (NSS) CAIN, CHRIS W Biomedical research support: optimum number of spreader insertions to produce homogenous mass of gutta percha
S07RR-05994-03 0294 (NSS) CILDERS, KYLE R Biomedical research support: stimulation of condylar growth with direct electric current
S07RR-05994-03 0295 (NSS) DICKENS, RICHARD L Biomedical research support: interproximal dental cavities: minimum radiographically detectable cavity volume
S07RR-05994-03 0296 (NSS) PABST, MICHAEL J Biomedical research support: serum factor requirements of response of neutrophils to lipopolysaccharide
S07RR-05995-04 (NSS) WISE, DAVID A NATL BUREAU OF ECONOMIC RESEAR 1050 MASSACHUSETTS AVENUE CAMBRIDGE, MA 02138 Biomedical research support grant
S07RR-05995-04 0049 (NSS) MURPHYM KEVIN Biomedical research support grant EMPIRICAL APPLICATIONS OF RATIONAL ADDICTION: SMOKING, ALCOHOL, ILLEGAL DRUG USE
S07RR-05995-04 0050 (NSS) JOHNSON, BRUCE D Biomedical research support grant DRUG USE & CRIME IN NEW YORK CITY
S07RR-05995-04 0051 (NSS) SHOVEN, JOHN B Biomedical research support grant REDISTRIB EFFECTS OF RANGE OF GOVT PROGRAMS ON DIFFER AGE GROUPS IN U.S.; AGING
S07RR-05995-04 0052 (NSS) WEIL, DAVID N Biomedical research support grant HOUSING WEALTH OF THE AGED
S07RR-05995-04 0053 (NSS) WOODBURY, RICHARD G Biomedical research support grant GOVERNMENT POLICY & SAVING & RETIREMENT IN NEW ZEALAND
S07RR-05995-04 0054 (NSS) HURD, MICHAEL D Biomedical research support grant HEALTH STATUS & WEALTH DEPLETION OF THE ELDERLY
S07RR-05996-04 (NSS) MORGAN, HOWARD E WEIS CENTER RESEARCH N. ACADEMY AVENUE DANVILLE, PA 17822-2601 Biomedical research support grant
S07RR-05996-04 0933 (NSS) MORGAN, HOWARD E Biomedical research support grant NO SUBPROJECTS
R03RR-05997-01A2 (BRC) NECKERS, DOUGLAS C BOWLING GREEN STATE UNIVERSTY CENTER FOR PHOTOCHEMICAL SCIS BOWLING GREEN, OH 43403 Three dimensional color imaging
S07RR-05997-04 (NSS) MARTINEZ-CARRION, MARINO UNIVERSITY OF MISSOURI SCHOOL OF BASIC LIFE SCIENCES KANSAS CITY , MO 64110 Biomedical research support grant
S07RR-05997-04 0817 (NSS) WATERBORG, JAKOB H Biomedical research support grant SITE SPECIFIC LYSINE ACETYLATION METHYLATION OF HISTONE H3
S07RR-05997-04 0818 (NSS) HIRSCHBERG, RONA Biomedical research support grant EIKENELLA CORRODENS PLASMIDS & TRANSFORMATION PLASMID; CHROMOSOMAL MARKERS
S07RR-05998-04 (NSS) FLOM, MERTON C UNIVERSITY OF HOUSTON 4800 CALHOUN HOUSTON, TX 77204 Biomedical research support grant
S07RR-05998-04 0029 (NSS) BARBEITO, RAPHAEL Biomedical research support grant EGOCENTRIC DIRECTIONALIZATION IN STRABISMICS
S07RR-05998-04 0030 (NSS) FOX, DONALD A Biomedical research support grant RETINAL CYCLIC GMP METABOLISM IN LEAD EXPOSED RATS
S07RR-05998-04 0031 (NSS) LOSHIN, DAVID S Biomedical research support grant DEVELOPMENT OF NON INVASIVE RETINAL IMAGE ASSESSMENT
S07RR-05998-04 0032 (NSS) WESTIN, ELIZABETH Biomedical research support grant PROTEIN ABSORPTION ON HYDROPHILIC CONTACT LENSES
S07RR-06002-04 (NSS) GILBERT, DAVID N PROVIDENCE MEDICAL CENTER 4805 NE GLISAN PORTLAND, OR 97213-2967 Biomedical research support grant
S07RR-06002-04 0822 (NSS) HINRICKS, DAVID J Biomedical research support grant IMMUNOREGULATION OF ANTILISTERIA IMMUNITY
S07RR-06002-04 0823 (NSS) HINRICKS, DAVID J Biomedical research support grant DEVELOPMENT & CONTROL OF ACTIVE & PASSIVE EAE
S07RR-06002-04 0824 (NSS) LEGGITT, JAMES Biomedical research support grant AZOTEMIA & EFFICACY OF INFREQUENT GENTAMICIN DOSING IN KLEBSIELLA PNEUMONIA

S07RR-06003-04 (NSS) RYMER, WILLIAM Z REHABILITATION INST OF CHICAGO 345 EAST SUPERIOR CHICAGO, ILLINOIS 60611 Biomedical research support grant
S07RR-06003-04 0368 (NSS) KING, ROSEMARY Biomedical research support grant ADAPTATION AFTER STROKE: PATIENT & SUPPORT PERSONNEL
S07RR-06003-04 0369 (NSS) RENTZ, DOREEN Biomedical research support grant INCIDENCE OF DEMENTIA AMONG GERIATRIC REHABILITATION PATIENTS
S07RR-06003-04 0370 (NSS) DEWALD, JULES Biomedical research support grant SENSORY INPUT CREATES ABNORMAL MUSCLE COACTIVATION PATTERNS; HEMIPLEGIC STROKE
S07RR-06004-04 (NSS) CATALANOTTO, FRANK A UMDNJ NEW JERSEY DENTAL SCH 110 BERGEN STREET NEWARK, N J 07103 Biomedical research support grant
S07RR-06004-04 0036 (NSS) FENESY, KIM E Biomedical research support grant CYTOKINES IN PATHOGENESIS OF HIV ASSOCIATED PERIODONTAL DISEASE
S07RR-06004-04 0037 (NSS) LIAU, YUN H Biomedical research support grant SULFATION IN SALIVARY MUCIN PROCESSING
S07RR-06004-04 0038 (NSS) MURTY, VARAHABHOTLA Biomedical research support grant SALIVARY LIPIDS & GLYCOPROTEINS IN ALCOHOLICS
S07RR-06004-04 0039 (NSS) WANG, SHOOU-LIH Biomedical research support grant ETHANOL ON EPIDERMAL GROWTH FACTOR RECEPTOR IN RAT BUCCAL MUCOSA
S07RR-06004-04 0040 (NSS) WANG, SHOOU-LIH Biomedical research support grant CIGARETTE SMOKING; EPIDERMAL GROWTH FACTOR RECEPTOR; HUMAN BUCCAL MUCOSA
S07RR-06004-04 0041 (NSS) WEINER, SAUL Biomedical research support grant MECHANORECEPTORS ADJACENT TO ENDOSSEOUS TITANIUM IMPLANTS; DOG MANDIBLE
S07RR-06004-04 0042 (NSS) WU-WANG, CHI-YING Biomedical research support grant PROSTAGLANDIN RESEARCH MOLECULAR APPROACH
S07RR-06004-04 0043 (NSS) ZIRVI, KARIMULLAH Biomedical research support grant EXTRACELLULAR MATRIX PROTEINS IN HUMAN COLON TUMOR METASTASIS
S07RR-06004-04 0033 (NSS) EHRLICH, JULIAN Biomedical research support grant AGE ASSOCIATED PROPERTIES OF HUMAN SALIVARY MUCIN
S07RR-06004-04 0034 (NSS) EHRLICH, JULIAN Biomedical research support grant AGING; PHYSICOCHEMICAL PROPERTIES OF SALIVARY MUCUS GLYCOPROTEINS
S07RR-06004-04 0035 (NSS) FELDMAN, CECILE A Biomedical research support grant HYPERMEDIA & MOUSE & TOUCH SCREEN TECHNOLOGY; DIAGNOSTIC CLINICAL DATA
S07RR-06005-04 (NSS) LEVIN, PETER J UNIV OF S FLORIDA, MHH-104 13301 BRUCE B DOWNS BLVD TAMPA, FL 33612-3899 Biomedical research support grant
S07RR-06005-04 0299 (NSS) MOREL, JORGE G Biomedical research support grant MIXTURE MODEL W/ APPLICATIONS TO TERATOLOGY & CLUSTER SAMPLING
S07RR-06005-04 0300 (NSS) RICHARDS, IRA S Biomedical research support grant ELECTROMECHANICAL PROPERTIES OF AIRWAY SMOOTH MUSCLE TRACHEOBRONCHIAL TREE
S07RR-06005-04 0301 (NSS) KWA, BOO H Biomedical research support grant DEVELOPMENT PF AN ATHYMIC NUDE MOUSE MODEL FOR ONCHOCERCOSIS
P41RR-06009-02 (SSS) ROSKIES, RALPH Z MELLON INSTITUTE 4400 FIFTH AVENUE PITTSBURGH, PA 15213 Supercomputing for biomedical research
P41RR-06009-02 0001 (SSS) BROOKS, CHARLES Supercomputing for biomedical research Workshop on free energy of biopolymers in aqueous solution
P41RR-06009-02 0002 (SSS) BRUNGER, AXEL Supercomputing for biomedical research Workshop on macromolecular X-ray crystallography--Phasing and refinement
P41RR-06009-02 9001 (SSS) BUCHANAN, BRUCE Supercomputing for biomedical research Core--An intelligent biomedical assistant
P41RR-06009-02 9002 (SSS) MURPHY, ROBERT Supercomputing for biomedical research Core--Analysis & modeling of intracellular organelle dynamics
P41RR-06009-02 9003 (SSS) BROOKS, CHARLES Supercomputing for biomedical research Core--Non-additive interactions in simulations of biological systems
P41RR-06009-02 9004 (SSS) NICHOLAS, HUGH Supercomputing for biomedical research Core--Context sensitive alignment and pattern matching
S07RR-06009-03 (NSS) YANCHICK, VICTOR A UNIVERSIY OF OKLAHOMA P O BOX 26901 OKLAHOMA CITY, OK 73190 Biomedical research support
S07RR-06009-03 0302 (NSS) LI, LUK C Biomedical research support SINTERING AS A METHOD FOR PREPARING CONTROLLED RELEASE TABLETS
S07RR-06009-03 0303 (NSS) SACHDEV, GORDON Biomedical research support BIOCHEMICAL & MOLECULAR BIOLOGICAL STUDIES OF AIRWAY MUCINS
S07RR-06011-02 (NSS) MCBRIDE, ANGELA B INDIANA UNIV SCH OF NURSING 1111 MIDDLE DRIVE INDIANAPOLIS, IN 46202-5107 Biomedical research support
S07RR-06012-03 (NSS) LARSON, ELAINE L JOHNS HOPKINS UNIVERSITY 600 N WOLFE STREET BALTIMORE, MD 21205 Biomedical research support
S07RR-06012-03 0304 (NSS) GOLDRICK, BARBARA A Biomedical research support CURRICULUM DEVELOPMENT FOR LONGTERM CARE: EDUCATIONAL RES, INFECTION CONTROL
S07RR-06012-03 0305 (NSS) ALLEN, JERI L Biomedical research support PSYCHOSOCIAL ADJUSTMENT IN SPOUSE PATIENT AFTER CORONARY BYPASS SURGERY
S07RR-06012-03 0306 (NSS) BUTZ, ARLENE M Biomedical research support IMMUNOGLOBULINS AS A MARKER TO HIV INFECTION IN HIV RISK INFANTS
S07RR-06012-03 0307 (NSS) KORNIEWICZ, DENISE Biomedical research support DOUBLE GLOVING IN CLINICAL PRACTICE
S07RR-06012-03 0308 (NSS) DELORENZO, LORI Biomedical research support NURSES TOWARD GRADUATE NURSES IN INTENSIVE CARE & SURGICAL SETTING
S07RR-06012-03 0309 (NSS) HILL, MARTHA N Biomedical research support PSYCH & SOCIAL PREDICTORS OF ENROLLMENTS, ADHERENCE, & OUTCOME
S07RR-06013-03 (NSS) FUNK, SANDRA G UNIVERSITY OF NORTH CAROLINA CB #7460, CARRINGTON HALL CHAPEL HILL, N C 27599 Biomedical research support
S07RR-06013-03 0826 (NSS) COOPER, MARY CAROLYN Biomedical research support OBSERVATIONS OF NURSING MORAL EXPERIENCE IN AN INTENSIVE CARE UNIT
S07RR-06013-03 0827 (NSS) RASCH, RANDOLPH F R Biomedical research support MULTIPLE CASE STUDY OF PATTERNS OF HEALTH IN MEN
S07RR-06013-03 0825 (NSS) CLOONAN, PATRICIA Biomedical research support HOME HEALTH CARE COORDINATION: STRATEGIES & OUTCOMES
S07RR-06014-03 (NSS) PADILLA, GERALDINE V UNIVERSITY OF CALIFORNIA 10833 LE CONTE AVE FACTOR BLDG LOS ANGELES, CA 90024-1702 Biomedical research support
S07RR-06014-03 0828 (NSS) LUDINGTON, SUSAN Biomedical research support PHYSIOLOGICAL IMPACT ON INFANTS OF SKIN TO SKIN CONTACT: REGULAR INFANTS
S07RR-06014-03 0829 (NSS) LUDINGTON, SUSAN Biomedical research support PHYSIOLOGICAL IMPACT ON INFANTS OF SKIN TO SKIN CONTACT: PREMATURE INFANTS
S07RR-06014-03 0830 (NSS) LUDINGTON, SUSAN Biomedical research support PHYSIOLOGICAL IMPACT ON INFANTS OF SKIN TO SKIN CONTACT: PREMATURE INFANTS B
S07RR-06014-03 0831 (NSS) PADILLA, GERALDINE Biomedical research support ILLNESS UNCERTAINTY & QUALITY OF LIFE IN WOMEN W/ CERVICAL CANCER
S07RR-06014-03 0832 (NSS) PADILLA, GERALDINE Biomedical research support SURVEY OF HOME NURSING SKILLS
S07RR-06014-03 0833 (NSS) LEWIS, CHARLES Biomedical research support PHYSICIANS PERCEPTION OF PAIN IN PEDIATRIC ORTHOPEDIC CHILDREN
S07RR-06014-03 0834 (NSS) LEWIS, CHARLES Biomedical research support PHYSICIAN FEEDBACK & PERCEPTION: PAIN IN PEDIATRIC ORTHOPEDIC CHILDREN
S07RR-06014-03 0835 (NSS) MCCARRICK, ANNE Biomedical research support LOG LINEAR MODELING OF PARENT PATIENT INTERACTIONS
S07RR-06014-03 0836 (NSS) KERR, JEAN Biomedical research support SURVEY OF MASTERS STUDENTS PERCEPTIONS & CHARACTERISTICS
S07RR-06014-03 0837 (NSS) GLAZNER, LINDA Biomedical research support HOT & COLD ENVIRONMENTS
S07RR-06014-03 0838 (NSS) GLAZNER, LINDA Biomedical research support FIREFIGHTERS JOB RELATED INJURIES: OCCUPATION
S07RR-06014-03 0839 (NSS) KEENAN, COLLEEN Biomedical research support ADVERSE REACTIONS TO DPT SHOTS IN CHILDREN
S07RR-06014-03 0840 (NSS) KONIAK-GRIFFIN, DEBO Biomedical research support TEENAGERS ADAPTATION TO MOTHERHOOD ROLE
S07RR-06014-03 0841 (NSS) SARNA, LINDA Biomedical research support WOMEN & LUNG CANCER
S07RR-06014-03 0842 (NSS) TICKEN, PATRICIA Biomedical research support HOME CAREGIVERS FOR CANCER PATIENTS
S07RR-06014-03 0843 (NSS) LINDSEY, ADA Biomedical research support NURSE MANAGED CLINIC FOR LA HOMELESS: PROBLEMS, NEEDS, SERVICES
S07RR-06014-03 0844 (NSS) LEWIS, MARY ANN Biomedical research support SURVEY OF MASTERS STUDENTS PERCEPTION OF EDUCATION
S07RR-06014-03 0845 (NSS) LEE, JAN Biomedical research support SELF CARE & COPING IN DIABETIC PTS
S07RR-06014-03 0846 (NSS) LEE, JAN Biomedical research support HLTH SERVICES FOR CHRONICALLY ILL VETERAN POP
S07RR-06014-03 0847 (NSS) KASPER, CHRISTINE Biomedical research support MUSCLE ATROPHY IN RATS
S07RR-06016-03 (NSS) BERNSTEIN, JAY WILLIAM BEAUMONT HOSP RES INST 3601 W THIRTEEN MILE ROAD ROYAL OAK, MI 48072 Biomedical research support
S07RR-06016-03 0371 (NSS) GRINES, CINDY Biomedical research support MYOCARDIAL ONCOGENESIS AFTER INFARCTION & REPERFUSION
P41RR-06017-02 (SSS) WESTBROOK, EDWIN M ARGONNE NATIONAL LABORATORY 9700 SOUTH CASS AVENUE ARGONNE IL 60439-4833 CCD area detector research resource
S07RR-06017-04 (NSS) CARLSON, GEORGE A MCLAUGHLIN RES. INSTITUTE 1625 3RD AVENUE NORTH GREAT FALLS, MT 59401 Biomedical research support
S07RR-06017-04 0044 (NSS) WETTSTEIN, PETER J Biomedical research support IMMUNOREGULATORY GENE FAMILY DIVERSITY & DIVERGENCE
S07RR-06018-03 (NSS) MCDOWELL, FLETCHER H THE WINNIFRED MASTERSON BURKE 785 MAMARONECK AVE WHITE PLAINS, N Y 10605 Biomedical research support
S07RR-06018-03 0310 (NSS) MCDOWELL, FLETCHER H Biomedical research support 44 RAT CAGES, COVERS, FILTER COVERS & BOTTLES
S07RR-06019-03 (NSS) KEANE, WILLIAM F HENNEPIN COUNTY MEDICAL CENTER 701 PARK AVENUE MINNEAPOLIS, MN 55415 Biomedical research support
S07RR-06019-03 0525 (NSS) KEANE, WILLIAM F Biomedical research support NO RESEARCH SUBPROJECTS
M01RR-06020-02 (SRC) MICHELS, ROBERT CORNELL UNIV MED COLL 1300 YORK AVE NEW YORK, NY 10021 General clinical research center
M01RR-06020-02 0442 (SRC) BOECK, MARJORIE A General clinical research center Energy expenditure in anorexia nervosa--Effects of refeeding
M01RR-06020-02 0443 (SRC) BOECK, MARJORIE A General clinical research center Effects of DHEAS administration on obesity and glucose utilization
M01RR-06020-02 0444 (SRC) GERTNER, JOSEPH M General clinical research center Safety and efficacy of growth hormone releasing factor I-29
M01RR-06020-02 0445 (SRC) SPEISER, PHYLLIS General clinical research center Hypothalamic-pituitary-gonadal axis in nonclassical 21-OHD--Fertility problems
M01RR-06020-02 0446 (SRC) NEW, MARIA I General clinical research center 21-OH activity in acquired and cryptic adrenal hyperplasia
M01RR-06020-02 0447 (SRC) SPEISER, PHYLLIS General clinical research center Glomerulosa function in congenital adrenal hyperplasia
M01RR-06020-02 0123 (SRC) GERTNER, JOSEPH General clinical research center Low renin hypertension of childhood
M01RR-06020-02 0126 (SRC) NEW, MARIA I General clinical research center Hypoadrenal and hyperadrenal states
M01RR-06020-02 0184 (SRC) HILGARTNER, MARGARET W General clinical research center Desferrioxamine therapy in iron overload
M01RR-06020-02 0306 (SRC) GERTNER, JOSEPH M General clinical research center Feedback control of growth hormone secretion

PROJECT NO., ORGANIZATIONAL UNIT., INVESTIGATOR, ADDRESS, TITLE

M01RR-06020-02 0354 (SRC) SPEISER, PHYLLIS General clinical research center Steroid 21-hydroxylase deficiency--Inborn error of steroid synthesis
M01RR-06020-02 0368 (SRC) GERTNER, JOSEPH M General clinical research center Diet on GH AND IGF's in childhood obesity
M01RR-06020-02 0382 (SRC) GERTNER, JOSEPH M General clinical research center Efficacy and safety of recombinant met-free growth hormone
M01RR-06020-02 0383 (SRC) GERTNER, JOSEPH M General clinical research center Growth hormone in familial hypophosphatemic rickets
M01RR-06020-02 0448 (SRC) CAHILL, PATRICK General clinical research center Alpha interferon for the treatment of non-A and B hepatitis in thalassemics
M01RR-06020-02 0449 (SRC) HILGARTNER, MARGARET General clinical research center Longitudinal evaluation of growth and development in children with hemophilia
M01RR-06020-02 0450 (SRC) GERTNER, JOSEPH M General clinical research center Energy intake and energy expenditure during growth hormone therapy
M01RR-06020-02 0451 (SRC) BUSSEL, JAMES General clinical research center Recombinant white cell stimulating factor of congenital aplastic anemia
M01RR-06020-02 0386 (SRC) NEW, MARIA I General clinical research center Evaluation of hormonal changes of abnormal puberty
M01RR-06020-02 0389 (SRC) GERTNER, JOSEPH M General clinical research center Adipocyte GH response as a predictor of somatic response
M01RR-06020-02 0391 (SRC) SPEISER, PHYLLIS General clinical research center Hypothalamic-pituitary-gonadal axis in nonclassical 21-OHD
M01RR-06020-02 0419 (SRC) GERTNER, JOSEPH M General clinical research center Growth and puberty in type I diabetes mellitus
M01RR-06020-02 0420 (SRC) GERTNER, JOSEPH M General clinical research center Safety and efficacy of protropin in GH-deficient children
M01RR-06020-02 0421 (SRC) BOECK, MARJORIE General clinical research center Childhood obesity--Energy expenditure and serotonin
M01RR-06020-02 0422 (SRC) BOECK, MARJORIE A General clinical research center Nutritional and estrogen effects on skeletal metabolism in anorexia nervosa
M01RR-06020-02 0423 (SRC) GERTNER, JOSEPH M General clinical research center Somatotropin to sustain catch-up growth in GH-deficient children
M01RR-06020-02 0425 (SRC) SPEISER, PHYLLIS General clinical research center Neuroendocrine evaluation in hypoadrenal disorders
M01RR-06020-02 0426 (SRC) GERTNER, JOSEPH M General clinical research center Methionyl hGH and oxandrolone in Turner's syndrome
M01RR-06020-02 0427 (SRC) SPEISER, PHYLLIS General clinical research center Hormonal changes in deslorelin therapy of precocious puberty
M01RR-06020-02 0428 (SRC) GERTNER, JOSEPH M General clinical research center Pregnancy and the 1-alpha hydroxylation of vitamin D
M01RR-06020-02 0431 (SRC) GERTNER, JOSEPH M General clinical research center Safety and efficacy of bio-hGH in GH-naive, GH-deficient children
M01RR-06020-02 0432 (SRC) SPEISER, PHYLLIS General clinical research center Factors regulating growth in congenital adrenal hyperplasia
M01RR-06020-02 0433 (SRC) GERTNER, JOSEPH M General clinical research center Safety and efficacy of protropin in naive, GH-deficient children
M01RR-06020-02 0434 (SRC) GERTNER, JOSEPH M General clinical research center Somatostatin in the modulation of growth hormone release
M01RR-06020-02 0435 (SRC) MCBRIDE, ANNE P General clinical research center Serotonergic function in psychiatric disorders
M01RR-06020-02 0436 (SRC) BOECK, MARJORIE General clinical research center Fluoxetine vs. placebo--Effects on weight loss and depression
M01RR-06020-02 0437 (SRC) GERTNER, JOSEPH M General clinical research center An indicator of bone elongation
M01RR-06020-02 0438 (SRC) GERTNER, JOSEPH M General clinical research center Humatrope and low dose estrogen in Turner syndrome
M01RR-06020-02 0439 (SRC) EDELSON, PAUL General clinical research center Clinical trial of IV gamma globulin in pediatric AIDS
M01RR-06020-02 0440 (SRC) DEBRUIN, WILLIAM General clinical research center Sequelae of ARDS in children
M01RR-06020-02 0441 (SRC) GERTNER, JOSEPH M General clinical research center Salt and water metabolism during therapy with human growth hormone
S07RR-06020-03 (NSS) HOWARD, BARBARA V MEDLANTIC RES FOUNDATION 108 IRVING STREET, N W WASHINGTON, D C 20010 Biomedical research support
S07RR-06020-03 0311 (NSS) OBEID, GEORGE Biomedical research support IBUPROFEN & ACETAMINOPHEN ON BONE & ARTICULAR CARTILAGE HEALING
S07RR-06020-03 0312 (NSS) DAVENPORT, NANCY Biomedical research support CORONARY VASCULAR RESPONSE TO ACETYLCHOLINE: ENDOTHELIN PROSTACYCLIN
M01RR-06021-02 (CLR) PECK, WILLIAM A WASHINGTON UNIVERSITY MED SCH 660 SOUTH EUCLID AVENUE ST LOUIS, MO 63110 General clinical research center
M01RR-06021-02 0429 (CLR) AVIOLI, LOUIS V General clinical research center Metabolic bone disease
M01RR-06021-02 0612 (CLR) BIER, DENNIS General clinical research center Abnormal growth study
M01RR-06021-02 0596 (CLR) SHACKELFORD, PENELOPE G General clinical research center Subclass and clonal diversity of antibodies to polysaccharide antigens
M01RR-06021-02 0613 (CLR) SANTIAGO, JULIO V General clinical research center Diabetes control and complications trial (DCCT)
M01RR-06021-02 0619 (CLR) PESTRONK, ALAN General clinical research center Collaborative investigation of Duchenne muscular dystrophy
M01RR-06021-02 0626 (CLR) POLMAR, STEPHEN H General clinical research center Immunodeficiency disorders--Pathogenetic mechanisms

PROJECT NO., ORGANIZATIONAL UNIT., INVESTIGATOR, ADDRESS, TITLE

M01RR-06021-02 0628 (CLR) ROTHBAUM, ROBERT J General clinical research center Vitamin deficiency and neurological disease in chronic fat malabsorption
M01RR-06021-02 0680 (CLR) SANTIAGO, JULIO V General clinical research center Diabetes center--Clinical research facility and training center
M01RR-06021-02 0684 (CLR) BIER, DENNIS M General clinical research center Leuprolide acetate in children with precocious puberty
M01RR-06021-02 0715 (CLR) VOLPE, JOSEPH J General clinical research center Positron emission tomography in cerebrovascular disorders of the newborn
M01RR-06021-02 1013 (CLR) VEHASKARI, VESA MATTI General clinical research center Growth failure in children with renal diseases
M01RR-06021-02 1014 (CLR) BIER, DENNIS M General clinical research center Insulin secretion and sensitivity in relatives of Type I diabetes
M01RR-06021-02 1015 (CLR) COLE, BARABARA R General clinical research center Cyclosporine toxicity in allograft recipients
M01RR-06021-02 1016 (CLR) POLMAR, STEPHEN H General clinical research center Allergireactions allegedly due to aspartame consumption
M01RR-06021-02 1017 (CLR) POLMAR, STEPHEN H General clinical research center Safety of Gammagard IGIV given at increased rates
M01RR-06021-02 1018 (CLR) STRUNK, ROBERT S General clinical research center Theophylline withdrawal on responsiveness of airways to adenosine
M01RR-06021-02 1019 (CLR) DOWTON, S BRUCE General clinical research center Organic Acidurias--Therapeutic trials related to management
M01RR-06021-02 1001 (CLR) BIER, DENNIS M General clinical research center Abnormalities in glucose homeostasis in infants and children
M01RR-06021-02 1003 (CLR) COLE, BARBARA R General clinical research center Evaluation of metabolic defects in patients w/ recurring nephrolithiasis
M01RR-06021-02 1004 (CLR) FJELD, CARLA R General clinical research center Metabolic effects of theophylline in newborn infants
M01RR-06021-02 1005 (CLR) STORCH, GREGORY A General clinical research center Ganciclovir (DHPG) for symptomatic congenital cytomegalovirus infection
M01RR-06021-02 1007 (CLR) POLMAR, STEPHEN H General clinical research center IgG subclass deficiencies & selective antibody deficiencies in children
M01RR-06021-02 1010 (CLR) PORTER, FRAN General clinical research center Neonatal vagal tone--Index of risk for respiratory illness
M01RR-06021-02 1011 (CLR) SANTIAGO, JULIO V General clinical research center Insulin requirements in adolescent diabetics
M01RR-06021-02 1012 (CLR) STORCH, GREGORY A General clinical research center Clinical trial to evaluate AZT with or without iv gamma globulin
M01RR-06022-02 (CLR) DONALDSON, ROBERT M YALE UNIVERSITY P O BOX 3333 NEW HAVEN, CT 06510 General clinical research center
M01RR-06022-02 0779 (CLR) WHITTEMORE, RUTH General clinical research center Children at risk for hyperlipidemia
M01RR-06022-02 0780 (CLR) RODIN, JUDITH General clinical research center Gravid food behavior
M01RR-06022-02 0205 (CLR) PEARSON, HOWARD A General clinical research center Iron chelating agent desferrioxamine in thalassemia major
M01RR-06022-02 0736 (CLR) MAYES, LINDA C General clinical research center Long-term effects of intrauterine cocaine exposure on infants
M01RR-06022-02 0738 (CLR) RAPPEPORT, JOEL M General clinical research center Allogenic bone marrow transplantation in leukemia and preleukemic syndromes
M01RR-06022-02 0739 (CLR) RIDDLE, MARK A General clinical research center Fluoxetine treatment of obsessive compulsive disorder
M01RR-06022-02 0740 (CLR) RIDDLE, MARK A General clinical research center Developmental phenomenology study of OCD and Tourette's syndrome in children
M01RR-06022-02 0741 (CLR) ROSEN, CAROL General clinical research center Respiratory disorders of sleep in children
M01RR-06022-02 0742 (CLR) ROSEN, CAROL General clinical research center Interferon alfa-2a for treatment of pulmonary hemangiomatosis
M01RR-06022-02 0744 (CLR) SEASHORE, JOHN H General clinical research center Postoperative apnea in young infants
M01RR-06022-02 0745 (CLR) SHAPIRO, EUGENE D General clinical research center Clinical trial of amoxicillin prophylaxis to prevent Lyme disease
M01RR-06022-02 0747 (CLR) SIEGEL, NORMAN J General clinical research center Follow-up of patients who have recovered from hemolytic uremic syndrome
M01RR-06022-02 0749 (CLR) SUCHY, FREDERICK J General clinical research center Vitamin E replacement in chronic cholestasis
M01RR-06022-02 0750 (CLR) TAMBORLANE, WILLIAM V General clinical research center Responses to hypoglycemia in insulin dependent diabetes mellitus
M01RR-06022-02 0751 (CLR) TAMBORLANE, WILLIAM V General clinical research center Effects of puberty on glucose kinetics
M01RR-06022-02 0752 (CLR) VAN HOFF, JACK General clinical research center Therapy for T-cell leukemia and advanced T-cell lymphoma
M01RR-06022-02 0755 (CLR) WHITTEMORE, RUTH General clinical research center Lovastatin treatment of hypercholesterolemia
M01RR-06022-02 0756 (CLR) EHRENKRANZ, RICHARD A General clinical research center Dietary iron availability in premature infants
M01RR-06022-02 0758 (CLR) GROSS, IAN General clinical research center Respiratory distress syndrome and multiple doses of surfactant
M01RR-06022-02 0763 (CLR) ANDIMAN, WARREN A General clinical research center Maternal behavior, medical history and outcome of HIV infection
M01RR-06022-02 0764 (CLR) BREGMAN, J D General clinical research center Treatment of fragile X syndrome with methylphenidate and clonidine
M01RR-06022-02 0765 (CLR) BERIS, SUSAN General clinical research center Benefits of local anesthesia for IV insertion
M01RR-06022-02 0766 (CLR) MAYES, LINDA C General clinical research

center Characteristics of infants with non-organic failure to thrive (FTT)
M01RR-06022-02 0767 (CLR) PEARSON, HOWARD A General clinical research center Use of recombinant human erythropoietin in homozygous beta thalassemia
M01RR-06022-02 0768 (CLR) RAPPEPORT, JOEL M General clinical research center Multiagent chemotherapy vs. autologous transplant for children with AML
M01RR-06022-02 0769 (CLR) RODIN, JUDITH General clinical research center Toddler eating behavior and weight gain
M01RR-06022-02 0770 (CLR) SEASHORE, MARGRETTA General clinical research center Hyperammonemia in carbamyl phosphate synthetase and OTC deficiency
M01RR-06022-02 0771 (CLR) SEASHORE, MARGRETTA General clinical research center Oral carnitine and glycine supplementation use in preventing metabolic acidosis
M01RR-06022-02 0772 (CLR) SHAPIRO, EUGENE D General clinical research center Immunogenicity of influenzae type B vaccine (PedvaxHIB) in infants and children
M01RR-06022-02 0773 (CLR) SIEGEL, NORMAN General clinical research center Magnetic resonance spectroscopy of the orthotopic human kidney
M01RR-06022-02 0774 (CLR) SNELLING, LINDA K General clinical research center The validation of non-verbal correlates of pain in critically ill children
M01RR-06022-02 0775 (CLR) VAN HOFF, JACK General clinical research center Pathologic variables in rhabdomyosarcoma
M01RR-06022-02 0776 (CLR) VAN HOFF, JACK General clinical research center Use of preoperative chemotherapy in osteogenic sarcoma
M01RR-06022-02 0777 (CLR) VAN HOFF, JACK General clinical research center Antiemetics in children receiving chemotherapy
M01RR-06022-02 0778 (CLR) VAN HOFF, JACK General clinical research center Rhabdomyosarcoma treatment by ifosfamide and radiation therapy
M01RR-06022-02 0345 (CLR) GENEL, MYRON General clinical research center Monitoring medullary carcinoma of the thyroid in a large kindred
M01RR-06022-02 0383 (CLR) CARPENTER, THOMAS O General clinical research center Adjunctive 24,25(OH)2D3 therapy in familial hypophosphatemic rickets
M01RR-06022-02 0480 (CLR) CHOHEN, DONALD J General clinical research center Autism, aphasia and other development disabilities--Biological studies
M01RR-06022-02 0550 (CLR) LECKMAN, JAMES General clinical research center Folic acid in fragile X syndrome
M01RR-06022-02 0591 (CLR) TAMBORLANE, WILLIAM V General clinical research center Mechanisms of glucose intolerance in children with IDDM
M01RR-06022-02 0592 (CLR) TAMBORLANE, WILLIAM General clinical research center Diabetes control and complication trial
M01RR-06022-02 0597 (CLR) COMITE, FLORENCE General clinical research center Therapy of precocious puberty with GnRH analogs
M01RR-06022-02 0599 (CLR) HELLEBRAND, WILLIAM General clinical research center Transcatheter closure of atrial septal defect and patent ductus arteriosus
M01RR-06022-02 0602 (CLR) VAN HOFF, JACK General clinical research center Evaluation of treatment regimens in childhood acute lymphoid leukemia
M01RR-06022-02 0604 (CLR) TAMBORLANE, WILLIAM V General clinical research center Growth hormone deficient children
M01RR-06022-02 0605 (CLR) TAMBORLANE, WILLIAM V General clinical research center Effect of biosynthetic growth hormone on growth and metabolism
M01RR-06022-02 0617 (CLR) TOWBIN, KENNETH General clinical research center Obsessive compulsive disorder and IV clorimipromine treatment
M01RR-06022-02 0624 (CLR) MENT, LAURA General clinical research center Randomized indomethacin GMH/intraventricular hemorrhage prevention trial
M01RR-06022-02 0649 (CLR) LECKMAN, JAMES General clinical research center Fragile X syndrome--Cognitive and language deficits
M01RR-06022-02 0661 (CLR) SHAPIRO, EUGENE D General clinical research center Immunogenicity of a conjugate vaccine against Hemophilus influenzae B
M01RR-06022-02 0663 (CLR) TAMBORLANE, WILLIAM V General clinical research center Effects of hospitalization on diabetes management
M01RR-06022-02 0665 (CLR) VAN HOFF, JACK General clinical research center Ifosfamide and VP-16 in children with resistant tumors
M01RR-06022-02 0697 (CLR) RIDDLE, MARK General clinical research center Fluoxetine in obsessive compulsive dis, Tourette's syn or multiple tics
M01RR-06022-02 0702 (CLR) VAN HOFF, JACK General clinical research center Phase II agents for osteosarcoma
M01RR-06022-02 0720 (CLR) ELEFTERIADES, J A General clinical research center Remote stimulation of the diaphragm by radiofrequency transmission
M01RR-06022-02 0723 (CLR) LECKMAN, JAMES F General clinical research center Neurobiology of Tourette's syndrome and related disorders
M01RR-06022-02 0734 (CLR) COHEN, DONALD J General clinical research center Clonidine double blind study
M01RR-06022-02 0735 (CLR) GRYBOSKI, JOYCE D General clinical research center Clostridium difficile infection and pepto-bismol treatment
S07RR-06022-02 (NSS) TODD, JAMES K CHILDREN'S HOSP KEMPE RES CTR 1056 E 19TH AVENUE DENVER, CO 80218 Biomedical research support
S07RR-06022-02 0848 (NSS) GARST, LYNN R Biomedical research support COGNITION IN PSYCHIATRICALLY HOSPITALIZED ADOLESCENTS
S07RR-06022-02 0849 (NSS) MORELLI, JOSEPH G Biomedical research support MELANOCYTE MIGRATION: CONTROL OF REPIGMENTATION IN HUMAN VITILIGO
S07RR-06022-02 0850 (NSS) ABMAN, STEVEN H Biomedical research support ENDOTHELIAL DERIVED PRODUCTS IN PERINATAL PULMONARY CIRCULATION
S07RR-06023-02 (NSS) CANALIS, ERNESTO ST FRANCIS HOSPITAL & MED CTR 114 WOODLAND ST HARTFORD, CT 06105 Biomedical research support
S07RR-06023-02 0526 (NSS) CANALIS, ERNESTO Biomedical research support NO RESEARCH SUBPROJECTS
S07RR-06024-03 (NSS) THOFT, RICHARD A THE EYE & EAR INSTITUTE 203 LOTHROP STREET PITTSBURGH, PA 15213 Biomedical research support grant
S07RR-06024-03 0851 (NSS) SANDO, ISAMU Biomedical research support grant HISTOPATHOLOGY OF OTITIS MEDIA IN HUMANS
S07RR-06024-03 0852 (NSS) BAKER, KAREN Biomedical research support grant NEURONS ON TYPE VII COLLAGEN EXPRESSION IN RABBIT CORNEAL EPITHELIAL
S07RR-06025-02 (NSS) HU, TEH W UNIV OF CALIFORNIA SCH OF PUB HLTH, WARREN HALL BERKELEY, CA 94720 Biomedical research support grant
S07RR-06025-02 0025 (NSS) SCHUFFLER, HELEN Biomedical research support grant ANALYSIS OF HEALTH PROMOTION & DISEASE PREVENTION POLICY UNDER MEDICARE
S07RR-06025-02 0026 (NSS) SCHWEITZER, STUART Biomedical research support grant SMALL AREA VARIATION IN HEALTH ACCESS & UTILIZATION IN INDONESIA
S07RR-06025-02 0027 (NSS) SIEGAL, JUDITH Biomedical research support grant FAMILY CONSTELLATION & MENT HLTH: SINGLE VS MARRIED MOTHERS, PARENT-CHILD RELAT
S07RR-06025-02 0028 (NSS) GUENDELMAN, SYLVIA Biomedical research support grant HEALTH PROMOTION STRATEGIES & INTERVENTIONS IN MAQUILADORAS; RISK TAKING BEHAV
S07RR-06025-02 0029 (NSS) GRAZIER, KYLE Biomedical research support grant RELATIONSHIP BETWEEN COST & QUALITY IN MENTAL HEALTH INSTITUTIONS
S07RR-06025-02 0030 (NSS) SPEAR ROBERT Biomedical research support grant ENVIRONMENTAL & OCCUPATIONAL HEALTH RESEARCH COLLABORATION IN INDONESIA
S07RR-06028-02 (NSS) BIRCH, DAVID G RETINA FOUNDATION OF SOUTHWEST 8230 WALNUT HILL LN DALLAS, TX 75231 Biomedical research support
S07RR-06028-02 0372 (NSS) BANE, MARK CHAPMAN Biomedical research support LOW VISION IN INFANTS
P41RR-06030-01A1 (SSS) POWERS, LINDA UTAH STATE UNIVERSITY LOGAN, UT 84322-4630 National center for the design of molecular function
P41RR-06030-01A1 9003 (SSS) POWERS, LINDA National center for the design of molecular function Core research--Applications
P41RR-06030-01A1 0001 (SSS) BUMPUS, JOHN A National center for the design of molecular function Enzymology of fungal and mammalian peroxidases
P41RR-06030-01A1 0002 (SSS) CALDWELL, KARIN D National center for the design of molecular function Protein adsorption from solution to solid phases
P41RR-06030-01A1 0003 (SSS) CHANCE, BRITTON National center for the design of molecular function Time-resolved X-ray absorption studies on heme proteins
P41RR-06030-01A1 0004 (SSS) CZERLINSKI, GEORGE National center for the design of molecular function Control of calmodulin function
P41RR-06030-01A1 0005 (SSS) DRATZ, E National center for the design of molecular function Mechanism of action of GTP-binding proteins in visual excitation
P41RR-06030-01A1 0006 (SSS) GREENBAUM, ELIAS National center for the design of molecular function In vivo enzyme synthesis studies using biochemical poise and pulsed laser spec
P41RR-06030-01A1 0007 (SSS) HOLLENBERG, PAUL F National center for the design of molecular function The mechanisms of peroxidase and cytochrome P-450 catalyzed reactions
P41RR-06030-01A1 0008 (SSS) LANCASTER, J R National center for the design of molecular function Bioenergetics of methanogens
P41RR-06030-01A1 0009 (SSS) PARKER, VERNON D National center for the design of molecular function Deprotonation of methylarene cation radicals
P41RR-06030-01A1 9001 (SSS) POWERS, LINDA National center for the design of molecular function Core research--Real-time time-resolved spectroscopic technology
P41RR-06030-01A1 9002 (SSS) POWERS, LINDA National center for the design of molecular function Core research--Data acquisition, analysis and visualization
S07RR-06031-02 (NSS) LANG, NORMA M UNIVERSITY OF WISCONSIN BOX 413 MILWAUKEE, WI 53201 Biomedical research support
S07RR-06031-02 0373 (NSS) COWLES, KATHY Biomedical research support EXPERIENCE OF SIGNIFICANT OTHERS W/ AIDS
S07RR-06031-02 0374 (NSS) DEVINE, ELIZABETH Biomedical research support EFFECTS OF PATIENT EDUCATION & PSYCHOSOCIAL SUPPORT
S07RR-06031-02 0375 (NSS) DIEKMANN, JUDY Biomedical research support PAIN INSTRUMENT DEVELOPMENT
S07RR-06031-02 0376 (NSS) HEIDRICH, SUSAN Biomedical research support PSYCHOSOCIAL ADAPTATION IN FRAIL ELDERLY
S07RR-06031-02 0377 (NSS) RLESCH, SUSAN Biomedical research support PARENTS & KIDS WHO LISTEN
S07RR-06032-02 (NSS) EYLAR, EDWARD H PONCE SCHOOL OF MEDICINE UNIVERISTY ST, PO BOX 7004 PONCE, PUERTO RICO 00732-7004 Biomedical research support
S07RR-06033-02 (NSS) ANDERS, THOMAS F EMMA PENDLETON BRADLEY HOSPITA 1011 VETERANS MEMORIAL PKWY EAST PROVIDENCE, RI 02915 Biomedical research support
S07RR-06033-02 0527 (NSS) ANDERS, THOMAS F Biomedical research support NO RESEARCH SUBPROJECTS
S07RR-06034-01 (NSS) ABBEY, JUNE C VANDERBILT UNIVERSITY 21ST AVE, SOUTH NASHVILLE, TN 37240 Biomedical research support grant
S07RR-06035-01 (NSS) GEVINS, ALAN S EEG SYSTEMS LABORATORY 51 FEDERAL STREET, STE 401 SAN FRANCISCO, CA 94107 Biomedical research support grant
S07RR-06036-01 (NSS) BOURDON, MARIO A CALIFORNIA INST OF BIOL RESEAR 11099 N TORREY PINES RD, STE 3 LA JOLLA, CA 92037 Biomedical research support grant
S07RR-06037-01 (NSS) STOOKEY, GEORGE K INDIANA UNIVERSITY 1121 WEST MICHIGAN STREET INDIANAPOLIS, IN 46202 Biomedical research support grant
S07RR-06038-01 (NSS) PAIRENT, FREDERICK W UNIVERSITYOF

PROJECT NO., ORGANIZATIONAL UNIT., INVESTIGATOR, ADDRESS, TITLE

WISCONSIN P O BOX 413 MILWAUKEE, WI 53201 Biomedical research support grant
S07RR-06039-01 (NSS) ISHIZAKA, KIMISHIGE LA JOLLA INST FOR ALLERGY/IMMU 11149 NORTH TORREY PINES ROAD LA JOLLA, CA 92037 Biomedical research support grant
S07RR-06040-01 (NSS) NIELSEN, DONALD W HOUSE EAR INSTITUTE 2100 WEST THIRD STREET LOS ANGELES, CA 90057 Biomedical research support grant
S07RR-06041-01 (NSS) MOSESSON, MICHAEL W SINAI SAMARITAN MEDICAL CENTER 950 NORTH 12TH STREET MILWAUKEE, WI 53233 Biomedical research support grant
U24RR-06042-03 (NSS) DUCAT, LEE Human cell, tissue and organ resource for research
S07RR-06043-01 (NSS) KAMINSKAS, EDVARDAS HEBREW REHABILITATION CENTER 1200 CENTRE STREET BOSTON, MA 02131 Biomedical research support grant
S07RR-06044-01 (NSS) TIPTON, CHARLES M UNIVERSITY OF ARIZONA GITTINGS BLDG, RM 108 TUCSON, AZZ 85721 Biomedical research support grant
S07RR-06045-01 (NSS) FLIESLER, STEVEN J BETHESDA EYE INSTITUTE 3655 VISTA AVENUE ST LOUIS, MO 63110 Biomedical research support grant
R24RR-06158-02 (AR) BARD, KIM A EMORY UNIVERSITY ATLANTA GA 30322 Behavioral interventions for nursery-reared chimpanzees
R01RR-06159-02 (AR) GORMUS, BOBBY J TULANE UNIVERSITY THREE RIVERS ROAD COVINGTON, LA 70433 A serologic determination of leprosy in chimpanzees
R01RR-06161-01 (AR) TAVARES, JAMES NATIONAL RESEARCH COUNCIL 2010 CONSTITUTION AVENUE, N.W. WASHINGTON, D.C. 20418 Nutrient requirements of laboratory animals
S10RR-06236-01 (SSS) KAVANAGH, TERRANCE J UNIVERSITY OF WASHINGTON DIV/PULMONARY/CRITICAL CARE ME SEATTLE, WA 98195 Anchored cell analysis and sorting cytometer
S10RR-06238-01 (SSS) GASKELL, SIMON J BAYLOR COLLEGE OF MEDICINE ONE BAYLOR PLAZA HOUSTON, TX 77030 Triple quadrupole electrospray mass spectrometer
S10RR-06239-01 (SSS) DE CROMBRUGGHE, BENOIT U OF TEXAS MD ANDERSON CANCER 1515 HOLCOMBE BLVD/BOX 11 HOUSTON, TX 77030 Automated DNA sequencer
S10RR-06240-01 (SSS) TAKEMOTO, LARRY J KANSAS STATE UNIVERSITY ACKERT HALL MANHATTAN, KS 66506 Protein sequencer, peptide synthesizer, DNA synthesizer, HPLC
S10RR-06243-01 (SSS) LAUTERBUR, PAUL C UNIVERSITY OF ILLINOIS 1307 WEST PARK ST URBANA, IL 61801 500 mhz nmr spectrometer
S10RR-06244-01 (SSS) LANSBURY, PETER T, JR MASSACHUSETTS INST OF TECH 77 MASSACHUSETTS AVE CAMBRIDGE, MA 02139 Mass spectrometry
S10RR-06245-01 (SSS) SCHULTZ, ARTHUR G RENSSELAER POLYTECHNIC INST 328 COGSWELL LABORATORY TROY, NY 12180-3590 400 MHz NMR spectrometer
S10RR-06246-01 (SSS) SARTORELLI, ALAN C YALE UNIVERSITY SCH OF MED 333 CEDAR ST, PO BOX 3333 NEW HAVEN, CT 06510 Triple quadrupole mass spectrometer
S10RR-06248-01 (SSS) SCHERAGA, HAROLD A CORNELL UNIVERSITY ITHACA, NY 14853-1301 500 MHz NMR spectrometer
S10RR-06250-01 (SSS) STALL, ALAN M HAMMER HEALTH SCIENCES 701 WEST 168TH STREET NEW YORK, NY 10032 Becton-dickinson facstar plus
S10RR-06252-01 (SSS) BRYANT, ROBERT G UNIVERSITY OF ROCHESTER 601 ELMWOOD AVENUE ROCHESTER, N Y 14642 400 mhz wide bore nmr spectrometer
S10RR-06254-01 (SSS) BLAIR, IAN A VANDERBILT UNIVERSITY MED CTR SCHOOL OF MEDICINE NASHVILLE, TN 37232 Acquisition of a high performance double focusing mass spectrometer
S10RR-06260-01 (SSS) AXEL, LEON UNIVERSITY OF PENNSYLVANIA 36TH ST & HAMILTON WALK PHILADELPHIA, PA 19104-6086 Clinical magnetic resonance imaging system for research
S10RR-06261-01 (SSS) KAN, LOU-SING JOHNS HOPKINS UNIVERSITY 615 NORTH WOLFE STREET BALTIMORE, MD 21205 A bruker AM-X console for a 300 MHz NMR spectrometer
S10RR-06262-01 (SSS) IRELAND, CHRIS M UNIVERSITY OF UTAH 308 SKAGGS HALL SALT LAKE CITY, UT 84112 500 MHz NMR spectrometer
S10RR-06264-01 (SSS) GORE, JOHN C YALE UNIVERSITY 155 WHITNEY AVENUE NEW HAVEN, CT 06510 Upgrade of NMR spectrometer for imaging and spectroscopy
S10RR-06276-01 (SSS) ADAMS, JEANETTE EMORY UNIVERSITY ATLANTA, GA 30322 High-resolution high-mass tandem mass spectrometer
S10RR-06280-01 (SSS) JAMES, J HOWARD UNIVERSITY OF CINCINNATI MED C 231 BETHESDA AVENUE CINCINNATI, OH 45267-0558 Purchase of amino acid analyzer
S10RR-06281-01 (SSS) OTVOS, LASZLO WISTAR INSTITUTE 36TH & SPRUCE STREETS PHILADELPHIA, PA 19104 Peptide synthetic and analytical workstation
S10RR-06282-01 (SSS) BACHOVCHIN, WILLIAM W TUFTS UNIVERSITY 136 HARRISON AVENUE BOSTON, MA 02111 Acquisition of NMR spectrometer
S10RR-06284-01 (SSS) PARKER, CHARLOTTE D UNIVERSITY OF MISSOURI COLUMBIA, MO 65212 Protein core facility
S10RR-06285-01 (SSS) KUNKEL, LOUIS M CHILDREN'S HOSPITAL 300 LONGWOOD AVENUE BOSTON, MA 02115 Automated DNA sequencer
S10RR-06286-01 (SSS) BERGMAN, ROBERT G UNIVERSITY OF CALIFORNIA COLLEGE OF CHEMISTRY BERKELEY, CA 94720 Double focusing mass spectrometer
S10RR-06287-01 (SSS) REINHOLD, VERNON N 665 HUNTINGTON AVENUE BOSTON, MA 02115 GC/SFC-MS instrument– triple quadrupole
S10RR-06294-01 (SSS) WILLIAMS, TODD D UNIVERSITY OF KANSAS MASS SPECTROMETRY LABORATORY LAWRENCE, KS 66045 Hybrid (EBQQ) mass spectrometer
S10RR-06296-01 (SSS) MARTINEZ-CARRION, M UNIVERSITY OF MISSOURI 5100 ROCKHILL RD KANSAS CITY, MO 64110-2499 Central protein facility
S10RR-06299-01 (SSS) RAUSHEL, FRANK M TEXAS A&M UNIVERSITY COLLEGE STATION, TX 77843 Purchase of 500 MHz NMR spectrometer
S10RR-06301-01 (SSS) SHOEMAKER, RICHARD K UNIVERSITY OF NEBRASKA LINCOLN, NE 68588-0304 300 and 500 MHz NMR spectrometers
S10RR-06312-01 (SSS) FLICKER, PAULA F VANDERBILT UNIVERSITY BOX 1820 STATION B NASHVILLE, TN 37235 Purchase of an electron microscope

PROJECT NO., ORGANIZATIONAL UNIT., INVESTIGATOR, ADDRESS, TITLE

S10RR-06313-01 (SSS) GUYRE, PAUL M DARTMOUTH MEDICAL SCHOOL HANOVER, NH 03756 Flow cytometer replacement for ortho 50hh
S10RR-06314-01 (SSS) SATTERLEE, JAMES D WASHINGTON STATE UNIVERSITY PULLMAN, WA 99164-4630 500 MHz NMR spectrometer
S10RR-06317-01 (SSS) WOLFENDEN, RICHARD V UNC AT CHAPEL HILL CB#7260, 413 FLOB CHAPEL HILL, NC 27599-7260 500 mhz nmr spectrometer
S10RR-06318-01 (SSS) CANTINO, MARIE E UNIVERSITY OF CONNECTICUT STORRS, CT 06269 Scanning/transmission microscope for multi-user facility
S10RR-06322-01 (SSS) KWOCK, LESTER UNIV NO CAROLINA/CB #7510 RES FACILITY (MED RES BLDG D) CHAPEL HILL, NC 27599 2 TESLA NMR spectrometer
S10RR-06327-01 (SSS) BRETSCHER, ANTHONY P CORNELL UNIVERSITY BIOTECHNOLOGY BUILDING ITHACA, NY 14853 Laser scanning confocal microscope
S10RR-06335-01 (SSS) HUBBARD, WALTER C JOHNS HOPKINS ASTHMA/ALLERGY C 301 BAYVIEW BLVD BALTIMORE, MD 21224 Finnegan MATT SSQ-700 with additional data system
S10RR-06337-01 (SSS) KENSLER, ROBERT W UNIVERSITY OF MISSOURI 2411 HOLMES ST RM M3-202 KANSAS CITY, MO 64108-2792 Electron microscope facility
S10RR-06338-01 (SSS) HYMAN, ROBERT A SALK INSTITUTE P O BOX 85800 SAN DIEGO, CA 92186-5800 FACStar plus cell sorter
S10RR-06351-01 (SSS) FURLONG, DEIRDRE B HARVARD MEDICAL SCHOOL 200 LONGWOOD AVE BOSTON, MA 02115 Shared conventional electron microscope proposal
S10RR-06352-01 (SSS) ORKIN, ROSLYN W MASSACHUSETTS GENERAL HOSPITAL 149 13TH ST CHARLESTOWN, MA 02129 Confocal fluorescence microscope
S10RR-06356-01 (SSS) GRANATH, WILLARD O, JR UNIVERSITY OF MONTANA MISSOULA, MT 59812 Electron microscope
S10RR-06357-01 (SSS) FERRELL, ROBERT E UNIVERSITY OF PITTSBURGH 130 DESOTO ST PITTSBURGH, PA 15261 Aks litm cytogenetic analysis system
S10RR-06358-01 (SSS) MARKWALD, ROGER R MEDICAL COLLEGE OF WISCONSIN 8701 WATERTOWN PLANK ROAD MILWAUKEE, WI 53226 Laser scanning confocal imaging system
S10RR-06359-01 (SSS) IDEN, CHARLES R STATE UNIVERSITY OF NEW YORK STONY BROOK, NY 11794-8651 Acquisition of a liquid chromatograph/mass spectrometer
S10RR-06363-01 (SSS) FAN, HUNG Y UNIVERSITY OF CALIFORNIA, IRVI IRVINE, CA 92717 Scanning electron microscope with BEI detector
S10RR-06369-01 (SSS) PEARLSON, GODFREY D JOHNS HOPKINS HOSPITAL 600 N WOLFE ST MEYER 3-166 BALTIMORE, MD 21205 Silicon Graphics, Inc. 4D240GTX graphics computer workstation
S10RR-06371-01 (SSS) SIDMAN, CHARLES L THE JACKSON LABORATORY 600 MAIN STREET BAR HARBOR, ME 04609-0800 Facstar plus flow cytometer
S10RR-06376-01 (SSS) BREW, KEITH UNIV OF MIAMI SCH OF MED PO BOX 016129 MIAMI, FL 33101 Peptide synthesis and amino acid analysis facility
S10RR-06380-01 (SSS) TEMPLETON, ALAN R WASHINGTON UNIVERSITY LINDELL-SKINKER BLVD ST LOUIS, MO 63130 Vax computer system for the biology department
S10RR-06381-01 (SSS) STONE, MICHAEL P VANDERBILT UNIVERSITY PO BOX 51 STATION B NASHVILLE, TN 37235 Scanning circular dichroism spectropolarimeter
S10RR-06383-01 (SSS) HARRISON, THERESA A MEDICAL COLLEGE OF GEORGIA AUGUSTA, GA 30912-2000 Bio-rad confocal microscope and 3-D analysis work station
S10RR-06387-01 (SSS) HARRELL, FRANK E DUKE UNIV MEDICAL CENTER BOX 3363 DURHAM, NC 27710 Biostatistical computing resource
S10RR-06390-01 (SSS) DEBRUNNER, PETER G LOOMIS LABORATORY OF PHYSICS 1110 WEST GREEN STREET URBANA, IL 61801 Sweeping super con magnet system for low temp VHF EPR
S10RR-06393-01 (SSS) DEY, RICHARD D WEST VIRGINIA UNIVERSITY 4052 HLTH SCIENCES CENTER NORT MORGANTOWN, WV 26506 Image analysis system
S10RR-06400-01 (SSS) KASHGARIAN, MICHAEL YALE UNIVERSITY 310 CEDAR ST, PO BOX 3333 NEW HAVEN, CT 06510 Transmission electron microscopy system
S10RR-06401-01 (SSS) TRINCHIERI, GIORGIO WISTAR INSTITUTE 36TH & SPRUCE STREETS PHILADELPHIA, PA 19104 Shared instrumentation/cell sorter
S10RR-06404-01 (SSS) CASKEY, CHARLES T BAYLOR COLLEGE OF MEDICINE ONE BAYLOR PLAZA HOUSTON, TX 77030 Automated DNA sequencing system
S10RR-06413-01 (SSS) GRAY, HARRY B CALIFORNIA INSTITUTE OF TECH 1201 E CALIFORNIA BLVD PASADENA, CA 91125 Laser spectroscopy laboratory
S10RR-06414-01 (SSS) TODD, ROBERT F, III UNIVERSITY OF MICHIGAN 102 OBSERVATORY DR ANN ARBOR, MI 48109-0724 Coulter elite flow cytometry system
S10RR-06420-01 (SSS) KING, MICHAEL A UNIV OF MASSACHUSETTS 55 LAKE AVENUE NORTH WORCESTER, MA 01655 Advanced spect imaging system
S10RR-06422-01 (SSS) CARABELLO, BLASE A MEDICAL UNIV OF SOUTH CAROLINA 171 ASHLEY AVENUE CHARLESTON, SC 29425-2221 Upgrade of angiographic facility
S10RR-06427-01 (SSS) CHASIN, LAWRENCE A COLUMBIA UNIVERSITY 912 FAIRCHILD CENTER NEW YORK, NY 10027 Molecular biology core instrumentation facility
S10RR-06433-01 (SSS) DOUGHTY, MICHAEL B UNIV OF KANSAS LAWRENCE, KS 66045-2506 Peptide synthesizer amino acid analyzer
S10RR-06434-01 (SSS) CRAIG, ROBERT G UNIV OF MICHIGAN SCH OF DENT 1011 N UNIVERSITY ANN ARBOR, MI 48109-1078 Instron 8501 digital servohydraulic testing instrument
S10RR-06445-01 (SSS) LAIDLAW, STEWART A HARBOR-UCLA MEDICAL CENTER 1000 W CARSON ST TORRANCE, CA 90509 Amino acid analyzer
S10RR-06448-01 (SSS) ZWEIER, JAY L JOHNS HOPKINS UNIVERSITY 301 BAYVIEW BLVD BALTIMORE, MD 21224 Multifrequency EPR spectrometer facility
S10RR-06449-01 (SSS) MEYER, THOMAS J UNIVERSITY OF NORTH CAROLINA CAMPUS BOX #3290 CHAPEL HILL, NC 27599-3290 Picosecond system for ultra fast transient spectroscopy

S10RR-06450-01 (SSS) PATERSON, YVONNE UNIV OF PENNSYLVANIA SCH OF ME 209 JOHNSON PAVILION PHILADELPHIA, PA 19104-6076 Circular dichroism spectrometer

S10RR-06453-01 (SSS) GRUNEWALD, GARY L UNIVERSITY OF KANSAS DEPT OF MEDICINAL CHEMISTRY LAWRENCE, KS 66045 High-performance molecular modeling and graphics system

S10RR-06456-01 (SSS) SIMPSON, LARRY UNIVERSITY OF CALIFORNIA 405 HILGARD AVENUE LOS ANGELES, CA 90024 Acquisition of a VAX computer system

S10RR-06458-01 (SSS) BROYDE, SUSE B NEW YORK UNIVERSITY 100 WASHINGTON SQUARE EAST NEW YORK, NY 10003 Iris model 4D220 VGX workstation

S10RR-06460-01 (SSS) DE CLARIS, NICHOLAS UNIV OF MARYLAND AT BALTIMORE 660 WEST REDWOOD ST BALTIMORE, MD 21201 Medical informatics network--A distributed computing facility

S10RR-06461-01 (SSS) SALSER, WINSTON A UNIVERSITY OF CALIFORNIA 405 HILGARD AVE LOS ANGELES, CA 90024 Automated DNA sequencing core facility

S10RR-06462-01 (SSS) WILLIARD, PAUL G DEPT OF CHEMISTRY BROWN UNIVERSITY PROVIDENCE, RI 02912 Upgrade of a nicolet single crystal x-ray diffractometer

S10RR-06468-01 (SSS) TOWNSEND, CRAIG A JOHNS HOPKINS UNIVERSITY CHARLES & 34TH STREETS BALTIMORE, MD 21218 500 MHz NMR instrumentation for shared use

S10RR-06472-01 (SSS) CAPRIOLI, RICHARD M UNIVERSITY OF TEXAS MED SCH P O BOX 20036 HOUSTON, TX 77225 Purchase of a laser desorption/time-of-flight mass spectrometer

S10RR-06474-01 (SSS) STROUD, ROBERT M UNIVERSITY OF CALIFORNIA, SF S-964 SAN FRANCISCO, CA 94143-0448 An area sensitive detector for protein crystallography

S10RR-06475-01 (SSS) BETZ, WILLIAM J UNIV OF COLORADO SCH OF MED 4200 EAST NINTH AVENUE DENVER, CO 80262 Multiuser confocal microscope facility

S10RR-06478-01 (SSS) LEWELLEN, THOMAS K UNIVERSITY OF WASHINGTON SEATTLE, WA 98195 Tofpet image reconstruction computer system

S10RR-06480-01 (SSS) BLACKBAND, STEPHEN J JOHNS HOPKINS UNIV HOSPITAL 600 N WOLFE ST/ MRI 110 BALTIMORE, MD 21205 Upgrade of a 4 7t/40cm GE CSI instrument

S10RR-06486-01 (SSS) SPUDICH, JOHN L ALBERT EINSTEIN COLLEGE OF MED 1300 MORRIS PARK AVENUE BRONX, N Y 10461 Multistation computerized motion analysis system

S10RR-06487-01 (SSS) DURANT, JOHN R UNIVERSITY OF ALABAMA AT BIRM UAB STATION BIRMINGHAM, AL 35294 Mass spectrometer for biomedical research

S10RR-06490-01 (SSS) OLIVER, JANET M UNIVERSITY OF NEW MEXICO 2701 FRONTIER, NE - SURGE BLDG ALBUQUERQUE, NM 87131 Spectrofluorometer to complete a fluorescence center

S10RR-06491-01 (SSS) MAUDSLEY, ANDREW A VA MEDICAL CENTER 4150 CLEMENT STREET (11M) SAN FRANCISCO, CA 94121 Instrumentation for NMR spectroscopic imaging in vivo

R01RR-06499-01 (SRC) CONNEELY, ORLA M BAYLOR COLLEGE OF MEDICINE ONE BAYLOR PLAZA HOUSTON, TX 77030 A novel host system to study steroid hormone action

R01RR-06500-02 (SRC) SARRAS, MICHAEL P, JR UNIVERSITY OF KANSAS MEDICAL C 39TH AND RAINBOW BLVD 66103-8410 A model for epithelial/basement membrane interactions

S10RR-06504-01 (SSS) NAPOLI, JOSEPH L STATE UNIV OF NEW YORK 3435 MAIN STREET BUFFALO, NY 14214 Protein sequencer/microbore HPLC

S10RR-06505-01 (SSS) SHACKLETON, CEDRIC H CHILDREN'S HOSP OAKL RES INST 747 52ND STREET OAKLAND, CA 94609 Electrospray HPLC/MS

S10RR-06506-01 (SSS) JACKSON, JAMES E MICHIGAN STATE UNIVERSITY EAST LANSING, MI 48824 Mass spectrometer for organic structure determination

S10RR-06507-01 (SSS) MC CRACKEN, ARDYTHE A UNIVERSITY OF NEVADA, RENO RENO, NV 89557 Bio-Rad MRC-600 confocal imaging system

S10RR-06509-01 (SSS) VAN ESSEN, DAVID C CALIFORNIA INST OF TECHNOLOGY 1201 E CALIFORNIA BLVD PASADENA, CA 91125 Confocal microscope and 3-D graphics workstation

S10RR-06513-01 (SSS) SIMONI, ROBERT D STANFORD UNIVERSITY STANFORD , CA 94305 Automated peptide synthesizer for molecular studies

S10RR-06516-01 (SSS) HELD, KATHRYN D MASSACHUSETTS GENERAL HOSPITAL FRUIT STREET BOSTON, MA 02114 X-ray generator

S10RR-06519-01 (SSS) PEARLMAN, JUSTIN D MASSACHUSETTS GENERAL HOSPITAL FRUIT STREET BOSTON, MA 02114 Parallel superscalar processing system for NMR research

S10RR-06520-01 (SSS) HESTER, RAYMOND B UNIVERSITY OF SOUTH ALABAMA COLLEGE OF MEDICINE MOBILE, AL 36688 ACAS 570 anchored-cell analyzer and sorter

S10RR-06521-01 (SSS) LECHENE, CLAUDE P LAB OF CELLULAR PHYSIOLOGY 221 LONGWOOD AVENUE BOSTON, MA 02115 Automated video microfluorometry and injection system

S10RR-06522-01 (SSS) WEISEL, JOHN W UNIVERSITY OF PENNSYLVANIA PHILADELPHIA, PA 19104-6058 Computer facility for rapid 3-D imaging

S10RR-06523-01 (SSS) BANDSTRA, EMMALEE S UNIVERSITY OF MIAMI PO BOX 016960 MIAMI, FL 33101 Ultrasonographic imaging system with color-flow doppler

S10RR-06524-01 (SSS) FOX, PETER T JOHNS HOPKINS MEDICAL INSTITUT 660 N WOLFE STREET, MEYER 8-15 BALTIMORE, MD 21205 150-dedicated radiochemistry system

S10RR-06525-01 (SSS) FUCHS, PHILIP L PURDUE UNIVERSITY WEST LAFAYETTE, IN 47907-3699 Rotating anode x-ray generator

S10RR-06527-01 (SSS) ANGELETTI, RUTH H ALBERT EINSTEIN COLL OF MEDICI 1300 MORRIS PARK AVE BRONX, NY 10461 Peptide synthesis and sequence-- Circular dichroism

S10RR-06533-01 (SSS) TALMAN, WILLIAM T UNIVERSITY OF IOWA HOSPS & CLI S209 GH IOWA CITY, IA 52242 High resolution image digitization and analysis system

S10RR-06541-01 (SSS) BRYANT, PETER J UNIVERSITY OF CALIFORNIA IRVINE, CA 92717 Interactive three-dimensional graphics computer system

R01RR-06555-01 (SRC) PERELSON, ALAN S UNIVERSITY OF CALIFORNIA PO BOX 1663, MAIL STOP K710 LOS ALAMOS, NM 87545 Mathematical models of immune networks

R01RR-06558-01 (SRC) HARRIS, THOMAS R VANDERBILT UNIVERSITY BOX 1724, STATION B NASHVILLE, TN 37235 Simulation and analysis of lung vascular system models

R01RR-06562-01 (SRC) RAO, GOVIND UNIV OF MARYLAND BALTIMORE CO TRC 227 BALTIMORE, MD 21228 In vivo oxidative DNA damage in cultured mammalian cells

R01RR-06564-02 (SRC) STIMERS, JOSEPH R UNIVERSITY OF ARKANSAS/MED SCI 4301 WEST MARKHAM STREET LITTLE ROCK, AR 72205 Modeling of Na/K pump activity in cardiac myocytes

R01RR-06565-02 (SRC) DORES, ROBERT M UNIVERSITY OF DENVER UNIVERSITY PARK DENVER, CO 80208-0178 Polypeptide hormone biosynthesis--Amphibian models

S10RR-06568-01 (SSS) GARAVITO, R MICHAEL UNIVERSITY OF CHICAGO 920 E 58TH STREET CHICAGO, ILLINOIS 60637 X-ray area detector for biomolecular research

S10RR-06578-01 (SSS) JAVITT, JONATHAN C CENTER FOR SIGHT 3800 RESERVOIR ROAD WASHINGTON, DC 20007 Shared Solbourne computer facility

S10RR-06579-01 (SSS) SCANU, ANGELO M UNIVERSITY OF CHICAGO 5841 S MARYLAND AVE, BOX 231 CHICAGO, IL 60637 Beckman optima xl analytical ultracentrifuge

R55RR-06587-01 (SRC) HLATKY, LYNN R NEW ENGLAND DEACONESS HOSP 50 BINNEY ST BOSTON, MA 02115 Modeling cell response to environmental heterogeneity

R01RR-06589-01 (SRC) STEPHENSON, JOHN L CORNELL UNIVERSITY MED COLL 1300 YORK AVE NEW YORK, NY 10021 Supercomputer simulation of the mammalian kidney

R01RR-06591-01A1 (AR) DAVIDSON, ERIC H CALIFORNIA INST OF TECHNOLOGY PASADENA, CALIF 91125 Homozygous sea urchin as a potential research resource

R01RR-06603-01 (SRC) KASAHARA, MASANORI UNIVERSITY OF MIAMI PO BOX 016960 MIAMI, FL 33101 Evolution of the major histocompatibility complex

S10RR-06605-01 (SSS) AKEY, CHRISTOPHER W BOSTON UNIVERSITY SCH OF MED 80 EAST CONCORD STREET BOSTON, MA 02118 Structural electron microscopy facility

S10RR-06606-01 (SSS) LEE, KUO-HSIUNG UNIVERSITY OF NORTH CAROLINA CB#7360 BEARD HALL CHAPEL HILL, N C 27599-7360 Low resolution gas chromatograph mass spectrometer

S10RR-06607-01 (SSS) GESTELAND, ROBERT C UNIVERSITY OF CINCINNATI CINCINNATI, OH 45267 Confocal microscope imaging system

R01RR-06610-01 (SRC) HOFFMANN, F MICHAEL UNIVERSITY OF WISCONSIN 1400 UNIVERSITY AVENUE MADISON, WI 53706 Functions of growth factors in Drosphila development

R01RR-06625-01 (SRC) HACKETT, PERRY B UNIVERSITY OF MINNESOTA 1445 GORTNER AVENUE ST PAUL, MN 55108-1095 Zebrafish as a model for biomedical research

R01RR-06627-02 (SRC) GILBERT, LAWRENCE I UNIV OF NORTH CAROLINA CB# 3280 CHAPEL HILL, NC 27599-3280 Hormonal regulation of Drosophila development

R01RR-06633-01 (SRC) CALLARD, IAN P BOSTON UNIVERSITY 5 CUMMINGTON STREET BOSTON, MA 02215 Regulation of apolipoprotein metabolism -- A turtle model

R01RR-06640-02 (SRC) MORSE, DANIEL E UNIVERSITY OF CALIFORNIA MARINE SCIENCE INSTITUTE SANTA, BARBARA, CA 93106 Control of metamorphosis in mollusc larvae

S10RR-06641-01 (SSS) BAKER, JOHN R UNIVERSITY OF ALABAMA UAB STATION 1808 7TH AVE SOUTH BIRMINGHAM, AL 35294 Protein/peptide sequencer and synthesizer

R01RR-06654-02 (SRC) THORGAARD, GARY H WASHINGTON STATE UNIVERSITY PULLMAN, W A 99164-4234 Homozygous clones of trout as models for biomedical research

S10RR-06662-01 (SSS) GERLT, JOHN A UNIVERSITY OF MARYLAND COLLEGE PARK, MD 20742 Autoradiograph imager

S10RR-06667-01 (SSS) ROHEIM, PAUL S LOUISIANA STATE UNIV MED CTR 1542 TULANE AVENUE/RM 638 NEW ORLEANS, LA 70112-2822 Radioanalytic imaging system

R01RR-06672-02 (SRC) KAUFMAN, LESLIE S NEW ENGLAND AQUARIUM CENTRAL WHARF BOSTON, MA 02110-3393 Mechanisms of bone growth in fish hyperostosis

S10RR-06679-01 (SSS) ABRAHAM, GEORGE N UNIV OF ROCHESTER 601 ELMWOOD AVE ROCHESTER, NY 14642 Molecular resources facility enhancement

S10RR-06691-01 (SSS) MASON, CAROL A COLUMBIA UNIV, HEALTH SCIENCES 630 WEST 168TH STREET NEW YORK, NY 10032 Electron microscope

S10RR-06692-01 (SSS) LEFURGEY, EDORIS A DUKE UNIVERSITY MEDICAL CENTER 347 NANALINE DUKE BLDG RES DR DURHAM, NC 27710 Analytical electron microscope

S10RR-06694-01 (SSS) KAGNOFF, MARTIN F UNIV OF CALIFORNIA, SAN DIEGO LA JOLLA, CA 92093 Multiparameter fluorescence flow cytometer

S10RR-06699-01 (SSS) GROGAN, W MC LEAN VIRGINIA COMMONWEALTH UNIV BOX 614 MCV STATION RICHMOND, VA 23298-0614 Acas interactive laser cytometer

S10RR-06703-01 (SSS) BASCH, ROSS S NEW YORK UNIVERSITY MED CENTER 550 FIRST AVE. NEW YORK, NY 10016 Shared flow cytometry facility

S10RR-06705-01 (SSS) LEWIS, JON C WAKE FOREST UNIVERSITY 300 SOUTH HAWTHORNE ROAD WINSTON-SALEM, NC 27103 Scanning electron microscope

S10RR-06706-01 (SSS) HILLE, CHARLES R OHIO STATE UNIVERSITY 1645 NEIL AVENUE COLUMBUS, OH 43210 Applications of a resonance Raman spectrometer

S10RR-06708-01 (SSS) MC INTOSH, THOMAS J DUKE UNIVERSITY MEDICAL CENTER BOX 3011 DURHAM, NC 27710 Purchase of rigaku rotating anode x-ray generator

S10RR-06709-01 (SSS) SCHEIDT, W ROBERT UNIVERSITY OF NOTRE DAME DEPARTMENT OF CHEMISTRY NOTRE DAME, IND 46556 Rotating anode x-ray diffraction system

S10RR-06710-01 (SSS) NELSON, JEFFREY W LOUISIANA STATE UNIVERSITY BATON ROUGE, LA 70803-1806 CD spectrometer

S10RR-06713-01 (SSS) JUNG, MICHAEL E UNIVERSITY OF CALIFORNIA

405 HILGARD AVENUE LOS ANGELES, CA 90024-1569 Purchase of a mass spectrometer

S10RR-06714-01 (SSS) SHEA, KENNETH J THE UNIVERSITY OF CALIFORNIA IRVINE, CA 92717 Purchase of a quadrupole mass spectrometer

S10RR-06716-01 (SSS) KISHI, YOSHITO HARVARD UNIVERSITY 12 OXFORD STREET CAMBRIDGE, MA 02138 High resolution and routine service mass spectrometers

S10RR-06725-01 (SSS) STRANGE, KEVIN CHILDREN'S HOSPITAL 300 LONGWOOD AVE/HUNNEWELL 3 BOSTON, MA 02115 Digital imaging fluorescence microscopy facility

S10RR-06726-01 (SSS) MERRICK, WILLIAM C CASE WESTERN RESERVE UNIV 2119 ABINGTON ROAD CLEVELAND, OH 44106 Purchase of a high sensitivity amino acid analyzer

S10RR-06727-01 (SSS) KAHN, C RONALD JOSLIN DIABETES CENTER, INC ONE JOSLIN PLACE BOSTON, MA 02215 Peptide/protein analysis facility

S10RR-06731-01 (SSS) TURNER, DOUGLAS H UNIVERSITY OF ROCHESTER ROCHESTER, N Y 14627 Computer graphics equipment

S10RR-06732-01 (SSS) PONZIO, NICHOLAS M UNIV OF MED & DENTISTRY 185 SOUTH ORANGE AVENUE NEWARK, N J 07103 Gamma irradiator

S10RR-06735-01 (SSS) SHEA, KENNETH J UNIVERSITY OF CALIFORNIA IRVINE, CA 92717 Purchase of an ESR spectrometer

S10RR-06736-01 (SSS) PHILLIPS, LINDA R UNIVERSITY OF ARIZONA TUCSON, AZ 87521 Research data acquisition and management network

S10RR-06739-01 (SSS) KOREEDA, MASATO UNIVERSITY OF MICHIGAN ANN ARBOR, MI 48109 500 MHz NMR spectrometer

S10RR-06741-01 (SSS) HEGYVARY, SUE T UNIVERSITY OF WASHINGTON SCHOOL OF NURSING, SC-72 SEATTLE, WA 98195 Computerized physiological data system

S10RR-06742-01 (SSS) HYDE, JAMES S MEDICAL COLLEGE OF WISCONSIN 8701 WATERTOWN PLANK RD MILWAUKEE, WI 53226 Medspec 3T/60cm imager spectroscopy scanner

R01RR-06753-01 (AR) NARAYAN, OPENDRA JOHNS HOPKINS UNIVERSITY 720 RUTLAND AVENUE BALTIMORE, MD 21205 Lentivirus replication in host macrophages is a prerequisite for disease

R13RR-06755-01 (AR) ANDERSON, PHILIP UNIVERSITY OF WISCONSIN 445 HENRY MALL MADISON, WI 53706 C. elegans meeting

R24RR-06758-01 (SSS) CRISSMAN, HARRY UNIVERSITY OF CALIFORNIA PO BOX 1663 MS M888 LOS ALAMOS, NM 87545 Flow cytometric analysis of multiple DNA fluorochromes

G20RR-06761-01 (AR) BJOTVEDT, GEORGE ARIZONA STATE UNIVERSITY TEMPE, AZ 85287-0608 Developing and improving institutional animal resources

G20RR-06762-01 (AR) HALL, ARTHUR S OREGON HEALTH SCIENCES UNIV 3181 SW SAM JACKSON PARK ROAD PORTLAND, OR 97201-3098 Animal resource improvement grant

G20RR-06763-01 (AR) MAUL, DONALD H COLORADO STATE UNIVERSITY PAINTER CENTER FORT COLLINS, CO 80523 Equipment request--Sheep pens and rodent Thoren cages

G20RR-06764-01 (AR) SOJKA, NICKOLAS J UNIVERSITY OF VIRGINIA BOX 450 CHARLOTTESVILLE, VA 22908 Animal resources development and improvement

G20RR-06768-01 (AR) WAGNER, JOSEPH L UNIVERSITY OF MIAMI PO BOX 016960 MIAMI, FL 33101 Developing and improving institutional animal resources

G20RR-06769-01 (AR) COOPER, PAUL S UNIVERSITY OF IOWA IOWA CITY, IA 52242 Developing and improving institutional animal resources

G20RR-06775-01 (AR) HENSON, PETER M NATIONAL JEWISH CENTER 1400 JACKSON STREET DENVER, CO 80206 Developing and improving institutional animal resources

G20RR-06776-01 (AR) MERRITT, DORIS H INDIANA UNIVERSITY 1120 SOUTH DRIVE INDIANAPOLIS, IN 46202-5114 Laboratory animal resource facility

G20RR-06777-01 (AR) HESSLER, JACK R WASHINGTON UNIVERSITY 660 S EUCLID AVENUE, BOX 8061 ST LOUIS, MO 63110 Developing and improving institutional animal resources

G20RR-06780-01 (AR) NADEL, ETHAN R JOHN B PIERCE FDN LAB, INC 290 CONGRESS AVE NEW HAVEN, CT 06519 Consolidation of Pierce Laboratory animal quarters

G20RR-06782-01 (AR) KOHN, DENNIS F COLUMBIA UNIVERSITY 630 WEST 168TH STREET NEW YORK, NY 10032 Development and improvement of an animal resource

G20RR-06785-01 (AR) STRANDBERG, JOHN D JOHNS HOPKINS UNIV SCHOOL OF M 720 RUTLAND AVENUE BALTIMORE, MD 21205 Renovation and improvement of animal resources

G20RR-06786-01 (AR) FERNER, WILLIAM T WASHINGTON STATE UNIVERSITY PULLMAN, WASHINGTON 99164-116 Developing and improving institutional animal resources

G20RR-06789-01 (AR) BAUMAN, DAVID H UNIVERSITY OF CINCINNATI 231 BETHESDA AVE ML 571 CINCINNATI, OH 45267-0671 Developing and improving institutional animal resources

R43RR-06801-01 (SSS) CAMPANA, JOSEPH E EXTREL FTMS 6416 SCHROEDER RD MADISON, WI 53711 Fourier transform mass spectrometer for bioscience

R43RR-06803-01 (REN) VOELKEL, STEVEN A GRANADA BIOSCIENCES, INC 100 RESEARCH PARK, SUITE 100 COLLEGE STATION, TX 77840 Nuclear transfer in non-human primates

R44RR-06807-03 (SSS) HOYT, CLIFFORD C CAMBRIDGE RES & INSTRUMTN INC 21 ERIE STREET CAMBRIDGE MA 02139 Image-preserving tunable filter for microscopy

R44RR-06809-03 (SSS) KLEIN, JAMES D EIC LABORATORIES INC 111 DOWNEY STREET NORWOOD MA 02062 Nonmagnetic biopsy needle for MRI environments

R03RR-06820-01 (BRC) MURPHY-BOESCH, JOSEPH FOX CHASE CANCER CENTER 7701 BURHOLME AVE PHILADELPHIA, PA 19111 A quadrature mode double-tuned probe for high-field NMR

R55RR-06841-01 (AR) GODENY, ELMER K GEORGIA STATE UNIVERSITY PO BOX 4010 ATLANTA, GA 30302 Enhanced SHFV diagnostics in non-human primate colonies

R03RR-06843-01 (BRC) BARBER, HERBERT B UNIVERSITY OF ARIZONA HEALTH SCIENCES CENTER TUCSON, AZ 85724 Semiconductor modular gamma cameras

R03RR-06845-01 (BRC) BARRETT, HARRISON H UNIVERSITY OF ARIZONA ARIZONA HEALTH SCIENCES CENTER TUCSON, AZ 85724 Multiplexed acoustic microscopy

R03RR-06846-01 (BRC) HO, PING-PEI CITY COLLEGE OF CUNY 138TH STREET & CONVENT AVE NEW YORK, NY 10031 Time gate ballistic imaging for mammograph

R03RR-06849-01 (BRC) MORGAN, JULIET UNIVERSITY OF CHICAGO 5841 SOUTH MARYLAND AVE BOX 40 CHICAGO, IL 60637 Light stimulated cardiac pacing and defibrillation

R24RR-06853-01 (SSS) BALLARD, DANA H UNIVERSITY OF ROCHESTER ROCHESTER, NY 14627 Resource for the study of neural models of behavior

R03RR-06854-01 (BRC) SCOTTO, ANTHONY W CORNELL UNIV MEDICAL COLLEGE 1300 YORK AVENUE NEW YORK, NY 10021 Glycosylated proteoliposomes--A new delivery vehicle

R03RR-06870-01 (BRC) WHEELER, BRUCE C UNIVERSITY OF ILLINOIS 1406 W GREEN ST URBANA, IL 61801 Patterned neuronal networks

R03RR-06876-01 (BRC) NATHANIELSZ, PETER W CORNELL UNIVERSITY ITHACA, NY 14853-6401 An electrical impedance imaging methods to monitor labor

R13RR-06884-01 (AR) GREENHOUSE, DOROTHY D NATIONAL ACADEMY OF SCIENCES 2101 CONSTITUTION, NW WASHINGTON, D C 20418 Definition, nomenclature, and conservation of rat strains

R01RR-06886-01 (AR) THRALL, MARY A COLORADO STATE UNIVERSITY COLLEGE VET/MED BIOMED SCIENCE FORT COLLINS, CO 80523 Characterization of feline model of Niemann-Pick type C

R55RR-06887-01 (SSS) TRAN, CHIEU D MARQUETTE UNIVERSITY MILWAUKEE, WI 53233 Bioanalytical applications of thermal lens spectrometry

P41RR-06892-01 (SSS) FRIESNER, RICHARD A COLUMBIA UNIVERSITY 116TH AND BROADWAY NEW YORK, NY 10027 Theoretical simulation of biological systems

P41RR-06892-01 0001 (SSS) BRESLOW, RONALD Theoretical simulation of biological systems Molecular recognition and understanding enzymatic reaction mechanisms

P41RR-06892-01 0002 (SSS) TURRO, NICHOLAS J Theoretical simulation of biological systems Interaction of DNA with metal complexes

P41RR-06892-01 0003 (SSS) HENDRICKSON, WAYNE Theoretical simulation of biological systems Biomolecular structure and dynamics from X-ray and NMR experiments

P41RR-06892-01 9001 (SSS) FRIESNER, RICHARD A Theoretical simulation of biological systems Core research--Electronic structure methods

P41RR-06892-01 9002 (SSS) FRIESNER, RICHARD A Theoretical simulation of biological systems Core research--Quantum dynamical methods

P41RR-06892-01 9003 (SSS) HONIG, BARRY Theoretical simulation of biological systems Core research--Electrostatic calculations

P41RR-06892-01 9004 (SSS) LEVY, R M Theoretical simulation of biological systems Core research--Spectroscopic calculations

P41RR-06892-01 9005 (SSS) FRIESNER, RICHARD Theoretical simulation of biological systems Core research--Classical simulation methods

R55RR-06904-01 (SSS) TURNER, JAMES N WADSWORTH CTR FOR LABS & RES PO BOX 509 ALBANY, NY 12201-0509 3d imaging of live neurons instrumentation and methods

R13RR-06913-01 (AR) GORDON, JON W MT SINAI SCHOOL OF MED 2056 ANNANBERG NEW YORK, NY 10029 FASEB conference transgenic animals

G20RR-06920-01 (AR) NEVILLE, JAMES A UNIVERSITY OF ALABAMA PO BOX 870326 TUSCALOOSA, AL 35487-0326 Animal facility improvement

G20RR-06921-01 (AR) UPHOUSE, LYNDA L TEXAS WOMAN'S UNIVERSITY P O BOX 23971 DENTON, TX 76204 Animal reduced improvement request for Texas Woman's University

G20RR-06922-01 (AR) PEARSON, THOMAS A MARY IMOGENE BASSETT HOSPITAL ONE ATWELL ROAD COOPERSTOWN, NY 13326 Improving animal resources at the Mary Imogene Bassett Hospital

G20RR-06925-01 (AR) DUBIN, STEPHEN E DREXEL UNIVERSITY 32ND & CHESTNUT STS (7-722) PHILADELPHIA, PA 19104 Improvement of institutional animal resources

G20RR-06928-01 (AR) COTTINGTON, ERIC M ALLEGHENY-SINGER RESEARCH INST 320 EAST NORTH AVENUE PITTSBURGH, PA 15212-9986 Animal resource improvement project

G20RR-06941-01 (AR) AGNEW, WILLIAM F HUNTINGTON MEDICAL RESEARCH IN 734 FAIRMOUNT AVE PASADENA, CA 91105 Upgrading of floor covering and cage sterilization

G20RR-06942-01 (AR) FARRIS, HAROLD E CLEMSON UNIVERSITY E-303 MARTIN HALL CLEMSON, SC 29634-5708 Animal resources improvement

G20RR-06944-01 (AR) ABDELAL, AHMED T GEORGIA STATE UNIVERSITY UNIVERSITY PLAZA ATLANTA, GA 30303 Animal facility improvements

G20RR-06945-01 (AR) NUWAYSER, ELIE S BIOTEK, INC 21-C OLYMPIA AVENUE WOBURN, MA 01801 Developing and improving Biotek's animal resources

G20RR-06950-01 (AR) IYPE, P THOMAS BIO RES FACULTY/FACILITY, INC 10075-20 TYLER PLACE IJAMSVILLE, MD 21754 Improvement of the animal facility at BRFF

G20RR-06951-01 (AR) BRETT, JAMES R CALIFORNIA STATE UNIVERSITY 1250 BELLFLOWER BOULEVARD LONG BEACH, CA 90840 CSU, Long Beach's animal facility renovation

G20RR-06952-01 (AR) PROZIALECK, WALTER C PHILADELPHIA COLLEGE OF OST ME 4150 CITY AVENUE PHILADELPHIA, PA 19131 Animal facility improvement project

R03RR-06953-01A1 (BRC) STEWART, BOB W UNIVERSITY OF CINCINNATI CINCINNATI, OH 45221-0011 Dual-wavelength accessory for simultaneous PDT and hyperthermia

G20RR-06958-01 (AR) BOWMAN, PHILIP J UNIVERSITY OF MONTANA PHARMACY/PSYCH RM 035 MISSOULA, MT 59801 University of Montana animal resource improvement

R13RR-06959-01 (AR) MORTON, WILLIAM R UNIVERSITY OF WASHINGTON SJ-50 SEATTLE, WA 98195 Nonhuman primate models for AIDS symposium

R03RR-06969-01 (BRC) SPELMAN, FRANCIS A UNIVERSITY OF WASHINGTON REGIONAL PRIMATE RESEARCH CTR SEATTLE, WA 98195 Biomagnetic imaging of cochlear stimulus currents

R03RR-06970-01 (BRC) BURROWS, CYNTHIA J STATE UNIVERSITY OF NEW YORK DEPARTMENT OF CHEMISTRY STONY BROOK, NY 11794-3400 Chemical

probes of protein secondary structure
R43RR-06983-01 (SSS) DEROSE, EUGENE F DYNAMICS TECHNOLOGY INC 1555 WILSON BLVD ARLINGTON, VA 22209-2405 Robust automatic shimming algorithm for NMR systems
R43RR-06984-01 (SSS) BLANC, JOSEPH PRINCETON X-RAY LASER INC PRINCETON CORPORATE PLAZA MONMOUTH JUNCTION, NJ 08852 Attractive atomic force microscopy for DNA sequencing
R03RR-07002-01 (AR) CHANG, JERJANG UNIVERSITY OF NORTH CAROLINA CHAPEL HILL, NC 27599 Clostridium difficile infection in aged hamsters
S07RR-07002-26 (NSS) CARTER, HERBERT E UNIVERSITY OF ARIZONA 601 ADMINISTRATION BLDG TUCSON, AZ 85721 Biomedical research support
S07RR-07002-26 0857 (NSS) ROBY, FRED B Biomedical research support PREDICTION OF MINIMAL BODY WEIGHT DIET
S07RR-07002-26 0858 (NSS) LITTLE, JOHN W Biomedical research support REGULATION OF HOMEOTIC GENE EXPRESSION DROSOPHILA
S07RR-07002-26 0870 (NSS) BULLER, DAVID B Biomedical research support SURVEY OF PRIMARY CARE PHYSICIANS
S07RR-07002-26 0871 (NSS) GILLIES, ROBERT J Biomedical research support BIOENERGETICS OF PROLIFERATION IN HYBRID CELLS
S07RR-07002-26 0872 (NSS) GILKEY, JOHN C Biomedical research support ULTRAMICROTOME FOR ELECTRON MICROSCOPE
S07RR-07002-26 0873 (NSS) MACKENZIE, NEIL E Biomedical research support NMR STUDIES OF INSECT APOLIPOPROTEIN
S07RR-07002-26 0874 (NSS) PARKER, ROY R Biomedical research support REGULATION OF NRNA STABILITY IN YEAST
S07RR-07002-26 0875 (NSS) STINI, WILLIAM A Biomedical research support BONE REMODELING IN OLD AGE
S07RR-07002-26 0876 (NSS) STAUSFELD, NICHOLAS Biomedical research support ACTIVATED NEURONAL ASSEMBLIES
S07RR-07002-26 0877 (NSS) VANETTEN, HANS D Biomedical research support PLANT PATHOGENIC FUNGUS NECTRIN HAEMATOCOCCA
S07RR-07002-26 0878 (NSS) WEINERT, TED A Biomedical research support CONTROL OF MITOSIS & DNA DAMAGE
S07RR-07002-26 0879 (NSS) ARKOWITZ, HAROLD S Biomedical research support RESISTANCE TO CHANGE IN DEPRESSION
S07RR-07002-26 0880 (NSS) BLOOM, PAUL Biomedical research support MEANING & FORM IN LANGUAGE DEVELOPMENT
S07RR-07002-26 0881 (NSS) BUCKNER, STEVEN W Biomedical research support PHOTODISSOCIATION SPECTROSCOPY
S07RR-07002-26 0882 (NSS) HENRIKSEN, ERIK J Biomedical research support VICINAL SULFHYDRYLS
S07RR-07002-26 0883 (NSS) ISTOCK, CONRAD Biomedical research support ECOLOGICAL & GENETIC ADAPTATION
S07RR-07002-26 0884 (NSS) MOREBECK, MARY ELLEN Biomedical research support BONE MINERALIZATION, MAINTENANCE, & LOSS IN CHIMPS
S07RR-07002-26 0885 (NSS) RAGHAVAN, SRINI Biomedical research support LYSIS KINETICS: MATERIALS SCI
S07RR-07002-26 0886 (NSS) THOMAS, JO ANN Biomedical research support PERIPHERAL GLUCOSE ON MEMORY STORAGE
S07RR-07002-26 0887 (NSS) TOLBERT, LESLIE P Biomedical research support FUNCTION OF OLFACTORY GLOMERULI
S07RR-07002-26 0888 (NSS) WIGLEY, DAVID E Biomedical research support AZIRIDINE SYNTHESIS
S07RR-07002-26 0889 (NSS) WYNN, KAREN Biomedical research support EARLY NUMERICAL KNOWLEDGE
S07RR-07002-26 0859 (NSS) TIMMERMANN, BARBARA Biomedical research support THERAPEUTIC AGENTS FROM HIGHER PLANTS: AIDS, HIV VIRUS
S07RR-07002-26 0860 (NSS) ADAMOWICZ, LUDWIK Biomedical research support MOLECULAR STRUCTURE OF ANTIVIRAL & MUTAGENIC AGENTS: TAUTOMERISM
S07RR-07002-26 0861 (NSS) PARK, DOUGLAS L Biomedical research support CHARACTERIZE CIGUATOXINS; GAMBIERDISCUS TOXINS, PROPROCENTRUM LIMA, ELISA
S07RR-07002-26 0862 (NSS) GLATTKE, THEODORE J Biomedical research support EFFERENT CONTROL IN COCHLEAS OF HUMAN EAR, HEARING
S07RR-07002-26 0863 (NSS) CALDER, WILLIAM A Biomedical research support NATURAL WEIGHT CONTROL MODEL
S07RR-07002-26 0864 (NSS) CUMMINS, DENISE D Biomedical research support REASONING DEDUCTIVELY ABOUT CAUSATION: LOGIC, THINKING
S07RR-07002-26 0865 (NSS) DOMINO, GEORGE Biomedical research support IMAGERY OF CANCER
S07RR-07002-26 0866 (NSS) ENRIQUEZ, F JAVIER Biomedical research support MODULATION OF IMMUNE RESPONSES
S07RR-07002-26 0867 (NSS) HARRIS, DAVID T Biomedical research support ANALYSIS OF TARGET CELL ANTIGEN: MK CELLS, IMMUNOLOGY, CANCER
S07RR-07002-26 0868 (NSS) HAWES, MARTHA C Biomedical research support CHARACTERIZATION OF ROOT LOCALIZED ENZYME: ROOT CAP
S07RR-07002-26 0869 (NSS) NADEL, LYNN Biomedical research support LIMBIC SYSTEM & SPATIAL LEARNING: HIPPOCAMPUS, SPATIAL MEMORY
S07RR-07003-26 (NSS) DAVIDSON, NORMAN R CALIFORNIA INST OF TECHNOLOGY 1201 E CALIFORNIA BLVD PASADENA, CA 91125 Biomedical research support
S07RR-07003-26 0326 (NSS) LAURENT, G Biomedical research support MEMBRANE PROPERTIES OF LOCUST NON SPIKING LOCAL INTERNEURONS
S07RR-07003-26 0327 (NSS) DAVIDSON, E Biomedical research support RANDOM ORDER AFFINITY CHROMATOGRAPHY FOR PURIFICATION OF GENE REGULATORY FACTORS
S07RR-07003-26 0328 (NSS) EMR, S Biomedical research support GOLGI TO LYSOSOME TRANSPORT & PROTEOLYTIC MATURATION OF A LYSOSOMAL HYDROLASE
S07RR-07003-26 0329 (NSS) KIRSCHVINK, J Biomedical research support PROBLEMS OF HUMAN BRAIN MAGNETITE & HIGH MAGNETIC FIELDS
S07RR-07003-26 0330 (NSS) KENNEDY, M Biomedical research support BRAIN CALCIUM & CALMODULIN DEPENDENT PROTEIN KINASE
S07RR-07003-26 0331 (NSS) REVEL, J P Biomedical research support PURCHASE OF CONFOCAL MICROSCOPE
S07RR-07003-26 0332 (NSS) LIDSTROM, M Biomedical research support DEVELOPMENT OF A SOLID STATE PRC ASSAY
S07RR-07003-26 0315 (NSS) PARKER, C Biomedical research support TRANSCRIPTION FACTORS FROM CULTURED DROSOPHILA & MAMMALIAN CELLS
S07RR-07003-26 0316 (NSS) CHAN, S Biomedical research support MULTINUCLEAR NMR OF PHOSPHOPHORYN
S07RR-07003-26 0333 (NSS) REVEL, J-P Biomedical research support COMPUTER SYSTEM FOR CONFOCAL MICROSCOPE TO BE LINKED TO ETHERNET
S07RR-07003-26 0317 (NSS) RICHARDS, J Biomedical research support COMPUTER GRAPHICS STUDIES OF BIOMOLECULAR STUDIES
S07RR-07003-26 0318 (NSS) KOCH, C Biomedical research support BIOPHYSICAL MECHANISMS UNDERLYING ASSOCIATIVE LEARNING IN MARINE NUDIBRANCH
S07RR-07003-26 0319 (NSS) CAMPBELL, J Biomedical research support CELL CYCLE STUDIES REQUIRING ELUTRIATOR CENTRIFUGE
S07RR-07003-26 0320 (NSS) ALLMAN, J Biomedical research support NEW APPROACHES TO PRIMATE VISUAL PERCEPTION
S07RR-07003-26 0321 (NSS) LESTER, H Biomedical research support PHYSIOLOGY OF GENE ACTIVATION
S07RR-07003-26 0322 (NSS) KENNEDY, M Biomedical research support MOLECULAR STRUCTURE OF POSTSYNAPTIC DENSITY
S07RR-07003-26 0323 (NSS) BOWER, J Biomedical research support MEASURING DISTRIBUTION OF ELECTRIC FIELDS GENERATED BY GNATHONEMUS PETERS
S07RR-07003-26 0324 (NSS) PINE, J Biomedical research support MULTIELECTRODE STUDIES
S07RR-07003-26 0325 (NSS) BOWER, J Biomedical research support MULTIUSER SILICON FABRICATION FACILITY
S07RR-07004-16 (NSS) NEEL, JAMES V SAN DIEGO STATE UNIVERSITY FDN 5178 COLLEGE AVENUE SAN DIEGO, CA 92182-1900 Biomedical research support
S07RR-07004-16 0045 (NSS) BREINDL, MICHAEL Biomedical research support RETROVIRAL INTEGRATION SITE & INSERTIONAL MUTATION; MURINE TYPE I COLLAGEN GENE
S07RR-07004-16 0046 (NSS) CLOUSE, STEVEN D Biomedical research support MOLECULAR ANALYSIS OF BRASSINOLIDE ACTION IN PLANT GROWTH & DEVELOPMENT
S07RR-07004-16 0047 (NSS) FREY, TERRENCE Biomedical research support ELECTRON MICROSCOPY OF CYTOCHROME OXIDASE CRYSTALS
S07RR-07004-16 0048 (NSS) HARRIS, GREG L Biomedical research support PHYSIOLOGICAL & MOLECULAR ANALYSIS OF PHOTOTRANSDUCTION IN DROSOPHILA
S07RR-07004-16 0049 (NSS) KRISANS, SKAIDRITE Biomedical research support PEROXISOMES IN CHOLESTEROL METABOLISM
S07RR-07004-16 0050 (NSS) MALCARNE, VANESSA Biomedical research support CHILDREN IN FAMILIES W/ PARENTAL ILLNESS
S07RR-07004-16 0051 (NSS) MCGUIRE, KATHLEEN L Biomedical research support HTLV 1 REGULATORY PROTEINS TAX & REX IN TRANSFORMATION; INTERLEUKIN 2
S07RR-07004-16 0052 (NSS) PAOLINI, PAUL J Biomedical research support 3 D RECONSTRUCTION OF SKELETAL FIBER SUBSTRUCTURE RELATIVE TO FORCE VS LENGTH
S07RR-07004-16 0053 (NSS) PERRAULT, JACQUES Biomedical research support VSV POLYMERASE REGULATION & DEFECTIVE INTERFERING PARTICLE REPLICATION
S07RR-07004-16 0054 (NSS) RILEY, EDWARD P Biomedical research support BEHAVIORAL EFFECTS OF NEONATAL ALCOHOL EXPOSURE
S07RR-07004-16 0055 (NSS) TSOUKAS, CONSTANTINE Biomedical research support GTP BINDING PROTEINS IN HUMAN T CELL ACTIVATION; BACTERIAL TOXINS
S07RR-07004-16 0056 (NSS) VALLE, RAMON Biomedical research support ASSESSMENT OF MEMORY DISORDERS ASSOCIATED W/ HISPANIC ALZHEIMERS DISEASE
S07RR-07005-26 (NSS) THOMAS, EWART A STANFORD UNIVERSITY BLDG. 1, 2070 STANFORD, CA 94305 Biomedical research support
S07RR-07005-26 0334 (NSS) DONIACH, SEBASTIAN Biomedical research support MONTE CARLO SIMULATION OF ANTIBODY LYSOZYME BINDING
S07RR-07005-26 0335 (NSS) DRUECKHAMMER, DALE G Biomedical research support ENZYMES AS CATALYSTS IN ORGANIC SYNTHESIS
S07RR-07005-26 0336 (NSS) FERNALD, RUSSELL Biomedical research support SOCIAL CONTROL OF GENE ACTION & EYE DEVELOPMENT
S07RR-07005-26 0344 (NSS) WANDELL, BRIAN A Biomedical research support SPATIO CHROMATIC PROPERTIES OF RETINAL GANGLION CELL RECEPTIVE FIELDS
S07RR-07005-26 0345 (NSS) WATT, WARD B Biomedical research support NATURAL GENETIC VARIATIONS: IN VIVO METABOLIC IMPACT
S07RR-07005-26 0337 (NSS) GRIFFIN, JOHN H Biomedical research support ANALYSIS & ENGINEERING OF PROTEINS & ENZYMES
S07RR-07005-26 0338 (NSS) HANAWALT, PHILIP C Biomedical research support REPAIR OF DNA DAMAGE CAUSED BY ENVIRONMENTAL CARCINOGENS
S07RR-07005-26 0339 (NSS) MACOVSKI, ALBERT Biomedical research support STORAGE & PROCESSING FOR NOVEL MAGNETIC RESONANCE IMAGING
S07RR-07005-26 0340 (NSS) MCCONNELL, SUSAN Biomedical research support DEVELOPMENT OF MAMMALIAN CENTRAL NERVOUS SYSTEM
S07RR-07005-26 0341 (NSS) PRATTO, FELICIA Biomedical research support AUTOMATIC EVALUATION
S07RR-07005-26 0342 (NSS) QUATE, CALVIN F Biomedical research support ATOMIC FORCE MICROSCOPY STUDIES OF MUSCLE PROTEIN STRUCTURE & DYNAMICS
S07RR-07005-26 0343 (NSS) REEVES, BYRON B Biomedical research support PSYCHOLOGY EXPERIMENTS ABOUT TELEVISION VIEWING
S07RR-07006-26 (NSS) ZUCKER, IRVING UNIVERSITY OF CALIF. 2111 BANCROFT WAY STE 530 BERKELEY, CA 94720 Biomedical research support
S07RR-07006-26 0890 (NSS) JOHNSON, NED K Biomedical research support PHYLOGENY OF HAWAIIAN HONEYCREEPERS AS REVEALED BY MTDNA BASE SEQUENCES
S07RR-07006-26 0891 (NSS) DELUMEN, BENITO O Biomedical research support ELUCIDATING FLATULENCE FACTOR IN BEANS: MOLECULAR APPROACH
S07RR-07006-26 0892 (NSS) BRUNS, THOMAS D Biomedical research support FUNGAL MITOCHONDRIAL INTRONS: MOLECULAR EVOLUTIONARY SURVEY
S07RR-07006-26 0893 (NSS) WANG, WILLIAM S-Y Biomedical research support TWIN STUDY OF ADULT FOREIGN LANGUAGE LEARNING ABILITY
S07RR-07006-26 0894 (NSS) MEYER, BARBARA J Biomedical research support ANALYSIS OF X CHROMOSOME ELEMENTS REQUIRED FOR DOSAGE COMPENSATION IN C ELEGANS
S07RR-07006-26 0895 (NSS) RINE, JASPER Biomedical research support GENETIC SUPPRESSION OF ONCOGENIC ALLELES OF RAS ONCOGENES
S07RR-07006-26 0896 (NSS) KANE, CAROLINE M Biomedical research support HIV REGULATION BY TRANSCRIPTION TERMINATION: HUMAN NUCLEAR

PROJECT NO., ORGANIZATIONAL UNIT., INVESTIGATOR, ADDRESS, TITLE

EXTRACTS
S07RR-07006-26 0897 (NSS) NELSON, HILLARY C M Biomedical research support TWO FOLD VERSUS THREE FOLD SYMMETRIC PROTEINS; IMPLICATIONS FOR DNA RECOGNITION
S07RR-07006-26 0898 (NSS) SCHLIWA, MANFRED Biomedical research support IMPROVED SHARED USE IMAGE ANALYSIS CAPABILITY FOR CAMPUS MICROSCOPISTS
S07RR-07006-26 0899 (NSS) BENTLEY, DAVID Biomedical research support CELL SURFACE PHOSPHATIDYLINOSITOL LINKED GLYCOPROTEINS & AXON GUIDANCE
S07RR-07006-26 0900 (NSS) WINOTO, ASTAR Biomedical research support CLONE & CHARACTER OF TCR ALPHA ENHANCER T CELL SPECIFIC TRANSCRIPTION FACTORS
S07RR-07006-26 0901 (NSS) WILLIAMS, MARY ANN Biomedical research support BILE ACID POOL SIZE IN RATS: ROLE OF ESSENTIAL FATTY ACIDS
S07RR-07006-26 0919 (NSS) WAKE, DAVID B Biomedical research support GENETICS OF HYBRIDIZING POPS: INTROGRESSION OF MITOCHONDRIAL DNA; SALAMANDERS
S07RR-07006-26 0920 (NSS) CALDWELL, ROY L Biomedical research support VISUAL PERFORMANCE IN STOMATOPOD CRUSTACEA
S07RR-07006-26 0902 (NSS) OACE, SUSAN M Biomedical research support ABSORPTION & DISTRIBUTION OF VITAMIN B12 IN RAT
S07RR-07006-26 0903 (NSS) FISCHER, ROBERT Biomedical research support GENETIC ANALYSIS OF MEGAGAMETOGENESIS IN ARABIDOPSIS THALIANA
S07RR-07006-26 0904 (NSS) SHIMAMURA, ARTHUR Biomedical research support NEUROBEHAVIORAL ANALYSIS OF AGE RELATED CHANGES IN MEMORY
S07RR-07006-26 0905 (NSS) JONES, ENRICO E Biomedical research support DEVELOPING TREATMENT MANUAL FOR PSYCHOLOGY OF DEPRESSION
S07RR-07006-26 0906 (NSS) HINSHAW, STEPHEN Biomedical research support ANALYSIS OF EXISTING DATA ON PRESCHOOLERS AT RISK FOR BEHAVIORAL DISORDERS
S07RR-07006-26 0907 (NSS) MAULDON, JANE Biomedical research support SOCIOECONOMIC CAUSES & CONSEQUENCES OF CHILDHOOD DISABILITY
S07RR-07006-26 0908 (NSS) MASON, MARY ANN Biomedical research support PATTERNS OF CIVIL COMMITMENT OF MINORS IN CALIFORNIA
S07RR-07006-26 0909 (NSS) MASON, MARY ANN Biomedical research support RACE & SOCIOECONOMIC FACTORS IN ADOLESCENTS: ACCESS TO PSYCHIATRIC HOSPITALS
S07RR-07006-26 0910 (NSS) MIDANIK, LORRAINE Biomedical research support TESTING TWO METHODS TO OBTAIN ACCURATE ESTIMATES OF ALCOHOL CONSUMPTION
S07RR-07006-26 0911 (NSS) ORGANISTA, KURT Biomedical research support MENTAL HLTH SERVICE USE & TREATMENT OUTCOME IN DEPRESSED MEDICAL PATIENT
S07RR-07006-26 0912 (NSS) BERRY, JANE Biomedical research support PHYSICAL & MENTAL HEALTH CORRELATES OF LIFE SATISFACTION ACROSS LIFESPAN
S07RR-07006-26 0913 (NSS) KEELER, THEODORE E Biomedical research support STATISTICAL ANALYSIS OF DETERMINANTS OF HOSPITAL COSTS
S07RR-07006-26 0914 (NSS) ARNOLD, JOHN Biomedical research support NOVEL SYNTHETIC ROUTES TO NEW TYPES OF METALLOPORPHYRINS
S07RR-07006-26 0915 (NSS) DAWSON, KENNETH A Biomedical research support COMPUTATIONAL STRATEGY FOR FOLDING PROTEINS
S07RR-07006-26 0916 (NSS) O'KONSKI, CHESTER Biomedical research support RESEARCH ON NICOTINIC ACETYLCHOLINE RECEPTOR
S07RR-07006-26 0917 (NSS) CAMPOS, JOSEPH J Biomedical research support LOCOMOTION IN VISUAL VESTIBULAR COORDINATION
S07RR-07006-26 0918 (NSS) LICHT, PAUL Biomedical research support NONMAMMALIAN MODEL FOR STUDY OF THYROID HORMONE BINDING PROTEINS IN PLASMA
S07RR-07007-26 (NSS) SHELTON, ROBERT N UNIVERSITY OF CALIFORNIA 275 MRAK HALL DAVIS, CA 95616 Biomedical research support
S07RR-07007-26 0921 (NSS) LA MAR, GERD N Biomedical research support DVLP 2D NMR METHOD TO STUDY PARAMAGNETIC PROTEINS: HEME PEROXIDASES
S07RR-07007-26 0922 (NSS) ROGERS, QUINTON R Biomedical research support NEUROCHEMISTRY OF FEEDING RESPONSE TO AMINO ACIDS
S07RR-07007-26 0923 (NSS) MAKI, AUGUST H Biomedical research support DESIGN & DNA BINDING OF PEPTIDE INTERCALATORS: ANTIBIOTIC, ANTITUMOR DRUGS
S07RR-07007-26 0924 (NSS) MEDRANO, JUAN F Biomedical research support IDENTIFY DNA POLYMORPHISMS IN IGF 1 GENE TO DETECT LINKAGE TO HIGHGROWTH GENE
S07RR-07007-26 0925 (NSS) SCHILLING, JAMES W Biomedical research support ACQUISITION OF DNA SYNTHESIZER & PROTEIN SEQUENCER
S07RR-07008-26 (NSS) FAN, HUNG UNIVERSITY OF CALIFORNIA SCHOOL OF BIOLOGICAL SCIENCES IRVINE, CALIF 92717 Biomedical research support
S07RR-07008-26 0057 (NSS) CALZONE, FRANK J Biomedical research support GENE EXPRESSION DURING EARLY DEVELOPMENT IN SEA URCHINS
S07RR-07008-26 0058 (NSS) FRANK, STEVEN A Biomedical research support EVOLUTION OF SOCIAL BEHAVIOR; SEX; GENETICS
S07RR-07008-26 0059 (NSS) FROSTIG, RONALD D Biomedical research support FUNCTIONAL ORGANIZATION OF PRIMATE VISUAL CORTEX OPTICAL IMAGING
S07RR-07008-26 0060 (NSS) GRAVES, JOSEPH L Biomedical research support EVOLUTION & PHYSIO AGING IN DROSOPHILA; CULTURAL DIVERSITY & STRUCTURE OF SCI
S07RR-07008-26 0061 (NSS) JAMES, ANTHONY A Biomedical research support MALARIA VECTORS; GENE EXPRESSION IN SALIVARY GLANDS OF MOSQUITOES
S07RR-07008-26 0062 (NSS) NEVE, RACHEL L Biomedical research support ALZHEIMERS DISEASE; GENETICS; NEURONAL GROWTH & PLASTICITY; LEARNING & MEMORY
S07RR-07008-26 0063 (NSS) OSBORNE, TIMOTHY F Biomedical research support EXPRESSION OF PROTEINS; CONTROL OF INTRACELLULAR CHOLESTEROL HOMEOSTATIS
S07RR-07008-26 0064 (NSS) CHAMBERLIN, RICHARD Biomedical research support NEUROTRANSMITTER RECEPTOR EXCITATION; MACROLACTONE ANTIBIOTICS
S07RR-07008-26 0065 (NSS) WEIS, ARTHUR E Biomedical research support EVOLUTIONARY ECOLOGY OF PLANT INSECT INTERACTIONS; PLANT POPULATION BIOLOGY
S07RR-07008-26 0066 (NSS) COLBY, BENJAMIN N Biomedical research support ADULT MALE URINE & RELATIONSHIP TO STRESS IN ELDERLY JAPANESE AMERICANS
S07RR-07009-26 (NSS) EISERLING, FREDERICK A UNIVERSITY OF CALIFORNIA 1312 MURPHY HALL LOS ANGELES, CALIF 90024 Biomedical research support
S07RR-07009-26 0938 (NSS) BAKER, BRUCE Biomedical research support SOCIAL SKILLS DEVELOPMENT IN YOUNG CHILDREN W/ DEVELOPMENTAL DISABILITIES
S07RR-07009-26 0939 (NSS) BEATTY, JACK Biomedical research support MAGNETIC RESONANCE IMAGERY
S07RR-07009-26 0926 (NSS) MCEWEN, JOAN Biomedical research support GENETIC ANALYSIS OF CYTOCHROME
S07RR-07009-26 0940 (NSS) MACKAY, DONALD Biomedical research support LANGUAGE & COGNITION
S07RR-07009-26 0941 (NSS) GREENFIELD, PATRICIA Biomedical research support NEURAL & COGNITIVE PROCESSING OF TELEVISION BY ADOLESCENTS
S07RR-07009-26 0942 (NSS) MAYS, VICKIE Biomedical research support AIDS BLACK GAY & BISEXUAL MEN AT RISK
S07RR-07009-26 0943 (NSS) HOLYOAK, KEITH Biomedical research support CONDITIONING & LEARNING W/ IN RULE BASED DEFAULT HIERARCHIES
S07RR-07009-26 0944 (NSS) SIMONS, ROBERT Biomedical research support AUTOMATED QUANTITATION OF BIOLOGICAL ASSAYS
S07RR-07009-26 0945 (NSS) MILLER, JEFFREY Biomedical research support MUTAGENESIS INDUCED BY ENVIRONMENTAL CARCINOGENS
S07RR-07009-26 0946 (NSS) NIERLICH, DONALD Biomedical research support SEQUENCE OF HUMAN R PROTEIN CDNA
S07RR-07009-26 0947 (NSS) ATKINSON, DANIEL Biomedical research support UREA SYNTHESIS IN PH HOMEOSTASIS IN MAMMALS
S07RR-07009-26 0948 (NSS) FOWLER, AUDREE Biomedical research support PROTEIN SEQUENCING
S07RR-07009-26 0949 (NSS) YOUNG, JANIS Biomedical research support PEPTIDE SYNTHESIS
S07RR-07009-26 0927 (NSS) VANVALKENBURGH, BLAI Biomedical research support PREDATORS & PREY THROUGH TIME
S07RR-07009-26 0928 (NSS) ENGELMANN, FRANZ Biomedical research support BINDING PROTEINS FOR JUVENILE HORMONES IN AN INSECT
S07RR-07009-26 0929 (NSS) KASAMATSU, HARUMI Biomedical research support CELLULAR PERMISSIVITY FACTOR & NUCLEAR RETENTION SIGNAL
S07RR-07009-26 0930 (NSS) ERICKSON, JEANNE Biomedical research support GENETICS & BIOCHEMISTRY OF CHLOROPLAST DNA SPLICING
S07RR-07009-26 0931 (NSS) CREWS, STEPHEN Biomedical research support CELL BIOLOGY OF DROSOPHILA DEVELOPMENT
S07RR-07009-26 0932 (NSS) BANERICE, UTBAL Biomedical research support NEUROBIOLOGY OF DROSOPHILA
S07RR-07009-26 0933 (NSS) WEISS, RICHARD Biomedical research support METABOLIC ORGANIZATION IN NEUROSPORA
S07RR-07009-26 0934 (NSS) GREGOR, ROBERT Biomedical research support MUSCULOSKELETAL MODELLING
S07RR-07009-26 0935 (NSS) SCANLAN, TARA Biomedical research support PSYCHO SOCIAL EFFECTS OF COMPETITION
S07RR-07009-26 0936 (NSS) CHANDLER, SCOTT Biomedical research support BRAINSTEM CONTROL OF RHYTHMICAL JAW MOVEMENTS
S07RR-07009-26 0937 (NSS) FELDMAN, JACK Biomedical research support NEURON IMAGING SYSTEM
S07RR-07010-26 (NSS) HOLTEN, DAROLD D UNIV OF CA, OFF OF RES AFF B-132 LIBRARY SOUTH RIVERSIDE, CA 92521-0217 Biomedical research support
S07RR-07011-26 (NSS) ATTIYEH, RICHARD E UNIV OF CALIF, SAN DIEGO GRAD STUDIES & RESEARCH Q-003 LA JOLLA, CALIF 92093 Biomedical research support
S07RR-07012-25 (NSS) PINGS, CORNELIUS J UNIV OF SOUTHERN CALIFORNIA UNIVERSITY PARK ADM 101 LOS ANGELES, CA 90089 Biomedical research support
S07RR-07012-25 0012 (NSS) BIRREN, JAMES E Biomedical research support AGING EFFECTS ON CNS INTEGRITY IDENTIFIED IN COMPONENTS OF PREHENSION
S07RR-07012-25 0013 (NSS) DAWSON, MICHAEL E Biomedical research support PET IMAGING & AUTONOMIC ORIENTING IN SCHIZOPHRENIA
S07RR-07012-25 0014 (NSS) DEONIER, RICHARD C Biomedical research support F PLASMID ORIT: STRUCTURE, FUNCTION, & PROTEIN BINDING: TRA OPERON
S07RR-07012-25 0015 (NSS) HEFTI, FRANZ F Biomedical research support ISOLATION OF DORAMINERGIC CELL SPECIFIC GENES PARKINSONS DISEASE, MPTP
S07RR-07012-25 0016 (NSS) LEFEVRE, JUDITH A Biomedical research support SOCIAL & ENDOCRINE EFFECT ON SEXUALITY IN MID LIFE: FEMALE SEXUALITY MENOPAUSAL
S07RR-07012-25 0017 (NSS) MCCLURE, WILLIAM Biomedical research support CNIDARIAN NEURO MUSCULAR SYSTEM
S07RR-07012-25 0018 (NSS) MCFALL-NAGAI, MARGAR Biomedical research support BACTERIAL SYMBIONTS IN HOST TISSUE MORPHOGENESIS: LUMINESCENCE, VIBRIO FISCHERI
S07RR-07012-25 0019 (NSS) MEDNICK, SARNOFF A Biomedical research support LINKAGE STUDIES IN SCHIZOPHRENIA: GENES
S07RR-07012-25 0020 (NSS) RAINE, ADRIAN Biomedical research support FRONTAL LOBE DISFUNCTION IN SCHIZOIDAL PERSONALITY DISORDER: PSYCHOPHYSIOLOGY
S07RR-07012-25 0021 (NSS) REARDON, KATHLEEN Biomedical research support DOCUMENTARY DEVELOPMENT BREAST CANCER RECOVERY
S07RR-07012-25 0022 (NSS) SAKAI, DENNIS D Biomedical research support GENE EXPRESSION IN IMMORTALIZED PITUITARY CELLS: PROLACTIN, GH, ONCOGENE
S07RR-07012-25 0023 (NSS) THOMPSON, RICHARD Biomedical research support NEURONAL PLASTICITY & MEMORY
S07RR-07012-25 0024 (NSS) ZELINSKY, ELIZABETH Biomedical research support PROCESSING RATE & LANGUAGE COMPREHENSION IN ELDERLY PSYCHOLINGUISTICS
S07RR-07012-25 0025 (NSS) ZEMKE, RUTH Biomedical research support KINEMATICS OF REACH IN INDIVIDUALS W/ CEREBRAL PALSY: MOTOR CONTROL VELOCITY
R03RR-07013-01 (AR) LA REGINA, MARIE C ST LOUIS UNIVERSITY 1402 S GRAND BLVD ST LOUIS, MO 63104-0250 Characterization of hereditary cerebellar ataxia in rats

S07RR-07013-26 (NSS) DUBIN, MARK W UNIVERSITY OF COLORADO CAMPUS BOX 40 BOULDER, COLO 80309 Biomedical research support
S07RR-07013-26 0950 (NSS) WINEY, MARK E Biomedical research support GENETIC ANALYSIS OF YEAST SPINDLE POLE BODY DUPLICATION
S07RR-07013-26 0951 (NSS) STORMO, GARY D Biomedical research support BIOCHEMICAL ANALYSIS OF PROTEIN & DNA INTERACTIONS
S07RR-07013-26 0952 (NSS) COPLEY, SHELLEY D Biomedical research support MECHANISTIC STUDIES OF 4 CHLOROBENZOATE DEHALOGENASE; ACINETOBACTER SP 4CB 1
S07RR-07013-26 0953 (NSS) FULKER, DAVID Biomedical research support COLORADO ADOPTION PROJECT: ADOLESCENT MENTAL HEALTH
S07RR-07013-26 0954 (NSS) POLSON, PETER Biomedical research support REAL TIME COMPUTER LABORATORY FOR COGNITIVE RESEARCH
S07RR-07013-26 0955 (NSS) MIKLOWITZ, DAVID J Biomedical research support FAMILY EXPRESSED EMOTION & RELATIVES & PATIENT ATTRIBUTES; BIPOLAR DISORDER
S07RR-07013-26 0956 (NSS) OLSON, RICHARD Biomedical research support COMPUTER BASED TRAINING FOR DISABLED READERS
S07RR-07013-26 0957 (NSS) BOGGIANO, ANN Biomedical research support OBSERVATION OF TEACHER STUDENT INTERACTIONS
S07RR-07013-26 0958 (NSS) VAN GERVEN, DENNIS Biomedical research support BIOMED EVAL; TRACE ELEMENT CONCENTRATIONS IN BONE; PATTERNS OF DIET & DISEASE
S07RR-07013-26 0959 (NSS) DUFOUR, DARNA Biomedical research support ACTIVITY MONITORS IN ASSESSMENT OF ENERGY EXPENDITURE; HEART RATE
S07RR-07013-26 0960 (NSS) RAMIREZ, E FRED Biomedical research support OPTICAL CONTROL OF FOREIGN PROTEIN PRODUCTION RECOMBINANT BACTERIA
S07RR-07013-26 0961 (NSS) BRADSHAW, GARY Biomedical research support JOINT SPEECH LAB; LINGUISTICS & PSYCHOLOGY & COMPUTER SCI
S07RR-07013-26 0962 (NSS) HAND, STEVEN C Biomedical research support BIOCHEMICAL & PHYSIOLOGICAL MECHANISMS OF INVERTEBRATE DORMANCY
S07RR-07013-26 0963 (NSS) BEKOFF, ANNE C Biomedical research support NEURAL BASIS OF DEVELOPMENT OF COORDINATED BEHAVIORS
S07RR-07013-26 0964 (NSS) HANKEN, JAMES Biomedical research support CRANIAL PATTERN FORMATION & MORPHOGENESIS
S07RR-07013-26 0965 (NSS) SNYDER, GREG Biomedical research support CAPILLARY GROWTH IN MUSCLE; CNS; MICRO CIRCULATION
S07RR-07013-26 0966 (NSS) EATON, ROBERT C Biomedical research support MECHANISMS FOR MOVEMENT COORDINATION IN HEALTH & TRAMA
S07RR-07013-26 0967 (NSS) MAZZEO, ROBERT S Biomedical research support INFLUENCE OF AGE ON EXTENT OF MUSCLE DAMAGE & INJURY FROM ECCENTRIC EXERCISE
S07RR-07013-26 0968 (NSS) PARSONS, DORABETH Biomedical research support 3 D RECONSTRUCTION OF CAPILLARY VASCULAR BED IN SKELETAL MUSCLE; EXERCISE
S07RR-07013-26 0969 (NSS) PARSONS, DORABETH Biomedical research support MOLECULAR BASIS FOR NU6 1 TUMORIGENICITY
S07RR-07014-26 (NSS) GIOLAS, THOMAS G UNIVERSITY OF CONNECTICUT U-133, 438 WHITNEY RD EXT STORRS, CT 06269 Biomedical research support
S07RR-07015-26 (NSS) ADELBERG, EDWARD A YALE UNIVERSITY 320 YORK ST, 117 HGS NEW HAVEN, CT 06520 Biomedical research support
S07RR-07015-26 0609 (NSS) REGAN, L Biomedical research support PROTEIN STRUCTURE & CATALYSIS
S07RR-07015-26 0598 (NSS) PATON, MARTHA Biomedical research support DEVELOPMENT OF VISUAL NEURAL SYSTEM IN VERTEBRATES
S07RR-07015-26 0599 (NSS) NELSON, TIMOTHY M Biomedical research support CELL SPECIFIC GENE EXPRESSION & REGULATORY GENES IN MAIZE DEVELOPMENT
S07RR-07015-26 0600 (NSS) SNYDER, MICHAEL Biomedical research support CHROMOSOME REPLICATION & SEGREGATION IN YEAST; YEAST & E COLI VECTORS
S07RR-07015-26 0601 (NSS) GOLDSMITH, MARY HELE Biomedical research support PLANT PHYSIOLOGY, HORMONE ACTION & TRANSPORT
S07RR-07015-26 0602 (NSS) DONEGAN, NELSON Biomedical research support PSYCHOBIOLOGY OF LEARNING
S07RR-07015-26 0603 (NSS) FORSCHER, PAUL Biomedical research support CYTOSKELETAL PROTEIN DYNAMICS & NEURONAL FUNCTION
S07RR-07015-26 0604 (NSS) SMITH, STEVEN Biomedical research support STRUCTURE & MECHANISM OF VISUAL PIGMENTS
S07RR-07015-26 0605 (NSS) TARR, MICHAEL Biomedical research support HUMAN VISUAL PERCEPTION
S07RR-07015-26 0606 (NSS) KAZDIN, ALAN Biomedical research support DEVELOPMENTAL PSYCHOPATHOLOGY IN CHILDHOOD DISORDERS
S07RR-07015-26 0607 (NSS) BROWNELL, K Biomedical research support EATING DISORDERS
S07RR-07015-26 0608 (NSS) GONDA, D Biomedical research support PROTEIN DEGRADATION
S07RR-07015-26 0610 (NSS) SHARP, P Biomedical research support PSYCHOBIOLOGY
S07RR-07015-26 0611 (NSS) RUDDLE, FRANK Biomedical research support TRANSGENIC ANIMALS
S07RR-07016-18 (NSS) STETSON, MILTON H UNIVERSITY OF DELAWARE LIFE & HLTH SCI 117 WOLF HALL NEWARK, DE 19716 Biomedical research support
S07RR-07016-18 0346 (NSS) BURNSIDE, JOAN Biomedical research support DEVELOPMENTAL EXPRESSION OF AVIAN GROWTH HORMONE RECEPTORS
S07RR-07016-18 0347 (NSS) WHITE, HAROLD B Biomedical research support STRUCTURE & FUNCTION OF VITAMIN TRANSPORT PROTEINS FROM EGGS
S07RR-07016-18 0348 (NSS) WHITE, HAROLD B Biomedical research support DIRECT TRANSFER OF DIETARY VITAMINS TO OOCYTE
S07RR-07016-18 0349 (NSS) TABER, DOUGLASS F Biomedical research support INTRAMOLECULAR DIENE CYCLOZIRCONATION
S07RR-07016-18 0350 (NSS) IZARD, CARROLL E Biomedical research support INFANTS EMOTION EXPRESSION STYLES & LATER COMPETENCE
S07RR-07016-18 0351 (NSS) IZARD, CARROLL E Biomedical research support INFANTS EMOTION EXPRESSION STYLES & LATER COMPETENCE
S07RR-07016-18 0352 (NSS) NORTHMORE, DAVID Biomedical research support TRACKING VISUAL RECOVERY DURING OPTIC NERVE REGENERATION
S07RR-07016-18 0353 (NSS) SIMONS, ROBERT F Biomedical research support FRONTAL & PARIETAL P300 RESPONSE IN PSYCHOSIS PRONE YOUNG ADULTS
S07RR-07016-18 0354 (NSS) ALLEN, DEBORAH E Biomedical research support ALPHA ADRENORECEPTORS IN COLD INDUCED DIURESIS
S07RR-07016-18 0355 (NSS) CIULLA, ANNA P Biomedical research support DIETARY INTAKE ON BONE DENSITY, BODY COMPOSITION & HORMONAL LEVELS
S07RR-07016-18 0356 (NSS) DELEON, PATRICIA A Biomedical research support MOTILITY KARYOTYPIC OF SPERM: "SUN UP" PROCEDURE
S07RR-07016-18 0357 (NSS) DELEON, PATRICIA A Biomedical research support KARYOTYPIC OF SPERM: FERTILIZING ABILITY IN VITRO & IN VIVO
S07RR-07016-18 0358 (NSS) MASER, RAELENE E Biomedical research support DIABETIC NEUROPATHY & MICROANGIOPATHY IN DIABETES MELLITUS
S07RR-07016-18 0359 (NSS) SCHMIEG, FLORENCE I Biomedical research support TRANSFORMATION RELATED PROPERTIES OF NORMAL & MUTATED P53 GENES
S07RR-07016-18 0360 (NSS) SCHOLZ, JOHN P Biomedical research support NEUROMUSCULAR COORDINATION: DYNAMIC PATTERN ANALYSIS OF MANUAL LIFTING
S07RR-07016-18 0361 (NSS) SNYDER-MACKLER, LYNN Biomedical research support ELECTRICAL STIMULATION EXERCISE TREATMENT IN PTS AFTER CRUCIATE LIGAMENT SURGERY
S07RR-07016-18 0362 (NSS) WILSON, DIANE Biomedical research support PEPTIDE TRANSPORT IN HUMAN INTESTINAL BRUSH BORDER MEMBRANE VESICLES
S07RR-07016-18 0363 (NSS) STETSON, MILTON H Biomedical research support SLHS CENTRAL ANIMAL
S07RR-07016-18 0364 (NSS) STETSON, MILTON H Biomedical research support BIOMED EQUIPMENT
S07RR-07019-26 (NSS) COATES, ANTHONY G GEORGE WASHINGTON UNIVERSITY 2121 I STREET NW RM 601 WASHINGTON, DC 20052 Biomedical research support
S07RR-07019-26 0067 (NSS) JASNOSKI, MARY L Biomedical research support RELAXATION IMAGERY & IMMUNE SYSTEM
S07RR-07019-26 0068 (NSS) CAPLAN, ROBERT D Biomedical research support ANTECEDENTS OF SOCIAL SUPPORT: FEASIBILITY STUDY: COUPLE INTERACTION
S07RR-07019-26 0069 (NSS) ABRAVANEL, EUGENE Biomedical research support COGNITIVE BEHAVIORAL SEQUELAE OF IN UTERO DRUG EXPOSURE: TERATOMA, INFANT
S07RR-07019-26 0070 (NSS) ROHRBECK, CYNTHIA Biomedical research support CHILD SELF CONTROL RATING: CHRONIC ILLNESSES & EXTERNALIZING MENTAL DISORDERS
G20RR-07020-01 (AR) DETOLLA, LOUIS J UNIVERSITY OF MARYLAND SCH OF MEDICINE/10 SOUTH PINE BALTIMORE, MD 21201 Developing and improving institutional animal resources
S07RR-07020-26 (NSS) JOHNSON, ROBERT M FLORIDA STATE UNIVERSITY 109 HERB MORGAN BUILDING TALLAHASSEE, FLA 32306 Biomedical research support
S07RR-07020-26 0528 (NSS) JOHNSON, ROBERT M Biomedical research support NO RESEARCH SUBPROJECTS
S07RR-07021-26 (NSS) WRAY, SUSAN D UNIVERSITY OF FLORIDA 219 GRINTER HALL GAINESVILLE, FL 32611 Biomedical research support
S07RR-07021-26 0629 (NSS) WRAY, SUSAN Biomedical research support NO RESEARCH SUBPROJECTS
S07RR-07022-24 (NSS) SCHNEIDERMAN, NEIL UNIVERSITY OF MIAMI BOX 248293 CORAL GABLES, FLA 33124 Biomedical research support
S07RR-07023-26 (NSS) STEVENS, ANN R EMORY UNIV, 303B SCH OF DENT 1462 CLIFTON ROAD, N E ATLANTA, GEORGIA 30322 Biomedical research support
S07RR-07023-26 0970 (NSS) GOODMAN, SHERRYL H Biomedical research support MATERNAL DEPRESSION ON CHILD DEVELOPMENT
S07RR-07023-26 0971 (NSS) HERNDON, JAMES G Biomedical research support GONADAL FUNCTION & SEXUAL BEHAVIOR IN MALE RHESUS MONKEY
S07RR-07023-26 0972 (NSS) HARZILLI, LUIGI G Biomedical research support SHARED DISK & TAPE BACK UP SYSTEM FOR CHEMISTRY
S07RR-07023-26 0973 (NSS) HEILL, DARRYL B Biomedical research support BRAIN REWARD SYSTEMS & STIMULANT DRUG ABUSE
S07RR-07023-26 0974 (NSS) PADUA, ALBERT Biomedical research support ACQUISITION OF SILICON GRAPHICS COMPUTER
S07RR-07023-26 0975 (NSS) TIGGES, JOHANNES V Biomedical research support AGE RELATED CHANGES IN MOTOR CORTEX OF RHESUS MONKEY
S07RR-07023-26 0976 (NSS) YUE, KWOK T Biomedical research support RAMAN STUDIES OF PHOSPHOLIPIDS
S07RR-07023-26 0977 (NSS) ELMER, WILLIAM A Biomedical research support CRYOSTAT
S07RR-07023-26 0978 (NSS) FAMILY, FEREYDOON Biomedical research support FRACTAL ANALYSIS OF MORPHOLOGY OF BACTERIAL & FUNGAL GROWTH ON AGAR PLATES
S07RR-07023-26 0979 (NSS) ELLIS, HILARY Biomedical research support PATTERN FORMATION DURING SENSORY ORGAN DEVELOPMENT IN DROSOPHILA
S07RR-07023-26 0980 (NSS) KLUMPP, SHERRY Biomedical research support DETERMINATION OF PATHOGENICITY OF GROUP 2 AEROTOLERANT CAMPYLOBACTER
S07RR-07023-26 0981 (NSS) WILSON, MARK Biomedical research support ACQUISITION OF EQUIPMENT FOR ASSAY SERVICES LABORATORY
S07RR-07023-26 0982 (NSS) BROWN, PETER Biomedical research support HPLC BASED ANALYSIS OF DIET, BEHAVIOR, & ENDOCRINE FUNCTION
S07RR-07023-26 0983 (NSS) LIEBESKIND, LANNY Biomedical research support REQUEST FOR ACQUISITION OF AUTOMATIC NMR SAMPLER DEVICE
S07RR-07023-26 0984 (NSS) NEILL, DARRYL Biomedical research support REQUEST FOR MICROCOMPUTER
S07RR-07024-26 (NSS) TORNABENE, THOMAS G GEORGIA INST OF TECHNOLOGY SCHOOL OF APPLIED BIOLOGY ATLANTA, GA 30332-0420 Biomedical research support
S07RR-07024-26 0039 (NSS) MILLARD-STAFFORD, ME Biomedical research support FLUID REQUIREMENTS IN MEN & WOMEN DURING PROLONGED RUNNING IN HEAT
S07RR-07024-26 0040 (NSS) GOKHALE, A M Biomedical research support DEVELOPMENT OF STEREOLOGICAL METHODS FOR BIOLOGICAL STRUCTURES
S07RR-07024-26 0041 (NSS) CHOI, JUNG H Biomedical research support ATTACHMENT OF AGROBACTERIUM TO COMPATIBLE & INCOMPATIBLE PLANT CELLS
S07RR-07024-26 0042 (NSS) GAUSS, PETER H Biomedical research support GENETIC & RECOMBINANT DNA ANALYSES OF E COLI DHG GENE
S07RR-07024-26 0043 (NSS) HALL, DWIGHT H Biomedical research

PROJECT NO., ORGANIZATIONAL UNIT., INVESTIGATOR, ADDRESS, TITLE

support GENETIC STUDIES OF CATALYTIC RNA: SELF SPLICING INTRONS OF BACTERIAL VIRUS T4
S07RR-07024-26 0044 (NSS) **JONES, WILLIAM J** Biomedical research support EVALUATION OF ANAEROBIC PATHWAYS FOR BIOCONVERSION OF TOXIC POLLUTANTS
S07RR-07024-26 0045 (NSS) **MUZZY, JOHN D** Biomedical research support PROSTHETIC INTERVERTEBRAL DISC
S07RR-07024-26 0046 (NSS) **IKEDA, RICHARD A** Biomedical research support RECOMBINANT HUMAN TRANSFERRIN STRUCTURE & FUNCTION RELATIONSHIP
S07RR-07024-26 0047 (NSS) **TOLBERT, LAREN M** Biomedical research support ENZYMATIC EPOXIDATION OF ARYLOLEFINS
S07RR-07024-26 0048 (NSS) **HUNT, WILLIAM D** Biomedical research support NOVEL ULTRASONIC SCHEME TO MONITOR CAROTID PLAQUE PROGRESSION
S07RR-07024-26 0049 (NSS) **PATTON, JAMES S** Biomedical research support ANALYSES OF DYNAMICS OF HUMAN SWALLOWING
S07RR-07024-26 0050 (NSS) **SPARLING, PHILLIP B** Biomedical research support COMPARISON OF BODY COMPOSITION METHODS IN BLACK & WHITE WOMEN
S07RR-07024-26 0051 (NSS) **WARTELL, ROGER M** Biomedical research support DETECTING BASE CHANGES IN DNA: TEMPERATURE GRADIENT GEL ELECTROPHORESIS
S07RR-07024-26 0052 (NSS) **CATRAMBONE, RICHARD** Biomedical research support ANALOGICAL REASONING
S07RR-07024-26 0026 (NSS) **CHOI, JUNG H** Biomedical research support CLONING POTENTIAL TYROSINE PROTEIN KINASE GENES IN PLANTS USING PCR
S07RR-07024-26 0027 (NSS) **DUSENBERY, DAVID** Biomedical research support SUBLETHAL TOXICITY OF METALLIC IONS IN SOIL
S07RR-07024-26 0028 (NSS) **EDMONDS, PAUL** Biomedical research support BACTERIAL ADHESION & INVASION OF ENDOTHELIAL CELLS IN VITRO
S07RR-07024-26 0029 (NSS) **HALL, DWIGHT H** Biomedical research support CLONING DIHYDROFOLATE REDUCTASE GENE OF PSEUDOMONAS MALTOPHILIA: ANTIBIOTIC THER
S07RR-07024-26 0030 (NSS) **JONES, WILLIAM J** Biomedical research support BIODEGRADATION OF TOXIC ORGANIC CHEMICALS UNDER ANAEROBIC CONDITIONS
S07RR-07024-26 0031 (NSS) **MATHIS, JAMES** Biomedical research support DEVELOPMENT OF A METHOD FOR DETECTION OF RARE FORMS OF CYSTIC FIBROSIS
S07RR-07024-26 0032 (NSS) **WARTELL, ROGER** Biomedical research support SCANNING TUNNELING MICROSCOPY OF TETHERED NUCLEIC ACIDS
S07RR-07024-26 0033 (NSS) **GELBAUM, LESLIE T** Biomedical research support STRUCTURE OF TELOMERIC DNA OLIGONUCLEOTIDES
S07RR-07024-26 0034 (NSS) **YOGANATHAN, AJIT** Biomedical research support VISUALIZATION OF INTRACARDIAC BLOOD FLOW
S07RR-07024-26 0035 (NSS) **BRIGGS, MARTHA** Biomedical research support MOLTEN GLOBULE STATE AS A MODEL FOR PROTEIN FOLDING INTERMEDIATES
S07RR-07024-26 0036 (NSS) **IKEDA, RICHARD** Biomedical research support RECOMBINANT HUMAN SERUM TRANSFERRIN
S07RR-07024-26 0037 (NSS) **LIOTTA, CHARLES** Biomedical research support ASYMMETRIC SYNTHESIS USING CHIRAL PHASE TRANSFER CATALYSIS
S07RR-07024-26 0038 (NSS) **MAY, SHELDON** Biomedical research support DISCOVERY OF A NEW ENZYME
S07RR-07024-26 0053 (NSS) **CORSO, GREGORY M** Biomedical research support COMPUTER INTERFACE FOR LEARNING IMPAIRED CHILD
S07RR-07024-26 0054 (NSS) **TORNABENE, THOMAS G** Biomedical research support BIOMEDICAL RESEARCH SUPPORT
S07RR-07025-26 (NSS) **KEY, JOE L** UNIVERSITY OF GEORGIA 608 GRADUATE STUDIES RES CTR ATHENS, GA 30602 Biomedical research support
S07RR-07025-26 0986 (NSS) **BERDANIER, CAROLYN D** Biomedical research support MEASURE O2 USE, CA, K NA, & PH CHANGE BY PREP OF ISOLATED MITOCHONDRIA
S07RR-07025-26 0987 (NSS) **BRODY, GENE H** Biomedical research support FAMILY PROCESSES & COMPETENCE IN RURAL BLACK FAMILIES
S07RR-07025-26 0988 (NSS) **CHU, CHUNG K** Biomedical research support SYNTHESIS & BIOTRANSFORMATION OF HIV PRODRUGS
S07RR-07025-26 0989 (NSS) **DAMIAN, RAYMOND T** Biomedical research support BABOON MODEL FOR ACUTE SCHISTOSOMIASIS
S07RR-07025-26 0990 (NSS) **KEY, JOE L** Biomedical research support DETAILED STUDY OF AUXIN DOWN REGULATED GENE EXPRESSION
S07RR-07025-26 0991 (NSS) **MARTIN, ROY J** Biomedical research support REGULATION OF ENERGY BALANCE NUTRITION
S07RR-07025-26 0992 (NSS) **MORIARTY, C MICHAEL** Biomedical research support CELLULAR TOXICITY OF LOW LEVEL ENVIRONMENTAL LEAD
S07RR-07025-26 0993 (NSS) **TARLETON, RICK L** Biomedical research support IMMUNOREGULATION IN EXPERIMENTAL CHAGAS DISEASE
S07RR-07025-26 0994 (NSS) **ZEICHNER, AMOS** Biomedical research support CIGARETTE SMOKING & NICOTINE: CARDIOVASCULAR RESPONSE & PAIN PERCEPTION
S07RR-07026-26 (NSS) **GIBBONS, BARBARA H** UNIVERSITY OF HAWAII 2540 MAILE WAY SPAULDING 255 HONOLULU, HAWAII 96822 Biomedical research support
S07RR-07026-26 0005 (NSS) **WOMERSLEY, CHRISTOPH** Biomedical research support METAB & CALORIES ON FLUORESCENT AGE PIGMENT ACCUMULATION; VERTEBRATE MYOCARDIUM
S07RR-07026-26 0006 (NSS) **BITTERMAN, M E** Biomedical research support IMPROVEMENT OF SHARED FACILITY
S07RR-07026-26 0000 (NSS) **LAU, ALAN F** Biomedical research support DEVELOPMENT OF AN IN VITRO ASSAY FOR TUMOR CELL INVASIVENESS
S07RR-07026-26 0001 (NSS) **PATTERSON, GREGORY M** Biomedical research support REPLACEMENT DRIVE MOTOR FOR SORVALL CENTRIFUGE, CULTURE FACILITY
S07RR-07026-26 0007 (NSS) **HARTLINE, DANIEL K** Biomedical research support PARTIAL SUPPORT FOR TUNABLE ARGON LASER
S07RR-07026-26 0008 (NSS) **PALUMBI, STEPHEN R** Biomedical research support BINDING IN FERTILIZATION FAILURE OF SEA URCHINS
S07RR-07026-26 0002 (NSS) **RUBEN, PETER C** Biomedical research support STEADY STATE VOLTAGE DEPENDENCE OF SODIUM CHANNEL ACTIVATION & SLOW INACTIVATION
S07RR-07026-26 0003 (NSS) **STARKUS, JOHN G** Biomedical research support SODIUM CONDUCTANCE CONTROL IN GIANT AXON
S07RR-07026-26 0004 (NSS) **TIUS, MARCUS A** Biomedical research support FUNCTIONALIZED CANNABINOIDS
S07RR-07026-26 0009 (NSS) **PATEK, PAUL Q** Biomedical research support SOMATIC EVOLUTION OF CANCER; IMMUNE SYSTEM IN PREVENTION OF TUMORIGENESIS
S07RR-07026-26 0010 (NSS) **SIMON, CHRIS** Biomedical research support DIRECT SEQUENCING OF MITOCHONDRIAL 12S GENE FROM ENZYMATICALLY AMPLIFIED DNA
S07RR-07026-26 0995 (NSS) **ALLEN, RICHARD D** Biomedical research support CYTOPLASMIC DYNEINS ROLE IN VESICULAR TRANSPORT
S07RR-07026-26 0996 (NSS) **COOKE, IAN M** Biomedical research support CULTURED PEPTIDERGIC NEURONS: ELECTRICAL & SECRETORY & MORPHOLOGICAL CORRELATES
S07RR-07026-26 0997 (NSS) **GIBBONS, BARBARA H** Biomedical research support PROPERTIES OF DYNEIN ISOENZYMES
S07RR-07026-26 0998 (NSS) **GIBBONS, IAN R** Biomedical research support STRUCTURAL BASIS OF SPERMATOZOAN MOTIVITY
S07RR-07026-26 0999 (NSS) **HADFIELD, MICHAEL G** Biomedical research support INDUCTION OF METAMORPHOSIS IN MOLLUSCAN LARVAE
S07RR-07027-26 (NSS) **WEBSTER, DALE A** ILLINOIS INST OF TECHNOLOGY 3300 S FEDERAL STREET CHICAGO, ILL 60616 Biomedical research support
S07RR-07027-26 0011 (NSS) **JAEGER, ROBERT J** Biomedical research support BIOMECHANICS & NEURAL CONTROL OF N LINK STRUCTURES
S07RR-07027-26 0012 (NSS) **LONGWORTH, JAMES W** Biomedical research support PHOTOSENSITIZATION OF AQUEOUS MODEL SYSTEMS BY HYPERICIN
S07RR-07027-26 0013 (NSS) **FILLER, ROBERT** Biomedical research support VARIABLE TEMPERATURE CONTROLLERS FOR NTC 300 NMR SPECTROMETER
S07RR-07027-26 0014 (NSS) **WEBSTER, DALE A** Biomedical research support ENERGY TRANSDUCTION BY NA+ MOTIVE CYTOCHROME O TERMINAL OXIDASE IN VITREOSCILLA
S07RR-07027-26 0015 (NSS) **BEISSINGER, RICHARD** Biomedical research support LIPOSOME ENCAPSULATED HEMOGLOBIN AS RED BLOOD CELL SUBSTITUTE
S07RR-07028-26 (NSS) **COHEN, DAVID H** NORTHWESTERN UNIVERSITY 633 CLARK STREET EVANSTON, IL 60208 Biomedical research support
S07RR-07028-26 0016 (NSS) **SCHWARTZ, NEENA B** Biomedical research support CENTER FOR REPRODUCTIVE SCIENCE
S07RR-07028-26 0017 (NSS) **KRAUS, NINA** Biomedical research support AUDITORY EVOKED POTENTIAL CORRELATES OF AUDITORY PROCESSING
S07RR-07028-26 0018 (NSS) **MATTESON, RANA L** Biomedical research support HEMISPHERIC DIFF IN PERCEPTUAL PROCESSING: VISUAL DISEMBEDDING & GESTALT CLOSURE
S07RR-07028-26 0019 (NSS) **RUNDELL, MARY K** Biomedical research support FUNCTION OF SIMIAN VIRUS 40 SMALL T ANTIGEN
S07RR-07028-26 0020 (NSS) **LOGEMANN, JERI A** Biomedical research support NEUROMUSCULAR CONTROL OF NORMAL & ABNORMAL SWALLOWING
S07RR-07028-26 0021 (NSS) **SCWARTZ, NEENA B** Biomedical research support ENVIRONMENTAL & HORMONAL INTERPLAY OF OVULATION
S07RR-07029-26 (NSS) **LAUMANN, EDWARD O** UNIVERSITY OF CHICAGO 1126 E 59TH STREET CHICAGO, IL 60637 Biomedical research support
S07RR-07029-26 0022 (NSS) **GROSSMAN, PETER** Biomedical research support BEHAVIORAL & METABOLIC EFFECTS OF CHRONIC BRAIN INFUSIONS OF INSULIN
S07RR-07029-26 0023 (NSS) **HERDT, GILBERT** Biomedical research support STABILITY & CHARGED IN SEXUAL IDENTITY
S07RR-07029-26 0024 (NSS) **SALLER, RICHARD** Biomedical research support SOCIAL & ECONOMIC RAMIFICATIONS OF ROMAN FAMILY LIFE
S07RR-07030-26 (NSS) **KONISKY, JORDAN** UNIVERSITY OF ILLINOIS 393 MORRILL HALL,505 S GOODWIN URBANA, ILL 61801-3794 Biomedical research support
S07RR-07030-26 0413 (NSS) **SEIGLER, DAVID S** Biomedical research support CYANIDE & CYANOGENIC METABOLISM IN MALACOSOMA AMERICANA
S07RR-07030-26 0378 (NSS) **BAUMGARDNER, DENNIS** Biomedical research support CULTURE OF BLASTOMYCES DERMATITIDIS FROM SOIL
S07RR-07030-26 0379 (NSS) **BELMONT, ANDREW S** Biomedical research support COMPUTATIONAL UNRAVELING OF CHROMOSOME STRUCTURE
S07RR-07030-26 0380 (NSS) **BLACKMAN, RONALD** Biomedical research support MOLECULAR ANALYSIS OF IMAGINAL DISK DEVELOPMENT IN DROSOPHILA
S07RR-07030-26 0414 (NSS) **STUCKI, JOSEPH W** Biomedical research support CHARACTERIZATION OF IRON CATALYSTS IN MINERAL INDUCED LUNG DISEASES
S07RR-07030-26 0381 (NSS) **BOHN, PAUL W** Biomedical research support OPTICAL CHARACTERIZATION OF MOLECULAR ASSEMBLIES
S07RR-07030-26 0382 (NSS) **BOILEAU, RICHARD A** Biomedical research support ENERGY EXPENDITURE IN ELDERLY WOMEN BY DOUBLY LABELED WATER METHOD
S07RR-07030-26 0383 (NSS) **COLES, MICHAEL G H** Biomedical research support FACILITY FOR SOURCE ANALYSIS OF EVENT RELATED BRAIN POTENTIALS
S07RR-07030-26 0415 (NSS) **UZZELL, THOMAS** Biomedical research support VERTEBRATE GENES USING PCR & PLUSED FIELD ELECTROPHORESIS OF DNA
S07RR-07030-26 0416 (NSS) **WAND, A JOSHUA** Biomedical research support PROTEIN STRUCTURE, DYNAMICS & FUNCTION
S07RR-07030-26 0417 (NSS) **WANG, ANDREW H J** Biomedical research support MOLECULAR RECOGNITION IN NUCLEIC ACID SYSTEMS
S07RR-07030-26 0418 (NSS) **WHEELER, BRUCE C** Biomedical research support MICROELECTRODE TECHNIQUES FOR CULTURED NEURONAL NETWORKS
S07RR-07030-26 0419 (NSS) **WHEELER, MATTHEW B** Biomedical research support REGULATION OF EXPRESSION OF MRNA FOR PROTEIN KINASE C IN OVARY
S07RR-07030-26 0420 (NSS) **WRAIGHT, COLIN A** Biomedical research support PHOTOSYNTHETIC REACTIN CENTER OF RHODOBACTER SPHAEROIDES & RHODOPSEUD VIRIDIS
S07RR-07030-26 0384 (NSS) **DELUCIA, EVAN H** Biomedical research support INSTRUMENT FOR MEASUREMENT OF FOLIAGE OPTICAL PROPERTIES & ENVIRONMENTAL LIGHT
S07RR-07030-26 0385 (NSS) **DENMARK, SCOTT E** Biomedical research support SYNTHESIS OF NEW ORGANIC SUBSTANCES
S07RR-07030-26 0386 (NSS) **DLOTT, DANA D** Biomedical research support ULTRAFAST CHEMICAL KINETICS OF SYNTHETIC HEME PROTEINS
S07RR-07030-26 0387 (NSS) **DOE, CHRIS** Biomedical research support DROSOPHILA NEUROGENETICS
S07RR-07030-26 0388 (NSS) **DRACKLEY, JAMES K** Biomedical research support LIPID METABOLISM IN NEONATE
S07RR-07030-26 0389 (NSS) **ESTER, ROBERT A** Biomedical research support NONRUMINANT ANIMAL NUTRITION
S07RR-07030-26 0390 (NSS) **FRIZZELL, LEON A** Biomedical research

support CAVITATION & DIAGNOSTIC ULTRASOUND
S07RR-07030-26 0391 (NSS) GETZ, LOWELL L Biomedical research support MATING SYSTEM OF PRAIRIE VOLE, MICROTUS OCHROGASTER
S07RR-07030-26 0392 (NSS) HAGER, LOWELL P Biomedical research support MICROFLUIDICS M 110T CELL DISRUPTOR
S07RR-07030-26 0393 (NSS) HELMAN, SANDY I Biomedical research support BLOCKER INSENSITIVE NA+ CHANNELS IN EPITHELIAL TISSUES
S07RR-07030-26 0394 (NSS) IRWIN, MICHAEL E Biomedical research support FLIGHT BEHAVIOR OF DISEASE TRANSMITTING INSECTS
S07RR-07030-26 0395 (NSS) JACOBSEN, ERIC N Biomedical research support CHIRAL CAPILLARY COLUMN FOR GAS CHROMATOGRAPHIC SEPARATION OF ENANTIOMERS
S07RR-07030-26 0396 (NSS) JI, LI L Biomedical research support HEART HYPERTROPHY & ISCHEMIC REPERFUSION INJURY
S07RR-07030-26 0397 (NSS) JURASKA, JANICE M Biomedical research support SEX DIFFERENCES IN STRUCTURE OF CEREBRAL CORTEX
S07RR-07030-26 0398 (NSS) KATZ, ABRAM Biomedical research support GLUTAMATE DEHYDROGENASE SYSTEM AS INDICATOR OF OXYGENATION STATE IN HUMAN MUSCLE
S07RR-07030-26 0399 (NSS) KATZENELLENBOGEN, BE Biomedical research support RADIOCHROMATOGRAPHY DETECTOR FOR ESTROGEN RECEPTOR & CYTOCHROMES P450
S07RR-07030-26 0400 (NSS) MILLER, CHARLES G Biomedical research support GENETICS & BIOCHEMISTRY OF INTRACELLULAR PROTEOLYSIS
S07RR-07030-26 0401 (NSS) NEWELL, K M Biomedical research support VISUALIZATION OF HUMAN MOVEMENT DYNAMICS
S07RR-07030-26 0402 (NSS) OAKLEY, BURKS, II Biomedical research support IONIC MECHANISM GLIAL ORIGINS; ELECTRO RETINOGRAM COMPONENTS VERTEBRATE RETINA
S07RR-07030-26 0403 (NSS) ORDAL, GEORGE W Biomedical research support SEQUENCING CHEMOTAXIS GENES FROM BACILLUS SUBTILIS
S07RR-07030-26 0404 (NSS) POTTER, SUSAN M Biomedical research support SULFUR AMINO ACIDS ON REGULATION OF CHOLESTEROL METABOLISM
S07RR-07030-26 0405 (NSS) RAMIREZ, VICTOR D Biomedical research support BIOLOGICAL EFFECTS OF A NOVEL DOPAMINE RELEASING PROTEIN
S07RR-07030-26 0406 (NSS) REIS, JANET Biomedical research support ADOLESCENTS CONCEPTUALIZATION OF DRUG USE
S07RR-07030-26 0407 (NSS) RESKIN, BARBARA Biomedical research support CHANGING SEX COMPOSITION OF HEALTH PROFESSIONALS: PHYSICIANS
S07RR-07030-26 0408 (NSS) RICCIO, GARY E Biomedical research support ENVIRONMENTAL CONSTRAINTS & ADAPTIVE CONTROL OF POSTURE
S07RR-07030-26 0409 (NSS) ROBERTSON, HUGH M Biomedical research support TRANSPOSABLE ELEMENTS IN INSECTS
S07RR-07030-26 0410 (NSS) ROBINSON, GENE E Biomedical research support GENETICS & PHYSIOLOGY OF HONEY BEE SOCIAL BEHAVIOR
S07RR-07030-26 0411 (NSS) ROBINSON, GENE E Biomedical research support MECHANISMS OF BEHAVIORAL PLASTICITY IN A MODEL SYSTEM
S07RR-07030-26 0412 (NSS) ROCHEFORD, TORBERT R Biomedical research support MARKERS OF GENES FOR RESISTANCE TO ASPERGILLUS FLAVUS & AFLATOXIN PRODUCTION
S07RR-07031-26 (NSS) ALBERTS, JEFFREY R INDIANA UNIVERSITY BRYAN HALL 104 BLOOMINGTON, IND 47405 Biomedical research support
S07RR-07031-26 0094 (NSS) KOCEJA, DAVID Biomedical research support CONDITIONING INFLUENCES ON MOTONEURON EXCITABILITY; YOUNG & OLD HUMAN
S07RR-07031-26 0095 (NSS) KOCH, ARTHUR L Biomedical research support ELASTICITY OF WALL OF GRAM NEGATIVE BACTERIUM
S07RR-07031-26 0096 (NSS) KRUSCHKE, JOHN K Biomedical research support CONNECTIONIST MODEL OF CATEGORY LEARNING
S07RR-07031-26 0097 (NSS) LIVELY, CURTIS M Biomedical research support GENETIC BASIS FOR INFECTION BY PARASITIC TREMATODES; SNAIL
S07RR-07031-26 0098 (NSS) MAHLBERG, PAUL G Biomedical research support THC & CBC LOCALIZATION IN MARIHUANA GLANDS; EM IMMUNOCYTOCHEM
S07RR-07031-26 0099 (NSS) MCCLURE, POLLEY A Biomedical research support THERMAL STRESS IN REGULATING MATERNAL & YOUNG INTERACTIONS
S07RR-07031-26 0100 (NSS) MILLER, WAYNE C Biomedical research support STABLE ISOTOPIC MEASUREMENT OF ENERGY EXPENDITURE IN OBESITY
S07RR-07031-26 0101 (NSS) POWELL, BRIAN Biomedical research support INTER SPECIALTY MOBILITY OF PHYSICIANS
S07RR-07031-26 0102 (NSS) RAGLIN, JOHN S Biomedical research support INFLUENCE OF EXERCISE INTENSITY ON MOOD STATE & PHYSIOLOGICAL AROUSAL
S07RR-07031-26 0103 (NSS) RICHMOND, ROLLIN C Biomedical research support DROSOPHILA MODEL SYSTEM DVMT; PSYCHOACTIVE DRUGS
S07RR-07031-26 0104 (NSS) RILEY, JAMES C Biomedical research support EUROPEAN MORTALITY DECLINE
S07RR-07031-26 0105 (NSS) SAXTON, WILLIAM M Biomedical research support MECHANISMS OF INTRACELLULAR MOTILITY; KINESIN HEAVY CHAIN; GENETICS
S07RR-07031-26 0106 (NSS) SCHMIDT, CHARLES Biomedical research support VOCAL ENDURANCE IN TRAINED & UNTRAINED SINGERS
S07RR-07031-26 0107 (NSS) SCHROEDER, DOLORES M Biomedical research support INTERCONNECTIONS OF MARGINAL NEURONS IN AMPHIBIAN SPINAL CORD
S07RR-07031-26 0108 (NSS) SMITH, LINDA B Biomedical research support PARTS & WHOLES IN INFANT PERCEPTION; CUES & SHAPE
S07RR-07031-26 0109 (NSS) STEINMETZ, JOSEPH E Biomedical research support CAUDATE NUCLEUS ACTIVITY & CLASSICAL EYELID CONDITIONING; RABBITS
S07RR-07031-26 0110 (NSS) STRYKER, JEFFREY M Biomedical research support CATALYTIC ASYMMETRIC HYDRIDE REDUCTION
S07RR-07031-26 0111 (NSS) WATSON, MAXINE Biomedical research support RESTRICTION FRAGMENT LENGTH POLYMORPHISMS; FIELD POPULATIONS OF MAYAPPLE
S07RR-07031-26 0112 (NSS) WIDLANSKI, THEODORE Biomedical research support SYNTHESIS & ACTIVITY; SULFONYL ANALOGS OF NUCLEOTIDES ANTI VIRAL AIDS; CANCER
S07RR-07031-26 0113 (NSS) ZOLAN, MIRIAM Biomedical research support MEIOSIS & DNA REPAIR IN COPRINUS CINERUS
S07RR-07031-26 0071 (NSS) BATES, JOHN E Biomedical research support PREPARING FOR 13 YEAR FOLLOW UP; DEPRESSION & AGGRESSION EARLY ADOLESCENTS
S07RR-07031-26 0072 (NSS) BENDER, ALAN D Biomedical research support GENETIC ANALYSIS OF POLARITY DVMT; YEAST; RAS; GTPASE ACTIVATING PROTEIN
S07RR-07031-26 0073 (NSS) BINGHAM, GEOFFREY Biomedical research support CHANGE OF PERSPECTIVE W/ EYEBALL ROTATION & NEAR SPACE PERCEPTION
S07RR-07031-26 0074 (NSS) BONNER, J JOSE Biomedical research support ANALYSIS OF DNA BINDING BY HEAT SHOCK FACTOR OF YEAST
S07RR-07031-26 0075 (NSS) CHOOI, YEAN W Biomedical research support MOLECULAR LEARNING & NEURAL PLASTICITY MEMORY; ALZHEIMERS; DM; PARKINSONS
S07RR-07031-26 0076 (NSS) COHEN, ASHER Biomedical research support COARSE LOCATION MECHANISM FOR FEATURE INTEGRATION IN VISUAL PERCEPTION
S07RR-07031-26 0077 (NSS) COKELY, JEFFREY A Biomedical research support EFFECTS OF AGE & HEARING LOSS ON AUDIOLOGIC MEASURES
S07RR-07031-26 0078 (NSS) COKELY, JEFFREY A Biomedical research support SCORING SPANISH WORD RECOGNITION MEASURES
S07RR-07031-26 0079 (NSS) CORNELL, L L Biomedical research support MORTALITY IN OLD AGE: EFFECT OF INTERGENERATIONAL RELATIONSHIPS
S07RR-07031-26 0080 (NSS) CREAGER, STEPHEN Biomedical research support TRANSPORT OF IONS & MOLECULES IN SUPPORTED MODEL MEMBRANES
S07RR-07031-26 0081 (NSS) CROUCH, MARTHA L Biomedical research support ENZYMES DURING FERTILIZATION IN LYCOPERSICON
S07RR-07031-26 0082 (NSS) DALEKE, DAVID Biomedical research support PHOSPHATIDYLSERINE IN NEUTOPHIL ACTIVATION; INFLAMMATION; ARTHRITIS; HUMAN
S07RR-07031-26 0083 (NSS) DELPH, LYNDA F Biomedical research support COST & TIMING OF REPRODUCTION IN PLANTS: SILENE
S07RR-07031-26 0084 (NSS) DELPH, LYNDA F Biomedical research support COST & TIMING OF REPRODUCTION IN PLANTS; SILENE
S07RR-07031-26 0085 (NSS) FAZIO, BARBARA Biomedical research support LANGUAGE IMPAIRED CHILDRENS MATH & ROTE SEQUENCING ABILITIES
S07RR-07031-26 0086 (NSS) FINN, PETER Biomedical research support SONS OF ALCOHOLICS: STRESS & PERCEPTUAL REACITIVITY & ALCOHOL SENSITIVITY
S07RR-07031-26 0087 (NSS) GAVANSKI, IGOR Biomedical research support NATURAL SAMPLE SPACES & ERRORS OF SUBJECTIVE PROBABILITY
S07RR-07031-26 0088 (NSS) GOH, EDWARD H Biomedical research support QUANTIFYING SERUM CHOLESTEROL TRANSPORT INTO ARTERY IN VITRO
S07RR-07031-26 0089 (NSS) HELLER, KENNETH Biomedical research support NETWORK REINFORCEMENT OF DEPRESSIVE APPRAISALS & COPING IN ELDERLY
S07RR-07031-26 0090 (NSS) HOLTZWORTH-MUNROE, A Biomedical research support IDENTIFYING SOCIAL SKILL DEFICIT IN MARITALLY VIOLENT MEN
S07RR-07031-26 0091 (NSS) JANSSEN, GARY R Biomedical research support TRANSLATION OF LEADERLESS APH TRANSCRIPT IN STREPTOMYCES
S07RR-07031-26 0092 (NSS) JONES, SUSAN SCANLON Biomedical research support MOTIVATIONAL BASES FOR OBJECT GIVING IN SECOND YEAR OF LIFE
S07RR-07031-26 0093 (NSS) JONES, SUSAN SCANLON Biomedical research support SMILING IN EARLY INFANCY
S07RR-07032-26 (NSS) ISOM, GARY E PURDUE UNIVERSITY DIV OF SPON PROG, HOVDE HALL WEST LAFAYETTE, IND 47907 Biomedical research support
S07RR-07032-26 0025 (NSS) RAY, WILLIAM J Biomedical research support MECHANISM OF ACTION OF PHOSPHOTRANSFERASE
S07RR-07032-26 0026 (NSS) MCDANIEL, MARK A Biomedical research support HUMAN MEMORY & CONCEPTUAL PROCESSES
S07RR-07032-26 0027 (NSS) SCHWARTZ, RICHARD G Biomedical research support CHILDRENS MOTOR CONTROL OF WORD PRODUCTION
S07RR-07032-26 0028 (NSS) LONG, GLENIS R Biomedical research support TIME CONSTANTS IN SUPPRESSION OF OTOACOUSTIC EMISSIONS
S07RR-07032-26 0029 (NSS) OTTINGER, DONALD R Biomedical research support DVMT AIDS & HIV PREVENTION PROGRAMS; INCARCERATED ADOLESCENTS
S07RR-07032-26 0030 (NSS) MASON, DANA R Biomedical research support STEREOTYPING BY NURSES OF HOMOSEXUALS & AIDS INTERVENTION
S07RR-07032-26 0031 (NSS) BEAVER, KATHRYN L Biomedical research support AIDS RELATED KNOWLEDGE & ATTITUDE & ANTICIPATED BEHAVIOR; EMERGEN MED PERSONNEL
S07RR-07032-26 0032 (NSS) SEEHAFER, ROGER W Biomedical research support COMPUTER BASED AIDS EDUCATION: USING ACTIVE LEARNING TOOL
S07RR-07032-26 0033 (NSS) GRAHAM, LINDA L Biomedical research support AIDS EDUCATION & PERSONS W/ SERIOUS MENTAL ILLNESS
S07RR-07032-26 0034 (NSS) LINDEN, KATHRYN W Biomedical research support AIDS RELATED KNOWLEDGE & ATTITUDE & ANTICIPATED BEHAVIOR; EMERGEN MED PERSONNEL
S07RR-07032-26 0036 (NSS) PROHOFSKY, EARL W Biomedical research support INTERBASE H BOND OPENING PROBABILITY FOR HELIX IN CONTACT W/ AN ENZYME
S07RR-07032-26 0037 (NSS) WIDDOWS, RICHARD Biomedical research support ECONOMIC IMPACT OF AIDS ON INDIANA FAMILIES
S07RR-07032-26 0035 (NSS) DOHERTY, MICHAEL J Biomedical research support COMPUTER BASED AIDS EDUCATION: USING ACTIVE LEARNING TOOL
S07RR-07032-26 0038 (NSS) DUNN, PETER E Biomedical research support REGULATION OF INSECT ANTIBACTERIAL GENE EXPRESSION
S07RR-07032-26 0039 (NSS) MURIANA, PETER M Biomedical research support BACTERIOCIN PRODUCING LACTIC ACID BACTERIA ISOLATED FROM RETAIL FOODS
S07RR-07032-26 0040 (NSS) LOWNEY, PATRICIA Biomedical research support EXPRESSION OF BRAIN TRANSCRIPTS; LEAN & OBESE ZUCKER RATS
S07RR-07032-26 0041 (NSS) MASON, HOLLY L Biomedical research support STEREOTYPING BY NURSES OF HOMOSEXUALS & AIDS INTERACTION
S07RR-07032-26 0042 (NSS) POWLEY, TERRY L Biomedical research support COMPUTER MEMORY UPGRADE FOR 3 D RECONSTRUCTION FACILITY
S07RR-07032-26 0043 (NSS) GANDOUR, JACKSON T Biomedical research support PROSODIC ASPECTS OF SPEECH AFTER BRAIN DAMAGE
S07RR-07032-26 0044 (NSS) LONG, GLENIS R Biomedical research support OTOACOUSTIC EMISSIONS & THRESHOLD MICROSTRUCTURE
S07RR-07032-26 0045 (NSS) SMITH, ANNE Biomedical research support APPLICATION OF COHERENCE ANALYSIS TO EMG
S07RR-07032-26 0046 (NSS) MORRISON, HARRY Biomedical research support CENTRAL SHARED RESEARCH RESOURCES
S07RR-07032-26 0047 (NSS) ALTERGOTT, KAREN Biomedical research support LIVING W/ CHRONIC ILLNESS: DAILY LIFE, WELL BEING & SOCIAL CONTEXT
S07RR-07032-26 0048 (NSS) HERMODSON, MARK A Biomedical research support FAST PROTEIN LIQUID CHROMATOGRAPHY SYSTEM
S07RR-07032-26 0049 (NSS) CRAMER, WILLIAM A Biomedical research

support TRANSPORT & ENERGY TRANSDUCTION IN ALL MEMBRANES
S07RR-07032-26 0050 (NSS) TAPAROWSKY, ELIZABET Biomedical research support ONCOGENE MEDIATED MULTISTEP TRANSFORMATION OF MAMMALIAN CELLS IN CULTURE
S07RR-07033-26 (NSS) HILLIARD, RICHARD A UNIVERSITY OF NOTRE DAME GRAD SCH - RES DIVISION NOTRE DAME, IN 46556 Biomedical research support
S07RR-07033-26 0051 (NSS) HYDE, DAVID R Biomedical research support DROSOPHILA GA TRANSDUCIN ANALOGUE
S07RR-07033-26 0052 (NSS) CHIBBER, BAKSHY A Biomedical research support MOLECULAR MODELING OF BIOMOLECULES
S07RR-07034-26 (NSS) SWAN, PATRICIA B IOWA STATE UNIVERSITY 211 BEARDSHEAR HALL AMES, IOWA 50011 Biomedical research support
S07RR-07034-26 0066 (NSS) PETRICH, JACOB Biomedical research support PROTEIN MOTIONS RELATED TO FUNCTION USING ULTRASHORT LIGHT PULSES
S07RR-07034-26 0067 (NSS) REDDING, WILLIAM Biomedical research support ADEQUAN & HEALING OF SURGICAL DEFECTS IN DIGITAL FLEXOR TENDONS
S07RR-07034-26 0068 (NSS) SHEN, SHELDON Biomedical research support ISOLATION OF PROTEIN KINASE C GENE(S) FROM SEA URCHIN EGGS
S07RR-07034-26 0063 (NSS) DARK, VERONICA Biomedical research support PARALLEL DISTRIBUTED PROCESSING SOFTWARE
S07RR-07034-26 0054 (NSS) FLATAU, ALISON Biomedical research support CHARACTERIZATION OF SOUND & VIBRATION LEVELS IN AN ARTIFICIAL HEART
S07RR-07034-26 0055 (NSS) GRIFFEN-PIERSON, SHA Biomedical research support COMPETITIVENESS IN WOMEN: IS ANXIETY FACTOR
S07RR-07034-26 0056 (NSS) HENDRICH, SUZANNE Biomedical research support DIETARY PREVENTION OF CANCER: PREDICTIVE MODEL
S07RR-07034-26 0057 (NSS) HSU, WALTER Biomedical research support CALCIUM IN INHIBITION OF EPINEPHRINE & INSULIN SECRETION
S07RR-07034-26 0058 (NSS) INGEBRITSEN, THOMAS Biomedical research support MOLECULAR BASIS FOR SUBSTRATE RECOGNITION BY PROTEIN TYROSINE PHOSPHATASES
S07RR-07034-26 0059 (NSS) JACOBSON, CAROL Biomedical research support IN SITU HYBRIDIZATION FOR MHC GENE TRANSCRIPTS
S07RR-07034-26 0060 (NSS) JERGENS, ALBERT E Biomedical research support HEMOSTATIC PARAMETERS & COLLOIDAL FOR RESUSCITATION OF DAY HEMORRHAGIC SHOCK
S07RR-07034-26 0069 (NSS) WARE, WENDY A Biomedical research support FUROSEMIDE VS FUROSEMIDE + CAPTOPRIL: SERUM, ERTHROCYTE & LYMPHOCYTE HT FAILURE
S07RR-07034-26 0070 (NSS) WITTE, SCOTT T Biomedical research support DIAGNOSTIC EVALUATION OF HYDROGEN SULFIDE EXPOSURE
S07RR-07034-26 0071 (NSS) YOUNGS, CURTIS R Biomedical research support DEVELOPMENT OF VITRIFICATION TECHNIQUES FOR CRYOPRESERVATION OF PORCINE EMBRYOS
S07RR-07034-26 0061 (NSS) JOHANSEN, JORGEN Biomedical research support MOLECULAR ANALYSIS OF AXON FASCICLE SPECIFIC SURFACE GLYCOPROTEINS
S07RR-07034-26 0062 (NSS) KING, DOUGLAS Biomedical research support EXERCISE INDUCED INCREASE IN INSULIN ACTION GLUCOSE TOLERANCE IN ELDERLY
S07RR-07034-26 0063 (NSS) KINTANAR, AGUSTIN Biomedical research support NMR STUDIES OF CU ZN SUPEROXIDE DISMUTASE FROM BRUCELLA ABORTUS
S07RR-07034-26 0064 (NSS) MCCLOSKEY, MICHAEL A Biomedical research support REGULATION OF ION CHANNELS IN MAST CELLS
S07RR-07034-26 0065 (NSS) MILLER-GRABER, PEGGY Biomedical research support CARNOSINE & ITS ROLE IN MUSCULAR BUFFERING CAPACITY
S07RR-07035-26 (NSS) MORRISON, JAMES D UNIVERSITYOF IOWA 201 GILMORE HALL IOWA CITY, IOWA 52242 Biomedical research support
S07RR-07035-26 0097 (NSS) CARPENTER, MARTHA Biomedical research support ETHICS IN ICUS
S07RR-07035-26 0098 (NSS) ZIMBA, LYNN D Biomedical research support CONTOUR INTERACTION AS FUNCTION OF AGE
S07RR-07035-26 0099 (NSS) MOBILY, PAULA R Biomedical research support EXPERIENCES OF CHRONIC BACK PAIN IN ELDERLY
S07RR-07035-26 0100 (NSS) ZEBROWSKI, PATRICIA Biomedical research support MATERNAL SPEECH RATE & CHILDHOOD STUTTERING
S07RR-07035-26 0072 (NSS) ELFENBEIN, JILL Biomedical research support DEVELOPMENTAL PATTERNS OF DURATION DISCRIMINATION
S07RR-07035-26 0073 (NSS) CHENG, CHI-LIEN Biomedical research support ARABIDOPSIS THALIANA & REGULATORY PATHWAY NITRATE REDUCTASE GENE TRANSCRIPTION
S07RR-07035-26 0074 (NSS) DELANEY, CONNIE Biomedical research support COMPUTERIZED DECISION SYSTEM DVMT; MINIMIZE PHLEBITIS: PHASE II
S07RR-07035-26 0075 (NSS) DULANEY, CONNIE Biomedical research support EVALUATE METHOD TO TRANSLATE COMPUTERIZED DATA INTO RESEARCH DATABASE
S07RR-07035-26 0076 (NSS) SIEBES, MARIA Biomedical research support HEMODYNAMIC EFFECT OF STENOSIS COMPLIANCE: CORONARY CIRCULATION FLOW MODEL
S07RR-07035-26 0077 (NSS) SCARPACI, JOSEPH L Biomedical research support PHYSICIANS ROLES IN SHAPING NATL HEALTH INSURANCE; ARGENTINA & URUGUAY
S07RR-07035-26 0078 (NSS) BECKERMANN, CHRISTOP Biomedical research support HEAT & MASS TRANSFER MEASUREMENTS; FREEZING OF BIOLOGICAL MATERIALS
S07RR-07035-26 0079 (NSS) MURHAMMER, DAVID W Biomedical research support HYBRIDOMA PROTEIN SYNTHESIS INCLUDING MABS; ANOXIC CONDITIONS
S07RR-07035-26 0080 (NSS) IRISH, ERIN E Biomedical research support MOLECULAR & DEVELOPMENTAL ANALYSIS OF MERISTEM DETERMINATION IN MAIZE
S07RR-07035-26 0081 (NSS) MURHAMMER, DAVID W Biomedical research support IMPROVE PROTEIN GLYCOSYLATION FIDELITY; BACULOVIRUS & INSECT CELL EXPRESSION
S07RR-07035-26 0082 (NSS) BULECHEK, GLORIA M Biomedical research support ADVENTITIOUS SOUNDS: INDICATOR OF NEED FOR TRACHEAL SUCTIONING
S07RR-07035-26 0083 (NSS) MYERS, GLENN A Biomedical research support DEVELOPMENT OF TOOLS FOR EARLY CLINICAL DETECTION OF VISUAL DEFICITS
S07RR-07035-26 0084 (NSS) SRINIVASAN, PADMINI Biomedical research support DESIGN OF SEMANTICALLY RICH CONCEPT SPACE FOR DIABETES LITERATURE
S07RR-07035-26 0085 (NSS) WEILER, KAY B Biomedical research support IOWA NURSES KNOWLEDGE OF PAIN MANAGEMENT
S07RR-07035-26 0086 (NSS) VERDOLINI-MARSTEN, K Biomedical research support EFFICACY OF TWO METHODS FOR BEHAVIORAL TREATMENT OF VOCAL NODULES
S07RR-07035-26 0087 (NSS) BLEGAN, MARY A Biomedical research support HEALTH CARE CLIENTS USE OF INFLUENCE TACTICS
S07RR-07035-26 0088 (NSS) DOVE, EDWIN L Biomedical research support MATHEMATICAL MODEL OF HEAT REGULATION IN PREMATURE INFANT
S07RR-07035-26 0089 (NSS) FASSLER, JAN Biomedical research support MOLECULAR ANALYSIS OF TRANSCRIPTION TERMINATION FACTORS IN YEAST
S07RR-07035-26 0090 (NSS) GLICK, ORPHA J Biomedical research support COMPUTERIZED HEALTH RISK APPRAISAL OF ELDERLY ADULTS
S07RR-07035-26 0091 (NSS) GREEN, STEVEN J Biomedical research support IDENTIFICATION OF GENES INVOLVED IN NEURONAL DIFFERENTIATION
S07RR-07035-26 0092 (NSS) RODGERS, VICTOR G J Biomedical research support EFFECTS OF TRANSMEMBRANE PRESSURE PULSING IN MICROFILTRATION
S07RR-07035-26 0093 (NSS) YOUNG, MARK A Biomedical research support INTERMOLECULAR INTERACTIONS OF OXYGEN & ARTIFICIAL BLOOD COMPOUNDS
S07RR-07035-26 0094 (NSS) BALON, THOMAS W Biomedical research support GLYCOPHOSTIDYLINOSITOL: MUSCLE METABOLISM IN POST EXERCISE STATE
S07RR-07035-26 0095 (NSS) BLEGAN, MARY A Biomedical research support NURSES JOB SATISFACTION: META ANALYSIS OF LITERATURE
S07RR-07035-26 0096 (NSS) GRASSIAN, VICKI H Biomedical research support SCANNING TUNNELLING MICROSCOPY OF BIOMOLECULES
S07RR-07036-26 (NSS) DONOGHUE, TIMOTHY R KANSAS STATE UNIVERSITY GRAD SCH, ANDERSON HALL 108 MANHATTAN, KANS 66506 Biomedical research support
S07RR-07036-26 0101 (NSS) FORTNER, W G Biomedical research support IMMUNE RESPONSE TO UV INDUCED TUMORS IN VERTEBRATES
S07RR-07036-26 0102 (NSS) JOHNSON, T C Biomedical research support NEUROPEPTIDES & CENTRAL NERVOUS SYSTEM DISEASE
S07RR-07036-26 0103 (NSS) WILSON, F E Biomedical research support PHYSIOLOGY OF HORMONE RESPONSE IN REPRODUCTION
S07RR-07036-26 0104 (NSS) CONSIGLI, R A Biomedical research support BIOLOGICAL FUNCTIONS OF VIRAL STRUCTURAL PROTEINS
S07RR-07036-26 0105 (NSS) WELTI, R Biomedical research support CHARACTERIZATION OF MEMBRANE LIPID DOMAIN
S07RR-07036-26 0106 (NSS) ULUG, E T Biomedical research support SIGNAL TRANSDUCTION IN TRANSFORMED & GROWTH FACTOR TREATED CELLS
S07RR-07036-26 0107 (NSS) FINGLAND, R B Biomedical research support VASCULAR ANATOMY OF CANINE TRACHEA
S07RR-07036-26 0108 (NSS) LAYNE, C Biomedical research support MICROGRAVITY ON CONTROL OF MOTOR RESPONSES TO POSTURAL PURTERBANCES
S07RR-07037-26 (NSS) BEARSE, ROBERT C UNIVERSITY OF KANSAS 226 STRONG HALL LAWRENCE, KANS 66045 Biomedical research support
S07RR-07037-26 0383 (NSS) KEMPER, SUSAN Biomedical research support GERIATRIC PSYCHOLINGUISTICS
S07RR-07037-26 0384 (NSS) GEGENHEIMER, PETER Biomedical research support ENZYMATIC RECOGNITION OF RNA: NOVEL ANALYTICAL APPROACHES
S07RR-07037-26 0385 (NSS) COLOMBO, JOHN Biomedical research support SIGNAL DETECTION APPROACH TO INFANT VISUAL RECOGNITION
S07RR-07037-26 0386 (NSS) SOUTHARD, MARYLEE Biomedical research support MATHEMATICAL SIMULATION OF RADIOLABELLED ESTRADIOL IN BREAST TUMOR DIAGNOSIS
S07RR-07037-26 0387 (NSS) KELLAS, GEORGE Biomedical research support AGING & MEANING PROCESS
S07RR-07037-26 0388 (NSS) BROWN, JOHN Biomedical research support MONOCLONAL RNA POLYMERASE I ANTIBODIES
S07RR-07037-26 0365 (NSS) EVERETT, GROVER W Biomedical research support TWO DIMENSIONAL NUCLEAR MAGNETIC RESONANCE STUDIES OF TETRAHYDROFOLATE SYNTHET
S07RR-07037-26 0366 (NSS) JUOLA, JAMES F Biomedical research support VOLUNTARY & INVOLUNTARY CONTROL OF ATTENTION
S07RR-07037-26 0367 (NSS) WEAVER, ROBERT E Biomedical research support CONTROL OF GENE EXPRESSION AT LEVEL OF TRANSCRIPTION
S07RR-07037-26 0368 (NSS) SHERMAN, JAMES Biomedical research support USING BAR CODE SCANNERS TO RECORD BEHAVIOR
S07RR-07037-26 0369 (NSS) SOUTHARD, MARYLEE Biomedical research support SHARED WATER PURIFICATION EQUIPMENT
S07RR-07037-26 0370 (NSS) FROST, SALLY K Biomedical research support HORMONAL STIMULATION OF CELL DIFFERENTIATION IN MUTANT & WILD TYPE AXOLOTLS
S07RR-07037-26 0371 (NSS) STETLER, DEAN A Biomedical research support ANTI NUCLEAR ANTIBODIES INDUCED IN MICE BY ORAL EXPOSURE
S07RR-07037-26 0372 (NSS) SCHLAGER, GUNTHER Biomedical research support CHROMOSOME LOCATION OF HYPERTENSIVE GENES
S07RR-07037-26 0373 (NSS) HIMES, RICHARD H Biomedical research support VINCA ALKALOID SITE IN TUBULIN W/ A PHOTOAFFINITY ANALOGUE
S07RR-07037-26 0374 (NSS) GAINES, MICHAEL S Biomedical research support POLYMERASE CHAIN REACTION TECHNIQUES IN DNA FINGERPRINTING OF PRAIRI
S07RR-07037-26 0375 (NSS) WILCOX, KIM Biomedical research support LOCALIZATION OF INFANT CRIES
S07RR-07037-26 0376 (NSS) ORR, JAMES Biomedical research support STIMULATION OF PULMONARY STRETCH RECEPTORS BY THROMBOXANE
S07RR-07037-26 0377 (NSS) WEAVER, ROBERT Biomedical research support STRUCTURE OF BACULOVIRUS EARLY PROMOTER
S07RR-07037-26 0378 (NSS) SCHNEIDER, CAROLE Biomedical research support ANABOLIC STEROID ADMINISTRATION ON MUSCLE ATROPHY DURING SIMULATED W
S07RR-07037-26 0379 (NSS) ALEXANDER, DAVID Biomedical research support CONSTRAINTS OF STRUCTURE & FUNCTION OF GAS EXCHANGE ORGANS
S07RR-07037-26 0380 (NSS) FAUTIN, DAPHNE G Biomedical research support TAXONOMY OF SEA ANEMONES
S07RR-07037-26 0381 (NSS) HOAGLAND, DONALD Biomedical research support POLYMERASE CHAIN REACTION TECHNIQUES IN SYNTHESIS OF RADIOACTIVITY
S07RR-07037-26 0382 (NSS) GEGENHEIMER, PETER A Biomedical research support PROTEIN ENGINEERING OF CATALYTIC SUBUNIT OF ATP SYNTHASE

PROJECT NO., ORGANIZATIONAL UNIT., INVESTIGATOR, ADDRESS, TITLE

S07RR-07039-20 (NSS) MC GLYNN, SEAN P LOUISIANA STATE UNIVERSITY 240 T BOYD HALL BATON ROUGE, LA 70803 Biomedical research support
S07RR-07040-24 (NSS) IDE, CHARLES F TULANE UNIVERSITY 6823 ST CHARLES AVENUE NEW ORLEANS, LA 70118 Biomedical research support
S07RR-07041-26 (NSS) BEER, MICHAEL JOHNS HOPKINS UNIVERSITY 34TH & CHARLES STREET BALTIMORE, MD 21218 Biomedical research support
S07RR-07041-26 0389 (NSS) NELSON, RANDY J Biomedical research support SEASONAL CHANGES IN IMMUNE FUNCTION
S07RR-07041-26 0390 (NSS) ANFINSEN, C B Biomedical research support ENZYMES OF HYPER THERMOPHILIC PYROCOCCUS FURIOSES
S07RR-07041-26 0391 (NSS) BRAND, LUDWIG Biomedical research support NANOSECOND TIME RESOLVED FLUORESCENCE INSTRUMENT: BIOLOGICAL MACROMOLECULES
S07RR-07041-26 0392 (NSS) SHEARN, ALLEN Biomedical research support IMMUNOLOCALIZATION OF DROSOPHILA & PROTEIN
S07RR-07041-26 0393 (NSS) SALTZMAN, W MARK Biomedical research support CONTROLLED RELEASE POLYMERS FOR IMMUNOPROTECTION
S07RR-07041-26 0394 (NSS) SCHROER, TRINA Biomedical research support MICROTUBULE BASED MEMBRANE TRANSPORT IN POLARIZED EPITHELIALS CELLS
S07RR-07041-26 0395 (NSS) KARLIN, KENNETH Biomedical research support BIOINORGANIC COPPER COORDINATION CHEMISTRY
S07RR-07041-26 0396 (NSS) HOYT, ANDREW M Biomedical research support FEEDBACK REGULATION OF MITOSIS
S07RR-07041-26 0397 (NSS) YANTIS, STEVEN Biomedical research support VISUAL ATTENTION & PERCEPTION OF OBJECTS
S07RR-07041-26 0398 (NSS) NIEDENTHAL, PAUL Biomedical research support PROTOTYPE MATCHING & EMOTION REGULATION
S07RR-07041-26 0399 (NSS) LEE, Y C Biomedical research support CANCER METASTASIS & OLIGOSACCHARIDE CHAINS OF LAMININ
S07RR-07041-26 0400 (NSS) BESA, WM Biomedical research support PHOSPHATIDYLINOSITOL CYCLE INVOLVEMENT IN VERTEBRATE PATTERN FORMATION
S07RR-07041-26 0401 (NSS) HARTMAN, PHILLIP E Biomedical research support DEVELOPMENT OF MUTAGEN TESTING STRAINS
S07RR-07041-26 0402 (NSS) HARRIS, ANDREW Biomedical research support PHYSIOLOGY OF RECONSTITUTED GAP JUNCTION CHANNELS
S07RR-07042-26 (NSS) VIJAY, INDER K UNIVERSITY OF MARYLAND ANIMAL SCIENCE BUILDING COLLEGE PARK, MD 20742 Biomedical research support
S07RR-07042-26 0403 (NSS) ALEXANDER, PAMELA Biomedical research support PARENT CHILD ATTACHMENT A PREDICTOR OF EFFECTS OF SEXUAL ABUSE
S07RR-07042-26 0404 (NSS) BENTLEY, WILLIAM Biomedical research support HETEROGENEITY OF PROTEIN EXPRESSION IN RECOMBINANT BACTERIAL SYSTEMS
S07RR-07042-26 0405 (NSS) CAPAGE, MICHAEL Biomedical research support GENETIC REGULATION EXOPOLYSACCHARDIE PRODUCTION IN XANTHOMONAS CAMPESTRIS
S07RR-07042-26 0406 (NSS) RUMPHO-KENNEDY, MARY Biomedical research support CHLOROPLAST BIOCHEMISTRY OF A MARINE SLUG ALGAL SYMBIOSIS
S07RR-07042-26 0407 (NSS) SARMIENTO, ULLA Biomedical research support DQ SUBREGION OF CANINE MAJOR HISTOCOMPATIBILITY COMPLEX
S07RR-07042-26 0408 (NSS) STRANEY, DAVID Biomedical research support REGULATION OF A VIRULENCE GENE IN NECTRIA HAENATOCCA
S07RR-07042-26 0411 (NSS) BENSON, SPENCER Biomedical research support HOEFER GS300 115V DENSITOMER
S07RR-07042-26 0412 (NSS) OLEK, ANTHONY Biomedical research support VIDEO SYSTEM
S07RR-07042-26 0413 (NSS) PENNER, MERRILYN Biomedical research support SPECIAL MICROPHONE
S07RR-07042-26 0409 (NSS) WOODSON, SARAH Biomedical research support MODEL HAIRPIN STUDIES OF TERIARY INTERACTION IN RNA
S07RR-07042-26 0410 (NSS) JARVIS, BRUCE Biomedical research support COUNTER CURRENT CHROMATOGRAPH
S07RR-07043-26 (NSS) MAKOWSKI, LEE BOSTON UNIVERSITY 5 CUMMINGTON MICROVAS RES LAB BOSTON, MASS 02215 Biomedical research support
S07RR-07043-26 0109 (NSS) FEDERSPIEL, WILLIAM Biomedical research support DETERMINATION OF PLASMA FLOW IN MICROVESSELS USING INJECTED TRACER
S07RR-07043-26 0110 (NSS) TRANIELLO, JAMES F A Biomedical research support MOLECULAR TEST OF INBREEDING HYPOTHESIS IN TERMITES
S07RR-07043-26 0111 (NSS) TOLAN, DEAN R Biomedical research support CELL CELL SIGNALLING IN CONTROL OF TISSUE SPECIFIC ALDOLASE GENE EXPRESSION
S07RR-07043-26 0112 (NSS) MONETTE, FRANCIS C Biomedical research support GROWTH FACTOR INDUCED EXPRESSION OF C MYC, C FOS PROTO ONCOGENES
S07RR-07043-26 0113 (NSS) BANSIL, RAMA Biomedical research support BIOPHYSICAL STUDIES OF GEL STRUCTURE & ELECTROPHORESIS IN GELS
S07RR-07043-26 0114 (NSS) LIEDERMAN, JACQUELIN Biomedical research support MALE PREVALENCE OF NEURODEVELOPMENTAL DISORDERS
S07RR-07043-26 0115 (NSS) KUNZ, THOMAS H Biomedical research support VARIABLE MATING SYSTEMS IN POLYGYNOUS BAT, MYOTIS ADVERSUS
S07RR-07043-26 0116 (NSS) WASSERMAN, FREDERICK Biomedical research support FUNCTION OF SONG IN WHITE THROATED SPARROWS
S07RR-07043-26 0117 (NSS) BENSON, THANE E Biomedical research support OLIVOCOCHLEAR BRANCH SYNAPSES IN GERBIL
S07RR-07043-26 0118 (NSS) BIFANO, THOMAS G Biomedical research support MEASURING BLOOD CELL DEFORMITY USING MICROMECHANICS & PRECISION ENGINEERING
S07RR-07043-26 0119 (NSS) CALLARD, IAN P Biomedical research support STEROID REGULATION OF YOLK PROTEIN SYNTHESIS IN LIVER MOLECULAR ASPECTS
S07RR-07043-26 0120 (NSS) HOLT, KENNETH G Biomedical research support TEACHING MINIMIZATION OF METABOLIC COST: APPLICATION TO PATIENT POPULATIONS
S07RR-07043-26 0121 (NSS) KALCKAR, HERMAN M Biomedical research support IS PHOSPHORYLATION CRUCIAL TO DOWN REGULATION OF HEXOSE TRANSPORT FOR D ALLOSE
S07RR-07043-26 0122 (NSS) MOREL, NICOLE Biomedical research support MEASUREMENT OF PERMEABILITY ACROSS AN ENDOTHELIAL MONOLAYER
S07RR-07043-26 0123 (NSS) BARBAS, HELEN Biomedical research support DISTRIBUTION OF DARPP 32 IN RHESUS MONKEY CORTEX

PROJECT NO., ORGANIZATIONAL UNIT., INVESTIGATOR, ADDRESS, TITLE

S07RR-07043-26 0124 (NSS) BROOKS, JAMES S Biomedical research support SCANNING TUNNELING MICROSCOPY OF BIOLOGICAL STRUCTURES
S07RR-07043-26 0125 (NSS) GOLUBIC, STJEPKO Biomedical research support MICROBIAL ROLE IN CACO3 DISSOLUTION & DESTRUCTION OF CALCIFIED TISSUES
S07RR-07043-26 0126 (NSS) HARRISON, J MICHAEL Biomedical research support STIMULUS NOVELTY; ACQUIRING QUALITY DIFFERENCE AUDITORY DISCRIMINATION
S07RR-07043-26 0127 (NSS) MOUNTAIN, DAVID C Biomedical research support SCANNING PROBE MICROSCOPY OF LIVING TISSUE
S07RR-07043-26 0128 (NSS) SCOTT, MICHELLE P Biomedical research support EVOLUTION OF COOPERATIVE BROOD CARE IN BURYING BEETLES
S07RR-07043-26 0129 (NSS) TAMARIN, ROBERT Biomedical research support PATERNITY DETERMINATION IN VOLES USING MINI SATELLITE DNA
S07RR-07043-26 0130 (NSS) WILLIAMS, SCOTT M Biomedical research support VARIATION IN HISTONE GENE FAMILY
S07RR-07043-26 0131 (NSS) PUGH, STEPHEN R Biomedical research support CONCEPTS & APPLICATIONS OF MOLECULAR BIOLOGY
S07RR-07043-26 0132 (NSS) MOHR, SCOTT C Biomedical research support SASP & DNA INTERACTION: RECIPROCAL CONFORMATION CHANGE
S07RR-07043-26 0133 (NSS) HAUSMAN, ROBERT E Biomedical research support EFFECT OF INSULIN ON CHOLINERGIC DIFFERENTIATION IN DEVELOPING CHICK RETINA
S07RR-07043-26 0134 (NSS) LUTCHEN, KENNETH R Biomedical research support TIME DOMAIN CHARACTERIZATION OF RESPIRATORY MECHANICS AT LOW FREQUENCIES
S07RR-07044-26 (NSS) COHEN, JOEL M BRANDEIS UNIVERSITY PO BOX 9110 WALTHAM, MA 02254 Biomedical research support
S07RR-07044-26 0115 (NSS) OPRIAN, DANIEL Biomedical research support RHODOPSIN VISUAL PIGMENTS; G PROTEINS; SITE DIRECTED MUTAGENESIS; GENE SYNTHESIS
S07RR-07044-26 0116 (NSS) HALPERN, DEBORA LYNN Biomedical research support INTERACTIONS BETWEEN DEPTH & MOTION PATHWAYS; VISUAL; NEURAL
S07RR-07044-26 0117 (NSS) GELLES, JEFF Biomedical research support MICROTUBULES; MECHANOENZYME ENERGY TRANSDUCTION; NANOMETER MOTION ANALYSIS
S07RR-07044-26 0118 (NSS) DAVIS, JAMES Biomedical research support PREPARATION & REACTIONS OF CO COMPLEXES OF BORON
S07RR-07044-26 0119 (NSS) SIMISTER, NEIL Biomedical research support INTESTINAL & PLACENTAL FC IMMUNOGLOBULIN G RECEPTORS; HUMAN; RATS; MICE; CLONE
S07RR-07044-26 0120 (NSS) BOLES, TRUETT CHRIST Biomedical research support DNA SUPERCOILING & GENETIC RECOMBINATION IN BACTERIA; E COLI
S07RR-07044-26 0114 (NSS) POCHAPSKY, THOMAS Biomedical research support ION PAIR SOLUTION STRUCTURES; DYNAMICS OF PUTIDAREDORIN BY NMR
S07RR-07045-01 (AR) SCHLEICHER, ROSEMARY L VAMC - RESEARCH SERVICE 1670 CLAIRMONT ROAD DECATUR, GA 30033 Optimization of antibody production in laying hens
S07RR-07046-26 (NSS) ROSOVSKY, HENRY HARVARD UNIVERSITY UNIVERSITY HALL 5 CAMBRIDGE, MASS 02138 Biomedical research support
S07RR-07046-26 0630 (NSS) ROSOVSKY, HENRY Biomedical research support NO RESEARCH SUBPROJECTS
S07RR-07047-26 (NSS) SMITH, KENNETH A MASS INSTITUTE OF TECHNOLOGY 77 MASSACHUSETTS AVE RM 3-240 CAMBRIDGE, MASS 02139 Biomedical research support
S07RR-07047-26 0135 (NSS) STELLER, HERMANN Biomedical research support ISOLATION OF GENES THAT DETERMINE NEURONAL SPECIFICITY IN DROSOPHILA
S07RR-07047-26 0136 (NSS) JORDAN, MICHAEL I Biomedical research support ACQUISITION OF SPEECH PRODUCTION
S07RR-07047-26 0137 (NSS) MACDONALD, MARYELLEN Biomedical research support SHORT TERM MEMORY IN LANGUAGE COMPREHENSION
S07RR-07047-26 0138 (NSS) POGGIO, THOMAS Biomedical research support OPTICAL RECORDING FROM CULTURED NEURONS
S07RR-07047-26 0139 (NSS) KEYSER, SAMUEL J Biomedical research support LEXICON
S07RR-07047-26 0140 (NSS) ROWELL, DEREK Biomedical research support DEVELOPMENT OF MEDICAL IMAGING FACILITY
S07RR-07047-26 0141 (NSS) WEDEEN, VAN J Biomedical research support PROTOTYPE NEUROANATOMY DATABASE
S07RR-07047-26 0142 (NSS) YANCH, JACQUELYN C Biomedical research support SCATTER ATTENUATION CORRECTION ALGORITHMS IN SINGLE PHOTON EMISSION TOMOGRAPHY
S07RR-07047-26 0143 (NSS) KAMM, ROGER D Biomedical research support DEVELOPMENT OF IMPLANTABLE OCULAR PRESSURE TRANDUCER
S07RR-07047-26 0144 (NSS) STEINER, LISA A Biomedical research support GENETIC BASIS FOR AN UNUSUAL HUMAN DISEASE PROTEIN
S07RR-07047-26 0145 (NSS) DURFEE, WILLIAM K Biomedical research support FUNCTIONAL ELECTRICAL STIMULATION AIDED PARAPLEGIC GAIT
S07RR-07047-26 0146 (NSS) DEWEY, C FORBES, JR Biomedical research support BIOMEDICAL IMAGING
S07RR-07047-26 0147 (NSS) YOUNG, LAURENCE R Biomedical research support HELMET MOUNTED DISPLAY
S07RR-07047-26 0148 (NSS) KIMSEY, PAUL Biomedical research support ALEUTIAN DISEASE IN FERRETS
S07RR-07047-26 0149 (NSS) RAULET, DAVID H Biomedical research support CHARACTERIZATION OF MUTANT MICE FOR MHC EXPRESSION
S07RR-07047-26 0150 (NSS) COHEN, DAVID Biomedical research support PROTOTYPE MAGNETIC STIMULATOR OF BRAIN
S07RR-07048-26 (NSS) CONTI, SAMUEL F UNIVERSITY OF MASSACHUSETTS 514 GOODELL BUILDING AMHERST, MA 01003 Biomedical research support
S07RR-07048-26 0664 (NSS) WOWER, JACEK Biomedical research support REPORTER PHOTOAFFINITY CROSS LINKING NEW APPROACH TO STUDY TRNA RIBSOME COMPLEX
S07RR-07048-26 0665 (NSS) WYSE, GORDON A Biomedical research support NEUROMODULATOR ACTION: DEMONSTRATION & FUNCTIONAL ROLES
S07RR-07048-26 0666 (NSS) ZIMMERMANN, ROBERT A Biomedical research support EXPRESS & ISOLATE RIBOSOMAL PROTEIN S8 FOR 2 DIMENSIONAL NMR STUDIES
S07RR-07048-26 0667 (NSS) ZUCKERMAN, BERT M Biomedical research support EFFECTS OF AGING & NUTRITION ON MUSCLE DEGENERATION

PROJECT NO., ORGANIZATIONAL UNIT., INVESTIGATOR, ADDRESS, TITLE

S07RR-07048-26 0627 (NSS) ANDERSON, DANIEL R Biomedical research support TELEVISION VIEWING BY CHILDREN W/ ATTENTION DEFICIT DISORDER
S07RR-07048-26 0628 (NSS) ANDERTON, DOUGLAS L Biomedical research support FAMILY FORMATION IN TRADITIONAL URBAN CHINA
S07RR-07048-26 0629 (NSS) BARNES, RAMON M Biomedical research support SIZE EXCLUSION CHROMATOGRAPHY OF LEAD PROTEINS
S07RR-07048-26 0630 (NSS) BERNATZKY, ROBERT Biomedical research support GENETIC & MOLECULAR MUTATION & CELL CELL RECOG: PLANT SEXUAL REPRODUCTION
S07RR-07048-26 0631 (NSS) BITTMAN, ERIC L Biomedical research support CIRCADIAN & HORMONAL FUNCTIONS OF SUPRACHIASMATIC GRAFTS
S07RR-07048-26 0632 (NSS) BRANDTS, JOHN F Biomedical research support DOMAIN INTERACTIONS IN FUNCTION OF PHOSPHOGLYCERATE KINASE
S07RR-07048-26 0633 (NSS) BUDNIK, VIVIAN Biomedical research support DEVELOPMENT OF MOTOR AXON TERMINALS IN DROSOPHILA MUTANTS & NEURONAL ACTIVITY
S07RR-07048-26 0634 (NSS) CARDE, RING T Biomedical research support ORGANIZATION OF RESPONSE TO PHEROMONE BLEND: CADRA CAUTELLA MODEL SYSTEM
S07RR-07048-26 0635 (NSS) CUNNINGHAM, ISABEL Biomedical research support CULTIVATE IN VITRO ENTIRE LIFE CYCLE OF TRYPANOSOMA BRUCEI SSPP
S07RR-07048-26 0636 (NSS) DASSARMA, S Biomedical research support CHARACTERIZE TRANSCRIPTION & TRANSLATION SIGNALS IN HALOPHILIC ARCHAEBACTERIA
S07RR-07048-26 0637 (NSS) DEVRIES, GEERT J Biomedical research support LINEAGE & NEUROTRANSMITTER CONTENT & SPECIFIC CONNECTIONS OF DEVELOPING NEURONS
S07RR-07048-26 0638 (NSS) DONAHOE, JOHN W Biomedical research support OPERANT CONDITIONING: EXPERIMENTS & SIMULATIONS
S07RR-07048-26 0639 (NSS) FITZGERALD-HAYES, MO Biomedical research support SCAFFOLD ATTACH & TOPIOSOMERASE II CLEAVAGE SITES IN CENTROMERE OF YEAST CHROM
S07RR-07048-26 0640 (NSS) GROSS, DAVID J Biomedical research support PATCH CLAMP RECORDING & MICROINJECTION APPARATUS
S07RR-07048-26 0641 (NSS) HELFER, KAREN S Biomedical research support SPEECH PERCEPTION IN REVERBERATION & NOISE: OLDER ADULTS W/ MINIMAL HEARING LOSS
S07RR-07048-26 0642 (NSS) HIXSON, STEPHEN S Biomedical research support PHOTOCHEMICAL PROBE OF BASE PAIRED SEGMENTS OF RNA
S07RR-07048-26 0643 (NSS) HONIGBERG, BRONISLAW Biomedical research support VIRULENCE DETERMINANTS ON SURFACES OF PARASITIC FLAGELLATE PROTOZOA
S07RR-07048-26 0644 (NSS) HUNTLEY, RUTH A Biomedical research support VOCAL AGE: SIMULATED VS ACTUAL PRODUCTIONS
S07RR-07048-26 0645 (NSS) LESSIE, THOMAS G Biomedical research support FORMATION OF ALGINIC ACID BY PSEUDOMONAS CEPACIA
S07RR-07048-26 0646 (NSS) MARONEY, MICHAEL J Biomedical research support PARAMAGNETIC 1H NMR INVESTIGATIONS OF MANGANOENZYMES
S07RR-07048-26 0647 (NSS) MARTIN, CRAIG T Biomedical research support SITE DIRECTED MUTAGENESIS OF CUA BINDING SITE IN CYTOCHROME C OXIDASE
S07RR-07048-26 0648 (NSS) MARTIN, CRAIG T Biomedical research support COORDINATION STRUCTURE & MECHANISM OF CUA CENTER IN CYTOCHROME C OXIDASE
S07RR-07048-26 0649 (NSS) MARTZ, ERIC Biomedical research support RESONANCE ENERGY TRANSFER STUDIES OF RECEPTOR MICROCLUSTERING
S07RR-07048-26 0650 (NSS) MASON, THOMAS L Biomedical research support GENETIC ENGINEERING OF INDUCIBLE TRANSCRIPTION SYSTEM FOR EUKARYOTIC ORGANELLES
S07RR-07048-26 0651 (NSS) NORDIN, JOHN H Biomedical research support YOLK PROTEIN GRANULES IN INSECT EMBYROGENESIS
S07RR-07048-26 0652 (NSS) NORKIN, LEONARD Biomedical research support FORMS OF SV40 T ANTIGEN IN TUMORS OF TRANSGENIC MICE INFECTED W/ SV40 OR JCV
S07RR-07048-26 0653 (NSS) OSBORN, BARBARA A Biomedical research support POLYMERASE CHAIN REACTION MACHINE
S07RR-07048-26 0654 (NSS) PHILLIS, RANDALL W Biomedical research support TRANSPOSABLE ELEMENTS & CHROMOSOME BREAKAGE IN DROSOPHILA MELANOGASTER
S07RR-07048-26 0655 (NSS) SMYTH, ROBERT J JR Biomedical research support VARIANT PHENOTYPIC EXPRESS OF AUTOIMMUNE AMELANOSIS IN VITILIGINOUS SMOOTH CHICK
S07RR-07048-26 0656 (NSS) STOFFOLANO, JOHN G J Biomedical research support RESEARCH ON OLDEST EXISTING PHORMIA COLONY IN U S
S07RR-07048-26 0657 (NSS) STOFFOLANO, JOHN G J Biomedical research support MALE ACCESSORY REPRODUC GLAND FLUID & FEMALE MATING BEHAV IN PHORMIA REGINA
S07RR-07048-26 0658 (NSS) UDEN, PETER Biomedical research support HPLC DETERMINATION OF FREE & METAL COMPLEXED TETRACYCLINES
S07RR-07048-26 0659 (NSS) WADSWORTH, PATRICIA Biomedical research support CELL CYCLE DEPENDENT REGULATION OF MICROTUBULE DYNAMICS
S07RR-07048-26 0660 (NSS) WEIS, ROBERT M Biomedical research support MOLECULAR BASIS OF CHEMOSENSORY BEHAVIOR IN BACTERIA
S07RR-07048-26 0661 (NSS) WEIS, ROBERT M Biomedical research support TRANSMEMBRANE SIGNALING BY ASPARTATE RECEPTOR OF SALMONELLA TYPHIMURIUM
S07RR-07048-26 0662 (NSS) WESTHEAD, E W Biomedical research support PATCH CLAMP WORK STATION
S07RR-07048-26 0663 (NSS) WOODCOCK, C L Biomedical research support CONFORMATION OF CHROMATIN IN VIVO & VITRO
S07RR-07049-26 (NSS) BREDECK, HENRY E MICHIGAN STATE UNIVERSITY 238 ADMINISTRATION BUILDING EAST LANSING, MI 48824-1046 Biomedical research support
S07RR-07049-26 0448 (NSS) SCHINDLER, MELVIN S Biomedical research support PREP & CHARACTER OF ANTIBODIES TO DEFINED AMINO ACID SEQ OF PLANT TYPE
S07RR-07049-26 0449 (NSS) STILLE, JOHN R Biomedical research support APPROACHES TO NITROGEN HETEROCYCLES
S07RR-07049-26 0421 (NSS) LUSTER, TOM Biomedical research support SOCIAL EMOTIONAL ADJUSTMENT OF CHILD BORN TO TEENAGE MOTHERS
S07RR-07049-26 0422 (NSS) SCHEMMEL, RACHEL A Biomedical research support FORCED RUNNING ON GROWTH, BONE DENSITY & IRON STATUS OF FEMALE RATS
S07RR-07049-26 0423 (NSS) YOKOYAMA, M T Biomedical research support COMPETITIVE ADHERENCE OF LACTIC ACID BACTERIA TO INTESTINAL MUCOSAL RECEPTORS
S07RR-07049-26 0424 (NSS) DUKELOW, W RICHARD Biomedical research support LAPAROSCOPIC ASSESSMENT OF UTERINE & OVARIAN FUNCTION
S07RR-07049-26 0425 (NSS) HELFERICH, WILLIAM Biomedical research support TRANSCRIPTION RATE OF SKELETAL MUSCLE DURING GROWTH & DEVELOPMENT IN PIGS
S07RR-07049-26 0426 (NSS) REVITTE, JOHN Biomedical research support SOCIOLOGY OF MSU EMPLOYEE PERCEPT OF OCCUPA SAFE HLTH HAZARD: PERS HLTH
S07RR-07049-26 0427 (NSS) DAVIS, GERALD L Biomedical research support INSULIN ON FIBRINOLYTIC POTENTIAL OF ENDOTHELIAL CELLS
S07RR-07049-26 0450 (NSS) ZIPSER, BIRTIT Biomedical research support SYNAPTIC PROJECTIONS EXPERIMENTALLY MANIPULATED VIA THEIR CARBOHYDRATE EPITOPES
S07RR-07049-26 0451 (NSS) KOPACHIK, WILL JOHN Biomedical research support DETECTION OF CELL DIVISION CYCLE MUTANTS IN DICTYOSTELIUM
S07RR-07049-26 0428 (NSS) ABELES, NORMAN Biomedical research support AGE ASSOCIATED MEMORY IMPAIRMENTS IN OLDER ADULTS
S07RR-07049-26 0429 (NSS) PERLSTADT, HARRY Biomedical research support PRACTITIONER INVOLVEMENT IN WEIGHT LOSS TREATMENT
S07RR-07049-26 0452 (NSS) NUNEZ, ANTONIO Biomedical research support CENTRAL VISUAL PATHWAYS & BEHAVIOR
S07RR-07049-26 0453 (NSS) FRIEDMAN, THOMAS B Biomedical research support GRADUATE SEMINAR PROGRAM IN GENETICS
S07RR-07049-26 0454 (NSS) KINGRY, MARGARET Biomedical research support HEALTH BELIEFS OF PREGNANT WOMEN
S07RR-07049-26 0430 (NSS) BURTON, ZACHARY FROM Biomedical research support NOVEL METHOD FOR CDNA AMPLIFICATION & CLONING
S07RR-07049-26 0431 (NSS) KANATZIDIS, MERCOURI Biomedical research support MODELING ACTIVE SITES OF METAL SULFIDE ENZYMES
S07RR-07049-26 0432 (NSS) MERRITT, RICHARD W Biomedical research support ECOLOGY OF LYME DIS IN MICH: LANDSCAPE, FOCALITY & VECTOR RELATIONSHIP
S07RR-07049-26 0433 (NSS) MURRY, MARCIA Biomedical research support CONSTRUCT OF SHUTTLE VECTORS FRANKIA ACTINORHIZAL SYMBIOSIS
S07RR-07049-26 0434 (NSS) UFFEN, ROBERT L Biomedical research support ANAEROBIC HYDROGEN METABOLISM IN RHODOCYCLUS GELATINOSUS
S07RR-07049-26 0435 (NSS) WALTON, JONATHAN Biomedical research support AMINO ACID SEQ OF XYLANASE & LICHENASE FROM COCHLIOBOLUS CARBONUM
S07RR-07049-26 0436 (NSS) WANG, C Y Biomedical research support MICROVASCULAR NETWORK MODELS
S07RR-07049-26 0437 (NSS) SISK, CHERYL L Biomedical research support QUANTITY OF NEURAL CORRELATES OF ENDOCRINE & BEHAV CHANGES IN PUBERTY
S07RR-07049-26 0438 (NSS) HEIDEMANN, STEVEN R Biomedical research support REGULATION OF NEURONAL GROWTH ON DIFFERING SUBSTRATES BY TENSION
S07RR-07049-26 0439 (NSS) BOND, JENNY T Biomedical research support FIBER SUPPLEMENT IN HEMODIALYSIS PATIENTS
S07RR-07049-26 0440 (NSS) MEYER, RONALD Biomedical research support SPECTROSCOPIC STUDIES OF SKELETAL MUSCLE RESPIRATION
S07RR-07049-26 0441 (NSS) HARRISON, MICHAEL J Biomedical research support CUBIC GROWTH OF AIDS: ITS INITIAL EMERGENCE FROM EARLY HIV INFECTION RATES
S07RR-07049-26 0442 (NSS) BENNETT, JAMES L Biomedical research support HMG COA REDUCTASE: TARGET FOR ANTISCHISTOSOMALS
S07RR-07049-26 0443 (NSS) HOGAN, ANDREW J Biomedical research support CANCER TREATMENT IN MICHIGAN: MICHIGAN MEDICAID POP
S07RR-07049-26 0444 (NSS) STRASBURG, GALE Biomedical research support CALMODULIN REGULATION OF CALCIUM CHANNELS
S07RR-07049-26 0445 (NSS) RODGERS, CAROL D Biomedical research support EXERCISE, DIET & DIABETES
S07RR-07049-26 0446 (NSS) BROMAN, CLIFFORD L Biomedical research support ALCOHOL & ALCOHOL RELATED PROBLEMS IN BLACK POP
S07RR-07049-26 0447 (NSS) ASHER, JAMES H Biomedical research support DEAFNESS IN HUMANS & MICE: WAARDENBURG SYNDROME WSI
S07RR-07050-26 (NSS) NEWMAN, SARAH W UNIVERSITY OF MICHIGAN 4080 ADMIN BLDG ANN ARBOR, MICH 48109 Biomedical research support
S07RR-07050-26 0121 (NSS) DONEEN, BRYON Biomedical research support EVOLUTION OF PROLACTIN & GROWTH HORMONE GENES
S07RR-07050-26 0122 (NSS) GLICK, GARY Biomedical research support CONFORMATIONALLY RESTRICTED PEPTIDE IMMUNOGENS
S07RR-07050-26 0123 (NSS) GRUBER, JAMES Biomedical research support FINNISH INSTITUTE OF OCCUPATIONAL HEALTH
S07RR-07050-26 0124 (NSS) HARDWICK, JANIS Biomedical research support SUPERCOMPUTER TO TEACH PROBLEMS IN MEDICAL STATISTICS
S07RR-07050-26 0125 (NSS) LANGMORE, JOHN Biomedical research support STRUCTURE OF SEA URCHIN EARLY HISTONE GENE CHROMATIN
S07RR-07050-26 0126 (NSS) MANGELSDORF, SARAH Biomedical research support INFANT TEMPERAMENT & MATERNAL CHARACTERISTICS IN PREDICTING ATTACHMENT
S07RR-07050-26 0127 (NSS) MARINO, JOSEPH Biomedical research support SYNTHETIC METHODS FOR SITE SPECIFIC & LATENT ANTITUMOR AGENTS
S07RR-07050-26 0128 (NSS) STEEL, DUNCAN Biomedical research support CIRCULARLY POLARIZED PHOSPHORIMETER FOR PROTEIN STRUCTURE
S07RR-07050-26 0129 (NSS) STEWART, ABIGAIL Biomedical research support SEPARATION & DIVORCE IN EARLY YEARS OF MARRIAGE
S07RR-07050-26 0130 (NSS) TSUBOTA, STUART Biomedical research support CIS ACTING & TRANS ACTING GENE REGULATORY SEQ
S07RR-07050-26 0131 (NSS) VERBRUGGE, LOIS Biomedical research support MUSCULOSKELETAL FUNCTIONING IN OLDER ADULTS
S07RR-07050-26 0132 (NSS) VILLEPONTEAU, BRYANT Biomedical research support GENE TARGETING TO IDENTIFY DNA ELEMENTS THAT PROMOTE ACTIVE CHROMATIN
S07RR-07050-26 0133 (NSS) VINOKUR, AMIRAM Biomedical research support HUSBANDS & WIVES LONG TERM ADJUSTMENT TO BREAST CANCER
S07RR-07050-26 0134 (NSS) WOLPOFF, MILFORD Biomedical research support EVOLUTIONARY CHANGES IN CRANIAL STRESS DISTRIBUTION
S07RR-07050-26 0135 (NSS) ZIMMERMAN, WILLIAM Biomedical research

PROJECT NO., ORGANIZATIONAL UNIT., INVESTIGATOR, ADDRESS, TITLE

support GENETIC POLYMORPHISMS & MOLECULAR SYSTEMATICS OF AZOLLA SYMBIOSIS
G20RR-07051-01 (AR) CLARKSON, THOMAS B WAKE FOREST UNIVERSITY 300 S HAWTHORNE ROAD WINSTON-SALEM, N C 27103 Developing and improving institutional animal resources
S07RR-07051-26 (NSS) HEBERLEIN, GARRETT T WAYNE STATE UNIVERSITY 4045 FAC ADM BLDG DETROIT, MI 48202 Biomedical research support
S07RR-07051-26 0727 (NSS) COMMISSARIS, RANDALL Biomedical research support PHARMACOLOGICAL EVALUATION OF AN ANIMAL MODEL FOR PANIC DISORDER
S07RR-07051-26 0728 (NSS) ARKING, ROBERT Biomedical research support ANTIOXIDANT REGULATION OF LONGEVITY IN DROSOPHILA
S07RR-07051-26 0729 (NSS) EDWARDS, DAVID J Biomedical research support INHIBITION OF OXIDATIVE METABOLISM BY QUINOLONE ANTIBIOTICS
S07RR-07051-26 0730 (NSS) HARI, V Biomedical research support LOCALIZE & CHARACTERIZE GENE TRANSCRIPTS & GENE PRODUCTS OF POLYVIRUSES
S07RR-07051-26 0731 (NSS) MOBASHERY, SHAHRIAR Biomedical research support INACTIVATORS FOR ZINC PROTEASE CARBOXYPEPTIDASE A
S07RR-07051-26 0732 (NSS) RUTLEDGE, DAVID R Biomedical research support RACIAL DIVERGENCE: C AMP IN LYMPHOCYTE BY ISOPROTERENOL & FORSKOLIN STIMULATION
S07RR-07051-26 0734 (NSS) LUCKINBILL, LEO Biomedical research support GENETICS OF LONGEVITY IN DROSOPHILA MELANOGASTER
S07RR-07051-26 0733 (NSS) LINDBLAD, WILLIAM Biomedical research support GLUCOCORTICOID STEROIDS IN SUPPRESSING HEPATOCELLULAR COLLAGEN BIOSYNTHESIS
S07RR-07051-26 0735 (NSS) MOBASHERY, SHAHRIAR Biomedical research support PURIFY & CHARACTERIZE AMINOGLYCOSIDE 3 PHOSPHOTRANSFERASE TYPE II & MUTANT ENZY
S07RR-07051-26 0736 (NSS) SLAUGHTER, RICHARD L Biomedical research support HEPATIC METABOLISM OF PROPRANOLOL IN UREMIA
S07RR-07051-26 0737 (NSS) TCHEN, T T Biomedical research support MELANOSOME GENESIS: A MOLECULAR BIOLOGICAL APPROACH
S07RR-07051-26 0738 (NSS) WHITMAN, R DOUGLAS Biomedical research support MEMORY DEFICITS IN WORKERS SUFFERING FROM HARD METAL DISEASE
S07RR-07051-26 0739 (NSS) WINTER, CHARLES H Biomedical research support USE OF HETEROCYCLIC DIENE COMPLEXES OF IRON IN ORGANIC SYNTHESIS
S07RR-07051-26 0740 (NSS) WOSTER, PATRICK J Biomedical research support SYNTHESIZE & BIOEVALUATE: INHIBITOR OF S ADENOSYLMETHIONINE DECARBOXYLASE
G20RR-07052-01 (AR) WOLF, ROBERT H UNIV OF TEXAS HLTH SCI CENTER 7703 FLOYD CURL DRIVE SAN ANTONIO, TX 78284-7859 Developing and improving institutional animal resources
S07RR-07052-26 (NSS) HOGENKAMP, HENRICUS P C UNV MINN, 417 JOHNSTON HALL 101 PLEASANT ST SE MINNEAPOLIS, MN 55455 Biomedical research support
S07RR-07052-26 0151 (NSS) ANDERSON, JOHN S Biomedical research support BIOSYNTHESIS OF TEICHURONIC ACID ATTACHMENT SITES ON PEPTIDOGLYCAN; BACTERIA
S07RR-07052-26 0152 (NSS) BAUER, PATRICIA J Biomedical research support EFFECTS OF TEMPORAL STRUCTURE ON YOUNG CHILDRENS MEMORY FOR EVENTS
S07RR-07052-26 0153 (NSS) CUNNINGHAM, WILLIAM Biomedical research support ULTRASTRUCTURAL IMMUNOCYTOCHEMISTRY OF LENS FIBER CELL GAP JUNCTIONAL PROTEINS
S07RR-07052-26 0154 (NSS) DEHART, SARA S Biomedical research support ALCOHOLISM IDENTIFICATION & PREVALENCE IN ELDERLY
S07RR-07052-26 0155 (NSS) FIRLING, CONRAD E Biomedical research support INFLUENCE OF ALUMINUM ON EMBRYONIC CHICK BONE MAINTAINED IN ORGAN CULTURE
S07RR-07052-26 0156 (NSS) GALLAHER, DANIEL D Biomedical research support REVERSIBILE OF GLOMERULAR BASEMENT MEMBRANE CHANGE IN DIAB; RENAL HYPERTROPHY
S07RR-07052-26 0157 (NSS) GLEASON, FLORENCE K Biomedical research support BIOACTIVE COMPOUNDS FROM FRESHWATER CYANOBACTERIA
S07RR-07052-26 0158 (NSS) HACKETT, PERRY Biomedical research support REGULATION OF MRNASRC TRANSLATION
S07RR-07052-26 0159 (NSS) HAYS, THOMAS S Biomedical research support PRIMARY STRUCTURE OF CYTOPLASMIC DYNEIN A MICROTUBULE MOTOR; DROSOPHILA
S07RR-07052-26 0160 (NSS) HOOPER, ALAN B Biomedical research support EVOLUTION OF BACTERIAL N OXIDE OXIDOREDUCTASES; PROTEIN SEQUENCE
S07RR-07052-26 0161 (NSS) KISS, ZOLTAN Biomedical research support ANALYSIS OF PHOSPHOPROTEINS & PROTEIN KINASE C
S07RR-07052-26 0162 (NSS) KURZER, MINDY S Biomedical research support DIETARY REGULATION OF IN VITRO ESTROGEN SYNTHESIS IN HUMAN FAT CELLS
S07RR-07052-26 0163 (NSS) MCLEOD, JANE D Biomedical research support SPOUSE RECOGNITION OF DEPRESSIVE DISORDERS
S07RR-07052-26 0164 (NSS) MESCE, KAREN A Biomedical research support METAMORPHOSIS OF AN INSECT NERVOUS SYSTEM
S07RR-07052-26 0165 (NSS) OPENSHAW, STEPHEN J Biomedical research support DNA METHYLATION PATTERNS IN ELITE MAIZE INBREDS & THEIR F1 HYBRIDS
S07RR-07052-26 0166 (NSS) QUE, LAWRENCE Biomedical research support MODELING DIOXYGEN BINDING & ACTIVATION BY DIIRON OXO PROTEINS
S07RR-07052-26 0167 (NSS) SADOWSKY, MICHAEL J Biomedical research support DNA PROBES TO DETERMINE SOYBEAN MODULATION COMPETITIVENESS; BRADYRHIZOBIUM
S07RR-07052-26 0168 (NSS) SCHLAUCH, ROBERT S Biomedical research support REFINING AUDIOLOGIC BEHAVIORAL TESTS
S07RR-07052-26 0169 (NSS) SERA, MARIA D Biomedical research support LINGUISTIC & CONCEPTUAL DIFFERENCES BETWEEN ENGLISH & SPANISH SPEAKERS; DVMTL
S07RR-07052-26 0170 (NSS) SHARROCK, WILLIAM J Biomedical research support TRANSGENIC DELETIONS IN YOLK LIPOPROTEINS
S07RR-07052-26 0171 (NSS) STUM, MARLENE S Biomedical research support ELDERLY FAMILY WELL BEING & LONG TERM CARE; IMPOVERISHMENT, CHRONIC ILLNESS

PROJECT NO., ORGANIZATIONAL UNIT., INVESTIGATOR, ADDRESS, TITLE

S07RR-07053-26 (NSS) SHERIDAN, JUDSON D UNIV OF MISSOURI-COLUMBIA 202 JESSE HALL COLUMBIA, MO 65211 Biomedical research support
S07RR-07053-26 0137 (NSS) HILL, GRETCHEN Biomedical research support EFFECT OF A1 ON CU UTILIZATION & BONE HEALTH
S07RR-07053-26 0138 (NSS) MUSTAPHA, SHERRY Biomedical research support DEPRESSION IN PERIMEOPAUSAL WOMEN
S07RR-07053-26 0139 (NSS) DEROOS, ROGER Biomedical research support BRAIN FUEL(S) OF SPINY DOGFISH SHARK
S07RR-07053-26 0140 (NSS) JEN, PHILLIP Biomedical research support AUDITORY SPATIAL SENSITIVITY & SOUND LOCALIZATION
S07RR-07053-26 0141 (NSS) SAGE, RICHARD Biomedical research support RETROVIRUS & MOUSE EVOLUTION IN HYBRID ZONE
S07RR-07053-26 0142 (NSS) HARRELSON, ALLAN Biomedical research support MONOCLONAL ANTIBODIES AGAINST DEVELOPING NERVOUS SYSTEM AXONS
S07RR-07053-26 0136 (NSS) WANG, RICHARD Biomedical research support TEMPERATURE SENSITIVE MUTANT DEFECTIVE IN MITOSIS
S07RR-07053-26 0143 (NSS) TRULL, TIMOTHY Biomedical research support INFLUENCE OF DEPRESSED & ANXIOUS MOODS REPORT OF PERSONALITY DISORDER SYMPTOMS
S07RR-07053-26 0144 (NSS) VOMSAAL, FREDERICK Biomedical research support LIBRARY RESEARCH FOR BOOK ON SEXUAL DIFFERENTIATION
S07RR-07053-26 0145 (NSS) COWAN, NELSON Biomedical research support MEMORY FOR ATTENDED & UNATTENDED SPEECH
S07RR-07053-26 0146 (NSS) WATTS, PARRIS Biomedical research support HEALTH BENEFITS OF MU HELP PROGRAM
S07RR-07053-26 0147 (NSS) CASH, DEREK Biomedical research support ULTRACENTRIFUGE ROTORS FOR BIOCHEMICAL DEPT; PROJECTS RELATED TO HUMAN HEALTH
S07RR-07053-26 0148 (NSS) SATTENSPIEL, LISA Biomedical research support POPULATION MOBILITY & DISEASE SPREAD IN DOMINICA
S07RR-07053-26 0149 (NSS) TWENTE, JOHN Biomedical research support REGULATION OF ALARM CLOCK THAT AROUSES HIBERNATING BATS
S07RR-07053-26 0150 (NSS) GERHARDT, H CARL Biomedical research support CODING BIOLOGICAL INFORMATION GRADED ACOUSTIC SIGNALS
S07RR-07053-26 0151 (NSS) KEISLER, DUANE Biomedical research support DIET & PHOTOPERIOD REGULATION OF PUBERTY IN EWE LAMBS
S07RR-07053-26 0152 (NSS) LAUGHLIN, M HAROLD Biomedical research support EFFECTS OF ENDOTOXEMIA ON CORONARY ARTERIOLAR FUNCTION
S07RR-07053-26 0153 (NSS) FIRMAN, JEFFRE Biomedical research support ELICITATION OF THIRST & SALT APPETITE IN DOMESTIC FOWL
S07RR-07053-26 0154 (NSS) BELL-DOLAN, DEBRA Biomedical research support COGNITIVE BEHAVIOR OF ANXIOUS CHILDREN
S07RR-07053-26 0155 (NSS) PETERSON-HOMER, LIZE Biomedical research support MICROANALYTIC ASSESSMENT OF CHILD INJURY PREVENTION
S07RR-07054-26 0156 (NSS) DAVID, JOHN Biomedical research support CLONING GENES FOR MYOBLAST SURFACES ANTIGENS
S07RR-07053-26 0157 (NSS) DAY, BILLY N Biomedical research support HORMONAL CONTROL OF BOVINE OVIDUCTAL SECRETORY PROTEINS
S07RR-07053-26 0158 (NSS) YAN, PEARLLY S Biomedical research support EVALUATION OF CHOLESTEROL OXIDE TRANSFER IN WISTAR RAT
S07RR-07053-26 0159 (NSS) TRULL, TIMOTHY J Biomedical research support CLINICAL DEPRESSION & SELF REPORT OF PERSONALITY
S07RR-07053-26 0160 (NSS) LOEPPKY, RICHARD N Biomedical research support IDENTIFICATION OF DNA NITROSAMINE ADDUCTS
S07RR-07053-26 0161 (NSS) PRATHER, RANDALL S Biomedical research support AMINO ACID TRANSPORT IN EARLY PIG EMBRYOS
S07RR-07053-26 0162 (NSS) HALL, ROBERT D Biomedical research support TICKS & LYME DISEASE IN MISSOURI
S07RR-07053-26 0163 (NSS) GLASER, RAINER Biomedical research support THEORETICAL STUDIES OF DEAMINATION REACTIONS PERTINENT TO CARCINOGENESIS
S07RR-07053-26 0164 (NSS) SCHACHTMAN, TODD R Biomedical research support CONTEXTUAL MODULATION OF BLOCKING POTENTIAL
S07RR-07053-26 0165 (NSS) STARK, WILLIAM Biomedical research support MAINTENANCE & FUNCTION OF DROSOPHILA VISUAL RECEPTORS
S07RR-07053-26 0166 (NSS) MCCLELLAN, ANDREW Biomedical research support BRAINSTEM COMMAND SYSTEMS FOR SWIMMING IN LAMPREY
S07RR-07053-26 0167 (NSS) ROBERTS, R MICHAEL Biomedical research support INTERACTION BETWEEN BLASTOCYST & UTERINE EPITHELIUM
G20RR-07054-01 (AR) BATTLES, AUGUST H ALBANY MEDICAL COLLEGE 47 NEW SCOTLAND AVENUE ALBANY, NY 12208 Animal resources improvement--Phase II
S07RR-07054-26 (NSS) DANFORTH, WILLIAM H WASHINGTON UNIVERSITY ONE BROOKINGS DRIVE, BOX 1192 ST LOUIS, MO 63130 Biomedical research support
S07RR-07055-26 (NSS) SONG, PILL-SOON UNIVERSITY OF NEBRASKA-LINCOLN 551 HAMILTON HALL LINCOLN, NE 68588-0118 Biomedical research support
S07RR-07055-26 0198 (NSS) DICKMAN, MARTIN Biomedical research support PATHOGENIC DETERMINANTS OF COLLETOTRICHUM TRIFOLII
S07RR-07055-26 0168 (NSS) VEOMETT, GEORGE Biomedical research support AMINO TERMINAL SEQUENCING OF PORCINE INSULIN LIKE GROWTH FACTOR BINDING PROTEIN
S07RR-07055-26 0169 (NSS) CONWAY, TYRRELL Biomedical research support CHARACTERIZATION OF GENES INVOLVED IN REGULATION OF GLYCOLYTIC CARBON FLUX
S07RR-07055-26 0170 (NSS) OSTERMAN, JOHN Biomedical research support CHARACTERIZE RDNA POLYMORPHISMS IN CLONAL SPECIES AMBROSIA PSILOSTACHYA
S07RR-07055-26 0171 (NSS) KELLEY, PHILIP Biomedical research support PROTEOLYTIC ACTIVATION OF ETHANOLIC FERMENTATION IN ANAEROBIC MAIZE ROOTS
S07RR-07055-26 0172 (NSS) MARKS, M DAVID Biomedical research support ANALYSIS OF MYB HOMOLOGS IN PLANTS
S07RR-07055-26 0173 (NSS) NICKERSON, KENNETH Biomedical research support MEMBRANE PHOSPHOLIPIDS & BACTERIAL DETERGENT RESISTANCE
S07RR-07055-26 0174 (NSS) SCHWARTZBACH, STEVEN Biomedical research support ID PROCESSING SITES IN LHCPII GENE OF EUGLENA
S07RR-07055-26 0175 (NSS) WADE, WILLIAM Biomedical research support CELL CYCLE & PROTEIN PHOSPHORALA & GENE TRANSCRIPT; TRANSMEMBRANE SIGNAL; MUTANT
S07RR-07055-26 0176 (NSS) PARDY, R L Biomedical research support

PROJECT NO., ORGANIZATIONAL UNIT., INVESTIGATOR, ADDRESS, TITLE

CELL WALL PROTEINS OF SYMBIOTIC ALGAE
S07RR-07055-26 0177 (NSS) GEORGE, T ADRIAN Biomedical research support NEW CATALYSTS: SYNTHESIS & CHARACTERIZATION
S07RR-07055-26 0178 (NSS) TAKACS, JAMES Biomedical research support NOVEL METHOD FOR ASYMMETRIC SYNTHESIS OF NITROGEN HETEROCYCLES
S07RR-07055-26 0179 (NSS) WHEELER, DESMOND M S Biomedical research support SYNTHESIS OF NAGILACTONE B & RELATED COMPOUNDS
S07RR-07055-26 0180 (NSS) DUSSAULT, PATRICK Biomedical research support FIRST STEREOSPECIFIC SYNTHESIS OF UNSATURATED HYDROPEROXIDES
S07RR-07055-26 0181 (NSS) HAGE, DAVID Biomedical research support COMPETITIVE BINDING TO IMMOBILIZED BIOCHEMICAL SUPPORT
S07RR-07055-26 0182 (NSS) WHEELER, DESMOND MS Biomedical research support SYNTHESIS OF DOXORUBICIN
S07RR-07055-26 0183 (NSS) PILL-SOON SONG Biomedical research support PHOTOSIGNAL TRANSDUCTION
S07RR-07055-26 0199 (NSS) MITRA, AMIT Biomedical research support DEVELOPMENT OF MAKE STERILE PLANTS
S07RR-07055-26 0200 (NSS) DONIS, RUBEN Biomedical research support MOLECULAR BASIS OF BOVINE VIRAL DIARRHEA VIRUS INDUCED CYTOPATHOLOGY
S07RR-07055-26 0201 (NSS) ROGERS, DOUGLAS Biomedical research support CHARACTERIZATION OF MOXAXELLA BOVIS HEMOLYSIN
S07RR-07055-26 0184 (NSS) HAGE, DAVID Biomedical research support CHROMATOGRAPHIC DETERMINATION OF HORMONE PROTEIN BINDING
S07RR-07055-26 0185 (NSS) WHEELER, DESMOND MS Biomedical research support DERIVATIVES OF DOXORUBICIN
S07RR-07055-26 0186 (NSS) DUSSAULT, PATRICK Biomedical research support MOLECULAR YARDSTICKS
S07RR-07055-26 0187 (NSS) HOUSH, TERRY Biomedical research support LACTATE RESPONSES; PHYSICAL WORKING CAPACITY OF FATIGUE THRESHOLD
S07RR-07055-26 0188 (NSS) JOHNSON, GLEN Biomedical research support VALIDATION OF FATIGUE THRESHOLD TEST
S07RR-07055-26 0189 (NSS) LEE, DONALD Biomedical research support GENETIC VARIATION IN SOYBEANS; POLYMERASE CHAIN REACTION
S07RR-07055-26 0190 (NSS) NISSEN, SCOTT Biomedical research support LEAFY SPURGE: ANALYSIS OF GENETIC VARIATION BY CPDNA CHARACTERIZATION
S07RR-07055-26 0191 (NSS) SPECHT, JAMES Biomedical research support USE OF NEAR ISOGENIC LINES IN CLONING OF DNA NEAR OR AT INTROGRESSED GENE LOCUS
S07RR-07055-26 0192 (NSS) KLUCAS, ROBERT Biomedical research support ACTIVE SITE SEQUENCE & HOMOLOGY INVESTIGATION OF FOUR FLAVOPROTEINS
S07RR-07055-26 0193 (NSS) WAGNER, FRED Biomedical research support CLONING & NUCLEOTIDE SEQUENCE OF AMINOPEPTIDASE FROM AEROMONAS PROTEOLYTICA
S07RR-07055-26 0194 (NSS) KRUEGER, RICK Biomedical research support ANALYSIS OF BIVALENT ACTH LIGAND BINDING TO RAT ADRENOCORTICAL CELLS
S07RR-07055-26 0195 (NSS) STANLEY-SAMUELSON, D Biomedical research support SEPARATIONS OF INSECT BLOOD CELLS FOR BIOCHEMICAL STUDIES OF PROSTOGLANDINS
S07RR-07055-26 0196 (NSS) ZEECE, MICHAEL Biomedical research support DEVELOPMENT OF ANTIBODY & CDNA PROBES FOR PROTEINASE INHIBITOR, CYSTATIN
S07RR-07055-26 0197 (NSS) SUMNER, SUSAN Biomedical research support EFFICACY OF LACTOPEROXIDASE SYSTEM AGAINST CLOSTRIDIUM PERFRINGENS
S07RR-07056-18 (NSS) WETTERHAHN, KAREN E DARTMOUTH COLLEGE 305 WENTWORTH HALL HANOVER, N H 03755 Biomedical research support
S07RR-07056-18 0202 (NSS) BORSZCZ, GEORGE S Biomedical research support COMPARISON OF SPINAL & SUPRASPINAL PAIN THRESHOLDS
S07RR-07056-18 0203 (NSS) GROSS, ROBERT H Biomedical research support RNA SPLICING & THERMOTOLERENCE IN DROSOPHILA
S07RR-07056-18 0204 (NSS) GRIBBLE, GORDON W Biomedical research support SYNTHESIS & BIOLOGICAL EVALUATION OF NOVEL ANTITUMOR ELLIPTICINE DERIVATIVES
S07RR-07056-18 0205 (NSS) HAMILTON, JOSHUA W Biomedical research support EFFECT OF CARCINOGEN INDUCED DNA DAMAGE ON GENE EXPRESSION IN VIVO
S07RR-07056-18 0206 (NSS) HANSEN, ERIC W Biomedical research support IMAGE FORMATION & PROCESSING IN OPTICAL MICROSCOPY
S07RR-07056-18 0207 (NSS) LYNCH, DANIEL R Biomedical research support COMPUTERIZED TREATMENT PLANNING FOR HYPERTHERMIA
S07RR-07056-18 0208 (NSS) SPENCER, THOMAS A Biomedical research support NOVEL INHIBITORS OF CHOLESTEROL BIOSYNTHESIS
S07RR-07056-18 0209 (NSS) WILCOX, DEAN E Biomedical research support MOLECULAR MECHANISM OF CHROMIUM(VI) CARCINOGENESIS
S07RR-07057-26 (NSS) FRESCO, JACQUES R PRINCETON UNIVERSITY LEWIS THOMAS LABORATORY PRINCETON, N J 08544 Biomedical research support
S07RR-07057-26 0631 (NSS) FRESCO, JACUES Biomedical research support NO RESEARCH SUBPROJECTS
S07RR-07058-26 (NSS) RUDCZYNSKI, ANDREW B RUTGERS UNIVERSITY ADMIN BLDG RM 123, BOX 1089 PISCATAWAY, NJ 08855 Biomedical research support
S07RR-07058-26 0172 (NSS) BAGNELL, CAROL A Biomedical research support INTERACTION OF RELAXIN & GROWTH FACTORS IN CONTROL OF OVARY
S07RR-07058-26 0173 (NSS) BAUM, JEAN Biomedical research support NMR STRUCTURE DETERMINATION OF TRIPLE HELICAL PEPTIDES
S07RR-07058-26 0174 (NSS) CONTRADA, RICHARD J Biomedical research support PSYCHOSOCIAL & PSYCHOPHYSIOLOGICAL FACTORS IN CORONARY ATHEROSCLEROSIS
S07RR-07058-26 0175 (NSS) EBRIGHT, RICHARD H Biomedical research support SEQ SPECIFIC DNA BINDING PROTEIN CONVERTED INTO SITE SPECIFIC DNA CLEAVAGE AGENT
S07RR-07058-26 0176 (NSS) FAGAN, JULIE M Biomedical research support TARGET PROTEASES IN FIBROBLASTS FOR BOWMAN BIRK INHIBITOR
S07RR-07058-26 0177 (NSS) GOLDMAN, ADRIAN Biomedical research support STRUCTURE OF LIGNINASE; XRAY CRYSTALLOGRAPHY
S07RR-07058-26 0178 (NSS) JOHN-ALDER, HENRY Biomedical research support PERIPHERAL THYROXINE METABOLISM
S07RR-07058-26 0179 (NSS) KATZ, LARRY S Biomedical research support LIVER MEDIATED REGULATION OF MATERNAL BEHAVIOR
S07RR-07058-26 0180 (NSS) KROGH-JESPERSEN, KAR Biomedical research support SIMULATIONS OF ELECTRONIC SPECTRA IN PROTEINS
S07RR-07058-26 0181 (NSS) MATSUMURA, FUMIO Biomedical research support MITOSIS SPECIFIC PHOSPHORYLATION OF MYOSIN LIGHT CHAIN KINASE
S07RR-07058-26 0182 (NSS) MONTELIONE, GAETANO Biomedical research support SOLUTION STRUCTURE OF HUMAN EPIDERMAL GROWTH FACTOR BY 2D & 3D NMR
S07RR-07058-26 0183 (NSS) PIETRUSZKO, REGINA Biomedical research support REQUEST FOR FUNDS FOR PEPTIDE SEQUENCING: ALCOHOL
S07RR-07058-26 0184 (NSS) TOMASEK, PAUL H Biomedical research support GENETIC REGULATION OF CARBOFURAN HYDROLASE
S07RR-07058-26 0185 (NSS) WEST, MARK O Biomedical research support BASAL GANGLIA; SENSORIMOTOR INTEGRATION
S07RR-07058-26 0186 (NSS) WHITE, EILEEN Biomedical research support ADENOVIRUS EIB ONCOGENE PRODUCT & CELL INTERMEDIATE FILAMENT PROTEINS COMPLEX
S07RR-07058-26 0187 (NSS) WIENCEK, JOHN Biomedical research support INFLUENCE OF PROTEIN PRIMARY STRUCTURE ON CRYSTAL GROWTH
S07RR-07059-26 (NSS) STEIN, DONALD G RUTGERS UNIV, HILL HALL RM 401 360 MARTIN LUTHER KING JR BLVD PISCATAWAY, NJ 08855 Biomedical research support
S07RR-07059-26 0829 (NSS) BUSH, DOUGLAS Biomedical research support ROLE OF CALCIUM IN SIGNAL TRANSDUCTION OF HORMONES
S07RR-07059-26 0830 (NSS) FEDER, HARVEY H Biomedical research support NORADRENERGIC REGULATION OF BEHAVIOR: REPRODUCTION, GUINEA PIGS
S07RR-07059-26 0831 (NSS) HART, RONALD P Biomedical research support PREPROTACHYKININ PROMOTER STRUCTURE: CNS
S07RR-07059-26 0832 (NSS) HUSKEY, WILLIAM P Biomedical research support ANALYSIS OF THE RATE CONTROLLING FEATURES OF A COMPLEX DEHYDROGENASE REACTION
S07RR-07059-26 0833 (NSS) JORDAN, FRANK Biomedical research support BIOPHYSICAL & BIO ORGANIC CHEMISTRY: LIPID PROTEIN: DRUG DESIGN
S07RR-07059-26 0834 (NSS) MCCASLIN, DARRELL R Biomedical research support MOLECULAR INTERACTIONS IN COMPONENTS OF VISUAL SYSTEM: RHODOPSIN, OPSIN KINASE
S07RR-07059-26 0835 (NSS) SMELTZER, SUZANNE C Biomedical research support EFFECTIVENESS OF COUGH IN MULTIPLE SCLEROSIS
S07RR-07059-26 0836 (NSS) WHIPPLE, BEVERLY Biomedical research support QUANTIFICATION OF MUSIC THERAPY AS A NON INVASIVE METHOD OF PAIN
S07RR-07059-26 0837 (NSS) MASON, DIANA J Biomedical research support CIRCADIAN RHYTHMS: OLDER ADULTS WITH & WITHOUT CONGESTIVE HEART FAILURE
S07RR-07059-26 0838 (NSS) SMELTZER SUZANNE C Biomedical research support MAXIMAL RESPIRATORY PRESSURES IN MULTIPLE SCLEROSIS: PULMONARY DYSFUNCTION
S07RR-07059-26 0839 (NSS) CARRITHERS, CAROLINE Biomedical research support ERRORS OF DEAF & DYSGRAPHIC SPELLERS: APHASIA, NEUROLINGUISTICS, PHONOLOGY
S07RR-07059-26 0840 (NSS) CHENG, MEI-FANG Biomedical research support BIOCHEMICAL BASIS OF BEHAVIOR
S07RR-07059-26 0841 (NSS) TEPPER, JAMES M Biomedical research support MICRODIALYSIS MEASUREMENT OF DOPAMINE RELEASE IN FREELY MOVING RATS
S07RR-07060-26 (NSS) HOOD, DONALD C COLUMBIA UNIVERSITY 406 SCHERMERHORN NEW YORK, NY 10027 Biomedical research support
S07RR-07060-26 0448 (NSS) PRYWES, RONALD Biomedical research support C FOS PROTO ONCOGENE MODEL FOR SIGNAL TRANSDUCTION IN GROWTH & CARCINOGENESIS
S07RR-07060-26 0449 (NSS) KRANTZ, DAVID Biomedical research support HUMAN REASONING
S07RR-07060-26 0450 (NSS) MANLEY, JAMES Biomedical research support CONTROL OF MRNA SYNTHESIS IN MAMMALIAN CELLS
S07RR-07060-26 0451 (NSS) PRIVES, CAROL Biomedical research support STRUCTURE & FUNCTION OF TUMOR ANTIGENS & TUMOR SUPPRESSOR PROTEINS
S07RR-07060-26 0452 (NSS) WRIGHT, CHARLES Biomedical research support GENERALIZED PROGRAMS IN WRITING, DRAWING, & AIMED MOVEMENTS
S07RR-07060-26 0453 (NSS) CHALFIE, MARTIN Biomedical research support GENETIC ANALYSIS OF NEMATOD CELL DIFFERENTIATION & DEGENERATION
S07RR-07061-26 (NSS) NESHEIM, MALDEN C CORNELL UNIVERSITY 300 DAY HALL ITHACA, N Y 14853 Biomedical research support
S07RR-07061-26 0188 (NSS) ANESHANSLEY, DANIEL Biomedical research support INTERDISCIPLINARY STUDY IN EXTREMELY LOW FREQUENCY MAGNETIC FIELDS & CANCER
S07RR-07061-26 0189 (NSS) MACINTYRE, ROSS J Biomedical research support NONSENSE MUTANTS & GLYCEROPHOSPHAGE DEHYDROGENASE LOCUS IN D MELANOGASTER: CDNA
S07RR-07061-26 0190 (NSS) RACKER, EFRAIM Biomedical research support IN VITRO RECONSTITUTIONS OF SIGNAL TRANSDUCTION PATHWAYS
S07RR-07061-26 0191 (NSS) STRUPP, BARBARA Biomedical research support NEONATAL BIOCHEMICAL DISTURBANCES & ADULT COGNITION: PKU, RETARDED
S07RR-07062-26 (NSS) STRAND, FLEUR NEW YORK UNIVERSITY 100 WASHINGTON SQUARE EAST NEW YORK, NY 10003 Biomedical research support
S07RR-07062-26 0210 (NSS) BOROWSKY, RICHARD Biomedical research support DNA FINGERPRINT ANALYSIS OF LOWER VERTEBRATE SPECIES; FISH XIPHOPHORUS VARIATUS
S07RR-07062-26 0211 (NSS) BRENNER, HENRY C Biomedical research support ODMR STUDIES OF BINDING OF ACETYLCHOLINE RECEPTOR PEPTIDES W/ NEUROTOXINS
S07RR-07062-26 0212 (NSS) CRAIG, RONALD G Biomedical research support XII COLLAGEN; PERIODONTAL MARKER; LIGAMENT SPECIFIC GENE EXPRESSION; WOUND HEAL
S07RR-07062-26 0213 (NSS) DEWAN, JOHN C Biomedical research support METAL INDUCED CHAIN SCISSIONS IN BIOMACRO MOLECULES; PROTEIN DYNAMICS
S07RR-07062-26 0215 (NSS) LANDY, MICHAEL S Biomedical research support SOFTWARE FOR MODELING VISUAL NEURAL TRANSFORMATIONS
S07RR-07062-26 0214 (NSS) LAFFERRIERE, GERARDO Biomedical research support DVMT NON LINEAR CONTROL MODEL; HUMAN UPPER TRUNK; BACK PAIN
S07RR-07062-26 0216 (NSS) MALLAT, STEPHANE Biomedical research support WAVELET THEORY APPLIED TO COMPUTER VISION IMAGE PROCESSING
S07RR-07062-26 0217 (NSS) LOBUE, JOSEPH Biomedical research support MEIOTIC STUDIES IN MICE BEARING TRANSPLANTABLE MONOMYELOCYTIC LEUKEMIA
S07RR-07062-26 0218 (NSS) MARKY, LUIS A Biomedical research support

VOLUME CHANGES IN NUCLEIC ACID HELIX FORMATION; DNA THERMODYNAMICS

S07RR-07062-26 0219 (NSS) MATTHEWS, T JAMES Biomedical research support APPLICATION OF NEW TECHNIQUE TO BEHAVIOR OF AUTISTIC CHILDREN

S07RR-07062-26 0220 (NSS) SHAPLEY, ROBERT Biomedical research support PROPORTIONS OF CONE PHOTORECEPTORS IN MACAQUE MONKEY RECEPTORS; VISION

S07RR-07062-26 0221 (NSS) MOVSHON, J ANTHONY Biomedical research support CORRELATED NEURONAL ACTIVITY IN VISUAL CORTEX

S07RR-07062-26 0222 (NSS) SPIELMAN, ANDREW I Biomedical research support PERIPHERAL MECHANISM OF MAMMALIAN BITTER TASTE

S07RR-07062-26 0223 (NSS) STITT, BARBARA Biomedical research support CLONING & SEQUENCING OF PROPOSED ANTITERMINATION FACTOR OF BACTERIOPHAGE T4

S07RR-07062-26 0224 (NSS) STITT, BARBARA Biomedical research support RHO RNA INTERACTIONS; TRANSCRIPTION TERMINATION

S07RR-07062-26 0225 (NSS) STOTZKY, GUENTHER Biomedical research support GENE TRANSFER BY TRANSFORMATION AMONG BACTERIA IN SOIL

S07RR-07062-26 0226 (NSS) WILSON, STEPHEN Biomedical research support SYNTH & DELIVERY OF INHIBITOR FOR CYTOCHROME P 450; ANTICANCER; ANTI CHOLESTEROL

S07RR-07062-26 0227 (NSS) GRUBMEYER, CHARLES Biomedical research support ENERGY COUPLING IN SALMONELL TYPHIMURIUM NICOTINATE PHOSPHORIBOSYL TRANSFERASE

S07RR-07062-26 0228 (NSS) AZMITIA, EFRAIN Biomedical research support FETAL NEURONAL TRANSPLANTATION INTO AGED BRAIN

S07RR-07062-26 0229 (NSS) BOROWSKY, RICHARD Biomedical research support GENETICS OF FEEDING BEHAVIOR IN SALT MARSH AMPHIPOD, GAMMARUS PALUSTRICS

S07RR-07062-26 0230 (NSS) MURPHY, RANDALL Biomedical research support PHARMACOLOGICAL CHARACTERIZATION OF SIGMA RECEPTOR; DRUGS OF ABUSE; NEUROLEPSY

S07RR-07064-24 (NSS) VERHAVE, THOM QUEENS COLLEGE OF THE CUNY 65-30 KISSENA BLVD FLUSHING, N Y 11367 Biomedical research support

S07RR-07064-24 0207 (NSS) SAFFRAN, WILMA Biomedical research support DNA CLEAVAGE BY PHOTOACTIVATED METALLOBLEOMYCINS

S07RR-07064-24 0208 (NSS) STREKAS, THOMAS C Biomedical research support BINDING OF ENANTIOMERIC RU(II) COMPLEXES TO DNA

S07RR-07064-24 0209 (NSS) SY, BON K Biomedical research support MODEL TO ASSESS DYSARTHRIC SPEECH SPEECH INTELLIGIBILITY & COMPUTERS RECOGNITION

S07RR-07064-24 0210 (NSS) SZALAY, JEANNE Biomedical research support LINOMIDE & 5DFUR ON MAMMARY TUMOR GROWTH, METASTASIS, HOST CELL IMMUNE RESPONSE

S07RR-07064-24 0211 (NSS) WASSERMAN, MARVIN Biomedical research support VITELLOGENINS (EGG PROTEINS) OF DROSOPHILA: VARIABILITY & REGULATION

S07RR-07064-24 0212 (NSS) WINNIK, WILMA Biomedical research support MEMORY DISSOCIATION IN NORMAL COMPARED TO HEAD INJURED PERSONS

S07RR-07064-24 0192 (NSS) AARONSON, SHELDON Biomedical research support USE OF FUNGI FOR FOOD OR MEDICINE BY ANCIENT & RECENT PEOPLES; PARASITES

S07RR-07064-24 0193 (NSS) BAKER, ARTHUR D Biomedical research support METAL COMPLEXES OF DIIMINES AS DNA PROBES

S07RR-07064-24 0194 (NSS) BODNAR, RICHARD J Biomedical research support SEROTONERGIC MODULATION OF OPIOID ANALGESIA W/ INTRACEREBRAL MICROINJECTION

S07RR-07064-24 0195 (NSS) BOROD, JOAN C Biomedical research support PERCEPTION OF FACIAL EMOTION IN SCHIZOPHRENIC & RIGHT BRAIN DAMAGED PATIENTS

S07RR-07064-24 0196 (NSS) BOSTOCK, ELIZABETH Biomedical research support NMDA ANTAGONIST MK 802 ON ENVIRONMENTALLY INDUCED PLASTICITY OF HIPPOCAMPUS

S07RR-07064-24 0197 (NSS) CALHOON, ROBERT E Biomedical research support GENETIC SUSCEPTABILITY: 7, 12 DIMETHYLBENZ A ANTHRACENE & MAMMARY CARCINOGENESIS

S07RR-07064-24 0198 (NSS) ENGEL, ROBERT Biomedical research support ANALOGUES OF INOSITOL PHOSPHATES

S07RR-07064-24 0199 (NSS) FARDY, PAUL S Biomedical research support PREVALENCE OF CORONARY ARTERY DISEASE RISK FACTORS IN ADOLESCENT MINORITIES

S07RR-07064-24 0200 (NSS) FRUMKES, THOMAS E Biomedical research support TONIC INHIBITION FROM DARK ADAPTED EYE ON VISION MEDIATED BY CONTRALATERAL EYE

S07RR-07064-24 0201 (NSS) GAFNEY, HARRY D Biomedical research support MECHANISM OF DNA CLEAVAGE BY PHOTOACTIVATED & PHOTOSENSITIZED METALLOBLEOMYCINS

S07RR-07064-24 0202 (NSS) HALPERIN, JEFFREY M Biomedical research support STIMULANT DRUG EFFECTS IN CHILDREN W/ ATTENTION DEFICIT HYPERACTIVITY DISORDER

S07RR-07064-24 0203 (NSS) HERSH, WILLIAM H Biomedical research support PHARMACEUTICAL SYNTHESIS ASYMMETRIC CATALYSIS OF DIELS ALDER REACTION

S07RR-07064-24 0204 (NSS) LUDMAN, ELAINE K Biomedical research support DIET RELATED FOLK MEDICINE PRACTICES OF KOREAN AMERICAN WOMEN IN PREGNANCY

S07RR-07064-24 0205 (NSS) RODBERG, LEONARD S Biomedical research support HEALTH & DISEASE INDICATORS VS SOCIAL ECONOMIC DATA FOR COMMUNITIES OF NY CITY

S07RR-07064-24 0206 (NSS) ROZE, ULDIS Biomedical research support MOSQUITO REPELLENT PROPERTIES OF PORCUPINE SKIN SECRETIONS

S07RR-07065-26 (NSS) BALTIMORE, DAVID ROCKEFELLER UNIVERSITY 1230 YORK AVENUE NEW YORK, NY 10021 Biomedical research support

S07RR-07065-26 0055 (NSS) BRESLOW, JAN L Biomedical research support GENETIC STUDIES OF LIPOPROTEINS; TRANSGENIC ANIMALS

S07RR-07065-26 0056 (NSS) BURLEY, STEPHEN K Biomedical research support X-RAY CRYSTALLOGRAPHIC STUDIES OF BIOLOGICAL MACROMOLECULES

S07RR-07065-26 0057 (NSS) CHAIT, BRIAN T Biomedical research support DVMT OF NEW MASS SPECTROMETRIC TOOLS FOR BIOMEDICAL RESEARCH SEQ

S07RR-07065-26 0058 (NSS) DARNELL, JAMES E Biomedical research support LIVER DIFFERENTIATION & MRNA REGULATION; TRANSCRIPTIONAL FACTORS

S07RR-07065-26 0059 (NSS) GOTSCHLICH, EMIL C Biomedical research support IMMUNOCHEMICAL & MOLECULAR STUDIES OF NEISSERIA: MENINGITIDIS, GONORRHOEAE

S07RR-07065-26 0060 (NSS) HEINTZ, NATHANIEL Biomedical research support BIOCHEMICAL GENETICS OF MICROTUBULES: CEREBELLUM GENE EXPRESSION

S07RR-07065-26 0061 (NSS) KAPPAS, ATTALLAH Biomedical research support ENV: HEME PATHWAY ENZYMES; CDNA CLONING & ERYTHROPOIETIC PROTOPORPHYRIA

S07RR-07065-26 0062 (NSS) KONARSKA, MARIA M Biomedical research support SPLICING OF MRNA PRECURSORS; REPLICATION OF HEPATITIS DELTA VIRUS

S07RR-07065-26 0063 (NSS) DEKABGEM TUTUA Biomedical research support CHROMOSOME FUNCTION IN VERTEBRATES

S07RR-07065-26 0064 (NSS) LUCK, DAVID Biomedical research support BIOCHEMICAL & GENETIC ANALYSIS OF MICROTUBULAR STRUCTURES

S07RR-07065-26 0065 (NSS) MANNING, JAMES M Biomedical research support CHEMICAL STUDIES ON SICKLE CELL HEMOGLOBIN; ANTI SICKLING AGENT

S07RR-07065-26 0066 (NSS) MCEWEN, BRUCE SW Biomedical research support HORMONAL REGULATION OF NEURAL GENE EXPRESSION

S07RR-07065-26 0067 (NSS) ISSCHE, SHEENAH Biomedical research support ROCKEFELLER UNIVERSITY PROTEIN SEQUENCING FACILITY

S07RR-07065-26 0068 (NSS) MILLER, ALAN D Biomedical research support CONTROL OF EMESIS: CANCER CHEMOTHERAPY INDUCED VOMITING, RESPIRATION

S07RR-07065-26 0069 (NSS) STARL, DENNIS M Biomedical research support HANDBOOK; TRAINING VIDEO; IN VITRO CYTOTOXICITY W/FISH HEPATOMA CELL LINE

S07RR-07066-26 (NSS) RENNIE, DONALD W SUNY AT BUFFALO 548 CAPEN HALL BUFFALO, NY 14260 Biomedical research support

S07RR-07066-26 0231 (NSS) ANGELO, JENNIFER K Biomedical research support COMPARING AUGMENTATIVE COMMUNICATION SCANNING MODES FOR PEOPLE W/ CEREBRAL PALSY

S07RR-07066-26 0232 (NSS) BALDWIN, IAN T Biomedical research support ALKALOIDS PHENOLICS IN RESISTANCE OF PLANTS TO ENHANCED UV B RADIATION

S07RR-07066-26 0233 (NSS) BEREZNEY, RONALD Biomedical research support IS P 200 NUCLEAR MATRIX ASSOCIATED MYOSIN LIKE PROTEIN?

S07RR-07066-26 0234 (NSS) BERMAN, CAROL M Biomedical research support GROUP SIZE, MATERNAL BEHAVIOR & INFANT SOCIAL NETWORKS

S07RR-07066-26 0235 (NSS) BERRY, JAMES O Biomedical research support MOLECULAR BIOLOGY OF C4 PHOTOSYNTHESIS IN GRAIN AMARANTH

S07RR-07066-26 0236 (NSS) BERRY, JAMES O Biomedical research support REGULAT EXPRESSION OF GENES ENCODING C4 MITROCHONDRIAL NAD MALIC ENZYME

S07RR-07066-26 0240 (NSS) BRUENN, JEREMY Biomedical research support ISOLATION OF CANDIDA ALBICANS GENES INVOLVED IN VIRULENCE

S07RR-07066-26 0241 (NSS) CADENHEAD, D ALLAN Biomedical research support DRUG INTERACTIONS W/ MODEL MEMBRANE

S07RR-07066-26 0242 (NSS) CHAKI, TARUN K Biomedical research support MECHANICAL PROPERTIES OF HYDROXYLAPATITE METAL COMPOSITES

S07RR-07066-26 0243 (NSS) CROCKER, JENNIFER Biomedical research support SELF ESTEEM & COPING AMONG HANDICAPPED

S07RR-07066-26 0244 (NSS) HASTRUP, JANICE L Biomedical research support ATTENTIONAL SHIFTS IN BRAIN FUNCTION: NATURAL STRESS & DICHOTIC LISTENING

S07RR-07066-26 0245 (NSS) HORVATH, PETER Biomedical research support DIFFERENTIATION OF COLON CANCER LINE BY SHORT CHAIN FATTY ACIDS

S07RR-07066-26 0237 (NSS) BOZARTH, MICHAEL A Biomedical research support INTRACRANIAL DYNORPHIN SELF ADMINISTRATION

S07RR-07066-26 0238 (NSS) BOZARTH, MICHAEL A Biomedical research support EVALUATION OF TWO NEW MEASURES OF BRAIN STIMULATION REWARD

S07RR-07066-26 0239 (NSS) BRIGHT, FRANK V Biomedical research support FIBER OPTIC BASED IMMUNOSENSORS

S07RR-07066-26 0246 (NSS) HULL, ELAINE M Biomedical research support GONADAL HORMONE INFLUENCE ON DOPAMINE METABOLISM & COPULATION IN MALE RATS

S07RR-07066-26 0247 (NSS) KOUDELKA, GERALD B Biomedical research support TRANSCRIPTIONAL ACTIVATION BY E COLI CAP

S07RR-07066-26 0248 (NSS) LASKER, HOWARD R Biomedical research support POPULATION GENETICS OF CLONAL INVERTEBRATES

S07RR-07066-26 0249 (NSS) LIN, TEIN-HSIANG Biomedical research support SOFTWARE DVMT; REAL TIME 3 D MICROIMAGING SYSTEM; SOFT XRAYS

S07RR-07066-26 0250 (NSS) LORETZ, CHRISTOPHER Biomedical research support STRETCH ACTIVATED ION CHANNELS

S07RR-07066-26 0251 (NSS) MAJOR, BRENDA N Biomedical research support COGNITIVE PREDICTORS OF EMOTIONAL SEQUELAE & DEPRESSION AFTER ABORTION

S07RR-07066-26 0252 (NSS) MORROW, JANET R Biomedical research support REAGENTS FOR SITE SPECIFIC RNA HYDROLYSIS

S07RR-07066-26 0253 (NSS) MORROW, JANET R Biomedical research support ARTIFICIAL RNA RESTRICTION ENZYMES

S07RR-07066-26 0254 (NSS) NAUGHTON, MICHAEL J Biomedical research support MAGNETIZATION STUDIES OF ANISOTROPHIC MACROMOLECULES

S07RR-07066-26 0255 (NSS) POLLOCK, DONALD K Biomedical research support DEPRESSION & ETHNICITY AMONG MEDICAL INPATIENTS

S07RR-07066-26 0256 (NSS) SALVI, RICHARD J Biomedical research support HAIR CELL REGENERATION & AUDITORY NERVE ACTIVITY AFTER AMINOGLYCOSIDE OTOTOXICI

S07RR-07066-26 0257 (NSS) SHAVER, PHILLIP R Biomedical research support ATTACHMENT STYLE AS MEDIATOR OF HEALTH RISK BEHAVIOR IN COUPLES

S07RR-07066-26 0258 (NSS) SHER, DAVID Biomedical research support QUANTITAT ANALYSIS & ERGONOMIC DISPLAY OF ELECTROCARDIOGRAPH DATA; STRESS TEST

S07RR-07066-26 0259 (NSS) TUROS, EDWARD Biomedical research support ORGANOMETALLIC APPROACH TO NOVEL POLYPROPIONATE ANTIBIOTICS

S07RR-07066-26 0260 (NSS) WHITE, SCOTT C Biomedical research support DISTRIBUTION OF JOINT STRESS DURING GAIT OF SUBJECT W/ HIP PAIN

S07RR-07066-26 0261 (NSS) YACK, H JOHN Biomedical research support IDENTIFYING FALLERS USING ACCELEROMETRY

PROJECT NO., ORGANIZATIONAL UNIT., INVESTIGATOR, ADDRESS, TITLE

S07RR-07067-26 (NSS) SCHNEIDER, ROBERT F STATE UNIV OF N Y STONY BROOK OFF OF RESEARCH SERVICES STONY BROOK, N Y 11794 Biomedical research support
S07RR-07067-26 0213 (NSS) CRULL, GEORGE Biomedical research support CALCIUM BINDING SITES OF HEME PROTEINS
S07RR-07067-26 0214 (NSS) FRANKLIN, NANCY Biomedical research support SPATIAL REPRESENTATION
S07RR-07067-26 0215 (NSS) DUDOCK, BERNARD S Biomedical research support MEDICAL RESEARCH & EDUCATION
S07RR-07067-26 0216 (NSS) FRICK, ROBERT Biomedical research support AUDITORY SHORT TERM MEMORY
S07RR-07067-26 0217 (NSS) GLASS, DAVID C Biomedical research support RELATIONSHIP BETWEEN DYSTHYMIA & CAREER BURNOUT
S07RR-07067-26 0218 (NSS) KLEIN, DANIEL N Biomedical research support EARLY ONSET CHRONIC DEPRESSION
S07RR-07067-26 0219 (NSS) LOBEL, MARCI Biomedical research support STRESS & BIRTH OUTCOMES
S07RR-07067-26 0220 (NSS) O'LEARY, K DANIEL Biomedical research support MARITAL CONFLICT
S07RR-07067-26 0222 (NSS) MENDELL, LORNE M Biomedical research support PHARMACOLOGY OF GABAERGIC TRANSMISSION; RETINA
S07RR-07067-26 0223 (NSS) PETRY, HEYWOOD Biomedical research support NEURAL MECHANISMS OF VISION
S07RR-07067-26 0224 (NSS) SIEBURTH, SCOTT Biomedical research support NEW METHODS FOR MATERIAL PRODUCT SYNTHESIS
S07RR-07067-26 0225 (NSS) STONE, ARTHUR Biomedical research support RELATIONSHIP BETWEEN STRESS & IMMUNITY
S07RR-07067-26 0226 (NSS) WEIDNER, GERDI Biomedical research support TYPE BEHAVIOR & LIFE & STRESS & CORONARY RISK IN FAMILIES
S07RR-07067-26 0227 (NSS) WOOD, JO ANNE Biomedical research support STRATEGIES OF SELF ENHANCEMENT
S07RR-07067-26 0221 (NSS) MAY, JACK Biomedical research support VISUAL PROJECTION IN GROUND SQUIRREL
S07RR-07068-26 (NSS) WARE, BENJAMIN R SYRACUSE UNIVERSITY 304 TOLLEY ADMIN BUILDING SYRACUSE, NY 13244-1100 Biomedical research support
S07RR-07068-26 0228 (NSS) BARLOW, ROBERT B Biomedical research support FUNCTIONAL ORGANIZATION OF VISUAL SYSTEM
S07RR-07068-26 0229 (NSS) BEEBER, LINDA S Biomedical research support FACTORS AFFECTING DEPRESSION IN YOUNG WOMEN:
S07RR-07068-26 0230 (NSS) BOLANOWSKI, STANLEY Biomedical research support MECHANOTRANSDUCTION IN PACINIAN CORPUSCLES: NEUROSCI REGENERATION
S07RR-07068-26 0231 (NSS) BORER, PHILIP N Biomedical research support NMR ANALYSIS OF RNA STRUCTURE & DYNAMICS
S07RR-07068-26 0232 (NSS) HOYER, WILLIAM Biomedical research support AGING, SKILL & KNOWLEDGE USE
S07RR-07068-26 0233 (NSS) LEVY, H RICHARD Biomedical research support STERIOD GLUCOSE 6 PHOSPHATE DEHYDROGENASE IN LIVERS OF AGING RATS
S07RR-07068-26 0234 (NSS) LIPSON, EDWARD Biomedical research support SYSTEM ANALYSIS OF PHYCOMYCES PHOTORESPONSES
S07RR-07068-26 0235 (NSS) MAINE, ELEANOR Biomedical research support GENETIC & MOLECULAR ANALYSIS OF DEVELOPMENT IN C ELEGANS
S07RR-07068-26 0236 (NSS) VAN DOREN, KEVIN Biomedical research support TRANS SPLICING IN NEMATODE CAENORHABDITIS ELEGANS
S07RR-07068-26 0237 (NSS) VERRILLO, RONALD T Biomedical research support INTENSITY EFFECTS ON AUDITORY & TACTILE SYSTEM
S07RR-07068-26 0238 (NSS) WITRAK, MARTHA Biomedical research support IMPACT OF RELOCATION ON DECISIONS AFFECTING PROFESSIONAL MOVES
S07RR-07069-26 (NSS) THOMPSON, BRIAN J UNIVERSITY OF ROCHESTER ROCHESTER, N Y 14627 Biomedical research support
S07RR-07069-26 0239 (NSS) SUPALLA, TED Biomedical research support CROSS LINGUISTIC STUDIES OF SIGNED LANGUAGE STRUCTURE
S07RR-07069-26 0240 (NSS) NEWPORT, ELISSA Biomedical research support EFFECTS OF AGE & INPUT ON ACQUISTION OF LANGUAGE
S07RR-07069-26 0241 (NSS) CARVER, S Biomedical research support DISCOVER ROCHESTER
S07RR-07069-26 0242 (NSS) KAYE, JEROME Biomedical research support TRANS ACTING FACTORS IN OVALBUMIN GENE EXPRESSION
S07RR-07069-26 0243 (NSS) SUPALLA, TED Biomedical research support TRAVEL EXPENSES, ETC ON CONFERENCE FOR CROSS LINGUISTIC RESEARCH
S07RR-07069-26 0244 (NSS) NORDEEN, KATHY Biomedical research support SPECIAL & GENERAL LEARNING IN SONG BIRDS
S07RR-07069-26 0245 (NSS) WU, J H DAVID Biomedical research support STRUCTURE & FUNCTION OF CELLULASE COMPONENTS
S07RR-07069-26 0246 (NSS) DOBSON, ANDREW Biomedical research support PRIMATE DEMOGRAPHY & GENETICS: MGMT OF CAPTIVE POPULATIONS USED IN MEDICINE
S07RR-07069-26 0247 (NSS) KNOX, ROBERT Biomedical research support MECHANISMS OF HPD PHOTOSENSITIZED SINGLET OXYGEN PRODUCTION
S07RR-07069-26 0248 (NSS) FRENCH, LUCIA Biomedical research support COMMUNICATION IN NURSERY SCHOOL
S07RR-07069-26 0249 (NSS) HALL, BARRY Biomedical research support MOLECULAR EVOLUTION
S07RR-07069-26 0250 (NSS) KOOL, ERIC Biomedical research support RECOGNITION OF PROTO ONCOGENE MRNA
S07RR-07070-26 (NSS) HOCHMUTH, ROBERT M DUKE UNIVERSITY 144A ENGINEERING BLDG DURHAM, N C 27706 Biomedical research support
S07RR-07070-26 0454 (NSS) CHERRY, ROBERT S Biomedical research support ACQUISITION OF A PARTICLE ANALYZER
S07RR-07070-26 0455 (NSS) NICHKLAS, BRUCE R Biomedical research support THREE DIMENSIONAL LIGHT MICROSCOPY OF LIVING CELLS IN REAL TIME
S07RR-07070-26 0456 (NSS) TOONE, ERIC J Biomedical research support ENZYME BASED CARBOHYDRATE SYNTHESIS
S07RR-07070-26 0457 (NSS) TOONE, ERIC J Biomedical research support PROTEIN CARBOHYDRATE INTERACTION
S07RR-07070-26 0458 (NSS) BOYNTON, JOHN E Biomedical research support SCANNING SPECTROFLUORIMETER FOR DCBM GROUP IN BIOLOGICAL SCIENCES
S07RR-07070-26 0459 (NSS) RUBIN, DAVID C Biomedical research support SUPPORT OF PSYCHOLOGY LABORATORY: MEMORY, SPATIAL & OBJECT IMAGERY
S07RR-07070-26 0460 (NSS) BEJAN, ADRIAN Biomedical research support HEAT TRANSFER FUNDAMENTALS OF SKIN BURNS
S07RR-07070-26 0461 (NSS) SMITH, STEPHEN W Biomedical research support IMPROVED ULTRASONIC IMAGING W/ NEW TRANSDUCERS: ULTRASOUND
S07RR-07071-26 (NSS) HODGSON, ERNEST NORTH CAROLINA STATE UNIV BOX 7633 RALEIGH, NC 27695-7633 Biomedical research support
S07RR-07071-26 0251 (NSS) BOSTON, REBECCA Biomedical research support FUNCTION OF MAIZE B 70 PROTEIN; HEAT SHOCK PROTEIN
S07RR-07071-26 0252 (NSS) KLAPES, N ARLENE Biomedical research support MAGAININ PEPTIDES BIOCIDAL ACTIVITY ON FOODBORNE PATHOGENS & SPOILAGE MICROORG
S07RR-07071-26 0253 (NSS) MAHAFFEY, JAMES W Biomedical research support ESTABLISHMENT OF HEAD SEGMENTATION DURING DROSOPHILA EMBRYOGENESIS II
S07RR-07071-26 0254 (NSS) LASTER, SCOTT M Biomedical research support RAS GENE MUTATIONS IN LUNG CANCER CELL RESISTANCE TO MACROPHAGE CYTOTOXICITY
S07RR-07071-26 0255 (NSS) LOMMEL, STEVEN A Biomedical research support HOST FACTORS INVOLVED IN RIBOSOMAL FRAMESHIFT REGULATION OF VIRAL POLYMERASE
S07RR-07071-26 0256 (NSS) LEBLANC, GERALD A Biomedical research support STEROL BINDING PROTEINS AS TARGET SITES FOR ANTI INFLAMMATORY DRUG ACTION
S07RR-07071-26 0257 (NSS) AGRIS, PAUL F Biomedical research support NEW PROTEIN SEQUENCER FOR SHARED RESEARCH RESOURCE
S07RR-07071-26 0258 (NSS) HARDIN, CHARLES C Biomedical research support ION DEPENDENT CONTROL OF GENE EXPRESSION: MODEL FOR C MYC ONCOGENE PROMOTER
S07RR-07071-26 0259 (NSS) KHALEDI, MORTEZA G Biomedical research support ORGANIZED MEDIA IN HIGH PERFORMANCE CAPILLARY ELECTROPHORESIS
G20RR-07072-01 (AR) GUERTIN, ROBERT P TUFTS UNIVERSITY 120 PACKARD AVENUE MEDFORD, MA 02155 Renovation for psychology research animal care facility
S07RR-07072-26 (NSS) COLEMAN, MARY SUE UNIVERSITY OF NORTH CAROLINA 02 S BLDG, CB #4000 CHAPEL HILL, N C 27599-4000 Biomedical research support
S07RR-07072-26 0274 (NSS) UDRY, RICHARD J Biomedical research support PURCHASE EQUIPMENT FOR CORE ACTIVITIES
S07RR-07072-26 0275 (NSS) WIGHTMAN, MARK R Biomedical research support CALCIUM FLUORESCENCE FROM ADRENAL CELLS
S07RR-07072-26 0262 (NSS) CHO, M J Biomedical research support PASSIVE DRUG TARGETING BY MEANS OF PARTICULATE DRUG CARRIERS
S07RR-07072-26 0263 (NSS) DEFRIESE, GORDON H Biomedical research support RURAL CENTER PROGRAM
S07RR-07072-26 0264 (NSS) DYKSTRA, LINDA A Biomedical research support BENZODIAZEPINES: TOLERANCES & ACUTE & CHRONIC DEPENDENCE
S07RR-07072-26 0265 (NSS) FORBES, MALCOLM D E Biomedical research support DIFFUSION IN PHOSPHOLIPID BILAYERS
S07RR-07072-26 0266 (NSS) GALLAGHER, MICHELA Biomedical research support HVS IMAGE; SOFTWARE; STUDY NERVOUS SYSTEM
S07RR-07072-26 0267 (NSS) KAY, BRIAN K Biomedical research support BIOGENESIS OF EUKARYOTIC HNRNP COMPLEX
S07RR-07072-26 0268 (NSS) KLECH, CATHY M Biomedical research support MODEL; TRANSPORT OF MACROMOLECULAR DRUGS ACROSS MICROPOROUS MEMBRANES
S07RR-07072-26 0269 (NSS) LYSLE, DONALD T Biomedical research support IMMUNE ALTERATIONS MEDIATED BY CONDITIONING
S07RR-07072-26 0270 (NSS) MILLEN, JANE Biomedical research support INHIBITORS OF COLLAGEN BIOSYNTHESIS
S07RR-07072-26 0271 (NSS) NEELON, VIRGINIA J Biomedical research support SLEEP APNEA & CONFUSION DVMT IN HOSPITALIZED ELDERLY
S07RR-07072-26 0272 (NSS) PICKER, MITCHELL J Biomedical research support BEHAVIORAL EFFECTS OF OPIOID
S07RR-07072-26 0273 (NSS) ROBERTS, JOANNE E Biomedical research support OTITIS MEDIA IN CHILDHOOD & LATER LANGUAGE LEARNING
S07RR-07074-26 (NSS) SWEENEY, THOMAS L OHIO ST UNIV RES & GRAD STUD 190 NORTH OVAL MALL COLUMBUS, OHIO 43210 Biomedical sciences support
S07RR-07074-26 0679 (NSS) KOLATTUKUDY, PAPPACH Biomedical sciences support ELASTASE DIRECTED APPROACH AGAINST ASPERGILLOSIS
G20RR-07075-01 (AR) JOHNSON, LAWRENCE L TRUDEAU INSTITUTE, INC P.O. BOX 59 SARANAC LAKE, NY 12983 Developing and improving institutional animal resources
S07RR-07075-17 (NSS) FRANK, ROBERT A UNIVERSITY OF CINCINNATI MAIL LOCATION #376 CINCINNATI, OH 45221 Biomedical research support
S07RR-07075-17 0260 (NSS) KANESHIRO, EDNA Biomedical research support UPTAKE & METABOLISM OF LIPIDS BY PNEUMOCYSTIS
S07RR-07075-17 0261 (NSS) ELDER, RICHARD Biomedical research support SUPPORT FOR DVMT OF BIOMED CHEM RESEARCH CNTR; MASS SPECT
S07RR-07075-17 0262 (NSS) GEHRKE, STEVIN H Biomedical research support BIORESPONSIVE POLYMERS FOR BIOMEDICAL APPLICATION
S07RR-07075-17 0263 (NSS) HEINEMANN, WM R Biomedical research support ELECTROCHEMICAL IMMUNOASSAY: SIMULTANEOUS DETERMINATION OF MULTIPLE ANALYTES
S07RR-07075-17 0264 (NSS) MEYER, RALPH R Biomedical research support STRUCTURE & FUNCTION RELATIONSHIPS; SINGLE STRANDED DNA BINDING PROTEIN; E COLI
S07RR-07075-17 0265 (NSS) DHAWAN, ATAM P Biomedical research support MULTI MODALITY MEDICAL IMAGING CORRELATION; KNOWLEDGE BASED IMAGE ANALYSIS
G20RR-07076-01 (AR) HOPPER, JOAN G IOWA STATE UNIVERSITY 1426 VETERINARY MEDICINE AMES, IOWA 50011 Iowa State University animal resource improvement
S07RR-07077-24 (NSS) DURHAM, NORMAN N OKLAHOMA STATE UNIVERSITY 101 WHITEHURST STILLWATER, OKLA 74078 Biomedical research support
S07RR-07077-24 0266 (NSS) LESSLEY, BRUCE A Biomedical research support METALLOPROTEASES OF MAMMALIAN SPERMATOZOA: IN VITRO FERTILIZATION
S07RR-07077-24 0267 (NSS) YATES, LAWRENCE Biomedical research support PATHWAYS I CALCIUM REGULATION OF MUSCLE CONTRACTION
S07RR-07077-24 0268 (NSS) SAUER, JOHN R Biomedical research support SALIVARY SECRETION IN BLOOD SUCKING ARTHROPOD

PROJECT NO., ORGANIZATIONAL UNIT., INVESTIGATOR, ADDRESS, TITLE

S07RR-07077-24 0269 (NSS) YU, CHANG-AN Biomedical research support
REACTION MECHANISM OF MYOCARDIAL UBIQUINONE BINDING PROTEINS
S07RR-07078-18 (NSS) SMITH, EDDIE C UNIVERSITY OF OKLAHOMA 1000 ASP AVENUE, RM 314 NORMAN, OKLA 73019 Biomedical research support
S07RR-07078-18 0455 (NSS) BLANK, C LEROY Biomedical research support MULTIELECTRODE ARRAY DETECTORS; LIQUID CHROMATOGRAPHY W/ ELECTROCHEM DETECTION
S07RR-07078-18 0456 (NSS) DEVENPORT, LYNN D Biomedical research support TYPE 2 CORTICOSTEROID RECEPTOR STIMULATIONS & FUEL DELIVER
S07RR-07078-18 0457 (NSS) NAGLE, DAVID P, JR Biomedical research support INHIBITION OF METHANE BACTERIA BY COENZYME ANALOGUE LUMAZINE
S07RR-07078-18 0458 (NSS) NELSON, DEBORAH I Biomedical research support CONTAMINATION IN HOMES OF LEAD WORKERS
S07RR-07078-18 0459 (NSS) OREAR, EDGAR A Biomedical research support THROMBOLYSIS W/ LIPOSOMAL ENCAPSULATED STREPTOKINASE: SIMULATION OF CLOTS
S07RR-07078-18 0460 (NSS) BASTIAN, JOSEPH A, J Biomedical research support MORPHOLOG, PHYSIOLOGICAL CHARACTER OF CENTRAL SENSORY NEURONS
S07RR-07078-18 0461 (NSS) DEVENPORT, LYNN D Biomedical research support EQUIPMENT FOR FEEDING & MEASURING METABOLISM, BODY COMP ENERGY REGULATION
S07RR-07078-18 0462 (NSS) DOWNARD, JOHN S Biomedical research support DNA SEQ OF MYXOCOCCUS XANTHUS GENES IN REGULATION OF DEVEL GENE EXPRESS
S07RR-07078-18 0463 (NSS) DRYHURST, GLENN Biomedical research support OXIDATION CHEMISTRY OF ABNORMAL CNS ALKALOIDS
S07RR-07078-18 0464 (NSS) DURICA, DAVID S Biomedical research support ACTIN GENE FUSIONS BY P ELEMENT MEDIATED GENE TRANSFER
S07RR-07078-18 0465 (NSS) LIU, MING-CHEH Biomedical research support BOVINE LIVER TYROSINE O SULFATE BINDING PROTEIN
S07RR-07078-18 0466 (NSS) TAYLOR, RICHARD A Biomedical research support IONOPHORE CATALYZED CATION TRANSPORT
G20RR-07079-01 (AR) MCPHERSON, CHARLES W NORTH CAROLINA STATE UNIVERSIT BOX 8401 RALEIGH, NC 27695-8401 Animal resource improvements
S07RR-07079-26 (NSS) MATHEWS, CHRISTOPHER K OREGON STATE UNIVERSITY DEPARTMENT OF ZOOLOGY CORVALLIS, OREGON 97331 Biomedical research support
S07RR-07079-26 0276 (NSS) HAYS, JOHN B Biomedical research support
TEMPERATURE SENSITIVITY OF PHOTOREACTIVATION OF UV DAMAGED DNA IN CROP PLANTS
S07RR-07079-26 0277 (NSS) REAM, WALT Biomedical research support
VIRD2 PROTEIN IN CROWN GALL TUMORIGENESES
S07RR-07079-26 0278 (NSS) ROHRMANN, GEORGE F Biomedical research support SPECIFIC BACULOVIRUS PROTEINS CHARACTERIZATION USING IMMUNOELECTRON MICROSCOPY
S07RR-07079-26 0279 (NSS) WHANGER, PHILIP D Biomedical research support ENCODING OF BOVINE GLUTATHIONE PEROXIDASE GENE IN BACTERIAL SYSTEM
S07RR-07079-26 0280 (NSS) HU, CHING YUAN Biomedical research support RAT ADIPOCYTE SITE SPECIFIC MABS PRODUCTION & CHARACTERIZATION
S07RR-07079-26 0281 (NSS) GAMBLE, WILBERT Biomedical research support MEVALONATE SHUNT & ROLE IN BIOSYNTHESIS OF N MEDIUM CHAIN DIACYL GLYCEROLS
S07RR-07079-26 0282 (NSS) SLABAUGH, MARY B Biomedical research support RETROVIRAL PROTEASE LIKE GENE ENCODED BY VACCINIA VIRUS
S07RR-07079-26 0283 (NSS) RIVIN, CAROL J Biomedical research support SPATIAL EXPRESSION OF MATURATION PHASE GENE DURING MAIZE EMBRYOGENESIS
S07RR-07079-26 0284 (NSS) GOULD, STEVEN J Biomedical research support BIOSYNTHESIS OF MICROBIAL METABOLITES FROM HYDROXYLATED ANTHRANILIC ACIDS
S07RR-07079-26 0285 (NSS) BAKALINSKY, ALAN T Biomedical research support SULFITE METABOLISM IN SACCHAROMYCES CEREVISIAE
S07RR-07079-26 0286 (NSS) MCGUIRE, JOSEPH M Biomedical research support PREADSORBED PROTEIN, LISTERIA MONOCYTOGENES TO HYDROPHILIC & PHOBIC SURFACES
S07RR-07079-26 0287 (NSS) SMITH, MARGARET M Biomedical research support COHORT OF PERSONS ARRESTED FOR DRIVING UNDER INFLUENCE OF INTOXICANTS
S07RR-07079-26 0288 (NSS) HARE, JANETTE M Biomedical research support FORMAL ADVANCE DIRECTIVES FOR HEALTH CARE AMONG PATIENTS & DECISION MAKERS
S07RR-07079-26 0289 (NSS) RICHARDS, LESLIE N Biomedical research support LONGITUDIAL STUDY OF GENERATIONS SINGLE PARENT STUDY
S07RR-07079-26 0290 (NSS) VUCHINICH, SAMUEL Biomedical research support ALLIANCES DURING FAMILY PROBLEM SOLVING: TEST FOR INHIBITING EFFECTS
S07RR-07079-26 0291 (NSS) WALKER, ALEXIS J Biomedical research support OBSERVATIONAL DATA IN FAMILY CAREGIVING
S07RR-07079-26 0292 (NSS) GELLER, BRUCE L Biomedical research support PROTEIN SECRETION FACTOR PURIFICATION
S07RR-07079-26 0293 (NSS) TREMPY, JANINE E Biomedical research support ACTIVITIES THAT SUPPRESS OVERPRODUCTION OF CAPSULAR POLYSACCHARIDE
S07RR-07079-26 0294 (NSS) CERKLEWSKI, FLORIAN Biomedical research support DIET, TISSUE CATABOLISM & ADRENAL GLUCOCORTICOID ACTIVITY RELATIONSHIP
S07RR-07079-26 0295 (NSS) MILLER, LORRAINE T Biomedical research support VITAMIN B 6 DEFICIENC EFFECT ON GROWTH KINETICS OF HUMAN BREAST CANCER CELL LINE
S07RR-07079-26 0296 (NSS) MUNAR, MYRNA Y Biomedical research support HEPATIC MARKERS USED TO PREDICT CYCLOSPORINE DISPOSITION
S07RR-07079-26 0297 (NSS) REED, MARJORIE A Biomedical research support SUBLEXIAL UNITS IN READING OF NORMAL & DISABLED READERS
S07RR-07079-26 0298 (NSS) DUFFEE, NICOLE E Biomedical research support INFLAMMATION ROLE IN RENAL REPERFUSION INJURY
S07RR-07079-26 0299 (NSS) FRANK, ANTHONY A Biomedical research support EMBRYO PROTECTION FROM ALKYLATION INDUCED INJURY
S07RR-07079-26 0300 (NSS) GIMLICH, ROBERT L Biomedical research support GAP JUNCTIONAL COMMUNICATIONS IN VERTEBRATE OVARIAN FOLLICLE
S07RR-07079-26 0301 (NSS) ROBERTS, PAUL A Biomedical research support LATE FUNCTIONS OF SALIVARY GLANDS IN DROSOPHILA

PROJECT NO., ORGANIZATIONAL UNIT., INVESTIGATOR, ADDRESS, TITLE

S07RR-07079-26 0302 (NSS) MEINTS, RUSSEL Biomedical research support TEMPERATURE SENSITIVITY OF UV DAMAGED DNA IN CROP PLANTS
S07RR-07079-26 0303 (NSS) MORAN, PATRICIA B Biomedical research support IMPACT OF DIVORCE ON CHILDREN DURING TRANSITION CHILDHOOD & ADOLESCENCE
S07RR-07080-26 (NSS) MOSELEY, JOHN T UNIVERSITY OF OREGON 120 CHAPMAN HALL EUGENE, ORE 97403 Biomedical research support
S07RR-07080-26 0304 (NSS) LANDE, RUSSELL Biomedical research support CORRELATED CHARACTERS IN COMPLEX GENETIC SYSTEMS
S07RR-07080-26 0305 (NSS) WOOD, MICHELLE Biomedical research support FLUORESCENT PROBES FOR INDIVIDUAL CELL HEALTH IN MICROBIAL POPULATIONS
S07RR-07080-26 0306 (NSS) SHAPIRO, LYNDA P Biomedical research support PHYSIOLOGY & ECOLOGY OF MARINE PHYTOPLANKTON
S07RR-07080-26 0307 (NSS) BARKAN, ALICE Biomedical research support
ROLES OF NUCLEAR GENE PRODUCTS IN PLASTID DEVELOPMENT
S07RR-07080-26 0308 (NSS) EISEN, JUDITH Biomedical research support
PATHFINDING BY IDENTIFIED NEURONS IN ZEBRAFISH
S07RR-07080-26 0309 (NSS) LOI, POH KENG Biomedical research support
NEUROBIOLOGY OF IDENTIFIED PEPTIDERGIC CELLS
S07RR-07080-26 0310 (NSS) ROBERTS, WILLIAM Biomedical research support ION CHANNELS AT NEUROMUSCULAR JUNCTION
S07RR-07080-26 0311 (NSS) WEEKS, JANIS Biomedical research support
HORMONALLY MEDIATED REORGANIZATION OF INSECT NERVOUS SYSTEM; METAMORPHOSIS
S07RR-07080-26 0312 (NSS) FREDERICK, SHERI Biomedical research support AFFECTING PRIMING OF POSITIVE & NEGATIVE TRAIT WORDS
S07RR-07080-26 0313 (NSS) FRISCH, DEBORAH Biomedical research support FRAMING EFFECTS IN DECISION MAKING
S07RR-07080-26 0314 (NSS) MARROCCO, RICHARD T Biomedical research support PSYCHOPHYSICAL STUDIES OF VISUAL NEURAL CHANNELS
S07RR-07080-26 0315 (NSS) MAURO, ROBERT Biomedical research support
EYEWITNESS IDENTIFICATION & INTERVIEWING
S07RR-07080-26 0316 (NSS) SIMONS, ANNE Biomedical research support
PSYCHOBIOLOGY OF RECOVERY IN DEPRESSION
S07RR-07080-26 0317 (NSS) SUNDBERG, NORMAN D Biomedical research support COMPARATIVE LIFE HISTORIES
S07RR-07081-26 (NSS) JORDAN, ANGEL G CARNEGIE MELLON UNIVERSITY 5000 FORBES AVENUE PITTSBURGH, PA 15213 Biomedical research support
G20RR-07082-01 (AR) LICHTMAN, MARSHALL A 601 ELMWOOD AVENUE P O BOX 706 ROCHESTER, NY 14642 University of Rochester animal resource improvements
S07RR-07082-26 (NSS) FERGUSON, FREDERICK G PENNSYLVANIA STATE UNIVERSITY CENTRALIZED BIO LAB UNIVERSITY PARK, PA 16802 Biomedical research support
S07RR-07082-26 0270 (NSS) AHERN, FRANK M Biomedical research support ALCOHOL & PRESCRIPTION DRUG INTERACTION AMONG ELDERLY
S07RR-07082-26 0271 (NSS) ARTECA, RICHARD N Biomedical research support PRODUCTION OF ANTITUMOR COMPOUNDS BY PLANT TISSUE CULTURES
S07RR-07082-26 0272 (NSS) BERNLOHR, ROBERT W Biomedical research support NUTRIENT SENSING AS GLOBAL CONTROL SIGNAL
S07RR-07082-26 0273 (NSS) CORNWELL, PAUL R Biomedical research support CATS HIPPOCAMPUS IN MEMORY
S07RR-07082-26 0274 (NSS) DANGLER, CHARLES A Biomedical research support HERPES VIRUSES IN PATHOGENESIS OF ATHEROSCLEROSIS
S07RR-07082-26 0275 (NSS) DEINES, PETER Biomedical research support
EXAM NUTRITION & HEALTH BY STABLE CARBON & NITROGEN ANALYSIS OF HUMAN BONE
S07RR-07082-26 0276 (NSS) DOORES, STEPHANIE Biomedical research support LISTERIOLYSIN IN INTRACELLULAR SURVIVAL & REPLICATION; LISTERIA MONOCYTOGENES
S07RR-07082-26 0277 (NSS) DUNSON, WILLIAM A Biomedical research support CLONAL FISH; RIVULUS MARMORATUS; ANIMAL MODEL; TOXICANT ACUTE & CHRONIC EFFECTS
S07RR-07082-26 0278 (NSS) FARRELL, PETER A Biomedical research support CENTRAL NERVOUS SYSTEM ENDORPHINS & OBESITY
S07RR-07082-26 0279 (NSS) FLORES, HECTOR E Biomedical research support METABOLISM & PRODUCTION OF SANGUINARINE IN HAIRY ROOT CULTURES
S07RR-07082-26 0280 (NSS) FOSMIRE, GARY J Biomedical research support EFFECTS OF MATERIALS OF LOW BIOAVAILABILITY OF ZINC ABSORPTION & UTILIZATION
S07RR-07082-26 0281 (NSS) FRANGOS, JOHN A Biomedical research support IN VITRO BONE INDUCTION
S07RR-07082-26 0282 (NSS) FREIVALDS, ANDRIS Biomedical research support QUANTIFICATION OF WRIST MOVEMENT IN CUMULATIVE TRAUMA DISORDERS
S07RR-07082-26 0283 (NSS) FRISQUE, RICHARD J Biomedical research support PRODUCE MABS & POLYCLONAL ANTIBODIES TO VIRAL ANTIGENS OF HUMAN POLYOMAVIRUS JCV
S07RR-07082-26 0284 (NSS) GAY, CAROL V Biomedical research support
PARATHYROID HORMONE RECEPTORS ON LIVING BONE CELLS
S07RR-07082-26 0285 (NSS) GILMOUR, DAVID S Biomedical research support MOLECULAR ARCHITECTURE OF HSP 70 HEAT SHOCK GENE PROMOTER OF DROSOPHILA
S07RR-07082-26 0286 (NSS) HAMMERSTEDT, ROY H Biomedical research support OFF SITE GRAPHICS & DATA ANALYSIS FOR FLOW CYTOMETER FACILITY
S07RR-07082-26 0287 (NSS) HILDENBRANDT, GEORGE Biomedical research support ANTINFLAMMATORY; DIHOMO Y LINOLENIC ACID; LIPOXYGENASE PATHWAY
S07RR-07082-26 0288 (NSS) HOOD, KATHRYN E Biomedical research support GENETIC & ENVIRON; ANIMAL MODEL OF INTERGENERATIONAL TRANSMISSION OF CHILD ABUSE
S07RR-07082-26 0319 (NSS) WOJCHOWSKI, DON M Biomedical research support MOLECULAR MECHANISMS OF ERTHROPOIETIN INDUCED RED BLOOD CELL DIFFERENTIATION
S07RR-07082-26 0320 (NSS) YEH, YU-YAN Biomedical research support
MECHANISMS OF HYPOCHOLESTEROLEMIC ACTION OF STEARIC ACID
S07RR-07082-26 0321 (NSS) ZARKOWER, ARIAN Biomedical research support DVMT MODEL; POLYUNSATURATED FATTY ACID EICOSANOID METABOLISM VS PULMONARY DIS
S07RR-07082-26 0289 (NSS) JONES, BARRY Biomedical research support
GENE SEQUENCE; SOMATICALLY RECOMBINED MHC CLASS II GENE; B CELL LYMPHOMA
S07RR-07082-26 0290 (NSS) JONES, BARRY Biomedical research support

PROJECT NO., ORGANIZATIONAL UNIT., INVESTIGATOR, ADDRESS, TITLE

INTRACISTERNAL A PARTICLE GENES W/ MOUSE MAJOR HISTOCOMPATABILITY COMPLEX
S07RR-07082-26 0291 (NSS) KAO, TEH-HUI Biomedical research support S PROTEIN RIBONUCLEASE ACTIVITY IN SELF RECOGNITION
S07RR-07082-26 0292 (NSS) KENNEY, EDWARD S Biomedical research support IMPROVED DETECTOR FOR MEDICAL & INDUSTRIAL PHOTON IMAGING
S07RR-07082-26 0293 (NSS) KENNEY, W LARRY Biomedical research support ESTROGEN SUPPLEMENT: POST MENOPAUSAL WOMEN; BODY FLUID BODY TEMP IN HOT ENVIRON
S07RR-07082-26 0294 (NSS) KEPHART, GEORGE C Biomedical research support CHANGES IN BREASTFEEDING & CONTRACEPTIVE PRACTICES ON INFANT MORTALITY
S07RR-07082-26 0295 (NSS) KILLIAN, GARY J Biomedical research support STUDIES ON SPERM CAPACITATION
S07RR-07082-26 0296 (NSS) KIM, KE CHUNG Biomedical research support VECTOR POTENTIAL OF TICKS IN LYME DISEASE EPIDEMIOLOGY
S07RR-07082-26 0297 (NSS) KNABEL, STEPHEN J Biomedical research support HEAT SHOCK PROTEINS IN PREVENTING OXYGEN RADICAL MEDIATED CYTOTOXICITY
S07RR-07082-26 0298 (NSS) LECOMTE, JULIETTE T Biomedical research support STRUCTURE OF APOCYTOCHROME B5 IN SOLUTION
S07RR-07082-26 0299 (NSS) MERZ, KENNETH M Biomedical research support SACCHARIDE CONFORMATION: STRUCTURAL & THEORETICAL STUDIES
S07RR-07082-26 0300 (NSS) MILAKOFSKY, LOUIS Biomedical research support TAURINE: BIOMARKER OF STRESS & AGING IN RATS
S07RR-07082-26 0301 (NSS) MITCHELL, ROBERT B Biomedical research support LONGITUDINAL AGING STUDY OF COLD TOLERANCE IN HS MICE
S07RR-07082-26 0302 (NSS) ORTH, ANNE B Biomedical research support MICROSOMAL LIPID PEROXIDATION: AROMATIC HYDROCARBON & DICARBOXIMIDE FUNGICIDES
S07RR-07082-26 0303 (NSS) PORTER, RONALD D Biomedical research support PROTEIN ENTRY IN FUNCTION OF RECOMBINATION HOT SPOTS
S07RR-07082-26 0304 (NSS) PUHL, SUSAN M Biomedical research support CARBON MONOXIDE DILUTION SYSTEM FOR DETERMIN BLOOD VOLUME; WOMEN
S07RR-07082-26 0305 (NSS) REDDY, A P Biomedical research support DOWNS SYNDROME REGION & OTHER LINKED GENES ON HUMAN CHROMOSOME 21
S07RR-07082-26 0306 (NSS) SEGAL, STEVEN S Biomedical research support CONDUIT BLOOD VESSEL RESPONSES TO HEMODYNAMIC STIMULI IN VITRO
S07RR-07082-26 0307 (NSS) SHALLOWAY, DAVID I Biomedical research support APPLICATION OF ADENOVIRUS EIA GENE IN CANCER IMMUNOTHERAPY
S07RR-07082-26 0308 (NSS) SMYER, MICHAEL Biomedical research support STRESS ADAPTION & SUCCESSFUL AGING: SELECTIVE OPTIMIZATION W/ COMPENSATION
S07RR-07082-26 0309 (NSS) STIFTER, CYNTHIA A Biomedical research support LONG TERM EFFECTS OF INFANT COLIC ON INFANT BEHAVIOR
S07RR-07082-26 0310 (NSS) STOUT, JOSEPH T Biomedical research support IMMUNE CYCLING IN SENESCENCE
S07RR-07082-26 0311 (NSS) STREIT, DONALD A Biomedical research support VARIABLE GRAVITY SYSTEM; ELDERLY; SPACE FLIGHT TRAINING; DESIGN & CONSTRUCT
S07RR-07082-26 0312 (NSS) TARBELL, JOHN M Biomedical research support AN IN VITRO STUDY OF SHEAR DEPENDENT ENDOTHELIAL PERMEABILITY
S07RR-07082-26 0313 (NSS) TU, CHEN-PEI D Biomedical research support DEFICIENCY OF HUMAN GLUTATHIONE S TRANSFERASE EXPRESSION & LUNG CANCER
S07RR-07082-26 0314 (NSS) ULTMAN, JAMES S Biomedical research support DYNAMIC RESPONSE; LOW BIRTH WEIGHT INFANT; NATURAL VARIAT IN ENVIRON CONDITIONS
S07RR-07082-26 0315 (NSS) VAN CAMPEN, HANA Biomedical research support TUMOR NECROSIS FACTOR & ENDOTOXIN RESISTANCE IN AVIAN SPECIES
S07RR-07082-26 0316 (NSS) VASILATOS-YOUNKEN, R Biomedical research support PLASMA GROWTH HORMONE CONCENTRATION CIRCULATING GH BINDING, SOMATIC GROWTH
S07RR-07082-26 0317 (NSS) WEDLER, FREDERICK C Biomedical research support REGULATION OF ENZYMES IN CNS BY MANGANESE II IONS
S07RR-07082-26 0318 (NSS) WILSON, RICHARD A Biomedical research support ID & EXPRESSION OF SHIGA LIKE TOXIN GENES; CYTOTOXIGENIC E COLI
S07RR-07083-26 (NSS) COOPERMAN, BARRY S UNIVERSITY OF PENNSYLVANIA 106 COLLEGE HALL/6381 PHILADELPHIA, PA 19104 Biomedical research support
S07RR-07083-26 0467 (NSS) BRASS, LAWRENCE F Biomedical research support PLATELET THROMBIN RECEPTORS IN XENOPUSLAEVIS OOCYTES
S07RR-07083-26 0468 (NSS) BUNIN, GRETA R Biomedical research support GEOGRAPHIC, SOCIOECON & RACIAL PATTERNS OF CHILD CANCER INCIDENCE
S07RR-07083-26 0469 (NSS) EBERWINE, JAMES H Biomedical research support CLONING & SEQ OF DOUBLE STRANDED NUCLEIC ACID
S07RR-07083-26 0470 (NSS) GIBSON, CAROLYN W Biomedical research support IMMORTALIZED CELL LINES FROM TRANSGENIC MICE; SV40 T ANTIGEN GENE
S07RR-07083-26 0471 (NSS) GRIMES, PATRICIA A Biomedical research support PERMEABILITY OF BLOOD VESSELS IN EXPERIMENTAL DIABETES
S07RR-07083-26 0472 (NSS) GUILD, GREGORY M Biomedical research support PRODUCTS ENCODED BY BROAD COMPLEX REGULATORY OF DROSOPHILA
S07RR-07083-26 0473 (NSS) KALLEN, ROLAND G Biomedical research support RECOMBINANT INSULIN RECEPTORS & PHOSPHATASES
S07RR-07083-26 0474 (NSS) KLIMAN, HARVEY Biomedical research support TPA & PAI 1 IN HUMAN TROPHOBLAST INVASION
S07RR-07083-26 0475 (NSS) MCCRAE, KEITH R Biomedical research support PLASMINOGEN ACTIVATOR ACTIVITY IN MALIGNANT & NORMAL TROPHOBLASTS
S07RR-07083-26 0476 (NSS) MEDOFF-COOPER, BARBA Biomedical research support EARLY INFANCY TEMPERMENT QUESTIONNAIRE
S07RR-07083-26 0477 (NSS) PORTNOY, DANIEL A Biomedical research support INTRACELLULAR GROWTH & SPREAD OF LISTERIA MONOCYTOGENES
S07RR-07083-26 0478 (NSS) QUILL, HELEN R Biomedical research support ANTIGEN SPECIFIC TOLERANCE IN AUTOREACTIVE EFFECTOR T CELLS
S07RR-07083-26 0479 (NSS) REED, JOHN C Biomedical research support MOLECULAR ANATOMY OF 6Q CHROMOSOMAL DELETION IN LEUKEMIAS
S07RR-07083-26 0480 (NSS) ROME, LAWRENCE C Biomedical research support DESIGN OF SKELETAL MUSCLE
S07RR-07083-26 0481 (NSS) RONCOLI, MARIANNE Biomedical research support ENERGY EXPENDITURE IN LBW INFANTS FOLLOWING TWO CARE PROTOCOLS
S07RR-07083-26 0482 (NSS) STAMBOLIAN, DWIGHT Biomedical research support GENETIC MAPPING OF NANCE HORAN SYNDROME & X LINKED CATARACTS
S07RR-07083-26 0483 (NSS) TANG, CHA-MIN Biomedical research support PATCH CLAMP RECORDING OF IDENTIFIABLE NEURONS DIRECTLY FROM BRAIN SLICES
S07RR-07083-26 0495 (NSS) SLOVITER, HENRY A Biomedical research support EMULSIONS OF PERFLUOROCARBONS AS BLOOD SUBSTITUTES
S07RR-07083-26 0496 (NSS) DIAMOND, ADELE Biomedical research support FRONTAL LOBE FUNCTION IN INFANTS & PRESCHOOLERS
S07RR-07083-26 0497 (NSS) TOMASZEWSKI, JOHN E Biomedical research support HLA CLASS II ANTIGEN ON RENAL EPITHELIA CELLS
S07RR-07083-26 0498 (NSS) WAYLAND, BRADFORD B Biomedical research support COENZYME B12 ORGANOMETALLIC MODEL STUDIES
S07RR-07083-26 0484 (NSS) TOPP, MICHAEL Biomedical research support LASER PHOTOLYSIS OF COENZYME B12 & MODEL COMPOUNDS
S07RR-07083-26 0485 (NSS) VANDERKOOI, JANE N Biomedical research support SITE SELECTION SPECTROSCOPY OF CYTOCHROME C
S07RR-07083-26 0486 (NSS) YEH, I-TIEN Biomedical research support NEW ONCOGENE EXPRESSION IN HUMAN BREAST TISSUE: A ESTROGEN, PROGESTERONE
S07RR-07083-26 0487 (NSS) GOLDFINE, HOWARD Biomedical research support STRUCTURE & FUNCTION OF BACTERIAL LIPIDS
S07RR-07083-26 0488 (NSS) SUYAMA, YOSHITAKA Biomedical research support NUCLEAR DNA ENCODED RNA INTO MITOCHONDRIA OF SACCHAROMYCES CEREBISIAE
S07RR-07083-26 0489 (NSS) REPETTI, RENA L Biomedical research support JOB STRESS & FAMILY INTERACTION
S07RR-07083-26 0490 (NSS) OPELLA, STANLEY J Biomedical research support PURCHASE OF PERDFUTERATED DETERGENT
S07RR-07083-26 0491 (NSS) ROTHSTEIN, ROBIN D Biomedical research support ELECTROGASTROGRAPHY IN PATIENTS W/ GASTROPARESIS
S07RR-07083-26 0492 (NSS) LALLY, EDWARD Biomedical research support CLONING ACTINOBACILUS
S07RR-07083-26 0493 (NSS) GLEITMAN, LILA Biomedical research support CLAUSE STRUCTURE & SEMANTICS OF VERBS
S07RR-07083-26 0494 (NSS) GLEITMAN, HENRY Biomedical research support INCONGRUITY RESOLUTION OF HUMOR
S07RR-07084-26 (NSS) BURGESS, DAVID R UNIVERSITY OF PITTSBURGH A234 LANGLEY HALL PITTSBURGH, PA 15260 Biomedical research support
S07RR-07084-26 0322 (NSS) DEFRANCO, DONALD B Biomedical research support V MOS ONCOPROTEINS & PROTEIN PHOSPHATASES & GLUCOCORTICOID RECEPTOR FUNCT
S07RR-07084-26 0323 (NSS) HATFULL, GRAHAM F Biomedical research support MOLECULAR BIOLOGY OF MYCOBACTERIOPHAGE L5: TUBERCULOSIS, LEPROSY, VACCINES
S07RR-07084-26 0324 (NSS) MANUCK, STEPHEN B Biomedical research support BEHAV INFLUENCES ON HYPERTENSION, ATHEROSCLEROSIS & IMMUNE FUNCT
S07RR-07084-26 0325 (NSS) PEEBLES, CRAIG L Biomedical research support MECHANISM OF MITOCHONDRIAL RNA SELF SPLICING SITE DIRECTED MUTAGENESIS
S07RR-07084-26 0326 (NSS) SAMULSKI, RICHARD J Biomedical research support AAV SPECIFIC INTEGRATION & RESCUE IN HUMAN CELLS: ADENO ASSOCIATED VIRUS
S07RR-07084-26 0327 (NSS) VANDYKE, TERRY Biomedical research support CELL SPECIFIC GENE REGULATION OF TRANSTHYRETIN: LIVER, GENE REGULATION
S07RR-07084-26 0328 (NSS) VAN DYKE, TERRY Biomedical research support TRANSTHYRETIN EXPRESSION IN ACUTE PHASE RESPIRATION: LIVER
S07RR-07084-26 0329 (NSS) WALSH, CHARLES J Biomedical research support ISOLATE & CHARACTERIZE OF NUCLEOLAR ANTIGENS; MABS YEAST MAMMALS
S07RR-07084-26 0330 (NSS) WANG, BI-CHENG Biomedical research support PURIFICATION OF DNA PRIMERSOME, PRIMASE, EXOTOXIN, GROWTH FACTORS
G20RR-07085-01 (AR) TAYLOR, JACK L UNIVERSITY OF UTAH 101 ANIMAL RESOURCES CENTER SALT LAKE CITY, UT 84112 Alterations and renovations--University of Utah Animal Resources Center
S07RR-07085-26 (NSS) MORSE, DOUGLASS H BROWN UNIVERSITY, BOX G DIV OF BIOLOGY & MEDICINE PROVIDENCE, R I 02912 Biomedical research support
S07RR-07085-26 0331 (NSS) ANDERSON, VERNON E Biomedical research support ISOLATION OF ENZYMES OF FATTY ACID OXIDATION
S07RR-07085-26 0332 (NSS) AU, TERRY K Biomedical research support CHILDRENS UNDERSTANDING OF DISEASE TRANSMISSION & INFECTION CONTROL
S07RR-07085-26 0333 (NSS) BROOKS, LISA D Biomedical research support VIABILITY & RECOMBINATION IN DROSOPHILIA MELANOGASTER
S07RR-07085-26 0334 (NSS) CANE, DAVID Biomedical research support DNA & PROTEIN SEQUENCE DATABASES
S07RR-07085-26 0335 (NSS) COLEMAN, JOHN Biomedical research support CELL LINEAGE & CONTROL OF SKELETAL MUSCLE CELL DIFFERENTIATION
S07RR-07085-26 0336 (NSS) DILL, ANN E P Biomedical research support SELF CARE ATTITUDES & PRACTICES OF ELDERLY PEOPLE
S07RR-07085-26 0337 (NSS) GAINES, STEVEN D Biomedical research support PILOT STUDY OF GENETIC VARIATION (MTDNA) IN MARINE INVERTEBRATES
S07RR-07085-26 0338 (NSS) HARRY, JASON D Biomedical research support SHAPE MEMORY ALLOYS IN MEDICAL DEVICES
S07RR-07085-26 0339 (NSS) MORGAN, JAMES L Biomedical research support UNITIZATION IN INFANT PERCEPTION OF CONTINUOUS MULTISYLLABIC SPEECH
S07RR-07085-26 0340 (NSS) MORGAN, JAMES L Biomedical research support PROSODIC CUES TO LINGUISTIC UNITS IN CHILD DIRECTED SPEECH
S07RR-07085-26 0341 (NSS) MORSE, DOUGLASS H Biomedical research support SPATIAL HETEROGENEITY IN HOST PARASITOID RELATIONSHIPS
S07RR-07085-26 0342 (NSS) PARKER, KATHLYN A Biomedical research support CHEMICAL SYNTHESIS OF TIBO R82150 & ANALOGS ENHANCED STRAND SCISSION
S07RR-07085-26 0343 (NSS) QUEVEDO, WALTER C, J Biomedical research support INFLUENCE OF MELANIN & MELANOGENESIS; UV LIGHT INDUCED DNA DAMAGE & CELL DEATH
S07RR-07085-26 0344 (NSS) WOOTEN, BILLY R Biomedical research

PROJECT NO., ORGANIZATIONAL UNIT., INVESTIGATOR, ADDRESS, TITLE

support LIGHTNESS PERCEPTION: CONTRAST RATIO, LUMINANCE, & RETINAL DISPARITY
S07RR-07086-15 (NSS) LUZZI, LOUIS A UNIVERSITY OF RHODE ISLAND COLLEGE OF PHARMACY KINGSTON, R I 02881-0809 Biomedical research support
S07RR-07086-15 0318 (NSS) COLLYER, CHARLES E Biomedical research support PERCEPTUAL MOTOR TIMING
S07RR-07086-15 0319 (NSS) NELSON, DAVID R Biomedical research support HEAT SHOCK RESPONSE OF B BURGDORFERI & RELATIONSHIP TO LYME DISEASE
S07RR-07086-15 0320 (NSS) SPERRY, JAY S Biomedical research support TOXIN PRODUCTION BY CLOSTRIDIUM DIFFICILE
S07RR-07086-15 0321 (NSS) RODGERS, ROBERT L Biomedical research support METABOLIC ASPECTS OF DIABETIC HYPERSENSITIVE CARDIOMYOPATHY
S07RR-07086-15 0322 (NSS) SHAIKH, ZAHIR Biomedical research support ID METAL BINDING PROTEINS IN MOUSE TISSUES & CULTURED CELLS
S07RR-07086-15 0323 (NSS) SHIMIZU, YUZURU Biomedical research support MOLECULAR BIOLOGICAL APPROACH TO HETEROGENEITY OF MARINE MICROORGANISMS
S07RR-07086-15 0324 (NSS) CHEN, CHING-SHIH Biomedical research support GENETICS & ENZYMOLOGY OF METABOLIC IBUPROFEN EPIMERIZATION
S07RR-07086-15 0325 (NSS) KISLALIOGLU, SERPIL Biomedical research support NONINVASIVE TRANSDERMAL DELIVERY OF POLYPEPTIDES VIA IONTOPHORESIS
S07RR-07086-15 0326 (NSS) CHICHESTER, CLINTON Biomedical research support QUANTIFICATION OF COLLAGEN TYPE II
S07RR-07086-15 0327 (NSS) TURCOTTE, JOSEPH G Biomedical research support DEVELOPMENT OF TWO NEW CLASSES OF EXPERIMENTAL ANTI AIDS DRUGS
S07RR-07086-15 0328 (NSS) NEEDHAM, THOMAS E Biomedical research support INTRANASAL DELIVERY OF POLYPEPTIDES
S07RR-07088-24 (NSS) COLLINS, THOMAS C UNIVERSITY OF TENNESSEE 404 ANDY HOLT TOWER KNOXVILLE, TN 37996-0140 Biomedical research support
S07RR-07088-24 0345 (NSS) SAVAGE, DWAYNE C Biomedical research support XRAY MACHINE FOR BIOLOGY CONSORTIUM
S07RR-07088-24 0346 (NSS) WICKS, WESLEY D Biomedical research support PROTEIN KINASE IN REGULATING PROTEIN SYNTHESIS
S07RR-07088-24 0347 (NSS) KOONTZ, JOHN W Biomedical research support INSULIN MEDIATED REGULATION OF GENE EXPRESSION
S07RR-07088-24 0348 (NSS) BECK, RAYMOND W Biomedical research support DISTINGUISHED LECTURER SERIES
S07RR-07088-24 0349 (NSS) HOWELL, ELIZABETH E Biomedical research support CONSTRUCT NOVEL SANDWICH PROTEIN BETWEEN CALMODULIN & DIHYDROFOLATE REDUCTASE
S07RR-07088-24 0350 (NSS) HALL, JIM C Biomedical research support NEURAL BASIS OF SOUND RECOGNITION: ROLE OF INHIBITORY MECHANISMS
S07RR-07088-24 0351 (NSS) BECKER, JEFFREY M Biomedical research support CELLULAR, MOLECULAR , & DEVELOPMENTAL BIOLOGY SEMINAR SERIES
S07RR-07088-24 0352 (NSS) PHILLIPS, PAUL J Biomedical research support PREPARE SPECIFIC DNAS & STUDY USING PHYSICAL METHODS: MATERIALS SCIENCE
S07RR-07088-24 0353 (NSS) WICKS, WESLEY D Biomedical research support PROTEIN KINASE IN REGULATING PROTEIN SYNTHESIS
S07RR-07088-24 0354 (NSS) WHITE, DAVID C Biomedical research support LOCALIZED ANALYSIS FOR MICROBIAL MATERIALS
S07RR-07088-24 0355 (NSS) BLOOR, JOHN E Biomedical research support SEED MONEY FOR THEORETICAL WORK ON STRUCTURE OF BIOPOLYMERS
G20RR-07089-01 (AR) WHITE, GARY L OKLAHOMA UNIV HEALTH SCIS CENT BIOMEDICAL SCIENCES BUILDING OKLAHOMA CITY, OK 73104 Animal resources upgrading program
S07RR-07090-26 (NSS) WILD, JAMES R TEXAS A&M UNIVERSITY DEPT OF BIOCHEMISTRY COLLEGE STATION, TEX 77843 Biomedical research support
S07RR-07090-26 0462 (NSS) LESSARD, CHARLES S Biomedical research support DESIGN OF ADAPTIVE ABOVE KNEE PROSTHESIS: ENERGY EXPENDITURE
S07RR-07090-26 0463 (NSS) BARNES, WILLIAM S Biomedical research support ETIOLOGY OF SKELETAL MUSCLE FATIGUE: ACID BASE BALANCE & ELECTROPHYSIOLOGY
S07RR-07090-26 0470 (NSS) ADAMS, THOMAS H Biomedical research support REGULATORY GENES FOR SPORULATION
S07RR-07090-26 0471 (NSS) FITZPATRICK, PAUL Biomedical research support MECHANISTIC STUDIES OF FLAVIN OXIDASE
S07RR-07090-26 0472 (NSS) KELLY, JEFFREY W Biomedical research support STRUCTURAL STUDIES OF HIV 1 PROTEASE
S07RR-07090-26 0473 (NSS) GIEDROC, DAVID P Biomedical research support RNA:RNA ANNEALING IN NUCLEOCAPSID PROTEIN
S07RR-07090-26 0474 (NSS) HARDING, KENN E Biomedical research support NOVEL APPLICATIONS OF CHIRAL LEWIS ACIDS
S07RR-07090-26 0475 (NSS) HARRIS, EDWARD D Biomedical research support GENETIC DEFECTS IN MENKES CELLS
S07RR-07090-26 0476 (NSS) LINDAHL, PAUL A Biomedical research support STRUCTURE OF CARBON MONOXIDE DEHASE
S07RR-07090-26 0477 (NSS) MCKNIGHT, THOMAS Biomedical research support VACUOLAR TARGETING IN TRANSGENIC PLANTS
S07RR-07090-26 0478 (NSS) SCHWEIKERT, EMILE A Biomedical research support FEASIBILITY OF SUB ATTOMOL IMMUNOASSAY
S07RR-07090-26 0479 (NSS) SMITH, MICHAEL Biomedical research support MEMORY RELATED ELECTRICAL FIELD POTENTIAL
S07RR-07090-26 0480 (NSS) TAYLOR, BRIAN H Biomedical research support ROOT DEVELOPMENT IN TOMATO
S07RR-07090-26 0481 (NSS) HONEYCUTT, RODNEY L Biomedical research support RODENT INSULIN GENES: STRUCTURE & FUNCTION MODIFICATIONS & GENE DUPLICATION
S07RR-07090-26 0482 (NSS) KLUNKEL, GARY R Biomedical research support STRUCTURE OF U4 U6 RIBONOCLEOPROTEIN
S07RR-07090-26 0483 (NSS) SAUER, HELMET W Biomedical research support IDENTIFY EMBRYO SPECIFIC GENES IN ACHETA, HOUSE CRICKET
S07RR-07090-26 0464 (NSS) BATES, GEORGE W Biomedical research support BETA CAROTENE DIOXYGENASE
S07RR-07090-26 0465 (NSS) CARRINGTON, JAMES C Biomedical research support PROTEIN PROTEIN INTERACTION & VIRAL PROTEINASE & POLYMERASE
S07RR-07090-26 0466 (NSS) CASSONE, VINCENT M Biomedical research support PINEAL HORMONE MELATONIN: GLUCOSE UTILIZATION & PROTEIN SYNTHESIS IN VITRO

PROJECT NO., ORGANIZATIONAL UNIT., INVESTIGATOR, ADDRESS, TITLE

S07RR-07090-26 0467 (NSS) STRANG, CANDACE J Biomedical research support OXIDATIVE CHANGES IN COLLAGEN AS ANTIGENIC DETERMINANTS IN AUTOIMMUNE ARTHRITIS
S07RR-07090-26 0468 (NSS) TAYLOR, BRIAN H Biomedical research support CDNA CLONES ASSOCIATED W/ ROOT DEVELOPMENT IN TOMATO
S07RR-07090-26 0469 (NSS) YOUNG, RY Biomedical research support CONTROL OF CELL PROLIFERATION: MUTATION OF NUCLEOLAR FUNCTION & REGULATION
S07RR-07091-26 (NSS) BOSE, HENRY R JR UNIVERSITY OF TEXAS AT AUSTIN DEAN OF GRADUATE STUDIES AUSTIN, TEXAS 78712 Biomedical research support
S07RR-07091-26 0763 (NSS) PANDY, MARCUS Biomedical research support OPTIMIZATION TECHNIQUE PREDICT INDIVIDUAL MUSCLE FORCES DURING HUMAN GAIT
S07RR-07091-26 0764 (NSS) POENIE, MARTIN F Biomedical research support NEW FLUORESCENT INDICATORS FOR CELL PHYSIOLOGY
S07RR-07091-26 0765 (NSS) REED, JULIA A Biomedical research support INTERVENTIONS IN THE TREATMENT OF BULIMIA
S07RR-07091-26 0766 (NSS) RICHARDS-KORTUM, REB Biomedical research support SCREENING FOR CERVICAL NEOPLASIA USING FLUORESCENCE SPECTROSCOPY
S07RR-07091-26 0746 (NSS) BEALE JOHN M Biomedical research support INFORMATIONAL AND MECHANISTIC STUDIES OF ORGANIC ACID BIOSYNTHESIS
S07RR-07091-26 0747 (NSS) BEMBENEK, MICHAEL E Biomedical research support CHARACTERIZATION OF A NOVEL ADENOSINE BINDING PROTEIN FROM BOVINE BRAIN
S07RR-07091-26 0748 (NSS) BRAND JERRY J Biomedical research support AUTOMATED GROWTH OF CYANOBACTERIA FOR PHARMACOLOGICAL SCREENING
S07RR-07091-26 0767 (NSS) ROBERTUS, JON D Biomedical research support REGULATION OF THE HDC OPERON: LACTOBACILLUS
S07RR-07091-26 0768 (NSS) SCHAUER, ALAN T Biomedical research support AN EFFICIENT DELIVERY STEM FOR STREPTOMYCES TRANSPOSON TN4556
S07RR-07091-26 0769 (NSS) SINGER, MICHAEL C Biomedical research support EVOLUTION OF INSECT DIET BREADTH: A STUDY OF MECHANISMS
S07RR-07091-26 0770 (NSS) STUIFBERGEN, ALEXA M Biomedical research support DEMANDS OF ILLNESS, TYPES, & SOURCES OF SUPPORT FOR MULTIPLE SCLEROSIS & SPOUSES
S07RR-07091-26 0771 (NSS) SZANISZLO, PAUL Biomedical research support CLONING & ANALYSIS OF CHITIN SYNTHASE OF WANGIELLA DERMATITIDIS
S07RR-07091-26 0772 (NSS) WILCOX, RICHARD E Biomedical research support BEHAVIORAL FACILITATION TO ANTI PARKINSON DRUGS: NEUROCHEMICAL BASIS
S07RR-07091-26 0773 (NSS) WINKLER, MATTHEW M Biomedical research support ID OF SEQ MOTIFS RESPONSIBLE FOR CLEAVAGE STAGE SPECIFIC BEHAVIOR OF MRNAS
S07RR-07091-26 0749 (NSS) CANNITO, MICHAEL P Biomedical research support SPEECH DIADOCHOKINESIS IN SPASMODIC DISPHONIA
S07RR-07091-26 0750 (NSS) CHAMPLIN, CRAIG A Biomedical research support HEARING THRESHOLDS OBTAINED W/ AUDITORY BRAINSTEM RESPONSE
S07RR-07091-26 0751 (NSS) DAVIS, PATRICK J Biomedical research support MICROBIAL MODELS OF MAMMALIAN METABOLISM
S07RR-07091-26 0752 (NSS) ERICKSON , CARLTON K Biomedical research support LOW DOSE ETHANOL EFFECTS ON CENTRAL BIOPEPTIDES
S07RR-07091-26 0753 (NSS) FREELAND-GRAVES, JEA Biomedical research support MANGANESE STATUS OF OSTEOPOROTIC, HEALTHY, AND CALCIUM SUPPLEMENTED INDIVIDUALS
S07RR-07091-26 0754 (NSS) GILLESPIE, WILLIAM R Biomedical research support DRUG RESPONSE GENETICS: METHODS FOR ANALYSIS TO EXPERIMENTAL DATA
S07RR-07091-26 0755 (NSS) GONZALES, RUEBEN A Biomedical research support EFFECTS OF D CYCLOSERINE ON SPATIAL LEARNING IN AGED RATS
S07RR-07091-26 0756 (NSS) HIRAIZUMI, YUICHIRO Biomedical research support SELECTION AT THE ABO LOCUS IN MAN & PREZYGOTIC SELECTION IN DROSOPHILA
S07RR-07091-26 0757 (NSS) KALTHOFF, KLAUS Biomedical research support HOMOLOGUE OF THE DROSOPHILA FUSHI TARAZU BONE IN THE MIDGE CHIRONOMUS SAMONESIS
S07RR-07091-26 0758 (NSS) LACLAIRE, JOHN W Biomedical research support NUCLEOTIDE SEQUENCING A PUTATIVE MYOSIN BONE FROM CHLAMYDOMONAS
S07RR-07091-26 0759 (NSS) LAGOW, RICHARD J Biomedical research support SYNTHETIC BONE MATERIALS & MATERIALS FOR ADVANCED MEDICAL & DENTAL PROSTHESES
S07RR-07091-26 0760 (NSS) LOCNISKAR, MARY Biomedical research support DIETARY FISH & VEGETABLE OILS & EXPRESSION AND MODULATION OF INTERLEUKIN I
S07RR-07091-26 0761 (NSS) MAKINO, SHINJI Biomedical research support IDENTIFICATION OF SEQUENCE IMPORT FOR PACKAGING OF CORONAVIRUS RNA
S07RR-07091-26 0762 (NSS) PAAP, CHRISTOPHER Biomedical research support PENTAMICIN NEPHROTOXICITY IN AN ISOLATED PERFUSED RAT KIDNEY MODEL
S07RR-07092-26 (NSS) GRAY, WILLIAM R UNIVERSITY OF UTAH 201 S BIOLOGY BLDG SALT LAKE CITY, UTAH 84112 Biomedical research support
S07RR-07092-26 0536 (NSS) WIENS, DELBERT Biomedical research support GENETICALLY MEDIATED SPONTANEOUS EMBRYO ABORTION IN ERIOGONUM
S07RR-07092-26 0484 (NSS) BEEBE, THOMAS P Biomedical research support DNA ANALYSIS BY SCANNING TUNNELING MICROSCOPY
S07RR-07092-26 0485 (NSS) CUELLAR, ORLANDO Biomedical research support TISSUE GRAFTING & COMPATIBILITY IN C VELOX
S07RR-07092-26 0486 (NSS) FOGEL, ALAN D Biomedical research support BEHAVIORAL STATES: FORMATION & DISSOLUTION
S07RR-07092-26 0487 (NSS) FRIEDRICH, FRANCES J Biomedical research support SPATIAL ATTENTION IN SCHIZOPHRENIC PATIENTS
S07RR-07092-26 0488 (NSS) GARD, DAVID L Biomedical research support ISOLATION & SEQUENCING OF XMAP PEPTIDES
S07RR-07092-26 0489 (NSS) GRANT, DAVID M Biomedical research support PROGRAMMABLE RF ATTENUATOR FOR NMR STUDIES OF BIOMEDICAL COMPOUNDS
S07RR-07092-26 0490 (NSS) GRISSOM, CHARLES B Biomedical research support MAGNETIC FIELD EFFECTS ON ENZYME CATALYZED REACTIONS
S07RR-07092-26 0491 (NSS) HLADY, VLADIMIR Biomedical research

PROJECT NO., ORGANIZATIONAL UNIT., INVESTIGATOR, ADDRESS, TITLE

support PROTEIN INTERACTIONS W/ CRYSTAL SURFACES
S07RR-07092-26 0537 (NSS) WIGHT, CHARLES A Biomedical research support OPTICAL PROBES OF AMORPHOUS SOLID STRUCTURES
S07RR-07092-26 0538 (NSS) ALLSOP, KENT G Biomedical research support DESIGN & FABRICATION OF LIGHT WEIGHT ORTHOTIC LEG BRACES
S07RR-07092-26 0539 (NSS) GARDNER, MICHAEL K Biomedical research support RECOVERABILITY OF ANALOGICAL REASONING IN ALCOHOLICS
S07RR-07092-26 0540 (NSS) GRISSOM, CHARLES B Biomedical research support EFFECT OF MAGNETIC FIELDS OF ENZYME RATES
S07RR-07092-26 0541 (NSS) GRISSOM, JANET W Biomedical research support SYNTHESIS OF INDOLE NATURAL PRODUCTS
S07RR-07092-26 0542 (NSS) WERNER, CAROL M Biomedical research support SMOKER & NONSMOKER INTERACTIONS: INCREASING NON SMOKER ASSERTIVENESS
S07RR-07092-26 0543 (NSS) TRUJILLO, EDWARD M Biomedical research support IMPROVED PERFLUOROCARBON MICROCARRIERS FOR CELL CULTURE
S07RR-07092-26 0544 (NSS) SHARP, M K Biomedical research support SCROLL PUMP: A NOVEL BLOOD PUMP FOR SHORT TERM EXTRACORPOREAL USE
S07RR-07092-26 0545 (NSS) POULTER, C DALE Biomedical research support TRANSFORMATION OF PROKARYOTIC & EUKARYOTIC CELLS BY ELECTROPORATION
S07RR-07092-26 0546 (NSS) MLADEJOVSKY, MICHAEL Biomedical research support MINIATURE IMPLANTABLE DRUG DELIVERY SYSTEM
S07RR-07092-26 0547 (NSS) BRAMBLE, DENNIS M Biomedical research support INTEGRATION OF CARDIOVASCULAR & RESPIRATORY SYSTEMS DURING HUMAN RUNNING
S07RR-07092-26 0548 (NSS) SYMKO, OREST Biomedical research support MAGNETIC ACTIVITY OF HEART, USING HIGH TEMPERATURE SUPERCONDUCTING MAGNETOMETER
S07RR-07092-26 0549 (NSS) OKUN, LAWRENCE M Biomedical research support SEPARATION OF NEURON TYPES IN VITRO
S07RR-07092-26 0550 (NSS) SHORTHILL, RICHARD W Biomedical research support MEASUREMENT OF ELECTRICAL CHARGE ON INDUSTRIAL AEROSOLS
S07RR-07092-26 0492 (NSS) ISABELLA, RUSSELL A Biomedical research support ORIGINS OF INFANT MOTHER ATTACHMENT
S07RR-07092-26 0493 (NSS) KUMPFER, KAROL Biomedical research support ANS HYPERREACTIVITY & ALCOHOLISM
S07RR-07092-26 0494 (NSS) LOYE, JENELLA E Biomedical research support PARASITE EFFECTS ON HOSTS
S07RR-07092-26 0495 (NSS) MOYER-MILEUR, LAURIE Biomedical research support GROWTH IN INFANTS W/ BRONCHOPULMONARY DYSPLASIA
S07RR-07092-26 0504 (NSS) ISABELLA, RUSSELL A Biomedical research support ORIGINS OF INFANT MOTHER ATTACHMENTS
S07RR-07092-26 0505 (NSS) HARRIS, JOEL M Biomedical research support PROTEIN ADSORPTION & CONFORMATION KINETICS AT LIQUID & SOLID INTERFACES
S07RR-07092-26 0496 (NSS) NEGUS, NORMAN C Biomedical research support PHOTOPERIOD & PINEAL SIZE IN MAMMALS
S07RR-07092-26 0497 (NSS) NIELSEN, LEWIS T Biomedical research support BIOLOGICAL CONTROL OF MOSQUITOES BY NEMATODES
S07RR-07092-26 0498 (NSS) RICHMOND, THOMAS G Biomedical research support PENDANT REDOX ACTIVE LIGANDS AS BIOCHEMICAL MODELS
S07RR-07092-26 0499 (NSS) ROWSEMITT, CAROL N Biomedical research support NEUROENDOCRINE & BEHAVIORAL PLASTICITY IN ROLES
S07RR-07092-26 0500 (NSS) TURNER, CHARLES W Biomedical research support QUALITY OF LIFE IN END STAGE RENAL DISEASE
S07RR-07092-26 0501 (NSS) MIZUMORI, SHERI J Biomedical research support NEUROPHYSIOLOGICAL BASIS OF ISCHEMIA INDUCED AMNESIA IN RATS
S07RR-07092-26 0502 (NSS) WOLTZ, DAN J Biomedical research support FORGETTING DIFFERENCES IN IMPLICIT & EXPLICIT MEMORY
S07RR-07092-26 0503 (NSS) SHERIDAN, SUSAN M Biomedical research support ATTENTION DEFICIENT HYPERACTIVE DISORDERED CHILDREN
S07RR-07092-26 0506 (NSS) GURNEY, THEODORE Biomedical research support UNSCHEDULED DNA REPLICATION IN SV440
S07RR-07092-26 0507 (NSS) DICKINSON, WILLIAM J Biomedical research support PATTERN FORMATION IN DROSOPHILA DEVELOPMENT
S07RR-07092-26 0508 (NSS) CROYLE, ROBERT T Biomedical research support PSYCHOLOGICAL EFFECTS OF CHOLESTEROL TEST RESULTS
S07RR-07092-26 0509 (NSS) KROPF, DARRYL L Biomedical research support CELL DIFFERENTIATION IN HIGHER PLANTS
S07RR-07092-26 0510 (NSS) WILLIAMS, CLAYTON C Biomedical research support ATOMIC FORCE MICROSCOPIC IMAGING OF BIOLOGICAL MOLECULES
S07RR-07092-26 0511 (NSS) CLINE, VICTOR B Biomedical research support EFFECTIVENESS OF VARIOUS TYPES OF MARITAL THERAPY
S07RR-07092-26 0512 (NSS) SANSONE, CAROL Biomedical research support INTRINSIC MOTIVATION: IMPLICATION FOR HEALTH CARE SETTING
S07RR-07092-26 0513 (NSS) CUELLAR, ORLANDO Biomedical research support GENETICS OF A PARTHENOGENETIC LIZARD
S07RR-07092-26 0514 (NSS) BERG, CYNTHIA A Biomedical research support PEOPLES INTUITIVE NOTIONS OF INTELLIGENCE
S07RR-07092-26 0515 (NSS) SPIKES, JOHN D Biomedical research support LASER ILLUMINATION OF PHOTOSENSITIZED REACTIONS IN BIOLOGY
S07RR-07092-26 0516 (NSS) ALVORD, LYNN S Biomedical research support EQUILIBRATION OF MIDDLE EAR PRESSURE BY GAS PRODUCING SUBSTANCES
S07RR-07092-26 0517 (NSS) KUMPFER, KAROL Biomedical research support VULNERABILITY TO DRUG ABUSE OR ALCOHOLISM IN CHILDREN OF SUBSTANCE ABUSERS
S07RR-07092-26 0518 (NSS) NIELSON, HAROLD C Biomedical research support MICRONUCLEUS ASSAY AS A MEASURE OF PSYCHOLOGICAL STRESS
S07RR-07092-26 0519 (NSS) EYRING, EDWARD M Biomedical research support CHEMICAL REACTIVATION OF CANCER INACTIVATED LYMPHOCYTES
S07RR-07092-26 0520 (NSS) HAYMET, ANTHONY D Biomedical research support WATER STRUCTURE IN BIOLOGICAL SYSTEMS
S07RR-07092-26 0521 (NSS) SANBONMATSU, DAVID M Biomedical research support ACCURACY IN SELF PERCEPTION
S07RR-07092-26 0522 (NSS) VARDENY, ZEEV V Biomedical research support OPTICAL STUDIES OF PHOTOSENSITIZERS
S07RR-07092-26 0523 (NSS) KIRCHER, JOHN C Biomedical research support ANXIETY DISORDERS OF CHILDHOOD
S07RR-07092-26 0524 (NSS) SMITH, TIMOTHY W Biomedical research support HOSTILITY & CORTISOL EXCRETION IN HUMANS
S07RR-07092-26 0525 (NSS) BERGER, PATRICIA J Biomedical research

PROJECT NO., ORGANIZATIONAL UNIT., INVESTIGATOR, ADDRESS, TITLE

support POST PARTUM ESTRUS IN RODENTS
S07RR-07092-26 0526 (NSS) BEEBE, THOMAS P Biomedical research support SCANNING TUNNELING MICROSCOPY OF DNA
S07RR-07092-26 0527 (NSS) MIZUMORI, SHERI J Biomedical research support AGE COMPARISONS OF SPATIAL MEMORY IN RATS
S07RR-07092-26 0528 (NSS) LARK, KARL G Biomedical research support REARRANGEMENTS OF BACTERIAL DNA
S07RR-07092-26 0529 (NSS) KESNER, RAYMOND P Biomedical research support CORTICAL PROJECTIONS TO BASAL FOREBRAIN IN RAT
S07RR-07092-26 0530 (NSS) BRAMBLE, DENNIS M Biomedical research support CINERADIOGRAPHIC OF CANINE THORACIC MOTION DURING NATURAL LOCOMOTION
S07RR-07092-26 0531 (NSS) RICHMOND, THOMAS G Biomedical research support TRANSITION METAL BASED REAGENTS FOR BIOLOGICAL MOLECULAR RECOGNITION
S07RR-07092-26 0532 (NSS) SHIMP, CHARLES P Biomedical research support COMPUTATIONAL PROCESSING MODEL FOR HUMAN & ANIMAL SPATIAL ATTENTION
S07RR-07092-26 0533 (NSS) STRASSBERG, DONALD S Biomedical research support GENDER RELATED DIFFERENCES IN RESPONSE TO SEXUALLY EXPLICIT MATERIAL
S07RR-07092-26 0534 (NSS) WEST, FREDERICK B Biomedical research support BIOLOGICAL IMPLICATIONS OF AMMONIUM DERIVED RADICAL PAIRS
S07RR-07092-26 0535 (NSS) VICKERY, ROBERT K Biomedical research support RFLP STUDY OF GENETIC POLYMORPHISM IN MIMULUS
S07RR-07093-24 (NSS) MACMAHON, JAMES A UTAH STATE UNIVERSITY DEAN COLLEGE OF SCIENCE LOGAN, UT 84322-4400 Biomedical research support
S07RR-07093-24 0774 (NSS) COULOMBE, ROGER A Biomedical research support PULMONARY TUMORS: ALFATOXIN B TREATED ANIMALS MUTATIONS IN LOCI OF KI RAS
S07RR-07093-24 0775 (NSS) KNAPP, GAYLE Biomedical research support TRNA SYNTHESIS IN YEAST: DURING MATURATION OF NUCLEUS
S07RR-07093-24 0776 (NSS) PIETTE, LAWRENCE H Biomedical research support BLOOD PRODUCTS: INCREASED MORTALITY W/ INFECTIOUS PERITONITIS POST SURGERY
S07RR-07093-24 0777 (NSS) WARREN, REED Biomedical research support DRUGS FOR IMMUNE RELATED DIS: AIDS, AUTISM, CANCER, DOWNS SYNDROME
S07RR-07094-26 (NSS) MILLER, OSCAR L UNIVERSITY OF VIRGINIA PO BOX 9025 WASHINGTON HALL CHARLOTTESVILLE, VA 22906 Biomedical research support
S07RR-07094-26 0356 (NSS) MCCARTY, RICHARD Biomedical research support DIETARY INFLUENCES ON HYPERTENSION
S07RR-07094-26 0357 (NSS) GAINER, JOHN L Biomedical research support EFFECT OF PLASMA RESISTANCE ON TISSUE OXYGEN CONSUMPTION
S07RR-07094-26 0358 (NSS) REBHUN, LIONEL I Biomedical research support ANALYSIS OF FUNCTIONAL ISOLATED SPINDLES
S07RR-07094-26 0359 (NSS) GOLD, PAUL E Biomedical research support BLOOD GLUCOSE, MEMORY, & AGING
S07RR-07094-26 0360 (NSS) RODEWALD, RICHARD D Biomedical research support EPITHELIAL TRANSPORT OF PROTEINS & PEPTIDES
S07RR-07094-26 0367 (NSS) CAFISO, DAVID S Biomedical research support STRUCTURE & ORGANIZATION OF PROTEINS
S07RR-07094-26 0368 (NSS) SUNDBERG, RICHARD J Biomedical research support DNA BINDING PROPERTIES OF HETEROAROMATIC CATIONS
S07RR-07094-26 0361 (NSS) FRANKFURTER, ANTHONY Biomedical research support CHARACTERIZATION OF BRAIN MICROTUBULES
S07RR-07094-26 0362 (NSS) DORNING, JOHN J Biomedical research support DYNAMICS ON NON LINEAR WAVES IN ACTIVE PHYSIOLOGICAL MEDIA
S07RR-07094-26 0363 (NSS) DUESER, RAYMOND P Biomedical research support SMALL MAMMAL ON DELMARVA PENINSULA
S07RR-07094-26 0364 (NSS) DORNING, JOHN J Biomedical research support DYNAMICS OF NON LINEAR WAVES
S07RR-07094-26 0365 (NSS) FINN, M G Biomedical research support CATALYTIC CHEMISTRY OF BIMETALLIC FISCHER CARBENE
S07RR-07094-26 0366 (NSS) JOHNSON, JACQUELINE Biomedical research support LANGUAGE PERMANENCE & RELATIONSHIP TO CRITICAL PERIOD
G20RR-07095-01 (AR) MONTREY, RICHARD D SOUTHERN ILLINOIS UNIVERSITY PO BOX 19230 SPRINGFIELD, IL 62794-9230 Developing and improving institutional animal resources
S07RR-07095-24 (NSS) RUTHERFORD, CHARLES L VA POLYTECHNIC INST / ST UNIV DEPARTMENT OF BIOLOGY BLACKSBURG, VA 24061 Biomedical research support
S07RR-07095-24 0369 (NSS) LICKLITER, ROBERT E Biomedical research support PRENATAL EXPERIENCE IN DVMT LATERALIZATION OF BRAIN FUNCTION
S07RR-07095-24 0370 (NSS) ENG, LUDEMAN A Biomedical research support SPERM RECEPTORS OF OOCYTE PLASMA MEMBRANE
S07RR-07095-24 0371 (NSS) RIMSTIDT, J DONALD Biomedical research support DISSOLUTION STUDIES OF ASBESTOSFORM AMPHIBOLES
S07RR-07095-24 0372 (NSS) TURNER, BRUCE J Biomedical research support ONCOGENE VARIATION IN HOMOZYGOUS CLONAL VERTEBRATE
S07RR-07095-24 0373 (NSS) WONG, ERIC A Biomedical research support MOLECULAR REGULATION OF OVINE INSULIN LIKE GROWTH FACTOR I GENE
S07RR-07095-24 0374 (NSS) GELLER, E SCOTT Biomedical research support DIRECTIVE VS NON PERSUASION: GET PIZZA DELIVERY DRIVER TO COME TO COMPLETE STOP
S07RR-07095-24 0375 (NSS) SOUTHARD, DOUGLAS R Biomedical research support EFFECT OF AEROBIC EXERCISE ON BLOOD PRESSURE RESPONSE TO NON EXERCISE STRESSORS
S07RR-07095-24 0376 (NSS) ANDERSON, MARK R Biomedical research support SPECTROSCOPIC STUDY OF IONIC TRANSPORT ACROSS LIQUID LIQUID INTERFACES
S07RR-07095-24 0377 (NSS) CRAWFORD, HELEN J Biomedical research support EEG BRAIN WAVE ACTIVITY CORRELATES OF HYPNOTIC ANALGESIA; NMR
S07RR-07095-24 0378 (NSS) FINNEY, JACK W Biomedical research support EMPIRICAL VALIDATION OF BEHAVIORAL TARGETS FOR DIABETES ADHERENCE; IDDM
S07RR-07095-24 0379 (NSS) DENBOW, DONALD M Biomedical research support REGULATION OF HMG COA REDUCTASE GENES IN CHICKEN; CHOLESTEROL; CDNA CLONING
S07RR-07095-24 0380 (NSS) GREGORY, EUGENE M Biomedical research support REGULATION OF SOD SYNTHESIS IN BACTEROIDES; SUPEROXIDE DISMUTASE: ANAEROBE

S07RR-07095-24 0381 (NSS) AMED, S A Biomedical research support INDUCTION OF RHEUMATIC DISORDER IN MICE
S07RR-07095-24 0382 (NSS) KOELLING, CHARLES P Biomedical research support HEARING CONSERVATION FOR MENTALLY DISADVANTAGED WORKER: OCCUPATION
G20RR-07096-01 (AR) LEHNER, NOEL D M EMORY UNIVERSITY 1510 CLIFTON RD NE ATLANTA, GA 30322 Developing and improving institutional animal resources
S07RR-07096-26 (NSS) JOHNSON, DALE E 201 ADMIN BLDG., UNIV OF WASH GRADUATE SCHOOL AG-10 SEATTLE, WA 98195 Biomedical research support
S07RR-07096-26 0067 (NSS) BEECHER, MICHAEL D Biomedical research support SIGNAL SYNTHESIS
S07RR-07096-26 0055 (NSS) STRATHMANN, RICHARD Biomedical research support PARENTAL INVESTMENT PER OFFSPRING, CONSEQUENCES, & EVOLUTIONAL IMPLICATIONS
S07RR-07096-26 0056 (NSS) DONG, FAYE M Biomedical research support PRODUCTION OF HIGH MONOUNSATURATED FISH
S07RR-07096-26 0057 (NSS) EDMONDS, ROBERT L Biomedical research support DOUGLAS FIR & GRAND FIR ON ALLUVIAL DEPOSITS IN WESTERN WASHINGTON
S07RR-07096-26 0058 (NSS) DUNCAN, S WAYNE Biomedical research support PARENTAL & MARITAL INFLUENCES ON CHILDRENS EMOTIONAL DEVELOPMENT
S07RR-07096-26 0059 (NSS) HUTTON, ROBERT S Biomedical research support GOLGI TENDON ORGAN REFLEXES & REGULATION OF FORCE IN HUMANS
S07RR-07096-26 0060 (NSS) WAKIMOTO, BARBARA T Biomedical research support GENES OF DROSOPHILA
S07RR-07096-26 0061 (NSS) GREENBERG, MARK T Biomedical research support SOCIAL COMPETENCE & ADAPTATION IN VISUALLY IMPAIRED CHILDREN
S07RR-07096-26 0062 (NSS) HANNAFORD, BLAKE Biomedical research support PROTOTYPE MICRO TELEMANIPULATION SYSTEM
S07RR-07096-26 0063 (NSS) BERG, CELESTE A Biomedical research support SCRAMBLED EGGS MUTANT DROSOPHILA AFFECTING FOLLICLE CELL MIGRATION & DEVELOPMENT
S07RR-07096-26 0064 (NSS) KUHL, PATRICIA K Biomedical research support CROSS LANGUAGE STUDY OF SPEECH PERCEPTION
S07RR-07096-26 0065 (NSS) KENAGY, GEORGE J Biomedical research support ENERGETICS OF MAMMALIAN REPRODUCTION & LIFE HISTORY
S07RR-07096-26 0066 (NSS) MELTZOFF, ANDREW Biomedical research support LANGUAGE & COGNITION IN DOWN SYNDROME CHILDREN
S07RR-07096-26 0068 (NSS) DALY, COLIN H Biomedical research support MECHANICAL STRESSES IN RESIDUAL LIMB TISSUES PROSTHETICS, BIOMECHANICS
S07RR-07096-26 0069 (NSS) FRANCIS, ROBERT C Biomedical research support OFFSHORE PACIFIC WHITING: A PARASITE STUDY
S07RR-07096-26 0070 (NSS) HILLE, MERRILL B Biomedical research support TRANSLATIONAL REGULATION DURING STARFISH MEIOTIC MATURATION
S07RR-07096-26 0071 (NSS) HWANG, JENQ-NENG Biomedical research support NEURAL NETWORKS TO CONTROL OF ARTIFICIAL LIMBS
S07RR-07096-26 0072 (NSS) LYE, DIANE N Biomedical research support BELOW REPLACEMENT FERTILITY IN INDUSTRIALIZED COUNTRIES
S07RR-07096-26 0073 (NSS) MANDOLI, DINA F Biomedical research support GENETICS & PATTERN FORMATION IN ACETABULARIA MEDITERRANEA
S07RR-07096-26 0074 (NSS) DIAZ, JAIME Biomedical research support NUTRITIONAL FACTORS DURING DEVELOPMENT AFFECT ADULT INSULIN RESISTENCE
S07RR-07096-26 0075 (NSS) PALMER, JOHN Biomedical research support PERCEPTION & MEMORY FOR OBJECTS & PARTS
S07RR-07096-26 0076 (NSS) DUNCAN, S WAYNE Biomedical research support ME MY FEELINGS QUESTIONNAIRE: MEASURE OF CHILDRENS EMOTIONAL COMPETENCE
G20RR-07097-01 (AR) MC LAUGHLIN, RONALD M UNIV OF MISSOURI/SCH OF MEDICI COLUMBIA, MO 65212 Animal resource improvement at the University of Missouri-Columbia
S07RR-07097-26 (NSS) SMITH, ROBERT V DEAN OF GRADUATE SCHOOL WASHINGTON STATE UNIVERSITY PULLMAN, WA 99164-5045 Biomedical research support
S07RR-07097-26 0383 (NSS) BARNES, C Biomedical research support AMINERGIC & PEPTIDERGIC SYSTEMS INTERACTION: LOCUS COERULEUS, RAPHE, MOTONEURONS
S07RR-07097-26 0384 (NSS) BARNES, C Biomedical research support ATTACHMENTS FOR MICROSCOPE MOLECULAR PURCHASED FOR IMMUNOHISTOCHEM RESEARCH
S07RR-07097-26 0385 (NSS) EATON, BRUCE Biomedical research support REVERSIBLE CROSS LINKING OF DNA; ALTERATION OF GENE EXPRESSION; CANCER; NMR
S07RR-07097-26 0386 (NSS) STONE, DIANA Biomedical research support CHROMOSOME FRAGILE SITE EXPRESSION & CANCER RISK IN DOG; AGING: LYMPHOCYTE
S07RR-07097-26 0387 (NSS) SCHROEDER, ALICE Biomedical research support RADIORESISTANT DNA SYNTHESIS: YEAST MODEL SYSTEM; ATAXIA; TELANGIECTASIA; HUMAN
S07RR-07097-26 0388 (NSS) FILBY, ROY Biomedical research support LABORATORY FOR BIOTECHNOLOGY & BIOANALYSIS II SPECTROMETRY
S07RR-07097-26 0389 (NSS) GILES, RICHARD E Biomedical research support MOLECULAR GENETICS OF SV40 MEDIATED CELL MUTAGENESIS; ONCOGENESIS
S07RR-07097-26 0390 (NSS) MEYERS, KENNETH Biomedical research support TREAT ANIMAL MODELS W/ BLOOD PRODUCTS; VON WILLEBRANDS DISEASE, HEMOPHILIA
G20RR-07098-01 (AR) SCHAEDLER, RUSSELL W THOMAS JEFFERSON UNIVERSITY 1020 LOCUST STREET PHILADELPHIA, PA 19107-6799 Animal room renovation to AAALAC standards
S07RR-07098-26 (NSS) SMITH, DEAN O 333 BASCOM HALL, UNIV WIS-MAD 500 LINCOLN DRIVE MADISON, WIS 53706 Biomedical research support
S07RR-07098-26 0339 (NSS) ANDREWS, JOHN H Biomedical research support EPIDEMIOLOGY OF SPOROTRICHOSIS: WISCONSIN SPHAGNUM MOSS
S07RR-07098-26 0340 (NSS) HAFERKAMP, CLAUDIA J Biomedical research support ATTRIBUTIONS & CONFLICT RESOLUTION STYLES AMONG DISTRESSED COUPLES
S07RR-07098-26 0341 (NSS) LAZARUS, JO-ANNE C Biomedical research support PATTERNS OF INHIBITORY CONTROL IN LEARNING DISABILITIES
S07RR-07098-26 0342 (NSS) CARTEE, GREGORY D Biomedical research support MEASUREMENT OF MUSCLE MEMBRANE GLUCOSE TRANSPORTER CONTENT
S07RR-07098-26 0343 (NSS) WHITALL, JILL Biomedical research support COORDINATION OF COGNITIVE & MOTORIC TASKS
S07RR-07098-26 0344 (NSS) STANLEY, WILLIAM C Biomedical research support REGULATION OF MYOCARDIAL CARBOHYDRATE METABOLISM
S07RR-07098-26 0345 (NSS) CAMERON, DOUGLAS C Biomedical research support METHYLGLYOXAL & GLYOXALASE ON MAMMALIAN CELLS GROWN IN CULTURE
S07RR-07098-26 0346 (NSS) MURPHY, REGINA M Biomedical research support MOLECULAR BASIS FOR VIRAL NEUTRALIZATION BY ANTIBODIES
S07RR-07098-26 0347 (NSS) STEVENSON, MARGUERIT Biomedical research support INTERACTIONAL ANALYSIS: YOUNG DOWN SYNDROME CHILDREN & MOTHERS
S07RR-07098-26 0348 (NSS) SCHOENINGER, MARGERE Biomedical research support NITROGEN METABOLISM UNDER RESTRICTED WATER & PROTEIN INTAKE
S07RR-07098-26 0349 (NSS) PRATT, SHEILA R Biomedical research support BACKGROUND NOISE, REVERBERATE & HIPASS FILTER ON SPEECH PERCEPT SKILL OF INFANT
S07RR-07098-26 0350 (NSS) GUBERNICK, DAVID J Biomedical research support HORMONAL CORRELATES OF FATHERHOOD IN MEN
S07RR-07098-26 0351 (NSS) MOFFITT, TERRI E Biomedical research support PERSONALITY & NEUROPSYCHOLOGICAL FUNCTIONING IN ADULT ARTHMETIC DISABILITY
S07RR-07098-26 0352 (NSS) NEWMAN, JOSEPH P Biomedical research support INFO PROCESSING CONSEQ OF BEHAVIOR ACTIVATION: IMPLICATIONS FOR PSYCHOPATHOLOGY
S07RR-07098-26 0353 (NSS) CASPI, AVSHALOM Biomedical research support LONGITUDINAL STUDY OF PERSONALITY DVMT AMONG INNER CITY KIDS
S07RR-07098-26 0354 (NSS) LAUGHLIN, NELLIE Biomedical research support LEAD INTAKE ON LATER AUDITORY PERCEPT & ATTENTION IN MONKEY IN KIDS
S07RR-07098-26 0355 (NSS) HIRT, EDWARD R Biomedical research support MULTI EXPLANATION: TECH TO IMPROVE RISK PERCEPTION IN MED DECISION MAKING TASK
S07RR-07098-26 0356 (NSS) TEST, MARY ANN Biomedical research support ARRESTS & OFFENSES OF YOUNG ADULTS W/ SCHIZOID DISORDERS IN COMMUNITY
S07RR-07098-26 0357 (NSS) GREENBERG, JAN Biomedical research support CAREGIVER BURDEN & SERVICES TO FAMILIES OF MENTALLY ILL IN DANE COUNTY
S07RR-07098-26 0358 (NSS) NEWMANN, JOY P Biomedical research support GENDER DIFFERENCES IN RISK FACTORS FOR DEPRESSION
S07RR-07098-26 0359 (NSS) ROBERTSON, JOAN F Biomedical research support ADOLESCENT & FAMILY ALCOHOL & DRUG TREATMENT
S07RR-07098-26 0329 (NSS) ESCALANTE, JORGE C Biomedical research support B12 BIOSYNTHESIS IN R SPHAEROIDES
S07RR-07098-26 0330 (NSS) SUTTIE, JOHN W Biomedical research support ISOLATION OF VITAMIN K DEPENDENT MITOCHONDRIAL PROTEIN
S07RR-07098-26 0331 (NSS) ADLER, JULIUS Biomedical research support RESPONSE OF BACTERIA TO ELECTRIC SHOCK
S07RR-07098-26 0332 (NSS) NELSON, DAVID L Biomedical research support GTP BINDING PROTEINS IN PARAMECIUM SECRETORY MUTANTS
S07RR-07098-26 0360 (NSS) STRETTON, ANTONY O Biomedical research support NEURONAL CONTROL OF LOCOMOTORY BEHAVIOR IN ASCARIS
S07RR-07098-26 0361 (NSS) PAWLEY, JAMES B Biomedical research support 1 NM GOLD LABELLING OF BIOLOGICAL SURFACES
S07RR-07098-26 0362 (NSS) BLAIR, SETH S Biomedical research support AXON GUIDANCE IN FRUIT FLY
S07RR-07098-26 0363 (NSS) HOLDEN, HAZEL M Biomedical research support XRAY CRYSTALLOGRAPH OF MOUSE EPIDERMAL GROWTH FACTOR BINDING PROTEIN
S07RR-07098-26 0364 (NSS) DEWAAL, FRANS B M Biomedical research support MULTIDISCIPLINE RES ON FEMALE RHESUS MONKEY W/ DOWNS LIKE SYNDROME
S07RR-07098-26 0365 (NSS) TERASAWA, EI Biomedical research support GROWTH & PUBERTY IN FEMALE RHESUS MONKEY
S07RR-07098-26 0366 (NSS) KEMNITZ, JOSEPH Biomedical research support CNS INSULIN IN CONTROL OF ENERGY BALANCE IN RHESUS MONKEYS
S07RR-07098-26 0367 (NSS) MATTERI, ROBERT Biomedical research support REGULATION OF LH & FSH ISOHORMONE SYNTHESIS & SECRETION
S07RR-07098-26 0368 (NSS) SHOLL, SAMUEL Biomedical research support MECHANISMS OF ANDROGEN ACTION IN FETAL BRAIN
S07RR-07098-26 0333 (NSS) SELMAN, BRUCE R Biomedical research support DO EUKARYNOTES PRODUCE METHANOL
S07RR-07098-26 0334 (NSS) SHEFFIELD, LEWIS G Biomedical research support POTENTIAL FOR GENE TRANSFER TO MAMMARY TISSUE IN SITU
S07RR-07098-26 0335 (NSS) GOODMAN, WALTER G Biomedical research support JUVENILE HORMONE TRANSPORT IN INSECT HEMOLYMPH
S07RR-07098-26 0336 (NSS) DASGUPTA, BIBHUTI R Biomedical research support BOTULINUM NEUROTOXIN AMINO ACID ANALYSIS & DERIVATIVES FOR STRUCT FUNC RELATION
S07RR-07098-26 0337 (NSS) RUTLEDGE, JACKIE J Biomedical research support SEASONS ON FOLLICULAR DYNAMICS SUPEROVULATORY RESPONSE IN MICE
S07RR-07098-26 0338 (NSS) NEY, DENISE M Biomedical research support TOTAL PARENTAL NUTRITION & SOMATOMEDIN RESPONSE
S07RR-07099-25 (NSS) ORIAS, EDUARDO UNIVERSITY OF CALIFORNIA DEPT OF BIOLOGICAL SCIENCES SANTA BARBARA, CALIF 93106 Biomedical research support
S07RR-07099-25 0391 (NSS) SINSHEIMER, ROBERT Biomedical research support SEA URCHIN; GENES HOMOLOGOUS TO HOMEOTIC GENES OF DROSOPHILA
S07RR-07099-25 0392 (NSS) SEARS, DUANE W Biomedical research support FC RECEPTOR FUNCTION OF NATURAL KILLERS
S07RR-07099-25 0393 (NSS) JACOBS, ROBERT Biomedical research support SITE & MECHANISM OF ACTION OF MARINE NATURAL PRODUCTS
S07RR-07099-25 0394 (NSS) ENGLESBERG, ELLIS Biomedical research support MECHANISM OF GENE REGULATION IN MAMMALIAN CELLS
S07RR-07099-25 0395 (NSS) LITTLE, R D Biomedical research support INTRAMOLECULAR DIYL TRAPPING IN ORGANIC SYNTHESIS
S07RR-07099-25 0396 (NSS) GERIG, J T Biomedical research support SIMULATION OF NMR EXPERIMENTS
S07RR-07099-25 0397 (NSS) DONNERSTEIN, EDWARD Biomedical research support MITIGATING EFFECTS OF MASS MEDIA & SEXUAL VIOLENCE
S07RR-07099-25 0398 (NSS) LYTLE, LOY D Biomedical research support MATURATIONAL CHANGES IN OPIATE DEPENDENT NOCICEPTION
S07RR-07099-25 0399 (NSS) MAYER, RICHARD E Biomedical research

support ILLUSTRATIONS & ANIMATIONS IN SCIENCE INSTRUCTION
S07RR-07099-25 0400 (NSS) ETTENBERG, AARON Biomedical research support MECHANISMS OF OPIATE & STIMULANT DRUG REWARD
S07RR-07099-25 0401 (NSS) BURGESS, TERESA L Biomedical research support COLOCALIZATION OF GOLGI APPARATUS & DETYROSINATED MICROTUBULES
S07RR-07099-25 0402 (NSS) FEINSTEIN, STUART C Biomedical research support ATTENDANCE AT ANNUAL MEETING OF SOCIETY FOR CELL BIOLOGY
S07RR-07099-25 0403 (NSS) HAIGH, JULIAN R Biomedical research support VESAMICOL BINDING IN RAT BRAIN SYNAPTIC VESICLES
S07RR-07099-25 0404 (NSS) MATSUMOTO, BRIAN Biomedical research support DEVELOPMENT OF MICROSCOPY FACILITY FOR NEUROSCIENCE RESEARCH INSTITUTE
S07RR-07099-25 0405 (NSS) NEITZ, MAUREEN E Biomedical research support MOLECULAR BIOLOGY OF RED GREEN COLOR VISION
G20RR-07100-01 (AR) HAYRE, MICHAEL D ROCKEFELLER UNIVERSITY 1230 YORK AVE BOX 257 NEW YORK, NY 10021-6399 Rockefeller University rodent health improvement program
S07RR-07100-13 (NSS) YOUNG, DAVID M MONTANA ST UNIV-VP RES 207 MONTANA HALL BOZEMAN, MONT 59717 Biomedical research support
G20RR-07101-01 (AR) ABEE, CHRISTIAN R UNIVERSITY OF SOUTH ALABAMA COLLEGE OF MEDICINE MOBILE, AL 36688 Renovation and centralization--Univ. of South Alabama animal research facilities
S07RR-07101-13 (NSS) MILLETT, FRANCIS S UNIVERSITY OF ARKANSAS DEPARTMENT OF CHEMISTRY FAYETTEVILLE, ARKANSAS 72701 Biomedical research support
S07RR-07101-13 0551 (NSS) BOTTJE, WALTER Biomedical research support DEVELOPMENT OF THERMAL PULSE DECAY PROBE ASSEMBLY CAPABILITIES
S07RR-07101-13 0552 (NSS) ROSE, JEROME Biomedical research support UNDERNUTRITION, MORBIDITY, & ENAMEL HISTORY
S07RR-07101-13 0553 (NSS) ETGES, WILLIAM Biomedical research support GENETIC BASIS OF ENERGY METABOLISM IN DROSOPHILA MOJAVENSIS
S07RR-07101-13 0554 (NSS) AMLANER, CHARLES Biomedical research support BIOTELEMETRY STUDIES OF SLEEP PHYSIOLOGY
S07RR-07101-13 0555 (NSS) KOEPPE, ROGER E Biomedical research support RNA PROTEIN INTERACTIONS
S07RR-07103-25 (NSS) MATTHEWS, KATHLEEN S RICE UNIVERSITY POST OFFICE BOX 1892 HOUSTON, TX 77251 Biomedical research support
S07RR-07103-25 0499 (NSS) WATKINS, MICHAEL J Biomedical research support EPISODIC MEMORY; RECOGNITION; SHORT TERM MEMORY
S07RR-07103-25 0500 (NSS) KING, GARRY C Biomedical research support NUCLEIC ACID RECOGNITION BY PROTEINS NMR
S07RR-07103-25 0501 (NSS) GLACKEN, MICHAEL W Biomedical research support CELL CELL ADHESION & CTL & TARGET CELL CONJUGATE STABILITY
S07RR-07103-25 0502 (NSS) SAN, KA-YIU Biomedical research support CELL CULTURING BIOREACTOR SYSTEMS
G20RR-07104-01 (AR) JACOBY, ROBERT O YALE UNIVERSITY SCHOOL OF MED 333 CEDAR STREET, P.O. BX 3333 NEW HAVEN, CT 06510 Renovation of the LSOG-5 and SHM-4 animal units
S07RR-07104-25 (NSS) PFAU, CHARLES J RENSSELAER POLYTECHNIC INST 125 COGSWELL LABORATORY TROY, NY 12180-3590 Biomedical research support
S07RR-07104-25 0556 (NSS) BELFORT, G Biomedical research support BIOREACTOR
S07RR-07104-25 0557 (NSS) BOYLEN, C W Biomedical research support E M FACILITY EQUIPMENT
S07RR-07104-25 0558 (NSS) DIWAN, J Biomedical research support PATCH CLAMPING EQUIPMENT
S07RR-07104-25 0559 (NSS) FRYE, L Biomedical research support ULTRA LOW DEEP FREEZE
S07RR-07104-25 0560 (NSS) NIERZWICKI-BAUER, S Biomedical research support PREPARATIVE ISO ELECTRIC FOCUSING APPARATUS
S07RR-07104-25 0561 (NSS) NIERZWICKI-BAUER, S Biomedical research support MICROSCOPE & DNA SYNTHESIZER
S07RR-07104-25 0562 (NSS) SAULNIER, G Biomedical research support 3D IMAGING EQUIPMENT
S07RR-07104-25 0563 (NSS) WALLACE, B A Biomedical research support XRAY SAFETY EQUIPMENT
S07RR-07104-25 0564 (NSS) WARDEN, J T Biomedical research support SPECTROSCOPY OF CRYSTALLINE SAMPLES
S07RR-07107-24 (NSS) LYNCH, CAROL B WESLEYAN UNIVERSITY DEAN'S OFF, 2ND FLR, N COLLEGE MIDDLETOWN, CONN 06457 Biomedical research support
S07RR-07107-24 0642 (NSS) LUKENS, LEWIS N Biomedical research support REGULATION OF COLLAGEN GENES W/ CHANGES IN CHONDROCYTE DIFFERENTIATION
S07RR-07108-19 (NSS) CHASTEEN, DENNIS N UNIVERSITY OF NEW HAMPSHIRE OFF OF SPON RES SVC BLDG DURHAM, NH 03824 Biomedical research support
S07RR-07108-19 0406 (NSS) CAREY, GALE B Biomedical research support LOCAL REGULATORS OF LIPOLYSIS VIA MICRO DIALYSIS
S07RR-07108-19 0407 (NSS) COLLINS, JOHN J Biomedical research support TISSUE SPECIFIC CONTROL OF TRANSPOSABLE GENETIC ELEMENTS
S07RR-07108-19 0408 (NSS) KANG, JAE O Biomedical research support METHYL RADICALS & DMH INDUCED COLON CARCINOGENESIS
S07RR-07108-19 0409 (NSS) MARGOLIN, AARON B Biomedical research support IN SITU ASSAY DEVELOPMENT FOR POLIOVIRUS DETECTION
S07RR-07108-19 0410 (NSS) TILLINGHAST, EDWARD Biomedical research support SPIDER WEB MUCOGLYCOPROTEINS ASSOCIATED PROTEINS
S07RR-07108-19 0411 (NSS) WATSON, WINSOR H Biomedical research support NEURAL NETWORK PATTERN GENERATION IN MELIBE LEONINA SWALLOWING
S07RR-07109-23 (NSS) RAPS, SHIRLEY HUNTER COLLEGE OF CUNY 695 PARK AVENUE NEW YORK, N Y 10021 Biomedical research support
S07RR-07109-23 0503 (NSS) CHAPPELL, RICHARD Biomedical research support NEURAL INTERACTION OF RETINA
S07RR-07109-23 0504 (NSS) DANNENBERG, JOSEPH Biomedical research support THEORETICAL ORGANIC CHEMISTRY
S07RR-07109-23 0505 (NSS) GOSS, DIXIE Biomedical research support REGULATION OF MRNA TRANSLATION
S07RR-07109-23 0506 (NSS) HARDING, CHERYL Biomedical research support HORMONAL ACTIVATION OF BEHAVIOR
S07RR-07109-23 0507 (NSS) HECHT, CHARLES Biomedical research support EXPONENTS FOR HIERARCHICAL LATTICE MODELS & LACTTICE PERCOLATION PROCESSES

S07RR-07109-23 0508 (NSS) MILLS, PAM Biomedical research support COMPUTER MODELING OF ELECTROSTATIC INTERACTION IN NUCLEIC ACID SOLUTIONS
S07RR-07109-23 0509 (NSS) RAPS, SHIRLEY Biomedical research support MOLECULAR PHYCOBILISOMES OF CYANOBACTERIUM MICROCYSTIS AERUGINOSA
S07RR-07109-23 0510 (NSS) SWEENEY, WILLIAM Biomedical research support CYSTEINYL RICH DOMAIN IN BLOOD CLOTTING FACTORS; IRON SULFUR PROTEIN STUDIES
S07RR-07109-23 0511 (NSS) TOMASZ, MARIA Biomedical research support INTERACTION OF DNA W/ MITOMYCINS
S07RR-07109-23 0512 (NSS) ZIEGLER, HARRIS PHIL Biomedical research support GRASPING MECHANISM NEURAL CONTROL IN PIGEONS
S07RR-07110-24 (NSS) ZIMMERMAN, WILLIAM F AMHERST COLLEGE P O BOX 2237 AMHERST, MA 01002 Biomedical research support
S07RR-07110-24 0369 (NSS) WILLIAMSON, PATRICK Biomedical research support PURIFICATION OF CHROMAFFIN GRANULE ATPASE II
S07RR-07110-24 0370 (NSS) ZIMMERMAN, WILLIAM F Biomedical research support PHOSPHOLIPID METABOLISM IN RETINA
S07RR-07110-24 0371 (NSS) HANSEN, DAVID E Biomedical research support MECHANISTIC ENZYMOLOGY & IMMUNOLOGY
S07RR-07111-12 (NSS) WINDER, WILLIAM W BRIGHAM YOUNG UNIVERSITY DEPT OF ZOOLOGY, 545 WIDB PROVO, UT 84602 Biomedical research support grant
S07RR-07111-12 0513 (NSS) ROWE, MARK J Biomedical research support grant MITOCHONDRIAL DNA POLYMORPHISMS IN MOLECULAR BIOLOGY OF INHERITED OBESITY
S07RR-07111-12 0514 (NSS) CONLEE, ROBERT K Biomedical research support grant EFFECTS OF COCAINE ON PHYSIOLOGY OF EXERCISE
S07RR-07111-12 0515 (NSS) SEEGMILLER, R E Biomedical research support grant EVAL TERATOGENIC POTENTIAL OF TOPICALLY APPLIED RETINOIC ACID IN MICE
S07RR-07111-12 0516 (NSS) WINDER, WILLIAM W Biomedical research support grant MUSCLE MALONYL COA RESPONSE TO EXERCISE
S07RR-07112-24 (NSS) MOSSMAN, KENNETH L ARIZONA STATE UNIVERSITY ADMINISTRATION BLDG RM 213 TEMPE, AZ 85287 Biomedical research support
S07RR-07112-24 0412 (NSS) WILLIAMS, ROBERT C Biomedical research support RHEUMATOID ARTHRITIS & HLA ANTIGENS IN PIMA INDIANS
S07RR-07112-24 0413 (NSS) HOFFMAN, STEVEN A Biomedical research support TISSUE CULTURE MODEL OF BRAIN REACTIVE AUTOANTIBODIES
S07RR-07112-24 0414 (NSS) SMITH, GEORGIA F Biomedical research support REGULATION OF C MYC ONCOGENE EXPRESSION BY INTERFERON
S07RR-07112-24 0415 (NSS) KILLEEN, PETER R Biomedical research support TUNING CURVES FOR REWARD
S07RR-07112-24 0416 (NSS) LANYON, RICHARD I Biomedical research support MEDICAL EXPERIENCE & SUCCESS OF DECEPTION
S07RR-07112-24 0417 (NSS) BURKE, WILLIAM F Biomedical research support TRACER PLASMIDS FOR MOSQUITOCIDAL STRAINS OF BACILLUS SPAERICUS
S07RR-07112-24 0418 (NSS) NAGOSHI, CRAIG T Biomedical research support ALCOHOL EXPECTATIONS & RESPONSES TO ALCOHOL
S07RR-07112-24 0419 (NSS) YAMAGUCHI, GARY T Biomedical research support HUMAN LOCOMOTION MODELS OF NORMAL & PATHOLOGICAL GAIT
S07RR-07112-24 0420 (NSS) ALLEN, JAMES P Biomedical research support CRYSTALLIZATION & CHARACTERIZATION OF MEMBRANE PROTEINS
S07RR-07112-24 0421 (NSS) SATTERLIE, RICHARD A Biomedical research support PEPTIDE SYNTHESIS IN IDENTIFIED NEURON EGG LAYING VIA MOLLUSC
S07RR-07112-24 0422 (NSS) MOORE, ANA L Biomedical research support CAROTENOPORPHYRINS AS DX TOOLS FOR DETECT OF NEOPLASM
S07RR-07112-24 0423 (NSS) BIEBER, ALLAN L Biomedical research support PARATHYROID PEPTIDES TWO D NMR
S07RR-07112-24 0424 (NSS) BRAVER, SANFORD L Biomedical research support AIDS & NEWLY DIVORCED
S07RR-07112-24 0425 (NSS) COLLINS, JAMES Biomedical research support SCINTILLATION COUNTER EQUIPMENT
S07RR-07112-24 0426 (NSS) BLANKENSHIP, ROBERT Biomedical research support BIOCHEMICAL & MOLECULAR BIOLOGY OF MEMBRANE BOUND
S07RR-07112-24 0427 (NSS) GOLDSTEIN, ELLIOTT S Biomedical research support MOLECULAR & GENETIC ANALYSIS OF JUN PROTO ONCOGENE
S07RR-07112-24 0428 (NSS) PIZZICONI, VINCENT B Biomedical research support FEASIBILITY STUDY OF NOVEL IMMUNOBIOSENSOR
S07RR-07112-24 0429 (NSS) PRESSON, CLARK C Biomedical research support STRATEGIES IN SPATIAL MEMORY
S07RR-07112-24 0430 (NSS) PRIMAS, PHYLLIS J Biomedical research support BREAKING CYCLE OF DISADVANTAGE: PILOT PROJECT
S07RR-07112-24 0431 (NSS) SMITH, ANDREW T Biomedical research support GENETIC ANALYSIS OF INBREEDING IN NATURAL POPULATION
S07RR-07112-24 0432 (NSS) KOMNENICH, PAULINE Biomedical research support NURSE OF 2000 PROJECT
S07RR-07113-24 (NSS) CULLIS, CHRISTOPHER A CASE WESTERN RESERVE UNIV 10900 EUCLID AVENUE CLEVELAND, OHIO 44106 Biomedical research support
S07RR-07113-24 0570 (NSS) GOLDSTEIN, MELVYN C Biomedical research support CHINAS ECONOMIC REFORMS ON ELDERLY: ETHNOGRAPHY
S07RR-07113-24 0565 (NSS) WEINBERGER, DANIEL A Biomedical research support FAMILY ENVIRON & EMOTIONAL REGULATION IN BEHAVIORALLY DISORDERED CHILDREN
S07RR-07113-24 0566 (NSS) BLACKWELL, JOHN Biomedical research support RHEOLOGICAL STUDIES OF MUCIN GLYCOPROTEINS: CYSTIC FIBROSIS
S07RR-07113-24 0567 (NSS) LIU, CHUNG-CHIUN Biomedical research support IMMUNOSENSOR FOR HIV ANTIBODIES: IMMUNOSENSOR
S07RR-07113-24 0568 (NSS) FOUKE, JANIE M Biomedical research support ACOUSTIC RHINOMETRY: DECONGESTANTS & POSTURE ON NASAL PATENCY
S07RR-07113-24 0569 (NSS) KICHER, THOMAS P Biomedical research support QUALITY CONTROL PROCEDURES FOR FES ELECTRODES: NEUROMUSCULAR STIMULATION
S07RR-07113-24 0571 (NSS) KLOPMANN, GILLES Biomedical research support PURCHASE OF HEWLETT PACKARD CC MASS SPECTROMETER
S07RR-07113-24 0572 (NSS) ZULL, JAMES E Biomedical research support CLONING OF PARATHYROID HORMONE RECEPTOR: CALCIUM CONCENTRATIONS
S07RR-07113-24 0573 (NSS) BURKE, MORRIS Biomedical research support STRUCTURAL BASIS OF MUSCLE CONTRACTION: MOTIVE
S07RR-07114-23 (NSS) CRAWFORD, EUGENE C UNIVERSITY OF KENTUCKY

101 T H MORGAN BUILDING LEXINGTON, KY 40506-0225 Biomedical research support
S07RR-07114-23 0433 (NSS) BERRY, DAVID T Biomedical research support GERIATRIC SLEEP APNEA SYNDROME: DEVELOPMENTAL ANALYSIS
S07RR-07114-23 0434 (NSS) BUZDYGON, BRUCE E Biomedical research support PHAGOCYTOSIS OF RETINAL PIGMENT EPITHELIAL CELLS IN CULTURE
S07RR-07114-23 0435 (NSS) DEKIN, MICHAEL S Biomedical research support SINGLE CHANNEL ANALYSIS OF PREMOTOR RESPIRATORY NEURONS
S07RR-07114-23 0436 (NSS) GRUBER, JOSEPH J Biomedical research support TISSUE DENSITY REFERENCE STANDARD DVMT; MRI; PARAPLEGICS
S07RR-07114-23 0437 (NSS) GUTHRIE, ROBERT D Biomedical research support RADICAL ANIONS & RADIOTHERAPY
S07RR-07114-23 0438 (NSS) HIRSCHHORN, RICKY R Biomedical research support GROWTH REGULATION OF CALCYCLIN
S07RR-07114-23 0439 (NSS) HIRSCHHORN, RICKY R Biomedical research support ANNEXIN II IN MATURATION OF XENOPUS OOCYTES
S07RR-07114-23 0440 (NSS) KRAEMER, PHILIPP J Biomedical research support RETRIEVAL PROCESSING IN ANIMALS
S07RR-07114-23 0441 (NSS) KRAEMER, PHILIPP J Biomedical research support ONTOGENETIC ANALYSIS OF OLFACTORY PROCESSING
S07RR-07114-23 0442 (NSS) LORCH, ELIZABETH P Biomedical research support ATTENTION TO & COMPREHENSION OF TV IN ADHD BOYS
S07RR-07114-23 0443 (NSS) LOTSHAW, DAVID P Biomedical research support CHANNELS IN REGULATION OF ALDOSTERONE SECRETION; ADRENAL GLOMERULOSA CELLS
S07RR-07114-23 0444 (NSS) MAJIDI, VAHID Biomedical research support RAPID DETERMINATION OF APOLIPOPROTEINS AI & AII & B CHOLESTEROL; HUMAN SERA
S07RR-07114-23 0445 (NSS) MCDOWELL, KAREN J Biomedical research support TIMING OF ACTIVATION OF GENES FOR CHORIONIC GONADOTROPIN
S07RR-07114-23 0446 (NSS) SCHLOSS, JEFFERY A Biomedical research support ALGAL SIGNAL TRANSDUCTION
S07RR-07114-23 0447 (NSS) SELEGUE, JOHN P Biomedical research support TRANSITION METAL COMPLEXES W/ OXIRANES: EPOXIDATION OF OLEFINS; MODEL
S07RR-07114-23 0448 (NSS) STABEN, CHARLES A Biomedical research support MUTAGENESIS OF NEUROSPORA CRASSA BY TRANSFORMING DNA; PCP; AIDS
S07RR-07114-23 0449 (NSS) TURNER, TERENCE J Biomedical research support COMPONENTIAL APPROACH TO BASIC EMOTIONS
S07RR-07114-23 0450 (NSS) WANG, YI-TIN Biomedical research support CHLORINATED ETHLYLENES & PHENOLS ON HYDROGEN UTILIZING METHANOGENS
S07RR-07114-23 0451 (NSS) WESTNEAT, DAVID F Biomedical research support PCR AMPLIFIED GENETIC MARKERS & RELATEDNESS; NATURAL POPULATIONS
S07RR-07115-24 (NSS) HILLMAN, RALPH TEMPLE UNIVERSITY PHILADELPHIA, PA 19122 Biomedical research support
S07RR-07115-24 0581 (NSS) BERSH, PHILIP Biomedical research support PAVLOVIAN OPERANT INTERACTIONS IN SELF CONTROL
S07RR-07115-24 0582 (NSS) BERSH, PHILIP Biomedical research support ENDORPHIN RECEPTORS INCREASED ALCOHOL CONSUMPTION AFTER EXPOSURE TO SHOCK
S07RR-07115-24 0583 (NSS) FAUBER, ROBERT Biomedical research support FAMILY STRESS & ADOLES ADJUST MECHANISMS & MODERATORS OF INFLUENCE
S07RR-07115-24 0584 (NSS) HANSON, CATHERINE Biomedical research support ROLE OF AGENTS, ACTIONS, & OBJECTS IN EVENT KNOWLEDGE
S07RR-07115-24 0585 (NSS) HINELINE, PHILIP N Biomedical research support DIMINISHING RETURNS IN A GAME LIKE EXPERIMENTAL PROCEDURE
S07RR-07115-24 0586 (NSS) HIRSH-PASEK, KATHRYN Biomedical research support AMERICAN INFANTS PERCEPTION OF BRITISH ENGLISH IN A SELECTIVE LISTENING PARADIGM
S07RR-07115-24 0587 (NSS) NEWCOMBE, NORA Biomedical research support EXPLICIT & IMPLICIT MEMORY IN EARLY
S07RR-07115-24 0588 (NSS) WEINRAUB, MARSHA Biomedical research support MATERNAL EMPLOYMENT ON PRESCHOOL CHILD: MATERNAL ROLE CONGRUENCE
S07RR-07115-24 0589 (NSS) WOODRUFF-PAK, DIANA Biomedical research support EYEBLINK CLASSICAL CONDITIONING IN PATIENTS W/ MULTI INFARCT DEMENTIA
S07RR-07115-24 0574 (NSS) FLORANT, GREGORY Biomedical research support FATTY ACID COMPOSITION OF PLASMA MEMBRANES IN HIBERANTORS
S07RR-07115-24 0575 (NSS) GRUBERG, EDWARD Biomedical research support STUDIES ON MEDULLA OBLONGATA OF FROG
S07RR-07115-24 0576 (NSS) HARVEY, WILLIAM Biomedical research support DELTA ENDOTOXIN CONDUCTANCE IN PATCH CLAMPED COLUMNAR CELLS
S07RR-07115-24 0577 (NSS) SHEFFIELD, JOE Biomedical research support DISTRIBUTION OF 1 C8 ANTIGEN IN EARLY CHICK EMBRYO
S07RR-07115-24 0578 (NSS) TOMPKINS, LAURIE Biomedical research support REVERSION ANALYSIS OF 1PHO, A GENE THAT AFFECTS LARVAL BEHAVIOR
S07RR-07115-24 0579 (NSS) TOMPKINS, LAURIE Biomedical research support ANALYSIS OF BEHAVIOR OF ADULTS EXPRESSING MUTATIONS IN 1PHO: LARVAL PHOTOTAXIS
S07RR-07115-24 0580 (NSS) MAYO, KEVIN Biomedical research support NMR STRUCTURES OF CELL ADHESION PROMOTING PEPTIDES FROM FIBRONECTIN
G20RR-07118-01 (AR) FORD, ELIZABETH W RES. INST. OF SCRIPPS CLINIC 10666 N TORREY PINES RD, MB18 LA JOLLA, CA 92037 Developing and improving institutional animal resources
S07RR-07118-22 (NSS) YOPP, JOHN H SOUTHERN ILLINOIS UNIVERSITY RESEARCH DEVELOPMENT & ADMIN CARBONDALE, IL 62901-4709 Biomedical research support
S07RR-07118-22 0372 (NSS) BARTKE, ANDRZEJ Biomedical research support RADIOIMMUNOLOGY LABORATORY
S07RR-07118-22 0373 (NSS) BARTKE, ANDRZEJ Biomedical research support MARIHUANA & MALE NEUROENDOCRINE & SEXUAL FUNCTIONING
S07RR-07118-22 0374 (NSS) COX, THOMAS Biomedical research support SINGLE CHANNEL KINETICS
S07RR-07118-22 0375 (NSS) ENGLERT, DUWAYNE Biomedical research support MORPHOGENESIS OF HOMEOTIC MUTATION
S07RR-07118-22 0376 (NSS) GUPTA, RAMESH Biomedical research support TRANSCRIPTION & RNA PROCESSING IN ARCHAEBACTERIA
S07RR-07118-22 0377 (NSS) HUVOS, PIROSKA Biomedical research support COMPARATIVE ANALYSIS OF DVMT GENOME REARRANGEMENTS IN CILIATED PROTOZOA
S07RR-07118-22 0378 (NSS) KOROPCHAK, JOHN Biomedical research support CHEMISTRY DEPARTMENT SPEAKER SERIES
S07RR-07118-22 0379 (NSS) MOLFESE, DENNIS L Biomedical research support EVOKED POTENTIAL STUDIES SIMULATED WEIGHTLESSNESS
S07RR-07118-22 0380 (NSS) MURPHY, LAURA Biomedical research support NEUROENDOCRINE MECHANISMS OF CANNABINOID ACTION
S07RR-07118-22 0381 (NSS) PARKER, JACK M Biomedical research support NEW SPECIES OF THERMOPHILIC PHOTOTROPIC GREEN BACTERIA
S07RR-07118-22 0382 (NSS) PARR, MARGARET Biomedical research support MUCOSAE IMMUNITY IN FEMALE GENITAL TRACT
S07RR-07118-22 0383 (NSS) PETERSON, RUDOLPH Biomedical research support ISOLATION OF SPERM PROTEIN
S07RR-07118-22 0384 (NSS) SHRIVER, JOHN Biomedical research support TRAVEL TO INTERNATIONAL NMR MEETING
S07RR-07118-22 0385 (NSS) STEVENS, WILLIAM Biomedical research support REPAIR OF NMR SPECTROMETER
S07RR-07119-20 (NSS) LEE, CHING-TSE BROOKLYN COLLEGE OF CUNY BROOKLYN, NY 11210 Biomedical research support
S07RR-07119-20 0466 (NSS) ABRAMOV, I Biomedical research support COLOR PERCEPTION
S07RR-07119-20 0467 (NSS) HAINLINE, L Biomedical research support VISUAL DEVELOPMENT IN INFANTS
S07RR-07119-20 0468 (NSS) OSMAN, E Biomedical research support HYPNOSIS & AUDITORY
S07RR-07119-20 0469 (NSS) SCARBOROUGH, D Biomedical research support TONALITY & MUSIC PERCEPTION
S07RR-07120-14 (NSS) GOLDSTEIN, BERNARD SAN FRANCISCO STATE UNIV 1600 HOLLOWAY AVENUE SAN FRANCISCO, CA 94132 Biomedical research support grant
S07RR-07121-13 (NSS) NEWKOME, GEORGE R UNIVERSITY OF SOUTH FLORIDA 4202 E FOWLER AVE, OFF RES TAMPA, FLA 33620 Biomedical research support
S07RR-07121-13 0470 (NSS) BAER, ROBERTA D Biomedical research support PROGRAM TO REDUCE RISK FROM USE OF LEAD BASED MEXICAN FOLK REMEDIES
S07RR-07121-13 0471 (NSS) LIM, DANIEL V Biomedical research support GROUP B STREPTOCOCCAL COLLAGENASE & PREMATURE RUPTURE OF MEMBRANES
S07RR-07121-13 0472 (NSS) WICKSTROM, ERIC Biomedical research support ANTISENSE DNA INHIBITION OF ONCOGENE EXPRESSION
S07RR-07121-13 0473 (NSS) WELLS, ALVIN F Biomedical research support TISSUE PATHOLOGY CAUSED BY BORRELIA BURGDORFERI
S07RR-07121-13 0474 (NSS) EDWARDS, SAMUEL Biomedical research support PROTEIN PHOSPHATASE IN PHOTORECEPTOR FUNCTION
S07RR-07122-23 (NSS) GULLAHORN, JEANNE E UNIVERSITY AT ALBANY, SUNY AD 227 ALBANY, NY 12222 Biomedical research support
S07RR-07122-23 0103 (NSS) BLANCHARD, EDWARD B Biomedical research support IRRITABLE BOWEL DISEASE RESEARCH
S07RR-07122-23 0104 (NSS) ISRAEL, ALLEN Biomedical research support CHILDHOOD OBESITY & ITS TREATMENT
S07RR-07122-23 0105 (NSS) JACCARD, JAMES J Biomedical research support DRUNK DRIVING PREVENTION, APPLIED PSYCHOLOGY
S07RR-07122-23 0106 (NSS) MCCAFFREY, ROBERT J Biomedical research support NEURAL BEHAVIORAL & DEVELOPMENT TOXICOLOGY
S07RR-07122-23 0107 (NSS) MCCAFFREY, ROBERT J Biomedical research support COGNITIVE ASPECTS OF MEDICAL CONDITIONS
S07RR-07122-23 0108 (NSS) ROSELLINI, ROBERT A Biomedical research support PSYCHOLOGICAL RESEARCH & DEVELOPMENT
S07RR-07122-23 0109 (NSS) GULLAHORN, JEANNE E Biomedical research support VP FOR RESEARCH GENERAL & DISCRETIONARY SUPPORT OF BIOMEDICAL RESFACILITY
S07RR-07122-23 0110 (NSS) VIDEKA-SHERMAN, LYNN Biomedical research support QUALITATIVE RESEARCH CONFERENCE
S07RR-07122-23 0111 (NSS) VIDEKA-SHERMAN, LYNN Biomedical research support HEALTH RESEARCH
S07RR-07122-23 0112 (NSS) MESSNER, STEVE F Biomedical research support HOMICIDE
S07RR-07122-23 0113 (NSS) SPITZE, GLENNA D Biomedical research support ALTERNATIVE CHILDBIRTH METHODS & MENTAL HEALTH
S07RR-07122-23 0114 (NSS) SPITZE, GLENNA D Biomedical research support TECHNOLOGY & STRESS AMONG LIBRARIANS
S07RR-07122-23 0115 (NSS) SPITZE, GLENNA D Biomedical research support MINORITY FAMILY NETWORKS & MENTAL HEALTH
S07RR-07122-23 0116 (NSS) TOLNAY, STEWART E Biomedical research support SOCIAL & DEMOGRAPHIC ANALYSIS OF FAMILIES
S07RR-07122-23 0117 (NSS) LOGAN, JOHN Biomedical research support WELL BEING IN URBAN CHINA
S07RR-07122-23 0118 (NSS) LOGAN, JOHN Biomedical research support SOCIAL INFLUENCES ON PHYSICAL & EMOTIONAL WELL BEING
S07RR-07122-23 0077 (NSS) JACKLET, JON W Biomedical research support BIOLOGICAL RESEARCH MACHINE USAGE
S07RR-07122-23 0078 (NSS) JACKLET, JON W Biomedical research support BIOLOGICAL RESEARCH SUPPORT SUPPLIES
S07RR-07122-23 0079 (NSS) JACKLET, JON W Biomedical research support BIOLOGICAL RESEARCH SUMMER SUPPORT GRADUATE STUDENTS
S07RR-07122-23 0080 (NSS) JACKLET, JON W Biomedical research support BIOLOGICAL RESEARCH
S07RR-07122-23 0081 (NSS) MILLIS, ALBERT Biomedical research support CELLULAR DIFFERENTIATION
S07RR-07122-23 0082 (NSS) SCHMIDT, JOHN T Biomedical research support NEUROBIOLOGICAL RESEARCH
S07RR-07122-23 0083 (NSS) SHUB, DAVID A Biomedical research support MOLECULAR GENETICS
S07RR-07122-23 0084 (NSS) TRAVIS, JEFFREY L Biomedical research support ELECTRON MICROSCOPY STUDIES
S07RR-07122-23 0085 (NSS) BANK, SHELTON Biomedical research support TEXACO NMR ACQUISITION
S07RR-07122-23 0086 (NSS) BLOCK, ERIC Biomedical research support CHEMICAL RESEARCH
S07RR-07122-23 0087 (NSS) BLOCK, ERIC Biomedical research support NMR REPAIR
S07RR-07122-23 0088 (NSS) HAUSER, FRANK Biomedical research support

PROJECT NO., ORGANIZATIONAL UNIT., INVESTIGATOR, ADDRESS, TITLE

SEMINAR & RECRUITMENT PROGRAM
S07RR-07122-23 0089 (NSS) HAUSER, FRANK Biomedical research support SYNTHESIS OF ANTI CANCER ANTIBIOTICS
S07RR-07122-23 0090 (NSS) KUIVILA, HENRY G Biomedical research support LEWIS ACID CHEMISTRY
S07RR-07122-23 0091 (NSS) SCHOLES, CHARLES P Biomedical research support SPECTROSCOPY & KINETICS OF ENDONUCLEASE III
S07RR-07122-23 0092 (NSS) ZUBIETA, JON Biomedical research support XRAY DEFRACTOMETER STUDIES
S07RR-07122-23 0093 (NSS) GAGE, TIMOTHY B Biomedical research support NUTRITION & MORTALITY PROJECT
S07RR-07122-23 0094 (NSS) SCHELL, LAWRENCE Biomedical research support ALBANY LEAD STUDY
S07RR-07122-23 0095 (NSS) SNOW, DEAN R Biomedical research support PRIMATE BRAIN MORPHOLOGY
S07RR-07122-23 0096 (NSS) VELLUTINO, FRANK R Biomedical research support TRAVEL FOR DATA COLLECTION FOR STUDY OF READING DISABLED
S07RR-07122-23 0097 (NSS) DUFFEE, DAVID E Biomedical research support CRIMINAL JUSTICE RESEARCH TRAVEL & CONFERENCE SUPPORT
S07RR-07122-23 0098 (NSS) MCDOWALL, DAVID Biomedical research support CRIMINAL JUSTICE RESEARCH PUBLICATIONS COSTS
S07RR-07122-23 0099 (NSS) GREEN, MICHAEL Biomedical research support DEVELOPMENTAL NEUROPSYCHOLOGY
S07RR-07122-23 0100 (NSS) GREEN, MICHAEL Biomedical research support BEHAVIOR RESEARCH & THERAPY
S07RR-07122-23 0101 (NSS) LANCE, TIMOTHY L Biomedical research support HEALTH RESEARCH PROJECTS
S07RR-07122-23 0102 (NSS) BARLOW, DAVID H Biomedical research support STRESS & ANXIETY RESEARCH
S07RR-07123-22 (NSS) DONLEY, ROSEMARY CATHOLIC UNIVERSITY OF AMERICA WASHINGTON, DC 20064 Biomedical research support
S07RR-07123-22 0590 (NSS) SEBRECHTS, MARC M Biomedical research support HYPERMEDIA AS AN INSTRUCTIONAL TOOL IN CARDIOLOGY
S07RR-07123-22 0591 (NSS) ROSS, BRUCE M Biomedical research support ECONOMIC & SOCIAL UNDERSTANDING IN CHILDREN
S07RR-07123-22 0592 (NSS) WAGNER, BARRY M Biomedical research support FOLLOW UP OF ADOLESCENT SUICIDE ATTEMPTERS
S07RR-07123-22 0593 (NSS) FURTH, HANS G Biomedical research support LEARNING ABOUT SOCIETY THROUGH CHILDREN AT PLAY
S07RR-07123-22 0594 (NSS) SLOANE, DOUGLAS M Biomedical research support BROKEN HOMES & ADOLESCENT DRUG USE
S07RR-07123-22 0595 (NSS) MCCARTHY, JOHN M Biomedical research support DYNAMICS OF CITIZENS MOVEMENT AGAINST DRUNK DRIVING
S07RR-07123-22 0596 (NSS) BUNCE, DIANE M Biomedical research support CONCEPTUAL APPROACH TO TEACHING & LEARNING CHEMISTRY
S07RR-07123-22 0597 (NSS) KOVACH, ILDIKO M Biomedical research support STRUCTURE & DYNAMICS OF SERINE HYDROLASE INHIBITION BY PHOSPHONATE ESTERS
S07RR-07123-22 0598 (NSS) BREWER, GREG Biomedical research support SYNTHESIS OF MAGNETIC RESONANCE IMAGING AGENTS
S07RR-07123-22 0599 (NSS) CARMINES, DAVID V Biomedical research support BIOMECHANICS LABORATORY IN BIOMEDICAL ENGINEERING PROGRAM
S07RR-07123-22 0600 (NSS) WHITE, JANE H Biomedical research support COGNITIVE BEHAVIORAL PROGRAM ON BULIMIA IN A GROUP OF WOMEN
R13RR-07124-01 (BRC) HALVORSON, HARLYN O MARINE BIOLOGICAL LABORATORY WOODS HOLE, MA 02543 Second international marine biotechnology conference
S07RR-07125-22 (NSS) BOND, LYNNE A UNIVERSITY OF VERMONT 85 S PROSPECT STREET BURLINGTON, VT 05405 Biomedical research support
S07RR-07125-22 0388 (NSS) HELD, JEAN M Biomedical research support RAT BRAIN TISSUE TRANSPLANTATION & LOCOMO RECOVERY & SENSORIMOTOR CORTEX DAMAGE
S07RR-07125-22 0386 (NSS) FORGAYS, DONALD G Biomedical research support PILOT STUDIES ON TYPE A BEHAVIOR
S07RR-07125-22 0387 (NSS) GILMARTIN, GREGORY M Biomedical research support REGULATION OF HIV MRNA 3 PROCESSING
S07RR-07125-22 0389 (NSS) HUOT, ANNE E Biomedical research support CELLULAR EFFECTS REACTIVE INTERMEDIATES BY J7741 CELLS EFFECTOR & TARGET CELL
S07RR-07125-22 0390 (NSS) IDE, HIROSHI Biomedical research support PROCESSING POTENTIALLY CARCINOGENIC MODIFIED BASES BY TRANSLESION DNA SYNTHESIS
S07RR-07125-22 0391 (NSS) KILPATRICK, C WILLIA Biomedical research support CONTROLLED BOTTLENECKS & GENETIC VARIABILITY; TWO RODENT SPECIES
S07RR-07125-22 0392 (NSS) LEITENBERG, HAROLD Biomedical research support RESTING METABOLIC RATE; BULIMIA NERVOSA
S07RR-07125-22 0393 (NSS) LINTILHAC, PHILIP M Biomedical research support MECHANICAL LOADING OF ISOLATED PLANT PROTOPLASTS
S07RR-07125-22 0394 (NSS) OTTER, TIMOTHY Biomedical research support CALCIUM BINDING PROTEINS IN SPERM FLAGELLA
S07RR-07125-22 0395 (NSS) PELL, ALICE N Biomedical research support ADHESION OF RUMINOCOCCUS ALBUS 8 & BACTEROIDES SUCCINOGES S85 TO CELLULOSE
S07RR-07125-22 0396 (NSS) PINTAURO, STEPHEN J Biomedical research support WHEAT GERM AGGLUTININ, INTESTINAL DRUG METABOLIZING ENZYME SYSTEMS: GUINEA PIG
S07RR-07125-22 0397 (NSS) RAPER, CHARLENE A Biomedical research support CHARACTERIZATION OF DNA PLASMID NATIVE TO SCHIZOPHYLLUM COMMUNE
S07RR-07125-22 0398 (NSS) ROSS, JANE K Biomedical research support LIGNIN & HEMICELLULOSE & PECTIN DIETS ON LIVER CHOLESTEROL & FECAL FATTY ACIDS
S07RR-07125-22 0399 (NSS) SCHAEFFER, WARREN I Biomedical research support CYTOPLASM IN MALIGNANCY
S07RR-07125-22 0400 (NSS) STRAND, EDYTHE A Biomedical research support LENGTH PHONETIC COMPLEXITY ON TEMPORAL ACOUSTIC MEASURES IN SPEAKERS
S07RR-07126-16 (NSS) GOLDSTEIN, SOLOMON GRAD SCH & UNIV CTR OF CUNY 33 WEST 42ND STREET NEW YORK, N Y 10036 Biomedical research support grant
R01RR-07127-01 (GEN) ROSE, ANN M UNIVERSITY OF BRITISH COLUMBIA 6174 UNIVERSITY BLVD VANCOUVER, CANADA V6T 1W5 A genetic toolkit for C elegans
S07RR-07127-23 (NSS) BENJAMIN, STEVEN A COLORADO STATE UNIVERSITY 206 ADMINISTRATION ANNEX FORT COLLINS, CO 80523 Biomedical research support
S07RR-07127-23 0475 (NSS) ACKLEY, R S Biomedical research support CISPLATIN INDUCED OTOTOXICITY IN YOUNG & OLD MICE: AGING EFFECTS
S07RR-07127-23 0476 (NSS) AVERY, DAVID Biomedical research support ANIMAL MODEL: COCAINE & ALCOHOL ON DIET SELF SELECT DURING PREGNANCY & LACTATION
S07RR-07127-23 0491 (NSS) LINDEN, JAMES Biomedical research support TAXOL, AN OVARIAN CANCER DRUG FROM PLANT CELL CULTURE
S07RR-07127-23 0492 (NSS) BAMBURG, JAMES R Biomedical research support REGULATION OF ACTIN ASSEMBLY IN MUSCLE & NERVE
S07RR-07127-23 0493 (NSS) DUESTER, GREGG Biomedical research support REGULATION OF GENES INVOLVED IN ALCOHOL & VITAMIN METABOLISM
S07RR-07127-23 0494 (NSS) ANDERSON, OREN Biomedical research support NEW MODELS FOR CYTOCHROME OXIDASE ACTIVE SITE
S07RR-07127-23 0495 (NSS) BARISAS, B GEORGE Biomedical research support GLYCOPROTEIN G63 IN ALLERGEN INDUCED DEGRANULATION BASOPHIL
S07RR-07127-23 0496 (NSS) CRANS, DEBBIE C Biomedical research support 2D 51V NMR SPECT KINETICS OF VANADATE EXCHANGE REACTIONS
S07RR-07127-23 0497 (NSS) DEBRUIN, KENNETH Biomedical research support USE OF MIXED IMIDES FOR STUDIES OF BIOMEDICAL PROCESSES
S07RR-07127-23 0498 (NSS) WILLIAMS, ROBERT M Biomedical research support DNA CROSS LINKING BY ANTI TUMOR ANTIBIOTIC FR 900482
S07RR-07127-23 0499 (NSS) NERGER, JANICE L Biomedical research support POLYMORPHISM OF HUMAN COLOR VISION
S07RR-07127-23 0500 (NSS) VOLBRECHT, VICKI Biomedical research support NEURAL PROCESSES MEDIATING ANOMALOUS COLOR VISION
S07RR-07127-23 0477 (NSS) AZARI, PARVIZ Biomedical research support ACTION OF TRANQUILIZERS ON LENS
S07RR-07127-23 0478 (NSS) BARBER, CLIFTON Biomedical research support EFFECT OF AGE ON OLFACTORY ACUITY
S07RR-07127-23 0479 (NSS) CRANS, DEBBIE Biomedical research support FREE TRACE LEVELS OF VANADIUM & V IN BIOLOGICAL & ENVIRON FLUIDS
S07RR-07127-23 0480 (NSS) HEYLIGER, PAUL Biomedical research support AN ANALYSIS OF FLUID INDUCED FRACTURE AT BONE CEMENT INTERFACE
S07RR-07127-23 0481 (NSS) HOSSNER, KIM Biomedical research support IGF I & II IN BOVINE TISSUES DURING FETAL DEVELOPMENT
S07RR-07127-23 0482 (NSS) MARQUARDT, W C Biomedical research support GENOMES OF PARASITIC PROTOZOA BY PULSED FIELD GEL ELECTROPHORESIS
S07RR-07127-23 0483 (NSS) MOORE, JANICE Biomedical research support BEHAVIOR OF MOSQUITOES INFECTED W/ DIROFILARIA IMMITIS
S07RR-07127-23 0484 (NSS) RAPPE, ANTHONY Biomedical research support HORMONES & NEUROTRANSMITTERS, ENKEPHALINS, OXYTOCIN VASOPRESSIN & SOMATOSTATIN
S07RR-07127-23 0485 (NSS) REARDON, KENNETH Biomedical research support CULTIVATION & PROTEIN PRODUCTION BY GENETICALLY MODIFIED BACTERIA
S07RR-07127-23 0486 (NSS) RANU, RAJINDER Biomedical research support REGULATION OF PROTEIN SYNTHESIS BY STEROIDS
S07RR-07127-23 0487 (NSS) SOCKLER, JAMES M Biomedical research support CHRONIC SWIM TRAINING ON PULMONARY VASCULAR REACTIVITY IN RATS
S07RR-07127-23 0488 (NSS) BARRETT, KAREN C Biomedical research support EMOTIONS IN TODDLER INTERGENERATIONAL TRANSMISSION OF PERSONALITY DISORDERS
S07RR-07127-23 0489 (NSS) MACPHEE, DAVID Biomedical research support COGNITIVE MEDIATORS OF CHILD ABUSE
S07RR-07127-23 0490 (NSS) THAUT, MICHAEL Biomedical research support AUDITORY RHYTHMIC STIMULI IN GAIT REHAB W/ STROKE & BRAIN INJURED PTS
S07RR-07129-22 (NSS) JARON, DOV DREXEL UNIVERSITY 32ND & CHESTNUT STREETS PHILADELPHIA, PA 19104 Biomedical research support
S07RR-07129-22 0501 (NSS) LOGAN, DAVID A Biomedical research support PATHOGENICITY OF CANDIDA ALBICANS: MOLECULAR APPROACH: AIDS RELATED
S07RR-07129-22 0502 (NSS) DUBIN, STEPHEN Biomedical research support NON INVASIVE MEASUREMENT OF BODY COMPOSITION IN ANIMALS
S07RR-07129-22 0503 (NSS) ZUCKERMAN, RALPH Biomedical research support COUPLING OF METABOLISM TO CELLULAR ACTIVATION
S07RR-07129-22 0504 (NSS) SUN, HUN H Biomedical research support NONLINEAR ANALYSIS OF POLARIZATION OF NOBLE METAL ELECTRODES
S07RR-07129-22 0505 (NSS) DINTER-GOTTLIEB, GAI Biomedical research support MUTAGENESIS OF RIBOZYME FROM HEPATITIS DELTA VIRUS: ANTI AIDS THERAPY
S07RR-07129-22 0506 (NSS) DICKSTEIN, REBECCA Biomedical research support ROOT NODULE SPECIFIC GENES OF MEDICAGO
S07RR-07129-22 0507 (NSS) MARTIN, PRESLEY F Biomedical research support SODIUM BUTYRATE & TISSUE SPECIFIC POSITION EFFECTS IN DROSOPHILA
S07RR-07131-22 (NSS) RILEY, MICHAEL V OAKLAND UNIVERSITY ROCHESTER, MI 48309-4401 Biomedical research support
S07RR-07131-22 0132 (NSS) LINDEMANN, CHARLES Biomedical research support PURCHASE OF OPTIMAS IMAGE ANALYSIS SYSTEMS
S07RR-07131-22 0133 (NSS) MOUDGIL, VIRINDER Biomedical research support GLUCOCORTICOID RECEPTORS IN MAMMALIAN HEART
S07RR-07131-22 0134 (NSS) MOUDGIL, VIRINDER Biomedical research support PHOSPHORYLATION OF AVIAN PROGESTERONE RECEPTOR
S07RR-07131-22 0135 (NSS) NAG, ASISH Biomedical research support ASSEMBLY OF CARDIAC MYOFIBRILS
S07RR-07131-22 0136 (NSS) NAG, ASISH Biomedical research support REPAIR OF MICROTOME
S07RR-07131-22 0137 (NSS) REDDY, VENKAT Biomedical research support EYE RESEARCH SUPPORT
S07RR-07131-22 0138 (NSS) SEVILLA, MICHAEL Biomedical research support PURCHASE OF 640 MBYTE HARD DISC & CONTROLLER PLUS ETHERNET CONNECTION
S07RR-07131-22 0139 (NSS) TAYLOR, CRAIG Biomedical research support PLATINUM & ARA C COMPLEX AS MULTIFUNCTIONAL ANTI VIRAL AND & OR ANTITUMOR AGENTS
S07RR-07131-22 0140 (NSS) TOMBOULIAN, PAUL Biomedical research

support CHEMISTRY SUPPORT
S07RR-07131-22 0141 (NSS) WALIA, SATISH Biomedical research support POLYCHLORINATED BIPHENYL DEGRADATION GENES IN BACTERIAL GENERA
S07RR-07131-22 0142 (NSS) WALIA, SATISH Biomedical research support GENETICALLY ENGINEERED PLASMIDS IN PATHOGENIC BACTERIA
S07RR-07131-22 0143 (NSS) ZEPELIN, HAROLD Biomedical research support INTENSITY OF SLEEP OVER HUMAN LIFE SPAN
S07RR-07131-22 0144 (NSS) BUTTERWORTH, FRANK Biomedical research support CELLULAR & MOLECULAR BIOLOGY OF PROTEIN SECRETION
S07RR-07131-22 0119 (NSS) BUTTERWORTH, FRANK Biomedical research support DNA AMPLIFICATION SYSTEM
S07RR-07131-22 0120 (NSS) BUTTERWORTH, FRANK Biomedical research support SYMPARTER UPGRADE & RENOVATION OF LKB KNIFEMAKER
S07RR-07131-22 0121 (NSS) BUTTERWORTH, FRANK Biomedical research support GENETIC REGULATION OF YOLK SECRETION
S07RR-07131-22 0122 (NSS) BUTTERWORTH, FRANK Biomedical research support BACTERIAL PHENYL CATECHOL DEGRADATION GENE IN A EUKARYOTIC GENOME
S07RR-07131-22 0123 (NSS) CALLEWAERT, DENIS Biomedical research support CYCLIC IMMUNOSUPPRESSANTS ON NATURAL KILLER CELLS
S07RR-07131-22 0124 (NSS) CHAUDHRY, RASUL Biomedical research support MOLECULAR GENETICS OF CATABOLISM OF CARBAMATES
S07RR-07131-22 0125 (NSS) CHAUDHRY, RASUL Biomedical research support CLONING & EXPRESSION OF GENES ENCODING BIOLOGICAL PESTICIDES
S07RR-07131-22 0126 (NSS) GORDON, SHELDON Biomedical research support TRANSFORMING GROWTH FACTOR BETA ON CORNEAL ENDOTHELIAL WOUND REPAIR
S07RR-07131-22 0127 (NSS) GORDON, SHELDON Biomedical research support PURCHASE OF SORVALL SHAKER
S07RR-07131-22 0128 (NSS) HANSEN-SMITH, FAYE Biomedical research support PSEUDOMONAS AERUGINOSA & BACTERIAL RESTRICTION ENDONUCLEASE DNA ANALYSIS
S07RR-07131-22 0129 (NSS) HEALY-MOORE, KATHLEE Biomedical research support REGULATORY EFFECTS OF OXALYL THIOL ESTERS ON ACYL COA METABOLISM
S07RR-07131-22 0130 (NSS) HARTZER, MICHAEL Biomedical research support PURCHASE OF SHIMADZU SPECTROPHOTOFLUOROMETER
S07RR-07131-22 0131 (NSS) HENRY, EGBERT Biomedical research support BIOMEDICAL RESEARCH SUPPORT
S07RR-07132-20 (NSS) LEVINE, LOUIS CITY COLLEGE OF CUNY 138TH ST & CONVENT AVE NEW YORK, N Y 10031 Biomedical research support
S07RR-07132-20 0401 (NSS) CALHOUN, DAVID Biomedical research support REGULATION OF GENE EXPRESSION BY AN ALLOSTERIC ENZYME
S07RR-07132-20 0402 (NSS) COICO, RICHARD Biomedical research support IMMUNOREGULATORY ACTIVITY OF IGD
S07RR-07132-20 0403 (NSS) GREEN, MICHAEL Biomedical research support SIMULATION OF ROLE OF WATER IN ION CHANNEL GATING
S07RR-07132-20 0404 (NSS) GUYDEN, JERRY Biomedical research support THYMIC NURSE CELL FUNCTIONS
S07RR-07132-20 0405 (NSS) LEV, MEIR Biomedical research support REGULATION OF BRAIN SULFOTRANSFERASE ACTIVITY BY VITAMIN K
S07RR-07132-20 0406 (NSS) LEVINE, LOUIS Biomedical research support NATURAL POPULATIONS LIVING NEAR NUCLEAR ENERGY PLANT
S07RR-07132-20 0407 (NSS) ROCKWELL, ROBERT Biomedical research support FITNESS DECLINES IN LESSER SNOW GEESE; AGRICULTURAL PESTICIDES
S07RR-07132-20 0408 (NSS) SIMMONS, GAIL Biomedical research support DNA SEQUENCE DIVERGENCE OF DROSOPHILA MOBILE ELEMENTS
S07RR-07132-20 0409 (NSS) TARTTER, VIVIEN Biomedical research support AUDITORY REGULATION & SPEECH PRODUCTION; COCHLEAR IMPLANT
S07RR-07132-20 0410 (NSS) YU, AMY WAN-HUA Biomedical research support ANDROGENIC REGULATION OF NEUTROPHIC ACTIVITIES
S07RR-07133-22 (NSS) GRAY, DONALD M UNIVERSITY OF TEXAS P O BOX 830688 M/S FO 3.1 RICHARDSON, TEX 75083-0688 Biomedical research support
S07RR-07133-22 0515 (NSS) WATKINS, RUTH W Biomedical research support MEASUREMENT ISSUES IN LANGUAGE SAMPLE ANALYSIS; CHILD
S07RR-07133-22 0508 (NSS) MARSH, ROBERT C Biomedical research support TECTONIN PROTEINS OF PHYSARUM & SACCHAROMYCES
S07RR-07133-22 0509 (NSS) FRIEL-PATTI, SANDY Biomedical research support LANGUAGE DEVELOPMENT OF OTITIS MEDIA; EARLY CHILDHOOD
S07RR-07133-22 0510 (NSS) HANNIG, ERNEST M Biomedical research support MOLECULAR ANALYSIS OF GCDII, NEGATIVE REGULATOR OF GCN4 IN YEAST; SEQ
S07RR-07133-22 0511 (NSS) YEE, THOMAS W Biomedical research support BRANCHED DNA RNA COPOLYMER OF MYXOCOCCUS XANTHUS
S07RR-07133-22 0512 (NSS) BARTLETT, JAMES C Biomedical research support HUMAN AGING & FACE MEMORY
S07RR-07133-22 0513 (NSS) SHERRY, A DEAN Biomedical research support CONFORMATION OF MACROMOLECULES W/ METAL IONS; MOLECULAR MODELING
S07RR-07133-22 0514 (NSS) REITZER, LAWRENCE J Biomedical research support CONTROL OF TOXIN EXPRESSION IN PSEUDOMONAS AERUGINOSA
S07RR-07133-22 0516 (NSS) GRAY, CARLA W Biomedical research support STRUCTURES, DYNAMICS, & FUNCTION OF VIRAL NUCLEOPROTEIN COMPLEXES; EM
S07RR-07134-15 (NSS) MURRAY, RAYMOND C UNIVERSITY OF MONTANA ROOM 116, MAIN HALL MISSOULA, MONTANA 59812 Biomedical research support
S07RR-07134-15 0517 (NSS) RAYMOND, KATHLEEN C Biomedical research support INSECT HOST RANGES AMONG DIFFERENT BACILLUS THURINGIENSIS SUBSPECIES
S07RR-07134-15 0518 (NSS) MITCHELL-OLDS, THOMA Biomedical research support MOLECULAR BIOCHEMICAL GENETICS OF DISEASE RESISTANCE; MYROSINASE
S07RR-07134-15 0519 (NSS) JOHNSTON, CRAIG Biomedical research support OXYTOCIN IN REGULATING PREOVULATORY SURGE OF LUTEINIZING HORMONE; NEURO
S07RR-07134-15 0520 (NSS) GREENE, ERICK Biomedical research support DIET INDUCED POLYMORPHISM IN CATERPILLAR NEMORIA ARIZONARIA; DVMT
S07RR-07135-21 (NSS) POODRY, CLIFTON A UNIVERSITY OF CALIFORNIA 1156 HIGH STREET SANTA CRUZ, CA 95064 Biomedical research support
S07RR-07135-21 0632 (NSS) POODRY, CLIFTON A Biomedical research support NO RESEARCH SUBPROJECTS
S07RR-07136-20 (NSS) BURRIS, JAMES J GEORGETOWN UNIVERSITY 3900 RESERVOIR RD, NW WASHINGTON, DC 20007 Biomedical research support
S07RR-07136-20 0608 (NSS) TANSEY, TERESE Biomedical research support MOLECULAR ANALYSIS OF TROPOMYOSIN: CONTRACTILE PROTEIN MUSCLE CELLS MYOPATHIES
S07RR-07136-20 0609 (NSS) JAMESON, GEOFFREY B Biomedical research support XRAY DIFFRACTION
S07RR-07136-20 0610 (NSS) BEAUCHAMP, TOM L Biomedical research support BIOETHICS
S07RR-07136-20 0611 (NSS) WEINSTEIN, MAXINE Biomedical research support MODEL OF AGE SPECIFIC MARITAL FERTILITY: MICRO SIMULATION
S07RR-07136-20 0612 (NSS) SOLDO, BETH J Biomedical research support HEALTH & FAMILY STATUS CHANGES OF OLDEST OLD: AGED
S07RR-07138-20 (NSS) COOMBE, ROBERT D UNIVERSITY OF DENVER 2101 E WESLEY AVE, UNIV PARK DENVER, COLO 80208 Biomedical research support
S07RR-07138-20 0521 (NSS) EATON, GARETH Biomedical research support S BAND MICROWAVE AMPLIFIER
S07RR-07138-20 0522 (NSS) DEWEY, GREGORY Biomedical research support ULTRAVIOLET VISUAL TRANSDUCTION BIOPHYSICAL TOOL
S07RR-07138-20 0523 (NSS) BENSON, JANETTE Biomedical research support THREE DIMENSIONAL RECONSTRUCTION & ANALYSIS OF INFANT LOCOMOTION
S07RR-07138-20 0524 (NSS) ROSSMAN, ROBBIE Biomedical research support CHILD DVMT & ADAPT IN MODERATING ESPOUSAL & CHILD MALTREAT EFFECT
S07RR-07138-20 0525 (NSS) MARKMAN, HOWARD Biomedical research support LONG TERM EFFECTS OF PREMARITAL INTERVENTION
S07RR-07138-20 0526 (NSS) FOGLEMAN, JAMES Biomedical research support DEVELOPMENT OF SOFTWARE LIBRARY FOR BACTERIAL IDENTIFICATION
S07RR-07138-20 0527 (NSS) BOWLER, BRUCE Biomedical research support PROTEIN STABILITY; SITE DIRECTED MUTAGENESIS IN YEAST ISO 1 CYTOCHROME C
S07RR-07138-20 0528 (NSS) SADLER, SUSAN Biomedical research support CAMP REGULATION IN XENOPUS OOCYTES
S07RR-07138-20 0529 (NSS) BOLGER, NIALL Biomedical research support MARITAL INTERACTION & RECOVERY FROM BREAST CANCER
S07RR-07138-20 0530 (NSS) DOWNEY, GERALDINE Biomedical research support STRESS, SOCIAL SUPPORT, & PARENTING IN FAMILIES W/ DEPRESSED PARENT
S07RR-07138-20 0531 (NSS) POTTS, GEORGE Biomedical research support SOFTWARE PACKAGE FOR ON LINE EXPERIMENT CONTROL
S07RR-07138-20 0532 (NSS) LINK, CHRISTOPHER Biomedical research support GLYCOSYLATION IN C ELEGANS
S07RR-07138-20 0533 (NSS) MARKMAN, HOWARD Biomedical research support LONG TERM EFFECTS OF PREMARITAL INTERVENTION
S07RR-07138-20 0534 (NSS) BOWLER, BRUCE Biomedical research support METAL ION ACTIVATION; SITE SPECIFIC CLEAVAGE OF DNA BY ECO RI ENDONUCLEASE
S07RR-07143-20 (NSS) FINE, SAMUEL NORTHEASTERN UNIVERSITY 360 HUNTINGTON AVENUE BOSTON, MASS 02115 Biomedical research support
S07RR-07143-20 0536 (NSS) WRIGHT, ANTHONY Biomedical research support AVIAN & PRIMATE CONCEPT LEARNING & MEMORY PROCESSING
S07RR-07143-20 0537 (NSS) BARBER, ROGER Biomedical research support MECHANISMS OF ADENYLATE CYCLASE ACTIVATION
S07RR-07143-20 0538 (NSS) CHAKRABORTY, RANAJIT Biomedical research support FAMILY HISTORY SCORE FOR CHRONIC DISEASE EPIDEMIOLOGY
S07RR-07143-20 0535 (NSS) WONG, WAI-HOI Biomedical research support DESIGN CONCEPT OF AN ULTRA HIGH RESOLUTION PET CAMERA
S07RR-07143-20 0539 (NSS) MARC, ROBERT Biomedical research support ENHANCEMENTS FOR ELECTRON MICROSCOPY
S07RR-07143-20 0637 (NSS) VOUROS, PAUL Biomedical research support GAS CHROMATOGRAPHIC MASS SPECTROMETRIC ANALYSIS OF BIOLOGICAL COMPOUNDS
S07RR-07143-20 0638 (NSS) WISE, DONALD L Biomedical research support BIODEGRADABLE POLYMER CARRIERS FOR CONTROLLED DRUG RELEASE
S07RR-07143-20 0639 (NSS) ZAMANSKY, HAROLD S Biomedical research support HYPNOSIS STUDIES
S07RR-07143-20 0540 (NSS) DOUGLAS, TOMMY Biomedical research support CONTROL OF ISOTOPE EXCLUSION BY ENHANCER ELEMENTS
S07RR-07143-20 0541 (NSS) HEWETT-EMMETT, DAVID Biomedical research support EVOLUTION & FUNCTION OF CARBONIC ANHYDRASE VII
S07RR-07143-20 0542 (NSS) SPERLING, HARRY G Biomedical research support CONSTRUCTION OF ERG DEVICE
S07RR-07143-20 0543 (NSS) LI, WEN-HSIUNG Biomedical research support STATISTICAL STUDIES OF DNA EVOLUTION
S07RR-07143-20 0613 (NSS) AYERS, JOSEPH L Biomedical research support PHYSIOLOGICAL ANALYSIS OF NEURAL CIRCUITS
S07RR-07143-20 0614 (NSS) BARABINO, GILDA A Biomedical research support SICKLE CELL ANEMIA
S07RR-07143-20 0615 (NSS) BERGMAN, KOSTIA Biomedical research support BACTERIAL PHYSIOLOGY STUDIES
S07RR-07143-20 0616 (NSS) BLOCK, MARTIN L Biomedical research support PSYCHOBIOLOGICAL PROCESSES UNDERLYING SOCIAL BEHAVIORS
S07RR-07143-20 0617 (NSS) BUUS, SOREN Biomedical research support AUDITORY STUDIES IN NORMAL & HEARING IMPAIRED
S07RR-07143-20 0618 (NSS) CHAMPION, PAUL M Biomedical research support CYTOCHROME BIOPHYSICAL STUDIES
S07RR-07143-20 0619 (NSS) CHENEY, DONALD P Biomedical research support GENETIC MODIFICATION IN SEAWEED BACTERIOLOGICAL & CELL CULTURE
S07RR-07143-20 0620 (NSS) COHEN, PERRIN S Biomedical research support AGGRESSION FRUSTRATION STUDIES
S07RR-07143-20 0621 (NSS) DAVIES, GEOFFREY Biomedical research support COPPER PEROXIDE COMPLEXES
S07RR-07143-20 0622 (NSS) DAVIS, FREDERICK C Biomedical research support CIRCADIAN RHYTHM STUDIES
S07RR-07143-20 0623 (NSS) FERRIER, LINDA J Biomedical research support STIMULATION FOR HANDICAPPED INFANT
S07RR-07143-20 0624 (NSS) FLORENTINE, MARY Biomedical research support AUDITORY STUDIES IN NORMAL & HEARING IMPAIRED
S07RR-07143-20 0625 (NSS) HALL, JUDITH A Biomedical research support DOCTOR PATIENT COMMUNICATION
S07RR-07143-20 0626 (NSS) HALPERN, ARTHUR M Biomedical research support PHOTOKINETICS & THERMODYNAMICS OF MOLECULES

PROJECT NO., ORGANIZATIONAL UNIT., INVESTIGATOR, ADDRESS, TITLE

S07RR-07143-20 0627 (NSS) KNOWLES, AILEEN F Biomedical research support HUMAN HEPATOMA CELLS BIOCHEMICAL STUDIES
S07RR-07143-20 0628 (NSS) KRULL, IRA S Biomedical research support CHROMATOGRAPHIC SEPARATION & ANALYSIS OF BIOLOGICAL COMPOUNDS
S07RR-07143-20 0629 (NSS) MACKAY, HARRY A Biomedical research support EMERGENT DISCRIMINATIVE BEHAVIOR
S07RR-07143-20 0630 (NSS) MESZOELY, CHARLES A Biomedical research support MALARIAL PARASITE ULTRASTRUCTURAL STUDIES
S07RR-07143-20 0631 (NSS) RAPPAPORT, CAREY M Biomedical research support MICROWAVE STERILIZATION STUDIES
S07RR-07143-20 0632 (NSS) REIFF, WILLIAM M Biomedical research support NUCLEAR GAMMA RESONANCE (MOSSBAUER EFFECT) CANCER RADIATION STUDIES
S07RR-07143-20 0633 (NSS) SCHEIRER, DANIEL C Biomedical research support CELLULAR LOCALIZATION OF LIGHT INDUCED CALCONE SYNTHASE
S07RR-07143-20 0634 (NSS) SHIFFMAN, CARL A Biomedical research support MAGNETIC RESONANCE FLOW STUDIES
S07RR-07143-20 0635 (NSS) SKAVENSKI, ALEXANDER Biomedical research support EFFECT OF FOVEAL SCOTOMA ON VISUAL IMPAIRMENT
S07RR-07143-20 0636 (NSS) STRAUSS, PHYLLIS R Biomedical research support TOPOISOMERASE & MITOCHONDRION OF TRYPANOSOMA BRUCEI
S07RR-07147-19 (NSS) LEVI, DENNIS M UNIVERSITY OF HOUSTON 4800 CALHOUN HOUSTON, TX 77204-2163 Biomedical research support
S07RR-07147-19 0640 (NSS) ALAM, MAKTOOB Biomedical research support REPAIR OF HIGH PRESSURE LIQUID CHROMATOGRAPH: MARINE INVERTEBRATES MARINE FUNGI
S07RR-07147-19 0641 (NSS) ALKADHI, KARIM A Biomedical research support RHYTHMIC ACTIVITIES IN GANGLIA BY EXPOSURE TO COLD TEMPS: CARDIOVASCULAR
S07RR-07147-19 0642 (NSS) BRAZEAU, GAYLE A Biomedical research support DRUG METABOLISM IN ANIMAL MODEL OF DUCHENNE MUSCULAR DYSTROPHY: HEPATIC
S07RR-07147-19 0643 (NSS) CERNUSZEWICZ, ROMAN Biomedical research support RESONANCE RAMAN STUDY OF ANION BINDING TO SUPEROXIDE DISMUTASES: SPECTROSCOPY
S07RR-07147-19 0644 (NSS) EICHBERG, JOSEPH Biomedical research support HYDROLYSIS OF PHOSPHATIDYLCHOLINE IN PERIPHERAL NERVE: NEUROTRANSMITTERS
S07RR-07147-19 0645 (NSS) ESKIN, ARNOLD Biomedical research support MESSENGER RNA EXPRESSION AS A RESULT OF LEARNING: APLYSIA CALIFORNICA
S07RR-07147-19 0646 (NSS) ESKIN, ARNOLD Biomedical research support BASIS OF REGULATION & TIMING OF CIRCADIAN RHYTHMS: APLYSIA CALIFORNICA
S07RR-07147-19 0647 (NSS) FOX, GEORGE E Biomedical research support EVOLUTIONARY CONSTRAINTS GOVERNING NUCLEOTIDE INSERTIONS IN RIBOSOMAL RNA: MODEL
S07RR-07147-19 0648 (NSS) FOX, GEORGE E Biomedical research support CANDIDATE TERTIARY INTERACTIONS IN RIBOSOMAL RNA: ARTIFICIAL GENE
S07RR-07147-19 0649 (NSS) GLOVER, JOHN R Biomedical research support CONTEXT BASED AUTOMATED DETECTION OF ABNORMAL EEG WAVES: EPILEPSY
S07RR-07147-19 0650 (NSS) JANSEN, BEN H Biomedical research support NONLINEAR MODELING OF EEG & VEP ANALYSIS: SOMOSENSORY STIMULUS
S07RR-07147-19 0651 (NSS) SHATTUCK, DAVID P Biomedical research support SPEED OF SOUND ESTIMATION IN LIVER DISEASE: FIBROSIS, CIRRHOSIS
S07RR-07147-19 0652 (NSS) STREET, JOSEPH P Biomedical research support ALKALINE PHOSPHATASE MODELS: METALLOPROTEIN, BINUCLEAR ZINC CONTAINING ENZYMES
S07RR-07147-19 0653 (NSS) TATE, CHARLOTTE A Biomedical research support MYOCARDIAL RESPONSE TO EXERCISE DURING SENSCENCE: SARCOPLASMIC RETICULUM
S07RR-07147-19 0654 (NSS) TU, SHIAO-CHUN Biomedical research support BACTERIAL LUCIFERASE VARIANTS TO STUDY ERRORS IN PROTEIN BIOSYNTHESIS: MUTAGEN
S07RR-07147-19 0655 (NSS) WELCH, STEVEN C Biomedical research support AN ENANTIOSELECTIVE SYNTHESIS OF ANTITUMOR AGENT ANDRIAMYCIN: CHIRAL SYNTHESIS
S07RR-07147-19 0656 (NSS) WELLS, DAN E Biomedical research support MAPPING A HUMAN DISEASE LOCUS BY IN SITU HYBRIDIZATION: LANGER GIEDION SYNDROME
S07RR-07147-19 0657 (NSS) WHITE, CATHERINE A Biomedical research support PHARMACOKINETIC OF LIPOSOMAL ENCAPSULATED CEFOTAXIME: RETICULOENDOTHELIAL
S07RR-07147-19 0658 (NSS) WIDGER, WILLIAM R Biomedical research support GENETIC ENGINEERING OF CORYNEBACTERIUM TO AID IN DECOMPOSITION OF SPILLED OIL
S07RR-07148-18 (NSS) BUTCHER, REGINALD W UNIV OF TEXAS HLTH SCIENCE CTR POST OFFICE BOX 20334 HOUSTON, TEXAS 77225 Biomedical research support
S07RR-07149-18 (NSS) SPEAR, NORMAN E SUNY BINGHAMTON PO BOX 6000 BINGHAMTON, NY 13902-6000 Biomedical research support
S07RR-07149-18 0411 (NSS) BATES, MARYANN S Biomedical research support BIOCULTURAL DIMENSIONS OF CHRONIC PAIN: PUERTO RICAN STUDY
S07RR-07149-18 0412 (NSS) CONNINE, CYNTHIA Biomedical research support LANGUAGE COMPREHENSION: PROCESSING OF NON LITERAL LANGUAGE
S07RR-07149-18 0418 (NSS) GAZZARA, RUSSELL A Biomedical research support EFFECTS OF PRENATAL COCAINE EXPOSURE ON DEV OF DOPAMINE NEUROTRANSMITTER SYSTEM
S07RR-07149-18 0419 (NSS) GAZZARA, RUSSELL A Biomedical research support ONTOGENY OF CALCIUM DEPENDENT DOPAMINE RELEASE EVOKED BY ELECTRICAL STIMULATION
S07RR-07149-18 0420 (NSS) HASTIE, SUSAN B Biomedical research support PHOTOAFFINITY LABELING ON COLCHICINE SITE ON TUBULIN
S07RR-07149-18 0421 (NSS) HORWATH, KATHLEEN L Biomedical research support CELL LINES FOR ANTIFREEZE PROTEIN PRODUCTION
S07RR-07149-18 0422 (NSS) HORWATH, KATHLEEN L Biomedical research support VERSONS GLAND PROTEIN PURIFICATION & ANTISERA PREPERATION
S07RR-07149-18 0423 (NSS) MICHAEL, SANDRA D Biomedical research support T CELL POPULATION IN MICE W/ NEONATAL THYMECTOMY INDUCED OVARIAN DIS
S07RR-07149-18 0424 (NSS) OH, TAEBOEM Biomedical research support FACE SELECTIVITY IN HETERO DIELS ALDER REACTIONS
S07RR-07149-18 0425 (NSS) PARIETTI, ELIZABETH Biomedical research support CAREGIVERS OF ALZHEIMERS PATIENTS
S07RR-07149-18 0413 (NSS) DI LORENZO, PATRICIA Biomedical research support COMPUTATIONAL ANALYSIS OF TASTE RESPONSES IN PONS: INTENSITY RESPONSE FUNCTIONS
S07RR-07149-18 0426 (NSS) TAN-WILSON, ANNA Biomedical research support MOLECULAR CLONING OF CYSTEINE PROTEINASE INHIBITOR FROM SOYBEAN
S07RR-07149-18 0427 (NSS) WILSON, KARL A Biomedical research support SUBCELLULAR COMPARTMENTALIZATION OF PROTEOLYSIS
S07RR-07149-18 0414 (NSS) DI LORENZO, PATRICIA Biomedical research support STIMULATION OF TASTE RELATED NEURAL AREAS: MODEL OF GUSTATORY NEURAL CODING
S07RR-07149-18 0415 (NSS) DIX, JAMES A Biomedical research support MAPPING MEMBRANE FLUIDITY
S07RR-07149-18 0416 (NSS) FRIEDMAN, ALICE Biomedical research support CHILDRENS APPRAISAL OF DANGER
S07RR-07149-18 0417 (NSS) FRIEDMAN, ALICE Biomedical research support IMPACT OF SITUATIONAL & FAMILY VARIABLES ON COPING
S07RR-07150-17 (NSS) ROGLER, LLOYD H FORDHAM UNIVERSITY HISPANIC RESEARCH CENTER BRONX, N Y 10458 Biomedical research support
S07RR-07150-17 0544 (NSS) AIELLO, EDWARD Biomedical research support REGULATION OF MUCOCILIARY ACTIVITY
S07RR-07150-17 0545 (NSS) BERMAN, WILLIAM H Biomedical research support BEHAVIORAL OBSERVATION OF ATTACHMENT BONDS IN ADULTS
S07RR-07150-17 0546 (NSS) BUSCH, NANCY Biomedical research support MASTERY MOTIVATION IN CRACK BABIES
S07RR-07150-17 0547 (NSS) GILBERT, ALLAN S Biomedical research support ASSESSMENT OF ORGANIC PRESERVATION IN ANCIENT ANIMAL BONES
S07RR-07150-17 0548 (NSS) HAMILTON, MARY Biomedical research support INTER DECAMERIC INTERACTIONS IN MOLLUSCAN HEMOCYANINS
S07RR-07150-17 0549 (NSS) MUKHERJEE, ASIT B Biomedical research support INVESTIGATIONS ON ASSOCIATION OF SEX CHROMOSOMAL ABERRATIONS & CELLULAR AGING
S07RR-07150-17 0550 (NSS) NORDSTROM, JEFFREY Biomedical research support MOLECULAR ARCHEOLOGY OF LEMURS: AMPLIFICATION & ANALYSIS OF DNA
S07RR-07150-17 0551 (NSS) POTTER, LLOYD Biomedical research support RACIAL VARIATION IN SOCIOECONOMIC CHARACTERISTICS OF HOMICIDE VICTIMS
S07RR-07150-17 0552 (NSS) ROSS, ROBERT Biomedical research support HUMAN NEUROBLASTOMA TRANSDIFFERENTIATION
S07RR-07150-17 0553 (NSS) VERNON, GRACE Biomedical research support ISOLATION OF METALLOTHIONEIN FROM HEPATOPANCREATIC TISSUE
S07RR-07151-13 (NSS) HARRISON, LYNDA L UNIVERSITY OF ALABAMA PO BOX 870118 TUSCALOOSA, AL 35487-0118 Biomedical research support
S07RR-07151-13 0517 (NSS) TIMKOVICH, RUSSELL Biomedical research support MOLECULAR MODELING OF PROTEINS & NATURAL PRODUCTS
S07RR-07151-13 0518 (NSS) PRENTICE-DUNN, STEVE Biomedical research support EVAL PROTECTION MOTIVATION THEORY & ALCOHOL USE AMONG OLDER ADULTS
S07RR-07151-13 0519 (NSS) THORN, BEVERLY E Biomedical research support DESCENDING PAIN INHIBITORY SYSTEMS OF MIDBRAIN
S07RR-07151-13 0520 (NSS) SLOAN, GARY L Biomedical research support EXTRACELL ENZYME PRODUCTION BY STAPHYLOCOCCUS SIMULANS BIOVAR STAPHYLOLYTICUS
S07RR-07151-13 0521 (NSS) TIMKOVICH, RUSSELL Biomedical research support STRUCTURE OF PROTEINS, NATURAL PRODUCTS & THERAPEUTIC COMPOUNDS
S07RR-07151-13 0522 (NSS) CHURCHILL, PERRY F Biomedical research support STRUCTURE & FUNCTION OF D HYDROXYBUTYRATE DEHYDROGENASE
S07RR-07151-13 0523 (NSS) RILEY, CAROL P Biomedical research support EFFECTS OF PULMONARY REHABILITATION
S07RR-07153-14 (NSS) FLANAGAN, PATRICK W UNIVERSITY OF LOUISVILLE RESEARCH & GRAD PROGRAMS LOUISVILLE, KY 40292 Biomedical research support
S07RR-07154-16 (NSS) MCCARTHY, CHARLOTTE M NEW MEXICO STATE UNIV BOX 3000 DEPARTMENT 3AF LAS CRUCES, NM 88003-0001 Biomedical research support
S07RR-07154-16 0555 (NSS) VELTEN, JEFF P Biomedical research support INTERMEDIATES OF POTATO SPINDLE TUBOR VIROID REPLICATION; TRANSGENIC PLANTS
S07RR-07154-16 0554 (NSS) VELTEN, JEFF P Biomedical research support DELETION SCANNING DISSECTI OF ADJACENT DIVERGENT PLANT TRANSCRIPTIONAL PROMOTERS
S07RR-07154-16 0556 (NSS) MCCARTHY, CHARLOTTE Biomedical research support CHARACTERIZATION OF PLASMIDS FROM MYCOBACTERIA
S07RR-07154-16 0557 (NSS) WANG, JOSEPH Biomedical research support RENEWABLE BIOSENSORS OBTAINED UTILIZING GRAPHITE EPOXY MATRICES
S07RR-07154-16 0558 (NSS) MCCARTHY, CHARLOTTE Biomedical research support INCORPORATION OF 5 FLUOROURACIL INTO RNA OF MYCOBACTERIUM AVIUM
S07RR-07154-16 0559 (NSS) MCCARTHY, CHARLOTTE Biomedical research support ANALYSIS OF MYCOBACTERIUM AVIUM COMPLEX BY MULTILOCUS ENZYME ELECTROPHORESIS
S07RR-07154-16 0560 (NSS) HERMAN, CEIL A Biomedical research support LEUKOTRIENE RECEPTORS IN BULLFROG HEART & LUNG
S07RR-07154-16 0561 (NSS) BOTSFORD, JAMES L Biomedical research support METABOLISM OF GLUTAMATE IN RHIZOBIUM MELILOTI
S07RR-07154-16 0562 (NSS) FIELDS, CHRISTOPHER Biomedical research support COMPARING SEQUENCES OF BINDING SITES BETWEEN SYSTEMS; MONOCOT & DICOT PLANTS
S07RR-07154-16 0563 (NSS) SENGUPTA-GOPALAN, CO Biomedical research support EXPRESSION OF GLUTAMINE SYNTHETASE GENES; SOYBEAN ROOT NODULE DVMT
S07RR-07154-16 0564 (NSS) SENGUPTA-GOPALAN, CH Biomedical research support CHARACTERIZATION OF "AT" BINDING DOMAINS OF NODULIN & SEED PROTEIN GENES
S07RR-07154-16 0565 (NSS) ROUBICEK, RUDOLF V Biomedical research support CENTRIFUGAL FILM BIOREACTOR; ENHANCED MASS TRANSFER
S07RR-07155-14 (NSS) ARLIAN, LARRY G WRIGHT STATE UNIVERSITY 235A BIOLOGICAL SCI BLDG DAYTON, OH 45435 Biomedical research support grant
S07RR-07156-16 (NSS) PETRI, WILLIAM H BOSTON COLLEGE 140 COMMONWEALTH AVENUE CHESTNUT HILL, MASS 02167 Biomedical research

support
S07RR-07156-16 0566 (NSS) KANTROWITZ, EVAN R Biomedical research support MECHANISMS OF COOPERATIVITY; RDNA TECHNIQUES TO STUDY PROTEINS
S07RR-07156-16 0567 (NSS) MCLAUGHLIN, LARRY W Biomedical research support FLUORESCENT LABELING OF NUCLEIC ACIDS; DETECT BIOPHYSICAL MEASUREMENTS
S07RR-07156-16 0568 (NSS) ROBERTS, MARY F Biomedical research support INTERFACIAL ACTIVATION OF WATER SOLUBLE PHOSPHOLIPASES & VARIAN VXR 500S: NMRS
S07RR-07156-16 0569 (NSS) FREEMAN, SCOTT Biomedical research support INSIDE MONEY & OPEN ECONOMY
S07RR-07156-16 0570 (NSS) MIZRACH, BRUCE Biomedical research support TIME SERIES ANALYSIS OF ERGODIC NON LINEAR DYNAMICAL SYSTEMS
S07RR-07157-16 (NSS) KSIR, CHARLES J, JR UNIVERSITY OF WYOMING PO BOX 3355 LARAMIE, WY 82071 Biomedical research support
S07RR-07157-16 0571 (NSS) GAVIN, WILLIAM J Biomedical research support GRAMMATICAL STRUCTURE OF LANGUAGE THERAPY GROUPS DIFFERING IN PRAGMATIC LOADING
S07RR-07157-16 0572 (NSS) CALDWELL, DANIEL R Biomedical research support ISOLATION & CHARACTERIZATION OF PLASMID DNA FROM RUMINOBACTER AMYLOPHILUS
S07RR-07157-16 0573 (NSS) RULE, DANIEL C Biomedical research support DIETARY LIPID ON HEPATIC & ADIPOSE TISSUE ACTIVITY IN FASTED REFED RATS
S07RR-07157-16 0574 (NSS) STAYTON, MARK M Biomedical research support INDUCTION OF PLANT DEFENSE RESPONSE IN TISSUE CULTURE
S07RR-07157-16 0575 (NSS) PETERSEN, NANCY S Biomedical research support GENE ENVIRONMENT INTERACTIONS FOR TERATOGENESIS
S07RR-07157-16 0576 (NSS) HANSEN, THOMAS R Biomedical research support UTERINE 28KD PROTEIN: COMMUNIC OF MOTHER & CONCEPTUS IN EARLY PREGNANCY; BOVINE
S07RR-07157-16 0577 (NSS) KLEE, THOMAS M Biomedical research support CHILDRENS EVENT KNOWLEDGE & LANGUAGE SAMPLING
S07RR-07157-16 0578 (NSS) THORSNESS, PETER E Biomedical research support SIGNAL TRANSDUCTION IN STARVATION RESPONSE OF YEAST
S07RR-07157-16 0579 (NSS) HARLOW, HENRY J Biomedical research support NEPHRON RECRUITMENT & ANTIDIURETIC HORMONE IN VAMPIRE BAT KIDNEY
S07RR-07157-16 0580 (NSS) AUSTIN, HARRIET B Biomedical research support EXTRACELLULAR MATRIX IN MULLERIAN DUCT REGRESSION IN AMERICAN ALLIGATOR
S07RR-07158-16 (NSS) HUSTON, RICHARD L UNIVERSITY OF ILLINOIS 1737 W POLK STREET CHICAGO, IL 60612 Biomedical research support
S07RR-07159-16 (NSS) YASBIN, RONALD E UNIV OF MD BALTIMORE CNTY BALTIMORE, MD 21228 Biomedical research support
S07RR-07159-16 0581 (NSS) SIEGMAN, ARON W Biomedical research support PSYCHOSOCIAL VARIABLES IN CARDIOVASCULAR REACTIVITY
S07RR-07159-16 0582 (NSS) HUMPHREY, JAY D Biomedical research support MICROMECHANICAL TEST DEVICE FOR BIOMATERIALS; VARIOUS SOFT TISSUE
S07RR-07160-16 (NSS) SODETZ, JAMES M UNIVERSITY OF SOUTH CAROLINA DEPARTMENT OF CHEMISTRY COLUMBIA, SC 29208 Biomedical research support
S07RR-07160-16 0583 (NSS) MILLER, GLORIA E Biomedical research support PARENT INFORMANT MEASURE OF CHILDRENS SELF CONTROL
S07RR-07160-16 0584 (NSS) BOWMAN, LEWIS Biomedical research support NUCLEAR MITOCHONDRIAL INTERACTIONS IN DEVELOPING MUSCLE
S07RR-07160-16 0585 (NSS) LAWTHER, ROBERT Biomedical research support ISOLEUCINE & VALINE METABOLISM
S07RR-07160-16 0586 (NSS) SILKS, LOUIS A Biomedical research support DESIGN OF OLIGONUCLEOTIDES CONTAINING TELLURIUM REPORTER GROUP
S07RR-07160-16 0587 (NSS) TOUR, JAMES M Biomedical research support MACROCYCLIZATIONS IN WATER
S07RR-07160-16 0588 (NSS) GALLINI, JOAN K Biomedical research support LEARNING PHYSICS FROM DIAGRAMS, COMPUTER ANIMATIONS & OBJECT MANIPULATION
S07RR-07160-16 0589 (NSS) DAWSON, JOHN H Biomedical research support CD SPECTROSCOPY AS PROBE OF HEME & CHLORIN IRON COORDINATION
S07RR-07160-16 0590 (NSS) LEBIODA, LUCASZ Biomedical research support CRYSTAL STUDIES OF ARRESTIN
S07RR-07160-16 0591 (NSS) THORPE, SUZANNE R Biomedical research support REGULATION OF PLASMA PROTEIN CATABOLISM
S07RR-07160-16 0592 (NSS) WEDELL, DOUGLAS H Biomedical research support ASSESSMENT AS FUNCTION OF JUDGEMENT PROCEDURE
S07RR-07160-16 0593 (NSS) APPEL, JAMES B Biomedical research support NEUROCHEMICAL SUBSTRATES OF BEHAVIORAL EFFECTS OF COCAINE & D AMPHETAMINE
S07RR-07160-16 0594 (NSS) COLEMAN, JAMES R Biomedical research support RECOVERY OF HEARING IN AGED RAT AFTER NEURAL GRAFTING INTO AUDITORY MIDBRAIN
S07RR-07160-16 0595 (NSS) COLEMAN, ROBERT S Biomedical research support ACYLKETONE (4+2) CYCLOADDITIONS: DE NOVO CARBOHYDRATE SYNTHESIS
S07RR-07160-16 0596 (NSS) DAWSON, WALLACE D Biomedical research support EVOLUTIONARY STABILITY OF MAMMALIAN GENOME
S07RR-07160-16 0597 (NSS) SCHERER, DAVID G Biomedical research support CHILDRENS PERCEPTION OF CHRONICALLY MENTALLY ILL PARENTS
S07RR-07160-16 0598 (NSS) YOCH, DUANE Biomedical research support FERREDOXIN GENE REGULATION IN PHOTOSYNTHETIC BACTERIUM
S07RR-07160-16 0599 (NSS) MORRIS, ROBIN K Biomedical research support EYE MOVEMENTS & LANGUAGE PROCESSING IN READING
S07RR-07160-16 0600 (NSS) SONO, MASANORI Biomedical research support SPECT PROTEIN MODEL STUDIES OF MYELOPEROXIDASE ACTIVE CENTER
S07RR-07160-16 0601 (NSS) WU, LICIA Biomedical research support BONE INDUCTION W/ TGF B + RETINOIC ACID IN GROWTH PLATE CARTLIAGE
S07RR-07161-14 (NSS) BLAKE, RICHARD D UNIVERSITY OF MAINE 238 HITCHNER HALL ORONO, MAINE 04469 Biomedical research support
S07RR-07161-14 0843 (NSS) HUNTER, SUSAN J Biomedical research support SPECTRIN LOCALIZATION IN ACTIVE & INACTIVE OSTEOCLASTS
S07RR-07161-14 0844 (NSS) ROSENWASSER, ALAN M Biomedical research support PSYCHOPHARMACOLOGY OF CIRCADIAN ACTIVITY RHYTHMS
S07RR-07161-14 0845 (NSS) BLAKE, RICHARD D Biomedical research support MICRODEGREE TEMP CONTROLLER FOR HIGH RESOLUTION THERMODYNAMIC ANALYSIS OF DNA
S07RR-07161-14 0846 (NSS) KASS, LEONARD Biomedical research support WHOLE CELL PATCH CLAMP RECORDINGS FROM LIMULUS PHOTORECEPTOR CELLS
S07RR-07161-14 0847 (NSS) DOWSE, HAROLD Biomedical research support PHASE SHIFTING OF CIRCADIAN CLOCK IN DROSOPHILA MAY ACTIVATE A PROTO ONCOGENE
S07RR-07161-14 0848 (NSS) BRUCE, ALICE E Biomedical research support MECHANISTIC STUDIES OF REACTIONS OF GOLD AND SULFUR COMPOUNDS
S07RR-07161-14 0849 (NSS) JELLISON, JODY Biomedical research support IRON CHELATING COMPOUNDS OF FUNGAL ORIGIN: EFFECT ON CHRONIC IRON TOXICITY
S07RR-07161-14 0850 (NSS) WALLACE, CHARLES R Biomedical research support EFFECTS OF OVINE PLACENTAL LACTOGEN ON VARIOUS SHEEP TISSUES IN VITRO
S07RR-07167-14 (NSS) JONES, FRED, JR MEHARRY MEDICAL COLLEGE 1005 D B TODD BLVD NASHVILLE, TENN 37208 Biomedical research support
S07RR-07167-14 0602 (NSS) HATCHER, FRANK Biomedical research support DEVELOPMENT OF HYBRIDOMA FACILITY FOR RESEARCH INFRASTRUCTURE: MABS
S07RR-07167-14 0603 (NSS) UNKNOWN Biomedical research support ELECTRON MICROSCOPY A RESEARCH RESOURCE FACILITY
S07RR-07169-07 (NSS) PATTERSON, WAYNE UNIVERSITY OF NEW ORLEANS LAKE FRONT CAMPUS AD 204 NEW ORLEANS, LA 70148 Biomedical research support grant
S07RR-07169-07 0169 (NSS) GITHENS, SHERWOOD Biomedical research support grant PURCHASE OF FLUOROMETER FOR FLUORIMETRIC ASSAYS
S07RR-07169-07 0170 (NSS) WILLIAMS, MARY C Biomedical research support grant COGNITIVE FACTORS RELATED TO SUBSTANCE ABUSE
S07RR-07169-07 0171 (NSS) THOMAS, JOCELYN Biomedical research support grant SEX DIFFERENCES IN DEVELOPMENT OF SPATIAL BEHAVIOR IN LEARNING DISABILITIES
S07RR-07170-15 (NSS) LAURENCE, KENNETH A UNIVERSITY OF IDAHO 111 MORRILL HALL MOSCOW, IDAHO 83843 Biomedical research support
S07RR-07170-15 0604 (NSS) MCKEAN, THOMAS A Biomedical research support INTRACELLULAR CALCIUM & CARDIAC MYOCYTE
S07RR-07170-15 0605 (NSS) TRUMBLE, WILLIAM R Biomedical research support CALCIUM REGULATION IN HEART USING NOVEL PROBES TO CARDIAC FOOT
S07RR-07170-15 0606 (NSS) MEAD, RODNEY A Biomedical research support IMMUNOCYTOCHEMISTRY LOCALIZATION OF TUBEROINFUNDIBULAR DOPAMINERGIC NEURONS; EM
S07RR-07170-15 0607 (NSS) BYERS, JOHN A Biomedical research support BIOLOGICAL EFFECTS OF LOCOMOTOR PLAY BEHAVIOR
S07RR-07170-15 0608 (NSS) YAMA, MARK F Biomedical research support LONG TERM CONSEQUENCES OF CHILDHOOD
S07RR-07171-08 (NSS) BAUMSTARK, ALFONS L GEORGIA STATE UNIVERSITY ATLANTA, GA 30303 Biomedical research support grant
S07RR-07171-08 0145 (NSS) ALBERS, H ELLIOT Biomedical research support grant HORMONAL BASIS OF SEX DIFFERENCES IN HAMSTER FLANK MARKING: SOCIAL COMMUNICATION
S07RR-07171-08 0146 (NSS) BARFUSS, DELON W Biomedical research support grant TRANSPORT & TOXICITY OF HG & CD IN RENAL PROXIMAL TUBULE
S07RR-07171-08 0147 (NSS) BARTNESS, TIMOTHY J Biomedical research support grant CNS MELATONIN RECEPTORS & RELATIONSHIP TO PHOTOPERIODIC & CIRCADIAN RHYTHMS
S07RR-07171-08 0148 (NSS) BAUMSTARK, ALFONS L Biomedical research support grant CH ACTIVATION REACTIONS OF DIMETHYLDIOXIRANE:CYCLIC PEROXIDES
S07RR-07171-08 0149 (NSS) BAUMSTARK, BARBARA R Biomedical research support grant SITE DIRECTED MUTAGENESIS OF PLCL GENE: FOREFINGER MOTIF WITHIN CL PROTEIN
S07RR-07171-08 0150 (NSS) BOYKIN, DAVID W Biomedical research support grant ANTI PCP AGENTS: DIARYLDIAMIDINES AS AGENTS FOR TREATMENT OF P CARINII PNEUMONIA
S07RR-07171-08 0151 (NSS) CHERNIAK, ROBERT Biomedical research support grant FINE STRUCTURE OF EXOPOLYSACCHARIDE OF C NEOFORMANS OF SEROGROUPS C & D
S07RR-07171-08 0152 (NSS) COOK, WARREN L Biomedical research support grant ENTEROTOXIC FACTOR IN NON TOXIGENIC V CHOLERAE W/ TUPHOA MUTAGENSIS: INTESTINE
S07RR-07171-08 0153 (NSS) DERBY, CHARLES Biomedical research support grant BIOCHEMICAL ANALYSIS OF OLFACTORY RECEPTOR BINDING
S07RR-07171-08 0154 (NSS) DIXON, DABNEY W Biomedical research support grant CONTROL OF ELECTRON TRANSFER IN BIOLOGICAL SYSTEMS:
S07RR-07171-08 0155 (NSS) FREY, TERRY K Biomedical research support grant PCR ASSAY TO DISCRIMINATE BETWEEN WILD TYPE & VACCINE STRAINS OF RUBELLA VIRUS
S07RR-07171-08 0156 (NSS) HOUGHTON, JOHN E Biomedical research support grant REGULATORY GENES IN BETA KETOODIPATE PATHWAY OF P PUTIDA
S07RR-07171-08 0157 (NSS) KENNEDY, G DAVON Biomedical research support grant BENZOCYCLOHEPTADRIENE AMIDES; POTENTIAL ANTIVIRAL AGENTS FOR TREATMENT OF AIDS
S07RR-07171-08 0158 (NSS) PATONAY, GABOR Biomedical research support grant NEAR IR DYE LABELED BIOMOLECULES ON POLYMER BEADS: DETECTION FOR PROTEINS
S07RR-07171-08 0159 (NSS) SMITH, JERRY C Biomedical research support grant MOLECULAR PROBES IN ENERGY TRANSDUCING MEMBRANES USING PICOSECOND SPECTROSCOPY
S07RR-07171-08 0160 (NSS) WALTHALL, W WILLIAM Biomedical research support grant MOLECULAR CLONING OF A GENE INVOLVED IN NEURONAL DIFFERENTIATION C ELEGANS
S07RR-07171-08 0161 (NSS) WRIGHT, KRISTINA Biomedical research support grant ACUTE PHASE INFLAMMATORY RESPONSE ON TESTOSTERONE SYNTHESIS: CYTOKINES
S07RR-07171-08 0162 (NSS) CHERNIAK, ROBERT Biomedical research support grant EXOPOLYSACCHARIDE OF C NEOFORMANS GC & MS FOR STUDY OF POLYSACCHARIDES
S07RR-07171-08 0163 (NSS) DIXON, DABNEY W Biomedical research support grant ELECTRON TRANSFER IN BIOLOGICAL SYSTEMS: CYTOCHROME C & B5
S07RR-07171-08 0164 (NSS) WILSON, W DAVID Biomedical research support grant BIOPHYSICAL STUDIES ON NUCLEIC ACIDS & DRUG BINDING UV & VIS SPECTROMETERS
S07RR-07172-01 (SSS) TARANTAL, ALICE F UNIVERSITY OF CALIFORNIA

PROJECT NO., ORGANIZATIONAL UNIT., INVESTIGATOR, ADDRESS, TITLE

DAVIS, CA 95616-8542 Ultrasound unit
S07RR-07173-10 (NSS) LASKER, JUDITH N LEHIGH UNIVERSITY 526 BRODHEAD AVENUE BETHLEHEM, PA 18015 Biomedical research support grant
S07RR-07175-15 (NSS) PERKINS, JOHN P UT SOUTHWESTERN MED CTR DALLAS 5323 HARRY HINES BLVD DALLAS, TEX 75235 Biomedical research support
S07RR-07175-15 0428 (NSS) AVERY, LEON Biomedical research support GENETICS OF FEEDING IN CAENORHABDITIS ELEGANS
S07RR-07175-15 0429 (NSS) CONDON, KEITH Biomedical research support NEURAL DETERMINATION OF POSTNATAL MUSCLE FIBER TYPES
S07RR-07175-15 0430 (NSS) CRAFT, CHERYL M Biomedical research support ISOLATION & SEQUENCING HUMAN RETINAL CDNA ENCODING N ACETYLTRANSFERASE
S07RR-07175-15 0431 (NSS) CORBETT, ARNOLD J Biomedical research support MULTINUCLEAR NMR STUDIES OF NEONATAL BRAIN METABOLISM
S07RR-07175-15 0432 (NSS) GALLAGHER, PATRICIA Biomedical research support CDNA ENCODING SMOOTH MUSCLE MYOSIN LIGHT CHAIN KINASE
S07RR-07175-15 0433 (NSS) GITOMER, BERNICE Y Biomedical research support CORRELATION OF IN VIVO 31P MRS DATA & PHOSPHORUS METABOLITES
S07RR-07175-15 0434 (NSS) HERRING, BRIAN PAUL Biomedical research support TISSUE REGULATORY ELEMENTS IN SKELETAL MUSCLE MYOSIN LIGHT CHAIN KINASE GENE
S07RR-07175-15 0435 (NSS) JEFFREY, MARK Biomedical research support SUBSTRATE UTILIZATION IN NORMOXIC & REPERFUSED RAT HEART
S07RR-07175-15 0436 (NSS) LI, JIA-LING Biomedical research support GENERATE NEW IMMUNOTOXIN W/ ANTI CD19; TREATMENT B CELL TUMORS
S07RR-07175-15 0437 (NSS) LUBY-PHELPS, KATHERI Biomedical research support CYTOMATRIX DYNAMICS IN LIVING VASCULAR ENDOTHELIAL CELLS
S07RR-07175-15 0438 (NSS) MCKEARIN, DENNIS M Biomedical research support GERMLINE STEM CELLS & ANTI PROLIFERATION GENES IN OOGENESIS & DROSOPHILA
S07RR-07175-15 0439 (NSS) MEEK (HASEMANN), KAT Biomedical research support DH SEGMENT PROMOTORS IN IMMUNOGLOBULIN REARRANGEMENT; RECOMBINATION
S07RR-07175-15 0440 (NSS) PERLMAN, PHILIP S Biomedical research support REVERSE TRANSCRIPTION IN YEAST MITOCHONDRIA
S07RR-07175-15 0441 (NSS) PFISTER, K KEVIN Biomedical research support DYNEIN; ORGANELLE MOTOR PROTEIN; MABS
S07RR-07175-15 0442 (NSS) ROTHBERG, KAREN G Biomedical research support ISOLATE & CHARACTERIZE NOVEL CHOLESTEROL SENSITIVE ENDOCYTIC COMPARTMENT
S07RR-07175-15 0443 (NSS) SHEN, GUO-LIANG Biomedical research support NEW IMMUNOTOXIN CONTAINING ANTI CD5; TREAT AUTO IMMUNE DISEASE
S07RR-07175-15 0444 (NSS) SLAUGHTER, CLIVE A Biomedical research support SEQUENCING N TERMINALLY BLOCKED PROTEINS; EDMAN DEGRADATION
S07RR-07175-15 0445 (NSS) STREET, NANCY E Biomedical research support CHARACTERIZE MURINE CD4+ T HELPER CELL PRECURSORS AT CELL & MOLECULAR LEVEL
S07RR-07175-15 0446 (NSS) WARD, ELIZABETH SALL Biomedical research support CLONING & EXPRESSION OF T CELL RECEPTORS; ESCHERICHIA COLI HOST
S07RR-07175-15 0447 (NSS) WILSON, JEAN D Biomedical research support GENETICS; ANDROGEN RECEPTOR EXPRESSIONS; ADULT; DEVELOPING TISSUE & CANCER
S07RR-07175-15 0448 (NSS) YIN, HELEN LU Biomedical research support STRUCTURE FUNCTION ANALYSIS OF GELSOLIN
S07RR-07176-14 (NSS) KRESHECK, GORDON C NORTHERN ILLINOIS UNIVERSITY DEKALB, ILL 60115 Biomedical research support
S07RR-07176-14 0531 (NSS) ALTSCHULER, MITCHELL Biomedical research support ISOLATION & CHARACTERIZATION OF PLANT LIPOXYGENASE USING PCR
S07RR-07176-14 0524 (NSS) GASSER, KENNETH W Biomedical research support REGULATION OF ELECTROLYTE TRANSPORT IN EXOCRINE SECRETION
S07RR-07176-14 0525 (NSS) NADLER, STEVE Biomedical research support MOLECULAR SYSTEMATICS OF BAYLISASCARIS PROCYONIS
S07RR-07176-14 0526 (NSS) CONWAY, SONYA Biomedical research support MSA IN MODIFYING GROWTH HORMONE RELEASE
S07RR-07176-14 0527 (NSS) BUJARSKI, JOZEF J Biomedical research support HOST SPECIFICITY OF THREE BROMOVIRUSES: APPLICATION TO CHIMERIC RNAS
S07RR-07176-14 0528 (NSS) HUBBARD, CHRISTOPHER Biomedical research support EFFECTS OF CYCLIC GMP ON OOCYTE DEVELOPMENT
S07RR-07176-14 0529 (NSS) HAHN, RICHARD Biomedical research support EVIDENCE OF DEMYELINATION IN MYOTONIC MICE
S07RR-07176-14 0530 (NSS) POLANS, NEIL O Biomedical research support MOLECULAR MARKERS FOR CONTROL OF PLASTID DNA TRANSMISSION IN PEA
S07RR-07178-14 (NSS) ROOZEN, KENNETH J UNIV OF ALABAMA IN BIRMINGHAM UNIVERSITY STATION BIRMINGHAM, ALA 35294 Biomedical research support
S07RR-07178-14 0669 (NSS) MARTIN, JAMES C Biomedical research support COMPUTATIONAL TOOLS TO SUPPORT BIOPHYSICAL LASER FACILITY: NORMAL MODE ANALYSIS
S07RR-07178-14 0670 (NSS) WRIGLEY, J MICHAEL Biomedical research support FACTORS RELATED TO REFERRAL OF SEVERELY INJURED PEOPLE TO REHABILITATION
S07RR-07178-14 0671 (NSS) WRIGLEY, J MICHAEL Biomedical research support RELATIONSHIP BETWEEN DOLLARS SPENT ON ACUTE CARE, REHABILITATION & OUTCOME
S07RR-07178-14 0672 (NSS) TUCKER, DIANE C Biomedical research support PACEMAKER DEVELOPMENT IN EMBRYONIC HEART: PACEMAKER HEART
S07RR-07179-14 (NSS) HO, SHUK-MEI TUFTS UNIVERSITY PAIGE HALL MEDFORD, MASS 02155 Biomedical research support
S07RR-07179-14 0673 (NSS) BUSHNELL, EMILY W Biomedical research support INTERACTIONS BETWEEN COGNITIVE PROCESSES & MOTOR BEHAVIOR DURING INFANCY
S07RR-07179-14 0674 (NSS) CHECHILE, RICHARD A Biomedical research support TOOLS FOR MODEL BASED DESIGN OF MEDICAL WORKSTATION
S07RR-07179-14 0675 (NSS) COCHRANE, DAVID E Biomedical research support PUTATIVE ANTAGONIST FOR NEUROTENSIN ON MAST CELLS
S07RR-07179-14 0676 (NSS) COOK, ROBERT Biomedical research support VISUAL & SPATIAL COGNITION IN ANIMALS
S07RR-07179-14 0677 (NSS) DEBOLD, JOSEPH Biomedical research support MEMBRANE SITES OF PROGESTERONE ACTION

PROJECT NO., ORGANIZATIONAL UNIT., INVESTIGATOR, ADDRESS, TITLE

S07RR-07179-14 0678 (NSS) EASTERBROOKS, ANN M Biomedical research support VULNERABILITY & RESILIENCE IN CHILDREN AT SOCIAL RISK
S07RR-07179-14 0679 (NSS) ERNST, SUSAN Biomedical research support HUMAN NUCLEAR ENCODED MITOCHONDRIA ISOFORM OF COX SUBUNIT IV
S07RR-07179-14 0680 (NSS) FELDBERG, ROSS S Biomedical research support MOLECULAR MODELLING OF MAST CELL ACTIVE PEPTIDES
S07RR-07179-14 0681 (NSS) HOLCOMB, PHILLIP Biomedical research support CROSS MODALITY LANGUAGE PROCESSING
S07RR-07179-14 0682 (NSS) KANAREK, ROBIN B Biomedical research support DIETARY MODULATION OF OPIATE ACTIVITY IN RATS
S07RR-07179-14 0683 (NSS) KENNY, JONATHAN Biomedical research support DYNAMICS OF ENZYME PHOTOINHIBITION
S07RR-07179-14 0684 (NSS) MICZEK, KLAUS Biomedical research support SOCIAL STRESS & NARCOTIC "CUE"
S07RR-07179-14 0685 (NSS) ROTHBAUM, FRED Biomedical research support PARENT CHILD RELATIONSHIP & LATER PROBLEM BEHAVIOR AT HOME & SCHOOL
S07RR-07179-14 0686 (NSS) SAMPSON, PHILIP B Biomedical research support MEASUREMENT OF HUMAN STRESS
S07RR-07179-14 0687 (NSS) WOLF, MARYANN Biomedical research support ASSESSMENT OF A PILOT INTERVENTION PROGRAM FOR CHILDREN W/ DYSLEXIA
S07RR-07179-14 0688 (NSS) CRIM, MARILYN C Biomedical research support EFFECT OF CALORIE RESTRICTION BY DIET OR EXERCISE ON NITROGEN BALANCE
S07RR-07179-14 0689 (NSS) DWYER, JOHANNA Biomedical research support AIDS: UNPROVEN NUTRITIONAL THERAPIES
S07RR-07179-14 0690 (NSS) GOLDBERG, JEANNE Biomedical research support EATING BEHAVIOR IN COLLEGE WOMEN A LONGITUDINAL STUDY: DIET, BODY IMAGE
S07RR-07179-14 0691 (NSS) MEYDANI, MOHSEN Biomedical research support DIETARY GLUTATHIONE ESTER SUPPLEMENTATION ON CATARACTOGENESIS
S07RR-07180-10 (NSS) POWELL, GARY L CLEMSON UNIVERSITY CLEMSON, SC 29634-1903 Biomedical research support grant
S07RR-07180-10 0624 (NSS) DIEHL, JOHN Biomedical research support grant EFFECT OF POLYAMINES ON OVULATION RATE & PREGNANCY
S07RR-07180-10 0625 (NSS) LILIEN, JACK Biomedical research support grant FODRIN: AN EXTRACELLULAR PROTEIN
S07RR-07180-10 0626 (NSS) KUNKEL, M E Biomedical research support grant GESTATIONAL CALCIUM DEFICIENCY EFFECT ON BONE PROTEINS
S07RR-07181-13 (NSS) KEULKS, GEORGE W UNIVERSITY OF WISCONSIN P O BOX 340 MILWAUKEE, WIS 53201 Biomedical research support
S07RR-07181-13 0533 (NSS) COOK, JAMES M Biomedical research support DETERMINE PHARMACOPHORE; BENZODIAZEPINE INVERSE AGONIST & ANTAGONIST BIND SITE
S07RR-07181-13 0534 (NSS) GREER, ANN L Biomedical research support EFFECTS OF COMPETITIVE POLICIES ON TECHNOLOGY ADOPTION BY DOCTORS & HOSPITALS
S07RR-07181-13 0535 (NSS) OTVOS, JAMES D Biomedical research support STRUCTURE & REACTIVITY OF METALLOTHIONEIN
S07RR-07181-13 0532 (NSS) BUNTIN, JOHN D Biomedical research support CHARACTERIZE BINDING PROPERTIES OF PROLACTIN RECEPTOR; RING DOVE NERVOUS SYSTEMS
S07RR-07181-13 0536 (NSS) PETERING, DAVID H Biomedical research support CADMIUM, ZINC, METALLOTHIONEIN & LIVER CYTOTOXICITY
S07RR-07181-13 0537 (NSS) RAGSDALE, STEPHEN W Biomedical research support MECHANISMS OF METHYL TRANSFERS IN ACETYL COA SYNTHESIS
S07RR-07181-13 0538 (NSS) WARREN, RICHARD M Biomedical research support MECHANISMS UNDERLYING PERCEPTION OF SPEECH
S07RR-07181-13 0539 (NSS) ZWEBEN, ALLEN Biomedical research support EFFICACY OF BRIEF INTERVENTION W/ PROBLEM DRINKERS
S07RR-07184-13 (NSS) LOEHR, THOMAS M OREGON GRADUATE INSTITUTE 19600 NW VON NEUMANN DR BEAVERTON, OR 97006-1999 Biomedical research support
S07RR-07184-13 0533 (NSS) LOEHR, THOMAS M Biomedical research support NO RESEARCH SUBPROJECTS
S07RR-07185-13 (NSS) RISSER, PAUL G UNIVERSITY OF NEW MEXICO 108 SCHOLES HALL ALBUQUERQUE, N MEX 87131 Biomedical research support
S07RR-07186-10 (NSS) RIERDAN, JILL WELLESLEY COLLEGE CENTER FOR RESEARCH ON WOMEN WELLESLEY, MASS 02181 Biomedical research support grant
S07RR-07186-10 0609 (NSS) BARNETT, ROSALIND C Biomedical research support grant UPGRADE PROJECT COMPUTER FACILITIES: FAMILY & WORK ROLE STRESS IN MEN
S07RR-07186-10 0610 (NSS) CLINCHY, BLYTHE MCV Biomedical research support grant FOLLOW UP STUDY OF EPISTEMOLOGICAL DVMT; UNDERGRADUATE WOMEN
S07RR-07186-10 0611 (NSS) GENERO, NANCY Biomedical research support grant MUTUAL PSYCHOLOG DVMT QUESTIONNAIRE: PERCEIVED MUTUALITY IN CLOSE RELATIONSHIPS
S07RR-07186-10 0612 (NSS) MARSHALL, NANCY Biomedical research support grant PURCHASE OF PERSONAL COMPUTER FOR INFANT DAY CARE PROJECT
S07RR-07186-10 0613 (NSS) RAYMAN, PAULA Biomedical research support grant HEALTH OUTCOMES; ADULT; WORKPLACE EDUCATION & HOMELESS SHELTER LITERACY PROGRAMS
S07RR-07186-10 0614 (NSS) RIERDAN, JILL Biomedical research support grant RESILIENCE IN ADOLESCENT GIRLS
S07RR-07187-13 (NSS) MILLER, SANFORD A UNIV OF TEXAS HLTH SCI CTR 7703 FLOYD CURL DRIVE SAN ANTONIO, TEX 78284 Biomedical research support
S07RR-07187-13 0692 (NSS) SCHWARTZ, JOYCE Biomedical research support REVISION OF ORAL GLUCOSE TOLERANCE TEST
S07RR-07187-13 0706 (NSS) VALENTE, ANTHONY J Biomedical research support STRUCTURE OF HUMAN MCP 1 RECEPTOR
S07RR-07187-13 0693 (NSS) LAM, Y W FRANCIS Biomedical research support PHARMACOGENETIC DIFFERENCES IN DRUG METABOLIZING CAPACITY OF DIABETIC PATIENTS
S07RR-07187-13 0707 (NSS) DAMON, DEBORAH H Biomedical research support INTERACTION OF SHR DERIVED ENDOTHELIUM & VASCULAR SMOOTH MUSCLE
S07RR-07187-13 0694 (NSS) DEB, SWATI Biomedical research support HERPES SIMPLEX VIRUS REPLICATION ROLE OF TRANSCRIPTION OF REPLICATION GENES

PROJECT NUMBER LISTING

PROJECT NO., ORGANIZATIONAL UNIT., INVESTIGATOR, ADDRESS, TITLE

S07RR-07187-13 0695 (NSS) WINBORN, WILLIAM B Biomedical research support IDENTIFICATION OF TRANSFERIN MRNA IN PRIMATES
S07RR-07187-13 0696 (NSS) OKORODUDU, ANGHONY O Biomedical research support INTRACELLULAR CALCIUM & HYDROGEN IONS IN PATHOGENESIS OF DIABETES
S07RR-07187-13 0697 (NSS) GAUNTT, CHARLES J Biomedical research support CHARACTERIZATION OF SUP TI CELL CLONES INFECTED W/ HIV 2
S07RR-07187-13 0698 (NSS) HEITMAN, DAVID W Biomedical research support DIETARY FIBER ON SERUM CHOLESTEROL & MINERAL RETENTION
S07RR-07187-13 0699 (NSS) MAXWELL, LEO C Biomedical research support ONSET OF DYSTROPHY IN MDX MOUSE DIAPHRAGM
S07RR-07187-13 0700 (NSS) SONG, CHUNG-SENG Biomedical research support AGE DEPENDENT REGULATION OF ALPHA 2 U GLOBULIN
S07RR-07187-13 0701 (NSS) WARD, WALTER R Biomedical research support INTERNALIZATION & DEGRADATION OF INSULIN BY RAT HEPATOCYTES
S07RR-07187-13 0702 (NSS) GREEN, GARY M Biomedical research support FEEDBACK REGULATION OF PANCREATIC SECRETION
S07RR-07187-13 0703 (NSS) HANSEN, JEFFREY C Biomedical research support MOLECULAR DETERMINANTS OF CHROMATIN STRUCTURE & STABILITY
S07RR-07187-13 0704 (NSS) LEACH, ROBIN J Biomedical research support CHARACTERIZATION OF HYBRIDS CONTAINING FRAGMENTS OF HUMAN CHROMOSOME 17
S07RR-07187-13 0705 (NSS) JAMIESON, MICHAEL J Biomedical research support INTERACTION OF SULFHYDRYL INHIBITORS & NITRIC OXIDE
S07RR-07189-12 (NSS) CHESNUT, T LLOYD OHIO UNIVERSITY CUTLER HALL ATHENS, OHIO 45701-2979 Biomedical research support
S07RR-07189-12 0634 (NSS) CHESNUT, T LLOYD Biomedical research support NO RESEARCH SUBPROJECTS
S07RR-07192-12 (NSS) DUNN, CHRISTOPHER S BOWLING GREEN STATE UNIVERSITY 120 MCFALL CTR, RES SVC OFF BOWLING GREEN, OHIO 43403 Biomedical research support
S07RR-07192-12 0615 (NSS) BINGMAN, VERNER Biomedical research support CONNECTIONS OF HOMING PIGEON NAVIGATIONAL FLEXIBILITY IN RNA
S07RR-07192-12 0616 (NSS) RANDALL, BARBARA Biomedical research support COMPUTERIZATION OF ANIMAL RESEARCH FACILITY
S07RR-07192-12 0617 (NSS) MESERVE, LEE Biomedical research support HORMONAL MECHANISMS BY WHICH PCB DEPRESSES GROWTH & NEURAL DVMT IN YOUNG RATS
S07RR-07192-12 0618 (NSS) DESHAYES, KURT Biomedical research support PHOTODYNAMIC DRUG TRANSPORT
S07RR-07192-12 0619 (NSS) DURA, JASON Biomedical research support CROSS SITE COMPARISON OF PROBLEM BEHAVIOR IN PEOPLE W/ MENTAL RETARDATION
S07RR-07192-12 0620 (NSS) JAMASBI, ROUDABEH Biomedical research support CELLULAR HETEROGENEITY & RADIATION SENSITIVITY OF HUMAN ESOPHAGEAL CARCINOMAS
S07RR-07192-12 0621 (NSS) BULLERJAHN, GEORGE Biomedical research support BLOTTING OF NUCLEIC ACIDS: CLONING W/ OLIGONUCLEOTIDES
S07RR-07192-12 0622 (NSS) FIORAVANTI, CARMEN Biomedical research support NADH DEHYDROGENASE IN PARASITIC HELMINTH ANAEROBIC ENERGY METABOLISM
S07RR-07194-09 (NSS) BUCHANAN, CHRISTINE E SOUTHERN METHODIST UNIVERSITY 220 FONDREN SCIENCE BLDG DALLAS, TEX 75275 Biomedical research support grant
S07RR-07194-09 0623 (NSS) BIEHL, EDWARD R Biomedical research support grant SYNTHESIS OF ANTICANCER DRUGS
S07RR-07194-09 0624 (NSS) BUYNAK, JOHN D Biomedical research support grant SYNTHETIC APPLICATION OF ALLENES IN ORGANIC CHEMISTRY
S07RR-07194-09 0625 (NSS) SOHAL, RAJINDAR S Biomedical research support grant CELLULAR AGING & OXYGEN FREE RADICALS
S07RR-07195-12 (NSS) SCHAFER, ROLLIE R UNIVERSITY OF NORTH TEXAS PO BOX 5446, NT STATION DENTON, TEX 76203 Biomedical research support
S07RR-07195-12 0708 (NSS) PIRTLE, ROBERT M Biomedical research support TRNA GENE LOCI FROM HUMAN CHROMOSOMES 19 & X
S07RR-07195-12 0709 (NSS) LOTT, JAMES R Biomedical research support LONG TERM MODERATE INTAKE OF ALCOHOL ON IMMUNE RESPONSE IN RATS
S07RR-07195-12 0710 (NSS) BRATERMAN, PAUL S Biomedical research support TARTAR PREVENTION ADDITIVES ON CALCIUM CARBONATE PRECIPITATION
S07RR-07195-12 0711 (NSS) MASARACCHIA, RUTHANN Biomedical research support RAPID PURIFICATION OF A UNIQUE S6 KINASE
S07RR-07195-12 0712 (NSS) WU, MING-CHI Biomedical research support GOPROTEIN IN REGULATION CSF SYNTHESIS
S07RR-07195-12 0713 (NSS) KUNZ, DANIEL A Biomedical research support CYANIDE ASSIMULATION IN BACTERIUM PSEUDOMONAS FLUORESCENS NCIMB 11764
S07RR-07195-12 0714 (NSS) EASOM, RICHARD A Biomedical research support PROTEIN KINASE C IN REGULATION OF INSULIN SECRETION
S07RR-07195-12 0715 (NSS) DONAHUE, MANUS Biomedical research support NOVEL 5 HT RECEPTOR PROTEIN IN ASCARIS SUUM MUSCLE
S07RR-07195-12 0716 (NSS) CORNELIUS, WILLIAM L Biomedical research support NEUROMUSCULAR FACILITATION STRETCHING TECHNIQUES ON ARTERIAL BLOOD PRESSURE
S07RR-07195-12 0717 (NSS) GOGGIN, NOREEN L Biomedical research support MUSCULAR ACTIVITY OF OLDER ADULTS WHILE PRODUCING BALLISTIC MOVEMENTS
S07RR-07195-12 0718 (NSS) ZIMMERMAN, EARL G Biomedical research support SEQUENCE DEVERGENCE IN MITOCHONDRIAL DNA IN RODENT MODELS
S07RR-07195-12 0719 (NSS) O'DONOVAN, GERARD A Biomedical research support SEQUENCING PYRB GENE FROM PSEUDOMONAS
S07RR-07196-11 (NSS) PIACSEK, BELA E MARQUETTE UNIVERSITY 530 NORTH 15TH STREET MILWAUKEE, WIS 53233 Biomedical research support
S07RR-07196-11 0626 (NSS) EDDINGER, THOMAS J Biomedical research support MYOSIN ISOFORMS IN SMOOTH MUSCLE: AORTA, UTERUS
S07RR-07196-11 0627 (NSS) MUELLER, REINHOLD D Biomedical research support DNA COMPONENTS IN B SUBTILIS NUCLEOSOME LIKE STRUCTURES: CHROMOSOME
S07RR-07196-11 0628 (NSS) TRAN, CHIEU Biomedical research support BIOANALYTICAL APPLICATIONS OF THERMAL LENS SPECTROMETRY
S07RR-07199-12 (NSS) SAFWAT, FUAD M UNIVERSITY OF MASSACHUSETTS HARBOR CAMPUS BOSTON, MASS 02125 Biomedical research support
S07RR-07199-12 0939 (NSS) BAWA, KAMAL S Biomedical research support DVMT OF DNA FINGERPRINTING & OTHER MOLECULAR MARKERS IN TROPICAL FOREST TREES
S07RR-07199-12 0940 (NSS) ARATHUZIK, MARY D Biomedical research support COGNITIVE BEHAV ON PAIN PERCEPT, PAIN CONTROL, & SELF ESTEEM IN BREAST CANCER
S07RR-07199-12 0941 (NSS) REISKIN, HELEN K Biomedical research support LOW INCOME, MINORITY WOMENS PERCEPT OF SELECTED SUBSTANCE ABUSE PREVENT FILMS
S07RR-07199-12 0942 (NSS) KALICK, SHELDON Biomedical research support PUBLIC SELF CONSCIOUSNESS & DESIRE FOR COSMETIC PLASTIC SURGERY
S07RR-07199-12 0943 (NSS) ADAMS, JANE Biomedical research support NEUROPSYCHOLOGY OF CHILDREN EXPOSED TO TERATOGENIC AGENTS IN UTERO
S07RR-07201-12 (NSS) REED, PETER W VANDERBILT UNIVERSITY 411 KIRKLAND HALL NASHVILLE, TENN 37240 Biomedical research support
S07RR-07201-12 0629 (NSS) BUTLER, J S Biomedical research support NUTRITIONAL ATTAINMENT OF ELDERLY POOR
S07RR-07201-12 0630 (NSS) CAVENER, DOUGLAS R Biomedical research support INITIATION & TERMINATION OF TRANSLATION IN EUKARYOTES
S07RR-07201-12 0631 (NSS) FLEISCHER, SIDNEY Biomedical research support EC COUPLING IN SKELETAL MUSCLE: MOLECULAR DEFINITION
S07RR-07201-12 0632 (NSS) FLICKER, PAULA Biomedical research support STRUCTURAL RELATIONSHIPS BETWEEN ACTIN & MYOSIN
S07RR-07201-12 0633 (NSS) FRIEDMAN, RICHARD N Biomedical research support OPTICAL RECORDING OF CARDIAC & NEURAL ELECTRICAL ACTIVITY
S07RR-07201-12 0634 (NSS) GARBER, JUDY Biomedical research support FAMILIAL PATTERNS OF AFFECTIVE ILLNESS & COGNITIVE STYLE
S07RR-07201-12 0635 (NSS) HARRIS, THOMAS M Biomedical research support SYNTHETIC APPROACHES TO CARCINOGEN LINKED DEOXYOLIGONUCLEOTIDES
S07RR-07201-12 0636 (NSS) JOHNSON, CARL Biomedical research support ESTIMATION OF INTRACELLULAR FREE CA 2+ BY IMMUNOFLUORESCENT METHODS
S07RR-07201-12 0637 (NSS) MOSIG, GISELA Biomedical research support DNA GYRASE IN DNA REPLICATION
S07RR-07201-12 0638 (NSS) RIESER, JOHN J Biomedical research support PERCEPTUAL LEARNING & CALIBRATION OF WALKING W/ OUT VISION
S07RR-07201-12 0639 (NSS) SEYFRED, MARK Biomedical research support CHROMATIN ASSEMBLY IN ESTROGEN INDUCED PROLACTIN GENE TRANSCRIPTION
S07RR-07201-12 0640 (NSS) TOMARKEN, ANDREW J Biomedical research support PSYCHOPHYSIOLOGY OF EXPOSURE THERAPY
S07RR-07201-12 0641 (NSS) WALDEN, TEDRA Biomedical research support CONTRIBUTIONS OF EMOTIONAL COMPETENCE OF PEER LIKING
S07RR-07201-12 0642 (NSS) WEISS, BAHR Biomedical research support SEQUENTIAL COMORBIDITY IN AGGRESSION & DEPRESSION
S07RR-07204-11 (NSS) SMITH, ELSKE V VA COMMONWEALTH UNIVERSITY BOX 2019 RICHMOND, VA 23284-2019 Biomedical research support
S07RR-07204-11 0449 (NSS) STEWART, JENNIFER K Biomedical research support REGULATION OF PNMT NRNA IN BRAIN & ADRENAL IN RAT: REGULATION, CDNA
S07RR-07204-11 0450 (NSS) TERNER, JAMES Biomedical research support RESONANCE RAMAN SPECTROSCOPY OF CHEMICAL TRANSIENTS
S07RR-07204-11 0451 (NSS) CREIGHTON-ZOLLAR, AN Biomedical research support INFANT MORTALITY IN RICHMOND, VA 1984 1988
S07RR-07205-11 (NSS) YIELDING, K LEMONE UNIV OF TEXAS MEDICAL BRANCH 301 UNIV BLVD, 528 ADMIN BLDG GALVESTON, TEX 77550-2774 Biomedical research support
S07RR-07205-11 0643 (NSS) TYPRING, STEPHAN K Biomedical research support CELLULAR IMMUNITY IN PATIENTS W/ SEVERE FORMS OF INHERITED EPIDERMOLYSIS BULLOSA
S07RR-07205-11 0644 (NSS) BROWN, DAVID B Biomedical research support ESTABLISH PARASEXUAL HYBRID CELL LINE USING MOUSE SOMATIC CELLS FUSED W/ HUMAN
S07RR-07205-11 0645 (NSS) SIMON, BRUCE Biomedical research support CALCIUM DEPENDENT INACTIVATION OF SR CALCIUM RELEASE CELLS FUSED W/ HUMAN SPERM
S07RR-07205-11 0646 (NSS) REUSS, LUIS Biomedical research support SALT TRANSPORT MECHANISM IN GALLBLADDER EPITHELIUM
S07RR-07205-11 0647 (NSS) CLOYD, MILES Biomedical research support PEPTIDES FOR POTENTIAL ANTI HIV THERAPY
S07RR-07205-11 0648 (NSS) SHEPPARD, LOUIS Biomedical research support MICROCOMPUTER BASED AUTOMATION & EXPERT SYSTEM DEVELOPMENT FOR AQUACULTURE
S07RR-07205-11 0649 (NSS) BUJALOWSKI, WLODZIMI Biomedical research support INTERACTIONS & CONFORMATIONS OF TRANSFER OF RIBONUCLEIC ACID IN SOLUTION
S07RR-07205-11 0650 (NSS) HSIE, ABRAHAM W Biomedical research support MOLECULAR MUTAGENESIS OF RADIATION & OXIDATIVE GENOTOXIC CHEMICALS;
S07RR-07205-11 0651 (NSS) SORDAHL, LOUIS A Biomedical research support NMR SPECTROSCOPY OF ISCHEMIC & REPERFUSED MYOCARDIUM
S07RR-07205-11 0652 (NSS) THOMPSON, AUBREY Biomedical research support HORMONAL REGULATION OF CELL PROLIFERATION; MALIGNANT CELLS
S07RR-07205-11 0653 (NSS) THOMPSON, WILLIAM Biomedical research support MICROTUBULE STRUCTURE & FUNCTION; CLEAVE TAXOL; MAKE MABS
S07RR-07205-11 0654 (NSS) WILLS, NANCY K Biomedical research support REGULATION OF NA+ & K+ TRANSPORT ACROSS EPITHELIA; ALDOSTERONE MECHANISM
S07RR-07205-11 0655 (NSS) BRODWICK, MALCOLM S Biomedical research support ELECTROPHYSIOLOGY OF VIRUS INFECTED CELLS
S07RR-07205-11 0656 (NSS) PAINTER, SHERRY D Biomedical research support CYTOCHEMICAL STUDIES OF BAY CELL PEPTIDE RECEPTORS IN CULTURED APLYSIA NEURONS
S07RR-07208-10 (NSS) ADAMS, WALTER C KENT STATE UNIVERSITY GRADUATE COLLEGE KENT, OHIO 44242 Biomedical research support
S07RR-07208-10 0662 (NSS) BLANK, JAMES L Biomedical research support IN VIVO ASSESSMENT OF NEUROTRANSMITTER EVENTS UNDERLYING PREOVULATORY LH SURGE
S07RR-07208-10 0663 (NSS) FOUNTAIN, STEPHEN B Biomedical research support DEVELOPMENT OF IN VITRO ASSAY FOR DETECTING CNS DYSFUNCTION
S07RR-07208-10 0664 (NSS) PARK, KATHRYN A Biomedical research support CORRELATES OF PARENT CHILD ATTACHMENT IN MIDDLE CHILDHOOD
S07RR-07208-10 0665 (NSS) SAMPSON, PAUL Biomedical research support SELECTIVE FLUORINATED CARBOCYLIC ANALOGUES OF FURANOSE & PYRANOSE CARBOHYDRATE

PROJECT NO., ORGANIZATIONAL UNIT., INVESTIGATOR, ADDRESS, TITLE

S07RR-07208-10 0666 (NSS) BRUOT, BRENT C Biomedical research support EFFECT OF MACROPHAGE SECRETORY PRODUCTS ON TESTOSTERONE SYNTHESIS
S07RR-07208-10 0667 (NSS) STALVEY, JOHN R D Biomedical research support ANDROGEN REGULATION OF LEYDIG CELL STEROIDOGENIC ENZYMES
S07RR-07208-10 0668 (NSS) WARD, STEVEN C Biomedical research support FUNCTIONAL CORRELATES OF CRANIOFACIAL DYSOTOSIS
S07RR-07208-10 0669 (NSS) BLANK, JAMES L Biomedical research support SEASONAL CONTROL OF REPRODUCTIVE & METABOLIC ADJUSTMENTS IN DEER MICE
S07RR-07208-10 0670 (NSS) STALVEY, JOHN R D Biomedical research support CHARACTERIZATION OF 3BHSD DNA CLONES
S07RR-07208-10 0671 (NSS) SAMPSON, PAUL Biomedical research support B RING SYSTEM OF TAXANE DITERPENES
S07RR-07208-10 0672 (NSS) STEPHENS, MARY ANN P Biomedical research support STRESS & WELL BEING IN MID LIFE WOMEN CARING FOR DEPENDENT OLDER FAMILY MEMBER
S07RR-07210-09 (NSS) FAY, RICHARD R LOYOLA UNIVERSITY 6525 N SHERIDAN RD CHICAGO, ILL 60626 Biomedical research support
S07RR-07210-09 0673 (NSS) NEW, JOHN Biomedical research support STRUCTURE & FUNCTION OF TELEOST OPTIC TECTUM
S07RR-07210-09 0674 (NSS) GRAHAM, DAN Biomedical research support SPECTROSCOPIC STUDY OF SPRAY CAST LIPIDS & PROTEINS
S07RR-07210-09 0675 (NSS) OLSEN, K Biomedical research support DEVELOPMENT OF HEMOGLOBIN BASED BLOOD SUBSTITUTES
S07RR-07210-09 0676 (NSS) OLSEN, K Biomedical research support XRAY STRUCTURES OF HORMONE & CARBOHYDRATE LECTIN COMPLEXES
S07RR-07210-09 0677 (NSS) SMARRELLI, J Biomedical research support REGULATION OF CONSTITUATIVE NADPH NITRATE REDUCTASE FROM SOYBEANS
S07RR-07210-09 0678 (NSS) DORUS, E Biomedical research support NMR STUDIES OF NA LI EXCHANGE IN RED BLOOD CELLS OF HYPERTENSIVE PTS
S07RR-07210-09 0679 (NSS) SHEFT, STANLEY Biomedical research support AMPLITUDE MODULATION IN AUDITORY SCENE ANALYSIS
S07RR-07210-09 0682 (NSS) WILEY, K Biomedical research support EVIDENCE OF ILLICIT DRUG USE & PREDICTIVE VALIDITY OF NURSES JUDGEMENTS
S07RR-07210-09 0680 (NSS) TENPENNY, P Biomedical research support HUMAN EPISODIC VISUAL MEMORY
S07RR-07210-09 0681 (NSS) MAECKER, H Biomedical research support CAUSES OF T CELL RECEPTOR VARIANTS IN HUMAN T LEUKEMIAS
S07RR-07210-09 0683 (NSS) MOTA DE FREITAS, D Biomedical research support MEASUREMENT OF LITHIUM TRANSPORT IN RBC FROM PSYCHIATRIC PATIENTS
S07RR-07210-09 0684 (NSS) JALOWIEC, ANNE Biomedical research support PREDICTORS OF QUALITY OF LIFE AFTER CARDIAC TRANSPLANT
S07RR-07210-09 0685 (NSS) SUTER, DIANE Biomedical research support DIFFERENTIAL SECRETION OF LH & FSH BY SINGLE CELLS
S07RR-07210-09 0686 (NSS) THOMPSON, C Biomedical research support CONSTRUCTION OF ANTIBODIES CAPABLE OF CATALYZING SPECIFIC PEPTIDE BONDS
S07RR-07210-09 0687 (NSS) RICHARDS, MARYSE Biomedical research support EARLY ADOLESCENT EXPERIENCE & ADJUSTMENT IN LATER ADOLESCENCE
S07RR-07210-09 0688 (NSS) PEREZ-WOODS, R Biomedical research support RELIABILITY & VALIDITY OF LOYOLA U NEONATAL SKIN ASSESSMENT SCALE
S07RR-07210-09 0689 (NSS) ZECHMEISTER, EUGENE Biomedical research support AGE RELATED CHANGES IN VOCABULARY KNOWLEDGE
S07RR-07210-09 0690 (NSS) MALLOW, J Biomedical research support OPTICAL DIGITIZED RADIOGRAPHY
S07RR-07214-03 (NSS) HOLLYDAY, MARGARET BRYN MAWR COLLEGE DEPARTMENT OF BIOLOGY BRYN MAWR, PA 19010 Biomedical research support
S07RR-07215-05 (NSS) CHAMBERS, JANICE E MISSISSIPPI STATE UNIVERSITY PO BOX DRAWER GY MISS STATE, MS 39762 Biomedical research support grant
S07RR-07215-05 0452 (NSS) WELLS-PARKER, ELIZAB Biomedical research support grant ACQUISITION OF ALCOHOL SAFETY ACTION PROJECTS ARCHIVES
S07RR-07215-05 0453 (NSS) CHAMBERS, HOWARD W Biomedical research support grant ORGANOPHOSPHATE DEGRADING ENZYMES IN HUMAN PLASMA
S07RR-07215-05 0454 (NSS) CHAMBERS, JANICE E Biomedical research support grant ORGANOPHOSPHATE INSECTICIDE METABOLISM & DISPOSITION IN MOSQUITOFISH
S07RR-07216-08 (NSS) RUDDON, RAYMOND UNIV OF NEBRASKA MED CTR 600 SOUTH 42ND STREET OMAHA, NE 68198-6805 Biomedical research support
S07RR-07216-08 0535 (NSS) RUDDON, RAYMOND Biomedical research support NO RESEARCH SUBPROJECTS
S07RR-07217-08 (NSS) WAYNER, MATTHEW J UNIVERSITY OF TEXAS DIV LIFE SCI,7000 LOOP 1604 NW SAN ANTONIO, TEX 78285-0662 Biomedical research support grant
S07RR-07217-08 0165 (NSS) SARDAR, DHIRAJ Biomedical research support grant OPTICAL PROPERTIES OF OCULAR TISSUES
S07RR-07217-08 0166 (NSS) ARMSTRONG, DEBORAH L Biomedical research support grant ETHANOL EFFECTS ON NMDA RECEPTOR CA2+ CHANNEL
S07RR-07217-08 0167 (NSS) DENNY, JOHN B Biomedical research support grant SORTING OF MEMBRANE PROTEINS IN NEURONS
S07RR-07217-08 0168 (NSS) URDANETA, MARIA-LUIS Biomedical research support grant MEXICAN & ANGLO ATTITUDES TOWARDS ORGAN DONATION & TRANSPLANTATION
S07RR-07218-05 (NSS) UPHOUSE, LYNDA L TEXAS WOMEN'S UNIVERSITY RES & GRANTS ADMIN DENTON, TX 76204 Biomedical research support grant
S07RR-07218-05 0455 (NSS) RUDICK, MICHAEL J Biomedical research support grant MECHANISM OF INTRACELLULAR TARGETING OF SECRETORY PROTEINS TO PROPER DESTINATION
S07RR-07218-05 0456 (NSS) DROGE, MICHAEL H Biomedical research support grant GENERATION OF MOTOR RHYTHM IN MAMMALIAN SPINAL CORD, IN VITRO
S07RR-07218-05 0457 (NSS) UPHOUSE, LYNDA L Biomedical research support grant NEUROREPRODUCTIVE EFFECTS OF CHLORINATED PESTICIDES; RATS
S07RR-07218-05 0458 (NSS) SANBORN, CHARLOTTE F Biomedical research support grant OSTEOBLAST/CLAST ACTIVITY PATTERNS; ADOLESCENT FEMALES W/ ANOREXIA NERVOSA

PROJECT NO., ORGANIZATIONAL UNIT., INVESTIGATOR, ADDRESS, TITLE

S07RR-07218-05 0459 (NSS) MILLS, NATHANIEL C Biomedical research support grant ETHANE DIMETHANE SULFONATE EFFECTS OF HEMICASTRATE TESTICULAR HYPERTROPHY
S07RR-07218-05 0460 (NSS) MEEUWSEN, HARRY J Biomedical research support grant CUTANEOUS FEEDBACK ON CONTROL GRIP FORCE
S07RR-07218-05 0461 (NSS) MCINTIRE, SARAH A Biomedical research support grant SOFTWARE FOR MOLECULAR BIOLOGY PROGRAM
S07RR-07218-05 0462 (NSS) JOHNSON, JAMES Biomedical research support grant CHEMISTRY OF COMPOUNDS THAT CONTAIN CARBON NITROGEN DOUBLE BOND
S07RR-07218-05 0463 (NSS) HSUEH, ANDIE Biomedical research support grant HIGH MENHADEN OIL CONSUMPTION; INITIAL STAGE OF CARCINOGENESIS; MAMMARY TUMORS
S07RR-07227-02 (NSS) MCBURNEY, WENDELL F INDIANA UNIVERSITY 620 UNION DRIVE, ROOM 618 INDIANAPOLIS, IN 46202-5167 Biomedical research support
S07RR-07228-02 (NSS) WILLETT, JAMES D GEORGE MASON UNIVERSITY 4400 UNIVERSITY DRIVE FAIRFAX, VA 22030-4444 Biomedical research support
S07RR-07229-06 (NSS) STUDEBAKER, GERALD A MEMPHIS STATE UNIVERSITY 807 JEFFERSON AVENUE MEMPHIS, TN 38105 Biomedical research support grant
S07RR-07229-06 0720 (NSS) GARTNER, T K Biomedical research support grant RGDS & LGGAKQAGDV BINDING SITES ON GPIIB & IIIA
S07RR-07229-06 0721 (NSS) LESSMAN, CHARLES A Biomedical research support grant OOCYTE MATURATION INDUCED BY DIFFERENT MEIOTOGENS
S07RR-07229-06 0722 (NSS) FAMILONI, BABAJIDE O Biomedical research support grant NEW ELECTRODE CONFIGURATION FOR ELECTROGASTROGRAPHY
S07RR-07229-06 0723 (NSS) UNKNOWN Biomedical research support grant PAYMENTS TO EXTERNAL REVIEWERS
S07RR-07232-05 (NSS) JENSEN, JAMES CALIF ST UNIV, LONG BEACH 1250 BELLFLOWER BLVD LONG BEACH, CA 90841-3903 Biomedical research support
S07RR-07232-05 0464 (NSS) ACEY, ROGER A Biomedical research support PHTHALATE ESTER INDUCED EMBRYOTOXICITY IN DEVELOPING ARTEMIA SALINA
S07RR-07232-05 0465 (NSS) COHLBERG, JEFFREY Biomedical research support ASSEMBLY & INTERACTION OF INTERMEDIATE NEUROFILAMENT PROTEINS
S07RR-07232-05 0466 (NSS) KINGSFORD, LAURA Biomedical research support NEUTRALIZATION OF LA CROSSE VIRUS
S07RR-07232-05 0467 (NSS) KHATRA, BALWANT Biomedical research support GLYCOGEN SYNTHASE PHOSPHATASE IN DIABETES
S07RR-07233-05 (NSS) BRUCE, JOHN I UNIVERSITY OF LOWELL 450 AIKEN STREET LOWELL, MA 01854 Biomedical research support universities
S07RR-07233-05 0169 (NSS) BRUCE, JOHN I Biomedical research support universities UPGRADING OF ANIMAL FACILITY FOR PRIMATES & RODENTS
S07RR-07234-05 (NSS) BALSAM, PETER D BARNARD COLLEGE 3009 BROADWAY, PSYCH DEPT NEW YORK, N Y 10027-6598 Biomedical research support
S07RR-07234-05 0851 (NSS) CHU, NATHAN Biomedical research support BIOCHEMICAL & GENETIC ANALYSIS OF MORPHOLOGICAL DEVELOPMENT
S07RR-07234-05 0852 (NSS) BALSAM, PETER Biomedical research support CONTEXT AND LEARNING
S07RR-07234-05 0853 (NSS) SILVER, RAE Biomedical research support FETAL BRAIN TRANSPLANT & RECOVERY CIRCADIAN RHYTHM
S07RR-07234-05 0854 (NSS) BRAINE, LILA Biomedical research support CHILDRENS CONFLICT WITH AUTHORITY
S07RR-07234-05 0855 (NSS) ABER, J LAWRENCE Biomedical research support PATHWAYS TO ADAPTATION & MALADAPTATION
S07RR-07235-03 (NSS) SCHLESINGER, HERBERT J NEW SCHOOL FOR SOCIAL RESEARCH 65 FIFTH AVE, RM 341 NEW YORK, N Y 10003 Biomedical research support grant
S07RR-07236-04 (NSS) WILLIAMSON, ALEX N N C A&T STATE UNIVERSITY 1601 E MARKET ST, CHEM DEPT GREENSBORO, N C 27411 Biomedical research support grant
S07RR-07236-04 0170 (NSS) ADENIYI, WILLIAM Biomedical research support grant ELECTROCHEMICAL OXIDATION OF INSOLUBLE INORGANIC SUBSTANCE IN AQUEOUS SUSPENSION
S07RR-07236-04 0171 (NSS) LAMB, CLAUDE Biomedical research support grant PC MODELS OF CYCLOPENTANONES & ENOL CONFORMERS
S07RR-07236-04 0172 (NSS) LISTON, HATTYE Biomedical research support grant DETERMIN BIOFEEDBACK USAGE FOR BEHAVIORAL & PHYSICAL DISORDERS BRAIN WAVE ACT
S07RR-07236-04 0173 (NSS) SCHUMACHER, SUSAN Biomedical research support grant HYPERTENSION IN GENETICALLY HYPERTENSIVE ANIMAL MODEL: PEPTIDERGIC VASOPRESSIN
S07RR-07236-04 0174 (NSS) SEGERSON, EDWARD Biomedical research support grant LYMPHOKINE ACTIVATED KILLER (LAK) CELL ACTIVITY BY BOVINE UTERINE PROTEIN
S07RR-07236-04 0175 (NSS) SHARMA, SARLA Biomedical research support grant ALCOHOL ABUSE PROGRAMS, ATTITUDES, & TRAINING NEEDS AT COLLEGES & UNIVERSITIES
S07RR-07237-04 (NSS) FUNK, MAX O UNIVERSITY OF TOLEDO DEPARTMENT OF CHEMISTRY TOLEDO, OH 43606 Biomedical research support grant
S07RR-07237-04 0745 (NSS) KOMUNIECKI, PATRICIA Biomedical research support grant AEROBIC ANAEROBIC TRANSITION IN ASCARIS SUUM
S07RR-07237-04 0741 (NSS) HAAF, ROBERT A Biomedical research support grant INFANT COGNITION CATEGORIZATION SOCIAL & COGNITIVE DVMT
S07RR-07237-04 0742 (NSS) MORGAN, ALAN R Biomedical research support grant PHOTODYNAMIC THERAPY: RAT BLADDER, TUMOR PURPURINS, VERDINS, BENZOCHLORINS
S07RR-07237-04 0743 (NSS) BULLOCK, WESLEY A Biomedical research support grant AD LIB CAFFEINE USE WITHDRAWAL CAFFEINE, SALIVA DEFECTION, PREMENSTRUAL SYNDROME
S07RR-07237-04 0744 (NSS) HEFFNER, HENRY E Biomedical research support grant BEHAVIORAL ANALYSIS OF THE ROLE OF AUDITORY CORTEX: PRIMATE MACAQUE
S07RR-07238-04 (NSS) GOODMAN, RICHARD H OREGON HEALTH SCIENCES UNIV 3181 SW SAM JACKSON PARK ROAD PORTLAND, OR 97201 Biomedical research support grant
S07RR-07238-04 0468 (NSS) HERSH, WILLIAM R Biomedical research support grant AUTOMATED INDEXING & NATURAL LANGUAGE RETRIEVAL OF

RELATED ABSTRACTS
S07RR-07238-04 0469 (NSS) BECK, J ROBERT Biomedical research support grant SET UP EXPERIMENTAL OFFICE MANAGEMENT SYSTEM ON LOCAL AREA NETWORK
S07RR-07238-04 0470 (NSS) THOMAS, GARY Biomedical research support grant CLONE OF RIN M5F CELL SOMATOSTATIN RECEPTOR USING RECOMBINANT VACCINIA VIRUS
S07RR-07238-04 0471 (NSS) FORTE, MICHAEL Biomedical research support grant DROSOPHILA GENES CODING FOR G PROTEIN COUPLED RECEPTORS
S07RR-07238-04 0472 (NSS) CIVELLI, OLIVIER Biomedical research support grant TECHNIQUE FOR RECEPTOR OPENING OF CA ACTIVATED CHLORIDE CHANNELS
S07RR-07238-04 0473 (NSS) WEBER, ECKARD Biomedical research support grant NMDA RECEPTORS IN ILEUM
S07RR-07238-04 0474 (NSS) WILKINSON, MILES Biomedical research support grant CHARACTERIZATION OF ANTI SENSE DNA EXPRESSED IN T CELLS
S07RR-07238-04 0475 (NSS) WILLIAMS, JOHN Biomedical research support grant 5 HT3 RECEPTORS IN BRAIN SLICE
S07RR-07238-04 0476 (NSS) JAHR, CRAIG Biomedical research support grant SYNAPTIC CONDUCTANCES IN ON CENTER BIPOLAR CELLS OF RETINA
S07RR-07238-04 0477 (NSS) SURPRENANT, ANN MARI Biomedical research support grant REGULATION OF RELEASE OF B ENDORPHIN FROM RAT INTERMEDIATE PITUITARY CELLS
S07RR-07238-04 0478 (NSS) BARKLIS, ERIC Biomedical research support grant FUSIONS OF MO MULV ENV PROTEIN
S07RR-07238-04 0479 (NSS) ADELMAN, JOHN Biomedical research support grant ISOLATE, CHARACTERIZE & EXPRESS CLONED ATP SENSITIVE K CHANNELS
S07RR-07238-04 0480 (NSS) ALLEN, CHARLES N Biomedical research support grant DEVELOPMENT OF TRANSGENIC B AMYLOID MOUSE
S07RR-07238-04 0481 (NSS) GOLD, BRUCE G Biomedical research support grant NGF PRODUCE ABERRANT NEUROFILAMENT PHOSPHORYLATION: SENSORY NEURONAL PERIKARYA
S07RR-07238-04 0482 (NSS) KISBY, GLEN E Biomedical research support grant RADIOLABELLING OF CYCASIN
S07RR-07238-04 0483 (NSS) LUDOLPH, ALBERT C Biomedical research support grant 3 NITROPROPIONIC ACID: PROBE OF ENERGY DYSFUNCTION OF NEURONAL DEGENERATION
S07RR-07238-04 0484 (NSS) ROY, DWIJENDRA N Biomedical research support grant CENTAUREA SPECIES & NIGROPALLIDAL ENCEPHALOMALACIA, ISOLATE ACTIVE PRINCIPLES
S07RR-07241-04 (NSS) ANGELAKOS, EVANGELOS T HAHNEMANN UNIVERSITY BROAD AND VINE MS 444 PHILADELPHIA, PA 19102-1192 Biomedical research support grant
S07RR-07241-04 0698 (NSS) CHOU, ROBIN Biomedical research support grant C MYC ONCOGENE STRUCTURES, NUCLEAR MATRIX ASSOCIATED REGION, INWARD K+ CHANNELS
S07RR-07241-04 0699 (NSS) MCLEAN, JUDITH Biomedical research support grant NMDA RECEPTORS IN PRIMARY VISUAL CORTEX OF ADULT CAT
S07RR-07241-04 0700 (NSS) NICOLELIS, MIGUEL A Biomedical research support grant GABAERGIC PROJECTIONS FROM ZONA INCERTA TO ENTIRE NEOCORTEX
S07RR-07241-04 0701 (NSS) SESSLER, FRANCIS Biomedical research support grant MODULATORY EFFECTS OF MONOAMINES & PEPTIDES ON CORTICAL SYNAPTIC TRANSMISSION
S07RR-07241-04 0702 (NSS) SOSLAU, GERALD Biomedical research support grant SITE DIRECTED MUTAGENESIS & ANALYSIS OF HSVGB
S07RR-07241-04 0703 (NSS) BRAMMUCCI, MICHAEL Biomedical research support grant EXPRESSION OF BACILLUS SUBTILIS GENES BACTERIOPHAGE ENHANCED SPORULATION
S07RR-07241-04 0704 (NSS) CHOU, ROBIN Biomedical research support grant MOLECULAR MECHANISMS OF HUMAN LEUKEMIC CELL
S07RR-07242-04 (NSS) DINGERSON, MICHAEL R UNIVERSITY OF MISSISSIPPI 126 SHOEMAKER HALL UNIVERSITY, MS 38677 Biomedical research support grant
S07RR-07242-04 0705 (NSS) BROWN, STANLEY Biomedical research support grant EFFECTS OF SHORT TERM AEROBIC TRAINING ON ANAEROBIC PERFORMANCES
S07RR-07242-04 0706 (NSS) CROWE, THOMAS Biomedical research support grant CENTRAL AUDITORY FUNCTION IN PRISONERS
S07RR-07242-04 0707 (NSS) DANIEL, STEVEN Biomedical research support grant GROWTH & ACETOGENESIS FROM OXALATE & GLYOXYLATE BY CLOSTRIDIUM THERMOACETICUM
S07RR-07242-04 0709 (NSS) FRATE, DENNIS Biomedical research support grant DIETARY CHANGES; CANCER PREVENTION & HEALTH CARE BLACKS; CORONARY HEART DISEASE
S07RR-07242-04 0708 (NSS) DINNO, MUMTAZ Biomedical research support grant EFFECTS OF ULTRASOUND ON SOLUBLE & MEMBRANE BOUND ENZYMES
S07RR-07244-03 (NSS) STARK, RUTH E COLLEGE OF STATEN ISLAND 130 STUYVESANT PLACE STATEN ISLAND, N Y 10301 Biomedical research support
S07RR-07244-03 0485 (NSS) CORIN, ROBERT E Biomedical research support INSULIN RECEPTOR HORMONAL REGULATION; ADIPOSE CELL DIFFERENTIATION EXPRESSION
S07RR-07244-03 0486 (NSS) FIELDS, LANNY Biomedical research support ALTERNATIVE PARADIGMS TO ESTABLISH EQUIVALENCE CLASSES
S07RR-07244-03 0487 (NSS) MEEHAN, EDWARD Biomedical research support ACQUISITION OF SECOND ORDER STIMULUS CONTROL OF MATCHING & ODDITY
S07RR-07244-03 0488 (NSS) MEEHAN, EDWARD Biomedical research support ACQUISITION OF SECOND ORDER STIMULUS CONTROL OF MATCHING & ODDITY
S07RR-07244-03 0489 (NSS) STARK, RUTH E Biomedical research support MOLECULAR BIOPHYSICS OF GASTROINTESTINAL TRACT
S07RR-07245-03 (NSS) KARCHMER, MICHAEL A GALLAUDET UNIVERSITY 800 FLA AVE, N E, FAY HOUSE WASHINGTON, D C 20002 Biomedical research support
S07RR-07245-03 0856 (NSS) REVOILE, SALLY G Biomedical research support PERCEPTION OF COMPLEX AUDITORY STIMULI BY THE DEAF & HEARING IMPAIRED
S07RR-07245-03 0857 (NSS) SEITZ, FRANZ P Biomedical research support ATTENTION & SPEECH PERCEPTION BY THE HEARING IMPAIRED: COGNITION
S07RR-07248-03 (NSS) MILLER, ROBERT L UNIV N C GREENSBORO GRAD SCH RM 241 MOSSMAN BLDG GREENSBORO, NC 27412-5001 Biomedical research support
S07RR-07248-03 0710 (NSS) MCINTOSH, MICHAEL K Biomedical research support ENERGY METABOLISM & OBESITY
S07RR-07249-03 (NSS) WODARSKI, JOHN S UNIVERSITY OF AKRON OFF ASSOC VP RES & GRAD STUD AKRON, OH 44325-2102 Biomedical research support
S07RR-07249-03 0724 (NSS) STULL, DONALD E Biomedical research support CARING FOR ELDERS: IMPACT OF SOCIAL SUPPORT & BURDEN: LONG TERM CARE, CAREGIVER
S07RR-07249-03 0725 (NSS) KITSON, GAY C Biomedical research support VIOLENT DEATH LIFE COURSE ADJUSTMENT FOR WIDOWS: MENTAL HEALTH SUICIDE HOMICIDE
S07RR-07249-03 0726 (NSS) VIOLA, RONALD E Biomedical research support MECHANISM & STRUCTURE OF L ASPARTASE: ENZYME MECHANISM
S10RR-07249-01 (SSS) JACOBBERGER, JAMES W CASE WESTERN RESERVE UNIVERSIT 2119 ABINGTON RD CLEVELAND, OH 44106 CWRU Cancer Research Center flow cytometer and cell sorter
S07RR-07253-02 (NSS) HENNEY, JANE E UNIVERSITY OF KANSAS MED CENTE 39TH AND RAINBOW BOULEVARD KANSAS CITY, KS 66103 Biomedical research support grant
S07RR-07254-03 (NSS) PROENZA, LUIS M UNIVERSITY OF ALASKA 306 SIGNERS HALL FAIRBANKS, AK 99775 Biomedical research support
S07RR-07254-03 0492 (NSS) BARNES, BRIAN Biomedical research support OPIOD SYSTEM IN HIBERNATION
S07RR-07254-03 0493 (NSS) DEVICHE, PIERRE Biomedical research support RADIOIMMUNOLOGICAL DETERMINATION OF S STEROIDAL HORMONES IN AVIAN PLASMA
S07RR-07254-03 0494 (NSS) CASTELLINI, MICHEL Biomedical research support BLOOD CHEMISTRY & HEALTH OF MARINE MAMMALS
S07RR-07254-03 0495 (NSS) SRINIVASAN, R Biomedical research support CATALYSIS OF REDOX STEP BY GLUTAMATE DEHYDROGENASE
S07RR-07254-03 0496 (NSS) PLUMLEY, GERALD Biomedical research support DIATOM PLASMID & ITS APPLICATION IN IN TRANSFORMATION
S07RR-07254-03 0497 (NSS) DUFFY, LAWRENCE Biomedical research support ANALYSIS OF CLINICAL POP OF ALCOHOLICS INCLUDING HOMELESS
S07RR-07254-03 0498 (NSS) FOLLMAN, ERICH H Biomedical research support ACQUIRED IMMUNITY TO RABIES VIRUS IN NATIVE ALASKAN TRAPPERS
S07RR-07254-03 0499 (NSS) JANIS (SCHMITT), MAR Biomedical research support BINDING OF DEHYDROEPIANDROSTERONE TO SPECIFIC RECEPTOR IN T LYMPHOCYTES
S07RR-07254-03 0500 (NSS) YORK, ALISON Biomedical research support LEARNING & NEUROSENESIS IN RAT HIPPOCAMPUS
S07RR-07255-02 (NSS) REEVE, THOMAS G AUBURN UNIVERSITY HEALTH & HUMAN PERFORMANCE AUBURN UNIVERSITY, AL 36849 Biomedical research support
S07RR-07255-02 0501 (NSS) AULL, JOHN L Biomedical research support NEW CLASS POTENTIAL ANTI CANCER DRUGS: THYMIDYLATE SYNTHASE INHIBITORS
S07RR-07255-02 0502 (NSS) VAUGHN, BRIAN E Biomedical research support ADULT ATTACHMENT RELATIONSHIPS; BELIEFS & VALUES & GOALS FOR CHILD REARING
S07RR-07256-02 (NSS) HOOPER, HENRY O NORTHERN ARIZONA UNIVERSITY BOX 4085 FLAGSTAFF, AZ 86011-4085 Biomedical research support
S07RR-07256-02 0070 (NSS) MARKLE, RONALD A Biomedical research support STUDIES OF AORTIC WALL SUBSTANCE P AND PERMEABILITY
S07RR-07256-02 0071 (NSS) OWENS, THOMAS L Biomedical research support EFFECT OF AGE ON COLD ACCLIMATION IN RATS: METABOLIC BEHAVIORAL
S07RR-07256-02 0072 (NSS) KEIM, PAUL Biomedical research support GENETIC MARKERS TO EVALUAT SOYBEAN BREEDING POPULATIONS; BIG GAME MGMT
S07RR-07257-02 (NSS) IRIARTE, ANA J UNIVERSITY OF MISSOURI 5100 ROCKHILL RD KANSAS CITY, MO 64110 Biomedical research support
S07RR-07257-02 0711 (NSS) GORSKI, JEFFREY Biomedical research support CLONING & SEQUENCING OF CDNA FOR RAT BONE ACIDIC GLYCOPROTEIN 75
S07RR-07258-02 (NSS) KELSO, J A FLORIDA ATLANTIC UNIVERSITY 500 NW 20TH ST, PO BOX 3019 BOCA RATON, FLORIDA 33431 Biomedical research support
S07RR-07258-02 0858 (NSS) DING, MINGZHOU Biomedical research support MATHEMATICAL MODELS OF PERCEPTION
S07RR-07260-02 (NSS) LONG, GERALD VILLANOVA UNIVERSITY VILLANOVA, PA 19085-1699 Biomedical research support
S07RR-07260-02 0547 (NSS) KRAUSS, STEVEN S Biomedical research support INTRA INDIVIDUAL VARIABILITY OF MOOD JUDGMENTS IN NON CLINICAL COLLEGE SAMPLE
S07RR-07260-02 0548 (NSS) SELINSKY, BARRY S Biomedical research support LIVER METABOLISM OF FLUORINATED INHALATION ANESTHETIC
S07RR-07260-02 0549 (NSS) ZAJAC, WALTER W Biomedical research support SELECTIVITY OF NITRONE FORMATION FROM SECONDARY AMINES W/ 2 SULFONYLOXARIDINES
S07RR-07260-02 0550 (NSS) KLIEGER, DOUGLAS M Biomedical research support AUTOMATED TEST DEVELOPMENT OF FEAR SURVEY SCHEDULE
S07RR-07260-02 0551 (NSS) REISER-DANNER, LORET Biomedical research support PHYSICAL ATTRACTIVENESS & BEHAVIORAL RATINGS OF INFANTS & PRE SCHOOLERS
S07RR-07261-02 (NSS) DICKEY, JOHN TRINITY UNIVERSITY 715 STADIUM DRIVE SAN ANTONIO, TX 78212 Biomedical research support grant
S07RR-07261-02 0712 (NSS) BLYSTONE, ROBERT V Biomedical research support grant ANALYSIS OF MACROPHAGES IN MICROWAVE ENVIRONMENT
S07RR-07261-02 0713 (NSS) BUSHEY, MICHELLE M Biomedical research support grant UTILIZING MECC W/ BILE SALT MICELLES FOR ANALYSIS OF BILE COMPONENTS
S07RR-07261-02 0714 (NSS) SHINKLE, JAMES R Biomedical research support grant INTRODUCING ELISA TECHNIQUE IN UNDERGRADUATE CELL & MOLECULAR BIOLOGY LAB
S07RR-07261-02 0715 (NSS) STONE, WILLIAM Biomedical research support grant RESTRICTION FRAGMENT ANALYSIS OF DNA
S07RR-07262-01 (NSS) OLIVER, JAMES H, JR GEORGIA SOUTHERN COLLEGE BOX 8042 STATESBORO, GA 30460 Biomedical research support grant
S07RR-07263-01 (NSS) LEE, HSIN-YI RUTGERS UNIVERSITY 311 N 5TH STREET CAMDEN, N J 08102 Biomedical research support grant
S07RR-07264-01 (NSS) THOMAS, STEPHEN J UNIVERSITY OF SOUTH

PROJECT NO., ORGANIZATIONAL UNIT., INVESTIGATOR, ADDRESS, TITLE

ALABAMA MOBILE, AL 36688 Biomedical research support grant
S10RR-07323-01 (SSS) HAGEN, KARL S EMORY UNIV ATLANTA, GA 30322 Small biomolecule high intensity diffractometer
S10RR-07383-01 (SSS) BELMONT, JOHN BAYLOR COLLEGE OF MEDICINE ONE BAYLOR PLAZA HOUSTON, TX 77030 Gammacell 40 self-contained irradiator
S10RR-07510-01 (SSS) LAKOWICZ, JOSEPH R UNIV OF MARYLAND AT BALTIMORE 660 WEST REDWOOD STREET BALTIMORE, MD 21201 Argon laser for time-and frequency-domain fluorescence
R43RR-07520-01 (SSS) BOTZ, EDUARD J MEDICAL & SCIENTIFIC ENTERPRIS 56 UNION AVE SUDBURY, MA 01776 X-ray fluorescence system for thyroid diagnosis
R43RR-07521-01 (SSS) ABILEAH, ADI OIS OPTICAL IMAGING SYSTEMS, I 1896 BARRETT STREET TROY, MI 48084 Spatially modulated radiographic illuminator
R43RR-07524-01 (SSS) SQUILLANTE, MICHAEL R RADIATION MONITORING DEVICES 44 HUNT STREET WATERTOWN, MA 02172 A low capacitance silicon photodetector for PET
R43RR-07527-01 (PSF) GREENBLATT, RICHARD D RG ASSOCIATES 675 MASSACHUSETTS AVE CAMBRIDGE, MA 02139 Concurrent voice and data telephone for out-patient use
R43RR-07528-01 (SSS) SHEN, SHIDA ANALYTICA OF BRANFORD, INC 29 BUSINESS PARK DRIVE BRANFORD, CT 06405 Electrospray with mechanical vibration assist
R43RR-07535-01 (SSS) DIGBY, WARD CTI, INC PO BOX 22999 KNOXVILLE, TN 37933-0999 A 2mm PET scintillation detector array
R43RR-07539-01 (SSS) ALLNUTT, F C THOMAS MARTEK CORPORATION 6480 DOBBIN ROAD COLUMBIA, MD 21045 Stable isotopically labeled ribonucleoside production
R43RR-07542-01 (SSS) DUNKEL, REINHARD SITAR, INC 7923 WILLOWCREST RD SALT LAKE CITY, UT 84121 Computer assisted analysis of 2D-INADEQUATE NMR spectra
R43RR-07544-01 (PSF) KNOTT, GARY D CIVILIZED SOFTWARE INC 7735 OLD GEORGETOWN RD #410 BETHESDA, MD 20814 Data acquistion and control via serial I/o
R43RR-07550-01 (PSF) BUNOW, BARRY J CIVILIZED SOFTWARE, INC 7735 OLD GEORGETOWN ROAD BETHESDA, MD 20814 MLAB-S--MLAB for supercomputers
R43RR-07554-01 (SSS) KEESE, CHARLES R APPLIED BIOPHYSICS, INC. SCIENCE CENTER 3W20 TROY, NY 12180-3590 Electrode arrays in tissue culture
R43RR-07555-01 (PSF) DIXON, WILFRID J DIXON STATISTICAL ASSOCIATES 1525 SEPULVEDA BOULEVARD LOS ANGELES, CA 90025 Design research for sample size and power software
R13RR-07557-01 (BRC) ARNOLD, MARK A UNIVERSITY OF IOWA IOWA CITY, IA 52242 Gordon research conference on bioanalytical sensors
R01RR-07558-01 (BLR) JARDETZKY, OLEG STANFORD UNIVERSITY STANFORD, CA 94305-5055 Protein dynamics and NMR--Solution structure
R43RR-07559-01 (SSS) RENSHAW, STEPHEN R AUTOMATED CONTROL SYSTEMS INC 290 N UNIVERSITY AVE SUITE 205 PROVO, UT 84601 Intelligent refrigerated automatic storage system
R25RR-07563-01 (SRCM) FLOYD, GARY L 484 W 12TH AVE COLUMBUS, OH 43210 Biosciences for low-income students and their teachers
R25RR-07573-01 (SSS) ELGIN, SARAH C WASHINGTON UNIVERSITY ONE BROOKINGS DRIVE, BOX 1137 ST LOUIS, MO 63130 Two units--Molecular genetics and environmental chemistry
R25RR-07582-01 (SSS) GOODELL, ESTELLE M MARY IMOGENE BASSETT HOSPITAL ONE ATWELL ROAD COOPERSTOWN, NY 13326 A rural partnership for science education
R25RR-07585-01 (SSS) POLLOCK, MARC WQED PITTSBURGH 4802 FIFTH AVE PITTSBURGH, PA 15213 "The Universe Within"
R25RR-07591-01 (SSS) FRANZBLAU, CARL BOSTON UNIVERSITY 80 EAST CONCORD STREET BOSTON, MA 02118 Citylab--Biotechnology learning laboratory
R25RR-07607-01 (SSS) FLEURY, DOUGLAS UNIVERSITY OF ARIZONA 410 FORBES BLDG TUCSON, AZ 85721 Using insects in elementary classrooms for early lessons in life
R25RR-07635-01 (SRCM) BLANKS, JANET C USC SCHOOL OF MEDICINE 1355 SAN PABLO ST LOS ANGELES, CA 90033 USC/BRAVO science partnership
R25RR-07642-01 (SSS) HENRY, SUSAN A CARNEGIE-MELLON UNIVERSITY 4400 FIFTH AVENUE PITTSBURGH, PA 15213 Science teachers workshops for computer training
R25RR-07654-01 (SSS) WILLETT, NORMAN P TEMPLE UNIVERSITY 3400 NORTH BROAD ST PHILADELPHIA, PA 19140 Research scientist-pre college educator partnership
R25RR-07674-01 (SSS) PLATT, JAMES E UNIVERSITY OF DENVER DENVER, CO 80208 Establishing a life sciences curriculum center
R25RR-07675-01 (SRCD) MATKOVICH, VELIMIR OHIO STATE UNIVERSITY 471 DODD DRIVE COLUMBUS, OH 43210 Nutrition and human growth-enhancing middle school science
R25RR-07690-01 (SSS) WEISS, MARTIN M NEW YORK HALL OF SCIENCE 47-01 111TH ST NEW YORK, NY 11368 National travelling AIDS exhibit and education program
R01RR-07716-03 (SSS) COHN, MELVIN THE SALK INSTITUTE P O BOX 85800 SAN DIEGO, CA 92186-5800 Evolutionary models of the immune response
R44RR-07751-02 (SSS) SHAPIRO, HOWARD M HOWARD M SHAPIRO, MD PC 283 HIGHLAND AVE WEST NEWTON, MA 02165 Improvements in flow cytometry of bacteria and viruses
Z01RR-10001-23 (BEI) DEDRICK, R L NCRR, NIH Pharmacokinetics
Z01RR-10034-14 (BEI) LEIGHTON, S B NCRR, NIH Three-dimensional histological reconstruction
Z01RR-10039-14 (BEI) LEWIS, M S NCRR, NIH Biophysical instrumentation and methodology
Z01RR-10097-11 (BEI) CHADWICK, R S NCRR, NIH Studies in cardiovascular dynamics
Z01RR-10098-11 (BEI) BONNER, R F NCRR, NIH Laser instrumentation for vitreous and cardiovascular microsurgery
Z01RR-10109-11 (BEI) LEVIN, R L NCRR, NIH Adjunctive heat treatment of cancer
Z01RR-10112-11 (BEI) BONNER, R F NCRR, NIH Analysis of microcirculatory blood flow by laser doppler scattering
Z01RR-10122-10 (BEI) CLEM, T R NCRR, NIH Microcomputer applications for the NIH bio-technology unit
Z01RR-10146-09 (BEI) LEIGHTON, S B NCRR, NIH Prosthetic urethral sphincter
Z01RR-10162-09 (BEI) TALBOT, T L NCRR, NIH Wound healing--Biology and rheology
Z01RR-10184-08 (BEI) LEWIS, M S NCRR, NIH Physical chemistry of biological macromolecules
Z01RR-10204-07 (BEI) LEIGHTON, S B NCRR, NIH Cell handling studies
Z01RR-10214-07 (BEI) SMITH, P D NCRR, NIH Photoradiation therapy
Z01RR-10225-07 (BEI) UNSER, M NCRR, NIH Processing of high resolution electron micrographs
Z01RR-10256-05 (BEI) TALBOT, T L NCRR, NIH Mechanical prosthetic heart valve tester
Z01RR-10257-05 (BEI) BONNER, R F NCRR, NIH Analysis of propagation of light in turbid biological tissues
Z01RR-10258-05 (BEI) BONNER, R F NCRR, NIH Photochemical inactivation of virus and bacteria in blood
Z01RR-10259-05 (BEI) CLEM, T R NCRR, NIH Visual target tracking-ability assesment system
Z01RR-10260-05 (BEI) GOLDSTEIN, S NCRR, NIH Real-time high-performance confocal laser scanning optical microscope
Z01RR-10270-05 (BEI) UNSER, M NCRR, NIH Computer-assisted analysis of echocardiograms
Z01RR-10272-04 (BEI) FRIAUF, W S NCRR, NIH Photometry for photodynamic therapy
Z01RR-10276-04 (BEI) DEDRICK, R L NCRR, NIH Microdialysis probe studies
Z01RR-10283-04 (BEI) MUDD, C P NCRR, NIH A microcomputer-based flow cytometry data collection and analysis system
Z01RR-10285-04 (BEI) MUDD, C P NCRR, NIH Calorimetric investigation of DNA/anthracycline drug interactions
Z01RR-10286-04 (BEI) MUDD, C P NCRR, NIH High-speed differential stopped-flow calorimeter
Z01RR-10296-04 (BEI) LEAPMAN, R D NCRR, NIH Experiments with a high resolution field-emission STEM
Z01RR-10303-03 (BEI) TALBOT, T L NCRR, NIH Assessment of scratching in biliary cirrhosis patients
Z01RR-10305-03 (BEI) LEVIN, R L NCRR, NIH Clinical Center image management system
Z01RR-10307-03 (BEI) ZHOU, G NCRR, NIH Pulse oximeter calibrator
Z01RR-10309-03 (BEI) MUDD, C P NCRR, NIH Signal conditioning & data acquisition system for sleep deprivation studies
Z01RR-10310-03 (BEI) MUDD, C P NCRR, NIH Microcalorimeter measurements of DNA-protein interactions
Z01RR-10313-03 (BEI) FRIAUF, W S NCRR, NIH High-speed multi-channel spectrophotometer
Z01RR-10314-03 (BEI) FRIAUF, W S NCRR, NIH Pulsed photodynamic therapy
Z01RR-10315-03 (BEI) ROTH, B J NCRR, NIH A model of magnetic stimulation of a nerve fiber
Z01RR-10316-03 (BEI) ROTH, B J NCRR, NIH Calculation of electric fields during magnetic stimulation
Z01RR-10317-03 (BEI) UNSER, M NCRR, NIH New algorithms for the processing of biomedical images
Z01RR-10318-03 (BEI) UNSER, M NCRR, NIH Apple Macintosh II-based image processing workstation
Z01RR-10319-03 (BEI) ROTH, B J NCRR, NIH Calculation of electrical activity in thick strands of cardiac tissue
Z01RR-10320-03 (BEI) ALDROUBI, A NCRR, NIH Computerized methods for analyzing 2-D agarose gel electrophoretograms
Z01RR-10322-03 (BEI) SWYT, C R NCRR, NIH Data acquisition system for ultrahigh-resolution STEM
Z01RR-10324-03 (BEI) LUTZ, R J NCRR, NIH In vitro hemodynamic models for cardiovascular studies
Z01RR-10325-03 (BEI) ROTH, B NCRR, NIH Noninvasive magnetic measurement of current in peripheral nerve
Z01RR-10327-04 (BEI) LEAPMAN, R D NCRR, NIH Mass mapping of macromolecule assemblies
Z01RR-10329-03 (BEI) EIDSATH, A NCRR, NIH Optimized mammography instrument
Z01RR-10331-02 (BEI) LEAPMAN, R D NCRR, NIH Microanalysis of rapidly-frozen tissue in the field emission STEM
Z01RR-10332-02 (BEI) LEAPMAN, R D NCRR, NIH Characterization of fluorine-labeled compounds by parallel EELS
Z01RR-10333-02 (BEI) SCHMITT, J M NCRR, NIH Applications of artificial neural networks in biomedical image processing
Z01RR-10335-02 (BEI) WALKER, E C NCRR, NIH Design and implementation of an equipment management program
Z01RR-10336-02 (BEI) MORRISON, P F NCRR, NIH Kinetics of folate metabolism
Z01RR-10337-02 (BEI) MARKOWITZ, A NCRR, NIH Nuclear medical imaging--Scintigraphic imaging system for small animals
Z01RR-10339-02 (BEI) LEVIN, R L NCRR, NIH Radiological science research and training program
Z01RR-10341-02 (BEI) CLEM, T R NCRR, NIH Muscle strength testing system
Z01RR-10342-02 (BEI) COLE, J W NCRR, NIH Computer based dual pump HPLC driver system
Z01RR-10343-02 (BEI) UNSER, M NCRR, NIH B-spline signal processing techniques
Z01RR-10344-02 (BEI) UNSER, M NCRR, NIH Computer analysis of ultrasound images of the tongue
Z01RR-10348-02 (BEI) CASCIO, H E NCRR, NIH An infrared strobe CCD television camera unit
Z01RR-10349-02 (BEI) SMITH, P D NCRR, NIH Image field modification for quantitative microscopy
Z01RR-10352-02 (BEI) ELLIS, J R NCRR, NIH Quantitative characterization of ciliated tracheal epithelial cell cultures
Z01RR-10353-01 (BEI) MORRISON, P F NCRR, NIH Drug transport in brain

PROJECT NO., ORGANIZATIONAL UNIT., INVESTIGATOR, ADDRESS, TITLE

Z01RR-10354-01 (BEI) BUNGAY, P M NCRR, NIH Kidney tubule and epithelial transport studies
Z01RR-10355-01 (BEI) PETERSON, J I NCRR, NIH Intratumoral PO2 measurements with photosensitizer
Z01RR-10356-01 (BEI) SWYT, C R NCRR, NIH Microdialysis program for the Macintosh computer
Z01RR-10357-01 (BEI) ROTH, B NCRR, NIH Electrode heating during magnetic stimulation
Z01RR-10358-01 (BEI) MUDD, C P NCRR, NIH Heat capacity effects in lipids during unicellular/multicellular phase changes
Z01RR-10359-01 (BEI) MARKOWITZ, A NCRR, NIH Flash photolysis apparatus
Z01RR-10360-01 (BEI) DONG, C NCRR, NIH Motility of tumor cell metastases
Z01RR-10361-01 (BEI) DONG, C NCRR, NIH Rheology of sickle erythrocytes
Z01RR-10362-01 (BEI) EIDSATH, A NCRR, NIH Binding forces in receptor mediated cell adhesion
Z01RR-10363-01 (BEI) ROTH, B NCRR, NIH Current dipole localization using EEG data, model
Z01RR-10364-01 (BEI) ALDROUBI, A NCRR, NIH Methods for the calculation of minimal electrophoresis time for DNA sequencing
Z01RR-10365-01 (BEI) SCHMITT, J M NCRR, NIH Study of polarized light propagation in scattering media
Z01RR-10366-01 (BEI) SCHMITT, J M NCRR, NIH Non-invasive measurement of arterial blood hematocrit
Z01RR-10367-01 (BEI) SCHMITT, J M NCRR, NIH Imaging of biological tissues using high-frequency intensity-modulated light
Z01RR-10368-01 (BEI) ZHOU, G NCRR, NIH Biopsy needle locator
Z01RR-10369-01 (BEI) CHEN, C-N NCRR, NIH Spatial distributions of chromosomes and molecular modeling of DNA
Z01RR-10370-01 (BEI) MATTIELLO, J NCRR, NIH Temperature dependence of magnetization transfer
Z01RR-10371-01 (BEI) ELLIS, J R NCRR, NIH Quantitative retinal atrophy
Z01RR-10372-01 (BEI) ELLIS, J R NCRR, NIH Development of a "CHAOS" PC resource at NIH
Z01RR-10373-01 (BEI) MOONEN, C NCRR, NIH Operation of the In Vivo NMR research center
Z01RR-10374-01 (BEI) MOONEN, C NCRR, NIH Functional magnetic resonance imaging and spectroscopy in medicine and biology
N01RR-12103-00 (**) SEIBEL, FREDERICK PROPHET systems support and enhancement
N01RR-12114-00 (**) MARRIOTT, BERNADETTE M Psychological well-being of nonhuman primates
N01RR-12115-00 (**) BULGER, RUTH Addressing career paths in clinical research
N01RR-62123-09 (**) WAGNER, JOSEPH L Provide services and a holding facility for new world primates
N01RR-92105-09 (**) STEVENSON, ROBERT Reference strains of microorganisms and cell cultures
N01RR-92113-02 (**) RIDDLE, DONALD L Operate a caenorhabditis genetic center
N01SP-01001-00 (**) ROW SCIENCES, INC(5515 SECURITY LANE SUITE 500 ROCKVILLE, MD 20852 Logistical for grant and contract review meetings
N01SP-01003-00 (**) U S SMALL BUSINESS ADMIN WASHINGTON DISTRICT OFFICE 1111 18TH STREET, NW 6TH FL WASHINGTON, D C 20036 Logistics and administrative support
N01SP-02004-00 (**) U S SMALL BUSINESS ADMIN WASHINGTON DISTRICT OFFICE 1111 18TH STREET, NW WASHINGTON, D C 20036 Technical assistance support for community partnership grantees
N01SP-02007-00 (**) MACRO SYSTEMS, INC 8630 FENTON STREET SILVER SPRING, MD 20910 Community prevention training
N01SP-03002-00 (**) (~RMACRO SYSTEM, INC 8630 FENTON STREET SILVER SPING, MD 20910 OSAP pregnant and postpartum demonstration project
N01SP-11002-00 (**) US SMALL BUSINESS ADMIN 409 - 3RD STREET, SW WASHINGTON, D C 20416 Logistical and administrative assistance for workshops, meetings & conferences
N01SP-11006-00 (**) CONWAL INC 520 N WASHINGTON ST SUITE 100 FALLS CHURCH, VA 22046 Management support services
N01SP-12001-00 (**) SUPER TEAMS OPERATING CO, INC 12 OVERTON AVENUE SAYVILLE, N Y 11782 National Volunteer Training Center for Substance Abuse Prevention
N01SP-12002-00 (**) US SMALL BUSINESS ADMIN 409 - 3RD STREET, SW WASHINGTON, D C 20416 DCPT logistical planning and management
N01SP-12003-00 (**) THE CDM GROUP, INC 5530 WISCONSIN AVENUE CHEVY CHASE, MD 20815 WASHINGTON, DC 20416 Technical and administrative support
N01SP-12004-00 (**) PACIFIC INST, RES & EVALUATION 7315 WISCONSIN AVE, SUITE 900E BETHESDA, MD 20814 Evaluation of the National Training System & technical assistance to communities
N01SP-13003-00 (**) CSR,INCORPORATED 1400 EYE STREET, NW - SUITE 60 WASHINGTON, D C 20005 Implementation and effectiveness of OSAP high risk youth demonstration grants
N01SP-13004-00 (**) LEWIN/ICF 1090 VERMONT AVE, NW - SUITE 7 WASHIGNTON, DC 20005 National Perinatal addiction prevention technical assistance & resource center
N01SP-14001-00 (**) EDITORIAL EXPERTS, INC 66 CANAL CENTER PLAZA, SUITE ALEXANDRIA, VA 22314-1538 Editorial Services Support
N01TI-10002-00 (**) NARCOTIC & DRUG RESEARCH INC 251 NEW KARNER ROAD ALBANY, NEW YORK 12205 Technical assistance and training services to prison drug treatment program
N01TI-10003-00 (**) ES, INC 1133 - 15TH ST, NW - SUTIE 550 WASHINGTON, DC 20005 Technical assistance for drug programs
N01TI-10004-00 (**) JOHNSON, BASSIN & SHAW, INC 8737 COLESVILLE, RD - SUITE 8 SILVER SPRING, MD 20910 Technical assistance in improving the methadone treatment services
N01TI-10005-00 (**) UNITED INFORMATION SYS, INC 4700 CORRIDOR PLACE, BLDG D BELTSVILLE, MD 20705 Logistical support services for pre and post review activities
N01TI-10006-00 (**) GLOBAL EXCHANGE, INC 4701 WILLARD DRIVE - SUITE 105 CHEVY CHASE, MD 20815 Logistical support for the national conference on primary care/substance abuse
N01TI-10007-00 (**) MACRO INTERNATIONAL, INC 8630 FENTON STREET SILVER SPRING, MD 20910 Technical assistance to on-site review for state substance abuse services
N01TI-10008-00 (**) JOHNSON, BASSIN AND SHAW, INC 8737 COLESVILLE RD - SUITE 800 SILVER SPRING, MD 20910 State alcohol and drug abuse system technical review program
N01TI-10011-00 (**) SOCIOTECHNICAL RES APPLS, INC 300 EYE STREET, NE WASHINGTON, D C 20002 Technical Assistance & Training Services to Demonstration Jail Drug Treatment Pro
N01TI-10013-00 (**) UNITED INFORMATION SYS, INC 4700 CORRIDOR PLACE, BLDG D BELTSVILLE, MD 20705 Technical assistance for treatment grants in critical & criminal justice program
N01TI-10015-00 (**) CALIBER ASSOCIATES 3998 FAIR RIDGE DR - SUITE 36 FAIRFAX, VA 22033-2907 Evaluation of Job Corps Demonstration Progam--Drug Teatment enrichment
N01TI-10016-00 (**) ES, INC 1133 - 15TH STREET, NW - SUITE WASHINGTON, DC 20005 Graduate schools of divinity model treatment training programs
N01TI-10018-00 (**) MAYATECH CORPORATION 1398 LAMBERTON DRIVE SILVER SPRING, MD 20902 Preparation for implementation of NTIES

PRINCIPAL INVESTIGATOR LISTING

AALBRECHT, P   Z01BF03011-01
AARONS, RALPH D   K08NS01315-04
AARONSON, DORIS R   R01MH16496-18
AARONSON, LAWRENCE R   R15GM45966-01
AARONSON, S A   Z01CP04940-24
AARONSON, S A   Z01CP05626-02
AARONSON, S A   Z01CP05627-02
AARONSON, S A   Z01CP05634-02
AARONSON, S A   Z01CP05644-02
AARONSON, SHELDON   S07RR07064-24 0192
AASLESTAD, HALVOR G   S07RR05358-30
AASLESTAD, HALVOR G   S15DK44703-01
AASLESTAD, HALVOR G   S15MH49307-01
ABASSI, Z   Z01HL03590-01
ABATE, MARIE A   R01LM05189-02
ABBAS, ABUL   P01CA39542-07 0005
ABBAS, ABUL K   R01AI22802-06
ABBAS, ABUL K   R01AI25022-05
ABBAS, PAUL A   P50DC00242-07 0005
ABBEY, ANTONIA   R24MH47181-02 0005
ABBEY, JUNE C   S07RR06034-01
ABBOTT, ELIZABETH F   S03RR03029-09
ABBOTT, ELIZABETH F   S03RR03241-08
ABBOTT, ELIZABETH F   S03RR03314-02
ABBOTT, ELIZABETH F   S03RR03560-01
ABBOTT, LOUISE C   S07RR05460-29 0363
ABBOTT, M   Z01ES61042-05
ABBOTT, MARY I   P01CA50084-03 0004
ABBOTT, PATRICK J   R18DA06953-02
ABBOTT, WILLIAM M   R01HL34780-07
ABBOUD, CAMILLE E   P01HL18208-17 0014
ABBOUD, CAMILLE N   R03CA53352-01
ABBOUD, FRANCOIS M   M01RR00059-30 0562
ABBOUD, FRANCOIS M   P01HL14388-20 0209
ABBOUD, FRANCOIS M   P01HL14388-20
ABBOUD, FRANCOIS M   P01HL14388-20 0185
ABBOUD, FRANCOIS M   P01HL14388-20 0244
ABBOUD, HANNA E   R01DK33665-08
ABBOUD, HANNA E   R01DK43988-01
ABBRUZZESE, JAMES L   R03CA53398-01
ABBS, JAMES H   P50DC00162-10S2
ABDEL-LATIF, ATA A   R01EY04387-10
ABDEL-LATIF, ATA A   R37EY04171-10
ABDEL-MONEM, MAHMOUD M   S07RR05686-11
ABDEL-MONEM, MAHMOUD M   S15CA55930-01
ABDEL-RAHMAN, ABDEL A   R29AA07839-04
ABDELAL, AHMED T   G20RR06944-01
ABDULNOUR-NAKHOUL, S   S07RR05812-12 0479
ABE, MIYAKO   S07RR05526-29 0071
ABEE, CHRISTIAN R   G20RR07101-01
ABEE, CHRISTIAN R   P40RR01254-11
ABEL, CARLOS   S07RR05566-28
ABEL, ERNEST   P50AA07606-04 9002
ABEL, ERNEST L   P50AA07606-04 0006
ABEL, FRANCIS   S07RR05815-12 0490
ABEL, LARRY   P30AG10133-01 0002
ABEL, LARRY   P50MH41684-07 0071
ABELE, LAWRENCE G   S15GM47048-01
ABELES, NORMAN   S07RR07049-26 0428
ABELES, ROBERT H   R37GM12633-28
ABELL, CREED W   R01NS24932-05
ABELL, CREED W   S15NS30112-01
ABELL, THOMAS   M01RR00211-27 0321
ABELL, THOMAS A   M01RR00211-27 0318
ABELL, THOMAS L   M01RR00211-27 0322
ABELL, THOMAS L   M01RR00211-27 0319
ABELMAN, WALTER H   M01RR01032-16 0260
ABELSON, JAMES C   M01RR00042-31 0523
ABELSON, JAMES L   M01RR00042-31 0550
ABELSON, JOHN N   R37GM32637-09
ABENDSCHEIN, DANA R   P50HL17646-17 0034
ABENDSCHEIN, DANA R   R01HL36274-05
ABER, J LAWRENCE   S07RR07234-05 0855
ABERCROMBIE, ELIZABETH D   P01NS19608-09 000
ABERCROMBIE, RONALD F   R01NS19194-10
ABERLE, DENISE R   P01CA51198-02 0003
ABERNATHY, ALEXIS D   M01RR00044-31 0379
ABERNATHY, ALEXIS D   M01RR00044-31 0373
ABERNETHY, ALEXIS D   M01RR00044-31 0351
ABERNETHY, DARRELL R   R01AG08226-03
ABIGAIL, ADAMS   S07RR05712-20 0095
ABIKOFF, HOWARD B   R01MH44848-03
ABILDSKOV, J A   R01HL35204-06
ABILEAH, ADI   R43RR07521-01
ABKOWITZ, JANIS L   M01RR00037-31 0481
ABKOWITZ, JANIS L   R01DK41934-03
ABKOWITZ, JANIS L   R01HL31823-08
ABKOWITZ, JANIS L   R01HL46598-01
ABLACK, IRA B   P01HD23315-05 0001
ABLASHI, D   Z01CP05063-13
ABLIN, ARTHUR R   U10CA17829-15
ABMAN, STEVEN   M01RR00069-29 0394
ABMAN, STEVEN H   K08HL01932-05
ABMAN, STEVEN H   R29HL41012-04
ABMAN, STEVEN H   S07RR06022-02 0850
ABNEY, THOMAS A   S07RR05365-30 0073
ABOOD, LEO G   R01DA00464-16
ABOOD, MARY E   P50DA05274-04 0010
ABOOD, MARY E   R29DA06867-01
ABOU-DONIA, MOHAMED B   R01ES05154-07
ABOU-DONIA, MOHAMED B   R01ES05071-02
ABOU-DONIA, MOHAMED B   R01OH00823-11A2
ABRAHAM, CARMELA   P01AG00001-17A2 0022
ABRAHAM, CARMELA R   P60AR20613-14 0025
ABRAHAM, CARMELA R   R01AG09905-01
ABRAHAM, DONALD   P30CA16059-15 9014
ABRAHAM, DONALD J   R01HL32793-08
ABRAHAM, EDATHARA C   R01EY07394-05
ABRAHAM, GEORGE N   P01AI29522-02 0003
ABRAHAM, GEORGE N   R01AG08177-04
ABRAHAM, GEORGE N   S07RR05403-30
ABRAHAM, GEORGE N   S10RR06679-01
ABRAHAM, GEORGE N   S15AG10230-01
ABRAHAM, JUDITH A   R43GM46166-01
ABRAHAM, ROBERT T   U01CA52995-02 0004
ABRAHAM, SAMUEL   S07RR05467-23 0023
ABRAHAM, SOMAN N   R01AI13550-16
ABRAHAM, WILLIAM   M01RR00051-30 0760
ABRAHAM, WILLIAM M   S03RR03371-07
ABRAHAM, WILLIAM M   S15HL47733-01
ABRAHAMSON, DALE   P50DK39258-05 0003
ABRAHAMSON, DALE R   R01DK34972-07
ABRAMOV, I   S07RR07119-20 0466
ABRAMOWSKY, CARLOS R   R01HD28549-01
ABRAMS, BARBARA F   R29HD27347-02
ABRAMS, CHARLES S   K11HL02464-02
ABRAMS, DAVID   P01CA50087-03 0002
ABRAMS, DAVID B   S07RR05818-12
ABRAMS, DAVID B   S15AR41247-01
ABRAMS, DONALD   M01RR00083-29 0217
ABRAMS, DONALD   M01RR00083-29 0238
ABRAMS, DONALD I   N01AI95035-06
ABRAMS, GARY W   U10EY02548-13
ABRAMS, GERALD   P30CA46592-04 9005
ABRAMS, JONATHAN   K07HL02677-01
ABRAMS, MARY   P60HL28391-09 0012
ABRAMS, RICHARD A   R29MH45145-02
ABRAMS, ROBERT M   R01HD20084-07
ABRAMS, THOMAS W   R01NS25788-04
ABRAMSON, ALLAN L   P01DC00203-09 0004
ABRAMSON, DAVID H   U10EY06899-06
ABRAMSON, FRED P   R01GM36143-05A2
ABRAMSON, JON S   R01AI20506-08
ABRAMSON, LYN Y   R01MH43866-02
ABRAMSON, NORMAN S   R01NS15295-12
ABRAMSON, STEVEN B   S07RR05399-30 0945
ABRAMSON, STEWART N   R55NS29951-01A1
ABRASS, CHRISTINE K   R01DK35142-06A2
ABRASS, CHRISTINE K   R01DK39871-04
ABRASS, ITAMAR B   K12AG00503-01
ABRAVANEL, EUGENE   S07RR07019-26 0069
ABREU, MARY E   R44MH44411-03
ABRIOLA, LINDA M   P42ES04911-03 0005
ABRIOLA, LINDA M   P42ES04911-03 0006
ABSHER, MARLENE   P50HL14212-20 0028
ABSHER, MARLENE   P50HL14212-20 9009
ABSHIRE, THOMAS   M01RR00069-29 0369
ABT ASSOCIATES, INC   N01DA02200-00
ABT ASSOCIATES, INC   N01DA88254-00
ABT, DONALD A   P40RR01333-12
ABU-SHAKRA, A   Z01ES21107-04
ABUMRAD, NADA A   R01DK33301-08
ABUMRAD, NAJI   M01RR00095-31 0318
ABUMRAD, NAJI   P60DK20593-13 9003
ABUMRAD, NAJI N   M01RR00095-31 0237
ABUMRAD, NAJI N   M01RR00095-31 0238
ABUMRAD, NAJI N   R01DK42562-01A1
ABUMRAD, NAJI N.   M01RR00095-31 0278
ABZUG, MARK J   R29HD27692-01A1
ACARA, MARGARET A   R01AA07854-03
ACCAVITTI, MARY ANN   P60AR20614-14 9001
ACCHIARDO, SERGIO S   M01RR00211-27 0254
ACCURSO, FRANK J   M01RR00069-29 0292
ACCURSO, FRANK J   M01RR00069-29 0453
ACCURSO, FRANK J   M01RR00069-29 0451
ACETO, MARIO D   R01DA06876-01
ACEY, ROGER A   S06GM08238-05 0008
ACEY, ROGER A   S07RR07232-05 0464
ACHARYA, SEETHARAMA A   P60HL38655-04 0005
ACHE, BARRY W   R03DC01042-01A1
ACHENBACH, THOMAS M   R01MH40305-07
ACHENBACH, THOMAS M   R01MH46093-02
ACITELLI, LINDA K   R29MH46567-01A1
ACKERMAN, E   Z01DK52011-07
ACKERMAN, EUGENE   P41RR01632-09 9015
ACKERMAN, EUGENE   P41RR01632-09 9009
ACKERMAN, JEROME L   P01CA48729-03 9001
ACKERMAN, JOSEPH J   R01CA40411-05
ACKERMAN, JOSEPH J   S15GM47100-01
ACKERMAN, ROBERT A   P01NS15654-13 0010
ACKERMAN, STEVEN J   R01AI25230-05
ACKERS, GARY K   P41RR04328-04 0003
ACKERS, GARY K   R01GM39343-04
ACKERS, GARY K   R37GM24486-15
ACKLES, PATRICK K   R29HD25345-03
ACKLEY, R S   S07RR07127-23 0475
ACKRELL, BRIAN A   P01HL16251-18 9001
ACKRELL, BRIAN A   P01HL16251-18 0002
ACOSTA, DANIEL, JR   S03RR03262-10
ACOTT, TED S   R01EY03279-12
ACOTT, TED S   R01EY07995-03
ACREDOLO, CURT R   R01HD27699-01
ACREDOLO, LINDA P   R01HD25476-03
ACTON, RONALD T   R01DK32767-09
ACTON, RONALD T   R01NS26795-02
ACTUARIAL RESEARCH CORP   N01DA98518-00
ADA, GORDON   P30AI28748-03
ADACHI, KAZUHIKO   R01HL32908-07
ADAIR, E   S07RR05692-22 0990
ADAIR, GERALD M   R01CA28711-10
ADAIR, LINDA   P01HD28076-01 0006
ADAIR, LINDA   P01HD28076-01 0007
ADAIR, STEVEN M   S07RR05795-14 0414
ADAIR, THOMAS H   K04HL02117-04
ADAIR, THOMAS H   R01HL42402-03
ADAIR, WINSTON L, JR   R01GM41003-11
ADAM, PETER A   P50HD11089-14 9003
ADAM, RODNEY D   R29AI28551-02
ADAMI, HANS-OLOV   N01CP85636-03
ADAMOWICZ, LUDWIK   S07RR07002-26 0860
ADAMS-CAMPBELL, LUCILE L   R03HL47208-01
ADAMS, ALISON E M   R01GM45288-01
ADAMS, ANTHONY J   R01EY02271-14
ADAMS, ANTHONY J   R01EY08893-01A1
ADAMS, ANTHONY J   S07RR05832-12 0189
ADAMS, BARBARA S   K11AI00768-05
ADAMS, BEVERLEY   M01RR00633-19 0325
ADAMS, BRIAN D   S07RR05429-30 0203
ADAMS, DAVID J   R01HL35422-06
ADAMS, DAVID S   S15GM47025-01
ADAMS, DOLPH O   P01CA29589-10
ADAMS, DOLPH O   P01CA29589-10 0001
ADAMS, DOLPH O   R01ES02922-10
ADAMS, HAROLD P, JR   R01NS27863-02
ADAMS, HARRY G   R01AI24916-03
ADAMS, JAMES A   R15ES05657-01
ADAMS, JAMES A.   S06GM08092-18 0012
ADAMS, JAMES D   S07RR05792-15 0939
ADAMS, JAMES M   R01HL29396-06
ADAMS, JANE   S07RR07199-12 0943
ADAMS, JEANETTE   S10RR06276-01
ADAMS, JERRY M   R01CA12421-20
ADAMS, JOE C   P50DC00422-05 0004
ADAMS, JOE C   R01DC00269-08
ADAMS, JOHN S   R01AR37399-05
ADAMS, JOHN S   R01DK33139-07
ADAMS, JOSE A   S07RR05662-18 0154
ADAMS, JULIAN P   R01GM30959-08
ADAMS, K   P50AA07378-04 0003
ADAMS, KENNETH G   S07RR05378-30 0986
ADAMS, KIRKWOOD   M01RR00046-31 0483
ADAMS, KIRKWOOD   M01RR00046-31 0469
ADAMS, KIRKWOOD   M01RR00046-31 0497
ADAMS, KIRKWOOD F   M01RR00046-31 0446
ADAMS, KIRKWOOD F   M01RR00046-31 0386
ADAMS, KIRKWOOD F   M01RR00046-31 0389
ADAMS, KIRKWOOD F   M01RR00046-31 0400
ADAMS, MICHAEL E   R01NS24472-05
ADAMS, MICHAEL R   P01HL45666-01 0002
ADAMS, MICHAEL R   P40RR00919-17 0006
ADAMS, MICHAEL R   P50HL14164-20 0051
ADAMS, MICHAEL R   R01HL46409-01
ADAMS, MICHAEL W   R01GM45597-01
ADAMS, NELSON   S06GM08040-21 0006
ADAMS, PERRIE M   S15MH49516-01
ADAMS, R   Z01CL40000-01
ADAMS, R G   Z01DK29017-12
ADAMS, R J   P01AI27297-04 9001
ADAMS, RALPH N   R01NS08740-25
ADAMS, ROBERT J   P01HL41544-04 0002
ADAMS, ROBERTA H   K11CA01443-03
ADAMS, SHERRILL L   R01AR41042-01
ADAMS, SHERRILL L   R01GM28840-11
ADAMS, THOMAS H   R01GM45252-01A1
ADAMS, THOMAS H   S07RR07090-26 0470
ADAMS, WALTER C   S03RR03333-07
ADAMS, WALTER C   S07RR07208-10
ADAMS, WALTER C   S15HD28777-01
ADAMSON, EILEEN D   R01HD21957-06
ADAMSON, EILEEN D   R01HD28025-01
ADAMSON, JOHN W   R01DK41937-04
ADAMSON, JOHN W   R01HL46524-01
ADAMSON, JOHN W   S07RR05688-23
ADASHI, ELI Y   R01HD19998-06
ADASHI, ELI Y   S07RR05379-30 0769
ADAY, LU ANN   R01LM05175-02

ADCOCK, GAYLE D R01AI24987-03
ADDISON, RANDOLPH S03RR03166-08
ADELBERG, EDWARD A S07RR07015-26
ADELBERG, EDWARD A S15GM47029-01
ADELMAN, ALAN M R01HS05705-02
ADELMAN, JOHN S07RR07238-04 0479
ADELMAN, JOHN P R01HD24562-03
ADELMAN, JOHN P R01NS28504-01A1
ADELMAN, JOHN P S07RR05412-30 0971
ADELMAN, MARK R S07RR05983-05 0346
ADELMAN, RICHARD C P30AG08808-03 9005
ADELSLEIN, R S Z01HL04219-01
ADELSTEIN, STANLEY J R01CA15523-18
ADELSTEIN, STANLEY J S07RR05381-30
ADELSTEIN, STANLEY J S15HD28736-01
ADENIYI, WILLIAM S07RR07236-04 0170
ADER, ROBERT K05MH06318-22
ADER, ROBERT R01MH42051-15
ADERA, TILAHUN S07RR05983-05 0347
ADEREM, ALAN A R01AI25032-05
ADES, PHILIP M01RR00109-28 0359
ADES, PHILIP A K08AG00426-04
ADES, PHILLIP A. M01RR00109-28 0315
ADESNIK, MILTON B R55GM30701-09A2
ADHYA, S L Z01CB08751-11
ADIBI, SIAMAK A R01DK15855-15A1
ADIBI, SIAMAK A R01DK15861-17
ADICKES, EDWARD D R29AA07358-05
ADKINS, BERNIE N01ES05296-01
ADKINS, REBECCA D S07RR05363-30 0818
ADKINS, WARREN P50DC00422-05 0002
ADKINSON, FRANKLIN U01AI31867-01 0013
ADKINSON, N FRANKLIN, JR N01HR16052-00
ADKINSON, N FRANKLIN, JR R01AI21073-08
ADKISON, KIMBERLY S07RR05635-18 0777
ADLER, ALICE J R01EY04368-09
ADLER, GAIL S07RR05899-10 0271
ADLER, GAIL K R29DK40475-05
ADLER, JOHN S07RR05353-30 0339
ADLER, JOHN R M01RR00070-29 0234
ADLER, JOSHUA P01HD23315-05 0004
ADLER, JOSHUA E P01AG03853-09 0015
ADLER, JULIUS R01AI08746-23
ADLER, JULIUS R01DK39121-05
ADLER, JULIUS S07RR07098-26 0331
ADLER, KARL P S07RR05398-30
ADLER, KENNETH B R01HL36982-05
ADLER, LAWRENCE M01RR00051-30 0765
ADLER, LAWRENCE E K01MH00728-04
ADLER, LAWRENCE E M01RR00051-30 0713
ADLER, LAWRENCE E M01RR00051-30 0698
ADLER, MARTIN W R01DA00376-18
ADLER, MARTIN W R01DA06650-01
ADLER, NANCY E R01HD23880-04
ADLER, PAUL N R01GM37163-06
ADLER, RUBEN R01EY04859-09
ADLER, RUBEN R01EY05404-07
ADLER, SHARON M01RR00425-22S3 0414
ADLER, SHARON G R29DK38451-04
ADLER, SHELDON R01NS26610-01A3
ADLER, STUART P R01AI17069-12
ADLER, STUART P R01AI27091-03
ADLER, STUART P R01AI27795-01A3
ADLER, STUART R S07RR05389-30 0627
ADLER, W H Z01AG00095-18
ADLER, W H Z01AG00104-15
ADLER, W H Z01AG00441-04
ADMAN, ELINOR T R01GM31770-08
ADRIAN, THOMAS E R01CA44799-02
ADRIAN, THOMAS E S15DK44708-01
ADROGUE, HORACIO M01RR00350-25 0469
ADVERTISING CNCL, INC N01DA88508-00
ADVOKAT, CLAIRE D R01DA02845-06
ADZICK, SCOTT N P50GM27345-11 0014
AEBISCHER, PATRICK R29NS26159-04
AFDAHL, NEZAM H S07RR05569-27 0107
AFDHAL, NEZAM W S07RR05569-27 0118
AFFLECK, GLENN G P60AR20621-13 0020
AFFONSO, DYANNE D R18NR02678-02
AFIFI, ABDELMONEM S03RR03232-06
AFIFI, ABDELMONEM S07RR05442-29
AFIFI, ABDELMONEM A S15CA55919-01
AFZAL, S M JAVED S07RR05918-08 0696
AGABIAN, NINA M R01AI21975-07
AGARD, DAVID P41RR00592-22 0030
AGARD, DAVID A R01GM31627-09
AGARWAL, KAN L R01DK21901-13
AGARWAL, RAM P R01AI29155-03
AGARWAL, VIJAY P M01RR00997-16 0380
AGAWAL, VIJAY S07RR05583-27 0620
AGER, JOEL P50AA07606-04 9003
AGGARWAL, ANEEL K R01GM44006-02
AGHAJANIAN, GEORGE K P01MH25642-18 0011
AGHAJANIAN, GEORGE K P01MH25642-18 9003
AGHAJANIAN, GEORGE K P01MH25642-18 0019
AGHAJANIAN, GEORGE K R37MH17871-22
AGILERA, G Z01HD00632-02
AGINS, ALAN P R29CA43914-05
AGIUS, MARK A K08NS01226-02
AGNELLO, VINCENT R01AR35487-07
AGNELUS, PAMELA A M01RR00997-16 0375
AGNEW, WILLIAM P01HL38156-05
AGNEW, WILLIAM F G20RR06941-01
AGNEW, WILLIAM F N01NS92326-03
AGNEW, WILLIAM S P01HL38156-05 0005
AGNEW, WILLIAM S P01HL38156-05 9002
AGNEW, WILLIAM S R01NS17928-10
AGRANOFF, BERNARD P50NS15655-12 0010
AGRANOFF, BERNARD W P01MH42652-05 9001
AGRANOFF, BERNARD W P01MH42652-05
AGRAS, W S R01DK39673-04
AGRAS, W STEWART R01HD25492-03
AGRAS, W STEWART R01MH38637-08
AGRAWAL, KRISHNA C R01AI25909-05
AGRE, PETER C R01HL33991-07
AGRE, PETER C R03AA09012-01
AGRESTI, ALAN R01GM43824-02
AGRIS, PAUL F S07RR07071-26 0257
AGUAYO, LUIS G R01AA08857-01
AGUILA, M CECILIA R29NS26821-01A3
AGUILERA, G Z01HD00631-02
AGUILO, FRANCISCO P40RR03640-05 0013
AGUIRRE, ALFREDO P50DE08240-05 0013
AGUIRRE, ALFREDO S07RR05330-30 0010
AGUIRRE, GUSTAVO D R01EY01244-19
AGUIRRE, GUSTAVO D R01EY07705-04
AGUIRRE, GUSTAVO D U01EY06855-05S1
AGURS, TANYA D R03AG10361-01
AHEARN, GREGORY A. S06GM08125-18 0041
AHEARN, JOSEPH M R29GM43803-02
AHEARN, MICHAEL J S03RR03170-10
AHERN, FRANK M R01AG08375-03
AHERN, FRANK M S07RR07082-26 0270
AHERN, GEOFFREY L S07RR05675-23 0940
AHERN, JOANN M01RR00125-28 0757
AHLQUIST, DAVID M01RR00585-20 0500
AHLQUIST, PAUL G R01GM35072-07
AHLSKOG, J E M01RR00585-20 0454
AHLSKOG, J E M01RR00585-20 0455
AHLSKOG, J ERIC M01RR00585-20 0442
AHMAD, FAZAL R01DK36739-05
AHMED, A RAZZAQUE R01DE09978-01
AHMED, A RAZZAQUE R01EY08379-02
AHMED, AHMED E R01ES01871-11
AHMED, KHALIL R37CA15062-18
AHMED, RAFI R01AI30048-02
AHMED, RAFI R01NS21496-07
AHMED, TAHIR S07RR05662-18 0150
AHMED, WISSAM W R43DC01172-01
AHN, SAMUEL S07RR05354-30 0423
AHRENS, PATRICIA B R29CA46956-04
AHRENS, RICHARD M01RR00059-30 0726
AHRENS, RICHARD M01RR00059-30 0733
AHRENS, RICHARD C M01RR00059-30 0625
AHRENS, RICHARD C M01RR00059-30 0698
AHRENS, RICHARD C M01RR00059-30 0703
AIELLO, EDWARD S07RR07150-17 0544
AIELLO, LLOYD M N01EY72145-21
AIGNER, T G Z01MH02039-01
AIKAWA, MASAMICHI P01AI15351-13 9003
AIKAWA, MASAMICHI R22AI10645-20
AIKEN, JUDD M R29AI29487-02
AIKEN, LINDA R01NR02754-02
AIKEN, LINDA H R01NR02280-02
AIKEN, LINDA H S07RR05948-05 0326
AIKEN, MARTHA L R29HL39702-04
AINE, CHERYL J R01EY08610-01A1
AIR, GILLIAN M P30CA13148-20 9017
AIR, GILLIAN M R01AI18203-09
AIR, GILLIAN M R01AI26718-04
AIR, GILLIAN M R37AI19084-09
AISEN, ALEX M01RR00042-31 0622
AISEN, PHILIP P41RR02583-07 0001
AISEN, PHILIP P41RR02583-07 0002
AISEN, PHILIP R01DK15056-21
AISEN, PHILIP R01DK37927-05
AISNER, JOSEPH U10CA31983-10
AITKEN, MICHAEL D S07RR05450-30 0328
AITKEN, MOIRA M01RR00037-31 0521
AITKEN, MOIRA L K08HL01920-05
AIZENMAN, ELIAS R01DA04975-04
AIZENMAN, ELIAS R01NS29365-01
AIZENMAN, ELIAS S07RR05416-30 0552
AJAYI, OLUADE S07RR05477-29 0429
AKABAS, MYLES P50DK41146-04 0005
AKABAS, MYLES H R03DC01019-01
AKESON, RICHARD A P01DC00347-06 0006
AKESON, RICHARD A R01EY08490-02
AKESON, RICHARD A R01HD21065-05
AKESON, WAYNE H R37AR34264-08
AKESSON, THOMAS R R29HD22869-04
AKEY, CHRISTOPHER W R01GM45377-01
AKEY, CHRISTOPHER W S10RR06605-01
AKHTAR, RASHID A R01EY05738-05
AKIL, HUDA M01RR00042-31 0494
AKIL, HUDA P01MH42251-05 0001
AKIL, HUDA P01MH42251-05 0002
AKIL, HUDA P30DK34933-06A1 9002
AKIL, HUDA R01DA02265-13
AKIN, DIANNE S07RR05308-30 0239
AKIN, JOHN P01HD28076-01 0005
AKIN, JOHN P01HD28076-01 0002
AKINS, DANIEL L S06GM08168-13 0020
AKINS, ROBERT S07RR05384-30 0774
AKINS, ROBERT A R01GM43309-02
AKIYAMA, TOSHIO . N01HC65061-07
AKPORIAYE, EMMANUEL T R29CA46809-05
AKSAMIT, ALLEN J R01NS29603-01
AKSAMIT, R R Z01MH00931-18
AL-AWQATI, QAIS R01DK39532-03
AL-AWQATI, QAIS P50DK41146-04
AL-AWQATI, QAIS P50DK41146-04 0001
AL-AWQATI, QAIS R37DK20999-14
AL-KATIB, AYAD M R29CA50715-02
ALAM, JAWED R01DK43135-01A1
ALAM, MAKTOOB S07RR07147-19 0640
ALAM, RAFEUL R29AI27864-02
ALAM, SYED Q R01DE05978-07A1
ALARCON, GRACEILA N01AR12207-01
ALARCON, RENATO D M01RR00032-31 0355
ALARIE, YVES C R01ES02747-09
ALAVA, M A Z01BH02012-03
ALAVI, ABASS M01RR00040-31 0418
ALAVI, ABASS P01AG03934-10 0003
ALAYASH, A I Z01BH01016-02
ALAYASH, A I Z01BH01017-02
ALAYASH, A I Z01BH01026-01
ALAYASH, A I Z01BH01027-01
ALAYASH, A I Z01BH01028-01
ALBA, RICHARD D R01HD25250-02
ALBANES, D Z01CN00100-09
ALBANES, D Z01CN00148-03
ALBANES, D Z01CN00154-01
ALBANO, JOANNE E R01EY07344-04
ALBELDA, STEVEN M R29HL46311-01
ALBERS, GREGORY S07RR05353-30 0340
ALBERS, H ELLIOT S07RR07171-08 0145
ALBERS, JOHN A P01HL30086-09 9001
ALBERS, JOHN J P01HL30086-09 0003
ALBERS, JOHN J P01HL30086-09
ALBERS, JOHN J R01HL44105-02
ALBERS, KATHRYN M R29AR40873-01
ALBERS, R W Z01NS00813-30
ALBERSHEIM, PETER P01AI27135-04
ALBERSHEIM, PETER P41RR05351-03
ALBERT, ARLENE D R01EY03328-09
ALBERT, DANIEL M R01EY01917-16
ALBERT, DANIEL M U10EY06284-04
ALBERT, DAVID E R43HL44794-01A1
ALBERT, K P30CA06927-29 9014
ALBERT, MARILYN P01AG04390-08 0005
ALBERT, MARILYN P01AG04953-08 9001
ALBERT, MARILYN S P01AG04953-08
ALBERT, MARILYN S P01AG04953-08 0001
ALBERT, MARILYN S U01MH46281-03
ALBERT, MARTIN P01DC00081-26 0016
ALBERT, MARTIN P01DC00081-26 0017
ALBERT, RICHARD K P01HL24163-13 0012
ALBERT, RICHARD K. P51RR00166-30 0134
ALBERT, ROY E P30ES00159-24S1
ALBERT, STEVEN S07RR05611-22 0711
ALBERTINE, KURT H. P01HL19737-15 9004
ALBERTINI, DAVID F R01HD20068-07
ALBERTINI, RICHARD J R01CA30688-09
ALBERTS, BRUCE M P01GM31286-09 0007
ALBERTS, BRUCE M R01GM23928-14
ALBERTS, BRUCE M R37GM24020-16
ALBERTS, DAVID S P01CA17094-16 0017
ALBERTS, DAVID S P01CA27502-11
ALBERTS, DAVID S P01CA41108-05 0001
ALBERTS, DAVID S P01CA41108-05 9004
ALBERTS, DAVID S P01CA41108-05
ALBERTS, DAVID S P01CA41183-05 0004
ALBERTS, JEFFREY R R01HD28246-01
ALBERTS, JEFFREY R R01MH46485-02
ALBERTS, JEFFREY R R37MH28355-16
ALBERTS, JEFFREY R S07RR07031-26
ALBERTS, MARK J K08NS01241-05
ALBERTSEN, PETER C R01HS06770-01
ALBIN, ROGER L K08NS01300-04
ALBIN, ROGER L P30AG08808-03 0003
ALBIN, ROGER L P50AG08671-03 0004
ALBINA, JORGE E R01GM42859-03
ALBINO, ANTHONY P R01CA37907-07
ALBINO, ANTHONY P S07RR05534-19 0530
ALBINO, JUDITH E N P50AA03527-14
ALBITAR, MAHER K11HL02229-04
ALBIZATI, KIM F R01GM38243-03
ALBIZATI, KIM F S06GM08167-13 0030
ALBO, VINCENT C U10CA36015-08
ALBRECHT, EUGENE D R01HD13294-11
ALBRECHT, MARY A K08AI01015-01
ALBRECHT, P Z01BF03010-01
ALBRECHT, RALPH P41RR00570-21 0006
ALBRECHT, RALPH M P01HL29586-09 0001
ALBRIGHT, JULIA W R01AG06278-06
ALBRIGHT, LELAND M01RR00084-29 0229
ALBRIGHT, MICHAEL J R43CA55434-01
ALBRO, P Z01ES50114-03
ALBRO, P W Z01ES30003-20
ALBUQUERQUE, EDSON X P50MH44211-03 0006
ALBUQUERQUE, EDSON X R01NS25296-04
ALCOFORADO, GILL A S07RR05321-30 0262
ALDAZ, CLAUDIO M R29CA48922-03
ALDER, MARDEN E S07RR05897-09 0266
ALDERETE, JOHN F P01AI22380-07 0001

ALDERETE, JOHN F R01AI18768-07A4
ALDERETE, JOHN F U01AI31498-01 0001
ALDERFER, JAMES L R01CA39027-07
ALDERMAN, BETH W R01HD28779-01
ALDERMAN, BETH W R29HD22831-05
ALDERMAN, EDWIN L R01HL28292-09
ALDERMAN, EDWIN L U01HL38642-05
ALDERMAN, MICHAEL H P50HL18323-17 0012
ALDRICH, JANE L R01DA05195-03
ALDRICH, MICHAEL S M01RR00042-31 0576
ALDRICH, MICHAELS P50AG08671-03 0005
ALDRICH, RICHARD W P50MH48108-01 0001
ALDRICH, RICHARD W R01NS23294-07
ALDRIDGE, JAMES W S03RR03221-08
ALDRIDGE, JAMES W S06GM08038-21 0005
ALDRIDGE, JAMES W S06GM08038-21
ALDROUBI, A Z01RR10320-03
ALDROUBI, A Z01RR10364-01
ALDWIN, CAROLYN S07RR05927-07 0965
ALDWIN, CAROLYN M R29AG07465-04
ALEDORT, LOUIS M M01RR00071-28A1 0202
ALEDORT, LOUIS M M01RR00071-28A1 0206
ALEDORT, LOUIS M M01RR00071-28A1 0186
ALEGRIA, ANTONIO E S06GM08216-09
ALEGRIA, ANTONIO E S06GM08216-09 0011
ALEJANDRO, RODOLFO M01RR05280-03 0001
ALEMI, FARROKH R18DA06913-02
ALENCAR, JOAQUIN E P01AI16305-13 0012
ALESSI, NORMAN E M01RR00042-31 0627
ALESSI, NORMAN E M01RR00042-31 0565
ALETTA, JOHN M P50AG08702-03 0005
ALEXANDER, DAVID S07RR07037-26 0379
ALEXANDER, ELAINE L M01RR00722-19 0192
ALEXANDER, GARRETT E R01NS17678-11
ALEXANDER, J WESLEY R01AI12936-15
ALEXANDER, J WESLEY R01HL38479-05
ALEXANDER, J WESLEY U01AI31449-01
ALEXANDER, JAMES F P50DA07697-01 0002
ALEXANDER, JOE, JR R29HL46344-01
ALEXANDER, KENNETH R R01EY08301-02
ALEXANDER, NANCY J P50HL14164-20 9011
ALEXANDER, NEIL B K01AG00519-01
ALEXANDER, NEIL B P30AG08808-03 0002
ALEXANDER, PAMELA S07RR07042-26 0403
ALEXANDER, R B Z01CM06667-01
ALEXANDER, R C Z01MH02455-03
ALEXANDER, R C Z01MH02456-03
ALEXANDER, STEVEN R M01RR00633-19 0423
ALEXOPOULOS, GEORGE S R01MH42819-03
ALFONSO, PETER S07RR05596-27 0135
ALFONSO, PETER J P01DC00121-29A1 0007
ALFORD, CHARLES A, JR P01HD10699-15
ALFORD, PETER T S07RR05404-30 0831
ALFRED, LAWRENCE J S06GM08140-17 0001
ALGASE, DONNA L P50AG08671-03 0008
ALGER, BRADLEY E R01NS22010-07
ALGER, BRADLEY E R01NS30219-01
ALGER, ELIZABETH R25CA19536-13
ALI-OSMAN, FRANCIS R29CA46410-04
ALI, I U Z01NS02814-02
ALI, I U Z01NS02815-02
ALI, I U Z01NS02840-01
ALKADHI, KARIM A S07RR07147-19 0641
ALKANA, RONALD L R01AA03972-12
ALKEMINDERS, LOUIS C S07RR05406-30 0878
ALKON, D L Z01NS02151-17
ALLAIRE, JANET H S07RR05431-30 0838
ALLAN JONATHAN S U01AI26462-04 0006
ALLAN, ANDREA M R01AA08219-03
ALLAN, ANDREA M R01DA06106-03
ALLAN, JANET R29NR02568-01A1
ALLAN, JONATHAN P30AI28696-01 9004
ALLAN, JONATHAN S R01AI28273-03
ALLAN, MAGGI P50HL21006-15 9005
ALLAN, MAGGI R55HL37023-04
ALLANSMITH, MATHEA R R01EY02882-13
ALLARD, ELIZABETH S07RR05664-24 0856
ALLDREDGE, ELHAM-EID N01HO09007-02
ALLEGA, C Z01CM06513-15
ALLEN-HOFFMANN, B LYNN R29AR40284-02
ALLEN, ANTON N01AG02109-01
ALLEN, ANTON N01AG92118-02
ALLEN, ANTON N01ES05279-02
ALLEN, CHARLES N P01NS19611-08 0005
ALLEN, CHARLES N S07RR07238-04 0480
ALLEN, DAVID B S07RR05435-30 0981
ALLEN, DEBORAH E S07RR07016-18 0354
ALLEN, DON L S07RR05970-06
ALLEN, GEORGE M01RR00095-31 0284
ALLEN, J Z01DE00441-05
ALLEN, JAMES P R01GM41300-04
ALLEN, JAMES P S07RR07112-24 0420
ALLEN, JANE P01AI31596-01 0002
ALLEN, JERI L S07RR06012-03 0305
ALLEN, JERILYN K K07NR00044-01
ALLEN, JOHN J R19DA06445-03
ALLEN, JULIAN L R29HL41132-04
ALLEN, JULIUS C R01HL24585-10A1
ALLEN, JULIUS C R01HL34280-07
ALLEN, KENNETH G R01HL39759-03
ALLEN, LOIS B S07RR05676-15 0952
ALLEN, MARY M S15GM47083-01
ALLEN, MICHAEL P R44HL41423-02
ALLEN, PAUL P01AI31238-01 0002
ALLEN, PAUL M R01AI24157-05
ALLEN, PAUL M R01AI28716-03
ALLEN, PHILIP A R29AG09282-01A1
ALLEN, RHIANNON P50MH43878-03 0014
ALLEN, RICHARD D S07RR07026-26 0995
ALLEN, ROBERT C U10EY06824-05
ALLEN, ROBERT H R37DK21365-15
ALLEN, STEVEN J K08HL01999-05
ALLEN, SUSAN P50MH42459-06 0011
ALLEN, SUSAN S07RR05387-30 0607
ALLEN, SUSAN A R01CA50847-03
ALLEN, SUSAN ANN R01AI23980-04
ALLERAND, DOMINIQUE P50HD05077-21 0032
ALLEWELL, NORMA R37DK17335-19
ALLEY, M Z01CM07193-01
ALLFREY, VINCENT G R01CA14908-17
ALLINGER, NORMAN L R01RR02165-07
ALLIS, CHARLES D R01GM40922-04
ALLIS, CHARLES D R01HD16259-10
ALLISON-COOKE, SHERRY R01HS06271-03
ALLISON, JAMES P R01AI26942-04
ALLISON, JAMES P R37CA40041-08
ALLISON, STUART A R55GM46516-01
ALLISON, T M01RR00585-20 0548
ALLISON, WILLIAM S R01GM16974-22
ALLMAN, J S07RR07003-26 0320
ALLMAN, RICHARD M R01AG07178-04
ALLMAN, RICHARD M. N01HC48053-11
ALLNUTT, F C THOMAS N44DK12259-00
ALLNUTT, F C THOMAS R43RR07539-01
ALLOWAY, KEVIN S07RR05680-23 0920
ALLOWAY, KEVIN D R29NS29363-01
ALLOY, LAUREN B P50MH41684-07 0083
ALLOY, LAUREN B R01MH48216-02
ALLRED, CRAIG P30CA54174-01 9004
ALLSOP, KENT G S07RR07092-26 0538
ALMERS, WOLFHARD R01GM39520-04
ALMERS, WOLFHARD R37AR17803-18
ALMOND, G W S07RR05911-08 0643
ALOIA, JOHN F P01DK42618-02 0001
ALOIA, JOHN F R01AR37520-05
ALONSO, JOSE R P01CA19138-15 9001
ALONSO, JOSE R R01CA56932-01
ALOSACHIE, IYAD J R43NS29298-01
ALPER, CHESTER A P01HD17461-08 0002
ALPER, CHESTER A P01HL29583-09
ALPER, CHESTER A R01DK26844-10
ALPER, CHESTER A R37AI14157-20
ALPER, CHESTER A S07RR05626-25 0669
ALPER, CHESTER A S07RR05626-25
ALPER, CHESTER A. P01HL29583-09 0006
ALPER, RICHARD S07RR05373-30 0710
ALPER, ROBERT P01AR20553-15 9001
ALPER, SETH L P50DK39249-05 0005
ALPER, SETH L R01DK43495-01
ALPERN, MATHEW R01EY00197-34
ALPERN, ROBERT P01DK20543-15 0011
ALPERN, ROBERT J R01DK39298-04A1
ALPERS, DAVID H P01DK33487-05
ALPERS, DAVID H P01DK33487-05 0005
ALPERS, DAVID H R37DK14038-22
ALPERT, BRUCE S M01RR00211-27 0333
ALPERT, BRUCE S M01RR00211-27 0316
ALPERT, BRUCE S M01RR00211-27 0329
ALPERT, BRUCE S M01RR00211-27 0251
ALPERT, BRUCE S M01RR00211-27 0246
ALPERT, BRUCE S R01HL35788-07
ALPERT, MURRY P50MH35976-10 9001
ALPERT, NATHANIEL P50NS10828-16 0029
ALPERT, NORMAN R P01HL28001-10 0001
ALPERT, NORMAN R P01HL28001-10
ALPERT, NORMAN R R01HL39303-05
ALPERT, STEPHEN E K08HL02430-02
ALSTER, DAVID K S07RR05377-30 0765
ALT, FRED P30CA13696-19 9023
ALT, FREDERICK W P01CA23767-13 0006
ALT, FREDERICK W R37AI20047-09
ALT, FREDERICK W U01AI31541-01 0001
ALTER, BLANCHE P P60HL38655-04 0003
ALTER, BLANCHE P R01DK26956-10
ALTER, CAROL L S07RR05393-30 0879
ALTER, GEORGE C R01AG09331-02
ALTER, GERALD M S07RR05794-15 0899
ALTER, H J Z01CL02005-22
ALTER, H J Z01CL02036-08
ALTER, H J Z01CL02038-08
ALTER, H J Z01CL02040-07
ALTER, MILTON R01NS22188-06
ALTERGOTT, KAREN S07RR07032-26 0047
ALTERMAN, ARTHUR R01AA07361-03
ALTERMAN, ARTHUR R01DA05858-02
ALTERMAN, ARTHUR I P50DA05186-05 0002
ALTERMAN, ARTHUR I R01AA08480-02
ALTIERE, RALPH S07RR05831-12 0974
ALTIERE, RALPH J K04HL02356-03
ALTIERE, RALPH J R01HL42584-02
ALTIERI, DARIO C R01HL43773-02
ALTIERI, JAMES S07RR05677-23 0973
ALTMAN, AMNON R01AI28197-04
ALTMAN, DENNIS I K08NS01335-03
ALTMAN, LEONARD C P50DE08229-05 0005
ALTMAN, NORMAN P30CA14395-18A1 9014
ALTMAN, NORMAN P30CA14395-18A1 9021
ALTMAN, NORMAN DR N01CM17533-00
ALTMAN, NORMAN H P30CA14395-18A1
ALTMAN, NORMAN H P40RR04326-04
ALTMAN, NORMAN H R01CA42003-08
ALTMAN, ROY R18AR21393-17 0005
ALTMAN, ROY R18AR21393-17 0027
ALTMAN, SIDNEY R37GM19422-20
ALTMANN, MICHAEL P41RR01632-09 9008
ALTMANN, MICHAEL P41RR01632-09 0025
ALTMANN, MICHAEL P41RR01632-09 9014
ALTMANN, MICHAEL P41RR01632-09 9003
ALTMANN, MICHAEL P41RR01632-09 9010
ALTMANN, MICHAEL P41RR01632-09 9011
ALTMANN, MICHAEL P41RR01632-09 9012
ALTOSE, MURRAY D. N01HR46020-16
ALTSCHULD, RUTH A R01HL36240-06
ALTSCHULER, MARSHA I R01HG00350-04
ALTSCHULER, MITCHELL S07RR07176-14 0531
ALTSCHULER, RICHARD A P01DC00274-08 0005
ALTSCHULER, RICHARD A P01DC00078-27 0038
ALTSCHULER, RICHARD A R01AG08885-02
ALTSCHULER, RICHARD A R01DC00383-05
ALTSCHULER, STEVEN M K08DK01747-05
ALTSHULER, BERNARD P30CA13343-18 9004
ALTURA, BURTON M R01AA08674-02
ALVARADO, JORGE A R01EY02068-14
ALVARADO, JORGE A R01EY08835-01
ALVARES, FREDERICK S06GM02721-07 0001
ALVAREZ-BUYLLA, ARTURO R29NS28478-02
ALVAREZ-GONZALEZ, RA S07RR05879-09 0598
ALVAREZ-LEEFMANS, FRANCISCO J R01NS29227-0
ALVAREZ, ROBERT E R43CA55430-01
ALVERSON, DALE C M01RR00997-16 0404
ALVERSON, DALE C M01RR00997-16 0347
ALVES, W P50NS10939-18A1S1 9003
ALVORD, LYNN S S07RR07092-26 0516
ALWARD, WALLACE L M U10EY08612-02
ALWIN, DUANE F R55AG04743-05A2
ALWINE, JAMES C R01CA28379-11
ALWINE, JAMES C R01GM45773-01
ALYONO, DAVID S07RR05359-30 0501
ALZERRECA, ARNALDO S06GM08159-13 0001
AMABILE, TERESA M R01MH44999-02
AMACHER, RICHARD N01CN05275-01
AMACHER, RICHARD N01CN95182-02
AMACHER, RICHARD N01LM83527-11
AMALFITANO, JOSEPH K15DE00322-01
AMAN, MICHAEL G R01MH44122-03
AMANN, RUPERT P R01HD14501-10A1
AMARA, SUSAN G R01GM42490-03
AMARAL, DAVID G R01NS16980-12
AMARAL, DAVID G R37MH41479-06
AMATRUDA, JOHN M M01RR00044-31 0357
AMATRUDA, JOHN M R01DK20948-13
AMATRUDA, JOHN M R01DK40816-03
AMBINDER, RICHARD F R01CA50131-03
AMBINDER, RICHARD F R01CA55529-01
AMBRE, JOHN J. M01RR00048-30 0119
AMBRON, RICHARD T R01NS22150-05
AMBRON, RICHARD T R01NS26638-02
AMBROS, VICTOR R R01GM34028-08
AMBROSINI, PAUL P50MH41684-07 0036
AMBROSINI, PAUL J P50MH41684-07 0080
AMBROSINO, DONNA M R01AI29623-01A1
AMBROSINO, DONNA M S07RR05526-29 0078
AMBRUS, CLARA M R43DK44394-01
AMBRUS, CLARA M R43HL47662-01
AMBRUS, JULIAN L S07RR05491-29 0452
AMBRUSO, DANIEL R K07HL02036-02
AMBRUSO, DANIEL R M01RR00069-29 0160
AMBRUSO, DANIEL R M01RR00069-29 0371
AMBRUSO, R DANIEL M01RR00069-29 0164
AMBUDKAR, I S Z01DE00438-04
AMDUR, MARY O P01ES02429-11
AMDUR, MARY O P01ES02429-11 0001
AMED, S A S07RR07095-24 0381
AMENTA, PETER S07RR05576-27 0616
AMER, HAROLD S07RR05468-29 0404
AMERO, SALLY A S07RR05431-30 0853
AMES, BRUCE N P30ES01896-13 9023
AMES, BRUCE N P30ES01896-13 9034
AMES, BRUCE N P30ES01896-13 9035
AMES, BRUCE N P30ES01896-13 9015
AMES, BRUCE N P30ES01896-13 9016
AMES, BRUCE N P30ES01896-13 9017
AMES, BRUCE N P30ES01896-13 9018
AMES, BRUCE N P30ES01896-13 9019
AMES, BRUCE N P30ES01896-13 9020
AMES, BRUCE N P30ES01896-13 9021
AMES, BRUCE N P30ES01896-13 9022
AMES, BRUCE N P30ES01896-13
AMES, BRUCE N P30ES01896-13 9014
AMES, BRUCE N R35CA39910-07
AMES, GENEVIEVE M P50AA06282-09 0004
AMES, GENEVIEVE M R01AA08989-01
AMES, GIOVANNA F R01DK43747-01
AMES, GIOVANNA F R01GM39415-02
AMES, GIOVANNA F R37DK12121-24
AMES, MATTHEW P30CA15083-18 9001

AMES, MATTHEW M N01CM97618-02
AMES, MATTHEW M P30CA15083-18 9004
AMES, MATTHEW M P30CA15083-18 0001
AMICO, JANET A M01RR00056-30 0352
AMIDON, GORDON L R01GM37188-06
AMIEL, DANIEL P01AG07996-03 9002
AMIEL, DAVID R01AR38159-03
AMINI-SERESHKI, LATIFEH R01NS20794-07
AMLANER, CHARLES S07RR07101-13 0554
AMMONS, WILLIAM S R01HL36378-06A2
AMORE, BENNY S07RR05635-18 0778
AMOS S07RR05380-30 0896
AMOS S07RR05380-30 0985
AMOS, JIM R R19MH46191-03
AMOSS, MAX S P01CA49488-01A2 9001
AMOSS, MAX S P01CA49488-01A2
AMOSS, MAX S P01CA49488-01A2 0003
AMSEL, ABRAM R01AA07052-05
AMSEL, ABRAM S15AA09255-01
AMSTERDAM, EZRA A K07HL01942-03
AMSTERDAM, JAY D M01RR00040-31 0312
AMTHOR, FRANKLIN R R01EY05070-08
AMZEL, L MARIO R01GM45540-01A1
AN, KAI-NAN R01AR26287-12
ANALYSIS & SIMULATION, INC N01AA10010-00
ANAND, RAJIV S07RR05426-30 0127
ANANTHAN, SUBRAMANIA S07RR05676-15 0969
ANANTHAN, SUBRAMANIAM R29DA06244-02
ANANTHASWAMY, HONNAVARA N R01CA51015-02
ANASETTI, CLAUDIO P01AI29518-02 0005
ANASETTI, CLAUDIO P01HL36444-11 0009
ANASTOPOULOS, ARTHUR S07RR05712-20 0043
ANATHAN, SUBRAMANIAM S07RR05676-15 0968
ANBAR, RAN D S07RR05506-29 0905
ANCOLI-ISRAEL, SONIA R01AG02711-13
ANCOLI-ISRAEL, SONIA R01AG08415-03
ANDELMAN, JULIAN B S07RR05451-30 0360
ANDERS, DAVID G R29AI31249-01
ANDERS, M W P30ES01247-17 0100
ANDERS, MARION W R01ES05407-02
ANDERS, MARION W R37ES03127-10
ANDERS, THOMAS F S07RR06033-02 0527
ANDERS, THOMAS F S07RR06033-02
ANDERSEN, DANA K R01DK39950-03
ANDERSEN, JANET S07RR05736-19 0213
ANDERSEN, MARCIA D U01DA06903-02
ANDERSEN, NANCY P50MH43271-05 9002
ANDERSEN, OLAF S R01GM21342-18
ANDERSEN, OLAF S R01GM40062-04
ANDERSEN, PHILIP R R44AI27605-03
ANDERSEN, RICHARD A R01EY05522-12
ANDERSEN, RICHARD A R01EY07492-05
ANDERSEN, RONALD M R01HS07084-01
ANDERSON, KARL E. M01RR00073-29 0265
ANDERSON, MARJORIE E. P51RR00166-30 0075
ANDERSON, PHILIP R13RR06755-01
ANDERSON, ALBERT F P30HD10003-16 9001
ANDERSON, AMEL S03RR03063-10
ANDERSON, BARBARA A P30HD10003-16
ANDERSON, BARBARA A R01HD19915-09
ANDERSON, BRADLEY D N01CM97585-02
ANDERSON, CAROLE A S07RR05944-04
ANDERSON, CAROLE A S15AG10563-01
ANDERSON, CHARLES B R01DK27895-09
ANDERSON, CLARK L R01CA44983-06
ANDERSON, CLARK L R01HL46652-01
ANDERSON, D E Z01AG00600-03
ANDERSON, D E Z01AG00604-03
ANDERSON, D E Z01AG00605-03
ANDERSON, DAN R19MH46178-03
ANDERSON, DANIEL C P51RR00165-31 0105
ANDERSON, DANIEL C P51RR00165-31 0200
ANDERSON, DANIEL R S07RR07048-26 0627
ANDERSON, DAVID C R01DA07428-01
ANDERSON, DAVID E R01CA29614-09
ANDERSON, DAVID J R01NS23476-06
ANDERSON, DEBRA F R01HL42893-02
ANDERSON, DONALD C P01HL42550-02 0002
ANDERSON, DONALD C R01AI23521-05
ANDERSON, DONALD C R37AI19031-10
ANDERSON, DONALD D S07RR05801-13 0446
ANDERSON, DOUGLAS R R01EY00031-20S1
ANDERSON, DWIGHT L R01DE08515-05
ANDERSON, DWIGHT L R01GM39931-04
ANDERSON, DWIGHT L R37DE03606-22
ANDERSON, ERLING A M01RR00059-30 0700
ANDERSON, ERLING A R29HL43514-02
ANDERSON, EVERETT P30HD06645-20 9004
ANDERSON, EVERETT P30HD06645-20 9005
ANDERSON, EVERETT R01HD14574-12
ANDERSON, GARTH R R01CA48828-02
ANDERSON, GENE C R01NR02444-01
ANDERSON, GERARD F R01HS07085-01
ANDERSON, GREGORY J R29DK40935-03
ANDERSON, H VERNON S07RR05745-19 0252
ANDERSON, HARRISON C R01DE05262-12
ANDERSON, HENRY A R01CA46883-04
ANDERSON, JAMES H R01CA36920-06
ANDERSON, JAMES H R01CA37870-06
ANDERSON, JAMES M R01HL33849-07
ANDERSON, JAMES M R01HL47300-01
ANDERSON, JAMES W P01HL36552-07 0009
ANDERSON, JOHN P01AI30548-01A1 9004
ANDERSON, JOHN E R01GM44473-02
ANDERSON, JOHN H P50DC00110-17 0020
ANDERSON, JOHN J B S07RR05450-30 0331
ANDERSON, JOHN N R01GM41708-03
ANDERSON, JOHN R K05MH00788-03
ANDERSON, JOHN R R01AI20245-09
ANDERSON, JOHN S S07RR07052-26 0151
ANDERSON, KAREN O S07RR05712-20 0044
ANDERSON, KAREN S R01GM45343-01A1
ANDERSON, KARL E M01RR00073-29 0282
ANDERSON, KARL E. M01RR00073-29 0281
ANDERSON, KATHRYN V R01GM35437-07
ANDERSON, KELLEY P R29HL40333-04
ANDERSON, KENNETH C R01CA50947-01A1
ANDERSON, KEVIN J R29AG08843-01A1
ANDERSON, L M Z01CP05352-09
ANDERSON, L M Z01CP05353-09
ANDERSON, LARRY D S07RR05896-09 0622
ANDERSON, LEE C S07RR05346-30 0322
ANDERSON, LEIGH C R01DE09065-03
ANDERSON, LEON JR S03RR03397-08
ANDERSON, M C Z01BA01001-10
ANDERSON, M C Z01BA01002-15
ANDERSON, M C Z01BA01003-06
ANDERSON, M C Z01BA01004-04
ANDERSON, M C Z01BA01005-02
ANDERSON, M C Z01BA01006-04
ANDERSON, M C Z01BA01019-01
ANDERSON, M C Z01BA01020-01
ANDERSON, M C Z01BA01021-01
ANDERSON, M W Z01ES35005-12
ANDERSON, MARJORIE E R01NS15017-12A1
ANDERSON, MARJORIE E. P51RR00166-30 0076
ANDERSON, MARK R S07RR07095-24 0376
ANDERSON, MARY E R29AI31804-01
ANDERSON, MARY E S07RR05396-30 0729
ANDERSON, NORMAN B M01RR00030-30 0464
ANDERSON, NORMAN B M01RR00030-30 0499
ANDERSON, NORMAN B M01RR00030-30 0467
ANDERSON, NORMAN B R01HL42660-03
ANDERSON, NORMAN G R43HG00440-01
ANDERSON, NORMAN G R44AI29285-02
ANDERSON, OREN S07RR07127-23 0494
ANDERSON, PAGE A R01HL20749-12
ANDERSON, PAGE A R01HL42250-04
ANDERSON, PAUL J R01CA53595-01
ANDERSON, PAUL M R01GM33842-06
ANDERSON, PAUL M R01NS27229-03
ANDERSON, PETER G R29HL40702-03
ANDERSON, PETER M R29CA53517-01
ANDERSON, PORTER N01AI05059-01
ANDERSON, PORTER W R01AI17938-11
ANDERSON, R V Z01HL05010-02
ANDERSON, RICHARD S07RR05656-24 0837
ANDERSON, RICHARD A R29GM38906-05
ANDERSON, RICHARD G P01HL20948-15 9002
ANDERSON, RICHARD G R01GM43169-02
ANDERSON, ROBERT P41RR01315-10 0037
ANDERSON, ROBERT A, JR R01AA06604-07
ANDERSON, ROBERT E R01EY00871-20
ANDERSON, ROBERT E R01EY04149-10
ANDERSON, ROBERT J S07RR05390-30 0653
ANDERSON, ROBERT J S07RR05390-30 0671
ANDERSON, ROBERT P R01GM30132-09
ANDERSON, ROBERT P R01GM41807-03
ANDERSON, RUSSELL D K08CA01616-01
ANDERSON, SALLY R19MH46200-03
ANDERSON, SHARON P01DK40839-03 0006
ANDERSON, SONIA R R01DK13912-18S1
ANDERSON, STEPHEN R01AG10462-01
ANDERSON, STEVEN M R29CA45241-05
ANDERSON, THOMAS M01RR00058-30 0253
ANDERSON, THOMAS N43ES11004-00
ANDERSON, THOMAS R N43DK12277-00
ANDERSON, THOMAS R N43DK12278-00
ANDERSON, TRUDY B R29AG08134-04
ANDERSON, V ELVING P50NS16308-12A1 0009
ANDERSON, VERNON E R01GM36562-06
ANDERSON, VERNON E S07RR07085-26 0331
ANDERSON, W B Z01CB08905-10
ANDERSON, W F Z01HL02216-12
ANDERSON, WAYNE F P01DK42502-02 0005
ANDERSON, WAYNE F S07RR05424-30 0069
ANDERSON, WAYNE K N01CM17569-00
ANDERSON, WAYNE K R01CA54507-01
ANDERSON, WAYNE K S15CA55948-01
ANDERSON, WILLIAM L S06GM08139-17 0068
ANDERSON, WINSTON A S06GM08016-21 0072
ANDERTON, DOUGLAS L S07RR07048-26 0628
ANDIMAN, WARREN A M01RR06022-02 0763
ANDIMAN, WARREN A R01AI32397-01
ANDIMAN, WARREN A R01DA05899-02
ANDORN, ANNE P50MH41684-07 0038
ANDRADE, JOSEPH D R01HL44538-02
ANDRADE, RODRIGO R29MH43985-04
ANDRADE, Z P01AI16305-13 0009
ANDRAGNA-LAUF, NORMA S07RR05794-15 0898
ANDRAKO, JOHN U76PE00235-01
ANDREASEN, N P01MH47200-02 0008
ANDREASEN, NANCY C K05MH00625-06
ANDREASEN, NANCY C P50MH43271-05 0002
ANDREASEN, NANCY C P50MH43271-05
ANDREASEN, NANCY C R01MH40856-06
ANDREEFF, MICHAEL P01CA20194-14 0021
ANDREOLI, ANTHONY J S06GM08101-20
ANDREOLI, ANTHONY J S06GM08101-20 0004
ANDRES, GIUSEPPE A R01DK36807-21
ANDRES, R Z01AG00218-01
ANDRES, ROBERT L S07RR05745-19 0258
ANDRESEN, MICHAEL C R01HL41119-01A1
ANDREW, E RAYMOND P41RR02278-06A1 9003
ANDREW, RICHARD N L S07RR05450-30 0349
ANDREWS, ROBERT G. P51RR00166-30 0077
ANDREWS, B S Z01NS02836-02
ANDREWS, DAVID W K11CA01514-02
ANDREWS, EDWIN J S07RR05464-29
ANDREWS, FRANK M R01HD21240-05
ANDREWS, FRANK M S07RR05845-11 0555
ANDREWS, GLEN K R01ES05704-01
ANDREWS, GLEN K R55ES04725-04A1
ANDREWS, JAMES P60DC01404-01 0005
ANDREWS, JAMES C R29DC00945-01
ANDREWS, JOHN H S07RR07098-26 0339
ANDREWS, LES S07RR05449-30 0318
ANDREWS, MATTHEW T R29HD24673-03
ANDREWS, NORMA W R29AI27260-04
ANDREWS, NORMA W S07RR05358-30 0489
ANDREWS, PETER W R01AI24943-04
ANDREWS, PETER W R01CA29894-10
ANDREWS, RICHARD V S07RR05390-30 0685
ANDREWS, ROBERT P01CA47748-03 0005
ANDREWS, ROBERT G N01AI85003-03
ANDREWS, S B Z01NS02610-08
ANDREWS, WALTER M01RR00633-19 0364
ANDREWS, WALTER S M01RR00633-19 0391
ANDREWS, WALTER S M01RR00633-19 0421
ANDREWS, WILLIAM M01RR00059-30 0737
ANDRIACCHI, THOMAS P50AR39239-05 0005
ANDRIACCHI, THOMAS P R01AR20702-13
ANDRIACCHI, THOMAS P R01AR39421-04
ANDROPHY, ELLIOT E P01CA24530-12 0010
ANDROPHY, ELLIOT J R01CA44174-05
ANDRYKOWSKI, MICHAEL S07RR05374-30 0739
ANDRYKOWSKI, MICHAEL A R01CA49431-02
ANESHANSLEY, DANIEL S07RR07061-26 0188
ANFINSEN, C B S07RR07041-26 0390
ANGELAKOS, E T S15AG10238-01
ANGELAKOS, EVANGELOS T S07RR07241-04
ANGELETTI, RUTH H R55NS22697-07
ANGELETTI, RUTH H S10RR06527-01
ANGELIDES, K S07RR05362-30 0804
ANGELIDES, KIMON J K04NS01218-05
ANGELIDES, KIMON J R01NS26733-02
ANGELIDES, KIMON J R01NS28072-02
ANGELL, WILLIAM W M01RR00833-17 0177
ANGELLO, DEBRA A S07RR05431-30 0854
ANGELO, JENNIFER K S07RR07066-26 0231
ANGERER, ROBERT C R01GM25553-13
ANGLE, CAROL R R01ES04762-02
ANGLE, MARCIA S07RR05406-30 0904
ANGLE, STEVEN R R01GM39354-04
ANGLIN, DOUGLAS S07RR05756-18 0314
ANGLIN, DOUGLAS S07RR05756-18 0299
ANGLIN, M DOUGLAS K02DA00146-02
ANGLIN, M DOUGLAS P50DA07699-01
ANGLIN, M DOUGLAS R01DA04268-04S1
ANGLIN, M DOUGLAS R01DA05589-04
ANGLIN, M DOUGLAS R18DA06250-03
ANGOLD, ADRIAN R01MH46323-03
ANGUS, C W Z01CL00082-02
ANGUS, C W Z01CL00083-02
ANHALT, GRANT J K04AR01686-05
ANHALT, GRANT J R01AR32490-09
ANHALT, GRANT J R01AR40018-01A2
ANHOLM, JAMES S07RR05352-30 0745
ANHOLT, ROBERT P50AG05128-08 0013
ANHOLT, ROBERT R R29DC00394-06
ANISFELD, ELIZABETH M01RR00645-20 0479
ANISFELD, ELIZABETH R29HD25126-04
ANJO, DENNIS M S06GM08238-05 0009
ANKEL, HELMUT K R01AI23450-05
ANKLESARIA, PERVIN S07RR05712-20 0077
ANN, DAVID K K04DE00292-02
ANN, DAVID K R29DE09175-03
ANNUNZIATO, ANTHONY T R01GM35837-05
ANSARI, AFTAB A M01RR00722-19 0242
ANSARI, AFTAB A P51RR00165-31 0195
ANSARI, AFTAB A P51RR00165-31 0107
ANSARI, AFTAB A P51RR00165-31 0204
ANSARI, AFTAB A P51RR00165-31 0205
ANSARI, AFTAB A P51RR00165-31 0206
ANSARI, AFTAB A P51RR00165-31 0207
ANSARI, AFTAB A P51RR00165-31 0208
ANSARI, AFTAB A P51RR00165-31 0196
ANSARI, AFTAB A R01AI25372-04
ANSARI, AFTAB A R01AI27057-04
ANSARI, AFTAB A R01HL47272-04
ANSARI, GHULAM A S R01OH02149-06
ANSARI, NASEEM H R29EY08547-01A1
ANSARI, NASEEM H S07RR05427-30 0157
ANSEL, JOHN C R01AR40678-01
ANSHER, S Z01BA03004-02
ANSHER, S Z01BA03005-02

ANTCZAK, DOUGLAS F R01HD15799-08
ANTELMAN, SEYMOUR P50AA08746-02 0001
ANTELMAN, SEYMOUR M R01MH24114-14
ANTHONISEN, NICHOLAS R. N01HR46017-18
ANTHONY, BASCOM F M01RR00425-22S3 0468
ANTHONY, CATHERINE T S07RR05424-30 0111
ANTHONY, DONNA T S07RR05650-25 0091
ANTHONY, DOUGLAS C K08NS01208-05
ANTHONY, DOUGLAS C R01ES05261-02
ANTHONY, JAMES C R01DA03992-04
ANTHONY, JAMES C R01DA04392-04
ANTHONY, LOWELL M01RR00095-31 0379
ANTHONY, MARY S P01HL45666-01 9006
ANTHONY, MARY S P50HL14164-20 9008
ANTICH, PETER P M01RR00633-19 0410
ANTIN, JOSEPH M01RR02635-07 0194
ANTIN, JOSEPH M01RR02635-07 0239
ANTIN, JOSEPH M01RR02635-07 0242
ANTIN, JOSEPH M01RR02635-07 0294
ANTIN, JOSEPH P01CA39542-07 9001
ANTMAN, KAREN P01CA38493-06S1 0001
ANTMAN, KAREN H P01CA38493-06S1 0006
ANTON, PETER A K11DK01879-03
ANTONARAKIS, STYLIANOS E P01HD24605-03 000
ANTONARAKIS, STYLIANOS E P01HG00373-04 000
ANTONARAKIS, STYLIANOS E R01HL38165-05
ANTONIADES, HARRY N P01HL29583-09 0002
ANTONIADES, HARRY N R01CA30101-09A1
ANTONIAN, LIDA S07RR05396-30 0772
ANTONUCCI, J P50DE09322-03 0002
ANTONUCCI, TONI C R01MH46549-01A1
ANTONUK, LARRY E R01CA51397-02
ANTONY, ASOK C R01AA08307-03
ANTONY, VEENA B R01AA08285-03
ANTONY, VEENA B R01HL44281-02
ANTZELEVITCH, CHARLES R01HL37396-05
ANUSAVICE, K P50DE09307-03 0004
ANUSAVICE, KENNETH J P50DE09307-03
ANUSAVICE, KENNETH J R01DE06672-09
ANVERSA, PIERO R01HL38132-05
ANVERSA, PIERO R01HL39902-03
ANVERSA, PIERO R01HL40561-03
ANVIA, FREDERICK R43GM46163-01
ANWER, MOHAMMED S R01DK33436-09
ANZANO, M A Z01CP05661-01
AOBA, TAKAAKI R01DE07623-06
AOBA, TAKAAKI R01DE08670-04
AOKI, CHIYE J R29EY08055-04
AOTIGLER, JOHN F M01RR02172-09 0175
APFEL, ROBERT E R01CA39374-06
APFEL, STUART C R01ES05752-01
APGAR, JOHN R R01GM42388-02
APICELLA, MICHAEL A R01AI18384-10
APICELLA, MICHAEL A R01AI24616-04
APICELLA, MICHAEL A R13AI31108-01
APKARIAN, A VANIA S07RR05402-30 0791
APKARIAN, ROBERT P51RR00165-31 9020
APONTE, GREGORY W R01DK38310-05
APOSHIAN, H V P42ES04940-02 0006
APOSHIAN, H VASKEN R01ES03356-08
APPEL, JAMES B R01DA02543-18
APPEL, JAMES B S07RR07160-16 0593
APPEL, MICHAEL C P30DK32520-08 9003
APPEL, MICHAEL C R01DK41090-03
APPEL, N Z01BB07006-01
APPEL, STANLEY H P50AG08664-03
APPELBAUM, FREDERICK P01CA44991-04 0003
APPELBAUM, FREDERICK R P01HL36444-11 0001
APPELBAUM, FREDERICK R R01CA18105-16
APPELLA, E Z01CB03229-23
APPENZELLER, OTTO M01RR00997-16 0248
APPENZELLER, OTTO M01RR00997-16 0135
APPERT, HUBERT E R01GM42647-01A3
APPERT, HUBERT E S07RR05700-22 0877
APPERT, HUBERT E S07RR05700-22 0861
APPLE, RIMA D R01LM05279-01
APPLE, THOMAS M R01GM40705-02
APPLEBAUM-BOWDEN, DE S07RR05404-30 0832
APPLEBAUM, FREDERICK P01CA18029-16 0035
APPLEBAUM, FREDERICK P01CA47748-03 0002
APPLEBAUM, FREDERICK P01CA47748-03 0003
APPLEBURY, MEREDITHE L R01EY04801-11
APPLEGATE, CRAIG D R29NS26865-04
APPLEGATE, DIANNE S07RR05653-24 0801
APPLEGATE, DIANNE E R29DK40154-04
APPLEGATE, MICHAEL E R35AG07914-03 0004
APPLEGATE, RAYMOND A R01EY08520-01A1
APPLEGATE, ROBERT J S07RR05404-30 0833
APPLEGATE, WILLIAM P60AG10484-01 0002
APPLEGATE, WILLIAM P60AG10484-01 0003
APPLEGATE, WILLIAM B U01HL37849-06
APPLEGATE, WILLIAM B U01HL44298-02
APPLEGATE, WILLIAM B. N01HC48067-11
APPLEMAN, JAMES R R29GM45367-01
APPLEQUIST, JON B R01GM13684-24
APPLETON, JUDITH A R01AI14490-13
APPLING, DEAN R K04DK01988-02
APPLING, DEAN R R01DK36913-05
APRILLE, JUNE R R01HD16936-08
APRISON, MORRIS H S07RR05371-30 0629
APSTEIN, CARL P01HL38189-04 0001
AQUADRO, CHARLES F R01GM36431-06
AQUAYO, SAMUEL M S07RR05357-30 0463
AQUILINO, WILLIAM S R01DA06614-02
AQUINO, DENNIS A P01NS23705-04A1 0006
ARAFAH, BAHA M M01RR00080-29 0560
ARAFAH, BAHA M M01RR00080-29 0373
ARAFAH, BAHA M M01RR00080-29 0337
ARAFAH, BAHA M M01RR00080-29 0340
ARAFAT, EL SAYED S14GM02866-07 0002
ARAFAT, ELSAYED S S14GM02866-07
ARAKAKI, RICHARD F K08DK02012-02
ARAKERE, G Z01BA02003-03
ARAKERE, G Z01BA02021-01
ARAM, CHOBANIAN S07RR05380-30
ARAM, DOROTHY M R01NS17366-11
ARAMANT, ROBERT B R01EY08519-01A1
ARANGO, VICTORIA P50MH46745-02 9004
ARANGO, VICTORIA R01AA09004-01
ARANT, BILLY S, JR R01DK32910-08
ARANYI, CATHERINE N01ES65132-13
ARANYI, CATHERINE N01ES65143-21
ARANYI, CATHERINE N01ES95266-12
ARASKIEWICZ, P S07RR05830-12 0964
ARATHUZIK, MARY D S07RR07199-12 0940
ARAUJO, FAUSTO U01AI30230-02 9001
ARBEIT, LAWRENCE S07RR05736-19 0168
ARBIB, MICHAEL A R01NS24926-06
ARCARI, RALPH N01LM13508-00
ARCE, RAFAEL S06GM08102-20 0034
ARCECI, ROBERT J R29GM38156-05
ARCECI, ROBERT J S07RR05526-29 0079
ARCH, STEPHEN W R01NS11149-17
ARCHBALD, LOUIS F S03RR03340-09
ARCHBOLD, PATRICIA G R01NR02088-02
ARCHER, GORDON L R01AI21772-06
ARCHER, PHILIP G P30CA46934-04 9001
ARCHER, STEPHEN L R29HL45735-01A1
ARCHER, SYDNEY R01DA01674-15
ARCHER, SYDNEY R01DA06786-02
ARCHIBALD, DAVID S07RR05317-21 0747
ARCHIBOLD, ERROL R S06GM45199-02 0001
ARCORIA, C J S07RR05915-08 0684
ARCORIA, C J S07RR05915-08 0668
ARD, MARCH D S07RR05386-30 0573
ARDMAN, BLAIR R01AI27729-03
ARDOIN, ROBIN K16DE00199-05S1 0001
ARENAZ, PABLO S06GM08012-21 0013
AREND, WILLIAM P R01AR39950-02
AREND, WILLIAM P R01AR40135-02
ARENSON, RONALD L R01HL33332-06
ARES, MANUEL K04GM00546-03
ARES, MANUEL R01GM40478-04
AREZZO, JOSEPH C P30HD01799-27 9009
AREZZO, JOSEPH C R01MH06723-29
ARGON, JUDITH K S15GM47043-01
ARGON, JUDITH K S15MH49290-01
ARGON, YAIR R01AI30178-02
ARGRAVES, W SCOTT R01GM42912-02
ARGUETA, R M01RR00585-20 0530
ARI, SITARAMAYYA R01EY07158-05
ARIAGNO, RONALD L M01RR00081-29 0087
ARIAGNO, RONALD L M01RR00081-29 0146
ARIAGNO, RONALD L M01RR00081-29 0139
ARIAGNO, RONALD L M01RR00081-29 0002
ARIAGNO, RONALD L R01HD24315-02
ARIANGO, RONALD L. M01RR00081-29 0121
ARIANO, MARJORIE A R01NS23079-06
ARIAS, IRWIN M R37DK35652-07
ARIEFF, ALLEN I R01AG08575-01A2
ARIEL, MICHAEL K02MH00815-03
ARIEL, MICHAEL R01EY05978-07
ARIMURA, AKIRA A R01DK09094-24A2
ARKIN, STEVEN M01RR00071-28A1 0205
ARKING, ROBERT S07RR07051-26 0728
ARKOWITZ, HAROLD S S07RR07002-26 0879
ARLIAN, LARRY G R01AI17252-07A3
ARLIAN, LARRY G S07RR07155-14
ARLINGHAUS, HEINRICH F R43CA54627-01
ARLINGHAUS, HEINRICH F R43HG00532-01
ARLINGHAUS, RALPH B P01CA49639-02 0003
ARLINGHAUS, RALPH B R01AI29308-02
ARLINGHAUS, RALPH B R01CA45125-05
ARLINGHAUS, RALPH B R01CA45217-05
ARMANT, DAVID R R01HD25795-02
ARMBRECHT, HARVEY J S07RR05388-30 0621
ARMITAGE, GARY C P01DE07946-05 0003
ARMITAGE, IAN M. P01GM40660-03 0003
ARMITAGE, JAMES P30CA36727-08 9009
ARMOUR, ELWOOD P R01CA53167-01
ARMSDEN, GAY S07RR05758-18 0242
ARMSTEAD, WILLIAM M R29HL42939-03
ARMSTRONG, BRENDA E P60HL28391-09 0003
ARMSTRONG, CLAY M R01NS12547-16
ARMSTRONG, D Z01ES80044-03
ARMSTRONG, D L Z01ES80043-04
ARMSTRONG, DANIEL W R01GM36292-05A2
ARMSTRONG, DAVID L P41RR01395-10 0001
ARMSTRONG, DAVID M R01AG08206-05
ARMSTRONG, DAWNA L P01HD24234-04 0006
ARMSTRONG, DEBORAH L S07RR07217-08 0166
ARMSTRONG, DONALD U01AI26056-05S1
ARMSTRONG, DONALD U01AI27669-05S2
ARMSTRONG, G R Z01BF01015-08
ARMSTRONG, MARK L P50HL14230-20 0094
ARMSTRONG, R DOUGLAS R29CA46550-06
ARMSTRONG, R WARWICK R01CA46567-02
ARMSTRONG, RICHARD N R01GM30910-10
ARMSTRONG, ROBERT D R01AA08967-02
ARMSTRONG, ROBERT W R29GM39512-04
ARMSTRONG, SANDRA K R29AI31088-01
ARMSTRONG, SANDRA K S07RR05812-12 0480
ARMSTRONG, WILLIAM E R01NS23941-06
ARMSTRONG, WILLIAM H R29GM38275-05
ARMSTRONG, WILLIAM M R01DK12715-22
ARNAOUT, AMIN P01AI28465-03
ARNAOUT, AMIN P01AI28465-03 0001
ARNAOUT, M AMIN R01AI21964-06
ARNAOUT, M AMIN R01DK42722-02
ARNASON, BARRY G W P01NS24575-04
ARNASON, BARRY G W P01NS24575-04 0001
ARNASON, BARRY G W P01NS24575-04 9001
ARNAUD, CLAUDE D R01DK21614-14
ARNDT, KIM T R01GM39892-04
ARNDT, KIM T R01GM45179-01
ARNETT, CAROL P50AG05136-08 0010
ARNHEIM, NORMAN R01GM36745-06
ARNHEIM, NORMAN R01HG00328-03
ARNHEITER, H Z01NS02742-05
ARNHEITER, H Z01NS02790-03
ARNOLD, ARTHUR P R01DC00217-08
ARNOLD, ARTHUR P R01HD15021-11
ARNOLD, BILL R S06GM08038-21 0007
ARNOLD, EDWARD R01AI27690-03
ARNOLD, EDWARD U01AI30238-02 0003
ARNOLD, JOHN S07RR07006-26 0914
ARNOLD, LUCY W K08HL02395-02
ARNOLD, MARK A R13RR07557-01
ARNOLD, R G P42ES04940-02 0011
ARNOLD, ROLAND R P01DE08917-02 9001
ARNOLD, ROLAND R R01DE06869-08
ARNOLD, ROLAND R S07RR05308-30 0240
ARNOLD, ROLAND R S07RR05333-30
ARNOLD, ROLAND R S15AR41227-01
ARNONE, ARTHUR R01GM40852-17
ARNOS, KATHLEEN S R03DC01338-01
ARNSDORF, MORTON F R37HL21788-12
ARNSTEIN, P Z01CP04930-20
ARNSTEN, AMY F R01AG06036-06
ARON, DAVID C R01DK41527-02
ARONSON, ARTHUR I R01GM34035-06A1
ARONSON, NATHAN N, JR R01DK33314-08A1
ARONSON, PETER S P01DK17433-18 0015
ARONSON, PETER S R01DK33793-08
ARONSON, RONALD S P01HL37412-04 0002
ARONSON, RONALD S R01HL32688-07
ARONSTAM, ROBERT S R55GM46408-01
ARORA, RAMESH P50MH41684-07 0035
ARORA, SANJEEV M01RR00054-30 0382
ARORA, SATISH K R01GM32690-08
ARQUILLA, EDWARD R S07RR05351-30 0030
ARRIGHI, J A Z01HL04874-01
ARRIGHI, J A Z01HL04875-01
ARRUDA, JOSE A R01DK36253-08
ARSLANIAN, SILVA M01RR00084-29 0228
ARSLANIAN, SILVA M01RR00084-29 0237
ARSLANIAN, SILVA R29HD27503-01
ART, JONATHAN J R01DC00454-04
ARTAVANIS-TSAKONAS, SPYRIDON R01GM29093-11
ARTAVANIS-TSAKONAS, SPYRIDON R01NS26084-04
ARTAVANIS-TSAKONAS, SPYRIDON P01GM39813-04
ARTAVANIS-TSAKONAS, SPYROS P01HG00365-04 0
ARTECA, RICHARD N S07RR07082-26 0271
ARTUN, JON S07RR05346-30 0311
ARTZ, STANLEY W R01GM27307-10A1
ARTZT, KAREN R01CA21651-15
ARTZT, KAREN R01HD10668-16
ARVAN, PETER R29DK40344-04
ARVIN, ANN M P01CA49605-03 0008
ARVIN, ANN M R01AI20459-09
ARVIN, ANN M R01AI22280-07
ARY, DENNIS V R01DA07389-01
ARYA, S Z01CP05539-05
ARZBAECHER, ROBERT S15HL47745-01
ARZBAECHER, ROBERT C R01HL32131-06
ARZBAECHER, ROBERT C R01HL35554-06
ASAL, NABIH R R01OH02391-03
ASANUMA, HIROSHI R01NS10705-19
ASARNOW, JOAN P01MH46981-01A1 0003
ASARNOW, ROBERT P01MH46981-01A1 0004
ASARNOW, ROBERT F R01NS26801-03
ASARNOW, ROBERT F R37MH45112-03
ASBURY, ARTHUR K S15HL47768-01
ASCENSAO, JOAO L R29DK42026-03
ASCH, ADAM S K04HL02541-01
ASCH, ADAM S P50HL18828-16 0009
ASCH, ADAM S R01HL44389-01A2
ASCH, ADAM S S07RR05396-30 0742
ASCH, BONNIE S07RR05648-25 0918
ASCH, BONNIE B R55CA32937-07A2
ASCH, DAVID R01HG00616-01
ASCH, DAVID R01HG00621-01
ASCHER, NANCY L N01DK02252-03
ASCHER, NANCY L P01DK13083-24 0188
ASCHER, NANCY L P01DK13083-24 0192
ASCHER, NANCY L R01AI28284-04

ASCHKENASY, JEANNIE S07RR05477-29 0427
ASCHNER, JUDITH L S07RR05394-30 0725
ASCHNER, MICHAEL R29ES05223-03
ASCOLI, MARIO P50HD13541-12 9002
ASCOLI, MARIO R01CA40629-08
ASEM, ELIKPLIMI K R29HD27354-02
ASH, DAVID E S07RR05417-30 0780
ASHBAUGH, JOHN W R43MH48610-01
ASHBY, BARRIE S07RR05417-30 0781
ASHBY, CHARLES R R03DA06870-01
ASHE, WARREN K S03RR03027-10
ASHE, WARREN K S06GM08244-05
ASHE, WARREN K S06GM08244-05 9001
ASHE, WARREN K S07RR05361-30
ASHE, WARREN K S15DE10072-01
ASHENDEL, CURTIS L K04CA01424-03
ASHENDEL, CURTIS L U01CA52995-02 0003
ASHER, JAMES H S07RR07049-26 0447
ASHER, SANFORD A R01GM30741-10
ASHER, SANFORD A R03RR05502-01A3
ASHIKAGA, TAKAMARU P50HL14212-20 9001
ASHLEY, GARY W R29GM42017-03
ASHLEY, KEVIN E S06GM08192-12 0016
ASHLEY, RHODA L P01AI30731-01A1 0003
ASHLEY, RHODA L P01AI30731-01A1 9001
ASHLINE, HERBERT C K14HL01991-04
ASHMAN, ROBERT F R01GM36261-10
ASHMEAD, DANIEL H P20DC01437-01 0001
ASHMEAD, DANIEL H R29HD23191-04
ASHRAF, MARY H M01RR00044-31 0353
ASHRAF, MUHAMMAD R01HL23597-10
ASHRAF, MUHAMMAD R01HL41358-03
ASHTON-MILLER, JAMES A R01NS24058-05
ASHWELL, G Z01DK17001-25
ASHWELL, J D Z01CM09290-06
ASHWELL, J D Z01CM09311-05
ASHWORTH, CAROLYN S S07RR05365-30 0074
ASIMOPOULOS, NIKOS R43DC01175-01
ASKARI, AMIR P01HL36573-06
ASKARI, AMIR P01HL36573-06 0001
ASKENASE, PHILIP W R01AI26689-03
ASKENASE, PHILIP W R37AI12211-18
ASLIN, RICHARD N R01HD20286-08
ASOFSKY, R Z01AI00134-29
ASPLIN, CHRISTOPHER M M01RR00847-18 0539
ASPLIN, CHRISTOPHER M M01RR00847-18 0422
ASPLIN, CHRISTOPHER M M01RR00847-18 0482
ASPLIN, CHRISTOPHER M M01RR00847-18 0483
ASPLIN, CHRISTOPHER M M01RR00847-18 0484
ASSEL, BARBARA M01RR00080-29 0559
ASSELIN, BARBARA M01RR00044-31 0365
ASSMANN, PETER F R29DC01258-01
ASSOIAN, RICHARD K R01HL38884-05
ASSOSIAN, RICHARD P50HD05077-21 0002
ASTER, RICHARD H P01HL44612-02 0003
ASTER, RICHARD H R37HL13629-22
ASTON-JONES, GARY S R01DA06214-03
ASTON-JONES, GARY S R01NS24698-04
ASTRIN, SUSAN M R01CA40636-06
ASWAD, DANA W R01NS17269-10
ASWAD, DANA W R01NS29421-01
ATASSI, M ZOUHAIR R01NS26280-03
ATAYA, KHALID M R01CA49081-01A3
ATCHISON, KATHRYN S07RR05304-30 0222
ATCHISON, KATHRYN S07RR05304-30 0220
ATCHISON, KATHRYN A R01HS06670-02
ATCHISON, MICHAEL S07RR05464-29 0370
ATCHISON, MICHAEL L R01GM42415-03
ATCHISON, WILLIAM D K04ES00178-04
ATCHISON, WILLIAM D R01ES03299-08
ATCHISON, WILLIAM D R01NS20683-04A1
ATCHISON, WILLIAM D S07RR05623-25 0716
ATCHLEY, HALL P01GM45344-01 0003
ATEMA, JELLE P01NS25915-04A1 0007
ATEN, MARILYN J, PHD S15HL47725-01
ATENCIO, ALONZO C S03RR03099-11
ATENCIO, ALONZO C S06GM08139-17
ATHANASIOU, K A S07RR05654-24 0115
ATHERTON, SALLY S R01EY06012-07
ATHERTON, SALLY S R01EY09169-01
ATHERTON, STEPHEN P41RR00886-16 0004
ATHERTON, STEPHEN P41RR00886-16 0003
ATKIN, CURTIS L R01DK39497-04
ATKIN, JOAN F M01RR00847-18 0463
ATKINS, DIANNE L R01HL43173-03
ATKINS, MARC S R29MH46820-02
ATKINS, MICHAEL M01RR00054-30 0377
ATKINS, MICHAEL M01RR00054-30 0420
ATKINS, MICHAEL M01RR00054-30 0426
ATKINS, MICHAEL M01RR00054-30 0423
ATKINS, MICHAEL A M01RR00054-30 0364
ATKINS, MICHAEL B M01RR00054-30 0378
ATKINS, MICHAEL B M01RR00054-30 0411
ATKINS, MICHAEL B M01RR00054-30 0412
ATKINS, MICHAEL B M01RR00054-30 0408
ATKINSON, ARTHUR J M01RR00048-30 0164
ATKINSON, DANIEL S07RR07009-26 0947
ATKINSON, DAVID P01HL26335-11A1 9001
ATKINSON, DAVID P01HL26335-11A1 0003
ATKINSON, E NEELY R01CA11430-25 0071
ATKINSON, E NEELY R01CA11430-25 0070
ATKINSON, J C Z01DE00332-09
ATKINSON, J C Z01DE00499-02
ATKINSON, J HAMPTON P50MH45294-03 9007
ATKINSON, MARK A L R29GM40423-04
ATKINSON, MARK D S07RR05958-06 0745
ATKINSON, PAUL H R01CA13402-19
ATKINSON, RICHARD L R01DK43250-01
ATKINSON, WILVERIA B S03RR03212-06
ATKINSON, WILVERIA B S06GM08040-21
ATKISON, ARTHUR J M01RR00048-30 0101
ATLAS, STEVEN A P50HL18323-17 0063
ATLAS, SUSAN J S07RR05378-30 0987
ATLEE, JOHN L, III R01GM25064-12
ATLURU, DURGAPRASADARAO R29CA46964-06
ATOR, NANCY A R01DA04133-06
ATTANASIO, ROBERTA S07RR05519-29 0510
ATTANASIO, VIRGINIA S07RR05393-30 0880
ATTARDI, BARBARA J AND DEFRANC P30HD08610-
ATTARDI, GIUSEPPE R01GM11726-28
ATTIE, ALAN D R01HL37251-05
ATTIE, MAURICE F M01RR00040-31 0366
ATTIE, MAURICE F P50AR39226-05 0006
ATTIYEH, RICHARD S06GM47165-01
ATTIYEH, RICHARD S15HL47773-01
ATTIYEH, RICHARD E S07RR07011-26
ATTKISSON, C CLIFFORD R01MH46122-03
ATUK, NUZHET O M01RR00847-18 0540
ATUK, NUZHET O M01RR00847-18 0056
ATURKKAN, JAYLAN S P50AG05146-09 0016
ATWAH, GEORGE P60HL16008-19 0027
ATWEH, GEORGE F R01HL42919-03
ATWOOD, JAN P01CA27502-11 9005
ATWOOD, JAN R P01CA41108-05 9003
AU, JESSIE L K04CA01497-02
AU, JESSIE L R01AI29133-03
AU, JESSIE L R01CA49816-03
AU, JESSIE L S07RR05607-25 0698
AU, TERRY K S07RR07085-26 0332
AU, WILLIAM W R01ES04926-02
AUBE, JEFFREY R29GM39402-04
AUBE, JEFFREY S07RR05606-25 0688
AUBORN, KAREN J P01DC00203-09 0008
AUCHINCLOSS, HUGH, JR R01HL36372-05
AUDESIRK, GERALD J R01ES05372-02
AUDUS, KENNETH L S07RR05606-25 0691
AUERBACH, ARLEEN D R01HL32987-06
AUERBACH, ROBERT R01EY03243-11
AUGENLICHT, LEONARD H R01CA41372-06
AUGENLICHT, LEONARD H R03CA53446-02
AUGENLICHT, LEONARD H S03RR03237-07
AUGUST, CHARLES S M01RR00240-27 0337
AUGUST, GERALD J R01MH46584-01
AUGUST, J THOMAS N01HD62915-08
AUGUST, J THOMAS P30AI28748-03 9003
AUGUST, PHYLLIS M01RR00047-31 0469
AUGUST, PHYLLIS M01RR00047-31 0470
AUGUST, PHYLLIS P50HL18323-17 0051
AUGUSTIN, ANDREI A P01AI22295-07 0002
AUGUSTIN, ANDREI A R01AI19775-10
AUGUSTINE, GEORGE J R01NS21624-07
AUKHIL, I S07RR05333-30 0864
AULAKH, C S Z01MH00332-13
AULL, JOHN L S07RR07255-02 0501
AULT, B Z01AG00123-11
AURBACH, G D Z01DK43002-26
AURBACH, G D Z01DK43006-16
AURELIAN, LAURE P01CA42762-05 0004
AURELIAN, LAURE P01NS26665-04 0004
AURELIAN, LAURE R01AI22192-07
AURELIAN, LAURE R01CA39691-04A1
AURIGEMMA, GERARD P S07RR05712-20 0078
AURIGEMMA, GERARD P S07RR05712-20 0105
AURON, PHILIP E R01AI27850-03
AURON, PHILIP E S07RR05486-29 0048
AUSIELLO, DENNIS P01DK38452-05 0001
AUSIELLO, DENNIS A P01DK38452-05
AUSIELLO, DENNIS A R37DK19406-15
AUSLANDER, WENDY P60DK20579-14 0030
AUSMAN, L M P51RR00168-30 0167
AUSMAN, LYNNE M P51RR00168-30 9013
AUSMAN, LYNNE M R01CA42352-05S1
AUSPRUNK, DIANNA H R01HL33022-09
AUST, ANN E R01ES05782-01
AUST, STEVEN D P42ES04922-03 9001
AUST, STEVEN D P42ES04922-03
AUST, STEVEN D P42ES04922-03 0001
AUST, STEVEN D R01ES05056-03
AUSTAD, STEVEN N R55AG09700-01
AUSTEN, K FRANK P01HL36110-07 0003
AUSTEN, K FRANK P01HL36110-07
AUSTEN, K FRANK R37AI22531-07
AUSTEN, K FRANK U01AI31599-01
AUSTIN, ARTHUR A P30AI28662-03 9006
AUSTIN, CHRISTOPHER P K11EY00321-01
AUSTIN, GREGORY A R01AA04570-09
AUSTIN, H A Z01DK43222-06
AUSTIN, H A Z01DK43224-05
AUSTIN, H A Z01DK43231-04
AUSTIN, HARRIET B S07RR07157-16 0580
AUSTIN, JOAN K R01NS22416-05
AUSTIN, MELISSA A R01HL46880-01
AUSTIN, MELISSA A R29HL38760-06
AUSTROM, MARY P30AG10133-01 9003
AUSUBEL, FREDERICK P01DK33506-08 0010
AUSUBEL, FREDERICK P01DK33506-08 9002
AVADHANI, NARAYAN G R01CA22762-14
AVADHANI, NARAYAN G S15AI32189-01
AVADHANI, NAVAYAN G R01GM34883-07
AVEN, LAURALEE G07LM05245-01
AVERILL, BRUCE A R01GM32117-09
AVERILL, DAVID B P01HL06835-30 9006
AVERILL, DAVID B P01HL06835-30 0087
AVERY, DAVID S07RR07127-23 0476
AVERY, DAVID H K01MH00493-05
AVERY, DAVID H M01RR00037-31 0465
AVERY, JAMES K S07RR05321-30 0258
AVERY, LEON S07RR07175-15 0428
AVERY, LEON B R01HL46154-01
AVERY, MARY E P50HL34616-07
AVERY05MARY ELLEN P50HL34616-07 0003
AVIGAN, J Z01HL00643-05
AVIGAN, MARK I R29CA54818-01
AVILA, VERNON L S06GM45765-01
AVIOLI, LOUIS V M01RR00036-31 0429
AVIOLI, LOUIS V M01RR06021-02 0429
AVIOLI, LOUIS V P01AR32087-09 0011
AVIOLI, LOUIS V P01AR32087-09
AVIRAM, URI P50MH43450-04 0010
AVIRAM, URI P50MH43450-04 0011
AVIS, NANCY R43AG09720-01
AVIS, NANCY E R43AG10082-01
AVIS, NANCY E R44HL43444-02
AVISON, MALCOLM J S07RR05358-30 0495
AVIV, ABRAHAM R01HL42856-02
AVIV, ABRAHAM S07RR05393-30 0881
AVNER, ELLIS D R01DK34891-07
AVNER, ELLIS D R01DK44875-01
AVOGARO, ANGELO P41RR00954-15 0023
AVORN, JEROME L P30AG08812-02 9003
AVORN, JEROME L R01AG09634-01
AVRAHAM, HAVA S07RR05591-27 0653
AVRAM, MICHAEL J R01GM43776-01A1
AVRAMIS, VASSILIOS I R01CA49843-03
AVRUCH, JOSEPH P50DK39249-05 0012
AVRUCH, JOSEPH R01DK17776-16A1
AVRUCH, JOSEPH R01DK41513-02
AVRUCH, JOSEPH R01DK41762-03
AW, TAK YEE S07RR05822-12 0500
AWASTHI, YOGESH C R01CA27967-12
AWASTHI, YOGESH C R01GM32304-07
AWASTHI, YOGESH C R55EY04396-09
AWBREY, BRIAN J K08AR01482-05
AWDEH, ZUHEIR P01HL29583-09 9004
AWDEH, ZUHEIR L. P01HL29583-09 0005
AWGULEWITSCH, ALEXANDER R29GM43334-03
AXEL, LEON R01HL43014-02
AXEL, LEON S10RR06260-01
AXEL, RICHARD P01CA23767-13 9001
AXEL, RICHARD P01CA23767-13
AXEL, RICHARD P01CA23767-13 0001
AXELROD, DANIEL R01NS14565-13
AXELROD, J Z01MH00434-10
AXELROD, LLOYD M01RR01066-14 0065
AXELROD, LLOYD P50DK39249-05 0011
AXENROD, T S06GM08168-13 0021
AXENROD, T S06GM08168-13 0021
AXLEY, M J Z01HL00265-05
AXSOM, DANNY K R29MH46965-01
AXTHELM, MICHAEL P51RR00163-32 9003
AXTHELM, MICHAEL P51RR00163-32 9006
AXTHELM, MICHAEL K P51RR00163-32 0039
AYALA, ALFRED R55GM46354-01
AYALA, FRANCISCO J P01GM42397-01A2 9001
AYALA, FRANCISCO J P01GM42397-01A2
AYDELOTTE, MARGARET B P50AR39239-05 0001
AYERS, CARLOS R M01RR00847-18 0541
AYERS, JOSEPH L S07RR07143-20 0613
AYLING, JUNE E R01NS26662-03
AYNSLEY, JOHN S R01CA55102-01
AYRES, S M S15HL47774-01
AYRES, STEPHEN M M01RR00065-29
AYRES, STEPHEN M S03RR03178-10
AYRES, STEPHEN M S07RR05430-30
AZAD, ABDU F R01AI17828-08A2
AZAR, SANDRA T R29MH46940-02
AZARI, PARVIZ S07RR07127-23 0477
AZEN, EDWIN A R37DE03658-27
AZEN, STANLEY P U10EY05571-07
AZIZKHAN, RICHARD G S07RR05406-30 0879
AZMITIA, EFRAIN S07RR07062-26 0228
AZNAVOORIAN, S Z01CB09185-02
AZRIN, NATHAN H R01DA05295-03
AZZIZ, RICARDO M01RR00032-31 0299
BAAS, PETER W R01NS28785-03
BABB, THOMAS L P01NS02808-30 0044
BABCOCK, DONNER F R01HD22973-05
BABCOCK, GERALD T R01GM25480-13
BABCOCK, GERALD T R01GM37300-06
BABCOCK, SUSAN K S07RR05357-30 0442
BABIARZ, BRUCE S R01HD20581-06
BABIGIAN, HAROUTUN M R01MH40053-05
BABIN, DONALD R S07RR05390-30 0662
BABIOR, BERNARD M M01RR00833-17 0166
BABIOR, BERNARD M R01AI28479-03
BABIOR, BERNARD M R01AI30742-01

BABIOR, BERNARD M R37AI24227-07
BABISS, LEE E R29CA48707-03
BABLER, W J S07RR05915-08 0690
BABLER, W J S07RR05915-08 0682
BABOR, THOMAS P50AA03510-14 0014
BABOR, THOMAS F R13AA09017-01
BABOR, THOMAS F U10AA08430-03
BABSON, JOHN R R29GM41496-04
BABU, JEGDISH P R29DE08030-05
BABU, V RAMESH R01CA48492-03
BABU, Y S R43AI31708-01
BACA, OSWALD P41RR01315-10 0033
BACALLAO, ROBERT L K11DK01777-05
BACCHE, ROBERT P01HL32427-06 9003
BACCHETTI, PETER R29AI31331-01
BACCHI, CYRUS J R01AI17340-11
BACH, FRITZ H P01DK13083-24 0189
BACH, FRITZ H P01DK13083-24 0183
BACH, FRITZ H P01HD19937-06 0005
BACH, FRITZ H R01AI19007-08
BACH, FRITZ H R01HL46802-01
BACH, RONALD R P01HL29019-10 0003
BACHARACH, S Z01CL00301-04
BACHARACH, S L Z01CL00304-03
BACHAS, LEONIDAS G R29GM40510-04
BACHE, ROBERT J P01HL32427-06 0004
BACHE, ROBERT J R01HL21872-14
BACHE, ROBERT J R37HL20598-16
BACHENHEIMOR, STEVEN L P01CA19014-14 0016
BACHEVALIER, J Z01MH02038-01
BACHORIK, PAUL S N01HV78102-06
BACHOVCHIN, WILLIAM W R01AI31866-01
BACHOVCHIN, WILLIAM W S10RR06282-01
BACHRACH, LAURA K R29DK40317-04
BACHVAROVA, ROSEMARY S07RR05396-30 0736
BACHVAROVA, ROSEMARY F R01HD06910-17
BACIC, ANTONY R01AI28962-01A1
BACIC, F Z01NS02777-03
BACIC, F Z01NS02795-03
BACK, ANTHONY L K08HL02637-01
BACKES, WAYNE L R29ES04344-04
BACKLUND, P S Z01MH00942-10
BACKLUND, STEPHEN J N01CM17545-00
BACON, ARTHUR L S03RR03247-09
BACON, ARTHUR L S14GM05966-02
BACON, BRUCE R S07RR05388-30 0623
BACON, SIDNEY P R29DC00424-05
BACUS, JAMES W R44CA50843-02A1
BADALAMENTE, MARIE A S07RR05736-19 0211
BADARO, ROBERTO P01AI16282-13 0004
BADARO, ROBERTO P01AI26506-04 0002
BADDOUR, LARRY S07RR05387-30 0603
BADEN, DANIEL G P30ES05705-01
BADEN, DANIEL G P30ES05705-01 9001
BADEN, DANIEL G P30ES05705-01 9002
BADEN, DANIEL G P30ES05705-01 9003
BADEN, DANIEL G P30ES05705-01 9004
BADEN, DANIEL G P30ES05705-01 9005
BADEN, DANIEL G P30ES05705-01 9006
BADEN, DANIEL G P30ES05705-01 9007
BADEN, DANIEL G P30ES05705-01 9008
BADEN, DANIEL G P30ES05705-01 9009
BADEN, SALLY T R03DE09573-01
BADER, DAVID M R01HL34318-06
BADER, DAVID M R01HL37675-06A1
BADER, JAMES D R01HS06669-02
BADERO, ROBERTO P50AI30639-01 0003
BADESCH, DAVID B K08HL02408-02
BADGER, LEE W R03MH45791-02
BADGER, TERRY S07RR05913-08 0664
BADGER, THOMAS M R01AA08213-02
BADGER, THOMAS M R01AA08645-02
BADR KAMAL F P01DK38226-06 0004
BADR, KAMAL P50DK39261-05 0002
BADR, KAMAL F R01DK43883-01
BADR, KAMAL F R29DK38667-05
BADR, M SAFWAN K08HL02588-01
BADWEY, JOHN A R01AI28342-02
BADWEY, JOHN A S07RR05711-21 0042
BAEHR, WOLFGANG R01EY08123-02
BAEHR, WOLFGANG S07RR05425-30 0727
BAEKKESKOV, STEINUNN P01DK41822-03 0002
BAEKKESKOV, STEINUNN R55DK41567-01A1
BAENZIGER, JACQUES U R01DK41738-03
BAENZIGER, JACQUES U R37CA21923-14
BAENZIGER, NANCY L R01HL33699-07
BAER, D M P01HD18955-07 0003
BAER, DONALD M P01HD26927-01A1 0002
BAER, JOHN S R01AA08632-01A1
BAER, RICHARD J R01CA46593-04
BAER, RICHARD J R01CA47975-04
BAER, ROBERTA D S07RR07121-13 0470
BAERTSCHI, ALEX J R01HL40553-01A4
BAERTSCHI, ALEX J R01NS27644-01A2
BAEZ, ADRIANA S06GM08102-20 0033
BAEZ, ADRIANA S06GM08224-07
BAEZ, ADRIANA S07RR05419-30
BAEZ, LUIS U10CA52667-02
BAGASRA, OMAR M01RR00349-25 0232
BAGASRA, OMAR S07RR05417-30 0782
BAGATELL, CARRIE J K08HD00890-02
BAGBY, G P01GM32654-08 9001
BAGBY, GREGORY J P01GM32654-08 0002
BAGBY, GROVER C R01CA36306-08
BAGBY, GROVER C R01DK41933-03
BAGDADE, JOHN D R01DK43227-01A1
BAGHDOYAN, HELEN A R29MH45361-03
BAGLEY, SUSAN T R01OH02611-03
BAGLIONI, CORRADO R01CA52541-01A1
BAGNATO, STEPHEN J M01RR00084-29 0246
BAGNELL, CAROL A S07RR07058-26 0172
BAGRAMIAN, ROBERT A S07RR05321-30 0259
BAHL, JOSEPH P01HL20984-15 9004
BAHL, OM P R01HD08766-25
BAHN, REBECCA S R01EY08819-01A1
BAHNSON, ROBERT R K08CA01490-02
BAHOU, WADIE S07RR05736-19 0198
BAHOU, WADIE F K08HL02431-03
BAHRICK, LORRAINE E R01HD25669-02
BAI, STEPHEN A R29HL39458-04
BAILEY, GEORGE S. P01ES04766-04 0001
BAILEY, CRAIG H R01MH37134-09
BAILEY, GEORGE S P01ES04766-04
BAILEY, GEORGE S P30ES03850-07
BAILEY, GEORGE S R01CA34732-08A1
BAILEY, GORDON B S06GM08248-05 0001
BAILEY, IAN L S07RR05832-12 0190
BAILEY, J J Z01CT00002-22
BAILEY, J J Z01CT00223-01
BAILEY, J M P01HL38079-05 0004
BAILEY, J MICHAEL R03MH47227-02
BAILEY, JEROME M S07RR05841-12 0241
BAILEY, LESLIE E. S06GM08125-18 0042
BAILEY, STEVEN C S07RR05591-27 0665
BAILEY, TIMOTHY S. M01RR00318-25 0225
BAILEY, WILLIAM C K07HL02327-03
BAILEY, WILLIAM C M01RR00032-31 0214
BAILEY, WILLIAM C N01HR46019-16
BAILEY, WILLIAM C R01HL31481-06
BAILLARGEON, RENEE L R01HD21104-06
BAIM, DONALD S U01HL38514-05
BAIN, RAYMOND R01DK39826-05
BAIN, RAYMOND P U01HD19897-07
BAINES, CAROL M U01CA52267-02
BAINTON, DOROTHY F R01DK10486-26
BAINTON, DOROTHY F R37HL31610-09
BAINTON, DOROTHY F S07RR05355-30 0429
BAIRD, ANDREW P01DK18811-17A1 0020
BAIRD, ANDREW P01DK18811-17A1 0017
BAIRD, ANDREW J P01DK18811-17A1
BAIRD, BARBARA P41RR04224-04 0001
BAIRD, BARBARA A R01AI18306-11
BAIRD, D D Z01ES47002-05
BAIRD, D D Z01ES49003-02
BAIRD, RICHARD A R29DC00355-05
BAIRD, SCOTT E R29GM46438-01
BAIRD, TERRY M U01HD29071-01
BAIRD, WILLIAM M P30CA23168-14
BAIRD, WILLIAM M R01CA40228-07
BAIRD, WILLIAM M R37CA28825-12
BAIRD, WILLIAM M. P30CA23168-14 9002
BAIRD, WILLIAM M. P30CA23168-14 9003
BAIRD, WILLIAM M. P30CA23168-14 9004
BAIRD, WILLIAM M. P30CA23168-14 9005
BAIRD, WILLIAM M. P30CA23168-14 9006
BAITCH, LAWRENCE WILLIAM R29EY08102-03
BAIZER, LAWRENCE R29NS26806-04
BAJAJ, S PAUL P50HL30572-08 0005
BAJAJ, S PAUL R55HL36365-07
BAJER, ANDREW S R01GM37543-04
BAJKOWSKI, ANDREW S R29CA44659-05
BAJORUNAS, D R P01CA29502-11A1 0052
BAK, M Z01NS01687-23
BAKALINSKY, ALAN T S07RR07079-26 0285
BAKAY, ROY A E P51RR00165-31 0090
BAKAY, ROY A E R01NS24340-03
BAKEMEIER, RICHARD F R25CA47905-04
BAKEMEIER, RICHARD F R25CA49981-03
BAKER, ARTHUR D S07RR07064-24 0193
BAKER, BILL J R15AI31256-01
BAKER, BRUCE S07RR07009-26 0938
BAKER, BRUCE S R37GM37731-07
BAKER, C C Z01CP05482-06
BAKER, CAROL S M01RR00188-27 0328
BAKER, DAVID C N01AI82680-07
BAKER, DAVID C N01CM17551-00
BAKER, DAVID C R01AI22296-06
BAKER, DEAN P30ES00928-18 9002
BAKER, DEAN B K07ES00216-01
BAKER, EDWARD N R01HD20859-05
BAKER, F M K07MH00816-01S1
BAKER, FRANK R01CA49218-03
BAKER, HARRIET D P01MH44043-04 0002
BAKER, HARRIET D R01AG09686-01
BAKER, HENRY V, II R29GM41330-03
BAKER, JAMES F P01NS17489-10 0005
BAKER, JAMES F P01NS17489-10 9002
BAKER, JAMES F R01EY05289-08
BAKER, JAMES F R01EY07342-05
BAKER, JAMES R, JR R29AI30501-02
BAKER, JAMES T P50AG05133-08 0012
BAKER, JEFFREY P R01LM05339-01
BAKER, JOHN C S07RR05623-25 0714
BAKER, JOHN E R29HL43030-03
BAKER, JOHN R R01AR39244-04
BAKER, JOHN R R55AG10070-01
BAKER, JOHN R S10RR06641-01
BAKER, KAREN S07RR06024-03 0852
BAKER, KENNETH M R01HL44379-01A2
BAKER, KENNETH M R01HL44883-02
BAKER, LAURENCE H P01CA46560-03
BAKER, LAURENCE H U10CA14028-18
BAKER, LAWRENCE H P30CA22453-14
BAKER, LESTER M01RR00240-27 0199
BAKER, LESTER M01RR00240-27 0096
BAKER, LESTER M01RR00240-27 0345
BAKER, LESTER M01RR00240-27 0342
BAKER, LESTER U01DK30619-09
BAKER, MARY S K07CA01468-03
BAKER, MAX T R29GM41121-02
BAKER, P J Z01AI00143-22
BAKER, P J Z01AI00144-27
BAKER, P J Z01AI00145-24
BAKER, RAYMOND D. P01CA21071-14 0016
BAKER, RICHARD S07RR05356-30 0440
BAKER, RICHARD E R29GM38566-05
BAKER, RICHARD E S07RR05712-20 0045
BAKER, ROBERT P01NS13742-15 0014
BAKER, RODNEY C R01AR39742-02
BAKER, THOMAS S07RR05583-27 0621
BAKER, VICKI V S07RR05408-30 0917
BAKKETEIG, LEIV S N01HD13127-00
BAKOS, MARY-ANN S07RR05427-30 0158
BALABAN, CAREY D R01DC00739-02
BALABAN, EVAN S R29MH47149-02
BALABAN, R S Z01HL04601-04
BALABAN, R S Z01HL04602-04
BALASUBRAMANIAM, AMBIKAIPAKAN R29GM38601-0
BALAZOVICH, KENNETH J R29AI25641-04
BALBER, ANDREW E R55AI28427-01A3
BALCER-KUBICZEK, ELIZABETH K R01CA50629-03
BALCERZAK, STANLEY P P30CA16058-17 9005
BALCERZAK, STANLEY P U10CA04920-32
BALCH, ALAN L R01GM26226-13
BALCH, CHARLES M P01AI30879-17 0003
BALCH, GEORGE I R01AA08537-01A1
BALCH, WILLIAM P01CA27489-12 0007
BALCH, WILLIAM E R01GM33301-09
BALCH, WILLIAM E R01GM42336-02
BALCZON, RONALD D R01GM46453-01
BALDASSARE, JOSEPH J R01HL40901-04
BALDERSTON, SCOTT M M01RR00069-29 0459
BALDESSARINI, ROSS J K05MH47370-17
BALDESSARINI, ROSS J P01MH31154-14 0019
BALDESSARINI, ROSS J P01MH31154-14 0015
BALDESSARINI, ROSS J P01MH31154-14 0017
BALDESSARINI, ROSS J P01MH31154-14 0018
BALDESSARINI, ROSS J P01MH31154-14 0012
BALDESSARINI, ROSS J R01MH34006-12
BALDESSARINI, ROSS J S07RR05484-29 0028
BALDREE, LOU A M01RR00211-27 0334
BALDWIN, JOHN C. P01HL13108-22 9001
BALDWIN, ALBERT S, JR R01CA52515-01A1
BALDWIN, ANN P01HL17421-18 0015
BALDWIN, BEVERLY S07RR05973-05 0783
BALDWIN, CLINTON T P01AR39740-03 9003
BALDWIN, CLINTON T R29AR40152-02
BALDWIN, D M S07RR05457-29 0999
BALDWIN, H S K11HL02197-04
BALDWIN, IAN T S07RR07066-26 0232
BALDWIN, JOHN C. P01HL13108-22 0032
BALDWIN, JOSEPH A R24MH48519-01 0001
BALDWIN, KENNETH M R01AR30346-10
BALDWIN, KENNETH M R01HL38819-05
BALDWIN, KENNETH M S07RR05351-30 0031
BALDWIN, R P41RR01209-12 0027
BALDWIN, ROBERT L R01GM31475-09
BALDWIN, ROBERT L R37GM19988-31
BALDWIN, THOMAS O R01GM42428-03
BALE, ALLEN E R01CA50497-03
BALENTINE, J DOUGLAS P01NS11066-17 0007
BALES, CONNIE W K01AG00420-04
BALES, CONNIE W S07RR05405-30 0868
BALES, R C P42ES04940-02 0001
BALFE, DENNIS M U01CA49088-03
BALFOUR, HENRY M01RR00400-23 0278
BALFOUR, HENRY H M01RR00400-23 0287
BALFOUR, HENRY H P01DK13083-24 0171
BALFOUR, HENRY H P01DK13083-24 0186
BALFOUR, HENRY H, JR U01AI27661-06
BALIAN, GARY P01DK40031-03 0003
BALIAN, GARY R01HL41038-04
BALICE-GORDON, RITA P50AG05681-08 0018
BALISH, EDWARD R01DE09659-01
BALK, DAVID E R03MH45044-02
BALKE, C WILLIAM K11HL02466-02
BALL, EDWARD D R01CA31888-09
BALL, EDWARD D R01CA37868-08
BALL, HARISON G M01RR00054-30 0417
BALL, HARRISON M01RR00054-30 0366
BALL, HARRISON G M01RR00054-30 0416
BALL, J Z01DA00106-01
BALL, KARLENE K R01AG05739-06
BALL, LAURENCE A R37AI18270-11
BALL, LOUISE S07RR05450-30 0337
BALL, MELVYN P30AG08017-02 9004

BALL, ROBERT S R19DA06435-03
BALL, WILLIAM D R01DE06635-07
BALL, WILLIAM J, JR R01HL32214-08
BALLABIO, ANDREA R01HD28333-01
BALLANTINE, DAVID L S06GM08103-18 0015
BALLANTYNE, CHRISTIE M K08HL02537-02
BALLARD, BILLY R S03RR03286-10
BALLARD, DANA H R24RR06853-01
BALLARD, HENRY H S06GM08094-17 0005
BALLARD, PHILIP L P01HL24075-13 0005
BALLARD, RICHARD S07RR05704-20 0003
BALLARD, ROBERT D S07RR05357-30 0445
BALLAS, SAMIR P60HL38632-04 9003
BALLATORI, NAZZARENO P01ES05197-01A1 0003
BALLATORI, NAZZARENO P30ES01247-17 0102
BALLATORI, NAZZARENO R29DK39165-05
BALLENGER, JAMES C M01RR01070-15 0148
BALLERMANN, BARBARA J P01DK40839-03 0001
BALLERMANN, BARBARA J P50DK39249-05 0001
BALLERMANN, BARBARA JUTTA R29DK40445-05
BALLESTER, OSCAR F S07RR05749-19 0266
BALLOU, STANLEY P K08AI01062-01
BALLOW, MARK R01HD25757-04
BALMES, JOHN R K07ES00219-01
BALMES, JOHN R R01CA47989-04
BALOGH-NAIR, V S06GM08168-13 0022
BALOGH-NAIR, V S06GM08168-13 0022
BALOGH-NAIR, VALERIA G12RR03060-07 0004
BALOH, ROBERT S07RR05354-30 0407
BALOH, ROBERT W P50DC00097-21 0001
BALOH, ROBERT W P60DC01404-01 0001
BALOH, ROBERT W R01AG09693-01
BALON, THOMAS W R29AR39974-02
BALON, THOMAS W S07RR07035-26 0094
BALOW, J E Z01DK43204-12
BALOW, J E Z01DK43205-14
BALSAM, PETER S07RR07234-05 0852
BALSAM, PETER D S07RR07234-05
BALSCHI, JAMES A R29HL46033-01A1
BALSHEM, MARTHA P01CA34856-09 0006
BALSTER, ROBERT L P50DA05274-04 0005
BALSTER, ROBERT L R01AA08473-01A1
BALSTER, ROBERT L R01DA01442-16
BALSTER, ROBERT L R01DA03112-07
BALTIMORE, DAVID P01HL43510-03 0003
BALTIMORE, DAVID R01CA51462-03
BALTIMORE, DAVID R01GM39458-05
BALTIMORE, DAVID R37AI22346-09
BALTIMORE, DAVID S07RR07065-26
BALTIMORE, DAVID U01AI26463-04 0002
BALTRUCKI, L Z01HL02220-91
BALTZELL, JANET K S07RR05992-04 0811
BALUDA, MARCEL A R01CA10197-24
BAMBARA, ROBERT A R01GM24441-12A2
BAMBURG, JAMES R P01NS28323-02 0001
BAMBURG, JAMES R R01GM35126-19
BAMBURG, JAMES R R01NS28338-02
BAMBURG, JAMES R S07RR07127-23 0492
BAME, KAREN J R15HD28210-01
BAME, SHERRY I R01DK43141-01
BAMFORD, OWEN S R03DE09488-01A1
BANASZAK, LEONARD J R01GM13925-27
BANCROFT, F CARTER R01GM36847-06
BAND, HAMID R29AI28508-03
BANDMAN, EVERETT R01AG08573-09
BANDSTRA, EMMALEE S M01RR05280-03 0018
BANDSTRA, EMMALEE S R01DA06556-02
BANDSTRA, EMMALEE S S07RR05363-30 0819
BANDSTRA, EMMALEE S S10RR06523-01
BANE, MARK CHAPMAN S07RR06028-02 0372
BANERICE, UTBAL S07RR07009-26 0932
BANERJEE, AMIYA K R01AI26585-04
BANERJEE, AMIYA K S07RR05674-23
BANERJEE, AMIYA K S07RR05674-23 0931
BANERJEE, AMIYA K S15HL47704-01
BANERJEE, ANIRBAN R29HL43696-02
BANERJEE, ANIRBAN S07RR05357-30 0443
BANERJEE, DEBENDRANATH R01HL36699-05
BANERJEE, DIPAK K S06GM08224-07 0001
BANERJEE, MUKUL R K14HL02138-04
BANERJEE, TARIT K U10CA35412-08
BANERJEE, UTPAL R01EY08152-02
BANERJI, MARY ANN M01RR00318-25 0184
BANERJI, MARY ANN M01RR00318-25 0218
BANES, ALBERT J R01AR38121-05
BANK, ARTHUR P60HL28381-09 0011
BANK, ARTHUR P60HL28381-09 0001
BANK, ARTHUR R37DK25274-26
BANK, BRUCE S07RR05393-30 0882
BANK, NORMAN R01DK32469-09
BANK, SHELTON S07RR07122-23 0085
BANKAITIS, VYTAS A R01GM44530-01A1
BANKER, GARY A R01NS17112-11
BANKER, GARY A R01NS23094-07
BANKERT, RICHARD B R01CA22786-14
BANKERT, RICHARD B R01CA25253-13
BANKERT, RICHARD B R01CA54491-01
BANKHURST, ARTHUR D R01CA24873-13
BANKIEWICZ, K Z01NS02781-04
BANKS, FLOYD W S06GM08043-21 0012
BANKS, MARTIN S R01HD19927-07
BANKS, MARTIN S S07RR05832-12 0191
BANKS, P M P30CA15083-18 9005
BANKS, S Z01BA02015-02
BANKS, S D Z01BA02022-01
BANKS, W L M01RR00065-29 0335
BANKS, WILLIAM L, JR R25CA22032-15
BANNER, RICHARD O U01CA52237-02
BANNON, MICHAEL S07RR05641-17 0849
BANNON, MICHAEL J R01MH43026-05
BANNON, MICHAEL JOHN R01DA06470-03
BANSAL, NAVIN S07RR05426-30 0128
BANSIL, RAMA S07RR07043-26 0113
BANTLE, JOHN P M01RR00400-23 0185
BANTLE, JOHN P M01RR00400-23 0289
BANTLE, JOHN P M01RR00400-23 0292
BANTLE, JOHN P M01RR00400-23 0211
BANTLE, JOHN P U01DK30626-09
BANZETT, ROBERT B R01HL35420-06
BANZETT, ROBERT B R01HL46690-01
BANZETT, ROBERT B. P50HL19170-15 0018
BAPNA, MAHENDRA S07RR05864-10 0933
BAR-SAGI, DAFNA R01CA55360-01
BAR-SAGI, DAFNA S07RR05717-21 0132
BAR, ROBERT S P30DK25295-12S1
BAR, ROBERT S P30DK25295-12S1 9001
BAR, ROBERT S P30DK25295-12S1 9007
BAR, ROBERT S R01DK25421-13
BARABAN, JAY M. P50DA00266-20 0012
BARABINO, GILDA A S07RR07143-20 0614
BARAFF, DAVID R R43CA55478-01
BARAJAS, LUCIANO R37HL18340-17
BARAM, TALLIE Z K08NS01307-04
BARAN, DANIEL T R01DK39085-04A1
BARAN, GEORGE R R01DE09530-02
BARANOSKI, MADELON V R01NR02352-01A1
BARANOWSKI, THOMAS J, JR R29AR36416-05
BARANSKI, BRUCE G S07RR05435-30 0985
BARANY, FRANCIS R01GM41337-03
BARANY, GEORGE R01GM42722-03
BARANY, GEORGE R01GM43552-02
BARANY, MICHAEL R01AR34602-17
BARAONA, E P50AA03508-14 0005
BARAONA, ENRIQUE P50AA03508-14 0045
BARATZ, K M01RR00585-20 0450
BARATZ, ROBERT S07RR05319-18 0621
BARBARESE, ELISA R01NS19943-06
BARBARESE, ELISE S07RR05678-23 0163
BARBARIN, OSCAR A R01HD23968-04
BARBAS, HELEN R01NS24760-05
BARBAS, HELEN S07RR07043-26 0123
BARBEE, EVELYN L S03RR03383-06
BARBEE, ROBERT A S07RR05675-23 0926
BARBEITO, RAPHAEL S07RR05998-04 0029
BARBER, B J R01AG10257-01
BARBER, BILLY J P01HL29587-09 9003
BARBER, BILLY J P01HL29587-09 0007
BARBER, BILLY J P01HL29587-09 9001
BARBER, CLIFTON S07RR07127-23 0478
BARBER, DIANE L R01DK41371-03
BARBER, DIANE L R29DK40259-05
BARBER, HERBERT B R03RR06843-01
BARBER, JACQUES P50MH45178-02 0006
BARBER, MICHAEL J R01GM32696-07
BARBER, ROGER S07RR07143-20 0537
BARBER, THOMAS W S07RR05569-27 0119
BARBER, W HENRY M01RR00032-31 0348
BARBER, WILLIAM D P01DK36289-06A1 0004
BARBER, WILLIAM D R01NS27972-02
BARBER, WILLIAM H K04AI00936-03
BARBER, WILLIAM H R01AI27985-02
BARBER, WILLIAM H U01AI31457-01
BARBIERI, JOSEPH T R01AI30162-02
BARBIERI, ROBERT M01RR02635-07 0273
BARBIERI, ROBERT L M01RR02635-07 0276
BARBIERI, ROBERT L R01HD24563-04
BARBOSA, GAIL A R03HS06930-01
BARBOSA, JOSE F P01DK13083-24 0169
BARBOSA, JOSE J M01RR00400-23 0075
BARBOSA, JOSE J M01RR00400-23 0294
BARBOSA, JOSE J M01RR00400-23 0220
BARBOSA, JOSE J M01RR00400-23 0126
BARBOUR, ALAN G R01AI24424-05
BARBOUR, ALAN G R01AI29731-02
BARBOUR, LINDA S07RR05357-30 0453
BARBOUR, MARILYN S07RR05862-10 0559
BARBUCCI,R P41RR01296-08 0003
BARBUL, ADRIAN R29GM38650-05
BARCAK, GERARD J R29AI30083-02
BARCAK, GERARD J S07RR05379-30 0759
BARCELLOS-HOFF, MARY H R29CA51841-01A1
BARCHAS, JACK D P50DA05010-05 0001
BARCHAS, JACK D P50DA05010-05 0002
BARCHAS, JACK D P50DA05010-05 0003
BARCHAS, JACK D P50DA05010-05
BARCHI, ROBERT L P01NS08075-21 0009
BARCHI, ROBERT L R01NS18013-10
BARCHOWSKY, AARON R01HL44454-02
BARCHOWSKY, AARON S07RR05414-30 0993
BARCOS, MAURICE P01CA41285-07 9004
BARCOS, MAURICE U10CA37055-08
BARD, KIM A P51RR00165-31 0152
BARD, KIM A P51RR00165-31 0154
BARD, KIM A R24RR06158-02
BARD, MARTIN R15GM45959-01
BARDACH, J P01DE05837-10 0004
BARDEN, L K Z01CT00231-01
BARDEN, NICHOLAS R01MH43448-03
BARDIN, CLYDE W P50HD13541-12
BARDIN, CLYDE W S07RR05860-11
BARDO, MICHAEL T P50DA05312-05 0001
BAREFOOT, JOHN C R01AG09276-02
BARENHOLZ, YECHEZKEL R01HL17576-15A1
BARFIELD, JAMES A K08NS01483-01
BARFIELD, RONALD J R01HD04484-20
BARFUSS, DELON W S07RR07171-08 0146
BARGE, FRANCES C S07RR05776-11 0385
BARGER, BRUCE P60AR20614-14 9003
BARGER, BRUCE O N01AI82513-08
BARGH, JOHN A R01MH43265-04
BARGIELLO, THADDEUS P01NS07512-23 0049
BARIBIERI, ROBERT M01RR02635-07 0138
BARIC, RALPH S S07RR05450-30 0332
BARIL, EARL F R01CA15187-15
BARILE, FRANK A. S06GM08153-16 0009
BARILE, M F Z01BA06001-08
BARILE, M F Z01BA06003-02
BARILE, M F Z01BA06004-04
BARILE, M F Z01BA06006-04
BARILE, M F Z01BA06009-01
BARILE, M F Z01BA06013-01
BARISAS, B GEORGE S07RR07127-23 0495
BARISH, MICHAEL E S07RR05841-12 0238
BARKA, TIBOR R01HL39419-02
BARKAN, ALICE S07RR07080-26 0307
BARKAN, ARIEL M01RR00042-31 0671
BARKAN, ARIEL L M01RR00042-31 0543
BARKAN, ARIEL L M01RR00042-31 0607
BARKAN, ARIEL L M01RR00042-31 0616
BARKAN, ARIEL L R29DK38449-05
BARKDOLL, A EDWIN, III R01EY08522-02
BARKER, ALLAN H N01HC65063-15
BARKER, CLYDE F R37DK26007-13
BARKER, J L Z01NS02019-19
BARKER, J L Z01NS02330-14
BARKER, JANE S07RR05545-29 0569
BARKER, JANE E R01DK27726-09
BARKER, JANE E R01HL29305-09
BARKER, KENNETH L R01HD16236-10
BARKER, KENNETH L S07RR05773-17
BARKER, WILLIAM H R01AG05188-02S1
BARKHORDAR, RAHMAT S07RR05305-30 0737
BARKLEY, MARY D R01GM42101-03
BARKLEY, MARY D S15GM47061-01
BARKLEY, RUSSEL A S07RR05712-20 0075
BARKLEY, RUSSELL A R01MH42181-03
BARKLEY, RUSSELL A R01MH45714-01A1
BARKLIS, ERIC R01CA47088-04A1
BARKLIS, ERIC R55CA53332-01
BARKLIS, ERIC S07RR05412-30 0973
BARKLIS, ERIC S07RR07238-04 0478
BARKMEIER, WAYNE W R13DE09956-01
BARLEY, ZOE A S07RR05809-06 0473
BARLOGIE, BART R01CA28771-12
BARLOGIE, BARTHEL P30CA16672-17 9015
BARLOGIE, BARTHEL U10CA37981-08
BARLOW, CLYDE H R44HL40775-03
BARLOW, CLYDE H R44HL43473-02
BARLOW, DAVID H R01MH33553-13
BARLOW, DAVID H R01MH36800-09
BARLOW, DAVID H R01MH39096-08
BARLOW, DAVID H R01MH45965-02
BARLOW, DAVID H R37MH34176-12
BARLOW, DAVID H S07RR07122-23 0102
BARLOW, ROBERT B S07RR07068-26 0228
BARLOW, ROBERT B, JR R01EY00667-19
BARLOW, STEVEN M R01DC00365-05A1
BARLOW, WILLIAM E P30EY01730-16 9005
BARMACK, NEAL H R01EY04778-10
BARMACK, NEAL H S03RR03556-01
BARMACK, NEAL H S07RR05593-24
BARMACK, NEAL H S15EY09452-01
BARMAN, SCOTT A R29HL47926-01
BARMAN, SUSAN M R01HL33266-08
BARMES, DAVID N01DE72570-07
BARMES, DAVID E R01HS05640-05
BARNA, BARBARA P R01CA49950-03
BARNARD, D Z01RR00087-02
BARNARD, D Z01RR00090-02
BARNARD, JOHN A K08DK01893-03
BARNARD, KATHYRN E S03RR03525-02
BARNARD, ROY J R01AG07592-03
BARNAS, GEORGE M R29HL44128-02
BARNATHAN, ELLIOT S R01HL47839-01
BARNATHAN, ELLIOT S R29HL44508-02
BARNEA, AYALLA R01DK25692-13
BARNES, BRIAN S07RR07254-03 0492
BARNES, BRIAN M R01HD23383-04A1
BARNES, C S07RR07097-26 0383
BARNES, C S07RR07097-26 0384
BARNES, CAROL A K02MH00897-02
BARNES, CAROL A R01AG03376-11
BARNES, CAROL A R01AG09219-01A1
BARNES, CHARLES D S15NS30129-01
BARNES, CHARLES L S06GM08102-20 0047
BARNES, DAVID W K04CA01226-05

BARNES, DAVID W P30ES00210-24 9008
BARNES, DAVID W R01CA40475-08
BARNES, EUGENE M P50NS11535-17 0020
BARNES, EUGENE M, JR R01DK17436-16A2
BARNES, EUGENE M, JR R01MH47715-01
BARNES, GRACE M R01AA06925-03
BARNES, KAREN P01HL06835-30 0085
BARNES, PETER F R01AI27285-03
BARNES, PETER F R22AI31066-01
BARNES, PETER J R01HL45947-02
BARNES, RAMON M S07RR07048-26 0629
BARNES, RANDALL B M01RR00055-30 0567
BARNES, WILLIAM S S07RR07090-26 0463
BARNETT, BETH R43CA56311-01
BARNETT, G OCTO N01LM13538-00
BARNETT, GUY O R01LM05200-02
BARNETT, GUY O R18HS06575-01
BARNETT, HENRY J R01NS24456-05
BARNETT, JEFF M01RR00042-31 0614
BARNETT, JEFFREY L M01RR00042-31 0612
BARNETT, JEFFREY L M01RR00042-31 0644
BARNETT, JOHN B R01ES02875-07A1
BARNETT, JOHN B R01ES04758-03
BARNETT, JOHN B S15ES05832-01
BARNETT, MAJORIE N01CP95612-06
BARNETT, RICHARD S07RR05736-19 0150
BARNETT, ROSALIND R01MH43222-03
BARNETT, ROSALIND C S07RR07186-10 0609
BARNHART, SCOTT K07HL02321-02
BARNSTABLE, COLIN J R01EY05206-09
BARNSTABLE, COLIN J R01EY07119-05
BARNSTABLE, COLIN J R01NS20483-08A1
BARNSTEINER, JANE S07RR05948-05 0333
BARNUM, SCOTT P60AR20614-14 0011
BARNUM, SCOTT R P01NS29719-01 0002
BARNWELL, JOHN W R22AI24710-05
BAROFSKY, DOUGLAS F P30ES00210-24 9001
BAROHN, RICHARD J S07RR05654-24 0123
BARON, ALAIN D M01RR00750-19 0286
BARON, ALAIN D M01RR00750-19 0279
BARON, ALAIN D M01RR00827-17 0509
BARON, ALAIN D R29DK42469-02
BARON, JOHN A R01AG07146-03
BARON, JOHN A R01CA53827-01A1
BARON, JOHN A U01CA46927-04
BARON, MARGARET H R01GM42413-03
BARON, MIRON K02MH00176-10
BARON, MIRON R01MH42535-05
BARON, MIRON R01MH43979-03
BARON, MIRON R01MH44115-03
BARON, ROLAND R13AR40812-01
BARON, ROLAND E R01AR40185-02
BARON, ROLAND E R01AR41339-01
BARON, ROLAND E R01DE04724-13
BARONAS-LOWELL, DIANE M R43AI31729-01
BARONDES, SAMUEL H R01MH47563-01
BARONDES, SAMUEL H S07RR05755-18
BARONDES, SAMUEL H S15HL47767-01
BARR, CHARLES E S07RR05886-08 0301
BARR, GORDON A R01DA06600-03
BARR, ROGER C P01HL11307-25 0005
BARR, STEPHEN C S07RR05462-29 0890
BARRACK, EVELYN R01CA16924-16A1
BARRACK, EVELYN R P01DK19300-16 0004
BARRACLOUGH, CHARLES A R01HD02138-30
BARRACO, ROBIN A R24MH47181-02
BARRACO, ROBIN A S06GM08167-13 0031
BARRAL-NETTO, MANOEL P50AI30639-01 0002
BARRANGER, JOHN A R01DK43709-02
BARRETT-CONNOR, ELIZABETH M01RR00827-17 04
BARRETT-CONNOR, ELIZABETH P60AR40770-01A1
BARRETT-CONNOR, ELIZABETH L U01HL40207-05
BARRETT-CONNOR, ELIZABETH L R37AG07181-05
BARRETT, ANTHONY G R01AI20644-07
BARRETT, ANTHONY G R01AI22252-07
BARRETT, ANTHONY G R01GM40949-03
BARRETT, D S07RR05362-30 0798
BARRETT, ELLEN F R01NS12404-17
BARRETT, EUGENE M01RR00125-28 0571
BARRETT, EUGENE M01RR00125-28 0758
BARRETT, EUGENE P30DK38942-04
BARRETT, HARRISON H R01CA52643-02
BARRETT, HARRISON H R03RR06845-01
BARRETT, HELEN R. S06GM08092-18 0013
BARRETT, J C Z01ES23002-01
BARRETT, J C Z01ES23003-01
BARRETT, J C Z01ES25001-14
BARRETT, J C Z01ES25031-05
BARRETT, JACK C R44HD23052-03
BARRETT, JACK D R01HL42636-03
BARRETT, JAMES E R01DA02873-11
BARRETT, JAMES E R01DA06828-02
BARRETT, JOHN N R01NS12207-17
BARRETT, KAREN C S07RR07127-23 0488
BARRETT, KATHLEEN J R01AR38821-06
BARRETT, KIM E R01DK28305-10
BARRETT, KIM E R13DK44466-01
BARRETT, KIM E R29AI24992-04
BARRETT, KIM E U01AI31595-01 0004
BARRETT, PAULA Q R01HL36977-05
BARRICK, DALE N01LM03514-06
BARRIERE, STEVE L M01RR00865-18 0356
BARRIERE, STEVEN L M01RR00865-18 0350
BARRINGTON, PEGGY L R29HL38909-04
BARRIO, JORGE R P01NS15654-13 0009
BARRIONUEVO, GERMAN K04NS01196-05
BARRIONUEVO, GERMAN R01NS24288-05
BARRIOS, NIOKA S07RR05377-30 0756
BARRON, BRUCE A U10EY07489-04
BARRON, RICHARD N01CO15642-00
BARRON, RICHARD N01CO15654-00
BARRON, SUSAN R29DA06049-03
BARRON, WILLIAM M. M01RR00055-30 0507
BARROW, WILLIAM W R01AI21946-07
BARROWS, HOWARD P30AG08014-02 9003
BARRY, ANITA S07RR05927-07 0961
BARRY, BRIDGETTE A R01GM43273-02
BARRY, MICHAEL A P01DC00168-10 0019
BARRY, MICHAEL J R01HS06540-01A1
BARRY, SUSAN R S07RR05383-30 0550
BARRY, WENDY C R29AI30136-02
BARRY, WILLIAM H R01HL30478-07
BARRY, WILLIAM H R01HL42535-01A1
BARSEVICK, ANDREA M R29NR01839-05
BARSH, GREGORY S R29HG00377-03
BARSHOP, BRUCE A M01RR00827-17 0488
BARSKY, ARTHUR J R01HL43216-03
BARSKY, ARTHUR J R01MH40487-06
BARSKY, SANFORD H K04CA01351-03
BARSKY, SANFORD H R01CA40225-07
BARSOTTI, ROBERT J R29HL40953-04
BARSS, VANESSA M01RR02635-07 0261
BARST, R M01RR00645-20 0408
BARST, R J M01RR00645-20 0415
BARST, ROBYN M01RR00645-20 0487
BARTEL, RONNDA L R43AR41110-01
BARTELS, PETER H P01CA38548-07
BARTELS, PETER H R35CA53877-01
BARTELS, STEPHEN P P30EY03790-11 9002
BARTELS, STEPHEN P R01EY04914-08
BARTELS, STEPHEN P S07RR05527-29 0519
BARTFAI, TAMAS P01AG10491-01 0004
BARTH, RICHARD P30CA11198-23 9023
BARTHOLD, STEPHEN P01AI30548-01A1 9001
BARTHOLD, STEPHEN P01AI30548-01A1 0003
BARTHOLD, STEPHEN W P01AI30548-01A1
BARTHOLD, STEPHEN W R01AI26815-04
BARTHOLD, STEPHEN W R01RR02039-08
BARTHOLDI, MARTY F P41RR01315-10 9001
BARTKE, ANDRZEJ R01DK42137-01A2
BARTKE, ANDRZEJ R01HD20001-08
BARTKE, ANDRZEJ R01HD20033-08
BARTKE, ANDRZEJ S07RR07118-22 0372
BARTKE, ANDRZEJ S07RR07118-22 0373
BARTLES, JAMES R R01CA53997-01
BARTLET, JOHN G M01RR00722-19 0193
BARTLET, JOHN G M01RR00722-19 0196
BARTLET, JOHN G M01RR00722-19 0195
BARTLET, JOHN GO M01RR00722-19 0194
BARTLETT, DONALD, JR R01HL19827-15
BARTLETT, JAMES C R01AG09965-01
BARTLETT, JAMES D S07RR07133-22 0512
BARTLETT, JIMMY D S07RR05807-13 0451
BARTLETT, JOHN A M01RR00030-30 0491
BARTLETT, JOHN A M01RR00030-30 0440
BARTLETT, JOHN A U01AI27662-06
BARTLETT, JOHN G U01AI27668-05S2
BARTLETT, KIRBY K N01CP05707-03
BARTLETT, PAUL A R01GM28965-09
BARTLETT, PAUL A R01GM46627-14
BARTLETT, PAUL A R37GM30759-16
BARTLETT, RICHARD J R35AG07922-04 0005
BARTLETT, ROBERT H M01RR00042-31 0638
BARTLETT, ROBERT H R01HD15434-11
BARTLEY, JAMES A S07RR05352-30 0755
BARTNESS, TIMOTHY J K02MH00841-02
BARTNESS, TIMOTHY J R01DK35254-08
BARTNESS, TIMOTHY J S07RR07171-08 0147
BARTO, ANDREW G P50MH48185-01 0002
BARTOLA, DAVID A. P01AG03991-08 0007
BARTOLUCCI, ALFRED H P01CA28103-13 9010
BARTON, BRUCE U01HL37948-05
BARTON, BRUCE A N01HC55023-19
BARTON, DEREK H R01GM37943-05
BARTON, JACQUELINE P01CA33620-08 0004
BARTON, JACQUELINE K R01GM33309-09
BARTON, N Z01NS02453-11
BARTON, N Z01NS02657-07
BARTON, N Z01NS02664-07
BARTOSHUK, LINDA M P01DC00168-10 0006
BARTOSHUK, LINDA M R01DC00283-07
BARTSCH, HELMUT R01CA47591-03
BARTSCH, HELMUT R13CA54157-01
BARTSCHAT, DIETER K R01NS21758-07
BARTSCHAT, DIETER K S15HD28750-01
BARTZOKIS, GEORGE P50MH30911-14 0033
BARTZOKIS, GEORGE S07RR05756-18 0305
BASAK, SUBHASH, C N01NS02398-03
BASAK, SUKLA R01AI28894-01A2
BASBAUM, ALLAN P50DE08973-02 0002
BASBAUM, ALLAN I P01NS16033-11 0007
BASBAUM, ALLAN I P01NS21445-07 0001
BASBAUM, ALLAN I R01NS14627-14
BASBAUM, CAROL B P01HL24136-13 0001
BASBAUM, CAROL B R01HL43762-02
BASCH, R P30CA16087-14 9009
BASCH, ROSS S P01AG04860-08 0004
BASCH, ROSS S S10RR06703-01
BASCO, MONICA R P50MH41115-05 0019
BASCOM, REBECCA R29HL40945-03
BASEL, RICHARD M R43CA54039-01
BASEMAN, JOEL B P01AI22380-07
BASEMAN, JOEL B P01AI22380-07 0002
BASEMAN, JOEL B R01AI27873-03
BASEMAN, JOEL B U01AI31498-01
BASEMAN, JOEL B U01AI31498-01 9004
BASEN-ENGQUIST, KARE S07RR05828-08 0533
BASERGA, RENATO P01CA56309-01 9001
BASERGA, RENATO P01CA56309-01
BASERGA, RENATO P01CA56309-01 0001
BASERGA, RENATO L P01AG00378-20 9002
BASERGA, RENATO L P01AG00378-20 0008
BASERGA, RENATO L R01CA53484-02
BASERGA, RENATO L R01GM33694-08
BASERGA, RENATO L R01GM42383-03
BASHEY, REZA I P01AR39740-03 9002
BASHEY, REZA I R01HL43564-03
BASHFORD, DONALD E R29GM45607-01
BASILE, DOMINICK S06GM08225-07 0003
BASILICO, CLAUDIO R35CA42568-06
BASILIO, CARLOS M S06GM08224-07 0002
BASINGER, SCOTT F R01EY01406-15
BASKIN, DENIS G P30DK17047-15 9004
BASKIN, GARY B P51RR00164-30 9009
BASKIN, GARY B P51RR00164-30 9010
BASKIN, GARY B P51RR00164-30 0011
BASS, BARBARA S07RR05359-30 0502
BASS, BARBARA L R29DK43356-01
BASS, BRENDA L R01GM44073-02
BASS, DAVID A P30CA12197-19 9012
BASS, DAVID A R01AI10732-20
BASS, DAVID A R01AI14929-12
BASS, NATHAN M P41RR01614-10 0006
BASS, NATHAN M R01DK32926-07
BASSETT, ARTHUR L R01HL19044-15
BASSETT, DANUTA N01CN85120-04
BASSETT, DAVID J R01ES05255-02
BASSETT, DAVID J R01HL34674-07
BASSETT, DAVID J P P30ES03819-06A1 9013
BASSETT, LAWRENCE P01CA50084-03 0005
BASSFORD, PHILIP J, JR R01AI17292-12
BASSIN, GAIL D N01AR02201-02
BASSIN, R H Z01CB04848-19
BASSINGTHWAIGHTE, J P41RR01243-10 0001
BASSINGTHWAIGHTE, J P41RR01243-10 0023
BASSINGTHWAIGHTE, J P41RR01243-10 0024
BASSINGTHWAIGHTE, J P41RR01243-10 0025
BASSINGTHWAIGHTE, J P41RR01243-10 0021
BASSINGTHWAIGHTE, J P41RR01243-10 0029
BASSINGTHWAIGHTE, JAMES B P01CA42045-06 90
BASSINGTHWAIGHTE, JAMES B P01HL38736-05 00
BASSINGTHWAIGHTE, JAMES B P41RR01243-10
BASSINGTHWAIGHTE, JAMES B P41RR01243-10 00
BASSINGTHWAIGHTE, JAMES B P41RR01243-10 00
BASSINGTHWAIGHTE, JAMES B R37HL19139-16
BASSUK, ELLEN L R01MH47312-01
BAST, ROBERT R01CA39930-08
BAST, ROBERT C P30CA14236-18 9014
BAST, ROBERT C S03RR03522-02
BAST, ROBERT C JR P01CA47741-02 0003
BAST, ROBERT C, JR P30CA14236-18
BASTACKY, SAMUEL J R01HL40521-04
BASTANI, BIJAN M01RR00080-29 0450
BASTANI, BIJAN P50MH41684-07 0053
BASTANI, ROSHAN P01CA50084-03 9001
BASTANI, ROSHAN P01CA50084-03
BASTANI, ROSHAN R29CA51142-02
BASTIA, DEEPAK P01CA30246-11 0002
BASTIA, DEEPAK R01AI19881-09
BASTIAN-ECHEVARRIA, WILLIAM K11DK02040-01
BASTIAN, JOSEPH A, J S07RR07078-18 0460
BASTIAN, JOSEPH A, JR R01NS12337-17
BASTIANI, MICHAEL J R29NS25387-04
BASTIAS, MARIA C S07RR05424-30 0079
BASTOW, KENNETH S07RR05967-04 0289
BASU, ASHIS K R01ES05695-01
BASU, HIRAK S R29CA49409-02
BASU, SUBHASH C R01NS18005-09
BASUK, PAUL M M01RR00827-17 0429
BATEMAN, ERIK A R29EY08706-02
BATEMAN, JAMES S07RR05424-30 0065
BATEMAN, JANE B R01EY08282-02
BATEMAN, ROBERT C JR R29DK41892-02
BATEMAN, ROBERT C, JR R03DA07181-01
BATES, ELIZABETH P50NS22343-06A1
BATES, ELIZABETH P50NS22343-06A1 9001
BATES, ELIZABETH R01DC00216-08
BATES, ELIZABETH A P01DC01289-01 0002
BATES, ELIZABETH A P01DC01289-01
BATES, ELIZABETH A R01DC00438-03
BATES, GEORGE W S07RR07090-26 0464
BATES, JOHN E S07RR07031-26 0071
BATES, MARSHA E P50AA08747-02 0006
BATES, MARYANN S S07RR07149-18 0411
BATES, S Z01CM06731-03

BATES, THEODORE R S06GM08061-17 0001
BATHON, JOAN M K08AR01856-01
BATICH, C P50DE09307-03 0001
BATICH, CHRISTOPHER P01DK20586-15 0006
BATKI, STEVEN L P50DA01696-12 0014
BATRA, PREM P S03RR03133-04
BATSFORD, WILLIAM M01RR00125-28 0756
BATSHAW, MARK L P01HD10981-14 0011
BATSHAW, MARK L P30HD26979-02
BATSHAW, MARK L R01NS28033-06
BATTAGLIA, F C M01RR00069-29 0389
BATTAGLIA, FREDERICK C K12HD00850-05
BATTAGLIA, FREDERICK C P01HD00781-27S1 003
BATTAGLIA, FREDERICK C P01HD00781-27S1
BATTAGLIA, FREDERICK C P01HD00781-27S1 004
BATTAGLIA, FREDERICK C P01HD00781-27S1 003
BATTAGLIA, FREDERICK C P50HD20761-06A1 000
BATTERSON, WILLIAM W R01DE09496-02
BATTERSON, WILLIAM W S07RR05970-06 0768
BATTEY, J Z01NS02753-03
BATTEY, J Z01NS02774-03
BATTEY, JAMES F S06GM08266-04 0005
BATTIE, MICHELLE C R01AR40857-01
BATTIFORA, HECTOR P30CA33572-11 9015
BATTIFORA, HECTOR A R01CA37194-08
BATTISTA, MICHAEL M01RR00080-29 0664
BATTLES, AUGUST H G20RR07054-01
BAUDRY, MICHEL R01NS18427-10
BAUER, CARL E R29GM40941-03
BAUER, CHARLES R U10HD21397-06
BAUER, EUGENE M01RR00070-29 0232
BAUER, EUGENE A R01AR41551-01 0001
BAUER, EUGENE A R01AR41551-01
BAUER, EUGENE A R37AR19537-16
BAUER, HAROLD R R03DA06804-01
BAUER, KENNETH M01RR01032-16 0443
BAUER, KENNETH A M01RR01032-16 0469
BAUER, KENNETH A M01RR01032-16 0470
BAUER, LANCE O R01DA05826-03
BAUER, MARK C S03RR03356-06
BAUER, MARK M M01RR00040-31 0417
BAUER, MARK S K11MH00720-04
BAUER, MARK S M01RR00040-31 0351
BAUER, MARK S M01RR00040-31 0404
BAUER, PATRICIA J R29HD28425-01
BAUER, PATRICIA J S07RR07052-26 0152
BAUER, RICHARD L R01AR39794-03
BAUER, RUSSELL M R01AA06203-04A1
BAUER, WILLIAM R R01GM37525-05
BAUGHMAN, ROBERT W R01EY03502-11
BAULDRY, SUE A R29AI30142-01A1
BAUM, ANDREW S R01MH40106-05
BAUM, B J Z01DE00336-09
BAUM, JEAN S07RR07058-26 0173
BAUM, JEAN S R29GM45302-01A1
BAUM, JULES L R01EY04034-09
BAUM, LINDA S07RR05366-30 0552
BAUM, LINDA G S07RR05354-30 0410
BAUM, MICHAEL J K02MH00392-10
BAUM, MICHEL G R01DK41612-01A2
BAUMAN, DAVID H G20RR06789-01
BAUMAN, KARL E S07RR05450-30 0343
BAUMAN, LAURIE J R29MH43379-04
BAUMAN, MARGARET L P01HD24448-04 0003
BAUMAN, RAQUEL S03RR03068-05
BAUMANN, HEINZ R01CA26122-13
BAUMANN, HEINZ R01DK33886-08
BAUMANN, MARGARET M P30AG08812-02 0004
BAUMANN, PAUL R01AI27090-03
BAUMANN, THOMAS K S07RR05412-30 0974
BAUMBACH, GARY L. P01NS24621-05 0005
BAUMBACH, GARY L R01HL22149-14
BAUMEISTER, ALAN A R01DA05907-03
BAUMEISTER, ALFRED P30HD15052-11 9011
BAUMEISTER, ALFRED A P01HD15051-11A1
BAUMEISTER, ALFRED A R01HD27336-02
BAUMEISTER, ROY F R01MH43826-01A2
BAUMGARDNER, ANN HUDSON R29MH43930-01A3
BAUMGARDNER, DENNIS S07RR07030-26 0378
BAUMGART, STEPHEN M01RR00240-27 0341
BAUMGART, STEPHEN M01RR00240-27 0326
BAUMGART, STEPHEN M01RR00240-27 0349
BAUMGARTEN, CLIVE M R01HL46764-01
BAUMGARTNER, RICHARD N R01AG08510-03
BAUMGARTNER, RUDOLF Z01HL00990-05
BAUMGARTNER, WILLIAM A R01HL41594-03
BAUMGOLD, JESSE R01NS28114-02
BAUMGOLD, JESSE S07RR05359-30 0503
BAUMRIND, SHELDON R01DE08713-04
BAUMSTARK, ALFONS L S07RR07171-08 0148
BAUMSTARK, ALFONS L S07RR07171-08
BAUMSTARK, ALFONS L S15NS30117-01
BAUMSTARK, BARBARA R S07RR07171-08 0149
BAUMSTARK, JOHN S S07RR05390-30 0667
BAUN, MARA M S03RR03507-03
BAUN, MARA M S07RR05942-06
BAUN, MARA M S07RR05942-06 0010
BAUN, MARA M S07RR05942-06 0011
BAUN, MARA M S15GM47073-01
BAUSHER, LARRY P R01EY07115-04
BAUSSERMAN, LINDA L S07RR05818-12 0158
BAUTCH, VICTORIA L R01HL43174-03

BAUTISTA, ABRAHAM P R29AA08846-01A1
BAVISTER, BARRY D P51RR00167-31 0048
BAVISTER, BARRY D R01HD14235-09A1
BAVISTER, BARRY D U01HD22023-07
BAVOIL, PATRIK M R01AI26280-04
BAWA, KAMAL S S07RR07199-12 0939
BAWDEN, JAMES W K16DE00165-07
BAWDEN, JAMES W R01DE07755-06
BAWDEN, JAMES W R13DE09772-01
BAX, A Z01DK29020-07
BAXLEY, NORMAN E R44MH43712-03
BAXTER-LOWE, LEE A R01AI28034-03
BAXTER-LOWE, LEE A R01HL47149-01
BAXTER, CHARLES R P50GM21681-27
BAXTER, CHARLES R P50GM21681-27 9001
BAXTER, JOHN D R01DK41842-03
BAXTER, JOHN D R01HL35706-06A1
BAXTER, LEWIS R K01MH00752-04
BAXTER, LEWIS R M01RR00865-18 0294
BAYER, BARBARA M R01DA07293-01
BAYER, MANFRED E P30CA06927-29 9009
BAYER, SHIRLEY A P01NS27613-01A2 0002
BAYLES, KATHRYN A P60DC01409-01 0008
BAYLES, KATHRYN A P60DC01409-01 0007
BAYLES, KATHRYN A R01MH43872-03
BAYLES, KENNETH W R03DE09799-01
BAYLEY, HAGAN P R01NS26760-03
BAYLIN, STEPHEN P30CA06973-29 9018
BAYLIN, STEPHEN B M01RR00722-19 0041
BAYLIN, STEPHEN B R01CA43318-06
BAYLIN, STEPHEN B R01CA48081-04
BAYLIN, STEPHEN B R01CA54396-01
BAYLINK, DAVID J R01AR31062-09
BAYLIS, CHRISTINE R01HL31933-08
BAYLIS, GORDON C R29NS27296-02
BAYLOR, DENIS A R01EY05750-07
BAYLOR, DENIS A R37EY01543-18
BAYLOR, STEPHEN M R01NS17620-10
BAYNE, CHRISTOPHER J R22AI16137-09
BAYNE, CHRISTOPHER J S15AI32216-01
BAYNE, K Z01RR00091-01
BAYNE, K Z01RR00092-01
BAYNE, K Z01RR00093-01
BAYNE, K Z01RR00094-01
BAYNE, STEPHEN C R01DE08561-03
BAYNES, JOHN W R37DK19971-15
BAYNES, KATHLEEN R29DC00811-04
BAYORH, MOHAMED S06GM08248-05 0002
BAZAN, HAYDEE E R01EY04928-09
BAZAN, HAYDEE E R01EY06635-05
BAZAN, NICOLAS G R01EY04428-08
BAZAN, NICOLAS G R01EY05121-08
BAZAN, NICOLAS G R01NS23002-06
BE MENT, SPENCER P01MH44337-03 0004
BEACH, DAVID H R01GM34517-07
BEACH, DAVID H R01GM34607-06
BEACH, DAVID H R01GM39620-04
BEACH, DAVID H R01HG00017-02
BEACH, JANIS N01CN75406-13
BEACH, JANIS N01CP05618-05
BEACH, JANIS A N01CM67810-12
BEACHY, ROGER N R01AI27161-03
BEAGLEY, KENNETH P01DK44240-01 0003
BEAK, PETER A R01GM18874-20
BEAL, M FLINT P01NS16367-12 0005
BEAL, M FLINT P50NS10828-16 0031
BEALE JOHN M S07RR07091-26 0746
BEALE, BRIAN S S07RR05788-15 0894
BEALE, ELMUS G R29GM39895-04
BEALE, JOHN S07RR05849-11 0251
BEALER, STEVEN L R01HL25877-10
BEALS, JANETTE R01MH42473-06 0001
BEALS, JANETTE L R03MH47377-01
BEAM, KURT G P01NS28323-02 0004
BEAM, KURT G, JR R01NS24444-06
BEAM, KURT G, JR R01NS26416-04
BEAMAN, BLAINE L R01AI20900-07A1
BEAMAN, KENNETH D R29HD23848-02
BEAMER, WESLEY S07RR05545-29 0575
BEAMER, WESLEY G R03CA54889-01
BEAMES, BURTON S07RR05519-29 0515
BEAN MICHAEL A S07RR05520-28 0827
BEAN, BARRY S03RR03382-07
BEAN, BRUCE P P01NS02253-32 0015
BEAN, BRUCE P R01HL35034-08
BEAN, FRANK D P30HD06160-20S1 9001
BEAN, JUDY A P01NS28059-01A1 9003
BEAN, MICHAEL P01HL36444-11 0012
BEANLANDS, DONALD S N01HC65059-15
BEAR, CHRISTINE P50DK41980-03 0005
BEAR, DAVID G S06GM08139-17 0035
BEAR, HARRY D R01CA48075-04
BEAR, MARK F R29EY06929-05
BEARD, DAVID V P01CA47982-04 0009
BEARD, DAVID V R01CA44060-04A1
BEARD, JOHN L R29DK39160-05
BEARDSLEY, G PETER R01CA50721-03
BEARDSLEY, G PETER U01CA52020-02 0002
BEARDSLEY, GEORGE P R01CA42300-06
BEARDSLEY, GEORGE P U10CA53127-01 0024
BEARDSLEY, GEORGE P U10CA53127-01 0044
BEARDSLEY, GEORGE P U10CA53127-01 0045

BEARDSLEY, GEORGE P U10CA53127-01 0025
BEARDSLEY, GEORGE P U10CA53127-01 0046
BEARDSLEY, GEORGE P U10CA53127-01 0047
BEARDSLEY, GEORGE P U10CA53127-01 0048
BEARDSLEY, GEORGE P U10CA53127-01 0049
BEARDSLEY, GEORGE P U10CA53127-01 0050
BEARDSLEY, GEORGE P U10CA53127-01 0051
BEARDSLEY, GEORGE P U10CA53127-01 0052
BEARDSLEY, GEORGE P U10CA53127-01 0053
BEARDSLEY, GEORGE P U10CA53127-01 0054
BEARDSLEY, GEORGE P U10CA53127-01 0055
BEARDSLEY, GEORGE P U10CA53127-01 0056
BEARDSLEY, GEORGE P U10CA53127-01 0057
BEARDSLEY, GEORGE P U10CA53127-01 0058
BEARDSLEY, GEORGE P U10CA53127-01 0059
BEARDSLEY, GEORGE P U10CA53127-01 0060
BEARDSLEY, GEORGE P U10CA53127-01 0026
BEARDSLEY, GEORGE P U10CA53127-01
BEARDSLEY, GEORGE P U10CA53127-01 0001
BEARDSLEY, GEORGE P U10CA53127-01 0002
BEARDSLEY, GEORGE P U10CA53127-01 0003
BEARDSLEY, GEORGE P U10CA53127-01 0027
BEARDSLEY, GEORGE P U10CA53127-01 0004
BEARDSLEY, GEORGE P U10CA53127-01 0005
BEARDSLEY, GEORGE P U10CA53127-01 0006
BEARDSLEY, GEORGE P U10CA53127-01 0007
BEARDSLEY, GEORGE P U10CA53127-01 0028
BEARDSLEY, GEORGE P U10CA53127-01 0029
BEARDSLEY, GEORGE P U10CA53127-01 0030
BEARDSLEY, GEORGE P U10CA53127-01 0031
BEARDSLEY, GEORGE P U10CA53127-01 0032
BEARDSLEY, GEORGE P U10CA53127-01 0008
BEARDSLEY, GEORGE P U10CA53127-01 0009
BEARDSLEY, GEORGE P U10CA53127-01 0010
BEARDSLEY, GEORGE P U10CA53127-01 0011
BEARDSLEY, GEORGE P U10CA53127-01 0012
BEARDSLEY, GEORGE P U10CA53127-01 0013
BEARDSLEY, GEORGE P U10CA53127-01 0033
BEARDSLEY, GEORGE P U10CA53127-01 0034
BEARDSLEY, GEORGE P U10CA53127-01 0035
BEARDSLEY, GEORGE P U10CA53127-01 0036
BEARDSLEY, GEORGE P U10CA53127-01 0037
BEARDSLEY, GEORGE P U10CA53127-01 0038
BEARDSLEY, GEORGE P U10CA53127-01 0039
BEARDSLEY, GEORGE P U10CA53127-01 0040
BEARDSLEY, GEORGE P U10CA53127-01 0041
BEARDSLEY, GEORGE P U10CA53127-01 0042
BEARDSLEY, GEORGE P U10CA53127-01 0043
BEARDSLEY, GEORGE P U10CA53127-01 0014
BEARDSLEY, GEORGE P U10CA53127-01 0015
BEARDSLEY, GEORGE P U10CA53127-01 0016
BEARDSLEY, GEORGE P U10CA53127-01 0017
BEARDSLEY, GEORGE P U10CA53127-01 0018
BEARDSLEY, GEORGE P U10CA53127-01 0019
BEARDSLEY, GEORGE P U10CA53127-01 0020
BEARDSLEY, GEORGE P U10CA53127-01 0021
BEARDSLEY, GEORGE P U10CA53127-01 0022
BEARDSLEY, GEORGE P U10CA53127-01 0023
BEARDSLEY, PATRICK M R29DA05712-04
BEARON, LUCILLE S07RR05405-30 0869
BEARSE, ROBERT C S07RR07037-26
BEARSE, ROBERT C S15DK44664-01
BEASLEY, DEBBIE S S07RR05487-29 0717
BEASLEY, JOHN M N01CN15374-00
BEASLEY, R PALMER S07RR05828-08
BEASLEY, VAL R R01ES05552-01
BEATTIE, CHARLES R01GM38177-04
BEATTIE, CRAIG W P01CA49488-01A2 0002
BEATTIE, DIANA S R01GM38433-06
BEATTIE, KENNETH L P30HG00210-01 0001
BEATTIE, MICHAEL S P50NS10165-20 0026
BEATTY, JACK S07RR07009-26 0939
BEATTY, PATRICK R18HL45265-02 0002
BEATTY, PATRICK G P01AI29518-02 0003
BEATY, BARRY J R01AI25629-04
BEATY, CHRISTOPHER D K08HL02622-01
BEATY, HARRY N M01RR00048-30
BEATY, HARRY N S07RR05370-30
BEAUCAGE, S L Z01BB07005-02
BEAUCAGE, S L Z01BB07008-01
BEAUCAGE, S L Z01BB07009-01
BEAUCAGE, S L Z01BB07010-01
BEAUCHAMP, GARY K P20DC01434-01
BEAUCHAMP, GARY K P50DC00214-06
BEAUCHAMP, GARY K R01DC00882-09
BEAUCHAMP, GARY K S07RR05825-12
BEAUCHAMP, GARY K S07RR05825-12 0508
BEAUCHAMP, GARY K S15NS30124-01
BEAUCHAMP, R DANIEL P01DK35608-06A1 9004
BEAUCHAMP, ROBERT DANIEL K11CA01309-06
BEAUCHAMP, TOM L S07RR07136-20 0610
BEAUDET, ARTHUR M01RR00188-27 0320
BEAUDET, ARTHUR L M01RR00188-27 0089
BEAUDET, ARTHUR L R01AI32177-01
BEAUDET, ARTHUR L. P30HD24064-04 9001
BEAUDRY, NORMAN N01HD13115-01
BEAUDRY, NORMAN N N01CB71010-06
BEAUDRY, NORMAN N N01HD02900-02
BEAUDRY, NORMAN N N01HD02907-03
BEAUDRY, NORMAN N N01HD13106-00
BEAUVAIS, FRED P50DA07074-02 0001
BEAUVAIS, FREDERICK R01AA08302-03

BEAUVAIS, FREDERICK R01DA03371-09
BEAVEN, M Z01HL00937-09
BEAVER, KATHRYN L S07RR07032-26 0031
BEAVIS, ANDREW D P01HL36573-06 0003
BEAVO, JOSEPH A P01HL44948-01A1 0005
BEAVO, JOSEPH A R01DK21723-14
BEAVO, JOSEPH A R01EY08197-03
BEAZOGLOU, TRYPHON N01DE12591-00
BEBRIN, WILLIAM R K15DE00240-04
BECHHOFER, DAVID H R29GM39516-04
BECHTOLD, CLIFFORD S07RR05390-30 0679
BECK, AARON T P50MH45178-02 0001
BECK, AARON T R01MH47383-01
BECK, CORNELIA P50MH48197-02 0003
BECK, CORNELIA M R01NR02367-02
BECK, DAVID P S03RR03416-07
BECK, DAVID P S15GM47038-01
BECK, J ROBERT S07RR07238-04 0469
BECK, JOHN P60AG10415-01 9003
BECK, JOHN C P60AG10415-01
BECK, JOHN R R13HS06904-01
BECK, KEITH C M01RR00425-22S3 0456
BECK, MELINDA A R29HL46195-01
BECK, RAYMOND W S07RR07088-24 0348
BECK, RAYMOND W S15AI32212-01
BECK, ROY W K11EY00316-01
BECK, ROY W U10EY07212-05
BECK, SHERYL G K02MH00880-02
BECK, SHERYL G R01NS28512-01A1
BECK, THOMAS J R29AG08713-02
BECK, WILLIAM T R01CA30103-11
BECK, WILLIAM T R01CA40570-07
BECK, WILLIAM T R01CA47941-03
BECKELHEIMER, MEL N01LM73509-07
BECKER, CHARLES P42ES04705-05 0010
BECKER, CHARLES E M01RR00083-29 0231
BECKER, CHARLES E M01RR00083-29 0224
BECKER, CHRISTOPHER H R01HG00174-02
BECKER, DAVID S R43CA52365-01A1
BECKER, DIANE M R01NR02241-01A1
BECKER, DONALD P R01NS27544-02
BECKER, DOROTHEA R01CA50189-03
BECKER, DOROTHY J M01RR00084-29 0214
BECKER, DOROTHY J M01RR00084-29 0240
BECKER, DOROTHY J M01RR00084-29 0199
BECKER, DOROTHY J M01RR00084-29 0203
BECKER, DOROTHY J M01RR00084-29 0003
BECKER, DOROTHY J M01RR00084-29 0055
BECKER, E D Z01DK29026-03
BECKER, E D Z01DK58000-47
BECKER, ELMER L R01AI09648-21
BECKER, FREDERICK F P30CA16672-17
BECKER, FREDERICK F P30CA16672-17 9010
BECKER, FREDERICK F P30CA16672-17 9014
BECKER, FREDERICK F R13CA52872-01
BECKER, FREDERICK F R13CA55015-01
BECKER, FREDERICK F S07RR05511-29
BECKER, FREDERICK F S15CA56008-01
BECKER, GARY M01RR00750-19 0296
BECKER, GARY S R37HD02054-06
BECKER, GAY R01AG09176-01A1
BECKER, GAYLENE R01AG08973-01A1
BECKER, HOWARD C R01AA07791-03
BECKER, JAMES S07RR05950-07 0995
BECKER, JAMES M M01RR00036-31 0984
BECKER, JAMES M M01RR02635-07 0278
BECKER, JAMES T R01MH45311-02
BECKER, JEFFREY M R01GM22087-15
BECKER, JEFFREY M R01GM46520-01
BECKER, JEFFREY M S07RR07088-24 0351
BECKER, JILL B R01NS22157-06
BECKER, JUDITH V P50MH43520-04 0004
BECKER, JUDITH V S07RR05650-25 0092
BECKER, LAURENCE E R01HD22713-05
BECKER, LEWIS C M01RR00035-31 0321
BECKER, LEWIS C P50HL17655-17 0030
BECKER, LEWIS C P50HL17655-17 9014
BECKER, LEWIS C R01HL33360-04A2
BECKER, MARK P R29CA53787-02
BECKER, MARSHALL H S03RR03404-07
BECKER, MICHAEL A R01DK28554-11
BECKER, PAMELA S K08HL02656-01
BECKER, PATRICIA T R01NR02701-01
BECKER, PATRICIA T S07RR05866-08 0985
BECKER, PATRICIA T S07RR05866-08 0986
BECKER, RICHARD C S07RR05712-20 0046
BECKER, ROBERT S07RR05368-30 0575
BECKER, ROBERT E P30AG08014-02
BECKER, ROBERT E R01MH41821-03
BECKER, SALLY A S07RR05390-30 0675
BECKER, STAN R R01HD27139-02
BECKER, THOMAS M R29CA48003-03
BECKERLE, MARY C R01HL41553-03
BECKERMANN, CHRISTOP S07RR07035-26 0078
BECKETT, WILLIAM S K07HL02316-03
BECKMAN, ALEXANDER L R01DA02254-10
BECKMAN, ANNA M P01CA42792-05 9001
BECKMAN, JEFFREY K R29DK40121-04
BECKMAN, JEFFREY K S07RR05424-30 0108
BECKMAN, JOSEPH S R01HL46407-01
BECKMAN, JOSEPH S S07RR05349-30 0750
BECKMANN, ANNA MARIE P01AI29363-02 9001
BECKNER, M Z01CB09352-01
BECKSTEAD, JAY P01HD24640-03 9005
BECKSTEAD, JAY H P01AI24286-05 0007
BECKSTEAD, ROBERT M R01NS24971-03
BECKSTEAD, ROBERT M S07RR05420-30 0036
BECKSTRAND, JANIS K R01NR01922-04
BECKWITH, JONATHAN R R01GM41883-03
BECKWITH, JONATHAN R R37GM38922-05
BECTON, DAVID N01HB77034-07
BEDELL, HAROLD E R01EY05068-07
BEDFORD, JOEL S R01CA49501-03
BEDFORD, JOEL S R37CA18023-17
BEDI, GURRINDER S R55DE09690-01A1
BEDI, GURRINDER S S07RR05330-30 0011
BEDIGIAN, HENDRICK G R01CA31102-10A2
BEDINGER, PATRICIA A R29GM38516-05
BEDNARSKI, MARK D R29GM43037-03
BEDROSIAN, CAMILLE L K08AI01022-02
BEEBE, D Z01BH07006-01
BEEBE, D Z01BH07007-02
BEEBE, D Z01BH07008-05
BEEBE, DAVID C R01EY04853-08
BEEBE, DAVID C R01EY07528-03
BEEBE, DAVID C S07RR05983-05 0348
BEEBE, DAVID C S07RR05983-05
BEEBE, G W Z01CP05279-08
BEEBE, G W Z01CP05280-08
BEEBE, G W Z01CP05329-08
BEEBE, THOMAS P S07RR07092-26 0526
BEEBE, THOMAS P S07RR07092-26 0484
BEEBER, LINDA S S07RR07068-26 0229
BEECHEM, JOSEPH M P41RR03155-06 0005
BEECHEM, JOSEPH M R01GM45990-01
BEECHER, CHRIS W W P01CA48112-01A3 9002
BEECHER, MICHAEL D S07RR07096-26 0067
BEECHERL, ERNEST S07RR05377-30 0772
BEEHLER, CONNIE J K08HL02369-02
BEEKEN, WARREN L. M01RR00109-28 0303
BEEKMAAN, ROBERT H M01RR00042-31 0655
BEEKMAN, ROBERT H M01RR00042-31 0566
BEEKMAN, ROBERT H M01RR00042-31 0459
BEELER, J Z01BF02005-01
BEELER, J Z01BF02006-01
BEELER, J A Z01BF02004-03
BEELER, TROY J S07RR05983-05 0349
BEEMON, KAREN L R01CA48746-03
BEEN, MICHAEL D R29GM40689-04
BEER, DAVID G R01CA46433-03
BEER, JANOS M P01ES01640-14 0017
BEER, MICHAEL S07RR07041-26
BEER, MICHAEL S15GM47099-01
BEER, WILLIAM M01RR01346-10 0135
BEERMAN, TERRY A R01CA28495-10
BEERMAN, TERRY A R01CA52682-02
BEERS, WILLIAM H S07RR05514-29 0507
BEERY, MADELINE P R43AI31748-01
BEESON, PETER G R19DA06405-03
BEESON, PETER G R19MH46230-03
BEEZHOLD, DONALD H R55CA53482-01A1
BEG, Z Z01HL02012-16
BEGENISICH, TED B R01NS14138-12
BEGG, COLIN P01CA38493-06S1 9001
BEGG, DAVID P41RR00592-22 0029
BEGG, DAVID A P30HD06645-20 9010
BEGG, DAVID A S07RR05381-30 0776
BEGG, LISA K07CA01397-04
BEGLEITER, HENRI R01AA05524-09
BEGLEITER, HENRI R37AA02686-15
BEGLEITER, HENRI U10AA08401-03
BEGLEITER, HENRI U10AA08403-03
BEGLEY, CAROLINE S07RR05962-05 0013
BEGLEY, TADHG P R01DK44083-01
BEGLEY, TADHG P R01GM40498-03
BEHAN, MARY R01EY04478-09
BEHAN, PETER O P01HD20806-05 0004
BEHAR, JOSE R01DK27389-07A2
BEHAR, KEVIN L R29NS26419-04
BEHAR, LENORE R01MH48053-01
BEHAR, LENORE R18MH48238-02
BEHBEHANI, MICHAEL M R01NS20643-07
BEHE, MICHAEL J R01GM36343-05A2
BEHE, MICHAEL J S15HD28746-01
BEHFOROUZ, MOHAMMAD R15CA54517-01
BEHM, FREDERICK G P01CA20180-14 9002
BEHRENS, B LYN S07RR05352-30
BEHRENS, B LYN S15HL47689-01
BEHRENS, PAUL N01CM97615-03
BEHRENS, PAUL W R44DK43174-02
BEHRENTS, ROLF G S07RR05994-03 0297
BEHRMAN, HAROLD R R01HD10718-15
BEIDEL, DEBORAH C R29MH43252-04
BEIDLER, LLOYD M R01AG06841-05
BEIER, DAVID S07RR05950-07 0012
BEIER, JOHN C R22AI29000-02
BEIER, JOHN C S07RR05445-30 0868
BEIERWALTES, WILLIAM H P01HL28982-10 0003
BEIERWALTES, WILLIAM H R01HL46683-01
BEIL, RICHARD E S06GM08043-21 0011
BEILKE, MARK S07RR05377-30 0771
BEINERT, HELMUT R01GM34812-07
BEINFELD, MARGERY C R01NS18667-08
BEIRNESS, DOUGLAS J P01AA07203-02 0002
BEISECKER, ANALEE P30AG10182-01 9003
BEISSINGER, RICHARD S07RR07027-26 0015
BEISSINGER, RICHARD L R29HL39856-03
BEITINS, INESE Z M01RR00042-31 0302
BEITZ, ALVIN J R01DA06687-02
BEITZ, ALVIN J R01DC01086-01
BEITZ, ALVIN J R01DE06682-08
BEITZ, ALVIN J S07RR05930-07 0719
BEJAN, ADRIAN S07RR07070-26 0460
BEJAR, RAUL F M01RR00827-17 0417
BEKHOR, ISAAC R01EY05406-07
BEKISZ, J Z01BD03004-02
BEKKEN, KAAREN E S07RR05486-29 0054
BEKOFF, ANNE C R01HD28247-01
BEKOFF, ANNE C S07RR07013-26 0963
BELARDETTI, FRANCESCO R29NS25186-05
BELARDINELLI, LUIZ R01HL35272-07
BELAS, MICHAEL R, JR R01AI27107-04
BELASCO, JOEL G R01GM35769-06
BELASCO, JOEL G R01GM42720-03
BELASCO, JOEL G S07RR05381-30 0785
BELCHER, JOHN P01CA50305-02 9002
BELCHER, JOHN D R01AA07838-03
BELFORD, R LINN P41RR01811-06A1 9002
BELFORT, G S07RR07104-25 0556
BELFORT, MARLENE R01GM39422-04
BELFORT, MARLENE R01GM44844-02
BELGRAVE, FAYE Z R03MH46048-01A1
BELINGER, LYNDA P51RR00168-30 9004
BELKNAP, JOHN K P01AA08621-02 0005
BELKNAP, JOHN K, JR R01AA06243-08
BELL-DOLAN, DEBRA S07RR07053-26 0154
BELL, DIANNE Y M01RR00030-30 0295
BELL, DIANNE Y P50HL14212-20 0036
BELL, DIANNE Y P50HL14212-20 0037
BELL, DONALD R R01HL26807-11
BELL, DOUGLAS A Z01ES46008-01
BELL, EDWARD M01RR00059-30 0716
BELL, EDWARD F M01RR00059-30 0403
BELL, EMMY K M01RR00032-31 0381
BELL, GREGORY M K11AI00999-02
BELL, JAMES N01OD12105-00
BELL, JAMES N01RG12113-00
BELL, LEONARD K11HL02351-03
BELL, LEONARD B R29HL42455-02
BELL, NORMAN H M01RR01070-15 0131
BELL, NORMAN H M01RR01070-15 0139
BELL, NORMAN H M01RR01070-15 0141
BELL, NORMAN H R01AR36066-06A2
BELL, PAUL B JR S03RR03387-08
BELL, PHILLIP D R01DK32032-08A2
BELL, ROBERT M R01GM20015-18
BELL, ROBERT M R01GM38737-05
BELL, ROBERT M R37DK20205-15
BELL, ROBERT M U01CA46738-05
BELL, ROBERT M U01CA46738-05 0002
BELL, ROBIN G R01AI17484-10
BELL, THEODORE S R29AG08959-01A1
BELL, THOMAS G R01HL31753-07
BELL, THOMAS G S07RR05623-25 0721
BELL, THOMAS W R01GM32937-06
BELL, THOMAS W R03AI30945-02
BELL, WILLIAM R R01HL36260-05
BELLACK, ALAN S R01MH41577-05
BELLACK, ALAN S R37MH38636-08
BELLACK, ALAN S U10MH39998-08
BELLAMY, H P41RR01209-12 0009
BELLAMY, MARY L R25AD00066-01
BELLAND, R J Z01AI00608-01
BELLANTI, JOSEPH P50AI26821-04 0001
BELLANTI, JOSEPH A P50AI26821-04
BELLDEGRUN, ARIE M01RR00865-18 0358
BELLDEGRUN, ARIE S07RR05354-30 0424
BELLDEGRUN, ARIE S R29CA52499-02
BELLEN, HUGO S07RR05425-30 0728
BELLER, DAVID I R01AI23668-05
BELLER, GEORGE A R01HL26205-11
BELLGRAU, DONALD P01DK40144-04 9001
BELLGRAU, DONALD P01DK40144-04 0001
BELLGUI, URSULA P01DC01289-01 0003
BELLI, JAMES A R01CA34269-08
BELLINGER, DAVID C R01HD25114-03
BELLINGER, DENISE L R29MH47783-01
BELLO-REUSS, ELSA R01DK38704-06
BELLOFATTO, VIVIAN M R01AI29478-01A1
BELLONI, FRANCIS L K04HL01770-05
BELLUGI, URSULA P50NS22343-06A1 0004
BELLUGI, URSULA R01DC00146-13
BELLUGI, URSULA R01DC00201-09
BELLUGI, URSULA R01HD26022-02
BELLUGI, URSULA R37HD13249-12
BELLVE, ANTHONY P50HD05077-21 9004
BELLVE, ANTHONY P50HD05077-21 0029
BELMONT, ANDREW S R29GM42516-02
BELMONT, ANDREW S S07RR07030-26 0379
BELMONT, JOHN S07RR05373-30 0711
BELMONT, JOHN S10RR07383-01
BELMONT, JOHN W R29HD22880-05
BELMONT, JOHN W U01AI30243-02 0001
BELMONT, JOHN W U01AI30243-02 9003
BELOTE, JOHN MADDOX R01GM36579-05
BELSHE, ROBERT N01AI05051-04

BELSHE, ROBERT N01AI05064-04
BELSITO, DONALD V P01AG04860-08 0002
BELSKY, JAY R01MH44604-02
BELSKY, JAY R01MH45527-02
BELSKY, JAY U10HD25420-02
BELT, JUDITH A P01CA23099-13 0013
BELT, JUDITH A R01CA55056-01
BELT, ROBERT J U10CA35176-08
BELTZ, BARBARA S P01NS25915-04A1 0005
BELTZ, BARBARA S P01NS25915-04A1 9001
BELTZ, GERALD P01GM39599-05 0002
BELTZ, W F P50HL14197-20 9004
BELZER, FOLKERT O R01DK33554-06
BELZER, FOLKERT O R37DK18624-16
BEMBENEK, MICHAEL E S07RR07091-26 0747
BEMBENEK, MIKE S07RR05849-11 0252
BEMPONG, MAXWELL A S06GM08033-21 0001
BEN DAVID, YAACOV R03CA54908-01
BEN-DOV, ISSAHAR S07RR05551-29 0964
BEN-JONATHAN, NIRA R01NS13243-13
BENACERRAF, BARUJ P30CA06516-28
BENACERRAF, BARUJ R35CA46967-05
BENACH, JORGE L R01AI27044-03
BENACH, JORGE L R01AR40445-02
BENADE, LEONARD E R29CA49258-04
BENARDO, LARRY K08NS01386-03
BENCA, RUTH M R29NS27730-02
BENDER, ALAN D R29GM46271-01
BENDER, ALAN D S07RR07031-26 0072
BENDER, DAVID B R01EY02254-12A2
BENDER, JAMES G R29CA40545-06
BENDER, JEFFREY R K08HL02328-04
BENDER, JEFFREY R R01HL43331-01A2
BENDER, ROBERT A R01GM47156-12
BENDER, STEVEN L R01AI29335-02
BENDER, TIMOTHY P P01CA40042-07 0006
BENDER, WELCOME W R01GM28630-11
BENDHEIM, PAUL E R01AG09694-01A1
BENDHEIM, PAUL E R29NS24720-04
BENDITT, EARL P P01HL03174-36 0014
BENDITT, EARL P R01HL40079-04
BENDITT, EARL P. P51RR00166-30 0135
BENEDEK, GEORGE B R37EY05127-09
BENEDETTI, JACQUELINE P01AI30731-01A1 9002
BENEDETTI, THOMAS J M01RR00037-31 0510
BENEDICT, CLAUDE R R01HL39916-06
BENEDICT, STEPHEN H R29GM40767-05
BENEDICT, WILLIAM F R01CA54672-14A1
BENEDICT, WILLIAM F R01EY02715-13S1
BENEDICT, WILLIAM F R01EY06195-07
BENES, FRANCINE M K02MH00423-10
BENES, FRANCINE M P01MH45212-02 0003
BENES, FRANCINE M R01MH42261-05
BENESCH, RUTH E R37HL05791-31
BENET, LESLIE Z P50GM26691-13
BENET, LESLIE Z P50GM26691-13 0004
BENET, LESLIE Z R01GM36633-04A2
BENFEY, PHILIP N R01GM43778-01A1
BENFORD, HELEN H S06GM08091-20 0026
BENGTSON, VERN L R37AG07977-09
BENIAN, GUY M R29AR39836-02
BENIGHT, ALBERT S R29GM39471-04
BENISEK, WILLIAM F R01DK14729-18
BENITZ, WILLIAM E M01RR00081-29 0138
BENITZ, WILLIAM E R55HL43222-01A1
BENJAMIN, BRUCE A R29HL41028-04
BENJAMIN, DAVID R01AI31262-02
BENJAMIN, DAVID C P30DK38942-04 9004
BENJAMIN, DAVID C R01AI20745-06
BENJAMIN, LENNETTE M01RR00102-28 0061
BENJAMIN, LENNETTE J P60HL38655-04 9003
BENJAMIN, LENNETTE J P60HL38655-04 0007
BENJAMIN, LENNETTE J P60HL38655-04 0008
BENJAMIN, SHELDON S07RR05712-20 0079
BENJAMIN, STEPHEN A S15GM47075-01
BENJAMIN, STEVEN A S07RR07127-23
BENJAMIN, THOMAS L R35CA44343-05
BENJAMIN, TOM N01LM93529-02
BENJAMIN, WILLIAM B S07RR05736-19 0203
BENJAMINS, JOYCE A R01NS13143-14
BENKOVIC, STEPHEN P41RR02583-07 0008
BENKOVIC, STEPHEN J R01GM13306-26
BENKOVIC, STEPHEN J R37GM24129-15
BENN, STEVEN I S07RR05424-30 0106
BENN, STEVEN I S07RR05424-30 0068
BENNET, G J Z01DE00509-02
BENNET, RICHARD S06GM08040-21 0007
BENNET, RICHARD S06GM08040-21 0007
BENNETT-CLARKE, CARO S07RR05700-22 0869
BENNETT-CLARKE, CAROL A R01EY08661-01A1
BENNETT, BARBARA A R01DA05073-02
BENNETT, BARBARA A S07RR05404-30 0834
BENNETT, C L S07RR05710-21 0026
BENNETT, CHARLES L R01HS06494-02
BENNETT, DAVID P30AG10161-01 9001
BENNETT, G J Z01DE00413-06
BENNETT, GEORGE N R01GM39420-03S1
BENNETT, GEORGE V R37DK29808-12
BENNETT, GUDRUN S R01NS24883-05
BENNETT, J E Z01AI00043-26
BENNETT, JAMES S07RR05772-17 0360
BENNETT, JAMES L P01AI16312-13 0006
BENNETT, JAMES L S07RR07049-26 0442
BENNETT, JAMES P M01RR00847-18 0381
BENNETT, JAMES P M01RR00847-18 0382
BENNETT, JOEL S P01HL40387-04 0001
BENNETT, JOEL S P01HL40387-04
BENNETT, JOHN M U10CA11083-24
BENNETT, L LEE, JR S03RR03000-11
BENNETT, L LEE, JR S07RR05676-15
BENNETT, LEE L P01CA34200-09 9003
BENNETT, MICHAEL P01NS07512-23 0047
BENNETT, MICHAEL R01CA36921-08
BENNETT, MICHAEL R01CA36922-08
BENNETT, MICHAEL V P01NS07512-23
BENNETT, MICHAEL V P01NS07512-23 9001
BENNETT, MICHAEL V P01NS07512-23 9002
BENNETT, MICHAEL V R01HD04248-22
BENNETT, P H Z01DK69006-21
BENNETT, P H Z01DK69009-26
BENNETT, P H Z01DK69024-05
BENNETT, P H Z01DK69037-02
BENNETT, PAUL B R29HL40608-03
BENNETT, RICHARD G M01RR02719-06 0130
BENNETT, ROBERT R29AA07276-02
BENNETT, ROBERT M R01AR34295-07
BENNETT, VICKIE DEE R29AR40184-03
BENNETT, WILLIAM M M01RR00334-25 0234
BENOIT, JOSEPH N P01DK43785-01 0003
BENOIT, JOSEPH N R01HL45559-01
BENOIT, JOSEPH N R29HL40963-03
BENOS, DALE J P50DK42017-03
BENOS, DALE J P50DK42017-03 0001
BENOS, DALE J R01DK37206-07
BENOVIC, JEFFERY L R01GM44944-02
BENOVIC, JEFFREY L R01HL45964-02
BENOVIC, JEFFREY L S07RR05417-30 0783
BENOWITZ, LARRY S07RR05484-29 0030
BENOWITZ, LARRY S07RR05484-29 0031
BENOWITZ, LARRY I R01EY05690-12
BENOWITZ, NEAL M01RR00083-29 0240
BENOWITZ, NEAL M01RR00083-29 0233
BENOWITZ, NEAL M01RR00083-29 0216
BENOWITZ, NEAL M01RR00083-29 0237
BENOWITZ, NEAL L M01RR00083-29 0226
BENOWITZ, NEAL L M01RR00083-29 0100
BENOWITZ, NEAL L M01RR00083-29 0154
BENOWITZ, NEAL L M01RR00083-29 0138
BENOWITZ, NEAL L M01RR00083-29 0212
BENOWITZ, NEAL L P30AI27763-04 9003
BENOWITZ, NEAL L P50DA01696-12 0012
BENOWITZ, NEAL L R01DA02277-13
BENOWITZ, NEAL T M01RR00083-29 0219
BENOWITZ, NEAL L M01RR00083-29 0215
BENSADOUN, ANDRE R01HL24873-12
BENSADOUN, ANDRE R01HL39239-05
BENSINGER, WILLIAM P01CA47748-03 0004
BENSINGER, WILLIAM P01CA47748-03 0010
BENSINGER, WILLIAM I P01CA18029-16 9004
BENSINGER, WILLIAM I P01CA18029-16 0038
BENSON, AL B M01RR00048-30 0166
BENSON, AL B U10CA17145-16
BENSON, BRYANT R01HD19521-06
BENSON, DENNIS P41LM05205-08 9001
BENSON, JANETTE S07RR07138-20 0523
BENSON, MERRILL P60AR20582-14 9004
BENSON, MERRILL D M01RR00750-19 0052
BENSON, MERRILL D R01DK42111-02
BENSON, PETER L R01MH42620-03
BENSON, SPENCER S07RR07042-26 0411
BENSON, THANE E S07RR07043-26 0117
BENTLER, PETER M K05DA00017-16
BENTLER, PETER M P01DA01070-18
BENTLEY, DAVID S07RR07006-26 0899
BENTLEY, DAVID R R01NS09074-22
BENTLEY, STUART A S07RR05406-30 0880
BENTLEY, WILLIAM S07RR07042-26 0404
BENTRUDE, WESLEY G R01CA11045-23
BENTZ, JOSEPH E R01GM31506-09
BENVENISTE, ETTY N P01NS29719-01 0001
BENVENISTE, ETTY N. P01AI27290-04 0005
BENVENISTE, R E Z01CP05414-08
BENVENISTE, R E Z01CP05620-03
BENYA, PAUL D R01AR16404-17
BENYAJATI, CHEEPTIP R01GM34850-07
BENZ, CHRISTOPHER C P01CA44768-05 0001
BENZ, CHRISTOPHER C R01CA36773-08
BENZ, EDWARD J, JR R01HL24385-13
BENZ, EDWARD J, JR R01HL44430-02
BENZ, EDWARD J, JR R01HL44985-02
BENZER, SEYMOUR P01GM40499-04
BENZER, SEYMOUR P01GM40499-04 0004
BENZER, SEYMOUR R01EY09278-01
BENZIGER, JACQUELINE P M01RR00997-16 0390
BERAN, MILOSALV R01CA51207-02
BERARD, JOHN P40RR03640-05 0023
BERBARI, EDWARD J R01HL44695-02
BERBAUM, KEVIN S R01CA42453-05
BERCHTOLD, GLENN A R01GM31958-09
BERCOVITCH, FRED B P40RR03640-05 0024
BERD, DAVID R01CA39248-07
BERDANIER, CAROLYN D S07RR07025-26 0986
BERDE, CHARLES P50GM15904-24 0025
BERDE, CHARLES P50GM15904-24 9003
BERDE, CHARLES S07RR05899-10 0273
BERECEK, KATHLEEN H R01HL31515-08
BEREITER, DAVID A R01NS26137-04
BERELOWITZ, MICHAEL S07RR05736-19 0201
BERENBAUM, SHERI S07RR05366-30 0553
BERENBERG, JEFFREY L U10CA32734-10
BERENDES, H W Z01HD00323-12
BERENDES, H W Z01HD00329-10
BERENDES, H W Z01HD00343-08
BERENDES, H W Z01HD01700-04
BERENDES, H W Z01HD01701-04
BERENDES, H W Z01HD01702-02
BERENDES, H W Z01HD01703-03
BERENDES, H W Z01HD01704-01
BERENHOLZ, GERRY R43CE00016-01
BERENS, MICHAEL E S07RR05872-08 0979
BERENSON, GERALD S R01HL02942-34
BERENSON, GERALD S R01HL38844-05 0019
BERENSON, GERALD S R01HL38844-05
BERENSON, GERALD S R01HL38844-05 0001
BERESFORD, SHIRLEY A R01CA49643-03
BERESFORD, SHIRLEY A R01HS06785-01
BERESFORD, SHIRLEY A A R01CA47749-03
BERESFORD, T P50AA07378-04 0001
BEREZNEY, RONALD R01GM23922-13
BEREZNEY, RONALD S07RR07066-26 0233
BERG, ANNE T R29NS27728-03
BERG, ANNE T S07RR05358-30 0496
BERG, CELESTE A R01GM45248-01
BERG, CELESTE A S07RR07096-26 0063
BERG, CYNTHIA A S07RR07092-26 0514
BERG, DARWIN P01NS25916-04 0002
BERG, DARWIN P01NS25916-04 9004
BERG, DARWIN K R01NS12601-16
BERG, DOUGLAS E R01HG00563-01
BERG, HOWARD C R37AI16478-12
BERG, JEREMY M R01GM46257-01
BERG, JEREMY M R29GM38230-05
BERG, KATHLEEN M R01DC00017-02
BERG, LEONARD P01AG03991-08 0005
BERG, LEONARD P01AG03991-08 9001
BERG, LEONARD P01AG03991-08
BERG, LEONARD P50AG05681-08
BERG, LEONARD P50AG05681-08 9006
BERG, LESLIE J R55AI29953-01A1
BERG, P Z01DK25045-08
BERG, PAUL P01AG02908-11
BERG, PAUL P01AG02908-11 0007
BERG, PAUL R37GM13235-25
BERG, RICHARD A R01AR31839-06A1
BERG, ROBERT A S07RR05675-23 0927
BERG, WILLIAM K R01MH46568-01A1
BERGA, SARAH M01RR00056-30 0365
BERGA, SARAH M01RR00056-30 0372
BERGELSON, JEFFREY M S07RR05526-29 0102
BERGER, ALAN R R01DA07055-01
BERGER, ALBERT J R01NS14857-13
BERGER, E Z01AI00538-04
BERGER, FRANKLIN G R01CA44013-05
BERGER, FRANKLIN G R01DK37265-06
BERGER, JEANNE N01LM93523-04
BERGER, JOSEPH P01NS25569-04 0001
BERGER, JOSEPH P01NS25569-04 9001
BERGER, JOSEPH R P01NS25569-04
BERGER, MELVIN M01RR00080-29 0447
BERGER, MELVIN P30DK27651-09 9009
BERGER, MELVIN R01AI22687-05
BERGER, MITCHEL S K08NS01253-04
BERGER, NATHAN P30CA43703-04A1 9010
BERGER, NATHAN A P01CA48735-02 0003
BERGER, NATHAN A P01CA51183-01A1
BERGER, NATHAN A P01CA51183-01A1 0003
BERGER, NATHAN A P30CA43703-04A1 9004
BERGER, NATHAN A P30CA43703-04A1
BERGER, PATRICIA J S07RR07092-26 0525
BERGER, PAUL S07RR05755-18 0238
BERGER, PETER E R43DK44409-01
BERGER, R L Z01HL01033-01
BERGER, R L Z01HL01034-01
BERGER, R L Z01HL01413-29
BERGER, R L Z01HL01414-19
BERGER, RALPH J R01DK38402-05
BERGER, S L Z01CB08212-17
BERGER, S PAUL R29DA07376-01
BERGER, THEODORE W K02MH00343-09
BERGER, THEODORE W P01NS19608-09 0008
BERGER, THEODORE W P50MH45156-02 0001
BERGERON, BRYAN P R29LM04715-04
BERGERON, RAYMOND J R01HL42817-03
BERGERON, RAYMOND J R13HL46912-01
BERGERON, RAYMOND J U01CA37606-08 0001
BERGET, SUSAN M R01GM38526-04
BERGET, SUSAN M R01HG00220-01
BERGET, SUSAN M R01HL44964-01A1
BERGEY, EARL J R01DE09562-02
BERGEY, EARL J R29DE08074-04
BERGGREN, ULF E R01DE08296-02
BERGHORN, KATHIE A S07RR05771-15 0336
BERGLUND, L S07RR05692-22 0983
BERGMAN, IRA M01RR00084-29 0249
BERGMAN, JACK P51RR00168-30 0116
BERGMAN, JACK P51RR00168-30 0117

BERGMAN, JACK P51RR00168-30 0118
BERGMAN, JACK R01DA03774-07
BERGMAN, KOSTIA S07RR07143-20 0615
BERGMAN, LAWRENCE WILLIAM R01GM41620-04
BERGMAN, RICHARD N R01DK29867-10
BERGMAN, RICHARD N U01HL47890-01
BERGMAN, ROBERT G R01GM45312-01A1
BERGMAN, ROBERT G R37GM25459-14
BERGMAN, ROBERT G S10RR06286-01
BERGMAN, THOMAS A P20NS30322-01 0001
BERGMANN, STEVEN R P50HL17646-17 0032
BERGMANN, STEVEN R R01HL46895-01
BERGSTRESSER, PAUL R R01AR35068-07
BERGSTRESSER, PAUL R R01AR40042-02
BERGSTROM, DONALD E R01GM45551-01
BERGSTROM, DONALD E U01AI26029-05
BERHANU, PAULOS R01DK32880-07
BERIS, SUSAN M01RR06022-02 0765
BERK, ARNOLD J R37CA25235-13
BERK, BRADFORD C R01HL44721-01A2
BERK, MICHAEL P01HD11725-13 0010
BERK, MICHAEL A P01HD11725-13 0007
BERK, MITCHELL L S07RR05870-10 0990
BERK, PAUL D R01DK26438-11A1
BERK, RICHARD S R01EY01935-11
BERKANOVIC, EMIL P60AR36834-05 0008
BERKE, GERALD S R01DC00855-02
BERKMAN, LISA M01RR00125-28 0759
BERKMAN, LISA P01CA42101-06 0012
BERKOVITZ, GARY D M01RR00052-30 0218
BERKOVITZ, ROBERT R43DC00998-01
BERKOVITZ, ROBERT R44DC00624-02A1
BERKOVITZ, ROBERT A R43DC01174-01
BERKOVITZ, ROBERT A R43DC01299-01
BERKOWER, I Z01BB06005-02
BERKOWER, I Z01BB06006-02
BERKOWITZ, GERTRUD S R29CA47053-05
BERKOWITZ, IRVING M U10CA45418-05
BERKOWITZ, MARVIN W R01DA06331-02
BERKSON, DAVID M N01HC48063-11
BERKSON, GERSHON B R01HD27184-01
BERKSON, GERSHON B R13HD23040-05
BERL, THOMAS M01RR00051-30 0753
BERLIN, CHARLES I P01DC00379-05
BERLIN, CHARLES I P01DC00379-05 0001
BERLIN, JOSHUA R R29HL43712-02
BERLINER, JUDITH P01HL30568-09 0006
BERLINER, LAWRENCE J R01GM40778-06
BERLINER, LAWRENCE J R01RR03126-04
BERLINER, NANCY R01DK42347-01A2
BERMAN, AARON M01RR01032-16 0437
BERMAN, CAROL M S07RR07066-26 0234
BERMAN, ELLIN R01CA52186-02
BERMAN, HARVEY A R01ES03085-09
BERMAN, HELEN M R01GM21589-17
BERMAN, JOAN W P01MH47667-02 0005
BERMAN, JUDITH G R29GM38626-04
BERMAN, K F Z01MH02576-01
BERMAN, MARLENE O R01AA07112-05
BERMAN, MICHAEL L R01CA50364-01A2
BERMAN, MICHAEL R R01HL38488-06
BERMAN, MONIQUE A R01AI28196-03
BERMAN, NANCY M01RR00425-2283 0443
BERMAN, NANCY E R01MH38399-08A1
BERMAN, ROBERT F S06GM08167-13 0032
BERMAN, STEPHEN M01RR00069-29 0416
BERMAN, STEPHEN M01RR00069-29 0449
BERMAN, STEPHEN M01RR00069-29 0456
BERMAN, STEPHEN M01RR00069-29 0424
BERMAN, WILLIAM H S07RR07150-17 0545
BERNACKI, RALPH J P01CA13038-19 0097
BERNACKI, RALPH J R01CA42898-05
BERNAL, SAMMUEL D P30CA06516-28 9013
BERNAL, SAMUEL D P01CA38493-06S1 0007
BERNAL, SAMUEL D R01CA45528-05A1
BERNANKE, DAVID H R29GM41667-03
BERNARD, DAVID N01CB71091-19
BERNARD, DAVID B M01RR00533-23 0210
BERNARD, DOFT U10EY08150-04
BERNARD, GEORGE S07RR05304-30 0231
BERNARD, GORDON R P50HL19153-15 0015
BERNARD, GORDON R P50HL19153-15 0006
BERNARD, GORDON R R01HL43167-02
BERNARD, LOUIS J P30CA49095-04
BERNARD, STEPHEN A M01RR00046-31 0437
BERNARDS, ANDRE R29NS28735-01A1
BERNARDS, RENE R01CA52756-01A1
BERNARDS, RENE S07RR05486-29 0049
BERNATH, ALBERT M U10CA35448-08
BERNATZKY, ROBERT S07RR07048-26 0630
BERNDT, RITA S R01DC00262-07
BERNDT, RITA S R01DC00699-03
BERNDT, WILLIAM O R01ES04803-04
BERNE, BRUCE J R01GM43340-01A1
BERNE, ROBERT M R01HL10384-26
BERNER, ETA S R01LM05125-02
BERNER, JAMES E U01CA52242-02
BERNER, Y P01CA29502-11A1 0050
BERNFIELD, MERTON S15DK44699-01
BERNFIELD, MERTON R N01HD02912-02
BERNFIELD, MERTON R R37HD06763-19
BERNHARD, WILLIAM A R37CA32546-16
BERNHEIM, B DOUGLAS P01AG05842-06 0002
BERNIER, GEORGE M JR M01RR00056-30
BERNIER, GEORGE M, JR S07RR05416-30
BERNIER, GEORGE M, JR S15HD28755-01
BERNIER, M Z01AG00213-01
BERNINGER, VIRGINIA W R01HD25858-03
BERNLOHR, DAVID A R01GM43199-02
BERNLOHR, ROBERT W S07RR07082-26 0272
BERNS, KENNETH I R01AI26122-04
BERNS, KENNETH I R37AI22251-08
BERNS, MICHAEL W P41RR01192-12
BERNS, MICHAEL W R01CA32248-09
BERNSTEIN, ALAN R01HD25850-03
BERNSTEIN, CAROL S07RR05675-23 0928
BERNSTEIN, DANIEL R29HL38741-04
BERNSTEIN, DANIEL S07RR05353-30 0341
BERNSTEIN, DAVID I K01OH00073-03
BERNSTEIN, DAVID I R01AI23482-05
BERNSTEIN, DAVID I S15AI32191-01
BERNSTEIN, EUGENE F M01RR00833-17 0178
BERNSTEIN, GERALD S N01HD13112-00
BERNSTEIN, GERALD S N01HD13109-00
BERNSTEIN, ILENE L R01DC00248-07
BERNSTEIN, IRWIN D P01CA44991-04 9001
BERNSTEIN, IRWIN D P01CA44991-04
BERNSTEIN, IRWIN D P30CA15704-18 9007
BERNSTEIN, IRWIN D R01CA39492-07
BERNSTEIN, IRWIN D R37CA26386-12
BERNSTEIN, JAIME S06GM08224-07 0003
BERNSTEIN, JAY S07RR06016-03
BERNSTEIN, JERALD J R01CA48956-02
BERNSTEIN, KENNETH E R01DK39777-04
BERNSTEIN, LESLIE P01CA17054-16 0001
BERNSTEIN, LESLIE R01CA44546-05
BERNSTEIN, LESLIE R R29DC00527-03
BERNSTEIN, LYNNE E R01DC00695-04
BERNSTEIN, MARVIN H S06GM08136-18 0003
BERNSTEIN, RICHARD P01DC00223-08 0005
BERNSTEIN, SANFORD I R01GM32443-09
BERNSTEIN, SOL S07RR05466-24
BERNSTEIN, SOL S15DK44700-01
BERNSTEIN, STANFORD I S06GM45765-01 0001
BERNSTEIN, ZALE S07RR05648-25 0919
BERNTSON, GARY G P51RR00165-31 0172
BERRIDGE, KENT C R01NS23959-06
BERRIDGE, MARC S R29HL43884-02
BERRY, C W S07RR05915-08 0679
BERRY, CAROLYNN S06GM08040-21 0008
BERRY, CAROLYNN S06GM08040-21 0008
BERRY, CHRISTINE A R01DK26142-11
BERRY, DAISILEE H R25CA49425-03
BERRY, DAISILEE H U10CA41188-06 0042
BERRY, DAISILEE H U10CA41188-06 0043
BERRY, DAISILEE H U10CA41188-06 0044
BERRY, DAISILEE H U10CA41188-06 0045
BERRY, DAISILEE H U10CA41188-06 0022
BERRY, DAISILEE H U10CA41188-06 0023
BERRY, DAISILEE H U10CA41188-06 0024
BERRY, DAISILEE H U10CA41188-06 0046
BERRY, DAISILEE H U10CA41188-06 0047
BERRY, DAISILEE H U10CA41188-06 0048
BERRY, DAISILEE H U10CA41188-06 0049
BERRY, DAISILEE H U10CA41188-06 0050
BERRY, DAISILEE H U10CA41188-06 0051
BERRY, DAISILEE H U10CA41188-06 0052
BERRY, DAISILEE H U10CA41188-06 0053
BERRY, DAISILEE H U10CA41188-06 0054
BERRY, DAISILEE H U10CA41188-06 0055
BERRY, DAISILEE H U10CA41188-06 0056
BERRY, DAISILEE H U10CA41188-06 0057
BERRY, DAISILEE H U10CA41188-06 0025
BERRY, DAISILEE H U10CA41188-06 0026
BERRY, DAISILEE H U10CA41188-06 0027
BERRY, DAISILEE H U10CA41188-06 0028
BERRY, DAISILEE H U10CA41188-06 0029
BERRY, DAISILEE H U10CA41188-06 0030
BERRY, DAISILEE H U10CA41188-06 0031
BERRY, DAISILEE H U10CA41188-06 0032
BERRY, DAISILEE H U10CA41188-06 0033
BERRY, DAISILEE H U10CA41188-06 0034
BERRY, DAISILEE H U10CA41188-06 0035
BERRY, DAISILEE H U10CA41188-06 0036
BERRY, DAISILEE H U10CA41188-06 0037
BERRY, DAISILEE H U10CA41188-06 0038
BERRY, DAISILEE H U10CA41188-06 0039
BERRY, DAISILEE H U10CA41188-06 0040
BERRY, DAISILEE H U10CA41188-06 0041
BERRY, DAISILEE H U10CA41188-06 0058
BERRY, DAISILEE H U10CA41188-06 0059
BERRY, DAISILEE H U10CA41188-06 0002
BERRY, DAISILEE H U10CA41188-06 0003
BERRY, DAISILEE H U10CA41188-06 0004
BERRY, DAISILEE H U10CA41188-06 0060
BERRY, DAISILEE H U10CA41188-06 0005
BERRY, DAISILEE H U10CA41188-06
BERRY, DAISILEE H U10CA41188-06 0001
BERRY, DAISILEE H U10CA41188-06 0006
BERRY, DAISILEE H U10CA41188-06 0007
BERRY, DAISILEE H U10CA41188-06 0008
BERRY, DAISILEE H U10CA41188-06 0009
BERRY, DAISILEE H U10CA41188-06 0010
BERRY, DAISILEE H U10CA41188-06 0011
BERRY, DAISILEE H U10CA41188-06 0012
BERRY, DAISILEE H U10CA41188-06 0013
BERRY, DAISILEE H U10CA41188-06 0014
BERRY, DAISILEE H U10CA41188-06 0015
BERRY, DAISILEE H U10CA41188-06 0016
BERRY, DAISILEE H U10CA41188-06 0017
BERRY, DAISILEE H U10CA41188-06 0018
BERRY, DAISILEE H U10CA41188-06 0019
BERRY, DAISILEE H U10CA41188-06 0020
BERRY, DAISILEE H U10CA41188-06 0021
BERRY, DAVID T S07RR07114-23 0433
BERRY, DONALD A R01HS06475-02
BERRY, GERARD T R01DK40382-04
BERRY, JAMES O S07RR07066-26 0235
BERRY, JAMES O S07RR07066-26 0236
BERRY, JANE S07RR07006-26 0912
BERRY, ROBERT W R01NS27150-02
BERRY, ROBERT W S07RR05370-30 0619
BERRY, SUSAN MD R01DK32817-08
BERS, DONALD M R01HL30077-09A1
BERS, DONALD M R01HL44583-01A1
BERSCHNEIDER, HELEN M R29DK42100-02
BERSETH, C M01RR00585-20 0462
BERSH, PHILIP S07RR07115-24 0582
BERSH, PHILIP S07RR07115-24 0581
BERSOF, THOMAS P M01RR00083-29 0204
BERSON, DAVID M R01EY06108-05
BERSON, ELIOT L R01EY00169-21
BERSON, ELIOT L U10EY02014-15
BERSON, ELLIOT L U10EY02014-15 0001
BERSON, ELLIOT L U10EY02014-15 0003
BERSON, JEROME A R37GM30787-09
BERSOT, THOMAS P M01RR00083-29 0115
BERTAKIS, KLEA D R18HS06167-02
BERTENTHAL, BENNETT I R01HD16195-10
BERTHOLD, PETER P50DE08239-04 9002
BERTICS, PAUL J R01CA47881-04
BERTIN, P Z01BB04001-02
BERTINO, JOSEPH P01CA25842-11 0003
BERTINO, JOSEPH P01CA47179-03 0003
BERTINO, JOSEPH R P01CA05826-29
BERTINO, JOSEPH R P01CA05826-29 9003
BERTINO, JOSEPH R P01CA08341-26 9001
BERTINO, JOSEPH R P01CA47997-03
BERTINO, JOSEPH R P01CA47997-03 0003
BERTINO, JOSEPH R R37CA08010-27
BERTOCCI, LOREN P01HL06296-31 9007
BERTOLAMI, CHARLES N R01DE07803-05A2
BERTOLAMI, CHARLES N R01DE09178-03
BERTOLINO, ARTHUR P R55AR40301-01A1
BERTORINI, TULIO M01RR00211-27 0294
BERTORINI, TULIO E M01RR00211-27 0339
BERTORININ, JULIO E M01RR00211-27 0305
BERTRAM, EDWARD S07RR05431-30 0835
BERTRAM, EDWARD H R01NS28073-02
BERTRAM, JOHN S R01CA39947-06A2
BERWICK, MARIANNE S07RR05443-30 0987
BERWICK, MARIANNE S07RR05443-30 0996
BERZOFSKY, J A Z01CB04020-14
BESA, WM S07RR07041-26 0400
BESCH, LYNN N01AI95032-06
BESCHORNER, WILLIAM E P01CA15396-18 9002
BESHARSE, JOSEPH C R01EY02414-15
BESHARSE, JOSEPH C R01EY03222-13
BESMER, PETER R37CA32926-07
BESS, FRED H P20DC01437-01
BESSEN, DEBRA E R01AI28944-02
BESSER, THOMAS E S07RR05465-29 0383
BESSEY, PALMER G M01RR00036-31 1032
BESSEY, PALMER Q R01GM41961-04
BESSMAN, MAURICE J R01GM18649-33
BEST, CATHERINE T K04DC00045-02
BEST, CATHERINE T R01DC00403-04A1
BEST, J ALLAN N01CN64093-10
BEST, J ALLAN R01HL36171-04
BESTEMAN, KARST U18DA07084-02
BESTOR, TIMOTHY H R01GM43565-02
BESTOR, TIMOTHY H S07RR05381-30 0777
BETH, ALBERT H R01HL34737-07
BETHEA, CYNTHIA L P30HD18185-08 9003
BETHEA, CYNTHIA L P51RR00163-32 0008
BETHEA, CYNTHIA L R01HD17269-09
BETHEA, CYNTHIA L. P51RR00166-30 0136
BETLEY, MARSHA J R01AI25574-04A1
BETRUS, PATRICIA A K07NR00010-05
BETTELHEIM, FREDERICK A R01EY02571-14
BETTS, ROBERT F M01RR00044-31 0367
BETZ, A LORRIS P01HL18575-16A1 0016
BETZ, A LORRIS R01NS23870-04A1
BETZ, WILLIAM J R01NS10207-20
BETZ, WILLIAM J R01NS23466-04A1
BETZ, WILLIAM J S10RR06475-01
BEUCHAT, CAROL A S07RR05675-23 0929
BEUCHAT, CAROL P S07RR05675-23 0898
BEUERMAN, ROGER W R01EY04074-11
BEUSEN, DENISE P01GM24483-12A1 0013
BEUSHAUSEN, S A Z01NS02842-01
BEUTLER, BRUCE P01DK42582-02 0005
BEUTLER, ERNEST M01RR00833-17 0175
BEUTLER, ERNEST M01RR00833-17 0173
BEUTLER, ERNEST M01RR00833-17 0156
BEUTLER, ERNEST M01RR00833-17 0168

BEUTLER, ERNEST M01RR00833-17 0089
BEUTLER, ERNEST M01RR00833-17
BEUTLER, ERNEST M01RR00833-17 0081
BEUTLER, ERNEST R01DK36639-06
BEUTLER, ERNEST R37HL25552-13
BEUTLER, J Z01CM07303-01
BEUTLER, J Z01CM07304-01
BEUTLER, LARRY E R01AA08970-02
BEVAN, JOHN A R01HL32383-08
BEVAN, JOHN A R37HL32985-08
BEVAN, MICHAEL J P01AI19499-08 0006
BEVAN, MICHAEL J P01CA25803-13 0001
BEVAN, MICHAEL J P01CA25803-13 9001
BEVAN, MICHAEL J R01AI29802-03
BEVAN, MICHAEL J R37AI19335-11
BEVENSON, RONALD P01CA47748-03 0006
BEVERIDGE, DAVID L R37GM37909-06
BEVERING, CARL S07RR05372-30 0706
BEVERLEY, STEPHEN M R01AI21903-07
BEVERLEY, STEPHEN M R01AI29646-02
BEVILACQUA, JOSEPH J R18MH49303-01
BEVILACQUA, MICHAEL S07RR05950-07 0997
BEVILACQUA, MICHAEL P P01HL36028-07 0009
BEYENE, YEWOUBDAR R01AG07618-03
BEYER-MEARS, ANNETTE R01EY03226-11
BEYER, ANN L R01GM39271-04
BEYER, ERIC C R01HL45466-02
BEYER, ERIC C R29EY08368-02
BEZANILLA, FRANCISCO J R01GM30376-11
BHAGAT, HITESH S07RR05770-13 0938
BHAGAVATI, SATYAKAM K08NS01351-03
BHAGWAT, ASHOK S K04HG00004-01
BHAGWAT, ASHOK S R01GM40576-03
BHALLA, DEEPAK K R01ES03521-07
BHALLA, KAPIL R29CA45671-05
BHALLA, VINOD K S07RR05365-30 0075
BHAN, ATUL P01DK33506-08 0008
BHAN, ATUL K P01HL18646-15 9002
BHANDARI, ANIL M01RR00043-31 0424
BHANDARI, JC N01ES85228-08
BHANDARI, JC N01ES85229-11
BHANDARY, KRISHNA P50DE08240-05 0002
BHANDARY, KRISHNA K R01GM22490-17
BHANSALI, KANTI G S06GM08061-17 0002
BHARDWAJ, NINA P60AR38520-04 0001
BHARDWAJ, NINA R29AR39552-03
BHARGAVA, HEMENDRA N R01DA02598-11
BHASIN, SHALENDAR M01RR00425-22S3 0459
BHASIN, SHALENDAR M01RR00425-22S3 0416
BHASIN, SHALENDER P30HD19445-05S1 0001
BHASIN, SHALENDER S07RR05551-29 0953
BHASKER, JOHN P30CA16086-17 9014
BHAT, GEETHA S07RR05408-30 0918
BHAT, K S Z01AI00609-01
BHAT, M Z01DE00538-01
BHAT, SURAJ P R01EY06044-08
BHAT, VENTATRAMANA N01CM97587-02
BHATIA, KISHORE P30CA51008-02 9007
BHATIA, SUBHASH C S06GM08241-07 0010
BHATNAGAR, ARUNI R29HL44676-02
BHATNAGAR, RAJENDRA P01DE09859-01 0004
BHATNAGAR, RAJENDRA S07RR05305-30 0730
BHATNAGER, RAVI S06GM08047-20S1 0030
BHATTACHARYA-CHATTERJEE, MALAY R01CA47860-
BHATTACHARYA, AMIT P01ES01566-13 0002
BHATTACHARYA, AMIT R01OH02794-01A1
BHATTACHARYA, JAHAR R01HL36024-07
BHATTACHARYA, SUNITA K08HL02483-02
BHATTACHARYA, SYAMAL K R01AR38540-04
BHATTACHARYYA, MOHIT L K14HL02480-02
BHATTACHARYYA, MOHIT L S06GM08037-20 0025
BHAVANANDAN, VEER P R01CA38797-05
BHAVANANDAN, VEER P R01HL42651-03
BHAVANANDAN, VEER P S07RR05680-23 0908
BHORJEE, JASWANT S S06GM08037-20 0049
BIA, MARGARET J M01RR00125-28 0734
BIAGGIONI, ITALO M01RR00095-31 0232
BIAGGIONI, ITALO P50HL14192-21 0017
BIAGLOW, JOHN E R37CA44982-05
BIANCANI, PIERO R01DK28614-11
BIANCO, JESUS A R01HL33514-06
BIANCONI, JOHN E R19DA06455-03
BIAS, WILMA B P01HG00373-04 9002
BIAS, WILMA B U10EY06156-07
BIBBO, MARLUCE R01CA37352-08
BIBEN, M Z01HD00054-17
BIBEN, M Z01HD01108-07
BIBER, MARGARET C R01NS14090-11
BIBER, THOMAS U R01DK26347-10
BICE, ALDEN N R29NS28758-02
BICE, THOMAS W S07RR05443-30 0988
BICKEL, WARREN K R01DA06205-02
BICKEL, WARREN K R01DA06526-02
BICKEL, WARREN K R18DA06969-02
BICKERS, DAVID R M01RR00080-29 0260
BICKERS, DAVID R P30AR39750-04
BICKERS, DAVID R R01ES01900-14
BICKFORD-WIMER, PAULA C P01AG04418-08 0006
BICKMAN, LEONARD R01MH46136-03
BICKNELL, WILLIAM S07RR05927-07 0966
BICSAK, THOMAS P01HD09690-18 0002
BIDANI, ANIL K R01DK40426-03
BIDDISON, WILLIAM E Z01NS02603-08
BIDDULPH, DAVID S07RR05404-30 0835
BIDEZ, MARTHA W P01DE08917-02 0003
BIDLACK, JEAN M R01DA03742-08
BIDLACK, JEAN M R01DA04355-03
BIEBER, ALLAN L R01GM34925-07
BIEBER, ALLAN L S07RR07112-24 0423
BIEBER, ALLAN L S15HL47747-01
BIEBER, LORAN S07RR05656-24 0827
BIEBER, LORAN L R01DK18427-14
BIEBER, LORAN L S07RR05656-24
BIEDERMAN, JOSEPH R01MH41314-04
BIEDLER, JUNE P01CA18856-16 0020
BIEDLER, JUNE L R01CA28595-10
BIEDLER, JUNE L R01CA41520-06
BIEGEL, JACLYN P01CA47983-04 9002
BIEGEL, JACLYN P50HG00425-01 9001
BIEGON, ANAT P30AG10129-01 0003
BIEHL, EDWARD R S07RR07194-09 0623
BIEK, DONALD P R29GM42746-03
BIEKER, JAMES J R29HD23250-03
BIELITZKI, JOSEPH T. P51RR00166-30 0166
BIELORY, LEONARD S07RR05393-30 0883
BIELSKI, BENON H J R01GM23656-14
BIEMAN, KLAUS P30ES02109-13 9002
BIEMANN, K P42ES04675-05 0004
BIEMANN, KLAUS P01ES01640-14 0012
BIEMANN, KLAUS P41RR00317-25 9001
BIEMANN, KLAUS P41RR00317-25
BIEMANN, KLAUS R37GM05472-33
BIENASZ, STANLEY S07RR05377-30 0757
BIER, DENNIS M01RR00036-31 0716
BIER, DENNIS M01RR00036-31 1003
BIER, DENNIS M01RR06021-02 0512
BIER, DENNIS M M01RR06021-02 1001
BIER, DENNIS M M01RR06021-02 1014
BIER, DENNIS M M01RR06021-02 0684
BIER, DENNIS M P01AG05562-07 0007
BIER, DENNIS M P01HD20805-05A1
BIER, DENNIS M P01HD20805-05A1 0001
BIER, DENNIS M P41RR00954-15
BIER, DENNIS M P41RR00954-15 9009
BIER, TRACY R18HL45265-02 0001
BIERER, BARBARA E R29AI28554-03
BIERER, LINDA M K08AG00408-04
BIERMAN, FREDRICK Z. P60HL28381-09 0009
BIERMAN, EDWIN L K12DK01964-02
BIERMAN, EDWIN L P01DK02456-33A1
BIERMAN, EDWIN L P01DK02456-33A1 0008
BIERMAN, EDWIN L P01HL18645-17 0010
BIERMAN, EDWIN L P30DK35816-06 9001
BIERMAN, EDWIN L P30DK35816-06 9002
BIERMAN, EDWIN L P30DK35816-06
BIERSDORF, WILLIAM R R01EY08097-02
BIEWENER, ANDREW A R01AR39828-01A1
BIFANO, THOMAS G S07RR07043-26 0118
BIGAZZI, PIERLUIGI U54HD29125-01 0003
BIGAZZI, PIERLUIGI E R01ES03230-04A2
BIGBY, MICHAEL E R29AR39795-01A1
BIGBY, TIMOTHY D K08HL01888-06
BIGEL INST FOR HLTH POLICY N01DA98516-01
BIGELOW, CAROLYN L S07RR05386-30 0574
BIGELOW, DOUGLAS A P50MH43458-04 0006
BIGELOW, GEORGE E K05DA00050-14
BIGELOW, GEORGE E P50DA05273-04
BIGELOW, GEORGE E R01DA04089-07
BIGELOW, GEORGE E R18DA06120-03
BIGELOW, L B Z01MH02476-04
BIGELOW, L B Z01MH02552-02
BIGELOW, L B Z01MH02553-02
BIGELOW, L B Z01MH02555-02
BIGELOW, L B Z01MH02574-01
BIGGART, NEAL W R29CA46818-04
BIGGER, J T M01RR00645-20 0420
BIGGER, J T M01RR00645-20 0427
BIGGER, J THOM M01RR00645-20 0452
BIGGER, JOHN T, JR R01HL41552-03
BIGGERS, J D P51RR00168-30 0178
BIGGERS, JOHN D R01HD21581-05
BIGGERS, JOHN D U01HD21988-07
BIGGERSTAFF, ROBERT H S03RR03467-05
BIGGIN, MARK D R01GM42387-03
BIGLAN, ANTHONY R01CA38273-07
BIGLAN, ANTHONY R01HD26249-02
BIGLAN, ANTHONY R01MH45651-02
BIGLER, ROBERT D R01AR40404-01A1
BIGLER, RODNEY E P01CA29502-11A1 9003
BIGLER, RODNEY E P01CA29502-11A1 0041
BIGLIERE, EDWARD G M01RR00083-29 0218
BIGLIERI, EDWARD G M01RR00083-29 0223
BIGLIERI, EDWARD G M01RR00083-29 0040
BIGLIERI, EDWARD G M01RR00083-29 0241
BIGLIERI, EDWARD G M01RR00083-29 0194
BIGLIERI, EDWARD G R01DK06415-30
BIGLIERI, EDWARD G. M01RR00083-29 0162
BIGLIERRI, EDWARD G M01RR00083-29 0230
BIGNAMI, GARY S R43CA52304-01A1
BIGNAMI, AMICO R01NS13034-17
BIGNAMI, GARY S R43CA54652-01
BIGNER, DARELL D P50NS20023-08 0005
BIGNER, DARELL D R01CA56115-01
BIGNER, DARRELL D P30CA14236-18 9010
BIGNER, DARRELL D P50NS20023-08
BIGNER, DARRELL D R37CA11898-21
BIGNER, SANDRA H P30CA14236-18 9018
BIGNER, SANDRA H P50NS20023-08 0008
BIGNER, SANDRA H R37CA43722-05
BIGOS, STANLEY J R01AR37507-05
BIGSBY, ROBERT M R29HD23244-06
BIHAIN, BERNARD E S07RR05376-30 0032
BIJUR, POLLY E R01HD28523-01
BIKLE, DANDIEL D M01RR00079-29 0391
BIKLE, DANIEL D R01AR38386-05
BIKLE, DANIEL D R01DK28116-11
BIKLE, DANIEL D. P01AR39448-04 0001
BIKOFF, ELIZABETH K R01AI19047-09
BIKOFF, ELIZABETH K R01HD25926-02
BILDERBACK, DONALD H P41RR01646-09
BILEZIKAIN, JOHN P P50AR39191-05 0003
BILEZIKIAN, JOHN P M01RR00645-20 0141
BILEZIKIAN, JOHN P P01HL28958-09 0003
BILEZIKIAN, JOHN P R01DK32333-08
BILGER, ROBERT C R01DC00174-09
BILGUTAY, NIHAT M P01CA52823-02 0003
BILL, ANDERS A R01EY00475-24
BILL, JEROME R R29AI31133-01
BILLADELLO, JOSEPH J R01HL38868-05
BILLER, JOSE M01RR00059-30 0721
BILLETT, HENNY H P60HL38655-04 0011
BILLIAR, TIMOTHY R R29GM44100-02
BILLIG, NATHAN R01MH42103-04
BILLINGHAM, MARGARET T P01HL13108-22 0003
BILLINGS, PAUL C R01CA45734-05
BILLINGS, PETER S07RR05878-09 0998
BILLINGS, RONALD J R01DE08946-01A2
BILLINGSLEY, MELVIN L R01ES05450-02
BILLINGTON, CHARLES J R01DK42698-01A2
BILLMAN, GEORGE E R01DA05917-02
BILLUPS, KEVIN K11DK02067-01
BILLY, JOHN O R01HD27620-01A1
BILTONEN, RODNEY L R01GM37658-04A1
BILWISE, DONALD P50MH40041-08 0007
BINA, MINOU R01AI29121-01A2
BINDER, HENRY M01RR00125-28 0760
BINDER, HENRY J R01DK14669-20
BINDER, LESTER I P01AG06569-05 0004
BINDER, LESTER I R01AG06969-04A1
BINDER, LESTER I R01AG09031-02
BINDER, MARC D R01NS26840-03
BINDER, RENEE S07RR05755-18 0233
BINDER, TERRI A K15DE00253-03
BINDER, TERRI A S07RR05331-28 0742
BINDON, JAMES R R21DK44565-01
BING, DAVID S07RR05479-29 0437
BING, DAVID H R44HL43441-02
BING, DAVID H S07RR05626-25 0671
BING, LI DR N01CP05634-02
BING, LI DR N01CP15622-00
BINGHAM, GEOFFREY S07RR07031-26 0073
BINGHAM, PAUL M R01GM32003-08
BINGMAN, VERNER S07RR07192-12 0615
BINKIEWICZ, ANNA M01RR00054-30 0399
BINKLEY, DAVID M R44CA49405-02A1
BINKLEY, PHILIP F. M01RR00034-31 0294
BIOMETRIC RESEARCH INC N01DA07300-00
BIRCH, DAVID G R01EY05235-07
BIRCH, DAVID G R01EY07188-05
BIRCH, DAVID G S07RR06028-02
BIRCH, DAVID G S15EY09458-01
BIRCH, EILEEN E R01EY05236-08
BIRCH, LEANN L R01HD19752-07
BIRCK, JONATHAN D R43DC01001-01
BIRD, EDWARD N01HD13139-00
BIRD, EDWARD P01NS16367-12 9002
BIRD, EDWARD D P50MH44866-04 9002
BIRD, EDWARD D R01MH31862-14
BIRD, HECTOR R P50MH43878-03 0005
BIRD, HECTOR R U01MH46718-03
BIRD, ROBERT E R43CA54662-01
BIRD, THOMAS D P50AG05136-08 0003
BIRDWELL, CHARLES R P30CA30199-11 9002
BIRGE, ROBERT R R01GM34548-07
BIRGE, STANLEY J P01AG05562-07 0006
BIRINYI, LOUIS K R01HL43771-02
BIRK, DAVID E R01AR37003-04A2
BIRK, DAVID E R01EY05129-08
BIRKE, RONALD L S06GM08168-13 0014
BIRKEDAL-HANSEN, HENNING P50DE08228-04
BIRKEDAL-HANSEN, HENNING P50DE08228-04 000
BIRKEDAL-HANSEN, HENNING S07RR05300-30
BIRKEDAL-HANSEN, HENNING S15DE10069-01
BIRKEN, STEVEN P01HD15454-11 0001
BIRKENBACH, MARK P K11CA01341-05
BIRKENMEIER, EDWARD S07RR05545-29 0576
BIRKENMEIER, EDWARD H R01DK34384-08
BIRKENMEIER, EDWARD H R01DK41082-03
BIRKENMEIER, THOMAS M K08HL02428-02
BIRKHAHN, RONALD H R01GM39329-03
BIRMAHER, BORIS R29MH46894-01A1
BIRNBAUM, EDWARD R S06GM08136-18 0017
BIRNBAUM, L S Z01ES21003-11
BIRNBAUM, L S Z01ES21004-11
BIRNBAUM, L S Z01ES21093-05
BIRNBAUM, MORRIS J R01DK39519-04

BIRNBAUMER, LUTZ P30DK27685-10 9003
BIRNBAUMER, LUTZ P30HD07495-19 9011
BIRNBAUMER, LUTZ R01HD09581-14
BIRNBAUMER, LUTZ R01HL45198-02
BIRNBAUMER, LUTZ R37DK19318-15
BIRNBAUMER, MARIEL R01DK41244-02
BIRNBOWNER, LUTZ P01HL37044-06 0007
BIRO, S Z01HL04896-01
BIRON, CHRISTINE A R01CA41268-06
BIROS, MICHELLE H P20NS30322-01 0002
BIROS, MICHELLE H P20NS30322-01 9001
BIRREN, JAMES E S07RR07012-25 0012
BIRRER, M J Z01CM07255-03
BIRSHSTEIN, BARBARA K P01AI10702-20 0006
BIRSHTEIN, BARBARA K R37AI13509-16
BIRT, DIANE F R01CA42986-06
BISGARD, GERALD E R37HL15473-17
BISHAYEE, SUBAL R29CA44441-06
BISHOP, COLIN E R01HD27584-01A1
BISHOP, D KEITH R29AI30104-02
BISHOP, D KEITH S07RR05428-30 0165
BISHOP, DAVID F R01DK40895-03
BISHOP, DONALD B R21DK44608-01
BISHOP, GAIL S07RR05372-30 0662
BISHOP, GAIL A R29AI28847-02
BISHOP, GEORGIA A R01NS18028-10
BISHOP, J M R35CA44338-05
BISHOP, MARK T R19DA06452-03
BISHOP, MICHAEL J P50HL30542-08 0003
BISHOP, PAUL P42ES04908-03 0004
BISHOP, SANFORD P P50HL17667-17 9006
BISHOP, SANFORD P R01HL36892-05
BISHOP, VERNON S P01HL36080-06
BISHOP, VERNON S P01HL36080-06 0001
BISHOP, VERNON S P01HL36080-06 0007
BISHOP, VERNON S R37HL12415-21
BISHOP, VERNON S S15AG10236-01
BISHOP, WARREN S07RR05372-30 0663
BISSELL, D MONTGOMERY P30DK26743-11 9002
BISSELL, DWIGHT M, JR R01DK31198-10
BISSELL, MINA J S07RR05918-08
BISSELL, MINA J S15HL47751-01
BISSETTE, GARTH R01MH45975-01
BISSONNETTE, BRUCE M K08DK02022-02
BISTRIAN, BRUCE R R01DK31933-09
BISTRIAN, BRUCE R R01DK40252-03
BISTRIAN, BRUCE R R01DK41128-03
BISWALL, NILAMBAR P50NS20022-08 0001
BISWAS, CHITRA R01CA38817-05
BISWAS, DEBAJIT K S07RR05318-30 0250
BISWAS, DEBAJIT K S07RR05318-30 0251
BISWAS, R Z01BG04001-02
BISWAS, R Z01BG04002-02
BISWAS, SUBHASIS B R01GM36002-05
BITAR, KHALIL N R01DK42876-01A1
BITAR, KHALIL N S07RR05383-30 0551
BITENSKY, MARK W R01EY06816-06
BITKUN, STEPHAN A S07RR05736-19 0174
BITTAR, E EDWARD R01ES05142-03
BITTERMAN, M E S07RR07026-26 0006
BITTERMAN, M. E. S06GM08125-18 0043
BITTERMAN, PETER M01RR00400-23 0264
BITTERMAN, PETER B R01HL39833-05
BITTL, JOHN M01RR02635-07 0280
BITTLE, JOYCE B M01RR00211-27 0338
BITTMAN, ERIC L R01MH44132-03
BITTMAN, ERIC L S07RR07048-26 0631
BITTMAN, ROBERT R37HL16660-18
BIXBY, JOHN L R01HD25154-02
BIXLER, EDWARD O R01HL40916-02
BIZZI, EMILIO R01NS09343-22
BIZZI, EMILIO R37AR26710-11
BIZZOZERO, OSCAR ANGEL R29NS28129-03
BJORKLUND, ANDERS R01NS06701-24
BJORKMAN, PAMELA J R01AI28931-02
BJORLING, DALE S07RR05912-08 0658
BJORLING, DALE S07RR05912-08 0647
BJORLING, DALE S07RR05912-08 0648
BJORNSON, ANN B N01HB87050-06
BJORNSON, ANN B R01AI20154-04
BJORNSON, ANN B R01GM45356-01A1
BJORNSON, ANN B S07RR05951-07 0737
BJORNSSON, THORIR D R01HL43183-02
BJORNSSON, THORIR D R01HL45593-01
BJORNSTI, MARY-ANN R29GM44810-02
BJOTVEDT, GEORGE G20RR06761-01
BLACHER, JANET B R01HD21324-05
BLACK, ALEXANDER C K11CA01566-01
BLACK, DENNIS D R29HD22551-05
BLACK, FRANKLIN O R01DC00205-10
BLACK, GORDON S R01DA06513-02
BLACK, GORDON S R01DA07041-02
BLACK, HENRY R K07HL02083-04
BLACK, HENRY R M01RR00125-28 0735
BLACK, HENRY R. N01HC48069-11
BLACK, HOMER S R01CA44383-03
BLACK, IRA B P01HD23315-05
BLACK, IRA B R01NS10259-21
BLACK, JOHN R M01RR00750-19 0274
BLACK, JOHN R M01RR00750-19 0258
BLACK, JOHN R M01RR00750-19 0255
BLACK, JOHN R U01AI25859-05 0004
BLACK, KEITH L P01NS25554-01A2S1 0004
BLACK, KEITH L R29NS26523-04
BLACK, LINDSAY W R37AI11676-17
BLACK, MARK M R01NS17681-09
BLACK, RONALD R35AG09014-01 0002
BLACK, RONALD S K08AG00504-01
BLACK, S Z01DK23140-33
BLACK, SHAUN D R29GM38261-04
BLACK, VIRGINIA H R01DK39671-02
BLACKARD, WILLIAM M01RR00065-29 0370
BLACKARD, WILLIAM M01RR00065-29 0341
BLACKARD, WILLIAM C. M01RR00065-29 0312
BLACKARD, WILLIAM G M01RR00065-29 0314
BLACKARD, WILLIAM G M01RR00065-29 0334
BLACKARD, WILLIAM G M01RR00065-29 0292
BLACKARD, WILLIAM G M01RR00065-29 0285
BLACKARD, WILLIAM G R01DK18903-15
BLACKBAND, STEPHEN J R29CA45308-05
BLACKBAND, STEPHEN J S10RR06480-01
BLACKBURN, ELIZABETH H P30ES01896-13 9024
BLACKBURN, ELIZABETH H R01GM32565-09
BLACKBURN, ELIZABETH H R37GM26259-14
BLACKBURN, HENRY W R01HL23727-13
BLACKBURN, JOHN G S07RR05420-30 0037
BLACKBURN, NINIAN J R01NS27583-03
BLACKFORD, JAMES T S07RR05845-11 0556
BLACKLOW, NEIL R U01AI25831-05 0003
BLACKLOW, ROBERT S S03RR03152-11
BLACKMAN, MARCIA A R29AI31489-01
BLACKMAN, RONALD S07RR07030-26 0380
BLACKSHEAR, PERRY J R01DK40408-04
BLACKWELL, JOHN S07RR07113-24 0566
BLAESE, R M Z01CB04015-15
BLAGBURN, JONATHAN P01NS07464-24 0050
BLAHUT, P S07RR05915-08 0670
BLAHUT, P S07RR05915-08 0688
BLAINE, G JAMES P41RR01380-10 9005
BLAINE, LOIS N01LM03508-02
BLAINE, LOIS D N01DE62562-16
BLAIR IAN A P01DK38226-06 0003
BLAIR, A Z01CP04480-16
BLAIR, D G Z01CP05295-10
BLAIR, D G Z01CP05571-04
BLAIR, D G Z01CP05595-03
BLAIR, D G Z01CP05672-01
BLAIR, D K Z01CP05572-04
BLAIR, IAN A P01GM31304-09 9001
BLAIR, IAN A P30DK26657-12 9003
BLAIR, IAN A P30ES00267-25 9006
BLAIR, IAN A P50DK39261-05 9001
BLAIR, IAN A P50GM15431-24 9001
BLAIR, IAN A S10RR06254-01
BLAIR, JAMES B S15ES05833-01
BLAIR, LESLIE A C R01CA51496-03
BLAIR, MARTHA L S07RR05403-30 0803
BLAIR, NORMAN P R01EY07794-04
BLAIR, OWEN P30CA51008-02 9004
BLAIR, ROBERT W R01HL29618-10
BLAIR, SETH S R01NS28202-02
BLAIR, SETH S S07RR07098-26 0362
BLAIR, STEVEN N R01AG06945-05
BLAIR, STEVEN N R03HL47478-01
BLAKE, BARBARA H S14GM44780-02 0003
BLAKE, CHARLES A R01HD22687-05
BLAKE, CHARLES A S15HL47702-01
BLAKE, DIANE A R01EY09092-01
BLAKE, MILAN S R01AI18637-09
BLAKE, MILAN S R01AI19469-08
BLAKE, R RANDOLPH R01EY07760-04
BLAKE, RICHARD D R01GM22827-13
BLAKE, RICHARD D S07RR07161-14 0845
BLAKE, RICHARD D S07RR07161-14
BLAKE, RICHARD H R01AA07683-03
BLAKELY, RANDY D R01DA07390-01
BLAKESLEE, JAMES S07RR05463-29 0369
BLAKLEY, GERALD A. P51RR00166-30 0167
BLAKLEY, SALLY S07RR05444-30 0257
BLALOCK, J EDWIN P01NS29719-01 0004
BLALOCK, JAMES E R01DK38024-06
BLALOCK, SUSAN J P60AR30701-10 0017
BLALOCK, SUSAN J P60AR30701-10 0021
BLANC, JOSEPH R43RR06984-01
BLANC, PAUL D K01OH00079-02
BLANCH, ANDREA K R18MH46140-04
BLANCH, ANDREA K R18MH47640-01
BLANCHARD-FIELDS, FREDDA H R01AG07607-02
BLANCHARD, CAROLINE D. S06GM08125-18 0044
BLANCHARD, D CAROLINE R01MH42803-03
BLANCHARD, D KAY R01AI26560-04
BLANCHARD, EDWARD B R01HL31189-04A3
BLANCHARD, EDWARD B R01MH48476-01
BLANCHARD, EDWARD B S07RR07122-23 0103
BLANCHARD, JAMES LEE P51RR00164-30 0012
BLANCHARD, JAMES LEE P51RR00164-30 0029
BLANCHARD, JAMES LEE P51RR00164-30 9013
BLANCHARD, JOHN S R01GM33449-07
BLANCHARD, ROBERT J. S06GM08125-18 0045
BLANCHETTE-MACKIE, E J Z01DK15404-07
BLANCK, GEORGE S07RR05749-19 0267
BLANCK, THOMAS J R01GM30799-10
BLAND, KIRBY M01RR00082-29 0453
BLAND, RICHARD D P01HL25816-11 0004
BLAND, RICHARD D R01HL40802-04
BLANE, HOWARD T S03RR03459-05
BLANE, HOWARD T S07RR05938-07 0312
BLANE, HOWARD T S07RR05938-07
BLANE, HOWARD T S07RR05938-07 0319
BLANE, HOWARD T S15AA09244-01
BLANE, HOWART T S07RR05938-07 0325
BLANER, WILLIAM S R01DK43097-01A1
BLANER, WILLIAM S S07RR05395-30 0821
BLANGERO, JOHN S07RR05519-29 0511
BLANK, C LEROY S07RR07078-18 0455
BLANK, JAMES L S07RR07208-10 0662
BLANK, JAMES L S07RR07208-10 0669
BLANK, KENNETH J P01CA15822-17 0010
BLANK, KENNETH J R01AI27766-04
BLANK, KENNETH J R01AI28715-03
BLANK, P S Z01AG00262-03
BLANKENHORN, DAVID H R01HL45005-01
BLANKENSHIP, JAMES E R01NS27314-03
BLANKENSHIP, ROBERT S07RR07112-24 0426
BLANKS, JANET C R25RR07635-01
BLANKS, JANET C. P50AG05142-08 0004
BLANKS, JANET M R01AG07891-03
BLANKS, JANET M R01EY03042-11
BLANTON, RICHARD E P01AI15351-13 9004
BLANTON, RONALD E R29AI27317-03
BLANTZ, ROLAND C R01DK28602-19
BLASCHKE, TERRENCE F M01RR00070-29 0233
BLASCHKE, TERRENCE F P30AI27762-03 9003
BLASCHKE, TERRENCE F R01AG05627-07
BLASCKE, TERRANCE M01RR00070-29 0225
BLASDEL, GARY G R01EY06586-04A2
BLASER, MARTIN J R01AI24145-04
BLASIE, J KENT P01HL18708-16 0017
BLASIE, J KENT P41RR01348-10 0001
BLASIE, J KENT P41RR01633-10 0004
BLASIE, J KENT P41RR01633-10
BLASIE, J KENT P41RR01633-10 9006
BLASIE, J KENT R01GM33525-08
BLASS, ELLIOTT M K05MH00524-08
BLASS, ELLIOTT M R01DA05724-03
BLASS, ELLIOTT M R01HD28245-01
BLASS, JOHN R35AG09014-01 0001
BLASS, JOHN P P01AG03853-09 9001
BLASS, JOHN P P01AG03853-09
BLASS, JOHN P P01AG03853-09 0011
BLASS, JOHN P R35AG09014-01
BLASZCZYK-THURIN, MAGDALENA R01CA45363-04
BLATT, JULIE M01RR00084-29 0245
BLATT, STEVEN D M01RR00084-29 0230
BLATTEIS, CLARK M R01NS22716-05
BLATTEIS, CLARK M S07RR05423-30 0048
BLATTNER, FREDERICK R R01AI27318-03
BLATTNER, FREDERICK R R01HG00504-01 0002
BLATTNER, FREDERICK R R01HG00504-01 0001
BLATTNER, FREDERICK R R01HG00301-04
BLATTNER, W A Z01CP05400-08
BLATZ, ANDREW L R29GM39731-03
BLAU, DAVID P01HD28076-01 0004
BLAU, HELEN M M01RR00081-29 0100
BLAU, HELEN M R01AG09521-05
BLAU, HELEN M R01HD18179-08
BLAUFOX, MORTON D N01HC48055-11
BLAUFOX, MORTON D R01HL40566-04
BLAUM, CAROLYN S07RR05490-29 0449
BLAUSTEIN, JEFFREY D K02MH00885-02
BLAUSTEIN, MORDECAI MD R01NS16285-11
BLAUSTEIN, MORDECAI P P50MH44211-03 0005
BLAUSTEIN, MORDECAI P R01HL45215-08
BLAUSTEIN, MORDECAI P R01NS16106-13
BLAYNEY, KEITH D S07RR05968-06
BLAYNEY, KEITH D S15CA55999-01
BLAZAR, BRUCE P01CA21737-14 0007
BLAZAR, BRUCE R N01AI85002-04
BLAZER, DAN N01AG12102-00
BLAZER, DAN N01AG42110-10
BLAZER, DAN G P30AG09463-01 9001
BLAZER, DAN G P50MH40159-08 0001
BLAZER, DAN G, II P50MH40159-08
BLAZER, DAN G, III R01DE08060-05
BLAZYNSKI, CHRISTINE R01EY02294-13
BLECK, THOMAS P S07RR05431-30 0864
BLEECKER, EUGENE R P01AG04402-09 9001
BLEECKER, MARGIT M01RR02719-06 0132
BLEECKER, MARGIT L P01AG04402-09 0007
BLEGAN, MARY A S07RR07035-26 0095
BLEGAN, MARY A S07RR07035-26 0087
BLEHM, KENNETH D S07RR05458-29 0824
BLEICHER, PAUL A K08AR01805-05
BLEIL, JEFFREY D R55HD27847-01
BLEIL, JEFFREY D U54HD29125-01 0004
BLEIWEIS, ARNOLD S R37DE08007-06
BLENIS, JOHN R01CA46595-05
BLESKE, BARRY E M01RR00042-31 0648
BLESS, DIANE M P60DC00976-02 0005
BLESSING, JOHN A U10CA37517-07
BLESSING, ROBERT S07RR05716-20 0144
BLESSING, ROBERT H R01GM34073-07
BLIGHT, ANDREW R R01NS21122-06
BLIGHT, ANDREW R S15NS30132-01
BLINKS, JOHN R R37HL12186-22
BLISARD, KAREN S S07RR05408-30 0919

BLISSARD, GARY W R29AI31130-01
BLITHE, D L Z01HD00627-02
BLIZZARD, DAVID S07RR05404-30 0836
BLIZZARD, ROBERT M M01RR00847-18 0563
BLIZZARD, ROBERT M M01RR00847-18 0424
BLIZZARD, ROBERT M M01RR00847-18 0426
BLIZZARD, ROBERT M M01RR00847-18 0427
BLIZZARD, ROBERT M M01RR00847-18 0428
BLIZZARD, ROBERT M M01RR00847-18 0429
BLIZZARD, ROBERT M M01RR00847-18 0385
BLIZZARD, ROBERT M M01RR00847-18 0167
BLIZZARD, ROBERT M M01RR00847-18 0338
BLIZZARD, ROBERT M M01RR00847-18 0552
BLIZZARD, ROBERT M M01RR00847-18 0547
BLOCH, ALEXANDER R01CA36241-08
BLOCH, CLIFFORD A M01RR00069-29 0422
BLOCH, CLIFFORD A M01RR00069-29 0448
BLOCH, DONALD B K08AR01866-01
BLOCH, GEORGE J R01HD27334-01
BLOCH, KENNETH D R29HL45895-01
BLOCH, KURT J P01DK33506-08 0003
BLOCH, ROBERT J R01NS17282-11
BLOCH, ROBERT J R01NS27171-03
BLOCK, BARBARA A R29AR40246-02
BLOCK, CARL S07RR05704-20 0008
BLOCK, CHRISTINE H P01HL06835-30 9003
BLOCK, EDWARD R R01HL35908-05
BLOCK, ERIC S07RR07122-23 0086
BLOCK, ERIC S07RR07122-23 0087
BLOCK, GENE D R01NS15264-13
BLOCK, GEOFFREY P50AA08746-02 0003
BLOCK, MARTIN L S07RR07143-20 0616
BLOCK, MICHAEL S R01DE08851-01A3
BLOCK, RONALD S07RR05662-18 0149
BLOCK, STEVEN M R29HD23847-04
BLOCK, TIMOTHY P01AI23968-06 0005
BLOEDEL, JAMES R R01NS21958-08
BLOEDEL, JAMES R S07RR05872-08
BLOEM, THOMAS A S07RR05321-30 0254
BLOMBERG, BONNIE B R01AI21870-05
BLONDER, LEE X M01RR02602-07 0054
BLONDER, LEE X S07RR05374-30 0733
BLOOM, ARTHUR D N01ES75185-13
BLOOM, BARRY P30CA13330-20 9004
BLOOM, BARRY R. P01AI26491-03 0002
BLOOM, BARRY R P01AI10702-20 0004
BLOOM, BARRY R P01AI26491-03
BLOOM, BARRY R R01AI07118-26
BLOOM, BARRY R R37AI23545-06
BLOOM, BARRY R U01AI28171-03 0004
BLOOM, BARRY R. P01AI26491-03 0001
BLOOM, BARRY R. P01AI26491-03 0004
BLOOM, BARRY R. P01AI26491-03 0005
BLOOM, E T Z01BD02017-01
BLOOM, E T Z01BD02018-01
BLOOM, FLOYD E P01NS22347-06
BLOOM, FLOYD E P01NS22347-06 0009
BLOOM, FLOYD E P50AA06420-08
BLOOM, FLOYD E P50AA06420-08 9001
BLOOM, FLOYD E P50AA06420-08 9005
BLOOM, FLOYD E P50AA06420-08 9006
BLOOM, FLOYD E P50MH47680-02
BLOOM, FLOYD E S15AA09252-01
BLOOM, JOHN W S07RR05675-23 0946
BLOOM, JOSEPH D P50MH43458-04 0003
BLOOM, KERRY S K04CA01175-05
BLOOM, KERRY S R01GM32238-09
BLOOM, M E Z01AI00085-14
BLOOM, M E Z01AI00263-10
BLOOM, PAUL S07RR07002-26 0880
BLOOM, RONALD S S06GM08140-17 0015
BLOOM, STEPHEN E R01ES03499-10
BLOOMER, JOSEPH R R01DK26466-13
BLOOMER, WILLIAM D R01CA37553-06
BLOOMFIELD, CLARA D U10CA37027-09
BLOOMFIELD, STEWART S07RR05399-30 0934
BLOOMFIELD, STEWART A R01EY07360-04
BLOOMFIELD, VICTOR A R01GM28093-11
BLOOMQUIST, EUNICE I R01HL35817-06
BLOOMSMITH, MOLLIE A R01RR03578-06
BLOOMSMITH, MOLLIE A R01RR05092-04
BLOOR, COLIN M P50HL17682-17 9004
BLOOR, COLIN M P50HL23584-13 9003
BLOOR, COLIN M R01HL32670-07
BLOOR, COLIN M R37HL20190-15
BLOOR, JOHN E S07RR07088-24 0355
BLOSSER, GABE F R44CA45913-03
BLOSSEY, BETTY P60AR20618-13 0016
BLOT, W J Z01CP04779-15
BLOUGH, NEIL V R55GM44966-01A1
BLOUIN, ROBERT A M01RR02602-07 0046
BLOUIN, ROBERT A R01GM42058-02
BLOUT, ELKAN R S03RR03069-11
BLOWERS, VIRGINIA K G07LM05391-01
BLUESTEIN, HARRY G R01AR30036-10
BLUESTONE, JEFFREY P01CA19266-14A1 0023
BLUESTONE, JEFFREY P01CA19266-14A1 9002
BLUESTONE, JEFFREY A P01AI29531-02
BLUESTONE, JEFFREY A P01AI29531-02 0001
BLUESTONE, JEFFREY A R01AI26847-04
BLUESTONE, JEFFREY A R01CA49260-04
BLUM, DAVID S07RR05756-18 0310
BLUM, JACOB J R01AI26534-03
BLUM, JACOB J R01NS25191-02
BLUM, JOANNE P40RR03624-05 0003
BLUM, JOANNE P40RR03624-05 9001
BLUM, MARIANN P01MH45212-02 0004
BLUM, RONALD M01RR00096-30A1 0292
BLUM, RONALD M01RR00096-30A1 0291
BLUM, RONALD M01RR00096-30A1 0285
BLUM, RONALD M01RR00096-30A1 0299
BLUM, RONALD M01RR00096-30A1 0258
BLUM, RONALD M01RR00096-30A1 0261
BLUM, RONALD M01RR00096-30A1 0313
BLUM, RONALD N01CM67895-01
BLUM, RONALD P30CA16087-14 9004
BLUM, RONALD H R25CA18002-13
BLUM, RONALD H U10CA16395-17
BLUM, TERRY C R01AA07192-05
BLUM, TERRY C R01AA07250-04
BLUM, TERRY C R01DA07417-01
BLUMBERG, BARUCH S U01CA48460-04
BLUMBERG, P M Z01CP05270-10
BLUMBERG, RICHARD S07RR05950-07 0991
BLUMBERG, RICHARD S K08DK01886-03
BLUME, KARL G P01CA49605-03
BLUME, KARL G P01CA49605-03 0001
BLUME, SCOTT K11CA01581-01
BLUMENBERG, MIROSLAV P30AR39749-04 9004
BLUMENFELD, JON M01RR00047-31 0460
BLUMENFELD, JON P50HL18323-17 0066
BLUMENFELD, OLGA O R01GM16389-22
BLUMENSTEIN, BRENT A P30CA15704-18 9017
BLUMENSTOCK, FRANK A P01GM40761-01A2 0003
BLUMENTHAL, DONALD K, II R29GM39290-05
BLUMENTHAL, JAMES A M01RR00030-30 0485
BLUMENTHAL, JAMES A M01RR00030-30 0450
BLUMENTHAL, JAMES A R01HL43028-03
BLUMENTHAL, KENNETH M R01HL41543-02
BLUMENTHAL, MALCOLM N M01RR00400-23 0091
BLUMENTHAL, R P Z01CB08303-18
BLUMENTHAL, ROSALYN D R55CA49995-01A2
BLUMENTHAL, THOMAS R01GM30870-10
BLUMER, KENDALL J R01GM44592-02
BLUMER, KENDALL J S07RR05389-30 0628
BLUMSTEIN, SHEILA E R01DC00142-13
BLUMSTEIN, SHEILA E R01DC00314-07
BLUSZTAJN S07RR05380-30 0900
BLUSZTAJN, JAN K P01AG09525-01
BLUSZTAJN, JAN K P01AG09525-01 0001
BLUSZTAJN, JAN K R01MH46095-01A2
BLUSZTAJN, JAN K S15MH49515-01
BLY, JAN E S07RR05386-30 0575
BLYDEN, GERSHWIN S06GM08111-19 0028
BLYDEN, GERSHWIN S06GM08111-19 0028
BLYDEN, GERSHWIN T G12RR03020-07 0003
BLYSTONE, ROBERT V S07RR07261-02 0712
BLYTHE, MARGARET J U01AI31494-01 9001
BOACKLE, ROBERT J R01DE08589-03
BOAT, THOMAS P50HL42384-04 0003
BOAT, THOMAS F P50HL19171-15 0018
BOAZ, RACHEL F R01AG10010-01
BOBBIN, RICHARD P P01DC00379-05 0003
BOBBIN, RICHARD P R01DC00722-01A1
BOBEK, LIBUSE P01DE07585-04 0002
BOBEK, LIBUSEA A S07RR05330-30 0012
BOBEK, MIROSLAV P01CA13038-19 0104
BOBIN, STEPHEN G12RR03037-07 9001
BOBO, R H Z01NS02812-02
BOBO, R H Z01NS02813-02
BOCCIA, MARIA L R01MH44131-04
BOCHNER, BARRY R R44AI22760-03
BOCHNER, BRUCE S R29AI27429-03
BOCIAN, DAVID F R01GM36243-06
BOCK, JAY L S07RR05736-19 0179
BOCK, PAUL E R29HL38779-06
BOCK, R DARRELL R01HD26031-03
BOCK, SUSAN P50HL45486-01 0004
BOCK, SUSAN C R01HL30712-09
BOCKMAN, JEFFREY S07RR05359-30 0504
BOCKMAN, R P01CA29502-11A1 0051
BOCKMAN, RICHARD S R01CA38645-07
BOCKRATH, RICHARD C R01GM21788-17
BOCKUS, BEVERLY J R29CA45310-04
BODDEN, MARTIN K K15DE00283-03
BODE, HANS R R01HD08086-18
BODE, HANS R R01HD24511-04
BODELL, WILLIAM P42ES04705-05 0003
BODELL, WILLIAM J P01CA13525-19 0023
BODEN, GUENHER M01RR00349-25 0209
BODEN, GUENTHER M01RR00349-25 0208
BODEN, GUENTHER M01RR00349-25 0238
BODEN, GUENTHER M01RR00349-25 0239
BODEN, GUENTHER M01RR00349-25 0236
BODEN, GUENTHER R01AG07988-02
BODINE, D Z01HL02335-04
BODINE, D M Z01HL02307-12
BODLEY, JAMES W R01GM26832-11
BODMER, WALTER F R13HG00275-02
BODNAR, RICHARD J R01DA04194-03
BODNAR, RICHARD J S07RR07064-24 0194
BODNER, ANNE J U01AI25697-05 0002
BODOR, NICHOLAS S P01AG10485-01 0003
BODY, SIMON S07RR05950-07 0994
BOECK, M P01CA29502-11A1 0044
BOECK, MARJORIE M01RR06020-02 0436
BOECK, MARJORIE M01RR06020-02 0421
BOECK, MARJORIE A M01RR06020-02 0422
BOECK, MARJORIE A M01RR06020-02 0442
BOECK, MARJORIE A M01RR06020-02 0443
BOECKMAN, ROBERT K, JR R01CA29108-10
BOECKMAN, ROBERT K, JR R01GM29290-11
BOEDY, ROBERT F S07RR05365-30 0076
BOEGEHOLD, MATTHEW ALAN R29HL44012-03
BOEHLECKE, BRIAN A K07HL02096-05
BOEHM, SUSAN S07RR05796-14 0423
BOEHNKE, MICHAEL L P30HG00209-02 9003
BOEHNKE, MICHAEL L R29HG00376-04
BOEHR, DIANE N01LM03503-01
BOEHRINGER, HANSRUEDI R29DE08412-04
BOEKE, JEF D P01CA16519-17 0010
BOEKE, JEF D R01GM36481-06
BOEKELHEIDE, KIM K04ES00193-03
BOEKELHEIDE, KIM R01ES05033-07
BOEPPLE, PAUL A M01RR01066-14 0022
BOEPPLE, PAUL A M01RR01066-14 0050
BOEPPLE, PAUL A M01RR01066-14 0110
BOEPPLE, PAUL A M01RR01066-14 0093
BOEPPLE, PAUL A M01RR01066-14 0094
BOERBOOM, LAWRENCE E R01HL41840-03
BOERNER, PAULA P01CA37497-07 0003
BOERWINKLE, E A M01RR00585-20 0396
BOERWINKLE, ERIC K04HL02453-01A1
BOERWINKLE, ERIC R29HL40613-04
BOETTIGER, DAVID E R01CA16502-17
BOETTIGER, DAVID E R01CA49866-03
BOEWN-POPE, DANIEL P01HL18645-17 0014
BOGARDDUS, C Z01DK69042-02
BOGARDUS, C Z01DK69015-09
BOGARDUS, C Z01DK69020-08
BOGARDUS, C Z01DK69021-10
BOGARDUS, C Z01DK69027-03
BOGARDUS, C Z01DK69033-03
BOGARDUS, C Z01DK69034-03
BOGARDUS, C Z01DK69035-03
BOGARDUS, C Z01DK69041-02
BOGARDUS, C Z01DK69044-01
BOGDANSKI, D F Z01HL03585-02
BOGENHAGEN, DANIEL P01ES04068-05 0003
BOGENHAGEN, DANIEL F R01GM29681-11
BOGENHAGEN, DANIEL F R01GM33321-08
BOGENMANN, EMIL R01EY04950-09
BOGENMANN, EMIL R01NS25795-03
BOGER, DALE L R01CA41101-07
BOGER, DALE L R01CA41986-08
BOGER, DALE L R01CA42056-08
BOGER, DALE L R01CA55276-01
BOGGARAM, VIJAYAKUMA S07RR05426-30 0129
BOGGIANO, ANN S07RR07013-26 0957
BOGGIANO, ANN K R01MH45566-02
BOGGS, SALLIE S S07RR05416-30 0553
BOGGS, WILLIAM S07RR05704-20 0011
BOGNER, ROBIN S07RR05743-14 0617
BOGNER, ROBIN S07RR05743-14 0615
BOGORAD, LAWRENCE R01GM41080-03
BOHACH, GREGORY A R29AI28401-03
BOHLEN, HAROLD G R01HL20605-14
BOHLEN, HAROLD G R01HL25824-12
BOHMAN, ROGER P01AR40919-01 9002
BOHN, MARTHA C S07RR05403-30 0804
BOHN, PAUL W S07RR07030-26 0381
BOHNSACK, JOHN S07RR05428-30 0166
BOHNSACK, JOHN F R29AI26733-02
BOHR, DAVID F P01HL18575-16A1 9001
BOHR, V Z01CM06186-05
BOICE, J D Z01CP04481-15
BOICE, J D Z01CP05368-08
BOILEAU, RICHARD A R01AG08513-03
BOILEAU, RICHARD A S07RR07030-26 0382
BOIME, IRVING R01HD23398-05
BOINEAU, JOHN P R01HL33722-06A1
BOISSE, N S07RR05830-12 0962
BOISSE, N S07RR05830-12 0966
BOISSE, NORMAN R R01DA05431-01A2
BOISSY, RAYMOND E S07RR05408-30 0920
BOK, DEAN R37EY00444-23
BOKOCH, GARY M R01GM39434-04
BOKOCH, GARY M R01GM44428-01A2
BOKOCH, GARY M R01HL48008-01
BOKOCH, GARY M R13CA54798-01
BOKOS, PETER J R18DA06086-03
BOLAMOS, BENJAMIN S06GM08224-07 0004
BOLAN, G P01AI21912-08 0004
BOLAN, GAIL U01AI31499-01 9002
BOLAND, C RICHARD R01CA39233-07
BOLANDER, FRANKLYN F, JR R01CA42009-05
BOLANOWSKI, STANLEY S07RR07068-26 0230
BOLDT, DAVID P30CA54174-01 9006
BOLDT, JEFFREY S07RR05394-30 0712
BOLE, G G P60AR20557-13 0063
BOLE, GILES G S15CA56021-01
BOLE, GILES G JR S03RR03075-10
BOLE, GILES G JR S07RR05383-30
BOLE, GILES G, JR M01RR00042-31
BOLEN, DAVID W R01GM22300-15
BOLEN, J B Z01CP05481-06

BOLEN, J B Z01CP05518-05
BOLENDER, DAVID L P01HD20743-05 9003
BOLES, TRUETT CHRIST S07RR07044-26 0120
BOLGER, NIALL S07RR07138-20 0529
BOLINGER, LIZANN P41RR02305-08 9001
BOLLA-WILSON, KAREN R29ES04427-05
BOLLA, KAREN M01RR02719-06 0016
BOLLEKENS, JACQUES A K11DK02018-01
BOLLENBACHER, WALTER E R01DK31642-09
BOLLI, ROBERTO P50HL42267-02 0005
BOLLI, ROBERTO R01HL43151-03
BOLOGNESI, DAN P N01AI15106-00
BOLOGNESI, DANI P P01CA43447-06
BOLOGNESI, DANI P P30AI28662-03
BOLT, ROBERT J U01HL37904-06
BOLTON, DAVID P01AG04220-07A1 0008
BOLTON, WARREN K M01RR00847-18 0387
BOLTON, WARREN K M01RR00847-18 0579
BOLTON, WARREN K R01DK44107-01
BOLUYT, M Z01AG00271-01
BOMALASKI, JOHN S R55AR39382-04
BOMSZTYK, KAROL P01GM42508-03 0002
BOMSZTYK, KAROL R01GM45134-01A1
BONA, CONSTANTIN A P01AI24460-04 0001
BONA, CONSTANTIN A P01AI24671-04 0001
BONA, CONSTANTIN A P01AI24671-04
BONA, CONSTANTIN A R01AI18316-11
BONA, CONSTANTIN A U01AI28666-03
BONACI, DAVID A P50MH40381-06 9002
BONADIO, JEFFREY F R01AR40679-01A1
BONANNO, JOSEPH A R01EY08834-01A1
BONANNO, JOSEPH A S07RR05832-12 0192
BONAVENTURA, JOSEPH P30ES01908-14
BONAVENTURA, JOSEPH P30ES01908-14 9001
BONAVIDA, BENJAMIN R01CA43121-04
BOND, GARY R K02MH00842-03
BOND, ISABEL E S03RR03037-10
BOND, JENNY T S07RR07049-26 0439
BOND, JUDITH S R37DK19691-16
BOND, LYNNE A S07RR07125-22
BOND, LYNNE A S15GM47049-01
BOND, MEREDITH P50HL33713-06 0014
BOND, MEREDITH R01HL41883-02
BONDADA, SUBBARAO K04AG00422-04
BONDADA, SUBBARAO R01AG05731-04A3
BONDADA, SUBBARAO R01AI21490-08
BONDER, BETTE R R01AG10646-01
BONDER, EDWARD M R01HD24649-03
BONDS, ALFRED B R01EY03778-09A2
BONDURANT, STUART M01RR00046-31
BONDURANT, STUART S07RR05406-30
BONDURANT, STUART S15AI32218-01
BONDY, C Z01HD00628-02
BONDY, C A Z01HD00629-02
BONDY, STEPHEN C R01AA08281-01A2
BONE, HENRY G R01AR40554-01A1
BONEWALD, LYNDA P01AR39529-02 0003
BONEWALD, LYNDA P01DE08569-03 0002
BONHAM, ANN S07RR05684-23 0172
BONHAUS, DOUGLAS W R29NS27311-03
BONHOMME, FRANCOIS S R01AI29834-02
BONIFACINO, J S Z01HD01607-01
BONILLA-ALVAREZ, MARISSA S06GM08216-09 0010
BONILLA, EDUARDO P01NS11766-17A1 0032
BONITO, ARTHUR N01DE82573-05
BONKOVSKY, HERBERT L M01RR00039-31 0426
BONKOVSKY, HERBERT L M01RR00039-31 0377
BONKOVSKY, HERBERT L M01RR00039-31 0378
BONKOVSKY, HERBERT L M01RR00039-31 0387
BONKOVSKY, HERBERT L M01RR00039-31 0375
BONKOVSKY, HERBERT L R01DK38825-07
BONKOVSKY, HERBERT L S07RR05712-20 0047
BONKOVSKY, HERBERT L. M01RR00039-31 0416
BONNER-WEIR, SUSAN P30DK36836-05 9002
BONNER, J JOSE S07RR07031-26 0074
BONNER, JAMES R P50AI23694-06 0001
BONNER, R F Z01RR10098-11
BONNER, R F Z01RR10112-11
BONNER, R F Z01RR10257-05
BONNER, R F Z01RR10258-05
BONNER, W Z01CM06140-15
BONNER, W Z01CM06192-03
BONNET, JOHN D U10CA28862-11
BONNEY, GEORGE E R29GM39573-05
BONOW, R O Z01HL04827-03
BONSETT, CHARLES A M01RR00750-19 0183
BONVENTRE, JOSEPH P01DK38452-05 0006
BONVENTRE, JOSEPH V P50NS10828-16 0025
BONVENTRE, JOSEPH V R01DK39773-07
BONVINI, E Z01BH02010-03
BOOCKFOR, FREDRIC R R01DK41652-03
BOOCKFOR, FREDRIC R R01HD25090-03
BOOKCHIN, R M P01HL21016-15 0021
BOOKCHIN, ROBERT M R01HL28018-24
BOOKSTEIN, FRED L R01GM37251-06
BOOKSTEIN, FRED L R01NS26529-03
BOOM, WILLEM H R01AI27243-03
BOONE, JOHN M R01CA55372-01
BOORD, ROBERT L R01NS11272-18
BOORSTEIN, ROBERT R29CA51060-02
BOORSTEIN, ROBERT S07RR05399-30 0942
BOOTH, ALAN R01AG04146-07A1
BOOTH, BRENDA M R01AA08732-02
BOOTH, CATHRYN L R01HD27806-05
BOOTH, CATHRYN L U10HD25447-02
BOOTH, DOROTHY S07RR05796-14 0424
BOOTH, FRANK W R37AR19393-15
BOOTHBY, JOHN T S06GM08192-12 0017
BOOTHBY, MARK R R29GM42550-03
BOOTHBY, MARK R S07RR05446-30 0264
BOOTHE, RONALD G P51RR00165-31 0091
BOOTHE, RONALD G R01EY05975-06
BOOTHE, THOMAS E S07RR05662-18 0152
BOOTHMAN, DAVID A S07RR05526-29 0069
BOOTHROYD, ARTHUR P01DC00178-10 0005
BOOTHROYD, ARTHUR P01DC00178-10 0004
BOOTHROYD, JOHN C R01AI21025-08
BOOTHROYD, JOHN C R01AI21423-06
BOOTHROYD, JOHN C U01AI30230-02 0003
BOOYSE, FRANCOIS M P50HL17667-17 0072
BOOZE, ROSEMARIE M P50DA06634-01A1 9003
BOOZE, ROSEMARIE M R01AG10747-01
BOOZE, ROSEMARIE M R01DA06638-01A1
BOOZER, CAROL N S07RR05771-15 0330
BORAKER, DAVID K R43AI30838-01
BORAKER, DAVID K R44AI26434-02
BORAL, LEONARD I S07RR05386-30 0576
BORCH, RICHARD F R01CA34619-10
BORCH, RICHARD F R01CA34620-09
BORCHARDT, RONALD T R01GM29332-18
BORCHARDT, RONALD T R01NS15692-13
BORCHARDT, RONALD T S07RR05606-25 0692
BORCHMAN, DOUGLAS R01EY07975-03
BORDELON, CASSIUS P30HD07495-19 9016
BORDEN, ERNEST M01RR00058-30 0266
BORDEN, ERNEST C M01RR03186-06 0056
BORDEN, ERNEST C P01CA20432-14 0034
BORDER, WAYNE A R01DK43609-02
BORDIGNON, CLAUDIA P01AI32918-09 0001
BOREJDO, JULIAN R01AR40095-03
BOREJDO, JULIAN S07RR05906-06 0633
BOREK, CARMIA P01CA12536-20 0009
BORELLI, MARIO S03RR03049-11
BORENSTEIN GRAVES, AMY R29AG08921-03
BORENSTEIN, MICHAEL T R44MH43083-03
BORER, PHILIP N R01GM32691-06
BORER, PHILIP N S07RR07068-26 0231
BORG, THOMAS K R01HL24935-11
BORGES, LAWRENCE F R01EY08264-02
BORGESE, THOMAS A S06GM08225-07 0013
BORHANI, NEMAT O. N01HC48054-16
BORISH, LARRY P50AI24848-05 0006
BORISY, GARY P41RR00570-21 0003
BORISY, GARY P41RR00570-21 0007
BORISY, GARY G R01GM30385-10
BORISY, GARY G R37GM25062-13
BORKMAN, RAYMOND F R01EY06800-05
BORKOVEC, THOMAS D R01MH39172-07
BORKOWSKI, JOHN G R01HD26456-01A2
BORKOWSKY, WILLIAM M01RR00096-30A1 0311
BORKOWSKY, WILLIAM M01RR00096-30A1 0263
BORKOWSKY, WILLIAM M01RR00096-30A1 0282
BORKOWSKY, WILLIAM M01RR00096-30A1 0306
BORKOWSKY, WILLIAM R01AI32427-01
BORKOWSKY, WILLIAM R01HD26613-02
BORKOWSKY, WILLIAM U01AI27553-04
BORLE, ANDRE B S07RR05416-30 0554
BORN, DAVID P30DE09737-02 9002
BORN, RICHARD T K11EY00320-01
BORN, WILLI K R01AI27903-03
BORNHEIM, LESTER M R01DA04265-05
BORNSTEIN, M H Z01HD01118-04
BORNSTEIN, M H Z01HD01119-04
BORNSTEIN, M H Z01HD01120-04
BORNSTEIN, M H Z01HD01122-04
BORNSTEIN, MURRAY B P50NS11920-17 0017
BORNSTEIN, MURRAY B P50NS11920-17 9001
BORNSTEIN, MURRAY B P50NS11920-17
BORNSTEIN, PAUL P01HL18645-17 0009
BORNSTEIN, PAUL P50DE08229-05 0004
BORNSTEIN, PAUL R37AR11248-25
BORNSTEIN, RICHARD S U10CA26730-12
BORNSTEIN, ROBERT A R01MH45649-03
BOROD, JOAN C R01MH42172-02
BOROD, JOAN C R03MH44889-01A2
BOROD, JOAN C S07RR07064-24 0195
BORON, WALTER F P01DK17433-18 0014
BORON, WALTER F R01DK30344-10
BORON, WALTER F R01NS18400-10
BOROS, DOV L R37AI12913-16
BOROUJERDI, M S07RR05830-12 0970
BOROWIEC, JAMES A R01AI29963-02
BOROWITZ, STEPHEN M S07RR05431-30 0842
BOROWSKY, RICHARD S07RR07062-26 0229
BOROWSKY, RICHARD S07RR07062-26 0210
BORRELLI, MICHAEL J R29CA49715-04
BORROW, KENNETH P60DK20595-14 0023
BORSON, D B R29HL38947-05
BORSOS, T Z01CB08552-25
BORST, JAMES R U10CA35178-08
BORSZCZ, GEORGE S R29NS27668-03
BORSZCZ, GEORGE S S07RR07056-18 0202
BORTIN, MORTIMER M P01CA40053-06
BORTIN, MORTIMER M P01CA40053-06 0001
BORTIN, MORTIMER M P01CA40053-06 0002
BORTIN, MORTIMER M P01CA40053-06 0003
BORYS, SUZANNE R19MH46181-03
BOS, TIMOTHY J R29CA51982-03
BOSCH, JUAN P U01DK39368-04
BOSE, HENRY R JR S07RR07091-26
BOSE, HENRY R, JR R01CA26169-13
BOSE, HENRY R, JR R01CA33192-07A2
BOSE, NRIPENDRA K S06GM08241-07 0007
BOSE, SUBIR K S07RR05388-30 0625
BOSELLI, BRUCE U10CA35435-08
BOSKEY, ADELE S07RR05495-29 0470
BOSKEY, ADELE L R01AR37661-05
BOSKEY, ADELE L R37DE04141-17
BOSLAND, MAARTEN C R01CA43151-06
BOSLAND, MAARTEN C R01CA48084-02
BOSLER, EDWARD S07RR05649-25 0788
BOSLEY, T P01NS14867-13 0008
BOSMA, MELVIN J R01AI13323-16
BOSMA, MELVIN J R37CA04946-30
BOSMA, MELVIN J S07RR05539-29 0548
BOSMAN, H BRUCE S07RR05369-30
BOSMANN, BRUCE H S15CA55992-01
BOSNICH, BRICE R01GM41043-03
BOSNICH, BRICE R01GM41598-03
BOSNJAK, ZELJKO J K04HL01901-05
BOSNJAK, ZELJKO J R01HL34708-06
BOSNJAK, ZELJKO J R01HL39776-04
BOSRON, WILLIAM F R01AA07117-05
BOSS, GERRY R P50HL17682-17 9007
BOSS, JEREMY M R01CA47953-03
BOSSE, RAYMOND R01AG02287-11
BOSSETTI, BRENDA M M01RR00034-31 0413
BOSSINGER, JUNE A R44GM41523-02
BOSTOCK, ELIZABETH S07RR07064-24 0196
BOSTON, REBECCA S07RR07071-26 0251
BOSTWICK, JAMES R P50AG08664-03 0002
BOSWELL, H SCOTT R01CA45571-05
BOSWELL, R P30AI28696-01 9005
BOTCHAN, MICHAEL R P30ES01896-13 9025
BOTCHAN, MICHAEL R R01CA42414-06
BOTCHAN, MICHAEL R R37CA30490-11
BOTHMER, A JAMES G07LM05151-02
BOTHNER-BY, AKSEL A P41RR00292-24S2
BOTHNER-BY, AKSEL A R01DK16532-17
BOTHWELL, ALFRED L M R01GM40924-03
BOTHWELL, MARK P50AG05136-08 0008
BOTHWELL, MARK A R01HL43397-03
BOTHWELL, MARK A R01NS23343-07
BOTHWELL, MARK A R55NS29582-01
BOTNEY, MITCHELL D K11HL02425-02
BOTO, WILLIAM G12RR03060-07 0003
BOTO, WILLIAM R01AI31852-01
BOTRINICK, ELIAS H P01HL25847-12 0008
BOTSFORD, JAMES L S07RR07154-16 0561
BOTSTEIN, DAVID P01HG00205-02
BOTSTEIN, DAVID P01HG00205-02 9001
BOTSTEIN, DAVID P01HG00205-02 9002
BOTSTEIN, DAVID P01HG00205-02 0002
BOTSTEIN, DAVID P01HG00205-02 9004
BOTSTEIN, DAVID R37GM46406-01
BOTTENSTEIN, JANE E K04NS01228-05
BOTTJE, WALTER S07RR07101-13 0551
BOTTJE, WALTER G S15DK46658-01
BOTTJER, SARAH W K04DC00058-02
BOTTJER, SARAH W R01DC00190-11
BOTTOMLY, KIM R01AI26791-04
BOTTOMLY, KIM R01CA38350-11
BOTTOMS, SIDNEY P50AA07606-04 0008
BOTTOMS, SIDNEY F U10HD27917-01
BOTVIN, GILBERT J N01CN65048-16
BOTVIN, GILBERT J P01CA50956-02 0005
BOTVIN, GILBERT J P50DA07656-01 0001
BOTVIN, GILBERT J P50DA07656-01
BOTVIN, GILBERT J R01DA06230-02
BOTZ, EDUARD J R43RR07520-01
BOUCEK, ROBERT J, JR R01CA48930-03
BOUCHER, RICHARD C P01HL34322-06
BOUCHER, RICHARD C P01HL34322-06 0005
BOUCHER, RICHARD C P50HL42384-04
BOUCHER, RICHARD C P50HL42384-04 0001
BOUCK, NOEL P R01CA27306-13
BOUCK, NOEL P R01CA52750-02
BOUGHMAN, JOANN A R01HL44069-02
BOULANGER, BRUNO P41RR01632-09 9016
BOULANT, JACK A R01NS14644-10A3
BOULPAEP, EMILE L P01DK17433-18 9004
BOULPAEP, EMILE L P01DK17433-18 0002
BOULT, CHARLES E K08AG00453-02
BOULWARE, DENNIS S07RR05377-30 0751
BOULWARE, SUSAN M01RR00125-28 0761
BOULWARE, SUSAN D S07RR05358-30 0483
BOUMA, SUSAN Z R43CA53984-01
BOUMPAS, D T Z01DK43239-01
BOUMPAS, D T Z01DK43240-01
BOUND, JOHN P30HD10003-16 9002
BOURASSA, MARTIAL G N01HC65034-08
BOURASSA, MARTIAL G U01HL38509-05
BOURASSA, MARTIAL G. N01HV18115-02
BOURDEAU, JAMES E R01DK35985-06
BOURDON, MARIO A R01CA52879-02
BOURDON, MARIO A S07RR06036-01

BOURGELAIS, DONNA B R43DE09787-01A1
BOURGEOIS-COHN, SUZANNE R01GM35751-06
BOURGEOIS-COHN, SUZANNE R37CA36146-18
BOURGEOIS, MICHELLE S R01AG09291-01A1
BOURGOIGNIE, JACQUES J R01DK19822-14
BOURGOIGNIE, JACQUES J R01DK40836-03
BOURGOIGNIE, JACQUES J U01DK39481-04
BOURGUIGNON, LILLY S07RR05363-30 0820
BOURGUIGNON, LILLY Y W R01GM36353-10A1
BOURNE, HENRY R R37GM27800-12
BOURNE, WILLIAM M R01EY02037-13
BOURNE, WILLIAM M R21EY08039-02
BOURQUE, DON P R01GM26937-13
BOUSCAREL, BERNARD S07RR05359-30 0505
BOUSFIELD, GEORGE R S07RR05511-29 0497
BOUSHEY, HOMER A P01HL24136-13 0008
BOUTROS, NASHAAT N S07RR05745-19 0233
BOVBJERB, DANA H S07RR05396-30 0743
BOVEE, KENNETH P01DK40555-04 0004
BOVEE, KENNETH C R01HL35435-06
BOVILLE, EDWIN M01RR00109-28 0367
BOVILLE, EDWIN M01RR00109-28 0349
BOVILLE, EDWIN G M01RR00109-28 0320
BOVILLE, EDWIN G M01RR00109-28 0299
BOWCOCK, ANNE M R01HG00461-01
BOWDEN, CHARLES L S15AA09264-01
BOWDEN, DONALD WARREN R01DK41269-04
BOWDEN, DOUGLAS M P40RR01240-12
BOWDEN, DOUGLAS M R01RR04515-04
BOWDEN, DOUGLAS M. P51RR00166-30 0168
BOWDEN, DOUGLAS M. P51RR00166-30 0169
BOWDEN, DOUGLAS M. P51RR00166-30 9023
BOWDEN, DOUGLAS M. P51RR00166-30 0053
BOWDEN, DOUGLAS M. P51RR00166-30 9024
BOWDEN, DOUGLAS M. P51RR00166-30 0052
BOWDEN, GEORGE T R01CA40584-07
BOWDEN, GEORGE T R01CA42239-06
BOWDEN, RALEIGH A R29HL38683-04
BOWDEN, VIRGINIA M G08LM05105-02
BOWDRE, JEAN H S07RR05406-30 0893
BOWEN-POPE, DANIEL F P01HL18645-17 9001
BOWEN-POPE, DANIEL F P50HL42270-02 0007
BOWEN-POPE, DANIEL F R01GM35501-05
BOWEN, DEBORAH J R29CA50858-01A1
BOWEN, JESSE W R29GM40568-04
BOWEN, MARY S07RR05522-29 0070
BOWEN, PHYLLIS N01CN05220-01
BOWEN, RAFAEL L P50DE09322-03 0008
BOWEN, RAFAEL L P50DE09322-03
BOWEN, RAFAEL L R37DE05129-14
BOWEN, RAFAEL L S03RR03041-11
BOWEN, WAYNE D R01DA03776-06
BOWEN, WAYNE D R01NS26746-03
BOWEN, WILLIAM H K16DE00159-07
BOWEN, WILLIAM H P50DE07003-08
BOWEN, WILLIAM H P50DE07003-08 0005
BOWEN, WILLIAM H R01DE07907-05
BOWER, ANNETTE S06GM08232-06
BOWER, ANNETTE S06GM08232-06 0008
BOWER, GORDON H R37MH47575-01
BOWER, J S07RR07003-26 0323
BOWER, J S07RR07003-26 0325
BOWERS, B Z01HL00419-11
BOWERS, BARBARA J R01NR02405-01A1
BOWERS, BARBARA J S07RR05866-08 0987
BOWERS, CHAUNCEY W S07RR05841-12 0247
BOWERS, CYRIL Y R01DK40202-03
BOWERS, JOHN L S07RR05591-27 0661
BOWERS, LARRY D R01AI25651-04
BOWERS, MALCOLM B P50MH30929-15 0032
BOWERS, MALCOLM B, JR P50MH30929-15
BOWERS, MALCOLM B, JR R01MH28216-16
BOWERS, ROGER R R15AR39905-01A2
BOWERS, ROGER R S06GM08101-20 0030
BOWIE, WALTER C R25HL37736-05
BOWKER, ROBERT S07RR05623-25 0723
BOWLER, BRUCE S07RR07138-20 0534
BOWLER, BRUCE S07RR07138-20 0527
BOWLES, C A M01RR00585-20 0430
BOWLES, NANCY L R01AG05972-06
BOWLES, W H S07RR05915-08 0680
BOWMAN, ARTHUR W S06GM08245-05
BOWMAN, BARBARA H P01AG06872-05
BOWMAN, BARBARA H P01AG06872-05 0001
BOWMAN, BARBARA H P30HD10202-15 9008
BOWMAN, BARRY J R01GM28703-11
BOWMAN, BARRY J S06GM08132-17
BOWMAN, BARRY J S06GM08132-17 0016
BOWMAN, DOUGLAS S07RR05700-22 0883
BOWMAN, GARY W S07RR05426-30 0130
BOWMAN, LEWIS S07RR07160-16 0584
BOWMAN, PHILIP J G20RR06958-01
BOWMAN, R L Z01HL01470-03
BOWMAN, ROBERT E R01ES01062-15
BOWNDS, M DERIC R01EY00463-23
BOWNE, SAMUEL F R29EY08700-01S1
BOWNS, TIMOTHY N01CO05725-01
BOWSER, BENJAMIN P50MH42459-06 0005
BOX, HAROLD C R01CA44808-04
BOX, HAROLD C R37CA25027-24
BOXER, LAURENCE A M01RR00042-31 0540
BOXER, LAURENCE A M01RR00042-31 0314
BOXER, LAURENCE A P01HL31963-08 0003
BOXER, LAURENCE A R01AI20065-10
BOXER, LAWRENCE A M01RR00042-31 0541
BOXER, STEVEN G P41RR01209-12 0004
BOXER, STEVEN G R01GM27738-12
BOYAN, BARBARA D R01DE05932-09
BOYAN, BARBARA D R01DE05937-10
BOYAN, BARBARA D R01DE08603-03
BOYARS, MICHAEL C M01RR00073-29 0308
BOYCE, ERIC G M01RR00040-31 0414
BOYCE, W M S07RR05457-29 0000
BOYCE, W THOMAS R01HD24718-03
BOYD, AUBREY E M01RR00350-25 0433
BOYD, AUBREY E M01RR00350-25 0467
BOYD, AUBREY E M01RR00350-25 0478
BOYD, AUBREY E M01RR00350-25 0446
BOYD, AUBREY E M01RR00350-25 0437
BOYD, AUBREY E P30DK27685-10 9001
BOYD, AUBREY E, III R01DK34447-09
BOYD, CAROL S07RR05796-14 0425
BOYD, CAROL J K20DA00150-02
BOYD, CHARLES D R01HL37438-05
BOYD, CHARLES D R01HL42798-12
BOYD, DALE D U42RR05093-04
BOYD, DOUGLAS DAVID R29CA51539-03
BOYD, FREDERICK T R03CA54952-01
BOYD, J A Z01ES23001-02
BOYD, KENNETH R R15AI29683-01A1
BOYD, LILLIE P01HL27430-10 0005
BOYD, LILLIE S06GM08049-20 0009
BOYD, NORMAN D R01DE09841-01
BOYD, NORMAN D R29NS25151-05
BOYD, ROBERT E S14GM44780-02 0004
BOYD, STEPHEN A P42ES04911-03 0003
BOYD, SUNNY K R29HD24653-04
BOYDEN, PENELOPE P01HL30557-08 0009
BOYDEN, PENELOPE A R01HL34477-05
BOYER, ARTHUR L R01CA43840-07
BOYER, DAN S07RR05313-30 0249
BOYER, HERBERT W R01GM31785-09
BOYER, JAMES L M01RR00125-28 0736
BOYER, JAMES L P30DK34989-08
BOYER, JAMES L P30DK34989-08 9003
BOYER, JAMES L P30DK34989-08 9004
BOYER, JAMES L P30DK34989-08 0014
BOYER, JAMES L P30ES03828-06 0002
BOYER, JAMES L R37DK25636-15
BOYER, MARCIA S07RR05313-30 0248
BOYER, PAUL D R01GM11094-29
BOYER, SAMUEL H R01DK38052-05
BOYER, SAMUEL H R01DK39888-05
BOYER, THOMAS D M01RR00083-29 0229
BOYER, THOMAS DAVID R01GM31555-09
BOYER, THOMAS E. P01AR39448-04 0002
BOYKIN, DAVID W S07RR07171-08 0150
BOYKIN, DAVID W U01AI27196-04 0003
BOYKIN, DAVID W U01AI27196-04
BOYKINS, R Z01BB02013-03
BOYKO, EDWARD J R21DK44561-01
BOYKO, EDWARD J R29DK39616-04
BOYLE, JAMES G R44MH46756-02
BOYLE, JOHN T R01HL35687-05
BOYLE, MARY B R01HD25909-02
BOYLE, MARY B R01HD26180-03
BOYLE, PATRICK M01RR00997-16 0366
BOYLE, PATRICK J M01RR00997-16 0397
BOYLE, PATRICK J M01RR00997-16 0417
BOYLE, PATRICK J M01RR00997-16 0378
BOYLE, PATRICK J M01RR00997-16 0373
BOYLE, RICHARD D R01NS27050-01A2
BOYLEN, C W S07RR07104-25 0557
BOYLES, JANET K. P01HL41633-03 0004
BOYNTON, ALTON L R01CA39745-07
BOYNTON, ALTON L R55CA57064-01
BOYNTON, ALTON L. S06GM08125-18 0046
BOYNTON, JOHN E R01GM19427-20
BOYNTON, JOHN E S07RR07070-26 0458
BOYSE, EDWARD A P30CA08748-26 9038
BOYSE, EDWARD A R35CA39827-08
BOYSON, SALLY M01RR00051-30 0766
BOYSON, SALLY J P01AG09417-01 0003
BOYSON, SALLY J P50NS09199-21 9003
BOYSON, SALLY J R01NS27170-02
BOYSON, SALLY J R01NS29203-01
BOZARTH, MICHAEL A R01DA02285-10
BOZARTH, MICHAEL A S07RR07066-26 0237
BOZARTH, MICHAEL A S07RR07066-26 0238
BOZELKA, BRIAN E P50HL15092-20 0021
BOZEMAN, PAULA M K11HL02373-02
BRAAS, KAREN M S07RR05429-30 0196
BRABEC, MICHAEL J R01ES05298-02
BRACE, ROBERT A R01HD20295-07A2
BRACE, ROBERT A R01HD21269-06
BRACE, ROBERT A R01HD23724-04
BRACHA, H STEFAN R29MH43537-06
BRACIALE, THOMAS J P01AI31238-01 0003
BRACIALE, THOMAS J R01HL33391-08
BRACIALE, THOMAS J R37AI15608-12
BRACIALE, THOMAS J R37AI28317-03
BRACKEN, MICHAEL B R01DA05484-05
BRACKEN, MICHAEL B R01NS15078-12
BRACKENBURY, ROBERT W R01CA45233-04
BRACKENBURY, ROBERT W R01NS27227-03
BRACKLEY, MARGARET H S07RR05654-24 0138
BRADBURN, NORMAN S07RR05901-07 0520
BRADBURN, NORMAN M S07RR05901-07
BRADBURY, DR RICHARD P N01CP15644-03
BRADBURY, E MORTON S07RR05919-08
BRADBURY, EDWIN M R01GM26901-11
BRADBURY, RICHARD N01AI05066-04
BRADBURY, RICHARD N01AI05067-03
BRADBURY, RICHARD N01AI05069-03
BRADBURY, RICHARD N01CP15657-00
BRADBURY, STEPHEN P S06GM08212-08 0012
BRADEN, CARRIE J R29NR01696-05
BRADEN, CARRIE JO R01CA48450-03
BRADEN, JEFFERY P S06GM08192-12 0018
BRADFIELD, CHRISTOPHER A R29ES05703-01
BRADFIELD, JAMES Y R01AI28368-03
BRADFORD, DAVID P50AR39255-05 0002
BRADFORD, M R18MH49379-01
BRADFORD, PETER G R29GM39588-05
BRADLEY, ALLAN R01HD24613-02
BRADLEY, ALLAN R01HD25326-03
BRADLEY, BRUCE E S07RR05321-30 0265
BRADLEY, DOUGLAS R R01GM20784-17
BRADLEY, JOHN D M01RR00750-19 0240
BRADLEY, JOHN D M01RR00750-19 0277
BRADLEY, MARGARET K S07RR05526-29 0068
BRADLEY, MATTHEWS O P01AG00378-20 0010
BRADLEY, ROBERT M R01DC00059-02
BRADLEY, ROBERT M R01DC00288-06
BRADLEY, SUZANNE F P30AG08808-03 0001
BRADLEY, WALTER M01RR00109-28 0351
BRADLEY, WALTER M01RR00109-28 0352
BRADLEY, WALTER M01RR00109-28 0357
BRADLEY, WALTER G. M01RR00109-28 0298
BRADLEY, WILLIAM A P60HL27341-10 9003
BRADLEY, WILLIAM A P60HL27341-10 0001
BRADLEY, WILLIAM A R01HL43373-03
BRADSHAW, BENJAMIN S P30HD06160-20S1 0001
BRADSHAW, BENJAMIN S P30HD06160-20S1 0002
BRADSHAW, BENJAMIN S R01HD24644-04
BRADSHAW, BENJAMIN S S07RR05828-08 0523
BRADSHAW, BENJAMIN S S07RR05828-08 0529
BRADSHAW, GARY S07RR07013-26 0961
BRADSHAW, RALPH A R01AG09735-10
BRADSHAW, RALPH A R01DK32465-09A1
BRADWAY, STEVEN D S07RR05928-06 0308
BRADY, ALLAN S07RR05354-30 0422
BRADY, HUGH R R29DK44380-01
BRADY, J Z01CP05254-10
BRADY, J Z01CP05605-03
BRADY, J Z01CP05691-01
BRADY, J Z01CP05692-01
BRADY, JOSEPH V K05DA00018-16
BRADY, JOSEPH V R18DA06949-02
BRADY, LINDA J R01DK39285-04A3
BRADY, R O Z01NS02770-04
BRADY, ROBERT J R01NS23071-06
BRADY, SCOTT T R01NS23320-07
BRADY, SCOTT T R01NS23868-06
BRADY, SUSAN P01HD01994-26A1 0014
BRADY, SUSAN S07RR05596-27 0133
BRADY, THOMAS J P01CA48729-03 0005
BRADY, THOMAS J P01CA48729-03
BRADY, THOMAS J R01CA54886-01
BRAELL, WILLIAM A R01GM34635-07
BRAFF, DAVID L R01MH42228-05
BRAGDON, ANDREW C S07RR05402-30 0802
BRAHAM, P Z01BB04002-02
BRAHIM, J S Z01DE00412-05
BRAHIM, J S Z01DE00502-02
BRAHN, ERNEST P01AR40919-01 0004
BRAHN, ERNEST P60AR36834-05 0001
BRAHN, ERNEST R29AR38844-04
BRAIDA, LOUIS D R01DC00117-16
BRAIN, ADRIENNE P01AI23287-06 0004
BRAIN, JOSEPH D P01HL43510-03 9002
BRAIN, JOSEPH D P30ES00002-29 0012
BRAIN, JOSEPH D P50HL19170-15
BRAIN, JOSEPH D P50HL19170-15 0004
BRAIN, JOSEPH D R01CA40696-06
BRAIN, JOSEPH D R37HL31029-09
BRAIN, JOSEPH D. P50HL19170-15 0019
BRAINE, HAYDEN P30CA06973-29 9019
BRAINE, HAYDEN G U01HL42810-03
BRAINE, LILA S07RR07234-05 0854
BRAITHWAITE, HAROLD R24MH47188-02 0001
BRALY, PATRICIA S S07RR05665-24 0880
BRAMBL, ROBERT M R01GM19398-16
BRAMBLE, DENNIS M S07RR07092-26 0530
BRAMBLE, DENNIS M S07RR07092-26 0547
BRAMHALL, JOHN S07RR05354-30 0391
BRAMMUCCI, MICHAEL S07RR07241-04 0703
BRAMSON, PAUL P30CA47904-04 9013
BRAMUCCI, MICHAEL S07RR05413-30 0991
BRANCH, MARC N R01DA04074-06
BRANCH, ROBERT M01RR00095-31 0358
BRANCH, ROBERT M01RR00095-31 0361
BRANCH, ROBERT A M01RR00095-31 0349
BRANCH, ROBERT A M01RR00095-31 0346
BRANCH, ROBERT A M01RR00095-31 0231
BRANCH, ROBERT A P01GM31304-09 0013

BRANCH, ROBERT A R01GM47124-01
BRANCH, ROBERT A. M01RR00095-31 0299
BRANCH, ROBERT A. M01RR00095-31 0319
BRAND JERRY J S07RR07091-26 0748
BRAND, JOSEPH G R01DC00356-06
BRAND, JOSEPH G S07RR05825-12 0520
BRAND, LUDWIG R01GM11632-29
BRAND, LUDWIG S07RR07041-26 0391
BRAND, PAUL H S07RR05700-22 0870
BRAND, RICHARD A R01AR40411-01A1
BRAND, STEPHEN P30DK43351-01 9001
BRAND, STEPHEN J R01DK42147-02
BRAND, STEPHEN J R29DK40543-04
BRANDA, RICHARD P30CA22435-11 9009
BRANDA, RICHARD F R01CA41843-04A2
BRANDEIS, GABRIEL H K08AG00499-01
BRANDES, M Z01DE00533-02
BRANDON, CHRISTOPHER J R01EY05601-06
BRANDRISS, MARJORIE C R01GM40751-04
BRANDSMA, ABIGAIL L P40RR00393-24 0008
BRANDSMA, JANET L P40RR00393-24 0002
BRANDSMA, JANET L R03CA54978-01
BRANDT-RAUF, PAUL W K01OH00076-03
BRANDT, CURTIS R R01EY07336-05
BRANDT, EDWARD JR S07RR05411-30
BRANDT, EDWARD N, JR S15HL47737-01
BRANDT, JASON P01NS15080-12 9007
BRANDT, JASON P01NS16375-11 0012
BRANDT, KENNETH D P50AR39250-05
BRANDT, KENNETH D P60AR20582-14
BRANDT, MARY P01DK44080-01 0003
BRANDT, NEIL R S07RR05363-30 0824
BRANDT, PHILIP W R01AR40300-01
BRANDTS, JOHN F R01GM42636-03
BRANDTS, JOHN F S07RR07048-26 0632
BRANN, BEN S M01RR00997-16 0334
BRANN, BENJAMIN S. M01RR00997-16 0252
BRANNON, BONNIE R R29AA08329-03
BRANNON, DIANE R01AG09984-01
BRANSFORD, JOHN D P01HD15051-11A1 0174
BRANT, DAVID A R01GM33062-08
BRANT, L J Z01AG00623-03
BRANT, L J Z01AG00637-02
BRANT, L J Z01AG00638-02
BRANTLY, M Z01HD00913-01
BRANTON, DANIEL R01GM39686-04
BRANTON, DANIEL R01HL17411-17
BRANTON, W DALE R01GM42829-01A1
BRANTON, WOODY D S07RR05385-30 0812
BRANZ, STEPHEN E. S06GM08192-12 0006
BRASCH, ROBERT C P01HL25847-12 0009
BRASCH, ROBERT C R01CA49786-03
BRASEL, JO ANNE M01RR00425-22S3 0411
BRASEL, JO ANNE M01RR00425-22S3 0357
BRASEL, JO ANNE M01RR00425-22S3 0312
BRASEL, JO ANNE M01RR00425-22S3 0466
BRASEL, JO ANNE M01RR00425-22S3 0454
BRASEL, JO ANNE M01RR00425-22S3 0401
BRASEL, JO ANNE P01CA42710-06A1 9004
BRASEL, JO ANNE S07RR05551-29 0969
BRASH, ALAN R P30HD05797-20 9007
BRASH, ALAN R P50GM15431-24 0129
BRASH, ALAN R R01DK35275-07
BRASH, ALAN R S07RR05424-30 0109
BRASH, DOUGLAS E S07RR05358-30 0484
BRASHEAR, HARRY R K08AG00407-04
BRASIER, ALLAN ROBERT R29HL45500-02
BRASITUS, T P30DK42086-02 9005
BRASITUS, T A P30DK26678-12 9013
BRASITUS, THOMAS A P30DK42086-02
BRASITUS, THOMAS A R01DK39573-03
BRASITUS, THOMAS A R37CA36745-09
BRASS, ERIC P R01DK36069-06
BRASS, LAWRENCE F P01HL40387-04 0004
BRASS, LAWRENCE F R01HL45181-02
BRASS, LAWRENCE F S07RR07083-26 0467
BRASS, LAWRENCE M R03HL47451-01
BRATER, CRAIG M01RR00750-19 0303
BRATER, D CRAIG M01RR00750-19 0295
BRATER, D CRAIG M01RR00750-19 0276
BRATER, D CRAIG M01RR00750-19 0294
BRATER, D CRAIG M01RR00750-19 0239
BRATER, D CRAIG M01RR00750-19 0259
BRATER, D CRAIG U01AI25859-05 9002
BRATER, DONALD C R01AG07631-04
BRATER, DONALD C R01DK37994-06
BRATERMAN, PAUL S S07RR07195-12 0710
BRATTAIN, MICHAEL G R01CA38173-04
BRATTAIN, MICHAEL G R01CA50457-02
BRATTAIN, MICHAEL G R01CA54807-01
BRATTAIN, MICHAEL G U01CA45967-05
BRAUCHT, GEORGE NICHOLAS U01AA08778-02
BRAULT, MARGO P30HD28263-01 9002
BRAUN, ANDREW N01ES05300-01
BRAUN, ANDREW N01ES05302-01
BRAUN, ANDREW N01ES15326-00
BRAUN, ANDREW N01ES95258-08
BRAUN, ANDREW N01ES95268-07
BRAUN, ANDREW N01ES95272-04
BRAUN, ANDREW G P01ES01640-14 9001
BRAUN, DANIEL K R29AI27960-02
BRAUN, JONATHAN P01CA12800-18A1 0056
BRAUN, JONATHAN R01CA49308-03
BRAUN, LUNDY A R29CA46617-04
BRAUN, ROBERT E R01HD27215-02
BRAUN, SHELDON R K07HL02097-01A4
BRAUN, THOMAS M01RR00051-30 0764
BRAUN, THOMAS J U10CA42777-04
BRAUNHUT, SUSAN J R29EY06726-05
BRAUNLICH, PETER F R44CA47644-03
BRAUNSCHWEIGER, PAUL G R01CA49143-03
BRAUNSTEIN, NED S R01GM39275-04
BRAUNWALD, EUGENE R01HL42311-02
BRAUNWALD, EUGENE R01HL42419-03
BRAUTH, STEVEN E R37MH40698-07
BRAUTIGAN, DAVID L R01GM35266-04A2
BRAVER, SANFORD L R01HD19383-06A1
BRAVER, SANFORD L S07RR07112-24 0424
BRAVERMAN, IRWIN M R01CA49414-12
BRAVERMAN, LEWIS E R01DK18919-17
BRAVO, EMMANUEL L P01HL06835-30 0091
BRAVO, EMMANUEL L P50HL33713-06 0015
BRAVO, MILAGROS R01MH36230-08
BRAY, GEORGE A. M01RR00043-31 0354
BRAY, GEORGE A M01RR00043-31 0463
BRAY, GEORGE A R01DK31988-09
BRAY, GEORGE A R01DK32089-10
BRAY, GEORGE A R01HD28020-01
BRAY, GORDON L N01HB77038-07
BRAY, GORDON L N01HB97055-03
BRAY, JAMES H R01HD22642-05
BRAY, NORMAN W, JR R01HD19426-06
BRAY, NORMAN W, JR R03DC01207-01
BRAY, PAUL F R29HL43020-03
BRAYDEN, JOSEPH E R01HL35911-06
BRAYDEN, ROBERT M R01MH38373-07
BRAYLAN, R S07RR05362-30 0782
BRAZEAU, GAYLE A S07RR07147-19 0642
BREAKEFIELD, XANDRA O P01NS24279-06
BREAKEFIELD, XANDRA O R01NS28384-01A1
BREAKEFIELD, XANDRA O R03AA08683-02
BREAKFIELD, XANDRA O P01NS24279-06 0005
BREAKFIELD, XANDRA O R01NS21921-09
BRECHA, NICHOLAS C R01EY04067-11
BRECHER, MARTIN L U10CA28383-12
BRECHER, MARTIN L U10CA28383-12 0026
BRECHER, MARTIN L U10CA28383-12 0027
BRECHER, MARTIN L U10CA28383-12 0001
BRECHER, MARTIN L U10CA28383-12 0002
BRECHER, MARTIN L U10CA28383-12 0003
BRECHER, MARTIN L U10CA28383-12 0004
BRECHER, MARTIN L U10CA28383-12 0028
BRECHER, MARTIN L U10CA28383-12 0029
BRECHER, MARTIN L U10CA28383-12 0030
BRECHER, MARTIN L U10CA28383-12 0031
BRECHER, MARTIN L U10CA28383-12 0032
BRECHER, MARTIN L U10CA28383-12 0033
BRECHER, MARTIN L U10CA28383-12 0034
BRECHER, MARTIN L U10CA28383-12 0035
BRECHER, MARTIN L U10CA28383-12 0036
BRECHER, MARTIN L U10CA28383-12 0037
BRECHER, MARTIN L U10CA28383-12 0038
BRECHER, MARTIN L U10CA28383-12 0039
BRECHER, MARTIN L U10CA28383-12 0040
BRECHER, MARTIN L U10CA28383-12 0041
BRECHER, MARTIN L U10CA28383-12 0042
BRECHER, MARTIN L U10CA28383-12 0043
BRECHER, MARTIN L U10CA28383-12 0044
BRECHER, MARTIN L U10CA28383-12 0045
BRECHER, MARTIN L U10CA28383-12 0005
BRECHER, MARTIN L U10CA28383-12 0006
BRECHER, MARTIN L U10CA28383-12 0007
BRECHER, MARTIN L U10CA28383-12 0008
BRECHER, MARTIN L U10CA28383-12 0009
BRECHER, MARTIN L U10CA28383-12 0010
BRECHER, MARTIN L U10CA28383-12 0011
BRECHER, MARTIN L U10CA28383-12 0012
BRECHER, MARTIN L U10CA28383-12 0013
BRECHER, MARTIN L U10CA28383-12 0014
BRECHER, MARTIN L U10CA28383-12 0015
BRECHER, MARTIN L U10CA28383-12 0016
BRECHER, MARTIN L U10CA28383-12 0017
BRECHER, MARTIN L U10CA28383-12 0018
BRECHER, MARTIN L U10CA28383-12 0019
BRECHER, MARTIN L U10CA28383-12 0020
BRECHER, MARTIN L U10CA28383-12 0021
BRECHER, MARTIN L U10CA28383-12 0022
BRECHER, MARTIN L U10CA28383-12 0023
BRECHER, MARTIN L U10CA28383-12 0024
BRECHER, MARTIN L U10CA28383-12 0025
BRECHER, MARTIN L U10CA28383-12 0046
BRECHER, MARTIN L U10CA28383-12 0047
BRECHER, MARTIN L U10CA28383-12 0048
BRECHER, MARTIN L U10CA28383-12 0049
BRECHER, MARTIN L U10CA28383-12 0050
BRECHER, MARTIN L U10CA28383-12 0051
BRECHER, MARTIN L U10CA28383-12 0052
BRECHER, MARTIN L U10CA28383-12 0053
BRECHER, MARTIN L U10CA28383-12 0054
BRECHER, MARTIN L U10CA28383-12 0055
BRECHER, MARTIN L U10CA28383-12 0056
BRECHER, MARTIN L U10CA28383-12 0057
BRECHER, MARTIN L U10CA28383-12 0058
BRECHER, MARTIN L U10CA28383-12 0059
BRECHER, MARTIN L U10CA28383-12 0060
BRECHER, PETER I R01HL31195-07
BREDECK, HENRY E S03RR03079-10
BREDECK, HENRY E S07RR07049-26
BREDECK, HENRY E S15AI32214-01
BREDESEN, DALE P30AG10123-01 0001
BREDESEN, DALE E R01AG10671-01
BREDESEN, DALE E R29NS27812-03
BREED, WARREN P50AA06282-09 0005
BREEDEN, LINDA L R29GM41073-03
BREEDLOVE, S MARC R01NS28421-02
BREEN, GAIL A R01GM41738-03
BREEN, PETER H R29HL42637-02
BREESE, GEORGE R P01HD23042-03
BREESE, GEORGE R P01HD23042-03 0005
BREESE, GEORGE R P50MH33127-13 0007
BREESE, GEORGE R R01AA08024-03
BREESE, GEORGE R R01MH39144-06
BREESE, GEORGE R R01NS26595-04
BREGMAN, BARBARA S K04NS01356-04
BREGMAN, BARBARA S R01NS19259-09
BREGMAN, BARBARA S R01NS27054-03
BREGMAN, J D M01RR06022-02 0764
BREHM, PAUL R01NS18205-11
BREIER, ALAN R01MH45074-02
BREINDL, MICHAEL S07RR07004-16 0045
BREITBART, ROGER E K11HL01650-05
BREITBART, WILLIAM R01MH45664-03
BREITENBERGER, CAROLINE A R29GM39498-04
BREITFELD, PHILIP P U10CA13809-19
BREITMAN, T R Z01CM07156-08
BREITMAYER, BONNIE J S07RR05776-11 0386
BREITMEYER, JAMES B. P30AI28691-03 9005
BREITNER, JOHN P50AG05128-08 0010
BREITNER, JOHN C R01AG08549-03
BREITNER, JOHN C S R35AG07922-04 0003
BREITWIESER, GERDA E R01HL41972-03
BREKKE, JOHN S R29MH43640-03
BREM, HENRY U01CA52857-02
BREM, HENRY U01CA52857-02 0001
BREMILLER, RUTH P01HD22486-05 9003
BREMNER, WILLIAM J M01RR00037-31 0512
BREMNER, WILLIAM J M01RR00037-31 0486
BREMNER, WILLIAM J M01RR00037-31 0472
BREMNER, WILLIAM J P50HD12629-12 9002
BREMNER, WILLIAM J P50HD12629-12 0001
BREMNER, WILLIAM J P50HD12629-12
BRENDEL, K P42ES04940-02 0005
BRENER, JASPER R01HL42366-03
BRENGELMANN, GEORGE L P01HL16910-18 9001
BRENGELMANN, GEORGE L. P01HL16910-18 0008
BRENNA, JAMES T R03HD29027-01
BRENNAN, JAMES K P01HL18208-17 9003
BRENNAN, M B Z01MH02579-01
BRENNAN, M B Z01MH02580-01
BRENNAN, M J Z01BA07015-03
BRENNAN, M J Z01BA07016-02
BRENNAN, M J Z01BA07017-04
BRENNAN, M J Z01BA07018-02
BRENNAN, M J Z01BA07025-01
BRENNAN, M J Z01BA07026-01
BRENNAN, MICHAEL J N01CN65035-18
BRENNAN, MICHAEL J P30CA22453-14 9012
BRENNAN, MURRAY P01CA47179-03 0001
BRENNAN, MURRAY P01CA47179-03 9001
BRENNAN, MURRAY R P01CA47179-03
BRENNAN, PATRICIA F R01AG08617-03
BRENNAN, PATRICK J N01AI05074-01
BRENNAN, PATRICK J R01AI27288-03
BRENNAN, PATRICK J R37AI18357-11
BRENNAN, PATRICK J U01AI30189-02 0001
BRENNAN, PATRICK J U01AI30189-02
BRENNAN, THOMAS M R01HG00323-03
BRENNEISE, CAROLE V S07RR05390-30 0677
BRENNEMAN, D Z01HD00709-05
BRENNEMAN, D E Z01HD00047-22
BRENNER, BARRY M M01RR02635-07 0141
BRENNER, BARRY M P01DK40839-03
BRENNER, BARRY M P01DK40839-03 0007
BRENNER, BARRY M P50DK39249-05
BRENNER, BARRY M R01DK35930-07
BRENNER, BARRY M R37DK30410-09
BRENNER, DAVID A R01GM41804-03
BRENNER, DAVID A R29DK39996-04
BRENNER, DAVID J P01CA12536-20 0018
BRENNER, DEAN E M01RR00042-31 0647
BRENNER, DEAN E. P01CA21071-14 0017
BRENNER, DOUGLAS M R43CA53987-01
BRENNER, HENRY C S07RR07062-26 0211
BRENNER, JOHN F R01NS15584-11
BRENNER, M Z01NS02677-07
BRENNER, MALCOLM S07RR05584-27 0647
BRENNER, MICHAEL P60AR36308-07 0014
BRENNER, MICHAEL B R01AI28973-02
BRENNER, MICHAEL B R01AR39582-04
BRENNER, MICHAEL B R01CA47724-04
BRENNER, PHYLLIS S07RR05809-06 0477
BRENNER, R M P51RR00163-32 0009
BRENNER, ROBERT M P30HD18185-08 9002
BRENNER, ROBERT M R01HD19182-07
BRENOWITZ, ELIOT A R29DC00487-05
BRENOWITZ, MICHAEL DAVID R29GM39929-04

BRENT, DAVID A P01MH41712-06 0002
BRENT, DAVID A P01MH41712-06 9001
BRENT, DAVID A R01MH43366-03
BRENT, DAVID A R01MH44711-03
BRENT, DAVID A R01MH46500-01A1
BRENT, LAWRENCE H S07RR05413-30 0988
BRENT, THOMAS P P01CA23099-13 0016
BRENT, THOMAS P R01CA14799-16A1
BRENT, THOMAS P R01CA36888-07
BRESHAN, DAVID B. M01RR00058-30 0218
BRESLAU, NAOMI K02MH00380-09
BRESLAU, NAOMI P50MH41684-07 0031
BRESLAU, NAOMI P50MH41684-07 0076
BRESLAU, NAOMI R01MH44586-02
BRESLAU, NEIL P01DK20543-15 0010
BRESLAU, NEIL A M01RR00633-19 0200
BRESLAU, NEIL A M01RR00633-19 0352
BRESLAU, NEIL A M01RR00633-19 0389
BRESLAU, NEIL A M01RR00633-19 0259
BRESLAU, NEIL A R01HD25860-03
BRESLAUER, KENNETH J R01GM23509-13
BRESLAUER, KENNETH J R01GM34469-07
BRESLER, HERBERT S R44AI26019-03
BRESLOW, ESTHER S07RR05396-30 0730
BRESLOW, ESTHER S07RR05396-30 0731
BRESLOW, ESTHER M R01GM17528-34
BRESLOW, J P41RR00862-18 0006
BRESLOW, JAN M01RR00102-28
BRESLOW, JAN L P01CA29502-11A1 9006
BRESLOW, JAN L R01HL32435-08
BRESLOW, JAN L R01HL33714-08
BRESLOW, JAN L R37HL36461-06
BRESLOW, JAN L S07RR07065-26 0055
BRESLOW, LESTER P30CA16042-17 9010
BRESLOW, MICHAEL J K08HL02018-05
BRESLOW, NORMAN E R01CA40644-07
BRESLOW, NORMAN E R01CA54498-01
BRESLOW, RONALD P41RR06892-01 0001
BRESLOW, RONALD C R01GM40401-04
BRESLOW, RONALD C R37GM18754-30
BRESNAHAN, JACQUELINE C P50NS10165-20 0025
BRESNICK, EDWARD P30CA36727-08 9010
BRESNICK, EDWARD R01CA36106-09
BRESNICK, EDWARD R01CA36679-09
BRESNICK, EDWARD R01ES03980-07
BRESNICK, EDWARD R25CA19379-15
BRESNICK, GEORGE H M01RR03186-06 0031
BRESNICK, GEORGE H U10EY06752-04
BRESNICK, GEORGE H U10EY07525-04
BRESNITZ, EDDY A K07HL02100-02
BRESSLER, NEIL M U10EY05958-06
BRESSLER, ROBERT B M01RR00350-25 0466
BRESSLER, ROBERT B R29AI27881-03
BRESSLER, STEVEN L R01MH43370-02
BRETAN, PETER S07RR05551-29 0966
BRETHERTON, INGE R01HD26766-01A1
BRETSCHER, ANTHONY P R01GM36652-06
BRETSCHER, ANTHONY P R01GM39066-04
BRETSCHER, ANTHONY P S10RR06327-01
BRETT, JAMES R G20RR06951-01
BREUHAUS, B A S07RR05911-08 0644
BREUNING, MARTIN H R01NS30152-01
BREW, KEITH P30CA14395-18A1 9016
BREW, KEITH R01GM21363-17A2 0001
BREW, KEITH R01GM21363-17A2 0002
BREW, KEITH R01GM21363-17A2 0004
BREW, KEITH R01GM21363-17A2
BREW, KEITH S07RR05363-30 0821
BREW, KEITH S10RR06376-01
BREWER, CURTIS F R01CA16054-15
BREWER, GARY A R01CA52443-02
BREWER, GARY A S07RR05404-30 0837
BREWER, GEORGE J M01RR00042-31 0621
BREWER, GEORGE J M01RR00042-31 0226
BREWER, GREG S07RR07123-22 0598
BREWER, H B Z01HL02010-20
BREY, ROBIN L K08NS01470-01A1
BREY, ROBIN L S07RR05654-24 0124
BREYER, JULIA A K11DK01660-05
BREYER, MATTHEW D P50DK39261-05 0005
BREYSSE, PATRICK N K01OH00087-02
BRIAN, ADRIENNE A R29GM39056-04
BRIAN, DAVID A R01AI14367-12
BRICE, SYLVIA L K08AR01860-01
BRICKER, JOHN T K07HL01940-05
BRIDGE, JOHN H B R01HL42357-03
BRIDGES, KENNETH R R01HL45794-01
BRIDGES, RICHARD R35AG07918-03 0003
BRIDGES, RICHARD J R01NS27056-03
BRIDGES, ROBERT P50DK42017-03 0004
BRIDGES, ROBERT S07RR05852-11 0260
BRIDGES, ROBERT S R01DA04291-04
BRIDGES, ROBERT S R01HD19789-08
BRIDGES, STANLEY LOUIS JR K11AR01867-01
BRIDGMAN, PAUL P01NS29343-01 9001
BRIDGMAN, PAUL C P01NS29343-01 0001
BRIDGMAN, PAUL C R01NS26150-04
BRIDSON, WILLIAM E. P51RR00167-31 9002
BRIEHL, ROBIN W R01HL07451-29
BRIELAND, JOAN K K01RR00040-04
BRIERLEY, GERALD P R01HL09364-27
BRIGELL, MITCHELL G R03EY09183-01
BRIGGAMAN, ROBERT A R37AR10546-26
BRIGGS, BRUCE C N01ES15323-00
BRIGGS, FRED N R55HL45957-01
BRIGGS, JOSEPHINE P50DK39255-05 0009
BRIGGS, JOSEPHINE P M01RR00042-31 0678
BRIGGS, JOSEPHINE PASHLER R01DK40042-04
BRIGGS, MARTHA S07RR07024-26 0035
BRIGGS, MARTHA S R29GM45616-01
BRIGGS, ROBERT C P30ES00267-25 9003
BRIGGS, ROBERT C S07RR05424-30 0121
BRIGGS, WINSLOW R S07RR05799-14 0686
BRIGHAM, KENNETH L P50HL19153-15
BRIGHAM, KENNETH L P50HL19153-15 0009
BRIGHAM, KENNETH L P50HL19153-15 9001
BRIGHAM, KENNETH L R01HL45151-02
BRIGHT, FRANK V S07RR07066-26 0239
BRIGHTMAN, VERNON J P50DE07118-07 0001
BRIGHTON, CARL T P50AR39226-05
BRIGHTON, CARL T P50AR39226-05 0001
BRIGHTON, CARL T R01AR13812-20A2
BRIGHTON, CARL T R37AR18033-18
BRILES, DAVID P01HD17812-09 0001
BRILES, DAVID E P60AR20614-14 0008
BRILES, DAVID E R01AI21548-08
BRILLIANT, MURRAY H R01GM43840-03
BRILLON, DAVID M01RR00047-31 0467
BRIMIJOIN, WILLIAM S R01NS18170-08
BRIMIJOIN, WILLIAM S R01NS29646-01
BRIN, MITCHELL M01RR00645-20 0357
BRIN, MITCHELL R01DC01139-02
BRINCKERHOFF, CONSTANCE E R01AR26599-12
BRINE, GEORGE A R01DA06317-03
BRINGHURST, F RICHAR S07RR05486-29 0055
BRINGHURST,F RICHARD P01DK11794-24 0006
BRINK, LELA W S07RR05426-30 0131
BRINK, PETER R R01HL31299-06
BRINKHOUS, KENNETH M R01HL01648-44
BRINKLEY, BILL P50DK42017-03 9001
BRINKLEY, BILL R R37CA41424-08
BRINKLEY, L S07RR05728-20 0192
BRINKLRY, B R P01DK38518-05 9001
BRINKMAN, E Z01HL04895-01
BRINSTER, RALPH L R01CA38635-07
BRINSTER, RALPH L R01HD19018-08
BRINSTER, RALPH L R37HD23657-04
BRINTON, ELIOT A K08HL02034-05
BRINTON, ELIOT A M01RR00102-28 0091
BRINTON, ELIOT A P01CA29502-11A1 0055
BRINTON, ELLIOT A M01RR00102-28 0144
BRINTON, L A Z01CP05526-05
BRINTON, MARGO A R01AI18382-08
BRINTON, MARGO A R01NS19013-09
BRINTON, ROBERTA E R29MH46036-02
BRINTON, ROBERTA E S03RR03011-08
BRINTON, ROBERTA E S07RR05792-15 0940
BRION, LUC P K08DK01984-02
BRISCO, M H P01HL25816-11 9004
BRISCOE, M P01HL24136-13 9002
BRISKI, KAREN P S07RR05465-29 0387
BRISTLOW, MICHAEL M01RR00064-27 0389
BRISTOL, D W Z01ES21161-01
BRISTOW, MICHAEL M01RR00064-27 0392
BRISTOW, MICHAEL R M01RR00064-27 0331
BRISTOW, MICHAEL R M01RR00064-27 0279
BRISTOW, MICHAEL R M01RR00064-27 0280
BRITIGAN, BRADLEY E P01AI28412-03 0002
BRITIGAN, BRADLEY E P01AI28412-03 9001
BRITIGAN, BRADLEY E R29HL44275-03
BRITT, STEVEN G K11EY00309-03
BRITT, WILLIAM P01HD10699-15 0016
BRITT, WILLIAM J R01AI30105-01A1
BRITTENHAM, GARY M M01RR00080-29 0354
BRITTENHAM, GARY M R01HL42439-02
BRITTENHAM, GARY M R01HL42814-03
BRIZZEE, KENNETH R P51RR00164-30 0035
BROACH, JAMES R P01CA41086-06 0004
BROACH, JAMES R R01GM34596-08
BROACH, JAMES R R13GM46575-01
BROADDUS, COURTNEY K08HL01893-05
BROADHEAD, WALTER E R01MH45750-01A1
BROADLEY, CAROLINE S07RR05424-30 0093
BROADNAX, STANLEY E R18DA05751-03S1
BROADUS, ARTHUR E M01RR00125-28 0733
BROADUS, ARTHUR E R01AR30102-11
BROADWELL-JACKSON, DEBRA R15NR02929-01
BROCK, D B Z01AG07030-03
BROCK, M A Z01AG00096-18
BROCK, TOMMY A R01HL41180-05
BROCK, TOMMY A R01HL45142-02
BROCK, WILLIAM A P01CA06294-30 0073
BROCK, WILLIAM A R01CA50192-03
BROCKBANK, KELVIN G R43CA53956-01
BROCKBANK, KELVIN G R43HL46607-01
BROCKERT, JOHN E N01HD02916-01
BROCKINGTON, KENNETH F R19DA06450-03
BROCKMAN, HERMAN E R15CA54488-01
BROCKMAN, HOWARD L, JR R01HL17371-16
BRODEUR, GARRETT M P01CA49712-03 0001
BRODEUR, GARRETT M R01CA39771-07
BRODEUR, PETER H R01GM36064-06
BRODFUEHRER, PETER D R15NS29509-01
BRODIE, ANGELA M R01CA27440-13
BRODIE, ANGELA M R01HD13909-11
BRODIE, JONATHAN D P01NS15638-13 0012
BRODIE, JONATHAN D P01NS15638-13 9002
BRODIE, JONATHAN D R01MH47277-01A1
BRODKIN , MARC A R15AI31194-01
BRODSKY, BARBARA M R01AR19626-13A1
BRODSKY, FRAN P60AR20684-14 0025
BRODSKY, FRANCES M P50GM26691-13 0017
BRODSKY, FRANCES M R01GM38093-04
BRODSKY, IRWIN M01RR00109-28 0365
BRODSKY, MICHAEL U10EY07685-04
BRODSKY, WILLIAM A R01DK16928-16
BRODWICK, MALCOLM S S07RR07205-11 0655
BRODY, A R Z01ES25030-05
BRODY, DAVID S R03MH46955-02
BRODY, ELAINE M P01MH43371-04 0001
BRODY, ELAINE M P50MH40380-07 0009
BRODY, GENE H S07RR07025-26 0987
BRODY, JEROME S P01HL19717-15 0023
BRODY, JEROME S R01HL34768-07
BRODY, MICHAEL J P01HL14388-20 9006
BRODY, MICHAEL J P01HL14388-20 0197
BRODY, MICHAEL J P01HL14388-20 0198
BRODY, MICHAEL J P01HL14388-20 0199
BRODY, MICHAEL J P01HL14388-20 0201
BRODY, MICHAEL J P01NS24621-05 9003
BRODY, MICHAEL J P50HL32295-07 0007
BRODY, WILLIAM R R01HL45090-02
BROEK, DANIEL L R01CA50261-03
BROEKMAN, M JOHAN R01HL29034-08
BROEN, PATRICIA A R01DC00533-02
BROERING, NAOMI C G08LM04392-06
BROGAN, DONNA P01AI19554-08S1 9004
BROGAN, DONNA R M01RR00039-31 0400
BROGAN, DONNA R M01RR00039-31 0394
BROIDE, DAVID H M01RR00827-17 0481
BROIDE, DAVID H R29AI29974-01A1
BROIDE, DAVID H U01AI31595-01 0003
BROITMAN, SELWYN A R01CA38177-06
BROITMAN, SELWYN A R01CA49227-03
BROKA, CHRIS A R01GM42987-03
BROKAW, CHARLES J R01GM18711-20
BROLIN, ROBERT E R01DK39035-03
BROMAN, CLIFFORD L S07RR07049-26 0446
BROMBERG, BARRY B R01EY04158-10
BROMBERG, JONATHAN S07RR05420-30 0038
BROMBERG, JUDITH P01DE09142-02 9001
BROMBERG, MARK B M01RR00042-31 0626
BROMBERGER-BARNEA, BARUCH P01ES03505-07 90
BROMET, EVELYN J R01MH44801-03
BRONER, CYNTHIA W S07RR05905-08 0631
BRONNER-FRASER, MARIANNE R01DE10066-01
BRONNER-FRASER, MARIANNE E R01HD25138-03
BRONNER-FRASER, MARIANNE E R01HD15527-11
BRONS, JOHN S07RR05336-29 0306
BRONSON, FRANKLIN H R01HD24177-04
BRONSON, FRANKLIN H R01HD26823-01A1
BRONSON, MAUREEN E R03DA06637-01A1
BRONSON, RODERICK T R01AG07747-04
BRONSON, RODERICK T R01NS30153-01
BRONTE-STEWART, HELEN K11EY00302-04
BROOK, JUDITH S R01DA03188-09
BROOK, JUDITH S R01DA05702-04
BROOK, JUDITH S R01DA05874-02
BROOKE, VIRGINIA K07NR00040-01
BROOKER, GARY R01HL28940-09
BROOKER, ROBERT J R01AI24204-05
BROOKES, NEVILLE R01ES03928-06
BROOKHART, MAURICE S R01GM28938-11
BROOKHOUSER, PATRICK E P60DC00982-02
BROOKHOUSER, PATRICK E P60DC00982-02 9003
BROOKMEYER, RONALD S R01CA48723-04A1
BROOKS-GUNN, JEANNE R01HD24770-03
BROOKS-GUNN, JEANNE R01HD26066-03
BROOKS, ANTONE L R01CA45590-04
BROOKS, B R Z01CT00232-01
BROOKS, B R Z01CT00233-01
BROOKS, B R Z01CT00234-01
BROOKS, BENJAMIN R M01RR03186-06 0030
BROOKS, CHARLES P41RR06009-02 0001
BROOKS, CHARLES P41RR06009-02 9003
BROOKS, CHARLES L K04DK01989-01A1
BROOKS, CHARLES L R01DK42604-01A2
BROOKS, CHARLES L, III R01GM37554-05
BROOKS, FREDERICK P, JR P41RR02170-08
BROOKS, G P01AI21912-08 0007
BROOKS, G P01AI21912-08 9004
BROOKS, GEO F P01AI21912-08
BROOKS, GEORGE A R01DK19577-10
BROOKS, JAMES S S07RR07043-26 0124
BROOKS, KATHRYN H R29AI24909-05
BROOKS, KATHY S07RR05656-24 0838
BROOKS, LISA D S07RR07085-26 0333
BROOKS, S C S06GM08167-13 0033
BROOKS, SAM C R01CA44771-04
BROOKS, SARAH R R19MH46246-03
BROOKS, STUART P30ES00159-24S1 0040
BROOM, ARTHUR D R01AI27692-03
BROOM, ARTHUR D R01CA37601-07
BROOME, PAMELA N01LM93502-08
BROONER, ROBERT K R01DA05569-03
BROOTEN, DOROTHY A R01NR02867-01

BROSIUS, FRANK C K08DK01956-02
BROSIUS, JURGEN R01MH38819-06
BROSNAN, CELIA F P50NS11920-17 0019
BROSNIHAN, K BRIDGET P01HL06835-30 0088
BROSSEAU, LISA M R03OH02938-01
BROSSI, A Z01DK58007-07
BROSSI, A Z01DK58010-06
BROSSI, A Z01DK58011-15
BROSSI, A Z01DK58017-02
BROSSI, A Z01DK58018-02
BROSTROM, CHARLES O R01DK35393-06
BROTHERS, LESLIE S07RR05756-18 0289
BROTHMAN, ARTHUR R R01CA46269-03S1
BROTT, THOMAS G N01NS02374-02
BROTT, THOMAS G R01NS26933-03
BROTZMAN, RICHARD W R43GM45646-01
BROUGHTON, GEORGE E S07RR05390-30 0684
BROUILLETTE, CHRISTIE G R01AI32687-01
BROUILLETTE, WAYNE J R01HL44668-01A1
BROUSSARD, DELMA M01RR00240-27 0338
BROUWER, KIM M01RR00046-31 0480
BROUWER, KIM L R01ES05774-01
BROUWER, KIM L R29GM41935-01A3
BROUWER, MARIUS R01ES04074-03
BROW, DAVID A R01GM44665-02
BROWER, DANNY L R01GM42474-03
BROWER, ROY G R29HL39435-04
BROWMAN, CATHERINE P P01DC00121-29A1 0001
BROWN UNIVERSITY N01AA10011-00
BROWN, MARK J. P01NS11037-18 0058
BROWN, ALICE B K11HD00837-04
BROWN, ANGELA M R29EY08083-05
BROWN, ANN L R37HD06864-18
BROWN, ANTHONY M C R29CA47207-04
BROWN, ARNOLD L S07RR05435-30
BROWN, ARTHUR C S07RR05336-29
BROWN, ARTHUR C S15EY09463-01
BROWN, ARTHUR M P01HL37044-06 0001
BROWN, ARTHUR M P01HL37044-06
BROWN, ARTHUR M R01HL39262-05
BROWN, ARTHUR M R01NS23877-06
BROWN, ARTHUR M MD PHD R01HL36930-06
BROWN, B GREG P01HL30086-09 0008
BROWN, B GREGORY M01RR00037-31 0336
BROWN, BARRY W P01CA06294-30 9007
BROWN, BARRY W P30CA16672-17 9007
BROWN, BARRY W R01CA11430-25 0069
BROWN, BARRY W R01CA11430-25 0072
BROWN, BRUCE N01HD13129-00
BROWN, BRUCE N01HD62905-16
BROWN, BURNELL R, JR R01GM45678-20
BROWN, BYRON W P01CA34233-09 0005
BROWN, BYRON W P01CA34233-09 9003
BROWN, BYRON W, JR P01CA49605-03 9001
BROWN, C C Z01CN00121-07
BROWN, C PERRY P30CA49095-04 9001
BROWN, CANDACE S M01RR00211-27 0310
BROWN, CAROLYN J R44DC00619-02A1
BROWN, CARTER N N01LM93508-02
BROWN, CHARLES H R01DC00164-12
BROWN, CHERRIE A P51RR00169-30 0107
BROWN, CLINTON D M01RR00318-25 0231
BROWN, COSTELLO L S06GM08101-20 0007
BROWN, DARRON R S07RR05371-30 0630
BROWN, DAVID B S07RR07205-11 0644
BROWN, DAVID M S03RR03085-10
BROWN, DAVID M S07RR05385-30
BROWN, DAVID M S15AI32198-01
BROWN, DAVID R S06GM08266-04 0002
BROWN, DAVID R S07RR05930-07 0717
BROWN, DENNIS P01DK38452-05 9001
BROWN, DENNIS P01DK38452-05 0004
BROWN, DENNIS R01DK42956-01A1
BROWN, DENNIS T R01AI19545-05
BROWN, DENNIS T R22AI14710-11
BROWN, DONALD S07RR05468-29 0406
BROWN, DONALD D R01GM22395-17
BROWN, DONALD D S07RR05799-14
BROWN, DONALD D S15GM47087-01
BROWN, EDWARD M M01RR02635-07 0248
BROWN, EDWARD M M01RR02635-07 0142
BROWN, EDWARD M M01RR02635-07 0277
BROWN, EDWARD M M01RR02635-07 0243
BROWN, EDWARD M M01RR02635-07 0297
BROWN, EDWARD M R01DK36796-06
BROWN, EDWARD M R01DK41415-03
BROWN, ELIZABETH R R18DA06365-03
BROWN, ERIC J R01GM38330-05
BROWN, ERIC J U01AI25903-05 0007
BROWN, F J Z01DE00031-23
BROWN, G Z01AA00233-09
BROWN, G Z01AA00257-07
BROWN, G Z01AA00276-03
BROWN, GAIL P R01HL37451-05
BROWN, GEORGE P30AG10163-01 0001
BROWN, GREGORY P01NS23393-06 0004
BROWN, GREGORY G P01NS23393-06 9004
BROWN, GREGORY G R01AG10677-01
BROWN, H MACK P01NS07938-22 0026
BROWN, H REAY U10EY06825-05
BROWN, HELENE N01CO03868-04
BROWN, IRENE S06GM08247-04 0001
BROWN, J MARTIN R01CA03352-35
BROWN, J MARTIN R01CA25990-13
BROWN, JAMES C S03RR03478-04
BROWN, JAMES K R01HL27669-11
BROWN, JAY C R01GM34036-08
BROWN, JEAN K M01RR00044-31 0364
BROWN, JERRY P30DK34914-06 0010
BROWN, JERRY P30DK34914-06 9008
BROWN, JERRY L R01HL37128-06
BROWN, JERRY L R01HL40203-05
BROWN, JOAN H R01GM36927-06
BROWN, JOAN H R01HL28143-10
BROWN, JOEL E R01EY05166-09
BROWN, JOHN S07RR07037-26 0388
BROWN, JOHN M R37CA15201-18
BROWN, JUDITH A S07RR05448-30 0293
BROWN, JUDITH E R01HD19724-03
BROWN, JUDITH K R01AG08269-02
BROWN, K W P42ES04917-03 0006
BROWN, L J Z01DE00475-04
BROWN, L J Z01DE00495-03
BROWN, L J Z01DE00496-03
BROWN, L J Z01DE00497-03
BROWN, L J Z01DE00515-02
BROWN, L J Z01DE00517-02
BROWN, L J Z01DE00542-01
BROWN, L J Z01DE00544-01
BROWN, L J Z01DE00545-01
BROWN, LAWRENCE N01AI05045-05
BROWN, LAWRENCE S JR R01DA05581-04
BROWN, LAWRENCE S, JR R18DA06142-03
BROWN, LOU ANN S R29HL38358-05
BROWN, LUCY L R01NS21356-06
BROWN, M CHRISTIAN R01DC01089-01
BROWN, MARIE ANNETTE S07RR05758-18 0243
BROWN, MARILYN M01RR00044-31 0272
BROWN, MARVIN R R01HL37716-07
BROWN, MARVIN R R01HL43154-03
BROWN, MARY M01RR00645-20 0488
BROWN, MARY B R29AI29084-02
BROWN, MARY B S15HD28743-01
BROWN, MELISSA A R29CA47992-04
BROWN, MICHAEL N01NS02384-42
BROWN, MICHAEL F R01EY03754-12
BROWN, MICHAEL F R01GM41413-04
BROWN, MICHAEL F R01MH45004-02
BROWN, MICHAEL S P01HL20948-15 0008
BROWN, MICHAEL S P01HL20948-15 0009
BROWN, MICHAEL S P01HL20948-15 0010
BROWN, MORTON B. P30HD18258-08 9009
BROWN, MYLES A K08CA01363-04
BROWN, NEAL C R01GM45330-01A1
BROWN, NEAL C S07RR05712-20 0048
BROWN, OLEN R R01ES02566-10
BROWN, PATRICK O R21HG00450-01
BROWN, PATRICK O. U01AI27205-04 0003
BROWN, PAUL B R01NS12061-13
BROWN, PETER S07RR07023-26 0982
BROWN, R STEVEN R13HG00270-01
BROWN, ROBERT M01RR01032-16 0451
BROWN, ROBERT D R29GM41470-04
BROWN, RONALD L N01AI05084-03
BROWN, RONALD L R44DK42753-02
BROWN, ROSALIND S S07RR05712-20 0080
BROWN, RUSSELL A K11CA01607-01
BROWN, S M01RR00042-31 0668
BROWN, SANDRA A P50MH30914-14 0059
BROWN, SANDRA A R01AA07033-06
BROWN, SCOTT M R43HL46036-01
BROWN, STANLEY S07RR07242-04 0705
BROWN, STANLEY A R01AR35590-07
BROWN, STEPHEN A K11HD00916-02
BROWN, STEPHEN J R43DK44402-01
BROWN, SUSAN N01LM13534-00
BROWN, T A S07RR05728-20 0204
BROWN, TERRY R R01DK43147-02
BROWN, THOMAS M01RR01346-10 0119
BROWN, THOMAS M01RR01346-10 0124
BROWN, THOMAS M01RR01346-10 0151
BROWN, THOMAS M01RR01346-10 0178
BROWN, THOMAS M01RR01346-10 0179
BROWN, THOMAS M01RR01346-10 0180
BROWN, THOMAS M01RR01346-10 0152
BROWN, THOMAS A K04DE00236-04
BROWN, THOMAS D R01AR35788-04
BROWN, THOMAS H R01NS27130-03
BROWN, TRUMAN R P01CA41078-05 0002
BROWN, TRUMAN R P01CA41078-05 0006
BROWN, TRUMAN R P01CA41078-05
BROWN, TRUMAN R P01HL22619-14 0013
BROWN, VALERIE S R03AG10362-01
BROWN, VIVIAN B R18DA06983-02
BROWN, W TED R13AG09316-02
BROWN, WALTER E R01HL30035-07A1
BROWN, WILLIAM P30HD15052-11 9004
BROWN, WILLIAM J R01DK37249-06
BROWN, ZANE A P01AI30731-01A1 0002
BROWNBILL, JOHN S07RR05322-30 0278
BROWNE, DOROTHY S07RR05450-30 0344
BROWNE, JERRY L P50MH33127-13 9004
BROWNE, JOHN M S06GM08247-04
BROWNE, JOHN S06GM08247-04 0002
BROWNELL, GORDON L R01CA32873-11
BROWNELL, HIRAM H R01NS27894-01A1
BROWNELL, K S07RR07015-26 0607
BROWNELL, WILLIAM E R01DC00354-05A1
BROWNER, CAROLE P01HD11944-12 0008
BROWNFIELD, MARK S07RR05912-08 0649
BROWNIE, ALEXANDER C R01HL39390-05
BROWNIE, ALEXANDER C R37HL06975-31
BROWNING, MICHAEL P01AG04418-08 0009
BROWNING, SCOTT M U10CA45374-03
BROWNLEE, MICHAEL A R01DK33861-07
BROWNSTEIN, DAVID G P40RR00393-24 0005
BROWNSTEIN, DAVID G P40RR00393-24 0006
BROWNSTEIN, DAVID G R24RR02053-08
BROWNSTEIN, M J Z01MH00424-16
BROXMEYER, HAL E R01HL46549-01
BROXMEYER, HAL E R37CA36464-08
BROYDE, SUSE B R01CA28038-11
BROYDE, SUSE B S10RR06458-01
BROYLES, R H Z01DK25071-04
BROYLES, STEVEN S R01AI28432-03
BROZE, GEORGE J P50HL14147-21 0025
BROZE, GEORGE J R01HL34462-07
BROZENA, SUSAN N01HC55006-07
BROZOVICH, FRANK V R29HL44181-02
BRSONAHAN, WILLIAM S07RR05372-30 0698
BRUBAKER, DAVID M01RR00425-22S3 0406
BRUBAKER, RICHARD F R37EY00634-21
BRUBAKER, ROBERT R R01AI19353-08
BRUCE, ALICE E S07RR07161-14 0848
BRUCE, ALICE E S15AR41232-01
BRUCE, CHARLES J R01EY04740-09
BRUCE, EUGENE N P01HL25830-11A1 0007
BRUCE, EUGENE N R01HL44889-01A1
BRUCE, JOCELYN B R29NS24853-06
BRUCE, JOHN I S07RR07233-05 0169
BRUCE, JOHN I S07RR07233-05
BRUCE, JOHN I S15HL47778-01
BRUCE, JOHN L N01AI05075-01
BRUCE, LAURA L S07RR05390-30 0663
BRUCE, MARGARET C R01HL31172-07
BRUCE, MARTHA L R29MH44984-03
BRUCE, ROBERT D R44DC00697-02
BRUCKNER, GEZA G P01HL36552-07 0010
BRUCKNER, GEZA G R01HL43311-03
BRUDER, GERALD P50MH43878-03 0013
BRUDER, GERARD S07RR05650-25 0093
BRUDER, GERARD E R01MH36295-08
BRUDVIG, GARY W R01GM32715-08
BRUDVIG, GARY W R01GM36442-05A1
BRUECKNER, MARTINA K11HL02492-02
BRUEGGEMEIER, ROBERT S07RR05607-25 0699
BRUEGGEMEIER, ROBERT W P30CA16058-17 9001
BRUEGGEMEIER, ROBERT W R01DK40255-04
BRUENN, JEREMY S07RR07066-26 0240
BRUER, LLOYD H P30HD03352-25 9004
BRUGGE, JOHN F. P01DC00116-16 9001
BRUGGE, JOAN S R01CA47572-04
BRUGGE, JOAN S R37CA27951-12
BRUGGE, JOHN F P01DC00116-16
BRUGGE, JOHN F R01DC00398-05
BRUGGE, JOHN F. P01DC00116-16 0019
BRUGGE, JOHN F. P01DC00116-16 0020
BRUGGEMAN, L Z01DE00481-03
BRUGNARA, CARLO P60HL15157-20 0026
BRUICE, THOMAS C R37DK09171-28
BRUIST, MICHAEL F R15GM45937-01
BRUMAGHIM, JOAN T R03MH45767-02
BRUNCK, TERENCE K R43HL46747-01
BRUNDEN, KURT R R29NS27587-04
BRUNELLE, J Z01DE00531-01
BRUNELLE, J A Z01DE00420-07
BRUNELLI, SUSAN S07RR05650-25 0094
BRUNENGRABER, HENRI R01DK35543-06A1
BRUNER, CATHY A R29HL45673-01A1
BRUNGER, AXEL P41RR06009-02 0002
BRUNHAM, ROBERT U01AI31448-01 0002
BRUNJES, PETER C R01DC00338-04A2
BRUNKEN, RICHARD C K08HL02022-05
BRUNKEN, WILLIAM J R01EY06776-05
BRUNNEMANN, KLAUS D P01CA29580-11 0006
BRUNNER, MARTHA J R29HL38316-04
BRUNO, ASKIEL M01RR00997-16 0338
BRUNO, DARRYL L R19DA06403-03
BRUNO, GERALD VINCENT S06GM08110-20 0009
BRUNS, GAIL P01HD18658-09 0013
BRUNS, GAIL A P R01HG00186-06
BRUNS, MARY E R55HD12335-13A1
BRUNS, THOMAS D S07RR07006-26 0892
BRUNSO-BECHTOLD, JUDY K R01DC00335-06
BRUNSWICK, ANN F R01DA05142-05
BRUNSWICK, M Z01BH02018-01
BRUNT, L MICHAEL S07RR05491-29 0453
BRUNT, MICHAEL M01RR00036-31 0599
BRUNTON, LAURENCE L R01HL41307-03
BRUNZELL, JOHN D M01RR00037-31 0297
BRUNZELL, JOHN D P01DK02456-33A1 0009
BRUNZELL, JOHN D P01HL30086-09 0001
BRUOT, BRENT C S07RR07208-10 0666
BRUSH, F ROBERT R01MH39230-05
BRUSHWOOD, DAVID B S07RR05573-13 0082
BRUSILOW, SAUL W M01RR00052-30 0087

BRUSILOW, SAUL W R01HD11134-14S1
BRUSILOW, SAUL W R01HD26358-02
BRUSILOW, WILLIAM S K04AI00882-05
BRUSKEWITZ, REGINALD C M01RR03186-06 0075
BRUSKEWITZ, REGINALD C R01DK41755-01A1
BRUST, JANNY D S07RR05448-30 0300
BRYAN, GEORGE T M01RR00073-29
BRYAN, GEORGE T S07RR05427-30
BRYAN, GEORGE T S15DK44697-01
BRYAN, GEORGE T U76PE00238-01
BRYAN, JOSEPH R01GM26091-13
BRYAN, JOSEPH R01HL26973-11
BRYAN, NICK P01HD24448-04 0006
BRYAN, NICK R N01HC15103-00
BRYAN, PHILIP N R01GM42560-02
BRYAN, R NICK R01CA54112-01
BRYAN, ROBERT M, JR R01HL41960-02
BRYANT-GREENWOOD, GILLIAN D R01HD24314-03
BRYANT, BRIAN R R44HD25355-03
BRYANT, BRUCE P R01DC00327-06
BRYANT, BRUCE P S07RR05825-12 0514
BRYANT, DONALD A R01GM31625-09
BRYANT, FLOYD R R01GM36516-06
BRYANT, PETER J S10RR06541-01
BRYANT, RICHARD R R01AA08477-01A1
BRYANT, ROBERT P30CA11198-23 9024
BRYANT, ROBERT G R01CA49004-03
BRYANT, ROBERT G R01GM34541-07
BRYANT, ROBERT G R55GM39309-04
BRYANT, ROBERT G S10RR06252-01
BRYANT, SHIRLEY P01HL22619-14 0017
BRYANT, SUSAN V R01HD25620-02
BRYLA, D A Z01HD00850-16
BRYLA, D A Z01HD00854-07
BRYSK, MIRIAM M R01DE08477-04A1
BRYSON, YVONNE J M01RR00865-18 0338
BRYSON, YVONNE J M01RR00865-18 0351
BRYSON, YVONNE J R01HD26621-02
BRYSON, YVONNE J U01AI27550-04
BUBLEY, GLENN J R29CA51438-01A2
BUCAN, MARIJA R01HD28410-01
BUCCAFUSCO, JERRY J R01HL30046-10
BUCCELLI, PAMELA S07RR05413-30 0989
BUCCI, ENRICO P41RR04328-04 0009
BUCCI, ENRICO R01HL13164-19
BUCCI, ENRICO R01HL33629-07
BUCHANAN THOMAS U01AI26503-04 0004
BUCHANAN, THOMAS A. M01RR00043-31 0407
BUCHANAN, BRUCE P41RR06009-02 9001
BUCHANAN, BRUCE G R01LM05104-03
BUCHANAN, BRUCE G R01LM05299-01
BUCHANAN, CHRISTINE E R01GM43564-08
BUCHANAN, CHRISTINE E S07RR07194-09
BUCHANAN, CHRISTINE E S15GM47051-01
BUCHANAN, D SCOTT R44NS24505-03
BUCHANAN, GEORGE N01HB77032-08
BUCHANAN, GEORGE R U10CA33625-09 0017
BUCHANAN, GEORGE R U10CA33625-09 0018
BUCHANAN, GEORGE R U10CA33625-09 0019
BUCHANAN, GEORGE R U10CA33625-09 0020
BUCHANAN, GEORGE R U10CA33625-09 0021
BUCHANAN, GEORGE R U10CA33625-09 0022
BUCHANAN, GEORGE R U10CA33625-09 0023
BUCHANAN, GEORGE R U10CA33625-09 0024
BUCHANAN, GEORGE R U10CA33625-09 0025
BUCHANAN, GEORGE R U10CA33625-09 0026
BUCHANAN, GEORGE R U10CA33625-09 0027
BUCHANAN, GEORGE R U10CA33625-09 0037
BUCHANAN, GEORGE R U10CA33625-09 0038
BUCHANAN, GEORGE R U10CA33625-09 0039
BUCHANAN, GEORGE R U10CA33625-09 0040
BUCHANAN, GEORGE R U10CA33625-09 0041
BUCHANAN, GEORGE R U10CA33625-09 0042
BUCHANAN, GEORGE R U10CA33625-09 0043
BUCHANAN, GEORGE R U10CA33625-09 0044
BUCHANAN, GEORGE R U10CA33625-09 0045
BUCHANAN, GEORGE R U10CA33625-09 0046
BUCHANAN, GEORGE R U10CA33625-09 0047
BUCHANAN, GEORGE R U10CA33625-09 0048
BUCHANAN, GEORGE R U10CA33625-09 0049
BUCHANAN, GEORGE R U10CA33625-09 0050
BUCHANAN, GEORGE R U10CA33625-09 0051
BUCHANAN, GEORGE R U10CA33625-09 0052
BUCHANAN, GEORGE R U10CA33625-09 0053
BUCHANAN, GEORGE R U10CA33625-09 0054
BUCHANAN, GEORGE R U10CA33625-09 0055
BUCHANAN, GEORGE R U10CA33625-09 0056
BUCHANAN, GEORGE R U10CA33625-09 0028
BUCHANAN, GEORGE R U10CA33625-09 0029
BUCHANAN, GEORGE R U10CA33625-09 0030
BUCHANAN, GEORGE R U10CA33625-09 0057
BUCHANAN, GEORGE R U10CA33625-09 0058
BUCHANAN, GEORGE R U10CA33625-09 0059
BUCHANAN, GEORGE R U10CA33625-09 0060
BUCHANAN, GEORGE R U10CA33625-09 0031
BUCHANAN, GEORGE R U10CA33625-09 0001
BUCHANAN, GEORGE R U10CA33625-09 0032
BUCHANAN, GEORGE R U10CA33625-09 0033
BUCHANAN, GEORGE R U10CA33625-09 0034
BUCHANAN, GEORGE R U10CA33625-09 0035
BUCHANAN, GEORGE R U10CA33625-09 0002
BUCHANAN, GEORGE R U10CA33625-09 0003
BUCHANAN, GEORGE R U10CA33625-09 0004
BUCHANAN, GEORGE R U10CA33625-09 0036
BUCHANAN, GEORGE R U10CA33625-09 0005
BUCHANAN, GEORGE R U10CA33625-09 0006
BUCHANAN, GEORGE R U10CA33625-09 0007
BUCHANAN, GEORGE R U10CA33625-09 0008
BUCHANAN, GEORGE R U10CA33625-09 0009
BUCHANAN, GEORGE R U10CA33625-09 0010
BUCHANAN, GEORGE R U10CA33625-09 0011
BUCHANAN, GEORGE R U10CA33625-09 0012
BUCHANAN, GEORGE R U10CA33625-09 0013
BUCHANAN, GEORGE R U10CA33625-09 0014
BUCHANAN, GEORGE R U10CA33625-09 0015
BUCHANAN, GEORGE R U10CA33625-09 0016
BUCHANAN, GEORGE R U10CA33625-09
BUCHANAN, JACK W P01HL27430-10 0008
BUCHANAN, JAMES T R29NS28369-03
BUCHANAN, JAMES T S15NS30120-01
BUCHANAN, JOAN S07RR05710-21 0025
BUCHANAN, ROBERT M R01GM45783-01
BUCHANAN, THOMAS A M01RR00043-31 0479
BUCHANAN, THOMAS A M01RR00043-31 0486
BUCHANAN, THOMAS A M01RR00043-31 0471
BUCHANAN, THOMAS A M01RR00043-31 0472
BUCHANAN, THOMAS S R29AR40408-02
BUCHANON, JO ANN P50MH48108-01 9001
BUCHER, NANCY L R R01CA39099-08
BUCHHALTER, JEFFREY R. P01NS27405-03 0004
BUCHMAN, TIMOTHY G K04GM00581-01
BUCHMAN, TIMOTHY G R29GM39756-03
BUCHMEIER, MICHAEL P50MH47680-02 0002
BUCHMEIER, MICHAEL J P01NS22347-06 0007
BUCHMEIER, MICHAEL J P01NS22347-06 9002
BUCHMEIER, MICHAEL J P50NS12428-17 0005
BUCHMEIER, NANCY A R01AI29566-02
BUCHNER, DAVID M U01AG09095-02
BUCHOLZ, KATHLEEN K P50AA03539-14 9008
BUCHSBAUM, DAVID G R01AA08278-02
BUCHSBAUM, DONALD J R01CA44173-06
BUCHSBAUM, MONTE P50MH30911-14 0023
BUCHSBAUM, MONTE P50MH30911-14 0018
BUCHSBAUM, MONTE P50MH30914-14 0054
BUCHSBAUM, MONTE P50MH44188-03 9004
BUCHSBAUM, MONTE S P50MH44188-03 0004
BUCHSBAUM, MONTE S P50MH44188-03 0003
BUCHSBAUM, MONTE S. P50AG05142-08 0007
BUCHWALD, DEDRA S U01AI32246-01 9002
BUCHWALD, HENRY R01HL15265-19
BUCHWALD, NATHANIAL S07RR05756-18 0295
BUCHWALD, NATHANIEL P30HD04612-21 9002
BUCHWALD, NATHANIEL A P01HD05958-20
BUCHWALD, NATHANIEL A P30HD04612-21
BUCHWALD, STEPHEN L R01GM34917-07
BUCK DAVID U01AI26462-04 0001
BUCK, CLAYTON A R01HL39023-04
BUCK, CLAYTON A R13GM46446-01
BUCK, CLAYTON A R37CA19144-17
BUCK, GREGORY P30CA16059-15 9012
BUCK, GREGORY A R01AI22946-04A2
BUCK, STEVEN L R01EY03221-10A1
BUCKALEW, VARDAMAN M, JR U01DK39366-04
BUCKBERG, GERALD D R01HL16292-18
BUCKELEW, SUSAN P R29AR39481-04
BUCKHEIT, ROBERT N01AI05087-02
BUCKHEIT, ROBERT W J S07RR05676-15 0953
BUCKLEY, CHARLES E M01RR00030-30 0507
BUCKLEY, EDWARD G M01RR00030-30 0441
BUCKLEY, EDWARD G U10EY07678-04
BUCKLEY, JOHN F S07RR05487-29 0687
BUCKLEY, JONATHAN D K04CA01152-05
BUCKLEY, KATHLEEN M R01NS27536-01A2
BUCKLEY, REBECCA H M01RR00030-30 0495
BUCKLEY, REBECCA H M01RR00030-30 0508
BUCKLEY, REBECCA H M01RR00030-30 0462
BUCKLEY, REBECCA H R01AI28414-03
BUCKLEY, REBECCA H R37AI18613-10
BUCKMAN, TRENT D R01NS25797-04
BUCKNER, C DEAN P01CA18029-16 0013
BUCKNER, C DEAN P01CA47748-03
BUCKNER, CARL K P50AI10404-21 0002
BUCKNER, DEAN C P01CA18029-16 0030
BUCKNER, STEVEN W S07RR07002-26 0881
BUCKPITT, A B P42ES04699-05 0004
BUCKPITT, ALAN R P51RR00169-30 0133
BUCKPITT, ALAN R P51RR00169-30 0132
BUCKPITT, ALAN R R01ES04311-05
BUCY, PAT P50AI23694-06 0009
BUCY, R P R01GM42751-03
BUCY, R PAT P01AR03555-32A1 0008
BUDA, ANDREW J R01HL34691-05A1
BUDD, G THOMAS P01CA48919-01A2 0001
BUDD, RALPH C R29AI28892-02
BUDD, RONALD R43EY09160-01
BUDDINGTON, ROGER W P51RR00165-31 9019
BUDELMANN, BERND U R01EY08312-03
BUDINGER, THOMAS P41RR05964-02 0005
BUDINGER, THOMAS F R37AG05890-07
BUDMAN, SIMON H R01MH40151-04S1
BUDMAN, SIMON H R01MH43908-02
BUDNIK, VIVIAN S07RR07048-26 0633
BUDZYNSKI, ANDREI S07RR05417-30 0784
BUENING, GERALD M S07RR05949-07
BUENING, GERALD M S15CA55976-01
BUESCHER, STEPHEN E P01HD13021-12 0010
BUETOW, K P01CA40737-06 0053
BUETOW, KENNETH H P50DE09164-03 0002
BUETOW, KENNETH H P50DE09164-03 9000
BUETOW, KENNETH H P50HG00206-01S1 0005
BUETOW, KENNETH H R29CA47816-04
BUFFINGTON, CHARLES W R01GM43074-01A2
BUGG, CHARLES E P30CA13148-20 9001
BUGGY, JAMES S07RR05815-12 0491
BUHI, WILLIAM C R01HD20553-06
BUHLER-WILKERSON, KAREN A R01NR02078-03
BUHLER, DONALD R. P01ES04766-04 0002
BUHLER, DONALD R P01ES00040-27 0078
BUHLER, DONALD R P30ES00210-24 9006
BUHLER, DONALD R R01ES05533-01
BUIST, A SONIA N01HR46016-17
BUIST, NEIL R M R01HD26360-02
BUJALOWSKI, WLODZIMI S07RR07205-11 0649
BUJARSKI, JOZEF R01AI26769-02
BUJARSKI, JOZEF J S07RR07176-14 0527
BUKOSKI, RICHARD P30DK40566-02 9004
BUKOSKI, RICHARD D R29HL41816-03
BUKOWSKI, RONALD M P01CA48919-01A2
BUKOWSKI, RONALD M R13CA54328-01
BULECHEK, GLORIA M S07RR07035-26 0082
BULGER, ROGER J R13HS06876-01
BULGER, RUTH N01RR12115-00
BULINSKI, JEANNETTE C R01CA39755-08
BULKLEY, GREGORY B R01DK31764-09
BULL, JOAN M R01CA43090-06
BULL, JOAN M C M01RR02558-07 0071
BULL, MARGARET J R01NR02249-01A2
BULL, ROBERT W K07HL02342-02
BULL, T E Z01BB03002-02
BULL, T E Z01BB03003-02
BULL, T E Z01BB03004-02
BULLAS, LEONARD S07RR05352-30 0746
BULLAS, LEONARD R S07RR05352-30 0761
BULLEN, BEVERLY A R01HD18999-07
BULLER, DAVID B S07RR07002-26 0870
BULLER, R M Z01AI00306-10
BULLERJAHN, GEORGE S07RR07192-12 0621
BULLESBACH, ERIKA E R29DK38348-04
BULLITT, ELIZABETH P01NS14899-13 0006
BULLOCK, JAMES O R01GM37396-06
BULLOCK, THEODORE H R01NS00021-43
BULLOCK, THEODORE H R01NS25963-04
BULLOCK, WARD E P01AI28392-02
BULLOCK, WESLEY S07RR05336-29 0304
BULLOCK, WESLEY A S07RR07237-04 0743
BUMP, RICHARD C U01AG05170-07 0003
BUMPASS, LARRY L R01HD21009-06
BUMPUS, JOHN A P41RR06030-01A1 0001
BUMPUS, JOHN A P42ES04922-03 0002
BUNAG, RUBEN D R01HL39383-05
BUNCE, DIANE M S07RR07123-22 0596
BUNCHMAN, TIMOTHY E S07RR05388-30 0619
BUNDY, KIRK J R01DE08222-02
BUNEGIN, LEONID S07RR05654-24 0125
BUNGAY, P M Z01RR10354-01
BUNGE, MARY BARLETT P01NS28059-01A1 9001
BUNGE, RICHARD P P01NS28059-01A1
BUNGE, RICHARD P R01NS09923-21
BUNGE, RICHARD P R01NS19923-09
BUNICK, GERARD J R01GM29818-10
BUNIN, GRETA R55HD28376-01
BUNIN, GRETA R S07RR07083-26 0468
BUNKER, CLAREANN H R01HL44413-01A1
BUNKER, CLAREANN H S07RR05451-30 0352
BUNKER, GRANT P41RR01633-10 9005
BUNKER, GRANT P41RR01633-10 0008
BUNKER, GRANT B R29GM39612-04
BUNN, H F M01RR02635-07 0262
BUNN, H FRANKLIN R01DK41234-03
BUNN, H FRANKLIN R37HL42949-03
BUNN, PAUL P30CA46934-04 9002
BUNN, PAUL P30CA46934-04 9004
BUNN, PAUL A M01RR00051-30 0775
BUNN, PAUL A M01RR00051-30 0612
BUNN, PAUL A M01RR00051-30 0729
BUNN, PAUL A M01RR00051-30 0682
BUNN, PAUL A P30CA46934-04 9010
BUNN, PAUL A U01CA46088-05 0002
BUNN, PAUL A, JR P30CA46934-04
BUNNELLE, WILLIAM H R01AI26259-01A2
BUNNETT, NIGEL W R01DK39957-05
BUNNEY, BENJAMIN S P01MH25642-18 0024
BUNNEY, BENJAMIN S P50MH44866-04 0005
BUNNEY, BENJAMIN S R37MH28849-15
BUNNEY, WILLIAM E P50MH44188-03 9003
BUNNEY, WILLIAM E P50MH44188-03
BUNOW, BARRY J R43CA52407-01A1
BUNOW, BARRY J R43CA53035-01A1
BUNOW, BARRY J R43CA54004-01
BUNOW, BARRY J R43HL47237-01
BUNOW, BARRY J R43RR07550-01
BUNTIN, JOHN D R37MH41447-06
BUNTIN, JOHN D S07RR07181-13 0532
BUNTING, ALISON N01LM13507-00
BUNTING, ALISON P30CA16042-17 9003
BUNTON, TRACIE P40RR00130-28 0112

BUONANNO, A Z01HD00710-03
BUONANNO, A Z01HD00711-02
BUONASSISI, VINCENZO R01HL38208-05
BUONASSISI, VINCENZO S07RR05863-11 0564
BURACK, ROBERT C R01CA54573-01
BURAKOFF, STEVEN J P01CA39542-07
BURAKOFF, STEVEN J P01CA39542-07 0003
BURAKOFF, STEVEN J P30CA06516-28 0024
BURAKOFF, STEVEN J R01AI17258-12
BURAKOFF, STEVEN J R01AI31868-09
BURATOWSKI, STEPHEN R29GM46498-01
BURBACHER, THOMAS M R01ES03745-05
BURBACHER, THOMAS M. P51RR00166-30 0078
BURBACHER, THOMAS M. P51RR00166-30 0079
BURBAUM, BEVERLY W R43NS29601-01
BURBECK, CHRISTINA A P01CA47982-04 0007
BURCH, JOHN B R01GM35535-07
BURCH, P A M01RR00585-20 0547
BURCHETT, SANDRA S07RR05655-21 0824
BURCHFIELD, DAVID J R01DA06866-01
BURCHINAL, MARGARET P01AG09973-01 9002
BURCKART, GILBERT J R01DK34475-06
BURD, GAIL D R01DC00446-04
BURD, GAIL D S07RR05675-23 0899
BURDEN, STEVEN J R01NS21579-08
BURDEN, STEVEN J R01NS27963-02
BURDETT, L A Z01CP05666-01
BURDETT, VICKERS R01AI15619-12
BURDETTE, BRYAN H S07RR05795-14 0415
BURDETTE, LINDA J R29MH45961-01A2
BURG, M Z01HL01283-04
BURGE, SANDRA K R01AA08604-02
BURGER, DOUGLAS E R43HL46628-01
BURGER, HAROLD U01AI25893-05 0002
BURGERS, PETER M R01GM32431-08
BURGESON, ROBERT E R01AR35532-08
BURGESON, ROBERT E R01AR35689-07
BURGESS, ANNE N01DA07401-01
BURGESS, BARBARA K R01GM43144-02
BURGESS, BARBARA K R01GM45209-01
BURGESS, DAVID R R01DK31643-11
BURGESS, DAVID R R01GM40086-05
BURGESS, DAVID R S07RR07084-26
BURGESS, DAVID R S15CA56027-01
BURGESS, ELIZABETH C R29AI24433-04
BURGESS, KEVIN R01AI28204-03
BURGESS, KEVIN R01DA06554-02
BURGESS, MARY JO R01HL34288-06A1
BURGESS, RICHARD R P01CA23076-14 0001
BURGESS, RICHARD R R01GM28575-11A1
BURGESS, TERESA L S07RR07099-25 0401
BURGESS, WILSON H P50HL44336-01 0003
BURGESS, WILSON H R01HL35762-05A1
BURGGRAAFF, BARBARA S07RR05372-30 0699
BURGHARDT, ROBERT C R01HD26182-03
BURGHARDT, THOMAS P R01AR39288-02
BURGHEN, GEORGE A M01RR00211-27 0332
BURGHEN, GEORGE A M01RR00211-27 0306
BURGHES, ARTHUR M R29AR40015-03
BURGIO, KATHRYN L K04AG00431-03
BURGIO, KATHRYN L R01AG08010-03
BURGIO, LOUIS D K01AG00491-02
BURGIO, LOUIS D R01NR02988-01
BURHOLT, DENNIS R S07RR05801-13 0445
BURING, JULIE E R01CA47988-01A1
BURING, JULIE E R01HL42441-02
BURING, JULIE E S07RR05381-30 0792
BURK, RAYMOND F, JR R01ES02497-13
BURK, RAYMOND F, JR R01HL36371-06
BURKA, L T Z01ES21075-08
BURKARD, ROBERT F R29DC00399-04
BURKE, BRIAN E R01GM38556-05
BURKE, D J R29GM40334-04
BURKE, DEBORAH M R01AG08835-02
BURKE, GEORGE W M01RR05280-03 0004
BURKE, GEORGE W S07RR05363-30 0823
BURKE, JAMES R K08NS01533-01
BURKE, JANICE M P30EY01931-15
BURKE, JANICE M R01EY04799-10
BURKE, JANICE M R01EY06664-04
BURKE, JOHN F P50GM21700-15
BURKE, JOHN F P50GM21700-15 0008
BURKE, JOHN F P50GM21700-15 9001
BURKE, JOHN M R01AI29892-02
BURKE, JOHN M R01AI30534-01
BURKE, JOHN M R01GM36981-05A2
BURKE, L Z01DK25078-01
BURKE, MORRIS R01NS15319-12
BURKE, MORRIS S07RR07113-24 0573
BURKE, R E Z01NS01686-23
BURKE, R E Z01NS02160-17
BURKE, RAE L R01AI29681-01A1
BURKE, ROBERT E R29NS26836-03
BURKE, STEVEN D R01GM28321-10
BURKE, T R Z01CM06198-02
BURKE, THOMAS P01DK35098-06A1 9001
BURKE, WILLIAM F S07RR07112-24 0417
BURKE, WILLIAM J R01AG09188-01A1
BURKHARDT, DWIGHT A R01EY00460-23
BURKHART, J G Z01ES61047-01
BURKHAUSER, RICHARD P01AG09743-01 0001
BURKHAUSER, RICHARD P01AG09743-01 9001
BURKHAUSER, RICHARD V P01AG09743-01
BURKS, ARVIL W JR R29AI26629-03
BURKS, CHRISTIAN R01GM37812-05
BURKS, THOMAS F R01DA02163-14
BURLEW, ANN K P60HL15996-19 0023
BURLEY, STEPHEN K S07RR07065-26 0056
BURLING, THOMAS A R01DA07426-01
BURLINGAME, A L P30DK26743-11 9006
BURLINGAME, A L P41RR01614-10 0002
BURLINGAME, A. P42ES04705-05 0006
BURLINGAME, ALMA L P41RR01614-10 9001
BURLINGAME, ALMA L P41RR01614-10
BURLINGHAM, WILLIAM J R01AI26941-03
BURMEISTER, LEON P50HL37121-05 9001
BURMER, GLENNA P01DK32971-08 9004
BURMER, GLENNA C R29AG07359-04
BURNAM, M AUDREY R01MH46121-03
BURNAM, M AUDREY U01AA08821-02
BURNATOWSKA-HLEDIN, MARIA R29DK38101-04
BURNE, ROBERT A S07RR05403-30 0805
BURNETT P41RR01646-09 0008
BURNETT, JOHN C, JR R01HL36634-05
BURNETT, ROGER M R01AI17270-12
BURNHAM, CHARLES E S07RR05408-30 0921
BURNHAM, NORA R P30CA15083-18 9006
BURNS, EDWARD M P01DC00520-04 0001
BURNS, EDWARD M. P01DC00520-04 9001
BURNS, TRUDY L. P50HL32295-07 9004
BURNS, ALASTAIR H S07RR05376-30 0034
BURNS, ALTON JAY S07RR05426-30 0132
BURNS, BARBARA J R01MH46624-03
BURNS, C P M01RR00059-30 0750
BURNS, C. P. M01RR00059-30 0593
BURNS, CHARLES P R01CA31526-10
BURNS, D L Z01BA07002-02
BURNS, D L Z01BA07011-07
BURNS, D L Z01BA07012-03
BURNS, D L Z01BA07019-02
BURNS, D L Z01BA07023-01
BURNS, FREDERIC J. P42ES04895-03 0008
BURNS, GREGORY L R29HL36811-05
BURNS, H DONALD P01CA32845-29 0020
BURNS, H DONALD P01CA32845-29 0022
BURNS, JAMES B R01NS27556-03
BURNS, JANE L R01AI23975-05
BURNS, LINDA S07RR05372-30 0673
BURNS, MARCELLINE M R01DA06466-02
BURNS, MARGARET S R01EY05979-05A1
BURNS, RISA B S07RR05487-29 0700
BURNS, STEPHEN A R01EY04395-11
BURNS, TRUDY P50HL42266-02 9001
BURNS, WILLIAM H P01CA15396-18 0007
BURNS, WILLIAM N S07RR05654-24 0145
BURNSIDE, BETH P41RR00592-22 0028
BURNSIDE, JOAN S07RR07016-18 0346
BURNSIDE, MARY B R37EY03575-11
BURNY, ARSENE L U01AI27136-03
BURR, BENJAMIN R01HG00372-04
BURR, DAVID B P40RR03640-05 0012
BURR, DAVID B R01AR39708-04
BURR, DAVID B R55AR40655-01A1
BURR, IAN P01DK39079-05 0007
BURR, IAN M P30HD28819-01
BURR, JOHN G R29CA47098-03
BURR, ROBERT L R55NR02429-01A1
BURRIDGE, KEITH W R01GM29860-11
BURRIDGE, KEITH W R01HL44918-01A1
BURRILL, PETER H R43GM45640-01
BURRILL, PETER H R43MH48241-01
BURRIS, JAMES F S07RR05360-30
BURRIS, JAMES F S15CA55971-01
BURRIS, JAMES F S15GM47089-01
BURRIS, JAMES F S15MH49510-01
BURRIS, JAMES J S07RR07136-20
BURRITT, M M01RR00585-20 0532
BURRITT, M F M01RR00585-20 0523
BURROW, GERARD N M01RR00827-17
BURROW, GERARD N P30CA23100-11
BURROW, GERARD N S07RR05665-24
BURROW, GERARD N S15DA07816-01
BURROWS, BENJAMIN P50HL14136-20
BURROWS, BENJAMIN P50HL14136-20 9006
BURROWS, BENJAMIN P50HL14136-20 0009
BURROWS, CYNTHIA J R01GM34841-06
BURROWS, CYNTHIA J R03RR06970-01
BURROWS, MALCOLM R01NS16058-11
BURRY, ARSENE U01AI27136-03 0001
BURSTEIN, DEBORAH R29HL38906-04
BURSTEIN, DEBORAH S07RR05479-29 0444
BURSTEIN, SAMUEL A R01HL29037-10
BURSTEIN, STEPHEN M01RR00211-27 0335
BURSTEIN, STEVEN M01RR00211-27 0289
BURSTEIN, SUMNER H K05DA00043-15
BURSTEIN, SUMNER H R01DA02043-15
BURSTEIN, SUMNER H R01DA02052-15
BURSZTAJN, SHERRY R01NS24377-05
BURT, BRIAN A N01DE12588-00
BURT, DAVID R R01AA07559-03
BURT, JANIS P01DK41006-03 9001
BURT, JANIS M R01HL31008-08
BURT, JANIS M R01HL39795-03
BURT, RANDALL M01RR00064-27 0137
BURT, RANDALL N01CN05321-01
BURT, RANDALL W P01CA48711-02 0002
BURTON, DEBORAH R18NR02685-02
BURTON, DEE P01CA42760-06 0005
BURTON, HAROLD R01DC00096-21
BURTON, HAROLD R01NS22012-06
BURTON, HAROLD W R29HL43796-02
BURTON, JAMES A R01AI29895-02
BURTON, JAMES A R01HL38212-05
BURTON, KAREN P R01HL30570-10
BURTON, LINDA M R29MH46057-02
BURTON, ROBERT W N01CP05625-04
BURTON, ZACHARY S07RR05772-17 0353
BURTON, ZACHARY F R01GM40708-01A2
BURTON, ZACHARY FROM S07RR07049-26 0430
BURZYNSKI, NORBERT J R25CA44789-02A2
BUSA, WILLIAM B R01HD27546-01
BUSA, WILLIAM B R29HD22879-05
BUSBEE, D L P42ES04917-03 0003
BUSBEE, DAVID L R01AG06347-05
BUSBEE, DAVID L R01AG07739-04
BUSBY, M. JANETTE M01RR02719-06 0124
BUSBY, MARJORIE M01RR00046-31 0502
BUSBY, MARJORIE M01RR00046-31 0517
BUSBY, MARJORIE M01RR00046-31 0518
BUSBY, MARY J K08AG00383-05
BUSBY, MARY J M01RR02719-06 0137
BUSBY, WILLIAM F P01ES01640-14 9003
BUSCAGLIA, MARINO P01DK18811-17A1 9005
BUSCH, BETSY K08NS01212-04
BUSCH, DARYLE H R01GM10040-28
BUSCH, HARRIS P01CA10893-23 9001
BUSCH, HARRIS P01CA10893-23
BUSCH, HARRIS P01CA10893-23 0047
BUSCH, NANCY S07RR07150-17 0546
BUSCHANG, P H S07RR05915-08 0676
BUSCHANG, P H S07RR05915-08 0669
BUSCHANG, P H S07RR05915-08 0674
BUSCHANG, P H S07RR05915-08 0675
BUSE, MARIA G R01DK02001-34
BUSE, MARIA G S07RR05420-30
BUSE, MARIA G S15EY09465-01
BUSEMEYER, JEROME R R01MH47126-01
BUSH, BRIAN P42ES04913-02 0007
BUSH, C ALLEN R01DE09445-03
BUSH, C ALLEN R01GM31449-09
BUSH, DOUGLAS S07RR07059-26 0829
BUSH, PATRICIA J R01DA04497-04
BUSH, TRUDY L R29HL39102-05
BUSH, TRUDY L U01HL40231-05
BUSHEY, MICHELLE M S07RR07261-02 0713
BUSHNELL, EMILY W S07RR07179-14 0673
BUSIJA, DAVID W R01HL30260-10
BUSIJA, DAVID W R01HL46558-01
BUSS, DAVID M R01MH44206-03
BUSS, JANICE E R01CA51890-02
BUSS, WILLIAM C R01AI25555-04
BUSSE, LAWRENCE J R44HL44230-02
BUSSE, WILLIAM M01RR03186-06 0057
BUSSE, WILLIAM P01HL42242-04 0005
BUSSE, WILLIAM W M01RR03186-06 0001
BUSSE, WILLIAM W M01RR03186-06 0039
BUSSE, WILLIAM W P50AI10404-21 0006
BUSSE, WILLIAM W R01AI23181-06
BUSSE, WILLIAM W R01AI26609-04
BUSSE, WILLIAM W R01HL44098-12
BUSSEL, JAMES M01RR06020-02 0451
BUSSEL, JAMES B M01RR00047-31 0423
BUSTAMANTE, CARLOS J R01GM32543-10
BUSTIN, M Z01CP04496-15
BUSTO, RAUL P01NS05820-26 0025
BUTCHER, EUGENE C P30DK38707-05 0002
BUTCHER, EUGENE C P30DK38707-05 0006
BUTCHER, EUGENE C R01AI19957-09
BUTCHER, EUGENE C R01GM37734-05
BUTCHER, EUGENE C R01GM41965-03
BUTCHER, LARRY L R01NS10928-15
BUTCHER, RAYMOND J S06GM08016-21 0025
BUTCHER, REGINALD W S07RR07148-18
BUTEL, JANET S R01CA22555-14
BUTEL, JANET S R01CA25215-13
BUTEL, JANET S R01CA33369-09
BUTEL, JANET S U01AI30243-02
BUTERBAUGH, GARY G S07RR05770-13 0935
BUTLER-SIMON, NANCY M01RR00069-29 0390
BUTLER, ALISON R29GM38130-04
BUTLER, ANDREW P R01CA52468-02
BUTLER, DAVID L R01AR38719-03
BUTLER, IAN J M01RR02558-07 0024
BUTLER, J D Z01HD00404-09
BUTLER, J S S07RR07201-12 0629
BUTLER, JAMES E R29HD24556-04
BUTLER, JAMES P P01HL33009-07 0001
BUTLER, JOHN M01RR00425-22S3 0446
BUTLER, JOHN P01HL24163-13 0002
BUTLER, JOHN P50HL30542-08 0004
BUTLER, KENNETH C N01HV88103-05
BUTLER, KENNETH C R01HL42303-03
BUTLER, KENNETH C R43HL46602-01
BUTLER, MERLIN G S07RR05424-30 0075
BUTLER, PETER C R29DK44341-01
BUTLER, REGINA P60HL38632-04 0007

BUTLER, ROBERT N. P50AG05138-08 9004
BUTLER, THOMAS C R03AI30994-02
BUTLER, THOMAS M P01HL15835-19 0030
BUTLER, VINCENT P, JR R01HL10608-25
BUTLER, WILLIAM T M01RR00350-25
BUTLER, WILLIAM T R01AR39273-05
BUTLER, WILLIAM T R37DE05092-14
BUTLERS, NELSON P50MH45294-03 0001
BUTOW, RONALD A R01GM22525-16
BUTOW, RONALD A R01GM35510-06A1
BUTOW, RONALD A R01GM41426-03
BUTTE, NANCY M01RR00350-25 0468
BUTTER, CHARLES M R01NS28330-01A1
BUTTERFIELD, EARL C R01HD26349-02
BUTTERS, NELSON M R01AG08204-04
BUTTERWORTH, FRANK S07RR07131-22 0122
BUTTERWORTH, FRANK S07RR07131-22 0119
BUTTERWORTH, FRANK S07RR07131-22 0120
BUTTERWORTH, FRANK S07RR07131-22 0121
BUTTERWORTH, FRANK S07RR07131-22 0144
BUTTERWORTH, JOHN F S07RR05404-30 0838
BUTTRICK, PETER M R29HL46034-01
BUTZ, ARLENE M S07RR06012-03 0306
BUUS, SOREN R29DC00437-04
BUUS, SOREN S07RR07143-20 0617
BUXBAUM, JOEL N R01DK34900-02
BUXTON, ALFRED E U01HL45700-01A1
BUXTON, IAIN P01DK41315-03 0005
BUXTON, IAIN P01DK41315-03 9001
BUXTON, IAIN L O R01HD26227-03
BUYNAK, JOHN D R01GM37774-04A1
BUYNAK, JOHN D S07RR07194-09 0624
BUZAID, ANTONIO M01RR00125-28 0762
BUZAID, ANTONIO M01RR00125-28 0763
BUZDYGON, BRUCE E S07RR07114-23 0434
BUZSAKI, GYORGY P01NS28121-01A1S1 0003
BUZSAKI, GYORGY R01NS27058-03
BUZSAKI, GYORGI S06GM08223-08 0026
BUZZARD, I MARILYN R01HL42165-03
BYERLEY, WILLIAM P50MH44212-03 0002
BYERLY, WILLIAM L R01NS28484-02
BYERS, BRECK E R01GM18541-20
BYERS, HUGH R R29CA45587-05
BYERS, JOHN A S07RR07170-15 0607
BYERS, MARGARET R R01DE05159-13
BYERS, PETER H P01AR21557-13 0002
BYLUND, DAVID B R01GM37664-05A1
BYLUND, DAVID B R01GM40784-07
BYLUND, DAVID B R01MH47354-01
BYNUM, DAVID P01CA28146-11 9001
BYRD, LARRY D P51RR00165-31 0067
BYRD, LARRY D R01DA01161-16
BYRD, LARRY D R01DA06264-02
BYRD, R A Z01BB03006-03
BYRN, RANDAL A P01HL43510-03 0002
BYRN, STEPHEN R P30AI27713-04
BYRN, STEPHEN R S07RR05586-24 0110
BYRNE, GERALD I R01AI19782-07
BYRNE, GERALD I U01AI31494-01 0003
BYRNE, J Z01CP05146-12
BYRNE, JOHN H R01NS19895-09
BYRNE, JOSEPH J S15DA07785-01
BYRNES, JOHN J R01CA55506-01
BYRNES, JOHN J R01HL42087-04
BYSTRITSKY, ALEXANDER R03MH45392-02
BYSTRYN, JEAN-CLAUDE P30AR39749-04 9003
BYSTRYN, JEAN-CLAUDE R01AR27663-11
BYSTRYN, JEAN-CLAUDE R03CA53468-01
BYYNY, RICHARD L M01RR00051-30 0727
BYYNY, RICHARD L. M01RR00051-30 0615
BZIK, DAVID J R29AI26651-04
BZIK, DAVID J S07RR05392-30 0689
CABALLERO, BENJAMIN M01RR00088-28 0275
CABALLERO, BENJAMIN M01RR00088-28 0276
CABALLERO, BENJAMIN M01RR00088-28 0277
CABALLERO, BENJAMIN S07RR05445-30 0869
CABASSO, ISRAEL R01DE06179-07
CABELLERO, BENJAMIN M01RR00088-28 0256
CABIB, E Z01DK17003-24
CABIRAC, HEWITT B P51RR00164-30 9008
CABOT, JOHN B R01HL24103-13
CABRAL, FERNANDO R R01CA52962-10
CABRAL, GUY A R01DA03647-06
CABRAL, GUY A R01DA05832-01A2
CADELL, DIANE N01CP71098-01
CADELL, DIANE N01CP85651-07
CADENAS, ENRIQUE R01ES05423-02
CADENAS, ENRIQUE S07RR05792-15 0941
CADENHEAD, D ALLAN S07RR07066-26 0241
CADET, JEAN L R29MH47509-01A1
CADILLA, CARMEN S07RR05419-30 0817
CADORET, R P50MH48165-02 0002
CADORET, REMI J R01DA05821-03
CAETANO, RAUL P50AA05595-11 0019
CAETANO, RAUL P50AA05595-11 0014
CAFFREY, JAMES L K04HL01658-05
CAFFREY, MARTIN D R01DK36849-05
CAFISO, DAVID S R01GM35215-06
CAFISO, DAVID S S07RR07094-26 0367
CAFRUNY, WILLIAM A R15AI27978-01A2
CAGGIANO, VINCENT U10CA45466-05
CAGGIULA, ANTHONY R R01MH48299-01
CAGGIULA, ARLENE W R01HL44160-03
CAGGIULA, ARLENE W U01DK40509-04
CAGLE, PHILIP T S07RR05425-30 0729
CAHALAN, MICHAEL D R01GM41514-07
CAHALAN, MICHAEL D R01NS14609-13
CAHALAN, MICHAEL D S15CA55990-01
CAHALAN, MICHAEL K P01AG03104-10 0007
CAHILL, JACK N01CN05221-01
CAHILL, PATRICK M01RR06020-02 0448
CAHN, FREDERICK R43HD27784-01A1
CAHOUR, A Z01AI00572-02
CAIL, STEPHEN N01CM97575-07
CAIL, STEPHEN P N01AG32103-21
CAIL, STEPHEN P N01AG52115-10
CAIN, BRIAN D R01GM43495-02
CAIN, CHARLES A R01CA44124-05
CAIN, CHARLES A R01CA55357-01
CAIN, CHRIS W S07RR05994-03 0293
CAIN, CHRISTOPHER D S07RR05352-30 0753
CAIN, MICHAEL E P50HL17646-17 0026
CAIN, STEPHEN M R01HL26927-11
CAIN, WILLIAM S R01DC00284-07
CAINE, DRURY S N01CM07335-02
CAINE, ERIC D P50MH40381-06
CAINE, ERIC D P50MH40381-06 0006
CAIRNS, J SCOTT S07RR05416-30 0555
CAIRNS, ROBERT B R01MH45532-03
CALA, PETER M R01HL21179-13
CALABRESE, LEONARD U01AI25879-04S2 0003
CALABRESE, RONALD L R01NS24072-07
CALABRESE, VINCENT P01NS25630-03 9003
CALABRESI, PAUL P30CA13943-19 9007
CALABRESI, PAUL P30CA13943-19 0010
CALABRESI, PAUL P30CA13943-19 9014
CALABRESI, PAUL P30CA13943-19 9015
CALABRESI, PAUL P30CA13943-19 9016
CALABRESI, PAUL P30CA13943-19 9011
CALABRETTA, BRUNO P01CA56309-01 0002
CALABRETTA, BRUNO R01CA46782-05
CALABRETTA, BRUNO R01DK44836-01
CALAME, KATHRYN L R01CA38571-07
CALAME, KATHRYN L R01GM29361-12
CALAME, KATHRYN L R01GM44300-01A1
CALAME, KATHRYN L R13GM46482-01
CALANCIE, BLAIR P01NS28059-01A1 0003
CALANCIE, BLAIR S07RR05363-30 0825
CALARCO, PATRICIA P01HD26732-01A1 9001
CALDER, WILLIAM A S07RR07002-26 0863
CALDERONE, RICHARD A R01AI25738-05
CALDERONE, RICHARD A R01HL21370-13
CALDERWOOD, STEPHEN B R29AI27329-03
CALDERWOOD, STUART K R01CA47407-04
CALDERWOOD, STUART K R29CA44940-05
CALDWELL, BETTYE U10HD25460-03
CALDWELL, DANIEL R S07RR07157-16 0572
CALDWELL, FRED T R01GM41293-03
CALDWELL, FRED T R01GM41694-03
CALDWELL, H D Z01AI00216-11
CALDWELL, JAMES H M01RR00034-31 0153
CALDWELL, JAMES H P01HL38736-05 0003
CALDWELL, JOHN H R01NS26505-03
CALDWELL, KARIN D P41RR06030-01A1 0002
CALDWELL, KARIN D R01GM38008-04
CALDWELL, MICHAEL D R01GM32224-08
CALDWELL, ROY L S07RR07006-26 0920
CALDWELL, STEVEN N01DE02578-04
CALENDAR, RICHARD L R37AI08722-23
CALHOON, LINDA L R03AA08582-01A1
CALHOON, ROBERT E S07RR07064-24 0197
CALHOUN, DAVID S07RR07132-20 0401
CALHOUN, DAVID A K11HL02568-01
CALHOUN, WILLIAM J K08HL01828-05
CALHOUN, WILLIAM J M01RR03186-06 0018
CALHOUN, WILLLIAM J M01RR03186-06 0058
CALIBER ASSOCIATES N01TI10015-00
CALIFANO, JOSEPH K16DE00151-05S2 0001
CALIFF, ROBERT M U01HL38516-05
CALIGIURI, MICHAEL A K11CA01572-02
CALIGIURI, MICHAEL P R29MH45959-01A2
CALKINS, RICHARD F R19DA06443-03
CALL, RICHARD P20DC01439-01 0004
CALL, RICHARD L U76PE00456-02
CALLAGHAN, JOHN R19MH46189-03
CALLAHAN, DANIEL R01HG00418-01
CALLAHAN, HUGH J R01DK38895-03
CALLAHAN, L Z01BD04013-03
CALLAHAN, LAWRENCE N01CO74103-16
CALLAHAN, LEIGH R18AR21393-17 0009
CALLAHAN, LISA A R29MH44258-04
CALLAHAN, PHYLLIS A R15AG09020-01
CALLAHAN, R Z01CB04829-17
CALLAHAN, R Z01CB05148-12
CALLANAN, MAUREEN A R29HD26228-04
CALLARD, GLORIA V R01HD16715-10
CALLARD, IAN P R01RR06633-01
CALLARD, IAN P S07RR07043-26 0119
CALLAWAY, ENOCH R01MH22149-17
CALLAWAY, ENOCH S07RR05755-18 0236
CALLE, ROBERTO A K08DK02054-01
CALLENDER, ROBERT H R01EY03142-13
CALLENDER, ROBERT H R01GM35183-07
CALLENDER, ROBERT H S06GM08168-13 0015
CALLERY, PATRICK S S15HL47770-01
CALLES-ESCANDON, JORGE K08DK01963-02
CALLES, JORGE M01RR00109-28 0354
CALLES, JORGE M01RR00109-28 0363
CALLES, JORGE M01RR00109-28 0360
CALLES, JORGE M01RR00109-28 0337
CALLEWAERT, DENIS S07RR07131-22 0123
CALLOW, ALLAN D R01HL36898-05
CALLOW, ALLAN D R01HL46514-02
CALOS, MICHELE P R01CA33056-09
CALVELLI, THERESA A R01AI32306-01
CALVET, JAMES S07RR05373-30 0712
CALVET, JAMES P R01DK37100-05
CALVO, JOSEPH M R01GM39496-04
CALZONE, FRANK J S07RR07008-26 0057
CAMA, VITIALIANO A U01AI30223-02 9001
CAMACHO, ELBER S S07RR05352-30 0757
CAMACHO, S ALBERT K08HL02448-02
CAMARATA, STEPHEN M P20DC01437-01 0002
CAMARGO, MARIA J P50HL18323-17 0064
CAMBIER, JOHN S07RR05842-12 0277
CAMBIER, JOHN C P01AI22295-07 0004
CAMBIER, JOHN C P01AI22295-07 9001
CAMBIER, JOHN C P01AI29903-02 9001
CAMBIER, JOHN C P01AI29903-02 0001
CAMBIER, JOHN C P01AI29903-02
CAMBIER, JOHN C R01AI20519-09
CAMBIER, JOHN C R01AI21768-07A1
CAMBRIA, RICHARD P R29HL39622-04
CAMERINI-OTERO, R D Z01DK52008-12
CAMERINI-OTERO, R D Z01DK52014-04
CAMERON, DON F S07RR05749-19 0268
CAMERON, DOUGLAS C S07RR07098-26 0345
CAMERON, DUKE E R01HL47191-01
CAMERON, G STRONG M01RR00585-20 0497
CAMERON, JOSEPH A S06GM08047-20S1 0024
CAMERON, JUDY L R01HD25929-03
CAMERON, JUDY L R01HD26888-02
CAMERON, MIRIAM L R03AI30973-02
CAMERON, WILLIAM E R01HD22703-07
CAMERON, WILLIAM E S07RR05570-20 0846
CAMERON, WILLIAM E S15HD28740-01
CAMILLERI, M M01RR00585-20 0558
CAMILLERI, M M01RR00585-20 0461
CAMILLERI, M M01RR00585-20 0550
CAMILLERI, M M01RR00585-20 0441
CAMILLERI, M M01RR00585-20 0412
CAMILLERI, M M01RR00585-20 0402
CAMILLERI, M M01RR00585-20 0408
CAMILLI, ANTHONY E K07HL02605-01
CAMINITI, BENELLA P51RR00166-30 9021
CAMITTA, BRUCE M U10CA32053-09
CAMITTA, BRUCE M U10CA32053-09 0051
CAMITTA, BRUCE M U10CA32053-09 0001
CAMITTA, BRUCE M U10CA32053-09 0002
CAMITTA, BRUCE M U10CA32053-09 0003
CAMITTA, BRUCE M U10CA32053-09 0004
CAMITTA, BRUCE M U10CA32053-09 0005
CAMITTA, BRUCE M U10CA32053-09 0006
CAMITTA, BRUCE M U10CA32053-09 0007
CAMITTA, BRUCE M U10CA32053-09 0008
CAMITTA, BRUCE M U10CA32053-09 0009
CAMITTA, BRUCE M U10CA32053-09 0010
CAMITTA, BRUCE M U10CA32053-09 0052
CAMITTA, BRUCE M U10CA32053-09 0011
CAMITTA, BRUCE M U10CA32053-09 0053
CAMITTA, BRUCE M U10CA32053-09 0054
CAMITTA, BRUCE M U10CA32053-09 0055
CAMITTA, BRUCE M U10CA32053-09 0056
CAMITTA, BRUCE M U10CA32053-09 0057
CAMITTA, BRUCE M U10CA32053-09 0012
CAMITTA, BRUCE M U10CA32053-09 0013
CAMITTA, BRUCE M U10CA32053-09 0014
CAMITTA, BRUCE M U10CA32053-09 0015
CAMITTA, BRUCE M U10CA32053-09 0016
CAMITTA, BRUCE M U10CA32053-09 0017
CAMITTA, BRUCE M U10CA32053-09 0018
CAMITTA, BRUCE M U10CA32053-09 0019
CAMITTA, BRUCE M U10CA32053-09 0020
CAMITTA, BRUCE M U10CA32053-09 0021
CAMITTA, BRUCE M U10CA32053-09 0022
CAMITTA, BRUCE M U10CA32053-09 0023
CAMITTA, BRUCE M U10CA32053-09 0024
CAMITTA, BRUCE M U10CA32053-09 0025
CAMITTA, BRUCE M U10CA32053-09 0026
CAMITTA, BRUCE M U10CA32053-09 0027
CAMITTA, BRUCE M U10CA32053-09 0028
CAMITTA, BRUCE M U10CA32053-09 0029
CAMITTA, BRUCE M U10CA32053-09 0030
CAMITTA, BRUCE M U10CA32053-09 0058
CAMITTA, BRUCE M U10CA32053-09 0059
CAMITTA, BRUCE M U10CA32053-09 0031
CAMITTA, BRUCE M U10CA32053-09 0060
CAMITTA, BRUCE M U10CA32053-09 0032
CAMITTA, BRUCE M U10CA32053-09 0033
CAMITTA, BRUCE M U10CA32053-09 0034
CAMITTA, BRUCE M U10CA32053-09 0035
CAMITTA, BRUCE M U10CA32053-09 0036
CAMITTA, BRUCE M U10CA32053-09 0037
CAMITTA, BRUCE M U10CA32053-09 0038
CAMITTA, BRUCE M U10CA32053-09 0039
CAMITTA, BRUCE M U10CA32053-09 0040

CAMITTA, BRUCE M U10CA32053-09 0041
CAMITTA, BRUCE M U10CA32053-09 0042
CAMITTA, BRUCE M U10CA32053-09 0043
CAMITTA, BRUCE M U10CA32053-09 0044
CAMITTA, BRUCE M U10CA32053-09 0045
CAMITTA, BRUCE M U10CA32053-09 0046
CAMITTA, BRUCE M U10CA32053-09 0047
CAMITTA, BRUCE M U10CA32053-09 0048
CAMITTA, BRUCE M U10CA32053-09 0049
CAMITTA, BRUCE M U10CA32053-09 0050
CAMMACK, RICHARD P41RR02583-07 0009
CAMMARATA, PATRICK R R01EY05570-05
CAMMER, WENDY P01NS23705-04A1 0002
CAMMER, WENDY R01NS12890-13
CAMP FIRE, INC N01MH90011-00
CAMP, BONNIE M01RR00069-29 0415
CAMP, BONNIE M01RR00069-29 0423
CAMP, BONNIE M01RR00069-29 0488
CAMP, BONNIE M01RR00069-29 0432
CAMP, BONNIE W M01RR00069-29 0218
CAMP, CAMERON J R01MH45389-02
CAMPAGNARI, ANTHONY A R01AI30006-01A1
CAMPAGNONI, A P30HD04612-21 9003
CAMPAGNONI, ANTHONY S07RR05756-18 0296
CAMPAGNONI, ANTHONY T P01HD25831-01A1 0003
CAMPAGNONI, ANTHONY T P01HD25831-01A1
CAMPAGNONI, ANTHONY T R01NS23022-06
CAMPAGNONI, ANTHONY T R01NS23322-06
CAMPANA, JOSEPH E R43RR06801-01
CAMPBELL, ALAN D M01RR00042-31 0680
CAMPBELL, ALLAN R13AI31581-01
CAMPBELL, ALLAN M R01AI08573-24
CAMPBELL, BENEDICT S07RR05387-30 0604
CAMPBELL, BEVERLY N01CP71114-05
CAMPBELL, BYRON A R01AA07641-04
CAMPBELL, BYRON A R37MH01562-33
CAMPBELL, BYRON A S15MH49282-01
CAMPBELL, COLIN S03RR03135-08
CAMPBELL, DAVID N01CO15603-00
CAMPBELL, DAVID S07RR05354-30 0392
CAMPBELL, DONALD T R01NS22577-07
CAMPBELL, EDWARD J R01HL46440-01
CAMPBELL, EMILY B S07RR05866-08 0988
CAMPBELL, FRANCES A R01HD24114-03
CAMPBELL, G Z01CT00111-10
CAMPBELL, G DOUGLAS S07RR05822-12 0503
CAMPBELL, J S07RR07003-26 0319
CAMPBELL, JACQUELYN C R01NR02571-02
CAMPBELL, JACQUELYN C R29NR01678-05
CAMPBELL, JAMES M01RR00722-19 0261
CAMPBELL, JAMES N R01NS14447-13
CAMPBELL, JAN L R18DA06954-02
CAMPBELL, JOHN S07RR05354-30 0382
CAMPBELL, JUDITH L R01GM25508-14
CAMPBELL, K P01HL14388-20 0254
CAMPBELL, K P01HL14388-20 9005
CAMPBELL, KATHLEEN C S07RR05843-11 0551
CAMPBELL, KATHLEEN C M K08DC00040-02
CAMPBELL, KENNETH B R01AR39583-03
CAMPBELL, KENNETH B R01HL21462-13A1
CAMPBELL, KENNETH B S07RR05465-29 0379
CAMPBELL, KEVIN P R01HL39265-05
CAMPBELL, MAGDA R01MH32212-12S1
CAMPBELL, MAGDA R01MH40177-04A2
CAMPBELL, MICHAEL J R29NS2?571-02
CAMPBELL, PAUL S R15HD2688?-01A1
CAMPBELL, PETER M01RR00095-31 0373
CAMPBELL, PETER P60DK20593-13 9002
CAMPBELL, PETER J R29DK41376-03
CAMPBELL, PHIL G R29CA54363-01
CAMPBELL, PRISCILL A P01AI29903-02 0004
CAMPBELL, PRISCILLA A R37AI11240-19
CAMPBELL, ROBERT M01RR00047-31 0456
CAMPBELL, ROBERT M01RR00047-31 0328
CAMPBELL, ROBERT G U01DK30627-08
CAMPBELL, SCOTT S07RR05387-30 0610
CAMPBELL, SCOTT S R01MH45067-04
CAMPBELL, SUSAN B R01MH40867-06
CAMPBELL, T COLIN R01CA54522-01
CAMPBELL, THOMAS F R03DC01328-01
CAMPBELL, THOMAS F S07RR05416-30 0556
CAMPBELL, THOMAS F S07RR05507-29 0474
CAMPBELL, WILLIAM B P50HL17669-17 0039
CAMPBELL, WILLIAM B R01HL21066-15
CAMPBELL, WILLIAM B R01HL37981-02
CAMPEAU, LUCIEN N01HC75075-08
CAMPER, SALLY M01RR00042-31 0666
CAMPER, SALLY ANN P60AR20557-13 0068
CAMPER, SALLY ANN R03MH46532-02
CAMPESE, VITO M. M01RR00043-31 0394
CAMPESE, VITO M M01RR00043-31 0450
CAMPESE, VITO M M01RR00043-31 0465
CAMPESE, VITO M R01HL47881-01
CAMPISI, JUDITH R01AG07114-05 0002
CAMPISI, JUDITH R01AG09909-02
CAMPISI, JUDITH R01AG10004-04
CAMPOCHIARO, PETER A R01EY05951-08
CAMPOS-OUTCALT, MD S07RR05675-23 0930
CAMPOS, JOSEPH J R01HD25066-03
CAMPOS, JOSEPH J R01MH47543-01
CAMPOS, JOSEPH J S07RR07006-26 0917
CAMRAS, CARL B R01EY07865-04

CANAANI, DAN R01CA53139-01
CANADA, ROBERT G S06GM08244-05 0020
CANAFAX, DANIEL P50DC00133-13 0012
CANALIS, ERNESTO S07RR06023-02
CANALIS, ERNESTO S07RR06023-02 0526
CANALIS, ERNESTO S15AR41241-01
CANALIS, ERNESTO M R01AR21707-11
CANALIS, ERNESTO M R01DK42424-03
CANALIS, ERNESTO M R01DK45227-01
CANCILLA, PASQUALE A P01NS25554-01A2S1 0002
CANCILLA, PASQUQLE A P30NS25554-01A2S1 9002
CANCRO, CAROL S07RR05664-24 0857
CANCRO, MICHAEL P S07RR05415-30 0000
CANCRO, ROBERT S07RR05651-24
CANDAGE, MELLEN N01CO03851-02
CANDE, W ZACHEUS P41RR05097-04
CANDE, WILLIAM Z R01GM23238-16
CANDELAS, GRACIELA C S06GM08102-20 0037
CANDIA, OSCAR A P30EY01867-15
CANDIA, OSCAR A R01EY04810-08
CANE, DAVID S07RR07085-26 0334
CANE, DAVID E R01GM22172-17
CANE, DAVID E R01GM30301-10
CANELLOS, GEORGE P P30CA06516-28 0020
CANELLOS, GEORGE P U10CA32291-10
CANESSA, MITZY S07RR05950-07 0008
CANESSA, MITZY L R01HL42120-03
CANESSA, MITZY L R55HL35664-06A1
CANFIELD, LOUISE M R01HD26715-02
CANFIELD, LOUISE M S07RR05675-23 0900
CANFIELD, ROBERT E M01RR00645-20 0143
CANFIELD, ROBERT E P01HD15454-11 0005
CANFIELD, ROBERT E P01HD15454-11
CANFIELD, ROBERT E S07RR05395-30 0822
CANFIELD, ROBERT E U10HD27006-02
CANFIELD, ROBERT E, P30CA13696-19 9019
CANGIANO, JOSE S06GM08102-20 0056
CANINO, GLORISA U01MH46732-03
CANNISTRA, STEPHEN A S07RR05526-29 0070
CANNITO, MICHAEL P S07RR07091-26 0749
CANNON-ALBRIGHT, LISA A P01CA48711-02 9001
CANNON-ALBRIGHT, LISA A R03CA54936-01
CANNON, DALE S R01AA07707-03
CANNON, GRANT M01RR00064-27 0385
CANNON, JANNE G R01AI23830-06
CANNON, JANNE G R01AI28807-02
CANNON, JANNE G U01AI31496-01 0002
CANNON, JOHN F R29GM40326-04
CANNON, JOSEPH G R01AR39595-03
CANNON, P M01RR00645-20 0424
CANNON, PAUL J P50HL21006-15 0013
CANNON, R Z01HL04825-03
CANNON, R Z01HL04840-01
CANNON, R Z01HL04842-02
CANNON, R O Z01HL04823-03
CANNON, R O Z01HL04836-01
CANNON, R O Z01HL04876-01
CANNON, R O Z01HL04877-01
CANNON, R O Z01HL04878-01
CANNON, R O Z01HL04879-01
CANNON, JOSEPH G P01AI26698-03S1 0004
CANT, NELL B R01DC00135-13
CANTER, JOSEPH R44EY08160-03
CANTERBURY, RANDOLPH J M01RR00847-18 0543
CANTEY, J ROBERT S07RR05767-17 0323
CANTILENA, LOUIS R S07RR05983-05 0350
CANTIN, EDOUARD S07RR05471-29 0587
CANTIN, EDOUARD M R01EY05588-06
CANTIN, EDOUARD M R01HL43594-03
CANTINO, MARIE E K04HL02142-03
CANTINO, MARIE E S10RR06318-01
CANTLEY, LEWIS P50DK39249-05 0014
CANTLEY, LEWIS C R01GM36624-06
CANTLEY, LEWIS C R01GM41890-02
CANTLEY, LEWIS C, JR R01GM36133-07
CANTLEY, LLOYD P50DK39249-05 0006
CANTONI, G L Z01MH02321-06
CANTONI, G L Z01MH02462-03
CANTOR, CHARLES P30CA13696-19 9014
CANTOR, CHARLES P41RR04224-04 0008
CANTOR, CHARLES R, R35CA39782-08
CANTOR, HARVEY I R01AI12184-16
CANTOR, HARVEY I R01AI13600-15
CANTRILL, HERBERT L U10EY08597-02
CANTWELL, DENNIS P P01MH46981-01A1
CANTWELL, DENNIS P P01MH46981-01A1 9001
CANTWELL, DENNIS P P01MH46981-01A1 0002
CANTZ, JOHN P01HL15194-20 0027
CAPAGE, MICHAEL S07RR07042-26 0405
CAPALBO, FRANK J N01LM93504-05
CAPALDI, ELIZABETH D R01MH39453-08
CAPALDI, RODERICK A R01HL22050-14
CAPALDI, RODERICK A R01HL24526-13
CAPARON, MICHAEL R29AI30643-01
CAPARON, MICHAEL G S07RR05389-30 0629
CAPCO, DAVID G R01AI32316-01
CAPDEVILA JORGE H P01DK38226-06 0002
CAPDEVILA JORGE H P01DK38226-06 9001
CAPDEVILA, JORGE H R01GM37922-05
CAPECCHI, MARIO R R01GM21168-18
CAPECCHI, MARIO R R01HD25395-03
CAPELLI, CHRISTOPHER C R43CA55422-01

CAPETANAKI, YASSEMI R01AR39617-04
CAPITAL CONSULTING CORPORATION N01DA10004-
CAPIZZI, ROBERT L P30CA12197-19
CAPIZZI, ROBERT L. P30CA12197-19 9007
CAPIZZI, ROBERT L. P30CA12197-19 9016
CAPLAN, ARNOLD P50AG08012-04 0004
CAPLAN, ARNOLD I R01AG08932-11
CAPLAN, ARNOLD I R01DE04008-16
CAPLAN, ARNOLD I R01DE07220-06
CAPLAN, DAVID P01DC00081-26 0015
CAPLAN, DAVID N R01DC00776-02
CAPLAN, DAVID N R01DC00942-01
CAPLAN, DAVID N R01NS29101-01A1
CAPLAN, DAVID N R03DC01198-01
CAPLAN, L Z01MH00682-05
CAPLAN, L Z01MH00684-04
CAPLAN, LOUIS M01RR00054-30 0430
CAPLAN, LOUIS M01RR00054-30 0431
CAPLAN, MICHAEL J R01GM42136-03
CAPLAN, ROBERT D R01MH47292-01A1
CAPLAN, ROBERT D S07RR07019-26 0068
CAPLAN, ROCHELLE S07RR05756-18 0301
CAPLE, G S06GM08215-09 0003
CAPLOW, MICHAEL R01GM46773-22
CAPON, DANIEL J U01AI31686-01 0001
CAPONE, GEORGE T K08NS01466-01A1
CAPONE, ROBERT J N01HC55013-10
CAPONE, ROBERT J. N01HC65060-08
CAPRA, DONALD J P01AI31229-01 0002
CAPRA, J D P50AR39169-05 0002
CAPRA, J DONALD P01AI23271-06 9001
CAPRA, J DONALD P01AI23271-06
CAPRA, J DONALD P01AI23271-06 0001
CAPRA, J DONALD P01DK42582-02 0006
CAPRA, J DONALD P01DK42582-02 9001
CAPRA, J DONALD P01GM31689-08 9002
CAPRA, J DONALD P01GM31689-08 9001
CAPRA, J DONALD P01GM31689-08
CAPRA, J DONALD P01GM31689-08 0001
CAPRA, J DONALD R01AI18499-10
CAPRA, J DONALD R37AI12127-17
CAPRA, J. DONALD P01AI11851-18 0019
CAPRA, NORMAN F R01DE06027-10
CAPRA, NORMAN F S15HD28739-01
CAPRANICA, ROBERT R R01DC00092-21
CAPRIO, SONIA R01HD28016-01
CAPRIOLI, JOSEPH R01EY07353-02
CAPRIOLI, JOSEPH R01EY09114-01
CAPRIOLI, JOSEPH U10EY06833-05
CAPRIOLI, RICHARD M R01GM43783-02
CAPRIOLI, RICHARD M S10RR06472-01
CAPUTA, LEWIS S07RR05795-14 0417
CARA, JOSE F M01RR00055-30 0575
CARABELLO, BLASE A R01HL38185-04
CARABELLO, BLASE A S10RR06422-01
CARADONNA, SALVATORE J R01CA42605-06A1
CARAGAY, ALEGRIA F N01CN05241-01
CARAMAZZA, ALFONSO R01DC00366-05
CARAMAZZA, ALFONSO R01NS22201-07
CARBALLEIRA, NESTER M S06GM08102-20 0058
CARBALLO-DIEGUEZ, ALEX R03MH47232-01A1
CARBON, JOHN A R01CA11034-23
CARBONE, PAUL P. P30CA14520-19 9015
CARBONE, PAUL P. P30CA14520-19 9014
CARBONE, KATHRYN M R01MH48948-01
CARBONE, KATHRYN M R29NS28599-02
CARBONE, KATHRYN M S07RR05378-30 0988
CARBONE, PAUL P M01RR03186-06 0061
CARBONE, PAUL P M01RR03186-06 0062
CARBONE, PAUL P M01RR03186-06 0051
CARBONE, PAUL P M01RR03186-06 0041
CARBONE, PAUL P M01RR03186-06 0063
CARBONE, PAUL P M01RR03186-06 0064
CARBONE, PAUL P M01RR03186-06 0010
CARBONE, PAUL P M01RR03186-06 0024
CARBONE, PAUL P M01RR03186-06 0009
CARBONE, PAUL P N01CN85109-01
CARBONE, PAUL P P01CA20432-14
CARBONE, PAUL P P30CA14520-19
CARD, JOSEFINA J N43HD13133-00
CARD, JOSEFINA J N44HD02910-02
CARD, JOSEFINA J R43DA07445-01
CARD, JOSEFINA J R44AG08895-02
CARDE, RING T S07RR07048-26 0634
CARDELINO, BEATRIZ H S06GM08241-07 0009
CARDELL, ROBERT R, JR R01DK27097-12
CARDELLI, JAMES A S07RR05822-12 0501
CARDELLINA, J Z01CM07300-01
CARDELLINA, J Z01CM07302-01
CARDELLINA, J H Z01CM07301-01
CARDEN, MARTIN J R01NS27418-03
CARDEN, SUSAN E K21DA00160-01
CARDIFF, ROBERT D R01AI29799-02
CARDIFF, ROBERT D R01CA54284-01
CARDIS, ELIZABETH N01ES95276-05
CARDONA, DOLORES S S03RR03187-08
CARDOSA, SERGIO S M01RR00211-27 0297
CARDULLO, RICHARD A R55HD27244-01A1
CAREW, THOMAS E P50HL14197-20 9005
CAREW, THOMAS E P50HL14197-20 9006
CAREW, THOMAS E P50HL14197-20 0019
CAREW, THOMAS J R37MH41083-05

CAREY, DAVID J R01NS21925-07
CAREY, GALE B S07RR07108-19 0406
CAREY, HANNAH V R29DK39668-05
CAREY, JAMES R P01AG08761-02 0003
CAREY, JANETTE R29GM43558-02
CAREY, JOHN C M01RR00064-27 0298
CAREY, JOHN T M01RR00080-29 0435
CAREY, JOHN T M01RR00080-29 0442
CAREY, K D P50HL36536-05 9001
CAREY, KATE B R29DA07635-01A1
CAREY, KENNETH D P01HL28972-10 9003
CAREY, MARTIN C P30DK34854-08 9003
CAREY, MARTIN C R37DK36588-07
CAREY, MICHAEL F R01GM46424-01
CAREY, R M P01HL19242-15 0014
CAREY, ROBERT J R01DA05366-05
CAREY, ROBERT M M01RR00847-18 0544
CAREY, ROBERT M M01RR00847-18 0545
CAREY, ROBERT M M01RR00847-18 0546
CAREY, ROBERT M M01RR00847-18 0389
CAREY, ROBERT M M01RR00847-18
CAREY, ROBERT M M01RR00847-18 0464
CAREY, ROBERT M R01HL32129-08
CAREY, ROBERT M S07RR05431-30
CAREY, ROBERT W U10CA12449-21
CAREY, TIMOTHY S R01HS06664-01A1
CARIGNAN, FOREST J R43AR40796-01
CARITIS, STEVE N U10HD21410-06
CARLETON, RICHARD A R01HL23629-12
CARLEY, DAVID W R29HL43860-02
CARLIN, CATHLEEN R R01CA49540-04
CARLISLE, EDITH M S07RR05442-29 0048
CARLOCK, LEON R R01NS24236-05A2
CARLSON, BRUCE M P01DE07687-09A1 0001
CARLSON, BRUCE M P01DE07687-09A1 9001
CARLSON, BRUCE M R01NS21108-06
CARLSON, CAROLYN E P01NR01413-04
CARLSON, CATHY S S07RR05404-30 0839
CARLSON, DAVID S R01DE08824-01A2
CARLSON, DON M R01DK36812-06
CARLSON, DON M R01HL41323-04
CARLSON, FRANCIS D R01AR12803-32
CARLSON, GARY P R01ES04362-05
CARLSON, GARY P S07RR05586-24 0120
CARLSON, GEORGE A P01NS14069-14 0009
CARLSON, GEORGE A P01NS22786-07 0001
CARLSON, GEORGE A R01AG10681-01
CARLSON, GEORGE A R01CA28231-10S1
CARLSON, GEORGE A S03RR03526-02
CARLSON, GEORGE A S07RR06017-04
CARLSON, GEORGE A S15CA56002-01
CARLSON, GERALD M R01DK32953-10
CARLSON, GERALD M S07RR05423-30 0049
CARLSON, HAROLD E S07RR05736-19 0187
CARLSON, JAMES R P30AI27732-04 9001
CARLSON, JOHN P01GM39813-04 0002
CARLSON, JOHN G R01NR02855-01
CARLSON, JOHN R R01GM36862-06
CARLSON, KAREN L M01RR00997-16 0369
CARLSON, KRISTIN R R01DA06539-02
CARLSON, KRISTIN R S07RR05712-20 0081
CARLSON, MARIAN B R01GM34095-08
CARLSON, MARY L R01MH40157-07
CARLSON, MICHAEL M01RR00095-31 0360
CARLSON, MICHAEL M01RR00095-31 0350
CARLSON, ROBERT M01RR00070-29 0229
CARLSON, ROBERT W P01CA44665-04 0002
CARLSON, RUSSELL W R01GM39583-05A1
CARLSON, SONIA L R29MH48644-01
CARLSON, STEVEN S R01NS22367-07
CARLSON, SUSAN E R01EY08770-02
CARLTON, SUSAN M P01NS11255-17 9005
CARLTON, SUSAN M P01NS11255-17 0025
CARLTON, SUSAN M R29NS27910-02
CARMAN, GEORGE M R01GM28140-11
CARMAN, GEORGE M R01GM35655-06
CARMAN, WENDY J R03AA08630-02
CARMEL, RALPH M01RR00043-31 0453
CARMEL, RALPH R01DK32640-07
CARMELLI, DORIT R01AA08925-01
CARMELLI, DORIT R03HL46115-02
CARMICHAEL, G P01HD22610-04 9001
CARMICHAEL, GORDON G R01CA45382-05
CARMINES, DAVID V S07RR07123-22 0599
CARNES, DAVID P01DE08569-03 0004
CARNES, MARY L M01RR03186-06 0045
CARNES, MARY L R29DK40759-03
CARNEY, ARLENE P60DC00982-02 0002
CARNEY, DARRELL H R01DK25807-13
CARNEY, PATRICIA S07RR05718-16 0145
CARNEY, ROBERT M R01HL42427-03
CARO, JAIME S07RR05414-30 0999
CARO, JOSE F P01DK36296-05
CARO, JOSE F P01DK36296-05 0001
CAROL COAN S07RR05301-21 0734
CAROME, EDWARD F R43AI30851-01
CAROME, M Z01DK43237-01
CARON, ALBERT J R01HD27120-03
CARON, JOHN P S07RR05623-25 0722
CARON, JOHN P S07RR05623-25 0715
CARON, MARC G P50MH44211-03 0001
CARON, MARC G R01NS19576-08
CARONE, FRANK A R01DK42304-02
CARP, RICHARD I P01AG09017-02
CARP, RICHARD I P01AG09017-02 0001
CARPENTER, CHARLES B P01AI23360-07
CARPENTER, CHARLES B P01AI23360-07 0002
CARPENTER, CHARLES B P50DK39249-05 0009
CARPENTER, DAVID P42ES04913-02 9001
CARPENTER, DAVID O P42ES04913-02
CARPENTER, DAVID O R01ES05203-03
CARPENTER, DAVID O R01NS23807-06
CARPENTER, GRAHAM P01CA43720-05 0002
CARPENTER, GRAHAM P01CA43720-05 0003
CARPENTER, GRAHAM P30HD05797-20 9004
CARPENTER, GRAHAM P50HL14214-20 0044
CARPENTER, GRAHAM F R01CA24071-13
CARPENTER, MARSHALL W P50HD11343-14A1 0018
CARPENTER, MARTHA S07RR07035-26 0097
CARPENTER, PATRICIA A K02MH00661-05
CARPENTER, SUSAN L R01AI30025-01A1
CARPENTER, THOMAS O K08AR01749-05
CARPENTER, THOMAS O M01RR06022-02 0383
CARPENTER, WILLIAM T P50MH40279-05 9004
CARPENTER, WILLIAM T P50MH40279-05 9001
CARPENTER, WILLIAM T P50MH44211-03 9001
CARPENTER, WILLIAM T, JR P50MH44211-03
CARPENTER, WILLIAM T, JR P50MH40279-05
CARPENTER, WILLIAM T, JR R37MH35996-10
CARPENTIER, ROBERT G S06GM08016-21 0073
CARPER, D Z01EY00201-07
CARPINO, LOUIS A R01GM09706-26
CARR, BRIAN I R29CA44602-05
CARR, BRUCE R M01RR00633-19 0385
CARR, CATHERINE E R29DC00436-04
CARR, DAISY M S06GM08140-17 0010
CARR, KENNETH D R01DA03956-06
CARR, KENNETH L R43HL46580-01
CARR, MARK S M01RR00032-31 0371
CARR, PETER W R01GM45988-01
CARR, STEVEN A P01GM39526-05 0005
CARR, STEVEN A P01GM39526-05
CARRASCO, NANCY R01DK41544-03
CARRASQUILLO, J A Z01CL00600-06
CARRASQUILLO, J A Z01CL00603-07
CARRASQUILLO, JA Z01CL00601-06
CARRAWAY, KERMIT L R01CA52498-01A1
CARRAWAY, ROBERT E R01DK28565-12
CARRERA, CARLOS J P60AR40770-01A1 0001
CARRERA, CARLOS J R29CA54892-01
CARRETERO, OSCAR A P01HL28982-10
CARRETERO, OSCAR A P01HL28982-10 0001
CARRETERO, OSCAR A. P01HL28982-10 0009
CARRIERI-KOHLMAN, VIRGINIA L R01NR02131-03
CARRIGAN, DONALD R P50NS20022-08 0003
CARRILLO, ALBERTO E S07RR05806-13 0904
CARRINGTON, JAMES C R29AI27832-03
CARRINGTON, JAMES C S07RR07090-26 0465
CARRITHERS, CAROLINE S07RR07059-26 0839
CARROLL, BERNARD J R01MH39593-07
CARROLL, DANA R01HL40186-05
CARROLL, F IVY U01CA46738-05 0001
CARROLL, FRANK I R01DA05477-04
CARROLL, FRANK I R01DA05721-03
CARROLL, FRANK I R01DA06302-02
CARROLL, JOHN L K08HL02543-01
CARROLL, MARILYN E R01DA02486-12
CARROLL, MARILYN E R37DA03240-09
CARROLL, MICHAEL C P01HD17461-08 0003
CARROLL, PAUL T R01NS21289-08
CARROLL, RAYMOND J R01GM39015-03
CARROLL, ROBERT B R01CA20802-15
CARROLL, WILLIAM L R29CA49986-02
CARROW, E W Z01BF04012-01
CARROW, E W Z01BF04013-01
CARRUTHERS, ANTHONY R01DK36081-07
CARSKADON, MARY A R01HL44138-02
CARSKADON, MARY A R01MH45945-02
CARSKADON, MARY A S15HL47705-01
CARSON, DANIEL D R01HD25235-03
CARSON, DANIEL D R03HD28072-01
CARSON, DENNIS M01RR00833-17 0004
CARSON, DENNIS A P60AR40770-01A1
CARSON, DENNIS A R01AI29151-03
CARSON, DENNIS A R01GM23200-16
CARSON, DENNIS A R37AR25443-13
CARSON, JEFFREY L R01HL41523-02
CARSON, JOHN H R01NS15190-12
CARSON, JOHNNY L P50HL19171-15 9002
CARSON, PAUL L R01DK42290-01A1
CARSON, R E Z01CL00801-01
CARSON, R E Z01CL00802-01
CARSON, SANDRA A U10HD27011-02
CARSON, STEVEN D K04HL02072-05
CARSON, STEVEN D R01HL31408-08A1
CARSON, VERNA S07RR05973-05 0789
CARSTENSEN, EDWIN L R01DK39796-04
CARSTENSEN, LAURA L R01AG08816-02
CARTEE, GREGORY D S07RR07098-26 0342
CARTER-DAWSON, LOVENIA S03RR03501-02
CARTER-SU P60AR20557-13 0062
CARTER-SU, CHRISTIN R01AR40740-01
CARTER-SU, CHRISTIN R01DK34171-07
CARTER, ANTHONY S07RR05430-30 0219
CARTER, ANTHONY D S07RR05697-22 0999
CARTER, B J Z01DK57501-15
CARTER, B J Z01DK57504-04
CARTER, BARRY L M01RR00350-25 0444
CARTER, BRIAN S M01RR00069-29 0434
CARTER, C SUE R01MH45836-01A3
CARTER, CAMERON S07RR05684-23 0176
CARTER, D M P01CA29502-11A1 0048
CARTER, D MARTIN M01RR00102-28 0032
CARTER, D MARTIN M01RR00102-28 0095
CARTER, D MARTIN M01RR00102-28 0096
CARTER, D MARTIN M01RR00102-28 0033
CARTER, D. MARTIN M01RR00102-28 0035
CARTER, DARRYL P30CA16359-17 9021
CARTER, DAVID S07RR05795-14 0416
CARTER, DEAN E P42ES04940-02
CARTER, DEAN E R01ES04616-04
CARTER, DEAN E R01ES05561-01A1
CARTER, HERBERT E S07RR07002-26
CARTER, JANETTE S R21DK44560-01
CARTER, LAURIE C S07RR05330-30 0013
CARTER, PHILIP B P30DK34987-06 9001
CARTER, TIMOTHY H S03RR03551-01
CARTER, W P30CA16059-15 9018
CARTER, WALTER H S07RR05697-22 0995
CARTER, WALTER H S07RR05697-22 0996
CARTER, WALTER H S07RR05724-20 0189
CARTER, WILLIAM G R01CA49259-03
CARTWRIGHT, CHRISTINE A R29DK43743-01
CARTWRIGHT, PETER P30HG00199-01 9002
CARTWRIGHT, PETER P30HG00199-01 9003
CARTWRIGHT, PETER S S07RR05424-30 0080
CARTWRIGHT, ROSALIND D R01MH40552-06S1
CARUSE, JOSEPH A P42ES04908-03 0005
CARUSI, EDWARD A S07RR05390-30 0664
CARUSO, JOSEPH A R01ES03221-09
CARUSO, R Z01EY00123-12
CARUSO, R Z01EY00144-10
CARUSO, R Z01EY00257-03
CARUSO, RITA L R29ES04424-05
CARUTHERS, MARVIN H R01GM21120-17
CARUTHERS, MARVIN H R01GM25680-13
CARUTHERS, MARVIN H R13CA53494-01
CARVALHO, EDGAR P01AI26506-04 0003
CARVALHO, EDGAR M P01AI16282-13 0005
CARVALHO, EDGAR M P50AI30639-01
CARVALHO, EDGAR M P50AI30639-01 0001
CARVER, S S07RR07069-26 0241
CARVEY, PAUL S07RR05477-29 0415
CASABURI, RICHARD M01RR00425-22S3 0299
CASADABAN, MALCOLM J R01GM45883-01
CASAGRANDE, VIVIEN A R01EY01778-15
CASALE, THOMAS B P50AI19093-08 0006
CASANOVA, M F Z01MH02472-03
CASAT, CHARLES D S07RR05745-19 0262
CASAZZA, ANN M U01CA50750-03 0002
CASAZZA, J P Z01AA00044-02
CASCIO, DUILIO P01GM39558-05 9001
CASCIO, H E Z01RR10348-02
CASCIO, WAYNE E K11HL01839-05
CASE, CASEY C R43DK44393-01
CASE, CASEY C R43HL46623-01
CASE, DAVID A P01GM38794-05 0001
CASE, DAVID A R01GM39914-04
CASE, DAVID A R01GM45811-01
CASEBOLT, DONALD B P40RR00463-23 0004
CASELLA, JAMES F R29HL38855-05
CASERO, ROBERT U01CA37606-08 0007
CASERO, ROBERT A S07RR05378-30 0989
CASERO, ROBERT A, JR R01CA51085-02
CASERO, ROBERT A, JR R29CA47492-04
CASEY, CAROL A R29AA07846-04
CASEY, DANIEL E R37MH36657-10
CASEY, M LINETTE R01DK40353-04
CASEY, M LINNETTE P50HD11149-14 0011
CASEY, MICHAEL P01AG06569-05 0008
CASEY, RICHARD S07RR05780-16 0970
CASEY, STEPHEN M N01LM13527-02
CASEY, STEVE N01LM83502-24
CASEY, TERENCE T S07RR05424-30 0070
CASGRANDE, JOHN T P30CA14089-16 9007
CASH, DEREK S07RR05387-30 0611
CASH, DEREK S07RR07053-26 0147
CASHDOLLAR, L WILLIA S07RR05434-30 0823
CASHEL, C M Z01HD00067-23
CASHMAN, JOHN R R01DK36398-04
CASHMAN, SUZANNE S07RR05927-07 0968
CASHMORE, ANTHONY R R01GM38409-06
CASIDA, JOHN E P01ES00049-27
CASIDA, JOHN E P01ES00049-27 0003
CASIDA, JOHN E P01ES00049-27 0013
CASIDA, JOHN E P01ES00049-27 0015
CASIDA, JOHN E P01ES00049-27 0029
CASIDA, JOHN E R01ES04863-04
CASILLAS, EDMUND R S06GM08136-18 0010
CASKEY, C THOMAS P50AG08664-03 0005
CASKEY, C. THOMAS P30HD24064-04 9005
CASKEY, CHARLES T P30HG00210-01
CASKEY, CHARLES T R01DK31428-10
CASKEY, CHARLES T R01DK42696-02
CASKEY, CHARLES T S10RR06404-01
CASNELLIE, JOHN E R01CA38821-07

CASPAR, DONALD L R35CA47439-04
CASPAR, EPHRIAM S P30CA08748-26 9036
CASPARY, DONALD M R01DC00151-12
CASPARY, DONALD M S07RR05843-11 0548
CASPARY, W Z01ES21106-04
CASPARY, W Z01ES21139-02
CASPI, AVSHALOM S07RR07098-26 0353
CASPI, R Z01EY00184-09
CASPI, R R Z01EY00258-03
CASSADY, JOHN M R01CA33326-09
CASSADY, JOHN M R01CA38151-07
CASSADY, JOHN M S07RR05607-25
CASSANO, PATRICIA A R29HL45731-01A1
CASSEDAY, JOHN H R01DC00287-07
CASSEL, CHRISTINE K K07AG00461-02
CASSEL, CHRISTINE K K12AG00488-01
CASSELBRANT, MARGARETHA M01RR00084-29 0243
CASSELL, GAIL H R01AI28279-03
CASSELL, GAIL H R01HD20928-05
CASSELL, GAIL H R01HL19741-16
CASSELL, GAIL H R01RR00959-16
CASSELL, MARTIN D R29NS25139-05
CASSIDY, JUDE A R03MH46572-02
CASSIDY, M M P01HL38079-05 9001
CASSIDY, MICHAEL J U10CA45461-03
CASSIDY, SUZANNE B S07RR05675-23 0901
CASSILETH, PETER A P30CA16520-16 9002
CASSILETH, PETER A R25CA40008-07
CASSIMERIS, LYNNE P41RR01219-10 0003
CASSIN, SIDNEY PHD MA R01HL10834-21
CASSIS, LISA A R29HL41954-03
CASSON, PETER R M01RR00211-27 0336
CASSONE, VINCENT M S07RR07090-26 0466
CASSORLA, F Z01HD00621-09
CASTAGNOLI, NEAL, JR R01NS28792-02
CASTEEL, DEE A S07RR05877-09 0591
CASTELLINI, MICHAEL A R29HL38675-05
CASTELLINI, MICHEL S07RR07254-03 0494
CASTELLINO, FRANCIS J R01HL19982-15
CASTELLINO, FRANCIS J R37HL13423-21
CASTELLOT, JOHN J, JR R01DK42420-09
CASTERLINE, JOHN B R01HD26706-02
CASTLE, J DAVID R01DE09655-01
CASTLE, JOHN D R01DE08941-03
CASTLE, VALERIE P K08CA01599-01
CASTLEBERRY, ROBERT P U10CA25408-13 0037
CASTLEBERRY, ROBERT P U10CA25408-13 0038
CASTLEBERRY, ROBERT P U10CA25408-13 0039
CASTLEBERRY, ROBERT P U10CA25408-13 0040
CASTLEBERRY, ROBERT P U10CA25408-13 0041
CASTLEBERRY, ROBERT P U10CA25408-13 0042
CASTLEBERRY, ROBERT P U10CA25408-13 0043
CASTLEBERRY, ROBERT P U10CA25408-13 0044
CASTLEBERRY, ROBERT P U10CA25408-13 0001
CASTLEBERRY, ROBERT P U10CA25408-13 0002
CASTLEBERRY, ROBERT P U10CA25408-13 0003
CASTLEBERRY, ROBERT P U10CA25408-13 0004
CASTLEBERRY, ROBERT P U10CA25408-13 0005
CASTLEBERRY, ROBERT P U10CA25408-13 0006
CASTLEBERRY, ROBERT P U10CA25408-13 0007
CASTLEBERRY, ROBERT P U10CA25408-13 0008
CASTLEBERRY, ROBERT P U10CA25408-13 0009
CASTLEBERRY, ROBERT P U10CA25408-13 0010
CASTLEBERRY, ROBERT P U10CA25408-13 0011
CASTLEBERRY, ROBERT P U10CA25408-13 0012
CASTLEBERRY, ROBERT P U10CA25408-13 0013
CASTLEBERRY, ROBERT P U10CA25408-13 0014
CASTLEBERRY, ROBERT P U10CA25408-13 0015
CASTLEBERRY, ROBERT P U10CA25408-13 0016
CASTLEBERRY, ROBERT P U10CA25408-13
CASTLEBERRY, ROBERT P U10CA25408-13 0045
CASTLEBERRY, ROBERT P U10CA25408-13 0057
CASTLEBERRY, ROBERT P U10CA25408-13 0058
CASTLEBERRY, ROBERT P U10CA25408-13 0046
CASTLEBERRY, ROBERT P U10CA25408-13 0047
CASTLEBERRY, ROBERT P U10CA25408-13 0048
CASTLEBERRY, ROBERT P U10CA25408-13 0049
CASTLEBERRY, ROBERT P U10CA25408-13 0050
CASTLEBERRY, ROBERT P U10CA25408-13 0051
CASTLEBERRY, ROBERT P U10CA25408-13 0052
CASTLEBERRY, ROBERT P U10CA25408-13 0053
CASTLEBERRY, ROBERT P U10CA25408-13 0054
CASTLEBERRY, ROBERT P U10CA25408-13 0055
CASTLEBERRY, ROBERT P U10CA25408-13 0056
CASTLEBERRY, ROBERT P U10CA25408-13 0059
CASTLEBERRY, ROBERT P U10CA25408-13 0017
CASTLEBERRY, ROBERT P U10CA25408-13 0060
CASTLEBERRY, ROBERT P U10CA25408-13 0018
CASTLEBERRY, ROBERT P U10CA25408-13 0019
CASTLEBERRY, ROBERT P U10CA25408-13 0020
CASTLEBERRY, ROBERT P U10CA25408-13 0021
CASTLEBERRY, ROBERT P U10CA25408-13 0022
CASTLEBERRY, ROBERT P U10CA25408-13 0023
CASTLEBERRY, ROBERT P U10CA25408-13 0024
CASTLEBERRY, ROBERT P U10CA25408-13 0025
CASTLEBERRY, ROBERT P U10CA25408-13 0026
CASTLEBERRY, ROBERT P U10CA25408-13 0027
CASTLEBERRY, ROBERT P U10CA25408-13 0028
CASTLEBERRY, ROBERT P U10CA25408-13 0029
CASTLEBERRY, ROBERT P U10CA25408-13 0030
CASTLEBERRY, ROBERT P U10CA25408-13 0031
CASTLEBERRY, ROBERT P U10CA25408-13 0032
CASTLEBERRY, ROBERT P U10CA25408-13 0033
CASTLEBERRY, ROBERT P U10CA25408-13 0034
CASTLEBERRY, ROBERT P U10CA25408-13 0035
CASTLEBERRY, ROBERT P U10CA25408-13 0036
CASTLEMAN, WILLIAM L P50AI10404-21 0010
CASTLEMAN, WILLIAM L R01HL33441-07
CASTONGUAY, THOMAS W R01DK42446-01A1
CASTOR, C WILLIAM R01AR10728-25
CASTOR, TREVOR P R43AI29829-01A1
CASTOR, TREVOR P R43CA56182-01
CASTRACANE, JAMES R43DC01000-01
CASTRIC, PETER A R15AI31197-01
CASTRO-MALASPINA, HUGO P01CA23766-14 0032
CASTRO, ANTHONY J R01NS13230-15
CASTRO, DAN J K08DC00031-04
CASTRO, FELIPE G R01CA57140-01
CASTRO, FELIPE G R18DA05661-05
CASTRO, GILBERT A R01AI11361-16
CASTRO, JOSE A R01DK13195-19A2
CASTRO, JOSE A R01ES05619-01
CASTRO, JOSEPH R P01CA19138-15 0004
CASTRO, JOSEPH R P01CA19138-15 0006
CASTRO, JOSEPH R P01CA19138-15
CASTRO, JOSEPH R P01CA19138-15 0007
CASTRONOVO, V Z01CB09353-01
CATALAND, SAMUEL M01RR00034-31 0201
CATALANO, CARLOS S07RR05831-12 0978
CATALANO, PATRICK M M01RR00109-28 0234
CATALANO, PATRICK M N01HD13125-00
CATALANO, PATRICK M R29HD22965-06
CATALANO, PATRICK M. M01RR00109-28 0318
CATALANO, RICHARD F R01DA05824-02
CATALANO, ROBERT P30CA06927-29 9026
CATALANOTTO, FRANK A S07RR06004-04
CATANESE, VERONICA S07RR05399-30 0915
CATANESE, VERONICA M R01DK43614-02
CATANIA, JOSEPH P50MH42459-06 0007
CATANIA, JOSEPH A R01MH43892-03
CATANIA, JOSEPH A R01MH48638-01
CATANIA, JOSEPH A R01MH48642-01
CATERSON, BRUCE R01AR40364-02
CATES, KATHRYN LYNN R01AI25938-04
CATHCART, EDGAR S R01AG06860-05
CATHCART, MARTHA K R01AI26121-03
CATHERWOOD, BAYARD D R01AR32196-07A1
CATLIN, ELIZABETH A R29HL46198-01
CATON, ANDREW R01AI24541-05
CATON, CAROL L R01MH44705-03S2
CATRAMBONE, RICHARD S07RR07024-26 0052
CATRAVAS, JOHN D R01HL31422-08
CATT, K J Z01HD00151-16
CATT, K J Z01HD00184-13
CATT, K J Z01HD00193-06
CATTAU, EDWARD M01RR00065-29 0336
CATTERAL, WILLIAM A P01NS20482-08 0013
CATTERALL, JAMES F P50HD13541-12 0005
CATTERALL, JAMES F S15HD28735-01
CATTERALL, JAMES F. P50HD13541-12 9005
CATTERALL, WILLIAM P01HL44948-01A1 0001
CATTERALL, WILLIAM A P01HL44948-01A1
CATTERALL, WILLIAM A R01NS15751-12
CATTERALL, WILLIAM A R01NS22625-06A1
CATTERALL, WILLIAM A R01NS25704-04
CAUCE, ANA M R29HD24056-04
CAUCE, ANA MARIE R18MH48087-02
CAUDILL, RICHARD S07RR05704-20 0016
CAUDY, MICHAEL A R01NS28652-01A1
CAUDY, MICHAEL A S07RR05396-30 0737
CAUFIELD, PAGE W R01DE09082-01A2
CAUGHEY, B Z01AI00580-02
CAUGHEY, THOMAS A R43EY09155-01
CAUGHMAN, GRETCHEN B R01AI22894-06
CAULEY, JANE A R01AR35582-06
CAULEY, JANE A R29HL40489-04
CAULFIELD, JOHN P30AR35907-07 9004
CAULFIELD, JOHN F P60AR36308-07 9006
CAULFIELD, JOHN P R22AI23083-07
CAULFIELD, MICHAEL J R01AI27573-01A3
CAUSEY, DENNIS M M01RR00043-31 0466
CAVA, MICHAEL P R01GM40967-03
CAVA, MICHAEL P R01GM44713-01
CAVALIERI, ERCOLE R01CA44686-04
CAVALIERI, ERCOLE R01CA49917-01A2
CAVALIERI, ERCOLE L P01CA49210-03
CAVALIERI, ERCOLE L P01CA49210-03 0001
CAVALIERI, STEPHEN J S07RR05390-30 0686
CAVALLI-SFORZA, LUIGI L P01GM28428-11 0001
CAVALLI-SFORZA, LUIGI L P01GM28428-11
CAVALLI-SFORZA, LUIGI L P01GM28428-11 9001
CAVALLI-SFORZA, LUIGI L P01MH39437-07 0005
CAVALLI-SFORZA, LUIGI L R01GM10452-28 0003
CAVALLI-SFORZA, LUIGI L R01GM20467-19
CAVALLO, TITO R01DK38644-05
CAVANAGH, H DWIGHT R01EY04604-06
CAVANAGH, H DWIGHT R01EY08277-03
CAVANAGH, PATRICK R01EY09258-01
CAVANAGH, PETER R R01AA07863-02
CAVANAGH, PETER R R01DK42912-01A1
CAVANAUGH, CHERYL S07RR05372-30 0707
CAVANAUGH, JOHN C R01AG09265-02
CAVENDER, DRUIE E R29AI27809-04
CAVENER, DOUGLAS R R01GM34170-07
CAVENER, DOUGLAS R S07RR07201-12 0630
CAVERT, H MEAD M01RR00400-23
CAVINESS, VERNE S P50NS20489-07 0004
CAVINESS, VERNE S S07RR05486-29 0062
CAVINESS, VERNE S, JR R01NS12005-17A1
CAYRE, YVON E R01CA43225-05A2
CDM GROUP, INC N01DA18205-00
CEASE, KEMP B R01AI26818-03
CEASE, KEMP B U01AI28681-03
CEBRA, JOHN J R01AI17997-12
CEBRA, JOHN J R01AI23970-06
CEBUL, RANDALL D R01HS06418-01A1
CECH, THOMAS R R37GM28039-12
CECI, STEPHEN J K04HD00801-04
CECI, STEPHEN J R01HD22839-04
CECI, STEPHEN J R01HD24775-02
CEDAR, HOWARD R01GM20483-18
CEDAR, HOWARD R01GM44669-01A1
CEDARBAUM, JESSE M M01RR00047-31 0419
CEDERBAUM, A P50AA03508-14 0004
CEDERBAUM, ARTHUR I R01AA03312-12
CEDERBAUM, ARTHUR I R37AA06610-07
CEDERBAUM, STEPHEN D P01HD06576-18 0008
CELADA, FRANCO R01AI28194-02
CELANO, PAUL R29CA51068-02
CELENTANO, DAVID D U01MH48019-02
CELLA, DAVID F R29CA51926-01A1
CELLO, JOHN P M01RR00083-29 0225
CENEDELLA, RICHARD J R01EY02568-14
CENSULLO, MEREDITH V R29NR02076-04
CENTER, DARIT M. P01HL19717-15 0050
CENTER, DAVID M R01AI28736-03
CENTER, DAVID M R01HL32802-07
CENTER, MELVIN S R01CA37585-08
CENTRELLA, MICHAEL R29AR39201-04
CEPKO, CONSTANCE L R01EY08064-03
CEPKO, CONSTANCE L R01NS23021-06
CEPLO, CONSTANCE P50NS16998-11 0005
CERAME-VIVAS, MAXIMO S06GM08239-06
CERAMI, ANTHONY R01AI21359-07
CERAMI, ANTHONY R22AI30660-01
CERAMI, ANTHONY R37AI19428-09
CERDA, JAMES J M01RR00082-29 0480
CERIANI, ROBERTO L R01CA39932-08
CERIANI, ROBERTO L R01CA39936-07
CERIANI, ROBERTO L S07RR05929-06 0281
CERILLI, G JAMES R01DK32088-07
CERIONE, RICHARD A R01EY06429-06
CERIONE, RICHARD A R01GM40654-04
CERKLEWSKI, FLORIAN S07RR07079-26 0294
CERKLEWSKI, FLORIAN L R01DE05628-10
CERLETTY, JAMES M M01RR00058-30 0072
CERMAK, LAIRD S P50NS26985-03
CERMAK, LAIRD S R01AA00187-19
CERNIACK, REUBEN M P01HL36577-06 0006
CERNUSZEWICZ, ROMAN S07RR07147-19 0643
CERNY, JAN R01AI23900-05
CERRA, D S07RR05362-30 0799
CETAS, THOMAS C R37CA29653-11
CEWIRTZ, ALAN M K04CA01324-05
CHA, JIN K K04GM00575-02
CHA, JIN K R01GM35956-06
CHACHOUA, ABRAHAM M01RR00096-30A1 0323
CHACHOUA, ABRAHAM P30AI27742-03 9006
CHACHOUA, ABRAHAM S07RR05399-30 0916
CHACKO, SAMUEL K R01DK39740-04
CHAD, F-F Z01HL02833-01
CHADA, KIRAN K R01GM38731-05
CHADER, GERALD J Z01EY00124-11
CHADER, GERALD J Z01EY00148-18
CHADWICK, R S Z01RR10097-11
CHAE, CHI-BOM R01DK39019-05
CHAE, CHI-BOM R01GM43814-01
CHAE, CHI-BOM R01HD20136-07
CHAET, ALFRED B R15GM46126-01
CHAFETZ, PAUL P50AG08013-04 0007
CHAFFIN, W LAJEAN S07RR05773-17 0362
CHAFFIN, WELDA L R01AI23416-04A2
CHAGANTI, RAJU P01CA05826-29 9004
CHAGANTI, RAJU S P01AI32918-09 9001
CHAGANTI, RAJU S P01CA23766-14 9007
CHAGANTI, RAJU S R01CA34775-08
CHAGANTI, RAJU S K P30CA08748-26 9035
CHAIKEN, ROCHELLE M01RR00318-25 0232
CHAIKEN, ROCHELLE L M01RR00318-25 0216
CHAIKEN, ROCHELLE L M01RR00318-25 0215
CHAISSON, RICHARD E M01RR00722-19 0150
CHAIT, ALAN M01RR00037-31 0493
CHAIT, ALAN P01DK02456-33A1 0015
CHAIT, ALAN P01HL30086-09 0006
CHAIT, BRIAN P41RR00862-18 9001
CHAIT, BRIAN T P41RR00862-18
CHAIT, BRIAN T S07RR07065-26 0057
CHAIT, LARRY D M01RR00055-30 0573
CHAIT, LARRY D P50DA00250-20 0028
CHAIT, LARRY D R01DA03517-08
CHAITIN, MICHAEL H R29EY06590-05
CHAITMAN, BERNARD R01HL42419-03 9002
CHAITMAN, BERNARD R R01HL42145-03
CHAITMAN, BERNARD R U01HL38504-05
CHAKI, TARUN K S07RR07066-26 0242
CHAKRABARTI, BIRESWA S07RR05527-29 0522

CHAKRABARTI, BIRESWAR R01EY05301-07
CHAKRABARTI, BIRESWAR R01EY04161-09A1
CHAKRABARTI, DEB P01AI28780-01A1 9001
CHAKRABARTY, ANANDA M R01ES04050-06
CHAKRABARTY, ANANDA M R37AI16790-12
CHAKRABARTY, SUBHAS R29CA47775-05
CHAKRABORTY, RANAJIT R01GM41399-02
CHAKRABORTY, RANAJIT S07RR07143-20 0538
CHAKRABURTTY, KALPAN S07RR05434-30 0818
CHAKRABURTTY, KALPANA R01GM29795-04A4
CHAKRAVARTI, ARAVINDA K04HD00774-05
CHAKRAVARTI, ARAVINDA M01RR00084-29 0239
CHAKRAVARTI, ARAVINDA R01HD28088-01
CHAKRAVARTI, ARAVINDA R01HG00344-07
CHAKRAVARTI, BULBUL P01AI28780-01A1 0004
CHALAZONITIS, ALCMENE R01NS26766-03
CHALFIE, MARTIN R01GM30997-10
CHALFIE, MARTIN R01GM34775-04
CHALFIE, MARTIN S07RR07060-26 0453
CHALKLEY, NEAL N01CO15740-00
CHALKLEY, NEAL N01CO15760-00
CHALKLEY, NEAL N01CO15763-00
CHALKLEY, NEAL N01CO15774-00
CHALKLEY, NEAL N01CO15779-00
CHALKLEY, ROGER P01DK42502-02
CHALKLEY, ROGER P01DK42502-02 0001
CHALKLEY, ROGER P01DK42502-02 9002
CHALKLEY, ROGER P60DK20593-13 0003
CHALLBERG, M Z01AI00445-08
CHALMERS, THOMAS C K10LM00092-01
CHALMERS, THOMAS C R01DA06323-02
CHALOVICH, JOSEPH M R01AR35216-07
CHALOVICH, JOSEPH M R01AR40540-01A1
CHALUPA, LEO M P51RR00169-30 0108
CHALUPA, LEO M R01EY03991-09
CHALUPA, LEO M R55EY08763-01A1
CHAMBERLAIN, JEFFREY P30HG00209-02 0001
CHAMBERLAIN, JEFFREY S P30HG00209-02 9002
CHAMBERLAIN, JEFFREY S R01AR40864-01
CHAMBERLAIN, PATRICIA R01MH47458-01
CHAMBERLAIN, ROBERT M P01CA52051-01A1 9005
CHAMBERLAIN, STEVEN C R55EY03446-10A1
CHAMBERLIN, ARTHUR R K04NS01227-05
CHAMBERLIN, ARTHUR R R01GM42708-01A2
CHAMBERLIN, ARTHUR R R01NS27600-02
CHAMBERLIN, MICHAEL J R01GM34963-06
CHAMBERLIN, MICHAEL J R37GM12010-28
CHAMBERLIN, RICHARD S07RR07008-26 0064
CHAMBERS JR, JOHN W R24MH48519-01 0002
CHAMBERS JR, JOHN W R24MH48519-01 0003
CHAMBERS, EDWARD L R01HD19126-07
CHAMBERS, HENRY F, III R29AI27406-03
CHAMBERS, HOWARD W S07RR07215-05 0453
CHAMBERS, JAMES P S06GM08194-12 0026
CHAMBERS, JANICE E K04ES00190-03
CHAMBERS, JANICE E R01ES04394-05
CHAMBERS, JANICE E S07RR07215-05
CHAMBERS, JANICE E S07RR07215-05 0454
CHAMBERS, JANICE E S15ES05843-01
CHAMBERS, JOHN W, JR R24MH48519-01
CHAMBERS, SETSUKO K R03HD27446-02
CHAMBERS, THOMAS J K08AI00973-02
CHAMBERS, TIMOTHY J R01AR39623-03
CHAMBLISS, GLENN H R01GM34324-07
CHAMNESS, GARY C P01CA30195-11 0011
CHAMNESS, GARY C P30HD10202-15 9005
CHAMPE, SEWELL P R01GM17020-23
CHAMPION, HOWARD R R01HS06721-01
CHAMPION, PAUL M R01DK35090-08
CHAMPION, PAUL M S07RR07143-20 0618
CHAMPION, VICTORIA L R01NR01843-04
CHAMPLIN, CRAIG A S07RR07091-26 0750
CHAMPLIN, RICHARD E M01RR00865-18 0117
CHAMPLIN, RICHARD E M01RR00865-18 0329
CHAMPLIN, RICHARD E M01RR00865-18 0273
CHAMPOUX, JAMES J R01CA51605-03
CHAN, ALBERT R01AA08771-02
CHAN, ARTHUR W K R01AA07794-02
CHAN, C C Z01EY00271-01
CHAN, C-C Z01EY00222-06
CHAN, C-C Z01EY00241-05
CHAN, C-C Z01EY00264-02
CHAN, CARCY L S03RR03399-07
CHAN, CARCY L S06GM08177-12
CHAN, CLARENCE S R01GM45185-01
CHAN, EDWARD K M01RR00833-17 0198
CHAN, GARY M01RR00064-27 0390
CHAN, GERTRUDE P50AI30601-01 0004
CHAN, HEANG-PING R01CA48129-05
CHAN, J P41RR01243-10 0022
CHAN, JAMES C R01DK31370-08
CHAN, JAMES C. M. M01RR00065-29 0278
CHAN, JAMES C.M. M01RR00065-29 0153
CHAN, JARVIS T S07RR05970-06 0769
CHAN, K-F Z01NS02969-06
CHAN, KELBY P01CA51198-02 0004
CHAN, KENNETH N01CM97620-02
CHAN, KENNETH K P30CA14089-16 9004
CHAN, KENNY H R29DC00561-03
CHAN, LAI-MAN S06GM08047-20S1 0025
CHAN, LAN BO P01CA44704-04A1 0005
CHAN, LAWRENCE C P60HL27341-10 0009
CHAN, LAWRENCE C R01HL45516-01
CHAN, LAWRENCE C R37HL16512-17
CHAN, LEE-NIEN L R01ES04132-03
CHAN, P C Z01ES21159-01
CHAN, PAK P50NS14543-14 0001
CHAN, PAK H P50NS14543-14 9001
CHAN, PAK HOO P50NS14543-14
CHAN, PAK HOO R01NS25372-04
CHAN, PUI-KWONG R01CA42476-06
CHAN, S S07RR07003-26 0316
CHAN, SUNNEY I R37GM22432-17
CHAN, TEH-SHENG R01GM27589-10
CHAN, THOMAS C R01AI29153-03
CHAN, TIMOTHY S07RR05792-15 0942
CHAN, TIMOTHY M R01DK31050-09
CHAN, TIMOTHY M R01ES05504-01
CHAN, WAI-YEE R01HD21793-05
CHAN, WALTER Y R01HD20839-06
CHAN, YUN LAI S07RR05369-30 0591
CHANCE, BRITTON P01HL18708-16 0009
CHANCE, BRITTON P41RR01348-10 0009
CHANCE, BRITTON P41RR01633-10 0009
CHANCE, BRITTON P41RR01633-10 9004
CHANCE, BRITTON P41RR01633-10 9002
CHANCE, BRITTON P41RR02305-08 9004
CHANCE, BRITTON P41RR06030-01A1 0003
CHANCE, BRITTON P50AA07186-06 0007
CHANCE, BRITTON R01HL44125-02
CHANCE, BRITTON R01NS27346-03
CHANCE, BRITTON R24RR05952-02
CHANCE, BRITTON S03RR03365-06
CHANCE, KENNETH S03RR03505-03
CHANCE, MARK R R29HL45892-01A1
CHANCE, PHILIP F K08NS01341-03
CHANDER, AVINASH P01HL19737-15 0012
CHANDER, AVINASH R01HL41644-02
CHANDERBHAN, RONALD S07RR05359-30 0506
CHANDLER, DAVID R01GM37307-06
CHANDLER, JOHN W P30EY01792-14
CHANDLER, JOHN W R01EY07011-06
CHANDLER, LAWRENCE J K21AA00127-02
CHANDLER, MARY H H M01RR02602-07 0048
CHANDLER, SCOTT S07RR07009-26 0936
CHANDLER, SCOTT H R01DE06193-09
CHANDLER, VICKI L R01GM35971-06
CHANDLER, WILLIAM K R01AR37643-24
CHANDRA, SURESH R U10EY03284-12
CHANDRAN, V C R43CA53951-01
CHANDRARATNA, P A N M01RR00043-31 0301
CHANDRASEGARAN, SRINIVASAN R29GM42140-03
CHANDRASEKARAN, K Z01AG00135-08
CHANDRASEKHARAN, RAMACHANDRAN R43AI30876-0[illegible]
CHANEY, EDWARD N01CM97565-03
CHANEY, RICHARD A R44NS26204-03
CHANEY, STEPHEN G R01CA55326-01
CHANEY, WILLIAM G R29CA47980-04
CHANG, A-LIEN L R01GM35132-07
CHANG, ALBERT S R01DA06743-01
CHANG, ALFRED E M01RR00042-31 0572
CHANG, ALFRED E M01RR00042-31 0552
CHANG, ALFRED E M01RR00042-31 0569
CHANG, ALFRED E R01CA51220-02
CHANG, BETTY LEE R01NR01297-06
CHANG, CHI K R01GM36520-06
CHANG, CHIA-CHENG R01CA50430-03
CHANG, CHING-JER R01CA44416-02
CHANG, CHING-JER R01CA55118-01
CHANG, CHING-JER U01CA50743-03
CHANG, E P30DK42086-02 9001
CHANG, ESTHER H P01CA42762-05 0003
CHANG, ESTHER H R01CA45158-05
CHANG, ESTHER H S07RR05983-05 0351
CHANG, EUGENE B R01DK38510-06
CHANG, EUGENE B R01DK40922-03
CHANG, GRACE S07RR05358-30 0471
CHANG, H K R01HL33274-06
CHANG, HOWARD T R01AG05944-05
CHANG, JEFFREY R P51RR00169-30 0109
CHANG, JEFFREY R P51RR00169-30 0110
CHANG, JERJANG R03RR07002-01
CHANG, KWANG-POO R01AI20486-08
CHANG, KWEN-JEN R01DA04240-06
CHANG, LONG-SHENG R29CA54323-01
CHANG, LONG-SHENG S07RR05905-08 0632
CHANG, LUCY M R01CA23365-13
CHANG, MING-DER S07RR05924-07 0999
CHANG, R JEFFREY U10HD26981-02
CHANG, ROBERT S P51RR00169-30 0171
CHANG, SANDRA P R29AI27130-03
CHANG, SHIH-WEN K08HL01966-05
CHANG, SHIH-WEN S07RR05370-30 0627
CHANG, SIMON H P01ES03347-08 0002
CHANG, SIMON H P01ES03347-08 0007
CHANG, SIMON H R01DK31676-07A1
CHANG, SULIE L R01DA05969-03
CHANG, SUSANNAH R01NS26519-03A2
CHANG, SUSANNAH S07RR05415-30 0001
CHANG, TA-MIN R01GM33754-04A2
CHANG, TA-YUAN R01HL36709-06
CHANG, TA-YUAN R01HL40822-04
CHANG, TAE GYU S06GM08092-18 0014
CHANG, TIEN-LAN K08AI00974-02
CHANG, WEI R01CA51329-02
CHANG, YI-HAN R01GM39102-04
CHANG, YUNG-FENG R01NS11822-14
CHANGARIS, DAVID G K08NS01164-04
CHANGIZ, CHEULA S07RR05479-29 0439
CHANH TRAN C U01AI26462-04 0003
CHANH, C P30AI28696-01 9001
CHANNING, M A Z01CL08001-04
CHANTLER, PETER D R01AR32858-06
CHAO, CONRAD R R29HD26600-02
CHAO, E Y M01RR00585-20 0411
CHAO, EDMUND Y R01CA40583-05A1
CHAO, EDMUND Y R37CA23751-13
CHAO, JULIE R01HL29397-09
CHAO, JULIE R01HL44083-02
CHAO, LEE P51RR00166-30 0137
CHAO, LEE R01DE09731-01
CHAO, LIN R01GM41005-03
CHAO, MOSES P01HD23315-05 0002
CHAO, MOSES P01HD23315-05 9001
CHAO, MOSES VICTOR R01NS21072-07
CHAPAR, GEORGE N P60HL38655-04 0010
CHAPATWALA, KIRIT D S06GM08169-13 0003
CHAPIN, JOHN K P01MH44337-03 0001
CHAPIN, JOHN K R01AA06965-06
CHAPIN, JOHN K R01NS26722-03
CHAPIN, R E Z01ES21127-02
CHAPIN, ROBERT E Z01ES21009-10
CHAPKIN, ROBERT S R29DK41693-03
CHAPLIN, DAVID D P50AI15322-14 0014
CHAPMAN, A L S15ES05835-01
CHAPMAN, ALGER B, III K11AI00986-02
CHAPMAN, ANNIE B R19DA06447-03
CHAPMAN, ARLENE S07RR05357-30 0464
CHAPMAN, ARLENE B M01RR00051-30 0754
CHAPMAN, ARLENE B M01RR00051-30 0683
CHAPMAN, ARLENE B M01RR00051-30 0690
CHAPMAN, C RICHARD P01CA38552-05A1
CHAPMAN, HAROLD A R01HL44712-01A1
CHAPMAN, HAROLD A. P50HL19170-15 0020
CHAPMAN, J DONALD R01CA52102-02
CHAPMAN, LOREN J K05MH00743-04
CHAPMAN, LOREN J R01MH44062-04
CHAPMAN, LOREN J R37MH31067-11
CHAPMAN, MARTIN D R29AI24687-04
CHAPMAN, ROBERT M R01MH40703-05
CHAPMAN, ROBIN S R01HD23353-04A1
CHAPMAN, SANDRA B R29AG09486-01A1
CHAPMAN, STANLEY W S07RR05386-30 0577
CHAPMAN, VERNE M R01GM33160-09
CHAPMAN, VERNE M R01HG00170-01
CHAPMAN, VERNE M R01HG00277-15
CHAPNICK, BARRY M R01HL34036-07
CHAPPEL, CYNTHIA M01RR00350-25 0475
CHAPPELL, CYNTHIA L R29AI24490-03
CHAPPELL, DAVID A K08HL02024-05
CHAPPELL, DAVID A P50HL14230-20 0095
CHAPPELL, PHILLIP B M01RR00125-28 0708
CHAPPELL, RICHARD S07RR07109-23 0503
CHAPPELOW, CECIL C P01DE09696-01 0001
CHAR, DEVRON H R01EY07504-04
CHARACHE, SAMUEL M01RR00035-31 0323
CHARACHE, SAMUEL M01RR00035-31 0381
CHARACHE, SAMUEL M01RR00722-19 0158
CHARACHE, SAMUEL M01RR00722-19 0197
CHARACHE, SAMUEL U01HL45692-01A1
CHARD, RONALD L, JR U10CA10382-25
CHAREST, NANCY J R29HD27306-02
CHARETTE, MARC F R43DE09486-01A1
CHARLES, C P41RR05959-02 9003
CHARLESWORTH, BRAIN S07RR05367-30 0566
CHARLSON, MARY P60AR38520-04 9003
CHARLTON, CLIVEL G S06GM08037-20 0043
CHARLTON, VALERIE E R01HD11109-13
CHARNAS, L R Z01HD00414-02
CHARNESS, MICHAEL E R01AA06662-07
CHARNEY, ALAN N P30ES03828-06 0003
CHARNEY, DENNIS S R01MH40140-05
CHARNEY, E Z01DK29006-21
CHARO, ISRAEL F R01HL42662-04
CHARON, NYLES W R01AI29743-02
CHARONIS, ARISTIDIS S R01DK43569-01
CHARRON, MAUREEN J S07RR05397-30 0789
CHASE, CHRISTOPHER H R25AD00059-01
CHASE, H PETER M01RR00069-29 0208
CHASE, HERBERT P50DK41146-04 0003
CHASE, HERBERT S, JR R01DK39154-05
CHASE, JOHN W U01AI25959-05 0005
CHASE, MICHAEL H R01NS09999-16
CHASE, MICHAEL H R01NS23426-05
CHASE, MICHAEL H R37AG04307-09
CHASE, PETER M01RR00069-29 0373
CHASE, PETER M01RR00069-29 0480
CHASE, PETER H M01RR00069-29 0349
CHASE, PETER H M01RR00069-29 0441
CHASE, SHEILA R01MH45161-01
CHASE, T N Z01NS02265-14
CHASIN, LAWRENCE A R01GM22629-17
CHASIN, LAWRENCE A S10RR06427-01
CHASIN, MARK U01CA52857-02 0005
CHASIS, JOEL A R55HL46224-01
CHASNOFF, IRA J R01DA04103-05

CHASNOFF, IRA J R01DA04822-05
CHASNOFF, IRA J R18DA06373-03
CHASSIN, LAURIE A R01DA05227-05
CHASTEEN, DENNIS N S07RR07108-19
CHASTEEN, NORMAN D R01GM20194-19
CHATILA, TALAL A R29AI30550-01
CHATILA, TALAL A U01AI31541-01 0004
CHATKUPT, SANSNEE R29NS29893-01
CHATKUPT, SANSNEE S07RR05393-30 0884
CHATOOR, IRENE K07MH00791-02
CHATTERJEE, BANDANA P01AG06872-05 0004
CHATTERJEE, BANDANA R01AG03527-09A1
CHATTERJEE, KANU M01RR00079-29 0404
CHATTERJEE, MALAYA P01CA57165-01 9003
CHATTERJEE, MALAYA P01CA57165-01 0001
CHATTERJEE, MOLLY S M01RR00997-16 0412
CHATTERJEE, MOLLY S M01RR00997-16 0408
CHATTERJEE, NANDO K R01DK33054-05
CHATTERJEE, SUBROTO B R01DK31722-05
CHATTERS, LINDA M R29AG07179-05
CHATTERTON, ROBERT T P01HD21921-04 9001
CHATTOPADHYAY, S K Z01AI00544-03
CHAU, VINCENT R01GM35803-07
CHAUDHARI, NIRUPA R01GM42652-03
CHAUDHRY, RASUL S07RR07131-22 0124
CHAUDHRY, RASUL S07RR07131-22 0125
CHAUDHURI, GAUTAM M01RR00865-18 0367
CHAUDHURI, GAUTAM R01HL40872-03
CHAUDHURI, GAUTAM R01HL46843-01
CHAUDRY, IRSHAD H R01GM37127-04
CHAUDRY, IRSHAD H R01GM39519-04
CHAUNCEY, JAMES BROWN M01RR00042-31 0603
CHAVEZ, ERNEST L P50DA07074-02 0002
CHAVEZ, ERNEST L R01DA04777-05
CHAVEZ, ERNEST L R01DA06293-02
CHAVEZ, PEDRO I S06GM08224-07 0005
CHAVKIN, CHARLES R01DA04123-04
CHAVKIN, CHARLES R01MH46501-01A1
CHAWLA, ANUPAMA S07RR05924-07 0000
CHAWLA, RAJENDER K R01AA08565-01
CHAZIN, WALTER J R29GM40120-04
CHEAL, EDWARD J R29AR38869-04
CHECHILE, RICHARD A S07RR07179-14 0674
CHEDEKEL, MILES ROBERT R01AR39420-06
CHEDID, ANTONIO R01AA08162-03
CHEEMA, IJAZ R. S06GM08119-18 0008
CHEESEMAN, SARAH H U01AI25831-05
CHEESEMAN, SARAH H U01AI25831-05 0001
CHEEVER, A W Z01AI00347-09
CHEEVER, A W Z01AI00487-05
CHEEVER, MARTIN A R01CA49850-02
CHEEVER, MARTIN A R01CA54561-01
CHEEVER, MARTIN A R37CA30558-11
CHEEVERS, WILLIAM P R01AR27680-11
CHEIRIF, JORGE M01RR00350-25 0360
CHEITLIN, MELVIN D R01HL41495-04
CHELBOWSKI, JAN F S07RR05430-30 0215
CHELBOWSKI, JAN F S07RR05724-20 0184
CHELLA, DAVID N01AI72650-07
CHELLADURAI, MOHANATHASAN R29CA49975-03
CHELMICKA-SCHORR, EWA R01NS18413-08
CHELMICKASCHORR, EVA M01RR00055-30 0576
CHEMTOB, SYLVAIN M01RR00059-30 0706
CHEMTOB, SYLVAN S07RR05372-30 0664
CHEN, ANDY N01CP05619-01
CHEN, BEN D R01CA47424-02
CHEN, BEN D M R01AI23499-06
CHEN, C-N Z01RR10369-01
CHEN, CHANG-HWEI S07RR05649-25 0791
CHEN, CHARLES S K08HL02522-02
CHEN, CHING-LING C R01DK34449-06
CHEN, CHING-SHIH R29GM39236-03
CHEN, CHING-SHIH S07RR07086-15 0324
CHEN, DAVID J R01CA50519-03
CHEN, FU-MING S06GM08092-18 0015
CHEN, GEORGE T P01CA19138-15 0005
CHEN, H C Z01HD00035-19
CHEN, H C Z01HD00146-17
CHEN, IRVIN P30AI28697-01 9005
CHEN, IRVIN P30AI28697-01 9009
CHEN, IRVIN P30AI28697-01 9004
CHEN, IRVIN S P30AI28697-01
CHEN, IRVIN S R01AI29107-03
CHEN, IRVIN S R01CA54551-01
CHEN, IRVIN S R01NS25508-04
CHEN, IRVIN S R37CA38597-07
CHEN, IRWIN S U01AI27221-03 0003
CHEN, JAN-KAN P01DK38639-04 0002
CHEN, JINQ-MAY R29CA55275-01
CHEN, JOHN C S07RR05487-29 0693
CHEN, KUANG Y R01CA49695-02
CHEN, KUEY C S07RR05374-30 0734
CHEN, LAN B P01CA22427-14 0004
CHEN, LAN B R01GM38318-05
CHEN, LAN BO P01CA19589-14A1 0033
CHEN, LAN BO P01HD24926-03 0005
CHEN, LAN BO S07RR05526-29 0072
CHEN, LAN SHU K08NS01411-02
CHEN, MEEI-SHIA K04DE00238-04
CHEN, MEEI-SHIA R01DE08693-03
CHEN, MOON S, JR R01HL44965-02
CHEN, POJEN P60AR40770-01A1 9002
CHEN, POJEN C M01RR00833-17 0194
CHEN, POJEN P R01AI32243-05
CHEN, PRISCILLA B R03DE09930-01
CHEN, PRISCILLA B S07RR05330-30 0014
CHEN, R F Z01HL01407-28
CHEN, SHIUAN P30CA33572-11 9013
CHEN, SHIUAN S07RR05841-12 0242
CHEN, SHIUAN S07RR05841-12 0231
CHEN, THOMAS T S03RR03379-07
CHEN, VIVIEN N01CN45175-11
CHEN, WEN TIEN P30CA51008-02 9003
CHEN, WEN-TIEN R01CA39077-08
CHEN, WEN-TIEN R01HL33711-09
CHEN, WINSTON W P01HD10981-14 0008
CHEN, XIAOHUAI S07RR05959-06 0023
CHEN, Y Z01DK29028-01
CHEN, YANG K S07RR05352-30 0767
CHEN, YIU-FAI R01HL44195-02
CHEN, YUAN T. M01RR00030-30 0265
CHEN, YUAN-TSONG R01DK39078-05
CHEN, YUNG-WU R29AI26113-03
CHENEVERT, THOMAS L M01RR00042-31 0625
CHENEY, CLARISSA M S07RR05389-30 0630
CHENEY, DONALD P S07RR07143-20 0619
CHENEY, ROSE A R18DA06989-02
CHENG, C Y P50HD13541-12 0004
CHENG, CHE PING R29HL45258-01
CHENG, CHI-LIEN R01GM46116-01
CHENG, CHI-LIEN S07RR07035-26 0073
CHENG, HONG P41RR00995-16 0001
CHENG, HONG-MING R01EY04424-09
CHENG, HONG-MING R01EY07620-04
CHENG, KWAN HON R29CA47610-06
CHENG, L Z01AG00267-02
CHENG, MEI-FANG R01MH47010-02
CHENG, MEI-FANG S06GM08223-08 0027
CHENG, MEI-FANG S07RR07059-26 0840
CHENG, S-Y Z01CB08752-11
CHENG, YUNG-CHI R35CA44358-05
CHENG, YUNG-CHI U01AI25697-05 0003
CHEPELINSKY, A B Z01EY00251-04
CHEPELINSKY, A B Z01EY00253-03
CHERAYIL, BOBBY P30DK43351-01 0004
CHERBAS, PETER T R01GM37813-06
CHEREK, DON R R01DA03166-08
CHEREK, DONALD R R01DA05154-02
CHERESH, DAVID A R01CA45726-04
CHERESH, DAVID A R01CA50286-03
CHERINGTON, VAN R29CA44761-03
CHERKSEY, BRUCE D P01AG09480-01 0002
CHERKSEY, BRUCE D R01EY08002-03
CHERLIN, ANDREW J R01HD25936-03
CHERN, YIJUANG E S07RR05591-27 0654
CHERNAUSEK, STEVEN D P50HD20748-06A1 0009
CHERNAUSEK, STEVEN D R29NS25354-05
CHERNIACK, NEIL S M01RR00080-29
CHERNIACK, NEIL S P01HL25830-11A1
CHERNIACK, NEIL S P01HL25830-11A1 0001
CHERNIACK, NEIL S P50HL37117-05 0002
CHERNIACK, NEIL S S07RR05410-30
CHERNIACK, NEIL S S15CA55974-01
CHERNIACK, NEIL S S15MH49293-01
CHERNIACK, REUBEN M P01HL36577-06 9003
CHERNIAK, ROBERT R01AI31769-01
CHERNIAK, ROBERT S07RR07171-08 0151
CHERNIAK, ROBERT S07RR07171-08 0162
CHERNY, RICHARD C K08CA01600-01
CHERPITEL, CHERYL P50AA05595-11 0018
CHERPITEL, CHERYL P50AA05595-11 0023
CHERRICK, HENRY M S07RR05304-30
CHERRINGTON, ALAN D R01DK18243-17
CHERRINGTON, ALAN D R01DK43706-01
CHERRY, ROBERT S S07RR07070-26 0454
CHERVENICK, PAUL A P30CA33572-11
CHESCHEIR, NANCY M01RR00046-31 0501
CHESEBRO, B Z01AI00074-19
CHESEBRO, B Z01AI00468-06
CHESEBRO, J H M01RR00585-20 0403
CHESEBRO, J H M01RR00585-20 0515
CHESEBRO, J H M01RR00585-20 0496
CHESEBRO, J. H. M01RR00585-20 0368
CHESEBRO, J.H. M01RR00585-20 0367
CHESEBRO, JAMES H M01RR00585-20 0352
CHESEBRO, JAMES H M01RR00585-20 0266
CHESEBRO, JAMES H M01RR00585-20 0540
CHESEBRO, JAMES H M01RR00585-20 0536
CHESEBRO, JAMES H M01RR00585-20 0556
CHESKIN, L J Z01DA00091-01
CHESKIN, L J Z01DA00100-01
CHESKIN, LAWRENCE J M01RR02719-06 0009
CHESLA, CATHERINE A S07RR05604-14 0674
CHESLER, MITCH P50NS10164-19 0023
CHESLER, MITCHELL P20NS30309-01 0001
CHESLER, MITCHELL R29NS27011-03
CHESNEY, MARGARET A P50MH42459-06 0010
CHESNEY, MARGARET A R01MH46805-02
CHESNEY, RUSSELL W R01DK37223-06A1
CHESNUT, ROBERT W R01AI25280-05
CHESNUT, ROBERT W R01CA49394-04
CHESNUT, T LLOYD S07RR07189-12 0534
CHESNUT, T LLOYD S07RR07189-12
CHESS, LEONARD P01AI26886-04 0001
CHESS, LEONARD P01AI26886-04
CHESS, LEONARD R01AI14969-14
CHESS, LEONARD R37AI24748-05
CHESSELET, MARIE-FRANCOISE P01GM34781-07 9
CHESSELET, MARIE-FRANCOISE P01MH48125-01 0
CHESSELET, MARIE-FRANCOISE S R01MH44894-03
CHESSELET, MARIE-FRANCOISE S R01NS29230-01
CHESTNUT, DAVID H R29GM40917-03
CHETTY, KOTHAPA N S06GM08094-17 0007
CHEUNG, ANDREW P N01CM17519-00
CHEUNG, ANTHONY W P51RR00169-30 0135
CHEUNG, CECILIA Y R01HD20299-07
CHEUNG, HERBERT C R01AR25193-13
CHEUNG, HERBERT C R01AR31239-06A2
CHEUNG, HERMAN S R01AR38421-04
CHEUNG, HOU T K01AG00390-04
CHEUNG, JOSEPH Y R01HL41582-01A2
CHEUNG, LAURENCE Y R01DK25998-14
CHEUNG, LAURENCE Y R01DK35191-06
CHEUNG, MARIAN P41RR02176-05 0002
CHEUNG, MARIAN C P01HL30086-09 0005
CHEUNG, NAI-KONG V R01CA53624-01A1
CHEUNG, NAI-KONG V P01CA33049-09 0007
CHEUNG, WAI Y R01GM36734-22
CHEVALIER, ROBERT P50DK44756-01 0004
CHEVALIER, ROBERT L R01DK40558-04
CHEVNG, ANTHONY T P51RR00169-30 0134
CHEW, CATHERINE S R01DK31900-11
CHEW, PAUL H M01RR02719-06 0138
CHEW, PAUL H M01RR02719-06 0142
CHEY, WILLIAM Y R01DK25962-11A1
CHI, EMIL Y P50HL30542-08 9001
CHIA, JOHN S07RR05468-29 0399
CHIAIA, NICHOLAS L P01DE07734-06 0005
CHIAIA, NICOLAS L R01DE08971-02
CHIANG, CHIA-MING R43GM43004-01A1
CHIANG, TAO R03DE10003-01
CHIANG, YAWEN L R43CA53938-01
CHIAO, JEN W R01CA53628-01A1
CHIAPPINELLI, VINCENT A R01EY06564-05
CHIAPPINELLI, VINCENT A R01NS17574-10
CHIARELLO, CHRISTINE L R29MH43868-04
CHIBBER, BAKSHY A S07RR07033-26 0052
CHICHESTER, CLINTON S07RR07086-15 0326
CHIEGO, DANIEL J JR S07RR05321-30 0268
CHIEL, HILLEL J P01HL25830-11A1 0012
CHIEN, KENNETH R P50HL17682-17 9008
CHIEN, KENNETH R P50HL17682-17 0043
CHIEN, KENNETH R R01HL45069-01A1
CHIEN, KENNETH R MD PHD R01HL36139-06
CHIEN, SHU P01HL43026-02
CHIEN, SHU P01HL43026-02 0004
CHIEN, SHU R01HL19454-16
CHIEN, SHU R37HL44147-03
CHIEN, YIE W N01HD13128-00
CHIEN, YIE W N01HD92909-03
CHIGBO, FRANCIS S06GM08047-20S1 0031
CHIGNELL, C F Z01ES50115-03
CHIGNELL, COLIN F Z01ES50046-13
CHIKARAISHI, DONA M R01NS22675-07
CHIKARAISHI, DONA M R01NS29679-01
CHIKARMANE, HEMANT S07RR05547-23 0073
CHIKAZAWA, DENNIS P51RR00165-31 9008
CHIKKAPPA, G S07RR05394-30 0719
CHILDERS, DONALD G R01DC00577-03
CHILDERS, KYLE R S07RR05994-03 0294
CHILDERS, NOEL S07RR05300-30 0209
CHILDERS, NOEL S07RR05300-30 0204
CHILDERS, STEVEN R P50DA06634-01A1 0001
CHILDERS, STEVEN R P50DA06634-01A1 9001
CHILDERS, STEVEN R R01DA02904-11
CHILDERS, STEVEN R R01DA06784-01
CHILDS, GEOFFREY J R01GM30333-10
CHILDS, GWEN V R01HD15472-10
CHILIAN, WILLIAM M P50HL17669-17 0036
CHILIAN, WILLIAM M R01HL32788-06
CHILIAN, WILLIAM M S15HL47714-01
CHILKOTI, A P41RR01296-08 0006
CHILTON, BEVERLY S R01HD20129-07
CHILTON, FLOYD HAROLD R01AI26771-04
CHILTON, FLOYD HAROLD R29AI24985-05
CHILUKURI, N R Z01CP05698-01
CHIN, DANIEL J R01AI30880-01A2
CHIN, G J Z01HD01204-01
CHIN, HEMIN R Z01NS02828-01
CHIN, LEE M R01CA50886-03
CHIN, TING FONG N01CM97577-02
CHIN, TING-FONG N01AI95040-02
CHIN, TING-FONG N01CM97572-02
CHIN, WILLIAM W K12DK01401-05S2
CHIN, WILLIAM W P30DK36836-05 9003
CHIN, WILLIAM W R01HD19938-08
CHIN, YEE HON R01AI23246-04
CHIN, YEE HON R01AI26761-01A2
CHINAULT, A CRAIG P30HG00210-01 9002
CHINAULT, ALAN C R01GM37187-04
CHINCHILLI, VERNON M R01DK32431-08
CHING, CLARA Y. S06GM08125-18 0047
CHING, WENDELL S07RR05468-29 0398
CHINKERS, MICHAEL R01HL47063-01
CHINN, J A P41RR01296-08 0004
CHINNADURAI, GOVINDASWAMY R01AI29200-01A1

CHINNADURAI, GOVINDASWAMY R01CA31719-10
CHINNADURAI, GOVINDASWAMY R01CA33616-12
CHINNDURAI, GOVINDASWAMY R01AI29541-02
CHINO, YUZO M R01EY08128-04
CHIODO, LOUIS A R01MH41557-06
CHIODO, LOUISE A S07RR05641-17 0850
CHIORAZZI, NICHOLAS R01AI10811-24A1
CHIORINI, J A Z01HL02227-02
CHIOU, GEORGE C R01EY07511-03
CHIPKIN, STUART R K08DK01902-02
CHIPKIN, STUART R M01RR00533-23 0206
CHIPKIN, STUART R M01RR00533-23 0204
CHIPMAN, STEWART D R01AR40926-02
CHIRALA, SUBRAHMANYAM S R01DK41872-02
CHIRGWIN, JOHN M P01AR39529-02 0002
CHIRGWIN, JOHN M P01CA40035-06 0007
CHIRIBOGA, CLAUDIA K08NS01528-01
CHISARI, FRANCIS V M01RR00833-17 0157
CHISARI, FRANCIS V R01AI20001-08
CHISARI, FRANCIS V R01CA54560-01
CHISARI, FRANCIS V R37CA40489-07
CHISHOLM, REX L R01GM39264-04
CHISOLM, GUY M P01HL29582-09 0001
CHISOLM, GUY M R01HL47852-01
CHISOLM, JULIAN M01RR00052-30 0210
CHITAMBAR, CHRISTOPHER R R01CA41740-07
CHITTUM, HAROLD S07RR05959-06 0026
CHITWOOD, DALE R01DA04433-05
CHIU-TSAO, SOU-TUNG R01EY08131-03
CHIU, ARLENE S07RR05841-12 0236
CHIU, ARLENE S07RR05841-12 0249
CHIU, ARLENE Y R01HD26810-01A1
CHIU, FUNG-CHOW A P01MH47667-02 0002
CHIU, FUNG-CHOW A R01NS23840-05
CHIU, FUNG-CHOW ALEX P01NS23705-04A1 0005
CHIU, ING-MING K04CA01369-02
CHIU, ING-MING R01CA45611-05
CHIU, JEN-FU R01CA25098-14
CHIU, SHING Y R01NS23375-06
CHIU, TED S07RR05700-22 0871
CHIU, WAH P41RR02250-06
CHIU, WAH P41RR02250-06 9001
CHIU, WAH P41RR02250-06 9002
CHIU, WAH P41RR02250-06 9003
CHIU, WAH P41RR02250-06 9004
CHIU, WAH R01GM41064-03
CHIU, WAH R01NS25877-06
CHIVEH, C C Z01MH02296-06
CHLEBOWSKI, JAN F S07RR05430-30 0218
CHLEBOWSKI, JAN F S07RR05430-30 0217
CHLEBOWSKI, ROWAN T M01RR00425-22S3 0451
CHLEBOWSKI, ROWAN T M01RR00425-22S3 0237
CHLEBOWSKI, ROWAN T M01RR00425-22S3 0325
CHLEBOWSKI, ROWAN T M01RR00425-22S3 0419
CHLEBOWSKI, ROWAN T R01DK40611-04
CHO-CHUNG, Y S Z01CB05216-20
CHO-CHUNG, Y S Z01CB08281-09
CHO, ARTHUR K R01DA02411-12
CHO, ARTHUR K R01DA04206-05
CHO, M J S07RR07072-26 0262
CHO, MOON P50DE08240-05 0010
CHO, MOON II S07RR05330-30 0015
CHOBANIAN, ARAM V P50HL47124-01 0005
CHOBANIAN, ARAM V P50HL47124-01
CHOBANIAN, ARAM V S15HL47708-01
CHOCA, JOSE S07RR05369-30 0592
CHOCK, P B Z01HL00202-20
CHOHEN, DONALD J M01RR06022-02 0480
CHOI, AUGUSTINE M K11AG00516-01
CHOI, DENNIS W R01NS26907-04
CHOI, DENNIS W R01NS30337-01
CHOI, EDMUND M R29AI24582-05
CHOI, JOHN U K15DE00302-01A1
CHOI, JUNG H S07RR07024-26 0026
CHOI, JUNG H S07RR07024-26 0041
CHOI, OKSOON Z01HL00993-05
CHOI, R W Z01HL04884-01
CHOI, SUNG C P01NS12587-16 9003
CHOI, THOMAS S07RR05448-30 0306
CHOI, YONG S R01CA42006-06
CHOJKIER, MARIO R01DK38652-05
CHOJKIER, MARIO S06GM47165-01 0021
CHOKHAVATIA, SITA S07RR05773-17 0380
CHOLE, RICHARD A R01DC00263-06
CHOLEWIAK, ROGER W R01DC00076-29
CHOMCZYNSKI, PIOTR R01DK41326-02
CHONG, ANITA S07RR05477-29 0414
CHONG, ANITA S R29CA53805-01A1
CHONG, LAWRENCE P R01HS06798-01
CHONG, PARKSON L S06GM08037-20 0044
CHONMAITREE, TASNEE M01RR00073-29 0322
CHOO, S YOON P01AI29518-02 0002
CHOOI, YEAN W S07RR07031-26 0075
CHOPKIN S07RR05380-30 0892
CHOPP, MICHAEL P01NS23393-06 0002
CHOPP, MICHAEL R01NS29463-01
CHOPRA, B K S06GM08022-20 0005
CHOPRA, BALDEO K S03RR03533-02
CHOPRA, BALDEO K S06GM08022-20
CHOPRA, DHARAM P R01DE09591-02
CHOPRA, DHARAM P R01HL33142-08
CHOPRA, DHARAM P R01HL41979-05
CHOPRA, DHARAM P S15ES05848-01
CHORNEY, MICHAEL S07RR05680-23 0917
CHORNEY, MICHAEL J R01CA53445-01A1
CHORY, JOANNE S07RR05595-27 0668
CHOU, B J N01ES85206-13
CHOU, BILL G N01ES05287-04
CHOU, BILLY N01ES15313-00
CHOU, BILLY N01ES15315-01
CHOU, BILLY N01ES15318-00
CHOU, BILLY N01ES95259-03
CHOU, BILLY J N01ES05291-03
CHOU, BILLY J N01ES75189-11
CHOU, BILLY J N01ES85207-07
CHOU, BILLY J N01ES85210-11
CHOU, BILLY J N01ES85211-16
CHOU, BILLY J N01ES85232-07
CHOU, BILLY J N01ES95239-07
CHOU, BILLY J N01ES95240-07
CHOU, BILLY J N01ES95262-06
CHOU, BILLY J N01ES95281-07
CHOU, BJ N01ES95241-07
CHOU, CHING-CHUNG S03RR03354-09
CHOU, CHUNG-KWANG R01CA56116-01
CHOU, IIH-NAN R01ES03543-05
CHOU, IIH-NAN R01ES04751-03
CHOU, J Y Z01HD00912-12
CHOU, ROBIN S07RR07241-04 0698
CHOU, ROBIN S07RR07241-04 0704
CHOU, T P01CA18856-16 9002
CHOU, TING-CHAO P01CA18856-16 0016
CHOU, WEN-GANG R01CA51064-02
CHOVNICK, ARTHUR R01GM09886-30
CHOW, L P50DE09322-03 0004
CHOW, LAURENCE C R01DE05354-14
CHOW, LAWRENCE C S07RR05689-23 0851
CHOW, LOUISE T R01CA36200-08
CHOW, MARIE R01AI22627-07
CHOW, SIEN-YAO R01NS21255-07
CHOW, SIEN-YAO R01NS21834-04
CHOWDHURY, ANISUZZAM S07RR05676-15 0957
CHOWDHURY, JAYANTA P30DK41296-03 9004
CHRAMBACH, A Z01HD00171-15
CHRISCHILLES, ELIZABETH A P20AG09682-01 0003
CHRISEY, LINDA A N01CM97637-04
CHRIST, GEORGE J S07RR05397-30 0788
CHRISTAKOS, SYLVIA R01NS20270-08
CHRISTAKOS, SYLVIA S R01AR41342-01
CHRISTAKOS, SYLVIA S R01DK38961-05
CHRISTENSEN, A KENT P01DK42718-02 9003
CHRISTENSEN, A KENT P30HD18258-08 9006
CHRISTENSEN, ALAN C R29GM38483-05
CHRISTENSEN, BRUCE M P01AI28781-02
CHRISTENSEN, BRUCE M P01AI28781-02 0005
CHRISTENSEN, BRUCE M R37AI19769-09
CHRISTENSEN, BURGESS N P01NS11255-17 0030
CHRISTENSEN, BURGESS N R01EY01897-14A1
CHRISTENSEN, JAMES R37DK11242-25
CHRISTENSEN, MERRILL J R29DK41647-02
CHRISTENSEN, ROBERT D R01HL44951-01A1
CHRISTENSEN, THOMAS G R01HL45588-01
CHRISTENSON, LISA R43DK43562-01A1
CHRISTERRSON, LARS A P50DE04898-14 0003
CHRISTIAN, CHARLES L P60AR38520-04
CHRISTIAN, FRED A S06GM08025-21 0009
CHRISTIAN, FREDERICK A S03RR03200-09
CHRISTIAN, FREDERICK A S06GM08025-21
CHRISTIAN, JOE M01RR00750-19 0252
CHRISTIAN, JOE C M01RR00750-19 0244
CHRISTIAN, JOE C M01RR00750-19 0198
CHRISTIAN, JOE C M01RR00750-19 0285
CHRISTIAN, JOE C P01AG05793-06 0002
CHRISTIAN, JOE C P50AA07611-04 9003
CHRISTIAN, JOE C R01AG08918-03
CHRISTIANI, DAVID C R01OH02421-02A2
CHRISTIANSEN, JAMES S07RR05372-30 0666
CHRISTIANSEN, SANDRA U01AI32834-01 0006
CHRISTIANSON, DAVID W R29GM45614-01A1
CHRISTIANSON, JON B R01MH45164-02
CHRISTIANSON, SANDRA M01RR00833-17 0130
CHRISTIANSON, THOMAS W R29GM46009-01
CHRISTIE, DOUGLAS J R01HL44917-02
CHRISTIE, NELWYN T. P42ES04895-03 0005
CHRISTMAN, JUDITH K R01CA45028-04
CHRISTMAN, JUDITH K R01CA50909-03
CHRISTMAN, NORMA J R29NR01830-04
CHRISTOFFEL, KATHERINE K R01HD25412-03
CHRONWALL, BIBIE M R01NS28019-02
CHROUSOS, G Z01HD02562-01
CHROUSOS, G P Z01HD00615-11
CHROUSOS, G P Z01HD00618-10
CHROUSOS, GEORGIA A U10EY07676-04
CHU, ALICE S07RR05425-30 0730
CHU, CHUNG K R01AI25899-05
CHU, CHUNG K S07RR07025-26 0988
CHU, CHUNG K U01CA52020-02 0003
CHU, E M Z01CT00218-02
CHU, ERNEST H P01CA26803-11 0003
CHU, GILBERT P01CA34233-09 0023
CHU, GILBERT R01CA44949-05
CHU, JOSEPH P01CA34847-09 0003
CHU, JOSEPH P01CA42792-05 0005
CHU, JOSEPH R01CA50795-02
CHU, JOSEPH S03RR03179-09
CHU, MON-LI H R01AR38912-05
CHU, NATHAN S07RR07234-05 0851
CHU, ROBERT L N01LM03513-02
CHU, SHIH HSI P30CA13943-19 9009
CHU, SHIH-HSI R01CA39427-05
CHU, WILLIAM T R01CA49562-03
CHUA-LIM, CHRISTINA P60HL38639-04 0006
CHUA, NAM-HAI R01GM44640-01A1
CHUANG, D M Z01MH02538-02
CHUANG, D M Z01MH02539-01
CHUANG, DAVID T R01DK37373-04A1
CHUANG, RONALD Y R01DA05901-02
CHUANG, RONALD Y S15DA07787-01
CHUANG, TSU-YI S07RR05435-30 0978
CHUCK, STEVEN L K11AI00951-02
CHUDLER, ERIC H S07RR05486-29 0037
CHUGANI, DIANE P01NS15654-13 0008
CHUGANI, HARRY T P01NS15654-13 0007
CHUI, HELENA P50AG05142-08 9004
CHUI, HELENA C R01AG07624-03
CHUMAKOV, K Z01BE03005-02
CHUN, LINDA L Y R01EY08125-03
CHUNG, ALBERT P30CA47904-04 9004
CHUNG, ALBERT E R01CA21246-13
CHUNG, ALBERT E R01GM25690-13
CHUNG, FRANK N01CN85095-06
CHUNG, FUNG-LUNG R01CA43159-06
CHUNG, FUNG-LUNG R01CA51830-02
CHUNG, JIN M P01NS11255-17 0027
CHUNG, JIN MO R01NS21266-08
CHUNG, KYUNGSOON P01NS11255-17 0018
CHUNG, LEE P30HD28048-01 9002
CHUNG, LELAND W R01CA56307-01
CHUNG, LELAND W R01DK38649-04
CHUNG, S I Z01DE00049-20
CHUNG, SU YUN R01NS26641-03
CHUONG, C JAMES M01RR00350-25 0482
CHUONG, CHENG-MING R01HD24301-04
CHURCH, AUSTIN T R29MH47343-01
CHURCH, FRANK C R01HL32656-06A2
CHURCH, MICHAEL W R01DA05536-04A2
CHURCH, ROBERT L P30EY06360-06 9001
CHURCH, ROBERT L R01EY08616-02
CHURCH, RUSSELL M R01MH44234-04
CHURCH, SUSAN L K08HD00885-03
CHURCH, WILLIAM P01HL46703-01 9001
CHURCH, WILLIAM R R29HL40467-03
CHURCHILL, LYNN R01DA06612-02
CHURCHILL, PAUL C R01HL24880-12
CHURCHILL, PERRY F S07RR07151-13 0522
CHURCHILL, RUSSELL J R44AG08407-02A1
CHURCHWARD, GORDON S07RR05364-30 0524
CHUSED, T M Z01AI00425-07
CHUTER, T A M01RR00645-20 0472
CHYTIL, FRANK P50HL14214-20 0023
CHYTIL, FRANK R01HD09195-16
CIACCIO, LEONARD A S03RR03553-01
CIANCIOTTO, NICHOLAS P R29AI30064-02
CIARANELLO, ROLAND D K05MH00219-12
CIARANELLO, ROLAND D P01MH39437-07
CIARANELLO, ROLAND D P01MH39437-07 9001
CIARANELLO, ROLAND D P01MH39437-07 0002
CIARDELLI, THOMAS L R01AI23398-06
CIARLO, JAMES A R01MH49114-01
CICCARELLI, RICHARD U01AI25721-05 9002
CICCHETTI, DANTE R37MH45027-01A1
CICERO, THEODORE J K05DA00095-09
CICERO, THEODORE J P01DA05951-03
CICERO, THEODORE J P50AA03539-14 9002
CICERO, THEODORE J R01AA07144-05
CICERO, THEODORE J R01DA03833-07
CICERO, THEODORE J S15DA07791-01
CICERONE, CAROL M R01EY08649-03
CIDLOWSKI, JOHN A R01DK32459-10
CIDLOWSKI, JOHN A R01DK32460-09
CIEMNECKI, ANNE N01CN85122-01
CIEPLAK, W Z01AI00552-03
CIEPLAK, W Z01AI00553-03
CIHLAR, RONALD L R01DE07168-07A1
CIMADEVILLA, JOSE M S03RR03485-03
CIMADEVILLA, JOSE M S06GM02721-07
CIMADEVILLA, JOSE M S06GM02721-07 0002
CIMENT, GARY S R01NS23883-06
CIMINO, GEORGE D R43AI30858-01
CIMINO, JAMES N01LM13536-00
CIMINO, WILLIAM G S07RR05569-27 0112
CINCIRIPINI, PAUL M R29DA04520-05
CINER, ELISE R03EY09287-01
CINES, DOUGLAS P01HL40387-04 0005
CINTI, DOMINICK L R01DK21633-14
CINTRON, CHARLES R01EY01199-18
CIOFFE, CHRISTINE J P40RR01180-14 0002
CIRAULO, DOMENIC A R01DA06328-03
CIRINCIONE, ULANA S07RR05311-30 0005
CISAR, J O Z01DE00254-14
CISNEROS, PAULINE S07RR05745-19 0227
CITI, SANDRA S07RR05396-30 0738
CITRI, YOAV R01NS28651-02
CITRON, MARK P41RR01861-07 0001
CIULLA, ANNA P S07RR07016-18 0355
CIVAN, MORTIMER P30DK19525-15 0019

CIVAN, MORTIMER M R01DK40145-04
CIVAN, MORTIMER M R01EY08343-02
CIVELLI, OLIVIER R01MH45614-03
CIVELLI, OLIVIER S07RR07238-04 0472
CIVIL, RICHARD P50AG08012-04 9002
CIVITELLI, ROBERTO S07RR05491-29 0454
CLABOUGH, DEBRA L K11AI00963-02
CLACK, JAMES W R01EY07523-04
CLACK, WILLIAM F R43DC01166-01
CLADARAS, CHRISTOS R29HL43909-02
CLAFLIN, J LATHAM R01AI12533-17
CLAIBORNE, BRENDA J R29AG07141-05
CLAIBORNE, BRENDA J S06GM08194-12 0022
CLAIBORNE, H ALEXANDER, JR R01GM35394-07
CLAMAN, HENRY M01RR00051-30 0761
CLAMAN, HENRY N R01CA47657-26
CLAMON, GERALD M01RR00059-30 0748
CLAMON, GERALD H U10CA47642-04
CLANCEY, ROBERT N01NS12315-00
CLANCY, ROBERT C M01RR00240-27 0319
CLAPHAM, DAVID E R01HL34873-08
CLAPHAM, DAVID E R01HL41303-04
CLAPP, JAMES F. P50HD11089-14 0022
CLAPP, CHARLES H R01GM37289-06
CLAPPER, DAVID L R44DK38271-03
CLAPPER, DAVID L R44GM42233-02
CLAPPER, DAVID L R44HL40280-03
CLAPPER, DAVID L R44HL42731-02
CLAPPER, MARGIE L S07RR05895-09 0616
CLAPPER, ROCK L R29DA07458-01
CLARDY, JON C R01CA24487-13
CLARDY, JON C U01CA50750-03
CLARDY, JON C U01CA50750-03 0001
CLARE-SALZLER, MICHAEL J K08DK01861-04
CLARK-CURTISS, JOSEPHINE E R01AI23470-05
CLARK-PEARSON, DANIEL P01CA47741-02 0002
CLARK, A P50DE09307-03 0002
CLARK, ALICE N01CP05621-06
CLARK, ALICE M N01AI72638-07
CLARK, ALICE M R01AI27094-03
CLARK, ALVIN J R37AI05371-29
CLARK, ANDREW G K04HD00743-05
CLARK, BARBARA M01RR01032-16 0433
CLARK, BARBARA M01RR01032-16 0456
CLARK, BARBARA M01RR01032-16 0455
CLARK, BARBARA M01RR01032-16 0475
CLARK, BARBARA M01RR01032-16 0476
CLARK, BARBARA M01RR01032-16 0477
CLARK, BARBARA M01RR01032-16 0478
CLARK, BARBARA A M01RR01032-16 0473
CLARK, BARBARA A P30AG08812-02 0006
CLARK, CHARLES C R01AR37560-03
CLARK, CHARLES M, JR P60DK20542-14
CLARK, CHRISTOPHER R35AG07922-04 0002
CLARK, CLARENCE W S06GM45199-02
CLARK, CLARENCE W S06GM45199-02 0002
CLARK, D JOSEPH R43CA51553-01A1
CLARK, DAVID C R01MH45501-02
CLARK, DONALD R S07RR05854-11 0917
CLARK, DUNCAN P50AA08746-02 0005
CLARK, EDWARD P01GM42508-03 0001
CLARK, EDWARD P51RR00166-30 9020
CLARK, EDWARD A P01GM42508-03
CLARK, EDWARD A P50DE08229-05 0003
CLARK, EDWARD A R01GM37905-05
CLARK, EDWARD A. P51RR00166-30 0152
CLARK, EDWARD A. P51RR00166-30 0183
CLARK, EDWARD A. P51RR00166-30 0184
CLARK, EDWARD A. P51RR00166-30 0185
CLARK, EDWARD A. P51RR00166-30 0054
CLARK, EDWARD A. P51RR00166-30 0055
CLARK, EDWARD A. P51RR00166-30 0186
CLARK, EDWARD B R01HL42151-04
CLARK, FRANCIS J R01NS24995-02
CLARK, GARY P30CA54174-01 9001
CLARK, GARY D K08NS01433-01A1
CLARK, GARY D S07RR05376-30 0033
CLARK, GARY M P01CA30195-11 0009
CLARK, GLENN T S15DE10073-01
CLARK, GRAEME M N01DC92400-04
CLARK, GRAEME M R01DC01282-07
CLARK, GRAEME M R01NS21027-06S1
CLARK, J M Z01ES65041-05
CLARK, JAMES H R01HD08436-18
CLARK, JEANETTE A P60HL15996-19 0007
CLARK, JEFFREY P30CA13943-19 0011
CLARK, JEFFREY R01CA50558-03
CLARK, JOAN P50HL30542-08 0007
CLARK, JOAN G P01CA18029-16 9008
CLARK, JOHN I R01EY04542-10
CLARK, JOHN T K14HL02482-02
CLARK, JOHN T S06GM08037-20 0045
CLARK, JUSTIN S R43HL44279-01A1
CLARK, JUSTIN S R44HL40752-03
CLARK, KENNETH E P50HD20748-06A1 0011
CLARK, KENNETH E R01HD18370-07
CLARK, KIM P01CA18029-16 9012
CLARK, LARRY C R01CA49764-04
CLARK, LEIGH B R01GM38575-05
CLARK, M Z01MH02459-02
CLARK, M Z01MH02460-03
CLARK, M Z01MH02461-02
CLARK, MARCUS R K08AR01864-02
CLARK, MARGARET R P60HL20985-14 0004
CLARK, MARGARET RUTH P51RR00164-30 0030
CLARK, MARY N01CP15750-00
CLARK, MARY N01CP85605-17
CLARK, NOREEN M R01HL38083-04
CLARK, RICHARD A P01HL36577-06 9001
CLARK, RICHARD A R01AG10143-09
CLARK, RICHARD B R01GM31208-07
CLARK, ROBERT K12DK01295-05S3
CLARK, ROBERT U01CA51908-02 0003
CLARK, ROBERT A P01AI28412-03
CLARK, ROBERT A P01AI28412-03 0001
CLARK, ROBERT A R37AI20866-08
CLARK, STEPHEN H P01HD22610-04 0004
CLARK, STEVEN S R29CA52142-01A1
CLARK, VANESSA R24MH47188-02 0002
CLARK, VERNESSA S06GM45199-02 0003
CLARK, VIRGINIA L R01AI11709-16
CLARK, VIRGINIA L R01DE08512-05
CLARK, W B P50DE08845-04 0003
CLARK, WALLACE H P01CA25874-12 0015
CLARK, WAYNE M K08NS01489-01
CLARK, WILLIAM B P50DE07117-07
CLARK, WILLIAM B R01DE05429-11
CLARK, WILLIAM R P30CA16042-17 9006
CLARK, WILLIAM R R01AI14747-18
CLARK, WILLIAM W R01OH02128-07
CLARKE-STEWART, K ALISON U10HD25456-02
CLARKE, ADELE E S07RR05604-14 0675
CLARKE, BERNARDINE A R01NR01939-03
CLARKE, BRENT P30AG08014-02 9001
CLARKE, CATHERINE F R01GM45952-01
CLARKE, DERRELL P01DK39079-05 0006
CLARKE, DONALD D S03RR03271-08
CLARKE, GREGORY N R03MH48118-01
CLARKE, JOHN R R01HS06740-01
CLARKE, LOUISE B R01GM33783-08
CLARKE, MARGARET R01GM29723-11
CLARKE, MARGARET RUTH P51RR00164-30 0021
CLARKE, MARGARET RUTH P51RR00164-30 9014
CLARKE, MICHAEL F R01CA46657-04
CLARKE, MICHAEL J R01GM26390-11
CLARKE, PAUL B R01DA05970-02
CLARKE, ROBERT P30CA51008-02 9001
CLARKE, ROBERT R55CA51782-01A1
CLARKE, STEPHEN H R01AI29576-02
CLARKE, STEPHEN H R29AI26844-04
CLARKE, STEVEN G R01GM26020-13
CLARKE, WILLIAM C M01RR00847-18 0488
CLARKE, WILLIAM L M01RR00847-18 0347
CLARKE, WILLIAM R P50HL14230-20 9005
CLARKE, WILLIAM R S07RR05432-30 0239
CLARKSON, ALLEN B, JR R01AI17899-04A5
CLARKSON, ALLEN B, JR R01AI27685-03
CLARKSON, BAYARD D P01CA05826-29 0150
CLARKSON, BAYARD D P01CA20194-14 9001
CLARKSON, BAYARD D P01CA20194-14 0024
CLARKSON, BAYARD D P01CA20194-14 9003
CLARKSON, BAYARD D P01CA20194-14
CLARKSON, BRIAN H R01DE09420-01A1
CLARKSON, CRAIG W K04HL02520-02
CLARKSON, CRAIG W R01HL36096-04A1
CLARKSON, JOHN G U10EY06749-04
CLARKSON, JOHN G U10EY06751-04
CLARKSON, MARSHA G R01HD16480-06
CLARKSON, ROBERT B P41RR01811-06A1 9008
CLARKSON, ROBERT B R01GM42208-02
CLARKSON, SARAH B. P60AR20684-14 0024
CLARKSON, THOMAS B G20RR07051-01
CLARKSON, THOMAS B N01HV53029-26
CLARKSON, THOMAS B P01HL45666-01
CLARKSON, THOMAS B P01HL45666-01 0001
CLARKSON, THOMAS B P40RR00919-17
CLARKSON, THOMAS B P50HL14164-20 0046
CLARKSON, THOMAS B R01HL38964-04
CLARKSON, THOMAS W P01ES05197-01A1
CLARKSON, THOMAS W P01ES05197-01A1 0002
CLARKSON, THOMAS W P30ES01247-17
CLARKSON, THOMAS W R01ES04400-05
CLARREN, STERLING K. P51RR00166-30 0080
CLASTER, SUSAN P60HL20985-14 0017
CLASTER, SUSAN N01HB97051-03
CLAUDE, PHILIPPA P51RR00167-31 0029
CLAUDIO, T P01HL38156-05 0004
CLAUDIO, T P01HL38156-05 9003
CLAUDIO, TONI R01NS21714-07
CLAUSEN, CHRIS S07RR05736-19 0148
CLAUSEN, JACK L M01RR00827-17 0369
CLAUSEN, JACK L M01RR00827-17 0370
CLAUSEN, JACK L R13HL48384-01
CLAUSEN, KATHRYN P U01CA44971-04
CLAWSON, GARY S07RR05359-30 0507
CLAWSON, GARY A R01CA40145-04A3
CLAY, J R Z01NS02608-08
CLAYBERGER, CAROL S07RR05353-30 0342
CLAYCAMP, H GREGG R01CA43324-07
CLAYCOMB, WILLIAM C R01HL43124-01A2
CLAYDON, FRANK J R15HL46511-01
CLAYTON, DAVID A R37GM33088-21
CLAYTON, DAVID FORREST R01NS25742-04
CLAYTON, LINDA P30CA49095-04 9003
CLAYTON, LINDA K R01AI31269-01
CLAYTON, LINDA K S07RR05526-29 0094
CLAYTON, PAUL D G08LM04419-06
CLAYTON, RICHARD R P50DA05312-05
CLAYTON, RICHARD R P50DA05312-05 0002
CLEARY, LEONARD S07RR05745-19 0247
CLEARY, MARGOT P R01HD25306-03
CLEARY, MICHAEL S07RR05353-30 0343
CLEARY, MICHAEL L P01CA34233-09 0019
CLEARY, MICHAEL L R01CA42971-06
CLEARY, MICHAEL L R01CA55029-01
CLEARY, P PATRICK R01AI16722-09
CLEARY, P PATRICK R01AI20016-08
CLEARY, PATRICIA A U10EY07460-05
CLEARY, PAUL D. P01NS25701-05 0003
CLEARY, STEPHEN F R01ES05417-01A1
CLEARY, STEPHEN F R01OH02148-07
CLEARY, THOMAS G P01HD13021-12 0009
CLEELAND, CHARLES S R01CA26582-11
CLEELAND, CHARLES S R01NS22677-04A2
CLEGG, DANIEL O M01RR00064-27 0308
CLEGG, DANIEL O M01RR00064-27 0263
CLEGG, DANIEL O N01AR12206-01
CLEGG, DENNIS O R29NS27356-03
CLEGG, MICHAEL T R01GM45144-01
CLEGG, SCOTT P01CA42745-05 0004
CLEGHORN, G DEAN U76PE00443-02
CLELAND, WALTER E, JR R15GM44335-01A1
CLELAND, WILLIAM W R37GM18938-20
CLEM, LESTER W R37AI19530-09
CLEM, T R Z01RR10122-10
CLEM, T R Z01RR10259-05
CLEM, T R Z01RR10341-02
CLEMENCE, SAMUEL P P42ES04913-02 0006
CLEMENDOR, ANTHONY A S03RR03231-10
CLEMENS, MARK G R01DK38201-05
CLEMENS, THOMAS P01DK42792-01A1 0001
CLEMENS, THOMAS P01DK42792-01A1 9001
CLEMENS, THOMAS L R01CA50906-03
CLEMENS,J E P01NS26643-04 0004
CLEMENT, LORAN S07RR05354-30 0377
CLEMENT, LORAN T P50AI15332-14 9002
CLEMENT, LORAN T P50AI15332-14 0015
CLEMENT, LORAN T R01CA42735-06
CLEMENTS, JANE R R29DE08185-06
CLEMENTS, JANICE S07RR05378-30 0990
CLEMENTS, JANICE E P30AI28748-03 9005
CLEMENTS, JANICE E R01NS23039-05
CLEMENTS, JANICE F. P01AI27297-04 0002
CLEMENTS, JOHN A P01HL24075-13 0006
CLEMENTS, JOHN A P01HL24075-13
CLEMENTS, JOHN A P01HL24075-13 9002
CLEMENTS, JOHN A P01HL24075-13 9003
CLEMENTS, JOHN D R01AI28835-02
CLEMENTS, MARY LOU N01AI05061-04
CLEMENTS, MARY LOU N01AI15095-00
CLEMENTS, MARY LOU N01AI62515-12
CLEMENTS, PHILIP J M01RR00865-18 0272
CLEMENTS, PHILIP J M01RR00865-18 0337
CLEMMMONS, DAVID R M01RR00046-31 0248
CLEMMONS, DAVID M01RR00046-31 0512
CLEMMONS, DAVID M01RR00046-31 0528
CLEMMONS, DAVID M01RR00046-31 0529
CLEMMONS, DAVID M01RR00046-31 0530
CLEMMONS, DAVID M01RR00046-31 0526
CLEMMONS, DAVID R P50HL26309-11 0003
CLEMMONS, DAVID R R01AG02331-11
CLEMMONS, DAVID R R01HD28081-01
CLEMONS, GISELA K R01HL22469-13
CLEVELAND, DON W P01NS22849-06 0007
CLEVELAND, DON W R01GM29513-11
CLEVELAND, DON W R01NS27036-03
CLEVELAND, JOHN L R01DK44158-01
CLEVELAND, PATRICK H R01EY08167-03
CLEVELAND, WILLIAM L U01AI25902-05 0003
CLEWELL, DON B R01AI10318-20
CLEWELL, DON B R01GM33956-07
CLICK, ROBERT E R01AI27331-02
CLIFFORD, ANDREW J R01DK43098-02
CLIFFORD, DAVID B M01RR00036-31 0966
CLIFFORD, DAVID B U01AI25903-05 0001
CLIFFORD, PHILIP S R29HL39712-03
CLIFT, ROBERT P01CA18029-16 0034
CLIFT, ROBERT P01CA18029-16 0032
CLIFTON, CHARLES E, JR R01HD18708-11
CLIFTON, G DENNIS M01RR02602-07 0041
CLIFTON, JAMES M01RR00059-30
CLIFTON, JAMES A S07RR05372-30
CLIFTON, JAMES A S15DK44715-01
CLIFTON, KELLY H R37CA13881-19
CLIFTON, RACHEL K K05MH00332-11
CLIFTON, RACHEL K R01HD27714-04A1
CLINCHY, BLYTHE MCV S07RR07186-10 0610
CLINE, HOLLIS S07RR05372-30 0649
CLINE, MARTIN J R01CA50275-03
CLINE, THOMAS W R01GM23468-15
CLINE, VICTOR B S07RR07092-26 0511
CLOGG, CLIFFORD C P30HD28263-01 9001
CLONINGER, C ROBERT P50MH31302-14
CLONINGER, CLAUDE R R01AA07982-04
CLONINGER, CLAUDE R R01AA08028-03
CLONINGER, CLAUDE R U01MH46276-03

CLONINGER, R P01MH47200-02 0009
CLOONAN, PATRICIA S07RR06013-03 0825
CLOPTON, BEN M P01DC00078-27 0039
CLOPTON, BEN M P01DC00274-08 0002
CLORE, G M Z01DK29023-04
CLORE, JOHN M01RR00065-29 0353
CLORE, JOHN M01RR00065-29 0360
CLORE, JOHN N M01RR00065-29 0338
CLORE, JOHN N R29DK43013-01A1
CLOUGH, RICHARD W R29HD24426-05
CLOUSE-STREBEL, K Z01BD03017-02
CLOUSE-STREBEL, K Z01BD03018-02
CLOUSE-STREBEL, K A Z01BD03035-01
CLOUSE-STREBEL, K A Z01BD03036-01
CLOUSE, MELVIN E R01DK43391-01A1
CLOUSE, STEVEN D S07RR07004-16 0046
CLOWES, ALEXANDER P01HL18645-17 0012
CLOWES, ALEXANDER W P50HL42270-02 0005
CLOWES, ALEXANDER W R01HL30946-08
CLOWES, ALEXANDER W. P51RR00166-30 0081
CLOYD, MILES S07RR07205-11 0647
CLOYD, MILES W M01RR00073-29 0294
CLOYD, MILES W R01AI32444-01
CLOYD, MILES W U01AI25722-05
CLOYD, MILES W U01AI25722-05 0003
CLUBB, FRED P40RR00890-16 0010
CLUBB, JEROME M P30AG04590-07
CLUM, GEORGE A R18MH48133-02
CLUSIN, WILLIAM T R01HL32093-08
CLYDE, WALLACE A, JR P50HL19171-15
CLYMAN, RONALD I P50HL27356-10 0003
COAKHAM, HUGH B P50NS20023-08 0017
COALSON, J J P50HL36536-05 9002
COALSON, JACQUELINE P50HL36536-05
COAN, CAROL R R01GM38073-04
COAST, DOUGLAS A S07RR05801-13 0444
COATE, DOUGLAS C R01AA08366-02
COATES, ANTHONY G S07RR07019-26
COATES, ANTHONY M R01AI27236-03
COATES, CAROLIE J R15NR02435-01A1
COATES, PAUL M R13DK44146-01
COATES, PENELOPE W R55HD22806-04A1
COATES, ROBERT M R01GM13956-26
COATES, THOMAS D R01AI23547-06
COATES, THOMAS J P50MH42459-06 0009
COATES, THOMAS J P50MH42459-06
COATES, THOMAS J R01HD24934-03
COATES, THOMAS J R01MH43911-03
COATES, VIVIAN N01LM13545-00
COBB, FREDERICK R M01RR00030-30 0376
COBB, FREDERICK R P50HL17670-17 0028
COBB, FREDERICK R P50HL17670-17 0040
COBB, FREDERICK R R01HL42562-03
COBB, MARGARET A M01RR00102-28 0145
COBB, MELANIE H K04DK01918-03
COBB, MELANIE H R01DK34128-07
COBB, MELANIE H R01GM44140-01A1
COBBETT, PETER S07RR05656-24 0849
COBBETT, PETER J R03MH47524-01
COBBETT, PETER J R29NS28206-02
COBIN, RHODA M01RR00071-28A1 0218
COBLE, MICHAEL J P30HD10003-16 9005
COBURN, RONALD F P01HL19737-15 0009
COBURN, RONALD F P01HL19737-15 0002
COBURN, RONALD F R37HL37498-05
COCA-PRADOS, MIGUEL R01EY04873-08
COCA-PRADOS, MIGUEL R01EY08672-02
COCCARO, EMIL F K02MH00951-01
COCCARO, EMIL F R01MH46948-01
COCHRAN, BRENT H P01CA42063-06 0004
COCHRAN, BRENT H R01GM44821-01
COCHRAN, DAVID S07RR05724-20 0191
COCHRAN, ELIZABETH P30AG10161-01 9003
COCHRAN, ELIZABETH J P01AG09466-01 9002
COCHRAN, GEORGE S07RR05649-25 0799
COCHRAN, GEORGE V R01AR39574-04
COCHRAN, SUSAN D K21MH00878-02
COCHRANE, CHARLES G P01AI17354-10S1 0002
COCHRANE, CHARLES G P01GM37696-05 0002
COCHRANE, CHARLES G P50HL23584-13 0001
COCHRANE, CHARLES G P50HL23584-13 9002
COCHRANE, DAVID E S07RR07179-14 0675
COCKERELL, GARY L R01CA43728-03
COCKERHAM, LORRIS G N01ES95278-07
COCKERHAM, ZENG P01GM45344-01 0001
CODA, BARBARA P01CA38552-05A1 0010
CODERRE, TERENCE P50DE08973-02 0003
CODY, DIANNA D R01AG10374-01
CODY, DIANNA D R29AG08776-02
CODY, ROBERT L M01RR00042-31 0599
CODY, ROBERT L M01RR00042-31 0571
CODY, VIVIAN R01CA34714-08
CODY, VIVIAN R01DK41009-03
COE, CHRIS P51RR00167-31 0041
COE, CHRISTOPHER L R01MH41659-07
COE, FREDRIC L P01DK33949-09
COE, J E Z01AI00262-10
COE, RODNEY M K07AG00302-06
COELHO, ANTHONY M, JR R01HL35136-06
COEN, DONALD M R01AI19838-09
COEN, DONALD M U01AI26077-05
COEN, RONALD W M01RR00827-17 0416
COFFEY, CHARLES E M01RR00030-30 0448
COFFEY, DONALD S P01DK19300-16 0007
COFFEY, DONALD S P01DK19300-16 9001
COFFEY, DONALD S P01DK19300-16
COFFEY, DONALD S R37CA15416-18
COFFEY, DONALD S R37DK22000-20
COFFEY, EDWARD P50MH40159-08 0007
COFFEY, J S07RR05728-20 0193
COFFEY, ROBERT J R01CA46413-04
COFFIN, JOHN M P01CA24530-12 0004
COFFIN, JOHN M P01CA24530-12
COFFIN, JOHN M R35CA44385-05
COFFIN, ROBERT W P51RR00163-32 9007
COFFINO, PHILIP R01CA29048-10
COFFINO, PHILIP R01GM45335-01
COFFMAN, JAY D R01HL26320-11
COFFMAN, JAY D S07RR05487-29
COFFMAN, JAY D S07RR05487-29 0703
COFFMAN, JAY D S15DK44704-01
COFFMAN, THOMAS M P01DK38108-04
COFFMAN, THOMAS M. M01RR00030-30 0447
COGAN, ALEXANDER S07RR05981-05 0803
COGAN, MARTIN G R01DK37423-05
COGAN, MARTIN G R01HL44341-01A1
COGAN, STUART F N43NS12311-00
COGGESHALL, RICHARD E R01NS10161-18
COGGESHALL, RICHARD E. P01NS11255-17 0024
COGGIN, JOSEPH H S03RR03003-11
COGGIN, JOSEPH H, JR R01CA39698-06
COGGIN, JOSEPH H, JR S07RR05774-17
COGGIN, JOSEPH H, JR S15HL47758-01
COGGINS, CECIL M01RR01066-14 0021
COHAN, CHRISTOPHER S R29NS25789-04
COHAN, FREDERICK M R29GM39501-04
COHEN-MANSFIELD, JISKA R01AG10642-01
COHEN-MANSFIELD, JISKA R01AG08675-06
COHEN, ADOLPH I R01EY00258-29
COHEN, ALAN P60HL38632-04 0004
COHEN, ALAN S P60AR20613-14 9001
COHEN, ALFRED M P01CA47997-03 0002
COHEN, ALLAN Y S07RR05932-07
COHEN, ALLEN B R01HL43650-02
COHEN, ALLEN B S07RR05958-06
COHEN, ASHER S07RR07031-26 0076
COHEN, AVIS H R01MH44809-03
COHEN, BENNETT J N01AG72102-05
COHEN, BENNETT J P30AG08808-03 9002
COHEN, BENNETT J P60DK20572-14 9004
COHEN, BERNARD R01EY02296-14
COHEN, BERNARD R01NS00294-37
COHEN, BERNARD R13DC01558-01
COHEN, BERNARD A M01RR00084-29 0247
COHEN, BERTRAM I S07RR05886-08 0300
COHEN, BERTRAM I S07RR05886-08 0299
COHEN, BEVERLY S R13OH02795-01
COHEN, BRIAN J P50DK39249-05 0008
COHEN, BRUCE M P50MH36224-08S2
COHEN, BRUCE M S07RR05484-29
COHEN, CARL I R01MH45780-03
COHEN, CARL M P01HL37462-05 0004
COHEN, CARL M R01HL24382-13
COHEN, CAROLYN R37AR17346-18
COHEN, DAVID R01NS27215-03
COHEN, DAVID S07RR07047-26 0150
COHEN, DAVID H S07RR07028-26
COHEN, DAVID J S07RR05654-24 0148
COHEN, DEBORAH A R29AA07360-04
COHEN, DEBRA P30CA16087-14 9012
COHEN, DONALD A R01AA08237-03
COHEN, DONALD J M01RR06022-02 0734
COHEN, DONALD J P01HD03008-24 0060
COHEN, DONALD M P01AI24010-05 0003
COHEN, EDWARD S07RR05369-30 0590
COHEN, FELISSA L S07RR05776-11 0387
COHEN, FERNAND S P01CA52823-02 0002
COHEN, FRANCES R01MH46788-02
COHEN, FRED E R01GM39900-03
COHEN, FREDRIC S R01GM27367-11
COHEN, GARY H P50DE08239-04 0005
COHEN, GARY H R01AI18289-11
COHEN, GARY N S07RR05400-30 0032
COHEN, GERALD R01NS23017-06
COHEN, GERALD R01NS28937-01A1
COHEN, HARTLEY M01RR00043-31 0351
COHEN, HARVEY J M01RR00030-30 0505
COHEN, HARVEY J P30AG00371-18
COHEN, HARVEY J P30AG09463-01
COHEN, HARVEY J R01AI19656-09
COHEN, HARVEY J R01DK33231-08
COHEN, HARVEY J R13AG09782-01
COHEN, IRA L S07RR05838-12 0270
COHEN, IRA S P01HL28958-09 0002
COHEN, IRA S MD PHD R37HL20558-15
COHEN, IRUN R R01AR32192-09
COHEN, IRWIN K R01GM20298-18
COHEN, ISAAC S07RR05370-30 0624
COHEN, J I Z01AI00621-01
COHEN, JEFFREY A K08NS01284-04
COHEN, JEFFREY A P01NS08075-21 0016
COHEN, JEROME N01HC65064-11
COHEN, JEROME D N01HV18120-03
COHEN, JEROME D U01HL37906-06
COHEN, JOEL S07RR05301-21 0731
COHEN, JOEL M S07RR07044-26
COHEN, JOEL M S15GM47090-01
COHEN, JOEL M S15MH49310-01
COHEN, JONATHAN P01NS29343-01 9003
COHEN, JONATHAN P01NS29343-01
COHEN, JONATHAN B P01NS29343-01 0002
COHEN, JONATHAN B R01NS19522-09
COHEN, JONATHAN D K11MH00673-05
COHEN, JONATHAN D P01MH47566-01 0002
COHEN, JONATHAN D R29MH47073-01A1
COHEN, JORDAN S03RR03261-05
COHEN, JORDAN J S07RR05736-19
COHEN, JORDAN J S15HL47781-01
COHEN, JUDITH B R01DA06393-02
COHEN, L A Z01DK31110-15
COHEN, L A Z01DK31111-21
COHEN, L A Z01DK31112-15
COHEN, L A Z01DK31114-09
COHEN, L A Z01DK31118-02
COHEN, L A Z01DK31119-02
COHEN, L A Z01DK31120-02
COHEN, L A Z01DK31121-01
COHEN, L A Z01DK31122-01
COHEN, LAWRENCE B R01NS08437-23
COHEN, LAWRENCE B R01NS28443-02
COHEN, LAWRENCE K R43AR41573-01
COHEN, LEE S P50MH43878-03 0017
COHEN, LEONARD A R01CA48741-03
COHEN, LESLIE S07RR05365-30 0103
COHEN, LESLIE B R01HD23397-05
COHEN, MAIMON M R13HD27123-02
COHEN, MARC M01RR00071-28A1 0227
COHEN, MARGO P R01DK38308-05
COHEN, MARGO P R43DK44386-01
COHEN, MARGO P R44HL44767-02
COHEN, MARK M01RR00069-29 0425
COHEN, MARK R35AG08992-01 0003
COHEN, MARK R35AG08992-01 0006
COHEN, MARTIN S07RR05366-30 0554
COHEN, MELVIN J P50NS10174-20 0014
COHEN, MICHAEL V R01HL17809-14
COHEN, MITCHELL B K08DK01908-03
COHEN, MITCHELL L K08DK01948-02
COHEN, MORTON I R01HL27300-10
COHEN, MYRON S R01AI23939-03
COHEN, MYRON S U01AI31496-01 0003
COHEN, MYRON S U01AI31496-01 9001
COHEN, NICHOLAS R01HD07901-24
COHEN, PATRICIA R R01MH44791-02
COHEN, PERRIN S S07RR07143-20 0620
COHEN, PHILIP P60AR30701-10 0011
COHEN, PHILIP L R01AR33887-07
COHEN, R Z01MH02594-01
COHEN, R M Z01MH00507-09
COHEN, RICHARD M01RR00088-28 0261
COHEN, RICHARD P50HL47124-01 0006
COHEN, RICHARD A R01HL31607-09
COHEN, RICHARD A R01HL38731-05
COHEN, RICHARD H P01NS07226-19A2 0003
COHEN, RICHARD J R01HL39291-03
COHEN, ROBERT P50HD05077-21 0030
COHEN, ROBERT E R01GM37666-05
COHEN, ROBERT E R29DE08448-04
COHEN, ROBERT L K11HL02329-03
COHEN, ROCHELLE S07RR05317-21 0748
COHEN, ROCHELLE S R01HD24553-04
COHEN, SAMUEL MONROE R01CA32513-08S2
COHEN, SARALE E R01HD27351-01A1
COHEN, SEYMOUR S03RR03115-10
COHEN, SEYMOUR S07RR05496-29
COHEN, SHEILA M01RR00081-29 0135
COHEN, SHELDON A K02MH00721-05
COHEN, SHELDON A R01MH47234-01A2
COHEN, STANLEY P01CA43720-05 9001
COHEN, STANLEY P01CA43720-05
COHEN, STANLEY R01HD00700-28
COHEN, STANLEY R35CA39723-06
COHEN, STANLEY N R01GM26355-11A3
COHEN, STANLEY N R01GM27241-10
COHEN, STANLEY N R01HG00325-03
COHEN, STANLEY N R37AI08619-24
COHEN, STEPHEN S07RR05425-30 0731
COHEN, STEPHEN M R15DE09434-01A1
COHEN, STUART J R01HS06992-01
COHEN, STUART J S07RR05894-09 0607
COHEN, THEODORE R01GM22760-16
COHEN, WILLIAM G12RR03037-07 9004
COHEN, WILLIAM D S06GM08176-12 0004
COHLBERG, JEFFREY S07RR07232-05 0465
COHLBERG, JEFFREY A S06GM08238-05 0004
COHN, BARBARA A R29AG08387-03
COHN, BARBARA A R55AG09250-01A1
COHN, DANIEL H R29AR39837-04
COHN, DAVID N01AI95033-06
COHN, DAVID V R01DK38296-06
COHN, DEIRDRE A S06GM08153-16 0003
COHN, JAY N N01HC55009-09
COHN, JAY N P01HL32427-06
COHN, JAY N P01HL32427-06 0005
COHN, JAY N P01HL32427-06 0007
COHN, JAY N P01HL32427-06 9002

COHN, JONATHAN A R29DK40701-04
COHN, KENNETH M01RR00318-25 0227
COHN, LAWRENCE R24MH47167-02 0001
COHN, MAJOR L S06GM08140-17 0016
COHN, MELVIN R01RR07716-03
COHN, MELVIN R37AI05875-27
COHN, SUSAN M01RR00046-31 0490
COHN, SUSAN M01RR00046-31 0506
COHN, SUSAN L R29CA51061-02
COHN, SUSAN L S07RR05370-30 0620
COHN, THEODORE E R01EY07606-04
COHN, THEODORE E S07RR05832-12 0193
COHN, ZANVIL P01AI24775-05 0001
COHN, ZANVIL A M01RR00102-28 0147
COHN, ZANVIL A P01AI24775-05
COHN, ZANVIL A R37AI07012-26
COHON, JARED L S15MH49291-01
COHRS, RANDALL J R01AI30462-02
COICO, RICHARD G12RR03060-07 0002
COICO, RICHARD S07RR07132-20 0402
COIE, JOHN D K05MH00797-03
COIE, JOHN D R01MH39140-08
COIE, JOHN D R18MH48043-02
COKELET, GILES R P01HL18208-17 0010
COKELY, JEFFREY A S07RR07031-26 0077
COKELY, JEFFREY A S07RR07031-26 0078
COLACCHIO, THOMAS ANTHONY R01CA48088-02
COLAIZZI, JOHN L S07RR05909-08
COLAMONICI, O R Z01CM06723-03
COLANERI, NICHOLAS F R43GM46584-01
COLBERN, DEBORAH L S15AA09260-01
COLBERT, JACK R19DA06410-03
COLBERT, MELISSA R N01LM93509-05
COLBURN, HARRY S R01DC00100-17
COLBURN, KEITH S07RR05352-30 0758
COLBURN, N H Z01CP05382-08
COLBURN, N H Z01CP05383-08
COLBY, ANNE R01MH40814-07
COLBY, BENJAMIN N S07RR07008-26 0066
COLDITZ, GRAHAM P01CA55075-01 0003
COLDITZ, GRAHAM A N01HD92913-03
COLDITZ, GRAHAM A R01AR41383-01
COLE-HARDING, SHIRLE S07RR05938-07 0311
COLE-HARDING, SHIRLE S07RR05938-07 0316
COLE, ANDREW J K08NS01360-03
COLE, BARABARA R M01RR06021-02 1015
COLE, BARBARA R M01RR06021-02 1003
COLE, BARRY C R01AI12103-14A1
COLE, BARRY C R01AR02255-31
COLE, CHARLES N R01CA39259-07
COLE, CHARLES N R01GM33998-07
COLE, DAVID P30ES01896-13 9026
COLE, GARRY T R01AI19149-06
COLE, GERALD P01NS26665-04 0002
COLE, GERALD A P01NS26665-04
COLE, GERALD A P50NS20022-08 0002
COLE, GREGORY J R01NS26087-03
COLE, GREGORY J R29EY07130-06
COLE, GREGORY M R01AG09009-02
COLE, HENRY P P50DA05312-05 0004
COLE, J W Z01RR10342-02
COLE, JONATHAN O R01MH32675-12
COLE, JONATHAN O S07RR05484-29 0036
COLE, KELLY J R01AR40199-02
COLE, LAURENCE A R01CA44131-06
COLE, LAURENCE A R01CA46828-04A1
COLE, MICHAEL P50AI26821-04 0003
COLE, MICHAEL D P01CA41086-06 0003
COLE, MICHAEL D R01CA39192-08
COLE, MICHAEL F R01DE08178-03
COLE, P M Z01MH02448-03
COLE, P M Z01MH02449-03
COLE, ROGER D R01GM20338-24
COLEBUNDERS, ROBERT P01AI26698-03S1 0001
COLECLOUGH, CHRISTOPHER P01AI31596-01 0005
COLELLA, RITA S07RR05375-30 0752
COLEMAN, M P N01CO84340-06
COLEMAN, C NORMAN R01CA42391-06A1
COLEMAN, DAVID P50NS27680-03 0003
COLEMAN, DAVID L S07RR05358-30 0472
COLEMAN, JAMES S07RR05649-25 0787
COLEMAN, JAMES R S07RR07160-16 0594
COLEMAN, JOHN S07RR07085-26 0335
COLEMAN, JOSEPH E R01DK09070-26
COLEMAN, JOSEPH E R01GM21919-17
COLEMAN, JOSEPH E R13GM47169-01
COLEMAN, MARY S R01CA19492-16A2
COLEMAN, MARY S R01CA26391-12
COLEMAN, MARY S S15DK44659-01
COLEMAN, MARY S S15MH49318-01
COLEMAN, MARY SUE S07RR07072-26
COLEMAN, PAUL P30AG08665-02 9003
COLEMAN, PAUL D P01AG03644-07 0007
COLEMAN, PAUL D P30AG08665-02
COLEMAN, PAUL D R01AG01121-12
COLEMAN, PAUL D R35AG09016-02
COLEMAN, PAUL D R35AG09016-02 0001
COLEMAN, PETER S R01GM36619-06
COLEMAN, R EDWARD P50HL17670-17 9001
COLEMAN, R EDWARD P50HL17670-17 0038
COLEMAN, R EDWARD R01CA54092-01
COLEMAN, ROBERT S S07RR07160-16 0595
COLEMAN, ROSALIND A R01HD19068-08
COLEMAN, ROSALIND A R01HD24570-04
COLEMAN, THOMAS G P01HL11678-24 0058
COLEMAN, THOMAS G P01HL11678-24 9001
COLEMAN, THOMAS G P01HL11678-24 0068
COLEMAN, W G Z01DK23330-13
COLENDA, CHRISTOPHER C III K07MH00787-02
COLERIDGE, JOHN C P01HL25847-12 0006
COLERIDGE, JOHN C R01HL42282-03
COLES, CLAIRE D R01AA08105-03
COLES, CLAIRE D R01DA07362-01
COLES, MICHAEL G R01MH41445-06
COLES, MICHAEL G H S07RR07030-26 0383
COLETTI, SHIRLEY D R18DA06369-03
COLGLAZIER, MERLE L G07LM05365-01
COLIGAN, J Z01AI00169-15
COLIGAN, J Z01AI00352-09
COLIGAN, J Z01AI00522-04
COLIGAN, J E Z01AI00172-13
COLIGAN, J E Z01AI00543-04
COLLARD, STEPHEN M S07RR05970-06 0770
COLLARD, STEPHEN M S07RR05970-06 0771
COLLAS, PHILLIPPE R44RR05269-02
COLLER, BARRY S R37HL19278-16
COLLETTI, RICHARD M01RR00109-28 0250
COLLEY, DANIEL G P01AI26505-03
COLLEY, DANIEL G R37AI11289-19
COLLEY, DANIEL G. P01AI26505-03 0001
COLLEY, NANSI J R29EY08768-02
COLLIE, NATHAN P30DK41301-02 0002
COLLIER, ALBERT C M01RR00046-31 0429
COLLIER, ALBERT M P50HL19171-15 0001
COLLIER, ANN C M01RR00037-31 0499
COLLIER, DAVID HARRIS M01RR00051-30 0686
COLLIER, E Z01DK47024-12
COLLIER, GEORGE H R01DK31016-10
COLLIER, ROBERT E S06GM08256-03
COLLIER, ROBERT J R01AI22848-06
COLLIER, ROBERT J R37AI22021-08
COLLIER, TIMOTHY P01NS24032-06 0005
COLLIER, TIMOTHY J R29AG08133-03
COLLIN-OSDOBY, PATRI S07RR05916-08 0305
COLLING, JOYCE C R01NR01554-04A1
COLLINS, ALLAN C K02DA00116-04
COLLINS, ALLAN C R01AA06391-07
COLLINS, ALLAN C R01DA03194-09
COLLINS, CARLEEN R29AI27907-02
COLLINS, CLARE E R01MH41766-05
COLLINS, DELWOOD C P51RR00165-31 0186
COLLINS, DELWOOD C R01DK41879-04
COLLINS, DELWOOD C R01HL43035-03
COLLINS, FRANCIS P30HG00209-02 9005
COLLINS, FRANCIS P30HG00209-02 0002
COLLINS, FRANCIS S M01RR00042-31 0539
COLLINS, FRANCIS S P01DK42718-02
COLLINS, FRANCIS S P30HG00209-02
COLLINS, FRANCIS S R01DK39690-04
COLLINS, FRANCIS S R01HG00244-07
COLLINS, FRANCIS S R01NS23410-06
COLLINS, FRANCIS S R13DK44376-01
COLLINS, FRANCIS S R13DK44904-01
COLLINS, FRANK L R01DA06503-03
COLLINS, FRANK M R01AI27156-03
COLLINS, FRANK M R22AI14065-15
COLLINS, J G R01GM29065-11
COLLINS, J G R01GM44954-01A1
COLLINS, JAMES S07RR07112-24 0425
COLLINS, JAMES M R01CA24158-13
COLLINS, JERRY C P30DK26657-12 9005
COLLINS, JIMMY H S06GM08033-21 0007
COLLINS, JOHN P01HL22619-14 0002
COLLINS, JOHN G K15DE00325-01
COLLINS, JOHN J S07RR07108-19 0407
COLLINS, LINDA M R01DA04111-05
COLLINS, MICHAEL D R29ES04402-05
COLLINS, NANCY H P01CA23766-14 9008
COLLINS, P L Z01AI00323-11
COLLINS, P L Z01AI00368-08
COLLINS, P L Z01AI00372-09
COLLINS, P L Z01AI00498-05
COLLINS, R LORRAINE R01AA07595-03S1
COLLINS, R LORRAINE R01DA05852-02
COLLINS, STEVEN J R01CA55397-01
COLLINS, THOMAS C S07RR07088-24
COLLINS, THOMAS J R01AG08249-01A2
COLLINS, TUCKER P01HL36028-07 0010
COLLINS, TUCKER R01HL35716-07
COLLINS, TUCKER R01HL45462-02
COLLINS, W ANDREW R01MH39267-07
COLLINS, W E P51RR00168-30 0148
COLLINS, WILLIAM E P51RR00165-31 0108
COLLINS, WILLIAM F, JR P50NS10174-20
COLLIVER, JERRY P30AG08014-02 9002
COLLMAN, JAMES P R37GM17880-21
COLLMAN, RONALD G K11HL02358-03
COLLUM, DAVID B R01GM39764-03
COLLYER, CHARLES E S07RR07086-15 0318
COLMAN, DAVID R R01NS20147-08
COLMAN, ROBERT W P50HL45486-01
COLMAN, ROBERT W P50HL45486-01 0001
COLMAN, ROBERTA F R01DK39075-05
COLOMBANI, PAUL M S07RR05378-30 0991
COLOMBE, BETH W P01AI29512-02 9002
COLOMBO, JOHN S07RR07037-26 0385
COLOMBOTOS, JOHN R01HS06359-03
COLON-URBAN, RITA S06GM08180-12 0002
COLON, EDWARD A M01RR00400-23 0273
COLSHER, PATRICIA L P20AG09682-01 0003
COLTEN, HARVEY R P01HD17461-08 0005
COLTEN, HARVEY R R01AI24836-06
COLTEN, HARVEY R R01HL37591-06
COLTEN, HARVEY R R37AI24739-05
COLTMAN, CHARLES P30CA54174-01 9009
COLTMAN, CHARLES A, JR P30CA54174-01
COLTMAN, CHARLES A, JR R01CA56138-01
COLTMAN, CHARLES A, JR R13CA54355-01
COLTMAN, CHARLES A, JR S07RR05956-06
COLTMAN, CHARLES A, JR S15CA55993-01
COLTMAN, CHARLES A, JR U10CA39091-07
COLTMAN, CHARLES A, JR U10CA37429-07
COLTMAN, CHARLES A, JR U10CA32102-11
COLTON, CLARK K R01HL21429-14
COLTON, RAYMOND H R01DC01131-02
COLTRERA, MARC D K08DC00035-03
COLUCCI, WILSON S R01HL42539-03
COLUCCIO, L S07RR05364-30 0525
COLUCCIO, LYNNE M R01GM44211-02
COLUMBO, JOHN P30HD02528-25A1 9015
COLVIN, MICHAEL U01CA52857-02 0004
COLVIN, O MICHAEL P01CA15396-18 0008
COLVIN, O MICHAEL R13CA55100-01
COLVIN, PERRY L, JR K08AG00437-02
COLVIN, ROBERT A R01NS30384-01
COLVIN, ROBERT B P01HL18646-15 9001
COLVIN, ROBERT B R37CA20822-14
COLWELL, CLIFFORD W M01RR00833-17 0205
COLWELL, CLIFFORD W M01RR00833-17 0179
COLWELL, CLIFFORD W M01RR00833-17 0180
COLWELL, CLIFFORD W M01RR00833-17 0182
COLWELL, JOHN A M01RR01070-15 0076
COLWELL, JOHN A U01DK30651-09
COMB, MICHAEL J K02DA00151-02
COMB, MICHAEL J R01DA05706-03
COMBER, ROBERT W S07RR05676-15 0970
COMBES, BURTON M01RR00633-19 0376
COMBES, BURTON M01RR00633-19 0417
COMBES, ROBERT N01ES05298-02
COMEROTA, ANTHONY J M01RR00349-25 0241
COMI, RICHARD J S07RR05392-30 0690
COMINELLI, FABIO R29DK42191-03
COMINGS, DAVID E S07RR05471-29
COMINGS, DAVID E S15AI32176-01
COMINS, DANIEL L R01GM34442-08
COMIS, ROBERT L U10CA27525-13
COMITE, FLORENCE M01RR00125-28 0709
COMITE, FLORENCE M01RR00125-28 0631
COMITE, FLORENCE M01RR06022-02 0597
COMITE, FLORENCE S07RR05358-30 0490
COMMISSARIS, RANDALL S07RR07051-26 0727
COMMISSARIS, RANDALL L R24MH47181-02 0007
COMO, DAVID M R19DA06401-03
COMP, PHILIP C R55HL30443-09
COMPANS, RICHARD W P30CA13148-20 9004
COMPANS, RICHARD W R01CA18611-16A1
COMPANS, RICHARD W R37AI12680-17
COMPANS, RICHARD W U01AI25784-05 0003
COMPANS, RICHARD W U01AI28147-03
COMPANS, RICHARD W. P01AI27290-04 0003
COMPANS, RICHARD W. U01AI28147-03 0001
COMPTON, MARGARET A R03HS06964-01
COMPUTECH, INC N01DA98337-00
COMSTOCK, GEORGE W K06HL21670-28
COMSTOCK, GEORGE W R01CA47503-04
CONARY, JON T P30HD28819-01 9005
CONAWAY, C CLIFFORD U01CA46589-05 0002
CONAWAY, RONALD C R01GM41628-04
CONBOY, JOHN G R01HL45182-02
CONCANNON, PATRICK P01DK41801-02 0004
CONCANNON, PATRICK J P01AI31241-01 0001
CONCANNON, PATRICK J R29DK41347-02
CONDEELIS, JOHN S R01GM25813-13
CONDEELIS, JOHN S R01GM38511-04
CONDEELIS, JOHN S R03CA54932-01
CONDIT, RICHARD C R01AI18094-11
CONDON, KEITH S07RR07175-15 0429
CONDON, ROBERT E M01RR00058-30 0240
CONDON, ROBERT E R01DK40966-02
CONE, E J Z01DA00002-05
CONE, E J Z01DA00023-05
CONE, E J Z01DA00306-04
CONE, E J Z01DA00310-02
CONE, E J Z01DA00327-03
CONE, E J Z01DA00328-02
CONE, RICHARD W R29AI30648-01
CONE, ROGER D R01DK43859-01
CONE, ROGER DAVID R29DK41921-04
CONFER, DENNIS N01HB97075-11
CONGER, JOHN P01DK35098-06A1 0007
CONGER, JOHN D R01DK41294-03
CONGER, RAND D P50MH48165-02
CONGER, RAND D R01DA05347-05
CONGER, RAND D R01MH43270-04
CONKLIN, BRUCE R K11HL02555-01
CONKLIN, JEFFREY L K08DK01750-05

CONKLIN, KATHLEEN F R01GM41571-03
CONKLIN, M H P42ES04940-02 0002
CONLAN, MAUREEN G M01RR02558-07 0070
CONLEE, JOHN W R01DC00498-02
CONLEE, ROBERT K R01DA04382-04A1
CONLEE, ROBERT K S07RR07111-12 0514
CONLEY, FRANCES K U01AI30230-02 9002
CONLEY, MARY N01HD92914-04
CONLEY, MARY E R01AI25129-05
CONLEY, SUSAN B M01RR02558-07 0068
CONN, P JEFFREY S07RR05364-30 0526
CONN, PAUL M R01HD19899-08
CONN, PETER J R29NS28405-02
CONNAGHAN, D G Z01CL10193-02
CONNALLY, PAUL P41RR00592-22 0020
CONNEALLY, MICHAEL P50AG05128-08 9006
CONNEALLY, P MICHAEL N01NS02385-01
CONNEELY, ORLA M R01RR06499-01
CONNEELY, ORLA M R55HD27965-01
CONNELL, JAMES P R01MH44449-03
CONNELL, KAREN P60AR30692-08 0003
CONNELL, KAREN P60AR30692-08 0015
CONNELL, KAREN J R43AR41076-01A1
CONNELLY, CAROLYN M R29HL38384-05
CONNELLY, DONALD P R01HL41086-02
CONNELLY, JULIA E S07RR05431-30 0834
CONNELLY, R R Z01CN00115-07
CONNER, MARY K S07RR05451-30 0358
CONNER, WILLIAM E M01RR00334-25 0263
CONNETT, JOHN E N01HR46002-22
CONNEY, ALLAN H R35CA49756-02
CONNINE, CYNTHIA S07RR07149-18 0412
CONNINE, CYNTHIA M R29DC00522-03
CONNOLLY, GREGORY N01CN15385-00
CONNOLLY, JANET M R01AI27568-03
CONNOLLY, JANET M S07RR05389-30 0631
CONNOLLY, MICHAEL L R01GM40958-03
CONNOR, EDWARD M U01AI25883-05
CONNOR, ELIZABETH A R01NS26879-03
CONNOR, JAMES R R01AG09063-02
CONNOR, JAMES R R01NS22671-05
CONNOR, WILLIAM M01RR00334-25 0287
CONNOR, WILLIAM M01RR00334-25 0300
CONNOR, WILLIAM E M01RR00334-25 0301
CONNOR, WILLIAM E M01RR00334-25 0256
CONNOR, WILLIAM E M01RR00334-25 0257
CONNOR, WILLIAM E M01RR00334-25 0260
CONNOR, WILLIAM E M01RR00334-25 0261
CONNOR, WILLIAM E M01RR00334-25 0262
CONNOR, WILLIAM E M01RR00334-25 0236
CONNOR, WILLIAM E M01RR00334-25 0266
CONNOR, WILLIAM E M01RR00334-25 0253
CONNORS, BARRY W R01NS25983-04
CONNORS, GERARD S07RR05938-07 0323
CONNORS, GERARD J R01AA08076-02
CONNORS, GERARD J U10AA08431-03
CONNORS, KENNETH A S07RR05456-29
CONNUCK, DAVID M K11HL02346-02
CONOVER, CHERYL A R29DK43258-01
CONRAD, DANIEL H R01AI18697-11
CONRAD, GARY W R01EY00952-20
CONRAD, KENDON J U01AA08818-02
CONRAD, MARCEL E R01DK36112-06
CONRAD, MARCEL E R25CA40021-07
CONRAD, MARCEL E U10CA52654-02
CONRAD, P A S07RR05457-29 0001
CONRAD, PATRICIA A P51RR00169-30 0136
CONRAD, ROBERT D P30CA36727-08 9001
CONRAD, STEVEN A S07RR05822-12 0505
CONRADI, EDWARD C M01RR01070-15 0145
CONROY, LORRAINE M K01OH00078-03
CONRY, JOHN P S07RR05322-30 0275
CONS, NAHAN C S07RR05313-30 0246
CONSIGLI, R A S07RR07036-26 0104
CONSIGLI, RICHARD A R01CA07139-28
CONSIGLI, RICHARD A S15EY09469-01
CONSOLI, AGOSTINO M01RR00056-30 0357
CONSOLI, AGOSTINO P41RR00954-15 0024
CONSTANTINI, FRANKLIN D. P30CA13696-19 9022
CONSTANTINO, ROSE E R01NR02108-01A2
CONTE, JOHN E M01RR00079-29 0392
CONTI-TRONCONI, BIANCA P01DA05695-03 0001
CONTI-TRONCONI, BIANCA M R01NS23919-05
CONTI, A Z01BH02013-02
CONTI, CLAUDIO J R01CA42157-06
CONTI, CLAUDIO J R01CA47105-02
CONTI, CLAUDIO J R01CA53123-01
CONTI, CLAUDIO J S07RR05511-29 0500
CONTI, SAMUEL F S03RR03250-09
CONTI, SAMUEL F S07RR07048-26
CONTRADA, RICHARD J R03MH46900-02
CONTRADA, RICHARD J S07RR07058-26 0174
CONTRERAS, PATRICIA C P50MH44188-03 0006
CONTRERAS, ROBERT J R01HL38630-06
CONTRERAS, ROBERT J R01NS11892-17
CONTURE, EDWARD G R01DC00523-01A2
CONVIT, ANTONIO S07RR05651-24 0142
CONVIT, ANTONIO J R29MH45060-01A2
CONVIT, JACINTO P01AI26491-03 0003
CONVIT, JACINTO P01AI26491-03 9001
CONWAL INC N01SP11005-00
CONWAY, KEVIN M R15HD26942-01A1
CONWAY, SONYA S07RR07176-14 0526
CONWAY, TYRRELL S07RR07055-26 0169
CONWAY, WILLIAM A. N01HR46015-16
CONWELL, YEATES K07MH00748-04
CONWELL, YEATES P50MH40381-06 0007
CONWILL, C M01RR00645-20 0449
COOK, BRIAN L M01RR00059-30 0704
COOK, C E N01HD92921-02
COOK, C EDGAR S07RR05791-15
COOK, C EDGAR U01CA46738-05 0004
COOK, CLARENCE EDGAR R01DA06282-03
COOK, DAVID M01RR00334-25 0273
COOK, DAVID M M01RR00334-25 0272
COOK, DAVID M M01RR00334-25 0282
COOK, DAVID M M01RR00334-25 0271
COOK, DAVID M M01RR00334-25 0171
COOK, EDWIN H, JR K07MH00822-02
COOK, EDWIN W S15AG10240-01
COOK, EDWIN W, III R03MH46701-01A1
COOK, GEORGE A R01HL40929-04
COOK, J C Z01HL00267-05
COOK, JAMES S07RR05842-12 0278
COOK, JAMES A R01GM27673-11
COOK, JAMES D R01DK39246-05
COOK, JAMES L R01CA43187-04
COOK, JAMES M R01MH36644-07
COOK, JAMES M R01MH46851-01A1
COOK, JAMES M S07RR07181-13 0533
COOK, JENNIFER M01RR00059-30 0731
COOK, JUDITH A R01MH44913-04
COOK, JULIA L S07RR05518-28 0507
COOK, NATHAN H S06GM08202-11
COOK, PAUL F R01GM36799-08
COOK, PAUL F S15HL47703-01
COOK, PAUL P S07RR05812-12 0481
COOK, RICHARD G R01AI17897-10
COOK, RICHARD G. P30HD24064-04 9006
COOK, ROBERT S07RR07179-14 0676
COOK, ROYER F R01DA05691-03
COOK, SANDRA M01RR02635-07 0251
COOK, SUSAN W S07RR05425-30 0732
COOK, WARREN L S07RR07171-08 0152
COOK, WILLIAM J R01NS30374-01
COOKE, DAVID B S06GM45199-02 0004
COOKE, HELEN J R01DK37237-05
COOKE, HELEN J R01DK37240-07
COOKE, IAN M S07RR07026-26 0996
COOKE, JOHN P K07HL02660-01
COOKE, NANCY E R01GM32035-08
COOKE, NANCY E R01HD25147-03
COOKE, ROGER A R01AR30868-10
COOKE, ROGER A R01HL32145-06
COOKE, WILLIAM J S07RR05771-15
COOLEY, LYNN R01GM43301-02
COOLEY, PHILIP C R01DA05152-04
COOMBE, ROBERT D S03RR03329-04
COOMBE, ROBERT D S07RR07138-20
COOMBS, ROBERT S07RR05756-18 0306
COOMBS, SHERYL P50DC00293-07 0004
COON, H G Z01CB05552-22
COON, MINOR J R01AA06221-08
COON, MINOR J R37DK10339-26
COON, PATRICIA J M01RR02719-06 0115
COON, PATRICIA J M01RR02719-06 0145
COON, PATRICIA J M01RR02719-06 0146
COONEY, NED L P50AA03510-14 0016
COONEY, NED L P50AA03510-14 0019
COONEY, ROBERT V R29ES04302-04
COONEY, TERESA M R29MH46946-02
COONEY, WILLIAM P R01AR17172-16
COONS, TERESA A R43AR41124-01
COOPER, ALLEN D P30DK38707-05 0007
COOPER, ALLEN D P30DK38707-05 0003
COOPER, ALLEN D R01DK36659-05
COOPER, ALLEN D R01DK38318-06
COOPER, ALLEN D S07RR05513-29
COOPER, ALLEN D S15AI32186-01
COOPER, ANNE LIGHTFOOT P30HD05876-21 9002
COOPER, ARTHUR R01DK16739-19A1
COOPER, ARTHUR J L P01AG03853-09 0013
COOPER, ARTHUR J L S07RR05396-30 0732
COOPER, B S07RR05728-20 0194
COOPER, BARRY J S07RR05462-29 0891
COOPER, BARRY J S07RR05462-29 0892
COOPER, BERNARD A U10CA31809-09
COOPER, BRIAN Y R01DE08701-03
COOPER, CARY W P01DK35608-06A1 0008
COOPER, DAN S07RR05551-29 0959
COOPER, DAN M R01HD26939-01A1
COOPER, DENNIS M01RR00125-28 0710
COOPER, DENNIS M01RR00125-28 0711
COOPER, DENNIS L P01CA08341-26 0077
COOPER, DENNIS L P30CA16359-17 0001
COOPER, DERMOT M R01NS28389-03
COOPER, DOUGLAS N W S07RR05755-18 0215
COOPER, EDWIN L S07RR05354-30 0386
COOPER, GARY P P30ES00159-24S1 0018
COOPER, GEOFFREY M R01CA18689-16
COOPER, GEOFFREY M R01HD26594-03
COOPER, GEORGE, IV R01HL37196-05
COOPER, H L Z01CB09006-09
COOPER, H L Z01CB09022-05
COOPER, HERBERT A U10CA42782-04
COOPER, J ALLEN D, JR M01RR00032-31 0321
COOPER, JACK R R01NS27672-01A1S1
COOPER, JAY M01RR00096-30A1 0201
COOPER, JAY S M01RR00096-30A1 0286
COOPER, JOEL D R01HL41281-02
COOPER, JOEL D R01HL41943-04
COOPER, JOHN A R01GM38542-03
COOPER, JONATHAN A R01CA41072-06
COOPER, JONATHAN A R01CA54786-01
COOPER, KEVIN D K08AR01770-05
COOPER, KIM E R29EY09636-01
COOPER, L C Z01HD00340-08
COOPER, L C Z01HD00363-04
COOPER, LOUIS R18DA06371-02
COOPER, M ROBERT R25CA52570-02
COOPER, M ROBERT U10CA03927-34
COOPER, MALCOLM R01NS30400-01
COOPER, MARY CAROLYN S07RR06013-03 0826
COOPER, MAX D M01RR00032-31 0025
COOPER, MAX D M01RR00032-31 0356
COOPER, MAX D P01AI18745-10 0004
COOPER, MAX D P01AI30879-17
COOPER, MAX D P01AI30879-17 0005
COOPER, MAX D P01AI30879-17 9001
COOPER, MAX D P30CA13148-20 9005
COOPER, MAX D P50AI23694-06
COOPER, MAX D. P01AI27290-04 0006
COOPER, MORRIS D R01AI20603-07
COOPER, NEIL R P01AI17354-10S1 0003
COOPER, NEIL R R01AI25016-05
COOPER, NEIL R R01CA52241-02
COOPER, NIGEL G F R01EY02708-14
COOPER, PAUL S G20RR06769-01
COOPER, PRISCILLA K S07RR05918-08 0697
COOPER, PRISCILLA K S07RR05918-08 0698
COOPER, RICHARD A M01RR00058-30
COOPER, RICHARD A S07RR05434-30
COOPER, RICHARD A S15CA56032-01
COOPER, RICHARD A S15DA07800-01
COOPER, RICHARD S R01HL45508-01
COOPER, RICHARD S R01HL47910-01
COOPER, RICHARD S R03HL46120-01
COOPER, ROBERT N01CN05322-01
COOPER, ROBERT A P30CA11198-23 9022
COOPER, ROBERT A, JR P30CA11198-23
COOPER, S L P41RR01296-08 0007
COOPER, SHELDON M R01AR40138-01A2
COOPER, STEPHEN R01GM44022-01A1
COOPER, STEPHEN S07RR05383-30 0552
COOPER, STUART L R01HL24046-12
COOPER, STUART L R01HL47179-01
COOPER, SUZANE C S07RR05417-30 0785
COOPER, TERRANCE G R01GM35642-07
COOPER, THOMAS P50MH30906-14 9007
COOPER, THOMAS S07RR05425-30 0733
COOPER, THOMAS A R29HL45565-01
COOPERMAN, BARRY S R01AG10599-01
COOPERMAN, BARRY S S03RR03144-09
COOPERMAN, BARRY S S07RR07083-26
COOPERMAN, BARRY S S15GM47033-01
COOPERMAN, BARRY S S15MH49277-01
COPE, TIMOTHY S07RR05413-30 0990
COPE, TIMOTHY C R01NS21023-07
COPELAND, DONNA R R01CA33097-09
COPELAND, ROBERT A R55GM44919-01A1
COPENHAGEN, DAVID R R01EY01869-15
COPLAN, JEREMY S07RR05650-25 0095
COPLEY, J BRIAN M01RR00750-19 0271
COPLEY, JOHN B S07RR05371-30 0631
COPLEY, SHELLEY D S07RR07013-26 0952
COPP, RICHARD P R01DK40049-02
COPP, RICHARD P S07RR05399-30 0933
COPPOLA, R Z01MH02360-05
CORAN, ARNOLD G M01RR00042-31 0620
CORAN, ARNOLD G M01RR00042-31 0613
CORASH, LAURENCE M R01HL43220-01A1
CORBETT, ADRIAN M R29NS28377-02
CORBETT, ARNOLD J S07RR07175-15 0431
CORBETT, JAMES R P50HL17669-17 0034
CORBETT, MICHAEL D R01ES03631-07
CORBETT, SCOTT S N44NS22319-00
CORBETT, THOMAS U01CA53001-02 0003
CORBETT, THOMAS H U01CA53001-02 0002
CORBETT, THOMAS H. P01CA46560-03 0001
CORBETT, THOMAS H. P01CA46560-03 0002
CORBIN, JACKIE D R01DK40029-03
CORBIN, JACKIE D R01GM41269-03
CORBIN, JACKIE D R13GM46260-01
CORCES, VICTOR G R01CA40540-07
CORCES, VICTOR G R01GM35463-06
CORCIA, AYUS S07RR05371-30 0632
CORDEIRO-STONE, MARILA P01CA42765-04 0005
CORDEIRO-STONE, MARILA R55CA55065-01
CORDELL, BARBARA R43AG09705-01
CORDELL, BARBARA L R01AG10665-01
CORDELL, GEOFFREY A R01CA20164-15
CORDELL, GEOFFREY A U01CA52956-02
CORDEN, JEFFRY L P01CA16519-17 0009
CORDINGLEY, JOHN S R29AI24531-04
CORDO, PAUL J K04AR01833-02
CORDO, PAUL J R01AR31017-08

CORDON-CARDO, CARLOS R01CA47538-03S1
COREY LAWRENCE U01AI26503-04 0005
COREY, DAVID P R01DC00304-06
COREY, DAVID P R13DC01229-01
COREY, ELIAS J R01GM18519-21
COREY, ELIAS J R37GM34167-17
COREY, LAWRENCE N01AI05065-04
COREY, LAWRENCE P01AI30731-01A1
COREY, LAWRENCE P01AI30731-01A1 0001
COREY, LAWRENCE P30AI27757-04 9002
COREY, LAWRENCE U01AI26503-04
COREY, LAWRENCE U01AI27664-05S3
COREY, LAWRENCE U01AI31448-01 0006
COREY, LINDA P01NS25630-03 0004
COREY, LINDA A R01HD26746-02
COREY, MARY P50DK41980-03 9001
COREY, SETH J K11HL02303-02
CORIN, ROBERT E S07RR07244-03 0485
CORK, LINDA P40RR00130-28 0114
CORK, LINDA C P50AG05146-09 0010
CORK, LINDA C P50NS20471-08 0005
CORK, LINDA C S07RR05378-30 0992
CORKEY, BARBARA E P41RR01395-10 0012
CORKEY, BARBARA E R37DK35914-08
CORKIN, SUZANNE M01RR00088-28 0274
CORKIN, SUZANNE M01RR00088-28 0246
CORKIN, SUZANNE P50AG05134-08 0012
CORKIN, SUZANNE H M01RR00088-28 0036
CORKIN, SUZANNE H R01AG08117-03
CORKIN, SUZANNE H R37AG06605-05
CORKIN, SUZANNE H. M01RR00088-28 0242
CORLESS, JOSEPH M P30EY05722-06A1 9002
CORLESS, JOSEPH M R01EY04922-08
CORLEY, RONALD B R01AI31209-01
CORLEY, RONALD B R01CA36642-11
CORLEY, RONALD B R55AI28539-01A2
CORLISS, DAVID A S07RR05807-13 0452
CORMIER, MILTON J R01GM46300-01
CORN, MORTON P30ES03819-06A1
CORNBLATH, D P01NS26643-04 0001
CORNELIUS, CHARLES E P51RR00169-30 0137
CORNELIUS, CHARLES E P51RR00169-30 0138
CORNELIUS, MARIE D R29AA08284-03
CORNELIUS, WILLIAM L S07RR07195-12 0716
CORNELL, L L S07RR07031-26 0079
CORNELL, RICHARD G N01AI95015-09
CORNELL, RICHARD G P30CA46592-04 9002
CORNELL, RICHARD G P60DK20572-14 9003
CORNETT, LAWRENCE E R01GM30669-08
CORNFORD, EAIN M P01NS25554-01A2S1 0003
CORNFORTH, MICHAEL N R29CA45141-05
CORNHILL, J FREDERICK R10HL45694-01
CORNHILL, J FREDRICK R10HL33760-07
CORNISH, JAMES W K20DA00144-02
CORNMAN, JANE S07RR05758-18 0244
CORNWALL, M CARTER R01EY01157-18
CORNWELL, ANNIE P01CA28103-13 9008
CORNWELL, DAVID G S07RR05409-30
CORNWELL, DAVID G S07RR05409-30 0503
CORNWELL, DAVID G S15CA56000-01
CORNWELL, DAVID G S15MH49302-01
CORNWELL, GIBBONS G, III U10CA04326-33
CORNWELL, MARILYN M R29CA51728-02
CORNWELL, MARILYN M S07RR05435-30 0979
CORNWELL, PAUL R S07RR07082-26 0273
COROMILAS, JAMES M01RR00645-20 0502
CORONADO, ROBERTO R01GM36852-07
CORPRON, RICHARD E R01DE09086-01A1
CORR, PETER B P41RR00954-15 9010
CORR, PETER B P50HL17646-17 0017
CORR, PETER B R01HL28995-09
CORREA, PELAYO P01CA28842-09 0009
CORREA, PELAYO P01CA28842-09 0011
CORREA, PELAYO P01CA28842-09
CORREA, PELAYO P01CA28842-09 0001
CORREA, PELAYO R01CA40095-06
CORREIA, JOHN A P50NS10828-16 9001
CORREIA, JOHN J R01GM41117-03
CORREIA, M ALMIRA P30DK26743-11 9007
CORREIA, MANNING J R01DC01273-01
CORREIA, MANNING J S07RR05427-30 0154
CORREIA, MARIA A R01GM44037-02
CORRELL, J M01RR00645-20 0508
CORRY, PETER M R37CA44550-05
CORSE, SARA J R29MH46363-04
CORSO, GREGORY M S07RR07024-26 0053
CORSO, PAUL J N02HI09503-08
CORSON, DAVID WESLEY R01EY07543-04
CORTES, PEDRO R01DK28081-10
CORTESE, D A M01RR00585-20 0543
CORTESE, D.A. M01RR00585-20 0361
CORTNER, JEAN A M01RR00240-27 0307
CORTNER, JEAN A M01RR00240-27 0214
CORUZZI, GLORIA M R01GM32877-08
CORWIN, JEFFREY T R01DC00200-09
CORWIN, MICHAEL J U01HD29067-01
CORY-SLECHTA, DEBORAH A P30ES01247-17 0079
CORY-SLECHTA, DEBORAH A R01ES05017-02
CORY-SLECHTA, DEBORAH A R55ES05903-01
CORY, SUZANNE R01CA43540-04A1
CORYELL, WILLIAM P50MH43271-05 0001
CORYELL, WILLIAM U01MH25416-18
CORYELL, WILLIAM H M01RR00059-30 0356
CORYELL, WILLIAM H R01MH38777-08
COSCAS, GABRIEL J U10EY06815-03S1
COSCIA, CARMINE J R01DA05412-05
COSCIA, CARMINE J R55GM41421-01A2
COSCIA, CARMINE J S07RR05388-30 0617
COSGROVE, JAMES S07RR05359-30 0508
COSIMI, A BENEDICT P01HL18646-15 0002
COSIMI, A BENEDICT P01HL18646-15 0001
COSIMI, BENEDICT A P01HL18646-15
COSIO, FERNANDO G R01DK43886-01
COSLETT, H BRANCH M01RR00349-25 0230
COSLETT, HARRY B R01AG08870-01A1
COSLETT, HARRY B R29NS26400-04
COSLOY, SHARON D S06GM08168-13 0011
COSS, RONALD A R01CA38656-07
COSTA, L S P42ES04696-05 0003
COSTA, LUCIO G R01AA08154-01A2
COSTA, LUCIO G S07RR05714-21 0130
COSTA, MAX P30ES00260-29 9008
COSTA, MAX P42ES04895-03
COSTA, MAX P42ES04895-03 0004
COSTA, MAX R01ES04715-03
COSTA, P T Z01AG00183-03
COSTA, P T Z01AG00184-03
COSTA, ROBERT H R01GM43241-02
COSTA, T Z01HD01407-02
COSTANTINI, FRANK P60HL28381-09 0012
COSTANTINI, F P01HL21016-15 0020
COSTANTINI, FRANKLIN D R01HD17704-09
COSTANZA, MARY E R25CA36762-07
COSTANZA, MICHAEL C P01CA46456-02 9001
COSTANZA, MICHAEL C P30CA22435-11 9012
COSTANZI, JOHN J N01CO15705-00
COSTELLO, ELIZABETH R01MH45244-03
COSTELLO, ELIZABETH J R01MH48085-01A1
COSTELLO, LESLIE C R01DK28015-09
COSTOFF, ALLEN S07RR05365-30 0077
COTANCHE, DOUGLAS A R29DC00412-04
COTE, LUCIEN P50AG08702-03 0007
COTE, RICHARD H R01EY05798-04A2
COTHERN, R P41RR02594-06 0004
COTHERN, R P41RR02594-06 0005
COTMAN, CARL P01AG00538-15 0017
COTMAN, CARL P01HD24236-03 0003
COTMAN, CARL P50MH44188-03 0002
COTMAN, CARL W P01AG00538-15
COTMAN, CARL W R01NS27320-03
COTMAN, CARL W R35AG07918-03
COTMAN, CARL W R35AG07918-03 0001
COTRAN, RAMZI S P01HL36028-07 9001
COTRAN, RAMZI S P01HL36028-07 0003
COTT, GARY S07RR05842-12 0279
COTTAM, GENE L R01DA07062-01A1
COTTEIRO, RICHARD A M01RR00054-30 0405
COTTER, ROBERT J R01GM33967-07
COTTINGTON, ERIC M G20RR06928-01
COTTLER, LINDA M R01DA05585-04
COTTLER, LINDA M R01DA05619-03
COTTLER, LINDA M R18DA06163-03
COTTON, ROBERT B P50HL14214-20 0047
COTTON, ROBERT B P50HL14214-20 9001
COTTON, THERESE M R01GM35108-09
COTTRELL, DARYL M01RR00034-31 0401
COTTRELL, DARYL M01RR00034-31 0402
COUCH, DAVID B R29DA07050-01A1
COUCH, ROBERT N01AI15103-00
COUCH, ROBT B N01AI72629-11
COUCHMAN, JOHN R P60AR20614-14 0009
COUCHMAN, JOHN R R01AR36457-06A1
COUCHMAN, JOHN R R01AR39741-03
COUCOUVANIS, DIMITRI N R01GM33080-09
COUGHLIN, JOHN M01RR01066-14 0087
COUGHLIN, RICHARD T R43AI30837-01
COUGHLIN, SHAUN R01HL43322-03
COUGHLIN, SHAUN R01HL44907-01A1
COUGHLIN, STEVEN S R29HL44904-02
COULL, BRUCE M01RR00334-25 0280
COULL, BRUCE M P01NS17493-08
COULL, BRUCE M P01NS17493-08 0009
COULOMBE, ROGER A S07RR07093-24 0774
COULSTON, ANN M01RR00070-29 0153
COULTAS, DAVID B K07HL02474-02
COULTAS, DAVID B R29HL40587-04
COULTER, DAVID L R01NS25801-04
COULTER, DOUGLAS E R01GM42621-01A2
COULTER, JOE D R01NS23783-06
COULTER, STEPHEN L N01HD13120-00
COULTON, CLAUDIA P60AR20618-13 0019
COUMAS, JAMES M S07RR05712-20 0094
COUNSELL, RAYMOND E R01CA08349-24A2
COURCHESNE, ERIC R01MH36840-08
COURCHESNE, ERIC R01NS19855-08
COURCHESNE, WILLIAM E U01AI31696-01 0003
COUREY, ALBERT J R01GM44522-02
COURTNEY, KENNETH R S07RR05513-29 0059
COURTNEY, RICHARD J R01AI29026-02
COURTNEY, RICHARD J R01CA42460-08
COURTS, F S07RR05728-20 0195
COURVAL, J M01RR00645-20 0471
COUSER, WILLIAM G R37DK34198-07
COUSIN, CAROLYN E S06GM08005-20 0005
COUSINS, JENNIFER H R01HD23991-04
COUSINS, JOSEPH P S07RR05394-30 0714
COUSINS, ROBERT J R01DK31127-10
COUSINS, SCOTT W K11EY00308-03
COUSINS, SCOTT W S07RR05363-30 0826
COUTTS, RICHARD D R01AR28467-10
COUTURE, JEAN U10CA41357-05
COUTURE, L Z01HL02221-91
COVAULT, JONATHAN M R29NS25264-05
COVELL, JAMES W P50HL17682-17 0039
COVELL, JAMES W P50HL17682-17 9001
COVELL, JAMES W R01HL32583-08
COVELL, JAMES W R01HL43617-03
COVERT, DAVID S S07RR05714-21 0131
COVEY, DOUGLAS F P50NS14834-13 0009
COVEY, DOUGLAS F R01HD19746-04
COVEY, ELLEN R01DC00607-02
COVI, L Z01DA00081-03
COVI, L Z01DA00098-02
COVI, L Z01DA00508-01
COWAN, K Z01CB09350-01
COWAN, K H Z01CM06516-10
COWAN, MARIE J R01NR01970-01A3
COWAN, MORTON P01HD24640-03 9004
COWAN, MORTON J M01RR01271-10 0065
COWAN, MORTON J P01AI29512-02 9001
COWAN, MORTON J P01AI29512-02
COWAN, MORTON J R01DA04331-05
COWAN, NELSON R01HD21338-06
COWAN, NELSON S07RR07053-26 0145
COWAN, NICHOLAS J R01AG09989-09
COWAN, NICHOLAS J R01NS25882-04
COWAN, PHILIP A R01MH31109-11
COWANS, E P Z01NS02831-01
COWARD, JAMES K U01CA37606-08 0002
COWARD, RAYMOND T P20AG09649-01
COWART, BEVERLY J P50DC00214-06 9001
COWBURN, DAVID A R01DK20357-11
COWDERY, JOHN S R01DK42418-02
COWELL, JULIA M R15NR02518-01A1
COWELL, JULIA M S07RR05776-11 0388
COWEN, MORTON J P01AI29512-02 0001
COWING, CAROL O R01AI23659-04A2
COWING, CAROL O R01AI24585-05
COWLES, KATHY S07RR06031-02 0373
COWLES, VERNE E S07RR05434-30 0821
COWLEY, ALLEN W P01HL29587-09 9002
COWLEY, ALLEN W P01HL29587-09 0001
COWLEY, ALLEN W P01HL29587-09 9004
COWLEY, ALLEN W, JR P01HL29587-09
COWLEY, BENJAMIN D S07RR05373-30 0713
COWLEY, DEBORAH S R29AA08161-03
COWLEY, MARIANNE S07RR05431-30 0856
COWLEY, MICHAEL J M01RR00065-29 0286
COWLEY, MICHAEL J U01HL38515-05
COWSERT, LEX M R43CA52391-01A2
COX, BRIAN M R01DA04953-04
COX, BRIAN M R37DA03102-10
COX, BRIAN M S15DA07786-01
COX, CHRISTOPHER P01ES05197-01A1 9001
COX, CHRISTOPHER P30ES01247-17 9007
COX, DANIEL J R01DK28288-10
COX, DAVID R P50HG00206-01S1 0002
COX, DAVID R R01HD24610-04
COX, DONALD S S07RR05778-16 0413
COX, EDWARD C R21HG00482-01
COX, EDWIN B P01CA42745-05 9003
COX, G W Z01CM09359-01
COX, GARY B U01AA08798-02
COX, JAMES A R15GM46137-01
COX, JAMES D U10CA21661-16
COX, JAMES D. P30CA13696-19 9025
COX, JAMES L R01HL32257-09
COX, JAMES L R01HL32257-09 0003
COX, JAMES L R01HL32257-09 0004
COX, JAMES L R01HL32257-09 0005
COX, KENNETH S07RR05566-28 0583
COX, L CLARKE S07RR05487-29 0710
COX, MARTHA J R01MH44763-03
COX, MARTHA J U10HD25445-03
COX, MICHAEL M R01GM32335-09
COX, MICHAEL M R01GM37835-05
COX, REBECCA A R01AI21431-08
COX, REBECCA A R01AI23555-05
COX, ROBERT H S07RR05874-10
COX, ROBERT H S15HL47691-01
COX, RODY P R01DK26758-13
COX, THOMAS S07RR07118-22 0374
COY, DAVID H R01DK30167-10
COY, DAVID H R55CA45153-04
COYLE, JOSEPH T P01MH46529-02 0004
COYLE, JOSEPH T P01MH46529-02
COYLE, JOSEPH T P01MH46529-02 9001
COYLE, JOSEPH T P01NS16375-11 0009
COYLE, JOSEPH T R01NS13584-15
COYLE, JOSEPH T R01NS18414-10
COYLE, PATRICIA K R01AR40470-02
COYLE, PATRICIA K S07RR05736-19 0209
COYLE, PETER P01HL18575-16A1 0008
COYNE, JAMES C R01MH43796-02
COYNE, JERRY A R01GM38462-05
COZINE, K M01RR00645-20 0445

COZZARELLI, NICHOLAS P30ES01896-13 9027
COZZARELLI, NICHOLAS R R01GM31655-09
COZZARELLI, NICHOLAS R R37GM31657-09
CRABB, DAVID W K02AA00081-08
CRABB, DAVID W M01RR00750-19 0270
CRABB, DAVID W P50AA07611-04 9002
CRABB, DAVID W R01AA06434-07
CRABB, JOHN W P01CA37589-08 9001
CRABB, JOHN W R01EY06603-06
CRABB, JOHN W S07RR05863-11 0565
CRABBE, JOHN C P01AA08621-02
CRABBE, JOHN C R01AA05828-08
CRABBE, JOHN C R01DA05228-03
CRABBE, JOHN C JR R01AA06498-06
CRABTREE, GERALD R R01CA39612-07
CRABTREE, GERALD R R01HL33942-07
CRABTREE, GERALD W P30CA13943-19 9008
CRABTREE, ROBERT H R01GM40974-03
CRAFT, CHERYL M R29NS28126-02
CRAFT, CHERYL M S07RR07175-15 0430
CRAFT, JOSEPH E R01AR40072-02
CRAFT, JOSEPH E R29AI26853-04
CRAFT, SUZANNE M01RR00036-31 1033
CRAFT, SUZANNE P50AG05681-08 0020
CRAGO, PATRICK E N01NS92356-03
CRAIG, ARTHUR D R01DA07402-01
CRAIG, ARTHUR D R01NS25616-04A1
CRAIG, ARTHUR D S07RR05872-08 0980
CRAIG, CAROL P01CA28103-13 9005
CRAIG, CHIE H K08DC00003-02
CRAIG, ELIZABETH A R01GM27870-12
CRAIG, ELIZABETH A R01GM31107-10
CRAIG, GEORGE B, JR R37AI02753-32
CRAIG, JAMES C R01DC00095-21
CRAIG, NANCY L R01AI21533-08
CRAIG, R G P50DE09296-03 0003
CRAIG, ROBERT G P50DE09296-03
CRAIG, ROBERT G S10RR06434-01
CRAIG, ROBERT M M01RR00048-30 0143
CRAIG, ROBERT M M01RR00048-30 0167
CRAIG, ROGER W R01AR34711-07
CRAIG, RONALD G P50DE08239-04 0011
CRAIG, RONALD G S07RR07062-26 0212
CRAIG, RUTH W R29CA54385-01
CRAIG, SUSAN W R01GM41605-15
CRAIGHEAD, JOHN E R01CA36993-07
CRAIGHEAD, JOHN E R13ES05632-01
CRAIGIE, R Z01DK36108-04
CRAIK, CHARLES S P01GM39552-05 0003
CRAIK, CHARLES S P41RR01614-10 0003
CRAIN, BARBARA P50AG05128-08 9003
CRAIN, BARBARA P50AG05128-08 0011
CRAIN, BARBARA J R01AG09216-01
CRAIN, ELLEN U01AI30777-01
CRAIN, JOHN P S07RR05401-30 0859
CRAIN, MARILYN J M01RR00032-31 0385
CRAIN, STANLEY M R01DA02031-12
CRAINE, BRIAN L R43AG09910-01
CRAINE, BRIAN L R43AR41123-01
CRAINE, ERIC R R43AR40799-01
CRAM, DONALD J R37GM12640-27
CRAM, L SCOTT P41RR01315-10
CRAM, L SCOTT P41RR01315-10 0021
CRAM, L SCOTT S15DK44656-01
CRAM, MICHAEL S07RR05372-30 0687
CRAMER, CAROLE L R29GM39549-04
CRAMER, DANIEL W R01HD23661-03
CRAMER, DONALD S07RR05468-29 0395
CRAMER, EVA B R01AI16480-09
CRAMER, RICHAARD D P01CA51993-01A1 0002
CRAMER, STEPHEN P R01GM44380-02
CRAMER, WILLIAM A R01GM18457-20
CRAMER, WILLIAM A R01GM38323-04A1
CRAMER, WILLIAM A S07RR07032-26 0049
CRANDALL, EDWARD D R01HL38621-06A1
CRANDALL, EDWARD D R37HL38578-07
CRANDALL, EDWARD D S07RR05396-30 0744
CRANE, FREDERICK L K06GM21839-28
CRANE, HEW S07RR05522-29 0065
CRANE, JOHN K S07RR05745-19 0249
CRANE, LAWRENCE N01AI95028-06
CRANE, LORI P01CA50084-03 0006
CRANE, MARTIN M S07RR05828-08 0534
CRANEFIELD, PAUL F R37HL14899-19
CRANFORD, CHARLES O U76PE00221-06
CRANIN, A N P41RR01296-08 0008
CRANMER, JOAN M R13ES05708-01
CRANS, DEBBIE S07RR07127-23 0479
CRANS, DEBBIE C R29GM40525-03
CRANS, DEBBIE C S07RR07127-23 0496
CRAPO, JAMES D P01HL31992-08
CRAPO, JAMES D P01HL31992-08 0002
CRAPO, JAMES D R01HL42609-03
CRAVEN, BRYAN M R01GM39513-04
CRAVEN, BRYAN M R01HL20350-14
CRAVEN, DONALD M01RR00533-23 0205
CRAVEN, DONALD E R01DA04750-05
CRAVISO, GALE L R01NS27550-03
CRAWFORD-BROWN, DOUG S07RR05450-30 0348
CRAWFORD-GREEN, CYNTHIA S06GM08244-05 0021
CRAWFORD, DANA R S07RR05712-20 0082
CRAWFORD, DANA R S07RR05712-20 0049
CRAWFORD, DOUGLAS S07RR05367-30 0567
CRAWFORD, EUGENE C S07RR07114-23
CRAWFORD, HELEN J S07RR07095-24 0377
CRAWFORD, JAMES M R29DK39512-03
CRAWFORD, MORRIS L R01NS19342-07
CRAWFORD, MORRIS L S15EY09476-01
CRAWFORD, NIGEL M R29GM40672-04
CRAWFORD, SUSAN Y S07RR05389-30 0632
CRAWFORD, THOMAS O K08NS01412-02
CRAWFORD, TIM B S07RR05465-29 0388
CRAWFORD, TIMOTHY B R01HL46651-01
CRAWFORD, WILLIAM H S07RR05303-30
CRAWLEY, ELIZABETH M01RR00997-16 0384
CREAGER, MARK A K04HL01768-05
CREAGER, MARK A K07HL02663-01
CREAGER, STEPHEN S07RR07031-26 0080
CREASEY, W N01CO84348-11
CREAVEN, PATRICK J P01CA21071-14 9002
CREAVEN, PATRICK J P01CA21071-14
CREAZZO, TONY L P01HL36059-06 0005
CREAZZO, TONY L R29HL39039-05
CREEKMORE, S P Z01CM09331-03
CREEKMORE, S P Z01CM09353-02
CREESE, IAN P50MH44211-03 0002
CREESE, IAN N K05MH00316-12
CREIGHTON-ZOLLAR, AN S07RR07204-11 0451
CREMO, CHRISTINE R R29AR40917-02
CRESPI, CHARLES N43ES11002-00
CRESPI, CHARLES N44ES12001-00
CRESSWELL, PETER R01AI15775-13
CRESSWELL, PETER R01AI23081-07
CREUTZ, CARL E P01CA40042-07 0003
CREUTZ, CARL E R01DK33151-08
CREVELING, C R Z01DK31101-22
CREWS, DAVID P K05MH00135-14
CREWS, DAVID P R01HD24976-03
CREWS, DAVID P R37MH41770-06
CREWS, DOUGLAS E S03RR03263-02
CREWS, FULTON J P01AG10485-01 0001
CREWS, FULTON T P01AG10485-01 9001
CREWS, FULTON T R01AA06069-08
CREWS, JAMES C S07RR05408-30 0922
CREWS, PHILLIP R01CA47135-03
CREWS, PHILLIP S06GM08132-17 0017
CREWS, PHILLIP U01CA52955-02 9001
CREWS, PHILLIP U01CA52955-02
CREWS, PHILLIP U01CA52955-02 0003
CREWS, STEPHEN S07RR07009-26 0931
CREWS, STEPHEN T R01HD25251-03
CRILL, WAYNE E R01NS16792-10
CRILL, WAYNE E. P01NS20482-08 0012
CRIM, MARILYN C S07RR07179-14 0688
CRIMMINS, EILEEN M R01AG05107-08
CRIMMINS, MICHAEL T R01GM38904-07A1
CRIPPEN, GORDON M R01DA06746-02
CRIPPEN, GORDON M R01GM37123-07
CRIQUI, MICHAEL H M01RR00827-17 0256
CRIQUI, MICHAEL H M01RR00827-17 0346
CRIQUI, MICHAEL H R01HL42973-02
CRISPE, IAN N R01AI30561-01
CRISSINGER, KAREN D P01DK43785-01 0002
CRISSINGER, KAREN D R29HD27528-02
CRISSINGER, KAREN D S07RR05822-12 0506
CRISSMAN, HARRY R24RR06758-01
CRISSMAN, ROBERT S S07RR05700-22 0872
CRIST, DOUGLAS M M01RR00997-16 0217
CRIST, KEITH A S07RR05700-22 0864
CRIST, WILLIAM M P01CA23099-13
CRISTOFALO, VINCENT J K07AG00532-01
CRISTOFALO, VINCENT J P01AG00378-20 9001
CRISTOFALO, VINCENT J P01AG00378-20 0003
CRISTOFALO, VINCENT J P01AG00378-20
CRISTOFALO, VINCENT J R13AG09985-01
CRITCHFIELD, THOMAS M01RR02719-06 0129
CRITCHLOW, B VAUGHN P51RR00163-32 0010
CRITCHLOW, B VAUGHN R01DK32442-09
CRITCHLOW, B VAUGHN S07RR05694-22
CRITCHLOW, B VAUGHN S15HD28761-01
CRITS-CHRISTOPH, PAUL K02MH00756-03
CRITS-CHRISTOPH, PAUL P50MH45178-02 0009
CRITS-CHRISTOPH, PAUL P50MH45178-02
CRITS-CHRISTOPH, PAUL P50MH45178-02 9002
CRITS-CHRISTOPH, PAUL P50MH45178-02 0002
CRITS-CHRISTOPH, PAUL U18DA07090-02
CRITSER, JOHN K R01HD25949-02
CRNIC, LINDA P30HD04024-23 9005
CRNIC, LINDA S K02MH00621-05
CRNIC, LINDA S R01MH44970-03
CROCE, CARLO P01AI25380-05 0004
CROCE, CARLO P30CA12227-20 9001
CROCE, CARLO P30CA12227-20 9010
CROCE, CARLO P30CA12227-20 9011
CROCE, CARLO P30CA12227-20 9002
CROCE, CARLO P30CA12227-20 9003
CROCE, CARLO P30CA12227-20 9004
CROCE, CARLO P30CA12227-20 9005
CROCE, CARLO P30CA12227-20 9006
CROCE, CARLO P30CA12227-20 9007
CROCE, CARLO P30CA12227-20 9008
CROCE, CARLO P30CA12227-20 9009
CROCE, CARLO M R35CA39860-07
CROCKER, JENNIFER S07RR07066-26 0243
CROCKETT-TORABI, ELAHE R29AI31436-01
CROEN, KENNETH D S07RR05408-30 0923
CROFFORD, OSCAR B P60DK20593-13
CROFT, JANET B R01HL38844-05 0015
CROFTS, ANTONY R R01GM26305-13
CROFTS, ANTONY R R01GM35438-06
CROGHAN, THOMAS WOODWARD K11AI00846-05
CROMPTON, DAVID A R19MH46229-03
CRONAN, JOHN E, JR R01AI15650-14
CRONAN, JOHN E, JR R01GM26156-12
CRONAN, THEREASA A R29AR40423-01A1
CRONIN, MARY E S07RR05434-30 0817
CRONKITE, EUGENE P R01HL42115-04
CRONSTEIN, BRUCE P01AG04860-08 0005
CROOK, RICHARD B R29EY07984-03
CROOKE, ROSANNE M R43AI30821-01
CROOKS, PETER A S07RR05857-11 0924
CROOP, JAMES M K08CA01227-05
CROOP, JAMES M R01CA48162-04
CROOP, JAMES M S07RR05526-29 0073
CROSA, JORGE H R01AI19018-10
CROSBY, GREGORY R01GM42466-03
CROSBY, LEANNA S07RR05913-08 0665
CROSBY, LEANNA S07RR05913-08 0663
CROSBY, LEANNA J S15CA55953-01
CROSS, GEORGE A R01AI21531-08
CROSS, GEORGE A R01AI26197-02
CROSS, GEORGE A R37AI21729-07
CROSS, GEORGE A M R01AI22229-06
CROSS, RICHARD L R01GM23152-14
CROSS, TIMOTHY A R01AI23007-05
CROSSEN, KARL S07RR05491-29 0455
CROTEAU, RODNEY B R01CA55254-01
CROTEAU, RODNEY B R01GM31354-07A1
CROTHERS, DONALD M P01AI28778-02 0004
CROTHERS, DONALD M R01GM21966-17
CROTHERS, DONALD M R01GM34205-07
CROUCH, EDMOND C P01CA49712-03 9001
CROUCH, EDMOND C P01HL29594-09 0002
CROUCH, EDMOND C P60DK20579-14 0031
CROUCH, EDMOND C S15HL47731-01
CROUCH, EDMOND C MD PHD R01HL44015-02
CROUCH, EDMUND A R01CA50726-01A1
CROUCH, EDMUND C P01HL29594-09 9002
CROUCH, MARTHA L S07RR07031-26 0081
CROUCH, R Z01HD00068-20
CROUCH, ROSALIE K R01EY04939-09
CROUSE, DAVID A R01CA46686-03
CROUSE, DENNIS T K11HL02109-04
CROUSE, GRAY F R01CA54050-02
CROUSE, J ROBERT S07RR05404-30 0840
CROUSE, JOHN R P50HL14164-20 0049
CROUSE, JOHN R R01HL46208-01
CROUSE, JOHN R U01HL44319-02
CROW, M Z01AG00273-01
CROW, MARY K R01AI28367-02
CROW, MICHAEL T S07RR05745-19 0222
CROW, PEGGY S07RR05495-29 0469
CROW, TERRY J R37MH40860-06
CROWE, RAYMOND P50MH43271-05 0003
CROWE, RAYMOND R K02MH00735-04
CROWE, RAYMOND R R01MH34728-07
CROWE, RAYMOND R R01MH43212-04
CROWE, RAYMOND R U10AA08402-03
CROWE, THOMAS S07RR07242-04 0706
CROWELL, DAVID H U01HD29073-01
CROWELL, J S Z01RR00071-07
CROWELL, JUDITH A S07RR05736-19 0183
CROWELL, RICHARD S07RR05583-27 0622
CROWELL, RICHARD E K11HL02016-05
CROWELL, RICHARD L R01AI03771-30
CROWLE, ALFRED J R01AI29810-02
CROWLE, PATRICIA K S06GM08218-08 0014
CROWLEY, JOHN S07RR05761-17 0208
CROWLEY, JOHN J P01CA53996-14 0004
CROWLEY, JOHN J P01CA53996-14 0003
CROWLEY, JOHN J U10CA38926-06
CROWLEY, MARK S07RR05583-27 0623
CROWLEY, THOMAS J R01DA03961-06
CROWLEY, THOMAS J R01DA05722-03
CROWLEY, THOMAS J R18DA06941-02
CROWLEY, THOMAS J U01DA06912-02
CROWLEY, WILLIAM M01RR01066-14 0027
CROWLEY, WILLIAM M01RR02172-09 0140
CROWLEY, WILLIAM F M01RR01066-14 0024
CROWLEY, WILLIAM F M01RR01066-14 0100
CROWLEY, WILLIAM F M01RR01066-14 0106
CROWLEY, WILLIAM F M01RR01066-14 0111
CROWLEY, WILLIAM F M01RR01066-14 0101
CROWLEY, WILLIAM F M01RR01066-14 0102
CROWLEY, WILLIAM F M01RR01066-14 0103
CROWLEY, WILLIAM F M01RR01066-14 0099
CROWLEY, WILLIAM F P30HD28138-01 9005
CROWLEY, WILLIAM F U54HD29164-01 0001
CROWLEY, WILLIAM F, JR P30HD28138-01
CROWLEY, WILLIAM F, JR R01HD18169-09
CROWLEY, WILLIAM F, JR R01HD15788-09S1
CROWLEY, WILLIAM F, JR R01HD15080-09A1
CROWLEY, WILLIAM F, JR U54HD29164-01
CROWLEY, WILLIAM R R01HD13703-12
CROWLEY, WILLIAM R R01HD20074-07
CROWN, M Z01AG00274-01

CROWNER, MARTHA S07RR05651-24 0144
CROWNER, MARTHA L R29MH44762-03
CROXTON, THOMAS L R29DK42786-03
CROYLE, ROBERT T R01HS06660-01
CROYLE, ROBERT T R01MH43097-02
CROYLE, ROBERT T S07RR07092-26 0508
CRUICKSHANKS, KAREN S07RR05357-30 0444
CRULL, GEORGE S07RR07067-26 0213
CRUM, CHRISTOPHER P R01CA47676-04
CRUM, EDWARD D M01RR00080-29 0457
CRUM, EDWARD D M01RR00080-29 0385
CRUM, EDWARD D M01RR00080-29 0423
CRUMPACKER, CLYDE S M01RR01032-16 0445
CRUMPACKER, CLYDE S, II R01AI29173-03
CRUTCHER, KEITH A R01NS17131-10
CRUZ, JULIO C S07RR05700-22 0860
CRUZ, LOURDES J R01NS27219-02
CRUZ, PONCIANO D S07RR05426-30 0133
CRUZ, PONCIANO D JR R29AI31649-01
CRUZE, ALVIN M S15AG10242-01
CRUZE, ALVIN M S15DA07776-01
CRYER, PHILIP M01RR00036-31 1035
CRYER, PHILIP E M01RR00036-31 1005
CRYER, PHILIP E M01RR00036-31 1007
CRYER, PHILIP E M01RR00036-31 1008
CRYER, PHILIP E M01RR00036-31 1009
CRYER, PHILIP E M01RR00036-31 0550
CRYER, PHILIP E M01RR00036-31 0503
CRYER, PHILIP E P01NS06833-25 0026
CRYER, PHILIP E P60DK20579-14 9001
CRYER, PHILIP E R01DK27085-11A1
CRYER, PHILIP E R55DK44235-01
CRYSTAL, HOWARD P01AG03949-10
CRYSTAL, HOWARD A P01AG03949-10 0001
CRYSTAL, R G Z01HL02407-17
CRYSTAL, R G Z01HL02533-07
CRYSTAL, R G Z01HL02536-01
CRYSTAL, STEPHEN P50MH43450-04 0022
CRYSTAL, STEPHEN R01HS06339-03
CSCHULLER, DAVID P30CA16058-17 9015
CSERR, HELEN F R01NS11050-19
CSONKA, LASZLO N R01GM31944-07A2
CSR, INC N01DA15305-00
CSR, INC N01DA98325-00
CSR, INCORPORATED N01DA02205-00
CSR,INCORPORATED N01SP13003-00
CSUKAS, STEPHEN C S07RR05375-30 0753
CTR FOR HUMAN TOXICOLOGY N01DA19205-00
CUDA, G Z01HL04217-01
CUELLAR, JOSE B R01AA08266-02
CUELLAR, ORLANDO S07RR07092-26 0513
CUELLAR, ORLANDO S07RR07092-26 0485
CUELLO, A CLAUDIO R01NS26415-03
CUENOUD, HENRI F S07RR05712-20 0106
CUFFEL, BRIAN P50MH48197-02 0002
CUFFIN, BENJAMIN N R01NS22703-04
CUKIERMAN, SAMUEL S S07RR05379-30 0773
CULBERTSON, MICHAEL R R01GM26217-12
CULBERTSON, MICHAEL R R01GM40310-04
CULLEN, BAGAN R P30AI28662-03 9001
CULLEN, BRYAN R R01AI29821-02
CULLEN, BRYAN R R29AI28233-03
CULLEN, J M S07RR05911-08 0645
CULLEN, JOHN K P01DC00379-05 0004
CULLEN, JOHN K P01DC00379-05 9001
CULLEN, KEVIN J R29CA55003-01
CULLEN, MARK R K07ES00227-01
CULLEN, MARK R R01CA48200-04
CULLER, FLOYD L M01RR00039-31 0443
CULLER, M D Z01ES70096-07
CULLIS, CHRISTOPHER S15GM47067-01
CULLIS, CHRISTOPHER A S07RR07113-24
CULLMAN, LOUIS C R43AI31707-01
CULLUM, C MUNRO S07RR05357-30 0454
CULLUM, MALFORD E R29CA45860-05
CULLUM, MALFORD E S15CA55934-01
CULOTTI, JOSEPH G R01HD26073-03
CULP, DAVID J P50DE07003-08 0012
CULP, DAVID J R01DE09599-02
CULP, DAVID J R03DE10005-01
CULP, LLOYD A R01CA27755-11
CULP, LLOYD A R01NS17139-11
CULPEPPER-MORGAN, JOAN P50DA05130-05 0006
CULPEPPER, MICHAEL M01RR00065-29 0354
CULPEPPER, MICHAEL M01RR00065-29 0345
CULPEPPER, ROY M R29DK38406-05
CUMMING, CHRISTOPHER S07RR05337-30 0768
CUMMINGS, JEFFREY L P30AG10123-01
CUMMINGS, JEFFREY L P50MH30911-14 0012
CUMMINGS, K MICHAEL N01CN64098-10
CUMMINGS, LESTER R S07RR05538-29 0539
CUMMINGS, RICHARD P01AI27135-04 0003
CUMMINGS, RICHARD P41RR05351-03 0003
CUMMINGS, RICHARD D R01CA37626-07
CUMMINGS, STEVEN R R01AG05407-06
CUMMINGS, TIMOTHY M01RR00054-30 0409
CUMMINS, DENISE D S07RR07002-26 0864
CUMSKY, MICHAEL G R01GM36675-06
CUNAWAN, SONNY S07RR05756-18 0281
CUNHA, GERALD R P01CA05388-31A1 0036
CUNHA, GERALD R R01CA49996-03
CUNHA, GERALD R R01HD17491-10
CUNHA, GERALD R R37DK32157-09
CUNNINGHAM-R, CHARLOTTE M01RR00071-28A1 02
CUNNINGHAM-RUNDLES, CHARLOTTE R03CA53341-02
CUNNINGHAM-RUNDLES, SUSANNA P01CA29502-11A
CUNNINGHAM-RUNDLES, SUSANNA P01CA29502-11A
CUNNINGHAM-RUNDLES, SUSANNA P01CA29502-11A
CUNNINGHAM-RUNDLES, SUSANNA R01HL43781-02
CUNNINGHAM, BRUCE A R01HD16550-09
CUNNINGHAM, BRUCE A R01NS28932-02
CUNNINGHAM, CAROL C R01AA02887-15
CUNNINGHAM, CAROL C R01AA08706-02
CUNNINGHAM, CHRISTOPHER L P01AA08621-02 00
CUNNINGHAM, CHRISTOPHER L R01AA07702-04
CUNNINGHAM, CHRISTOPHER L R01DA03608-05
CUNNINGHAM, DENNIS P01AG00538-15 0014
CUNNINGHAM, DENNIS D R01AG10598-09
CUNNINGHAM, DIANA N01LM13502-02
CUNNINGHAM, GLENN R P30DK27685-10 9002
CUNNINGHAM, ISABEL S07RR07048-26 0635
CUNNINGHAM, JAMES M R29CA47075-04
CUNNINGHAM, KATHRYN A R01DA06511-02
CUNNINGHAM, KATHRYN A R29DA05708-03
CUNNINGHAM, M Z01ES21119-03
CUNNINGHAM, M W S07RR05411-30 0967
CUNNINGHAM, MADELEINE W K04HL01913-05
CUNNINGHAM, MADELEINE W R01HL35280-06
CUNNINGHAM, MICHAEL J K08HL02387-04
CUNNINGHAM, SUSAN S07RR05656-24 0847
CUNNINGHAM, SUSANNA L R25AD00052-01
CUNNINGHAM, TIMOTHY J R01NS16487-11
CUNNINGHAM, WALTER R R01AG04337-07A3
CUNNINGHAM, WILLIAM S07RR07052-26 0153
CUNNION, R E Z01CL00076-03
CUNNION, R E Z01CL00077-03
CUNNION, R E Z01CL00084-02
CUNNION, R E Z01CL00085-02
CUPP, EDDIE W R01AI29971-01A1
CUPP, EDDIE W R01AI31075-01
CUPPLES, HOWARD P R01HS06799-01
CUPPOLETTI, JOHN P01HD11725-13 0008
CUPPOLETTI, JOHN R01DK43377-01A1
CUPPOLETTI, JOHN R01DK43816-01
CURB, J. DAVID N01HC05102-07
CURCIO, CHRISTINE A R01EY06109-07
CURD, JOHN G M01RR00833-17 0120
CURET, LUIS N01HD13124-00
CURET, LUIS B M01RR00997-16 0354
CURIEL, DAVID T S07RR05406-30 0894
CURLEY, MICHAEL G R44HL42199-03
CURLEY, ROBERT W, JR R01CA49837-01A2
CURNUTT, JOHN T M01RR00833-17 0164
CURNUTTE, JOHN T, III R01AI24838-06
CURPHEY, THOMAS J R01CA51106-02
CURRAN, DENNIS P K04AI00813-05
CURRAN, DENNIS P R01GM31678-07A2
CURRAN, DENNIS P R01GM33372-08
CURRAN, DENNIS P R01GM34862-06
CURRAN, JAMES P51RR00168-30 9006
CURRELL, DOUGLAS L S06GM08101-20 0008
CURRIE, JULIA R S07RR05838-12 0269
CURRIE, RICHARD A S07RR05357-30 0461
CURRY, FITZ-ROY E R01HL28607-10
CURRY, FITZ-ROY E R01HL44485-01A1
CURRY, SUSAN J R01DA04447-06
CURRY, THOMAS E, JR R29HD23195-03
CURTHOYS, NORMAN P R01DK37124-06
CURTHOYS, NORMAN P R01DK43704-01
CURTI, B D Z01CM09363-01
CURTIN, HUGH D U01CA54016-01
CURTIN, PETER T K11HL02060-04
CURTIS, LAWRENCE R. P01ES04766-04 0003
CURTIS, JEFFREY P60AR20684-14 0022
CURTIS, JOHN J M01RR00032-31 0290
CURTIS, JOHN J M01RR00032-31 0233
CURTIS, JOHN J M01RR00032-31 0372
CURTIS, JOHN J M01RR00032-31 0376
CURTIS, JOHN J P50DK39258-05 0008
CURTIS, LAWRENCE R R01ES05543-01
CURTIS, PETER R18CA52748-02
CURTIS, PETER S07RR05540-29 0551
CURTIS, PETER U01CA51958-02 0001
CURTIS, PETER J R01HL33884-07
CURTIS, ROY R01AI28487-02
CURTIS, TOMMIE G N01AI05088-01
CURTIS, TOMMIE G N01CM17532-00
CURTISS, LINDA K R01HL35297-06
CURTISS, LINDA K R01HL43815-02
CURTISS, ROY U54HD29099-01 9003
CURTISS, ROY, III R01AI24533-05
CURTISS, ROY, III R37DE06673-09
CURTSINGER, JAMES W P01AG08761-02 0004
CURTSINGER, JAMES W R01GM40907-03
CUSANOVICH, MICHAEL A R01GM21277-16
CUSH, JOHN J M01RR00633-19 0401
CUSHION, MELANIE T R01AI29839-01A1
CUSHION, MELANIE T S07RR05408-30 0924
CUSHION, MELANIE T U01AI31702-01 0001
CUSHMAN, LAURA A R29AG08256-01A2
CUSHMAN, MARK S N01CM17512-00
CUSHMAN, MARK S N01CM17513-00
CUSHMAN, S W Z01DK55012-09
CUSICK, CATHERINE G R01EY08906-01A1
CUSICK, MICHAEL E S07RR05814-12 0142
CUSICK, MICHAEL E S07RR05814-12 0147
CUSSON, REGINA S07RR05973-05 0784
CUSTER, PHILIP P30CA06927-29 9008
CUTHBERTSON, R A Z01EY00259-02
CUTHBERTSON, R A Z01EY00273-01
CUTILLO, ANTONIO G R01HL31216-07A1
CUTLER, CHRISTOPHER W K15DE00214-06
CUTLER, G B Z01HD00610-11
CUTLER, G B Z01HD00623-08
CUTLER, JIMMY E R01AI24912-04
CUTLER, JIMMY E S06GM08218-08 0012
CUTLER, R G Z01AG00303-07
CUTRONEO, KENNETH R R01HL45138-02
CUTTER, GARY S07RR05584-27 0648
CUTTER, GARY R N01HD92920-04
CUTTING, COURT B R01DE09560-01A1
CUTTING, GARRY R R01DK44003-01
CUTTLER, LEONA R29DK40221-05
CUTTNER, JANET M01RR00071-28A1 0238
CUZE, BARRY S07RR05756-18 0282
CVITANIC, MARILYN S07RR05710-21 0024
CWI, JOAN S N01CP15602-00
CYAPO, JAMES D P01HL42444-02 0005
CYBULSKY, MYRON I R01HL45563-01
CYGNUS CORPORATION N01DA15302-00
CYGNUS CORPORATION N01DA18104-00
CYRLIN, MARSHALL N U10EY06834-05
CYSYK, R Z01CM06163-07
CZAJA, A M01RR00585-20 0420
CZAJA, A M01RR00585-20 0421
CZAJA, A M01RR00585-20 0502
CZAJA, A J M01RR00585-20 0499
CZAJA, MARK P30DK41296-03 0002
CZAJA, MARK J K08DK01792-05
CZECH, MICHAEL P P01CA39240-07
CZECH, MICHAEL P P01CA39240-07 0001
CZECH, MICHAEL P R01DK30648-11
CZECH, MICHAEL P R01DK30898-11
CZEISLER, CHARLES M01RR02635-07 0150
CZEISLER, CHARLES P01AG09975-01 0003
CZEISLER, CHARLES A M01RR02635-07 0295
CZEISLER, CHARLES A M01RR02635-07 0293
CZEISLER, CHARLES A M01RR02635-07 0290
CZEISLER, CHARLES A M01RR02635-07 0263
CZEISLER, CHARLES A M01RR02635-07 0264
CZEISLER, CHARLES A P01AG09975-01
CZEISLER, CHARLES A P01AG09975-01 0001
CZEISLER, CHARLES A R01AG06072-07
CZEISLER, CHARLES A R01MH45130-03
CZERLINSKI, GEORGE P41RR06030-01A1 0004
CZERNIK, ANDREW J P01AG09464-01 9001
CZINN, STEVEN J M01RR00080-29 0439
CZINN, STEVEN J R29AI25818-04
CZOP, JOYCE S07RR05950-07 0989
CZOP, JOYCE K R01AI23542-05
CZUPRYNSKI, CHARLES J R01AI21343-07A1
CZUPRYNSKI, CHUCK S07RR05912-08 0650
D'AGOSTINO, RALPH B R55HL40423-04
D'ALESSIO, DAVID A M01RR00037-31 0501
D'ALESSIO, DONN J R01DK36904-05
D'AMBROSIO, STEVEN M R01ES05727-01
D'AMORE, PATRICIA A P01CA45548-05 9003
D'AMORE, PATRICIA A P01CA45548-05 0003
D'AMORE, PATRICIA A R01EY05318-09
D'AMORE, PATRICIA A R01EY05985-07
D'ANNA, JOE P41RR01315-10 0032
D'AQUILA, RICHARD T R01AI29193-02
D'ARGENIO, DAVID Z P41RR01861-07 9002
D'ERASMO, MARTHA J R43AG10150-01
D'ERCOLE, A JOSEPH R01HD08299-18
D'EUSTACHIO, PETER G R01HG00300-09
D'ONOFRIO, CAROL N R01CA41733-05S1
D'SOUZA, RENA N S07RR05970-06 0775
D'SOUZA, STANLEY E R29HL43721-01A1
DABBOUS, MUSTAFA K S07RR05994-03
DABESTANI, R Z01ES50087-05
DACEY, DENNIS M R01EY06678-06
DACEY, DENNIS M. P51RR00166-30 0138
DACEY, RALPH C P01HL03174-36 0017
DACEY, RALPH G, JR R01HL37983-05
DACHEUX, RAMON F R01EY03011-12A1
DADA, M OLUBUNMI S07RR05815-12 0492
DAE, MICHAEL W R29HL38105-04
DAGER, S. R. P51RR00166-30 0082
DAGER, STEPHEN R S07RR05432-30 0236
DAHL, ALAN R R01ES04422-05
DAHL, RONALD E P01MH41712-06 9002
DAHL, RONALD E P01MH41712-06 0004
DAHL, RONALD E P01MH41712-06 0005
DAHL, RONALD E R29MH46510-02
DAHLBERG, ALBERT E R01GM19756-20
DAHLBERG, JAMES E R01GM30220-09
DAHLQUIST, FREDERICK W R01AI17808-11
DAHMS, A STEPHEN S06GM45765-01 0003
DAHMS, NANCY M S07RR05434-30 0802
DAHMS, WILLIAM T M01RR00080-29 0197
DAHMUS, MICHAEL E R01GM33300-05
DAIGER, STEPHEN P R01EY07142-03
DAIL, WILLIAM G R01NS19839-09
DAIL, WILLIAM G S06GM08139-17 0038
DAILEY, HARRY A R01DK32303-09

DAILEY, HARRY A R01DK35898-05
DAILEY, LISA A R29CA49472-03
DAILEY, MORRIS O R01AI22730-06
DAINIAK, NICHOLAS R01DK27071-12
DAINIAK, NICHOLAS R01DK31060-08A2
DAIRE, JOHN S07RR05704-20 0010
DAISEY, JOAN M R01HL42490-02
DAL CANTO, MAURO P01NS23349-06 9001
DAL CANTO, MAURO C R01NS13011-16
DALAKAS, M C Z01NS02038-18
DALAKAS, M C Z01NS02531-10
DALDAL, FEVZI R01GM38237-06
DALE, DAVID C. M01RR00037-31 0423
DALE, BEVERLY A K16DE00161-05S2
DALE, BEVERLY A P01AR21557-13 0001
DALE, BEVERLY A R13AR41036-01
DALE, BEVERLY A R37DE04660-16
DALE, BEVERLY A S07RR05346-30 0325
DALE, DAVID C M01RR00037-31 0491
DALE, DAVID C M01RR00037-31 0487
DALE, DAVID C R01DK18951-14A2
DALE, GEORGE KL R01AG08545-04
DALE, GEORGE L R01DK35220-07
DALE, GRADY, JR S07RR05770-13 0936
DALE, JAMES B R55AI10085-28
DALE, PETER A P01AI24760-05 0001
DALEKE, DAVID S07RR07031-26 0082
DALEN, JAMES E S15CA55942-01
DALEN, JAMES P S07RR05675-23
DALESSANDRO, ANTHONY S07RR05435-30 0983
DALGARD, DAN N01CP05622-05
DALHOUSE, DERICK A S06GM08047-20S1 0026
DALING, JANET R N01CP95671-03
DALING, JANET R P01CA42792-05 0003
DALING, JANET R P01CA42792-05 0004
DALING, JANET R R01CA52656-01A1
DALING, JANET R R01HD25959-02
DALING, JANET R S07RR05714-21 0121
DALING, JANET R S07RR05714-21 0120
DALL, OWEN B R43AG09719-01
DALLA-FAVERA, RICCARDO R01CA37165-08
DALLA-FAVERA, RICCARDO R01CA44029-05
DALLA-FAVERA, RICCARDO R37CA37295-08
DALLAS, WILLIAM J R01CA49261-03
DALLEY, ROBERT W U01CA54011-01
DALLMAN, MARY F R37DK28172-11
DALLMAN, PETER R R37DK13897-22
DALLOS, PETER J R01DC00089-21
DALLOS, PETER J R01DC00708-02
DALSKY, GAIL P U01AG10382-01
DALTON, ARTHUR J R01AG08849-01A1
DALTON, WILLIAM S P01CA17094-16 0028
DALTON, WILLIAM S P01CA41183-05 0005
DALVI, RAMESH R S06GM08091-20 0010
DALY, BARBARA R01NR02248-01A1
DALY, COLIN H S07RR07096-26 0068
DALY, DANIEL L S03RR03254-02
DALY, DOUGLAS N01CM17546-00
DALY, J W Z01DK31100-26
DALY, J W Z01DK31102-21
DALY, J W Z01DK31108-03
DALY, KATHLEEN A R01DC01242-01
DALY, WALTER J S07RR05371-30
DALY, WALTER J S15DK44677-01
DAMASIO, ANTONIO R M01RR00059-30 0447
DAMASIO, ANTONIO R P01NS19632-09 0008
DAMASIO, ANTONIO R P01NS19632-09 0004
DAMASIO, ANTONIO R P01NS19632-09
DAMASIO, HANNA C P01NS19632-09 9001
DAMASSA, DAVID A R01HD16535-08
DAMBACH, GEORGE E S07RR05384-30
DAMBACH, GEORGE E S15CA56011-01
DAMBACH, GEORGE E S15DA07835-01
DAMBROSIA, J M Z01NS02490-11
DAMBROSIA, J M Z01NS02652-07
DAME, JOHN B S07RR05788-15 0891
DAMIAN, RAYMOND T S07RR07025-26 0989
DAMIANO, RALPH S07RR05430-30 0221
DAMJANOV, IVAN P01HD21355-04 0005
DAMJANOV, IVAN P50AA07186-06 0015
DAMMANN, JOHN F M01RR00847-18 0489
DAMMKOEHLER, R A P01GM24483-12A1 0010
DAMON, DEBORAH H P01HL36080-06 0010
DAMON, DEBORAH H S07RR07187-13 0707
DAMSKY, CAROLINE S07RR05305-30 0733
DAMSKY, CAROLINE H P01HD26732-01A1 0001
DAMSKY, CAROLINE H R01CA42032-07
DAMSKY, CAROLINE H R01HD22210-06
DAMSKY, CAROLYN S07RR05305-30 0726
DANCIS, JOSEPH R01AI28256-03
DANCIS, JOSEPH R01AI29349-02
DANCIS, JOSEPH R01AI32298-01
DANCY, BARBARA L S07RR05776-11 0389
DANDEKAR, SATYA P51RR00169-30 0185
DANDEKAR, SATYA R01AI30377-02
DANDEKAR, SATYA R29NS27338-04
DANDLIKER, RENE P01DC00316-06 0004
DANEO-MOORE, LOLITA R01DE05180-10A3
DANEO-MOORE, LOLITA R01DE08942-03
DANEO-MOORE, LOLITA S07RR05417-30 0786
DANFORTH, D N Z01CM06663-02
DANFORTH, ELLIOT M01RR00109-28 0356
DANFORTH, ELLIOT M01RR00109-28 0368
DANFORTH, ELLIOT M01RR00109-28 0369
DANFORTH, ELLIOT, JR R01DK18535-11
DANFORTH, WILLIAM H S07RR07054-26
DANG, CHI V R29CA51497-02
DANGENBERG, PATRICIA P01CA42760-06 9003
DANGLER, CHARLES A S07RR07082-26 0274
DANGMAN, KENNETH H R01HL24354-12
DANHAUSER, LYNN L R29CA45620-05
DANHEISER, RICK L R01GM28273-11A1
DANI, JOHN S07RR05425-30 0734
DANI, JOHN A R01NS21229-07A1
DANIEL, CHARLES W R01HD27845-05
DANIEL, D G Z01MH02436-04
DANIEL, D G Z01MH02478-04
DANIEL, D G Z01MH02554-02
DANIEL, ELNORA R24MH47187-02 0003
DANIEL, GREGORY B S07RR05845-11 0552
DANIEL, L N Z01CP05674-01
DANIEL, LARRY W R01CA43297-05
DANIEL, LARRY W R01CA48995-03
DANIEL, M D P51RR00168-30 0109
DANIEL, M D P51RR00168-30 0160
DANIEL, M D P51RR00168-30 0153
DANIEL, M D P51RR00168-30 0154
DANIEL, M D P51RR00168-30 0157
DANIEL, MICHAEL A K15DE00287-04
DANIEL, PETER P01NS24279-06 0007
DANIEL, SALHA P50HD13063-12 0010
DANIEL, STEVEN S07RR07242-04 0707
DANIEL, THOMAS P30HD28819-01 9003
DANIEL, THOMAS M P01AI26482-03S1 0002
DANIEL, THOMAS O P50DK39261-05 0003
DANIEL, THOMAS O R01DK38517-04A1
DANIELE, RONALD P R01HL43002-03
DANIELL, LAURA C R01AA08166-03
DANIELL, WILLIAM S07RR05714-21 0132
DANIELS, CHRISTOPHER K R01AG08552-03
DANIELS, DONNA L R01GM35682-09A1
DANIELS, M P Z01HL00153-04
DANIELS, NORMAN R01LM05005-03
DANIELS, ROBERT S07RR05704-20 0013
DANIELS, ROBERT S S07RR05376-30
DANIELS, ROBERT S S15DA07802-01
DANIELS, ROBERT S S15DK44667-01
DANIELS, STEPHEN R R01HL34698-06
DANIELSEN, MARK R01DK42552-02
DANILO, PETER P50HD13063-12 0004
DANILOFF, JOANNE K R29NS25102-05
DANIS, MARION R01HS06655-02
DANIS, RONALD P S07RR05371-30 0633
DANISH, ELIZABETH S07RR05410-30 0946
DANISHEFSKY, ISIDORE R01HL16955-18
DANISHEFSKY, SAMUEL J R01AI16943-12
DANISHEFSKY, SAMUEL J R01CA28824-12
DANISHEFSKY, SAMUEL J R01HL25848-12
DANNALS, ROBERT F P01NS15080-12 9003
DANNEMAN, PEGGY J K01RR00052-03
DANNEMILLER, JAMES L R01HD23247-05
DANNENBERG, A M P30ES03819-06A1 9019
DANNENBERG, ANDREW J K08DK01992-02
DANNENBERG, ANDREW L R01MH47756-02
DANNENBERG, ANDREW L S07RR05445-30 0870
DANNENBERG, JOSEPH S07RR07109-23 0504
DANNER, D B Z01AG00705-06
DANNER, DEAN J R01DK38320-06
DANNER, R L Z01CL00064-03
DANNER, R L Z01CL00065-03
DANNER, R L Z01CL00067-03
DANNER, R L Z01CL00068-03
DANNER, R L Z01CL00069-03
DANNER, R L Z01CL00070-03
DANNER, R L Z01CL00090-02
DANNIES, PRISCILLA S R01DK40343-02
DANNIES, PRISCILLA S R01HD11487-14A1
DANOFF, ANN K08DK01894-03
DANSEREAU, DONALD F R01DA04987-03
DANTZLER, WILLIAM P01DK41006-03 0001
DANTZLER, WILLIAM H P01DK41006-03
DANTZLER, WILLIAM H R01DK16294-17
DANZEISEN, RICHARD N01CO03861-02
DANZIGER, ROGER M01RR00240-27 0350
DAR, M SAEED R01AA07101-03
DARBA, PRASHANTH P41RR02301-07 0007
DARBA, PRASHANTH P41RR02301-07 0009
DARBY, CHARLES A N01CO94382-05
DARBY, JOSEPH M P20NS30318-01 9002
DARENSBOURG, MARCETTA Y R01GM44865-01A1
DARITY, WILLIAM A N01CN65028-17
DARK, VERONICA S07RR07034-26 0053
DARKO, DENIS F M01RR00827-17 0482
DARKO, DENIS F P50MH30914-14 0058
DARKO, DENIS F R29MH42762-04
DARLAND, CELIA M01RR01346-10 0125
DARLING, DOUGLAS S R29DK44332-01
DARLING, WARREN G R01AR40217-02
DARLINGTON, DANIEL N R55GM46540-01
DARLINGTON, GRETCHEN P01DK44080-01 0002
DARLINGTON, GRETCHEN J P01AG07123-04 0003
DARLINGTON, GRETCHEN J P01AG07123-04 9003
DARLINGTON, GRETCHEN J R01GM32111-10
DARNELL, JAMES E R01AI32489-01
DARNELL, JAMES E R01CA16006-18
DARNELL, JAMES E S07RR07065-26 0058
DARNELL, ROBERT B K08NS01461-02
DARRAS, BASIL THEODORE K08NS01367-03
DARTEL, DONATA P01DC00116-16 0021
DARTT, DARLENE A R01EY06177-07
DARTT, DARLENE A R01EY09057-01
DARUNA, JORGE H R01AA07548-03
DARZYNKIEWICA, Z P41RR01315-10 0040
DARZYNKIEWICZ, ZBIGNIEW R01CA28704-12
DARZYNKIEWICZ, ZBIGNIEW R37CA23296-15
DAS SARMA, SHILADITYA R01GM41980-03
DAS, ANATH R01GM37555-04A2
DAS, ANATHBANDHU R01GM42557-03
DAS, ASIS K R01GM28946-11
DAS, DIPAK K R01HL34360-04A1
DAS, GOKUL C R29CA47611-05
DAS, GOPAL D R01NS08817-21
DAS, JOHN B S07RR05475-26 0053
DAS, KIRON M R01DK44314-01
DAS, SALIL S06GM08198-10 0009
DASANAYAKE, ANADA P S07RR05829-09 0957
DASGUPTA, ASIM R01AI18272-10
DASGUPTA, ASIM R01AI27451-03
DASGUPTA, BIBHUTI R R01NS17742-09
DASGUPTA, BIBHUTI R R01NS24545-03S1
DASGUPTA, BIBHUTI R S07RR07098-26 0336
DASHEIFF, RICHARD M R01HS06752-01
DASQUPTA, ARUNANSU S07RR05576-27 0601
DASSARMA, S S07RR07048-26 0636
DATILES, M B Z01EY00187-08
DATILES, M B Z01EY00188-08
DATILES, M B Z01EY00212-06
DATILES, MB Z01EY00062-15
DATTA-GUPTA, NIRMALENDU S06GM08060-21
DATTA-GUPTA, NIRMALENDU S06GM08060-21 0001
DATTA, MUKUL C S06GM08091-20 0019
DATTA, PRASANTA K R01GM21436-17
DATTA, SYAMAL K R01AR39157-03
DATTA, SYAMAL K R01CA31789-13
DATTELL, RONNIE P01HD24640-03 9001
DATTWYLER, RAYMOND P50AI16337-13 0004
DAUBE-WITHERSPOON, M E Z01CL04001-01
DAUBEN, WILLIAM G R01DK00709-38
DAUBENSPECK, JOHN A R01HL29068-10
DAUDISTEL, HOWARD R24MH47167-02 0002
DAUGHADAY, WILLIAM H P01HD20805-05A1 0002
DAUGHERTY, ROBERT M, S07RR05813-12 0515
DAUGHERTY, ROBERT M, JR S07RR05813-12
DAUGHERTY, ROBERT M, JR U76PE00215-06
DAUSSET, JEAN R24RR05056-03
DAUTERMAN, WALTER P01ES00044-26 0002
DAVANIPOUR, ZOREH R01AG08567-01A2
DAVANIPOUR, ZOREH R01NS26732-02
DAVANZO, JULIE P01HD28372-01 0008
DAVANZO, JULIE P01HD28372-01 0002
DAVANZO, JULIE P01HD28372-01 0001
DAVANZO, JULIE S P01HD28372-01
DAVANZO, JULIE S R01AG08189-03S1
DAVAR, GUDARZ K08NS01497-01
DAVENPORT, MARSHA L R29HD28447-01
DAVENPORT, NANCY S07RR06020-03 0312
DAVENPORT, PAUL W R01HL37596-03
DAVES, G DOYLE, JR R01AI26261-04
DAVID, CHELLA S P50HD09140-16 9003
DAVID, CHELLA S R01AR30752-08
DAVID, CHELLA S R01AR39875-03
DAVID, CHELLA S R01CA24473-14
DAVID, CHELLA S R37AI14764-15
DAVID, GLENN P50MH41684-07 0077
DAVID, HENRY P R01HD25574-01A1
DAVID, JOHN S07RR07053-26 0156
DAVID, JOHN D S03RR03087-07
DAVID, JOHN R P01AI16305-13 9001
DAVID, JOHN R P01AI16305-13
DAVID, JOHN R R01AI22532-07
DAVID, JOHN R R13AI31013-01
DAVID, JOHN R S07RR05446-30 0270
DAVID, LARRY L R29EY07755-03
DAVID, RAPHAEL M01RR00096-30A1 0209
DAVID, RAPHAEL M01RR00096-30A1 0317
DAVID, RAPHAEL M01RR00096-30A1 0168
DAVIDOFF, AMY J S07RR05874-10 0583
DAVIDOFF, ROBERT A R01NS17577-10
DAVIDORF, FREDERICK H U10EY06257-07
DAVIDOVITCH, ZEEV R01DE08428-03
DAVIDOVITCH, ZEEV R13DE09458-01S1
DAVIDSON, ANNE K08AR01806-04
DAVIDSON, E S07RR07003-26 0327
DAVIDSON, ERIC H R01RR06591-01A1
DAVIDSON, ERIC H R37HD05753-22
DAVIDSON, ERNEST R R01GM34081-08
DAVIDSON, EUGENE A R01HL42332-04
DAVIDSON, GESTUR P41RR01632-09 9017
DAVIDSON, JEFFREY M R01AG06528-06A1
DAVIDSON, JEFFREY M R01GM37387-06
DAVIDSON, JOHN P S06GM08091-20 0024
DAVIDSON, JONATHAN R R01MH47448-01A1
DAVIDSON, JULIAN M R37AG01437-11
DAVIDSON, MAUREEN K P40RR00463-23 0002
DAVIDSON, MICHAEL M01RR00071-28A1 0214
DAVIDSON, MICHAEL R01MH37922-08

DAVIDSON, MICHAEL R01MH46436-02
DAVIDSON, N P30DK42086-02 9002
DAVIDSON, NANCY E R29CA49634-03
DAVIDSON, NICHOLAS O K04HL02166-04
DAVIDSON, NICHOLAS O R01HL38180-05
DAVIDSON, NORMAN R S07RR07003-26
DAVIDSON, NORMAN R S15NS30130-01
DAVIDSON, RICHARD J K02MH00875-02
DAVIDSON, RICHARD J R01MH43454-03
DAVIDSON, RICHARD J S15MH49316-01
DAVIDSON, RICHARD L R01CA31781-11
DAVIDSON, ROBERT M R29DE09662-01A1
DAVIDSON, ROBIN S07RR05756-18 0302
DAVIDSON, SANDRA S06GM08248-05 0014
DAVIDSON, TERRY L R01HD28792-01
DAVIDSON, VICTOR L R01GM41574-04
DAVIDSON, W Z01CB08953-01
DAVIDSON, WILLIAM S II R01MH44849-03
DAVIE, EARL R01HL16919-18 0020
DAVIE, EARL R01HL16919-18 0017
DAVIE, EARL R01HL16919-18 0018
DAVIE, EARL R01HL16919-18 0019
DAVIE, EARL R01HL16919-18 0016
DAVIE, EARL R01HL16919-18 0021
DAVIE, EARL R01HL16919-18 0022
DAVIE, EARL W R01HL16919-18 0009
DAVIE, EARL W R01HL16919-18
DAVIE, EARL W. P01HL03174-36 0022
DAVIE, JOSEPH M P01AI15353-13 9003
DAVIES, ALBERT O R01DK41780-03
DAVIES, D R Z01DK34002-27
DAVIES, D R Z01DK34003-23
DAVIES, D R Z01DK36109-04
DAVIES, DAVID L R29AA07145-05
DAVIES, DONALD S R01CA40895-06
DAVIES, GEOFFREY S07RR07143-20 0621
DAVIES, HUW M R01DA06301-01A2
DAVIES, HUW M L P50DA06634-01A1 0004
DAVIES, K MICHAEL P50AR39221-05 9002
DAVIES, KELVIN J R13CA53492-01S1
DAVIES, KELVIN JAMES ANTHONY R01ES03598-08
DAVIES, PETER P01AG06803-05 9001
DAVIES, PETER P01AG06803-05
DAVIES, PETER P01AG06803-05 0001
DAVIES, PETER P01MH47667-02 0001
DAVIES, PETER R37MH38623-12
DAVIES, PETER F P01HL36028-07 0005
DAVIES, PETER F R01HL36049-07
DAVIES, PETER F R13HL46857-01
DAVIES, PETER J R01DK27078-11
DAVIES, R WYNE U01AI27221-03 0004
DAVIES, RICHARD P50HL42236-04 0002
DAVIES, RICHARD F. N01HV18117-02
DAVIES, RICHARD J R01CA55331-01
DAVIES, TERRY F R01DK35764-06
DAVILA-ROMAN, VICTOR S07RR05491-29 0456
DAVILA, ENRIQUE U10CA45564-05
DAVIS, ALVIN E P01HD17461-08 9001
DAVIS, ALVIN E P30HD28827-01 9002
DAVIS, ALVIN E, III R01HD22082-06
DAVIS, B P30DK42086-02 0001
DAVIS, BARRY J R01DC00245-07
DAVIS, BARRY J R01DC00451-04
DAVIS, BARRY J S07RR05349-30 0749
DAVIS, BARRY R R01HL40072-04
DAVIS, BARRY R S07RR05828-08 0525
DAVIS, BERNARD H P30DK26678-12 0005
DAVIS, BERNARD H R29DK40223-03
DAVIS, BERTHA R24MH47187-02 0002
DAVIS, BRIAN R R01HL42105-04
DAVIS, BRIAN R R01HL42283-04
DAVIS, C WILLIAM P01HL34322-06 9004
DAVIS, CINDA-SUE G R25AD00077-01
DAVIS, CLARENCE E N01HC55000-16
DAVIS, CLARENCE E U01HL44311-02
DAVIS, DAN J S03RR03297-10
DAVIS, DENNIS S07RR05305-30 0721
DAVIS, DIANE H R29NR01894-04
DAVIS, DUANE L R01HD26762-01A1
DAVIS, EDWARD R24MH47181-02 0003
DAVIS, EDWARD M R43GM46592-01
DAVIS, ELAINE J S06GM08016-21 0074
DAVIS, ELAINE J S06GM08049-20 0010
DAVIS, ELDRED J R01DK13939-20
DAVIS, FAITH G S07RR05871-03 0577
DAVIS, FRANKLIN A R01GM34014-07
DAVIS, FREDERICK P01AG09975-01 0002
DAVIS, FREDERICK C R01HD18686-06
DAVIS, FREDERICK C S07RR07143-20 0622
DAVIS, GARY L M01RR00082-29 0296
DAVIS, GEORGE MORGAN R22AI11373-17
DAVIS, GERALD L S07RR07049-26 0427
DAVIS, GERALD S P50HL14212-20 0031
DAVIS, GERALD S P50HL14212-20 0029
DAVIS, GERALD S P50HL14212-20 0035
DAVIS, GERALD S P50HL14212-20 9007
DAVIS, GLENN J S07RR05746-19
DAVIS, JACQUELINE K K11DE00310-01
DAVIS, JAMES N01CN15377-00
DAVIS, JAMES S07RR07044-26 0118
DAVIS, JAMES N P50NS06233-25
DAVIS, JAMES N P50NS06233-25 0042
DAVIS, JANET H S07RR05776-11 0390
DAVIS, JANET L M01RR05280-03 0017
DAVIS, JOHN A S03RR03425-06
DAVIS, JOHN D R01DK41563-02
DAVIS, JOHN R P01CA41183-05 9003
DAVIS, JOHN S M01RR00847-18 0549
DAVIS, JOHN S M01RR00847-18 0006
DAVIS, JOHN S R01HD22248-05A2
DAVIS, JOHN W S06GM08174-13 0005
DAVIS, JOSEPH H S15AG10233-01
DAVIS, JOSEPH H S15DA07792-01
DAVIS, KATHRYN A R01HL38941-04
DAVIS, KATHRYN B N01HV78100-08
DAVIS, KATHRYN B U01HL42824-03
DAVIS, KEITH R R29GM45570-01
DAVIS, KENNETH M01RR00071-28A1 0148
DAVIS, KENNETH M01RR00071-28A1 0144
DAVIS, KENNETH L M01RR00071-28A1 0139
DAVIS, KENNETH L P01MH45212-02
DAVIS, KENNETH L P50AG05138-08
DAVIS, KENNETH L. P50AG05138-08 0010
DAVIS, KENNETH M K08AG00455-02
DAVIS, KENNETH M P30AG08812-02 0002
DAVIS, L N S07RR05333-30 0865
DAVIS, LARRY E S06GM08139-17 0039
DAVIS, LAWRENCE W P01CA23113-13
DAVIS, LOIS S07RR05710-21 0028
DAVIS, MARADEE P60AR20684-14 0029
DAVIS, MARADEE A R37AG05284-06
DAVIS, MARGARET S07RR05635-18 0779
DAVIS, MARK P01AI19512-09 0008
DAVIS, MARK M R01AI22511-07
DAVIS, MATTHEW D N01EY02130-01
DAVIS, MATTHEW D R21EY08107-03
DAVIS, MATTHEW D U10EY08067-04
DAVIS, MATTHEW D U10EY08210-03
DAVIS, MICHAEL K05MH00004-17
DAVIS, MICHAEL P01MH25642-18 0015
DAVIS, MICHAEL P01MH25642-18 0016
DAVIS, MICHAEL P01MH25642-18 0017
DAVIS, MICHAEL P01MH25642-18 0018
DAVIS, MICHAEL P01MH25642-18 0014
DAVIS, MICHAEL R37MH47840-01
DAVIS, MICHAEL I S06GM08012-21 0014
DAVIS, MICHAEL J R29HL38104-05
DAVIS, MICHEAL P01MH25642-18 0013
DAVIS, PAMELA B P30DK27651-09
DAVIS, PAMELA B R01DK43999-01
DAVIS, PATRICK J S07RR07091-26 0751
DAVIS, PAUL J R01AG07736-05
DAVIS, RICHARD L R01CA50210-03
DAVIS, ROBIN M01RR00997-16 0411
DAVIS, ROGER P30DK34914-06 9002
DAVIS, ROGER A R01HL37195-07
DAVIS, ROGER A R01HL41624-03
DAVIS, ROGER J P01CA39240-07 9002
DAVIS, ROGER J P01CA39240-07 0004
DAVIS, ROGER J R01GM37845-05
DAVIS, RONALD P01HG00205-02 9003
DAVIS, RONALD P01HG00205-02 0001
DAVIS, RONALD L R01GM47680-01
DAVIS, RONALD L R01NS19904-09
DAVIS, RONALD W P01AG02908-11 0011
DAVIS, RONALD W P01GM28428-11 0007
DAVIS, RONALD W R01AI27076-04
DAVIS, RONALD W R37HG00198-17
DAVIS, ROWLAND H R01GM35120-07
DAVIS, SALLY M U01CA52283-02
DAVIS, SALLY M PHD R01HL32021-06
DAVIS, SCOTT K04CA01374-04
DAVIS, SCOTT S07RR05714-21 0122
DAVIS, SCOTT S07RR05761-17 0207
DAVIS, STEPHEN M01RR00095-31 0377
DAVIS, STEVEN P R19DA06429-03
DAVIS, STEVEN P R19MH46192-03
DAVIS, THOMAS P01DK36289-06A1 0011
DAVIS, THOMAS E S07RR05920-08
DAVIS, THOMAS E S07RR05920-08 0522
DAVIS, THOMAS P P01HD26013-01A2 0002
DAVIS, TRISHA N R01GM40506-04
DAVIS, W K P60AR20557-13 0064
DAVIS, WAYNE K P60DK20572-14 9009
DAVIS, WILLIAM C R01CA50141-03
DAVISON-FAIRBURN, BILLIE B K01RR00075-01
DAVISON, A P41RR00317-25 0005
DAVISON, PETER F S07RR05711-21 0039
DAVISSON, MURIEL T N01HD02913-01
DAVISSON, MURIEL T N01HD13131-00
DAVISSON, MURIEL T N01HD52917-10
DAVISSON, MURIEL T P40RR01183-14
DAVISSON, V JO R01GM45756-01
DAVITZ, MICHAEL A S07RR05399-30 0927
DAVY, DWIGHT T R01AR40004-03
DAW, NIGEL W P01NS29343-01 0003
DAW, NIGEL W R01EY00053-22
DAWES, LILLIAN G S07RR05370-30 0623
DAWICKI, DOLORETTA S07RR05862-10 0560
DAWID, I B Z01HD01001-09
DAWID, I B Z01HD01002-10
DAWID, I B Z01HD01007-02
DAWKINS, CECILIA S07RR05796-14 0426
DAWSON-HUGHES, BESS M01RR00054-30 0418
DAWSON-HUGHES, BESS U01AG10353-01
DAWSON, CHANDLER R U10EY07479-04
DAWSON, CHRISTOPHER A R37HL19298-16
DAWSON, CHRISTOPHER A U01CA46088-05 0003
DAWSON, DAVID C P30ES03828-06 0004
DAWSON, DAVID C R01DK29786-10
DAWSON, DEAN S R01GM40452-04
DAWSON, DEBORAH P50AG05128-08 0009
DAWSON, DEBORAH V R35AG07922-04 0004
DAWSON, DOUGLAS S07RR05372-30 0667
DAWSON, DOUGLAS A R01ES05405-01A1
DAWSON, GERALDINE R01MH47117-01
DAWSON, GLYN P01HD09402-16 0009
DAWSON, GLYN P01HL18577-16 9003
DAWSON, GLYN R01DA02575-12
DAWSON, GLYN R01HD06426-20
DAWSON, GLYN R01NS28549-01A1
DAWSON, JEFFREY R R01CA42890-06
DAWSON, JOHN H R01GM39287-04
DAWSON, JOHN H S07RR07160-16 0589
DAWSON, KENNETH A S07RR07006-26 0915
DAWSON, M P41RR05964-02 0007
DAWSON, MARCIA N01CM17502-00
DAWSON, MARCIA S07RR05522-29 0071
DAWSON, MARCIA I P01CA51993-01A1
DAWSON, MARCIA I P01CA51993-01A1 0001
DAWSON, MICHAEL E P50MH30911-14 0025
DAWSON, MICHAEL E R01MH46433-02
DAWSON, MICHAEL E S07RR07012-25 0013
DAWSON, NEAL V R01HS06754-01
DAWSON, PAUL A S07RR05404-30 0841
DAWSON, RALPH, JR S07RR05573-13 0088
DAWSON, ROBERT C S07RR05424-30 0090
DAWSON, WALLACE D S07RR07160-16 0596
DAWSON, WILLIAM W P40RR03640-05 0004
DAWSON, WILLIAM W R01EY04460-08
DAX, E Z01DA00021-04
DAX, E M Z01DA00014-04
DAX, E M Z01DA00017-02
DAX, E M Z01DA00018-02
DAX, E M Z01DA00019-01
DAX, E M Z01DA00020-04
DAX, E M Z01DA00022-04
DAX, E M Z01DA00110-03
DAX, E M Z01DA00111-03
DAX, E M Z01DA00113-03
DAY, ROGER S. P30CA47904-04 9001
DAY, BILLY N S07RR07053-26 0157
DAY, EDMUND P R01GM32394-08
DAY, HARRY R R43DA05987-01A1
DAY, LOREN A R01GM42286-23
DAY, MELVIN N01LM83508-07
DAY, NANCY L K02AA00115-09
DAY, NANCY L R01AA06666-07
DAY, NANCY L R01DA03874-05
DAY, NOORBIBI K R01CA40931-07
DAY, PHILLIP S07RR05583-27 0624
DAY, RICHARD A R01GM42697-01A2
DAY, ROBERT W N01CO03870-05
DAY, ROBERT W P30CA15704-18 9014
DAY, ROBERT W P30CA15704-18
DAY, ROBERT W S07RR05761-17
DAY, ROBERT W S15CA55923-01
DAY, RUFUS S III R01CA49936-03
DAYAL, BISHAMBAR S07RR05393-30 0885
DAYAL, HARI P01CA34856-09 9001
DAYAN, JEAN S06GM08225-07 0018
DAYNES, RAYMOND A R01CA33065-10
DAYNES, RAYMOND A R37CA25917-12
DAYTON, A Z01AI00587-02
DAYTON, MERRIL T M01RR00064-27 0353
DDONOHUE-ROLFE, ARTHUR P01AI26698-03S1 000
DE ANGELIS, CATHERINE M01RR00052-30 0237
DE ARMOND, STEPHEN J. P01AG02132-11 0004
DE BLAS, ANGEL L R01NS17708-10
DE BUSTROS, ANDREE C R01CA49938-03
DE CAMILLI, PIETRO R01AI30248-02
DE CAMILLI, PIETRO R01MH45191-02
DE CAPRIO, ANTHONY P R01ES05172-02
DE CASTRO, AURORA F R44AI27006-02A2
DE CASTRO, AURORA F R44DK41601-03
DE CASTRO, JOHN M R01DK39881-03
DE CLARIS, NICHOLAS S10RR06460-01
DE CLERCK, YVES A R01CA42919-04A2
DE CLERCK, YVES A R03CA54861-01
DE COURSEY, THOMAS E K04HL01928-05
DE COURSEY, THOMAS E R01HL37500-05
DE CROMBRUGGHE, BENOIT R01AR40335-02
DE CROMBRUGGHE, BENOIT R01CA49515-03
DE CROMBRUGGHE, BENOIT R01HL41264-04
DE CROMBRUGGHE, BENOIT S10RR06239-01
DE FABO, EDWARD C R01CA53793-01
DE FERRA, FRANCESCA P50NS11036-18 0051
DE FRANCO, ANTHONY L R01AI20038-08
DE FRANCO, DONALD B K04CA01608-01
DE FRANCO, DONALD B R01CA43037-04A1
DE FREITAS, ELAINE C P50NS11036-18 0052
DE FREITAS, ELAINE C R01CA48184-03
DE FRIES, JOHN C P50HD27802-01S1
DE FRIES, JOHN C P50HD27802-01S1 0001
DE FRIES, JOHN C R01HD10333-15
DE FRIES, JOHN C S15AA09259-01

DE FRIES, JOHN C S15GM47062-01
DE FRONZO, RALPH A R01DK24092-12
DE GENNARO, LOUIS J P50AG05134-08 0015
DE GRAW, JOSEPH I R01CA28783-12
DE GROAT, WILLIAM C R01DK37241-06
DE GROAT, WILLIAM C R01DK42369-02
DE GROOT, LESLIE J R01DK13377-23
DE GROOT, LESLIE J R01DK27384-11
DE GRUTTOLA, VICTOR R29AI28905-02
DE HASETH, PIETER L R01GM31808-08
DE JONG, WILFRIED W R01EY08202-03
DE JUAN, EUGENE R01EY07576-01A2
DE LA CADENA, RAUL A K08HL02681-01
DE LA CADENA, RAUL A S07RR05417-30 0787
DE LA CHAPELLE, ALBERT R01NS27103-02
DE LA CRUZ, VIDAL F U01AI28171-03 9001
DE LA MAZA, LUIS M R01AI26807-03
DE LA MONTE, SUZANNE M K11AG00425-04
DE LA MONTE, SUZANNE M R01NS29793-01
DE LANDER, GARY E R01NS27639-02
DE LANEROLLE, NIHAL C R01NS27081-03
DE LANEROLLE, PRIMAL K04HL02411-02
DE LANEROLLE, PRIMAL R01HL35808-06
DE LANEY, T F Z01CM06388-04
DE LEO, VINCENT A R01AR33663-07A1
DE LEON, GEORGE P50DA07700-01
DE LEON, GEORGE P50DA07700-01 0001
DE LEON, GEORGE P50DA07700-01 9001
DE LEON, GEORGE R01DA05192-04
DE LEON, GEORGE R18DA06131-03
DE LEON, MONY J R01MH43965-04
DE LIA, JULIAN E M01RR00064-27 0369
DE LISLE, ROBERT C R29GM41388-04
DE LISSOVOY, GREGORY R01HS06138-03
DE LONG, MAHLON R R01NS15417-11
DE LONG, MAHLON R R01NS23160-06
DE LORENZO, ROBERT J P01NS25630-03
DE LORENZO, ROBERT J R01NS23350-07
DE LUCA, DOMINICK R01AI29407-06
DE LUCA, HECTOR F P01DK14881-21
DE LUCA, HECTOR F P01DK14881-21 0001
DE LUCA, HECTOR F P01DK14881-21 0012
DE LUCA, NEAL A R01AI27431-03
DE MARS, ROBERT I R01AI15486-13
DE MEDINACELI, L Z01MH02541-02
DE MONASTERIO, F Z01EY00065-14
DE MONASTERIO, F Z01EY00122-11
DE MOSS, JOHN A R01GM19511-20
DE NARDIN, ERNESTO R29DE07926-05
DE NARDO, SALLY J P01CA47829-04 0002
DE PABLO, F Z01DK47002-04
DE PAOLI- ROACH, ANNA A. P01HL06308-31 0046
DE PAULO, BELLA M K02MH00709-04
DE PEYSTER, ANN S03RR03524-02
DE PINHO, RONALD A R01EY09300-01
DE PINHO, RONALD A R01HD28317-01
DE ROBERTIS, EDWARD M R01HD27700-01A1
DE ROBERTIS, EDWARD M R01HD21502-06
DE ROCHEMONT, L PIERRE R43ES05687-01
DE SANTIS, FRANK J S15HD28762-01
DE SHONG, PHILIP R R01GM39815-03
DE SIMONE, DOUGLAS W R01HD26402-02
DE SIMONE, JOHN A R01DC00122-14
DE SIMONE, JOSEPH R01DK40093-02
DE SMET, M D Z01EY00218-06
DE SMET, M D Z01EY00266-02
DE SMET, M D Z01EY00267-02
DE SOMBRE, EUGENE R R01CA49906-02
DE SOUSA, E B Z01DA00311-02
DE SOUZA, E B Z01DA00302-03
DE SOUZA, E B Z01DA00303-03
DE SOUZA, E B Z01DA00304-03
DE SOUZA, E B Z01DA00305-03
DE SOUZA, E B Z01DA00308-03
DE SOUZA, E B Z01DA00309-03
DE VALOIS, RUSSELL L R01EY00014-24
DE VELLIS, JEAN P01HD06576-18
DE VELLIS, JEAN P01HD06576-18 0018
DE VELLIS, JEAN P30HD04612-21 9004
DE VELLIS, JEAN R01NS29220-01
DE VITO, JUNE L P51RR00166-30 9019
DE VITO, JUNE L. P51RR00166-30 0056
DE VITO, WILLIAM J R29NS26343-03
DE VIVO, DARRYL C M01RR00645-20 0500
DE VOE, ROBERT D S07RR05962-05
DE VOE, ROBERT D S15EY09453-01
DE VOOGD, TIMOTHY J R01HD21033-06
DE VRIES, GEERT J R01MH47538-01
DE VRIES, GEORGE H R01NS10821-18
DE VRIES, GEORGE H R01NS15408-13
DE WAAL, FRANS B R01RR05276-03
DE WAAL, FRANS B M P51RR00165-31 0173
DE WEER, PAUL J R01NS11223-20
DE WIT, HARRIET M01RR00055-30 0545
DE WIT, HARRIET M01RR00055-30 0546
DE WIT, HARRIET M01RR00055-30 0533
DE WIT, HARRIET P50DA00250-20 0027
DE WIT, HARRIET R01DA02812-11
DE WIT, HARRIET R01DA06176-02
DEA, PHOEBE K S06GM08101-20 0021
DEACON, DIANA R01DC00895-02
DEADWYLER, SAMMUAL A P01MH44337-03 0002
DEADWYLER, SAMUEL A K05DA00119-04
DEADWYLER, SAMUEL A P50DA06634-01A1 0003
DEADWYLER, SAMUEL A R01DA04441-05
DEADWYLER, SAMUEL A R37DA03502-08
DEAK, SUSAN B R29HL39869-04
DEAL, E CHANDLER P01HL25830-11A1 0006
DEAN-BERNHOFT, CARON S07RR05434-30 0805
DEAN-JOHNSON, BARBARA A R18MH46082-03
DEAN, A Z01DK15508-04
DEAN, ALFRED R01MH41781-06
DEAN, DEBORAH A K11EY00310-01A1
DEAN, DONALD H R01AI29092-03
DEAN, DOUGLAS C R01CA49438-02
DEAN, DOUGLAS C R01HL43418-03
DEAN, GARY P01AI28392-02 0001
DEAN, GARY E R01GM39555-04
DEAN, J Z01DK15506-08
DEAN, PHILLIP N R01GM42817-01A1
DEANFIELD, JOHN E. N01HV18125-02
DEANS, ROBERT J P01NS18146-10 0004
DEANS, ROBERT J P01NS26991-02 0002
DEAR, KEITH B G S07RR05526-29 0086
DEARBORN, DORR P30DK27651-09 9012
DEARBORN, DORR G R01DK41331-03
DEARDEN, KIRK A S07RR05829-09 0954
DEARMOND, STEPHEN J P01NS14069-14 0012
DEASE, D Z01CP05618-03
DEATHERAGE, J P41RR02250-06 0008
DEATHERAGE, JAMES F R01AR33141-06
DEATON, JEFFERY L. M01RR00109-28 0311
DEATRICK, JANET A S07RR05948-05 0327
DEB, SWATI S07RR07187-13 0694
DEB, SWATI P U01AI31498-01 0003
DEBAKEY, MICHEAL E M01RR00350-25 0364
DEBAS, HAILE T R01DK37173-06A1
DEBAUCHE, DAVID M S07RR05386-30 0578
DEBELL, K Z01BH02014-03
DEBIASI, SILVIA R01NS27827-02
DEBOLD, JOSEPH S07RR07179-14 0677
DEBOLD, ROWAN M01RR00095-31 0353
DEBOLD, ROWAN S07RR05424-30 0097
DEBROY, CHITRITA R03AI32253-01
DEBRUIN, KENNETH S07RR07127-23 0497
DEBRUIN, WILLIAM M01RR06020-02 0440
DEBRUNNER, PETER G R01GM16406-22
DEBRUNNER, PETER G S10RR06390-01
DEBS, ROBERT J R01AI26128-04
DEBS, ROBERT J R01AI27681-02
DEBUS, RICHARD J R01GM43496-02
DEBUSK, ROBERT F R01HL36734-05
DEBUSK, ROBERT F R01HL46260-01
DECAMILLA, JOHN J R44HL38588-03
DECAMILLI, PIETRO P01DK43078-02 9003
DECAPRIO, JAMES K11CA01385-04
DECARLI, C Z01AG00132-09
DECARLO, ARTHUR S07RR05300-30 0214
DECASTRO, CARLOS M K11HL02643-01
DECHERNEY, ALAN H U10HD26975-02
DECHOW, PAUL C R01DE07761-06
DECI, EDWARD L R01HD19914-04A2
DECI, EDWARD L R01MH47293-01
DECKARD, LINDSAY A S07RR05676-15 0950
DECKELBAUM, RICHARD M01RR00645-20 0362
DECKELBAUM, RICHARD J P01AI26497-03
DECKELBAUM, RICHARD J P50HL21006-15 0012
DECKELBAUM, RICHARD J R01HL40404-04
DECKER, MICHAEL P01AG10481-01 9004
DECKER, ROBERT S R01HL33616-08
DECOSTER, THOMAS A S07RR05583-27 0625
DECRESCITO, VINCENT P50NS10164-19 9001
DEDMAN, JOHN R R01AR41309-01
DEDMAN, JOHN R R01DK41740-04
DEDMAN, JOHN R R01GM29323-09
DEDRICK, DALE K K11AR01793-05
DEDRICK, R L Z01RR10001-23
DEDRICK, R L Z01RR10276-04
DEEG, JOACHIM, H P01CA18029-16 0031
DEEMS, DANIEL A. P01DC00161-11 0012
DEEN, DARWIN D JR R01CA32241-09
DEEN, DENIS P01CA13525-19 9001
DEEN, DENNIS P01CA13525-19 0025
DEEN, WILLIAM M P01CA26731-12 0006
DEEN, WILLIAM M R01DK41641-01A1
DEEN, WILLIAM M R37DK20368-14
DEEPE, GEORGE S K04AI00856-05
DEEPE, GEORGE S R01AI23017-06
DEERING, REGINALD A R01GM16620-22
DEERY, WILLIAM R01DK26088-12
DEES, W LES K02AA00104-05
DEES, W LES R01AA07216-06
DEFELICE, LOUIS J P01HL27385-11 0002
DEFELICE, LOUIS J P01HL27385-11 9002
DEFENDI, VITTORIO P30CA16087-14 9008
DEFENDI, VITTORIO P30CA16087-14
DEFFEBACH, MARK E K08HL02383-03
DEFFENBACHER, JERRY L P50DA07074-02 0003
DEFILIPPES, F Z01AI00126-19
DEFOE, DENNIS M S07RR05365-30 0078
DEFRANCO, DONALD B S07RR07084-26 0322
DEFRIESE, GORDON H P20AG09648-02
DEFRIESE, GORDON H S07RR07072-26 0263
DEFRONZO, RALPH A M01RR01346-10 0153
DEFRONZO, RALPH A M01RR01346-10 0154
DEFRONZO, RALPH A M01RR01346-10 0155
DEFRONZO, RALPH A M01RR01346-10 0157
DEFRONZO, RALPH A M01RR01346-10 0158
DEFRONZO, RALPH A M01RR01346-10 0181
DEFRONZO, RALPH A M01RR01346-10 0182
DEFRONZO, RALPH A M01RR01346-10 0183
DEFRONZO, RALPH A M01RR01346-10 0184
DEFRONZO, RALPH A M01RR01346-10 0185
DEFRONZO, RALPH A M01RR01346-10 0186
DEFRONZO, RALPH A M01RR01346-10 0187
DEFRONZO, RALPH A M01RR01346-10 0156
DEFTOS, LEONARD J M01RR00827-17 0461
DEFTOS, LEONARD J R01AR15888-18
DEFTOS, LEONARD J R01CA47373-04
DEFTOS, LEONARD J R01CA49474-02
DEFUSCO, PATRICIA A U10CA43652-05
DEGEN, JAY L R29CA44611-05
DEGEN, SANDRA J R29HL38232-05
DEGENNARO, LOUIS J R01NS27833-03
DEGIROLAMI, UMBERTO S07RR05712-20 0083
DEGOWIN, RICHARD L M01RR00059-30 0684
DEGRAFFENREID, LINDA N01CM17503-02
DEGRAFFENREID, LINDA N01LM93514-10
DEGROEN, P M01RR00585-20 0520
DEGRUY, FRANK V, III R29MH45441-02
DEHAAN, ROBERT L P01HL27385-11 9001
DEHAAN, ROBERT L P01HL27385-11 0009
DEHAAN, ROBERT L P01HL27385-11
DEHAAN, ROBERT L P01HL27385-11 0008
DEHART, SARA S S07RR07052-26 0154
DEHASETH, PETER P30CA43703-04A1 9002
DEHMER, GREGORY J P50HL26309-11 9001
DEIBLER, G E Z01MH00903-14
DEICH, ROBERT A R01AI27007-03
DEINES, PETER S07RR07082-26 0275
DEININGER, PRESCOTT S07RR05518-28 0506
DEININGER, PRESCOTT S07RR05518-28 0509
DEININGER, PRESCOTT L R01HG00340-10
DEINZER, MAX L P01ES00040-27 0075
DEINZER, MAX L P30ES00210-24 9005
DEISSEROTH, ALBERT P01CA49639-02 0004
DEISSEROTH, ALBERT B P01CA49639-02
DEISSEROTH, ALBERT B P01CA49639-02 0001
DEISSEROTH, ALBERT B P01CA49639-02 9001
DEITCH, EDWIN A R01GM36376-05
DEITRICH, RICHARD S07RR05831-12 0977
DEITRICH, RICHARD A K05AA00093-06
DEITRICH, RICHARD A P50AA03527-14 0019
DEITRICH, RICHARD A R01AA05868-09
DEITRICH, RICHARD A S15AA09261-01
DEJARNETTE, WAYNE T R44CA49166-03
DEJESUS, ONOFRE T R29NS26621-03
DEKABGEM TOTUA S07RR07065-26 0063
DEKERNION, JEAN M01RR00865-18 0340
DEKIN, MICHAEL S K04HL02314-03
DEKIN, MICHAEL S P01HL40369-03 0005
DEKIN, MICHAEL S S07RR07114-23 0435
DEKKER, EUGENE E R01DK03718-32
DEKOSKY, STEVEN T P20NS30318-01 0004
DEKRUYFF, ROSMARIE H R01AI24571-06
DEL CASTILLO, JOSE K06NS14938-30
DEL CASTILLO, JOSE P01NS07464-24 0046
DEL CERRO, MANUEL R01EY05262-08
DEL GROSSO, A V Z01BB01006-05
DEL GROSSO, A V Z01BB01007-06
DEL GROSSO, A V Z01BB01008-04
DEL LLANO, ANA M S06GM08216-09 0013
DEL NIDO, PEDRO J S07RR05507-29 0475
DEL ZOPPO, GREGORY J M01RR00833-17 0174
DEL ZOPPO, GREGORY J R01NS26945-03
DELAFONTAINE, PATRICE R29HL45317-02
DELAFONTAINE, PATRICK R01HL47035-01
DELAFUENTE, JEFFREY S07RR05573-13 0087
DELAMATER, JOHN D R01MH48630-01
DELAMERE, NICHOLAS A R01EY06915-06
DELANEY, CONNIE S07RR07035-26 0074
DELANEY, JAYNE E R01DE07457-06
DELANEY, T F Z01CM06379-05
DELANEY, T F Z01CM06393-02
DELANO, BARBARA M01RR00318-25 0213
DELANO, BARBARA M01RR00318-25 0226
DELAYRE, JOHN L R43CA55421-01
DELBECCARO, MARK S07RR05655-21 0812
DELCERVO, DIANE N01LM13542-00
DELCLOS, GEORGE M01RR00350-25 0389
DELEMOS, ROBERT A P50HL36536-05 0001
DELEO, J M Z01CT00204-02
DELEO, J M Z01CT00221-01
DELEO, JOYCE A S07RR05392-30 0691
DELEON, M Z01DE00526-01
DELEON, MONY J P01NS15638-13 0013
DELEON, PATRICIA A S07RR07016-18 0356
DELEON, PATRICIA A S07RR07016-18 0357
DELEUSE, BETSEY W S15CA55921-01
DELEUSE, BETSEY W S15MH49279-01
DELFS, JOHN R R01NS27685-02
DELGADO-ESCUETA, ANTONIO V P01NS21908-06A1
DELGADO-ESCUETA, ANTONIO V P01NS21908-06A1
DELGADO-ESCUETA, ANTONIO V P01NS21908-06A1
DELGADO, RAFAEL E R43NS28280-01A1
DELGUTTE, BERTRAND P01DC00361-05S1 0005

DELISI, CHARLES R01AI27471-03
DELISI, CHARLES R01AI30535-01
DELISI, LYNN E R01MH44233-02
DELISI, LYNN E R01MH44245-01A4
DELISLE, ROBERT C S07RR05373-30 0714
DELIVORIA-PAPADOPOULOS, MARIA R01HD20337-0
DELL, RALPH B P50HL21006-15 9003
DELLAPORTA, STEPHEN L R01GM38148-06
DELLSPERGER, KEVIN C K08HL02198-03
DELLSPERGER, KEVIN C P50HL32295-07 0001
DELLSPERGER, KEVIN C MD PHD R01HL20827-14
DELMAR, MARIO P01HL39707-02 0002
DELMONICO, FRANCIS L U01AI31440-01
DELOACHE, JUDY S R01HD25271-03
DELOMOS, ROBERT A P50HL36536-05 0004
DELONG, MAHLON R P50NS20471-08 0003
DELONG, MAHLON R P50NS20471-08 0001
DELONG, RALPH P30DE09737-02 9000
DELONG, STEPHEN E S15CA55944-01
DELONG, STEPHEN E S15MH49289-01
DELORENZO, LORI S07RR06012-03 0308
DELORENZO, ROBERT J P01NS25630-03 0001
DELORI, FRANCOIS C R01EY08511-02
DELORI, FRANCOIS C S07RR05527-29
DELPH, LYNDA F S07RR07031-26 0083
DELPH, LYNDA F S07RR07031-26 0084
DELSON, DAVID A N01HD13111-00
DELUCA, HECTOR F P01DK14881-21 0014
DELUCA, L M Z01CP04798-21
DELUCIA, ANGELO L S07RR05806-13 0903
DELUCIA, EVAN H S07RR07030-26 0384
DELUMEN, BENITO O S07RR07006-26 0891
DELVALLE, JOHN K08DK01823-04
DEMAREST, JEFFREY R01DK38664-05
DEMARIA, ANTHONY N N01HC65069-12
DEMARIA, THOMAS R01DC00090-21
DEMARIA, THOMAS R13DC01085-01
DEMARTINO, GEORGE N P01HL06296-31 0015
DEMBO, JEFFREY B S07RR05374-30 0748
DEMBO, MICAH R01AI21002-06
DEMBO, RICHARD R01DA06657-02
DEMBY, K Z01ES21163-01
DEMCHAK, PAUL A M01RR00082-29 0474
DEMELLO, WALMOR S07RR05419-30 0818
DEMELLO, WALMOY C S06GM08224-07 0006
DEMENAIS, FLORENCE M R01CA55772-01
DEMENAIS, FLORENCE M R01GM41885-03
DEMENT, WILLIAM C K05MH05804-22
DEMENT, WILLIAM C P01MH39437-07 0003
DEMENT, WILLIAM C P50NS23724-06 0009
DEMENT, WILLIAM C P50NS23724-06 0003
DEMENT, WILLIAM C P50NS23724-06
DEMENT, WILLIAM C P50NS23724-06 9001
DEMENT, WILLIAM C P50NS23724-06 0008
DEMENT, WILLIAM C R01AG06066-05
DEMENT, WILLIAM C R01AG10643-01
DEMENT, WILLIAM C R01NS15184-12
DEMENT, WILLIAM C R01NS27710-03
DEMENT, WILLIAM C R37AG06490-06
DEMER, JOSEPH L R01EY08313-01A2
DEMER, JOSEPH L R01EY08656-02
DEMER, LINDA L R29HL43379-03
DEMERS, LAWRENCE P01CA40011-07 9002
DEMETER, STEVEN R01NS26908-01A2
DEMETRIOU, ACHILLES A R01DK38763-06
DEMETS, DAVID P30CA14520-19 9010
DEMETS, DAVID L P01CA20432-14 9002
DEMETS, DAVID L P30CA14520-19 9003
DEMETS, DAVID L R01CA18332-17
DEMIRJIAN, DAVID C R43GM46600-01
DEMITRACK, MARK U54HD29184-01 0002
DEMLING, ROBERT H P50GM36428-07 0005
DEMLING, ROBERT H R01GM31662-09
DEMMLER, GAIL M01RR00188-27 0337
DEMMLER, GAIL J M01RR00188-27 0314
DEMOPOULOS, RITA P30CA16087-14 9006
DEMPLE, BRUCE P01ES03926-07 0001
DEMPLE, BRUCE R01CA37831-07
DEMPSEY, EDWARD C S07RR05357-30 0469
DEMPSEY, JEROME P01HL42242-04 9001
DEMPSEY, JEROME A P01HL42242-04 0002
DEMPSEY, JEROME A P01HL42242-04
DEMPSEY, JEROME A P01HL42242-04 9003
DEMPSEY, JEROME A R37HL15469-19
DEMPSEY, MARY E R01HL28176-08
DEMPSEY, NORAH S07RR05611-22 0708
DEMPSEY, ROBERT J R01NS28000-02
DEMPSTER, D M01RR00645-20 0438
DEMPSTER, D W S07RR05649-25 0789
DEMPSTER, DAVID W P50AR39191-05 0001
DEMPSTER, DAVID W P50AR39191-05 9002
DEMPSTER, PHILIP T R44DK42396-02
DEMULDER, E Z01MH02487-02
DENARDIN, ERNESTO G S07RR05330-30 0016
DENARDIN, ERNESTO G S07RR05330-30 0017
DENARDO, GERALD L P01CA47829-04 0001
DENARDO, GERALD L P01CA47829-04 9001
DENARDO, GERALD L P01CA47829-04 9002
DENARDO, GERALD L P01CA47829-04
DENARDO, SALLY J P01CA47829-04 9003
DENARDO, SALLY J P01CA47829-04 9004
DENARDO, SALLY J P01CA47829-04 9005

DENARO, F J S07RR05773-17 0363
DENBESTEN, PAMELA K R01DE08706-03
DENBESTEN, PAMELA K R01DE09389-02
DENBOW, DONALD M S07RR07095-24 0379
DENBURG, JEFFREY L P01NS15350-13
DENBURG, JEFFREY L P01NS15350-13 9002
DENBURG, JEFFREY L P01NS15350-13 9003
DENBURG, JEFFREY L P01NS15350-13 0010
DENCKLA, MARTHA B P50HD25806-02
DENEKE, SUSAN M R01HL32824-08
DENENBERG, VICTOR H P01HD20806-05 0003
DENENNO, LEANNE N01CB85607-21
DENERIS, EVAN S R01NS29123-01A1
DENHARDT, DAVID T R01AG07972-03
DENHARDT, DAVID T R01CA50183-02
DENHARDT, DAVID T R01DC01295-01
DENHOLM, ELIZABETH M R29HL42622-02
DENIS, CLYDE L R01GM41215-02
DENIS, KATHLEEN A R43AI31285-01
DENISON, MARK R R29AI26603-04
DENKE, MARGO A K08HL02456-02
DENKE, MARGO A M01RR00633-19 0413
DENKE, MARGO A M01RR00633-19 0397
DENLINGER, DAVID L R01AI26178-03
DENMARK, SCOTT E R01GM30938-10
DENMARK, SCOTT E R01GM45532-01
DENMARK, SCOTT E S07RR07030-26 0385
DENNE, SCOTT C M01RR00750-19 0304
DENNE, SCOTT C M01RR00750-19 0305
DENNE, SCOTT C M01RR00750-19 0306
DENNE, SCOTT C M01RR00750-19 0307
DENNE, SCOTT C M01RR00750-19 0308
DENNERT, GUNTHER R01CA37706-07
DENNERT, GUNTHER R01CA39623-06
DENNERY, PHYLLIS A M01RR00081-29 0142
DENNING, STEPHEN M P30AI28662-03 9004
DENNIS, COOPER L. P30CA16359-17 9023
DENNIS, EDWARD A R01GM20501-17
DENNIS, EDWARD A R01HD26171-03
DENNIS, GARY C S06GM08244-05 0022
DENNIS, KAREN E K08NR00021-03
DENNIS, KAREN E M01RR02719-06 0121
DENNIS, SHANE R19DA06448-03
DENNIS, VINCENT W M01RR00030-30 0474
DENNIS, VINCENT W U01DK39486-04
DENNISON, BARBARA P01CA29502-11A1 0040
DENNISON, BARBARA S07RR05396-30 0773
DENNISON, DAVID K S03RR03500-03
DENNISON, DAVID K S07RR05970-06 0772
DENNISON, KATHRYN F R44AG06259-03
DENNISON, KATHRYN F R44HL34242-02A5
DENNY, CHRISTOPHER P01CA12800-18A1 0055
DENNY, CHRISTOPHER T R01CA50443-03
DENNY, JOHN B S07RR07217-08 0167
DENNY, PAUL C R01DE04960-13
DENNY, PAUL C R01DE06892-08
DENSEN, PETER R01AI20880-08
DENSNICK, ROBERT J M01RR00071-28A1 0216
DENTLER, WILLIAM L R01GM32556-09
DENYES, MARY J R01NR02101-02
DEONIER, RICHARD C S07RR07012-25 0014
DEPALO, LOUIS R K08HL02584-01
DEPAOLA, PAUL F N01DE02581-02
DEPAOLA, PAUL F P50DE07009-08
DEPAOLI-ROACH, ANNA A K04DK01690-05
DEPAOLI-ROACH, ANNA A R01DK36569-06
DEPAOLO, LOUIE V. P01AG01188-13 0010
DEPAOLO, LOUIS P01HD09690-18 0003
DEPAOLO, LOUIS P01HD09690-18 9003
DEPARTMENT OF PSYCHIATRY N01AA00013-00
DEPAUL, ROXANNE R29DC00921-01
DEPAULO, J RAYMOND, JR R01MH42243-04
DEPAULO, J RAYMOND, JR U01MH46274-03
DEPHILIP, ROBERT M R01HD19735-06
DEPINHO, RONALD P30CA13330-20 9017
DEPP, RICHARD, III U01HD21363-06S1
DEQUATTRO, VINCENT M01RR00043-31 0476
DEQUATTRO, VINCENT M01RR00043-31 0477
DER, CHANNING J R01CA42978-05
DER, CHANNING J R01CA52072-02
DER, CHANNING J R01CA55008-01
DERBY, CHARLES S07RR07171-08 0153
DERBY, CHARLES D K04DC00002-02
DERBY, CHARLES D R01DC00312-06
DEREN, SHERRY R18DA05746-03S1
DEREN, SHERRY U01DA07286-01
DERENDOFF, HARTMUT M01RR00082-29 0478
DERENZO, STEVE E R01CA48002-02
DERIEL, JON K S07RR05417-30 0788
DERMODY, TERENCE S K11AI00865-05
DEROOS, ROGER S07RR07053-26 0139
DEROSE, EUGENE F R43RR06983-01
DEROSIER, DAVID J R01GM26357-13
DEROSIER, DAVID J R37GM35433-07
DEROSIERS, RONALD C U01AI26463-04 0003
DEROUEN, TIMOTHY U01AI31448-01 9001
DEROUEN, TIMOTHY A P30DE09743-02 9001
DEROVEN, TIMOTHY A P01AI24756-05 9003
DERRYBERRY, DOUGLAS A R01MH45360-01A1
DERSE, D Z01CP05528-05
DERSE, D Z01CP05583-04
DERSE, D Z01CP05683-01

DERUBEIS, ROBERT P50MH45178-02 0003
DERUBERTIS, FREDERICK R R01CA31680-10
DERVAN, PETER B R01GM35724-06
DERVAN, PETER B R01HG00329-03
DES JARLAIS, DON C R01DA03574-08
DESAI, ASHOK N01CM97571-03
DESAI, PRAFUL R01CA48717-03
DESCADA, MYRA N01CN15384-00
DESCH, CHRISTOPHER E U10CA52784-02
DESCHENES, ROBERT J R01CA50211-02
DESCHEPPER, CHRISTIAN F P01HL29714-29 0007
DESCHEPPER, CHRISTIAN F R29HL38774-05
DESCHRYVER, KATHERINE P01DK33487-05 9002
DESHARNAIS, SUSAN I R01HM47720-01A1
DESHAYES, KURT S07RR07192-12 0618
DESHAZO, RICHARD D P50HL15092-20 0020
DESHMUKH, DIWAKAR S R01GM40366-01A2
DESIDERIO, DOMINIC M R01GM26666-13
DESIDERIO, STEPHEN V P01CA16519-17 0008
DESIMONE, R Z01MH02036-01
DESJARDINS, CLAUDE R01HD20876-02A2
DESMOND, MARY E R01HD24710-02
DESMOND, NANCY L R01NS26645-03
DESNICK, ROBERT J M01RR00071-28A1 0171
DESNICK, ROBERT J R01DK26824-12
DESNICK, ROBERT J R01DK34045-08
DESPOMMIER, DICKSON D R01AI10627-20S1
DESROSIERS, RONALD C P51RR00168-30 0156
DESROSIERS, RONALD C P51RR00168-30 0164
DESROSIERS, RONALD C P51RR00168-30 0165
DESROSIERS, RONALD C P51RR00168-30 0162
DESROSIERS, RONALD C P51RR00168-30 0155
DESROSIERS, RONALD C P51RR00168-30 0111
DESROSIERS, RONALD C R01AI25328-04
DESROSIERS, RONALD C R01CA31363-10
DESROSIERS, RONALD C U01AI26507-03 0003
DESSEM, DEAN R01DE10132-01
DESSEM, DEAN S07RR05916-08 0304
DESSEM, DEAN S07RR05916-08 0306
DESSEM, DEAN A S07RR05317-21 0745
DESTACHE, CHRISTOPHE S07RR05390-30 0669
DETELES, ROGER P30AI28697-01 9008
DETELS, ROGERS N01AI72631-16
DETERA-WADLEIGH, S D Z01MH02237-07
DETH, RICHARD C R01HL29847-09
DETHLEFSEN, LYLE A P30CA42014-06 9001
DETHLEFSEN, LYLE A R01CA22188-12
DETHLEFSEN, LYLE A S07RR05428-30 0167
DETITTA, GEORGE T R01DK19856-15
DETKE, SIEGFRIED S15DK44670-01
DETMERS, PATRICIA A R01GM40791-03
DETOLEDO-MORRELL, LEYLA P01AG09466-01
DETOLEDO-MORRELL, LEYLA P01AG09466-01 0001
DETOLEDO-MORRELL, LEYLA R01AG08794-03
DETOLLA, LOUIS J G20RR07020-01
DETRANO, ROBERT C R01HL43277-03
DETRE, KATHERINE P50AG05133-08 9004
DETRE, KATHERINE M N01DK02251-05
DETRE, KATHERINE M R01HL44284-02
DETRE, KATHERINE M U01HL33292-07
DETRE, KATHERINE M U01HL38610-05
DETTO, GIAN-PAOLO P01CA16038-18 0020
DETWILER, PETER B R01EY02048-15
DETWILER, THOMAS C R37HL37250-05
DEUEL, THOMAS F P01CA49712-03
DEUEL, THOMAS F P01CA49712-03 0002
DEUEL, THOMAS F P50HL14147-21 0020
DEUEL, THOMAS F R37HL31102-09
DEUTCH, ARIEL Y P01MH25642-18 0021
DEUTCH, ARIEL Y P01MH25642-18 0022
DEUTCH, ARIEL Y P01MH25642-18 0023
DEUTCH, ARIEL Y P01MH25642-18 0025
DEUTCH, ARIEL Y P01MH25642-18 0026
DEUTCH, ARIEL Y R01MH45124-03
DEUTSCH, CAROL J R01GM36433-04A2
DEUTSCH, CAROL J R01GM41467-12
DEUTSCH, DALE G R03DA07318-01
DEUTSCH, DAN R01DE05780-08
DEUTSCH, EDWARD A R01HL21276-13
DEUTSCHER, MURRAY P R01GM16317-24
DEVANAND, DAVANGERE P R29MH44176-03
DEVASKAR, SHERIN U R29HD25024-03
DEVELLIS, ROBERT P60AR30701-10 0018
DEVELOPMENT ASSOC. INC N01AA10009-00
DEVENPORT, LYNN D S07RR07078-18 0461
DEVENPORT, LYNN D S07RR07078-18 0456
DEVEREUX, RICHARD M01RR00047-31 0475
DEVEREUX, RICHARD B M01RR00047-31 0455
DEVEREUX, RICHARD B P50HL18323-17 0055
DEVERS, KELLY JEAN R03HS06952-01
DEVI, LAKSHMI A R29NS26880-03
DEVICHE, PIERRE S07RR07254-03 0493
DEVINE, ELIZABETH S07RR06031-02 0374
DEVINE, ELIZABETH C R01NR01539-04
DEVINE, ELIZABETH C S15HL47728-01
DEVINE, JAMES R24MH47167-02 0003
DEVITA, VINCENT T S07RR05753-19 0513
DEVIVO, DARRYL C. P60HL28381-09 0013
DEVIVO, D M01RR00645-20 0433
DEVLIN, JOHN M01RR00109-28 0361
DEVLIN, JOHN M01RR00109-28 0355
DEVLIN, JOHN T K08DK01554-06

DEVLIN, JOHN T R01DK44889-01
DEVLIN, JOHN T. M01RR00109-28 0314
DEVLIN, MICHAEL S07RR05650-25 0096
DEVOLL, ROBERT E K15DE00309-01
DEVOR, ERIC P50MH31302-14 0024
DEVOUS, MICHAEL D P50MH41115-05 0024
DEVREOTES, PETER N R01GM28007-12
DEVREOTES, PETER N R01GM34933-05
DEVRIES, GEERT J S07RR07048-26 0637
DEVRIES, Y Z01BB02011-02
DEVRIES, Y L Z01BB02008-02
DEW, MARY A R29MH45020-03
DEWAAL, FRANS P51RR00167-31 0030
DEWAAL, FRANS B M S07RR07098-26 0364
DEWALD, GORDON W P30CA15083-18 9012
DEWALD, J P S07RR05915-08 0689
DEWALD, JULES S07RR06003-04 0370
DEWALT, KATHLEEN M P20NR02979-01
DEWAN, JOHN C S07RR07062-26 0213
DEWEY, C FORBES P01HL36028-07 9004
DEWEY, C FORBES, JR S07RR07047-26 0146
DEWEY, GREGORY S07RR07138-20 0522
DEWEY, KATHRYN G R01HD24112-03
DEWEY, WILLIAM C R01CA31808-11
DEWEY, WILLIAM C R37CA31813-11
DEWEY, WILLIAM L P50DA05274-04 0009
DEWEY, WILLIAM L R01DA01647-15
DEWHIRST, FLOYD E R01DE07378-07
DEWHIRST, MARK W P01CA42745-05
DEWHIRST, MARK W R01CA40355-07
DEWHURST, STEPHEN R01AI31342-01A1
DEWHURST, STEPHEN S07RR05403-30 0806
DEWILLE, JAMES W S15AI32185-01
DEWITT, CHARLES W P30CA42014-06 9005
DEWITT, DAVID L R01GM40713-04
DEWJI, NAZNEEN N R01NS27580-03
DEWS, PETER B R01MH45641-03
DEY, RICHARD D K04HL02125-04
DEY, RICHARD D S10RR06393-01
DEY, SUDHANSU K R01DA06668-02
DEY, SUDHANSU K R01HD12304-11
DEYKIN, DANIEL R01DK39624-04
DEYKIN, EVA Y R01DA05834-03
DEYO, RICHARD A P01HS06344-03
DEYO, RICHARD A P01HS06344-03 0001
DEYO, RICHARD A P01HS06344-03 0002
DEYO, RICHARD A P01HS06344-03 0003
DEYO, RICHARD A P01HS06344-03 0004
DEYOE, EDGAR A S07RR05434-30 0807
DEYOE, EDGAR A, III R01EY08406-02
DEZFULIAN, MANOUCHER R15AI31234-01
DHANARAJAN, ZACHARIAH S06GM08111-19 0023
DHAR, R Z01CP05643-02
DHAWAN, ATAM P R29CA49976-04
DHAWAN, ATAM P S07RR07075-17 0265
DHEANDHANNO, SEKSAN R43MH48273-01
DI BERARDINO, MARIE A R01GM23635-13
DI BONA, GERALD F P01HL14388-20 0222
DI BONA, GERALD F R01DK15843-18A2
DI BONA, GERALD F R01HL40222-05
DI CIOCCIO, RICHARD A R01DK32161-04A3
DI FIORE, P P Z01CP05630-02
DI GIROLAMO, MARIO R01DK39326-04
DI LORENZO, PATRICIA S07RR07149-18 0413
DI LORENZO, PATRICIA S07RR07149-18 0414
DI MARCO, ANTHONY F R01HL34143-06
DI RUSSO, CONCETTA C R29GM38104-03
DI SILVESTRO, ROBERT A R29DK39604-04
DI STEFANO, ANTHONY F S07RR05978-04
DI STEFANO, JOSEPH J, III R01DK34839-06
DIAKUN, KATE R R29CA45316-05
DIAMOND, ADELE S07RR07083-26 0496
DIAMOND, ADELE D R01MH41842-05
DIAMOND, ALAN D R43HL47225-01
DIAMOND, ALAN M R01CA54364-01
DIAMOND, BETTY A P01AI10702-20 0005
DIAMOND, BETTY A P30CA13330-20 9008
DIAMOND, BETTY A R01AR32371-09
DIAMOND, DON J R01CA52177-02
DIAMOND, DONALD S07RR05841-12 0222
DIAMOND, FLORENCE P50MH35976-10 9006
DIAMOND, FRANK S07RR05749-19 0278
DIAMOND, HOWARD R43HL45402-01
DIAMOND, IRVING T R01MH04849-30
DIAMOND, IVAN P01AA08353-03 0002
DIAMOND, IVAN P01AA08353-03
DIAMOND, IVAN R01AA06451-07
DIAMOND, IVAN S07RR05980-05
DIAMOND, IVAN S07RR05980-05 0292
DIAMOND, IVAN S15HL47784-01
DIAMOND, JACK R01AG07732-04
DIAMOND, JARED M R01DK42973-02
DIAMOND, JARED M R37GM14772-24
DIAMOND, JONATHAN P01DK40839-03 0003
DIAMOND, JONATHAN R R29DK38394-05
DIAMOND, L S Z01AI00094-32
DIAMOND, LOUIS S07RR05831-12
DIAMOND, LOUIS S15CA56014-01
DIAMOND, MICHAEL M01RR00125-28 0678
DIAMOND, MICHAEL M01RR00125-28 0679
DIAMOND, MICHAEL M01RR00125-28 0764
DIAMOND, MICHAEL M01RR00125-28 0765
DIAMOND, MICHAEL P M01RR00125-28 0718
DIAMOND, RICHARD D P01AI28408-02
DIAMOND, RICHARD D P01AI28408-02 0001
DIAMOND, RICHARD D R01AI15338-13A1
DIAMONDIS, PETER J R43ES05385-01A1
DIANA, JOHN N P01HL36552-07 0001
DIANA, JOHN N P01HL36552-07
DIASIO, ROBERT B M01RR00032-31 0347
DIASIO, ROBERT B M01RR00032-31 0312
DIASIO, ROBERT B M01RR00032-31 0315
DIASIO, ROBERT B R37CA40530-08
DIAUGUSTINE, R Z01ES48005-04
DIAUGUSTINE, R P Z01ES70069-09
DIAZ, ANA M S07RR05419-30 0819
DIAZ, CLEMENTE N01AI85005-10
DIAZ, EMILIO S06GM08103-18 0016
DIAZ, JAIME S07RR07096-26 0074
DIAZ, LUIS A R01AR32599-09
DIAZ, LUIS A R37AR32081-10
DIAZ, MANUEL O R01CA49133-03
DIAZ, MANUEL O R55CA38725-04A1
DIAZ, PAMELA S K08AI01029-01
DIBENNARDO, ROBERT R15AR39887-01A2
DIBENNARDO, ROBERT S06GM08225-07 0016
DIBIANCA, FRANK A R01AR41376-01
DIBIANCA, FRANK A R01CA55378-01
DICARLO, STEPHEN E R29HL45245-02
DICARLO, STEPHEN E S15HL47763-01
DICARLSO, STEPHEN E S07RR05806-13 0910
DICE, JAMES F, JR R01AG07472-04
DICE, JAMES F, JR R01NS30148-01
DICE, JAMES F, JR R37AG06116-07
DICHEK, D Z01HL02219-03
DICHEK, D Z01HL02224-02
DICHIRO, G Z01NS02073-18
DICHIRO, G Z01NS02315-14
DICHTER, MARC P50NS16998-11 9001
DICHTER, MARC A R01NS24927-05
DICICCO-BLOOM, EMANU S07RR05576-27 0588
DICK, MACDONALD M01RR00042-31 0601
DICKENS, RICHARD L S07RR05994-03 0295
DICKERMAN, HERBERT S07RR05649-25
DICKERMAN, HERBERT W S03RR03101-11
DICKERSON, DEBORAH R19DA06426-03
DICKERSON, IAN S07RR05363-30 0827
DICKERSON, RICHARD E P01GM31299-09 9001
DICKERSON, RICHARD E P01GM31299-09
DICKERSON, RICHARD E P01GM31299-09 0001
DICKERSON, RICHARD E P01GM39558-05 0003
DICKEY, BURTON F R01HL43161-04
DICKEY, JOHN S07RR07261-02
DICKINSON, CHRIS J K08DK01903-02
DICKINSON, DOUGLAS P R01DE08902-03
DICKINSON, DOUGLAS P R01EY08172-03
DICKINSON, WILLIAM J S07RR07092-26 0507
DICKMAN, J DAVID S07RR05386-30 0579
DICKMAN, MARTIN S07RR07055-26 0198
DICKSON, DENNIS P01AG06803-05 0003
DICKSON, DENNIS P01MH47667-02 0003
DICKSON, EDGAR R R01DK34238-06
DICKSON, ROBERT B U01CA51908-02 0005
DICKSON, ROBERT C R01GM22749-16
DICKSON, ROBERT C R01GM41302-03
DICKSTEIN, REBECCA S07RR07129-22 0506
DICLEMENTE, CARLO C U10AA08432-03
DICORLETO, PAUL E P01HL29582-09 9001
DICORLETO, PAUL E P01HL29582-09 0004
DICORLETO, PAUL E R01HL34727-07
DIDIER, PETER J P51RR00164-30 0028
DIDLAKE, RALPH S07RR05386-30 0580
DIECKMANN, CAROL L R01GM34893-06
DIEDERICH, FRANCOIS N R01GM40989-03
DIEDRICH, DANA L R01GM34838-05
DIEHL, ANNA M E R29AA08260-03
DIEHL, JOHN S07RR07180-10 0624
DIEHL, RANDY L R01DC00427-04
DIEHL, RUTH R19DA06599-03
DIEHL, SCOTT R R01DC00038-02
DIEHL, SCOTT R R01MH45390-03
DIEKMANN, JUDY S07RR06031-02 0375
DIELMAN, TEDDY E R01AA06324-08
DIELMAN, TEDDY E R01AA08447-01A2
DIEM, MAX R01GM28619-09
DIEM, MAX S06GM08176-12 0022
DIEM, MAX S15GM47036-01
DIEMER, RICHARD S07RR05916-08 0303
DIENSTAG, JULES L M01RR01066-14 0097
DIENSTAG, JULES L M01RR01066-14 0053
DIENSTBIER, RICHARD A R01MH43974-02
DIERSCHKE, DONALD P51RR00167-31 0031
DIETER, M P Z01ES21050-08
DIETER, M P Z01ES21097-05
DIETER, M P Z01ES21143-02
DIETER, M P Z01ES21144-02
DIETER, M P Z01ES21145-02
DIETERICH, DOUGLAS M01RR00096-30A1 0294
DIETRICH, ALLEN J R01CA52631-01A1
DIETRICH, ALLEN J R01CA54300-01
DIETRICH, KIM N P01ES01566-13 0001
DIETRICH, W DALTON P01NS05820-26 0020
DIETRICH, W DALTON P50NS30291-01 0002
DIETRICH, W DALTON R01NS27127-02
DIETRICK, JOHN A S07RR05700-22 0865
DIETSCHY, JOHN M R01HL09610-27
DIETZ, JOHN R R01HL44868-01A1
DIETZ, WILLIAM M01RR00088-28 0271
DIETZ, WILLIAM M01RR00088-28 0265
DIETZ, WILLIAM H M01RR00088-28 0177
DIETZ, WILLIAM H. M01RR00088-28 0154
DIETZ, WILLIAM H. M01RR00088-28 0250
DIETZ, WILLIAM H, JR R01HD25579-03
DIETZSCHOLD, BERNHARD R01MH45174-03
DIFIGLIA, MARIAN P01NS16367-12 0007
DIFINO, SANTO M U10CA45389-05
DIFIORE, P P Z01CP05457-07
DIGBY, WARD R43RR07535-01
DIGGINS, MAUREEN R R15HD26929-01A1
DIGIACOMO, ENZO V R43CA53022-01A1
DIGIACOMO, RONALD F S07RR05432-30 0244
DIGIOVANNI, JOHN R01CA36979-08
DIGIOVANNI, JOHN R01CA37111-09
DIGIROLAMO, MARIO M01RR00039-31 0412
DIGIROLAMO, MARIO M01RR00039-31 0428
DIGNAM, JOHN D R01DE09669-01
DIGNAN, MARK B U01CA52256-02
DIKMEN, SUREYYA S R01HS06497-01
DIKMEN, SUREYYA S S07RR05432-30 0230
DIKSIC, MIRKO R01NS28220-01A2
DILGER, JAMES P R01GM42095-03
DILL, ANN E P S07RR07085-26 0336
DILL, JOHN RICHARD S03RR03483-04
DILL, KEN A R01GM34993-06
DILL, KEN A R01GM40692-04
DILL, KEN A R01GM46628-01
DILLEHAY, LARRY P01CA43791-04A1 0001
DILLER, KENNETH R P50GM21681-27 0001
DILLMAN, WOLFGANG H P50HL17682-17 0041
DILLMANN, WOLFGANG H R01HL25022-12A1
DILLON, JAMES P41RR00886-16 0008
DILLON, JAMES P R01EY08883-01
DILLON, KENNETH H S07RR05829-09 0953
DILLON, MARK E R43HL46608-01
DILLON, PATRICK S07RR05772-17 0347
DILLON, PATRICK F R01DK42268-02
DILLON, STEPHEN M. P01HL30557-08 0011
DILMANIAN, F AVRAHAM P01DK42618-02 9001
DILORETO, DAVID A S07RR05376-30 0041
DILSIZIAN, V Z01HL04869-01
DILTS, ROGER P S07RR05812-12 0482
DIMAGNO, E P M01RR00585-20 0457
DIMAGNO, E.P. M01RR00585-20 0378
DIMAGNO, EUGENE N01CB95601-07
DIMAGNO, EUGENE P M01RR00585-20 0519
DIMAIO, DANIEL C R01CA37157-08
DIMARCO, ANTHONY F M01RR00080-29 0422
DIMAURO, SALVATORE P01NS11766-17A1 0023
DIMENT, STEPHANIE R29AI28552-03
DIMENT, STEPHANIE S07RR05399-30 0914
DIMICCO, JOSEPH A S07RR05371-30 0634
DIMITROV, NIKOLAY N01CN85104-02
DIMITROV, NIKOLAY V U10CA28837-11
DIMLICH, RUTH V R29NS25635-04
DIMLICH, RUTH V W S07RR05408-30 0925
DIMSDALE, JOEL E M01RR00827-17 0422
DIMSDALE, JOEL E M01RR00827-17 0380
DIMSDALE, JOEL E M01RR00827-17 0341
DIMSDALE, JOEL E R01HL36005-08
DIMSDALE, JOEL E R01HL40102-05
DIMSDALE, JOEL E R01HL44915-01A1
DINARELLO, CHARLES A R37AI15614-13
DINAUER, MARY C K08HL02253-03
DINAUER, MARY C R01HL45635-01
DINDZANS, VINCENTS J S07RR05416-30 0557
DINES, KRIS A R44CA45915-02A1
DING, AIHAO R29AI30165-02
DING, MINGZHOU S07RR07258-02 0858
DINGERSON, MICHAEL R S07RR07242-04
DINGES, DAVID F M01RR00040-31 0388
DINGES, DAVID F M01RR00040-31 0359
DINGES, DAVID F P01MH44193-03
DINGES, DAVID F P50HL42236-04 0005
DINGES, DAVID F. P01MH44193-03 0005
DINGES, DAVID F. P01MH44193-03 0001
DINGES, DAVID F. P01MH44193-03 9002
DINGLEDINE, RAYMOND J P01NS17771-10 0003
DINGLEDINE, RAYMOND J R01NS27452-03
DINICH, DAVID R18MH49374-01
DINKLAGE, DAVID S07RR05712-20 0050
DINNO, MUMTAZ S07RR07242-04 0708
DINTER-GOTTLIEB, GAI S07RR07129-22 0505
DIODATI, J G Z01HL04871-01
DIODATI, J G Z01HL04872-01
DIODATI, J G Z01HL04873-01
DIOKNO, ANANIAS C R37AG08511-03
DIOKNO, ANANIAS C U01DK45013-01
DION, ARNOLD S S07RR05903-08 0278
DIONNE, R Z01DE00132-17
DIONNE, R A Z01DE00286-12
DIONNE, VINCENT E R01DC00256-08
DIPAOLO, J A Z01CP04629-26
DIPERSIO, JOHN F R01GM41097-03
DIPERSIO, JOHN F S07RR05403-30 0807
DIPETTE, DONALD J R01HL44277-01A1
DIPIETRO, JANET A R29HD27592-01A1

DIPIETRO, JOSEPH A S07RR05460-29
DIPIETRO, JOSEPH A S15HD28765-01
DIRIENZO, JOSEPH M. P50DE07118-07 0006
DIRITA, VICTOR J R29AI31645-01
DIRKS, DONALD D R01DC00094-17
DIRKSEN, THOMAS R S03RR03035-11
DIRKSEN, THOMAS R S07RR05795-14
DIRKSEN, THOMAS R S15DE10084-01
DIRKX, PATIENCE P30HD24051-03 9002
DISALVO, JOSEPH P01HL22619-14 0008
DISCIPIO, RICHARD G R01AI22415-06
DISCIULLO, STEVEN O R43AI30847-01
DISHION, THOMAS J R01DA07031-01
DISMUKES, GERARD C R01GM39932-04
DISMUKES, WILLIAM M01RR00032-31 0366
DISMUKES, WILLIAM M01RR00032-31 0367
DISMUKES, WILLIAM M01RR00032-31 0368
DISMUKES, WILLIAM E M01RR00032-31 0369
DISMUKES, WILLIAM E M01RR00032-31 0316
DISMUKES, WILLIAM E M01RR00032-31 0311
DISMUKES, WILLIAM E M01RR00032-31 0361
DISMUKES, WILLIAM E M01RR00032-31 0357
DISMUKES, WILLIAM E M01RR00032-31 0362
DISMUKES, WILLIAM E M01RR00032-31 0358
DISMUKES, WILLIAM E M01RR00032-31 0349
DISMUKES, WILLIAM E M01RR00032-31 0341
DISMUKES, WILLIAM E M01RR00032-31 0365
DISMUKES, WILLIAM E M01RR00032-31 0360
DISMUKES, WILLIAM E M01RR00032-31 0296
DISMUKES, WILLIAM E M01RR00032-31 0216
DISMUKES, WILLIAM E N01AI15082-00
DISMUKES, WILLIAM E. M01RR00032-31 0259
DISTELHORST, CLARK W R01CA42755-07
DISTELHORST, CLARK W R01DK39599-03
DISTERHOFT, JOHN F R01AG08796-02
DITORO, DOMINIC M. P42ES04895-03 0012
DITTA, GARY S R01GM44400-01A1
DITTAMI, JAMES P R29GM37939-05
DITTMAN, WILLIAM A P50HL26309-11 0007
DIVEN, KINTA N01CB85608-09
DIVENYI, PIERRE L R01AG07998-03
DIWAN, J S07RR07104-25 0558
DIWAN, JOYCE J R01GM20726-13
DIX, JAMES A S07RR07149-18 0415
DIX, RICHARD P01NS25569-04 0003
DIX, THOMAS A R01GM40338-02
DIXIT, VISHVA M R01CA51888-01A1
DIXIT, VISHVA M R01HL39037-05
DIXIT, VISHVA M R01HL45351-02
DIXIT, VISHVA MITRA M01RR00042-31 0650
DIXON, ANDREW S07RR05304-30 0230
DIXON, ANDREW S07RR05304-30 0218
DIXON, BRADLEY S R29HL42377-04
DIXON, D Z01ES21130-02
DIXON, DABNEY W S07RR07171-08 0163
DIXON, DABNEY W S07RR07171-08 0154
DIXON, DABNEY W U01AI27196-04 0001
DIXON, DENNIS O R01CA11430-25 0073
DIXON, DONNA L S07RR05313-30 0244
DIXON, EARL K14HL01994-04
DIXON, EARL S06GM08091-20 0011
DIXON, FRANK J P01AG01743-12 0006
DIXON, FRANK J P01CA27489-12 0004
DIXON, J SCOTT P01GM39526-05 0002
DIXON, JACK E P60DK20542-14 9009
DIXON, JACK E R01DK18849-16
DIXON, JACK E R37DK18024-16
DIXON, JACK E. U01AI27310-04 0002
DIXON, KATHLEEN P01ES05652-01 0005
DIXON, KATHLEEN R01ES05400-02
DIXON, SUZANNE P01DC01289-01 0004
DIXON, WALTER R S03RR03053-11
DIXON, WALTER R S07RR05606-25 0689
DIXON, WILFRID J R43RR07555-01
DIZ, DEBRA I P01HL06835-30 0086
DIZ, DEBRA I R29HL38535-04
DJAKIEW, DANIEL R01CA50229-03
DJEU, JULIE Y R01AI24699-05
DJEU, JULIE Y R01CA46820-04
DJEU, JULIE Y R01DA05575-04
DLOTT, DANA D S07RR07030-26 0386
DLOUGHY, STEPHEN R S07RR05371-30 0635
DLUHY, RICHARD A R29GM40117-05
DLUHY, ROBERT G M01RR02635-07 0235
DLUHY, ROBERT G M01RR02635-07 0254
DLUHY, ROBERT G R01HL45321-02
DLUZEN, DEAN E S07RR05806-13 0911
DMITROVSKY, ETHAN R01CA54494-01
DMYTRENKO, GEORGE M K08NS01255-04
DOANE, DAVID G U76PE00236-01
DOANE, MARSHALL G R01EY07526-04
DOBBINS, DOROTHY C S03RR03529-02
DOBBINS, JOHN W R01DK31969-09
DOBBS, LELAND G P01HL24075-13 0004
DOBBS, LELAND G R01HL41958-03
DOBIE, DORCAS K12AG00503-01 0001
DOBIE, ROBERT A R01DC00337-07
DOBKE, MAREK K S07RR05665-24 0896
DOBKIN, CARL S R01HG00079-02
DOBKIN, JAY F M01RR00645-20 0503
DOBS, ADRIAN S M01RR00035-31 0395
DOBS, ADRIAN S M01RR00722-19 0198
DOBS, ADRIAN S M01RR00722-19 0243
DOBSON S07RR05380-30 0894
DOBSON, ANDREW S07RR07069-26 0246
DOBSON, DEBORAH R01AG07114-05 0004
DOBSON, G P Z01AA00045-02
DOBSON, G P Z01AA00046-02
DOBSON, G P Z01AA00054-01
DOBSON, G P Z01AA00055-01
DOBSON, JAMES G, JR R37HL22828-14
DOBSON, MARGARET V R01EY05804-07
DOBSON, MARGARET V U10EY08176-03
DOCHEUX, RAMON F S07RR05381-30 0778
DOCKERY, DOUGLAS W R01ES01108-18
DOCTOR, VASANT M S06GM08094-17 0002
DOCTROW, SUSAN R R44NS28256-02
DODD, DEBRA A S07RR05424-30 0114
DODD, JANE R01NS27113-02
DODDS, MICHAEL W S07RR05897-09 0267
DODDS, W JEAN R01HL09902-26A1
DODDS, WYLIE J M01RR00058-30 0059
DODDS, WYLIE J R01DC00669-03
DODDS, WYLIE J R01DK25731-13
DODGE, HAROLD R01HL42419-03 9001
DODGE, KENNETH A K04HD00806-05
DODGE, KENNETH A R01MH42498-05
DODGSON, JERRY B R01GM41394-03
DODGSON, SUSANNA J R01DK38041-05
DODRILL, CARL B R01NS24823-05
DODSON, THOMAS S07RR05305-30 0740
DODSON, WILLIAM C S07RR05680-23 0921
DODSWORTH, ROBERT P51RR00167-31 9010
DOE, CHRIS S07RR07030-26 0387
DOE, CHRIS Q R01HD27056-02
DOEG, KENNETH A S03RR03025-10
DOELLGAST, GEORGE J P30CA12197-19 9008
DOELLGAST, GEORGE J R43HL46064-01
DOERING, WILLIAM V R01CA41325-06
DOETCH, PAUL P30AG10130-01 0003
DOETSCH, PAUL W K04CA01441-03
DOETSCH, PAUL W R01CA42607-06
DOETSCHMAN, T P01ES05652-01 0003
DOETSCHMAN, THOMAS P01ES05652-01 9001
DOETSCHMAN, THOMAS P01HL41496-03 0012
DOETSCHMAN, THOMAS P01HL46826-01 9001
DOETSCHMAN, THOMAS P01HL46826-01 9002
DOETSCHMAN, THOMAS C R01HD26471-02
DOETSCHMAN, TOM P01HL46826-01 0002
DOETSCHMAN, TOMAS P01HL41496-03 9003
DOFT, BERNARD H U10EY08614-02
DOHANICS, JANOS K08DK02014-01
DOHERTY, DENNIS P50HL27353-10 0010
DOHERTY, DENNY S07RR05842-12 0293
DOHERTY, MICHAEL J S07RR07032-26 0035
DOHERTY, PETER P01AI31596-01 0004
DOHERTY, PETER P01AI31596-01 9002
DOHERTY, PETER C P01AI31596-01
DOHERTY, PETER C R01AI29579-02
DOHM, GERALD L P01DK36296-05 0002
DOHM, GERALD L R01DK38416-05
DOHRENWEND, BRUCE P R01DE05989-07A2
DOHRENWEND, BRUCE P R01MH30710-10A1
DOHWENREND, BRUCE S07RR05650-25 0097
DOI, KUNIO R01CA24806-12
DOI, KUNIO R01CA47043-05
DOIRON, DANIEL R N44CM07261-02
DOIRON, DANIEL R R43CA55446-01
DOIRON, DANIEL R R43EY09003-01
DOIRON, DANIEL R R44CA48541-03
DOKAS, LINDA S07RR05700-22 0878
DOLAN, JAMES G R01HS06391-01A1
DOLAN, MARY E R29CA47228-04
DOLAN, TERRENCE R P30HD03352-25
DOLBER, PAUL C. P01HL11307-25 9002
DOLCE, JEFFREY J R01HL42489-02
DOLCE, PETER J G12RR03032-07 9001
DOLE, W P P01HL14388-20 0253
DOLIN, RAPHAEL M01RR00044-31 0368
DOLIN, RAPHAEL M01RR00044-31 0366
DOLIN, RAPHAEL N01AI05063-05
DOLIN, RAPHEAL N01AI05049-06
DOLINSKY, ZELIG P50AA03510-14 0017
DOLINSKY, ZELIG P50AA03510-14 0018
DOLINSKY, ZELIG S07RR05678-23 0160
DOLNICK, BRUCE J P01CA13038-19 0113
DOLNICK, BRUCE J P30CA14520-19 9009
DOLNICK, BRUCE J R01CA34301-08
DOLPHIN, DAVID H R01DK17989-16
DOMAR, ALICE D R03MH45591-02
DOMER, JUDITH E R01AI12806-13A1
DOMESICK, VALERIE S07RR05484-29 0025
DOMINEY, LAWRENCE A R44HL43465-02
DOMINGUE, GERALD J R01DK44812-01
DOMINO, EDWARD F R01DA01531-07A5
DOMINO, GEORGE S07RR07002-26 0865
DOMINO, KAREN B K08HL02507-02
DOMJAN, MICHAEL R01MH39940-05
DON, MANUEL R01DC00043-02
DONAHOE, JOHN W S07RR07048-26 0638
DONAHOE, PATRICIA K P30HD28138-01 9003
DONAHOE, PATRICIA K R01CA17393-17
DONAHOE, ROBERT M R01DA04400-03S2
DONAHOE, ROBERT M R01DA04498-04A1
DONAHUE, MANUS S07RR07195-12 0715
DONAHUE, R Z01HL02338-01
DONAHUE, RICHARD P R03HL46211-01A1
DONAHUE, THOMAS F R01GM32263-10
DONALDSON, DEIRDRE H K11AG00452-02
DONALDSON, DONALD J R01AR27940-09A1
DONALDSON, DONALD J S07RR05423-30 0050
DONALDSON, G P01CA38552-05A1 9002
DONALDSON, MILTON H U10CA48743-03
DONALDSON, ROBERT M01RR00125-28
DONALDSON, ROBERT M M01RR06022-02
DONALDSON, SARAH S P01CA34233-09 0004
DONALDSON, SUE K P20NR02300-03
DONALDSON, SUE K R01AR35132-06
DONALDSON, VIRGINIA H R01HL15690-19
DONALDSON, WILLIAM A R01GM42641-03
DONALDSON, WILLIAM F M01RR00084-29
DONATO, NICHOLAS J R29CA48906-03
DONDERO, RICHARD S R43DE09767-01A1
DONEEN, BRYON S07RR07050-26 0121
DONEGAN, NELSON S07RR07015-26 0602
DONEHOWER, LAWRENCE A R01AI28741-02
DONEHOWER, LAWRENCE A U01AI30243-02 0002
DONEHOWER, ROSS N01CM07302-02
DONEHOWER, ROSS C M01RR00035-31 0396
DONEHOWER, ROSS C M01RR00035-31 0397
DONEHOWER, ROSS C M01RR00035-31 0417
DONEHOWER, ROSS C M01RR00035-31 0398
DONELSON, JOHN E P30DK25295-12S1 9011
DONEY, KRISTINE P01CA18029-16 0033
DONEY, KRISTINE P01CA47748-03 0001
DONEY, KRISTINE C P01HL36444-11 0002
DONG, C Z01RR10360-01
DONG, C Z01RR10361-01
DONG, FAYE M S07RR07096-26 0056
DONG, WILLIE K R01NS29459-01A1
DONIACH, S P41RR01209-12 0026
DONIACH, SEBASTIAN P41RR01209-12 0005
DONIACH, SEBASTIAN S07RR07005-26 0334
DONIGER, JAY N S07RR05360-30 0774
DONIS-KELLER, HELEN R01HG00100-02
DONIS-KELLER, HELEN R01HG00304-04S1
DONIS-KELLER, HELEN R01HG00469-01
DONIS, RUBEN S07RR07055-26 0200
DONKERSLOOT, J A Z01DE00043-22
DONLEY, ROSEMARY S07RR07123-22
DONLON, TIMOTHY S07RR05353-30 0344
DONLON, TIMOTHY A R01HD28015-01
DONLY, KEVIN J S07RR05970-06 0773
DONLY, KEVIN J S07RR05970-06 0774
DONNELLY, DAVID F R01HL33783-06
DONNELLY, R P Z01BD03032-01
DONNENBERG, ALBERT D R03CA54856-01
DONNENBERG, ALBERT D R55CA44887-04
DONNENBERG, ALBERT D. P01AI27297-04 0003
DONNENBERG, MICHAEL P01AG04393-07 0008
DONNER, DAVID B P01CA29502-11A1 0056
DONNER, DAVID B R01CA44747-04
DONNERSTEIN, EDWARD S07RR07099-25 0397
DONOFF, R BRUCE S07RR05318-30
DONOGHUE, DANIEL J R01CA34456-08
DONOGHUE, DANIEL J R01CA40573-07
DONOGHUE, JOHN P R01NS22517-06
DONOGHUE, JOHN P R01NS25074-05
DONOGHUE, TIMOTHY R S07RR07036-26
DONOHEW, ROBERT L P50DA05312-05 0003
DONOHEW, ROBERT L R01DA04887-03
DONOHEW, ROBERT L R01DA06892-02
DONOHOUE, PATRICIA A R29DK41260-04
DONOHUE-ROLFE, ARTHUR M R01AI20325-08
DONOHUE, TIMOTHY J R01GM37509-04
DONOSO, LARRY A R01EY05095-08
DONOSO, LARRY A R01EY07737-04
DONOSO, LARRY A S07RR05510-28
DONOSO, LARRY A S07RR05510-28 0058
DONOSO, LARRY A S15EY09460-01
DONOVAN-PELUSO, MARYANN A R29HL45621-01A1
DONOVAN, JOHN E R01AA08007-03
DONOVAN, MAUREEN D S07RR05877-09 0592
DONOW, CAROLYN F S03RR03293-05
DONOWITZ, MARK P30DK34928-07 9003
DONOWITZ, MARK R01DK26523-12
DONZANTI, BRUCE A S07RR05806-13 0906
DOODY, RACHELLE S P50AG08664-03 0006
DOOLEY, CORNELIUS M01RR00043-31 0455
DOOLEY, DAVID P41RR02583-07 0010
DOOLEY, DAVID C R01AA08379-02
DOOLEY, DAVID M R01GM27659-12
DOOLING, ROBERT J R01DC00198-09
DOOLITTLE, RUSSELL F R37HL26873-11
DOOMES, EARL S06GM08025-21 0010
DOORES, STEPHANIE S07RR07082-26 0276
DOPPELT, SAMUEL H M01RR01066-14 0089
DOREIAN, PATRICK R01MH41948-04
DORES, ROBERT M R01RR06565-02
DOREY, C KATHLEEN R01EY08121-02
DOREY, C KATHLEEN S07RR05527-29 0520
DORF, MARTIN E R35CA39790-07
DORFMAN, N Z01DE00535-01
DORGAN, J Z01CN00153-02
DORIN, RICHARD I M01RR00997-16 0405
DORIN, RICHARD I S07RR05583-27 0626

DORINSKY, PAUL M R29HL41366-01A2
DORIS, PETER A S07RR05773-17 0375
DORMAN, JANICE S R01DK42316-02
DORMAN, JANICE S R29DK39125-05
DORMAN, MICHAEL F R01DC00654-02
DORMAN, NANCY J S07RR05386-30 0581
DORMER, KENNETH J R01HL39105-02
DORNBURG, RALPH S07RR05576-27 0597
DORNING, JOHN J S07RR07094-26 0362
DORNING, JOHN J S07RR07094-26 0364
DOROSHOW, JAMES S07RR05471-29 0591
DOROSHOW, JAMES H U10CA46368-04
DORR, ROBERT T P30CA23074-14 9006
DORRIS, R L S07RR05915-08 0681
DORSA, DANIEL M R01NS20311-08
DORSET, D P41RR02250-06 0005
DORSET, DOUGLAS L S07RR05716-20 0141
DORSHKIND, KENNETH A K04AI00843-05
DORSHKIND, KENNETH A R01AI21256-08
DORSHKIND, KENNETH A R01HL36591-06
DORSKY, DAVID I R29AI29009-03
DORUS, E S07RR07210-09 0678
DORUS, WALTER R01DA04337-05
DORWART, ROBERT A K20MH00848-03
DORY, LADISLAV R01HL45513-01A1
DOSIK, HARVEY N01HB07085-01
DOSTROVSKY, JONATHAN O R01DE05404-12
DOTSON, JAMES N01CN05243-05
DOTTERS, DEBORAH M01RR00046-31 0511
DOTTIN, ROBERT G12RR03037-07 0002
DOTTIN, ROBERT P R01GM27310-13
DOTTO, GIAN-PAOLO R01AR39190-03S1
DOTY, GORDON L U10CA45377-05
DOTY, RICHARD P30AG10124-01 0004
DOTY, RICHARD S07RR05337-30 0769
DOTY, RICHARD L P01DC00161-11
DOTY, RICHARD L P01DC00161-11 0001
DOTY, RICHARD L P01DC00161-11 0009
DOTY, RICHARD L R01AG08148-03
DOTY, ROBERT W R01NS20052-08
DOUG, DEAN F P01HD23042-03 0003
DOUGHERTY, CHARLES S06GM08225-07 0019
DOUGHERTY, DENNIS A R01GM43936-02
DOUGHERTY, JOSEPH S07RR05576-27 0594
DOUGHERTY, JOSEPH P R29CA50777-03
DOUGHERTY, MOLLY C R01NR01115-07
DOUGHERTY, THOMAS J R01CA16717-17
DOUGHTY, CLYDE C S07RR05369-30 0589
DOUGHTY, MICHAEL S07RR05606-25 0697
DOUGHTY, MICHAEL B R29GM38722-04
DOUGHTY, MICHAEL B S10RR06433-01
DOUGLAS, EDWIN C. P30CA21765-14 9010
DOUGLAS, ENGEL J P01HL45168-01A1 0001
DOUGLAS, GORDON C R01AI32307-01
DOUGLAS, J S07RR05692-22 0992
DOUGLAS, JAMES S R01HL28274-09
DOUGLAS, JANICE G P01HL41618-03
DOUGLAS, JANICE G P01HL41618-03 0001
DOUGLAS, JANICE G P01HL41618-03 9001
DOUGLAS, M A Z01CT00003-21
DOUGLAS, M A Z01CT00042-14
DOUGLAS, MICHAEL G R01GM36536-08
DOUGLAS, MICHAEL G R01GM36537-07
DOUGLAS, MICHAEL G R01GM41758-04
DOUGLAS, RICHARD N01HD62941-12
DOUGLAS, STEVEN D R03MH47422-02
DOUGLAS, TOMMY S07RR07143-20 0540
DOUGLAS, WILLIAM H P50DE08240-05 0003
DOUGLAS, WILLIAM W R01NS09137-21
DOUGLASS, JAMES O R01DA04154-06
DOUGLASS, JAMES O R01HD25970-02
DOUPLE, EVAN B P30CA23108-14 9008
DOUPLE, EVAN B R01CA40500-05
DOURADO, HEITOR V P01AI16305-13 0007
DOUSA, THOMAS P R37DK30759-10
DOUVAS, ANGELINE M01RR00043-31 0488
DOVE, EDWIN L S07RR07035-26 0088
DOVE, S BRENT K11AG00371-05
DOVE, WILLIAM F P01CA23076-14 0002
DOVE, WILLIAM F P01CA23076-14
DOVE, WILLIAM F P01CA23076-14 9001
DOVE, WILLIAM F R01CA50585-03
DOVE, WILLIAM F R01DK40393-03
DOVER, GEORGE J R01HL28028-10
DOVICHI, NORMAN J P30HG00199-01 0002
DOW-EDWARDS, DIANA L R01DA04118-05
DOW, STEVEN W K11AI00952-03
DOWD, FRANK J R01DE06115-07
DOWD, PAUL R01GM19906-14A1
DOWD, PAUL R01GM39825-04
DOWELL, RUSSELL P01HL36552-07 0012
DOWHAN, WILLIAM R01GM20478-19
DOWHAN, WILLIAM R01GM35143-06
DOWLING, GLENNA S07RR05604-14 0676
DOWLING, GLENNA A R01NR02968-01
DOWLING, JOHN E R01EY00824-21
DOWLING, JOHN E R37EY00811-20
DOWLING, JOHN N S07RR05416-30 0558
DOWLING, PETER C S07RR05393-30 0886
DOWMAN, ROBERT R29NS28797-02
DOWNARD, JOHN S S07RR07078-18 0462
DOWNES, HALL P01NS17493-08 9001
DOWNEY, GERALDINE S07RR07138-20 0530
DOWNEY, H FRED R01HL35027-06A2
DOWNEY, H FRED S07RR05879-09 0599
DOWNEY, JAMES M R01HL20648-12A2
DOWNEY, KATHLEEN U01AI25696-05 0004
DOWNING, ARTHUR N01LM13501-00
DOWNING, DONALD R01AR22083-12S1
DOWNING, DONALD T R01AR32374-08
DOWNING, JAMES R K08CA01429-03
DOWNING, KENNETH H P01GM36884-06 0001
DOWNING, KENNETH H S07RR05918-08 0700
DOWNING, ROBERT P01AI26482-03S1 9002
DOWNING, S EVANS R01HL38034-05
DOWNS, ROBERT M01RR00065-29 0340
DOWNS, ROBERT M01RR00065-29 0049
DOWNS, ROBERT M01RR00065-29 0368
DOWNS, ROBERT M01RR00065-29 0225
DOWNS, ROBERT M01RR00065-29 0369
DOWNS, ROBERT M01RR00065-29 0364
DOWNS, STEPHEN M R01HD25291-03
DOWSE, HAROLD S07RR07161-14 0847
DOWSE, HAROLD B R01NS26412-03
DOWTON, S BRUCE M01RR06021-02 1019
DOWTON, S BRUCE R01AI24835-06
DOXSEE, KENNETH M R29GM39494-04
DOYLE, CAROLYN F R29GM46391-01
DOYLE, DARRELL J R01CA38773-07S1
DOYLE, DONALD D R01HL44004-02
DOYLE, LAURIE G P51RR00169-30 0139
DOYLE, MARILYN S07RR05745-19 0260
DOYLE, MARILYN G M01RR02558-07 0061
DOYLE, MARILYN G M01RR02558-07 0062
DOYLE, MARILYN G M01RR02558-07 0063
DOYLE, MICHAEL P R01GM46503-01
DOYLE, RONALD J R01DE07199-06
DOZIER, MARY R29MH44691-03
DRABKIN, HARRY P01HD17449-08 0006
DRABKIN, HARRY A R01HD23826-04
DRABKIN, HARRY A R01HG00358-04
DRACH, JOHN N01AI72641-09
DRACH, JOHN C U01AI25739-04
DRACH, JOHN C U01AI31718-01 0002
DRACHMAN, DANIEL B M01RR00035-31 0399
DRACHMAN, DANIEL B R01NS23719-06
DRACKLEY, JAMES K S07RR07030-26 0388
DRACOPOLI, NICHOLAS C R01HG00395-01
DRACUP, KATHLEEN A R01NR02434-01A1
DRAGALIN, DAN P01AI19554-08S1 0002
DRAGER, URSULA C R01EY01938-15
DRAKE, DAVID S07RR05313-30 0243
DRAKE, DAVID R P30DE10126-01 0001
DRAKE, DAVID R R03DE09373-01A1
DRAKE, DAVID R R29DE09316-02
DRAKE, J W Z01ES65042-04
DRAKE, J W Z01ES65045-05
DRAKE, J W Z01ES65054-04
DRAKE, J W Z01ES65071-01
DRAKE, MILES E M01RR00034-31 0365
DRAKE, NEIL P41LM05205-08 9003
DRAKE, ROBERT E K02MH00839-03
DRAKE, ROBERT E R01AA08341-03
DRAKE, ROBERT E R01DK41859-03
DRAKE, ROBERT E R18MH46072-03
DRAKE, ROBERT E R18MH47650-02
DRAKE, ROBERT E U01AA08840-02
DRANOFF, GLENN K11HL02221-03
DRAPER, DAVID E R01GM29048-11
DRAPER, DAVID E R01GM37005-06
DRAPER, ROCKFORD K R01GM34297-06A2
DRAPER, ROCKFORD K R01GM43612-01A1
DRAPER, WILLIAM P42ES04705-05 0007
DRASH, ALAN M01RR00084-29 0180
DRASH, ALLAN L M01RR00056-30 0227
DRASH, ALLAN L R01DK24021-13
DRASH, ALLAN L U01DK30665-09
DRASH, ALLAN L. M01RR00084-29 0196
DRATMAN, MARY P01MH44210-03 0004
DRATMAN, MARY B R01MH45252-03
DRATZ, E P41RR06030-01A1 0005
DRATZ, EDWARD A R01EY06913-06
DRATZ, EDWARD A S15AI32215-01
DRAY, SHELDON R01CA30088-11
DRAYER, BURTON P P60HL28391-09 0002
DRAZEN, JEFFERY M P01HL33009-07 0003
DRAZEN, JEFFREY M M01RR01032-16 0472
DRAZEN, JEFFREY M P01HL36110-07 0002
DRAZEN, JEFFREY M P01HL36110-07 0008
DRAZEN, JEFFREY M R01HL39827-04
DRAZEN, JEFFREY M U01AI31599-01 0001
DRAZEN, JEFFREY M. P50HL19170-15 0016
DRECHSLER-PARKS, DEBORAH M R01HL45915-01
DREESEN, THOMAS D R55GM44586-01A1
DREIFUSS, FRITZ E M01RR00847-18 0550
DREIFUSS, FRITZ E M01RR00847-18 0390
DREIFUSS, FRITZ E M01RR00847-18 0535
DREIFUSS, FRITZ E M01RR00847-18 0491
DREIFUSS, FRITZ E M01RR00847-18 0433
DREIFUSS, FRITZ E N01NS72313-01
DRESCHER, DENNIS G R01DC00156-12
DRESKIN, STEPHEN C R01GM45578-01A1
DRESSER, MICHAEL E R29GM45250-01
DRESSLER, G R Z01HD01800-03
DRESSMAN, JENNIFER M01RR00042-31 0453
DRESSMAN, JENNIFER B M01RR00042-31 0639
DRESSMAN, JENNIFER B M01RR00042-31 0652
DRESSMAN, JENNIFER B M01RR00042-31 0646
DREVETS, WAYNE C K20MH00928-01
DREYER, EVAN B K08NS01395-03
DREYER, RICHARD F N01EY02126-02
DREYER, WILLIAM J R01HL47163-01
DREYER, WILLIAM J R01EY07752-03S1
DREYFUS, CHERYL P01HD23315-05 0005
DREYFUS, LAWRENCE A R01AI32736-01
DREYFUS, LAWRENCE A R29AI24684-05
DREYFUSS, GIDEON R01GM31888-09
DREZNER, MARC K M01RR00030-30 0266
DREZNER, MARC K R01AR27032-12
DREZNER, MARC K R01DK38015-05
DRICKAMER, KURT R01GM42628-03
DRILLER, JACK S07RR05853-11 0983
DRILLER, JACK S07RR05853-11 0984
DRINKWATER, NORMAN R P01CA22484-14 0006
DRINKWATER, NORMAN R R01CA37166-07
DRISCOLL, B F Z01MH02308-06
DRISCOLL, B F Z01MH02570-01
DRISCOLL, CATHERINE S07RR05396-30 0774
DRISCOLL, DONNA S07RR05519-29 0513
DRISCOLL, DONNA M R29HL45478-01
DRISCOLL, W S Z01DE00070-19
DRISCOLL, W S Z01DE00310-11
DRISCOLL, W S Z01DE00523-02
DRISKA, STEVEN P S07RR05417-30 0789
DRITSCHILO, ANATOLY P01CA52066-02 0001
DRITSCHILO, ANATOLY P01CA52066-02
DRITSCHILO, ANATOLY R01CA45408-05
DROBNY, GARY P01GM32681-08 0006
DROBNY, GARY P R01CA45643-03
DROBYSKI, WILLIAM K08CA01534-01A1
DROGE, MICHAEL S06GM08256-03 0004
DROGE, MICHAEL H R29NS25250-05
DROGE, MICHAEL H S07RR07218-05 0456
DROSSMAN, DOUGLAS M01RR00046-31 0478
DROSSMAN, DOUGLAS A M01RR00046-31 0394
DROSSMAN, DOUGLAS A R01MH46959-01A1
DROZDOWICZ, ZBIGNIEW R43CA54670-01
DRUBIN, DAVID G R01GM42759-03
DRUCKER, ERNEST R18DA06925-02
DRUECKHAMMER, DALE G R29GM45831-01
DRUECKHAMMER, DALE G S07RR07005-26 0335
DRUELINGER, MELVIN L S06GM08197-10 0010
DRUELINGER, MELVIN L S06GM08197-10 0010
DRUES, MICHAEL E R03OH02932-01
DRUKER, BRIAN J K08CA01422-02
DRUKER, DAVID G P60DC00976-02 9002
DRUMMOND, JAMES L R01DE07979-02
DRUSE-MANTEUFFEL, MARY J R01AA03490-12
DRUSIN, R M01RR00645-20 0291
DRUY, MARK A R43OH02906-01
DRUZGALA, PASCAL J R43EY09168-01
DRYER, STUART E R29NS27013-03
DRYHURST, GLENN R01GM32367-09
DRYHURST, GLENN S07RR07078-18 0463
DRYJA, THADDEUS P R01EY05321-09
DRYJA, THADDEUS P R01EY08088-03
DRYJA, THADDEUS P R01EY08683-02
DRZYZGULA, CATHY N01CP05609-02
DU CLOS, TERRY W R29AI28358-02
DUANE, WILLIAM C R01DK42433-02
DUAX, WILLIAM L R01GM32812-08
DUAX, WILLIAM L R37DK26546-24
DUAX, WILLIAM L S03RR03103-06
DUBACH, MARK F. P51RR00166-30 0083
DUBE, WILLIAM V P01HD25995-03 0001
DUBE, WILLIAM V R29HD25488-01A2
DUBEAU, LOUIS R29CA51167-02
DUBELL, W Z01AG00258-03
DUBIN, MARK J S03RR03019-11
DUBIN, MARK W S07RR07013-26
DUBIN, NEIL I R01AI29184-03
DUBIN, NORMAN H S07RR05378-30 0993
DUBIN, STEPHEN S07RR07129-22 0502
DUBIN, STEPHEN E G20RR06925-01
DUBINETT, STEVE S07RR05354-30 0402
DUBINSKY, JANET M R01AG10034-01
DUBINSKY, WILLIAM P P01DK38518-05 0003
DUBNAU, DAVID A R01AI10311-21
DUBNAU, DAVID A R01GM43756-01
DUBNO, JUDY R R01DC00184-10
DUBOIS-DALCQ, M Z01NS02034-19
DUBOIS-DALCQ, M Z01NS02789-03
DUBOIS, A S07RR05692-22 0985
DUBOIS, PAUL P51RR00167-31 9011
DUBOSE, COIT M S07RR05538-29 0540
DUBOSE, THOMAS D, JR R01DK30603-12
DUBOWY, RONALD L U10CA41721-06 0028
DUBOWY, RONALD L U10CA41721-06 0008
DUBOWY, RONALD L U10CA41721-06 0029
DUBOWY, RONALD L U10CA41721-06 0030
DUBOWY, RONALD L U10CA41721-06 0009
DUBOWY, RONALD L U10CA41721-06 0010
DUBOWY, RONALD L U10CA41721-06 0031
DUBOWY, RONALD L U10CA41721-06 0032
DUBOWY, RONALD L U10CA41721-06 0033
DUBOWY, RONALD L U10CA41721-06 0034

DUBOWY, RONALD L U10CA41721-06 0035
DUBOWY, RONALD L U10CA41721-06 0036
DUBOWY, RONALD L U10CA41721-06 0037
DUBOWY, RONALD L U10CA41721-06 0011
DUBOWY, RONALD L U10CA41721-06 0012
DUBOWY, RONALD L U10CA41721-06 0013
DUBOWY, RONALD L U10CA41721-06 0014
DUBOWY, RONALD L U10CA41721-06 0015
DUBOWY, RONALD L U10CA41721-06 0016
DUBOWY, RONALD L U10CA41721-06 0017
DUBOWY, RONALD L U10CA41721-06 0018
DUBOWY, RONALD L U10CA41721-06 0019
DUBOWY, RONALD L U10CA41721-06 0020
DUBOWY, RONALD L U10CA41721-06 0021
DUBOWY, RONALD L U10CA41721-06 0022
DUBOWY, RONALD L U10CA41721-06 0023
DUBOWY, RONALD L U10CA41721-06 0038
DUBOWY, RONALD L U10CA41721-06 0039
DUBOWY, RONALD L U10CA41721-06 0040
DUBOWY, RONALD L U10CA41721-06 0041
DUBOWY, RONALD L U10CA41721-06 0042
DUBOWY, RONALD L U10CA41721-06 0024
DUBOWY, RONALD L U10CA41721-06 0025
DUBOWY, RONALD L U10CA41721-06 0026
DUBOWY, RONALD L U10CA41721-06 0027
DUBOWY, RONALD L U10CA41721-06 0043
DUBOWY, RONALD L U10CA41721-06
DUBOWY, RONALD L U10CA41721-06 0001
DUBOWY, RONALD L U10CA41721-06 0002
DUBOWY, RONALD L U10CA41721-06 0003
DUBOWY, RONALD L U10CA41721-06 0004
DUBOWY, RONALD L U10CA41721-06 0044
DUBOWY, RONALD L U10CA41721-06 0045
DUBOWY, RONALD L U10CA41721-06 0046
DUBOWY, RONALD L U10CA41721-06 0047
DUBOWY, RONALD L U10CA41721-06 0005
DUBOWY, RONALD L U10CA41721-06 0006
DUBOWY, RONALD L U10CA41721-06 0007
DUBOWY, RONALD L U10CA41721-06 0048
DUBOWY, RONALD L U10CA41721-06 0049
DUBOWY, RONALD L U10CA41721-06 0050
DUBOWY, RONALD L U10CA41721-06 0051
DUBOWY, RONALD L U10CA41721-06 0052
DUBOWY, RONALD L U10CA41721-06 0053
DUBOWY, RONALD L U10CA41721-06 0054
DUBOWY, RONALD L U10CA41721-06 0055
DUBOWY, RONALD L U10CA41721-06 0056
DUBOWY, RONALD L U10CA41721-06 0057
DUBOWY, RONALD L U10CA41721-06 0058
DUBOWY, RONALD L U10CA41721-06 0059
DUBOWY, RONALD L U10CA41721-06 0060
DUBROW, ROBERT M01RR00125-28 0738
DUBROW, ROBERT P01CA42101-06 0008
DUBROW, ROBERT S07RR05443-30 0989
DUBROW, ROBERT D K07CA01463-03
DUBYAK, GEORGE R R01GM36387-05
DUCAT, LEE U24RR06042-03
DUCH, DANIEL S R01GM41102-05
DUCHEYNE, PAUL P50AR39226-05 0005
DUCHEYNE, PAUL R01AR40194-01A1
DUCK, STEPHEN C. M01RR00058-30 0217
DUCKETT, LAURA J R01NR01938-03
DUCKLES, SUE P R01AG06912-05
DUCKROW, ROBERT B R01NS24109-05
DUCLOS, TERRY W S07RR05583-27 0627
DUDEK, BRUCE C R01AA09038-01
DUDEK, F EDWARD P01HD05958-20 0012
DUDEK, FRANCIS E R01NS16683-10
DUDGEON, DAVID L S07RR05378-30 0994
DUDLEY, DONALD J K08HD00964-01
DUDLEY, JAQUELIN P R01CA34780-07
DUDLEY, WALTER C S06GM08073-20 0010
DUDOCK, BERNARD S S07RR07067-26 0215
DUDYCZ, LECH W S07RR05712-20 0084
DUEKER, DAVID S07RR05387-30 0609
DUELAND, RUDOLPH S07RR05912-08 0656
DUESBERG, PETER H R35CA39915-07
DUESER, RAYMOND P S07RR07094-26 0363
DUESTER, GREGG S07RR07127-23 0493
DUESTER, GREGG L K02AA00119-03
DUESTER, GREGG L R01AA07261-06
DUFAU, M L Z01HD00147-16
DUFAU, M L Z01HD00150-16
DUFF, THOMAS A R01NS20637-07
DUFFEE, DAVID E S07RR07122-23 0097
DUFFEE, DOUGLAS S07RR05959-06 0021
DUFFEE, NICOLE E S07RR07079-26 0298
DUFFEL, MICHAEL W R01CA38683-08
DUFFEY, MICHAEL E R01DK38026-02
DUFFIELD, RICHARD M S06GM08016-21 0027
DUFFY, FRANK H P01AG04953-08 0002
DUFFY, JOHN P30CA23074-14 9015
DUFFY, LAWRENCE S07RR07254-03 0497
DUFFY, PAM R R01HS06448-02
DUFFY, SUSAN A R03MH46855-02
DUFOUR, DARNA S07RR07013-26 0959
DUGAN, WILLIAM M, JR U10CA52384-02
DUGGAN, DAVID B U10CA21060-15
DUIGNAN, MICHAEL T R43GM45660-01A1
DUKE, LINDA P30AG10163-01 0002
DUKE, RICHARD C R01AI29553-02
DUKELOW, W RICHARD P42ES04911-03 0008
DUKELOW, W RICHARD S07RR07049-26 0424
DUKER, NAHUM J P01AG00378-20 0009
DUKES, GEORGE M01RR00046-31 0489
DUKES, PETER P S07RR05469-29
DUKES, PETER P S15CA56026-01
DULANEY, CONNIE S07RR07035-26 0075
DULBECCO, RENATO P30CA14195-18 0035
DULCAN, MINA K U01MH46725-03
DULCHAVSKY, SCOTT A S07RR05736-19 0181
DULING, BRIAN R P01HL19242-15 0012
DULING, BRIAN R R37HL12792-22
DUMAN, RONALD S R29MH45481-03
DUMAS, RHETAUGH G S03RR03077-11
DUMENCO, LUBA L K08ES00244-01
DUMONT, MARK E R55GM44685-01A1
DUN, NAE J R01NS18710-10
DUN, NAE J R01NS24226-05
DUNAIF, ANDREA M01RR00071-28A1 0128
DUNAIF, ANDREA R01DK40605-03
DUNAWAY-MARIANO, DEBRA R01GM36260-06
DUNAWAY-MARIANO, DEBRA R01GM28688-11
DUNAWAY, GEORGE A R01HD16666-07
DUNAWAY, GEORGE A S07RR05843-11 0549
DUNBAR-JACOB, JACQUELINE M P20NR02334-03
DUNBAR, BONNIE P30HD07495-19 9019
DUNBAR, JACQUELINE M R01NR02107-02
DUNBAR, JOSEPH C S06GM08167-13 0034
DUNBAR, JOSEPH C S06GM08167-13
DUNBAR, ROBERT C P01CA48735-02 9001
DUNCAN, CRAIG H P60HL15996-19 0019
DUNCAN, DONALD D P01NS07226-19A2 0004
DUNCAN, EDGAR N S03RR03446-05
DUNCAN, GARY E R55DC00918-01A1
DUNCAN, IAN S07RR05912-08 0657
DUNCAN, IAN D R01NS23124-05
DUNCAN, IAN W R01GM32318-09
DUNCAN, JAMES P30CA06927-29 9025
DUNCAN, JAMES S R29HL38333-04
DUNCAN, MARILYN JEAN R29DK42056-03
DUNCAN, R P P50DE08845-04 0001
DUNCAN, ROBERT U01AI25696-05 9005
DUNCAN, ROGER S07RR05792-15 0950
DUNCAN, ROGER F R29GM42644-03
DUNCAN, S WAYNE S07RR07096-26 0076
DUNCAN, S WAYNE S07RR07096-26 0058
DUNCAN, W C Z01MH02294-07
DUNCAN, W C Z01MH02405-04
DUNCAN, W C Z01MH02430-05
DUNHAM, G Z01CT00001-21
DUNHAM, PHILIP B R01DK33640-09
DUNIPACE, ANN J P01DE09835-01A1 9002
DUNIPACE, ANN J P01DE09835-01A1 0002
DUNIPACE, ANN J R03DE09773-01
DUNKEL, EDMUND C N01AI15100-00
DUNKEL, EDMUND C R01EY06584-06
DUNKEL, REINHARD R43RR07542-01
DUNLAP, JAY C R01GM34985-06
DUNLAP, JAY C R01MH44651-03
DUNLAP, KATHLEEN R01NS28815-02
DUNLAP, KATHLEEN L R01NS16483-10
DUNLAP, MARILYN R. S06GM08125-18 0038
DUNLAP, NANCY E M01RR00032-31 0330
DUNLAP, R BRUCE R01CA15645-16
DUNLEVY, MAUREEN E S07RR05390-30 0678
DUNLOP, DAVID S07RR05651-24 0141
DUNLOP, SILBA CUNNINGHAM N01CO84338-10
DUNN, ADRIAN J R01MH46261-03
DUNN, BEN M R01AI28571-03
DUNN, BEN M U01AI31934-01
DUNN, CHRISTOPHER S S03RR03123-11
DUNN, CHRISTOPHER S S07RR07192-12
DUNN, DAVID L K04GM00517-04
DUNN, DAVID L R01GM32414-09
DUNN, FLOYD R01CA45689-04
DUNN, FLOYD R01HD21692-04A1
DUNN, FREDERICK L M01RR00030-30 0493
DUNN, FREDERICK L M01RR00030-30 0473
DUNN, FREDERICK L. M01RR00030-30 0406
DUNN, JAMES F M01RR01346-10 0044
DUNN, JOHN T R01DK11043-22
DUNN, JUDITH F R01HD23158-04
DUNN, JUDITH F R03MH46535-02
DUNN, LAWRENCE A R29MH47503-01
DUNN, MICHAEL S07RR05576-27 0610
DUNN, MICHAEL F R01DK42124-02
DUNN, MICHAEL J P50HL37117-05 9001
DUNN, MICHAEL J R01DK41684-03
DUNN, MICHAEL J R37HL22563-15
DUNN, PETER E R01GM41753-03
DUNN, PETER E S07RR07032-26 0038
DUNN, SUSAN M J R01GM42375-03
DUNN, TERESA M R01GM46495-01
DUNN, WILLIAM A, JR R01DK33326-07
DUNN, WILLIAM A, JR R01NS30161-01
DUNNICK, WESLEY A R01CA39068-11
DUNNING, JEREMY D S03RR03048-10
DUNNY, GARY M R01AI19310-09
DUNPHY, WILLIAM G R01GM43974-02
DUNSMORE, MARLENE N01CB95600-04
DUNSON, WILLIAM A S07RR07082-26 0277
DUNST, CARL J R01HD23038-05
DUNWIDDIE, THOMAS V R01DA02702-12
DUNWIDDIE, THOMAS V R01NS29173-01A1
DUPAUL, GEORGE J S07RR05712-20 0051
DUPONT, BO P01AI32918-09 0002
DUPONT, BO P01CA23766-14 0030
DUPONT, BO R01CA49096-03
DUPONT, GERRY P01CA25874-12 0011
DUPONT, HERBERT L R55AI31356-01A1
DUPONT, RENEE P50MH45294-03 0002
DUPONT, RENEE R01MH42575-03
DUPONT, RENEE M M01RR00827-17 0467
DUPONT, RENEE M P50MH30914-14 0053
DUPONT, WILLIAM D R01CA50468-02
DUPRE, JOHN U01DK30666-09
DUQUESNOY, RENE J N01AI15115-00
DUQUESNOY, RENE J R01AI23467-05
DUQUETTE, PETER H R43DA07450-01
DUQUETTE, PETER H R44HD25357-02
DURA, JASON S07RR07192-12 0619
DURACK, DAVID M01RR00030-30 0393
DURAKO, STEPHEN N01AI15123-00
DURAKO, STEPHEN J N01HD82913-13
DURAKO, STEVEN N01HD72925-28
DURAN, LISE W N43DK12272-00
DURAN, LISE W R44AI28125-02
DURAN, WALTER N R01HL43146-01A2
DURAN, WALTER N S07RR05393-30 0887
DURAND, DAVID B S07RR05429-30 0190
DURANT, JOHN R S10RR06487-01
DURAY, PAUL P30CA06927-29 9015
DURBAN, ELISA M R01DE07766-05
DURBIN, PATRICIA W R01ES02698-09
DURE, LEON S K11HD00983-01
DURFEE, WILLIAM K S07RR07047-26 0145
DURHAM, DIANNE P01DC00520-04 0003
DURHAM, JOHN P41RR01395-10 0018
DURHAM, NORMAN N S07RR07077-24
DURICA, DAVID S S07RR07078-18 0464
DURIE, PETER P50DK41980-03 0002
DURING, MATTHEW J R29NS28227-02
DURKIN, MAUREEN S R29NS27971-02
DURNAM, DIANE P01CA18029-16 0025
DURNAM, DIANE M R01CA53866-02
DUROJAIYE, MUSTAPHA A S06GM45913-01 0003
DURUM, S K Z01CM09287-07
DUSDIEKER, LOIS B M01RR00059-30 0458
DUSDIEKER, LOIS B M01RR00059-30 0546
DUSENBERY, DAVID S07RR07024-26 0027
DUSENBURY, LINDA P50DA07656-01 0004
DUSSAULT, PATRICK S07RR07055-26 0180
DUSSAULT, PATRICK S07RR07055-26 0186
DUSSAULT, PATRICK H R29GM45571-01A1
DUTCHER, SUSAN K P41RR00592-22 0027
DUTCHER, SUSAN K R01GM32843-08
DUTT, KAMLA S06GM08248-05 0003
DUTTA, SISIR K S06GM08016-21 0083
DUTTON, JONATHAN J U10EY06848-06
DUTTON, P LESLIE P41RR01348-10 0002
DUTTON, P LESLIE R37GM27309-13
DUTTON, PETER L R01GM41048-03
DUTTON, RICHARD P01AI23287-06 0006
DUTTON, RICHARD W P01AI23287-06
DUTTON, RICHARD W P01AI23287-06 0002
DUTTON, RICHARD W R37AI08795-23
DUVALL, ARNDT J P50DC00110-17 0023
DUVALL, ARNDT J, III P50DC00110-17
DUVALL, MICHAEL D K11DK01935-02
DUVIC, MADELEINE R01AR39915-03
DUVIC, MADELEINE R01AR40520-02
DUVIC, MADELEINE R01HD24427-02
DUVOISIN, ROGER C P01NS21469-07
DUZGUNES, NEJAT A R01AI25534-05
DVORAK, ANN M R01CA28834-12
DVORAK, HAROLD F R01CA28471-12
DVORAK, HAROLD F R01CA50453-03
DVORAK, J A Z01AI00099-21
DWORKIN, BARRY R R01HL40837-03
DWORKIN, GERALD E M01RR00349-25 0237
DWORKIN, MARTIN R01GM19957-19
DWORKIN, S F P01DE08773-03 0004
DWORKIN, S F P01DE08773-03 0001
DWORKIN, SAMUEL F P01DE08773-03
DWORKIN, SAMUEL F P30DE09743-02 9003
DWORKIN, STEVEN I P50DA06634-01A1 0002
DWORKIN, STEVEN I P50DA06634-01A1 9004
DWOSKIN, LINDA S07RR05857-11 0925
DWYER, D M Z01AI00162-15
DWYER, JAMES H R01HL42932-01A1
DWYER, JOHANNA S07RR07179-14 0689
DYALOWICH, JACK C P01CA23099-13 0014
DYBVIG, KEVIN F R01AI31144-01
DYBVIG, KEVIN F R29AI25640-03
DYCK, PETER J P01NS14304-13
DYCK, PETER J P01NS14304-13 0037
DYCK, PETER J. P01NS14304-13 0036
DYE, EARL S R01CA50891-02
DYE, RAYMOND P50DC00293-07 0001
DYER, ALAN R P60AR30692-08 9001
DYER, CHERYL A R01HD27167-01A1
DYER, DAVID P50DE08240-05 0007
DYER, DAVID W R01AI23357-05A2
DYKE, BENNETT P01HL45522-01A1 9002
DYKE, BENNETT R01RR02229-08

DYKSTRA, CHRISTINE C S07RR05406-30 0881
DYKSTRA, LINDA A K05DA00033-15
DYKSTRA, LINDA A R37DA02749-16
DYKSTRA, LINDA A S07RR07072-26 0264
DYM, MARTIN R01HD16260-09A2
DYNAN, WILLIAM S R01GM35866-06
DYNAN, WILLIAM S R55CA44958-04A1
DYSON, HELEN J R01GM43238-01A2
DZAU, VICTOR J R01HL35252-06
DZAU, VICTOR J R01HL35610-07A1
DZAU, VICTOR J R01HL46631-02
DZIAK, ROSEMARY P50DE08240-05 0009
DZIAK, ROSEMARY R01AR25271-13
DZIDA, FRANKLIN J S07RR05654-24 0153
DZIELAK, DAVID J S07RR05386-30 0582
Eisenberg, E Z01HL00516-05
Elliot, S Z01DK43227-04
EAGON, PATRICIA K R01AA06971-04S1
EAGON, PATRICIA K R01AA08914-01
EAKER, ERVIN Y K08DK02007-01
EALICK, STEVEN E R29GM38823-05
EANES, E D Z01DE00088-18
EANES, WALTER F R01GM45247-01A1
EARL, NANCY L M01RR00030-30 0496
EARLS, FELTON J P50MH31302-14 0014
EARNEST, DAVID J R29NS24661-05
EARNEST, DAVID L P01CA41108-05 0002
EARNEST, DAVID L P50AA08037-04 0003
EARNSHAW, WILLIAM C R01GM30985-09
EARNSHAW, WILLIAM C R01GM35212-07
EARP, H SHELTON S07RR05406-30 0905
EARP, H SHELTON, III R01DK30002-08A2
EARP, H SHELTON, III R01DK31683-09
EARY, JANET F P01CA44991-04 9003
EARY, JANET F R29CA47430-03
EASOM, RICHARD A S07RR07195-12 0714
EAST, DAWN P30CA14395-18A1 9009
EASTELL, RICHARD M M01RR00585-20 0514
EASTELL, RICHARD M. M01RR00585-20 0372
EASTER, STEPHEN S, JR R01EY00168-22
EASTERBROOKS, ANN M S07RR07179-14 0678
EASTERLING, THOMAS R M01RR00037-31 0478
EASTERLING, THOMAS R M01RR00037-31 0390
EASTERLING, THOMAS R S07RR05432-30 0242
EASTMAN-ONEILL, ALLI S07RR05394-30 0721
EASTMAN, ALAN P30CA36727-08 9007
EASTMAN, ALAN R55CA50224-01A2
EASTMAN, CHARMANE I R01MH42768-04
EASTMAN, CHARMANE I R01NS23421-06
EASTMAN, M S06GM08215-09 0004
EASTMAN, R Z01DK47009-04
EASTMAN, R Z01DK47027-06
EASTWOOD, GREGORY L S07RR05365-30
EATOCK, RUTH A R29DC00414-05
EATON, BRUCE S07RR07097-26 0385
EATON, D P42ES04696-05 0001
EATON, DAVID L P42ES04696-05
EATON, DAVID L R01ES03933-04
EATON, DAVID L R01ES05780-04
EATON, DOUGLAS C R01DK37963-05
EATON, DOUGLAS C R01DK38830-06
EATON, DOUGLAS C R01DK44017-01
EATON, ELIZABETH G08LM05012-02
EATON, GARETH S07RR07138-20 0521
EATON, GARETH R R01GM21156-15A2
EATON, GORDON G R01RR05355-03
EATON, GORDON J P30CA06927-29 9007
EATON, GRAY G P51RR00163-32 0011
EATON, JOHN W R13GM46944-01
EATON, R P M01RR00997-16 0085
EATON, R PHILIP M01RR00997-16 0379
EATON, ROBERT C R01NS22621-06
EATON, ROBERT C S07RR07013-26 0966
EATON, ROBERT P M01RR00997-16 0150
EATON, ROBERT P M01RR00997-16 0218
EATON, ROBERT P M01RR00997-16 0361
EATON, ROBERT P M01RR00997-16 0340
EATON, ROBERT P M01RR00997-16 0309
EATON, ROBERT P M01RR00997-16 0324
EATON, SANDRA P01AG10446-01 0002
EATON, W A Z01DK29010-19
EATON, WILLIAM A P41RR01348-10 0003
EAVES, LINDON J R01AG04954-08
EBBERT, LARRY P U10CA45553-03
EBBESSON, SVEN O E R21DK44592-01
EBBESSON, SVEN O E R55NS25289-04A1
EBELING, P M01RR00585-20 0470
EBENHOLTZ, SHELDON M S15EY09444-01
EBERHARD, MARK L P51RR00165-31 0188
EBERHARDT, MANFRED K S06GM08224-07 0007
EBERHARDT, NORMAN L R01DK41206-04
EBERHART, ROBERT C R01HL28690-09
EBERLE, RICHARD W S03RR03523-02
EBERLEIN, TIMOTHY J M01RR02635-07 0250
EBERLEIN, TIMOTHY J R01CA45484-03
EBERSOLE, JEFFREY L R01DE08521-05
EBERSTEIN, ISAAC W R01MH47246-02
EBERT, ELLEN C R01DK42166-02
EBERT, THOMAS M01RR00058-30 0261
EBERT, THOMAS J R29HL38349-04
EBERWINE, JAMES R01AG09900-01
EBERWINE, JAMES H P01GM34781-07 9002
EBERWINE, JAMES H S07RR07083-26 0469
EBERWINE, JIM P30AG10124-01 0003
EBIHARA, LISA MD PHD R29HL45377-02
EBLING, FANNY P60AR36834-05 9001
EBNER, FORD F R01NS13031-15
EBNER, FORD F R01NS25907-03
EBNER, TIMOTHY J R01NS18338-10
EBNER, TIMOTHY J R01NS27210-03
EBON RESEARCH SYSTEMS N01MH80026-00
EBREY, THOMAS G R01EY01323-19
EBRIGHT, RICHARD H R01GM41376-03
EBRIGHT, RICHARD H S07RR07058-26 0175
EBY, RONALD J N01AI82689-07
ECCLES, CHRISTINE U R03DA06195-02
ECCLES, CHRISTINE U S07RR05770-13 0933
ECCLES, JACQUELYNNE S R01HD17553-06
ECHEL, ROBERT H M01RR00051-30 0677
ECHEVERRIA, DIANA R01OH02719-02
ECHOLS, HARRISON P30ES01896-13 9028
ECHOLS, HARRISON R01CA41655-07
ECHOLS, HARRISON R01GM17078-23
ECHOLS, RICHARD E S06GM08025-21 0003
ECHT, DEBRA S R29HL40396-03
ECHTELER, STEPHEN M R29DC00493-02
ECKARDT, M Z01AA00231-09
ECKARDT, M Z01AA00250-08
ECKARDT, M Z01AA00267-06
ECKARDT, M Z01AA00268-06
ECKARDT, M Z01AA00275-03
ECKARDT, M J Z01AA00239-08
ECKARDT, M J Z01AA00240-12
ECKBERG, WILLIAM R S06GM08016-21 0075
ECKEL, ROBERT M01RR00051-30 0471
ECKEL, ROBERT H M01RR00051-30 0441
ECKEL, ROBERT H M01RR00051-30 0707
ECKEL, ROBERT H M01RR00051-30 0687
ECKEL, ROBERT H M01RR00051-30 0711
ECKEL, ROBERT H M01RR00051-30 0767
ECKEL, ROBERT H M01RR00051-30 0768
ECKEL, ROBERT H M01RR00051-30 0752
ECKEL, ROBERT H M01RR00051-30 0678
ECKEL, ROBERT H R01DK26356-12
ECKEL, ROBERT H R01DK42266-02
ECKELS, DAVID D K04AI00799-05
ECKELS, DAVID D P01HL44612-02 0006
ECKELS, DAVID D P01HL44612-02 9002
ECKELS, DAVID D R01AI22832-06
ECKENSTEIN, FELIX P01NS17493-08 0011
ECKENSTEIN, FELIX P R29AG07424-04
ECKER, JOSEPH R R01HG00322-03
ECKER, JOSEPH R R29GM38894-05
ECKERMAN, CAROL O. P01HD21354-05 0003
ECKERT, J KEVIN R01AG04895-06
ECKERT, RICHARD L R01GM43751-01A1
ECKFELDT, JOHN H R01HL40848-04
ECKHARDT, LAUREL A R01AI30653-02
ECKHART, WALTER P30CA14195-18 9002
ECKHART, WALTER P30CA14195-18 0005
ECKHART, WALTER P30CA14195-18
ECKHART, WALTER P30CA14195-18 9003
ECKHART, WALTER P30CA14195-18 9004
ECKHART, WALTER P30CA14195-18 9005
ECKHART, WALTER P30CA14195-18 9006
ECKHART, WALTER P30CA14195-18 9001
ECKHART, WALTER R37CA13884-19
ECKHART, WALTER S07RR05595-27
ECKHAUSER, FREDERIC E M01RR00042-31 0510
ECKHAUSER, FREDERICK E M01RR00042-31 0578
ECKHERT, CURTIS P01CA42710-06A1 9007
ECKHOFF, DONALD G S07RR05357-30 0465
ECKSTEIN, EUGENE C R01HL33100-07
ECONOMOU, JAMES S R29CA50780-03
EDDINGER, THOMAS J S07RR07196-11 0626
EDDLESTONE, GEOFFREY T R01DK39652-02
EDDY, E M Z01ES70076-07
EDDY, E M Z01ES70077-05
EDDY, HUBERT A S07RR05379-30 0775
EDELHAUSER, HENRY F P30EY06360-06
EDELHAUSER, HENRY F R01EY00933-20
EDELL, DAVID J N01NS02399-02
EDELMAN, ARTHUR M R29NS24738-04
EDELMAN, GERALD M R37AG09326-02
EDELMAN, GERALD M R37DK04256-32
EDELMAN, GERALD M R37HD09635-16
EDELMAN, NORMAN H R37HL16022-18
EDELMAN, NORMAN H S03RR03096-10
EDELSOHN, GAIL K07MH00789-03
EDELSON, PAUL M01RR06020-02 0439
EDELSON, PAUL J R01AI19888-06
EDELSON, RICHARD L R01CA43058-06
EDENBERG, HOWARD J R01AA06460-08
EDENS, NEILE K R29DK41380-02
EDER, HOWARD A P60DK20541-14 9003
EDER, JOSEPH P K08CA01412-03
EDER, WARREN N01LM93521-03
EDER,HOWARD P60DK20541-14 0027
EDERER, FRED U10EY07057-05
EDERERI, FRED N01EY02127-02
EDGE, ALBERT S P30DK36836-05 0001
EDGELL, CORA-JEAN S P01HL06350-30 0022
EDGELL, CORA-JEAN S R01HL37653-05
EDGERTON, MIRA K11DE00213-05
EDGERTON, MIRA R03DE09931-01
EDGERTON, ROBERT P01HD11944-12 0004
EDGERTON, ROBERT B P01HD11944-12
EDGERTON, V REGGIE P01NS16333-11S1
EDGERTON, V REGGIE P01NS16333-11S1 0009
EDGERTON, V REGGIE P01NS16333-11S1 9001
EDGINGTON, THOMAS P50MH47680-02 0008
EDGINGTON, THOMAS S M01RR00833-17 0207
EDGINGTON, THOMAS S P01HL16411-18
EDGINGTON, THOMAS S P01HL16411-18 0003
EDGINGTON, THOMAS S P01HL16411-18 9004
EDIDIN, MICHAEL A R37AI14584-25
EDIDIN, MICHAEL E P41RR04328-04 0004
EDISON, LIU P30CA16086-17 9013
EDITORIAL EXPERTS, INC N01SP14001-00
EDLIND, THOMAS D S07RR05418-30 0023
EDMAN, JEFFREY C R01AI27128-03
EDMAN, JEFFREY C R01AI29312-02
EDMAN, JEFFREY C U01AI30261-02 0001
EDMOND, JOHN P01HD06576-18 0016
EDMONDS, PAUL S07RR07024-26 0028
EDMONDS, PETER D R01CA34398-07
EDMONDS, ROBERT L S07RR07096-26 0057
EDMONDSON, DALE E R01GM29433-10
EDMUNDS, L HENRY, JR R01HL19055-16
EDMUNDS, L HENRY, JR R01HL36308-06
EDMUNDS, L HENRY, JR R01HL47186-01
EDMUNDS, LELAND N S07RR05736-19 0210
EDMUNDSON, ALLEN B R37CA19616-17
EDSON, CLARK MC WHORTER R01AI21674-07
EDWARD, CORWIN M01RR00064-27 0380
EDWARDS S07RR05380-30 0890
EDWARDS, BRIAN F R01GM33192-08
EDWARDS, BRIAN F R01GM40630-04
EDWARDS, BRUCE S R01CA51130-02
EDWARDS, CHARLES S07RR05749-19
EDWARDS, CHARLES S15CA56012-01
EDWARDS, CHARLES A R29MH44100-03
EDWARDS, CYNTHIA A R01AI29856-01A1
EDWARDS, DAVID J S07RR07051-26 0729
EDWARDS, DAVID V R18MH49380-01
EDWARDS, DEAN P P01CA30195-11 0008
EDWARDS, DEAN P P01CA30195-11 0012
EDWARDS, DEAN P P01CA30195-11 9001
EDWARDS, DEAN P P30CA46934-04 9009
EDWARDS, DEAN P R01CA41386-06
EDWARDS, DEAN P R01CA46938-04
EDWARDS, EMMELINE S07RR05736-19 0204
EDWARDS, GAYLEN L R29DK42533-01A1
EDWARDS, JOHN E U01AI31696-01 0002
EDWARDS, JOHN E, JR R01AI19990-07
EDWARDS, JOHN S R01NS07778-24
EDWARDS, KATHRYN M01RR00095-31 0364
EDWARDS, KATHRYN M01RR00095-31 0363
EDWARDS, KATHRYN M01RR00095-31 0291
EDWARDS, KATHRYN M01RR00095-31 0219
EDWARDS, KATHRYN M01RR00095-31 0109
EDWARDS, KATHRYN M M01RR00095-31 0331
EDWARDS, KIAH S06GM08061-17 0010
EDWARDS, MATTHEW E S06GM08206-10
EDWARDS, MICHAEL A R01HD21018-06
EDWARDS, MORVEN S R01AI19800-09
EDWARDS, PETER A P01HL30568-09 0005
EDWARDS, ROBERT P30AG10123-01 0002
EDWARDS, RUTH W P50DA07074-02 0004
EDWARDS, S P41RR01209-12 0012
EDWARDS, SAMUEL S07RR07121-13 0474
EDWARDS, SAMUEL C R29EY08765-02
EDWARDS, W THOMAS R01AR33066-09
EDWORTHY, STEVEN R18AR21393-17 0015
EDWORTHY, STEVEN R18AR21393-17 0018
EELLS, JANIS THANE R29ES05006-03
EERNISSE, DOUGLAS J M01RR00042-31 0677
EFFROS, RICHARD M R01HL18606-16
EFFROS, RITA B K04AG00427-04
EFFROS, RITA B R01AG05309-05
EFRON, BRADLEY R01GM21215-16
EFSTRATIADIS, ARGIRIS P20HG00424-01
EFSTRATIADIS, ARGIRIS P20HG00424-01 0001
EFSTRATIADIS, ARGIRIS P20HG00424-01 9001
EFSTRATIADIS, ARGIRIS P30CA13696-19 9020
EFSTRATIADIS, ARGIRIS R01DK32085-08
EFSTRATIADIS, ARGIRIS R01HD28342-01
EFSTRATIADIS, ARGIRIS R01HG00362-04
EGAN, BRENT M01RR00058-30 0267
EGAN, BRENT M01RR00058-30 0259
EGAN, BRENT M01RR00058-30 0260
EGAN, BRENT M M01RR00058-30 0246
EGAN, BRENT M M01RR00058-30 0241
EGAN, BRENT M R01HL43164-01A2
EGAN, BRENT M S07RR05434-30 0800
EGAN, BRENT M. M01RR00058-30 0219
EGAN, J Z01AG00214-01
EGAN, M F Z01MH02257-07
EGAN, MICHAEL F Z01MH02373-05
EGELAND, BYRON R R01MH40864-06
EGELAND, BYRON R R01MH41879-05
EGELAND, JANICE A R01MH28287-15
EGELMAN, EDWARD H R01GM35269-05
EGER, EDMOND I P01AG03104-10
EGETH, HOWARD E S03RR03062-11
EGGER, MARLENE J P30CA42014-06 9007

EGGERMAN, THOMAN L Z01HL02033-01
EGGERS, PHILIP E R43CA54646-01
EGGERT, LEONA L R01DA04530-04
EGGERT, LEONA L R18MH48139-02
EGGLESTON, PEYTON A M01RR00052-30 0239
EGGLESTON, PEYTON A M01RR00052-30 0213
EGGLESTON, PEYTON A M01RR00052-30 0227
EGGLESTON, PEYTON A U01AI30773-01
EGGLETON, GORDON L S03RR03265-10
EGGLETON, GORDON L S06GM08003-21 0006
EGHBALI, MAHBOUBEH R01HL42666-02
EGHBALI, MAHBOUBEH R01HL43557-03
EGOROV, IGOR K R01GM28017-11
EGWUAGU, C E Z01EY00262-02
EHLERS, CINDY M01RR00833-17 0132
EHLERS, CINDY L K02AA00098-06
EHLERS, CINDY L M01RR00833-17 0161
EHLERS, CINDY L R01AA06059-07
EHLERT, FREDERICK J K04NS01396-03
EHLERT, FREDERICK J R29NS26511-04
EHMAN, RICHARD L R01CA51124-01A2
EHRENFELD, ELVERA R R01AI12387-17
EHRENFELD, ELVERA R R01AI17386-10
EHRENKRANZ, RICHARD A M01RR06022-02 0756
EHRENKRANZ, RICHARD A U10HD27871-01
EHRENSTEIN, G Z01NS02709-06
EHRHARDT, ANKE A P50MH43520-04
EHRHART, ALLEN P01HL29582-09 0005
EHRKE, M JANE P01CA13038-19 0115
EHRLICH, BARBARA E P01HL33026-07 0007
EHRLICH, BARBARA E R29GM39092-04
EHRLICH, H PAUL R01GM32705-07
EHRLICH, JULIAN S07RR06004-04 0033
EHRLICH, JULIAN S07RR06004-04 0034
EHRLICH, MICHELLE P01MH40899-07 0006
EHRLICH, MICHELLE E K02MH00945-01
EHRLICH, MICHELLE E R29MH47028-02
EHRMAN, RONALD N P50DA05186-05 0006
EHRMAN, RONALD N P50DA07705-01 0003
EHRMANN, DAVID M01RR00055-30 0542
EHSANI, ALI A P01AG05562-07 0002
EICHACKER, P Q Z01CL00075-03
EICHACKER, P Q Z01CL00078-02
EICHACKER, P Q Z01CL00111-01
EICHBERG JORG W U01AI26462-04 0007
EICHBERG, JORG P30AI28696-01 9002
EICHBERG, JORG W U01AI26471-04 0004
EICHBERG, JOSEPH R01DK30577-10
EICHBERG, JOSEPH S07RR07147-19 0644
EICHELE, GREGOR R01HD20209-08
EICHENBAUM, HOWARD P01AG09973-01 0005
EICHENBAUM, HOWARD B R01NS26402-04
EICHER, EVA M R01GM20919-18
EICHHORN, ERIC J P50HL17669-17 0031
EICHHORN, G Z01AG00044-18
EICHLER, DUANE C S07RR05749-19 0269
EICHMILLER, F C P50DE09322-03 0007
EICHMILLER, FREDERICK C S15DE10082-01
EICK, J DAVID P01DE09696-01
EICK, J DAVID P01DE09696-01 9001
EICK, J DAVID P01DE09696-01 9002
EICK, J DAVID P01DE09696-01 9003
EICK, J DAVID R01DE08223-04
EICKBUSH, THOMAS H R01GM31867-08
EIDELBERG, EDUARDO S07RR05654-24 0122
EIDELS, LEON P01HD22766-05 0002
EIDEN, JOSEPH J R29AI24922-04
EIDEN, L E Z01MH02386-05
EIDEN, L E Z01MH02387-05
EIDEN, M V Z01MH02591-01
EIDEN, M V Z01MH02592-01
EIDSATH, A Z01RR10329-03
EIDSATH, A Z01RR10362-01
EIGLER, NEAL L R01HL40865-04
EIGNER, TONI S07RR05336-29 0301
EIKENBURG, DOUGLAS C R29HL38767-05
EILBER, FREDERICK R P01CA29605-10 0002
EILBERT, JAMES L P41RR01638-07 9002
EIMAS, PETER D R01HD05331-21
EINHORN, LAWRENCE M01RR00750-19 0261
EINHORN, LAWRENCE H M01RR00750-19 0302
EINHORN, LAWRENCE H M01RR00750-19 0284
EINHORN, LAWRENCE H M01RR00750-19 0159
EINHORN, LAWRENCE H R35CA39844-07
EINHORN, LAWRENCE H U10CA49883-03
EINHORN, THOMAS A R55AR40701-01A1
EINHORN,LAWRENCE H. M01RR00750-19 0213
EINSTEIN, ALBERT B, JR U10CA35192-08
EINSTEIN, GILLIAN R29EY07840-03
EIPPER, ELIZABETH A K05DA00098-08
EIPPER, ELIZABETH A P50DA00266-20 0011
EIPPER, ELIZABETH A R37DK32949-09
EISEN, ANDREW S07RR05397-30 0787
EISEN, ARTHUR Z R37AR12129-24
EISEN, HARVEY A R01AI23010-05
EISEN, HARVEY A R01AI27803-02
EISEN, HERMAN N R35CA42504-06
EISEN, JUDITH P01HD22486-05 0001
EISEN, JUDITH S07RR07080-26 0308
EISEN, JUDITH S K04NS01476-01
EISEN, JUDITH S R01NS23915-06
EISENACH, JAMES C R01GM35523-06A1
EISENACH, KATHLEEN R01AI27284-03
EISENBARTH, GEORGE M01RR02635-07 0270
EISENBARTH, GEORGE S R01DK32083-10
EISENBARTH, GEORGE S S15DK44713-01
EISENBERG, DALE M01RR00645-20 0470
EISENBERG, DAVID P01GM31299-09 0002
EISENBERG, DAVID P01GM39558-05
EISENBERG, DAVID P01GM39558-05 0001
EISENBERG, JOHN M R18HS07080-01
EISENBERG, MICKEY S R18HS06473-01
EISENBERG, MOISES P01CA47995-02 0003
EISENBERG, MOSHE P01ES04068-05 0006
EISENBERG, NANCY K02MH00903-01
EISENBERG, PAUL R P50HL17646-17 0035
EISENBERG, PETER U10CA52420-02
EISENBERG, RICHARD M R01DA07186-01
EISENBERG, ROBERT A P60AR30701-10 0014
EISENBERG, ROBERT A R01AR26574-11
EISENBERG, ROBERT A R01AR34156-07
EISENBERG, ROBERT A R01AR40620-02
EISENHAUER, PATRICIA S07RR05354-30 0404
EISENMAN, GEORGE R01GM24749-22
EISENMAN, JOSEPH S S07RR05653-24
EISENMAN, JOSEPH S S15AA09265-01
EISENMAN, JOSEPH S S15DK44714-01
EISENMAN, LEONARD M R01NS22093-06
EISENMAN, ROBERT N R01CA57138-01
EISENMAN, ROBERT N R37CA20525-15
EISENMANN, DALE R S07RR05864-10
EISENSTARK, ABRAHAM R01ES04889-04
EISENSTEIN, BARRY I R01AI24731-05
EISENSTEIN, BARRY I R01AI24734-06
EISENSTEIN, REUBEN R01EY07732-02
EISERLING, FREDERICK A P01GM39558-05 0002
EISERLING, FREDERICK A P30CA16042-17 9002
EISERLING, FREDERICK A R01AI25319-05
EISERLING, FREDERICK A S03RR03502-03
EISERLING, FREDERICK A S07RR07009-26
EISERLING, FREDERICK A S15CA55998-01
EISINGER, JOSEF P01HL21016-15 9004
EISINGER, JOSEF R01RR05272-03
EISMAN, JOHN A R01AR41409-01
EISNER, ALVIN R01EY05047-08
EISNER, THOMAS R01AI02908-33
EISSENBERG, JOEL C R01GM40732-03
EKERDT, DAVID J R01AG08882-02
EKMAN, PAUL K05MH06092-15
EKMAN, PAUL S07RR05755-18 0229
EL KOUNI, MAHMOUD HAMDI R01AI29848-03
EL-BAYOUMY, KARAM U01CA46589-05 0001
EL-BAYOUMY, KARAM E R01CA35519-08
EL-DAHR, SAMIER S07RR05377-30 0766
EL-FAKAHANY, ESAM E R01NS25743-04
EL-MALLAKH, R S Z01MH02545-02
EL-MALLAKH, R S Z01MH02546-02
EL-MALLAKH, R S Z01MH02547-02
EL-MALLAKH, R S Z01MH02548-02
EL-MALLAKH, R S Z01MH02567-01
EL-SADR, WAFAA N01AI95029-06
EL-SHERIF, NABIL E N01HC65067-09
ELAHI, DARIUSH M01RR01032-16 0468
ELAHI, DARIVSH P30AG08812-02 9004
ELASHOFF, ROBERT P01CA42710-06A1 9008
ELASHOFF, ROBERT P01CA43461-05 9001
ELASHOFF, ROBERT P01CA50084-03 9002
ELASHOFF, ROBERT P30AI28697-01 9006
ELASHOFF, ROBERT M P30CA16042-17 9001
ELBADAWI, AHMAD P50DK39257-05
ELBADAWI, AHMED P50DK39257-05 0002
ELBAUM, DANEK R43DA07014-01
ELBEIN, ALAN D P01HL26890-09 0006
ELBEIN, ALAN D R01DK21800-15
ELBEIN, ALAN D R01HL17783-18
ELBEIN, STEVEN C M01RR00064-27 0309
ELBEIN, STEVEN C M01RR00064-27 0371
ELBEIN, STEVEN C R29DK39311-04
ELBER, RON R01GM41905-03
ELBER, RON R29GM40698-04
ELBERGER, ANDREA J R01EY08466-02
ELBERT, MARY R01DC00260-07
ELBLE, RODGER J R01NS20973-07
ELBLE, RODGER J S07RR05843-11 0550
ELDE, ROBERT P01DA05695-03 0006
ELDE, ROBERT P R37DA06299-02
ELDEFRAWI, AMIRA T R01ES02594-16
ELDEFRAWI, MOHYEE E R01DA03680-06A1
ELDEFRAWI, MOHYEE E R01ES04977-03
ELDER, FREDERICK S07RR05745-19 0229
ELDER, GLEN H, JR K05MH00567-07
ELDER, GLEN H, JR R01MH41327-05
ELDER, JAMES T R29AR40016-03
ELDER, JOHN P50MH47680-02 0001
ELDER, JOHN R01CA44921-05
ELDER, JOHN H R01AI25825-05
ELDER, RICHARD S07RR07075-17 0261
ELDER, ROBERT T R01HD19252-08
ELDRED, GRAIG E R01EY06458-06
ELDRED, WILLIAM D R01EY04785-10
ELDRIDGE, JOHN H. U01AI28147-03 0002
ELDRIDGE, BRUCE F R01AI26154-04
ELDRIDGE, CHARLES J R01DA06218-02
ELDRIDGE, FREDERIC L R37HL17689-19
ELDRIDGE, JOHN P60AR20614-14 9002
ELDRIDGE, R Z01NS01924-21
ELDRIDGE, R Z01NS01927-21
ELDRIDGE, R Z01NS02167-17
ELEFTERIADES, J A M01RR00125-28 0720
ELEFTERIADES, J A M01RR06022-02 0720
ELFARRA, ADNAN A R29GM40375-04
ELFENBEIN, JILL S07RR07035-26 0072
ELFORD, HOWARD L R43AR40948-01
ELGAVISH, ADA R01DK44835-01
ELGAVISH, GABRIEL A P50HL17667-17 0070
ELGEBALY, SALWA A R01HL42654-02
ELGIN, SARAH C R01GM31532-09
ELGIN, SARAH C R01HD23844-04
ELGIN, SARAH C R25RR07573-01
ELIAS, JACK A R01HL36708-05
ELIAS, JACK A R01HL41216-05
ELIAS, LAURENCE R01CA42520-05
ELIAS, MERRILL F R37AG03055-10
ELIAS, PETER P01AR39448-04 0003
ELIAS, PETER M P01AR39448-04
ELIAS, PETER M R01AR19098-16
ELIAS, SHERMAN N01HD82904-07
ELICEIRI, GEORGE L R01CA50387-03
ELICEIRI, GEORGE L R01GM44588-01A1
ELICES, MARIANO J S07RR05526-29 0095
ELIN, R J Z01CL10001-17
ELIN, R J Z01CL10010-16
ELIN, R J Z01CL10190-02
ELING, T E Z01ES80008-16
ELING, T E Z01ES80035-16
ELKAYAM, URI M01RR00043-31 0491
ELKAYAM, URI M01RR00043-31 0305
ELKIND-HIRSCH, KAREN M01RR00350-25 0418
ELKIND-HIRSCH, KAREN M01RR00350-25 0451
ELKIND, MORTIMER M R35CA47497-04
ELKINS, RALPH L R01DA05121-04
ELKON, KEITH S07RR05495-29 0468
ELKON, KEITH B K04AR01792-05
ELKON, KEITH B P60AR38520-04 0010
ELKON, KEITH B R01AR38915-04
ELLEDGE, STEPHEN S07RR05425-30 0735
ELLEDGE, STEPHEN J R01GM44664-02
ELLEDGE, STEPHEN J R21HG00463-01
ELLERTON, JOHN A U10CA35421-08
ELLINGSON, JOHN S P50AA07186-06 0012
ELLINWOOD, EVERETT H P50DA05303-03 0001
ELLINWOOD, EVERETT H P50DA05303-03 9002
ELLINWOOD, EVERETT H R01DA01883-11
ELLINWOOD, EVERETT H R01DA06519-02
ELLINWOOD, EVERETT H, JR P50DA05303-03
ELLIOT, JOHN F P01ES02429-11 0002
ELLIOT, S Z01DK43221-06
ELLIOTT, DELBERT S R01AA08203-03
ELLIOTT, DELBERT S R01MH41761-05
ELLIOTT, I WESLEY S06GM08062-21
ELLIOTT, IRVIN W S06GM08062-21 0001
ELLIOTT, JOHN F P01ES01640-14 0018
ELLIOTT, LUCINDA H S07RR05374-30 0738
ELLIOTT, MARK S R29CA45213-05
ELLIOTT, ROBERT D P01CA34200-09 9001
ELLIOTT, ROBERT D S07RR05676-15 0967
ELLIOTT, STEPHEN J K08HL02595-01
ELLIOTT, THOMAS A R01GM40403-04
ELLIOTT, WILLIAM C R43NS29301-01A1
ELLIOTT, WILLIAM H S07RR05388-30 0626
ELLIS WEISMER, SUSAN R29DC01101-01
ELLIS, AVERY K S07RR05400-30 0033
ELLIS, CHARLES N M01RR00042-31 0538
ELLIS, CHARLES N M01RR00042-31 0632
ELLIS, DARREL L S07RR05424-30 0078
ELLIS, DAVID D R01CA55106-01
ELLIS, EARL E. P01NS12587-16 0020
ELLIS, EARL F P01NS12587-16 0008
ELLIS, EARL F P50DA05274-04 0007
ELLIS, EARL F R01HL41788-03
ELLIS, EARL F R01NS27214-03
ELLIS, EILEEN N S07RR05350-30 0330
ELLIS, GARY N01HD92925-04
ELLIS, HILARY S07RR07023-26 0979
ELLIS, J R Z01RR10352-02
ELLIS, J R Z01RR10371-01
ELLIS, J R Z01RR10372-01
ELLIS, JOHN R01AG05214-07
ELLIS, LELAND R01DK40511-04
ELLIS, NANCY B P30AG10124-01 9003
ELLIS, PAUL D R01GM26295-11
ELLIS, STEVEN R R29GM40632-04
ELLIS, THOMAS M R01CA48069-02
ELLIS, WALTHER R, JR R29GM43507-02
ELLIS, WILLIAM P30AG10129-01 9002
ELLISMAN, M P41RR04050-03 9003
ELLISMAN, MARK H P41RR04050-03
ELLISMAN, MARK H R01NS14718-12
ELLISMAN, MARK H R01NS26739-03
ELLISMAN, MARK H S06GM47165-01 0022
ELLISON, GAYLORD D R01MH39961-07A1
ELLISON, J S Z01BA04009-01
ELLISON, JAMES S07RR05305-30 0718
ELLISON, MARK P41RR00592-22 0008
ELLISON, ROBERT C R01HL35653-07
ELLISON, ROSE R P30CA13696-19 9008

ELLISON, ROSE R P30CA13696-19 9009
ELLNER, JERROLD M01RR00080-29 0437
ELLNER, JERROLD J P01AG04391-09 0005
ELLNER, JERROLD J R01AI18471-09
ELLNER, JERROLD J R01AI25799-05
ELLNER, JERROLD J R22AI24298-04
ELLNER, JERROLD J U01AI30189-02 0004
ELLSWORTH, ALVORD P30HD02274-24 9007
ELLSWORTH, JEFF L S07RR05513-29 0062
ELLSWORTH, MARY L R29HL39226-05
ELMAN, MICHAEL J N01EY02114-02
ELMAN, MICHAEL L M01RR00035-31 0355
ELMER, G I Z01DA00101-05
ELMER, G I Z01DA00102-05
ELMER, GARY W P30DK35816-06 0001
ELMER, PATRICIA P01CA50305-02 9001
ELMER, PATRICIA S07RR05448-30 0285
ELMER, PATRICIA S07RR05448-30 0312
ELMER, PATRICIA J P01CA50305-02 0003
ELMER, PATRICIA J S07RR05448-30 0296
ELMER, PATRICIA PHD R01HL44141-03
ELMER, WILLIAM A S07RR07023-26 0977
ELMETS, CRAIG A K04AR01765-05
ELMETS, CRAIG A R01AR32593-07A1
ELMETS, CRAIG A R01CA48763-03
ELOVIC, ARAM E K11DE00323-01
ELOVIC, REBECCA P K15DE00277-02
ELSAS, LOUIS J M01RR00039-31 0317
ELSAS, LOUIS J M01RR00039-31 0274
ELSAS, LOUIS J M01RR00039-31 0442
ELSAS, LOUIS J M01RR00039-31 0433
ELSAS, LOUISE J. M01RR00039-31 0417
ELSBACH, PETER R37DK05472-30
ELSE, JAMES P51RR00165-31 9009
ELSNER, ANN E R29EY07624-05
ELSON, CHARLES P01DK44240-01 9001
ELSON, CHARLES P01DK44240-01 0001
ELSON, CHARLES O P01DK44240-01
ELSON, CHARLES O R01DK28623-10
ELSON, ELLIOT L R01GM38838-05
ELSON, H F Z01HL04218-01
ELSTAD, MARK R R29AI30735-01
ELSTEIN, ARTHUR S R01LM04583-06
ELSTON, ROBERT C P41RR03655-05
ELSTON, ROBERT C R01GM28356-12
ELSTON, ROBERT C R01HL38844-05 0016
ELTA, GRACE H M01RR00042-31 0628
ELWOOD, L Z01CB09178-03
ELWOOD, L Z01CB09186-02
ELWOOD, L Z01CB09351-01
ELWOOD, P C Z01CM06718-03
ELY, BERT R01GM34765-06A1
ELY, KATHRYN R P01CA51993-01A1 0004
ELZINGA, LAWRENCE P30DK40566-02 0006
EMANCIPATOR, STEVEN N R55AI31230-01A1
EMANUEL, BEVERLY P01CA47983-04 0003
EMANUEL, BEVERLY P50HG00425-01 0002
EMANUEL, BEVERLY S P50HG00425-01
EMANUEL, BEVERLY S R01CA39926-07
EMANUEL, BEVERLY S R01CA46274-03
EMANUEL, BEVERLY S R13HG00448-01
EMANUEL, DAVID P01CA23766-14 0034
EMANUEL, IRVIN S07RR05714-21 0123
EMANUELE, MARY A R01AA08661-02
EMANUELE, MARY ANN R01AA06755-06
EMANUELE, NICHOLAS V R01DK39361-04
EMBREY, THOMAS P41RR05964-02 0006
EMBURY, STEPHEN H P60HL20985-14 0005
EMDE, ROBERT N K05MH36808-14
EMDE, ROBERT N R37MH22803-18
EMERMAN, MICHAEL R01AI30927-01A1
EMERSON, BEVERLY M P01CA54418-01 0003
EMERSON, BEVERLY M R01GM38760-04A1
EMERSON, CHARLES P01DK40031-03 0002
EMERSON, CHARLES P, JR R01HD07796-19
EMERSON, RONALD G R01NS26612-04
EMERSON, SCOTT S R29CA53449-01
EMERSON, STEPHEN G P01CA49639-02 0005
EMERSON, STEPHEN G P01DK42718-02 0004
EMERSON, STEPHEN G R01DK39586-05
EMERSON, STEPHEN G R01HL42096-04
EMERSON, SUZANNE Z01AI00569-02
EMERY, CHARLES F R29HL45290-01A1
EMERY, DENNIS G R03MH45604-02
EMERY, OLGA P50MH41684-07 0081
EMERY, THOMAS F R01AI09580-17
EMLEN, JAMES W R01AR24015-14
EMMETT-OGLESBY, MICHAEL W R01DA04137-05
EMMETT-OGLESBY, MICHAEL W R01DA03521-06
EMMONS, ROBERT A R03MH47263-01
EMMONS, SCOTT W R01GM38174-05
EMORY, EUGENE K K01MH00660-03
EMORY, EUGENE K R03MH47712-01
EMORY, LEE E M01RR00073-29 0173
EMOTO, S E Z01NS02483-11
EMPEY, MARGE S07RR05336-29 0299
EMR, S S07RR07003-26 0328
EMR, SCOTT D R01GM32703-08
EMRIE, PHILIP S07RR05842-12 0280
EMSLIE, GRAHAM J R01MH39188-04A1
ENDEMANN, GERDA C R43HL47220-01
ENDERS, ALLEN C R01HD10342-16
ENDERS, ALLEN G P51RR00169-30 0111
ENDERS, GEORGE C R29HD26639-03
ENDICOTT, JEAN P50MH30906-14 9006
ENDICOTT, JEAN P50MH30906-14 9001
ENDICOTT, JEAN R01HD23512-04
ENDICOTT, JEAN U01MH23864-19
ENDOW, SHARYN A R01GM46225-01
ENDRES, R P50AR39166-05 0003
ENDRES, ROBERT P50AR39166-05 9001
ENG, CALVIN P01HL37412-04 0005
ENG, ELAINE S07RR05924-07 0001
ENG, HOWARD S07RR05573-13 0090
ENG, LAWRENCE P50MH40041-08 0006
ENG, LAWRENCE F R01NS11632-17
ENG, LUDEMAN A S07RR07095-24 0370
ENGEL, ANDREW G R01NS06277-26
ENGEL, B T Z01AG00063-23
ENGEL, B T Z01AG00072-06
ENGEL, B T Z01AG00603-02
ENGEL, B T Z01AG00606-01
ENGEL, DANIEL A S07RR05431-30 0862
ENGEL, JAMES D R01GM28896-08
ENGEL, JAMES D R01HL24415-13
ENGEL, JAMES D R01HL42536-02
ENGEL, JEROME P01NS02808-30 9001
ENGEL, JEROME P01NS02808-30 0005
ENGEL, JEROME JR P01NS02808-30
ENGEL, JOANNE N S07RR05355-30 0425
ENGEL, L DAVID P30DE09743-02 9000
ENGEL, ROBERT S07RR07064-24 0198
ENGEL, ROBERT R R01GM40441-03
ENGELHARD, VICTOR H R01AI20963-08
ENGELHARD, VICTOR H R01AI21393-08
ENGELHARDT, SUSAN M01RR02719-06 0127
ENGELKE, DAVID P30HG00209-02 9006
ENGELKE, DAVID P30HG00209-02 0003
ENGELKE, DAVID R R01GM34869-06
ENGELMAN, DONALD M P01GM22778-16 0002
ENGELMAN, DONALD M P01GM39546-05 9001
ENGELMAN, DONALD M P01GM39546-05
ENGELMAN, DONALD M P01GM39546-05 0001
ENGELMAN, EDGER P30AI27762-03 9002
ENGELMAN, KARL M01RR00040-31 0415
ENGELMAN, KARL M01RR00040-31 0372
ENGELMAN, KARL M01RR00040-31 0390
ENGELMAN, KARL M01RR00040-31 0378
ENGELMAN, RICHARD M R01HL22559-11
ENGELMANN, FRANZ S07RR07009-26 0928
ENGELMANN, GARY L R01HL42218-04
ENGELS, WILLIAM R R01GM30948-09
ENGER, M DUANE R01ES03863-06
ENGERMAN, RONALD L R01EY00300-26
ENGLAND, BARRY G P60DK20572-14 9005
ENGLAND, JOHN D K08NS01272-04
ENGLAND, JOHN D P01AG09417-01 0005
ENGLAND, SANDRA J R55HL45520-01
ENGLANDER, S WALTER P41RR01348-10 0004
ENGLANDER, S WALTER R01DK11295-25A1
ENGLANDER, S WALTER R01GM31847-08
ENGLE, I. DAVID P01DE08555-03 0002
ENGLEBERG, N CARY R01AI26232-02
ENGLEMAN, EDGAR P01AI29796-08 0006
ENGLEMAN, EDGAR G P50HL33811-06 0003
ENGLEMAN, EDGAR G P50HL33811-06 9003
ENGLEMAN, EDGAR G R37CA24607-13
ENGLEMAN, EDGAR G U01AI25922-05 0001
ENGLEMAN, EDGAR G U01AI25922-05
ENGLEMAN, EDGAR G U01AI25922-05 9001
ENGLER, H D Z01CL10197-01
ENGLER, H D Z01CL10198-01
ENGLER, H D Z01CL10199-01
ENGLER, JEFFREY A P30AI27767-04 9004
ENGLER, JEFFREY A P30CA13148-20 9016
ENGLER, JEFFREY A R01AI20408-08
ENGLER, JEFFREY A R01GM38234-04
ENGLER, THOMAS A R01GM39820-03
ENGLERT, DUWAYNE S07RR07118-22 0375
ENGLES, WILLIAM R01HG00504-01 9001
ENGLESBERG, ELLIS S07RR07099-25 0394
ENGLISH, ARTHUR W R01NS20545-06
ENGLISH, DENIS R55AI25656-05A1
ENGLISH, HUGH R P01CA40011-07 0004
ENGLISH, JAMIE L M01RR00069-29 0429
ENGLISH, KATHLEEN P01NS07938-22 0032
ENGLUND, PAUL T R01AI21334-08
ENGLUND, PAUL T R37GM27608-23
ENGSTROM, P F N01CO03864-06
ENGSTROM, PAUL F P01CA34856-09
ENGSTROM, PAUL F R01CA45834-05
ENGVALL, EVA S P01CA28896-11 0003
ENGVALL, EVA S P30CA30199-11 9001
ENGVALL, EVA S R01DK30051-11
ENIGBOKAN, MOFOLRUNSO A S06GM08061-17 0003
ENKE, CHRISTIE G R01GM44077-01A1
ENNIS, BRUCE W R03CA54942-01
ENNIS, BRUCE W S07RR05424-30 0119
ENNIS, FRANCES A P30DK32520-08 9002
ENNIS, FRANCIS A R01AI29375-03
ENNIS, FRANCIS A U01AI25831-05 0002
ENNIS, JACQUELINE M R19MH47697-02
ENNS, CAROLINE A R01DK40608-04
ENOCH, JAY M S03RR03259-08
ENOCH, JAY M S07RR05832-12
ENOCH, JAY M S07RR05832-12 0194
ENOCH, JAY M S15EY09449-01
ENOKA, ROGER M R01AG09000-02
ENOKA, ROGER M R01NS20544-08
ENRIETTO, PAULA P01CA28146-11 0007
ENRIETTO, PAULA R01CA51792-02
ENRIGHT, PAUL L. N01HR46018-16
ENRIQUEZ, F JAVIER S07RR07002-26 0866
ENSEL, WALTER M R29MH43723-04
ENSINCK, JOHN W. M01RR00037-31 0427
ENSINCK, JOHN W M01RR00037-31 0457
ENSINCK, JOHN W R01DK34397-08
ENSINCK, JOHN W. P51RR00166-30 0084
ENSLEY, JOHN F R03CA53293-02
ENSMINGER, MARGARET E R01DA06630-01A1
ENSMINGER, WILLIAM D M01RR00042-31 0615
ENSMINGER, WILLIAM D M01RR00042-31 0649
ENSMINGER, WILLIAM D M01RR00042-31 0418
ENSMINGER, WILLIAM D M01RR00042-31 0506
ENSMINGER, WILLIAM D M01RR00042-31 0670
ENSMINGER, WILLIAM D M01RR00042-31 0636
ENSMINGER, WILLIAM D M01RR00042-31 0619
ENSMINGER, WILLIAM D M01RR00042-31 0637
ENSMINGER, WILLIAM D M01RR00042-31 0580
ENSMINGER, WILLIAM D M01RR00042-31 0574
ENSMINGER, WILLIAM D R01CA33825-08
ENTERLINE, JOHN P30CA06973-29 9015
ENTERLINE, JOHN P P30CA06973-29 9008
ENTERTAINMENT INDUSTRIES, INC N01DA98544-0
ENTINE, GERALD N44CM07601-02
ENTINE, GERALD R43CA53944-01
ENTINE, GERALD R44CA52370-02
ENTMAN, MARK L P01HL42550-02 0001
ENTMAN, MARK L P01HL42550-02
ENTMAN, MARK L R37HL13870-22
ENTWISLE, BARBARA P01HD28076-01 0003
ENTWISLE, DORIS R R01HD23738-04
ENTWISLE, DORIS R R01HD23943-04
ENWONWU, CYRIL O R01DE09653-01A1
ENWONWU, CYRIL O R13CA55089-01
ENYEART, JOHN J R29DK40131-04
EPP, EDWARD R R01CA18614-15
EPPIG, JANAN S07RR05545-29 0570
EPPIG, JANAN T P01HG00330-03 0002
EPPIG, JOHN J P30CA34196-09 9013
EPPIG, JOHN J R01HD20575-07
EPPIG, JOHN J R01HD23839-04
EPPIG, JOHN J U01HD21970-07
EPPS, CHARLES H G12RR03048-07
EPPS, THOMAS H S14GM44814-02
EPSTEIN, ALAN L R01CA49987-01A2
EPSTEIN, ALAN N P01MH43787-03 0003
EPSTEIN, ALAN N P01MH43787-03 9001
EPSTEIN, ALAN N P01MH43787-03
EPSTEIN, ALAN N R01HD25857-03
EPSTEIN, ALAN N R01NS03469-30
EPSTEIN, ARNOLD M R01HS06239-03
EPSTEIN, CHARLES P01HD26732-01A1 9002
EPSTEIN, CHARLES J P01AG08938-07
EPSTEIN, CHARLES J P01HD26732-01A1 0005
EPSTEIN, CHARLES J R37HD03132-23
EPSTEIN, DAVID L R01EY01894-15
EPSTEIN, ERVIN H, JR R01AR28069-11
EPSTEIN, ERVIN H, JR R01AR39959-03
EPSTEIN, FRANKLIN H M01RR01032-16 0454
EPSTEIN, FRANKLIN H P30ES03828-06 0007
EPSTEIN, FRANKLIN H P50DK39249-05 0007
EPSTEIN, FRANKLIN H R01DK18078-18
EPSTEIN, FRANKLIN H R13DK44067-01
EPSTEIN, HENRY P50HL42267-02 0001
EPSTEIN, HENRY F R01GM33223-07
EPSTEIN, J S Z01BG06035-01
EPSTEIN, J S Z01BG06036-01
EPSTEIN, J S Z01BG06037-01
EPSTEIN, JOHN H R01CA15605-15
EPSTEIN, LEON G R01AI32305-01
EPSTEIN, LEON G R01NS28754-05
EPSTEIN, LEON G R03EY09217-01
EPSTEIN, LEONARD H R01HD20829-06
EPSTEIN, LEONARD H R01HD23713-03
EPSTEIN, LEONARD H R01HD25997-03
EPSTEIN, LLOYD M R29GM38791-05
EPSTEIN, LOIS B M01RR01271-10 0105
EPSTEIN, LOIS B R01CA44446-05
EPSTEIN, LOIS B R37CA27903-16
EPSTEIN, MARK H R03HS06639-01
EPSTEIN, N D Z01HL02330-05
EPSTEIN, S L Z01BB06001-04
EPSTEIN, S L Z01BB06002-03
EPSTEIN, S L Z01BB06003-06
EPSTEIN, SEYMOUR K05MH00363-07
EPSTEIN, SEYMOUR R37MH01293-31
EPSTEIN, SUSAN D U01CA50116-02
EPSTEIN, WOLFGANG R01GM22323-17
ERBAN, JOHN K K08HL02542-01
ERCOLANI, LOUIS P50DK39249-05 0013
ERCOLANI, LOUIS R01DK42543-01A1
ERDOS, ERVIN G R01HL36081-05
ERDOS, ERVIN G R01HL36082-05
ERDOS, ERVIN G R37HL36473-06
ERECINSKA, MARIA P50NS10939-18A1S1 0028

ERECINSKA, MARIA R01DK35808-07
ERECINSKA, MARIA R01NS28329-02
ERESHEFSKY, LARRY M01RR01346-10 0140
EREXSON, GREGORY N01ES15312-00
ERFURT, JOHN C R01DA05934-02
ERGUN, GULCHIN A M01RR00047-31 0424
ERIAN, RALPH F S07RR05654-24 0121
ERICKSON , CARLTON K S07RR07091-26 0752
ERICKSON-LAMY, KRISTINE A R01EY07321-03
ERICKSON, BRUCE W R01GM42031-03
ERICKSON, CARL S07RR05849-11 0253
ERICKSON, CARLTON K R01DA07355-01
ERICKSON, CHRISTOPHER M01RR00188-27 0317
ERICKSON, HAROLD P P30CA14236-18 9025
ERICKSON, HAROLD P R01CA47056-12
ERICKSON, HAROLD P R01GM28553-11
ERICKSON, HELEN L R01NR03032-01
ERICKSON, JEANNE S07RR07009-26 0930
ERICKSON, JOHN W U01AI27220-04 0004
ERICKSON, KENNETH R R29AG07933-03
ERICKSON, KENT L R01CA47050-04
ERICKSON, LEONARD C R01CA45628-05
ERICKSON, LEONARD C R01CA47929-03
ERICKSON, PAMELA R K15DE00224-05
ERICKSON, ROBERT P R01HD20670-06
ERICKSON, ROBERT P R01HD26454-03
ERICKSON, ROBERT P. P30HD18258-08 9010
ERIKSEN, CHARLES W K06MH22014-29
ERIKSEN, CHARLES W R01MH01206-36
ERIKSEN, MICHAEL P U01CA51671-03
ERIKSON, RAYMOND L R35CA42580-06
ERKI, RUOSLAHTI P30CA30199-11 9008
ERLANGER, BERNARD F R01DA06333-02
ERLANGER, BERNARD F R01NS15581-11S1
ERLANGER, BERNARD F R55CA55159-01
ERLENMEYER-KIMLING, L R37MH19560-20
ERLICH, HENRY A R01AI29042-02
ERLICH, HENRY A R01HL47170-01
ERLICHMAN, CHARLES R01CA52182-02
ERLICHMAN, JACK R01DK27736-11
ERLIJ, DAVID J R01DK33612-08
ERMAK, THOMAS H R01DK38550-05
ERMAN, JAMES E R15DK43944-01
ERNHART, CLAIRE B P50AA07606-04 0001
ERNHART, CLAIRE B R01AA06571-09
ERNSBERGER, PAUL P01HL25830-11A1 9006
ERNSBERGER, PAUL R R29HL44514-01A1
ERNST, FREDERICK A K14HL02140-01A3
ERNST, JEROME N01AI95038-05
ERNST, JOEL D. P60AR20684-14 0023
ERNST, STEPHEN A S07RR05383-30 0553
ERNST, SUSAN S07RR07179-14 0679
ERNSTOFF, MARC S P01CA08341-26 9002
ERNSTOFF, MARC S R01CA52166-02
ERRECART, MICHAEL T R43CA53979-01
ERRECART, MICHAEL T R43CA53967-01
ERREDE, BEVERLY J R01GM30619-10
ERREDE, BEVERLY J R01GM39852-04
ERSENMAN, ROBERT N. P01AI27291-04 0002
ERSHLER, WILLIAM B K07AG00485-02
ERSHLER, WILLIAM B R01AG07831-03
ERSKINE, MARY S R01HD21802-06
ERTL, HILDEGUND R01AI27435-03
ERVIN, M GORE R29HD22914-05
ERVIN, NAOMI E S07RR05776-11 0391
ERWIN, ROLAND J R29MH45113-03
ERWIN, V GENE K02AA00079-08
ERWIN, V GENE P01DA07171-01 0002
ERWIN, V GENE P50AA03527-14 9001
ERWIN, V GENE P50AA03527-14 0021
ERWIN, V GENE R01AA07330-05
ERWIN, V GENE S07RR05831-12 0972
ERZINE, SANDI N01CP71096-02
ES, INC N01TI10003-00
ES, INC N01TI10016-00
ESA, AHMED H R29AI24682-04
ESAU, SHARON A S07RR05431-30 0850
ESCABI, JOSE R S03RR03270-07
ESCALANTE-SEMERENA, JORGE C R01GM40313-04
ESCALANTE, JORGE C S07RR07098-26 0329
ESCALONA DE MOTTA, GLADYS S06GM08102-20
ESCHBACH, JOSEPH W M01RR00037-31 0411
ESCHBACH, JOSEPH W, JR R01DK33488-08
ESCHENBACH, DAVID A P01AI24756-05 0001
ESCHENBACH, DAVID A R01AI31871-04
ESCOBALES, NELSON S06GM08224-07 0008
ESCOBEDO, JAIME A P01HL43821-02 9003
ESDAILE, JOHN R18AR21393-17 0025
ESEKOWITZ, R ALAN P01HL43510-03 0001
ESFANDIARI, ADELPH S07RR05780-16 0971
ESKAY, R Z01AA00287-01
ESKIN, ARNOLD R01MH41979-05A1
ESKIN, ARNOLD R01NS28462-01A1
ESKIN, ARNOLD S07RR07147-19 0645
ESKIN, ARNOLD S07RR07147-19 0646
ESKIN, SUZANNE G R01HL23016-13
ESKIN, SUZANNE G R01HL47876-01
ESKIN, THOMAS A R01NS26598-04
ESKO, JEFFREY D R01CA46462-02
ESKO, JEFFREY D R01GM33063-08
ESLINGER, PAUL J. P50NS26985-03 0003
ESMON, CHARLES T R01HL29807-10
ESMON, CHARLES T R37HL30340-09
ESPELAND, MARK A R01AG09773-01A1
ESPOSITO, DIANE S07RR05395-30 0823
ESPOSITO, ROCHELLE E R01GM29182-11
ESSANI, KARIM R15GM46025-01
ESSELMAN, WALTER S07RR05656-24 0834
ESSELMAN, WALTER S07RR05656-24 0842
ESSELMAN, WALTER S07RR05772-17 0350
ESSELMAN, WALTER J R01GM35774-05
ESSER, A P41RR02250-06 0007
ESSER, ALFRED F R01AI19478-10
ESSEX, MYRON P50HL33774-06 0001
ESSEX, MYRON E R35CA39805-07
ESSIG, DAVID A R29AR39872-03
ESSIGMANN, JOHN M P01ES03926-07 0003
ESSIGMANN, JOHN M R35CA52127-02
ESSNER, EDWARD S R01EY04831-09
ESSOCK, SUSAN M R18MH46062-03
ESSOCK, SUSAN M R19MH46306-03
ESTELLE, MARK A R01GM43644-03
ESTER, ROBERT A S07RR07030-26 0389
ESTES, CARROLL L R01HS06860-01
ESTES, JAMES E R01GM32007-07
ESTES, KERRY S R43NS28954-01A1
ESTES, MARY K R01AI24998-05
ESTES, MARY K R01DK30144-11
ESTES, MARY K R13AI30488-01
ESTES, MARY K U01AI30448-02
ESTESS PILA U01AI26462-04 0002
ESTRIN, JORGE A M01RR00400-23 0244
ESTROFF, SUE E R01MH40314-06
ETCHISON, DIANE R01AI24356-06
ETCOFF, NANCY L R29DC00565-03
ETGEN, ANNE M K02MH00636-06
ETGEN, ANNE M R37MH41414-07
ETGES, WILLIAM S07RR07101-13 0553
ETH, SPENCER P50MH30911-14 0017
ETHIER, STEPHEN P R01CA40064-06
ETINGIN, ORLI R K08HL01687-05
ETLINGER, JOSEPH D R01AR37145-04
ETO, ISAO S07RR05968-06 0339
ETTENBERG, AARON R01DA05041-04
ETTENBERG, AARON S07RR07099-25 0400
ETTENSOHN, CHARLES A R29HD24690-03
ETTER, MARGARET C R01GM42148-03
ETTINGER, DAVID S N01CO03862-05
ETTINGER, DAVID S U10CA16116-18
ETTINGER, RONALD P30DE10126-01 9002
ETTINGER, RONALD P30DE10126-01 0004
ETTINGER, WALTER P60AG10484-01 9004
ETTINGER, WALTER H K07AG00421-04
ETTINGER, WALTER H P60AG10484-01 0001
ETTINGHAUSEN, S E Z01CM06668-01
ETZLER, MARILYNN E R01GM21882-16
ETZWILER, DONNELL D U01DK30598-09
EUNPU, DEBORAH L R13HG00401-01A1
EVA, A Z01CP05062-13
EVANOCHKO, WILLIAM P50HL17667-17 9005
EVANS, AUDREY P41RR02305-08 0016
EVANS, C H Z01CP04673-20
EVANS, C H Z01CP05552-04
EVANS, D FENNELL R01GM34341-06
EVANS, DALE B R43HL45398-01A1
EVANS, DAN R19DA06414-03
EVANS, DAVID S07RR05664-24 0858
EVANS, DAVID A R01GM43912-02
EVANS, DAVID A R37GM33328-09
EVANS, DAVID H P30ES03828-06 0001
EVANS, DAVID H P30ES03828-06
EVANS, DAVID R R01GM47399-12
EVANS, DAVID S N43DK12271-00
EVANS, DENIS P30AG10161-01 0001
EVANS, DENIS A P30AG10161-01
EVANS, DENIS A R01AG09966-01
EVANS, DWIGHT M01RR00046-31 0470
EVANS, DWIGHT L M01RR00046-31 0391
EVANS, DWIGHT L P50MH33127-13 0011
EVANS, DWIGHT L R01MH44618-03
EVANS, EVAN A R01HL45099-05
EVANS, GLEN P01HG00202-02 9005
EVANS, GLEN A P01HG00202-02 9004
EVANS, GLEN A P01HG00202-02
EVANS, GLEN A P01HG00202-02 0001
EVANS, GLEN A P30CA14195-18 0049
EVANS, GLEN A R01GM33868-08
EVANS, GLEN A R13HG00518-01
EVANS, HELEN P30CA43703-04A1 9001
EVANS, HELEN H R37CA15901-17
EVANS, HERBERT S07RR05697-22 0997
EVANS, HUGH P42ES04895-03 0007
EVANS, JANE C R15NR02768-01
EVANS, JEREMY N R01GM43215-01A2
EVANS, JOHN N R01HL38924-05
EVANS, JOHN N R01HL41213-02
EVANS, JOHN W P01HL17731-17 9002
EVANS, L H Z01AI00266-10
EVANS, LOIS K R01AG08324-02
EVANS, MARILYN I R29HD26339-02
EVANS, MARY E R18MH48072-02
EVANS, MILES S K08NS01503-01
EVANS, PRINCILLA S S06GM08062-21 0002
EVANS, R SCOTT R18HS06028-03
EVANS, RICHARD I R01CA41722-05
EVANS, RICHARD, III U01AI30756-01
EVANS, ROBERT R01CA27523-11
EVANS, ROBERT S07RR05545-29 0574
EVANS, ROBERT M R01GM42770-03
EVANS, RONALD M P01CA54418-01 0004
EVANS, RONALD M P30CA14195-18 0038
EVANS, RONALD M R01HD27183-02
EVANS, RONALD M R37GM26444-13
EVANS, SHARON S R29CA46645-04
EVANS, STANLEY L G12RR03032-07 0002
EVANS, THOMAS G S07RR05428-30 0168
EVANS, TODD R R01DK44167-01
EVANS, W JAMES K08DC00033-02
EVANS, WILLIAM P01CA23099-13 0012
EVANS, WILLIAM E P01CA20180-14 0010
EVANS, WILLIAM E R37CA36401-08
EVANS, WILLIAM E. P30CA21765-14 9006
EVANS, WILLIAM J P01DK42618-02 0004
EVANS, WILLIAM S M01RR00847-18 0466
EVANS, WILLIAM S M01RR00847-18 0485
EVANS, WILLIAM S M01RR00847-18 0551
EVANS, WILLIAM S M01RR00847-18 0564
EVANS, WILLIAM S M01RR00847-18 0580
EVANS, WILLIAM S M01RR00847-18 0581
EVANS, WILLIAM S M01RR00847-18 0559
EVANS, WILLIAM S M01RR00847-18 0557
EVANS, WILLIAM S M01RR00847-18 0568
EVANS, WILLIAM S M01RR00847-18 0578
EVANS, WILLIAM S M01RR00847-18 0435
EVANS, WILLIAM S M01RR00847-18 0437
EVANS, WILLIAM S M01RR00847-18 0392
EVANS, WILLIAM S M01RR00847-18 0304
EVANS, WILLIAM S M01RR00847-18 0356
EVARTS, C MC COLLISTER S07RR05680-23
EVARTS, C MC COLLISTER S15HL47749-01
EVARTS, R P Z01CP05262-10
EVELHOCH, JEFFREY L R01CA43926-03
EVERETT, GROVER W S07RR07037-26 0365
EVERETT, JAMES S06GM08049-20 0008
EVERS, ALEX S P01DK38111-05 0003
EVERS, ALEX S R01GM37846-05
EVERSOLE, L ROY S07RR05304-30 0232
EVERSON, C Z01MH02426-04
EVERSON, GREGORY M01RR00051-30 0730
EVERSON, GREGORY P30DK34914-06 9006
EVERSON, GREGORY P30DK34914-06 0009
EVERSON, GREGORY T M01RR00051-30 0515
EVERSON, GREGORY T M01RR00051-30 0755
EVERSON, GREGORY T P01DK34039-06A1 0004
EVERSON, GREGORY T. M01RR00051-30 0330
EVERSON, LLOYD U10CA52385-02
EVERSON, WILLIAM V R29HD27603-01A1
EVERSON, WILLIAM V S07RR05408-30 0926
EVINGER, LESLIE C R01EY07391-05
EVINGER, MARIAN J R01GM46588-01
EWALD, SANDRA J R01AA07010-06
EWART, CRAIG K R01HL45139-01A1
EWASKOW, SANDRA P S07RR05390-30 0654
EWENS, WARREN J R01GM21135-18
EWENSTEIN, BRUCE S07RR05950-07 0996
EWERT, DONALD L R01CA53058-02
EWIGMAN, BERNARD G U01HD21140-05
EWING, ANDREW G R01GM37621-04A1
EWING, JAMES R P01NS23393-06 0001
EWING, JAMES R P01NS23393-06 9003
EWING, JAMES R P01NS23393-06 9005
EWING, LARRY L P01AG08321-03 0001
EWING, LARRY L P01DK19300-16 0003
EXPOSITO, LORENZA N01HD13140-00
EXPOSITO, LORENZO N01AI15108-00
EXPOSITO, LORENZO F N01CB05689-01
EXPOSITO, LORENZO F N01HD72918-05
EXTON, JOHN H R01GM40919-03
EY, JOHN L S07RR05675-23 0903
EYLAR, EDWARD H P40RR03640-05 0028
EYLAR, EDWARD H S07RR06032-02
EYLAR, EDWARD H S15GM47052-01
EYLER, FONDA DAVIS R01DA05854-01A2
EYMAN, RICHARD K R01HD21056-04
EYRE, DAVID R R01AR36794-06
EYRE, DAVID R R01AR37318-06
EYRE, HARMON J N01CO03877-06
EYRE, HARMON T P30CA42014-06 9008
EYRING, EDWARD M S07RR07092-26 0519
EYSTER, KATHLEEN M R29HD26640-03
EYSTER, KATHLEEN M S15HL47734-01
EYSTER, M ELAINE U01AI25928-05
EYZAGUIRRE, CARLOS E P01NS07938-22 0019
EYZAGUIRRE, CARLOS E P01NS07938-22 9001
EZEKOWITZ, ALAN M01RR02172-09 0190
EZEKOWITZ, R ALAN B R01AI23786-04A2
EZQUERRA, NORBERTO F R29LM04692-05
FABER, DONALD S R01NS15335-12
FABER, DONALD S R01NS21848-06
FABER, DONALD S R01NS27144-03
FABER, J JOB R01HD27452-01A1
FABER, JAMES E K04HL02377-03
FABER, JAMES E R01HL38783-05
FABER, JAMES E S07RR05406-30 0906
FABER, LEE E R01DK41881-03
FABER, LEE E R03HD28034-01

FABISIAK, JAMES P S07RR05416-30 0559
FABRICIUS, WILLIAM V R01HD28796-01
FABRY, M P01HL21016-15 0019
FABRY, MARY E P60HL38655-04 0012
FABRY, MARY E P60HL38655-04 0009
FACEY, MARIA R N01CN15389-00
FACTOR, STEPHEN M P01HL37412-04 0004
FACTOR, STEPHEN M P01HL37412-04 9002
FADAVI, SHAHRBANOO S07RR05864-10 0934
FADEN, ALAN I R01NS27849-03
FADEN, HOWARD S R01HD19679-06
FADEN, RUTH R R01HD24816-04
FADULU, SUNDAY O S06GM08061-17 0017
FAGAN, DIANA S07RR05468-29 0407
FAGAN, JOHN B K04CA01557-01
FAGAN, JOHN B R01CA38655-06
FAGAN, JULIE M R29AR38867-04
FAGAN, JULIE M S07RR07058-26 0176
FAGEN, JEFFREY W R01MH39449-03A2
FAGIN, JAMES P01DK42792-01A1 0003
FAGIN, JAMES A R29CA50706-03
FAGOT, BEVERLY I R01HD19739-05
FAGOT, BEVERLY I R01MH37911-09
FAHEY, JOHN L P30CA16042-17 9007
FAHEY, JOHN L P50AI15332-14 0006
FAHEY, JOHN L P50AI15332-14
FAHEY, JOHN L P50AI15332-14 0016
FAHEY, ROBERT C R01CA39582-07
FAHEY, THOMAS J N01CO03866-05
FAHEY, THOMAS J R25CA20449-15
FAHEY, THOMAS J JR S03RR03107-10
FAHEY, THOMAS J JR S07RR05753-19
FAHL, WILLIAM E P01CA22484-14 0007
FAHL, WILLIAM E R37CA42024-07
FAHN, STANLEY M01RR00645-20 0326
FAHN, STANLEY M01RR00645-20 0328
FAHN, STANLEY M01RR00645-20 0484
FAHN, STANLEY M01RR00645-20 0456
FAHN, STANLEY M01RR00645-20 0457
FAHN, STANLEY M01RR00645-20 0505
FAHN, STANLEY R01NS26656-03
FAHNESTOCK, MARGARET P01AG03644-07 0009
FAHNESTOCK, MARGARET S07RR05522-29 0068
FAHRBACH, SUSAN E R29HD24637-03
FAHRENBACH, W H P51RR00163-32 9009
FAHRENBACH, WOLF H P51RR00163-32 0027
FAIL, PAT N01ES65141-22
FAIN, GORDON L R01EY07568-04
FAIN, GORDON L R37EY01844-15
FAIN, JOHN N R01DK37004-06
FAIN, PAMELA R R01HG00360-04
FAIN, PAMELA R R13HG00505-01
FAINGOLD, CARL L R55NS21281-07
FAIR, DARYL S07RR05958-06 0748
FAIRBANK, JOHN A R01MH45827-02
FAIRCHILD, BEATRICE M P60HL28381-09 0007
FAIRCLOUGH, ROBERT P01NS24304-05 0006
FAIRCLOUGH, ROBERT P01NS24304-05 0001
FAIRHURST, CARL W R37DE06374-10
FAISAL, MOHAMED R01ES05534-01
FAJTOVA, VERA T K08DK02020-01
FALANGA, VINCENT R29AR39658-02
FALANY, CHARLES N R01GM40440-04
FALANY, CHARLES N R29GM38953-06
FALBO, TONI R01HD25257-03
FALCK JOHN RUSSELL P01DK38226-06 0006
FALCK JOHN RUSSELL P01DK38226-06 9002
FALCK-PEDERSEN, ERIK R01GM41967-02
FALCK, JOHN R R01GM31278-08
FALCONE, DOMENICK S07RR05396-30 0769
FALCONE, DOMENICK J K04HL01962-05
FALCONE, DOMENICK J P01HL46403-01 0005
FALCONE, DOMENICK J R01HL40819-02
FALCONE, JEFFREY C S07RR05814-12 0148
FALEK, ARTHUR R01DA01451-15
FALES, H M Z01HL01003-19
FALES, H M Z01HL01030-03
FALES, H M Z01HL01035-01
FALGOUT, B Z01AI00500-05
FALGOUT, B Z01AI00531-04
FALK, CATHERINE T R01GM29177-11
FALK, JOHN L K05DA00142-02
FALK, JOHN L R01DA03117-10
FALK, JOHN L R01DA05305-05
FALK, RODNEY M01RR00533-23 0189
FALK, RODNEY M01RR00533-23 0203
FALK, RONALD J M01RR00046-31 0424
FALK, RONALD J R01DK40208-03
FALK, RONALD J S07RR05406-30 0907
FALKE, JOSEPH J R01GM40731-04
FALKOW, STANLEY R01AI26195-04
FALKOW, STANLEY R37AI23945-06
FALLER, DOUGLAS V R01CA50459-03
FALLER, DOUGLAS V R01HL45940-02
FALLER, JOHN W R01GM37513-02
FALLER, LARRY D R01DK36873-06
FALLETTA, JOHN M U10CA15525-18 0019
FALLETTA, JOHN M U10CA15525-18 0059
FALLETTA, JOHN M U10CA15525-18 0020
FALLETTA, JOHN M U10CA15525-18 0060
FALLETTA, JOHN M U10CA15525-18 0021
FALLETTA, JOHN M U10CA15525-18 0039
FALLETTA, JOHN M U10CA15525-18 0040
FALLETTA, JOHN M U10CA15525-18 0041
FALLETTA, JOHN M U10CA15525-18 0042
FALLETTA, JOHN M U10CA15525-18 0043
FALLETTA, JOHN M U10CA15525-18 0022
FALLETTA, JOHN M U10CA15525-18 0023
FALLETTA, JOHN M U10CA15525-18 0024
FALLETTA, JOHN M U10CA15525-18 0025
FALLETTA, JOHN M U10CA15525-18 0026
FALLETTA, JOHN M U10CA15525-18 0027
FALLETTA, JOHN M U10CA15525-18 0028
FALLETTA, JOHN M U10CA15525-18 0029
FALLETTA, JOHN M U10CA15525-18 0030
FALLETTA, JOHN M U10CA15525-18 0031
FALLETTA, JOHN M U10CA15525-18 0032
FALLETTA, JOHN M U10CA15525-18 0033
FALLETTA, JOHN M U10CA15525-18 0034
FALLETTA, JOHN M U10CA15525-18 0035
FALLETTA, JOHN M U10CA15525-18 0036
FALLETTA, JOHN M U10CA15525-18 0037
FALLETTA, JOHN M U10CA15525-18 0038
FALLETTA, JOHN M U10CA15525-18 0044
FALLETTA, JOHN M U10CA15525-18
FALLETTA, JOHN M U10CA15525-18 0045
FALLETTA, JOHN M U10CA15525-18 0046
FALLETTA, JOHN M U10CA15525-18 0047
FALLETTA, JOHN M U10CA15525-18 0048
FALLETTA, JOHN M U10CA15525-18 0049
FALLETTA, JOHN M U10CA15525-18 0050
FALLETTA, JOHN M U10CA15525-18 0051
FALLETTA, JOHN M U10CA15525-18 0052
FALLETTA, JOHN M U10CA15525-18 0053
FALLETTA, JOHN M U10CA15525-18 0054
FALLETTA, JOHN M U10CA15525-18 0055
FALLETTA, JOHN M U10CA15525-18 0056
FALLETTA, JOHN M U10CA15525-18 0057
FALLETTA, JOHN M U10CA15525-18 0058
FALLETTA, JOHN M U10CA15525-18 0001
FALLETTA, JOHN M U10CA15525-18 0002
FALLETTA, JOHN M U10CA15525-18 0003
FALLETTA, JOHN M U10CA15525-18 0004
FALLETTA, JOHN M U10CA15525-18 0005
FALLETTA, JOHN M U10CA15525-18 0006
FALLETTA, JOHN M U10CA15525-18 0007
FALLETTA, JOHN M U10CA15525-18 0008
FALLETTA, JOHN M U10CA15525-18 0009
FALLETTA, JOHN M U10CA15525-18 0010
FALLETTA, JOHN M U10CA15525-18 0011
FALLETTA, JOHN M U10CA15525-18 0012
FALLETTA, JOHN M U10CA15525-18 0013
FALLETTA, JOHN M U10CA15525-18 0014
FALLETTA, JOHN M U10CA15525-18 0015
FALLETTA, JOHN M U10CA15525-18 0016
FALLETTA, JOHN M U10CA15525-18 0017
FALLETTA, JOHN M U10CA15525-18 0018
FALLON, ANN M R01AI20385-09
FALLON, JAMES H R01NS15321-12
FALLON, JOHN D P01HD20743-05 0004
FALLON, MICHAEL B K11DK02030-01
FALLON, ROBERT J R29DK42081-02
FALLOON, IAN P50MH30911-14 9009
FALLOON, J Z01CL00051-03
FALLOON, J Z01CL00080-02
FALLOON, J Z01CL00081-02
FALLOON, J Z01CL00113-01
FALLS, DOUGLAS L K11HD00777-06
FALLS, WILLIAM S07RR05772-17 0352
FALLS, WILLIAM S07RR05772-17 0359
FAMBROUGH, DOUGLAS M P01HL27867-10 0007
FAMBROUGH, DOUGLAS M R01NS23241-07
FAMILONI, BABAJIDE O S07RR07229-06 0722
FAMILY, FEREYDOON S07RR07023-26 0978
FAN-HAVARD, PATTY S07RR05909-08 0953
FAN, HUNG S03RR03351-09
FAN, HUNG S07RR07008-26
FAN, HUNG Y N01ES05301-02
FAN, HUNG Y R01CA32455-11
FAN, HUNG Y S10RR06363-01
FAN, HUNG Y S15NS30110-01
FANANAPAZIR, L Z01HL04870-01
FANAROFF, AVROY A U10HD21364-06
FANBURG, BARRY L R01HL14456-20
FANBURG, BARRY L R01HL42376-03
FANBURG, BARRY L R37HL32723-08
FAND, IRWIN R01CA43455-06
FANG, MEIKA A S07RR05354-30 0400
FANGER, MICHAEL W P30CA23108-14 9011
FANGER, MICHAEL W R01AI19053-11
FANGER, MICHAEL W R01CA44794-05
FANGMAN, WALTON L R01GM18926-20
FANGMAN, WALTON L R01GM43847-02
FANNING-HEIDECKER, G Z01CP05533-05
FANNING-HEIDECKER, G Z01CP05654-02
FANNON, LEWIS D, JR K15DE00251-04
FANOS, JOANNA H R01HG00639-01
FANSELOW, MICHAEL S R01MH39786-06
FANT, JANE P30CA13330-20 9001
FANT, MICHAEL E R29HD22993-03
FANTA, CHRISTOPHER H K07HL02091-04
FANTA, CHRISTOPHER H U01AI31599-01 0002
FANTEL, ALAN G R01ES05623-02
FANTL, J ANDREW U01AG05170-07 0002
FANTL, JOHN A U01AG05170-07
FANTONE, JOSEPH P50DK39255-05 0003
FANTONE, JOSEPH C P01DK38149-04 0002
FANTONE, JOSEPH C R01HL44085-02
FARABAUGH, PHILIP JAMES R01GM29480-10
FARACH-CARSON, MARY S07RR05970-06 0776
FARACI, FRANK M R29HL38901-05
FARAH, MARTHA J K04NS01405-03
FARAH, MARTHA J R01MH48274-01
FARAHBAKHSH, NASSER A R01EY06969-04
FARAS, ANTHONY J N01AI82688-04
FARAS, ANTHONY J R01AI28758-02
FARAS, ANTHONY J R01CA18303-16
FARAS, ANTHONY J R01CA25462-12
FARAS,ANTHONY S07RR05385-30 0802
FARB, DAVID H R01NS22116-08
FARB, DAVID H R01NS23140-06
FARBER, DEBORA B R01EY08285-03
FARBER, DEBORA B R37EY02651-14
FARBER, HARRISON P01HL19717-15 0049
FARBER, JAY P R01HL37318-04A1
FARBER, JOHN L P50AA07186-06 0017
FARBER, JOHN L R01DK38305-06
FARBER, JOSHUA M R01CA52001-01A1
FARBER, LEN H M01RR00833-17 0190
FARBER, ROSANN A R01CA49039-03
FARBER, SAUL J M01RR00096-30A1
FARBER, SAUL J S07RR05399-30
FARBER, SAUL J S15CA55932-01
FARBER, SAUL J S15MH49284-01
FARBMAN, ALBERT I P01DC00347-06 0002
FARBMAN, ALBERT I R01DC00080-23
FARBMAN, ALBERT I R03DC01033-01
FARDE, LARS F R01MH41205-06
FARDY, PAUL S S07RR07064-24 0199
FAREL, PAUL B P01NS14899-13 0001
FARIS, PATRICIA L R01MH47189-02
FARISS, MARC W R01ES05452-01A1
FARKAS, GASPAR A R01HL43865-02
FARLEY, DONNA P01HL14388-20 9002
FARLEY, GLENN P50DC00215-08 0007
FARLEY, JOSEPH R01NS26106-03
FARLEY, MONICA S07RR05364-30 0550
FARLEY, ROBERT A R01GM28673-10
FARLEY, ROBERT A R01HL39295-05
FARLOW, MARTIN P30AG10133-01 9001
FARMER, GAIL C R01CA49553-03
FARMER, J DOYNE R01MH47184-02
FARNHAM, PEGGY J P01CA23076-14 0007
FARNHAM, PEGGY J R29CA45240-05
FARNSWORTH, NORMAN R R01CA33047-06
FARNSWORTH, NORMAN R U01CA52956-02 0001
FARNSWORTH, PATRICIA N R55EY05787-07
FAROOQUI, MOHAMMED Y S06GM08038-21 0008
FARQUHAR, DAVID R01AI28213-03
FARQUHAR, JOHN W K07HL02268-03
FARQUHAR, JOHN W R01AA08497-02
FARQUHAR, JOHN W R01HL21906-14
FARQUHAR, JOHN W R01HL32185-07
FARQUHAR, LYNDA J S15DK44675-01
FARQUHAR, MARILYN G P01CA46128-04 0001
FARQUHAR, MARILYN G P01CA46128-04 9001
FARQUHAR, MARILYN G P30DK34989-08 0011
FARQUHAR, MARILYN G R01DK17724-18
FARQUHAR, MARILYN GIST R37DK17780-19
FARR, ANDREW G R01AG04360-09
FARR, ANDREW G R01AI24137-05
FARR, BARRY M S07RR05431-30 0831
FARR, LYNNE A R01NR02235-02
FARR, SPENCER B R01GM43799-01A1
FARR, SPENCER B S07RR05446-30 0281
FARRAN, CAROL P30AG10161-01 9002
FARRAR, DAVID J R01HL45608-01
FARRAR, W L Z01CM09254-09
FARRAR, WILLIAM B R25CA18016-13
FARRELL, JAY P R01AI27828-01A3
FARRELL, JOAN M R03MH46451-01A1
FARRELL, JOHN N01CN15381-00
FARRELL, KEVIN W R01GM41751-03
FARRELL, PETER A S07RR07082-26 0278
FARRELL, PHILIP M M01RR03186-06 0005
FARRELL, PHILIP M R01DK34108-06A1
FARRELL, RICHARD A R01EY01019-18
FARRER, LINDSAY A R01AG09029-01A1
FARRER, LINDSAY A R29NS26454-04
FARRIS, HAROLD E G20RR06942-01
FARRUKH, IMAD S S07RR05428-30 0161
FARWELL, JACQUELINE R. M01RR00037-31 0428
FARWELL, ALAN P K08DK02005-02
FARWELL, JACQUELINE M01RR00037-31 0509
FARWELL, JACQUELINE R M01RR00037-31 0471
FARWELL, JACQUELINE R R01NS24641-03
FARZADEGAN, HAMAYOON P30AI28748-03 9004
FARZADEGAN, HOMAYOON P01AI26499-03S1 9001
FARZADEGAN, HOMAYOON R01AI28264-03
FASCO, MICHAEL S07RR05649-25 0792
FASMAN, GERALD D R01AG10002-01
FASS, ROBERT M01RR00034-31 0341
FASS, ROBERT J M01RR00034-31 0426
FASS, ROBERT J M01RR00034-31 0404
FASS, ROBERT J M01RR00034-31 0405
FASS, ROBERT J M01RR00034-31 0406

FASS, ROBERT J M01RR00034-31 0407
FASS, ROBERT J M01RR00034-31 0408
FASS, ROBERT J M01RR00034-31 0409
FASS, ROBERT J M01RR00034-31 0410
FASS, ROBERT J M01RR00034-31 0411
FASS, ROBERT J U01AI25924-05
FASSENDEN, PETER P01CA44665-04 0003
FASSLER, JAN S07RR07035-26 0089
FASSLER, JAN S R29GM40306-04
FATHMAN, C GARRISON P01AI29796-08 0005
FATHMAN, C GARRISON P01AI29796-08 0002
FATHMAN, C GARRISON P60AR20610-14 9002
FATHMAN, C GARRISON R01AI27989-03
FATHMAN, CHARLES G R01DK39959-04
FAUBER, ROBERT S07RR07115-24 0583
FAUCETT, JULIA S07RR05604-14 0677
FAUCI, A S Z01AI00537-04
FAUGHT, R EDWARD N01NS72312-02
FAULKNER, D JOHN R01CA49084-18
FAULKNER, D JOHN U01CA50750-03 0003
FAULKNER, JOHN A P01DE07687-09A1 0005
FAULKNER, JOHN A P01DE07687-09A1
FAULKNER, JOHN A R01AG06157-05
FAULMAN, ERVIN L W J S07RR05700-22 0879
FAUST, IRVING M P30DK26687-11 9001
FAUSTMAN, E P42ES04696-05 0005
FAUSTMAN, ELAINE S07RR05714-21 0133
FAUSTMAN, ELAINE S07RR05714-21 0134
FAUSTMAN, ELAINE M R01ES03157-09
FAUSTO-STERLING, ANN S07RR05664-24 0861
FAUSTO, NELSON R01CA23226-20
FAUSTO, NELSON R01CA35249-07
FAUTIN, DAPHNE G S07RR07037-26 0380
FAVA, MAURIZIO M01RR01066-14 0068
FAVA, MAURIZIO M01RR01066-14 0109
FAVA, ROY A S07RR05424-30 0120
FAVUS, MURRAY J R01DK35065-08
FAVUS, MURRAY J. M01RR00055-30 0498
FAWAZ, KARIM M01RR00054-30 0424
FAWCETT, JAN A R01AA07645-02
FAWCETT, JAN A U01MH29957-15
FAWCETT, NEWTON C R15GM46098-01
FAXON, DAVID P U01HL38525-05
FAY, FRED S07RR05712-20 0076
FAY, FREDRIC S R37HL14523-20
FAY, JOSEPH P01CA41081-06A1 0004
FAY, PHILIP J R01AI27054-03
FAY, PHILIP J R01HL38199-04
FAY, RICHARD R P50DC00293-07 0002
FAY, RICHARD R S07RR07210-09
FAYNOR, STEVEN S07RR05433-30 0250
FAZIO, BARBARA S07RR07031-26 0085
FAZIO, RUSSELL H K02MH00452-05
FAZIO, RUSSELL H R37MH38832-08
FAZLEABAS, ASGERALLY T R01HD21991-06
FEAGIN, JEAN E R29AI25513-04
FEAGIN, JEAN E S07RR05939-07 0723
FEARON, DOUGLAS T R01AI22833-08
FEARON, DOUGLAS T R01AI28191-04
FEATHERSTONE, JOHN D S07RR05548-26 0582
FEATHERSTONE, JOHN D S07RR05548-26 0581
FEATHERSTONE, JOHN D S15DE10083-01
FECHTEL, KIM S07RR05373-30 0715
FECHTER, LAURENCE P30ES03819-06A1 9018
FECHTER, LAURENCE D R01ES02852-08
FEDDE, KENTON N S07RR05491-29 0457
FEDDE, KENTON N. P01AR32087-09 0010
FEDDER, DONALD O S07RR05770-13 0937
FEDER, HARVEY H R01HD04467-20
FEDER, HARVEY H S06GM08223-08 0028
FEDER, HARVEY H S07RR07059-26 0830
FEDER, N Z01DK58004-24
FEDEROFF, HOWARD J R29HD27116-02
FEDERSPIEL, WILLIAM S07RR07043-26 0109
FEDIO, P Z01NS00200-39
FEDIO, P Z01NS01245-25
FEDIO, P Z01NS01424-25
FEDIO, P Z01NS01658-24
FEDOR, MARTHA J R55GM46422-01
FEDOROFF, NINA V R37GM34296-08
FEDSON, DAVID S R01AG09145-02
FEE, JAMES A P41RR02231-08
FEE, JAMES A P41RR02231-08 9001
FEE, JAMES A P41RR02231-08 9002
FEE, JAMES A P41RR02231-08 9003
FEE, JAMES A R01GM35342-07
FEE, JAMES A S07RR05919-08 0715
FEENEY, ANN J R01AI29672-01A2
FEENEY, DENNIS M S06GM08139-17 0042
FEFER, ALEXANDER P01CA47748-03 0009
FEHER, GEORGE R37GM13191-27
FEIG, LARRY A R29CA47391-04
FEIG, STEPHEN A U10CA27678-12
FEIGAL, DAVID S07RR05665-24 0891
FEIGAL, DAVID W P01DE07946-05 0001
FEIGAL, DAVID W P30AI27763-04 9001
FEIGAL, ELLEN G R01CA55513-01
FEIGAL, ROBERT J S07RR05322-30 0274
FEIGEL, DAVID P01AI24286-05 9002
FEIGENBAUM, SETH L K08HD00883-02
FEIGENSON, GERALD W R01HL18255-16
FEIGIN, RALPH D M01RR00188-27
FEIGIN, RALPH D P30HD27823-02
FEIGL, ERIC O P01HL16910-18 9002
FEIGL, ERIC O P01HL16910-18 0002
FEIGL, ERIC O P41RR02176-05 0007
FEIGL, ERIC O. P51RR00166-30 0085
FEIGON, JULI F R01GM37254-05
FEIN, ALAN R01EY03793-11
FEIN, FREDERICK P01HL37412-04 9003
FEIN, GEORGE R01AA08968-01
FEIN, GEORGE R01MH45680-02
FEIN, HARRY R44GM43725-02
FEIN,FREDERICK P60DK20541-14 0028
FEINBERG, ANDREW P M01RR00042-31 0665
FEINBERG, ANDREW P R01CA48932-03
FEINBERG, ANDREW P R01CA54358-01
FEINBERG, MICHAEL P50MH40380-07 0007
FEINBERG, RONALD F S07RR05415-30 0004
FEINBERG, WILLIAM M S07RR05675-23 0931
FEINGLOS, MARK N M01RR00030-30 0497
FEINGLOS, MARK N M01RR00030-30 0502
FEINGLOS, MARK N M01RR00030-30 0488
FEINGLOS, MARK S M01RR00030-30 0498
FEINGOLD, KENNETH R R01AR39639-01A3
FEINMARK, STEVEN J R29HL38312-03
FEINSTEIN, CARL B K07MH00766-03
FEINSTEIN, MAURICE B R37HL37422-05
FEINSTEIN, STEVEN B R01HL39794-03
FEINSTEIN, STUART C S07RR07099-25 0402
FEINSTONE, S M Z01BF05001-03
FEINSTONE, S M Z01BF05002-04
FEINSTONE, S M Z01BF05003-03
FEISS, MICHAEL G R01AI12851-16
FEISTNER, GOTTFRIED S07RR05841-12 0243
FEITELSON, MARK A R29CA48656-05
FEJES-TOTH, GEZA P01HL28982-10 0002
FEJES-TOTH, GEZA R01DK39523-04
FEKE, GILBERT S07RR05527-29 0517
FEKE, GILBERT T P30EY03790-11 9005
FEKE, GILBERT T R01EY01303-15
FELD, MICHAEL S P41RR02594-06
FELD, MICHAEL S P41RR02594-06 9002
FELD, MICHAEL S P41RR02594-06 9003
FELD, MICHAEL S P41RR02594-06 9001
FELD, MICHAEL S R01CA53717-01
FELD, RONALD M01RR00059-30 0749
FELD, RONALD D M01RR00059-30 0670
FELDBERG, ROSS S S07RR07179-14 0680
FELDBUSH, THOMAS P30DK25295-12S1 9012
FELDBUSH, THOMAS L S15GM47057-01
FELDER, MICHAEL R R01AA06608-07
FELDER, ROBIN A R29DK42185-02
FELDER, TYRONE B S06GM08061-17 0004
FELDHERR, CARL M R01GM43065-06
FELDMAN , MARK R01DK16816-18
FELDMAN, HENRY P30ES00002-29 9004
FELDMAN, ARTHUR M R29HL39719-03
FELDMAN, BRUCE H M01RR00997-16 0396
FELDMAN, CECILE A S07RR06004-04 0035
FELDMAN, DAVID R01DK41246-02
FELDMAN, DAVID R01DK42482-01A1
FELDMAN, EVA L K08NS01381-03
FELDMAN, G Z01BD03028-01
FELDMAN, G Z01BD03029-01
FELDMAN, HENRY A. P50HL19170-15 9002
FELDMAN, HORALD I R29DK42907-02
FELDMAN, JACK S07RR07009-26 0937
FELDMAN, JACK L R01NS24742-05
FELDMAN, JACK L R01NS28805-02
FELDMAN, JACK L R37HL37941-06
FELDMAN, JONATHAN D K11AR01870-01
FELDMAN, JUDITH N01CN15375-00
FELDMAN, JUDITH R01CA52958-02
FELDMAN, LAURIE R29DK41395-03
FELDMAN, LAWRENCE A S03RR03094-11
FELDMAN, LAWRENCE T R01AI20953-07
FELDMAN, LAWRENCE T R01AI28338-03
FELDMAN, MARCUS W R01GM28016-12
FELDMAN, MARTIN L R01AG06217-05
FELDMAN, MICHAEL R01CA28139-11
FELDMAN, PETER D R29NS29458-02
FELDMAN, R J Z01CT00235-01
FELDMAN, R J Z01CT00236-01
FELDMAN, R J Z01CT00237-01
FELDMAN, RICARDO A R29CA55293-01
FELDMAN, RICARDO A S07RR05379-30 0767
FELDMAN, ROSS D P30DK25295-12S1 0009
FELDON, STEVEN E S07RR05810-13 0021
FELEPPA, ERNEST J S07RR05853-11
FELEPPA, ERNEST J S15EY09474-01
FELICE, MARIANNE E M01RR00827-17 0408
FELICE, MARIANNE E M01RR00827-17 0420
FELICE, MARIANNE E M01RR00827-17 0421
FELLER, DANIEL J R29AA07573-03
FELLER, DENNIS R N01CM97619-04
FELLOWS, ROBERT E, JR S03RR03455-05
FELSBURG, PETER J R01AI26103-02
FELSEN, DIANE R01DK42367-03
FELSENFELD, G Z01DK34001-26
FELSENSTEIN, JOSEPH R01GM41716-03
FELSON, DAVID P60AR20613-14 9002
FELSON, DAVID T P60AR20613-14 0023
FELSON, DAVID T P60AR20613-14 0024
FELSON, DAVID T R01AG07861-04
FELSON, DAVID T R01AG09300-01A1
FELSON, DAVID T R01AR41221-01
FELSTED, R L Z01CM06167-07
FELTEN, DAVID L P50MH40381-06 0008
FELTEN, DAVID L P50MH40381-06 9003
FELTEN, DAVID L R37AG06060-06
FELTEN, DAVID L R37MH42076-06
FELTEN, SUZANNE Y K02MH00899-02
FELTEN, SUZANNE Y R01NS25223-05
FELTES, TIMOTHY S07RR05425-30 0736
FELTON, JAMES S R01CA40811-05
FELTON, JAMES S S07RR05917-08 0692
FELTON, JEFFREY R R29DE08207-05
FENDER, DEREK H R01GM41635-03
FENDRICH, MICHAEL P50MH43878-03 0008
FENDRICH, ROBERT P01NS17778-10 0008
FENDRICK, JAMES L S07RR05350-30 0336
FENESY, KIM E S07RR06004-04 0036
FENG, ALBERT S R01DC00663-02
FENICAL, WILLIAM U01CA50750-03 0004
FENICAL, WILLIAM H R01CA44848-05
FENICHEL, GERALD M01RR00095-31 0288
FENN, JOHN B R01GM31660-06S1
FENNELL, PEARLIE N01CO94393-03
FENNELL, PEARLIE M S06GM08061-17 0012
FENNERTY, BRIAN S07RR05675-23 0904
FENNESSEY, PAUL P30HD04024-23 9003
FENNESSEY, PAUL V P50HD20761-06A1 9002
FENNEWALD, MICHAEL S07RR05366-30 0555
FENNEWALD, SUSAN M R43CI00004-01
FENNINGTON, BRUCE P30HD04024-23 9004
FENOGLIO, JOHN J P01HL30557-08 9002
FENSELAU, CATHERINE C R01GM21248-16
FENSTERMACHER, JOSEPH D R01NS26004-04
FENTERS, JAMES D S07RR05744-14
FENTON, JOHN W, II R01HL13160-21
FENTON, MATTHEW J R01AI29088-02
FENTON, MATTHEW J S07RR05487-29 0701
FENTON, R G Z01CM09364-01
FENTON, WAYNE A R01DK12579-23
FERAMISCO, JAMES P01CA46370-04 0005
FERAMISCO, JAMES R P01CA50528-03
FERAMISCO, JAMES R P01CA50528-03 9001
FERAMISCO, JAMES R P01CA50528-03 0001
FERAMISCO, JAMES R R01CA39811-07
FERDINAND, BARBARA R19MH46228-03
FERDINAND, PATRICA E S06GM08171-11 0008
FERENCZ, CHARLOTTE R37HL25629-12
FERGUSON-MILLER, SHELAGH M F R01GM26916-13
FERGUSON, APRIL R24MH47187-02 0005
FERGUSON, DONALD G R01HL34779-04A1
FERGUSON, DONALD G S07RR05408-30 0927
FERGUSON, DUNCAN C R01DK38814-05
FERGUSON, FREDERICK G S07RR07082-26
FERGUSON, GARY S07RR05842-12 0281
FERGUSON, GARY T K08HL02225-02
FERGUSON, JAMES A G12RR03059-04
FERGUSON, JAMES E, I S07RR05431-30 0857
FERGUSON, JAMES M R19DA06427-03
FERGUSON, JAMES M R19MH46193-03
FERGUSON, RONALD M R01AI24676-04
FERGUSON, T BRUCE, JR R29HL46287-01
FERGUSON, THOMAS A R01EY06765-05
FERGUSON, THOMAS A R01EY08972-01
FERIN, MICHEL P50HD05077-21 0022
FERIN, MICHEL P50HD05077-21 9002
FERIN, MICHEL J R01DK39144-05
FERINDE, JOHN N01AI87248-19
FERKETICH, SANDRA S07RR05913-08 0660
FERKETICH, SANDRA L R18HS06801-02
FERL, ROBERT J R01GM40061-03
FERNALD, ANNE R01HD24349-03
FERNALD, ANNE R01MH41511-06
FERNALD, RUSSELL S07RR07005-26 0336
FERNALD, RUSSELL D R01HD23799-03
FERNANDES, DANIEL J R29CA44597-05
FERNANDES, GABRIEL P01AG01188-13 0009
FERNANDES, GABRIEL R01AG03417-11
FERNANDEZ-REPOLLET, EMMA D S06GM08224-07 0
FERNANDEZ, CESAR R01DC00070-35 0001
FERNANDEZ, CESAR R01DC00070-35 0003
FERNANDEZ, JUAN R G12RR03641-06
FERNANDEZ, JULIO M R29GM38857-05
FERNANDEZ, SALVADOR M R44HD26217-02
FERNANDO, Q P42ES04940-02 0004
FERNANDO, Q P42ES04940-02 9002
FERNBACH, DONALD J U10CA03161-34 0037
FERNBACH, DONALD J U10CA03161-34 0017
FERNBACH, DONALD J U10CA03161-34 0038
FERNBACH, DONALD J U10CA03161-34 0018
FERNBACH, DONALD J U10CA03161-34 0019
FERNBACH, DONALD J U10CA03161-34 0020
FERNBACH, DONALD J U10CA03161-34 0021
FERNBACH, DONALD J U10CA03161-34 0022
FERNBACH, DONALD J U10CA03161-34 0023
FERNBACH, DONALD J U10CA03161-34 0024
FERNBACH, DONALD J U10CA03161-34 0025
FERNBACH, DONALD J U10CA03161-34 0026
FERNBACH, DONALD J U10CA03161-34 0027
FERNBACH, DONALD J U10CA03161-34 0028
FERNBACH, DONALD J U10CA03161-34 0029

FERNBACH, DONALD J U10CA03161-34 0030
FERNBACH, DONALD J U10CA03161-34 0031
FERNBACH, DONALD J U10CA03161-34 0032
FERNBACH, DONALD J U10CA03161-34 0033
FERNBACH, DONALD J U10CA03161-34 0034
FERNBACH, DONALD J U10CA03161-34 0035
FERNBACH, DONALD J U10CA03161-34 0036
FERNBACH, DONALD J U10CA03161-34 0039
FERNBACH, DONALD J U10CA03161-34 0057
FERNBACH, DONALD J U10CA03161-34 0058
FERNBACH, DONALD J U10CA03161-34 0059
FERNBACH, DONALD J U10CA03161-34 0060
FERNBACH, DONALD J U10CA03161-34 0040
FERNBACH, DONALD J U10CA03161-34 0001
FERNBACH, DONALD J U10CA03161-34 0002
FERNBACH, DONALD J U10CA03161-34 0003
FERNBACH, DONALD J U10CA03161-34 0004
FERNBACH, DONALD J U10CA03161-34 0005
FERNBACH, DONALD J U10CA03161-34 0006
FERNBACH, DONALD J U10CA03161-34 0007
FERNBACH, DONALD J U10CA03161-34 0008
FERNBACH, DONALD J U10CA03161-34 0009
FERNBACH, DONALD J U10CA03161-34 0010
FERNBACH, DONALD J U10CA03161-34 0011
FERNBACH, DONALD J U10CA03161-34 0041
FERNBACH, DONALD J U10CA03161-34 0042
FERNBACH, DONALD J U10CA03161-34 0043
FERNBACH, DONALD J U10CA03161-34 0044
FERNBACH, DONALD J U10CA03161-34 0045
FERNBACH, DONALD J U10CA03161-34 0046
FERNBACH, DONALD J U10CA03161-34 0047
FERNBACH, DONALD J U10CA03161-34 0048
FERNBACH, DONALD J U10CA03161-34 0049
FERNBACH, DONALD J U10CA03161-34 0050
FERNBACH, DONALD J U10CA03161-34 0051
FERNBACH, DONALD J U10CA03161-34 0052
FERNBACH, DONALD J U10CA03161-34 0053
FERNBACH, DONALD J U10CA03161-34 0054
FERNBACH, DONALD J U10CA03161-34 0055
FERNBACH, DONALD J U10CA03161-34 0056
FERNBACH, DONALD J U10CA03161-34 0012
FERNBACH, DONALD J U10CA03161-34 0013
FERNBACH, DONALD J U10CA03161-34 0014
FERNBACH, DONALD J U10CA03161-34 0015
FERNBACH, DONALD J U10CA03161-34 0016
FERNBACH, DONALD J U10CA03161-34
FERNER, WILLIAM T G20RR06786-01
FERNSTROM, JOHN P50AA08746-02 0002
FERNSTROM, JOHN D K05MH00254-12
FERNSTROM, JOHN D R01HD24730-04
FERNSTROM, MADELYN H R01MH41644-03S1
FERRANS, V J Z01HL05212-01
FERRANS, V J Z01HL05213-01
FERRANS, V J Z01HL05214-01
FERRANS, V J Z01HL05215-01
FERRANS, V J Z01HL05216-01
FERRANS, V J Z01HL05217-01
FERRANS, V J Z01HL05218-01
FERRANS, V J Z01HL05219-01
FERRANS, V J Z01HL05220-01
FERRANS, V J Z01HL05221-01
FERRARIO, CARLOS M P01HL06835-30 0090
FERRARIO, CARLOS M P01HL06835-30
FERRARIO, CARLOS M P01HL06835-30 9005
FERRARIS, RONALDO S07RR05393-30 0888
FERRELL, BETTY R R03NR02798-01
FERRELL, JAMES E R01GM46383-01
FERRELL, ROBERT C P01CA34936-08 0002
FERRELL, ROBERT E R01HL44682-01A2
FERRELL, ROBERT E S10RR06357-01
FERRELL, ROBERT S M01RR00082-29 0290
FERRENDELLI, JAMES A P50NS14834-13
FERRENDELLI, JAMES A P50NS14834-13 0010
FERRETTI, J A Z01HL01027-09
FERRETTI, JOSEPH J R01AI19304-07S1
FERRETTI, JOSEPH J R01DE08191-05
FERRICK, DAVID A R55GM46412-01
FERRIER, LINDA J S07RR07143-20 0623
FERRIERI, PATRICIA R01AI13926-14
FERRIERO, DONNA M K08NS01222-05
FERRIS, CRAIG F S07RR05712-20 0097
FERRIS, S H P50MH43486-03 0001
FERRIS, S H P50MH43486-03 9001
FERRIS, S H P50MH43486-03 9002
FERRIS, S H P50MH43486-03 9003
FERRIS, STEVEN H P30AG08051-02
FERRIS, STEVEN H P50MH43486-03
FERRIS, STEVEN H R01MH42216-05
FERRIS, STEVEN H U01AG10483-01 0002
FERRO-NOVICK, SUSAN S07RR05358-30 0497
FERRO-NOVICK, SUSAN S R01GM45431-01
FERRONE, FRANK A R01DK30239-08
FERRONE, FRANK A R01HL28102-10
FERRONE, SOLDANO R01CA37959-08
FERRONE, SOLDANO R01CA51814-01A2
FERRY, GEORGE M01RR00188-27 0340
FERRY, LINDA H S07RR05352-30 0756
FERSTER, DAVID L R01EY04726-08
FERSTL, SONDRA M S15NS30289-01
FESIK, STEPHEN W R01GM45351-01
FESIK, STEPHEN W U01AI27220-04 0005
FESIK, STEPHEN W U01AI30183-02 9002
FESSENDEN, PETER P01CA44665-04 0004
FESSLER, HENRY E K08HL02194-04
FESSLER, JOHN H R01AG02128-11
FESTOFF, BARRY P30AG10182-01 0003
FETCHER, NED S06GM08102-20 0052
FETCHO, JOSEPH R R29NS26539-04
FETROW, JACQUELYN S R29GM44829-01A1
FETTEN, JAMES V K08CA01487-02
FETTERMAN, J GREGOR R01MH48359-01
FETZ, EBERHARD E P51RR00166-30 0038
FETZ, EBERHARD E R01NS12542-17
FETZ, EBERHARD E. P51RR00166-30 0057
FETZ, EBERHARD E. P51RR00166-30 0058
FEUERSTEIN, BURT G R29CA41757-05
FEUERSTEIN, I P41RR01296-08 0002
FEUERSTEIN, NILI S07RR05415-30 0002
FEUERSTEIN, NILI H R29CA48667-04
FEUSTEL, PAUL J P20NS30303-01 0002
FEVOLD, H RICHARD S06GM08218-08 0024
FEX, J Z01DC00001-03
FEY, EDWARD G R01CA51945-02
FEY, EDWARD G S07RR05712-20 0085
FEY, GEORG H M01RR00833-17 0200
FEY, GEORG H P01AI17354-10S1 0006
FEY, GEORG H R01AI22166-06
FEY, MICHAEL S R44HL42738-02
FEYEREISEN, RENE R01DK34549-07
FEYEREISEN, RENE' R01GM39014-06
FFRENCH-CONSTANT, RICHARD H R29NS29623-01
FIALA, EMERICH S R01ES03257-07
FIALA, EMERICH S U01CA46589-05 0005
FIALKOW, PHILIP J M01RR00037-31
FIALKOW, PHILIP J R37CA16448-17
FIATARONE, MARIA A U01AG09078-02
FICK, ROBERT P50HL37121-05 0003
FICKLIN, FRED L S03RR03334-10
FIDLER, ISAIAH J R35CA42107-05
FIDONE, SALVATORE J P01NS07938-22 0030
FIDONE, SALVATORE J P01NS07938-22
FIDONE, SALVATORE J R01NS12636-17
FIEDOREK, FREDERICK T, JR R01DK44074-01
FIEKERS, JEROME F R01NS27319-03
FIELD, C S M01RR00585-20 0438
FIELD, C S M01RR00585-20 0464
FIELD, ELIZABETH M01RR00059-30 0745
FIELD, ELIZABETH M01RR00059-30 0740
FIELD, ELIZABETH E M01RR00059-30 0545
FIELD, ELIZABETH H R29CA45541-05
FIELD, F JEFFREY P50HL14230-20 0102
FIELD, F JEFFREY P50HL14230-20 9001
FIELD, JAMES B P30DK27685-10 0008
FIELD, LOREN J R01HL45453-03
FIELD, LOREN J R01HL46555-02
FIELD, LOREN J R29HL38605-05
FIELD, MICHAEL P50DK41146-04 0002
FIELD, MICHAEL R01DK35183-08
FIELD, MICHAEL R01DK39515-04
FIELD, RUTH B R29DE08699-04
FIELD, TIFFANY M R01HD27003-01A1
FIELD, TIFFANY M R01HD27157-01A1
FIELD, TIFFANY M R18DA06900-02
FIELD, TIFFANY M R37MH46586-01A1
FIELDER, DAVID R S15CA55920-01
FIELDING, CHRISTOPHER J P50HL14237-20 0002
FIELDING, CHRISTOPHER J P50HL14237-20 0009
FIELDING, CHRISTOPHER J R01HL41224-04
FIELDING, PHOEBE E P50HL14237-20 0008
FIELDS, ALAN P R29GM43186-02
FIELDS, BARRY L R29HL41845-03
FIELDS, BERNARD N P50NS16998-11
FIELDS, BERNARD N P50NS16998-11 0001
FIELDS, BERNARD N R37AI13178-16
FIELDS, CHRISTOPHER S07RR07154-16 0562
FIELDS, HOWARD L P01NS21445-07
FIELDS, HOWARD L P01NS21445-07 0002
FIELDS, HOWARD L R37DA01949-14
FIELDS, JEREMY Z R01NS26449-03
FIELDS, LANNY S07RR07244-03 0486
FIELDS, STANLEY R01CA54699-01
FIERER, JOSHUA P01DK35108-07 0006
FIERKE, CAROL A R29GM40602-04
FIESE, BARBARA H R03MH47367-01A1
FIETKAU, RONALD S06GM08003-21 0008
FIFE, F R P50AR39250-05 0002
FIFE, KENNETH H M01RR00750-19 0288
FIFE, KENNETH H M01RR00750-19 0290
FIFE, KENNETH H M01RR00750-19 0291
FIFE, KENNETH H M01RR00750-19 0267
FIFE, KENNETH H M01RR00750-19 0268
FIFE, KENNETH H U01AI25859-05 0001
FIFE, KENNETH H U01AI31494-01 0004
FIG, LORRAINE M01RR00042-31 0597
FIG, LORRAINE M01RR00042-31 0545
FIGLEWICZ, DIANNE P30DK35816-06 0002
FIGUEROA, JORGE P R29HD25175-04
FIGURSKI, DAVID H R01GM29085-11
FIHN, STEPHAN D R01DK41341-01A2
FIKE, CANDICE D R29HL42883-03
FIKE, CANDICE D S07RR05428-30 0178
FIKE, JOHN R P01CA13525-19 0022
FILBIN, MARIE T R29NS26242-05
FILBY, ROY S07RR07097-26 0388
FILDERMAN, ANDREW E S07RR05591-27 0662
FILIPEK, PAULINE P01NS24279-06 9005
FILIPOVICH, ALEXANDRA P01CA21737-14 0006
FILLER, ROBERT S07RR07027-26 0013
FILLEY, CHRISTOPHER P01AG09417-01 0002
FILLING-KATZ, M Z01AA00290-01
FILLINGAME, ROBERT H R01GM23105-16
FILLIT, HOWARD P01AI24671-04 0004
FILLIT, HOWARD M R01AI24876-02
FILLIT, HOWARD M. P50AG05138-08 0012
FILLMORE, KAYE R01AA07034-06
FILLMORE, KAYE M K02AA00073-08
FILLOUX, FRANCIS M K08HD00912-02
FILSTEAD, WILLIAM J R01AA08455-01A1
FILUTOWICZ, MARCIN S R01GM40314-03
FINBERG, ROBERT W R01AI20382-09
FINBERG, ROBERT W R01CA34979-08
FINBLOOM, D S Z01BD03019-03
FINCH, CALEB P01AG09793-01 0004
FINCH, CALEB E P01AG09793-01 9001
FINCH, CALEB E P50AG05142-08
FINCH, CALEB E R35AG07909-03
FINCH, CALEB E R35AG07909-03 0001
FINCH, DAVID M R01NS16721-09
FINCH, DAVID M R01NS23074-06
FINCHAM, FRANCIS D R01MH44078-03
FINDLEY, SALLY S07RR05449-30 0327
FINDLING, JAMES W R01DK41015-03
FINE, BETH A R01HG00411-01
FINE, HOWARD A K11CA01467-01A2
FINE, JAMES R18DA06360-03
FINE, JO D. M01RR00032-31 0254
FINE, JO-DAVID M01RR00046-31 0508
FINE, JO-DAVID R01AR34861-04A3
FINE, KENNETH D S07RR05906-06 0634
FINE, MARK A R15HD28198-01
FINE, RICHARD E R01AG05894-19
FINE, RICHARD E R01EY08535-02
FINE, RICHARD M R43GM45651-01
FINE, RICHARD N M01RR00865-18 0322
FINE, SAMUEL S07RR07143-20
FINE, SAMUEL S15HD28753-01
FINE, STUART L U10EY06266-07
FINEBERA, S EDWIN M01RR00750-19 0272
FINEBERG, JAOMI S P60DK20542-14 9001
FINEBERG, S EDWIN P60DK20542-14 9002
FINEGOLD, DAVID N M01RR00084-29 0241
FINEGOLD, MILTON P01DK44080-01 9003
FINEMAN, NORMAN R03HS06984-01
FINER-MOORE, JANET S R01CA41323-06
FINERMAN, GERALD A R13AR40962-01
FINGAR, VICTOR H R01CA51771-02
FINGER, THOMAS E P01DC00244-07
FINGER, THOMAS E P01DC00244-07 0003
FINGER, THOMAS E P20DC01439-01
FINGER, THOMAS E P20DC01439-01 0001
FINGER, THOMAS E P41RR00592-22 0010
FINGER, THOMAS E P50NS09199-21 0032
FINGER, THOMAS E R01DC00147-13
FINGERMAN, MILTON R13HD28530-01
FINGEROTH, JOYCE D R29AI26835-04
FINGEROTH, JOYCE D S07RR05526-29 0074
FINGLAND, R B S07RR07036-26 0107
FINGOLD, DAVID N M01RR00084-29 0235
FINI, M ELIZABETH R01EY08408-03
FINK, ANTHONY L R01GM45316-01
FINK, B RAYMOND R01GM31710-07A1
FINK, DAVID J P60DK20572-14 0041
FINK, DAVID J R29NS27771-03
FINK, GERALD R R01GM40266-08
FINK, GERALD R R37GM35010-08
FINK, GERALD R S07RR05937-07
FINK, GERALD R S07RR05937-07 0523
FINK, GREGORY D R01HL24111-13
FINK, J STEPHEN R01NS27514-03
FINK, JORDAN N M01RR00058-30 0010
FINK, MARY L R15GM46123-01
FINK, MITCHELL P R29GM37631-05
FINK, PAMELA J R29AI27417-04
FINKBEINER, WALTER E P50HL42368-04 9002
FINKE, JAMES H P01CA48919-01A2 0002
FINKE, RICHARD G R01DK26214-13
FINKEL, SANFORD I K07MH00793-02
FINKEL, TERRI H R01AI30575-01
FINKELMAN, FRED D R01AI21328-07
FINKELMAN, RICHARD D S07RR05352-30 0759
FINKELSTEIN, ALAN R01GM29210-14
FINKELSTEIN, DANIEL U10EY06750-04
FINKELSTEIN, DIANNE M R01AI30885-01
FINKELSTEIN, JACOB P50HL36543-05 0001
FINKELSTEIN, JACOB N P30ES01247-17 0097
FINKELSTEIN, JACOB N P50HL36543-05 0003
FINKELSTEIN, JAMES D R01DK13048-23
FINKELSTEIN, JUDITH S07RR05806-13 0907
FINKELSTEIN, MARCIA A R01EY08654-02
FINKELSTEIN, RICHARD A R22AI16776-13
FINKELSTEIN, SETH P P01AG02126-11 0014
FINKELSTEIN, STANLEY M R55NR02128-01A3
FINKLESTEIN, JACOB P30ES01247-17 9010
FINKLESTEIN, JERRY Z U10CA14560-18
FINKLESTEIN, SETH P50NS10828-16 0028
FINKLESTEIN, SETH P R01AG08207-04

FINLAY, BARBARA L R01NS19245-08
FINLAY, CATHY A R01CA55036-01
FINLAY, MARY F S03RR03216-08
FINLAY, MARY F S06GM08117-18
FINLAYSON-PITTS, BARBARA J R01ES03484-07
FINLAYSON-PITTS, BARBARA J S06GM08258-02 0002
FINLAYSON, BIRDWELL P01DK20586-15 9002
FINLAYSON, BIRDWELL P01DK20586-15 0001
FINLAYSON, BRUCE P41RR01243-10 0007
FINLEY, DANIEL J R01GM43601-02
FINLEY, RICHARD W S07RR05386-30 0583
FINN, FRANCES M R01DK42019-01A2
FINN, M G S07RR07094-26 0365
FINN, OLIVERA J R01CA56103-01
FINN, PATRICIA K11HL02054-04
FINN, PETER S07RR07031-26 0086
FINN, T Z01BA07024-01
FINN, WILLIAM F M01RR00046-31 0404
FINN, WILLIAM F M01RR00046-31 0448
FINNEGAN, ALISON R29AI26173-04
FINNEGAN, KEVIN T R29DA07239-01A1
FINNEY, JACK W S07RR07095-24 0378
FINNEY, JOHN W JR R01AA08689-02
FIOCCHI, CLAUDIO R01DK30399-09
FIORAVANTI, CARMEN S07RR07192-12 0622
FIORE, MICHAEL C K07CA01541-02
FIQUERAS, JOHN R43CA52374-01A1
FIRE, ANDREW Z R01GM37706-05
FIREK, A F M01RR00585-20 0528
FIREK, A J M01RR00585-20 0349
FIREMAN, MARIAN M01RR00334-25 0305
FIREMAN, PHILIP M01RR00084-29 0197
FIREMAN, PHILIP R01AI19262-08
FIREMAN, PHILIP A M01RR00084-29 0099
FIREMAN, PHILLIP M01RR00084-29 0252
FIRESTEIN, GARY U01AI31595-01 9001
FIRESTEIN, GARY S R01AR40525-02
FIRESTEIN, GARY S R29AR39576-04
FIRESTEIN, GARY S S07RR05665-24 0887
FIRESTEIN, STUART R01DC00920-01
FIRESTONE, GARY L P01CA05388-31A1 0035
FIRESTONE, GARY L R01DK42799-02
FIRESTONE, LEONARD L R29GM35900-06
FIRLING, CONRAD E S07RR07052-26 0155
FIRMAN, JEFFRE S07RR07053-26 0153
FIRTEL, RICHARD R01GM37830-06
FIRTEL, RICHARD A R01GM24279-15
FIRTEL, RICHARD A R01GM30693-10
FISCH, BRUCE J S07RR05376-30 0040
FISCHBACH, GERALD D R01NS18458-12
FISCHBACH, MICHAEL S07RR05654-24 0126
FISCHBACH, RUTH L S07RR05381-30 0787
FISCHBARG, JORGE R01EY06178-06
FISCHBECK, KENNETH H P01NS08075-21 0014
FISCHEL-GHODSIAN S07RR05468-29 0410
FISCHELL, TIM A K08HL02001-05
FISCHER, ALLAN G S03RR03344-06
FISCHER, E. P01GM42508-03 0005
FISCHER, EDMOND H R01DK07902-29
FISCHER, ITZHAK R29NS24725-05
FISCHER, JAMES B R44MH45735-03
FISCHER, JOSEF E R01DK37908-04A2
FISCHER, KENNETH N01HD13105-01
FISCHER, LAWRENCE J P42ES04911-03 9002
FISCHER, LAWRENCE J P42ES04911-03
FISCHER, PAMELA J R01MH46106-03
FISCHER, RANDY S R43AI31753-01
FISCHER, ROBERT S07RR07006-26 0903
FISCHER, ROBIN M01RR00109-28 0366
FISCHER, STUART G S07RR05395-30 0824
FISCHER, SUSAN M R01CA34443-08
FISCHER, SUSAN M R01CA42211-05
FISCHER, SUSAN M R55CA46886-04
FISCHER, THOMAS H K04HL02521-02
FISCHER, WOLFGANG P01DK26741-12 9004
FISCHER, WOLFGANG P01HD13527-12 9002
FISCHER, WOLFGANG H P01CA54418-01 9002
FISCHETTI, VINCENT A R37AI11822-18
FISCHHOFF, BARUCH R01AA08381-02
FISCHINGER, PETER J M01RR01070-15
FISCHL, MARGARET A R01AI25773-05
FISCHL, MARGARET A R37CA34988-09
FISCHL, MARGARET A U01AI27675-05S2
FISCHMAN, DONALD A R01AR32147-10
FISCHMAN, DONALD A R01HL45458-02
FISCHMAN, DONALD A S07RR05396-30 0739
FISCHMAN, MARIAN W M01RR00035-31 0324
FISCHMAN, MARIAN W R01DA03476-09
FISCHMAN, MARIAN W R01DA06234-02
FISCHMAN, MARIAN W R37DA03818-08
FISER, DEBRA H R01MH48590-01
FISH, ALFRED M01RR00400-23 0288
FISH, GARY E U10EY06239-06
FISH, STEPHEN E R15NS29566-01
FISH, STEPHEN E S07RR05870-10 0991
FISHBEIN, JAMES C R01CA52881-02
FISHER, ARON B P01HL19737-15 0001
FISHER, ARON B R01HL26710-10
FISHER, ARON B R01HL41939-04
FISHER, BERNARD R03CA53282-02
FISHER, BERNARD U10CA12027-20
FISHER, BERNARD U10CA12028-20
FISHER, BERNARD U10CA37377-07
FISHER, BERNARD U10CA39086-07
FISHER, D S07RR05830-12 0961
FISHER, D S07RR05830-12 0971
FISHER, DELBERT A M01RR00425-22S3 0425
FISHER, DELBERT A R01HD06335-18
FISHER, DELBERT A R37HD04270-23
FISHER, DENNIS G U01DA07290-01
FISHER, DENNIS M R01GM37795-03
FISHER, EDWARD A S07RR05418-30 0024
FISHER, EDWIN B P60DK20579-14 9006
FISHER, EDWIN B, JR R01HL43555-03
FISHER, EDWIN B, JR R01HL45293-02
FISHER, FRANKLIN G N01AI15127-00
FISHER, GARY J R29AR39691-03
FISHER, GEORGE H S06GM45455-01 0001
FISHER, HARVEY F R01GM15188-23
FISHER, JAMES H R01HL41320-04
FISHER, JEFFREY D R01MH46224-03
FISHER, JOSEPH N M01RR00211-27 0292
FISHER, JOSEPH N M01RR00211-27 0308
FISHER, L W Z01DE00074-19
FISHER, LISA J P01AG10435-01 0002
FISHER, LLOYD P01CA47748-03 9001
FISHER, LLOYD P30DK17047-15 9007
FISHER, LLOYD D P01AI29363-02 9003
FISHER, LLOYD D P30AI27757-04 9004
FISHER, M T Z01HL00273-02
FISHER, MARILYN R01NS25350-04
FISHER, MARK J R01NS20989-08
FISHER, MARYE S07RR05656-24 0831
FISHER, PAUL P01ES04068-05 0004
FISHER, PAUL A R01GM33132-07
FISHER, PAUL B R01CA35675-08
FISHER, PAUL B R01CA43208-05
FISHER, PRUDENCE P50MH43878-03 0020
FISHER, R P30HD04612-21 9005
FISHER, R S P01HD05958-20 0013
FISHER, RACHEL A R01HD27125-01A1
FISHER, RICHARD I R01CA55509-01
FISHER, RICHARD I U10CA46282-04
FISHER, ROBERT H S07RR05812-12 0483
FISHER, ROBERT S M01RR00035-31 0382
FISHER, ROBIN S R29NS24596-04
FISHER, RORY A R29HL41071-03
FISHER, SEYMOUR R01MH39661-08
FISHER, STANLEY E R01AA07284-05
FISHER, STEPHEN K P01MH42652-05 0002
FISHER, STEPHEN K R01NS23831-06
FISHER, STEVEN K R37EY00888-20
FISHER, SUSAN P01HD24180-04 0001
FISHER, SUSAN P41RR01614-10 0011
FISHER, SUSAN H R01AI23168-07
FISHER, SUSAN J N01HD82903-07
FISHER, SUSAN J P01HD26732-01A1 0002
FISHER, SUSAN J R01DE07244-06
FISHER, WALDO R M01RR00082-29 0445
FISHER, WALDO R M01RR00082-29 0471
FISHMAN, ALFRED P R01HL39775-04
FISHMAN, GLENN I K11HL02391-02
FISHMAN, JAY A K08HL01916-05
FISHMAN, JAY A P01HL43510-03 9003
FISHMAN, MYER M S03RR03209-10
FISHMAN, MYER M S06GM08168-13
FISHMAN, P H Z01NS01309-26
FISHMAN, P H Z01NS02366-14
FISK, ARTHUR D R01AG07654-04A1
FISKE, ALAN P R29MH43857-04
FISKE, SUSAN T R01MH41801-06
FISKE, SUSAN T S15MH49321-01
FISLER, JANIS S R01DK45066-01
FITCH, FRANK W P01AI29531-02 9002
FITCH, FRANK W P01AI29531-02 0002
FITCH, FRANK W P01CA19266-14A1 9003
FITCH, FRANK W P01CA19266-14A1 0020
FITCH, FRANK W P50HL15062-20 0030
FITCH, FRANK W R35CA44372-05
FITCH, JOHN N01LM03516-01
FITCH, WALTER M P01GM42397-01A2 0001
FITCHEN, JOHN H R01CA37881-06
FITCHETT, JAMES E, JR K11DE00208-05
FITE, KATHERINE V R01EY07370-05
FITHIAN, JANET P60HL38632-04 0008
FITTS, DOUGLAS A R55NS22274-06A1
FITTS, ROBERT H R01AR39894-02
FITZ, ANNETTE E M01RR00059-30 0689
FITZ, JOHN G R01DK43278-01
FITZGERALD-BOCARSLY, S07RR05393-30 0889
FITZGERALD-BOCARSLY, PATRICIA R01AI26806-0
FITZGERALD-HAYES, MO S07RR07048-26 0639
FITZGERALD-HAYES, MOLLY K04GM00528-03
FITZGERALD-HAYES, MOLLY R01GM32257-09
FITZGERALD, ROBERT S. P01HL10342-26 0033
FITZGERALD, D J Z01CB08757-04
FITZGERALD, DAVID M S07RR05404-30 0842
FITZGERALD, DESMOND J R29HL40056-04
FITZGERALD, E A Z01BE03001-09
FITZGERALD, E A Z01BE03002-10
FITZGERALD, EDWARD F P42ES04913-02 0001
FITZGERALD, EDWARD F R03CA55168-01
FITZGERALD, GARRET M01RR00095-31 0362
FITZGERALD, GARRET M01RR00095-31 0365
FITZGERALD, GARRET M01RR00095-31 0266
FITZGERALD, GARRET M01RR00095-31 0283
FITZGERALD, GARRET M01RR00095-31 0187
FITZGERALD, GARRET A P50GM15431-24 0131
FITZGERALD, GARRET A P50GM15431-24 0134
FITZGERALD, GARRET A R01HL30400-08
FITZGERALD, GWEN H N01AR82200-04
FITZGERALD, MARK S07RR05321-30 0264
FITZGERALD, PAUL G R01EY08747-02
FITZGERALD, PAUL G R29EY07074-05
FITZGERALD, ROBERT H, JR R01AR26928-11
FITZGERALD, THOMAS J S07RR05896-09 0624
FITZMAURICE, M P41RR02594-06 0006
FITZPATRICK, DAVID R01EY06661-06
FITZPATRICK, DAVID R01EY06821-04A1
FITZPATRICK, FRANK A P01HL34303-07 0007
FITZPATRICK, FRANK A R01GM41026-03
FITZPATRICK, JOYCE J S15NR02931-01
FITZPATRICK, L A M01RR00585-20 0531
FITZPATRICK, LORRAINE A R01DK42572-03
FITZPATRICK, LORRAINE A R55DK42802-01A1
FITZPATRICK, PATRICIA G M01RR00044-31 0383
FITZPATRICK, PAUL S07RR07090-26 0471
FITZSIMMONS, JEFFREY R P41RR02278-06A1 900
FITZSIMONS, KATHLEEN H S03RR03479-04
FIVES-TAYLOR, PAULA R03DE09671-01
FIVES-TAYLOR, PAULA M R01DE05606-11
FIVUSH, BARBARA M01RR00052-30 0236
FIXMAN, MARSHALL R01GM27945-12
FJELD, CARLA R M01RR06021-02 1004
FJELD, CARLA R P41RR00954-15 0022
FLACK, JOHN M S07RR05448-30 0310
FLACK, YREANA-RENEE S03RR03119-07
FLAGLER, SUSAN S07RR05758-18 0245
FLAHERTY, LORRAINE A R01GM37947-04A2
FLAHERTY, LORRAINE A R37AI12603-17
FLAJNIK, MARTIN F R29AI27877-03
FLAKOLL, PAUL J R29DK43290-01
FLAM, MARSHALL S U10CA35283-07A1
FLAMM, MICHAEL K08HL02547-01
FLANAGAN, KATE S07RR05664-24 0859
FLANAGAN, PATRICK W S07RR07153-14
FLANAGAN, STEVEN S07RR05841-12 0229
FLANAGAN, STEVEN D R01MH45908-02
FLANAGAN, STEVEN D S07RR05841-12 0248
FLANAGAN, THOMAS D R01AI26800-04
FLANDERS, K Z01CP05624-02
FLANDERS, K C Z01CP05550-04
FLANDERS, MARTHA R01NS27484-03
FLANEGAN, JAMES B R01AI15539-13
FLANIGAN, MICHAEL J M01RR00059-30 0659
FLANIGAN, TIMOTHY P K08AI01085-01
FLANNERY, JOHN T P01CA42101-06 9003
FLATAU, ALISON S07RR07034-26 0054
FLATT, JEAN-PIERRE R01DK33214-08
FLAVAHAN, NICHOLAS A R29HL43365-02
FLAVELL, JOHN H R37MH40687-07
FLAVELL, RICHARD P01AI30548-01A1 0004
FLAVELL, RICHARD P01DK43078-02 0003
FLAVELL, RICHARD A R01AI29902-02
FLAVIN, KAREN P60DK20579-14 0029
FLAVIN, M Z01HL00517-01
FLAY, BRIAN R R01DA06307-01A1
FLECKMAN, PHILIP P01AR21557-13 0004
FLEG, J Z01AG00265-02
FLEG, J L Z01AG00228-08
FLEGE, JAMES E R01DC00257-08
FLEISCHER, NORMAN S P60DK20541-14
FLEISCHER, NORMAN S P60DK20541-14 9002
FLEISCHER, S P41RR01219-10 0005
FLEISCHER, SIDNEY R01HL32711-07
FLEISCHER, SIDNEY S07RR07201-12 0631
FLEISCHMAN, JULIAN B R03EY09266-01
FLEISCHMANN, AMOS R03MH46711-01A1
FLEISCHMANN, WILLIAM R, JR R01CA50752-02
FLEISHER, DAVID R29NS24616-05
FLEISHER, GARY S07RR05899-10 0274
FLEISHER, LLOYD N R01EY08688-02
FLEISHER, T A Z01CL10139-06
FLEISHER, T A Z01CL10140-06
FLEISHER, T A Z01CL10162-04
FLEISHER, T A Z01CL10164-04
FLEISSNER, ERWIN S03RR03410-07
FLEISSNER, ERWIN S06GM08176-12
FLEISSNER, ERWIN J P01CA16599-17 0018
FLEISSNER, ERWIN J P01CA16599-17 9001
FLEIT, HOWARD B R01CA38055-07
FLEMING, C R M01RR00585-20 0295
FLEMING, DAVID W U01DA07302-01
FLEMING, JOHN T R29HL42447-02
FLEMING, LORA E P30ES05705-01 0001
FLEMING, MICHAEL R19MH46214-03
FLEMING, MICHAEL F M01RR03186-06 0055
FLEMING, MICHAEL F R01AA08512-01A1
FLEMING, NEIL S07RR05684-23 0177
FLEMING, T P Z01CP05631-02
FLEMING, THOMAS R R01AI29168-03
FLEMING, WILLIAM W R01DA03773-06
FLEMING, WILLIAM W R01GM29840-22
FLESNESS, NATHAN R R01RR03576-06
FLESS, GUNTHER M P01HL18577-16 0014
FLETCHER, H PATRICK S07RR05586-24 0118

FLETCHER, J E Z01CT00045-14
FLETCHER, J E Z01CT00173-05
FLETCHER, J E Z01CT00224-01
FLETCHER, JACK M P01HD21888-04 9001
FLETCHER, JACK M R01HD27597-01
FLETCHER, JOHN R S07RR05774-17 0384
FLETCHER, JONATHAN A K11CA01498-02
FLETCHER, JONATHON S07RR05950-07 0006
FLETCHER, MADILYN P01AG04393-07 0009
FLETCHER, PAUL W S07RR05394-30 0715
FLETCHER, WILLIAM S U10CA46113-04
FLETTERICK, ROBERT J P01HL43821-02 0005
FLETTERICK, ROBERT J R01DK26081-13
FLETTERICK, ROBERT J R01DK32822-08
FLETTERICK, ROBERT J R01DK39304-04
FLEURY, DOUGLAS R25RR07607-01
FLEXNER, CHARLES W K08AI00982-02
FLEXNER, CHARLES W M01RR00035-31 0400
FLEXNER, CHARLES W M01RR00722-19 0244
FLICKENGER, CHARLES P30CA44579-04A1 9002
FLICKER, PAUL L S07RR05426-30 0134
FLICKER, PAULA S07RR07201-12 0632
FLICKER, PAULA F S10RR06312-01
FLICKINGER, CHARLES J U54HD29099-01 9001
FLICKINGER, GEORGE L P01HD06274-20 0009
FLIER, JEFFERY M01RR01032-16 0462
FLIER, JEFFERY M01RR01032-16 0464
FLIER, JEFFREY S R01DK28082-10
FLIESLER, STEVEN J R01EY06045-09
FLIESLER, STEVEN J S07RR06045-01
FLINN, CHRISTOPHER J R01HD28409-01
FLINT, PAUL W S07RR05432-30 0240
FLINT, SARAH J R01AI17265-11
FLINT, SARAH J R01AI24545-05
FLINT, SARAH J R01GM37705-05
FLOM, MERTON C P30EY07551-04
FLOM, MERTON C S07RR05998-04
FLOMENBERG, NEAL P01AI32918-09 9002
FLOMENBERG, NEAL P01AI32918-09 0010
FLOMENBERG, NEAL P01CA23766-14 0022
FLOMENBERG, NEAL P01CA23766-14 9009
FLOMENBERG, NEAL R01AI28449-03
FLOMENBERG, NEAL P01NS25701-05 9002
FLOOD, DOROTHY G P01AG03644-07 0006
FLOOD, JAMES F R01AG09321-01A1
FLOOD, P S07RR05333-30 0879
FLOOD, PATRICK M R01DE09426-01A1
FLOOR, ERIK R01NS24890-06
FLORANT, GREGORY S07RR07115-24 0574
FLORENTINE, MARY R01DC00187-08
FLORENTINE, MARY S07RR07143-20 0624
FLORES, ESTEVAN T U01CA52903-02
FLORES, HECTOR E S07RR07082-26 0279
FLORES, J Z01AI00346-09
FLORES, J Z01AI00446-07
FLORES, J Z01AI00558-03
FLORINI, JAMES R R37HL11551-24
FLORKIEWICZ, ROBERT P01DK18811-17A1 9006
FLORKIEWICZ, ROBERT P01DK18811-17A1 0018
FLORMAN, HARVEY P41RR00570-21 0017
FLORMAN, HARVEY M R29HD22615-05
FLOROS, JOANNA R01HL34788-08
FLOROS, JOANNA R01HL38288-05
FLOSS, HEINZ G R01AI20264-09
FLOSS, HEINZ G R01GM32333-09
FLOSS, HEINZ G R01GM32910-08
FLOSS, HEINZ G R01GM41363-03
FLOSS, HEINZ G R01GM43345-02
FLOURET, GEORGE R N01HD13103-00
FLOWERS, NANCY C R55HL33692-07
FLOYD, C P41RR05959-02 9005
FLOYD, C P41RR05959-02 9006
FLOYD, FRANK J R01HD24205-04
FLOYD, GARY L R25RR07563-01
FLOYD, JOHN C M01RR00042-31 0557
FLOYD, ROBERT A R01AG09690-01
FLOYD, ROBERT A R01CA42854-05
FLOYD, ROBERT A R01NS23307-04A2
FLUCHER, B E Z01NS02834-01
FLUCK, MICHELE M R01CA29270-10
FLUCK, RICHARD A P41RR01395-10 0017
FLUG, FRANCES S07RR05399-30 0946
FLUGELMAN, M Y Z01HL04880-01
FLUGELMAN, M Y Z01HL04881-01
FLUGELMAN, M Y Z01HL04882-01
FLUHARTY, ARVAN L S07RR05756-18 0297
FLUORNOY, N P01CA18029-16 9003
FLUSBERG, ALLEN M R43DK43556-01
FLYE, M WAYNE P01AI24854-05 0004
FLYE, M WAYNE R01AI28480-02
FLYER, DAVID S07RR05680-23 0918
FLYER, DAVID C R01CA44633-06
FLYNN, BRIAN S P01CA46456-02 9002
FLYNN, CHERYL S07RR05651-24 0147
FLYNN, DONNA D R01NS19065-08
FLYNN, DONNA D S07RR05363-30 0828
FLYNN, FRANCIS W R01NS24879-05
FLYNN, MICHAEL S07RR05450-30 0346
FLYNN, MICHAEL S07RR05490-29 0451
FLYNN, MICHAEL R R01OH02710-02
FLYNN, MICHAEL R R01OH02858-01
FLYNN, PATRICK J U10CA35267-08
FLYTZANIS, CONSTANTIN N R01HD22055-04A2
FOA, E P01MH47200-02 0006
FOA, EDNA B R01MH42178-06
FOA, EDNA B R01MH45404-02
FOCHTMANN, LAURA J R29MH46040-02
FOE, VICTORIA E R01GM36263-07
FOEGH, MARIE L. P01HL40069-04 0001
FOEGH, MARIE L. P01HL40069-04 0002
FOEHRING, ROBERT C R29NS27180-02
FOGEL, ALAN D S07RR07092-26 0486
FOGEL, BARRY S R01MH47572-01
FOGEL, BERNARD J M01RR05280-03
FOGEL, BERNARD J S07RR05363-30
FOGEL, BERNARD J S15AI32192-01
FOGEL, BERNARD J S15DA07779-01
FOGEL, SEYMOUR N01ES95283-04
FOGEL, SEYMOUR R01GM17317-22
FOGELMAN, ALAN M M01RR00865-18 0184
FOGELMAN, ALAN M P01HL30568-09 0007
FOGELMAN, ALAN M P01HL30568-09 0002
FOGELMAN, ALAN M P01HL30568-09
FOGLEMAN, JAMES S07RR07138-20 0526
FOGO, AGNES B R29DK42131-02
FOILES, PETER R01ES05787-01
FOJO, A T Z01CM06732-03
FOJO, S S Z01HL02028-07
FOJO, S S Z01HL02035-02
FOJO, S S Z01HL02036-01
FOJO, S S Z01HL02037-01
FOK, AGNES K. S06GM08125-18 0048
FOKER, JOHN E R01HL26640-10
FOLBERG, ROBERT R01EY07043-05
FOLDS, JAMES U01AI25868-05 9001
FOLEY, KATHLEEN M R01CA32897-09
FOLEY, MICHAEL R M01RR00034-31 0414
FOLEY, THOMAS P M01RR00084-29 0176
FOLEY, THOMAS P M01RR00084-29 0177
FOLEY, THOMAS P M01RR00084-29 0178
FOLEY, THOMAS P. M01RR00084-29 0096
FOLK, J E Z01DE00001-39
FOLK, JAMES C U10EY02553-13
FOLK, WILLIAM R R01CA38538-08
FOLK, WILLIAM R R01CA45033-04
FOLK, WILLIAM R R01GM34537-06
FOLKERS, KARL N01HD13101-01
FOLKINS, JOHN W P60DC00976-02 0003
FOLKMAN, JUDAH P01CA45548-05 9002
FOLKMAN, JUDAH P01CA45548-05 0006
FOLKMAN, M JUDAH R37CA37395-10
FOLKMAN, MOSES J P01CA45548-05
FOLKMAN, SUSAN P50MH42459-06 9002
FOLKMAN, SUSAN R01MH44045-03
FOLKS, DAVID P30AG10163-01 9001
FOLKS, DAVID G P01AG06569-05 0006
FOLLIS, FABRIZIO S07RR05583-27 0628
FOLLMAN, ERICH H S07RR07254-03 0498
FOLSOM, RICHARD C. P01DC00520-04 0004
FOLSOM, AARON R R01CA39742-07
FOLSOM, AARON R. N01HC55019-10
FOLSTEIN, MARSHAL F P50AG05146-09 9004
FOLSTEIN, MARSHAL F P50AG05146-09 9001
FOLSTEIN, MARSHAL F U01MH46290-03
FOLSTEIN, SUSAN E M01RR00035-31 0401
FOLSTEIN, SUSAN E M01RR00722-19 0184
FOLSTEIN, SUSAN E P01NS16375-11 9001
FOLSTEIN, SUSAN E P01NS16375-11
FOLSTEIN, SUSAN E P01NS16375-11 9003
FOLSTEIN, SUSAN E R01MH39936-06
FOLTIN, RICHARD W R01DA04130-06
FOLTS, JOHN D P01HL29586-09 0003
FOLTZ, C M Z01DK58003-17
FOLTZ, RODGER L R01DA05860-03
FOLTZ, RODGER L R43DA07045-01
FOMON, SAMUEL J P41RR00954-15 0021
FONG, CHIN-TO S07RR05389-30 0633
FONG, DUNNE R01CA49359-03
FONG, HARRY H S P01CA48112-01A3 0001
FONG, HENRY K W R01EY08364-02
FONSECA, RAYMOND S07RR05337-30
FONSECA, RAYMOND J S03RR03147-06
FONTANA, EDUARDO R43HD28542-01
FONZI, WILLIAM A R01GM38778-03
FOOD, AMASA B P01AG04391-09 9001
FOON, KENNETH P01CA57165-01
FOON, KENNETH R03CA53503-02
FOON, KENNETH A P01CA57165-01 0003
FOON, KENNETH A P01CA57165-01 9001
FOOTE, CHRISTOPHER S R01GM20080-18
FOOTE, ROBERT H U01HD21939-07
FOOTE, STEPHEN P50MH47680-02 0014
FOOTE, STEPHEN L P50AA06420-08 0007
FORBES, DOUGLASS J R01GM33279-08
FORBES, GILBERT M01RR00044-31 0331
FORBES, GILBERT B K06HD18454-30
FORBES, GILBERT B M01RR00044-31 0371
FORBES, GILBERT B M01RR00044-31 0226
FORBES, GILBERT B. M01RR00044-31 0300
FORBES, GILBERT B. M01RR00044-31 0302
FORBES, M S P01HL19242-15 9005
FORBES, MALCOLM D E S07RR07072-26 0265
FORBUSH, BLISS P01DK17433-18 0021
FORBUSH, BLISS, III R01GM31782-09
FORBUSH, MARI P30HD24051-03 9004
FORBUSH, MARI P30HD24051-03 9001
FORCE, THOMAS L K08DK01986-02
FORCHETTI, CONCETTA S07RR05477-29 0426
FORD, AMASA B P01AG04391-09
FORD, AMASA B P01AG04391-09 0004
FORD, AMASA B R01AG07195-03S1
FORD, DANIEL E M01RR00722-19 0203
FORD, DANIEL E R29MH46967-02
FORD, DAVID A P41RR00954-15 0031
FORD, DAVID A R29HL42665-03
FORD, DOUGLAS M01RR00069-29 0493
FORD, DOUGLAS M S07RR05357-30 0446
FORD, ELIZABETH W G20RR07118-01
FORD, JANET R18MH48036-02
FORD, JEAN K08CA01643-01
FORD, KATHLEEN R01HD26250-02
FORD, LINCOLN E P01HL20592-15 9002
FORD, LINCOLN E R01HL44398-02
FORD, RICHARD J P30CA16672-17 9018
FORD, RICHARD J, JR R01CA52778-02
FORD, RICHARD J, JR R01CA55526-01
FORD, SUSAN H S06GM08043-21 0005
FORDTRAN, JOHN S R37DK37172-07
FORDTRAN, JOHN S S07RR05906-06
FORDTRAN, JOHN S S15AR41240-01
FORDYCE, MARIANNA K K04HL01862-05
FOREHAND, CYNTHIA J K04NS01344-03
FOREHAND, CYNTHIA J S07RR05429-30 0201
FOREHAND, JOHN R S07RR05506-29 0906
FOREMAN, MARQUIS D R29NR02231-01A1
FOREMAN, ROBERT D R01HL42321-02
FOREMAN, SPENCER S07RR05499-29
FOREMAN, SPENCER S07RR05499-29 0506
FORERO, ENRIQUE N01CM17547-00
FOREYT, JOHN M01RR00350-25 0483
FOREYT, JOHN P R01DK43109-01A1
FORGAC, MICHAEL D R01GM34478-07
FORGAC, MICHAEL D R01GM44828-02
FORGAYS, DONALD G S07RR07125-22 0386
FORGET, BERNARD G R01DK19482-16
FORGET, BERNARD G R01DK44058-01
FORGEY, MARY A R43DA07010-01
FORKER, E LEE R37DK27623-12
FORMAN, EDWIN N U10CA29293-11 0043
FORMAN, EDWIN N U10CA29293-11
FORMAN, EDWIN N U10CA29293-11 0001
FORMAN, EDWIN N U10CA29293-11 0044
FORMAN, EDWIN N U10CA29293-11 0045
FORMAN, EDWIN N U10CA29293-11 0046
FORMAN, EDWIN N U10CA29293-11 0047
FORMAN, EDWIN N U10CA29293-11 0048
FORMAN, EDWIN N U10CA29293-11 0049
FORMAN, EDWIN N U10CA29293-11 0050
FORMAN, EDWIN N U10CA29293-11 0051
FORMAN, EDWIN N U10CA29293-11 0052
FORMAN, EDWIN N U10CA29293-11 0053
FORMAN, EDWIN N U10CA29293-11 0054
FORMAN, EDWIN N U10CA29293-11 0055
FORMAN, EDWIN N U10CA29293-11 0056
FORMAN, EDWIN N U10CA29293-11 0057
FORMAN, EDWIN N U10CA29293-11 0058
FORMAN, EDWIN N U10CA29293-11 0059
FORMAN, EDWIN N U10CA29293-11 0002
FORMAN, EDWIN N U10CA29293-11 0060
FORMAN, EDWIN N U10CA29293-11 0003
FORMAN, EDWIN N U10CA29293-11 0023
FORMAN, EDWIN N U10CA29293-11 0024
FORMAN, EDWIN N U10CA29293-11 0025
FORMAN, EDWIN N U10CA29293-11 0026
FORMAN, EDWIN N U10CA29293-11 0027
FORMAN, EDWIN N U10CA29293-11 0028
FORMAN, EDWIN N U10CA29293-11 0029
FORMAN, EDWIN N U10CA29293-11 0030
FORMAN, EDWIN N U10CA29293-11 0031
FORMAN, EDWIN N U10CA29293-11 0032
FORMAN, EDWIN N U10CA29293-11 0033
FORMAN, EDWIN N U10CA29293-11 0004
FORMAN, EDWIN N U10CA29293-11 0005
FORMAN, EDWIN N U10CA29293-11 0006
FORMAN, EDWIN N U10CA29293-11 0007
FORMAN, EDWIN N U10CA29293-11 0008
FORMAN, EDWIN N U10CA29293-11 0009
FORMAN, EDWIN N U10CA29293-11 0010
FORMAN, EDWIN N U10CA29293-11 0011
FORMAN, EDWIN N U10CA29293-11 0012
FORMAN, EDWIN N U10CA29293-11 0013
FORMAN, EDWIN N U10CA29293-11 0014
FORMAN, EDWIN N U10CA29293-11 0015
FORMAN, EDWIN N U10CA29293-11 0016
FORMAN, EDWIN N U10CA29293-11 0017
FORMAN, EDWIN N U10CA29293-11 0018
FORMAN, EDWIN N U10CA29293-11 0019
FORMAN, EDWIN N U10CA29293-11 0020
FORMAN, EDWIN N U10CA29293-11 0021
FORMAN, EDWIN N U10CA29293-11 0022
FORMAN, EDWIN N U10CA29293-11 0034
FORMAN, EDWIN N U10CA29293-11 0035
FORMAN, EDWIN N U10CA29293-11 0036
FORMAN, EDWIN N U10CA29293-11 0037
FORMAN, EDWIN N U10CA29293-11 0038
FORMAN, EDWIN N U10CA29293-11 0039

FORMAN, EDWIN N U10CA29293-11 0040
FORMAN, EDWIN N U10CA29293-11 0041
FORMAN, EDWIN N U10CA29293-11 0042
FORMAN, HENRY J R01ES05511-01
FORMAN, HENRY J R01HL37556-06A1
FORMAN, JAMES P01AI11851-18 0020
FORMAN, JAMES P01AI11851-18 9002
FORMAN, JAMES M R01AI28332-03
FORMAN, MERVYN M01RR00095-31 0372
FORMAN, MERVYN B R01HL40892-04
FORMAN, MERVYN B R29HL38294-05
FORMAN, STEPHEN J P01CA30206-10
FORMAN, STEPHEN J P01CA30206-10 0001
FORMAN, WALTER B M01RR00997-16 0409
FORMICOLA, ALLAN J S15GM47068-01
FORMICOLA, ALLEN J S07RR05331-28
FORMOSA, TIMOTHY G R29GM43424-02
FORNACE, A J Z01CM07184-02
FORNACE, A J Z01CM07186-02
FORNACE, A J Z01CM07187-02
FORNACE, A J Z01CM07188-02
FORNACE, A J Z01CM07309-01
FORNEY, JAMES D R29GM43357-02
FORREST, GERALD P30CA33572-11 9003
FORREST, GERALD P30CA33572-11 9009
FORREST, GERALD S07RR05841-12 0235
FORREST, GERALD S07RR05841-12 0225
FORREST, JOHN P01DK17433-18 9005
FORREST, JOHN N R01DK34208-08
FORREST, KAREN R29DC00783-02
FORREST, KATHERINE A R01HD26243-01A2
FORSAYETH, JOHN R01NS28062-02
FORSCHER, PAUL R01NS28695-02
FORSCHER, PAUL S07RR07015-26 0603
FORSE, ROBERT A R01GM44200-02
FORST, STEVEN A R29GM44671-01A1
FORSTER-BLOUIN, SHAR S07RR05788-15 0895
FORSTER, JEAN S07RR05448-30 0287
FORSTER, MICHAEL J S07RR05879-09 0600
FORSTER, PETER S07RR05755-18 0212
FORSTER, ROBERT E P01HL19737-15 0004
FORSTER, ROBERT E P01HL19737-15 9001
FORSTER, ROBERT E, II P01HL19737-15
FORT, BRUCE H S06GM08023-20 0004
FORTE, GERTRUDE M P01HL18574-16 0004
FORTE, JOHN G R01DK10141-25A2
FORTE, JOHN G R01DK38972-05
FORTE, LEONARD S07RR05387-30 0608
FORTE, MICHAEL S07RR07238-04 0471
FORTE, MICHAEL A R01GM35759-06
FORTE, MICHAEL A R01NS27684-03
FORTENBERRY, JAMES D K11HD00858-03
FORTES, P A GEORGE S06GM47165-01 0003
FORTINI, MARY-ELLEN R29AA07749-04
FORTMANN, STEPHEN P R01HL39770-04
FORTMANN, STEPHEN P R01HL46782-01
FORTNER, W G S07RR07036-26 0101
FORTUNE, JOHN B P20NS30303-01 0003
FOSKETT, JAMES P50DK41980-03 0003
FOSMIRE, GARY J S07RR07082-26 0280
FOSS, F Z01CM07258-03
FOSSLIEN, EGIL S07RR05369-30 0579
FOSTER, CAROL M M01RR00042-31 0469
FOSTER, CAROL M R55DK43513-01A1
FOSTER, CAROL M U54HD29184-01 0007
FOSTER, CHARLES S R01EY06008-07
FOSTER, DANIEL W M01RR00633-19 0310
FOSTER, DANIEL W R37DK18573-30
FOSTER, DAVID P41RR02176-05 9003
FOSTER, DAVID P41RR02176-05 9002
FOSTER, DAVID A R29CA46677-03
FOSTER, DAVID M P01HL30086-09 9004
FOSTER, DAVID M P41RR02176-05
FOSTER, DOUGLAS L R01HD18394-08
FOSTER, DOUGLAS L. P30HD18258-08 9007
FOSTER, EMILY S R29DK40129-04
FOSTER, HENRY W S06GM08198-10
FOSTER, HENRY W S07RR05422-30
FOSTER, JOHN W R55GM39018-01A3
FOSTER, JUDITH A R01HL30061-09
FOSTER, JUDITH A R01HL46100-02
FOSTER, KELLI C R44HD23432-02
FOSTER, KENNETH W R01GM34218-09
FOSTER, MARTHA A R18MH47958-02
FOSTER, MARY H K08DK01904-03
FOSTER, NORMAN L M01RR00042-31 0608
FOSTER, NORMAN L P50AG08671-03 9001
FOSTER, NORMAN L R01MH47144-02
FOSTER, PATRICIA L R01CA37880-07
FOSTER, PAUL A K11HL02064-05
FOSTER, ROGER M01RR00109-28 0371
FOSTER, ROGER P30CA22435-11 9014
FOSTER, ROGER P30CA22435-11 9015
FOSTER, ROGER S, JR P30CA22435-11
FOSTER, ROGER S, JR U10CA20203-15
FOSTER, WILLIAM M R01HL31429-07
FOTOS, PETE G R03DE09381-01A1
FOUAD-TARAZI, FEDNAT P50HL33713-06 9006
FOUKE, JANIE M S07RR07113-24 0568
FOULDS, J Z01DK57002-17
FOULKES, ERNEST C P30ES00159-24S1 0033
FOULKES, ERNEST C R01ES02453-12
FOULKES, ERNEST C R01ES04840-03
FOULKES, M A Z01NS02516-10
FOULKES, M A Z01NS02810-02
FOULKES, MARY A Z01NS02598-09
FOULKS, GARY N U10EY06116-07
FOUNG, STEVEN P50HL33811-06 0007
FOUNG, STEVEN K H P50HL33811-06 9001
FOUNG, STEVEN K H R01AI22557-07
FOUNG, STEVEN K H R01DA06596-02
FOUNG, STEVEN K H U01AI26031-03S1
FOUNTAIN, STEPHEN B R03MH48402-01
FOUNTAIN, STEPHEN B S07RR07208-10 0663
FOURMAN, STUART B S07RR05736-19 0191
FOURMAN, STUART B S07RR05736-19 0192
FOURNIER, ARTHUR M U76PE00219-06
FOURNIER, MAURILLE J, JR R01GM19351-19
FOURNIER, RAYMOND E R01GM26449-14
FOUSER, LAURIE S K11HD00939-01
FOUSHEE, DORETHA B S06GM08019-21 0005
FOWLER, ANNE E S07RR05596-27 0134
FOWLER, AUDREE S07RR07009-26 0948
FOWLER, B O Z01DE00012-29
FOWLER, BRUCE A R01ES04979-02
FOWLER, C L Z01CL10179-02
FOWLER, C L Z01CL10180-02
FOWLER, CAROL A P01HD01994-26A1 0012
FOWLER, FRANK W R01DA06272-02
FOWLER, GEORGE N01CM17501-02
FOWLER, HARRY R01MH24115-15
FOWLER, JOANNA S P01NS15638-13 0001
FOWLER, JOHN C R01NS28027-03
FOWLER, JOHN F P01CA52686-02 0004
FOWLER, JOHN F P01CA52686-02 9001
FOWLER, JOHN F R01CA50937-02
FOWLER, ROBERT G R15GM45938-01
FOWLER, ROBERT G. S06GM08192-12 0007
FOWLER, STANLEY D R01HL42496-03
FOWLER, STANLEY D S07RR05815-12
FOWLER, STEPHEN C R01MH43429-04
FOWLER, VELIA M P01GM46006-01 0002
FOWLER, VELIA M R01GM34225-07
FOWLKES, B J Z01AI00486-05
FOWLKES, DANA M R01HL31012-08
FOX, AARON P R01GM43560-01A2
FOX, AARON P R29NS26189-04
FOX, BARBARA S R29CA48664-04
FOX, BARBARA S U01AI28718-03
FOX, C FRED R13AI31222-01
FOX, C FRED R13AI31270-01
FOX, C FRED R13AI31277-01
FOX, C FRED R13AR40910-01
FOX, C FRED R13AR40911-01
FOX, C FRED R13AR40927-01
FOX, C FRED R13CA54489-01
FOX, C FRED R13CA54777-01
FOX, C FRED R13CA54779-01
FOX, C FRED R13CA54780-01
FOX, C FRED R13CA54781-01
FOX, C FRED R13CA56114-01
FOX, C FRED R13CA56142-01
FOX, C FRED R13DK44100-01
FOX, C FRED R13GM46112-01
FOX, C FRED R13GM46188-01
FOX, C FRED R13HL47232-01
FOX, C FRED R25CA09353-13
FOX, DAVID P60AR20557-13 0057
FOX, DAVID P60AR20557-13 9002
FOX, DAVID A M01RR00042-31 0634
FOX, DAVID A R01AR38477-06
FOX, DONALD A S07RR05998-04 0030
FOX, EBEN S R29DK44305-01
FOX, EBEN S S07RR05591-27 0666
FOX, GEORGE E S07RR07147-19 0647
FOX, GEORGE E S07RR07147-19 0648
FOX, HOWARD S R29AR40981-01
FOX, IRA J R55AI31641-01
FOX, IRVING P60AR20557-13 0059
FOX, JACOB P01AG09466-01 9001
FOX, JAMES P40RR01046-16 0001
FOX, JAMES P40RR01046-16 0002
FOX, JAMES P40RR01046-16 0003
FOX, JAMES G P01CA26731-12 0008
FOX, JAMES G P40RR01046-16
FOX, JAMES R P01CA26731-12 9002
FOX, JAY W P30CA44579-04A1 9003
FOX, JAY W R55GM31289-09A2
FOX, JEFFREY L R01DE06552-07
FOX, JEFFREY L S07RR05738-20 0219
FOX, JOAN E R01HL30657-09
FOX, KEVIN R01NS27759-03
FOX, LYNDA M S03RR03474-04
FOX, MARYE P41RR00886-16 0002
FOX, MARYE P41RR00886-16 0001
FOX, MARYE A P41RR00886-16
FOX, MAURICE S R37AI05388-29
FOX, MICHAEL H R01CA25636-10
FOX, MICHAEL H S07RR05458-29 0825
FOX, NATHAN A R01HD17899-07
FOX, NATHAN A R01HD26768-01A2
FOX, P C Z01DE00337-09
FOX, PAUL LOUIS R29HL40352-04
FOX, PETER T S10RR06524-01
FOX, RAYMOND N01CO15649-00
FOX, RAYMOND N01CO15662-00
FOX, ROBERT P01HD15051-11A1 0175
FOX, ROBERT R01HD27716-01A1
FOX, ROBERT A R01AG08353-03
FOX, ROBERT I R01AR33983-11
FOX, ROBERT L M01RR00833-17 0160
FOX, ROBERT O R01AI23923-04
FOX, SARAH A R01CA45003-05
FOX, STEVEN E R01NS17095-09A1
FOX, THOMAS D R01GM29362-11
FOXALL, MARTHA S07RR05942-06 0007
FOXMAN, BETSY R01DK35368-04A2
FOZARD, J L Z01AG00015-33
FOZARD, J L Z01AG00624-02
FOZARD, J L Z01AG00626-02
FOZARD, J L Z01AG00635-02
FOZZARD, HARRY A P01HL20592-15
FOZZARD, HARRY A P01HL20592-15 0004
FRACICA, PHILIP J P01HL31992-08 0005
FRADET, YVES R01CA47526-03S1
FRAENKEL-CONRAT, HEINZ R01AA08854-02
FRAENKEL, DAN G R01GM21098-18
FRAIL, DONALD P01AG10481-01 0004
FRAIRE, ARMANDO E S07RR05425-30 0737
FRAKER, PAMELA S07RR05772-17 0342
FRALEY, SANDRA M R29EY07206-04
FRAM, ROBERT J S07RR05712-20 0099
FRAMBACH, DONALD A R01EY05422-08
FRAME, ANNE D S03RR03443-06
FRAME, ANNE D S06GM08159-13
FRAME, LAWRENCE H R01HL38386-04
FRAME, PAUL S R01HS06283-02
FRAME, PETER U01AI25897-05 9001
FRAME, PETER T U01AI25897-05
FRANCE, CHARLES P P50DA00254-20 0012
FRANCE, CHARLES P R01DA05018-04
FRANCES, ALLEN P01MH47200-02
FRANCES, CHARLES W P01HL30616-09 0001
FRANCESCHI, RENNY T R01DK35317-05A2
FRANCHESCHI, RENNY T S07RR05970-06 0777
FRANCHINI, G Z01CP05645-02
FRANCIS SCOTT KEY MED CTR N01DA92009-00
FRANCIS, ANDREW S07RR05736-19 0169
FRANCIS, CHARLES W. P01HL30616-09 9003
FRANCIS, CHARLES W. P01HL30616-09 0008
FRANCIS, ISAAC R U01CA49077-03
FRANCIS, JOSEPH R29AG08568-04
FRANCIS, ROBERT C S07RR07096-26 0069
FRANCIS, RUPERT A U76PE00035-08
FRANCIS, RUPERT A U76PE00447-02
FRANCK, J.E. P01NS20482-08 0011
FRANCK, JO ANN E R29NS25155-04
FRANCK, RICHARD W R01CA39351-05
FRANCK, RICHARD W S06GM08176-12 0023
FRANCKE, UTA R01HG00298-14
FRANCKE, UTA R01HG00314-03
FRANCO, CHARLES D S07RR05393-30 0890
FRANCO, ROBERT S P60HL15996-19 0028
FRANCOMANO, CLAIR A M01RR00052-30 0238
FRANCOMANO, CLAIR A M01RR00052-30 0243
FRANCOMANO, CLAIR A M01RR00722-19 0245
FRANCOMANO, CLAIR A P41HG00586-01 0002
FRANCUS, TOVA S07RR05396-30 0745
FRANGIONE, BLAS P01AG10491-01 0001
FRANGIONE, BLAS R01AG05891-07
FRANGIONE, BLAS R01AG08721-02
FRANGIONE, BLAS R01NS30455-01
FRANGIONE, BLAS R37AR02594-33
FRANGOS, JOHN A R29HL40696-04
FRANGOS, JOHN A S07RR07082-26 0281
FRANK, ANTHONY A S07RR07079-26 0299
FRANK, ARLENE F U01DA07663-01
FRANK, DARA W R29AI31665-01
FRANK, DARA W S07RR05434-30 0806
FRANK, DEBORAH A R01DA06532-02
FRANK, ELLEN R01MH29618-13S1
FRANK, ERIC R01NS24373-06
FRANK, GAIL C R01HL38844-05 9003
FRANK, HARRY A R01GM30353-05
FRANK, JOACHIM P41RR01219-10 9004
FRANK, JOACHIM R01GM29169-10
FRANK, JOACHIM R01GM40165-04
FRANK, JOACHIM R13GM46434-01
FRANK, JOY S P01HL30568-09 0008
FRANK, JOY S R01HL28791-10
FRANK, JOY S S07RR05354-30
FRANK, JOY S S15EY09473-01
FRANK, JOY S S15MH49305-01
FRANK, M M Z01AI00045-23
FRANK, M M Z01AI00048-21
FRANK, MARION E P01DC00168-10 0013
FRANK, MARION E P01DC00168-10
FRANK, MARION E R01DC00058-02
FRANK, MARION E R01DC00853-02
FRANK, MARK BARTON P01AI21568-07 0006
FRANK, MARTIN R13DK39306-05
FRANK, P P41RR01209-12 0014
FRANK, R. S. P01HL18208-17 0016
FRANK, RICHARD G12RR03037-07 0001
FRANK, ROBERT R03OH02856-01
FRANK, ROBERT A S07RR07075-17

FRANK, ROBERT N R01EY01857-15
FRANK, STEVEN A R29GM42403-02
FRANK, STEVEN A S07RR07008-26 0058
FRANKEL, ALAN D R01AI29135-03
FRANKEL, ARTHUR E R01CA54116-02
FRANKEL, JACK S S06GM08016-21 0076
FRANKEL, JOSEPH R37HD08485-17
FRANKEL, KENNETH A S07RR05918-08 0711
FRANKER, COLIN S07RR05304-30 0233
FRANKFURT, OSKAR S R01CA50677-03
FRANKFURTER, ANTHONY R01NS21142-04A2
FRANKFURTER, ANTHONY S07RR07094-26 0361
FRANKL, SPENCER S07RR05989-04
FRANKL, SPENCER N S15DE10071-01
FRANKL, SPENCER W S07RR05989-04 0524
FRANKLIN, CLAIRE N01ES05285-07
FRANKLIN, DAVID R44DC00621-03
FRANKLIN, DAVID R44DC00796-02
FRANKLIN, DEAN R01HL32800-05
FRANKLIN, ERNEST W U10CA45450-05
FRANKLIN, JOHN E U01AA08783-01S1
FRANKLIN, NANCY S07RR07067-26 0214
FRANKLIN, RUDOLPH MICHAEL R01EY03028-14
FRANKLIN, WILBUR S07RR05357-30 0449
FRANKLIN, WILLIAM A R29CA52025-02
FRANKMANN, SANDRA P R01DK39180-05A1
FRANKMANN, SANDRA P S07RR05396-30 0782
FRANKS, PETER N R01GM41609-03
FRANKS, R Z01DE00471-04
FRANKS, RONALD D S07RR05896-09
FRANKS, RONALD D S15AI32196-01
FRANOMANO, CLAIR A P01HG00373-04 0004
FRANTZ, CHRISTOPHER N R01NS22039-08
FRANTZ, RITA A R01NR01657-04
FRANZ, MICHAEL R R29HL40483-04
FRANZA, B ROBERT, JR R01AI32028-01A1
FRANZA, B ROBERT, JR R01CA40512-05
FRANZBLAU, CARL P01HL13262-19 0027
FRANZBLAU, CARL P01HL13262-19 9002
FRANZBLAU, CARL P01HL19717-15 0001
FRANZBLAU, CARL P01HL19717-15
FRANZBLAU, CARL R25RR07591-01
FRANZBLAU, SCOTT G R29AI26265-04
FRANZINI-ARMSTRONG, CLARA P01HL15835-19 00
FRANZUSOFF, ALEX P30DK34914-06 0011
FRASER-REID, BERTRAM O R01GM41071-02
FRASER-REID, BERTRAM O R01GM32569-07
FRASER, B A Z01BB05001-10
FRASER, C M Z01AA00483-02
FRASER, C M Z01AA00484-02
FRASER, GARY S07RR05352-30 0747
FRASER, GARY E R01AG08961-01A2
FRASER, MALCOLM J K04AI01006-01
FRASER, MALCOLM J, JR R01AI22610-05
FRASER, MARY E R18MH46070-02
FRASER, NIGEL W P01AI23968-06
FRASER, NIGEL W P01AI23968-06 0001
FRASER, NIGEL W P50NS11036-18 0035
FRASER, NIGEL W R01NS29390-01
FRASER, ROBERT P01NS17111-11 0016
FRASER, ROBERT B R43HL47233-01
FRASER, SCOTT E R01EY08363-02
FRASER, SCOTT E R01HD29304-01
FRATANTONI, J C Z01BH01024-01
FRATE, DENNIS S07RR07242-04 0709
FRATE, DENNIS A R01CA49578-03
FRATIELLO, ANTHONY S06GM08101-20 0011
FRATKIN, JONATHAN D S07RR05772-17 0354
FRAUENFELDER, HANS R01GM18051-20
FRAUENHOFFER, ELIZAB S07RR05680-23 0922
FRAUTSCHY, SALLY A R01AG10685-01
FRAWLEY, LEO S R01DK38215-07
FRAZER DE LLADO, TERESA S06GM08239-06 0004
FRAZER, ALAN P01MH48125-01
FRAZER, ALAN P01MH48125-01 0004
FRAZER, ALAN R37MH29094-15
FRAZER, TERESA G12RR03050-07 0003
FRAZIER, DONALD S07RR05374-30 0751
FRAZIER, DONALD T P01HL40369-03
FRAZIER, DONALD T P01HL40369-03 9001
FRAZIER, DONALD T P01HL40369-03 0001
FRAZIER, DONALD T S03RR03309-10
FRAZIER, JOHN M P40RR05236-03
FRAZIER, L W S07RR05915-08 0673
FRAZIER, MARSHA L R01CA49667-03
FRAZIER, WILLIAM A P50HL14147-21 0024
FRAZIER, WILLIAM A, III R01HD27712-14A1
FREAKE, HEDLEY C R29DK41705-03
FRECHET, JEAN M J R01GM44885-02
FREDBERG, JEFFREY J P01HL33009-07
FREDBERG, JEFFREY J P01HL33009-07 0004
FREDBERG, JEFFREY J P50HL34616-07 0004
FREDDO, THOMAS F R01EY04567-09
FREDERICH, ROBERT C K08HL02564-01
FREDERICK, CHRISTIN P01GM37641-05 0004
FREDERICK, SHERI S07RR07080-26 0312
FREDERIKSEN, LEE W R43CA52419-01A1
FREDERIKSEN, LEE W R43DA06698-01A1
FREDERIKSEN, LEE W R43HL44260-01A2
FREDERIKSEN, N L S07RR05915-08 0683
FREDIN, LEIF G R43EY09315-01
FREDMAN, STEVEN M R01NS28199-01A2

FREDMAN, STEVEN M S06GM08037-20 0046
FREDRICKSON, H A Z01CT00203-02
FREE, K Z01MH02408-04
FREE, K Z01MH02442-03
FREE, K Z01MH02443-03
FREED, ARTHUR N R29HL39406-05
FREED, CURT R R01HL30722-08
FREED, CURT R R01NS18639-07A2
FREED, CURT R R01NS23918-04
FREED, JACK H R01GM25862-13A1
FREED, JOHN P01AI22295-07 9002
FREED, JOHN S07RR05842-12 0294
FREED, JOHN H R01AI26880-02
FREED, JOHN H R01CA36700-09
FREED, W J Z01MH02252-07
FREED, W J Z01MH02253-07
FREEDBERG, IRWIN M P30AR39749-04
FREEDBERG, IRWIN M R01AR30682-10
FREEDLENDER, ARTHUR E P30DK38942-04 9001
FREEDMAN, ARNOLD S R01CA55207-01
FREEDMAN, DANIEL S07RR05756-18 0321
FREEDMAN, DANIEL X S07RR05756-18 0322
FREEDMAN, DANIEL X S07RR05756-18
FREEDMAN, DANIEL X S15NS30116-01
FREEDMAN, DAVID P01AI28780-01A1 0003
FREEDMAN, ELIZABETH S07RR05664-24 0860
FREEDMAN, JONATHAN E R29MH48545-01
FREEDMAN, LYNN S07RR05449-30 0325
FREEDMAN, ROBERT M01RR00051-30 0655
FREEDMAN, ROBERT P50AA03527-14 0016
FREEDMAN, ROBERT P50MH44212-03 0005
FREEDMAN, ROBERT P50MH44212-03 0001
FREEDMAN, ROBERT P50MH44212-03
FREEDMAN, ROBERT R01DA02429-12
FREEDMAN, ROBERT R01MH38321-08
FREEDMAN, ROBERT R R01AG05233-04
FREEDMAN, ROBERT R R01HL30604-08
FREEDMAN, ROGER A R29HL39175-05
FREEDY, JOHN R R03MH49485-01
FREELAND-GRAVES, JEA S07RR07091-26 0753
FREELING, MICHAEL R R01GM42610-03
FREEMAN, ARTHUR P50MH45178-02 0005
FREEMAN, ARTHUR S R01DA07844-01
FREEMAN, BRUCE A R01HL40458-03
FREEMAN, BRUCE A R01NS24275-05
FREEMAN, DANIEL H P30CA23108-14 9001
FREEMAN, DAVID S07RR05464-29 0371
FREEMAN, ELAINE K P60DC00979-02 9002
FREEMAN, ELLEN W M01RR00040-31 0402
FREEMAN, ELLEN W R01HD18633-07
FREEMAN, H P41RR01209-12 0008
FREEMAN, HAROLD P P01CA50956-02 9003
FREEMAN, HAROLD P R01CA50520-03
FREEMAN, JAMES W R29CA49633-02
FREEMAN, JOHN A R01EY01117-19
FREEMAN, MARC E R01HD11669-13
FREEMAN, MASON R01HL45098-02
FREEMAN, MICHAEL L R55CA38079-08
FREEMAN, PETER K P01ES00040-27 0076
FREEMAN, RALPH D P30EY03176-11
FREEMAN, RALPH D R01EY01175-19
FREEMAN, RALPH D S07RR05832-12 0195
FREEMAN, RONALD H R01HL10612-25
FREEMAN, ROY M01RR01032-16 0448
FREEMAN, SCOTT S07RR07156-16 0569
FREEMAN, WALTER J R37MH06686-29
FREEMAN, WILLIAM R R01EY07366-04
FREEMARK, MICHAEL S K04HD00901-02
FREEMARK, MICHAEL S R01HD24192-04
FREER, RICHARD P50AI28532-03 0001
FREER, RICHARD P50AI28532-03 0002
FREGIEN, NEVIS L R01CA49926-02
FREGIEN, NEVIS L R29AR38872-05
FREGLY, MELVIN J R01HL39154-05
FREGOSI, RALPH F R29HL41790-02
FREI, BLAZ B S07RR05446-30 0266
FREI, EMIL P01CA19589-14A1 0015
FREI, EMIL P01CA38493-06S1 0003
FREI, EMIL P01CA38493-06S1 9005
FREI, EMIL P30CA06516-28 0016
FREI, EMIL P30CA06516-28 0022
FREI, EMIL P30CA06516-28 9009
FREI, EMIL, III P01CA19589-14A1
FREI, EMIL, III P01CA38493-06S1
FREI, JOHN K, SR S06GM45455-01
FREIMER, NELSON P50MH43878-03 0025
FREIMER, NELSON S07RR05355-30 0430
FREIMER, NELSON S07RR05755-18 0239
FREIMER, NELSON S07RR05755-18 0231
FREIMER, NELSON B K21MH00916-01
FREIRE, ERNESTO I P41RR04328-04 9001
FREIRE, ERNESTO I P41RR04328-04
FREIRE, ERNESTO I P41RR04328-04 9002
FREIRE, ERNESTO I P41RR04328-04 0001
FREIRE, ERNESTO I R01GM37911-06A1
FREIRE, ERNESTO I R01NS24520-06
FREIREICH, EMIL J R35CA39809-07
FREISHEIM, JAMES H R01CA41461-07
FREIVALDS, ANDRIS S07RR07082-26 0282
FRELINGER, JEFFREY A N01AI72651-10
FRELINGER, JEFFREY A R01AI29324-02
FRELINGER, JEFFREY A R37AI20288-09

FRENCH, DEBORAH L S07RR05736-19 0184
FRENCH, EDARD D S07RR05675-23 0939
FRENCH, EDWARD D P50MH44211-03 0007
FRENCH, EDWARD D R01DA03876-05
FRENCH, FRANK S P30HD18968-08
FRENCH, FRANK S R01HD04466-21
FRENCH, J E Z01ES21162-01
FRENCH, JOHN R18DA05286-03S1
FRENCH, JOHN R18DA05289-03S1
FRENCH, JOHN R18DA05755-04
FRENCH, JOHN R19DA06409-03
FRENCH, LUCIA S07RR07069-26 0248
FRENCH, SAMUEL W R01AA08116-03
FRENCH, WILLIAM S07RR05551-29 0963
FRENCHICK, GARY S07RR05656-24 0832
FRENCK, ROBERT S07RR05745-19 0228
FRENDEWEY, DAVID ALLYN R01GM38242-06
FRENDL, GYORGY S07RR05487-29 0707
FRENKEL, GERALD D R01ES04087-06
FRENKEL, JACOB K R01AI23730-05
FRENKEL, KRYSTYNA P42ES04895-03 0011
FRENKEL, KRYSTYNA R01CA37858-06S1
FRENKEL, KRYSTYNA R01CA49798-02
FRENKEL, N Z01AI00540-04
FRENKEL, N Z01AI00620-01
FRENKEL, NIZA P01AI24009-05 0004
FRENZ, DOROTHY A R29DC00881-01A1
FRERMAN, FRANK E. P01HD08315-16 0021
FRESCHI, JOSEPH E R01NS22628-06
FRESCO, JACQUES R R01GM42936-03
FRESCO, JACQUES R S03RR03097-10
FRESCO, JACQUES R S07RR07057-26
FRESCO, JACQUES R S15DK44660-01
FRESCO, JACUES S07RR07057-26 0531
FRESTON, JAMES S07RR05678-23 0166
FRETER, ROLF G R01AI20387-07
FREUND, DEBORAH A P01HS06432-02
FREUND, KAREN M S07RR05487-29 0690
FREUND, YVONNE R S07RR05513-29 0061
FREUNDLICH, MARTIN R01GM17152-22
FREUNDLICH, MARTIN R01GM36339-06
FREVERT, CHARLES E K11HL02374-03
FREY, KIRK A P01MH42652-05 0001
FREY, KIRK A P50NS15655-12 0011
FREY, MAUREEN S07RR05796-14 0427
FREY, MAUREEN A R29NR02243-03
FREY, PERRY A R01GM30480-11
FREY, PERRY A R37DK28607-11
FREY, TERRENCE S07RR07004-16 0047
FREY, TERRY K S07RR07171-08 0155
FREY, TERYL K K04AI00923-03
FREY, TERYL K R01AI21389-07A1
FREYD, JENNIFER J K02MH00780-03
FREYD, JENNIFER J R01MH39784-07
FREYER, JAMES P P41RR01315-10 0041
FREYER, JAMES P R01CA51150-01A2
FREYTAG, SVEND O R01CA51748-03
FRIAUF, W S Z01RR10272-04
FRIAUF, W S Z01RR10313-03
FRIAUF, W S Z01RR10314-03
FRIBERG, THOMAS R N01EY02125-02
FRICK, G PETER S07RR05712-20 0052
FRICK, ROBERT S07RR07067-26 0216
FRICKE, THOMAS E R01HD22543-05
FRICKE, W Z01BH07009-05
FRICKE, W Z01BH07010-01
FRICKE, W Z01BH07011-01
FRICKER, FREDERICK J S07RR05507-29 0476
FRICKER, LLOYD D R01DA04494-05
FRIDLAND, ARNOLD R01AI27652-09
FRIDLAND, ARNOLD R01AI31145-04
FRIED, DEBORAH S07RR05358-30 0473
FRIED, JERROLD P01CA20194-14 9006
FRIED, JOSEF P30CA14599-18 9004
FRIED, L P Z01AG00636-02
FRIED, LINDA N01AG12112-00
FRIED, LINDA P M01RR00722-19 0246
FRIED, LINDA P N01HC85081-06
FRIED, PETER A R01DA04874-04
FRIED, SUSAN K R01DK43442-02
FRIED, VICTOR A. P30CA21765-14 9013
FRIED, WALTER S15AR41237-01
FRIEDBERG, DOROTHY M01RR00096-30A1 0314
FRIEDBERG, ERROL C R01CA44247-06
FRIEDBERG, ERROL C R37CA12428-22
FRIEDBERG, FELIX R01MH43797-03
FRIEDELL, GILBERT H N01CO03869-05
FRIEDEN, CARL P41RR00954-15 0032
FRIEDEN, CARL R37DK13332-23
FRIEDHOFF, ARNOLD J K05MH14024-24
FRIEDHOFF, ARNOLD J P01MH08618-27
FRIEDHOFF, ARNOLD J P01MH08618-27 0099
FRIEDHOFF, ARNOLD J P50MH35976-10
FRIEDHOFF, ARNOLD J R13NS29346-01
FRIEDLAND, GERALD H R01DA04347-05
FRIEDMAN-KIEN, ALVIN M01RR00096-30A1 0169
FRIEDMAN, ALAN D K11CA01326-04
FRIEDMAN, ALAN H M01RR00071-28A1 0231
FRIEDMAN, ALFRED S R01DA05259-02
FRIEDMAN, ALICE S07RR07149-18 0416
FRIEDMAN, ALICE S07RR07149-18 0417
FRIEDMAN, CHARLES P R01LM04843-04

FRIEDMAN, DAVID K02MH00510-08
FRIEDMAN, DAVID N01OD12100-00
FRIEDMAN, DAVID R01AG05213-06
FRIEDMAN, DAVID R01AG09988-01
FRIEDMAN, DAVID I R01AI11459-19
FRIEDMAN, DAVID J S07RR05654-24 0116
FRIEDMAN, EILEEN A R01CA50645-02
FRIEDMAN, EITAN P01DA06871-01 0003
FRIEDMAN, EITAN R01AG07700-04
FRIEDMAN, EITAN R01MH45166-03
FRIEDMAN, EITAN R01NS29514-01A1
FRIEDMAN, EMILY D K08NS01449-02
FRIEDMAN, F K Z01CP05318-09
FRIEDMAN, GARY N01CN05316-01
FRIEDMAN, GARY D R35CA49761-03
FRIEDMAN, HARVEY M R01HL28220-10
FRIEDMAN, HENRY S P50NS20023-08 0018
FRIEDMAN, HERMAN R01AI16618-09
FRIEDMAN, HERMAN R01DA03646-08
FRIEDMAN, HOWARD S R01AG08825-02
FRIEDMAN, JACQUELINE ELISE R29NS27102-03
FRIEDMAN, JEFFREY M R01DK41096-03
FRIEDMAN, JEFFREY M R01HG00316-03
FRIEDMAN, JULIUS J R01HL44881-02
FRIEDMAN, KAREN LEE R43NS29918-01
FRIEDMAN, KENNETH D M01RR00997-16 0418
FRIEDMAN, KENNETH D M01RR00997-16 0415
FRIEDMAN, KENNETH D S07RR05583-27 0629
FRIEDMAN, KIEN, ALVIN E. P30AI27742-03 900
FRIEDMAN, LEE P50MH41684-07 0066
FRIEDMAN, LEE P50MH41684-07 0067
FRIEDMAN, LEE P50MH41684-07 0069
FRIEDMAN, LEE R03MH47574-01
FRIEDMAN, MARK I P50DC00214-06 0001
FRIEDMAN, PAUL A P01HL33014-07 0007
FRIEDMAN, PETER A R01GM34399-07
FRIEDMAN, PETER A S07RR05392-30 0692
FRIEDMAN, RICHARD M01RR00047-31 0445
FRIEDMAN, RICHARD S07RR05736-19 0160
FRIEDMAN, RICHARD N S07RR07201-12 0633
FRIEDMAN, ROBERT H R01HL40076-03
FRIEDMAN, ROBERT M R01CA37351-07
FRIEDMAN, S J Z01CM07190-01
FRIEDMAN, SAMUEL S07RR05859-09 0929
FRIEDMAN, SAMUEL R R01DA06723-02
FRIEDMAN, SCOTT L R01DK37340-05
FRIEDMAN, STANLEY S03RR03047-11
FRIEDMAN, STEVEN P60AR38520-04 9002
FRIEDMAN, STEVEN M R01CA49283-08
FRIEDMAN, THOMAS S07RR05656-24 0826
FRIEDMAN, THOMAS B S07RR07049-26 0453
FRIEDMANN, NAOMI K R01DK36916-05
FRIEDMANN, THEODORE P01CA51495-02 0003
FRIEDMANN, THEODORE R01HD20034-07
FRIEDMANN, THEODORE R01HG00309-03
FRIEDMANN, THEODORE R01HL47119-01
FRIEDRICH, FRANCES J S07RR07092-26 0487
FRIEL-PATTI, SANDY S07RR07133-22 0509
FRIEL, PATRICK P01NS17111-11 0014
FRIELLE, THOMAS S07RR05417-30 0790
FRIES, BRANT E P30AG08808-03 9003
FRIES, JAMES R18AR21393-17 0022
FRIES, JAMES R18AR21393-17 0006
FRIES, JAMES R18AR21393-17 0004
FRIES, JAMES F P60AR20610-14 0004
FRIES, JAMES F P60AR20610-14 0016
FRIES, JAMES F P60AR20610-14 9001
FRIES, JAMES F R01HS06211-03
FRIES, JAMES F R18AR21393-17
FRIESEN, HENRY G R01HD07843-16A1
FRIESEN, PAUL D R29AI25557-04
FRIESEN, WOLFGANG O R01NS21778-07
FRIESINGER, GOTTLIEB N01HC65037-10
FRIESNER, RICHARD P41RR06892-01 9005
FRIESNER, RICHARD A K04GM00527-04
FRIESNER, RICHARD A P41RR06892-01
FRIESNER, RICHARD A P41RR06892-01 9002
FRIESNER, RICHARD A P41RR06892-01 9001
FRIESNER, RICHARD A R01GM40526-04
FRIGOLETTO, FREDRIC D R01HD26813-02
FRIGOLETTO, FREDRIC D U01HD21017-05
FRISBIE, W PARKER R01HD24643-04
FRISCH, DEBORAH S07RR07080-26 0313
FRISCH, STEVEN M R29GM44573-02
FRISCH, STEVEN M S07RR05389-30 0634
FRISHMAN, LAURA J R01EY06671-04A2
FRISHMAN, LAURA J S15EY09466-01
FRISINA, ROBERT D R29DC00408-04
FRISQUE, RICHARD J R01CA38789-07
FRISQUE, RICHARD J R01CA44970-05
FRISQUE, RICHARD J S07RR07082-26 0283
FRISSE, MARK E R01HG00223-01
FRISTROM, JAMES W R01GM19937-19
FRITSCHE, HERBERT A P01CA52051-01A1 9003
FRITSCHE, THOMAS R R03AI30985-02
FRITZ, GREGORY K R01HL45157-01A1
FRITZ, JO U42RR03602-06
FRITZ, LAWRENCE C R44GM42268-03
FRITZ, MARC A S07RR05983-05 0352
FRITZ, MICHAEL E P01DE08917-02 9000
FRITZ, MICHAEL E P01DE08917-02
FRITZ, ROBERT B R01AI30605-17

FRIZZELL, LEON A S07RR07030-26 0390
FRIZZELL, RAYMOND A P01DK38518-05
FRIZZELL, RAYMOND A P01DK38518-05 0001
FRIZZELL, RAYMOND A R01DK31091-11
FRIZZELL, RAYMOND A R01DK41330-03
FRIZZELL, RAYMOND A R13DK44288-01
FROBERG, DEBRA S07RR05448-30 0302
FRODEL, JOHN S07RR05372-30 0668
FROEHLICH, J P Z01AG00266-02
FROEHLICH, JANICE C P01AA08553-02 0005
FROEHLICH, JANICE C R29AA08312-03
FROEHNER, STANLEY C R01NS14871-13
FROEHNER, STANLEY C R01NS27504-03
FROELICH, CHRISTOPHE S07RR05629-22 0137
FROHMAN, LAWRENCE A R37DK30667-11
FROIMOWITZ, MARK R01DA04762-03
FROIMOWITZ, MARK R01DA06681-02
FROM, ROBERT P M01RR00059-30 0751
FROM, ROBERT P M01RR00059-30 0598
FROMKIN, VICTORIA P01NS19632-09 0005
FROMM, GERHARD H R01NS19889-04
FROMM, HERBERT J R01NS10546-25
FRONDOZA, CARMELITA S07RR05445-30 0871
FRONDOZA, CARMELITA G R29CA45640-03
FRONEK, ZDENKA S07RR05665-24 0885
FROST, J JAMES P01NS15080-12 0010
FROST, J JAMES P01NS15080-12 0011
FROST, J JAMES R01AG08740-02
FROST, JAMES P50MH44211-03 0010
FROST, JAMES D P50NS11535-17 0002
FROST, JAMES D, III R43HG00410-01
FROST, PHILIP R01CA41525-06
FROST, PHILIP R37CA39853-08
FROST, PHILIP H M01RR00079-29 0342
FROST, PHILIP H M01RR00079-29 0382
FROST, PHILIP H M01RR00079-29 0387
FROST, SALLY K S07RR07037-26 0370
FROST, SUSAN C R29DK39135-04
FROST, WILLIAM R29MH48536-01
FROST, WILLIAM N S07RR05745-19 0244
FROSTHOLM, ADRIENNE M R29NS27784-03
FROSTIG, RONALD D S07RR07008-26 0059
FRUGONI, P Z01BD04003-03
FRUMKES, THOMAS E S07RR07064-24 0200
FRY, DONALD L R01HL29095-10
FRY, DONALD L R01HL41225-04
FRY, KEITH R R01EY06469-04A2
FRY, KIRK U01AI25922-05 0003
FRYBACK, DENNIS G R01HS06491-02
FRYBURG, DAVID M01RR00125-28 0766
FRYBURG, DAVID A K08AR01881-01
FRYE, BARBARA S07RR05352-30 0763
FRYE, GERALD D K02AA00101-05
FRYE, GERALD D R01AA06322-08
FRYE, L S07RR07104-25 0559
FRYE, LEAH L R01GM44127-01A1
FRYE, LEAH L R01HL45287-02
FRYER, ALLISON D R29HL44727-01A2
FRYER, JOHN P60AR30701-10 9004
FRYER, REGINA K G08LM05197-02
FRYER, RODNEY I S06GM08223-08 0029
FRYSINGER, ROBERT P01NS02808-30 9002
FU ITA-YAMAGUCHI, YO S07RR05841-12 0237
FU, PAUL R01MH47193-02 0002
FU, PAUL C S03RR03018-11
FU, S JOSEPH R01EY01156-14
FU, S JOSEPH R01EY05437-07
FU, SHU MAN R01AR39254-05
FU, SHU MAN R01CA34546-11
FU, XINYU R43CA53963-01A2
FUCHS, ALBERT F P51RR00166-30 0060
FUCHS, ALBERT F R37EY00745-21
FUCHS, ALBERT F. P51RR00166-30 0061
FUCHS, ALBERT F. P51RR00166-30 0062
FUCHS, ALBERT F. P51RR00166-30 0063
FUCHS, ALBERT F. P51RR00166-30 0064
FUCHS, ALBERT F. P51RR00166-30 0065
FUCHS, ALBERT F. P51RR00166-30 0059
FUCHS, BRUCE A R01DA07292-01
FUCHS, BRUCE A R29MH45931-03
FUCHS, ELAINE V R01AR27883-11
FUCHS, ELAINE V R01AR31737-09
FUCHS, FRANKLIN R01AR10551-26
FUCHS, HENRY P01CA47982-04 0001
FUCHS, JAMES A R01GM40775-04
FUCHS, JANNON L R29MH41865-05
FUCHS, PAUL A R01DC00276-07
FUCHS, PHILIP L R01GM32693-08
FUCHS, PHILIP L R01GM42295-13
FUCHS, PHILIP L S10RR06525-01
FUENTES, FRANCISCO K07HL02435-02
FUERST, THOMAS R R44GM43638-02
FUERST, THOMAS R U01AI28171-03 0003
FUHR, JOSEPH E S15CA55966-01
FUJII, A M P51RR00168-30 0133
FUJIMOTO, JAMES M R01DA00451-18
FUJIMOTO, WILFRED Y M01RR00037-31 0526
FUJIMOTO, WILFRED Y M01RR00037-31 0516
FUJIMOTO, WILFRED Y M01RR00037-31 0500
FUJIMOTO, WILFRED Y M01RR00037-31 0321
FUJIMOTO, WILFRED Y P30DK17047-15 9006
FUJIMURA, OSAMU R55DC00015-01A1

FUJINAMI, ROBERT S R01NS23162-06
FUJIOKA, GEORGE R18MH49373-01
FUJITA-YAMAGUCHI, YO S07RR05841-12 0246
FUJITA-YAMAGUCHI, YO S07RR05841-12 0224
FUJITA-YAMAGUCHI, YOKO R01DK34427-06
FUKADA, KEIKO R29NS26175-04
FUKAGAWA, NAOMI M01RR00088-28 0284
FUKAGAWA, NAOMI K M01RR01032-16 0438
FUKAGAWA, NAOMI K M01RR01032-16 0439
FUKAGAWA, NAOMI K M01RR01032-16 0400
FUKAGAWA, NAOMI K M01RR01032-16 0467
FUKAMAUCHI, F Z01MH02298-06
FUKS, ZVI R01CA52462-02
FUKUDA, MICHIKO N R01DK37016-04A1
FUKUDA, MINORU P30CA30199-11 9005
FUKUDA, MINORU R01CA33000-11
FUKUDA, MINORU R01CA33895-09
FUKUDA, MINORU R01CA48737-03
FUKUI, YOSHIO R01GM39548-03
FUKUNAGA, NINA M01RR00042-31 0675
FUKUTO, JON S07RR05354-30 0415
FUKUYAMA, KIMIE R37AR12433-24
FUKUYAMA, TOHRU R01CA28119-11
FULCHER, CAROL A R01HL35090-07
FULCO, ARMAND J R01GM23913-14
FULGINITI, VINCENT A M01RR05096-02
FULGINITI, VINCENT A S07RR05377-30
FULKER, DAVID S07RR07013-26 0953
FULKER, DAVID W R01HD18426-08
FULKER, DAVID W R01HD19802-06
FULKER, DAVID W R01MH43899-04
FULLARD, RODERICK J S07RR05807-13 0453
FULLARD, RODERICK J S07RR05807-13 0454
FULLER, A OVETA R29AI28378-02
FULLER, BARBARA S07RR05809-06 0474
FULLER, BARBARA F R01NR01468-04
FULLER, BARBARA F R01NR02044-02
FULLER, CARL W R43HG00191-01A1
FULLER, CHARLES A P51RR00169-30 0140
FULLER, CHARLES A P51RR00169-30 0141
FULLER, CHARLES A P51RR00169-30 0142
FULLER, CHARLES A P51RR00169-30 0143
FULLER, CHARLES A P51RR00169-30 0144
FULLER, CHARLES A P51RR00169-30 0145
FULLER, DWAIN G U10EY06276-07
FULLER, GERALD P50DK42017-03 0002
FULLER, GERALD M R01HL43155-02
FULLER, JAMES L S07RR05313-30 0247
FULLER, MARC S R29NS26222-05
FULLER, MARGARET P41RR00592-22 0026
FULLER, MARGARET T R01HD18127-09
FULLER, SHERRILYNNE G08LM05050-02
FULLER, SHERRILYNNE N01LM13506-00
FULLER, THOMAS C P01HL18646-15 0011
FULLERTON, DWIGHT S S07RR05738-20
FULLILOVE, ROBERT E S03RR03375-06
FULLMER, CURTIS S R01ES04072-06
FULOP, GEORGE R29MH43378-03
FULTON, AMY M R01CA51326-03
FULTON, ANNE B R01EY05325-09
FULTON, ANNE B R01EY05329-09
FULTON, ROBERT J R43AI30839-01
FULTS, DANIEL W R29CA52855-02
FULTZ, MICHAEL N01LM03511-11
FULTZ, MICHAEL N01LM93530-06
FULTZ, MICHAEL J N01LM83532-26
FULTZ, PATRICIA N U01AI27136-03 0003
FULWILER, CARL E K20MH00898-02
FUNDER, DAVID C R01MH42427-06
FUNDERBURG, FIONA M R01HL40563-03
FUNG, P41RR02024-08 9003
FUNG, P41RR02024-08 9004
FUNG, BERNARD K R01EY05895-07
FUNG, BERNARD K R13EY09046-01
FUNG, HO-LEUNG R01GM42850-03
FUNG, HO-LEUNG R37HL22273-14
FUNG, HO-LEUNG S07RR05454-29 0884
FUNG, LESLIE W R01HL38361-05
FUNG, SEK-CHUNG R44AI26971-03
FUNG, YUAN-CHENG P01HL43026-02 0006
FUNG, YUAN-CHENG B R01HL26647-11
FUNG, YUEN K R01EY07846-04
FUNG, YUEN K R29CA44754-05
FUNK, COLIN D R01HL46017-01
FUNK, COLIN D S07RR05454-29 0124
FUNK, MAX O S07RR07237-04
FUNK, MAX O S15GM47079-01
FUNK, RAYMOND L R01GM28663-12
FUNK, SANDRA G S07RR06013-03
FUNKHOUSER, EDWARD A S03RR03468-05
FUNKHOUSER, JANE D R01HL38750-04
FUNKHOUSER, JANE D R01HL42330-03
FUQUA, SUZANNE A R29CA52351-02
FURANO, A V Z01DK23580-28
FURBERG, CURT D N01HC85080-08
FURBERG, CURT D P01NS27500-01A2 9003
FURBERG, CURT D R01HL38194-04
FURBISH, F S N01NS92360-02
FURBISH, F SCOTT N01NS92365-04
FURBISH, SCOTT F N01NS92358-04
FURCHGOTT, ROBERT F R37HL21860-31
FURCHT, LEO T R01CA29995-11

FURCHT, LEO T R01EY09065-01
FURCHT, LEO T R37CA21463-14
FURIE, BARBARA P01HL42443-03 0002
FURIE, BARBARA C R37HL18834-17
FURIE, BRUCE M01RR00054-30 0466
FURIE, BRUCE P01HL42443-03
FURIE, BRUCE P01HL42443-03 0005
FURIE, BRUCE P01HL42443-03 0003
FURIE, BRUCE P01HL42443-03 9001
FURIE, BRUCE R37HL38216-05
FURIE, MARTHA B S07RR05736-19 0156
FURLANETTO, RICHARD W R01CA38981-08
FURLONG, CLEMENT EUGENE R01ES05194-03
FURLONG, DEIRDRE B S10RR06351-01
FURLONG, STEPHEN T R29AI24570-02
FURMAN, JOSEPH S07RR05416-30 0560
FURMAN, JOSEPH M R01AG10009-01
FURMAN, JOSEPH M R29DC01317-05
FURMAN, WYNDOL C R01MH45830-02
FURMANSKI, PHILIP R01AI30376-01A1
FURNEAUX, HENRY M R01NS29682-01
FURNEAUX, RICHARD H N01CM07340-04
FURNESS, JOHN B R01NS28316-01A1
FURSHPAN, EDWIN J P01NS02253-32 0002
FURSHPAN, EDWIN J P01NS02253-32 9004
FURSHPAN, EDWIN J P01NS02253-32
FURSPAN, PHILIP P01HL18575-16A1 0017
FURTH, HANS G S07RR07123-22 0593
FURTHMAYR, HEINZ R01AR30556-10
FURTHMAYR, HEINZ R01AR41551-01 0006
FUSELER, JOHN W S07RR05822-12 0504
FUSON, MICHAEL M R15GM46102-01
FUSTER, JOAQUIN M K05MH25082-21
FUTCHER, BRUCE A R01GM39978-04
FUTCHER, BRUCE A R01GM45410-01
FUZESSERY, ZOLTAN M R29DC00054-02
FYER, ABBEY P01MH37592-08 0004
FYER, ABBY P01MH37592-08 0007
FYER, ABBY J R01MH44175-03
FYFFE, ROBERT E R01NS25547-04A1
FYHRIE, DAVID P R29AR40776-01A1
FYRBERG, ERIC A R01GM29357-11
GAASTERLAND, DOUGLAS E U10EY06835-05
GABA, DAVID S07RR05353-30 0345
GABBAY, FRANCES H R01DA07110-01
GABBAY, KENNETH H M01RR00188-27 0324
GABBAY, KENNETH H R01DK41113-03
GABEL, JOSEPH R01HL36635-06
GABER, AHMED M01RR00211-27 0301
GABER, RICHARD F R01GM45739-01
GABIG, THEODORE G R01AI21961-07
GABIG, THEODORE G R01CA45677-06
GABIG, THEODORE G R01CA54432-01
GABOW, PATRICIA M01RR00069-29 0301
GABOW, PATRICIA P01DK34039-06A1 0007
GABOW, PATRICIA A M01RR00051-30 0413
GABOW, PATRICIA A P01DK34039-06A1 9001
GABOW, PATRICIA A P01DK34039-06A1
GABRIEL, ABRAM K11AI00803-05
GABRIEL, STEVEN M P50AG05138-08 0013
GABRIEL, STEVEN M R01MH45480-03
GABRIELI, JOHN P30AG10161-01 0004
GABRIELI, JOHN D P01AG09466-01 0002
GABRIELI, JOHN D. E. P50NS26985-03 0002
GABRILOV, JANICE N01CM87270-04
GABUZDA, DANA H K08AI01017-01
GAD, MARSHA P60HL20985-14 0020
GADO, MOKHTAR H. U01AG06790-06 0003
GADOW, KENNETH D R01MH45358-01A1
GADOW, KENNETH D S07RR05736-19 0177
GADSBY, DAVID C R01HL36783-05
GAENSLER, EDWARD A K06HL01173-28
GAERTNER, DIANE J P40RR00393-24 0007
GAFFNEY, BETTY J R01GM36232-06
GAFFNEY, KATHLEEN F R29NR02713-01
GAFNEY, HARRY D S07RR07064-24 0201
GAFNI, ARI R01AG09761-02
GAGE, FRED P01AG10435-01 0001
GAGE, FRED H P01AG10435-01
GAGE, FRED H P01NS28121-01A1S1 0002
GAGE, FRED H R01AG06088-05A1
GAGE, FRED H R01AG08514-03
GAGE, FRED H S06GM47165-01 0017
GAGE, TIMOTHY B R01HD25346-03
GAGE, TIMOTHY B S07RR07122-23 0093
GAGEL, ROBERT M01RR00350-25 0471
GAGEL, ROBERT M01RR00350-25 0410
GAGINELLA, TIMOTHY S U01AI25924-05 0003
GAHL, W A Z01HD00131-17
GAIL, M H Z01CP04500-14
GAIL, M H Z01CP05498-06
GAINER, H Z01NS02723-05
GAINER, H Z01NS02724-05
GAINER, JOHN L S07RR07094-26 0357
GAINES, KENNETH J N01NS02380-03
GAINES, KENNETH J R01NS29627-01
GAINES, LAWRENCE S R01AA08763-01A1
GAINES, MICHAEL S S07RR07037-26 0374
GAINES, STEVEN D S07RR07085-26 0337
GAITHER, T Z01AI00275-10
GAJDUSEK, D C Z01NS00969-27
GAJDUSEK, D C Z01NS01282-28
GAL, REUVEN R01MH44997-02
GALABURDA, ALBERT M P01HD20806-05 0001
GALABURDA, ALBERT M P01HD20806-05
GALABURDA, ALBERT M R01NS27119-02
GALAN, JORGE S07RR05736-19 0185
GALAN, JORGE E R29AI30492-01
GALANTE, JORGE O R01AR39310-03
GALANTER, MARC R18DA06122-03
GALAU, GLENN A R01GM29495-11
GALBRAITH, RICHARD M01RR00102-28 0160
GALBRAITH, RICHARD A P01CA29502-11A1 0057
GALBRAITH, ROBERT M R01DK33082-06
GALE, ELLIOT N R01DE04358-15
GALE, HENRY H S07RR05390-30 0672
GALE, JAMES L S07RR05714-21 0124
GALE, KAREN N P01NS28130-02 0004
GALE, KAREN N R01DA02206-10
GALE, KAREN N R01NS20576-08
GALE, THOMAS F S07RR05365-30 0079
GALILI, URI R01AG06299-07
GALINSKI, MARK S R01AI26256-05
GALINSKI, MARY S07RR05399-30 0911
GALINSKY, RAYMOND E R29AG07135-05
GALIVAN, JOHN H R01CA25933-12
GALIZIO, J MARK R01DA07380-01
GALL, CHRISTINE P01AG00538-15 0015
GALL, CHRISTINE P01HD24236-03 0002
GALL, CHRISTINE M R01NS26748-03
GALL, JOSEPH G R37GM33397-08
GALLA, JOHN H P01AI18745-10 0002
GALLAGER, DOROTHY W R01NS23321-06
GALLAGHER-THOMPSON, DOLORES E R01MH43407-0
GALLAGHER, DOLORES E P50MH40041-08 0005
GALLAGHER, J C P50AR39221-05 0001
GALLAGHER, J C P50AR39221-05 9003
GALLAGHER, J C P50AR39221-05 9004
GALLAGHER, J C P50AR39221-05 0007
GALLAGHER, J CHRISTOPHER R01AG10358-01
GALLAGHER, J CHRISTOPHER U01AG10373-01
GALLAGHER, JOEL P R01MH39163-04A3
GALLAGHER, KIM P R01HL32043-07A1
GALLAGHER, KIM P R01HL45578-01
GALLAGHER, MICHELA K02MH00406-10
GALLAGHER, MICHELA P01AG09973-01 9001
GALLAGHER, MICHELA P01AG09973-01
GALLAGHER, MICHELA P01AG09973-01 0002
GALLAGHER, MICHELA R01MH35554-11
GALLAGHER, MICHELA S07RR07072-26 0266
GALLAGHER, PATRICIA S07RR07175-15 0432
GALLAGHER, PATRICIA E R29CA47457-05
GALLAGHER, ROBERTA P01DC00081-26 9001
GALLAHER, DANIEL D S07RR07052-26 0156
GALLAHER, EDWARD J P01AA08621-02 0003
GALLANT, JONATHAN A R01GM13626-25
GALLANT, SHERYLE J R01HL42583-01A3
GALLATIN, W MICHAEL P01AI27291-04 0006
GALLATIN, W. MICHAEL P51RR00166-30 0086
GALLATIN, WILLIAM M R01CA40272-08
GALLE, OMER R P30HD06160-20S1
GALLER, JAMINA R S07RR05487-29 0688
GALLER, JANINA R P01HD22539-04
GALLER, JANINA R P01HD22539-04 0001
GALLETTI, PIERRE M S07RR05664-24
GALLETTI, PIERRE M S15AA09304-01
GALLETTI, PIERRE M S15EY09464-01
GALLI, STEPHEN J R01AI22674-06
GALLI, STEPHEN J R01AI23990-06
GALLIE, THOMAS M P01HL11307-25 9001
GALLIGAN, JAMES J R29DK40210-02
GALLIMORE, RONALD P01HD11944-12 0007
GALLIMORE, RONALD G R01HD19124-06
GALLIN, J I Z01AI00155-16
GALLIN, J I Z01AI00521-04
GALLINI, JOAN K S07RR07160-16 0588
GALLO, R C Z01CP05534-05
GALLO, R C Z01CP07148-05
GALLOP, PAUL M R01AG07723-04
GALLOWAY, DARRELL R K04AI00876-04
GALLOWAY, DARRELL R R01AI23429-04
GALLOWAY, DENISE A P01AI29363-02
GALLOWAY, DENISE A P01AI29363-02 0003
GALLOWAY, DENISE A P01CA42792-05 0001
GALLOWAY, DENISE A R01CA26001-13
GALLOWAY, DENISE A R01CA35568-08
GALLOWAY, DENISE A U01AI31448-01 0005
GALLOWAY, MATTHEW P R01DA04120-05
GALLOWAY, ROBERT L, JR R29NS28602-01A1
GALOTTI, KATHLEEN M R15HD28177-01
GALPER, JONAS B R01HL36014-07
GALT, SPENCER W S07RR05392-30 0693
GALTON, VALERIE A R01HD09020-16
GALTON, VALERIE A R01HD27706-02
GALUN, RACHEL N01AI22668-26
GALVAO, PAULO AYROZA P01AI26506-04 0001
GAMBAL, DAVID S07RR05390-30 0676
GAMBASSI, G Z01AG00269-02
GAMBASSI, G Z01AG00275-01
GAMBETTI, PIERLUIGI P50AG08012-04 9004
GAMBETTI, PIERLUIGI R01NS14509-14
GAMBETTI, PIERLUIGI R35AG08992-01
GAMBETTI, PIERLUIGI R35AG08992-01 0001
GAMBETTI, PIERLUIGI R35AG08992-01 0005
GAMBETTI, PIERLUIGI R37AG08155-03
GAMBLE, VANESSA N R01LM05310-01
GAMBLE, WILBERT S07RR07079-26 0281
GAMCSIK, MICHAEL P R29CA51229-01A1
GAMELLI, RICHARD L R01GM42577-03
GAMETCHU, BAHIRU R29CA49297-04
GAMLIN, PAUL D R01EY07558-03
GAMLIN, PAUL D R S07RR05807-13 0455
GAMLIN, PAUL D R S07RR05807-13 0456
GAMLIN, PAUL D R S15EY09445-01
GAMMON, MARILIE S07RR05449-30 0323
GAMMON, WALTER R R01AR30475-09
GAMPER, HOWARD B R43AI31007-01A1
GAMPER, HOWARD B R43AI31315-01
GAN, L P41RR02594-06 0007
GANAPATHI, RAM N R01CA35531-07
GANAPATHY, VADIVEL R01HD22103-05
GANAPATHY, VADIVEL R01HD24451-03
GANCHER, STEPHEN T M01RR00334-25 0290
GANCHER, STEPHEN T M01RR00334-25 0250
GANCHER, STEPHEN T M01RR00334-25 0313
GANCHER, STEPHEN T S07RR05412-30 0979
GAND, H DANANA S07RR05487-29 0704
GANDA, OM P P30DK36836-05 0002
GANDHI, OM P R01ES03329-07
GANDHI, VARSHA R03CA53311-02
GANDOLFI, A JAY P01DK41006-03 0003
GANDOLFI, A JAY R01ES05790-05
GANDOLFI, A JAY R01GM34788-06
GANDOUR, JACKSON R01DC00515-04
GANDOUR, JACKSON T S07RR07032-26 0043
GANDOUR, RICHARD D R01GM42016-02
GANDY, JAY R29ES05318-03
GANDY, SAMUEL S07RR05651-24 0138
GANDY, SAMUEL E P01AG09464-01 0002
GANDY, SAMUEL E P01AG10491-01 0002
GANEM, BRUCE R01GM24054-13
GANEM, BRUCE R01GM35712-06A1
GANEM, DONALD P30DK26743-11 9009
GANEM, DONALD E R01AI18782-10
GANEM, DONALD E R01AI22503-07
GANEM, DONALD E R01AI24436-04
GANESAN, ADAYAPALAM T R01GM14108-24
GANETZKY, BARRY S R01GM43100-02
GANETZKY, BARRY S R01NS15390-12
GANEY, PATRICIA S07RR05656-24 0854
GANEY, PATRICIA E R29ES05722-01
GANGADHARAM, PATTISAPU R R01AI21897-07
GANGJEE, ALEEM R55AI30900-01
GANGULI, MARY R01AG07562-03
GANGULI, MARY R01AG09202-01A1
GANGULI, ROHAN K01MH00626-05
GANGULI, ROHAN R01MH41883-05
GANI, JOSEPH M R01AI29426-02
GANIATS, THEODORE G R01HS06098-03
GANJU-KRISHAN, AWTAR R01CA29360-09
GANJU-KRISHAN, AWTAR R01CA44737-05
GANJU-KRISHAN, AWTAR U01AI25696-05 0006
GANJU-KRISHAN, AWTAR U01AI25696-05
GANJU-KRISHAN, AWTAR U01AI25696-05 9002
GANN, DONALD S R01DK26831-12
GANN, DONALD S R01GM27946-13
GANNETT, PETER M R15GM46067-01
GANNON, DAVID E K08HL02627-01
GANNON, MARY C R01DK43018-01A1
GANONG, LAWRENCE H R01NR01522-02
GANONG, WILLIAM F P01HL29714-29 0004
GANONG, WILLIAM F P01HL29714-29
GANS, BRUCE M01RR00054-30 0386
GANS, BRUCE M01RR00054-30 0387
GANS, BRUCE M01RR00054-30 0388
GANS, BRUCE M01RR00054-30 0389
GANS, BRUCE M01RR00054-30 0390
GANS, BRUCE M01RR00054-30 0385
GANS, BRUCE M01RR00054-30 0467
GANSCHOW, ROGER E R01DK14770-19
GANSOW, O A Z01CM06353-09
GANTER, PHILLIP F S06GM45455-01 0002
GANTHER, HOWARD P01CA45164-04A1 0002
GANTHER, HOWARD E R01DK14184-21
GANTT, JAMES S R29GM38769-04
GANTZ, BRUCE J M01RR00059-30 0498
GANTZ, BRUCE J P50DC00242-07
GANTZ, BRUCE J P50DC00242-07 9001
GANTZ, IRA M01RR00042-31 0635
GANZ, PATRICIA A P01CA43461-05 0001
GANZ, PETER K04HL02566-01
GANZ, TOMAS R01HL35640-06A1
GAO, X-M Z01MH02468-03
GAO, ZHIRONG S07RR05970-06 0778
GARA, MICHAEL A R01MH42935-03
GARABRANT, DAVID H K07CA01291-06
GARANT, PHILIAS S03RR03552-01
GARANT, PHILIAS R S07RR05778-16
GARANT, PHILIAS R S15DE10077-01
GARAVITO, MICHAEL R P01HL30121-08 0006
GARAVITO, R MICHAEL R01GM39550-04
GARAVITO, R MICHAEL S10RR06568-01
GARAY, GABRIEL L R43AI30854-01A1
GARBER, ALAN J M01RR00350-25 0465
GARBER, ALAN M P01AG05842-06 0005
GARBER, ALAN M R01HL46297-01

GARBER, ALAN M R29AG07651-04
GARBER, DAVID W R29HL38329-05
GARBER, JUDY R29MH45458-01A1
GARBER, JUDY S07RR07201-12 0634
GARBERN, JAMES Y K08NS01464-02
GARBERS, DAVID L P30HD05797-20 9006
GARBERS, DAVID L R01HD10254-16
GARBO, GRETA P01CA48733-02 0002
GARBUTT, JAMES C P50MH33127-13 0001
GARCEA, ROBERT L P01CA50661-03 0003
GARCEA, ROBERT L R01CA37667-08
GARCIA-ARRARAS, JOSE E S06GM08102-20 0053
GARCIA-BLANCO, MARIANO A R55GM46474-01
GARCIA-CASTINEIRAS, SIXTO S03RR03339-09
GARCIA-RILL, EDGAR E R01NS20246-08
GARCIA, CHARLES A U10EY06237-06
GARCIA, EMILIO S07RR05917-08 0694
GARCIA, ERNEST V R01HL42052-03
GARCIA, FERNANDO V S07RR05424-30 0083
GARCIA, G E Z01HL00266-03
GARCIA, GEORGE A R55GM45968-01
GARCIA, JOE G K08HL02312-04
GARCIA, JOE G R29HL44746-02
GARCIA, MARTHA C S07RR05771-15 0335
GARCIA, PATRICIA M01RR00048-30 0170
GARCIA, RAUL I R29DE09088-01A2
GARCIA, RAYMOND E S06GM08101-20 0031
GARD, ANTHONY L R55NS29648-01
GARD, ANTHONY L S07RR05774-17 0383
GARD, DAVID L R29GM38475-05
GARD, DAVID L S07RR07092-26 0488
GARDIN, JULIUS M N01HC95100-02
GARDINE, ROBERTA R18MH49193-01
GARDINE, ROBERTA R19MH46205-03
GARDINER, KATHELEEN K04HG00001-02
GARDINER, KATHELEEN P01HD17449-08 0005
GARDINER, KATHELEEN R01HG00378-04
GARDINER, KATHELEEN S07RR05964-06 0767
GARDINER, KATHELEEN S07RR05964-06 0759
GARDINER, KATHELEEN S07RR05964-06 0755
GARDINER, KATHELEEN S07RR05964-06 0760
GARDNER, CAROLE S07RR05909-08 0948
GARDNER, CHRISTOPHER M01RR00083-29 0235
GARDNER, DAVID G P01HL29714-29 0009
GARDNER, DAVID G R01HL35753-07
GARDNER, ESTHER P R01NS11862-14
GARDNER, FRANK H M01RR00073-29 0102
GARDNER, FRED A R43AI31313-01
GARDNER, I A S07RR05457-29 0002
GARDNER, J D Z01DK53001-21
GARDNER, J D Z01DK53004-19
GARDNER, JANE D S07RR05446-30 0268
GARDNER, JEFFREY S07RR05393-30 0891
GARDNER, JEFFREY F R01GM28717-11
GARDNER, JEFFREY P R29HL44196-01A2
GARDNER, JUDITH M R01HD21784-07
GARDNER, LAURA B R03HS06642-01
GARDNER, MICHAEL K S07RR07092-26 0539
GARDNER, MURRAY B P30AI27732-04
GARDNER, MURRAY B P51RR00169-30 0097
GARDNER, MURRAY B P51RR00169-30 0098
GARDNER, MURRAY B P51RR00169-30 0099
GARDNER, MURRAY B P51RR00169-30 0100
GARDNER, MURRAY B U01AI26471-04
GARDNER, MURRY B U01AI26471-04 0001
GARDNER, PAUL D R01NS30243-01
GARDNER, PHYLLIS I R01DK41324-02
GARDNER, RICK M S03RR03361-09
GARDNER, SUSAN N01CP95608-03
GARDNER, TIMOTHY J R01HL19414-14
GAREN, ALAN P01GM39813-04 0003
GAREWAL, HARINDER P01CA27502-11 0017
GARFINKEL, DAVID P41RR01861-07 0009
GARG, ABHIMANYU M01RR00633-19 0380
GARG, ABHIMANYU S07RR05426-30 0135
GARG, L S07RR05362-30 0788
GARG, RAMESH C S06GM08091-20 0027
GARGES, S Z01CB08750-11
GARGUS, JOHN J P01HL27385-11 0010
GARGUS, JOHN J R01GM34436-07
GARGUS, JOHN J R01GM34939-06
GARIEPY, JEAN R01AI26152-03
GARIN, EDUARDO H S07RR05749-19 0279
GARLAND, D L Z01EY00189-07
GARLICK, JONATHAN A K11DE00263-03
GARLID, KEITH D P01HL36573-06 0002
GARLID, KEITH D R01HL43814-02
GARNER, CHARLES M R15GM46075-01
GARNER, JUDY A R01NS22402-07
GARNER, M M Z01HD01408-01
GARNER, MARGARET H R01EY07010-06
GARNER, PHILIP P R01GM35557-06
GARNETT, JOHN E P50DK39250-05 0002
GARNICK, DEBORAH W R03MH47577-01A1
GARNIER, PHILIP C R03MH46841-01
GARON, C F Z01AI00488-05
GARON, C F Z01AI00554-03
GARRAHLE S07RR05380-30 0887
GARRARD, JUDITH K01AG00434-03
GARRARD, JUDITH S07RR05448-30 0301
GARRARD, WILLIAM T P01GM31689-08 0003
GARRARD, WILLIAM T R01GM22201-17
GARRARD, WILLIAM T R01GM29935-10
GARRELL, ROBIN L R29GM42977-02
GARRELS, JAMES I P41RR02188-07
GARRETT, CARLETON T R01CA47994-03
GARRETT, K M S07RR05411-30 0958
GARRETT, MERRILL F P60DC01409-01 0003
GARRETT, STEPHEN R01GM44666-01A1
GARRISON, CAROL Z R01MH40363-05
GARRISON, JAMES C P01CA40042-07 0004
GARRISON, JAMES C, II R01DK19952-15
GARRISON, MARK W S07RR05686-11 0981
GARRO, ANTHONY J P50AA03508-14 0032
GARRY, PHILIP M01RR00997-16 0221
GARRY, PHILIP J R37AG02049-12
GARRY, ROBERT F, JR R01AI28048-03
GARSON, ARTHUR M01RR00188-27 0244
GARSON, ARTHUR, JR R01HL24916-11
GARST, LYNN R S07RR06022-02 0848
GART, J J Z01CP04265-26
GART, J J Z01CP04267-26
GARTE, SEYMOUR P30ES00260-29 9007
GARTE, SEYMOUR J R01CA36342-08
GARTE, SEYMOUR J R01CA43199-05
GARTE, SEYMOUR J R01CA52925-02
GARTE, SEYMOUR J. P42ES04895-03 0003
GARTLAN, STEVE P51RR00167-31 0032
GARTLER, STANLEY M K06GM03874-28
GARTLER, STANLEY M R37HD16659-09
GARTNER, T K S07RR07229-06 0720
GARTNER, THEODORE K R01HL46152-01
GARVER, FRED A P01HL41544-04 0004
GARVEY, ARTHUR J R01DA06183-01A2
GARVEY, TIMOTHY M01RR00750-19 0287
GARVEY, TIMOTHY M01RR00750-19 0297
GARVEY, W TIMOTHY R29DK38765-05
GARVIN, ABBOTT J R01CA37887-07A1
GARWOOD, MICHAEL G R29CA50703-03
GARZA, CUTBERTO R01HD21049-06
GASCOIGNE, NICHOLAS R R29GM39476-04
GASCON, PEDRO R01AI29328-02
GASH, A GRAHAM P01CA47982-04 9003
GASH, DON M R01NS15109-13
GASIEWICZ, THOMAS P30ES01247-17 9009
GASIEWICZ, THOMAS A P30ES01247-17 0031
GASIEWICZ, THOMAS A R01ES02515-11
GASIEWICZ, THOMAS A R01ES04862-02
GASKELL, SIMON J S10RR06238-01
GASKILL, HAROLD V, I S07RR05654-24 0128
GASKIN, FELICIA R01AG06348-05A1
GASKIN, FELICIA R01NS24489-05A1
GASPARI, ANTHONY A R29AR40933-01
GASPER, PETER W R29CA46371-04
GASPER, PETER W S07RR05458-29 0826
GASS, DONALD M U10EY02549-13
GASSER, DAVID L P50DE09164-03
GASSER, KENNETH W S07RR07176-14 0524
GASSMAN, PAUL G R01GM35962-06
GASSON, JUDITH C R01CA40163-07
GASSSER, D L P50DE09164-03 0005
GASTON, LOUISE R01MH47118-01
GATCHEL, ROBERT J R01DE08414-02
GATCHEL, ROBERT J R01MH46452-01A2
GATELEY, ANN M01RR02558-07 0064
GATES, ALLEN H P30ES01247-17 9005
GATEWOOD, LAEL C P41RR01632-09
GATEWOOD, LAEL C P41RR01632-09 9018
GATEWOOD, LAEL C P41RR01632-09 9007
GATEWOOD, LAEL C P41RR01632-09 9013
GATTONE, VINCENT H, II R03MH46511-02
GATZ, MARGARET J R01AG08724-02
GAULTON, GLEN N R01AI25535-03
GAULTON, GLEN N R01GM42626-01A2
GAUNTT, CHARLES J R01HL45979-01
GAUNTT, CHARLES J S07RR07187-13 0697
GAUSE, WILLIAM C S07RR05983-05 0353
GAUSE, WILLIAM C U01AI32247-01 0003
GAUSS, PETER H S07RR07024-26 0042
GAUTAM, ANIL P30DK34989-08 9001
GAUTHIER, VERLENE J R29DK43050-01A1
GAUWERKY, CHARLOTTE K11CA01279-07
GAVALCHIN, JERRIE R29AI26710-04
GAVALER, JUDITH S R01AA06772-07
GAVANSKI, IGOR S07RR07031-26 0087
GAVIN, WILLIAM J S07RR07157-16 0571
GAVISH, DOV M01RR00102-28 0092
GAVRAS, HARALAMBOS S07RR05487-29 0714
GAWIN, FRANK H R01DA06289-03
GAWLEY, ROBERT E R01GM37985-03
GAY, CAROL V R01DE04345-16
GAY, CAROL V R01DE09459-01A1
GAY, CAROL V S07RR07082-26 0284
GAY, ROY P60HL38632-04 9004
GAY, THOMAS J R01DC00848-03
GAY, THOMAS J R01DC00993-01
GAYDA, RANDALL C R01GM36414-05
GAYESKI, THOMAS R01HL03290-35
GAYNON, PAUL S U10CA05436-25
GAYNOR, JEFFREY P01CA47179-03 9004
GAYNOR, MARTIN S R29MH45841-02
GAYNOR, RICHARD B R01AI25288-05
GAYNOR, RICHARD B R01AI29167-03
GAYNOR, RICHARD B R01CA30981-11
GAZDAR, A Z01CM06589-07
GAZZANIGA, MICHAEL S P01NS17778-10
GAZZANIGA, MICHAEL S P01NS17778-10 9001
GAZZANIGA, MICHAEL S R01NS22626-07
GAZZARA, RUSSELL A S07RR07149-18 0418
GAZZARA, RUSSELL A S07RR07149-18 0419
GAZZINELLI, GIOVANNI P01AI26505-03 0001
GAZZINELLI, GIOVANNI P01AI26505-03 9001
GEACINTOV, NICHOLAS E R01CA20851-14
GEAHLEN, ROBERT L R01CA37372-08
GEAHLEN, ROBERT L R55CA45667-04
GEAR, ADRIAN R R01HL27014-09
GEARD, CHARLES R P01CA12536-20 0011
GEARD, CHARLES R P01CA49062-02 0005
GEARD, CHARLES R R01CA49672-03
GEARHART, JOHN P01MH46529-02 0001
GEARHART, JOHN D P01HD24605-03
GEARHART, JOHN D P01HD24605-03 0004
GEARHART, JOHN D R01HD25863-03
GEARHART, JOHN P S07RR05378-30 0995
GEARHART, PATRICIA J R01GM42975-08
GEARY, NORCROSS D R01DK32448-10
GEBALLE, ADAM P R29AI26672-04
GEBALLE, ADAM P. P01AI27291-04 0005
GEBBER, GERARD L R37HL13187-22
GEBHARDT, BRYAN M R01EY08701-02
GEBHART, GERALD F P50HL32295-07 0012
GEBHART, GERALD F R01DA02879-15
GEBHART, GERALD F R01NS19912-09
GEBHART, SUZANNE M01RR00039-31 0446
GEBHART, SUZANNE M01RR00039-31 0427
GEBHART, SUZANNE S M01RR00039-31 0447
GEDDES, J W R35AG08974-01 0008
GEDDES, JAMES R35AG07918-03 0002
GEDDES, JAMES W R01AG10678-01
GEDDES, JIM W P01AG00538-15 9001
GEDEN, ELIZABETH A R01NR01282-04
GEE, A S07RR05362-30 0789
GEE, KELVIN W R01NS25986-03
GEE, KELVIN W R29NS24645-04
GEE, MARLYS H R01HL34014-05A2
GEER, BILLY W R01AA06702-09
GEERS, ANN E R01DC00443-04
GEERTSEN, DENNIS C R19MH46186-03
GEFFNER, MITCHELL E M01RR00865-18 0360
GEFFNER, MITCHELL E M01RR00865-18 0293
GEFFNER, MITCHELL E M01RR00865-18 0232
GEFFNER, MITCHELL E M01RR00865-18 0334
GEFFNER, MITCHELL E M01RR00865-18 0292
GEFTER, MALCOLM L P01GM37641-05 0002
GEFTER, MALCOLM L R37AI13357-16
GEFTER, WARREN B R01HL43286-02
GEGENHEIMER, PETER S07RR07037-26 0384
GEGENHEIMER, PETER A S07RR07037-26 0382
GEHA, RAIF P01AI28046-03 0001
GEHA, RAIF P01AI28046-03 0002
GEHA, RAIF S M01RR02172-09 0180
GEHA, RAIF S M01RR02172-09 0035
GEHA, RAIF S P01CA39542-07 0004
GEHA, RAIF S R01AI27411-02
GEHA, RAIF S R01AI29906-02
GEHA, RAIF S U01AI31541-01
GEHA, RAIF S U01AI31541-01 0002
GEHAN, EDMUND A U10CA30138-11
GEHLSEN, KURT R R01CA57202-01
GEHR, LYNNE M01RR00065-29 0359
GEHR, TODD M01RR00065-29 0326
GEHR, TODD M01RR00065-29 0330
GEHR, TODD W D S07RR05430-30 0222
GEHRKE, LEE R01GM42504-03
GEHRKE, STEVIN H S07RR07075-17 0262
GEHRZ, RICHARD P01HD19937-06 9004
GEHRZ, RICHARD C P01HD19937-06
GEHRZ, RICHARD C P01HD19937-06 0003
GEHSHAN, MICHELE L R13HS06776-01
GEIB, ROY W R29CA47944-04
GEIDUSCHEK, E PETER R01GM39418-04
GEIDUSCHEK, E PETER R37GM18386-22
GEINISMAN, YURI P01AG09466-01 0003
GEISBUHLER, TIMOTHY P R29HL39025-05
GEISELMAN, PAULA J K04DK01897-04
GEISLER, C. DANIEL P01DC00116-16 0017
GEISLER, WILSON S R01EY02688-13
GEISSER, SEYMOUR R01GM25271-13A1
GEISSLER, EDWIN N R01GM45311-01
GEJMAN, P V Z01MH02465-03
GELATO, MARIE C S07RR05736-19 0202
GELB, LAWRENCE M01RR00036-31 0968
GELB, LAWRENCE M01RR00036-31 0641
GELB, LAWRENCE M01RR00036-31 1010
GELB, LAWRENCE D U01AI25903-05 0004
GELB, MICHAEL H K04GM00562-02
GELB, MICHAEL H R01CA52874-01A1
GELB, MICHAEL H R01HL36235-06
GELBART, WILLIAM M P01GM29301-11 0002
GELBART, WILLIAM M R01GM28669-11
GELBAUM, LESLIE T S07RR07024-26 0033
GELBER, RICHARD P01CA34183-08 9001
GELBERG, LILLIAN R01HS06696-01
GELBERMAN, RICHARD H R01AR33097-13
GELBOIN, H V Z01CP05436-07
GELEHRTER, THOMAS D R01HL39085-05

GELEHRTER, THOMAS D R37CA22729-14
GELERNTER, JOEL K20MH00931-01
GELFAND, DONNA M R37MH41474-05
GELFAND, ERWIN W P01HL36577-06 0011
GELFAND, ERWIN W R01AI26490-03
GELFAND, ERWIN W R01AI29704-02
GELFAND, JEFFREY A P50GM21700-15 0011
GELINAS, CELINE R29CA54999-01
GELINAS, RICHARD P01DK31232-10 0003
GELINAS, RICHARD P41RR01315-10 0044
GELLER, BARBARA R01DA04844-03
GELLER, BARBARA R01MH40273-08
GELLER, BARBARA R01MH45486-03
GELLER, BRUCE L S07RR07079-26 0292
GELLER, E SCOTT S07RR07095-24 0374
GELLER, HERBERT M P01NS21469-07 0007
GELLER, HERBERT M R01NS25168-04A1
GELLER, NANCY P01CA05826-29 9002
GELLERT, M Z01DK33000-25
GELLERT, M Z01DK33001-07
GELLES, JEFF R01GM43369-01A1
GELLES, JEFF S07RR07044-26 0117
GELLMAN, SAMUEL H R29GM41825-02
GELMANN, EDWARD P R01CA50355-02
GELPI, R J P51RR00168-30 0137
GELTMAN, EDWARD M P50HL17646-17 0036
GEMMILL, ROBERT P30CA46934-04 9003
GEMMILL, ROBERT S07RR05964-06 0761
GEMMILL, ROBERT S07RR05964-06 0765
GEMMILL, ROBERT M R13HG00428-01
GEMSON, DONALD R01HS07076-01
GENANT, HARRY K R01AR27926-10
GENANT, HARRY K R01AR37562-04
GENCO, CAROLINE S07RR05308-30 0236
GENCO, CAROLINE A R01AI30797-01A1
GENCO, CAROLINE A R01DE09161-01A2
GENCO, ROBERT J K16DE00158-07
GENCO, ROBERT J P50DE04898-14
GENCO, ROBERT J P50DE08240-05 0008
GENCO, ROBERT J S07RR05330-30 0018
GENCO, ROBERT J S07RR05330-30 0019
GENDREAU, MARK P01AG08777-01 9001
GENEL, MYRON M01RR06022-02 0345
GENERO, NANCY S07RR07186-10 0611
GENNARELLI, THOMAS A M01RR00040-31 0335
GENNARELLI, THOMAS A P01NS08803-20A1 0009
GENNARELLI, THOMAS A P01NS08803-20A1 0010
GENNARELLI, THOMAS A P01NS08803-20A1 0011
GENNARELLI, THOMAS A P01NS08803-20A1 9001
GENNARELLI, THOMAS A P01NS08803-20A1
GENNARO, MARIA L R55GM45774-01
GENNARO, SUSAN R01NR02085-02
GENNARO, SUSAN S07RR05948-05 0332
GENNIS, ROBERT B R01HL16101-18
GENSLER, HELEN L P01CA27502-11 0012
GENSLER, HELEN L R29CA44504-05
GENTILE, DOUGLAS A S07RR05424-30 0095
GENTRY-WEEKS, C R Z01DE00512-02
GENTRY, LARRY E R29CA48091-04
GENTRY, R T P50AA03508-14 0051
GENUTH, SAUL M U01DK30628-09
GEOFFRION, CHARLES A S15NS30131-01
GEORG, GUNDA I R01CA52790-02
GEORG, GUNDA I S07RR05606-25 0685
GEORGE, ALFRED L K08AR01862-01
GEORGE, CINDY L R43HD27411-01
GEORGE, D Z01AA00249-08
GEORGE, D Z01AA00265-06
GEORGE, D Z01AA00266-06
GEORGE, D Z01AA00273-03
GEORGE, D Z01AA00274-03
GEORGE, D Z01AA00278-02
GEORGE, D Z01AA00286-02
GEORGE, DONNA L R01NS30025-01
GEORGE, EDWIN B K08NS01504-01
GEORGE, FRANK R R01AA07754-04
GEORGE, FREDRICK W K04HD00845-04
GEORGE, FREDRICK W R01HD21966-04A1
GEORGE, JEANNE W P51RR00169-30 0146
GEORGE, JEANNE W P51RR00169-30 0147
GEORGE, LINDA K P30AG09463-01 9003
GEORGE, LINDA K P50MH40159-08 0008
GEORGE, MATTHEW S06GM08016-21 0077
GEORGE, ROBERT S07RR05354-30 0413
GEORGE, SAMUEL S07RR05425-30 0738
GEORGE, SAMUEL E K08HL02433-02
GEORGE, STEPHEN N01CO03874-05
GEORGE, STEPHEN P01CA29582-10A1 9002
GEORGE, STEPHEN L P01CA23099-13 9002
GEORGE, STEPHEN L P30CA14236-18 9012
GEORGE, STEPHEN L U10CA33601-12
GEORGE, STEPHEN L. P30CA21765-14 9003
GEORGE, T ADRIAN R01GM38613-05
GEORGE, T ADRIAN S07RR07055-26 0177
GEORGE, VARGHESE T R29HG00374-04
GEORGE, WILLIAM H R01AA06776-06
GEORGIEV, ALEXANDER S07RR05420-30 0039
GEORGIEV, VASSIL S N01CM97591-03
GEORGITIS, JOHN W R29AI24598-05
GEORGOPOULOS, ANGELIKI M01RR00722-19 0204
GEORGOPOULOS, APOSTOLOS P50MH48185-01 0001
GEORGOPOULOS, APOSTOLOS P P01NS07226-19A2 0001
GEORGOPOULOS, APOSTOLOS P R01NS17413-11
GEORGOPOULOS, CONSTANTINE P R01AI21029-08
GEORGOPOULOS, CONSTANTINE P R37GM23917-15
GEPPERT, EUGENE F K07HL02098-05
GEPPERT, THOMAS D M01RR00633-19 0419
GERACE, LAINA M S07RR05776-11 0392
GERACE, LARRY P01GM46006-01 0003
GERACE, LARRY R R01GM28521-12
GERACE, LARRY R R01GM41955-02
GERACE, TERENCE A P01HL36588-06 9002
GERACI, JOSEPH P R01DK35129-05
GERACIOTI, THOMAS M01RR00095-31 0368
GERAETS, DOUGLAS R S07RR05877-09 0595
GERAGHTY, DANIEL P01AI29518-02 0001
GERAGHTY, DANIEL E R01AI31873-01
GERARD-STIMLER, NORMA P R01HL41587-03
GERARD, CRAIG S07RR05899-10 0275
GERARD, CRAIG J R01HL41277-04
GERARD, NORMA P PHD R01HL36162-07
GERARD, ROBERT D R01GM38886-05
GERARD, ROBERT D R01HL42398-02
GERARDI, DONNA N01CO44027-10
GERATZ, JOACHIM D R01AR39460-04
GERBA, C P P42ES04940-02 0003
GERBER, JOHN G M01RR00051-30 0726
GERBER, JOHN G R01DK38504-02
GERBER, L H Z01CL60011-01
GERBER, LINDA M P50HL18323-17 9002
GERBERT, BARBARA P50MH42459-06 0006
GERBI, SUSAN A R01GM20261-18
GERBI, SUSAN A R01GM35929-03
GERD, GRIENINGER S07RR05688-23 0597
GERDES, ANTHONY M R01HL30696-09
GERFEN, C R Z01MH02497-02
GERGELY, JOHN R37HL05949-31
GERGELY, JOHN S07RR05711-21 0038
GERGELY, JOHN S07RR05711-21
GERGEN, JOHN P R01HD22448-05
GERHARD, DANIELA S R01NS26854-03
GERHARD, GLENN S K11AG00523-01
GERHARD, WALTER R37AI13989-15
GERHARDT, GREG A K04AG00441-03
GERHARDT, GREG A P20DC01439-01 0003
GERHARDT, GREG A P50NS09199-21 0035
GERHARDT, H CARL S07RR07053-26 0150
GERHARDT, HOWARD C K02MH00757-03
GERHARDT, PHILIPP S07RR05772-17 0337
GERHART, JOHN P41RR00570-21 0011
GERHART, JOHN C R01GM19363-28
GERICH, JOHN M01RR00056-30 0356
GERICH, JOHN M01RR00056-30 0359
GERICH, JOHN M01RR00056-30 0373
GERICH, JOHN E M01RR00056-30 0344
GERICH, JOHN E M01RR00056-30 0297
GERICH, JOHN E M01RR00056-30 0298
GERICH, JOHN E M01RR00056-30 0327
GERICH, JOHN E M01RR00056-30 0354
GERICH, JOHN E M01RR00056-30 0340
GERICH, JOHN E M01RR00056-30 0320
GERICH, JOHN E M01RR00056-30 0346
GERICH, JOHN E P41RR00954-15 9012
GERICH, JOHN E R37DK20411-16
GERIG, J T R01GM44558-02
GERIG, J T S07RR07099-25 0396
GERIG, JOHN T R01GM25975-10A2
GERIN, JOHN L N01AI72623-38
GERKEN, THOMAS P30DK27651-09 0009
GERKEN, THOMAS A R29DK39918-05
GERLT, JOHN A R01GM34572-08
GERLT, JOHN A R01GM34573-08
GERLT, JOHN A R01GM40570-03
GERLT, JOHN A S10RR06662-01
GERMAIN, R N Z01AI00349-09
GERMAIN, R N Z01AI00403-08
GERMAIN, R N Z01AI00520-04
GERMAIN, R N Z01AI00545-03
GERMAINE, GREG R R01DE08514-05
GERMAN, DWIGHT C P50AG08013-04 0005
GERMAN, DWIGHT C R01DA05314-03
GERMAN, DWIGHT C. P51RR00166-30 0087
GERMAN, JAMES L, III R01CA50897-03
GERMAN, JAMES L, III R01HD04134-23
GERMAN, REBECCA S07RR05916-08 0302
GERMAN, REBECCA Z R01DE08697-04
GERMANE, NICHOLAS S07RR05795-14 0418
GERMERAAD, SUSAN E S06GM08192-12 0019
GERNER, EUGENE P30CA23074-14 9010
GERNER, EUGENE W R01CA47396-04
GERNSBACHER, MORTON A K04NS01376-03
GERNSBACHER, MORTON A R01NS29926-01
GERONE, PETER J P51RR00164-30 9015
GERONIMUS, ARLINE T R01HD24122-04
GEROSKI, D H P30EY06360-06 9003
GEROSKI, DAYLE H R01EY05609-07
GERR, FREDRIC E K01OH00098-02
GERRARD, MEG P50MH48165-02 0005
GERRARD, T L Z01BD03010-03
GERRITSEN, MARY E R01HL35739-04A2
GERRITY, LAURETTA P40RR00890-16 0008
GERRITY, ROSS G R01HL46312-01
GERSHENGORN, MARVIN C R01DK43036-02
GERSHFELD, N L Z01AR27004-22
GERSHON, ANNE A R01AI24021-06A2
GERSHON, ANNE A R01AI27187-02
GERSHON, ANNE A U01AI27562-05
GERSHON, E S Z01MH00086-16
GERSHON, MICHAEL D R01NS12969-16
GERSHON, MICHAEL D R01NS15547-12
GERSHON, MICHAEL D R01NS22637-06
GERSHON, MICHAEL D R13DK44261-01
GERSHON, SAMUEL P50AA08746-02
GERSHWIN, ERIC M P51RR00169-30 0112
GERSHWIN, M ERIC P30DK35747-06 9003
GERSHWIN, M ERIC P51RR00169-30 0067
GERSHWIN, MERRILL E R01AR36867-05
GERSHWIN, MERRILL E R01CA20816-16
GERSHWIN, MERRILL E R01DK39588-04
GERSHWIN, MERRILL E R01HD14388-11
GERSON, STANLEY S07RR05864-10 0938
GERSON, STANTON P30CA43703-04A1 9012
GERSON, STANTON L P01CA51183-01A1 0004
GERSON, STANTON L R03MH47440-01
GERSTEIN, GEORGE L R37MH46428-02
GERSTENBLITH, GARY P50HL17655-17 0033
GERSTENFELD, LOUIS C R01AR39405-04
GERSTENFELD, LOUIS C R01HD22400-05
GERSTNER, GEOFFREY E K15DE00205-05
GERSTNER, JAMES B U10CA35113-08
GERSTNER, PATSY G08LM05160-02
GERT, BERNARD R01HG00130-02
GERTHOFFER, WILLIAM P01DK41315-03 0007
GERTLER, PAUL P01HD28372-01 9001
GERTLER, PAUL P01HD28372-01 0007
GERTLER, PAUL P01HD28372-01 0004
GERTLER, PAUL P50HD12639-12 0017
GERTLER, PAUL J P01AG08291-03 0004
GERTNER, JOSEPH M01RR06020-02 0123
GERTNER, JOSEPH M M01RR06020-02 0306
GERTNER, JOSEPH M M01RR06020-02 0450
GERTNER, JOSEPH M M01RR06020-02 0444
GERTNER, JOSEPH M M01RR06020-02 0437
GERTNER, JOSEPH M M01RR06020-02 0438
GERTNER, JOSEPH M M01RR06020-02 0441
GERTNER, JOSEPH M M01RR06020-02 0423
GERTNER, JOSEPH M M01RR06020-02 0389
GERTNER, JOSEPH M M01RR06020-02 0433
GERTNER, JOSEPH M M01RR06020-02 0434
GERTNER, JOSEPH M M01RR06020-02 0368
GERTNER, JOSEPH M M01RR06020-02 0382
GERTNER, JOSEPH M M01RR06020-02 0383
GERTNER, JOSEPH M M01RR06020-02 0426
GERTNER, JOSEPH M M01RR06020-02 0419
GERTNER, JOSEPH M M01RR06020-02 0420
GERTNER, JOSEPH M M01RR06020-02 0428
GERTNER, JOSEPH M M01RR06020-02 0431
GERTNER, JOSEPH M P01CA29502-11A1 0043
GERTNER, JOSEPH M P01CA29502-11A1 0058
GERTON, GEORGE L R01HD22899-04
GERWECK, LEO E R37CA22860-14
GERWICK, WILLIAM U01CA52955-02 0002
GERWIN, B I Z01CP05611-03
GERY, I Z01EY00069-14
GESSERT, CHARLES E U76PE00234-01
GEST, THOMAS R S07RR05365-30 0080
GESTELAND, RAYMOND F P30HG00199-01
GESTELAND, RAYMOND F P30HG00199-01 9004
GESTELAND, RAYMOND F P30HG00199-01 9005
GESTELAND, RAYMOND F. U01AI27205-04 0002
GESTELAND, ROBERT C P01DC00347-06 0001
GESTELAND, ROBERT C S10RR06607-01
GETCHELL, THOMAS V R01DC00159-12
GETHING, MARY-JANE H R01AI23594-07
GETTES, LEONARD S P01HL27430-10 9001
GETTES, LEONARD S P01HL27430-10
GETTES, LEONARD S P01HL27430-10 0002
GETTES, LEONARD S R37HL38885-05
GETTINS, PETER R01HD28187-01
GETTINS, PETER R01HL32595-06
GETTLEMAN, LAWRENCE R15DE09865-01
GETTO, CARL J M01RR03186-06
GETTYS, THOMAS W R29DK42486-02
GETZ, GODFREY S P30DK26678-12 9007
GETZ, GODFREY S P50HL15062-20
GETZ, GODFREY S P50HL15062-20 9003
GETZ, GODFREY S P50HL15062-20 0009
GETZ, GODFREY S P50HL15062-20 0024
GETZ, GODFREY S R01HL04442-33
GETZ, GODFREY S. P01HL28972-10 9006
GETZ, LOWELL L S07RR07030-26 0391
GETZ, MICHAEL J R01CA33643-09
GETZ, MICHAEL J R01CA51852-01A1
GETZOFF, ELIZABETH D P01AI19499-08 0008
GETZOFF, ELIZABETH D R01GM37684-05
GEVINS, ALAN S R01MH43324-04
GEVINS, ALAN S R01NS23558-05
GEVINS, ALAN S R44MH43075-02
GEVINS, ALAN S R44NS27392-02
GEVINS, ALAN S S07RR06035-01
GEWIRTZ, ALAN M M01RR00349-25 0229
GEWIRTZ, ALAN M R01CA36896-08A1
GEWIRTZ, ALAN M R01CA54384-01
GEYER, J RUSSELL K08CA01451-03
GEYER, MARK A K02MH00188-08
GEYER, MARK A R01DA02925-10

GEYER, MARK A R01DA06325-02
GEYER, PAMELA S07RR05372-30 0650
GEYER, PAMELA K R01GM42539-01A2
GEYER, S J Z01BG06026-04
GEYER, S J Z01BG06030-02
GEYER, S J Z01BG06031-02
GEYER, S J Z01BG06033-02
GEYER, S J Z01BG06056-01
GHAFARI, JOSEPH G R01DE08722-04
GHANAYEM, B I Z01ES21084-06
GHANAYEM, B I Z01ES21109-04
GHANAYEM, B I Z01ES21117-03
GHANAYEM, B I Z01ES21138-02
GHANBARI, HOSSEIN P01AG10481-01 0002
GHAZZI, MAHMOUD U54HD29184-01 0006
GHAZZI, MAHMOUD N K11HD00828-05
GHETTI, BERNARDINO P01NS27613-01A2
GHETTI, BERNARDINO P01NS27613-01A2 0001
GHETTI, BERNARDINO P01NS27613-01A2 9002
GHETTI, BERNARDINO P01NS27613-01A2 9001
GHETTI, BERNARDINO P30AG10133-01 9002
GHETTI, BERNARDINO P30AG10133-01
GHETTI, BERNARDINO R01NS14426-11
GHETTI, BERNARDINO R01NS29822-01
GHIO, ANDREW J K11HL02655-01
GHISHAN, FAYEZ K P30DK26657-12 9004
GHISHAN, FAYEZ K R01DK33209-08
GHISHAN, FAYEZ K R01DK41274-04
GHODSI, ABDI S S07RR05372-30 0688
GHONEUM, MAMDOOH S07RR05780-16 0972
GHOSH, DEBABRATA S06GM08061-17 0016
GHOSH, DEBASHIS S07RR05716-20 0142
GHOSH, SANTIBRATA R01NS30091-01
GHOSH, SOUMITRA S R43HL46629-01
GIACOMINI, JOHN P N01DK92250-06
GIACOMINI, KATHLEEN M P50GM26691-13 0016
GIACOMINI, KATHLEEN M R01GM36780-06
GIACOMINI, KATHLEEN M R01GM42230-01A2
GIAM, C S P42ES04917-03 0001
GIAM, CHOU-ZEN R01AI29327-03
GIAM, CHOU-ZEN R01CA48709-04
GIAMBRA, L M Z01AG00189-01
GIAMMARA, BEVERLY L S15HD28754-01
GIANG, DANIEL M01RR00044-31 0343
GIANNINI, EDWARD M01RR00350-25 0384
GIANTURCO, SANDRA H M01RR00032-31 0323
GIANTURCO, SANDRA H P60HL27341-10 0008
GIANTURCO, SANDRA H R01HL44480-01A1
GIARDIELLO, FRANCIS M U01CA53801-01
GIARDIELLO, FRANK M M01RR00722-19 0205
GIARDINA, E M01RR00645-20 0426
GIARDINA, ELSA M01RR00645-20 0372
GIARDINA, ELSA G M01RR00645-20 0495
GIARDINA, P V P01CA29502-11A1 0046
GIBALDI, MILO S03RR03448-04
GIBALDI, MILO S07RR05635-18
GIBAS, ALEXANDRA M01RR00080-29 0444
GIBB, JAMES W R01DA00869-17
GIBB, JAMES W R01DA04222-06
GIBB, JAMES W S03RR03558-01
GIBBON, JOHN R01MH41649-06
GIBBONS, BARBARA H R01HD06565-25
GIBBONS, BARBARA H S07RR07026-26 0997
GIBBONS, BARBARA H S07RR07026-26
GIBBONS, BARBARA H S15CA56018-01
GIBBONS, IAN R R01GM30401-15
GIBBONS, IAN R S07RR07026-26 0998
GIBBONS, ROBERT D R01MH44826-01A2
GIBBONS, RONALD P01DE02847-23 0024
GIBBONS, RONALD P01DE02847-23 0025
GIBBONS, RONALD P01DE02847-23 0026
GIBBONS, RONALD P01DE02847-23 0027
GIBBONS, RONALD J S07RR05483-29
GIBBONS, RONALD J S15DE10078-01
GIBBONS, WALTER R R01HL14614-20
GIBBS, JAMES P30DK26687-11 9008
GIBBS, JAMES G, JR R55DK33248-07
GIBBS, RICHARD S07RR05425-30 0739
GIBBS, RICHARD A P30HG00210-01 9003
GIBBS, RICHARD A P30HG00210-01 0003
GIBBS, RICHARD A U01AI30243-02 9002
GIBBS, ROBERT B R01NS28896-01A1
GIBBS, RONALD S P01AI22380-07 9003
GIBBS, VERNA P30DK26743-11 9010
GIBLIN, FRANK J R01EY02027-15
GIBORI, GEULA R01HD12356-10A1
GIBORI, GEULA R37HD11119-14
GIBSON, ALAN R R01NS24042-06
GIBSON, ALAN R S07RR05872-08 0981
GIBSON, ALAN R S07RR05872-08 0982
GIBSON, ALAN R S07RR05872-08 0983
GIBSON, BRADFORD W P41RR01614-10 0009
GIBSON, C P50DE09164-03 0003
GIBSON, CAROLYN P50DE08239-04 9001
GIBSON, CAROLYN W S07RR07083-26 0470
GIBSON, D WADE R01AI13718-15
GIBSON, D WADE R01AI22711-07
GIBSON, DAVID R R01DA07310-02
GIBSON, DAVID T R01GM29909-11
GIBSON, GAIL S S06GM08250-04 0001
GIBSON, GARY P01MH44043-04 0003
GIBSON, GARY E P01AG03853-09 0012
GIBSON, GARY E P01NS03346-31 0030
GIBSON, ILENE K P30EY03790-11 9001
GIBSON, JAMES J P01AI19554-08S1 0004
GIBSON, K MICHAEL S07RR05906-06 0636
GIBSON, KEVIN F K11HL01963-05
GIBSON, MARIE J R01NS20335-07A2
GIBSON, MARIE J R55HD19077-07
GIBSON, MARK M01RR00109-28 0301
GIBSON, MARK M01RR00109-28 0310
GIBSON, MARK M01RR00109-28 0108
GIBSON, NEIL W R01CA52949-02
GIBSON, NEIL W R29CA47844-04
GIBSON, QUENTIN H R01GM14276-27
GIBSON, ROGER M R43AI31739-01
GIBSON, WILLIAM A R44CA45869-03
GIBSON, WILLIAM A S03RR03464-05
GIBSON, WILLIAM A S07RR05915-08
GICK, GREGORY S07RR05401-30 0860
GIDDENS, DON P P50HL15062-20 0031
GIDDINGS, J CALVIN R01GM10851-34
GIEBEL, GREGORY R01CA49619-02
GIEBINK, G SCOTT P50DC00133-13 0009
GIEBINK, G SCOTT P50DC00133-13
GIEBINK, G. SCOTT P50DC00133-13 0015
GIEBISCH, GERHARD H P01DK17433-18 0001
GIEBISCH, GERHARD H P01DK17433-18
GIEDROC, DAVID P R29GM42569-01A2
GIEDROC, DAVID P S07RR07090-26 0473
GIERASCH, LILA M R01GM27616-12
GIERASCH, LILA M R01GM34962-08
GIERHART, DENNIS L R43CA53991-01A1
GIERTHY, JOHN F R01ES03561-07
GIERUT, JUDITH A R29DC00433-05
GIESE, ROGER W R01HG00029-01A1
GIESE, ROGER W R01OH02792-01
GIESLER, GLENN J, JR R01NS29276-01A1
GIETZEN, DOROTHY W R29DK42274-01A2
GIFFARD, RONA G K08NS01425-02
GIFFORD, ROBERT H S03RR03024-11
GIFFORD, ROBERT R S07RR05680-23 0926
GIFT, AUDREY S07RR05973-05 0787
GIFT, H Z01DE00530-01
GIGER, MARYELLEN L R01CA48985-02
GIGER, URS K07HL02355-03
GIGER, URS R55DK37602-04A1
GIGLI, IRMA P01DK35108-07 0004
GIGLI, IRMA R37AI20067-08
GIGLI, IRMA U01AI31595-01 0005
GIGLIOTTI, FRANCIS R01AI23302-06
GIL, GREGORIO R01DK44218-01
GIL, KAREN M R29HL39124-05
GILAD, G M Z01MH02483-03
GILBARD, JEFFREY P R01EY03373-11
GILBERT, ALLAN S S07RR07150-17 0547
GILBERT, CHARLES D R01EY07968-03
GILBERT, D L Z01NS02218-16
GILBERT, DANIEL T K02MH00939-01
GILBERT, DAVID G R01DA05361-03
GILBERT, DAVID N S07RR06002-04
GILBERT, DOROTHY A R15NR02460-01A1
GILBERT, G S07RR05728-20 0196
GILBERT, GARY E K08HL02587-01
GILBERT, HARRIET S P60HL38655-04 9002
GILBERT, HIRAM F R01GM40379-04
GILBERT, HIRAM F R01HL28521-09
GILBERT, ILEEN A R29HL44495-02
GILBERT, JAY S07RR05737-20 0216
GILBERT, JEFFREY M P01MH31154-14 0014
GILBERT, JEREMY L R03DE09866-01
GILBERT, LAWRENCE I R01RR06627-02
GILBERT, LAWRENCE I R37DK30118-11
GILBERT, MARK K08NS01339-03
GILBERT, RAYMOND D R01HD22190-05
GILBERT, RICHARD J R29AI25635-04
GILBERT, SUSAN H R01AR37277-03
GILBERT, WALTER R01EY08397-02
GILBERT, WALTER R01GM37997-05
GILBERT, WALTER R01GM41895-03
GILBERT, WALTER R01HG00124-02
GILBOA, ELI P01AI32918-09 0013
GILBOA, ELI R01AI28771-03
GILCHER, RONALD N01HB97078-03
GILCHREST, BARBARA A R01AG07114-05 9001
GILCHREST, BARBARA A R01AG07114-05 0001
GILCHREST, BARBARA A R01AG07114-05
GILCHREST, BARBARA A R01HD24538-03
GILCHRIST, ALAN L S06GM08223-08 0030
GILCHRIST, GERALD S U10CA28882-11
GILDEN, DONALD P01NS11037-18 0055
GILDEN, DONALD H P01AG07347-04
GILDEN, DONALD H R01AG06127-05
GILDEN, JANICE S07RR05366-30 0556
GILDEN, RAYMOND V N01CO74102-45
GILDENBERG, PHILIP M01RR02558-07 0041
GILES, DONNA E R01MH39531-07
GILES, RICHARD E S07RR07097-26 0389
GILHAM, PETER T P30AI27713-04 9001
GILHAM, PETER T R01GM11518-26
GILHAM, PETER T R01GM19395-20
GILHAM, PETER T R01GM45109-02
GILINSKY, ALBERTA S R01AG07812-02
GILKESON, GARY S K08AR01847-02
GILKEY, JOHN C S07RR07002-26 0872
GILKEY, ROBERT H R01DC00786-03
GILL, DONALD L R01NS19304-08
GILL, GORDON N R37DK13149-24
GILL, PARKASH S07RR05356-30 0432
GILL, PARKASH S R01CA51621-03
GILL, SARJEET S R01ES03298-08
GILL, STANLEY C R01GM44276-02
GILL, THOMAS J, III R01CA18659-19
GILL, THOMAS J, III R01HD08662-16
GILL, THOMAS J, III R01HD09880-14
GILL, V J Z01CL10200-01
GILLAM, RONALD B K08DC00063-01
GILLES, FLOYD H R01CA49532-03
GILLESPIE, M JANE R29DE09661-01A1
GILLESPIE, MARGARET S07RR05330-30 0020
GILLESPIE, MARK N K04HL02174-04
GILLESPIE, MARK N R01HL38495-04A1
GILLESPIE, MARK N R01HL43831-01A2
GILLESPIE, WILLIAM R S07RR07091-26 0754
GILLETT, PATRICIA A R29NR02087-02
GILLETT, WILL D R01HG00180-02
GILLETTE, EDWARD P01CA29582-10A1 0006
GILLETTE, EDWARD L P01CA29582-10A1 9001
GILLETTE, EDWARD L P01CA29582-10A1
GILLETTE, EDWARD L R01CA29117-10
GILLETTE, EDWARD L U01CA46088-05 0004
GILLETTE, MARTHA U R01NS22155-06
GILLETTE, PAUL C R01HL43842-02
GILLETTE, PETER N N01HB97068-03
GILLETTE, RHANOR R01NS26838-02
GILLEY, DAVID P30AG10161-01 0002
GILLEY, DAVID W R01AG10647-01
GILLIAM, CONRAD P50MH30906-14 9008
GILLIAM, THOMAS R01NS28877-02
GILLIAM, THOMAS C R01HG00462-01
GILLIES, DEE A S07RR05776-11 0393
GILLIES, ROBERT J R01GM43046-03
GILLIES, ROBERT J S07RR07002-26 0871
GILLIES, STEPHEN D N01CM87253-02
GILLIES, STEPHEN D U01CA51946-02 0001
GILLIGAN, ANN R01HD23291-05
GILLIGAN, PETER S07RR05406-30 0908
GILLIN, FRANCES P01DK35108-07 0003
GILLIN, FRANCES D R01AI19863-08
GILLIN, FRANCES D R01AI24285-04
GILLIN, J CHRISTIAN P50AG05131-08 0001
GILLIN, J CHRISTIAN P50MH30914-14
GILLIN, J CHRISTIAN P50MH30914-14 0046
GILLIN, J CHRISTIAN P50MH30914-14 9001
GILLIN, J CHRISTIAN P50MH30914-14 9002
GILLIN, J CHRISTIAN P50MH30914-14 9003
GILLIN, J CHRISTIAN P50MH30914-14 0051
GILLIN, J CHRISTIAN P50MH30914-14 0052
GILLIN, J CHRISTIAN R01MH38738-08
GILLIS, C NORMAN R01HL13315-21
GILLIS, N P41RR01209-12 0028
GILLIS, RICHARD A P01NS28130-02
GILLIS, RICHARD A P01NS28130-02 0005
GILLIS, RICHARD A R01DA05333-05
GILLIS, THOMAS P R22AI26305-03
GILLMORE, MARY L R U01AI31448-01 0009
GILLMORE, MARY R R01MH47241-02
GILLY, WILLIAM F R01NS17510-10
GILMAN-SACHS, ALICE S07RR05366-30 0557
GILMAN, ALFRED G R37GM34497-11
GILMAN, MICHAEL P01CA46370-04 0003
GILMAN, MICHAEL Z R01CA45642-05
GILMAN, SID P01NS19613-07
GILMAN, SID P01NS19613-07 0001
GILMAN, SID P50AG08671-03
GILMAN, SID P50AG08671-03 0001
GILMAN, SID P50NS15655-12 0003
GILMARTIN, GREGORY M S07RR07125-22 0387
GILMORE, G C P50MH41684-07 0079
GILMORE, GROVER C P01AG04391-09 0006
GILMORE, JAMES R R01GM35687-07
GILMORE, JAMES R R01GM43768-02
GILMORE, MICHAEL S R01EY08289-03
GILMORE, SHIRLEY A R01NS04761-28
GILMORE, THOMAS D R29CA47763-04
GILMOUR, DAVID S S07RR07082-26 0285
GILMOUR, ROBERT F JR R01HL40800-03
GILMOUR, SUSAN K R29CA55066-01
GILOVICH, THOMAS D R01MH45531-02
GILSDORF, JANET R R01AI25630-01A3
GILULA, NORTON B R01GM37907-03
GILULA, NORTON B R37GM37904-05
GILULA, NORTON B S03RR03010-09
GIMBLE, JEFFREY M R29CA50898-03
GIMBRONE, MICHAEL A P01HL36028-07 0001
GIMBRONE, MICHAEL A P01HL36028-07 9002
GIMBRONE, MICHAEL A, JR P01HL36028-07
GIMBRONE, MICHAEL A, JR R01HL35013-07
GIMLICH, ROBERT L S07RR07079-26 0300
GINDER, GORDON D R01CA45634-06
GINDER, GORDON D R01DK29902-12
GINGERICH, RONALD P60DK20579-14 9002
GINGRAS, JEANNINE L R03DA07247-01
GINGRICH, ROGER D M01RR00059-30 0666
GINNS, E I Z01MH02340-06
GINNS, E I Z01MH02341-06

GINNS, E I Z01MH02343-06
GINSBERG-FELLNER, FREDDA V R01DK39286-05
GINSBERG, BARRY H P30DK25295-12S1 9006
GINSBERG, BARRY H P30DK25295-12S1 9002
GINSBERG, HAROLD S P01AI26886-04 0003
GINSBERG, HAROLD S P01AI26886-04 9001
GINSBERG, HAROLD S R01AI12052-18
GINSBERG, HENRY N M01RR00645-20 0499
GINSBERG, HENRY N M01RR00645-20 0294
GINSBERG, HENRY N M01RR00645-20 0485
GINSBERG, HENRY N P50HL21006-15 0010
GINSBERG, HENRY N P50HL21006-15 9002
GINSBERG, HENRY N P50HL21006-15 9001
GINSBERG, HENRY N R01HL36000-07
GINSBERG, HENRY N U01HL45460-02
GINSBERG, MARK M01RR00833-17 9001
GINSBERG, MARK H M01RR00833-17 0203
GINSBERG, MARK H P01GM37696-05 0005
GINSBERG, MARK H P01HL16411-18 0004
GINSBERG, MARK H P01HL31950-08 0007
GINSBERG, MARK H R01HL28235-10
GINSBERG, MARK H R37AR27214-11
GINSBERG, MYRON D P01NS05820-26 9002
GINSBERG, MYRON D P01NS05820-26 0024
GINSBERG, MYRON D P01NS05820-26
GINSBERG, MYRON D P01NS05820-26 9001
GINSBERG, MYRON D P50NS30291-01
GINSBERG, MYRON D R01NS22603-07
GINSBURG, A Z01HL00204-24
GINSBURG, DAVID R01HL39137-05
GINSBURG, DAVID R01HL39693-03
GINSBURG, V Z01DK57000-26
GINTZLER, ALAN R R01HD18448-05
GIOIA, PETER J R29LM05268-02
GIOLAS, THOMAS G S07RR07014-26
GIOLAS, THOMAS G S15AI32171-01
GIOLAS, THOMAS G S15MH49509-01
GIORDANO, PEGGY C R01MH46410-01A1
GIORGI, J V P50AI15332-14 9001
GIORGI, JANIA V N01AI72656-09
GIORGI, JANIS P30AI28697-01 9003
GIORGIO, TODD D R29GM41082-01A1
GIOVANELLA, BEPPINO P01CA34936-08 9002
GIOVANELLA, BEPPINO C P01CA50529-01A2 0004
GIOVANNI, MARAINI N01EY92108-03
GIPSON, ILENE K P30EY03790-11
GIPSON, ILENE K R37EY03306-13
GIRI, SHRI N R01HL27354-11
GIROTTI, ALBERT W P01CA49089-03
GIROTTI, ALBERT W P01CA49089-03 9001
GIROTTI, ALBERT W P01CA49089-03 0002
GIRSON, ANDREW D R43HD27771-01
GISOLFI, CARL V R01HL38959-04A1
GISSENDANNER, BEVERLY S03RR03359-09
GITELMAN, HILLEL J R01DK40891-03
GITHENS, SHERWOOD S07RR07169-07 0169
GITLIN, JONATHAN D R01HL41536-03
GITOMER, BERNICE Y S07RR07175-15 0433
GITSCHIER, JANE M R01HL42968-03
GITTES, RUBEN P01DK42717-02 9001
GIUDICE, GEORGE J R29AR40410-02
GIUDICE, GEORGE J S07RR05434-30 0804
GIUDICE, LINDA C R03HD28079-01
GIUDICE, LINDA C R29HD25220-02
GIULIAN, DANA P50NS23327-07 0006
GIULIAN, DANA J R01MH48652-01
GIULIAN, DANA J R01NS23113-06
GIULIAN, DANA J R01NS25637-04
GIVEN, CHARLES W R01AG06584-06
GIVENS, CAROLYN R K11DK02043-01
GIVNER, LAURENCE B R29AI25019-05
GIZZI, MARTIN S K11EY00306-03
GJERSET, GEORGE F R01HL43512-02
GLABE, CHARLES G R01HD21379-07
GLACKEN, MICHAEL W S07RR07103-25 0501
GLADDEN, L BRUCE R01AR40342-03
GLADDEN, L BRUCE S15AR41233-01
GLAESER, ROBERT M P01GM36884-06
GLAESER, ROBERT M P01GM36884-06 9001
GLAESER,ROBERT M P01GM36884-06 0002
GLAGOV, SEYMOUR P50HL15062-20 0020
GLANT, TIBOR T R01AR40310-02
GLANTZ, STANTON A M01RR00079-29 0401
GLANTZ, STANTON A M01RR00079-29 0403
GLANTZ, STANTON A R01HL25869-10
GLANZER, MURRAY R01MH44938-03
GLAROS, ALAN G S03RR03548-01
GLASER, RAINER S07RR07053-26 0163
GLASER, RONALD P01MH44660-04
GLASER, RONALD P01MH44660-04 0001
GLASER, RONALD R01MH40787-07
GLASER, SALLY L R29CA50381-03
GLASGOW, RUSSELL E R01HL45548-01
GLASKY, ALVIN J R43AG09911-01
GLASS, ANDREW N01CN05317-01
GLASS, ANDREW N01CP95648-01
GLASS, ANDREW DR N01CP95675-05
GLASS, ANDREW G U10CA20148-15
GLASS, CHRISTOPHER K R01CA52599-01A1
GLASS, DAVID S07RR05364-30 0527
GLASS, DAVID C S07RR07067-26 0217
GLASS, DAVID N R01AR39979-03
GLASS, JONATHAN R01DK41279-03
GLASS, PENNY R01NS26805-02
GLASS, RICHARD S R01HL15104-18
GLASSER, LEWIS S07RR05675-23 0905
GLASSER, LOREN M01RR00188-27 0246
GLASSER, STANLEY R P30HD07495-19 9009
GLASSER, STANLEY R R01HD22785-04A1
GLASSER, STANLEY R R01HD25189-03
GLASSER, STEPHAN W S07RR05408-30 0928
GLASSMAN, ALEXANDER H R01DA04732-03
GLASSROTH, JEFFREY N01HR76035-05
GLATSTEIN, E Z01CM00650-36
GLATSTEIN, E Z01CM06357-08
GLATT, SANDER P30AG10182-01 9001
GLATT, SANDER P30AG10182-01 0001
GLATTKE, THEODORE J P60DC01409-01 0006
GLATTKE, THEODORE J S07RR07002-26 0862
GLAUDEMANS, C P J Z01DK59701-19
GLAUERT, HOWARD P R01CA43719-04A1
GLAZE, DANIEL M01RR00188-27 0274
GLAZE, DANIEL G P01HD24234-04 0003
GLAZER, GARY M P30CA46592-04 9006
GLAZER, ROBERT I R01CA54231-01
GLAZER, WILLIAM M R01MH39665-07
GLAZNER, LINDA S07RR06014-03 0837
GLAZNER, LINDA S07RR06014-03 0838
GLEASON, FLORENCE K S07RR07052-26 0157
GLEASON, WALLACE A M01RR02558-07 0049
GLEDHILL, BARTON L S07RR05917-08
GLEED, KENT M01RR00059-30 0752
GLEESON, KEVIN K08HL01959-05
GLEICH, G J M01RR00585-20 0399
GLEICH, G J M01RR00585-20 0432
GLEICH, GERALD J R01AI15231-14
GLEICH, GERALD J R01AI31155-01
GLEICH, GERALD J R01HD22924-04
GLEICH, GERALD J R37AI09728-21
GLEITMAN, HENRY S07RR07083-26 0494
GLEITMAN, LILA S07RR07083-26 0493
GLEMBOTSKI, CHRISTOPHER C R01NS25037-05
GLENDE, ERIC A, JR R01ES01821-35
GLENDENNING, KAREN R01DC00197-09
GLENN, MICHAEL G S07RR05432-30 0238
GLENNER, GEORGE G R01AG09411-01
GLENNER, GEORGE G R37AG05683-07
GLENNEY, JOHN P30CA14195-18 0047
GLENNEY, JOHN R R01CA49298-03
GLENNEY, JOHN R R01GM32866-09
GLENNON, RICHARD A R01DA01642-11
GLENNON, RICHARD A R01MH45225-01A2
GLENNON, TERRENCE M01RR00350-25 0476
GLENNY, ROBB W K08HL02625-01
GLEW, ROBERT H R01DK31357-11
GLEZEN, PAUL N01AI15126-00
GLICK, DAVID S07RR05547-23 0074
GLICK, GARY S07RR07050-26 0122
GLICK, IRA D U10MH40007-08
GLICK, JANE P01HL22633-14 0006
GLICK, JOHN H P30CA16520-16
GLICK, JOHN H U10CA15488-19
GLICK, MARY C R01CA37853-07
GLICK, MARY C R01CA52526-01A1
GLICK, ORPHA J S07RR07035-26 0090
GLICK, STANLEY D P01HD20806-05 0002
GLICK, STANLEY D R01AA08599-02
GLICK, STANLEY D R01DA03817-07
GLICKMAN, BARRY W N01ES75197-10
GLICKMAN, ROBERT M P50HL21006-15 0008
GLICKMAN, STEPHEN E R01MH39917-07S1
GLICKSMAN, ALLEN S07RR05611-22 0709
GLICKSMAN, ARVIN S U10CA29511-12
GLICKSON, JERRY D R01CA51935-01A2
GLICKSON, JERRY D R01CA51950-01A1
GLICKSON, JERRY D R01HL35079-06
GLICKSON, JERRY D S07RR05378-30 0996
GLIDEN, DONALD H P01AG07347-04 0001
GLIDER, PEGGY J R18DA05748-03S1
GLIESSMAN, PERRY M P51RR00163-32 9015
GLIMCHER, LAURIE A U01AI31541-01 0005
GLIMCHER, LAURIE H R01AI21569-08
GLIMCHER, LAURIE H R01AI28907-02
GLIMCHER, LAURIE H R01AI32412-06
GLIMCHER, MELVIN J R37AR34081-07
GLINDMEYER, HENRY W P50HL15092-20 9005
GLISH, GARY L R01GM45372-01A1
GLISKY, ELIZABETH L R01AG09195-01A1
GLISSON, BONNIE S S07RR05511-29 0499
GLISSON, CHARLES A R01MH46124-03
GLITZ, DOHN G R01GM32769-06
GLOBAL EXCHANGE, INC N01TI10006-00
GLOBUS, MORDECAI R01NS26784-03
GLOBUS, MORDECAI Y R13NS29348-01
GLOBUS, MORDECAI Y T P50NS30291-01 0001
GLOBUS, MORDECAI Y-T P01NS05820-26 0026
GLODE, L MICHAEL M01RR00051-30 0460
GLODE, MARY P M01RR00069-29 0259
GLODE, MARY P M01RR00069-29 0444
GLODE, MICHAEL M01RR00051-30 0747
GLOER, JAMES B K04CA01571-02
GLOER, JAMES B R01AI27436-02
GLOER, JAMES B R29CA46612-04
GLOMSET, JOHN A P51RR00166-30 0040
GLOMSET, JOHN A. P51RR00166-30 0066
GLORIOSO, JOSEPH C P01NS19608-09 0010
GLORIOSO, JOSEPH C R01AG09470-01
GLORIOSO, JOSEPH C R01AI26937-04
GLORIOSO, JOSEPH C R01GM34534-11
GLOSSER, GUILA S07RR05611-22 0710
GLOVER, CLAIBORNE V R01GM33237-08
GLOVER, JOHN R S07RR07147-19 0649
GLOVER, THOMAN P30HG00209-02 9004
GLOVER, THOMAS W R01CA43222-05
GLOVER, THOMAS W R55DK44130-01
GLOVER, THOMAS W S07RR05383-30 0554
GLOVINSKY, D Z01MH02450-03
GLOVINSKY, D Z01MH02544-02
GLOWACKI, JULIANNE P01CA45548-05 0005
GLOWACKI, JULIANNE S07RR05950-07 0003
GLOWACKI, JULIEANNE R01AR31330-08
GLUCK, STEPHEN P01AR32087-09 0013
GLUCK, STEPHEN P01DK09976-27 0019
GLUCK, STEPHEN L R01DK38848-05
GLUCKSBERG, SAM R01HD25826-03
GLUECKSOHN-WAELSCH, SALOME R01GM27250-36
GLUM, DIETER M01RR00109-28 0364
GLUSKER, JENNY P R01CA10925-42
GLUSKER, JENNY P R01GM44360-02
GLUSKER, JENNY P S07RR05539-29 0549
GLUSKER, ROBERT P30CA06927-29 9010
GLUSMAN, MURRAY M01RR00645-20 0493
GLUSMAN, MURRAY R01HL42532-02
GLUZMAN, YAKOV P01CA13106-20 0013
GLYNN-BARNHART, ANNE S07RR05831-12 0975
GLYNN, ROBERT J R03HL46163-01
GNADT, JAMES W R01EY08217-02
GNEGY, MARGARET E R01DA05066-03
GNEGY, MARGARET E R01MH36044-11
GO, RODNEY C U01MH46373-03
GO, VAY LIANG S07RR05354-30 0398
GOCKE, DAVID J U01AI25914-04S2
GOCKE, DAVID J U01AI25914-04S2 0001
GODBOLD, JAMES P30CA08748-26 9010
GODDARD-FINEGOLD, JAN R01NS28388-03
GODENY, ELMER K R55RR06841-01
GODFREY, DONALD A R01DC00172-11A1
GODFREY, DONALD A S07RR05700-22 0885
GODFREY, EARL W P01HD20743-05 0003
GODFREY, EARL W R01NS27218-03
GODFREY, HENRY P R01CA34141-10
GODFREY, L R P51RR00168-30 0175
GODLESKI, JOHN J R01HL31021-07
GODLEY, PAUL M01RR00046-31 0522
GODLEY, PAUL A R01CA55760-01
GODSCHALK, MICHAEL M01RR00065-29 0323
GODSEY, T S07RR05333-30 0866
GODSON, G NIGEL R22AI21496-08
GODT, ROBERT E P01HL36059-06 0008
GODT, ROBERT E R01AR31636-09
GOEBL, MARK G R29GM45460-01
GOEDERS, NICHOLAS E R01DA04293-04A2
GOEDERS, NICHOLAS E R01DA06013-02
GOEL, VIJAY K R01AR40166-01A2
GOELZ, M F Z01ES22109-03
GOERKE, JON P01HL24075-13 0001
GOETINCK, PAUL F P01HD25938-02
GOETINCK, PAUL F R01HD22016-07
GOETINCK, PAUL F R01HD22050-06
GOETINCK, PAUL F. P01HD25938-02 0003
GOETINCK, PAUL F. P01HD25938-02 9002
GOETINCK, PAUL F. P01HD25938-02 9001
GOETZ, FREDERICK G R01DK33225-07
GOETZ, FREDERICK W, JR R01HD25924-01A2
GOETZL, EDWARD J R01HL31809-09
GOFF, CLINTON R19DA06434-03
GOFF, HAROLD M R01GM28831-11
GOFF, JOHN M01RR00051-30 0751
GOFF, STEPHEN P01AI26886-04 0004
GOFF, STEPHEN P P01CA23767-13 0008
GOFF, STEPHEN P P01GM38125-04 0001
GOFF, STEPHEN P R37CA30488-11
GOFF, STEPHEN P U01AI24845-06 0009
GOFF, STEVE P01CA21111-15 0010
GOFFMAN, T Z01CM06386-04
GOFFMAN, T Z01CM06391-02
GOFFMAN, T Z01CM06392-02
GOGGIN, JUDITH R24MH47167-02 0004
GOGGIN, JUDITH P R24MH47167-02
GOGGIN, JUDITH P S06GM08012-21 0011
GOGGIN, NOREEN L S07RR07195-12 0717
GOGUEN, JON D R01AI22176-06
GOH, EDWARD H S07RR07031-26 0088
GOING, SCOTT B R29AG06810-05
GOITEIN, M P01CA21239-15 0003
GOITEIN, M P01CA21239-15 9001
GOITEIN, MICHAEL R01CA50628-03
GOITEIN, MICHAEL R01CA56931-01
GOKEL, GEORGE W R01GM36262-06
GOKHALE, A M S07RR07024-26 0040
GOLAB, THOMAS J R44RR03801-03
GOLAN, DAVID E P60HL15157-20 0025
GOLAN, DAVID E R01HL32854-08
GOLAND, ROBIN P50HD13063-12 0001
GOLAND, ROBIN S M01RR00645-20 0397
GOLAND, ROBIN S S07RR05395-30 0825

GOLBUS, MITCHELL P01AI29512-02 0002
GOLBUS, MITCHELL S. P01HD24640-03 0001
GOLD, AVRAM R01ES03433-09
GOLD, AVRAM S07RR05736-19 0196
GOLD, BARRY I R01CA29088-08
GOLD, BARRY I R01CA38976-07
GOLD, BRUCE G P01NS19611-08 0002
GOLD, BRUCE G S07RR07238-04 0481
GOLD, DAVID V R01CA43218-05
GOLD, DAVID V S15CA55947-01
GOLD, DEBORAH T S07RR05405-30 0870
GOLD, ELLEN B K04ES00202-02
GOLD, GEOFFREY H R01DC00505-04
GOLD, JEFFREY R01HL44719-01A1
GOLD, LAWRENCE M R01GM28685-11
GOLD, LAWRENCE M R37GM19963-19
GOLD, LESLIE S07RR05399-30 0918
GOLD, LESLIE I R01CA49507-03
GOLD, LOIS S P30ES01896-13 9013
GOLD, LOIS S S07RR05918-08 0699
GOLD, P W Z01MH02583-01
GOLD, P W Z01MH02584-01
GOLD, P W Z01MH02586-01
GOLD, PAUL E R01AG07648-02
GOLD, PAUL E S07RR07094-26 0359
GOLD, WARREN M P01HL24136-13 0006
GOLDBAUM, MICHAEL H R01EY05996-05
GOLDBERG, A JON R01DE09126-02
GOLDBERG, ALAN M S03RR03060-09
GOLDBERG, ALAN M S07RR05445-30
GOLDBERG, ALAN M S15GM47076-01
GOLDBERG, ALFRED L R13GM45969-01
GOLDBERG, ALLAN R P40RR01180-14 0004
GOLDBERG, ANDREW S07RR05379-30 0761
GOLDBERG, ANDREW P M01RR02719-06 0143
GOLDBERG, ANDREW P P01AG04402-09 0002
GOLDBERG, ANDREW P R01AG07660-05
GOLDBERG, ANDREW P. M01RR02719-06 0007
GOLDBERG, BARRY B P01CA52823-02 9001
GOLDBERG, BARRY B R01HD21678-05
GOLDBERG, BURTON D R01AR38174-05
GOLDBERG, DANIEL E R29AI31615-01
GOLDBERG, DANIEL J R01NS25161-04A1
GOLDBERG, EDWARD B R01GM13511-26
GOLDBERG, ERWIN P30HD28048-01 9004
GOLDBERG, ERWIN R01HD05863-20
GOLDBERG, ERWIN R01HD23771-04
GOLDBERG, ERWIN U54HD29099-01 0002
GOLDBERG, ERWIN U54HD29099-01 9004
GOLDBERG, GREGORY I R01AR39472-03
GOLDBERG, HERBERT S S07RR05387-30
GOLDBERG, HERBERT S S15DK44706-01
GOLDBERG, IRA J R01HL45095-01A1
GOLDBERG, IRVING H R01GM12573-27
GOLDBERG, IRVING H R35CA44257-04
GOLDBERG, IRWIN S S06GM02721-07 0003
GOLDBERG, IVAN D R01GM41086-03
GOLDBERG, JAY M R01DC00070-35 0002
GOLDBERG, JAY M R01DC00070-35
GOLDBERG, JAY M R01DC00070-35 0004
GOLDBERG, JEANNE S07RR07179-14 0690
GOLDBERG, JOANNA B R29AI30050-01A1
GOLDBERG, LEWIS R R01MH39077-08
GOLDBERG, LOUIS J R37DE04166-22
GOLDBERG, M E Z01EY00049-13
GOLDBERG, MICHAEL L R01GM31935-08
GOLDBERG, MORTON F P30EY01765-16
GOLDBERG, NELSON D R01GM28818-25
GOLDBERG, ROBERT J R01HL32821-08
GOLDBERG, ROBERT J R01HL35434-05
GOLDBERG, S J P42ES04940-02 0007
GOLDBERG, S R Z01DA00001-06
GOLDBERG, S R Z01DA00003-06
GOLDBERG, STEPHEN J R01EY07924-02
GOLDBERG, T E Z01MH02573-01
GOLDBERG, VICTOR M R01AR30833-10
GOLDBERG, VICTOR M R01AR37726-06
GOLDBERG,IRA J P50HL21006-15 0011
GOLDBERGER, ARY L P01DA06306-01A1 0004
GOLDBERGER, ARY L R01HL42172-03
GOLDBERGER, GERALD N S03RR03044-09
GOLDBERGER, MICHAEL P01NS24707-05 0004
GOLDBERGER, MICHAEL E P01NS24707-05
GOLDBERGER, MICHAEL E R01NS16629-10
GOLDBERGER, MICHAEL E R01NS28081-02
GOLDE, DAVID W R01HL42107-04
GOLDE, DAVID W R37CA30388-11
GOLDEN, DAVID B U01AI31867-01 0015
GOLDEN, GERALD S M01RR00211-27 0326
GOLDEN, JAMES W R01GM36890-06
GOLDEN, ROBERT P30HD01799-27 9012
GOLDEN, ROBERT N P50MH33127-13 0014
GOLDEN, ROBERT N R01MH42145-05
GOLDEN, ROBERT N. M01RR00046-31 0300
GOLDEN, SUSAN S R01GM37040-06
GOLDENBERG, DAVID M R35CA39841-07
GOLDENBERG, DAVID M S07RR05903-08
GOLDENBERG, DAVID P R01GM42494-03
GOLDENBERG, ROBERT L N01HD13116-00
GOLDENBERG, ROBERT L N01HD42811-09
GOLDENBERG, ROBERT L R01HD27289-02
GOLDENGERG, KIM S07RR05794-15

GOLDENHERSH, MARGARET J M01RR00865-18 0318
GOLDENRING, JAMES R R29DK43405-01
GOLDENRING, JAMES R S07RR05358-30 0491
GOLDFARB, DAVID S R29GM40362-04
GOLDFARB, JOHANNA P01AI26482-03S1 0001
GOLDFARB, JOSEPH R01DA04507-03
GOLDFARB, MITCHELL P R01CA48054-04
GOLDFARB, MITCHELL P R01HD27198-02
GOLDFARB, RONALD H R01CA49114-03
GOLDFARB, ROY D S07RR05394-30 0727
GOLDFARB, STANLEY M01RR00040-31 0297
GOLDFARB, STANLEY M01RR00040-31 0385
GOLDFARB, STANLEY M01RR00040-31 0397
GOLDFARB, STANLEY R01CA51549-06
GOLDFELD, ANNE E K11AI00683-05
GOLDFIEN, ROBERT D R29AI30559-01
GOLDFINE, HOWARD R01AI31537-01
GOLDFINE, HOWARD S07RR07083-26 0487
GOLDFINE, IRA D R01DK26667-11
GOLDFINE, IRA D R01DK44834-01
GOLDFINGER, STEPHEN M R18MH48080-02
GOLDFISCHER, SIDNEY P30DK41296-03 9003
GOLDFRIED, MARVIN R R01MH40196-07
GOLDGABER, DMITRY Y R01AG09320-02
GOLDGAR, DAVID P01CA48711-02 9002
GOLDHABER, SAMUEL Z M01RR02635-07 0274
GOLDHABER, SAMUEL Z M01RR02635-07 0256
GOLDHOR, RICHARD S R43DC01225-01
GOLDIN-MEADOW, SUSAN J R01DC00491-04
GOLDIN, ALAN L R01NS26729-03
GOLDIN, L R Z01MH02463-03
GOLDIN, STANLEY M R01GM35423-13
GOLDING, B Z01BH02008-02
GOLDING, B Z01BH02009-02
GOLDING, H Z01BF01006-04
GOLDING, H Z01BF01007-02
GOLDING, H Z01BF01008-02
GOLDING, H Z01BF01013-01
GOLDINGER, JAMES M R01DK18918-15
GOLDMAN-RAKIC, PATRICIA A P50MH44866-04 0006
GOLDMAN-RAKIC, PATRICIA S K05MH00298-12
GOLDMAN-RAKIC, PATRICIA S P50MH44866-04 9000
GOLDMAN-RAKIC, PATRICIA S P50MH44866-04
GOLDMAN-RAKIC, PATRICIA S P50MH44866-04 0000
GOLDMAN-RAKIC, PATRICIA S R37MH38546-12
GOLDMAN, ANNE P01CA21737-14 9001
GOLDMAN, ADRIAN S07RR07058-26 0177
GOLDMAN, ALLEN S07RR05369-30 0598
GOLDMAN, D Z01AA00280-02
GOLDMAN, D Z01AA00282-02
GOLDMAN, D Z01AA00283-02
GOLDMAN, DANIEL J R29NS25153-05
GOLDMAN, DANIEL W R01AI24283-05
GOLDMAN, DAVID P30CA16059-15 9020
GOLDMAN, DAVID P30CA16059-15 9021
GOLDMAN, DAVID P30CA16059-15 9011
GOLDMAN, DAVID P30CA16059-15 9015
GOLDMAN, EMANUEL R01GM27711-11
GOLDMAN, EMANUEL S07RR05393-30 0892
GOLDMAN, FREDERICK D K08AI01039-01
GOLDMAN, HARVEY P01CA44704-04A1 9004
GOLDMAN, HOWARD H P50MH49454-01
GOLDMAN, HOWARD H P50MH49454-01 0001
GOLDMAN, HOWARD H P50MH49454-01 0002
GOLDMAN, HOWARD H P50MH49454-01 0003
GOLDMAN, I DAVID P30CA16059-15
GOLDMAN, ISRAEL D R35CA39807-07
GOLDMAN, JAMES E P01AG07232-03 9002
GOLDMAN, JAMES E R01EY09331-01
GOLDMAN, JAMES E R01NS17125-10
GOLDMAN, JAMES M P50AG08702-03 9002
GOLDMAN, JEFFREY S07RR05371-30 0636
GOLDMAN, LEE R01HS06573-01
GOLDMAN, MARK S R01AA08333-01A1
GOLDMAN, MARLENE B R29HD23718-04
GOLDMAN, MORRIS B M01RR00055-30 0565
GOLDMAN, MORRIS B M01RR00055-30 0568
GOLDMAN, MORRIS B M01RR00055-30 0564
GOLDMAN, MORRIS B R29MH43618-03
GOLDMAN, N Z01BB02006-09
GOLDMAN, N Z01BB02007-04
GOLDMAN, N Z01BB02009-02
GOLDMAN, N Z01BB02010-02
GOLDMAN, ROBERT D R01CA31760-10
GOLDMAN, ROBERT D R01GM36806-06
GOLDMAN, STEVEN P01HL20984-15 0007
GOLDMAN, STEVEN P01HL20984-15 9003
GOLDMAN, STEVEN A K08NS01316-04
GOLDMAN, WILLIAM E R01AI22243-05
GOLDMAN, WILLIAM F R01HL43091-01A2
GOLDMAN, YALE P01HL15835-19 0032
GOLDMAN, YALE E P01HL15835-19
GOLDMAN, YALE E R01AR26846-12
GOLDMAN,D Z01AA00281-02
GOLDRICK, BARBARA A S07RR06012-03 0304
GOLDRING, MARY P01AR03564-32 0002
GOLDRING, STEVEN P01AR03564-32 0022
GOLDRING, STEVEN R R01AR39515-04
GOLDSCHEIDER, FRANCES K P30HD28251-01
GOLDSCHEIDER, FRANCIS K P50HD12639-12 0015
GOLDSCHMIDT, MICHAEL S07RR05464-29 0372
GOLDSCHMIDT, MILLICE S07RR05970-06 0779

GOLDSCHNEINER, IRVIN S07RR05678-23 0155
GOLDSMITH, LOWELL A R01AR30965-11
GOLDSMITH, MARY HELE S07RR07015-26 0601
GOLDSMITH, PAUL C P30HD11979-13 9003
GOLDSMITH, PAUL C R01HD10907-13A2
GOLDSMITH, TIMOTHY H R01EY00222-31
GOLDSON, ALFRED L U10CA52652-02
GOLDSTEIN, ALLEN P41RR01243-10 0004
GOLDSTEIN, BARRY J R01DK43396-01A1
GOLDSTEIN, BARRY M R29CA45145-04
GOLDSTEIN, BERNARD S07RR07120-14
GOLDSTEIN, BERNARD S15AR41243-01
GOLDSTEIN, BERNARD D P30ES05022-04
GOLDSTEIN, BERNARD D R13ES03820-05
GOLDSTEIN, BRAHAM M01RR00044-31 0380
GOLDSTEIN, BRAHM S07RR05403-30 0808
GOLDSTEIN, BYRON B R01GM35556-07
GOLDSTEIN, D S Z01NS02839-01
GOLDSTEIN, DAVID E U01DK30590-09
GOLDSTEIN, ELLIOT R01AI22745-07
GOLDSTEIN, ELLIOTT S S07RR07112-24 0427
GOLDSTEIN, GARY S03RR03353-08
GOLDSTEIN, GARY W R01ES02380-13
GOLDSTEIN, GARY W S07RR05808-13
GOLDSTEIN, GARY W S15HD28757-01
GOLDSTEIN, IRA M P01HL25816-11 0018
GOLDSTEIN, IRA M P50HL19155-15 0013
GOLDSTEIN, IRA M P50HL19155-15 9001
GOLDSTEIN, IRA M P60AR20684-14
GOLDSTEIN, IRWIN J R01CA20424-15
GOLDSTEIN, IRWIN J R01GM29470-26
GOLDSTEIN, J A Z01ES21024-10
GOLDSTEIN, JOSEPH L P01HL20948-15
GOLDSTEIN, JOSEPH L P01HL20948-15 0011
GOLDSTEIN, JOSEPH L P01HL20948-15 9001
GOLDSTEIN, JULIUS L R01DC00737-02
GOLDSTEIN, LARRY P41LM05205-08 0001
GOLDSTEIN, LARRY B K08NS01162-05
GOLDSTEIN, LAWRENCE S P01GM29301-11 0009
GOLDSTEIN, LAWRENCE S R01GM35252-07
GOLDSTEIN, LEON P30ES03828-06 0008
GOLDSTEIN, M P41RR02250-06 0009
GOLDSTEIN, MARGARET A R55HL17376-16
GOLDSTEIN, MARION Z R01MH45048-03
GOLDSTEIN, MELVYN C S07RR07113-24 0570
GOLDSTEIN, MENEK P01MH43230-04
GOLDSTEIN, MENEK P50MH35976-10 9004
GOLDSTEIN, MICHAEL G P01CA50087-03 0003
GOLDSTEIN, MICHAEL G R01DA05623-03
GOLDSTEIN, MICHAEL J P50MH30911-14 0036
GOLDSTEIN, MICHAEL J P50MH30911-14 0005
GOLDSTEIN, MICHAEL J P50MH30911-14 9002
GOLDSTEIN, MICHAEL J P50MH30911-14 0034
GOLDSTEIN, MICHAEL J R37MH42556-03
GOLDSTEIN, PAUL J R01DA04017-05S1
GOLDSTEIN, RICHARD R01GM40419-01A2
GOLDSTEIN, RICHARD S07RR05569-27 0120
GOLDSTEIN, RONALD H. P01HL19717-15 0047
GOLDSTEIN, S Z01RR10260-05
GOLDSTEIN, SAMUEL R01AG08708-02
GOLDSTEIN, SIDNEY N01HC65052-09
GOLDSTEIN, SIDNEY N01HV18121-02
GOLDSTEIN, SOLOMON S07RR07126-16
GOLDSTEIN, SOLOMON S15AG10235-01
GOLDSTEIN, STEVEN P60AR20557-13 9005
GOLDSTEIN, STEVEN A R01AR31793-06A3
GOLDSTEIN, STEVEN A R01AR34399-06
GOLDSTEIN, STEVEN A R01AR41349-01
GOLDTHWAIT, DAVID A K06GM21444-28
GOLDWASSER, EUGENE P01HL30121-08
GOLDWASSER, EUGENE P01HL30121-08 0004
GOLDWASSER, EUGENE R01DK40250-17
GOLDWASSER, EUGENE R37HL21676-15
GOLDWHITE, HAROLD S06GM08101-20 0039
GOLDYNE, MARK P50DE08973-02 9000
GOLDYNE, MARK E. P01AR39448-04 0004
GOLENBOCK, DOUGLAS T K11AI00840-05
GOLENBOCK, DOUGLAS T S07RR05569-27 0121
GOLIGORSKY, MICHAEL S07RR05736-19 0164
GOLIGORSKY, MICHAEL S R29DK41573-03
GOLIN, JOHN E S15DK44662-01
GOLISZEK, ANDREW G S06GM08019-21 0006
GOLLAHON, KATHERINE S07RR05939-07 0724
GOLLAMUDI, RAMACHANDER R01HL22236-12
GOLLAN, JOHN L R01DK36887-07
GOLLIN, SUSANNE M S07RR05451-30 0356
GOLOMB, E Z01HL03591-01
GOLOMB, E Z01HL03592-01
GOLOMB, FREDERICK M01RR00096-30A1 0272
GOLOMB, FREDERICK M01RR00096-30A1 0320
GOLOMB, FREDERICK M01RR00096-30A1 0324
GOLOMB, FREDERICK M01RR00096-30A1 0325
GOLOS, THADDEUS P51RR00167-31 0049
GOLOS, THADDEUS G R01AI32339-01
GOLOS, THADDEUS G R29HD26458-02
GOLPER, THOMAS A S07RR05375-30 0754
GOLTZMAN, DAVID R01CA37126-07
GOLUB, ELLIS P50DE08239-04 9003
GOLUB, ELLIS E R01DE06533-09
GOLUB, HOWARD L N01HD62930-07
GOLUB, LORNE M R37DE03987-17
GOLUB, MARI S P51RR00169-30 0093

GOLUB, MARI S P51RR00169-30 0094
GOLUB, MARI S R01ES04190-05
GOLUB, MARI S R01GM32920-06A1
GOLUB, SIDNEY H P01CA12582-19 0016
GOLUB, SIDNEY H R01CA34442-08
GOLUBIC, STJEPKO S07RR07043-26 0125
GOMBERG, E P50AA07378-04 0002
GOMER, CHARLES J R37CA31230-09
GOMER, RICHARD H R01GM42604-03
GOMEZ-SANCHEZ, CELSO E R01HL27737-09A2
GOMEZ-SANCHEZ, CELSO E R01HL27255-11
GOMEZ, CHRISTOPHER M S07RR05385-30 0804
GOMEZ, MANUEL S03RR03358-07
GOMEZ, MARK A S07RR05357-30 0457
GOMEZ, R ARIEL P50DK44756-01 0003
GOMEZ, ROBERTO A K04HL02307-03
GOMEZ, ROBERTO A R01HL41899-03
GONATAS, NICHOLAS K R01NS05572-27
GONATAS, NICHOLAS K R01NS26882-03
GONCHAROFF, PAUL S07RR05331-28 0738
GONDA, D S07RR07015-26 0608
GONDA, DAVID K R01GM45314-01A1
GONDA, DAVID KEITH S07RR05358-30 0485
GONIAS, STEVEN L K04HL02272-03
GONIAS, STEVEN L R01HL45786-02
GONNELLA, JOSEPH S S07RR05414-30
GONNELLA, JOSEPH S S15HL47787-01
GONYEA, WILLIAM J R01AR40056-03
GONZALES-FERNANDEZ, J M Z01DK13002-19
GONZALES, L S07RR05411-30 0965
GONZALES, RUEBEN A R01AA08484-01A1
GONZALES, RUEBEN A S07RR07091-26 0755
GONZALEZ-LIMA, FRANCISCO R01MH43353-05
GONZALEZ-REDONDO, J S07RR05365-30 0081
GONZALEZ-SCARANO, F. P01NS27405-03 0001
GONZALEZ-SCARANO, FRANCISCO R29AI24888-05
GONZALEZ, ALFONSO S07RR05428-30 0172
GONZALEZ, F Z01CP05561-04
GONZALEZ, F Z01CP05562-04
GONZALEZ, F J Z01CP05521-05
GONZALEZ, F J Z01CP05651-02
GONZALEZ, FERNANDO R24MH47188-02 0003
GONZALEZ, FRANK M01RR00080-29 0402
GONZALEZ, R GILBERTO R01AG10679-01
GOOD, BYRON J S07RR05381-30 0788
GOOD, DAVID W K04DK01745-05
GOOD, DAVID W R01DK38217-05
GOOD, MARY-JO S07RR05381-30 0789
GOOD, ROBERT A R01AG05633-07A1
GOOD, ROBERT A R37AG05628-07
GOODALL, ELEANOR R43AR40958-01
GOODCHILD, JOHN P30CA12708-21 9005
GOODCHILD, JOHN R01AI29819-02
GOODELL, ESTELLE M R25RR07582-01
GOODENOUGH, DANIEL A R01EY02430-14
GOODENOUGH, DANIEL A R01GM28932-11
GOODENOUGH, DANIEL A R37GM18974-20
GOODENOUGH, URSULA W R01GM26150-12
GOODENOW, MAUREEN M R01AI28210-02
GOODENOW, ROBERT A R01AI27853-03
GOODENOW, ROBERT A R01CA37099-08
GOODFRIEND, THEODORE P01HL42242-04 0004
GOODGAL, SOL H S07RR05415-30 0003
GOODGLASS, HAROLD P01DC00081-26
GOODGLASS, HAROLD P01DC00081-26 0001
GOODIN, DAVID B R29GM41049-03
GOODING, LINDA R R01CA48219-04
GOODING, LINDA R U01AI26035-03S1
GOODKIN, KARL R01MH48628-01
GOODMAN MARC T P01CA33619-09 0008
GOODMAN, ALAN H R15DE09863-01
GOODMAN, ALLEN C R01AA07694-03
GOODMAN, ARNOLD L S07RR05378-30 0997
GOODMAN, BARBARA E R29HL38310-04
GOODMAN, COREY S R01NS18366-10
GOODMAN, COREY S R37HD21294-07
GOODMAN, DE WITT S P50HL21006-15
GOODMAN, DE WITT S P50HL21006-15 0003
GOODMAN, DE WITT S R37DK05968-31
GOODMAN, DE WITT S R37DK05968-31 0001
GOODMAN, DE WITT S R37DK05968-31 0003
GOODMAN, GARY E P01CA34847-09 0002
GOODMAN, J CLAY P01NS27616-02S1 9002
GOODMAN, JAMES A G12RR03034-06
GOODMAN, JAY I R01ES05299-02
GOODMAN, JESSE L R01AR40448-02
GOODMAN, JESSE L R29AI27440-03
GOODMAN, JOEL S03RR03349-09
GOODMAN, JOEL M R01GM31859-07A2
GOODMAN, JOEL W R01AI05664-28
GOODMAN, MAJOR M P01GM45344-01 0005
GOODMAN, MARC T R01CA55700-01
GOODMAN, MICHAEL G R01AI15284-13
GOODMAN, MORRIS R01HL33940-07
GOODMAN, MURRAY R01DA05539-02
GOODMAN, MURRAY R01DA06254-03
GOODMAN, MURRAY R01DE05476-10
GOODMAN, MURRAY R01DK15410-20
GOODMAN, MURRAY R01GM18694-16
GOODMAN, MYRON F R01GM21422-15
GOODMAN, MYRON F R01GM42554-03
GOODMAN, R J S07RR05576-27 0609
GOODMAN, RICHARD H P30DK34928-07 9002
GOODMAN, RICHARD H R01CA37370-09
GOODMAN, RICHARD H S07RR07238-04
GOODMAN, RICHARD H S15DK44707-01
GOODMAN, ROBERT L R01HD17864-07A1
GOODMAN, SHERRYL H M01RR00039-31 0399
GOODMAN, SHERRYL H S07RR07023-26 0970
GOODMAN, STEPHEN M01RR00069-29 0485
GOODMAN, STEPHEN P01HD08315-16 0024
GOODMAN, STEPHEN P30HD04024-23 9002
GOODMAN, STEPHEN I P01HD08315-16
GOODMAN, STEPHEN I P30HD04024-23
GOODMAN, STEPHEN I. P01HD08315-16 0020
GOODMAN, STEVEN R R01NS26536-05
GOODMAN, WALTER G S07RR07098-26 0335
GOODNER, CHARLES J R55DK30992-09A1
GOODNER, CHARLES J. P51RR00166-30 0088
GOODNER, CJ P30DK17047-15 0046
GOODNOW, CHRISTOPHER P01AI19512-09 0009
GOODRICH, RAYMOND P R43HL46507-01
GOODRIDGE, ALAN G R01DK21594-15
GOODRIDGE, ALAN G R03AA08738-01A1
GOODSITT, MITCHELL M S07RR05432-30 0245
GOODWIN, CAROL E. M01RR00039-31 0421
GOODWIN, CLEON W P50GM26145-13
GOODWIN, CLEON W P50GM26145-13 0006
GOODWIN, DAVID A R01CA28343-12
GOODWIN, DONALD W R01AA08176-03
GOODWIN, JAMES A U10EY07689-04
GOODWIN, SHEILA D M01RR00030-30 0503
GOODWIN, W JARRAD P01CA42101-06 0010
GOODWIN, WENDALL J U10CA45560-05
GOODWIN, WILLIAM J S15AI32182-01
GOODWIN, WILLIAM J. N01HB77029-07
GOOGINS, BRADLEY R01AA07624-02
GOORHA, RAKESH M R01CA43237-04
GOORHA, RAKESH M R01GM23638-14
GOOSBY, ERIC M01RR00083-29 0236
GOOTMAN, PHYLLIS M R01HD28931-01
GOPALAKRISHNA, RAYUDU R29CA47142-05
GOPALAN, ARAVAMUDAN S S06GM08136-18 0022
GOPE, MOHAN L S07RR05390-30 0673
GOPE, RAJALAKSHMI S07RR05390-30 0674
GORBACH, SHERWOOD L M01RR00054-30 0433
GORBACH, SHERWOOD L M01RR00054-30 0403
GORBACH, SHERWOOD L R25CA49612-02
GORBACH, SHERWOOD L R37CA45128-06
GORDEN, P Z01DK47005-19
GORDEN, P Z01DK47019-14
GORDON-LICKEY, BARBARA R01EY04050-10
GORDON-SALANT, S Z01AG00628-02
GORDON-SALANT, SANDRA M R01AG09191-01
GORDON, ADRIENNE S P01AA08353-03 0001
GORDON, ADRIENNE S R01AA07827-04
GORDON, ADRIENNE S R01NS25537-03
GORDON, ALBERT M P01HL31962-08 0004
GORDON, ALBERT M P01HL31962-08 0005
GORDON, ALBERT M P01HL31962-08 9004
GORDON, ALBERT M R01NS08384-23
GORDON, ANDREW S R15GM44101-01A1
GORDON, BARRY R01NS26553-03
GORDON, CHRISTOPHER N01CO74115-03
GORDON, DAVID P50HL42270-02 0003
GORDON, DAVID P50HL42270-02 9001
GORDON, DAVID R01HL42119-03
GORDON, DAVID S M01RR00039-31 0432
GORDON, DAVID S M01RR00039-31 0380
GORDON, DOROTHY L R01NR02091-03
GORDON, ELLEN R P30DK34989-08 9002
GORDON, ELLEN R P30DK34989-08 0012
GORDON, FRANK J R01HL36907-05
GORDON, GARY P01CA44530-05 0003
GORDON, JEFFREY I P01HL18577-16 0016
GORDON, JEFFREY I R01DK30292-10
GORDON, JEFFREY I R01DK37960-05
GORDON, JEFFREY I U01AI27179-04
GORDON, JEFFREY I U01AI30188-02
GORDON, JON W P01AI24460-04 0003
GORDON, JON W R01CA42103-04A1
GORDON, JON W R01HD20484-06
GORDON, JON W R01HD25136-02
GORDON, JON W R13RR06913-01
GORDON, LEO I R01CA55518-01
GORDON, MARION K R01EY09056-01
GORDON, NEIL F R29AR39715-03
GORDON, SHELDON S07RR07131-22 0126
GORDON, SHELDON S07RR07131-22 0127
GORDON, TERRY R01ES04947-03
GORDON, THOMAS P P51RR00165-31 0069
GORDON, THOMAS P P51RR00165-31 0209
GORDON, THOMAS R S07RR05358-30 0474
GORDON, Y JEROLD R01EY05232-07
GORDON, Y JEROLD R01EY08227-01A1
GORE, DENNIS M01RR00065-29 0371
GORE, JOHN C R01CA40675-05
GORE, JOHN C S10RR06264-01
GORE, ROBERT W R37HL13437-22
GORE, SUSAN L R01MH42909-05
GORECKI, MARIAN N01AI82696-05
GORELICK, D Z01DA00147-01
GORELICK, D A Z01DA00139-01
GORELICK, D A Z01DA00140-01
GORELICK, FRED P30DK34989-08 0015
GORELICK, PHILIP B R01AG10102-01
GOREN, MARSHALL P R01CA49529-03
GORENSTEIN, DAVID G P30AI27713-04 9003
GORENSTEIN, DAVID G R01AI27744-03
GORES, GREGORY J R29DK41876-03
GORESKY, C A P41RR01243-10 0015
GOREVIC, PETER P50AI16337-13 0005
GOREVIC, PETER D S07RR05736-19 0151
GORIN, M B Z01EY00246-04
GORIN, MICHAEL B R01EY09192-01
GORKIN, LARRY R43HL46071-01
GORLEN, K E Z01CT00139-08
GORLIN, JED B K11HL02158-04
GORMAN, DENNIS P50MH43450-04 0017
GORMAN, JACK P01MH37592-08 0001
GORMAN, JACK P01MH37592-08 0002
GORMAN, JACK P01MH37592-08 0003
GORMAN, JACK P50MH30906-14 9005
GORMAN, JACK M K02MH00416-10
GORMAN, JACK M P50MH43520-04 0005
GORMAN, JACK M R01MH41778-04A1
GORMAN, JACK M R01MH43977-02
GORMAN, JACK M R01MH45963-02
GORMAN, MARK S07RR05656-24 0840
GORMAN, MARK S07RR05772-17 0346
GORMLEY, GLENN J M01RR00865-18 0291
GORMUS, BOBBY J R01RR06159-02
GORMUS, BOBBY J R22AI19302-06
GORMUS, ROBERT J P51RR00164-30 0006
GORMUS, ROBERT J P51RR00164-30 0015
GORMUS, ROBERT J P51RR00164-30 0016
GORMUS, ROBERT J P51RR00164-30 0017
GOROSPE, WILLIAM C R29HD25262-03
GOROVSKY, MARTIN A R01GM26973-13
GORRAY, KENNETH C R29DK38917-03
GORRAY, KENNETH C S07RR05496-29 0903
GORRY, ANTHONY G N01LM13516-00
GORRY, G ANTHONY G08LM04905-04
GORSKI, JACK P01HL44612-02 0005
GORSKI, JACK P01HL44612-02 9003
GORSKI, JACK R01CA18110-17
GORSKI, JACK R37HD08192-19
GORSKI, JEFFREY S07RR07257-02 0711
GORSKI, JEFFREY P R15AR40923-01
GORSKI, JEROME L R01NS30771-04
GORSKI, JEROME L S07RR05383-30 0555
GORSKI, ROGER S07RR05354-30 0388
GORSKI, ROGER A P01HD25831-01A1 0005
GORSKI, ROGER A R01HD01182-29
GORSKI, ROGER A S07RR05354-30 0384
GORTMAKER, STEVEN L P01AI26487-03S1 0002
GORZIGLIA, M Z01AI00582-02
GORZIGLIA, M Z01AI00601-01
GORZIGLIA, M Z01AI00602-01
GORZIGLIA, M Z01AI00603-01
GOSHGARIAN, HARRY G R01NS14705-11
GOSHORN, JEANNE N01LM83517-03
GOSLOW, GEORGE E S07RR05664-24 0862
GOSNELL, BLAKE A M01RR00042-31 0465
GOSNELL, BLAKE A R01DA05471-04
GOSPE, SIDNEY M JR R03DA06665-02
GOSPODAROWICZ, DENIS J R01EY02186-14
GOSPODAROWICZ, DENIS J R01HL20197-15
GOSS, DIXIE S06GM08176-12 0024
GOSS, DIXIE S07RR07109-23 0505
GOTAY, CAROLYN C N01CM17507-01
GOTH-GOLDSTEIN, REGI S07RR05918-08 0704
GOTLIN, RONALD W M01RR00069-29 0296
GOTLIN, RONALD W M01RR00069-29 0417
GOTSCHLICH, EMIL C R01AI10615-21
GOTSCHLICH, EMIL C R37AI26558-04
GOTSCHLICH, EMIL C S07RR07065-26 0059
GOTSHALL, ROBERT W S07RR05794-15 0900
GOTTESFELD, JOEL M R01GM26453-12A1
GOTTESFELD, JOEL M S07RR05882-09 0606
GOTTESFELD, ZEHAVA S07RR05745-19 0245
GOTTESMAN, M Z01CB05598-02
GOTTESMAN, M M Z01CB08705-15
GOTTESMAN, M M Z01CB08715-13
GOTTESMAN, M M Z01CB08754-08
GOTTESMAN, MAX R01GM37219-06
GOTTESMAN, MAX E P50DK41146-04 0004
GOTTESMAN, MAXWELL E P01CA23767-13 0009
GOTTESMAN, S Z01CB08714-14
GOTTESMAN, SUSAN R P01AG04860-08 0003
GOTTESMAN, SUSAN R S S07RR05399-30 0929
GOTTHEIL, EDWARD R18DA06166-03
GOTTLIEB, DAVID I P50AG05681-08 0017
GOTTLIEB, DAVID I R01NS12867-16
GOTTLIEB, GARY P30AG10124-01 9001
GOTTLIEB, GERALD L R01AR33189-08
GOTTLIEB, GERALD L R01NS28176-01A2
GOTTLIEB, GILBERT R01MH44813-03
GOTTLIEB, LAWRENCE J P30DK26678-12 0006
GOTTLIEB, NELL H K07CA01286-05
GOTTLIEB, PAUL D R01CA30147-12
GOTTLIEB, SIDNEY O P01AG04402-09 0005
GOTTLIEB, SIDNEY O P50HL17655-17 9013
GOTTLIEB, SIDNEY O P50HL17655-17 9012
GOTTLIEB, SIDNEY O P50HL17655-17 0035
GOTTMAN, JOHN M K05MH00257-13

GOTTMAN, JOHN M R01MH42722-05
GOTTMAN, JOHN M R37MH42484-04
GOTTO, ANTONIO M01RR00350-25 0474
GOTTO, ANTONIO M01RR00350-25 0481
GOTTO, ANTONIO M M01RR00350-25 0361
GOTTO, ANTONIO M, JR P30DK27685-10
GOTTO, ANTONIO M, JR P60HL27341-10
GOTTSCHALL, JEROME L K07HL01631-05
GOTTSCHLING, DANIEL E R01GM43893-01A1
GOULD, K LANCE R01HL26862-10
GOULD, K LANCE R01HL42453-03
GOULD, KENNETH P51RR00165-31 0052
GOULD, KENNETH G R01HD26076-03
GOULD, KENNETH G R01RR03587-06
GOULD, KENNETH G R01RR05994-02
GOULD, MADELYN P50MH43878-03 0019
GOULD, MADELYN P50MH43878-03 0006
GOULD, MADELYN P50MH43878-03 0007
GOULD, MADELYN S P50MH43878-03 0043
GOULD, MADELYN S R01MH47559-01
GOULD, MICHAEL N P01CA52686-02 0001
GOULD, MICHAEL N R01CA28954-10
GOULD, MICHAEL N R01CA30295-11
GOULD, MICHAEL N R01CA38128-06
GOULD, MICHAEL N R01CA44387-05
GOULD, MICHAEL N R01CA52475-01
GOULD, ROBERT M R01NS13980-14
GOULD, STEVEN J R01GM31715-09
GOULD, STEVEN J R01GM32110-09
GOULD, STEVEN J S07RR07079-26 0284
GOULETTE, ROBERT P P01HL28001-10 9001
GOULIAN, MEHRAN R01CA11705-21A1
GOURAS, PETER R01EY03854-09S2
GOURAS, PETER R01EY04138-08
GOURDIN, THEODORE S07RR05569-27 0122
GOURSE, RICHARD L K04AI00935-04
GOURSE, RICHARD L R01GM37048-05
GOUSTIN, ANTON S R01HD27444-01
GOUZOULES, HAROLD T P51RR00165-31 0174
GOVINDAN, MELEDATH S03RR03536-02
GOVINDAN, MELEDATH S06GM08266-04 0006
GOVINDAN, MELEDATH S06GM08266-04
GOWATY, PATRICIA A K02MH00706-02
GOWER, WILLIAM S07RR05749-19 0277
GOWN, ALLEN M R01CA36250-08
GOY, MICHAEL F P01NS25915-04A1 9002
GOY, MICHAEL F P01NS25915-04A1 0004
GOY, MICHAEL F R01GM45568-01A1
GOY, MICHAEL F S07RR05406-30 0882
GOY, ROBERT P51RR00167-31 0034
GOYAL, HARI O S06GM08091-20 0028
GOYAL, RAJ K R37DK31092-11
GOYAN, JERE E S07RR05453-29
GOYAN, JERE E S07RR05453-29 0504
GOYCOOLEA, MARCOS P50DC00133-13 0017
GOYERT, SANNA M R01AI23859-07
GOZZO, J S07RR05830-12 0969
GOZZO, JAMES J R01AI29650-02
GOZZO, JAMES J R01DK33466-11
GOZZO, JAMES J S07RR05830-12
GOZZO, JAMES J S15CA55936-01
GRAAE, FLEMING S07RR05650-25 0098
GRABBE, LINDA L R03HS06925-01
GRABER, GLENN C R13HG00580-01
GRABER, MARTHA L K11DK01945-02
GRABOWSKI, ERIC F R01HL33095-06
GRABOWSKI, GEORGE A M01RR00071-28A1 0217
GRABOWSKI, GREGORY A M01RR00071-28A1 0236
GRABOWSKI, GREGORY A R01DK36729-06
GRABOWSKI, JOHN R18DA06143-03
GRABOWSKI, PAULA J R01GM39695-05
GRABOWY, RICHARD S R43CA52345-01A2
GRABOWY, RICHARD S R44CA44249-03
GRABOWY, RICHARD S R44HL38564-03
GRACCO, CAROL K08DC00044-01A1
GRACCO, VINCENT L P01DC00121-29A1 0004
GRACCO, VINCENT L R01DC00594-03
GRACCO, VINCENT L S15HD28758-01
GRACE, ANTHONY A P01NS19608-09 0007
GRACE, ANTHONY A P50MH45156-02 0003
GRACE, ANTHONY A R01MH42217-04A1
GRACE, JEANNE T S07RR05952-06 0738
GRACE, MARCELLUS G12RR05075-04
GRACEFFA, PHILIP J R01AR30917-08
GRACELY, R H Z01DE00133-17
GRACY, ROBERT W R37AG01274-13
GRAD, RONI S07RR05675-23 0906
GRADY, C Z01AG00131-08
GRADY, GEORGE F N01HD82917-07
GRADY, H SHELTON S07RR05520-28 0828
GRADY, JOHN K R43HL46578-01
GRADY, KATHLEEN E R01CA36798-08
GRADY, MICHAEL S K08NS01371-03
GRAEFF, RON S07RR05372-30 0700
GRAF, WERNER M R01DC00239-08
GRAF, WERNER M R01EY04613-09
GRAFE, MARJORIE R K08NS01442-02
GRAFF-RADFORD, STEVE S07RR05304-30 0234
GRAFFEO, ANTHONY N01ES95277-04
GRAFMAN, J Z01NS02792-03
GRAFMAN, J Z01NS02793-03
GRAFSTEIN, BERNICE R01NS09015-21
GRAHAM, BARNEY S M01RR00095-31 0336
GRAHAM, BARNEY S. M01RR00095-31 0297
GRAHAM, DAN S07RR07210-09 0674
GRAHAM, DAVID M01RR00350-25 0419
GRAHAM, DAVID Y M01RR00350-25 0420
GRAHAM, DAVID Y M01RR00350-25 0322
GRAHAM, DAVID Y M01RR00350-25 0414
GRAHAM, DAVID Y M01RR00350-25 0429
GRAHAM, DAVID Y M01RR00350-25 0480
GRAHAM, DAVID Y M01RR00350-25 0462
GRAHAM, DAVID Y M01RR00350-25 0447
GRAHAM, DAVID Y R01DK39919-05
GRAHAM, DOYLE G R37ES02611-11
GRAHAM, FRANCES K R01MH42465-06
GRAHAM, GLENN G R03HS06905-01
GRAHAM, JOE S S06GM08107-18 0007
GRAHAM, JOHN B P01HL06350-30 0015
GRAHAM, KATHERINE S07RR05758-18 0246
GRAHAM, LINDA L S07RR07032-26 0033
GRAHAM, LINDA M R01HL41178-03
GRAHAM, MARTIN F R01DK34151-08
GRAHAM, MARY B K11AI01086-01
GRAHAM, MICHAEL M P01CA42045-06 9004
GRAHAM, MICHAEL M P01CA42045-06 0004
GRAHAM, MICHAEL M P01HL24163-13 9005
GRAHAM, NEIL M H M01RR00722-19 0206
GRAHAM, NORMA V R01EY08459-02
GRAHAM, ROBERT M P01HL38070-05 0003
GRAHAM, ROBERT M P50HL33713-06 0013
GRAHAM, ROBERT M P50HL33713-06
GRAHAME, D A Z01HL00261-06
GRAINGER, ROBERT M R01EY06675-06
GRALLA, JAY D R01GM35754-06
GRALNICK, H R Z01CL10012-23
GRALNICK, H R Z01CL10013-24
GRALNICK, H R Z01CL10105-08
GRALNICK, H R Z01CL10117-08
GRAMMAS, PAULA R01NS30457-01
GRANATH, WILLARD O, JR R01AI23700-04A1
GRANATH, WILLARD O, JR S10RR06356-01
GRAND, RICHARD J M01RR00054-30 0413
GRAND, RICHARD J P30DK34928-07 9004
GRAND, RICHARD J R01DK32658-08
GRANDE, DANIEL R29AR40959-02
GRANDGENETT, DUANE P R01AI31334-01
GRANDGENETT, DUANE P R01CA16312-18
GRANELLI-PIPERNO, ANGELA P01AI24775-05 000
GRANGER, DANIEL N P01DK43785-01 0004
GRANGER, DANIEL N P01DK43785-01
GRANGER, DANIEL N R01DK33594-07
GRANGER, DANIEL N R01HL26441-11A1
GRANGER, HARRIS J R37HL21498-15
GRANGER, JOEY P R01HL38499-05
GRANGER, NOELLE A R01NS18114-11
GRANNEMAN, JAMES R01DK37006-07
GRANNER, DARYL K P01DK42502-02 0002
GRANNER, DARYL K R37DK35107-08
GRANOFF, DAN M R01AI17962-10
GRANOT, ESTHER P01AI26497-03 0002
GRANT MARIA M01RR00082-29 0450
GRANT, ANDREW J M01RR00073-29 0309
GRANT, AUGUSTUS O P50HL17670-17 0035
GRANT, AUGUSTUS O R01HL32708-08
GRANT, BARBARA W M01RR00109-28 0231
GRANT, DAVID M R01GM08521-31
GRANT, DAVID M S07RR07092-26 0489
GRANT, GEORGE C S06GM08033-21 0008
GRANT, GREG P01DK33487-05 9001
GRANT, GREGORY A P41RR00954-15 0030
GRANT, GREGORY A P60DK20579-14 9007
GRANT, GREGORY A R01NS28447-02
GRANT, IGOR P50MH45294-03
GRANT, IGOR R01MH42840-03S1
GRANT, J ANDREW R01AI22940-05
GRANT, JAMES W K08HL01902-06
GRANT, JOHN P. M01RR00030-30 0415
GRANT, K A Z01AA00400-06
GRANT, K A Z01AA00707-03
GRANT, KENNETH W R29DC00792-01A1
GRANT, LESLIE A U01AG10328-01
GRANT, MARCIA M R25CA09486-08
GRANT, MARIA B R29EY07739-03
GRANT, STEPHAN M01RR00065-29 0325
GRANT, STEPHEN R S07RR05879-09 0601
GRANT, STEVEN J R03MH45610-02
GRANTHAM, D WESLEY R01DC00185-07
GRANTHAM, JARED J R01DK13476-22
GRANTHAM, JARED J R01DK38980-05
GRASSIAN, VICKI H S07RR07035-26 0096
GRASSL, STEVEN M R29DK37907-01A2
GRATT, BARTON S07RR05304-30 0227
GRATTON, ENRICO P41RR03155-06
GRATTON, ENRICO P41RR03155-06 9001
GRATTON, ENRICO P41RR03155-06 9004
GRATTON, ENRICO P41RR03155-06 9005
GRATZ, EDWARD P01NS26665-04 0005
GRATZNER, H G N43ES11003-00
GRAVALLESE, ELLEN M K08AR01824-03
GRAVEL, JUDITH S P01DC00223-08 0001
GRAVENSTEIN, STEFAN R01AG09632-01A1
GRAVES, BARBARA J R29GM38663-05
GRAVES, DANA T K04DE00254-04
GRAVES, DANA T R01DE07559-08
GRAVES, DANA T R01DE09581-02
GRAVES, DAVID E S15CA55952-01
GRAVES, DONALD C R01AI20940-07
GRAVES, DONALD J R01GM09587-29A2
GRAVES, JOSEPH L S07RR07008-26 0060
GRAVES, KAREN P01CA50305-02 0002
GRAVES, MICHAEL C R01AI25650-04
GRAVES, STEVEN M01RR02635-07 0296
GRAVES, STEVEN W R01HD24499-04
GRAVETT, MICHAEL G S07RR05412-30 0977
GRAVISH, DOV M01RR00102-28 0157
GRAY, BARRY M P01HD17812-09 0002
GRAY, BARRY M P01HD17812-09
GRAY, BARRY M P01HD17812-09 9001
GRAY, CARLA W S07RR07133-22 0516
GRAY, CHARLES M R29EY08686-01A1
GRAY, CHARLES M S07RR05595-27 0672
GRAY, DAVID S M01RR00043-31 0440
GRAY, DIANA L M01RR00036-31 0987
GRAY, DIANA L M01RR00036-31 0988
GRAY, DIANA L M01RR00036-31 0989
GRAY, DONALD M R01GM19060-19
GRAY, DONALD M S07RR07133-22
GRAY, DONALD M S15GM47032-01
GRAY, GARY M P30DK38707-05
GRAY, GARY M P30DK38707-05 0001
GRAY, GARY M R01DK11270-23S1
GRAY, GARY R R01CA15325-17A2
GRAY, GARY R R01GM34710-07
GRAY, H P41RR01209-12 0021
GRAY, HARRY B R01DK19038-13
GRAY, HARRY B S10RR06413-01
GRAY, JOE W R01HD17665-10
GRAY, KENNETH T M01RR00046-31 0455
GRAY, KENNEY M01RR00046-31 0503
GRAY, LINCOLN C R01DC00018-02
GRAY, LINCOLN C R01DC00243-07
GRAY, LINCOLN C R01HD28261-01
GRAY, LLOYD S R29CA47401-04
GRAY, MARK S07RR05382-30 0868
GRAY, MARK R R01HG00126-02
GRAY, MARK R R01HL43203-03
GRAY, MICHAEL A R01DK43956-01
GRAY, RICHARD S07RR05425-30 0740
GRAY, RICHARD A R55NS29871-01
GRAY, RICHARD J N01HC75072-06
GRAY, RICHARD W S07RR05434-30 0808
GRAY, ROBERT M R01CA49697-02
GRAY, SARAH D R01HL42463-02
GRAY, STEVEN DEAN K08DC00036-04
GRAY, T KENNEY M01RR00046-31 0419
GRAY, WAYNE L R29AI26070-04
GRAY, WESLEY P01DK38181-05 9001
GRAY, WILLIAM R S07RR07092-26
GRAY, WILLIAM R S15HL47721-01
GRAYBIEL, ANN M R01EY02866-12
GRAYBIEL, ANN M R01NS25529-04
GRAYBILL, JOHN RICHARD M01RR01346-10 0159
GRAYBILL, JOHN RICHARD M01RR01346-10 0188
GRAYBILL, JOHN RICHARD M01RR01346-10 0049
GRAYHACK, JOHN T P50DK39250-05 0003
GRAYHACK, JOHN T P50DK39250-05
GRAYSON, STEPHEN P01AR39448-04 0005
GRAYSON, STEPHEN P01AR39448-04 9002
GRAYSTON, J THOMAS R01AI21885-07
GRAYSTON, J THOMAS R01EY00219-30
GRAYSTON, J THOMAS U10EY05239-06S1
GRAZIADEI, PASQUALE P R01DC00253-08
GRAZIADEI, PASQUALE P R01DC01071-01
GRAZIANI, LEONARD J R01HD21453-03
GRAZIANI, LEONARD J R01NS27463-03
GRAZIANO, FRANK M P50AI10404-21 0007
GRAZIANO, FRANK M R01HL33237-07
GRAZIANO, JOSEPH M01RR00645-20 0481
GRAZIANO, JOSEPH H R01ES03460-07
GRAZIANO, JOSEPH H R01ES05025-03
GRAZIANO, STEPHEN L R03CA53444-02
GRAZIER, KYLE S07RR06025-02 0029
GRDINA, DAVID J R01CA37435-09
GREASER, MARION P41RR00570-21 0016
GREAVES, IAN S07RR05448-30 0313
GREAVES, WAYNE L U01AI31107-02
GREBB, JACK A K01MH00671-05
GRECO, WILLIAM R P01CA21071-14 9005
GRECO, WILLIAM R R01CA46732-03
GREDEN, J P50AA07378-04 0004
GREDEN, JOHN F P50AA07378-04
GREELEY, GEORGE P01DK35608-06A1 0010
GREELEY, GEORGE H P01DK35608-06A1 9001
GREEN, ALLAN R01DK40061-04
GREEN, ANNETTE R18DA05761-03S1
GREEN, ARTHUR S07RR05650-25 0099
GREEN, BARRY G R01DC00249-08
GREEN, BARRY G R01ES04356-05
GREEN, DANIEL G R01EY00379-24
GREEN, DANIEL M U10CA42326-07
GREEN, DAVID R01HL43758-01A1
GREEN, DAVID M R01DC00334-07
GREEN, DOUGLAS R R01AI31591-01
GREEN, GARY M R01DK37482-04A1
GREEN, GARY M S07RR07187-13 0702

GREEN, GLORIA A R29HL38096-04
GREEN, HOWARD R35CA40029-07
GREEN, J E Z01CP05607-03
GREEN, J E Z01CP05670-01
GREEN, J E Z01CP05671-01
GREEN, JEFFREY A M01RR00080-29 0414
GREEN, JERRY F R01HL31979-08
GREEN, K Z01AI00343-10
GREEN, K Z01AI00507-05
GREEN, K Z01AI00533-04
GREEN, K Z01AI00573-02
GREEN, KEITH R01EY04558-09
GREEN, KERRY P P60DC01409-01 0002
GREEN, KERRY P R29DC00510-05
GREEN, LEE A R01HS06409-02
GREEN, M V Z01CL00400-04
GREEN, M V Z01CL00401-03
GREEN, MARK A R01CA46909-06
GREEN, MARK R M01RR00827-17 0507
GREEN, MARK R M01RR00827-17 0389
GREEN, MARK R U10CA11789-21
GREEN, MAURICE K06AI04739-30
GREEN, MAURICE R01AI28201-03
GREEN, MAURICE R01CA29561-33A1
GREEN, MAURICE R01CA54703-01
GREEN, MAURICE S07RR05388-30 0622
GREEN, MICHAEL M01RR00084-29 0234
GREEN, MICHAEL M01RR00084-29 0254
GREEN, MICHAEL R01GM41602-03
GREEN, MICHAEL S07RR07122-23 0099
GREEN, MICHAEL S07RR07122-23 0100
GREEN, MICHAEL S07RR07132-20 0403
GREEN, MICHAEL E S06GM08168-13 0016
GREEN, MICHAEL F P50MH30911-14 0020
GREEN, MICHAEL F P50MH30911-14 0024
GREEN, MICHAEL F R29MH43292-04
GREEN, MICHAEL R R01AI31272-02
GREEN, MICHAEL R R01AI31938-01
GREEN, MICHAEL R R01GM33977-08
GREEN, MICHAEL R R01GM35490-07
GREEN, MICHAEL R R01GM41304-04
GREEN, MICHEAL M01RR00084-29 0219
GREEN, N S07RR05362-30 0791
GREEN, NEIL S07RR05424-30 0125
GREEN, PETER M M01RR00645-20 0510
GREEN, PHILIP S R01CA41579-06
GREEN, PHILIP S R01GM44902-01A1
GREEN, PHILLIP S07RR05522-29 0066
GREEN, REZA R29GM38501-04
GREEN, RICHARD D R01HL40583-02
GREEN, ROBERT P30AG10130-01 9001
GREEN, ROBERT S07RR05364-30 0528
GREEN, S B Z01CN00116-08
GREEN, S B Z01CN00119-08
GREEN, STEVEN J S07RR07035-26 0091
GREEN, TERRENCE R R01AI27880-03
GREEN, TERRY J. S06GM08119-18 0009
GREEN, WILLIAM R K04CA01112-05
GREEN, WILLIAM R R01CA36860-09
GREEN, WILLIAM R R01CA43475-06
GREEN, WILLIAM R R01CA50157-02
GREENAMYRE, J T S07RR05403-30 0809
GREENAMYRE, JOHN T K08NS01487-01
GREENBAUM, ELIAS P41RR06030-01A1 0006
GREENBAUM, IRA F R01GM27014-10
GREENBERG PHIL U01AI26503-04 0003
GREENBERG, BARRY H N01HC55011-11
GREENBERG, CHARLES S P50HL26309-11 0008
GREENBERG, CHARLES S R01HL38245-03
GREENBERG, DANIELLE R29DK38757-04
GREENBERG, DAVID M01RR00071-28A1 0229
GREENBERG, DAVID A R01AA07032-07
GREENBERG, DAVID A R01DK31775-09
GREENBERG, DAVID A R01NS27941-02
GREENBERG, E ROBERT U01CA32934-10
GREENBERG, E ROBERT U01CA37287-08
GREENBERG, EDWARD S R01AA08669-01A1
GREENBERG, HARRY B P30DK38707-05 0004
GREENBERG, HARRY B P30DK38707-05 9001
GREENBERG, HARRY B R03AI30346-02
GREENBERG, HARRY B R22AI21362-08
GREENBERG, HARRY S M01RR00042-31 0617
GREENBERG, J P50NS10939-18A1S1 0030
GREENBERG, JAMES M K08CA01254-03
GREENBERG, JAN S07RR07098-26 0357
GREENBERG, JAN R R01MH45988-02
GREENBERG, JAN S R03MH46564-02
GREENBERG, JAY R R01GM38351-07
GREENBERG, JOEL P01NS14867-13 0005
GREENBERG, JOEL H S07RR05415-30 0005
GREENBERG, LESLIE S R01MH45040-01A2
GREENBERG, MARK T R01MH42131-04
GREENBERG, MARK T S07RR07096-26 0061
GREENBERG, MICHAEL P01CA43447-06 9003
GREENBERG, MICHAEL E R01CA43855-05
GREENBERG, MICHAEL E R01NS28829-02
GREENBERG, MICHAEL J R37HL28440-10
GREENBERG, MICHAEL L R01AI32393-01
GREENBERG, MIRIAM L R01GM37723-05
GREENBERG, MIRIAM L S07RR05383-30 0556
GREENBERG, PHILIP P30AI27757-04 9001
GREENBERG, PHILIP U01AI30238-02 0005
GREENBERG, PHILIP D R37CA33084-09
GREENBERG, RAYMOND N01CN05227-09
GREENBERG, RAYMOND S R25CA17998-16
GREENBERG, ROBERT E M01RR00997-16 0414
GREENBERG, STEPHEN B M01RR00350-25 0401
GREENBERG, STEVEN R29DC00502-04
GREENBERG, STEVEN M K08HL02641-01
GREENBERGER, JOEL S R01DE08798-03
GREENBERGER, JOEL S R37CA39851-08
GREENBERGER, PAUL A P50AI11403-19 0009
GREENBLATT, DAVID M01RR00054-30 0427
GREENBLATT, DAVID M01RR00054-30 0374
GREENBLATT, DAVID J R01DA05258-04A1
GREENBLATT, RICHARD D R43RR07527-01
GREENBLATT, RICHARD E R43MH48270-01A1
GREENBURGH, R S07RR05362-30 0793
GREENE, ARTHUR E N01AG62109-08
GREENE, BRUCE P01AI28780-01A1 0001
GREENE, BRUCE M P01AI28780-01A1
GREENE, BRUCE M P51RR00165-31 0117
GREENE, BRUCE M R01EY03318-11
GREENE, CAROL M01RR00069-29 0442
GREENE, CAROL M01RR00069-29 0177
GREENE, CAROL M01RR00069-29 0178
GREENE, DOUGLAS A M01RR00042-31 0546
GREENE, DOUGLAS A P60DK20572-14
GREENE, DOUGLAS A R01DK38304-06
GREENE, ERICK S07RR07134-15 0520
GREENE, GEOFFREY L R01CA02897-35
GREENE, H LEON R01HL31472-05
GREENE, HARRY M01RR00095-31 0352
GREENE, HARRY L M01RR00095-31 0329
GREENE, HARRY L P30DK26657-12
GREENE, HARRY L S07RR05675-23 0907
GREENE, HENRY A R44EY08327-02
GREENE, JAMES J R01CA48641-03
GREENE, JOHN C S07RR05305-30
GREENE, LLOYD P50NS27680-03 0001
GREENE, LLOYD A P50NS27680-03
GREENE, LLOYD A R01NS16036-14
GREENE, MARK P50NS16998-11 0006
GREENE, MARK I P01CA15822-17
GREENE, MARK I P30CA16520-16 9020
GREENE, MARK I R01EY06778-06
GREENE, MARK I R01EY08191-06
GREENE, MARK I R01EY09332-06
GREENE, R L S06GM08022-20 0010
GREENE, ROBERT M R01DE05550-10A2
GREENE, ROBERT M R01DE08199-04
GREENE, ROBERT M R01DE09540-01A1
GREENE, VERNON L R18HS06757-01A1
GREENE, WARNER C R01AI28240-03
GREENE, WARNER C R01AI29117-03
GREENER, ALAN L R43AI31761-01
GREENER, EVAN S07RR05311-30 0001
GREENER, EVAN H S07RR05311-30
GREENES, ROBERT A R01LM04572-04A1
GREENES, ROBERT G N01LM13539-00
GREENFIELD, JOSEPH C, JR R37HL18468-16
GREENFIELD, PATRICIA S07RR07009-26 0941
GREENFIELD, SHELDON R01HS06665-02
GREENFIELD, THOMAS K R01AA08557-02
GREENGARD, JUDITH S M01RR00833-17 0196
GREENGARD, PAUL P01AG09464-01 0001
GREENGARD, PAUL P01AG09464-01
GREENGARD, PAUL P01AG10491-01
GREENGARD, PAUL P01MH40899-07
GREENGARD, PAUL P01MH40899-07 0004
GREENGARD, PAUL R01MH39327-09
GREENGARD, PAUL R01NS21550-08
GREENHILL, LARRY P50MH43878-03 0036
GREENHOUSE, DOROTHY N01CM07316-01
GREENHOUSE, DOROTHY D R13RR06884-01
GREENHOUSE, JOEL B P50MH30915-15 9020
GREENHOUSE, JOEL B R01CA54852-01
GREENLEAF, ARNO L R01GM28078-12
GREENLEAF, JAMES F R01CA43920-04A1
GREENLEAF, JAMES F R01HL41046-03
GREENLEE, DONALD V S07RR05356-30 0431
GREENLEY, JAMES R P50MH43555-04
GREENOUGH, WILLIAM P41RR05964-02 0004
GREENOUGH, WILLIAM T R01AG10154-04
GREENOUGH, WILLIAM T R01MH40631-06
GREENOUGH, WILLIAM T R37MH35321-09
GREENSPAN, DANIEL S R29GM38544-05
GREENSPAN, JOHN P01AI24286-05 9003
GREENSPAN, JOHN S P01DE07946-05 0002
GREENSPAN, JOHN S P01DE07946-05
GREENSPAN, JOHN S P30AI27763-04 9002
GREENSPAN, NEIL S R29AI26561-03
GREENSPAN, PHILLIP R01HL43794-02
GREENSPAN, SUSAN L M01RR01032-16 0441
GREENSPAN, SUSAN L M01RR01032-16 0401
GREENSPAN, SUSAN L P30AG08812-02 0001
GREENSTEIN, JEFFREY M01RR00349-25 0233
GREENSTEIN, JEFFREY M01RR00349-25 0234
GREENSTEIN, JEFFREY M01RR00349-25 0235
GREENSTEIN, JEFFREY I M01RR00349-25 0192
GREENWALD, BLAINE S. P50AG05138-08 9003
GREENWALD, GILBERT S R01HD00596-29
GREENWALD, IVA S R01GM37602-05
GREENWALD, JAMES E K08HL02196-03
GREENWALD, JAMES E S07RR05389-30 0635
GREENWALT, TIBOR J R01HL44897-02
GREENWOOD, CHARLES R P01HD03144-24
GREENWOOD, CHARLES R P01HD03144-24 0029
GREENWOOD, CHARLES R P30HD02528-25A1 9014
GREENWOOD, FREDERICK C S03RR03036-11
GREENWOOD, FREDERICK C S06GM08125-18
GREENWOOD, MARY R R01HD12637-12
GREER, ANN L S07RR07181-13 0534
GREER, CHARLES A R01DC00210-07A1
GREER, CHARLES A. P50NS10174-20 0026
GREER, CHARLES G P41RR00592-22 0032
GREER, CHRISTOPHER L R01GM35955-06
GREER, JONATHAN P01AG10481-01 9005
GREER, MONTE A R01DK01447-35
GREER, WILLIAM E N01NS02388-05
GREER, WILLIAM E U42RR03583-06
GREFFE, BRIAN M01RR00069-29 0436
GREGER, JANET L M01RR03186-06 0036
GREGER, JANET L R01DK41116-02
GREGER, JANET L R01DK41940-02
GREGER, RAINER F P30ES03828-06 0005
GREGERSEN, PETER K R29AI29113-02
GREGERSON, DALE S R01EY09207-01
GREGERSON, KAREN A K04DK02019-01
GREGERSON, KAREN A R29DK40336-04
GREGG, RON G P30HD03352-25 0001
GREGOR, ROBERT S07RR07009-26 0934
GREGOR, ROBERT J P01NS16333-11S1 0008
GREGORIADES, ANASTASIA R01AI23446-05
GREGORY, DOUGLAS S R01EY05078-07
GREGORY, EUGENE M S07RR07095-24 0380
GREGORY, MARTIN C M01RR00064-27 0346
GREGORY, MARTIN C M01RR00064-27 0347
GREGORY, MARTIN C M01RR00064-27 0285
GREGORY, RICHARD L S07RR05308-30
GREGORY, RICHARD L S07RR05308-30 0238
GREIDER, CAROL S07RR05717-21 0127
GREIDER, CAROL W R01AG09383-01A1
GREIDER, CAROL W R01GM43080-02
GREIG, N H Z01AG00120-14
GREINER, DALE L R01DK36024-07
GREINER, J W Z01CB09009-10
GREISLER, HOWARD P R01HL41272-04
GREKIN, ROGER J M01RR00042-31 0402
GREKIN, ROGER J P01HL18575-16A1 0012
GREKIN, ROGER J P01HL18575-16A1 9002
GREMBOWSKI, DAVID E R01DE08227-03
GRESS, R E Z01CB09287-04
GRESS, R E Z01CB09288-04
GREVER, MICHAEL R P30CA16058-17 9004
GREY, HOWARD M P01AI22295-07 0005
GREY, HOWARD M R01AI18634-09
GREY, MARGARET R29DK38397-03
GREY, MARGARET S07RR05948-05 0328
GRIBBIN, THOMAS E K08CA01499-02
GRIBBLE, GORDON W S07RR07056-18 0204
GRIDER, JOHN R R01DK34153-08
GRIECO, M M01RR00645-20 0441
GRIECO, MICHAEL H U01AI25902-05
GRIECO, PAUL A R01GM33605-12
GRIECO, PAUL A R37CA28865-13
GRIENDLING, KATHY K R29HL38206-06
GRIEPP, RANDALL B R01HL45636-01
GRIFFEN-PIERSON, SHA S07RR07034-26 0055
GRIFFEN, ANN L R03DE09807-01
GRIFFEN, CAROL N01CN95127-02
GRIFFIN, C P30CA06973-29 9012
GRIFFIN, D E P01NS26643-04 0003
GRIFFIN, DIANE E R01AI23047-05S1
GRIFFIN, DIANE E R01NS18596-09
GRIFFIN, DIANE E R01NS29234-01
GRIFFIN, JAMES D P01CA34183-08 0003
GRIFFIN, JAMES D R01CA36167-08
GRIFFIN, JAMES D R01DK43904-01
GRIFFIN, JAMES D S07RR05526-29 0089
GRIFFIN, JOHANNA A P50AI23694-06 0004
GRIFFIN, JOHN H M01RR00833-17 0216
GRIFFIN, JOHN H P01HL31950-08 0008
GRIFFIN, JOHN H P01HL31950-08
GRIFFIN, JOHN H R01HL21544-15
GRIFFIN, JOHN H S07RR07005-26 0337
GRIFFIN, JOHN W P01NS22849-06
GRIFFIN, JOHN W P01NS22849-06 0008
GRIFFIN, JOHN W P01NS22849-06 9001
GRIFFIN, JOHN W R01NS14784-14
GRIFFIN, ROBERT G R01GM23289-16
GRIFFIN, ROBERT G R01GM25505-14
GRIFFIN, ROBERT G R01GM38352-05
GRIFFIN, ROBERT G R37GM23403-15
GRIFFIN, WILMA S R01NS27414-02
GRIFFING, GEORGE T R01HL40123-03
GRIFFIS, M P01AI21912-08 0008
GRIFFISS, J MCLEOD R01AI21171-06
GRIFFISS, J MCLEOD R01AI21620-08
GRIFFISS, MCLEOD P41RR01614-10 0014
GRIFFITH, JACK P01CA19014-14 9002
GRIFFITH, JACK P30CA16086-17 9002
GRIFFITH, JACK R01GM42342-03
GRIFFITH, JEFFREY K P41RR01315-10 0049
GRIFFITH, JEFFREY K S07RR05583-27 0630
GRIFFITH, LAWRENCE S C M01RR00722-19 0100

GRIFFITH, O HAYES R01CA11695-22
GRIFFITH, O HAYES R01GM25698-25
GRIFFITH, OWEN W R01DK26912-11
GRIFFITH, OWEN W S07RR05396-30 0733
GRIFFITH, PAMELA J N01NS72398-10
GRIFFITH, WILLIAM H, III R01AG07805-03
GRIFFITHS, ROLAND R R01DA01147-17
GRIFFITHS, ROLAND R R01DA03889-08
GRIFFITHS, ROLAND R R01DA03890-08
GRIFFITHS, T DANIEL R01CA32579-10
GRIGG, PETER R01NS10783-19
GRIGGS, DOUGLAS M, JR R37HL11876-24
GRIGGS, ROBERT P60AG10463-01 9004
GRIGGS, ROBERT C M01RR00044-31 0370
GRIGGS, ROBERT C M01RR00044-31 0229
GRIGGS, ROBERT C M01RR00044-31 0361
GRIGGS, ROBERT C R01NS22099-06
GRIGGS, THOMAS R P50HL26309-11 9002
GRIGGS, THOMAS R P50HL26309-11 0002
GRILL, HARVEY J R01DK21397-14
GRIM, CLARENCE E K07HL02680-01
GRIM, CLARENCE E R01HL47923-01
GRIMES, PATRICIA A S07RR07083-26 0471
GRIMES, SHEILA S07RR05623-25 0719
GRIMES, WILLIAM J R01CA49743-02
GRIMM, RICHARD H R01AG05394-06
GRIMM, RICHARD H JR N01HC48062-10
GRIMM, RICHARD H JR R01HL34767-06
GRIMM, RICHARD H, JR S07RR05448-30 0311
GRIMSHAW, CHARLES E M01RR00833-17 0185
GRIMSHAW, CHARLES E R01DK43595-02
GRINDLEY, NIGEL D R01GM28550-12
GRINDLEY, NIGEL D R37GM28470-12
GRINES, CINDY S07RR06016-03 0371
GRINES, CINDY L M01RR02602-07 0030
GRINNELL, ALAN D R01NS06232-27
GRINNELL, FREDERICK P50GM21681-27 0008
GRINNELL, FREDERICK L R01CA14609-18
GRINNELL, FREDERICK L R01GM31321-08A1
GRISHAM, J W P01CA42765-04 0001
GRISHAM, J W R37CA29323-11
GRISHAM, JOE W R01CA24144-13
GRISHAM, MATTHEW B P01DK43785-01 9002
GRISHAM, MATTHEW B P01DK43785-01 0006
GRISHAM, MATTHEW B R29DK39168-04
GRISSO, JEANE A R01AR35409-05
GRISSO, JEANE A R01AR39807-02
GRISSO, THOMAS R01MH44623-02
GRISSOM, CHARLES B S07RR07092-26 0540
GRISSOM, CHARLES B S07RR07092-26 0490
GRISSOM, GRANT R R43DA06688-01A1
GRISSOM, GRANT R R43DA07438-01
GRISSOM, GRANT R R44DA05395-03
GRISSOM, JANET W S07RR07092-26 0541
GRISTINA, ANTHONY G R01AR26957-06
GRISWOLD, D P JR N01CM07315-01
GRISWOLD, MICHAEL D R01HD10808-14
GRISWOLD, MICHAEL D R01HD25846-03
GRISWOLD, MICHAEL D R01HD26298-02
GRISWOLD, MICHAEL D S15HD28769-01
GRITZ, ELLEN R P01CA43461-05 0003
GRITZ, ELLEN R P01CA43461-05
GRITZ, ELLEN R P01CA43461-05 9002
GRITZ, ELLEN R P01CA43461-05 9003
GRITZ, ELLEN R R01HL43608-03
GRITZMACHER, CHRISTINE A R29AI25086-05
GRIZZLE, JAMES E P30DK34987-06 9002
GRIZZLE, JAMES E U01CA51688-03
GRIZZLE, JAMES G P01ES01104-16 9003
GRIZZLE, WILLIAM E N01CN15340-01
GRIZZLE, WILLIAM E P30CA13148-20 9011
GRIZZLE, WILLIAM E U01CA44968-04
GROBE, SUSAN R29NR01483-04
GROBER, ELLEN P01AG03949-10 0005
GRODSKY, GEROLD M R37DK01410-33
GRODY, WAYNE W R01HD29337-01
GRODZICKER, TERRI I P01CA13106-20 0006
GRODZICKER, TERRI I R13CA02809-36
GRODZICKER, TERRI I R13GM30337-12
GRODZICKER, TERRI I R13GM46427-01
GRODZICKER, TERRI I R13NS29824-01
GRODZICKER, TERRI I R25CA09481-10
GRODZINSKY, ALAN J R01AR33236-08
GRODZINSKY, YOSEF P01DC00081-26 0013
GROESBECK, LOIS J P30HD10003-16 9004
GROFFEN, JOHN H R55CA47456-04
GROGAN, W MC LEAN S10RR06699-01
GROGAN, WILLIAM M. P01DK38030-05 0003
GROGGEL, GERALD C K08DK01603-06
GROLLMAN, ARTHUR P P01CA47995-02
GROLLMAN, ARTHUR P P01CA47995-02 0002
GROLLMAN, ARTHUR P P01ES04068-05 0002
GROLLMAN, ARTHUR P P01ES04068-05
GROLLMAN, ARTHUR P R01CA17395-17
GROLLMAN, E F Z01DK18007-12
GROLLMAN, EDWIN M K11AG00396-05
GROMPE, MARKUS R03HD28585-01
GRONEBORN, A M Z01DK29022-04
GRONENBORN, A M Z01DK29025-03
GRONER, YORAM R01HD21229-06
GRONICH, JOSEPH K08DK01933-03
GRONOWICZ, GLORIA P60AR20621-13 0026
GRONOWICZ, GLORIA A R29AR38636-04
GRONOWITZ, GLORIA S07RR05678-23 0165
GROOD, EDWARD S R01AR21172-13
GROOD, EDWARD S R01AR39703-03
GROOPMAN, JEROME E P50HL33774-06 0005
GROOPMAN, JEROME E R01HL42112-04
GROOPMAN, JEROME E R01HL46668-01
GROOPMAN, JEROME E U01AI31686-01 0002
GROOPMAN, JEROME E U01AI31686-01
GROOPMAN, JOHN P30ES03819-06A1 9014
GROOPMAN, JOHN D K04CA01517-03
GROOPMAN, JOHN D R01CA54114-02
GROOPMAN, JOHN D U01CA48409-05
GROOTHIUS, JESSIE M01RR00069-29 0490
GROOTHIUS, JESSIE R M01RR00069-29 0378
GROOTHIUS, JESSIE R M01RR00069-29 0411
GROOTHUIS, DENNIS S07RR05629-22
GROOTHUIS, DENNIS R R01NS12745-15
GROOTHUIS, DENNIS R S03RR03045-05
GROOTHUIS, DENNIS R S15GM47115-01
GROOTHUIS, JESSIE R M01RR00069-29 0364
GROOTHUIS, JESSIE R M01RR00069-29 0443
GROOVER, KATHLEEN N01CM07317-01
GROSE, CHARLES F R01AI22795-06A1
GROSHEN, SUSAN P01AI32918-09 9003
GROSHEN, SUSAN P01CA23766-14 9002
GROSS DE NUNEZ, GAYLE R43AA09059-01
GROSS DE NUNEZ, GAYLE R43DA06570-01A1
GROSS, ALAN M R01DE08641-03
GROSS, CAROL A R01AI19635-09
GROSS, CAROL A R01GM36278-06
GROSS, CHARLES G R01MH19420-21
GROSS, CORDELL E P20NS30324-01 9002
GROSS, CORDELL E P20NS30324-01 0004
GROSS, CORDELL E R55NS28708-01A1
GROSS, DAVID J S07RR07048-26 0640
GROSS, DAVID R S07RR05374-30 0750
GROSS, DAVID S R01GM45842-01
GROSS, DAVID S S07RR05822-12 0498
GROSS, DEBORAH A R29NR02013-03
GROSS, GARRETT J R01HL08311-26A2
GROSS, HOWARD M U10CA35090-08
GROSS, IAN M01RR06022-02 0758
GROSS, J B M01RR00585-20 0443
GROSS, J. B. M01RR00585-20 0370
GROSS, JOSEPH F P01HL17421-18 0002
GROSS, KENNETH W R01HL35792-07
GROSS, KENNETH W S07RR05648-25 0920
GROSS, MARTIN P01HL30121-08 0005
GROSS, MICHAEL L. P01CA49210-03 0002
GROSS, MYRON S07RR05448-30 0295
GROSS, NICHOLAS J R01HL45782-01
GROSS, RICHARD W R01HL34839-06A1
GROSS, RICHARD W R01HL35864-06
GROSS, RICHARD W R01HL41250-04
GROSS, ROBERT A P01NS19613-07 0005
GROSS, ROBERT H S07RR07056-18 0203
GROSS, SAMUEL U10CA29281-11
GROSS, SAMUEL U10CA29281-11 0001
GROSS, SAMUEL U10CA29281-11 0004
GROSS, SAMUEL U10CA29281-11 0005
GROSS, SAMUEL U10CA29281-11 0006
GROSS, SAMUEL U10CA29281-11 0007
GROSS, SAMUEL U10CA29281-11 0008
GROSS, SAMUEL U10CA29281-11 0002
GROSS, SAMUEL U10CA29281-11 0003
GROSS, SAMUEL U10CA29281-11 0009
GROSS, SAMUEL U10CA29281-11 0010
GROSS, SAMUEL U10CA29281-11 0011
GROSS, SAMUEL U10CA29281-11 0012
GROSS, SAMUEL U10CA29281-11 0044
GROSS, SAMUEL U10CA29281-11 0045
GROSS, SAMUEL U10CA29281-11 0046
GROSS, SAMUEL U10CA29281-11 0047
GROSS, SAMUEL U10CA29281-11 0048
GROSS, SAMUEL U10CA29281-11 0049
GROSS, SAMUEL U10CA29281-11 0050
GROSS, SAMUEL U10CA29281-11 0051
GROSS, SAMUEL U10CA29281-11 0052
GROSS, SAMUEL U10CA29281-11 0053
GROSS, SAMUEL U10CA29281-11 0054
GROSS, SAMUEL U10CA29281-11 0013
GROSS, SAMUEL U10CA29281-11 0014
GROSS, SAMUEL U10CA29281-11 0015
GROSS, SAMUEL U10CA29281-11 0016
GROSS, SAMUEL U10CA29281-11 0017
GROSS, SAMUEL U10CA29281-11 0018
GROSS, SAMUEL U10CA29281-11 0019
GROSS, SAMUEL U10CA29281-11 0020
GROSS, SAMUEL U10CA29281-11 0021
GROSS, SAMUEL U10CA29281-11 0022
GROSS, SAMUEL U10CA29281-11 0023
GROSS, SAMUEL U10CA29281-11 0055
GROSS, SAMUEL U10CA29281-11 0056
GROSS, SAMUEL U10CA29281-11 0057
GROSS, SAMUEL U10CA29281-11 0058
GROSS, SAMUEL U10CA29281-11 0024
GROSS, SAMUEL U10CA29281-11 0025
GROSS, SAMUEL U10CA29281-11 0026
GROSS, SAMUEL U10CA29281-11 0027
GROSS, SAMUEL U10CA29281-11 0028
GROSS, SAMUEL U10CA29281-11 0029
GROSS, SAMUEL U10CA29281-11 0030
GROSS, SAMUEL U10CA29281-11 0031
GROSS, SAMUEL U10CA29281-11 0032
GROSS, SAMUEL U10CA29281-11 0033
GROSS, SAMUEL U10CA29281-11 0059
GROSS, SAMUEL U10CA29281-11 0060
GROSS, SAMUEL U10CA29281-11 0034
GROSS, SAMUEL U10CA29281-11 0035
GROSS, SAMUEL U10CA29281-11 0036
GROSS, SAMUEL U10CA29281-11 0037
GROSS, SAMUEL U10CA29281-11 0038
GROSS, SAMUEL U10CA29281-11 0039
GROSS, SAMUEL U10CA29281-11 0040
GROSS, SAMUEL U10CA29281-11 0041
GROSS, SAMUEL U10CA29281-11 0042
GROSS, SAMUEL U10CA29281-11 0043
GROSS, STEVEN S07RR05396-30 0779
GROSS, STEVEN S P01HL46403-01 0002
GROSSCHEDL, RUDOLF R01GM37701-05
GROSSI, CARLOS E P30CA13148-20 9018
GROSSMAN, ALAN D R01GM41934-03
GROSSMAN, ARTHUR S07RR05799-14 0683
GROSSMAN, ARTHUR S07RR05799-14 0685
GROSSMAN, ARTHUR R R01GM33436-07
GROSSMAN, LAWRENCE R01GM31110-10
GROSSMAN, LAWRENCE R37GM22846-17
GROSSMAN, M P50NS10939-18A1S1 0032
GROSSMAN, MARK H R29NS24066-05
GROSSMAN, MICHAEL R01AA08359-03
GROSSMAN, MURRAY K08DC00039-02
GROSSMAN, MURRAY M01RR00040-31 0412
GROSSMAN, MURRAY R01AG09399-01
GROSSMAN, NEIL J N01HB77040-07
GROSSMAN, PAUL S07RR05372-30 0701
GROSSMAN, PETER S07RR07029-26 0022
GROSSMAN, ROBERT G P01NS27616-02S1
GROSSMAN, ROBERT G P01NS27616-02S1 0001
GROSSMAN, ROBERT I R01NS29029-01A1
GROSSMAN, WILLIAM P01HL38189-04
GROSSMANN, ANGELIKA R01AG08102-03
GROSSMANN, ANGELIKA S07RR05432-30 0237
GROSSNIKLAUS, H P30EY06360-06 9002
GROSSO, LEONARD E S07RR05491-29 0458
GROSSWEINER, LEONARD I R01GM20117-28
GROSVENOR, CLARK E R37HD04358-31
GROTBERG, JAMES B MD PHD K04HL01818-05
GROTENDORST, GARY ROBERT R01GM37223-06
GROTEVANT, HAROLD D R01HD28296-01
GROTHAUS, PAUL G R44CA53060-02
GROTTA, JAMES C N01NS02381-03
GROTTA, JAMES C R01NS23979-04A1
GROUDINE, MARK R01CA57156-01 0008
GROUDINE, MARK T P01DK31232-10 0002
GROUDINE, MARK T R01CA54337-01
GROUDINE, MARK T R01CA57156-01
GROUDINE, MARK T. P01AI27291-04 0003
GROUTAS, WILLIAM C R01HL38048-05
GROVER-MCKAY, MALEAH S07RR05372-30 0676
GROVER, ROBERT F P01HL14985-20 9003
GROVER, SCOTT D S06GM08101-20 0032
GROVES, BERTRON M M01RR00051-30 0476
GROVES, JOHN T R01GM36298-06
GROVES, PHILIP M K05DA00079-19
GROVES, PHILIP M R37DA02854-12
GROVES, PHILIP M S06GM47165-01 0023
GROWDON, JOHN U01AG10483-01 0003
GROWDON, JOHN H M01RR01066-14 0080
GROWDON, JOHN H M01RR01066-14 0107
GROWDON, JOHN H M01RR01066-14 0056
GROWDON, JOHN H M01RR01066-14 0066
GROWDON, JOHN H P50AG05134-08 0016
GROWDON, JOHN H P50AG05134-08 9001
GROWDON, JOHN H P50AG05134-08
GROWDON, JOHN H R01AG07906-03
GRUBB, ROBERT L P01NS06833-25 0028
GRUBBS, CLINTON N01CN85062-02
GRUBBS, CLINTON N01CN95156-04
GRUBBS, CLINTON J P01CA28103-13 9007
GRUBBS, CLINTON J P01CA28103-13 9009
GRUBE, JOEL S07RR05932-07 0005
GRUBE, JOEL W R01AA08097-02
GRUBER, BARRY S07RR05736-19 0170
GRUBER, JAMES S07RR07050-26 0123
GRUBER, JOSEPH J S07RR07114-23 0436
GRUBER, KENNETH A S07RR05419-30 0820
GRUBER, M Z01BD03012-02
GRUBER, MARTIN A S07RR05736-19 0188
GRUBER, WILLIAM M01RR00095-31 0378
GRUBERG, EDWARD S07RR07115-24 0575
GRUBERG, EDWARD R R01EY04366-07
GRUBMEYER, CHARLES S07RR07062-26 0227
GRUDER, CHARLES L P01CA42760-06 0003
GRUEN, WILLIAM R44MH44943-03
GRUENER, RAPHAEL S07RR05675-23 0908
GRUENERT, DIETER C R01HL41928-04
GRUENEWALD, DAVID K12AG00503-01 0002
GRUENEWALD, GARY L S07RR05606-25 0686
GRUENEWALD, PAUL J R01AA08395-03
GRUENEWALD, PAUL J R01AA08663-02
GRUENEWALD, PAUL J S15AA09262-01
GRUENSTEIN, ERIC I R01HL40113-05
GRUENSTEIN, ERIC I R01NS27814-02

GRUETTER, CARL A R01HL35711-07
GRUFT, J M01RR00645-20 0507
GRUM, CYRIL M K08HL01930-05
GRUMBACH, MELVIN M R01HD02335-26
GRUMET, CARL P01AI29796-08 0004
GRUMET, CARL P50NS23724-06 0011
GRUMET, F CARL P50HL33811-06 0006
GRUMET, FRANK C P50HL33811-06
GRUMET, MARTIN H R01NS21629-07
GRUNBAUM, JO ANNE S07RR05828-08 0532
GRUNBERG, STEVEN M M01RR00043-31 0482
GRUNBERG, STEVEN M M01RR00043-31 0461
GRUNBERGER, DEZIDER P01CA21111-15 0002
GRUNBERGER, DEZIDER P01CA49062-02 0003
GRUNBERGER, DEZIDER R01CA39547-07
GRUND, VERNON R R15AI31232-01
GRUNDBACHER, FRED J S07RR05369-30 0580
GRUNDER, HERMANN A P01CA19138-15 0002
GRUNDFEST, WARREN P41RR01861-07 0002
GRUNDKE-IGBAL, INGE P01AG04220-07A1 0007
GRUNDKE-IQBAL, INGE R01NS18105-10A2
GRUNDY, SCOTT M M01RR00633-19 0415
GRUNDY, SCOTT M M01RR00633-19 0358
GRUNDY, SCOTT M M01RR00633-19 0368
GRUNDY, SCOTT M M01RR00633-19 0398
GRUNDY, SCOTT M M01RR00633-19 0396
GRUNDY, SCOTT M M01RR00633-19 0386
GRUNDY, SCOTT M M01RR00633-19 0388
GRUNDY, SCOTT M M01RR00633-19 0382
GRUNDY, SCOTT M M01RR00633-19 0407
GRUNDY, SCOTT M M01RR00633-19 0314
GRUNDY, SCOTT M M01RR00633-19 0408
GRUNDY, SCOTT M M01RR00633-19 0402
GRUNDY, SCOTT M P50HL17669-17 0030
GRUNDY, SCOTT M R13HL46543-01
GRUNDY, SCOTT M R37HL29252-10
GRUNER, JOHN A P50NS10164-19 0024
GRUNER, SOL M P41RR01633-10 0005
GRUNER, SOL M R01GM32614-12
GRUNEWALD, GARY L R01HL34193-07
GRUNEWALD, GARY L S10RR06453-01
GRUNFELD, CARL R01DK40990-03
GRUNHAUS, LEON M01RR00042-31 0343
GRUNSTEIN, MICHAEL R01GM23674-15
GRUNSTEIN, MICHAEL R01GM42421-03
GRUNSTEIN, MICHAEL R13GM45759-01
GRUNSTEIN, MICHAEL M R01HL31467-07
GRUNSTEIN, MICHAEL M R01HL45063-02
GRUNWALD, DAVID J S07RR05428-30 0186
GRUNWALD, GERALD B R01EY06658-04A2
GRUNWALD, JUAN M01RR00040-31 0318
GRUNWALD, JUAN E R01EY05775-07
GRUNWERG, BARRY K11DE00203-03
GRUOL, DONNA P50MH47680-02 0011
GRUOL, DONNA L R01AA06665-06
GRUOL, DONNA L R01NS21777-07
GRUPPUSO, PHILIP P50HD11343-14A1 0021
GRUPPUSO, PHILIP A R01HD24455-03
GRUTZNER, JOHN B R01GM41645-03
GRYBOSKI, JOYCE D M01RR06022-02 0735
GRZANNA, REINHARD S07RR05378-30 0998
GRZYWACZ, NORBERTO M R01EY08921-01A1
GU, HONG S07RR05874-10 0584
GU, JIANG R01HL42975-02
GU, JIANG R01HL44916-02
GU, X X Z01BA02012-02
GU, X X Z01BA02013-02
GUADALUPE, ANA R S06GM08102-20 0049
GUALTIERI, C THOMAS P01HD23042-03 0002
GUALTIERI, C THOMAS P50MH33127-13 0010
GUARE, JOHN M01RR00056-30 0355
GUARENTE, LEONARD P R01GM30454-10
GUARINO, LINDA A R01GM44055-02
GUARINO, LINDA A R29AI27450-03
GUARNACCIA, PETER P50MH43450-04 0016
GUARNACCIA, PETER J R29MH45789-02
GUARNIERI, THOMAS M01RR00035-31 0402
GUARNIERI, THOMAS R29HL38210-05
GUBA, SUSAN C K08DK02115-01
GUBERNICK, DAVID J S07RR07098-26 0350
GUCCIONE, ANDREW A K01AG00567-01
GUDAS, LORRAINE P01HD24926-03 0002
GUDAS, LORRAINE J P01CA22427-14 0007
GUDAS, LORRAINE J R01CA39036-08
GUDAS, LORRAINE J R01HD24319-05
GUDELSKY, GARY P50MH41684-07 0056
GUDELSKY, GARY P50MH41684-07 0057
GUDELSKY, GARY P50MH41684-07 0058
GUDELSKY, GARY P50MH41684-07 0059
GUDELSKY, GARY S07RR05410-30 0947
GUDEMAN, HOWARD R19MH46231-03
GUDEWICZ, PAUL W P01GM40761-01A2 0004
GUEBELI, THOMAS P R43GM45087-01
GUELLEMINAULT, CHRISTIAN P50MH40041-08 000
GUENDELMAN, SYLVIA S07RR06025-02 0028
GUENGERICH, F PETER P30ES00267-25
GUENGERICH, F PETER P30ES00267-25 9007
GUENGERICH, F PETER R01ES02205-13
GUENGERICH, F PETER R35CA44353-05
GUENTHNER, THOMAS M K04CA01287-05
GUENTHNER, THOMAS M R01CA51218-02
GUERCI, ALLAN D P50HL17655-17 0034
GUERRA, NANCY G R18MH48034-02
GUERRANT, RICHARD L P01AI26512-03 0001
GUERRANT, RICHARD L P01AI26512-03
GUERRERO, MARTIN S07RR05773-17 0382
GUERRIERO, VINCE, JR R01HL43651-02
GUERRY, DUPONT M01RR00040-31 0379
GUERRY, DUPONT P30CA16520-16 9015
GUERRY, DUPONT R01CA29200-10
GUERTIN, ROBERT P G20RR07072-01
GUESS, HARRY A R03CA54156-01
GUEVARA, JUAN S07RR05425-30 0741
GUEVIN, RAYMOND M U10CA25769-12
GUEVREMONT, DAVID C S07RR05712-20 0053
GUFFEY, STEVEN E S07RR05714-21 0135
GUGGINO, SANDRA E R01DK43423-01A1
GUGGINO, WILLIAM B R01HL40178-05
GUGGINO, WILLIAM B R01HL47122-01
GUGGINO, WILLIAM B R37DK32753-09
GUGINO, LAVERN S07RR05950-07 0007
GUGLIELMI, GUIDO R01HL46286-01
GUHA, ARABINDA P01HL29019-10 9001
GUIDERA, SHARON L R19MH47693-02
GUIDOTTI, ALESSANDRO P01NS28130-02 0001
GUIDOTTI, GUIDO R01DK27626-10S1
GUIDOTTI, GUIDO R01HL08893-27
GUIDRY, MARIJA S07RR05704-20 0012
GUIGO, RODERIC P41LM05205-08 9011
GUILARTE, TOMAS R R01HD20939-06
GUILD, GREGORY M S07RR07083-26 0472
GUILFORD, JAMES S06GM08061-17 0014
GUILFOYLE, THOMAS J R01GM37950-06
GUILKEY, DAVID K P01HD28076-01 9002
GUILLEMINAULT, CHRISTIAN M01RR00070-29 022
GUILLEMINAULT, CHRISTIAN P50NS23724-06 001
GUILLEMINAULT, CHRISTIAN R01AG07772-04
GUILLETTE, LOUIS J P41RR02278-06A1 0011
GUILLON, CHRISTINA M P50MH41115-05 0020
GUINAN, EVA M01RR02172-09 0178
GUINAN, JOHN J, JR R01DC00235-07A2
GUINAN, JOHN T P01DC00119-16 0006
GUINEY, DONALD P01DK35108-07 9003
GUINEY, DONALD G R01AI16463-12
GUINEY, DONALD G R01GM28924-10A2
GUIRE, PATRICK R44DK41171-03
GUIRE, PATRICK E R44CA42670-03
GUITTON, DANIEL R01EY08216-02
GULATI, ADARSH K R01NS24834-04
GULATI, DUSHYANT N01ES05286-02
GULATI, DUSHYANT N01ES95249-03
GULBRANDSEN, CHRISTI S07RR05599-25 0509
GULBRANDSEN, CHRISTIAN L S07RR05599-25
GULICK, ELSIE E S06GM08223-08 0031
GULIG, PAUL A R29AI28421-02
GULLAHORN, JEANNE E S07RR07122-23 0109
GULLAHORN, JEANNE E S07RR07122-23
GULLANS, STEVEN R P01DK40839-03 0004
GULLANS, STEVEN R R01DK36031-05
GULLBERG, GRANT T R01HL39792-04
GULLEY, MARGARET L K08CA01615-01
GULLION, DAVID S R01HL31305-08
GUMBINER, BARRY P30DK26743-11 0011
GUMBINER, BARRY M R01GM37432-05
GUMERLOCK, PAUL S07RR05684-23 0167
GUMMIT, ROBERT J P50NS16308-12A1 9001
GUMNIT, ROBERT J P50NS16308-12A1
GUMPORT, RICHARD I R01GM25621-12
GUMUCIO, JORGE J R01DK32842-08
GUNDBERG, CAREN M K04AR01789-05
GUNDBERG, CAREN M R01AR38460-06
GUNDERSEN, CAMERON S07RR05354-30 0414
GUNDERSEN, GREGG G R01GM42026-03
GUNDERSON, VIRGINIA M. P51RR00166-30 0089
GUNG, BENJAMIN W R15GM44260-01A1
GUNION, MARK W R01NS20660-07
GUNN, MICHAEL D K11HL02388-03
GUNN, ROBERT B R37HL28674-10
GUNN, SCOTT J S06GM08038-21 0009
GUNNAR, MEGAN R K02MH00946-01
GUNNAR, MEGAN R R01HD16494-10
GUNNESS-HEY, MICHELE P01AR38933-05 0006
GUNSALUS, IRWIN C R01DK00562-37
GUNSALUS, ROBERT P R01AI21678-06
GUNSALUS, ROBERT P R01GM29456-10
GUNSOLLEY, JOHN C R01DE09155-01A2
GUNTER, THOMAS S07RR05403-30 0810
GUNTHER, STEPHEN S07RR05384-30 0775
GUNTUPALLI, JAYARAMA S07RR05745-19 0225
GUO, PEIXUAN S07RR05910-08 0642
GUO, SHUMEI R29HD27063-02
GUPTA, CHHANDA R01HD22781-05A1
GUPTA, KAILASH C R01AI30517-01
GUPTA, MADHU R29NS24291-07
GUPTA, MADHU S07RR05375-30 0755
GUPTA, NABA K R01GM22079-15A2
GUPTA, NABA K R01GM37504-01A4
GUPTA, PHALGUNI R55AI30937-01A1
GUPTA, RAJ K P30CA13330-20 9011
GUPTA, RAJ K R01DK32030-10
GUPTA, RAMESH S07RR07118-22 0376
GUPTA, RISHAB K P01CA12582-19 0003
GUPTA, SALIL K M01RR00059-30 0694
GUPTA, SAMIR K P50DA05303-03 0006
GUPTA, SANJEEV K08DK01909-03
GUR, DAVID R01CA51248-02
GUR, DAVID R01HL39299-05
GUR, RAQUEL E K02MH00586-07
GUR, RAQUEL E M01RR00040-31 0383
GUR, RAQUEL E M01RR00040-31 0260
GUR, RAQUEL E P30MH48539-01
GUR, RAQUEL E P50MH43880-04
GUR, RAQUEL E P50MH43880-04 9004
GUR, RAQUEL E R37MH42191-05
GUR, REGUEL E P50MH43880-04 9001
GUR, RUBEN C P01MH44210-03 0002
GUR, RUBEN C P01NS14867-13 0006
GUR, RUBEN C P30MH48539-01 9003
GUR, RUBEN C P50MH43880-04 9002
GUR, RUBEN C P50MH43880-04 9003
GURALNICK, MICHAEL J P30HD02274-24
GURICH, RICHARD W R29DK39331-03
GURLAND, BARRY J P01AG07232-03 0001
GURLAND, BARRY J P50AG08702-03 0006
GURLAND, BARRY J P50AG08702-03 9003
GURLEY, WILLIAM B R01GM38278-04
GURLEY, WILLIAM B R01GM39732-04
GURNEY, MARK E P50NS21442-07 0005
GURNEY, THEODORE S07RR07092-26 0506
GUROFF, G Z01HD00093-17
GURPIDE, ERLIO R01HD07197-19
GURRI GLASS, GREGORY S07RR05445-30 0872
GURRI GLASS, GREGORY E R55AI30042-01A1
GURTNER, GAIL H P01HL43023-01A2 0003
GURTOO, HIRA L R01CA25362-11
GURWITZ, JERRY H K08AG00510-01
GURWITZ, JERRY H P30AG08812-02 0005
GUSELLA, JAMES F P01NS16367-12 0012
GUSELLA, JAMES F P01NS16367-12
GUSELLA, JAMES F P01NS24279-06 0001
GUSELLA, JAMES F R01HG00169-09
GUSELLA, JAMES F R01HG00317-03
GUSELLA, JAMES F R01NS22224-07
GUSOVSKY, F Z01DK31109-02
GUSSIN, GARY N R01AI17508-11
GUST, DEBORAH A P51RR00165-31 0175
GUST, DEBORAH A R03MH46676-02
GUSTAFSON, DAVID H R18HS06177-02
GUSTAFSON, ERIC L P01AG09464-01 0003
GUSTAFSON, ERIC L P01MH40899-07 0005
GUSTAFSON, GWEN E R01HD22871-04
GUSTAFSON, K Z01CM07307-01
GUSTAFSON, THOMAS A R29DK44093-01
GUSTAFSON, THOMAS A S07RR05379-30 0771
GUSTAFSSON, JAN-AKE R01ES03954-06
GUTCHER, GARY M01RR00065-29 0288
GUTCHER, GARY M01RR00065-29 0317
GUTGESELL, MARGARET M01RR00847-18 0393
GUTGESELL, MARGARET S07RR05431-30 0830
GUTH, LLOYD R01NS21460-06
GUTH, PAUL P30DK41301-02 9003
GUTH, PAUL S R01DC00303-06
GUTH, PAUL S R01DC00712-02
GUTHRIE, BARBARA S07RR05796-14 0428
GUTHRIE, BARBARA J P20NR02962-01 0001
GUTHRIE, CHRISTINE R37GM21119-18
GUTHRIE, DONALD P30HD04612-21 9007
GUTHRIE, FRANK E P01ES00044-26 0007
GUTHRIE, GORDON JR. N01HC48058-13
GUTHRIE, GORDON P M01RR02602-07 0042
GUTHRIE, GORDON P M01RR02602-07 0043
GUTHRIE, GORDON P M01RR02602-07 0038
GUTHRIE, GORDON P M01RR02602-07 0039
GUTHRIE, PETER B R01NS29747-01
GUTHRIE, ROBERT D S07RR07114-23 0437
GUTIERREZ-HARTMANN, ARTHUR R01DK37667-05
GUTIERREZ, CARLOS S06GM08101-20 0023
GUTIERREZ, CARLOS G R15GM46086-01
GUTIERREZ, MARY S07RR05792-15 0943
GUTIN, PHILIP P01CA13525-19 0026
GUTKNECHT, JOHN W R01GM28844-11
GUTMAN, FRONCIE A U10EY07813-04
GUTSCHE, C DAVID R01GM23534-15
GUTTERMAN, ELAINE P50MH43450-04 0020
GUY, H R Z01CB08363-09
GUY, J S07RR05362-30 0783
GUY, J S07RR05362-30 0784
GUY, JOHN P41RR02278-06A1 0012
GUY, JOHN R M01RR00082-29 0280
GUY, JOHN R R01EY07982-02
GUY, JOHN R U10EY07671-04
GUY, RICHARD P01HD24180-04 0004
GUY, RICHARD H R01HD27839-02
GUYDEN, JERRY S07RR07132-20 0404
GUYENET, PATRICE G R01HL28785-10
GUYENET, PATRICE G R01HL39841-05
GUYRE, PAUL M P30CA23108-14 9007
GUYRE, PAUL M R01DK33100-08
GUYRE, PAUL M S10RR06313-01
GUYTON, ARTHUR C P01HL11678-24 9003
GUYTON, JOHN R K04HL02114-04
GUYTON, JOHN R R01HL29680-09
GUYTON, JOHN R R01HL45619-01A1
GUZE, BARRY S07RR05756-18 0300
GUZE, BARRY H K07MH00912-01
GUZE, SAMUEL B P50AA03539-14

GUZE, SAMUEL B P50AA03539-14 9009
GUZELIAN, PHILIP S, JR R01ES05744-06
GUZICK, DAVID M01RR00056-30 0378
GUZICK, DAVID S S07RR05570-20 0847
GUZICK, DAVID S U10HD27009-02
GUZIEC, FRANK N01CM17528-00
GUZIEC, FRANK S S06GM08136-18 0015
GUZMAN, ANGEL L S07RR05419-30 0827
GWADZ, R W Z01AI00248-10
GWATHMEY, JUDITH K R29HL39091-05
GWINNE, JOHN M01RR00046-31 0505
GWINNETT, A JOHN S07RR05778-16 0411
GWIRTZ, PATRICIA A PHD R01HL34172-05
GWOSDOW, ANDREA R R29DK41419-02
GWYNNE, JOHN T M01RR00046-31 0371
GWYNNE, JOHN T M01RR00046-31 0451
GWYTHER, LISA P50AG05128-08 9005
GYARFAS, IVAN N01HC48051-10
GYERMEK, LAZSLO P51RR00169-30 0148
GYULAI, LASZLO P30MH48539-01 0001
GYULAI, LASZLO P41RR02305-08 0020
Hudson, L D Z01NS02528-10
HAACKE, E M R01HL38698-02
HAAF, ROBERT A S07RR07237-04 0741
HAAGENSON, DARROW M01RR00036-31 1046
HAAN, MARY R29AG09785-01
HAAS, ARTHUR L R01GM34009-08
HAAS, GABRIEL P R01CA55763-01
HAAS, GRETCHEN L P50MH46745-02 9005
HAAS, GRETCHEN L P50MH46745-02 0002
HAAS, GRETCHEN L R01MH48492-01
HAAS, GRETCHEN L R29MH43613-06
HAAS, MARTIN R01CA34151-09S1
HAAS, MARTIN S07RR05665-24 0889
HAAS, RICHARD H R01NS29504-01
HAAS, ROBERT P42ES04705-05 0005
HAASE, ASHLEY T R01NS21423-08
HAASE, ASHLEY T R01NS21580-08
HAASE, ASHLEY T R01NS23446-05
HAASE, ASHLEY T R37AI28246-03
HABEEB, AHMED S06GM08224-07 0010
HABENER, JOEL F R01DK25532-13
HABENER, JOEL F R01DK30457-10
HABENER, JOEL F R01DK30834-09
HABER, BARBARA A K11DK01905-03
HABER, JAMES E R01GM20056-19
HABER, JAMES E R01GM29736-09
HABER, JAMES E R01GM39739-03
HABER, MICHAEL J M01RR00039-31 0398
HABER, RALPH N R01EY07801-02
HABER, RICHARD S R01DK41674-01A2
HABER, SUZANNE R01NS22511-05
HABER, SUZANNE R37MH45573-03
HABERLAND, MARGARET P01HL30568-09 9001
HABERLAND, MARGARET E P01HL30568-09 0001
HABERLY, LEWIS B R01NS19865-09
HABIB, JUBRAN B M01RR00350-25 0458
HABICHT, GAIL S R01AR36028-06
HABLITZ, JOHN J R01NS18145-09
HABLITZ, JOHN J R01NS22373-07
HACHEY, DAVID M01RR00188-27 0330
HACK, MAUREEN R01HD26554-02
HACKEL, ANDREA P30AG09463-01 0001
HACKEL, ANDREA J M01RR00030-30 0456
HACKENBROCK, CHARLES R R55GM28704-10A1
HACKER, MILES P K04CA01205-05
HACKER, MILES P P30CA22435-11 9003
HACKERT, MARVIN L R01GM30105-09
HACKETT, CHARLES J R01AI14162-14
HACKETT, JOHN T R01NS25669-02
HACKETT, NEIL R R29HG00349-04
HACKETT, NEIL R S07RR05396-30 0763
HACKETT, PERRY S07RR07052-26 0158
HACKETT, PERRY B R01RR06625-01
HACKETT, RAYMOND L P01DK20586-15 0003
HACKETT, RAYMOND L P01DK20586-15
HACKLEY, STEVEN A R29MH47746-01
HACKMAN, BELA B M01RR00211-27 0281
HACKNEY, DAVID R01NS25921-04
HACKNEY, DAVID D R01NS28562-02
HACKSTADT, T Z01AI00567-01
HADDAD, GABRIEL G R01HD15736-11
HADDAD, GABRIEL G R01HD28940-01
HADDAD, GABRIEL G R01HL39924-05
HADDAD, JOHN G P50AR39226-05 0002
HADDAD, JOHN G, JR R01AR28292-11
HADDOX, MARI K R01DK44331-01
HADFIELD, MICHAEL G S07RR07026-26 0999
HADLEY, ROBERT D S07RR05420-30 0040
HAEBERLE, JOE R P01HL28001-10 0009
HAEBERLE, JOE R R01AR40259-02
HAEBERLE, JOSEPH R S07RR05429-30 0197
HAEGER, ELISABETH B K11AI00984-02
HAEGERSTROM-PORTNOY, GUNILLA R01EY07345-01
HAEGERTROM-PORTNOY, S07RR05832-12 0199
HAERTZEN, C A Z01DA00013-05
HAFERKAMP, CLAUDIA J S07RR07098-26 0340
HAFFAJEE, ANNE D P50DE04881-14 0003
HAFFAJEE, ANNE D P50DE04881-14 0004
HAFLER, DAVID A R01NS24247-04A1
HAFNER, GARY S S07RR05962-05 0014
HAFTER, ERVIN R R01DC00087-23

HAGAN, MICHAEL D S07RR05374-30 0749
HAGE, DAVID S07RR07055-26 0184
HAGE, DAVID S07RR07055-26 0181
HAGE, DAVID S R29GM44931-01A1
HAGEDORN, CURT H R01GM40219-03
HAGEDORN, HENRY H R01HD24869-03
HAGEL-BRADWAY, SUSAN S07RR05330-30 0021
HAGEMAN, GILBERT R R01HL37289-04
HAGEMAN, GREGORY S R01EY06463-06
HAGEMAN, GREGORY S. P51RR00166-30 0139
HAGEMAN, JAMES H S06GM08136-18 0002
HAGEN, KARL S R01GM46506-01
HAGEN, KARL S S10RR07323-01
HAGEN, PER-OTTO F R01HL15448-18
HAGEN, SUSAN J R55DK44287-01
HAGER, G Z01CP04986-15
HAGER, G L Z01CP05450-07
HAGER, G L Z01CP05601-03
HAGER, G L Z01CP05660-02
HAGER, LOWELL P R01GM07768-32
HAGER, LOWELL P S07RR07030-26 0392
HAGER, STEPHEN R S07RR05434-30 0820
HAGERMAN, PAUL J R01GM28293-12
HAGERMAN, PAUL J R01GM35305-07
HAGERMAN, RANDI M01RR00069-29 0486
HAGERMAN, RANDI M01RR00069-29 0484
HAGERMAN, RANDI J R01MH45916-02
HAGERTY, BONNIE S07RR05796-14 0429
HAGERTY, BONNIE S07RR05796-14 0430
HAGGER, JODY A R43NR02591-01A1
HAGGERTY, DONALD F P01HD06576-18 0014
HAGGERTY, JOHN M01RR00046-31 0521
HAGGERTY, JOHN J M01RR00046-31 0373
HAGGERTY, JOHN J M01RR00046-31 0375
HAGGERTY, JOHN J P50MH33127-13 0013
HAGGERTY, JOHN J, JR S07RR05406-30 0883
HAGGIS, GEOFFREY P41RR00570-21 0008
HAGHBIN, MAHROO R25CA48010-03
HAGINS, W A Z01DK29011-20
HAGLER, HERBERT K P50HL17669-17 9003
HAGSTROM, NATE M01RR00109-28 0347
HAHIN, RICHARD S07RR07176-14 0529
HAHN, ANN N01LM13541-00
HAHN, BEATRICE H P01AI27290-04
HAHN, BEATRICE H R01AI25291-05
HAHN, BEATRICE H. P01AI27290-04 0001
HAHN, BEVRA P60AR36834-05 0004
HAHN, BEVRA H P01AR40919-01
HAHN, BEVRA H P01AR40919-01 0002
HAHN, BEVRA H P60AR36834-05
HAHN, BEVRA H R01AR33962-07
HAHN, ELLIOT F R44AI28124-03
HAHN, GEORGE M P01CA44665-04 0007
HAHN, GEORGE M P01CA44665-04 9001
HAHN, GEORGE M P01CA44665-04
HAHN, GEORGE M R01CA19386-15
HAHN, GEORGE M R01CA32827-09
HAHN, PETER J R29CA46880-04
HAHN, RICHARD P41RR05351-03 0004
HAHN, RICHARD G U10CA13650-19
HAHN, STEVEN M R01GM42551-03
HAHN, THEODORE P60AG10415-01 9002
HAHN, WILLIAM E R01NS10813-18
HAI, TSONWIN R29GM46218-01
HAIGH, JULIAN R S07RR07099-25 0403
HAIGHT, BARBARA K R29MH45323-02
HAILE, ROBERT W R01CA36387-08
HAILE, ROBERT W R01CA51923-01A1
HAINES, JONATHAN P01NS24279-06 9004
HAINES, JONATHAN L R01HG00324-03
HAINES, MICHAEL R R01HD24106-03
HAINES, RICHARD M01RR00042-31 0585
HAINFIELD, JAMES F U01CA51958-02 0003
HAINLINE, L S07RR07119-20 0467
HAINLINE, LOUISE D R01EY03957-10
HAIRE-JOSHU, DEBRA M01RR00036-31 1011
HAIT, WILLIAM N P01CA08341-26 9003
HAIT, WILLIAM N P01CA08341-26 9004
HAIT, WILLIAM N P01CA08341-26
HAIT, WILLIAM N P01CA08341-26 0075
HAIT, WILLIAM N R01CA43888-04A1
HAITH, MARSHALL M K05MH00367-10
HAITH, MARSHALL M R01HD20026-05
HAJDU, J P41RR01209-12 0011
HAJDU, JOSEPH R01GM41452-02
HAJDU, STEVEN P01CA47179-03 9002
HAJDUCZOK, ZINA M01RR00059-30 0712
HAJDUK, STEPHEN L R01AI21401-08
HAJDUK, STEPHEN L R01AI27316-03
HAJJAR, DAVID P P01HL46403-01
HAJJAR, DAVID P P01HL46403-01 9001
HAJJAR, DAVID P P01HL46403-01 0007
HAJJAR, DAVID P P50HL18828-16 0006
HAJJAR, DAVID P R01HL39701-04
HAJJAR, DAVID P R01HL45343-02
HAJJAR, DAVID P S07RR05396-30 0735
HAJJAR, KATHERINE A P01HL46403-01 0004
HAJJAR, KATHERINE A R01HL42493-03
HAJRA, AMIYA K R01NS15747-12
HAK, LAWRENCE M01RR00046-31 0523
HAK, LAWRENCE M01RR00046-31 0474
HAK, LAWRENCE M01RR00046-31 0498

HAK, LAWRENCE M01RR00046-31 0481
HAKAN, ROBERT L R29DA06498-02
HAKES, THOMAS B P01CA52477-01A1 0001
HAKIM, RAYMOND M R01HL36015-07A1
HAKOMORI, SEN-ITIROH P01DK31232-10 0005
HAKOMORI, SEN-ITIROH R35CA42505-07
HALABAN, RUTH R01AR39848-02
HALABAN, RUTH R29CA44542-04
HALARIS, ANGELOS P50MH41684-07 0039
HALARIS, ANGELOS E R01MH42859-03
HALBAN, PHILIPPE A R01DK35292-07
HALBEEK, H P41RR05351-03 0001
HALBERG, FRANZ K06GM13981-30
HALBHERR, THERESA P01CA40737-06 9005
HALBREICH, URIEL R01MH45242-02
HALBREICH, URIEL R01MH46901-01
HALBROOK, KAREN A P01AR21557-13
HALDER, KASTURI S07RR05353-30 0346
HALE, CALVIN C S07RR05949-07 0732
HALE, KATHY M01RR00069-29 0492
HALE, PAUL D R43HL46095-01
HALE, PAUL D R44DK42379-02
HALEGOUA, SIMON R01NS18218-09
HALENDA, STEPHEN P R29HL38406-04
HALES, BRIAN J R01GM33965-07
HALES, CHARLES A R01HL36829-04A1
HALES, CHARLES A S07RR05486-29 0061
HALEY, NANCY J. P30CA17613-17 9011
HALEY, BOYD E R01GM35766-07A1
HALEY, E C, JR N01NS02376-02
HALEY, JOHN D R43CA55438-01
HALEY, JOHN D R43DK44056-01
HALEY, JOHN D R44CA49337-02A1
HALEY, NANCY J P01CA29580-11 0009
HALEY, PAUL E R43HL46576-01
HALEY, WILLIAM P30AG10163-01 9002
HALEY, WILLIAM E P01AG06569-05 0005
HALFTER, WILLI S07RR05416-30 0561
HALGREN, ERIC R01NS18741-09
HALHONEN, MARILYN J P50HL14136-20 9003
HALIKAS, JAMES A R18DA05763-03S1
HALIKAS, JAMES A R18DA06975-02
HALKETT, IAN W N01LM93511-02
HALL, ALAN K R01CA49422-03
HALL, ARTHUR S G20RR06762-01
HALL, BARRY S07RR07069-26 0249
HALL, BRUCE P01AI29796-08 0003
HALL, BRUCE P01AI29796-08 9003
HALL, CAROLINE B M01RR00044-31 0372
HALL, COLIN M01RR00046-31 0513
HALL, COLIN D M01RR00046-31 0422
HALL, COLIN D P01NS26680-04A1
HALL, COLIN D P01NS26680-04A1 0001
HALL, COLIN D P01NS26680-04A1 9001
HALL, COLIN D P01NS26680-04A1 0005
HALL, CRAIG G K08CA01486-02
HALL, DAVID J R29CA51170-02
HALL, DWIGHT H S07RR07024-26 0043
HALL, DWIGHT H S07RR07024-26 0029
HALL, ELIZABETH R P50NS23327-07 0005
HALL, ERIC J P01CA12536-20
HALL, ERIC J P01CA12536-20 0003
HALL, ERIC J P01CA12536-20 9001
HALL, ERIC J P01CA28881-07A1 0005
HALL, ERIC J P01CA49062-02
HALL, ERIC J P01CA49062-02 0001
HALL, ERIC J P01CA49062-02 9001
HALL, ERIC J R01CA43194-05
HALL, FREDERICK L S07RR05469-29 0411
HALL, GORDON C R01MH45700-01A1
HALL, HAROLD E R44HD24403-03
HALL, JAMES A R18DA06911-02
HALL, JAMES E R01EY05661-07
HALL, JAMES E R13EY09132-01
HALL, JANET E M01RR01066-14 0026
HALL, JANET E U54HD29164-01 0002
HALL, JEAN P30DK40566-02 0007
HALL, JEFFREY C P01GM33205-08 0001
HALL, JEFFREY C R01GM21473-17
HALL, JIM C S07RR07088-24 0350
HALL, JOHN P01HL11678-24
HALL, JOHN E P01HL11678-24 0064
HALL, JOHN E R01HL23502-12
HALL, JOHN E R01HL39399-05
HALL, JOSEPH W R01DC00397-06
HALL, JOSEPH W R01DC00418-06
HALL, JUDITH A R01HS06999-01
HALL, JUDITH A S07RR07143-20 0625
HALL, KARYL M S03RR03539-01
HALL, LINDA M R01NS16204-13
HALL, LINDA M S07RR05454-29 0880
HALL, LYNNE A K07NR00038-01
HALL, MARGRUETTA N01DE02582-03
HALL, MICHAEL O R01EY00046-22
HALL, NICHOLAS R K02DA00158-01
HALL, NICHOLAS R R01DA05723-03
HALL, R VANCE P01HD03144-24 0028
HALL, ROBERT D S07RR07053-26 0162
HALL, RUSSELL P, III R01AR34718-07
HALL, S L Z01AI00327-10
HALL, S PAIGE R03HS06944-01
HALL, SHARON M R01DA02538-12

HALL, SHARON M R01DA03082-07
HALL, STEPHEN D R29DK39546-04
HALL, SUSAN H R01HD24628-02
HALL, THOMAS C U10CA52743-02
HALL, W DALLAS M01RR00039-31 0440
HALL, W DALLAS M01RR00039-31 0445
HALL, W DALLAS N01HC48056-12
HALL, WARREN G K02MH00571-05
HALL, WILLIAM P60AG10463-01 0002
HALL, WILLIAM C R01EY08233-03
HALL, WILLIAM W R01CA51012-02
HALL, ZACH W P01NS16033-11
HALL, ZACH W P01NS16033-11 0002
HALL, ZACH W P01NS16033-11 9001
HALL, ZACH W R01NS13521-16
HALLBERG, RICHARD L R01GM46302-01
HALLETT, M Z01NS02667-08
HALLETT, M Z01NS02669-07
HALLETT, M Z01NS02675-07
HALLETT, M Z01NS02711-06
HALLETT, M Z01NS02712-07
HALLGREN, RICHARD S07RR05772-17 0351
HALLICK, LESLEY M S15MH49328-01
HALLICK, RICHARD B R01GM35625-07
HALLICK, RICHARD B R01GM35665-07
HALLINE, ALLAN S07RR05369-30 0597
HALLOCK, JAMES A S07RR05812-12
HALLOCK, JAMES A S15HL47713-01
HALLORAN, BERNARD P M01RR00079-29 0343
HALLORAN, MARY E R29AI31057-01
HALLS, LINDA M R01HL39369-06
HALLSTROM, ALFRED P R18HS06152-02
HALM, DAN R R29DK39007-06
HALME, JOUKO K R01HD21546-06
HALMI, KATHERINE M01RR00047-31 0462
HALMI, KATHERINE M01RR00047-31 0429
HALMI, KATHERINE A K02MH00516-06A1
HALMI, KATHERINE A R01DK40961-03
HALONEN, MARILYN J R01HL22582-14
HALPERIN, HENRY R P50HL17655-17 0032
HALPERIN, HENRY R P50HL17655-17 0037
HALPERIN, HENRY R R01HL44092-02
HALPERIN, JEFFREY M01RR00071-28A1 0228
HALPERIN, JEFFREY M01RR00071-28A1 0232
HALPERIN, JEFFREY M R01MH46448-02
HALPERIN, JEFFREY M S07RR07064-24 0202
HALPERN, ALLAN C R01CA25298-13
HALPERN, ALLEN C N01CP05682-02
HALPERN, ARTHUR M S07RR07143-20 0626
HALPERN, DEBORA LYNN S07RR07044-26 0116
HALPERN, GEORGES S07RR05684-23 0168
HALPERN, HOWARD J R29CA50679-03
HALPERN, J L Z01BA03001-02
HALPERN, JACK R37DK13339-23
HALPERN, MIMI N R01DC00104-17
HALPERN, MIMI N R13DC01244-01
HALPERT, JAMES R R01ES03619-07
HALPERT, JAMES R R01ES04995-03
HALSEY, JAMES H, JR M01RR00032-31 0342
HALSEY, JAMES H, JR R01AG06432-05
HALSEY, JAMES H, JR R01NS28518-01A1
HALSEY, NEAL A R01AI26521-04
HALSEY, NEAL A R01AI32468-01
HALSEY, NEAL A R01MH45237-04
HALSTED, CHARLES H P30DK35747-06
HALSTED, CHARLES H P30DK35747-06 9006
HALSTED, CHARLES H R01AA06938-06
HALTER, JEFFREY P60DK20572-14 9007
HALTER, JEFFREY B M01RR00042-31 0288
HALTER, JEFFREY B M01RR00042-31 0502
HALTER, JEFFREY B M01RR00042-31 0586
HALTER, JEFFREY B P30AG08808-03
HALTER, SUSAN A S07RR05424-30 0081
HALTERMAN, BARBARA N01CO15660-00
HALTERMAN, RONALD L R29GM42735-02
HALUSHKA, PERRY V R01HL36838-05A1
HALVERSON, JOHN D. M01RR00036-31 0607
HALVORSEN, STANLEY S07RR05454-29 0881
HALVORSON, HARLYN O R13GM31136-12
HALVORSON, HARLYN O R13HD07098-15
HALVORSON, HARLYN O R13NS20478-09
HALVORSON, HARLYN O R13RR07124-01
HALVORSON, HARLYN O S07RR05547-23
HALVORSON, HARLYN O S15EY09456-01
HAM, RICHARD G R01AR39860-03
HAMBIDGE, K MICHAEL M01RR00069-29 0264
HAMBIDGE, K MICHAEL M01RR00069-29 0129
HAMBIDGE, K MICHAEL M01RR00069-29 0446
HAMBIDGE, K MICHAEL R01DK12432-23
HAMBIDGE, K MICHAEL R01HD23855-04
HAMBIDGE, MICHAEL M01RR00069-29 0462
HAMBIDGE, MICHAEL K M01RR00069-29 0421
HAMBRICK-DIXON, PRISCELLA J S06GM08225-07
HAMBRIDGE, MICHAEL M01RR00069-29 0469
HAMBURG, CHERYL N01LM03505-01
HAMBURGER, ANNE W R01HL42069-04
HAMEL, E Z01CM07102-16
HAMEL, E Z01CM07179-06
HAMEL, FREDERICK G R01DK42470-01A1
HAMER, D H Z01CB05262-11
HAMERA, EDNA K R03MH46650-01A1
HAMERMAN, DAVID K07AG00359-05
HAMERMAN, DAVID P01AG03949-10 0002
HAMERNIK, ROGER P R01OH02317-07
HAMES, CURTIS G R37HL03341-35
HAMIL, ROBERT P30AG08665-02 9001
HAMILL, DELPHIA F S06GM08170-11A2
HAMILL, ROBERT W P01AG03644-07
HAMILL, ROBERT W P01AG03644-07 0008
HAMILL, ROBERT W P60AG10463-01
HAMILL, ROBERT W R01NS20832-09A1
HAMILL, ROBERT W R01NS22103-05
HAMILL, ROBERT W R35AG09016-02 0007
HAMILTON, ANDREW D R01GM35208-06
HAMILTON, ARCHIE C R44GM39641-03
HAMILTON, BRIAN L R01AI30997-09
HAMILTON, BRIAN L S07RR05363-30 0822
HAMILTON, CHARLES R01MH34770-10
HAMILTON, DAVID L R37MH40058-07
HAMILTON, DAVID W R01HD11962-13
HAMILTON, GLENYS A S07RR05712-20 0086
HAMILTON, GORDON A R01DK13448-23
HAMILTON, GORDON A R55GM45542-01
HAMILTON, JAMES A P01HL26335-11A1 0007
HAMILTON, JAMES A R01HL41904-01A2
HAMILTON, JOHN D P01DK38108-04 0003
HAMILTON, JOSHUA W R29CA49002-03
HAMILTON, JOSHUA W S07RR07056-18 0205
HAMILTON, KAREN K K11HL01749-05
HAMILTON, KATHRYN ANN R01DC00300-08
HAMILTON, MARY S07RR07150-17 0548
HAMILTON, RICHARD T R01HD24990-03
HAMILTON, ROBERT L P50HL14237-20 0004
HAMILTON, ROBERT L R01HL44710-01A1
HAMILTON, STANLEY P30CA06973-29 9021
HAMILTON, SUSAN L K04HL02063-04
HAMILTON, SUSAN L P01HL37044-06 0008
HAMILTON, SUSAN L R01HL37028-07
HAMILTON, THOMAS R01CA51228-02
HAMILTON, THOMAS A R01CA39621-08
HAMILTON, THOMAS ALAN P01CA48919-01A2 0003
HAMILTON, THOMAS A P01HL29582-09 0006
HAMKALO, BARBARA P41RR01315-10 0043
HAMLETT, WILLIAM C S07RR05700-22 0873
HAMLIN, JOYCE L P30DK38942-04 9002
HAMLIN, JOYCE L R01CA52559-02
HAMLIN, JOYCE L R01GM26108-13
HAMLYN, JOHN M S07RR05379-30 0774
HAMM, HEIDI E R01EY06062-07
HAMM, JOHN T U10CA33622-09
HAMM, L LEE P01DK09976-27 0018
HAMM, L LEE R01DK34394-08
HAMM, MICHAEL W R29HL38223-04
HAMM, ROBERT J. P01NS12587-16 0018
HAMM, THOMAS P40RR03624-05 0004
HAMM, THOMAS E P40RR03624-05
HAMM, THOMAS E, JR P40RR03624-05 9002
HAMM, THOMAS M R01NS22454-06
HAMMAD, YEHIA Y P50HL15092-20 9004
HAMMAD, YEHIA Y P50HL15092-20 0019
HAMMAN, R F M01RR00069-29 0426
HAMMAN, RICHARD F R01DK30747-09
HAMMAN, RICHARD F R01DK32493-09
HAMMARSKJOLD, MARIE L U01AI25721-05 0001
HAMMARSKJOLD, MARIE-LOUISE R01AI25304-05
HAMMEL, EUGENE A R01HD25841-02
HAMMER, C H Z01AI00595-01
HAMMER, J A Z01HL00514-08
HAMMER, RONALD P., JR. S06GM08125-18 0049
HAMMER, RONALD P., JR. S06GM08125-18 0049
HAMMER, RONALD P, JR K04NS01161-05
HAMMER, RONALD P, JR R01DA06645-01
HAMMER, SCOTT M P01HL43510-03 0006
HAMMERLING, ULRICH N01AI72620-06
HAMMERLING, ULRICH G R01CA38351-14
HAMMERLING, ULRICH G R01CA49933-03
HAMMERMAN, MARC R P01DK09976-27 0021
HAMMERMAN, MARC R R01DK42958-02
HAMMERMAN, MARC R R37DK27600-12
HAMMERSCHLAG, MARGARET R. M01RR00318-25 02
HAMMERSCHLAG, RICHARD R01HD26956-01A1
HAMMERSCHLAG, RICHARD R01NS27173-03
HAMMERSTEDT, ROY H S07RR07082-26 0286
HAMMOCK, B D P42ES04699-05 0005
HAMMOCK, BRUCE D P42ES04699-05
HAMMOCK, BRUCE D R01ES02710-11
HAMMOND, DAVID N K08NS01244-05
HAMMOND, DENMAN U10CA13539-19
HAMMOND, DENMAN U10CA37400-08
HAMMOND, DONNA L R01DA06736-01
HAMMOND, DONNA LOUISE R01DA07004-02
HAMMOND, JAMES M R01HD24565-04
HAMMOND, JAMES M R01HD25034-02
HAMMOND, PAUL B P01ES01566-13
HAMMOND, PAUL B P01ES01566-13 9001
HAMMOND, PAUL B R01ES05660-01
HAMMOND, WILLIAM P R01DK42083-01A1
HAMMOND, WILLIAM P S07RR05432-30 0246
HAMMONS, GEORGE J S14GM02716-05
HAMMONS, GEORGE J S14GM02716-05 0001
HAMOS, JAMES E P50AG05134-08 0013
HAMOSH, MARGIT R01HD10823-13
HAMOSH, MARGIT R01HD15631-08A1
HAMPEL, ARNOLD E R01AI29870-02
HAMPSEY, D MICHAEL R29GM39484-04
HAMPSON, SARAH E R01AG08837-02
HAMRA, MARY M S07RR05425-30 0742
HAMRELL, BURT B P01HL28001-10 9002
HAMRELL, BURT B S07RR05429-30 0191
HAMRICK, JOSEPH T S07RR05444-30
HAN, DENNIS P S07RR05434-30 0799
HAN, DENNIS P U10EY08596-02
HAN, GRACE S06GM45199-02 0005
HAN, JI-SHENG R01DA03983-05
HAN, MOON-CHULL P01CA48112-01A3 9001
HANACHI, FARID S07RR05704-20 0006
HANAFUSA, HIDESABURO R35CA44356-05
HANAHAN, DONALD J R01DK33538-08
HANAHAN, DOUGLAS P01DK41822-03
HANAHAN, DOUGLAS P01DK41822-03 9001
HANAHAN, DOUGLAS P01DK41822-03 0001
HANAHAN, DOUGLAS P30CA45508-05 9001
HANAHAN, DOUGLAS R01CA45234-06
HANAHAN, DOUGLAS R01CA47632-05
HANAHAN, DOUGLASS P01CA46370-04 0002
HANAS, JAY S R29GM40670-04
HANASH, SAMIR M P01CA26803-11
HANASH, SAMIR M P01CA26803-11 0004
HANASH, SAMIR M P01CA26803-11 9001
HANASH, SAMIR M P60HL16008-19 0024
HANAUSEK-WALASZEK, MARGARET R01CA54296-01
HANAWALT, PHILIP C P01AG02908-11 0012
HANAWALT, PHILIP C R35CA44349-05
HANAWALT, PHILIP C S07RR07005-26 0338
HANBAUER, I Z01HL03563-05
HANBAUER, I Z01HL03567-04
HANCHARD, BARRIE DR N01CP31006-25
HANCK, DOROTHY A P01HL20592-15 0017
HANCOCK, LARRY W R29DK38593-05
HANCOCK, ROBERT S06GM08202-11 0006
HANCOCK, ROBERT A S03RR03477-04
HANCOCK, STEVEN S07RR05353-30 0347
HAND, PETER J R01NS22283-05
HAND, STEVEN C S07RR07013-26 0962
HANDE, KENNETH M01RR00095-31 0321
HANDE, KENNETH R R01CA49186-03
HANDELSMAN, LEONARD R01DA05971-02
HANDEN, BENJAMIN L R29HD26186-02
HANDFORTH, ADRIAN S07RR05756-18 0283
HANDFORTH, ADRIAN S07RR05756-18 0320
HANDFORTH, ADRIAN S07RR05756-18 0309
HANDIN, ROBERT I P01HL33014-07 0005
HANDIN, ROBERT I R37HL34787-07
HANDLER, JOSEPH S R01DK42479-02
HANDLER, MICHAEL P30AG10182-01 9002
HANDMAN, EMANUELA R01AI19347-08
HANDSCHUMACHER, ROBERT E P01GM40660-03
HANDSCHUMACHER, ROBERT E P01CA08341-26 007
HANDSCHUMACHER, ROBERT E R01CA45303-05
HANDSCHUMACHER, ROBERT E R25CA47883-04
HANDSFIELD, H HUNTER R01NS25183-05
HANDSFIELD, H HUNTER U01AI31448-01 9003
HANDSHUMACHER, ROBERT E. P01GM40660-03 000
HANDWERGER, BARRY S R01AI27885-02
HANDWERGER, SANDRA R55AI31612-01
HANDWERGER, STUART R01HD07447-17
HANDWERGER, STUART R37HD15201-12
HANDY, RW N01ES15307-01
HANFT, RUTH S R13HS06877-01
HANGARTNER, THOMAS N R01AR40231-01A2
HANGAUER, DAVID S07RR05454-29 0885
HANGAUER, DAVID G R01CA52800-01A1
HANGHTON, JANET A P01CA23099-13 0015
HANGHTON, PETER J P01CA23099-13 9004
HANGHTON, PETER J P01CA23099-13 0008
HANIFIN, JOHN M01RR00334-25 0289
HANIGAN, MARIE H S07RR05431-30 0843
HANIS, CRAIG L K04DK01748-05
HANIU, MITSURU S07RR05841-12 0226
HANKEN, JAMES S07RR07013-26 0964
HANKER, J S07RR05333-30 0880
HANKIN, JANET R R01AA08561-02
HANKIN, JANET R R24MH47181-02 0006
HANKIN, JEAN P01CA33619-09 0006
HANKIN, MARK H R01NS26777-04
HANKINS, DAVID W R43HL47259-01
HANKS, C P50DE09296-03 0004
HANKS, CARL T S15DE10080-01
HANKS, GERALD E N01CM87275-07
HANKS, JOHN B M01RR00847-18 0494
HANKS, JOHN B M01RR00847-18 0553
HANKS, JOHN B R01DK39595-04A1
HANKS, STEVEN K R01HD28375-01
HANKS, STEVEN K R29GM38793-05
HANKS, STEVEN K S07RR05424-30 0117
HANLEY, BARBARA E R01HS06404-02
HANLEY, DANIEL F M01RR00035-31 0384
HANLEY, JEROME H R18MH48136-01A1
HANLEY, MICHAEL S07RR05357-30 0450
HANLEY, MICHAEL E K08HL02201-04
HANLON, JOSEPH T R01AG08380-02
HANLON, ROGER T P40RR01024-15
HANLON, ROGER T R24RR04226-04
HANLON, THOMAS E S07RR05546-26
HANMOSFIELD, H HUNTER P30AI27757-04 9003
HANN, STEPHEN R R01CA47399-04

HANNA, JAMES M01RR00065-29 0365
HANNA, JAMES M01RR00065-29 0366
HANNA, MICHELLE M R01GM47493-01
HANNA, PATRICK E R01GM39783-03
HANNA, PATRICK E R55CA55334-01
HANNAFORD, BLAKE S07RR07096-26 0062
HANNIG, ERNEST M S07RR07133-22 0510
HANNIGAN, JOHN H K21AA00140-01
HANNIGAN, JOHN H R01AA06721-06
HANNO, PHILIP M R01DK39086-06
HANNUN, YUSEL U01CA46738-05 0003
HANNUN, YUSUF P01CA47741-02 0005
HANNUN, YUSUF A R01GM43825-01A1
HANNUN, YUSUF A R01HL43707-02
HANRAHAN, JOHN P50DK41980-03 0004
HANRAHAN, JOHN W R01DK44006-01
HANS, SYDNEY L P50MH30911-14 0027
HANS, SYDNEY L R01DA05396-03
HANS, SYDNEY L R01MH45208-02
HANSELL, PHYLLIS S R01NR02903-01
HANSEN-SMITH, FAYE S07RR07131-22 0128
HANSEN, BARBARA C R01AG10612-06
HANSEN, C T Z01RR00001-21
HANSEN, DAVID E R29GM39758-04
HANSEN, DAVID E R29HL44555-02
HANSEN, DAVID E S07RR05424-30 0091
HANSEN, DAVID E S07RR07110-24 0371
HANSEN, ERIC J P01HD22766-05 0003
HANSEN, ERIC J R01AI17621-11
HANSEN, ERIC J R01AI23366-06
HANSEN, ERIC W R01GM36594-04A1
HANSEN, ERIC W S07RR07056-18 0206
HANSEN, J NORMAN R55AI24454-04A1
HANSEN, JAMES M01RR00059-30 0729
HANSEN, JAMES R K08HD00869-03
HANSEN, JEFFREY C R29GM45916-01
HANSEN, JEFFREY C S07RR07187-13 0703
HANSEN, JOHN S07RR05761-17 0202
HANSEN, JOHN S07RR05761-17 0203
HANSEN, JOHN S07RR05761-17 0205
HANSEN, JOHN A P01AI29518-02
HANSEN, JOHN A P01CA18029-16 0021
HANSEN, JOHN A P01HL36444-11 0007
HANSEN, JOHN A R01AR39153-04
HANSEN, MARC F R01CA50331-02
HANSEN, MARC F R03CA53318-02
HANSEN, PETER J R01HD26421-02
HANSEN, RANALD D R01MH45388-01A2
HANSEN, ROBERT J S03RR03006-04
HANSEN, TED H R01AI19687-09
HANSEN, TED H R01AI27123-03
HANSEN, THOMAS R S07RR07157-16 0576
HANSEN, ULLA M R01CA38038-05
HANSEN, WILLIAM B R01AA06201-07
HANSEN, WILLIAM B R01DA07030-02
HANSFORD, R Z01AG00231-07
HANSFORD, R G Z01AG00249-05
HANSON-PAINTON, O S07RR05411-30 0959
HANSON, CATHERINE S07RR07115-24 0584
HANSON, CINDY L R29DK41969-03
HANSON, DAVID P01CA40007-06A1 9001
HANSON, DOUGLAS B R29ES05064-02
HANSON, JAMES P50DE09170-03 0001
HANSON, KATHLEEN S S07RR05776-11 0394
HANSON, LOUISE N01CP05683-01
HANSON, R S07RR05830-12 0965
HANSON, RICHARD W R01DK25541-14
HANSON, RICHARD W R37DK21859-13
HANSON, STEPHEN R P01HL31950-08 9001
HANSON, STEPHEN R P01HL31950-08 0001
HANSON, STEPHEN R P51RR00165-31 0194
HANSON, STEPHEN R R01HL31469-09
HANSON, WILLIAM F U10CA10953-24
HANSON, WILLIAM F U10EY06291-07
HANTZ, EDWIN C R01DC00674-01A2
HANZLIK, ROBERT P R01GM21784-17
HANZLIK, ROBERT P R01GM31910-06
HANZLIK, ROBERT P S07RR05606-25 0687
HANZLIK, ROBERT P S07RR05606-25 0696
HAPONIK, EDWARD F K07HL02479-01A1
HAPP, GEORGE M R01AI15662-12
HAQQI, TARIQ P60AR20618-13 0022
HAQQI, TARIQ M R29AR40672-01
HARA, SABURO S06GM08198-10 0010
HARALAMBOS, GAVRAS P50HL47124-01 9001
HARALAMBOS, GAVRAS P50HL47124-01 0003
HARALSON, MICHAEL A P50HL14214-20 0038
HARAMATI, AVIAD R01DK36111-04A3
HARASAKI, HIROAKI R01HL41888-03
HARBER, PHILIP P60AR36834-05 0005
HARBISON, GERARD S R29GM39071-04
HARBOUR, DEBORAH V R01NS28069-02
HARBOUR, DEBORAH V R29NS27546-03
HARD, ROBERT P R01HL45650-01
HARDEN, T KENDALL P01HL34322-06 0007
HARDEN, T KENDALL R01GM29536-14
HARDEN, T KENDALL R01GM38213-05
HARDER, DAVID R P01HL29587-09 0008
HARDER, DAVID R R37HL33833-07
HARDIES, STEPHEN C R01HG00190-04A1
HARDIN, CHARLES C S07RR07071-26 0258
HARDIN, JOHN A K12DK01423-05S2
HARDIN, JOHN A R01AR32549-08
HARDIN, SALLY B R01MH47551-02
HARDING, CHERYL S07RR07109-23 0506
HARDING, CHERYL F R01HD15191-09
HARDING, CHERYL F R03MH48406-01
HARDING, CHERYL F S06GM08176-12 0018
HARDING, CLIFFORD V S07RR05389-30 0636
HARDING, JOSEPH W S07RR05465-29 0386
HARDING, KENN E S07RR07090-26 0474
HARDING, MATTHEW W S07RR05358-30 0475
HARDING, SHIRLEY S07RR05772-17 0339
HARDING, SUSAN M K11HL02195-04
HARDISON, ROSS C K04DK01589-05
HARDISON, ROSS C R01DK27635-11
HARDISTY, JERRY F N01ES95254-09
HARDISTY, JERRY F N01ES95260-09
HARDS, ROBERT G R44HL42214-02A1
HARDWICK, J MARIE R01CA43532-05
HARDWICK, JAMES P R01DK42671-02
HARDWICK, JAMES P S07RR05806-13 0908
HARDWICK, JANIS S07RR07050-26 0124
HARDY, CHERYL L S07RR05386-30 0584
HARDY, DEVON J R18MH47910-02
HARDY, KENNETH J P60AR20614-14 0010
HARDY, LARRY W R01GM43023-03
HARDY, LARRY W S07RR05712-20 0054
HARDY, MARK A R01CA52678-02
HARDY, MARK A R01DK34232-08
HARDY, MARK A R01DK35228-06
HARDY, RICHARD R R01AI26782-02
HARDY, ROBERT E S06GM08198-10 0011
HARDY, ROBERT J S07RR05828-08 0522
HARDY, ROBERT J U10EY05897-07
HARDY, W DAVID M01RR00865-18 0349
HARDY, W DAVID M01RR00865-18 0347
HARE, JANETTE M S07RR07079-26 0288
HAREL, SHAUL R13HD25480-01A2
HAREVEN, TAMARA K R13AG09382-01
HARFORD, ANTONIA M01RR00997-16 0337
HARFORD, ANTONIA M M01RR00997-16 0283
HARFORD, J B Z01HD01601-07
HARGRAVE, PAUL A P30EY08571-02
HARGRAVE, PAUL A R01EY04590-08
HARGRAVE, PAUL A R01EY06225-07
HARGRAVE, PAUL A R37EY06226-07
HARGREAVES, KENNETH S07RR05322-30 0272
HARGREAVES, MARGARET S06GM08198-10 0012
HARGREAVES, WILLIAM A K05MH00900-01
HARGREAVES, WILLIAM A P50MH43694-04 0016
HARGREAVES, WILLIAM A R01MH48141-02
HARGREAVES, WILLIAM A R01MH47056-01
HARGREAVES, WILLIAM A U10MH40042-08
HARGROVE, JAMES P41RR00317-25 0003
HARGROVE, JAMES L R01DK39329-04
HARI, V S07RR07051-26 0730
HARIG, JAMES M P30DK26678-12 0004
HARIK, SAMI I P50AG08012-04 0001
HARIK, SAMI I R01HL35617-07
HARINDRANATH, N Z01DE00467-04
HARING, JOHN H P01DE07734-06 0007
HARKEN, ALDEN H R01HL44186-02
HARKER, LAURENCE A P01HL31950-08 0002
HARKER, LAURENCE A P51RR00165-31 0193
HARKER, LAURENCE ARDELL R37HL41619-04
HARKER, LAURENCE ARDELL R55HL41357-04
HARKER, LAWRENCE M01RR00039-31 0439
HARLAN, JOHN P01HL18645-17 0013
HARLAN, JOHN M P01HL03174-36 0015
HARLAN, JOHN M P50HL30542-08 0002
HARLAN, RICHARD E R01DA06194-02
HARLAN, RICHARD E R01NS24148-06
HARLAN, RICHARD E S15DK44710-01
HARLAND, RICHARD M R01GM42341-07
HARLESTON, BERNARD W G12RR03060-07
HARLEY, JOHN B P01AI21568-07 9002
HARLEY, JOHN B P01AI21568-07 0002
HARLEY, JOHN B R01AI24717-05
HARLEY, JOHN B R01AI31584-01
HARLEY, JOHN B R01AR39577-03
HARLOW, EDWARD P01CA13106-20 0011
HARLOW, EDWARD E P30CA45508-05 9003
HARLOW, EDWARD E R01CA54696-01
HARLOW, EDWARD E R01CA55339-01
HARLOW, HENRY J S07RR07157-16 0579
HARLOW, SIOBAN S07RR05450-30 0350
HARMAN, S M Z01AG00013-16
HARMAN, S M Z01AG00023-15
HARMAN, S M Z01AG00281-01
HARMAN, S MITCHELL M01RR02719-06 0126
HARMAN, S MITCHELL M01RR02719-06 0144
HARMAN, S MITCHELL M01RR02719-06 0141
HARMATZ, PAUL P01DK33506-08 0006
HARMON, JEFFREY M R01CA32226-10
HARMON, WILLIAM M01RR02172-09 0181
HARMONY, JUDITH P01HL41496-03 0011
HARMONY, JUDITH A R37HL27333-12
HARMSEN, ALLEN G R01AI28354-02
HARN, DONALD A R22AI27448-01A3
HARO, LUIS S R01HD24617-04
HARO, LUIS S S07RR05876-09 0589
HAROSI, FERENC S07RR05547-23 0075
HAROSI, FERENC I R01EY04876-08
HAROUTUNIAN, VAHRAM P50AG05138-08 0001
HARPEL, PETER C P50HL18828-16 9001
HARPEL, PETER C P50HL18828-16 0003
HARPER, JEFFREY W R01AI29833-02
HARPER, JEFFREY W U01AI30243-02 0003
HARPER, JOHN R R29CA45626-05
HARPER, KAREN J M01RR01346-10 0189
HARPER, KRISTINE D M01RR00044-31 0388
HARPER, MICHAEL J R01HD25224-03
HARPER, RONALD M P01NS02808-30 0046
HARPER, RONALD M R01HD22506-05
HARPER, RONALD M R01HD22695-06
HARPER, RONALD M R01HL22418-14
HARPER, SEAN E K11CA01609-01
HARRELL, FRANK E S10RR06387-01
HARRELL, JOANNE S R01NR01837-02
HARRELL, JULES R24MH47199-02 0002
HARRELL, JULES P S06GM08016-21 0052
HARRELL, LINDY M01RR00032-31 0189
HARRELL, LINDY E P01AG06569-05
HARRELL, LINDY E P01AG06569-05 9001
HARRELL, LINDY E P01AG06569-05 0010
HARRELL, LINDY E P30AG10163-01
HARRELL, ROBERT L, JR S03RR03061-09
HARRELL, WILLIAM B S06GM08061-17 0005
HARRELL, WILLIAM E, JR R43DE09619-01A1
HARRELSON, ALLAN S07RR07053-26 0142
HARRELSON, ALLAN L R01HD26482-02
HARRIMAN, ANTHONY M R01CA53619-01
HARRINGTON, DAVID U10CA23318-15
HARRINGTON, DAVID P R01CA39929-07
HARRINGTON, MARY E R29NS26496-04
HARRINGTON, MAUREEN A R29GM43972-03
HARRINGTON, WILLIAM F R37AR04349-32
HARRIS RAYMOND C P01DK38226-06 0005
HARRIS-HOOKER, SANDRA S06GM08248-05 0004
HARRIS-WARRICK, RONALD M P01NS25915-04A1 0
HARRIS-WARRICK, RONALD M R01NS17323-10
HARRIS, ANDREW S07RR07041-26 0402
HARRIS, ANDREW L R01GM36044-04A3
HARRIS, BEN G R01AI24155-06
HARRIS, BEN G S03RR03377-08
HARRIS, BEN G S07RR05879-09
HARRIS, BENJAMIN S H III N01CP85649-09
HARRIS, C C Z01CP05505-07
HARRIS, C C Z01CP05543-04
HARRIS, CRAIG R29ES05235-02
HARRIS, DAVID A K08NS01200-05
HARRIS, DAVID T R01CA48085-05
HARRIS, DAVID T S07RR05675-23 0941
HARRIS, DAVID T S07RR07002-26 0867
HARRIS, DOROTHY S07RR05477-29 0425
HARRIS, E NIGEL S07RR05375-30 0756
HARRIS, EDWARD D R01DK41682-03
HARRIS, EDWARD D S07RR07090-26 0475
HARRIS, EMILY S07RR05353-30 0348
HARRIS, EMILY S K20MH00864-03
HARRIS, EVETTE P60HL15996-19 9006
HARRIS, G SHYAMALA S07RR05918-08 0706
HARRIS, GREG L S07RR07004-16 0048
HARRIS, JAMES O U76PE00233-01
HARRIS, JAMES P R19DA06418-03
HARRIS, JEFFREY P P20DC01433-01
HARRIS, JEFFREY P R01DC00193-09
HARRIS, JEFFREY P R13DC01232-01
HARRIS, JOEL M S07RR07092-26 0505
HARRIS, JOHN S07RR05410-30 0948
HARRIS, JOHN JR R01NS25699-03
HARRIS, JOHN W K06DK14370-30
HARRIS, JULES E U10CA25988-13
HARRIS, KATHERINE S P01DC00121-29A1
HARRIS, LOUIS S R01DA00490-16
HARRIS, LOUIS S R13DA07113-01
HARRIS, LOUIS S S03RR03517-03
HARRIS, MARJORIE R P60DC01404-01 0006
HARRIS, MARY C M01RR00240-27 0340
HARRIS, MARY C M01RR00240-27 0348
HARRIS, MARY C M01RR00240-27 0332
HARRIS, MARY C M01RR00240-27 0323
HARRIS, R ADRON P50AA03527-14 0018
HARRIS, RANDALL E N01CO03873-07
HARRIS, RANDALL E P01CA32617-09A1 0008
HARRIS, ROBERT A R01DK19259-13A3
HARRIS, ROBERT A R01DK40441-04
HARRIS, ROBERT A R37AA06399-09
HARRIS, ROBERT B R01NS24933-03
HARRIS, ROBERT B S07RR05724-20 0186
HARRIS, RUTH M R01DA07288-01
HARRIS, SHYAMALA S07RR05918-08 0701
HARRIS, STEPHEN E P01DK38639-04 0003
HARRIS, THOMAS M P01ES05355-01A1 9001
HARRIS, THOMAS M P01ES05355-01A1 0001
HARRIS, THOMAS M P01ES05355-01A1
HARRIS, THOMAS M P30ES00267-25 9001
HARRIS, THOMAS M R01ES03755-06
HARRIS, THOMAS M R01ES05509-01
HARRIS, THOMAS M S07RR07201-12 0635
HARRIS, THOMAS R P50HL19153-15 0005
HARRIS, THOMAS R P50HL19153-15 9002
HARRIS, THOMAS R R01HL39155-01A3
HARRIS, THOMAS R R01RR06558-01
HARRIS, TIMOTHY J U01CA52956-02 0005

HARRIS, W A P01NS25916-04 9001
HARRIS, WILLIAM S07RR05373-30 0716
HARRIS, WILLIAM A P01NS25916-04 0003
HARRIS, WILLIAM A R01HD14490-12
HARRIS, WILLIAM S R29HL40832-04
HARRISON, DAVID E R01AG06232-05
HARRISON, DAVID E R01HL46536-01
HARRISON, DAVID G R01HL32717-08
HARRISON, DAVID G R01HL39006-04
HARRISON, GAIL G R25CA53459-01A1
HARRISON, GEORGE H R55CA52681-01A1
HARRISON, J MICHAEL S07RR07043-26 0126
HARRISON, LEE H S07RR05445-30 0873
HARRISON, LYNDA L S07RR07151-13
HARRISON, MADALINE B K08NS01454-02
HARRISON, MICHAEL J S07RR07049-26 0441
HARRISON, MICHAEL R P01AI29512-02 0003
HARRISON, MICHAEL R R01HD25505-02
HARRISON, MICHAEL R R01HL39875-04
HARRISON, NEIL L R01GM45129-01A1
HARRISON, RICHARD M P51RR00164-30 0037
HARRISON, ROBERT L R29HL39661-02
HARRISON, ROBERT W R01CA42091-04A2
HARRISON, STEADMAN P01CA34200-09 9009
HARRISON, STEADMAN D JR N01CM97553-05
HARRISON, STEPHEN C R01AI30361-02
HARRISON, STEPHEN C R01CA13202-20
HARRISON, STEVE P41RR01646-09 0009
HARRISON, THERESA A R29DC00690-03
HARRISON, THERESA A S10RR06383-01
HARROLD, MARC W R15GM46068-01
HARROW, MARTIN P50MH41684-07 0082
HARROW, MARTIN R01MH26341-16
HARRY, G J Z01ES21154-01
HARRY, G J Z01ES21155-01
HARRY, JASON D S07RR07085-26 0338
HARSCH, HAROLD M01RR00058-30 0238
HARSH, GRIFFITH R K08NS01281-04
HARSHEY, RASIKA M R01GM33247-08
HART, B P01HD18955-07 0004
HART, BENJAMIN L P51RR00169-30 0149
HART, BETH A R01ES03098-07A2
HART, BETH A S07RR05429-30 0200
HART, C N01CP15641-00
HART, DAVID J R01GM27647-12
HART, GERALD W R01CA42486-06
HART, GERALD W R01HD13563-12
HART, HAROLD R01GM15997-21
HART, MICHAEL P01NS24621-05 0001
HART, MICHAEL N P01NS24621-05 9002
HART, MICHAEL N P50HL14230-20 0099
HART, RONALD D U10CA45400-03
HART, RONALD P K02MH00855-02
HART, RONALD P S07RR07059-26 0831
HART, THOMAS K16DE00151-05S2 0002
HART, WILLIAM M P41RR01380-10 0004
HARTE, PETER J R01GM39255-04
HARTENSTEIN, VOLKER R01NS29367-01
HARTER, SUSAN R01HD09613-15
HARTIG, PAUL R R43DA07455-01
HARTIG, PAUL R R44NS27789-02
HARTIG, PAUL R R44NS27797-02
HARTL, DANIEL L R01GM33741-08
HARTL, DANIEL L R01HG00357-04
HARTLEY, CRAIG J R37HL22512-14
HARTLEY, J W Z01AI00284-10
HARTLEY, J W Z01AI00286-10
HARTLEY, JOELLEN T S06GM08238-05 0010
HARTLEY, R W Z01DK15102-31
HARTLEY, WILLIAM R S07RR05444-30 0258
HARTLINE, DANIEL K S07RR07026-26 0007
HARTMAN, BARRY J U01AI25917-04 0004
HARTMAN, BOYD K R01NS12311-17
HARTMAN, JUDITH M01RR00034-31 0423
HARTMAN, MARK L M01RR00847-18 0496
HARTMAN, MARK L M01RR00847-18 0554
HARTMAN, MARK L M01RR00847-18 0468
HARTMAN, MARK L M01RR00847-18 0570
HARTMAN, MARK L M01RR00847-18 0572
HARTMAN, N Z01CM06197-02
HARTMAN, PHILIP S R01ES05772-01
HARTMAN, PHILLIP E S07RR07041-26 0401
HARTMAN, RAYMOND N01CO15685-01
HARTMANN, WILLIAM M R01DC00181-10
HARTSFIELD, JAMES K JR K11DE00243-03
HARTSHORN, KEVAN L R29AI29550-02
HARTSHORNE, DAVID J P01HL20984-15 0006
HARTSHORNE, DAVID J R01HL23615-14
HARTWELL, LELAND H R37GM17709-22
HARTWELL, TYLER D N01CN64096-09
HARTWELL, TYLER D R01DA07250-01
HARTWELL, TYLER D U01MH48008-02
HARTWIG, JOHN H P01DK38452-05 0002
HARTWIG, JOHN H R01HL47874-01
HARTY, KATHLEEN N01CN15378-00
HARTZ, STUART C N01HD92912-03
HARTZELL, H CRISS P01HL27385-11 0004
HARTZELL, H CRISS, JR R37HL21195-15
HARTZER, MICHAEL S07RR07131-22 0130
HARTZER, MICHAEL K R01EY06520-06
HARVATH, L Z01BH01001-02
HARVATH, L Z01BH01003-05
HARVATH, L Z01BH01006-07
HARVATH, L Z01BH01007-03
HARVATH, L Z01BH01029-01
HARVER, ANDREW R R03MH45731-02
HARVEY, DANIEL F R29GM41984-03
HARVEY, DANIEL F S06GM47165-01 0024
HARVEY, JOHN P01DA06871-01 9001
HARVEY, JOHN A P01DA06871-01 0004
HARVEY, JOHN A P01DA06871-01
HARVEY, JOHN A R01DA04944-05
HARVEY, JOHN A R37MH16841-24
HARVEY, JOHN W S07RR05788-15 0892
HARVEY, RICHARD P R01HD26024-03
HARVEY, ROBERT D R29HL45141-02
HARVEY, RONALD G R01CA36097-08
HARVEY, RONALD G R01ES04266-05
HARVEY, RONALD G R01ES04732-04
HARVEY, STEPHEN C R01GM34015-07
HARVEY, WILLIAM S07RR07115-24 0576
HARVEY, WILLIAM R R01AI30464-01
HARVISON, PETER J R29ES05189-02
HARWERTH, RONALD S R01EY01139-17
HARWOOD, PATRICIA M P30CA06973-29 9002
HARZILLI, LUIGI G S07RR07023-26 0972
HASAN, TAYYABA R29AR38918-01A3
HASCALL, V C Z01DE00134-17
HASDAY, JEFFREY DAVID R29CA52741-02
HASEGAWA, BRUCE H R01CA50539-03
HASELGROVE, JOHN C P50DE08239-04 0010
HASELKORN, ROBERT R01GM21823-17
HASELKORN, ROBERT R01GM40685-03S1
HASELTINE, WILLIAM P01AI27135-04 0001
HASELTINE, WILLIAM P01GM39599-05 0003
HASELTINE, WILLIAM A R01AI28785-06
HASELTINE, WILLIAM A R01AI29873-02
HASELTINE, WILLIAM A R01AI29333-02
HASELTINE, WILLIAM A R01CA36974-08
HASELTINE, WILLIAM A R01CA44460-05
HASELTINE, WILLIAM A U01AI24845-06
HASELTINE, WILLIAM A U01AI24845-06 0007
HASELTON, FREDERICK R R01HL40554-04
HASEMAN, J K Z01ES45001-11
HASH, JOHN H M01RR00095-31
HASH, JOHN H S03RR03473-04
HASH, JOHN H S07RR05424-30
HASH, JOHN H S07RR05424-30 0126
HASH, JOHN H S15HL47719-01
HASHER, LYNN A R01AG04306-06
HASHIM, GEORGE A R01NS21466-07
HASHIM, GEORGE A S07RR05840-13 0275
HASHIMOTO, FRED M01RR00997-16 0349
HASHIMOTO, YASHUHIRO S07RR05415-30 0006
HASHIMOTO, YASUHIRO R01AR39910-02
HASHISAKI, GEORGE T K08DC00051-01
HASHTROUDI, SHAHIN R01AG09253-02
HASIN, DEBORAH S R01AA08159-02
HASKELL, JOYCE F R29HL38442-06
HASKELL, WILLIAM L R55AG09991-01
HASKETT, ROGER F M01RR00042-31 0594
HASKILL, STEPHEN P30DK34987-06 0006
HASKILL, STEPHEN R01AI26774-03
HASKINS, KATHRYN P01DK40144-04 0002
HASKINS, KATHRYN P01DK40144-04 9002
HASKINS, KATHRYN R55DK44132-01
HASKINS, MARK R01DK25759-13
HASLAM, SANDRA S07RR05656-24 0836
HASLAM, SANDRA Z R01CA40104-07
HASLER, WILLIAM M01RR00042-31 0656
HASLER, WILLIAM P30DK34933-06A1 0011
HASSELGREN, GUNNAR S07RR05331-28 0737
HASSELL, JOHN R R01EY08104-03
HASSELL, JOHN R R01GM45380-02
HASSELL, T S07RR05728-20 0197
HASSELL, THOMAS M R01DE09177-01A1
HASSER, EILEEN M R01HL43700-02
HASSETT, DANIEL J S07RR05406-30 0895
HASSETT, JOSEPH M01RR00071-28A1 0207
HASSETT, JOSEPH M01RR00071-28A1 0244
HASSETT, JOSEPH M01RR00071-28A1 0240
HASSID, AVIV P01HL34300-07 9003
HASSID, AVIV R01HL44761-03
HASSID, AVIV I R01HL33769-08
HASSOLD, JERRY M01RR00039-31 0436
HASSOLD, JERRY J M01RR00039-31 0437
HASSOLD, TERRY J N01HD92907-04
HASSOLD, TERRY J R01HD21341-07
HASSOUN, PAUL M K08HL02133-04
HASSTEDT, SANDRA J R01HD17463-08
HASTIE, SUSAN B S07RR07149-18 0420
HASTINGS, ALAN M R01GM32130-09
HASTINGS, JOHN W R01GM19536-17
HASTINGS, JOHN W R37MH46660-02
HASTINGS, LLOYD R01ES04099-04
HASTRUP, JANICE L S07RR07066-26 0244
HASTY, DAVID L R01DE07218-06
HASTY, KAREN A R01AI22603-06A1
HATADA, M P41RR01209-12 0007
HATCH, C Z01CM06170-07
HATCH, FRED E M01RR00211-27 0325
HATCH, FRED E M01RR00211-27 0320
HATCH, MAUREEN M01RR00645-20 0476
HATCH, MAUREEN C R01HD24659-02S1
HATCH, MAUREEN C R01OH02885-01
HATCHELL, DIANE L P30EY05722-06A1 9001
HATCHELL, DIANE L R01EY02903-14
HATCHER, CHARLES R P51RR00165-31
HATCHER, FRANK G12RR03032-07 0003
HATCHER, FRANK S07RR07167-14 0602
HATCHER, FRANK M S06GM08037-20 0047
HATCHER, VICTOR B S15CA56009-01
HATEFI, YOUSSEF R37DK08126-28
HATFIELD, ALAN K U10CA35195-08
HATFIELD, D L Z01CP05317-08
HATFIELD, D L Z01CP05555-04
HATFULL, GRAHAM F R29AI28927-02
HATFULL, GRAHAM F S07RR07084-26 0323
HATHAWAY, DAVID R P01HL06308-31
HATHAWAY, DAVID R P01HL06308-31 0041
HATHAWAY, DONNA K K08NR00029-02
HATHAWAY, RONALD R S07RR05426-30 0136
HATHAWAY, WILLIAM E M01RR00069-29 0189
HATHAWAY, WILLIAM E M01RR00069-29 0419
HATSUKAMI, DOROTHY M01RR00400-23 0290
HATSUKAMI, DOROTHY K R01DA05013-05
HATTEN, MARY E R01NS15429-13A1
HATTEN, MARY E R01NS21097-07
HATTMAN, STANLEY M R01GM29227-20
HATTON, DANIEL P30DK40566-02 0005
HATTON, GLENN I R01NS09140-21
HATTON, GLENN I R01NS16942-11
HAUCK, WALTER W U10EY07483-04
HAUFT, SHERRIE M K08HD00955-01
HAUG, MARIE R R37AG08557-01A2
HAUG, PETER J R01LM05323-01
HAUG, PETER J S15HL47710-01
HAUGLAND, RICHARD P R44CA49328-02
HAUN, FOREST A S07RR05418-30 0031
HAUN, FORREST A R01MH44734-03
HAUN, FORREST A R01NS28856-02
HAUN, STEVEN E K08NS01523-01
HAUPTMAN, HERBERT A S07RR05716-20
HAUPTMAN, HERBERT A S15DK44674-01
HAUSCHKA, PETER R01DE08519-05
HAUSCHKA, PETER V R01AR38349-05
HAUSCHKA, PETER V R01AR41392-01
HAUSCHKA, STEPHEN D R01AR18860-15
HAUSCHKA, STEPHEN D R01HL39070-05
HAUSER, CRAIG A R29HD28525-01
HAUSER, FRANK S07RR07122-23 0088
HAUSER, FRANK S07RR07122-23 0089
HAUSER, FRANK M R01CA18141-16
HAUSER, KURT F R01DA06204-02
HAUSER, ROBERT M P30HD05876-21 9003
HAUSER, ROBERT M R01AG09775-01
HAUSER, STEPHEN L R01NS26799-03
HAUSER, STUART T K05MH70178-08
HAUSER, STUART T R01MH44934-03
HAUSER, WILLIAM E P01AI28408-02 0005
HAUSMAN, ROBERT E S07RR07043-26 0133
HAUSMANN, ERNEST R01DE08544-04
HAUSSLER, MARK R R01DK33351-08
HAUSSLER, MARK R R37AR15781-20
HAUSWIRTH, WILLIAM W R01EY07864-03
HAUSWIRTH, WILLIAM W R01GM34825-07
HAUT, ROGER S07RR05772-17 0358
HAUTH, JOHN C N01HD13122-00
HAUTH, JOHN C R01HD24496-04
HAUTH, JOHN C U10HD27869-01
HAVASSY, BARBARA E R18DA05582-03
HAVEL, RICHARD J P50HL14237-20
HAVEL, RICHARD J P50HL14237-20 0001
HAVEL, RICHARD J P50HL14237-20 9002
HAVEL, RICHARD J P50HL14237-20 0005
HAVEL, TIMOTHY F R01GM38221-07
HAVELL, EDWARD A R01AI23544-05
HAVERKAMP, LANNY S07RR05425-30 0743
HAWES, MARTHA C S07RR07002-26 0868
HAWES, ROBERT H M01RR00750-19 0247
HAWFOOD, SAMUEL P01HL24075-13 0007
HAWIGER, JACK J R01HL30648-09
HAWIGER, JACK J R01HL45994-02
HAWIGER, JACK J R37HL30647-09
HAWK, C TERRANCE K01RR00064-02
HAWKEN, MICHAEL J R01EY08300-02
HAWKINS, BARBARA S U10EY05995-06
HAWKINS, BARBARA S U10EY06287-07
HAWKINS, C MORTON N01HC48052-18
HAWKINS, C MORTON S15HL47736-01
HAWKINS, H P41RR02250-06 0011
HAWKINS, HAROLD K P01HL42550-02 9001
HAWKINS, JOHN D R01DA03721-07
HAWKINS, LAWRENCE J S07RR05538-29 0541
HAWKINS, LAWRENCE J S07RR05538-29 0542
HAWKINS, MORTON C R01HL35528-05
HAWKINS, RICHARD A R01NS16389-11
HAWKINS, ROBERT D R01MH26212-18
HAWORTH, ROBERT A R01HL33652-08
HAWROT, EDWARD S07RR05664-24 0863
HAWRYLEWICZ, ERVIN J R01CA50264-02
HAWTHORN, MARK H R29AA08182-02
HAWTHORN, MARK H S15AA09243-01
HAWTHORNE, M FREDERICK R01CA31753-09
HAWTHORNE, M FREDERICK R01CA53870-01
HAXBY, J V Z01AG00130-01

HAY, DON I P50DE07009-08 0003
HAY, DONALD I R01DE08601-04
HAY, DONALD I R37DE03915-18
HAY, ELIZABETH D R01HD00143-31A1
HAY, JOHN R01AI25376-03
HAY, JOHN U01AI32247-01 0002
HAY, JOHN I S07RR05983-05 0354
HAY, REGINE E R29EY08044-02
HAY, RICK P50HL15062-20 0027
HAY, RICK P50HL15062-20 9002
HAY, ROBERT J N01CP05684-02
HAY, ROBERT J N01HD62906-14
HAY, WILLIAM M01RR00069-29 0267
HAY, WILLIAM W P01HD00781-27S1 0031
HAY, WILLIAM W P50HD20761-06A1 0001
HAY, WILLIAM W JR M01RR00069-29 0455
HAY, WILLIAM W, JR P50HD20761-06A1
HAY, WILLIAM W, JR R01DK35836-07
HAYASHI, JUN P01CA37589-08 0006
HAYASHI, JUN P01DK38639-04 0004
HAYASHI, JUN S07RR05863-11 0566
HAYASHI, MASAKI R01GM12934-27
HAYASHI, MASANDO R01AG09199-01
HAYCOCK, JOHN W R03MH46653-01A1
HAYCOCK, JOHN W R29NS25134-05
HAYDAY, ADRIAN P01DK43078-02 0002
HAYDAY, ADRIAN C R01GM37759-05
HAYDEN, WILLIAM J JR R01HS06786-01
HAYDON, PHILIP G R01NS24233-05
HAYDON, PHILIP G R01NS26650-03
HAYE, KEITH R S06GM08170-11A2 0001
HAYEK, ALBERTO R01DK39087-03
HAYEK, ALBERTO S07RR05876-09 0586
HAYEK, ALBERTO S15DK44705-01
HAYER, LEON W S07RR05737-20 0215
HAYES, BARBARA E S06GM08061-17 0015
HAYES, COLLEEN E R01AI27790-03
HAYES, D L M01RR00585-20 0479
HAYES, DANIEL R03CA53336-01
HAYES, DONALD J R44NS26571-03
HAYES, H M Z01CP04411-15
HAYES, KENNETH C R01DK35375-07
HAYES, KENNETH C R01EY07103-05
HAYES, LEON S07RR05737-20 0214
HAYES, M Z01BD03008-03
HAYES, MARK P Z01BD03021-01
HAYES, RONALD L P01NS12587-16 0012
HAYES, RONALD L. P01NS12587-16 0015
HAYES, RONALD LAWRENCE R01NS21458-07
HAYES, WILSON C R01AR39760-03
HAYES, WILSON C R01AR40321-01A1
HAYES, WILSON C R01CA40211-06
HAYES, WILSON C R01CA41295-04A1
HAYHOE, MARY M R01EY05729-08
HAYMAN, LAURA L R01NR01822-04
HAYMAN, MICHAEL P01CA28146-11 0008
HAYMAN, MICHAEL J R01CA42573-06
HAYMET, ANTHONY D S07RR07092-26 0520
HAYMOND, M W M01RR00585-20 0567
HAYMOND, M W M01RR00585-20 0508
HAYMOND, M W M01RR00585-20 0445
HAYMOND, M W M01RR00585-20 0471
HAYMOND, MOREY W M01RR00585-20 0400
HAYMOND, MOREY W M01RR00585-20 0373
HAYMOND, MOREY W R01DK26989-12
HAYNE, HARLENE K21AA00125-03
HAYNES, BARTON F P01CA43447-06 0007
HAYNES, BARTON F P30CA14236-18 0929
HAYNES, BARTON F P50AR39162-05
HAYNES, BARTON F R01CA28936-11
HAYNES, BARTON F. P50AR39162-05 0001
HAYNES, DUNCAN H R01HL38228-03
HAYNES, JOHN K S06GM45199-02 0006
HAYNES, JOHNSON, JR K08HL02352-03
HAYNES, MARGARET L S03RR03336-08
HAYNES, ROBERT B R01LM04696-05
HAYNES, S Z01HD01008-02
HAYNOR, DAVID R P01CA42045-06 0008
HAYRE, MICHAEL P40RR01180-14
HAYRE, MICHAEL D G20RR07100-01
HAYREH, SOHAN M01RR00059-30 0708
HAYREH, SOHAN S R01EY01576-17
HAYS, DANIEL M R01CA44133-05
HAYS, DANIEL M R25CA23146-13
HAYS, ELIZABETH T S06GM45455-01 0003
HAYS, ESTHER F P30CA16042-17 9008
HAYS, JAMES H S07RR05417-30 0791
HAYS, JOHN B S07RR07079-26 0276
HAYS, RICHARD M R01DK03858-30
HAYS, RONALD S07RR05710-21 0022
HAYS, RONALD S07RR05710-21 0023
HAYS, RONALD D R01AA07852-02
HAYS, STEVEN R K08DK01859-04
HAYS, THOMAS R S06GM08107-18 0008
HAYS, THOMAS S R01GM44757-02
HAYS, THOMAS S S07RR07052-26 0159
HAYSLETT, JOHN P R01DK18061-17
HAYWARD, ANTHONY M01RR00069-29 0478
HAYWARD, ANTHONY P01DK40144-04 0006
HAYWARD, ANTHONY R M01RR00069-29 0420
HAYWARD, ANTHONY R M01RR00069-29 0303
HAYWARD, GARY S R01AI24576-05
HAYWARD, GARY S R01CA28473-11
HAYWARD, GARY S R37CA22130-14
HAYWARD, JAMES N S07RR05406-30 0896
HAYWARD, MARK D R01AG09338-02
HAYWARD, PATRICIA C R25AD00027-01
HAYWARD, S DIANE R01CA42245-06
HAYWARD, S DIANE R37CA30356-10
HAYWARD, WILLIAM P01CA16599-17 0017
HAYWARD, WILLIAM S P01CA16599-17
HAYWOOD, JOSEPH R P01HL36080-06 0002
HAZELBAUER, GERALD L R01GM29963-10
HAZELKORN, HERBERT M R01HS06149-02
HAZEN-MARTIN, DEBRA S07RR05420-30 0041
HAZEN-MARTIN, DEBRA J R29ES04413-04
HAZEN-SWANN, NANCY L R29HD23261-05
HAZEN, KEVIN C R29AI31048-02
HAZINSKI, THOMAS A P50HL14214-20 0046
HAZLETT, LINDA D P30EY04068-10
HAZLETT, LINDA D R01EY02986-13
HAZUDA, HELEN P R01AG10444-01
HAZZARD, WILLIAM R P60AG10484-01
HEACOCK, ANNE M P01MH42652-05 0003
HEAD, JAMES F R01NS20357-06
HEAD, JANET A U76PE00225-04
HEAD, JUDITH R R01HD18717-05
HEAGY, WYRTA R01AI29657-01A1
HEALY-MOORE, KATHLEE S07RR07131-22 0129
HEALY, DENNIS P R01HL42585-03
HEALY, JOHN P60AR38520-04 0007
HEANEY, ROBERT P P50AR39221-05 9001
HEANEY, ROBERT P P50AR39221-05 0004
HEANEY, ROBERT P P50AR39221-05 0005
HEANEY, ROBERT P R01AR07912-26
HEARING, JANET S07RR05736-19 0171
HEARING, PATRICK P01CA28146-11 0004
HEARING, PATRICK R01AI29427-02
HEARING, PATRICK R01CA44673-05
HEARING, V J Z01CB09100-06
HEARST, JOHN E R01GM41911-03
HEARST, NORMAN P50MH42459-06 0002
HEASLEY, SUSAN G R43AG10083-01
HEASLEY, VICTOR L R15ES05671-01
HEATH-CHIOZZI, MARGO M01RR01032-16 0446
HEATH-CHIOZZI, MARGO E U01AI31089-02
HEATH-MONNIG, ELLEN P01HD20805-05A1 9001
HEATH-MONNIGS, ELLEN M01RR00036-31 1047
HEATH, ANDREW C P50AA03539-14 9003
HEATH, ANDREW C R01AA07535-04
HEATH, ANDREW C R01AA07728-04
HEATH, HUNTER M01RR00585-20 0394
HEATH, HUNTER M01RR00585-20 0535
HEATH, HUNTER M01RR00585-20 0209
HEATH, HUNTER, III R01DK38855-05
HEATH, HUNTER, III R03DK44292-01
HEATH, J P41RR02250-06 0010
HEATH, JOHN M S07RR05402-30 0792
HEATH, JULIAN P30HD07495-19 9017
HEATHCOCK, CLAYTON H R37AI15027-14
HEATON, ROBERT P50MH45294-03 9004
HEAVEN, TIM S07RR05300-30 0200
HEBBEL, ROBERT P R01HL30160-08
HEBBEL, ROBERT P R01HL37528-05
HEBDEN, JEREMY C R29CA54223-01
HEBDEN, JEREMY G S07RR05428-30 0179
HEBER-KATZ, ELLEN P50NS11036-18 0046
HEBER-KATZ, ELLEN R01AI22528-06
HEBER, DAVID M01RR00425-22S3 0247
HEBER, DAVID M01RR00865-18 0346
HEBER, DAVID M01RR00865-18 0354
HEBER, DAVID P01CA42710-06A1 9002
HEBER, DAVID P01CA42710-06A1
HEBER, DAVID P01CA43461-05 0004
HEBER, DAVID R01CA51165-02
HEBER, DAVID S07RR05354-30 0397
HEBERLEIN, GARRETT T S07RR07051-26
HEBERT, JAMES R P50DA05321-04 0001
HEBERT, JAMES R S07RR05712-20 0087
HEBERT, LEE A M01RR00034-31 0421
HEBERT, LEE A M01RR00034-31 0422
HEBERT, LEE A R01HL25404-10
HEBERT, LEE A U01DK39485-04
HEBERT, PATRICIA R R03HL46923-01
HEBERT, STEVEN C R01DK36803-06
HEBERT, STEVEN C R01DK37605-04A1
HECHT, CHARLES S07RR07109-23 0507
HECHT, GAIL A K08DK02013-01
HECHT, JACQUELINE T R29DE09954-01
HECHT, NORMAN B R01HD11878-13
HECHT, NORMAN B R01HD28832-12
HECHT, SIDNEY U01CA50771-03 0003
HECHT, SIDNEY M R01CA27603-13
HECHT, SIDNEY M R01GM43328-02
HECHT, SIDNEY M R35CA53913-01
HECHT, SIDNEY M R37CA38544-07
HECHT, SIDNEY M U01CA50771-03
HECHT, STEPHEN S P01CA29580-11 0001
HECHT, STEPHEN S R35CA44377-05
HECHT, STEPHEN S U01CA46535-05
HECHT, SUSAN N01HC65045-07
HECHTMAN, HERBERT B R01GM24891-14
HECHTMAN, HERBERT B R01GM35141-06
HECHTMAN, LILY R01MH44842-03
HECK, D A P50AR39250-05 9002
HECK, GERARD S07RR05430-30 0220
HECKROTH, JOHN A S07RR05371-30 0637
HECOX, KURT E R01DC00163-11
HEDGE, GEORGE A S03RR03445-05
HEDGE, GEORGE A S07RR05433-30
HEDGE, GEORGE A S15HL47706-01
HEDIGER, MATTHIAS A R01DK43171-02
HEDIGER, MATTHIAS A R01DK43632-02
HEDLEY-WHYTE, E TESSA P50AG05134-08 9002
HEDLUND, BO E R43CA55452-01
HEDLUND, L P41RR05959-02 9007
HEDMAN, B P41RR01209-12 0013
HEDREEN, JOHN P01NS16375-11 9002
HEDRICH, STEPHEN P01CA51495-02 0005
HEDRICK, JERRY L R01HD04906-22
HEDRICK, STEPHEN M P01AI23287-06 0003
HEDRICK, STEPHEN M R01AI21372-08
HEDRICK, STEPHEN M R01AI29990-01A1
HEDRICK, STEPHEN M R01GM35880-07
HEDSTROM, OLAF R P30ES00210-24 9002
HEE, TOM T S07RR05390-30 0682
HEEG, MARY P30CA22453-14 9003
HEESCH, CHERYL M R01HL36245-06
HEFFERNAN, EDWIN J K08AI01043-01
HEFFNER, HENRY E S07RR07237-04 0744
HEFFNER, RICKYE S R01DC00179-10
HEFFRON, FRED R01AI22933-06
HEFFRON, FRED L R01GM33808-08
HEFNER, JAMES A G12RR03033-06
HEFT, M W P50DE08845-04 0002
HEFT, MARC W N01DE12587-00
HEFT, MARC W P50DE08845-04
HEFTA, STANLEY A S07RR05841-12 0244
HEFTI, ARTHUR R01DE07481-04A2
HEFTI, FRANZ P01AG09793-01 0001
HEFTI, FRANZ F P01AG09793-01
HEFTI, FRANZ F P01AG10480-01 0002
HEFTI, FRANZ F P01AG10480-01
HEFTI, FRANZ F R01NS22933-05
HEFTI, FRANZ F S07RR07012-25 0015
HEGAZY, MOHAMMED S07RR05700-22 0882
HEGEDUS, LOUIS S R01GM26178-13
HEGGENHOUGEN, KRISTI S07RR05381-30 0790
HEGYVARY, SUE T S07RR05758-18
HEGYVARY, SUE T S10RR06741-01
HEGYVARY, SUE T S15HD28774-01
HEI, TOM K P01CA49062-02 0002
HEI, TOM K R29ES05801-01
HEIDARAN, M A Z01CP05633-02
HEIDEMAN, WARREN R29GM42406-03
HEIDEMANN, STEVEN S07RR05772-17 0341
HEIDEMANN, STEVEN R R01GM36894-04A1
HEIDEMANN, STEVEN R S07RR05772-17 0355
HEIDEMANN, STEVEN R S07RR07049-26 0438
HEIDENREICH, RANDALL S07RR05506-29 0907
HEIDENREICH, RANDALL A K08HD00855-03
HEIDRICH, SUSAN S07RR06031-02 0376
HEIKKILA, RICHARD E P01NS21469-07 0001
HEILBRUN, LANCE K. P01CA46560-03 9001
HEILBRUN, PETER M01RR00064-27 0311
HEILIG, CHARLES W K08DK01953-03
HEILIGENBERG, WALTER F R01NS22244-06
HEILIGENBERG, WALTER F R37MH26149-16
HEILL, DARRYL B S07RR07023-26 0973
HEIM, WILLIAM J U10CA45558-04A1
HEIMARK, RONALD L R01HL45335-03
HEIMARK, RONALD L. P01HL03174-36 9002
HEIMARK, RONALD L. P01HL03174-36 0021
HEIMBERG, MURRAY S07RR05423-30 0051
HEIMBERG, RICHARD G R01MH44119-04
HEIMBURGER, DOUGLAS R25CA47888-04
HEIMBURGER, DOUGLAS C P01CA28103-13 9003
HEIMER, LENNART R01NS17743-11
HEIN, DAVID W R01CA34627-08A1
HEIN, JOHN W S07RR05483-29 0505
HEINDEL, J J Z01ES21089-05
HEINDEL, J J Z01ES21110-04
HEINDEL, J J Z01ES21118-03
HEINECKE, JAY W K11HD00798-05
HEINEMAN, WILLIAM R R01CA42179-06
HEINEMANN, J Z01AI00568-02
HEINEMANN, STEPHEN F R01NS11549-18
HEINEMANN, STEPHEN F R01NS28709-02
HEINEMANN, WM R S07RR07075-17 0263
HEINEN, STEPHEN J R55EY09260-01
HEINER, DOUGLAS C M01RR00425-22S3 0423
HEINER, DOUGLAS C M01RR00425-22S3 0367
HEINER, DOUGLAS C M01RR00425-22S3 0430
HEINER, DOUGLAS C M01RR00425-22S3 0431
HEINICKE, CHRISTOPH M R01MH45722-01A2
HEINONEN, OLLI P N01CN45165-17
HEINRICH, GERHARD R01NS22422-04A2
HEINRICH, GERHARD S07RR05487-29 0696
HEINSTEIN, PETER S07RR05586-24 0108
HEINTZ, NATHANIEL R01GM32544-08S1
HEINTZ, NATHANIEL S07RR07065-26 0060
HEINTZ, NICHOLAS H R01GM45891-01
HEINTZ, NICHOLAS H S07RR05429-30 0206
HEINTZELMAN, M D Z01BE01004-03
HEINY, JUDITH A R01AR40243-02
HEINZ-BROSS, KARL P30CA22453-14 9004

HEINZEL, FREDERICK P R29AI27461-03
HEIRD, W M01RR00645-20 0403
HEIRD, W C M01RR00645-20 0409
HEIRD, W C M01RR00645-20 0410
HEISE, EUGENE R S07RR05404-30 0843
HEISEY, RICHARD S07RR05656-24 0835
HEISS, GERARDO N01HC55018-11
HEISS, GERARDO U01HL45467-02
HEISTAD, DONALD D. P01NS24621-05 0007
HEISTAD, DONALD D P01HL14388-20 0180
HEISTAD, DONALD D P01NS24621-05
HEISTAD, DONALD D P01NS24621-05 0004
HEISTAD, DONALD D P50HL14230-20 0101
HEISTAD, DONALD D R37HL16066-18
HEISTERKAMP, NORA C R01CA50248-01A1
HEITER, PHILIP P01HG00373-04 0001
HEITJAN, DANIEL F S07RR05680-23 0911
HEITKEMPER, MARGARET S07RR05758-18 0247
HEITKEMPER, MARGARET M K07NR00007-05
HEITKEMPER, MARGARET M R01NR01094-07A1
HEITMAN, DAVID W S07RR07187-13 0698
HEIZER, WILLIAM D M01RR00046-31 0454
HEJTMANCIK, J F Z01EY00272-01
HELBERG, JUNE L R29NR02000-03
HELD, JEAN M S07RR07125-22 0388
HELD, KATHRYN D R01CA42167-07
HELD, KATHRYN D S10RR06516-01
HELD, PHILIP N01DK82234-05
HELD, RICHARD M R01EY01191-18
HELD, WILLIAM A R01CA50675-02
HELENIUS, ARI H P01CA46128-04 0003
HELENIUS, ARI H R01GM38346-10
HELENIUS, ARI H R37AI18599-10
HELFAND, STEPHEN S07RR05677-23 0971
HELFAND, STUART C S07RR05912-08 0651
HELFER, KAREN S S07RR07048-26 0641
HELFERICH, WILLIAM S07RR07049-26 0425
HELFMAN, DAVID P01CA46370-04 0004
HELFMAN, DAVID M R01GM43049-06
HELFRICK, JOHN F R01HS07079-01
HELGERSON, SAM L R55CA54950-01
HELINSKI, DONALD R R01AI07194-26
HELKE, CINDA J R01NS20991-06
HELKE, CINDA J R01NS24876-05
HELLEBRAND, WILLIAM M01RR06022-02 0599
HELLEKANT, GORAN S07RR05912-08 0652
HELLER, ALFRED R01MH28942-13
HELLER, ALFRED R37MH42134-05
HELLER, GARY S07RR05862-10 0558
HELLER, H CRAIG P50NS23724-06 0010
HELLER, H CRAIG R25AD00006-01
HELLER, KENNETH S07RR07031-26 0089
HELLER, LOUIS I S07RR05712-20 0055
HELLER, MORTON A S06GM08040-21 0005
HELLER, RICHARD F S03RR03206-09
HELLER, RICHARD F S06GM08174-13
HELLER, RICHARD F S06GM08174-13 0003
HELLERSTEIN, MARC M01RR00083-29 0234
HELLERSTEIN, MARC M01RR00083-29 0228
HELLERSTEIN, MARC M01RR00083-29 0213
HELLERSTEIN, MARC M01RR00083-29 0201
HELLERSTEIN, MARC R01DK40995-03
HELLMAN, DAVID B M01RR00722-19 0208
HELLMAN, SAMUEL M01RR00055-30
HELLMAN, SAMUEL S03RR03504-03
HELLMAN, SAMUEL S07RR05367-30
HELLMAN, SAMUEL S15CA55961-01
HELLSTROM, WAYNE S07RR05377-30 0767
HELLUMS, JESSE D P50NS23327-07 0004
HELLUMS, JESSE D R01HL19824-13
HELLUMS, JESSE D R37HL18584-15
HELM-ESTABROOKS, NANCY P01DC00081-26 0012
HELM-ESTABROOKS, NANCY P60DC01409-01 0005
HELM, EDWARD G S03RR03436-06
HELM, JAMES F R29DK39208-05
HELM, RICKI M S07RR05350-30 0338
HELMAN, L Z01CM06892-02
HELMAN, SANDY I S07RR07030-26 0393
HELMKAMP, G M JR S07RR05373-30 0717
HELMS, JILL K16DE00157-05S2 0003
HELMS, RONALD P30HD03110-24 9004
HELMS, RONALD W P50HL19171-15 0013
HELMS, RONALD W P50HL19171-15 9001
HELMS, SHERRON R K11HD00799-05
HELMSTETTER, CHARLES E R01GM26429-26
HELMY, FATMA M S06GM08182-12 0001
HELPER, DEBRA J K11DK01682-05
HELPER, DEBRA J S07RR05371-30 0638
HELPER, LLOYD C S03RR03046-07
HELQUIST, PAUL R01GM47227-04
HELSON, RAVENNA M R01MH43948-03
HELVEY, WILLIAM N01LM13512-00
HELZER, J P01MH47200-02 0010
HELZER, JOHN E P01AA07203-02 0004
HELZER, JOHN E P50MH31302-14 0015
HELZLSOUER, KATHY J K07CA01522-02
HELZLSOUER, KATHY J R55CA36390-07
HEMBREE, WYLIE M01RR00645-20 0376
HEMBREE, WYLIE P50HD05077-21 9001
HEMENWAY, DAVID R P50HL14212-20 0030
HEMENWAY, DAVID R P50HL14212-20 9008
HEMLER, MARTIN E R01CA42368-06
HEMLER, MARTIN E R01GM38903-05
HEMLER, MARTIN E R01GM46526-01
HEMLER, MARTIN E S07RR05526-29 0090
HEMMES, DON E S06GM08073-20 0005
HEMMINGSEN, EDWARD A R01HL16855-14A2
HEMPEL, JOHN D R01AA06985-05
HEMPLE, JOHN P30CA47904-04 9014
HEMPLEMAN, STEVEN C K04HL02071-04
HEMPSTEAD, BARBARA L S07RR05396-30 0746
HEMSTREET, GEORGE P, III R01OH02647-01S2
HENCH, KAHLER P M01RR00833-17 0152
HENDELES, LESLIE G M01RR00082-29 0461
HENDELY, DALE E M01RR00048-30 0165
HENDERSHOT, LINDA M R01GM43576-07
HENDERSON, ANN S R01ES05735-01
HENDERSON, BARBARA W R01CA42278-06
HENDERSON, BRIAN E P30CA14089-16
HENDERSON, BRIAN E P30CA14089-16 9012
HENDERSON, D Z01CL10182-02
HENDERSON, DONALD R01OH01152-10A2
HENDERSON, EARL N01LM84716-16
HENDERSON, EARL E R01AI28761-03
HENDERSON, EARL E R01CA49608-02
HENDERSON, ERIC R R29GM41023-03
HENDERSON, FREDERICK W P50HL19171-15 0004
HENDERSON, FREDERICK W P50HL19171-15 0016
HENDERSON, GEORGE I K02AA00121-03
HENDERSON, GEORGE I R01HD26707-02
HENDERSON, JAMES H S03RR03190-10
HENDERSON, JOHN M M01RR00039-31 0292
HENDERSON, JOHN M R01DK41571-03
HENDERSON, JOHN MICHAEL M01RR00039-31 0381
HENDERSON, JOHN MICHAEL M01RR00039-31 0435
HENDERSON, JOHN MICHAEL M01RR00039-31 0430
HENDERSON, JOHN MICHEAL M01RR00039-31 0404
HENDERSON, LAURA N01DK22200-14
HENDERSON, LESLIE P R01NS28668-02
HENDERSON, LESLIE P S07RR05392-30 0694
HENDERSON, MAUREEN N01CN64100-11
HENDERSON, MAUREEN S07RR05761-17 0204
HENDERSON, MAUREEN H S03RR03531-02
HENDERSON, MAUREEN M P01CA34847-09
HENDERSON, MAUREEN M R13CA53712-01
HENDERSON, RICHARD M01RR00046-31 0500
HENDERSON, VICTOR W. P50AG05142-08 9007
HENDERSON, WILLIAM P50DK41978-03 0005
HENDERSON, WILLIAM R M01RR00037-31 0518
HENDERSON, WILLIAM R P50HL30542-08 0001
HENDLER, R W Z01HL00401-25
HENDLER, R W Z01HL00418-11
HENDLER, ROSA M01RR00125-28 0575
HENDLER, ROSA G M01RR00125-28 0740
HENDLEY, EDITH D R01NS26390-03
HENDREN, ROBERT L M01RR00997-16 0389
HENDREN, ROBERT L R01MH45838-01A1
HENDRICH, CHESTER E S07RR05365-30 0082
HENDRICH, SUZANNE S07RR07034-26 0056
HENDRICK, E P30CA46934-04 9008
HENDRICKS, JERRY D. P01ES04766-04 0004
HENDRICKS, ANDREW G N01HD82909-07
HENDRICKS, ANDREW G P30AI27732-04 9002
HENDRICKS, JERRY P30ES03850-07 9002
HENDRICKS, JERRY D P30ES00210-24 9007
HENDRICKS, JOAN S07RR05464-29 0373
HENDRICKS, JOAN C P50HL42236-04 0003
HENDRICKS, JOAN C R01HL41371-04
HENDRICKS, JOHN B R44CA51576-02
HENDRICKS, JON R01AA08559-02
HENDRICKS, JON A P50DA05312-05 0005
HENDRICKS, ROBERT L R01EY05945-06
HENDRICKSON-SMITH, JANET P30HD28263-01 900
HENDRICKSON, ANITA P51RR00166-30 0140
HENDRICKSON, ANITA P51RR00166-30 0141
HENDRICKSON, ANITA P51RR00166-30 0090
HENDRICKSON, ANITA E P30EY01730-16 9003
HENDRICKSON, ANITA E R01EY04536-09
HENDRICKSON, BARBARA A K11AI01035-01
HENDRICKSON, DAVID N R37HL13652-21
HENDRICKSON, ROY V P51RR00169-30 9010
HENDRICKSON, WAYNE P41RR06892-01 0003
HENDRICKSON, WAYNE A R01GM34102-08
HENDRICKX, ANDREW G P51RR00169-30 0113
HENDRICKX, ANDREW G P51RR00169-30 0114
HENDRICKX, ANDREW G P51RR00169-30 0060
HENDRICKX, ANDREW G P51RR00169-30 0115
HENDRICKX, ANDREW G P51RR00169-30 9021
HENDRICKX, ANDREW G P51RR00169-30 0116
HENDRICKX, ANDREW G P51RR00169-30 0117
HENDRICKX, ANDREW G P51RR00169-30 0118
HENDRICKX, ANDREW G P51RR00169-30 0119
HENDRICKX, ANDREW G P51RR00169-30 0150
HENDRICKX, ANDREW G R01HD25528-02
HENDRIE, HUGH C R01AG09956-01
HENDRIX, MARY J R03CA54984-01
HENDRIX, ROGER W R01AI12227-16S1
HENDRIX, ROGER W R01GM47795-17
HENDRIX, SUSAN S07RR05772-17 0345
HENDRY, STEWARD P01DC00450-04 0006
HENDRY, WILLIAM J, III R03HD28074-01
HENIKOFF, LEO M S07RR05477-29
HENIKOFF, STEVEN R01GM29009-11
HENINGER, GEORGE R P01MH25642-18
HENINGER, GEORGE R P50MH30929-15 9001
HENINGER, GEORGE R R01MH36229-10
HENKART, P A Z01CB09251-21
HENKART, P A Z01CB09263-10
HENKE, CURTIS P60AR20684-14 0032
HENKE, CURTIS K P60AR20684-14 0030
HENKEL, CRAIG K R01DC00813-02
HENKEL, CRAIG K S07RR05404-30 0844
HENKEN, D B Z01NS02804-02
HENKER, BARBARA A R01HD27035-02
HENKIN, ROBERT I P41RR02176-05 0006
HENKIN, TINA M R29GM40650-04
HENLE, KURT J R01CA33405-11
HENLE, KURT J S07RR05350-30 0335
HENLEY, CHARLES M R29DC00656-03
HENLEY, KEITH M01RR00042-31 0653
HENN, FRITZ A P01NS15638-13 9003
HENNEKENS, CHARLES H R01CA40360-07
HENNEKENS, CHARLES H R01EY08427-02
HENNEKENS, CHARLES H R01HL34594-07
HENNEKENS, CHARLES H R01HL34595-07
HENNEKENS, CHARLES H R01HL43851-01A2
HENNEKENS, CHARLES H S07RR05381-30 0793
HENNEKENS, CHARLES H U01HL37852-06
HENNEMAN, CAROL P01CA50084-03 0001
HENNER, WILLIAM D R01CA35767-08
HENNER, WILLIAM D R01CA55232-01
HENNER, WILLIAM D S07RR05412-30 0980
HENNEY, JANE E N01CO15704-00
HENNEY, JANE E S07RR07253-02
HENNIG, BERNHARD P01HL36552-07 0008
HENNIGHAUSEN, L Z01DK17009-06
HENNING, SUSAN J R37HD14094-13
HENNINGFIELD, J E Z01DA00004-05
HENNINGFIELD, J E Z01DA00005-05
HENNINGFIELD, J E Z01DA00006-04
HENNINGFIELD, J E Z01DA00007-05
HENNINGFIELD, J E Z01DA00008-04
HENNINGFIELD, J E Z01DA00010-06
HENNINGFIELD, J E Z01DA00011-05
HENNINGFIELD, J E Z01DA00024-03
HENNINGFIELD, J E Z01DA00025-03
HENNINGFIELD, J E Z01DA00026-02
HENNINGFIELD, J E Z01DA00028-02
HENNINGFIELD, J E Z01DA00029-02
HENNINGFIELD, J E Z01DA00030-02
HENNINGFIELD, J E Z01DA00031-02
HENNINGFIELD, J E Z01DA00033-02
HENNINGFIELD, J E Z01DA00034-02
HENNINGFIELD, J E Z01DA00035-02
HENNINGFIELD, J E Z01DA00036-06
HENNINGFIELD, J E Z01DA00037-01
HENNINGFIELD, J E Z01DA00040-01
HENNINGFIELD, J E Z01DA00041-01
HENNINGFIELD, J E Z01DA00042-01
HENNINGFIELD, J E Z01DA00044-01
HENNINGFIELD, J E Z01DA00045-01
HENNINGFIELD, J E Z01DA00046-01
HENNINGFIELD, J E Z01DA00047-01
HENNINGFIELD, J E Z01DA00048-03
HENNINGFIELD, J E Z01DA00213-07
HENOCH, NEIL F S03RR03406-07
HENRETTA, JOHN C R01AG07849-03
HENRICH, JANET B S07RR05358-30 0498
HENRICKSON, KELLY J S07RR05434-30 0812
HENRICKSON, ROY V P51RR00169-30 9011
HENRICKSON, ROY V P51RR00169-30 9007
HENRICKSON, ROY V P51RR00169-30 9018
HENRIKSEN, ERIK J S07RR07002-26 0882
HENRIKSEN, RUTH A R29HL45194-01A1
HENRIKSEN, STEVEN P50MH47680-02 0012
HENRIKSEN, STEVEN J K02DA00131-04
HENRIKSEN, STEVEN J P50AA06420-08 0009
HENRIKSEN, STEVEN J R01AA07365-03
HENRIQUES, HORACE S07RR05359-30 0509
HENRY, C A S07RR05915-08 0677
HENRY, CAROLL E S06GM08043-21 0010
HENRY, E R Z01DK29021-06
HENRY, EGBERT S07RR07131-22 0131
HENRY, EGBERT W S03RR03081-11
HENRY, MICHAEL A K11DE00219-05
HENRY, MITCHELL L R29AI28478-03
HENRY, PATRICK H U10CA35128-08
HENRY, PHILIP D P50HL42267-02 0006
HENRY, PHILIP D R01HL36894-05
HENRY, ROBERT R M01RR00827-17 0377
HENRY, ROBERT R M01RR00827-17 0470
HENRY, ROBERT R M01RR00827-17 0378
HENRY, ROBERT R M01RR00827-17 0381
HENRY, ROBERT R R29DK38949-04
HENRY, SUSAN A R25RR07642-01
HENRY, SUSAN A R37GM19629-20
HENRY, WALTER L S07RR05351-30
HENSCHEN, AGNES H R01HL42412-03
HENSHAW, EDGAR C P30CA11198-23 9015
HENSHAW, EDGAR C R01CA21663-15
HENSKI, ELIZABETH P K08NS01571-01
HENSON, LINDSEY C M01RR00425-22S3 0441
HENSON, O'DELL W, JR R01DC00114-15
HENSON, PETER P50HL27353-10 0008
HENSON, PETER M G20RR06775-01
HENSON, PETER M P01HL34303-07 0004

HENSON, PETER M P01HL34303-07 9004
HENSON, PETER M S07RR05842-12
HENSON, PETER M S15AI32163-01
HENTALL, IAN D R29NS26116-04
HENTALL, IAN D S06GM08224-07 0011
HENTOSH, PATRICIA R01CA55414-01
HEPPEL, LEON P41RR04224-04 0003
HEPPEL, LEON A R01AG07429-03
HEPPNER, GLORIA P30CA22453-14 0003
HEPPNER, GLORIA H R01CA27419-13
HEPPNER, GLORIA H S03RR03294-10
HEPPNER, GLORIA H S07RR05529-29
HEPPNER, GLORIA H S07RR05529-29 0524
HERBERMAN, RONALD P30CA47904-04 9015
HERBERMAN, RONALD P30CA47904-04 9005
HERBERMAN, RONALD P30CA47904-04 9019
HERBERMAN, RONALD B P01CA47445-03
HERBERMAN, RONALD B P01CA47445-03 9001
HERBERMAN, RONALD B P30CA47904-04
HERBERT, JOSEPH R29NS26892-03
HERBERT, LEE A M01RR00034-31 0282
HERBETTE, LEO P41RR01633-10 0011
HERBETTE, LEO G P01HL33026-07 0003
HERBST, ARTHUR N01ES95267-02
HERD, DENISE A R29AA09002-01
HERD, J ALAN M01RR00350-25 0438
HERD, J ALAN N01HC75071-06
HERDMAN, SUSAN J K08DC00032-04
HERDMAN, SUSAN J P60DC00979-02 0006
HERDT, GILBERT S07RR07029-26 0023
HERDT, THOMAS H S07RR05623-25 0713
HEREK, GREGORY M R01MH43253-06
HERGENROEDER, ALBERT M01RR00188-27 0275
HERING, THOMAS M R29AR40829-01
HERKENHAM, M Z01MH01090-14
HERLIHY, JEREMIAH T. P01AG01188-13 0011
HERLYN, DOROTHEE P01CA25874-12 0007
HERLYN, DOROTHEE R03CA53411-02
HERLYN, DOROTHEE M R03CA54851-01
HERLYN, MEENHARD P01CA25874-12
HERLYN, MEENHARD P01CA25874-12 0004
HERLYN, MEENHARD R01CA44877-05
HERLYN, MEENHARD R01CA47159-03
HERMALIN, ALBERT I R37AG07637-03
HERMAN-BONERT, VIVIE S07RR05468-29 0393
HERMAN-BONERT, VIVIEN S K08DK01949-01A1
HERMAN, A A Z01HD00380-02
HERMAN, BARBARA H R01HD25849-01A1
HERMAN, BRIAN P30CA16086-17 9015
HERMAN, BRIAN S07RR05406-30 0916
HERMAN, BRIAN A R01AG07218-05
HERMAN, BRIAN A R01AG10104-01
HERMAN, CEIL A S07RR07154-16 0560
HERMAN, CEIL ANN S06GM08136-18 0016
HERMAN, D J S07RR05333-30 0867
HERMAN, GABOR P41RR02305-08 9009
HERMAN, GABOR T R01HL28438-11
HERMAN, GAIL E R01AR39499-01A3
HERMAN, GAIL E R01HG00131-01A1
HERMAN, IRA M R01HL35570-07
HERMAN, IRA M S07RR05382-30 0869
HERMAN, MICHAEL V N01HC65035-09
HERMAN, MICHAEL V U01HL38524-05
HERMAN, ROBERT K R01GM22387-16
HERMAN, SANDRA E R19MH46307-03
HERMAN, TERENCE S R01CA50174-01A2
HERMAN, WILLIAM H M01RR00042-31 0560
HERMODSON, MARK A S07RR07032-26 0048
HERMSMEYER, KENT P01HL14388-20 0168
HERMSMEYER, R KENT R01HL38537-06
HERMSMEYER, R KENT S15HL47788-01
HERNANDEZ-AVILA, MANUEL L S06GM08103-18
HERNANDEZ, LINDA L R01DA06676-02
HERNANDEZ, M ROSARIO R01EY06416-06
HERNANDEZ, NOURIA R01GM38810-05
HERNANDEZ, NOURIA T R01AI31826-01
HERNANDEZ, TERESITA N44CN05310-02
HERNDON, CAROL D S03RR03295-10
HERNDON, DAVID N M01RR00073-29 0304
HERNDON, JAMES G P51RR00165-31 0093
HERNDON, JAMES G S07RR07023-26 0971
HERNDON, ROBERT P30AG08017-02 9001
HERNESS, M SCOTT R29DC00401-05
HERNING, R I Z01DA00509-01
HERNING, R I Z01DA02001-05
HERNING, R I Z01DA02101-05
HERNING, R I Z01DA03101-05
HERNING, R I Z01DA05801-04
HERNING, R I Z01DA06801-04
HEROLD, BETSY C K11AI00945-03
HEROLD, KEVAN C K08DK01938-02
HEROLD, KEVAN C M01RR00055-30 0577
HEROS, DEBORAH M01RR00054-30 0365
HEROS, ROBERTO C R01NS23682-06
HERR, JOHN U54HD29099-01 0003
HERR, JOHN C P30CA44579-04A1 9005
HERR, JOHN C R01HD23789-04A1
HERR, JOHN C U54HD29099-01
HERR, JOHN C. P51RR00166-30 0142
HERR, WINSHIP P01CA13106-20 0014
HERR, WINSHIP R13GM46652-01
HERRERA, ALBERT A R01NS24805-04A1
HERRERA, ALBERT A R01NS27209-02
HERRERA, VICTORIA L K11HL01967-05
HERRERA, VICTORIA L M P50HL47124-01 0007
HERRICK, GLENN A R01GM25203-14
HERRICK, RICHARD C S07RR05425-30 0744
HERRING, BRIAN PAUL S07RR07175-15 0434
HERRING, SUSAN W R01DE08513-06
HERRINGTON, DAVID M S07RR05404-30 0845
HERRMANN, JOHN U01AI28167-02 0002
HERRMANN, SCOTT J S06GM08197-10 0006
HERRMANN, STEVEN H R01CA47718-05
HERROD, HENRY G M01RR00211-27 0247
HERRON, JAMES N R01AI22898-05
HERRUP, KARL P30HD04147-22A1 9013
HERRUP, KARL R01NS18381-11
HERRUP, KARL R01NS20591-08A1
HERS, HENRI-GERY R01DK09235-26
HERSCHMAN, HARVEY R R01GM24797-14
HERSCHMAN, HARVEY R R01NS28660-01A1
HERSCOVICS, ANNETTE A R01GM31265-09
HERSCOVITCH, P Z01CL03002-01
HERSCOVITCH, P Z01CL03003-01
HERSCOWITZ, HERBERT B R01HL25478-09A2
HERSEY, STEPHEN S07RR05364-30 0529
HERSEY, STEPHEN J R01DK14752-21
HERSH, ALICE S R13HS06190-03
HERSH, EVAN P30CA23074-14 9014
HERSH, EVAN M R01AI27689-02
HERSH, EVANS M P01CA17094-16 0026
HERSH, LOUIS B P50AG08013-04 0001
HERSH, LOUIS B R01AG05893-12
HERSH, LOUIS B R01DA02243-14
HERSH, WILLIAM H S07RR07064-24 0203
HERSH, WILLIAM R R29LM05307-01
HERSH, WILLIAM R S07RR07238-04 0468
HERSHEY, JOHN W R01GM22135-17
HERSHEY, JOHN W R01GM40082-04
HERSHFIELD, MICHAEL S R01DK20902-14
HERSHKO, AVRAM R01DK25614-12
HERSHKO, CHAIM R01HL34062-06
HERSHKOWITZ, NORMAN K08NS01460-02
HERSHON, DAVE P01NS23393-06 9002
HERSHOW, RONALD C S07RR05871-03 0578
HERSKOWITZ, AHVIE M01RR00722-19 0211
HERSKOWITZ, AHVIE R01HL41514-04
HERSKOWITZ, IRA P01GM31286-09 0004
HERSKOWITZ, IRA R37AI18738-11
HERTZ-PICCIOTTO, IRVA R01ES05738-01
HERTZ-PICCIOTTO, IRVA R03CA55637-01
HERTZ, ROGER H. P50HD11089-14 0019
HERTZ, MARSHALL M01RR00400-23 0245
HERTZ, MARSHALL I M01RR00400-23 0286
HERTZ, SUSAN R R43DC01305-01
HERTZBERG, ELLIOT L R01GM30667-11
HERTZBERG, VICKI P01HD11725-13 9001
HERWALDT, LOREEN A K08AI01032-01
HERWEIJER, JANTIEN A S07RR05330-30 0022
HERZ, FRITZ R01CA47512-03
HERZBERG, MARK P30DE09737-02 9001
HERZBERG, MARK C K16DE00270-02
HERZBERG, MARK C R01DE05501-10
HERZBERG, MARK C R01DE08590-02
HERZBERG, OSNAT R01AI27175-03
HERZENBERG, LEONARD P01AI19512-09 0010
HERZENBERG, LEONARD A R35CA42509-06
HERZENBERG, LEONORE R01LM04836-03
HERZENBERG, LEONORE A R01HD01287-28
HERZFELD, JUDITH R01GM36810-07
HERZFELD, JUDITH R01HL36546-06
HERZLINGER, DORIS A R01DK45218-01
HERZOG, A REGULA P01AG05561-06A1 0001
HERZOG, ANNA R R01AG02038-09A1
HERZOG, DAVID B R01MH38333-05
HERZON, GARRETT S07RR05370-30 0626
HESELTINE, PETER N. M01RR00043-31 0420
HESELTINE, PETER N M01RR00043-31 0470
HESS, ALLAN D P01CA15396-18 0003
HESS, ALLAN D R01AI24319-05
HESS, ARTHUR S07RR05576-27 0589
HESS, DAVID P51RR00163-32 9012
HESS, DAVID L P30HD18185-08 9001
HESS, G P P41RR04224-04 0005
HESS, G P P41RR04224-04 0007
HESS, GEORGE P R01GM04842-36
HESS, H H Z01EY00135-19
HESS, MICHAEL M01RR00065-29 0373
HESS, MICHAEL M01RR00065-29 0084
HESS, PETER R01HL37124-06
HESS, REX A R29ES05214-03
HESS, THOMAS M R01AG05552-05A1
HESSELBROCK, VICTOR P50AA03510-14 0013
HESSELBROCK, VICTOR P50AA03510-14 0020
HESSELBROCK, VICTOR P50AA03510-14 0021
HESSELINK, JOHN P50MH45294-03 9005
HESSLER, JACK R G20RR06777-01
HESTER, RAYMOND B S10RR06520-01
HESTER, ROBERT L R29HL43089-02
HESTON, LEONARD L R01MH43240-04
HESTON, WARREN D W P01CA29502-11A1 9002
HESTRIN, SHAUL R01EY07507-04
HESTRIN, SHAUL R01EY09120-01
HETENYI, GEZA P41RR02176-05 0005
HETH, CYNTHIA A R01EY08091-03
HEUER, DALE K U10EY06806-06
HEUSER, JOHN E R01GM29647-11
HEWETT-EMMETT, DAVID S07RR07143-20 0541
HEWETT, JOHN E R01GM42584-02
HEWITT, JOHN K R01AA08672-02
HEWITT, JOHN K R01MH45268-03
HEWLETT, EDMOND S07RR05304-30 0225
HEWLETT, ERIK L R01AI18000-10
HEWLETT, ERIK L R01AI31119-01
HEWLETT, I Z01BG06015-02
HEWLETT, I K Z01BG06016-02
HEWLETT, I K Z01BG06017-03
HEWLETT, I K Z01BG06018-03
HEWLETT, I K Z01BG06021-02
HEWLETT, I K Z01BG06022-02
HEWLETT, I K Z01BG06038-01
HEWLETT, I K Z01BG06039-01
HEWLETT, I K Z01BG06040-01
HEWLETT, I K Z01BG06041-01
HEWLETT, I K Z01BG06042-01
HEXUM, TERRY D R01NS26479-01A2
HEYES, M P Z01MH02384-05
HEYLIGER, PAUL S07RR07127-23 0480
HEYMAN, ALBERT K06NS16677-29
HEYMAN, ALBERT P50NS06233-25 0041
HEYMAN, ALBERT R37AG08937-01
HEYMAN, ALBERT U01AG06790-06
HEYMAN, BARRY N01CO15698-01
HEYMAN, GENE M R03AA08731-01A1
HEYMAN, MELVIN B M01RR01271-10 0110
HEYMAN, MELVIN B M01RR01271-10 0070
HEYMANN, MICHAEL A R01HL40473-04
HEYMANN, PETER W R29AI24261-05
HEYMSFIELD, STEVE P01DK42618-02 0003
HEYMSFIELD, STEVEN P30DK26687-11 9010
HEYNER, SUSAN R01HD23511-05A1
HEYWORTH, MARTIN F P30AI27763-04 9005
HIATT, ROBERT A R01CA54605-01
HIATT, ROBERT DR N01CP95606-04
HIBBARD, LISA B S06GM08241-07 0008
HIBBARD, LYNDON S P50AG05681-08 9005
HIBBERT, JACQULINE M01RR00073-29 0318
HICKEY, J E Z01DA00507-01
HICKEY, ROBERT W M01RR00084-29 0248
HICKEY, TERRY L S03RR03001-11
HICKEY, TERRY L S03RR03002-11
HICKEY, TERRY L S03RR03233-07
HICKEY, TERRY L S03RR03235-10
HICKEY, TERRY L S03RR03400-08
HICKEY, TERRY L S03RR03449-05
HICKOK, NOREEN J R29AR40022-02
HICKS, JANICE M R55GM46258-01
HICKS, KENNETH W S06GM08019-21 0007
HICKS, LESLIE H R24MH47199-02
HICKS, MELVIN L S03RR03106-09
HICKS, PAULINE G12RR03020-07 9001
HICKS, RICHARD E R43CI00017-01
HICKS, ROBERT A S06GM08192-12
HICKS, ROBERT A. S06GM08192-12 0008
HICKSON, ROBERT C R01AR39496-03
HICKSTEIN, DENNIS D R29DK43530-01
HIDALGO, HUMBERTO A S07RR05654-24 0139
HIDER, ROBERT C R01HL42800-02
HIENZ, ROBERT D R01DA02490-12
HIENZ, ROBERT D R01DA04731-04
HIESIGER, EMILE M P01NS15638-13 0010
HIETER, PHILIP P01HD24605-03 0001
HIETER, PHILIP A P01CA16519-17 0006
HIGASHIJIMA, TSUTOMU R01GM40676-02
HIGASHIKUBO, RYUJI P01CA51116-02 9001
HIGGINBOTHAM, D JEFFERY K08DC00034-03
HIGGINS, EARL B S03RR03163-01
HIGGINS, EDWARD TORY R37MH39429-08
HIGGINS, GERALD A P30ES01247-17 0096
HIGGINS, GERALD A R35AG09016-02 0002
HIGGINS, GLORIA C K08AR01863-01
HIGGINS, JANE A R18MH47644-01A1
HIGGINS, KENT E R01EY07886-02
HIGGINS, MAUREEN S07RR05834-12 0536
HIGGINS, MICHAEL L R01AI10971-20
HIGGINS, PAUL J R43AI31712-01
HIGGINS, R J S07RR05457-29 0003
HIGGINS, ROBERT P51RR00169-30 0151
HIGGINS, ROBERT H S06GM08206-10 0005
HIGGINS, ROBERT H S06GM08206-10 0005
HIGGINS, STEPHEN M01RR00109-28 0353
HIGGINS, STEPHEN M01RR00109-28 0278
HIGGINS, STEPHEN T R18DA06113-03
HIGGINS, STEPHEN T R29DA04545-05
HIGGINS, WILLIAM E R29CA53607-01
HIGH, KATHERINE A K08HL01922-05
HIGHET, R J Z01HL01006-20
HIGHLANDER, SARAH S07RR05425-30 0745
HIGHSMITH, ROBERT F R01HL31543-07
HIGHSMITH, STEFAN R01AR37499-04
HIGHSMITH, STEFAN S07RR05301-21
HIGHSMITH, STEFAN S07RR05301-21 0736
HIGHSMITH, STEFAN S15HL47766-01
HIGHSTEIN, STEPHEN M P01NS17763-10 0011
HIGHSTEIN, STEPHEN M R01DC01425-09
HIGHTOWER, KENNETH R R01EY03681-11

HIGLEY, J Z01AA00277-03
HIGSON, HOWARD S07RR05301-21 0730
HIGUCHI, WILLIAM I R01DK32472-07
HIGUCHI, WILLIAM I R01GM43181-02
HILAL, SADEK K P01CA28881-07A1 9001
HILAL, SADEK K P01CA28881-07A1
HILAL, SADEK K P01CA28881-07A1 0001
HILDEBOLT, CHARLES F R29DE08173-04
HILDEBRAND, JOHN G P01NS28495-02
HILDEBRAND, JOHN G P01NS28495-02 0001
HILDEBRAND, JOHN G R01DC00348-06
HILDEBRAND, JOHN G R37AI23253-07
HILDEBRANDT, JOHN P30CA12708-21 9006
HILDEBRANDT, JOHN P30CA12708-21 9007
HILDEBRANDT, JOHN D R01DK37219-05
HILDEBRANDT, NANCY R29DC00462-03
HILDEBRANDT, PAUL N01ES95270-02
HILDENBRANDT, GEORGE S07RR07082-26 0287
HILDRETH, JAMES E R01AI31806-01
HILE, MATTHEW G R29MH43439-03
HILF, RUSSELL R01CA16660-14
HILF, RUSSELL R01CA36856-08
HILF, RUSSELL R01HD24459-02
HILGARTNER, MARGARET M01RR06020-02 0449
HILGARTNER, MARGARET W M01RR06020-02 0184
HILGARTNER, MARGARET W R01HL43027-03
HILGARTNER, STEPHEN R01HG00417-01
HILGEMANN, DONALD W R29HL45240-02
HILL, ANNA B R29CA47547-03
HILL, BRUCE C S07RR05513-29 0060
HILL, CHARLES E, III R43DC01168-01
HILL, CHARLES W R01GM16329-24
HILL, COLIN K R01CA42808-07
HILL, DAVID L R01DC00407-06
HILL, DEBORAH P50DE08240-05 0014
HILL, DONALD N01CM87285-04
HILL, DONALD L P01CA34200-09 9007
HILL, DONALD L. U01AI25739-04 0003
HILL, ESTHER P P01HL17731-17 0016
HILL, ESTHER P P01HL17731-17 0010
HILL, GENE E N01LM13525-01
HILL, GEORGE C R01AI21159-06A3
HILL, GEORGE C R13AI31424-01
HILL, GEORGE C S03RR03384-03
HILL, GERALD L S03RR03490-04
HILL, GOERGE S06GM08037-20 0050
HILL, GRETCHEN S07RR07053-26 0137
HILL, HARLAN P01CA38552-05A1 0005
HILL, HARLAN P01CA38552-05A1 9003
HILL, HARLAN F R01DA05513-03
HILL, HARLAN F R01DA07313-01
HILL, HARRY R R01AI13150-14
HILL, J DONALD S07RR05566-28 0584
HILL, JAMES M01RR00095-31 0280
HILL, JAMES M01RR00095-31 0369
HILL, JAMES M01RR00095-31 0371
HILL, JAMES M01RR00095-31 0376
HILL, JAMES P30DK26657-12 9007
HILL, JAMES M R01EY06311-06
HILL, JAMES M R01EY08871-01
HILL, JAMES O M01RR00095-31 0344
HILL, JAMES O R01DK38088-06
HILL, JAMES O R01DK42549-02
HILL, JAMES O. M01RR00095-31 0279
HILL, JAMES O. M01RR00095-31 0306
HILL, JAMES R M01RR00082-29 0291
HILL, JOSEPH A K11HD00815-05
HILL, JOSEPH O R01AI31344-01
HILL, KELVIN A W S07RR05352-30 0760
HILL, KENNETH H R01HD28411-01
HILL, MARTHA N S07RR06012-03 0309
HILL, MICHAEL R01HL33324-07
HILL, MICHAEL A S07RR05814-12 0149
HILL, MICHAEL A S07RR05814-12 0141
HILL, NICHOLAS S R01HL45050-01A1
HILL, PAMELA D R15NR02764-01
HILL, PAMELA D S07RR05776-11 0395
HILL, RICHARD M S07RR05969-05
HILL, ROBERT U01AG10483-01 9001
HILL, ROBERT L R37GM25766-31
HILL, ROGER P30CA15704-18 9018
HILL, SHIRLEY Y R01AA05909-08
HILL, SHIRLEY Y R01AA08082-02
HILL, STEVEN M R29CA54152-01
HILL, THOMAS M R29GM43193-02
HILL, WALTER E R01GM35717-06
HILL, WALTER E S06GM08218-08 0015
HILLABRANT, WALTER J R43PS00001-01
HILLAR, MARIAN S06GM08061-17 0011
HILLARD, CECILIA J R29DA04800-04
HILLE, BERTE P50HD12629-12 0010
HILLE, BERTIL R01NS08174-23
HILLE, CHARLES R R01AR38917-04
HILLE, CHARLES R S10RR06706-01
HILLE, MERRILL B S07RR07096-26 0070
HILLEMEIER, ALFRED C R01HD20054-07
HILLER, JACOB M R01AG08945-03
HILLHOUSE, GREGORY L R01GM41650-02
HILLIARD, JULIA K P40RR05062-03
HILLIARD, JULIA K R01RR03163-06
HILLIARD, RICHARD A S07RR07033-26
HILLIER, SHARON L U01AI31448-01 0004
HILLIS, ARGYE U10EY06797-04
HILLMAN, DEAN E P01AG09480-01 0003
HILLMAN, DEAN E P01NS13742-15 0003
HILLMAN, JEFFREY D R01DE04529-13A2
HILLMAN, RALPH S07RR07115-24
HILLMAN, RALPH S15GM47042-01
HILLMAN, ROBERT E R01DC00266-07
HILLSON, JAN L R29AR40239-02
HILLYARD, ROBERT S07RR05551-29 0952
HILLYARD, STEVEN A P01NS17778-10 0007
HILLYARD, STEVEN A R37MH25594-18
HILLYER, GEORGE V P40RR03640-05 0030
HILLYER, GEORGE V S06GM08102-20 0001
HILT, DANA P01HD16596-08 0007
HILTNER, P ANNE R01HL25239-10
HILTON, CHARLES W S07RR05376-30 0036
HILTON, MICHAEL P50AA05595-11 0015
HILTON, MICHAEL P50AA05595-11 0012
HILTON, MICHAEL P50AA05595-11 0013
HILVERT, DONALD M R01GM38273-06
HIMES, JOHN S07RR05448-30 0314
HIMES, JOHN H R01HD24684-03
HIMES, RICHARD H R01DK07140-26
HIMES, RICHARD H S07RR07037-26 0373
HIND, JOSEPH E. P01DC00116-16 0015
HINDER, RONALD A R01DK40381-03
HINDMAN, BRADLEY J R01HL47159-01
HINDS, JOSEPH E K07HL02678-01
HINDS, JOSEPH E S07RR05422-30 0047
HINDS, PAMELA S R01CA48432-02
HINDSGAUL, OLE R01CA50542-03
HINE, A BROMFIELD S06GM08224-07 0012
HINE, R JEAN M01RR00032-31 0384
HINELINE, PHILIP N S07RR07115-24 0585
HINES, DEBORAH H S03RR03315-08
HINES, JOHN N01CM73714-05
HINES, MELISSA M R01HD24542-02
HINES, MICHAEL L R01NS11613-16
HINES, RONALD N R01CA53106-01A1
HINES, RONALD N R01ES03832-07
HINGERTY, BRIAN E R01GM34687-05
HINGSON, RALPH W R01AA07536-04
HINK, ROBERT F R43DA07276-01
HINK, ROBERT F R44DA05889-02
HINKES, MICHAEL T K11AR01816-04
HINKLE, PATRICIA M R01DK19974-15
HINNEBUSCH, A G Z01HD01004-08
HINOJOSA, RAUL R01DC00301-07
HINRICHS, DAVID J R01AI23455-05
HINRICHS, JAMES P30DE09737-02 0003
HINRICHS, JAMES E S07RR05322-30 0280
HINRICHS, STEVEN H P30AI27732-04 9004
HINRICHS, STEVEN H R29CA49624-03
HINRICHSEN, ROBERT D R13GM46322-01
HINRICKS, DAVID J S07RR06002-04 0823
HINRICKS, DAVID J S07RR06002-04 0822
HINSHAW, STEPHEN S07RR07006-26 0906
HINSHAW, STEPHEN P R29MH45064-02
HINSHAW, VIRGINIA S R29AI24902-04
HINTON, BARRY T S07RR05431-30 0861
HINTON, D E P42ES04699-05 0002
HINTON, D M Z01DK23750-05
HINTON, DAVID P01NS26991-02 9001
HINTON, DAVID E R01CA45131-05
HINTON, LADSON S07RR05755-18 0214
HINTON, MARY ANN R19DA06430-03
HINTON, R J S07RR05915-08 0686
HINTZ, RAYMOND L R01DK24085-12
HINTZE, THOMAS H P01HL43023-01A2 0005
HIRAIZUMI, YUICHIRO R01GM19770-18A1
HIRAIZUMI, YUICHIRO S07RR07091-26 0756
HIRAMOTO, RAYMOND N R01CA37570-05
HIRATA, FUSAO R01ES04802-04
HIROMI, YASUSHI R01NS29662-01
HIROSHI, MIZUKAMI S06GM08167-13 0041
HIRS, WERNER C M P30CA46934-04 9007
HIRSCH, ALAN T K08HL02429-03
HIRSCH, ALAN T M01RR02635-07 0257
HIRSCH, ALAN T M01RR02635-07 0268
HIRSCH, JULES M01RR00102-28 0158
HIRSCH, JULES M01RR00102-28 0004
HIRSCH, JULES M01RR00102-28 0159
HIRSCH, MARTIN S R01CA12464-21
HIRSCH, MARTIN S R01CA35020-09
HIRSCH, MARTIN S R01CA54741-01
HIRSCH, MARTIN S U01AI27659-05S2
HIRSCH, P F S07RR05333-30 0868
HIRSCH, RHODA E R01DK41253-02
HIRSCHBERG, CARLOS B R01GM34396-08
HIRSCHBERG, CARLOS B R37GM30365-17
HIRSCHBERG, RONA S07RR05997-04 0818
HIRSCHEL, MARK D R44AI28654-02A1
HIRSCHEL, MARK D U24RR05991-02
HIRSCHHORN, KURT P30HD28822-01
HIRSCHHORN, RICKY R S07RR07114-23 0438
HIRSCHHORN, RICKY R S07RR07114-23 0439
HIRSCHHORN, ROCHELLE R37AI10343-20
HIRSCHMAN, CHARLES R01HD26330-02
HIRSCHMAN, JODI E S07RR05712-20 0103
HIRSCHMANN, RALPH F R01GM41821-02
HIRSCHMANN, RALPH F R01GM45611-01
HIRSCHOWITZ, BASIL I M01RR00032-31 0309
HIRSH-PASEK, KATHRYN S07RR07115-24 0586
HIRSH, DAVID I R01GM37823-06
HIRSH, IRA J S07RR05987-05 0024
HIRSH, JAY R01GM27318-12
HIRSHAUT, YASHAR P01CA20194-14 9002
HIRSHBERG, LINDA R44AA07661-02A3
HIRSHFIELD, ANNE N R01HD27194-02
HIRSHFIELD, IRVIN N R15GM44097-01A1
HIRSHMAN, CAROL P01HL10342-26 0028
HIRSHMAN, CAROL A P50HL37119-05 0002
HIRSHMAN, CAROL A R01HL45974-02
HIRST, WILLIAM C R01MH42064-02
HIRT, EDWARD R S07RR07098-26 0355
HIRTH, RICHARD A R03HS06934-01
HISKEY, RICHARD G R37HL20161-15
HISS, ROLAND G P60DK20572-14 9008
HITCHCOCK-DEGREGORI, SARAH E R01GM36326-06
HITCHCOCK-DEGREGORI, SARAH E R01HL35726-04
HITCHCOCK, PETER F R01EY07060-05
HITRI, A Z01MH02484-03
HITRI, A Z01MH02543-02
HITRI, A Z01MH02568-01
HITTELMAN, WALTER N P01CA06294-30 0068
HITTELMAN, WALTER N R01CA27931-11
HITTLEMAN, WALTER N P01CA52051-01A1 0004
HITZEMAN, ROBERT S07RR05736-19 0157
HITZIG, BERNARD M R01HL43819-01A2
HITZIG, BERNARD M S07RR05486-29 0056
HITZIG, BERNARD M S07RR05486-29 0050
HIXON, LEE J S07RR05675-23 0909
HIXON, THOMAS J P60DC01409-01
HIXON, THOMAS J P60DC01409-01 0001
HIXON, THOMAS J R01DC00281-07
HIXSON, DOUGLAS C R01CA42714-06
HIXSON, DOUGLAS C R01CA42715-06
HIXSON, DOUGLAS C R03CA54877-01
HIXSON, JAMES E P01HL45522-01A1 0002
HIXSON, JAMES E R01HL39913-04
HIXSON, STEPHEN S S07RR07048-26 0642
HIZI, AMNON R01AI27035-03
HJELLE, BRIAN L R01CA55480-01
HJELMELAND, LEONARD M R01EY06473-06
HLADY, VLADIMIR S07RR07092-26 0491
HLASTALA, MICHAEL P51RR00166-30 0091
HLASTALA, MICHAEL P P01HL24163-13
HLASTALA, MICHAEL P P01HL24163-13 0007
HLASTALA, MICHAEL P R37HL12174-23
HLATKY, LYNN R R55RR06587-01
HNATOWICH, DONALD J N01CM97570-02
HNN, STEPHEN R P01CA48799-03 0003
HO, BENG T S07RR05511-29 0502
HO, CHIEN P41RR03631-04
HO, CHIEN R01GM26874-13
HO, CHIEN R37HL24525-13
HO, DAVID D R01AI28747-04
HO, E E K07CA01353-05
HO, ING K R01DA04264-05
HO, ING K R01DA04480-05
HO, ING K S15DA07818-01
HO, ING KANG R01DA05828-03
HO, MENGFEI S07RR05454-29 0886
HO, MONTO M01RR00056-30 0329
HO, MONTO M01RR00056-30 0361
HO, MONTO M01RR00056-30 0380
HO, MONTO P01CA47445-03 0001
HO, MONTO U01AI27672-05S1
HO, PING-PEI R03RR06846-01
HO, RODNEY J R01AI32332-01
HO, RODNEY J R29AI31854-01
HO, SHUK-MEI S07RR07179-14
HO, SHUK-MEI S15HD28778-01
HO, SIU-CHEONG R01GM45200-01
HO, TIMOTHY W K11HD00810-05
HO, YE-SHIH P01HL31992-08 0008
HO, YE-SHIH R01HL39585-05
HO, YE-SHIH R01HL44571-02
HO, YEE-KIN R01EY05788-05
HOAGLAND, DONALD S07RR07037-26 0381
HOAGLAND, MAHLON B P30CA12708-21 9001
HOARD, RICHARD S07RR05304-30 0217
HOARE, GEOFFREY A S07RR05714-21 0129
HOATH, STEVEN P50HD20748-06A1 0008
HOBAR, P CRAIG S07RR05426-30 0137
HOBBINS, MELODY S07RR05405-30 0871
HOBBS, HELEN H M01RR00633-19 0405
HOBBS, PATRICIA J M01RR00064-27 0312
HOBERMAN, ALEJANDRO M01RR00084-29 0253
HOBERMAN, ALEJANDRO M01RR00084-29 0250
HOBERMAN, HARRY M R01MH47786-02
HOBFOLL, STEVAN E R01HD24901-02
HOBFOLL, STEVAN E R01MH45669-02
HOBSON, J ALLAN R01MH13923-23
HOBSON, MARVIN S06GM08169-13 0004
HOCH, CAROLINE C P50AG05133-08 0010
HOCH, CAROLYN C K07MH00792-03
HOCH, JAMES A M01RR00833-17 0197
HOCH, JAMES A R01GM19416-20
HOCH, SALLIE O R01AI21083-09
HOCH, SALLIE O R01AR40601-01A1
HOCHBERG, MARC R18AR21393-17 0016
HOCHBERG, MARK C M01RR00035-31 0403
HOCHBERG, RICHARD B R01CA29591-12

HOCHGESCHWENDER, U Z01MH02578-01
HOCHHAUS, GUENTHER S07RR05573-13 0086
HOCHMAN, JACOB D R01CA48146-03
HOCHMUTH, ROBERT M P60HL28391-09 0006
HOCHMUTH, ROBERT M R01HL23728-12
HOCHMUTH, ROBERT M S07RR07070-26
HOCHSCHILD, ANN R01GM44025-02
HOCHSCHILD, ANN S07RR05381-30 0786
HOCHSTEIN, H D Z01BE01001-09
HOCHSTEIN, PAUL S07RR05792-15
HOCHSTEIN, PAUL S15DK44690-01
HOCHSTER, HOWARD M01RR00096-30A1 0321
HOCHSTER, HOWARD M01RR00096-30A1 0290
HOCHSTER, HOWARD P01CA50529-01A2 9001
HOCHSTER, HOWARD S R01CA56129-01
HOCHSTRASSER, ROBIN M P41RR01348-10 9001
HOCHSTRASSER, ROBIN M P41RR01348-10
HOCHSTRASSER, ROBIN M R01GM12592-27
HOCK, ELLEN I R01MH46003-02
HOCK, JANET M R01DE07272-07
HOCK, JANET M S15AI32209-01
HOCKBERGER, PHILIP P01NS17489-10 0013
HOCKBERGER, PHILIP E R29NS26915-03
HOCKENSMITH, JOEL W R29GM43569-02
HOCKFIELD, SUSAN P01NS22807-07 0002
HOCKFIELD, SUSAN R01EY06511-07
HOCKMEYER, WAYNE T U01AI28171-03 0001
HOD, YEACOV S07RR05736-19 0208
HODAPP, ROBERT M P01HD03008-24 0062
HODES, M E S07RR05371-30 0639
HODES, MARION E P01NS27613-01A2 0004
HODES, R J Z01CB09258-13
HODES, R J Z01CB09265-10
HODES, R J Z01CB09266-09
HODES, R J Z01CB09281-06
HODGE, FELICIA U01CA52279-02
HODGE, LON S07RR05365-30 0083
HODGE, SUSAN E R55DK31813-09
HODGES, MORRISON N01HC65056-08
HODGSON, CLAGUE P R29GM41314-04
HODGSON, ERNEST P01ES00044-26 0004
HODGSON, ERNEST P01ES00044-26
HODGSON, ERNEST S03RR03427-05
HODGSON, ERNEST S07RR07071-26
HODGSON, K P41RR01209-12 9002
HODGSON, K P41RR01209-12 9003
HODGSON, KEITH P41RR01209-12 9001
HODGSON, KEITH O P41RR01209-12 0001
HODGSON, KEITH O P41RR01209-12
HODGSON, S F M01RR00585-20 0291
HODNICKI, DONNA R R03HS06954-01
HODOS, WILLIAM R01EY00735-20
HODSON, ALAN W. P51RR00166-30 0092
HODSON, WILLIAM A P01HL39157-05
HODSON, WILLIAM A P01HL39157-05 0001
HOEBEL, BARTLEY G R01DA03597-06
HOECK, JOANNES B P50AA07186-06 0005
HOEFFLER, JAMES P R29GM45872-01
HOEFFLER, JAMES P S07RR05357-30 0462
HOEG, J M Z01HL02022-11
HOEHN-SARIC, RUDOLPH R01MH42579-03A1
HOEK, JOANNES B P01AA07215-06 0001
HOEK, JOANNES B R01AA08714-01A1
HOEKSTRA, MERL F P01HG00202-02 0003
HOEL, D G Z01ES43010-06
HOELDTKE, ROBERT D M01RR00349-25 0226
HOELDTKE, ROBERT D M01RR00349-25 0194
HOELDTKE, ROBERT D R01DK32239-09
HOELDTKE, ROBERT D. M01RR00349-25 0206
HOENER, BETTY A R01AI27796-01A3
HOENIG, MARGARETHE E R29DK41869-03
HOERR, ROBERT A. M01RR00088-28 0251
HOEVET, GAIL L S07RR05654-24 0144
HOF, LISELOTTE B R01NS25355-03
HOFER, KURT G R01CA21673-11
HOFER, MYRON A K05MH38632-14
HOFER, MYRON A R37MH40430-08
HOFF, ANNE L S07RR05736-19 0175
HOFF, HENRY F P01HL29582-09 9002
HOFF, HENRY F P01HL29582-09
HOFF, HENRY F P01HL29582-09 0003
HOFF, JULIAN T R01NS17760-11
HOFFEE, PATRICIA A R01DK12152-23
HOFFER, BARRY J K05MH00289-12
HOFFER, BARRY J P01AG04418-08 0004
HOFFER, BARRY J P01AG04418-08 9001
HOFFER, BARRY J P01AG04418-08
HOFFER, BARRY J P01MH44337-03 0003
HOFFER, BARRY J P50AA03527-14 0005
HOFFER, BARRY J P50NS09199-21
HOFFER, BARRY J P50NS09199-21 0024
HOFFMAN, A S P41RR01296-08 0010
HOFFMAN, A S P41RR01296-08 0011
HOFFMAN, ALAN S. P51RR00166-30 0093
HOFFMAN, ALLAN S R01GM40111-04
HOFFMAN, ANDREW R R01DK36054-04A2
HOFFMAN, BRIAN M01RR00070-29 0219
HOFFMAN, BRIAN B R01AG09597-01
HOFFMAN, BRIAN B R01HL41315-04
HOFFMAN, BRIAN F P01HL30557-08
HOFFMAN, BRIAN F P01HL30557-08 0004
HOFFMAN, BRIAN F P01HL30557-08 0006
HOFFMAN, BRIAN F R37HL08508-28
HOFFMAN, BRIAN M R37HL13531-19
HOFFMAN, CHARLES S R29GM46226-01
HOFFMAN, DOUGLAS W R01GM40858-04
HOFFMAN, DOUGLAS W S15AA09256-01
HOFFMAN, ERIC A R01HL42672-04
HOFFMAN, ERIC A S07RR05415-30 0007
HOFFMAN, ERIC P R01NS29525-01
HOFFMAN, ERIC PAUL R01AR41025-01
HOFFMAN, G S Z01AI00213-11
HOFFMAN, GARY N01LM93505-06
HOFFMAN, GLORIA E R01NS28477-01A1
HOFFMAN, GLORIA E R01NS28730-01A1
HOFFMAN, H J Z01HD00801-16
HOFFMAN, H J Z01HD00802-16
HOFFMAN, H J Z01HD00803-07
HOFFMAN, H J Z01HD00860-11
HOFFMAN, H J Z01HD00861-09
HOFFMAN, H J Z01HD00871-07
HOFFMAN, H J Z01HD00872-07
HOFFMAN, JEFFREY A R18DA06168-03
HOFFMAN, JOSEPH F R01HL09906-26
HOFFMAN, JULIEN I P01HL25847-12
HOFFMAN, JULIEN I P01HL25847-12 0003
HOFFMAN, LESLIE M01RR00056-30 0376
HOFFMAN, LESLIE A R01NR01086-06
HOFFMAN, LOREN H P30HD05797-20 9003
HOFFMAN, LOREN H R01HD18123-08
HOFFMAN, MICHAEL P01AI32918-09 0009
HOFFMAN, NEIL S07RR05799-14 0684
HOFFMAN, NEIL F R29GM42609-03
HOFFMAN, P Z01AA00700-07
HOFFMAN, P Z01AA00702-07
HOFFMAN, P Z01AA00703-07
HOFFMAN, P Z01AA00705-05
HOFFMAN, PAUL N P01NS22849-06 0006
HOFFMAN, PAULA L R01AA09005-01
HOFFMAN, RAYMOND M01RR00058-30 0258
HOFFMAN, ROBERT M01RR00059-30 0725
HOFFMAN, ROBERT M01RR00059-30 0732
HOFFMAN, ROBERT P01HL43026-02 9001
HOFFMAN, ROBERT S07RR05372-30 0651
HOFFMAN, ROBERT M R01CA27564-10
HOFFMAN, ROBERT P M01RR00059-30 0741
HOFFMAN, ROBERT V R01GM44529-01
HOFFMAN, ROBERT W R29AR41051-01
HOFFMAN, RONALD R01CA34841-10
HOFFMAN, RONALD R01CA45279-03
HOFFMAN, RONALD R01HL42674-03
HOFFMAN, RONALD R01HL46548-01
HOFFMAN, STANLEY R R01HL37641-06
HOFFMAN, STEVEN A S07RR07112-24 0413
HOFFMAN, T Z01BH02001-02
HOFFMAN, T Z01BH02002-02
HOFFMAN, T Z01BH02017-01
HOFFMAN, T Z01BH02019-01
HOFFMAN, W Z01CL00089-02
HOFFMAN, W D Z01CL00109-01
HOFFMAN, WILLIAM R01NS23560-04S1
HOFFMAN, WILLIAM F R29MH43586-05
HOFFMANN, DIETRICH P01CA29580-11
HOFFMANN, F MICHAEL R01CA49582-03
HOFFMANN, F MICHAEL R01RR06610-01
HOFFMANN, MICHAEL K R01AI29869-02
HOFKOSH, DENA M01RR00084-29 0217
HOFKOSH, DENA M01RR00084-29 0222
HOFMAN, FLORENCE M R01EY08144-03
HOFMAN, WENDELL F R01HL40488-04
HOFMANN, KLAUS P30CA47904-04 9009
HOFMANN, ALAN F M01RR00827-17 0463
HOFMANN, ALAN F R01DK21506-14
HOFRICHTER, J Z01DK29016-15
HOGAN, ANDREW J S07RR07049-26 0443
HOGAN, ANDY S07RR05656-24 0845
HOGAN, BRIGID L R01HD25580-03
HOGAN, BRIGID L.M. P01CA48799-03 0004
HOGAN, BRIGID L.M. P01CA48799-03 9003
HOGAN, DENNIS P P20AG09646-02
HOGAN, DENNIS P P30HD28263-01
HOGAN, DENNIS P R01HD26070-02
HOGAN, EDWARD L P01NS11066-17 0008
HOGAN, KEVIN T R29AI29574-02
HOGAN, KEVIN T S07RR05434-30 0797
HOGAN, MICHAEL C R29AR40155-01A1
HOGAN, MICHAEL E R01CA39527-07
HOGAN, NEVILLE R01AR40029-03
HOGAN, PATRICK G R29NS25078-05
HOGAN, PERRY M P01HL28542-10 9001
HOGAN, PERRY M P01HL28542-10 0004
HOGAN, YVONNE H S06GM08061-17 0008
HOGANSON, GEORGE S07RR05369-30 0587
HOGARTY, GERARD E R37MH30750-14
HOGENKAMP, H P C S07RR05385-30 0813
HOGENKAMP, HARRY P C S03RR03082-11
HOGENKAMP, HENRICUS P R01GM33776-08
HOGENKAMP, HENRICUS P S15DA07794-01
HOGENKAMP, HENRICUS P S15HD28747-01
HOGENKAMP, HENRICUS P C S07RR07052-26
HOGG, EVELYN N01CB95621-10
HOGGAN, M D Z01AI00437-07
HOGLE, JAMES P41RR01646-09 0010
HOGLE, JAMES P50NS12428-17 0011
HOGLE, JAMES M P01GM38794-05 0002
HOGLE, JAMES M R01AI20566-09
HOGLE, JAMES M R01AI30580-01
HOGLE, JAMES M U01AI32480-01
HOGNESS, DAVID S R01GM45355-01
HOGNESS, DAVID S R37GM31409-09
HOHMANN, CHRISTINE F P01MH46529-02 0003
HOHMANN, PHILLIP S07RR05648-25 0921
HOIDAL, JOHN R M01RR00064-27 0370
HOIDAL, JOHN R R01HL37615-05
HOISETH, SUSAN K R29AI26148-04
HOIT, JEANNETTE D K08DC00030-04
HOJIMA, YOSHIO P01AR38188-07 0001
HOJNACKI, JEROME L R01AA06636-07
HOKAMA, YOSHITSUGI S06GM08125-18 0050
HOKAMA, YOSHITSUGI S06GM08125-18 0050
HOKE, GLENN D R43GM45061-01A1
HOKIN, LOWELL E R01GM33850-08
HOKIN, LOWELL E R01HL16318-33
HOLBROOK, C TATE N01HB77033-07
HOLBROOK, KAREN P01AR21557-13 9001
HOLBROOK, KAREN A R37HD17664-09
HOLBROOK, KAREN A S07RR05432-30
HOLBROOK, KAREN A S15HL47687-01
HOLBROOK, N J Z01AG00713-04
HOLBROOK, N J Z01AG00719-03
HOLBROOK, N J Z01AG00721-01
HOLCOMB, HENRY H P50MH44211-03 0013
HOLCOMB, PHILLIP S07RR07179-14 0681
HOLCOMB, PHILLIP J R29HD25889-03
HOLCOMBE, RANDALL F K08HL02467-03
HOLDEN, GEORGE W R01HD26574-01A1
HOLDEN, HAZEL R29GM39082-05
HOLDEN, HAZEL M R01HL42322-03
HOLDEN, HAZEL M S07RR07098-26 0363
HOLDEN, JOSEPH S07RR05841-12 0240
HOLDEN, JOSEPH T S07RR05841-12
HOLDEN, JOSEPH T S15CA55928-01
HOLDER, HAROLD D P50AA06282-09
HOLDER, HAROLD D R01AA08765-02
HOLDER, HAROLD D R01AA09146-01
HOLERS, V MICHAEL R01CA53615-01A1
HOLETS, VICKY R P01NS28059-01A1 9002
HOLETS, VICKY R R01AR41347-01
HOLFORD, THEODORE R R01CA30931-10
HOLGUIN, ALFONSO H S07RR05828-08 0530
HOLIAN, ANDRIJ M01RR02558-07 0029
HOLIAN, ANDRIJ R01ES04804-03
HOLIAN, ANDRIJ R01HL42030-03
HOLICK, MICHAEL F M01RR00533-23 0211
HOLICK, MICHAEL F M01RR00533-23 0209
HOLICK, MICHAEL F M01RR00533-23 0212
HOLICK, MICHAEL F M01RR00533-23 0213
HOLICK, MICHAEL F P01AG04390-08 0003
HOLICK, MICHAEL F R01AR36963-06
HOLICK, MICHAEL F R01ES04814-05
HOLICK, MICHAEL F R37AG06079-08
HOLICK, MICHAEL F. M01RR00533-23 0187
HOLLAND, AUDREY L P60DC01409-01 0004
HOLLAND, AUDREY L R01AG07886-04
HOLLAND, CHRISTIE A R01CA41510-05
HOLLAND, CHRISTIE A S07RR05712-20 0107
HOLLAND, HENRY K R01CA57034-01
HOLLAND, JAMES F U10CA04457-32
HOLLAND, JOHN J R37AI14627-24
HOLLAND, LOUIS E N01AI05077-03
HOLLAND, MICHAEL J R01GM30307-11
HOLLAND, O BRYAN M01RR00073-29 0147
HOLLAND, SCOTT K S07RR05358-30 0476
HOLLAND, THOMAS S07RR05384-30 0779
HOLLAND, THOMAS C K04AI00875-04
HOLLANDER, CHARLES M01RR00096-30A1 0175
HOLLANDER, CHARLES M01RR00096-30A1 0301
HOLLANDER, CHARLES M01RR00096-30A1 0315
HOLLANDER, CHARLES M01RR00096-30A1 0176
HOLLANDER, CHARLES M01RR00096-30A1 0181
HOLLANDER, CHARLES S M01RR00096-30A1 0109
HOLLANDER, CHARLES S M01RR00096-30A1 0287
HOLLANDER, ERIC K01MH00750-04
HOLLANDER, ERIC P50MH43878-03 0033
HOLLANDER, ERIC S07RR05650-25 0100
HOLLANDER, WILLIAM P01HL13262-19
HOLLANDER, WILLIAM P01HL13262-19 0026
HOLLANDER, WILLIAM P01HL13262-19 9001
HOLLEN, PATRICIA J R29CA55202-01
HOLLEN, PATRICIA J S07RR05952-06 0739
HOLLENBECK, PETER J R01NS27073-02
HOLLENBECK, PETER J S07RR05381-30 0779
HOLLENBERG, NORMAN P01CA41167-06 0007
HOLLENBERG, NORMAN K M01RR02635-07 0279
HOLLENBERG, NORMAN K P01CA41167-06
HOLLENBERG, PAUL F P41RR06030-01A1 0007
HOLLENBERG, PAUL F R37CA16954-16
HOLLENDER, LARS P30DE09743-02 9002
HOLLEY, JEREAL W R19DA06420-03
HOLLEY, ROBERT W P30CA14195-18 0051
HOLLIDAY, MALCOLM A M01RR01271-10 0116
HOLLIDAY, MALCOLM A M01RR01271-10 0113
HOLLIDAY, MALCOLM A. M01RR01271-10 0099
HOLLINGER, BLAINE N01AI82517-08
HOLLINGSHEAD, M N01AI05086-02
HOLLINGSHEAD, MELINDA N01CM17542-00

HOLLINGSWORTH, MICHAEL A R01DK44762-01
HOLLINGSWORTH, PEGGI S07RR05383-30 0557
HOLLIS, JACK N01DE12589-00
HOLLIS, JACK F U01HL37899-06
HOLLISTER, ALAN S M01RR00095-31 0348
HOLLISTER, ALAN S P50HL14192-21 9002
HOLLOMAN, WILLIAM K R01GM42482-03
HOLLOMAN, WILLIAM K R01GM42548-02
HOLLOSZY, JOHN M01RR00036-31 0661
HOLLOSZY, JOHN O P01AG05562-07 0008
HOLLOSZY, JOHN O P01AG05562-07 9001
HOLLOSZY, JOHN O P01AG05562-07
HOLLOSZY, JOHN O R01DK18986-15
HOLLOSZY, JOHN O R37AG00425-27
HOLLOSZY, JOHN O. M01RR00036-31 0673
HOLLOWAY, FRANK A R01AA08338-02
HOLLOWAY, FRANK A R01DA04444-05
HOLLOWAY, PETER W R01GM23858-13
HOLLOWAY, PETER W S07RR05431-30 0866
HOLLOWAY, WILLIAM N01AI05046-05
HOLLY, ELIZABETH N01CP05681-03
HOLLY, ELIZABETH A R01CA45614-04
HOLLYDAY, MARGARET R01NS25340-05
HOLLYDAY, MARGARET S07RR07214-03
HOLLYFIELD, JOE G R01EY02363-15
HOLM, BRUCE A K04HL02629-01
HOLM, BRUCE A R01HL45170-01A1
HOLM, CONNIE R01GM36510-06
HOLM, KARYN R55NR01453-05
HOLM, KARYN S07RR05776-11 0396
HOLM, LARS E N01CP15652-00
HOLM, RICHARD H R37GM28856-12
HOLMAN, B LEONARD S07RR05950-07 0999
HOLMAN, B LEONARD S07RR05950-07 0984
HOLMAN, HALSTED R P60AR20610-14 0013
HOLMAN, HALSTED R P60AR20610-14
HOLMAN, HALSTED R R01HS06680-01
HOLMAN, LEONARD B P01AG04953-08 0005
HOLMAN, WILLIAM L R29HL43213-02
HOLMES, D R M01RR00585-20 0456
HOLMES, D R M01RR00585-20 0534
HOLMES, D R M01RR00585-20 0526
HOLMES, DOUGLAS U01AG10330-01
HOLMES, EDWARD W JR R37DK12413-25
HOLMES, EDWARD W, JR R01CA47631-04
HOLMES, ERIC H K04CA01343-04
HOLMES, ERIC H R01CA41521-06
HOLMES, GREGORY L R01NS27984-01A2
HOLMES, K L Z01AI00484-05
HOLMES, K L Z01AI00523-04
HOLMES, KATHRYN V R01AI25231-04
HOLMES, KATHRYN V S07RR05983-05 0366
HOLMES, KATHRYN V U01AI26075-05
HOLMES, KING K P01AI24756-05
HOLMES, KING K P01AI24756-05 9002
HOLMES, KING K P01AI29363-02 0001
HOLMES, KING K P30AI27757-04
HOLMES, KING K R01CA34493-08
HOLMES, KING K R01HD23412-04
HOLMES, KING K U01AI31448-01 0008
HOLMES, KING K U01AI31448-01
HOLMES, LEWIS B R01NS24125-04A2
HOLMES, RANDALL K R01AI14107-15
HOLMES, TALMAGE S07RR05656-24 0841
HOLMES, WALTER M R01GM25871-13
HOLMGREN, ROBERT A R01NS28472-02
HOLMQUIST, GERALD P R01CA54773-01
HOLMQUIST, GERALD P S07RR05841-12 0245
HOLOHAN, PETER D R01GM41265-03
HOLOHAN, PETER D R01HL02835-34
HOLOSHITZ, JOSEPH M01RR00042-31 0674
HOLOSHITZ, JOSEPH R01AR40544-02
HOLOWAY, E J N01CP85625-02
HOLOWKA, DAVID A R01AI22449-06
HOLSAPPLE, MICHAEL P R01ES02520-09
HOLST, RUTH G07LM05145-01S1
HOLSTEIN-RATHLOU, NIELS-HENRIK R29HL45623-01A1
HOLSTEIN, GAY R R29NS24656-05
HOLT, CHRISTINE R01NS23780-05
HOLT, JEFFREY T R01CA49052-03
HOLT, JEFFREY T R01CA51735-02
HOLT, JEFFRY T. P01CA48799-03 9002
HOLT, KENNETH G S07RR07043-26 0120
HOLT, ROBERT G S06GM08037-20 0027
HOLT, STANLEY C K16DE00152-07
HOLT, STANLEY C P01DE08569-03
HOLT, STANLEY C P01DE08569-03 0001
HOLT, STANLEY C R01DE07267-07
HOLTEN, DAROLD D S03RR03343-08
HOLTEN, DAROLD D S07RR07010-26
HOLTEN, DAROLD D S15DK44681-01
HOLTEN, DEWEY R01GM34685-07
HOLTGRAVES, THOMAS M R03MH45847-01A2
HOLTOM, G R P41RR01348-10 9003
HOLTON, ROBERT A R01CA42031-07
HOLTZER, ALFRED M R01GM20064-17
HOLTZER, HOWARD P01HL15835-19 0009
HOLTZMAN, DAVID P41RR00995-16 0002
HOLTZMAN, DAVID M K11AG00445-03
HOLTZMAN, ERIC R01EY03168-22
HOLTZMAN, MICHAEL J R01HL40078-04
HOLTZMAN, MICHAEL J S07RR05389-30 0637
HOLTZMAN, NEIL A R01HG00026-02
HOLTZMAN, NEIL A R01HG00481-01
HOLTZMAN, STEPHEN G K05DA00008-17
HOLTZMAN, STEPHEN G R01DA03413-08
HOLTZMAN, STEPHEN G R37DA00541-18
HOLTZWORTH-MUNROE, A S07RR07031-26 0090
HOLTZWORTH-MUNROE, AMY R29MH46927-02
HOLYOAK, KEITH S07RR07009-26 0943
HOLZ, G P41RR00317-25 0007
HOLZ, RONALD W R01DK27959-11
HOLZBACH, R THOMAS R01DK17562-18
HOLZEMER, WILLIAM L R01NR02215-03
HOLZEMER, WILLIAM L S03RR03278-10
HOLZEMER, WILLIAM L S07RR05604-14
HOLZEMER, WILLIAM L S15NR02933-01
HOLZMAN, LAWRENCE B K11DK01924-03
HOLZMAN, PHILIP S P01MH31154-14
HOLZMAN, PHILIP S P01MH31154-14 0021
HOLZMAN, PHILIP S P50MH44866-04 0002
HOLZMAN, PHILIP S R01MH31340-15
HOLZMAN, PHILIP S R37MH44876-03
HOLZMAN, THOMAS P01AG10481-01 0003
HOM, JAMES M01RR00633-19 0420
HOMAN, M M01RR00585-20 0522
HOMANDBERG, GENE A U01AI27220-04 0002
HOMCY, CHARLES J P01HL38070-05 0002
HOMER, CHARLES J U01AI31541-01 0007
HOMES, TERRYL L M01RR00080-29 0426
HOMSHER, E Z01HL04215-01
HOMSHER, EARL E R01AR30988-10
HONDA, CHRISTOPHER N R29NS25658-04
HONDA, CHRISTOPHER N S07RR05385-30 0800
HONDALUS, MARY K K11AI01001-01A1
HONEYCUTT, RODNEY L S07RR07090-26 0481
HONG, BARRY A U01AI25903-05 0003
HONG, BARRY A U01AI25903-05 0010
HONG, CHUNG I R01AI27697-01A1
HONG, H L Z01ES21098-05
HONG, H L Z01ES21113-04
HONG, H L Z01ES21115-04
HONG, H L Z01ES21125-02
HONG, H L Z01ES21126-02
HONG, H L Z01ES21147-01
HONG, J S Z01ES90049-05
HONG, J S Z01ES90056-03
HONG, JEN-SHIANG R01GM29843-10
HONG, JEN-SHIANG S07RR05711-21 0036
HONG, RICHARD M01RR03186-06 0046
HONG, RICHARD P50AI10404-21 9001
HONG, RICHARD P50AI10404-21 0009
HONG, RICHARD P50AI10404-21
HONG, SUK E P01HL28542-10
HONG, SUK KI P01HL28542-10 0005
HONG, WAUN K P01CA52051-01A1 0001
HONG, WAUN K U01CA48369-04
HONG, WAUN KI P01CA52051-01A1
HONIG, BARRY P41RR06892-01 9003
HONIG, BARRY H R01GM30518-10
HONIG, BARRY H R01GM41371-03
HONIG, BARRY H. P30CA13696-19 9006
HONIG, WERNER K R01MH47260-01
HONIGBERG, BRONISLAW S07RR07048-26 0643
HONN, KENNETH V P30CA22453-14 0002
HONN, KENNETH V R01CA29997-09
HONRUBIA, VICENTE P50DC00097-21
HONRUBIA, VICENTE P50DC00097-21 0009
HONRUBIA, VICENTE P60DC01404-01 0002
HONRUBIA, VICENTE P60DC01404-01 0003
HONRUBIA, VICENTE P60DC01404-01 0004
HONRUBIA, VICENTE P60DC01404-01
HOOBER, KENNETH S07RR05417-30 0792
HOOBER, KENNETH S07RR05417-30 0793
HOOD, DONALD C R01EY02115-15
HOOD, DONALD C R01EY09076-01
HOOD, DONALD C S07RR07060-26
HOOD, KATHRYN E S07RR07082-26 0288
HOOD, LEROY P01NS22786-07 0004
HOOD, LEROY R13HG00546-01
HOOD, LEROY E P01NS14069-14 0008
HOOD, LEROY E P30CA32911-08
HOOD, LEROY E P30CA32911-08 9001
HOOD, LEROY E P30CA32911-08 9002
HOOD, LEROY E P30CA32911-08 9003
HOOD, LEROY E R01AI17565-11
HOOD, LEROY E R01AI19624-09
HOOD, LEROY E R01HG00084-02
HOOD, LEROY E R01HG00356-04
HOOD, VIRGINIA L R21DK44598-01
HOOD, WILLIAM B JR N01HC55014-10
HOOD, WILLIAM B. M01RR00044-31 0305
HOOFNAGLE, J H Z01CL02010-17
HOOFNAGLE, J H Z01DK53509-13
HOOGWERF, BYRON J. N01HC75073-07
HOOK, EDWARD P01AI26499-03S1 9002
HOOK, EDWARD W, III R01AI27727-03
HOOK, EDWARD W, III R01AI29508-03
HOOK, G R Z01ES25020-09
HOOK, G R Z01ES25027-08
HOOK, MAGNUS R01AI20624-07
HOOK, MAGNUS R01AR27807-12
HOOK, MAGNUS R01HL47313-01
HOOK, REUEL R S07RR05949-07 0733
HOOK, REUEL R, JR R15AI31187-01
HOOK, VIVIAN Y H R01DA04271-05
HOOK, VIVIAN Y H R01NS24553-05
HOOKER, KAREN A R03MH46637-01A2
HOOKS, J J Z01EY00232-06
HOOKS, J J Z01EY00233-06
HOOKS, J J Z01EY00240-05
HOOLEY, JILL M R01MH42782-04A1
HOOP, BERNARD S07RR05486-29 0038
HOOPER, ALAN B S07RR07052-26 0160
HOOPER, DAVID C R01AI23988-06
HOOPER, HENRY O S07RR07256-02
HOOPER, JOAN E R29GM45396-01
HOOPES, LAURA L R15AG09034-01A1
HOOTS, W KEITH M01RR02558-07 0048
HOOTS, W KEITH M01RR02558-07 0058
HOOVER, EDWARD A N01AI05079-02
HOOVER, EDWARD A N01AI72663-09
HOOVER, EDWARD A R01CA43216-06
HOOVER, EDWARD A R01CA48594-04
HOOVER, HERBERT C, J S07RR05486-29 0039
HOOVER, R N Z01CP04378-16
HOOVER, RICHARD G R01CA41165-07
HOOVER, RICHARD L R55HL36526-07
HOPEWELL, PHILIP C. N01HR76034-04
HOPFER, ROY L S07RR05406-30 0884
HOPFER, ULRICH P01HL41618-03 0003
HOPFER, ULRICH P30DK27651-09 9010
HOPFER, ULRICH R01DK39658-03
HOPKINS, CARL D R37MH37972-09
HOPKINS, LINTON M01RR00039-31 0425
HOPKINS, NANCY H R01CA19308-15
HOPKINS, PAUL B K04AG00417-04
HOPKINS, PAUL B R01GM45804-01
HOPKINS, PAUL N M01RR00064-27 0348
HOPKINS, WALTER J R55DK44378-01
HOPKINS, WILLIAM D R55NS29574-01
HOPP, THOMAS P R43AI31722-01
HOPPE, RICHARD T P01CA34233-09 9007
HOPPEL, CHARLES L M01RR00080-29 0456
HOPPEL, CHARLES L P01CA51183-01A1 9002
HOPPENBROUWERS, TOKE T U01HD29060-01
HOPPER, ANITA K R01GM27930-12
HOPPER, JAMES E R01GM27925-12
HOPPER, JOAN G G20RR07076-01
HOPPIN, FREDERIC G S15HL47769-01
HOPPIN, FREDERIC G, JR R37HL26863-10
HOPPIN, FREDERIC G, JR S07RR05862-10
HOPS, HYMAN R01DA03706-08
HOPS, HYMAN R01DA06316-02
HOPS, HYMAN R01MH43311-04A1
HOPS, HYMAN S07RR05612-19
HOPS, HYMAN S15MH49313-01
HOPWOOD, NANCY J M01RR00042-31 0624
HOPWOOD, NANCY J M01RR00042-31 0404
HOPWOOD, NANCY J M01RR00042-31 0631
HOPWOOD, NANCY J M01RR00042-31 0102
HORACEK, MARK J R29HD28330-01
HORAK, FAY B R01AG06457-06
HORAK, I D Z01CM06728-03
HORAN, LEO G R01HL33715-05
HORAN, PAUL K R44AI28600-02
HORBETT, THOMAS A R01DK30770-07
HORBETT, THOMAS A R01HL19419-15A1
HORCH, KENNETH W R01NS27371-03
HORD, ALLEN H M01RR00039-31 0441
HORDINSKY, MARIA P01GM22167-16 0008
HOREL, JAMES A R01NS18291-10
HORGAN, GERARD M01RR00069-29 0468
HORGAN, MICHAEL J S07RR05394-30 0723
HORII, YOSHIYUKI P60DC00976-02 0006
HORIKOSHI, MASAMI R29GM45258-01
HORITA, AKIRA R01DA04907-03
HORIUCHI, KAZUMI R29HL44640-02
HORIUCHI, KAZUMI S07RR05506-29 0908
HORN-ROSS, PAMELA L R29CA49499-02
HORN, GLENN T R44HD25348-03
HORN, JOHN L R01AG09936-01
HORN, JOHN P K04NS01427-02
HORN, JOHN P R01NS21065-07A2
HORN, JOHN R M01RR00037-31 0504
HORN, PATRICK P01GM22220-15 0006
HORNBECK, PETER S07RR05379-30 0762
HORNBECK, PETER V R29AI30822-01A1
HORNBROOK, MARK C U01AG09089-02
HORNBY, PAMELA J R29DK42714-01A2
HORNBY, PAMELA J S07RR05376-30 0038
HORNE, DONALD W R01DK32189-08
HORNE, M K Z01CL10192-02
HORNER, JAMES R S07RR05700-22 0884
HORNER, JENNIFER R01AG10648-01
HORNER, MARCIA E G07LM05146-01S1
HORNICK, CONRAD A P01HL25596-12 0001
HORNIK, JOHN A R19MH46210-03
HORNING, SANDRA P01CA34233-09 0002
HORNING, SANDRA J P01CA34233-09 0021
HORNING, SANDRA J P01CA49605-03 0002
HORNSBY, PETER J R37AG06108-07
HORNSTEIN, GAIL A R01LM05067-02
HORNUNG, DAVID G P01DC00220-08 0006
HOROHOV, DAVID W R29AI28542-03
HOROWICZ, PAUL R01AR31814-09

HOROWITZ, BERNARD R01HL41221-04
HOROWITZ, BURTON R01DK42505-01A2
HOROWITZ, JACK R01GM45546-01
HOROWITZ, JONATHAN M R01CA53248-01
HOROWITZ, M E Z01CM06891-03
HOROWITZ, MARK C R01AR40073-03
HOROWITZ, MARK C R01AR40507-01A1
HOROWITZ, PAUL M R01ES05729-01
HOROWITZ, PAUL M R01GM25177-12A3
HOROWITZ, STEVEN H N01NS02379-03
HOROWITZ, ZEBULON D S07RR05408-30 0929
HORROCKS, LLOYD A P50NS10165-20 0017
HORROCKS, LLOYD A R01NS29441-01
HORROCKS, WILLIAM D, JR R01GM23599-15
HORSEMAN, NELSON D R01DK42461-02
HORTIN, GLEN L R29GM38280-05
HORTON, EDWARD S R01DK26317-11
HORTON, JOHN R25CA17971-15
HORTON, JOHN L P01CA06294-30 9005
HORTON, JURETA P50GM21681-27 0004
HORTON, RICHARD M01RR00043-31 0484
HORTON, RICHARD M01RR00043-31 0158
HORTON, RICHARD M01RR00043-31 0435
HORTON, TONYA LYNETTE R03AG10376-01
HORTON, WILLIAM A R01HD20691-05A1
HORVATH, CSABA G R37GM20993-17
HORVATH, PETER S07RR07066-26 0245
HORVITZ, H ROBERT R37GM24663-14
HORWATH, KATHLEEN L S07RR07149-18 0421
HORWATH, KATHLEEN L S07RR07149-18 0422
HORWICH, ARTHUR L R01GM34433-07
HORWICH, ARTHUR L R01HD27533-01
HORWITZ, DAVID M01RR00043-31 0409
HORWITZ, ALAN F R01GM23244-17
HORWITZ, ALLAN P50MH43450-04 0015
HORWITZ, ALLEN L R01HD24119-04
HORWITZ, B Z01AG00404-05
HORWITZ, BARBARA A R01AG06665-04
HORWITZ, BARBARA A R01DK32907-07
HORWITZ, DAVID M01RR00043-31 0315
HORWITZ, DAVID A P30CA14089-16 9002
HORWITZ, DAVID A R01AR29846-10
HORWITZ, JOSEPH P30EY00331-25
HORWITZ, JOSEPH R01EY03897-11
HORWITZ, KATHRYN B R01CA26869-12
HORWITZ, LAWRENCE D R01HL41661-03
HORWITZ, MARCUS A R01AI22421-06
HORWITZ, MARCUS A R01AI28825-02
HORWITZ, MARCUS A R01AI31338-01
HORWITZ, MARSHALL S R01AI27199-03
HORWITZ, MARSHALL S R01CA11512-22
HORWITZ, SARAH M R01MH48456-01
HORWITZ, SARAH M S07RR05443-30 0990
HORWITZ, SARAH M S07RR05443-30 0992
HORWITZ, SUSAN P30DK41296-03 0003
HORWITZ, SUSAN B R35CA39821-07
HOSCH, HARMON R24MH47167-02 0005
HOSENPUD, JEFFREY D R01HL43369-02
HOSENPUD, JEFFREY D S07RR05412-30 0981
HOSEY, M MARLENE R01HL23306-13
HOSEY, M MARLENE R01HL31601-08
HOSEY, M MARLENE S07RR05370-30 0621
HOSFORD, DAVID A K08NS01232-05
HOSHINO, Y Z01AI00339-10
HOSHINO, Y Z01AI00340-10
HOSHINO, Y Z01AI00604-01
HOSICK, HOWARD L R01CA46885-03
HOSKINS, DALE D P51RR00163-32 0013
HOSKINS, DALE D R01HD18737-08
HOSKINS, DALE D R01HD25908-03
HOSKINS, LANSING C R01HL45659-01
HOSKINS, SALLY G R29NS25042-06
HOSKINS, WILLIAM J P01CA52477-01A1
HOSODA, JUNKO S07RR05918-08 0713
HOSS, WAYNE P R01DA06258-02
HOSSLI, JOHN N01CO15735-00
HOSSNER, KIM S07RR07127-23 0481
HOSTETLER, KARL Y R01GM24979-14
HOSTETTER, MARGARET K M01RR00400-23 0269
HOSTETTER, MARGARET K R01AI24162-05
HOSTETTER, MARGARET K R01AI25827-04
HOSTETTER, THOMAS M01RR00400-23 0261
HOSTETTER, THOMAS H R01DK31437-08
HOTSON, JOHN R R01EY03387-11
HOTTENDORF, GIRARD H R01GM42615-01A1
HOTTORI, MASAKAZU P30DK36836-05 9009
HOTZ, V JOSEPH P30HD18288-08
HOTZ, V JOSEPH S15HD28764-01
HOUGH, C Z01MH01532-13
HOUGH, LINDSAY B R01DA03816-08
HOUGH, RICHARD R18MH48095-02
HOUGHTEN, RICHARD P01CA27489-12 9001
HOUGHTEN, RICHARD A P01HL31950-08 9003
HOUGHTEN, RICHARD A R43DA07018-01
HOUGHTON, ALAN N01CM97609-05
HOUGHTON, ALAN N P01CA33049-09 0005
HOUGHTON, JANET A P01CA23099-13 0011
HOUGHTON, JANET A R01CA32613-09
HOUGHTON, JOHN E S07RR07171-08 0156
HOUGHTON, PETER J R01CA51949-02
HOUK, JAMES C P01NS17489-10 0014
HOUK, JAMES C P50MH48185-01 0003
HOUK, JAMES C P50MH48185-01 0004
HOUK, JAMES C P50MH48185-01
HOUK, JAMES C P50MH48185-01 9001
HOUK, JAMES C R01NS21015-07
HOUK, KENDALL N R01GM36688-06
HOUK, KENDALL N R01GM36700-06
HOUK, KENDALL N R01GM40544-04
HOULDSWORTH, JANE R29CA53511-01
HOULE, JOHN D R01NS26380-04
HOUPT, JEFFREY L M01RR00039-31
HOUPT, JEFFREY L S07RR05364-30
HOUPT, THOMAS R R01DK41383-03
HOUSE, JAMES S P01AG05561-06A1 0003
HOUSE, JAMES S P01AG05561-06A1
HOUSE, STEVEN D R29HL44914-02
HOUSER, CAROLYN S07RR05354-30 0389
HOUSER, CAROLYN R P01NS21908-06A1 0006
HOUSER, CAROLYN R R01NS29231-01
HOUSER, STEVEN R R01HL33921-07
HOUSER, WALLACE D P51RR00167-31 9003
HOUSER, WILLIAM H R29ES05440-02
HOUSH, CYNTHIA H P30HD10003-16 9003
HOUSH, TERRY S07RR07055-26 0187
HOUSMAN, DAVID P01CA42063-06 0002
HOUSMAN, DAVID P01HL41484-03 0007
HOUSMAN, DAVID E P01CA26712-11S1 0007
HOUSMAN, DAVID E R01HG00299-12
HOUSMAN, DAVID E R37CA17575-17
HOUSMANS, PHILIPPE R R01GM36365-04A1
HOUSTON, CLIFFORD W R01AI21075-05
HOUSTON, L L U01CA51880-02
HOUSTON, LOU L U01CA51880-02 0002
HOUTS, ARTHUR C R01HD21736-04
HOUTS, PETER S S07RR05680-23 0904
HOVELL, MELBOURNE F R01HD25021-03
HOVEN, CHRISTINA W R01MH46310-01A1
HOVERSLAND, ROGER C R01HD26638-02
HOWARD, B H Z01HD08719-11
HOWARD, BARBARA V R01HL43660-02
HOWARD, BARBARA V S07RR06020-03
HOWARD, BARBARA V S15HL47740-01
HOWARD, BARBARA V U01HL41642-04
HOWARD, BRUCE D R37MH38633-08
HOWARD, CHARLES F P40RR03640-05 0005
HOWARD, CHARLES F P51RR00163-32 0037
HOWARD, CHERYL R24MH47167-02 0006
HOWARD, DARLENE V R37AG02751-10
HOWARD, DEXTER H R01AI22963-06
HOWARD, DONALD R S03RR03122-11
HOWARD, EUGENE F S07RR05365-30 0084
HOWARD, GEORGE U01HL47887-01
HOWARD, JOGAYLE K01RR00045-04
HOWARD, JONATHON R01AR40593-02
HOWARD, JUDD L M01RR00865-18 0359
HOWARD, JUDY R18DA06380-03
HOWARD, KENNETH I K05MH00924-01A1
HOWARD, KENNETH I R01MH42901-04
HOWARD, MARTHE J R55HD28184-01
HOWARD, PAUL C R55ES03648-07
HOWARD, PHILLIP N01LM13529-00
HOWARD, RANDALL F R29AI24520-04
HOWARD, RANDALL F S07RR05939-07 0731
HOWARD, RANDALL F S07RR05939-07 0725
HOWARD, RANDY L K11DK02116-01
HOWARD, THOMAS H R01AI25214-04
HOWARD, TODD S07RR05468-29 0400
HOWARDS, STUART S R01HD18825-07A1
HOWE, CHIN C R01GM37762-04A1
HOWE, CHIN C R01HD25078-03
HOWE, JOHN G R29CA52754-02
HOWELL, ALEXANDRA L S07RR05392-30 0695
HOWELL, DAVID S R01AR08662-26
HOWELL, ELIZABETH E R01GM35308-08
HOWELL, ELIZABETH E S07RR07088-24 0349
HOWELL, JOEL D M01RR00042-31 0588
HOWELL, KATHRYN P30DK34914-06 9005
HOWELL, KATHRYN E R01GM42629-02
HOWELL, LEONARD L R29DA05346-03
HOWELL, NEIL P01HD08315-16 0023
HOWELL, NEIL R01GM33683-07
HOWELL, ROGER W R13CA53064-01
HOWELL, ROGER W R29CA54891-01
HOWELL, STEPHEN B M01RR00827-17 0500
HOWELL, STEPHEN B M01RR00827-17 0441
HOWELL, STEPHEN B M01RR00827-17 0427
HOWELL, STEPHEN B P30CA23100-11 9003
HOWELLS, RICHARD D R01DA05819-03
HOWERDE, E SAUBERLICH P01CA28103-13 9002
HOWES, PAUL W R03MH48077-01
HOWETT, MARY K P01CA27503-12 0006
HOWIE, VIRGIL M R01HD20988-04
HOWLAND, HOWARD C R01EY02994-13
HOWLAND, JONATHAN R01AA08320-01A2
HOWLAND, JONATHON S07RR05927-07 0962
HOWLAND, JONATHON S07RR05927-07 0972
HOWLAND, JONATHON S07RR05927-07 0960
HOWLAND, REBEKAH S07RR05756-18 0284
HOWLETT, ALLYN C R01DA03690-08
HOWLETT, ALLYN C R01DA06312-03
HOWLEY, P M Z01CP00543-13
HOWLEY, P M Z01CP00898-08
HOWSON, CHRISTOPHER N01AI95041-03
HOWZE, GWENDOLYN B S06GM08061-17 0009
HOXIE, JAMES A P01AI25380-05 0002
HOXIE, JAMES A P01HL40387-04 9001
HOXIE, JAMES A R01AI28208-03
HOY, RONALD R R01DC00103-19
HOYE, THOMAS R R01GM34492-06
HOYE, THOMAS R R01GM39339-01A3
HOYER, LEON W P50HL44336-01 0006
HOYER, LEON W P50HL44336-01
HOYER, LEON W R01HL36099-05
HOYER, LEON W S07RR05737-20
HOYER, LEON W S15HL47700-01
HOYER, PATRICIA S07RR05675-23 0932
HOYER, PATRICIA B K04HD00907-01
HOYER, PATRICIA B R01HD26778-01A2
HOYER, PAULETTE S07RR05796-14 0431
HOYER, WILLIAM S07RR07068-26 0232
HOYER, WILLIAM J R01AG06041-04A3
HOYT, ANDREW M S07RR07041-26 0396
HOYT, CLIFFORD C R44RR06807-03
HOYT, D P20AG09682-01 0004
HOYT, DONALD F R15AR39893-01A2
HOYT, MYLES A R01GM40714-04
HOYT, RICHARD F, JR R01HL19379-14
HOYTE, ROBERT M S06GM08180-12
HOYTE, ROBERT M S06GM08180-12 0001
HOYUMPA, ANASTACIO M01RR01346-10 0161
HOZA, BETSY R29MH47390-01
HOZIER, JOHN N01ES05305-04
HRACHOVY, RICHARD A P50NS11535-17 0018
HRACHOVY, RICHARD A R01NS25884-04
HRESHCHYSHYN, MYROSL S07RR05400-30 0034
HRNCIR, ELIZABETH J R29HD22799-05
HRUBY, DENNIS E R01AI21335-08
HRUBY, DENNIS E R01AI29367-02
HRUBY, VICTOR J P01DA06284-03
HRUBY, VICTOR J P01DK36289-06A1 0006
HRUBY, VICTOR J R01DA04248-05
HRUBY, VICTOR J R01DK17420-18
HRUBY, VICTOR J R01NS19972-08
HRUBY, VICTOR J R37DK21085-15
HRUSHESKY, WILLIAM J R01CA50749-02
HRUSHESKY, WILLIAM J M R01CA31635-07A3
HRUSKA, KEITH A P01AR32087-09 0012
HRUSKA, KEITH A P01DK09976-27 0009
HRUSKA, KEITH A R01AR39561-04
HSER, YIH-ING K01DA00139-03
HSER, YIH-ING P50DA07699-01 0001
HSER, YIH-ING R01DA07382-01
HSIA, CONNIE CW M01RR00633-19 0375
HSIA, JAMES R43GM45661-01
HSIA, JAMES R44EY08019-03
HSIA, JAMES C R43EY09156-01
HSIA, JAMES C R44AR38987-03
HSIA, JUDITH R01HL41507-04
HSIAO, HENRY S P01HL34322-06 9001
HSIAO, HENRY SHIH-HAN P01HL27430-10 9004
HSIAO, KAREN R35AG08967-02 0002
HSIAO, KAREN K K08NS01419-02
HSIAO, LUKE Y N01CM07341-02
HSIAO, LUKE Y N01CM97626-02
HSIE, ABRAHAM W S07RR07205-11 0650
HSIEH, CHUNG P01AI30795-02 9002
HSIEH, CHUNG-CHENG R01CA44683-03
HSIEH, CHUNG-CHENG R03CA52560-01A1
HSIEH, P Z01DK52015-03
HSIEH, TAO-SHIH R01GM29006-11
HSIUNG, GUEH-DJEN R01AI28241-03
HSU, BETTY P01DK40555-04 0006
HSU, CHUNG Y P01NS11066-17 0012
HSU, CHUNG Y R01NS25545-03S1
HSU, CHUNG Y R01NS28995-02
HSU, KATHERINE S07RR05664-24 0864
HSU, L K GEORGE R01HD24777-04
HSU, MING-CHU U01AI27397-04
HSU, MING-CHU U01AI27397-04 0001
HSU, PEI-LING S07RR05745-19 0259
HSU, WALTER S07RR07034-26 0057
HSU, WALTER H R01ES05641-01
HSU, YU-CHIH R01HD20347-06
HSUEH, AARON P01HD13527-12 0007
HSUEH, AARON J W R01HD23273-06
HSUEH, ANDIE S06GM08256-03 0001
HSUEH, ANDIE S07RR07218-05 0463
HSUEH, WEI R01DK34574-08
HSUEH, WILLA A M01RR00043-31 0278
HSUEH, WILLA A M01RR00043-31 0483
HSUEH, WILLA A M01RR00043-31 0489
HSUEH, WILLA A M01RR00043-31 0388
HSUEH, WILLA A M01RR00043-31 0481
HSUEH, WILLA A R37DK30254-09
HU SHU-LOK U01AI26503-04 0001
HU, CHIA-LING R43MH46761-01A1
HU, CHIA-LING R44HD24034-03
HU, CHING Y R29DK42536-01A1
HU, CHING YUAN S07RR07079-26 0280
HU, EDDIE M01RR00043-31 0462
HU, FUPEI R43CA53950-01
HU, HOWARD M01RR02635-07 0229
HU, HOWARD M01RR02635-07 0286
HU, HOWARD R01ES05257-01A1
HU, HOWARD S07RR05446-30 0274

HU, JAMES W R01DE09559-01
HU, MING S07RR05686-11 0978
HU, PING-CHUAN P50HL19171-15 0015
HU, PING-CHUAN P50HL19171-15 9004
HU, R Q Z01BD03002-02
HU, R Q Z01BD03030-01
HU, R Q Z01BD03031-01
HU, TEH W S07RR06025-02
HU, TEH-WEI P50MH43694-04 0014
HU, TEH-WEI R01MH47063-01A1
HU, TEH-WEI S15MH49345-01
HU, VALERIE S07RR05359-30 0510
HU, VALERIE S07RR05359-30 0511
HUA, DUY H R01CA51794-02
HUA, DUY H R01GM36336-06
HUANG, ADA J K08HL02202-04
HUANG, ALICE S R37AI20896-10
HUANG, ALICE S U01AI25934-05 9002
HUANG, BESSIE P R01GM38113-04
HUANG, C Y Z01HL00224-14
HUANG, CHI-KUANG R01AI20943-08
HUANG, CHING-HSIEN R01GM17452-20
HUANG, CHUN-MING R43CA53939-01
HUANG, CHUN-MING R44CA48534-03
HUANG, DIANA D R29AI26064-04
HUANG, ENG SHANG P01CA19014-14 9003
HUANG, ENG SHANG P01CA19014-14 0017
HUANG, ENG-SHANG R01CA21773-12
HUANG, ENG-SHANG U01AI25868-05 0004
HUANG, H K P01CA51198-02
HUANG, H K P01CA51198-02 9001
HUANG, H K R01CA40456-06
HUANG, HENRY R01AI26763-04
HUANG, JUNG S R01CA38808-07
HUANG, JUNG S R01HL41782-03
HUANG, K-P Z01HD00187-13
HUANG, L M01RR00058-30 0237
HUANG, LEAF R01AI29893-03
HUANG, LEAF R01CA24553-12
HUANG, LI Y M P01NS11255-17 0026
HUANG, LI-YEN M K04NS01050-05
HUANG, LI-YEN M R01NS23061-06
HUANG, MANLEY T R43AI30289-01A1
HUANG, P C R01GM32606-08
HUANG, RU C R01AI32301-01
HUANG, RU-CHIH C R01CA48263-07
HUANG, S Z01DK25077-02
HUANG, SHOEI K STEPH S07RR05712-20 0088
HUANG, SHU-ZHEN R44HL44095-02
HUANG, WAI M R01GM21960-16
HUANG, WU-HSIUNG R01HL45554-01
HUBBARD, ANN L R01GM29185-12
HUBBARD, CHRISTOPHER S07RR07176-14 0528
HUBBARD, WALTER C S10RR06335-01
HUBBELL, F ALLAN R01CA52931-01A1
HUBBELL, JEFFREY A R29HL39714-04
HUBBELL, WAYNE L R37EY05216-09
HUBBLE, JEAN S07RR05373-30 0718
HUBEL, DAVID H R37EY00605-32
HUBEL, KENNETH A M01RR00059-30 0603
HUBER, BRIGITTE T R01AI14910-12A1
HUBER, PAUL W R29GM38200-05
HUBER, PAUL W S15HL47723-01
HUBER, SALLY A R01HL28833-11
HUBERMAN, JOEL P01GM44119-02 0001
HUBERMAN, JOEL A P01GM44119-02
HUBERT, HELEN R18AR21393-17 0001
HUBERT, HELEN R18AR21393-17 0002
HUBIG, STEPHEN P41RR00886-16 0006
HUBIG, STEPHEN P41RR00886-16 0007
HUBMAYR, ROLF D R29HL38107-04
HUDGEL, DAVID W P01AG04391-09 0007
HUDGEL, DAVID W P50HL42215-04 9001
HUDGEL, DAVID W P50HL42215-04 0002
HUDGINS, JOHN R24MH47187-02 0001
HUDGINS, JOHN L R24MH47187-02
HUDIG, DOROTHY R01CA38942-07
HUDIG, DOROTHY R01GM42212-02
HUDLICKY, TOMAS R01GM40648-02
HUDSON, BILLY G R01DK18381-18
HUDSON, BILLY G R01DK43507-01
HUDSON, BRUCE S R01GM36578-06
HUDSON, J P01HL25816-11 9005
HUDSON, JAMES I R01HS06658-02
HUDSON, JAMES I U76PE00425-02
HUDSON, JAMES I U76PE00475-01
HUDSON, JERRY L P30CA46592-04 9010
HUDSON, LEONARD D P50HL30542-08 9002
HUDSON, LEONARD D P50HL30542-08
HUDSON, LEONARD D P50HL30542-08 0006
HUDSON, M'LISS A R29CA54277-01
HUDSON, RANDALL L R29AR39700-04
HUDSON, RICHARD R P01GM42397-01A2 0002
HUDSON, RICHARD R R01GM42447-03
HUDSPETH, ALBERT J R01DC00317-07
HUDSPETH, ALBERT JAMES R01DC00241-10
HUEBNER, KAY F P01CA21124-14 0006
HUENNEKENS, FRANK M R35CA39836-07
HUERTA, MICHAEL F R29NS25874-04
HUESMANN, L ROWELL R01MH47474-01
HUESTIS, M A Z01DA00329-02
HUESTIS, WRAY H R01HL23787-13
HUFF, JOHN S07RR05477-29 0432
HUFF, STEVEN N01LM13526-01
HUFF, THOMAS P50AI28532-03 0004
HUFF, THOMAS F K04AI00948-03
HUFF, THOMAS F R01AI25537-04
HUFFAKER, TIM C R01GM40479-04
HUFFMAN, ANN P60HL15996-19 9003
HUFFORD, DAVID J S07RR05680-23 0905
HUG, CARL C M01RR00039-31 0444
HUGANIR, RICHARD L R01NS24418-06
HUGENBERG, STEVEN T P60AR20582-14 0004
HUGHES, ALISON M R13HS06991-01
HUGHES, AUSTIN L R01GM43940-03
HUGHES, BRET A R01EY08850-01
HUGHES, BRET A S07RR05383-30 0558
HUGHES, HOWARD C P01NS17778-10 0009
HUGHES, JANET M P50HL15092-20 9003
HUGHES, JOHN R K02DA00109-07
HUGHES, KELLY T R01GM43149-02
HUGHES, LARRY F P01DC00379-05 9002
HUGHES, MARK R R01DK41427-03
HUGHES, MARY O N01CN75405-12
HUGHES, RICHARD A R03DA06841-02
HUGHES, ROBERT G, JR S07RR05648-25 0922
HUGHES, SUSAN L P60AR30692-08 0006
HUGHES, THOMAS A M01RR00211-27 0324
HUGHES, THOMAS A M01RR00211-27 0276
HUGHES, THOMAS A M01RR00211-27 0312
HUGHES, THOMAS E R01EY08362-02
HUGHES, WALTER T R01AI20673-09
HUGHEY, BARBARA J R43CA53953-01
HUGHEY, REBECCA P R01DK26012-11
HUGLI, TONY P01DK42717-02 0004
HUGLI, TONY E P01AI17354-10S1 0004
HUGLI, TONY E P01HL16411-18 0005
HUGLI, TONY E R01HL25658-11
HUGLI, TONY E U01AI32834-01 0003
HUI, DAVID Y R01DK40917-02
HUI, KA KIT M01RR00865-18 0345
HUI, KOON-SEA R01DA06271-01A1
HUI, SEK-WEN R01GM28120-11
HUI, SEK-WEN R01GM30969-09
HUI, SIU L P01AG05793-06 9001
HUI, SIU LUI R01AG04518-08
HUISMAN, TITUS H P01HL41544-04 9001
HUISMAN, TITUS H P01HL41544-04
HUISMAN, TITUS H P01HL41544-04 0001
HUISMAN, TITUS H R01HL29604-10
HUIZINGA, DAVID H R01DA05183-04
HULETT, F MARION R01GM33471-07
HULETTE, CHRISTINE M K08AG00446-03
HULKA, BARBARA S P30CA16086-17 9007
HULKA, BARBARA S R03CA52447-02
HULKA, BARBARA S R03CA54179-01
HULL, ALAN P60AR20618-13 9001
HULL, BARBARA DR N01CP61022-11
HULL, BARBARA E R01AR39297-04
HULL, BARBARA E S15CA55929-01
HULL, ELAINE M S07RR07066-26 0246
HULL, MAGDALEN S07RR05736-19 0154
HULL, MARGARET M S07RR05944-04 0977
HULL, RICHARD A R01AI18462-09
HULL, SHEILA I R01AI21009-07A1
HULL, WALTER J R19DA06416-03
HULLETT, DEBRA A R01DK35446-06A1
HULLEY, STEPHEN B R01AA08238-02
HULLEY, STEPHEN B S15MH49288-01
HULSEBOSCH, CLAIRE E K04NS01217-04
HULSEBOSCH, CLAIRE E. P01NS11255-17 0017
HULTGREN, SCOTT J R01AI29549-01A1
HULTQUIST, DONALD E R01AG07046-25
HUMAYUN, M ZAFRI R01CA47234-04
HUME, JOSEPH P01DK41315-03 0003
HUME, JOSEPH R R01HL30143-10
HUME, RICHARD I R01NS25782-04
HUMENICK, SHARRON S R01NR02297-01A1
HUMES, DAVID P50DK39255-05 0008
HUMES, H DAVID R01DK30879-10
HUMES, LARRY E R01AG08293-02
HUMMELL, DONNA P30DK26657-12 0028
HUMMERT, MARY L R29AG09433-01A1
HUMPHREY, ALLEN L R01EY06459-07
HUMPHREY, DONALD R N01NS12308-00
HUMPHREY, DONALD R R01NS28858-01
HUMPHREY, DONALD R S15DK44711-01
HUMPHREY, JAY D R29HL41130-04
HUMPHREY, JAY D S07RR07159-16 0582
HUMPHREY, MOSS S07RR05780-16 0973
HUMPHREY, PETER A P50NS20023-08 0015
HUMPHREY, PETER A R29NS29955-01
HUMPHREY, RONALD M R01CA04484-33
HUMPHREYS-BEHER, M S07RR05728-20 0202
HUMPHREYS-BEHER, MICHAEL G K04DE00291-03
HUMPHREYS-BEHER, MICHAEL G R01DE08778-04
HUMPHREYS, MICHAEL H R01DK31623-06
HUMPHRIES, ARTHUR L S07RR05365-30 0085
HUMPHRIES, ERIC H R01CA41450-06
HUMPHRIES, FREDERICK S G12RR03020-07
HUMPHRIES, JOHN E K11HL02592-01
HUMPHRIES, LAURIE L K07MH00767-03
HUMPHRIES, LAURIE L M01RR02602-07 0004
HUNDER, GENE R18AR21393-17 0021
HUNG, DAVID T K11HL02487-02
HUNKER, CHAUNCEY J R03DC01028-01
HUNNINGHAKE, DONALD M01RR00400-23 0230
HUNNINGHAKE, DONALD M01RR00400-23 0243
HUNNINGHAKE, DONALD B M01RR00400-23 0271
HUNNINGHAKE, DONALD B U01HL44327-02
HUNNINGHAKE, DONALD B. N01HC75074-07
HUNNINGHAKE, GARY W M01RR00059-30 0579
HUNNINGHAKE, GARY W P30ES05605-02 9004
HUNNINGHAKE, GARY W P50AI19093-08 0002
HUNNINGHAKE, GARY W P50HL37121-05
HUNNINGHAKE, GARY W P50HL37121-05 0001
HUNNINGHAKE, GARY W P50HL37121-05 0002
HUNNINGHAKE, GARY W R01HL43883-02
HUNSICKER, LAWRENCE G M01RR00059-30 0687
HUNSICKER, LAWRENCE G M01RR00059-30 0651
HUNSICKER, LAWRENCE G M01RR00059-30 0331
HUNSICKER, LAWRENCE G U01AI31490-01
HUNSICKER, LAWRENCE G U01DK34495-07
HUNT, CARL E U01HD29056-01
HUNT, CARLTON C P01NS17763-10 0012
HUNT, CARLTON C R01NS07907-24
HUNT, CARLTON C R01NS27643-03
HUNT, CHRISTINE M M01RR00030-30 0482
HUNT, CLAYTON R R29CA50503-03
HUNT, DONALD F R01GM37537-05
HUNT, GAIL G R43AG10087-01
HUNT, JOAN S R01HD26429-02
HUNT, JOAN S R29HD24212-03
HUNT, L W M01RR00585-20 0560
HUNT, MARGARET S07RR05815-12 0493
HUNT, PATRICIA A R29HD27393-02
HUNT, PATRICIA A S07RR05364-30 0530
HUNT, R D P51RR00168-30 0168
HUNT, RICHARD C R01EY06164-05
HUNT, RONALD P30DK43351-01 9004
HUNT, RONALD U42RR05091-04
HUNT, RONALD D P01DK36350-05S1 9001
HUNT, RONALD D P01HL38070-05 9001
HUNT, RONALD D P30HD06645-20 9002
HUNT, STEPHEN P60AR30701-10 0010
HUNT, STEPHEN W, III R29GM43528-02
HUNT, STEVEN C R01HL44738-02
HUNT, THOMAS K P50GM27345-11
HUNT, THOMAS K P50GM27345-11 0010
HUNT, THOMAS K P50GM27345-11 9001
HUNT, WILLIAM D S07RR07024-26 0048
HUNTER, ANTHONY R P30CA14195-18 0009
HUNTER, ANTHONY R R35CA39780-07
HUNTER, DALE D R01NS29785-01
HUNTER, DAVID J P01CA55075-01 0004
HUNTER, E S Z01ES21152-01
HUNTER, E S Z01ES21153-01
HUNTER, ELLEN B S07RR05424-30 0088
HUNTER, ERIC P01AI27290-04 0002
HUNTER, ERIC P30AI27767-04
HUNTER, ERIC R37CA27834-11
HUNTER, ERIC R37CA29884-11
HUNTER, ERIC U01AI25784-05 0001
HUNTER, JAMES H K08HL02455-02
HUNTER, NANCY S07RR05487-29 0715
HUNTER, ROBERT L, JR U01AI28676-03
HUNTER, ROBERT M R44HD24009-03
HUNTER, ROY P30CA49095-04 9002
HUNTER, SAUNDRA M R01HL38844-05 0017
HUNTER, SUSAN J S07RR07161-14 0843
HUNTER, TIM S07RR05372-30 0702
HUNTER, TONY P30CA14195-18 0039
HUNTER, WILLIAM C R01HL18912-12
HUNTER, WILLIAM C R01HL30552-07
HUNTLEY, RUTH A S07RR07048-26 0644
HUNTSMAN, LEE L P01HL31962-08 9001
HUNTSMAN, LEE L P01HL31962-08 0002
HUNZICKER-DUNN, MARY P01HD21921-04 0001
HUOT, ANNE E S07RR07125-22 0389
HUPKA, ARTHUR G12RR03050-07 0005
HUPPERT, MICHAEL E U76PE00441-02
HUPPERT, MICHAEL E U76PE00442-02
HUPPERT, MICHAEL E U76PE00468-01
HUPPERT, MICHAEL E U76PE00469-01
HUQUE, TAUFIQUL S07RR05825-12 0518
HUQUE, TAUFIQUL S07RR05825-12 0511
HURD, DAVID P01CA21737-14 0004
HURD, MICHAEL D S07RR05995-04 0054
HURD, WILLIAM W R29DA06490-01A2
HURD, WILLIAM W S07RR05383-30 0559
HURDLIK, PAUL F S06GM08016-21 0035
HURKO, OREST P01HG00373-04 0005
HURKO, OREST P01NS16375-11 0014
HURLBERT, ANDREA P01CA41167-06 9002
HURLEY, ANN C R03NR02829-01
HURLEY, CAROLYN P30CA51008-02 9005
HURLEY, CAROLYN K P01CA52066-02 9001
HURLEY, CAROLYN K R01AI26899-03
HURLEY, JAMES B R01EY06641-06
HURLEY, LAURENCE H R35CA49751-03
HURLEY, LAURENCE H S07RR05849-11
HURLEY, MARJA S07RR05678-23 0164
HURLEY, MARJA M S03RR03362-08
HURLEY, THOMAS W R01DE07341-07
HURST, DEBORAH P60HL20985-14 9003
HURST, AGNETA S07RR05792-15 0944

HURST, JAMES K R01AI15834-11
HURST, SUSAN S07RR05635-18 0780
HURT, HALLAM R01DA04965-02
HURT, MAURE JR N01CM25606-16
HURT, R D M01RR00585-20 0440
HURTIG, HOWARD I M01RR00040-31 0406
HURTIG, HOWARD I P01AG09215-02 9001
HURTIG, HOWARD L M01RR00040-31 0336
HURWITZ, ARYEH R01AG07980-01A3
HURWITZ, ARYEH S07RR05373-30 0719
HURWITZ, JERARD P30CA08748-26 9032
HURWITZ, JERRAD R37GM34559-08
HURWITZ, MARY Y R29DK09079-03
HURWITZ, RICHARD L R01EY06656-04A2
HUSAIN, AHSAN P50HL33713-06 0012
HUSAIN, AHSAN R01HD23925-04
HUSAIN, S S P50GM15904-24 9002
HUSAIN, ZAHEED S07RR05526-29 0096
HUSAINI, BAQAR A. S06GM08092-18 0016
HUSKEY, WILLIAM P S07RR07059-26 0832
HUSO, DAVID L R55AI31340-01A1
HUSSAIN, TAHIR S07RR05812-12 0484
HUSSAIN, ZAMIRUL M P50GM27345-11 0013
HUSSEIN, CARLESSIA A R19DA06408-03
HUSSEIN, WEDAD R S06GM08047-20S1 0027
HUSSEY, ROBERT G S03RR03252-08
HUSTON, ALETHA C U10HD25430-02
HUSTON, BUTCH M S07RR05372-30 0689
HUSTON, JAMES S R43CA52323-01A1
HUSTON, JAMES S U01CA51880-02 0001
HUSTON, RICHARD L S07RR07158-16
HUSTON, RICHARD L S15HL47692-01
HUSZAR, GABOR B R01HD19505-04A2
HUTCHINGS, DONALD E R01DA03544-07
HUTCHINS, B S07RR05915-08 0671
HUTCHINS, GARY D. P50NS15655-12 9006
HUTCHINS, JAMES B R01EY08228-02
HUTCHINS, JAMES B S07RR05386-30 0585
HUTCHINS, JAMES B S07RR05386-30 0586
HUTCHINS, PHILLIP M R01HL13936-18
HUTCHINS, ROBERT J R29EY06977-05
HUTCHINS, SANDRA E R44HD24848-03
HUTCHINSON, CHARLES R R01GM25799-12
HUTCHINSON, CHARLES R R01GM31925-07
HUTCHINSON, G Z01CT00011-18
HUTCHINSON, RAYMOND J M01RR00042-31 0470
HUTCHINSON, RAYMOND J U10CA02971-35
HUTCHINSON, RICHARD G. N01HC55021-13
HUTCHINSON, WILLIAM B S07RR05520-28
HUTCHINSON, WILLIAM B S15CA55950-01
HUTCHISON, ALASTAIR MB R29HL39858-04
HUTCHISON, CLYDE A, III R01GM21313-17
HUTCHISON, CLYDE A, III R37AI08998-23
HUTCHISON, FLORENCE N M01RR01070-15 0151
HUTCHISON, FLORENCE N R01DK43186-02
HUTCHISON, NANCY J R01GM34873-07
HUTH, JAMES F R25CA17973-17
HUTSON, JAMES C R01HD26733-02
HUTSON, PAUL R M01RR03186-06 0068
HUTSON, SUSAN S07RR05404-30 0846
HUTSON, SUSAN M R01DK34738-08
HUTT-FLETCHER, LINDSEY M R01AI20662-08
HUTTENLOCHER, JANELLEN R01MH45402-03
HUTTENLOCHER, PETER R R01NS23960-04
HUTTENLOCHER, PETER R R01NS28726-01A1
HUTTER, JOHN J S07RR05675-23 0902
HUTTLINGER, K S06GM08215-09 0005
HUTTO, SUSAN C R01HD26619-02
HUTTON, JOHN S07RR05305-30 0742
HUTTON, JOHN S07RR05305-30 0734
HUTTON, JOHN J R01HD19919-08
HUTTON, JOHN J JR S15HL47762-01
HUTTON, JOHN J, JR S07RR05408-30
HUTTON, LYNN R19MH46187-03
HUTTON, ROBERT S S07RR07096-26 0059
HUVOS, PIROSKA S07RR07118-22 0377
HUXLEY, HUGH E R01AR38899-05
HUXLEY, VIRGINIA H R01HL42528-02
HUXTABLE, RYAN J R01HL25258-12
HUYNH, BOI H R01GM32187-08
HWANG, BANG H R29NS25087-05
HWANG, DANIEL H R01DK41868-03
HWANG, JENQ-NENG S07RR07096-26 0071
HWANG, KOU U01AI25922-05 9003
HWANG, YU-WEN R29CA53782-01
HYATT, DAVID E R43OH02913-01
HYDE, DALLAS M P01ES00628-19 0010
HYDE, DALLAS M P51RR00169-30 0163
HYDE, DAVID R R01EY08058-03
HYDE, DAVID R S07RR07033-26 0051
HYDE, JAMES S P41RR01008-16
HYDE, JAMES S P41RR01008-16 9001
HYDE, JAMES S P41RR01008-16 9002
HYDE, JAMES S P41RR01008-16 9003
HYDE, JAMES S P41RR01008-16 9004
HYDE, JAMES S P41RR01008-16 9005
HYDE, JAMES S P41RR01008-16 9006
HYDE, JAMES S R01CA41464-06
HYDE, JAMES S R01GM27665-13
HYDE, JAMES S R03EY09243-01
HYDE, JAMES S R37GM22923-16
HYDE, JAMES S S10RR06742-01
HYDE, JANET S R01MH44340-03
HYERS, THOMAS M P50HL30572-08
HYERS, THOMAS M P50HL30572-08 9002
HYLAND, KEITH S07RR05906-06 0635
HYLANDER, WILLIAM L R37DE04531-13
HYLEMON, PHILLIP B P01DK38030-05 9001
HYLEMON, PHILLIP B R01DK40986-03
HYLEMON, PHILLIP B. P01DK38030-05 0004
HYMAN, ALBERT L R01HL11802-23
HYMAN, BRADLEY T R29AG08487-03
HYMAN, EDWARD D R43CA53925-01
HYMAN, LESLIE G R01EY05653-04S1
HYMAN, PAUL E M01RR00425-22S3 0371
HYMAN, PAUL E M01RR00425-22S3 0420
HYMAN, PAUL E M01RR00425-22S3 0463
HYMAN, PAUL E M01RR00425-22S3 0437
HYMAN, PAUL E R29HD22912-05
HYMAN, ROBERT A P30CA14195-18 0040
HYMAN, ROBERT A P30CA14195-18 0010
HYMAN, ROBERT A R37CA13287-20
HYMAN, ROBERT A S10RR06338-01
HYMAN, STEVEN E K02MH00892-02
HYMAN, STEVEN E R01DA07134-01
HYMAN, STEVEN E R29MH44160-04
HYMEL, L S07RR05377-30 0761
HYMOWITZ, NORMAN N01CN64099-11
HYNDIUK, ROBERT A U10EY07496-04
HYNES, HENRY E U10CA35431-08
HYNES, JAMES T R01GM41332-03
HYNES, RICHARD P01HL41484-03 0006
HYNES, RICHARD O P01CA26712-11S1 9001
HYNES, RICHARD O P01CA26712-11S1
HYNES, RICHARD O P01CA26712-11S1 0002
HYNES, RICHARD O P30CA14051-20
HYNES, RICHARD O R01CA17007-16
HYNYNEN, KULLERVO H R01CA48939-01A2
HYNYNEN, KULLERVO H R29CA46627-04
HYSLOP, NEWTON E, JR U01AI27674-06
HYSON, RICHARD L R29DC00858-02
IACONO, VINCENT J S07RR05778-16 0403
IACOVITTI, LORRAINE M R01NS24204-04
IADAROLA, M J Z01DE00414-07
IADECOLA, CONSTANTIN S07RR05385-30 0803
IAMS, JAY D M01RR00034-31 0415
IANDOLO, JOHN J R37AI17474-11
IANNACCONE, PHILIP M R01CA29078-11
IANNACONE, PHILIP P01AG10481-01 9003
IANNOTTI, JOSEPH P P50AR39226-05 9002
IANNOTTI, RONALD J R01MH47252-02
IANNOTTI, RONALD J R03HL47388-01
IANNUZZI, MICHAEL C P01DK42718-02 0002
IANZANO, JOHN A S07RR05778-16 0412
IBER, RICHARD I R13AI32476-01
IBERS, JAMES A R01HL13157-21
IBRAHIM, MICHEL S07RR05450-30
IBRAHIM, MICHEL A S15AI32173-01
ICHIKAWA, IEKUNI R01DK37868-06
ICHIKAWA, IEKUNI R55DK37869-06A1
ICHIKAWA, IEKUNI P50DK39261-05 0001
IDE, CHARLES F S07RR07040-24
IDE, CHARLES F S15AI32213-01
IDE, HIROSHI S07RR07125-22 0390
IDEKER, RAYMOND E P50HL17670-17 0027
IDEKER, RAYMOND E R01HL28429-10
IDEKER, RAYMOND E R01HL42760-03
IDEKER, RAYMOND E R01HL44066-02
IDELL, STEVEN R01HL37770-06
IDELL, STEVEN R01HL45018-01A1
IDELL, STEVEN S07RR05958-06 0749
IDEN, CHARLES P01ES04068-05 9001
IDEN, CHARLES R P01CA47995-02 9001
IDEN, CHARLES R S10RR06359-01
IDLER, ELLEN L R29AG07480-04
IDZERDA, REJEAN P50HD12629-12 9004
IDZERDA, REJEAN L P01HL44948-01A1 9001
IEZZONI, LISA I R01HS06512-02
IEZZONI, LISA I R01HS06742-01
IGARASHI, PETER R01DK42921-01A1
IGLEHART, J DIRK R01CA40640-04A2
IGLEWSKI, BARBARA H R01AI25669-04
IGNARRO, LOUIS J R01HL40922-02
IGNOTZ, RONALD A S07RR05712-20 0056
IGUCHI, MARTIN YONEO R18DA06096-03
IGWE, ORISA J R29AR41606-01
IHDE, D C Z01CM03024-22
IHLE, JAMES N P01CA20180-14 0012
IHLE, JAMES N R01CA51020-02
IHLE, JAMES N R01DK42932-02
IIKIW, ROMA M01RR00188-27 0326
IIT RESEARCH INST N01DA19201-00
IKEBE, MITSUO R01AR38888-05
IKEDA-SAITO, MASAO R01GM39359-04
IKEDA-SAITO, MASAO R01GM39492-09
IKEDA, KAZUO R01NS18856-11
IKEDA, RICHARD S07RR07024-26 0036
IKEDA, RICHARD A R29AI24905-03
IKEDA, RICHARD A S07RR07024-26 0046
IKEDA, STEPHEN R R29HL43242-03
IKEGAMI, MACHIKO M01RR00425-22S3 0436
IKLE, DAVID S07RR05842-12 0292
ILAN, JOSEPH R01HD25004-03
ILAN, JUDITH R01HD18271-06
ILDSTAD, SUZANNE T R01AI30615-01A1
ILDSTAD, SUZANNE T R55DK43901-01
ILDSTAD, SUZANNE T S07RR05416-30 0562
ILEANA, QUINTAS N01AI85006-07
ILIAKIS, GEORGE R01CA42026-07
ILIAKIS, GEORGE R01CA45557-05
ILIAKIS, GEORGE R55CA52715-01A1
ILINSKY, IGOR R01NS24188-04A2
ILLANES, OSCAR G S07RR05854-11 0919
ILLINGSWORTH, ROGER P30DK40566-02 9003
ILLINGWORTH D. ROGER M01RR00334-25 0224
ILLINGWORTH, D ROGER M01RR00334-25 0212
ILLINGWORTH, D ROGER M01RR00334-25 0295
ILLINGWORTH, D ROGER M01RR00334-25 0169
ILLINGWORTH, D ROGER M01RR00334-25 0298
ILLINGWORTH, D ROGER M01RR00334-25 0311
ILLINGWORTH, D ROGER M01RR00334-25 0237
ILLINGWORTH, D ROGER M01RR00334-25 0233
ILLINGWORTH, D ROGER M01RR00334-25 0297
ILLINGWORTH, D ROGER R01HL28399-08
ILLINGWORTH, D ROGER R01HL37940-05
ILLINGWORTH, ROGER M01RR00334-25 0244
ILLNER, HANA P R01GM37045-05
ILLSLEY, NICHOLAS P R01HD23498-04
ILLSLEY, NICHOLAS P R01HD26392-02
ILTZSCH, MAX H U01AI31702-01 0003
ILYAS, AMJAD A R29NS29668-01
ILYAS, AMJAD A S07RR05393-30 0893
IM, MIE-JAE R01GM45985-01
IMBER, STANLEY D U01MH33753-09S1
IMBODEN, JOHN B R01AI26644-04
IMBODEN, JOHN B R01CA52669-02
IMBRA, RICHARD J S07RR05399-30 0944
IMIG, THOMAS J R01DC00173-10
IMPERATO-MCGINLEY, J S07RR05396-30 0747
IMPERATO-MCGINLEY, JULIANNE L R01HD09421-1
IMPERATO, JULIANNE M01RR00047-31 0421
IMPERIALE, MICHAEL J M01RR00042-31 0664
IMPERIALE, MICHAEL J R01CA19816-16
IMPERIALE, MICHAEL J R01GM34902-07
IMPERIALI, BARBARA R29GM39334-05
INADA, YORITARO U01AI25902-05 0004
INAGAMI, TADASHI P50HL14192-21
INAGAMI, TADASHI P50HL14192-21 0004
INAGAMI, TADASHI R01HL35323-06
INANA, GEORGE R01EY08904-01
INBODY, STEVEN B P50AG08664-03 9002
INCFEY, GENEVIEVE S P01AI32918-09 0006
INCIARDI, JAMES A R18DA06124-03
INCIARDI, JAMES A R18DA06948-02
INDRA, PRAKASH N01CM17509-00
INESI, GIUSEPPE P01HL27867-10
INESI, GIUSEPPE P01HL27867-10 0002
INFANTE, ANTHONY S07RR05654-24 0152
INFANTE, ANTHONY J R01NS29093-01A1
INFELD, MICHAEL P30DK27651-09 0010
ING, PAUL P60DC00982-02 9002
INGBER, DONALD P01CA45548-05 0001
INGBER, DONALD P01CA45548-05 0002
INGEBRITSEN, THOMAS S07RR07034-26 0058
INGENITO, EDWARD P R29HL45687-01
INGERSOLL, GAIL L U01NR02156-04
INGHAM, KENNETH P50HL44336-01 0002
INGHAM, KENNETH P50HL44336-01 9002
INGHAM, KENNETH C R01HL21791-14
INGHAM, ROGER J R01DC00060-01A1
INGOGLIA, NICHOLAS A S07RR05393-30 0894
INGRAM, D P01HL14388-20 9007
INGRAM, D K Z01AG00302-08
INGRAM, ROLAND H P01HL36110-07 0010
INGWALL, JOANNE P41RR02305-08 0017
INGWALL, JOANNE S P01HL38189-04 9001
INGWALL, JOANNE S P01HL38189-04 0003
INGWALL, JOANNE S R01HL43170-03
INMAN, J K Z01AI00035-18
INMAN, ROSS B R01GM14711-25
INNERARITY, THOMAS L. P01HL41633-03 9001
INNES, ROGER W R29GM46451-01
INNIS, ROBERT B P01MH25642-18 9006
INNIS, ROBERT B P50DA04060-06 0010
INNIS, ROBERT B P50MH44866-04 0004
INOUE, SHINYA R37GM31617-10
INOUE, TAN R01GM35755-06
INOUYE, MASAYORI R01GM44012-02
INOUYE, MASAYORI R37GM19043-20
INOUYE, SHARON K K08AG00524-01
INOUYE, SUMIKO R01GM26843-12
INSEL, PAUL A P50HL17682-17 0042
INSEL, PAUL A R01GM31987-09
INSEL, PAUL A R01GM40781-04
INSEL, RICHARD A P01AI29522-02 0001
INSEL, T R Z01MH00797-05
INSEL, T R Z01MH02219-08
INSELBURG, JOSEPH W R22AI22038-07
INSOGNA, KARL M01RR00125-28 0767
INSOGNA, KARL M01RR00125-28 0722
INSOGNA, KARL L M01RR00125-28 0741
INSOGNA, KARL L R01AR39571-03
INTERSYSTEMS, INC N01AA10008-00
INTURRISI, CHARLES E P50DA05130-05 0002
INTURRISI, CHARLES E R01DA01457-16
INTURRISI, CHARLES E S07RR05396-30 0780

INVERIUS, PER-HENRIK M01RR00064-27 0313
IOANNIDES, CONSTANTI S07RR05511-29 0486
IORIO, RONALD M R01AI12467-14
IORIO, RONALD M R29AI24770-05
IORIO, RONALD M S07RR05712-20 0057
IOZZO, RENATO V R01CA39481-07
IOZZO, RENATO V R01CA47282-02
IP, CLEMENT P01CA45164-04A1 0001
IP, CLEMENT C Y P01CA45164-04A1
IP, CLEMENT C Y R01CA27706-11
IP, MARGOT M R01CA33240-09
IP, WALLACE S R01AR35973-07
IPP, ELI M01RR00425-22S3 0353
IPP, ELI M01RR00425-22S3 0376
IPP, ELI M01RR00425-22S3 0403
IPP, ELI M01RR00425-22S3 0422
IPP, ELI M01RR00425-22S3 0442
IPP, ELI M01RR00425-22S3 0455
IPP, ELI M01RR00425-22S3 0450
IPP, ELI S07RR05551-29 0947
IPPEN-IHLER, KARIN A R01AI14426-15
IPPOLITI, ANDREW M01RR00865-18 0361
IQBAL, KHALID R01AG05892-10
IQBAL, KHALID R01AG08076-01A3
IRELAND, CHRIS M K04CA01179-05
IRELAND, CHRIS M R01CA36622-09
IRELAND, CHRIS M S10RR06262-01
IRELAND, CHRIS M U01CA50750-03 0005
IRELAND, ROBERT C R15HD26867-01A1
IRELAND, ROBERT E R01GM39998-04
IRELAND, ROBERT E R01GM41983-02
IRIARTE, ANA J S07RR07257-02
IRIARTE, ANA J S15GM47074-01
IRIE, REIKO F P01CA12582-19 0017
IRIE, REIKO F P01CA29605-10 0003
IRIMURA, TATSURO R01CA39319-06
IRIMURA, TATSURO R01CA50231-03
IRISH, ERIN E S07RR07035-26 0080
IRONSON, GAIL P01HL36588-06 0005
IRVIN, CHARLES G P01HL36577-06 0012
IRVING, STEVEN G S07RR05360-30 0775
IRWIN, MICHAEL P50MH30914-14 0057
IRWIN, MICHAEL E S07RR07030-26 0394
IRWIN, MICHAEL R M01RR00827-17 0484
IRWIN, MICHAEL R R29MH44275-04
ISAAC, LAWRENCE P20NS30295-01 0004
ISAACS, JOHN P30CA06973-29 9001
ISAACS, JOHN T R01CA42954-05
ISAACS, JOHN T R01CA50601-02
ISAACS, WILLIAM B R29CA55231-01
ISAACSON, GLENN S07RR05507-29 0477
ISABELLA, RUSSELL A S07RR07092-26 0492
ISABELLA, RUSSELL A S07RR07092-26 0504
ISACKSON, PAUL P01AG00538-15 0016
ISACKSON, PAUL R35AG07918-03 0005
ISACKSON, PAUL J R29NS24747-05
ISACSON, E PETER P30ES05605-02 9001
ISACSON, OLE P01NS16367-12 0016
ISACSON, OLE R29NS29178-01A1
ISAHAKIA, MOHAMED P51RR00165-31 0111
ISAKSON, PETER C R01AI29976-02
ISALES, CARLOS M K11DK01825-04
ISBERG, RALPH R R01AI23538-05
ISBERG, RALPH R R01AI29719-02
ISEMAN, MICHAEL D N01AI72636-06
ISENBERG, J NEVIN M01RR00073-29 0315
ISENBERG, J NEVIN M01RR00073-29 0316
ISENBERG, J NEVIN M01RR00073-29 0292
ISENBERG, J NEVIN M01RR00073-29 0212
ISENBERG, J. NEVIN M01RR00073-29 0278
ISENBERG, JON I R01DK33491-07
ISENBERG, KEITH E P50AA03539-14 9007
ISENBERG, SHERWIN J M01RR00425-22S3 0464
ISENBERG, SHERWIN J M01RR00425-22S3 0424
ISHAQ, M Z01NS02827-01
ISHIDA, ANDREW T R29EY08120-03
ISHIHARA, S Z01NS02144-17
ISHII, DOUGLAS N P01NS28323-02 0003
ISHII, DOUGLAS N R01NS24327-05
ISHII, H Z01NS02623-08
ISHIZAKA, KIMISHIGE R01AI11202-19
ISHIZAKA, KIMISHIGE R37AI14784-15
ISHIZAKA, KIMISHIGE S07RR06039-01
ISHIZAKA, KIMISHIGE U01AI32834-01 0004
ISHIZAKA, TERUKO R01AI10060-21
ISMAIL-BEIGI, FARAMARZ R01GM39835-04
ISMAIL-BEIGI, GARAMARZ R01HL39300-04
ISOKAWA-AKESSON, MASAKO P01NS02808-30 0002
ISOM, GARY E R01ES04140-06
ISOM, GARY E S07RR05586-24 0116
ISOM, GARY E S07RR07032-26
ISOM, GARY E S15DK44661-01
ISOM, GARY E S15MH49292-01
ISOM, HARRIET C P01CA27503-12 0002
ISOM, HARRIET C R01CA23931-14
ISON-FRANKLIN, ELEANOR L S06GM08016-21 0078
ISRAEL, ALLEN S07RR07122-23 0104
ISRAEL, ESTER J M01RR01066-14 0108
ISRAEL, ESTHER J K08HD00938-01
ISRAEL, MERVYN R01CA37082-08
ISRAEL, MERVYN R01CA37209-06
ISRAEL, MERVYN S07RR05423-30 0052
ISRAELE, VICTOR S07RR05468-29 0405
ISSARAGRISIL, SURAPOL R01HL35068-04
ISSCHE, SHEENAH S07RR07065-26 0067
ISSELBACHER, KURT J P01DK36350-05S1 0004
ISSELBACHER, KURT J R37DK01392-35
ISSELL, BRIAN F K07CA01642-01
ISSELL, BRIAN F N01CO15624-01
ISSENBERG, PHILLIP P30CA36727-08 9003
ISSEROFF, ROSLYN-RIVKAH K04AR01803-04
ISTOCK, C A P42ES04940-02 0009
ISTOCK, CONRAD S07RR07002-26 0883
ISTVAN, JOSEPH A R29HL38414-05
ITO, JAMES S07RR05471-29 0593
ITO, JOEL P51RR00163-32 9011
ITO, Y Z01HL01031-02
ITO, Y Z01HL01032-01
ITO, Y Z01HL01462-05
ITO, Y Z01HL01463-05
ITOH, KYOGO R01CA47891-03
ITOH, KYOGO S07RR05511-29 0491
ITTMANN, MICHAEL M R29GM40560-04
ITZKOWITZ, STEVEN H R01CA42981-06
ITZKOWITZ, STEVEN H R01CA52491-02
IUVONE, PAUL M R01EY04864-09
IUVONE, PAUL MICHAEL P51RR00165-31 0095
IVASHKIV, LIONEL B K08AR01852-01
IVERIUS, PER-HENRIK R29HL39595-04
IVERSEN, PATRICK L R01CA49135-03
IVERSON, LINDA E P01NS18858-09A2 0015
IVERSON, LINDA E R29NS28135-02
IVES, DAVID H R01CA47828-03
IVES, HARLAN E R01DK34127-07
IVES, HARLAN E R01HL41210-04
IVRY, RICHARD R29NS30256-01
IVY, JOHN M R43HL46043-01
IWAMOTO, EDGAR T R01NS28847-02
IWAMOTO, GARY A K04HL01910-06
IWAMOTO, HARRIET P50HD20748-06A1 0010
IWANCZYK, JAN S R01GM37161-07
IWANIJ, VICTORIA R01DK43794-01
IWAOKA, WAYNE S06GM08125-18 0039
IWASA, K Z01NS02609-08
IWASA, K Z01NS02799-03
IWAZUMI, TATSUO R01HL45906-02
IYENGAR, SATISH P01MH41712-06 9003
IYENGAR, SRINIVAS R R01CA44998-05
IYENGAR, SRINIVAS R R01DK38761-06
IYER, RATHYI V N01HB77043-07
IYPE, P THOMAS G20RR06950-01
IYPE, P THOMAS N01CP15628-00
IYPE, P THOMAS DR N01CP71025-09
IZANT, JONATHAN G R55CA47629-04
IZARD, CARROLL E S07RR07016-18 0351
IZARD, CARROLL E S07RR07016-18 0350
IZUMO, SEIGO R01HL45903-01
IZUTSU, KENNETH T R01DE09271-05A1
IZUTSU, KENNETH T R01DE09812-01
IZYDORE, ROBERT S06GM08049-20 0011
JAARDA, MERLE J S07RR05321-30 0261
JABBAR, MOHAMED A R29AI25009-06
JABS, DOUGLAS A M01RR00035-31 0404
JABS, DOUGLAS A M01RR00722-19 0247
JABS, DOUGLAS A U10EY08052-04
JABS, ETHYLIN W P01HG00373-04 0003
JABS, KATHY M01RR02172-09 0187
JACCARD, JAMES J R01HD25522-02
JACCARD, JAMES J R01HD28434-01
JACCARD, JAMES J S07RR07122-23 0105
JACGUES, S P41RR02594-06 0002
JACHIKAWA, HIROYASU S06GM08047-20S1 0028
JACK, CLIFFORD R R55NS28374-01A1
JACK, RICHARD P60AR36308-07 9005
JACK, RICHARD S07RR05950-07 0998
JACK, RICHARD M R01AI26292-03
JACKLET, JON W S07RR07122-23 0077
JACKLET, JON W S07RR07122-23 0078
JACKLET, JON W S07RR07122-23 0079
JACKLET, JON W S07RR07122-23 0080
JACKMAN, SUSAN H S07RR05870-10 0992
JACKMAN, WARREN M R01HL39670-04
JACKNOWITZ, LINDA G08LM05047-04
JACKOWSKI, SUZANNE R01GM45737-01
JACKSON, ANDREW C R01HL31248-07
JACKSON, BENJAMIN T R01DK39178-05
JACKSON, CARL W R01HL31598-08
JACKSON, CHARLES V P60DK20572-14 0038
JACKSON, CYNTHIA L R29HG00044-02
JACKSON, EDWIN K P50HL14192-21 0016
JACKSON, EDWIN K R01HL35909-05
JACKSON, EDWIN K R01HL40319-05
JACKSON, F ROB R01NS30386-01
JACKSON, F ROB R29NS25914-04
JACKSON, GARY L R01HD13037-13
JACKSON, GARY L R01HD27453-01
JACKSON, GEORGE A S03RR03484-04
JACKSON, HENRY P S03RR03465-05
JACKSON, IVOR M R01DK34540-07
JACKSON, J EDWARD P50AG05131-08 9003
JACKSON, JAMES D R03AG10372-01
JACKSON, JAMES E S10RR06506-01
JACKSON, JAMES S P01AG05561-06A1 0002
JACKSON, JAMES S R01MH47182-02
JACKSON, JANIS H R01CA54298-01
JACKSON, JAY B R01AI32395-01
JACKSON, JOSEPH E M01RR00750-19 0282
JACKSON, JULIUS H G12RR03062-07
JACKSON, MARIAN S07RR05425-30 0746
JACKSON, MARIAN J R55CA54849-01
JACKSON, MARY E R01AG10641-01
JACKSON, MEYER B R01NS23512-05
JACKSON, REBECCA D K11HD00772-04
JACKSON, RICHARD A P30DK36836-05 0003
JACKSON, RICHARD A P30DK36836-05 9004
JACKSON, RICHARD D P01DE09835-01A1 0001
JACKSON, RICHARD L P01HL22619-14 0011
JACKSON, ROBERT M R29HL39147-05
JACKSON, RODWIN A R01AG07057-02
JACKSON, RUDOLPH E P20AI29360-02
JACKSON, SUSAN P30AI27767-04 9005
JACKSON, SUSAN R01AI23952-05
JACKSON, SUSAN R01DK40117-03
JACKSON, THOMAS S07RR05405-30 0872
JACKSON, THOMAS E N01HD13113-00
JACKSON, TIMOTHY K S07RR05433-30 0256
JACKSON, VALERIE P R01CA48004-03
JACKSON, W DANIEL S07RR05428-30 0177
JACKSON, WILLIAM FREDERICK R01HL32469-09
JACOB-LABARRE, JEAN T R01EY08539-02
JACOB-LABARRE, JEAN T R55EY08669-01A1
JACOB, ROLF G P01HL40962-04 9002
JACOB, ROLF G P01HL40962-04 0003
JACOB, HARRY S R37HL28935-23
JACOB, MICHELE H R01NS21725-08
JACOB, SAMSON T R01CA25078-13
JACOB, SAMSON T R01CA31894-10
JACOB, THEODORE R01AA08098-02
JACOB, THEODORE R37AA03037-14
JACOBBERGER, JAMES P30CA43703-04A1 9003
JACOBBERGER, JAMES W R01HL41945-04
JACOBBERGER, JAMES W S10RR07249-01
JACOBOWITZ, D M Z01MH00382-03
JACOBOWITZ, D M Z01MH00388-15
JACOBOWITZ, D M Z01MH00396-13
JACOBOWITZ, D M Z01MH00397-13
JACOBOWITZ, D M Z01MH02377-05
JACOBOWITZ, D M Z01MH02565-01
JACOBS-LORENA, MARCELO R01AI31478-01
JACOBS, BARRY L R01MH23433-18
JACOBS, BERTRAM L R01AI30349-01A1
JACOBS, BERTRAM L R29CA48654-04
JACOBS, DANNY O P50GM36428-07 0007
JACOBS, DANNY O R29GM42224-03
JACOBS, DAVID R S07RR05448-30 0289
JACOBS, ELIZABETH R K08HL01924-04
JACOBS, GERALD H R01EY02052-12A2
JACOBS, GWEN A R29NS29847-01
JACOBS, HARVEY P50MH30911-14 0021
JACOBS, HARVEY E P50MH30911-14 0029
JACOBS, JERRY M01RR00645-20 0482
JACOBS, JOHN R R01CA46764-04
JACOBS, JOHN W P01CA40035-06 9001
JACOBS, LAWRENCE D R01NS26321-02
JACOBS, LUCIA F R03MH45617-03
JACOBS, MARC S07RR05755-18 0224
JACOBS, MARK R15GM46024-01
JACOBS, ROBERT S07RR07099-25 0393
JACOBS, ROBERT R S07RR05829-09 0952
JACOBS, RUSSELL E R01HD25390-03
JACOBS, WILLIAM R R01AI27235-03
JACOBS, WILLIAM R U01AI30189-02 0002
JACOBS, WILLIAM R, JR R22AI26170-03
JACOBSEN, DAVID W P01HL06835-30 9004
JACOBSEN, ERIC N R01GM43214-01A1
JACOBSEN, ERIC N S07RR07030-26 0395
JACOBSEN, LAWRENCE P51RR00167-31 9012
JACOBSEN, STEPHEN J M01RR00827-17 0487
JACOBSON HARRY R P01DK38226-06 0001
JACOBSON, A E Z01DK59502-05
JACOBSON, ALAN M R01DK27845-10
JACOBSON, ALAN M R01DK42315-01A1
JACOBSON, ALAN M U01DK30633-09
JACOBSON, ALLAN S R01GM27757-12
JACOBSON, ALLAN S R01GM38642-05
JACOBSON, ANN B S07RR05736-19 0212
JACOBSON, ANTONE G R01HD25902-03
JACOBSON, BRUCE S R01GM29127-11
JACOBSON, CAROL S07RR07034-26 0059
JACOBSON, EUGENE D R01DK37050-07
JACOBSON, GARY R R01GM28226-09
JACOBSON, HARRY R P01DK38226-06
JACOBSON, HARRY R P50DK39261-05
JACOBSON, HARRY R R01DK37097-07
JACOBSON, HERBERT I R01CA47969-02
JACOBSON, HERBERT I S15CA56017-01
JACOBSON, IRA M01RR00047-31 0459
JACOBSON, JED J S03RR03076-10
JACOBSON, JED J S07RR05321-30 0255
JACOBSON, JOSEPH P50AA07606-04 0002
JACOBSON, JOSEPH L R01ES05483-01
JACOBSON, JOSEPH L S06GM08167-13 0035
JACOBSON, K Z01DK31115-08
JACOBSON, K Z01DK31116-04
JACOBSON, K Z01DK31117-04
JACOBSON, KENNETH A R01GM35325-06

JACOBSON, KENNETH A R01GM41402-03
JACOBSON, LINDA B P30CA23168-14 9001
JACOBSON, MARCUS R01HD26460-02
JACOBSON, MARK M01RR00083-29 0189
JACOBSON, MARK M01RR00083-29 0227
JACOBSON, MYRON K R01CA43894-06
JACOBSON, NEIL S K02MH00868-02
JACOBSON, NEIL S R01MH43101-03
JACOBSON, NEIL S R37MH44063-03
JACOBSON, S Z01NS02817-02
JACOBSON, SAMUEL G R01EY05627-06
JACOBSON, SANDRA W P50AA07606-04 0003
JACOBSON, SHAROL F R01NR02618-01
JACOBUS, WILLIAM E P01NS20020-08 9002
JACOBUS, WILLIAM E S07RR05700-22 0874
JACOBY, DAVID B R29HL47126-01
JACOBY, JEAN R01EY06232-06
JACOBY, JEAN S07RR05399-30 0935
JACOBY, LEE B R01CA51410-01A2
JACOBY, LEE B S07RR05486-29 0040
JACOBY, ROBERT O G20RR07104-01
JACOBY, ROBERT O P40RR00393-24
JACOBY, ROBERT O P40RR00393-24 0003
JACOBY, ROBERT O R24RR04047-04
JACOX, ADA K R01NR02376-03
JACQUES, S P41RR02594-06 0001
JACQUES, STEVEN L R29HL45045-01A1
JACQUEZ, GEOFFREY M R44CA50800-02
JACQUEZ, JOHN P41RR02176-05 9001
JACQUIN, MARK F P01DE07734-06
JACQUIN, MARK F P01DE07734-06 0004
JACQUIN, MARK F R01DE07662-07
JADHAV, ARUN L S06GM08061-17 0006
JAECKLE, KURT A M01RR00064-27 0314
JAECKLE, KURT A M01RR00064-27 0354
JAECKLE, KURT A R01NS29697-01
JAEGER, CHRISTINE B R01NS27694-03
JAEGER, JUDITH S07RR05399-30 0937
JAEGER, ROBERT J S07RR07027-26 0011
JAEHNING, JUDITH A K04AI00874-04
JAEHNING, JUDITH A R01GM36692-07
JAEHNING, JUDITH A R01GM38101-05
JAENISCH, RUDOLF R35CA44339-05
JAENISCH, RUDOLF S15HD28756-01
JAENISH, RUDOLF P01HL41484-03 0005
JAESCHKE, HARTMUT W R29GM42957-03
JAFEK, BRUCE P01DC00244-07 9002
JAFEK, BRUCE W P01DC00244-07 0004
JAFFE, ALLAN S P50HL17646-17 0015
JAFFE, BERNARD M M01RR00318-25 0182
JAFFE, CONRADE C R01LM05007-02
JAFFE, E S Z01CB00550-11
JAFFE, E S Z01CB00855-09
JAFFE, EILEEN K R01ES03654-09
JAFFE, EILEEN K R01GM41913-03
JAFFE, ERIC A P50HL18828-16 0002
JAFFE, ERIC A S07RR05396-30 0748
JAFFE, KENNETH M S07RR05655-21 0819
JAFFE, LAURINDA A R01HD14939-10
JAFFE, LIONEL F P41RR01395-10
JAFFE, LIONEL F P41RR01395-10 9003
JAFFE, LIONEL F P41RR01395-10 9004
JAFFE, LIONEL F P41RR01395-10 9005
JAFFE, M J Z01MH02262-07
JAFFE, RICHARD S07RR05353-30 0349
JAFFE, ROBERT M01RR00079-29 0395
JAFFE, ROBERT M01RR00079-29 0396
JAFFE, ROBERT B P30HD11979-13
JAFFE, ROBERT B R01HD08478-17
JAGACINSKI, RICHARD J R01AG09179-02
JAGADEESWARAN, PUDUR P01AG06872-05 9001
JAGADEESWARAN, PURDUR P01AG06872-05 0003
JAGGER, PAUL I M01RR00827-17 0430
JAGIELLO, GEORGIANA M P50HD05077-21
JAGIELLO, GEORGIANA M R01HD18735-08
JAGUS, ROSEMARY R01GM33631-08
JAGUST, WILLIAM J P30AG10129-01
JAGUST, WILLIAM J R01AA09042-01
JAGUST, WILLIAM J R01AG07793-04
JAHAN-PARWAR, BEHRUS P42ES04913-02 0003
JAHN, CAROLYN L R01GM37661-05
JAHOOR, FAROOK M01RR00073-29 0228
JAHOOR, FAROOK R29DK41764-03
JAHR, CRAIG S07RR07238-04 0476
JAHR, CRAIG E R01EY09139-01
JAHR, CRAIG E R01NS21419-08
JAHR, JONATHAN S07RR05377-30 0762
JAHR, JONATHAN S07RR05377-30 0773
JAIN, AVANINDRA M01RR00046-31 0347
JAIN, RAKESH K R01CA36902-08
JAIN, RAKESH K R01CA37239-06
JAIN, RAKESH K R01CA49792-02
JAINCHILL, NANCY P50DA07700-01 0002
JAISWAL, ANIL K R29GM47466-01
JAKAB, GEORGE J R01ES05429-02
JAKEN, SUSAN P01CA37589-08 0008
JAKEN, SUSAN R01CA53841-01
JAKEN, SUSAN S07RR05863-11 0567
JAKINOVICH, WILLIAM S06GM08225-07 0006
JAKOBIEC, FREDERICK A S07RR05485-29
JAKOBS, THOMAS R43DC01008-01
JAKOBSSON, ERIC G R01GM32356-06S1
JAKOBY, W B Z01DK17002-21
JAKOWLEW, S B Z01CP05622-02
JAKSCHIK, BARBARA A R01HL31922-08
JAKUBOWSKI, HENRY V R15HL46475-01
JALIFE, JOSE P01HL39707-02
JALIFE, JOSE P01HL39707-02 0001
JALIFE, JOSE R01HL29439-10
JALOWIEC, ANNE S07RR07210-09 0684
JALOWIEC, ANNE M R01NR01693-05
JAMASBI, ROUDABEH S07RR07192-12 0620
JAMES, ANTHONY A R01AI29746-03
JAMES, ANTHONY A S07RR07008-26 0061
JAMES, CHARLES D R01CA55728-01
JAMES, DAVID E R01DK42503-02
JAMES, EDWARD P50MH44188-03 9002
JAMES, ERIC R R01EY06462-05
JAMES, GARY M01RR00047-31 0471
JAMES, J HOWARD S10RR06280-01
JAMES, L STANLEY P50HD13063-12
JAMES, L STANLEY P50HD13063-12 9002
JAMES, MARGARET O R01ES05781-05
JAMES, MARK S07RR05444-30 0259
JAMES, ROBERT C R01ES05216-03
JAMES, S P Z01AI00354-09
JAMES, S P Z01AI00432-06
JAMES, THARAPPEL C R01GM42813-01A2
JAMES, THOMAS L R01GM39247-04
JAMES, THOMAS L R01GM41639-01A1
JAMESON, BRADFORD P50HL45486-01 9001
JAMESON, BRADFORD A R01AI30395-02
JAMESON, C W Z01ES21123-03
JAMESON, GEOFFREY B S07RR07136-20 0609
JAMESON, J LARRY U54HD29164-01 0004
JAMESON, JAMES L P30HD28138-01 9001
JAMESON, JAMES L R01DK42144-01A1
JAMESON, JAMES L R01HD23519-04
JAMIESON, GORDON A, S07RR05408-30 0930
JAMIESON, GRAHAM A R01HL40858-03
JAMIESON, GRAHAM A R37HL39438-04
JAMIESON, JAMES D P01CA46128-04 0004
JAMIESON, JAMES D P01CA46128-04
JAMIESON, JAMES D R37DK17389-19
JAMIESON, MICHAEL J S07RR07187-13 0705
JAMIESON, PATRICK W R29LM05074-02S1
JAMPOL, LEE M U10EY06844-06
JAMRICH, M A Z01BB07001-03
JAN, LILY K P01NS16033-11 0008
JAN, LILY K R01NS15963-11
JAN, LILY Y P50MH48200-01
JAN, LILY Y P50MH48200-01 0001
JAN, LILY Y P50MH48200-01 9001
JAN, YUH NUNG P50MH48200-01 0002
JANCZEWSKI, A Z01AG00226-09
JANDA, KIM D R29GM43858-02
JANERICH, DWIGHT N01CN05226-06
JANERICH, DWIGHT P30CA16359-17 9015
JANERICH, DWIGHT T P01CA42101-06 0001
JANEWAY, CHARLES A P01DK43078-02 0001
JANEWAY, CHARLES A, JR P01DK43078-02
JANEWAY, CHARLES A, JR R01AI26810-03
JANEWAY, CHARLES A, JR R01AI27855-03
JANEWAY, CHARLES A, JR R37AI14579-13
JANGHORBANI, MORTEZA P30DK26678-12 9006
JANICAK, PHILIP G R29MH45465-02
JANICKI, BERNARD S07RR05526-29
JANICKI, BERNARD W P30AI28691-03
JANICKI, BERNARD W S07RR05526-29 0093
JANICKI, BERNARD W S15AI32197-01
JANICKI, JOSEPH S R01HL46461-02
JANIK, J E Z01CM09329-03
JANIK, J E Z01CM09357-02
JANIK, J E Z01CM09362-01
JANIS (SCHMITT), MAR S07RR07254-03 0499
JANKELEVICH, SHIRLEY K11AI00983-02
JANKOVIC, JOSEPH M01RR00350-25 0335
JANKOWSKA, J S07RR05362-30 0797
JANMEY, PAUL A R01AR38910-04A1
JANNE, OLLI A P50HD13541-12 0001
JANOFF, ANDREW S U01AI31696-01 9003
JANOFF, EDWARD N R29AI31373-01
JANOWSKY, AARON J R01AA08465-01A1
JANOWSKY, DAVID M01RR00046-31 0516
JANSEN, BEN H S07RR07147-19 0650
JANSEN, D L Z01BA07020-39
JANSSEN, GARY R S07RR07031-26 0091
JANUARY, CRAIG P01HL20592-15 0020
JANUARY, CRAIG T R01HL38927-03
JANZEN, EDWARD G P41RR05517-01A1
JANZEN, EDWARD G P41RR05517-01A1 9001
JAP, BING K P01GM36884-06 0004
JAP, BING K S07RR05918-08 0708
JARCHO, JOHN A K08HL02371-02
JARCHO, SAUL R01LM05139-02
JARDETZKY, OLEG P41RR02300-05S1
JARDETZKY, OLEG R01GM33385-07
JARDETZKY, OLEG R01RR07558-01
JARDINE, DAVID S07RR05655-21 0807
JARDINE, JOHN H P30CA16672-17 9008
JARDINES, LORI S07RR05415-30 0008
JAREO, PATTI W S07RR05390-30 0687
JARESKO, GEORGE S07RR05792-15 0945
JARET, DAVID M01RR00056-30 0264
JARETT, LEONARD P30DK19525-15 9004
JARETT, LEONARD R01DK28143-11A1
JARETT, LEONARD R01DK28144-12
JARJOUR, NIZAR N M01RR03186-06 0073
JARON, DOV S03RR03143-09
JARON, DOV S07RR07129-22
JARON, DOV S15GM47058-01
JARRELL, MAUREEN A M01RR00109-28 0316
JARRETT, DAVID B K02MH00327-10
JARRETT, HARRY W R01GM43609-04
JARRETT, ROBIN B P50MH41115-05 0022
JARRETT, ROBIN B R01MH45043-03
JARROLL, EDWARD L R15AI29591-01A1
JARVIS, BRUCE S07RR07042-26 0410
JARVIS, BRUCE B R01GM43724-11
JASIN, HUGO E R01AR16209-18
JASKI, BRIAN M01RR00827-17 0414
JASMER, DOUGLAS P R29AI26157-04
JASNOSKI, MARY L S07RR07019-26 0067
JASON, LEONARD A R01HL42987-02
JASPAN, JONATHAN B M01RR00055-30 0525
JASPAN, JONATHAN B M01RR00055-30 0570
JASPAN, JONATHAN B M01RR00055-30 0543
JASTREBOFF, PAWEL J R01DC00299-07
JASTREBOFF, PAWEL J R01DC00445-03
JASZCZAK, RONALD J R01CA33541-09
JATLOW, PETER P50DA04060-06 0007
JATLOW, PETER P50MH30929-15 9003
JAUCH, DIANA P50MH44211-03 0008
JAUCH, DIANA A K11MH00727-03
JAVEL, ERIC P50DC00215-08 0001
JAVEL, ERIC P50DC00215-08 0002
JAVEL, ERIC R01DC00138-11
JAVITCH, JONATHAN S07RR05650-25 0101
JAVITT, DANIEL C R03MH46962-02
JAVITT, JONATHAN C R01EY08805-02
JAVITT, JONATHAN C S10RR06578-01
JAVITT, NORMAN B R01DK32995-09
JAVITT, NORMAN B. P30AI27742-03 9005
JAVOIS, LORETTE C R29HD23275-05
JAVOR, GEORGE T S07RR05352-30 0764
JAVORS, MARTIN A S07RR05654-24 0149
JAY, DANIEL G R01NS29007-01A1
JAY, GILBERT P50HL44336-01 0005
JAY, GILBERT R01CA51779-02
JAY, GILBERT R01CA51886-02
JAY, GILBERT R01CA53633-02
JAY, GILBERT R01CA54564-01
JAY, JAMES M S06GM08167-13 0036
JAY, MICHAEL J S03RR03471-04
JAY, SUSAN M R01CA34871-09
JAY, SUSAN S K07NR00032-01A1
JAYARAM, HIREMAGALUR N R01CA51770-01A1
JAYARAM, MAKKUNI R01GM35654-06
JAZWINSKI, S MICHAL R01AG06168-06
JAZWINSKI, S MICHAL R01AG08504-02
JEANG, K-T Z01AI00547-03
JEDERLINIC, PETER J S07RR05712-20 0093
JEDZINIAK, JUDITH A R55EY03565-11
JEE, WEBSTER SHEW S R01AR38346-05
JEFCOATE, COLIN R R01CA16265-16A1
JEFCOATE, COLIN R R01DK18585-16
JEFFCOAT, A ROBERT N01ES15329-00
JEFFCOAT, A ROBERT N01ES65137-05
JEFFCOAT, MARJORIE K K16DE00279-02
JEFFCOAT, MARJORIE K P01DE08917-02 0002
JEFFERIES, LEIGH S07RR05415-30 0009
JEFFERIES, LEIGH C K07HL02673-01
JEFFERS, WILLIAM Q R44EY07803-03
JEFFERSON, DOUGLAS M R01DK44861-01
JEFFERSON, DOUGLAS M R55DE09596-01A1
JEFFERSON, LEONARD S S07RR05680-23 0909
JEFFERSON, LEONARD S, JR R01DK15658-21
JEFFERSON, LEONARD S, JR R37DK13499-23
JEFFERSON, MARGARET C S06GM08101-20 0025
JEFFERY, ROBERT W R01DK42201-02
JEFFERY, ROBERT W R01HL34740-05
JEFFERY, ROBERT W R01HL41332-03
JEFFERY, WILLIAM R R01HD13970-12
JEFFREY, ALAN P30CA13696-19 9017
JEFFREY, ALAN M P01CA21111-15 0001
JEFFREY, ALAN M P01ES05294-02 0002
JEFFREY, ALLAN S07RR05449-30 0319
JEFFREY, JOHN J R01HD05291-19
JEFFREY, MARK S07RR07175-15 0435
JEFTINIJA, SRDIJA R01NS27751-03
JEGASOTHY, BRIAN V M01RR00056-30 0348
JEGASOTHY, BRIAN V M01RR00056-30 0331
JEKEL, JAMES U01AA08774-02
JELLEY, DAVID M01RR00069-29 0487
JELLIES, JOHN A R01NS28603-03
JELLISON, JODY S07RR07161-14 0849
JELOVSEK, FREDERICK R R01ES05307-03
JEMERIN, JOHN M S07RR05755-18 0219
JEMMERSON, RONALD S07RR05385-30 0817
JEMMOTT, JOHN B, III R01HD24921-03
JEMMOTT, JOHN B, III R01MH45668-01A2
JEN-JACOBSON, LINDA R01GM29207-10
JEN, KAI-LIN C R29DK40046-04
JEN, KAI-LIN CATHERINE S06GM08167-13 0037
JEN, PHILIP S07RR07053-26 0140
JENCKS, WILLIAM P R37GM20888-34

JENDEN, DONALD J R01GM37816-05
JENDEN, DONALD J R01MH17691-22
JENDRESEN, MALCOLM D P01DE09859-01 0001
JENDRISAK, MARTIN D R29DK40454-04
JENIKE, MICHAEL M01RR01066-14 0095
JENIKE, MICHAEL A R01MH45133-03
JENISON, STEVE A K11CA01391-03
JENISTA, JERI ANN M01RR00042-31 0553
JENISTA, JERRI A R01LM05281-01
JENKINS, ALVERNA P60HL15996-19 0006
JENKINS, DAVID J R01HL39689-03
JENKINS, JANIS H R29MH47920-02
JENKINS, JESSE J. P30CA21765-14 9011
JENKINS, LARRY W R01NS19550-05
JENKINS, LAWRENCE P01NS12587-16 0016
JENKINS, MARC K R01AI27998-03
JENKINS, MARC K R01AI28365-03
JENKINS, MARC K S07RR05385-30 0816
JENKINS, ROBERT B U01CA50905-03
JENNES, LOTHAR S07RR05794-15 0901
JENNES, LOTHAR H R01HD24697-03
JENNESS, DUANE D R01GM34719-07
JENNESS, DUANE D S07RR05712-20 0091
JENNINGS, J RICHARD P01HL40962-04 9001
JENNINGS, J RICHARD R37MH40418-07
JENNINGS, LINDA W P50AG08013-04 9003
JENNINGS, LISA K R29HL38171-05
JENNINGS, MARK T K08NS00986-06
JENNINGS, MICHAEL L R01GM26861-13
JENNINGS, MICHAEL L R01HL37479-04A2
JENNINGS, MYRA B P51RR00169-30 0101
JENNY, RICHARD J R43HL46035-01
JENNY, RICHARD J R44HL42232-03
JENSEN, DENNIS P30DK41301-02 9001
JENSEN, DENNIS M R01DK33273-08
JENSEN, FRANCES E K11HD00807-05
JENSEN, JAMES S07RR07232-05
JENSEN, JAMES B P01AI16312-13
JENSEN, JAMES L S06GM08238-05
JENSEN, JAMES L S06GM08238-05 0005
JENSEN, JAMES L S15GM47044-01
JENSEN, LYLE H R01GM39610-03
JENSEN, M D M01RR00585-20 0465
JENSEN, MICHAEL D M01RR00585-20 0521
JENSEN, MICHAEL D M01RR00585-20 0176
JENSEN, MICHAEL D M01RR00585-20 0524
JENSEN, MICHAEL D M01RR00585-20 0371
JENSEN, MICHAEL D M01RR00585-20 0516
JENSEN, MICHAEL D M01RR00585-20 0517
JENSEN, MICHAEL D M01RR00585-20 0518
JENSEN, MICHAEL D R29DK40484-04
JENSEN, OLE M R01CA47812-02
JENSEN, PAMELA J P01AR39674-03 9002
JENSEN, PAMELA J P01AR39674-03 0003
JENSEN, PETER E R01AI30554-01A1
JENSEN, PETER E R29CA46667-05
JENSEN, R T Z01DK53100-03
JENSEN, R T Z01DK53101-03
JENSEN, RALPH J R29EY07318-05
JENSEN, ROBERT E S07RR05378-30 0999
JENSEN, RON S07RR05917-08 0695
JENSEN, ROY A R01DK38309-06
JENSEN, THOMAS E S06GM08225-07 0007
JENSEN, WAYNE A K11AI00924-03
JENSON, A BENNETT R01CA50182-03
JENSON, JAMES B P01AI16312-13 0002
JENTOFT, JOYCE E P60AR20618-13 0018
JERDAN, JANICE A R01EY06888-05
JERGENS, ALBERT E S07RR07034-26 0060
JERGER, JAMES F R01AG08958-01A1
JERGER, SUSAN W R29DC00421-03
JERINA, D M Z01DK31104-23
JERINA, D M Z01DK31106-04
JERMMOTT, LORETTA SWEET S06GM08223-08 0033
JERNIGAN, HOWARD M, JR R01EY07938-03
JERNIGAN, J S07RR05362-30 0802
JERNIGAN, R L Z01CB08320-15
JERNIGAN, R L Z01CB08370-08
JERNIGAN, R L Z01CB08371-08
JERNIGAN, TERRY L P50NS22343-06A1 0001
JEROME, CHRISTOPHER P P40RR00919-17 9001
JERRELL, JEANETTE M R01MH45072-03
JERRELL, JEANETTE M R01MH46331-03
JERRELLS, THOMAS R K02AA00129-02
JERRELLS, THOMAS R R01AA07731-05
JERRELLS, THOMAS R R01AI27858-04
JESAITIS, ALGIRADAS JOSEPH R01AI26711-05
JESAITIS, ALGIRDAS J R01AI22735-06
JESSELL, THOMAS M R01NS24880-06
JESSEN, JOHN W R44HD21856-03
JESSOP, J J Z01BH02003-03
JESSUP, J MILBURN P01CA44704-04A1 0008
JESSUP, J MILBURN S07RR05591-27 0660
JESTE, DILIP V P50AG05131-08 0019
JESTE, DILIP V P50MH45294-03 0006
JESTE, DILIP V R01MH45131-03
JESTE, DILIP V R37MH43693-04
JESTEADT, WALT P50DC00215-08 0004
JESTEADT, WALT P50DC00215-08
JESTEADT, WALT P60DC00982-02 9001
JESTEADT, WALT R01DC00136-14
JESTEADT, WALT S07RR05834-12
JESTEADT, WALT S07RR05834-12 0537
JESTEADT, WALT S07RR05834-12 0538
JESTEADT, WALT S15NS30123-01
JESTER, JAMES V R01EY07348-05
JESTY, JOLYON R01HL45955-02
JETER, ELAINE K K07HL02530-01A1
JETT, JAMES H P41RR01315-10 9009
JETTE, ALAN M R01AG07139-04
JETTE, ALAN M R43AG09715-01
JETTE, DAVID R01CA41490-08
JETTEN, A M Z01ES25021-08
JEWELL, NICHOLAS P R01AI29162-03
JEWETT, DON L R01DC00328-06
JEWETT, SANDRA L R15DK41460-01A2
JHANWAR, SURESH C N01CP71126-04
JHAVERI, SONAL R01EY05504-08
JHAVERI, SONAL R01NS27678-02
JHUNJHUNWALA, JAGADI S07RR05700-22 0886
JI, LI L S07RR07030-26 0396
JI, TAE H R01AG10559-01
JI, TAE H R01HD18702-15
JIALAL, ISHWARLAL M01RR00633-19 0411
JIALAL, ISHWARLAL M01RR00633-19 0412
JIANG, BAI-CHUAN R29EY08862-01
JIANG, K S S14GM05231-04 0001
JIDEAMA, NATHAN S06GM08247-04 0014
JIMENEZ-RIVERA, CARLOS A R03DA07175-01
JIMENEZ, BRAULIO D S07RR05419-30 0821
JIMENEZ, SERGIO A P01AR39740-03 0002
JIMENEZ, SERGIO A P01AR39740-03
JIMENEZ, SERGIO A R01AR19616-15
JIMENEZ, SERGIO A R01AR32564-07
JIMENEZ, SERGIO A R01HL41214-04
JIMERSON, DAVID M01RR01032-16 0450
JIMERSON, DAVID S07RR05479-29 0436
JIMERSON, DAVID C R01MH45466-01A2
JINKS-ROBERTSON, SUE R29GM38464-05
JINKS, MARTIN J R01AG09568-01
JIRTLE, RANDY L P30CA14236-18 0928
JIRTLE, RANDY L R01CA25951-11
JIRTLE, RANDY L R01CA40172-05
JOACHIM, CATHERINE L R35AG07911-04 0004
JOAD, JESSE S07RR05684-23 0170
JOBE, ALAN H R01HD12714-13
JOBE, ALAN H R01HD20618-06
JOBE, ALAN H R37HD11932-13
JOBE, PHILLIP C R01NS22672-04
JOCHIMSEN, PETER R U10CA12036-19
JOCOBS, JOHN W P01CA30195-11 0010
JOE, JENNIE R R21DK44586-01
JOEKEL, COREY S S07RR05390-30 0655
JOFFE, ALAIN M01RR00722-19 0248
JOH, TONG H P01MH44043-04
JOH, TONG H P01MH44043-04 0001
JOH, TONG H P50AG08702-03 0003
JOH, TONG H R37MH24285-16
JOHANSEN, ERLING S07RR05319-18
JOHANSEN, JORGEN R29NS28857-02
JOHANSEN, JORGEN S07RR07034-26 0061
JOHANSON, CHRIS E R01DA06030-02
JOHANSON, CHRIS-ELLYN R01DA06175-02
JOHANSON, CONRAD E R01NS27601-03
JOHANSON, NORMAN P60AR38520-04 0006
JOHLIN, FREDERICK S07RR05372-30 0652
JOHN-ALDER, HENRY S07RR07058-26 0178
JOHN, A MEREDITH R01HD27044-01A1
JOHN, A MEREDITH R29AI29418-03
JOHN, ROBBINS N01HC85083-09
JOHNS HOPKINS UNIV N01DA07408-00
JOHNS HOPKINS UNIV N01DA98146-00
JOHNS HOPKINS UNIVERSITY N01DA68113-02
JOHNS, DEARING W R01DK41117-03
JOHNS, DONALD R K08NS01359-03
JOHNS, G Z01CM07181-06
JOHNS, JAMES A K11HL02076-04
JOHNS, MICHAEL E M01RR00035-31
JOHNS, MICHAEL E M01RR00052-30
JOHNS, MICHAEL E M01RR00722-19
JOHNS, MICHAEL E M01RR02719-06
JOHNS, MICHAEL E S07RR05378-30
JOHNS, MICHAEL E S15HL47724-01
JOHNS, NELLIE O P51RR00165-31 9012
JOHNS, RICHARD J P01NS07226-19A2
JOHNS, ROGER A R29HL39706-04
JOHNSON JR, ROBERT L P01HL06296-31 9001
JOHNSON, A K P01HL14388-20 0251
JOHNSON, ALEXANDER D R01GM37049-06
JOHNSON, ALEXANDER D R01GM44532-01A1
JOHNSON, ARMEAD N01AI82514-07
JOHNSON, ARMEAD H R01AI23371-05
JOHNSON, ARNOLD R01HL48406-01
JOHNSON, ARTHUR E R01GM26494-13
JOHNSON, ARTHUR E R01HL32934-07
JOHNSON, ARTHUR E S15GM47104-01
JOHNSON, B E Z01CM06594-06
JOHNSON, B E Z01CM06596-05
JOHNSON, BARBARA P30CA15704-18 9004
JOHNSON, BARBARA DEAN R18MH47686-02
JOHNSON, BASSIN & SHAW, INC N01TI10004-00
JOHNSON, BASSIN AND SHAW, INC N01TI10008-00
JOHNSON, BRUCE D R01DA05126-03
JOHNSON, BRUCE D R01DA06615-01
JOHNSON, BRUCE D S07RR05995-04 0050
JOHNSON, CANDACE SUE R01CA45674-05
JOHNSON, CAREY K R29GM40071-03
JOHNSON, CARL P01HL22619-14 9003
JOHNSON, CARL S07RR07201-12 0636
JOHNSON, CARL H R29MH43836-04
JOHNSON, CARL R R01CA37806-07
JOHNSON, CHRIS A R01EY03424-11
JOHNSON, CHRISTOPHER M01RR00058-30 0250
JOHNSON, CHRISTOPHER M R01HL32752-07
JOHNSON, COLLEEN L R37AG06559-04
JOHNSON, CURTIS A M01RR03186-06 0067
JOHNSON, CURTIS A M01RR03186-06 0043
JOHNSON, DALE E P01HL31962-08 0003
JOHNSON, DALE E P01HL31962-08 9002
JOHNSON, DALE E S07RR07096-26
JOHNSON, DALE E S15HL47783-01
JOHNSON, DANIEL E R01HG00081-02
JOHNSON, DAVID K04NS01383-03
JOHNSON, DAVID N01AI82683-09
JOHNSON, DAVID A R01ES04999-02
JOHNSON, DAVID H U10CA49957-03
JOHNSON, DAVID L N01CM87249-09
JOHNSON, DAVID R R01MH44317-03
JOHNSON, DAVID W S14GM04303-03
JOHNSON, DEBORAH L R01GM45299-01A1
JOHNSON, DEBORAH L R29GM40623-04
JOHNSON, DON H R01MH46453-01A1
JOHNSON, DONALD C R01ES03950-04A1
JOHNSON, DONALD G R43GM47164-01
JOHNSON, DORTHEA A R01DE06000-10
JOHNSON, DOUGLAS H R01EY07065-05
JOHNSON, E Z01ES49001-03
JOHNSON, EDWARD M R01HL37130-06
JOHNSON, EDWARD M R55CA55219-01
JOHNSON, ERIC F M01RR00833-17 0188
JOHNSON, ERIC F R01GM31001-10
JOHNSON, ERIC F R37HD04445-22
JOHNSON, ERIC R R15GM40056-01A3
JOHNSON, EUGENE M P50AG05681-08 0006
JOHNSON, EUGENE M, JR R01NS24679-05
JOHNSON, F M Z01ES61050-01
JOHNSON, FRANCIS P01CA47995-02 0001
JOHNSON, FRANCIS P01ES04068-05 0001
JOHNSON, FRANCIS U01AI25993-05 0002
JOHNSON, G P41RR05959-02 9001
JOHNSON, G ALLAN P41RR05959-02
JOHNSON, G ALLAN R01ES04187-04A1
JOHNSON, GAIL P01AG06569-05 0009
JOHNSON, GAIL V R29NS27538-03
JOHNSON, GARY L P01CA39240-07 0003
JOHNSON, GARY L R01DK37871-10
JOHNSON, GARY L R01GM30324-11
JOHNSON, GEORGE O S07RR05448-30 0316
JOHNSON, GIBBES R Z01BD01010-01
JOHNSON, GLEN S07RR07055-26 0188
JOHNSON, GLYN P01CA28881-07A1 0002
JOHNSON, GLYN P01CA28881-07A1 0003
JOHNSON, HOWARD M R01AI25904-04
JOHNSON, HOWARD M R01CA38587-07
JOHNSON, HOWARD M R01HD26006-02
JOHNSON, J P01NS26665-04 0001
JOHNSON, J DAVID R01DK33727-07
JOHNSON, JACK P41RR01646-09 0007
JOHNSON, JACQUELINE S07RR07094-26 0366
JOHNSON, JACQULINE U S06GM08250-04 0002
JOHNSON, JAMES S06GM08256-03 0005
JOHNSON, JAMES S07RR07218-05 0462
JOHNSON, JAMES E R29EY07584-05
JOHNSON, JEAN E R01NR02541-01A1
JOHNSON, JEFFREY A U76PE00486-01
JOHNSON, JEFFREY V R29HL39633-04
JOHNSON, JERRY D R55GM43975-01A2
JOHNSON, JOHN P01NS26665-04 9001
JOHNSON, JOHN D M01RR00997-16 0342
JOHNSON, JOHN E R01AI18764-10
JOHNSON, JOHN E R01GM34220-07
JOHNSON, JOHN E. U01AI27310-04 0003
JOHNSON, JOHN M P01HL36080-06 0009
JOHNSON, JOHN M R01HL20663-13
JOHNSON, JOHN P R01DA04312-05
JOHNSON, JON W K02MH00944-01
JOHNSON, JON W R29MH45817-02
JOHNSON, KAREN M R01HL43615-03
JOHNSON, KARL N01AI15104-02
JOHNSON, KATHERIN P30CA54174-01 9008
JOHNSON, KEITH A K08NS01325-04
JOHNSON, KEITH R R29GM41116-04
JOHNSON, KENNETH S07RR05831-12 0979
JOHNSON, KENNETH A R01GM26726-13
JOHNSON, KENNETH A R01GM44613-01A1
JOHNSON, KENNETH H R01DK36734-06
JOHNSON, KENNETH H S07RR05930-07 0718
JOHNSON, KENNETH M, JR R01DA02073-13
JOHNSON, KENNETH M, JR R01DA05159-03
JOHNSON, KENNETH O P01NS07226-19A2 0001
JOHNSON, KENNETH O R01NS18787-09
JOHNSON, KENNETH P P50NS20022-08
JOHNSON, KENT P50DK39255-05 9002
JOHNSON, KENT J P01HL31963-08 9002
JOHNSON, KENT J P50DK39255-05 0004
JOHNSON, KENT J R01HL42607-03

JOHNSON, KURT S07RR05359-30 0512
JOHNSON, LARRY K04AG00465-01
JOHNSON, LARRY S07RR05854-11 0923
JOHNSON, LAWRENCE L G20RR07075-01
JOHNSON, LAWRENCE L R01AI27791-03
JOHNSON, LAWRENCE W S06GM08153-16 0008
JOHNSON, LEE F R01GM29356-11
JOHNSON, LEONARD R R37DK16505-20
JOHNSON, MAHLON D S07RR05424-30 0100
JOHNSON, MARCIA K R01AG09744-01A1
JOHNSON, MARK R01AG08289-02
JOHNSON, MARK D R29CA49916-03
JOHNSON, MARK D S07RR05370-30 0611
JOHNSON, MARY A R01EY05118-07
JOHNSON, MARY K R01EY00424-19
JOHNSON, MARY K S07RR05377-30 0753
JOHNSON, MARY P S07RR05675-23 0910
JOHNSON, MELVIN A, JR R24AA09294-02
JOHNSON, MICHAEL E R01HL45977-01
JOHNSON, MICHAEL E S03RR03042-10
JOHNSON, MICHAEL E S07RR05564-13
JOHNSON, MICHAEL E S07RR05564-13 0916
JOHNSON, MICHAEL K R01GM33806-09
JOHNSON, MICHAEL L P01DK34039-06A1 9002
JOHNSON, MICHAEL L P30DK38942-04 9003
JOHNSON, MICHAEL L R01DK44833-01 9002
JOHNSON, MICHAEL P S07RR05445-30 0874
JOHNSON, MICHAEL T R43NS28633-01A2
JOHNSON, MITZI M R29AG09976-01
JOHNSON, NED K S07RR07006-26 0890
JOHNSON, PATRICIA J R01AI30537-01A1
JOHNSON, PATRICIA JEAN R29AI27857-03
JOHNSON, PATRICK B R01AA08008-03
JOHNSON, PAUL C P01HL17421-18
JOHNSON, PAUL C P01HL17421-18 0014
JOHNSON, PAUL C R01HL15390-23
JOHNSON, PETER C R01DK38163-05
JOHNSON, PETER C R29HL45891-01A1
JOHNSON, PETER C S07RR05416-30 0563
JOHNSON, PETER C U01CA50931-03
JOHNSON, PHILIP P51RR00165-31 0201
JOHNSON, PHILIP P51RR00165-31 0129
JOHNSON, PHILIP C M01RR02558-07 0043
JOHNSON, R Z01NS02794-03
JOHNSON, R E Z01DA00090-02
JOHNSON, R T P01NS26643-04 0002
JOHNSON, RANDALL U01CA50771-03 0001
JOHNSON, REID C R01GM38509-05
JOHNSON, RICHARD P30AI28748-03 9007
JOHNSON, RICHARD D P01NS27511-03 0005
JOHNSON, RICHARD J R01DK43422-01A1
JOHNSON, RICHARD J R29DK39068-05
JOHNSON, RICHARD T P01NS26643-04
JOHNSON, ROBERT E M01RR00109-28 0345
JOHNSON, ROBERT E P01AI19554-08S1 0006
JOHNSON, ROBERT H S06GM08171-11 0009
JOHNSON, ROBERT H S06GM08171-11
JOHNSON, ROBERT J M01RR00109-28 0348
JOHNSON, ROBERT J R01AR40174-02
JOHNSON, ROBERT L, JR R01HL35914-05
JOHNSON, ROBERT L, JR R01HL40070-04
JOHNSON, ROBERT M P60HL16008-19 0025
JOHNSON, ROBERT M S07RR07020-26
JOHNSON, ROBERT M S07RR07020-26 0528
JOHNSON, RODNEY D S06GM08212-08 0014
JOHNSON, RODNEY L R01NS20036-07A2
JOHNSON, ROGER A R01DK38828-05A1
JOHNSON, ROGER A S07RR05736-19 0207
JOHNSON, ROGER B R03DE10047-01
JOHNSON, ROSS G R01CA28548-11
JOHNSON, ROSS G R55GM46277-01
JOHNSON, RUSSELL A S07RR05417-30 0794
JOHNSON, RUSSELL C R01AI29739-02
JOHNSON, RUSSELL C R01AR34744-07
JOHNSON, RUSSELL C R01AR41522-01
JOHNSON, SAMUEL V R43OH02780-01A1
JOHNSON, STEVEN A R01AG10673-01
JOHNSON, STEVEN A R35AG07909-03 0005
JOHNSON, STEVEN W K08NS01423-02
JOHNSON, SUZANNE P01DK39079-05 0002
JOHNSON, SUZANNE B M01RR00082-29 0402
JOHNSON, SUZANNE B R01HD13820-10
JOHNSON, T C S07RR07036-26 0102
JOHNSON, THOMAS E K04AG00369-05
JOHNSON, THOMAS E R01AG10248-01
JOHNSON, THOMAS E R13AG09968-01
JOHNSON, THOMAS E R55AG08322-04
JOHNSON, TIMOTHY A P01HL27430-10 9003
JOHNSON, V G Z01BA03006-01
JOHNSON, VICTORIA A R29AI32794-01
JOHNSON, WALTER C, JR R01GM21479-17
JOHNSON, WALTER C, JR R01GM43133-02
JOHNSON, WARREN D, JR P01AI16282-13
JOHNSON, WARREN D, JR P01AI26506-04
JOHNSON, WARREN D, JR R37AI22624-07
JOHNSON, WAYNE S07RR05372-30 0670
JOHNSON, WAYNE A R01NS28743-02
JOHNSON, WILLIAM R01AI26532-04
JOHNSON, WILLIAM S R01DK03787-32
JOHNSTON, BRIAN H R29GM41423-03
JOHNSTON, C CONRAD P01AG05793-06 0001
JOHNSTON, C CONRAD JR M01RR00750-19 0248
JOHNSTON, C CONRAD, JR P01AG05793-06
JOHNSTON, CONRAD C. M01RR00750-19 0218
JOHNSTON, CRAIG S07RR07134-15 0519
JOHNSTON, CRAIG A R03MH48252-02
JOHNSTON, CRAIG A R29MH48228-02
JOHNSTON, DANIEL P50AG08664-03 0001
JOHNSTON, DANIEL P50NS11535-17 0012
JOHNSTON, DANIEL R01MH48432-01
JOHNSTON, DANIEL R37MH44754-03
JOHNSTON, DAVID E R29DK42161-01A2
JOHNSTON, DENNIS A R01CA11430-25 0058
JOHNSTON, HENRY M R01GM32540-08
JOHNSTON, J. O'NEAL P51RR00166-30 0143
JOHNSTON, JOHN M P01HD13912-12
JOHNSTON, JOHN M P01HD13912-12 0001
JOHNSTON, JOHN M P50HD11149-14 0004
JOHNSTON, KENNETH H S07RR05376-30 0031
JOHNSTON, KENT J P01DK38149-04 9002
JOHNSTON, LLOYD D R01DA01411-17
JOHNSTON, LYSLE E, JR R01DE08716-04
JOHNSTON, MICHAEL R U01CA46088-05
JOHNSTON, MICHAEL R U01CA46088-05 0001
JOHNSTON, MICHAEL V R01NS28208-02
JOHNSTON, RICHARD B, JR R01AI24782-06
JOHNSTON, ROBERT E R01AI22186-06
JOHNSTON, ROBERT E R01NS26681-04
JOHNSTON, ROBERT E S07RR05406-30 0897
JOHNSTON, ROGER G R01GM38287-03
JOHNSTON, STEPHEN A R01GM40700-05
JOHNSTON, TIMOTHY C R15GM45967-01
JOHNSTON, VICKI M01RR00080-29 0661
JOHNSTON, WILLIAM E R01HL44944-01A1
JOHNSTON, WILLIAM E R29HL40395-04
JOHNSTON, WILLIAM M R29DE08003-04
JOHNSTONE, BRIAN S07RR05406-30 0886
JOHNSTONE, BRYAN M R29AA08475-03
JOHNSTONE, DAVID E. N01HC55005-11
JOHO, ROLF P50HL42267-02 0003
JOHO, ROLF H P01HL37044-06 0009
JOHO, ROLF H R01NS28407-02
JOHSTON, A P50DE09322-03 0003
JOINER, CLINTON H R55HL37515-04A1
JOINER, KEITH A R01AI30060-02
JOINER, KEITH A U01AI31808-01
JOINER, KEITH A U01AI31808-01 9002
JOINER, KEITH A U01AI31808-01 0003
JOINER, KEITH A U01AI31808-01 0004
JOINES, WILLIAM T P01CA42745-05 9004
JOKLIK, WOLFGANG K P01CA30246-11 0003
JOKLIK, WOLFGANG K P01CA30246-11
JOKLIK, WOLFGANG K P01CA30246-11 9001
JOKLIK, WOLFGANG K P30CA14236-18 9002
JOKLIK, WOLFGANG K R01AI08909-23
JOLESSZ, FERENC P01CA41167-06 0006
JOLESZ, FERENC P01AG04953-08 0004
JOLESZ, FERENC A R01CA45743-04
JOLLIE, WILLIAM P S07RR05724-20 0185
JOLLOW, DAVID J R01HL30038-09
JOLLY, DOUGLAS J R43AI31295-01
JOLLY, PAUL N01OD72108-07
JOLLY, ROBERT D R01NS11238-17
JONAKAIT, G MILLER R01DA05964-02
JONAS, ADAM J R01DK44220-01
JONAS, ALBERT S07RR05367-30 0568
JONAS, ANA R01HL16059-18
JONAS, ELIZABETH A K11AG00486-02
JONAS, JIRI R01GM42452-03
JONAS, MAUREEN M S07RR05363-30 0829
JONES, ALBERT L P30DK26743-11 9004
JONES, ALBERT L R01DK25878-13
JONES, ALBERT L R01DK38436-05
JONES, ALBERT M P30CA34196-09 9010
JONES, ALBERT M P30CA34196-09 9011
JONES, ALLAN W R37HL15852-18
JONES, ALUN G R01CA34970-13
JONES, ANNE H S07RR05427-30 0155
JONES, BARRY S07RR07082-26 0289
JONES, BARRY S07RR07082-26 0290
JONES, BETH A R03HS06910-01
JONES, BETTY R S06GM45913-01
JONES, BETTY R S06GM45913-01 0001
JONES, BYRON C P01DA07171-01 0001
JONES, BYRON C R01AA08454-03
JONES, C MICHAEL R01CA39441-05
JONES, CARL E R01HL19232-06A3
JONES, CAROL P01HD17449-08 0003
JONES, CAROL R25CA09496-07
JONES, CAROL A R01CA18734-15A1
JONES, CLINTON J R29CA47872-05
JONES, CLINTON J S15GM47065-01
JONES, COLETTE S07RR05942-06 0009
JONES, DAN B P30EY02520-13
JONES, DAN B U10EY07480-04
JONES, DAVY R01GM33995-08
JONES, DEAN S07RR05364-30 0531
JONES, DEAN P R01HL39968-04A1
JONES, E A Z01DK53501-18
JONES, E A Z01DK53503-17
JONES, E A Z01DK53510-12
JONES, E A Z01DK53511-12
JONES, E A Z01DK53514-07
JONES, E A Z01DK53516-02
JONES, EDWARD G R01NS21377-08
JONES, EDWARD G R01NS22317-08
JONES, ELAINE G R29NR02665-02
JONES, ELIZABETH W R01DK18090-18
JONES, ELIZABETH W R01GM29713-11
JONES, ENRICO E S07RR07006-26 0905
JONES, FRED, JR S07RR07167-14
JONES, G S07RR05830-12 0959
JONES, G S07RR05830-12 0963
JONES, GRACE M R01DK39197-04A1
JONES, GRACE M S15GM47028-01
JONES, J M Z01AA00047-02
JONES, JAMES F M01RR00069-29 0405
JONES, JANICE L R01HL24606-13
JONES, JEFFERY S07RR05403-30 0811
JONES, JOHN I, III K11DK02024-01
JONES, JONATHAN S07RR05311-30 0007
JONES, JONATHAN C R R01GM38470-04
JONES, KATHERINE A P01CA54418-01 0002
JONES, KATHERINE A P01CA54418-01 9004
JONES, KATHERINE A R01GM38166-05
JONES, KATHRYN J R01NS28238-02
JONES, KEITH S07RR05731-20 0147
JONES, KENNETH L M01RR00827-17 0363
JONES, KENNETH L M01RR00827-17 0276
JONES, KENNETH L M01RR00827-17 0278
JONES, KENNETH L M01RR00827-17 0503
JONES, KENNETH L M01RR00827-17 0462
JONES, KENNETH L. P01AG07996-03 9001
JONES, KENNETH LEE M01RR00827-17 0375
JONES, LARRY R P01HL06308-31 9002
JONES, LARRY R P01HL06308-31 0040
JONES, LARRY R R01HL28556-09
JONES, LESLIE S R29NS27903-02
JONES, LOVELL A R13CA55586-01
JONES, M Z01HL02714-11
JONES, M DOUGLAS P01NS20020-08 0002
JONES, MARGARET Z R01NS16886-11
JONES, MARK M R01ES02638-11
JONES, MARSHALL B S07RR05680-23 0906
JONES, MARY S07RR05372-30 0653
JONES, MICHAEL P R29CA55212-01
JONES, PATRICIA P01AI19512-09 0012
JONES, PATRICIA P R01AI15732-13
JONES, PATRICIA P R01AI19964-07
JONES, PETER R01HD19821-07
JONES, PETER A R35CA49758-03
JONES, REESE T K05DA00053-15
JONES, REESE T P50DA01696-12 9002
JONES, REESE T P50DA01696-12
JONES, RICHARD E R01HD27122-01A1
JONES, RICHARD H R01GM38519-05
JONES, RICHARD J R01CA54203-01
JONES, RICHARD S R01GM46567-01
JONES, RICHARD T R01HL20142-15
JONES, ROBERT B U01AI25859-05
JONES, ROBERT B U01AI25859-05 9001
JONES, ROBERT B U01AI31494-01
JONES, ROBERT B U01AI31494-01 9003
JONES, ROBERT E R01HD26899-02
JONES, ROBERT H P50HL17670-17 0015
JONES, ROBERT L M01RR00102-28 0120
JONES, ROBERT L M01RR00102-28 0064
JONES, ROBERT N P50HL15092-20 0018
JONES, ROGER A R01GM31483-09
JONES, ROSEMARY C R01HL34552-06
JONES, SIAN K11AI01031-01
JONES, STANLEY T S03RR03518-02
JONES, STEPHEN W R01NS24471-06
JONES, STEVEN E P30CA23074-14 9001
JONES, SUSAN S R03MH46977-01A1
JONES, SUSAN SCANLON S07RR07031-26 0092
JONES, SUSAN SCANLON S07RR07031-26 0093
JONES, T Z01HL01029-04
JONES, THOMAS M01RR00046-31 0514
JONES, THOMAS M P01HD24234-04 0004
JONES, THOMAS W R01ES05436-02
JONES, WILLIAM J S07RR07024-26 0030
JONES, WILLIAM J S07RR07024-26 0044
JONG, AMBROSE Y R29GM39436-03
JONSEN, ALBERT R R01HG00477-01
JOPE, RICHARD S P01AG06569-05 0001
JOPE, RICHARD S R01MH38752-08
JORDAN, COLIN P01CA21737-14 0010
JORDAN, ANGEL G S07RR07081-26
JORDAN, ANGEL G S15HL47782-01
JORDAN, B KATHLEEN R01DA06387-02
JORDAN, CHESTER L S03RR03542-01
JORDAN, CHESTER L S14GM04531-03
JORDAN, FRANK S06GM08223-08 0020
JORDAN, FRANK S07RR07059-26 0833
JORDAN, LYNDA M K14HL02338-03
JORDAN, LYNDA M S06GM08019-21 0008
JORDAN, M COLIN U01AI30456-02
JORDAN, MICHAEL I S07RR07047-26 0136
JORDAN, PAMELA L K07NR00030-02
JORDAN, PETER C R01GM28643-11
JORDAN, STANLEY S07RR05468-29 0408
JORDAN, V CRAIG P30CA14520-19 9007
JORDAN, VIRGIL C R01CA32713-10
JORGENSEN, E VERENA K08DK01980-01A1
JORGENSEN, TIMOTHY J R29CA48716-03

JORGENSEN, WILLIAM L   R01GM32136-09
JORGENSON, TIMOTHY J   P01CA52066-02 0003
JORNS, MARILYN S   R01GM31704-10
JOSE, PEDRO   P50DK44756-01 0002
JOSE, PEDRO A   R01DK39308-04A2
JOSE, PEDRO A   R01HL23081-11
JOSEPH, DAVID   P30HD18968-08 9005
JOSEPH, DAVID R   R01HD21744-05
JOSEPH, J A   Z01AG00306-03
JOSEPH, LOREN J   R29CA50774-02
JOSEPH, PETER M   R01CA44580-05
JOSEPH, SHIRLEY A   R01NS21323-06
JOSEPH, SURESH K   R01DK34804-06
JOSEPHS, ROBERT   P01HL30121-08 9001
JOSEPHS, ROBERT   P01HL30121-08 0001
JOSEPHS, ROBERT   R01HL22654-12A1
JOSEPHS, STEVEN F   N01CP95626-08
JOSEPHSON, IRA R   R01HL45624-01A1
JOSEPHSON, LEE   R44DK40664-03
JOSHI, HARISH C   S07RR05364-30 0532
JOSHI, J B   Z01MH02587-01
JOSHI, MADHUSUDAN S   S07RR05407-30 0048
JOSHI, SAROJ   S07RR05711-21 0034
JOSHI, SHARMISHTHA   S07RR05390-30 0656
JOSIASSEN, RICHARD C   R01MH42769-05A1
JOULLIE, MADELEINE M   R01CA40081-05A2
JOURDIAN, GEORGE W   R01AR10531-26
JOVE, RICHARD   R29CA47809-04
JOYCE, GERALD F   R01AI30882-01
JOYCE, JEFFREY M   P01NS08803-20A1 0008
JOYCE, JEFFREY N   P01AG09215-02 0001
JOYCE, JEFFREY N   R29MH43852-04
JOYCE, NANCY C   R01EY05767-07
JOYNER, M J   M01RR00585-20 0539
JOYNER, RONALD W   P01HL27385-11 0011
JOYNER, RONALD W   R01HL22562-10A2
JOZEFOWICZ, RALPH F   M01RR00044-31 0387
JU, SHYR-TE   P60AR20613-14 0019
JUAREZ, RUMALDO   S06GM08038-21 0010
JUCHAU, MONT R   R01ES04041-06
JUDD, B H   Z01ES65036-07
JUDD, B H   Z01ES65037-07
JUDD, HOWARD L   U01HL40273-05
JUDD, RALPH C   K04AI00834-04
JUDD, RALPH C   R01AI21236-06S2
JUDKINS, DAVID   N01DE62560-10
JUHN, S.K.   P50DC00133-13 9005
JUHN, STEVEN K   P50DC00133-13 0005
JUKES, THOMAS H   R01HG00312-03
JULIAN, BRUCE A   M01RR00032-31 0282
JULIAN, BRUCE A.   M01RR00032-31 0250
JULIANO, RUDOLPH   P30CA16086-17 9016
JULIANO, RUDOLPH L   R01GM26165-11
JULIANO, SHARON L   R01NS24014-05
JULIANO, SHARON L   R01NS26658-03
JULIANO, SHARON L   S07RR05983-05 0356
JULIN, DOUGLAS A   R29GM39777-03
JULIUS, DAVID J   P50MH48200-01 0003
JULIUS, DAVID J   R01GM44298-02
JULIUS, MARA   R01HL41796-01A1
JULIUS, STEVO   R37HL37464-05
JUMBLATT, JAMES E   R01EY05246-09
JUMP, DONALD B   R01DK43220-01A1
JUNCK, LARRY   P50NS15655-12 0008
JUNCK, LARRY   R01CA54104-01
JUNE, CARL H   R01AI29331-02
JUNEJA, HARINDER S   R29CA47346-04
JUNG, LAWRENCE   S07RR05712-20 0058
JUNG, MICHAEL E   R01GM31349-09A1
JUNG, MICHAEL E   R01GM41592-03
JUNG, MICHAEL E   R01GM47228-04
JUNG, MICHAEL E   S10RR06713-01
JUNGALWALA, FIROZE   P30HD04147-22A1 9012
JUNGALWALA, FIROZE B   P01AG02126-11 0010
JUNGALWALA, FIROZE B   P01HD05515-21 0051
JUNGALWALA, FIROZE B   R01NS24405-04A1
JUNGE, DOUGLAS   S07RR05304-30 0215
JUNGER, WILLIAM J   S07RR05736-19 0159
JUNGINGER, JOHN A   R03MH47005-02
JUNGMANN, RICHARD A   R01HD12046-12
JUNI, ELLIOT   S07RR05383-30 0560
JUOLA, JAMES F   S07RR07037-26 0366
JURASKA, JANICE M   S07RR07030-26 0397
JURGENSON, JAMES E   R15GM42206-01A2
JURIVICH, DONALD A   K11AG00509-01
JURNAK, FRANCES A   R01GM26895-10
JUSCZYK, PETER W   R01HD15795-11
JUSKO, WILLIAM J   R01GM24211-15
JUSKO, WILLIAM J   R01GM41037-03
JUST, MARCEL A   K02MH00662-05
JUST, MARCEL A   R01MH29617-12
JUSTEMENT, LOUIS B   R29GM46524-01
JUSTER, F T   R01AG08270-03
JUSTER, F THOMAS   U01AG09740-02
JYONOUCHI, HARUMI   R29AI25062-03
KAAS, JON H   R01EY02686-17
KAAS, JON H   R01NS16446-11
KAATARRI, STEPHEN L   P30ES03850-07 0004
KAATTARI, STEPHEN L   R01ES05783-01
KABALEH, M BASHAR   M01RR01070-15 0140
KABAT, DAVID   R01AI28572-03
KABAT, DAVID   R01CA25810-13
KABAT, DAVID   R01CA54149-01
KABAT, ELVIN A   R01AI19042-07A2
KABAT, ELVIN A   R01AI25616-04
KABAT, ELVIN A   R01AI27508-03
KABAT, GEOFFREY C   P01CA32617-09A1 0001
KABISCH, WILLIAM T   S07RR05843-11
KABISCH, WILLIAM T   S15AG10232-01
KACHAR, B   Z01DC00002-03
KACINSKI, BARRY M   R03HD28095-01
KACINSKI, BARRY M   R29CA47292-04
KACZMAREK, L K   P01HL38156-05 9001
KACZMAREK, LEONARD K   R01NS18492-09
KADDEN, RONALD M   P50AA03510-14 0011
KADDEN, RONALD M   U10AA08438-03
KADEKARO, MASSAKO   R01NS23055-06
KADISH, ALAN H   M01RR00042-31 0595
KADISH, ALAN H   R29HL40667-05
KADISH, KARL M   R01GM25172-14
KADNER, ROBERT J   R01GM19078-19
KADNER, ROBERT J   R01GM38681-05
KADO, CLARENCE I   R01GM45550-21A1
KADONAGA, JAMES T   R01GM41249-03
KADOR, P   Z01EY00003-19
KADOWAKI, HIROKO   R01NS23354-05A2
KADOWITZ, PHILIP J   R01HL15580-15
KAELBER, NANCY   N01LM93531-04
KAELIN, WILLIAM G, JR   K11CA01528-02
KAEMPF, JOSEPH   M01RR00069-29 0400
KAESBERG, PAUL J   R01AI01466-35
KAESBERG, PAUL J   R37AI23742-06
KAETZEL, CHARLOTTE S   R29CA51998-02
KAFATOS, FOTIS C   P01GM29301-11
KAFATOS, FOTIS C   P01GM29301-11 9001
KAFATOS, FOTIS C   P01GM29301-11 0005
KAGAN, BRUCE L   R29MH43433-04
KAGAN, HERBERT M   P01HL13262-19 0028
KAGAN, HERBERT M   P01HL19717-15 0004
KAGAN, HERBERT M   R37AR18880-15
KAGAN, JACOB   S07RR05511-29 0487
KAGNOFF, MARTIN F   P01DK35108-07
KAGNOFF, MARTIN F   P01DK35108-07 0002
KAGNOFF, MARTIN F   P01DK35108-07 0001
KAGNOFF, MARTIN F   P01DK35108-07 9001
KAGNOFF, MARTIN F   P01DK35108-07 9002
KAGNOFF, MARTIN F   R01DK40582-04
KAGNOFF, MARTIN F   S10RR06694-01
KAGUNI, JON M   R01GM33992-08
KAGUNI, LAURIE S   R01GM45295-01
KAHAN, BARRY D   M01RR02558-07 0053
KAHAN, BARRY D   M01RR02558-07 0054
KAHAN, BARRY D   R01AI22664-07
KAHAN, BARRY D   R01DK38016-05
KAHAN, BARRY D   R37CA29592-11
KAHANA, EVA F   R37AG07823-03
KAHL, STEPHEN B   R01CA37961-06S1
KAHL, STEPHEN B   R01CA53901-01
KAHN, ANDREW M   R29HL40480-04
KAHN, ARNOLD J   R01AR37716-05
KAHN, ARNOLD J   S15AR41235-01
KAHN, C RONALD   P30DK36836-05
KAHN, C RONALD   R01DK31036-10
KAHN, C RONALD   R01DK33201-08
KAHN, C RONALD   S07RR05673-22
KAHN, C RONALD   S10RR06727-01
KAHN, HENRY S   R01HL40844-02
KAHN, JAMES   M01RR00083-29 0220
KAHN, JAMES   M01RR00083-29 0206
KAHN, JAMES O   M01RR00083-29 0221
KAHN, JAMES O   M01RR00083-29 0242
KAHN, KATHERINE L   R01HS06546-01
KAHN, MICHAEL S   R01GM38260-04
KAHN, MIRIAM   S07RR05780-16 0974
KAHN, R A   Z01CM06181-06
KAHN, STUART J   R03HD28586-01
KAHNE, DANIEL E   R01GM42733-02
KAHRILAS, PETER J   R01DC00646-02
KAIGHN, M EDWARD   R43CA55469-01
KAIGHN, ME   N44ES02001-03
KAIKAUS, RAJA M   K08DK02056-01
KAIL, ROBERT   R01HD19947-07
KAIRISS, EDWARD W   R03MH47826-01
KAISER-KUPFER , M I   Z01EY00060-14
KAISER-KUPFER, M I   Z01EY00011-17
KAISER-KUPFER, M I   Z01EY00083-14
KAISER-KUPFER, M I   Z01EY00163-09
KAISER-KUPFER, M I   Z01EY00211-06
KAISER, A DALE   R01GM23441-15
KAISER, ANN P   P01HD15051-11A1 0177
KAISER, ANN P   R01HD27583-01A1
KAISER, E   P41RR00862-18 0003
KAISER, EMIL T   P01HL18577-16 0005
KAISER, LANA   K08HL01842-05
KAISER, LANA   R01HL25779-12
KAJANDER, KEITH C   R55NS29567-01
KAJANDER, KEITH C   S07RR05322-30 0269
KAKAR, FAIZ   P51RR00166-30 0094
KALANT, HAROLD   R01AA08212-03
KALANTAR, RAY   N01CO94381-15
KALAYOGLU, MUNCI   S07RR05435-30 0984
KALB, ROBERT G   K08NS01247-05
KALB, VERNON F   U01AI31702-01 0005
KALCKAR, HERMAN M   S07RR07043-26 0121
KALDAHL, WAYNE B   R01DE06103-08
KALDERON, DANIEL D   R01GM41815-03
KALE, PURUSHOTTAM G   S03RR03497-03
KALE, PURUSHOTTAM G   S06GM08250-04 0003
KALE, PURUSHOTTAM G   S06GM08250-04
KALE, RANJINI P   S06GM08250-04 0004
KALEIDA, PHILLIP H   S07RR05507-29 0478
KALET, ADINA   S07RR05406-30 0909
KALET, IRA J   N01CM97566-06
KALET, IRA J   R01LM04174-06
KALEY, GABOR   P01HL43023-01A2
KALEY, GABOR   P01HL43023-01A2 0004
KALHAN, SATISH C   M01RR00080-29 0438
KALHAN, SATISH C   P50HD11089-14
KALHAN, SATISH C   P50HD11089-14 0021
KALIA, MADHU   P50AA07186-06 0014
KALIA, MADHU   R01HL40270-05
KALICHMAN, MICHAEL W   R29NS24833-05
KALICK, SHELDON   S07RR07199-12 0942
KALID, SYED   P41RR01633-10 9003
KALIL, KATHERINE   R01NS14428-14
KALIL, RONALD E   R01EY01331-16
KALIN, NED H   R01MH40855-05
KALIN, NED H   R01MH43986-03
KALIN, NED H   R01MH46729-02
KALINA, ROBERT E   P30EY01730-16
KALINER, M A   Z01AI00154-17
KALINER, M A   Z01AI00279-10
KALINER, M A   Z01AI00429-07
KALINER, M A   Z01AI00495-06
KALINOSKI, DARLINE L   R01DC01228-01
KALINOSKI, DARLINE L   S07RR05825-12 0512
KALINOSKI, DARLINE L   S07RR05825-12 0517
KALINYAK, KAREN   N01HB77045-06
KALINYAK, KAREN   P60HL15996-19 0025
KALINYAK, KAREN A   P60HL15996-19 9001
KALISH, LESLIE   P01CA19589-14A1 9003
KALISH, RICHARD S   R29AI26580-04
KALIVAS, PETER W   K02DA00153-02
KALIVAS, PETER W   R01DA03906-08
KALIVAS, PETER W   R01MH40817-07
KALK, DOUGLAS F   P01NS17111-11 9003
KALKWARF, KENNETH L   S07RR05897-09
KALLEN, ROLAND G   S07RR05415-30 0010
KALLEN, ROLAND G   S07RR07083-26 0473
KALLENBACH, NEVILLE R   R01CA24101-12A1
KALLENBACH, NEVILLE R   R01GM40746-03
KALLMAN, MARY J   R01DA05253-03
KALLMAN, ROBERT F   R01CA03353-34
KALLMAN, ROBERT F   R01CA34544-08
KALLMERTEN, JAMES L   R01GM39990-02
KALLOO, ANTHONY N   M01RR00035-31 0405
KALMAN, THOMAS   S07RR05454-29 0887
KALMAN, THOMAS I   R01AI27251-03
KALMAN, THOMAS I   R01CA35212-07
KALMAR, JOHN   S07RR05308-30 0237
KALMUSS, DEBRA   R01HD23915-04
KALONIA, DEVENDRA   S07RR05743-14 0618
KALOUSEK, FRANTISEK   R01DK09527-27
KALRA, PUSHPA S   R01DK37273-06
KALRA, PUSHPA S   R01HD11362-11
KALRA, SATYA P   R01HD08634-15
KALSOW, CAROLYN M   R01EY06866-06
KALTENBACH, JAMES   S07RR05384-30 0776
KALTENBACH, KAROL   R18DA06363-03
KALTER, SEYMOUR S   R44AI29317-02
KALTHOFF, KLAUS   S07RR07091-26 0757
KALTHOFF, L   M01RR00585-20 0498
KALU, DIKE N   P01AG01188-13 0007
KALU, DIKE N   R01AG07572-04
KALUZNY, ARNOLD D   N01CN75435-08
KALUZNY, ARNOLD D   R01CA54343-01
KALYANARAMAN, BALARAMAN   P01CA49089-03 0001
KALYANARAMAN, BALARAMAN   R01HL45048-02
KALYANARAMAN, BALARAMAN   R01HL47250-01
KAM, WING   R29DK40556-03
KAMBOH, MOHAMMAD I   R01HL44672-01A1
KAMBOH, MOHAMMAD I   S07RR05451-30 0357
KAMEN, BARTON A   R01CA52625-02
KAMEN, GARY P   R01AG09662-01
KAMENTSKY, LOUIS A   R43CA55413-01
KAMHOLZ, JOHN   P01NS11037-18 0057
KAMHOLZ, JOHN   P01NS08075-21 0017
KAMIL, ALAN C   R01MH44200-04
KAMINSKA, GRAZYNA M   S07RR05426-30 0138
KAMINSKAS, EDVARDAS   P01AG04390-08 0008
KAMINSKAS, EDVARDAS   S07RR06043-01
KAMINSKI, DONALD L   R01DK27695-07A2
KAMINSKI, DONALD L   S07RR05388-30 0618
KAMINSKI, HENRY J   R03EY09186-01
KAMINSKI, MARK S   M01RR00042-31 0511
KAMINSKI, MARK S   R01CA52298-02
KAMINSKY, LAWRENCE   S07RR05649-25 0793
KAMM, KRISTINE E   R01HL32607-07
KAMM, ROGER D   P01HL33009-07 0007
KAMM, ROGER D   P01HL33009-07 0008
KAMM, ROGER D   R01EY05503-08
KAMM, ROGER D   R01HL45679-01
KAMM, ROGER D   S07RR07047-26 0143
KAMMER, GARY M   M01RR00080-29 0381
KAMMERER, CANDACE   P01HL28972-10 0009
KAMMERER, CANDACE M   P01HL45522-01A1 0003

KAMMERER, CANDACE M R01HL45323-02
KAMOUN, MALEK R01AI20846-07
KAN-MITCHELL, JUNE R01EY09031-01
KAN, LOU-SING S10RR06261-01
KAN, YUET W R37DK16666-19
KANAGAWA, OSAMI R01AI30803-02
KANALAS, JOHN J R29DK40189-03
KANAREK, ROBIN B S07RR07179-14 0682
KANATZIDIS, MERCOURI S07RR07049-26 0431
KANDA PATRICK U01AI26462-04 0004
KANDA, P P30AI28696-01 9003
KANDA, PATRICK R29AI25151-05
KANDARPA, KRISHNA S07RR05950-07 0990
KANDEEL, FOUAD M01RR00425-22S3 0400
KANDEEL, FOUAD M01RR00425-22S3 0453
KANDEEL, FOUAD R M01RR00425-22S3 0380
KANDEL, DENISE P50MH43878-03 0010
KANDEL, DENISE B K05DA00081-11
KANDEL, DENISE B R01DA04866-04
KANDEL, ERIC R P50AG08702-03 0001
KANDEL, ERIC R R37MH45923-02
KANDROTAS, ROBERT J S07RR05738-20 0218
KANDUTSCH, ANDREW A R37CA02758-35
KANE, AGNES B R01ES03189-09
KANE, AGNES B R01ES03721-07
KANE, AGNES B R55ES05712-01
KANE, CAROLINE M S07RR07006-26 0896
KANE, CATHERINE F S07RR05952-06 0740
KANE, JOHN M P50MH41960-05S1
KANE, JOHN M P50MH41960-05S1 0001
KANE, JOHN M P50MH41960-05S1 0006
KANE, JOHN M P50MH41960-05S1 9001
KANE, JOHN M P50MH41960-05S1 9002
KANE, JOHN M P50MH41960-05S1 9003
KANE, JOHN M R01MH40015-05A1
KANE, JOHN M R01MH42929-05
KANE, JOHN M R37MH32369-13
KANE, JOHN M U10MH39992-08
KANE, JOHN P M01RR00079-29 0383
KANE, JOHN P P50HL14237-20 0003
KANE, JOHN P P50HL14237-20 0006
KANE, JOHN P P50HL14237-20 9001
KANE, MADELEINE A R55CA54502-01
KANE, ROBERT L S07RR05712-20 0089
KANE, ROBERT L S07RR05712-20 0090
KANE, SUSAN S07RR05471-29 0577
KANE, WILLIAM H R01HL43106-01A2
KANEKO, CHRIS R R01EY06558-05
KANESHIRO, EDNA S07RR07075-17 0260
KANESHIRO, EDNA S R01AI29316-02
KANESHIRO, EDNA S S03RR03126-05
KANESHIRO, EDNA S S15CA55981-01
KANESHIRO, EDNA S U01AI31702-01 0002
KANG, ANDREW H P50AR39166-05
KANG, CHANG-YUIL R43AI31310-01
KANG, DAVID S R01HL36135-04
KANG, ELLEN S S07RR05423-30 0053
KANG, JAE O R15CA54443-01
KANG, JAE O S07RR07108-19 0408
KANG, REBECCA S07RR05758-18 0248
KANG, UN J K11AG00406-04
KANG, YOHN S S06GM08110-20 0005
KANGARLOO, HOOSHANG P01CA51198-02 0001
KANGARLOO, HOOSHANG R01CA39063-07
KANKEL, DOUGLAS R P01GM39813-04
KANKEL, DOUGLAS R R01NS11788-18
KANKI, PHYLLIS P01AI30795-02 0003
KANKI, PHYLLIS P01AI30795-02 9001
KANKI, PHYLLIS J P01AI26487-03S1 9001
KANKI, PHYLLIS J P01AI26487-03S1 9003
KANKI, PHYLLIS J P01AI30795-02
KANNEL, DOUGLAS P01GM39813-04 0004
KANNEL, DOUGLAS P01GM39813-04 9001
KANNER, ANDRES M M01RR03186-06 0053
KANNER, ANDRES M M01RR03186-06 0069
KANNER, ANDRES M M01RR03186-06 0070
KANNER, RICHARD E M01RR00064-27 0270
KANNER, RICHARD E. N01HR46014-16
KANO-SUEOKA, TAMIKO R01CA30545-07
KANOF, MARJORIE E R29DK40918-03
KANOST, MICHAEL R R29GM41247-03
KANT, JEFFREY A P30CA16520-16 9019
KANTER, PETER M P01CA13038-19 0101
KANTOR, FRED P01AI30548-01A1 0001
KANTOR, GEORGE J R01CA49411-03
KANTOR, GLENDA K R01AA08269-02
KANTOR, HOWARD L P01CA48729-03 0002
KANTOR, HOWARD L R01HL39371-05
KANTOR, J Z01CB09028-01
KANTROWITZ, EVAN R R01GM26237-13
KANTROWITZ, EVAN R R01GM42833-03
KANTROWITZ, EVAN R S07RR07156-16 0566
KANWAR, YASHPAL S R01DK28492-11
KANWISHER, NANCY G R29MH45245-03S1
KAO, CHIEN-YUAN R01DK39731-05
KAO, FA-TEN P01HD17449-08 0004
KAO, HENRY W P30DK36200-05S1 0003
KAO, JOSEPH P S07RR05379-30 0772
KAO, KENNETH R P41RR00954-15 0026
KAO, KUO-JANG R01HL35124-06
KAO, KUO-JANG U01HL42811-03
KAO, RICHARD S07RR05305-30 0739
KAO, RICHARD S07RR05305-30 0728
KAO, TEH-HUI S07RR07082-26 0291
KAO, WINSTON P01HL41496-03 0005
KAO, WINSTON W R01EY05629-06
KAPATOS, GREGORY R01NS26081-05
KAPCALA, LEONARD P R01NS23317-07
KAPELANSKI, DAVID S07RR05372-30 0669
KAPER, JAMES B R03AI30344-02
KAPER, JAMES B R22AI19716-09
KAPER, JAMES B R22AI21657-06
KAPIKIAN, A Z Z01AI00333-10
KAPIKIAN, A Z Z01AI00341-10
KAPIKIAN, A Z Z01AI00342-10
KAPIKIAN, A Z Z01AI00605-01
KAPILA, SUNIL S07RR05305-30 0738
KAPLAN, JAY R P01HL40962-04 0001
KAPLAN, ALAN M R01CA34052-08
KAPLAN, ALAN M R13AI31620-01
KAPLAN, ALLEN P P50AI16337-13
KAPLAN, ALLEN P P50AI16337-13 0001
KAPLAN, ALLEN P P50AI16337-13 0002
KAPLAN, ALLEN P R01HL23714-12
KAPLAN, BARRY P01NS19608-09 0004
KAPLAN, BARRY P50MH30915-15 9018
KAPLAN, BARRY B R01NS30715-04
KAPLAN, BRUCE E P30CA33572-11 9008
KAPLAN, CHARLES S N01AI05054-05
KAPLAN, DAVID N01AR12203-01
KAPLAN, DAVID R R01AI28923-02
KAPLAN, EHUD R01EY04888-07
KAPLAN, ELLEN M01RR00047-31 0478
KAPLAN, FREDERICK S M01RR00040-31 0394
KAPLAN, GARY M01RR00054-30 0379
KAPLAN, GEORGE A R01HL44199-02
KAPLAN, GILLA R22AI22616-06
KAPLAN, HAROLD S S03RR03112-11
KAPLAN, HENRY J P30EY02687-13
KAPLAN, HENRY J R01EY03723-11
KAPLAN, HENRY J R01EY08915-01
KAPLAN, HOWARD B K05DA00136-03
KAPLAN, HOWARD B R01DA02497-12
KAPLAN, JACK H R01GM39500-04
KAPLAN, JACK H R01HL30315-09
KAPLAN, JAY R P01HL45666-01 0003
KAPLAN, JAY R P50HL14164-20 0047
KAPLAN, JERRY R01DK30534-10
KAPLAN, JERRY R01HL26922-11
KAPLAN, JOHN E P01GM40761-01A2
KAPLAN, JOHN E P01GM40761-01A2 0001
KAPLAN, JOHN E P01GM40761-01A2 9001
KAPLAN, JOSEPH P60HL16008-19 0019
KAPLAN, KAREN L P50HL21006-15 0009
KAPLAN, LAWRENCE D R01CA55514-01
KAPLAN, LEE MICHAEL R29DK42189-02
KAPLAN, MARSHALL M01RR00054-30 0363
KAPLAN, MARSHALL M01RR00054-30 0337
KAPLAN, MARSHALL M M01RR00054-30 0252
KAPLAN, MARSHALL M M01RR00054-30 0375
KAPLAN, MARSHALL M M01RR00054-30 0402
KAPLAN, MARSHALL M M01RR00054-30 0407
KAPLAN, MARSHALL M M01RR00054-30 0429
KAPLAN, MICHAEL W S07RR05593-24 0125
KAPLAN, N L Z01ES44002-15
KAPLAN, PAIGE M01RR00240-27 0330
KAPLAN, PAUL P01CA22427-14 0012
KAPLAN, PETER S R01HD19143-07
KAPLAN, RICHARD P50AA03510-14 0003
KAPLAN, ROBERT M P60AR40770-01A1 0006
KAPLAN, ROBERT M R01HL34732-07
KAPLAN, ROBERT M U01CA52948-02
KAPLAN, RONALD S R29GM38785-05
KAPLAN, SAMUEL R01GM15590-25A1
KAPLAN, SAMUEL R01GM31667-09
KAPLAN, SAMUEL L. N01HR96038-06
KAPLAN, SANDRA J R01MH43772-03
KAPLAN, SELNA L M01RR01271-10 0012
KAPLAN, SELNA L M01RR01271-10 0040
KAPLAN, SELNA L M01RR01271-10 0115
KAPLAN, SELNA L M01RR01271-10 0044
KAPLAN, SELNA L M01RR01271-10 0050
KAPLAN, SELNA L M01RR01271-10 0101
KAPLAN, SELNA L M01RR01271-10 0081
KAPLAN, SELNA L M01RR01271-10 0107
KAPLAN, SELNA L M01RR01271-10 0109
KAPLAN, SELNA L. M01RR01271-10 0093
KAPLAN, SHERRIE P60AR36834-05 0006
KAPLAN, SHERRIE H R01HS06897-01
KAPLITE, PAUL V U01AI27221-03 0005
KAPLOWITZ, LISA M01RR00065-29 0348
KAPLOWITZ, LISA M01RR00065-29 0329
KAPLOWITZ, NEIL R01DK30312-10
KAPLOWITZ, NEIL R13DK44465-01
KAPLOWITZ, PAUL B. M01RR00065-29 0305
KAPOOR, SHIV C S07RR05417-30 0795
KAPOOR, WISHWA N K04HL01899-05
KAPOOR, WISHWA N R01HL36735-05
KAPOOR, WISHWA N R01HS06468-02
KAPP-PIERCE, JUDITH A R01AI13987-14
KAPP, DANIEL S P01CA44665-04 0006
KAPP, DANIEL S P01CA44665-04 0001
KAPPAS, ATTALLAH M01RR00102-28 0119
KAPPAS, ATTALLAH M01RR00102-28 0005
KAPPAS, ATTALLAH S07RR07065-26 0061
KAPPES, JOHN C R29AI31816-01
KAPPLER, FRANCIS P01CA41078-05 9002
KAPPLER, JOHN W R01AI18785-10
KAPPLER, JOHN W R37AI17134-12
KAPPS, ATTALLAH N01HD02901-03
KAPTEIN, ELAINE M M01RR00043-31 0474
KAPTEIN, ELAINE M M01RR00043-31 0357
KAPUR, KRISHAN K R01DE09085-02
KAPUR, KRISHAN K R01DE09401-01A1
KARAM, ELIE G R03MH48887-01
KARAM, JIM D R01GM18842-18
KARAM, JOHN M01RR00079-29 0394
KARANIAN, J Z01AA00285-02
KARASEC, MARVIN A R01AR41551-01 9001
KARASEK, MARVIN A R01AR41551-01 0003
KARASIC, RAYMOND B S07RR05507-29 0479
KARATHANASIS, SOTIRIOS K R01HL32032-08
KARBON, EDWARD W, JR R43MH47213-01A1
KARBON, EDWARD W, JR R43NS29906-01
KARCHMER, MICHAEL A S07RR07245-03
KARCZMAR, GREGORY S R29CA52008-01A1
KARDINAL, CARL G U10CA35272-08
KARDON, RANDY S07RR05372-30 0675
KARGACIN, GARY J R29AR39678-03
KARGER, BARRY L R01HG00023-02
KARGER, BARRY L R37GM15847-22
KARI, BRUCE P01HD19937-06 0006
KARI, BRUCE E P01HD19937-06 9001
KARI, F Z01ES21149-01
KARI, F W Z01ES21046-08
KARI, F W Z01ES21124-03
KARIN, MICHAEL P01CA50528-03 0002
KARIN, MICHAEL R01DK38527-05
KARIN, MICHAEL R01ES04151-06
KARINO, TAKESHI R01HL41187-04
KARJALA, DENNIS S R13HG00265-01
KARL, IRENE M01RR00036-31 0991
KARL, LESLIE M01RR00036-31 1031
KARL, PETER I S07RR05924-07 0002
KARLAN, BETH S07RR05468-29 0402
KARLE, ISABELLA L R01GM30902-10
KARLER, RALPH R01DA00346-18
KARLIN, ARTHUR R01NS07065-25
KARLIN, KENNETH S07RR07041-26 0395
KARLIN, KENNETH D R01GM28962-11
KARLIN, KENNETH D R01GM45971-01
KARLIN, SAMUEL R01GM10452-28
KARLIN, SAMUEL R01GM10452-28 0001
KARLIN, SAMUEL R01GM10452-28 0002
KARLIN, SAMUEL R01HG00335-04
KARLINER, JOEL S P01HL25847-12 0005
KARLINER, JOEL S P01HL25847-12 9004
KARLISH, STEVEN J R01GM32286-07
KARLOWICZ, KAREN A R13DK44731-01
KARLSON, KARL H S07RR05350-30 0332
KARLSSON, S Z01NS02730-05
KARLSSON, S Z01NS02731-05
KARLSSON, S Z01NS02785-03
KARMEL, BERNARD Z R01DA06644-02
KARNES, WILLIAM P30DK41301-02 0001
KARNIK, PRATIMA S P30DK34854-08 0011
KARNO, MARVIN P50MH30911-14 0035
KARNO, MARVIN S07RR05756-18 0290
KARNO, MARVIN S07RR05756-18 0293
KARNO, MARVIN S07RR05756-18 0313
KARNOVSKY, MANFRED L R01AI03260-32
KARNOVSKY, MORRIS J R01DE08507-05
KARNOVSKY, MORRIS J R01HL43318-03
KARNOVSKY, MORRIS J R37HL17747-17
KAROL, MERYL H R01ES01532-14
KAROLY, LYNN P50HD12639-12 0019
KAROUM, F Z01MH02259-07
KAROUM, F Z01MH02420-04
KAROUM, F Z01MH02453-03
KAROUNOS, DENNIS M01RR00350-25 0391
KAROUNOS, DENNIS S07RR05425-30 0747
KARP, DANIEL D U10CA44067-05
KARP, DANIELS D U10CA07190-28
KARP, HERBERT R P30AG10130-01 9003
KARP, JOEL P30MH48539-01 9002
KARP, MARSHA W R29HL43312-03
KARP, RICHARD D R01GM39398-03
KARPAS, A B Z01BA04003-08
KARPATKIN, SIMON R01DA04315-06
KARPEN, JEFFREY W R01EY09275-01
KARPIAK, STEPHEN E S07RR05650-25 0102
KARPLUS, MARTIN P01GM39589-05 0003
KARPLUS, MARTIN R37GM30804-21
KARPLUS, PAUL A R01GM43566-01A1
KARR, JAMES P S15CA56023-01
KARR, ROBERT W R01AI24138-04
KARR, ROBERT W R01AI27214-03
KARRER, FREDERICK M01RR00069-29 0472
KARRER, FREDERICK M M01RR00069-29 0447
KARRER, FREDERICK M M01RR00069-29 0458
KARSCH, FRED J R01HD18337-08
KARSON, CRAIG N R01MH45729-01A1
KARSON, SAMUEL U18DA07160-02
KARTEN, HARVEY J R01EY06890-07
KARTEN, HARVEY J R01NS24560-05
KARUKSTIS, KERRY K R15GM46090-01

KARUNA-KARAN, ARTHUR R43DE10018-01
KARVALY, BELA S06GM08047-20S1 0032
KARWOSKI, CHESTER J R01EY03526-12
KASAHARA, MASANORI R01HD25493-03
KASAHARA, MASANORI R01RR06603-01
KASAIAN, MARION P30CA13943-19 0014
KASAMATSU, HARUMI R01CA50574-02
KASAMATSU, HARUMI S07RR07009-26 0929
KASAMATSU, TAKUJI R01EY06733-05
KASAMATSU, TAKUJI S07RR05981-05 0809
KASAMATSU, TAKUJI S07RR05981-05 0797
KASARSKIS, EDWARD M01RR02602-07 0055
KASCSAK, RICHARD J P01AG09017-02 0003
KASE, NATHAN G M01RR00071-28A1
KASHGARIAN, MICHAEL P01DK17433-18 0012
KASHGARIAN, MICHAEL P01DK17433-18 9002
KASHGARIAN, MICHAEL S10RR06400-01
KASHKET, SHELBY R01DE05253-09A4
KASHMIRI, S Z01CB09023-05
KASID, USHA N P01CA52066-02 0002
KASID, USHA N R29CA46641-04
KASIM, SIDIKA E R29HL41991-02
KASINATH, BALAKUNTALAM S R01DK41517-03
KASINATHAN, CHINNASWAMY R15DE09874-01
KASL, STANISLAV V P01CA42101-06 0003
KASLOVSKY, ROBERT A S07RR05394-30 0716
KASLOW, D Z01AI00240-10
KASLOW, HARVEY R R01AI24320-05
KASPER, CHARLES B P01CA22484-14 0005
KASPER, CHRISTINE S07RR06014-03 0847
KASPER, CHRISTINE E R29NR02204-04
KASPER, DENNIS L R01AI23339-07
KASPER, DENNIS L R01AI30628-01A1
KASPER, LLOYD H K04AI00932-03
KASPER, LLOYD H R01AI30000-02
KASPEREK, GEORGE J R01AR39299-03
KASPRZAK, K S Z01CP04582-16
KASS, IRA S R29GM38866-05
KASS, LEONARD S07RR07161-14 0846
KASS, LEONARD J R29EY07570-04
KASS, MICHAEL A U10EY05436-07
KASS, ROBERT S R01HL21922-14
KASSELL, NEAL F R01NS24806-05
KASSIS, AMIN P01CA41167-06 0004
KASSIS, J A Z01BB04006-02
KASSIS, J A Z01BB04007-02
KASSIS, J A Z01BB04009-03
KASSOFF, AARON N01EY02119-02
KASTNER, D L Z01AR41083-02
KASULE, OMAR M. N01HB17088-00
KATER, STANLEY P01NS28323-02 0002
KATER, STANLEY P41RR01395-10 0013
KATER, STANLEY B P01NS28323-02
KATER, STANLEY B P01NS28323-02 9002
KATER, STANLEY B R01NS24683-06
KATER, STANLEY B R01NS26819-03
KATER, STANLEY B S07RR05458-29 0827
KATES, WENDY G S07RR05808-13 0913
KATHOL, ROGER P50MH43271-05 0007
KATHOL, ROGER G M01RR00059-30 0504
KATHOL, ROGER G M01RR00059-30 0551
KATHRYN LEARY S07RR05418-30 0025
KATON, WAYNE J R01MH41739-04A1
KATONA, ILDY M R29AI26150-03
KATOOT, MOHAMMAD W R44NS26978-03
KATOVICH, MICHAEL J R01HD18133-07A1
KATOVICH, MICHAEL J S03RR03452-05
KATSOYANNIS, PANAYOTIS G R01DK12925-22
KATTAN, MEYER M01RR00071-28A1 0230
KATTAN, MEYER U01AI30772-01
KATTAN, MEYER L. N01HR96042-06
KATULA, KAREN S R29GM38652-04
KATUSIC, ZVONIMIR S R29HL44116-02
KATYAL, SIKANDAR L R01HL28193-07
KATZ, ABRAM S07RR07030-26 0398
KATZ, ARNOLD M P01HL33026-07
KATZ, ARNOLD M P01HL33026-07 0001
KATZ, B P50AR39250-05 9004
KATZ, B P U01AI25859-05 9003
KATZ, BARRETT P50AG05131-08 0016
KATZ, BARRETT U10EY07695-05
KATZ, BARRY P P01DE09835-01A1 9001
KATZ, BARRY P P60AR20582-14 9006
KATZ, BARRY P U01AI31494-01 9002
KATZ, BEN A S07RR05443-30 0994
KATZ, BILL N01CO15693-00
KATZ, D A Z01CB09145-07
KATZ, D J P42ES04699-05 0008
KATZ, DAVID F R01ES03614-05
KATZ, DAVID M P01HL25830-11A1 0014
KATZ, DAVID M P01HL25830-11A1 9005
KATZ, DAVID M R01HL42131-03
KATZ, FLORA R01EY09298-01
KATZ, HOWARD P60AR36308-07 9003
KATZ, HOWARD R P30AR35907-07 9002
KATZ, HOWARD R R29AI23430-05
KATZ, IRA P50MH40380-07 0006
KATZ, IRA R P50MH40380-07
KATZ, IRA R. P01AG03934-10 0006
KATZ, J L Z01DA00103-01
KATZ, J L Z01DA00105-01
KATZ, JACQUELINE P01AI31596-01 0003
KATZ, JANNET K11DE00232-04
KATZ, JAY L U10EY06830-05
KATZ, JOSEPH R01DK36449-06
KATZ, LARRY S S07RR07058-26 0179
KATZ, LAWRENCE C R01EY07960-03
KATZ, MARTIN L R01EY03274-13
KATZ, MARTIN L R01EY08813-01
KATZ, MARTIN L R01NS30155-01
KATZ, PHYLLIS A R01HD22929-04
KATZ, RICHARD J N01HC65068-10
KATZ, ROBERT M01RR00997-16 0406
KATZ, ROBERT W M01RR00997-16 0376
KATZ, RONALD W K11DE00301-02
KATZ, S I Z01CB03657-17
KATZ, SOLOMON H N01HD72909-09
KATZ, VERN M01RR00046-31 0475
KATZ, VERN L M01RR00046-31 0415
KATZ, WILLIAM N01CO15629-00
KATZ, WILLIAM N01CO15771-01
KATZE, JON R S07RR05423-30 0054
KATZE, MICHAEL G R01AI22646-07
KATZE, MICHAEL G. P51RR00166-30 0067
KATZEFF, HARVEY L R01DK38337-04
KATZEL, LESLIE I K08AG00497-03
KATZENELLENBOGEN, BE S07RR07030-26 0399
KATZENELLENBOGEN, BENITA S R37CA18119-15
KATZENELLENBOGEN, BENITA S R01CA51482-05
KATZENELLENBOGEN, JOHN A R01CA25836-12
KATZENELLENBOGEN, JOHN A R37DK15556-21
KATZENSTEIN, PAUL L K11AR01872-01
KATZENSTEIN, PAUL L S07RR05745-19 0255
KATZKA, DAVID A K08DK01839-04
KATZMAN, MICHAEL R29AI30759-01A1
KATZMAN, ROBERT P01AG03949-10 9001
KATZMAN, ROBERT P50AG05131-08 9002
KATZMAN, ROBERT P50AG05131-08
KATZMANN, JOHN A P30CA15083-18 9007
KAUER, JOHN S R01DC00228-10
KAUFFMAN, CHARLES W R01OH01122-09
KAUFFMAN, FRED P30ES05022-04 9002
KAUFFMAN, FREDERICK S07RR05909-08 0949
KAUFFMAN, FREDERICK C R01CA20807-12
KAUFFMAN, GORDON L JR, MD R01HL18995-16
KAUFMAN, B Z01BH05012-02
KAUFMAN, B T Z01DK15200-31
KAUFMAN, CAROL P50MH30915-15 9011
KAUFMAN, DAVID G P01CA42765-04
KAUFMAN, DAVID G P01CA42765-04 0002
KAUFMAN, DAVID G P01CA42765-04 0003
KAUFMAN, DAVID G P01CA42765-04 9001
KAUFMAN, DAVID G P30CA16086-17 9006
KAUFMAN, DAVID G R01CA31733-10
KAUFMAN, DAVID I U10EY07680-04
KAUFMAN, DAVID W R01HL31768-07
KAUFMAN, E C Z01MH02414-04
KAUFMAN, E E Z01MH00881-35
KAUFMAN, FRANCINE R R01HD26401-02
KAUFMAN, HERBERT E P30EY02377-13
KAUFMAN, HERBERT E R01EY02672-14
KAUFMAN, HERBERT E R37EY02580-14
KAUFMAN, LARYSSA S07RR05772-17 0348
KAUFMAN, LEE D S07RR05736-19 0158
KAUFMAN, LEON R01HL39171-05
KAUFMAN, LESLIE S R01RR06672-02
KAUFMAN, MARC P R01HL30710-09
KAUFMAN, MARC P R01HL40910-04
KAUFMAN, PAUL L R01EY02698-13
KAUFMAN, PETER A K11CA01458-03
KAUFMAN, RUSSEL E R01DK38699-05
KAUFMAN, RUSSEL E. P50AR39162-05 9002
KAUFMAN, RUSSELL E P60HL28391-09 0004
KAUFMAN, RUSSELL E P60HL28391-09 0010
KAUFMAN, S Z01MH01031-23
KAUFMAN, S Z01MH01032-23
KAUFMAN, S Z01MH01038-23
KAUFMAN, S Z01MH01040-23
KAUFMAN, S Z01MH02563-01
KAUFMAN, STEPHEN B R43NR02645-01A1
KAUFMAN, STEPHEN J R01GM28842-10A1
KAUFMAN, THOMAS C R01GM24299-15
KAUFMAN, WILLIAM K P01CA42765-04 0004
KAUFMANN, CAROLINE L R01MH45218-03
KAUFMANN, CHARLES A K11MH00682-05
KAUFMANN, CHARLES A U01MH46289-03
KAUFMANN, HORACIO M01RR00071-28A1 0235
KAUFMANN, HORACIO M01RR00071-28A1 0211
KAUFMANN, SCOTT H R01CA50435-03
KAUGARS, GEORGE E R01DE09523-01A1
KAUL, D K P01HL21016-15 0018
KAUL, D K P01HL21016-15 9003
KAUL, DHANANJAYA K R01HL45931-02
KAUL, KAREN L S07RR05370-30 0609
KAUL, SANJIV R29HL38345-05
KAUMAYA, PRAVIN T P R29AI25790-05
KAUSHANSKY, KENNETH P51RR00166-30 0095
KAUSHANSKY, KENNETH R01CA31615-10
KAUSLER, DONALD H R01AG08214-03
KAUWELL, GAIL P A M01RR00082-29 0475
KAVANAGH, RON S07RR05635-18 0781
KAVANAGH, TERRANCE J P01AG01751-13 0009
KAVANAGH, TERRANCE J R01HL39594-05
KAVANAGH, TERRANCE J S10RR06236-01
KAVANAH, MAUREEN T U10CA22489-14
KAVANAUGH, WILLIAM M K11HL02410-02
KAVATHAS, PAULA S07RR05358-30 0486
KAVEY, RAE-ELLEN W K07HL02078-02
KAVOUSSI, LOUIS R S07RR05491-29 0459
KAWAI, K Z01NS02833-01
KAWAMOATO, S Z01HL01665-16
KAWANISHI, DAVID T M01RR00043-31 0369
KAWANISHI, HIDERNORI R01AG07603-04
KAWAOKA, YOSHIHIRO R01AI29599-02
KAWAS, CLAUDIA H R01AG08325-02
KAWAS, CLAUDIA H. M01RR02719-06 0116
KAY, BRIAN K S07RR07072-26 0267
KAY, CHRISTOPHER J R01GM43911-02
KAY, EUNDUCK P R01EY06431-08
KAY, EUNDUCK P S07RR05810-13 0020
KAY, M M B R01AG08574-04
KAY, MARGUERITE M B R01AG08444-04
KAY, STEVE A R55GM43884-01A1
KAY, THOMAS P20NS30309-01 9001
KAYDEN, HERBERT J R01HL30842-09
KAYE, CELIA I S07RR05654-24 0146
KAYE, D P01AG03934-10 0000
KAYE, DONALD P01AG03934-10
KAYE, DONALD P01AG03934-10 0001
KAYE, DONALD P01AG03934-10 9001
KAYE, EDWARD M K08NS01390-02
KAYE, F J Z01CM07256-03
KAYE, JEFFREY P30AG08017-02 9002
KAYE, JEROME S07RR07069-26 0242
KAYE, JONATHAN G R29AI31231-02
KAYE, WALTER H M01RR00084-29 0238
KAYE, WALTER H R01AA08983-01
KAYE, WALTER H R01MH46001-02
KAYES, STEPHEN G R01AI19968-08
KAYNE, HERBERT S07RR05927-07 0956
KAYSEN, GEORGE A R01DK42297-02
KAZAK, LESLIE P P30CA34196-09 9008
KAZAZIAN, HAIG H, JR R01GM45398-01
KAZAZIAN, HAIG H, JR R37DK13983-22
KAZDIN, ALAN S07RR07015-26 0606
KAZDIN, ALAN E K05MH00353-10
KAZDIN, ALAN E R37MH35408-11
KAZER, RALPH R M01RR00048-30 0161
KAZER, RALPH R M01RR00048-30 0144
KAZER, RALPH R M01RR00048-30 0162
KAZMIERCZAK, STEVEN S07RR05812-12 0485
KAZURA, JAMES P01AI26482-03S1 0003
KAZURA, JAMES W P01AI15351-13
KAZURA, JAMES W P50HL37117-05 0005
KEAN, EDWARD L R01EY00393-24
KEAN, EDWARD L R01EY03685-10
KEAN, MARY-LOUISE R35AG07918-03 0008
KEANA, JOHN F R01GM27137-12
KEANE, ANNE R01MH45139-02
KEANE, WILLIAM S15DA07774-01
KEANE, WILLIAM F R21DK44587-01
KEANE, WILLIAM F S07RR06019-03
KEANE, WILLIAM F S07RR06019-03 0525
KEANE, WILLIAM F S15GM47102-01
KEARNEY, CHERRI L N01CO84343-11
KEARNEY, CHERRI L. N01HO09009-03
KEARNEY, EDNA B P01HL16251-18 0003
KEARNEY, EDNA B P01HL16251-18 0004
KEARNEY, JOHN F P01AI30879-17 0002
KEARNEY, JOHN F R01AI14782-14
KEARNS, D Z01BE01005-01
KEARNS, DAVID R R01GM35177-06
KEARNS, DAVID R R01GM40635-04
KEARNS, M K Z01DE00536-01
KEATH, ELIZABETH J R29AI28950-02
KEATING, MARK T R29HL46401-01
KEATING, MARK T S07RR05428-30 0169
KEATS, BRONYA J R01HG00343-07
KECK, GARY E R01CA52834-02
KECK, GARY E R01GM28961-11
KEDAR, AMOS M01RR00082-29 0455
KEDES, LAURENCE P50DE09165-03 0002
KEDES, LAURENCE H P30DK38707-05 9002
KEECH, RONALD S07RR05372-30 0671
KEEF, KATHLEEN P01DK41315-03 0001
KEEF, KATHLEEN D R01HL40399-04A1
KEEFE, DOUGLAS H. P01DC00520-04 0002
KEEFE, FRANCIS J P50AR39162-05 0006
KEEFE, FRANCIS J R01AR35270-06A1
KEEFE, MAUREEN R R29NR01620-05
KEEFER, L K Z01CP04542-19
KEEFER, L K Z01CP05673-01
KEEFER, MICHAEL C M01RR00044-31 0381
KEEFER, MICHAEL C M01RR00044-31 0358
KEEFOVER, ROBERT R01AG09519-01
KEELER, EMMETT P60AG10415-01 9001
KEELER, THEODORE E S07RR07006-26 0913
KEELEY, FRED W R13HL46864-01
KEELING, MICHAEL E P30CA16672-17 9012
KEELING, MICHALE E U42RR03589-06
KEELING, MICHALE E U42RR05080-04
KEEN, CARL L R01HD01743-26
KEEN, CARL L R01HD26777-02
KEENAN, BRUCE S. M01RR00073-29 0261
KEENAN, BRUCE S. M01RR00073-29 0260
KEENAN, BRUCE M01RR00073-29 0207

KEENAN, BRUCE S M01RR00073-29 0107
KEENAN, BRUCE S M01RR00073-29 0300
KEENAN, COLLEEN S07RR06014-03 0839
KEENAN, THOMAS W R01GM31244-10
KEENE, JACK D P01CA30246-11 0004
KEENE, JACK D R01AI16099-12
KEENS, THOMAS G R01HD22696-03
KEEPING, HUGH S R01HD25272-03
KEESE, CHARLES R R43RR07554-01
KEEVER, CAROLYN A P01CA23766-14 0033
KEEVER, CAROLYN A R55CA57134-01
KEFALIDES, NICHOLAS A P01AR20553-15 0003
KEFALIDES, NICHOLAS A P01AR20553-15
KEFALIDES, NICHOLAS A R01HL29492-09
KEFALIDES, NICHOLAS A R13AR40831-01
KEFALIDES, NICHOLAS A S03RR03145-09
KEFALIDES, NICHOLAS A S07RR05415-30
KEFALIDES, NICHOLAS A S07RR05823-12
KEFALIDES, NICHOLAS A S15HL47750-01
KEGELES, SUSAN M R01MH46816-02
KEHL, LOIS J K15DE00225-03
KEHRER, JAMES P R01HL35689-05
KEHRER, JAMES P R01HL40695-03
KEHRER, JIM S07RR05849-11 0254
KEHRL, J H Z01AI00210-11
KEIDERLING, TIMOTHY A R01GM30147-10
KEIL, FRANK C R01HD23922-04
KEIL, JULIAN E R01HL31397-08
KEIM, PAUL S07RR07256-02 0072
KEIRN, PHILIP A R43AG09727-01
KEISER, H R Z01HL03593-01
KEISLER, DUANE S07RR07053-26 0151
KEITEL, WENDY M01RR00350-25 0454
KEITEL, WENDY A M01RR00350-25 0460
KEITH, INGEGERD S07RR05912-08 0653
KEITH, INGEGERD M R01HL42362-03
KEITH, J M Z01DE00518-02
KEITH, L DONALD P01AA08621-02 0004
KEITH, TIM P R01HG00460-01
KEITHLEY, ELIZABETH M R29DC00405-05
KEIVER, CAROLYN A P01AI32918-09 0012
KELCH, ROBERT P M01RR00042-31 0235
KELCH, ROBERT P M01RR00042-31 0681
KELCH, ROBERT P P30HD28820-01
KELCH, ROBERT P R01HD16000-10
KELLAM, SHEPPARD G P50MH38725-07
KELLAM, SHEPPARD G R01MH42968-03
KELLAR, KENNETH J R01DA06486-02
KELLAS, GEORGE S07RR07037-26 0387
KELLAWAY, PETER P50NS11535-17
KELLAWAY, PETER A P50NS11535-17 0019
KELLAWAY, PETER A P50NS11535-17 0017
KELLAWAY, PETER A P50NS11535-17 9001
KELLEHER-WALSH, BARBARA J R43HD27777-01
KELLEHER, CATHERINE P R01NR02262-02
KELLEHER, JOANNE K K01AG00412-04
KELLEHER, JOANNE K R01GM33536-07
KELLEHER, JOLEEN P30CA15704-18 9013
KELLEHER, KELLY P50MH48197-02 0001
KELLEHER, PETER J R43EY09021-01A1
KELLEHER, PETER J R43EY09022-01
KELLEHER, PETER J R43EY09324-01
KELLEHER, PHILIP C R01CA50267-01A2
KELLEMS, RODNEY E R01AI25255-05
KELLEMS, RODNEY E R01GM30204-10
KELLER-WOOD, MAUREEN E K04DK01898-03
KELLER, A M01RR00645-20 0447
KELLER, ALAN M U10CA45459-05
KELLER, BRADLEY B K11HL02498-02
KELLER, EDWARD L R01EY06860-06
KELLER, EDWARD L S07RR05981-05 0793
KELLER, EDWARD L S07RR05981-05 0794
KELLER, EDWARD L S07RR05981-05 0795
KELLER, GORDON S07RR05842-12 0285
KELLER, GORDON M R01DK43285-01
KELLER, JOHN C K04DE00234-03
KELLER, JOHN C R01DE08540-03
KELLER, M P01MH47200-02 0005
KELLER, MARGARET S07RR05551-29 0956
KELLER, MARK W K08HL02419-02
KELLER, MARTIN B U01MH25478-18
KELLER, MARY L R01NR02253-03
KELLER, RAYMOND E R01HD25594-03
KELLER, RICHARD M01RR02172-09 0183
KELLER, RICHARD W R01DA06199-02
KELLER, ROBERT B R18HS06813-01
KELLER, RONALD K R01EY07361-04
KELLER, RONALD K R01HL43111-03
KELLER, STEVEN E R01MH44142-04
KELLER, STEVEN E. P01MH44193-03 9003
KELLERMAN, PAUL S07RR05684-23 0169
KELLEY, ANN E R29DA04788-05
KELLEY, C A Z01HL04210-04
KELLEY, DARCY P41RR00592-22 0035
KELLEY, DARCY B R01NS19949-09
KELLEY, DARCY B R01NS23684-11
KELLEY, DAVID M01RR00056-30 0366
KELLEY, DAVID M01RR00056-30 0367
KELLEY, J A Z01CM03581-22
KELLEY, J A Z01CM06177-06
KELLEY, J A Z01CM06178-06
KELLEY, JASON P50HL14212-20 0034
KELLEY, JIM L P01HL26890-09 0003
KELLEY, KEITH W R01AG06246-06
KELLEY, KEVIN A R01DK43973-01
KELLEY, MARK A M01RR00040-31 0410
KELLEY, PHILIP S07RR07055-26 0171
KELLEY, VICKI M01RR02635-07 0232
KELLEY, VICKI E P01DK40839-03 0005
KELLEY, VICKI E R01DK36149-07
KELLEY, WILLIAM N M01RR00040-31
KELLMAN, RAYMOND S06GM08192-12 0009
KELLNER, CHARLES H K07MH00821-03
KELLOGG, CAROL K K02MH00651-05
KELLOGG, CAROL K R01DA07080-02
KELLY, ALAN M P01HL15835-19 0010
KELLY, ANDREW B R01HL47181-01
KELLY, CAROLYN J R01DK42155-02
KELLY, CIARAN P S07RR05487-29 0702
KELLY, DANIEL P S07RR05389-30 0638
KELLY, DAVID M01RR00056-30 0368
KELLY, EDWARD I N01LM13522-00
KELLY, H WILLIAM M01RR00997-16 0399
KELLY, JEFFREY A R01MH41800-07
KELLY, JEFFREY A R01MH42908-04
KELLY, JEFFREY A R01MH44149-04
KELLY, JEFFREY A S07RR05386-30 0587
KELLY, JEFFREY A U01MH49055-01
KELLY, JEFFREY W S07RR07090-26 0472
KELLY, JOSEPH A. N01HO89004-08
KELLY, K Z01CB09171-07
KELLY, K Z01CB09356-01
KELLY, K Z01CB09357-01
KELLY, K Z01CB09358-01
KELLY, K A M01RR00585-20 0415
KELLY, K A M01RR00585-20 0511
KELLY, KAREN L K11CA01408-02
KELLY, KATHLEEN J R44DA06580-02
KELLY, KEITH A R37DK18278-17
KELLY, KEITH A. M01RR00585-20 0377
KELLY, KEVIN M K08NS01472-02
KELLY, MARTIN J K04HD00718-05
KELLY, MARTIN J R01DA05158-04
KELLY, MICHAEL R29HD23385-05
KELLY, MICHAEL J N01GM72110-20
KELLY, PAUL T R01NS22452-07
KELLY, REGIS P01DK41822-03 0003
KELLY, REGIS B P01NS16033-11 0005
KELLY, REGIS B R01NS09878-21
KELLY, REGIS B R01NS15927-12
KELLY, SANDRA J R29AA08080-03
KELLY, SHEILA S07RR05654-24 0140
KELLY, T ROSS R01GM44470-02
KELLY, THADDEUS E M01RR00847-18 0556
KELLY, THOMAS H R29AA07302-04
KELLY, THOMAS J R01CA40414-07
KELLY, THOMAS J R01GM42780-03
KELLY, THOMAS J JR P01CA16519-17 0001
KELLY, THOMAS J JR P01CA16519-17 9001
KELLY, THOMAS J, JR P01CA16519-17
KELLY, WILLIAM C S03RR03074-10
KELLY, WILLIAM R P30HD06160-20S1 0003
KELMAN, EUGENIA G S03RR03105-11
KELNER, MICHAEL J R01ES04989-02
KELNER, MICHAEL J S06GM47165-01 0025
KELSEN, DAVID N01CM07311-04
KELSEN, DAVID P R01CA49784-03
KELSEN, DAVID P R01CA56125-01
KELSEN, STEVEN G R01HL40295-05
KELSEY, JENNIFER M01RR00645-20 0492
KELSEY, JENNIFER L P50AR39191-05 0004
KELSEY, JENNIFER L R01AG10454-01
KELSEY, KARL T K01OH00110-01
KELSEY, RICK G R01CA55151-01
KELSEY, SHERYL F U10EY08151-03
KELSO, J A R01MH42900-05
KELSO, J A S07RR07258-02
KELSO, J A S15NS30122-01
KELSO, STEPHEN R R01NS24591-06
KELSOE, GARNETT H R01AI24335-05
KELSOE, GARNETT H R55AG08192-04
KELSOE, JOHN R M01RR00827-17 0499
KELSOE, JOHN R S07RR05665-24 0895
KELTNER, JOHN L U10EY07461-04
KELVIN, D J Z01CM09369-01
KEMENY, MARGARET E K01MH00820-03
KEMENY, MARGARET E R01MH42918-05
KEMENY, NANCY P01CA47997-03 0001
KEMNITZ, JOSEPH P51RR00167-31 0035
KEMNITZ, JOSEPH S07RR07098-26 0366
KEMP, ALAN M01RR00054-30 0381
KEMP, DANIEL S R01GM40547-04
KEMP, DANIEL S R37GM13453-26
KEMP, ROBERT G R01DK19912-15
KEMP, W. MICHAEL P01AI26505-03 0003
KEMPER, BYRON W R01GM35897-06
KEMPER, BYRON W R01GM39360-04
KEMPER, SUSAN K04AG00443-02
KEMPER, SUSAN P30AG10182-01 0002
KEMPER, SUSAN S07RR07037-26 0383
KEMPER, THOMAS P01AG00001-17A2 0015
KEMPER, THOMAS A P01HD22539-04 0003
KEMPFF, MAYA P30CA22453-14 9001
KEMPHUES, KENNETH J R01HD27689-01
KEMPNER, E S Z01AR27003-32
KEMPNER, K M Z01CT00138-08
KEMPNER, K M Z01CT00199-02
KEMPPAINEN, B.W. P51RR00166-30 0144
KEMPSON, STEPHEN A R01DK32148-10
KENAGY, GEORGE J S07RR07096-26 0065
KENDALL, DEBRA A R01GM37639-05
KENDALL, JOHN S03RR03140-10
KENDALL, JOHN W S15NS30119-01
KENDALL, JOHN W, JR M01RR00334-25
KENDALL, JOHN W, JR S07RR05412-30
KENDE, ANDREW S R01CA18846-16
KENDIG, JAMES P50HL36543-05 0006
KENDIG, JOAN J R01NS13108-15
KENDLER, KENNETH P50MH41960-05S1 0005
KENDLER, KENNETH S R01MH40828-06
KENDLER, KENNETH S R01MH41953-05
KENDLER, KENNETH S R03MH46944-02
KENDRICK & COMPANY N01MH80023-00
KENDRICK, KATHLEEN E R01GM40681-03
KENG, PETER C R01CA44723-05
KENIMER, J G Z01BA04001-06
KENNA, MARGARET A R29DC00465-05
KENNEDY RONALD U01AI26462-04 0005
KENNEDY, ANN R R37CA22704-15
KENNEDY, C Z01MH02590-01
KENNEDY, EUGENE P R01GM22057-17
KENNEDY, EUGENE P R37GM19822-32
KENNEDY, F P M01RR00585-20 0513
KENNEDY, F P M01RR00585-20 0444
KENNEDY, F P M01RR00585-20 0478
KENNEDY, G DAVON S07RR07171-08 0157
KENNEDY, JAMES E S07RR05677-23
KENNEDY, JOHN I M01RR00032-31 0293
KENNEDY, JOHN IRA, JR M01RR00032-31 0333
KENNEDY, JOHN M R29AA08716-02
KENNEDY, KATHERINE A R01CA36946-07A1
KENNEDY, M S07RR07003-26 0322
KENNEDY, M S07RR07003-26 0330
KENNEDY, MARY B R01NS17660-11
KENNEDY, MARY B R01NS28710-02
KENNEDY, PHILIP R P51RR00165-31 0178
KENNEDY, PHILIP R R01NS24602-03
KENNEDY, R P30AI28696-01 9006
KENNEDY, ROBERT D R01AG10644-01
KENNEDY, RONALD C P01AI22380-07 0005
KENNEDY, RONALD C P30AI28696-01
KENNEDY, RONALD C R01AI22307-06
KENNEDY, RONALD C U01AI26462-04
KENNEDY, SUSAN S07RR05507-29 0480
KENNEDY, THOMAS P P01HL42444-02 0002
KENNEDY, WILLIAM R R01NS26348-03
KENNELL, DAVID E R01GM34127-15
KENNELL, JOHN H R01HD16915-07
KENNELLY, PETER J R29GM45368-01
KENNERLY, DONALD A R01AI22277-07
KENNETT, ROGER P30DK19525-15 9005
KENNETT, ROGER H P30CA16520-16 9014
KENNEY, DIANNE M P01HL29583-09 0001
KENNEY, EDWARD S S07RR07082-26 0292
KENNEY, MALCOLM E P01CA48735-02 0001
KENNEY, MARIA C R01EY06807-05
KENNEY, SHANNON U01AI25868-05 0003
KENNEY, SHANNON C K08CA01229-05
KENNEY, W LARRY S07RR07082-26 0293
KENNEY, WILLIAM L R29AG07004-05
KENNISON, J Z01HD01005-04
KENNY, ALEXANDER D S03RR03393-07
KENNY, JOHN T P50MH41684-07 0074
KENNY, JOHN T P50MH41684-07 0078
KENNY, JONATHAN S07RR07179-14 0683
KENSHALO, D Z01DE00329-10
KENSIL, CHARLOTTE A R43AI30290-01A1
KENSLER, ROBERT W R01AR30442-11
KENSLER, ROBERT W S10RR06337-01
KENSLER, THOMAS P01CA44530-05 0002
KENSLER, THOMAS W K04CA01230-05
KENSLER, THOMAS W R01CA39416-06
KENT, CLAUDIA R01CA52574-02
KENT, CLAUDIA M R01HD10580-13
KENT, CLAUDIA M R13HD27920-01
KENT, JOHN N K16DE00199-05S1
KENT, KARLA S07RR05336-29 0303
KENT, RAYMOND D R01DC00319-07
KENT, THOMAS A R03MH49552-01
KENTER, AMY L R01GM45718-01
KENTER, AMY L S07RR05369-30 0601
KENYON, CYNTHIA P01GM31286-09 0008
KENYON, CYNTHIA J R01GM37053-06
KENYON, GEORGE L P01GM39552-05
KENYON, GEORGE L P41RR01614-10 0013
KENYON, GEORGE L R37AR17323-19
KENYON, JAMES P01DK41315-03 0004
KENYON, JAMES P01DK41315-03 9003
KENYON, KENNETH R R01EY05799-06
KEOGH, JAMES P K07ES00209-01
KEOGH, JAMES P R01CA48196-04
KEPHART, GEORGE C S07RR07082-26 0294
KEPLER, J A N01CM17511-00
KEPLER, JOHN A N01CM97561-02
KERBEL, ROBERT S R01CA41233-06
KERBEL, ROBERT S R13CA54796-01

KERBER, RICHARD E P50HL32295-07 0002
KERBER, RICHARD E R01HL43098-03
KERBESHIAN, LYNN S07RR05407-30 0045
KERCSMAR, CAROLYN M U01AI30751-01
KERGDER, JOHN W N01AI82687-03
KERKERING, THOMAS N01AI95034-04
KERKVLIET, NANCY I P01ES00040-27 0080
KERKVLIET, NANCY I P30ES00210-24 9009
KERKVLIET, NANCY I R01ES03966-05
KERN, DAVID S07RR05862-10 0561
KERN, DAVID F R01HL36763-05
KERN, DAVID F S07RR05959-06
KERN, DAVID F S15HL47785-01
KERN, EARL R N01AI15098-00
KERN, EARL R N01AI82518-03
KERN, EARL R U01AI31718-01 9001
KERN, FRANCIS G R01CA50376-03
KERN, FRED, JR R01DK31765-09
KERN, LAWRENCE N01CO03852-01
KERNAN, KEITH T P01HD11944-12 0003
KERNAN, NANCY A P01CA23766-14 0031
KERNER, JON F R01CA53083-02
KERNS, JAMES S07RR05477-29 0416
KERR, DOUGLAS S. P50HD11089-14 0026
KERR, DOUGLAS S07RR05410-30 0949
KERR, JEAN S07RR06014-03 0836
KERR, JOANNE T S06GM08192-12 0021
KERRIGAN, JAMES R K08HD00926-02
KERSEY, JOHN H. P01CA21737-14 9002
KERSEY, JOHN H P01CA21737-14
KERSEY, JOHN H R35CA49721-03
KERSHAW, GLENN R S07RR05712-20 0059
KERTESZ, ANDREW E R01EY01055-18
KERTZNER, ROBERT S07RR05650-25 0103
KERWIN, JAMES L R01AI22993-04A3
KESHAVAN, MATCHERI S R01MH45203-01A1
KESHISHIAN, HAIG P01GM39813-04 0005
KESHNER, EMILY A R29DC01125-01
KESNER, RAYMOND P R01DA06169-02
KESNER, RAYMOND P R01NS20771-07A1
KESNER, RAYMOND P S07RR07092-26 0529
KESSEL, DAVID P01CA48733-02 0003
KESSEL, DAVID H R01CA23378-12
KESSEL, DAVID H R01CA52997-02
KESSEL, RAYMOND R25AD00064-01
KESSIN, RICHARD H R01GM33136-09
KESSLER, BEATRICE N01DE92576-09
KESSLER, JOHN P30HD01799-27 9006
KESSLER, JOHN A P01NS07512-23 0043
KESSLER, JOHN A P30HD01799-27 9010
KESSLER, JOHN A R01NS20013-08
KESSLER, JOHN A R01NS27778-08
KESSLER, MARKUS R01NS21860-06
KESSLER, MATT J N01AI05057-04
KESSLER, MATTHEW J P40RR03640-05 9001
KESSLER, MATTHEW J P40RR03640-05
KESSLER, PAUL D K11HL02379-03
KESSLER, ROBERT M R01MH46943-02
KESSLER, RONALD C K02MH00507-08
KESSLER, RONALD C R01MH41135-05
KESSLER, RONALD C R01MH46376-03
KESSLER, RONALD C R37MH42714-05
KESSLER, S SIM N01LM13524-00
KESSLER, SHEILA N01LM83509-06
KESTER, MARK R29AR40225-02
KESTERSON, LEE S07RR05583-27 0631
KESTLER, DANIEL P S07RR05371-30 0640
KETNER, GARY W R01AI26239-01A2
KETTERING, JAMES S07RR05352-30 0748
KETTMAN, JOHN P01AI11851-18 9003
KETTMAN, JOHN P01AI11851-18 0012
KETTMAN, JOHN P01AI11851-18 0021
KETTMAN, JOHN P01AI11851-18 0011
KETY, S S Z01MH02288-07
KETY, SEYMOUR S P01MH31154-14 0005
KETY, SEYMOUR S P01MH31154-14 0006
KETY, SEYMOUR S P01MH31154-14 0007
KEULKS, GEORGE W S07RR07181-13
KEUSCH, GERALD T P01AI26698-03S1
KEUSCH, GERALD T R01AI16242-10
KEUTMANN, HENRY T P30HD28138-01 9004
KEUTMANN, HENRY T R01HD12851-12
KEUTMANN,HENRY T P01DK11794-24 9002
KEVETTER, GOLDA A K04DC00052-01
KEW, RICHARD R S07RR05736-19 0197
KEY, CHARLES N01CN05228-08
KEY, JOE L R01GM30317-11
KEY, JOE L S07RR07025-26
KEY, JOE L S07RR07025-26 0990
KEY, L LYNDON, JR R01AR41463-01
KEYES, MELVIN H R44HL39342-04
KEYES, P LANDIS S07RR05383-30 0561
KEYL, PENELOPE M R01AG08327-03
KEYNTON, ROBERT S R03AG10398-01
KEYOMARSI, KHANDAN S07RR05526-29 0083
KEYS, RICHARD T S06GM08101-20 0033
KEYSER, KENT T R01EY07845-03
KEYSER, SAMUEL J S07RR07047-26 0139
KEYSERLING, HARRY P01AI19554-08S1 0009
KEYSERLING, HARRY P01AI19554-08S1 9002
KEYSERLING, HARRY L P51RR00165-31 0192
KEYZER, HENDRIK S03RR03192-11

KEZDY, FERENC P01NS24304-05 0005
KHAKOO, YUSUF N01HB97058-03
KHALEDI, MORTEZA G R29GM38738-03
KHALEDI, MORTEZA G S07RR07071-26 0259
KHALID, SYED R43CA54657-01
KHALILI, KAMEL R01AI28272-02
KHALILI, KAMEL R29CA47996-04
KHALKHALI, IRAJ S07RR05551-29 0968
KHALSA, HARI K P50DA07699-01 0003
KHAN-DAWOOD, FIRYAL S R01HD24928-03
KHAN, A Z01AI00588-02
KHAN, A S Z01AI00353-09
KHAN, SAEED R R01DK41434-01A2
KHAN, SALEEM P30CA47904-04 9018
KHAN, SALEEM A K04AI00742-05
KHAN, SALEEM A R01GM31685-10
KHAN, SHABBIR A P01AI25380-05 9001
KHAN, SHABBIR A R01AI27422-03
KHAN, SHAHID M R01GM36936-06
KHAN, SOHAIB A R01HD22918-04A1
KHAN, SOHAIB A S07RR05408-30 0931
KHANDEKAR, JANARDAN D U10CA35199-08
KHANDERIA, B K M01RR00585-20 0564
KHANNA, SHYAM P01DC00316-06 0005
KHANNA, SHYAM P01DC00316-06 0006
KHANNA, SHYAM P01DC00316-06 0002
KHANNA, SHYAM M P01DC00316-06
KHATRA, BALWANT S07RR07232-05 0467
KHATRA, BALWANT S S06GM08238-05 0011
KHAW, BAN-AN R01CA50505-02
KHOKHAR, ABDUL R R01CA41581-06
KHOO, MICHAEL P41RR01861-07 9010
KHOO, MICHAEL C K04HL02536-02
KHOOBEHI, BAHRAM R01EY08137-03
KHOOR, ANDRAS S07RR05424-30 0099
KHORANA, HAR G R01AI11479-17
KHORANA, HAR G R37GM28289-11
KHOSLA, MAHESH C P01HL06835-30 0089
KHOT, V Z01MH02458-03
KHOURI, ROGER K S07RR05389-30 0639
KHOURY, EMILIO S07RR05305-30 0732
KHRAIBI, ALI A R29HL41533-02
KIANG, DAVID T R01CA51487-02
KIANG, NELSON Y P01DC00119-16 9001
KIANG, NELSON Y P01DC00119-16
KIANG, NELSON Y P01DC00119-16 0003
KICHER, THOMAS P S07RR07113-24 0569
KIDD, GARY R R29DC00545-01A3
KIDD, GERALD D, JR R01DC00597-03
KIDD, KENNETH K P01HG00365-04 0002
KIDD, KENNETH K P50MH30929-15 9005
KIDD, KENNETH K R01CA32066-08
KIDD, KENNETH K R37MH39239-08
KIDD, VINCENT P50AI23694-06 0008
KIDD, VINCENT J R01GM44088-02
KIDOKORO, YOSHIAKI R01NS23753-06
KIEBURTZ, KARL D M01RR00044-31 0389
KIECKHEFER, GAIL S07RR05758-18 0249
KIECOLT-GLASER, JANICE M01RR00034-31 0397
KIECOLT-GLASER, JANICE K P01MH44660-04 0001
KIECOLT-GLASER, JANICE K R01MH42096-05
KIEFER, DAVID J N43DK12279-00
KIEFF, ELLIOTT D R35CA47006-05
KIEHART, DANIEL P R01GM33830-08
KIEL, DOUGLAS P R01AR41398-01
KIELIAN, MARGARET C R01GM38743-05
KIEN, C LAWRENCE M01RR00034-31 0368
KIEN, CRAIG L R01HD19773-08
KIENZLE, MICHAEL G M01RR00059-30 0634
KIER, ANN P01ES05652-01 9004
KIER, ANN B R01AI29654-01A1
KIERAS, FRED J S07RR05838-12 0266
KIERNAN, FRANK H. P51RR00165-31 9013
KIERSZENBAUM, ABRAHAM L R01HD11884-13
KIERSZENBAUM, FELIPE R01AI24874-03
KIERSZENBAUM, FELIPE R01AI26542-03
KIESEL, BRUCE N01LM13540-00
KIESEWETTER, D O Z01CL09002-01
KIESLER, SARA B K02MH00533-07
KIESSLING, ANN A R01CA53899-02
KIHLSTROM, JOHN F R37MH35856-12
KIICK, DENNIS M R29GM43307-02
KIJEWSKI, MARIE P01CA41167-06 0001
KIJEWSKI, MARIE S07RR05950-07 0004
KILBERG, MICHAEL S R01DK28374-10A1
KILBERG, MICHAEL S R01DK31580-09
KILBOURN, MICHAEL A. P50NS15655-12 9005
KILBOURN, MICHAEL R P50NS15655-12 9002
KILBOURN, MICHAEL R P50NS15655-12 0009
KILBOURN, MICHAEL R R01MH47611-01A1
KILBRIDE, PAUL E R43EY08791-01A1
KILBURN, DANNY N01CO15780-00
KILDUFF, MICHAEL N01LM93528-05
KILENY, PAUL R M01RR00042-31 0473
KILENY, PAUL R P01DC00274-08 0006
KILEY, PATRICIA J R01GM45844-01
KILLARY, ANN M R01HG00042-02
KILLARY, ANN M R29GM37999-06
KILLEEN, MAUREEN R K07MH00764-03
KILLEEN, PETER R S07RR07112-24 0415
KILLEN, PAUL P01HL31963-08 0006
KILLEN, PAUL D R01DK44848-01

KILLIAN, GARY J S07RR07082-26 0295
KILLIANY, DENNIS M R29DE08165-02
KILLIEN, MARCIA G R01NR01920-03
KILLINGSWORTH, CHERYL R K11HL01900-05
KILLINGSWORTH, MARK R R01HS06854-01
KILLION, CHERYL M R01NR02030-03
KILPATRICK, C WILLIA S07RR07125-22 0391
KILPATRICK, D P01MH47200-02 0007
KILPATRICK, DANIEL L R01DK36468-06
KILPATRICK, DAVID S07RR05357-30 0452
KILPATRICK, DEAN G R01DA05220-03
KILPATRICK, DEAN G R01MH47508-01A1
KILTS, CLINTON D P50DA05303-03 0002
KILTS, CLINTON D R01MH39967-06
KIM, BENJAMIN S07RR05428-30 0182
KIM, BYUNG S P60AR30692-08 0017
KIM, BYUNG S R01AI15446-09
KIM, BYUNG S R01NS28752-02
KIM, C H M01RR00585-20 0551
KIM, CHARLES S07RR05736-19 0153
KIM, CHRISTINE P30HD24051-03 9006
KIM, DO HAN P01HL33026-07 0006
KIM, DONGHEE R29HL40586-05
KIM, DUCK O R01DC00360-07A1
KIM, H Y Z01AA00284-02
KIM, HELEN R01AG09683-01
KIM, I H Z01DK25074-04
KIM, JAE H R01CA53114-01A1
KIM, JAE HO P01CA29502-11A1 0039
KIM, JANICE J R29AI28871-02
KIM, JIN K P01DK19928-13 0018
KIM, JIN K P01DK19928-13 9001
KIM, JONG HWAN P01NS28059-01A1 0005
KIM, JUNG H P01AG03106-09 0002
KIM, JUNG-JA P R01GM29076-09
KIM, KE CHUNG S07RR07082-26 0296
KIM, KI-HAN R01CA46882-04
KIM, KWAN H R29HD25094-03
KIM, KWANG C R01HL47125-01
KIM, KWANG S R01NS26310-04
KIM, KWANG-JIN R01HL38658-04
KIM, KYUNGMANN R01EY09252-01
KIM, KYUNGMANN R29CA52733-02
KIM, PETER S R01GM41307-03
KIM, PETER S R01GM44162-02
KIM, R Y Z01EY00274-01
KIM, S W P41RR01296-08 0009
KIM, STUART S07RR05353-30 0350
KIM, STUART K R01GM43977-01A1
KIM, SUN KEE M01RR00042-31 0667
KIM, SUNG W R01HL17623-17A1
KIM, SUNG W R01HL44539-04A1
KIM, SUNG-HOU R01AI30725-01
KIM, SUNG-HOU R01CA45593-05
KIM, SUNG-HOU R01DC00145-12
KIM, SUNG-WAN R01DK36598-06
KIM, SUNG-WAN R01HL20251-14
KIM, SUNYOUNG R29AI30897-01
KIM, SYNGCUK R13DE09917-01
KIM, SYNGYCK S07RR05331-28 0741
KIM, YONG I R01NS18607-09
KIM, YOON H K11AR01850-01A1
KIM, YOUNG D R01GM42045-01A2
KIM, YOUNG J R01HD19145-08
KIM, YOUNG S R01CA24321-13
KIM, YOUNG S R37DK17938-18
KIM, YOUNG W R44AI28151-02
KIMBALL, ALLYN W P01NS15080-12 9008
KIMBALL, ALLYN W P30HD06268-18 9004
KIMBALL, PAMELA S07RR05745-19 0242
KIMBERLING, WILLIAM P01DK34039-06A1 0006
KIMBERLING, WILLIAM P50DC00215-08 0006
KIMBERLING, WILLIAM S07RR05834-12 0539
KIMBERLING, WILLIAM J R01DC00677-02
KIMBERLY, ROBER S07RR05495-29 0471
KIMBERLY, ROBERT P60AR38520-04 0003
KIMBERLY, ROBERT P R01AR33062-08
KIMBLE, JUDITH E R01GM31816-09
KIMBLE, JUDITH E R01HD24663-04
KIMELBERG, HAROLD K P20NS30303-01
KIMELBERG, HAROLD K P20NS30303-01 0001
KIMELBERG, HAROLD K R01NS19492-08
KIMELBERG, HAROLD K R01NS23750-05
KIMELMAN, DAVID R01HD27262-02
KIMES, A S Z01DA00210-05
KIMLER, BRUCE F R01NS16694-09
KIMMEL, A R Z01DK15503-10
KIMMEL, CHARLES P01HD22486-05 0003
KIMMEL, CHARLES P01HD22486-05 9001
KIMMEL, CHARLES B R01NS17963-10
KIMMEL, DANIEL B P50AR39221-05 9005
KIMMEL, DONALD B P50AR39221-05 0003
KIMMEL, PAUL S07RR05359-30 0513
KIMMEL, PAUL L R01DK40811-03
KIMMICH, GEORGE A R01DK15365-20
KIMSEY, PAUL S07RR07047-26 0148
KIMURA, JAMES H P50AR39239-05 9001
KIMURA, JAMES H R01AR38650-04
KIMURA, ROBERT S R01DC00073-30
KIMURA, S Z01CP05522-06
KINASEWITZ, GARY T R01HL27999-08
KINBERLY, ROBERT P60AR38520-04 9001

KINCADE, PAUL W R01AI19884-10
KINCADE, PAUL W R37AI20069-09
KINCAID, DWIGHT T S06GM08225-07 0008
KINCAID, JAMES R R01DK35153-07
KINCAID, R L Z01AA00404-04
KINCAID, STEVEN A R15AR40913-01
KINDER, BARBARA K S07RR05358-30 0492
KINDER, DAVID H S07RR05686-11 0980
KINDER, DAVID H S07RR05686-11 0977
KINDER, SUSAN A K11DE00212-05
KINDMAN, L ALLEN K11HL02361-02
KINDT, T J Z01AI00166-14
KINDT, T J Z01AI00168-14
KINDT, T J Z01AI00171-14
KINDT, T J Z01AI00180-13
KINDWALL, ERIC M01RR00058-30 0262
KINET, J Z01AI00594-02
KING-SMITH, P EWEN R01EY04948-08
KING, ABBY C K01AG00440-03
KING, ALBERT I R01NS28994-14
KING, ANNE M01RR00065-29 0367
KING, BARRY F R01HD11658-15
KING, BARRY F R01HD24491-04
KING, BRYAN H K20MH00917-01
KING, CHARLES P30CA22453-14 0001
KING, CHARLES P60AR20618-13 0015
KING, CHARLES H R29AI24645-05
KING, CHARLES M R37CA23386-14
KING, CHARLES R R44CA50077-03
KING, CHARLES R R44CA50811-02
KING, CHERYL A S07RR05383-30 0562
KING, DAVID K U10CA35262-08
KING, DONNA S07RR05366-30 0558
KING, DOUGLAS S07RR07034-26 0062
KING, GARRY C R29GM42913-01A2
KING, GARRY C S07RR07103-25 0500
KING, GEORGE L P30DK36836-05 9001
KING, GEORGE L R01EY05110-08
KING, GREGORY J R01DE08659-03
KING, GREGORY J R01DE08715-02
KING, JAMES C R01AI29816-02
KING, JAMES S R55NS08798-19
KING, JANET C P30HD22224-05S1 0001
KING, JANET C R01DK41732-03
KING, JOAN C R01HD19803-05
KING, JONATHAN A R37GM17980-22
KING, LLOYD E, JR R01DK26518-12
KING, M MARGARET S07RR05538-29 0543
KING, MARITA M R01GM42535-03
KING, MARY C R01CA27632-12
KING, MARY C R01DC01076-01
KING, MARY C R01HD25792-03
KING, MARY C R01HG00263-01
KING, MARY-CLAIRE P01GM28428-11 0008
KING, MICHAEL A R01CA42165-04A1
KING, MICHAEL A R01CA50641-02
KING, MICHAEL A S10RR06420-01
KING, N W P51RR00168-30 0140
KING, N W P51RR00168-30 0141
KING, NORVAL W P01DK36350-05S1 0001
KING, NORVAL W P51RR00168-30 9005
KING, NORVAL W P51RR00168-30 0177
KING, NORVAL W P51RR00168-30 9015
KING, NORVAL W P51RR00168-30 0100
KING, PETER C P30CA11198-23 9018
KING, PETER C P30CA11198-23 9019
KING, R P41RR01243-10 0027
KING, R P41RR01243-10 9005
KING, RAY J R43CA53941-01
KING, RICHARD A P01GM22167-16 0004
KING, RICHARD A P01GM22167-16
KING, RICHARD B P01HL38736-05 9002
KING, RICHARD B P41RR01243-10 0010
KING, RICHARD B P41RR01243-10 0003
KING, RICHARD J P50HL36536-05 0002
KING, RICHARD J R01HL40986-02
KING, RICHARD J R01HL43704-02
KING, ROSEMARIE B R01NR02416-01A1
KING, ROSEMARY S07RR06003-04 0368
KING, ROY J R29DA04789-04
KING, ROYCE G R19MH46235-03
KING, SPENCER B M01RR00039-31 0384
KING, SPENCER B R01HL33965-05
KING, STEPHEN S07RR05384-30 0778
KING, TALMADGE E P50HL27353-10 0007
KING, TE PIAO R01AI17021-12
KING, THOMAS P30CA13943-19 0013
KING, THOMAS C S07RR05818-12 0157
KING, THOMAS J R13CA40577-06
KING, THOMAS S P30HD10202-15 9006
KING, THOMAS S R01DA06039-02
KING, WILLIAM M R01EY04045-09
KINGHORN, A DOUGLAS P01CA48112-01A3 0002
KINGHORN, A DOUGLAS U01CA52956-02 0002
KINGHORN, ALAN D R01DE08937-01A2
KINGHORN, ALAN D S15CA55963-01
KINGMAN, A Z01DE00519-02
KINGMAN, A Z01DE00520-02
KINGMAN, A Z01DE00521-02
KINGMAN, A Z01DE00522-02
KINGRY, MARGARET S07RR05772-17 0344
KINGRY, MARGARET S07RR07049-26 0454
KINGSBURY, MILDRED E G07LM05275-01
KINGSFORD, LAURA S06GM08238-05 0006
KINGSFORD, LAURA S07RR07232-05 0466
KINGSLEY, PETER B R29HL42168-03
KINGSTON, DAVID G R01CA48974-02
KINGSTON, DAVID G R01CA55131-01
KINGSTON, DAVID G U01CA50771-03 0002
KINGSTON, ROBERT E R01GM43901-01A1
KINGSTON, WILLIAM J R29AR38193-05
KINKADE, JOSEPH M, JR R01CA22294-14
KINLAW, WILLIAM B R01DK43142-03
KINNAMON, J C P41RR00592-22 0019
KINNAMON, JOHN C P41RR00592-22 0009
KINNAMON, JOHN C R01DC00285-05A2
KINNAMON, SUE C P01DC00244-07 0005
KINNAMON, SUE C R01DC00766-02
KINNE, ROLF P30ES03828-06 0009
KINNE, SUSAN P01CA34847-09 9009
KINNEY, DENNIS P01MH31154-14 0008
KINNEY, DENNIS K R01MH46479-01A1
KINNEY, DENNIS K S07RR05484-29 0027
KINNEY, DENNIS K S07RR05484-29 0035
KINNEY, HANNAH C P30HD18655-10 9007
KINNEY, HANNAH C R01HD20991-06
KINNEY, JOHN H P01DE09859-01 0003
KINNEY, JOHN M P01CA29502-11A1 0059
KINNEY, MARSHA C S07RR05424-30 0116
KINNEY, ROLAND W N01OD62107-27
KINNEY, ROOSEVELT L R19DA06474-03
KINNEY, THOMAS R N01HB77036-07
KINNEY, THOMAS R P60HL28391-09 0001
KINNI, MARK S07RR05304-30 0216
KINNIBURGH, ALAN J P01CA41285-07 0005
KINNUNEN, PAULA M R29HL42032-03
KINON, BRUCE J P50MH41960-05S1 0002
KINOSIAN, BRUCE R55AG09837-01
KINSBOURNE, MARCEL P01DC00081-26 0018
KINSBOURNE, MARCEL R01MH37578-08
KINSELLA, J Z01AG00277-01
KINSELLA, TIMOTHY J P01CA52686-02 0002
KINSELLA, TIMOTHY J P01CA52686-02
KINSELLA, TIMOTHY J P01CA52686-02 0005
KINSELLA, TIMOTHY J R01CA50595-02
KINSEY, WILLIAM H R01HD14846-11
KINSMAN, STEPHEN L K08NS01455-02
KINTANAR, AGUSTIN S07RR07034-26 0063
KINTER, MICHAEL S07RR05431-30 0847
KINTNER, BARBARA A U42RR05081-03S1
KINTNER, CHRIS R R01HD23891-04
KINTSCH, WALTER R37MH15872-24
KINZIE, ROBERT A. S06GM08125-18 0051
KINZIE, ROBERT A. S06GM08125-18 0051
KINZIG, BARBARA J P01DE09696-01 0002
KIORPES, LYNNE P51RR00166-30 0096
KIORPES, LYNNE P51RR00166-30 0097
KIORPES, LYNNE R01EY05864-07
KIPLE, KENNETH F R01LM05320-01
KIPNIS, DAVID M P60DK20579-14
KIPPS, THOMAS J M01RR00833-17 0192
KIPPS, THOMAS J R01CA49870-04
KIPPS, THOMAS J R01CA54755-01
KIPPS, THOMAS J R55AG04100-08A1
KIPPS, THOMAS J. P01CA37497-07 0007
KIRASIC, KATHLEEN C R01AG06806-04
KIRBY, EDWARD P R01HL27993-07A2
KIRBY, EDWARD P S07RR05417-30 0796
KIRBY, MARGARET L P01HL36059-06 9001
KIRBY, MARGARET L P01HL36059-06
KIRBY, MARGARET L P01HL36059-06 0001
KIRCH, D G Z01MH02263-07
KIRCH, D G Z01MH02282-07
KIRCHBERGER, MADELEINE A R01HL15764-18
KIRCHER, JOHN C S07RR07092-26 0523
KIRCHGESSNER, ANNETTE L R01NS27645-03
KIRCHHAUSEN, TOMAS R01GM36548-05
KIRCHHAUSEN, TOMAS L S07RR05381-30 0780
KIRCHHOFF, LOUIS V R29AI24711-05
KIRCHNER, KENT A S07RR05386-30 0588
KIRCHNER, KENT A U01HL37854-06
KIRK, DAVID L R01GM27215-12
KIRK, DAVID N N01DK42201-08
KIRK, K L Z01DK31113-15
KIRK, KATHERINE A P50HL17667-17 9004
KIRK, KEVIN L P01DK38518-05 0004
KIRK, KEVIN L R01DK43974-01
KIRK, MARK DOUGLAS R29NS24662-06
KIRKCONNELL, SHIRLEY U01CA50121-03
KIRKEGAARD, KARLA A R29AI25166-05
KIRKLAND, JOHN L M01RR00188-27 0310
KIRKLAND, JOHN L M01RR00188-27 0189
KIRKLAND, JOHN L M01RR00188-27 0308
KIRKLAND, REBECCA T M01RR00188-27 0293
KIRKLIN, JOHN W P50HL17667-17 0073
KIRKMAN, ROBERT N01AI82512-08
KIRKMAN, ROBERT L P01AI23360-07 0005
KIRKNESS, E F Z01AA00485-02
KIRKPATRICK, BRIAN K20MH00925-01A1
KIRKPATRICK, CHARLES S07RR05842-12 0282
KIRKPATRICK, JOEL B P50AG08664-03 9003
KIRKPATRICK, MARK A R55GM45226-01
KIRKPATRICK, MARK, III R43AG09358-01A1
KIRKWOOD, JOHN M01RR00056-30 0362
KIRKWOOD, JOHN M U10CA39229-07
KIRLEY, TERENCE L K04AR01841-01A1
KIRLEY, TERENCE L R01AR38576-03
KIRLIN, WARD G S07RR05907-08 0637
KIRN, JOHN R R55NS29843-01
KIRON, RAVI S07RR05396-30 0749
KIRSCH, GLENN E R01NS29473-01A1
KIRSCH, I R Z01CM06579-08
KIRSCH, I R Z01CM06587-07
KIRSCH, JACK F R01GM35393-07
KIRSCH, JEFFREY R K08NS01225-05
KIRSCHNER, DANIEL A P30HD18655-10 9002
KIRSCHNER, DANIEL A R01AG08572-03
KIRSCHNER, DANIEL A R01NS20824-09
KIRSCHNER, MARC P01HL43821-02 0003
KIRSCHNER, MARC A K08NS01342-03
KIRSCHNER, MARC W P01GM31286-09 9001
KIRSCHNER, MARC W P01GM31286-09 0005
KIRSCHNER, MARC W P01GM31286-09
KIRSCHNER, MARC W R01GM39023-04
KIRSCHNER, MARC W R37GM26875-13
KIRSCHVINK, J S07RR07003-26 0329
KISBY, GLEN E S07RR07238-04 0482
KISBY, GLENN E P01NS19611-08 0004
KISH, STEPHEN J R01DA07182-01
KISH, STEPHEN J R01NS26034-04
KISHI, YOSHITO R01CA55148-01
KISHI, YOSHITO R01NS12108-17
KISHI, YOSHITO R37CA22215-14
KISHI, YOSHITO S10RR06716-01
KISHIMOTO, YASUO P01HD10981-14 0007
KISHIMOTO, YASUO R01NS13559-17A1
KISHORE, VIMAL S06GM08008-21 0016
KISIEL, WALTER R01HL35246-06
KISILEVSKY, ROBERT R01NS30361-01
KISKER, THOMAS C M01RR00059-30 0688
KISLALIOGLU, SERPIL S07RR07086-15 0325
KISLIUK, ROY L S07RR05382-30 0870
KISS, ZOLTAN S07RR07052-26 0161
KISSEBAH, AHMED M01RR00058-30 0254
KISSEBAH, AHMED M01RR00058-30 0256
KISSEBAH, AHMED H M01RR00058-30 0248
KISSIN, IGOR R01GM35135-06
KISSIN, IGOR R01GM39344-03
KISTLER, J PHILIP R01HL33233-07
KISTLER, W STEPHEN R01HD10793-14
KISZKISS, DAVID S07RR05591-27
KISZKISS, DAVID F S15CA55978-01
KITA, HITOSHI P01NS26473-04 0002
KITA, HITOSHI P41RR00592-22 0031
KITA, HITOSHI R01NS25783-04
KITABCHI, ABBAS M01RR00211-27 0237
KITABCHI, ABBAS E M01RR00211-27 0203
KITABCHI, ABBAS E M01RR00211-27 0311
KITABCHI, ABBAS E M01RR00211-27 0328
KITABCHI, ABBAS E S07RR05423-30 0063
KITABCHI, ABBAS E S07RR05423-30 0064
KITABCHI, ABBAS E U01DK30625-09
KITAHATA, LUKE M R01NS09871-20
KITAI, STEPHEN T P01NS26473-04
KITAI, STEPHEN T P01NS26473-04 0001
KITAI, STEPHEN T R01NS20702-09
KITCHELL, BARBARA E K11CA01561-01
KITCHINGMAN, GEOFFREY R R01AI17654-08
KITCHINGMAN, GEOFFREY R R01CA52259-01A2
KITOS, PAUL P30HD02528-25A1 9016
KITSON, GAY C S07RR07249-03 0725
KITT, CHERYL A P01HD24448-04 0002
KITTERMAN, JOSEPH A P50HL27356-10 0001
KITTNER, STEVEN J K08NS01319-04
KITTNER, STEVEN J P01NS16332-09A2 0001
KITTRELL, E. MELANIE P01AG06836-04 0004
KITTUR, DILIP S R29AI25550-03
KITZES, LEONARD P01DC00450-04 0002
KITZES, LEONARD M P01DC00450-04
KITZES, LEONARD M. P01DC00450-04 9001
KITZMAN, DALANE P30AG09463-01 0003
KITZMILLER, JOHN P01HD24180-04 0005
KIVIAT, NANCY P01AI29363-02 9002
KIVIAT, NANCY P01CA42792-05 9002
KIVIAT, NANCY R01CA50738-03
KIVIAT, NANCY R01CA50856-02
KIYAK, ASUMAN P30DE09743-02 0012
KIYAK, H ASUMAN N01DE12586-00
KIYAK, H ASUMAN R01DE07889-03
KIYONO, HIROSHI K04DE00237-04
KIYONO, HIROSHI R01AI19674-07
KIYONO, HIROSHI R01AI30366-02
KIYONO, HIROSHI R01DE09837-01
KIZER, JOHN S P50MH33127-13 0005
KJELSBERG, MARCUS O R01HL43232-02
KJERULFF, KRISTEN H R01HS06865-01
KLAASSEN, CURTIS D R01ES01142-17
KLAASSEN, CURTIS D R01ES03192-21
KLAFF, LESLIE P30DK17047-15 9002
KLAG, MICHAEL J R01AG01760-11
KLAG, MICHAEL J R01DK41837-01A2
KLAGSBRUN, MICHAEL R13CA54155-01
KLAGSBRUN, MICHAEL R37CA37392-10
KLAHR, DAVID R01HD25211-02
KLAHR, SAULO P01DK09976-27
KLAHR, SAULO P01DK09976-27 0014

KLAHR, SAULO P01DK09976-27 9001
KLAHR, SAULO R01DK40321-04
KLAHR, SAULO S07RR05491-29
KLAIBER, EDWARD L R01AG08751-02
KLAMEN, DEBRA S07RR05369-30 0595
KLAPES, N ARLENE S07RR07071-26 0252
KLAPPER, DAVID G R01AI14908-13
KLASS, MICHAEL P01AG10481-01 9002
KLASSEN, DEIDRE R01MH45484-02
KLASSEN, LYNELL W R01AA07818-03
KLAUS, ROBERT J N01DE02580-03
KLAUSNER, MITCHELL R43AR40797-01
KLAUSNER, MITCHELL R43MH48296-01S1
KLAUSNER, MITCHELL R44GM44418-02
KLAUSNER, R D Z01HD01602-07
KLAUSNER, R D Z01HD01605-05
KLAUSNER, R D Z01HD01606-04
KLEBAN, MORTON S07RR05611-22 0712
KLEBANOFF, M A Z01HD00334-09
KLEBANOFF, M A Z01HD00346-07
KLEBANOFF, M A Z01HD00366-04
KLEBANOFF, M A Z01HD00369-03
KLEBANOFF, M A Z01HD00370-03
KLEBANOFF, M A Z01HD00379-02
KLEBANOFF, M A Z01HD00382-01
KLEBANOFF, M A Z01HD00383-01
KLEBANOFF, SEYMOUR J R01AI17758-10
KLEBANOFF, SEYMOUR J R37AI07763-25
KLEBE, KELLY P30HD24051-03 9003
KLEBE, ROBERT J R01DE08144-04
KLECH, CATHY M S07RR07072-26 0268
KLECKNER, NANCY E R01GM44794-02
KLECKNER, NANCY E R37GM25326-14
KLEE, C B Z01CB05231-17
KLEE, THOMAS M S07RR07157-16 0577
KLEE, W A Z01MH00934-19
KLEEBERGER, STEVEN R P01ES03505-07 0005
KLEEMAN, CHARLES S07RR05468-29 0409
KLEENE, STEVEN J R55DC00926-01A1
KLEEREKOPER, MICHAEL R01AR39657-03
KLEEREKOPER, MICHAEL U01AG10407-01
KLEI, THOMAS R R22AI19199-08
KLEIMAN, NORMAN J R01EY08750-01A1
KLEIN , GEORGE R01CA30264-10
KLEIN-SZANTO, ANDRE J R01CA53713-01
KLEIN-SZANTO, ANDRES S07RR05895-09 0611
KLEIN-SZANTO, ANDRES J R01CA44980-06
KLEIN-SZANTO, ANDRES J R01CA44981-05
KLEIN, SAM M01RR00073-29 0258
KLEIN, BARBARA E R01EY08012-03
KLEIN, BRADLEY G R01DE08966-02
KLEIN, BRUCE S K11AI00905-04
KLEIN, BRUCE S R29AI31479-01
KLEIN, CHERYL L S06GM08008-21
KLEIN, CHERYL L S06GM08008-21 0017
KLEIN, CLAUDETTE R01GM34561-06
KLEIN, D C Z01HD00094-21
KLEIN, D C Z01HD00095-21
KLEIN, DANIEL N R01MH45757-01A1
KLEIN, DANIEL N S07RR07067-26 0218
KLEIN, DAVID J R01DK39786-05
KLEIN, DAVID J S07RR05385-30 0808
KLEIN, DONALD F P01MH37592-08
KLEIN, DONALD F P50MH30906-14
KLEIN, ERIC A P01CA48919-01A2 9002
KLEIN, EVA R01CA25250-12
KLEIN, GEORGE R01CA14054-18
KLEIN, GEORGE R01CA52225-02
KLEIN, HANNAH S07RR05399-30 0910
KLEIN, HANNAH L R01GM30439-10
KLEIN, JAMES D R44RR06809-03
KLEIN, JAN R01AI23667-06
KLEIN, JERRY P01CA43791-04A1 0002
KLEIN, JOHN P R01CA54706-01
KLEIN, JOHN P R13CA54325-01
KLEIN, JOHN R R01DK35566-07
KLEIN, JON B S07RR05375-30 0757
KLEIN, JONATHON S07RR05372-30 0654
KLEIN, KENNETH B M01RR00046-31 0411
KLEIN, LARRY L U01AI30183-02 0001
KLEIN, MARC R01MH45397-03
KLEIN, MICHAEL R01GM40712-04
KLEIN, MICHAEL L U10EY06488-07
KLEIN, MICHAEL L U10EY06777-04
KLEIN, NORMAN W R01ES04312-05
KLEIN, PAUL P01DK39079-05 9002
KLEIN, PETER M01RR00350-25 0484
KLEIN, RACHEL P50MH43878-03 0001
KLEIN, RACHEL P50MH43878-03 0022
KLEIN, RACHEL P50MH43878-03 0034
KLEIN, RACHEL P50MH43878-03 0023
KLEIN, RACHEL P50MH43878-03 0030
KLEIN, RACHEL G P01MH37592-08 0005
KLEIN, RACHEL G R01MH18579-19
KLEIN, RACHEL G R37MH35779-07
KLEIN, ROBERT F S07RR05412-30 0969
KLEIN, ROBERT S R01CA24634-12
KLEIN, RONALD R01EY03083-13
KLEIN, RONALD U10EY06594-05
KLEIN, SAMUEL M01RR00073-29 0280
KLEIN, SAMUEL M01RR00073-29 0295
KLEIN, SAMUEL M01RR00073-29 0320
KLEIN, SAMUEL R29CA50330-02
KLEIN, STANLEY A R01EY04776-08
KLEIN, STANLEY A S07RR05832-12 0196
KLEIN, STEVEN L R03DC01196-01
KLEIN, STEVEN L R29HD23324-05
KLEIN, THOMAS W R01DA05568-02
KLEIN, WILLIAM P01AG10481-01 0005
KLEIN, WILLIAM S07RR05511-29 0495
KLEIN, WILLIAM H R01HD22619-07
KLEIN, WILLIAM L R01AG09337-01A1
KLEIN, WILLIAM L R01NS21234-07
KLEINBERG, DAVID M01RR00096-30A1 0276
KLEINBERG, DAVID M01RR00096-30A1 0185
KLEINBERG, DAVID M01RR00096-30A1 0300
KLEINBERG, DAVID M01RR00096-30A1 0186
KLEINBERG, MICHAEL S07RR05379-30 0763
KLEINBERG, MICHAEL L P30CA08748-26 9037
KLEINERMAN, EUGENIE S R01CA42992-06
KLEINFELD, ALAN M R01GM44171-01A1
KLEINFELD, ALAN M R43HL44818-01A2
KLEINHENZ, MARY E K07HL02099-05
KLEINMAN, H Z01DE00482-03
KLEINMAN, H K Z01DE00230-16
KLEINMAN, J E Z01MH02399-06
KLEINMAN, STEVEN N01HB97080-04
KLEINSCHMIDT, JOCHEN R01EY05213-07
KLEINSCHMIDT, JOCHEN S07RR05399-30 0921
KLEINSTEIN, BRUCE N01LM13523-00
KLEINSTEIN, BRUCE N01LM83507-03
KLEINSTEIN, ROBERT N S07RR05807-13 0457
KLEINZELLER, ARNOST P30ES03828-06 0010
KLEINZELLER, ARNOST S07RR05415-30 0011
KLEMP, SUZANNE G S07RR05357-30 0447
KLEMPNER, MARK S P50AI24848-05 0005
KLEMPNER, MARK S R01AI16732-11
KLEMPNER, MARK S R01AR41500-01
KLEPINGER, DANIEL H R55HD28427-01
KLEPPER, JOHN RICHARD S15CA56010-01
KLERMAN, GERALD L U01MH43077-05
KLESGES, ROBERT C R01HL39332-04
KLESGES, ROBERT C R03HL46117-02
KLESGES, ROBERT C R18HL45057-01A1
KLESSIG, DANIEL F R01AI23591-07
KLETZIEN, ROLF F R01AA06728-05
KLETZKY, OSCAR A M01RR00425-22S3 0458
KLEVECZ, ROBERT P30CA33572-11 9004
KLEVECZ, ROBERT R R01CA49203-08
KLEVECZ, ROBERT R S07RR05841-12 0239
KLEVIT, RACHEL P01GM32681-08 0005
KLEVIT, RACHEL E R01DK35187-07
KLIAUGA, PAUL P01CA12536-20 0016
KLIBANSKI, ANNE M01RR01066-14 0071
KLIBANSKI, ANNE M01RR01066-14 0086
KLIBANSKI, ANNE M01RR01066-14 0035
KLIBANSKI, ANNE R01DK40947-03
KLIBANSKI, ANNE R55HD21204-04A2
KLIEGER, DOUGLAS M S07RR07260-02 0550
KLIEGMAN, ROBERT M R01HD20851-04A3
KLIGER, DAVID S R01EY00983-19
KLIGER, DAVID S R01GM35158-07
KLIGER, DAVID S R01GM38549-05
KLIGER, DAVID S S15GM47030-01
KLIKS, SRISAKUL C R01AI32446-01
KLIMAN, HARVEY S07RR05415-30 0012
KLIMAN, HARVEY S07RR07083-26 0474
KLIMPEL, GARY R01AI23731-04
KLIMPEL, GARY R01AI31519-01
KLINE, DOUGLAS W R01HD26032-04
KLINE, JENNIE P50MH43520-04 0001
KLINE, JENNIE K R55AG10251-01
KLINE, KIMBERLY R29CA45422-04
KLINE, LAWRENCE M01RR00833-17 0006
KLINE, LEWIS P50HL42236-04 9002
KLINE, LEWIS R M01RR00040-31 0340
KLINE, RICHARD P R01HL42353-01A3
KLINENBERG, JAMES R S07RR05468-29
KLINENBERG, JAMES R S15DK44695-01
KLING, O RAY S15AA09263-01
KLING, PAMELA M01RR00059-30 0714
KLINGENSMITH, GEORGEANNA M01RR00069-29 023
KLINGENSMITH, GEORGEANNA M01RR00069-29 032
KLINGER, HAROLD P R01CA51395-02
KLINGER, KATHERINE W R01DK44853-01
KLINGER, MARTIN J S07RR05676-15 0962
KLINGER, ROCHELLE M01RR00065-29 0349
KLINMAN, D M Z01BF04003-03
KLINMAN, JUDITH P P41RR01614-10 0005
KLINMAN, JUDITH P R01GM39296-04
KLINMAN, JUDITH P R37GM25765-14
KLINMAN, NORMAN R M01RR00833-17 0201
KLINMAN, NORMAN R P01AG01743-12 9001
KLINMAN, NORMAN R P01AG01743-12 0002
KLINMAN, NORMAN R P01AG01743-12
KLINMAN, NORMAN R P01AI19499-08 0003
KLINMAN, NORMAN R P01AI19499-08 9001
KLINMAN, NORMAN R P01AI19499-08
KLINMAN, NORMAN R R37AI15797-14
KLINNERT, MARY D R01MH44729-01A2
KLINTWORTH, GORDON K P30EY05722-06A1
KLINTWORTH, GORDON K R01EY00146-20
KLINTWORTH, GORDON K R01EY08249-03
KLIONSKY, DANIEL J R01DK43684-01
KLISH, WILLIAM M01RR00188-27 0335
KLISH, WILLIAM J M01RR00188-27 0307
KLISH, WILLIAM J M01RR00188-27 0311
KLITZMAN, BRUCE M P01HL36552-07 9001
KLITZMAN, BRUCE M P01HL42444-02 0004
KLOBUTCHER, LAWRENCE A R01GM33277-07A1
KLOCKE, FRANCIS J P01HL15194-20 0001
KLOCKE, FRANCIS J P01HL15194-20 9001
KLOCKE, FRANCIS J P01HL15194-20 9002
KLOCKE, ROBERT A R01HL46013-01
KLOPFENSTEIN, HAROLD S R01HL42254-04
KLOPMANN, GILLES S07RR07113-24 0571
KLOPOTEK, PETER J R43EY09017-01
KLORMAN, RAFAEL R01MH38118-05
KLORMAN, RAFAEL R01MH47333-01A1
KLOSE, K JOHN P01NS28059-01A1 0001
KLOSE, KATHLEEN P41LM05205-08 9010
KLOTMAN, M E Z01CP05689-01
KLOTMAN, P Z01DK00508-02
KLOTMAN, PAUL E P01DK38108-04 9001
KLOTMAN, PAUL E P01DK38108-04 0001
KLOTZ, JOAN S07RR05354-30 0393
KLOTZ, JOAN L P01AR40919-01 0003
KLUCAS, ROBERT S07RR07055-26 0192
KLUEBER, KATHLEEN R29DK41553-04
KLUENDER, KEITH R R29DC00719-02
KLUG, THOMAS N43DK12274-00
KLUGER, ALAN R29MH44697-03
KLUGER, MATTHEW J R01AI27556-01A3
KLUGER, MATTHEW J R01MH48609-01
KLUMPP, SHERRY S07RR07023-26 0980
KLUMPP, SHERRY A P51RR00165-31 0183
KLUNK, W E R35AG08974-01 0005
KLUNK, WILLIAM E P50AG05133-08 0009
KLUNKEL, GARY R S07RR07090-26 0482
KLUVE-BECKERMAN, BARBARA P60AR20582-14 900
KLUVE-BECKERMAN, BARBARA R29DK42657-02
KLUVE-BECKMAN, BARBARA P60AR20582-14 0002
KLYCE, STEPHEN D R01EY03311-12S1
KMETZ, DONALD R S07RR05375-30
KNABEL, STEPHEN J S07RR07082-26 0297
KNAFL, KATHLEEN A R01NR01594-05
KNAFL, KATHLEEN A S03RR03411-07
KNAFL, KATHLEEN A S07RR05776-11
KNAFL, KATHLEEN A S15AG10562-01
KNAPE, KELLY G S07RR05654-24 0129
KNAPP, ANDREW G R43NS29907-01
KNAPP, CHARLES F M01RR02602-07 0037
KNAPP, DANIEL R R01EY08239-03
KNAPP, GAYLE S07RR07093-24 0775
KNAPP, HOWARD M01RR00095-31 0374
KNAPP, HOWARD R P50GM15431-24 0130
KNAPP, HOWARD R R01HL35380-06
KNAPP, ROBERT M01RR02635-07 0228
KNAPP, ROGER D P60HL27341-10 9001
KNAPP, STUART E S06GM08218-08 0025
KNAPPENBERGER, ROBERT R19DA06424-03
KNATTERUD, GENELL L N01HC75076-13
KNATTERUD, GENELL L N01HV18114-04
KNATTERUD, GENELL L R01HL41384-03
KNATTERUD, GENELL L R01HL42428-03
KNAUER, DANIEL J R01GM34001-07
KNAUF, PHILIP A P01HL18208-17 0013
KNAUF, PHILIP A R01DK27495-12
KNAUS, WILLIAM A R01HS05787-04
KNAZEK, RICHARD A R43CA54694-01
KNECHT, DAVID A R01GM40599-04
KNEPPER, JANICE E R29CA52853-02
KNEPPER, M A Z01HL01282-05
KNESEVICH, JOHN W P50MH31302-14 0023
KNIGHT, BRUCE W, JR R01EY01428-16
KNIGHT, D R P51RR00168-30 0135
KNIGHT, HERBERT S07RR05431-30 0833
KNIGHT, KATHERINE L R01AI16611-12
KNIGHT, KATHERINE L R37AI11234-20
KNIGHT, KENDALL L R01GM44772-01A1
KNIGHT, KENDALL L S07RR05712-20 0060
KNIGHT, LINDA C R01AA07735-03
KNIGHT, PAUL R, III R01GM28911-10
KNIGHT, PAUL R, III R01GM39227-01A2
KNIGHT, RAYMOND A R01MH32309-10
KNIGHT, ROBERT P50AG05142-08 9009
KNIGHT, ROBERT T R01NS21135-06
KNIGHTON, ROBERT W P30EY02180-14
KNIGHTON, ROBERT W R01EY08684-02
KNIPE, DAVID P01AI24010-05 0002
KNIPE, DAVID M R01AI20530-08
KNIPE, DAVID M R01AI31500-01
KNIPE, DAVID M R37CA26345-12
KNOBIL, ERNST R37HD17438-10
KNOBLER, ROBERT L R01NS22145-04
KNOCHEL, PAUL R01GM41908-03
KNOKE, JAMES N01HD13121-00
KNOPF, PAUL M R22AI31224-01
KNOPMAN, DAVID M01RR00400-23 0279
KNOPP, ROBERT H M01RR00037-31 0514
KNOPP, ROBERT H M01RR00037-31 0284
KNOPP, ROBERT H R01HL44878-01A1
KNOPP, ROBERT H U01HL44299-02
KNOTT, GARY R44CA44076-03
KNOTT, GARY D R43LM05343-01
KNOTT, GARY D R43RR07544-01

KNOWLER, W C Z01DK69000-26
KNOWLER, W C Z01DK69025-05
KNOWLER, W C Z01DK69028-03
KNOWLER, W C Z01DK69036-02
KNOWLER, W C Z01DK69038-02
KNOWLER, W C Z01DK69039-02
KNOWLER, W C Z01DK69040-02
KNOWLES, AILEEN F S07RR07143-20 0627
KNOWLES, B B P01HD21355-04 0002
KNOWLES, BARBARA B P01CA21124-14 0010
KNOWLES, BARBARA B P01HD21355-04
KNOWLES, BARBARA B R01CA18470-15
KNOWLES, BARBARA B R01CA37225-07
KNOWLES, DANIEL P01AI26886-04 9002
KNOWLES, DANIEL M R01CA48236-04
KNOWLES, DANIEL M R01EY06337-08
KNOWLES, JEREMY R R01GM37007-06
KNOWLES, JEREMY R R37GM21659-17
KNOWLES, JEREMY R S15GM47070-01
KNOWLES, MICHAEL M01RR00046-31 0472
KNOWLES, MICHAEL M01RR00046-31 0525
KNOWLES, MICHAEL R M01RR00046-31 0326
KNOWLES, MICHAEL R M01RR00046-31 0232
KNOWLES, MICHAEL R P01HL34322-06 0006
KNOWLES, MICHEAL R. M01RR00046-31 0304
KNOWLTON, ANNE A K11HL01853-05
KNOWLTON, KIRK U K08HL02618-01
KNOWLTON, KIRK U M01RR00827-17 0412
KNOWLTON, ROBERT G P01AR39740-03 0001
KNOX, BARRY E S07RR05402-30 0799
KNOX, CRAIG P50AG05144-08 9001
KNOX, FRANKLYN G R01DK19715-14A1
KNOX, FRANKLYN G R01HL14133-21
KNOX, ROBERT S07RR07069-26 0247
KNUDSEN, ERIC I R01DC00155-12
KNUDSEN, ERIC I R01NS27687-02
KNUDSEN, KAREN A R01AR37945-05
KNUDSEN, THOMAS B R29HD25143-04
KNUDSON, ALFRED G R01CA43211-06
KNUDSON, CHERYL B R29AR39507-01A3
KNUDSON, RONALD J P50HL14136-20 0001
KNUDSON, RONALD J P50HL14136-20 9002
KNUEPFER, MARK M R01DA05180-03
KNULL, HARVEY S07RR05407-30 0049
KNUTSON, J R Z01HL01452-08
KNUTSON, JOHN P50DC00242-07 0002
KNUTSON, KRISTINE R01HD23000-04A2
KO, DAIJIN P01NS25630-03 9001
KO, LI-WEN P01AG03853-09 9002
KO, WEN H P41RR02024-08 9002
KOBASA, SUZANNE P60AR38520-04 0008
KOBAYASHI, GEORGE S N01AI72640-10
KOBAYASHI, GEORGE S R01AI29609-02
KOBAYASHI, KAZUMI R44GM41547-03
KOBILKA, BRIAN K R01NS28471-02
KOBLER, JAMES B R29DC01294-01
KOBLIKA, BRIAN K P50HL17670-17 0033
KOBLIN, DONALD D P01AG03104-10 0008
KOBZIK, LESTER S07RR05446-30 0275
KOCEJA, DAVID S07RR07031-26 0094
KOCH, ALISA E. P60AR30692-08 0011
KOCH, ARTHUR L S07RR07031-26 0095
KOCH, C S07RR07003-26 0318
KOCH, CAMERON J R01CA49498-03
KOCH, RICHARD N01HD43807-14
KOCH, TAD H R01CA24665-13
KOCH, TIMOTHY R. M01RR00058-30 0223
KOCH, WILLIAM S07RR05430-30 0223
KOCHANEK, PATRICK M S07RR05416-30 0564
KOCHANSKA, G Z01MH02369-05
KOCHANSKA, G Z01MH02444-03
KOCHANSKA, G Z01MH02489-02
KOCHERSBERGER, GARY S07RR05405-30 0873
KOCHEVAR, IRENE E R01GM30755-11
KOCHHAR, DEVENDRA M R37HD20925-06
KOCHHAR, T S S14GM05231-04 0002
KOCHHAR, TEJINDER S S14GM05231-04
KOCIBA, GARY J R01DK41939-03
KOCSIS, JAMES M01RR00047-31 0476
KOCSIS, JAMES H R01MH37103-07
KODA, LEONARD Y P50AA06420-08 0002
KODADEK, THOMAS J R01GM39393-04
KODAMA, VICKI N01LM93532-03
KOECHEL, DANIEL S07RR05700-22 0875
KOEFFLER, H PHILIP P01CA42710-06A1 9006
KOEFFLER, H PHILIP P01DK42792-01A1 0005
KOEFFLER, H PHILIP R01CA26038-12
KOEFFLER, PHILLIP H R01CA33936-09
KOEFFLER, PHILLIP H R01DK41936-03
KOEGEL, PAUL P50MH30911-14 0016
KOEGEL, ROBERT L R01MH28210-14A1
KOEHLER, KENNETH J R01CA51831-01A1
KOEHLER, RAYMOND C P01NS20020-08 9001
KOEHLER, RAYMOND C P01NS20020-08 0005
KOEHLER, RAYMOND C R01HL38285-05
KOEHLER, RAYMOND C R01NS25275-05
KOEHNKE, JANET D R29DC00428-05
KOELLING, CHARLES P S07RR07095-24 0382
KOEN, JOHN B R44DE08877-02
KOENEMAN, JAMES B R01AR40558-01A1
KOENIG, HAROLD R01NS18047-10
KOENIG, JAMES I R01DK40788-04
KOENIG, JANE Q R01ES02366-11
KOENIG, JANE Q S07RR05714-21 0136
KOENIG, JOYCE S07RR05425-30 0748
KOENIG, RONALD J M01RR00042-31 0641
KOENIG, RONALD J R01DK44155-01
KOENIG, RONALD J R29DK40095-03
KOENIG, S Z01AI00586-02
KOENIGSBERG, HAROLD W R01MH42805-03
KOEPPE, ROBERT E. P50NS15655-12 9007
KOEPPE, ROGER E S07RR07101-13 0555
KOEPPE, ROGER E, II R01GM34968-11
KOEPSELL, THOMAS P01CA34847-09 0020
KOEPSELL, THOMAS D N01HD62914-05
KOEPSELL, THOMAS D S07RR05714-21 0128
KOERBER, H RICHARD R01NS23725-07
KOERBER, H RICHARD S07RR05416-30 0565
KOERKER, DONNA J P30DK17047-15 9001
KOERKER, DONNA J. P51RR00166-30 0098
KOERKER, DONNA J. P51RR00166-30 0099
KOERKER, DONNA J. P51RR00166-30 0100
KOERNER, THEODORE S07RR05372-30 0678
KOERNER, THEODORE A JR R29HL42395-03
KOESTER, CHARLES P01DC00316-06 0003
KOESTER, JOHN D R01NS19328-07
KOESTNER, ADALBERT S07RR05772-17 0356
KOETZLE, THOMAS F R01RR03120-06
KOFIE, VINCENT Y U01CA50137-03
KOGAN, BARRY A M01RR01271-10 0064
KOGAN, BARRY A M01RR01271-10 0117
KOGAN, BARRY A R01DK43687-01
KOGOMA, TOKIO R01GM22092-16
KOH, DONALD B S07RR05469-29 0412
KOH, HOWARD K K07CA01380-04
KOH, SHAY-WHEY M R29EY06961-05
KOHANSKI, RONALD A R29DK38893-05
KOHL, STEVE P01HD13021-12 0002
KOHL, STEVE R01AI32384-01
KOHLER, BEN N01CO05714-01
KOHLER, BEN N01CO15625-00
KOHLER, BEN N01CO15626-00
KOHLER, BEN N01CO15627-00
KOHLER, BEN N01CO15634-00
KOHLER, BEN N01CO15640-00
KOHLER, BEN N01CO15645-00
KOHLER, BEN N01CO15656-00
KOHLER, BEN N01CO15658-00
KOHLER, BEN N01CO15664-00
KOHLER, BEN N01CO15666-00
KOHLER, BEN N01CO15694-00
KOHLER, BEN N01CO15710-00
KOHLER, BEN N01CO15725-01
KOHLER, BEN N01CO15733-00
KOHLER, BEN N01CO15741-00
KOHLER, BEN N01CO15745-00
KOHLER, BEN N01CO15755-00
KOHLER, BEN N01CO15758-00
KOHLER, BEN N01CO15777-00
KOHLER, BEN N01CO15778-00
KOHLER, BRYAN E R01EY06466-07
KOHLER, HEINZ P01CA57165-01 0002
KOHLER, HEINZ R01AG04180-09
KOHLER, HEINZ R01CA51434-02
KOHLER, HEINZ R01CA56701-01
KOHLER, HEINZ R43AI31724-01
KOHLER, PETER O P51RR00163-32
KOHLER, PETER O P51RR00163-32 9014
KOHLHAW, GUNTER B R01GM15102-24
KOHN, DAVID H S07RR05321-30 0263
KOHN, DENNIS F G20RR06782-01
KOHN, DONALD B P01NS26991-02 0005
KOHN, DONALD B R01AI29125-03
KOHN, DONALD B R01DK42694-01A1
KOHN, DONALD B U01AI25959-05 0006
KOHN, E C Z01CB09163-03
KOHN, HAROLD L R01GM37934-06
KOHN, JOACHIM B K04GM00550-02
KOHN, JOACHIM B R29GM39455-04
KOHN, K W Z01CM06172-07
KOHN, ROBERT N01HC55012-11
KOHN, SUSAN E R29DC00447-05
KOHORN, BRUCE D R29GM39696-04
KOHOUT, F P30DE10126-01 9001
KOHRMAN, ARTHUR F R01MH48290-01
KOHRT, WENDY M R29AR40705-01
KOHTZ, DONALD S R01HL43583-03
KOHTZ, DONALD S R29HL40659-04
KOHUT, ROBERT I R01DC00589-03
KOHWI-SHIGEMATSU, TERUMI R01CA39681-07
KOHWI, YOSHINORI R01CA51377-01A1
KOKIKO, ELAINE N01LM53523-06
KOLACHANA, B S Z01MH02575-01
KOLATTUKUDY, P E R01GM18278-22
KOLATTUKUDY, PAPPACH S07RR07074-26 0679
KOLB, HELGA E R01EY03323-12
KOLB, HELGA E R01EY04855-09
KOLDOVSKY, OTAKAR P01HD26013-01A2
KOLDOVSKY, OTAKAR P01HD26013-01A2 9002
KOLDOVSKY, OTAKAR R01DK27624-12
KOLDOVSKY, OTAKAR S07RR05675-23 0911
KOLE, RYSZARD R01GM32994-08A1
KOLENBRANDER, P E Z01DE00273-13
KOLESNICK, RICHARD N R01CA42385-06
KOLHOUSE, J FRED R01GM26486-13
KOLKO, DAVID J R01MH39976-06A1
KOLLAR, EDWARD J K16DE00157-05S2
KOLLER, AKOS R29HL46813-01
KOLLER, WILLIAM C P30AG10182-01
KOLLMAN, PETER A R01GM29072-10
KOLLROS, JERRY J P01NS15350-13 0011
KOLOBOW, T Z01HL01404-23
KOLODNER, RICHARD P01HD24926-03 9001
KOLODNER, RICHARD U01AI27336-04 0004
KOLODNER, RICHARD D R01GM26017-13
KOLODNER, RICHARD D R01GM29383-09
KOLODNER, RICHARD D R01HG00305-04
KOLODNER, RICHARD D. P30AI28691-03 9003
KOLODNY, EDWIN H S07RR05730-20 0512
KOLODNY, GERALD S07RR05479-29 0435
KOLONEL, LAURENCE N N01CN05223-06
KOLONEL, LAURENCE N P01CA33619-09 9001
KOLONEL, LAURENCE N P01CA33619-09
KOLONEL, LAURENCE N P01CA33619-09 0001
KOLP, LISA S07RR05431-30 0860
KOLP, LISA A K08HD00943-01
KOLSTAD, R S07RR05915-08 0685
KOLTER, ROBERTO G R01AI25944-03
KOLTERMAN, ORVILLE G M01RR00827-17 0405
KOLTERMAN, ORVILLE G M01RR00827-17 0390
KOLTERMAN, ORVILLE G M01RR00827-17 0443
KOLTERMAN, ORVILLE G M01RR00827-17 0283
KOLTERMAN, ORVILLE G M01RR00827-17 0447
KOLTERMAN, ORVILLE G M01RR00827-17 0493
KOLTERMAN, ORVILLE G M01RR00827-17 0469
KOLTERMAN, ORVILLE G M01RR00827-17 0466
KOLTERMAN, ORVILLE G U01DK37828-06
KOMAROFF, ANTHONY L R01AI26788-03
KOMAROFF, ANTHONY L R01AI27314-02
KOMAROFF, ANTHONY L U01AI32246-01 9001
KOMAROFF, ANTHONY L U01AI32246-01
KOMAROFF, ANTHONY L U01AI32246-01 0001
KOMAROMY, MICHAEL C R29HL39362-04
KOMISARUK, BARRY R S06GM08223-08
KOMISARUK, BARRY R. S06GM08223-08 0021
KOMM, BARRY S R01DK41317-03
KOMNENICH, PAULINE S07RR07112-24 0432
KOMOLY, S Z01NS02808-02
KOMORIYA, AKIRA Z01BD01011-01
KOMOROSKI, EVA M S07RR05350-30 0331
KOMUNIECKI, PATRICIA S07RR07237-04 0745
KOMUNIECKI, RICHARD W R01AI18427-10
KON, H Z01DK29007-20
KON, VALENTINA R01DK42159-02
KON, VALENTINA R29DK39547-04
KONARSKA, MARIA M S07RR07065-26 0062
KONDO, NORMAN S S03RR03194-10
KONDO, NORMAN S S06GM08005-20
KONDO, NORMAN S S06GM08005-20 0003
KONE, BRUCE C K08DK01885-04
KONEFAL, JANET R18DA06212-03
KONIAK-GRIFFIN, DEBO S07RR06014-03 0840
KONIECZNY, STEPHEN F R01HD25518-03
KONIECZNY, STEPHEN F R29HD24489-04
KONIGSBERG, PAULA J R43AI31287-01
KONIGSBERG, PAULA J R43AR41094-01
KONIGSBERG, WILLIAM H P01HL29019-10 0004
KONIGSBERG, WILLIAM H R01GM12607-27
KONISHI, MASAKAZU R01DC00134-14
KONISKY, JORDAN R01GM41587-03
KONISKY, JORDAN S07RR07030-26
KONISKY, JORDAN S15GM47080-01
KONKLE, BARBARA A R29HL44956-02
KONNO, KUNIO U01AI27280-03 0002
KONO, TETSURO R01DK06725-29
KONO, TETSURO R01DK19925-15
KONOPELSKI, JOSEPH P R01GM45015-02
KONOPKA, A K Z01CB08394-03
KONRAD, THOMAS R R01HS06544-01S1
KONSTAM, MARVIN M01RR00054-30 0395
KONSTAM, MARVIN A M01RR00054-30 0421
KONSTAN, MICHAEL P30DK27651-09 0011
KONSTAN, MICHAEL W M01RR00080-29 0315
KONSTAN, MICHAEL W M01RR00080-29 0384
KONTOS, HERMES P01NS25630-03 0003
KONTOS, HERMES A R01NS19316-09
KONTOS, HERMES A R37HL21851-14
KOO, EDWARD H R35AG07914-03 0003
KOOB, GEORGE P50MH47680-02 0016
KOOB, GEORGE F P01DK26741-12 0004
KOOB, GEORGE F P50AA06420-08 0008
KOOB, GEORGE F R01AA08459-02
KOOB, GEORGE F R01DA04043-06
KOOB, GEORGE F R01DA04398-05
KOOCHER, GERALD P R01MH41791-04
KOOL, ERIC S07RR07069-26 0250
KOOL, ERIC T R01GM46625-01
KOOMEY, J MICHAEL M01RR00042-31 0676
KOOMEY, J MICHAEL R29AI27837-03
KOONTZ, JOHN W S07RR07088-24 0347
KOONTZ, MARGARET A R01EY08053-03
KOOP, DENNIS P01HL41618-03 0002
KOOP, DENNIS R R01AA08608-03
KOOP, EVERETT C R13CA54094-01
KOOPMAN, JAMES S P41RR02176-05 0010
KOOPMAN, JAMES S R01AI29876-02

KOOPMAN, WILLIAM J M01RR00032-31 0375
KOOPMAN, WILLIAM J P01AR03555-32A1 0003
KOOPMAN, WILLIAM J P60AR20614-14
KOOS, BRIAN J R01HD18478-06
KOOS, ROBERT D R01CA45055-09
KOOS, ROBERT D R03HD28055-01
KOOTZ, RUSTY N01CO15762-00
KOOYMAN, GERALD L P01HL17731-17 0003
KOPACHIK, WILL JOHN S07RR07049-26 0451
KOPCHICK, JOHN P01ES05652-01 9003
KOPECEK, JINDRICH R01DK39544-04
KOPELL, NANCY R01MH47150-02
KOPELMAN, R M01RR00645-20 0434
KOPF, GREGORY S R01HD22732-05
KOPIA, GREGORY A R43HL46626-01
KOPIN, ALAN S K08DK01934-03
KOPIN, I J Z01NS02717-06
KOPITO, RON R R01DK43994-01
KOPITO, RON R R01GM38543-05
KOPLOWITZ, LISA M01RR00065-29 0310
KOPP, CLAIRE B R01HD26773-02
KOPPEL, LOUIS N R43CA53030-01A1
KOPPENHEFFER, THOMAS L S15HD28752-01
KOPPLE, JOEL D M01RR00425-22S3 0382
KOPPLE, JOEL D M01RR00425-22S3 0410
KOPPLE, JOEL D M01RR00425-22S3 0384
KOPPLE, JOEL D M01RR00425-22S3 0396
KOPPLE, JOEL D M01RR00425-22S3 0462
KOPPLE, JOEL D M01RR00425-22S3 0461
KOPPLE, JOEL D U01DK34513-07
KOPPLEMAN, MICHELLE M01RR02635-07 0269
KOPROWSKI, HILARY P01AI25380-05 0003
KOPROWSKI, HILARY P01CA21124-14
KOPROWSKI, HILARY P01CA21124-14 0013
KOPROWSKI, HILARY P30CA10815-24 9005
KOPROWSKI, HILARY P30CA10815-24 9008
KOPROWSKI, HILARY P30CA10815-24 9010
KOPROWSKI, HILARY P30CA10815-24 9011
KOPROWSKI, HILARY P30CA10815-24 9012
KOPROWSKI, HILARY P30CA10815-24
KOPROWSKI, HILARY P50NS11036-18 9003
KOPROWSKI, HILARY P50NS11036-18
KOPROWSKI, HILARY R37AI09706-21
KOPROWSKI, HILARY S07RR05540-29
KOPROWSKI, HILIARY P01CA21124-14 9001
KOPUN, JUDY S07RR05834-12 0540
KORACH, K S Z01ES70065-15
KORAL, KENNETH F R01CA38790-07
KORAN, A P50DE09296-03 0002
KORBA, BRENT E R44AI25983-03
KORC, MURRAY R01CA40162-07
KORC, MURRAY R01DK32561-06
KORCHAK, HELEN M R01AI24840-05
KORDOWER, JEFFREY H P01AG09466-01 0004
KORDOWER, JEFFREY H R01NS25655-04
KOREEDA, MASATO R01CA25185-13
KOREEDA, MASATO R01DK30025-14
KOREEDA, MASATO S10RR06739-01
KOREN, GIDEON R01HL46005-01A1
KOREN, MARY J R01AG10645-01
KORENBERG, JULIE R R29HG00037-02
KORENBROT, JUAN I R01EY05498-07
KORENBROT, JUAN I R01EY08306-03
KORENEK, NANCY S07RR05845-11 0557
KORENMAN, STANLEY S07RR05354-30 0405
KORETSKY, ALAN P P41RR03631-04 9002
KORETSKY, ALAN PAUL R29HL40354-03
KORETZ, JANE F R01EY02195-13
KORETZ, JANE F R01EY07853-03
KORETZKY, GARY A R29CA56843-01
KORF, BRUCE P30HD18655-10 9011
KORFHAGEN, THOMAS R P50HD20748-06A1 0005
KORITNIK, DONALD R P50HL14164-20 9007
KORITNIK, DONALD R S07RR05404-30 0847
KORMAN, NEIL J R55AR41008-01
KORN, DAVID M01RR00070-29
KORN, DAVID S07RR05353-30
KORN, DAVID S15AG10243-01
KORN, E D Z01HL00501-18
KORN, E D Z01HL00506-16
KORN, JANE E S07RR05712-20 0101
KORN, JOSEPH H R01AR32343-08
KORNBERG, ARTHUR P01AG02908-11 0001
KORNBERG, ARTHUR R37GM07581-31
KORNBERG, ROGER D R01AI21144-08
KORNBERG, ROGER D R01GM36659-06
KORNBERG, THOMAS B P01GM31286-09 0006
KORNBERG, THOMAS B R01GM30637-10
KORNBLUM, SYLVAN R01MH43287-03
KORNBLUTH, RICHARD S R01AI25316-04A1
KORNBLUTH, RICHARD S R01HL43523-03
KORNECKI, ELIZABETH H K04HL02412-02
KORNECKI, ELIZABETH H P01HL28001-10 9003
KORNER, ANNELIESE F M01RR00081-29 0098
KORNETSKY, CONAN K05DA00099-08
KORNETSKY, CONAN R01AA05950-08
KORNETSKY, CONAN R01DA02326-12
KORNETSKY, CONAN R01DA05100-03
KORNFELD, HARDY R01HL44846-02
KORNFELD, ROSALIND H R13GM45446-01
KORNFELD, STEPHEN B M01RR00827-17 0497
KORNFELD, STUART A R37CA08759-25
KORNGOLD, ROBERT R01AI26653-04
KORNGOLD, ROBERT R01CA38951-08
KORNHAUSER, DAVID D M01RR00035-31 0406
KORNHAUSER, DAVID D M01RR00722-19 0249
KORNIEWICZ, DENISE S07RR06012-03 0307
KOROLY, M S07RR05362-30 0796
KORONES, SHELDON B U10HD21415-06
KOROPCHAK, JOHN S07RR07118-22 0378
KOROSHETZ, WALTER J K08NS01276-04
KOROSHETZ, WALTER J P50NS10828-16 0026
KORSMEYER, STANLEY J P01CA49712-03 0003
KORSMEYER, STANLEY J P01CA49712-03 9002
KORSMEYER, STANLEY J R01CA50239-03
KORSTEN, M P50AA03508-14 0052
KORSZUN, Z RICHARD R01GM41822-03
KORTE, GARY E R01EY08284-03
KORTHUIS, RONALD J R01HL36069-06
KORYTKOWSKI, MARY T S07RR05416-30 0566
KORYTOKOWSKI, MARY M01RR00056-30 0369
KORZEKWA, K Z01CP05676-01
KORZEKWA, K Z01CP05677-01
KOSCH, PHILIP C S07RR05788-15
KOSER, UGER N01LM93519-07
KOSHER, ROBERT P01HD22610-04 0001
KOSHER, ROBERT A R01HD22896-05
KOSHLAND, DANIEL E R37DK09765-26 0005
KOSHLAND, DANIEL E R37DK09765-26 0007
KOSHLAND, DANIEL E R37DK09765-26 0008
KOSHLAND, DANIEL E, JR R37DK09765-26
KOSHLAND, DOUGLAS S07RR05799-14 0681
KOSHLAND, DOUGLAS E R01GM41718-01A1
KOSHLAND, GAIL F R01AR40835-01
KOSHLAND, MARIAN E R37AI07079-26
KOSHY, MABEL N01HB97062-03
KOSIK, KENNETH P41RR00317-25 0004
KOSIK, KENNETH S R01AG06601-05
KOSIK, KENNETH S R01NS29031-01A1
KOSIK, KENNETH S R35AG07911-04 0006
KOSIK, KENNETH S R35AG07911-04 0008
KOSIK, KENNETH S R35AG07911-04 0003
KOSKI, CAROL L P50NS20022-08 0005
KOSLOW, MAXIM R01CA46788-03S1
KOSNETT, MICHAEL J K01OH00108-01
KOSS, JOAN D R01DA07381-01
KOSS, MARY P K02MH00827-01A2
KOSS, MARY P R01MH47194-01A1
KOSS, MARY P S07RR05675-23 0912
KOSSIAKOFF, ANTHONY A R01GM33571-06
KOSSLYN, STEPHEN M P01NS17778-10 0010
KOSTEN, THERESE A P50DA04060-06 0009
KOSTEN, THOMAS R K02DA00112-05
KOSTEN, THOMAS R M01RR00125-28 0685
KOSTEN, THOMAS R P50DA04060-06
KOSTEN, THOMAS R R01DA05626-04
KOSTEN, THOMAS R R18DA06190-02
KOSTENBAUDER, HARRY B S07RR05857-11
KOSTER, FREDERICK T M01RR00997-16 0352
KOSTER, FREDERICK T S07RR05583-27 0632
KOSTERLITZ, HANS W R01DA00662-16
KOSTIS, JOHN B N01HC65032-07
KOSTIS, JOHN B R01HL33960-05
KOSTIS, JOHN B. N01HC48066-11
KOSTREVA, DAVID R S07RR05434-30 0813
KOSTRZEWA, RICHARD M R15NS29505-01
KOSTYK, SANDRA K K11EY00311-03
KOSTYO, JACK P60DK20572-14 9001
KOSTYO, JACK L S07RR05383-30 0563
KOTARSKI, MICHAEL A R29EY09311-01
KOTB, MALAK R29GM38530-04
KOTLER, DONALD P P01DK42618-02 0002
KOTLER, DONALD P R01AI21414-06
KOTLIAR, ABRAHAM M R44RR05077-03
KOTLIKOFF, LAURENCE J P01AG05842-06 0004
KOTLIKOFF, LAURENCE J R01AG06380-03
KOTLIKOFF, MICHAEL I R29HL41084-04
KOTLIKOFF, MICHAEL, IV R01HL45239-02
KOTLOFF, KAREN L R01AI28711-03
KOTLOFF, KAREN L R01HD26691-03
KOTRANSKI, LYNNE C R18DA04841-03S1
KOTRANSKI, LYNNE C U01DA06919-02
KOTTKE, BRUCE A M01RR00585-20 0495
KOTTKE, BRUCE A M01RR00585-20 0525
KOTTKE, BRUCE A M01RR00585-20 0490
KOTTKE, BRUCE A M01RR00585-20 0492
KOTTKE, THOMAS P41RR01632-09 0027
KOTTKE, THOMAS E P41RR01632-09 9019
KOTZIN, BRIAN L P01DK40144-04 0005
KOTZIN, BRIAN L R01AI28495-03
KOUDELKA, GERALD B R29GM42138-03
KOUDELKA, GERALD B S07RR07066-26 0247
KOUDELKA, GERALD B S15GM47081-01
KOUP, RICHARD ALAN R01AI30358-02
KOUREMBANAS, STELLA K08HL02394-03
KOURI, RICHARD E R43HG00524-01
KOUROSH, SOHRAB S07RR05426-30 0139
KOURY, MARK J R01DK31513-09
KOURY, STEPHEN T R29DK43058-01
KOUSOULAS, KONSTANTIN G R29AI27886-02
KOUSVELARI, E Z01DE00458-03
KOUTCHER, JASON A P01CA47997-03 0005
KOUTSKY, LAURA ANN P01AI29363-02 0002
KOVACH, ILDIKO M S07RR07123-22 0597
KOVACH, JOHN S N01CM07309-01
KOVACH, JOHN S P01CA31224-06S1 0004
KOVACH, JOHN S P30CA15083-18
KOVACH, JOHN S P30CA15083-18 9011
KOVACH, JOSEPH K R01HD06770-18
KOVACS, ANDREA M01RR00043-31 0493
KOVACS, ANDREA M01RR00043-31 0494
KOVACS, ANDREA M01RR00043-31 0495
KOVACS, ANDREA M01RR00043-31 0496
KOVACS, CHARLES J R01CA48172-02
KOVACS, GREGORY T A R03DC01318-01
KOVACS, J A Z01CL00034-04
KOVACS, J A Z01CL00035-04
KOVACS, J A Z01CL00036-04
KOVACS, J A Z01CL00037-04
KOVACS, J A Z01CL00049-03
KOVACS, J A Z01CL00087-02
KOVACS, J A Z01CL00088-02
KOVACS, J A Z01CL00098-01
KOVACS, J A Z01CL00099-01
KOVACS, MARIA R01DK25568-11A1
KOVACS, MARIA R37MH33990-12
KOVACS, SHIRLEY A R15AI27975-01A2
KOVAK, JOEL N01AI82500-09
KOVAL, THOMAS M R01CA34158-11
KOVALEVSKY, GEORGE S07RR05664-24 0865
KOW, YOKE W R01GM37216-06
KOWAL, JEROME R01AG08332-01A1
KOWALCZYKOWSKI, STEPHEN C R01AI18987-11
KOWALCZYKOWSKI, STEPHEN C R01GM41347-04
KOWALKOWSKI, STAN R19DA06404-03
KOWALL, NEIL W P50AG05134-08 0014
KOWALL, NEIL W R29NS25588-04
KOWALSKI, CHARLES J R01DE08730-04
KOWALSKI, DAVID P01GM44119-02 0002
KOWALSKI, DAVID R01GM30614-09
KOWARSKI, ALLEN A U01DK37834-06
KOWATCH, ROBERT A S07RR05426-30 0140
KOZAK, C Z01AI00301-10
KOZAK, C A Z01AI00300-10
KOZAK, LESLIE P R01HD08431-17
KOZAK, MARILYN S R01GM33915-09
KOZAK, R W Z01BD02016-01
KOZARICH, JOHN W R01GM34454-07
KOZARICH, JOHN W R01GM35066-08
KOZARICH, JOHN W R01GM37210-06
KOZBOR, DANUTA B R01HD27107-03
KOZEK, WIESLAW J S06GM08224-07 0013
KOZEL, THOMAS R R01AI14209-13
KOZEL, THOMAS R U01AI31696-01 0004
KOZIK, MARIUSZ R15CA54462-01
KOZIKOWSKI, ALAN P R01AG07591-03S1
KOZIKOWSKI, ALAN P R01CA50175-04
KOZINER, BENJAMIN P01CA20194-14 0025
KOZIOL, JAMES A R01CA41582-06
KOZLOVSKIS, PATRICIA L R01HL40711-03
KOZLOWSKI, GERALD P R01AA06014-08
KOZLOWSKI, JAMES M N01CM97628-04
KOZLOWSKI, JAMES M P50DK39250-05 0001
KOZLOWSKI, P B P01AG04220-07A1 9002
KOZLOWSKI, PIOTR R01HD24884-03
KOZLOWSKI, PIOTR B S15AG10241-01
KOZULIN S07RR05380-30 0883
KRABELBURD, EDMUNDO N S06GM08224-07 0014
KRADIN, RICHARD L R01CA51345-01A1
KRADIN, RICHARD L R01HL43827-02
KRAEMER, FREDRIC B R01HL42865-03
KRAEMER, K H Z01CP04517-15
KRAEMER, PAUL M P41RR01315-10 0001
KRAEMER, PHILIPP J S07RR07114-23 0440
KRAEMER, PHILIPP J S07RR07114-23 0441
KRAFFT, GRANT P01AG10481-01 0001
KRAFFT, GRANT A P01AG10481-01
KRAFFT, MARIE E R29GM40693-04
KRAFT, ANDREW S R01CA42533-06
KRAFT, KENNETH A R29HL40967-04
KRAG, MARTIN H R01AR38630-04
KRAG, SHARON S R01CA20421-15
KRAG, SHARON S R01GM36570-04A1
KRAGIE, LAURA K11DK01456-04
KRAHN, DEAN D R01DA06791-01
KRAHN, DEAN D R01DA06827-02
KRAHN, GLORIA L R29HD23014-04
KRAIG, ELLEN B R01AI22181-07
KRAINER, ADRIAN S07RR05717-21 0135
KRAINER, ADRIAN R R01GM42699-03
KRAISELBURD, EDMUNDO P40RR03640-05 0029
KRAKOFF, IRWIN H N01CM07310-01
KRAKOW, JOSEPH G12RR03037-07 9003
KRAKOW, JOSEPH S R01GM22619-15A1
KRAKOWKA, GEORGE S R01DK39570-02
KRAKOWSKI, MENACHEM I R29MH45454-02
KRALY, F SCOTT R01NS19133-04A2
KRAMER, ALFRED V P01CA32845-29 0025
KRAMER, ARTHUR F R01AG08435-01A2
KRAMER, B S Z01CM07250-05
KRAMER, FRED R R01HL43521-03
KRAMER, GARY W P01HD23042-03 0004
KRAMER, GEORGE C R01HL34151-07
KRAMER, GEORGE C R01HL40296-04
KRAMER, J P41RR02594-06 0009
KRAMER, JAMES M K04HD00900-01

KRAMER, JAMES M R01HD22028-07
KRAMER, JAMES M R01HD27211-02
KRAMER, JAN L S07RR05396-30 0728
KRAMER, RANDALL H R01CA33834-09
KRAMER, RANDALL H R01CA51884-02
KRAMER, ROBERT A R29CA50473-03
KRAMER, STEVEN G P30EY02162-14
KRAMER, THOMAS P01DK36289-06A1 0009
KRAMSCH, DIETER M R01HL41074-04
KRANE, ELLIOT S07RR05655-21 0809
KRANE, STEPHEN P01AR03564-32 9004
KRANE, STEPHEN P01AR03564-32 0001
KRANE, STEPHEN M P01AR03564-32
KRANE, STEVEN P01AR03564-32 0019
KRANGEL, MICHAEL S R01GM41052-03
KRANIAS, EVANGELIA G R01HL26057-11
KRANTZ, DAVID S07RR07060-26 0449
KRANTZ, SANFORD B M01RR00095-31 0218
KRANTZ, SANFORD B R01DK15555-20
KRANTZ, SANFORD B. M01RR00095-31 0273
KRANZ, DAVID M R29AI24635-05
KRANZ, ROBERT G R29GM39106-04
KRANZLER, HENRY R P50DA04060-06 0006
KRASINSKI, KEITH M01RR00096-30A1 0239
KRASINSKI, KEITH M01RR00096-30A1 0289
KRASINSKI, KEITH P30AI27742-03 9003
KRASINSKI, KEITH M R01DA04791-04
KRASNE, FRANKLIN B R01NS08108-24
KRASNE, SALLY J R01DK44023-01
KRASNEY, JOHN A P01HL28542-10 0002
KRASNEY, JOHN A R01HL36126-05
KRASNOW, MARK S07RR05353-30 0351
KRASNOW, MARK A R01GM47735-01
KRASNOW, MARK A R01HD25624-03
KRATZ, KENNETH E S07RR05376-30 0042
KRAUS, GEORGE A R01GM33604-07
KRAUS, JAN P01HD08315-16 0025
KRAUS, JAN P R01HD26651-03
KRAUS, JESS F R01OH02872-01
KRAUS, LEWIS R43CA53980-01
KRAUS, LEWIS E R43AI31349-01
KRAUS, LORRAINE M S07RR05423-30 0055
KRAUS, M H Z01CP05366-08
KRAUS, NINA R01DC00264-07
KRAUS, NINA S07RR07028-26 0017
KRAUS, VIRGINIA B K11CA01358-04
KRAUSE, DUNCAN C K04AI00968-02
KRAUSE, DUNCAN C R01AI23362-06
KRAUSE, JAMES E P01NS29343-01 0004
KRAUSE, JAMES E R01NS21937-08
KRAUSE, KURT L K08DK01928-03
KRAUSE, NEAL M R01AG08491-02
KRAUSE, NEAL M R01AG09221-01A1
KRAUSKOPF, JOHN R01EY06638-06
KRAUSMAN, DAVID T R43HL46078-01
KRAUSMAN, DAVID T R43MH49009-01
KRAUSS, RONALD M P01HL18574-16
KRAUSS, RONALD M P01HL18574-16 0006
KRAUSS, RONALD M R01HL33577-07
KRAUSS, STEVEN S S07RR07260-02 0547
KRAUT, JOSEPH R01CA17374-17
KRAUT, JOSEPH R01GM10928-29
KRAUTER, KENNETH P30DK41296-03 0001
KRAUTER, KENNETH S R01CA39553-07
KRAVITZ, EDWARD A P01NS02253-32 9003
KRAVITZ, EDWARD A P01NS02253-32 0014
KRAVITZ, EDWARD A P01NS25915-04A1 9003
KRAVITZ, EDWARD A P01NS25915-04A1
KRAVITZ, EDWARD A P01NS25915-04A1 0001
KRAVITZ, EDWARD A P01NS25915-04A1 0003
KRAWITT, EDWARD L R55DK42643-01A1
KRAYBILL, WILLIAM M01RR00036-31 0993
KREAM, BARBARA E P01AR38933-05 0002
KREAM, BARBARA E R01AR29850-11
KREAM, RICHARD M R01DA04128-05
KREAM, RICHARD M S07RR05382-30 0871
KREBS, EDWIN P01GM42508-03 0003
KREBS, EDWIN G R01DK42528-02
KREBS, NANCY M01RR00069-29 0481
KREDICH, NICHOLAS M K12DK01965-02
KREDICH, NICHOLAS M R01DK12828-24
KREEK, MARY J K05DA00049-14
KREEK, MARY J M01RR00102-28 0050
KREEK, MARY J M01RR00102-28 0053
KREEK, MARY J M01RR00102-28 0148
KREEK, MARY J M01RR00102-28 0054
KREEK, MARY J M01RR00102-28 0055
KREEK, MARY J P50DA05130-05
KREEK, MARY JEANNE M01RR00102-28 0121
KREEK, MARY JEANNE M01RR00102-28 0161
KREEK, MARY JEANNE M01RR00102-28 0162
KREEK, MARY JEANNE P50DA05130-05 0007
KREEK, MARY JEANNE P50DA05130-05 0004
KREEK, MARY JEANNE P50DA05130-05 0005
KREEK, MARY L M01RR00102-28 0149
KREIBICH, GERT R01GM21971-17
KREIDER, JOHN P01CA27503-12 0009
KREIDER, JOHN W R01CA47622-04
KREIDER, MARGARET S P01MH44210-03 9001
KREIG, PAUL A R01HD25179-02
KREISBERG, JEFFREY I R01DK29787-10
KREISMAN, NORMAN S07RR05377-30 0768

KREISS, JOAN K R29AI25024-04
KREISS, KATHLEEN K07ES00214-01
KREISS, KATHLEEN R01ES04843-04
KREITMAN, MARTIN E R01GM39355-04
KRELL, WILLANE S K08HL01954-05
KREMENAK, C R P01DE05837-10 0002
KRENSKY, ALAN M P01CA34233-09 0018
KRENSKY, ALAN M P01CA49605-03 0006
KRENSKY, ALAN M R01CA47609-04
KRENSKY, ALAN M R01DK35008-08
KRESGE, ALEXANDER J R01GM43210-02
KRESHECK, GORDON C S03RR03043-10
KRESHECK, GORDON C S07RR07176-14
KRESHECK, GORDON C S15GM47095-01
KRESINA, THOMAS F R01AI29102-02
KRESS, LAWRENCE F R01HL22996-14
KRESSEL, HERBERT Y R01CA47354-03
KRESSEL, HERBERT Y R01CA50985-01A1
KRETCHMER, NORMAN M01RR00083-29 0161
KRETCHMER, NORMAN P30HD22224-05S1
KRETCHMER, NORMAN P30HD22224-05S1 9001
KRETCHMER, NORMAN P30HD22224-05S1 9002
KRETCHMER, NORMAN P30HD22224-05S1 9003
KRETCHMER, NORMAN P30HD22224-05S1 9004
KRETSINGER, ROBERT H P41RR01135-14
KREULEN, DAVID L P01DK36289-06A1 0003
KREULEN, DAVID L R01HL27781-11
KREUTZER, DONALD S07RR05678-23 0161
KREUTZER, DONALD L R01EY04131-08
KREUTZER, DONALD L R01HL25015-10
KREUZER, KENNETH N R01GM34622-07
KREVSKY, BENJAMIN R01CA56121-01
KREVSKY, BENJAMIN S07RR05417-30 0797
KREY, LEWIS C R01HD19236-05A2
KRICHEVSKY, ALEXANDER P01HD15454-11 9002
KRICKER, M C Z01ES65056-03
KRICKER, M C Z01ES65058-02
KRIEBEL, DAVID R01ES04202-05
KRIEBEL, DAVID R01OH02820-01
KRIEG-KOWALD, MARIANNE R29CA50733-03
KRIEGER, JOHN N R01DK38955-05
KRIEGER, JOHN N R01DK40747-04
KRIEGER, MONTY P01HL41484-03 0003
KRIEGER, MONTY R01HL32459-07
KRIEGER, NEIL R R01GM42672-03
KRIEGSTEIN, ARNOLD R P50NS12151-17 0017
KRIEGSTEIN, ARNOLD R R01NS21223-07
KRIER, JACOB R01DK29920-11
KRIGMAN, MARTIN R P01ES01104-16 0004
KRIGMAN, MARTIN R P01ES01104-16 9001
KRIMES, PETER E S07RR05487-29 0695
KRIMMER, EDWARD C S07RR05806-13 0905
KRINSKY, NORMAN I R01CA51506-02
KRIPKE, DANIEL F K05MH00117-15
KRIPKE, DANIEL F M01RR00827-17 0490
KRIPKE, DANIEL F M01RR00827-17 0479
KRIPKE, DANIEL F M01RR00827-17 0397
KRIPKE, DANIEL F P50MH30914-14 0047
KRIPKE, DANIEL F R01HL40930-02
KRIPKE, MARGARET L R01CA52457-02
KRIPKE, MARGARET L R55ES04875-04
KRISANS, SKAIDRITE R01DK44350-01
KRISANS, SKAIDRITE S07RR07004-16 0049
KRISCHER, JEFFREY P U10CA29139-11
KRISCHER, JEFFREY P U10CA37379-07 0053
KRISCHER, JEFFREY P U10CA37379-07 0054
KRISCHER, JEFFREY P U10CA37379-07 0055
KRISCHER, JEFFREY P U10CA37379-07 0056
KRISCHER, JEFFREY P U10CA37379-07 0057
KRISCHER, JEFFREY P U10CA37379-07 0058
KRISCHER, JEFFREY P U10CA37379-07 0033
KRISCHER, JEFFREY P U10CA37379-07 0034
KRISCHER, JEFFREY P U10CA37379-07 0035
KRISCHER, JEFFREY P U10CA37379-07 0036
KRISCHER, JEFFREY P U10CA37379-07 0037
KRISCHER, JEFFREY P U10CA37379-07 0038
KRISCHER, JEFFREY P U10CA37379-07 0039
KRISCHER, JEFFREY P U10CA37379-07 0040
KRISCHER, JEFFREY P U10CA37379-07 0041
KRISCHER, JEFFREY P U10CA37379-07 0042
KRISCHER, JEFFREY P U10CA37379-07 0043
KRISCHER, JEFFREY P U10CA37379-07 0044
KRISCHER, JEFFREY P U10CA37379-07 0059
KRISCHER, JEFFREY P U10CA37379-07 0060
KRISCHER, JEFFREY P U10CA37379-07 0045
KRISCHER, JEFFREY P U10CA37379-07
KRISCHER, JEFFREY P U10CA37379-07 0001
KRISCHER, JEFFREY P U10CA37379-07 0002
KRISCHER, JEFFREY P U10CA37379-07 0003
KRISCHER, JEFFREY P U10CA37379-07 0004
KRISCHER, JEFFREY P U10CA37379-07 0005
KRISCHER, JEFFREY P U10CA37379-07 0006
KRISCHER, JEFFREY P U10CA37379-07 0007
KRISCHER, JEFFREY P U10CA37379-07 0046
KRISCHER, JEFFREY P U10CA37379-07 0047
KRISCHER, JEFFREY P U10CA37379-07 0048
KRISCHER, JEFFREY P U10CA37379-07 0049
KRISCHER, JEFFREY P U10CA37379-07 0050
KRISCHER, JEFFREY P U10CA37379-07 0051
KRISCHER, JEFFREY P U10CA37379-07 0052
KRISCHER, JEFFREY P U10CA37379-07 0008
KRISCHER, JEFFREY P U10CA37379-07 0009

KRISCHER, JEFFREY P U10CA37379-07 0010
KRISCHER, JEFFREY P U10CA37379-07 0011
KRISCHER, JEFFREY P U10CA37379-07 0013
KRISCHER, JEFFREY P U10CA37379-07 0014
KRISCHER, JEFFREY P U10CA37379-07 0012
KRISCHER, JEFFREY P U10CA37379-07 0015
KRISCHER, JEFFREY P U10CA37379-07 0016
KRISCHER, JEFFREY P U10CA37379-07 0017
KRISCHER, JEFFREY P U10CA37379-07 0018
KRISCHER, JEFFREY P U10CA37379-07 0019
KRISCHER, JEFFREY P U10CA37379-07 0020
KRISCHER, JEFFREY P U10CA37379-07 0021
KRISCHER, JEFFREY P U10CA37379-07 0022
KRISCHER, JEFFREY P U10CA37379-07 0023
KRISCHER, JEFFREY P U10CA37379-07 0024
KRISCHER, JEFFREY P U10CA37379-07 0025
KRISCHER, JEFFREY P U10CA37379-07 0026
KRISCHER, JEFFREY P U10CA37379-07 0027
KRISCHER, JEFFREY P U10CA37379-07 0028
KRISCHER, JEFFREY P U10CA37379-07 0029
KRISCHER, JEFFREY P U10CA37379-07 0030
KRISCHER, JEFFREY P U10CA37379-07 0031
KRISCHER, JEFFREY P U10CA37379-07 0032
KRISHAN, AWTAR P30CA14395-18A1 9015
KRISHAN, AWTAR P30CA14395-18A1 9017
KRISHAN, AWTAR P30CA14395-18A1 9019
KRISHAN, AWTAR P30CA14395-18A1 9020
KRISHNA, G Z01HL04410-01
KRISHNA, G Z01HL04411-01
KRISHNA, G GOPAL S07RR05417-30 0798
KRISHNA, GOPAL M01RR00349-25 0227
KRISHNA, GOPAL M01RR00349-25 0228
KRISHNA, N RAMA P30CA13148-20 9002
KRISHNA,GOPAL M01RR00349-25 0197
KRISHNAN, H RANGA P50DA05303-03 9001
KRISHNAN, RANGA R R01MH44716-03
KRISHNAN, SURESH P R03OH02880-01
KRISHNARAJ, RAJABATHER R01AG05717-07
KRISHNASWAMY, SRIRAM R29HL38337-06
KRISKA, ANDREA M R29DK43394-01
KRISKA, ANDREA M S07RR05451-30 0355
KRISTAL, ALAN P01CA34847-09 9005
KRISTAL, MARK B R01DA04586-03
KRISTAN, W P01NS25916-04 9002
KRISTAN, WILLIAM B P01NS25916-04 0004
KRISTAN, WILLIAM B, JR R01MH43396-04A1
KRITCHEVSKY, DAVID K06HL00734-30
KRITCHEVSKY, DAVID R01CA43856-03
KRIVIT, WILLIAM P01CA21737-14 0009
KRIVIT, WILLIAM R01NS29099-01A1
KROENKE, KURT K S07RR05983-05 0357
KROGH-JESPERSEN, KAR S07RR07058-26 0180
KROGSTAD, DONALD J R22AI25136-01A4
KROGSTAD, DONALD J U01AI25903-05 0008
KROGSTAD, DONALD J U01AI25903-05 9003
KROHN, K P41RR01243-10 9003
KROHN, KENNETH P01HL38736-05 9001
KROHN, KENNETH A P01CA42045-06 0007
KROHN, KENNETH A P01CA42045-06
KROHN, KENNETH A P01CA42045-06 9001
KROHN, MARIJANE A R29HD26377-02
KROLEWSKI, ANDRZEJ S P50DK39249-05 0017
KROLEWSKI, ANDRZEJ S R01DK41526-02
KROLICK, KEITH A R01NS28172-02
KROLICK, KEITH A R55NS24954-04A1
KROLL, JUDITH F R01MH44246-03
KROLL, M H Z01CL10085-09
KROLL, M H Z01CL10125-07
KROLL, M H Z01CL10170-03
KROLL, M H Z01CL10194-01
KROLL, MICHAEL S07RR05425-30 0749
KROLL, MICHAEL HOWARD K08HL02311-04
KROM, R A M01RR00585-20 0473
KRON, MICHAEL S07RR05772-17 0349
KRON, MICHAEL A K11AI01019-01
KRONAUER, RICHARD E P01AG09975-01 9001
KRONAUER, RICHARD E R01EY01808-15
KRONAUGE, JAMES S07RR05950-07 0983
KRONENBERG, AMY R29GM43178-02
KRONENBERG, AMY S07RR05918-08 0702
KRONENBERG, F M01RR00645-20 0001
KRONENBERG, F M01RR00645-20 0435
KRONENBERG, HENRY M P01DK11794-24 0002
KRONENBERG, HENRY M R01DK36597-05
KRONENBERG, MITCHELL E R01CA52511-01A1
KRONFOL, ZIAD A R01MH42988-04
KRONMAL, RICHARD N01HC85079-10
KRONMAL, RICHARD A R01DK40940-03
KRONMILLER, JAN E K11DE00286-03
KRONTIRIS, THEODORE G R01CA45052-05
KRONTIRIS, THEODORE G R01CA51985-01A1
KRONTOL, ZIAD P50AA07378-04 0005
KROOK, JAMES E U10CA35269-08
KROOS, LEE R R29GM43585-02
KROPF, DARRYL L S07RR07092-26 0509
KROSS, BURTON C N01CP95602-02
KROSS, BURTON C P20AG09682-01 0001
KRUEGER, BRUCE K R01AG10686-01
KRUEGER, JAMES M R01NS25378-06A1
KRUEGER, JAMES M R01NS27250-03
KRUEGER, JOHN W P01HL37412-04 0003
KRUEGER, KARL E R29MH44284-03

KRUEGER, RICK   S07RR07055-26 0194
KRUG, EDWARD L   R01HL44928-01A1
KRUG, EDWARD L   S07RR05434-30 0811
KRUG, ROBERT M   R37AI11772-19
KRUGER, LAWRENCE   R01NS05685-27
KRUGER, PHILIP B   R01EY05901-06
KRUGH, THOMAS R   R01CA35251-08
KRUGLANSKI, ARIE W   R01MH46412-02
KRUGMAN, RICHARD D   M01RR00051-30
KRUGMAN, RICHARD D   M01RR00069-29
KRUGMAN, RICHARD D   S07RR05357-30
KRUH, G   Z01CP05469-06
KRUISBEEK, A M   Z01CM09310-05
KRUISBEEK, A M   Z01CM09323-04
KRUKOWSKI, MARILYN   R01DE09100-03
KRULL, IRA S   S07RR07143-20 0628
KRULWICH, TERRY A   R01GM28454-10
KRUMDIECK, CARLOS L   P01CA28103-13
KRUMDIECK, CARLOS L   P01CA28103-13 9011
KRUMMEL, THOMAS M   R01GM41343-03
KRUPIN, THEODORE   R01EY05240-10
KRUPIN, THEODORE   R01EY09268-01
KRUPINSKI, JOHN   R29GM46395-01
KRUPP, LAUREN B   S07RR05736-19 0186
KRUSCHKE, JOHN K   S07RR07031-26 0096
KRUSE, CAROL A   K04NS01401-02
KRUSE, CAROL A   R01NS28905-02
KRUSKAL, JONATHAN B   S07RR05591-27 0663
KRUSKALL, MARGOT S   K07HL02033-05
KRUTH, H S   Z01HL02834-01
KRUTH, H S   Z01HL02835-01
KRYSTAL, MARK R   R29AI26663-04
KRYTER, KARL D   R01OH02904-01
KRZANOWSKI, JOSEPH J   S15MH49511-01
KSANDER, BRUCE R   R29EY08122-03
KSIEZAK-REDING, HANNA   P01AG06803-05 0005
KSIR, CHARLES J, JR   R01DA04126-03
KSIR, CHARLES J, JR   S07RR07157-16
KSIR, CHARLES J, JR   S15HD28773-01
KU, DAVID D   P50HL17667-17 0056
KU, DAVID N   R29HL39437-05
KUBIE, JOHN L   R01NS20686-06
KUBO, SPENCER H   M01RR00400-23 0257
KUBOVY, MICHAEL   R01MH47317-01
KUCERA, JAN   R55NS25796-03A2
KUCERA, LOUIS S   P30CA12197-19 9004
KUCERA, LOUIS S   S07RR05404-30 0848
KUCHERLAPATI, RAJU S   R01GM33943-08
KUCHERLAPATI, RAJU S   R01GM36565-06
KUCHERLAPATI, RAJU S   R01HG00380-01
KUCZENSKI, RONALD T   R01DA04157-07
KUCZMARSKI, EDWARD R   R01GM31907-09
KUDLOW, JEFFREY E   R01DK43652-01
KUEHL, LEROY R   S07RR05428-30 0183
KUEHL, W M   Z01CM06581-08
KUEHN, GLENN D   S03RR03100-08
KUEHN, GLENN D   S06GM08136-18
KUEHN, GLENN D   S06GM08136-18 0008
KUEHN, MICHAEL R   R01HD25109-03
KUEHNE, MARTIN E   R01CA12010-29
KUEMPEL, PETER L   R01GM32968-08
KUEPPERS, FRIEDRICH   R01HL41522-03
KUETTNER, KLAUS   P50AR39239-05 0003
KUETTNER, KLAUS E   P50AR39239-05
KUETTNER, KLAUS E   S03RR03253-06
KUFE, DONALD W   P01CA19589-14A1 0031
KUFE, DONALD W   P01CA34183-08 0005
KUFE, DONALD W   R01CA29431-11
KUFE, DONALD W   R01CA42802-05
KUFE, DONALD W   R03CA53414-01
KUFF, E L   Z01CB00366-20
KUHAR, M J   Z01DA00107-05
KUHAR, M J   Z01DA00108-04
KUHAR, M J   Z01DA00112-04
KUHAR, MICHAEL J   P01NS15080-12 9005
KUHL, PATRICIA K.   P01DC00520-04 0005
KUHL, PATRICK K.   P01DC00520-04 9002
KUHL, DAVID E   P50NS15655-12
KUHL, DAVID E   R01NS24896-06
KUHL, PATRICIA K   S07RR07096-26 0064
KUHL, PATRICIA K.   P51RR00166-30 0101
KUHL, STEVE A   S07RR05675-23 0933
KUHLS, THOMAS L   R29AI31360-01
KUHN, CYNTHIA M   R01DA02739-10
KUHN, CYNTHIA M   R01DK41777-03
KUHN, DONALD M   R01DA06219-01A2
KUHN, JOHN   P30CA54174-01 9003
KUHN, RAYMOND E   R37AI13128-14
KUHN, ROBERT W   P30HD11979-13 9005
KUHR, WERNER G   R01GM44112-01A1
KUIVANIEMI, S HELENA   R01HL45996-01A1
KUIVILA, HENRY G   S07RR07122-23 0090
KUJUBU, DEAN A   K11DK01815-04
KUKI, ATSUO   R29GM39576-04
KUKULKA, CARL G   R29NS24991-05
KUKULL, WALTER A   R01AG07584-04
KUKURUZINSKA, MARIA A   R29GM41365-03
KULAGA, H   Z01MH02549-02
KULESZ-MARTIN, MOLLY   P01CA13038-19 0114
KULESZ-MARTIN, MOLLY F   R01CA31101-10
KULIK, JAMES A   R01HL43654-02
KULIK, JAMES A   R01HS06348-02
KULIK, THOMAS J   K08HL02226-03
KULIK, THOMAS J   R01HL42908-03
KULIKOWSKI, CASIMIR   P41RR02230-06S1 0019
KULIKOWSKI, CASIMIR   P41RR02230-06S1
KULIKOWSKI, CASIMIR   P41RR02230-06S1 0020
KULIKOWSKI, CASIMIR   P41RR02230-06S1 0021
KULIKOWSKI, CASIMIR   P41RR02230-06S1 0017
KULIKOWSKI, CASIMIR   P41RR02230-06S1 0018
KULIKOWSKI, CASIMIR   P41RR02230-06S1 0022
KULIKOWSKI, CASIMIR   P41RR02230-06S1 0023
KULIKOWSKI, CASIMIR   P41RR02230-06S1 0024
KULIKOWSKI, CASIMIR   P41RR02230-06S1 0025
KULIKOWSKI, CASIMIR   P41RR02230-06S1 0026
KULIN, HOWARD E   R01HD26636-01A2
KULJIS, RODRIGO   S07RR05372-30 0677
KULJIS, RODRIGO O   R01NS29856-01
KULKARNI, A   Z01NS02771-04
KULKARNI, PRASAD S   R01EY02861-14
KULKOSKY, PAUL J   S06GM08197-10 0007
KULLBERG, RICHARD W   R01NS24078-04
KULLER, LEWIS H   N01HC85082-09
KULLER, LEWIS H   R01AR35858-06
KULLER, LEWIS H   R01HL28266-09
KULLER, LEWIS H   R37HL30793-08
KULLER, LEWIS H   S07RR05451-30 0353
KULLER, LEWIS H   U01HL37853-06
KULLER, LEWIS H.   N01HC48065-10
KUMAMOTO, CAROL A   R01GM36415-06
KUMANYIKA, SHIRIKI S   R01HL46778-01
KUMAR, AJIT   R55AI25531-04A1
KUMAR, AJIT   S07RR05359-30 0514
KUMAR, AJIT   S15CA55949-01
KUMAR, ANAND   P30MH48539-01 0003
KUMAR, ASHOK   P50HL18323-17 0067
KUMAR, ASHOK   R01HL44137-04
KUMAR, GYANENDRA   R29GM38228-06
KUMAR, GYANENDRA   S06GM08167-13 0038
KUMAR, KUSUM   R29NS26489-01A3
KUMAR, MAHENDRA   P01HL36588-06 9004
KUMAR, MAHENDRA   P01NS25569-04 0004
KUMAR, NIRBHAY   R29AI24704-05
KUMAR, RAJIV   R01DK25409-12
KUMAR, RAJIV   R01DK42971-02
KUMAR, SUBODH   R01ES03346-06
KUMAR, VINAY   R01AI20451-07
KUMMER, MARK A   M01RR00059-30 0679
KUMPFER, KAROL   S07RR07092-26 0517
KUMPFER, KAROL   S07RR07092-26 0493
KUNA, SAMUEL   M01RR00073-29 0231
KUNA, SAMUEL T   K04HL02353-03
KUNA, SAMUEL T   M01RR00073-29 0310
KUNA, SAMUEL T   M01RR00073-29 0089
KUNA, SAMUEL T   R01HL27520-07
KUNA, SAMUEL T   R13AG09454-01
KUNCL, RALPH W   R01ES05750-01
KUNDEL, HAROLD L   R01CA32870-11
KUNG, CHING   R01GM22714-17
KUNG, CHING   R01GM36386-06
KUNG, FAITH H   U10CA28439-12
KUNG, FAITH H   U10CA28439-12 0045
KUNG, FAITH H   U10CA28439-12 0046
KUNG, FAITH H   U10CA28439-12 0005
KUNG, FAITH H   U10CA28439-12 0006
KUNG, FAITH H   U10CA28439-12 0007
KUNG, FAITH H   U10CA28439-12 0008
KUNG, FAITH H   U10CA28439-12 0009
KUNG, FAITH H   U10CA28439-12 0010
KUNG, FAITH H   U10CA28439-12 0047
KUNG, FAITH H   U10CA28439-12 0048
KUNG, FAITH H   U10CA28439-12 0049
KUNG, FAITH H   U10CA28439-12 0050
KUNG, FAITH H   U10CA28439-12 0051
KUNG, FAITH H   U10CA28439-12 0052
KUNG, FAITH H   U10CA28439-12 0053
KUNG, FAITH H   U10CA28439-12 0054
KUNG, FAITH H   U10CA28439-12 0055
KUNG, FAITH H   U10CA28439-12 0056
KUNG, FAITH H   U10CA28439-12 0057
KUNG, FAITH H   U10CA28439-12 0058
KUNG, FAITH H   U10CA28439-12 0059
KUNG, FAITH H   U10CA28439-12 0060
KUNG, FAITH H   U10CA28439-12 0025
KUNG, FAITH H   U10CA28439-12 0026
KUNG, FAITH H   U10CA28439-12 0027
KUNG, FAITH H   U10CA28439-12 0028
KUNG, FAITH H   U10CA28439-12 0029
KUNG, FAITH H   U10CA28439-12 0030
KUNG, FAITH H   U10CA28439-12 0031
KUNG, FAITH H   U10CA28439-12 0032
KUNG, FAITH H   U10CA28439-12 0033
KUNG, FAITH H   U10CA28439-12 0034
KUNG, FAITH H   U10CA28439-12 0035
KUNG, FAITH H   U10CA28439-12 0011
KUNG, FAITH H   U10CA28439-12 0012
KUNG, FAITH H   U10CA28439-12 0013
KUNG, FAITH H   U10CA28439-12 0014
KUNG, FAITH H   U10CA28439-12 0015
KUNG, FAITH H   U10CA28439-12 0016
KUNG, FAITH H   U10CA28439-12 0036
KUNG, FAITH H   U10CA28439-12 0037
KUNG, FAITH H   U10CA28439-12 0038
KUNG, FAITH H   U10CA28439-12 0039
KUNG, FAITH H   U10CA28439-12 0040
KUNG, FAITH H   U10CA28439-12 0041
KUNG, FAITH H   U10CA28439-12 0042
KUNG, FAITH H   U10CA28439-12 0043
KUNG, FAITH H   U10CA28439-12 0044
KUNG, FAITH H   U10CA28439-12 0001
KUNG, FAITH H   U10CA28439-12 0002
KUNG, FAITH H   U10CA28439-12 0003
KUNG, FAITH H   U10CA28439-12 0004
KUNG, FAITH H   U10CA28439-12 0017
KUNG, FAITH H   U10CA28439-12 0018
KUNG, FAITH H   U10CA28439-12 0019
KUNG, FAITH H   U10CA28439-12 0020
KUNG, FAITH H   U10CA28439-12 0021
KUNG, FAITH H   U10CA28439-12 0022
KUNG, FAITH H   U10CA28439-12 0023
KUNG, FAITH H   U10CA28439-12 0024
KUNG, H   Z01CM09299-04
KUNG, H   Z01CM09300-05
KUNG, H   Z01CM09301-05
KUNG, H   Z01CM09302-05
KUNG, H   Z01CM09312-05
KUNG, H   Z01CM09315-05
KUNG, H   Z01CM09316-04
KUNG, HANK F   P01MH48125-01 0006
KUNG, HANK F   P01MH48125-01 9003
KUNG, HANK F   P30MH48539-01 9001
KUNG, HANK F   R01NS18509-09
KUNG, HANK F   R01NS24538-06
KUNG, HSING-JIEN   R01CA46613-04
KUNG, HSING-JIEN   R37CA39207-07
KUNG, JOHN T   R01CA41982-06
KUNG, ROBERT T V   N01HV88104-04
KUNICKI, THOMAS J   P01HL44612-02
KUNICKI, THOMAS J   P01HL44612-02 9004
KUNICKI, THOMAS J   P01HL44612-02 0001
KUNICKI, THOMAS J   R01HL32279-07
KUNIO, MISONO   P30HD05797-20 9010
KUNITAKE, STEVEN T   R01HL31210-08
KUNITZ, SELMA   N01NS12318-00
KUNITZ, STEPHEN J   R01AA08153-02
KUNKEL, LOUIS   P01HD18658-09 0015
KUNKEL, LOUIS   S07RR05899-10 0277
KUNKEL, LOUIS M   P01HD18658-09
KUNKEL, LOUIS M   P30HD18655-10 9012
KUNKEL, LOUIS M   P30HD18655-10 9004
KUNKEL, LOUIS M   P30HD18655-10 9006
KUNKEL, LOUIS M   R01NS23740-06
KUNKEL, LOUIS M   S10RR06285-01
KUNKEL, M E   S07RR07180-10 0626
KUNKEL, STEVEN   P01DK38149-04 0004
KUNKEL, STEVEN   P50DK39255-05 0002
KUNKEL, STEVEN L   P01HL31963-08 0002
KUNKEL, STEVEN L   P01HL31963-08 9001
KUNKEL, STEVEN L   R01HL31237-07
KUNKEL, STEVEN L   R01HL35276-05
KUNKEL, T A   Z01ES65046-05
KUNKEL, T A   Z01ES65047-05
KUNKEL, T A   Z01ES65070-01
KUNOS, G   Z01AA00401-04
KUNOS, G   Z01AA00402-04
KUNOS, G   Z01AA00403-04
KUNTZ, IRWIN D   P01GM39552-05 0002
KUNTZ, IRWIN D   P41RR01081-14 0004
KUNTZ, IRWIN D   U01AI30261-02 0003
KUNTZ, IRWIN D JR   R24RR01695-07
KUNTZ, IRWIN D, JR   R01GM31497-09A1
KUNTZBERG, JOANNE   P30CA14236-18 0931
KUNZ, DANIEL A   S07RR07195-12 0713
KUNZ, THOMAS H   S07RR07043-26 0115
KUNZE, DIANA L   R01HL36840-06
KUO, CHO-CHOU   R01AI22082-05
KUO, CHO-CHOU   S07RR05714-21 0117
KUO, JYH-FA   R01CA36777-08
KUO, JYH-FA   R37HL15696-19
KUO, LIH   S07RR05814-12 0143
KUO, LIH   S07RR05814-12 0150
KUO, WEN   R01MH47460-01A1
KUO, WU-NAN   S06GM08119-18 0010
KUPERSMIDT, JANIS B   R03MH48101-01
KUPERSMITH, MARK   M01RR00096-30A1 0257
KUPERSMITH, MARK J   U10EY07673-04
KUPERSZTOCH, YANKEL   P01HD22766-05 0004
KUPFER, ABRAHAM   R01AI23764-06
KUPFER, C   Z01EY00084-13
KUPFER, DAVID   R01ES00834-17
KUPFER, DAVID J   P50MH30915-15
KUPFER, DAVID J   P50MH30915-15 0001
KUPFER, DAVID J   P50MH30915-15 0002
KUPFER, DAVID J   P50MH30915-15 0003
KUPFER, DAVID J   P50MH30915-15 9016
KUPFER, DAVID J   P50MH30915-15 9017
KUPFER, DAVID J   R37MH24652-17
KUPFER, DAVID J   S15MH49274-01
KUPFER, STUART R   K08HD00963-01
KUPFERMANN, IRVING   P01GM32099-09
KUPFERMANN, IRVING   P01GM32099-09 0009
KUPFERMANN, IRVING   P01GM32099-09 0010
KUPFERMANN, IRVING   P01GM32099-09 0011
KUPFERMANN, IRVING   P01GM32099-09 0017
KUPFERMANN, IRVING   R37MH35564-18
KUPIEC-WEGLINSKI, JERZY W   R01AI23847-04

KUPKE, DONALD W R01GM34938-06
KUPPER, THOMAS S M01RR00036-31 1037
KUPPER, THOMAS S R01AR40124-03
KUPPER, THOMAS S R29AI25082-05
KURACHI, KOTOKU P01DK42718-02 0005
KURACHI, KOTOKU R01HL38644-06
KURACINA, THOMAS C R43AI31782-01
KURAMITSU, HOWARD K R01DE08293-05
KURAMITSU, HOWARD K R03DE09864-01
KURAMITSU, HOWARD K R37DE03258-20
KURAMITSU, HOWARD K S15DE10076-01
KURANE, ICHIRO R01AI30624-01
KURANTSIN-MILLS, JOSEPH R29HL38521-05
KURET, JEFFREY A R01GM42816-03
KURET, JEFFREY A R01GM44806-01A1
KURITZKES, DANIEL S07RR05357-30 0459
KURITZKES, DANIEL R K11AI00929-04
KURIYAMA, RYOKO R01GM41350-03
KURIYAN, JOHN R01GM45547-01
KURIYAN, JOHN R29GM43094-02
KURJAN, JANET A R01GM47176-01
KURJAN, JANET ANN R01GM40585-05
KURKINEN, MARKKU T R01GM34090-08
KURKINEN, MARKKU T R01HD24442-03
KURL, RABINDER N R29ES05303-02
KURLAN, ROGER M M01RR00044-31 0390
KURLAN, ROGER M M01RR00044-31 0322
KURLAN, ROGER M M01RR00044-31 0356
KURLAN, ROGER M R01NS24278-05
KURLAN, ROGER M. M01RR00044-31 0306
KURLAN, ROGER M. M01RR00044-31 0307
KURLAND, LEONARD T P01AG08802-02
KURLAND, LEONARD T P01AG08802-02 0001
KURLAND, LEONARD T P01AG08802-02 9001
KURLAND, LEONARD T P30AG08031-02
KURLAND, LEONARD T P50NS16308-12A1 0008
KURLAND, LEONARD T P50NS17750-10 9001
KURLAND, LEONARD T P50NS17750-10
KURLAND, LEONARD T P50NS17750-10 0001
KURLAND, LEONARD T U01AG06786-06
KURLANDER, ROGER J R01AI18073-10A1
KURNICK, JAMES T R01AR39993-03
KURNICK, JAMES T R01HL43793-02
KURODA, MITZI I R01GM45744-01
KUROSKY, ALEXANDER R01NS29261-01
KURT-JONES, EVELYN A R29AI24952-04
KURTH, M J P42ES04699-05 0006
KURTH, M J P42ES04699-05 9002
KURTH, MARK J K04ES00182-03
KURTH, MARK J S15HL47780-01
KURTIN, PAUL M01RR00054-30 0400
KURTTI, TIMOTHY J R01AR37909-04
KURTZ, DONALD M, JR K04HL02207-04
KURTZ, IRA R01DK41212-01A3
KURTZ, PERRY N01ES05293-01
KURTZ, PERRY N01ES05295-04
KURTZ, PERRY N01ES15308-00
KURTZ, PERRY N01ES15314-00
KURTZ, PERRY N01ES15320-02
KURTZ, PERRY N01ES15322-00
KURTZBERG, DIANE P01DC00223-08 0004
KURTZBERG, DIANE P50NS20489-07 0003
KURZ, LINDA C R01GM33851-07
KURZER, MINDY S S07RR07052-26 0162
KUSAKAWA, ISOA S07RR05507-29 0481
KUSANO, K Z01NS02757-04
KUSEWITT, D F S07RR05900-06 0627
KUSHI, LARRY S07RR05448-30 0291
KUSHI, LAWRENCE H R01HL46781-01
KUSHMERICK, MARTIN J P01HL31962-08 0006
KUSHMERICK, MARTIN J R01AR36281-07A1
KUSHMERICK, MARTIN J R01AR38782-06
KUSHNER, IRVING R01AG02467-10
KUSHNER, JAMES P M01RR00064-27 0190
KUSHNER, JAMES P M01RR00064-27 0155
KUSHNER, JAMES P M01RR00064-27 0319
KUSHNER, JAMES P R01DK20503-14
KUSHNER, JAMES P R01DK20630-13
KUSHNER, MICHAEL J M01RR00040-31 0283
KUSHNER, ROBERT M01RR00055-30 0581
KUSHNER, ROBERT M01RR00055-30 0563
KUSHNER, SIDNEY R R01GM27997-12
KUSHNER, SIDNEY R R01GM28760-10
KUSHWAHA, RAMPRATAP S P01HL28972-10 0001
KUSHWAHA, RAMPRATAP S R01HL41256-04
KUSTU, SYDNEY G R01GM38361-06
KUSZAK, JEROME P50AR39239-05 9002
KUSZAK, JEROME R R01EY06642-05S1
KUTAS, MARTA R01AG08313-02
KUTAS, MARTA R01HD22614-05
KUTNER, NANCY M01RR00039-31 0393
KUTNER, NANCY G R01DK42949-02
KUTNER, NANCY G U01AG10306-01
KUTTY, R K Z01HL04409-01
KUTZBERG, DIANE P30HD01799-27 9011
KUWADA, JOHN Y R01NS24848-05
KUWADA, SHIGEYUKI R01NS18027-10
KUYK, THOMAS S07RR05807-13 0465
KUZIRIAN, ALAN S07RR05547-23 0080
KUZIRIAN, ALAN M P40RR03820-03S1
KUZURA, JAMES W P01AI15351-13 0005
KVALE, PAUL N01HR76033-04
KVEDAR, JOSEPH C K08AR01804-04
KVIETYS, PETER R P01DK43785-01 9001
KVIETYS, PETER R P01DK43785-01 0005
KVIETYS, PETER R R01DK41399-02
KVIZ, FREDERICK J. P01CA42760-06 0002
KWA, BOO H S07RR06005-04 0301
KWAN, SAU-PING K04AI01044-01
KWAN, SAU-PING R01AI25117-05
KWIATKOWSKI, DAVID J R01HG00598-01
KWIRAM, ALVIN L S15MH49330-01
KWITEROVICH, PETER O M01RR00052-30 0230
KWITEROVICH, PETER O, JR R01HL31497-08
KWITEROVICH, PETER O, JR U01HL37975-05
KWOCK, LESTER R01CA39633-07
KWOCK, LESTER S10RR06322-01
KWOH, C KENT R29AR39366-03
KWOH, KENT M01RR00056-30 0358
KWOK, CHEUK SANG R01CA50872-03
KWOK, SIMON C R29HD24599-04
KWOK, WILLIAM R29DK40964-03
KWON-CHUNG, K J Z01AI00057-18
KWON, BYOUNG S R01AR40248-02
KYLE, ANDREW C R44EY06874-03S1
KYLE, DAVID J R43CA55474-01
KYLE, DAVID J R43HL47286-01
KYLE, DAVID J R44DK41962-02
KYLE, DAVID J R44DK41963-02
KYRIAKIS, JOHN M R29GM46577-01
KYTE, JACK E R01GM33962-07
L|MUMBY, MARC C P50HL17669-17 0043
L'HERNAULT, STEVEN W R29GM40697-04
LA BELLE, EDWARD F, JR R01HL37413-06
LA BRECQUE, DOUGLAS R R01CA29101-09S1
LA CELLE, PAUL L P01HL18208-17
LA DU, BERT N JR R01GM44887-02
LA LANDE, MARC P01HD18658-09 0012
LA MANNA, JOSEPH P50HL42215-04 0004
LA MAR, GERD N R37HL16087-18
LA MAR, GERD N S07RR07007-26 0921
LA MOTTE, CAROLE C P50NS10174-20 0024
LA MOTTE, CAROLE C R01NS13335-13
LA MOTTE, CAROLE C R01NS28876-02
LA MOTTE, ROBERT H R01NS14624-13
LA MOTTE, ROBERT H R01NS15888-12
LA PORTE, DAVID C K04DK01722-04
LA PORTE, DAVID C R01DK40486-04
LA PORTE, DAVID C R01GM33927-07S1
LA PORTE, RONALD E R01AR39541-03
LA PORTE, RONALD E R01DK35905-05A1
LA REGINA, MARIE C R03RR07013-01
LA ROSA, JOHN C U01HL40185-05
LA ROSA, JOHN C U01HL44315-02
LA RUSSO, NICHOLAS F R37DK24031-13
LA VAIL, JENNIFER H R01EY08773-14
LA VAIL, MATTHEW M R37EY01919-15
LA VAIL, MATTHEW M U01EY06842-05S1
LA VOIE, EDMOND J R01ES02338-11
LA VOIE, EDMOND J R37ES02030-13
LABARTHE, DARWIN R R01HL38429-05
LABARTHE, DARWIN R S07RR05828-08 0524
LABARTHE, DARWIN R U01HL41166-02
LABERGE, MARTINE S15AR41250-01
LABHART, PAUL R01GM46938-01
LABIB, RAMZY S S07RR05378-30 0000
LABIG, CHALMER E, JR R03DA06793-01A1
LABOUVIE-VIEF, GISELA R01AG09203-01A1
LABOV, WILLIAM R01AG07806-02
LABRECQUE, DOUGLAS M01RR00059-30 0730
LABRECQUE, DOUGLAS R M01RR00059-30 0652
LABRECQUE, DOUGLAS R M01RR00059-30 0332
LACEY, DAVID L R29AI26814-04
LACEY, LORETTA F R01CA54403-01
LACEY, STEPHEN W K11DK01860-04
LACHENBRUCH, PETER A P01HL14388-20 9004
LACHIN, JOHN M N01DK22206-37
LACHIN, JOHN M S15DK44668-01
LACHMAN, LAWRENCE B R01CA38043-08
LACKNER, ANDREW P51RR00169-30 0184
LACKNER, ANDREW A K01RR00039-05
LACKNER, ANDREW A P51RR00169-30 0172
LACKS, SANFORD A R01GM29721-11
LACKS, SANFORD A R37AI14885-14
LACLAIRE, JOHN W S07RR07091-26 0758
LACROIX, KAROL A R15HL44602-01A1
LACY, ALTON S07RR05305-30 0736
LACY, CLIFTON R S07RR05576-27 0598
LACY, ELIZABETH H R01AI30502-01
LACY, ELIZABETH H R01HD20919-06
LACY, ELIZABETH H R01NS25129-05
LACY, ERIC R R01DK39074-04
LACY, JILL R29CA51449-02
LACY, PAUL P01AI24854-05 0003
LACY, PAUL E R01DK01226-35
LAD, PRAMOD M S07RR05521-29 0066
LAD, THOMAS E R01CA56117-01
LAD, THOMAS E U10CA52651-02
LADENSON, PAUL W M01RR00035-31 0408
LADENSON, PAUL W M01RR00035-31 0407
LADENSON, PAUL W M01RR00035-31 0409
LADENSON, PAUL W M01RR00722-19 0250
LADISCH, STEPHAN K R01CA42361-06
LAEMLE, LOIS K S07RR05393-30 0895
LAFER, EILEEN M K04NS01536-01
LAFER, EILEEN M R01NS29051-05
LAFFERRIERE, GERARDO S07RR07062-26 0214
LAFFERTY, KEVIN P01DK40144-04 0003
LAFFERTY, KEVIN J P01DK40144-04
LAFFERTY, KEVIN J R01DK33470-08
LAFFREY, SHIRLEY C S07RR05604-14 0679
LAFLEUR, ARTHUR L P01ES01640-14 9002
LAFORCE, E MARC M01RR00044-31 0375
LAFRANCHI, STEPHEN M01RR00334-25 0247
LAFRATTA, J P01NS02253-32 9001
LAFUSE, WILLIAM P R01GM41786-02
LAGAKOS, STEPHEN N01AI95030-06
LAGAKOS, STEPHEN W R01AI24643-05
LAGAKOS, STEPHEN W R01CA39640-07
LAGE, JANICE S07RR05950-07 0002
LAGOW, RICHARD J S07RR07091-26 0759
LAGUNOFF, DAVID P50HL30572-08 0006
LAGUNOFF, DAVID S03RR03549-01
LAGUNOFF, DAVID S15HL47688-01
LAGUNOFF, WILLIAM J P50HL30572-08 9003
LAHEY, B P01MH47200-02 0003
LAHEY, MARGARET R01DC00676-02
LAHIRI, DEBOMOY P30AG10133-01 0001
LAHIRI, SUKHAMAY P01HL19737-15 0011
LAHIRI, SUKHAMAY R01HL43413-03
LAHMEYER, HENRY S07RR05369-30 0607
LAHUE, ROBERT S R01GM44824-02
LAHUE, ROBERT S S07RR05712-20 0061
LAI-FOOK, STEPHEN J P01HL25816-11 0017
LAI-FOOK, STEPHEN J P01HL36552-07 0007
LAI-FOOK, STEPHEN J R01HL36597-06
LAI-FOOK, STEPHEN J R01HL40362-05
LAI, CHEE K R43CA55423-01
LAI, CHING-SAN R01GM35719-06
LAI, ERIC H C S07RR05406-30 0885
LAI, HENRY C R01ES03712-07
LAI, JOSEPHINE S07RR05675-23 0913
LAI, MICHAEL M R01AI19244-10
LAI, MICHAEL M R01AI26741-04
LAI, MICHAEL M C P01NS18146-10 0006
LAI, WAYNE P40RR00890-16 0007
LAI, YIH-LOONG P01HL40369-03 0006
LAIBSON, PETER R S07RR05510-28 0056
LAIDLAW, STEWART A S10RR06445-01
LAIMING, VIRGINIA DR N01CP05623-05
LAIMINS, LAIMONIS R01CA49670-03
LAINE, GLEN A R01HL36115-06
LAINE, RICHARD M R01DE09839-01
LAING, RONALD A R01EY01990-08
LAING, TIMOTHY J M01RR00042-31 0591
LAIPIS, PHILIP J R01GM33537-06
LAIRD, CHARLES D R01GM19179-19
LAIRD, NAN M R01GM29745-11
LAIRSON, DAVID R S07RR05828-08 0528
LAIRSON, PAUL D S07RR05521-29
LAIRSON, PAUL D S15HL47715-01
LAKATTA, E Z01AG00264-02
LAKATTA, E Z01AG00270-02
LAKATTA, E G Z01AG00243-05
LAKATTA, E G Z01AG00268-02
LAKE-BAKAAR, GERONE S07RR05736-19 0205
LAKE, JAMES A R01GM24034-15
LAKE, JEFFREY P P01AI15353-13 9001
LAKE, JOHN R K08DK01858-03
LAKE, WILLIAM H N01NS92325-04
LAKE, WILLIAM, JR N01CN15371-00
LAKEMAN, FRED D U01AI30451-02
LAKOSKI, JOAN M K04AG00450-03
LAKOWICZ, JOSEPH R R01GM35154-07
LAKOWICZ, JOSEPH R R01GM39617-04
LAKOWICZ, JOSEPH R S10RR07510-01
LAKSHMAN, RAJ R01AA08149-04
LAKSHMANAN, MARK C K08DK01870-03
LAL, HARBANS R01AA06890-06
LAL, HARBANS R01AG07695-04
LALANDE, MARC P30HD18655-10 9009
LALANDE, MARC E R55HG00177-01
LALLEMANT, MARC P01AI30795-02 0001
LALLY, EDWARD P50DE07118-07 0008
LALLY, EDWARD P50DE08239-04 9004
LALLY, EDWARD S07RR07083-26 0492
LALLY, EDWARD T R01DE09517-02
LALLY, EDWARD T R25CA28297-12
LALONDE, BERNADETTE S07RR05758-18 0250
LALOUEL, JEAN-MARC R01HL45325-02
LALOUEL, JEAN-MARC R01HL45753-01
LAM, DOMINIC M R01EY02423-15
LAM, ERIC R01GM45574-01
LAM, KWOK-WAI R01EY08213-03
LAM, LUKE K R43CA54037-01A1
LAM, LUKE K T R43CA52378-01A1
LAM, LUKE K T R44CA47720-03
LAM, SI-HOI N01AI95031-06
LAM, STEPHEN C T R29HL41793-04
LAM, STEPHEN C T S07RR05369-30 0584
LAM, Y W FRANCIS M01RR01346-10 0190
LAM, Y W FRANCIS S07RR07187-13 0693
LAMANNA, JOSEPH C R01NS22077-06
LAMARRE, YVES R13NS30146-01
LAMARTINIERE, CORAL S07RR05829-09 0958
LAMARTINIERE, CORAL A R01ES04360-06

LAMARTINIERE, CORAL A S15AI32202-01
LAMASTERS, PAUL R N01CO15743-00
LAMASTERS, PAUL R N01CO15746-00
LAMASTERS, PAUL R N01CO15756-00
LAMASTERS, PAUL R N01CO15769-00
LAMASTERS, PAUL R N01CO15776-00
LAMASTERS, PAUL R N01CO15782-00
LAMB, CLAUDE S07RR07236-04 0171
LAMB, DAVID M01RR00034-31 0416
LAMB, M A Z01BH07001-02
LAMB, M A Z01BH07002-01
LAMB, M A Z01BH07003-01
LAMB, M E Z01HD01112-05
LAMB, M E Z01HD01113-05
LAMB, M E Z01HD01114-04
LAMB, M E Z01HD01115-04
LAMB, M E Z01HD01116-04
LAMB, MARVIN R01NS27902-03
LAMB, ROBERT A R01AI23173-06
LAMB, ROBERT A R37AI20201-09
LAMB, ROBERT G R01AA08758-01A1
LAMBERT, H MICHAEL U10EY08588-02
LAMBERT, PAUL F R29CA55048-01
LAMBERT, SCOTT R P51RR00165-31 0179
LAMBERT, SCOTT R R01EY08544-02
LAMBETH, J DAVID R01CA46508-05
LAMBETH, JOHN D R01AI22809-06
LAMBETH, JOHN D R01DK27373-12
LAMBOWITZ, ALAN M R01GM37949-06
LAMBOWITZ, ALAN M R01GM37951-06
LAMBRIS, JOHN P30CA16520-16 9018
LAMBROZA, ARNON M01RR00047-31 0463
LAMM, MICHAEL E P50HL37117-05 0004
LAMM, MICHAEL E R01AI26449-11
LAMMERS, PETER J S06GM08136-18 0018
LAMMIE, PATRICK P51RR00165-31 0189
LAMON, EDDIE W R01CA38008-05
LAMON, EDDIE W R01CA49609-02
LAMONT, JOHN T R01DK28195-11
LAMONT, JOHN T R01DK34583-08
LAMONT, RICHARD S07RR05346-30 0314
LAMONT, RICHARD J P30DE09743-02 0018
LAMONT, RICHARD J R29DE09439-01A2
LAMONTAGNE, LYNDA L R29NR02673-02
LAMORTE S07RR05380-30 0898
LAMPERT, PETER W P50NS12428-17 0008
LAMPING, KATHRYN G R29HL39050-05
LAMPPA, GAYLE K R01GM36419-06
LAMPSON, LOIS A R01NS24878-06
LAMSON, MYLES L R44RR03565-03
LAMSTER, IRA B P01DE09545-01A1 9001
LAMSTER, IRA B P01DE09545-01A1 0002
LAMSTER, IRA B P01DE09545-01A1
LAMURAGLIA, GLENN M K08HL02583-01
LAMY, PETER P S03RR03059-10
LAMY, PETER P S07RR05770-13
LAN, KK GORDON R01CA55098-01
LAN, M Z01DE00423-06
LANCASTER, FRANCINE E R29AA08009-03
LANCASTER, J R P41RR06030-01A1 0008
LANCASTER, WAYNE D R01CA32638-11
LANCE-JONES, CYNTHIA R01HD25676-03
LANCE, MICHAEL P R29DK43649-02
LANCE, TIMOTHY L S07RR07122-23 0101
LANCLOS, KENNETH D S07RR05365-30 0086
LANCZ, GERALD J R01DA05794-03
LAND, GARLAND N01HD02915-01
LAND, GARLAND N01HD62916-07
LAND, PETER W S07RR05416-30 0567
LAND, VITA J U10CA05587-31
LAND, VITA J U10CA05587-31 0001
LAND, VITA J U10CA05587-31 0002
LAND, VITA J U10CA05587-31 0032
LAND, VITA J U10CA05587-31 0033
LAND, VITA J U10CA05587-31 0034
LAND, VITA J U10CA05587-31 0035
LAND, VITA J U10CA05587-31 0036
LAND, VITA J U10CA05587-31 0037
LAND, VITA J U10CA05587-31 0038
LAND, VITA J U10CA05587-31 0039
LAND, VITA J U10CA05587-31 0040
LAND, VITA J U10CA05587-31 0041
LAND, VITA J U10CA05587-31 0042
LAND, VITA J U10CA05587-31 0043
LAND, VITA J U10CA05587-31 0044
LAND, VITA J U10CA05587-31 0045
LAND, VITA J U10CA05587-31 0046
LAND, VITA J U10CA05587-31 0047
LAND, VITA J U10CA05587-31 0048
LAND, VITA J U10CA05587-31 0003
LAND, VITA J U10CA05587-31 0004
LAND, VITA J U10CA05587-31 0005
LAND, VITA J U10CA05587-31 0006
LAND, VITA J U10CA05587-31 0007
LAND, VITA J U10CA05587-31 0008
LAND, VITA J U10CA05587-31 0009
LAND, VITA J U10CA05587-31 0010
LAND, VITA J U10CA05587-31 0011
LAND, VITA J U10CA05587-31 0049
LAND, VITA J U10CA05587-31 0052
LAND, VITA J U10CA05587-31 0053
LAND, VITA J U10CA05587-31 0054
LAND, VITA J U10CA05587-31 0055
LAND, VITA J U10CA05587-31 0056
LAND, VITA J U10CA05587-31 0057
LAND, VITA J U10CA05587-31 0058
LAND, VITA J U10CA05587-31 0059
LAND, VITA J U10CA05587-31 0060
LAND, VITA J U10CA05587-31 0050
LAND, VITA J U10CA05587-31 0012
LAND, VITA J U10CA05587-31 0013
LAND, VITA J U10CA05587-31 0014
LAND, VITA J U10CA05587-31 0051
LAND, VITA J U10CA05587-31 0015
LAND, VITA J U10CA05587-31 0016
LAND, VITA J U10CA05587-31 0017
LAND, VITA J U10CA05587-31 0018
LAND, VITA J U10CA05587-31 0019
LAND, VITA J U10CA05587-31 0020
LAND, VITA J U10CA05587-31 0021
LAND, VITA J U10CA05587-31 0022
LAND, VITA J U10CA05587-31 0023
LAND, VITA J U10CA05587-31 0024
LAND, VITA J U10CA05587-31 0025
LAND, VITA J U10CA05587-31 0026
LAND, VITA J U10CA05587-31 0027
LAND, VITA J U10CA05587-31 0028
LAND, VITA J U10CA05587-31 0029
LAND, VITA J U10CA05587-31 0030
LAND, VITA J U10CA05587-31 0031
LANDALE, NANCY S R29HD25859-03
LANDAU, BERNARD R R37DK14507-22
LANDAU, EMMANUAL M P01MH45212-02 0007
LANDAU, EMMANUEL M R01AA06659-06
LANDAY, ALAN L R01AI32478-01
LANDE, RUSSELL S07RR07080-26 0304
LANDE, RUSSELL S R01GM27120-12
LANDEFELD, C SETH R01AG09657-01
LANDEFELD, THOMAS D P60DK20572-14 0039
LANDEFELD, THOMAS D S07RR05383-30 0564
LANDER, ARTHUR D R01NS26862-02
LANDER, ERIC S P50HG00098-02
LANDESBERG, REGINA R29DE09832-01
LANDESMAN, SHELDON H M01RR00318-25 0214
LANDESMAN, SHELDON H N01AI95014-05
LANDESMAN, SHELDON H R01HD25714-03
LANDFEAR, SCOTT M R01AI25920-04
LANDFIELD, PHILIP W R01AG04542-07
LANDFIELD, PHILIP W R01AG07767-04
LANDFIELD, PHILIP W R01DA03637-08
LANDICK, ROBERT C R29GM38660-05
LANDIS, CLARK R29GM39417-05
LANDIS, CLAUDIA K11DK01845-04
LANDIS, DENNIS M R01NS22614-06
LANDIS, DENNIS M R01NS23641-06
LANDIS, J RICHARD R01HL33407-08
LANDIS, RICHARD P01CA40011-07 9003
LANDIS, STORY C R01HD25681-03
LANDIS, STORY C R01NS23678-07
LANDIS, SUZANNE U01AI25868-05 0006
LANDIS, SUZANNE E S07RR05450-30 0335
LANDMESSER, LYNN T R01NS19640-09
LANDO, HARRY A R01HL44992-02
LANDOWNE, DAVID R01NS26651-02
LANDRETH, GARY E R01GM34908-05
LANDRETH, GARY E R01NS28744-02
LANDRETH, KENNETH S R01AI23950-06
LANDRIGAN, PHILIP J P30ES00928-18
LANDRIGAN, PHILIP J R01OH02717-02
LANDRIGAN, PHILLIP J M01RR00071-28A1 0215
LANDRIGAN, PHILLIP J P30ES00928-18 9014
LANDRY, SUSAN H R01HD25128-01A3
LANDRY, SUSAN H R29HD23800-05
LANDSBERG, LEWIS M01RR01032-16 0463
LANDSBERG, LEWIS M01RR01032-16 0427
LANDSBERG, LEWIS M01RR01032-16 0368
LANDSBERG, LEWIS M01RR01032-16 0407
LANDSBERG, LEWIS R01DK20378-15
LANDSVERK, JOHN A R01MH46078-03
LANDY, ARTHUR R01GM33928-07
LANDY, ARTHUR R37AI13544-15
LANDY, MICHAEL S R01EY08266-03
LANDY, MICHAEL S S07RR07062-26 0215
LANE, ALFRED T M01RR00081-29 0140
LANE, ALFRED T R01AR41551-01 0005
LANE, DAVID A P01AG08761-02 9002
LANE, H C Z01AI00390-08
LANE, HARLAN L P01DC00361-05S1 0002
LANE, HC Z01AI00585-02
LANE, JAMES D R01DA06857-01A1
LANE, JOSEPH M P01CA29502-11A1 9008
LANE, JOSEPH M S07RR05495-29
LANE, LOIS K P01HL22619-14 0001
LANE, M DANIEL R01DK14575-23
LANE, M DANIEL R01DK38418-05
LANE, M DANIEL R37DK14574-22
LANE, MICHAEL J R01HG00318-03
LANE, RICHARD D P01HL36573-06 9002
LANE, RICHARD D S07RR05366-30 0559
LANE, RICHARD D S07RR05700-22 0876
LANE, ROBERT S R01AI22501-07
LANFORD, ROBERT E R01CA39390-08
LANFORD, ROBERT E R01CA53246-01
LANFORD, ROBERT E. P01HL28972-10 0008
LANG, BRIEN R R01DE06720-08
LANG, C MAX P40RR00469-23
LANG, CHARLES H R29GM38032-05
LANG, NORMA M S07RR06031-02
LANG, PETER J R01AG09779-04
LANG, PETER J R01MH43975-04
LANG, PETER J R37MH37757-10
LANG, W PAUL S07RR05321-30 0256
LANG, Z E S07RR05477-29 0418
LANGA, KENNETH M R03HS06948-01
LANGAN, THOMAS J K08NS01361-03
LANGE, BEVERLY M01RR00240-27 0309
LANGE, CHRISTOPHER S R01CA39045-05
LANGE, CHRISTOPHER S R01GM43374-02
LANGE, DALE J M01RR00645-20 0378
LANGE, DAVID G R01ES03386-05
LANGE, DAVID G R01EY08132-02
LANGE, LOUIS G K05AA00139-01
LANGE, LOUIS G, III R01AA06989-06
LANGE, LOUIS G, III R01AA08247-02
LANGE, W R Z01DA00212-03
LANGE, YVONNE P50HL15062-20 0033
LANGE, YVONNE R01HL28448-11
LANGENBACH, R Z01ES21121-03
LANGENBACH, R Z01ES21133-02
LANGENBACH, R Z01ES21158-01
LANGENBUCHER, JAMES R01DA05688-03
LANGER, GLENN A R01HL28539-10
LANGER, PAMELA J R29AI25031-05
LANGER, ROBERT U01CA52857-02 0002
LANGER, ROBERT U54HD29125-01 0006
LANGER, ROBERT D R01HL44689-01A1
LANGER, ROBERT S R01EY05333-09
LANGER, ROBERT S R01GM25810-13
LANGER, ROBERT S R01GM26698-12
LANGER, ROBERT S R01GM44884-01
LANGHOFF, ERIC S07RR05526-29 0080
LANGHOFF, ERIK R01AI28734-01A3
LANGLAIS, PHILIP J P50AG05131-08 0017
LANGLAIS, PHILIP J R01NS29481-01
LANGLEY, RICKY L S07RR05812-12 0486
LANGLOIS, ALPHONSE J P01CA43447-06 9002
LANGLOIS, JUDITH H R01HD21332-06
LANGMORE, JOHN S07RR07050-26 0125
LANGMORE, JOHN P R01GM44403-01A2
LANGMORE, SUSAN P01DE09142-02 0004
LANGMUIR, MARGARET E R44HL47175-02
LANGMUIR, MARGARET E R44MH45278-02A1
LANGMUIR, VIRGINIA K R29CA52285-03
LANGNESS, LEWIS P01HD11944-12 0005
LANGOIS, JUDITH H P30HD06160-20S1 0004
LANGRIDGE, ROBERT P41RR01081-14 0015
LANGRIDGE, ROBERT P41RR01081-14 0016
LANGRIDGE, ROBERT P41RR01081-14 0017
LANGRIDGE, ROBERT P41RR01081-14 0018
LANGRIDGE, ROBERT P41RR01081-14 0019
LANGRIDGE, ROBERT P41RR01081-14 9001
LANGRIDGE, ROBERT P41RR01081-14 9002
LANGRIDGE, ROBERT P41RR01081-14 9003
LANGRIDGE, ROBERT P41RR01081-14 9004
LANGRIDGE, ROBERT P41RR01081-14 9005
LANGRIDGE, ROBERT P41RR01081-14 9006
LANGRIDGE, ROBERT P41RR01081-14
LANGSTON, AMELIA A K11HD00936-02
LANGSTON, DEBORAH P R55EY08851-01A1
LANGSTON, J WILLIAM R01AG09121-02
LANGSTON, J WILLIAM R01NS27365-03
LANIER, STEPHEN M R29NS24821-05
LANNER, MICHAEL S03RR03066-11
LANNERS, H NORBERT P51RR00164-30 0026
LANNERS, H NORBET P51RR00164-30 0024
LANNERS, H NORBET P51RR00164-30 0025
LANNOM, LINDA N01CP05626-07
LANNON, CAROLE S07RR05406-30 0910
LANNON, RICHARD P50DA01696-12 0013
LANOUE, KATHRYN F R01DK44070-01
LANSBURY, PETER T JR R01AG08470-03
LANSBURY, PETER T JR R29HL42416-02
LANSBURY, PETER T, JR S10RR06244-01
LANSDALE, SHARON N01CN15383-00
LANSDORP, PETER M R01AI29524-02
LANSER, MARC E R01GM36258-07
LANSKA, DOUGLAS S07RR05374-30 0741
LANSKA, MARY JO S07RR05374-30 0740
LANSKY, SHIRLEY B N01CO03878-06
LANSKY, SHIRLEY B P30CA21742-13
LANSKY, SHIRLEY B R01CA44140-05
LANSKY, SHIRLEY B S03RR03433-06
LANSKY, SHIRLEY B S15CA55925-01
LANTIGUA, RAFAEL R01AG10489-01
LANTZ, MARILYN S07RR05300-30 0210
LANTZ, MARILYN S R01DE07256-08
LANTZ, ROBERT C R03AA08530-02
LANYI, JANOS K R01GM29498-11
LANYON, RICHARD I S07RR07112-24 0416
LANZA-JACOBY, SUSAN R01GM31828-06
LAOURI, MARIANNE R03HS06916-01
LAPHAM, LOWELL P30AG08665-02 9002
LAPHAM, LOWELL W P01AG03644-07 9003
LAPHAM, LOWELL W P30ES01247-17 9003
LAPHAM, SANDRA C U01AA08815-02
LAPIN, GREGORY D S07RR05370-30 0612

LAPOSATA, MICHAEL R01DK43159-02
LAPP, DAVID F S07RR05365-30 0087
LAPP, WILLIAM M S07RR05938-07 0313
LAPPIN, JOSEPH S R01EY05926-06
LAPPIN, MICHAEL R S07RR05458-29 0828
LARAGH, JOHN H P50HL18323-17
LARAMEY, CHARLENE R01CA46587-05
LARDY, HENRY A R01DK10334-26
LARDY, HENRY A R01DK20678-13
LARGE, THOMAS S07RR05410-30 0950
LARGE, THOMAS H R01EY08885-01
LARGENT, BRIAN LEE M01RR00042-31 0663
LARGMAN, COREY R01HL25408-13
LARIMER, JAMES L R01NS05423-25
LARISH, DOUGLAS D R29AG07352-04
LARK, KARL G R01GM42337-14
LARK, KARL G S07RR07092-26 0528
LARKINS, BRIAN A R01GM36970-06
LARNER, A Z01BD03020-04
LARNER, JOSEPH R37DK14334-23
LAROCCA, DAVID S07RR05929-06 0280
LAROCHELLE, W J Z01CP05546-04
LAROCK, RICHARD C R01GM40036-04
LAROS, RUSSEL P01HD24180-04 9001
LAROSA, JOHN C S07RR05359-30
LARRABEE, MARTIN G R01NS00702-35
LARRALDE, G Z01AI00574-02
LARRICK, JAMES W R44AI28127-02
LARSEN, ERIC C K08HL02611-02
LARSEN, GARY P01HL36577-06
LARSEN, GARY L P01HL36577-06 0001
LARSEN, JENNIFER L R29DK40752-03
LARSEN, PHILIP R R01DK36256-07
LARSEN, RANDY J K01MH00704-05
LARSEN, RANDY J R01MH42057-06
LARSEN, ULLA M R01HD27610-01
LARSON-PRIOR, LINDA J R29NS30759-01
LARSON, ERIC B. M01RR00037-31 0431
LARSON, ALICE A K02DA00124-04
LARSON, ALICE A R01DA04090-06
LARSON, ALICE A R01DA04190-05
LARSON, CHARLES R R01DC00207-09
LARSON, DOUGLAS F S07RR05675-23 0914
LARSON, DRENA D R29GM41899-03
LARSON, ELAINE L S03RR03527-02
LARSON, ELAINE L S07RR06012-03
LARSON, ELAINE L S15DK44678-01
LARSON, ERIC B R01AG09769-01
LARSON, ERIC B U01AG06781-05
LARSON, J R01NR01428-05
LARSON, JANET S07RR05518-28 0508
LARSON, JANET E K11HD00880-01A1
LARSON, MARTIN P60AR36308-07 9001
LARSON, REED W R01MH38324-07
LARSON, RICHARD P01CA40046-05S2 9001
LARSON, SIGNE M01RR00071-28A1 0152
LARTEY, PAUL A U01AI30183-02
LARTEY, PAUL A U01AI31808-01 9001
LARUSSO, N F M01RR00585-20 0431
LARUSSO, NICHOLAS F M01RR00585-20 0179
LASANSKY, A Z01NS01659-23
LASATER, ERIC P01NS07938-22 0028
LASATER, ERIC M R01EY05972-06
LASEK, RAYMOND J R01AG08887-03
LASEK, RAYMOND J R01NS14900-13
LASH, LAWRENCE H R29DK40725-04
LASH, ROBERT S07RR05379-30 0764
LASHER, ROBERT S P20DC01439-01 0002
LASHNER, BRET M01RR00055-30 0571
LASHOF, JOYCE C S07RR05441-30
LASHOF, JOYCE C S15ES05842-01
LASITER, PHILLIP S R01DC00732-02
LASKA, EUGENE S07RR05651-24 0139
LASKA, EUGENE M R01MH42959-04
LASKER, HOWARD R S07RR07066-26 0248
LASKER, J P50AA03508-14 0044
LASKER, JUDITH N S07RR07173-10
LASKER, LORRAINE S15CA55945-01
LASKI, FRANK A R01GM40451-04
LASKIN, DEBRA L R01ES04738-03
LASKIN, DEBRA L R01GM34310-07
LASKIN, JEFFREY D R01ES03647-06
LASKOW, DAVID A M01RR00032-31 0332
LASKOWSKI, MICHAEL, JR R01GM10831-32
LASLEY, B P42ES04699-05 0009
LASLEY, BILL L P51RR00169-30 0120
LASLEY, STEPHEN S07RR05369-30 0594
LASSER, ELLIOTT C R01CA46675-04
LASSER, NORMAN L U01HL37884-06
LASSER, NORMAN L U01HL37966-05
LAST, JEROLD A R01HL32690-07
LAST, ROBERT L R29GM43134-02
LASTER, SCOTT M S07RR07071-26 0254
LASTRA, ANSELMO P50AG05128-08 0015
LASZIO, ANDREI P01CA51116-02 0003
LASZLO, ANDREI R01CA49018-03
LATERRA, JOHN J K08NS01329-03
LATERRA, JOHN J S07RR05808-13 0912
LATIES, ALAN M S07RR05610-24
LATIES, ALAN M S07RR05610-24 0932
LATIES, VICTOR G R01DA04925-03
LATIFPOUR, JAMSHID R29DK42530-02
LATINA, MARK A K11EY00292-05
LATORRE, RAMON R01GM35981-06
LATOV, NORMAN P01NS11766-17A1 0035
LATOV, NORMAN R01NS25187-04A1
LATRENTA, GREGORY S07RR05396-30 0784
LATTEMANN, DIANNE F R01DK40963-04
LATTIME, EDMUND C R01CA42908-05A1
LATTMAN, EATON E R01GM35171-07
LATTMAN, EATON E R01GM36358-05
LAU, ALAN F R01CA52098-01A1
LAU, ALAN F S07RR07026-26 0000
LAU, BENJAMIN S07RR05352-30 0749
LAU, EDUARDO P50DE09165-03 0003
LAU, JOSEPH T R01GM38193-05
LAU, KIN-HING W R01AR40614-01A1
LAU, KIN-HING W R01DE08681-02
LAU, LEE MIN R03HS06947-01
LAU, LESTER F R01CA46565-05
LAU, LESTER F R01CA52220-02
LAU, SERRINE S R29GM39338-04
LAU, YUN-FAI C R01HD24384-04
LAU, YUN-FAI C R01HD27392-02
LAUBE, BETH U01AI31867-01 0012
LAUBE, BETH L M01RR00722-19 0251
LAUBE, BETH L M01RR00722-19 0252
LAUDENSLAGER, MARK L R01MH37373-09
LAUDER, JEAN M P01HD23042-03 0007
LAUDER, JEAN M R01HD22052-05
LAUE, LOUISA S07RR05360-30 0776
LAUER, BRIAN A N01AI82520-04
LAUER, RONALD M01RR00059-30 0747
LAUER, RONALD P50HL42266-02 0001
LAUER, RONALD M M01RR00059-30 0648
LAUER, RONALD M P50HL14230-20 0088
LAUER, RONALD M P50HL42266-02
LAUER, RONALD M U01HL37962-05
LAUFFENBURGER, DOUGLAS A R01GM41476-04
LAUFFER, RANDALL A P01CA48729-03 9003
LAUFMAN, LESLIE R U10CA35261-08
LAUG, WALTER E R01CA50559-03
LAUGHLIN, JOHN S P30CA08748-26 9031
LAUGHLIN, M HAROLD S07RR07053-26 0152
LAUGHLIN, MAURICE H R01HL36088-05
LAUGHLIN, MAURICE H R01HL36531-05A2
LAUGHLIN, NELLIE S07RR07098-26 0354
LAUGHLIN, NELLIE K R01ES04860-01A3
LAUMANN, EDWARD O S07RR07029-26
LAUMANN, EDWARD O S15GM47094-01
LAUMANN, EDWARD O S15MH49287-01
LAURENCE, JEFFREY C R01AI29119-02
LAURENCE, KENNETH A S07RR07170-15
LAURENT, G S07RR07003-26 0326
LAURENT, GILLES J R01NS29194-01
LAURIE, GORDON W S07RR05431-30 0849
LAUSCH, ROBERT N R01EY05099-08
LAUSCH, ROBERT N R01EY07564-04
LAUSE, DAVID B S07RR05365-30 0088
LAUTENBERGER, J A Z01CP05120-12
LAUTENBERGER, J A Z01CP05564-04
LAUTENBERGER, J A Z01CP05570-04
LAUTENBERGER, J A Z01CP05587-03
LAUTERBUR, PAUL P41RR05964-02 0003
LAUTERBUR, PAUL C P41RR05964-02
LAUTERBUR, PAUL C S10RR06243-01
LAUTERIO, THOMAS J R29DK40982-03
LAVALLEE, DAVID K S06GM08176-12 0025
LAVEIST, THOMAS A S07RR05445-30 0875
LAVELLE, DONALD S07RR05369-30 0581
LAVELLE, WILLIAM G S07RR05712-20 0092
LAVERGNE, JULIO A S06GM08224-07 0015
LAVIN, THOMAS M01RR00079-29 0400
LAVIN, THOMAS N R01DK39998-03
LAVIZZO-MOUREY, RISA K08AG00363-05
LAVKER, ROBERT M P01AR39674-03 0002
LAVKER, ROBERT M R01EY06769-04
LAVOIE, EDMOND J P01CA29580-11 0004
LAVOIE, LAWRENCE U01AI25696-05 9004
LAW, JOHN H R01GM29238-11
LAW, MARTHA P01HD17449-08 0002
LAW, PETER K R01NS26185-04
LAW, PING Y R01DA05945-03
LAW, PING Y R01DA07339-01
LAW, PING-YEE P01DA05695-03 0004
LAWELLIN, DAVID W S03RR03540-01
LAWELLIN, DAVID W S15CA55964-01
LAWLER, JAMES E R01HL19680-13
LAWLER, JOHN W P01HL42443-03 0006
LAWLER, JOHN W R01HL28749-11
LAWLESS, HARRY T R01DC00902-01A1
LAWLESS, HARRY T R03DC01192-01
LAWLEY, THOMAS J R01AR39632-03
LAWLOR, BRIAN M01RR00071-28A1 0242
LAWRENCE, CHARLES B P30HG00210-01 9004
LAWRENCE, CHARLES B R24LM05207-07
LAWRENCE, CHARLES B. P30HD24064-04 9007
LAWRENCE, CHRISTOPHER W R01GM21858-17
LAWRENCE, CHRISTOPHER W R01GM32885-08
LAWRENCE, CLINTON E M01RR00350-25 0407
LAWRENCE, CLINTON E M01RR00350-25 0405
LAWRENCE, DAVID A R01ES03179-09
LAWRENCE, DAVID A R01ES03778-07
LAWRENCE, DAVID A R01ES05020-01A3
LAWRENCE, DAVID S R01GM45989-01
LAWRENCE, E CLINTON M01RR00350-25 0246
LAWRENCE, H SHERWOOD P30AI27742-03
LAWRENCE, HUGH J R01CA47866-03
LAWRENCE, IRA P50AI11403-19 0011
LAWRENCE, JEANNE B K04HG00002-02
LAWRENCE, JEANNE B R01HG00251-03
LAWRENCE, JOHN C, JR R01DK28312-11
LAWRENCE, JOHN H K11HL02639-01
LAWRENCE, K SILBART R01CA47132-04
LAWRENCE, LEONARD E S03RR03304-10
LAWRENCE, PAUL J R43AI31738-01
LAWRENCE, PAUL J R44AI28148-03
LAWRENCE, RENEE H R29AG09344-02
LAWRENCE, ROBERT M K11HD00826-05
LAWRENCE, THEODORE P30CA46592-04 9013
LAWRENCE, THEODORE S M01RR00042-31 0508
LAWRENCE, THEODORE S R29CA53440-01
LAWS, EDWARD R P50NS17750-10 0018
LAWSON, DAN S07RR05431-30 0851
LAWSON, DAVID M S06GM08167-13 0039
LAWSON, EDWARD E R01HL34919-06
LAWSON, RUSSELL K R01DK31063-10
LAWSON, WILLIAM M01RR00095-31 0298
LAWSON, WILLIAM E K07HL02086-04
LAWTHER, ROBERT S07RR07160-16 0585
LAWTON, ANDREW W S07RR05376-30 0039
LAWTON, M POWELL P01MH43371-04
LAWTON, M POWELL P01MH43371-04 0003
LAWTON, M POWELL P01MH43371-04 9001
LAWTON, M POWELL P50MH40380-07 0012
LAWTON, M POWELL R37AG07001-05
LAWTON, M POWELL S07RR05611-22
LAWTON, M POWELL S15AG10244-01
LAWTON, M POWELL U01AG10304-01
LAWTON, TERI A R43EY09166-01
LAWTON, WILLIAM P01HL14388-20 0242
LAWTON, WILLIAM J M01RR00059-30 0462
LAXER, KENNETH D N01NS72333-01
LAXMANAN, SEETHALAKSHMI R29DK39003-05
LAYCHOCK, SUZANNE GALE R01DK25705-14
LAYNE, C S07RR07036-26 0108
LAYTON, HAROLD E R29DK42091-02
LAZAR, HAROLD L S07RR05487-29 0691
LAZAR, HAROLD L S07RR05487-29 0692
LAZAR, MITCHELL A R01DK43806-01
LAZAR, RICHARD B R01DC00550-03
LAZAROW, PAUL B R37DK19394-15
LAZAROWITZ, SONDRA G R01AI27449-04
LAZARUS, BRUCE S07RR05862-10 0562
LAZARUS, GERALD S M01RR00040-31 0371
LAZARUS, GERALD S P01AR39674-03 0004
LAZARUS, GERALD S P01AR39674-03
LAZARUS, HERBERT U01AI25696-05 9001
LAZARUS, HILLARD P01CA51183-01A1 0006
LAZARUS, HILLARD M M01RR00080-29 0441
LAZARUS, J MICHAEL U01DK37072-06
LAZARUS, JO-ANNE C S07RR07098-26 0341
LAZARUS, L H Z01ES90053-04
LAZEN, AL N01CP71128-08
LAZO, JOHN S R01CA43917-06
LAZZARA, RALPH R01HL35047-03
LAZZARINI, ROBERT A R01NS29056-01
LAZZARINI, ROBERT A. P50AG05138-08 0006
LE BEAU, MICHELLE M R01CA41644-06
LE BRETON, GUY C R01HL24530-12
LE DOUX, JOSEPH E, JR R01MH46516-01A1
LE DOUX, JOSEPH E, JR R37MH38774-07
LE DUC, LOUISE E R01DK40222-02
LE GALL, JEAN R01GM41482-03
LE GRICE, STUART F R01GM46623-01
LE GRICE, STUART F J R01AI31147-01
LE MARCHAND, LOIC P01CA33619-09 0009
LE MARCHAND, LOIC P01CA33619-09 0007
LE MARCHAND, LOIC R01CA55874-01
LE MARCHAND, LOIC R03CA52505-02
LE MASTER, DAVID M R01GM38779-04
LE THI, B-T Z01DE00529-01
LE VAY, SIMON R01EY05551-07
LE WINTER, MARTIN M R01HL35309-06
LE WINTER, MARTIN M R01HL45116-02
LE, C.T. P50DC00133-13 9003
LE, DIEM D R43DK44414-01
LE, DZUNG A R01AA08254-01A1
LE, JUNMING R01AI28993-02
LEA, ARDEN O R01AI17297-12
LEACH, CHARLES T S07RR05654-24 0130
LEACH, ROBIN J R03DE09933-01
LEACH, ROBIN J R29AR40689-01A1
LEACH, ROBIN J S07RR07187-13 0704
LEADERER, BRIAN P R01ES05410-02
LEADON, STEVEN A S07RR05918-08 0703
LEADON, STEVEN ANTHONY R01CA40453-06
LEAF, ALEXANDER U01HL40548-03
LEAF, PHILIP J R01MH40603-05
LEAF, PHILIP J R01MH41638-05
LEAHY, JOHN L P30DK36836-05 0004
LEAHY, JOHN L R01DK38543-06
LEAKE, PATRICIA A N01DC12400-00
LEAKE, PATRICIA A R01DC00160-10
LEAKE, ROSEMARY D M01RR00425-22S3 0426
LEAPMAN, R D Z01RR10296-04

LEAPMAN, R D Z01RR10327-04
LEAPMAN, R D Z01RR10331-02
LEAPMAN, R D Z01RR10332-02
LEAR, JAMES LOUIS R01NS26657-03
LEARNED, ROBERT M R29GM44074-01A1
LEARY, JAMES F R01HD20601-07
LEARY, MARY R18CA43521-05
LEATHERBURY, LINDA P01HL36059-06 0003
LEAV, IRWIN R01CA15776-14
LEAVITT, BRUCE J S07RR05429-30 0210
LEAVITT, DENNIS D R01CA46562-04
LEAVITT, DENNIS D R01CA52585-01A1
LEAVITT, JOHN S15EY09448-01
LEAVITT, JOHN C R01CA34763-08
LEAVITT, JOHN C S07RR05768-12
LEBEAU, MICHELLE P01CA40046-05S2 0003
LEBER, STEVEN M K08NS01524-01
LEBIEN, TUCKER P01CA21737-14 0001
LEBIEN, TUCKER W R01CA31685-10
LEBIODA, LUCASZ S07RR07160-16 0590
LEBKOWSKI, JANE S R43HL46618-01
LEBLANC, ANDREA R35AG08992-01 0002
LEBLANC, DONALD J R01DE08915-03
LEBLANC, GERALD A S07RR07071-26 0256
LEBMAN, DEBORAH A R29DK42982-01A1
LEBOEUF, RENE P01DK02456-33A1 0014
LEBOEUF, RENEE C R29HL42333-04
LEBOEUF, ROBERT D R29CA54290-01A1
LEBOUTON, ALBERT V P01HD26013-01A2 9001
LEBOVITZ, HAROLD E M01RR00318-25 0219
LEBOVITZ, ROBERT M R01NS26899-03
LEBOVITZ, RUSSELL M R29CA49845-03
LEBOWITZ, MICHAEL D P50HL14136-20 9001
LEBOWITZ, MICHAEL D P50HL14136-20 0019
LEBOWITZ, PAUL R01CA49238-03
LEBOY, PHOEBE S P50DE08239-04 0009
LEBOY, PHOEBE S R01AR40075-02
LEBWOHL, DAVID K11DK01799-05
LECH, JOHN J R01ES01080-17
LECH, JOHN J R01ES05773-01
LECH, JOHN J R01GM37498-06
LECHAGO, JUAN P01DK42582-02 9003
LECHAGO, JUAN P30DK36200-05S1 9003
LECHAN, RONALD M R01DK37021-06
LECHENE, CLAUDE P S10RR06521-01
LECHNER, J F Z01CP05541-04
LECKMAN, JAMES M01RR06022-02 0649
LECKMAN, JAMES M01RR06022-02 0550
LECKMAN, JAMES F M01RR00125-28 0723
LECKMAN, JAMES F M01RR06022-02 0723
LECKMAN, JAMES F R01MH44843-03
LECLERC, PAUL G12RR03037-07 9002
LECLERC, PAUL G12RR03037-07
LECLERC, PAUL G12RR03037-07 9005
LECLERC, PAUL G12RR03037-07 0003
LECOMTE, JULIETTE T S07RR07082-26 0298
LECOMTE, JULIETTE T J R29HG43101-02
LEDBETTER, DAVID H P30HG00210-01 9001
LEDBETTER, DAVID H R01HD20619-06
LEDBETTER, DAVID H R01HG00259-02
LEDBETTER, JEFFREY P01GM42508-03 0006
LEDDO, JOHN M R43HD27781-01
LEDDY, JOHN P P01AI29522-02 0004
LEDDY, JOHN P P01AI29522-02
LEDDY, JOHN P R01AG08178-04
LEDEEN, ROBERT W R01NS04834-29
LEDEEN, ROBERT W R01NS16181-12
LEDEEN, ROBERT W R01NS24172-06
LEDERER, SUSAN E R01LM05326-01
LEDERER, WILLIAM J R01HL25675-12
LEDERER, WILLIAM J R01HL36974-05
LEDERMAN, HOWARD M01RR00052-30 0235
LEDERMAN, HOWARD M S07RR05378-30 0001
LEDERMAN, MICHAEL U01AI25879-04S2 0001
LEDERMAN, MICHAEL M M01RR00080-29 0443
LEDERMAN, MICHAEL M M01RR00080-29 0394
LEDERMAN, MICHAEL M M01RR00080-29 0455
LEDERMAN, MICHAEL M M01RR00080-29 0395
LEDERMAN, MICHAEL M M01RR00080-29 0405
LEDERMAN, MICHAEL M M01RR00080-29 0453
LEDERMAN, MICHAEL M U01AI25879-04S2
LEDET, EARL G R43HL45376-01
LEDLEY, FRED P01DK44080-01 9001
LEDLEY, FRED D R29HD24186-04
LEDLEY, ROBERT S P41LM05206-08
LEDLEY, ROBERT S S15CA55989-01
LEE WILLIAM R P01ES03347-08 9001
LEE-HUANG, SYLVIA R55AI31343-01A1
LEE-HUANG, SYLVIA S07RR05399-30 0925
LEE-PARRITZ, D E P51RR00168-30 0169
LEE, A W Z01HL02333-04
LEE, AMY S R01GM31138-08
LEE, AMY S R37CA27607-12
LEE, B Z01CT00130-07
LEE, B Z01CT00158-06
LEE, B Z01CT00176-08
LEE, B Z01CT00225-01
LEE, BELLE L M01RR00083-29 0239
LEE, C J Z01BA02020-02
LEE, C J Z01BA02023-01
LEE, C J Z01BA02024-01
LEE, CHIA S07RR05373-30 0720
LEE, CHING-TSE S07RR07119-20
LEE, CHING-TSE S15DK44665-01
LEE, CHUAN-PU R01NS23384-05
LEE, CHUNG P50DK39250-05 0004
LEE, CHUNG P50DK39250-05 9001
LEE, DAVID P30CA16086-17 9012
LEE, DAVID C R01CA43793-05
LEE, DAVID R R01AI31129-01A1
LEE, DOH-YEEL M01RR00042-31 0542
LEE, DONALD S07RR07055-26 0189
LEE, ELISA T R21DK44567-01
LEE, ELISA T U01HL41654-04
LEE, ERNEST Y R01DK18512-17
LEE, EVA Y H PAN R29CA49649-04
LEE, FRANCIS K R01AI32456-01
LEE, FRANK S07RR05403-30 0812
LEE, GLORIA R29GM39300-04
LEE, GLORIA R35AG07911-04 0002
LEE, GLORIA R35AG07911-04 0007
LEE, HENRY J G12RR03020-07 0002
LEE, HON C R01HD17484-09
LEE, HON-CHI R29HL43710-02
LEE, HSIN-YI S07RR07263-01
LEE, J Z01MH02566-01
LEE, JAMES C R01DK21489-12
LEE, JAMES C R01GM45579-01
LEE, JAMES E K01MH00719-03
LEE, JAN S07RR06014-03 0845
LEE, JAN S07RR06014-03 0846
LEE, JANET S R29GM39698-04
LEE, JEAN C R01AI23244-06A2
LEE, JEAN C R01AI29040-02
LEE, JIN S P01CA52051-01A1 9004
LEE, JOHN N01CL72105-07
LEE, JOHN W R01GM28139-12
LEE, KATHRYN A R29NR02247-03
LEE, KERRY L P50HL17670-17 9004
LEE, KERRY L U01HL45726-01A1
LEE, KEVIN SCOTT R01NS24782-04
LEE, KUO-HSIUNG R01CA17625-15
LEE, KUO-HSIUNG R01CA54508-01
LEE, KUO-HSIUNG S10RR06606-01
LEE, LU-YUAN P01HL40369-03 0003
LEE, MARIETTA Y R01AI29158-03
LEE, MARIETTA Y R01GM31973-09
LEE, MATTHEW P20NS30309-01 0002
LEE, MINAKO Y R01AR40820-01
LEE, MINAKO Y R01CA38189-07
LEE, MING-SHENG P01CA49639-02 0002
LEE, MING-SHENG R01CA49443-03
LEE, MYUNG P50MH41684-07 0051
LEE, MYUNG P50MH41684-07 0052
LEE, NANCY L R01GM14652-24
LEE, NANCY M K05DA00020-14
LEE, NANCY M P01DA05695-03 0008
LEE, NANCY M R01DA02643-11
LEE, NANCY M R01DA06011-02
LEE, PAULINE M01RR00833-17 0217
LEE, PETER A M01RR00084-29 0158
LEE, PHILIP D M01RR00069-29 0427
LEE, PHILIP R P50MH42459-06 9004
LEE, PIN CHEUNG S07RR05434-30 0816
LEE, RANDALL J K11AR01829-02
LEE, RICHARD E, JR R15DK43958-01
LEE, RICHARD T K11HL01835-05
LEE, ROBERT S03RR03090-11
LEE, RONALD D R01HD24982-03
LEE, SE-JIN S07RR05799-14 0680
LEE, SOO-YOUNG R01CA51324-02
LEE, STEPHANIE L R29DK41321-02
LEE, SUM P50DK41978-03 0004
LEE, SUM P R01DK41678-02
LEE, TERRY R01DK33155-08
LEE, TERRY D P30CA33572-11 9012
LEE, THERESA M R01HD24575-04
LEE, THOMAS H, JR R01HS06452-02
LEE, TONY J R01HL27763-08A1
LEE, TUN-HOU P50HL33774-06 0006
LEE, TUN-HOU R01HL43561-03
LEE, VINCENT H R01DK34013-07
LEE, VINCENT H R01EY03816-09
LEE, VINCENT H R01EY07389-04
LEE, VIRGINIA M R01NS18616-10
LEE, VIRGINIA M-Y P01AG09215-02 9003
LEE, VIRGINIA M-Y P01AG09215-02 0003
LEE, W PAUL S07RR05551-29 0948
LEE, WEN-HWA P01CA51495-02
LEE, WEN-HWA P01CA51495-02 0001
LEE, WEN-HWA P01CA51495-02 0002
LEE, WEN-HWA P01CA51495-02 0004
LEE, WEN-HWA P01CA51495-02 9002
LEE, WEN-HWA R01EY05758-08
LEE, WILLIAM R P01ES03347-08 0003
LEE, WILLIAM R P01ES03347-08
LEE, WILLIAM R P01ES03347-08 0001
LEE, Y C S07RR07041-26 0399
LEE, YUAN C P41RR04328-04 0005
LEE, YUAN C R37DK09970-26
LEEB-LUNDBERG, L M R29GM41659-04
LEECH, JAMES H R01AI29882-01A2
LEEDOM, JOHN M M01RR00043-31 0439
LEEDOM, JOHN M U01AI27673-05S2
LEEF, JAMES N01AI95016-08
LEEK, MARJORIE R R01DC00626-03
LEEMAN, SUSAN E R01DK29876-12
LEES, ALAN W U10CA44064-05
LEES, MARJORIE P30HD04147-22A1 9009
LEES, MARJORIE B R01NS13649-15
LEES, MARJORIE B R01NS16945-11
LEES, SIDNEY R01AG02325-10
LEETE, EDWARD R01GM13246-32A3
LEFEBVRE, CAROL S07RR05795-14 0419
LEFEBVRE, CRAIG N01CO03859-13
LEFEBVRE, PAUL A R01GM34437-06
LEFER, ALLAN M R01GM45434-01A1
LEFER, ALLAN M R01HL25575-11
LEFEVRE, JUDITH A S07RR07012-25 0016
LEFEVRE, MICHAEL P01HL25596-12 0004
LEFF, ALAN R R01HL32495-07
LEFF, ALAN R R01HL35718-06
LEFF, ALAN R R01HL46368-01
LEFF, JONATHON A S07RR05357-30 0468
LEFF, STUART S07RR05353-30 0352
LEFF, STUART E K04NS01404-03
LEFF, STUART E R29GM40125-04
LEFF, TODD R01HL45394-01A1
LEFFALL JR, LASALLE D S06GM08244-05 0012
LEFFERT, HYAM L R01DK28215-11
LEFFLER, CHARLES W R01HL34059-07
LEFFLER, CHARLES W R01HL42851-01A2
LEFFLER, H P41RR01614-10 0007
LEFFLER, HAKON S07RR05755-18 0216
LEFKOWITH, JAMES A R01DK37879-05
LEFKOWITH, JAMES B R01AI27457-03
LEFKOWITZ, LEWIS M01RR00095-31 0334
LEFKOWITZ, ROBERT J R37HL16037-19
LEFRAK, EDWARD A N02HI09502-05
LEFURGEY, EDORIS A S10RR06692-01
LEGAN, SANDRA J R01HD23347-02
LEGATO, MARIANNE J P01HL28958-09 9002
LEGATT, ALAN D R29NS25041-05
LEGEROS, RACQUEL Z R01DE07223-04A2
LEGEROS, RACQUEL Z S15DE10079-01
LEGGE, GORDON E R01EY02857-12
LEGGE, GORDON E R37EY02934-12
LEGGITT, JAMES S07RR06002-04 0824
LEGUIRE, LAWRENCE E S03RR03442-06
LEHMAN, ANTHONY F R01DA05114-05
LEHMAN, ANTHONY F R18MH48070-02
LEHMAN, I R R01AI26538-04
LEHMAN, I R R37GM06196-33
LEHMAN, I ROBERT P01AG02908-11 0006
LEHMAN, MICHAEL N R01HD21968-07
LEHMAN, MICHAEL N R01NS28175-02
LEHMAN, WAYNE R01DA04390-03
LEHMANN, PAUL S07RR05700-22 0880
LEHMANN, RUTH E R01GM40704-04
LEHMANN, RUTH E R01HD27549-01
LEHNER, NOEL D M G20RR07096-01
LEHNERT, BRUCE P41RR01315-10 0028
LEHR, JOHN L P01HL33009-07 9001
LEHRER, PAUL M R01HL44097-02
LEHRER, ROBERT I R01AI22839-06
LEHRER, ROBERT I R01AI25693-05
LEHRER, ROBERT I R01AI29595-02
LEHRER, SAMUEL B R01AI20331-07A1
LEHRER, SHERWIN S R01HL22461-12
LEHRER, STEVEN P R01CA49506-03
LEHRMAN, MARK A R01GM38545-05
LEHTO, MARK R R01AA08382-02
LEIBACH, FREDERICK H R01DK28389-08
LEIBACH, FREDERICK H R01DK42069-02
LEIBACH, FREDERICK H S15HD28760-01
LEIBEL, RUDOLPH L P30DK26687-11 9005
LEIBEL, RUDOLPH L R01DK30583-09
LEIBEL, RUDOLPH L R01HD28047-01
LEIBENLUFT, E Z01MH02502-02
LEIBENLUFT, E Z01MH02503-02
LEIBO, STANLEY P S07RR05425-30 0750
LEIBOLD, ELIZABETH A R01GM45201-01
LEIBOVICH, SAMUEL J R01GM29135-09
LEIBOVITZ, ALBERT P01CA41183-05 9002
LEIBOVITZ, ALBERT P30CA23074-14 9011
LEIBOWITZ, ARLEEN P50HD12639-12 0012
LEIBOWITZ, HOWARD M R01EY07574-04
LEIBOWITZ, SARAH F R01MH43422-04
LEIBSON, CYNTHIA R29AG08729-02
LEIBSON, PAUL J R01CA47752-02
LEICHNER, PETER K P01CA43791-04A1 0003
LEICKLY, FREDERICK E U01AI30779-01
LEIDEN, JEFFREY M P01DK42718-02 0006
LEIDEN, JEFFREY M R01AI29673-02
LEIFER, DANA K11HD00888-03
LEIFERMAN, KRISTIN M R01AR36008-06
LEIGH, BARBARA C R01AA08461-01A1
LEIGH, J R18AR21393-17 0003
LEIGH, J PAUL R01AG10410-01
LEIGH, JOHN P41RR02305-08 9010
LEIGH, JOHN A R01GM39785-04
LEIGH, JOHN S P41RR02305-08
LEIGH, RICHARD J R01EY06717-05
LEIGHTON, J M01RR00645-20 0379
LEIGHTON, S B Z01RR10034-14
LEIGHTON, S B Z01RR10146-09

LEIGHTON, S B   Z01RR10204-07
LEIM, RONALD   P50NS27680-03 0002
LEIN, ELIZABETH A   S07RR05390-30 0688
LEIN, JOHN N   P51RR00166-30
LEININGER, E   Z01BA04004-03
LEININGER, E   Z01BA04005-02
LEININGER, E   Z01BA04006-02
LEININGER, E   Z01BA04007-02
LEININGER, JOEL   N01ES95269-05
LEINWAND, LESLIE A   P01HL37412-04 0008
LEINWAND, LESLIE A   R01GM29090-11
LEIRER, VON O   R44AG06957-03
LEIS, JONATHAN P   R01CA38046-08
LEISCHOW, SCOTT J   R29DA06679-02
LEISSINGER, CINDY A   R55HL46670-01
LEITENBERG, HAROLD   M01RR00109-28 0308
LEITENBERG, HAROLD   S07RR07125-22 0392
LEITER, EDWARD H   R01DK27722-11
LEITER, EDWARD H   R01DK36175-06A1
LEITER, JAMES C   K08HL01998-05
LEITER, JAMES C   S07RR05392-30 0696
LEITH, JOHN T   R01CA50350-03
LEITMAN, S   Z01CL02062-02
LEITMAN, S F   Z01CL02045-06
LEITMAN, S F   Z01CL02050-05
LEITMAN, S F   Z01CL02055-04
LEITMAN, S F   Z01CL02056-04
LEITMAN, S F   Z01CL02057-04
LEITMAN, S F   Z01CL02063-01
LEITMAN, S F   Z01CL02065-01
LEJEMTEL, THIERRY H.   N01HC55002-10
LELAND,NANCY L   S07RR05448-30 0299
LELEIKO, NEAL S   M01RR00071-28A1 0210
LELLA, VIJAYA M   K04HL02590-01
LELLA, VIJAYA M   R01HL42813-03
LEMANN, JACOB   M01RR00058-30 0249
LEMANN, JACOB   M01RR00058-30 0225
LEMANN, JACOB   M01RR00058-30 0164
LEMANN, JACOB   M01RR00058-30 0207
LEMANN, JACOB   M01RR00058-30 0211
LEMANN, JACOB JR   R37DK15089-22
LEMANN, JACOB JR.   M01RR00058-30 0209
LEMANN, JACOB JR.   M01RR00058-30 0220
LEMANSKE, ROBERT F   P50AI10404-21 0008
LEMANSKE, ROBERT F, JR   K07AI00995-02
LEMANSKI, LARRY F   P01HL39707-02 9002
LEMASTERS, JOHN J   R01DK37034-06
LEMBERGER, AUGUST P   S03RR03183-10
LEMEN, RICHARD J   P50HL14136-20 0018
LEMIRE, JACQUES M   M01RR02558-07 0069
LEMIRE, JACQUES M   R29DK39024-04
LEMISCHKA, IHOR R   R01CA45339-05
LEMISCHKA, IHOR R   R01DK42989-02
LEMKAU, HENRY L, JR   G08LM05168-02
LEMKE, GREG E   R01NS23896-06
LEMKE, GREG E   R55NS29186-01
LEMKE, JON H   P60DC00976-02 9001
LEMKIN, P   Z01CB08381-08
LEMMON, VANCE P   R01EY05285-10
LEMON, STANLEY   U01AI25868-05 0001
LEMONS, JACK E   P01DE08917-02 0001
LEMONS, JAMES A   R01HD14820-10
LEMONS, JAMES A   U10HD27856-01
LEMOS, JOSE R   R01NS29470-01
LEMP, MICHAEL A   R21EY07744-04
LEMPERS, JACQUES D   R03MH48954-01
LENARD, JOHN   R01AI13002-16
LENARD, JOHN   R01DK39502-03
LENARDO, M   Z01AI00565-02
LENARDO, M   Z01AI00566-02
LENCER, WAYNE   P01AI26698-03S1 9003
LENCER, WAYNE   P01AI26698-03S1 9002
LENCER, WAYNE I   K08DK01848-03
LENGENFELDER, JAMES T   R19MH46213-03
LENGYEL, JUDITH A   R01HD09948-15
LENGYEL, PETER   P01CA16038-18 0018
LENGYEL, PETER   R37AI12320-17
LENNARZ, WILLIAM J   R01GM33184-08
LENNARZ, WILLIAM J   R01HD18590-10
LENNARZ, WILLIAM J   R37GM33185-10
LENNIE, PETER   P30EY01319-17
LENNIE, PETER   R01EY04440-10
LENNON, MARY CLARE   R29MH42974-04
LENTZ, BARRY R   R01GM32707-08
LENTZ, BARRY R   R01HL45916-01
LENTZ, THOMAS L   R01NS21896-05
LENZ, ELIZABETH R   S03RR03544-01
LENZ, ELIZABETH R   S07RR05973-05
LENZ, FREDERICK   S07RR05378-30 0002
LENZ, FREDERICK A   K08NS01384-03
LENZ, FREDERICK ARTHUR   R29NS28598-02
LENZ, HEINZ J   K08DK01998-02
LENZ, JOHN R   R01CA44822-05
LENZENWEGER, MARK FRANCIS   R29MH45448-02
LEO, M A   P50AA03508-14 0048
LEOF, EDWARD B   R01CA42836-06
LEON, GLORIA R   R01HD24700-02
LEON, JOEL   U01AG10317-01
LEON, MICHAEL   P01HD24236-03 0001
LEON, MICHAEL   R35AG07918-03 0006
LEON, MICHAEL A   K02MH00371-10
LEON, MICHAEL A   P01HD24236-03
LEON, MICHAEL A   P01HD24236-03 9001
LEON, MICHAEL A   R01DA07425-01
LEON, MICHAEL A   R01MH45353-02
LEON, MICHAEL A   R01MH48950-01
LEON, MICHAEL A   S15MH49319-01
LEONARD E F   P41RR01296-08 0005
LEONARD, BARBARA J   S07RR05448-30 0307
LEONARD, CHRISTOPHER S   R55NS27881-01A2
LEONARD, E J   Z01CB08575-18
LEONARD, EDWARD F   R01HL38306-03
LEONARD, EDWARD F   R01HL44535-01A1
LEONARD, JACK L   R01DK38772-06
LEONARD, JANET L   R29MH43302-04
LEONARD, JOHN P   R29NS26432-04
LEONARD, KENNETH E   R01AA07183-04
LEONARD, KENNETH E   R01AA08128-02
LEONARD, KENNETH E   S07RR05938-07 0318
LEONARD, LAURENCE B   R01DC00458-04
LEONARD, REBECCA J   K04CA01125-05
LEONARD, ROBERT   P01NS11255-17 9003
LEONARD, W J   Z01HD01604-06
LEONARDI, CRAIG L   S07RR05363-30 0830
LEONE, LOUIS A   S07RR05644-19
LEONE, MICHAEL R   S07RR05412-30 0978
LEONE, PETER A   K11HL02123-04
LEONG, DENIS A   R01DK35937-06
LEONG, KAM W   R01NS27961-02
LEONG, SALLY A   R01GM33716-05
LEONTIS, NEOCLES B   R01GM41454-03
LEOPOLD, DONALD A   P01DC00220-08 9001
LEOPOLD, DONALD A   P01DC00220-08 0003
LEPKOWSKI, JAMES   P01AG05561-06A1 9001
LEPOCK, JAMES R   R01CA40251-06
LEPOR, HERBERT   R29DK43148-02
LEPPER, MARK R   R01HD25258-02
LEPPERT, MARK F   P30HG00199-01 9001
LEPPIK, ILO E   N01NS72337-02
LEPPIK, ILO E   P50NS16308-12A1 0014
LEPPLA, S   Z01DE00537-01
LEPPLA, S H   Z01DE00514-02
LEPPO, JEFFREY A   R01HL34199-06
LEQUIRE, VIRGIL S   P50HL14214-20 9004
LERANTH, CSABA   P50MH44866-04 0003
LERANTH, CSABA   R01HD23830-03
LERANTH, CSABA   R01NS26068-03
LERCHE, NICHOLAS W   P51RR00169-30 0102
LERCHE, NICHOLAS W   P51RR00169-30 0103
LEREA, CONNIE L   R29EY09112-01
LERER, BERNARD   R01MH48470-01
LERESCHE, L A   P01DE08773-03 0003
LERESCHE, LINDA   P30DE09743-02 0004
LERESCHE, LINDA   R01DE06219-08
LERMAN, BRUCE B   R01HL44747-03
LERMAN, CARYN   S07RR05895-09 0617
LERMAN, CARYN E   K07CA01604-01
LERMAN, LEONARD S   R37HG00345-07
LERMAN, PAUL   P50MH43450-04 0021
LERMAN, STEPHEN P   R01CA52603-02
LERNER, AARON B   R01AR39869-03
LERNER, HARVEY J   U10CA20187-15
LERNER, LAURA E   R29AR39801-03
LERNER, NEIL   N44HD02909-02
LERNER, NEIL D   R43AG09907-01
LERNER, NEIL D   R44AG08151-02
LERNER, RICHARD A   M01RR00833-17 0171
LERNER, RICHARD A   P01AI19499-08 0002
LERNER, RICHARD A   P01CA27489-12
LERNER, RICHARD A   P01CA27489-12 0006
LERNER, RICHARD A   S07RR05514-29
LERNER, RICHARD A   S15HL47777-01
LERNER, RICHARD M   R01HD23229-03
LERNMARK, AKE   P01DK41801-02 0005
LERNMARK, AKE   P01DK41801-02
LERNMARK, AKE   R01DK26190-09
LERNMARK, AKE   R01DK33873-07
LERNMARK, AKE   R01DK42654-01A1
LEROITH, D   Z01DK47001-10
LEROITH, D   Z01DK47018-14
LEROY, E CARWILE   R01AR30431-10
LEROY, EDWARD C   M01RR01070-15 0100
LERTRATANANGKOON, KHINGKAN   R29ES04857-04
LESH, MICHAEL D   R29HL45664-01
LESH, RYAN E   K11AR01871-01
LESIECKI, MICHAEL   R43DE09765-01
LESIECKI, MICHAEL   R44AR40278-02
LESIECKI, MICHAEL   R44NS28279-02
LESKAWA, KENNETH C   R01NS21057-07
LESKE, M CRISTINA   R01EY08291-03
LESKE, M CRISTINA   R21EY07722-04
LESKE, M CRISTINA   U10EY07625-05
LESKO, LYNNA M   R01MH46475-01A1
LESLIE, CATHERINE A   K11MH00708-05
LESLIE, CHRISTINA C   P01HL34303-07 9003
LESLIE, CHRISTINA C   P01HL34303-07 0003
LESLIE, FRANCES   P01DC00450-04 0005
LESLIE, KEVIN O   P50HL14212-20 9006
LESLIE, STEVEN W   R01AA05809-10
LESLIE, STEVEN W   R01AA08104-03
LESNAW, JUDITH A   R01AI13574-14
LESSARD, CHARLES S   S07RR07090-26 0462
LESSARD, J L   P01HL46826-01 0003
LESSARD, JAMES   P30HD28827-01 9003
LESSARD, JAMES   S07RR05535-29 0532
LESSER, IRA M   R01MH43960-01A3
LESSER, RONALD P   M01RR00035-31 0410
LESSEY, BRUCE A   S07RR05415-30 0013
LESSICK, MIRA   S07RR05477-29 0422
LESSIE, THOMAS G   S07RR07048-26 0645
LESSIN, LAWRENCE S   R01HL42498-02
LESSIN, STUART R   R29CA55017-01
LESSLEY, BRUCE A   S07RR07077-24 0266
LESSMAN, CHARLES A   S07RR07229-06 0721
LESTER, BRUCE   P30HD24051-03 9007
LESTER, BRUCE   P30HD24051-03 9008
LESTER, H   S07RR07003-26 0321
LESTER, HENRY A   R01GM29836-10A1
LESTER, HENRY A   R01NS11756-17
LESTER, ROGER G   R01HD14198-15
LETINSKY, MICHAEL   S07RR05354-30 0416
LETINSKY, MICHAEL   S07RR05354-30 0417
LETO, T L   Z01AI00614-01
LETOURNEAU, PAUL C   R01HD19950-07
LETOURNEAU, PAUL C   R01NS28807-01A1
LETSINGER, ROBERT L   R37GM10265-29
LETVIN, NORMAN   P30DK43351-01 9003
LETVIN, NORMAN L   P01DK36350-05S1 0002
LETVIN, NORMAN L   R01AI20729-08
LETVIN, NORMAN L   R01AI27747-03
LETVIN, NORMAN L   R01CA50139-03
LEUCHTAG, H R   S06GM08061-17 0018
LEUCHTER, ANDREW   P30AG10123-01 9001
LEUCHTER, ANDREW   S07RR05756-18 0311
LEUCHTER, ANDREW F   R01MH40705-06
LEUNG, BENJAMIN S   R01AA07733-03
LEUNG, CHRISTOPHER   S07RR05393-30 0896
LEUNG, DONALD   P01HL36577-06 0010
LEUNG, DONALD Y   R01HL37260-05
LEUNG, LAWRENCE L   R01HL42943-03
LEUNG, MICHAEL   R24MH47392-02 0002
LEUNG, PATRICK   P30DK35747-06 0011
LEUNG, PATRICK   S07RR05684-23 0171
LEUNG, WAI-CHOI   R01AI31828-01
LEUSSING, DANIEL L   R01GM40179-02
LEV, MEIR   S07RR07132-20 0405
LEVANDOWSKI, R A   Z01BF02002-05
LEVANDOWSKI, R A   Z01BF02003-03
LEVANDOWSKI, R A   Z01BF02007-01
LEVAV, ITZHAK   R03MH48979-01
LEVEN, ROBERT M   R29HL38248-05
LEVENBOOK, I S   Z01BE03007-02
LEVENE, RICHARD   S07RR05527-29 0521
LEVENKRON, JEFFREY C   R01HL41097-03
LEVENS, D L   Z01CB09168-03
LEVENSON, RICHARD   S07RR05405-30 0874
LEVENSON, ROBERT   R01CA38992-07
LEVENSON, ROBERT   R01HL39263-05
LEVENSON, ROBERT W   R01AG07476-04
LEVENSON, SUZETTE   S07RR05927-07 0963
LEVENSTEIN, SUSAN B   R01DK41084-02
LEVENTHAL, AUDIE G   R01EY04951-08
LEVENTHAL, AUDIE G   R01EY08523-01A1
LEVENTHAL, BRIGID   P30CA06973-29 9014
LEVENTHAL, BRIGID G   U10CA28476-12
LEVENTHAL, BRIGID G   U10CA28476-12 0022
LEVENTHAL, BRIGID G   U10CA28476-12 0023
LEVENTHAL, BRIGID G   U10CA28476-12 0001
LEVENTHAL, BRIGID G   U10CA28476-12 0024
LEVENTHAL, BRIGID G   U10CA28476-12 0025
LEVENTHAL, BRIGID G   U10CA28476-12 0026
LEVENTHAL, BRIGID G   U10CA28476-12 0027
LEVENTHAL, BRIGID G   U10CA28476-12 0028
LEVENTHAL, BRIGID G   U10CA28476-12 0029
LEVENTHAL, BRIGID G   U10CA28476-12 0030
LEVENTHAL, BRIGID G   U10CA28476-12 0031
LEVENTHAL, BRIGID G   U10CA28476-12 0042
LEVENTHAL, BRIGID G   U10CA28476-12 0043
LEVENTHAL, BRIGID G   U10CA28476-12 0044
LEVENTHAL, BRIGID G   U10CA28476-12 0045
LEVENTHAL, BRIGID G   U10CA28476-12 0046
LEVENTHAL, BRIGID G   U10CA28476-12 0047
LEVENTHAL, BRIGID G   U10CA28476-12 0048
LEVENTHAL, BRIGID G   U10CA28476-12 0032
LEVENTHAL, BRIGID G   U10CA28476-12 0033
LEVENTHAL, BRIGID G   U10CA28476-12 0034
LEVENTHAL, BRIGID G   U10CA28476-12 0035
LEVENTHAL, BRIGID G   U10CA28476-12 0036
LEVENTHAL, BRIGID G   U10CA28476-12 0037
LEVENTHAL, BRIGID G   U10CA28476-12 0038
LEVENTHAL, BRIGID G   U10CA28476-12 0039
LEVENTHAL, BRIGID G   U10CA28476-12 0040
LEVENTHAL, BRIGID G   U10CA28476-12 0041
LEVENTHAL, BRIGID G   U10CA28476-12 0049
LEVENTHAL, BRIGID G   U10CA28476-12 0050
LEVENTHAL, BRIGID G   U10CA28476-12 0051
LEVENTHAL, BRIGID G   U10CA28476-12 0052
LEVENTHAL, BRIGID G   U10CA28476-12 0002
LEVENTHAL, BRIGID G   U10CA28476-12 0003
LEVENTHAL, BRIGID G   U10CA28476-12 0004
LEVENTHAL, BRIGID G   U10CA28476-12 0005
LEVENTHAL, BRIGID G   U10CA28476-12 0006
LEVENTHAL, BRIGID G   U10CA28476-12 0007
LEVENTHAL, BRIGID G   U10CA28476-12 0008
LEVENTHAL, BRIGID G   U10CA28476-12 0009
LEVENTHAL, BRIGID G   U10CA28476-12 0010

LEVENTHAL, BRIGID G U10CA28476-12 0011
LEVENTHAL, BRIGID G U10CA28476-12 0012
LEVENTHAL, BRIGID G U10CA28476-12 0013
LEVENTHAL, BRIGID G U10CA28476-12 0014
LEVENTHAL, BRIGID G U10CA28476-12 0015
LEVENTHAL, BRIGID G U10CA28476-12 0016
LEVENTHAL, BRIGID G U10CA28476-12 0017
LEVENTHAL, BRIGID G U10CA28476-12 0018
LEVENTHAL, BRIGID G U10CA28476-12 0019
LEVENTHAL, BRIGID G U10CA28476-12 0020
LEVENTHAL, BRIGID G U10CA28476-12 0021
LEVENTHAL, BRIGID G U10CA28476-12 0053
LEVENTHAL, BRIGID G U10CA28476-12 0054
LEVENTHAL, BRIGID G U10CA28476-12 0055
LEVENTHAL, BRIGID G U10CA28476-12 0056
LEVENTHAL, BRIGID G U10CA28476-12 0057
LEVENTHAL, BRIGID G U10CA28476-12 0058
LEVENTHAL, BRIGID G U10CA28476-12 0059
LEVENTHAL, BRIGID G U10CA28476-12 0060
LEVENTHAL, ELAINE A P50AA08747-02 0004
LEVENTHAL, HOWARD R37AG03501-10
LEVER, JULIA E R37DK27400-11
LEVERETT, DENNIS H N01DE32441-17
LEVERETT, DENNIS H R01DE09109-03
LEVEY, ALLAN I K08NS01387-03
LEVEY, ALLAN I R01NS30454-01
LEVEY, ANDREW S M01RR00054-30 0401
LEVEY, ANDREW S U01DK34516-07
LEVI, DENNIS M R01EY01728-16
LEVI, DENNIS M S03RR03239-09
LEVI, DENNIS M S07RR07147-19
LEVI, ROBERTO R01HL34215-17
LEVIN, ANDREW E R43CI00015-01
LEVIN, ARTHUR G N01CP85603-07
LEVIN, BARRY N01CN15352-01
LEVIN, BARRY E R01DK30066-10
LEVIN, BRUCE R R01GM33782-07
LEVIN, D L Z01CN00142-07
LEVIN, DANIEL H R01GM24825-13
LEVIN, DAVID S07RR05445-30 0876
LEVIN, DAVID N R01CA51245-01A1
LEVIN, EUGENE G R01HL40435-02
LEVIN, HARVEY S R01NS21889-08
LEVIN, I W Z01DK29001-19
LEVIN, J G Z01HD00069-19
LEVIN, JEFFREY S R29AG09462-01
LEVIN, KENNETH H R43GM45075-01A1
LEVIN, LINDA G K11DE00300-01
LEVIN, MARC S R29DK43029-02
LEVIN, MARVIN S07RR05336-29 0307
LEVIN, MYRON M01RR00069-29 0396
LEVIN, MYRON R03AI30345-02
LEVIN, MYRON J M01RR00069-29 0438
LEVIN, MYRON J P01AG07347-04 0003
LEVIN, PETER J S07RR06005-04
LEVIN, R L Z01RR10109-11
LEVIN, R L Z01RR10305-03
LEVIN, R L Z01RR10339-02
LEVIN, ROBERT M P50DK39257-05 0003
LEVIN, ROBERT M R01DK26508-11
LEVIN, ROBERT M R01DK33559-07
LEVIN, ROBERT M S03RR03264-08
LEVIN, ROBERT M S07RR05569-27
LEVIN, ROBERT M S15AI32187-01
LEVIN, VICTOR A U01CA53617-02
LEVINE, A S Z01HD01500-09
LEVINE, ALAN E R01CA49127-04
LEVINE, ALEXANDRA M R01CA50850-03
LEVINE, ALEXANDRA M R01CA55510-01
LEVINE, ALLEN S R01DA03999-05
LEVINE, ARNOLD J P01CA41086-06 0005
LEVINE, ARNOLD J R01CA49271-03
LEVINE, ARNOLD J R13CA54109-01
LEVINE, ARNOLD J R37CA38757-07
LEVINE, BARBARA P01CA29502-11A1 0034
LEVINE, BENJAMIN D S07RR05426-30 0141
LEVINE, DAVID M R01HL43604-03
LEVINE, DOUGLAS P01DK32971-08 0005
LEVINE, ELLIOT M R13AG09962-01
LEVINE, JOEL M R01NS21198-08
LEVINE, JON P50DE08973-02 0004
LEVINE, JON D P50DE08973-02
LEVINE, JON D R01AR32634-09
LEVINE, JON D R01NS21647-06
LEVINE, JON E K04HD00879-03
LEVINE, JON E P01HD21921-04 0004
LEVINE, JON E R01HD20677-06
LEVINE, LOUIS S07RR07132-20 0406
LEVINE, LOUIS S07RR07132-20
LEVINE, LOUIS S15HL47786-01
LEVINE, MICHAEL A R01DK34281-07
LEVINE, MICHAEL A. M01RR00722-19 0163
LEVINE, MICHAEL J P01DE07585-04
LEVINE, MICHAEL J P01DE07585-04 0001
LEVINE, MICHAEL J P50DE08240-05
LEVINE, MICHAEL J P50DE08240-05 0001
LEVINE, MICHAEL J S07RR05330-30 0023
LEVINE, MICHAEL S P01HD05958-20 0001
LEVINE, MICHAEL S R01GM34431-08
LEVINE, MICHAEL S R01GM46638-01
LEVINE, MYRON R01AI18228-10
LEVINE, MYRON M N01AI15096-00
LEVINE, MYRON M N01AI62528-18
LEVINE, MYRON M N01AI62553-14
LEVINE, MYRON M R01AI29471-02
LEVINE, PAUL A S07RR05431-30 0832
LEVINE, R J Z01HD00373-03
LEVINE, R L Z01HL00225-14
LEVINE, RHEA J P01HL15835-19 0007
LEVINE, RICHARD B P01NS28495-02 0002
LEVINE, RICHARD B P01NS28495-02 9002
LEVINE, ROBERT A P01DC00119-16 0008
LEVINE, ROBERT A R01AG10687-01
LEVINE, ROBERT A R29HL38176-05
LEVINE, ROY A R01HL43395-03
LEVINE, SEYMOUR R01MH47573-01A1
LEVINE, SEYMOUR R37MH45006-03
LEVINE, STEPHANIE M S07RR05654-24 0150
LEVINE, STEPHEN P60AR20618-13 0020
LEVINE, STEVEN S07RR05373-30 0721
LEVINE, STEVEN R N01NS02373-03
LEVINE, SUSAN C R01NS26871-02
LEVINE, WILLIAM S N01DC12116-00
LEVINGER, LOUIS F R15GM46030-01
LEVINSON, ARNOLD I R01NS19546-09
LEVINSON, CHARLES R01CA32927-08
LEVINSON, DOUGLAS F R01MH45097-02
LEVINSON, S F Z01CL60012-01
LEVINSON, SIMON R R01NS15879-12
LEVINTHAL, FRANCOISE R01GM31540-08
LEVIS, ROBERT J R01HG00485-01
LEVIS, ROBERT W R01GM38259-04A2
LEVISON, HENRY N01HR16047-00
LEVISON, MATTHEW E R55HD26239-01A2
LEVITAN, EDWIN S R29NS29804-01
LEVITAN, IRWIN B R01NS17910-10
LEVITAN, IRWIN B R01NS25366-04
LEVITAN, KAREN B N44CN05308-03
LEVITAN, KAREN B R43CA54040-01
LEVITON, ALAN R01NS26093-01A2S1
LEVITON, ALAN R01NS27306-02
LEVITSKY, HYAM I K08CA01595-01
LEVITSKY, LYNNE L P60DK20595-14 9008
LEVITSKY, LYNNE L R01HD22891-07
LEVITSKY, SIDNEY R01HL29077-10
LEVITT, ALEXANDRA S07RR05399-30 0912
LEVITT, ALEXANDRA M R01AI30066-01A1
LEVITT, ANDREA G R15HD28173-01
LEVITT, HARRY P01DC00178-10 0010
LEVITT, HARRY P01DC00178-10 0002
LEVITT, HARRY P01DC00178-10
LEVITT, HARRY R01DC00507-04
LEVITT, LEE J K04HL02213-04
LEVITT, LEE J R01HL35774-06
LEVITT, MICHAEL P01GM30387-10
LEVITT, MICHAEL P01GM30387-10 0009
LEVITT, MICHAEL R01GM41455-03
LEVITT, MICHAEL D R01DK13309-23
LEVITT, PAT P01DA06871-01 0002
LEVITT, PAT P01NS24707-05 9001
LEVITT, PAT R R01AG10560-01
LEVITT, PAT R R37MH45507-03
LEVITT, RALPH U10CA37417-08
LEVITT, ROY C R01GM47145-01
LEVITZ, MORTIMER R01CA02071-38
LEVITZ, STUART M P01AI28408-02 0003
LEVITZ, STUART M R01AI25780-05
LEVKOFF, SUE E K01AG00508-01
LEVY , H RICHARD R01GM41085-03
LEVY WILSON, BEATRIZ P01HL41633-03 0006
LEVY, ALEJANDRO S07RR05651-24 0145
LEVY, ALEJANDRO V R01MH44832-02
LEVY, DANIEL R01DK25836-12
LEVY, DAVID P01NS03346-31 9001
LEVY, DAVID S07RR05399-30 0928
LEVY, DAVID E R01AI28900-02
LEVY, GERALD N K01OH00081-02
LEVY, H B Z01AI00020-16
LEVY, H RICHARD S07RR07068-26 0233
LEVY, HARVEY L M01RR02172-09 0189
LEVY, HARVEY L N01HD42809-21
LEVY, JAY P01HD24640-03 9002
LEVY, JAY A P01AI24286-05 0001
LEVY, JAY A P01AI24286-05 0002
LEVY, JAY A R01AI29394-03
LEVY, JAY A R01AI30350-02
LEVY, JAY A U01AI26471-04 0002
LEVY, JUDITH R18DA06994-02
LEVY, LAURA S R01CA48801-02
LEVY, LEON H R01MH43843-03
LEVY, MATTHEW N R37HL10951-24
LEVY, MATTHEW N S07RR05658-24
LEVY, MATTHEW N S07RR05658-24 0929
LEVY, R M P41RR06892-01 9004
LEVY, RENE H P01GM32165-09 0003
LEVY, RENE H P01NS17111-11 0009
LEVY, RICHARD S K11DK01931-02
LEVY, ROBERT J R01HL38118-04A2
LEVY, ROBERT J R01HL41663-03
LEVY, RONALD P01CA34233-09
LEVY, RONALD P01CA34233-09 0010
LEVY, RONALD P01CA34233-09 0017
LEVY, RONALD P01CA49605-03 0007
LEVY, RONALD R37CA33399-10
LEVY, RONALD M R01GM30580-10
LEVY, SANDRA P01CA47445-03 0004
LEVY, STEVEN S07RR05313-30 0242
LEVY, STEVEN M P30DE10126-01 0003
LEVY, STEVEN M R01DE09551-01A1
LEVY, STEVEN M R03DE09770-01
LEVY, STUART B R01AI16756-09
LEVY, STUART B R01AI30646-01
LEVY, STUART B S07RR05382-30 0872
LEVY, SUSAN R R01MH45470-03
LEVY, WILLIAM B R01MH48161-01
LEVY, WILLIAM B R01NS15488-13
LEW, DUKHEE B R29HL47022-01
LEWELLEN, THOMAS K P01CA42045-06 9002
LEWELLEN, THOMAS K R01CA42593-05
LEWELLEN, THOMAS K S10RR06478-01
LEWICKI, JOHN N44DK12253-01
LEWICKI, PAWEL R01MH42715-05
LEWIN/ICF N01SP13004-00
LEWIN, ANITA H R01NS27859-02
LEWIN, JOHN C R18DA05745-03S1
LEWIN, LEWIS M R01MH45188-02
LEWIN, PETER A P01CA52823-02 0007
LEWINE, RICHARD R J R37MH44151-03
LEWINSOHN, PETER M R01MH41278-06
LEWINSOHN, PETER M S07RR05612-19 0136
LEWINTER, MARTIN P01HL28001-10 0006
LEWIS, A M Z01AI00013-28
LEWIS, AARON P41RR04224-04 0009
LEWIS, ARTHUR S S06GM08171-11 0010
LEWIS, BARBARA A R29DC00528-03
LEWIS, BENJAMIN F R01DA05615-02
LEWIS, BENJAMIN F R18DA06151-03
LEWIS, BENJAMIN M K06HL02182-29
LEWIS, CAROL A R01NS27016-03
LEWIS, CHARLES S07RR06014-03 0833
LEWIS, CHARLES S07RR06014-03 0834
LEWIS, COLLINS E R01AA07582-03
LEWIS, CORA E R21DK44595-01
LEWIS, DARRELL V R01DA06735-01
LEWIS, DARRELL V, JR R01NS27488-02
LEWIS, DAVID P50AG05133-08 0008
LEWIS, DAVID A K02MH00519-07
LEWIS, DAVID A P01NS19608-09 9002
LEWIS, DAVID A P50MH45156-02 0002
LEWIS, DAVID B R29AI26940-04
LEWIS, DEBORAH L R29NS28894-02
LEWIS, DOROTHY E P01AI21289-08 9001
LEWIS, DOROTHY E U01AI30243-02 9001
LEWIS, DOUGLAS S R01HD23327-05
LEWIS, EDMUND J R01DK39908-05
LEWIS, EDWARD P01GM40499-04 0003
LEWIS, EDWARD P01GM40499-04 9001
LEWIS, EDWARD B R01HD06331-20
LEWIS, EDWIN R R01DC00112-16
LEWIS, ELAINE J R29GM38696-05
LEWIS, FRANCES S07RR05758-18 0251
LEWIS, FRED A N01AI15112-00
LEWIS, FRED A R22AI16006-12
LEWIS, FRED A R22AI27777-02
LEWIS, GEORGE P01NS26665-04 0003
LEWIS, HENRY III G12RR03045-06
LEWIS, HENRY III S03RR03225-06
LEWIS, HUGH B S07RR05910-08
LEWIS, JACK P50AR39255-05 0003
LEWIS, JACK P50AR39255-05 9001
LEWIS, JACK L R01AR38398-05
LEWIS, JAMES A S06GM08194-12 0028
LEWIS, JAMES G P01CA29589-10 9005
LEWIS, JAMES G R29CA44734-05
LEWIS, JANNET F K14HL01984-05
LEWIS, JILL S07RR05795-14 0420
LEWIS, JOHN W R01DA07315-01
LEWIS, JON C P30CA12197-19 9010
LEWIS, JON C P41RR02722-05
LEWIS, JON C P50HL14164-20 0044
LEWIS, JON C P50HL14164-20 9010
LEWIS, JON C R01HL41990-03
LEWIS, JON C S10RR06705-01
LEWIS, K C Z01CN00162-01
LEWIS, LESLIE A S03RR03441-06
LEWIS, LESLIE A S06GM08153-16
LEWIS, LESLIE A S06GM08153-16 0005
LEWIS, LINDA S07RR05758-18 0252
LEWIS, M S Z01RR10039-14
LEWIS, M S Z01RR10184-08
LEWIS, MARK H R01MH45371-01A2
LEWIS, MARY ANN R01MH45754-03
LEWIS, MARY ANN S07RR06014-03 0844
LEWIS, MARYANN R18AI30151-01A1
LEWIS, MEMORY E S07RR05916-08 0307
LEWIS, MICHAEL I K08HL01907-05
LEWIS, MICHAEL I S06GM08016-21 0039
LEWIS, MICHAEL L R01HD18511-06A1
LEWIS, MITCHELL P01GM39526-05 0003
LEWIS, MITCHELL R01GM44617-02
LEWIS, NEIL J R43HL46614-01
LEWIS, R M Z01BH07004-02
LEWIS, R M Z01BH07005-01
LEWIS, RICHARD M01RR00350-25 0479
LEWIS, RICHARD S07RR05353-30 0353
LEWIS, RICHARD M M01RR02558-07 0052

LEWIS, RICHARD S R01GM45374-01A1
LEWIS, ROBERT A R01DA06514-01A1
LEWIS, ROBERT A R18DA06932-02
LEWIS, ROBERT B S03RR03330-05
LEWIS, ROBERT E R29DK41896-02
LEWIS, ROBERT M S07RR05416-30 0568
LEWIS, RUTH S07RR05814-12 0144
LEWIS, SHARON L K08NR00001-05
LEWIS, SIMON A R01DK33243-08
LEWIS, SIMON A R01DK44821-01
LEWIS, STEPHEN F M01RR00633-19 0316
LEWIS, STEVEN F P01HL06296-31 0012
LEWIS, SUSAN N01ES95273-03
LEWISTON, NORMAN J P50HL42368-04 9001
LEWITT, ROBERT M R01CA56356-01
LEWITT, PETER A R01NS27892-02
LEWKOWICZ, DAVID S07RR05838-12 0271
LEWONTIN, RICHARD C P01GM29301-11 0006
LEWONTIN, RICHARD C R01GM21179-18
LEWS, JON P40RR00919-17 0013
LEWY, ALFRED J K02MH00703-05
LEWY, ALFRED J M01RR00334-25 0214
LEWY, ALFRED J M01RR00334-25 0299
LEWY, ALFRED J M01RR00334-25 0303
LEWY, ALFRED J M01RR00334-25 0274
LEWY, ALFRED J M01RR00334-25 0279
LEWY, ALFRED J M01RR00334-25 0292
LEWY, ALFRED J R01MH40161-07
LEX, BARBARA W R01AA06794-07
LEX, BARBARA W R01DA04870-03
LEY, RONALD D R01ES05180-03
LEY, RONALD D S15CA55979-01
LEY, TIMOTHY J P01CA49712-03 0004
LEY, TIMOTHY J R01DK38682-05
LEYASMEYER, EDITH D S07RR05448-30
LEYASMEYER, EDITH D S15HL47775-01
LEYH, THOMAS S R01DK43003-02
LEYH, THOMAS S S07RR05397-30 0790
LEYKO, MARIE A N01CM17531-00
LEYKO, MARIE ANN N01CM73710-11
LEYKO, MARY ANN N01CM17541-01
LI, BAOGUANG Z01AI00583-02
LI, CHRISTINE R01HD25212-02
LI, ELLEN R29DK40172-03
LI, F P Z01CP04400-26
LI, GLORIA C R01CA56909-01
LI, GLORIA C R37CA31397-10
LI, J Z01BA02017-02
LI, JIA-LING S07RR07175-15 0436
LI, JIAN-MING S07RR05712-20 0062
LI, JONATHAN J R01CA22008-14
LI, JONATHAN J R13CA55109-01
LI, JONATHAN J R55CA41387-04A2
LI, JOSEPH K P42ES04922-03 0003
LI, LINGNA R43CA53995-01A1
LI, LUK C S07RR06009-03 0302
LI, S S Z01ES61043-01
LI, S S Z01ES61044-01
LI, S S Z01ES61045-01
LI, S S Z01ES61046-01
LI, S-H Z01DE00501-02
LI, TING-KAI P01AA07203-02 0003
LI, TING-KAI P01AA08553-02
LI, TING-KAI P01AA08553-02 0001
LI, TING-KAI P50AA07611-04
LI, TING-KAI R37AA02342-16
LI, TING-KAI S15MH49331-01
LI, VIRGINIA C R25CA49565-03
LI, WEIYE R01EY06563-05
LI, WEN-HSIUNG R01GM30998-08
LI, WEN-HSIUNG R55GM45670-01
LI, WEN-HSIUNG S07RR07143-20 0543
LI, YEN R01CA50146-03
LI, YEN R29AI25108-05
LI, YU-TEH R01NS09626-21
LIAN, ERIC C R01HL27007-09
LIAN, ERIC C-Y M01RR05280-03 0007
LIAN, JANE B R01AR33920-08
LIAN, JANE B R01AR35166-06
LIANG, BRUCE T R29HL44188-03
LIANG, BRUCE T S07RR05415-30 0014
LIANG, CHANG-SENG M01RR00044-31 0363
LIANG, CHANG-SENG M01RR00044-31 0310
LIANG, CHANG-SENG M01RR00044-31 0386
LIANG, CHANG-SENG R01HL35194-05
LIANG, CHANG-SENY M01RR00044-31 0355
LIANG, JACK J R01EY05803-06
LIANG, JAKE T K08DK01952-02
LIANG, JAN C P01CA49639-02 9002
LIANG, JAN C R01CA43585-05
LIANG, JEROME Z R29HL44194-02
LIANG, JERSEY R01AG08094-03
LIANG, JERSEY R37AG06643-05
LIANG, KUNG-YEE R29GM39261-04
LIANG, MATTHEW H P60AR36308-07
LIANG, MATTHEW H P60AR36308-07 0013
LIANG, MATTHEW H R01AR39921-01A1
LIANG, SHU MEI Z01BD03022-03
LIANG, SHU-MEI Z01BD03023-01
LIANG, SHU-MEI Z01BD03025-01
LIANG, SHU-MEI Z01BD03026-01
LIANG, SM Z01BD03027-01

LIANG, T JAKE R01CA54524-01
LIANOS, ELIAS A R01DK34793-07
LIANOS, K S07RR05333-30 0869
LIAO, JAMES K K11HL02508-02
LIAO, JAMES T F N01CM87256-10
LIAO, MARTHA S07RR05964-06 0766
LIAO, SHUTSUNG R01DK37694-06
LIAO, SHUTSUNG R01DK41670-03
LIAO, WARREN S S07RR05511-29 0496
LIAO, WARREN S-L R29AR38858-05
LIARAKOS, CHARLES D R01GM41257-03
LIARD, JEAN-FRANCOIS P01HL29587-09 0009
LIAU, GENE K04HL02449-02
LIAU, GENE R01HL37510-04
LIAU, YUN H S07RR06004-04 0037
LIAW, YUN-LONG S06GM08110-20 0010
LIBBY, PETER R01HL34636-08
LIBBY, PETER R01HL43364-03
LIBBY, PETER R01HL47840-01
LIBBY, R DANIEL R15GM42078-01A2
LIBER, HOWARD L R01CA49696-03
LIBERMAN, M CHARLES R01DC00188-10
LIBERMAN, MORTON S07RR05755-18 0230
LIBERMAN, ROBERT P50MH30911-14 0022
LIBERMAN, ROBERT S07RR05756-18 0288
LIBERMAN, ROBERT S07RR05756-18 0318
LIBERMAN, ROBERT S07RR05756-18 0298
LIBERMAN, ROBERT P P50MH30911-14
LIBERMAN, ROBERT P P50MH30911-14 0014
LIBERMAN, ROBERT P P50MH30911-14 0015
LIBERMAN, ROBERT P P50MH30911-14 9008
LIBERTI, PAUL A R43GM45658-01A1
LIBERTI, PAUL A R43HL46073-01
LIBURDY, ROBERT P R01CA53711-01
LICHT, JONATHAN D K11CA01272-05
LICHT, JONATHAN D S07RR05526-29 0097
LICHT, PAUL S07RR07006-26 0918
LICHTEN, M Z01CB05268-03
LICHTENBERGER, LENARD M R01DK33239-08A1
LICHTENSTEIN, ALICE M01RR00054-30 0448
LICHTENSTEIN, EDWARD N01CN64094-09
LICHTENSTEIN, EDWARD L U01CA52230-02
LICHTENSTEIN, LAWRENCE M P50HL37119-05 9001
LICHTENSTEIN, LAWRENCE M R01AI07290-26
LICHTENSTEIN, LAWRENCE M R37AI08270-24
LICHTENSTEIN, LAWRENCE M U01AI31867-01 9001
LICHTER, DANIEL T R01HD26321-01A1
LICHTER, PAUL R P30EY07003-05
LICHTER, WOLF P30CA14395-18A1 9013
LICHTLER, ALEX P01AR38933-05 0007
LICHTLER, ALEX P01HD22610-04 0003
LICHTLER, ALEXANDER R01AR29983-08A3
LICHTMAN, ANDREW H R29CA43651-05
LICHTMAN, JEFF W P01NS29343-01 9002
LICHTMAN, JEFF W P01NS29343-01 0005
LICHTMAN, JEFF W R01NS20364-08
LICHTMAN, MARSHALL A G20RR07082-01
LICHTMAN, MARSHALL A M01RR00044-31
LICHTMAN, MARSHALL A P01HL18208-17 9001
LICHTMAN, MARSHALL A P01HL18208-17 9002
LICHTMAN, MARSHALL A P01HL18208-17 9004
LICHTMAN, MARSHALL A P01HL18208-17 0001
LICHTMAN, STEVEN N R29DK44233-01
LICHU, MON P01AR38188-07 0004
LICKLITER, ROBERT E R01MH48949-01
LICKLITER, ROBERT E S07RR07095-24 0369
LICKO, VOJTECH P30DK26743-11 9008
LIDDLE, HOWARD A P50DA07697-01
LIDDLE, HOWARD A P50DA07697-01 0001
LIDDLE, RODGER A R01DK38626-05
LIDDLE, ROGER A M01RR00030-30 0475
LIDOFSKY, STEVEN D K08DK01987-02
LIDOW, MICHAEL P01NS22807-07 0004
LIDSKY, THEODORE I R01NS21418-08
LIDSTROM, M S07RR07003-26 0332
LIDSTROM, MARY E R01GM36296-07
LIDSTROM, MARY E R01GM40859-03
LIDZ, CHARLES W P50MH30915-15 9015
LIDZ, CHARLES W R01MH40030-07
LIEBER, CHARLES S P50AA03508-14 9002
LIEBER, CHARLES S P50AA03508-14 9003
LIEBER, CHARLES S P50AA03508-14 9004
LIEBER, CHARLES S P50AA03508-14 0047
LIEBER, CHARLES S P50AA03508-14
LIEBER, CHARLES S R01AA05934-08
LIEBER, CHARLES S R01AA07802-04
LIEBER, MICHAEL P01AG02908-11 0013
LIEBER, MICHAEL S07RR05353-30 0354
LIEBER, MICHAEL S07RR05353-30 0355
LIEBER, MICHAEL R P01CA34233-09 0022
LIEBER, MICHAEL R R01CA51105-02
LIEBER, MICHAEL R R01GM43236-02
LIEBER, RICHARD L R01AR35192-06
LIEBER, RICHARD L R01AR40050-03
LIEBERMAN, ELLICE S S07RR05446-30 0269
LIEBERMAN, HARRIS M01RR00088-28 0272
LIEBERMAN, HOWARD B R29CA54044-02
LIEBERMAN, JEFFREY A K02MH00537-06
LIEBERMAN, JEFFREY A R01MH38880-07
LIEBERMAN, JEFFREY A R01MH45122-02
LIEBERMAN, JUDY K08CA01449-02
LIEBERMAN, JUDY R01AI30926-01A1

LIEBERMAN, MELVYN R01HL27105-11
LIEBERMAN, MELVYN S07RR05405-30 0867
LIEBERMAN, MICHAEL P50HD20748-06A1 0007
LIEBERMAN, MICHAEL W R01CA40263-07
LIEBERMAN, MICHAEL W R01CA50684-03
LIEBERMAN, MICHAEL W R13CA54129-01
LIEBERMAN, MICHAEL W R37CA39392-08
LIEBERMAN, MORTON S07RR05755-18 0209
LIEBERMAN, MORTON A K05MH20342-15
LIEBERMAN, SEYMOUR R01DK00110-40
LIEBERMAN, SEYMOUR S07RR05840-13
LIEBERMAN, SEYMOUR S15AI32188-01
LIEBERMANN, DAN A R01CA43618-02
LIEBERT, MONICA R01DK44804-01
LIEBESKIND, JOHN C R01NS07628-24
LIEBESKIND, LANNY S07RR07023-26 0983
LIEBESKIND, LANNY S R01CA40157-08
LIEBESKIND, LANNY S R01CA44404-05
LIEBESKIND, LANNY S R01GM43107-02
LIEBLER, DANIEL C R29CA47943-04
LIEBMAN, HOWARD M01RR00533-23 0197
LIEBMAN, HOWARD S07RR05569-27 0108
LIEBMAN, HOWARD A R29HL39665-05
LIEBMAN, PAUL A P30EY01583-17
LIEBMAN, PAUL A R01EY00012-28
LIEBOVITCH, LARRY S R01EY06234-06
LIEBOW, E Z01MH00680-08
LIEBOWITZ, MICHAEL P50MH30906-14 9009
LIEBOWITZ, MICHAEL R R01MH40121-08
LIEBOWITZ, MICHAEL R R01MH43845-03
LIEBOWITZ, MICHAEL R R01MH45436-02
LIEBOWITZ, MICHAEL R R01MH46439-02
LIEBSON, IRA A M01RR02719-06 0023
LIEBSON, IRA A M01RR02719-06 0013
LIEBSON, PAUL P30CA15083-18 9014
LIECHTY, EDWARD A K04HD00865-03
LIECHTY, EDWARD A R01HD19089-08
LIECHTY, MELISSA N44ES92003-05
LIEDERMAN, JACQUELIN S07RR07043-26 0114
LIEDERMAN, JACQUELINE R03MH47409-01A1
LIEDTKE, A JAMES R01HL41914-03
LIEDTKE, CAROLE M R01HL43907-07
LIEHR, JOACHIM P01DK42788-01 0002
LIEHR, JOACHIM P01DK42788-01 9001
LIEHR, JOACHIM G R01CA43232-06
LIEHR, JOACHIM G R01CA44069-06
LIEHR, JOACHIM G R37CA43233-07
LIEM, RONALD K R01NS15182-13
LIEM, RONALD K R01NS29224-01
LIEN, ERIC S07RR05792-15 0946
LIENHARD, GUSTAV E R01DK25336-13
LIENHARD, GUSTAV E R01DK42816-02
LIEPNIEKS, JURIS J P60AR20582-14 0003
LIERMAN, LETHA S07RR05758-18 0253
LIESVELD, JANE L K11HL02385-02
LIETMAN, PAUL S M01RR00035-31 0386
LIETMAN, PAUL S M01RR00035-31 0368
LIETMAN, PAUL S M01RR00035-31 0371
LIETMAN, PAUL S M01RR00035-31 0387
LIEW, C C P01HL37412-04 0007
LIFF, JONATHAN N01CP95604-07
LIFSCHITZ, MEYER D M01RR01346-10 0163
LIFSCHITZ, MEYER D U01DK39479-04
LIFSON, JEFFREY U01AI25922-05 9002
LIFSON, JEFFREY U01AI25922-05 0002
LIGGETT, PETER E R01EY08001-02
LIGGETT, PETER E U10EY06270-07
LIGGETT, STEPHEN B R01HL45967-02
LIGHT, ALAN R R01DA04420-05
LIGHT, ALAN R R01NS16433-12
LIGHT, JIMMY A U01AI31442-01
LIGHT, KATHLEEN C M01RR00046-31 0322
LIGHT, KATHLEEN C R01HL18976-12
LIGHT, KATHLEEN C R01HL31533-08
LIGHT, KIM E R01AA06483-04A1
LIGHT, LEAH L R37AG02452-12
LIGHTFOOT, EDWIN N P41RR01243-10 0012
LIGHTNER, DAVID A R01HD17779-09
LIKE, ARTHUR A R37DK19155-17
LIKE, ARTHUR A R37DK19155-17 0001
LIKE, ARTHUR A R37DK19155-17 0002
LIKE, ARTHUR A R37DK19155-17 0004
LIKE, ARTHUR A R37DK19155-17 0006
LIKE, ROBERT P50MH43450-04 0014
LILIEN, JACK S07RR07180-10 0625
LILIEN, JACK E R01EY05860-10
LILIEN, JACK E R01EY08888-02
LILIS, RUTH P30ES00928-18 9003
LILJA, HERMAN N01ES95256-10
LILJA, HERMAN S N01ES55111-19
LILJA, HERMAN S N01ES75146-08
LILJA, HERMAN S N01ES85212-12
LILJEMARK, WILLIAM F R37DE04614-15
LILLARD, LEE P01HD28372-01 0010
LILLARD, LEE P50HD12639-12 0013
LILLARD, LEE P50HD12639-12 9001
LILLARD, LEE S07RR05710-21 0020
LILLARD, LEE A P01AG08291-03
LILLARD, LEE A P01AG08291-03 0001
LILLARD, LEE A P01AG08291-03 9001
LILLARD, LEE A R37AG08346-02
LILLEMOE, KEITH D R01CA49776-03

LILLEMOE, KEITH D R29DK41889-03
LILLEY, GEORGE W, JR R01MH48239-01
LILLEY, GEORGE WOOD, JR R18MH46145-03
LILLO-MARTIN, DIANE R01DC00183-09
LILLY, FRANK R01CA19931-13A3
LILLY, FRANK R01CA52621-02
LILLY, JOHN R M01RR00069-29 0428
LILLY, JOHN R M01RR00069-29 0285
LILLY, JOHN R M01RR00069-29 0248
LILLY, K Z01HL02836-01
LIM, BING R29DK44099-01
LIM, DANIEL V S07RR07121-13 0471
LIM, DONGBIN S07RR05399-30 0941
LIM, HENRY P30AR39749-04 9001
LIM, PETER N01CM73715-05
LIM, ROBERT W R29AR40682-01A1
LIM, VICTORIA M01RR00059-30 0696
LIM, VICTORIA M01RR00059-30 0743
LIM, VICTORIA S M01RR00059-30 0511
LIM, WILMA M01RR00046-31 0504
LIMA, ALDO P01AI26512-03 9001
LIMA, JOHN J M01RR00034-31 0419
LIMA, NOELIA P01AI26512-03 0004
LIMACHER, MARIAN C K07HL01717-05
LIMACHER, MARIAN C M01RR00082-29 0479
LIMANDRI, BARBARA P50MH43458-04 0004
LIMBIRD, LEE E R01HL25182-11A1
LIMBIRD, LEE E R37HL43671-02
LIMENTANI, STEVEN A K11HL02504-02
LIN JUNG-CHUNG P01CA19014-14 0019
LIN, CHARLES N43NS12309-00
LIN, CHI-WEI R01CA32259-09
LIN, CHIA-SHENG P50NS06233-25 0040
LIN, CHIA-SHENG R01NS29161-01
LIN, CHING-SHWUN R01CA49423-03
LIN, EDMUND C R01GM11983-28
LIN, EDMUND C R01GM39693-04
LIN, EDMUND C R01GM40993-03
LIN, HSIU-SAN P01CA51116-02 0004
LIN, JIM J P50HL42266-02 0004
LIN, JIM JUNG-CHIN P01HD18577-08 0004
LIN, JIM JUNG-CHING R01GM40580-04
LIN, KEH-MING M01RR00425-22S3 0449
LIN, KEH-MING R01MH47193-02
LIN, KEH-MING R01MH47193-02 0001
LIN, KEH-MING R01MH47355-01
LIN, KUANG-TZU D S03RR03426-05
LIN, L Z01BB02014-01
LIN, LILY R43AI30818-01A1
LIN, LILY R43AI31300-01
LIN, LILY R43AI31714-01
LIN, MING-FONG R29CA52112-02
LIN, NAN R01AA07600-03
LIN, RENEE C P50AA07611-04 0003
LIN, S M01RR00585-20 0559
LIN, SHIN R01GM22289-17
LIN, SUE-HWA R01GM43189-01A1
LIN, TAI-SHUN R01AI29430-02
LIN, TEIN-HSIANG S07RR07066-26 0249
LIN, TSU M01RR00188-27 0231
LIN, TSU M01RR00188-27 0260
LIN, TSU-HUI M01RR00188-27 0302
LIN, TSU-HUI M01RR00188-27 0303
LIN, TSU-HUIBECCA T M01RR00188-27 0188
LIN, TSUE-MING R44AI26965-03
LIN, TU R01HD25641-03
LIN, VICTOR K S07RR05426-30 0142
LIN, W-W Z01MH02467-03
LINAS, STUART P01DK35098-06A1 0008
LINAS, STUART L P50HL40784-03 0003
LINAS, STUART L R01HL37694-04A1
LINCK, RICHARD W R01GM35648-07
LINCOLN, MICHAEL J R29LM05260-01
LINCOLN, THOMAS M R01HL34646-07
LIND, STUART E R01HL42457-03
LINDAHL, LASSE A R01AI15286-14
LINDAHL, PAUL A S07RR07090-26 0476
LINDAHL, RONALD G R01CA21103-10A3
LINDAY, BRUCE D S07RR05389-30 0640
LINDBERG, IRIS K04DK01868-04
LINDBERG, IRIS R01DA05084-04
LINDBERG, IRIS R01DK35199-06
LINDBLAD, WILLIAM S07RR07051-26 0733
LINDELL, THOMAS J S03RR03495-03
LINDEMAN, DAVID P30AG10129-01 9003
LINDEMAN, DAVID A U01AG10311-01
LINDEMAN, KAREN S K11HL02417-02
LINDEMAN, ROBERT D M01RR00997-16 0374
LINDEMANN, CHARLES S07RR07131-22 0132
LINDEMANN, JON P P01HL06308-31 0043
LINDEMANN, ROBERT S07RR05304-30 0223
LINDEMANN, ROBERT A R29DE09174-03
LINDEMANN, ROBERT A S03RR03535-02
LINDEN, JAMES S07RR07127-23 0491
LINDEN, JOEL M R55HL37942-06
LINDEN, KATHRYN W S07RR07032-26 0034
LINDENFELD, JO A M01RR00051-30 0762
LINDENMAYER, GEORGE MD PHD R01HL42040-03
LINDENZWEIG, BOB N01CO15753-00
LINDENZWEIG, C R N01CO15655-00
LINDENZWEIG, C R N01CO15691-00
LINDENZWEIG, C R N01CO15706-01
LINDENZWEIG, C R N01CO15721-00
LINDENZWEIG, C R N01CO15726-01
LINDENZWEIG, C R N01CO15749-00
LINDENZWEIG, C R N01CO15765-00
LINDENZWEIG, C R N01CO15768-00
LINDENZWEIG, C R N01CO15772-00
LINDENZWEIG, C R N01CO15781-00
LINDER, MARIA C S06GM08258-02 0002
LINDERMAN, RUSSELL J. P01ES00044-26 0008
LINDGREN, CLARK A R15NS29520-01
LINDGREN, FRANK T P01HL18574-16 9001
LINDGREN, SCOTT M01RR00059-30 0717
LINDMAYER, JOSEPH R44CA50916-02
LINDOR, K D M01RR00585-20 0494
LINDOR, KEITH D M01RR00585-20 0437
LINDQUIST, SUSAN L R01GM25874-13
LINDSAY, HARRIET A R19DA06453-03
LINDSAY, JAMES A R01HD24714-03
LINDSAY, KAREN L M01RR00865-18 0368
LINDSAY, ROBERT P50AR39191-05
LINDSAY, ROBERT P50AR39191-05 9003
LINDSAY, ROBERT R01DK42892-02
LINDSAY, ROBERT S07RR05649-25 0800
LINDSEY, ADA S07RR06014-03 0843
LINDSEY, BRUCE G R01NS19814-07A1
LINDSEY, BRUCE G S07RR05749-19 0270
LINDSEY, DELWIN R01EY07078-05
LINDSEY, J RUSSELL N01ES05280-01
LINDSEY, J RUSSELL P40RR00463-23
LINDSEY, JONATHAN S R01GM36238-05
LINDSEY, THOMAS K N01LM13515-00
LINDSTEDT, STAN L S15HL47771-01
LINDSTEN, TULLIA R29CA54521-01
LINDSTROM, DANIEL P P50HL14214-20 9003
LINDSTROM, DANIEL P R01HL38354-04A1
LINDSTROM, JON M R01NS11323-18
LINEHAN, JOHN H R01HL24349-13
LINEHAN, MARSHA M R01MH34486-10
LINEHAN, W M Z01CM06659-09
LINENBERGER, MICHAEL L K08HL02396-03
LING, BRIAN S07RR05364-30 0533
LING, C CLIFTON R01CA52713-02
LING, FRANK W M01RR00211-27 0330
LING, JACK S07RR05444-30 0260
LING, NICHOLAS P01HD09690-18 0001
LING, NICHOLAS C P01DK18811-17A1 9003
LING, NICHOLAS C P01HD09690-18 9002
LING, NICHOLAS C S07RR05876-09 0590
LING, NICHOLAS CHI-KWAN P01HD09690-18
LING, VICTOR R01CA37130-08
LING, WALTER R18DA06082-03
LINGAPPA, VISHWANATH P30DK26743-11 0010
LINGAPPA, VISHWANATH R P01AG02132-11 0005
LINGAPPA, VISHWANATH R R01HL45480-01
LINGEN, MARK W K15DE00313-01
LINGREL, JERRY P01HL41496-03 0001
LINGREL, JERRY P01HL41496-03 9001
LINGREL, JERRY B P01HL41496-03
LINGREL, JERRY B P60HL15996-19 0020
LINGREL, JERRY B R01HL28573-09
LINGREL, JERRY B R37DK39585-04
LINGREL, JERRY B. P01HL22619-14 0016
LINHARDT, ROBERT J R01GM38060-04
LINIAL, MAXINE L P01AI27291-04
LINIAL, MAXINE L R01CA18282-16
LINIAL, MAXINE L. P01AI27291-04 0001
LINIAL, MAXINE L. P01AI27291-04 9001
LINK, CHRISTOPHER S07RR07138-20 0532
LINK, CHRISTOPHER D R29HD26087-03
LINK, MICHAEL P U10CA33603-09
LINK, MICHAEL P U10CA33603-09 0014
LINK, MICHAEL P U10CA33603-09 0015
LINK, MICHAEL P U10CA33603-09 0016
LINK, MICHAEL P U10CA33603-09 0001
LINK, MICHAEL P U10CA33603-09 0002
LINK, MICHAEL P U10CA33603-09 0003
LINK, MICHAEL P U10CA33603-09 0017
LINK, MICHAEL P U10CA33603-09 0004
LINK, MICHAEL P U10CA33603-09 0005
LINK, MICHAEL P U10CA33603-09 0006
LINK, MICHAEL P U10CA33603-09 0007
LINK, MICHAEL P U10CA33603-09 0008
LINK, MICHAEL P U10CA33603-09 0009
LINK, MICHAEL P U10CA33603-09 0010
LINK, MICHAEL P U10CA33603-09 0011
LINK, MICHAEL P U10CA33603-09 0012
LINK, MICHAEL P U10CA33603-09 0013
LINK, MICHAEL P U10CA33603-09 0018
LINK, MICHAEL P U10CA33603-09 0054
LINK, MICHAEL P U10CA33603-09 0019
LINK, MICHAEL P U10CA33603-09 0055
LINK, MICHAEL P U10CA33603-09 0056
LINK, MICHAEL P U10CA33603-09 0020
LINK, MICHAEL P U10CA33603-09 0021
LINK, MICHAEL P U10CA33603-09 0057
LINK, MICHAEL P U10CA33603-09 0058
LINK, MICHAEL P U10CA33603-09 0059
LINK, MICHAEL P U10CA33603-09 0060
LINK, MICHAEL P U10CA33603-09 0022
LINK, MICHAEL P U10CA33603-09 0034
LINK, MICHAEL P U10CA33603-09 0035
LINK, MICHAEL P U10CA33603-09 0036
LINK, MICHAEL P U10CA33603-09 0023
LINK, MICHAEL P U10CA33603-09 0024
LINK, MICHAEL P U10CA33603-09 0025
LINK, MICHAEL P U10CA33603-09 0026
LINK, MICHAEL P U10CA33603-09 0027
LINK, MICHAEL P U10CA33603-09 0028
LINK, MICHAEL P U10CA33603-09 0029
LINK, MICHAEL P U10CA33603-09 0030
LINK, MICHAEL P U10CA33603-09 0031
LINK, MICHAEL P U10CA33603-09 0032
LINK, MICHAEL P U10CA33603-09 0033
LINK, MICHAEL P U10CA33603-09 0037
LINK, MICHAEL P U10CA33603-09 0038
LINK, MICHAEL P U10CA33603-09 0039
LINK, MICHAEL P U10CA33603-09 0040
LINK, MICHAEL P U10CA33603-09 0041
LINK, MICHAEL P U10CA33603-09 0042
LINK, MICHAEL P U10CA33603-09 0043
LINK, MICHAEL P U10CA33603-09 0044
LINK, MICHAEL P U10CA33603-09 0045
LINK, MICHAEL P U10CA33603-09 0046
LINK, MICHAEL P U10CA33603-09 0047
LINK, MICHAEL P U10CA33603-09 0048
LINK, MICHAEL P U10CA33603-09 0049
LINK, MICHAEL P U10CA33603-09 0050
LINK, MICHAEL P U10CA33603-09 0051
LINK, MICHAEL P U10CA33603-09 0052
LINK, MICHAEL P U10CA33603-09 0053
LINKER-ISARAELI, MAR S07RR05468-29 0391
LINKS, JONATHAN M P01NS15080-12 9004
LINN, JAMES G. S06GM08092-18 0017
LINN, STUART P30ES01896-13 9029
LINN, STUART M R01GM30415-10
LINN, STUART M R37GM19020-23
LINNEBACH, ALBAN J P01CA25874-12 0009
LINNEKIN, D M Z01CM09360-01
LINNER, KRISTIN M R29DA07068-01
LINNEY, ELWOOD A P30CA14236-18 9026
LINNEY, ELWOOD A R01CA39066-08
LINNEY, ELWOOD A R01HD24130-04
LINNOILA, I Z01CM06595-05
LINNOILA, I Z01CM07259-02
LINNOILA, M Z01AA00238-09
LINNOILA, M Z01AA00258-07
LINNOILA, M Z01AA00272-04
LINSCHEID, RONALD L R01AR40242-01A2
LINSENMAYER, THOMAS P01HD23681-04 0002
LINSENMAYER, THOMAS F R37EY05191-09
LINSENMEIER, ROBERT A R01EY05034-09
LINSTER, MICHELLE L R24AA08671-02 0002
LINSTER, MICHELLE L S14GM44780-02 0001
LINTHICUM, DARWIN S R01DA07240-01
LINTILHAC, PHILIP M S07RR07125-22 0393
LINZ, JOHN E R01CA52003-01A1
LINZ, JOHN E R01GM41216-01A3
LINZER, DANIEL I P30HD28048-01 9001
LINZER, DANIEL I R01GM34238-07
LINZER, DANIEL I R01HD24518-04
LINZER, MARK M01RR00054-30 0422
LIONBERGER, DAVID A M01RR00350-25 0323
LIOTTA, CHARLES S07RR07024-26 0037
LIOTTA, DENNIS C R01AI28731-03
LIOTTA, DENNIS C R01AI31827-01
LIOU, GREGORY I R01EY03829-12
LIOY, PAUL L P30ES05022-04 9004
LIPINSKI, JOSEPH F P01MH31154-14 0022
LIPINSKI, JOSEPH F P01MH31154-14 0023
LIPINSKI, JOSEPH F P01MH31154-14 0024
LIPINSKI, JOSEPH F P01MH31154-14 0025
LIPKE, PETER N R01GM43762-02
LIPKE, PETER N S06GM08176-12 0019
LIPKIN, EDWARD W M01RR00037-31 0347
LIPKIN, EDWARD W R01AR39688-02
LIPKIN, EDWARD W. P51RR00166-30 0102
LIPKIN, MARTIN N01CN15363-01
LIPKIN, WALTER I K08NS01026-05
LIPKIN, WALTER I R01NS29425-01
LIPKOWITZ, MICHAEL S K08DK01856-04
LIPMAN, JONATHAN M01RR00095-31 0355
LIPMAN, JONATHAN M01RR00095-31 0324
LIPOWSKI, EARLENE E S07RR05573-13 0084
LIPOWSKY, HERBERT H P60HL28381-09 0005
LIPOWSKY, HERVERT H R01HL39286-06
LIPPARD, STEPHEN P41RR00317-25 0008
LIPPARD, STEPHEN J R37CA34992-09
LIPPARD, STEPHEN J R37GM32134-10
LIPPE, BARBARA M M01RR00865-18 0128
LIPPERT, MARGUERITE C M01RR00847-18 0498
LIPPMAN, MARC E P30CA51008-02
LIPPMAN, MARC E U01CA51908-02
LIPPMAN, SCOTT M P01CA52051-01A1 0003
LIPPMAN, STEPHEN S R01DK40923-02
LIPPMANN, MORTON P30ES00260-29 9010
LIPPMANN, MORTON R01ES00881-18
LIPSCHITZ, DAVID A R01AG09458-01A1
LIPSCHULTZ, STEPHEN M. N01HR96041-06
LIPSCOMB, JOHN D R01GM24689-14
LIPSCOMB, JOHN D R01GM40466-04
LIPSCOMB, MARY F R01AI21951-07
LIPSCOMB, WILLIAM N R37GM06920-32
LIPSHITZ, HOWARD P01GM40499-04 0001
LIPSHITZ, HOWARD P01GM40499-04 9002

LIPSHUTZ, BRUCE H R01GM40287-01A3
LIPSICK, JOSEPH P01CA50528-03 0003
LIPSICK, JOSEPH P01CA50528-03 9002
LIPSICK, JOSEPH S P01CA28146-11 0010
LIPSICK, JOSEPH S R01CA43592-05
LIPSICK, JOSEPH STEVEN K04CA01457-04
LIPSITZ, LEWIS M01RR01032-16 0331
LIPSITZ, LEWIS M01RR01032-16 0466
LIPSITZ, LEWIS A P01AG04390-08
LIPSITZ, LEWIS A P30AG08812-02 9001
LIPSITZ, LEWIS A P50AG05134-08 9004
LIPSIUS, STEPHEN L R01HL27652-07
LIPSKA, B Z01MH02352-05
LIPSKY, P P50AR39169-05 0004
LIPSKY, P E P50AR39169-05 0006
LIPSKY, P. P01AR09989-27 0025
LIPSKY, P. P01AR09989-27 0026
LIPSKY, PETER P01AR09989-27 9003
LIPSKY, PETER P01AR09989-27 9004
LIPSKY, PETER E M01RR00633-19 0400
LIPSKY, PETER E P01AI31229-01
LIPSKY, PETER E P01AI31229-01 0001
LIPSKY, PETER E P01AI31229-01 9001
LIPSKY, PETER E P01AR09989-27
LIPSKY, PETER E P01AR09989-27 0001
LIPSKY, PETER E P50AR39169-05
LIPSKY, PETER E R01AI17653-10
LIPSKY, PETER E R13AR40817-01
LIPSON, EDWARD S07RR07068-26 0234
LIPSON, EDWARD D R01GM29707-09
LIPSON, KENNETH L P01CA56309-01 0003
LIPSON, STEVEN P60AR36308-07 0015
LIPTON, DOUGLAS S S07RR05859-09
LIPTON, DOUGLAS S S15DA07780-01
LIPTON, HELENE L R01AG09611-01
LIPTON, HELENE L R01HS06443-02
LIPTON, HOWARD L P01NS23349-06 0007
LIPTON, HOWARD L R01NS21913-16
LIPTON, JAMES M R01NS10046-17
LIPTON, JEFFREY M M01RR00071-28A1 0241
LIPTON, JEFFREY M U10CA38859-05S1
LIPTON, MARTIN S07RR05367-30 0569
LIPTON, STUART S07RR05899-10 0276
LIPTON, STUART A R01EY05477-08
LIPTON, STUART A R01EY09024-01
LIPUMA, JOHN J R29AI28833-01A2
LIPUMA, JOHN J S07RR05418-30 0029
LIS, JOHN T R01GM25232-14
LIS, JOHN T R01GM40918-03
LISANSKY, EDGAR J M01RR00997-16 0223
LISBERGER, STEPHEN G R37EY03878-11
LISCUM, LAURA R01DK36505-05
LISHKO, VALERYI K R44CA43444-03
LISKAY, ROBERT M R01GM32741-08
LISKAY, ROBERT M R01GM45413-01
LISMAN, JOHN E R01NS27337-03
LISMAN, JOHN E R37EY01496-18
LISSNER, LAUREN R03MH47775-02
LIST, MARCY A P01CA40007-06A1 0005
LIST, MARCY A U10CA37423-07
LISTER, PHILIP D S07RR05390-30 0670
LISTERUD, JOHN R29HL45179-01A1
LISTON, HATTYE S07RR07236-04 0172
LISTOWSKY, IRVING R01CA42448-05
LITCHY, WILLIAM J P50NS17750-10 0023
LITMAN, BURTON J R01EY00548-20
LITMAN, GARY W R01AI23338-07
LITMAN, GARY W R01GM38656-05
LITOSCH, IRENE R01DK37007-04A3
LITOSCH, IRENE S07RR05363-30 0831
LITSKY, ALAN S R29AR39684-03
LITSTER, J DAVID S15EY09461-01
LITT, LAWRENCE R01GM34767-06
LITT, MARK S07RR05677-23 0975
LITT, MARK D R01DE09211-01A2
LITT, MICHAEL R01HG00022-02
LITTAU, L W S06GM08022-20 0009
LITTLE, JOHN B. P30ES00002-29 9005
LITTLE, CHARLES D R01HL45348-02
LITTLE, J RUSSELL P01AI15353-13 9004
LITTLE, J RUSSELL R01AI27466-03
LITTLE, JOHN B P30ES00002-29
LITTLE, JOHN B P30ES00002-29 9002
LITTLE, JOHN B P30ES00002-29 0014
LITTLE, JOHN B R35CA47542-04
LITTLE, JOHN W R01GM24178-14A1
LITTLE, JOHN W S07RR07002-26 0858
LITTLE, R D S07RR07099-25 0395
LITTLE, RODERICK J A R01MH37188-08
LITTLE, STEPHEN E P41RR01243-10 0002
LITTLE, WILLIAM C R01HL42364-02
LITTLEFIELD, L GAYLE R01CA51388-02
LITTLETON, GEORGE K S06GM08016-21
LITTLETON, RAY S07RR05490-29 0450
LITTMAN, DAN R R01AI23513-05
LITTMAN, DON R P01AI24286-05 0003
LITWACK, GERALD R01DK13531-22
LITWACK, GERALD R01DK42353-03
LITWIN, SAMUEL P30CA06927-29 9005
LITZ, CRAIG E S07RR05385-30 0815
LITZINGER, MARCIA J K08HD00886-02
LIU-CHEN, LEE-YUAN R29DA04745-04

LIU, BRIAN C S R01CA51968-01A1
LIU, CHIEN K06AI01826-29
LIU, CHUNG-CHIUN P41RR02024-08 9005
LIU, CHUNG-CHIUN P41RR02024-08 9006
LIU, CHUNG-CHIUN P41RR02024-08
LIU, CHUNG-CHIUN S07RR07113-24 0567
LIU, EDISON S07RR05406-30 0911
LIU, EDISON T N01ES15327-00
LIU, EDISON T R01CA49240-03
LIU, FU-TONG M01RR00833-17 0218
LIU, FU-TONG R01AI19747-10
LIU, FU-TONG R01AI20958-08
LIU, FU-TONG U01AI32834-01 0005
LIU, HUNG-WEN K04GM00559-02
LIU, HUNG-WEN R01GM35906-06
LIU, HUNG-WEN R01GM40541-03
LIU, JAMES H P50HD12303-13 0006
LIU, JOHN H K R01EY07544-04
LIU, KATHERINE JUNG-MEI R29CA50710-04
LIU, LEO X K11AI00965-02
LIU, LEROY F P01CA50529-01A2 0002
LIU, LEROY F R01CA39662-07
LIU, LEROY F R01GM27731-12
LIU, MARK C U01AI31867-01 0010
LIU, MAW-SHUNG R01GM31664-07
LIU, MING-CHEH S07RR07078-18 0465
LIU, PAUL P60HL38639-04 0010
LIU, ROBERT S R37DK17806-17
LIU, SAMMY H R01EY04444-10
LIU, SHIH-CHUN D P01HL37462-05 0003
LIU, SONG YUAN Z01HD01003-03
LIU, T Z01BB02015-01
LIU, YUNG-NAN P01HD19937-06 9002
LIU, YUNG-NAN P01HD19937-06 0002
LIUZZI, FRANCIS J S07RR05771-15 0332
LIVE, DAVID H R03DK44666-01
LIVE, DAVID H R29DK38676-04
LIVELY, CURTIS M S07RR07031-26 0097
LIVELY, MARK O P30CA12197-19 9011
LIVESEY, JOHN C R01EY07028-06
LIVINGSTON, DAVID H S07RR05393-30 0897
LIVINGSTON, DAVID M P01CA50661-03 0004
LIVINGSTON, DAVID M P01CA50661-03 9001
LIVINGSTON, DAVID M P01CA50661-03 9002
LIVINGSTON, DAVID M P01CA50661-03
LIVINGSTON, DAVID M P30CA06516-28 9007
LIVINGSTON, DAVID M P30CA06516-28 0023
LIVINGSTON, DAVID M P30CA06516-28 9011
LIVINGSTON, DAVID M R01CA24715-13
LIVINGSTON, DAVID M R01CA49530-03
LIVINGSTON, DAVID M R37CA15751-18
LIVINGSTON, JAMES N R01DK40394-04
LIVINGSTON, PHILIP O P01CA33049-09 0004
LIVINGSTON, PHILIP O R01CA40532-04A2
LIVNY, MIRON R01HG00504-01 0005
LIVOLSI, VIRGINIA A P30CA16520-16 9021
LIVOLSI, VIRGINIA A U01CA44974-04
LIZZI, FREDERIC L R01CA38400-11
LJUNG, BRITT-MARIE P01CA44768-05 9001
LJUNGDAHL, LARS G R01DK27323-12
LLINAS, MIGUEL R01HL29409-10
LLINAS, RODOLFO R P01AG09480-01
LLINAS, RODOLFO R P01AG09480-01 9001
LLINAS, RODOLFO R P01AG09480-01 0001
LLINAS, RODOLFO R P01NS13742-15
LLINAS, RODOLFO R P01NS13742-15 0006
LLINAS, RODOLFO R P01NS13742-15 9001
LLOYD, CYNTHIA A R43AG10076-01
LLOYD, K P41RR00862-18 0004
LLOYD, KENNETH G P01CA33049-09 0006
LLOYD, KENNETH O P01CA52477-01A1 0004
LLOYD, KENNETH O P01CA52477-01A1 9001
LLOYD, KENNETH O R01CA21445-15
LLOYD, MARK L K08DK01789-05
LLOYD, PHILIP E R01NS23569-06
LLOYD, R STEPHEN P30ES00267-25 9005
LLOYD, RICARDO V M01RR00042-31 0673
LLOYD, RICARDO V R01CA42951-06
LLOYD, RICHARD E R01AI27914-03
LLOYD, ROBERT S R01ES04091-05
LLOYD, STEPHEN R P01ES05355-01A1 0002
LLOYD, THOMAS A R01HD25973-02
LO, BERNARD P50MH42459-06 9003
LO, CECILIA P01HD21355-04 0003
LO, DAVID R01AI29689-02
LO, KWOK M K11CA01505-02
LO, S C Z01CL02058-03
LO, SHAW-HWA S07RR05449-30 0317
LO, SHYH-CHING R01AI31830-01
LO, WARREN D K08NS01235-04
LO, WOO-KUEN R01EY05314-09
LOACH, PAUL A R01GM11741-24
LOATS, HARRY L P01NS15080-12 9006
LOATS, HARRY L R43ES05872-01
LOATS, HARRY L R44NS26548-03
LOBB, CRAIG J R01AI23052-06
LOBBAN, CHRISTOPHER S S06GM44796-02 0001
LOBECK, CHARLES C S03RR03184-11
LOBEL, MARCI S07RR07067-26 0219
LOBEL, PETER S07RR05576-27 0613
LOBIONDO-WOOD, GERI S07RR05942-06 0006
LOBO, PETER ISSAC R01CA50342-02

LOBO, ROGERIO A M01RR00043-31 0490
LOBO, ROGERIO A M01RR00043-31 0459
LOBRUTTO, RUSSELL R01GM25052-15
LOBUE, JOSEPH S07RR07062-26 0217
LOBUGLIO, ALBERT F M01RR00032-31 0320
LOBUGLIO, ALBERT F N01CM97611-05
LOBUGLIO, ALBERT F P30CA13148-20
LOBUGLIO, ALBERT F R01AI20792-09
LOBUGLIO, ALBERT F. M01RR00032-31 0263
LOCALIO, ARTHUR R R01HS07067-01
LOCK, RICHARD B R29CA53184-01
LOCKARD, JOAN S R01HD26556-01A3
LOCKARD, JOAN S R01NS30767-04
LOCKE, F B Z01CN00113-08
LOCKE, KENNETH W R43MH47618-01A1
LOCKE, PATRICK R19MH46206-03
LOCKER, JOSEPH D R01CA43909-04A1
LOCKETT, WILLIAM R19MH46180-03
LOCKLEY, ORA S06GM08023-20 0005
LOCKSHIN, RICHARD A R01AG10101-01
LOCKSLEY, RICHARD M R01AI26918-04
LOCKSLEY, RICHARD M R01AI30663-01
LOCKWOOD, DEAN H R55DK20129-14A2
LOCKYER, JEAN S07RR05377-30 0763
LOCNISKAR, MARY S07RR07091-26 0760
LODDER, ROBERT A R29HL45143-01A1
LODISH, HARVEY P01HL41484-03 0002
LODISH, HARVEY F P01HL32262-10 0007
LODISH, HARVEY F R01GM35012-07
LODISH, HARVEY F R01GM40916-03
LODMELL, D L Z01AI00072-20
LOE, H Z01DE00410-07
LOEB, D S M01RR00585-20 0545
LOEB, GERALD E R01NS27193-03
LOEB, JOHN N R37HD05506-20
LOEB, LAURENCE A P01AG01751-13 0007
LOEB, LAWRENCE A R35CA39903-07
LOEBER, ROLF R01MH42529-05
LOECHLER, EDWARD L R01CA50432-02
LOEFFLER, HERBERT H R43AI29778-01A1
LOEGERING, DANIEL J R01GM26102-12
LOEHR, THOMAS M R01GM34468-07
LOEHR, THOMAS M S07RR07184-13
LOEHR, THOMAS M S07RR07184-13 0533
LOEHR, THOMAS M S15AI32195-01
LOENING-BAUCKE, VERA M01RR00059-30 0746
LOENING-BAUCKE, VERA A M01RR00059-30 0513
LOEPPKY, RICHARD N R01ES03953-06
LOEPPKY, RICHARD N R37CA26914-11
LOEPPKY, RICHARD N S07RR07053-26 0160
LOESCHE, WALTER J P01DE09142-02
LOESCHE, WALTER J P01DE09142-02 0002
LOEW, FRANKLIN M S03RR03389-05
LOEW, FRANKLIN M S07RR05852-11
LOEW, GILDA H R01DA06304-03
LOEW, GILDA H R01GM27943-10A2
LOEW, LESLIE M R01GM35063-08
LOEWENSTEIN, WERNER R R01CA14464-18
LOEWY, ARTHUR D R37HL25449-16
LOFQVIST, ANDERS R01DC00865-02
LOFTUS, GEOFFREY R R37MH41637-06
LOFTUS, JOSEPH C R29HL42977-02
LOGAN, BARBARA N S07RR05776-11 0397
LOGAN, DAVID A S07RR07129-22 0501
LOGAN, HENRIETTA L R01DE09419-01A2
LOGAN, HENRIETTA L S07RR05313-30 0245
LOGAN, JOHN S07RR07122-23 0117
LOGAN, JOHN S07RR07122-23 0118
LOGAN, JOY L R01DK41485-02
LOGEMANN, JERI A S07RR07028-26 0020
LOGEMANN, JERILYN A P01CA40007-06A1
LOGEMANN, JERILYN A P01CA40007-06A1 0002
LOGEMANN, JERILYN A P01CA40007-06A1 0003
LOGEMANN, JERILYN A R01NS28525-02
LOGHMAN-ADHAM, MAHMO S07RR05428-30 0176
LOGIN, GARY R K11DE00210-05
LOGIN, IVAN S S07RR05431-30 0840
LOGSDON, CRAIG D R01DK35912-05A2
LOGSDON, CRAIG D R01DK41350-03
LOGSDON, CRAIG D S07RR05383-30 0565
LOH, DENNIS P50AI15322-14 0013
LOH, EVAN K11HL02514-02
LOH, HORACE H K05DA70554-19
LOH, HORACE H P01DA05695-03
LOH, HORACE H P01DA05695-03 9001
LOH, HORACE H P01DA05695-03 0002
LOH, HORACE H R01DA00564-19
LOH, HORACE H R37DA01583-14
LOH, IH-HOUNG R44NS27793-03
LOH, Y P Z01HD00056-16
LOH, Y P Z01HD01202-04
LOHKA, MANFRED J R29GM40658-04
LOHMAN, TIMOTHY G R01AR39559-03
LOHMAN, TIMOTHY M R01GM30498-10
LOHMAN, TIMOTHY M R01GM45948-01
LOHMEIER, THOMAS E P01HL11678-24 0027
LOHMEIER, THOMAS E P01HL11678-24 9002
LOHR, CHARLES P51RR00166-30 0170
LOHR, JAMES B R29MH45142-03
LOHR, JAMES W S07RR05400-30 0035
LOI, POH KENG S07RR07080-26 0309
LOIKE, JOHN D R29DK39110-04

LOIZZI, ROBERT F S07RR05369-30 0578
LOJEWSKI, FRANK P51RR00169-30 9005
LOKER, ERIC S R01AI24340-05
LOKER, ERIC S S15AR41236-01
LOLLAR, JOHN S R01HL40921-04
LOLLEY, RICHARD N R01EY00395-23
LOLLEY, RICHARD N R01EY07860-03
LOMBARD, JULIAN H P01HL29587-09 0010
LOMBARD, JULIAN H R01HL37374-05
LOMBARD, KENNETH M01RR00059-30 0692
LOMBARD, KENNETH M01RR00059-30 0718
LOMBARDI, ANTHONY S07RR05664-24 0866
LOMBARDI, BENITO R01CA23449-13
LOMBROSO, PAUL J K20MH00856-02
LOMMEL, STEVEN A S07RR07071-26 0255
LONBERG, NILS R43AI31003-01
LONDON, E D Z01DA00200-05
LONDON, E D Z01DA00202-07
LONDON, E D Z01DA00312-01
LONDON, ERWIN R01GM31986-08
LONDON, IRVING M R01DK16272-19
LONDON, J Z01DE00454-05
LONDON, J P Z01DE00498-02
LONDON, JILL A P01DC00168-10 0020
LONDON, PERRY R01DA06844-02
LONDON, R Z01ES50110-03
LONDON, R Z01ES50111-03
LONDON, R Z01ES50112-03
LONDON, R E Z01ES10004-12
LONDON, R E Z01ES50104-05
LONDON, W P01CA40737-06 0052
LONDON, W THOMAS P01CA40737-06
LONDON, W THOMAS P01CA40737-06 0043
LONDON, W THOMAS P01CA40737-06 0044
LONDON, W THOMAS R01CA43217-05
LONDOS, C Z01DK15505-14
LONEY, JAN R01MH41695-05
LONG, CAROLE A R01AI21089-06
LONG, DAVID M R01CA32857-12
LONG, DONLIN M R01NS21718-06
LONG, E Z01AI00170-14
LONG, E O Z01AI00525-04
LONG, GEORGE L P01AG08777-01 0003
LONG, GEORGE L P01HL46703-01 0002
LONG, GEORGE L R01HL38899-05
LONG, GERALD S07RR07260-02
LONG, GLENIS R R01DC00307-06
LONG, GLENIS R S07RR07032-26 0044
LONG, GLENIS R S07RR07032-26 0028
LONG, MARGARET S07RR05365-30 0104
LONG, MICHAEL W P01AG08777-01 0004
LONG, MICHAEL W R01HL35255-04
LONG, SHARON R R01GM30962-10
LONG, WILLIAM S07RR05407-30 0050
LONG, WILLIAM J R01HL33041-07
LONGABAUGH, RICHARD H R01AA07812-04
LONGABAUGH, RICHARD H U10AA08443-03
LONGBOTHAM, HAROLD G S06GM08194-12 0033
LONGCOPE, CHRISTOPHER P01AG05793-06 9002
LONGCOPE, CHRISTOPHER P01HD20290-06A1
LONGCOPE, CHRISTOPHER L P01HD20290-06A1 0002
LONGENECKER, GESINA P60HL38639-04 0003
LONGHURST, JOHN C MD PHD R01HL36527-08
LONGINI, IRA M M01RR00039-31 0392
LONGLEY, BRUCE J R29AR40514-01A1
LONGMAN, ALICE S07RR05913-08 0661
LONGMORE, WILLIAM J R37HL13405-22
LONGNECKER, DANIEL S R01CA47327-04
LONGNECKER5, MATTHEW S07RR05442-29 0045
LONGO, D L Z01CM09335-03
LONGO, D L Z01CM09336-03
LONGO, D L Z01CM09337-03
LONGO, D L Z01CM09339-03
LONGO, D L Z01CM09340-03
LONGO, D L Z01CM09341-03
LONGO, D L Z01CM09342-03
LONGO, D L Z01CM09352-02
LONGO, D L Z01CM09367-01
LONGO, FRANK P41RR00570-21 0005
LONGO, FRANK J R01HD15510-10
LONGO, FRANK J R01HD22085-04A1
LONGO, FRANK M R01AG09873-01
LONGO, LAWRENCE D K12HD00849-04
LONGO, LAWRENCE D R01HD03807-22
LONGSHORE, DOUGLAS P50DA07699-01 0002
LONGSTRETH, W T, JR R01NS27880-02
LONGWELL, JOHN P P01ES01640-14 0009
LONGWELL, JOHN P P30ES02109-13 9001
LONGWORTH, JAMES W R43CA53917-01
LONGWORTH, JAMES W R43CA54629-01
LONGWORTH, JAMES W S07RR07027-26 0012
LONIGRO, ANDREW J P50HL30572-08 0003
LONIGRO, ANDREW J P50HL30572-08 9001
LONKY, NEAL M M01RR00425-22S3 0434
LONNERDAL, BO R01DK43850-01
LONSBURY-MARTIN, BRENDA L R01ES03500-09
LOO, TI L U01AI25697-05
LOO, TI LI U01AI25697-05 0006
LOOK, A THOMAS P01CA20180-14 0001
LOOK, ALFRED T, JR P01CA20180-14
LOOK, ALFRED T, JR R01CA42804-06
LOOK, THOMAS A P01CA23099-13 0017
LOOK, THOMAS A P01CA23099-13 9003
LOOK, THOMAS A. P30CA21765-14 9009
LOOMIS, RONALD E K04DE00229-04
LOOMIS, RONALD E R01DE07760-06
LOOMIS, WILLIAM F R01GM23822-12
LOOMIS, WILLIAM F R01HG00096-02
LOON, JOEL S07RR05359-30 0515
LOONEY, DAVID U01AI30238-02 9001
LOONEY, J R P30ES01247-17 0098
LOOP, MICHAEL S S07RR05807-13 0458
LOOP, MICHAEL S S07RR05807-13 0459
LOOSE, DAVID S R29DK38965-05
LOOSE, MICHAEL D R29NS29970-01
LOOSEN, PETER T M01RR00095-31 0326
LOOSEN, PETER T R01AA07732-03
LOPACHIN, RICHARD M R01ES03830-05
LOPATIN, DENNIS P01DE09142-02 0003
LOPER, JOHN C P42ES04908-03
LOPER, JOHN C P42ES04908-03 0001
LOPEZ-GARRIGA, JUAN S06GM08103-18 0017
LOPEZ-S, ALFREDO R25CA47877-04
LOPEZ, DIANA M R37CA25583-13
LOPEZ, F J Z01ES90062-02
LOPEZ, F J Z01ES90063-02
LOPEZ, GENARO A S06GM08101-20 0034
LOPEZ, J S Z01EY00248-04
LOPEZ, JOSE A K08HL02463-02
LOPEZ, JOSE A U10CA52757-02
LOPEZ, LARRY M M01RR00082-29 0288
LOPEZ, LAUREEN S07RR05450-30 0338
LOPEZ, MARCO A S06GM08238-05 0012
LOPREST, LORRAINE P30AG09463-01 0004
LOPRESTI, JONATHAN S. M01RR00043-31 0414
LOPRESTI, JONATHAN S. M01RR00043-31 0281
LOPRESTI, JONATHAN S M01RR00043-31 0436
LOPRESTI, JONATHAN S M01RR00043-31 0454
LORAND, LASZLO K06HL03512-29
LORAND, LASZLO P01HL45168-01A1
LORAND, LASZLO P01HL45168-01A1 0005
LORAND, LASZLO R01DK25412-13
LORAND, LASZLO R01EY03942-10
LORAND, LASZLO R01HL02212-36
LORAND, LASZLO R37HL16346-21
LORANGER, ARMAND W R01MH40340-05S1
LORCH, ELIZABETH P S07RR07114-23 0442
LORD, CATHERINE R01MH46865-01
LORD, EDITH M R01CA28332-11
LORD, SUSAN T R01HL31048-08
LORD, SUSAN T S07RR05406-30 0887
LORELL, BEVERLY P01HL38189-04 0002
LORENZ, F P50MH48165-02 0001
LORENZ, RODNEY M01RR00095-31 0354
LORENZ, RODNEY A M01RR00095-31 0210
LORENZ, RODNEY A U01DK30620-09
LORENZ, RODNEY A. M01RR00095-31 0316
LORENZI, MARA R01EY09122-06
LORENZO, JOSEPH A P01AR38933-05 0005
LORENZO, JOSEPH A R01AR31263-10
LORETZ, CHRISTOPHER S07RR07066-26 0250
LORIA, ROGER M S07RR05697-22 0993
LORIA, ROGER M S07RR05724-20 0183
LORIG, TYLER S R03DC01323-01
LORING, RALPH HARROP R01NS22472-08
LORING, STEPHEN P50HL19170-15 0017
LORING, STEPHEN H P01HL33009-07 0006
LORISH, CHRISTOPHER P60AR20614-14 0005
LORTON, DIANNE R29MH49050-01
LORY, STEPHEN R01AI21451-06
LOSCALZO, JOSEPH K04HL02273-02
LOSCALZO, JOSEPH R01HL40411-04
LOSE, EDWARD J K11HL02445-02
LOSHIN, DAVID S S07RR05998-04 0031
LOSICK, RICHARD M R37GM18568-19
LOSKUTOFF, DAVID J M01RR00833-17 0181
LOSKUTOFF, DAVID J P01HL16411-18 9005
LOSKUTOFF, DAVID J P01HL16411-18 0013
LOSKUTOFF, DAVID J P01HL31950-08 0006
LOSKUTOFF, DAVID J R01HL22289-13
LOTAN, REUBEN P01CA52051-01A1 0006
LOTHMAN, ERIC W R01NS21671-07
LOTHMAN, ERIC W R01NS25605-04
LOTHROP, CLINTON D, JR R01HL15647-18
LOTKE, PAUL A M01RR00040-31 0341
LOTLIKAR, PRABHAKAR S07RR05417-30 0799
LOTLIKAR, PRABHAKAR D R01CA31641-07A2
LOTSHAW, DAVID P S07RR07114-23 0443
LOTT, JAMES R S07RR07195-12 0709
LOTTENBERG, RICHARD R01HL41898-03
LOTZ, MARTIN P01AG07996-03 0003
LOTZ, MARTIN P01DK42717-02 0006
LOTZ, MARTIN K R01AR39799-01A2
LOTZ, MARTIN K R01CA51406-02
LOUDON, G MARC S07RR05586-24 0121
LOUDON, G MARC S15ES05846-01
LOUGH, JOHN W, JR R01HL39829-04
LOUGHLIN, SANDRA E R01NS26761-03
LOUGHRAN, THOMAS P P01CA18221-16 0010
LOUGHRAN, THOMAS P, JR R01CA46903-02
LOUGHRAN, THOMAS P, JR R01CA54552-01
LOUIE, DEXTER STEPHEN R29DK39356-05
LOUIE, STANLEY S07RR05792-15 0947
LOUIS, CHARLES S07RR05930-07 0720
LOUIS, CHARLES F R01EY05684-07
LOUIS, CHARLES F R01GM31382-08
LOUIS, THOMAS S07RR05448-30 0315
LOUIS, THOMAS A P01AG08761-02 9001
LOUNIBOS, LEON P R22AI31034-01
LOURY, MARK C K11AG00470-01A1
LOUTZENHISER, RODGER S07RR05363-30 0832
LOVALLO, WILLIAM R R01HL32050-07
LOVATO, CHRIS Y S06GM45765-01 0004
LOVE, BRIAN E R01DA06310-03
LOVE, ERIKA G08LM05286-01
LOVE, RICHARD S07RR05959-06 0025
LOVE, RICHARD C R25CA47785-04
LOVE, RICHARD R R13CA54318-01
LOVELAND-CHERRY, CAR S07RR05796-14 0432
LOVELAND, KATHERINE A R01DC00357-06
LOVELESS, MARK O M01RR00334-25 0314
LOVELL, DANIEL R18AR21393-17 0013
LOVELL, KATHRYN S07RR05656-24 0855
LOVELL, KATHRYN L R01NS20254-04
LOVELY, RICHARD H R01MH47649-01
LOVERDE, PHILIP T R22AI18867-09
LOVERDE, PHILIP T R22AI27219-03
LOVETT, DAVID H R01DK39776-05
LOVETT, MICHAEL R01HG00368-04
LOVETT, MICHAEL R44HG00508-02
LOVETT, MICHAEL S07RR05354-30 0394
LOVETT, MICHAEL A R01AI21352-08
LOVETT, MICHAEL A R01AI29733-02
LOVETT, PAUL S R01GM42925-03
LOVETT, PAUL S S03RR03335-09
LOVETT, SUSAN T R01GM43889-02
LOVINGER, DAVID M R01AA08986-01
LOW, DAVID A K04AI00881-04
LOW, DAVID A R01AI23348-04A2
LOW, DAVID A R55GM45379-01
LOW, MALCOLM J R01HD28367-01
LOW, MALCOLM JAMES R01DK40457-05
LOW, MARTIN G R01GM35873-07
LOW, MARTIN G R01GM40083-03
LOW, P A M01RR00585-20 0488
LOW, PHILIP S R01GM24417-12
LOW, PHILIP S R01GM40983-03
LOW, PHILLIP A P01NS14304-13 0031
LOW, PHILLIP A R01NS22352-07
LOW, ROBERT S15AR41239-01
LOW, ROBERT B P50HL14212-20
LOW, ROBERT B P50HL14212-20 0032
LOW, ROBERT B S15MH49308-01
LOWE, ANSON S07RR05353-30 0356
LOWE, ANSON W R29DK43294-01
LOWE, IRVING J P41RR03631-04 9001
LOWE, JACK W S15GM47071-01
LOWE, JANE M01RR00997-16 0345
LOWE, JOHN M R03HS06949-01
LOWE, MARK EVAN R29DK42120-02
LOWE, NANCY K S07RR05944-04 0978
LOWENSTEIN, CHARLES J K11HL02451-02
LOWENSTEIN, DANIEL H K08NS01424-02
LOWENSTEIN, JOHN M R01GM07261-31
LOWENSTEIN, LINDA J P51RR00169-30 0174
LOWENSTINE, LINDA J P51RR00169-30 0173
LOWERY, BARBARA J R01NR01840-03
LOWERY, BARBARA J S07RR05948-05
LOWERY, BARBARA J S07RR05948-05 0336
LOWERY, BARBARA J S15NS30118-01
LOWEY, SUSAN R37AR17350-19
LOWLEY, SUSAN M01RR02558-07 0055
LOWNDES, HERBERT E P30ES05022-04 9005
LOWNDES, HERBERT E R01NS23325-07
LOWNEY, PATRICIA S07RR07032-26 0040
LOWRANCE, JOHN L R44RR04384-02A1
LOWRIE, PATRICIA M S03RR03080-11
LOWRIE, ROBERT C P51RR00164-30 0022
LOWRIE, ROBERT C P51RR00164-30 0023
LOWRY, OLIVER H R01NS08862-22
LOWRY, OLIVER H R01NS24719-05
LOWRY, ROBIN P R01AI30732-01A1
LOWRY, STEPHEN M01RR00047-31 0464
LOWRY, STEPHEN E M01RR00047-31 0443
LOWRY, STEPHEN F M01RR00047-31 0420
LOWRY, STEPHEN F M01RR00047-31 0454
LOWRY, STEPHEN F R01GM34695-07
LOWY, D R Z01CB03663-15
LOWY, MARTIN T P50MH41684-07 0047
LOWY, MARTIN T P50MH41684-07 0054
LOWY, MARTIN T P50MH41684-07 0048
LOWY, MARTIN T R29MH44699-03
LOY, GARY L M01RR00055-30 0574
LOY, REBEKAH P01AG09525-01 0002
LOY, REBEKAH R01AG09231-02
LOYD, JAMES E R01HL41952-04
LOYE, JENELLA E S07RR07092-26 0494
LOZANO, GUILLERMINA R29CA47296-04
LOZOFF, BETSY R01HD14122-10A1
LU, C S Z01BA02018-02
LU, CHRISTOPHER Y K04HD00862-04
LU, CHRISTOPHER Y R01DK43634-02
LU, CHRISTOPHER Y R01HD24797-04
LU, JIAN-YU R29CA54212-01
LU, JOHN K R37AG04810-08
LU, LEE-JANE W R01CA56273-01

LU, PONZY P30CA16520-16 0001
LU, PONZY P30CA16520-16 9017
LU, PONZY R55GM32987-07A1
LU, RENNE C R01AR28401-09A1
LU, RENNE C S15GM47091-01
LU, SHELLY S07RR05468-29 0394
LU, Y P40RR00890-16 0009
LU, Y P40RR00890-16 0011
LUANDE, JEFF N01CN07344-20
LUBAN, JEREMY K11AI00988-02
LUBEN, RICHARD A R01AR39241-03
LUBER-NAROD, J S07RR05712-20 0063
LUBET, R A Z01CP05299-11
LUBIN, BERTRAM H. P60HL20985-14 0016
LUBIN, BERTRAM H R01HL27059-11
LUBIN, BERTRAM H R01HL43048-02
LUBIN, BERTRAM H S03RR03015-11
LUBIN, BERTRAM H S07RR05467-23
LUBLIN, DOUGLAS P50AI15322-14 0015
LUBLIN, DOUGLAS M R01GM41297-02
LUBMAN, DAVID P30HG00209-02 0004
LUBORSKY, JUDITH L N01HD52934-16
LUBORSKY, LESTER P50MH45178-02 0004
LUBORSKY, LESTER P50MH45178-02 9001
LUBORSKY, LESTER B K05MH40710-22
LUBORSKY, LESTER B U18DA07085-02
LUBORSKY, MARK R P50MH40380-07 0011
LUBORSKY, MARK R R01AG09065-01A1
LUBRANO, GLENN J R44AA07772-03
LUBRANO, GLENN J R44NS28275-02
LUBRECHT, JODY R18MH47951-02
LUBS, HERBERT A P01HD21885-05
LUBS, HERBERT A R01HD26202-02
LUBY-PHELPS, KATHERI S07RR07175-15 0437
LUCAS, ALEXANDER H R01AI25008-06
LUCAS, ALEXANDER R P50NS17750-10 0002
LUCAS, CAROL L R01HL35389-06
LUCAS, CAROL L R01HL42075-03
LUCAS, JEN H R01NS29683-01
LUCAS, JOHN J R01AI05802-27
LUCAS, JOHN J R01GM43111-02
LUCAS, JOHN J R01HD09046-15
LUCAS, JOHN J S07RR05402-30
LUCAS, JOHN J S15HL47695-01
LUCCHESI, BENEDICT R R01HL19782-13
LUCCHESI, BENEDICT R R37HL05806-31
LUCCHESI, JOHN C R01GM15691-24
LUCE, PAUL A R29DC00879-02
LUCERO, MARY E R43AG09368-01A1
LUCEY, JEROLD F. M01RR00109-28 0305
LUCHER, LYNNE A R15CA52091-01A1
LUCHI, ROBERT J K07AG00368-05
LUCHINS, DANIEL P50MH41684-07 0070
LUCHTEL, DANIEL L P01HL24163-13 0014
LUCHTEL, DANIEL L R01ES05650-01
LUCIER, G Z01ES46004-07
LUCIER, RICHARD E N01LM83531-03
LUCIW, PAUL P30AI27732-04 9003
LUCIW, PAUL P51RR00169-30 0183
LUCIW, PAUL A R01AI28580-03
LUCIW, PAUL A R01HL43609-03
LUCK, DAVID S07RR07065-26 0064
LUCK, DAVID J L R01GM17132-22
LUCK, EDWARD E R43CA54089-01
LUCKER, G WILLIAM R24MH47167-02 0007
LUCKEY, MARY K04AI00800-05
LUCKI, IRWIN P01MH48125-01 0005
LUCKI, IRWIN P01MH48125-01 9002
LUCKI, IRWIN P50DA05186-05 0005
LUCKI, IRWIN R37MH36262-10
LUCKINBILL, LEO S07RR07051-26 0734
LUCKING, STEVEN E S07RR05680-23 0924
LUCKY, ANNE W R01HL38170-05
LUDBROOK, PHILIP A P50HL17646-17 0027
LUDDEN, PAUL W R01GM35332-05
LUDINGTON, SUSAN S07RR06014-03 0828
LUDINGTON, SUSAN S07RR06014-03 0829
LUDINGTON, SUSAN S07RR06014-03 0830
LUDINGTON, SUSAN M R01NR02251-01A1
LUDLOW, C L Z01DC00004-03
LUDLOW, C L Z01DC00005-03
LUDLOW, C L Z01DC00006-03
LUDLUM, DAVID B R01CA44499-06
LUDMAN, ELAINE K S07RR07064-24 0204
LUDOLPH, ALBERT C S07RR07238-04 0483
LUDUENA, RICHARD F R01CA26376-12
LUDUENA, RICHARD F R01GM23476-11
LUDWICK, ADRIANE G S06GM08091-20 0016
LUEDERS, K K Z01CB05264-10
LUEPKER, RUSSELL V R01HL25523-12
LUEPKER, RUSSELL V S07RR05448-30 0305
LUEPKER, RUSSELL V S07RR05448-30 0286
LUFKIN, ROBERT B P01CA51198-02 0002
LUFT, BENJAMIN J R01AI32454-01
LUFT, BENJAMIN J U01AI25893-05 0004
LUFT, BENJAMIN J U01AI31808-01 0001
LUFT, FREDERICH C M01RR00750-19 0262
LUFT, HAROLD S R01HS06216-02
LUGGEN, MICHAEL R18AR21393-17 0023
LUGGEN, MICHAEL R18AR21393-17 0024
LUGINBUHL, WILLIAM H M01RR00109-28
LUGINBUHL, WILLIAM H S07RR05429-30
LUGO-GARCIA , NIDZA P01NS07464-24 0044
LUHRS, CAROL A K08DK01726-05
LUI, MARK D M01RR02719-06 0003
LUIDENS, MARY K K11DK02031-01
LUINE, VICTORIA N R01HD12011-13A1
LUK, GORDON D R01CA51206-02
LUK, GORDON D U01CA50399-03
LUKAS, ANTON R29HL43148-03
LUKAS, J M Z01BE01002-06
LUKAS, SCOTT E K02DA00115-05
LUKAS, SCOTT E R01DA03994-05
LUKAS, VICTOR P40RR03624-05 0001
LUKASIEWICZ, PETER D R01EY08922-01
LUKASIEWICZ, PETER D S07RR05389-30 0641
LUKATELA, GEORGIJE L R01HD27709-01
LUKEHART, SHEILA A R01AI18988-08
LUKEHART, SHEILA A U01AI31448-01 0003
LUKENS, JOHN N U10CA26270-11
LUKENS, LEWIS N S07RR07107-24 0842
LUKERT, BARBARA S07RR05373-30 0722
LUM, CALIANN T S07RR05654-24 0117
LUM, GARY M01RR00069-29 0395
LUM, LAWRENCE P01AI32918-09 0011
LUMENG, LAWRENCE P50AA07611-04 0002
LUMENG, LAWRENCE P50AA07611-04 9001
LUMENG, LAWRENCE R01AA07647-05
LUMPKIN, CHARLES K JR R29AA07550-04
LUMPKIN, MICHAEL D R01NS23036-06
LUNA, ELIZABETH J R01GM33048-09
LUNA, ELIZABETH J R55CA54885-01
LUND, JENNIFER S R01EY05282-09
LUND, P P30DK34987-06 9004
LUND, PAULINE K R01DK01022-36
LUND, PAULINE K R01DK40247-03
LUND, RAYMOND D R01EY05308-09
LUND, RAYMOND D R37EY05283-09
LUNDBLAD, ROGER L R01DE08671-03
LUNDERGAN, CONOR S07RR05359-30 0516
LUNDQUIST, R E Z01BF03002-06
LUNDQUIST, R E Z01BF03003-08
LUNDQUIST, R E Z01BF03012-01
LUNDRIGAN, MICHAEL D S07RR05386-30 0589
LUNTE, CRAIG E R01GM44900-01A1
LUNTE, CRAIG E R01GM45566-01
LUO, MING P01NS23349-06 0006
LUO, MING R29AI27518-03
LUO, MING U01AI31888-01
LUPAN, DAVID M U01AI31696-01 9001
LUPERCIO, RAFAEL S07RR05372-30 0708
LUPERCIO, RAFAEL S07RR05372-30 0690
LUPINETTI, FLAVIAN M R01HL42426-04
LUPSKI, JAMES R R01NS27042-02
LUPSKI, JAMES R S07RR05425-30 0751
LUPU, RUTH R01CA55406-01
LURIA, SALVADOR E P30CA14051-20 9001
LURIA, SALVADOR E P30CA14051-20 9002
LURIA, SALVADOR E P30CA14051-20 9003
LURIE, ALAN G R01DE08518-05
LURIE, KEITH G K11HL01674-05
LUSCHEI, ERICH S P60DC00976-02 0002
LUSE, DONAL S P01HL41496-03 0008
LUSE, DONAL S P60HL15996-19 0021
LUSE, DONAL S R01GM29487-11
LUSHBAUGH, WILLIAM B S07RR05386-30 0590
LUSHER, JEANNE N01AI82678-09
LUSIS, ALDONS J P01HL28481-09 0003
LUSIS, ALDONS J P01HL28481-09 9005
LUSIS, ALDONS J P01HL30568-09 9002
LUSIS, ALDONS J P01HL30568-09 0009
LUSIS, ALDONS J R01HL42488-03
LUSK, EDWARD J P30CA16520-16 9011
LUSK, SALLY L R01NR02050-03
LUSKEY, KENNETH P01DK42582-02 0004
LUSKEY, KENNETH L M01RR00633-19 0406
LUSKIN, MARLA B R01NS28380-02
LUSKIN, MARLA B S07RR05364-30 0534
LUSKY, MONIKA D R01CA51127-02
LUSSO, FRANCES M P50HL14164-20 9004
LUST, GEORGE R01AR35664-06
LUST, WESLEY D R01NS22254-07
LUST, WESLEY D R01NS22571-04A1
LUSTBADER, EDWARD D P01CA40737-06 0050
LUSTBADER, EDWARD D P01CA40737-06 9001
LUSTER, M I Z01ES30106-17
LUSTER, TOM S07RR07049-26 0421
LUSTIG, ROBERT H S07RR05435-30 0986
LUSTMAN, PATRICK J R01DK36452-06
LUSTY, CAROL J R01GM25846-12
LUTCHEN, KENNETH R S07RR07043-26 0134
LUTFI, ROBERT A R01DC01262-01
LUTHER, JERRY P30CA21765-14 9002
LUTHIN, GARY R R01NS23006-06
LUTHRA, H S M01RR00585-20 0429
LUTKENHAUS, JOSEPH F R01GM29764-11
LUTTGEN, PATRICIA J S07RR05458-29 0829
LUTTY, GERARD A R01HL45922-02
LUTZ, CHARLES T R29AI27879-02
LUTZ, HARRY A. P01NS12587-16 9006
LUTZ, R J Z01RR10324-03
LUX, ROBERT L R01HL42388-03
LUX, SAMUEL E K12DK01977-02
LUX, SAMUEL E P01HL32262-10 0003
LUX, SAMUEL E, IV R37DK34083-10
LUZZI, LOUIS A S07RR07086-15
LUZZI, LOUIS A S15CA56029-01
LWEBUGA-MUKASA, JAMSON S R01HL41854-02
LYDEN, PATRICK D N01NS02377-02
LYDEN, PATRICK D R29NS26783-03
LYDERS, RICHARD N01LM13505-00
LYDIARD, R BRUCE M01RR01070-15 0149
LYDIARD, R BRUCE R01AA07825-03
LYDIC, RALPH R01HL40881-03
LYDIC, RALPH S07RR05680-23 0903
LYE, DIANE N S07RR07096-26 0072
LYERLY, AMANDA P01HD28076-01 9001
LYETH, BRUCE P01NS12587-16 0017
LYETH, BRUCE P01NS12587-16 9007
LYKKEN, DAVID T R01DA05147-05
LYKKEN, DAVID T R01MH37860-07
LYLES, DOUGLAS S R01AI20778-08
LYLES, DOUGLAS S R55AI15892-13
LYLES, KENNETH W K08AG00367-05
LYLES, KENNETH W M01RR00030-30 0472
LYMAN, JOHN T P01CA19138-15 0001
LYMAN, WILLIAM D P01MH47667-02
LYMAN, WILLIAM D P01MH47667-02 9001
LYMAN, WILLIAM D P01MH47667-02 0004
LYMAN, WILLIAM D R01DA05583-03
LYMAN, WILLIAM D R37MH46815-02
LYNAUGH, JOAN E S07RR05948-05 0335
LYNCH-SAUER, JUDITH S07RR05796-14 0433
LYNCH, CARL, III R01GM31144-07A1
LYNCH, CAROL B S07RR07107-24
LYNCH, CHARLES N01CN05229-08
LYNCH, CHARLES P30ES05605-02 9005
LYNCH, CHARLES F K07CA01181-05
LYNCH, CHARLES F N01CP85626-02
LYNCH, CHRISTOPHER J R29DK43402-01
LYNCH, DANIEL R R01CA37245-08
LYNCH, DANIEL R S07RR07056-18 0207
LYNCH, DENNIS C P01HL33014-07 0009
LYNCH, DENNIS C R01HL31311-08
LYNCH, DENNIS C R01HL41222-04
LYNCH, GARY P01HD24236-03 0004
LYNCH, GARY S K05MH00358-11
LYNCH, GARY S P01AG00538-15 0009
LYNCH, HENRY T R01CA48802-03
LYNCH, JAMES C R01EY04159-12
LYNCH, KATHRYN J S07RR05983-05 0358
LYNCH, KEVIN R P01HL19242-15 0017
LYNCH, KEVIN R P30DK38942-04 9005
LYNCH, KEVIN R R01DA07216-01
LYNCH, KEVIN R S07RR05431-30 0837
LYNCH, MARY C R01EY07067-05
LYNCH, MICHAEL R R01GM36827-04
LYNCH, RICHARD G R01CA49228-03
LYNCH, ROBERT E R01HL42992-03
LYNCH, RONALD M S07RR05675-23 0942
LYNCH, SAMUEL E R44DE08878-02A1
LYNCH, THOMAS J R01DA05998-02
LYNCH, THOMAS J R43DA07007-01
LYNESS, W H S07RR05773-17 0381
LYNN, ANNE M. P51RR00166-30 0103
LYNN, DORCAS J R01HS07075-01
LYNN, MICHAEL J U10EY03752-11
LYNN, RICHARD B K08DK02094-01
LYON, JOSEPH N01ES85236-03
LYON, JOSEPH L R01ES04855-04
LYON, KAREN S N01DK02255-03
LYON, MARY K R29GM40735-04
LYSLE, DONALD T R01MH46284-04
LYSLE, DONALD T S07RR07072-26 0269
LYSS, ALAN P U10CA47546-04
LYTE, MARK R29MH45246-04
LYTLE, LOY D S07RR07099-25 0398
LYTTLE, CECIL R R01HD20025-07
LYTTON, JONATHAN R01DK42879-02
LYTTON, WILLIAM K11AG00382-05
MA, AVERIL K11DK01831-04
MA, DIN-POW R15GM46039-01
MA, HONG S07RR05717-21 0134
MA, HONG S07RR05717-21 0136
MA, HONG S07RR05717-21 0137
MA, N S F P51RR00168-30 0144
MA, N S F P51RR00168-30 0145
MA, N S F P51RR00168-30 0146
MA, N S F P51RR00168-30 0147
MA, POKEY M R03MH47368-01A1
MA, SHAU P K08AR01714-05
MA, TERENCE P S07RR05386-30 0591
MA, TSUN S07RR05346-30 0316
MAACK, THOMAS P50HL18323-17 0065
MAACK, THOMAS M R01DK14241-21
MAAS, JAMES W R01MH40935-05
MAAS, WERNER K K06GM15129-28
MAAS, WERNER K R01GM06048-33
MAASSAB, H F N01AI05053-01
MAAYANI, SAUL R01GM34852-06
MABRY, TOM J R01GM35710-25
MAC DERMOTT, AMY B R29NS25215-05
MAC DERMOTT, RICHARD P JR R37DK21474-14
MAC DONALD, MICHAEL J R01DK28348-11
MAC DONALD, MICHAEL J R01DK42176-01A1
MAC DONALD, PAUL P50HD11149-14 0014

MAC DONALD, RAYMOND J R01DK27430-12
MAC KENZIE, MALCOLM R P51RR00169-30 0175
MAC KENZIE, MALCOLM R P51RR00169-30 0176
MACAGNO, EDUARDO R R01HD20954-05
MACAGNO, EDUARDO R R01NS20336-08A1
MACARA, IAN G P30ES01247-17 0069
MACARA, IAN G R01CA43551-05
MACARA, IAN G R01CA56300-01
MACARA, IAN GREGORY R01CA38888-08
MACARAK, EDWARD J R01HL34005-06A2
MACCHIARULO, PATRICIA A R03DE10000-02
MACCLUER, JEAN W P01HL28972-10 0004
MACCLUER, JEAN W P01HL45522-01A1
MACCLUER, JEAN W P01HL45522-01A1 0001
MACCLUER, JEAN W R01GM31575-09
MACCLUER, JEAN W R01HG00336-03
MACCONNELL, WILLIAM P R43HG00293-01
MACDERMOTT, RICHARD P01DK33487-05 9003
MACDERMOTT, RICHARD P P01DK33487-05 0004
MACDONALD, GREGORY P K08NS01331-03
MACDONALD, KEVIN B R03MH46493-01A1
MACDONALD, MARNIE L R29GM42549-02
MACDONALD, MARYELLEN S07RR07047-26 0137
MACDONALD, PAUL C P50HD11149-14
MACDONALD, PAUL M R01GM42612-03
MACDONALD, RAYMOND J P01GM31689-08 0004
MACDONALD, ROBERT C P01HL45168-01A1 0004
MACDONALD, ROBERT C R01GM38244-04
MACDONALD, ROBERT L P01NS19613-07 0003
MACDONALD, ROBERT L R01DA04122-06
MACDONALD, STEVEN C R03HS06980-01
MACDONALD, SUSAN M K11AI00804-05
MACDONALD, TIMOTHY L R01CA54347-01
MACDONALD, TIMOTHY L R55CA55111-01
MACDOUGALL, MARY B R29DE09875-01
MACEWEN, E GREGORY S07RR05912-08 0654
MACFALL, J P41RR05959-02 9002
MACFARLANE, RONALD D R01GM26096-14
MACGLASHAN, DONALD W R01AI27906-02
MACGLASHAN, DONALD W, JR R01AI20253-07
MACGREGOR, DOUGLAS N K11CA01419-03
MACGREGOR, JAMES N01AI15111-00
MACGREGOR, ROB R R01DA05876-02
MACGREGOR, RONAL S07RR05373-30 0723
MACHAMER, CAROLYN E R01GM42522-03
MACHEN, J BERNARD S07RR05321-30
MACHEN, TERRY E R01DK19520-13
MACHER, BRUCE A R01CA32826-10
MACHER, BRUCE A R01GM40205-04A1
MACHIDA, CURTIS P51RR00163-32 0028
MACHIDA, CURTIS A R29HL42358-03
MACIAG, THOMAS P50HL44336-01 0004
MACIAG, THOMAS R01AG07450-03
MACIAG, THOMAS R01HL32348-08
MACIAG, THOMAS R01HL35627-08
MACIAS, WILLIAM L K11DK01851-04
MACINTYRE, ROSS J S07RR07061-26 0189
MACINTYRE, STEPHEN S R01AR34313-07
MACIUNAS, ROBERT J S07RR05424-30 0087
MACK, G S07RR05692-22 0991
MACK, GARY W R29HL39818-04
MACK, ROBERT W S06GM08047-20S1
MACK, THOMAS M R35CA42581-06
MACKALL, J Z01BA05005-02
MACKAY, A R Z01CP05608-03
MACKAY, A R Z01CP05609-03
MACKAY, A R Z01CP05699-01
MACKAY, BRUCE C N01NS02378-02
MACKAY, DON G R01AG09755-01
MACKAY, DONALD S07RR07009-26 0940
MACKAY, HARRY A P01HD25995-03 0004
MACKAY, HARRY A S07RR07143-20 0629
MACKAY, K Z01DK43234-02
MACKAY, LANGLEY P01GM45344-01 0004
MACKAY, TRUDY F R01GM45146-01
MACKEL, ROBERT G R01NS26288-03
MACKEM, S Z01CB09170-04
MACKENZIE, CHARLES S07RR05656-24 0850
MACKENZIE, IAN C R01DE05395-11
MACKENZIE, IAN C S15AR41248-01
MACKENZIE, NEIL E S07RR07002-26 0873
MACKENZIE, PETER B R01GM40546-04
MACKENZIE, PETER B R29GM37996-05
MACKERSIE, ROBERT C S07RR05665-24 0886
MACKERT, J R, JR R01DE07806-06
MACKEY, MARLENE C R15NR02144-01A2
MACKICHAN, JANIS J M01RR00034-31 0395
MACKIE, A P01CA38552-05A1 0002
MACKIE, HUGH R44AI28650-02
MACKIE, THOMAS R R01CA52692-02
MACKIE, THOMAS R R29CA48902-03
MACKINNON, CAROL E R01MH44268-02
MACKINNON, DAVID POTER R01AA08547-03
MACKINNON, RODERICK R01GM43949-02
MACKLIN, WENDY B P01HD25831-01A1 0002
MACKLIN, WENDY B R01NS25304-05
MACKLIS, JEFFREY D R29HD28478-01
MACKLIS, ROGER M R29CA49017-03
MACLACHLAN, N J S07RR05457-29 0004
MACLAREN, NOEL K M01RR00082-29 0466
MACLAREN, NOEL K P01DK39079-05
MACLAREN, NOEL K R01HD19469-08
MACLAREO, NOEL K P01DK39079-05 0001
MACLAUGHLIN, DAVID T S07RR05486-29 0041
MACLEAN, P D Z01MH00796-05
MACLEAN, P D Z01MH02482-03
MACLEISH, PETER R R01EY05201-09
MACLEISH, PETER R R01EY08273-03
MACLENNAN, ALEXANDER J R29DA07244-01
MACLENNAN, DAVID H R01AR39280-04
MACLEOD, CAROL L R01CA37778-07
MACLEOD, CAROL L S07RR05665-24 0893
MACLEOD, DONALD I R01EY01711-16
MACLEOD, MICHAEL C R01CA35581-08
MACLEOD, ROBERT M R01CA07535-28
MACMAHON, BRIAN P30ES00002-29 0034
MACMAHON, BRIAN R01CA47305-04
MACMAHON, JAMES A S07RR07093-24
MACMAHON, JAMES A S15ES05845-01
MACNAB, ROBERT M R01AI12202-18
MACNAB, ROBERT M R01GM40335-04
MACOSKA, JILL S07RR05529-29 0525
MACOVSKI, ALBERT R01CA48269-02
MACOVSKI, ALBERT R01CA50948-02
MACOVSKI, ALBERT R01HL39297-05
MACOVSKI, ALBERT S07RR07005-26 0339
MACPHEE, DAVID S07RR07127-23 0489
MACPHERSON, JANE M R01NS29025-01A1
MACRAE, SCOTT S07RR05412-30 0972
MACRIDES, FOTEOS R01NS12344-17
MACRINA, FRANCIS L R01DE09035-09
MACRINA, FRANCIS L R37DE04224-17
MACRO INTERNATIONAL, INC N01TI10007-00
MACRO SYSTEM, INC N01AA60003-00
MACRO SYSTEMS, INC N01DA88227-00
MACRO SYSTEMS, INC N01SP02007-00
MACWHINNEY, BRIAN J R01HD17790-07
MACWHINNEY, BRIAN J R01HD23998-04
MADAIO, MICHAEL P R01AI27915-04
MADAIO, MICHAEL P R01DK33694-08
MADARA, JAMES P01DK33506-08 0007
MADARA, JAMES L R01DK35932-07
MADDAHI, JAMSHID R01HL41628-03
MADDAHI, JAMSHID R01HL42020-03
MADDEN, CAROLYN W R01HS06062-04
MADDEN, DAVID J R01AG02163-10
MADDEN, DAVID J R01AG05110-06
MADDEN, JOHN J R01DA05002-04A1
MADDEN, JOHN, IV R29MH43426-04
MADDEN, MICHAEL C R01ES04951-03
MADDEN, P A Z01MH02577-01
MADDIESON, IAN R01DC00642-03
MADDON, PAUL J R43AI31743-01
MADDOX, ANNE-MARIE R29CA47428-05
MADDUX, JAMES F R18DA06128-03
MADELIAN, VERGINE R03MH47965-01
MADER, SCOTT L K08AG00387-05
MADHOK, THELMA C R29DA04446-05
MADISON, DANIEL S07RR05353-30 0357
MADISON, ROGER R01NS22404-06
MADISON, V DANIEL P50NS12151-17 0016
MADL, JAMES E R29NS28824-01A1
MADOFF, LAWRENCE C K11AI00981-02
MADRAS, B K P51RR00168-30 0120
MADRAS, B K P51RR00168-30 0121
MADRAS, B K P51RR00168-30 0122
MADRAS, B K P51RR00168-30 0123
MADRI, JOSEPH A R01HL28373-10
MADSEN, JOSEPH R K08NS01471-02
MADSEN, ROBERT R S06GM08218-08 0026
MADTES, DAVID K K08HL02460-02
MAECKER, H S07RR07210-09 0681
MAEDA, NOBUYO R01GM37567-06
MAEDA, NOBUYO R01HL42630-03
MAEDA, NOBUYO S07RR05406-30 0912
MAEDKE, JAMES M R19MH46197-03
MAESTRE, MARCOS F R01AI08427-23
MAESTRE, MARCOS F S07RR05918-08 0712
MAFFEO, CARLA E N01CP95605-05
MAGANA, J RAUL U01MH49070-01
MAGARIAN, ROBERT A R01CA40458-05
MAGASANIK, BORIS R01DK13894-22
MAGASANIK, BORIS R01GM07446-33
MAGAZINER, JAY R01AG06322-03
MAGAZINER, JAY R01AG08211-01A1
MAGAZINER, JAY R01AG09902-01
MAGAZINER, JAY R55AG09901-01
MAGE, M G Z01CB05203-23
MAGE, R G Z01AI00036-26
MAGE, R G Z01AI00226-10
MAGEE, FRANK P R43AR40673-01A1
MAGEE, MITCHELL S07RR05654-24 0132
MAGEE, PAUL T R01AI16567-10
MAGEE, PETER N R37CA43342-05
MAGEN, JED S07RR05656-24 0848
MAGEN, JED S07RR05772-17 0340
MAGGIO, CAROL A R01DK25141-09
MAGGIO, JOHN R01NS22961-06
MAGGIO, JOHN E P50GM15904-24 0024
MAGHSOUDI, RAHBAR S06GM02721-07 0004
MAGID, NORMAN M R29HL40679-04
MAGID, NORMAN M S07RR05396-30 0750
MAGILAVY, DANIEL B R29AI26735-04
MAGILVY, JOAN S07RR05809-06 0472
MAGILVY, JOAN K R01NR02006-03
MAGIN, RICHARD L R13CA54368-01
MAGLEBY, KARL L R37AR32805-09
MAGLOTT, DONNA R R01HG00326-03
MAGNESS, RONALD R R01HD24971-04
MAGNUS, PHILIP D R01CA50512-02
MAGNUS, PHILIP D R01GM32718-10
MAGNUSON, M A P01DK42502-02 9001
MAGNUSON, MARK A R01DK42612-02
MAGNUSON, TERRY P60AR20618-13 0017
MAGNUSON, TERRY R R01HD24462-02
MAGNUSON, TERRY R R01HD26722-02
MAGNUSSON, N INGVAR P50DE07117-07 0001
MAGOFFIN, CAROLE J R03HS06803-01
MAGOFFIN, DENNIS S07RR05468-29 0396
MAGOVERN, GEORGE J R01HL38078-04
MAGRATH, I T Z01CM06890-13
MAGUIRE, GEORGE P K07HL02318-02
MAGUIRE, HELEN S07RR05373-30 0724
MAGUIRE, M HELEN R01HD14888-08
MAGUIRE, MAUREEN G U10EY06146-07
MAGUIRE, MICHAEL E P01HL18708-16 0018
MAGUIRE, MICHAEL E R01GM39447-01A1
MAGUN, BRUCE E R01CA39360-08
MAGUN, BRUCE E R01CA47404-04
MAGURA, STEPHEN R01DA05942-02
MAGURA, STEPHEN R18DA06959-02
MAGYARI, PATRICIA A R43DK44794-01
MAHADIK, SAHEBARAO P R03MH46546-01A1
MAHAFFEY, JAMES W R01AG01739-11
MAHAFFEY, JAMES W S07RR07071-26 0253
MAHAJAN, SATISH C S14GM04564-03
MAHAN, C S07RR05362-30 0800
MAHAN, CLAIRE P50DA05321-04 9002
MAHAN, JOHN D R29DK39628-01A3
MAHAN, KENT I S06GM08197-10 0008
MAHDAVI, VIJAK R01HL35576-06
MAHDAVI, VIJAK R01HL45425-02
MAHER, JACQUELYN J R01AA07810-04
MAHER, JAMES W R01DK41323-01A2
MAHER, PAMELA P01DK18811-17A1 0019
MAHER, PAMELA A R01HD25005-04
MAHER, VERONICA M R01CA21253-15
MAHER, VERONICA M R01CA48066-03
MAHESH, VIRENDRA B R01DK32046-10
MAHESH, VIRENDRA B R01HD16688-10
MAHESH, VIRENDRA B R01HD24488-02
MAHLBERG, PAUL G S07RR07031-26 0098
MAHLER, DAVID B R01DE02936-23
MAHLEY, ROBERT W P01HL41633-03
MAHLEY, ROBERT W S07RR05880-09
MAHLEY, ROBERT W S07RR05880-09 0518
MAHMOUD, ADEL A P01AI15351-13 0001
MAHNENSMITH, REX S07RR05818-12 0160
MAHON, K A Z01HD01801-02
MAHONEY, JOHN F R43GM45656-01
MAHONEY, MARTIN S07RR05649-25 0796
MAHONY, CHERYL R01HL38904-03
MAHOWALD, ANTHONY P R01HD17607-11
MAHOWALD, ANTHONY P R01HD17608-09S1
MAHOWALD, MAREN L R01AR39148-03
MAHUT, HELEN R01NS20805-07
MAIBACH, EDWARD W U01MH49062-01
MAIER, KATHERINE T S07RR05425-30 0752
MAIER, ROBERT J R01GM40079-04
MAIER, RONALD V R01GM45873-01
MAIER, STEVEN F K05MH00314-11
MAIER, STEVEN F R01MH45045-03
MAIER, TOM J R29CA49024-04
MAIHLE, NITA J R01CA51197-02
MAIHLE, NITA J S07RR05530-29 0527
MAILLIARD, MARK E K08DK01832-03
MAILLY, TIMOTHY R19DA06436-03
MAILMAN, RICHARD P30HD03110-24 9003
MAILMAN, RICHARD B P01ES01104-16
MAILMAN, RICHARD B P01ES01104-16 0003
MAILMAN, RICHARD B P50MH33127-13 0012
MAILMAN, RICHARD B R01ES05279-02
MAILMAN, RICHARD B R01MH40537-07
MAIMAN, L A Z01HD00876-01
MAIMAN, L A Z01HD00877-01
MAIN, DENISE P01HD24180-04 0002
MAIN, ELLIOTT K R01HD24495-05
MAIN, ELLIOTT K. P01HD24640-03 0002
MAINARDI, CARLO P50AR39166-05 0005
MAINARDI, CARLO P50AR39166-05 0006
MAINE, ELEANOR S07RR07068-26 0235
MAINES, MAHIM P30ES01247-17 0101
MAINES, MAHIN D R01ES03968-07
MAINES, MAHIN D R01ES04066-06
MAINES, MAHIN D R37ES04391-05
MAINIGI, KUSUM K R44AR40512-02A2
MAINS, RICHARD E K05DA00097-08
MAINS, RICHARD E P50DA00266-20 0010
MAINS, RICHARD E R37DK32948-10
MAIO, JOSEPH J R01AI27111-04
MAIR, ROBERT G R01NS26855-03
MAISEL, HARRY R01EY01417-18
MAISEL, HARRY S06GM08167-13 0040
MAISIAK, RICHARD P60AR20614-14 0007
MAITRA, SUBIR R S07RR05736-19 0195
MAITRA, UMADAS R01GM15399-21

MAIXNER, WILLIAM M01RR00046-31 0510
MAIXNER, WILLIAM M01RR00046-31 0342
MAIXNER, WILLIAM R29DE08013-05
MAIZEL, ABBY S07RR05765-17
MAIZEL, ABBY S07RR05765-17 0210
MAIZEL, ABBY S15CA55946-01
MAIZEL, ABBY L P30CA13943-19
MAIZEL, ABBY L R37CA45148-06
MAIZEL, J V Z01CB08380-07
MAIZELS, NANCY R01GM39799-04
MAIZELS, NANCY R01GM41712-02
MAJERUS, PHILIP W P50HL14147-21
MAJERUS, PHILIP W P50HL14147-21 0019
MAJERUS, PHILIP W R37HL16634-26
MAJIDI, VAHID S07RR07114-23 0444
MAJNO, GUIDO R01HL25973-11
MAJOCHA, RONALD E P01AG02126-11 9001
MAJOR, BRENDA N S07RR07066-26 0251
MAJOR, E O Z01NS01983-20
MAJORS, JOHN E R01CA38994-07
MAJUMDAR, ADHIP N R01AG08438-01A2
MAJZOUB, JOSEPH S07RR05899-10 0272
MAJZOUB, JOSEPH A R01DK40170-05
MAJZOUB, JOSEPH A R01HD24704-03
MAJZOUB, JOSEPH A R01NS29384-01
MAK, GILBERT K K11DE00293-02
MAK, TAK W U01AI27221-03
MAK, TAK W U01AI27221-03 0001
MAKDAD, BONNIE M01RR00065-29 0320
MAKHLOUF, GABRIEL M R01DK28300-11
MAKHLOUF, GABRIEL M R37DK15564-20
MAKI, AUGUST H R01ES02662-11
MAKI, AUGUST H S07RR07007-26 0923
MAKI, RICHARD A R01AI30656-01
MAKI, TAKASHI R01AI20686-08
MAKI, TAKASHI R01DK41255-03
MAKIELSKI, JONATHAN C P01HL20592-15 0019
MAKINEN, MARVIN W R01AA06374-08
MAKINEN, MARVIN W R01GM21900-16
MAKINO, SHINJI R01AI29984-02
MAKINO, SHINJI S07RR07091-26 0761
MAKKER, SUDESH P R01DK33941-08
MAKLAN, DAVID N01HD13118-00
MAKMAN, MAYNARD H R01DA04512-02
MAKOUS, WALTER L R01EY04885-08
MAKOWKA, LEONARD P41RR03631-04 0001
MAKOWSKI, L P41RR01633-10 0012
MAKOWSKI, LEE R01GM29829-11
MAKOWSKI, LEE R01GM34343-07
MAKOWSKI, LEE S07RR07043-26
MAKOWSKI, LEE S15HL47754-01
MAKRIYANNIS, ALEXANDROS K02DA00152-02
MAKRIYANNIS, ALEXANDROS R01DA03801-07
MALAMUD, DANIEL P50DE08239-04 0006
MALAMUD, DANIEL R01DE09569-02
MALAMUTH, NEIL M R01MH45058-02S1
MALAMY, MICHAEL S07RR05382-30 0873
MALAMY, MICHAEL H R01AI19497-08
MALAND, LYNN R43CA55451-01
MALARKEY, WILLIAM B M01RR00034-31 0360
MALARKEY, WILLIAM B M01RR00034-31 0383
MALARKEY, WILLIAM B P01MH44660-04 0003
MALASPINA, DOLORES K07MH00824-03
MALATHY-SHEKHAR, PV R03CA54944-01
MALATY, RAGA R01EY07213-04
MALAVE-LOPEZ, JOSE S03RR03386-07
MALAWISTA, STEPHEN M01RR00125-28 0768
MALAWISTA, STEPHEN P01AI30548-01A1 0002
MALAWISTA, STEPHEN E R01AR10493-25
MALAWISTA, STEPHEN E R01AR40452-02
MALAWISTA, STEVEN E M01RR00125-28 0724
MALBON, CRAIG C R01DK25410-13
MALCARNE, VANESSA S07RR07004-16 0050
MALCHOFF, CARL D R29DK42840-01
MALCOM, SHIRLEY M R25AD00035-01
MALDONADO, FILOMENO G S03RR03168-10
MALDONADO, YVONNE S07RR05353-30 0358
MALDONADO, YVONNE S07RR05353-30 0359
MALECH, H L Z01AI00481-06
MALEJKA-GIGANTI, DANUTA R37CA28000-12
MALEK, EMILE A K06AI18424-29
MALEK, THOMAS R R01CA45957-05
MALEK, THOMAS R R01CA46096-05
MALENKA, ROBERT C K02MH00942-01
MALENKA, ROBERT C R29MH45334-03
MALENKA, ROBERT C S07RR05355-30 0428
MALEQUE, MOHAMMED A. S06GM08037-20 0034
MALEY, FRANK R35CA44355-05
MALHOTRA, VIVEK R01GM46224-01
MALIK, ASRAR B R01HL45638-01
MALIK, ASRAR B R37HL27016-11
MALIK, KAFAIT U R37HL19134-17
MALINOW, M RENE S07RR05694-22 0856
MALINOW, RENE P51RR00163-32 0036
MALINOW, ROBERTO S07RR05372-30 0655
MALIZIA, ANTHONY P51RR00165-31 0121
MALKIN, RICHARD R01GM20571-18
MALKINSON, ALVIN S07RR05831-12 0980
MALKINSON, ALVIN S07RR05831-12 0981
MALKINSON, ALVIN M R01CA33497-08
MALKINSON, ALVIN M R01ES02370-11
MALKOWITZ, DENISE S07RR05418-30 0033
MALLAT, STEPHANE S07RR07062-26 0216
MALLAVIA, LOUIS P R01AI20190-09
MALLAVIA, LOUIS P R01AI27180-03
MALLER, JAMES L R01DK28353-10
MALLER, JAMES L R01GM26743-12
MALLEY, A P51RR00163-32 0038
MALLEY, ARTHUR R01AI28570-02
MALLEY, ARTHUR R01HD27143-01A1
MALLEY, ARTHUR S07RR05694-22 0857
MALLEY, J D Z01CT00039-15
MALLEY, J D Z01CT00189-01
MALLING, H V Z01ES65033-08
MALLORY, BRENDA N01NS92367-02
MALLOUK, THOMAS E R01GM43844-02
MALLOW, J S07RR07210-09 0690
MALLOY, CRAIG P50HL17669-17 0033
MALLOY, CRAIG R01HL27472-08
MALLOY, LAURA G R15HL46542-01
MALLOY, M H Z01HD00344-08
MALLOY, M H Z01HD00365-05
MALLOY, M H Z01HD00368-05
MALLOY, M H Z01HD00381-02
MALLUCHE, HARTMUT H R01AR35837-04A2
MALMGREN, LESLIE T R01AG09186-01A1
MALONE, JOHN I U01DK37857-06
MALONE, ROBERT E R01GM36846-06
MALONEY, PETER C R01DK44015-01
MALONEY, PETER C R01GM24195-15
MALOUF, ALFRED T R29NS28650-01A1
MALOY, STANLEY R R01GM34715-07
MALOY, W LEE R44DK41947-02
MALPELI, JOSEPH G R01EY02695-13
MALSPEIS, L Z01CM07198-01
MALT, RONALD A R37DK12769-26
MALTAS, CAROLYN N S07RR05484-29 0026
MALTER, JAMES S R01AG10675-01
MALTER, JAMES S R01DK45213-01
MALTESE, WILLIAM A R01CA34569-09
MALVEAUX, FLOYD R01HL45312-02
MALVEAUX, FLOYD J U01AI30780-01
MALVEAUX, FLOYD J U01AI31867-01 0014
MALVIN, G S07RR05900-06 0630
MALVIN, GARY M R29HL38942-05
MAMTANI, RAVINDER R25CA48094-02
MANAK, MARK M R01HL43560-03
MANAKER, SCOTT R29HL41169-03
MANASCO, P K Z01ES90064-02
MANASCO, P K Z01ES90065-02
MANASCO, PENELOPE M01RR00046-31 0493
MANCE, ROSALIND M. M01RR00039-31 0423
MANCHESTER, D M01RR00069-29 0382
MANCI, ELIZABETH A. N01HB07086-02
MANCLARK, C R Z01BA07021-24
MANCO-JOHNSON, MARILYN M01RR00069-29 0461
MANCO-JOHNSON, MARILYN M01RR00069-29 0327
MANCO-JOHNSON, MARILYN M01RR00069-29 0471
MANCO-JOHNSON, MARILYN M01RR00069-29 0489
MANCO-JOHNSON, MARILYN M01RR00069-29 0483
MANCO-JOHNSON, MARILYN M01RR00069-29 0465
MANCO-JOHNSON, MARILYN M01RR00069-29 0473
MANCO-JOHNSON, MARILYN E M01RR00069-29 045
MANCO-JOHNSON, MARILYN J M01RR00069-29 044
MANCO-JOHNSON, MARILYN J R01HL44586-02
MANCUSO, ANTHONY A U01CA54026-01
MANDARINO, LAWRENCE M01RR00056-30 0364
MANDARINO, LAWRENCE J R01DK41075-03
MANDARINO, LAWRENCE J R01EY08391-01A2
MANDEL, DR JACK N01CB95613-08
MANDEL, FREDERIC P01HL22619-14 0006
MANDEL, GAIL R01NS22518-07
MANDEL, IRWIN D S07RR05331-28 0740
MANDEL, JACK N01CB61005-09
MANDEL, JACK S N01CP15673-00
MANDEL, LAZARO J R01DK26816-12
MANDEL, NEIL S R01DK30579-08
MANDELBLATT, JEANNE S K08AG00471-03
MANDELL, GERALD L R37AI09504-21
MANDELL, WALLACE R01DA06326-02
MANDLER, RAUL L S07RR05583-27 0633
MANDLER, RAUL N R29NS27698-02
MANDOLI, DINA F S07RR07096-26 0073
MANECKE, GERARD R, J S07RR05736-19 0206
MANES, COLE U01HD22847-06
MANESS, PATRICIA F K04HD00652-05
MANESS, PATRICIA F R01EY08975-01
MANESS, PATRICIA F R01NS26620-07
MANFREDI, CLARA P01CA42760-06 0004
MANFREDI, K Z01CM07305-01
MANFREDI, K Z01CM07306-01
MANGAN, KENNETH F S07RR05417-30 0800
MANGANIELLO, V C Z01HL00634-11
MANGANO, DENNIS T R01HL36744-05
MANGEL, STUART C R01EY05102-08
MANGEL, WALTER F U01AI26049-05
MANGELSDORF, SARAH S07RR07050-26 0126
MANGINO, ARLENE D G07LM05341-01
MANGKORNKARN, CHUTMA S07RR05304-30 0224
MANGOLD, JAMES S07RR05743-14 0616
MANGUN, GEORGE R K21MH00930-01
MANHEIM, LARRY P60AR30692-08 0018
MANHEIM, LARRY M R01HS06250-02
MANIATIS, THOMAS P P01GM29301-11 0008
MANIATIS, THOMAS P R01GM29379-11
MANIATIS, THOMAS P R01GM42231-11
MANIATIS, THOMAS P R37AI20642-08
MANIS, PAUL B K04DC00048-02
MANIS, PAUL B P60DC00979-02 0003
MANIS, PAUL B R01DC00425-04
MANISCALCO, WILLIAM M P50HL36543-05 0002
MANISCHEWITZ, J F Z01BF01004-02
MANISCHEWITZ, J F Z01BF01005-02
MANISCHEWITZ, J F Z01BF01014-01
MANKAD, VIPUL N P60HL38639-04 0007
MANKAD, VIPUL N P60HL38639-04
MANKAD, VIPUL N P60HL38639-04 0005
MANKES, RUSSELL F R01AA08150-02
MANKES, RUSSELL F S15AA09246-01
MANKIN, HENRY J R01AR16265-17A3
MANLEY, JAMES S07RR07060-26 0450
MANLEY, JAMES L P01CA33620-08 0002
MANLEY, JAMES L R01CA46121-05
MANLEY, JAMES L R01GM28983-11
MANLEY, JAMES L R01GM37971-05
MANN, D L Z01CP05326-09
MANN, D L Z01CP05328-09
MANN, D L Z01CP05434-07
MANN, DAVID R P51RR00165-31 0162
MANN, DAVID R P51RR00165-31 0163
MANN, DAVID R R01HD23295-04A1
MANN, DAVID R R01HD26423-02
MANN, DOUGLAS K08HL02010-06
MANN, HENRY M01RR00400-23 0233
MANN, J JOHN M01RR00047-31 0434
MANN, J JOHN P50MH46745-02
MANN, J JOHN P50MH46745-02 0001
MANN, J JOHN P50MH46745-02 0004
MANN, J JOHN P50MH46745-02 9002
MANN, J JOHN R01MH40695-05
MANN, JOSEPH J R01MH40210-08
MANN, KENNETH G P01AG04875-08 0004
MANN, KENNETH G P01AG08777-01
MANN, KENNETH G P01AG08777-01 0001
MANN, KENNETH G P01AG08777-01 0006
MANN, KENNETH G P01HL46703-01
MANN, KENNETH G P01HL46703-01 0001
MANN, KENNETH G R01HL38460-06
MANN, KENNETH G R01HL42940-03
MANN, KENNETH G R01HL46973-01
MANN, KENNETH G R37HL34575-07
MANN, RICHARD A R29DK40504-04
MANN, ROBERT W R01AR40036-01A1
MANNE, JOSEPH S07RR05496-29 0902
MANNI, ANDREA P01CA40011-07 0009
MANNI, ANDREA P01CA40011-07 0002
MANNI, ANDREA P01CA40011-07 0001
MANNICK, JOAN B K11AI00996-02
MANNICK, JOHN A P50GM36428-07 0006
MANNICK, JOHN A R01GM35633-07
MANNIE, MARK D S07RR05812-12 0487
MANNIK, MART R01AR11476-24
MANNIK, MART R37AR12849-23
MANNING, D S Z01AI00612-01
MANNING, DAVID R P01GM34781-07 0004
MANNING, DAVID R P01MH48125-01 0003
MANNING, DAVID R R01CA39712-07
MANNING, GERALD S R01GM36284-06
MANNING, JAMES E S07RR05406-30 0888
MANNING, JAMES M R37HL18819-20
MANNING, JAMES M S07RR07065-26 0065
MANNING, JERRY E R01AI18873-09
MANNING, MAURICE R01GM25280-20
MANNING, R DAVIS P01HL11678-24 0070
MANNING, R DAVIS P01HL11678-24 0001
MANNING, WARREN J P30AG08812-02 0003
MANNINO, FRANK L M01RR00827-17 0411
MANNINO, RAPHAEL J U01AI28171-03 0002
MANNINO, RAPHAEL J U01AI28702-03
MANNION, JOHN D R01HL41918-03
MANNISI, JOHN A S07RR05736-19 0155
MANNO, BARBARA R R01DA05850-02
MANNY, RUTH E R01EY05113-08
MANOHAR, MURLI R01AR39787-01A2
MANOIL, COLIN C R01GM46493-01
MANOLAGA, STAVROS M01RR00750-19 0257
MANOLAGAS, STAVROS C R01AI21761-06
MANOLAGAS, STAVROS C R01AR41313-01
MANON-ESPAILLAT, RAMON M01RR00349-25 0240
MANOS, PATRICIA S07RR05756-18 0285
MANOWITZ, PAUL R01AA07799-02
MANSBACH, CHARLES M, II R01DK38760-05
MANSBACH, ROBERT S R03MH46631-02
MANSER, TIMOTHY L R01AI23739-04A3
MANSFIELD, JOHN M P01AI28781-02 0001
MANSFIELD, JOHN M R01AI22441-07
MANSKE, CONNIE L M01RR00400-23 0246
MANSKI, CHARLES F R01HD25842-03
MANSON, MICHAEL D R01GM39736-04
MANSON, SPERO M K02MH00833-02
MANSON, SPERO M R01AA08474-01A1
MANSON, SPERO M R01DA06076-02
MANSON, SPERO M R01MH42473-06
MANSOUR, EDWARD G U10CA14548-17
MANSOUR, TAG E R01AI16501-11
MANSOUR, TAG E U01AI30230-02 0002

MANSSON-RAHEMTULLA, BRITTA R01DE07076-06
MANSSON, PER-ERIK P01CA37589-08 9002
MANTE, FRANCIS S07RR05337-30 0770
MANTELL, JOANNE E R01DA05995-02
MANTIATIS, THOMAS P P01GM29301-11 0010
MANTON, KENNETH G R01AG01159-15
MANTON, KENNETH G R01AG07469-04
MANTON, KENNETH G R37AG07025-05
MANTON, KENNETH G R37AG07198-05
MANTYH, PATRICK W R01NS23970-06
MANTZOURANIS, EVANGELIA C R29AR38551-05
MANUCK, STEPHEN P01HL40962-04 0004
MANUCK, STEPHEN B P01HL40962-04 0002
MANUCK, STEPHEN B P01HL40962-04
MANUCK, STEPHEN B S07RR07084-26 0324
MANUELIDES, LAURA P01AG03106-09 0007
MANUELIDIS , LAURA P01AG03106-09 9001
MANUELIDIS, ELIAS E P01AG03106-09 0001
MANUELIDIS, ELIAS E P01AG03106-09 0003
MANUELIDIS, ELIAS E R01NS12674-16
MANUELIDIS, LAURA P01AG03106-09 0004
MANUELIDIS, LAURA P01AG03106-09 0006
MANUELIDIS, LAURA P01AG03106-09
MANUELIDIS, LAURA M R01CA15044-18
MAO, JEN-I R01HG00122-01A1
MAO, JEN-I R01HG00520-01
MAO, JEN-I R43HG00295-01
MAO, JEN-I R43HG00491-01
MAO, JENRI N01NS02387-01
MAPLE, TERRY P51RR00165-31 0055
MAPOLES, JOHN P30DK34914-06 0008
MAQUAT, LYNNE E R01DK33938-08
MAR, E C Z01ES90061-02
MARAIA, R J Z01HD00412-04
MARANGOS, PAUL J R43NS29908-01
MARANTO, ANTHONY S07RR05587-20 0651
MARANTZ, PAUL R P01AG03949-10 0006
MARASCO, WAYNE A K08CA01507-03
MARATOS-FLIER, ELEFTHERIA P30DK36836-05 0002
MARATOS-FLIER, ELEFTHERIA R01AI28971-02
MARBAN, EDUARDO P50HL17655-17 0031
MARBAN, EDUARDO R01HL44065-02
MARBAN, EDUARDO MD PHD R01HL36957-06
MARBURY, MARIAN C R29ES04787-03
MARC, ROBERT S07RR07143-20 0539
MARC, ROBERT E R01EY02576-14
MARCANTONIO, EUGENE E R01GM44585-02
MARCELLETTI, JOHN F R43AI30843-01A1
MARCELO, CYNTHIA L R01AR26009-11
MARCH, PAUL E R29GM40087-03
MARCHALONIS, JOHN J R01CA42049-08
MARCHALONIS, JOHN J R01GM42437-03
MARCHANT, ROGER E R29HL40047-04
MARCHASE, RICHARD P50DK42017-03 0003
MARCHASE, RICHARD B P50NS06233-25 0037
MARCHASE, RICHARD B R01EY06714-06
MARCIAL-ROJAS, RAUL G12RR03035-06
MARCIANI, DANTE U01AI28167-02 0001
MARCIANO-CABRAL, FRANCINE R01AI25111-03
MARCOVICH, ROBERT S07RR05664-24 0867
MARCU, KENNETH B R01CA36246-08
MARCU, KENNETH B R01GM26939-13
MARCUS-SEKURA, C J Z01BF01009-02
MARCUS-SEKURA, C J Z01BF01001-07
MARCUS-SEKURA, C J Z01BF01002-02
MARCUS-SEKURA, C J Z01BF01003-02
MARCUS, AARON J P01HL46403-01 0001
MARCUS, AARON J P50HL18828-16 0008
MARCUS, AARON J R01HL47073-01
MARCUS, AARON J S07RR05396-30 0751
MARCUS, AARON J S07RR05396-30 0752
MARCUS, ALBERT C P01CA43461-05 0002
MARCUS, ALFRED C P01CA50084-03 0002
MARCUS, ALFRED C S07RR05894-09 0608
MARCUS, BESS H S07RR05818-12 0164
MARCUS, BETH A R43OH02907-01
MARCUS, CRAIG B R29ES05311-02
MARCUS, CRAIG B S07RR05586-24 0123
MARCUS, DANIEL C P01DC00384-05 0003
MARCUS, DANIEL C R01DC00212-09
MARCUS, DONALD M R37AI17712-12
MARCUS, MELVIN L P01HL14388-20 0216
MARCUS, MICHELE R01HD24618-03
MARCUS, S E Z01DE00540-01
MARCUS, S E Z01DE00541-01
MARCUS, SAMUEL N S07RR05569-27 0109
MARCUS, SAMUEL N S07RR05569-27 0117
MARCY, S MICHAEL S07RR05521-29 0067
MARCZYNSKI, THAD S07RR05369-30 0596
MARDER, EVE E R01MH46742-02
MARDER, EVE E R01NS17813-10
MARDER, KAREN M01RR00645-20 0509
MARDER, STEPHEN R P50MH30911-14 0007
MARDER, STEPHEN R P50MH30911-14 0030
MARDER, STEPHEN R P50MH30911-14 0031
MARDER, STEPHEN R P50MH30911-14 9004
MARDER, VICTOR J P01HL30616-09
MARDER, VICTOR J P01HL30616-09 0004
MARDINI, ISSAM A S07RR05417-30 0801
MARE, ROBERT D P30HD05876-21
MARE, ROBERT D R01HD25749-03
MARECI, THOMAS H P41RR02278-06A1
MARECI, THOMAS H P41RR02278-06A1 9002
MARECI, THOMAS H R01NS29362-01
MAREK, KENNETH L K08NS01168-05
MAREK, MIROSLAV I R01DE07754-06
MAREN, THOMAS H R01EY02227-14
MARFURT, CARL F R01EY05717-05
MARGERUM, DALE W R01GM12152-27
MARGHERIO, RAYMOND R N01EY02115-02
MARGHERIO, RAYMOND R S15EY09455-01
MARGHERIO, RAYMOND R U10EY02563-12
MARGHERIO, RAYMOND R U10EY06289-07
MARGHERIO, RAYMOND R U10EY08589-02
MARGIOTTA, JOSEPH F R01NS24417-06
MARGO, GEOFFREY M S07RR05402-30 0794
MARGOLESE, RICHARD G U10CA20156-15
MARGOLIASH, EMANUEL R01GM19121-21
MARGOLIASH, EMANUEL R01GM29001-11
MARGOLIASH, EMANUEL R37AI12001-15
MARGOLICK, JOSEPH B P30AI28748-03 9002
MARGOLICK, JOSEPH B R29AI25184-05
MARGOLIES, MICHAEL N R01CA24432-29
MARGOLIN, AARON B S07RR07108-19 0409
MARGOLIN, ARTHUR P50DA04060-06 0005
MARGOLIN, GAYLA R01MH36595-08
MARGOLIS, DAVID M K11AI01027-01
MARGOLIS, HENRY C R01DE07493-05
MARGOLIS, RENEE K R01NS09348-21
MARGOLIS, RICHARD U K05MH00129-10
MARGOLIS, RICHARD U R01NS13876-14
MARGOLIS, RICHARD U R01NS26283-03
MARGOLIS, ROBERT LEWIS R01GM32022-08
MARGOLIUS, HARRY S R01HL17705-17
MARGOLIUS, HARRY S R01HL44671-01A1
MARGULIES, D H Z01AI00394-08
MARGULIES, LOLA R01CA35580-07S1
MARHSALL, ROSEMARIE S06GM08101-20 0028
MARIAM, YITBAREK S06GM08247-04 0005
MARIANO, PATRICK S R01GM27251-12
MARIANS, KENNETH J P30CA08748-26 9034
MARIANS, KENNETH J R01GM34558-08
MARIANS, KENNETH J R01GM34557-08
MARIASH, CARY N R01DK32885-07
MARICQ, HILDEGARD R R01AR31283-09
MARIN-PADILLA, MIGUEL R01NS22897-06
MARIN, BARBARA A R01MH46777-03
MARIN, BARBARA A R01MH46789-01A1
MARIN, DEBORAH M01RR00047-31 0477
MARIN, GERARDO R01AA08545-02
MARINA, MANUEL G12RR03051-06
MARINETTI, TIMOTHY D R01GM32955-07
MARINI, J C Z01HD00408-08
MARINI, MARGARET M R01HD27598-01
MARINO, CHRISTOPHER R K08DK01910-03
MARINO, JOSEPH S07RR07050-26 0127
MARINO, JOSEPH P R01CA22237-12
MARINO, LUCYNDIA R R01HD25983-01A3
MARINO, THOMAS A R01HL29351-07
MARINUS, MARTIN G R01GM33233-07
MARINUS, MARTIN G S07RR05712-20 0064
MARION, DONALD W P20NS30318-01
MARION, DONALD W P20NS30318-01 0001
MARION, DONALD W P20NS30318-01 0005
MARION, TONY S07RR05423-30 0056
MARION, TONY N R01AI26833-04
MARIOTTI, A S07RR05728-20 0203
MARISCALCO, MARY S07RR05425-30 0753
MARK, ALLYN M01RR00059-30 0722
MARK, ALLYN L M01RR00059-30 0701
MARK, ALLYN L M01RR00059-30 0702
MARK, ALLYN L M01RR00059-30 0580
MARK, ALLYN L M01RR00059-30 0705
MARK, ALLYN L M01RR00059-30 0301
MARK, ALLYN L P01HL14388-20 0208
MARK, ALLYN L P01HL14388-20 0184
MARK, ALLYN L P01HL14388-20 0248
MARK, ALLYN L R37HL24962-12
MARK, DANIEL B R18HS05635-05
MARK, ROGER G M01RR00088-28
MARK, YVONNE S07RR05664-24 0868
MARKAVERICH, BARRY M R01CA35480-07
MARKEL, DORENE P30HG00209-02 9001
MARKEL, KARLA J S03RR03444-06
MARKELL, MARIANA S M01RR00318-25 0230
MARKESBERG, WILLIAM R P01AG05119-07 9001
MARKESBERY, WILLIAM R P01AG05119-07
MARKESBERY, WILLIAM R P01AG05119-07 0003
MARKESBERY, WILLIAM R P50AG05144-08
MARKESBERY, WILLIAM R P50AG05144-08 9002
MARKESBERY, WILLIAM R R01AG10664-01
MARKEY, S P Z01MH00274-17
MARKEY, S P Z01MH00279-09
MARKHAM, BRUCE E R01HL43662-02
MARKHAM, CHARLES P41RR01861-07 0003
MARKHAM, GEORGE R01CA11196-22
MARKHAM, GEORGE D R01GM31186-10
MARKHAM, JOANNE P50HL17646-17 9002
MARKHAM, P D N01CP73725-08
MARKHAM, PHILLIP D DR N01CP87213-11
MARKHAM, RICHARD B P30AI28748-03 9001
MARKHAM, RICHARD B R01AI22456-06
MARKHAM, RICHARD B R01AI29163-03
MARKIDES, KYRIAKOS S R01AG08633-01A2
MARKLE, RONALD A S07RR07256-02 0070
MARKLEY, JOHN P41RR02301-07 0005
MARKLEY, JOHN P41RR02301-07 0008
MARKLEY, JOHN P41RR02301-07 9001
MARKLEY, JOHN P41RR02301-07 9002
MARKLEY, JOHN P41RR02301-07 9003
MARKLEY, JOHN P41RR02301-07 9004
MARKLEY, JOHN L P41RR02301-07
MARKLEY, JOHN L R01LM04958-04
MARKLEY, JOHN L R37GM35976-07
MARKMAN, HOWARD S07RR07138-20 0525
MARKMAN, HOWARD S07RR07138-20 0533
MARKMAN, HOWARD J R01MH35525-09A2
MARKOFF, EDITH R01DK35679-05A2
MARKOFF, EDITH S07RR05535-29 0533
MARKOFF, L Z01AI00501-05
MARKOFF, L Z01AI00502-05
MARKOFF, L J Z01AI00557-03
MARKOLF, KEITH L R01AR40330-01A2
MARKOV, ANGEL R01HL36771-05
MARKOVAC, ANICA N01CM17510-00
MARKOVAC, ANICA PHD N01CM97592-02
MARKOVITS, JUDIT M P51RR00169-30 0152
MARKOVITZ, DAVID M K08CA01479-02
MARKOVITZ, DAVID M R29AI30924-01A1
MARKOW, THERESE A R03MH48999-01
MARKOWITZ, A Z01RR10337-02
MARKOWITZ, A Z01RR10359-01
MARKOWITZ, SANFORD P01CA51183-01A1 0005
MARKOWITZ, SANFORD D R29CA51504-02
MARKS, GARY S R01MH42023-05
MARKS, GILBERT L K11AI00922-03
MARKS, JAY W R01DK37080-05
MARKS, LAWRENCE E R01DC00271-08
MARKS, LAWRENCE E R01DC00818-02
MARKS, LLOYD S07RR05417-30 0802
MARKS, M DAVID S07RR07055-26 0172
MARKS, MELVIN I R01AI24841-06
MARKS, PAUL A P30CA08748-26
MARKS, PAUL A P30CA08748-26 9023
MARKS, SANDY C, JR R01AR39737-01A1
MARKS, SANDY C, JR R01DE05996-07A2
MARKS, SANDY C, JR R01DE07444-06
MARKS, SANDY C, JR R01DE08952-02
MARKS, W B Z01NS02079-18
MARKUS, GABOR S07RR05648-25 0923
MARKUS, HAZEL R01AG08279-01A2
MARKWALD, ROGER R P01HD20743-05
MARKWALD, ROGER R P01HD20743-05 0001
MARKWALD, ROGER R R37HL33756-08
MARKWALD, ROGER R S10RR06358-01
MARKY, LUIS A R01GM42223-03
MARKY, LUIS A S07RR07062-26 0218
MARLAN, RICHARD M01RR00069-29 0439
MARLARKEY, WILLIAM B M01RR00034-31 0299
MARLATT, G ALAN K05AA00113-05
MARLATT, G ALAN R37AA05591-09
MARLER, PETER P40RR03640-05 0025
MARLER, PETER ROBERT R37MH14651-25
MARLETT, JUDITH A R01DK21712-12A1
MARLETT, JUDITH A U01CA46339-04
MARLETTA, MICHAEL A P01CA26731-12 0007
MARLETTA, MICHAEL A R01CA50414-03
MARLEY, R J Z01DA00012-02
MARLEY, SUSAN S07RR05372-30 0709
MARLINK, RICHARD P01AI30795-02 0002
MARMAR, CHARLES R R01MH47382-02
MARMARELIS, VASILIS Z P41RR01861-07
MARMARELIS, VASILIS Z P41RR01861-07 9004
MARMAROU, ANTHONY P01NS12587-16 0011
MARMAROU, ANTHONY P01NS12587-16 0013
MARMAROU, ANTHONY R01NS19235-07
MARMOR S07RR05380-30 0888
MARMOR, MICHAEL R01DA06001-01A1
MARMOR, MICHAEL F R01EY01678-16
MARMOR, MICHAEL P30AI27742-03 9004
MARMOT, MICHAEL G N01HD02914-01
MARMOT, MICHAEL G R01HL36310-06
MARMOT, MICHAEL G R01HS06516-02
MARMUR, JULIUS R01GM28572-10
MARNETT, LAWRENCE J R35CA47479-04
MAROM, ZVI M01RR00071-28A1 0198
MAROM, ZVI M R01HL37254-03
MARON, B Z01HL04860-02
MARON, B J Z01HL04885-01
MARON, B J Z01HL04886-01
MARON, B J Z01HL04887-01
MARON, B J Z01HL04888-01
MARON, B J Z01HL04889-01
MARON, B J Z01HL04890-01
MARON, B J Z01HL04891-01
MARON, B J Z01HL04892-01
MARON, MICHAEL B R01HL31070-09
MARONEY, MICHAEL J R29GM38829-05
MARONEY, MICHAEL J S07RR07048-26 0646
MARONI, BRAD S07RR05364-30 0535
MARONI, GUSTAVO P R01ES02654-10
MARONPOT, R R Z01ES21080-07
MARONPOT, R R Z01ES21129-02
MARONPOT, R R Z01ES21131-02
MARONPOT, R R Z01ES21132-02
MAROTTA, CHARLES A P01AG02126-11 0009

MAROTTA, CHARLES A P01AG02126-11 0011
MAROTTA, CHARLES A P01AG02126-11
MARQUARDT, DIANA L K07AI00961-02
MARQUARDT, DIANA L R55AI25507-04
MARQUARDT, W C S07RR07127-23 0482
MARQUES, JANICE R19MH46391-03
MARQUES, PAUL R R18DA06379-03
MARQUEZ, V E Z01CM06173-06
MARQUEZ, V E Z01CM06174-06
MARQUEZ, V E Z01CM06175-06
MARQUEZ, V E Z01CM06176-07
MARQUIS, JUDITH N01ES15330-00
MARQUIS, ROBERT E P50DE07003-08 0001
MARQUIS, ROBERT E R01DE06127-09
MARR, ALLEN G S03RR03005-04
MARR, THOMAS G R01HG00203-01A1
MARR, THOMAS G R01LM04965-02S1
MARRACK, PHILIPPA C P01AI22295-07 0001
MARRACK, PHILIPPA C P01AI22295-07
MARRACK, PHILIPPA C P01AI29903-02 0003
MARRERO-CORLETTO, ROBERTO S06GM08216-09 00
MARRION, NEIL V R55NS29806-01
MARRIOTT, BERNADETTE P40RR03640-05 0026
MARRIOTT, BERNADETTE M N01RR12114-00
MARROCCO, RICHARD T S07RR07080-26 0314
MARROW, GARY R M01RR00044-31 0362
MARRS, CARL F R01EY07125-05
MARSANO, LUIS S M01RR02602-07 0053
MARSCHARK, MARC E K04DC00028-04
MARSCHARK, MARC E R01NS27243-02
MARSDEN, PHILIP D. P01AI16282-13 0007
MARSH, DAVID G R01AI20059-09
MARSH, DAVID G R55AI19727-09
MARSH, DONALD P41RR01861-07 0004
MARSH, DONALD J R01DK33729-07
MARSH, DONALD J R37DK15968-20
MARSH, GAIL P50MH40159-08 0009
MARSH, GAIL R P30AG09463-01 9005
MARSH, GENE S07RR05809-06 0475
MARSH, JAMES D R01HL35781-07
MARSH, JULIAN B P01HL22633-14 0001
MARSH, LORRAINE R01GM43365-02
MARSH, MARY E R01AR36239-08
MARSH, RICHARD F R01AG10669-01
MARSH, RICHARD L R29AR39318-04
MARSH, ROBERT C S07RR07133-22 0508
MARSHAK-ROTHSTEIN, ANN K04AR01684-05
MARSHAK-ROTHSTEIN, ANN R01AR35230-06
MARSHAK, DANIEL R P30CA45508-05 9007
MARSHAK, DAVID P51RR00166-30 0146
MARSHAK, DAVID W R01EY06472-05
MARSHAK, DAVID W S07RR05745-19 0221
MARSHALL, ALAN G R01GM31683-08A1
MARSHALL, B D JR P50MH30911-14 0013
MARSHALL, BARRY J S07RR05431-30 0848
MARSHALL, BRUCE C K08HL02370-03
MARSHALL, BRYAN E R01GM29628-10
MARSHALL, GARLAND P01GM24483-12A1 0015
MARSHALL, GARLAND P01GM24483-12A1 0016
MARSHALL, GARLAND R N01HD13104-00
MARSHALL, GARLAND R P01GM24483-12A1
MARSHALL, GARLAND R U01AI27302-04
MARSHALL, GARLAND R U01AI27302-04 0001
MARSHALL, GORDON S07RR05336-29 0300
MARSHALL, GRAYSON S07RR05305-30 0735
MARSHALL, GRAYSON S07RR05305-30 0722
MARSHALL, GRAYSON W P01DE09859-01 0002
MARSHALL, GRAYSON W R01DE06563-08
MARSHALL, JAMES N01CN05319-01
MARSHALL, JAMES A R01CA34247-09
MARSHALL, JAMES A R01GM29475-11
MARSHALL, JAMES R R13CA54182-01
MARSHALL, JOHN C M01RR00042-31 0400
MARSHALL, JOHN C R01HD11489-15
MARSHALL, JOHN C R01HD23736-04
MARSHALL, JOHN F P50MH44188-03 0005
MARSHALL, JOHN F R01NS22698-06
MARSHALL, JOHN F R01NS28846-02
MARSHALL, LAWRENCE P01NS14899-13 0010
MARSHALL, MILTON VIRGIL R01CA49401-04
MARSHALL, NANCY S07RR07186-10 0612
MARSHALL, SALLY S07RR05305-30 0723
MARSHALL, SALLY S07RR05305-30 0720
MARSHALL, SALLY J P01DE09859-01
MARSHALL, STEPHEN S07RR05423-30 0057
MARSHALS, DANIEL R P01CA13106-20 0012
MARSON, LESLEY R29NS29420-01A1
MARSTAD, ANDREW T. P51RR00166-30 0145
MARTELL, ARTHUR E R01HL42780-02
MARTENS, LESLIE V S07RR05322-30 0273
MARTENSEN, T M Z01AA00405-04
MARTHA, PAUL M JR K08HD00868-04
MARTHAS, MARTA L R01AI31383-01A1
MARTI, BERNSTEIN N01LM93512-15
MARTI, G E Z01BB04005-03
MARTI, GERARDO R03AG10396-01
MARTIENNSSEN, ROB S07RR05717-21 0128
MARTIN-STANLEY, CHARLES R24AA09294-02 0002
MARTIN, A Z01MH02588-01
MARTIN, A KEITH S07RR05992-04 0812
MARTIN, ARNOLD R R01NS16605-10
MARTIN, B Z01MH02344-06

MARTIN, BILLY R P50DA05274-04 9001
MARTIN, BILLY R P50DA05274-04 0008
MARTIN, BILLY R P50DA05274-04
MARTIN, BILLY R R01DA03672-08
MARTIN, CHRISTOPHER S07RR05425-30 0754
MARTIN, CRAIG T S07RR07048-26 0647
MARTIN, CRAIG T S07RR07048-26 0648
MARTIN, DANIEL S P01CA25842-11
MARTIN, DANIEL S P01CA25842-11 0001
MARTIN, DAVID R03AA08727-02
MARTIN, DAVID E P51RR00165-31 0164
MARTIN, DAVID L R37MH35664-12
MARTIN, DENNIS P60DK20572-14 9002
MARTIN, DOUGLAS K R18HS06173-03
MARTIN, DWIGHT W S07RR05736-19 0152
MARTIN, G R Z01AG00720-02
MARTIN, G STEVEN R01GM44173-02
MARTIN, G STEVEN R37CA17542-16
MARTIN, GAIL R P01HL43821-02 0002
MARTIN, GAIL R P01HL43821-02 9002
MARTIN, GAIL R R01HD25331-03
MARTIN, GEORGE P50AG05136-08 0011
MARTIN, GEORGE F P50NS10165-20 0027
MARTIN, GEORGE F R01NS25095-05
MARTIN, GEORGE M P01AG01751-13 0006
MARTIN, GEORGE M P01AG01751-13 9001
MARTIN, GEORGE M P01AG01751-13
MARTIN, GEORGE M P50AG05136-08
MARTIN, GEORGE M R37AG08303-03
MARTIN, GLEN KAY R01DC00613-04
MARTIN, HOWARD D S07RR05458-29 0830
MARTIN, HUNTER S07RR05874-10 0585
MARTIN, J H P01GM32099-09 0015
MARTIN, J R Z01NS02549-10
MARTIN, JAMES C R01GM36844-06
MARTIN, JAMES C S07RR07178-14 0669
MARTIN, JOEL F P50HL17682-17 0045
MARTIN, JOHN C P41RR01315-10 9006
MARTIN, JOHN C P41RR01315-10 9003
MARTIN, JOHN C R13AI31935-01
MARTIN, JOHN E R01AG08476-02
MARTIN, JOHN L K02MH00779-01A1
MARTIN, JOHN L R01MH39557-08
MARTIN, JOHN R R15HL44531-01A1
MARTIN, JOHN SAMUEL S07RR05417-30 0803
MARTIN, JOSEPH B M01RR00079-29
MARTIN, JOSEPH B M01RR00083-29
MARTIN, JOSEPH B M01RR01271-10
MARTIN, JOSEPH B S07RR05355-30
MARTIN, JOSEPH B S15GM47114-01
MARTIN, KAREN S R01NR02192-03
MARTIN, KATHY A R15GM45976-01
MARTIN, KEVIN J P01DK09976-27 0007
MARTIN, LEE J P50AG05146-09 0015
MARTIN, LOUIS N01AI15119-00
MARTIN, LYNN D S07RR05378-30 0003
MARTIN, M A Z01AI00190-13
MARTIN, M A Z01AI00415-08
MARTIN, MARK E R01HD27200-02
MARTIN, MARY B R01CA50445-03
MARTIN, MARY BETH U01CA51908-02 0001
MARTIN, NANCY C R01GM27597-14
MARTIN, NANCY C R01GM42454-03
MARTIN, OLIVIER R R01DK35766-05
MARTIN, OLIVIER R S15DK44712-01
MARTIN, PAUL P01AI29518-02 0004
MARTIN, PAUL P01AI29518-02 9001
MARTIN, PAUL P01CA47748-03 9002
MARTIN, PAUL J P01CA18029-16 0037
MARTIN, PAUL J P01HL25830-11A1 0008
MARTIN, PAUL J R01AI27951-02
MARTIN, PAUL J R01HL22484-14
MARTIN, PETER M01RR00095-31 0359
MARTIN, PETER R R01AA08492-02
MARTIN, PRESLEY F S07RR07129-22 0507
MARTIN, R G Z01DK36113-02
MARTIN, RANDI C R01DC00218-08
MARTIN, RICHARD P01HL36577-06 0008
MARTIN, RONALD L R43CA52337-01A1
MARTIN, ROY J R01HD18447-08
MARTIN, ROY J S07RR07025-26 0991
MARTIN, SANDRA L R29GM40367-04
MARTIN, STEPHEN F R01CA50991-02
MARTIN, STEPHEN F R01GM31077-07A2
MARTIN, STEPHEN F R01GM42763-01A2
MARTIN, STEPHEN F R01GM43473-01A2
MARTIN, THOMAS P41RR00570-21 0015
MARTIN, THOMAS P50HL30542-08 0008
MARTIN, THOMAS F R01DK40428-04
MARTIN, THOMAS F R37DK25861-12
MARTIN, THOMAS R K11HL02240-02
MARTIN, THOMAS R R01AI29103-02
MARTIN, WADE M01RR00036-31 1038
MARTIN, WADE H R01HL41290-03
MARTIN, WILLIAM J R01HL43524-03
MARTIN, WILLIAM J II R01HL36124-06
MARTIN, WILLIAM J, II R01HL46647-01
MARTIN, WILLIAM R R01DA02195-12
MARTINEZ-CARRION, M S10RR06296-01
MARTINEZ-CARRION, MARINO P01NS24304-05 000
MARTINEZ-CARRION, MARINO R01GM38184-04
MARTINEZ-CARRION, MARINO R01GM38341-05

MARTINEZ-CARRION, MARINO S07RR05997-04
MARTINEZ-CARRION, MARINO S15DK44701-01
MARTINEZ-CRUZADO, J C S06GM08103-18 0018
MARTINEZ-MAZA, OTONIEL K04CA01588-01
MARTINEZ-MAZA, OTONIEL R29AI24691-05
MARTINEZ, ANDREW O S06GM08194-12 0029
MARTINEZ, DANIEL S07RR05372-30 0691
MARTINEZ, EDWIN R24MH47392-02 0003
MARTINEZ, J RICARDO R01DE04897-11
MARTINEZ, J RICARDO R01DE09270-06
MARTINEZ, J RICARDO S07RR05900-06
MARTINEZ, JOE L R01DA06192-02
MARTINEZ, JOE L JR R01DA04195-05
MARTINEZ, JOSE R01HL20092-15
MARTINEZ, P Z01MH02490-02
MARTINEZ, P E Z01MH02493-02
MARTINIUK, FRANK T R01DK39669-04
MARTINO, R L Z01CT00148-07
MARTINO, R L Z01CT00200-02
MARTINS, JAMES B M01RR00059-30 0552
MARTINS, JAMES B P50HL32295-07 0004
MARTON, LAWRENCE J P01CA13525-19 0020
MARTORELL, REYNALDO R22HD22440-04
MARTUZA, ROBERT P01NS24279-06 0006
MARTYN, J JEEVENDRA R01GM31569-08
MARTZ, ERIC S07RR07048-26 0649
MARUCHA, PHILIP K16DE00157-05S2 0004
MARUCHA, PHILIP K16DE00199-05S1 0002
MARUCHA, PHILIP T S07RR05928-06 0309
MARUCHA, PHILLIP T R29DE09942-01
MARUNIAK, JOEL A R01DC00400-04
MARUSICH, MICHAEL P01HD22486-05 9002
MARVER, DIANA R01DK21576-11
MARVIN, JANET S07RR05758-18 0254
MARVIN, ROBERT S R01HD26911-02
MARVIN, WILLIAM J P01HL14388-20 0235
MARX, PRESTON A P51RR00169-30 0177
MARX, PRESTON A P51RR00169-30 0178
MARX, PRESTON A P51RR00169-30 0179
MARX, PRESTON A P51RR00169-30 0180
MARX, PRESTON A R01AI27698-02
MARX, PRESTON A U42RR03582-05A1
MARX, S J Z01DK43003-26
MARX, S J Z01DK43008-10
MARX, S J Z01DK43009-06
MARZETTA, CAROL A. P51RR00166-30 0147
MARZILLI, LUIGI G R01GM29222-11
MARZLUF, GEORGE A R01GM23367-15
MARZLUFF, WILLIAM F, JR R01GM27789-12
MARZLUFF, WILLIAM F, JR R01GM29832-15
MAS, MARIA P30CA33572-11 9014
MAS, MARIA S07RR05841-12 0227
MAS, MARIA T R01GM37715-05
MAS, MARIA T R01GM41360-03
MASAMUNE, SATORU R01CA48175-04
MASAMUNE, SATORU R01GM35879-06
MASARACCHIA, RUTHANN S07RR07195-12 0711
MASARACCHIA, RUTHANN A R01GM32350-09
MASARYK, THOMAS J R01HL43812-02
MASCARENHAS, MARIA R S07RR05576-27 0607
MASCHARAK, PRADIP K R29CA53076-02
MASCHARAK, PRADIP K S06GM08132-17 0018
MASELLI, RICARDO S07RR05367-30 0570
MASER, RAELENE E S07RR07016-18 0358
MASH, DEBORAH C R01DA06227-02
MASH, DEBORAH C R29NS25785-05
MASHAL, ROBERT D K11CA01556-01
MASKER, WARREN E R01GM34614-08
MASLAK, PRZEMYSLAW R01GM41489-03
MASLAND, RICHARD H R01EY05747-07
MASLAND, RICHARD H R37EY01075-18
MASLAR, ILA P51RR00163-32 0032
MASLAR, ILA A S03RR03291-10
MASLIAH, ELIEZER R01AG10689-01
MASON, ANDREW Z S06GM08238-05 0013
MASON, ANNE B S07RR05429-30 0194
MASON, BARBARA J R01AA08111-02
MASON, CAROL A R01NS16951-11
MASON, CAROL A R01NS27615-03
MASON, CAROL A S10RR06691-01
MASON, DANA R S07RR07032-26 0030
MASON, DIANA J S07RR07059-26 0837
MASON, GEORGE A P50MH33127-13 9001
MASON, GEORGE A R01AA07809-02
MASON, GREGORY M01RR00425-22S3 0392
MASON, GREGORY R M01RR00425-22S3 0418
MASON, HOLLY L S07RR07032-26 0041
MASON, J M Z01ES21051-08
MASON, J M Z01ES21053-08
MASON, JAMES I R01AG08175-04
MASON, JAY M01RR00064-27 0381
MASON, JAY W M01RR00064-27 0293
MASON, JAY W R01HL34071-06
MASON, JAY W R01HL34744-04
MASON, JILL S07RR05336-29 0302
MASON, JILL S07RR05336-29 0309
MASON, JOHN W R01MH41125-03
MASON, MARY ANN S07RR07006-26 0908
MASON, MARY ANN S07RR07006-26 0909
MASON, R Z01ES50109-03
MASON, R P Z01ES50088-05
MASON, R P Z01ES50090-05

MASON, R P Z01ES50117-01
MASON, R P Z01ES50118-01
MASON, ROBERT J P50HL27353-10 0004
MASON, ROBERT J P50HL27353-10
MASON, ROBERT J R37HL29891-09
MASON, THERESA H R18DA07003-02
MASON, THOMAS J S03RR03381-05
MASON, THOMAS L S07RR07048-26 0650
MASON, WILLIAM S07RR05539-29 0547
MASON, WILLIAM A P51RR00169-30 0095
MASON, WILLIAM A P51RR00169-30 0089
MASON, WILLIAM A P51RR00169-30 0088
MASON, WILLIAM S R01AI18641-10
MASORO, EDWARD J K07AG00469-02
MASORO, EDWARD J P01AG01188-13 9001
MASORO, EDWARD J. P01AG01188-13 0014
MASOUD, ASAAD U01AI25696-05 9003
MASS, HOWARD S06GM08239-06 0005
MASS, HOWARD J G12RR03050-07 0001
MASSA, PAUL T S07RR05402-30 0800
MASSAGUE, JOAN P01CA39240-07 0002
MASSAGUE, JOAN R01CA34610-09
MASSAGUE, JOAN R01CA53559-01
MASSAQUE, JOAN P01CA39240-07 9005
MASSARO, DOMINIC W R01DC00236-10
MASSARO, DONALD J R01HL41610-04
MASSARO, DONALD J R37HL20366-16
MASSERANO, JOSEPH M R01MH41551-03
MASSEY, DOUGLAS S P30HD18288-08 9004
MASSEY, DOUGLAS S P30HD18288-08 9005
MASSEY, DOUGLAS S R37HD24047-05
MASSEY, GITA S07RR05430-30 0224
MASSEY, MARILYN N01CN05295-03
MASSEY, STEPHEN C R55EY06515-07
MASSEY, VINCENT R37GM11106-29
MASSIE, BARRIE P01HL25847-12 0007
MASSOF, ROBERT W R01EY01791-15A2
MASSOF, ROBERT W R01EY05675-07
MASSOTH, DONNA S07RR05346-30 0313
MASSRY, SHAUL G M01RR00043-31 0367
MASSRY, SHAUL G R55DK29955-11
MASSRY, SHAUL G U01DK39819-04
MAST, JOELLE K11HD00819-04
MAST, JOELLE S07RR05396-30 0775
MASTERS, BARRY R R01EY06958-04
MASTERS, BETTIE S R01GM31296-11
MASTERS, BETTIE S R37HL30050-10
MASTERS, MARY N N01DE12592-00
MASTERS, PAUL S R29AI31622-01
MASTERS, W MITCH R01DC01251-01
MASTERTON, R BRUCE R01NS07726-24S1
MASTRANGELO, MICHAEL J N01CM67902-01
MASTRIANNI, DAVID M K11CA01602-01
MASTRO, ANDREA M R01CA24385-12
MASTROIANNI, FRANK P30CA08748-26 9016
MASTROIANNI, LUIGI P01HD06274-20 9001
MASTROIANNI, LUIGI JR U10HD27049-02
MASTRONARDE, DAVID P41RR00592-22 0015
MASTRONARDE, DAVID N P41RR00592-22 0021
MASUDA, T Z01AA00048-02
MASUKAWA, LEONA M R01NS23077-07
MASUR, SANDRA K R03EY09244-01
MATA, MARINA P50AG08671-03 0006
MATALON, REUBEN N01HD42808-14
MATALON, SADIS R01HL31197-08
MATANOSKI, GENEVIEVE M P30ES03819-06A1 900
MATANOSKI, GENEVIEVE M R01OH02730-02
MATAS, ARTHUR J M01RR00400-23 0276
MATAS, ARTHUR J U01AI31559-01
MATES, ROBERT E P01HL15194-20 9003
MATES, ROBERT E P01HL15194-20 9004
MATES, ROBERT E P01HL15194-20
MATES, ROBERT E P01HL15194-20 0026
MATES, SHARON N01HD92908-11
MATHENY, ADAM P, JR R01HD21395-05
MATHENY, ADAM P, JR R01HD22637-05
MATHENY, ADAM P, JR R01MH39772-06
MATHER, FRANCES S07RR05444-30 0261
MATHER, THOMAS N R29AI30733-01
MATHERLY, SANDRA C R43NR02824-01
MATHERNE, GAYNELL P, JR K08HL02457-02
MATHES, LAWRENCE E R01CA40714-06
MATHESON, N W P41HG00586-01 9001
MATHEW, MATHAI R01DE05030-13
MATHEW, OOMMEN P R01HL32921-08
MATHEWS, CHRISTOPHER K R01GM37508-05
MATHEWS, CHRISTOPHER K S07RR07079-26
MATHEWS, F P41RR01209-12 0006
MATHEWS, F SCOTT R01GM20530-19
MATHEWS, F SCOTT R01GM31611-09
MATHEWS, KATHERINE S07RR05372-30 0679
MATHEWS, MICHAEL S07RR05717-21 0138
MATHEWS, MICHAEL B P01CA13106-20
MATHEWS, MICHAEL B P01CA13106-20 9002
MATHEWS, MICHAEL B P01CA13106-20 0001
MATHEWS, MICHAEL B P01CA13106-20 0015
MATHEWS, MICHAEL B R13GM30579-07
MATHEY-PREVOT, BERNARD R01DK41758-02
MATHIAS, RICHARD T R01EY06391-07
MATHIES, RICHARD A R01GM44801-02
MATHIES, RICHARD A R37EY02051-15
MATHIEU-COSTELLO, ODILE P01HL17731-17 0019
MATHIEU-COSTELLO, ODILE P01HL17731-17 9001
MATHIEU-COSTELLO, ODILE A S06GM47165-01 00
MATHIS, CHESTER P30AG10129-01 0001
MATHIS, CHESTER A R01NS22899-06
MATHIS, CHESTER A R01NS28867-01A1
MATHIS, JAMES S07RR07024-26 0031
MATHISON, DAVID A M01RR00833-17 0162
MATHISON, JOHN C M01RR00833-17 0208
MATHUR, AMBIKA R29AI31662-01
MATHUR, AMBIKA S07RR05322-30 0270
MATHUR, RAVINDRA L S07RR05393-30 0898
MATIN, ABDUL R01GM42159-03
MATIS, L A Z01CM09358-01
MATKOVIC, VELIMIR M01RR00034-31 0403
MATKOVIC, VELMIR M01RR00034-31 0393
MATKOVICH, VELIMIR R01AR40736-01A1
MATKOVICH, VELIMIR R25RR07675-01
MATLIB, MOHAMMED A R01HL34664-07
MATLIN, KARL S S07RR05381-30 0781
MATON, P N Z01DK53200-02
MATON, P N Z01DK53201-02
MATRISIAN, LYNN M P01CA48799-03 0002
MATRISIAN, LYNN M R01CA46843-04
MATSCHINSKY, FRANZ M P30DK19525-15 9002
MATSCHINSKY, FRANZ M P30DK19525-15
MATSCHINSKY, FRANZ M R37DK22122-14
MATSON, DAVID M01RR00188-27 0333
MATSON, DAVID D S07RR05425-30 0755
MATSON, DAVID O R29AI28544-03
MATSON, STEVEN W R01GM33476-07
MATSUDA, RYOICHI S07RR05863-11 0569
MATSUDAIRA, P P41RR02250-06 0003
MATSUDAIRA, PAUL P01CA44704-04A1 0003
MATSUDAIRA, PAUL P01CA44704-04A1 9005
MATSUDAIRA, PAUL T R01CA55621-01
MATSUDAIRA, PAUL T R01DK35306-07
MATSUEDA, GARY R R01HL28015-10
MATSUI, SUZANNE M K11DK01811-05
MATSUMOTO, BRIAN R29EY07191-04
MATSUMOTO, BRIAN S07RR07099-25 0404
MATSUMOTO, HIROYUKI R01EY06595-06
MATSUMOTO, STEVEN S07RR05336-29 0305
MATSUMOTO, STEVEN G R29NS25644-05
MATSUMURA, FUMIO K04CA01304-04
MATSUMURA, FUMIO R01ES03575-07
MATSUMURA, FUMIO R01ES05233-02
MATSUMURA, FUMIO R37CA42742-07
MATSUMURA, FUMIO S07RR07058-26 0181
MATSUMURA, PHILIP R01AI18985-10
MATSUO, FUMISUKE N01NS72321-01
MATSUOKA, YUMIKO N44AI05083-04
MATSUURA, HIDEMITSU R29CA49435-02
MATSUYA, H Z01CM07220-01
MATT, DENNIS W R29AG07452-04
MATTA, KHUSHI L R01AI29326-01A3
MATTA, KHUSHI L R01CA35329-06
MATTERI, ROBERT P51RR00167-31 0050
MATTERI, ROBERT S07RR07098-26 0367
MATTES, RICHARD D M01RR00040-31 0408
MATTES, RICHARD D P50DC00214-06 0002
MATTES, RICHARD D R01CA37298-07
MATTES, RICHARD D S07RR05825-12 0521
MATTESON, DONALD S R01GM39063-02
MATTESON, DONALD S R01GM44995-02
MATTESON, MARY A R01NR02998-01
MATTESON, MARY A S07RR05654-24 0136
MATTESON, RANA L S07RR07028-26 0018
MATTHAY, KATHERINE K M01RR01271-10 0111
MATTHAY, KATHERINE K R01CA39448-06
MATTHAY, MICHAEL P01HL25816-11 0002
MATTHEW, WILLIAM D P01NS02253-32 0013
MATTHEWS, BRIAN W R01GM21967-17
MATTHEWS, BRIAN W R37GM20066-19
MATTHEWS, CHARLES R R01GM23303-16
MATTHEWS, DAVID A P01GM39599-05
MATTHEWS, DAVID A P01GM39599-05 0001
MATTHEWS, DWIGHT M01RR00047-31 0411
MATTHEWS, DWIGHT P30DK26687-11 9009
MATTHEWS, DWIGHT E P50GM26145-13 0013
MATTHEWS, DWIGHT E R01DK38429-06
MATTHEWS, GARY G R01EY03821-11
MATTHEWS, GARY G R01EY08673-02
MATTHEWS, H B Z01ES21038-09
MATTHEWS, J Z01BA01007-02
MATTHEWS, J Z01BA01010-02
MATTHEWS, J Z01BA01017-01
MATTHEWS, J Z01BA01018-01
MATTHEWS, JAMES L R01HL43421-03
MATTHEWS, KAREN A R01HL25767-12
MATTHEWS, KAREN A R37HL38712-05
MATTHEWS, KATHLEEN S R01GM22441-16
MATTHEWS, KATHLEEN S S07RR07103-25
MATTHEWS, KATHLEEN S S15HL47741-01
MATTHEWS, ROWENA G R37GM24908-14
MATTHEWS, T JAMES S07RR07062-26 0219
MATTHEWS, THOMAS J P01CA43447-06 0008
MATTHEWS, THOMAS J R01AI30411-02
MATTHYSSE, STEVEN W P01MH31154-14 0010
MATTIELLO, J Z01RR10370-01
MATTISON, DONALD R S07RR05451-30
MATTISON, DONALD R S15HL47722-01
MATTLINGLY, STEPHEN J P01AI22380-07 0003
MATTOON, JAMES R S15AR41244-01
MATTOX, DOUGLAS E P60DC00979-02 0005
MATTREY, ROBERT F K04CA01319-04
MATTREY, ROBERT F M01RR00827-17 0506
MATTREY, ROBERT F R01CA36799-07
MATTS, ROBERT L R29ES04299-05
MATTSON, MARK P P50AG05144-08 0005
MATTSON, MARK P R01NS29001-01
MATTSON, RICHARD H M01RR00125-28 0689
MATTSON, RICHARD H M01RR00125-28 0690
MATUSCHAK, GEORGE M R01GM43153-02
MATYAS, MICHAEL N01CO03887-47
MATZINGER, P Z01AI00581-02
MATZUK, MARTIN M K11HD00960-01
MAUCHER, PETER N01LM63521-09
MAUDSLEY, ANDREW A R01CA48815-03
MAUDSLEY, ANDREW A S10RR06491-01
MAUE, ROBERT A R29NS28767-01A1
MAUE, ROBERT A S07RR05392-30 0697
MAUER, ALVIN M M01RR00211-27 0327
MAUER, ALVIN M N01HB97070-04
MAUER, ALVIN M S07RR05423-30 0058
MAUER, ALVIN M U10CA47555-04
MAUER, MICHAEL S M01RR00400-23 0277
MAUER, S MICHAEL M01RR00400-23 0209
MAUER, S MICHEAL M01RR00400-23 0275
MAUGHAN, DAVID W R01AR38980-08
MAUGHAN, DAVID W R01AR40234-02
MAUK, ARTHUR G R01GM33804-07
MAUK, MICHAEL DEAN S07RR05745-19 0246
MAUL, DIANA M N43ES11001-00
MAUL, DONALD H G20RR06763-01
MAUL, GERD G P30CA10815-24 9003
MAULDON, JANE R55HD27715-01
MAULDON, JANE S07RR07006-26 0907
MAUNSELL, JOHN H R01EY05911-06
MAURELLI, ANTHONY T R01AI24656-03
MAURER, ERIK S07RR05417-30 0806
MAURER, HAROLD M U10CA24507-13
MAURER, HAROLD M U10CA28530-12
MAURER, HELEN N01HB87049-05
MAURER, R P01HL14388-20 0250
MAURER, RICHARD A R01DK36407-06
MAURER, RUSSELL A R01GM47111-09
MAURICE, DAVID M R01EY04863-09
MAURICE, DAVID M R37EY00431-22
MAURO, ROBERT S07RR07080-26 0315
MAURO, THEODORA S07RR05684-23 0178
MAURO, THEODORA M K08AR01853-01
MAURY, W Z01AI00418-08
MAUSNER, LEONARD U01CA51958-02 0002
MAUST, ANN P N01OD02135-04
MAUTONE, ALAN J R29HL38303-04
MAUZERALL, DAVID C R01GM25693-13
MAVISSAKALIAN, MATIG R R01MH42730-05
MAVROTHALASSITIS, G J Z01CP05593-03
MAVROVOUNIOTIS, MICHAEL L R29LM05278-01
MAWE, GARY M R29NS26995-04
MAWE, GARY M S07RR05429-30 0193
MAWHINNEY, MICHAEL S07RR05433-30 0251
MAWHINNEY, THOMAS P R01HL32026-08
MAWHORTER, LINDA M01RR00997-16 0327
MAX, E E Z01BD04008-03
MAX, E E Z01BD04019-01
MAX, M Z01DE00366-09
MAX, STEPHEN P01HD16596-08 0008
MAX, STEPHEN R R01DK41022-03
MAXFIELD, FREDERICK R R01DK27083-13
MAXFIELD, FREDERICK R R01GM34770-07
MAXIN, LENORA N01CO15684-00
MAXON, HARRY R R01CA32863-12
MAXON, ROBERT P50DE09165-03 0001
MAXSON, ROBERT E, JR R01HD18582-09
MAXSON, ROBERT E, JR R01HD22416-04A2
MAXWELL, ANNA K S07RR05788-15 0896
MAXWELL, GERALD D R01NS16115-10A2
MAXWELL, IAN H R01CA42354-05
MAXWELL, IAN H R01CA50285-02
MAXWELL, JANE C R19DA06415-03
MAXWELL, LEO C S07RR07187-13 0699
MAY, BRADFORD J R29DC00954-01
MAY, GREGORY S R01GM41626-03
MAY, J C Z01BB01001-14
MAY, J C Z01BB01002-17
MAY, J C Z01BB01003-16
MAY, J C Z01BB01004-11
MAY, J C Z01BB01005-07
MAY, J C Z01BB01009-13
MAY, J C Z01BB01010-01
MAY, JACK S07RR07067-26 0221
MAY, JAMES M R01DK38794-04A2
MAY, KATHARYN A R01NR02377-02
MAY, KATHLEEN S07RR05913-08 0659
MAY, MICHAEL E R29DK40910-02
MAY, PATRICK C R35AG07909-03 0003
MAY, PAUL J R29EY07166-05
MAY, ROBERT C R29DK38953-03
MAY, SHELDON S07RR07024-26 0038
MAY, SHELDON W R01HL28167-10
MAY, STERLING R R44GM42312-03
MAY, STERLING R R44HL44233-02
MAY, STRATFORD S07RR05378-30 0004

MAY, VICTOR R01HD27468-01A1
MAY, VICTOR S07RR05429-30 0195
MAY, WILLIAM S JR R01CA44649-04A1
MAYALL, BRIAN H P01CA44768-05 9003
MAYALL, BRIAN H R01CA47537-03
MAYATECH CORPORATION N01TI10018-00
MAYBEE, DAVID A U10CA28572-10S1
MAYBERG, HELEN S R29MH49553-01
MAYBERG, MARC R K08NS01191-05
MAYBERG, MARC R R01HL44458-01A1
MAYBERRY, RACHEL I R01DC00231-05
MAYER, CECILIA C R01AI25284-05
MAYER, CECILIA C R01AI29857-02
MAYER, CECILIA C R29NS25007-05
MAYER, D LUISA R01EY05685-07
MAYER, D LUISA U10EY07776-03
MAYER, EMERAN A R01DK40919-03
MAYER, JOSEPH H K20DA00143-02
MAYER, KENNETH H R01AI25828-05
MAYER, LLOYD P01AI24671-04 0003
MAYER, LLOYD P01AI24671-04 9002
MAYER, LLOYD F R01AI23504-04A1
MAYER, LLOYD F R01CA41583-06
MAYER, M L Z01HD00707-06
MAYER, MELANIE J R01EY07557-03
MAYER, RICHARD E S07RR07099-25 0399
MAYER, STEVEN E R01GM44295-01A1
MAYER, STEVEN E S07RR05424-30 0086
MAYERI, EARL P01NS16033-11 0010
MAYERI, EARL R01NS16490-11
MAYERS, GEORGE P01CA41285-07 9003
MAYERSOHN, MICHAEL R01DA06775-02
MAYES, LINDA C M01RR06022-02 0766
MAYES, LINDA C M01RR06022-02 0736
MAYEUX, PHILIP R R29DK44716-01
MAYEUX, R M01RR00645-20 0425
MAYEUX, RICHARD M01RR00645-20 0501
MAYEUX, RICHARD M01RR00645-20 0489
MAYEUX, RICHARD M01RR00645-20 0383
MAYEUX, RICHARD M01RR00645-20 0464
MAYEUX, RICHARD M01RR00645-20 0465
MAYEUX, RICHARD M01RR00645-20 0466
MAYEUX, RICHARD M01RR00645-20 0467
MAYEUX, RICHARD P50AG08702-03 9001
MAYEUX, RICHARD P50MH43520-04 9003
MAYEUX, RICHARD P M01RR00645-20 0299
MAYEUX, RICHARD P M01RR00645-20 0300
MAYEUX, RICHARD P P01AG07232-03 0003
MAYEUX, RICHARD P P01AG07232-03
MAYEUX, RICHARD P R01MH44959-03
MAYFIELD, JOHN E S06GM08049-20 0012
MAYFIELD, STEPHEN P M01RR00833-17 0213
MAYFIELD, STEPHEN P R01GM41353-03
MAYHAN, WILLIAM G. P01NS24621-05 0002
MAYHAN, WILLIAM GERARD K04HL02124-05
MAYNE, RICHARD R01AR30481-10
MAYNER, R Z01BG06051-01
MAYO, KELLY E K04HD00920-01
MAYO, KELLY E P01HD21921-04 0006
MAYO, KELLY E P30HD28048-01 9003
MAYO, KELLY E R01HD27491-01
MAYO, KEVIN S07RR07115-24 0580
MAYO, KEVIN H R01HL43194-02
MAYS, LAWRENCE E R01EY03463-12
MAYS, VICKIE S07RR07009-26 0942
MAYS, VICKIE M R01MH42584-04S1
MAYS, VICKIE M R01MH44345-03
MAZANEC, MARY B K08HL02002-05
MAZE, MERVYN R01GM30232-07
MAZIS, MICHAEL B R01AA08383-03
MAZUR, ERIC M S07RR05818-12 0161
MAZZAFERRI, ERNEST L M01RR00034-31 0361
MAZZAFERRI, ERNEST L M01RR00034-31 0334
MAZZE, ROGER S P60DK20541-14 9004
MAZZE,ROGER P60DK20541-14 0029
MAZZEO, ROBERT S R29AG07180-05
MAZZEO, ROBERT S S07RR07013-26 0967
MAZZIOTTA, JOHN P30AG10123-01 9002
MAZZIOTTA, JOHN C M01RR00865-18 0223
MAZZIOTTA, JOHN C P01NS15654-13 0006
MAZZONE, THEODORE P50HL15062-20 9004
MAZZONE, THEODORE P50HL15062-20 0025
MAZZUCA, STEVEN P60AR20582-14 9007
MAZZUCA, STEVEN A P60DK20542-14 9004
MC AFEE, JOHN G R01DK33357-22
MC AFEE, PAUL C R29AR38489-05
MC ALISTER-HENN, L LEE R01GM33218-07
MC ALISTER, ALFRED L U01CA52939-02
MC ALLISTER, MARY E P60HL28391-09 0009
MC ALLISTER, WILLIAM T R01GM38147-05
MC ARDLE, J JACK R01AG07137-05
MC ARTHUR, WILLIAM P S07RR05728-20
MC AULEY, EDWARD R29AG07907-05
MC AULIFFE, WILLIAM E R01DA04418-06
MC AULIFFE, WILLIAM E R01DA07063-01
MC AULIFFE, WILLIAM E R01DA07296-01
MC AULIFFE, WILLIAM E R18DA05271-03S1
MC AVOY, JOHNSTON W R01EY03177-13
MC BRIDE, JOHN T R01HL29842-07
MC BRIDE, PATRICK E K07HL01936-05
MC BRIDE, WILLIAM H R01CA44384-05
MC BURNETT, ROBERT K R03MH48951-01
MC CABE, EDWARD R P30HD04024-23 0014
MC CABE, EDWARD R P30HD24064-04
MC CABE, EDWARD R R01HD22563-04
MC CABE, PHILIP M P01HL36588-06 0004
MC CALL, ANTHONY L R13NS29022-01A1
MC CALL, CHARLES E R01AI09169-19
MC CALL, CHARLES E R01HL29293-10
MC CALLUM, RICHARD W M01RR00847-18 0402
MC CALLUM, RICHARD W M01RR00847-18 0306
MC CALLUM, RICHARD W M01RR00847-18 0403
MC CAMAN, RICHARD E R03DA07328-01
MC CAMMON, JAMES A R01GM31749-09
MC CANN, BARBARA S R01HL41657-03
MC CANN, BARBARA S R01HL45707-01
MC CANN, SAMUEL M R01DK10073-24
MC CANN, SAMUEL M R01DK40994-03
MC CARLEY, ROBERT W R01MH40799-05
MC CARLEY, ROBERT W R37MH39683-08
MC CARN, DAVIS B N01LM93518-07
MC CARN, DAVIS B N01LM93520-05
MC CARREY, JOHN R K04HD00829-04
MC CARREY, JOHN R P01AG08321-03 0004
MC CARRON, DAVID A P30DK40566-02
MC CARTER, ROGER J P01AG01188-13 0005
MC CARTHY, CHARLOTTE M S15HD28775-01
MC CARTHY, GREGORY R01MH05286-29
MC CARTHY, JAMES B R01CA43924-04
MC CARTHY, JAMES B R55CA54263-01
MC CARTHY, JOHN F P01ES02429-11 9001
MC CARTHY, KEN D P01ES01104-16 0009
MC CARTHY, KEN D R01NS29471-01
MC CARTHY, KENNY D R01NS20212-08
MC CARTHY, SUSAN A R55AI31644-01
MC CARTNEY, KATHLEEN U10HD25451-03
MC CARTON, CECELIA M R01HD27344-01A1
MC CAUL, MARY E R18DA06897-02
MC CLAIN, DONALD A R29DK43526-02
MC CLAIN, WILLIAM H R01GM42123-19
MC CLANE, BRUCE A R01AI19844-09
MC CLAY, DAVID R, JR R01HD14483-12
MC CLAY, DAVID R, JR R01HD24199-04
MC CLAY, DAVID R, JR R01HD27299-02
MC CLEARN, GERALD E S15AA09254-01
MC CLELLAN, ANDREW D R01NS29043-01A1
MC CLELLAND, JAMES L K02MH00385-11
MC CLELLAND, JAMES L P01MH47566-01 9001
MC CLELLAND, JAMES L P01MH47566-01
MC CLELLAND, JAMES L P01MH47566-01 0001
MC CLELLAND, MICHAEL R01HG00106-02
MC CLELLAND, MICHAEL R55HG00456-01
MC CLESKEY, EDWIN W R01DA07415-01
MC CLESKEY, EDWIN W R29GM38178-05
MC CLOSKEY, JAMES A R01GM21584-17
MC CLOSKEY, JAMES A R01GM29812-17
MC CLOSKEY, MICHAEL E R01NS21047-06
MC CLUER, ROBERT H P01HD05515-21
MC CLUER, ROBERT H P01HD05515-21 0049
MC CLUER, ROBERT H P01HD05515-21 9001
MC CLUER, ROBERT H R01NS15037-10A1
MC CLUER, ROBERT H R01NS16447-10
MC CLUER, ROBERT H S03RR03437-06
MC CLUER, ROBERT H S15NS30113-01
MC CLURE, JOAN N01LM93525-04
MC CLURE, WILLIAM R R01GM30375-11
MC COLLUM, GIN R01NS23209-06
MC CONATHY, WALTER J R01HL46967-01
MC CONKIE, GEORGE W R01HD28181-01
MC CONNELL, KEVIN R K11DK01946-02
MC CORMACK, FRANCIS X K08HL02423-02
MC CORMACK, RICHARD P50MH41684-07 0055
MC CORMICK, DANIEL J R29NS24694-05
MC CORMICK, DAVID A R29NS26143-04
MC CORMICK, DAVID L R01CA40874-06
MC CORMICK, DONALD B R01DK38940-05
MC CORMICK, DONALD B R01DK43005-02
MC CORMICK, J JUSTIN S15CA55924-01
MC CORMICK, PAULETTE J R01CA49466-02
MC CORMICK, PAULETTE J R01HD23402-03
MC CORMICK, RICK N01LM13514-00
MC COY, CLYDE B U01DA06910-02
MC COY, GEORGE D R01CA32126-05
MC COY, GEORGE D R01CA49384-03
MC COY, KATHERINE O S15DA07819-01
MC COY, KATHLEEN L R29AI28422-03
MC CRACKEN, ARDYTHE A S10RR06507-01
MC CRACKEN, GEORGE H P01HD22766-05
MC CRACKEN, JAMES T K11MH00722-05
MC CRACKEN, JAMES T R03MH46915-02
MC CRACKEN, JOHN A P01HD20290-06A1 0004
MC CRACKEN, JOHN A R01HD08129-13A2
MC CRACKEN, JOHN L R29GM45795-01
MC CRADY, BARBARA S P50AA08747-02 0003
MC CRADY, BARBARA S P50AA08747-02 9001
MC CRADY, BARBARA S P50AA08747-02
MC CRADY, BARBARA S R01AA07070-04
MC CRAE, KEITH R K08HD00882-02
MC CRARY, JOHN A, III U10EY07679-04
MC CREA, ROBERT A R01EY08041-03
MC CULLEY, JAMES P R01EY03650-09A1
MC CULLOCH, ANDREW D R29HL41603-03
MC CULLOCH, DAVID K R01DK40627-02
MC CULLOCH, JOHN H U10CA35119-08
MC CUNE, MICHAEL J N01AI05080-03
MC CUSKEY, ROBERT S S15AA09241-01
MC CUTCHAN, J ALLEN M01RR00827-17 0337
MC DANIEL, JOE R R44CA47241-03
MC DANIEL, MARTHA D R03HS06675-01S1
MC DANIEL, MICHAEL L R01DK06181-30
MC DEVITT, HUGH O P01AI19512-09
MC DEVITT, HUGH O R01AI28896-02
MC DEVITT, HUGH O R01DK33880-08
MC DEVITT, HUGH O R01HG00346-12
MC DEVITT, HUGH O R35CA49734-03
MC DEVITT, HUGH O R37AI07757-25
MC DONAGH, ANTONY F R01DK26307-12
MC DONAGH, JAN P01HL33014-07 0002
MC DONALD, CLEMENT J R18HS05626-04
MC DONALD, CURTIS W S06GM08061-17
MC DONALD, DONALD M P01HL24075-13 9001
MC DONALD, DONALD M P01HL24136-13 9001
MC DONALD, DONALD M P01HL24136-13 0012
MC DONALD, GREGORY A R29AI30127-02
MC DONALD, JOHN A P01HL29594-09 0001
MC DONALD, JOHN A P01HL29594-09 9001
MC DONALD, JOHN A R01GM38276-07
MC DONALD, JOHN A R01HL39894-05
MC DONALD, MELISENDA J R01HL38456-06
MC DONALD, R H P30HD02274-24 9003
MC DONALD, ROGER B K01AG00429-03
MC DONALD, TED P R01HL14637-17
MC DONALD, TED P S15HL47716-01
MC DONALD, THOMAS V K11HL02397-02
MC DONNELL, DONALD P R29DK43267-01
MC DONNELL, SUE M K04NS01537-01
MC DONOUGH, ALICIA A R01DK34316-07
MC DONOUGH, KATHLEEN H R01AA07747-03
MC DOUGALL, JAMES K P01CA42792-05
MC DOUGALL, JAMES K R13CA55253-01
MC DOWELL, ELIZABETH M R01HL37640-05
MC DOWELL, FLETCHER H S15AG10246-01
MC DOWELL, THOMAS D R01DE07077-04A4
MC ELLIGOTT, DAVID L R29HL45993-01
MC ELLIGOTT, JAMES G R01DC01094-01
MC ENTEE, KEVIN R01GM29558-10
MC ENTEE, KEVIN R01GM38456-05
MC EVER, RODGER P R01HL34363-07
MC EVER, RODGER P R01HL45510-01
MC EVOY, ROBERT C R01DK43675-01
MC EWEN, BRUCE S P01MH43787-03 0002
MC EWEN, BRUCE S R01MH41256-06
MC EWEN, BRUCE S R01NS07080-25
MC FADDEN, DANIEL L P01AG05842-06 9001
MC FADDEN, DANIEL L P01AG05842-06 0003
MC FADDEN, DENNIS R01DC00153-12
MC FADDEN, E REGIS P01HL36110-07 0001
MC FADDEN, E REGIS, JR R01HL44920-01A1
MC FADDEN, EDWARD R, JR P50HL37117-05
MC FARLANE, WILLIAM R R18MH47642-02
MC GAHAN, MARY C R01EY04900-09
MC GARR, NANCY M P01DC00178-10 0001
MC GARRITY, THOMAS J R29CA45468-04
MC GARVEY, GLENN J R01AI17595-11
MC GARVEY, STEPHEN T R01AG09375-02
MC GAUGH, JAMES L R37MH12526-24
MC GHEE, JERRY R R01AI18958-10
MC GHEE, JERRY R R37DE04217-17
MC GIFF, JOHN C P01HL34300-07
MC GIFF, JOHN C R37HL25394-13
MC GILL, HENRY C. JR. N01HV53030-30
MC GILL, HENRY C, JR P01HL28972-10
MC GILL, HENRY C, JR S07RR05519-29
MC GILLIS, JOSEPH P R29NS29038-01A1
MC GINN, MICHAEL D K04DC00057-01
MC GINNIS, JAMES F R01EY06085-06
MC GINNIS, JAMES F R01EY06639-06
MC GINNIS, MICHAEL E R29NS26251-04
MC GINNIS, WILLIAM P01GM39813-04 0006
MC GINNIS, WILLIAM J R01HD28315-01
MC GINTY, JACQUELINE F R01DA03982-08
MC GIVERN, ROBERT F R01AA06478-06
MC GIVERN, ROBERT F R01DA04490-02
MC GLAVE, PHILIP B R01CA45814-04
MC GLYNN, KATHERINE A K07CA01591-01
MC GLYNN, SEAN P S07RR07039-20
MC GOWAN, EDWARD J R44AG07522-02
MC GOWAN, RICHARD S R29DC01247-01
MC GOWAN, STEPHEN E R01HL45135-01A1
MC GRAW, THOMAS P P51RR00169-30 0104
MC GRAW, THOMAS P P51RR00169-30 0105
MC GRAW, THOMAS P P51RR00169-30 0106
MC GUE, MATTHEW K R01AG06886-05
MC GUFFEE, LINDA J R01HL37015-04
MC GUIGAN, JAMES E R01DK13711-20
MC GUIRE, BARBARA A R01EY06792-05
MC GUIRE, JOHN J R01CA43500-06
MC GUIRE, PAUL G R29HL46865-01
MC GUIRE, THOMAS G K05MH00832-03
MC GUIRE, TRAVIS C R01AI24291-04A1
MC GUIRE, WILLIAM L P01CA30195-11
MC GUIRE, WILLIAM L P01CA30195-11 0007
MC GUIRE, WILLIAM L P01CA30195-11 9002
MC GUIRE, WILLIAM L R37CA11378-22
MC HUGH, KIRK M R29HD27252-02
MC HUGH, WILLIAM D S07RR05548-26

MC ILVANE, WILLIAM J R01HD28141-01
MC ILWAIN, DAVID L R01NS12103-15
MC ILWAIN, JAMES T R01EY02505-19
MC INTIRE, LARRY V P50NS23327-07 0008
MC INTIRE, LARRY V R01HL31588-07
MC INTIRE, LARRY V R37HL18672-14
MC INTOSH, J M K20MH00929-01
MC INTOSH, JOHN R R01GM33787-07
MC INTOSH, JOHN R R01GM36663-06
MC INTOSH, KENNETH U01AI25934-05
MC INTOSH, KENNETH U01AI25934-05 0001
MC INTOSH, MARK A R01GM40565-03
MC INTOSH, THOMAS J R01GM27278-10
MC INTOSH, THOMAS J S10RR06708-01
MC INTOSH, TRACY K R01GM34690-07
MC INTOSH, TRACY K R01NS26818-03
MC INTYRE, O ROSS P30CA23108-14
MC INTYRE, O ROSS P30CA23108-14 9012
MC INTYRE, O ROSS P30CA23108-14 9013
MC INTYRE, O ROSS U10CA39097-07
MC INTYRE, THOMAS M R01HL35828-06
MC IVER, ROBERT T, JR R01GM43910-01A1
MC KAY, DAVID B R01AI30606-02
MC KAY, DAVID B R01GM39928-05
MC KAY, DAVID B R01GM42938-03
MC KAY, DENNIS B R29NS24813-05
MC KAY, RONALD D R01NS21991-08
MC KEAN, DAVID J R01CA26297-12
MC KEARIN, DENNIS M R01GM45820-01
MC KEARNEY, JAMES W R01DA01015-17
MC KEE, ANN C K08NS01368-03
MC KEE, BRUCE D K04GM00522-04
MC KEE, BRUCE D R01GM40489-04
MC KEE, SUZANNE P P30EY06883-06
MC KEE, SUZANNE P R01EY06644-06
MC KEE, SUZANNE P U10EY07657-03
MC KEEHAN, WALLACE L P01CA37589-08 0005
MC KEEHAN, WALLACE L P01CA37589-08
MC KEEHAN, WALLACE L R01DK35310-06
MC KEEHAN, WALLACE L R01DK40739-03
MC KEEHAN, WALLACE L S07RR05863-11
MC KENNA, KEVIN P01NS17489-10 9003
MC KENNA, KEVIN E R01NS26157-03
MC KENNA, OLIVIA C S06GM08168-13 0018
MC KENZIE, FAUSTINO P01NS07464-24 9001
MC KENZIE, JAMES C R29HL45241-02
MC KEON, FRANK D R01GM37977-04
MC KEOWN-LONGO, PAULA J R01CA37785-07S1
MC KEOWN, MICHAEL B R01GM36549-05
MC KINLAY, JOHN B R37AG07182-05
MC KINLAY, SONJA M U01HL47098-01
MC KNIGHT, GEORGE S R01GM32875-08
MC KNIGHT, JENNIFER L R01AI26539-04
MC KOON, GAIL A R01DC01240-01
MC LACHLAN, ALAN R01DK33445-09
MC LAFFERTY, FRED W R01GM16609-23
MC LAUGHLIN, BARBARA J R01EY02853-13A1
MC LAUGHLIN, JERRY L R01CA30909-08
MC LAUGHLIN, LARRY W R01GM37065-06
MC LAUGHLIN, RONALD M G20RR07097-01
MC LAUGHLIN, STEVEN D R01AG09295-01A1
MC LAUGHLIN, STUART G R01GM24971-14
MC LELLAN, A THOMAS P50DA07705-01
MC LELLAN, A THOMAS R01DA05634-03
MC LENDON, GEORGE L R01GM33881-05
MC LEOD, RIMA L R01AI16945-10
MC LEOD, RIMA L R01AI27530-03
MC LOON, STEVEN C R01EY05371-07
MC LOYD, VONNIE C R01MH44662-04
MC MACKEN, ROGER L R01GM32253-09
MC MACKEN, ROGER L R01GM36526-06
MC MAHAN, C ALEX R10HL45719-01
MC MAHAN, UEL J R01NS14506-15
MC MAHON, DOUGLAS G R29EY09256-01
MC MAHON, LAURENCE F R01HS06486-02
MC MAHON, LILLIAN P60HL15157-20 9001
MC MAHON, LILLIAN P60HL15157-20
MC MAHON, LILLIAN P60HL15157-20 0001
MC MAHON, LILLIAN P60HL15157-20 0002
MC MAHON, LILLIAN P60HL15157-20 0003
MC MAHON, MICHAEL J R19DA06431-03
MC MAHON, ROBERT C R01DA05433-04
MC MANAMAN, JAMES R01NS23058-06
MC MANUS, LINDA M R01DE08000-05
MC MANUS, THOMAS J P60HL28391-09 0007
MC MICHAEL, ROBERT F S03RR03418-07
MC MILLAN, DONALD E R01DA02251-13A1
MC MILLAN, DONALD E S15MH49512-01
MC MILLAN, JAMES A S06GM08218-08 0004
MC MILLAN, MINNIE R01GM36804-09
MC MILLAN, PAUL N S15DK44672-01
MC MILLAN, ROBERT R01HL37945-19
MC MORRIS, ARTHUR P50NS11036-18 0015
MC MORRIS, F ARTHUR R01NS26119-04
MC MULLEN, NATHANIEL T R03DC01210-01
MC MURRAY, DAVID N R01AI15495-10A1
MC MURRAY, DAVID N R01AI27204-02
MC NALLY, RICHARD J R29MH43809-03
MC NAMARA, DONALD J R01HD22954-01A3
MC NAMARA, JAMES O P01NS17771-10 0001
MC NAMARA, JAMES O P01NS17771-10 9001
MC NAMARA, JAMES O P01NS17771-10
MC NAMARA, JAMES O P50NS06233-25 0045
MC NAMARA, JAMES O R01NS24448-05
MC NAMARA, JOHN P R29HD24529-04
MC NAMARA, PAMELA P01DK40555-04 0005
MC NAMARA, PAMELA P01DK40555-04 9001
MC NAMEE, MARK G R01NS13050-16
MC NEIL, BARBARA J U01CA45256-04S2
MC NEIL, BARBARA J U01CA54019-01
MC NEILL, THOMAS H P01AG03644-07 0005
MC NEILL, THOMAS H R01NS30426-01
MC PHEE, STEPHEN J R01CA54569-01
MC PHERSON, ALEXANDER R01GM40706-04
MC QUEEN, CHARLENE A S15ES05839-01
MC REA, JAMES C R43HL47257-01
MC REE, DUNCAN E R29GM44841-02
MC REYNOLDS, JOHN S R01EY01653-15
MC ROBERTS, JAMES A R01DK42874-01A1
MC VEIGH, ELLIOT R R29HL45683-01A1
MC WHORTER, WILLIAM P U01CA53807-01
MCADOO, DAVID J P01NS11255-17 9002
MCADOO, DAVID J P01NS11255-17 0029
MCAFEE, JOHN G R01CA32853-15
MCALARNEY, MONA S07RR05331-28 0739
MCALISTER, ALFRED L S07RR05828-08 0527
MCALPINE, JAMES B U01AI30183-02 9001
MCARDLE, JOSEPH J R01AA08025-03
MCARTHUR, J P01NS26643-04 9001
MCARTHUR, JUSTIN C M01RR00722-19 0226
MCARTHUR, WILLIAM P. P50DE07117-07 0003
MCBRIDE, A A Z01CP05662-01
MCBRIDE, ANGELA B S07RR06011-02
MCBRIDE, ANNE P M01RR06020-02 0435
MCBRIDE, DUNCAN S07RR05551-29 0954
MCBRIDE, JOHN T S07RR05403-30 0813
MCBRIDE, MOLLY M01RR00350-25 0372
MCBRIDE, O W Z01CB05202-24
MCBRIDE, P ANNE R29MH44177-03
MCBRIDE, WILLIAM J P01AA08553-02 0003
MCBURNEY, ROBERT N R44NS27381-03
MCBURNEY, WENDELL F S07RR07227-02
MCCABE, EDWARD P30HG00210-01 9005
MCCABE, JOSEPH T R01NS25913-04
MCCACHREN, S SPENCE P50AR39162-05 0003
MCCAFFREY, ROBERT J S07RR07122-23 0106
MCCAFFREY, ROBERT J S07RR07122-23 0107
MCCAFFREY, RONALD P U01CA48626-04 0002
MCCAFFREY, RONALD P U01CA52020-02
MCCAFFREY, RONALD P U01CA52020-02 0001
MCCAFFREY, TIMOTHY S07RR05396-30 0753
MCCAFFREY, TIMOTHY A P01HL46403-01 0006
MCCAFFREY, TIMOTHY A R29HL42606-02
MCCALL, ANTHONY L P01NS17493-08 0010
MCCALL, ANTHONY L R01NS22213-05
MCCALL, JOHN N01AI15107-00
MCCALL, MARK B S07RR05918-08 0705
MCCALLIE, DAVID P30HD18655-10 9008
MCCALLUM, RICHARD W M01RR00847-18 0445
MCCALLUM, RICHARD W M01RR00847-18 0560
MCCALLUM, RICHARD W M01RR00847-18 0561
MCCALLUM, RICHARD W M01RR00847-18 0558
MCCALLUM, RICHARD W M01RR00847-18 0499
MCCAMAN, MARILYN W R01NS23273-06
MCCANCE, DENNIS J R01AI30798-02
MCCANN, FRANCES V S07RR05392-30 0698
MCCANN, MARGARET F S07RR05450-30 0341
MCCANNAL, C A M01RR00585-20 0466
MCCAREY, BERNARD E P51RR00165-31 0123
MCCARRICK, ANNE S07RR06014-03 0835
MCCARRON, R M Z01NS02324-14
MCCARRON, R M Z01NS02776-03
MCCARRON, R M Z01NS02780-04
MCCARRON, R M Z01NS02801-03
MCCARRON, R M Z01NS02802-03
MCCARTER, LINDA L R29GM43196-02
MCCARTER, ROGER P01AG01188-13
MCCARTHY, BRIAN J. P01HL41633-03 9003
MCCARTHY, BRIAN J. P01HL41633-03 0007
MCCARTHY, CHARLOTTE S07RR07154-16 0558
MCCARTHY, CHARLOTTE S07RR07154-16 0559
MCCARTHY, CHARLOTTE S07RR07154-16 0556
MCCARTHY, CHARLOTTE M S07RR07154-16
MCCARTHY, DENNIS J R01HL41889-03
MCCARTHY, DONNA R29NR02258-03
MCCARTHY, DONNA O S07RR05866-08 0989
MCCARTHY, JOHN M S07RR07123-22 0595
MCCARTHY, MICHELINE S07RR05745-19 0257
MCCARTHY, PHILIP L K08AI00926-03
MCCARTHY, SUSAN A S07RR05416-30 0569
MCCARTHY, WALTER J S07RR05370-30 0628
MCCARTNEY-FRANCIS, N L Z01DE00424-05
MCCARTON, CECELIA P30HD01799-27 9001
MCCARTY, DENNIS R19DA06449-03
MCCARTY, RICHARD S07RR07094-26 0356
MCCASLIN, DARRELL R S07RR07059-26 0834
MCCASLIN, PATRICK P R29DA05737-02
MCCHESNEY, JAMES D R01CA55127-01
MCCLAIN, C J M01RR02602-07 0045
MCCLAIN, CRAIG J M01RR02602-07 0047
MCCLANAHAN, MARK M01RR00065-29 0361
MCCLAY, EDWARD F M01RR00827-17 0465
MCCLAY, EDWARD F M01RR00827-17 0471
MCCLAY, EDWARD F R01CA52151-02
MCCLEARN, GERALD E P01DA07171-01
MCCLEARN, GERALD E P01DA07171-01 0003
MCCLEARN, GERALD E R01AA08125-03
MCCLEARN, GERALD E R01AG08861-02
MCCLEARN, GERALD E R01AG09333-02
MCCLELLAN, ANDREW S07RR07053-26 0166
MCCLELLAN, LINDA P60HL38737-04 0005
MCCLISH, DONNA K U01AG05170-07 9001
MCCLOSKEY, JAMES A. P30CA42014-06 9011
MCCLOSKEY, JOANNE C R01NR02079-02
MCCLOSKEY, MICHAEL A S07RR07034-26 0064
MCCLUER, ROBERT H P30HD04147-22A1
MCCLUER, ROBERT H S07RR05730-20
MCCLURE, HAROLD M P51RR00165-31 0124
MCCLURE, HAROLD M P51RR00165-31 0198
MCCLURE, HAROLD M P51RR00165-31 0202
MCCLURE, HAROLD M P51RR00165-31 0203
MCCLURE, HAROLD M P51RR00165-31 0127
MCCLURE, HAROLD M P51RR00165-31 0181
MCCLURE, HAROLD M P51RR00165-31 0182
MCCLURE, HAROLD M P51RR00165-31 0131
MCCLURE, HAROLD M P51RR00165-31 0210
MCCLURE, HAROLD M P51RR00165-31 0132
MCCLURE, HAROLD M P51RR00165-31 0133
MCCLURE, HAROLD M P51RR00165-31 0134
MCCLURE, HAROLD M. P51RR00165-31 9002
MCCLURE, MARCELLA A R01AI28309-02
MCCLURE, POLLEY A S07RR07031-26 0099
MCCLURE, SHEILA A S06GM08241-07 0004
MCCLURE, SUZANNE M01RR00073-29 0324
MCCLURE, WILLIAM S07RR07012-25 0017
MCCLUSKEY, ROBERT T P01DK38452-05 0005
MCCOMBIE, W R Z01NS02837-01
MCCOMBS, ROBERT M S03RR03176-09
MCCONNAHA, DEBRA L S07RR05962-05 0015
MCCONNEL, FRED P01CA40007-06A1 0001
MCCONNEL, FRED P01CA40007-06A1 0004
MCCONNELL, DAVID S07RR05772-17 0361
MCCONNELL, HARDEN M R37AI13587-16
MCCONNELL, ROSE S06GM08211-09 0010
MCCONNELL, ROSE S06GM08211-09 0010
MCCONNELL, SUSAN S07RR07005-26 0340
MCCONNELL, SUSAN K R01EY08411-03
MCCOOL, FRANKLIN D R01HL39811-03
MCCORD, JEFFREY D S07RR05460-29 0368
MCCORKLE, RUTH P50NR02324-03
MCCORMACK, JOHN N01CM87286-04
MCCORMICK, DANIEL J P50HD09140-16 0008
MCCORMICK, DAVID A P01NS22807-07 0005
MCCORMICK, DAVID L S07RR05744-14 0140
MCCORMICK, FRANK U01CA51992-02 0001
MCCORMICK, FRANK P U01CA51992-02
MCCORMICK, J J N01ES65152-11
MCCORMICK, J JUSTIN S07RR05772-17
MCCORMICK, J JUSTIN S07RR05772-17 0343
MCCORMICK, K A Z01AG00601-03
MCCORMICK, K A Z01AG00602-03
MCCORQUODALE, D JAME S07RR05700-22 0862
MCCORQUODALE, D JAME S07RR05700-22 0887
MCCOWN, DARLENE E S07RR05952-06
MCCOY, PHILIP J. P30CA47904-04 9008
MCCOY, BRUCE S07RR05795-14 0421
MCCOY, CLYDE B R18DA05349-03S1
MCCOY, KATHLEEN L S07RR05430-30 0216
MCCOY, KATHLEEN L S07RR05724-20 0180
MCCRACKEN, GEORGE H M01RR00633-19 0366
MCCRACKEN, GEORGE H P01HD22766-05 9001
MCCRACKEN, GEORGE H P01HD22766-05 9002
MCCRACKEN, JAMES T M01RR00425-22S3 0448
MCCRACKEN, JAMES T M01RR00425-22S3 0412
MCCRACKEN, JOHN P01HD20290-06A1 9001
MCCRACKEN, M C S07RR05333-30 0870
MCCRAE, KEITH R S07RR07083-26 0475
MCCRAE, R R Z01AG00180-05
MCCRARY, JOHN A M01RR00350-25 0403
MCCRAY, JOSEPH W S06GM45199-02 0007
MCCRIMMON, DONALD P01NS17489-10 0009
MCCRIMMON, DONALD R R01HL40336-03
MCCRONE, SUSAN S07RR05973-05 0786
MCCUBBIN, JAMES A M01RR02602-07 0051
MCCUBBIN, JAMES A R01HL32738-06
MCCUBBIN, MARILYN A R29NR02563-02
MCCULLOCH, ANDREW P01HL43026-02 9002
MCCULLOCH, CHRISTOPHER A G P40RR03640-05 0
MCCULLOUGH, DOUGLAS R44AI26430-03
MCCULLOUGH, J JEFFREY U01HL42802-03
MCCULLY, KEVIN S07RR05418-30 0026
MCCUMBEE, WILLIAM D S07RR05870-10 0993
MCCUNE, CRAIG S M01RR00044-31 0385
MCCUNE, JOSEPH M01RR00042-31 0509
MCCUNE, JOSEPH M R01AI29323-03
MCCUNE, W JOSEPH M01RR00042-31 0549
MCCUNE, W JOSEPH M01RR00042-31 0592
MCCURDY, PAUL R N01CL62104-18
MCCURLEY, THOMAS L S07RR05424-30 0115
MCCUSKER, KEVIN T S07RR05428-30 0162
MCCUSKEY, R P50AA08037-04 0001
MCCUSKEY, ROBERT P01HD26013-01A2 0004
MCCUTCHAN, J ALLEN P50MH45294-03 9001
MCCUTCHAN, T Z01AI00208-11
MCDANIEL, ANTONIO R01HD27485-01
MCDANIEL, KEITH D S07RR05403-30 0814

MCDANIEL, LARRY S R01AI27201-03
MCDANIEL, MARK A S07RR07032-26 0026
MCDANIEL, NANCY L S07RR05431-30 0844
MCDAVID, WILLIAM D S07RR05897-09 0268
MCDEVITT, DAVID S07RR05464-29 0374
MCDEVITT, HUGH P01AI19512-09 0013
MCDEVITT, HUGH P01AI19512-09 9001
MCDEVITT, HUGH O P50NS23724-06 0001
MCDIARMID, R Z01DK29008-20
MCDONAGH, JAN R01HL29512-11
MCDONALD, A BRUCE P01AI24760-05 0003
MCDONALD, ALEXANDER J R01NS19733-08
MCDONALD, CURTIS W S06GM08061-17 0013
MCDONALD, DOUGLAS J S07RR05388-30 0616
MCDONALD, GEORGE B P01CA18029-16 9010
MCDONALD, ISABEL P51RR00163-32 9010
MCDONALD, J KEN S07RR05767-17 0324
MCDONALD, JOHN K R01HD24701-03
MCDONALD, JOHN K R01HD26833-01A1
MCDONALD, KENT L P41RR00592-22 0011
MCDONALD, KENT L P41RR00592-22 0012
MCDONALD, KENT L P41RR00592-22 0013
MCDONALD, L J Z01HL00655-01
MCDONALD, MARGUERITE B R01EY08101-03
MCDONALD, MARGUERITE B R01EY03635-11
MCDONALD, ROBERT L P01NS19613-07 9002
MCDONNELL, JAN M R01EY08889-02
MCDONOUGH, STEPHEN L U01CA50133-03
MCDOUGALL, JAMES E P01CA42792-05 0002
MCDOUGALL, JAMES K P01AI29363-02 0004
MCDOUGALL, JAMES K P01CA42792-05 9003
MCDOUGALL, S S07RR05354-30 0380
MCDOWALL, A P41RR02250-06 0012
MCDOWALL, DAVID S07RR07122-23 0098
MCDOWD, JOAN M R29AG07991-02
MCDOWELL, FLETCHER H S07RR06018-03
MCDOWELL, FLETCHER H S07RR06018-03 0310
MCDOWELL, KAREN J S07RR07114-23 0445
MCDOWELL, THOMAS D S06GM08139-17 0047
MCDOWELL, WILLIAM H P42ES04913-02 0004
MCDUFFIE, MARCIA P01DK40144-04 9003
MCDUFFIE, MARCIA P01DK40144-04 0004
MCEACHRON, D L P41RR01638-07 0024
MCEACHRON, D L P41RR01638-07 0026
MCELLIGOTT, DAVID P01HG00202-02 9003
MCELLIGOTT, DAVID P01HG00202-02 9001
MCELLIGOTT, DAVID L P01HG00202-02 9002
MCEVOY, CATHY L R01MH45207-03
MCEVOY, K M M01RR00585-20 0544
MCEWEN, BRUCE SW S07RR07065-26 0066
MCEWEN, JOAN S07RR07009-26 0926
MCEWEN, JOAN E R01GM36192-04A2
MCFADDEN, E REGIS JR M01RR00080-29 0558
MCFADDEN, E R M01RR00080-29 0327
MCFADDEN, E R, JR R01HL33791-08
MCFADDEN, E REGIS M01RR00080-29 0353
MCFADDEN, E REGIS M01RR00080-29 0427
MCFADDEN, E REGIS JR M01RR00080-29 0451
MCFADDEN, E REGIS JR M01RR00080-29 0403
MCFADDEN, EDWARD R, JR P50HL37117-05 0001
MCFALL-NAGAI, MARGAR S07RR07012-25 0018
MCFARLAND, BENTSON H P50MH43458-04
MCFARLAND, BENTSON H R01MH45015-02
MCFARLAND, H F Z01NS02205-16
MCFARLAND, JANICE G U01HL42832-03
MCFARLIN, D E Z01NS02202-16
MCFARLIN, D E Z01NS02204-16
MCGADNEY, BRENDA F R03AG10390-01
MCGAGHIE, WILLIAM C P60AR30701-10 0016
MCGANITY, P L J S07RR05654-24 0118
MCGARRITY, MICHAEL R19DA06425-03
MCGARRITY, THOMAS J S07RR05680-23 0912
MCGARRY, J DENIS P01DK42582-02 0003
MCGEE, DANIEL P01CA41108-05 9001
MCGEE, DANIEL P01CA41183-05 9001
MCGEE, DANIELLE P01CA17094-16 9002
MCGEE, MARIA P R01HL42812-03
MCGEE, ZELL A M01RR00064-27 0365
MCGHEE, JERRY N01AI15128-00
MCGHEE, JERRY P01DK44240-01 0002
MCGIFF, JOHN C P01HL34300-07 0001
MCGILL JR, HENRY C P01HL28972-10 0007
MCGILL, JANET M01RR00036-31 1013
MCGILL, JANET M01RR00036-31 1014
MCGILL, JANET M01RR00036-31 1015
MCGILL, JANET M01RR00036-31 1016
MCGILLIS, JOSEPH S07RR05374-30 0747
MCGINNIS, ETHELEEN K14HL02334-03
MCGINNIS, ETHELENE S06GM08037-20 0052
MCGINNIS, MARILYN Y S07RR05653-24 0802
MCGLAVE, PHILIP P01CA21737-14 0005
MCGLOTHIN, MARK W N01HD13110-00
MCGLYNN, KATHERINE A S07RR05895-09 0609
MCGONIGLE, PAUL P01GM34781-07 0002
MCGONIGLE, PAUL R29MH43821-04
MCGOVERN, PATRICIA MARIE R03HS06950-01
MCGOWAN, JOHN J N01AI72662-12
MCGRATH, CHARLES M R44CA51595-02
MCGRATH, MARGARET M R29NR02263-03
MCGRATH, MICHAEL P01AI24286-05 0004
MCGRATH, MICHAEL P01AI24286-05 0006
MCGRATH, MICHAEL S R01CA54743-01
MCGRAW, SARAH A R18CA39304-05S1
MCGUE, MATTHEW P41RR01632-09 0028
MCGUFFEE, LINDA J S06GM08139-17 0048
MCGUINNESS, GAIL A. M01RR00059-30 0613
MCGUINNESS, OWEN P60DK20593-13 0002
MCGUIRE, DEBORAH P30CA06973-29 9016
MCGUIRE, EDWARD J P50DK39257-05 0001
MCGUIRE, JOHN J P01CA13038-19 0112
MCGUIRE, JOSEPH M S07RR07079-26 0286
MCGUIRE, JOSEPH S R01AR41551-01 0004
MCGUIRE, KATHLEEN L S07RR07004-16 0051
MCGUIRE, MICHAEL J S07RR05426-30 0143
MCGUIRE, TRAVIS C S07RR05465-29 0381
MCGUIRE, WILLIAM J R01MH32588-11
MCGURN, WEALTHA P20NR03039-01 0002
MCGURN, WEALTHA C P20NR03039-01
MCGURN, WEALTHA C S07RR05654-24 0127
MCHALE, PHILIP A S03RR03342-09
MCHENRY, CHARLES S R01AI26600-03
MCHENRY, CHARLES S R01GM35695-06A1
MCHENRY, CHARLES S R01GM36255-07
MCHUGH, E Z01BB07002-02
MCHUGH, KIRK M S07RR05414-30 0996
MCILROY, MALCOLM B P50HL27356-10 0006
MCILROY, PATRICK J R01HD22791-03
MCILVANE, WILLIAM J P01HD25995-03 9001
MCILVANE, WILLIAM J P01HD25995-03 9002
MCILVANE, WILLIAM J P01HD25995-03 0002
MCILVANE, WILLIAM J P30HD04147-22A1 9014
MCILWRAITH C WAYNE S07RR05458-29 0831
MCINTIRE, SARAH A S07RR07218-05 0461
MCINTOSH, J RICHARD P41RR00592-22 0014
MCINTOSH, J RICHARD P41RR00592-22 0022
MCINTOSH, J RICHARD P41RR00592-22
MCINTOSH, J RICHARD P41RR00592-22 0016
MCINTOSH, KENNETH M01RR02172-09 0165
MCINTOSH, KENNETH M01RR02172-09 0191
MCINTOSH, KENNETH M01RR02172-09 0173
MCINTOSH, KENNETH M01RR02172-09 0186
MCINTOSH, KENNETH M01RR02172-09 0192
MCINTOSH, KENNETH U01AI25934-05 9001
MCINTOSH, MICHAEL K S07RR07248-03 0710
MCINTOSH, NANCY A M01RR00042-31 0604
MCINTYRE, O ROSS U10CA37447-08
MCINTYRE, ROSS O U10CA31946-10
MCINTYRE, THOMAS M R01HL44513-02
MCIVOR, R S R01AI27416-03
MCIVOR, R S R29CA46878-04
MCKANNA, JAMES P01CA43720-05 0006
MCKAY, CHARLES S07RR05372-30 0680
MCKAY, DAVID P01GM30387-10 0010
MCKAY, JUDITH M01RR00865-18 0365
MCKAY, JUDITH M01RR00865-18 0366
MCKEAN, D J P01CA31224-06S1 0005
MCKEAN, DAVID J P30CA15083-18 0002
MCKEAN, DAVID J P30CA15083-18 9010
MCKEAN, DAVID J S03RR03555-01
MCKEAN, THOMAS A S07RR07170-15 0604
MCKEARIN, DENNIS M S07RR07175-15 0438
MCKEE, DAPHNE P50MH33127-13 9002
MCKEE, SUZANNE P S07RR05981-05 0802
MCKEEHAN, WALLACE L P01DK38639-04 0001
MCKEEHAN, WALLACE L S07RR05863-11 0568
MCKEEL, DANIEL W JR P50AG05681-08 9004
MCKEEL, DANIEL W. P01AG03991-08 9003
MCKEEVER, PAUL E R29CA47558-04
MCKEITHAN, TIMOTHY W R01CA55356-01
MCKEITHAN, TIMOTHY WAYNE R29CA49207-03
MCKENNA, CHARLES E U01AI25697-05 0001
MCKENNA, KEVIN E P01NS17489-10 0010
MCKENNA, KEVIN E P20NS30295-01 0003
MCKENNA, WILLIAM G R01CA51149-02
MCKENNEY, PATRICIA S07RR05487-29 0713
MCKENNY, JAMES M01RR00065-29 0350
MCKENZIE, R Z01AI00469-06
MCKEON, C Z01DK47028-02
MCKEOWN-LONGO, PAULA J P01GM40761-01A2 000
MCKERROW, JAMES H R01AI20452-08
MCKIM, JAMES M S06GM08212-08 0013
MCKINLAY, JOHN B R01HD25026-03
MCKINLAY, SONJA M N01AI05072-06
MCKINLAY, SONJA M N01HB97073-08
MCKINLAY, SONJA M N01HD82908-10
MCKINLEY, MICHAEL P P01AG02132-11 0006
MCKINNEY, MICHAEL P01AG09973-01 0004
MCKINNEY, ROSS E U01AI27535-03 0002
MCKNIGHT, A JAMES R01AA08370-02
MCKNIGHT, G STANLEY P50DK41978-03 0002
MCKNIGHT, G STANLEY P50HD12629-12 0009
MCKNIGHT, THOMAS S07RR07090-26 0477
MCKUSICK, VICTOR A M01RR00035-31 0388
MCKUSICK, VICTOR P41HG00586-01 0003
MCKUSICK, VICTOR A P01HG00373-04
MCLACHLAN, ALAN M01RR00833-17 0186
MCLACHLAN, ALAN M01RR00833-17 0187
MCLACHLAN, ALAN R01AI30070-01A1
MCLACHLAN, ALAN R29AI25183-05
MCLACHLAN, J A Z01ES70060-18
MCLAIN, ROGER N01CN15387-00
MCLANAHAN, SARA S R01HD19375-08
MCLANE, JERRY A R01AA07399-03
MCLARTY, JERRY W U01CA34290-08
MCLAUGHLIN-TAYLOR, E S07RR05471-29 0586
MCLAUGHLIN-TAYLOR, ELIZABETH P01CA30206-10
MCLAUGHLIN, A C Z01AA00038-04
MCLAUGHLIN, A C Z01AA00039-04
MCLAUGHLIN, A C Z01AA00040-04
MCLAUGHLIN, A C Z01AA00042-03
MCLAUGHLIN, A C Z01AA00051-02
MCLAUGHLIN, A C Z01AA00052-01
MCLAUGHLIN, A C Z01AA00053-01
MCLAUGHLIN, A C Z01AA00056-01
MCLAUGHLIN, GERALD LEE R01EY08205-04
MCLAUGHLIN, JERRY L S07RR05586-24 0117
MCLAUGHLIN, JOHN S07RR05655-21 0806
MCLAUGHLIN, JOHN F R01NS27867-01A2
MCLAUGHLIN, LARRY W S07RR07156-16 0567
MCLAUGHLIN, MARGARET S07RR05408-30 0932
MCLEAN, J E P01HD18955-07 0006
MCLEAN, JUDITH S07RR07241-04 0699
MCLEAN, ROBERT H M01RR00722-19 0227
MCLELLAN, A THOMAS P50DA05186-05 0004
MCLELLAN, A THOMAS P50DA07705-01 0001
MCLELLAN, A THOMAS P50DA07705-01 9001
MCLELLAN, A THOMAS P50DA07705-01 0004
MCLEOD, JANE D R29MH48211-01
MCLEOD, JANE D S07RR07052-26 0163
MCLOON, LINDA P30HD24051-03 9005
MCLOON, LINDA K R01EY07935-03
MCMACKEN, R P30ES03819-06A1 9020
MCMAHAN, C ALEX P01HL28972-10 9004
MCMAHON-PRATT, DIANE M R01AI23004-07
MCMAHON-PRATT, DIANE M R01AI27811-03
MCMAHON, J Z01CM07191-01
MCMAHON, KATHRYN S07RR05773-17 0364
MCMAHON, L F P60AR20557-13 0065
MCMANUS, C Z01DE00044-21
MCMICHAEL, THOMAS S07RR05704-20 0004
MCMILLAN, CAMPBELL W M01RR00046-31 0363
MCMILLAN, CAMPBELL W M01RR00046-31 0440
MCMILLAN, MINNIE P01NS18146-10 0008
MCMILLAN, MINNIE P01NS26991-02 0004
MCMILLAN, MINNIE P01NS26991-02 9002
MCMILLAN, MINNIE P30CA14089-16 9001
MCMILLIAN, M Z01ES90059-02
MCMILLIAN, M K Z01ES90067-01
MCMILLIN, DAVID P41RR02583-07 0011
MCMORRIS, TREVOR C S06GM47165-01 0004
MCMULLEN, NATANIEL T S07RR05675-23 0915
MCMURRAY, CYNTHIA T S07RR05530-29 0528
MCMURRAY, MARTHA P M01RR00064-27 0294
MCMURRAY, MARTHA P M01RR00064-27 0343
MCMURRY, T Z01CM06390-03
MCMURTY , IVAN F. P01HL14985-20 0025
MCNABB, WYLIE P60DK20595-14 9007
MCNAIL, BARBARA J P01HS06341-03 0002
MCNAIR, DAVID S03RR03267-10
MCNAMARA, A M Z01CL10195-01
MCNAMARA, A M Z01CL10196-01
MCNAMARA, ROBERT M S07RR05418-30 0028
MCNAMEE, MARK G R01NS22941-04A1
MCNAUGHTON, BRUCE R01MH46823-02
MCNAUGHTON, BRUCE L R01NS20331-09
MCNEAL, MERYL U76PE00038-08
MCNEARNEY, TERRY ANN K11AI00972-02
MCNEIL, BARBARA J P01HS06341-03
MCNEIL, BARBARA J P01HS06341-03 0001
MCNEIL, DALE S07RR05755-18 0227
MCNEIL, PAUL L R01CA42275-05
MCNEILL, BARBARA P01CA41167-06 9003
MCNEILL, THOMAS H P01AG09793-01 0002
MCNULTY, WILBUR P P51RR00163-32 9002
MCNUTT, ROBERT A R01HS06125-02
MCPHAIL, LINDA C R01AI22564-07
MCPHEE, RICHARD S07RR05321-30 0257
MCPHERSON, C P30DK34987-06 9003
MCPHERSON, CHARLES W G20RR07079-01
MCPHERSON, ROBERT W P01NS20020-08 9003
MCPHIE, P Z01DK17004-23
MCQUEEN, CHARLENE A R01ES05174-03
MCQUEEN, CHARLENE A R01GM39390-05
MCQUEEN, NANCY L R15AI31191-01
MCQUILLEN, DANIEL P K11AI01061-01
MCQUILLEN, DANIEL P S07RR05569-27 0123
MCSHERRY, SUSAN M01RR00046-31 0487
MCVARY, KEVIN T S07RR05370-30 0622
MCWHORTER, WILLIAM M01RR00064-27 0388
MCWHORTER, WILLIAM N01CN05222-08
MCWHORTER, WILLIAM P. P30CA42014-06 9010
MCWILLIAMS, BENNIE M01RR00997-16 0377
MCWILLIAMS, BENNIE M01RR00997-16 0346
MCWILLIAMS, BENNIE C N01HR16046-00
MCWILLIAMS, BETTY J M01RR00084-29 0251
MEACCI, E Z01HL00652-02
MEAD, KEITH T R15GM46141-01
MEAD, RODNEY A R01HD06556-19
MEAD, RODNEY A S07RR07170-15 0606
MEAD, RODNEY A S15ES05838-01
MEADE, B D Z01BA07001-23
MEADE, B D Z01BA07003-03
MEADE, B D Z01BA07005-08
MEADE, B D Z01BA07006-02
MEADE, MICHAEL S07RR05755-18 0240
MEADOR-WOODRUFF, JAMES H K01MH00818-02

MEADOWS, ANNA T U10CA11796-22
MEADOWS, GARY G K02AA00138-01
MEADOWS, GARY G R01AA07293-05
MEADOWS, GARY G R01CA42465-04A2
MEADOWS, HAROLD L R19DA06433-03
MEAGHER, RICHARD B R01GM36397-06
MEANEY, MICHAEL J R01AG09488-01
MEANS, ANTHONY R P30HD07495-19 9015
MEANS, ANTHONY R R01DK43071-02
MEANS, ANTHONY R R01GM33976-08
MEARES, CLAUDE F P01CA47829-04 0004
MEARES, CLAUDE F R01GM25909-13
MEARES, CLAUDE F R37CA16861-17
MEBERT, CAROLYN J R29HD23351-05
MECHAM, ROBERT P P01HL29594-09 0005
MECHAM, ROBERT P R01HL26499-10
MECHAM, ROBERT P R01HL41926-03
MECHANIC, DAVID P50MH43450-04 0012
MECHANIC, DAVID P50MH43450-04
MECHANIC, DAVID P50MH43450-04 0008
MECHOULAM, RAPHAEL R01DA06481-02
MECK, WARREN H P01AG09525-01 0003
MECK, WARREN H R29NS24794-04
MECKSTROTH, DIANE M01RR00069-29 0460
MEDEIROS, DENIS M R01HL34286-05
MEDFORD, RUSSELL M R55HL45933-01A1
MEDIADORA, SANIEL P50AI30601-01 9001
MEDIADORA, SANIEL P50AI30601-01 9002
MEDINA, DANIEL P01CA45164-04A1 0003
MEDINA, DANIEL R01CA11944-19
MEDINA, DANIEL R01CA47112-04
MEDINA, DANIEL R13CA55154-01
MEDINA, FREDDY R S06GM08159-13 0004
MEDINA, MIGUEL A S03RR03305-09
MEDNICK, SARNOFF P50MH44188-03 0001
MEDNICK, SARNOFF P50MH44188-03 9001
MEDNICK, SARNOFF A K05MH00619-06
MEDNICK, SARNOFF A R01MH46014-02
MEDNICK, SARNOFF A S07RR07012-25 0019
MEDOF, M P01DK38181-05 0001
MEDOF, M EDWARD R01AI23598-06
MEDOFF-COOPER, BARBA S07RR05948-05 0329
MEDOFF-COOPER, BARBA S07RR07083-26 0476
MEDOFF-COOPER, BARBARA S R01NR02093-03
MEDOFF, GERALD U01AI25903-05 0009
MEDOFF, GERALD U01AI25903-05 0005
MEDRANO, JUAN F S07RR07007-26 0924
MEDSGER, THOMAS M01RR00056-30 0363
MEDSGER, THOMAS R18AR21393-17 0028
MEDVECAKY, PETER G S07RR05749-19 0271
MEDVECZKY, PETER R01CA43264-06
MEDZIHRADSKY, FEDOR P50DA00254-20 0009
MEDZIHRADSKY, FEDOR R01DA04087-05
MEEDEL, THOMAS H S07RR05547-23 0077
MEEHAN, EDWARD S07RR07244-03 0487
MEEHAN, EDWARD S07RR07244-03 0488
MEEHAN, THOMAS D R01CA40598-08
MEEK (HASEMANN), KAT S07RR07175-15 0439
MEEK, ALLEN G S07RR05736-19 0194
MEEK, KATHERYN D P01AI31229-01 0003
MEEKER, TIMOTHY C K08CA01102-06
MEEKS, SUZANNE R29MH44787-02
MEENAN, ROBERT F P60AR20613-14
MEENAN, ROBERT F P60AR20613-14 0011
MEENHARD, HERLYN P01CA25874-12 9001
MEERS S07RR05380-30 0891
MEERS, PAUL R R29GM41790-02
MEEUWSEN, HARRY J S07RR07218-05 0460
MEEZAN, ELIAS R01DK34949-07
MEFFORD, I N Z01MH01860-01
MEFFORD, I N Z01MH02322-01
MEGIBOW, ALEC J U01CA49079-03
MEHANDRU, PERM M01RR00080-29 0663
MEHDI, BOROUJERDI S07RR05830-12 0967
MEHRABAN, FUAD P60AR20618-13 9004
MEHROTRA, BAM D S06GM08110-20 0008
MEHTA, CYRUS R R01CA33019-09
MEHTA, CYRUS R R44CA46973-03
MEHTA, RAJENDRE N01CN95173-03
MEHTA, RAJESHWARI R N01CM97567-05
MEHTA, RAJESHWARI R R29CA46423-04
MEHTA, RAVINDRA L R01HS06466-02
MEIER, DIANE M01RR00071-28A1 0141
MEIER, DIANE E K08AG00358-05
MEIER, DIANE E R01AG07113-05
MEIER, GUY P R29AI28559-03
MEIER, KATHRYN P01GM42508-03 0004
MEIER, PAULA P R29NR01935-04
MEIKLE, A WAYNE M01RR00064-27 0377
MEIKLE, A WAYNE M01RR00064-27 0167
MEIKLE, A WAYNE R55DK43344-01
MEIKLE, WAYNE M01RR00064-27 0384
MEILLER, TIMOTHY F K15DE00168-05
MEINCKE-REZA, JEFF S07RR05372-30 0692
MEINERS, NORWOOD P51RR00164-30 9011
MEINERT, CURTIS L U10EY08057-04
MEINERT, CURTIS L U10EY09152-02
MEINERTZHAGEN, IAN A R01EY03592-11
MEINHOLD, CHARLES B R01CA18001-25
MEININGER, CYNTHIA J S07RR05814-12 0151
MEINKOTH, JUDY L S07RR05665-24 0897
MEINTS, RUSSEL S07RR07079-26 0302
MEINWALD, JERROLD R01AI12020-19
MEIRI, KARINA F R29NS26091-04
MEIROVITCH, EVA R43GM46614-01
MEIS, PAUL J U10HD27860-01
MEISCH, RICHARD A K05DA00159-01
MEISCH, RICHARD A R01DA04972-03
MEISCH, RICHARD A R01DA06324-02
MEISEL, MARTIN S15GM47077-01
MEISEL, ROBERT L R01HD21478-04A3
MEISELMAN, HERBERT J R01HL41341-03
MEISELMAN, HERBERT J R37HL15722-19
MEISENHELDER, JANICE S07RR05591-27 0657
MEISLEER, MIRIAM P60DK20572-14 0046
MEISLER, MIRIAM P30DK34933-06A1 0010
MEISLER, MIRIAM H P30DK34933-06A1 9001
MEISLER, MIRIAM H R01DK36089-07
MEISLER, MIRIAM H R01GM24872-14
MEISLER, NEIL R18MH46061-02
MEISSNER, GERHARD P01HL27430-10 0001
MEISSNER, GERHARD W R37AR18687-16
MEISTER, ALTON R37DK12034-25
MEISTRICH, MARVIN L R01CA17364-14
MEISTRICH, MARVIN L R01HD16843-08
MEIZEL, STANLEY R01HD23098-02
MEKALANOS, JOHN J R01AI26289-04
MEKALANOS, JOHN J R37AI18045-11
MELAMED, MYRON R P30CA08748-26 9022
MELAMED, MYRON R R01CA14134-20
MELANCON, PAUL R R01GM43378-02
MELARA, ROBERT D R29NS28617-02
MELBY, JAMES M01RR00533-23 0200
MELBY, JAMES C R01DK41016-03
MELBY, JAMES C R37DK12027-24
MELBY, PETER S07RR05654-24 0151
MELCHIOR, CHRISTINE L R01AA08709-02
MELCHIOR, DONALD L S07RR05712-20
MELCHIOR, DONALD L S15AR41230-01
MELCHIOR, DONALD L S15MH49309-01
MELENEY, JANET N01CM07314-04
MELERA, PETER W R01CA44678-06
MELERA, PETER W R01CA49538-02
MELESE, TERI R01GM44901-01A1
MELETIOU, STEVEN D S07RR05372-30 0693
MELIN, SUSAN M01RR00046-31 0484
MELLAMN, IRA P01CA46128-04 9002
MELLENCAMP, MARTHA A R29AA09173-01
MELLER, EMANUEL R01NS22589-05
MELLER, EMANUEL R01NS23618-05
MELLER, EMANUEL S07RR05399-30 0924
MELLER, STEPHEN T R29NS29844-01
MELLER, WILLIAM M01RR00400-23 0274
MELLGREN, RONALD L P01HL36573-06 0006
MELLINS, ELIZABETH S07RR05655-21 0810
MELLINS, ELIZABETH D R29AI28809-02
MELLINS, ROBERT B R01HL28907-10
MELLINS, ROBERT B R01HL45304-02
MELLINS, ROBERT B. N01HR96043-07
MELLITIS, E DAVID P01CA15396-18 9004
MELLMAN, IRA P01CA46128-04 0005
MELLMAN, IRA P30DK34989-08 0013
MELLMAN, IRA S R01GM29765-11
MELLMAN, IRA S R01GM33904-07
MELLO, NANCY K K05DA00101-08
MELLO, NANCY K R01AA04368-12
MELLO, NANCY K R01DA02519-10
MELLON, CHARLES DAVID K20MH00869-02
MELLON, ISABEL R29GM45535-01
MELLON, PAMELA L R01DK44838-01
MELLON, PAMELA L R01HD20377-07
MELLON, PAMELA L R01HD23818-04
MELLON, PAMELA L S07RR05595-27 0669
MELLON, SYNTHIA H R01HD27970-01
MELMAN, ARNOLD R01DK42027-03
MELMED, SHLOMO P01DK42792-01A1
MELMED, SHLOMO P01DK42792-01A1 0004
MELMED, SHLOMO R01DK34824-07
MELMED, SHLOMO R01DK41906-02
MELMON, KENNETH L R01AI23463-06
MELNER, MICHAEL H P51RR00163-32 0033
MELNER, MICHAEL H R01DK41035-03
MELNICK, ELAINE N01DK92242-07
MELNICK, GLENN A R01HS06490-02
MELNICK, STEVEN J S07RR05662-18 0153
MELNYKOVYCH, GEORGE R01CA08315-27
MELTON, DOUGLAS A R01GM32921-08
MELTON, DOUGLAS A R01GM44653-02
MELTON, JOSEPH E R29HL44678-02
MELTON, JOSEPH L. P01AG04875-08 0002
MELTON, L JOSEPH R01AR30582-26
MELTON, LEE JOSEPH R01AR27065-12
MELTZER, HEBERT Y. M01RR00080-29 0331
MELTZER, HERBERT Y K05MH47808-17
MELTZER, HERBERT Y M01RR00080-29 0306
MELTZER, HERBERT Y M01RR00080-29 0452
MELTZER, HERBERT Y M01RR00080-29 0662
MELTZER, HERBERT Y M01RR00080-29 0307
MELTZER, HERBERT Y M01RR00080-29 0357
MELTZER, HERBERT Y M01RR00080-29 0425
MELTZER, HERBERT Y M01RR00080-29 0407
MELTZER, HERBERT Y M01RR00080-29 0448
MELTZER, HERBERT Y M01RR00080-29 0449
MELTZER, HERBERT Y P50MH41684-07 0049
MELTZER, HERBERT Y P50MH41684-07 0032
MELTZER, HERBERT Y P50MH41684-07 0060
MELTZER, HERBERT Y P50MH41684-07 0061
MELTZER, HERBERT Y P50MH41684-07 0062
MELTZER, HERBERT Y P50MH41684-07 0063
MELTZER, HERBERT Y P50MH41684-07 0064
MELTZER, HERBERT Y P50MH41684-07 0065
MELTZER, HERBERT Y P50MH41684-07 0046
MELTZER, HERBERT Y P50MH41684-07 0034
MELTZER, HERBERT Y P50MH41684-07
MELTZER, HERBERT Y P50MH41684-07 0014
MELTZER, HERBERT Y. M01RR00080-29 0328
MELTZER, PAUL S P01CA41183-05 0001
MELTZER, STEPHEN S07RR05379-30 0765
MELTZOFF, ANDREW S07RR07096-26 0066
MELTZOFF, ANDREW N R01HD22514-05
MELVIN, JAMES E P50DE07003-08 0011
MELVIN, JAMES E R01DE08921-03
MELVIN, JAMES E R01DE09692-01
MELVOLD, ROGER N01CM87257-04
MELVOLD, ROGER W P01NS23349-06 0005
MELVOLD, ROGER W R01AI16919-13
MEMOLI, VINCENT A P30CA23108-14 9004
MENAGHAN, ELIZABETH G R01HD26047-02
MENAKER, MICHAEL R01HD13162-11
MENARD, MICHELE S07RR05465-29 0384
MENASHE, VICTOR D S03RR03557-01
MENDEL, CARL M R29DK40355-03
MENDELL, JERRY M01RR00034-31 0289
MENDELL, JERRY M01RR00034-31 0412
MENDELL, JERRY R M01RR00034-31 0390
MENDELL, JERRY R M01RR00034-31 0391
MENDELL, LORNE P01NS14899-13 0005
MENDELL, LORNE M P01NS14899-13 0011
MENDELL, LORNE M R01NS16996-12
MENDELL, LORNE M S07RR07067-26 0222
MENDELMAN, PAUL M R01AI24630-05
MENDELSOHN, JOHN P30CA23100-11 9004
MENDELSOHN, JOHN P30CA23100-11 9001
MENDELSOHN, JOHN R37CA42060-07
MENDELSOHN, JOHN U01CA37641-07 0003
MENDELSOHN, JOHN U01CA37641-07
MENDELSOHN, MICHAEL E M01RR02635-07 0291
MENDELSOHN, MICHAEL EDWARD K08HL02154-03
MENDELSOHN, RICHARD R01GM29864-10
MENDELSOHN, RICHARD S06GM08223-08 0022
MENDELSON, BRUCE S07RR05350-30 0337
MENDELSON, CAROLE R P01HD13912-12 0003
MENDELSON, CAROLE R R01DK31206-08
MENDELSON, JACK H K05DA00064-12
MENDELSON, JACK H R01AA06252-09
MENDELSON, JACK H R18DA06116-03
MENDELSON, NEIL H R01GM34180-05
MENDELSON, ROBERT A, JR R01AR39710-03
MENDELSON, WALLACE B R01MH47769-01
MENDICINO, JOSEPH F R01HL26858-10
MENDOW, LOUIS P51RR00164-30 9003
MENDOZA, RICARDO S07RR05551-29 0965
MENDOZA, SALLY P P51RR00169-30 0096
MENDRICK, DONNA L R01DK38995-02
MENEELY, PHILIP M R01HD24324-02
MENGER, FREDRIC M R01GM21457-15
MENICK, DONALD R R01HL44202-02
MENKEN, JANE P30HD10379-15
MENN, LISE R01DC00730-02
MENNELLA, JULIE A S03RR03141-11
MENON, ANANT K R01AI28858-01A2
MENON, JAIRAM K R01HD06656-17A1
MENON, MANI R01DK43184-01
MENSAH, EDWARD K S07RR05871-03 0579
MENT, LAURA M01RR06022-02 0624
MENT, LAURA R R01NS27116-03
MENTZER, WILLIAM C. P60HL20985-14 9001
MENTZER, WILLIAM C. P60HL20985-14 9002
MENTZER, WILLIAM C. P60HL20985-14 9004
MENTZER, ROBERT M, JR R01HL34579-07
MENTZER, STEVEN S07RR05950-07 0009
MENTZER, WILLIAM C, JR P60HL20985-14
MENYUK, PAULA R01DC00537-03
MEONS, ROBERT S07RR05649-25 0797
MERCADO, CARMEN M S06GM08239-06 0006
MERCADO, T I Z01AI00097-33
MERCER, DOROTHY L R01MH48987-01
MERCER, EDWARD S07RR05417-30 0804
MERCER, ROBERT R P01HL42444-02 9001
MERCER, ROBERT W P01HL36573-06 0008
MERCER, ROBERT W R29GM39746-04
MERCER, ROBERT W S07RR05389-30 0642
MERCHANT, J A P50AI19093-08 0007
MERCHANT, JAMES P30ES05605-02 9003
MERCHANT, JAMES P50HL37121-05 0004
MERCHANT, JAMES A P30ES05605-02
MERCHANT, ROBERT K K08ES00196-02
MERCHANT, SABEEHA R29GM42143-03
MERCHENTHALER, I Z01ES90055-03
MERCHLINSKY, M Z01AI00123-25
MERCIER, MICHEL U01ES02617-12
MERCOLA, DANIEL A R01CA49963-03
MERCOLA, MARK K R01HD28460-01
MERCURIO, ARTHUR P01CA44704-04A1 0002
MERCURIO, ARTHUR M R01CA42276-06
MEREDITH STEPHEN C P50HL15062-20 0028

MEREDITH, MICHAEL R01DC00906-01
MEREDITH, MICHAEL J R01ES03272-06
MEREDITH, RUBY F M01RR00032-31 0370
MEREDITH, S P30DK42086-02 9004
MEREDITH, STEPHEN C P50HL15062-20 0007
MEREDITH, STEVEN S06GM08202-11 0007
MEREDITH, TRAVIS N01EY02116-03
MEREDITH, TRAVIS A R01EY05794-05
MERENSTEIN, GERALD M01RR00069-29 0476
MERENSTEIN, GERALD M01RR00069-29 0470
MEREZHINSKAYA, N Z01DK25070-03
MERGNER, WOLFGANG J R10HL45693-01
MERIGAN, THAOMS C M01RR00070-29 0235
MERIGAN, THOMAS C M01RR00070-29 0230
MERIGAN, THOMAS C M01RR00070-29 0211
MERIGAN, THOMAS C M01RR00070-29 0231
MERIGAN, THOMAS C M01RR00070-29 0226
MERIGAN, THOMAS C P30AI27762-03
MERIGAN, THOMAS C P30AI27762-03 9001
MERIGAN, THOMAS C R01AI28733-02
MERIGAN, THOMAS C R37AI05629-29
MERIGAN, THOMAS C U01AI27666-05S1
MERIGAN, THOMAS C U01AI28685-03
MERIGAN, WILLIAM H P30ES01247-17 0039
MERIGAN, WILLIAM H R01EY08898-01A1
MERIKANGAS, KATHLEEN R K02MH00499-07
MERIKANGAS, KATHLEEN R R01DA05348-05
MERIMEE, THOMAS J M01RR00082-29 0464
MERIMEE, THOMAS J R01DK18130-18
MERINO, M Z01CB09192-01
MERINO, M Z01CB09193-02
MERINO, M Z01CB09194-01
MERINO, M Z01CB09359-01
MERINO, M Z01CB09360-01
MERINO, M Z01CB09361-01
MERINO, M J Z01CB00853-38
MERLIE, JOHN P R01NS19910-10
MERLIE, JOHN P R01NS29172-01
MERLINO, G T Z01CB08756-04
MERMELSTEIN, ROBIN J R01HL42485-03
MERRIAM, JOHN R R01LM04896-04
MERRICK, WILLIAM C R01GM26796-12
MERRICK, WILLIAM C S10RR06726-01
MERRIFIELD, R P41RR00862-18 0002
MERRIFIELD, ROBERT B R01DK01260-36
MERRIFIELD, ROBERT B R01DK24039-14
MERRIGAN, DANIEL S07RR05927-07 0959
MERRIL, C R Z01MH00935-24
MERRIL, C R Z01MH00941-11
MERRILL, ALFRED H, JR R01GM33369-07
MERRILL, ALFRED H, JR R01GM46368-01
MERRILL, EDWARD C R29HD23325-05
MERRILL, GARY F R01GM34432-07
MERRILL, JEAN E P01HD25831-01A1 0004
MERRILL, M Z01NS02708-06
MERRILL, M J Z01NS02707-06
MERRILL, WILLIAM W M01RR00125-28 0651
MERRIMAN, WILLIAM E R29HD25958-03
MERRITT, DORIS H G20RR06776-01
MERRITT, DORIS H M01RR00750-19
MERRITT, RICHARD W R01AI21884-07
MERRITT, RICHARD W S07RR07049-26 0432
MERRITT, T ALLEN P50HL23584-13 0008
MERRYFIELD, MARGARET S06GM08238-05 0014
MERRYMAN, CARMEN F R01EY07610-04
MERTELSMANN, ROLAND H P01CA20194-14 0026
MERTES, KRISTIN B R01GM33922-08
MERTZ-FAIRHURST, EVA J R55DE06112-09A1
MERTZ, GREGORY J M01RR00997-16 0391
MERTZ, JANET E P01CA22443-14 0002
MERUELO, DANIEL R01CA31346-09
MERUELO, DANIEL R01CA35482-07
MERUELO, DANIEL R37CA22247-14
MERVIS, CAROLYN B R01HD26892-03
MERVIS, CAROLYN B R01HD27042-03
MERWIN, ELIZABETH S07RR05431-30 0845
MERWIN, G S07RR05362-30 0785
MERYMAN, HAROLD T R01GM17959-19
MERZ, KENNETH M S07RR07082-26 0299
MERZ, KENNETH M, JR R29GM44974-01A1
MERZENICH, MICHAEL N01DC02401-01
MERZENICH, MICHAEL M R01NS10414-19S1
MESA-TEJADA, RICHARD P30CA13696-19 9013
MESCE, KAREN A R29HD26175-03
MESCE, KAREN A S07RR07052-26 0164
MESCHER, MATTHEW F R01AI26950-03
MESCHER, MATTHEW F R01AI31524-01
MESCHIA, GIACOMO P01HD00781-27S1 0035
MESCHIA, GIACOMO R37HD01866-26
MESELSON, MATTHEW S P01GM29301-11 0007
MESELSON, MATTHEW S R01GM22274-16A1
MESERVE, LEE S07RR07192-12 0617
MESHNICK, STEVEN R G12RR03060-07 0001
MESHNICK, STEVEN R R22AI26848-02
MESHULAM, TOVA P01AI28408-02 9002
MESSANA, JOSEPH M M01RR00042-31 0618
MESSANA, JOSEPH M M01RR00042-31 0593
MESSENHEIMER, JOHN M01RR00046-31 0485
MESSENHEIMER, JOHN M01RR00046-31 0476
MESSENHEIMER, JOHN A M01RR00046-31 0463
MESSENHEIMER, JOHN A M01RR00046-31 0449
MESSENHEIMER, JOHN A M01RR00046-31 0407
MESSENHEIMER, JOHN A M01RR00046-31 0395
MESSENHEIMER, JOHN A P01NS26680-04A1 0004
MESSENHEIMER, JOHN A. M01RR00046-31 0306
MESSER, WILLIAM S, JR K04NS01493-01
MESSER, WILLIAM S, JR S15NS30121-01
MESSINA, ANTHONY M01RR00047-31 0473
MESSINA, JOSEPH L R01DK40456-03
MESSINA, LOUIS M M01RR00042-31 0530
MESSING, ALBEE R01NS22475-06
MESSING, EDWARD M P01CA51987-02
MESSING, EDWARD M P01CA51987-02 0003
MESSING, JOACHIM W R01GM43261-02
MESSING, ROBERT P01AA08353-03 0004
MESSING, ROBERT O P01AA08353-03 9002
MESSING, ROBERT O R01AA08117-02
MESSNER, RONALD P R01AA08848-01
MESSNER, RONALD P R01AI31101-02
MESSNER, STEVE F S07RR07122-23 0112
MESTECKY, JIRI F P01AI18745-10 9001
MESTECKY, JIRI F P01AI18745-10
MESTECKY, JIRI F P01AI18745-10 0001
MESTECKY, JIRI F R01DK28537-10
MESULAM, MAREK-MARSEL M01RR01032-16 0447
MESULAM, MAREK-MARSEL P50AG05134-08 0005
MESULAM, MAREK-MARSEL R01NS20285-07
MESZOELY, CHARLES A S07RR07143-20 0630
METCALF, AMANDA S07RR05372-30 0672
METCALF, DONALD R01CA22556-14
METCALF, DONALD R01CA25972-11
METCALF, ELEANOR S R01AI22436-05
METCALF, ZUBIE W S03RR03121-11
METCALFE, D D Z01AI00249-10
METCALFE, D D Z01AI00513-04
METCALFE, D D Z01AI00514-04
METCALFE, JANET A R29MH48066-02
METCALFE, WALTER K R29NS27122-03
METEVIA, LOUIS A S06GM08025-21 0018
METHENY, NORMA A R01NR01669-03A2
METTER, E J Z01AG00622-04
METTER, E J Z01AG00629-02
METTER, E J Z01AG00630-02
METTER, E J Z01AG00631-02
METTER, E J Z01AG00632-02
METTER, E J Z01AG00633-02
METZ, JOHN P50MH41684-07 0068
METZ, JOHN P50MH41684-07 0072
METZ, KENNETH R S07RR05591-27 0664
METZ, STEWART A R01DK37312-07
METZENBERG, ROBERT L, JR R37GM08995-30
METZGAR, RICHARD S P51RR00165-31 0135
METZGER, BOYD M01RR00048-30 0159
METZGER, BOYD E R01DK10699-24
METZGER, DAVID S P50DA07705-01 0005
METZGER, DAVID S P50DA07705-01 0002
METZGER, DENNIS W P30CA21765-14 9005
METZGER, H Z01AR41025-20
METZLER, DAVID E R01DK01549-34
MEULLER, HERBERT S07RR05689-23 0854
MEULLER, NANCY E P01AI26487-03S1 9002
MEULLER, NANCY E P01AI26487-03S1 0003
MEUNIER, FRANCOISE U10CA11488-21
MEYD, CONSTANCE R01AG08494-03
MEYDANI, MOHSEN S07RR07179-14 0691
MEYDANI, SIMIN N R01AG09140-02
MEYER-BAHLBURG, HEIN S07RR05650-25 0104
MEYER-BAHLBURG, HEINO P50MH43520-04 9002
MEYER, ALEXANDRA S07RR05664-24 0869
MEYER, BARBARA J R01GM30702-11
MEYER, BARBARA J S07RR07006-26 0894
MEYER, BERND P41RR05351-03 0002
MEYER, BRUCE S07RR05745-19 0241
MEYER, CHARLES R R01CA52709-01A1
MEYER, DAVID I R01GM38538-05
MEYER, EDWIN M P01AG10485-01 0002
MEYER, EDWIN M R01AG06226-05
MEYER, FREDRIC B R01NS26301-03
MEYER, JERROLD S R01DA06495-01A1
MEYER, LAURENCE J M01RR00064-27 0355
MEYER, LAURENCE J P01CA48711-02 0001
MEYER, LAURENCE J S07RR05428-30 0187
MEYER, LAURENCE J U01CA50298-03
MEYER, RALPH R S07RR07075-17 0264
MEYER, RICHARD J R01GM37462-05
MEYER, ROGER E P50AA03510-14
MEYER, ROGER F U10EY06158-07
MEYER, RONALD S07RR07049-26 0440
MEYER, RONALD A R01AR38972-04A1
MEYER, RONALD L R01EY07466-12
MEYER, RONALD L R01NS26750-03
MEYER, THOMAS J R01GM32296-09
MEYER, THOMAS J S10RR06449-01
MEYER, TIMOTHY W R01DK42093-02
MEYER, TIMOTHY W R01DK43597-01
MEYER, WALTER J M01RR00073-29 0311
MEYERHOFF, MARK E R01GM28882-10A1
MEYEROWITZ, CYRIL P50DE07003-08 0010
MEYEROWITZ, ELLIOT M R01GM45697-01
MEYERS-WALLEN, VICKI N R01HD19393-07
MEYERS, ALAN S07RR05569-27 0113
MEYERS, ALBERT I R01GM33200-08
MEYERS, ALBERT I R01GM34275-07
MEYERS, ALLEN R S07RR05417-30
MEYERS, BARNETT S R29MH43856-04
MEYERS, CHESTER A P01GM39526-05 0001
MEYERS, DEBORAH A P01HG00373-04 9003
MEYERS, FREDERICK J U10CA46441-04
MEYERS, JOEL P01CA18029-16 0036
MEYERS, JOEL D P01HL36444-11 0008
MEYERS, KENNETH S07RR07097-26 0390
MEYERS, KENNETH M K07HL02146-04
MEYERS, MARIAN B R29CA41375-05
MEYERS, WILLIAM C M01RR00030-30 0384
MEYERS, WILLIAM C R01DK35490-07
MEYERTHOLEN, EDWARD P R15EY08572-01A1
MEYN, M STEPHEN S07RR05358-30 0477
MEYN, RAYMOND E P01CA06294-30 0033
MEYN, RAYMOND E R01CA26312-10A1
MEYRICK, BARBARA O P50HL19153-15 9003
MEYRICK, BARBARA O P50HL19153-15 0013
MEYRICK, BARBARA O R01HL34208-07
MEYSKENS, FRANK JR U01CA51610-03
MEYSKENS, FRANK L P01CA41108-05 0004
MEYSKENS, FRANK L JR R01CA52596-01A1
MEZEI, MIHALY R55GM43500-01A1
MEZEY, ESTEBAN R01AA00626-17
MEZEY, ESTEBAN R01AA06865-06
MEZZICH, ADA P50AA08746-02 0006
MEZZICH, ADA C R01DA05952-02
MEZZICH, JUAN P50AA08746-02 9002
MIA, ABDUL J K14HL01730-06
MIAN, ABDUL MOHSIN U01AI25696-05 0001
MICELI, MICHAEL V R01EY06782-04A1
MICEVYCH, PAUL S07RR05354-30 0383
MICEVYCH, PAUL S07RR05354-30 0385
MICEVYCH, PAUL E R01NS21220-08
MICHAEL, ALFRED F R01AI10704-31
MICHAEL, JOHN R K04HL02297-03
MICHAEL, LLOYD P01HL42550-02 9002
MICHAEL, LLOYD P50HL42267-02 9002
MICHAEL, RICHARD P R01MH19506-17
MICHAEL, ROBERT T P30HD18288-08 9003
MICHAEL, ROBERT T R01HD27150-03
MICHAEL, SANDRA D R55HD27506-01A1
MICHAEL, SANDRA D S07RR07149-18 0423
MICHAELIS, ELIAS K R37AA04732-11
MICHAELIS, ELIAS K S07RR05606-25
MICHAELIS, ELIAS K S07RR05606-25 0695
MICHAELIS, ELIAS K S15GM47059-01
MICHAELIS, SUSAN D R01GM41223-03
MICHAELS, DAN F R43GM47226-01
MICHAELS, DONALD C P01HL39707-02 9001
MICHAELS, DONALD C P01HL39707-02 0003
MICHAELS, G Z01CT00228-01
MICHAELS, G Z01CT00229-01
MICHAELS, G Z01CT00230-01
MICHAELSON, JAMES S R01CA37374-10
MICHAIL, ANTOUN D S07RR05419-30 0826
MICHALEK, SUZANNE M P50DE08228-04 0001
MICHALEK, SUZANNE M R01DE08182-04
MICHALEK, SUZANNE M R01DE09081-02
MICHALOPOULOS, GEORGE K R01CA35373-09
MICHALOPOULOS, GEORGE K R01CA30241-12
MICHALOPOULOS, GEORGE K R01CA43632-06
MICHALOWICZ, BRYAN P30DE09737-02 0002
MICHEL, JAMES L R29AI28500-02
MICHELS, CORINNE A R01GM28216-16
MICHELS, CORINNE A S15GM47046-01
MICHELS, ROBERT M01RR00047-31
MICHELS, ROBERT M01RR06020-02
MICHELS, VIRGINIA V R01HL36879-05
MICHELSON, ALAN D R29HL38138-05
MICHELSON, LARRY R01MH46747-03
MICHENFELDER, JOHN D R01GM44486-01A1
MICHIELUTTE, ROBERT N01CN65034-19
MICHIGAN STATE UNIV N01MH80011-00
MICHL, JOSEF R01CA22682-12S1
MICHOD, RICHARD E R01GM36410-06
MICHOD, RICHARD E R01HD19949-07
MICKENS, RONALD S06GM08247-04 0006
MICKLE, P S07RR05362-30 0786
MICKLE, P S07RR05362-30 0795
MICZEK, KLAUS S07RR07179-14 0684
MICZEK, KLAUS A R01AA05122-10
MICZEK, KLAUS A R01DA02632-13
MIDANIK, LORRAINE S07RR07006-26 0910
MIDDAUGH, LAWRENCE D R01AA06611-06
MIDDAUGH, LAWRENCE D S15AA09266-01
MIDDAUGH, SUSAN J M01RR01070-15 0137
MIDDLEBROOKS, JOHN C R29DC00420-05
MIDGLEY, A REES U54HD29184-01 0005
MIDGLEY, A REES, JR P30HD18258-08
MIDGLEY, A REES, JR R01HD18018-06
MIDGLEY, A. REES, JR. P30HD18258-08 9005
MIEDEMA, B W M01RR00585-20 0469
MIEDEMA, B W M01RR00585-20 0554
MIEDEMA, B W M01RR00585-20 0561
MIELER, WILLIAM F U10EY06279-07
MIER, JAMES W R01CA43950-05
MIES, G Z01NS02821-02
MIESFELD, ROGER L R01GM40738-04
MIETUS-SNYDER, MICHELE K11HL02111-04
MIFFLIN, STEVEN W P01HL36080-06 0008
MIFFLIN, STEVEN W R29HL41894-04
MIGEON, BARBARA R R01HD05465-21

MIGEON, CLAUDE J R01DK00180-40A1
MIGLIOZZI, JOSEPH S07RR05394-30 0717
MIHICH, ENRICO P01CA13038-19
MIHICH, ENRICO P01CA13038-19 9001
MIHICH, ENRICO R01CA15142-18
MIHOVILOVIC, MIRTA P01NS26630-03 0005
MIKE, VALERIE P01CA20194-14 9004
MIKI, T Z01CP05548-04
MIKKELSEN, ROSS B R22AI24307-04A1
MIKLOWITZ, DAVID J R29MH43931-01A2
MIKLOWITZ, DAVID J S07RR07013-26 0955
MIKSICEK, RICHARD J R29CA47384-03
MILAKOFSKY, LOUIS S07RR07082-26 0300
MILAM, ANN E P30EY01730-16 9004
MILAM, ANN H P30EY01730-16 9002
MILAM, ANN H R01EY01311-18
MILANICK, MARK A K04DK02006-02
MILANICK, MARK A R01DK37512-06
MILAS, LUKA P01CA06294-30 9003
MILAVETZ, GARY S07RR05877-09 0596
MILBRANDT, JEFFREY D P01CA49712-03 9003
MILBRANDT, JEFFREY D P01CA49712-03 0005
MILBRANDT, JEFFREY D R01NS26224-03
MILBY, JESSE B U01AA08819-02
MILCAREK, CHRISTINE A R01CA36606-09
MILDER, FREDRIC L R43AR40954-01
MILDVAN, ALBERT S R37DK28616-11
MILEDI, RICARDO R01MH48358-01
MILEDI, RICARDO R01NS23284-06
MILES, E W Z01DK24140-25
MILES, F A Z01EY00153-09
MILES, H T Z01DK35000-27
MILES, J M M01RR00585-20 0553
MILES, JOHN M R01DK38092-05
MILES, KATHRYN R29NS29356-01
MILES, LINDSEY A R01HL45934-02
MILES, LINDSEY A R29HL38272-04
MILES, MICHAEL P01AA08353-03 9001
MILES, MICHAEL F P01AA08353-03 0003
MILES, MICHAEL F R29AA07750-03
MILES, MICHAEL FRANCIS K02AA00118-04
MILES, STEVEN P30AI28697-01 9001
MILES, TONI P R01AG10430-01
MILETIC, VJEKOSLAV R01NS21278-07
MILETIC, VJEKOSLAV R01NS26850-03
MILETICH, JOSEPH P P50HL14147-21 0026
MILETICH, JOSEPH P R01HL41963-03
MILEWICH, LEON S07RR05426-30 0144
MILGROM, PETER P30DE09743-02 0014
MILGROM, PETER S07RR05346-30 0326
MILGROM, PETER S07RR05346-30 0324
MILGROM, PETER M R01DE06950-03A2
MILGROM, PETER M R01HS06554-01A1
MILGROM, PETER M R03DE09804-01
MILICH, DAVID R R01AI20720-07A1
MILL, JOHN Z01NS02825-01
MILLAN, JOSE L R01CA42595-06
MILLAN, JOSE L. P01HD25938-02 0004
MILLAR, MICHELLE M R01GM36308-06
MILLAR, STEPHEN J S07RR05970-06 0780
MILLARD-STAFFORD, ME S07RR07024-26 0039
MILLARD, P J P41RR04224-04 0002
MILLARD, RONALD W P01HL22619-14 9001
MILLARD, RONALD W P01HL22619-14 0014
MILLARD, WILLIAM J P01AG10485-01 9002
MILLEN, JANE S07RR07072-26 0270
MILLER-CHISHOLM, A Z01DE00503-02
MILLER-CHISHOLM, A Z01DE00506-02
MILLER-GRABER, PEGGY S07RR07034-26 0065
MILLER-GRAZIANO, CAROL L R01GM36214-06
MILLER-HANCE, WANDA C K08HL02712-01
MILLER, A. DUSTY P01AI27291-04 0004
MILLER, ALAN D R55NS20585-07
MILLER, ALAN D S07RR07065-26 0068
MILLER, ALAN M R29CA44838-05
MILLER, ALBERT B S06GM08182-12 0002
MILLER, ALEXANDER P01AR40919-01 9001
MILLER, ANDREW H K01MH00680-04
MILLER, ANDREW H R01MH47674-01
MILLER, ARTHUR P01HL36444-11 0010
MILLER, ARTHUR D R01HL41212-03
MILLER, BAILA H R01AG09416-01A1
MILLER, BARBARA A R29HL40576-03
MILLER, BARNEY P01AG10481-01 9001
MILLER, BARRY S07RR05505-18
MILLER, BARRY S15HL47694-01
MILLER, BRENDA S07RR05938-07 0321
MILLER, BRENDA A R01AA07554-04
MILLER, BRENDA A S07RR05938-07 0317
MILLER, BRUCE P30AG10123-01 0003
MILLER, BRUCE L R01NS29919-01
MILLER, BUELL A R01HS06121-03
MILLER, CARL W P01CA42710-06A1 0001
MILLER, CAROL A P50AG05142-08 9001
MILLER, CAROL A R37MH39145-08
MILLER, CASS T S07RR05450-30 0351
MILLER, CASS T S07RR05450-30 0340
MILLER, CHARLES G R01AI10333-21
MILLER, CHARLES G S07RR07030-26 0400
MILLER, CHARLES W S03RR03021-11
MILLER, CHARLES W S03RR03022-09
MILLER, CHARLES W S07RR05458-29 0832
MILLER, CHRISTOPHER R37GM31768-09
MILLER, CORINNE E R03DE09889-01
MILLER, D CRAIG R01HL29589-09
MILLER, D CRAIG R01HL37499-05
MILLER, D M Z01BD03005-03
MILLER, D S Z01ES80047-02
MILLER, D S Z01ES80048-01
MILLER, DALE T R01MH44069-03
MILLER, DAVID P01AG04220-07A1 0005
MILLER, DAVID A R15GM42153-01S1
MILLER, DAVID M R29NS26115-05
MILLER, DENNIS L R01GM44223-02
MILLER, DONALD M R01CA42664-07
MILLER, DONALD M R55CA54380-01
MILLER, DOROTHY L S07RR05902-05
MILLER, DOROTHY L S07RR05902-05 0521
MILLER, DOROTHY L S15HD28767-01
MILLER, DOUGLAS P30AG08051-02 9002
MILLER, DOUGLAS K R01AG10436-01
MILLER, DOUGLAS L R01CA42947-07
MILLER, DUANE D R01NS17907-08
MILLER, DUNCAN A S07RR05424-30 0066
MILLER, EDWARD J P50DE08228-04 0002
MILLER, EDWARD J R01DE08520-04
MILLER, EDWARD J R10HL33728-07
MILLER, ELIZABETH C P01CA22484-14 9001
MILLER, ELIZABETH C P30CA07175-28 0001
MILLER, ELIZABETH C P30CA07175-28 9010
MILLER, ELIZABETH C P30CA07175-28 9005
MILLER, ERIC S R29GM38659-05
MILLER, F P30CA12708-21 9004
MILLER, F W Z01BB06007-01
MILLER, FRED R R01CA28366-12
MILLER, FRED R R03CA54926-01
MILLER, FREDERICK N R43DK44057-01
MILLER, GARY J P30CA46934-04 9006
MILLER, GERALD R43HG00296-01
MILLER, GERALDINE P R01DK41312-02
MILLER, GLORIA E S07RR07160-16 0583
MILLER, GREGORY A R01MH39628-05
MILLER, GREGORY A S15MH49296-01
MILLER, HERMAN T S06GM08202-11 0003
MILLER, I GEORGE P01CA16038-18 0006
MILLER, I GEORGE, JR R01CA52228-02
MILLER, I GEORGE, JR R37AI22959-06
MILLER, I GEORGE, JR R37CA12055-20
MILLER, INGLIS J, JR R01DC00230-07
MILLER, IVAN W R01MH44778-02
MILLER, J PHILIP P50AG05681-08 9001
MILLER, J PHILIP U01AG09098-02
MILLER, J PHILIP U01AI25903-05 9005
MILLER, J Z M01RR00750-19 0201
MILLER, JACQUES F R01AI29385-01A1
MILLER, JAMES N01CM87276-06
MILLER, JAMES A P01CA22484-14 0001
MILLER, JAMES D R01DC00296-07
MILLER, JAMES D R13DC00909-01
MILLER, JAMES D S07RR05987-05
MILLER, JAMES D S15EY09462-01
MILLER, JAMES F R01DK42857-01A1
MILLER, JAMES F R01GM42071-04
MILLER, JAMES G P50HL17646-17 0024
MILLER, JAMES G R01HL40302-04
MILLER, JAMES N R01AI12601-15
MILLER, JEAN N01LM63505-14
MILLER, JEANNETTE C P01MH08618-27 0100
MILLER, JEANNETTE C P01MH08618-27 0102
MILLER, JEFFERY F R29AI31548-01
MILLER, JEFFERY O S06GM47165-01 0027
MILLER, JEFFREY S07RR05354-30 0395
MILLER, JEFFREY S07RR07009-26 0945
MILLER, JEFFREY B R01HD25394-03
MILLER, JEFFREY B R01HL45429-02
MILLER, JEFFREY H R01GM32184-09
MILLER, JEFFREY H R01GM43827-01A1
MILLER, JOAN G R01MH42940-04
MILLER, JOANNE L R01DC00130-14
MILLER, JOEL M P30EY06883-06 9002
MILLER, JOEL M R01EY06973-06
MILLER, JOEL M R01EY08399-02
MILLER, JOEL M S07RR05981-05 0798
MILLER, JOEL M S07RR05981-05 0799
MILLER, JOEL M S07RR05981-05 0800
MILLER, JOEL M S07RR05981-05 0801
MILLER, JOHN W P50NS14834-13 0012
MILLER, JON F P30HD03352-25 9012
MILLER, JON F R01HD22393-04
MILLER, JONATHAN L R01HL32853-06
MILLER, JOSEF M P01DC00274-08
MILLER, JOSHUA R01DK25243-13
MILLER, JUDY Z P01AG05793-06 0004
MILLER, KATHRYN G R29GM43607-02
MILLER, KEITH W P50GM15904-24
MILLER, KEITH W P50GM15904-24 0014
MILLER, KEITH W R01AA07040-05
MILLER, KENNETH EUGENE R29NS27213-04
MILLER, KURT W S07RR05983-05 0359
MILLER, L H Z01AI00108-20
MILLER, L H Z01AI00241-10
MILLER, LARRY D R18MH46060-03
MILLER, LARRY R S07RR05404-30 0849
MILLER, LAURENCE J R01DK32878-09
MILLER, LAWRENCE G R01DA06327-01A2
MILLER, LAWRENCE G R01MH47598-01
MILLER, LEO R01HD24438-04
MILLER, LESLIE M R25AD00004-01
MILLER, LOIS K R37AI23719-06
MILLER, LORRAINE T S07RR07079-26 0295
MILLER, M J Z01CP05263-09
MILLER, M J Z01CP05675-01
MILLER, MARCIA S07RR05841-12 0250
MILLER, MARCIA S07RR05841-12 0232
MILLER, MARCIA MADSEN R01AI21736-07
MILLER, MARILYN S07RR05393-30 0899
MILLER, MARILYN M R01AG07795-02
MILLER, MARTHA J R01HL41814-03
MILLER, MARVIN J R01AI30988-01
MILLER, MARVIN J R01GM25845-12A1
MILLER, MICHAEL K07HL02263-03
MILLER, MICHAEL H R01EY08977-01A1
MILLER, MICHAEL I P41RR01380-10 9004
MILLER, MICHAEL I R01DC00333-06
MILLER, MICHAEL L S07RR05654-24 0131
MILLER, MICHAEL W P01DE07734-06 0003
MILLER, MICHAEL W R01AA06916-08
MILLER, MORTON W R01CA39230-17
MILLER, MYRON M01RR00071-28A1 0243
MILLER, MYRON M01RR00071-28A1 0184
MILLER, NEIL R U10EY07659-04
MILLER, OSCAR L R01GM21020-15
MILLER, OSCAR L S07RR07094-26
MILLER, PAUL S P01CA42762-05 9001
MILLER, PAUL S P01CA42762-05 0001
MILLER, PAUL S R01GM45012-02
MILLER, PERRY N01LM13537-00
MILLER, PERRY L R01HG00175-01
MILLER, PERRY L R01LM05044-03
MILLER, R Z01AI00314-11
MILLER, R Z01AI00570-02
MILLER, R Z01CM06382-05
MILLER, R Z01CM06383-05
MILLER, R DWAYNE R01GM41909-02
MILLER, R H Z01AI00530-04
MILLER, RALPH R R01MH33881-10
MILLER, RANDOLPH N01LM13535-00
MILLER, RANDOLPH A R01LM04622-04
MILLER, RAYMOND R R29AR39396-03
MILLER, RICHARD P01ES05197-01A1 9003
MILLER, RICHARD S07RR05346-30 0318
MILLER, RICHARD A R01AG03978-10
MILLER, RICHARD A R01AG07114-05 0003
MILLER, RICHARD A R37AG09801-02
MILLER, RICHARD A R44CA41846-03
MILLER, RICHARD E S15DA07817-01
MILLER, RICHARD J K02DA00106-06
MILLER, RICHARD J R01DA02121-13
MILLER, RICHARD J R01NS27539-03
MILLER, RICHARD J R37MH40165-07
MILLER, RICHARD K R01AI32319-01
MILLER, RICHARD K R01ES02774-09
MILLER, RICHARD T R29DK41726-03
MILLER, ROBERT N01CM07320-03
MILLER, ROBERT F P01NS17763-10 0003
MILLER, ROBERT F R01EY07376-05
MILLER, ROBERT F R37EY03014-15
MILLER, ROBERT H R01NS25597-04
MILLER, ROBERT L S07RR07248-03
MILLER, RODNEY N01CN95166-04
MILLER, RONALD D P01AG03104-10 0009
MILLER, S Z01NS02816-02
MILLER, S P Z01NS02162-17
MILLER, S P Z01NS02163-17
MILLER, SAMUEL I K11AI00917-03
MILLER, SAMUEL I R01AI30479-01
MILLER, SAMUEL O P50DA05321-04 9003
MILLER, SAMUEL O P50DA05321-04 0002
MILLER, SANFORD A S07RR07187-13
MILLER, SCOTT N01HB77035-07
MILLER, SCOTT N01HB97069-03
MILLER, SCOTT C R01CA47659-04
MILLER, SCOTT C R01DE06007-09
MILLER, SHELDON L R01NS26844-01A4
MILLER, SHELDON S R37EY02205-14
MILLER, SHELDON S S07RR05832-12 0197
MILLER, STEPHEN P01NS23349-06 0001
MILLER, STEPHEN D P01NS23349-06
MILLER, STEPHEN D R01NS26543-04
MILLER, SUZANNE M R01CA46591-02
MILLER, TERRY L P01ES00040-27 0077
MILLER, THOMAS A P50GM38529-04 0004
MILLER, THOMAS A P50GM38529-04 9001
MILLER, THOMAS A R55DK25838-13
MILLER, THOMAS B P30DK32520-08
MILLER, THOMAS B, JR R01DK18269-17
MILLER, THOMAS B, JR R37HL20476-15
MILLER, THOMAS P U10CA13612-18
MILLER, TOM R R01HL42884-02
MILLER, VIRGINIA L R01AI27342-03
MILLER, VIRGINIA M R29HL42614-03
MILLER, WALTER L R01DK37922-05
MILLER, WALTER L R01DK42154-02
MILLER, WARREN B R01HD23900-04
MILLER, WAYNE C S07RR07031-26 0100
MILLER, WEBB C R01LM05110-03

MILLER, WESLEY J M01RR00400-23 0293
MILLER, WILLIAM U54HD29184-01 0004
MILLER, WILLIAM R K05AA00133-02
MILLER, WILLIAM R R01AA07564-04
MILLER, WILLIAM R R13AA09051-01
MILLER, WILLIAM R U10AA08435-03
MILLER, YORK E R01HL45745-01
MILLETT, FRANCIS S R01GM20488-19
MILLETT, FRANCIS S S07RR07101-13
MILLETTE, CLARKE F P30HD06645-20 9009
MILLETTE, CLARKE F R01HD15269-11
MILLETTE, CLARKE F R01HD27581-01
MILLEY, JOHN R R01HD27455-01
MILLHORN, DAVID E R01HD28948-01
MILLHORN, DAVID E R01HL33831-07
MILLIGAN, RONALD A R01AR39155-04
MILLIGAN, SHARON P60AR20618-13 0021
MILLINER, D M01RR00585-20 0434
MILLINGTON, WILLIAM R R29DA04598-04
MILLIS, ALBERT S07RR07122-23 0081
MILLIS, ALBERT J R01AG09279-01
MILLIS, ALBERT J R01HL40417-02
MILLMAN, IRVING P01CA40737-06 9004
MILLMAN, ROBERT B R18DA06153-03
MILLS, BARBARA G R01AR19980-11
MILLS, J H P50DC00422-05 0001
MILLS, J L Z01HD00325-10
MILLS, J L Z01HD00331-08
MILLS, JOHN R01DK41059-03
MILLS, JOHN U01AI27663-05S2
MILLS, JOHN H P50DC00422-05
MILLS, JOHN H R01ES01301-16
MILLS, JOY R19MH46207-03
MILLS, NATHANIEL C S07RR07218-05 0459
MILLS, PAM S07RR07109-23 0508
MILLS, PAUL J R29HL47074-01
MILLS, RICHARD P. P51RR00166-30 0127
MILLS, STEPHEN A P01NS27500-01A2 0002
MILLSTEIN, JEFFREY A R43AI30864-01
MILNE, G W Z01CM06194-03
MILNER, ERIC P01DK41801-02 0003
MILNER, ERIC C R29AR39918-03
MILNER, ERIC C B P01AI31241-01 0004
MILNER, JOEL S R01MH34252-08
MILNER, PAUL F. N01HB97060-04
MILNER, PETER G S07RR05491-29 0460
MILNER, ROBERT P01NS22347-06 0006
MILNER, ROBERT P50MH47680-02 0004
MILNER, ROBERT J M01RR00833-17 0191
MILNER, ROBERT J R01NS20728-07
MILNER, TERESA A R01MH42834-05
MILO, GEORGE E P30CA16058-17 9002
MILO, GEORGE E R01ES04623-04
MILSTIEN, S Z01MH01039-23
MILSTIEN, S Z01MH02564-01
MILSTONE, LEONARD M01RR00125-28 0770
MILSTONE, LEONARD M R01AR37594-06
MILTON, DONALD K S07RR05446-30 0276
MILTON, JOHN G R01MH47542-01
MILTON, RICHARD L R01AR40801-02
MIMOUNI, FRANCIS P01HD11725-13 0004
MIMS, MARTHA P S07RR05425-30 0756
MINA, MINA R01DE08682-04
MINAKER, KENNETH M01RR01032-16 0430
MINAKER, KENNETH M01RR01032-16 0431
MINAKER, KENNETH P01AG04390-08 0006
MINAKER, KENNETH L M01RR01032-16 0362
MINAKER, KENNETH L M01RR01032-16 0465
MINAKER, KENNETH L P30AG08812-02 9006
MINAKER, KENNETH L. P01AG04390-08 0007
MINDICH, LEONARD E R01GM31709-25
MINDICH, LEONARD E R01GM34352-06A2
MINDICH, LEONARD E S07RR05533-29 0529
MINGUELL, JOSE J S07RR05386-30 0592
MINION, F CHRIS K04AI01021-01
MINION, F CHRIS R01AI24428-06
MINION, F CHRIS S15CA55926-01
MINK, C M Z01BA07004-03
MINK, C M Z01BA07010-04
MINKE, BARUCH R01EY03529-11
MINKIN, CEDRIC R01AR40176-02
MINKOFF, ROBERT R01DE07674-04A1
MINNEAR, FRED P41RR01219-10 0001
MINNEMA, DANIEL J S07RR05408-30 0933
MINNEMAN, KENNETH P R01NS21325-08
MINOCHA, ANIL S07RR05656-24 0843
MINOR, RONALD R R01AR20793-11
MINOR, THOMAS R R01MH41170-03
MINSHEW, NANCY J R01MH40858-04
MINSHEW, NANCY J R35AG08974-01 0006
MINTH, CAROLYN A R29NS28496-02
MINTON, A P Z01DK24150-20
MINTZ, BEATRICE R35CA42560-05
MINTZ, DANIEL H R01DK25802-12
MINTZ, ERIC A S06GM08247-04 9001
MINTZ, ERIC A S06GM08247-04 0015
MINTZ, JAMES P50MH30911-14 9006
MIODOVNIK, MENACHEM P01HD11725-13 0001
MIODOVNIK, MENACHEM U10HD27905-01
MION, LORRAINE C R03HS06923-01
MIRA-Y-LOPEZ, RAFAEL R29CA54273-01
MIRALDI, FLORO D M01RR00080-29 0445
MIRAND, EDWIN A N01CO03872-05
MIRAND, EDWIN A R25CA18201-16
MIRAND, EDWIN A S03RR03102-10
MIRANDA, ARMAND P01NS11766-17A1 0036
MIRANDA, JEANNE R29MH47855-02
MIRANDA, MARIA S06GM08159-13 0002
MIRCHEFF, AUSTIN K R01EY05801-07
MIRDA, DANIEL P K11AI01037-01
MIRELS, LILY R01DE09428-02
MIRKES, PHILIP E R01HD16287-08
MIRKES, PHILIP E R01HD22095-04
MIRKIN, BERNARD L S07RR05475-26
MIROCHNICK, MARK M01RR00533-23 0201
MIROCHNICK, MARK S07RR05569-27 0124
MIRRA, SUZANNE S P30AG10130-01 9002
MIRRA, SUZANNE S P30AG10130-01
MIRRA, SUZANNE S. U01AG06790-06 0004
MIRRO, JOSEPH P01CA20180-14 0009
MIRRO, ROBERT K08HL01996-05
MIRRO, ROBERT R29HL42875-03
MIRSALIS, JON C N01CN05267-01
MIRSKY, A F Z01MH00471-36
MIRSKY, A F Z01MH00503-11
MIRSKY, A F Z01MH00508-09
MIRSKY, A F Z01MH00509-09
MIRSKY, A F Z01MH02295-06
MIRSKY, A J Z01MH02404-05
MIRSKY, ISRAEL P01HL38070-05 0004
MIRSKY, ISREAL S07RR05950-07 0987
MIRTH, D B Z01DE00282-13
MIRVIS, DAVID M S07RR05423-30 0059
MISCHEL, WALTER R01MH45994-02
MISCHEL, WALTER R37MH39349-08
MISELIS, RICHARD R R01GM27739-10
MISER, J S M01RR00585-20 0472
MISER, J S M01RR00585-20 0481
MISER, J S M01RR00585-20 0506
MISER, JAMES S M01RR00585-20 0447
MISHKIN, M Z01MH00478-01
MISHLER, R S06GM08066-20 0006
MISKIEL, EDWARD R43DC01004-01
MISKIMINS, WILSON KEITH R01GM43976-03
MISLER, STANLEY R01DK37380-05
MISLER, STANLEY R01NS27983-02
MISONO, KUNIO P50HL33713-06 9005
MISRA, DHARITRI N01LM03512-05
MISRA, HEMANT K S07RR05712-20 0065
MISRA, TAPAN K R29GM36722-04
MISTRETTA, CHARLES A R01CA50382-03
MISTRETTA, CHARLOTTE M R01DC00456-04
MISTRETTA, CHARLOTTE M S15CA56001-01
MISTSIALIS S07RR05380-30 0889
MITANI, GLADYS S07RR05792-15 0948
MITCH, WILLIAM E M01RR00039-31 0448
MITCH, WILLIAM E P50DK39249-05 0002
MITCH, WILLIAM E R01DK37175-07
MITCH, WILLIAM E R01DK40907-02
MITCH, WILLIAM E U01DK39488-04
MITCHELL-OLDS, THOMA S07RR07134-15 0518
MITCHELL, AARON P R01GM39531-04
MITCHELL, ALLEN A R01OH02598-02
MITCHELL, ANN D R44CA45903-03
MITCHELL, BEVERLY S R01AI24012-06
MITCHELL, BEVERLY S R01CA34085-09
MITCHELL, C L Z01ES90043-06
MITCHELL, C L Z01ES90044-06
MITCHELL, C L Z01ES90057-02
MITCHELL, CHARLES D R03AI30219-02
MITCHELL, DAVID B R29AG07854-04
MITCHELL, DAVID R R01GM44228-02
MITCHELL, EDITH S03RR03086-11
MITCHELL, GORDON S R01HL36780-05
MITCHELL, HERMAN E R43CA53068-01A1
MITCHELL, J B Z01CM06321-12
MITCHELL, J B Z01CM06351-09
MITCHELL, JERE H P01HL06296-31
MITCHELL, JERE H P01HL06296-31 0007
MITCHELL, JOHN J P50HL14212-20 0033
MITCHELL, JOHN L R01GM33841-07
MITCHELL, MALCOLM N01CM47675-01
MITCHELL, MALCOLM S R01CA36233-08
MITCHELL, MARVIN L R01HD11959-11
MITCHELL, MURRAY D R01HD20747-07
MITCHELL, PAMELA H R01NR02343-01A1
MITCHELL, RICHARD W R01HL42758-03
MITCHELL, ROBERT B S07RR07082-26 0301
MITCHELL, SUSAN J S07RR05402-30 0793
MITCHELL, THOMAS G R01AI25783-05
MITCHELL, THOMAS G R01AI28836-01A2
MITCHELL, W J Z01NS02803-02
MITCHELL, WILLIAM M R01AI29398-03
MITCHISON, TIMOTHY J R01GM39565-04
MITLER, MERRILL M01RR00833-17 0158
MITLER, MERRILL P50MH47680-02 0017
MITLER, MERRILL M M01RR00833-17 0109
MITLER, MERRILL M R03AA08235-02
MITRA, AMIT S07RR07055-26 0199
MITRA, SANKAR R01CA31721-10
MITRA, SANKAR R01CA53791-01
MITSCHER, LESTER A R01CA43713-03
MITSHER, LESTER A U01AI30183-02 0004
MITSIALIS, ALEX S R29GM44520-02
MITSUYA, H Z01CM07218-01
MITSUYA, H Z01CM07219-01
MITSUYA, H Z01CM07221-01
MITSUYA, H Z01CM07222-01
MITSUYA, H Z01CM07223-01
MITSUYASU, RONALD T U01AI27660-05S2
MITTAG, THOMAS W R01EY02619-14
MITTAG, THOMAS W R01EY07400-05
MITTAL, RAVINDER K R29DK40027-03
MITTLEMAN, MARY P30AG08051-02 9003
MITTMAN, BRIAN S R29AG07676-02
MITZNER, WAYNE A. P01HL10342-26 0029
MITZNER, WAYNE A. P01HL10342-26 9001
MITZNER, WAYNE P30ES03819-06A1 9016
MITZNER, WAYNE A P01HL10342-26
MITZNER, WAYNE A P30ES03819-06A1 9021
MIVECHI, NAHID F R29CA54093-02
MIX, THOMAS W R44DK40661-02A2
MIYAI, KATSUMI S06GM47165-01 0014
MIYAMOTO, MICHAEL D R01NS22457-03
MIYAMOTO, RICHARD T R01DC00064-02
MIYAMOTO, S Z01HL02226-02
MIYASAKI, KENNETH T K04DE00282-03
MIYATA, H Z01AG00276-01
MIZE, RICHARD R R01EY02973-11
MIZE, SUSAN G R13HD28134-01
MIZE, SUSAN G R44HD25354-03
MIZEL, STEVEN B R01AI25836-04
MIZEL, STEVEN B R01AI27163-03
MIZIORKO, HENRY M R37DK21491-14
MIZRACH, BRUCE S07RR07156-16 0570
MIZRAHI, ELI N01NS12316-00
MIZUKAMI, HIROSHI P60HL16008-19 0017
MIZUMORI, SHERI J S07RR07092-26 0501
MIZUMORI, SHERI J S07RR07092-26 0527
MIZUUCHI, K Z01DK33006-13
MLADEJOVSKY, MICHAEL S07RR07092-26 0546
MLADENOVIC, JEANETTE R01HL42142-04
MMERMAN, KATHERINE L S07RR05983-05 0355
MOAK, JEFFREY M01RR00188-27 0331
MOAWAD, ATEF H U10HD27861-01
MOBARHAN, SOHRAB U01CA53799-01
MOBASHERY, SHAHRIAR S07RR07051-26 0735
MOBASHERY, SHAHRIAR S07RR07051-26 0731
MOBASSALEH, MUNIR R29DK39120-03
MOBBS, CHARLES V R01HD25543-03
MOBILY, PAULA R S07RR07035-26 0099
MOBLEY, HARRY L R01AI23328-06
MOBLEY, HARRY L R01AI25567-03
MOBLEY, HARRY L T P01AG04393-07 0004
MOBLEY, WILLIAM C R01AG10672-01
MOBLEY, WILLIAM C R01NS24054-06
MOBRAATEN, LARRY E N01AI95024-03
MOBRAATEN, LARRY E P01HG00330-03 0003
MOBRAATEN, LARRY E P30CA34196-09 9007
MOBRAATEN, LARRY E P40RR01262-10
MOCARSKI, EDWARD S P50HL33811-06 0002
MOCARSKI, EDWARD S R01AI30363-01A1
MOCARSKI, EDWARD S, JR R01AI20211-08
MOCARSKI, EDWARD S, JR R01AI28341-01A2
MOCARSKI, EDWARD S, JR R13AI31416-01
MOCCHETTI, ITALO R01NS29664-01
MOCHAN, EUGENE R01DE09218-02
MOCHLY-ROSEN, DARIA P01AA08353-03 0005
MOCHLY-ROSEN, DARIA D R01HL43380-03
MOCK, DONALD A M01RR00059-30 0673
MOCK, DONALD M K04DK01810-05
MOCK, DONALD M R01DK36823-07
MOCK, DONALD M R01HD27061-02
MOCK, M B M01RR00585-20 0397
MOCK, MICHAEL B U01HL38493-05
MOCK, WILLIAM L R01GM39740-03
MOCKEL, M P41RR02594-06 0008
MOCZYDLOWSKI, EDWARD P01HL38156-05 0003
MOCZYDLOWSKI, EDWARD G R01AR38796-06
MODAK, MUKUND J R01AI26652-03
MODAK, MUKUND J R01GM36307-05
MODAN, BARUCH R01AG05885-03S1
MODAN, BARUCH R01CA51117-02
MODELL, HAROLD P01HL38736-05 9003
MODELL, HAROLD I P01CA42045-06 9007
MODELL, HAROLD I R43DK44064-01
MODELL, JACK G M01RR00042-31 0633
MODEST, EDWARD J R01CA41314-06
MODIANO, MANUEL R R13CA55083-01
MODLIN, IRVIN M R01DK38063-03
MODLIN, JOHN M01RR00052-30 0231
MODLIN, JOHN M01RR00052-30 0217
MODLIN, JOHN F M01RR00052-30 0234
MODLIN, ROBERT L R01AR40312-02
MODLIN, ROBERT L R22AI22553-08
MODRICH, PAUL L P30CA14236-18 9024
MODRICH, PAUL L R01GM45190-01
MODRICH, PAUL L R37GM23719-16
MODY, ISTVAN P50NS12151-17 0015
MODY, ISTVAN R01NS27528-02
MOE, AARON J R29HD27258-02
MOE, ORSON W S07RR05426-30 0145
MOEHRING, THOMAS J R01AI09100-22
MOELLER, KEVIN D P01GM24483-12A1 0017
MOEN, LAURA K R29AI29311-02
MOENCH, M D P01NS26643-04 0005

MOERLAND, TIMOTHY S R29DK41908-02
MOERLEIN, STEPHEN M R29NS26788-03
MOERSCHBAECHER, JOSEPH M R01DA04775-05
MOERSCHBAECHER, JOSEPH M R01DA03573-09
MOERTEL, CHARLES G P01CA31224-06S1 0003
MOERTEL, CHARLES G P01CA31224-06S1 9002
MOERTEL, CHARLES G P01CA31224-06S1
MOERTEL, CHARLES G U10CA25224-12
MOERTEL, CHARLES G U10CA37404-07
MOFFAT, JOHN K P41RR01646-09 9001
MOFFAT, JOHN K P41RR01646-09 9002
MOFFAT, JOHN K P41RR01646-09 9003
MOFFAT, JOHN K P41RR01646-09 9004
MOFFAT, JOHN K P41RR01646-09 9005
MOFFAT, JOHN K P41RR01646-09 9006
MOFFAT, JOHN K R01GM36452-06
MOFFITT, ROBERT A R01HD27248-02
MOFFITT, TERRI E S07RR07098-26 0351
MOFFITT, TERRIE E R01MH45070-03
MOFFITT, TERRIE E R01MH45548-03
MOGHADAM, BEHJAT KH R15DE09023-01A2
MOGHISSI, KAMRAN U54HD29184-01 0001
MOHAGHEGHPOUR, NAHID R01AI30939-01A1
MOHAGHEGHPOUR, NAHID R22AI22653-06
MOHAMED, ABDUL S06GM08047-20S1 0013
MOHAMMAD, SYED F R01HL42555-02
MOHAN, OLGA S07RR05551-29 0962
MOHANAKUMAR, THALACHALLOUR R01AI23902-03
MOHANAKUMAR, THALACHALLOUR R01AI28356-03
MOHANAKUMAR, THALACHALLOUR R01DK32253-09
MOHANTY, PRAMOD M01RR00065-29 0376
MOHL, NORMAN D S07RR05330-30 0024
MOHLER, JAMES P R29HD22751-04
MOHR, F C S07RR05457-29 0005
MOHR, J P P01AG07232-03 0002
MOHR, JAY P M01RR00645-20 0344
MOHR, SCOTT C S07RR07043-26 0132
MOHRAZ, MANIJEH R01GM35399-07
MOHRAZ, MANIJEH S07RR05399-30 0909
MOHS, RICHARD C P01AG02219-11
MOHS, RICHARD C P01MH45212-02 0001
MOHS, RICHARD C. P50AG05138-08 0011
MOHS, RICHARD C. U01AG06790-06 0002
MOHSENIN, V S07RR05692-22 0988
MOIR, DONALD T R43GM43697-01A1
MOISE, ALICIA S07RR05425-30 0757
MOISE, N SYDNEY S07RR05462-29 0893
MOISE, NANCY S R01HD28938-01
MOISEFF, ANDREW R01DC00277-06
MOISES, HYLAN C R01AG10667-01
MOISES, HYLAN C R01DA03365-08
MOJSOV, SVETLANA R29DK40083-05
MOKHTARIAN, FOROOZAN R29NS24688-06
MOKLER, DAVID J R03DA07316-01
MOKYR, MARGALIT B K04CA01350-04
MOLANDER, GARY A R01GM35249-07
MOLD, CAROLYN R01AI24720-06
MOLDAWER, LYLE L R01CA52108-02
MOLDAWER, LYLE L R01GM40586-04
MOLDAY, ROBERT S R01EY02422-14
MOLDOVEANUA, ZINA R43AI31008-01
MOLE, JOHN E P30DK32520-08 9001
MOLER, FRANK W M01RR00042-31 0476
MOLER, FRANK W M01RR00042-31 0537
MOLFESE, DENNIS L R01HD17860-06
MOLFESE, DENNIS L S07RR07118-22 0379
MOLINARI, HELEN H R55NS29771-01
MOLINE, MARGARET L S07RR05396-30 0783
MOLINEUX, IAN J R01GM32095-09
MOLINOFF, PERRY B P01GM34781-07 0005
MOLINOFF, PERRY B P01GM34781-07
MOLINOFF, PERRY B P01MH48125-01 0001
MOLINOFF, PERRY B R01NS18479-10
MOLINOFF, PERRY B R01NS18591-10
MOLINSKI, TADEUSZ F R29AI31660-01
MOLITCH, MARK E M01RR00048-30 0163
MOLITCH, MARK E M01RR00048-30 0171
MOLITCH, MARK E M01RR00048-30 0150
MOLITCH, MARK E M01RR00048-30 0153
MOLITCH, MARK E U01DK37859-06
MOLITOR, THOMAS W S07RR05930-07 0721
MOLITORIS, BRUCE A R01DK41126-02
MOLL, GEORGE W, JR M01RR00039-31 0368
MOLL, PATRICIA P R01HL46292-01
MOLLER, AAGE R R01DC00272-08
MOLLER, DAVID R29HL45115-02
MOLLER, DAVID R M01RR00722-19 0253
MOLLIVER, MARK E R01DA04431-05
MOLLIVER, MARK E R01NS15199-11
MOLLOI, SABEE R29HL42435-03
MOLNAR, CHARLES E R01DC00282-07
MOLNAR, JANOS S07RR05369-30 0577
MOLOF, MARTIN J R01AA08404-03
MOLONY, DONALD A S07RR05745-19 0223
MOLS, OLE P30CA22453-14 9002
MONACO, ANTHONY P R01AI14551-15
MONACO, JOHN J R29GM38774-05
MONACO, JOHN J S07RR05697-22 0000
MONAFO, WILLIAM W R01GM33770-08
MONAGHAN, DANIEL T R29NS28966-01
MONCLA, BERNARD J. P01DE08555-03 0004
MOND, JAMES J R01AI27465-03
MONDER, CARL R01DK37094-06
MONDER, CARL S07RR05860-11 0931
MONDINO, BARTLY J R01EY04606-10
MONDINO, BARTLY J R01EY04607-10
MONDRAGON, ALFONSO R29GM43187-01A1
MONDRAGON, ALFONSO S15HL47761-01
MONEIM, MOHEB S07RR05583-27 0634
MONESTIER, MARC R29AI26665-04
MONETTE, FRANCIS C S07RR07043-26 0112
MONFORT, STEVEN L K08HD00903-02
MONGINI, PATRICIA K R01GM35174-06
MONK, TIMOTHY H P01AG06836-04 9001
MONK, TIMOTHY H P01AG06836-04
MONK, TIMOTHY H. P01AG06836-04 9002
MONK, TIMOTHY H. P01AG06836-04 0002
MONK, TIMOTHY H. P01AG06836-04 0003
MONKS, TERRANCE J R01ES04662-05
MONNAT, RAYMOND P50AG05136-08 0012
MONNAT, RAYMOND J P01AG01751-13 0008
MONNAT, RAYMOND J, JR R29CA48022-04
MONNIER, VINCENT M R01AG05601-07
MONNIER, VINCENT M R01EY07099-05
MONOHAR, V Z01BH02006-03
MONROE, JOHN G R01AI23568-05
MONROE, JOHN G S07RR05415-30 0015
MONROE, SCOTT E P30HD11979-13 9001
MONROE, SCOTT E P30HD11979-13 9004
MONSON, RICHARD P30ES00002-29 0038
MONSOUR, ALFRED P30DK34933-06A1 0009
MONT, DANIEL M R29HD27529-01
MONTAL, S MAURICIO K05MH00778-03
MONTAL, S MAURICIO R01GM42340-03
MONTAL, S MAURICIO R01MH44638-03
MONTALI, RICHARD J R01AI27203-03
MONTAMAT, STEPHEN C K08AG00525-01
MONTANO, DANIEL S07RR05758-18 0255
MONTANO, DANIEL E R01MH47059-02
MONTE-WICHER, VICTORIA R01AI21833-06
MONTEALEGRE, FEDERICO J S06GM08239-06 0007
MONTEALEGRE, FEDERICO G12RR03050-07 0006
MONTECALVO, MARISA S07RR05569-27 0114
MONTEFIORI, DAVID C R01AI29377-01A1
MONTELARO, RONALD C R01AI25850-05
MONTELARO, RONALD C R01CA49296-04
MONTELARO, RONALD C. U01AI28243-03 0003
MONTELIONE, GAETANO S07RR07058-26 0182
MONTELL, CRAIG R01EY08117-03
MONTELL, DENISE J R29GM46425-01
MONTER, PAUL M01RR00997-16 0419
MONTERO, VICENTE M R01EY02877-11
MONTGOMERY, DAVID W R29DK40519-04
MONTGOMERY, GARY T S06GM08038-21 0011
MONTGOMERY, MARK R R01AG07801-04
MONTGOMERY, PAUL C R01DE09658-01A1
MONTGOMERY, PAUL C R01EY05133-07A2
MONTGOMERY, RHONDA J R01MH45840-01A1
MONTGOMERY, RHONDA J U01AG10318-01
MONTGOMERY, RICHARD S07RR05889-09 0519
MONTGOMERY, ROBERT R P01HL44612-02 9001
MONTGOMERY, ROBERT R P01HL44612-02 0004
MONTGOMERY, ROBERT R R01HL33721-08
MONTGOMERY, ROBERT R S15HL47764-01
MONTGOMERY, ROBERT R, JR S07RR05889-09
MONTI, PETER M R01AA07850-04
MONTI, PETER M R01AA08734-01A1
MONTI, PETER M R01DA04859-04
MONTMINY, MARC R P01CA54418-01 0001
MONTMINY, MARC R R01GM37828-05
MONTMINY, MARC R S07RR05595-27 0670
MONTOYA, HELEN MARIE R03AG10405-01
MONTOYA, JEAN P R43HL46613-01
MONTRELLA, MARY M01RR00065-29 0344
MONTREY, RICHARD D G20RR07095-01
MONTROSE, MARSHALL S07RR05378-30 0005
MONTROSE, MARSHALL H R01DK42457-01A1
MOOD, DARLENE W R01NR01089-07
MOOD, DARLENE W S03RR03341-06
MOOD, DARLENE W S07RR05718-16
MOOD, DARLENE W S15CA55955-01
MOODY, DAVID E R29DA05102-04
MOODY, DIXON M P01NS27500-01A2 0003
MOODY, DIXON M R01NS20618-08
MOODY, FRANK G P50GM38529-04
MOODY, FRANK G P50GM38529-04 0001
MOODY, SALLY A K04NS01373-03
MOODY, SALLY A R01NS23158-06
MOODY, TERRY W R01CA48071-03
MOODY, TERRY W R01CA53477-01
MOOLGAVKAR, SURESH P01CA53996-14 0002
MOOLGAVKAR, SURESH H R01CA47658-04
MOON, DUDLEY G R29HL40615-02
MOON, DUDLEY J P01GM40761-01A2 0002
MOON, JERALD B P60DC00976-02 0004
MOON, JERRY B P01DE05837-10 0003
MOON, RANDALL T K04AR01837-02
MOON, RANDALL T R01AR40089-03
MOON, RANDALL T R01HD27525-01
MOON, RICHARD N01CN85097-11
MOON, RICHARD N01CN95151-08
MOON, RICHARD C P01CA48112-01A3 0005
MOON, RICHARD C S07RR05744-14 0139
MOON, RICHARD C S15CA55941-01
MOON, THOMAS E P01CA27502-11 9002
MOON, THOMAS E P01CA27502-11 0015
MOON, THOMAS E P01CA27502-11 0016
MOON, THOMAS E P30CA23074-14 9002
MOON, THOMAS E U01CA34256-08
MOONEN, C Z01RR10373-01
MOONEN, C Z01RR10374-01
MOONEY, RICHARD D R01EY08015-03
MOONEY, ROBERT A R01DK38138-04A1
MOORADIAN, ARSHAG D S07RR05675-23 0934
MOORE, JOHN J. P50HD11089-14 0024
MOORE, STEVEN A. P01NS24621-05 0006
MOORE, ALBERT L R01ES03437-08
MOORE, ANA L S07RR07112-24 0422
MOORE, ANTONY S07RR05852-11 0259
MOORE, BETTY P30CA13696-19 9007
MOORE, BLAKE W R01AA07569-03
MOORE, CAROLYN A R24AA08671-02 0001
MOORE, CHRISTOPHER A R29DC00822-01A1
MOORE, CLAIRE L R01GM41752-03
MOORE, CLAIRE L R01GM42760-03
MOORE, DAVID M01RR00046-31 0473
MOORE, DAVID D R01DK43382-01A1
MOORE, DEXTER S S06GM08016-21 0079
MOORE, DONALD E M01RR00037-31 0470
MOORE, DONALD E M01RR00037-31 0502
MOORE, E NEIL R01HL28393-10
MOORE, EDWARD W R01DK32130-09
MOORE, FRANCIS D R29AI24139-05
MOORE, G WAYNE R01NS27461-03
MOORE, HAROLD W R01GM36312-05
MOORE, HSIAO-PING H R01GM35239-07
MOORE, IDA K S07RR05913-08 0666
MOORE, IDA M R01NR02557-02
MOORE, JANICE S07RR07127-23 0483
MOORE, JOAN W R01DA07128-01
MOORE, JOHN W R01NS03437-31
MOORE, KENNETH E R01NS15911-23
MOORE, KENNETH E R37MH42802-25
MOORE, KRISTIN A N01HD92919-04
MOORE, L V P01DE08972-03 0003
MOORE, LARRY J R43AR40807-01
MOORE, LARRY J R43HL46046-01A1
MOORE, LEE E R01MH45796-01A2
MOORE, LEON C R01DK26341-10
MOORE, LORNA G P01HL14985-20 0029
MOORE, LORNA G P01HL14985-20 0002
MOORE, LORNA G. P01HL14985-20 0031
MOORE, MALCOLM A P01CA20194-14 0023
MOORE, MALCOLM A P01CA23766-14 0003
MOORE, MALCOLM A R01DK42693-02
MOORE, MALCOLM A R01HL46546-01
MOORE, MARK W R29HD27242-02
MOORE, MARY L R01NR02410-02
MOORE, MELVIN R U10CA52735-02
MOORE, MICHAEL DR N01CP95670-04
MOORE, MICHAEL R S07RR05870-10 0994
MOORE, P F S07RR05457-29 0006
MOORE, P F S07RR05457-29 0998
MOORE, PAUL A N01DE12590-00
MOORE, PETER B P01GM22778-16 0007
MOORE, PETER B R01GM41651-03
MOORE, PETER B R37AI09167-23
MOORE, PETER D R01GM45141-01
MOORE, PETER D S07RR05369-30 0604
MOORE, R BLAINE P60HL38639-04 0001
MOORE, R BLAINE P60HL38639-04 0002
MOORE, RICHARD U01CA53001-02 0001
MOORE, RICHARD E R01CA12623-18
MOORE, ROBERT M R43HL46038-01
MOORE, ROBERT N R01DK43229-01
MOORE, ROBERT Y R01AG08172-04
MOORE, ROBERT Y R01NS16304-11A1
MOORE, RUSSELL L R01HL40306-02
MOORE, RUSSELL L R01HL44146-02
MOORE, SHEILA G U01CA54009-01
MOORE, STEPHEN P01CA41167-06 0002
MOORE, STEVEN A R01NS27914-01A2
MOORE, THOMAS J M01RR02635-07 0184
MOORE, THOMAS J M01RR02635-07 0267
MOORE, THOMAS J M01RR02635-07 0247
MOORE, THOMAS R M01RR00827-17 0456
MOORE, V Z01AA00279-02
MOORE, WILLIAM G R29DE08580-03
MOORHEAD, JOHN P30DK34914-06 9007
MOORMAN, JOSEPH R R29HL46573-02
MOORMAN, M P Z01ES21031-07
MOOS, M Z01BB07004-02
MOOS, M Z01BB07011-01
MOOS, RUDOLF P60AR20610-14 0006
MOOS, RUDOLPH H R01AA06699-06
MOOS, RUDOLPH H R37AA02863-12
MOOSEKER, MARK S R01DK25387-13
MOOSEKER, MARK S R01GM37556-04A1
MOOSER, GREGORY R01DE03739-19
MOOSSY, JOHN P50AG05133-08 9002
MOR, VINCENT R01HS06214-03
MOR, VINCENT R01HS06795-01
MORAD, MARTIN R01HL16152-19
MORAFKA, DAVID J S06GM08156-15 0005
MORAHAN, PAGE S07RR05418-30 0027
MORAHAN, PAGE S R01AI25751-05

MORAHAN, PAGE S R01CA35961-07
MORALES, MANUEL F R37HL44200-03
MORALES, REGINALD S06GM08102-20 0019
MORALES, T I Z01DE00510-03
MORAN, CHARLES P, JR K04AI00760-05
MORAN, CHARLES P, JR R01AI20319-09
MORAN, CHARLES P, JR R01GM39917-04
MORAN, DAVID T P01DC00244-07 0001
MORAN, ELIZABETH R01CA53592-01A1
MORAN, ELIZABETH R01CA55330-01
MORAN, ELIZABETH R29CA46436-04
MORAN, FRANK X N01CP95618-08
MORAN, PATRICIA B S07RR07079-26 0303
MORAN, RICHARD G R01CA27605-11
MORAN, RICHARD G R01CA36054-09
MORAN, RICHARD G R01CA39687-07
MORAN, THOMAS P01AI24671-04 9001
MORAN, TIMOTHY H R01DK19302-16
MORANDI, MARIA T S07RR05828-08 0531
MORAVEK, JOSEF N43CM17566-00
MORAWETZ, RICHARD B M01RR00032-31 0283
MORAWETZ, RICHARD B M01RR00032-31 0325
MORAWETZ, RICHARD B M01RR00032-31 0326
MORAWETZ, RICHARD B M01RR00032-31 0285
MORAWETZ, RICHARD B M01RR00032-31 0286
MORAWETZ, RICHARD B M01RR00032-31 0287
MORAWETZ, RICHARD B M01RR00032-31 0291
MORAWETZ, RICHARD B M01RR00032-31 0302
MORDAN, LAWRENCE J R01CA51498-02
MORDEN, KATHLEEN M R29GM38137-05
MORDES, JOHN P R01DK41235-03
MORE, FREDERICK G S07RR05321-30 0260
MOREAU, DONNA P50MH43878-03 0029
MOREAU, DONNA P50MH43878-03 0028
MOREAU, DONNA P50MH43878-03 0011
MOREAU, DONNA L P50MH43878-03 0009
MOREAU, DONNA L P50MH43878-03 0016
MOREAU, DONNA L R03MH47849-01
MOREBECK, MARY ELLEN S07RR07002-26 0884
MOREL, ANNE E R01DC00922-01A1
MOREL, DIANE W R29HL45306-02
MOREL, FRANCOIS M M P30ES02109-13 9004
MOREL, JORGE G S07RR06005-04 0299
MOREL, NICOLE S07RR07043-26 0122
MOREL, PENELOPE A R01AI29027-01A1
MOREL, PENELOPE A R01AI31427-01
MORELAND, ROBERT S R01HL37956-07
MORELL, PIERRE P01ES01104-16 0007
MORELL, PIERRE R01NS11615-19
MORELLI, JOSEPH G K08AR01828-02
MORELLI, JOSEPH G S07RR06022-02 0849
MORENO, EDGARD C P50DE07009-08 0005
MORENO, EDGARD C R37DE03187-20
MORENS, DAVID M R01NS30371-01
MOREST, D KENT R01NS29613-01
MORETON, J EDWARD R01DA03173-07
MOREY, DAVID N01CO15663-00
MOREY, DAVID N01CO15697-01
MOREY, DAVID N01CO15724-00
MOREY, DAVID B N01CO15711-00
MORGAN, ALAN R P01CA48733-02
MORGAN, ALAN R P01CA48733-02 0001
MORGAN, ALAN R S07RR07237-04 0742
MORGAN, D L Z01ES21090-06
MORGAN, D L Z01ES21136-02
MORGAN, D L Z01ES21137-02
MORGAN, DAVID P01AG09793-01 0005
MORGAN, DAVID G R01AG07892-03
MORGAN, DAVID G R35AG07909-03 0002
MORGAN, DAVID L R01AG08273-01A1
MORGAN, DAVID O R01CA52481-02
MORGAN, DAVID O S07RR05355-30 0427
MORGAN, EDWARD THOMAS R29DK39968-04
MORGAN, HOWARD E S07RR05996-04
MORGAN, HOWARD E S07RR05996-04 0933
MORGAN, HOWARD E S15HL47686-01
MORGAN, JAMES L S07RR07085-26 0339
MORGAN, JAMES L S07RR07085-26 0340
MORGAN, JAMES P P01DA06306-01A1
MORGAN, JAMES P P01DA06306-01A1 0001
MORGAN, JAMES P R01DA05171-05
MORGAN, JAMES P R01HL31117-08
MORGAN, JULIET R03RR06849-01
MORGAN, KATHLEEN G R01HL31704-08
MORGAN, KATHLEEN G R01HL42293-03
MORGAN, LEE ROY R44CA49310-02
MORGAN, LESLIE S07RR05336-29 0308
MORGAN, P Z01AA00288-01
MORGAN, PATRICIA R01DA06853-01
MORGAN, PHILIP G R01GM45402-01A1
MORGAN, R Z01HL02218-03
MORGAN, R Z01HL02225-02
MORGAN, SARAH L S07RR05968-06 0338
MORGAN, STEVEN H S06GM08062-21 0003
MORGAN, TIMOTHY P60AG10484-01 9002
MORGAN, TIMOTHY M P01HL45666-01 9007
MORGAN, WILLIAM T R01HL37570-05A2
MORGAN, WILLIAM W R01GM43763-01A1
MORGANE, PETER J P01HD22539-04 0002
MORGANSTEIN, WARREN M S07RR05317-21
MORGENSTERN, HAL R03OH02765-02
MORGENSTERN, JONATHAN P50AA08747-02 0005
MORHENN, VERA B K04AR01782-05
MORHENN, VERA B R01AR38658-05
MORIARTY, C MICHAEL S03RR03032-11
MORIARTY, C MICHAEL S07RR07025-26 0992
MORIARTY, C MICHAEL S15AI32164-01
MORIARTY, ROBERT M P01CA48112-01A3 0006
MORIMOTO, CHIKAO P01AI29530-02 0002
MORIMOTO, CHIKAO R01AR33713-07
MORIMOTO, RICHARD I R01GM38109-05
MORIN, CHARLES M R29MH47020-02
MORIN, FREDERICK C, III R01HL41387-02
MORIN, LAWRENCE S07RR05736-19 0161
MORIN, LAWRENCE S07RR05736-19 0172
MORIN, LAWRENCE P R01NS22168-06
MORIN, ROBERT J S07RR05551-29 0949
MORING, JILL K21AA00126-02
MORISHIMA, A M01RR00645-20 0411
MORISHIMA, HISAYO O R01DA06648-02
MORISKY, DONALD E S07RR05442-29 0047
MORITA, H P51RR00168-30 0138
MORITA, MICHIO R01CA47409-03
MORIZONO, TETSUO P50DC00133-13 0013
MORKIN, EUGENE P01HL20984-15 0001
MORKIN, EUGENE MS BS P01HL20984-15
MORLEY, BARBARA P60DC00982-02 0005
MORLEY, BARBARA J R03DA06482-01A1
MORLEY, BARBARA J S07RR05834-12 0541
MORLOCK, LAURA L R01HS06735-01
MORRA, MARION P01CA42101-06 9001
MORRE, D JAMES R01GM44675-02
MORRE, D JAMES S07RR05586-24 0119
MORRELL, JOAN I R01HD22983-05A2
MORRILL, GENE A R01HD10463-09
MORRIS, ALAN S07RR05471-29 0589
MORRIS, CHRISTOPHER L K08HL02128-05
MORRIS, CYNTHIA N01HD13123-00
MORRIS, CYNTHIA P30DK40566-02 0002
MORRIS, CYNTHIA P30DK40566-02 9001
MORRIS, CYNTHIA D R29HL39052-05
MORRIS, D Z01BB07007-01
MORRIS, DAVID P01GM42508-03 0007
MORRIS, DAVID J R01DK21404-10
MORRIS, DAVID R P50DE08229-05 0002
MORRIS, DAVID R R01CA39053-08
MORRIS, HUGHLETT L P01DE05837-10
MORRIS, J GLENN R22AI28856-02
MORRIS, JOHN S07RR05743-14 0619
MORRIS, JOHN B S15ES05837-01
MORRIS, JOHN C M01RR00036-31 0970
MORRIS, JOHN C P50AG05681-08 9002
MORRIS, JOHN C. M01RR00036-31 0702
MORRIS, JOHN C. P01AG03991-08 0006
MORRIS, JOHN C. U01AG06790-06 0001
MORRIS, JOHN C, III R29DK42008-01A2
MORRIS, JOHN E R01HD19530-05
MORRIS, JOHN GLENN JR R01AI25634-03
MORRIS, JOHN N P01AG04390-08 0004
MORRIS, JOHN N R01AG07820-02
MORRIS, JOHN N R01NR02054-03
MORRIS, JOHN N U01AG10305-01
MORRIS, MARIANA R01HL43178-02
MORRIS, MARILYN E R29GM40551-03
MORRIS, MICHAEL D R01GM37006-06
MORRIS, MICHAEL D R01NS26160-03
MORRIS, N RONALD R01GM29228-11
MORRIS, N RONALD R01GM34711-07
MORRIS, N RONALD S07RR05576-27
MORRIS, N RONALD S07RR05576-27 0586
MORRIS, N RONALD S15AI32206-01
MORRIS, NICHOLAS P R29GM39862-04
MORRIS, PATRICIA L S07RR05860-11 0932
MORRIS, R CURTIS, JR R01HL47943-01
MORRIS, R D P51RR00165-31 0170
MORRIS, RANDAL E R01HL40987-03
MORRIS, REBECCA J R29CA45293-05
MORRIS, ROBIN P01HD06016-21 0009
MORRIS, ROBIN P50NS20489-07 9002
MORRIS, ROBIN K S07RR07160-16 0599
MORRIS, S L Z01BA05001-04
MORRIS, S L Z01BA05003-03
MORRIS, S L Z01BA05004-03
MORRIS, SIDNEY M R01DK33144-08
MORRIS, STEPHEN J R15GM44071-01A1
MORRISETT, JOEL D M01RR00350-25 0473
MORRISETT, JOEL D P60HL27341-10 9002
MORRISETT, JOEL D P60HL27341-10 0005
MORRISETT, JOEL D R01HL32971-07
MORRISON-PLUMMER, JANICE P01AI22380-07 900
MORRISON, ADRIAN R P50HL42236-04 0001
MORRISON, ADRIAN R, JR R37MH42903-05
MORRISON, ALAN S R01DK35402-06
MORRISON, ALAN S R01DK42202-02
MORRISON, AUBERY R P01DK38111-05 0004
MORRISON, AUBERY R P01DK38111-05 9001
MORRISON, AUBREY P01DK38111-05
MORRISON, AUBREY R P01DK09976-27 0002
MORRISON, DAVID C R37AI23447-06
MORRISON, DIANE M R01AI29507-03
MORRISON, DIANE M U01AI31448-01 0007
MORRISON, FRANCIS S K07HL02032-03
MORRISON, FREDERICK J R01HD27176-01
MORRISON, G H P41RR04224-04 0004
MORRISON, GEORGE H R01GM24314-15
MORRISON, GRACE M K15DE00262-03
MORRISON, HARRY S07RR07032-26 0046
MORRISON, HARRY A R01AR39286-04
MORRISON, JAMES D S03RR03051-11
MORRISON, JAMES D S07RR07035-26
MORRISON, JAMES D S15GM47098-01
MORRISON, JOHN C R01EY09117-01
MORRISON, JOHN H P01MH45212-02 0002
MORRISON, JOHN H P50AG05131-08 0003
MORRISON, JOHN H R01AG06647-04A1
MORRISON, JOHN H R01MH48603-01
MORRISON, JOHN H. P50AG05138-08 0007
MORRISON, LYNNE H R29AR39761-03
MORRISON, MARCELLE R R01HD14886-11
MORRISON, MARCELLS P50AG08013-04 0004
MORRISON, P F Z01RR10336-02
MORRISON, P F Z01RR10353-01
MORRISON, PETER S07RR05710-21 0021
MORRISON, R P Z01AI00519-04
MORRISON, RICHARD STEVEN R29NS26125-05
MORRISON, SHAUN P20NS30295-01 0002
MORRISON, SHAUN F R01HL47196-01
MORRISON, SHERIE L R01AI29470-01A1
MORRISON, SHERIE L R01CA16858-18
MORRISON, SHERIS P30CA13696-19 9015
MORRISON, SIDONIE A U01AI25893-05 0007
MORRISON, TRUDY G R01AI30572-01
MORRISON, TRUDY G R01GM37745-14
MORRISON, TRUDY G S07RR05712-20 0108
MORRISS, FRANK H, JR P30HD27748-02
MORRISSEY, JAMES H P01HL16411-18 0017
MORRISSEY, JAMES H R01HL44225-03
MORRISSEY, JEREMIAH J P01DK09976-27 0016
MORRISSEY, JEREMIAH J R01DK30178-10
MORROW, A LESLIE R01AA09013-01
MORROW, CARY J S06GM08139-17 0027
MORROW, CASEY P30AI27767-04 9003
MORROW, CASEY D R01AI25005-05
MORROW, CASEY D. P01AI27290-04 0004
MORROW, DANIEL G R01AG08521-03
MORROW, GARY R R01NR01905-11
MORROW, GARY R U10CA37420-07
MORROW, GRANT, III S07RR05905-08
MORROW, GRANT, III S15CA56013-01
MORROW, JANET R R29GM46539-01
MORROW, JANET R S07RR07066-26 0252
MORROW, JANET R S07RR07066-26 0253
MORROW, JON S R01DK43812-01
MORROW, JON S R01HL28560-09
MORROW, JON S R01NS29611-01
MORROW, LESTER G S03RR03128-11
MORROW, LESTER G S03RR03129-11
MORROW, LESTER G S03RR03130-11
MORROW, LESTER G S03RR03131-11
MORROW, LESTER G S03RR03488-04
MORROW, LESTER G S03RR03554-01
MORROW, LEWIS U76PE00462-01
MORROW, LEWIS B U76PE00429-02
MORROW, LEWIS B U76PE00430-02
MORROW, LEWIS B U76PE00433-02
MORROW, LISA A R29MH43846-03
MORROW, PHILLIP R R43CA56961-01
MORROW, WILLIAM J R43AI31284-01
MORSE, BRENDA S R43HL46096-01
MORSE, DANIEL E R01CA53105-01
MORSE, DANIEL E R01RR06640-02
MORSE, DOUGLASS H S07RR07085-26
MORSE, DOUGLASS H S07RR07085-26 0341
MORSE, DOUGLASS H S15GM47092-01
MORSE, GARY ANDREW R18MH46160-03
MORSE, H C Z01AI00465-06
MORSE, JANICE M R01NR02130-03
MORSE, STEPHEN S P40RR01180-14 0001
MORSE, STEPHEN S R24RR03121-05
MORSE, WILLIAM H P51RR00168-30 0119
MORSE, WILLIAM H P51RR00168-30 0088
MORSE, WILLIAM H R37MH07658-28
MORSTAD, ANDREW T S07RR05322-30 0277
MORTENSEN, RICHARD F R01CA30015-11
MORTENSON, LEONARD E R01GM40067-04
MORTIMER, JEYLAN T R01MH42843-04
MORTIMER, JOHN T N01NS02395-01
MORTIMER, ROBERT K P40RR04231-05
MORTIMER, ROBERT K R01GM30990-08
MORTIMORE, GLENN E R01DK21624-14
MORTOLA, JOSEPH M01RR01032-16 0471
MORTOLA, JOSEPH P50HD12303-13 0004
MORTOLA, JOSEPH F M01RR00827-17 0388
MORTOLA, JOSEPH F M01RR00827-17 0431
MORTON WILLIAM U01AI26503-04 0002
MORTON, CYNTHIA C R01DC00871-02
MORTON, DAVID B R29NS29740-01
MORTON, DONALD L P01CA12582-19
MORTON, DONALD L P01CA12582-19 0004
MORTON, DONALD L P01CA29605-10
MORTON, DONALD L P01CA29605-10 0001
MORTON, DONALD L P01CA29605-10 9001
MORTON, DONALD L. P01CA12582-19 9001
MORTON, KATHRYN A R29CA49275-03
MORTON, LAURENCE L U01CA37606-08 0006
MORTON, MARK J R01HL40041-05

MORTON, RICHARD E P01HL29582-09 0007
MORTON, RICHARD E P01HL29582-09 9003
MORTON, ROSCOE F U10CA35101-08
MORTON, STEVEN G R43CA54689-01
MORTON, THOMAS H S03RR03180-08
MORTON, WILLIAM B P51RR00166-30 9016
MORTON, WILLIAM P P51RR00166-30 9014
MORTON, WILLIAM R N01AI15094-00
MORTON, WILLIAM R P51RR00166-30 9015
MORTON, WILLIAM R R13RR06959-01
MORTON, WILLIAM R U01AI30238-02 0004
MORTON, WILLIAM R. P51RR00166-30 0153
MORTON, WILLIAM R. P51RR00166-30 0171
MORTON, WILLIAM R. P51RR00166-30 0172
MORTON, WILLIAM R. P51RR00166-30 0173
MORTON, WILLIAM R. P51RR00166-30 0174
MORTON, WILLIAM R. P51RR00166-30 0175
MORTON, WILLIAM R. P51RR00166-30 0154
MORTON, WILLIAM R. P51RR00166-30 0155
MORTON, WILLIAM R. P51RR00166-30 0156
MORTON, WILLIAM R. P51RR00166-30 0157
MORTON, WILLIAM R. P51RR00166-30 0158
MORTON, WILLIAM R. P51RR00166-30 0159
MORYKWAS, MICHAEL J S07RR05404-30 0850
MORZYCHA-WROBLEWSKA, S07RR05665-24 0888
MOSBACH, ERWIN H R37HL24061-13
MOSBACH, ERWIN H S03RR03385-07
MOSBACH, ERWIN H S07RR05886-08 0298
MOSBACH, ERWIN H S07RR05886-08
MOSBACH, ERWIN H S15HL47693-01
MOSBAUGH, DALE W R01GM32823-09
MOSBERG, HENRY I K02DA00118-03
MOSBERG, HENRY I P50DA00254-20 9002
MOSBERG, HENRY I R01DA03910-06
MOSCA, JOSEPH D R29AI24489-05
MOSCATELLI, DAVID A R01CA42229-04
MOSCICKI, BARBARA R01CA51323-02
MOSCICKI, RICHARD P01DK33506-08 9001
MOSCICKI, RICHARD A R01DC00824-01A1
MOSCICKI, RICHARD A S07RR05486-29 0042
MOSCONA, ANNE K11AI00739-05
MOSELEY, JOHN T S07RR07080-26
MOSELEY, JOHN T S15HL47727-01
MOSELEY, JOHN T S15MH49283-01
MOSELEY, POPE L R01AR40771-01A1
MOSELEY, POPE L R29HL40349-04
MOSELEY, RAY E R01HG00402-01
MOSELEY, RICHARD H R29DK39167-04
MOSELEY, STEPHEN L R01AI23771-04A1
MOSER-VEILLON, PHYLIS B R01HD28033-01
MOSER, HUGH M01RR00035-31 0350
MOSER, HUGO M01RR00052-30 0232
MOSER, HUGO W M01RR00035-31 0389
MOSER, HUGO W M01RR00722-19 0228
MOSER, HUGO W M01RR00722-19 0229
MOSER, HUGO W M01RR00722-19 0230
MOSER, HUGO W M01RR00722-19 0231
MOSER, HUGO W P01HD10981-14 0009
MOSER, HUGO W P01HD10981-14
MOSER, HUGO W P01HD24448-04
MOSER, HUGO W P30HD24061-04
MOSER, HUGO W R01HD26371-02
MOSER, KENNETH M M01RR00827-17 0293
MOSER, KENNETH M P50HL23584-13
MOSER, STEPHEN A R01AI29213-02
MOSES, ALAN C. M01RR01032-16 0391
MOSES, HAMILTON M01RR00035-31 0359
MOSES, HAMILTON M01RR00722-19 0164
MOSES, HAROLD L R35CA42572-06
MOSES, KEVIN R01EY09299-01
MOSES, ROBB E P01AG07123-04 0004
MOSES, ROBB E R01GM24711-14
MOSES, ROBB E S07RR05412-30 0983
MOSESSON, MICHAEL W R01HL47000-01
MOSESSON, MICHAEL W S07RR06041-01
MOSHANG, THOMAS M01RR00240-27 0347
MOSHANG, THOMAS M01RR00240-27 0204
MOSHANG, THOMAS M01RR00240-27 0289
MOSHANG, THOMAS M01RR00240-27 0290
MOSHANG, THOMAS JR M01RR00240-27 0329
MOSHE, SOLOMON L R01NS20253-06
MOSHER, DEANE F P01HL29586-09 0002
MOSHER, DEANE F, JR P01HL29586-09
MOSHER, DEANE F, JR R01HL21644-14
MOSHER, LOREN R R18MH49102-01
MOSIER, DONALD P01AI24526-05
MOSIER, DONALD E R01AI22871-06
MOSIER, DONALD E R01AI27703-03
MOSIER, DONALD E R01AI29182-03
MOSIER, DONALD E S07RR05882-09
MOSIER, DONALD E S15AI32169-01
MOSIER, DONALD E U01AI30238-02 0006
MOSIER, DONALD E U01AI31686-01 0003
MOSIER, STEPHEN R S15HD28770-01
MOSIG, GISELA R01GM13221-27
MOSIG, GISELA S07RR07201-12 0637
MOSIMANN, J E Z01CT00013-18
MOSIMANN, J E Z01CT00132-08
MOSKO, SARAH S R55HD27482-01
MOSKOWITZ, JOEL M P50AA06282-09 0003
MOSKOWITZ, MICHAEL A P50NS10828-16
MOSKOWITZ, MICHAEL A P50NS10828-16 0030
MOSKOWITZ, MICHAEL A P50NS10828-16 9002
MOSKOWITZ, MICHAEL A R01NS21558-07
MOSKOWITZ, MICHAEL A R01NS26782-03
MOSKOWITZ, MICHAEL A R55NS26361-04
MOSKOWITZ, ROLAND W P60AR20618-13
MOSKOWITZ, ROLAND W R01AR30134-13
MOSKOWITZ, WILLIAM B R29HL38878-03
MOSLEY, JAMES W. N01HB97074-09
MOSS, ALBERT A U01CA49078-03
MOSS, ANDREW R R01DA04363-05A1
MOSS, ANDREW R R03DA07067-01
MOSS, ANDREW R U01AI31499-01 9003
MOSS, ARTHUR J R01HL38702-04
MOSS, B Z01AI00298-10
MOSS, B Z01AI00307-10
MOSS, B Z01AI00416-08
MOSS, B Z01AI00539-04
MOSS, DENIS J R01CA52250-02
MOSS, DONALD R24MH47167-02 0008
MOSS, DONALD E S03RR03222-09
MOSS, HOWARD N01CM17529-00
MOSS, HOWARD N01CM87263-09
MOSS, J Z01HL00622-14
MOSS, JONATHAN R01NS27185-03
MOSS, LARRY G R29DK43129-02
MOSS, LARRY G S07RR05425-30 0758
MOSS, MARK P01HL13262-19 0035
MOSS, MARK B P01AG00001-17A2 9003
MOSS, MARK B P01AG00001-17A2 0020
MOSS, MIRIAM S07RR05611-22 0704
MOSS, RICHARD L R01AR31806-09A1
MOSS, RICHARD L R01HL25861-12
MOSS, ROBERT L R01MH41784-05
MOSS, ROBERT L R01MH47418-01
MOSS, SHARON E S06GM08016-21 0080
MOSS, STUART B R01HD25524-04
MOSS, STUART B S07RR05417-30 0805
MOSS, THOMAS S07RR05468-29 0401
MOSSER, DAVID M R29AI24313-06
MOSSEY, JANA M R01NR02642-01
MOSSMAN, BROOKE T P50HL14212-20 0038
MOSSMAN, BROOKE T R01HL39469-05
MOSSMAN, KENNETH L S03RR03320-04
MOSSMAN, KENNETH L S07RR07112-24
MOSTELLER, FREDERICK R01HS05936-04
MOSTER, MARK L K08NS01357-02
MOSTOV, KEITH P30DK26743-11 0012
MOSTOV, KEITH E R01AI25144-05
MOSTOV, KEITH E S07RR05355-30 0426
MOSTWIN, JACEK L R01DK38466-06
MOSTWIN, JACEL P01DK19300-16 0010
MOTA DE FREITAS, D S07RR07210-09 0683
MOTA DE FREITAS, DUARTE E R29MH45926-02
MOTE, CLAYTON D, JR R01AR26446-09
MOTICKA, EDWARD J R01EY06926-02
MOTIL, KATHLEEN M01RR00188-27 0327
MOTIL, KATHLEEN L M01RR00188-27 0301
MOTT, FRANK L R01HD23160-03
MOTT, GLEN E P01HL28972-10 9001
MOTT, GLEN E R01HD24308-03
MOTTER, BRAD C R01EY07059-05
MOTTET, N KARLE R01ES05011-03
MOTTET, N. KARLE P51RR00166-30 0104
MOTTLEY, JACK G M01RR00044-31 0378
MOTULSKY, ARNO G P01HL30086-09 0002
MOTULSKY, ARNO G P01HL30086-09 9005
MOTULSKY, ARNO G R01EY08395-02
MOUDGIL, VIRINDER S07RR07131-22 0133
MOUDGIL, VIRINDER S07RR07131-22 0134
MOUDRIANAKIS, EVANGELOS N P41RR04328-04 00
MOUL, JUDD W S07RR05983-05 0360
MOULDER, JOHN E R01CA24652-13
MOULT, JOHN R01GM41034-03
MOULT, JOHN R01LM05102-03
MOULTON, KAREN K11HL02563-01
MOULTON, PETER F R43EY08794-01A1
MOULTON, PETER F R43EY09154-01
MOUNT, DAVID W R01GM24496-14
MOUNT, STEPHEN M R01GM37991-04A1
MOUNTAIN, DAVID C S07RR07043-26 0127
MOUNTCASTLE, VERNON B R01NS27776-03
MOUNTFORD, CAROLYN E R01CA51054-02
MOUNTY, JUDITH L R43DC01011-01
MOUNTZ, JOHN P50AI23694-06 0010
MOUNTZ, JOHN D P01AR03555-32A1 0007
MOUNTZ, JOHN D R01AI30744-01A1
MOURADIAN, M M Z01NS02826-01
MOUSSAVI, M Z01HL04216-01
MOVSHON, J ANTHONY S07RR07062-26 0221
MOW, V C M01RR00645-20 0506
MOW, VAN C R01AR38728-04
MOWBRAY, CAROL T R18MH46081-03
MOWER, GEORGE D R01NS25216-05
MOXLEY, RICHARD T, III R01AR38894-03
MOY, JAMES S07RR05477-29 0431
MOYE-ROWLEY, W SCOTT S07RR05372-30 0681
MOYER-MILEUR, LAURIE M01RR00064-27 0367
MOYER-MILEUR, LAURIE S07RR07092-26 0495
MOYER, CAROLYN F P01HL45666-01 9004
MOYER, CAROLYN F P50HL14164-20 9003
MOYER, MARY P P30CA54174-01 9007
MOYER, MARY S R29GM42673-03
MOYER, RICHARD W R01AI15722-13
MOYER, SUE A R01AI14594-15
MOYLE, WILLIAM R P01HD15454-11 0003
MOYLE, WILLIAM R R01HD14907-08
MOYLE, WILLIAM R R01HD24650-03
MOYNIHAN, JAN A R01MH45681-03
MOZELL, MAXWELL M P01DC00220-08 0004
MOZELL, MAXWELL M P01DC00220-08
MOZELL, MAXWELL M R01DC00072-26
MPTP, MITOLCHONDRIA AND AGING P01NS21469-0
MRAZEK, DAVID A K12MH00991-01
MRAZEK, DAVID A M01RR00069-29 0383
MROCZKOWSKI, BARBARA P01CA43720-05 9002
MROCZKOWSKI, BARBARA S07RR05424-30 0076
MROEKOWSKI, BARBARA P01CA43720-05 0001
MROZ, EDMUND A P01DC00119-16 0007
MROZ, EDMUND A R01DC00033-02
MRUTHINTI, SATYANARA S07RR05365-30 0089
MUALLEM, SHMUEL R01DK38938-06
MUCHLINSKI, ALAN E. S06GM08101-20 0040
MUCHMORE, A V Z01CB04018-15
MUCHMORE, ELAINE A R29GM43165-02
MUDD, C P Z01RR10283-04
MUDD, C P Z01RR10285-04
MUDD, C P Z01RR10286-04
MUDD, C P Z01RR10309-03
MUDD, C P Z01RR10310-03
MUDD, C P Z01RR10358-01
MUDZINSKI, STANLEY P R29ES04020-06
MUECKLER, MICHAEL M P60DK20579-14 0032
MUECKLER, MIKE M R01DK38495-05
MUECKLER, MIKE M R01DK43695-01
MUEHLLEHNER, G P01NS14867-13 9001
MUEHLLEHNER, GERD R44CA52342-02
MUEHLLEHNER, GERD R44NS26549-03
MUELLER, BETH A R01HD25230-03
MUELLER, DANIEL L R29AI31669-01
MUELLER, FRANCO B P50HL18323-17 9004
MUELLER, GERALD C K06CA00685-31
MUELLER, GERALD C P01CA23076-14 0004
MUELLER, GERALD C P30CA07175-28 0003
MUELLER, GERALD C R01AA07849-03
MUELLER, HILTRUD N01HV18122-02
MUELLER, HOWARD W S07RR05745-19 0253
MUELLER, KATHYRNE J R01DA05817-03
MUELLER, KEITH J R01HS05760-03
MUELLER, LUCIANO P01GM39526-05 0004
MUELLER, NANCY E P01AI26487-03S1 0001
MUELLER, NANCY E P01AI26487-03S1
MUELLER, NANCY E R01CA44578-04
MUELLER, NANCY E R37CA38450-06
MUELLER, REINHOLD D S07RR07196-11 0627
MUELLER, ROBERT A P01HD23042-03 0006
MUELLER, STEPHEN N R01HL41891-03
MUENKE, MAXIMILIAN S07RR05506-29 0909
MUENTER, M D M01RR00585-20 0448
MUENTER, M D M01RR00585-20 0428
MUENZ, LARRY P01MH44210-03 9002
MUENZ, LARRY P50MH45178-02 9003
MUENZENMAIER, KRISTI S07RR05650-25 0105
MUENZER, JOSEPH M01RR00042-31 0658
MUENZER, JOSEPH R29DK38383-05
MUFSON, ELLIOT P30AG10161-01 0003
MUFSON, ELLIOTT J R01AG10668-01
MUFSON, ELLIOTT J R01NS26146-03
MUFTI, SIRAJ I R01CA51088-02
MUGANDA-OJIKAU, PERPETUA S06GM08012-21 001
MUGGIA, FRANCO M M01RR00043-31 0449
MUGGIA, FRANCO M R01CA50412-02
MUGGIA, FRANCO M R03CA53280-02
MUGNAINI, ENRICO R01NS09904-20
MUIR, MARIEL M S06GM08102-20 0007
MUIZELAAR, J PAUL R01NS29412-01A1
MUKENGE, IDA R R24MH47188-02
MUKHERJEE, A B Z01HD00415-01
MUKHERJEE, A B Z01HD00416-01
MUKHERJEE, A B Z01HD00910-12
MUKHERJEE, ASIT B S07RR07150-17 0549
MUKHERJEE, SUKDEB S07RR05650-25 0106
MUKHTAR, HASAN P01CA48735-02 0004
MUKHTAR, HASAN R01CA51802-02
MULCAHY, R TIMOTHY P01CA52686-02 0003
MULCAHY, R TIMOTHY P30CA14520-19 9006
MULCAHY, R TIMOTHY R01CA42325-07
MULDER, KATHLEEN M R29CA51452-03
MULDROW, LYCURGUS L R29AI26813-03
MULDROW, LYCURGUS L S06GM08241-07 0005
MULE, J J Z01CM06665-02
MULHOLLAND, JOY I R03HD28122-01
MULHOLLAND, MICHAEL W R01DK41204-03
MULHOLLAND, MICHAEL W R01DK43225-01
MULIVOR, RICHARD A N01AG12101-00
MULIVOR, RICHARD A N01GM92102-09
MULLEN, HELEN B R01AI28540-03
MULLEN, HELEN B R01DK35527-07
MULLEN, KEVIN D R29MH43524-03
MULLEN, PATRICIA D R01HL44898-02
MULLEN, PATRICIA D S07RR05828-08 0535
MULLEN, ROD R18DA06918-02
MULLEN, YOKO S R01DK20827-13A2
MULLENIX, PHYLLIS J R01CA53858-02
MULLER-EBERHARD, HANS J P01AI17354-10S1 90

MULLER-EBERHARD, HANS J P01AI17354-10S1 00
MULLER-EBERHARD, URSULA R01DK30203-10
MULLER-EBERHARD, URSULA R01DK30664-10A1
MULLER-SIEBURG, CHRISTA E R01DK41214-03
MULLER, BARBARA M U01CA51946-02 9001
MULLER, DC Z01AG00217-01
MULLER, ERIC G R01GM45448-01
MULLER, J Z01BF03005-02
MULLER, JAMES M01RR02635-07 0281
MULLER, JAMES M01RR02635-07 0282
MULLER, JAMES E M01RR02635-07 0223
MULLER, JAMES E R01HL41016-03
MULLER, KEITH E P01CA47982-04 9002
MULLER, KENNETH J R01NS20607-09
MULLER, MARK T R01AI28362-03
MULLER, MARY E S07RR05944-04 0976
MULLER, WILLIAM A R01HL46849-01
MULLET, JOHN E R01GM37987-05
MULLIGAN, EILEEN M R01HL43410-03
MULLIGAN, LOUIS T N01ES65147-02
MULLIGAN, LOUIS T N01ES75178-08
MULLIGAN, LOUIS T N01ES95242-06
MULLIGAN, MARK J K11AI00912-04
MULLIGAN, RICHARD P01HL41484-03 0008
MULLIGAN, RICHARD C R01HL37569-05
MULLIN, JAMES M R01CA48121-04
MULLINS, DON J N01OD92111-11
MULLINS, JAMES I R01AI25273-05
MULLINS, JAMES I U01AI27136-03 0002
MULLINS, JOHN R01HL45468-02
MULLIS, KARY B R01HL43532-03
MULLIS, KARY B R43AI31933-01
MULLONEY, BRIAN R01NS26742-03
MULROW, CYNTHIA D U01AG09117-02
MULROY, MICHAEL J P01HL36059-06 0007
MULROY, MICHAEL J R01DC00309-07
MULSHINE, J L Z01CM06597-05
MULSHINE, J L Z01CM06598-05
MULVIHILL, SEAN J R29HD24773-02
MUMA, NANCY A P50AG05146-09 9005
MUMA, NANCY A R35AG07914-03 0002
MUMBY, MARC C R01CA54726-01
MUMBY, MARC C R01HL31107-08
MUNAR, MYRNA Y S07RR07079-26 0296
MUNCH, PAUL A R29HL44675-02
MUNCK, ALLAN U R01DK03535-32A1
MUNCK, ECKARD R01GM22701-16
MUNDY, BRADFORD P S06GM08218-08 0027
MUNDY, GREGORY P01AR39529-02 9001
MUNDY, GREGORY P01AR39529-02 0001
MUNDY, GREGORY R M01RR01346-10 0164
MUNDY, GREGORY R P01AR39529-02
MUNDY, GREGORY R P01CA40035-06 0005
MUNDY, GREGORY R P01CA40035-06
MUNDY, GREGORY R P01DE08569-03 9001
MUNDY, GREGORY R R37AR28149-12
MUNEOKA, KEN R29HD23921-04
MUNFORD, ROBERT S P01HD22766-05 0001
MUNFORD, ROBERT S R01AI18188-11
MUNGAS, DAN P30AG10129-01 0002
MUNGER, K Z01CP00565-09
MUNGER, MARK M01RR00080-29 0412
MUNIR, KERIM K07MH00826-03
MUNNERLYN, CHARLES R R43EY08320-01A1
MUNOX, RICARDO S07RR05755-18 0207
MUNOZ, ALVARD N01AI72676-11
MUNOZ, ALVARO P01AI26499-03S1 9003
MUNOZ, JOSE L R29AI28104-04
MUNOZ, RICARDO S07RR05755-18 0217
MUNRO, BARBARA S07RR05948-05 0334
MUNROE-BLUM, HEATHER R01MH43323-04
MUNSAT, THEODORE L M01RR00054-30 0326
MUNSAT, THEODORE L M01RR00054-30 0398
MUNSAT, THEODORE L M01RR00054-30 0471
MUNSAT, THEODORE L M01RR00054-30 0475
MUNSAT, THEODORE L M01RR00054-30 0432
MUNSAT, THEODORE L M01RR00054-30 0380
MUNSAT, THEODORE L M01RR00054-30 0384
MUNSON, ALBERT E N01ES05288-04
MUNSON, BENJAMIN S07RR05648-25 0924
MUNSON, JOHN B P01NS27511-03 0002
MUNSON, JOHN B R01NS15913-11
MUNSON, P J Z01CT00226-01
MUNSON, P J Z01CT00227-01
MUNSON, P J Z01HD00040-16
MUNSON, ROBERT S R01AI17572-11
MUNTZ, KATHRYN H P50HL17669-17 0038
MUNTZ, KATHRYN H R01HL45326-02
MURA, UMBERTO R01EY07832-02
MURAD, FERID R01DK30787-11
MURAD, FERID R01HL28474-10
MURAKAMI, KENTARO S07RR05454-29 0882
MURASKO, DONNA M R01AG07719-04
MURASKO, DONNA M R01AG08659-02
MURATA, PAUL S07RR05354-30 0406
MURAYAMA, M Z01AR27005-09
MURGOLA, EMANUEL J R01GM21499-15
MURHAMMER, DAVID W S07RR07035-26 0079
MURHAMMER, DAVID W S07RR07035-26 0081
MURIANA, PETER M S07RR07032-26 0039
MURLAS, CHRISTOPHER G K01OH00060-04
MURLAS, CHRISTOPHER G K04HL01965-07
MURLAS, CHRISTOPHER G R01HL34228-09
MURONO, EISUKE S07RR05815-12 0494
MURPH, JODY R R01HD22136-06
MURPHEY-CORB, MICHAEL N01AI15093-00
MURPHEY-CORB, MICHAEL P51RR00164-30 0019
MURPHEY-CORB, MICHAEL A R01AI32302-01
MURPHEY-CORB, MICHAEL A U01AI28243-03
MURPHEY-CORB, MICHAEL A. U01AI28243-03 000
MURPHEY-CORB, MICHAEL A. U01AI28243-03 900
MURPHEY, RODNEY K R01NS15571-13
MURPHY-BOESCH, JOSEP S07RR05895-09 0615
MURPHY-BOESCH, JOSEPH P01CA41078-05 9001
MURPHY-BOESCH, JOSEPH R03RR06820-01
MURPHY-ULLRICH, JOANNE R01HL44575-02
MURPHY, ALEXANDER S07RR05301-21 0733
MURPHY, ALEXANDER J R01GM31083-07
MURPHY, B R Z01AI00324-10
MURPHY, B R Z01AI00325-09
MURPHY, B R Z01AI00326-10
MURPHY, B R Z01AI00345-10
MURPHY, CAROL A S07RR05650-25 0107
MURPHY, CLAIRE L R01AG08203-04
MURPHY, CLAIRE L R37AG04085-08
MURPHY, CLAIRE L S03RR03451-05
MURPHY, D L Z01MH00336-12
MURPHY, D L Z01MH00337-12
MURPHY, DONAL B P30CA16359-17 9020
MURPHY, DONAL B R01AI14349-13
MURPHY, DOUGLAS B R01GM33171-08
MURPHY, DOUGLAS B R13GM41434-03
MURPHY, DOUGLAS B R55GM45745-01
MURPHY, E HAZEL P01DA06871-01 0001
MURPHY, E HAZEL P01NS24707-05 0001
MURPHY, E HAZEL S07RR05418-30 0032
MURPHY, EDWARD N01HB97077-03
MURPHY, EDWIN C, JR R01CA34734-08
MURPHY, EDWIN C, JR R01ES05323-02
MURPHY, FREDERICK A P51RR00169-30
MURPHY, FREDERICK A S07RR05457-29
MURPHY, FREDERICK A S15ES05841-01
MURPHY, GEORGE F P01AR39674-03 9001
MURPHY, GERALD P P30CA16056-16 9014
MURPHY, GREGORY L R01MH41704-04
MURPHY, H CLAIRE S07RR05390-30 0659
MURPHY, JAMES P40RR01046-16 0004
MURPHY, JAMES J S07RR05362-30 0779
MURPHY, JAMES M P01AA08553-02 0002
MURPHY, JANE M R01MH39576-07
MURPHY, JANE M S07RR05486-29 0057
MURPHY, JANE M S07RR05486-29 0043
MURPHY, JOHN R R01AI21628-07A1
MURPHY, JOHN R R01CA41746-06
MURPHY, JOHN R U01CA48626-04
MURPHY, JOHN R U01CA48626-04 0001
MURPHY, JOSEPH K R01HL44847-03
MURPHY, JOSEPH K S07RR05818-12 0155
MURPHY, JUNEANN W R01AI15716-12
MURPHY, JUNEANN W R37AI18895-10
MURPHY, KENNETH M P01AI31238-01 0004
MURPHY, LAURA S07RR07118-22 0380
MURPHY, LAURA LYNN R29DA05452-03
MURPHY, MICHAEL B P01GM22220-15 0008
MURPHY, MICHAEL B P01GM22220-15
MURPHY, P Z01AI00615-01
MURPHY, PATRICIA A R01CA56308-01
MURPHY, PETER N01CM07322-02
MURPHY, R MAUREEN S07RR05408-30 0934
MURPHY, RANDALL S07RR07062-26 0230
MURPHY, RANDALL B R01DA05728-02
MURPHY, REGINA M S07RR07098-26 0346
MURPHY, RICHARD A P01HL19242-15 0016
MURPHY, RICHARD A P01HL19242-15
MURPHY, ROBERT P41RR06009-02 9002
MURPHY, ROBERT C P01HL34303-07
MURPHY, ROBERT C P01HL34303-07 0001
MURPHY, ROBERT C P01HL34303-07 0006
MURPHY, ROBERT C P50AA03527-14 0003
MURPHY, ROBERT C R37HL25785-13
MURPHY, ROBERT F R01GM32508-07A2
MURPHY, ROBERT J P41RR01315-10 0042
MURPHY, ROBERT P U10EY02556-13
MURPHY, SEAN P R01NS29226-01A1
MURPHY, SHARON B R01CA55507-01
MURPHY, SHARON B U10CA07431-28 0016
MURPHY, SHARON B U10CA07431-28 0017
MURPHY, SHARON B U10CA07431-28 0056
MURPHY, SHARON B U10CA07431-28 0057
MURPHY, SHARON B U10CA07431-28 0058
MURPHY, SHARON B U10CA07431-28 0059
MURPHY, SHARON B U10CA07431-28 0060
MURPHY, SHARON B U10CA07431-28 0018
MURPHY, SHARON B U10CA07431-28 0019
MURPHY, SHARON B U10CA07431-28 0020
MURPHY, SHARON B U10CA07431-28 0021
MURPHY, SHARON B U10CA07431-28 0001
MURPHY, SHARON B U10CA07431-28 0002
MURPHY, SHARON B U10CA07431-28 0003
MURPHY, SHARON B U10CA07431-28 0004
MURPHY, SHARON B U10CA07431-28 0005
MURPHY, SHARON B U10CA07431-28 0006
MURPHY, SHARON B U10CA07431-28 0007
MURPHY, SHARON B U10CA07431-28 0008
MURPHY, SHARON B U10CA07431-28 0009
MURPHY, SHARON B U10CA07431-28 0010
MURPHY, SHARON B U10CA07431-28 0011
MURPHY, SHARON B U10CA07431-28 0012
MURPHY, SHARON B U10CA07431-28 0013
MURPHY, SHARON B U10CA07431-28 0014
MURPHY, SHARON B U10CA07431-28 0015
MURPHY, SHARON B U10CA07431-28
MURPHY, SHARON B U10CA07431-28 0022
MURPHY, SHARON B U10CA07431-28 0036
MURPHY, SHARON B U10CA07431-28 0037
MURPHY, SHARON B U10CA07431-28 0038
MURPHY, SHARON B U10CA07431-28 0039
MURPHY, SHARON B U10CA07431-28 0040
MURPHY, SHARON B U10CA07431-28 0041
MURPHY, SHARON B U10CA07431-28 0042
MURPHY, SHARON B U10CA07431-28 0043
MURPHY, SHARON B U10CA07431-28 0044
MURPHY, SHARON B U10CA07431-28 0045
MURPHY, SHARON B U10CA07431-28 0046
MURPHY, SHARON B U10CA07431-28 0047
MURPHY, SHARON B U10CA07431-28 0048
MURPHY, SHARON B U10CA07431-28 0049
MURPHY, SHARON B U10CA07431-28 0050
MURPHY, SHARON B U10CA07431-28 0051
MURPHY, SHARON B U10CA07431-28 0052
MURPHY, SHARON B U10CA07431-28 0053
MURPHY, SHARON B U10CA07431-28 0054
MURPHY, SHARON B U10CA07431-28 0055
MURPHY, SHARON B U10CA07431-28 0023
MURPHY, SHARON B U10CA07431-28 0024
MURPHY, SHARON B U10CA07431-28 0025
MURPHY, SHARON B U10CA07431-28 0026
MURPHY, SHARON B U10CA07431-28 0027
MURPHY, SHARON B U10CA07431-28 0028
MURPHY, SHARON B U10CA07431-28 0029
MURPHY, SHARON B U10CA07431-28 0030
MURPHY, SHARON B U10CA07431-28 0031
MURPHY, SHARON B U10CA07431-28 0032
MURPHY, SHARON B U10CA07431-28 0033
MURPHY, SHARON B U10CA07431-28 0034
MURPHY, SHARON B U10CA07431-28 0035
MURPHY, SHARON E P01CA32617-09A1 0007
MURPHY, SHIRLEY M01RR00997-16 0313
MURPHY, SHIRLEY R01HL45279-02
MURPHY, SHIRLEY S07RR05758-18 0256
MURPHY, SHIRLEY A R01NR01926-01A2
MURPHY, TIMOTHY F R01AI19641-09
MURPHY, TIMOTHY F R01AI28304-03
MURPHY, TIMOTHY F S07RR05400-30 0036
MURPHY, W J Z01CM09368-01
MURPHYM KEVIN S07RR05995-04 0049
MURRAY, ANDREW W R01GM43987-02
MURRAY, BARBARA E R01AI27249-02
MURRAY, BRENNAN P01CA47179-03 0002
MURRAY, CHRISTOPHER J R29GM43251-02
MURRAY, DAVID R01CA51870-01A1
MURRAY, DAVID R29CA49477-02
MURRAY, HENRY M01RR00047-31 0479
MURRAY, HENRY M01RR00047-31 0457
MURRAY, HENRY M01RR00047-31 0458
MURRAY, HENRY W M01RR00047-31 0439
MURRAY, HENRY W M01RR00047-31 0451
MURRAY, HENRY W P01CA29502-11A1 0037
MURRAY, HENRY W R01AI16963-12
MURRAY, HENRY W U01AI25917-04 9001
MURRAY, HENRY W U01AI25917-04 0001
MURRAY, HENRY W U01AI25917-04
MURRAY, J D S07RR05457-29 0007
MURRAY, JAMES L R01CA43544-03
MURRAY, JEFFERY P50DE09170-03 0002
MURRAY, JEFFREY C P50HG00206-01S1 0004
MURRAY, JEFFREY C R01DE08559-04
MURRAY, JEFFREY C R01HG00355-04
MURRAY, JEFFREY C R13HG00262-02
MURRAY, JOHN F P50HL19155-15
MURRAY, JOHN F P50HL19155-15 0001
MURRAY, JOHN J S07RR05424-30 0071
MURRAY, JOHN J S07RR05424-30 0102
MURRAY, KATHERINE T K11HL02363-02
MURRAY, LEE N01CM97610-07
MURRAY, LOUANN P01HD22657-05 0003
MURRAY, MARION P01NS24707-05 0002
MURRAY, MARION P01NS24707-05 0003
MURRAY, MARION R01NS16556-12
MURRAY, MARY K R29HD24998-01A3
MURRAY, PATRICIA A K04DE00231-05
MURRAY, PAUL A R01HL38291-04
MURRAY, PAUL A R01HL40361-03
MURRAY, PETER M M01RR00059-30 0693
MURRAY, RAYMOND C S07RR07134-15
MURRAY, RICHARD K K08HL02424-02
MURRAY, ROBERT D R29HD21295-05
MURRAY, ROBERT W R37ES01984-13
MURRAY, RONALD S P01AG07347-04 0006
MURRAY, SANDRA A S07RR05416-30 0570
MURRAY, THOMAS F P30ES03850-07 0005
MURRAY, THOMAS F R01DA07218-01
MURRAY, THOMAS H R01HG00503-01
MURRAY, TIMOTHY G U10EY06275-07
MURRE, CORNELIS R01CA54198-01
MURRILL, EVELYN N01AI05056-03

MURRILL, EVELYN N01CM73713-05
MURRILL, EVELYN N01CM87228-03
MURRILL, EVELYN A N01ES15306-00
MURRIN, LEONARD C R01NS23975-04A2
MURRO, ANTHONY M S07RR05365-30 0090
MURRY, MARCIA S07RR07049-26 0433
MURTAGH, J Z01HL00638-09
MURTHY, LEELAVATTI R R03MH47428-02
MURTI, KURUGANTI G. P30CA21765-14 9004
MURTY, VARAHABHOTLA S07RR06004-04 0038
MUSACCHIO, JOSE M K05MH17785-15
MUSCH, M P30DK42086-02 0002
MUSCHEL, RUTH J R01CA46830-04
MUSCI, THOMAS J R03HD27449-01A1
MUSEMECHE, CATHERINE S07RR05745-19 0265
MUSEN, MARK S07RR05353-30 0360
MUSEN, MARK A R29LM05157-02
MUSEY, PAUL N01CN15331-00
MUSHAK, PAUL P01ES01104-16 9002
MUSHINSKI, J F Z01CB08727-14
MUSKAVITCH, MARC A T R01GM33291-08
MUSLINER, THOMAS A P01HL18574-16 0007
MUSLOW, IKE S03RR03302-10
MUSLOW, IKE S07RR05822-12
MUSLOW, IKE S15DA07783-01
MUSLOW, IKE S15DK44691-01
MUSTAFA, MOHAMMED G S07RR05442-29 0046
MUSTAFA, S JAMAL R01HL27339-09
MUSTAPHA, SHERRY S07RR07053-26 0138
MUSTARI, MICHAEL J R01EY06069-07
MUSTO, NEAL A P50HD13541-12 0002
MUSTOE, THOMAS R29GM41303-04
MUTHEN, BENGT O R01AA08651-02
MUTTER, GEORGE S07RR05950-07 0981
MUTTER, GEORGE L R29CA49859-03
MUTTER, SHARON A R29AG10047-01
MUZYCZKA, NICHOLAS P01CA28146-11 0009
MUZYCZKA, NICHOLAS R01GM35723-06
MUZZY, JOHN D S07RR07024-26 0045
MYATT, LESLIE R01HD26167-03
MYATT, LESLIE R01HL40029-05
MYER, EDWIN M01RR00065-29 0355
MYERS, ADAM K. P01HL40069-04 9001
MYERS, ADAM K R01HL43160-02
MYERS, ALAN M R29GM39254-04
MYERS, ALLEN M01RR00349-25
MYERS, ALLEN R P30CA12227-20
MYERS, ALLEN R S15HL47742-01
MYERS, ANDREW G R01GM43327-02
MYERS, ANDREW G R29CA47148-04
MYERS, ANNE B R55GM39724-04
MYERS, BRENT M S07RR05431-30 0867
MYERS, BRYAN D M01RR00070-29 0212
MYERS, BRYAN D M01RR00070-29 0214
MYERS, BRYAN D M01RR00070-29 0162
MYERS, BRYAN D M01RR00070-29 0191
MYERS, BRYAN D N01DK72291-09
MYERS, BRYAN D R01DK29985-10
MYERS, BRYAN D R01DK40800-04
MYERS, C E Z01CM06524-01
MYERS, C E Z01CM06730-03
MYERS, DAVID D P30CA08748-26 9029
MYERS, DAVID D P30CA08748-26 9017
MYERS, DONALD R R43CE00011-01
MYERS, GARY J P01ES05197-01A1 0001
MYERS, GEORGE C R01AG08523-01A2
MYERS, GLENN A S07RR07035-26 0083
MYERS, J C P01AR20553-15 0010
MYERS, JEANNE CAROL R01HL41882-03
MYERS, JOHN A S06GM08049-20 0007
MYERS, L K P50AR39166-05 0002
MYERS, LINDA K R29AR40595-01A1
MYERS, MARTIN G N01AI15101-00
MYERS, RICHARD P01NS16367-12 0014
MYERS, RICHARD M P01NS14069-14 0011
MYERS, RICHARD M P50HG00206-01S1
MYERS, RICHARD M P50HG00206-01S1 0001
MYERS, RICHARD M P50HG00206-01S1 9001
MYERS, RICHARD M R01NS26237-04
MYERS, ROBERT R R01NS18715-08
MYERS, RONALD E P01CA34856-09 0007
MYERS, STEPHEN P50AR39250-05 0004
MYERS, STUART I P50GM38529-04 0003
MYERS, STUART I R29DK38342-05
MYERS, TERRY O R29HL44715-02
MYKLES, DON L P01NS28323-02 9001
MYLES-WORSLEY, MARINA M01RR00064-27 0344
MYLES-WORSLEY, MARINA M01RR00064-27 0386
MYLES-WORSLEY, MARINA R29MH45195-03
MYLES-WORSLEY, MARINA S15MH49276-01
MYLES, DIANA G R01HD16580-10
MYLES, DIANA G U54HD29125-01 0002
MYLROIE, AUGUSTA A S03RR03323-09
MYONES, BARRY L P60AR30692-08 0016
MYONES, BARRY L S07RR05475-26 0054
MYSLINSKI, NORBERT R S03RR03457-05
NABEL, ELIZABETH G R01DK42706-02
NABEL, GARY J R01AI29179-03
NABEL, GARY J R29AI26865-03
NABELEK, ANNA K R01DC00107-15
NACHBAR, JAMES M S07RR05583-27 0635
NACHMAN, RALPH L P50HL18828-16
NACHMAN, RALPH L P50HL18828-16 0001
NACHMAN, RALPH L S07RR05396-30 0754
NACHMIAS, VIVIAN T S07RR05415-30 0016
NACHMIAS, VIVIANNE T P01HL15835-19 0004
NACHMIAS, VIVIANNE T R01AR40840-01
NACLERIO, ROBERT M P50HL37119-05 0001
NACLERIO, ROBERT M R01AI31335-07
NADAL-GINARD, BERNARDO R01AR36865-06
NADAL-GINARD, BERNARDO R01GM33577-09
NADAL-GINARD, BERNARDO R01HL33730-09A1
NADEAU, JOHN H P50HL14192-21 0019
NADEAU, JOHN H P50HL14192-21 9001
NADEAU, JOHN H. M01RR00095-31 0230
NADEAU, JOSEPH H P01HG00330-03 9001
NADEAU, JOSEPH H P01HG00330-03
NADEAU, JOSEPH H P01HG00330-03 0001
NADEAU, JOSEPH H R01HD25389-03
NADEAU, JOSEPH H R01HG00189-04
NADEAU, JOSEPH H R13HD27947-01
NADEAU, JOSEPH H R13HG00521-01
NADEAU, LISA S07RR05664-24 0870
NADEL, E S07RR05692-22 0984
NADEL, E S07RR05692-22 0986
NADEL, E S07RR05692-22 0987
NADEL, ETHAN R G20RR06780-01
NADEL, ETHAN R R01HL20634-14
NADEL, ETHAN R S07RR05692-22
NADEL, ETHAN R S15HL47743-01
NADEL, JAY A P01HL24136-13
NADEL, JAY A P01HL24136-13 0007
NADEL, JAY A P01HL24136-13 0013
NADEL, JAY A P01HL24136-13 0011
NADEL, LYNN S07RR07002-26 0869
NADELMAN, ROBERT B R01AR41508-01
NADEMANEE, KOONLAWEE R01DA05485-04
NADER, MICHAEL A R01DA06829-01
NADER, PHILIP R U01HL39870-05
NADLER, JERRY L. M01RR00043-31 0411
NADLER, J VICTOR P01NS17771-10 0005
NADLER, J VICTOR P50NS06233-25 0044
NADLER, J VICTOR R01NS16064-12
NADLER, JERRY L M01RR00043-31 0287
NADLER, JERRY L M01RR00043-31 0333
NADLER, LEE M P01CA34183-08 0010
NADLER, LEE M R01CA40216-07
NADLER, RONALD P51RR00165-31 0185
NADLER, RONALD D P51RR00165-31 0184
NADLER, RONALD D P51RR00165-31 0077
NADLER, STEVE S07RR07176-14 0525
NADOL, JOSEPH B P01DC00361-05S1 9001
NADOL, JOSEPH B P01DC00361-05S1 0004
NADOL, JOSEPH B, JR P01DC00361-05S1
NADOL, JOSEPH B, JR R01DC00152-12
NAESER, MARGARET P01DC00081-26 0019
NAESER, MARGARET P01DC00081-26 9002
NAESER, MARGARET A P01DC00081-26 0007
NAEVE, CLAYTON W P30CA21765-14 9012
NAEVE, CLAYTON W R29AI27497-02
NAFIE, LAURENCE A R01GM23567-14
NAFTEL, JOHN P R01DE09137-01A1
NAFTILAN, ALLAN J R01HL47152-01
NAFTILAN, ALLAN J R29HL43052-03
NAFTOLIN, FREDERICK R01HD13587-11
NAFTOLIN, FREDERICK R01HD22970-04
NAG, ABHIJIT R43HL46606-01
NAG, ASISH S07RR07131-22 0135
NAG, ASISH S07RR07131-22 0136
NAGAMANI, MANUBAI M01RR00073-29 0263
NAGAMI, GLENN T R01DK44122-01
NAGARAJAN, LALITHA R29CA49765-04
NAGARAJAN, SRIDHER N01CM17543-00
NAGASAWA, HERBERT T R01AA07317-03
NAGASE, HIDEAKI R01AR39189-04
NAGASE, HIDEAKI R01AR40994-01
NAGEL, DONALD L P30CA36727-08 9005
NAGEL, GLENN M S06GM08258-02 0003
NAGEL, JOACHIM H P01HL36588-06 0006
NAGEL, JOACHIM H P01HL36588-06 9006
NAGEL, RONALD L P01HL21016-15 9001
NAGEL, RONALD L P01HL21016-15 0017
NAGEL, RONALD L P01HL21016-15
NAGEL, RONALD L P60HL38655-04 9001
NAGEL, RONALD L P60HL38655-04
NAGEL, WALTER O R15HL44564-01A1
NAGGAN, LECHAIM P01AI26497-03 0001
NAGLE, DAVID P, JR S07RR07078-18 0457
NAGLE, JOHN F R01GM44976-02
NAGLER-ANDERSON, CAT S07RR05486-29 0063
NAGLER-ANDERSON, CATHRYN P30DK43351-01 0001
NAGOSHI, CRAIG T S07RR07112-24 0418
NAGOSHI, RODNEY N R01GM45843-01
NAGPAL, MADAN S07RR05815-12 0495
NAGY, AGNES K P01NS21908-06A1 9002
NAHIN, R L Z01DE00460-04
NAHM, MOON H R01AI31473-01
NAHMAN, N STANLEY M01RR00034-31 0375
NAHMIAS, ANDRE J P01AI19554-08S1 0008
NAHMIAS, ANDRE J P01AI19554-08S1
NAHMIAS, ANDRE J R01AI32341-01
NAHMIAS, ANDRE J R01HD26634-02
NAIDER, FRED R R01GM22086-15
NAIDES, STANLEY J M01RR00059-30 0660
NAIDES, STANLEY J R29AR40854-01
NAIDU, SRILATA S07RR05664-24 0871
NAIDU, YATHI M S07RR05356-30 0433
NAIGLES, LETITIA G R29HD26595-02
NAIL, STEVEN L S07RR05586-24 0122
NAIR, K SREE M01RR00109-28 0334
NAIR, K SREE M01RR00109-28 0358
NAIR, K SREE M01RR00109-28 0370
NAIR, K SREEKUMRAN R01DK41973-03
NAIR, K STREE M01RR00109-28 0330
NAIR, MADHAVAN G R01CA27101-11
NAIR, PRASANNA R01DA07432-01
NAIR, RAMACHANDRAN M S R01AI28975-01A2
NAIR, VASU R01AI29842-02
NAIR, VELAYUDHAN S07RR05366-30
NAIRN, A P41RR00862-18 0007
NAIRN, ANGUS C P01MH40899-07 0001
NAIRN, RODNEY S R01CA36361-08
NAIRN, RODNEY S R01CA55245-01
NAJAFI, KHALIL N01NS12314-00
NAJARIAN, JOHN S P01DK13083-24
NAJARIAN, JOHN S P01DK13083-24 9001
NAJI, ALI R01DK34878-06
NAJI, ALI R01DK44309-01
NAKA, KEN P41RR01861-07 0005
NAKA, KEN-ICHI R01EY07738-04
NAKA, KEN-ICHI S07RR05399-30 0922
NAKAJIMA, MOTOWO R01CA41524-06
NAKAJIMA, SHIGEHIRO R01NS24711-05
NAKAJIMA, STEVEN M01RR00109-28 0344
NAKAJIMA, STEVEN M01RR00109-28 0362
NAKAJIMA, STEVEN T M01RR00109-28 0336
NAKAJIMA, STEVEN T M01RR00109-28 0333
NAKAJIMA, STEVEN T M01RR00109-28 0285
NAKAJIMA, STEVEN T M01RR00109-28 0286
NAKAJIMA, STEVEN T M01RR00109-28 0287
NAKAJIMA, YASUKO R01AG06093-19
NAKAMOTO, JON M K11DK01997-02
NAKAMOTO, TETSUO S07RR05704-20 0015
NAKAMURA, ICHIRO R01CA52519-01A1
NAKAMURA, KENNETH T R29HL45220-02
NAKANISHI, KOJI R01AI10187-21
NAKANISHI, KOJI R01GM36564-18
NAKANISHI, KOJI R37GM34509-22
NAKAO, MARTA S P60DK20595-14 0020
NAKATANI, Y Z01NS02829-01
NAKATSUKASA, H Z01CP05599-03
NAKAYAMA, KEN R01EY06522-08
NAKEFF, ALEXANDER P30CA22453-14 9009
NAKHASI, H L Z01BB02002-02
NAKHOUL, NAZIH L S07RR05812-12 0488
NALCIOGLU, ORHAN P50AG05142-08 0005
NALCIOGLU, ORHAN R01CA45229-04A1
NALCIOGLU, ORHAN R35AG07918-03 0007
NALL, BARRY T R01GM32980-08
NAMBIAR, KRISHNAN P R29GM39822-02
NANCE, W E P01DE08972-03 0001
NANCE, W E P01DE08972-03 0002
NANCE, WALTER E R13DC01226-01
NANCOLLAS, G H P01DE07585-04 0004
NANCOLLAS, GEORGE H R37DE03223-21
NANDI, SATYABRATA P01CA05388-31A1
NANDI, SATYABRATA P01CA05388-31A1 0030
NANDI, SATYABRATA P01CA05388-31A1 9001
NANDI, SATYABRATA R01CA40160-07
NANDI, SATYABRATA R01CA49374-03
NANDI, STAYABRATA P01CA05388-31A1 9002
NANES, MARK S S07RR05364-30 0536
NANNA, IFENDU A S06GM08167-13 0042
NANNEY, LILLIAN B R01GM40437-04
NAPIER, TAVYE C R01DA05255-02
NAPIER, TAVYE C R29MH45180-02
NAPLES, NANCY P50MH48165-02 0003
NAPOLI, JOSEPH L R01DK36870-07
NAPOLI, JOSEPH L S10RR06504-01
NAPOLITANO, LEONARD M M01RR00997-16
NAPOLITANO, LEONARD M S07RR05583-27
NAPOLITANO, LEONARD M U76PE00209-07
NAPOM, BARBARA S P01AI31241-01 0003
NAPPI, ANTHONY J R01AI24199-03
NAPPI, BRUCE R43HG00528-01
NAQVI, ALI M R01HD24995-03
NAQVI, REHAN H N01HD13130-01
NAQVI, SYED M S06GM08025-21 0015
NARA, P L Z01CP05614-03
NARA, P L Z01CP05616-03
NARA, P L Z01CP05690-01
NARAHASHI, TOSHIO R01AA07836-04
NARAHASHI, TOSHIO R01NS14143-15
NARAHASHI, TOSHIO R01NS14144-15
NARAY-FEJES-TOTH, ANIKO R01DK41841-04
NARAYAMAN, A SAMPATH P50DE08229-05 0006
NARAYAN, O. P01AI27297-04 0001
NARAYAN, O. P01AI27297-04 9002
NARAYAN, OPENDRA P01AI27297-04
NARAYAN, OPENDRA R01AI29382-03
NARAYAN, OPENDRA R01NS12127-17
NARAYAN, OPENDRA R01RR06753-01
NARAYAN, RAJ K P01NS27616-02S1 0003
NARAYANAN, THOMAS K S07RR05365-30 0091
NARAYANAN, VINODH K08NS01282-05
NARAYANASWAMY, B S07RR05373-30 0725

NARCOTIC & DRUG RESEARCH INC N01TI10002-00
NARDIN, ELIZABETH H R29AI25085-05
NARENBERG, MICHAEL P50MH47680-02 0009
NARINS, PETER M R01DC00222-08
NARINS, ROBERT G S07RR05417-30 0807
NARKEWICS, MICHAEL M01RR00069-29 0482
NARKEWICZ, MICHAEL S07RR05357-30 0460
NARKEWICZ, MICHAEL R R03HD27448-02
NARLA, MOHANDAS R01DK26263-13
NARLA, MOHANDAS R01HL31579-10
NARLA, MOHANDAS R13HL46948-01
NASCA, PHILIP C R01CA46586-05
NASH, H A Z01MH01035-22
NASH, H A Z01MH02228-06
NASH, J FRANK R03DA06491-02
NASH, JAY P50MH41684-07 0050
NASH, T E Z01AI00161-14
NASH, T E Z01AI00350-09
NASI, ENRICO R01EY07559-04
NASJLETTI, ALBERTO P01HL34300-07 0002
NASJLETTI, ALBERTO R01HL36670-06
NASJLETTI, ALBERTO R37HL18579-17
NASR, SAMYA M01RR00042-31 0640
NAT'L ASIAN PACIFIC AM FAMILIE N01MH90004-
NAT'L COALITION OF HISPANIC HL N01MH90005-
NAT'L OPINION RESEARCH CTR N01DA18321-00
NATALE, RONALD B P30CA46592-04 9001
NATALE, RONALD B U10CA27057-12
NATANSON, C Z01CL00044-03
NATANSON, C Z01CL00045-03
NATANSON, C Z01CL00073-03
NATANSON, C Z01CL00108-01
NATARAJAN, VISWANATH S07RR05371-30 0641
NATELSON, BENJAMIN H U01AI32247-01
NATELSON, BENJAMIN H U01AI32247-01 0001
NATELSON, BENJAMIN H U01AI32247-01 9001
NATH, CARL M01RR00400-23 0229
NATH, KARL A R01DK43346-01A1
NATH, KARL A R29DK38767-04
NATH, RAVINDER R01CA44537-05
NATH, RAVINDER R01CA49469-03
NATHAN, CARL F M01RR00047-31 0427
NATHAN, CARL F P01AI24775-05 0005
NATHAN, CARL F P01CA33049-09 0008
NATHAN, CARL F R01CA43610-06A1
NATHAN, CARL F R01CA45218-05
NATHAN, DAVID G M01RR02172-09
NATHAN, DAVID G P01CA39542-07 0001
NATHAN, DAVID G P01HL32262-10 0006
NATHAN, DAVID G P01HL32262-10
NATHAN, DAVID G S07RR05899-10
NATHAN, DAVID M M01RR01066-14 0105
NATHAN, DAVID M M01RR01066-14 0059
NATHAN, DAVID M M01RR01066-14 0040
NATHAN, DAVID M M01RR01066-14 0085
NATHAN, DAVID M M01RR01066-14 0083
NATHAN, DAVID M U01DK30643-09
NATHANIELSZ, PETER W P01HD21350-05
NATHANIELSZ, PETER W P01HD21350-05 0001
NATHANIELSZ, PETER W P01HD21350-05 0003
NATHANIELSZ, PETER W P01HD21350-05 9001
NATHANIELSZ, PETER W R01HD26203-02
NATHANIELSZ, PETER W R03RR06876-01
NATHANS, DANIEL P01CA16519-17 0007
NATHANS, JEREMY H R29EY07828-03
NATHANSON, CONSTANCE A P30HD06268-18
NATHANSON, JAMES A R01AI29533-02
NATHANSON, JAMES A R01EY05077-08
NATHANSON, NEAL P01NS27405-03 0003
NATHANSON, NEAL P01NS27405-03
NATHANSON, NEAL R01NS20904-11
NATHANSON, NEIL M P01HL44948-01A1 0003
NATHANSON, NEIL M R01HL30639-08
NATHANSON, NEIL M R01NS26920-03
NATHENSON, STANLEY G P01AI10702-20 0002
NATHENSON, STANLEY G P01AI10702-20
NATHENSON, STANLEY G P30AI27741-04 9003
NATHENSON, STANLEY G R37AI07289-26
NATHWANI, BHARAT N R01CA51729-01A1
NATIONAL ACADEMY OF SCIENCES N01DA08203-00
NATIONAL ACADEMY OF SCIENCES N01MH80025-00
NATIONAL CAPITOL SYSTEMS, INC N01DA88238-0
NATIONS, MARILYN K P01AI26512-03 0003
NATL ACADEMY OF SCIENCES N01MH00003-00
NATL PARENTS' RESOURCE INST N01MH90006-00
NATOLI, C P41RR01209-12 0020
NATTIE, EUGENE E R01HL28066-11
NATTINGER, ANN B R01CA54676-01
NAUGHTON, JOHN P S07RR05400-30
NAUGHTON, MICHAEL J S07RR07066-26 0254
NAUSEEF, WILLIAM M P01AI28412-03 0003
NAUSEEF, WILLIAM M R01HL34327-07
NAUTA, WALLE J P01MH31154-14 0001
NAVALKAR, RAMCHANDRA S06GM08248-05 0008
NAVALKAR, RAMCHANDRA G R22AI27189-03
NAVAR, L GABRIEL P50DK39258-05 0002
NAVAR, L GABRIEL R01HL26371-10
NAVAR, L GABRIEL R37HL18426-18
NAVARRO, JAVIER V K04AR01810-04
NAVARRO, JAVIER V R01AR39602-04
NAVIA, BRADFORD A K08NS01510-01
NAVIA, JUAN M S07RR05829-09
NAVIA, MANUEL A R43GM46164-01
NAVRAN, STEPHEN S R29HL40624-04
NAVRE, MARC E R01HL43399-03
NAYAK, DEBI P R01AI12749-16
NAYAK, DEBI P R01AI16348-12
NAYAR, J K R01AI27774-01A2
NAYER, RAM S06GM08119-18 0011
NAYLOR, MARY D R01NR02095-03
NAYLOR, SUSAN P30CA54174-01 9005
NAYLOR, SUSAN L R01HG00315-03
NAYLOR, SUSAN L R01HG00490-01
NAYLOR, SUSAN L R13HG00692-01
NAYLOR, SUSAN L R29CA44764-05
NAZ, RAJESH K R29HD24425-03
NAZIAN, STANLEY J S07RR05749-19 0272
NEALE, E A Z01HD00704-07
NEALE, E A Z01HD00708-07
NEALE, JOHN M R01MH44116-03
NEALE, JOSEPH H P01NS28130-02 0006
NEALE, JOSEPH H R01DA02297-12
NEAME, PETER J R01AR35322-06
NEARY, TIMOTHY J S07RR05390-30 0681
NEATON, JAMES D N01AI05073-02
NEATON, JAMES D R01HL28715-10
NEAVES, WILLIAM B S07RR05426-30
NEAVES, WILLIAM B S15DK46676-01
NEBELING, LINDA C M01RR00080-29 0454
NEBERT, DANIEL W R01AG09235-02
NEBES, ROBERT D P50AG05133-08 0006
NEBES, ROBERT D R37AG04791-08
NECKERS, DOUGLAS C R03RR05997-01A2
NECKERS, L M Z01CM06525-01
NECKERS, L M Z01CM06526-01
NEDEAU, JOHN G S15EY09457-01
NEDERGAARD, MAIKEN S07RR05396-30 0765
NEDJAR, S Z01BG04004-02
NEDJAR, S Z01BG04008-01
NEEDHAM, DAVID R29GM40162-03
NEEDHAM, THOMAS E S07RR07086-15 0328
NEEDLEMAN, HERBERT L R01ES05015-02
NEEDLEMAN, LAURENCE R01HD22560-04
NEEDLEMAN, PHILIP R01HL20787-15
NEEDLEMAN, PHILLIP P01DK38111-05 0001
NEEDLEMAN, RICHARD B R01GM32558-07
NEEFE, JOHN R M01RR02602-07 0052
NEEFE, JOHN R U10CA46136-04
NEEL, BENJAMIN R01CA49152-03
NEEL, JAMES V S07RR07004-16
NEEL, JAMES W S15AA09251-01
NEEL, JAMES W S15DK44702-01
NEELON, VIRGINIA J R01NR01339-06
NEELON, VIRGINIA J S07RR07072-26 0271
NEELON, VIRGINIA J S15AG10561-01
NEELY, CONSTANCE F R29HL44434-02
NEELY, STEPHEN T R01DC00251-05
NEELY, STEPHEN T S07RR05834-12 0542
NEER, EVA S07RR05950-07 0992
NEER, EVA J R01GM46370-01
NEER, EVA J R37GM36259-07
NEER, ROBERT M M01RR01066-14 0104
NEER, ROBERT M M01RR01066-14 0091
NEER, ROBERT M M01RR01066-14 0092
NEER, ROBERT M M01RR01066-14 0044
NEER, ROBERT M M01RR01066-14 0039
NEER, ROBERT M M01RR01066-14 0012
NEERHOUT, ROBERT C U10CA26044-13
NEET, KENNETH E R01NS24380-05
NEET, KENNETH E S15CA56004-01
NEFF-DANIELS, MARIANNE R18MH49378-01
NEFF, DONNA L R01DC00925-01
NEFF, JOHN M S07RR05655-21
NEFF, NORTON H R01MH43374-03
NEGENDANK, WILLIAM G P30CA22453-14 9008
NEGENDANK, WILLIAM G P30CA22453-14 9010
NEGENDANK, WILLIAM G R01CA56960-01
NEGENDANK, WILLIAM G. P01CA46560-03 9002
NEGISHI, EI-ICHI R01GM36792-05
NEGISHI, M Z01ES80040-08
NEGLIA, JOSEPH P K08CA01240-05
NEGRIN, ROBERT S07RR05353-30 0361
NEGRO-VILAR, A Z01ES70090-08
NEGRO-VILAR, A Z01ES70092-08
NEGRO-VILAR, A Z01ES90058-03
NEGUS, NORMAN C S07RR07092-26 0496
NEHLSEN-CANNARELLA, S07RR05352-30 0765
NEI, MASATOSHI R01GM20293-20
NEIDERS, MIRDZA P50DE08240-05 0012
NEIDHARDT, FREDERICK C M01RR00042-31 0669
NEIDHARDT, FREDERICK C R01GM17892-22
NEIDHART, JAMES A M01RR00997-16 0330
NEIDHART, JAMES A U10CA12213-20
NEIDLINGER, SUSAN H S07RR05604-14 0680
NEIGHBOR, WILLIAM E R01HS06574-02
NEIGHBORS, HAROLD K02MH00919-01
NEIL, JEFFREY J K08NS01453-02
NEILANDS, JOHN B P30ES01896-13 9030
NEILANDS, JOHN B R01AI04156-30
NEILL, DARRYL S07RR07023-26 0984
NEILS, JEAN M R29DC00741-02
NEILSON, ERIC G P01AR20553-15 0008
NEILSON, ERIC G R01DK41110-03
NEILSON, ERIC G R37DK30280-10
NEIMAN, PAUL E R01CA20068-16
NEIMANN, WENDELL P30CA13696-19 9002
NEIMARK, HAROLD S07RR05401-30 0861
NEIMS, ALLEN H M01RR00082-29
NEIMS, ALLEN H S07RR05362-30 0780
NEIMS, ALLEN H S07RR05362-30
NEITZ, MAUREEN E R01EY09303-01
NEITZ, MAUREEN E S07RR07099-25 0405
NEL, ANDRE E S07RR05354-30 0399
NELKIN, BARRY D R01CA47480-04
NELKIN, DOROTHY R01HG00447-01
NELP, WIL B R01CA29639-10
NELP, WILL B P01CA44991-04 0004
NELSEN, STEPHEN F R01GM29549-09
NELSESTUEN, GARY L R01GM38819-05
NELSESTUEN, GARY L R01HL15728-19
NELSON, ALAN C P50HL42270-02 9002
NELSON, CHRISTIAN R01DK44282-01
NELSON, CHRISTOPHER E R43CA54685-01
NELSON, D L Z01CB04017-13
NELSON, DANIEL A R01DK41898-03
NELSON, DAVID S07RR05425-30 0759
NELSON, DAVID A P50DC00110-17 0017
NELSON, DAVID A R01DC00149-13
NELSON, DAVID A R15AR39940-01A2
NELSON, DAVID L R01GM34906-06
NELSON, DAVID L S07RR07098-26 0332
NELSON, DAVID R S07RR07086-15 0319
NELSON, DEBORAH I S07RR07078-18 0458
NELSON, DEBORAH J P01NS24304-05 0003
NELSON, DEBORAH J P01NS24575-04 0006
NELSON, DON H M01RR00064-27 0334
NELSON, DONALD M R29HD22913-05
NELSON, DOROTHY A R01AR41319-01
NELSON, DOUGLAS L R01MH16360-22
NELSON, FRED R S S06GM08047-20S1 0014
NELSON, HILLARY C R01GM44086-02
NELSON, HILLARY C M S07RR07006-26 0897
NELSON, J ARLY R01DK41606-01A2
NELSON, JAMES F R01AG09220-01
NELSON, JAY A P01AG04342-09 0006
NELSON, JAY A R01AI21640-07
NELSON, JAY A R01AI24178-04
NELSON, JAY A R01CA50151-03
NELSON, JEFFREY W R29GM39615-04
NELSON, JEFFREY W S10RR06710-01
NELSON, JUDITH L R29AR39282-04
NELSON, K B Z01NS02243-15
NELSON, K B Z01NS02715-06
NELSON, K B Z01NS02746-06
NELSON, K B Z01NS02747-05
NELSON, K B Z01NS02748-05
NELSON, K B Z01NS02819-02
NELSON, K G Z01ES70062-04
NELSON, KARL M S07RR05992-04 0813
NELSON, KEITH E R01DC00508-03
NELSON, KENRAD M01RR00722-19 0186
NELSON, KENRAD P01AI26499-03S1 0004
NELSON, KENRAD E R01DA05911-03
NELSON, L M Z01HD00633-01
NELSON, MARK T R01HL44455-01A1
NELSON, NORMAN C S07RR05386-30
NELSON, P G Z01HD00064-15
NELSON, PATRICIA M01RR00036-31 1017
NELSON, R Z01NS02631-08
NELSON, RALPH A R01HD26945-01A1
NELSON, RANDALL J P01NS26473-04 0003
NELSON, RANDY J S07RR07041-26 0389
NELSON, RICHARD G R01AI29886-02
NELSON, ROBERT D R01AI22374-12A2
NELSON, ROBERT D R01AI25816-04
NELSON, ROBERT G R21DK44564-01
NELSON, S P01GM32654-08 0005
NELSON, SHARON H R01HL38876-01A3
NELSON, SIDNEY D P01GM32165-09 0004
NELSON, SIDNEY D R01ES02728-10
NELSON, SIDNEY D R01GM25418-13
NELSON, STANLEY P30AG10182-01 0004
NELSON, STANLEY F K11HD00929-01
NELSON, STEVE R29AA07710-04
NELSON, T Z01MH02431-04
NELSON, THOMAS E R01GM23875-12A1
NELSON, THOMAS O R01MH32205-11
NELSON, TIMOTHY M R01GM33984-06
NELSON, TIMOTHY M S07RR07015-26 0599
NELSON, W JAMES R01GM35527-07
NELSON, WENDEL L R01DA06675-02
NELSON, WILLIAM H R01CA36810-06
NEMAZEE, DAVID R01GM44809-02
NEMAZEE, DAVID S07RR05842-12 0289
NEMER, MARTIN J R01HD04367-30
NEMEROFF, CHARLES P50MH40159-08 0005
NEMEROFF, CHARLES B P50DA05303-03 0003
NEMEROFF, CHARLES B R01MH40524-06
NEMEROFF, CHARLES B R01MH42088-05
NEMEROFF, CHARLES B R01MH49523-01
NEMEROFF, CHARLES B R37MH39415-08
NEMEROW, GLEN R M01RR00833-17 0199
NEMEROW, GLEN R R01CA36204-07
NEMEROW, GLEN R U01AI31883-01
NEMERSON, YALE R P01HL29019-10
NEMERSON, YALE R P01HL29019-10 0001

NEMETH, PATTI M R01NS20762-06
NEMETHY, GEORGE R37AG00322-17
NEMIR, DAVID C R43DE09481-01A1
NEPOM, BARBARA S R29AR38883-05
NEPOM, GERALD P01DK41801-02 0002
NEPOM, GERALD P01DK41801-02 9001
NEPOM, GERALD T P01AI31241-01
NEPOM, GERALD T P01AI31241-01 0002
NEPOM, GERALD T P01AI31241-01 9001
NEPOM, GERALD T R01AR37296-06
NEPOM, GERALD T R01DK42732-02
NEPOM, GERALD T S07RR05588-25 0652
NEPOM, GERALD T S15AR41228-01
NERBONNE, JEANNE M R01HL34161-05
NEREM, ROBERT M P01HL26890-09 0002
NERENBERG, MICHAEL P50NS12428-17 0010
NERENBERG, MICHAEL I K08NS01330-03
NERENBERG, MICHAEL I R01CA50234-02
NERGER, JANICE L S07RR07127-23 0499
NESHEIM, MALDEN C S07RR07061-26
NESHEIM, MICHAEL P01HL46703-01 0003
NESS, GENE C R01HL18094-15A3
NESS, GENE C S07RR05749-19 0273
NESS, KENNETH S07RR05392-30 0699
NESS, ROBERTA R03HL46168-01A1
NESSON, H RICHARD M01RR02635-07
NESSON, H RICHARD S07RR05950-07
NESSON, H RICHARD S15HL47759-01
NESTADT, GERALD R29MH45999-02
NESTER, EUGENE W R01GM32618-20
NESTLER, ERIC J P01MH25642-18 9005
NESTLER, ERIC J R01DA07359-01
NESTLER, ERIC J R29DA05490-03
NESTLER, JOHN M01RR00065-29 0358
NESTLER, JOHN E M01RR00065-29 0269
NESTOR, J P41RR01209-12 0010
NETSELL, RONALD P50DC00215-08 9001
NETSELL, RONALD P50DC00215-08 9002
NETSELL, RONALD P50DC00215-08 0005
NETT, TERRY M R01HD07841-14
NETTESHEIM, P Z01ES25023-08
NETTESHEIM, P Z01ES25032-02
NETTLEMAN, MARY S07RR05372-30 0674
NEU, HAROLD C P50MH43520-04 9004
NEU, JOSEF M01RR00082-29 0294
NEU, JOSEF M01RR00082-29 0473
NEUBERG, STEVEN L R01MH45719-02
NEUBIG, RICHARD M01RR00042-31 0679
NEUBIG, RICHARD R R01GM39561-03
NEUBIG, RICHARD R S07RR05383-30 0566
NEUDORF, STEVEN R29AI28282-03
NEUFELD, ELIZABETH F R01DK38857-05
NEUFELD, ELIZABETH F R01NS22376-07
NEUGUT, A M01RR00645-20 0388
NEUHAUS, FRANCIS C R01AI04615-30
NEUHAUS, JOHN M R29AI28995-02
NEUMAN, MICHAEL R N01NS92355-02
NEUMANN, LILY P01AI26497-03 9002
NEUMANN, R Z01CL00604-01
NEUMAYER, LEIGH A S07RR05675-23 0943
NEUMEYER, JOHN L R43GM46605-01
NEUMEYER, JOHN L R44MH45692-03
NEUMEYER, JOHN L R44MH46152-02
NEUMEYER, JOHN L R44MH48243-03
NEURATH, A ROBERT R01CA43315-05
NEURATH, A ROBERT S15CA56030-01
NEURATH, ALEXANDER R R01AI29373-03
NEURATH, HANS R55HL36114-04A3
NEURINGER, LEO P41RR00995-16 0003
NEURINGER, LEO P41RR00995-16 9001
NEURINGER, LEO J P41RR00995-16
NEURINGER, MARTHA D R01DK29930-11
NEUTRA, MARIAN R R01DK21505-15
NEUTRA, MARIAN R R37HD17557-10
NEUTRA, MARIAN R R55AI29378-01A1
NEUWELT, EDWARD A R01CA31770-09
NEUWELT, EDWARD A R01NS27757-02
NEUWIRTH, B R S07RR05333-30 0871
NEVA, F A Z01AI00102-17
NEVA, F A Z01AI00257-10
NEVE, KIM A R01MH45372-03
NEVE, RACHAEL L R01NS28406-02
NEVE, RACHAEL L R01NS28965-01A1
NEVE, RACHAEL L. P01HD18658-09 0014
NEVE, RACHEL L S07RR07008-26 0062
NEVELS, HAROLD S06GM08198-10 0013
NEVID, JEFFREY S R01HL43606-03
NEVILLE, D M Z01MH01037-23
NEVILLE, HELEN P01DC01289-01 0005
NEVILLE, HELEN P50NS22343-06A1 0007
NEVILLE, HELEN J P50AA06420-08 0010
NEVILLE, HELEN J R01DC00128-13
NEVILLE, HELEN J R01DC00481-04
NEVILLE, HELEN J R01NS29561-01
NEVILLE, JAMES A G20RR06920-01
NEVILLE, JAMES A S15GM47066-01
NEVILLE, MARGARET C R01HD19547-07
NEVIN, DAVID N K11HL02162-04
NEVINS, JOSEPH R R01GM35894-07
NEVINS, THOMAS M01RR00400-23 0232
NEVIT, MICHAEL P60AR20684-14 0028
NEVITT, MICHAEL C R01AR40431-02

NEW YORK UNIVERSITY N01DA07403-00
NEW, JOHN S07RR07210-09 0673
NEW, JOHN G R29NS30194-01
NEW, MARIA M01RR00047-31 0468
NEW, MARIA I M01RR06020-02 0126
NEW, MARIA I M01RR06020-02 0446
NEW, MARIA I M01RR06020-02 0386
NEW, MARIA I R01HD00072-28
NEW, PAMELA Z M01RR01346-10 0165
NEWBERNE, PAUL M R01CA40080-05
NEWBERNE, PAUL M R01CA46288-03
NEWBOWER, RONALD S S07RR05486-29
NEWBOWER, RONALD S S15DK44696-01
NEWBOWER, RONALD S S15MH49513-01
NEWBURGER, JANE M01RR02172-09 0188
NEWBURGER, JANE M01RR02172-09 0160
NEWBURGER, JANE W R01HL41786-03
NEWBURGER, PETER E R01CA38325-08
NEWBURGER, PETER E R01DK41625-03
NEWCOM, SAMUEL S07RR05364-30 0537
NEWCOM, SAMUEL R R01CA50739-02
NEWCOMB, ELIZABETH P30CA16087-14 9010
NEWCOMB, ELIZABETH W R01CA40533-07
NEWCOMB, ELIZABETH W R01CA53572-01A1
NEWCOMB, POLLY A R01CA47147-04
NEWCOMB, ROBERT S06GM08125-18 0052
NEWCOMB, ROBERT S06GM08125-18 0052
NEWCOMBE, NORA S07RR07115-24 0587
NEWCOMBE, NORA S R01HD25137-03
NEWCOMER, MARCIA E R29DK41891-01A2
NEWCOMER, MARICA E S07RR05424-30 0123
NEWELL-MORRIS, LAURA L. P51RR00166-30 0128
NEWELL, GUY R R13CA54776-01
NEWELL, JONATHAN C R01GM42935-03
NEWELL, JONATHAN C S15GM47086-01
NEWELL, K M S07RR07030-26 0401
NEWELL, KARL M R01HD21212-04A1
NEWGARD, CHRISTOPHER P01DK42582-02 0002
NEWGARD, CHRISTOPHER B R29DK40734-03
NEWHOUSE, JOSEPH P R01HS06414-02
NEWHOUSE, PAUL M01RR00109-28 0335
NEWHOUSE, PAUL A R29MH46625-02
NEWKIRK, DEBORAH P30CA23074-14 9013
NEWKIRK, ROBERT F S03RR03394-08
NEWKIRK, ROBERT F. S06GM08092-18 0018
NEWKIRK, ROBERT G S06GM08092-18
NEWKOME, GEORGE R S07RR07121-13
NEWKOME, GEORGE R S15EY09471-01
NEWLAND, M CHRISTOPHER R03DA06499-02
NEWLIN, D B Z01DA00500-01
NEWLIN, D B Z01DA00501-01
NEWLIN, D B Z01DA00502-01
NEWLIN, D B Z01DA00504-01
NEWLIN, D B Z01DA00506-01
NEWLIN, D B Z01DA10701-02
NEWLON, CAROL S R01GM35679-07
NEWLON, CAROL S S07RR05393-30 0900
NEWMAN, ANITA NADINE K08DC00029-04
NEWMAN, ANNE B R29AG08047-02
NEWMAN, CONNIE M01RR00096-30A1 0319
NEWMAN, ERIC A R01EY04077-11
NEWMAN, J D Z01HD01123-01
NEWMAN, J D Z01HD01124-01
NEWMAN, JOHN H R01HL39952-04
NEWMAN, JOHN H R01HL45107-02
NEWMAN, JOSEPH P S07RR07098-26 0352
NEWMAN, LEE S K11ES00173-05
NEWMAN, MARK U01AI28167-02 0003
NEWMAN, MARK J U01AI28167-02
NEWMAN, MARK J. U01AI28243-03 0002
NEWMAN, PETER J P01HL44612-02 0002
NEWMAN, PETER J R01HL40926-04
NEWMAN, R Z01CL00101-01
NEWMAN, ROLAND A R43AI31730-01
NEWMAN, ROSEMARY K S06GM08218-08 0017
NEWMAN, SAMMYE S07RR05430-30 0214
NEWMAN, SAMMYE S07RR05697-22 0998
NEWMAN, SAMMYE S07RR05724-20 0181
NEWMAN, SAMMYE S07RR05724-20 0182
NEWMAN, SANDRA J R01MH46097-02
NEWMAN, SARAH S15MH49329-01
NEWMAN, SARAH W R01NS20629-08
NEWMAN, SARAH W S07RR07050-26
NEWMAN, SARAH W S15HD28771-01
NEWMAN, SIMON P01AI28392-02 0002
NEWMAN, SIMON L R01AI23985-04A1
NEWMAN, STUART A R01HD22564-04A2
NEWMAN, WILLIAM P R01HL38844-05 0018
NEWMAN, WILLIAM P, III R01HL42082-03
NEWMANN, JOY P S07RR07098-26 0358
NEWMARK, RICHARD D S07RR05918-08 0709
NEWMEYER, DONALD D R01GM42642-02
NEWMEYER, JOHN A R18DA06145-03
NEWPORT, ELISSA S07RR07069-26 0240
NEWPORT, ELISSA L R01DC00167-11
NEWPORT, JOHN W R01GM33523-08
NEWPORT, JOHN W R01GM44656-01A1
NEWPORT, MARY LYNN S07RR05773-17 0365
NEWSOME, DAVID A R01EY06677-05
NEWSOME, WILLIAM T R01EY05603-07
NEWTON, ALEXANDRA C R01EY08820-01A1
NEWTON, ALEXANDRA C R01GM43154-02

NEWTON, AUSTIN R01GM22299-17
NEWTON, BRUCE W S07RR05350-30 0334
NEWTON, CHARLES D S03RR03146-05
NEWTON, EDWARD R U01AI31498-01 9002
NEWTON, SHEILA R01CA45290-04A1
NEWTON, SHEILA A R25CA19376-15
NEWTON, WILLIAM A, JR U01CA54021-01
NEWTON, WILLIAM E R01DK37255-06A2
NEY, DENISE M R29DK42835-02
NEY, DENISE M S07RR07098-26 0338
NG, STEPHEN P50DA07656-01 9002
NG, STEPHEN K R01DA05730-03
NG, THIAN C R01CA47227-04
NG, YUK-CHOW R29HL39723-04
NGO, FRANK Q R01CA51515-02
NGUYEN, N Y Z01BD03009-02
NGUYEN, QUOC V S07RR05712-20 0066
NGUYEN, THAI D R01EY08905-01
NGUYEN, TOAN D P30DK38707-05 0008
NGUYEN, TOAN D R29DK40506-04
NIAURA, RAYMOND S07RR05818-12 0163
NIAURA, RAYMOND S R01HL32318-06A1
NICHAMAN, MILTON Z P01CA52051-01A1 9006
NICHKLAS, BRUCE R S07RR07070-26 0455
NICHOL, CLAUD E S07RR05429-30 0211
NICHOLAS, HUGH P41RR06009-02 9004
NICHOLAS, JOHANNA G R29DC01259-01
NICHOLAS, JOHN M. N01HC65033-10
NICHOLAS, KENNETH M R01GM34799-06
NICHOLAS, ROBERT A R01AI27039-03
NICHOLS, ALEX V P01HL18574-16 0005
NICHOLS, ALEXANDER V R01HL46281-01
NICHOLS, ANDREW W U76PE00036-08
NICHOLS, ANDREW W U76PE00445-02
NICHOLS, ANDREW W U76PE00482-01
NICHOLS, BARBARA A R01EY08168-03
NICHOLS, BRIAN P R01GM44199-02
NICHOLS, COLIN G R01HL45742-02
NICHOLS, D K Z01RR00095-01
NICHOLS, DAVID E R01DA02189-12
NICHOLS, DAVID E R01DA04758-04
NICHOLS, DAVID E R01MH42705-08
NICHOLS, MICHAEL F N43NS12312-00
NICHOLS, MICHAEL F R44HL43476-02
NICHOLS, NANCY R R35AG07909-03 0004
NICHOLS, RUTHANN R03MH49538-01
NICHOLS, STUART E P50DA05321-04 9004
NICHOLS, T RICHARD R01NS20855-09
NICHOLSON-WELLER, AN S07RR05479-29 0443
NICHOLSON-WELLER, ANNE R01HL33768-08
NICHOLSON, ALLEN W R29GM41283-03
NICHOLSON, BRUCE J R01CA48049-03
NICHOLSON, CHARLES P01NS13742-15 0001
NICHOLSON, CHARLES R01NS28642-02
NICHOLSON, GARTH L P30CA16672-17 9016
NICHOLSON, WAYNE S07RR05879-09 0602
NICHOLSON, WILLIAM P30ES00928-18 9010
NICHOLSON, WILLIAM J R01ES05079-03
NICHTER, MARK R01HD24737-04
NICK, HARRY S R01HL39593-05
NICKEL, JENNIE T R01NR02281-03
NICKELL, STEVEN P R29AI27171-03
NICKENS, HERBERT W R13HS06772-01
NICKENS, HERBERT W R25AD00076-01
NICKERSON, DEBORAH A R01HG00464-01
NICKERSON, JOHN M Z01EY00196-09
NICKERSON, KENNETH S07RR07055-26 0173
NICKLAS, JOHN M M01RR00042-31 0561
NICKLAS, JOHN M M01RR00042-31 0630
NICKLAS, JOHN M M01RR00042-31 0532
NICKLAS, JOHN M M01RR00042-31 0533
NICKLAS, JOHN M M01RR00042-31 0534
NICKLAS, R BRUCE R01GM13745-26
NICKLAS, WILLIAM J R01NS17360-11
NICKLAS, WILLIAM J R01NS21752-07
NICKOL, ALLEN D R44AI24832-03
NICKOL, J Z01DK36110-04
NICKOL, J Z01DK36111-03
NICKOLOFF, BRIAN J K04AR01823-03
NICKOLOFF, BRIAN J R01AR40065-03
NICKOLOFF, BRIAN J R01AR40488-01A1
NICKOLOFF, JAC A R29CA54079-02
NICKOLOFF, JAC A S07RR05446-30 0265
NICKOLS, SHARON Y S07RR05460-29 0367
NICOD, PASCAL H M01RR00827-17 0364
NICOD, PAUL P50HL17682-17 0046
NICOLAIDIS, STELIO P01MH43787-03 0004
NICOLAOU, KYRIACOS C R01CA46446-05
NICOLAOU, KYRIACOS C R01GM26879-12
NICOLAOU, KYRIACOS C R01GM31398-10
NICOLAOU, KYRIACOS C R01GM32192-09
NICOLELIS, MIGUEL A S07RR07241-04 0700
NICOLINI, HUMBERTO S07RR05756-18 0286
NICOLL, CHARLES S R01HD14661-10
NICOLL, ROGER A K05MH00437-09
NICOLL, ROGER A P50MH48200-01 0004
NICOLL, ROGER A R01NS24205-05
NICOLL, ROGER A R37MH38256-08
NICOLOFF, JOHN T R01DK11727-20A2
NICOLOSI, ROBERT J R01HL39385-04
NICOLSON, GARTH L R35CA44352-05
NICOSIA, ROBERTO F R29HL43392-03

NIEBAUER, GERT, DR S07RR05464-29 0375
NIEDENTHAL, PAUL S07RR07041-26 0398
NIEDENTHAL, PAULA M R29MH44811-02
NIEDER, GARY L R01HD25236-03
NIEDERHUBER, JOHN S07RR05378-30 0006
NIEDERKORN, JERRY Y R01CA30276-11
NIEDERKORN, JERRY Y R01EY05631-07
NIEDERKORN, JERRY Y R01EY07641-04
NIEDZWEICKI, DONNA P01CA47997-03 9001
NIEFORTH, KARL A S03RR03311-10
NIEFORTH, KARL A S07RR05743-14
NIEKRASH, CHRISTINE S07RR05677-23 0974
NIELD, MARGARET S07RR05758-18 0257
NIELL, HARVEY B S07RR05423-30 0060
NIELSEN, D Z01AA00234-09
NIELSEN, DONALD W S07RR06040-01
NIELSEN, HEBER C R01HL43407-03
NIELSEN, LEWIS T S07RR07092-26 0497
NIELSON, DENNIS W R01HL28165-09
NIELSON, HAROLD C S07RR07092-26 0518
NIEMAN, L K Z01HD00626-03
NIEMCRYCK, STEVE N01CN15348-00
NIEMCRYK, STEVE J N01CN95162-03
NIENHUIS, A W Z01HL02208-17
NIENHUIS, A W Z01HL02313-09
NIENHUIS, A W Z01HL02320-08
NIENHUIS, A W Z01HL02336-04
NIERENBERG, DAVID W R01CA51479-02
NIERLICH, DONALD S07RR07009-26 0946
NIERMAN, WILLIAM N01HD13132-01
NIERMAN, WILLIAM C N01HD52944-19
NIERZWICKI-BAUER, S S07RR07104-25 0560
NIERZWICKI-BAUER, S S07RR07104-25 0561
NIES, ALAN S M01RR00051-30 0557
NIES, ALAN S M01RR00051-30 0750
NIES, ALAN S M01RR00051-30 0746
NIES, ALAN S M01RR00051-30 0745
NIES, ALAN S M01RR00051-30 0774
NIES, ALAN S M01RR00051-30 0770
NIESEL, DAVID W R29AI24677-04
NIEUWKOOP, ANTHONY J R15GM45991-01
NIEVES, ILEANA S06GM08216-09 0015
NIEWIAROWSKI, STEFAN P50HL45486-01 0005
NIEWIAROWSKI, STEFAN R01HL15226-19
NIGHTINGALE, STEPHEN D M01RR00633-19 0403
NIGIDA, STEVE P01AI19554-08S1 9003
NIHIRA, KAZUO P01HD11944-12 0006
NIKAIDO, HIROSHI R37AI09644-22
NIKAIDO, TOSHIO R29CA52835-01A1
NIKODEM, V M Z01DK45033-08
NIKODEM, V M Z01DK45038-04
NIKODEM, VA Z01DK45040-03
NIKOLETSEAS, MICHAEL S07RR05419-30 0822
NIKOLICS, KAROLY P01AG10480-01 0001
NIKOSKELAINEN, EEVA K R01EY09040-01
NILAND, JOYCE C P01CA30206-10 9001
NILAND, JOYCE C P30CA33572-11 9006
NILES, EDWARD G R01AI28824-02
NILES, EDWARD G S07RR05400-30 0037
NILES, RICHARD P01HL19717-15 0048
NILES, RICHARD M R01HL44647-02
NILGES, MARK J P41RR01811-06A1 9009
NILSEN-HAMILTON, MARIT R13CA55093-01
NILSEN, TIMOTHY W R01AI28799-02
NILSEN, TIMOTHY W R01GM31528-08
NILSON, JOHN H R01DK28559-11
NILSON, JOHN H R01DK43039-01A1
NIMER, STEPHEN D R01DK43025-02
NIMNI, MARCEL E R37AG02577-09
NIMS, JUDITH C G07LM05256-01A1
NINAN, PHILIP T U10MH40597-07
NING, RUOLA S07RR05403-30 0815
NIRENBERG, M Z01HL00009-17
NISENBAUM, JAN R18MH49376-01
NISENGARD, RUSSELL J R01DE07227-06
NISHI, RAE R01NS25767-03
NISHIDA, TOSHIRO R37HL17597-18
NISHIKURA, KAZUKO R01CA46676-04A1
NISHIKURA, KAZUKO R01GM40536-01A4
NISHIKURA, KAZUKO S07RR05540-29 0558
NISHIMOTO, SATORU K R01AR35056-07
NISHIMURA, DWIGHT G R29NS29434-01
NISHIMURA, HIROKO R01HL29364-08
NISHIMURA, ICHIRO R29EY08219-03
NISHIMURA, JONATHAN S R01GM17534-21
NISHIMURA, R A M01RR00585-20 0565
NISHIOKA, DAVID J R01HD19054-06
NISHIOKA, KENJI R13CA54176-01
NISONOFF, ALFRED R37AI24272-06
NISSEN, SCOTT S07RR07055-26 0190
NISSENSON, ROBERT R01DK42146-01A1
NISSENSON, ROBERT A R01DK35323-07
NISSIM, ITZHAK P01DK40555-04 0002
NISSIM, ITZHAK R01DK39348-04
NISSIM, ITZHAK S07RR05506-29 0910
NISSINEN, MIRJA A R01AG08762-01A1
NISSLEY, S P Z01CB04016-18
NISULA, B C Z01HD00616-11
NISWENDER, GORDON D R37HD11590-13
NISWENDER, GORDON D S07RR05458-29
NITECKA, L Z01NS02832-01
NITISS, JOHN L R01CA52814-02
NITISS, JOHN L S07RR05469-29 0413
NITSCHKE, RUPRECHT U10CA11233-23 0056
NITSCHKE, RUPRECHT U10CA11233-23 0036
NITSCHKE, RUPRECHT U10CA11233-23 0037
NITSCHKE, RUPRECHT U10CA11233-23 0057
NITSCHKE, RUPRECHT U10CA11233-23 0038
NITSCHKE, RUPRECHT U10CA11233-23 0039
NITSCHKE, RUPRECHT U10CA11233-23 0040
NITSCHKE, RUPRECHT U10CA11233-23 0041
NITSCHKE, RUPRECHT U10CA11233-23 0058
NITSCHKE, RUPRECHT U10CA11233-23 0059
NITSCHKE, RUPRECHT U10CA11233-23 0060
NITSCHKE, RUPRECHT U10CA11233-23 0042
NITSCHKE, RUPRECHT U10CA11233-23 0043
NITSCHKE, RUPRECHT U10CA11233-23
NITSCHKE, RUPRECHT U10CA11233-23 0001
NITSCHKE, RUPRECHT U10CA11233-23 0002
NITSCHKE, RUPRECHT U10CA11233-23 0003
NITSCHKE, RUPRECHT U10CA11233-23 0004
NITSCHKE, RUPRECHT U10CA11233-23 0005
NITSCHKE, RUPRECHT U10CA11233-23 0006
NITSCHKE, RUPRECHT U10CA11233-23 0007
NITSCHKE, RUPRECHT U10CA11233-23 0008
NITSCHKE, RUPRECHT U10CA11233-23 0009
NITSCHKE, RUPRECHT U10CA11233-23 0010
NITSCHKE, RUPRECHT U10CA11233-23 0011
NITSCHKE, RUPRECHT U10CA11233-23 0012
NITSCHKE, RUPRECHT U10CA11233-23 0013
NITSCHKE, RUPRECHT U10CA11233-23 0014
NITSCHKE, RUPRECHT U10CA11233-23 0015
NITSCHKE, RUPRECHT U10CA11233-23 0044
NITSCHKE, RUPRECHT U10CA11233-23 0045
NITSCHKE, RUPRECHT U10CA11233-23 0046
NITSCHKE, RUPRECHT U10CA11233-23 0016
NITSCHKE, RUPRECHT U10CA11233-23 0017
NITSCHKE, RUPRECHT U10CA11233-23 0018
NITSCHKE, RUPRECHT U10CA11233-23 0019
NITSCHKE, RUPRECHT U10CA11233-23 0020
NITSCHKE, RUPRECHT U10CA11233-23 0021
NITSCHKE, RUPRECHT U10CA11233-23 0022
NITSCHKE, RUPRECHT U10CA11233-23 0023
NITSCHKE, RUPRECHT U10CA11233-23 0024
NITSCHKE, RUPRECHT U10CA11233-23 0025
NITSCHKE, RUPRECHT U10CA11233-23 0026
NITSCHKE, RUPRECHT U10CA11233-23 0027
NITSCHKE, RUPRECHT U10CA11233-23 0028
NITSCHKE, RUPRECHT U10CA11233-23 0029
NITSCHKE, RUPRECHT U10CA11233-23 0030
NITSCHKE, RUPRECHT U10CA11233-23 0031
NITSCHKE, RUPRECHT U10CA11233-23 0032
NITSCHKE, RUPRECHT U10CA11233-23 0033
NITSCHKE, RUPRECHT U10CA11233-23 0034
NITSCHKE, RUPRECHT U10CA11233-23 0035
NITSCHKE, RUPRECHT U10CA11233-23 0047
NITSCHKE, RUPRECHT U10CA11233-23 0048
NITSCHKE, RUPRECHT U10CA11233-23 0049
NITSCHKE, RUPRECHT U10CA11233-23 0050
NITSCHKE, RUPRECHT U10CA11233-23 0051
NITSCHKE, RUPRECHT U10CA11233-23 0052
NITSCHKE, RUPRECHT U10CA11233-23 0053
NITSCHKE, RUPRECHT U10CA11233-23 0054
NITSCHKE, RUPRECHT U10CA11233-23 0055
NITTROUER, SUSAN R29DC00633-04
NITTROUER, SUSAN S07RR05834-12 0543
NIXON, B TRACY R55GM40404-04
NIXON, C S07RR05728-20 0198
NIXON, JOSEPH E P01ES00040-27 0079
NIXON, RALPH R37AG05604-06
NIXON, RALPH A P01AG02126-11 0006
NIXON, RALPH A P01AG02126-11 0013
NIXON, RALPH A R01AG08278-10
NIXON, RALPH A S07RR05484-29 0029
NIXON, RAPLH A P50AG05134-08 0006
NIXON, SARA J K21AA00134-02
NIYOGI, SALIL K R01CA50735-03
NOBLE, BERNICE R01DK41218-02
NOBLE, ERNEST P R01AA07653-04
NOBLE, ERNEST P R01AA08020-03
NOBLE, LINDA J P50NS14543-14 0015
NOBLE, LINDA J R01NS23324-06A1
NOBURI, TSUTOMU M01RR00833-17 0193
NOCK, BRUCE P01GM24483-12A1 0014
NOCK, BRUCE L K02DA00157-01
NOCK, BRUCE L R01DA05816-02
NODA, HIROHARU R01EY04063-10
NODEN, DREW M R01DE06632-08
NOE, DENNIS P30CA06973-29 9013
NOE, ERIC A S06GM08047-20S1 0015
NOEBELS, JEFFREY L R01NS29709-01
NOEBELS, JEFFREY L. P30HD24064-04 9008
NOEL, GARY J R29AI30063-02
NOELKER, LINDA S R01MH45918-01A1
NOELL, JOHN S15CA55958-01
NOELLE, RANDOLPH J R01AI26296-02
NOELLE, RANDOLPH J R01AI28468-03
NOELLE, RANDOLPH J R01ES05252-02
NOETZEL, MICHAEL P50AG05681-08 0019
NOGUCHI, C T Z01DK25021-16
NOGUCHI, C T Z01DK25061-06
NOGUICHI, M Z01HL02228-02
NOKTA, MOSTAFA A R29AI29908-01A1
NOLAN, CHARLES S S03RR03089-10
NOLAN, THOMAS E S07RR05365-30 0092
NOLAND, MELODY P20NR02979-01 0001
NOLEN-HOEKSEMA, SUSAN KAY R01MH43760-03
NOLL, HANS R01GM38984-04
NOLL, WALTER W R01CA46806-04A1
NOLLER, HARRY F, JR R37GM17129-21
NOMEIR, AMIN A N01CM87284-05
NOMURA, ABRAHAM M R01CA33644-09
NOMURA, MASAYASU R37GM35949-07
NONNER, WOLFGANG F R55GM30377-10
NONOYAMA, MEIHAN R01CA31949-08A3
NONOYAMA, MEIHAN U01AI27280-03 0001
NONOYAMA, MEIHAN U01AI27280-03
NOODLEMAN, LOUIS R01GM43278-01A1
NOON, GEORGE M01RR00350-25 0390
NOONAN, FRANCES P R01CA53765-01
NOONAN, FRANCES P R29AR38850-05
NOONAN, LINDA R R29MH46442-02
NORBECK, JANE S R01NR01459-05
NORBERG, ROBERT N01CM97623-04
NORCIA, ANTHONY R01EY06579-06
NORCIA, ANTHONY S07RR05981-05 0804
NORCIA, ANTHONY S07RR05981-05 0805
NORCIA, ANTHONY S07RR05981-05 0806
NORCIA, ANTHONY S07RR05981-05 0807
NORCIA, ANTHONY S07RR05981-05 0810
NORCROSS, M A Z01BD04011-03
NORCROSS, M A Z01BD04012-03
NORCROSS, M A Z01BD04018-01
NORCUM, MONA T R29GM40521-03
NORD, EDWARD P R01DK36351-04A2
NORDAHL, THOMAS E R29MH46990-01A1
NORDAN, R P Z01CM06722-03
NORDEEN, ERNEST J R01MH45096-03
NORDEEN, KATHY S07RR07069-26 0244
NORDEEN, KATHY W R29NS24862-05
NORDEEN, STEVEN K R01DK37061-05
NORDEN, JEANETTE J R01NS25150-03
NORDIN, A A Z01AG00093-19
NORDIN, JOHN H S07RR07048-26 0651
NORDLANDER, RUTH H R01NS18773-10
NORDLIE, ROBERT C R01DK07141-28
NORDLIE, ROBERT C S07RR05407-30
NORDSTROM, JEFFREY S07RR07150-17 0550
NORDSTROM, JEFFREY L R01GM33410-09
NORENBERG, MICHAEL D P50NS30291-01 0003
NORENBERG, MICHAEL D R01DK38153-05
NORGARD, MICHAEL V R01AI16692-11
NORGARD, MICHAEL V R01AI29735-02
NORGREN, RALPH P01MH43787-03 0005
NORGREN, RALPH S07RR05680-23 0907
NORGREN, RALPH E K05MH00653-06
NORGREN, RALPH E R01DC00240-09
NORGREN, ROBERT B S07RR05408-30 0935
NORIN, ALLEN J R01CA47548-03
NORINS, NAN A S07RR05434-30 0822
NORK, T MICHAEL R01EY08724-02
NORKIN, LEONARD S07RR07048-26 0652
NORKIN, LEONARD C R01CA50532-03
NORLING, BARRY K S07RR05897-09 0270
NORMAN, ANDREW B R03MH45253-01A2
NORMAN, ANTHONY W R37DK09012-27
NORMAN, ANTHONY W S07RR05816-12
NORMAN, ANTHONY W S07RR05816-12 0516
NORMAN, ANTHONY W S15AR41242-01
NORMAN, JILL R01DK34049-08
NORMAN, MARK M01RR00079-29 0402
NORMAN, PHILIP S U01AI31867-01 0004
NORMAN, PHILLIP S R37AI04866-29
NORMAN, PHILLIP S U01AI31867-01
NORMAN, REID L R01HD18591-08
NORMAN, ROGER A P01HL11678-24 0069
NORMARK, STAFFAN R01GM44655-02
NORMILE, HOWARD J R24MH47181-02 0004
NORMILE, HOWARD J R29AG07069-05
NORMILE, HOWARD J S06GM08167-13 0043
NORNES, HOWARD O R01NS21309-05
NORR, KATHLEEN F R01AG10499-02
NORR, KATHLEEN F R55NR01956-01A3
NORRIS, DAVID A M01RR00051-30 0525
NORRIS, FRAN H R01MH45069-02
NORRIS, JAMES S R01CA52085-02
NORRIS, JEANETTE R01AA07271-03
NORRIS, STEVEN J R01AI20006-08
NORRIS, STEVEN J R01AR41507-01
NORROD, E PININA S15AI32201-01
NORROD, ERMINIA P R01AI20850-07
NORTH, RICHARD A R01DA03161-11
NORTH, RICHARD A R37DA03160-12
NORTH, ROBERT J R01CA16642-17
NORTH, ROBERT J S07RR05705-22
NORTH, ROBERT J S07RR05705-22 0511
NORTH, ROBERT J S15AI32194-01
NORTH, THOMAS W R55AI28189-04
NORTH, WILLIAM G R01AG07771-05
NORTH, WILLIAM G R01CA19613-14
NORTH, WILLIAM G R01CA46551-04
NORTHCUTT, RICHARD G R01DC01081-01
NORTHCUTT, RICHARD G R01NS24869-06
NORTHCUTT, RICHARD G R01NS24669-04A1
NORTHMORE, DAVID S07RR07016-18 0352
NORTHOUSE, LAUREL L R29NR02019-03

NORTHRUP, DORIS R N01CP15600-00
NORTHRUP, HOPE M01RR02558-07 0066
NORTHRUP, HOPE S07RR05745-19 0261
NORTHRUP, SCOTT H R01GM34248-05
NORTON, J A Z01CM06657-09
NORTON, JOHN N K11HD00908-02
NORTON, MARY A P20NR02962-01 0002
NORTON, MARY ANN S07RR05796-14 0434
NORTON, PAMELA A R29GM46402-01
NORTON, PEGGY A K11AG00454-02
NORTON, SUSAN J R01DC00599-03
NORTON, THOMAS T P30EY03039-13
NORTON, THOMAS T R01EY05922-06
NORTON, THOMAS T S07RR05807-13 0460
NORTON, THOMAS T S07RR05807-13 0461
NORTON, WILLIAM T P01NS23705-04A1 0004
NORTON, WILLIAM T P01NS23705-04A1
NORTON, WILLIAM T P01NS23705-04A1 9001
NORTON, WILLIAM T R01NS02476-32
NORUSIS, MARIJA J P01AG09466-01 9003
NORWOOD, THOMAS H P01AG01751-13 0001
NORWOOD, THOMAS H P50AG05136-08 9004
NOSEK, THOMAS M R55AR40598-01A1
NOSOFSKY, ROBERT M R01MH48494-01
NOSSAL, GUSTAV J R01AI03958-30
NOSSAL, N G Z01DK24260-25
NOSSAL, R Z01CT00017-19
NOTARIO-RUIZ, VICENTE R29CA49858-03
NOTARIO-RUIZ, VINCENTE P01CA52066-02 0004
NOTIDES, ANGELO C P30ES01247-17 0030
NOTIDES, ANGELO C R01HD06707-19
NOTTEBOHM, FERNANDO R01DC00182-09
NOTTEBOHM, FERNANDO R37MH18343-21
NOTTELMANN, E Z01MH02409-04
NOTTELMANN, E Z01MH02410-04
NOTTELMANN, E Z01MH02411-03
NOTTELMANN, E Z01MH02561-01
NOTTELMANN, E D Z01MH02231-07
NOTTELMANN, E D Z01MH02446-02
NOTTENBURG, CAROL P01CA18221-16 0001
NOTTER, ROBERT H P50HL36543-05 0004
NOTTER, ROBERT H P50HL36543-05
NOTTER, ROBERT H MD PHD R01HL37388-05
NOTTINGHAM, LAMONT D U76PE00426-02
NOVA RESEARCH COMPANY N01DA08405-00
NOVA RESEARCH COMPANY N01DA18407-00
NOVA RESEARCH COMPANY N01DA88231-00
NOVA RESEARCH COMPANY, INC N01DA08401-00
NOVACK, NANCY S07RR05389-30 0643
NOVAK, JOEL W N01CM17506-01
NOVAK, M A P51RR00168-30 0174
NOVAK, M A P51RR00168-30 0172
NOVAK, MICHAEL J S07RR05897-09 0269
NOVAK, RAYMOND F R01ES02521-10
NOVAK, RAYMOND F R01ES03656-05
NOVAK, RAYMOND F R01GM42620-03
NOVICK, ANDREW C P50HL33713-06 0007
NOVICK, DAVID P50DA05130-05 0008
NOVICK, LLOYD F N01CN15379-00
NOVICK, PETER P01CA46128-04 9003
NOVICK, PETER J R01GM35370-07
NOVICK, RICHARD P R01AI22159-07
NOVICK, RICHARD P R01AI30138-01A1
NOVICK, RICHARD P R01GM14372-25
NOVICK, RICHARD P S07RR05533-29
NOVICK, SUSAN F P01CA46128-04 0002
NOVIKOFF, PHYLLIS P01DK41918-02 9001
NOVIKOFF, PHYLLIS M R01CA06576-28
NOVOTNY, CHARLES P R01GM34023-06
NOVOTNY, EDWARD J R29NS28790-02
NOVOTNY, JOROSLAV N01AI05055-01
NOVOTNY, MILOS V R01DK44347-01
NOVOTNY, MILOS V R01GM24349-12
NOVOTNY, WILLIAM F K08HL02515-02
NOVY, MILES J P51RR00163-32 0014
NOVY, MILES J R37HD06159-19
NOWAK, LINDA M R01NS24467-05
NOWAK, MICHAEL S07RR05678-23 0158
NOWAK, ROMANA S07RR05950-07 0005
NOWAK, T S Z01NS02720-05
NOWAK, THOMAS R01DK17049-19
NOWAKOWSKI, RICHARD S R01NS28061-02
NOWAKOWSKI, RODNEY W S07RR05807-13 0462
NOWELL, PETER C P01CA15822-17 0007
NOWELL, PETER C R35CA42232-06
NOWICKI, PHILIP T R01HD25256-01A2
NOWICKI, STEPHEN R29DC00402-05
NOWJACK-RAYMER, R E Z01DE00439-05
NOWOTNY, ALOIS H R01CA24628-08
NOWYCKY, MARTHA C R01NS22281-07
NOY, NOA R01DK42601-01A1
NOY, NOA R01EY09296-01
NOY, NOA S07RR05396-30 0755
NOYES, CLAUDIA M P01HL06350-30 9001
NOYES, DAVID H P50NS10165-20 0028
NOZICKA, GEORGE J N01OD02108-04
NOZZA, ROBERT S07RR05507-29 0482
NTAMBI, JAMES M R01DK42825-02
NUCCITELLI, RICHARD L R01HD19966-06
NUDO, RANDOLPH J R29NS27974-02
NUECHTERLEIN, KEITH H P50MH30911-14 9007
NUECHTERLEIN, KEITH H P50MH30911-14 0019
NUECHTERLEIN, KEITH H P50MH30911-14 0009
NUECHTERLEIN, KEITH H P50MH30911-14 9003
NUECHTERLEIN, KEITH H R01MH37705-08
NUGENT, DIANE J R01DK33345-07
NULL, DONALD M JR P50HL36536-05 9003
NUMMIKOSKI, PIRKKA V R03DE09463-01A1
NUNAMAKER, DAVID M R01AR40393-01A1
NUNES, EDWARD V K20DA00154-01
NUNEZ, ANTONIO S07RR07049-26 0452
NUNEZ, ELADIO A R01DK19743-14A1
NUNEZ, PAUL L R01NS24314-05
NURCO, DAVID N R01DA03766-07
NURCO, DAVID N R01DA04346-05
NURCO, DAVID N R01DA06680-01
NURCO, DAVID N R18DA06988-02
NURNANE, ROBERT D S07RR05460-29 0364
NURNBERGER, JOHN I, JR M01RR00750-19 0250
NURNBERGER, JOHN I, JR R01MH43325-02
NURNBERGER, JOHN I, JR U01MH46282-03
NURNBERGER, JOHN JR. M01RR00750-19 0225
NURSE, COLIN A R01HL43412-03
NUSBAUM, HOWARD C R01DC00601-03
NUSBAUM, MICHAEL P R01NS29436-01
NUSSBAUM, GILBERT H R01CA41635-04
NUSSBAUM, O Z01HL02223-02
NUSSBAUM, ROBERT P50HG00425-01 0003
NUSSBAUM, ROBERT L P50HG00425-01 9003
NUSSBAUM, ROBERT L R01EY06566-05
NUSSBAUM, ROBERT L R01HD23245-05
NUSSBAUM, SAMUEL M01RR01066-14 0096
NUSSBAUM, SAMUEL R P01DK11794-24 0005
NUSSENBLATT, R Z01EY00075-13
NUSSENBLATT, R Z01EY00115-13
NUSSENWEIG, VICTOR P41RR04224-04 0006
NUSSENZWEIG, VICTOR R37AI08499-24
NUTMAN, T B Z01AI00197-12
NUTMAN, T B Z01AI00512-04
NUTT, JOHN G M01RR00334-25 0161
NUTT, JOHN G M01RR00334-25 0310
NUTT, JOHN G R01NS21062-08
NUTTALL, ALFRED L R01DC00105-17
NUTTALL, ALFRED L R01DC00141-12
NUTTER, LOUISE M R29CA52618-01A1
NUTTER, LOUISE M S07RR05385-30 0807
NUWAYSER, E S N43NS12310-00
NUWAYSER, ELIE S G20RR06945-01
NUWAYSER, ELIE S R43HD27380-01A1
NUWAYSER, ELIE S R43HD27387-01A1
NUWAYSER, ELIE S R44DA05400-03
NUWAYSER, ELIE S R44DA06573-02
NWEKE, ANRHONY C S06GM08033-21 0009
NY, TOR P50HD12303-13 0007
NYAMATHI, ADELINE M R01DA05565-04
NYAMATHI, ADELINE M R01DA06719-01
NYBORG, JENNIFER K R55CA55035-01
NYCE, JONATHAN W R29CA47217-04
NYDEGGER, CORINNE N R01AG07778-02
NYE, C S06GM08215-09 0006
NYE, JEFFREY S K08NS01516-01
NYE, PATRICK W S07RR05596-27 0128
NYE, PATRICK W S07RR05596-27 0129
NYGAARD, TORBJOERN G K08HD00914-02
NYHAN, DANIEL K08HL02426-02
NYHAN, DANIEL S07RR05378-30 0007
NYHAN, WILLIAM L M01RR00827-17 0406
NYHAN, WILLIAM L M01RR00827-17 0366
NYHAN, WILLIAM L M01RR00827-17 0235
NYHAN, WILLIAM L M01RR00827-17 0016
NYHAN, WILLIAM L M01RR00827-17 0045
NYHAN, WILLIAM L P01HD23042-03 0001
NYHAN, WILLIAM L P50NS22343-06A1 0006
NYLES, CHARON S07RR05433-30 0249
NYMAN, JOHN A R01HS07018-01
NYMAN, JOHN A S07RR05448-30 0292
NYSTROM, ANGELA L S07RR05372-30 0694
NYSTROM, GERALD A S07RR05352-30 0744
O, CHUN-SING S07RR05426-30 0146
O' BRIEN, WILLIAM A R29AI29894-02
O' LEARY, DENNIS D M R01EY07025-06
O'BRIAN, CATHERINE A R29CA52460-02
O'BRIEN-PENNEY, BILL C R01CA51071-02
O'BRIEN, ALISON D R22AI20148-09
O'BRIEN, CAROLEEN J R03MH45640-01A1
O'BRIEN, CHARLES P K12DA00172-01
O'BRIEN, CHARLES P P50DA05186-05
O'BRIEN, CHARLES P R18DA06107-02
O'BRIEN, CHARLES P R37DA03008-09
O'BRIEN, CHRISTOPHER B M01RR00040-31 0344
O'BRIEN, CHRISTOPHER B M01RR00040-31 0375
O'BRIEN, DEBORAH A R01HD26485-01A2
O'BRIEN, DONOUGH M01RR00069-29 0321
O'BRIEN, JAMES P01CA18856-16 0022
O'BRIEN, JOHN S R01NS08682-22
O'BRIEN, MARY E R01NR02068-03
O'BRIEN, PETER C P01AG08802-02 9002
O'BRIEN, REBECCA L R01AI31588-01
O'BRIEN, RICHARD F. P01HL14985-20 9004
O'BRIEN, RICHARD L S07RR05390-30
O'BRIEN, RICHARD T U10CA10198-21
O'BRIEN, S Z01CP05652-02
O'BRIEN, S Z01CP05678-01
O'BRIEN, S Z01CP05679-01
O'BRIEN, THOMAS F R01AI23474-06
O'BRIEN, THOMAS G R01ES01664-15
O'BRIEN, THOMAS G R37CA36353-09
O'BRIEN, THOMAS W R01GM15438-22
O'BRIEN, TIMOTHY J R01CA40406-06
O'BRIEN, W J P50DE09296-03 0001
O'BRIEN, WILLIAM E R55EY07612-04
O'BRIEN, WILLIAM J R01DE05423-10
O'CALLAGHAN, DENNIS J R01AI22001-08
O'CONNELL, ANNA P P01CA40737-06 9003
O'CONNELL, MARY ANN S06GM08136-18 0028
O'CONNELL, MARY E R55AG09566-01
O'CONNELL, MICHAEL J P01CA31224-06S1 0001
O'CONNELL, MICHAEL J P30CA15083-18 0004
O'CONNELL, P G Z01CL60013-01
O'CONNER, BRIAN P50AR39250-05 9001
O'CONNOR, BRIAN P50AR39250-05 0003
O'CONNOR, BRIAN K M01RR00042-31 0590
O'CONNOR, CLARE M R01AG08109-07
O'CONNOR, GERALD T R29LM04667-04
O'CONNOR, JOHN F P01HD15454-11 0004
O'CONNOR, JOHN F R01HD28632-01
O'CONNOR, JOSEPH M S06GM47165-01 0028
O'CONNOR, JOSEPH M. P42ES04895-03 0009
O'CONNOR, MICHAEL B R01GM42546-03
O'CONNOR, MICHAEL D L M01RR00079-29 0397
O'CONNOR, MICHEAL D L M01RR00079-29 0384
O'CONNOR, SALLY E S06GM08008-21 0021
O'DAY, DENIS M R01EY01621-16
O'DONNELL, JAMES M R01MH40694-07
O'DONNELL, MARTHA E R01HL45674-01A1
O'DONNELL, MICHAEL E R01CA53525-01
O'DONNELL, MICHAEL E R01GM38839-04
O'DONNELL, PAUL P01CA16599-17 0019
O'DONOVAN, ANDREW R19DA06446-03
O'DONOVAN, GERARD A S07RR07195-12 0719
O'DONOVAN, M J Z01NS02787-03
O'DONOVAN, MICHAEL J P01NS15350-13 0012
O'DORISIO, MARY S R01CA41997-07
O'DORISIO, SUE M R01DK36061-07
O'DORSIO, THOMAS M01RR00034-31 0263
O'DOWD, DIANE K R29NS27501-03
O'DWYER, PETER R01CA49820-02
O'FALLON, JUDITH R P01CA31224-06S1 9001
O'FALLON, JUDITH R P30CA15083-18 9003
O'FALLON, WILLIAM M P01AG04875-08 9001
O'FARRELL, PATRICK P01GM31286-09 0009
O'FARRELL, PATRICK P01HL43821-02 0008
O'FARRELL, PATRICK H R01GM37193-06
O'FARRELL, TIMOTHY J R01AA08637-01A1
O'FLAHERTY, JOSEPH T R01HL26257-11
O'FLAHERTY, JOSEPH T R01HL27799-11
O'FOGHLUDHA, FEARGHUS R44CA50826-02
O'GRADY, KEVIN P50MH40279-05 9002
O'GRADY, MAUREEN P R01DK41025-03
O'HALLORAN, JAMES P R44MH43072-03
O'HALLORAN, JAMES P R44MH44946-02
O'HALLORAN, THOMAS V R01GM45972-01
O'HALLORAN, THOMAS V R29GM38784-05
O'HANLEY, PETER P30DK38707-05 0010
O'KEEFE, EDWARD J R01AR25871-13
O'KEEFE, S J M01RR00585-20 0507
O'KONSKI, CHESTER S07RR07006-26 0916
O'LEARY, ANN M R01MH45238-04
O'LEARY, ANN M U01MH48013-02
O'LEARY, DENNIS P41RR01861-07 9011
O'LEARY, DENNIS D M P01NS17763-10 0009
O'LEARY, DONAL S R29HL45038-01A1
O'LEARY, JAMES J R01AG02338-09
O'LEARY, JAMES J R01AG09246-01A1
O'LEARY, K DANIEL R01MH42488-01A1
O'LEARY, K DANIEL S07RR07067-26 0220
O'LEARY, MARION H R01GM43043-03
O'LEARY, TIMOTHY J S03RR03541-01
O'MALLEY, BERT P30HD07495-19 9020
O'MALLEY, BERT W P30HD07495-19
O'MALLEY, BERT W R01HD08188-20
O'MALLEY, BERT W R37HD07857-20
O'MALLEY, KAREN L P01NS29343-01 0006
O'MALLEY, KAREN L R01MH45530-03
O'MALLEY, STEPHANIE S R01AA08033-03
O'NEIL, CAROL E P50HL15092-20 9002
O'NEIL, ROGER G R03DK28231-10
O'NEILL, R R Z01NS02769-04
O'NEILL, R R Z01NS02782-03
O'NEILL, WILLIAM E R01DC00267-07
O'RAND, MICHAEL G R01HD23755-04
O'RAND, MICHAEL G U54HD29099-01 0001
O'REAR, JULIAN S07RR05576-27 0595
O'REAR, JULIAN S07RR05576-27 0596
O'REILLY, RICHARD J P01AI32918-09
O'REILLY, RICHARD J P01AI32918-09 0008
O'REILLY, RICHARD J P01CA23766-14
O'REILLY, RICHARD J P01CA23766-14 0023
O'REILLY, RICHARD J P01CA23766-14 0024
O'SHAUGHNESSY, J A Z01CM06735-01
O'SHEA, J Z01CM09349-02
O'SULLIVAN, MARY J R01HD23698-04
O'TOOLE, E P41RR00592-22 0017
O'TOOLE, EILEEN P41RR00592-22 0018
O'TOOLE, RICHARD E R01MH47719-01
O'TOUSA, JOSEPH E R01EY06808-05

O'VIDEEN, TOM P01NS06833-25 9004
Odenwald, W F Z01NS02698-06
OACE, SUSAN M S07RR07006-26 0902
OAKES, DAVID R01CA52572-02
OAKES, JOHN E R01EY03621-11
OAKLEY, BERL R R01GM31837-09
OAKLEY, BRUCE R01DC00083-25
OAKLEY, BURKS, II S07RR07030-26 0402
OAKLEY, DEBORAH J R01NR01887-03
OAKLEY, F Z01CL06014-04
OAS, TERRENCE G R29GM45322-01
OATES, JOHN A M01RR00095-31 0159
OATES, JOHN A P50GM15431-24
OBEID, GEORGE S07RR06020-03 0311
OBER, CAROLE R01HD21244-07
OBER, RICHARD R U10EY08595-02
OBERDOERSTER, GUENTER P30ES01247-17 0063
OBERDOERSTER, GUENTER R01ES04872-04
OBERHARDT, BRUCE J R43HL47223-01
OBERKOTTER, LINDA V R01HD27068-02
OBERLEY, LARRY W R01CA41267-04A3
OBERMAN, ALBERT R01HL37597-05
OBERMAN, ALBERT U01HL37907-06
OBERST, MARILYN T S07RR05866-08
OBERST, MARILYN T S15HL47729-01
OBIRI, GODWIN U S07RR05829-09 0956
OBLINGER, MONICA M R01NS21571-07
OBLITAS, JAIME N01CL12108-00
OBLON, DAVID J M01RR00082-29 0285
OBLON, DAVID J M01RR00082-29 0292
OBLON, DAVID J M01RR00082-29 0293
OBLON, DAVID J U10CA49952-01A2
OBRIEN, S J Z01CP05367-07
OBRIEN, S J Z01CP05384-08
OBRIEN, S J Z01CP05385-08
OBRIEN, S J Z01CP05389-08
OBRIG, TOM G R01AI24431-05
OBRIST, WALTER D P20NS30318-01 0002
OBRIST, WALTER D R01HL39588-03S1
OCHMAN, HOWARD R01GM40995-03
OCHOA, JOSE L R01NS24766-05
OCHOA, JOSE L R01NS28747-02
OCHS, HANS D. M01RR00037-31 0433
OCHS, BURT D R43NS28627-01A1
OCHS, HANS D M01RR00037-31 0473
OCHS, HANS D M01RR00037-31 0450
OCHS, HANS D M01RR00037-31 0490
OCHS, HANS D M01RR00037-31 0310
OCHS, HANS D R01AI32317-01
OCHS, HANS D R01HD17427-25
OCHS, MARLEEN T P20DC01437-01 0003
OCHS, MARLEEN T S07RR05424-30 0082
OCKENE, IRA S K07HL01943-05
OCKENE, IRA S R01HL44492-01A1
OCKENE, IRA S S07RR05712-20 0096
OCKENE, JUDITH K N01CN64091-10
OCKNER, ROBERT K P30DK26743-11
OCKNER, ROBERT K R37DK13328-22
OCONNOR, SEAN S07RR05678-23 0157
ODA, DOLPHINE R03DE09890-01
ODA, DOROTHY S R01HS06510-01
ODDIS, CHESTER R18AR21393-17 0020
ODEGAARD, BILLI R18DA05753-03S1
ODELL, GERARD B R01DK21668-13A2
ODELL, WILLIAM D M01RR00064-27 0322
ODENWALD, W F Z01NS02820-02
ODOM, M JANELLE P01HD13912-12 0004
ODOM, ROBERT W R44GM39005-03
ODONNELL, MICHAEL S07RR05396-30 0764
ODONOGHUE, D L S07RR05411-30 0964
ODOROFF, CHARLES L P30CA11198-23 9017
ODOWD, DIANE K S07RR05351-30 0028
ODYA, CHARLES E R01HL38833-04
OEGEMA, T. R. P50AR39255-05 9002
OEGEMA, THEODORE R, JR R01AR32145-08A2
OELBERG, DAVID G K08HL02292-03
OERTEL, DONATA R01DC00176-10
OESTENSTAD, RIEDAR K K01OH00085-02
OETTGEN, HERBERT F P01CA33049-09 9001
OETTGEN, HERBERT F P01CA33049-09
OETTGEN, HERBERT F S15CA55967-01
OETTING, WILLIAM S R29AR40001-03
OFFENBACHER, STEVEN P51RR00165-31 0190
OFFENBACHER, STEVEN R01HD26652-03
OFFERMAN, MARGARET S07RR05364-30 0538
OFFIT, PAUL A K04AI00889-04
OFFIT, PAUL A P30DK38707-05 0009
OFFIT, PAUL A R01AI26251-02
OFFNER S07RR05380-30 0899
OFFNER, ELSA N S07RR05372-30 0695
OFFNER, GWYNNETH D R29DK40538-03
OFFNER, HALINA R01NS23444-05
OFNER, PETER S07RR05382-30 0874
OFNER, PETER S07RR05446-30 0282
OFOSU, GUSTAV A S03RR03280-05
OFOSU, GUSTAV A S06GM08182-12 0003
OFOSU, MILDRED D S06GM08182-12
OFOSU, MILDRED D S06GM08182-12 0005
OGATA, RONALD T R01GM29831-10
OGATA, RONALD T R01GM36960-05A1
OGAWA, MAKIO R01DK32294-09
OGDEN, THOMAS E P30EY03040-12
OGDEN, THOMAS E S07RR05810-13
OGDEN, THOMAS E S15EY09459-01
OGILVIE, GREGORY K S07RR05458-29 0833
OGILVIE, ROBERT W S07RR05411-30 0957
OGLE, THOMAS F S07RR05365-30 0093
OGNIBENE, F P Z01CL00050-03
OGNIBENE, F P Z01CL00086-02
OGNIBENE, F P Z01CL00105-01
OGNIBENE, F P Z01CL00106-01
OGNIBENE, F P Z01CL00107-01
OGNIBENE, PETER J R43AG08195-01A1
OGRA, PEARAY L P30HD27841-02
OGRA, PEARAY L R01AI15939-12
OGSTON, CHARLES W R01CA57035-01
OGSTON, WALTER S07RR05477-29 0424
OH, CHANG-HYUH P01CA28881-07A1 0004
OH, JANG O R01EY08037-03
OH, MYUNG-HI KIM M01RR00032-31 0382
OH, MYUNG-HI KIM M01RR00032-31 0383
OH, TAE HWAN R01NS15013-13
OH, TAEBOEM S07RR07149-18 0424
OH, WILLIAM P50HD11343-14A1 0020
OH, WILLIAM P50HD11343-14A1
OH, WILLIAM U10HD27904-01
OHAR, JILL A K08HL01931-05
OHARA, JUN-ICHI R01AI26884-04
OHARA, JUNICHI S07RR05357-30 0455
OHARA, PETER T R01NS26488-02
OHDE, RALPH N R01DC00464-02
OHENE-FREMPONG, KWAKU N01HB97056-03
OHENE-FREMPONG, KWAKU P60HL38632-04
OHENE-FREMPONG, KWAKU P60HL38632-04 0006
OHENE-FREMPONG, KWAKU P60HL38632-04 0010
OHENE-FREMPONG, KWAKU P60HL38632-04 9001
OHENE-FREMPONG, KWAKU P60HL38632-04 9002
OHI, SEIGO G12RR03032-07 0004
OHI, SEIGO K14HL01989-05
OHI, SEIGO P60HL38737-04 0001
OHLENDORF, DOUGLAS H R01GM46436-01
OHLSON-WILHELM, BETSY P01CA40011-07 0007
OHLSSON-WILHELM, BETSY P01CA40011-07 9001
OHMAN, DENNIS E R01AI19146-08
OHMAN, JOHN P50AI24848-05 0001
OHMAN, JOHN L JR R01AI28586-03
OHMORI, TETSURO P50MH41684-07 0045
OHMORI, TETSURO P50MH41684-07 0033
OHNISHI, TOMOKO R01GM30736-09
OHRBACH, RICHARD K11DE00280-03
OHSFELDT, ROBERT L R01HS06685-01
OIE, SVEIN R01GM35192-07
OJEDA, SERGIO P51RR00163-32 0029
OJEDA, SERGIO R R01HD24870-04
OJEDA, SERGIO R R01HD25123-02
OJEMANN, GEORGE A P01NS17111-11
OJEMANN, GEORGE A P01NS20482-08 0009
OJEMANN, GEORGE A R01NS21724-07
OJIMA, IWAO R01GM39226-04
OJIMA, IWAO R01GM42798-02
OKA, T Z01DK57502-18
OKABE, T S07RR05915-08 0667
OKABE, TORU R01DE07644-06
OKABE, TORU S15EY09451-01
OKAMURA, MELVIN Y R01GM41637-03
OKAMURO, JACK K R29GM46309-01
OKAZAKI, HAROU P30AG08031-02 9002
OKEEFE, STEPHEN J S07RR05526-29 0091
OKEN, BARRY S R01AG08714-01A2
OKITA, RICHARD T R01ES03771-07
OKITA, RICHARD T R01HD21765-05
OKORODUDU, ANGHONY O S07RR07187-13 0696
OKUDA, ROY K R29GM38040-05
OKULICZ, WILLIAM C P01HD20290-06A1 0002
OKUN, LAWRENCE M S07RR07092-26 0549
OKUNEWICK, JAMES P R01AI28425-01A2
OKUNEWICK, JAMES P R01CA49437-03
OKUNEWICK, JAMES P S07RR05801-13
OKUNEWICK, JAMES P S15AI32190-01
OKUNIEFF, PAUL R29CA48096-04
OLAH, GEORGE A R01GM24832-14
OLBRIGHT, WILLIAM P01HL18208-17 0015
OLDAKOWSKI, R J Z01DE00539-01
OLDFIELD, E H Z01NS02454-11
OLDFIELD, E H Z01NS02697-07
OLDFIELD, E H Z01NS02739-05
OLDFIELD, E H Z01NS02811-02
OLDFIELD, ERIC R01GM40426-04
OLDHAM, JOHN S03RR03281-09
OLDHAM, JOHN S07RR05650-25
OLDHAM, JOHN M S15HD28768-01
OLDHAM, JOHN M S15MH49304-01
OLDHAM, KEITH T R29GM41745-03
OLDS-CLARKE, PATRICIA J R01HD15045-09
OLDS, DAVID L R01NR01691-04
OLDS, G RICHARD S07RR05818-12 0162
OLDSTONE, MICHAEL P50MH47680-02 0006
OLDSTONE, MICHAEL B P01AG04342-09 9001
OLDSTONE, MICHAEL B P01AG04342-09
OLDSTONE, MICHAEL B P01AG04342-09 0001
OLDSTONE, MICHAEL B P50NS12428-17 9001
OLDSTONE, MICHAEL B P50NS12428-17
OLDSTONE, MICHAEL B P50NS12428-17 0001
OLDSTONE, MICHAEL B R37AI09484-22
OLEFSKY, JERROLD M M01RR00827-17 0372
OLEFSKY, JERROLD M M01RR00827-17 0439
OLEFSKY, JERROLD M M01RR00827-17 0483
OLEFSKY, JERROLD M M01RR00827-17 0480
OLEFSKY, JERROLD M M01RR00827-17 0299
OLEFSKY, JERROLD M M01RR00827-17 0475
OLEFSKY, JERROLD M R01DK33651-09
OLEFSKY, JERROLD M R37DK33649-09
OLEINICK, NANCY P30CA43703-04A1 9007
OLEINICK, NANCY L P01CA48735-02 0002
OLEINICK, NANCY L P01CA48735-02
OLEINICK, NANCY L R37CA15378-18
OLEK, ANTHONY S07RR07042-26 0412
OLER, JACQUELINE P50DE07118-07 0009
OLERUD, JOHN E P01AR21557-13 0003
OLERUD, JOHN E R01AR39818-03
OLESKE, DENISE P30CA14599-18 9005
OLIFF, ALLEN P01CA16599-17 0020
OLIN, PATRICK N01AI15125-00
OLIPHANT, ARNOLD S07RR05428-30 0173
OLIVARI, MARIA-TERES S07RR05426-30 0147
OLIVE, DAVID S07RR05654-24 0114
OLIVE, PEGGY L R01CA37879-08
OLIVER, C Z01DE00199-15
OLIVER, CONNIE P41RR00570-21 0013
OLIVER, DONALD B R01GM42033-03
OLIVER, DOUGLAS L R01DC00189-10
OLIVER, JAMES H, JR R01AI09556-21
OLIVER, JAMES H, JR R01AI24899-05
OLIVER, JAMES H, JR R01AI30026-02
OLIVER, JAMES H, JR S07RR07262-01
OLIVER, JANET M P41RR01315-10 0045
OLIVER, JANET M S10RR06490-01
OLIVER, NOELYNN P01HD23681-04 0004
OLIVER, NOELYNN A R01CA43860-05
OLIVERA, BALDOMERO M R01GM22737-13
OLIVERA, BALDOMERO M R37GM25654-13
OLIVIER, N B K11HL01950-05
OLIVO, PAUL D S07RR05389-30 0644
OLLAPALLY, ABRAHAM S06GM08111-19 0024
OLLAPALLY, PHILIP J. S06GM08092-18 0019
OLLER, D KIMBROUGH R01DC00484-04
OLLINGER, JOHN M R01CA54959-01
OLMSTED, JOANNA B R01GM22214-16
OLMSTED, R Z01AI00370-08
OLNESS, KAREN N R01NS28631-02
OLNEY, JOHN W K05MH38894-14
OLNEY, JOHN W P50AG05681-08 0004
OLNEY, JOHN W R01DA05072-05
OLNEY, JOHN W R01EY08089-02
OLSCHOWKA, JOHN S07RR05403-30 0816
OLSCHOWKA, JOHN A R01NS29400-01
OLSEN, BJORN R P01HL33014-07 0010
OLSEN, BJORN R R01AR36819-07
OLSEN, BJORN R R01AR36820-07
OLSEN, BJORN R R01EY07334-05
OLSEN, DON B R01HL32816-06
OLSEN, DONALD B N01HV88106-04
OLSEN, ELISE A M01RR00030-30 0367
OLSEN, ELISE A M01RR00030-30 0512
OLSEN, GEORGE D R01DA04905-03
OLSEN, GEORGE D S07RR05412-30 0968
OLSEN, JAMES R P01CA42745-05 0003
OLSEN, JOHN C R01HL47121-01
OLSEN, K S07RR07210-09 0675
OLSEN, K S07RR07210-09 0676
OLSEN, MARGARET A S07RR05390-30 0665
OLSEN, MARY L S07RR05745-19 0256
OLSEN, NANCY M01RR00095-31 0332
OLSEN, NANCY M01RR00095-31 0347
OLSEN, NANCY J R01DK41053-03
OLSEN, RICHARD W R01NS22071-07
OLSEN, RICHARD W R01NS28772-02
OLSEN, WARD A R01DK13927-22
OLSHAN, ANDREW F R01CA57004-01
OLSHANSKY, ELLEN S07RR05758-18 0258
OLSHEN, RICHARD P50MH45294-03 9009
OLSHEN, RICHARD A R01CA55325-01
OLSHEN, RICHARD A. P01CA37497-07 9003
OLSHO, LYNNE W. P01DC00520-04 0006
OLSON, A KENNETH M01RR00032-31 0329
OLSON, ARDIS L S07RR05392-30 0700
OLSON, ARTHUR J P01GM38794-05 9001
OLSON, ARTHUR J P01GM38794-05
OLSON, ARTHUR J P01GM38794-05 0003
OLSON, CARL ROGER R01NS27287-04
OLSON, ERIC N R01AR39849-03
OLSON, ERIC N R01AR40339-02
OLSON, GARY E P30HD05797-20 9002
OLSON, GARY E R01HD20419-07
OLSON, JACK W K04HL02055-04
OLSON, JACK W R01HL36404-06
OLSON, JACK W R01HL44084-02
OLSON, JACK W S15HL47765-01
OLSON, JAMES A R01CA46406-04
OLSON, JAMES A R01DK39733-04
OLSON, JAMES A R01HD27994-01
OLSON, JAMES A R13DK44225-01
OLSON, JAMES E R01NS23218-05A1
OLSON, JOAN C S07RR05767-17 0325
OLSON, JOHN S R01GM35649-17A1
OLSON, JOHN S R01HL47020-01

OLSON, L D Z01BA06005-04
OLSON, L D Z01BA06007-02
OLSON, L D Z01BA06008-01
OLSON, L D Z01BA06010-01
OLSON, L D Z01BA06011-01
OLSON, L D Z01BA06012-01
OLSON, LARS P01AG04418-08 0011
OLSON, LARS P50NS09199-21 0036
OLSON, LEONARD P51RR00163-32 9004
OLSON, LEONARD P51RR00163-32 9005
OLSON, LYNNE E K04HL02122-04
OLSON, LYNNE E R01HL38243-05
OLSON, MAYNARD V P41RR01380-10 0006
OLSON, MERLE S R01DK19473-16
OLSON, NEIL C DVM PHD R01HL32726-07
OLSON, RICHARD S07RR07013-26 0956
OLSON, RICHARD K P50HD27802-01S1 0005
OLSON, RICHARD K P50HD27802-01S1 0002
OLSON, RICHARD K R01HD22223-05
OLSON, STEPHEN C R29MH43650-04
OLSON, STEVEN T R29HL39888-04
OLSON, WILMA K R01GM34809-07
OLSON, WILMA K R37GM20861-18
OLSSON, RAY A R01HL30391-08
OLSTER, DEBORAH H R29HD23483-05
OLSWANG, LESLEY B R29DC00431-04
OLSZEWSKI, NEIL E R29GM40553-04
OLTON, DAVID S R01AG07735-04
OLTON, DAVID S R01AG10015-01
OLUBADEWO, JOSEPH O K14HL02134-03
OLVEDA, REMIGIO P50AI30601-01 0001
OLVERA DE LA CRUZ, MONICA R29GM40684-04
OLWIN, BRADLEY B R29AR39467-04
OMAR, RAWHI S07RR05433-30 0252
OMDAHL, JOHN L S06GM08139-17 0006
OMENN, GILBERT S P01CA34847-09 0001
OMENN, GILBERT S S03RR03363-09
OMENN, GILBERT S S07RR05714-21
OMENN, GILBERT S S15AI32204-01
OMERY, ANNA K R03NR02831-01
OMIECINSKI, C I P42ES04696-05 0004
OMIECINSKI, CURTIS J R01ES04978-03
OMIECINSKI, CURTIS J R01GM32281-07
OMIECINSKI, CURTIS J S07RR05714-21 0137
OMNELL, KARL-AKE S07RR05346-30
OMNELL, KARL-AKE S07RR05346-30 0315
OMNELL, KARL-AKE S07RR05346-30 0319
OMNELL, KARL-AKE S15DE10085-01
OMURA, GEORGE A U10CA47545-04
ONAK, THOMAS P S06GM08101-20 0014
ONDERDONK, ANDREW P01AI26698-03S1 9001
ONDRIAS, MARK R R01GM33330-08
ONDRIAS, MARK R S06GM08139-17 0050
ONEIL, GARY M01RR00350-25 0363
ONEILL, IAN K R01CA39417-06
ONEILL, J PATRICK S07RR05429-30 0207
ONG, DAVID E R01DK32642-08
ONG, DAVID E R01HD25206-02
ONG, DAVID E R01HD25286-03
ONGERTH, JERRY E R01AI28110-01A2
ONO, JOYCE K R15NS29570-01
ONO, JOYCE K S06GM08258-02 0004
ONODA, JAMES M R01CA50465-02
ONTELL, MARCIA B R01AR36294-15
ONTELL, MARCIA B R01HD25630-02
ONTKO, JOSEPH A R01AA09325-01
ONTKO, JOSEPH A R01HL32609-08
OOKHTENS, MURAD R01AG07467-05
OPARIL, SUZANNE R01HL22544-13
OPAVA-STITZER, SUSAN C S06GM08224-07 0020
OPELLA, STANLEY J R01AI20770-07
OPELLA, STANLEY J R01GM24266-15
OPELLA, STANLEY J R01GM29754-10
OPELLA, STANLEY J R24RR05976-01A1
OPELLA, STANLEY J S07RR07083-26 0490
OPENSHAW, STEPHEN J S07RR07052-26 0165
OPHAUG, ROBERT H R01DE08766-03
OPHIR, JONATHAN R01CA38515-06
OPITZ, JOHN M R13NS29690-01
OPP, MARK R R03MH47103-02
OPPENHEIM, FRANK G R01DE07652-06
OPPENHEIM, FRANK G R37DE05672-09
OPPENHEIM, J J Z01CM09289-06
OPPENHEIM, RONALD W R01NS20402-09
OPPENHEIMER, JACK H M01RR00400-23 0295
OPPENHEIMER, JACK H R01DK19812-16
OPPENHEIMER, NANCY P01AR09989-27 0004
OPPENHEIMER, NORMAN J R01GM22982-16
OPPENHEIMER, VALERIE K R01HD27955-01
OPRIAN, DANIEL S07RR07044-26 0115
OPRIAN, DANIEL D R01EY07965-03
OPTICAN, L M Z01EY00256-03
ORAM, JOHN P01DK02456-33A1 9001
ORAM, JOHN F P41RR02176-05 0003
ORAM, JOHN F R01HL31194-07
ORCHARD, TREVOR J R01DK34818-07
ORCHARD, TREVOR J S07RR05451-30 0354
ORCKLAND S07RR05380-30 0882
ORDAHL, CHARLES P01HL43821-02 0004
ORDAHL, CHARLES P R01GM32018-08
ORDAHL, CHARLES P R01HL35561-07
ORDAL, GEORGE W R01AI20336-09
ORDAL, GEORGE W S07RR07030-26 0403
ORDWAY, GEORGE A P01HL06296-31 9002
ORDWAY, GREGORY A R01MH46692-01A2
OREAR, EDGAR A S07RR07078-18 0459
OREGON HLTH SCIENCES UNIV N01DA07405-00
OREM, JOHN M R01HL21257-15
OREN, D A Z01MH02206-07
OREN, D A Z01MH02501-02
OREN, MOSHE R01CA40099-07
ORENSTEIN, DAVID M M01RR00084-29 0221
ORENSTEIN, DAVID M R01HL35334-04
ORENSTEIN, JAN M N01DE12585-00
ORENSTEIN, SUSAN M01RR00084-29 0190
ORENSTEIN, SUSAN R M01RR00084-29 0242
ORGANISCIAK, DANIEL T R01EY01959-15
ORGANISTA, KURT S07RR07006-26 0911
ORGEBIN-CRIST, MARIE-CLAIRE P30HD05797-20
ORGEBIN-CRIST, MARIE-CLAIRE R37HD03820-22
ORGEL, LESLIE E R01AI29850-02
ORGEL, LESLIE E R01GM33023-08
ORIANI, JULIA M01RR02719-06 0131
ORIANS, GORDON H R01MH44609-03
ORIAS, EDUARDO S07RR07099-25
ORIAS, EDUARDO S15EY09470-01
ORIGITANO, THOMAS C S07RR05368-30 0574
ORIGONI, REGINA N01LM13528-01
ORIOL, NANCY E P01DA06306-01A1 9002
ORIS, JAMES T R01ES05536-01
ORKAND, PAULA P01NS07464-24 9004
ORKAND, RICHARD K P01NS07464-24
ORKIN, BRUCE S07RR05359-30 0517
ORKIN, ROSLYN W R01AR25527-10
ORKIN, ROSLYN W S10RR06352-01
ORKIN, STUART H P01CA39542-07 0002
ORKIN, STUART H P01HL32262-10 0009
ORKIN, STUART H P01HL32262-10 0002
ORKIN, STUART H R01HL32259-10
ORKIN, STUART H R37HD18661-09
ORKLAND, RICHARD K. P01NS07464-24 0051
ORLANDI, MARIO N01CN64095-09
ORLANDI, MARIO A P01CA50956-02 0003
ORLANDI, MARIO A P50DA07656-01 0003
ORLANDO, ROY C R01DK36013-06
ORLEAN, PETER A R01GM46220-01
ORLEANS, TRACY P01CA34856-09 0005
ORLICKY, DAVID J R01HD25961-03
ORLOFF, JOHN J K08DK01936-02
ORLOFF, MARSHALL J R01DK30825-08
ORLOFF, MARSHALL J R01DK41920-02
ORLOW, SETH S07RR05399-30 0920
ORLOWSKI, CRAIG C S07RR05403-30 0817
ORLOWSKI, MARIAN R01DK25377-13
ORME-JOHNSON, WILLIAM P41RR01633-10 0003
ORME-JOHNSON, WILLIAM H, III R01GM30943-09
ORME-JOHNSON, WILLIAM H, III R01GM28358-12
ORME, I M U01AI30189-02 0003
ORME, IAN M R01AG06946-05A2
ORME, IAN M S07RR05458-29 0834
ORNDORFF, PAUL E R01AI22223-07
ORNE, MARTIN T P01MH44193-03 0003
ORNE, MARTIN T P01MH44193-03 0004
ORNE, MARTIN T P01MH44193-03 9001
ORNE, MARTIN T. P01MH44193-03 0002
ORNISH, DEAN R01HL42554-04
ORNITZ, EDWARD M R01HD14193-08
ORNSTEIN, PETER A R01MH43904-03
OROSZ, CHARLES G R01DK34774-06
OROURKE, FLAVIA A R29HL42454-03
ORR-WEAVER, TERRY L R29GM39341-04
ORR, CLIFTON S06GM08211-09 0007
ORR, CLIFTON S06GM08211-09 0007
ORR, DONALD P U01AI31494-01 0007
ORR, HARRY T P50NS16308-12A1 0017
ORR, HARRY T R01AI18124-11
ORR, JAMES S07RR07037-26 0376
ORR, SUEZANNE T R01HD25754-03
ORRINGER, EUGENE M01RR00046-31 0465
ORRINGER, EUGENE M01RR00046-31 0486
ORRINGER, EUGENE M01RR00046-31 0499
ORRINGER, EUGENE M01RR00046-31 0479
ORRINGER, EUGENE M01RR00046-31 0519
ORRINGER, EUGENE M01RR00046-31 0520
ORRINGER, EUGENE P M01RR00046-31 0457
ORRINGER, EUGENE P M01RR00046-31 0358
ORSINI, JAMES S07RR05464-29 0376
ORSULAK, PAUL J P50MH41115-05 0023
ORTABASI, ILSE M R43GM46208-01
ORTALDO, J R Z01CM09247-11
ORTALDO, J R Z01CM09256-09
ORTEGA, JORGE A U10CA02649-35
ORTENBERG, JOSEPH S07RR05377-30 0764
ORTH, ANNE B S07RR07082-26 0302
ORTH, DAVID H N01EY02124-02
ORTH, DAVID H U10EY03288-12
ORTH, DAVID H U10EY06730-04
ORTH, DAVID N M01RR00095-31 0001
ORTH, DAVID N P30HD05797-20 9001
ORTH, DAVID N P50HL14214-20 0040
ORTH, DAVID N R01CA11685-21
ORTH, DAVID N R01DK41043-03
ORTH, JOANNE M R01HD15563-11
ORTIZ DE MONTELLANO, PAUL R R37GM25515-14
ORTIZ DE MONTELLANO, PAUL R P01GM39552-05
ORTIZ DE MONTELLANO, PAUL R R01GM32488-09
ORTIZ DE MONTELLANO, PAUL R R01DK30297-10
ORTIZ-MARCALES, MARGARITA S06GM08216-09 00
ORTIZ, CHARLES L S06GM08132-17 0009
ORTIZ, JOSE G S06GM08224-07 0017
ORTMAN, LANCE F S07RR05330-30 0025
ORTNER, DAVID L R43HL46037-01
ORTWERTH, BERYL J R01EY02035-15
ORTWERTH, BERYL J R01EY07070-05
ORVIG, CHRISTOPHER E R01CA48964-03
ORWOLL, ERIC M01RR00334-25 0307
ORWOLL, ERIC M01RR00334-25 0291
ORWOLL, LUCINDA J P30AG08808-03 0006
ORY, PETER A K08AR01819-03
ORZECHOWSKI, BEVERLY J R43NR02838-01
OSAWA, SHOJI S07RR05406-30 0889
OSAWA, Y Z01HL00967-09
OSAWA, YOSHIO R37HD04945-21
OSAWA, YOSHIO S07RR05716-20 0139
OSAWA, YOSHIO S07RR05716-20 0140
OSBAKKEN, MARY D R01HL39208-05
OSBERGER, MARY J R01DC00423-05
OSBORN, BARBARA A S07RR07048-26 0653
OSBORN, JEFFREY L P01HL29587-09 0005
OSBORN, JEFFREY L R01HL40137-03
OSBORN, JOHN W, JR R29HL39619-05
OSBORN, JUNE E S07RR05447-30
OSBORN, JUNE E S15ES05831-01
OSBORN, LARRY A M01RR00997-16 0288
OSBORN, MARY J R01AI31646-01
OSBORN, MARY J R01GM42339-03
OSBORNE, BARBARA A R01GM36344-06
OSBORNE, SUSAN S R29HD24167-04
OSBORNE, TIMOTHY F S07RR07008-26 0063
OSBORNE, WILLIAM R R01DK38531-03
OSDOBY, PHILIP A R01AR32927-08
OSDOBY, PHILIP A R01DE06891-06
OSDOBY, PHILIP A S07RR05916-08
OSDOBY, PHILIP A S15AR41251-01
OSEAS, RONALD S M01RR00425-22S3 0391
OSEI, KWAME M01RR00034-31 0301
OSEI, KWAME M01RR00034-31 0382
OSEI, KWAME M01RR00034-31 0304
OSEROFF, A P41RR02594-06 0003
OSEROFF, ALLAN R R01CA45767-06
OSGANIAN, STAVROULA R43HL47256-01
OSGOOD, PATRICIA F S07RR05486-29 0044
OSHENOFF, MORRILL, R N01NS82316-04
OSHEROFF, NEIL P01CA43720-05 0005
OSHEROFF, NEIL R01DK43325-01
OSHEROFF, NEIL R01GM33944-08
OSHIMA, ROBERT G R01CA42302-06
OSKI, FRANK A P30HD27799-02
OSLEY, MARY A R01GM40118-04
OSMAN, E S07RR07119-20 0468
OSMANI, STEPHEN A R01GM42564-03
OSMANI, STEPHEN A S07RR05425-30 0760
OSOL, GEORGE R01HL17335-17
OSOL, GEORGE R01HL38231-04
OSOL, GEORGE J S07RR05429-30 0192
OSSOWSKI, LILIANA R01CA40758-05
OSTEEN, KEVIN G R03HD28128-01
OSTEEN, KEVIN G S07RR05424-30 0074
OSTER-GRANITE, MARY LOU P01MH46529-02 0002
OSTERGAARD, ARNE L P50AG05131-08 0018
OSTERGAARD, ARNE L R29AG06849-04
OSTERHOLM, MICHAEL T R01AI21842-05
OSTERMAN, JOHN S07RR07055-26 0170
OSTFELD, ADRIAN N01AG02105-23
OSTLUND, RICHARD M01RR00036-31 0675
OSTLUND, RICHARD E P41RR00954-15 9014
OSTLUND, RICHARD E P60DK20579-14 9004
OSTLUND, RICHARD E, JR R01HL29229-08
OSTMAN, PONTUS S07RR05372-30 0656
OSTRAND-ROSENBERG, SUZANNE R01CA52527-02
OSTRANDER, GARY K R29CA54590-02
OSTREA, ENRIQUE M, JR R01DA06821-01A1
OSTRER, HARRY R01EY08076-03
OSTRONSKI, M C P01CA30246-11 0005
OSTROUR, JEFFREY M N01AI82685-09
OSTROWSKI, MICHAEL C R01CA53271-01
OSTROWSKI, MICHAEL C R01GM34615-06
OSTWALD, SHARON K S07RR05448-30 0304
OSUCH, JANET S07RR05656-24 0833
OSWALD, ROBERT S07RR05346-30 0317
OSWALD, ROBERT E R01NS18660-07A2
OSWALD, ROBERT E S07RR05462-29 0894
OSWALD, THOMAS H S06GM08110-20 0004
OSWEILER, GARY D R15ES05659-01
OTHMER, HANS G R01GM29123-12
OTRAKJI, CHRISTIAN P30CA14395-18A1 9012
OTT, COBERN S07RR05374-30 0746
OTT, JURG P20HG00424-01 0003
OTT, JURG R01HG00008-02
OTT, JURG R01MH44292-03
OTT, MARY JANE M01RR01271-10 0112
OTTER, BRIAN A P30CA08748-26 9012
OTTER, BRIAN A R01CA36517-07A1
OTTER, TIMOTHY S07RR07125-22 0394
OTTERSON, MARY F R29DK43104-02
OTTERY, FAITH P01CA41078-05 0007

OTTESEN, E A Z01AI00253-10
OTTESEN, E A Z01AI00255-10
OTTESEN, E A Z01AI00439-07
OTTINGER, DONALD R S07RR07032-26 0029
OTTO, DAVID A S07RR05992-04
OTTO, DAVID A S15CA55977-01
OTVOS, JAMES D R01ES04036-07
OTVOS, JAMES D R01HL43230-03
OTVOS, JAMES D S07RR07181-13 0535
OTVOS, LASZLO R01AG10670-01
OTVOS, LASZLO R01GM45011-02
OTVOS, LASZLO S07RR05540-29 0552
OTVOS, LASZLO S10RR06281-01
OU, JING-HSIUNG J R01AI26244-04
OU, JING-HSIUNG J R01CA54533-01
OU, LO-CHANG R01HL21159-13
OUIMET, CHARLES C R01NS27096-03
OURIEL, KENNETH M01RR00044-31 0354
OURIEL, KENNETH R29HL40889-03
OUSLANDER, JOSEPH G R37AG08678-02
OUTENREATH, ROBERT S07RR05755-18 0220
OUYANG, ANN M01RR00040-31 0306
OUYANG, ANN R01DK34148-06
OUYANG, PAMELA S07RR05378-30 0008
OVARY, ZOLTAN R01AI03075-30A3
OVERALL, JOHN E R01MH32457-13
OVERBAUGH, JULIE M R01CA51080-02
OVERBECK, HENRY W R01HL23312-14
OVERBEEK, PAUL P30HD07495-19 9021
OVERBEEK, PAUL P30HD24064-04 9004
OVERBEEK, PAUL A R01EY06762-05
OVERBEEK, PAUL A R01HD25340-03
OVERBEEK, PAUL A R29HD24306-04
OVERBY, LYNNETTE Y S06GM08016-21 0081
OVERHAUSER, JOAN M R01HG00236-01A1
OVERHAUSER, JOAN M R29HG00167-03
OVERHAUSER, JOAN M S07RR05414-30 0994
OVERMAN, LARRY E R01GM30859-10
OVERMAN, LARRY E R01HL25854-12
OVERMAN, LARRY E R01NS12389-17
OVERPECK, M D Z01HD00361-05
OVERPECK, M D Z01HD00378-03
OVERPECK, M D Z01HD00832-08
OVERSTREET, JAMES W P51RR00169-30 0121
OVERSTREET, JAMES W P51RR00169-30 0122
OVERSTREET, JAMES W P51RR00169-30 0123
OVERSTREET, JAMES W R01HD25907-03
OVERSTREET, JAMES W U54HD29125-01 9001
OVERSTROM, ERIC W S15CA55957-01
OVERTON, DONALD A R01DA02403-12
OVERTON, DONALD A R01DA04725-03
OVERTON, G CHRISTIAN P50HG00425-01 9004
OVERTON, G CHRISTIAN R01RR04026-05
OWASOYO, JOSEPH S06GM08211-09 0008
OWASOYO, JOSEPH S06GM08211-09 0008
OWEN-SCHAUB, LAURIE B R29CA55195-01
OWEN, WILLIAM F P01HL36110-07 0007
OWEN, WILLIAM F U01AI31599-01 0003
OWEN, WILLIAM G R01EY03785-10
OWENS, ALBERT P30CA06973-29 9024
OWENS, ALBERT H, JR P30CA06973-29
OWENS, G P30CA44579-04A1 9012
OWENS, G K P01HL19242-15 0013
OWENS, G K P01HL19242-15 9004
OWENS, GARY K R01HL38854-05
OWENS, GREGORY R K07HL02102-04
OWENS, GREGORY R. N01HR46013-21
OWENS, I S Z01HD00137-17
OWENS, JOHN W S06GM08025-21 0019
OWENS, S MICHAEL R01DA04136-06
OWENS, THOMAS L S07RR07256-02 0071
OWERBACH, DAVID R29DK39965-05
OWNBY, CHARLOTTE L R01AI26923-04
OWNBY, DENNIS R R01AI24156-05
OWNBY, HELEN P30CA22453-14 9005
OWSLEY, CYNTHIA R01AG04212-09
OWSLEY, CYNTHIA R13AG09942-01
OWYANG, CHUNG M01RR00042-31 0507
OWYANG, CHUNG M01RR00042-31 0250
OWYANG, CHUNG P30DK34933-06A1 9007
OWYANG, CHUNG R01DK32838-09
OWYANG, CHUNG R01DK39199-02
OXENDER, DALE P01DK42718-02 9001
OXENDER, DALE P60AR20557-13 9003
OXENDER, DALE L P30CA46592-04 9007
OXENDER, DALE L R01GM20737-18
OXFORD, GERRY S R01NS18788-10
OXMAN, THOMAS E R01MH35779-02
OYASU, RYOICHI R01CA14649-18
OYASU, RYOICHI R01CA33511-07A1
OZATO, K Z01HD01310-04
OZCAN, GURHAN M01RR00350-25 0459
OZER, HARVEY L R01AG04821-09
OZER, HOWARD R01CA43201-07
OZER, HOWARD U10CA47559-01A1
OZOLS, JURIS B R01GM26351-13
OZOLS, ROBERT F R01CA51175-02
OZOLS, ROBERT F R01CA52181-02
OZONOFF, DAVID S07RR05927-07 0964
OZTURK, MEHMET R01CA54567-01
OZTURK, MEHMET R29CA49832-03
PAAP, CHRISTOPHER S07RR05849-11 0255
PAAP, CHRISTOPHER S07RR07091-26 0762
PABO, CARL P41RR04328-04 0006
PABO, CARL O R01GM31471-09
PABO, CARL O R13GM46419-01
PABST, MICHAEL J R01DE05494-11
PABST, MICHAEL J S07RR05994-03 0296
PACE, CARLOS N R01GM37039-06
PACE, NATHAN L M01RR00064-27 0323
PACE, NORMAN R R01GM34527-08
PACE, WILLIAM S07RR05372-30 0696
PACHNER, ANDREW R R01AR40476-02
PACHTER, BRUCE R R01NS25624-03
PACIFIC INST FOR RESEARCH & EV N01DA98252-
PACIFIC INST, RES & EVALUATION N01SP12004-
PACIFICI, MAURIZIO R01AR39705-03
PACIFICI, ROBERTO M01RR00036-31 1018
PACIFICI, ROBERTO R01AR41412-01
PACIFICI, ROBERTO R29AR39706-02
PACIFICO, ANTONIO M01RR00350-25 0368
PACK, ALLAN M01RR00040-31 0413
PACK, ALLAN I M01RR00040-31 0360
PACK, ALLAN I P01AG03934-10 0005
PACK, ALLAN I P50HL42236-04
PACK, ALLAN I P50HL42236-04 0004
PACK, ALLEN M01RR00040-31 0286
PACK, GEORGE R R01GM29079-10
PACKARD, B Z01BD01004-03
PACKER, LESTER R55CA53812-01A1
PACKER, MIHON M01RR00071-28A1 0172
PACKER, MILTON R01HL25055-10
PACKER, SAMUEL R01EY08560-02
PACKER, SAMUEL U10EY06288-07
PACKMAN, SEYMOUR M01RR01271-10 0062
PACKO, KIRK H U10EY08599-02
PACOLD, IVAN V K07HL01944-05
PADBURY, JAMES F M01RR00425-22S3 0345
PADBURY, JAMES F M01RR00425-22S3 0429
PADBURY, JAMES F M01RR00425-22S3 0467
PADBURY, JAMES F M01RR00425-22S3 0432
PADBURY, JAMES F R01HD18014-08
PADEN, CHARLES M K04NS01318-04
PADEN, CHARLES M R03MH48413-01
PADEN, CHARLES M S06GM08218-08 0018
PADGETT, DUDLEY N01LM13513-00
PADGETT, RICHARD A R01GM45371-01
PADGITT, PATRICIA J S07RR05390-30 0668
PADIAN, NANCY S U01AI31499-01 0003
PADILLA, GEORGE P50AG05128-08 0014
PADILLA, GERALDINE S07RR06014-03 0831
PADILLA, GERALDINE S07RR06014-03 0832
PADILLA, GERALDINE V S07RR06014-03
PADILLA, GERALDINE V S15NR02930-01
PADLAN, E A Z01DK36114-01
PADLAN, E A Z01DK36115-01
PADMANABHAN, RADHA K R01CA33099-07
PADMANABHAN, VASANTHA U54HD29184-01 0003
PADUA, ALBERT S07RR07023-26 0974
PADULA, STEVEN P60AR20621-13 0027
PADULA, STEVEN J R29AR39361-04
PADWA, ALBERT R01CA26750-13
PADWA, ALBERT R01CA26751-12
PADYKULA, HELEN A P01HD20290-06A1 0001
PAE, WALTER E, JR R29HL39872-04
PAFFENBARGER, RALPH S, JR R01HL34174-07
PAFFENBARGER, RALPH S, JR R01CA49446-03
PAGAN, ELI F S03RR03463-04
PAGANELLI, CHARLES V P01HL28542-10 0006
PAGANINI- HILL, ANNLIA R01CA32197-10
PAGANO RICHARD E S07RR05799-14 0682
PAGANO, JOSEPH U01AI25868-05 0002
PAGANO, JOSEPH S P01CA19014-14
PAGANO, JOSEPH S P01CA19014-14 0007
PAGANO, JOSEPH S P30CA16086-17 9011
PAGANO, JOSEPH S P30CA16086-17 9003
PAGANO, JOSEPH S P30CA16086-17
PAGANO, JOSEPH S P30CA16086-17 9009
PAGANO, JOSEPH S R01AI17205-12
PAGANO, MARCELLO R01AI28076-03
PAGANO, RICHARD E R37GM22942-16
PAGANO, ROBERT R P01NS19608-09 9005
PAGANS, J S P30CA16086-17 9008
PAGE, DAVID C R01HD22532-05
PAGE, DAVID C R01HG00257-01
PAGE, ERNEST P01HL20592-15 0006
PAGE, ERNEST P01HL20592-15 9001
PAGE, ERNEST R37HL10503-26
PAGE, JIMMY D S07RR05417-30 0808
PAGE, JOHN N01CN95170-02
PAGE, JOHN B R01MH49047-01
PAGE, JOHN G N01CM87259-11
PAGE, JOHN G N01CM97574-05
PAGE, NORBERT P N01LM83511-08
PAGE, RODNEY L P01CA29582-10A1 0002
PAGE, RODNEYES E P01CA42745-05 0002
PAGE, ROY C P01DE08555-03
PAGE, ROY C P30DE09743-02
PAGE, ROY C P50DE08229-05
PAGE, ROY C P50DE08229-05 0001
PAGE, ROY C. P01DE08555-03 0001
PAGE, ROY C. P01DE08555-03 9001
PAGE, ROY C. P51RR00166-30 0105
PAGLIA, DONALD E R01HL12944-22
PAGRATIS, NIKOS C R44GM43039-02
PAHWA, SAVITA R01AI28281-03
PAHWA, SAVITA R01DA05161-03
PAHWA, SAVITA R01HD26606-02
PAIETTA, JOHN V R29GM38671-04
PAIGEN, BEVERLY J R01HL32087-07
PAIGEN, KENNETH P30CA34196-09
PAIGEN, KENNETH P30CA34196-09 9015
PAIGEN, KENNETH P30CA34196-09 9016
PAIGEN, KENNETH S03RR03347-07
PAIGEN, KENNETH S07RR05545-29
PAIK, WOON K R01DK09602-22
PAINE, PHILIP L R01GM44390-03
PAINE, PHILIP L S15DK44663-01
PAINE, PHILLIP L P30CA22453-14 9007
PAINE, ROBERT, III K08HL02415-02
PAINTER, MICHAEL J R01NS26946-02
PAINTER, RICHARD G R01AI26386-03
PAINTER, RICHARD G R01HL39040-05
PAINTER, RICHARD G R01HL39943-05
PAINTER, SHERRY D R01HD28500-01
PAINTER, SHERRY D S07RR07205-11 0656
PAIRENT, FREDERICK W S07RR06038-01
PAJAK, THOMAS F P01CA52051-01A1 9001
PAJAK, THOMAS F U10CA32115-10
PAK, CHARLES M01RR00633-19 0330
PAK, CHARLES M01RR00633-19 0332
PAK, CHARLES M01RR00633-19 0334
PAK, CHARLES P01DK20543-15 0016
PAK, CHARLES P01DK20543-15 0017
PAK, CHARLES P01DK20543-15 0013
PAK, CHARLES Y M01RR00633-19 0345
PAK, CHARLES Y M01RR00633-19 0281
PAK, CHARLES Y M01RR00633-19 0340
PAK, CHARLES Y M01RR00633-19 0393
PAK, CHARLES Y M01RR00633-19 0238
PAK, CHARLES Y M01RR00633-19 0240
PAK, CHARLES Y P01DK20543-15 9001
PAK, CHARLES Y P01DK20543-15
PAK, CHARLES Y R01AR16061-20A1
PAK, CHARLES Y C M01RR00633-19 0186
PAK, CHARLES Y C M01RR00633-19
PAK, CHARLES Y C M01RR00633-19 0379
PAK, CHARLES Y C M01RR00633-19 0305
PAK, CHARLES Y C M01RR00633-19 0317
PAK, CHARLES Y C M01RR00633-19 0394
PAK, CHARLES Y C M01RR00633-19 0399
PAK, CHARLES Y C M01RR00633-19 0395
PAK, CHARLES Y C M01RR00633-19 0387
PAK, CHARLES YC M01RR00633-19 0367
PAK, WILLIAM L R01EY04767-09
PAK, WILLIAM L R37EY00033-22
PAKES, STEVEN P P40RR00890-16
PAKRASI, HIMADRI B R01GM45797-01
PAKRASI, HIMADRI B R29GM41841-03
PALADE, GEORGE E P01CA46128-04 0006
PALADE, GEORGE E R37HL17080-18
PALADE, GEORGE E S15AI32207-01
PALADE, PHILIP T R01AR34377-06
PALADE, PHILIP T R01HL42527-03
PALASCAK, JOSEPH E P60HL15996-19 9002
PALAZZO, ROBERT E R01GM43264-02
PALCZEWSKI, KRZYSZTOF R29EY08061-04
PALEFSKY, J P01AI21912-08 0005
PALEFSKY, JOEL S07RR05305-30 0725
PALEFSKY, JOEL M R01CA54053-01A1
PALEFSKY, JOEL M U01AI31499-01 0001
PALEK, JIRI P01HL37462-05
PALEK, JIRI P01HL37462-05 0001
PALEK, JIRI P60HL15157-20 0023
PALEK, JIRI R37HL27215-11
PALEK, JIRI S07RR05587-20
PALELLA, THOMAS D P01DK42718-02 0003
PALELLA, THOMAS D P60AR20557-13
PALESE, PETER P01AI24460-04 9001
PALESE, PETER P01AI24460-04 0002
PALESE, PETER M P01AI24460-04
PALESE, PETER M R01AI11823-18
PALESE, PETER M R37AI18998-10
PALFREY, CLIVE H P01HL30121-08 0007
PALFREY, CLIVE H P60DK20595-14 0018
PALFREY, HUGH C R01GM42715-03
PALIS, JAMES R29HL45573-01
PALKER, THOMAS J P01CA43447-06 0010
PALKER, THOMAS J P30AI28662-03 9002
PALKER, THOMAS J R01CA40660-06
PALLAS, DAVID C R29CA45285-05
PALLAVICINI, MARIA G R01AI27909-03
PALLER, AMY S K08AR01811-02
PALLER, AMY S S07RR05370-30 0618
PALLONE, THOMAS L R29DK42495-02
PALLOTTA, BARRY S R01GM42399-01A1
PALLOTTA, BARRY S R01NS29881-01
PALLOTTA, JOHANNA A M01RR01032-16 0360
PALMA, GLORIA I P50AI30603-01 9002
PALMENBERG, ANN C R01AI17331-11
PALMENBERG, ANN C R01AI30566-01
PALMER, JERRY P. M01RR00037-31 0435
PALMER, JERRY P. M01RR00037-31 0436
PALMER, ALAN M P20NS30318-01 0003
PALMER, ALAN M P50AG05133-08 0007
PALMER, ALAN M R35AG08974-01 0007

PALMER, CAROLINE M R29MH45764-02
PALMER, CHARLES S07RR05680-23 0925
PALMER, EARL A U10EY05874-07
PALMER, EARL A U10EY06395-07
PALMER, EDWARD P01AI22295-07 0006
PALMER, EDWARD R01AI22259-07
PALMER, EDWARD R01AR37070-06
PALMER, GRAHAM P41RR02583-07 0012
PALMER, GRAHAM A R37GM21337-17
PALMER, JEFFREY B K08DC00024-05
PALMER, JEFFREY DONALD R01GM35087-08
PALMER, JEFFREY M R29DK39647-04
PALMER, JERRY P01DK02456-33A1 0013
PALMER, JERRY P01DK41801-02 0006
PALMER, JERRY P M01RR00037-31 0511
PALMER, JERRY P M01RR00037-31 0525
PALMER, JERRY P P30DK17047-15 9003
PALMER, JERRY P U01DK30604-09
PALMER, JOHN S07RR07096-26 0075
PALMER, JULIE R01CA52223-02
PALMER, JULIE R R01CA55766-01
PALMER, LARRY A R01EY07112-04A1
PALMER, LAWRENCE G R01DK27847-11
PALMER, MICHAEL R K02AA00102-05
PALMER, MICHAEL R R01AA05915-09
PALMER, R HEATHER R01HS06469-02
PALMER, ROBERT M01RR00997-16 0353
PALMER, STEPHEN E R01MH46141-02
PALMITER, RICHARD D R37HD09172-17
PALOMBO, JOHN S07RR05591-27 0667
PALSSON, BERNHARD O R29DK39256-05
PALTA, MARI P01HL42242-04 9002
PALTA, MARI R01HL38149-05
PALTER, KAREN B R29GM41000-03
PALTIEL, A D S07RR05710-21 0027
PALUMBI, STEPHEN R S07RR07026-26 0008
PAMER, ERIC G K08AI00937-03
PAMUKCU, RIFA S07RR05408-30 0936
PAN, BIN-TAO S07RR05374-30 0745
PAN, PERCY S N01AI95012-07
PAN, SUEIHUA S07RR05576-27 0614
PANASCI, LAWRENCE C R01NS22230-05
PANDE, AJAY K R01EY09521-01
PANDE, HEMA S07RR05841-12 0233
PANDEY, GHANSHYAM N R01MH36169-08A2
PANDEY, JANARDAN P S07RR05420-30 0042
PANDEY, KAILASH N R29HD25527-03
PANDEY, KAILASH N S07RR05424-30 0098
PANDIAN, NATESA M01RR00054-30 0468
PANDIANI, JOHN A R19MH46203-03
PANDINA, ROBERT J R01DA03395-08
PANDOL, STEPHEN J R01DK33010-08
PANDURANGI, ANAND M01RR00065-29 0352
PANDY, MARCUS S07RR07091-26 0763
PANDYA, DEEPAK N R01NS16841-11
PANEK, JAMES S R29CA47249-04
PANETH, NIGEL S R03AA09008-01
PANETTIERI, REYNOLD A K08HL02647-01
PANG, K SANDY R01GM38250-04
PANG, KAM YEE P30DK36200-05S1 0004
PANG, KEUM Y S06GM08244-05 0023
PANG, SONGYA R01HD24360-04
PANGANIBAN, ANTONITO P01CA22443-14 0005
PANGANIBAN, ANTONITO T R01CA49741-02
PANGBURN, MICHAEL K R01DK35081-07
PANGBURN, MICHAEL K S15HL47789-01
PANGE, JENNY N01LM03520-01
PANICALI, DENNIS L R44AI26028-03
PANICALI, DENNIS L U01AI26507-03
PANICEK, DAVID M U01CA54046-01
PANINI, SANKHAVARAM S07RR05964-06 0757
PANINI, SANKHAVARAM S07RR05964-06 0758
PANINI, SANKHAVARAM R R01DK42270-02
PANITCH, HOWARD S07RR05417-30 0809
PANJABI, MANOHAR M R01AR39209-02
PANJWANI, NOORJAHAN A R01EY07088-05
PANKIEWICZ, KRYSTOF W R01GM42010-01A2
PANKO, WALTER B G08LM05329-01
PANNELL, KEITH H S06GM08012-21 0008
PANNELL, L Z01DK31107-04
PANT, H C Z01NS02725-06
PANTALOS, GEORGE M R29HL41777-03
PANTUCK, EUGENE M01RR00645-20 0455
PANZA, J A Z01HL04883-01
PANZER, ROBERT P60AG10463-01 9001
PAOLINI, PAUL J S07RR07004-16 0052
PAPACONSTANTINOU, JOHN R01CA31472-07
PAPADOPOULOS, VASSILIOS R55DK43358-01A1
PAPAHADJOPOULOS, P DEMETRIOS R01CA25526-09
PAPAHADJOPOULOS, P DEMETRIOS R01GM28117-10
PAPAIOANNOU, VIRGINIA E R01HD25225-03
PAPAIOANNOU, VIRGINIA E R01HD27295-02
PAPANICOLAOU, ANDREW C R01NS29540-01
PAPARELLA, M.M. P50DC00133-13 9004
PAPARELLA, MICHAEL M P50DC00133-13 9002
PAPARELLA, MICHAEL M. P50DC00133-13 0016
PAPAS, ATHENA S07RR05319-18 0620
PAPAS, T S Z01CP05441-07
PAPAS, T S Z01CP05443-07
PAPAS, T S Z01CP05591-03
PAPAS, T S Z01CP05667-01
PAPAS, T S Z01CP05669-01
PAPASOZOMENOS, SOZOS CH P50AG08664-03 0003
PAPAVASILIOU, S07RR05333-30 0872
PAPAYANNOPOULOU, THALIA P01DK31232-10 9002
PAPAYANNOPOULOU, THALIA P51RR00166-30 0106
PAPAYANNOPOULOU, THALIA R01HL46557-01
PAPAYANNOPOULOU, THALIA R37DK30852-10
PAPAZIAN, DIANE S07RR05354-30 0420
PAPAZIAN, DIANE M R01GM43459-02
PAPE, LINDA A S07RR05712-20 0104
PAPE, RICHARD P51RR00167-31 9009
PAPERMASTER, DAVID S R01EY06891-04
PAPILE, LU-ANN U10HD27881-01
PAPKA, RAYMOND E R01NS22526-06
PAPLANUS, P P01CA38548-07 0001
PAPLAUSKAS, LEONARD P S15AR41253-01
PAPLAUSKAS, LEONARD P S15GM47054-01
PAPOLOS, DEMETRI F K20MH00873-01A2
PAPP, LASZLO A K20MH00858-01A1
PAPPANO, ACHILLES J R01HL42512-01A2
PAPPANO, ACHILLES J R37HL13339-21
PAPPAS, CAROL D R01AI31079-01
PAPPAS, GEORGE D R01NS28931-05
PAPPAS, THEODORE N R29DK40790-03
PAPPO, JACQUES R01DK36563-06
PAPPONE, PAMELA A R01GM44840-02
PAPSIDERO, LAWRENCE D R44AI26983-03
PAQUETTE, EDMOND S07RR05664-24 0872
PAQUETTE, LEO A R01CA12115-21
PAQUETTE, LEO A R01GM28468-12
PAQUETTE, LEO A R01GM30827-09
PAQUETTE, LEO ARMAND R01AI11490-18
PARA, MICHAEL F U01AI25924-05 0001
PARADISE, JACK L M01RR00084-29 0244
PARADISE, JACK L R01HD26026-01A2
PARADISE, JACK L S07RR05507-29 0483
PARADISE, LOIS J R03DA07303-01A1
PARADISO, ANTHONY M R01HL44173-02
PARASURAMAN, RAJA R01AG07569-03
PARCEL, GUY S S07RR05828-08 0526
PARCEL, GUY S U01HL39927-05
PARCEL, TOBY L R01HD23467-03
PARCHMENT, RALPH E R01CA51325-03
PARDEE, ARTHUR B P01CA22427-14 9001
PARDEE, ARTHUR B P01CA22427-14
PARDEE, ARTHUR B P01CA22427-14 0003
PARDEE, ARTHUR B R01CA50608-01A1
PARDEE, JOEL D R01GM32458-08
PARDES, HERBERT S07RR05395-30
PARDI, ARTHUR K04AI01051-01
PARDI, ARTHUR R01AI27026-04
PARDI, ARTHUR R01AI30726-01
PARDINI, BENET J R29HL38137-05
PARDO, JOSE V S07RR05389-30 0645
PARDOLL, DREW M R01AI27992-02
PARDRIDGE, WILLIAM M P01NS25554-01A2S1 900
PARDRIDGE, WILLIAM M P01NS25554-01A2S1
PARDRIDGE, WILLIAM M P01NS25554-01A2S1 000
PARDRIDGE, WILLIAM M R01AI28760-03
PARDUE, HARRY L R01GM13326-24
PARDUE, MARY LOU R01GM21874-17
PARDY, R L S07RR07055-26 0176
PARENTAEAU, NANCY L R43EY09014-01
PARENTEAU, G L Z01HL02777-05
PARFITT, A MICHAEL P01AG07542-05
PARFITT, A MICHAEL R01AG10381-01
PARHAM, PETER P01GM30387-10 0008
PARHAM, PETER R37AI17892-11
PARHAM, PETER R R01AI22039-07
PARHAM, PETER R R01AI31168-01
PARHAM, PETER R R01HL47153-01
PARHAM, PETER R R55AI24258-06
PARIETTI, ELIZABETH S07RR07149-18 0425
PARIKH, INDU R43DA07437-01
PARIS, DIANE M01RR00069-29 0452
PARISE, LESLIE V R01HL45923-02
PARISE, LESLIE V R29HL38405-06
PARISE, LESLIE V S07RR05406-30 0898
PARISE, LESLIE V S07RR05406-30 0899
PARISH, HARLIE A R43HL46621-01
PARISH, HARLIE A R44AR39427-02A2
PARISI, RICHARD A R29HL42445-02
PARISIEN, MAY R01AR41386-01
PARK, BERNADETTE M R01MH45049-01A2
PARK, CHUN S S07RR05712-20 0067
PARK, DENISE C R01AG06265-06A1
PARK, DONG H P01MH44043-04 0004
PARK, DONG H P01MH44043-04 9001
PARK, DOUGLAS L S07RR07002-26 0861
PARK, I W P51RR00168-30 0161
PARK, JAMES T R01GM40768-04
PARK, JAMES T R37AI05090-29
PARK, JANIE C R03DC01043-01
PARK, KATHRYN A S07RR07208-10 0664
PARK, KINAM R01HL39081-05
PARK, KINAM S07RR05586-24 0111
PARK, M H Z01DE00311-11
PARK, NO-HEE S07RR05304-30 0229
PARK, R E S07RR05710-21 0030
PARK, ROBERT C U10CA27469-11
PARK, S S Z01CP05086-11
PARK, S S Z01CP05125-11
PARK, TAE S R01NS21045-08
PARKE, JAMES C, JR N01HD92927-02
PARKER, BARBARA S07RR05973-05 0785
PARKER, BARBARA A M01RR00827-17 0504
PARKER, BARBARA A. P01CA37497-07 9001
PARKER, C S07RR07003-26 0315
PARKER, CARL P01GM40499-04 0002
PARKER, CARL S R01GM42671-02
PARKER, CHARLES J K04DK01942-02
PARKER, CHARLES J R55DK35830-07
PARKER, CHARLES R, JR R01HD22969-05
PARKER, CHARLES W P50AI15322-14 0009
PARKER, CHARLOTTE D R01AI25055-03
PARKER, CHARLOTTE D S10RR06284-01
PARKER, CHRISTINA M K11AI00903-03
PARKER, DAVID C R01AI24303-05
PARKER, DAVID C R01AI29544-01A1
PARKER, DAVID C R13AI31012-01
PARKER, DAVID C S07RR05712-20 0113
PARKER, DAVIS M01RR00069-29 0263
PARKER, IAN R29GM39831-04
PARKER, JACK M S07RR07118-22 0381
PARKER, JAMES C R01HL24571-13
PARKER, JANET L R01HL36079-05
PARKER, JOHN C R01DK11356-25
PARKER, KATHLYN A R01AI29900-01A2
PARKER, KATHLYN A R01CA50720-01A2
PARKER, KATHLYN A S07RR07085-26 0342
PARKER, LINDA A R01DA06559-03
PARKER, M Z01CL00091-02
PARKER, M M Z01CL00032-04
PARKER, MARY H R43AG08910-01
PARKER, R I Z01CL10191-02
PARKER, ROY R R01GM45443-01
PARKER, ROY R S07RR07002-26 0874
PARKER, VERNON D P41RR06030-01A1 0009
PARKER, W DAVIS M01RR00069-29 0386
PARKER, W DAVIS P01AG09417-01 0001
PARKER, WILLIAM B P01CA34200-09 0011
PARKER, WILLIAM B R01AI29157-03
PARKER, WILLIAM B S15CA56019-01
PARKER, WILLIAM D, JR P01AG10446-01
PARKER, WILLIAM D, JR R01NS25382-04
PARKER, WILLIAM DAVIS P01AG10446-01 0001
PARKHURST, LAWRENCE J R01DK36288-19
PARKINS, CHARLES W R01NS20680-08
PARKINSON, ANDREW R01ES03765-06
PARKINSON, ANDREW R01ES04996-03
PARKINSON, ANDREW R01GM37044-04
PARKINSON, DAVID P50AG05681-08 0014
PARKINSON, JOHN S R01GM19559-19
PARKINSON, JOHN S R01GM43098-02
PARKMAN, ROBERTSON P01NS26991-02 0001
PARKS, DALE A R29DK38681-05
PARKS, JOHN M01RR00039-31 0321
PARKS, JOHN S R01HD24960-03
PARKS, JOHN S. M01RR00039-31 0371
PARKS, LEO W R01DK37222-06A1
PARKS, ROBERT E, JR R01CA07340-28
PARKS, THOMAS N R01DC00144-13
PARKS, WADE P01NS25569-04 0002
PARKS, WILLIAM C R29HL41040-04
PARLOW, ALBERT F N01DK02256-03
PARLOW, ALBERT F N01DK12269-00
PARLOW, ALBERT F P30HD19445-05S1 9003
PARMELEE, D C Z01CP05559-04
PARMELEE, PATRICIA A P50MH40380-07 0010
PARMELY, MICHAEL S07RR05373-30 0726
PARMLEY, RICHARD T U10CA52771-02
PARMS, CLIFFORD A R43CA54719-01
PARMS, CLIFFORD A R44AI26387-03
PARNES, HERBERT S R01AG07973-03
PARNES, HOWARD L R13CA53161-01
PARNES, JANE P01AI19512-09 0011
PARNES, JANE R R01AI30155-02
PARNES, JANE R R01CA46507-05
PARNES, JANE R R01GM34991-06A1
PARODI, ARMANDO J R01GM44500-02
PARR, EARL L R01HD24450-03
PARR, MARGARET S07RR07118-22 0382
PARR, MARGARET B R01HD17337-09
PARRIS, B Z01AI00607-01
PARRIS, DEBORAH S R01GM34930-06
PARRISH, COLIN R R01AI28385-02
PARRISH, COLIN R S07RR05462-29 0895
PARRISH, JOHN P30HD26979-02 9005
PARRISH, JOHN A R01AR25395-11
PARRISH, MARK S07RR05684-23 0173
PARRISH, RICHARD K U10EY05473-07
PARRY, BARBARA M01RR00827-17 0387
PARRY, BARBARA L P50MH30914-14 0048
PARRY, BARBARA L R29MH42831-03
PARRY, D M Z01CP04377-20
PARRY, D M Z01CP05139-12
PARRY, RONALD J R01CA25142-10A3
PARRY, RONALD J R01GM26166-13
PARRY, RONALD J R01GM26569-12
PARRYM GARETH J S07RR05376-30 0037
PARS, HARRY N01CN15359-01
PARSEGIAN, V Z01CT00026-16
PARSEGIAN, V A Z01DK18013-04
PARSLOW, TRISTRAM G R01AI29313-02
PARSLOW, TRISTRAM G R01GM43574-06

PARSONNET, JEFFREY R29AI25608-04
PARSONNET, JULIE R01CA55764-01
PARSONNET, JULIE S07RR05353-30 0362
PARSONS, C L R01DK39239-05
PARSONS, C LOWELL U01DK45026-01
PARSONS, DONALD S07RR05649-25 0785
PARSONS, DORABETH S07RR07013-26 0968
PARSONS, DORABETH S07RR07013-26 0969
PARSONS, J THOMAS P01CA40042-07
PARSONS, J THOMAS R01CA27578-11
PARSONS, J THOMAS R01CA29243-11
PARSONS, JACK N01CM17544-00
PARSONS, MARILYN R01AI22635-05
PARSONS, MARILYN S07RR05939-07 0726
PARSONS, OSCAR A R01AA06135-08
PARSONS, OSCAR A R01AA08650-02
PARSONS, OSCAR A R01DA05175-05
PARSONS, POLLY P50HL40784-03 0004
PARSONS, POLLY P50HL40784-03 9003
PARSONS, REGIS R19MH46179-03
PARSONS, RODNEY L R01NS23978-06
PARSONS, SARAH J R01CA39438-07
PARSONS, SARAH J R01DK44199-01
PARSONS, STANLEY M R01NS15047-12
PARSONS, STANLEY M R01NS26168-04
PARSONS, THOMAS J P01CA40042-07 0002
PARTHASARATHY, SAMPATH P50HL14197-20 9003
PARTHASARATHY, SAMPATH P50HL14197-20 0010
PARTRIDGE, EDWARD E M01RR00032-31 0374
PARTRIDGE, NICOLA C R01AR39743-03
PARTRIDGE, NICOLA C R01AR40661-01
PARYSEK, LINDA M R01HD25752-03
PASCAL, ROBERT ANTHONY, JR R01AI24146-05
PASCUAL, VIRGINIA H S07RR05992-04 0814
PASHLER, HAROLD E R29MH45584-03
PASHLEY, DAVID H R01DE06427-10
PASPUALE, ELENA B R29HD26351-03
PASQUALE, ELENA B S07RR05803-13 0449
PASQUE, MICHAEL K R29HL44511-02
PASS, H I Z01CM06662-05
PASS, KENNETH S07RR05649-25 0784
PASS, ROBERT P01HD10699-15 0015
PASS, ROBERT F P01HD10699-15 0013
PASS, ROBERT F P01HD10699-15 0004
PASS, ROBERT F R01HD17966-09
PASS, THEODORE M R43HL44280-01A2
PASSMORE, HOWARD C R01GM46641-13
PASTAN, I Z01CB08000-21
PASTAN, I Z01CB08753-09
PASTER, BRUCE J R01DE08303-03
PASTERNACK, BERNARD P30CA16087-14 9005
PASTERNACK, BERNARD S P30ES00260-29 9005
PASTERNACK, BERNARD S R01CA34588-07
PASTERNACK, BERNARD S. P30AI27742-03 9008
PASTERNACK, GARY R R55CA54404-01
PASTERNACK, MARK S07RR05486-29 0047
PASTERNACK, MARK S R29CA45658-05
PASTERNAK, GAVRIL W K02DA00138-03
PASTERNAK, GAVRIL W P50DA05130-05 0001
PASTERNAK, GAVRIL W R01DA02615-12
PASTERNAK, GAVRIL W R01DA06241-02
PASTERNAK, GAVRIL W R01DA07242-01
PASTERNAK, RICHARD M01RR01032-16 0457
PASTERNAK, RICHARD M01RR01032-16 0459
PASTERNAK, RICHARD M01RR01032-16 0460
PASTERNAK, RICHARD C M01RR01032-16 0458
PASTERNAK, TATIANA R01EY06175-06
PASTOR, R W Z01BB03005-07
PASTUSZKO, ANNA R01NS27543-02
PASYK, KRYSTYNA P30HG00209-02 0005
PATAKI, CAROLY S07RR05736-19 0176
PATARCA, ROBERTO S07RR05526-29 0081
PATCH, LYNNE S07RR05655-21 0808
PATE, EDWARD F R01AR39643-03
PATEK, PAUL Q S07RR07026-26 0009
PATEL, MULCHAND S. P50HD11089-14 0027
PATEL, DINSHAW P01CA21111-15 0008
PATEL, DINSHAW P01CA47995-02 0004
PATEL, DINSHAW J R01CA46533-04
PATEL, DINSHAW J R01CA46778-04
PATEL, DINSHAW J R01CA49982-02
PATEL, DINSHAW J R01GM34504-07
PATEL, GORDHAN N R44CA49347-03
PATEL, MULCHAND S R01DK20478-12
PATEL, MULCHAND S R01DK42885-02
PATEL, PRAGNA P30HD24064-04 9003
PATEL, PRAGNA I S07RR05425-30 0761
PATEL, RAMON S06GM08140-17 0017
PATEL, TARUN B K04DK01742-05
PATEL, TARUN B R01DK35713-06
PATEL, VASISHTA M01RR00350-25 0477
PATEL, VIKRAM P P01HL45168-01A1 0002
PATEL, VIKRAM P R01DK41386-03
PATENAUDE, ANDREA FARKAS N01CO84331-01
PATERSON, B M Z01CB05258-12
PATERSON, CHRISTOPHER A R01EY06918-05
PATERSON, YVONNE R01GM31841-08
PATERSON, YVONNE S10RR06450-01
PATHAK, MADHUKAR A R01CA05003-33
PATHAK, SEN P01CA34936-08 9001
PATIERNO, STEVEN S07RR05359-30 0518
PATIERNO, STEVEN R R01ES05304-02

PATINO, REYNALDO R29HD27729-01A1
PATLAK, JOSEPH B R01AR37606-05
PATO, MARTIN L R01GM24270-13S1
PATON, MARTHA S07RR07015-26 0598
PATON, MARTHA C R01EY08760-02
PATON, MARTHA C R37EY06039-08
PATONAY, GABOR R01AI28903-01A2
PATONAY, GABOR S07RR07171-08 0158
PATRICK, JAMES W R01DA04077-05
PATRICK, JAMES W R01NS13546-16
PATSCH, JOSEF R P60HL27341-10 0006
PATSCH, WOLFANG M01RR00350-25 0435
PATSCH, WOLFGANG P N01HC55016-10
PATSCH, WOLFGANG P R01HL41199-04
PATTERSON, A P Z01HL02034-01
PATTERSON, B Z01CN00107-09
PATTERSON, BRADFORD W N01CO03871-06
PATTERSON, C ANNE P51RR00165-31 0138
PATTERSON, DAVID P01HD17449-08
PATTERSON, DAVID P01HD17449-08 0001
PATTERSON, DAVID P01HD17449-08 9001
PATTERSON, DAVID P01HD17449-08 9002
PATTERSON, DAVID P01HD17449-08 9003
PATTERSON, DAVID R01AG00029-17
PATTERSON, DAVID R01HD22720-05S1
PATTERSON, DAVID R01HG00406-01
PATTERSON, DAVID R13HG00427-01
PATTERSON, DAVID S07RR05964-06 0754
PATTERSON, DAVID S07RR05964-06
PATTERSON, DAVID R R01GM42725-02
PATTERSON, DONALD F P40RR02512-07
PATTERSON, DONALD F R37HL18848-16
PATTERSON, GERALD R R37MH37940-10
PATTERSON, GREGORY M S07RR07026-26 0001
PATTERSON, HERBERT J M01RR00046-31 0427
PATTERSON, HERBERT J M01RR00046-31 0452
PATTERSON, JOAN M S07RR05448-30 0294
PATTERSON, JOHN L P01NS12587-16 0009
PATTERSON, JOHN W R01EY06457-06
PATTERSON, KEN R19DA06407-03
PATTERSON, PAUL H R01NS20916-09
PATTERSON, RICHARD B U10CA53128-01
PATTERSON, RICHARD B U10CA53128-01 0023
PATTERSON, RICHARD B U10CA53128-01 0024
PATTERSON, RICHARD B U10CA53128-01 0025
PATTERSON, RICHARD B U10CA53128-01 0026
PATTERSON, RICHARD B U10CA53128-01 0027
PATTERSON, RICHARD B U10CA53128-01 0028
PATTERSON, RICHARD B U10CA53128-01 0001
PATTERSON, RICHARD B U10CA53128-01 0002
PATTERSON, RICHARD B U10CA53128-01 0029
PATTERSON, RICHARD B U10CA53128-01 0043
PATTERSON, RICHARD B U10CA53128-01 0044
PATTERSON, RICHARD B U10CA53128-01 0045
PATTERSON, RICHARD B U10CA53128-01 0046
PATTERSON, RICHARD B U10CA53128-01 0047
PATTERSON, RICHARD B U10CA53128-01 0048
PATTERSON, RICHARD B U10CA53128-01 0049
PATTERSON, RICHARD B U10CA53128-01 0050
PATTERSON, RICHARD B U10CA53128-01 0051
PATTERSON, RICHARD B U10CA53128-01 0052
PATTERSON, RICHARD B U10CA53128-01 0053
PATTERSON, RICHARD B U10CA53128-01 0054
PATTERSON, RICHARD B U10CA53128-01 0055
PATTERSON, RICHARD B U10CA53128-01 0056
PATTERSON, RICHARD B U10CA53128-01 0057
PATTERSON, RICHARD B U10CA53128-01 0058
PATTERSON, RICHARD B U10CA53128-01 0059
PATTERSON, RICHARD B U10CA53128-01 0060
PATTERSON, RICHARD B U10CA53128-01 0030
PATTERSON, RICHARD B U10CA53128-01 0031
PATTERSON, RICHARD B U10CA53128-01 0003
PATTERSON, RICHARD B U10CA53128-01 0004
PATTERSON, RICHARD B U10CA53128-01 0005
PATTERSON, RICHARD B U10CA53128-01 0006
PATTERSON, RICHARD B U10CA53128-01 0007
PATTERSON, RICHARD B U10CA53128-01 0032
PATTERSON, RICHARD B U10CA53128-01 0033
PATTERSON, RICHARD B U10CA53128-01 0034
PATTERSON, RICHARD B U10CA53128-01 0035
PATTERSON, RICHARD B U10CA53128-01 0036
PATTERSON, RICHARD B U10CA53128-01 0037
PATTERSON, RICHARD B U10CA53128-01 0008
PATTERSON, RICHARD B U10CA53128-01 0009
PATTERSON, RICHARD B U10CA53128-01 0010
PATTERSON, RICHARD B U10CA53128-01 0011
PATTERSON, RICHARD B U10CA53128-01 0012
PATTERSON, RICHARD B U10CA53128-01 0013
PATTERSON, RICHARD B U10CA53128-01 0038
PATTERSON, RICHARD B U10CA53128-01 0039
PATTERSON, RICHARD B U10CA53128-01 0040
PATTERSON, RICHARD B U10CA53128-01 0041
PATTERSON, RICHARD B U10CA53128-01 0042
PATTERSON, RICHARD B U10CA53128-01 0014
PATTERSON, RICHARD B U10CA53128-01 0015
PATTERSON, RICHARD B U10CA53128-01 0016
PATTERSON, RICHARD B U10CA53128-01 0017
PATTERSON, RICHARD B U10CA53128-01 0018
PATTERSON, RICHARD B U10CA53128-01 0019
PATTERSON, RICHARD B U10CA53128-01 0020
PATTERSON, RICHARD B U10CA53128-01 0021
PATTERSON, RICHARD B U10CA53128-01 0022

PATTERSON, RODNEY S S03RR03392-08
PATTERSON, RODNEY S S03RR03391-08
PATTERSON, ROSALYN M S06GM45199-02 0008
PATTERSON, ROY P50AI11403-19
PATTERSON, ROY R01AI20060-09
PATTERSON, THOMAS P50MH45294-03 0004
PATTERSON, THOMAS R01MH46255-02
PATTERSON, WAYNE S07RR07169-07
PATTILLO, WALTER H, JR S06GM08049-20
PATTON, CURTIS L R01AI21862-07
PATTON, CURTIS L S07RR05443-30 0995
PATTON, DOROTHY L P01AI24756-05 0002
PATTON, DOROTHY L. P51RR00166-30 0109
PATTON, DOROTHY L. P51RR00166-30 0107
PATTON, DOROTHY L. P51RR00166-30 0108
PATTON, DOROTHY L. P51RR00166-30 0110
PATTON, DOROTHY L. P51RR00166-30 0148
PATTON, JAMES S S07RR07024-26 0049
PATTON, JOHN T K04AI00990-02
PATTON, JOHN T R22AI21478-06
PATTON, JOHN T S07RR05363-30 0833
PATWARDHAN, NILIMA A S07RR05712-20 0068
PATZ, SAMUEL R01HL39035-04
PATZ, SAMUEL S07RR05950-07 0000
PATZ, SAMUEL S07RR05950-07 0986
PAUERSTEIN, CARL J P30HD10202-15
PAUERSTEIN, CARL J U01HL40154-05
PAUKER, STEVEN M01RR00054-30 0476
PAUL, ARA G S03RR03073-11
PAUL, ARA G S07RR05571-27
PAUL, ARA G S07RR05571-27 0917
PAUL, ARA G S15CA55935-01
PAUL, B P30CA16056-16 9017
PAUL, DAVID L R01GM37751-05
PAUL, DAVID L S07RR05381-30 0782
PAUL, DENNIS S07RR05376-30 0043
PAUL, RHEA R01DC00793-02
PAUL, RICHARD P01HL22619-14 0020
PAUL, RICHARD H U10HD21434-06
PAUL, SUDHIR K04HL02217-03
PAUL, SUDHIR R01HL40348-04
PAUL, SUDHIR R01HL44126-02
PAUL, VALERIE J R29GM38624-05
PAUL, VALERIE J S06GM44796-02
PAUL, VALERIE J S06GM44796-02 0003
PAUL, W E Z01AI00030-23
PAUL, W E Z01AI00493-05
PAULAUSKIS, JOSEPH D S07RR05446-30 0277
PAULE, MARVIN R R01GM22580-16
PAULE, MARVIN R R01GM26059-12
PAULE, MARVIN R R01GM39901-04
PAULES, R S Z01ES21157-01
PAULI, BENDICHT U R01CA48642-04
PAULS, DAVID L K02MH00508-08
PAULS, DAVID L P01HD21888-04 0005
PAULS, DAVID L R01NS16648-12
PAULSEN, DOUGLAS S06GM08248-05 0015
PAULSEN, ELSA P M01RR00847-18 0502
PAULSEN, KEITH D R29CA45357-06
PAULSON, DONALD R S06GM08101-20 0015
PAULSON, GEORGE M01RR00034-31 0343
PAULSON, GEORGE M01RR00034-31 0342
PAULSON, JAMES C R01AI16165-13
PAULSON, JAMES C R01GM27904-13
PAULSON, ROBERT I R01MH44839-03
PAULUS, HENRY S07RR05711-21 0032
PAULUS, HENRY P R55GM45879-01
PAULY, JOHN S07RR05648-25 0925
PAULY, MARK V R01AA08345-02
PAULY, R Z01AG00278-01
PAUSHTER, DAVID M U01CA45226-03S1
PAVAN, PETER R U10EY08605-02
PAVLIK, EDWARD J R01CA52774-02
PAVLIN, DUBRAVKO K11DE00239-04
PAVLOU, SPYROS M01RR00095-31 0370
PAVLOU, SPYROS M01RR00095-31 0366
PAVLOU, SPYROS M01RR00095-31 0166
PAWLEY, JAMES B S07RR07098-26 0361
PAX, RALPH A R01AI30465-01A1
PAXTON, RALPH R29DK39263-04
PAXTON, RAYMOND P30CA33572-11 9005
PAYAMI, HAYDEH S07RR05412-30 0976
PAYAN, DONALD G R01NS21710-07
PAYNE S07RR05380-30 0902
PAYNE-JOHNSON, JOAN C S06GM08016-21 0071
PAYNE, ANITA H M01RR00042-31 0662
PAYNE, ANITA H R01HD08358-15
PAYNE, ANITA H R01HD17916-09
PAYNE, ANITA H R13HD28311-01
PAYNE, BERTRAM R R01MH44647-03
PAYNE, BRUCE D P01HL25847-12 9001
PAYNE, CLAIRE M S07RR05675-23 0947
PAYNE, EDWARD A R19MH46208-03
PAYNE, GREGORY S R01GM39040-04
PAYNE, SUSAN S07RR05927-07 0971
PAYNE, SUSAN L R01CA50168-02
PAYNE, SUSAN L S07RR05410-30 0955
PAYVAR, FARHANG S07RR05388-30 0613
PAYZA, K Z01MH02572-01
PAZ, MERCEDES A R01DE08649-04
PAZNER, ZOLLASUSAN N01AI72658-08
PEABODY, CECILIA S07RR05745-19 0236

PEABODY, DAVID S R01GM42901-01A1
PEACE, DAVID J K08CA01299-05
PEACH, MICHAEL J P01HL19242-15 0008
PEACH, MICHAEL J S15HL47738-01
PEACHEY, LEE D P41RR02483-05S1
PEACOCK, J Z01HL04856-02
PEACOCK, MUNRO M01RR00750-19 0226
PEACOCK, MUNRO M01RR00750-19 0227
PEACOCK, MUNRO M01RR00750-19 0280
PEACOCK, MUNRO M01RR00750-19 0281
PEACOCK, MUNRO M01RR00750-19 0251
PEACOCK, MUNRO P01AG05793-06 9003
PEACOCK, MUNRO P01AG05793-06 0005
PEACOCK, THOMAS D S06GM08212-08
PEACOCK, THOMAS D S06GM08212-08 0011
PEACOCK, TOM S03RR03402-08
PEACOCKE, MONICA R29AG09927-02
PEAKE, WILLIAM T P01DC00119-16 0001
PEARCE, DAVID K11DK01877-04
PEARCE, FREDERICK J R01GM30095-08
PEARCE, JOHN P01CA50084-03 0003
PEARCE, T ELDER K11HL02444-02
PEARCE, WILLIAM J R01HL41347-04
PEARL, RONALD G. P01HL13108-22 0031
PEARL, DENNIS K P01MH44660-04 9001
PEARLIN, LEONARD I R01MH42122-05
PEARLIN, LEONARD I R01MH44600-02
PEARLMAN, ALAN L R01EY00621-17
PEARLMAN, JUSTIN D P01CA48729-03 9002
PEARLMAN, JUSTIN D R29HL41287-04
PEARLMAN, JUSTIN D S10RR06519-01
PEARLSON, GODFREY M01RR00722-19 0161
PEARLSON, GODFREY D M01RR00035-31 0370
PEARLSON, GODFREY D R01DA05317-05
PEARLSON, GODFREY D R01MH43326-03
PEARLSON, GODFREY D R01MH43775-04
PEARLSON, GODFREY D S10RR06369-01
PEARSE, WARREN H G08LM04915-02
PEARSON-WHITE, SONIA H R01HD27202-02
PEARSON, ANTHONY J R01GM36925-04A2
PEARSON, BETTY D R01NR01857-03
PEARSON, DAVID S06GM08101-20 0035
PEARSON, DEOBRAH S07RR05745-19 0237
PEARSON, GARY R R01CA39617-08
PEARSON, GLENN F R44AR40113-02
PEARSON, HELEN S07RR05417-30 0810
PEARSON, HOWARD A M01RR06022-02 0767
PEARSON, HOWARD A M01RR06022-02 0205
PEARSON, HOWARD A N01HB97072-04
PEARSON, J W Z01CM09288-06
PEARSON, JOHN P50MH35976-10 9005
PEARSON, PETER L P41HG00586-01
PEARSON, PETER REES P41HG00586-01 0001
PEARSON, PETER REES P41HG00586-01 9002
PEARSON, RICHARD D P01AI26512-03 0005
PEARSON, THOMAS A G20RR06922-01
PEARSON, THOMAS A R01HL42734-04
PEARSON, THOMAS A R01HL44177-03
PEARSON, THOMAS A S03RR03537-02
PEARSON, THOMAS A S07RR05498-22
PEARSON, WILLIAM H R01GM35572-07
PEARSON, WILLIAM R R01LM04969-04
PEASE, LARRY R R01AI22420-07
PEASE, LARRY R R01AI28320-02
PEBLEY, ANNE R R01HD27361-02
PECHNICK, ROBERT R01DA04113-05
PECHNICK, ROBERT NELSON R29DA05448-04
PECK, AMMON P01DK39079-05 9001
PECK, AMON B P01DK39079-05 0005
PECK, CAROL R01NS21238-07
PECK, HARRY D JR R01GM34903-06A1
PECK, JEFFREY W R01CA47756-04
PECK, LAWRENCE J R01GM46232-01
PECK, WILLIAM A M01RR00036-31
PECK, WILLIAM A M01RR06021-02
PECK, WILLIAM A P01AG06815-05
PECK, WILLIAM A P01AR32087-09 9001
PECK, WILLIAM A S07RR05389-30
PECK, WILLIAM A S15DK44682-01
PECKER, MARK S M01RR00047-31 0426
PECKHAM, PAUL H R01NS29549-01
PECORARO, VINCENT L R01GM39406-04
PECORARO, VINCENT L R01GM42703-02
PEDERSEN, CORT A P50MH33127-13 0008
PEDERSEN, CORT A R01HD24086-02
PEDERSEN, CORT A R01HD25255-02
PEDERSEN, LEE G R01HL27995-07
PEDERSEN, NIELS C R01AI25802-05
PEDERSEN, NIELS C R01CA50179-03
PEDERSEN, PETER L R01CA32742-09
PEDERSEN, PETER L R01DK43962-01
PEDERSEN, PETER L R37CA10951-24
PEDERSEN, ROBERT C R01DK18141-17
PEDERSEN, ROGER A P01HD26732-01A1
PEDERSEN, ROGER A P01HD26732-01A1 0006
PEDERSEN, ROGER A R01HD25387-02
PEDERSEN, STEEN S07RR05425-30 0762
PEDERSEN, STEEN E P01HL37044-06 9004
PEDERSEN, STEEN E R29NS28879-02
PEDERSEN, STEVEN F R01GM38735-04
PEDERSON, NIELS C P51RR00169-30 0181
PEDERSON, NIELS C P51RR00169-30 0182
PEDERSON, THORU P30CA12708-21 9002
PEDERSON, THORU P30CA12708-21
PEDERSON, THORU R01GM21595-17
PEDERSON, THORU S07RR05528-29
PEDERSON, THORU S07RR05528-29 0508
PEDERSON, THORU S15GM47078-01
PEEBLES, CRAIG L S07RR07084-26 0325
PEEKE, HARMAN V S S07RR05755-18 0221
PEEPLES, MARK E K04AI00908-04
PEEPLES, MARK E R01AI25586-04
PEEPLES, MARK E R01AI29606-02
PEERCE, BRIAN E R01DK34807-08
PEERCE, BRIAN E R01DK39944-05
PEERSCHKE, ELLINOR I B R01HL28183-10
PEETERS, GEORGE A S07RR05428-30 0180
PEFFLEY, DENNIS M R01HL44006-02
PEGELOW, CHARLES H N01HB77039-07
PEGG, ANTHONY E R01GM26290-13
PEGG, ANTHONY E R37CA18137-16
PEGG, ANTHONY E R37CA18138-16
PEGG, ANTHONY E U01CA37606-08 0004
PEINADO, SANDRA S07RR05948-05 0330
PEIPER, STEPHEN C R01DK45242-01
PEISACH, JACK P41RR02583-07
PEISACH, JACK P41RR02583-07 9001
PEISACH, JACK P41RR02583-07 9003
PEISACH, JACK P41RR02583-07 9004
PEISACH, JACK P41RR02583-07 9005
PEISACH, JACK R37GM40168-29
PEITZ, BETSY S06GM08101-20 0029
PELAYO, JUAN C R01DK37706-07
PELCHAT, MARCIA L S07RR05825-12 0509
PELEG, SARA S07RR05425-30 0763
PELHAM, WILLIAM E R01AA06267-05
PELHAM, WILLIAM E R42MH48157-01
PELI, ELIEZER R01EY05957-06
PELIKAN, PETER M01RR00425-22S3 0447
PELKER, RICHARD R R29AR39854-03
PELL, ALICE N S07RR07125-22 0395
PELLEG, AMIR R01HL43006-02
PELLEGRINI, MARIA C R01GM40857-02
PELLEY, JOHN S07RR05773-17 0366
PELLEY, JOHN S07RR05773-17 0377
PELLEY, ROBERT J K08CA01199-05
PELLEYMOUNTER, MARY A R03MH49541-01
PELLI, DENIS G R01EY04432-09
PELLICER, ANGEL G R01CA36327-08
PELLICER, ANGEL G R01CA50434-03
PELLING, JILL C K04CA01382-04
PELLING, JILL C R01CA40847-07
PELLIS, NEAL R S07RR05511-29 0489
PELLOCK, JOHN M01RR00065-29 0343
PELLOCK, JOHN M01RR00065-29 0372
PELLOCK, JOHN M N01NS72318-02
PELOQUIN, CHARLES S07RR05842-12 0291
PELTON, STEPHEN M01RR00533-23 0202
PELTON, STEPHEN I U01AI27557-04
PELUS, LOUIS M R01CA33225-10
PELUSO, RICHARD W R01AI22116-06
PEMBERTON, J H M01RR00585-20 0555
PEMBERTON, J H M01RR00585-20 0549
PEMBERTON, JOHN H M01RR00585-20 0552
PEMBERTON, JOHN H. M01RR00585-20 0365
PENA, JOSE M R01DA06798-01A1
PENAR, PAUL L P20NS30324-01 0003
PENDER, EMILY SMITH S07RR05386-30 0593
PENDER, NOLA J P20NR02962-01
PENDER, NOLA J S07RR05796-14
PENDERGAST, DAVID R P01HL28542-10 0001
PENDERGRAST, ROBERT S07RR05365-30 0094
PENDERSEN, NEILS P51RR00169-30 0186
PENDRYS, DAVID G R29DE08939-02
PENEFSKY, HARVEY S R01GM21737-26
PENG, CHIN-TZU R01CA33537-08
PENG, HSIAO-MING B R01NS23583-07
PENG, ISAAC S07RR05576-27 0587
PENG, ISSAC R29AR40839-01
PENG, YEI-MEI P01CA27502-11 9003
PENG, YEI-MEI R01CA51477-02
PENIX, LEROY S07RR05756-18 0307
PENK, WALTER E R01MH46335-03
PENK, WALTER E R18MH49169-01
PENMAN, SHELDON R37CA08416-26
PENMAN, SHELDON S. R01CA45480-05
PENN, AUDREY S R01NS17904-10
PENN, JOHN S R29EY07533-05
PENN, NOLAN E S07RR05665-24 0881
PENN, RICHARD D R01NS15630-12
PENN, STEPHEN M R44ES05151-02
PENNER-HAHN, JAMES E R01GM45205-01A1
PENNER-HAHN, JAMES E R29GM38047-05
PENNER, J P41RR01633-10 0010
PENNER, MERRILYN S07RR07042-26 0413
PENNER, MERRILYNN J R01DC00068-02
PENNEY, DAVID P R01HL39949-05
PENNEY, JOHN B M01RR00042-31 0481
PENNEY, JOHN B P01NS19613-07 9001
PENNEY, JOHN B P50AG08671-03 0002
PENNEY, JOHN B P50AG08671-03 9002
PENNING, TREVOR M K04CA01335-04
PENNING, TREVOR M R01CA39504-06
PENNING, TREVOR M R01GM33464-07
PENNINGTON, BRUCE F K02MH00419-09
PENNINGTON, BRUCE F P50HD27802-01S1 0003
PENNINGTON, BRUCE F R37MH38820-09
PENNINGTON, MARGARET R18MH49327-01
PENNINGTON, MARGARET A R18MH46065-03
PENNINGTON, MARGARET A R19MH47698-02
PENNISTON, JOHN T P50HD09140-16 0014
PENNISTON, JOHN T R01GM28835-11
PENNO, MARGARET B R29CA46418-04
PENNY, DAVID P P30CA11198-23 9020
PENNY, DAVID P P30CA11198-23 9011
PENNYBACKER, MARGARET N01ES05284-10
PENNYBACKER, MARGARET N01ES45067-29
PENNYPACKER, K R Z01ES90066-01
PENRY, J KIFFIN S03RR03366-08
PENRY, J KIFFIN S07RR05404-30
PENRY, J KIFFIN S15DA07782-01
PENRY, J KIFFIN S15HL47772-01
PENTCHEV, P G Z01NS00815-31
PENTECOST, BRIAN T R29DK41706-03
PENTLAND, ALICE P K04AR01849-02
PENTLAND, ALICE P P01DK38111-05 0002
PENTLAND, ALICE P R01AR40574-02
PENTNEY, ROBERTA J R01AA05592-08
PENTZ, MARY A R01DA03976-07
PEPE, FRANK A P01HL15835-19 9001
PEPE, FRANK A R01AR39590-01A3
PEPE, MARGARET S P01HL36444-11 9008
PEPINE, CARL J M01RR00082-29 0286
PEPINE, CARL J N01HC65031-09
PEPINE, CARL J N01HV18119-03
PEPOSE, JAY S R01EY08143-02
PEPPAS, NIKOLAOS A R01GM43337-02
PEPPAS, NIKOLAOS A R01GM45027-01A1
PEPPER, I L P42ES04940-02 0010
PEPPERBERG, DAVID S07RR05369-30 0602
PEPPERBERG, DAVID R R01EY05494-08A1
PERACCHIA, CAMILLO R01GM20113-18
PERACHIO, ADRIAN A R01DC00385-04A1
PERALTA, ERNEST G R01DK44025-01
PERALTA, ERNEST G R01GM42843-03
PERANTONI, A O Z01CP05093-13
PERCIVAL, SUSAN S R29DK43518-01A1
PERCY, ALAN M01RR00188-27 0280
PERCY, ALAN P01HD24234-04 0001
PERCY, ALAN K P01HD24234-04
PERCY, ALAN K P01HD24234-04 9001
PERDEW, GARY H R29ES04869-03
PERDUE, JAMES F R01CA47150-03
PERDUE, MARY H R01NS29536-01
PERDUE, SONDRA T U01AI31498-01 9003
PEREDNIA, DOUGLAS A R01CA56159-01
PEREIRA-SMITH, OLIVIA M P01AG07123-04 0002
PEREIRA-SMITH, OLIVIA M R01AG05333-07
PEREIRA, GILBERTA R. M01RR00240-27 0292
PEREIRA, GILBERTO R. M01RR00240-27 0243
PEREIRA, H ANNE R01AI28018-02
PEREIRA, LENORE P01AI19554-08S1 0001
PEREIRA, LENORE R01AI30873-05
PEREIRA, MICHAEL N01CN85096-01
PEREIRA, MICHAEL A N01ES65167-09
PEREIRA, MICHAEL E R29HD23243-04
PEREIRA, MIERCIO E R01AI24837-06
PEREIRA, MIERCIO E R01HL46659-01
PEREL, JAMES M P50AG05133-08 0011
PEREL, JAMES M P50MH30915-15 9019
PEREL, JULIUS R44RR05079-03
PERELSON, ALAN S R01AI28433-02
PERELSON, ALAN S R01RR06555-01
PERENTESIS, JOHN P K11AI00793-05
PERERA, FREDERICA S07RR05449-30 0320
PERERA, FREDERICA P P01ES05294-02 9001
PERERA, FREDERICA P R01ES05294-02
PERERA, FREDERICA P R01CA51196-02
PERETZ, BERTRAM R01AG07547-03
PEREZ FONTAN, J J R29HL38916-03
PEREZ-ARMENDARIZ, ELIA M R29DK38529-05
PEREZ-CHIESA, YVETTE S06GM08102-20 0054
PEREZ-REYES, EDWARD R55HL46702-01
PEREZ-REYES, MARIO R01DA04484-05
PEREZ-SOLER, ROMAN R01CA45423-03
PEREZ-SOLER, ROMAN R01CA50270-01A2
PEREZ-STABLE, ELISEO J R01CA50030-03
PEREZ-STABLE, ELISEO J R18CA39260-07
PEREZ-WOODS, R S07RR07210-09 0688
PEREZ, GEORGE N01AI95039-06
PEREZ, HECTOR D R01AI28290-03
PEREZ, HECTOR D R01AR28566-12
PEREZ, JOHN C S06GM08107-18
PEREZ, JOHN C S06GM08107-18 0002
PEREZ, JULIO E P50HL17646-17 0038
PEREZ, LAUTARO G R29AI28566-03
PEREZ, MARITZA I M01RR00125-28 0744
PERFECT, JOHN R R01AI28388-01A2
PERGOLIZZI, ROBERT G S03RR03461-05
PERIASAMY, MUTHU P01HL28001-10 0010
PERIASAMY, MUTHU R29HL38355-05
PERICAK-VANCE, MARGARET A P01NS26630-03
PERICAK-VANCE, MARGARET A. P01NS26630-03 9
PERINI, CHARLES S07RR05756-18 0291
PERINI, CHARLES S07RR05756-18 0292
PERINI, FULVIO P60AR20557-13 9004

PERIS, JOANNA K02AA00135-02
PERIS, JOANNA R01AA08262-03
PERKELL, JOSEPH P R01DC01291-01
PERKETT, ELIZABETH A K08HL02276-03
PERKINS, DAVID D R37AI01462-36
PERKINS, DAVID L R29AI31527-01
PERKINS, JOHN P S07RR07175-15
PERKINS, JOHN P S15GM47050-01
PERKINS, KENNETH A R01DA04174-06
PERKINS, KENNETH A R01DA05807-03
PERKINS, LAURA N01HC95095-10
PERKINS, LAURA L S07RR05829-09 0951
PERKINS, MARGARET E R22AI19585-09
PERKINS, S N Z01CN00160-01
PERKINS, SHERRIE S07RR05491-29 0461
PERL, ANDRAS S07RR05648-25 0926
PERL, DANIEL P P01AG08802-02 0002
PERL, DANIEL P P01AG08802-02 0003
PERL, DANIEL P P01MH45212-02 9001
PERL, DANIEL P. P50AG05138-08 0009
PERL, DANIEL P. P50AG05138-08 9002
PERL, EDWARD R P01NS14899-13 9005
PERL, EDWARD R P01NS14899-13 0012
PERL, EDWARD R P01NS14899-13
PERL, EDWARD R R01NS10321-20
PERLIN, DAVID S R01GM38225-05
PERLIN, MARK W R29LM04707-05
PERLIN, MICHAEL H R01AI26579-02
PERLMAN, JEFFREY M01RR00036-31 1048
PERLMAN, PHILIP R01GM31480-09
PERLMAN, PHILIP S S07RR07175-15 0440
PERLMAN, ROBERT P01HD09402-16 0008
PERLMAN, STANLEY K04NS01369-03
PERLMAN, STANLEY R01NS24401-05
PERLMAN, WILLIAM N01LM13544-00
PERLMUTT, M ALAN M01RR00036-31 0972
PERLMUTTER, DAVID H R01HL37784-06
PERLMUTTER, JOEL M01RR00036-31 0708
PERLMUTTER, LYNN S R29AG07127-06
PERLMUTTER, MARION P30AG08808-03 9004
PERLMUTTER, MARION R01AG07466-02
PERLMUTTER, ROGER M R01CA45682-05
PERLSTADT, HARRY S07RR07049-26 0429
PERMAN, JAY A M01RR00052-30 0242
PERMUTT, M ALAN M01RR00036-31 1036
PERMUTT, M ALAN M01RR00036-31 0995
PERMUTT, MARSHALL ALAN R37DK16746-19
PERMUTT, SOLBERT P01HL10342-26 0008
PERMUTT, SOLBERT P50HL37119-05
PERMUTT, SOLBERT P50HL37119-05 0003
PERNEGER, THOMAS R03HS06978-01
PERNIS, BENVENUTO G R01AI30033-02
PEROT, PHANOR L P01NS11066-17 9001
PEROT, PHANOR L, JR P01NS11066-17
PERR, HILARY A K08DK01849-04
PERR, HILARY A S07RR05430-30 0225
PERRAULT, JACQUES R01AI21572-06A3
PERRAULT, JACQUES S07RR07004-16 0053
PERRIMON, NORBERT R55HD23684-04
PERRIN, JAMES M R01HS06060-02
PERRINE, SUSAN P60HL20985-14 0018
PERRINE, KIMBERLY S07RR05794-15 0902
PERRINE, MERVYN W P01AA07203-02 9001
PERRINE, MERVYN W P01AA07203-02
PERRINE, MERVYN W P01AA07203-02 0001
PERRINE, MERVYN W R01AA06926-06
PERRINE, MERVYN W R01AA07876-04
PERRINE, SUSAN P R01HL37118-07
PERRINO, FRED W S07RR05404-30 0851
PERRONE-BIZZOZERO, NORA I R29NS30255-01
PERROTT, DAVID S07RR05305-30 0724
PERROTT, DAVID R S06GM08101-20 0037
PERRY, BRUCE D P50DA00250-20 0029
PERRY, CHERYL L R01AA08596-02
PERRY, CHERYL L U01HL39852-05
PERRY, DAVID S07RR05359-30 0519
PERRY, EDWARD H R15HD28216-01
PERRY, GARY W R01EY06449-07
PERRY, GEORGE K04AG00415-04
PERRY, GEORGE P50AG08012-04 0005
PERRY, GEORGE R01AG07552-04
PERRY, GEORGE R01AG09287-02
PERRY, GEORGE R35AG08992-01 0008
PERRY, GEORGE R35AG08992-01 0004
PERRY, GREG A R29AI25222-05
PERRY, H MITCHELL, JR R03HL47677-01
PERRY, HORACE M, III R03AA08634-01A1
PERRY, JACQUELIN R01AR41018-01
PERRY, JACQUELIN S15AR41234-01
PERRY, JAMES M01RR00188-27 0281
PERRY, L L Z01AI00524-04
PERRY, L L Z01AI00550-03
PERRY, L L Z01AI00551-03
PERRY, L L Z01AI00610-01
PERRY, MICHAEL C U10CA12046-19
PERRY, MITCHELL H JR N01HC48068-13
PERRY, NATHAN W S07RR05933-07 0310
PERRY, NATHAN W S15HD28759-01
PERRY, NATHAN W, JR S07RR05933-07
PERRY, PAUL J M01RR00059-30 0735
PERRY, R E M01RR00585-20 0433
PERRY, ROBERT D R29AI25098-04
PERRY, ROBERT P R01AI17330-11
PERRY, SAMUEL W P50GM26145-13 0010
PERRY, SAMUEL W R01MH42277-06
PERRY, SAMUEL W R01MH46250-02
PERRY, STANTON B K08HL02246-02
PERRY, WILLIAM M R01HD22025-05
PERRY, WILLIAM M R01HD27246-02
PERRY, WILLIAM M S07RR05511-29 0493
PERRYMAN, LANCE E R01AI25731-05
PERRYMAN, LANCE E S07RR05465-29
PERSECHINI, ANTHONY S07RR05403-30 0818
PERSHING, LYNN K R29AR39021-03
PERSING, DAVID H R01AI32403-01
PERSING, DAVID H R01AR41497-01
PERSON, WILLIS B R01GM32988-07
PERSSON, ANDERS V R29HL45058-02
PERSSON, ROGER P01DE08555-03 0003
PERSSON, RUTGER P30DE09743-02 0017
PERSSONS, ANDERS S07RR05491-29 0462
PERT, A Z01MH02531-02
PERT, A Z01MH02532-02
PERT, A Z01MH02533-02
PERT, A Z01MH02534-02
PERT, A Z01MH02535-02
PERTSCHUK, MICHAEL J R01AR39514-03
PERUCHO, MANUEL R01CA33021-10
PERUCHO, MANUEL R01CA38579-08
PERUMAL, NARAYANAN S07RR05801-13 0448
PERUSSIA, BICE R01CA37155-07
PERUSSIA, BICE R01CA45284-04
PERUTZ, MAX F R01HL31461-08
PESCOSOLIDO, BERNICE A K01MH00849-03
PESCOSOLIDO, BERNICE A R29MH44780-03
PESCOVITZ, ORA H K04DK02042-01
PESCOVITZ, ORA H R01DK41899-02
PESHOCK, RONALD M P50HL17669-17 0032
PESSAH, I M S07RR05457-29 0008
PESSAH, ISAAC N R29ES05002-03
PESSIN, JEFFREY P30DK25295-12S1 0014
PESSIN, JEFFREY E K04DK01822-04
PESSIN, JEFFREY E R01DK33823-08
PESSIN, JEFFREY E R01DK42452-01A1
PESTKA, JAMES J R01ES03358-07
PESTKA, SIDNEY R01CA46465-04
PESTKA, SIDNEY U01AI25914-04S2 0003
PESTKA, SIDNEY U01AI25914-04S2 0004
PESTRONK, ALAN M01RR06021-02 0619
PETER, WILLIAM P30CA14236-18 0930
PETERING, DAVID H P30ES04184-05
PETERING, DAVID H R01ES04026-05
PETERING, DAVID H S07RR07181-13 0536
PETERING, DAVID H S15ES05849-01
PETERKOFSKY, A Z01HL00151-21
PETERKOFSKY, B Z01CB00945-18
PETERLIN, BORIS M R01AI29954-02
PETERS, ALAN P01AG00001-17A2 0016
PETERS, ALAN P01AG00001-17A2
PETERS, ALAN R01NS07016-25
PETERS, ARTHUR N01ES85227-10
PETERS, ARTHUR C N01ES85213-12
PETERS, ARTHUR C N01ES85226-08
PETERS, B P30DK34987-06 0007
PETERS, B Z01DK25076-02
PETERS, BARRY P R01CA41359-05
PETERS, CHARLES S07RR05372-30 0682
PETERS, DONNA P41RR00570-21 0014
PETERS, DONNA P R01EY08540-01A1
PETERS, H ELIZABETH R01HD26555-01A2
PETERS, KEVIN K11HL02309-02
PETERS, KEVIN R01HL22325-14
PETERS, LEONARD K S15MH49514-01
PETERS, LESTER J N01CM57775-12
PETERS, LESTER J P01CA06294-30
PETERS, LESTER J P01CA06294-30 0079
PETERS, MARION M01RR00036-31 1039
PETERS, MARION G R01DK43020-01A1
PETERS, ROBERT N01AI72622-08
PETERS, ROBERT W N01HC65053-13
PETERS, RUTH K P01CA17054-16 0003
PETERS, RUTH K R01CA44401-05
PETERS, THEODORE F R01HG00487-01
PETERS, WILLIAM P M01RR00030-30 0478
PETERS, WILLIAM P P01CA47741-02 9001
PETERS, WILLIAM P P01CA47741-02 0004
PETERS, WILLIAM P P01CA47741-02 0001
PETERS, WILLIAM P P01CA47741-02
PETERSEN, ANNE C R01MH38142-09
PETERSEN, BARBARA J N01CN95177-05
PETERSEN, BARBARA J R44CA50045-02
PETERSEN, DENNIS R K02AA00106-05
PETERSEN, DENNIS R P50AA03527-14 0009
PETERSEN, MARTA J K08AR01787-05
PETERSEN, MARTA J S07RR05428-30 0175
PETERSEN, NANCY S S07RR07157-16 0575
PETERSEN, PAMELA R19DA06444-03
PETERSEN, RONALD C R01NS29059-01A1
PETERSEN, SANDRA S07RR05387-30 0605
PETERSEN, STEVEN E R01EY08775-05
PETERSON-HOMER, LIZE S07RR07053-26 0155
PETERSON-HOMER, LIZETTE R01HD25414-03
PETERSON, ARTHUR P01CA34847-09 0018
PETERSON, ARTHUR V R01CA38269-08
PETERSON, BARRY W P01NS17489-10 0004
PETERSON, BARRY W P01NS17489-10
PETERSON, BARRY W P01NS17489-10 9001
PETERSON, BARRY W P50MH48185-01 0005
PETERSON, BARRY W R01EY06485-06
PETERSON, BARRY W R01NS22490-06
PETERSON, BRUCE A U10CA16450-17
PETERSON, CHRISTINE R29AG07855-04
PETERSON, CHRISTINE R35AG07918-03 0004
PETERSON, DANIEL D R29ES05607-01
PETERSON, DARRELL L R01AI15955-10A2
PETERSON, DARRYL R R01DK42331-01A1
PETERSON, DAVID O R01CA32695-08
PETERSON, DAVID O R01CA48041-04
PETERSON, DENTON R P41RR01632-09 9020
PETERSON, DENTON R P41RR01632-09 9006
PETERSON, ELLENA M R01AI30499-01A1
PETERSON, ELLENGENE H R01DC00618-02
PETERSON, GARY M01RR00046-31 0432
PETERSON, GLORIA M P30DK36200-05S1 0002
PETERSON, J I Z01RR10355-01
PETERSON, JAMES L R43MH48261-01
PETERSON, JERRY A S07RR05929-06
PETERSON, JERRY A S07RR05929-06 0279
PETERSON, JERRY A S15CA55970-01
PETERSON, JOHN L P50MH42459-06 0008
PETERSON, JOHN R R55CA57139-01
PETERSON, JOHN W R01HL44554-02
PETERSON, JOHNNY W R01AI18401-10
PETERSON, JULIAN A R01GM43479-02
PETERSON, K LINNEA S07RR05372-30 0703
PETERSON, KENNETH M R29AI28502-03
PETERSON, NEAL S07RR05755-18 0232
PETERSON, PER P01CA27489-12 0005
PETERSON, PER A P01AI17354-10S1
PETERSON, PER A P01NS22347-06 0008
PETERSON, PER A R01AI26610-04
PETERSON, PER A R01DK37915-04
PETERSON, PER A R01GM46411-01
PETERSON, PHILLIP K R01DA04381-05
PETERSON, RICHARD E R01GM41131-03
PETERSON, RONALD C P30AG08031-02 9001
PETERSON, ROSE P60HL38639-04 0009
PETERSON, RUDOLPH S07RR07118-22 0383
PETERSON, STEVEN E P01NS06833-25 0030
PETERSON, STEVEN L R29NS24566-05
PETERSON, THOMAS A R01GM39832-04
PETERSON, THOMAS V R01HL31987-07
PETERSON, WARD D N01CP85645-08
PETES, THOMAS D R01GM24110-15
PETHEL, M Z01AI00571-02
PETICOLAS, WARNER L R01GM15547-25
PETICOLAS, WARNER L R01GM33825-07
PETITO, CAROL K P01NS03346-31 9002
PETITO, CAROL K P01NS03346-31 0045
PETITO, CAROL K R01NS27416-03
PETITO, CAROL K S07RR05396-30 0770
PETITTI, DIANA N01HD13108-00
PETITTI, DIANA B R01HL47043-01
PETRA, PHILIP H R01HD13956-11
PETRAKIS, NICHOLAS L R01CA54239-01A1
PETRASH, J MARK R55EY05856-08A1
PETRI, MICHELLE M01RR00722-19 0068
PETRI, MICHELLE R29HL47080-01
PETRI, MICHELLE A M01RR00035-31 0390
PETRI, WILLIAM A, JR R01AI26649-03
PETRI, WILLIAM H S07RR07156-16
PETRICH, JACOB S07RR07034-26 0066
PETRIKOVSKY, BORIS S07RR05736-19 0190
PETROLL, WALTER M R03EY09667-01
PETROSKI, RICHARD J R13GM46515-01
PETROVITCH, HELEN N01HC48064-11
PETRUSZ, PETER P30DK34987-06 9005
PETRUSZ, PETER P30HD18968-08 9002
PETRUSZ, PETER R01NS27679-03
PETRUSZ, PETER S07RR05406-30 0913
PETRY, HEYWOOD S07RR07067-26 0223
PETRY, HEYWOOD M R29EY07113-05
PETRYSHYN, RAYMOND A S07RR05402-30 0798
PETSKO, GREGORY A R01GM26788-12
PETSKO, GREGORY A R01GM32415-10
PETTEGREW, JAY R35AG08974-01 0001
PETTEGREW, JAY R35AG08974-01 0002
PETTEGREW, JAY R35AG08974-01 0003
PETTEGREW, JAY R35AG08974-01 0004
PETTEGREW, JAY W P01AG09017-02 0004
PETTEGREW, JAY W P50AG05133-08
PETTEGREW, JAY W P50AG05133-08 0001
PETTEGREW, JAY W P50MH45156-02 0004
PETTEGREW, JAY W R01AG08371-03
PETTEGREW, JAY W R01MH46614-02
PETTEGREW, JAY W R35AG08974-01
PETTENGILL, OLIVE S S07RR05392-30 0701
PETTERBORG, LARRY S07RR05387-30 0602
PETTERS, ROBERT M U01HD21937-06
PETTI, PAULA L R01CA48900-03
PETTIGREW, CHENITS JR S03RR03159-11
PETTIGREW, LUTHER C K08NS01505-01
PETTIGREW, RODERIC I R01HL42021-02
PETTIJOHN, DAVID E R01GM18243-20
PETTINATI, HELEN M P50AA08747-02 0002
PETTINATI, HELEN M R01AA07831-04

PETTINGER, WILLIAM A R01HL30339-10
PETTIT, GEORGE R R35CA44344-03
PETTIT, GEORGE R U01AI25696-05 0002
PETTITT, D J Z01DK69001-22
PETTIWAY, LEON E R01DA05672-03
PETTO, A J P51RR00168-30 0176
PETTO, A J P51RR00168-30 0171
PETTO, A J P51RR00168-30 0173
PETTO, ANDREW J P51RR00168-30 9010
PETTO, ANDREW J P51RR00168-30 0114
PETTY, BRENT G M01RR00035-31 0413
PETTY, BRENT G M01RR00035-31 0414
PETTY, BRENT G M01RR00035-31 0415
PETTY, BRENT G M01RR00035-31 0373
PETTY, BRENT G M01RR00722-19 0254
PETTY, BRENT G M01RR00722-19 0233
PETTY, BRENT G M01RR00722-19 0222
PETTY, FREDERICK R01AA07234-03
PETTY, FREDERICK R01MH37899-04A2
PETTY, HOWARD R R01AI27409-03
PETZ, LAWRENCE D K07HL02151-03
PEULER, JACOB D R29HL38135-04
PEUSNER, KENNA D R01DC00970-01
PEYMAN, GHOLAM A R01EY07541-03
PEZACKA, EWA H R29DK42122-01A2
PEZUTTO, JOHN M P01CA48112-01A3 0003
PEZZOLLA, PETER A R19DA06457-03
PEZZUTO, JOHN M P01CA48112-01A3
PEZZUTO, JOHN M S07RR05564-13 0914
PEZZUTO, JOHN M U01CA52956-02 0003
PFAFF, DONALD W R01HD05751-19S1
PFAFF, DONALD W R01MH38273-06
PFAFF, WILLIAM W M01RR00082-29 0476
PFAHL, MAGNUS P01CA51993-01A1 0003
PFAHL, MAGNUS R01CA50676-02
PFAHL, MAGNUS R01DK35083-07
PFAU, CHARLES J S07RR07104-25
PFEFFER, B A Z01EY00243-05
PFEFFER, LAWRENCE M R01GM36716-06
PFEFFER, MARC M01RR02635-07 0206
PFEFFER, MARC A M01RR02635-07 0292
PFEFFER, SUZANNE R R01DK37332-06
PFEFFERBAUM, ADOLF P50MH30854-14 9001
PFEFFERBAUM, ADOLF P50MH30854-14
PFEFFERBAUM, ADOLF P50MH30854-14 0015
PFEFFERBAUM, ADOLF P50MH30854-14 0016
PFEFFERBAUM, ADOLF P50MH40041-08 0002
PFEFFERBAUM, ADOLF R01AA05965-09
PFEFFERBAUM, ADOLF S15MH49320-01
PFEFFERBAUN, ADOLF P50MH30854-14 0017
PFEFFERKORN, ELMER R R01AI25817-04
PFEFFERKORN, ELMER R U01AI30279-02 0003
PFEFFERKORN, LORRAINE C R29AI29455-01A1
PFEIFFER, STEVEN E R01NS10861-17
PFENDER, ELLEN S07RR05505-18 0473
PFENNINGER, KARL H R01NS24676-05
PFENNINGER, KARL H R01NS24672-06
PFINGST, BRYAN E P01DC00274-08 0001
PFINGST, BRYAN E R01DC00560-03
PFISTER, K KEVIN S07RR07175-15 0441
PFISTER, ROSWELL R R01EY04716-08
PFLUGFELDER, STEPHEN C R01EY08711-02
PFOHL, BRUCE P50MH43271-05 0005
PHAIR, JOHN P U01AI25915-05
PHAIRE-WASHINGTON, LINDA S06GM08091-20 9001
PHAIRE-WASHINGTON, LINDA S06GM08091-20 0007
PHALEN, ROBERT F R01HL39682-04
PHAN, SEM P50DK39255-05 0001
PHAN, SEM H P01DK38149-04 0001
PHAN, SEM H P01HL31963-08 0004
PHAN, SEM HIN R01HL28737-09
PHAN, SEM HIN R01HL39925-05
PHANG, J M Z01CN00157-01
PHARR, PAMELA P R01CA50244-03
PHAU, JOHN P N01AI32535-38
PHELAN, JOAN A P01DE09545-01A1 0001
PHELAN, SAM N01CM17549-00
PHELAN, SAMUEL N01ES95265-02
PHELEY, ALFRED P20NS30322-01 9002
PHELPS, CAROL J R01NS25987-04
PHELPS, CHARLES E R01AA08393-02
PHELPS, CHARLES E R01HS06366-02
PHELPS, CHRISTOPHER P R01MH46808-02
PHELPS, DALE L P50HL36543-05 0005
PHELPS, DALE L U10EY06354-07
PHELPS, DAVID S R01HL48006-01
PHELPS, MICHAEL S07RR05354-30 0381
PHELPS, MICHAEL E P01NS15654-13 9001
PHELPS, MICHAEL E P01NS15654-13
PHELPS, MICHAEL E P01NS15654-13 0004
PHELPS, MICHAEL E R01MH37916-09
PHEMISTER, ROBERT D S07RR05462-29
PHEMISTER, ROBERT D S15CA55931-01
PHIBBS, RODERIC H P50HL27356-10 0004
PHILBRICK, JOHN T S07RR05431-30 0836
PHILIPP, DAVID P R01HD27331-02
PHILIPPS, ANTHONY F S07RR05675-23 0935
PHILIPPS, ANTHONY F S07RR05675-23 0916
PHILIPS, LAURA A R29NS27039-03
PHILIPSON, ELLIOT H. P50HD11089-14 0020
PHILIPSON, KENNETH D R01HL27821-10
PHILLIP, C Z01HL04214-02
PHILLIP, JUDI P01CA41167-06 0003
PHILLIPP, MANFRED S06GM08225-07 0010
PHILLIPS-QUAGLIATA, S07RR05399-30 0917
PHILLIPS, ANTHONY F P01HD26013-01A2 0005
PHILLIPS, BARBARA A K07HL02322-03
PHILLIPS, BRENDA M01RR00059-30 0720
PHILLIPS, CLYDE N01CN75415-19
PHILLIPS, CONSTANCE L S03RR03545-01
PHILLIPS, DAVID H R01CA21959-15
PHILLIPS, DAVID M P50HD13541-12 9003
PHILLIPS, DAVID M R01HD27433-01
PHILLIPS, DAVID R R37HL28947-12
PHILLIPS, DEBORAH A U10HD25449-03
PHILLIPS, DWIGHT E R01AA07042-06
PHILLIPS, DWIGHT E S06GM08218-08 0019
PHILLIPS, G P41RR02250-06 0006
PHILLIPS, GEORGE JR M01RR00030-30 0511
PHILLIPS, GEORGE N, JR R01AR40252-02
PHILLIPS, GEORGE N, JR R01AR32764-08
PHILLIPS, GREGORY J R15GM45942-01
PHILLIPS, J THEODORE M01RR00633-19 0381
PHILLIPS, JAMES L S03RR03127-11
PHILLIPS, JOHN M01RR00095-31 0367
PHILLIPS, JOHN A M01RR00095-31 0340
PHILLIPS, JOHN A III P30HD28819-01 9001
PHILLIPS, JOHN A, III R01DK35592-08
PHILLIPS, JOHN A, III R01HG00638-01
PHILLIPS, JOSEPH T R29DK39526-04
PHILLIPS, LAWRENCE S M01RR00039-31 0411
PHILLIPS, LAWRENCE S. M01RR00039-31 0419
PHILLIPS, LINDA R R01NR01323-06
PHILLIPS, LINDA R S07RR05913-08
PHILLIPS, LINDA R S10RR06736-01
PHILLIPS, M IAN R01HL27334-12
PHILLIPS, MARION S03RR03120-11
PHILLIPS, MARK H R01CA51076-02
PHILLIPS, MARTIN D R55HL46981-01
PHILLIPS, MICHAEL C P01HL22633-14
PHILLIPS, MICHAEL C P01HL22633-14 0004
PHILLIPS, NELSON B R29AI30497-01A1
PHILLIPS, NONA K R29HD22893-04
PHILLIPS, NONA K. P51RR00166-30 0111
PHILLIPS, NONA K. P51RR00166-30 0112
PHILLIPS, PAUL D R01AG09778-02
PHILLIPS, PAUL J S07RR07088-24 0352
PHILLIPS, PETER C K08NS01279-05
PHILLIPS, ROBERT M01RR00071-28A1 0212
PHILLIPS, ROBERT S R01GM42588-03
PHILLIPS, ROLAND P01CA17054-16 9001
PHILLIPS, RUSSELL S07RR05479-29 0441
PHILLIPS, S F M01RR00585-20 0541
PHILLIPS, S F M01RR00585-20 0393
PHILLIPS, S F M01RR00585-20 0557
PHILLIPS, S F M01RR00585-20 0503
PHILLIPS, S F M01RR00585-20 0476
PHILLIPS, S MICHAEL R22AI15193-12
PHILLIPS, SIDNEY F R01DK32121-09
PHILLIPS, T D P42ES04917-03 0004
PHILLIPS, TAMARA J P01AA08621-02 0002
PHILLIPS, TANIA M01RR00533-23 0208
PHILLIPS, THEODORE L P01CA19138-15 0008
PHILLIPS, TOM M01RR00833-17 0212
PHILLIS, JOHN W R01NS26912-03
PHILLIS, RANDALL W S07RR07048-26 0654
PHILP, ELIZABETH S07RR05404-30 0852
PHILP, NANCY J R01EY05508-08
PHILPOT, R M Z01ES80001-19
PHILPOTT, GORDON W R01CA44728-04
PHINNEY, JEAN S S06GM08101-20 0041
PHINNEY, STEPHEN D P30DK35747-06 9004
PHIPPS, GRANT T S03RR03369-08
PHIPPS, GRANT T S07RR05330-30
PHIPPS, GRANT T S07RR05330-30 0026
PHIPPS, GRANT T S15DE10068-01
PHIPPS, KATHY R R55DE09983-01
PHIPPS, RICHARD P R01CA42739-06
PHIPPS, RICHARD P R01CA55305-01
PHIPPS, SU AN R15NR02719-01
PHIPPS, TIMOTHY P51RR00165-31 9015
PHIZACKERLEY, PAUL R P41RR01209-12 0002
PHIZICKY, ERIC S07RR05403-30 0819
PHOENIX, C N P51RR00163-32 0015
PHONG, LE T R01AR34808-07
PI-SUNYER, F XAVIER M01RR00645-20 0459
PI-SUNYER, F XAVIER P30DK26687-11 9003
PI-SUNYER, F XAVIER P30DK26687-11
PI-SUNYER, F XAVIER R55DK35911-05A2
PIACENTINI, JOHN P50MH43878-03 0012
PIACENTINI, JOHN P50MH43878-03 0041
PIACENTINI, JOHN S07RR05650-25 0108
PIACSEK, BELA E S07RR07196-11
PIAN, MARK S K08HL02157-04
PIANTADES, CLAUDE A P01HL42444-02 0001
PIANTADOSI, CLAUDE A P01HL31992-08 0006
PIANTADOSI, CLAUDE A P01HL42444-02
PIATIGORSKY, J Z01EY00126-10
PIATT, JOSEPH H, JR S07RR05412-30 0975
PICKARD, GARY E R01MH47501-01
PICKARD, GARY E R01NS21165-07
PICKART, CECILE M K04DK02026-01
PICKEL, VIRGINIA M K05MH00078-16
PICKEL, VIRGINIA M R01DA04600-03
PICKEL, VIRGINIA M R37MH40342-07
PICKEN, ROGER N R01AR41517-01
PICKENS, DAVID R R01NS27966-01A2
PICKENS, DAVID R S07RR05424-30 0096
PICKER, LOUIS J R29AI31545-01
PICKER, MITCHELL J R29DA07327-01
PICKER, MITCHELL J S07RR07072-26 0272
PICKERING, LARRY E P01HD13021-12 0011
PICKERING, LARRY K M01RR02558-07 0047
PICKERING, LARRY K M01RR02558-07 0060
PICKERING, LARRY K P01HD13021-12 9002
PICKERING, LARRY K P01HD13021-12 9003
PICKERING, LARRY K P01HD13021-12
PICKERING, S Z01CL60015-01
PICKERING, THOMAS G M01RR00047-31 0447
PICKERING, THOMAS G M01RR00047-31 0274
PICKERING, THOMAS G M01RR00047-31 0399
PICKERING, THOMAS G P50HL18323-17 9005
PICKERING, THOMAS G P50HL18323-17 0052
PICKERING, THOMAS G R01HL30605-07
PICKERING, THOMAS G R01HL40567-04
PICKETT, CAROL L R29AI27908-02
PICKLE, LINDA P30CA51008-02 9002
PICKOFF, ARTHUR S07RR05377-30 0759
PICKOFF, ARTHUR S R01HD28929-01
PICKUP, D J P01CA30246-11 0006
PICKUP, DAVID J R01AI23886-06
PICKWORTH, W B Z01DA00038-01
PICKWORTH, W B Z01DA00039-01
PICOU, DAVID R13AR41073-01
PIDGEON, CHARLES S07RR05586-24 0115
PIEGORSCH, W W Z01ES48001-04
PIEKUT, DIANE T R01NS18626-08
PIELAK, GARY J R29GM42501-03
PIEPER, RUSSELL O R29CA55064-01
PIER, GERALD B R01AI22535-07
PIER, GERALD B R01AI22806-06
PIER, GERALD B R01AI23335-05
PIERCE, CARL W P01AI15353-13
PIERCE, CARL W R01AI13915-16
PIERCE, DONALD A P30ES00210-24 9004
PIERCE, DONALD A R01CA51007-02
PIERCE, G BARRY R01CA47369-04
PIERCE, IRVING U10CA35281-08
PIERCE, J Z01CP05164-11
PIERCE, JOSEPH F N01CM97596-05
PIERCE, L Z01CM06396-01
PIERCE, PENNY S07RR05796-14 0435
PIERCE, PENNY S07RR05796-14 0436
PIERCE, SUSAN K P01HL45168-01A1 0003
PIERCE, SUSAN K P01HL45168-01A1 9001
PIERCE, SUSAN K R01AI27957-02
PIERCE, SUSAN K R37AI18939-08
PIERCE, WILLIAM S R01HL13426-22
PIERCE, WILLIAM S R01HL20356-15
PIERRO, LOUIS P01HD22610-04 9002
PIERSCHBACHER, MICHAEL D P01CA28896-11 000
PIERSCHBACHER, MICHAEL D P30CA30199-11 900
PIERSCHBACHER, MICHAEL D R13CA53709-01
PIERSON, DOROTHY E S07RR05357-30 0470
PIERSON, MARTHA G R01DA07213-01
PIERSON, RICHARD N, S07RR05840-13 0276
PIERSON, RICHARD N, JR P01DK42618-02
PIETRA, GIUSEPPE G R01HL32482-08
PIETRANTONI, MARCELL S07RR05675-23 0944
PIETRUSZKO, REGINA K05AA00046-13
PIETRUSZKO, REGINA R01AA00186-19
PIETRUSZKO, REGINA S07RR07058-26 0183
PIETRYGA, DANIEL S07RR05535-29 0534
PIETTE, JOHN R03HS06914-01
PIETTE, LAWRENCE H S07RR07093-24 0776
PIFOT, HENRY C P30CA07175-28 9012
PIGGOT, PATRICK J R01GM43577-05
PIHLSTROM, BRUCE L P30DE09737-02
PIHLSTROM, BRUCE L P50DE08489-04
PIJOAN, CARLOS S07RR05930-07
PIJOAN, CARLOS B S15DK44669-01
PIKE, JOHN W R01DK38130-06
PIKE, LINDA J R29GM41729-03
PIKE, MALCOLM C R01CA48774-03
PIKE, MARILYN P01AI28465-03 0002
PIKE, MARILYN C R01AI28386-03
PIKE, MARTIN M R29HL45684-01A1
PIKUS, A Z01DC00007-03
PIKUS, A Z01DC00008-04
PILAND, NEILL F N01CN64101-09
PILAR, GUILLERMO R R01NS10338-18
PILARO, A M Z01CM09322-03
PILATI, CHARLES F R29HL43245-03
PILBEAM, CAROL S07RR05678-23 0159
PILCH, PAUL F R01DK30425-10
PILCH, PAUL F R01DK36424-06
PILCHER, WEBSTER S07RR05403-30 0820
PILKINGTON, THEO C P01HL11307-25 0007
PILKINGTON, THEO C R01HL40092-04
PILKIS, SIMON J R37DK38354-06
PILKONIS, PAUL A R01MH44672-02
PILL-SOON SONG S07RR07055-26 0183
PILLAI, SHIV S R29AI27835-03
PILLEMER, KARL A R01MH42163-04
PILOTTE, N S Z01DA00015-02
PILOTTE, N S Z01DA00016-02

PILOTTE, N S   Z01DA00049-02
PILZ, RENATE B   K08CA01548-02
PINCH, WINIFRED J   R03NR02819-01
PINCHERT, JAMES   P60DK20593-13 9007
PINCKARD, R NEAL   R01AI21818-08
PINCUS, MATTHEW R   R01CA42500-05A2
PINCUS, S H   Z01AI00516-04
PINCUS, STEPHANIE   S07RR05400-30 0038
PINCUS, STEPHANIE H   P50AI24848-05 0004
PINCUS, STEVEN M   R43AG09716-01
PINCUS, THEODORE   R18AR21393-17 0010
PINCUS, THEODORE   R18AR21393-17 0011
PINE, J   S07RR07003-26 0324
PINE, JEROME   N01NS02383-02
PINE, STANLEY H   S06GM08101-20 0020
PINGS, CORNELIUS J   S07RR07012-25
PINGS, CORNELIUS J   S15MH49285-01
PINGS, CORNELIUS J   S15NS30134-01
PINK, F   S07RR05728-20 0199
PINKEL, DANIEL   R01CA45919-04
PINKEL, DANIEL   S15HD28737-01
PINKEL, DONALD   U10CA03713-33S1
PINKER, STEVEN   R01HD18381-09
PINKERT, CARL   N01ES95253-04
PINKERTON, KENT E   P01ES00628-19 0012
PINKOWSKI, BEN   R15DC01122-01
PINKSTON, PAULA   P01HL43510-03 9001
PINNELL, SHELDON R   R01AR28304-09
PINNELL, SHELDON R   R37AR17128-19
PINNICK, HAROLD W   R03DA06792-02
PINON, RAMON R, JR   S03RR03348-09
PINSKY, PETER M   R01EY09284-01
PINSON, DAVID M   K01RR00037-06
PINTADO, MARIA   P30DE09737-02 0004
PINTAR, JOHN   P50HD05077-21 0031
PINTAR, JOHN E   R01HD18592-09
PINTAR, JOHN E   R01NS21970-06
PINTAURO, STEPHEN J   S07RR07125-22 0396
PINTEL, DAVID J   K04AI00934-03
PINTEL, DAVID J   R01AI21302-07
PINTER, ABRAHAM   P30AI27742-03 9001
PINTER, ABRAHAM   R01AI23884-06
PINTER, ABRAHAM   R01CA42129-06
PINTER, MARTIN   P01NS24707-05 0006
PINTO DE SILVA, P   Z01CB08387-04
PINTO, LAWRENCE H   R01EY01221-19
PINTO, NEAL B   P60DC00976-02 0010
PIOMELLI, SERGIO   P60HL28381-09 9002
PIOMELLI, SERGIO   P60HL28381-09
PIOMELLI, SERGIO   P60HL28381-09 0008
PIOMELLI, SERGIO   U10CA03526-34
PION, PAUL D   K11HL02107-04
PIOTROWSKI, JOSEPH   S07RR05410-30 0951
PIOUS, DONALD   P01DK41801-02 0001
PIOUS, DONALD A   R01AI30527-01
PIOUS, DONALD A   R01HG00243-27
PIOUS, DONALD A   R37AI16689-12
PIPAS, JAMES M   R37CA40586-07
PIPER, DOUGLAS L   R01DA05038-06
PIPER, DOUGLAS L   R01DA06224-02
PIPER, JAMES R   R01CA25236-12
PIPER, JAMES R   U01AI30279-02
PIPER, JAMES R   U01AI30279-02 0001
PIPER, WALTER N   R01ES02424-09
PIPERNO, GIANNI   R01GM44467-02
PIPPIN, C G   Z01CM06395-02
PIRIE, PHYLLIS   S07RR05448-30 0308
PIRISI, LUCIA A   R29CA48990-03
PIROFSKI, LIISE-ANNE   K11AI00877-04
PIROFSKY, BERNARD   M01RR00334-25 0048
PIROFSKY, BERNARD   M01RR00334-25 0308
PIROFSKY, BERNARD   M01RR00334-25 0309
PIROFSKY, BERNARD   M01RR00334-25 0283
PIRROTTA, VINCENZO   R01GM34630-07
PIRROTTA, VINCENZO   R01HG00311-03
PIRRUNG, MICHAEL C   R01GM43816-01A1
PIRTLE, ROBERT M   S07RR07195-12 0708
PISANO, ETTA D   P01CA47982-04 0008
PISARRA, VIRGINIA   N02HI19505-00
PISCHEL, KEN D   R29AI24624-05
PISETSKY, DAVID S   M01RR00030-30 0501
PISETSKY, DAVID S.   P50AR39162-05 0005
PISONI, DAVID B   R01DC00111-15
PISONI, RONALD L   R29DK40323-04
PITAS, ROBERT E   R01NS25678-04
PITHA-ROWE, P   P30CA06973-29 9023
PITHA-ROWE, PAULA M   R01AI19737-09
PITHA-ROWE, PAULA M   R01CA50158-03
PITHA-ROWE, PAULA M   R37AI26123-04
PITHA-ROWE, PAULA M.   P01AI27297-04 0004
PITHA, J   Z01AG00046-21
PITLER, THOMAS A   R01NS27968-02
PITMAN, ROGER K   R01MH42872-04
PITOT, HENRY C   P01CA22484-14
PITOT, HENRY C   P01CA22484-14 0004
PITOT, HENRY C   P30CA07175-28 9004
PITOT, HENRY C   P30CA07175-28
PITOT, HENRY C   P30CA07175-28 9006
PITOT, HENRY C   R01CA45700-05
PITRAK, DAVID L   S07RR05369-30 0582
PITT, BRUCE R   R01HL32154-09
PITT, COLIN G   R01DA03616-07
PITT, HENRY A   R55DK44279-01
PITT, JANE   M01RR00645-20 0469
PITT, JANE   M01RR00645-20 0486
PITT, JANE   N01AI82506-09
PITT, MARK M   P30HD28251-01 9001
PITTELKOW, MARK R   R01AR39547-01A3
PITTMAN, JAMES A, JR   M01RR00032-31
PITTMAN, JAMES A, JR   S07RR05349-30
PITTMAN, JAMES A, JR   S15HD28742-01
PITTMAN, RANDALL N   R01NS22663-05
PITTMAN, RAY C   P50HL14197-20 0014
PITTMAN, RAY C   P50HL14197-20 9001
PITTMAN, ROLAND N   R01HL18292-16A1
PITTS, DAVID K   R29MH47857-01
PIWNICA-WORMS, DAVID R   R29HL42966-02
PIWNICA-WORMS, HELEN   S07RR05382-30 0875
PIWNICA-WORMS, HELEN M   R29CA50767-03
PIXLEY, SARAH K   P01DC00347-06 0007
PIZER, LEWIS I   P01AG07347-04 0004
PIZER, STEPHEN M   P01CA47982-04
PIZER, STEPHEN M   P01CA47982-04 0002
PIZZICONI, VINCENT B   S07RR07112-24 0428
PIZZIMENTI, BRUCE   N01LM13509-00
PIZZO, P   Z01CM06830-21
PIZZO, SALVATORE   P01CA29589-10 0006
PIZZO, SALVATORE   P30CA14236-18 9023
PIZZO, SALVATORE V   P50NS20023-08 0013
PIZZO, SALVATORE V   R01HL24066-13
PIZZO, SALVATORE V   R01HL31932-06A1
PIZZO, SALVATORE V   R01HL43339-03
PIZZUTILLO, PETER D   S07RR05414-30 0997
PLACKE, MICHAEL E   N01CM97617-04
PLAEGER-MARSHALL, SUSAN F   R01AI32440-01
PLAEGER-MARSHALL, SUSAN F   R29AI26098-04
PLAEGER/MARSHALL S   S07RR05354-30 0376
PLAGEMANN, PETER G   R01AI15267-21
PLAGEMANN, PETER G   R01AI27320-03
PLAITAKIS, ANDREAS   M01RR00071-28A1 0196
PLAITAKIS, ANDREAS   M01RR00071-28A1 0185
PLAITAKIS, ANDREAS   R01NS16871-11
PLANT, TONY M   P30HD08610-17
PLANT, TONY M   P30HD08610-17 9001
PLANT, TONY M   R01HD16851-08
PLANT, TONY M   S07RR05416-30 0571
PLANTE, DENNIS A   M01RR00109-28 0341
PLAPP, BRYCE V   R01AA00279-19
PLAPP, BRYCE V   R01AA06223-08
PLATIA, EDWARD V.   N01HC65066-11
PLATO, C C   Z01AG00021-28
PLATO, C C   Z01AG00022-15
PLATO, C C   Z01AG00028-15
PLATSOUCAS, CHRIS D   R01AI24669-03
PLATSOUCAS, CHRIS D   R01AR41003-01
PLATSOUCAS, CHRIS D   R01CA52308-01A1
PLATT, JAMES E   R25RR07674-01
PLATT, JANE E   R03MH47090-01A1
PLATT, JANE E   S07RR05399-30 0938
PLATT, JEFFREY L   R01HL46810-01
PLATT, JEROME J   R18DA06986-02
PLATT, JEROME J   S07RR05908-08
PLATT, MARK W   S07RR05583-27 0636
PLATT, ORAH S   P60HL15157-20 0020
PLATT, TERRY   R01GM35658-07
PLATTNER, JACOB   U01AI27220-04
PLATTNER, JACOB J   U01AI27220-04 0003
PLATTS-MILLS, THOMAS A   M01RR00847-18 0446
PLATTS-MILLS, THOMAS A   M01RR00847-18 0562
PLATTS-MILLS, THOMAS A   M01RR00847-18 0214
PLATTS-MILLS, THOMAS A   M01RR00847-18 0584
PLATTS-MILLS, THOMAS A   R01AI30840-01
PLATTS-MILLS, THOMAS A   R01AI20565-08
PLATZ, MATTHEW S   R01GM34823-06
PLATZ, MATTHEW S   R01GM36489-05
PLAUCHE, WARREN C   U76PE00222-04
PLAUT, ANDREW   P30DK34928-07 9001
PLAUT, ANDREW G   P30DK34928-07
PLAUT, ANDREW G   R01DE09677-01
PLAUT, MARSHALL   P50HL37119-05 0004
PLAYER, DENIFIELD W   S07RR05362-30 0813
PLAYER, DENIFIELD W   S07RR05362-30 0814
PLAYER, DENIFIELD W   S07RR05362-30 0815
PLAYER, DENIFIELD W   S07RR05362-30 0816
PLAYER, DENIFIELD W   S07RR05362-30 0817
PLEASS, CHARLES M   R01GM42012-03
PLEASURE, DAVID   P01CA47983-04 0004
PLEASURE, DAVID   P30HD26979-02 9004
PLEASURE, DAVID E   P01NS08075-21
PLEASURE, DAVID E   P01NS08075-21 0004
PLEASURE, DAVID E   R01NS25044-05
PLEDGER, JACK W   P01CA43720-05 0004
PLEDGER, WARREN J   P01CA48799-03
PLEDGER, WARREN J   P01CA48799-03 0001
PLEDGER, WARREN J   R01CA42713-07
PLESH, OCTAVIA   R03DE09810-01
PLESH, OCTAVIA   S07RR05305-30 0743
PLEZIA, PATRICIA M   P01CA27502-11 0009
PLISKHER, GORDON A   P50NS11535-17 0013
PLISZKA, STEVEN R   K11MH00731-04
PLOFNICK, LESLIE P   M01RR00052-30 0219
PLOMIN, ROBERT   P01DA07171-01 9001
PLOMIN, ROBERT   R01HD27694-01A1
PLOMIN, ROBERT   R37AG08055-03 0001
PLONSEY, ROBERT   R01HL40609-04
PLOPPER, CHARLES G   P01ES00628-19
PLOPPER, CHARLES G   P01ES00628-19 0003
PLOPPER, CHARLES G   R01HL43032-03
PLOTH, DAVID W   P50DK39258-05 0006
PLOTKIN, DANIEL A   K07MH00823-03
PLOTKIN, SHIRLEY   M01RR00240-27 0322
PLOTKIN, STANLEY   P01AI25380-05 9002
PLOTNICK, L   M01RR00052-30 0194
PLOTNICK, L.   M01RR00052-30 0193
PLOTNICK, LESLIE P   M01RR00052-30 0149
PLOTNICK, LESLIE P   M01RR00052-30 0244
PLOTNICK, LESLIE P   M01RR00052-30 0206
PLOTNICK, LESLIE P   M01RR00052-30 0240
PLOTNICK, LESLIE P   M01RR00052-30 0241
PLOTSKY, PAUL M   P01HD13527-12 0006
PLOTSKY, PAUL M   R01MH45216-03
PLOTZ, P H   Z01AR41074-04
PLOTZ, P H   Z01AR41076-04
PLOTZ, P H   Z01AR41080-03
PLOUFFE, LEO   S07RR05365-30 0095
PLOUZEK, C A   Z01CN00156-01
PLOW, EDWARD F   P01HL16411-18 0012
PLOW, EDWARD F   R01HL17964-17
PLOW, EDWARD F   R01HL38292-05
PLUDE, DANA JEFFREY   R01AG08060-03
PLUM, FRED   P01NS03346-31 0043
PLUM, THOMAS B   R18MH49377-01
PLUMB, VANCE J   M01RR00032-31 0298
PLUMB, VANCE J   M01RR00032-31 0335
PLUMLEY, GERALD   S07RR07254-03 0496
PLUMMER, FRANK   U01AI31448-01 0001
PLUMMER, T H, JR   R01GM30471-09
PLUNKETT, PATRICK F   S03RR03321-08
PLUNKETT, R J   Z01NS02729-05
PLUNKETT, ROBERT J   S07RR05400-30 0039
PLUNKETT, WILLIAM K   R01CA28596-11
PLUNKETT, WILLIAM K   R01CA32839-09
PLUZNIK, D H   Z01BD01006-03
PLUZNIK, D H   Z01BD01007-03
PO, HENRY N   S06GM08238-05 0015
POBER, JORDAN S   P01HL36028-07 0007
POBER, JORDAN S   R01HL36003-07
POCHAPSKY, THOMAS   S07RR07044-26 0114
POCHAPSKY, THOMAS C   R29GM44191-02
POCKROS, PAUL   M01RR00833-17 0138
POCKROS, PAUL J   M01RR00833-17 0176
PODACK, ECKHARD R   R01CA39201-08
PODGORSKI, CAROL   P60AG10463-01 0005
PODOLASKY, DAVID K   P01DK36350-05S1 0003
PODOLSKY, DANIEL   P30DK43351-01 9005
PODOLSKY, DANIEL K   P01DK36350-05S1
PODOLSKY, DANIEL K   P30DK43351-01
PODOLSKY, DANIEL K   R01DK34422-08
PODOLSKY, R J   Z01AR27000-29
PODUSLO, SHIRLEY   S07RR05773-17 0367
PODUSLO, J.F.   P01NS14304-13 0038
PODUSLO, JOSEPH F   R01NS20551-07A2
PODUSLO, SHIRLEY E   R03DA07366-01
POEHLMAN, ERIC   M01RR00109-28 0350
POEHLMAN, ERIC   M01RR00109-28 0327
POEHLMAN, ERIC   M01RR00109-28 0338
POEHLMAN, ERIC T   R29AG07857-04
POENIE, MARTIN F   R01GM40605-04
POENIE, MARTIN F   S07RR07091-26 0764
POERTNER, GRACE C S   R03HS06627-01S1
POFFENBERGER, K   Z01BG06043-01
POFFENBERGER, K   Z01BG06044-01
POFFENBERGER, K   Z01BG06045-01
POGGIO, GIAN F   R01EY02966-12
POGGIO, THOMAS   S07RR07047-26 0138
POGREL, M ANTHONY   S07RR05305-30 0741
POGUE-GEILE, MICHAEL F   R29MH43666-03
POGWIZD, STEVEN M   R29HL46929-01
POGWIZD, STEVEN M   S07RR05389-30 0646
POH-FITZPATRICK, MAUREEN B   R01AR18549-16A1
POHL, CLIFFORD R   P30HD08610-17 9003
POHORECKY, LARISSA A   R01AA08499-01A1
POHOST, GERALD M   P50HL17667-17
POHOST, GERALD M   P50HL17667-17 0062
POIESZ, BERNARD   U01AI27310-04 9001
POIESZ, BERNARD J   R01HL43602-03
POINDEXTER, ALFRED N   M01RR00350-25 0440
POIRIER, M C   Z01CP05177-10
POIZNER, HOWARD   R01NS28665-02
POIZNER, HOWARD   R29NS25149-05
POKORNY, JOEL M   R01EY00901-18
POKORNY, LOIS J   R19MH46324-03
POLAKOSKI, KENNETH L   R01HD12863-13
POLAKOWSKA, RENATA R   R29AR39724-03
POLAND, ALAN   P01CA22484-14 0008
POLAND, ALAN P   R37ES01884-15
POLAND, RUSSELL E   K02MH00534-05
POLAND, RUSSELL E   M01RR00425-22S3 0305
POLAND, RUSSELL E   R01DA06863-02
POLAND, RUSSELL E   R01MH47193-02 0003
POLAND, RUSSELL E   R37MH34471-10A2
POLANS, ARTHUR S   R29EY07089-05
POLANS, NEIL O   S07RR07176-14 0530
POLANSKY, JON R   R01EY02477-12
POLANSKY, JON R   R01EY03980-09
POLAREK, JAMES W   R44GM42278-03

POLEDNAK, ANTHONY P P01CA42101-06 0007
POLGAR, PETER R R01HL25776-10
POLICH, JOHN P50MH45294-03 9006
POLICH, JOHN P50MH47680-02 0018
POLICH, JOHN M P50MH45294-03 0003
POLICH, JOHN M R01AG10604-01
POLINSKY, R J Z01NS02115-18
POLINSKY, R J Z01NS02630-08
POLIS, M A Z01CL00103-01
POLIS, M A Z01CL00104-01
POLISKY, BARRY A R01GM24212-15
POLISKY, BARRY A R01GM31745-08
POLISSON, RICHARD P M01RR00030-30 0509
POLISSON, RICHARD P M01RR00030-30 0353
POLISSON, RICHARD P M01RR00030-30 0510
POLITINO, M Z01HL00275-02
POLITOFF, ALBERTO L S07RR05407-30 0044
POLK, B FRANK P01AI26499-03S1 0001
POLK, DAVID B S07RR05424-30 0113
POLLACK, BRIAN P30CA12197-19 9014
POLLACK, GERALD H P01HL31962-08
POLLACK, GERALD H P01HL31962-08 0001
POLLACK, GERALD H P01HL31962-08 9003
POLLACK, GERALD H R01HL18676-16
POLLACK, MARILYN S P01AI21289-08 0004
POLLACK, MARILYN S P01AI21289-08 9002
POLLACK, MARILYN S R01AI28086-03
POLLACK, PAUL S07RR05745-19 0231
POLLACK, RALPH M R01GM38155-04A1
POLLACK, ROBERT E P01CA33620-08 9001
POLLACK, ROBERT E P01CA33620-08 0003
POLLACK, SOLOMON P50AR39226-05 0003
POLLACK, SYLVIA B R01CA32553-10
POLLACK, SYLVIA B R01HD28031-01
POLLAK, GEORGE D R01DC00268-08
POLLARD, H B Z01DK21019-09
POLLARD, JEFFREY W R01HD25074-03
POLLARD, KENNETH P60AR40770-01A1 0002
POLLARD, RICHARD B M01RR00073-29 0283
POLLARD, RICHARD B M01RR00073-29 0325
POLLARD, RICHARD B M01RR00073-29 0323
POLLARD, THOMAS D R01GM26338-14
POLLARD, THOMAS D R37GM26132-14
POLLEN, DANIEL A R01EY05156-09
POLLOCK, ALLAN S R01DK31398-07A2
POLLOCK, DONALD K S07RR07066-26 0255
POLLOCK, JERRY J R01DE07441-06
POLLOCK, JERRY J S07RR05778-16 0410
POLLOCK, JERRY J S07RR05778-16 0408
POLLOCK, MARC R25RR07585-01
POLLOCK, RAPHAEL E R29CA51512-02
POLLOCK, ROBERTA R R29AI30020-02
POLLOCK, VICKI E R01AA08031-02
POLMAR, STEPHEN H M01RR06021-02 0626
POLMAR, STEPHEN H M01RR06021-02 1007
POLMAR, STEPHEN H M01RR06021-02 1016
POLMAR, STEPHEN H M01RR06021-02 1017
POLMAR, STEPHEN H U01AI25903-05 9002
POLMAR, STEPHEN S M01RR00036-31 1040
POLOGE, LAURA S07RR05399-30 0913
POLONSKY, K P30DK42086-02 0003
POLONSKY, KENNETH S M01RR00055-30 0547
POLONSKY, KENNETH S M01RR00055-30 0410
POLONSKY, KENNETH S M01RR00055-30 0549
POLONSKY, KENNETH S P30DK26678-12 9011
POLONSKY, KENNETH S R01DK31842-09
POLSE, KENNETH A R01EY04930-06
POLSE, KENNETH A R01EY07728-03
POLSE, KENNETH A S07RR05832-12 0198
POLSON, PETER S07RR07013-26 0954
POLTORAK, M Z01MH02428-04
POLVERINI, PETER S07RR05311-30 0006
POLVERINI, PETER J R01HL39926-04
POLYMEROPOULOS, M H Z01MH02571-01
POMARA, NUNZIO R01MH42499-03
POMARA, NUNZIO R01MH44194-03
POMERANTZ, ROGER J K11AI00930-04
POMERANTZ, STEVEN M R01HD25145-01A3
POMERLEAU, OVIDE F M01RR00042-31 0654
POMERLEAU, OVIDE F R01CA42730-07
POMERLEAU, OVIDE F R01DA06529-02
POMEROY, JOHN S07RR05736-19 0165
POMEROY, SCOTT R01NS27773-04
POMEROY, SCOTT L S07RR05389-30 0647
POMMIER, Y Z01CM06150-10
POMMIER, Y Z01CM06161-08
POMPEIANO, OTTAVIO R01NS07685-22
POMREHN, PAUL N01CN64092-13
POMREHN, PAUL R01HL32847-08
PONCZ, MORTIMER P01HL40387-04 0002
PONCZ, MORTIMER R01HL17419-05
POND, FINN R R15GM46045-01
PONDER, JAY P01GM24483-12A1 0012
PONDER, JAY W S07RR05389-30 0648
PONDER, SPEPHEN W M01RR00073-29 0317
PONNAPPA, BIDDANDA C R29AA07571-03
PONNAPPAN, USHA S07RR05373-30 0727
PONS, T P Z01MH02037-01
PONTEN, JAN N01CO94383-03
PONZIO, NICHOLAS M S10RR06732-01
PONZY, LU P41RR01348-10 0005
POO, MU-MING R01NS22764-08
POO, MU-MINGY P41RR01395-10 0014
POODRY, CLIFTON A S06GM08132-17 0019
POODRY, CLIFTON A S07RR07135-21
POODRY, CLIFTON A S07RR07135-21 0532
POOL, JAMES L M01RR00350-25 0417
POOL, JEREMY D R43CA55418-01
POOLE, KENNETH W. N01HR76029-04
POON, LEONARD W R01MH43435-04
POORE, E ROBIN P01HD21350-05 9002
POPE, ALFRED P01MH31154-14 0002
POPE, ANDREW N01AI15110-00
POPE, ANDREW N01LM93513-03
POPE, CLYDE R P50MH43458-04 0005
POPE, HARRISON G, JR R01DA06543-02
POPE, HARRISON G, JR R01DA06522-01A1
POPE, MALCOLM H R01AR39213-04
POPE, RICHARD M P60AR30692-08
POPESCU, N C Z01CP05499-05
POPKIN, BARRY M P01HD28076-01
POPKIN, BARRY M P01HD28076-01 0001
POPKIN, BARRY M R01HD19983-06
POPKIN, BARRY M R01HD23416-02
POPKO, BRIAN J R29NS27336-03
POPLACK, D G Z01CM06840-16
POPLACK, D G Z01CM06880-13
POPOFF, STEVEN N R29AR39876-01A3
POPP, RAYMOND A R01HL43375-03
POPPELE, RICHARD E R01NS21143-06
POPS, MARTIN A S03RR03415-05
PORCELLI, STEVEN A K08AR01854-01
PORER, JOHN M M01RR00334-25 0270
PORETSKY, LEONID R29HD22738-05
PORGES, STEPHEN W R01HD22628-07
PORRECA, FRANK P01DK36289-06A1 0010
PORRECA, FRANK F R01DK33547-07
PORRINO, L Z01NS02760-04
PORRINO, L Z01NS02761-03
PORRINO, L Z01NS02762-04
PORRINO, L J Z01MH02216-08
PORTALE, ANTHONY A M01RR00079-29 0309
PORTE, DANIEL M01RR00037-31 0437
PORTE, DANIEL, JR P30DK17047-15
PORTE, DANIEL, JR R01DK12829-23
PORTENOY, RUSSELL K P01CA52477-01A1 0002
PORTER, CARL W R01CA22153-15
PORTER, CARL W R01CA51524-02
PORTER, CARL W R13CA55370-01
PORTER, CARL W U01CA37606-08 0005
PORTER, CARL W U01CA37606-08
PORTER, CORNELIA S07RR05796-14 0437
PORTER, CORNELIA P P20NR02962-01 0004
PORTER, FRAN M01RR06021-02 1010
PORTER, FRAN L R01HD20414-04
PORTER, FRANKLIN I R01EY06394-05
PORTER, JOHN M01RR00334-25 0296
PORTER, JOHN C P50HD11149-14 0012
PORTER, JOHN C R01AG08173-04
PORTER, JOHN C R01DK01237-36
PORTER, JOHN C R37AG04344-08
PORTER, JOHN M M01RR00334-25 0302
PORTER, JOHN M M01RR00334-25 0293
PORTER, JOHN M M01RR00334-25 0264
PORTER, JOHN M M01RR00334-25 0306
PORTER, JOHN M M01RR00334-25 0188
PORTER, JOHN M M01RR00334-25 0286
PORTER, LINDA L R29NS27038-03
PORTER, MARY E S07RR05385-30 0814
PORTER, NED A R01HL17921-17
PORTER, RONALD D S07RR07082-26 0303
PORTER, TODD D R01GM47615-01
PORTERFIELD, SUSAN P S07RR05365-30 0096
PORTIER, C J Z01ES48002-04
PORTIS, J L Z01AI00086-15
PORTMAN, RONALD J M01RR02558-07 0051
PORTNER, ALAN P01AI31596-01 0001
PORTNER, ALLEN P01AI31596-01 9001
PORTNER, ALLEN R01AI11949-17
PORTNER, PEER N01HV98107-04
PORTNOY, DANIEL A R01AI29619-02
PORTNOY, DANIEL A R29AI27655-04
PORTNOY, DANIEL A S07RR07083-26 0477
PORTNOY, JAY M R29AI31213-02
PORTOGHESE, PHILIP P01DA05695-03 0003
PORTOGHESE, PHILIP S R01DA01533-16
PORTOGHESE, PHILIP S R01DA02659-08
PORTOGHESE, PHILIP S R01DA06251-03
PORUSH, JEROME G U01DK39367-04
POSAKONY, JAMES W R01GM41100-04
POSER, JAMES W P01DE08569-03 0003
POSES, ROY M R01HS06274-02
POSEY, ISADORA S06GM08005-20 0009
POSNER, BARBARA S07RR05927-07 0967
POSNER, BARBARA M R01HL39144-03
POSNER, GARY H P01CA44530-05 0004
POSNER, GARY H R01GM30052-09
POSNER, JEROME B R01NS26064-04
POSNER, JOEL P41RR02305-08 0018
POSNER, JOEL D P01AG03934-10 0004
POSNER, MARSHALL R R01CA50054-03
POSNER, MICHAEL I U01AI25903-05 0002
POSNETT, DAVID N R01AI31140-01
POSNETT, DAVID N R01CA42046-06
POSNETT, DAVID N S07RR05396-30 0756
POSNETT, DAVID N S07RR05396-30 0757
POSSIDENTE, BERNARD P, JR R15DC00760-01A1
POST, CAROL B R29GM39478-01A3
POST, CAROL B S07RR05586-24 0109
POST, MARTIN R01HL43416-03
POST, R M Z01MH02509-02
POST, R M Z01MH02510-02
POST, R M Z01MH02511-02
POST, R M Z01MH02512-02
POST, R M Z01MH02513-02
POST, R M Z01MH02514-03
POST, THEODORE W K08DK02046-01
POSTLE, KATHLEEN R01GM42146-01A1
POSTLETHWAIT, EDWARD M R29ES04952-03
POSTLETHWAIT, JOHN H R01AI26734-04
POSTLETHWAITE, A E P50AR39166-05 0004
POSTLETHWAITE, ARNOLD E R01AR26034-11
POSTON, J M Z01HL00268-05
POTASH, LOUIS N01AI15129-01
POTASH, LOUIS N01AI82681-06
POTASHNER, STEVEN J R01DC00199-08
POTE, KENNETH GENE R29DC00929-02
POTEETE, ANTHONY R R01AI18234-11
POTEETE, ANTHONY R R01AI24083-04
POTEGAL, MICHAEL S07RR05650-25 0109
POTEMPA, KATHLEEN R01NR02096-02
POTKIN, STEVEN G R01MH45962-02
POTMESIL, MILAN P01CA50529-01A2
POTMESIL, MILAN P01CA50529-01A2 0003
POTTALA, E W Z01CT00004-21
POTTER, BARRY J R01AA06860-06
POTTER, BARRY J R01AA08742-02
POTTER, DAVID A K08CA01562-01
POTTER, DAVID D P01NS02253-32 0011
POTTER, DAVID D R01DA04582-10
POTTER, DAVID E R01EY06338-06A1
POTTER, HUNTINGTON P01NS25915-04A1 0006
POTTER, HUNTINGTON P01NS25915-04A1 9004
POTTER, HUNTINGTON R01AG08084-03
POTTER, HUNTINGTON R01AG09665-06A1
POTTER, JAMES D P01HL22619-14 0005
POTTER, JAMES D R01AR40727-01A1
POTTER, JAMES D R37HL42325-03
POTTER, JANE F K07AG00474-02
POTTER, JOHN D P01CA50305-02
POTTER, JOHN D P01CA50305-02 0001
POTTER, JOHN D R01CA51932-02
POTTER, JOHN D S07RR05448-30 0309
POTTER, JOSEPH E R01HD22798-01A2
POTTER, LINCOLN T R01AG06170-06
POTTER, LLOYD S07RR07150-17 0551
POTTER, M Z01CB05596-22
POTTER, S STEVEN P30HD28827-01 9004
POTTER, S STEVEN P60HL15996-19 9005
POTTER, STANLEY S R01HD24517-04
POTTER, STEVEN P01HL41496-03 9002
POTTER, STEVEN P01HL41496-03 0009
POTTER, SUSAN M S07RR07030-26 0404
POTTER, TERRY S07RR05842-12 0283
POTTER, TERRY A P01AI29903-02 0002
POTTER, TERRY A R01AI28115-04
POTTER, W Z Z01MH01850-01
POTTER, W Z Z01MH02486-01
POTTICK, KATHLEEN P50MH43450-04 0019
POTTS, ALBERT M R44HD26209-02A1
POTTS, GEORGE S07RR07138-20 0531
POTTS, JOHN T P01DK11794-24 9001
POTTS, JOHN T, JR K12DK01410-07
POTTS, JOHN T, JR M01RR01066-14
POTTS, JOHN T, JR P01DK11794-24
POTTS, RUSSELL O R13AR40999-01
POU, SOVITZ S07RR05770-13 0934
POUDRIER, DON N01CO05733-01
POUDRIER, DON N01CO15631-01
POUDRIER, DON N01CO15633-00
POUDRIER, DON N01CO15653-00
POUDRIER, DON N01CO15687-00
POUDRIER, DON N01CO15738-00
POULEUR, HUBERT N01HC65030-10
POULOS, THOMAS L R01GM33688-07
POULOS, THOMAS L R01GM42614-03
POULSON, CLAIRE L R01HD22070-03
POULTER, C DALE S07RR07092-26 0545
POULTER, CHARLES D R01GM21328-17
POULTER, CHARLES D R01GM25521-12
POUNDS, JOEL G R01ES04040-04A1
POUNDS, JOEL G R01ES05548-01A1
POUR, PARVIZ M P30CA36727-08 9004
POURCHO, ROBERTA G R01EY02267-13
POVIRK, LAWRENCE F R01CA40615-07
POVLISHOCK, JOHN T P01NS12587-16 0005
POVLISHOCK, JOHN T R01NS20193-08
POVLISHOCK, JOHN T R01NS29469-01
POVLISHOCK, JOHN T R13NS29625-01
POVLISHOCK, JOHN T. P01NS12587-16 0019
POWDERLY, WILLIAM M01RR00036-31 1041
POWDERLY, WILLIAM M01RR00036-31 1042
POWDERLY, WILLIAM M01RR00036-31 1020
POWDERLY, WILLIAM M01RR00036-31 1022
POWDERLY, WILLIAM M01RR00036-31 1019
POWELL, A JAMES S03RR03296-09

POWELL, ALICE M S14GM44779-02
POWELL, BARBARA J R01AA07386-04
POWELL, BAYARD L. P30CA12197-19 9015
POWELL, BRIAN S07RR07031-26 0101
POWELL, DAVID R R01DK38773-06
POWELL, DON W P30DK34987-06
POWELL, DON WATSON R37DK15350-21
POWELL, DONALD A R01AG08522-03
POWELL, FRANK L P01HL17731-17 0017
POWELL, GARY L R01HL38190-05
POWELL, GARY L S07RR07180-10
POWELL, GERALDINE K. M01RR00073-29 0285
POWELL, HENRY C R01NS14162-14
POWELL, J I Z01CT00206-02
POWELL, J I Z01CT00207-02
POWELL, JEANNE A R15AR40914-01
POWELL, KEITH R M01RR00044-31 0384
POWELL, LYNDA H S07RR05443-30 0997
POWELL, MARIANNE B R29CA51971-02
POWELL, RICHARD D R43CA55432-01
POWELL, SAUL S07RR05924-07 0003
POWELL, THOMAS J R24MH46399-03
POWER, GORDON G R01HD16827-09
POWER, KAREN L R03HS06961-01
POWER, ROBERT L R44CA49164-03
POWER, THOMAS G R01AA07740-02
POWERS-LEE, SUSAN G R01DK33460-09
POWERS, ALVIN C R01DK43736-01
POWERS, ALVIN C S07RR05424-30 0084
POWERS, CLAUD A R01DK32783-07
POWERS, EDWARD L P41RR00886-16 9001
POWERS, JAMES C R01HL34035-04A3
POWERS, LINDA P41RR06030-01A1 9001
POWERS, LINDA P41RR06030-01A1 9002
POWERS, LINDA P41RR06030-01A1 9003
POWERS, LINDA P41RR06030-01A1
POWERS, LINDA S P42ES04922-03 0004
POWERS, MAUREEN K P30EY08126-03
POWERS, MAUREEN K R01EY08256-02
POWERS, MICHAEL R K11EY00318-01
POWERS, R SCOTT R01GM41258-03
POWERS, RANDALL K R29NS25206-06
POWERS, RICHARD P01AG06569-05 9002
POWERS, RICHARD P01AG06569-05 0007
POWERS, RICHARD P30AG10163-01 9003
POWERS, ROBERT E R29DK40472-04
POWERS, SCOTT S07RR05576-27 0591
POWERS, STEPHEN M01RR00046-31 0468
POWERS, STEPHEN M01RR00046-31 0509
POWERS, STEPHEN M01RR00046-31 0466
POWERS, STEPHEN K M01RR00046-31 0439
POWERS, STEPHEN K M01RR00046-31 0409
POWERS, STEPHEN K M01RR00046-31 0324
POWERS, STEPHEN K M01RR00046-31 0325
POWERS, STEPHEN K M01RR00046-31 0318
POWERS, STEPHEN K M01RR00046-31 0327
POWERS, STEPHEN K M01RR00046-31 0330
POWERS, STEPHEN K M01RR00046-31 0331
POWERS, STEPHEN K M01RR00046-31 0319
POWERS, STEPHEN K M01RR00046-31 0321
POWERS, WILLIAM P01NS06833-25 0029
POWERS, WILLIAM J R01NS28700-02
POWIN, GARTH U01CA52995-02 0005
POWIS, GARTH N01ES05304-02
POWIS, GARTH R01CA42286-04A2
POWIS, GARTH R01CA48725-02
POWIS, GARTH U01CA52995-02
POWIS, GARTH U01CA52995-02 0002
POWLEY, TERRY L R01DK27627-12S1
POWLEY, TERRY L R01NS26632-03
POWLEY, TERRY L S07RR07032-26 0042
POWNALL, HENRY M01RR00350-25 0470
POWNALL, HENRY J P60HL27341-10 0003
POWNALL, HENRY J R01HL30914-08
POWNALL, HENRY J R01HL33914-05
POWNALL, HENRY J R01HL39312-05
POYTON, ROBERT O R01GM39324-01A4
POZZATTI, RUDY O R29CA52140-01A1
PRABHAKAR, NANDURI R R29HL38986-04
PRABHAKAR, RISBOOD N01CM17517-00
PRADOS, MICHAEL P01CA13525-19 0015
PRAGER, DIANE K08DK02023-01
PRAHALADA, SRINIVASA P51RR00169-30 9019
PRAISSMAN, MELVIN S07RR05736-19 0189
PRAKASH, CHANDRA S07RR05424-30 0104
PRAKASH, LOUISE R01GM19261-19
PRAKASH, LOUISE S07RR05403-30 0821
PRAKASH, OM R01DA06502-03
PRAKASH, SATYA R01CA35035-09
PRAKASH, SATYA R01CA41261-06
PRALINSKY, KAREN P51RR00165-31 9007
PRALINSKY, KAREN P51RR00165-31 9006
PRAMMER, MANFRED P41RR02305-08 9008
PRANGE, ARTHUR J, JR K05MH22536-22
PRANGE, ARTHUR J, JR P50MH33127-13
PRANZATELLI, MICHAEL M01RR00645-20 0491
PRASAD, KEDAR N R01DE09589-02
PRASAD, VINAYAKA R R01AI30861-01A1
PRASAD, VINAYAKA R S07RR05397-30 0786
PRATHER, RANDALL S S07RR07053-26 0161
PRATLEY, RICHARD E K08AG00494-03
PRATT, CHARLES P01CA23099-13 0001
PRATT, CHARLES B P01CA23099-13 0010
PRATT, CRAIG M M01RR00350-25 0472
PRATT, CRAIG M M01RR00350-25 0463
PRATT, CRAIG M M01RR00350-25 0464
PRATT, CRAIG M M01RR00350-25 0249
PRATT, CRAIG M M01RR00350-25 0336
PRATT, CRAIG M M01RR00350-25 0427
PRATT, CRAIG M P50HL42267-02 9003
PRATT, CRAIG M. N01HV18123-02
PRATT, HOWARD M01RR00750-19 0292
PRATT, JOHN H R01HL35795-06
PRATT, KAREN R R29AI29354-02
PRATT, MICHAEL F S07RR05771-15 0331
PRATT, PHILIP C P01HL31992-08 9001
PRATT, RAYMOND D R55DK44299-01
PRATT, REX F R01AI17986-10
PRATT, RICHARD E R01HL42663-04
PRATT, SHEILA R S07RR07098-26 0349
PRATT, WILLIAM B R01CA28010-12
PRATT, WILLIAM B R01DK31573-10
PRATTO, FELICIA S07RR07005-26 0341
PRAZMA, JIRI S07RR05406-30 0914
PRAZMA, JIRI S07RR05406-30 0915
PRCHAL, JOSEF T P01HL37462-05 0002
PRCHAL, JOSEF T R01EY08468-02
PREIRE, ERNESTO I P41RR04328-04 9003
PREISLER, HARVEY D P01CA21071-14 0006
PREISLER, HARVEY D P01CA41285-07 0001
PREISLER, HARVEY D P01CA41285-07
PREISLER, HARVEY D P01CA41285-07 0004
PREISS, JACK R37AI22835-07
PREJEAN, J DAVID N01ES85217-09
PREJEAN, J DAVID N01ES85233-06
PREJEAN, JD N01ES05289-01
PREJEAN, JD N01ES85222-09
PREJEAN, JD N01ES85234-06
PREJEAN, JD N01ES95271-05
PREJEAN, JOE N01ES15328-00
PREJEAN, JOE DAVID N01ES85219-07
PRELL, GEORGE D R29NS28012-02
PREMINGER, GLENN P01DK20543-15 0014
PREMINGER, GLENN P01DK20543-15 0015
PRENDERGAST, FRANKLYN G M01RR00585-20
PRENDERGAST, FRANKLYN G R01GM34847-07
PRENDERGAST, FRANKLYN G S07RR05530-29
PRENDERGAST, FRANKLYN G S15HL47730-01
PRENDERGAST, FRAUKLYN G P30CA15083-18 0003
PRENTICE-DUNN, STEVE S07RR07151-13 0518
PRENTICE, ROSS N01CN15343-00
PRENTICE, ROSS S07RR05761-17 0206
PRENTICE, ROSS L P01CA53996-14
PRENTICE, ROSS L P01CA53996-14 0001
PRESANT, CARY A U10CA35200-08
PRESCOTT, DAVID M R01GM19199-19A1
PRESCOTT, STEPHEN M R01HL34127-07
PRESS, JOAN L R01AI13725-13A2
PRESS, MICHAEL F R01CA48780-04
PRESS, MICHAEL F R01CA50589-01A1
PRESS, OLIVER W P01CA44991-04 0001
PRESS, OLIVER W R29CA46134-05
PRESS, RICHARD D K08NS01551-01
PRESSER, ADOLPH R43EY09000-01
PRESSIN, J P01HL14388-20 0249
PRESSLEY, THOMAS A K04HL02305-03
PRESSLEY, THOMAS A R29HL39846-04
PRESSMAN, BERTON C R01GM38920-03
PRESSMAN, MARK R P50MH40380-07 0008
PRESSON, CLARK C S07RR07112-24 0429
PRESTEGARD, JAMES H R01GM32243-09
PRESTEGARD, JAMES H R01GM33225-07
PRESTON-MARTIN, SUSAN P01CA17054-16 0005
PRESTON-MARTIN, SUSAN P01CA17054-16 0006
PRESTON-MARTIN, SUSAN R01CA47082-04
PRESTON, ALAN M S06GM08224-07 0018
PRESTON, ALLAN M S07RR05419-30 0828
PRESTON, BRADLEY D R29CA48174-04
PRESTON, J S07RR05362-30 0790
PRESTON, JAMES B R01NS02957-31
PRESTON, KENDALL, JR R43CA56511-01
PRESTON, KENDALL, JR R43GM44424-01A1
PRESTON, KENZIE L R01DA05196-05
PRETI, GEORGE P50DC00214-06 9002
PRETLOW, THERESA P R01CA48032-04
PRETLOW, THOMAS P30CA43703-04A1 9011
PRETLOW, THOMAS G, II U01CA54031-01
PREUSS, HARRY G R01AG06929-05
PREZANT, DAVID J K08HL02165-04
PREZIO, JOSEPH A S07RR05400-30 0040
PRICE-WILLIAMS, DOUG S07RR05756-18 0287
PRICE, CAROLYN M R29GM41803-03
PRICE, CATHERINE J N01ES95255-07
PRICE, CHESTER W R01GM42077-07
PRICE, D L P01NS26643-04 9002
PRICE, DAVID N01CL82107-07
PRICE, DONALD D R01NS28595-02
PRICE, DONALD L P01AG10480-01 0003
PRICE, DONALD L P01AG10491-01 0003
PRICE, DONALD L P50AG05146-09 0012
PRICE, DONALD L P50AG05146-09
PRICE, DONALD L P50AG05146-09 0008
PRICE, DONALD L P50NS20471-08
PRICE, DONALD L P50NS20471-08 0004
PRICE, DONALD L P50NS20471-08 0006
PRICE, DONALD L P50NS20471-08 0002
PRICE, DONALD L R01NS10580-16
PRICE, DONALD L R35AG07914-03
PRICE, DONALD L R35AG07914-03 0001
PRICE, DONALD L R35AG07914-03 0005
PRICE, DONALD L R35AG07914-03 0006
PRICE, DONALD R S15MH49299-01
PRICE, JAMES C N01CM73712-06
PRICE, JAMES G S07RR05373-30
PRICE, JANET E R29CA51053-02
PRICE, JOEL M S07RR05749-19 0274
PRICE, JOSEPH L P50AG05681-08 0016
PRICE, JOSEPH L R01DC00093-21
PRICE, JOSEPH L. P01AG03991-08 0009
PRICE, JOSEPH M R29MH48192-01
PRICE, LAWRENCE H M01RR00125-28 0695
PRICE, LAWRENCE H P01MH25642-18 9002
PRICE, LAWRENCE H P50DA04060-06 0008
PRICE, PAUL A R01AR25921-12A1
PRICE, PAUL A R37AR27029-12
PRICE, R ARLEN P01MH44210-03 0003
PRICE, R ARLEN R01DK44073-01
PRICE, R ARLEN R29MH43409-04
PRICE, RAY M R29DE09219-02
PRICE, RICHARD H P50MH38330-08
PRICE, RICHARD H R01DA03272-08
PRICE, RICHARD W P01NS25701-05
PRICE, RICHARD W. P01NS25701-05 0001
PRICE, RICHARD W. P01NS25701-05 0005
PRICE, S R Z01HL00656-01
PRICE, STUART B R15AI31211-01
PRICE, THOMAS R N01NS02375-02
PRICE, THOMAS R P01NS16332-09A2 0003
PRICE, THOMAS R P01NS16332-09A2
PRICE, THOMAS R. N01HC48059-08
PRICE, V HUGH S07RR05822-12 0496
PRICHARD, JAMES W P01DK34576-06 0001
PRICHARD, JAMES W R01NS21708-07
PRICHARD, JAMES W R01NS27883-02
PRIDHAM, KAREN F M01RR03186-06 0074
PRIDHAM, KAREN F R01NR02348-02
PRIDHAM, KAREN F R01NR02875-01
PRIESS, JAMES R, JR R29AR39722-03
PRIEST, DAVID G M01RR01070-15 0150
PRIEST, DAVID G R01CA22754-14
PRIETO, JOSE A S06GM08102-20 0050
PRIEUR, DAVID J S03RR03368-08
PRIMAKOFF, PAUL R01HD21989-06
PRIMAKOFF, PAUL U54HD29125-01
PRIMAKOFF, PAUL U54HD29125-01 0001
PRIMAS, PHYLLIS J S07RR07112-24 0430
PRIMERANO, DONALD A S07RR05870-10 0995
PRINCE, CHARLES W K04DE00247-04
PRINCE, CHARLES W R01DE06739-07
PRINCE, CHARLES W S07RR05968-06 0337
PRINCE, CHRISTOPHER L R43CA55456-01
PRINCE, DAVID A P50NS12151-17
PRINCE, DAVID A P50NS12151-17 0001
PRINCE, DAVID A P50NS12151-17 9001
PRINCE, DAVID A R01NS06477-26
PRINEAS, RONALD J R01HL44600-01A1
PRINGLE, JOHN R R01GM31006-09
PRINS, GAIL S R29DK40890-03
PRINZ, PATRICIA N M01RR00037-31 0290
PRINZ, PATRICIA N R37MH33688-12
PRINZ, RONALD J R01MH38667-06
PRINZ, RONALD J R18MH48018-02
PRIOLA, DONALD V S06GM08139-17 0018
PRIOR, D S06GM08215-09 0007
PRIORE, ROGER L P01CA41285-07 9002
PRITCHARD, DAVID G P01HD17812-09 0003
PRITCHARD, J B Z01ES80031-15
PRITCHARD, THOMAS C R01DC00246-07
PRITCHETT, DOLAN P01MH48125-01 9001
PRITCHETT, DOLAN B R01DA07130-01A1
PRITCHETT, DOLAN B S07RR05506-29 0911
PRITCHETT, EDWARD L M01RR00030-30 0297
PRITCHETT, EDWARD L R01HL40392-03
PRITCHETT, EDWARD L C P50DA05303-03 0005
PRITSOS, CHRIS A R29CA43660-04
PRITZKER, KENNETH P H P40RR03640-05 0009
PRIVALSKY, MARTIN L R01CA38823-07
PRIVALSKY, MARTIN L R01CA53394-01
PRIVES, CAROL P01CA33620-08 0001
PRIVES, CAROL S07RR07060-26 0451
PRIVES, CAROL L P01CA33620-08
PRIVES, CAROL L R01CA26905-12
PRIVITERA, MICHAEL D N01NS82306-02
PRIVITERA, PHILIP J R01HL41921-02
PRIVITERA, PHILIP J S07RR05420-30 0043
PROBER, C M01RR00081-29 0078
PROBER, CHARLES G K07AI00884-04
PROBER, CHARLES G R01AI31872-10
PROBER, CHARLES G R01HD16080-09S1
PROBST, P G Z01BA04008-01
PROCHASKA, JAMES O P01CA50087-03
PROCHASKA, JAMES O P01CA50087-03 0001
PROCHASKA, JAMES O R01CA27821-11
PROCHOWNIK, EDWARD V R01HL33741-08
PROCKOP, DARWIN J P01AR38188-07 9001
PROCKOP, DARWIN J P01AR38188-07 9003

PROCKOP, DARWIN J P01AR38188-07
PROCKOP, DARWIN J P01AR38188-07 0002
PROCKOP, DARWIN J P01AR38188-07 0003
PROCKOP, DARWIN J P01AR39740-03 0003
PROCKOP, DARWIN J P01AR39740-03 0004
PROCKOP, DARWIN J P50AA07186-06 0016
PROCTOR, ENOLA K R01HS06406-02
PROCTOR, KENNETH G R01HL30663-07
PRODOUZ, K N Z01BH01008-08
PRODOUZ, K N Z01BH01009-03
PRODOUZ, K N Z01BH01010-05
PRODOUZ, K N Z01BH01011-04
PRODOUZ, K N Z01BH01012-02
PRODOUZ, K N Z01BH01013-02
PRODOUZ, K N Z01BH01025-01
PROENZA, LUIS M S07RR07254-03
PROENZA, LUIS M S15AG10239-01
PROFFIT, WILLIAM R R01DE08708-04
PROFFIT, WILLIAM R R37DE05215-13
PROFY, ALBERT T R43AI31713-01
PROGRAIS, LAWRENCE P60HL38737-04 0003
PROGULSKE-FOX, A S07RR05728-20 0200
PROGULSKE-FOX, ANN R01DE07496-06
PROHASKA, JOSEPH R S07RR05896-09 0626
PROHASKA, JOSEPH R S07RR05896-09 0620
PROHASKA, OTTO P41RR02024-08 9007
PROHASKA, THOMAS R S07RR05871-03 0580
PROHOFSKY, EARL W S07RR07032-26 0036
PROHOVNIK, ISAK P50AG08702-03 0008
PROHOVNIK, ISAK R01AG10638-01
PROHOVNIK, ISAK A R01AG05433-06
PROIA, ALAN D R01EY05883-07
PROIA, R L Z01DK52012-07
PROKOPCZYK, BOGDAN P01CA29580-11 0007
PROPPE, DUANE W R01HL27504-09
PROROK, P C Z01CN00105-09
PROROK, P C Z01CN00106-08
PROSPECT ASSOCIATES, LTD N01MH90001-00
PROSS, SUSAN H R01DA06385-02
PROTEAU, PAUL N01CM07353-01
PROTEAU, PAUL N01CM97600-04
PROTEAU, PAUL R N01CM17508-01
PROTHERO, JOHN W R01HL29761-09
PROTHERO, JOHN W. P51RR00166-30 0149
PROUD, DAVID R01HL32272-07
PROUD, DAVID S07RR05378-30 0009
PROUD, VIRGINIA S07RR05387-30 0600
PROUDFIT, HERBERT K R01DA03980-10
PROUGH, DONALD S P01NS27500-01A2
PROUGH, RUSSELL A R01ES04244-06
PROUTY, LEONARD A S07RR05822-12 0507
PROUTY, MURIEL S06GM08005-20 0010
PROVAN, KEITH G R01MH43783-01A3
PROVVEDINI, DIEGO M R29AI24252-05
PROZIALECK, WALTER C G20RR06952-01
PROZIALECK, WALTER CHARLES R15ES05656-02
PRUCHNO, RACHEL A P01MH43371-04 0002
PRUETT, TIMOTHY L R29AI28954-02
PRUITT, RONALD C R29GM42921-03
PRUITT, STEVEN P01GM44119-02 0003
PRUITT, STEVEN C R01HD25419-03
PRUSINER, STANLEY P41RR01614-10 0004
PRUSINER, STANLEY B P01AG02132-11
PRUSINER, STANLEY B P01AG02132-11 0001
PRUSINER, STANLEY B P01AG02132-11 9001
PRUSINER, STANLEY B P01NS14069-14
PRUSINER, STANLEY B P01NS14069-14 0010
PRUSINER, STANLEY B P01NS22786-07
PRUSINER, STANLEY B P01NS22786-07 0005
PRUSINER, STANLEY B P01NS22786-07 9001
PRUSINER, STANLEY B P01NS22786-07 9002
PRUSINER, STANLEY B R35AG08967-02 0006
PRUSINER, STANLEY B R35AG08967-02
PRUSINER, STANLEY B R35AG08967-02 0001
PRUSINER, STANLEY B R35AG08967-02 0005
PRUSOFF, WILLIAM H R01CA05262-31
PRYOR, DAVID B P01HS06503-02
PRYOR, DAVID B P01HS06503-02 0001
PRYOR, DAVID B P01HS06503-02 0002
PRYOR, STEPHEN C S06GM08180-12 0009
PRYOR, WILLIAM A R01HL25820-10
PRYOR, WILLIAM AUSTIN R37HL16029-17
PRYSTOWSKY, JANET H K08AR01838-01A1
PRYSTOWSKY, MICHAEL B P30CA16520-16 9012
PRYSTOWSKY, MICHAEL B R01CA48648-07
PRYSTOWSKY, MICHAEL B R01GM41226-03
PRYSTOWSKY, MICHAEL B R01HL42090-04
PRYWES, RON M R01CA50329-03
PRYWES, RONALD S07RR07060-26 0448
PRYZWANSKY, KATHERIN S07RR05406-30 0900
PSATY, BRUCE S07RR05714-21 0125
PSATY, BRUCE M R01HL43201-01A2
PSATY, BRUCE M R29HL40628-04
PTACEK, LOUIS J K11HD00940-01
PTASHNE, MARK S R01GM29109-11
PTASHNE, MARK S R01GM32308-09
PTASHNE, MARK S R37GM22526-15
PUBLICOVER, NELSON P01DK41315-03 0006
PUBLICOVER, NELSON P01DK41315-03 9002
PUBLICOVER, NELSON G R01DK32176-09
PUBLICOVER, NELSON G R01DK40162-04
PUBOLS, BENJAMIN H, JR R01NS19486-09

PUCK, JENNIFER M R01HD23679-04
PUCK, JENNIFER M R01HG00233-01
PUCKETT, CARMIE K08NS01163-05
PUENTES, STEPHEN S07RR05551-29 0944
PUETT, J DAVID R01DK33973-08A1
PUGH, EDWARD N, JR R01EY02660-13
PUGH, EDWARD N, JR R01EY08206-03
PUGH, JACQUELINE M01RR01346-10 0149
PUGH, JACQUELINE A R01DK38392-04
PUGH, REGINALD P U10CA35117-08
PUGH, STEPHEN R S07RR07043-26 0131
PUHL, SUSAN M S07RR07082-26 0304
PUHVEL, S MADLI R01ES03597-07
PUI, CHING-HON U10CA31566-10 0022
PUI, CHING-HON U10CA31566-10 0002
PUI, CHING-HON U10CA31566-10 0003
PUI, CHING-HON U10CA31566-10 0004
PUI, CHING-HON U10CA31566-10 0005
PUI, CHING-HON U10CA31566-10 0006
PUI, CHING-HON U10CA31566-10 0007
PUI, CHING-HON U10CA31566-10 0008
PUI, CHING-HON U10CA31566-10 0009
PUI, CHING-HON U10CA31566-10 0010
PUI, CHING-HON U10CA31566-10 0011
PUI, CHING-HON U10CA31566-10 0012
PUI, CHING-HON U10CA31566-10 0013
PUI, CHING-HON U10CA31566-10 0014
PUI, CHING-HON U10CA31566-10 0015
PUI, CHING-HON U10CA31566-10 0016
PUI, CHING-HON U10CA31566-10 0017
PUI, CHING-HON U10CA31566-10 0018
PUI, CHING-HON U10CA31566-10 0019
PUI, CHING-HON U10CA31566-10 0023
PUI, CHING-HON U10CA31566-10 0024
PUI, CHING-HON U10CA31566-10 0025
PUI, CHING-HON U10CA31566-10 0026
PUI, CHING-HON U10CA31566-10 0027
PUI, CHING-HON U10CA31566-10 0028
PUI, CHING-HON U10CA31566-10 0029
PUI, CHING-HON U10CA31566-10 0030
PUI, CHING-HON U10CA31566-10 0031
PUI, CHING-HON U10CA31566-10 0032
PUI, CHING-HON U10CA31566-10 0033
PUI, CHING-HON U10CA31566-10 0034
PUI, CHING-HON U10CA31566-10 0035
PUI, CHING-HON U10CA31566-10 0036
PUI, CHING-HON U10CA31566-10 0037
PUI, CHING-HON U10CA31566-10 0038
PUI, CHING-HON U10CA31566-10 0039
PUI, CHING-HON U10CA31566-10 0040
PUI, CHING-HON U10CA31566-10 0041
PUI, CHING-HON U10CA31566-10 0020
PUI, CHING-HON U10CA31566-10 0042
PUI, CHING-HON U10CA31566-10 0043
PUI, CHING-HON U10CA31566-10 0044
PUI, CHING-HON U10CA31566-10 0045
PUI, CHING-HON U10CA31566-10 0046
PUI, CHING-HON U10CA31566-10 0047
PUI, CHING-HON U10CA31566-10 0048
PUI, CHING-HON U10CA31566-10 0049
PUI, CHING-HON U10CA31566-10 0050
PUI, CHING-HON U10CA31566-10 0051
PUI, CHING-HON U10CA31566-10 0052
PUI, CHING-HON U10CA31566-10 0053
PUI, CHING-HON U10CA31566-10 0054
PUI, CHING-HON U10CA31566-10 0055
PUI, CHING-HON U10CA31566-10 0056
PUI, CHING-HON U10CA31566-10 0057
PUI, CHING-HON U10CA31566-10 0058
PUI, CHING-HON U10CA31566-10 0059
PUI, CHING-HON U10CA31566-10 0060
PUI, CHING-HON U10CA31566-10 0021
PUI, CHING-HON U10CA31566-10
PUI, CHING-HON U10CA31566-10 0001
PUIZ, JAIME S06GM08239-06 0008
PULIAFITO, CARMEN A U10EY08587-02
PULLARKAT, RAJU K S07RR05838-12 0268
PULLEN, D JEANETTE U10CA15989-17
PULLEN, D JEANETTE U10CA15989-17 0012
PULLEN, D JEANETTE U10CA15989-17 0013
PULLEN, D JEANETTE U10CA15989-17 0001
PULLEN, D JEANETTE U10CA15989-17 0002
PULLEN, D JEANETTE U10CA15989-17 0003
PULLEN, D JEANETTE U10CA15989-17 0004
PULLEN, D JEANETTE U10CA15989-17 0005
PULLEN, D JEANETTE U10CA15989-17 0006
PULLEN, D JEANETTE U10CA15989-17 0007
PULLEN, D JEANETTE U10CA15989-17 0014
PULLEN, D JEANETTE U10CA15989-17 0015
PULLEN, D JEANETTE U10CA15989-17 0016
PULLEN, D JEANETTE U10CA15989-17 0017
PULLEN, D JEANETTE U10CA15989-17 0018
PULLEN, D JEANETTE U10CA15989-17 0019
PULLEN, D JEANETTE U10CA15989-17 0020
PULLEN, D JEANETTE U10CA15989-17 0021
PULLEN, D JEANETTE U10CA15989-17 0022
PULLEN, D JEANETTE U10CA15989-17 0023
PULLEN, D JEANETTE U10CA15989-17 0024
PULLEN, D JEANETTE U10CA15989-17 0025
PULLEN, D JEANETTE U10CA15989-17 0008
PULLEN, D JEANETTE U10CA15989-17 0009
PULLEN, D JEANETTE U10CA15989-17 0010

PULLEN, D JEANETTE U10CA15989-17 0011
PULLEN, D JEANETTE U10CA15989-17 0026
PULLEN, D JEANETTE U10CA15989-17 0027
PULLEN, D JEANETTE U10CA15989-17 0028
PULLEN, D JEANETTE U10CA15989-17 0029
PULLEN, D JEANETTE U10CA15989-17 0030
PULLEN, D JEANETTE U10CA15989-17 0031
PULLEN, D JEANETTE U10CA15989-17 0032
PULLEN, D JEANETTE U10CA15989-17 0052
PULLEN, D JEANETTE U10CA15989-17 0053
PULLEN, D JEANETTE U10CA15989-17 0054
PULLEN, D JEANETTE U10CA15989-17 0055
PULLEN, D JEANETTE U10CA15989-17 0056
PULLEN, D JEANETTE U10CA15989-17 0057
PULLEN, D JEANETTE U10CA15989-17 0058
PULLEN, D JEANETTE U10CA15989-17 0059
PULLEN, D JEANETTE U10CA15989-17 0060
PULLEN, D JEANETTE U10CA15989-17 0033
PULLEN, D JEANETTE U10CA15989-17 0034
PULLEN, D JEANETTE U10CA15989-17 0035
PULLEN, D JEANETTE U10CA15989-17 0036
PULLEN, D JEANETTE U10CA15989-17 0037
PULLEN, D JEANETTE U10CA15989-17 0038
PULLEN, D JEANETTE U10CA15989-17 0039
PULLEN, D JEANETTE U10CA15989-17 0040
PULLEN, D JEANETTE U10CA15989-17 0041
PULLEN, D JEANETTE U10CA15989-17 0042
PULLEN, D JEANETTE U10CA15989-17 0043
PULLEN, D JEANETTE U10CA15989-17 0044
PULLEN, D JEANETTE U10CA15989-17 0045
PULLEN, D JEANETTE U10CA15989-17 0046
PULLEN, D JEANETTE U10CA15989-17 0047
PULLEN, D JEANETTE U10CA15989-17 0048
PULLEN, D JEANETTE U10CA15989-17 0049
PULLEN, D JEANETTE U10CA15989-17 0050
PULLEN, D JEANETTE U10CA15989-17 0051
PULLMAN, JAMES M S07RR05712-20 0109
PULLMAN, THOMAS W P30HD06160-20S1 0005
PULSINELLI, WILLIAM P01NS03346-31
PULSINELLI, WILLIAM P01NS03346-31 0042
PULSINELLI, WILLIAM A P01NS03346-31 0044
PULST, STEFAN M K08NS01428-02
PULVER, ANN E R01MH45588-03
PUMFORD, N R Z01HL00962-09
PUMO, DOROTHY E R01GM42563-03
PUMPLIN, DAVID W R01NS15513-11
PUNCH, JERRY L R03DC01045-01
PUNNETT, LAURA R01OH02741-02
PUPPIONE, DONALD L P01HL28481-09 9004
PURCELL, R H Z01AI00311-11
PURDON, D Z01AG00134-08
PURDY, JAMES A N01CM97564-03
PURE, ELLEN R01AI25185-05
PURI, J Z01BH02005-02
PURI, J Z01BH02007-02
PURI, R Z01BD02002-03
PURI, R Z01BD02003-03
PURI, R Z01BD02004-03
PURI, R Z01BD02012-01
PURI, RAJINDER N S07RR05417-30 0811
PURICH, DANIEL L R01GM44823-01A1
PURO, DONALD G R29EY06931-06
PUROHIT, SARLA P01AI29512-02 0004
PURPURA, DOMINICK P S07RR05397-30
PURPURA, DOMINICK P S15GM47060-01
PURPURA, DOMINICK P S15MH49294-01
PURTLE, RONALD R19MH46225-03
PURVES, DALE R01NS29187-01
PUSZKIN, SAUL R01NS12467-16
PUSZKIN, SAUL R01NS26113-04
PUTKEY, JOHN A K04AR01831-02
PUTKEY, JOHN A R01AR39218-04
PUTMAN, DONALD N01ES95252-04
PUTNAM, CHARLES W R01DK42279-01A2
PUTNAM, DAVID L R43GM46161-01
PUTNAM, F Z01MH02366-05
PUTNAM, F W Z01MH02365-05
PUTNAM, F W Z01MH02367-05
PUTNAM, F W Z01MH02368-05
PUTNAM, FRANK W R01DK19221-16
PUTNAM, ROBERT W R29AR38881-04
PUTNAM, ROBERT W S15AR41238-01
PUTNEY, J W Z01ES80042-05
PUTNEY, SCOTT D R01AI29825-02
PUTNEY, SCOTT D. U01AI28243-03 0004
PUTTEN, THEODORE VAN P50MH30911-14 0032
PYERITZ, REED E M01RR00722-19 0152
PYERITZ, REED E R01HL35877-06
PYTELA, ROBERT R01CA53250-01
P15606271 U01AI25902-05 0001
Quadri, Syed P01CA43791-04A1 9001
QASBA, P K Z01CB08386-05
QASBA, P K Z01CB08389-04
QAVI, HAMIDA B R01EY08082-03
QIAN, Y Z01AI00534-04
QUADE, DANA P50MH33127-13 9005
QUADRI, SYED M R01CA51161-01A2
QUAID, KIMBERLY A P50AG05146-09 0017
QUANDT, SARA A R01AG07999-03
QUARANTA, VITO R01CA47858-04
QUARLES, DARRYL L R01AR37308-04A2
QUARLES, R H Z01NS01808-22

QUARLES, R H Z01NS02786-03
QUARLES, R H Z01NS02805-02
QUARLESS, SHELLY A S07RR05425-30 0764
QUARONI, ANDREA R01DK32656-09
QUAST, MICHAEL J S07RR05427-30 0159
QUATE, CALVIN F S07RR07005-26 0342
QUATRANO, RALPH S R01GM44288-01A1
QUAYHAGEN, MARY P R01NR01931-03
QUE HEE, SHANE S07RR05442-29 0044
QUE, LAWRENCE P41RR02583-07 0013
QUE, LAWRENCE S07RR07052-26 0166
QUE, LAWRENCE, JR R01GM38767-04A1
QUE, LAWRENCE, JR R01GM43315-01
QUEBBEMAN, EDWARD J M01RR00058-30 0263
QUEENER, SHERRY N01AI87240-09
QUENCER, ROBERT M P01NS28059-01A1 0002
QUENZER, ROANDL W S07RR05583-27 0637
QUERTERMOUS, THOMAS R01HL46994-01
QUESENBERRY, PETER P01DK40031-03 0001
QUESENBERRY, PETER P01DK40031-03 9001
QUESENBERRY, PETER J P01DK40031-03
QUESENBERRY, PETER J R01AI23869-05
QUESENBERRY, PETER J R01CA27466-13
QUESENBERRY, PETER J R01DK27424-12
QUEST INTERNATIONAL N01MH90008-00
QUEVEDO, WALTER C, J S07RR07085-26 0343
QUICK, DONALD C S07RR05322-30 0271
QUIGG, RICHARD J, JR R29DK41873-03
QUIGLEY, GARY JOSEPH R01GM41359-03
QUIGLEY, HARRY A R01EY02120-15
QUIGLEY, HARRY A R13EY02143-15
QUIGLEY, JAMES P R01CA16740-16
QUILL, HELEN R R29AI28186-04
QUILL, HELEN R S07RR07083-26 0478
QUILLEY, JOHN P01HL34300-07 0003
QUILLIGAN, EDWARD J S07RR05351-30 0029
QUINLAN, DONALD P50MH30929-15 9007
QUINLAN, JOHN G S07RR05408-30 0937
QUINLAN, MARGARET P R01CA50540-02
QUINN, DANIEL M R01NS21334-08
QUINN, F R Z01CM07183-05
QUINN, GRAHAM E U10EY06363-07
QUINN, JAMES S07RR05704-20 0014
QUINN, JOHN A R01HL38680-03
QUINN, MICHAEL R S07RR05838-12 0267
QUINN, PATRICK G R01DK43871-01
QUINN, STEPHEN J R01HL42354-02
QUINN, T C Z01AI00358-10
QUINN, T C Z01AI00361-09
QUINN, THOMAS H S07RR05390-30 0680
QUINONES, SUSAN R R29DK42514-02
QUINT, LESLIE E U01CA45205-04S1
QUINTANS, JOSE P01CA19266-14A1 0022
QUINTILES, INC N01DA19400-00
QUINTON, PAUL M R01DK41329-03
QUIOCHO, FLORANTE A R01GM21371-17
QUISSELL, DAVID O R01DE07201-05
QUISSELL, DAVID O R01DK33835-08
QUIST, EUGENE E R01HL35433-03
QUITKIN, FREDERIC M R01AA08030-03
QUITKIN, FREDERIC M R18DA06140-03
QUITTNER, ALEXANDRA L R29HL47064-01
QUIVEY, ROBERT P50DE07003-08 0003
QUIVEY, ROBERT G, JR R01DE07777-04
QUOCK, RAYMOND S07RR05369-30 0588
QUOCK, RAYMOND M R01DE06894-04A4
QUYYUMI, A A Z01HL04864-01
QUYYUMI, A A Z01HL04865-01
QUYYUMI, A A Z01HL04866-01
QUYYUMI, A A Z01HL04867-01
QUYYUMI, A A Z01HL04868-01
QWARNSTROM, EVA E R29DE08172-04
RAAB- TRAUB, NANCY P01CA19014-14 0021
RAAB-TRAUB, NANCY R01CA32979-07
RAAB-TRAUB, NANCY J R01CA52406-02
RAABE, OTTO G R01CA46296-04
RAAM, SHANTHI R01CA37944-06
RAAPHORST, G PETER R01CA54184-01
RABADJIJA, LUKA S07RR05318-30 0252
RABANUS, JORG-PETER S07RR05305-30 0727
RABBANI, LEROY E K11HL02578-01
RABE, C S Z01AA00706-03
RABEN, DANIEL M R01HL39086-03
RABENSTEIN, DALLAS L R01GM37000-06
RABIN, BRUCE S R01MH43411-05
RABIN, LINDA R43AI30301-01A1
RABIN, RICHARD A R01AA06207-06
RABINOVITCH, PETER P01DK32971-08 9003
RABINOVITCH, PETER S P01AG01751-13 0003
RABINOVITCH, PETER S P01AG01751-13 9003
RABINOVITZ, M Z01CM07189-01
RABINOWE, STEVEN M01RR02635-07 0191
RABINOWE, STEVEN L R01AI30987-02
RABINOWITZ, JESSE C R01DK02109-34
RABINOWITZ, WILLIAM M P01DC00361-05S1 0001
RABINS, PETER V R01MH40843-04
RABKIN, JUDITH G R01MH45652-03
RABKIN, MITCHELL T M01RR01032-16
RABKIN, MITCHELL T S07RR05479-29
RABKIN, MITCHELL T S15AI32203-01
RABKIN, RALPH R01DK32342-08
RABON, EDD C R01DK34286-08
RABSON, ARNOLD B R01AI30901-01
RABSON, ARNOLD B R01CA55487-01
RABY, KHETHER E K08HL02553-01A1
RACANIELLO, VINCENT R P01GM38125-04 0002
RACANIELLO, VINCENT R R01AI20017-09
RACE, R E Z01AI00265-10
RACEVSKIS, JANIS P01CA16599-17 0021
RACHAL, J VALLEY R18DA07262-02
RACHLIN, HOWARD R01MH44049-03
RACHLIN, JOSEPH S06GM08225-07 0011
RACKER, EFRAIM R01CA08964-24A1
RACKER, EFRAIM S07RR07061-26 0190
RACUSEN, LORRAINE C S07RR05378-30 0010
RACZYNSKI, JAMES M R01HL43041-02
RADANY, ERIC H K08CA01590-01
RADDA, GEORGE P01HL18708-16 0020
RADDING, CHARLES M R01GM33504-08
RADDING, CHARLES M R01HG00338-03
RADER, D J Z01HL02038-01
RADER, D J Z01HL02039-01
RADER, D J Z01HL02040-01
RADER, DANIEL Z01HL02019-13
RADHAKRISHNAMURTHY, B R01HL38844-05 0014
RADICH, JERALD P K08CA01612-01
RADKE-YARROW, M Z01MH02361-05
RADKE-YARROW, M Z01MH02370-05
RADKE-YARROW, M Z01MH02372-05
RADKE-YARROW, M Z01MH02381-05
RADKE-YARROW, M Z01MH02491-02
RADKE-YARROW, M Z01MH02560-01
RADKE, KATHRYN R55CA46374-04
RADOLF, JUSTIN D R29AI26756-04
RADOSEVICH, JAMES A S07RR05370-30 0613
RADTKE, RICHARD L. S06GM08125-18 0053
RADTKE, RICHARD L. S06GM08125-18 0053
RADWIN, ROBERT G K01OH00107-01
RAE, JAMES L R01EY06005-07
RAE, JAMES L R37EY03282-13
RAEL, EPPI D S06GM08012-21 0012
RAEL, EPPIE D S06GM08012-21
RAESE, JOACHIM P50AG08013-04 0003
RAFAL, ROBERT D R01MH41544-04
RAFERTY, MICHAEL P01DA05695-03 0007
RAFF, ELIZABETH C R01HD16739-09A1
RAFF, HERSHEL R01DK43577-02
RAFF, HERSHEL R01HL39103-05A1
RAFF, RUDOLF A R01HD21337-06
RAFFELD, M Z01CB09182-03
RAFFELD, M Z01CB09191-02
RAFFERTY, NANCY S R01EY00698-21
RAFFIN, THOMAS A R01HL45533-01
RAFLA, SAMEER U10CA57137-01
RAFOLS, JOSE S06GM08167-13 0044
RAFTERY, MICHAEL A R01NS10294-20
RAGAB, ABDELSALAM H U10CA20549-15
RAGAN, HARVEY A N01ES55073-15
RAGAN, HARVEY A N01ES55105-42
RAGHAVAN, SRINI S07RR07002-26 0885
RAGHOW, R P50AR39166-05 0008
RAGHU, GANESH R01HL39854-05
RAGLIN, JOHN S S07RR07031-26 0102
RAGNI, MARGARET V R01CA50849-03
RAGSDALE, STEPHEN W R01GM39451-05
RAGSDALE, STEPHEN W S07RR07181-13 0537
RAHAV, MICHAEL R18DA06968-02
RAHEMTULLA, BRITTA S07RR05300-30 0203
RAHEMTULLA, BRITTA S07RR05300-30 0212
RAHEMTULLA, FIROZ S07RR05300-30 0211
RAHMANI, MUNIR A S06GM08119-18
RAHMANI, MUNIR A. S06GM08119-18 0012
RAHWAN, RALF S07RR05607-25 0700
RAI, KANTI R U10CA11028-24
RAI, KARAMJIT S R01AI21443-08
RAIBLE, DONALD S07RR05413-30 0984
RAICH, PETER N01CO03863-06
RAICHLE, MARCUS M01RR00036-31 1023
RAICHLE, MARCUS E P01AG03991-08 0003
RAICHLE, MARCUS E P01HL13851-29 0004
RAICHLE, MARCUS E P01NS06833-25
RAICHLE, MARCUS E P01NS06833-25 9002
RAICHLE, MARCUS E P41RR01380-10 0009
RAICHLE, MARCUS E R01AG08377-03
RAIJMAN, LUISA J R01GM44638-01A1
RAIKHEL, ALEXANDER S R01AI24716-05A1
RAIKHEL, ALEXANDER S R01AI32154-05
RAINE, ADRIAN R01MH46435-01A1
RAINE, ADRIAN S07RR07012-25 0020
RAINE, CEDRIC S P50NS11920-17 0006
RAINE, CEDRIC S R01NS08952-23
RAINES, RONALD T R01GM44783-02
RAINEY, PETRIE M R01AI27382-03
RAINWATER, DAVID L P01HL45522-01A1 0005
RAINWATER, DAVID L R29HL40637-04
RAINWATER, LEE P P01AG07669-03
RAINWATER, LEE P. P01AG07669-03 0001
RAINWATER, LEE P. P01AG07669-03 0003
RAINWATER, LEE P. P01AG07669-03 9001
RAISZ, LAWRENCE G P01AR38933-05 9001
RAISZ, LAWRENCE G P01AR38933-05
RAISZ, LAWRENCE G P01AR38933-05 0001
RAISZ, LAWRENCE G R01AR18063-17A2
RAITI, SALVATORE N01HD02919-01
RAIZADA, M S07RR05362-30 0787
RAIZADA, M S07RR05362-30 0801
RAIZADA, MOHAN K R01HL33610-06
RAIZMAN, MICHAEL B K11EY00296-04
RAIZNER, ALBERT E M01RR00350-25 0422
RAIZNER, ALBERT E M01RR00350-25 0355
RAJ, J USHA R01HL38438-04
RAJ, J USHA S07RR05551-29 0960
RAJ, N BABU S07RR05378-30 0011
RAJA, SRINIVASA N R01NS26363-03
RAJAGOPALAN, K V R01GM00091-46
RAJAGOPALAN, K V R01GM44283-02
RAJALAKSHMI, S R01CA45361-05
RAJAN, ARUN S07RR05425-30 0765
RAJAN, THIRUCHANDURAI V P01AI10702-20 0001
RAJAN, THIRUCHANDURAI V R22AI30046-02
RAJANNA, BETTAIYA S06GM08169-13
RAJANNA, BETTAIYA S06GM08169-13 0002
RAJAVASHISTH, TRIPAT S07RR05551-29 0955
RAJBHANDARY, UTTAM L R01GM17151-22
RAKELA, J M01RR00585-20 0309
RAKFAL, SUSAN M S07RR05812-12 0489
RAKIC, PASKO T P01NS22807-07
RAKIC, PASKO T P01NS22807-07 0001
RAKIC, PASKO T P01NS22807-07 9001
RAKIC, PASKO T R01NS14841-14
RAKIC, PASKO T R13HD28647-01
RAKOWSKI, ROBERT F R01NS22979-07
RAKOWSKI, WILLIAM P01CA50087-03 0004
RALEIGH, JAMES A R01CA50995-02
RALL, STANLEY C. P01HL41633-03 0001
RALL, STANLEY C. P01HL41633-03 9002
RALL, W Z01DK13001-18
RALLISON, MARVIN L M01RR00064-27 0324
RALLISON, MARVIN L M01RR00064-27 0016
RALLISON, MARVIN L M01RR00064-27 0379
RALPH, RUTH O R18MH46059-03
RALSTON, E Z01NS02835-02
RALSTON, HENRY P50DE08973-02 0001
RALSTON, HENRY J P01NS21445-07 0004
RALSTON, HENRY J P01NS21445-07 9001
RALSTON, HENRY J, III R01NS23347-18
RAM, C VENKATA M01RR00633-19 0416
RAMABHADRAN, T P01AG10491-01 9001
RAMACHANDRAN, JANAKIRAMAN R44DA05984-02
RAMACHANDRAN, JANAKIRAMAN R43NS29300-01
RAMAKRISHNAN, SUNDARAM R01CA48068-04
RAMAKRISHNAN, VENKATRAMAN R R01GM42796-03
RAMAMURTHY, N S S07RR05778-16 0405
RAMAN, RAMAS V R43AR40787-01
RAMANATHAN, JAYASHREE R44HL42208-03
RAMASWAMY, KRISHNAMURTHY R01DK33349-08
RAMEY, CRAIG P30HD03110-24 9005
RAMIG, LORRAINE O P60DC00976-02 0007
RAMIG, LORRAINE O R01DC01150-02
RAMIG, ROBERT F R22AI16687-12
RAMIG, ROBERT F R22AI21494-08
RAMIREZ-RONDA, CARLOS H S06GM08102-20 0022
RAMIREZ, BERNADETTE P50AI30601-01 0002
RAMIREZ, CARLOS A S06GM08103-18 0011
RAMIREZ, E FRED S07RR07013-26 0960
RAMIREZ, FRANCESCO P01HD22657-05 0002
RAMIREZ, FRANCESCO R01AR38648-06
RAMIREZ, FRANCESCO R01GM41849-02
RAMIREZ, FRANCESCO R01HL41104-05
RAMIREZ, FRANCESCO B R13AR40887-01
RAMIREZ, ISRAEL R01DC01107-01
RAMIREZ, LUIS C M01RR00633-19 0414
RAMIREZ, MARIA E R29DK38702-04
RAMIREZ, VICTOR D R55HD14625-10A1
RAMIREZ, VICTOR D S07RR07030-26 0405
RAMON, FIDEL R01NS26127-03
RAMOS, DANIEL M K15DE00242-04
RAMOS, KENNETH S R01ES04849-05
RAMOS, KENNETH S S07RR05854-11 0921
RAMOS, R Z01BE01003-03
RAMPINO, N J Z01HD01413-01
RAMSAY, NORMA K. C. P01CA21737-14 0003
RAMSAY, DAVID J R01HL41156-03
RAMSAY, DAVID J S03RR03017-07
RAMSAY, DOUGLAS S R29DA07391-01
RAMSAY, RONA R P01HL16251-18 0015
RAMSAY, RONA R R01DK41572-03
RAMSDELL, JOE S07RR05665-24 0892
RAMSDELL, JOE W M01RR00827-17 0458
RAMSDELL, JOHN S R29DK43107-02
RAMSEY-GOLDMAN, ROSALIND R29AR41607-01
RAMSEY, PAUL G R01HS06454-02
RAMSINGH, ARLENE S07RR05649-25 0795
RAMWELL, PETER W. P01HL40069-04 0003
RAMWELL, PETER W P01HL40069-04
RAMWELL, PETER W R01HL36802-05
RANCE, MARK A R01GM40089-04
RANCE, NAOMI E P50AG05146-09 0014
RANCE, NAOMI E R29AG09214-01A1
RANCK, JAMES B, JR R01NS14497-13
RAND, JACOB H R01HL32200-06
RAND, JAMES B R01GM38679-05
RAND, LAWRENCE L P30DK36836-05 9006
RAND, LAWRENCE L P30DK36836-05 9007
RAND, LAWRENCE L P30DK36836-05 9008
RAND, WILLIAM P01AI26698-03S1 9004

RANDALL, BARBARA S07RR07192-12 0616
RANDALL, CARRIE L U10AA08428-03
RANDALL, LINDA L R01GM29798-11
RANDALL, OTELIO S K07HL02269-02
RANDALL, PATRICK K R01DA06201-01A1
RANDALL, PATRICK K R01MH44799-03
RANDALL, WALTER C R01HL27595-10
RANDALL, WILLIAM R R29NS26885-03
RANDERATH, K P42ES04917-03 0005
RANDERATH, KURT R01AG07750-04
RANDERATH, KURT R37CA32157-10
RANDICH, ALAN R01NS22966-06
RANDLE, MICHEL R19DA06412-03
RANDO, R F Z01DE00534-01
RANDO, ROBERT R R01EY03624-11
RANDO, ROBERT R R01HL34346-06
RANDO, ROBERT R R37EY04096-10
RANELLI, PAUL L S07RR05573-13 0083
RANGAN, S R S P51RR00164-30 0020
RANGAN, S R S P51RR00164-30 0027
RANGAN, S R S P51RR00164-30 0018
RANGE, NAOMI E S07RR05675-23 0917
RANGNEKAR, VIVEK M R29CA52837-01A1
RANK, ROGER G R01AI23044-06
RANK, ROGER G R01AR39726-03
RANKIN, GARY O R01ES04954-02
RANKIN, GARY O S03RR03338-09
RANKIN, GARY O S07RR05870-10
RANKIN, GARY O S15ES05847-01
RANKIN, J SCOTT P50HL17670-17 0030
RANKIN, J SCOTT R01HL29436-09
RANKIN, JOCELYN A G07LM05377-01
RANKIN, JOHN A M01RR00125-28 0747
RANKIN, SALLY S07RR05604-14 0681
RANNELS, D EUGENE, JR R01HL20344-15
RANNELS, D EUGENE, JR R01HL31560-09
RANNELS, STEPHEN R R01HL42482-03
RANSCHT, BARBARA P01HD25938-02 0002
RANSCHT, BARBEL R29NS25194-05
RANSEEN, JOHN D S07RR05374-30 0736
RANSOHOFF, JOSEPH P20NS30309-01
RANSOHOFF, RICHARD M K08NS01265-05
RANSOM, BRUCE R R01NS15589-13
RANSOM, JANET N01CM87236-09
RANSOM, JANET H N01CM17505-01
RANSOM, JANET H. N01HI79500-09
RANU, RAJINDER S07RR07127-23 0486
RANZ, JULES R01MH46698-01A2
RAO, A KONETI M01RR00349-25 0223
RAO, A VIJAYA N01AI42532-14
RAO, ANJANA R01AI22900-06
RAO, ANJANA R01CA42471-06
RAO, ANJANA R01GM46227-01
RAO, B D NAGESWARA R01GM43966-03
RAO, CH V R01HD25510-02
RAO, CH V R01HD26173-03
RAO, DABEERU C R01GM28719-12
RAO, DAMANNA R S06GM08250-04 0005
RAO, G N Z01ES21141-02
RAO, GOVIND R01RR06562-01
RAO, IRUVANTI M S07RR05365-30 0097
RAO, KAVITHA S07RR05755-18 0226
RAO, NARSING A R01EY05662-07
RAO, NARSING A R01EY09088-01
RAO, P SYAMASUNDAR M01RR03186-06 0054
RAO, PEMMARAJU N N01HD13137-00
RAO, POTU N S07RR05511-29 0488
RAO, R HARSHA S07RR05592-21 0124
RAO, RAMACHANDRA S07RR05780-16 0975
RAO, RAYASAM H R29HL46348-01
RAO, SEKHARA B K14HL01986-05
RAO, SEKHARA B S14GM44780-02 0002
RAO, STEPHEN M01RR00058-30 0229
RAO, STEPHEN M K04NS01055-05
RAO, STEPHEN M R01NS22128-06
RAO, VELIDI R01AR40046-01A1
RAPACZ, JAN R01HL44900-01A1
RAPAPORT, HENRY P41RR01237-09 9004
RAPAPORT, SAMUEL I R37HL27234-11
RAPER, CHARLENE A S07RR07125-22 0397
RAPER, STEVEN E R29DK42485-02
RAPHAEL, KAREN P50MH43878-03 0042
RAPHAN, THEODORE R01EY04148-09
RAPIN, ISABELLE P50NS20489-07
RAPIN, ISABELLE P50NS20489-07 0001
RAPIN, ISABELLE P50NS20489-07 9003
RAPKIN, ANDREA M01RR00865-18 0348
RAPKIN, BRUCE D R01HS06415-01A1
RAPOPORT, BASIL R01DK19289-16
RAPOPORT, BASIL R01DK36182-07
RAPOPORT, BASIL R01EY09498-01
RAPOPORT, DAVID M01RR00096-30A1 0189
RAPOPORT, DAVID M01RR00096-30A1 0296
RAPOPORT, HENRY P41RR01237-09 0005
RAPOPORT, HENRY P41RR01237-09 0006
RAPOPORT, HENRY P41RR01237-09 0007
RAPOPORT, HENRY R01GM28994-10
RAPOPORT, J L Z01MH00153-14
RAPOPORT, J L Z01MH02240-07
RAPOPORT, J L Z01MH02581-01
RAPOPORT, S Z01AG00406-01
RAPOZA, PETER S07RR05435-30 0980
RAPP, FRED P01CA27503-12 0001
RAPP, FRED P01CA27503-12 9001
RAPP, JOHN P R01HL20176-15
RAPP, JOHN P R01HL45341-02
RAPP, JOSEPH H R29HL41470-04
RAPP, LAURENCE M R01EY04554-08
RAPP, PAUL E R01NS19716-07
RAPP, PETER R P01AG09973-01 0001
RAPP, U Z01CP05684-01
RAPP, U Z01CP05685-01
RAPP, U Z01CP05686-01
RAPP, U Z01CP05687-01
RAPP, U R Z01CP05417-07
RAPP, U R Z01CP05531-05
RAPP, U R Z01CP05582-04
RAPP, U R Z01CP05655-02
RAPP, U R Z01CP05656-02
RAPPAPORT, CAREY M S07RR07143-20 0631
RAPPAPORT, ERIC F S07RR05506-29 0912
RAPPAPORT, JAY F R29AI31823-01
RAPPAPORT, MAURICE S07RR05755-18 0222
RAPPAPORT, STEPHEN M R01OH02221-04
RAPPAPORT, VALERIE S07RR05468-29 0397
RAPPE, ANTHONY S07RR07127-23 0484
RAPPEPORT, JOEL M M01RR06022-02 0768
RAPPEPORT, JOEL M M01RR06022-02 0738
RAPRAEGER, ALAN C R01HD21881-07
RAPS, SHIRLEY S07RR07109-23 0509
RAPS, SHIRLEY S07RR07109-23
RAPUANO, BRUCE EDWARD R29AR40253-02
RAREY, KYLE E R01DC00716-02
RAREY, KYLE E R55DC00426-04A1
RASCH, RANDOLPH F R S07RR06013-03 0827
RASCHKE, WILLIAM C R01GM32017-08
RASE Z10CL00007-
RASENICK, MARK M K02MH00699-05
RASENICK, MARK M R01MH39595-07A1
RASEY, JANET S P01CA42045-06 0006
RASEY, JANET S R01CA36485-08
RASEY, JANET S R37CA34570-09
RASEY, JANET S S07RR05432-30 0229
RASGADO-FLORES, HECTOR F R29AR39522-05
RASH, JOHN E R01GM39503-03
RASH, JOHN E S15NS30114-01
RASKA, KAREL U01AI25914-04S2 9002
RASKIN, PHILIP M01RR00633-19 0319
RASKIN, PHILIP M01RR00633-19 0103
RASKIN, PHILIP M01RR00633-19 0284
RASKIN, PHILIP M01RR00633-19 0254
RASKIN, PHILIP M01RR00633-19 0306
RASKIN, PHILIP U01DK30611-09
RASKIND, MURRAY P50AG05136-08 0006
RASKIND, MURRAY A R01AG08419-03
RASKIND, MURRY P50AG05136-08 9002
RASKIND, WENDY P01DK32971-08 9005
RASMINSKY, MICHAEL R13NS20032-09
RASMUSSEN, DENNIS D P50HD12303-13 0005
RASMUSSEN, HOWARD R37DK19813-16
RASMUSSEN, HOWARD MD PHD R01HL35849-06
RASMUSSEN, RONALD E R01HL44523-02
RASO, VICTOR S07RR05711-21 0040
RASO, VICTOR A R01CA49254-03
RASO, VICTOR A R01CA49856-02
RASOOL, N Z01AI00576-02
RASPA, ROBERT F S07RR05983-05 0361
RAST, JAMES P01HD26927-01A1 0003
RATAIN, MARK J N01CM07301-03
RATCLIFF, GRAHAM G R01MH46643-02
RATCLIFF, ROGER K02MH00871-02
RATCLIFF, ROGER R01MH44640-03
RATCLIFF, ROGER S15MH49300-01
RATCLIFFE, ANTHONY R01AR40032-03
RATECH, HOWARD K08CA01501-03
RATHBUN, WILLIAM B R01EY01197-18
RATHBUN, WILLIAM B. P51RR00166-30 0150
RATHOD, PRADIPSINH K R29AI26912-03
RATLIFF, TIMOTHY L R01CA37926-08
RATLIFF, TIMOTHY L R55CA44426-04
RATNASINGHE, DUMINDA S07RR05959-06 0019
RATNER, BUDDY D P41RR01296-08
RATNER, BUDDY D P41RR01296-08 9001
RATNER, BUDDY D P41RR01296-08 9002
RATNER, BUDDY D P41RR01296-08 9003
RATNER, BUDDY D P41RR01296-08 9004
RATNER, BUDDY D P41RR01296-08 9005
RATNER, BUDDY D P41RR01296-08 9006
RATNER, BUDDY D R01HL25951-11
RATNER, LEE R01AI24745-05
RATNER, LEE U01AI25903-05
RATNER, LEE U01AI25903-05 0006
RATNER, LEE U01AI25903-05 9004
RATNER, LEE U01AI27302-04 0003
RATNER, NANCY R01NS28840-02
RATNOFF, OSCAR D R01HL01661-40A1
RATTAN, SATISH C R01DK35385-08
RATTAZZI, MARIO C S07RR05924-07
RATTAZZI, MARIO C S15AI32166-01
RATTE, DONNA J R43CE00015-01
RAUCH, HELENE C S06GM08167-13 0046
RAUCY, JUDY L R29AA08139-04
RAUDENBUSH, BRIAN N01CO15699-00
RAUH, VIRGINIA S07RR05449-30 0324
RAUH, VIRGINIA A K04HD00872-03
RAULET, DAVID H R01AI21069-09
RAULET, DAVID H R01AI30171-03
RAULET, DAVID H R01AI31650-01
RAULET, DAVID H S07RR07047-26 0149
RAUM, WILLIAM J P30HD19445-05S1 9002
RAUM, WILLIAM J S07RR05551-29 0951
RAUSCH, H REBECCA P01NS02808-30 0045
RAUSCH, JEFFREY L M01RR00827-17 0491
RAUSCH, JEFFREY L R29MH43388-04
RAUSCH, ROBERT L S07RR05714-21 0119
RAUSCHER, FRANK J P01CA47983-04 0005
RAUSCHER, FRANK J P01CA52009-01A1 0003
RAUSHEL, FRANK M R01DK30343-10
RAUSHEL, FRANK M R01GM33894-07
RAUSHEL, FRANK M R13GM46420-01
RAUSHEL, FRANK M S10RR06299-01
RAVDIN, JONATHAN I R01AI18841-09
RAVDIN, PETER M01RR01346-10 0175
RAVDIN, PETER M R29CA49675-03
RAVECHE', ELIZABETH S R01AI29740-03
RAVEN, PETER B R01HL43202-03
RAVETCH, JEFFREY V R01GM36306-06
RAVETCH, JEFFREY V R01GM39256-04
RAVICH, WILLIAM J M01RR00035-31 0416
RAVIDA, MARK N01CO15661-00
RAVINDRA, RUDRAVAJHA S07RR05365-30 0098
RAVINDRANATH, YADDANAPUDI U10CA29691-11 00
RAVINDRANATH, YADDANAPUDI U10CA29691-11 00
RAVINDRANATH, YADDANAPUDI U10CA29691-11
RAVINDRANATH, YADDANAPUDI U10CA29691-11 00
RAVINDRANATH, YADDANAPUDI U10CA29691-11 00
RAVINDRANATH, YADDANAPUDI U10CA29691-11 00
RAVINDRANATH, YADDANAPUDI U10CA29691-11 00
RAVINDRANATH, YADDANAPUDI U10CA29691-11 00
RAVINDRANATH, YADDANAPUDI U10CA29691-11 00
RAVINDRANATH, YADDANAPUDI U10CA29691-11 00
RAVINDRANATH, YADDANAPUDI U10CA29691-11 00
RAVINDRANATH, YADDANAPUDI U10CA29691-11 00
RAVINDRANATH, YADDANAPUDI U10CA29691-11 00
RAVINDRANATH, YADDANAPUDI U10CA29691-11 00
RAVINDRANATH, YADDANAPUDI U10CA29691-11 00
RAVINDRANATH, YADDANAPUDI U10CA29691-11 00
RAVINDRANATH, YADDANAPUDI U10CA29691-11 00
RAVINDRANATH, YADDANAPUDI U10CA29691-11 00
RAVINDRANATH, YADDANAPUDI U10CA29691-11 00
RAVINDRANATH, YADDANAPUDI U10CA29691-11 00
RAVINDRANATH, YADDANAPUDI U10CA29691-11 00
RAVINDRANATH, YADDANAPUDI U10CA29691-11 00
RAVINDRANATH, YADDANAPUDI U10CA29691-11 00
RAVINDRANATH, YADDANAPUDI U10CA29691-11 00
RAVINDRANATH, YADDANAPUDI U10CA29691-11 00
RAVINDRANATH, YADDANAPUDI U10CA29691-11 00
RAVINDRANATH, YADDANAPUDI U10CA29691-11 00
RAVINDRANATH, YADDANAPUDI U10CA29691-11 00
RAVINDRANATH, YADDANAPUDI U10CA29691-11 00
RAVINDRANATH, YADDANAPUDI U10CA29691-11 00
RAVINDRANATH, YADDANAPUDI U10CA29691-11 00
RAVINDRANATH, YADDANAPUDI U10CA29691-11 00
RAVINDRANATH, YADDANAPUDI U10CA29691-11 00
RAVINDRANATH, YADDANAPUDI U10CA29691-11 00
RAVINDRANATH, YADDANAPUDI U10CA29691-11 00
RAVINDRANATH, YADDANAPUDI U10CA29691-11 00
RAVINDRANATH, YADDANAPUDI U10CA29691-11 00
RAVINDRANATH, YADDANAPUDI U10CA29691-11 00
RAVINDRANATH, YADDANAPUDI U10CA29691-11 00
RAVINDRANATH, YADDANAPUDI U10CA29691-11 00
RAVINDRANATH, YADDANAPUDI U10CA29691-11 00
RAVINDRANATH, YADDANAPUDI U10CA29691-11 00
RAVINDRANATH, YADDANAPUDI U10CA29691-11 00
RAVINDRANATH, YADDANAPUDI U10CA29691-11 00
RAVINDRANATH, YADDANAPUDI U10CA29691-11 00
RAVINDRANATH, YADDANAPUDI U10CA29691-11 00
RAVINDRANATH, YADDANAPUDI U10CA29691-11 00
RAVINDRANATH, YADDANAPUDI U10CA29691-11 00
RAVINDRANATH, YADDANAPUDI U10CA29691-11 00
RAVINDRANATH, YADDANAPUDI U10CA29691-11 00
RAVINDRANATH, YADDANAPUDI U10CA29691-11 00
RAVINDRANATH, YADDANAPUDI U10CA29691-11 00
RAVINDRANATH, YADDANAPUDI U10CA29691-11 00
RAVINDRANATH, YADDANAPUDI U10CA29691-11 00
RAVINDRANATH, YADDANAPUDI U10CA29691-11 00
RAVINDRANATH, YADDANAPUDI U10CA29691-11 00
RAVINDRANATH, YADDANAPUDI U10CA29691-11 00
RAVINDRANATH, YADDANAPUDI U10CA29691-11 00
RAVINDRANATH, YADDANAPUDI U10CA29691-11 00
RAVINDRANATH, YADDANAPUDI U10CA29691-11 00
RAVINDRANATH, YADDANAPUDI U10CA29691-11 00
RAVIOLA, ELIO R01EY01344-17
RAWLINS, DAN R R01AI22881-05
RAWLS, HENRY R R03DE09730-01
RAWSON, RICHARD R18DA06185-03
RAWSON, RICHARD R43AA08971-01
RAWSON, RICHARD R44DA05778-03
RAWSON, RICHARD A R43DA07641-01
RAY, ANURADHA R01AI31137-01
RAY, BRUCE W N01CO15736-00
RAY, C GEORGE P50HL14136-20 9005
RAY, DAN S P30CA16042-17 9005
RAY, DAN S R01AI20080-09
RAY, DANIEL W K08HL02376-04
RAY, JASODHARA P01AG10435-01 9001

RAY, OAKLEY S R13MH48199-01
RAY, PAUL D R01DK41631-03
RAY, RATNA R29CA52799-01A1
RAY, WILLIAM J S07RR07032-26 0025
RAY, WILLIAM J, JR R01GM08963-29
RAYA, THOMAS E S07RR05675-23 0936
RAYBOULD, HELEN R29DK41004-03
RAYCHAUDHURI, PRADIP R01CA55279-01
RAYCHAUDHURI, PRADIP S07RR05369-30 0606
RAYCHAUDHURI, SYAMAL R43CA51568-01A1
RAYFORD, PHILLIP L R01DK30415-09
RAYFORD, PHILLIP L R01DK43746-01
RAYHUL, RAY P41RR00317-25 0001
RAYMAN, PAULA S07RR07186-10 0613
RAYMENT, IVAN R01AR35186-07
RAYMER, JAMES H N01ES05290-01
RAYMOND, C HARRIS P50DK39261-05 0004
RAYMOND, KATHLEEN C S07RR07134-15 0517
RAYMOND, KATHLEEN C S15AI32183-01
RAYMOND, KENNETH N R01AI11744-17
RAYMOND, KENNETH N R01DK32999-12
RAYMOND, LYNN A K08NS01525-01
RAYMOND, PAMELA A R01EY04318-09
RAYNER, KEITH R01HD17246-06
RAYNER, KEITH R01HD26765-02
RAYPORT, STEPHEN G K01MH00705-04
RAYPORT, STEPHEN G R29MH44736-03
RAYSON, BARBARA M R01DK33352-06
RAYSON, JACK H S07RR05704-20
RAZ, AVRAHAM R01CA51714-01A2
RAZA, AZRA P01CA41285-07 0002
RAZDAN, RAJ K R01DA05488-04
RAZZAQUE, A Z01BF01010-02
RAZZAQUE, A Z01BF01011-02
RAZZAQUE, A Z01BF01012-02
RAZZOOG, MICHAEL E R13DE09808-01A1
RAZZOOG, MICHAEL E R13HS06902-01
RBONEWALD, LINDA F P01CA40035-06 0001
RE, RICHARD N S07RR05518-28
RE, RICHARD N S15CA56028-01
REA, ROBERT F M01RR00059-30 0695
READ, GEORGE S, JR R01AI21501-08A1
READ, LEANNA C P51RR00169-30 0124
READ, PAGE F R44HD23420-02
READING, ROGERS, W S07RR05962-05 0016
READY, DONALD F R01AG09302-02
REAGAN, DAVID R S07RR05959-06 0028
REAM, LARRY J S03RR03132-11
REAM, LLOYD W K04AI00838-05
REAM, WALT S07RR07079-26 0277
REAMAN, GREGORY R03CA53543-02
REAMAN, GREGORY U10CA03888-34
REAME, NANCY E R01NR01373-05
REAME, NANCY E U54HD29184-01
REAMS, R RENEE S06GM08232-06 0009
REAMS, R RENEE S06GM08232-06 0009
REARDON, C P30DK42086-02 0007
REARDON, KATHLEEN S07RR07012-25 0021
REARDON, KENNETH S07RR07127-23 0485
REAVEN, EVE P R01HL33881-07
REAVEN, GERALD M M01RR00070-29 0192
REAVEN, GERALD M R01HL08506-28
REBAR, ROBERT W P01HD21921-04 0005
REBEC, GEORGE V R01DA02451-11
REBECCHI, MARIO S07RR05736-19 0162
REBECCHI, MARIO J R29GM43422-02
REBEK, JULIUS JR R01GM25912-14
REBEK, JULIUS, JR R01GM27932-11
REBEK, JULIUS, JR R01GM45002-02
REBHUN, LIONEL I S07RR07094-26 0358
REBOIS, R V Z01NS02784-03
REBOLI, ANNETTE C S07RR05413-30 0985
REBOUCHE, CHARLES J M01RR00059-30 0739
REBOUCHE, CHARLES J M01RR00059-30 0628
RECH, RICHARD S07RR05656-24 0839
RECHLER, M M Z01DK55006-18
RECHSTEINER, MARTIN C R01GM27159-12
RECHTSCHAFFEN, ALLAN K05MH18428-25
RECHTSCHAFFEN, ALLAN R37MH04151-32
RECKER, ROBERT R P50AR39221-05 0006
RECKER, ROBERT R P50AR39221-05
RECKER, ROBERT R P50AR39221-05 0002
RECKER, ROBERT R R01AR40832-01
RECORD, M THOMAS JR R01GM34351-07
RECORD, M THOMAS, JR R01GM23467-15
RECTOR, THOMAS H P01HL32427-06 9001
RECTOR, WILLIAM G M01RR00051-30 0689
RECTOR, WILLIAM G, JR R29AA07832-05
REDBURN, DIANNA A R01EY01655-14
REDBURN, DIANNA A S15NS30126-01
REDD, WILLIAM H K02MH00882-02
REDD, WILLIAM H R01MH45157-03
REDDA, KEN S06GM08111-19
REDDA, KINFE S06GM08111-19 0025
REDDA, KINFE S06GM08111-19 0025
REDDA, KINFE K S03RR03196-10
REDDAN, JOHN R R01EY00362-23
REDDI, A H Z01DE00204-15
REDDING, WILLIAM S07RR07034-26 0067
REDDY, A P S07RR07082-26 0305
REDDY, BANDARU S U01CA46589-05
REDDY, BANDARU S U01CA46589-05 0003
REDDY, CHILEKAMPALLI A R01GM39032-04
REDDY, CHINTHAMANI C R01HL31245-08
REDDY, E PREMKUMAR R01CA55492-01
REDDY, E SHYAM P R01CA57157-01
REDDY, E SHYAM P S07RR05417-30 0812
REDDY, JANARDAN K R01DK37958-05
REDDY, JANARDAN K R37GM23750-16
REDDY, M NARAHARI S07RR05434-30 0803
REDDY, MICHAEL S07RR05300-30 0202
REDDY, MOLAKALA S R01AI27401-03
REDDY, PREMAKUR P01CA21124-14 0014
REDDY, PREMKUMAR S07RR05540-29 0553
REDDY, PREMKUMAR E P01AI25380-05
REDDY, PREMKUMAR E P01AI25380-05 0001
REDDY, PREMKUMAR E P01CA52009-01A1 0001
REDDY, PREMKUMAR E P01CA52009-01A1
REDDY, PREMKUMAR E R01CA47937-04
REDDY, RAMACHANDRA P01CA10893-23 0049
REDDY, RAMACHANDRA R R01GM38320-04
REDDY, RAVINDER D R03MH47002-01A1
REDDY, S NARASIMHA S07RR05551-29 0950
REDDY, SATYANARAYANA G R29DK39138-05
REDDY, VEMURI B R44HD25349-02A1
REDDY, VENKAT S07RR07131-22 0137
REDDY, VENKAT N P30EY05230-07
REDDY, VENKAT N R37EY00484-24
REDEI, EVA R01AA07389-02
REDEI, EVA R01MH45862-02
REDFERN, MARK S K01AG00463-01
REDFIELD, ALFRED U01CA51992-02 0004
REDFIELD, ALFRED G R37GM20168-19
REDFORD-BADWAL, DEBORAH A K15DE00276-03
REDING, MICHAEL J R01DC00885-02
REDLINE, SUSAN R01HL46380-02
REDLINE, SUSAN S07RR05765-17 0209
REDMAN, COLVIN M R01HL33841-07
REDMAN, COLVIN M R01HL37457-05
REDMAN, RICHARD W S07RR05796-14 0438
REDMOND, DONALD E P01NS24032-06 0003
REDMOND, DONALD E P01NS24032-06 9001
REDMOND, DONALD E, JR K05MH00643-12
REDMOND, DONALD E, JR P01NS24032-06
REDMOND, NINFA N01CM87202-08
REDMOND, T M Z01EY00260-02
REDPATH, JOHN L R01CA39312-06
REECE, ELENA R S06GM08244-05 0024
REED, BARBARA D R29AI29648-03
REED, C E M01RR00585-20 0426
REED, CHARLES E R01AI21255-08
REED, CHARLOTTE M R01DC00126-12
REED, CHRISTOPHER A R01GM23851-11
REED, DONALD J P01ES00040-27
REED, DONALD J P01ES00040-27 0071
REED, DONALD J P30ES00210-24
REED, DONALD J P30ES00210-24 9003
REED, DONALD J R37ES01978-14
REED, E Z01CM06716-04
REED, E Z01CM06736-01
REED, GEORGE H R01GM35752-06
REED, GREGORY S07RR05373-30 0728
REED, GREGORY A R01ES04092-04A1
REED, GUY L K08HL02348-03
REED, JOHN C R01CA47956-04
REED, JOHN C R01CA54957-01
REED, JOHN C S07RR07083-26 0479
REED, JULIA A S07RR07091-26 0765
REED, LESTER J R01GM06590-32A1
REED, MARJORIE A S07RR07079-26 0297
REED, MELVIN L N01CO15702-00
REED, MICHAEL W R43GM46143-01
REED, NORMAN D R01AI29001-02
REED, PETER W S07RR07201-12
REED, PETER W S15EY09472-01
REED, PETER W S15MH49312-01
REED, RANDALL R R01MH47506-01
REED, RANDALL R R13DK45023-01
REED, RICHARD S07RR05675-23 0937
REED, ROBERTA G S15HL47720-01
REED, ROBIN E R01GM43375-02
REED, SHARON L R01AI28035-02
REED, STEVEN G P01AI16282-13 0006
REED, STEVEN G R01AI22726-06
REED, STEVEN G R01AI25038-04A1
REED, STEVEN G R01AI27711-02
REED, STEVEN G S07RR05939-07 0727
REED, STEVEN I P01GM46006-01 9001
REED, STEVEN I P01GM46006-01 9002
REED, STEVEN I P01GM46006-01
REED, STEVEN I P01GM46006-01 0001
REED, STEVEN I R01GM38328-05
REED, STEVEN I R01GM39429-04
REED, WILLIAM P60AR30701-10 0015
REEDER, RONALD H R01GM26624-13
REEDER, RONALD H R01GM41792-02
REEDERS, STEPHEN T R01DK40703-03
REEDY, MICHAEL K R01AR14317-20
REEM, GABRIELLE H R01AI26483-04
REEMTSMA, KEITH R01HL14799-18
REES, DOUGLAS C P01GM39558-05 0004
REES, DOUGLAS C R01GM45162-01
REESE, BENJAMIN E R01EY08415-01A1
REESE, T S Z01NS01442-25
REESE, T S Z01NS01881-21
REESE, T S Z01NS02551-11
REEVE, JOSEPH R, JR R01DK33850-06
REEVE, THOMAS G S07RR07255-02
REEVES, BYRON B S07RR07005-26 0343
REEVES, JOHN T P01HL14985-20 0017
REEVES, JOHN T P01HL14985-20 0024
REEVES, JOHN T. P01HL14985-20 0030
REEVES, RAYMOND R01GM46352-01
REEVES, ROBERT B P01HL28542-10 0003
REEVES, ROGER H P01HD24605-03 0002
REEVES, ROGER H R01HG00405-01
REEVES, WESTLEY H R01AR40391-02
REEVES, WESTLEY H. M01RR00102-28 0139
REEVES, WILLIAM C N01CP41026-06
REFETOFF, SAMUEL M01RR00055-30 0407
REFETOFF, SAMUEL M01RR00055-30 0520
REFETOFF, SAMUEL M01RR00055-30 0544
REFETOFF, SAMUEL R37DK15070-20
REFOJO, MIGUEL F R01EY00327-26
REGALDO, MICHAEL S07RR05780-16 0976
REGAN, DAVID R01EY07569-04
REGAN, JOHN W R29EY09355-01
REGAN, L S07RR07015-26 0609
REGEN, STEVEN L R01AI28220-02
REGEN, STEVEN L R01GM43787-02
REGENSTEINER, JUDITH S07RR05357-30 0451
REGEZI, JOSEPH S07RR05321-30 0267
REGGIA, JAMES A R01NS29414-02
REGISTER, THOMAS C S07RR05404-30 0853
REGNIER, FRED E R01GM25431-14
REH, THOMAS A R01NS28308-03
REHG, JEROLD E P30CA21765-14 9001
REICH, EVA-PIA P01DK43078-02 9001
REICH, GWENDOLYN G R29AA07551-04
REICH, NANCY S07RR05736-19 0173
REICH, NANCY C R29CA50773-02
REICH, NORBERT O R01GM46333-01
REICH, THEODORE R01MH45522-02
REICH, THEODORE U01MH46280-03
REICHARD, GEORGE A, JR S07RR05585-19
REICHARDT, LOUIS F P01NS16033-11 0011
REICHARDT, LOUIS F P50MH48200-01 0005
REICHARDT, LOUIS F R01NS19090-09
REICHEK, NATHANIEL R01HL42958-02
REICHEL, RONALD S07RR05366-30 0560
REICHEL, RONALD S07RR05366-30 0561
REICHENBECHER, VERNO S07RR05870-10 0996
REICHERT, LEO E, JR R01HD13938-13
REICHERT, WILLIAM M R01HL32132-06
REICHERT, WILLIAM M R01HL44972-02
REICHLIN, MORRIS P01AI21568-07 0005
REICHLIN, MORRIS P01AI21568-07
REICHLIN, MORRIS R01AR31133-09A1
REICHLIN, MORRIS R01AR32214-07
REICHLIN, SEYMOUR M01RR00054-30 0184
REICHLIN, SEYMOUR R37DK16684-20
REICHMAN, LEE B K07HL02095-05
REICHMAN, LEE B. N01HR76032-05
REICHMAN, RICHARD C N01AI82509-04
REICHMAN, RICHARD C U01AI27658-05S1
REID, BRAIN J S07RR05432-30 0234
REID, BRIAN P01DK32971-08 0004
REID, BRIAN R P01GM32681-08 9001
REID, BRIAN R P01GM32681-08 0002
REID, BRIAN R P01GM32681-08
REID, BRIAN R R01GM42896-03
REID, DARRELL N01LM13530-01
REID, DEBORAH L R29HL44447-01A1
REID, IAN A P01HL29714-29 0006
REID, IAN A P01HL29714-29 9002
REID, JAMES D R03MH46430-02
REID, JOHN S07RR05839-10 0927
REID, JOHN B P50MH46690-02
REID, JOHN B P50MH46690-02 0001
REID, JOHN B P50MH46690-02 0002
REID, JOHN B P50MH46690-02 0003
REID, JOHN B P50MH46690-02 0004
REID, JOHN B P50MH46690-02 9001
REID, JOHN B S07RR05839-10
REID, JOHN B S15HD28763-01
REID, JOHN M P01CA52823-02
REID, JOHN M P01CA52823-02 9002
REID, K Z01DE00532-01
REID, LOLA P30DK41296-03 9002
REID, MARY K R01HD24116-04
REID, MICHAEL S07RR05425-30 0766
REIDENBERG, MARCUS M M01RR00047-31 0394
REIDY, MICHAEL A P01HL03174-36 9001
REIDY, MICHAEL A P50HL42270-02 0006
REIDY, MICHAEL A R01HL41103-04
REIDY, MICHAEL A. P01HL03174-36 0018
REIER, PAUL J P01NS27511-03
REIER, PAUL J P01NS27511-03 0001
REIER, PAUL J P01NS27511-03 9001
REIER, PAUL J P41RR02278-06A1 0010
REIF, JOHN S S07RR05458-29 0835
REIFF, WILLIAM M S07RR07143-20 0632
REIFFEL, JAMES A M01RR00645-20 0308
REIFFEL, JAMES A M01RR00645-20 0347
REIGEL, CHARLES S07RR05773-17 0368
REIGHLIN, SEYMOUR M01RR00054-30 0414

REILLY, JOHN J K08HL02554-01
REILLY, JUDY S R29DC00539-03
REILLY, JUDY S S06GM45765-01 0006
REILLY, ROBERT F K11DK01816-04
REIMANN, ERWIN M P01HL36573-06 9001
REIMANN, K A P51RR00168-30 0149
REIMANN, KEITH A K01RR00055-03
REIMER, KEITH A P50HL17670-17 9002
REIMER, KEITH A R01HL27416-10
REIMER, NEIL S. S06GM08125-18 0040
REIMERS, THOMAS P01HD21350-05 0002
REIN, MITCHELL S07RR05950-07 0988
REINACH, PETER S R01EY04795-10
REINARD, GREGORY R P40RR01180-14 0003
REINBERG, DANNY S07RR05576-27 0590
REINBERG, DANNY F R01GM37120-07
REINER, ANTON J R01EY05298-08
REINER, ANTON J R01NS19620-09
REINER, ANTON J R01NS28721-02
REINERS, JOHN J, JR R01CA40823-07
REINERS, JOHN J, JR R01CA49935-03
REINES, DANIEL R01GM46331-01
REINES, DANIEL S07RR05364-30 0539
REINES, DAVID M01RR00065-29 0362
REINGOLD, STEPHEN C R13NS20758-07
REINHARDT, JOANN P R03MH46596-01A1
REINHART, FREDERICK P30DK34854-08 0012
REINHART, GREGORY D R01GM33216-08
REINHART, HARALD S07RR05384-30 0777
REINHERZ, ELLIS L R01AI19807-09
REINHERZ, ELLIS L R01AI21226-08
REINHERZ, ELLIS L R01CA49232-04
REINHERZ, ELLIS L U01AI27336-04 9001
REINHERZ, ELLIS L U01AI27336-04
REINHERZ, ELLIS L U01AI27336-04 0001
REINHERZ, HELEN Z R01MH41569-05
REINHOLD, RANDOLPH B M01RR00054-30 0469
REINHOLD, VERNON N R01AI28215-03
REINHOLD, VERNON N R01GM45781-01
REINHOLD, VERNON N S10RR06287-01
REINISCH, JUNE M R01DA05056-03
REINKE, LESTER A R01AA07337-04
REINKE, ROSEMARY R01EY08396-02
REINLIB, L Z01AA00486-01
REINSCHMIDT, JULIAN U76PE00229-02
REIS, ARTHUR H, JR S03RR03373-08
REIS, DONALD J P01NS03346-31 0041
REIS, JANET S07RR07030-26 0406
REIS, MOSHE S07RR05479-29 0448
REIS, ROBERT J S07RR05350-30 0329
REISBERG, BARRY P30AG08051-02 9001
REISBERG, BARRY R01AG03051-08
REISBERG, BARRY R01AG09127-02
REISER-DANNER, LORET S07RR07260-02 0551
REISER, HANS R29AI30169-01A1
REISER, KAREN M P51RR00169-30 0164
REISER, KAREN M P51RR00169-30 0165
REISER, KAREN M P51RR00169-30 0166
REISER, KAREN M R01AG05324-07
REISER, KAREN M R01AG07711-04
REISER, PETER J R29AR39652-03
REISFELD, RALPH A R35CA42508-06
REISFELD, RALPH A U01CA51946-02
REISFELD, RALPH A U01CA51946-02 0002
REISINE, SUSAN T P60AR20621-13 0022
REISINE, SUSAN T P60AR20621-13 0023
REISINE, TERRY D R01MH45533-03
REISINE, TERRY D R01MH48518-01
REISKIN, HELEN K S07RR07199-12 0941
REISLER, EMIL R01AR22031-14
REISS, ALLAN L K11MH00726-05
REISS, CAROL S P30CA06516-28 9002
REISS, CAROL S R01AI18083-11
REISS, CAROL S S07RR05526-29 0075
REISS, DAVID R01MH43373-05
REISS, DAVID R01MH48825-01
REISS, DAVID R37MH43417-04
REISS, MICHAEL R01CA41556-05
REIST, ELMER N01AI72643-09
REIST, ELMER N01CN05270-02
REIST, ELMER J N01CP71108-06
REITE, MARTIN M01RR00051-30 0744
REITE, MARTIN L K05MH46335-21
REITE, MARTIN L P50MH44212-03 0004
REITE, MARTIN L R01MH47476-01
REITH, MAARTEN E R01DA03025-08
REITZ, M Z01CP05538-06
REITZ, M S Z01CP07149-08
REITZER, LAWRENCE J R29GM38877-05
REITZER, LAWRENCE J S07RR07133-22 0514
REITZES, DONALD C R01AG07410-01A3
REIVICH, MARTIN M01RR00040-31 0407
REIVICH, MARTIN P01NS14867-13
REIVICH, MARTIN P01NS14867-13 0009
REIVICH, MARTIN P50NS10939-18A1S1
REIVICH, MARTIN P60HL38632-04 0003
REKOSH, DAVID U01AI25721-05 0003
REKOSH, DAVID M R01AI30399-02
REKOSH, DAVID M U01AI25721-05
REKOW, E DIANNE R29DE08455-05
RELLING, MARY V R29CA51001-02
REMBOLD, CHRISTOPHER M R55HL38918-05A1
REMERS, WILLIAM A R01CA49875-02
REMEZ, ROBERT E R01DC00308-07
REMICK, DANIEL G R01DK42455-01A1
REMICK, DANIEL G R01GM44918-02
REMINGTON, JACK S R37AI04717-30
REMINGTON, JACK S U01AI30230-02 0001
REMINGTON, JACK S U01AI30230-02
REMINGTON, PATRICK N01CN15373-00
REMINGTON, STEPHEN J R01GM42618-01A1
REMMEL, RORY P R01AI28236-03
REMMERS, JOHN E R01HL42470-03
REMOLD-O'DONNELL, EI S07RR05626-25 0670
REMOLD-O'DONNELL, EILEEN R01HL41579-07
REMOLD-O'DONNELL, EILEEN R01AI29880-02
REMOLD, HEINZ G P01HL43510-03 0004
REMOLD, HEINZ G R01AI31006-01A2
REN, K Z01DE00440-05
RENAUD, FERNANDO L S06GM08102-20 0018
RENDER, JOANN R01HD27328-03
RENEGAR, RANDALL H R29HD23481-03
RENEHAN, WILLIAM E P01DE07734-06 0002
RENKIN, EUGENE M R01HL18010-17
RENLUND, DALE M01RR00064-27 0387
RENNARD, STEPHEN I R01HL43922-01A1
RENNIE, DONALD W S03RR03268-10
RENNIE, DONALD W S07RR07066-26
RENNKE, HELMUT G P01DK40839-03 0002
RENNKE, HELMUT G R01DK35931-07
RENSHAW, STEPHEN R R43RR07559-01
RENSTROM, PER S07RR05429-30 0208
RENTHAL, ROBERT D S06GM08194-12 0004
RENTZ, DOREEN S07RR06003-04 0369
REPASKE, R Z01AI00218-10
REPASKY, ELIZABETH P30CA16056-16 9018
REPASKY, ELIZABETH A R01AI30131-02
REPETTI, RENA L R29MH48593-01
REPETTI, RENA L S07RR07083-26 0489
REPIK, PATRICIA M R29AI24989-05
REPINE, JOHN E P50HL40784-03
REPINE, JOHN E P50HL40784-03 0001
REPKA, MICHAEL X U10EY08221-03
REPKE, JOHN T M01RR00722-19 0255
REPP, BRUNO H S07RR05596-27 0131
REPP, BRUNO H S07RR05596-27 0132
REPPERT, STEVEN M R01DK42125-02
REPPERT, STEVEN M R01HD14427-11
RES & EVALUATION ASSOC, INC N01DA08201-00
RES FDN FOR MENTAL HYGIENE, IN N01AA10007-
RES TRIANGLE INST N01DA98542-00
RESARCH/EVALUATION ASSOC, INC N01DA98525-0
RESCH, RICHARD I S15HD28766-01
RESCORLA, LESLIE A R01DC00807-02
RESEARCH BIOCHEMICALS, INC N01MH00007-00
RESEARCH TRIANGLE INST N01DA98532-00
RESEARCH TRIANGLE INST N01DA98160-00
RESEARCH TRIANGLE INST N01DA08200-00
RESEARCH TRIANGLE INST N01DA14306-00
RESEARCH TRIANGLE INST N01DA98333-00
RESEARCH TRIANGLE INST N01DA98340-00
RESEARCH TRIANGLE INST N01DA98158-00
RESEARCH TRIANGLE INST N01DA98149-00
RESEARCH TRIANGLE INSTITUTE N01DA88310-00
RESEARCH TRIANGLE INSTITUTE N01DA98233-00
RESH, MARILYN D R01CA52405-02
RESICK, PATRICIA A R01MH46992-01A1
RESING, KATHERYN A R29AR39730-03
RESKIN, BARBARA S07RR07030-26 0407
RESKO, JOHN A P51RR00163-32 0016
RESKO, JOHN A R01HD16022-10
RESKO, JOHN A R01HD18196-08
RESNICK, LAWRENCE M P50HL18323-17 0068
RESNICK, LIONEL R01DE09563-02
RESNICK, LIONEL S07RR05662-18 0151
RESNICK, LIONEL U01AI25696-05 0003
RESNICK, M A Z01ES21016-10
RESNICK, M A Z01ES21091-06
RESNICK, M A Z01ES21122-03
RESNICK, M A Z01ES65072-01
RESNICK, M A Z01ES65073-01
RESNICK, MARTIN I M01RR00080-29 0446
RESNICK, MICHAEL D S07RR05448-30 0297
RESNICK, NEIL M P01AG04390-08 0002
RESNICK, NEIL M P30AG08812-02 9002
RESNICK, OSCAR P01HD22539-04 9001
RESNICK, STACI S07RR05664-24 0873
RESNICK, SUSAN M P30AG10124-01 0002
RESNICK, SUSAN M P50MH43880-04 9005
RESSETAR, H G Z01NS02807-02
REST, RICHARD F R01AI20897-07
RESTREPO, DIEGO R01GM42495-03
RESTREPO, DIEGO S07RR05825-12 0513
RESTREPO, DIEGO S07RR05825-12 0519
RESTUCCIA, JOSEPH D R01HS06048-02
RETCHIN, SHELDON P30CA16059-15 9019
RETCHIN, SHELDON M R01HS06589-01A1
RETIEF, HUGO S07RR05300-30 0207
RETIEF, HUGO S07RR05300-30 0208
RETTENMIER, CARL W R29HL40603-03
RETTIE, ALLAN E R29GM43511-02
REUBEN, ADRIAN M01RR00125-28 0696
REUBEN, ADRIAN R01DK40914-03
REUBEN, DAVID P60AG10415-01 0003
REUHL, KENNETH R R01ES04976-03
REUS, WILLIAM F, III S07RR05392-30 0702
REUSS, LUIS R01DK38734-06
REUSS, LUIS S07RR07205-11 0646
REVEILLE, JOHN D M01RR02558-07 0046
REVEILLE, JOHN D R29AR39325-04
REVEL, HELEN R R01GM35268-07
REVEL, J P S07RR07003-26 0331
REVEL, J-P S07RR07003-26 0333
REVELETTE, W ROBERT P01HL40369-03 0002
REVELEY, ADRIANNE M R01MH44359-03
REVENIS, MARY S07RR05515-28 0064
REVENSON, TRACEY P60AR38520-04 0009
REVES, J G R01AG09663-01
REVITTE, JOHN S07RR07049-26 0426
REVOILE, SALLY G R01DC00077-26
REVOILE, SALLY G S07RR07245-03 0856
REVOILE, SALLY G S15NS30125-01
REVZIN, ARNOLD R01GM25498-13
REWERS, MARIAN J U01HL47892-01
REX, DOUGLAS K M01RR00750-19 0293
REYES-CINTRON, ZELIDETH E S06GM08216-09 00
REYES, EDWARD R01AA08072-01A2
REYES, EDWARD R13NS25952-04
REYES, EDWARD S06GM08139-17 0014
REYES, PHILLIP S07RR05583-27 0638
REYLAND, MARY R01HL32868-08
REYNOLDS, ALBERT S07RR05584-27 0649
REYNOLDS, C P01MH47200-02 0004
REYNOLDS, CHARLES F P50MH30915-15 9021
REYNOLDS, CHARLES F. P01AG06836-04 0001
REYNOLDS, CHARLES F, III K05MH00295-12
REYNOLDS, CHARLES F, III R01MH40023-07
REYNOLDS, CHARLES F, III R01MH37869-09
REYNOLDS, CHARLES F, III R37MH43832-03
REYNOLDS, CHARLES P S03RR03530-02
REYNOLDS, ELWOOD E R01HL48478-01
REYNOLDS, FRED H R44CA49338-02
REYNOLDS, GARY A P50HL17669-17 0040
REYNOLDS, HERBERT S07RR05772-17 0357
REYNOLDS, IAN J S07RR05416-30 0572
REYNOLDS, KEVIN A S07RR05770-13 0930
REYNOLDS, KIM D R03AA08531-02
REYNOLDS, LAWRENCE P R01HD22559-04A2
REYNOLDS, NANCY R R03HS06971-01
REYNOLDS, RICHARD J R01CA55019-01
REYNOLDS, RICHARD J S07RR05919-08 0714
REYNOLDS, S Z01ES46005-07
REYNOLDS, TELFER B M01RR00043-31 0478
REYNOLDS, THOMAS C R43CA54647-01
REYNOLDS, WANDA F R01GM34888-07
REZAIE, BAHMAN S06GM02721-07 0005
REZEK, DONALD L P50AG05133-08 9001
REZNIKOFF, CATHERINE A P01CA51987-02 0001
REZNIKOFF, CATHERINE A P01CA51987-02 9001
REZNIKOFF, CATHERINE A R01CA29525-11
RFFY, RODOLPHE S07RR05428-30 0181
RFRANCHINI, G Z01CP05688-01
RHEAD, WILLIAM J R01DK33289-08
RHEE, S G Z01HL00263-06
RHEINWALD, JAMES G P01CA22427-14 0008
RHEINWALD, JAMES G R01CA26656-14
RHEUBAN, KAREN S S07RR05431-30 0829
RHIM, J S Z01CP05060-13
RHINE, WILLIAM D K08HD00891-02
RHINE, WILLIAM D M01RR00081-29 0143
RHOADES, ROBERT W P01DE07734-06 0001
RHOADES, ROBERT W R01EY04170-11
RHOADES, ROBERT W R01NS28888-02
RHOADES, RODNEY A R01HL36745-05
RHOADES, RODNEY A R01HL40894-02
RHOADS, DENNIS E R01AA07848-02
RHOADS, J P30DK34987-06 0008
RHOADS, JON M K08HD00945-02
RHOADS, ROBERT E R01GM20818-17
RHODE, WILLIAM P01DC00116-16 0018
RHODE, EDWARD A P51RR00169-30 9020
RHODE, SOLON P30CA36727-08 9008
RHODE, SOLON L, III R01AI25552-02
RHODE, WILLIAM P01DC00116-16 0016
RHODES, BUCK A R44CA50788-02
RHODES, FEN R18DA05747-03S1
RHODES, FEN U01DA07474-01
RHODES, JUDITH P01AI28392-02 0003
RHODES, PHILIP S07RR05387-30 0601
RHODES, R K S06GM08022-20 0007
RHODES, RATHBUN K R44DK40657-02
RHOTEN, WILLIAM B S07RR05393-30 0901
RHYNE, CRAIG S07RR05773-17 0378
RHYNE, CRAIG S07RR05773-17 0379
RIBAK, CHARLES E R01NS15669-11
RIBBLE, JOHN C M01RR02558-07
RIBBLE, JOHN C S07RR05745-19
RIBEIRO, JOSE M C R01AI18694-08
RIBERA, ANGELES B K04NS01531-01
RIBERA, ANGELES B R29NS25217-04
RIBERA, ANGELES B S07RR05357-30 0466
RIBLET, ROY J R01AI23548-07
RICAURTE, GEORGE A M01RR02719-06 0128
RICAURTE, GEORGE A R01DA05938-03
RICAURTE, GEORGE A R01DA06275-01A2
RICAURTE, GEORGE A R29DA05707-03

RICCARDI, VINCENT M M01RR00188-27 0136
RICCIARDI, ROBERT P P01CA52009-01A1 0004
RICCIARDI, ROBERT P R01AI29362-02
RICCIARDI, ROBERT P R01CA29797-10
RICCIARDI, ROBERT P R01CA44960-05
RICCIO, DAVID C R37MH37535-11
RICCIO, GARY E S07RR07030-26 0408
RICE, ANDREW P R01AI25308-04A1
RICE, CHARLES L R01GM42686-02
RICE, CHARLES L. P51RR00166-30 0113
RICE, CHARLES L. P51RR00166-30 0114
RICE, CHARLES M R01AI24134-05
RICE, CHARLES M R01AI31501-01
RICE, DALE P41RR01861-07 0011
RICE, DOROTHY P R01AG07425-04
RICE, DOROTHY P R01AG08145-03S1
RICE, GRACE E R01AG05963-05
RICE, J M Z01CP05092-14
RICE, J M Z01CP05399-08
RICE, JOHN A P60AR40770-01A1 9001
RICE, JOHN P R01MH37685-09
RICE, JOHN P U01MH25430-18
RICE, K C Z01DK59501-05
RICE, MABEL L R29DC00485-04
RICE, MARGARET S07RR05399-30 0919
RICE, MARGARET E R29NS28480-01A1
RICE, PETER A P01AI24760-05 0002
RICE, PETER A P01AI24760-05
RICE, PETER A P01AI24760-05 9001
RICE, PETER J S07RR05959-06 0022
RICE, ROBERT H R01AR27130-11
RICE, ROBERT R U01AI25924-05 9002
RICE, THOMAS A U10EY08603-02
RICE, WARD R R01HL46653-01
RICE, WARD R R29HL38764-05
RICE, WILLIAM G R01DE09575-02
RICH, ALEXANDER P01GM37641-05 0005
RICH, ALEXANDER R37CA04186-33
RICH, DANIEL H R01AI24650-04
RICH, DANIEL H R01AR32007-09
RICH, DANIEL H R01GM40092-04
RICH, DANIEL H S15GM47040-01
RICH, DANIEL H U01AI27302-04 0002
RICH, ELIZABETH A K11HL01829-05
RICH, ELIZABETH A M01RR00080-29 0434
RICH, ELIZABETH A M01RR00080-29 0338
RICH, ELIZABETH A R01HL43571-03
RICH, KENNETH N01AI82505-11
RICH, MICHAEL W R29HL44739-02
RICH, ROBERT R P01AI21289-08 0002
RICH, ROBERT R P01AI21289-08
RICH, ROBERT R R01AI18882-09
RICH, ROBERT R R01AI30036-01A1
RICH, ROBERT R R37AI15394-13
RICH, ROBERT R S07RR05425-30
RICH, ROBERT R S15GM47026-01
RICH, STEPHEN S P41RR01632-09 0030
RICH, STEPHEN S P41RR01632-09 9021
RICH, STEPHEN S P41RR01632-09 0031
RICH, STEPHEN S P41RR01632-09 9022
RICH, STUART N01HC55007-11
RICH, SUSAN S P01AI21289-08 0001
RICH, SUSAN S R01AI21420-08
RICH, TYVIN A P01CA06294-30 0080
RICHARD, CHARLES W K11MH00802-03
RICHARD, J MARTIN P01HL25830-11A1 0003
RICHARD, JOHN P R29GM39754-04
RICHARD, M P30CA30199-11 9007
RICHARD, SHEILA A N01DC12104-00
RICHARDS-KORTUM, REB S07RR07091-26 0766
RICHARDS, DAVID K16DE00157-05S2 0005
RICHARDS, ERIC J R01GM43518-02
RICHARDS, ERNEST W S07RR05992-04 0815
RICHARDS, FRANK F P01AI28778-02
RICHARDS, FRANK F P01AI28778-02 0002
RICHARDS, FRANK F R01AI24194-05
RICHARDS, FRANK F R13AI31447-01
RICHARDS, FREDERIC M P01GM22778-16
RICHARDS, FREDERIC M P01GM22778-16 9001
RICHARDS, FREDERIC M P01GM22778-16 0004
RICHARDS, FREDERIC M P01GM39546-05 0002
RICHARDS, GAIL E M01RR00073-29 0219
RICHARDS, IRA S S07RR06005-04 0300
RICHARDS, J S07RR07003-26 0317
RICHARDS, JOANNE S R01HD16229-10
RICHARDS, JOANNE S R01HD16272-10
RICHARDS, JOHN E R01HD18942-06S1
RICHARDS, JOHN H R01GM16424-21
RICHARDS, JON M M01RR00055-30 0569
RICHARDS, LESLIE N S07RR07079-26 0289
RICHARDS, MARYSE S07RR07210-09 0687
RICHARDS, RICHARD D R21EY07766-04
RICHARDS, RICHARD D S07RR05379-30
RICHARDS, RICHARD D S15HL47776-01
RICHARDS, ROBERT S07RR05656-24 0844
RICHARDS, TODD L R29NS24622-05
RICHARDS, TODD L. P51RR00166-30 0115
RICHARDS, TONI R01HS06567-01
RICHARDS, VIRGINIA MARIE R29DC00526-04
RICHARDS, WILLIAM O M01RR00095-31 0328
RICHARDSON, ARLAN G R01AG01548-08A1
RICHARDSON, ARLAN G R13AG09763-01
RICHARDSON, BARRY L S03RR03136-10
RICHARDSON, BRUCE M01RR00042-31 0573
RICHARDSON, BRUCE P60AR20557-13 0060
RICHARDSON, BRUCE C R01AI25526-04
RICHARDSON, CHARLES A R01HL26176-08
RICHARDSON, CHARLES C R37AI06045-28
RICHARDSON, CHARLES P R43HL46625-01
RICHARDSON, DANIEL P01HL36552-07 0011
RICHARDSON, DAVID N01HC65055-10
RICHARDSON, DAVID C R01GM15000-22
RICHARDSON, DAVID E R01GM42637-01A2
RICHARDSON, DOUGLAS K R01HS06123-03
RICHARDSON, G S07RR05333-30 0873
RICHARDSON, GALE A R01DA06839-01
RICHARDSON, GALE A R29DA05460-04
RICHARDSON, JAMES K S07RR05383-30 0567
RICHARDSON, JOHN P R37AI10142-21
RICHARDSON, KATHLEEN R22AI23417-04A2
RICHARDSON, R L M01RR00585-20 0449
RICHARDSON, RONALD L N01CM07304-01
RICHARDSON, STEPHEN A R01HD23012-05
RICHARDSON, THOMAS M R01EY02655-13
RICHARDSON, THOMAS O S03RR03195-10
RICHARDSON, VELMA B S06GM08091-20 0022
RICHARDSON, WILLIAM G P50MH33127-13 9003
RICHELSON, ELLIOTT R01MH27692-17
RICHERSON, H B P30ES05605-02 9007
RICHERSON, HAL B M01RR00059-30 0675
RICHERSON, HAL B M01RR00059-30 0333
RICHERSON, HAL B P50AI19093-08
RICHERSON, HAL B P50AI19093-08 0005
RICHERSON, HAL B. P50HL37121-05 0005
RICHERT, JOHN P50AI26821-04 0004
RICHERT, JOHN R R01AI26675-04
RICHES, DAVID W R01CA50107-03
RICHFIELD, ERIK K R35AG09016-02 0003
RICHIE, ELLEN R R01CA37912-06
RICHIE, ELLEN R R01CA50604-03
RICHIE, JOHN P P01CA32617-09A1 0009
RICHIE, JOHN P, JR R01DE09514-01A2
RICHIE, JOHN P, JR R03AA08479-02
RICHMAN, DAVID P P01NS24304-05 9001
RICHMAN, DAVID P P01NS24304-05
RICHMAN, DAVID P P01NS24304-05 0004
RICHMAN, DAVID P R01NS15462-12
RICHMAN, DAVID P R01NS19779-08
RICHMAN, DOUGLAS D M01RR00827-17 0450
RICHMAN, DOUGLAS D M01RR00827-17 0452
RICHMAN, DOUGLAS D R01AI29164-03
RICHMAN, DOUGLAS D U01AI30457-02
RICHMAN, JUDITH A R01AA07311-05
RICHMAN, L C P01DE05837-10 0005
RICHMAN, ROBERT A P01DC00220-08 0005
RICHMAN, ROBERT A S07RR05402-30 0795
RICHMOND, ANN R01CA34590-10
RICHMOND, B J Z01MH02032-01
RICHMOND, ROBERT H S06GM44796-02 0002
RICHMOND, ROLLIN C S07RR07031-26 0103
RICHMOND, THOMAS G S07RR07092-26 0498
RICHMOND, THOMAS G S07RR07092-26 0531
RICHTER, CONRAD P30AI28662-03 9005
RICHTER, JOEL D R01CA40189-07
RICHTER, JOEL E M01RR00032-31 0378
RICHTER, JOEL E R01DK42428-03
RICHTER, M S07RR05333-30 0874
RICK, M E Z01CL10035-11
RICK, M E Z01CL10058-12
RICK, PAUL D R01AI21309-08
RICK, ROGER P50DK39258-05 0004
RICK, ROGER P50DK39258-05 9002
RICKELS, KARL M R37MH08957-27
RICKETTS, THOMAS C R18HS06706-01
RICKOLL, WAYNE L R15GM46131-01
RICO-HESSE, REBECA R29AI27779-03
RICO, M JOYCE K08AR01808-02
RIDALL, AMY L K15DE00218-04
RIDDIFORD, LYNN M R01AI12459-16
RIDDLE, DONALD L N01RR92113-02
RIDDLE, DONALD L R01HD11239-15
RIDDLE, MARK M01RR00125-28 0697
RIDDLE, MARK M01RR00125-28 0771
RIDDLE, MARK M01RR00125-28 0769
RIDDLE, MARK M01RR06022-02 0697
RIDDLE, MARK A M01RR00125-28 0748
RIDDLE, MARK A M01RR06022-02 0739
RIDDLE, MARK A M01RR06022-02 0740
RIDDLE, MATTHEW M01RR00334-25 0276
RIDDLE, MATTHEW C M01RR00334-25 0315
RIDDLE, MATTHEW C M01RR00334-25 0312
RIDEOUT, DARRYL C R29CA44505-04
RIDEOUT, DARRYL C R55AI28202-01A2
RIDER, EVELYN D K08HD00933-02
RIDER, LISA S07RR05655-21 0821
RIDER, LISA G S07RR05655-21 0813
RIDER, LISA G S07RR05655-21 0814
RIDER, SUSAN H P50HG00206-01S1 0003
RIDER, VIRGINIA C R03HD28038-01
RIDER, VIRGINIA C R29HD23896-03
RIDGE, J Z01BE03008-02
RIDGEWAY, ELI CHESTER M01RR00051-30 0696
RIDGEWAY, LISA M01RR00069-29 0413
RIDGWAY, CHESTER E R01CA47411-04
RIDGWAY, CHESTER E R01DK36843-07
RIDGWAY, E C M01RR00051-30 0632
RIDGWAY, E CHES M01RR00051-30 0666
RIED, L DOUGLAS R01AG07433-03
RIEDER, CONLY P41RR01219-10 9001
RIEDER, CONLY L P41RR01219-10
RIEDER, CONLY L R01GM40198-07
RIEDER, RONALD F R01DK12401-23
RIEDERER, STEPHEN J R01CA37993-08
RIEDESEL, MARVIN M01RR00997-16 0179
RIEDESEL, MARVIN L M01RR00997-16 0394
RIEDESEL, MARVIN L M01RR00997-16 0365
RIEDESEL, MARVIN L M01RR00997-16 0413
RIEGEL, ANNA T R29DK43127-02
RIEGEL, ILSE L P30CA07175-28 9008
RIEKE, REUBEN D R01GM35153-06
RIEKER, PATRICIA P S07RR05526-29 0098
RIELY, CAROLINE A P30DK34989-08 9006
RIEMER, ROBERT K R01HD26152-03
RIENHOFF, HUGH Y, JR K11AR01537-05
RIERDAN, JILL S07RR07186-10 0614
RIERDAN, JILL S07RR07186-10
RIES, ANDREW L K07HL02215-04
RIES, RICHARD K R01DA04864-03
RIESER, JOHN J R01HD24554-04
RIESER, JOHN J S07RR07201-12 0638
RIESNER, DETLEV P01NS22786-07 0003
RIESZ, P Z01CM06358-08
RIETHER, A. M. M01RR00039-31 0420
RIETHMAN, HAROLD R01HG00567-01
RIFKIN, BARRY R R01DE09576-02
RIFKIN, DANIEL B R01CA23753-14
RIFKIN, DANIEL B R01CA34282-08
RIFKIN, MARY R R01GM37778-05
RIFKIN, MATTHEW D U01CA45254-04S1
RIFKIND, ARLEEN B R01ES03606-06
RIFKIND, ARLEEN B S07RR05396-30 0781
RIFKIND, J M Z01AG00047-21
RIFKIND, RICHARD A S03RR03260-09
RIFKIND, RICHARD A S07RR05534-19
RIGAS, BASIL R01HG00385-01
RIGBY, JAMES H R01CA36543-05
RIGBY, JAMES H R01GM30771-07A3
RIGBY, WILLIAM F K04AI00910-04
RIGBY, WILLIAM F C R01AI24348-04A2
RIGBY, WILLIAM FC S07RR05392-30 0703
RIGGS, ARTHUR D R01AG08196-04
RIGGS, AUSTEN F, II R01GM35847-06
RIGGS, B L M01RR00585-20 0385
RIGGS, B L M01RR00585-20 0409
RIGGS, B L M01RR00585-20 0422
RIGGS, B L M01RR00585-20 0423
RIGGS, B L M01RR00585-20 0459
RIGGS, B L M01RR00585-20 0453
RIGGS, B L M01RR00585-20 0487
RIGGS, B L M01RR00585-20 0505
RIGGS, B L M01RR00585-20 0509
RIGGS, B L M01RR00585-20 0563
RIGGS, B LAWRENCE M01RR00585-20 0314
RIGGS, B LAWRENCE M01RR00585-20 0212
RIGGS, B. L. M01RR00585-20 0383
RIGGS, B. LAWRENCE P01AG04875-08 0006
RIGGS, BYRON L P01AG04875-08
RIGGS, CHARLES E M01RR00059-30 0655
RIGGS, JOHN L N01CP51001-09
RIGGS, LAWRENCE B. P01AG04875-08 0001
RIGGS, MICHAEL W U01AI30223-02 9002
RIGGS, MICHAEL W U01AI30223-02 0002
RIGGS, ROBERT S07RR05857-11 0926
RIIS, RONALD S07RR05462-29 0896
RIKANS, LORA E R01AG04984-06
RIKER, ROBERT J R44NS28265-02
RIKIHISA, YASUKO R01AI30010-02
RILEY, CAROL P S07RR07151-13 0523
RILEY, CHRIS M S07RR05606-25 0693
RILEY, CRYSTAL P50MH43458-04 0007
RILEY, DANNY A P01HD20743-05 9004
RILEY, DAVID J R01HL24264-13
RILEY, DAVID J R01HL44081-02
RILEY, DONALD A R01MH44746-03
RILEY, EDWARD P R01AA06902-07
RILEY, EDWARD P R01DA04275-05
RILEY, EDWARD P R37AA03249-15
RILEY, EDWARD P S07RR07004-16 0054
RILEY, JAMES C S07RR07031-26 0104
RILEY, LELA K R29RR04568-03
RILEY, MICHAEL V R01EY00541-22
RILEY, MICHAEL V S07RR07131-22
RILEY, RICHARD S07RR05363-30 0834
RILEY, RICHARD L R01AI23350-05
RILEY, WILLIAM P01DK39079-05 0004
RILEY, WILLIAM J M01RR00082-29 0405
RILLEMA, JAMES A R01HD06571-20
RILLEMA, JAMES A S06GM08167-13 0047
RILLING, HANS C R01DK43055-02
RIMAR, STEPHEN S07RR05358-30 0478
RIMER, BARBARA P01CA34856-09 0002
RIMER, BARBARA P01CA34856-09 9002
RIMM, ALFRED A P01CA40053-06 9001
RIMM, ALFRED A R03CA54801-01
RIMMER, JEFFREY M S07RR05429-30 0209
RIMNAC, CLARE M R01AR40191-03

RIMNAC, CLARE M R29AR38007-05
RIMOIN, DAVID L M01RR00425-22S3 0322
RIMOIN, DAVID L P01HD22657-05
RIMOIN, DAVID L P01HD22657-05 0001
RIMOIN, DAVID L P01HD22657-05 9001
RIMSTIDT, J DONALD S07RR07095-24 0371
RINALDO, CHARLES N01AI72632-15
RINALDO, CHARLES R, JR R01AI28721-01A2
RINALDO, PIERO S07RR05358-30 0487
RINALDY, AUGUSTINUS R01CA43769-05
RINCHIK, EUGENE M R01HG00370-04
RINDER, CHRISTINE ST S07RR05358-30 0479
RINDFUSS, RONALD R R01HD24325-04
RINDFUSS, RONALD R R01HD25934-01
RINDFUSS, RONALD R R01HD27690-01
RINDLER, MICHAEL J R01DK44238-01
RINE, JASPER S07RR07006-26 0895
RINE, JASPER D P30ES01896-13 9031
RINE, JASPER D R01GM31105-10
RINE, JASPER D R01GM35827-06
RINEHART, CLIFFORD A S07RR05406-30 0890
RINEHART, JOHN J R55CA51160-01A2
RINEHART, KENNETH L R01AI01278-35
RINEHART, KENNETH L R01AI04769-30
RINEHART, KENNETH L R01GM27029-20A1
RINGER, DANIEL C N01CP95663-06
RINGLER, D J P51RR00168-30 0142
RINGLER, D J P51RR00168-30 0143
RINGLER, DANIEL H P40RR00200-28
RINGLER, DOUGLAS J R01AI29855-02
RINGLER, DOUGLAS J R01AI32309-01
RINGLER, DOUGLAS J R29AI25644-04
RINGNALDA, MURCO N R43GM46160-01
RINGO, JAMES L R01NS26526-04
RINGO, JAMES L R29NS24217-05
RINGOLD, GORDON M R01GM25821-13
RINGWALT, CHRISTOPHER L R01DA07037-02
RINTOUL, DAVID A R01EY06493-06
RINZEL, J Z01DK13004-18
RIO, DONALD C R01HD28063-01
RIO, DONALD C R29HD22857-05
RIORDAN, JOHN P50DK41980-03 0001
RIORDAN, JOHN R P50DK41980-03
RIOS, EDUARDO R01AR32808-09
RIPICH, DANIELLE P50AG08012-04 0003
RIPKA, WILLIAM C R43HL46584-01
RIPKA, WILLIAM C R43HL47260-01
RIPPS, HARRIS P41RR01395-10 0015
RIPPS, HARRIS R01EY06516-07
RIPS, LANCE J R01MH39633-05
RIS, HANS P41RR00570-21 0009
RIS, M DOUGLAS S07RR05535-29 0535
RISBY, EMILE M01RR00039-31 0434
RISBY, EMILE D K20MH00870-01A1
RISCH, NEIL J R01HG00348-04
RISLEY, TODD R P01HD03144-24 0027
RISO, RONALD R R01NS27456-03
RISSER, PAUL G S07RR07185-13
RISSER, REX P01CA22443-14 0003
RISSER, REX G P30CA07175-28 9011
RISSING, J PETER S07RR05365-30 0099
RITCHIE, B S07RR05692-22 0989
RITCHIE, BRENDA B R01HL30026-09
RITCHIE, J MURDOCH R01NS08304-23A1
RITCHIE, J MURDOCH R01NS12327-17
RITENBAUGH, CHERYL P01CA27502-11 9004
RITENBAUGH, CHERYL P01CA41108-05 9002
RITMAN, ERIK L R01HL43025-01A2
RITTENBERG, MARVIN B R01AI26827-04
RITTENHOUSE, SUSAN E R01HL38622-06
RITTENHOUSE, SUSAN E. M01RR00109-28 0297
RITTER, ROBERT C R01NS20561-08
RITTER, W SUE R01DK40498-03
RITTER, WALTER P R01NS30029-14
RITTMAN, BARRY R R29DE09083-04
RITZ, JEROME P01AI29530-02
RITZ, JEROME P01AI29530-02 0001
RITZ, JEROME P01AI29530-02 0003
RITZ, JEROME P01AI29530-02 9001
RITZ, JEROME P01CA34183-08 0013
RITZ, JEROME P01CA34183-08 9002
RITZ, JEROME P30CA06516-28 9014
RITZ, JEROME R01CA41619-04
RITZ, LOUIS A P01NS27511-03 0004
RITZI, EARL S07RR05773-17 0369
RITZMANN, ROY E R01NS17411-10
RIVA, CHARLES E R01EY03242-13
RIVA, CHARLES E R01EY08413-02
RIVENSON, ABRAHAM P01CA29580-11 9002
RIVENSON,ABRAHAM S. P01CA29580-11 9001
RIVERA-COLON, MARITZA S06GM08267-04 0001
RIVERA, AUDELIO S07RR05745-19 0230
RIVERA, WARREN C S07RR05795-14 0422
RIVERS, RICHARD J K11HL01654-05
RIVIER, CATHERINE P01HD13527-12 9003
RIVIER, CATHERINE P01HD13527-12 0002
RIVIER, CATHERINE R01AA08924-01
RIVIER, CATHERINE R01DA05602-02
RIVIER, CATHERINE S07RR05595-27 0671
RIVIER, CATHERINE L P01DK26741-12 0009
RIVIER, CATHERINE L P01DK26741-12 9001
RIVIER, JEAN P01CA54418-01 9001
RIVIER, JEAN P01DK26741-12 0010
RIVIER, JEAN R01HL41910-03
RIVIER, JEAN E N01HD13100-01
RIVIER, JEAN E P01DK26741-12 9003
RIVIER, JEAN E P01HD13527-12 0005
RIVIER, JEAN E P01HD13527-12 9001
RIVIN, CAROL J S07RR07079-26 0283
RIVKEES, SCOTT A K08HD00924-02
RIVKIN, SAUL E U10CA20319-15
RIVLIN, RICHARD S P01CA29502-11A1
RIXON, F P41RR02250-06 0002
RIZZA, R A M01RR00585-20 0115
RIZZA, R A M01RR00585-20 0398
RIZZA, R A M01RR00585-20 0406
RIZZA, R A M01RR00585-20 0401
RIZZA, R A M01RR00585-20 0512
RIZZA, R A M01RR00585-20 0562
RIZZA, ROBERT A M01RR00585-20 0344
RIZZA, ROBERT A M01RR00585-20 0529
RIZZA, ROBERT A R01DK29953-10
RIZZINO, ARNOLD A R01HD19837-05
RIZZO, JOSEPH F III K11EY00281-05
RIZZO, MATTHEW P01NS19632-09 0001
RIZZO, THOMAS A S07RR05370-30 0614
RIZZO, WILLIAM M01RR00065-29 0357
RIZZO, WILLIAM M01RR00065-29 0375
RIZZO, WILLIAM B M01RR00065-29 0228
RIZZO, WILLIAM B M01RR00065-29 0337
RIZZO, WILLIAM B R01DK41843-03
RIZZO, WILLIAM R M01RR00065-29 0332
RIZZOLO, LAWRENCE J R01EY08694-01A1
RKING, R P41RR01243-10 0019
RLESCH, SUSAN S07RR06031-02 0377
ROA, VEENA S07RR05417-30 0813
ROACH, PETER J R01DK27221-13
ROACH, PETER J R01DK42576-01A1
ROACHE, JOHN D R29DA05716-03
ROBAIRE, BERNARD R13HD27948-01
ROBAKIS, NIKOLAOS K P01MH45212-02 0005
ROBAKIS, NIKOLAOS K. P50AG05138-08 0008
ROBAKIS, NILOLAOS K R01AG08200-04
ROBB, JAMES A M01RR00833-17 0183
ROBBIN, A R Z01DK18009-12
ROBBINS, DAVID C M01RR00109-28 0340
ROBBINS, DICK S07RR05684-23 0175
ROBBINS, DICK L R01AR39831-01A1
ROBBINS, FREDERICK C P01AI26482-03S1
ROBBINS, FREDERICK C P01AI26482-03S1 9001
ROBBINS, J Z01BB07003-03
ROBBINS, J Z01DK45000-24
ROBBINS, J Z01DK45009-24
ROBBINS, J Z01DK45020-15
ROBBINS, J Z01DK45028-13
ROBBINS, J B Z01HD01304-09
ROBBINS, J H Z01CB03638-22
ROBBINS, JEFFREY P01HL22619-14 0019
ROBBINS, JEFFREY P01HL41496-03 0007
ROBBINS, JEFFREY P01HL46826-01
ROBBINS, JEFFREY P01HL46826-01 0001
ROBBINS, JOANNE R01NS24427-05
ROBBINS, K C Z01DE00479-03
ROBBINS, K C Z01DE00480-03
ROBBINS, KENNETH C R01HL34276-07
ROBBINS, LEE N. P01AG03991-08 0008
ROBBINS, NORMAN R01AG06641-05
ROBBINS, NORMAN R01AG08886-03
ROBBINS, NORMAN S07RR05410-30 0952
ROBBINS, P Z01CB09021-05
ROBBINS, PAUL D R01CA55227-01
ROBBINS, PHILLIPS W P01CA26712-11S1 0003
ROBBINS, PHILLIPS W R01GM45188-01
ROBBINS, PHILLIPS W R37GM31318-29
ROBBINS, RICHARD M01RR00125-28 0656
ROBBINS, RICHARD J R01NS26362-03
ROBBINS, RICHARD J R01NS27989-02
ROBBINS, TERRY J S06GM08061-17 0007
ROBBLEE, LOIS S N01NS12300-00
ROBERSTON, JAMES M01RR00211-27 0307
ROBERSTON, MARJORIE J R01MH46104-03
ROBERT-GUROFF, M Z01CP05536-05
ROBERTS, A Z01CP05617-03
ROBERTS, A B Z01CP05051-13
ROBERTS, ALAN H M01RR00833-17 0184
ROBERTS, BEVERLY L R01NR02575-01A1
ROBERTS, BRYAN E U01AI26507-03 0001
ROBERTS, D D Z01CB09172-03
ROBERTS, D D Z01CB09173-03
ROBERTS, D D Z01CB09174-03
ROBERTS, D D Z01CB09175-03
ROBERTS, DRUCILLA J K11CA01573-01
ROBERTS, EUGENE L, JR R29AG08710-02
ROBERTS, HAROLD M01RR00046-31 0507
ROBERTS, HAROLD R M01RR00046-31 0428
ROBERTS, HAROLD R P01HL06350-30
ROBERTS, HAROLD R P01HL06350-30 0018
ROBERTS, HAROLD R P50HL26309-11
ROBERTS, INGRAM S07RR05359-30 0520
ROBERTS, INGRAM M R29DK38729-04
ROBERTS, JAMES P01HD24180-04 0003
ROBERTS, JAMES A P51RR00164-30 0031
ROBERTS, JAMES A P51RR00164-30 0032
ROBERTS, JAMES A P51RR00164-30 0033
ROBERTS, JAMES A P51RR00164-30 0034
ROBERTS, JAMES A P51RR00164-30 0036
ROBERTS, JAMES A R01DK14681-22
ROBERTS, JAMES A R13DK44447-01
ROBERTS, JAMES L P01MH45212-02 0006
ROBERTS, JAMES L P01MH45212-02 9002
ROBERTS, JAMES M P01HD24180-04
ROBERTS, JAMES M R01HD21785-05
ROBERTS, JAMES M R29CA48718-03
ROBERTS, JAY P01DA06871-01 0005
ROBERTS, JEANETTE C S07RR05738-20 0220
ROBERTS, JEANETTE C S07RR05738-20 0217
ROBERTS, JEFFREY A P51RR00169-30 0153
ROBERTS, JEFFREY A P51RR00169-30 0154
ROBERTS, JEFFREY W R01GM21941-17
ROBERTS, JOANNE E S07RR07072-26 0273
ROBERTS, JOHN W S06GM08156-15 0007
ROBERTS, KENNETH S07RR05834-12 0544
ROBERTS, KENNETH R R01HD27276-01A1
ROBERTS, L JACKSON P50GM15431-24 0128
ROBERTS, L JACKSON R01GM42056-03
ROBERTS, MARILYN C R01AI24136-05
ROBERTS, MARILYN C S07RR05714-21 0118
ROBERTS, MARK S R01HS06728-01
ROBERTS, MARY F R01GM26762-12
ROBERTS, MARY F S07RR07156-16 0568
ROBERTS, MARY F S15GM47103-01
ROBERTS, MICHAEL H R29NS26272-04
ROBERTS, MICHELLE M K08DK01954-02
ROBERTS, NEAL M01RR00065-29 0351
ROBERTS, NORBERT J, JR R01AI23774-05
ROBERTS, PAUL A S07RR07079-26 0301
ROBERTS, R MICHAEL S07RR07053-26 0167
ROBERTS, RICHARD B M01RR00047-31 0449
ROBERTS, RICHARD B U01AI25917-04 0003
ROBERTS, RICHARD J P01CA13106-20 0007
ROBERTS, RICHARD J P30CA45508-05
ROBERTS, RICHARD J P30CA45508-05 9002
ROBERTS, RICHARD J P30CA45508-05 9004
ROBERTS, RICHARD J R01GM46127-01
ROBERTS, RICHARD J R01HG00303-04
ROBERTS, RICHARD J R01LM04971-04
ROBERTS, RICHARD J R13HG00049-02
ROBERTS, RICHARD J S07RR05717-21
ROBERTS, RICHARD J S15GM47039-01
ROBERTS, ROBERT P50HL42267-02
ROBERTS, ROBERT P50HL42267-02 0002
ROBERTS, ROBERT P50HL42267-02 9001
ROBERTS, ROBERT J P50HL36536-05 0003
ROBERTS, ROBERT J R01HL42057-03
ROBERTS, ROBERT M R01HD21980-07
ROBERTS, ROBERT M R37HD21896-06
ROBERTS, STEPHEN M R01DA06893-01A1
ROBERTS, STEVEN M S07RR05458-29 0836
ROBERTS, THOMAS P01HD24926-03 0003
ROBERTS, THOMAS M P01CA50661-03 0001
ROBERTS, THOMAS M R01CA30002-10
ROBERTS, THOMAS M R01CA43803-05
ROBERTS, THOMAS M R01GM29994-10
ROBERTS, W C Z01HL03994-01
ROBERTS, W C Z01HL03995-01
ROBERTS, W C Z01HL03996-01
ROBERTS, W C Z01HL03997-01
ROBERTS, W C Z01HL03998-01
ROBERTS, W C Z01HL03999-01
ROBERTS, W C Z01HL04000-01
ROBERTS, W C Z01HL05201-01
ROBERTS, W C Z01HL05202-01
ROBERTS, W C Z01HL05203-01
ROBERTS, W C Z01HL05204-01
ROBERTS, W C Z01HL05205-01
ROBERTS, W C Z01HL05206-01
ROBERTS, W C Z01HL05207-01
ROBERTS, W C Z01HL05208-01
ROBERTS, W C Z01HL05209-01
ROBERTS, W C Z01HL05210-01
ROBERTS, W C Z01HL05211-01
ROBERTS, W C Z01HL05222-01
ROBERTS, W EUGENE R01DE09237-02
ROBERTS, WILLIAM S07RR07080-26 0310
ROBERTS, WILLIAM J R01NS13447-10A1
ROBERTS, WILLIAM M K08CA01546-02
ROBERTS, WILLIAM M R29NS27142-02
ROBERTSON, STEVEN S. P50HD11089-14 0025
ROBERTSON, ABEL L R10HL33758-07
ROBERTSON, ANNE D R19DA06440-03
ROBERTSON, CLAUDIA P01NS27616-02S1 0004
ROBERTSON, CLAUDIA S P01NS27616-02S1 9001
ROBERTSON, CLAUDIA S P01NS27616-02S1 0002
ROBERTSON, DAVID P50AG05128-08 0016
ROBERTSON, DAVID P50HL14192-21 0018
ROBERTSON, DAVID G K11DK01872-04
ROBERTSON, DAVID H R01HL44589-02
ROBERTSON, DENNIS M U10EY06253-07
ROBERTSON, ELIZABETH J R01HD25335-03
ROBERTSON, ELIZABETH J R01HD25208-03
ROBERTSON, FREDIKA M R01CA51443-02
ROBERTSON, FREDIKA M R01CA55211-01
ROBERTSON, GARY L M01RR00048-30 0168
ROBERTSON, GARY L M01RR00048-30 0169
ROBERTSON, GARY L M01RR00055-30 0579
ROBERTSON, GARY L M01RR00055-30 0550

ROBERTSON, GARY L P60DK20595-14 0024
ROBERTSON, GARY L R01DK36467-05
ROBERTSON, GARY L. M01RR00055-30 0463
ROBERTSON, H THOMAS P01HL24163-13 9004
ROBERTSON, H THOMAS P01HL24163-13 0013
ROBERTSON, H THOMAS P01HL38736-05 0002
ROBERTSON, HUGH D P50DA05130-05 0003
ROBERTSON, HUGH D U01AI31876-01
ROBERTSON, HUGH M S07RR07030-26 0409
ROBERTSON, J DAVID R01NS26853-01A2
ROBERTSON, JOAN F S07RR07098-26 0359
ROBERTSON, JOHN M M01RR00042-31 0643
ROBERTSON, PAUL K P01CA20180-14 9001
ROBERTSON, PAUL R M01RR00400-23 0255
ROBERTSON, R PAUL M01RR00400-23 0291
ROBERTSON, R PAUL M01RR00400-23 0206
ROBERTSON, RICHARD T. P01DC00450-04 0004
ROBERTSON, RODERICK P R01DK38325-06
ROBERTSON, RODERICK P R01DK39994-03
ROBERTSON, ROSE M01RR00095-31 0305
ROBERTSON, ROSE M01RR00095-31 0357
ROBERTSON, ROSE MARIE M01RR00095-31 0294
ROBERTUS, JON D R01GM30048-13
ROBERTUS, JON D S07RR07091-26 0767
ROBESON, BONNIE L N01CM97569-03
ROBEY, F A Z01DE00433-05
ROBEY, F A Z01DE00434-05
ROBEY, F A Z01DE00437-05
ROBEY, P G Z01DE00380-08
ROBIDOUX, ANDRE U10CA44066-05
ROBILLARD, JEAN P50DK44756-01 9001
ROBILLARD, JEAN P50DK44756-01 0001
ROBILLARD, JEAN E P01HL14388-20 0238
ROBILLARD, JEAN E P50DK44756-01
ROBILLARD, JEAN E R01DK43961-06
ROBIN, DONALD A R03DC01182-01
ROBINETTE, C DENNIS N01CP15690-00
ROBINETTE, C L S07RR05911-08 0646
ROBINOVITCH, MURRAY S07RR05346-30 0323
ROBINS, DIANE M R01GM31546-10
ROBINS, DIANE M R01GM42597-04
ROBINS, H IAN M01RR03186-06 0020
ROBINS, H IAN P01CA20432-14 0033
ROBINS, JAMES M K04ES00180-04
ROBINS, LEE N P50AA03539-14 9005
ROBINS, LEE N P50AA03539-14 9006
ROBINS, SANDER J R01DK28640-08
ROBINS, THOMAS G R01OH02761-02
ROBINSON, ALAN G M01RR00056-30 0041
ROBINSON, ALAN G M01RR00056-30 0152
ROBINSON, ARTHUR M01RR00069-29 0025
ROBINSON, ARTHUR R01HD10032-15
ROBINSON, BRUCE P01GM32681-08 0009
ROBINSON, CECIL H R01HD11840-13
ROBINSON, D L Z01EY00045-13
ROBINSON, DAVID A R37EY00598-23
ROBINSON, DWIGHT P01AI28465-03 0003
ROBINSON, DWIGHT P01AR03564-32 0024
ROBINSON, FARREL R, JR R29EY07991-03
ROBINSON, GENE E R29MH47374-01
ROBINSON, GENE E S07RR07030-26 0410
ROBINSON, GENE E S07RR07030-26 0411
ROBINSON, GERRY P01NS14867-13 9002
ROBINSON, GLADYS P60HL28391-09 0008
ROBINSON, HARRIET L P01CA39240-07 0005
ROBINSON, HARRIET L R01CA23086-14
ROBINSON, HARRIET L R01CA27223-12
ROBINSON, J P41RR02250-06 0004
ROBINSON, J DANIEL R43AI30863-01
ROBINSON, JACK L S06GM08003-21
ROBINSON, JAMES C R01HS06580-01
ROBINSON, JAMES E R01AI24030-05
ROBINSON, JOHN A S07RR05368-30
ROBINSON, JOHN A S15AA09250-01
ROBINSON, JOHN A S15AI32193-01
ROBINSON, JOSEPH D R01NS05430-25
ROBINSON, JOSEPH P R29GM38827-06
ROBINSON, KENNETH R R01NS28154-02
ROBINSON, M A Z01AI00389-08
ROBINSON, MITCHELL E R29DK38660-05
ROBINSON, N EDWARD S07RR05623-25
ROBINSON, NEAL C R01GM24795-14
ROBINSON, NORMAN E S15GM47093-01
ROBINSON, RICHARD B P01HL28958-09 0004
ROBINSON, RICHARD B P01HL28958-09 9001
ROBINSON, RICHARD B P01HL30557-08 9003
ROBINSON, ROBERT G P01NS15080-12 0008
ROBINSON, ROBERT G R01MH40355-05
ROBINSON, SUSAN P50DA05274-04 0003
ROBINSON, SUSAN E R01DA04746-02
ROBINSON, TERRY E R01DA04294-04
ROBINSON, W A M01RR00051-30 0660
ROBINSON, WILLIAM A M01RR00051-30 0708
ROBINSON, WILLIAM A M01RR00051-30 0763
ROBINSON, WILLIAM A M01RR00051-30 0688
ROBINSON, WILLIAM A M01RR00051-30 0605
ROBINSON, WILLIAM A M01RR00051-30 0692
ROBINSON, WILLIAM A M01RR00051-30 0714
ROBINSON, WILLIAM A M01RR00051-30 0681
ROBINSON, WILLIAM A M01RR00051-30 0716
ROBINSON, WILLIAM A M01RR00051-30 0728
ROBINSON, WILLIAM A M01RR00051-30 0740
ROBINSON, WILLIAM A M01RR00051-30 0743
ROBINSON, WILLIAM E, JR R01AI31326-01
ROBINSON, WILLIAM S P30AI27762-03 9004
ROBINSON, WILLIAM S P30DK38707-05 0011
ROBINSON, WILLIAM S P50HL33811-06 0004
ROBINSON, WILLIAM S R01AI20551-08
ROBINSON, WILLIAM S R37AI13526-16
ROBISHAW, JANET D R29GM39867-04
ROBISON, ALICE N01CP15665-00
ROBISON, LESLIE P01CA21737-14 0011
ROBISON, LESLIE L R01CA48051-04
ROBISON, LESLIE L R01CA49450-03
ROBISON, W G Z01EY00149-18
ROBITAILLE, PIERRE-MARIE L R55HL45120-01A1
ROBKIN, MAURICE A S07RR05714-21 0138
ROBLES, LAURA J S03RR03450-05
ROBLES, LAURA J S06GM08156-15
ROBLES, RAFAELA R R18DA05743-03S1
ROBLES, RAFAELA R R18DA06993-02
ROBLES, RAFAELA R U01DA07287-01
ROBOTHAM, JAMES R01HL39138-04A1
ROBRISH, S A Z01DE00382-09
ROBSON, ALAN U01HL38110-06
ROBSON, JOHN A R01EY03490-08
ROBY, FRED B S07RR07002-26 0857
ROBYT, JOHN F R01DE03578-18A1
ROCCHINI, ALBERT P M01RR00042-31 0570
ROCCHINI, ALBERT P M01RR00042-31 0431
ROCHA, VICTOR S06GM08132-17 0011
ROCHE, JAMES K S07RR05431-30 0865
ROCHE, PATRICK C R29HD22735-04
ROCHEFORD, TORBERT R S07RR07030-26 0412
ROCK, CHARLES O R01GM28035-12
ROCK, CHARLES O R01GM34496-07
ROCK, IRVIN K05MH00707-05
ROCK, KENNETH L R01AI20248-09
ROCK, KENNETH L R01AI31337-01
ROCK, KENNETH L R01GM38515-04
ROCKHOLD, ROBIN W R01HL39387-05
ROCKHOLD, ROBIN W S15HL47707-01
ROCKHOLD, ROBIN WILL S07RR05386-30 0594
ROCKLAND, KATHLEEN S R01EY07058-06
ROCKSWOLD, GAYLAN L P20NS30322-01
ROCKSWOLD, GAYLAN L P20NS30322-01 0003
ROCKWAY, SUSIE S07RR05477-29 0419
ROCKWELL, KENNETH M01RR00030-30 0370
ROCKWELL, ROBERT S07RR07132-20 0407
ROCKWELL, SARA C R01CA35215-08
RODARTE, JOSEPH R R01HL46230-01
RODBELL, M Z01ES80045-03
RODBERG, LEONARD S S07RR07064-24 0205
RODDAN, PAULINE P51RR00169-30 9003
RODEBUSH, WILLIAM E S07RR05959-06 0020
RODECK, ULRICH P01CA25874-12 0013
RODEHAFFER, R J M01RR00585-20 0542
RODEHEFFER, R J M01RR00585-20 0483
RODEN, DAN M M01RR00095-31 0351
RODEN, DAN M M01RR00095-31 0335
RODEN, DAN M N01HC65065-09
RODEN, DAN M R01HL32694-07
RODEN, DAN M. M01RR00095-31 0314
RODEN, DAN M. M01RR00095-31 0292
RODEN, DAN M. M01RR00095-31 0313
RODEN, LENNART R01DE08252-05
RODEN, LENNART R01NS27353-03
RODER, HEINRICH R01GM35926-07
RODER, HEINRICH R01GM44881-03
RODERICK, THOMAS H R01GM19656-20
RODEWALD, RICHARD D S07RR07094-26 0360
RODGERS, CAROL D S07RR07049-26 0445
RODGERS, CHRISTINE M S07RR05357-30 0458
RODGERS, DON N01LM13546-00
RODGERS, FRANK G S15AI32167-01
RODGERS, G P Z01DK25028-13
RODGERS, G P Z01DK25058-06
RODGERS, G P Z01DK25063-05
RODGERS, GEORGE M S07RR05428-30 0189
RODGERS, JOSEPH L R01HD21973-05A1
RODGERS, KATHLEEN E R29ES04337-06
RODGERS, MICHAEL P41RR00886-16 0005
RODGERS, MICHAEL A R01GM24235-14
RODGERS, MICHAEL A J S15CA55982-01
RODGERS, ROBERT L S07RR07086-15 0321
RODGERS, VICTOR G J S07RR07035-26 0092
RODIECK, ROBERT W R01EY02923-13
RODIER, PATRICIA M P01ES05197-01A1 9002
RODIER, PATRICIA M R01AA08666-02
RODIER, PATRICIA M R01NS24287-04A2
RODIN, JUDITH M01RR00125-28 0772
RODIN, JUDITH M01RR06022-02 0769
RODIN, JUDITH M01RR06022-02 0780
RODIN, JUDY P01DC00168-10 0016
RODMAN, JOHN P41RR01861-07 0006
RODMAN, PETER S P51RR00169-30 0080
RODNEY, H ELAINE R24AA09294-02 0001
RODNITZKY, ROBERT L M01RR00059-30 0629
RODRIGUEZ DEL VALLE, S07RR05419-30 0823
RODRIGUEZ-BOULAN, ENRIQUE J R01EY08538-01A
RODRIGUEZ-BOULAN, ENRIQUE J R01GM41771-02
RODRIGUEZ-BOULAN, ENRIQUE J R01GM34107-08
RODRIGUEZ-DEL VALLE, NURI S06GM08102-20 00
RODRIGUEZ, ELOY R01AI18398-09
RODRIGUEZ, ELOY R01AI24779-01A3
RODRIGUEZ, GLADYS M01RR01346-10 0191
RODRIGUEZ, JOSE R S07RR05419-30 0824
RODRIGUEZ, MOSES R01NS24180-05
RODRIGUEZ, ORLANDO R01MH30569-14
RODRIGUEZ, PAUL H S03RR03243-10
RODRIQUEZ-BOULAN, E S07RR05396-30 0740
RODRIQUEZ, ORLANDO R01AA07544-04
RODU, BRAD P30CA13148-20 9012
RODU, BRAD S07RR05300-30 0201
RODWELL, VICTOR W R01HL47113-01
RODY, NANCY G07LM05238-01A1
ROE, BRUCE A R01HG00313-03
ROE, CHARLES R M01RR00030-30 0352
ROE, CHARLES R R01HD24908-03
ROEDER, G S R01GM28904-11
ROEDER, ROBERT G R35CA42567-06
ROEDER, ROBERT G U01AI27397-04 0003
ROEHRS, TIMOTHY A R01AA07147-04
ROEHRS, TIMOTHY A R01DA05086-04
ROEMER, RICHARD A R01DA06728-01A1
ROEMER, ROBERT B R01CA33922-08
ROEMER, ROBERT B R01CA36428-07
ROESKE, ROGER W N01HD13102-00
ROESKE, WILLIAM R P01HL20984-15 0005
ROESS, DEBORAH A R29HD23236-05
ROESSLER, BLAKE J R01DK38932-04
ROFFLER-TARLOV, SUZA S07RR05382-30 0876
ROFFLER-TARLOV, SUZANNE K R01NS20181-07A2
ROFFMAN, ROGER A R01DA03586-06
ROFFMAN, ROGER A R01MH46792-01A2
ROFFWARG, HOWARD P P50MH41115-05 0021
ROGALSKI, ADRIENNE A R01GM36802-06
ROGAN, ELEANOR G P30CA36727-08 9002
ROGAN, W J Z01ES43002-15
ROGART, RICHARD P01HL20592-15 0018
ROGART, RICHARD B R01HL37217-03
ROGART, RICHARD B R01NS23360-04
ROGAWSKI, M Z01NS02733-06
ROGAWSKI, M A Z01NS02772-04
ROGERS, ADRIANNE E P01ES02429-11 0004
ROGERS, ADRIANNE E S07RR05883-07
ROGERS, ALAN RAY R29GM39593-05
ROGERS, ANDREI R13AG09737-01
ROGERS, ANN S07RR05796-14 0439
ROGERS, ANN E R29NS29378-02
ROGERS, ANNE T P01NS27500-01A2 0001
ROGERS, BARBARA P S06GM08218-08 0020
ROGERS, BEVERLY J S07RR05424-30 0072
ROGERS, BONNIE, DR S07RR05450-30 0333
ROGERS, DOUGLAS S07RR07055-26 0201
ROGERS, DUKE S R15GM46016-01
ROGERS, GARY L U10EY06323-07
ROGERS, J S07RR05728-20 0206
ROGERS, JOHN C R55DK44219-01
ROGERS, JOSEPH R01AG07367-04
ROGERS, JOSEPH R01AG08374-01A2
ROGERS, KATHRYN E R35AG09016-02 0005
ROGERS, MARK C P01NS20020-08 0003
ROGERS, PAUL U10CA29013-11
ROGERS, QUINTON R S07RR07007-26 0922
ROGERS, RICHARD C R01NS24530-06
ROGERS, ROBERT M01RR00056-30 0379
ROGERS, ROBERT M M01RR00056-30 0282
ROGERS, ROBERT M R01HL33269-05
ROGERS, SANDRA A R43DA07020-01
ROGERS, SHERRY L K04NS01352-03
ROGERS, SHERRY L R01NS23368-07
ROGERS, SHERRY L S06GM08139-17 0072
ROGERS, TERRY B R01HL28138-10
ROGERS, THOMAS J R01AI28372-02
ROGERS, TINA S S07RR05676-15 0955
ROGERS, W LESLIE R01CA32846-21
ROGERS, W LESLIE R01CA54362-01
ROGERS, WILLIAM J M01RR00032-31 0225
ROGERS, WILLIAM J M01RR00032-31 0313
ROGERS, WILLIAM J M01RR00032-31 0300
ROGERS, WILLIAM J M01RR00032-31 0301
ROGERS, WILLIAM J U01HL38512-05
ROGERS, WILLIAM J. M01RR00032-31 0268
ROGERS, WILLIAM J. M01RR00032-31 0260
ROGERS, WILLIAM J. N01HC55001-13
ROGERS, WILLIAM J. N01HV18116-02
ROGLER, CHARLES P30DK41296-03 9001
ROGLER, CHARLES E R01CA37232-08
ROGLER, LLOYD H S07RR07150-17
ROGNSTAD, ROBERT A R01DK42725-03
ROGNSTAD, ROBERT A R01DK43409-01
ROGOFF, BARBARA R01HD16973-07
ROGOL, ALAN M01RR00847-18 0362
ROGOL, ALAN D M01RR00847-18 0364
ROGOL, ALAN D M01RR00847-18 0367
ROGOL, ALAN D M01RR00847-18 0565
ROGOL, ALAN D M01RR00847-18 0566
ROGOL, ALAN D M01RR00847-18 0577
ROGOL, ALAN D M01RR00847-18 0272
ROGOL, ALAN D M01RR00847-18 0447
ROGOL, ALAN D M01RR00847-18 0548
ROGOL, ALAN D M01RR00847-18 0404
ROGOL, ALAN D M01RR00847-18 0405
ROGOL, ALAN D M01RR00847-18 0504
ROGOL, ALAN D M01RR00847-18 0505

ROH, MARK S K11CA01423-01A3
ROHEIM, PAUL S P01HL25596-12 9003
ROHEIM, PAUL S P01HL25596-12 0005
ROHEIM, PAUL S P01HL25596-12
ROHEIM, PAUL S S10RR06667-01
ROHOWSKY-KOCHAN, CHRISTINE M R29NS25625-04
ROHRBECK, CYNTHIA S07RR07019-26 0070
ROHRER, JAMES E R29AG08674-03
ROHRMANN, GEORGE F R01AI21973-12
ROHRMANN, GEORGE F S07RR07079-26 0278
ROHRSCHNEIDER, LARRY R R01CA40987-07
ROHRSCHNEIDER, LARRY R R01CA20551-15
ROISEN, FRED J P01DE07734-06 0006
ROIZAN, NANCY J M01RR00055-30 0537
ROIZEN, MICHAEL F M01RR00055-30 0548
ROIZEN, RON P50AA05595-11 0017
ROIZMAN, BERNARD P01AI24009-05 0002
ROIZMAN, BERNARD P01AI24009-05
ROIZMAN, BERNARD P30CA14599-18 9007
ROIZMAN, BERNARD P30CA14599-18 9002
ROIZMAN, BERNARD R01AI15488-13
ROIZMAN, BERNARD R35CA47451-04
ROJKIND, M P50AA03508-14 0046
ROJKIND, MARCOS P01DK41918-02 0003
ROJKO, JENNIFER L R01DK41066-03
ROJKO, JENNIFER L U01AI25722-05 0001
ROJKO, JENNIFER L U01AI25722-05 0002
ROJO, JAVIER S06GM08012-21 0016
ROKEACH, LUIS A R29AR40159-02
ROKEY, ROXANN K11HL02009-04
ROLE, LORNA W R01NS22061-07
ROLE, LORNA W R01NS29071-01
ROLF, JON E R01AA08578-02
ROLF, L L, JR S07RR05411-30 0960
ROLFE, RIAL D S15AI32165-01
ROLL, FREDRICK J R01AA06092-08
ROLLAND, R M P51RR00168-30 0170
ROLLER, P P Z01CM06195-03
ROLLINS VAN, MIKE P01HL28982-10 0007
ROLLINS-SMITH, LOUIS S07RR05424-30 0103
ROLLINS, BARRETT J P01CA19589-14A1 0032
ROLLINS, BARRETT J R01CA53091-01
ROLLINS, BARRETT J S07RR05526-29 0099
ROLLINS, BARRETT J S07RR05526-29 0082
ROLLS, BARBARA J R01DK39177-05
ROLLS, BARBARA J R01DK40968-04
ROLLS, BARBARA J S07RR05378-30 0012
ROLPH, ELIZABETH S R13HS06878-01
ROLPH, JOHN E R01HS06419-02
ROM, WILLIAM M01RR00096-30A1 0307
ROMAGNANO, MARYANN A R01NS27197-03
ROMAIN, PAUL L R29AI29417-03
ROMAN, ANN U01AI31494-01 0005
ROMAN, G C Z01NS02240-15
ROMAN, G C Z01NS02297-15
ROMAN, G C Z01NS02299-15
ROMAN, G C Z01NS02301-15
ROMAN, G C Z01NS02307-15
ROMAN, G C Z01NS02370-13
ROMAN, G C Z01NS02838-01
ROMAN, JESSE S07RR05389-30 0649
ROMAN, RICHARD J P01HL29587-09 0003
ROMAN, RICHARD J R01HL36279-06
ROMAN, SHEILA M01RR00071-28A1 0234
ROMAN, SHEILA M01RR00071-28A1 0239
ROMANHA, ALVARO J. P01AI26505-03 0004
ROMANO, LOUIS J R01CA40605-06
ROMANOSKI, ALAN J R29DA06605-02
ROME, L P30HD04612-21 9006
ROME, LAWRENCE C R29AR38404-06
ROME, LAWRENCE C S07RR07083-26 0480
ROME, LEONARD H P01HD06576-18 0017
ROME, LEONARD H R01GM38097-05
ROMEO, TONY S07RR05879-09 0603
ROMERO, GUILLERMO G R29DK40753-03
ROMERO, JUAN C R01HL16496-17
ROMERO, ROBERTO J K11HD00728-05
ROMERO, ROBERTO J U10HD21366-06
ROMNEY, SEYMOUR L R01CA55781-01
ROMNEY, SEYMOUR L U01CA53818-01
ROMOFF, JEFFREY A G08LM05261-01
ROMRELL, L S07RR05362-30 0794
ROMSKI, MARY ANN P01HD06016-21 0001
ROMSOS, DALE R R37DK15847-21
RONAI, ZEEV A R29CA51995-01A1
RONCOLI, MARIANNE S07RR07083-26 0481
RONEY, DAVID N01CN75401-15
RONG, YANG Z01BD03024-01
RONINSON, IGOR B R01CA39365-07
RONINSON, IGOR B R01CA40333-07
RONNER, PETER P30DK19525-15 9001
RONNER, PETER S07RR05415-30 0017
RONNET, GABRIELE V S07RR05378-30 0013
RONNETT, GABRIELE V R29DC00872-02
ROO, DABEERU C P50MH31302-14 0016
ROO, DABEERU C P50MH31302-14 0022
ROODMAN, G DAVID P01AR39529-02 0004
ROODMAN, G DAVID P01CA40035-06 0004
ROODMAN, GARSON D R01AR35188-05
ROODMAN, GARSON D R01AR41336-01
ROOF, DOROTHY J R01EY06514-06A1
ROOM, ROBIN P50AA05595-11 9003
ROOM, ROBIN G P50AA05595-11
ROONEY, J F Z01DE00421-07
ROONEY, SEAMUS A R01HL31175-08
ROONEY, SEAMUS A R01HL43320-16
ROOP, DENNIS R R01AI30283-02
ROOP, DENNIS R R01AR40240-02
ROOP, DENNIS R R01CA52607-02
ROOP, DENNIS R R01HD25479-03
ROOP, ROY M S07RR05350-30 0333
ROOP, ROY M, II R29AI28867-02
ROOPENIAN, DERRY C R01AI28802-02
ROOPENIAN, DERRY C R29AI24544-05
ROOS, ALBERT R01HL00082-43
ROOS, DAVID S R01AI28724-03
ROOS, DAVID S U01AI31808-01 0002
ROOS, KENNETH P R01HL47065-01
ROOS, RAYMOND P50NS21442-07 0003
ROOS, RAYMOND P M01RR00055-30 0478
ROOS, RAYMOND P P01NS24575-04 0004
ROOS, RAYMOND P P50NS21442-07
ROOSA, MARK W P50MH39246-07 0005
ROOSA, MARK W P50MH39246-07 0004
ROOSA, ROBERT A S15CA56006-01
ROOZEN, KENNETH J S07RR07178-14
ROPER, STEPHEN D P01DC00244-07 0002
ROPER, STEPHEN D R01AG06557-06
ROPER, STEPHEN D R01DC00374-04
ROPER, STEPHEN D R01DC01238-01
ROPPOLO, JAMES R N01NS92366-03
RORIE, DUANE K R01GM41797-03
RORIE, DUANE K R01HL23217-12
RORKE, ELLEN A R01ES05227-02
RORKE, ELLEN A R01HD25135-03
RORKE, LUCY P30HD26979-02 9003
RORKE, LUCY B P50NS11036-18 9002
ROSA, P A Z01AI00549-03
ROSA, ROBERT M M01RR01032-16 0411
ROSAN, BURTON P50DE07118-07 0007
ROSAN, BURTON R01DE03180-20
ROSAN, BURTON S07RR05337-30 0771
ROSARIO, OSVALDO S06GM08102-20 0046
ROSAZZA, JOHN P R01HD06380-18
ROSBASH, MICHAEL M P01GM33205-08 9001
ROSBASH, MICHAEL M P01GM33205-08
ROSBASH, MICHAEL M P01GM33205-08 0005
ROSBASH, MICHAEL M R01GM23549-15
ROSCIOLI, N A Z01BE03004-03
ROSCIOLI, N E Z01BE03003-07
ROSE, ANN M R01RR07127-01
ROSE, ERIC M01RR00645-20 0490
ROSE, GEORGE D R01GM29458-11
ROSE, GEORGE D R55GM41484-04A2
ROSE, GREGORY M P50MH44212-03 0003
ROSE, GREGORY M R01AG10755-01
ROSE, IRWIN A R37GM20940-28
ROSE, J A Z01AI00294-10
ROSE, J A Z01AI00295-10
ROSE, J A Z01AI00296-10
ROSE, J A Z01AI00297-10
ROSE, J A Z01AI00564-03
ROSE, J B ALEXANDER S07RR05653-24 0803
ROSE, JAMES C R37HD11210-12
ROSE, JAMES C S07RR05404-30 0854
ROSE, JAMES D R01NS13748-16
ROSE, JED E R01DA02665-12
ROSE, JEROME S07RR07101-13 0552
ROSE, JOHN K P01CA46128-04 0007
ROSE, JOHN K P30CA14195-18 0041
ROSE, JOHN K R01AI30374-01A1
ROSE, JOHN K R13AI31565-01
ROSE, JOHN K R37AI24345-05
ROSE, JOSEPH L P01CA52823-02 0005
ROSE, LYNN M. P51RR00166-30 0016
ROSE, LYNN M. P51RR00166-30 0117
ROSE, MARK D R01GM37739-05
ROSE, MICHAEL D S07RR05393-30 0902
ROSE, MICHAEL R R01AG06346-04S1
ROSE, NOEL R P30ES03819-06A1 9017
ROSE, NOEL R R01HL33878-07
ROSE, NOEL R R13HL46157-01
ROSE, RICHARD J R01AA08315-02
ROSE, RICHARD M P01HL43510-03
ROSE, RICHARD M P01HL43510-03 0005
ROSE, RICHARD M R01HL41312-04
ROSE, SETH D R01CA49729-02
ROSE, SUSAN M01RR00997-16 0400
ROSE, SUSAN A R01HD13810-08A2
ROSE, SUSAN R M01RR00997-16 0401
ROSE, TIMOTHY L R44NS26976-03
ROSELLI, CHARLES E R29HD23293-05
ROSELLI, ROBERT J P50HL19153-15 0004
ROSELLI, ROBERT J R01HL41129-03
ROSELLINI, ROBERT A S07RR07122-23 0108
ROSEMAN, SAUL P41RR04328-04 0002
ROSEMAN, SAUL R01GM38927-05
ROSEMAN, SAUL R37GM38759-05
ROSEMEIER, RONALD G R43ES05681-01
ROSEMEIER, RONALD G R43GM46154-01
ROSEMERGY, JANET P30HD15052-11 9001
ROSEN, BARRY P R01AI19793-08
ROSEN, BARRY P R01CA54141-01
ROSEN, BRUCE R P01CA48729-03 0001
ROSEN, BRUCE R R01CA40303-06
ROSEN, CAROL M01RR06022-02 0741
ROSEN, CAROL M01RR06022-02 0742
ROSEN, CRAIG A U01AI27397-04 0002
ROSEN, DAVID I R43GM43676-01A1
ROSEN, ELIOT M R01CA50516-03
ROSEN, FRED S P01HD17461-08
ROSEN, FRED S P01HD17461-08 0001
ROSEN, FRED S S07RR05626-25 0668
ROSEN, FRED S S15HL47744-01
ROSEN, FRED S U01AI31541-01 0006
ROSEN, GERALD M R01HL33550-06
ROSEN, GLENN D K08HL02558-01
ROSEN, HENRY R01AI25606-04
ROSEN, J Z01MH02523-02
ROSEN, J Z01MH02524-02
ROSEN, J Z01MH02525-02
ROSEN, J Z01MH02526-02
ROSEN, JEFFREY M R13DK44290-01
ROSEN, JEFFREY M R37CA16303-16
ROSEN, JOHN F R01ES04039-06
ROSEN, JOHN F R37ES01060-16
ROSEN, MARK J. N01HR76031-04
ROSEN, MICHAEL R P01HL28958-09
ROSEN, MICHAEL R P01HL28958-09 0001
ROSEN, MICHAEL R P01HL28958-09 0005
ROSEN, MICHAEL R R01HL43731-02
ROSEN, NEAL R01CA50377-03
ROSEN, ORA M P30CA08748-26 9033
ROSEN, STEPHEN G P60DK20572-14 0040
ROSEN, STEVEN P60AR20684-14 0020
ROSEN, STEVEN D R01GM23547-15
ROSEN, STEVEN T M01RR00048-30 0172
ROSEN, STEVEN T M01RR00048-30 0151
ROSEN, TOVE S R01DA06171-01A2
ROSEN, WARREN D S07RR05745-19 0264
ROSENBAUM, DANIEL M K08NS01484-01
ROSENBAUM, GEROLD P41RR01633-10 9001
ROSENBAUM, JAMES T R01EY06477-07
ROSENBAUM, JAMES T R01EY06484-06
ROSENBAUM, JAMES T R01EY07373-03
ROSENBAUM, JOEL L R01GM14642-24
ROSENBAUM, MARSHA R01DA05277-02
ROSENBAUM, MARSHA R01DA05332-03
ROSENBAUM, MARSHA R01DA06832-01A1
ROSENBAUM, MICHAEL K08DK01983-01A1
ROSENBERG, JOHN M. P30CA47904-04 9010
ROSENBERG, A Z01BD02007-03
ROSENBERG, ADAM M01RR00069-29 0494
ROSENBERG, ADAM A M01RR00069-29 0454
ROSENBERG, ADAM ARTHUR R01HL36301-06
ROSENBERG, GERSON N01HV88105-04
ROSENBERG, HELENE F K11HL02288-03
ROSENBERG, HOWARD C R01DA02194-13A1
ROSENBERG, JOHN M R01GM25671-14
ROSENBERG, LAWRENCE C R01AR34614-07
ROSENBERG, LAWRENCE C R37AR21498-14
ROSENBERG, LYNN R01HL42483-03
ROSENBERG, LYNN R37CA45762-04
ROSENBERG, LYNN S07RR05927-07 0970
ROSENBERG, MARK E R29DK43075-01A1
ROSENBERG, MARTIN U01AI24845-06 0010
ROSENBERG, NAOMI E P01CA24530-12 0007
ROSENBERG, NAOMI E R01CA24220-13
ROSENBERG, NAOMI E R01CA33771-09
ROSENBERG, NEIL L R01DA05311-03
ROSENBERG, PAUL A R01NS26830-03
ROSENBERG, PHILIP R01NS14521-14
ROSENBERG, RICHARD S S07RR05370-30 0625
ROSENBERG, ROBERT M01RR01032-16 0442
ROSENBERG, ROBERT P01HL41484-03 0001
ROSENBERG, ROBERT C S06GM08016-21 0044
ROSENBERG, ROBERT D P01HL33014-07
ROSENBERG, ROBERT D P01HL33014-07 0001
ROSENBERG, ROBERT D P01HL41484-03
ROSENBERG, ROBERT D R37HL39753-04
ROSENBERG, ROBERT L R29NS26660-03
ROSENBERG, ROGER N P50AG08013-04
ROSENBERG, S A Z01CM03800-21
ROSENBERG, S A Z01CM03801-21
ROSENBERG, S A Z01CM03811-17
ROSENBERG, SAUL A P01CA34233-09 0001
ROSENBERRY, TERRONE L P01DK38181-05 0002
ROSENBERRY, TERRONE L R01NS16577-12
ROSENBLATT, DORRIE E P30AG08808-03 0004
ROSENBLATT, JAY S R01MH45891-01A1
ROSENBLATT, JAY S. S06GM08223-08 0024
ROSENBLATT, JOSEPH D K11CA01314-05
ROSENBLATT, JOSEPH D R01CA52410-02
ROSENBLATT, JOSEPH D R01CA53632-02
ROSENBLATT, JOSEPH D R55CA54718-01
ROSENBLATT, ROGER A R01HS06166-03
ROSENBLOOM, ARLAN M01RR00082-29 0449
ROSENBLOOM, ARLAN L M01RR00082-29 0279
ROSENBLOOM, ARLAN L M01RR00082-29 0470
ROSENBLOOM, JOEL P01AR20553-15 0001
ROSENBLOOM, JOEL P50DE08239-04 0008
ROSENBLOOM, JOEL P50DE08239-04
ROSENBLOOM, JOEL S15AR41249-01
ROSENBLUM, BARNETT B S07RR05369-30 0583
ROSENBLUM, JERRY P01DK33487-05 0006
ROSENBLUM, LEONARD A R01MH15965-18

ROSENBLUM, LEONARD A R01RR05321-03
ROSENBLUM, NORMAN D K11DK01900-03
ROSENBLUM, NORMAN D M01RR02172-09 0193
ROSENBLUM, WILLIAM I R01HL35935-07
ROSENBLUM, WILLIAM I R01HL45617-01
ROSENBLUTH, JACK R01NS07495-23
ROSENBLUTH, RICHARD J U10CA35096-08
ROSENE, DOUGLAS P01AG00001-17A2 9002
ROSENE, DOUGLAS L P01AG00001-17A2 0017
ROSENE, DOUGLAS L P01HD22539-04 0004
ROSENFELD, CHARLES R P01HD13912-12 0007
ROSENFELD, CHARLES R R01HD08783-17
ROSENFELD, JOEL P R01DA06971-05
ROSENFELD, MICHAEL P30DK35816-06 0003
ROSENFELD, MICHAEL E R29HL42617-03
ROSENFELD, MICHAEL G P01DK26741-12 0005
ROSENFELD, MICHAEL G R01DK18477-16A1
ROSENFELD, MICHAEL G R01MH47137-02
ROSENFELD, MICHAEL G R37DK39949-10
ROSENFELD, RON G R01DK28229-11
ROSENFELD, STEVEN S K08NS01500-01
ROSENFIELD, ALLAN S07RR05449-30
ROSENFIELD, ALLAN S15HD28772-01
ROSENFIELD, ROBERT L M01RR00055-30 0524
ROSENFIELD, ROBERT L R01HD06308-19
ROSENFIELD, ROBERT L. M01RR00055-30 0446
ROSENFIELD, ROBERT L. M01RR00055-30 0491
ROSENFIELD, SARAH P50MH43450-04 0009
ROSENGARTEN, HELEN P01MH08618-27 0101
ROSENKRANTZ, MARK S07RR05697-22 0994
ROSENKRANTZ, MARK S R01GM41889-01A2
ROSENMAN, JULIAN G P01CA47982-04 0004
ROSENMAN, MARTIN R24MH47188-02 0004
ROSENMAN, MARTIN F S06GM45199-02 0009
ROSENQUIST, ALAN C R01EY02654-13
ROSENQUIST, GLENN C S07RR05515-28
ROSENQUIST, GLENN C S15CA55940-01
ROSENQUIST, THOMAS H P01HL36059-06 0002
ROSENQUIST, THOMAS H R01HL42164-04
ROSENQUIST, THOMAS H R01HL45337-02
ROSENSTEIN, BARRY S R01CA45078-06
ROSENSTEIN, JEFFREY M R01NS17468-09
ROSENSTIEL, STEPHEN F R01DE09119-03
ROSENSTOCK, LINDA K07ES00237-01
ROSENSTREICH, DAVID L R01AI29871-01A2
ROSENTHAL, CONSTANTIN J U10CA52772-02
ROSENTHAL, DANIEL I U01CA54022-01
ROSENTHAL, ERIC T R29HD23130-05
ROSENTHAL, FRANK S R01HL36530-07
ROSENTHAL, G J Z01ES21135-02
ROSENTHAL, G L Z01ES21148-01
ROSENTHAL, J THOMAS U01AI31492-01
ROSENTHAL, JEANNE N01CP15672-03
ROSENTHAL, LEON K20MH00860-02
ROSENTHAL, LEONARD J R01CA37259-05
ROSENTHAL, MIRIAM D R01DK42615-01A1
ROSENTHAL, MIRIAM D S06GM08033-21 0003
ROSENTHAL, MIRIAM D S07RR05771-15 0334
ROSENTHAL, MYRON P01NS05820-26 0019
ROSENTHAL, MYRON R01NS14325-13
ROSENTHAL, N E Z01MH02402-05
ROSENTHAL, NADIA A R01AG08920-06
ROSENTHAL, PHILIP J K11AI00870-04
ROSENTHAL, RAOUL S R01AI14826-13
ROSENTHAL, RICHARD N R01MH46327-03
ROSENWASSER, ALAN M S07RR07161-14 0844
ROSENWASSER, LANNY P01HL36577-06 0009
ROSENWASSER, LANNY J P50AI24848-05
ROSENWASSER, LARRY P50AI24848-05 0007
ROSENZWEIG, ANTHONY K11HL02228-03
ROSENZWEIG, MARK R R01DA04795-04A1
ROSENZWEIG, MARK R R01HD23343-05
ROSENZWEIG, MARK R R01HD26089-02
ROSENZWEIG, MARK R R01HD26384-02
ROSENZWEIG, STEVEN A R01DK34389-09
ROSENZWEIG, STEVEN A R01EY06581-04
ROSES, ALLEN P50AG05128-08 9001
ROSES, ALLEN D M01RR00030-30 0463
ROSES, ALLEN D P30AG09463-01 9004
ROSES, ALLEN D P50AG05128-08
ROSES, ALLEN D R01NS19999-08S1
ROSES, ALLEN D R35AG07922-04
ROSES, ALLEN D R35AG07922-04 0001
ROSES, ALLEN S. M01RR00030-30 0407
ROSEVEAR, PAUL R R01GM41232-03
ROSIELLO, ARTHUR P S07RR05487-29 0712
ROSIER, RANDY N R29AR38945-05
ROSIER, RANDY N R55AR40325-01A1
ROSKAMP, ERIC J R29GM42732-01A2
ROSKIES, RALPH Z P41RR06009-02
ROSLER, HEINZ S07RR05770-13 0931
ROSMAN, A P50AA03508-14 0001
ROSMAN, NORMAN P R01NS24620-06
ROSMARIN, ALAN G K11CA01283-05
ROSNER, BERNARD A R01CA50597-03
ROSNER, BERNARD A R01EY08103-03
ROSNER, BERNARD A R01HL40619-04
ROSNER, BERNARD A R03HL46212-01
ROSNER, BERNARD A S07RR05381-30 0794
ROSNER, GARY P01CA47741-02 9002
ROSNER, INGRID S07RR05396-30 0776
ROSNER, J L Z01DK36003-07
ROSNER, MARSHA R R01CA35541-08
ROSNER, WILLIAM R01DK36714-05
ROSOFF, PHILIP M R01GM41076-04A1
ROSOVSKY, HENRY S07RR07046-26
ROSOVSKY, HENRY S07RR07046-26 0530
ROSOWSKI, JOHN R01DC00194-09
ROSOWSKY, ANDRE P01CA19589-14A1 9002
ROSOWSKY, ANDRE P01CA19589-14A1 0005
ROSOWSKY, ANDRE P30AI28691-03 9004
ROSOWSKY, ANDRE R01AI25715-04
ROSOWSKY, ANDRE R01AI29904-02
ROSOWSKY, ANDRE R01CA25394-11
ROSS, A. CATHERINE P01HL22633-14 0007
ROSS, ALTA C R01AG09839-01
ROSS, ALTA C R01DK41479-03
ROSS, ALTA C R01HD16484-10
ROSS, BRIAN D R03CA53527-02
ROSS, BRUCE M S07RR07123-22 0591
ROSS, CHARLES D R03DC01223-01
ROSS, CHRISTOPHER P01NS16375-11 0013
ROSS, CHRISTOPHER A P50AG05146-09 0011
ROSS, CHRISTOPHER A R29MH43040-05
ROSS, CHRISTOPHER R R15HL46476-01
ROSS, DAVID R01CA51210-02
ROSS, DAVID R01ES04112-05
ROSS, DAVID S07RR05831-12 0973
ROSS, DONALD C P50MH30906-14 9002
ROSS, DONALD R R43LM05349-01
ROSS, DOUGLAS S M01RR01066-14 0081
ROSS, DOUGLAS S M01RR01066-14 0084
ROSS, DOUGLAS T R01NS28852-02
ROSS, DOUGLAS T S07RR05415-30 0018
ROSS, E EDWARDS S07RR05487-29 0709
ROSS, ELLIOTT S07RR05407-30 0051
ROSS, ELLIOTT M R01GM30355-11
ROSS, ELLIOTT M R13GM46458-01
ROSS, F PATRICK S07RR05491-29 0463
ROSS, GORDON P60AR30701-10 9003
ROSS, GORDON D R01AI27771-12
ROSS, GORDON D S15AI32208-01
ROSS, HELEN J K11CA01660-01
ROSS, J B ALEXANDER R01GM39750-04
ROSS, JAMES G R43CA53977-01
ROSS, JANE K S07RR07125-22 0398
ROSS, JEFFREY P01CA23076-14 0005
ROSS, JEFFREY P30CA07175-28 9003
ROSS, JOHN P50HL17682-17 0015
ROSS, JOHN R01GM40972-03
ROSS, JOHN, JR P50HL17682-17
ROSS, JUDITH L R01NS29857-01
ROSS, LEE D R01MH44321-03
ROSS, LEONARD S15AG10234-01
ROSS, LEONARD S15MH49311-01
ROSS, LEONARD L S07RR05418-30
ROSS, MARGARET E S07RR05385-30 0805
ROSS, MARGARET E S07RR05385-30 0806
ROSS, MICHAEL G M01RR00425-22S3 0465
ROSS, MICHAEL G R01DK43311-01A1
ROSS, MICHAEL G R01HL40899-03
ROSS, MURIEL D R01MH47305-01A1
ROSS, NATHAN S R29HD25299-04
ROSS, P D Z01DK36104-10
ROSS, PHILIP D R01AG10412-01
ROSS, RICHARD F S07RR05885-06
ROSS, RICHARDUS P01HD11725-13 0011
ROSS, RICHARDUS P01HD11725-13 0005
ROSS, ROBERT S07RR07150-17 0552
ROSS, ROBERT G S06GM08267-04
ROSS, RONALD K P01CA17054-16 0002
ROSS, RONALD K P01CA17054-16
ROSS, RONALD K R01CA43092-05
ROSS, RUSSELL P01HL03174-36 0019
ROSS, RUSSELL P01HL18645-17
ROSS, RUSSELL P01HL18645-17 0001
ROSS, RUSSELL P01HL18645-17 0006
ROSS, RUSSELL P51RR00166-30 0118
ROSS, RUSSELL P51RR00166-30 9025
ROSS, RUSSELL S07RR05432-30 0247
ROSS, SAMUEL M P01HL30557-08 9001
ROSS, SUSAN R R01CA45954-08
ROSS, WILLIAM N R01NS16295-11
ROSSANT, JANET R01HD25334-03
ROSSAVIK, I K S07RR05411-30 0966
ROSSE, CORNELIUS R01HD25069-03
ROSSE, CORNELIUS R01LM04925-03
ROSSE, WENDELL N01HB97059-03
ROSSE, WENDELL F P60HL28391-09
ROSSE, WENDELL F R01HL30270-08
ROSSE, WENDELL F R37DK31379-10
ROSSE, WENDELL F U01HL42805-03
ROSSEN, ROGER D R01AI28071-03
ROSSEN, ROGER D R01HL41408-04
ROSSER, ROY J R43GM45644-01
ROSSETTI, L S07RR05654-24 0119
ROSSETTI, LUCIANO R29DK45024-01
ROSSI, HUMBERTO S07RR05664-24 0874
ROSSI, JOHN S07RR05841-12 0234
ROSSI, JOHN J R01AI29329-02
ROSSI, JOHN J U01AI25959-05 0001
ROSSIGNOL, P P41RR00317-25 0002
ROSSINI, ALDO A R37DK25306-14
ROSSKY, PETER J R01GM30452-10
ROSSMAN, MICHAEL G P30AI27713-04 9004
ROSSMAN, MICHAEL G. U01AI27310-04 0001
ROSSMAN, ROBBIE S07RR07138-20 0524
ROSSMAN, TOBY G R01CA29258-10
ROSSMAN, TOBY G. P42ES04895-03 0006
ROSSMANN, MICHAEL P41RR01646-09 0006
ROSSMANN, MICHAEL G R37AI11219-19
ROSSMANN, MICHAEL G U01AI27310-04
ROST, KATHRYN M R01MH49116-01
ROSTAMI, A M M01RR00040-31 0411
ROSTAMI, ABDOLMOHAMMAD P01NS08075-21 0013
ROSTAMI, ABDOLMOHAMMAD R29AR39489-03
ROSVOLD, ELIZABETH S07RR05895-09 0618
ROSZMAN, THOMAS L R01CA18234-14
ROSZMAN, THOMAS L R01MH47679-01
ROSZMAN, THOMAS L R01NS17423-10
ROTE, NEAL S R01HD23697-04
ROTE, NEAL S R01HD24490-04
ROTH, ALAN M U10EY06330-07
ROTH, B Z01RR10325-03
ROTH, B Z01RR10357-01
ROTH, B Z01RR10363-01
ROTH, B J Z01RR10315-03
ROTH, B J Z01RR10316-03
ROTH, B J Z01RR10319-03
ROTH, DAVID A K11HL02574-01
ROTH, DAVID L R01MH46988-01A1
ROTH, DEE R19MH46348-03
ROTH, EUGENE F P60HL38655-04 0002
ROTH, G S Z01AG00301-08
ROTH, G S Z01AG00304-05
ROTH, GERALD J R01HL39947-04
ROTH, JACK A R37CA45187-05
ROTH, JAMES A R01CA50159-03
ROTH, JEROME A R01ES04249-05
ROTH, JOHN R R01GM27068-12
ROTH, JOHN R R01GM34804-07
ROTH, JOHN R R37GM23408-15
ROTH, LOIS S07RR05788-15 0890
ROTH, MARK B R29GM42786-03
ROTH, MARK S R29DK43470-01
ROTH, MICHAEL D K08CA01549-02
ROTH, MICHAEL G R01GM37547-05
ROTH, MICHAEL G R01GM41050-03
ROTH, MONICA S07RR05576-27 0592
ROTH, MONICA J R01CA49932-02
ROTH, RICHARD A R01DK41765-03
ROTH, RICHARD A R37DK34926-08
ROTH, ROBERT P50MH30929-15 9006
ROTH, ROBERT A P42ES04911-03 0007
ROTH, ROBERT A, JR R37ES02581-11
ROTH, ROBERT H P01MH25642-18 9004
ROTH, ROBERT H P01NS24032-06 0002
ROTH, ROBERT H R37MH14092-24
ROTH, ROBERT I R01DK43102-01
ROTH, WALTON T R01MH40052-06
ROTHBART, MARY K R01MH43361-04A1
ROTHBART, MYRON R37MH40662-07
ROTHBAUM, FRED S07RR07179-14 0685
ROTHBAUM, ROBERT J M01RR00036-31 1049
ROTHBAUM, ROBERT J M01RR06021-02 0628
ROTHBERG, KAREN G S07RR07175-15 0442
ROTHBERG, PAUL G R29CA50246-03
ROTHBLAT, GEORGE H P01HL22633-14 9001
ROTHBLAT, GEORGE H P01HL22633-14 0002
ROTHBLUM, LAWRENCE P01CA10893-23 0048
ROTHE, CARL F R37HL07723-28
ROTHENBERG, ELLEN R01AI19752-09
ROTHENBERG, ELLEN R01CA39605-07
ROTHENBERG, MARTIN R44DC00623-03
ROTHENBERG, SHELDON P R01CA32369-09
ROTHENBERG, SHELDON P R01DK28561-10
ROTHERAM-BORUS, MARY J R18MH48059-02
ROTHERAM-BORUS, MARY J U01MH49059-01
ROTHERAM, MARY J P50MH43878-03 0032
ROTHERAN, MARYJANE P50MH43520-04 0003
ROTHERMAN, MARY J P50MH43878-03 0031
ROTHERMEL, CONSTANCE S07RR05396-30 0758
ROTHERT, MARILYN L R01NR01245-04A2
ROTHFIELD, LAWRENCE I R01AI22183-07
ROTHFIELD, LAWRENCE I R01GM41978-03
ROTHFIELD, NAOMI S07RR05678-23 0162
ROTHFIELD, NAOMI F P60AR20621-13
ROTHFIELD, NAOMI F R01AR37986-05
ROTHGARN, ERIC P51RR00169-30 9004
ROTHMAN-DENES, LUCIA B R01AI12575-17
ROTHMAN-DENES, LUCIA B R01GM35170-07
ROTHMAN-DENES, LUCIA B R01GM38416-05
ROTHMAN-DENES, LUCIA B R13GM46640-01
ROTHMAN, ABRAHAM S07RR05665-24 0879
ROTHMAN, ALAN L K11AI00971-02
ROTHMAN, BARRY S K04NS01177-05
ROTHMAN, JAMES E R01CA47767-04
ROTHMAN, JAMES E R37GM25662-15
ROTHMAN, R B Z01MH02429-04
ROTHMAN, STEVEN P50NS14834-13 0011
ROTHMAN, STEVEN M R01NS19988-08
ROTHMAN, TAUBE P R01HD20470-05
ROTHMAN, TAUBE P R01HD21032-06
ROTHMN, JAMES E R01DK27044-14
ROTHSCHILD, ANTHONY J R29MH47457-01A1
ROTHSCHILD, KENNETH J R01EY05499-08

ROTHSTEIN, DAVID M K08DK02011-01A1
ROTHSTEIN, GERALD M01RR00064-27 0326
ROTHSTEIN, JEFFREY D K08NS01355-03
ROTHSTEIN, MARCOS M01RR00036-31 1043
ROTHSTEIN, MARCOS M01RR00036-31 0611
ROTHSTEIN, MARCOS M01RR00036-31 0977
ROTHSTEIN, MARK A R13HG00160-01S1
ROTHSTEIN, ROBIN D M01RR00040-31 0389
ROTHSTEIN, ROBIN D S07RR07083-26 0491
ROTHSTEIN, RODNEY J P01CA21111-15 0009
ROTHSTEIN, RODNEY J R01GM34587-08
ROTHSTEIN, RODNEY J R01HG00452-01
ROTHSTEIN, THOMAS L R01AI23454-05
ROTHSTEIN, THOMAS L R01AI29690-02
ROTHSTEIN, THOMAS L S07RR05487-29 0699
ROTHSTEIN, THOMAS R S07RR05487-29 0716
ROTHWELL, BRUCE R P30DE09743-02 0011
ROTI ROTI, JOSEPH L P01CA51116-02
ROTI ROTI, JOSEPH L R01CA43198-05
ROTI, JOSEPH P01CA51116-02 0001
ROTTENBERG, DAVID A. P01NS25701-05 0004
ROTTENBERG, HAGAI R01GM28173-11
ROTTER, ANDREJ R01NS18089-09
ROTTER, ANDREJ R03AA08520-02
ROTTER, JEROME I P01HL28481-09 9006
ROTTER, JEROME I P30DK36200-05S1 9004
ROTTMAN, FRITZ M R01CA31810-11
ROTTMAN, FRITZ M R01DK32770-09
ROTTMAN, GERALD A K11DK01841-04
ROTTMAN, JEFFREY N K11HL02488-03
ROTUNDO, RICHARD L K04NS01292-04
ROTUNDO, RICHARD L R01AG05917-07
ROTWEIN, PETER M01RR00036-31 0997
ROTWEIN, PETER P01HD20805-05A1 0004
ROTWEIN, PETER S R01DK37449-06
ROTWEIN, PETER S R01DK42748-01A1
ROUBICEK, RUDOLF V S07RR07154-16 0565
ROUDIER, JEAN M01RR00833-17 0195
ROUFA, DONALD J R01GM23013-13
ROUFA, DONALD J R01GM38932-05
ROULLET, JB P30DK40566-02 0004
ROUNDS, SHARON I S R01HL34009-05A3
ROUNSAVILLE, BRUCE J K05DA00089-09
ROUNSAVILLE, BRUCE J K12DA00167-01
ROUNSAVILLE, BRUCE J P50AA03510-14 0015
ROUNSAVILLE, BRUCE J R01DA04029-06
ROUNSAVILLE, BRUCE J R01DA05592-04
ROUNSAVILLE, BRUCE J R18DA05758-03S1
ROUNSAVILLE, BRUCE J R18DA06963-02
ROUSE, BARRY T R01AI14981-14
ROUSE, BARRY T R01AI24762-05
ROUSE, BARRY T R01EY05093-08
ROUSE, BOBBY M N01HD43810-12
ROUSE, D A Z01BA05002-03
ROUSE, WILLIAM R R01GM26782-13
ROUSE, WILLIAM R R01GM38436-04
ROUSE, WILLIAM R R01GM38907-04
ROUSLAHTI, ERKKI I P01CA28896-11 0005
ROUSLIN, WILLIAM R01HL30926-07A1
ROUTTENBERG, ARYEH R37MH25281-18
ROVAINEN, CARL M R01HL41075-04
ROVEE-COLLIER, CAROLYN K05MH00902-01
ROVEE-COLLIER, CAROLYN K R37MH32307-13
ROVERA, GIOVANNI P01CA21124-14 0011
ROVERA, GIOVANNI P01CA47983-04
ROVERA, GIOVANNI P01CA47983-04 0001
ROVERA, GIOVANNI P01CA52009-01A1 0002
ROVERA, GIOVANNI S07RR05540-29 0560
ROVETTO, MICHAEL J R01HL27336-10A1
ROVIN, BRAD S07RR05491-29 0464
ROVNER, BARRY W R01MH45293-03
ROW SCIENCE, INC N01AA80003-00
ROW SCIENCES, INC N01DA88010-00
ROW SCIENCES, INC N01DA98016-00
ROW SCIENCES, INC{ N01SP01001-00
ROWBOTHAM, MICHAEL C P50DA01696-12 0015
ROWE, BRIAN P R15HL46504-01
ROWE, DAVID C R01DA06287-02
ROWE, DAVID W P01AR38933-05 0003
ROWE, DAVID W P01HD22610-04
ROWE, DAVID W P01HD22610-04 0006
ROWE, DAVID W R01AR30426-10
ROWE, H. ALAN S06GM08033-21 0006
ROWE, HENRY A S03RR03226-05
ROWE, JOHN W P01AG04390-08 0001
ROWE, MARK J S07RR07111-12 0513
ROWE, MICHAEL H R01EY08038-03
ROWE, THOMAS C R29GM38859-05
ROWELL, DEREK S07RR07047-26 0140
ROWELL, LORING B P01HL16910-18 0006
ROWINSKY, ERIC K R01CA55133-01
ROWITZ, LOUIS S07RR05871-03
ROWLAND, LEWIS P M01RR00645-20 0309
ROWLAND, LEWIS P P01NS11766-17A1
ROWLAND, RANDAL S07RR05724-20 0190
ROWLAND, RANDAL W R29DE09408-01A1
ROWLES, GRAHAM D R01AG08475-01A2
ROWLEY, ANNE H S07RR05370-30 0617
ROWLEY, DONALD A R37AI10242-30
ROWLEY, JANET D R35CA42557-06
ROWLEY, PETER T R01NR03125-01
ROWLEY, ROY S07RR05428-30 0174
ROWLEY, SCOTT D P01CA15396-18 9003
ROWND, ROBERT H R01GM30731-12
ROWSEMITT, CAROL N S07RR07092-26 0499
ROY-BURMAN, PRADIP R01CA51485-02
ROY-CHOWDHURY, JAYANTA R01DK34357-08
ROY-CHOWDHURY, NAMITA R01DK39137-05
ROY, ARUN K R37DK14744-22
ROY, DENIS N01HC65057-11
ROY, DEODUTTA R29CA52584-02
ROY, DWIJENDRA N S07RR07238-04 0484
ROY, GREG S07RR05704-20 0001
ROY, POLLY R01AI26879-04
ROY, ROLAND R P01NS16333-11S1 0003
ROYCE, JACQUELINE M P01CA50956-02 0001
ROYDS, ROBERT B N01CM87208-03
ROYER, CATHERINE A P41RR03155-06 0004
ROYER, CATHERINE A R29GM39969-05
ROYER, CATHERINE A S07RR05456-29 0361
ROYER, ROBERT E R29AI25869-05
ROYER, WILLIAM E, JR R01DK43323-01
ROYER, WILLIAM E, JR S07RR05712-20 0069
ROYSTON, IVOR P01CA37497-07 9002
ROYSTON, IVOR P01CA37497-07 0001
ROYSTON, IVOR P01CA37497-07 0008
ROYSTON, IVOR P01CA37497-07
ROYSTON, IVOR P01CA37497-07 0006
ROYSTON, IVOR P30CA23100-11 0003
ROYSTON, IVOR R13CA55284-01
ROZANSKI, GEORGE J R29HL38917-05
ROZE, ULDIS S07RR07064-24 0206
ROZENTAL, JACK M M01RR03186-06 0019
RUBEL, EDWIN W P01DC00520-04
RUBEL, EDWIN W R01DC00395-06
RUBEN, LAWRENCE S R01AI24627-05
RUBEN, PETER C R01NS29204-01A1
RUBEN, PETER C S07RR07026-26 0002
RUBEN, PHILIP P01DC00121-29A1 9001
RUBEN, ROBERT J P01DC00223-08
RUBEN, ROBERT J P01DC00223-08 9001
RUBENS, CRAIG E R01AI22498-07
RUBENS, CRAIG E R01AI30068-02
RUBENSTEIN, ARTHUR H P60DK20595-14 9003
RUBENSTEIN, ARTHUR H P60DK20595-14
RUBENSTEIN, IRWIN R01GM24756-13
RUBENSTEIN, JOHN L P01MH39437-07 0006
RUBENSTEIN, LORETTA R03DE10002-01
RUBENSTEIN, PETER A P01HL14388-20 0236
RUBENSTEIN, PETER A R01GM33689-07
RUBENSTEIN, RICHARD P01AG09017-02 0002
RUBENSTEIN, RICHARD R29NS25308-04
RUBIN, EDWARD M. P60HL20985-14 0015
RUBIN, ALLEN J S07RR05576-27 0600
RUBIN, B I Z01EY00263-02
RUBIN, BERISH Y R01CA38661-09
RUBIN, BERISH Y S15CA55995-01
RUBIN, CHARLES S P60DK20541-14 9001
RUBIN, CHARLES S R01DK21248-14
RUBIN, CHARLES S R01GM22792-14
RUBIN, CLINTON T R01AR39278-04A1
RUBIN, CLINTON T R55AR41040-01
RUBIN, CYRUS P01DK32971-08 0006
RUBIN, CYRUS E P01DK32971-08 9002
RUBIN, CYRUS E P01DK32971-08
RUBIN, DAVID B R29HL41155-04
RUBIN, DAVID C S07RR07070-26 0459
RUBIN, DEBORAH C K08HD00946-02
RUBIN, DEBORAH C S07RR05491-29 0465
RUBIN, E M P01HL18574-16 0008
RUBIN, EMANUEL P01AA07215-06
RUBIN, EMANUEL P01AA07215-06 9001
RUBIN, EMANUEL P50AA07186-06
RUBIN, EUGENE H M01RR00036-31 0998
RUBIN, GARY S R01EY06380-06
RUBIN, GERALD M R37GM33135-09
RUBIN, HARRY R01CA15744-16
RUBIN, J S Z01CP05596-03
RUBIN, JEFFREY P50MH43450-04 0018
RUBIN, JEFFREY P50MH43450-04 0013
RUBIN, JEFFREY P50MH43450-04 0023
RUBIN, JEFFREY P50MH43450-04 0024
RUBIN, KAREN P01AR38933-05 0008
RUBIN, LEE L R01NS21767-07
RUBIN, LEONA J S07RR05949-07 0734
RUBIN, LESLIE R S07RR05371-30 0642
RUBIN, MICHAEL M01RR00047-31 0472
RUBIN, PHILIP M01RR00044-31 0377
RUBIN, PHILIP R01CA27791-10A1
RUBIN, PHILIP E S07RR05596-27 0126
RUBIN, RAPHAEL K02AA00123-02
RUBIN, ROBERT S07RR05551-29 0946
RUBIN, ROBERT L M01RR00833-17 0147
RUBIN, ROBERT L R01AG09574-01
RUBIN, ROBERT L R01AR34358-08
RUBIN, ROBERT T K05MH47363-10
RUBIN, ROBERT T R01MH28380-13S1
RUBIN, ROBERT W S03RR03510-03
RUBIN, RONALD P R01DE05764-10
RUBIN, RONALD P R01DK28029-12
RUBIN, STEPHEN C P01CA52477-01A1 0003
RUBIN,CHARLES P60DK20541-14 0026
RUBINO, JOSEPH S07RR05967-04 0291
RUBINO, JOSEPH T N01CM97627-03
RUBINOW, D R Z01MH00180-09
RUBINOW, D R Z01MH00181-02
RUBINOW, D R Z01MH00182-08
RUBINOW, D R Z01MH02537-02
RUBINSON, KALMAN S07RR05399-30 0930
RUBINSTEIN, ARYE P30AI27741-04 9001
RUBINSTEIN, ARYE P30AI27741-04
RUBINSTEIN, ARYE R01AI20671-08
RUBINSTEIN, ARYE R01AI20671-08 0001
RUBINSTEIN, ARYE R01AI20671-08 0002
RUBINSTEIN, ARYE R01AI20671-08 9001
RUBINSTEIN, ARYE R01AI20671-08 9002
RUBINSTEIN, ARYE U01AI27533-03
RUBINSTEIN, DANIEL B K08AG00537-01
RUBINSTEIN, JOAN E K11MH00747-04
RUBINSTEIN, JOAN E S07RR05736-19 0193
RUBINSTEIN, L Z01BA02005-06
RUBINSTEIN, NEAL A R01NS14332-11
RUBINSTEIN, ROBERT L R01AG08481-03
RUBINSTEIN, ROBERT L R01AG08836-01A2
RUBINSTEIN, Y R Z01BA02002-03
RUBLE, DIANE N K02MH00484-08
RUBLE, DIANE N R37MH37215-09
RUBY, JOHN D K11DE00257-03
RUCHKIN, DANIEL S R01NS11199-16
RUCKDESCHEL, JOHN C S07RR05394-30 0720
RUCKDESCHEL, JOHN C U10CA06594-27A1
RUCKER, HUBERT K. S06GM08037-20 0036
RUCKER, ROBERT B R01HL15965-18
RUCKNAGEL, DONALD L P60HL15996-19
RUCKNAGEL, DONALD L P60HL15996-19 0029
RUCKNAGEL, DONALD L P60HL15996-19 0027
RUDA, M Z01DE00288-12
RUDCZYNSKI, ANDREW B S03RR03234-10
RUDCZYNSKI, ANDREW B S07RR07058-26
RUDCZYNSKI, ANDREW B S15GM47045-01
RUDCZYNSKI, ANDREW B S15MH49301-01
RUDD, CHRISTOPHER E R01AI25505-04
RUDD, CHRISTOPHER E R01CA51887-02
RUDD, COLETTE J P01CA51993-01A1 9001
RUDD, COLLETTE N01CN95175-03
RUDD, M DAVID R18MH48097-02
RUDDELL, ALANNA S07RR05403-30 0822
RUDDERS, RICHARD A R01CA40725-07
RUDDLE, FRANK S07RR07015-26 0611
RUDDLE, FRANK H P01HG00365-04
RUDDLE, FRANK H P01HG00365-04 0001
RUDDLE, FRANK H P01HG00365-04 9001
RUDDLE, FRANK H R37GM09966-30
RUDDLE, NANCY H R01AR40416-02
RUDDLE, NANCY H R01CA16885-16
RUDDLE, NANCY H R01CA47878-04
RUDDON, RAYMOND S03RR03408-07
RUDDON, RAYMOND S07RR07216-08
RUDDON, RAYMOND S07RR07216-08 0535
RUDDON, RAYMOND W P30CA36727-08
RUDDON, RAYMOND W R01CA32949-09
RUDDON, RAYMOND W S15CA55994-01
RUDDY, SHAUN P50AI28532-03
RUDE, ROBERT K M01RR00043-31 0094
RUDE, ROBERT K M01RR00043-31 0373
RUDE, ROBERT K M01RR00043-31 0460
RUDE, ROBERT K M01RR00043-31 0480
RUDEEN, PAUL K K02AA00107-05
RUDEL, LAWRENCE L P01HL45666-01 9002
RUDEL, LAWRENCE L P50HL14164-20 0033
RUDEL, LAWRENCE L P50HL14164-20 9002
RUDEL, LAWRENCE L R01HL24736-12
RUDEL, LAWRENCE L R01HL41135-04
RUDERMAN, JOAN V R01HD23696-05
RUDERMAN, NEIL B R01DK19514-13A1
RUDERMAN, NEIL B R01DK39814-04
RUDERMAN, NEIL B R01DK42621-02
RUDICK, MICHAEL S06GM08256-03 0002
RUDICK, MICHAEL J S07RR07218-05 0455
RUDIKOFF, S Z01CB05553-22
RUDMAN, DANIEL M01RR00058-30 0264
RUDMAN, DANIEL U01AG10383-01
RUDNER, LAWRENCE N44CN15392-00
RUDNER, RIVKA S06GM08176-12 0026
RUDNEY, HARRY R01DK12402-23
RUDNEY, JOEL D R01DE07233-06
RUDNEY, JOEL D R01DE08505-05
RUDNICKI, MARKET S07RR05498-22 0472
RUDOFSKY, ULRICH H R01DK41923-01A1
RUDOLPH, ABRAHAM M P50GM26691-13 0011
RUDOLPH, ABRAHAM M R37HL35842-06
RUDOLPH, FREDERICK B S03RR03494-03
RUDOMIN, PEDRO N R01NS09196-18
RUDY, BERNARDO R01GM26976-09
RUDY, DAVID W M01RR00750-19 0264
RUDY, DELBERT C S07RR05745-19 0238
RUDY, ELLEN B M01RR00080-29 0424
RUDY, ELLEN B R01NR01525-06
RUDY, ELLEN B R01NR01596-04
RUDY, ELLEN B S07RR05947-07
RUDY, THOMAS E R01AR38698-05
RUDY, THOMAS E R01DE07514-06
RUDY, YORAM R01HL33343-07
RUECKERT, ROLAND R R01AI24939-05
RUECKERT, ROLAND R R37AI22813-25
RUEFLI, TERRY S07RR05938-07 0320

RUEGG, CHARLES E R43ES05784-01
RUEGGEBERG, FREDERICK A R29DE09418-01A1
RUEHL, BILL P40RR03624-05 0002
RUEHL, WILLIAM S07RR05353-30 0363
RUEHL, WILLIAM W S07RR05353-30 0364
RUEHLE, PAUL N01CP71007-07
RUEHLMAN, LINDA S R44MH44010-02A1
RUFF, CHRISTOPHER B R01AG09412-02
RUFF, HOLLY A K02MH00652-05
RUFF, HOLLY A R55HD27570-01
RUFF, ROBERT R01NS26661-03
RUGGERI, ZAVERIO M M01RR00833-17 0163
RUGGERI, ZAVERIO M P01HL31950-08 0004
RUGGERI, ZAVERIO M R01HL42846-03
RUGGERO, MARIO A P50DC00110-17 0005
RUGGERO, MARIO A R01DC00419-05
RUGGIERI, MICHAEL R R01DK42890-01A1
RUGGIERI, MICHAEL R R01DK43333-01A1
RUGGIERO, DAVID A R01NS28200-02
RUGGLES, STEVEN R01HD25839-02
RUGH, JOHN D R01DE09630-02
RUIZ-OPAZO, NELSON R01HL39267-05
RUIZ-PALACIOIS, GUILLERMO P01HD13021-12 00
RUIZ, PHILLIP S07RR05363-30 0835
RUIZ, RICHARD S U10EY06258-07
RULE, DANIEL C S07RR07157-16 0573
RULE, GORDON S S07RR05431-30 0858
RULE, GORDON S S07RR05431-30 0839
RULEY, EARL P01HL41484-03 0004
RULEY, HENRY E P01CA42063-06 0005
RULEY, HENRY E R01CA40602-07
RULFS, JILL R15DK43923-01
RULIN, MARVIN C S07RR05570-20
RUMBAUGH, DUANE M P01HD06016-21 0008
RUMBAUGH, DUANE M P01HD06016-21
RUMBAUGH, DUANE M P51RR00165-31 0079
RUMBAUGH, SUE S P01HD06016-21 0004
RUMPHO-KENNEDY, MARY S07RR07042-26 0406
RUMSEY, J M Z01MH00178-08
RUNDELL, JAMES R S07RR05983-05 0362
RUNDELL, MARY K P01NS23349-06 0008
RUNDELL, MARY K R01CA21327-14
RUNDELL, MARY K S07RR07028-26 0019
RUNGE-MORRIS, MELISSA A K11ES00170-06
RUNGE, MARSCHALL S K04HL02414-02
RUNGE, MARSCHALL S R01HL44307-03
RUNNEGAR, MARIA T R01ES05678-02
RUNYAN, RAYMOND P50HL42266-02 0003
RUOHO, ARNOLD E R01GM33138-17
RUOSLAHTI, ERKKI P30CA30199-11
RUOSLAHTI, ERKKI I P01CA28896-11
RUOSLAHTI, ERKKI I P01CA28896-11 0001
RUOSLAHTI, ERKKI I P01CA28896-11 9001
RUOSLAHTI, ERKKI I R35CA42507-06
RUOSLAHTI, ERKKI I S07RR05803-13
RUOSLAHTI, ERKKI I S15CA55922-01
RUPP, W DEAN R01GM31399-09
RUPPENTHAL, GERALD C P30HD02274-24 9004
RUPPENTHAL, GERALD C. P51RR00166-30 0176
RUPPENTHAL, GERALD C. P51RR00166-30 0177
RUPPENTHAL, GERALD C. P51RR00166-30 0178
RUPRECHT, RUTH M R01AI29797-02
RUPRECHT, RUTH M R01AI32330-01
RUPRECHT, RUTH M S07RR05526-29 0076
RUPRECHT, RUTH M U01AI24845-06 0011
RUPRECHT, RUTH M. P30AI28691-03 9002
RUSBULT, CARYL E R01MH45417-02
RUSCETTI, F W Z01CM09251-09
RUSCETTI, F W Z01CM09264-09
RUSCETTI, S K Z01CP05657-02
RUSCH, NANCY J R29HL40474-04
RUSCKOWSKI, MARY R29AI25570-04
RUSH, AUGUSTUS J P50MH41115-05
RUSH, BENJAMIN F, JR R01GM37060-05
RUSH, JOHN V S03RR03298-10
RUSLING, JAMES F R01ES03154-09
RUSSELL, ANN N01LM13549-00
RUSSELL, BRENDA R MD PHD R01HL40880-05
RUSSELL, CHARLOTTE S S06GM08168-13 0007
RUSSELL, DANIEL W P01AG07094-05 0003
RUSSELL, DAVID F R01NS23028-06
RUSSELL, DAVID G R01AI26889-02
RUSSELL, DAVID H R01GM33780-05
RUSSELL, DAVID W R01GM43753-02
RUSSELL, GARY P30DK43351-01 0002
RUSSELL, GARY J K08DK02010-01
RUSSELL, H F S06GM08022-20 0008
RUSSELL, I R18AR21393-17 0014
RUSSELL, J Z01HD00705-10
RUSSELL, J ERIC K11HL02623-01
RUSSELL, J T Z01HD01203-01
RUSSELL, JAMES N01ES95264-03
RUSSELL, JAMES S06GM08037-20 0041
RUSSELL, JAMES A R01HL28630-10
RUSSELL, JAMES D N01CM97624-03
RUSSELL, JAMES D N01ES95274-03
RUSSELL, JAMES D R01CA17229-14S2
RUSSELL, JAMES D S15AI32222-01
RUSSELL, JOHN R01DK34822-06
RUSSELL, JOHN H R01CA28533-12
RUSSELL, JOHN M R01NS11946-18
RUSSELL, MARCIA R01AA05702-07
RUSSELL, MICHAEL W R01DE06746-08
RUSSELL, MICHAEL W R01DE09691-01
RUSSELL, P Z01EY00237-06
RUSSELL, P Z01EY00252-03
RUSSELL, PAUL R P01GM46006-01 0004
RUSSELL, PAUL R R01GM41281-03
RUSSELL, PAUL S R01HL43340-03
RUSSELL, PERCY J S03RR03009-11
RUSSELL, PERCY J S07RR05665-24 0883
RUSSELL, ROBERT G R24RR03123-05
RUSSELL, ROBERT J N01AG12117-00
RUSSELL, ROBERT J N01CM23911-52
RUSSELL, ROBERT M P01AI26698-03S1 0002
RUSSELL, ROBERT M R01CA49195-01A3
RUSSELL, SHIRLEY B S06GM08037-20 0029
RUSSELL, STEPHEN W R01CA31199-11
RUSSELL, STEPHEN W R01CA38779-06
RUSSELL, THOMAS M01RR00058-30 0247
RUSSELL, WILLIAM E R01DK44557-01
RUSSELL, WILLIAM E S07RR05486-29 0045
RUSSO, A P50DE09170-03 9000
RUSSO, A Z01CM06320-12
RUSSO, A Z01CM06361-07
RUSSO, A Z01CM06387-04
RUSSO, ANDREW S07RR05372-30 0665
RUSSO, ANDREW F R01HD25969-01A1
RUSSO, CARLO S07RR05396-30 0759
RUSSO, JOSE R01CA38921-07
RUSSO, JOSE R01CA48927-02
RUSSO, T Z01AI00589-02
RUSSO, T A Z01AI00617-01
RUSSO, T A Z01AI00618-01
RUSTGI, ANIL K K08CA01586-01
RUSTIN, TERRY A S07RR05745-19 0263
RUSTIONI, ALDO R01NS12440-16
RUSTIONI, ALDO R01NS16264-12
RUSTUM, YOUCEF M P01CA13038-19 0111
RUSTUM, YOUCEF M P01CA21071-14 0001
RUSTUM, YOUCEF M P01CA21071-14 0015
RUTA, M Z01BG06024-03
RUTA, M Z01BG06052-01
RUTA, M Z01BG06053-01
RUTA, M Z01BG06054-01
RUTA, M Z01BG06055-01
RUTECKI, PAUL A R29NS28580-01A1
RUTH, GEORGE R S07RR05930-07 0716
RUTHERFORD, CHARLES L R01AG00677-14
RUTHERFORD, CHARLES L S07RR07095-24
RUTHERFORD, CHARLES L S15GM47037-01
RUTISHAUSER, URS S R01EY06107-06
RUTISHAUSER, URS S R01HD18369-08
RUTKIN, B P01HL24136-13 9003
RUTKOWSKI, J LYNN P50AG05146-09 0013
RUTKOWSKI, MONICA M01RR00096-30A1 0269
RUTLEDGE, CHARLES O S07RR05586-24
RUTLEDGE, DAVID R S07RR07051-26 0732
RUTLEDGE, JACKIE J S07RR07098-26 0337
RUTLEDGE, JOHN C K11HL02112-02
RUTLEDGE, ROBERT R01HS06527-01
RUTSTEIN, RICHARD M M01RR00240-27 0346
RUTSTEIN, ROBERT P S07RR05807-13 0463
RUTSTEIN, ROBERT P S07RR05807-13 0464
RUTTER, WILLIAM P01DK41822-03 0004
RUTTER, WILLIAM J R37AI19744-10
RUTTER, WILLIAM J R37DK21344-15
RUVKUN, GARY B R01GM44619-01A1
RUWE, WILLIAM D R29NS26045-04
RUYECHAN, WILLIAM T R01AI18449-10
RUYECHAN, WILLIAM T R01AI22468-07
RUYMANN, FREDERICK B U10CA03750-34
RUZICKA, GLEN N01LM13548-00
RUZICKA, JAROMIR R01GM45260-01
RYALS, BRENDA M R01DC01245-01
RYAN, ALLEN F R01DC00129-13
RYAN, ALLEN F R01DC00139-12
RYAN, CAROLINE A K08AI00938-03
RYAN, CHRISTOPHER M R01DK39629-04
RYAN, JAMES P R01AI28520-03
RYAN, JAMES P R01HD21047-05
RYAN, JAMES W R01EY07135-05
RYAN, JAMES W R01HL39684-04
RYAN, JAMES W R55HL46689-01
RYAN, KATHLEEN D P30HD08610-17 9004
RYAN, KENNETH J P30HD06645-20
RYAN, LAWRENCE J R01MH45341-03
RYAN, LAWRENCE M R01AR38656-05
RYAN, LOUISE R29CA48061-04
RYAN, NEAL D P01MH41712-06
RYAN, NEAL D P01MH41712-06 0001
RYAN, NEAL D R01MH45424-02
RYAN, RICHARD M R01RR00054-30
RYAN, RICHARD M, JR S07RR05382-30
RYAN, RITA S07RR05403-30 0823
RYAN, RITA M K08HL02630-01
RYAN, ROBERT O R01HL34786-07
RYAN, STEPHEN J M01RR00043-31
RYAN, STEPHEN J R01EY01545-15
RYAN, STEPHEN J R01EY02061-14
RYAN, UNA S R01HL46029-02
RYAN, UNA S R37HL21568-15
RYBAK, LEONARD P R01DC00321-07
RYBICKI, ANNE C R29HL41382-04
RYCHNOVSKY, SCOTT D R01GM43854-02
RYCHTARIK, ROBERT G R01AA07712-02
RYDEN, MURIEL B R01NR02965-01
RYDER, KEVIN R01CA52752-02
RYDMAN, ROBERT J S07RR05871-03 0581
RYER, HELENA I R29NS25512-04
RYKOWSKI, MARY C R01GM44855-01
RYKOWSKI, MARY C S07RR05675-23 0918
RYMASZEWSKI, ZBIGNIE S07RR05408-30 0938
RYMER, W ZEV P01NS17489-10 0011
RYMER, WILLIAM Z P20NS30295-01
RYMER, WILLIAM Z P20NS30295-01 0001
RYMER, WILLIAM Z P20NS30295-01 9001
RYMER, WILLIAM Z R01AR40425-01A1
RYMER, WILLIAM Z R01NS19331-08
RYMER, WILLIAM Z R01NS28076-02
RYMER, WILLIAM Z S07RR06003-04
RYMER, WILLIAM Z S15AR41254-01
RYMOND, BRIAN C R29GM42476-03
RYSER, HUGUES J R01CA14551-16A4
RYU, JAI H S07RR05404-30 0855
RYU, JUNICHI S07RR05352-30 0750
RYU, JUNICHI S07RR05352-30 0762
RYUGO, DAVID K P01DC00119-16 0004
RYUGO, DAVID K P60DC00979-02 0002
RYUGO, DAVID K R01DC00232-07
RZEDZIAN, RICHARD R R43CA55449-01
ROGAWSKI, M Z01NS02732-05
Schapiro, M Z01AG00126-11
SAAD, MOHAMMED F U01HL47902-01
SAAG, MICHAEL S M01RR00032-31 0352
SAAG, MICHAEL S M01RR00032-31 0379
SAAG, MICHAEL S M01RR00032-31 0373
SAAG, MICHAEL S M01RR00032-31 0305
SAAG, MICHAEL S M01RR00032-31 0317
SAAG, MICHAEL S. P01AI27290-04 9001
SAAH, ALFRED J M01RR00722-19 0235
SAAH, ALFRED J P01AI26499-03S1
SAAH, ALFRED J P01AI26499-03S1 0002
SAAH, ALFRED J P01AI26499-03S1 0003
SAAH, ALFRED J P30AI28748-03 9006
SAAH, ALFRED J R01HD22496-04
SAAH, ALFRED J R01HD25785-03
SAAL, ALFRED N01AI72634-14
SAARI, JOHN C R01EY02317-15
SAARI, JOHN E P30EY01730-16 9001
SAAVEDRA, J M Z01MH00433-11
SAAVEDRA, RAUL A R29AR41046-01
SABA, GEORGE P III M01RR00722-19 0236
SABA, THOMAS M R01GM21447-17
SABATINI, DAVID D R01GM20277-19
SABATINI, DAVID D R01GM43583-11A1
SABATINI, SANDRA R01DK36119-07
SABBAHI, MOHAMED S06GM08256-03 0006
SABBAN, ESTHER L K04NS01121-05
SABBAN, ESTHER L R01NS28869-02
SABET, TAWFIK S07RR05864-10 0935
SABINA, RICHARD L R01AR40766-01A1
SABISTON, DAVID C JR R01HL09315-27A1
SABOL, S L Z01HL00018-14
SABRY, Z I N01HC55024-10
SACCHETTINI, JAMES C R01GM45859-01A1
SACCO, RALPH L R01NS27517-03
SACHDEV, GORDON S07RR06009-03 0303
SACHDEV, GOVERDHAN P R01HL34012-08
SACHDEV, GOVERDHAN P R01HL41200-04
SACHS, ALAN BRUCE R29GM43164-02
SACHS, BENJAMIN D R01HD08933-16
SACHS, D H Z01CB05021-20
SACHS, D H Z01CB05023-20
SACHS, DAVID H N01HI19054-00
SACHS, DAVID H R01AI31046-01
SACHS, DAVID H R01HL46532-01
SACHS, DAVID P R01DA04986-04
SACHS, DAVID P R01DA06861-01
SACHS, DAVID P R44DA06567-02
SACHS, FREDERICK P41RR01219-10 0002
SACHS, GEORGE P30DK41301-02 9004
SACHS, GEORGE R01DK40615-04
SACHS, JOHN R R01DK19185-14
SACHS, MARTIN M R01GM34740-07
SACHS, MURRAY B P60DC00979-02 0004
SACHS, MURRAY B P60DC00979-02 9001
SACHS, MURRAY B P60DC00979-02
SACHS, MURRAY B P60DC00979-02 9003
SACHS, MURRAY B R01DC00109-17
SACK, ANDREW P30HD02274-24 9002
SACK, BRADLEY R03AI30993-01
SACK, ROBERT M01RR00334-25 0285
SACK, ROBERT M01RR00334-25 0278
SACK, ROBERT L M01RR00334-25 0277
SACK, ROBERT L R01MH47089-01
SACK, WILLIAM H R01MH42927-03
SACKEIM, HAROLD A R01MH44779-03
SACKEIM, HAROLD A R37MH35636-10
SACKELLARES, C JAMES M01RR00042-31 0645
SACKELLARES, J CHRIS M01RR00042-31 0642
SACKELLARES, J CHRIS M01RR00042-31 0623
SACKELLARES, J CHRIS M01RR00042-31 0600
SACKELLARES, J CHRIS M01RR00042-31 0512
SACKELLARES, J CHRIS P50NS15655-12 0012
SACKETT, GENE P. P51RR00166-30 0179

SACKETT, GENE P. P51RR00166-30 0068
SACKETT, GENE P. P51RR00166-30 0069
SACKETT, GENE P. P51RR00166-30 0070
SACKETT, GENE P. P51RR00166-30 0071
SACKETT, GENE P. P51RR00166-30 0072
SACKIN, HENRY J R55DK38596-04
SACKNER, MARVIN A S07RR05662-18
SACKS, D Z01AI00494-05
SACKS, D L Z01AI00256-10
SACKS, DAVID B K11DK01680-06
SACKS, FRANK M01RR02635-07 0198
SACKS, FRANK M R01HL34593-05
SACKS, FRANK M R01HL36392-05
SACKS, HENRY M01RR00071-28A1 0201
SACKS, HENRY M01RR00071-28A1 0177
SACKS, HENRY M01RR00071-28A1 0219
SACKS, HENRY M01RR00071-28A1 0220
SACKS, HENRY M01RR00071-28A1 0221
SACKS, HENRY M01RR00071-28A1 0222
SACKS, HENRY M01RR00071-28A1 0223
SACKS, HENRY M01RR00071-28A1 0224
SACKS, HENRY M01RR00071-28A1 0225
SACKS, HENRY M01RR00071-28A1 0226
SACKS, HENRY M01RR00071-28A1 0179
SACKS, HENRY M01RR00071-28A1 0180
SACKS, HENRY S R01AI32457-01
SACKS, HENRY S R01MH45686-01A2
SACKS, HENRY S U01AI27554-04
SACKS, HENRY S U01AI27667-06
SACKS, MICHAEL H R01MH45647-03
SACKS, PETER G R01CA57166-01
SACKTOR, TODD C K08NS01515-02
SADEE, WOLFGANG R01DA04166-06
SADEE, WOLFGANG R01GM43102-02
SADEE, WOLFGANG R13DA07194-01
SADLER, J EVAN P50HL14147-21 0023
SADLER, SUSAN S07RR07138-20 0528
SADLER, SUSAN E R01CA42426-05
SADLER, THOMAS W R01HD19593-07
SADOVE, RICHARD C S07RR05374-30 0737
SADOWSKY, DONALD R01DE08417-03
SADOWSKY, MICHAEL J S07RR07052-26 0167
SADRZADEH, S M HOSSE S07RR05591-27 0655
SADUN, ALFREDO A R01EY08145-03
SAENZ DE TEJADA, I R01DK39080-05
SAENZ DE TEJADA, INIGO R01DK40487-04
SAEZ, JUAN P01NS07512-23 0048
SAEZ, JUAN C R01DK41368-02
SAFA, AHMAD R R29CA47652-05
SAFAR, PETER P20NS30318-01 0006
SAFAR, PETER S07RR05416-30 0573
SAFE, S H P42ES04917-03 0002
SAFE, STEPHEN H P42ES04917-03
SAFE, STEPHEN H R01ES03554-07
SAFE, STEPHEN H R01ES03843-06
SAFE, STEPHEN H R01ES04176-03
SAFER, B Z01HL02213-15
SAFER, B Z01HL02229-02
SAFER, DANIEL R29AR38976-05
SAFFER, HENRY R01AA08349-02
SAFFER, HENRY R01DA07111-01A1
SAFFIOTTI, U Z01CP04491-15
SAFFIOTTI, U Z01CP05274-10
SAFFIOTTI, U Z01CP05276-10
SAFFITZ, JEFFREY E P50HL17646-17 9003
SAFFITZ, JEFFREY E P50HL17646-17 0025
SAFFRAN, ELEANOR M R01DC00191-10
SAFFRAN, WILMA S07RR07064-24 0207
SAFRAN, CHARLES R01HS06288-02
SAFRAN, HOWARD S07RR05487-29 0705
SAFWAT, FUAD M S07RR07199-12
SAFWAT, FUAD M S15AI32172-01
SAGAR, STEPHEN M R01NS27448-02
SAGAR, STEPHEN M R01NS27864-02
SAGE, E HELENE R01GM40711-04
SAGE, E HELENE R01HL41196-04
SAGE, HELENE P01HL03174-36 0020
SAGE, HELENE P50HD12629-12 0011
SAGE, RICHARD S07RR07053-26 0141
SAGE, RICHARD D R01AI29800-02
SAGEN, JACQUELINE R01NS25054-04A1
SAGER, ALAN S07RR05927-07 0969
SAGER, ALAN S07RR05927-07 0958
SAGER, RUTH P01CA22427-14 0009
SAGER, RUTH R35CA39814-07
SAGI, ABRAHAM R01HD25975-01A1
SAHAGIAN, GARABED G R01DK36632-05
SAHLEY, CHRISTIE L R01MH44789-01A2
SAHN, DAVID J R01HL36472-04
SAHN, DAVID J R01HL43287-02
SAHNI, SURESH K R43DK44411-01
SAID, SAMI I R01HL30450-10
SAIER, MILTON H JR R01AI14176-14
SAIER, MILTON H, JR R01AI21702-07
SAIGO, PATRICIA E P01CA52477-01A1 9003
SAINT MARIE, RICHARD L R01DC00726-02
SAINT-COME, CLAUDE S06GM08025-21 0020
SAITO, HARUO R01AI26598-04
SAITO, HARUO R01CA51132-02
SAITO, MARIKO S07RR05651-24 0148
SAITO, MITSUO S07RR05651-24 0140
SAITO, NI Z01NS02822-02
SAITOH, TSUNAO P01NS28121-01A1S1 0004
SAITOH, TSUNAO P50AG05131-08 0012
SAITOH, TSUNAO R01AG08205-04
SAITTA, MICHAEL R K11AR01825-03
SAKAI, DENNIS D S07RR07012-25 0022
SAKAI, HIROKO S07RR05399-30 0923
SAKAI, HIROKO M R01EY08848-01
SAKAI, SHARLEEN S07RR05656-24 0851
SAKAI, SHARLEEN S07RR05656-24 0828
SAKALA, ELMAR S07RR05352-30 0743
SAKANARI, JUDY A R29AI29457-01A1
SAKANO, HITOSHI R01AI18790-10
SAKAR, HEMANTA K P01HL37044-06 9003
SAKATANI, KAORU P50NS10164-19 0026
SAKHAEE, KHASAYAR M01RR00633-19 0373
SAKHAEE, KHASHAYAR M01RR00633-19 0347
SAKHAEE, KHASHAYAR M01RR00633-19 0320
SAKHAEE, KHASHAYAR M01RR00633-19 0321
SAKHAEE, KHASHAYAR P01DK20543-15 0012
SAKHAEE, KHASHAYER M01RR00633-19 0279
SAKHAEE, KHASHAYER M01RR00633-19 0348
SAKHAEE, KHASHAYER M01RR00633-19 0377
SAKKUBAI, NAIDU P01HD24448-04 0001
SALA, LUIS F G12RR03050-07
SALA, LUIS F G12RR03050-07 9001
SALAFSKY, BERNARD P S07RR05369-30 0593
SALAFSKY, BERNARD P S07RR05369-30 0585
SALAMA, GUY R55AR40836-01
SALAMONE, JOHN D R03MH47520-01
SALAMY, ALAN S07RR05755-18 0218
SALAMY, ALAN S07RR05755-18 0237
SALAND, LINDA C R01NS21256-05
SALAND, LINDA C S06GM08139-17 0057
SALANT, DAVID J R01DK30932-09
SALAS, MARGARITA R01GM27242-12
SALATA, ROBERT A P01AI15351-13 9002
SALAZAR, NELIA P50AI30601-01 0003
SALE, GEORGE P01CA47748-03 9004
SALE, GEORGE E P01CA18029-16 9005
SALE, GEORGE E P01HL36444-11 9001
SALE, GEORGE E P30CA15704-18 9001
SALE, GEORGE E P30CA15704-18 9012
SALE, WINFIELD S R01HD20497-07
SALEH, MANSOOR N M01RR00032-31 0364
SALEH, MANSOOR N R29HL38910-03
SALEM, DEEB N01HC55010-09
SALEM, N Z01AA00235-09
SALEM, N Z01AA00262-09
SALEMI, JOSEPH N01CO94392-11
SALEN, GERALD R01DK18707-15
SALEN, GERALD R37HL17818-18
SALHANY, KEVIN E S07RR05424-30 0089
SALING, PATRICIA U54HD29125-01 0005
SALING, PATRICIA M K04HD00816-05
SALING, PATRICIA M R01HD18201-07
SALISBURY, JEFFREY L R01GM35258-07
SALKEVER, DAVID S R01AA08364-02
SALKEVER, DAVID S R01AA08371-02
SALKOFF, LAWRENCE B R01NS24785-05
SALLAN, STEPHEN E U10CA41573-06 0057
SALLAN, STEPHEN E U10CA41573-06 0058
SALLAN, STEPHEN E U10CA41573-06 0059
SALLAN, STEPHEN E U10CA41573-06 0060
SALLAN, STEPHEN E U10CA41573-06
SALLAN, STEPHEN E U10CA41573-06 0001
SALLAN, STEPHEN E U10CA41573-06 0037
SALLAN, STEPHEN E U10CA41573-06 0038
SALLAN, STEPHEN E U10CA41573-06 0039
SALLAN, STEPHEN E U10CA41573-06 0002
SALLAN, STEPHEN E U10CA41573-06 0003
SALLAN, STEPHEN E U10CA41573-06 0004
SALLAN, STEPHEN E U10CA41573-06 0005
SALLAN, STEPHEN E U10CA41573-06 0006
SALLAN, STEPHEN E U10CA41573-06 0007
SALLAN, STEPHEN E U10CA41573-06 0008
SALLAN, STEPHEN E U10CA41573-06 0009
SALLAN, STEPHEN E U10CA41573-06 0010
SALLAN, STEPHEN E U10CA41573-06 0011
SALLAN, STEPHEN E U10CA41573-06 0012
SALLAN, STEPHEN E U10CA41573-06 0013
SALLAN, STEPHEN E U10CA41573-06 0014
SALLAN, STEPHEN E U10CA41573-06 0015
SALLAN, STEPHEN E U10CA41573-06 0016
SALLAN, STEPHEN E U10CA41573-06 0040
SALLAN, STEPHEN E U10CA41573-06 0017
SALLAN, STEPHEN E U10CA41573-06 0041
SALLAN, STEPHEN E U10CA41573-06 0042
SALLAN, STEPHEN E U10CA41573-06 0043
SALLAN, STEPHEN E U10CA41573-06 0044
SALLAN, STEPHEN E U10CA41573-06 0045
SALLAN, STEPHEN E U10CA41573-06 0046
SALLAN, STEPHEN E U10CA41573-06 0018
SALLAN, STEPHEN E U10CA41573-06 0019
SALLAN, STEPHEN E U10CA41573-06 0020
SALLAN, STEPHEN E U10CA41573-06 0021
SALLAN, STEPHEN E U10CA41573-06 0022
SALLAN, STEPHEN E U10CA41573-06 0023
SALLAN, STEPHEN E U10CA41573-06 0024
SALLAN, STEPHEN E U10CA41573-06 0025
SALLAN, STEPHEN E U10CA41573-06 0026
SALLAN, STEPHEN E U10CA41573-06 0027
SALLAN, STEPHEN E U10CA41573-06 0028
SALLAN, STEPHEN E U10CA41573-06 0029
SALLAN, STEPHEN E U10CA41573-06 0030
SALLAN, STEPHEN E U10CA41573-06 0031
SALLAN, STEPHEN E U10CA41573-06 0032
SALLAN, STEPHEN E U10CA41573-06 0033
SALLAN, STEPHEN E U10CA41573-06 0034
SALLAN, STEPHEN E U10CA41573-06 0035
SALLAN, STEPHEN E U10CA41573-06 0036
SALLAN, STEPHEN E U10CA41573-06 0047
SALLAN, STEPHEN E U10CA41573-06 0048
SALLAN, STEPHEN E U10CA41573-06 0049
SALLAN, STEPHEN E U10CA41573-06 0050
SALLAN, STEPHEN E U10CA41573-06 0051
SALLAN, STEPHEN E U10CA41573-06 0052
SALLAN, STEPHEN E U10CA41573-06 0053
SALLAN, STEPHEN E U10CA41573-06 0054
SALLAN, STEPHEN E U10CA41573-06 0055
SALLAN, STEPHEN E U10CA41573-06 0056
SALLEE, FLOYD R R01MH46673-02
SALLEE, FLOYD R R03DA06510-02
SALLER, RICHARD S07RR07029-26 0024
SALLIS, JAMES F R01HL44467-03
SALMON, DAVID P P50AG05131-08 0013
SALMON, EDWARD D R01GM24364-13
SALMON, JANE P60AR38520-04 0004
SALMON, JANE EVA R01AR38889-03
SALMON, MARLA S07RR05450-30 0336
SALMON, SYDNEY P01CA41183-05
SALMON, SYDNEY E P01CA17094-16
SALMON, SYDNEY E P01CA17094-16 0019
SALMON, SYDNEY E P01CA17094-16 0029
SALMON, SYDNEY E P30CA23074-14
SALMON, SYDNEY E P30CA23074-14 9012
SALO, WILMAR L S07RR05896-09 0625
SALO, WILMAR L S07RR05896-09 0621
SALOMON, D S Z01CB09003-09
SALOMON, DANIEL R K08DK01820-04
SALOMON, GAVRIEL R01HD27628-01
SALONER, DAVID A R29HL42506-03
SALOVEY, PETER P01CA42101-06 0011
SALPETER, MIRIAM M R01GM10422-29
SALPETER, MIRIAM M R01NS09315-22
SALSER, WINSTON A R01CA32186-17
SALSER, WINSTON A S10RR06461-01
SALT, ALEC N P01DC00384-05 0001
SALTER, DAVID R S07RR05430-30 0226
SALTHOUSE, TIMOTHY A R37AG06826-06
SALTIEL, ALAN R R01DK33804-08
SALTMAN, PAUL D R01DK12386-24
SALTON, STEPHEN R R01AG10676-01
SALTON, STEPHEN R R55GM41227-01A2
SALTZ, ROBERT P50AA06282-09 0001
SALTZBERG, BERNARD P01HD21888-04 0003
SALTZMAN, BERNARD E P30ES00159-24S1 0041
SALTZMAN, ELLIOT P01DC00121-29A1 0010
SALTZMAN, GLENN S07RR05806-13
SALTZMAN, MARK U01CA52857-02 0003
SALTZMAN, W MARK S07RR07041-26 0393
SALTZMAN, WILLIAM M R01GM43873-02
SALUSKY, ISIDRO S07RR05354-30 0379
SALUSKY, ISIDRO B M01RR00865-18 0357
SALUSKY, ISIDRO B R01DK35423-05
SALVATERRA, PAUL E P01NS18858-09A2 0011
SALVATERRA, PAUL M R55NS19482-09
SALVATO, MARIA S R29AI25522-05
SALVATORE, R P01CA29502-11A1 0047
SALVESEN, GUY S R01GM38860-01A2
SALVI, RICHARD J S07RR07066-26 0256
SALYERS, ABIGAIL A R01AI17876-11
SALYERS, ABIGAIL A R01AI22383-06
SALZ, HELEN K S07RR05410-30 0953
SALZBERG, BRIAN M R01NS16824-11
SALZER, JAMES L R01NS26001-04
SALZMAN, EDWIN W P01HL33014-07 0003
SALZMAN, EDWIN W R01HL13754-21
SALZMAN, EDWIN W R01HL37610-05
SALZMAN, GARY C R01CA54518-01
SALZMAN, LEONARD P50MH40381-06 9001
SALZMAN, LEONARD F P50MH40381-06 9004
SALZMAN, NORMAN N01AI05058-07
SALZMAN, NORMAN P R01AI29372-03
SAMAREL, ALLEN M R01HL34328-07
SAMAREL, ALLEN M R01HL43582-03
SAMBROOK, JOSEPH P50HL17669-17
SAMBROOK, JOSEPH F P50HL17669-17 0041
SAMBROOK, JOSEPH F P50HL17669-17 0042
SAMBROOK, JOSEPH F R01GM37829-06
SAMBROOK, JOSEPH F R01HL45944-02
SAMELSON, L E Z01HD01600-07
SAMEROFF, ARNOLD J R01MH39588-05
SAMEROFF, ARNOLD J R01MH44755-03
SAMET, JONATHAN R01CA55730-01
SAMET, JONATHAN M R03HS06879-01
SAMET, JONATHON R01HL43153-03
SAMLOWSKI, WOLFRAM M01RR00064-27 0358
SAMLOWSKI, WOLFRAM M01RR00064-27 0376
SAMLOWSKI, WOLFRAM M01RR00064-27 0382
SAMLOWSKI, WOLFRAM M01RR00064-27 0359
SAMLOWSKI, WOLFRAM M01RR00064-27 0360
SAMLOWSKI, WOLFRAM M01RR00064-27 0361
SAMLOWSKI, WOLFRAM M01RR00064-27 0362
SAMLOWSKI, WOLFRAM M01RR00064-27 0363

SAMLOWSKI, WOLFRAM E R29CA45354-04
SAMO, JILL M01RR00082-29 0282
SAMOLLOW, PAUL B R01HD26962-03
SAMOLS, DAVID R R01AR40765-01A1
SAMOSZUK, MICHAEL K R29CA48713-03
SAMOWITZ, WADE S S07RR05428-30 0171
SAMPLE, PAMELA A R01EY08208-02
SAMPLES, JOHN M01RR00334-25 0275
SAMPLES, JOHN R R01EY07111-02
SAMPSELLE, CAROLYN S07RR05796-14 0440
SAMPSELLE, CAROLYN M M01RR00042-31 0629
SAMPSELLE, CAROLYN M R29NR01950-02
SAMPSON, H M01RR00052-30 0198
SAMPSON, H WAYNE S07RR05814-12 0152
SAMPSON, HUGH A R01AI24439-05
SAMPSON, JAMES H N01AI95037-06
SAMPSON, MICHAEL G U01AI25893-05 0005
SAMPSON, PAUL S07RR07208-10 0665
SAMPSON, PAUL S07RR07208-10 0671
SAMPSON, PHILIP B S07RR07179-14 0686
SAMS, W MITCHELL, JR N01AR62271-08
SAMSON, HERMAN H R01AA06845-06
SAMSON, HERMAN H R01AA07404-03
SAMSON, LEONA P01ES03926-07 0004
SAMSON, LEONA D R01CA55042-01
SAMUEL, CHARLES E R01AI20611-08
SAMUEL, CHARLES E R37AI12520-17
SAMUELS, BRIAN L M01RR00055-30 0535
SAMUELS, HERBERT M01RR00096-30A1 0308
SAMUELS, HERBERT H R01DK41093-03
SAMUELS, HERBERT H R37DK16636-19
SAMUELS, MARY M01RR01346-10 0166
SAMUELS, MARY H M01RR01346-10 0192
SAMUELS, MARY H S07RR05654-24 0133
SAMUELS, SHELDON W R13HG00449-01
SAMUELSON, JOHN C R29AI28395-03
SAMUELSON, JOHN C S07RR05446-30 0271
SAMUELSON, LINDA C R01DE09598-02
SAMUELSON, LINDA C S07RR05383-30 0568
SAMULSKI, R JUDE R01DK42701-02
SAMULSKI, R JUDE R29AI25530-04
SAMULSKI, RICHARD J S07RR07084-26 0326
SAMY, T P30CA14395-18A1 9011
SAN AGUSTIN, MUTYA R01MH46132-02
SAN, KA-YIU S07RR07103-25 0502
SAN, RICHARD N01CP05620-02
SANADI, D RAO S07RR05711-21 0035
SANBONMATSU, DAVID M S07RR07092-26 0521
SANBORN, BARBARA M R01HD09618-14
SANBORN, BARBARA M R01HD17795-07
SANBORN, CHARLOTTE F S07RR07218-05 0458
SANCAR, AZIZ R01GM31082-09
SANCAR, AZIZ R01GM32833-08
SANCAR, GWENDOLYN B R01GM35123-07
SANCHEZ, LORRAINE K08CA01641-01
SANCHEZ, RICHARD S S03RR03098-09
SANDBERG, A L Z01DE00061-20
SANDBERG, AVERY A N01CP71018-06
SANDBERG, AVERY A P01CA41183-05 0006
SANDBERG, AVERY A P01CA41285-07 9001
SANDBERG, AVERY A S15CA56022-01
SANDBERG, MICHAEL A R01EY08398-02
SANDBORG, CHRISTY IRENE R01AI28214-03
SANDEDERS, V M Z01ES21151-01
SANDELL, JULIE H R29EY09081-02
SANDELL, LINDA J R01AR36994-05
SANDELOWSKI, MARGARETE J R01NR01707-04
SANDER, LINDA D. S06GM08037-20 0037
SANDER, M Z01ES61049-01
SANDERS-BUSH, ELAINE R01MH34007-12
SANDERS, BRENDA S06GM08238-05 0016
SANDERS, DONALD B. M01RR00030-30 0458
SANDERS, IRA R01DC01143-02
SANDERS, KENTON P01DK41315-03 0002
SANDERS, KENTON M P01DK41315-03
SANDERS, KENTON M R01DK40569-04
SANDERS, MICHEL M R29DK40082-04
SANDERS, PATRICIA C R01CA55382-01
SANDERS, PAULETTA E S07RR05362-30 0805
SANDERS, PAULETTA E S07RR05362-30 0806
SANDERS, PAULETTA E S07RR05362-30 0807
SANDERS, PAULETTA E S07RR05362-30 0808
SANDERS, PAULETTA E S07RR05362-30 0809
SANDERS, PAULETTA E S07RR05362-30 0810
SANDERS, PAULETTA E S07RR05362-30 0811
SANDERS, PAULETTA E S07RR05362-30 0812
SANDISON , GEORGE A R01CA53113-01
SANDLER, D P Z01ES43004-14
SANDLER, D P Z01ES46002-07
SANDLER, D P Z01ES47001-05
SANDLER, IRWIN N P50MH39246-07 0003
SANDLER, IRWIN N P50MH39246-07
SANDLER, IRWIN N P50MH39246-07 0001
SANDLER, RIVKA B R01AR39234-03
SANDLER, ROBERT S M01RR00046-31 0406
SANDLER, ROBERT S R01CA44684-04
SANDLOW, LESLIE S07RR05476-29
SANDMAIER, BRENDA M K08CA01483-02
SANDMAN, CURT A R01MH41446-03
SANDMEYER, SUZANNE B R01GM33281-08
SANDO, GLORIA N P50HL14230-20 0100
SANDO, ISAMU R01DC00123-15
SANDO, ISAMU S07RR05416-30 0574
SANDO, ISAMU S07RR06024-03 0851
SANDO, JULIANNE P01DK40031-03 0004
SANDO, JULIANNE J P01CA40042-07 0005
SANDO, JULIANNE J R01GM31184-09
SANDOR, P P50NS10939-18A1S1 0031
SANDOR, TAMAS P01AG04953-08 0003
SANDOR, TAMAS P01AG04953-08 9002
SANDOR, TAMAS P01CA41167-06 9001
SANDOW, BRUCE A S07RR05571-27 0333
SANDRA, ALEXANDER P30DK25295-12S1 9013
SANDRI-GOLDIN, ROZANNE M K04AI00878-04
SANDRI-GOLDIN, ROZANNE M R01AI21515-08
SANDS, DAVID C S06GM08218-08 0021
SANDS, JEFF M01RR00039-31 0431
SANDS, JEFF M R29DK41707-03
SANDS, LAURA S07RR05611-22 0705
SANDS, RICHARD H R01GM32785-08
SANDS, STEPHEN F N01NS12317-00
SANDSON, JOHN I M01RR00533-23
SANDSTEAD, HAROLD H M01RR00073-29 0312
SANDY, JOHN D R01AR38580-06
SANES, DAN H R29DC00540-03
SANES, JEROME N R01AG10634-01
SANES, JOSHUA R R01NS19195-09
SANES, JOSHUA R R01NS29169-01
SANETO, RUSSELL P51RR00163-32 0030
SANFILIPPO, ALFRED P P01DK38108-04 0002
SANFORD, BARBARA A R01AI17242-10
SANFORD, GARY S06GM08248-05 0021
SANFORD, GARY L R29HL38944-05
SANFORD, GERRY P30CA30199-11 9004
SANFORD, GORDON P30CA06973-29 9022
SANFORD, K K Z01CP04976-14
SANFORD, KEAT M S03RR03023-10
SANGAMESWAREN, LAKSHMI P30AG10133-01 0003
SANGEORZAN, BRUCE J S07RR05432-30 0243
SANGER, JOSEPH W P01HL15835-19 0029
SANI, BRAHMA P S07RR05676-15 0956
SANIEL, MEDIADORA C P50AI30601-01
SANOVICH, E Z01NS01805-23
SANSOM, STEVE S07RR05745-19 0224
SANSOM, STEVEN C S07RR05745-19 0250
SANSONE, CAROL S07RR07092-26 0512
SANT, ANDREA P01CA19266-14A1 0021
SANT'AMBROGIO, GIUSEPPE R01HL20122-14
SANTAGO, PETER S07RR05404-30 0856
SANTAMORE, WILLIAM P R01HL40327-04
SANTAMORE, WILLIAM P S15HL47752-01
SANTELLA, REGINA P01CA21111-15 0007
SANTELLA, REGINA S07RR05449-30 0321
SANTELLA, REGINA M P01ES05294-02 0001
SANTELLA, REGINA M R01ES05116-02
SANTELLA, REGINA M R01OH02622-03
SANTEN, R P01CA40011-07 0005
SANTEN, RICHARD J P01CA40011-07
SANTI, DANIEL V R01AI19358-10
SANTI, DANIEL V R01AI32784-01
SANTI, DANIEL V R37CA14394-19
SANTI, DANIEL V U01AI30261-02
SANTI, DANIEL V U01AI30261-02 0002
SANTI, PETER A P50DC00110-17 0004
SANTIAGO, JULIO V M01RR00036-31 0613
SANTIAGO, JULIO V M01RR06021-02 0680
SANTIAGO, JULIO V M01RR06021-02 1011
SANTIAGO, JULIO V M01RR06021-02 0613
SANTIAGO, JULIO V U01DK30653-09
SANTIAGO, TEODORO V R01HL23315-13
SANTOLI, DANIELA R01CA47589-04
SANTONI, TIMOTHY W R19MH47695-02
SANTORO, NANETTE F K08HD00923-02
SANTORO, SAMUEL A R01HL40506-04
SANTORO, THOMAS J R29AI26284-04
SANTOS-BUCH, CHARLES S07RR05396-30 0771
SANTOS-BUCH, CHARLES A R01HL34221-06
SANTOS-SACCHI, JOSEPH R R01DC00273-09
SANTOS, GEORGE W P01CA15396-18
SANTOS, GEORGE W P01CA15396-18 0001
SANTOSHAM, MATHURAM R01AI20738-06
SANYAL, MRINAL K R01ES05337-03
SANZ, IGNACIO R29AI29003-02
SAPARETO, STEPHEN A R01CA51189-03
SAPER, CLIFFORD B P01AG09466-01 0005
SAPER, CLIFFORD B R01NS22835-06
SAPIN, ROBERT S07RR05838-12 0273
SAPIR, SHIMON R29DC00591-01A1
SAPIRSTEIN, VICTOR S S15MH49275-01
SAPOLSKY, ROBERT M R01AG06633-05
SAPRU, HREDAY N R01HL24347-11
SAR, MADHABANANDA R01NS17479-08
SARAFIAN, THEODORE A R29ES04722-04
SARAL, REIN S07RR05378-30 0014
SARANGAPANI, S R43HL47238-01
SARANGAPANI, S R44DK39923-03
SARANGAPANI, SRINIVASAN R44DK39278-02A2
SARASON, IRWIN P01CA34847-09 9007
SARASON, IRWIN G P01CA34847-09 0015
SARASON, IRWIN G R01HL33091-07
SARAVIA, NANCY G P50AI30603-01 0003
SARAVIA, NANCY G P50AI30603-01 0004
SARAVIA, NANCY G P50AI30603-01
SARAVOLATZ, LOUIS N01AI95036-04
SARDAR, DHIRAJ S07RR07217-08 0165
SARELIUS, I. H. P01HL18208-17 0017
SAREMBOCK, IAN J R01HL47849-01
SARGENT, PETER S07RR05305-30 0729
SARGENT, PETER B R01NS24207-07
SARGENT, T Z01HD01006-03
SARGENT, THORNTON, III R01MH36801-07A1
SARID, JACOB R01NS28662-01A1
SARIN, P S Z01CP05535-05
SARIS, S Z01NS02778-04
SARKAR, DIPAK K R01AA08757-01A1
SARKAR, NILIMA R01GM26517-11
SARKAR, NURUL H R01CA45127-06
SARKAR, SATYAPRIYA P01HD23681-04 0005
SARKAR, SATYAPRIYA S07RR05852-11 0258
SARMA, BALA S07RR05366-30 0562
SARMA, J S M S07RR05471-29 0592
SARMA, RAMASWAMY H R01GM29787-18
SARMA, RAMASWAMY H R13GM46361-01
SARMIENTO, ULLA S07RR07042-26 0407
SARNA, GREGORY P M01RR00865-18 0362
SARNA, GREGORY P M01RR00865-18 0323
SARNA, GREGORY P P30CA16042-17 9009
SARNA, LINDA S07RR06014-03 0841
SARNA, SUSHIL K M01RR00058-30 0239
SARNA, SUSHIL K R01DK32346-08
SARNGADHARAN, DR M G N01CP15643-02
SARNGADHARAN, MANGALAS G N01CP73722-09
SARNGADHARAN, MANGALAS G N01CP73723-13
SARNGADHARAN, MANGALAS G N01CP87214-14
SARNO, MARTHA T R01DC00432-04
SARNOW, PETER P01AG07347-04 0005
SARNOW, PETER P30DK34914-06 0012
SARNOW, PETER R29AI25105-05
SAROFF, H A Z01DK24590-21
SAROFIM, ADEL F P01ES01640-14 0010
SAROFIM, ADEL F P01ES02429-11 0003
SAROSIEK, JERZY S07RR05431-30 0863
SARR, MICHAEL G R01DK39337-03
SARRAS, MICHAEL P, JR R01RR06500-02
SARRAS, MICHAEL P, JR R03DK43651-01
SARRAS, SARRAS, JR S07RR05373-30 0729
SARRO, TONY N01CO15635-01
SARTER, MARTIN F R01AG10173-01
SARTER, MARTIN F R03MH46869-01A1
SARTHY, VIJAY P R01EY03664-12
SARTOR, O Z01CM06527-01
SARTOR, RYAN B R01DK40249-03
SARTORELLI, A N01CO03867-05
SARTORELLI, ALAN C P01CA08341-26 0072
SARTORELLI, ALAN C P01CA42101-06
SARTORELLI, ALAN C P30CA16359-17 9005
SARTORELLI, ALAN C P30CA16359-17
SARTORELLI, ALAN C R01CA02817-35
SARTORELLI, ALAN C R01CA43659-05
SARTORELLI, ALAN C S10RR06246-01
SARTORELLI, ALLAN C. P30CA16359-17 9022
SARTORELLI, ALLAN C. P30CA16359-17 9024
SARTORIS, DAVID J. P01AG07996-03 0002
SARTORIUS, NORMAN U01MH35883-09
SARVENTNICK, NORA P50MH47680-02 0010
SARVETNICK, NORA P01DK41801-02 0007
SARVEY, JOHN M S07RR05983-05 0363
SASAKI, CLARENCE T R01DC01147-02
SASAME, HENRY Z01HL04408-01
SASSA, SHIGERU R01DK32890-09
SASSA, SHIGERU R01DK39264-01A3
SASSO, ERIC H R29AR40561-01A1
SASSON S07RR05380-30 0897
SATCHER, DAVID G12RR03032-07
SATCHER, DAVID R01HS07074-01
SATEL, SALLY L P50DA04060-06 0011
SATHYAMOORTHY, N Z01CN00161-01
SATINOFF, EVELYN R01MH41138-06
SATIR, BIRGIT H R01GM32767-08
SATIR, BRIGIT P30DK41296-03 0005
SATLIN, ANDREW R01AG09301-02
SATO, GORDON P01DK38639-04 9001
SATO, GORDON P01DK38639-04 9002
SATO, GORDON S07RR05863-11 0570
SATO, GORDON H P01CA37589-08 0003
SATO, GORDON H P01DK38639-04
SATO, GORDON H S15CA55988-01
SATO, J DENRY S07RR05863-11 0571
SATO, KENZO R01AR25339-14
SATO, KENZO R01DK27857-11
SATO, S Z01DK45041-02
SATO, S Z01DK45042-02
SATTENSPIEL, LISA S07RR07053-26 0148
SATTERFIELD, WILLIAM C N01AI05060-02
SATTERLEE, JAMES D S10RR06314-01
SATTERLIE, RICHARD A R01NS27951-01A1
SATTERLIE, RICHARD A S07RR07112-24 0421
SATTLER, FRED R M01RR00043-31 0487
SATTLER, FRED R M01RR00043-31 0485
SATYASWAROOP, P G P01CA40011-07 0003
SATYASWAROOP, P G P01CA40011-07 0008
SATYASWAROOP, P G R01CA46349-03
SATZ, PAUL P50MH30911-14 0026
SATZ, PAUL R01DA06597-01A1
SAUBERMANN, ALBERT J R01NS21455-07
SAUDEK, CHRISTOPHER M01RR00035-31 0353

SAUER, HELMET W S07RR07090-26 0483
SAUER, JOHN R R01AI26158-04
SAUER, JOHN R R01AI31460-01
SAUER, JOHN R S07RR07077-24 0268
SAUER, LEONARD A R01CA27809-11
SAUER, ROBERT T P01GM37641-05 0003
SAUER, ROBERT T R01AI15706-13
SAUER, ROBERT T R01AI16892-12
SAUK, JOHN J R01DE08648-04
SAUL, JEROME P K08HL02380-02
SAULNIER, G S07RR07104-25 0562
SAUNDERS, C S07RR05333-30 0875
SAUNDERS, ALEX M R44DK41597-03
SAUNDERS, GRADY F P01CA34936-08 0003
SAUNDERS, GRADY F R01CA46720-04
SAUNDERS, JAMES C R01DC00531-03
SAUNDERS, JAMES C R01DC00710-02
SAUNDERS, JUDITH M K08NR00033-01
SAUNDERS, MICHELE J P20NR03039-01 0003
SAUNDERS, PRISCILLA P R01CA48945-01A2
SAUNDERS, RICHARD P01HD26927-01A1 9001
SAUNDERS, RICHARD P01HD26927-01A1 0001
SAUSVILLE, E Z01CM06528-01
SAUSVILLE, E Z01CM06529-01
SAUSVILLE, E Z01CM06530-01
SAUSVILLE, EDWARD A U01CA51908-02 0002
SAUTTER, FREDERIC J R03MH46530-01A1
SAUVE, MARY J R01NR02515-01A2
SAVAGE, DANIEL D S06GM08139-17 0058
SAVAGE, DANIEL D, II R01AA06548-06
SAVAGE, DWAYNE C S07RR07088-24 0345
SAVAGE, EDWARD W R01CA45847-05
SAVAGEAU, MICHAEL A R01GM30054-09
SAVARESE, TODD M K04CA01241-05
SAVEDRA, MARILYN R01NR01045-05
SAVIN, SAMUEL M P50HD11089-14 9002
SAVIN, VIRGINIA S07RR05373-30 0730
SAVIN, VIRGINIA J R01DK22040-11A2
SAVINO, PETER J S07RR05510-28 0055
SAVINO, PETER J U10EY07674-04
SAVITZ, DAVID S07RR05450-30 0345
SAVITZ, DAVID A R29HD23862-04
SAWADA, STEPHEN M01RR00750-19 0300
SAWADOGO, MICHELE R01GM38212-05A1
SAWATARI, TAKEO R43HL47277-01
SAWCHENKO, PAUL E R01HL35137-06
SAWCHENKO, PAUL E R01NS21182-07
SAWCHUK, RONALD J R01NS27019-03
SAWCZUK, IHOR S R29DK40832-03
SAWHNEY, RAJINDER S R01EY08079-02
SAWICKI, DOROTHEA L R01AI15123-14
SAWICKI, JANET A R01CA40402-06
SAWICKI, STANLEY S07RR05700-22 0863
SAWICKI, STANLEY G R01AI28506-02
SAWUSCH, JAMES R R01DC00219-09
SAWYER, ELSPETH H S07RR05944-04 0973
SAWYER, L A Z01BF03006-02
SAWYER, L A Z01BF03008-02
SAWYER, L A Z01BF03013-01
SAWYER, L A Z01BF03014-01
SAWYER, L A Z01BF03015-01
SAWYER, L A Z01BF04011-01
SAWYER, RICHARD T S15AI32217-01
SAWYER, ROBERT S P01CA25842-11 0002
SAWYER, STANLEY R01GM44889-02
SAWYER, STEPHEN T R01DK39781-05
SAWYERS, CHARLES L K11CA01551-02
SAX, HARRY C M01RR00044-31 0321
SAXE, CHARLES S07RR05364-30 0540
SAXENA, SUNITA B S06GM08244-05 0025
SAXINGER, W C Z01CP05537-05
SAXON, ANDREW M01RR00865-18 0352
SAXON, ANDREW M01RR00865-18 0353
SAXON, ANDREW P01CA12800-18A1 0057
SAXON, ANDREW P30AI28697-01 9002
SAXON, ANDREW P50AI15332-14 0014
SAXON, ANDREW R01AI15251-13
SAXTON, MICHAEL J R01GM38133-04
SAXTON, WILLIAM M R01GM46295-01
SAXTON, WILLIAM M S07RR07031-26 0105
SAYA, HIDEYUKI S07RR05511-29 0492
SAYED, ATEF S07RR05433-30 0254
SAYEED, MOHAMMED M R01GM32288-05A2
SAYEED, VILAYAT N01CM97590-02
SAYERS, STEVEN L R03MH47834-01
SAYERS, STEVEN L S07RR05418-30 0030
SAYKIN, ANDREW J R01NS28813-01A1
SAYLOR, TILLMAN N01CM87245-04
SAYRE, LAWRENCE M K04NS01184-05
SAYRE, LAWRENCE M R55NS22688-07
SAZ, HOWARD J R01AI09483-22
SCADDEN, DAVID T R01CA55520-01
SCADDEN, DAVID T R01HL44851-01
SCADUTO, RUSSELL C, JR R01HL43215-01A2
SCADUTO, RUSSELL C, JR R29DK40069-03
SCALARONE, GENE M R01AI23140-02A3
SCALETTI, JOSEPH V S15HL47690-01
SCALLEN, TERENCE J S06GM08139-17 0008
SCALZO, FRANK M R29DA06319-02
SCAMMELL, JONATHAN G R29DK40593-04
SCANDRETT-HIBDON, SHARON L R15NR02114-01A2
SCANLAN, JAMES M R03MH48827-01
SCANLAN, TARA S07RR07009-26 0935
SCANLON, KEVIN S07RR05471-29 0582
SCANLON, KEVIN J R01CA50618-01A2
SCANLON, MARY S06GM08248-05 0016
SCANU, ANGELO S07RR05367-30 0572
SCANU, ANGELO M M01RR00055-30 0541
SCANU, ANGELO M P01HL18577-16 0017
SCANU, ANGELO M P01HL18577-16 9001
SCANU, ANGELO M P01HL18577-16
SCANU, ANGELO M R01HL43344-03
SCANU, ANGELO M S10RR06579-01
SCARATA, SUZANNE S07RR05396-30 0760
SCARBOROUGH, D S07RR07119-20 0469
SCARBOROUGH, DAVID E S07RR05822-12 0499
SCARBOROUGH, GENE A R01GM24784-15
SCARLATA, SUZANNE FRANCES R29GM39924-05
SCARPA, ANTONIA P01HL41618-03 9002
SCARPA, ANTONIO P01HL18708-16
SCARPA, ANTONIO P01HL18708-16 0019
SCARPA, ANTONIO R01HL41206-04
SCARPACE, P P50DE08845-04 0004
SCARPACI, JOSEPH L S07RR07035-26 0077
SCARPELLI, DANTE G P40RR00301-26
SCARPELLI, DANTE G R01CA34051-09
SCARPULLA, RICHARD C R01GM32525-09
SCARR, SANDRA W R01HD27383-03
SCHAACK, JEROME B R01GM42555-01A2
SCHAAL, STEPHEN F M01RR00034-31 0399
SCHAAPER, R M Z01ES60147-08
SCHAAPER, R M Z01ES65034-07
SCHABTACH, E P01HD22486-05 9000
SCHACHAT, ANDREW N01EY02111-02
SCHACHAT, ANDREW P U10EY06260-07
SCHACHAT, ANDREW P U10EY07617-04S1
SCHACHAT, FREDERICK H R01AR39603-03
SCHACHAT, FREDERICK H R01AR37344-09
SCHACHER, SAMUEL M R01NS27541-03
SCHACHMAN, HOWARD K R37GM12159-28
SCHACHT, JOCHEN P01DC00078-27 0041
SCHACHT, JOCHEN P01DC00078-27
SCHACHT, JOCHEN R01DC00124-14
SCHACHTELE, CHARLES S07RR05322-30 0281
SCHACHTELE, CHARLES F P50DE08489-04 0003
SCHACHTELE, CHARLES F S07RR05322-30
SCHACHTELE, CHARLES F S15DE10075-01
SCHACHTER, BETH S R01HD27557-01A1
SCHACHTER, DAVID R01DK01483-32
SCHACHTER, JULIUS P01AI24768-05 0002
SCHACHTER, JULIUS R01AI28481-03
SCHACHTER, JULIUS U01AI31499-01 9001
SCHACHTER, JULIUS U01AI31499-01
SCHACHTMAN, TODD R S07RR07053-26 0164
SCHACTER, DANIEL L R01AG08441-03
SCHACTER, J P01AI21912-08 9001
SCHACTER, NEIL E M01RR00071-28A1 0203
SCHAD, GERHARD A R01AI22662-05
SCHAD, GERHARD A S07RR05464-29 0377
SCHADE, DAVID S M01RR00997-16 0410
SCHADE, DAVID S M01RR00997-16 0385
SCHADE, DAVID S M01RR00997-16 0184
SCHADE, DAVID S U01DK37825-06
SCHADE, DAVID S. M01RR00997-16 0262
SCHADE, ROBERT N01CN05320-01
SCHADE, SYLVIA S07RR05477-29 0423
SCHAECHTER, MOSELIO R01GM34132-20
SCHAEDLER, RUSSELL W G20RR07098-01
SCHAEFER, ERNST J M01RR00054-30 0410
SCHAEFER, ERNST J M01RR00054-30 0419
SCHAEFER, ERNST J R01HL39326-05
SCHAEFER, JACOB R01GM40634-04
SCHAEFER, PAUL U10CA35415-08
SCHAEFER, SAUL K08HL02131-05
SCHAEFFER, ANTHONY J R01DK42648-02
SCHAEFFER, ANTHONY J U01DK45021-01
SCHAEFFER, ERIC P01AG09464-01 0004
SCHAEFFER, STEPHEN W R29GM42472-03
SCHAEFFER, WARREN I P30CA22435-11 9011
SCHAEFFER, WARREN I S07RR05429-30 0205
SCHAEFFER, WARREN I S07RR07125-22 0399
SCHAFER, ANDREW I P01HL36028-07 0008
SCHAFER, ANDREW I R01HL36045-08
SCHAFER, JAMES A P50DK39258-05 0001
SCHAFER, JAMES A R01DK25519-13
SCHAFER, MARK E R43DK43166-01A1
SCHAFER, ROLLIE R S07RR07195-12
SCHAFER, ROLLIE R S15GM47072-01
SCHAFFER, PRISCILLA A P01AI24010-05 9001
SCHAFFER, PRISCILLA A P01AI24010-05
SCHAFFER, PRISCILLA A P30CA06516-28 9003
SCHAFFER, PRISCILLA A R01AI28537-03
SCHAFFER, PRISCILLA A R37CA20260-15
SCHAFFER, PRISCILLA A. P01AI24010-05 0004
SCHAFFER, RICHARD P01HL17421-18 9002
SCHAFFER, STEPHEN W R01DK36440-06
SCHAFFER, WILLIAM M R01AI23534-04
SCHAFFHAUSEN, BRIAN S P01CA24530-12 0011
SCHAFFHAUSEN, BRIAN S P01CA50661-03 0005
SCHAFFHAUSEN, BRIAN S R37CA34722-09
SCHAFFLER, MITCHELL B. P01AG07996-03 9003
SCHAFFNER, CARL P R01CA46785-03
SCHAIE, K WARNER R13AG09787-01
SCHAIE, K WARNER R37AG08055-03
SCHAIE, K. WARNER R37AG08055-03 0002
SCHAIE, K. WARNER R37AG08055-03 0004
SCHALCH, DON S M01RR03186-06 0071
SCHALL, JEFFREY D R01EY08890-01
SCHALLERT, TIMOTHY J R01NS23964-06
SCHALLY, ANDREW V R01CA40003-06
SCHALLY, ANDREW V R01CA40004-06
SCHALLY, ANDREW V R01CA40077-06
SCHAMBELAN, MORRIS M01RR00083-29 0164
SCHAMBELAN, MORRIS M01RR00083-29 0178
SCHANBERG, SAUL M R01MH13688-25
SCHANLER, RICHARD M01RR00188-27 0338
SCHANTZ, STIMSON P01CA52051-01A1 0002
SCHANTZ, STIMSON P R01CA57155-01
SCHANTZ, STIMSON P R13CA54775-01
SCHANTZ, STIMSON P R29CA46251-04
SCHANZLIN, DAVID J R01EY04609-09
SCHAPIRA, MARC S07RR05424-30 0077
SCHAPIRA, MARC M R01HL40875-04
SCHAPIRA, RALPH M K08ES00239-02
SCHAPIRA, RALPH M S07RR05434-30 0814
SCHAPIRO, M Z01AG00403-06
SCHAPIRO, M B Z01AG00140-08
SCHARF, BERTRAM R01DC00084-16
SCHARF, STEVEN S07RR05496-29 0901
SCHARFF, MATTHEW D P30AI27741-04 9002
SCHARFF, MATTHEW D P30CA13330-20 9009
SCHARFF, MATTHEW D P30CA13330-20 9016
SCHARFF, MATTHEW D P30CA13330-20 9015
SCHARFF, MATTHEW D P30CA13330-20
SCHARFF, MATTHEW D R35CA39838-07
SCHARP, DAVID M01RR00036-31 0650
SCHARP, DAVID P60DK20579-14 9008
SCHARP, DAVID W R01DK40465-04
SCHARRER, BERTA V R01NS22344-06
SCHARSCHMIDT, BRUCE F R01DK26270-12
SCHATTEN, G P41RR00570-21 0001
SCHATTEN, G P41RR00570-21 9001
SCHATTEN, G P41RR00570-21 9002
SCHATTEN, GERALD P41RR00570-21 9003
SCHATTEN, GERALD P41RR00570-21 0010
SCHATTEN, GERALD P P41RR00570-21
SCHATTEN, GERALD P R01HD22902-05
SCHATZ, GOTTFRIED R01GM37803-05
SCHATZKIN, A Z01CN00146-03
SCHATZKIN, A Z01CN00147-03
SCHATZKIN, A Z01CN00151-03
SCHAUB, DEBORAH L R01HD23468-02
SCHAUER, ALAN T S07RR07091-26 0768
SCHAUWECKER, DONALD S R01AR36460-06
SCHECHTER, A N Z01DK25016-18
SCHECHTER, DIANNE E R03MH46551-01A1
SCHECHTER, ISHAIAHU S07RR05964-06 0763
SCHECHTER, ISHAIAHU S07RR05964-06 0764
SCHECHTER, JOEL E R01DK35904-07
SCHECHTER, MARTIN D R03AA08598-02
SCHECHTER, NISSON R01EY05212-09
SCHECHTER, NORMAN M P01AR39674-03 9003
SCHECHTER, NORMAN M P01AR39674-03 0001
SCHECTMAN, GORDAN O M01RR00058-30 0189
SCHECTMAN, GORDON M01RR00058-30 0222
SCHECTMAN, GORDON M01RR00058-30 0252
SCHECTMAN, GORDON M01RR00058-30 0265
SCHEDL, PAUL R01GM25976-13
SCHEDL, PAUL R01GM43432-02
SCHEDL, TIM B R01HD25614-03
SCHEELE, GEORGE A R01DK18532-18
SCHEFF, PETER A S07RR05871-03 0582
SCHEFF, STEPHEN W P50AG05144-08 0003
SCHEFFLER, IMMO E R01GM18835-21
SCHEFFLER, IMMO E R01GM33752-07
SCHEFFLER, RICHARD M P50MH43694-04
SCHEID, CHERYL R R01HL41188-04
SCHEID, CHERYL R S07RR05712-20 0070
SCHEIDT, W ROBERT R01GM38401-19
SCHEIDT, W ROBERT S10RR06709-01
SCHEIER, MICHAEL F R01HL44436-01A1
SCHEIFER, MARTIN P30CA06927-29 9006
SCHEIMAN, JAMES M M01RR00042-31 0651
SCHEIN, STANLEY J R01EY06096-05
SCHEINBERG, DAVID A R01CA55349-01
SCHEINER, LEWIS B P01AG03104-10 9001
SCHEINER, PETER S06GM08153-16 0007
SCHEINER, STEVE R01GM29391-11
SCHEINER, STEVE R01GM36912-05
SCHEINMAN, JON I M01RR00030-30 0469
SCHEINMAN, JON I R01DK40834-03
SCHEIRER, DANIEL C S07RR07143-20 0633
SCHEKMAN, RANDY W R01GM26755-13
SCHELBERT, HEINRICH R R01HL33177-07
SCHELD, W MICHAEL R01AI17904-06
SCHELL, LAWRENCE S07RR07122-23 0094
SCHELL, RONALD F R01AI22199-08
SCHELLER, RICHARD H P50MH48108-01 0003
SCHELLER, RICHARD H R01MH38710-06
SCHELLING, MARGARET E R29HL41378-05
SCHELLMAN, JOHN A R01GM20195-34
SCHEMIN, RICHARD J S07RR05487-29 0689
SCHEMMEL, RACHEL A S07RR07049-26 0422
SCHENCK, CRAIG C K04GM00536-03
SCHENCK, CRAIG C R29GM38214-04
SCHENEIDER, MARTIN F P01HL27867-10 0008

SCHENGRUND, CARA L R01AI23721-04A2
SCHENGRUND, CARA L R01NS26126-03
SCHENK, DALE B R44AG08406-03
SCHENK, SUSAN R01DA06825-01A1
SCHENK, SUSAN R29DA05548-04
SCHENKEIN, DAVID P K08CA01554-02
SCHENKEIN, HARVEY A K16DE00151-05S2
SCHENKEIN, HARVEY A P01DE08972-03
SCHENKEIN, HARVEY A P01DE08972-03 0005
SCHENKEIN, HARVEY A R01DE07606-04A2
SCHENKEIN, HARVEY A S07RR05724-20
SCHENKEIN, HARVEY A S15DE10081-01
SCHENKER, M B P42ES04699-05 9003
SCHENKER, STEVEN R01AA07514-05
SCHENKMAN, JOHN B R01GM26114-14
SCHENSUL, JEAN R18DA05750-03S1
SCHER, ALLEN M P01HL16910-18
SCHER, ALLEN M P01HL16910-18 0005
SCHER, CHARLES D P01CA47983-04 0006
SCHER, MARK S R01NS26793-03
SCHERAGA, HAROLD A P01HL30616-09 0002
SCHERAGA, HAROLD A R01DK08465-25
SCHERAGA, HAROLD A R01GM14312-36
SCHERAGA, HAROLD A S10RR06248-01
SCHERER, DAVID G S07RR07160-16 0597
SCHERER, PETER W R01HL33891-06
SCHERER, RONALD P60DC00976-02 0008
SCHERER, RONALD C P60DC00976-02 0009
SCHERER, STEWART R01AI23850-04A2
SCHERER, STEWART S07RR05385-30 0818
SCHERL, DONALD J S07RR05401-30
SCHERR, PAUL A S07RR05712-20 0102
SCHERRMAN, JAYNE S07RR05704-20 0009
SCHETKY, L R43DE10016-01
SCHEUER, JAMES P01HL37412-04 9001
SCHEUER, JAMES R01HL15498-19
SCHEVING, LAWRENCE A K08DK01929-03
SCHEYER, RICHARD D M01RR00125-28 0743
SCHHOLEY, ROBERT T M01RR00051-30 0772
SCHIAVI, RAUL C R01AA08214-02
SCHIAVONE, MARC T R29NS26804-03
SCHICK, BARBARA P R01HL29282-09
SCHICK, BRENDA S R29DC00952-01
SCHICK, BRENDA S S07RR05834-12 0545
SCHICK, PAUL K R01HL25455-11A2
SCHICK, PAUL K R01HL39238-06
SCHIEBER, MARC H R01NS27686-03
SCHIEBINGER, RICK J R01HL42209-03
SCHIEKEN, RICHARD M R01HL31010-09
SCHIEWE, M C Z01RR00088-02
SCHIFF, GILBERT M S07RR05951-07
SCHIFF, LESLIE A S07RR05385-30 0819
SCHIFF, RICHARD I M01RR00030-30 0486
SCHIFF, RICHARD I M01RR00030-30 0487
SCHIFF, RICHARD I M01RR00030-30 0489
SCHIFF, RICHARD I M01RR00030-30 0490
SCHIFFENBAUER, JOEL R01AI27324-02
SCHIFFER, CHARLES A R01CA52178-02
SCHIFFER, CHARLES A U01HL42815-03
SCHIFFER, MARIANNE R01GM36598-06
SCHIFFERLE, ROBERT E R29DE09602-01A1
SCHIFFMAN, ERIC L R29DE08668-01A2
SCHIFFMAN, ERIC L S07RR05322-30 0276
SCHIFFMAN, GERALD N01AI82699-03
SCHIFFMAN, JOYCE U10EY05480-07
SCHIFFMAN, SUSAN P50AG05128-08 0008
SCHIFFMAN, SUSAN S R37AG00443-17
SCHILDKRAUT, JOSEPH J R01MH15413-23
SCHILLER, J T Z01CB09052-03
SCHILLER, JOAN H M01RR03186-06 0065
SCHILLER, JOAN H M01RR03186-06 0052
SCHILLER, JOAN H P01CA20432-14 0032
SCHILLER, PETER H P30EY02621-14
SCHILLER, PETER H R01EY08502-01A1
SCHILLER, PETER H R37EY00676-21
SCHILLER, PETER W R01DA04443-05
SCHILLER, PETER W R01DA06252-02
SCHILLHORN VAN VEEN, S07RR05623-25 0726
SCHILLING, JAMES W S07RR07007-26 0925
SCHILLING, ROBERT F P01CA50956-02 0002
SCHILLING, ROBERT F P50DA05321-04 0004
SCHILLING, ROBERT F R01DA05356-04
SCHILLING, ROBERT F R01DA07059-01
SCHILLING, ROBERT F U01MH49058-01
SCHILLING, WILLIAM P R29HL44119-02
SCHILSKY, MICHAEL K08DK01925-03
SCHILSKY, RICHARD L M01RR00055-30 0421
SCHILSKY, RICHARD L P30CA14599-18
SCHILSKY, RICHARD L U10CA44691-07
SCHILSKY, RICHARD LEWIS R01CA49150-04
SCHIMENTI, JOHN C R01HD24374-04
SCHIMERLIK, MICHAEL I R01HL23632-12
SCHIMKE, JOEL T N44CN15402-00
SCHIMKE, ROBERT T R01CA16318-17
SCHIMKE, ROBERT T R01CA54346-01
SCHIMKE, ROBERT T R01GM14931-25
SCHIMMEL, PAUL P01GM37641-05 9001
SCHIMMEL, PAUL P01GM37641-05
SCHIMMEL, PAUL P01GM37641-05 0001
SCHIMMEL, PAUL R01GM23562-15
SCHIMMEL, PAUL R37GM15539-24
SCHIMMEL, RICHARD J R01DK36090-07
SCHIMMEL, RICHARD J S15DK44671-01
SCHINAZI, RAYMOND U01AI27196-04 9001
SCHINAZI, RAYMOND F R01CA53892-01
SCHINDLER, C W Z01DA00009-04
SCHINDLER, JAY P41RR01632-09 9023
SCHINDLER, MELVIN S S07RR07049-26 0448
SCHINI, VALERIE B R29HL46356-01
SCHINKE, STEVEN P P01CA50956-02 0004
SCHINKE, STEVEN P P01CA50956-02 9001
SCHINKE, STEVEN P P50DA05321-04 9001
SCHINKE, STEVEN P P50DA05321-04
SCHINKE, STEVEN P P50DA05321-04 0003
SCHINKE, STEVEN P P50DA07656-01 9001
SCHINKE, STEVEN P P50DA07656-01 0002
SCHINKE, STEVEN P R01CA44903-04
SCHINKE, STEVEN P R01DA03277-07
SCHINKE, STEVEN P U01CA52251-02
SCHINNAR, ARIE P R01MH44325-02
SCHIPMA, PETER B R44CA50842-02A1
SCHIRCH, LAVERNE G S07RR05430-30 0213
SCHIRCH, VERNE G R01GM28143-12
SCHIRGER, ALEXANDER M01RR00585-20 0418
SCHLAEPFER, WILLIAM W R01NS15722-14
SCHLAG-REY, MADELEINE L R01EY02305-13
SCHLAG, JOHN D R01EY05879-28
SCHLAGER, GUNTHER S07RR07037-26 0372
SCHLAGER, KENNETH J R43HL46079-01A1
SCHLANT, ROBERT C. N01HC65049-14
SCHLAUCH, ROBERT S S07RR07052-26 0168
SCHLECHTE, JANET M01RR00059-30 0724
SCHLECHTE, JANET A M01RR00059-30 0395
SCHLECHTE, JANET A M01RR00059-30 0410
SCHLECHTE, JANET A M01RR00059-30 0525
SCHLECHTE, JANET A. M01RR00059-30 0235
SCHLEEF, RAYMOND R R01HL45954-02
SCHLEGEL, RICHARD R01CA53371-01
SCHLEGEL, ROBERT R01CA49749-02
SCHLEGEL, ROBERT S07RR05446-30 0283
SCHLEGEL, ROBERT A R01AI26641-04
SCHLEICH, THOMAS W R01EY04033-10
SCHLEICHER, ROSEMARY L R01DK41418-03
SCHLEICHER, ROSEMARY L R03RR07046-01
SCHLEIF, ROBERT FERBER R01GM18277-22
SCHLEIFER, LEONARD S P01HD23315-05 0003
SCHLEIFER, STEVEN J R01AA08195-02
SCHLEIMER, ROBERT P R01AR31891-09
SCHLEIMER, ROBERT P U01AI31867-01 0002
SCHLEMMER, R FRANCIS S07RR05564-13 0915
SCHLENDER, KEITH K P01HL36573-06 0004
SCHLENKER, EVELYN H S07RR05421-27 0977
SCHLESINGER, DAVID H P30CA16087-14 9007
SCHLESINGER, DAVID H R01DE06159-08
SCHLESINGER, HERBERT J R01MH46005-02
SCHLESINGER, HERBERT J S07RR07235-03
SCHLESINGER, MARK J R03MH47371-01
SCHLESINGER, MARK J S07RR05381-30 0791
SCHLESINGER, MICHAEL P01AI26497-03 9001
SCHLESINGER, MILTON J R01AI19494-19
SCHLESINGER, MILTON J U01AI31889-01
SCHLESINGER, RICHARD P30ES00260-29 9009
SCHLESINGER, SONDRA R37AI11377-18
SCHLESSELMAN, JAMES J R01CA50193-03
SCHLESSELMAN, SARAH E U01AI25867-05 9001
SCHLESSINGER, DAVID P50HG00201-02
SCHLESSINGER, DAVID R01HG00247-03
SCHLESSINGER, RICHARD H R01GM31256-15
SCHLIER, ROBERT R43EY09002-01
SCHLIEVERT, PATRICK M R01HL36611-06
SCHLIWA, MANFRED S07RR07006-26 0898
SCHLOERB, PAUL R R01DK36969-05
SCHLOM, J Z01CB05190-11
SCHLOM, J Z01CB09008-10
SCHLOM, J Z01CB09018-07
SCHLONDORFF, DETLEF O R01DK22036-13
SCHLONDORFF, DETLEF O R01DK41566-03
SCHLOSS, JEFFERY A S07RR07114-23 0446
SCHLOSSMAN, STUART F P01AI23360-07 0004
SCHLOSSMAN, STUART F P01CA34183-08
SCHLOSSMAN, STUART F P01CA34183-08 0017
SCHLOSSMAN, STUART F P30CA06516-28 9012
SCHLOSSMAN, STUART F R37AI12069-17
SCHLUCHTER, MARK D P50HL33713-06 9002
SCHLUCHTER, MARK D. N01HR96037-07
SCHLUNDT, DAVID P60DK20593-13 9006
SCHLUSSEL, YVETTE M01RR00047-31 0466
SCHMADER, KEN S07RR05405-30 0875
SCHMADER, KENNETH E K08AG00526-01
SCHMADER, KENNETH E P30AG09463-01 0002
SCHMAIER, ALVIN P50HL45486-01 0002
SCHMAIER, ALVIN H K04HL01615-05
SCHMAIER, ALVIN H R01HL35553-05
SCHMALE, MICHAEL C R01CA53313-01
SCHMALE, MICHAEL C R01NS21997-07
SCHMALL, B Z01CL07002-03
SCHMALZ, M M01RR00058-30 0244
SCHMECHEL, DONALD E P50AG05128-08 0012
SCHMECHEL, DONALD E R01AG07671-04
SCHMEDTJ, JOHN M01RR00065-29 0311
SCHMEITZEL, LYNN S07RR05845-11 0553
SCHMELZER, MICHAEL P41LM05205-08 9007
SCHMID-SCHOENBEIN, GEERT W R01HL10881-26
SCHMID-SCHONBEIN, G W P50HL17682-17 0044
SCHMID-SCHONBEIN, GEERT W P01HL43026-02 00
SCHMID, CARL W R01GM21346-18
SCHMID, HAROLD H. O. P01NS14304-13 0009
SCHMID, PHILLIP P01HL14388-20 0252
SCHMID, PHILLIP G P01HL14388-20 0183
SCHMID, SANDRA L R01GM42455-03
SCHMID, STEVEN M S07RR05676-15 0965
SCHMIDHAUSER, THOMAS J R29GM45282-01
SCHMIDT, CHARLES S07RR07031-26 0106
SCHMIDT, E M Z01NS01688-23
SCHMIDT, GERHARD S07RR05471-29 0583
SCHMIDT, GERHARD S07RR05471-29 0584
SCHMIDT, JAKOB R01NS20233-06
SCHMIDT, JOHN T R01EY03736-11
SCHMIDT, JOHN T S07RR07122-23 0082
SCHMIDT, K Z01MH02569-01
SCHMIDT, LAURA P50AA05595-11 0020
SCHMIDT, MARTIN C R29GM46443-01
SCHMIDT, P M Z01RR00077-07
SCHMIDT, ROBERT E R01DK19645-14
SCHMIDT, ROBERT J R29GM41286-03
SCHMIDT, ROBERT S R01DC00082-26
SCHMIDT, SUSAN Y U10EY02014-15 0002
SCHMIEDT, R A P50DC00422-05 9001
SCHMIEDT, R A P50DC00422-05 9002
SCHMIEDT, RICHARD A P50DC00422-05 0003
SCHMIEG, FLORENCE I S07RR07016-18 0359
SCHMITT, EDWARD E R43GM46156-01
SCHMITT, J M Z01RR10333-02
SCHMITT, J M Z01RR10365-01
SCHMITT, J M Z01RR10366-01
SCHMITT, J M Z01RR10367-01
SCHMITT, MADELINE H R01AG08957-01A1
SCHMITT, MADELINE H S07RR05952-06 0741
SCHMITZ, FRANCIS U01CA52955-02 0001
SCHMITZ, JOHN P K15DE00249-03
SCHMITZ, JOY M S07RR05745-19 0235
SCHMUCKER, DOUGLAS L P51RR00169-30 0155
SCHMUCKER, DOUGLAS L P51RR00169-30 0156
SCHNAAR, RONALD L R01HD14010-12
SCHNAITMAN, CARL A R01GM39087-05
SCHNAPF, JULIE L R01EY07642-04
SCHNAPP S07RR05380-30 0881
SCHNAPP, BRUCE J R01NS26846-03
SCHNECK, JONATHAN P R01AI29575-01A1
SCHNECK, STUART A P01AG09417-01 9001
SCHNECK, STUART A P01AG09417-01
SCHNEEBERGER, EVELINE E R01HL25822-12
SCHNEEBERGER, EVELINE E R01HL36781-06
SCHNEEMAN, BARBARA O R01DK20446-09S2
SCHNEERSON, R Z01HD01301-08
SCHNEIDER, ARTHUR B R37CA21518-15
SCHNEIDER, BRUCE S P50MH41960-05S1 0004
SCHNEIDER, CAROLE S07RR07037-26 0378
SCHNEIDER, DANIEL J S07RR05538-29 0544
SCHNEIDER, DONALD L S07RR05392-30 0704
SCHNEIDER, EDWARD G R01DK40253-04
SCHNEIDER, ELIZABETH S07RR05390-30 0661
SCHNEIDER, GARY B R01DE06065-10
SCHNEIDER, GERALD E R01EY00126-22
SCHNEIDER, JAY S R01MH46531-01A2
SCHNEIDER, JERRY A M01RR00827-17 0134
SCHNEIDER, JERRY A M01RR00827-17 0258
SCHNEIDER, JERRY A N01HD62927-11
SCHNEIDER, LINDA H R29NS24781-05
SCHNEIDER, LON S S07RR05356-30 0434
SCHNEIDER, MARTIN F R01NS23346-07
SCHNEIDER, MARTIN J R44GM38355-03
SCHNEIDER, MICHAEL D R01HL39141-04
SCHNEIDER, ROBERT M01RR00059-30 0727
SCHNEIDER, ROBERT F S03RR03482-02
SCHNEIDER, ROBERT F S07RR07067-26
SCHNEIDER, ROBERT F S15HD28748-01
SCHNEIDER, ROBERT F S15MH49286-01
SCHNEIDER, ROBERT J R01CA42357-05
SCHNEIDER, ROBERT J R01CA54525-01
SCHNEIDER, STEPHEN P R01NS25771-04
SCHNEIDER, T D Z01CB08396-03
SCHNEIDER, VICTOR S M01RR02558-07 0065
SCHNEIDER, VICTOR S M01RR02558-07 0011
SCHNEIDERMAN, E D S07RR05915-08 0687
SCHNEIDERMAN, LAWRENCE J R18HS06912-01
SCHNEIDERMAN, MARTIN H R01CA41270-07
SCHNEIDERMAN, NEIL P01HL36588-06
SCHNEIDERMAN, NEIL P01HL36588-06 0001
SCHNEIDERMAN, NEIL P01NS05820-26 9004
SCHNEIDERMAN, NEIL S07RR07022-24
SCHNEIDERMAN, NEIL S15HL47757-01
SCHNEIER, FRANK P50MH30906-14 9010
SCHNEIER, FRANKLIN R R29MH47831-01
SCHNELL, VICKI L S07RR05427-30 0160
SCHNELLE, JOHN F P60AG10415-01 0002
SCHNELLE, JOHN F R01NR02795-02
SCHNELLE, JOHN F R55AG10064-01
SCHNELLER, STEWART W N01AI72645-10
SCHNELLMANN, RICKY G R29ES04410-05
SCHNERMANN, JURGEN B R01DK37448-06
SCHNEYER, ALAN L R01HD25941-02
SCHNEYER, ALAN L U54HD29164-01 0006
SCHNEYER, CHARLOTTE A R01DE02110-27
SCHNIPPER, LOWELL P01CA38493-06S1 0004
SCHNITZER, JAN E R29HL43278-04

SCHNOLL, SIDNEY M01RR00065-29 0346
SCHNOLL, SIDNEY M01RR00065-29 0347
SCHNOLL, SIDNEY H R18DA06094-03
SCHNOOR, JERALD P30ES05605-02 9002
SCHNUR, DAVID B R03MH46632-01A1
SCHNUR, PAUL S06GM08197-10
SCHNUR, PAUL S06GM08197-10 0009
SCHNUR, RHONDA E K11EY00298-04
SCHNUR, RHONDA E S07RR05506-29 0913
SCHODT, CAROLYN S07RR05948-05 0331
SCHOEB, TRENTON R P40RR00463-23 0001
SCHOEB, TRENTON R R24RR05363-01A1
SCHOELLER, DALE A M01RR00055-30 0566
SCHOELLER, DALE A M01RR00055-30 0578
SCHOELLER, DALE A P30DK26678-12 9005
SCHOELLER, DALE A R01DK30031-09
SCHOELLER, DALE A R01HL45574-01
SCHOEN, ROBERT R01HD28443-01
SCHOENBERG, DANIEL R R01GM38277-05
SCHOENBERG, DANIEL R S15GM47027-01
SCHOENBERG, JANET B N01CP95672-04
SCHOENBERG, M Z01AR27001-17
SCHOENBERGER, JAMES A N01HC65062-09
SCHOENER, EUGENE P R24MH47181-02 0002
SCHOENFELD, FRANK B R01MH45364-01A2
SCHOENFIELD, LESLIE J P30DK36200-05S1 9005
SCHOENINGER, MARGERE S07RR07098-26 0348
SCHOENWOLF, GARY C R01NS18112-10
SCHOEPHOERSTER, RICHARD T R15HL46444-01
SCHOFF, PATRICK K R29HD26604-02
SCHOFIELD, GEOFFREY G R29HL43656-02
SCHOLD, S CLIFFORD P50NS20023-08 0010
SCHOLD, STANLEY C M01RR00030-30 0500
SCHOLD, STANLEY C, JR R01NS20581-08
SCHOLER-JAQUISH, ALW S07RR05973-05 0788
SCHOLES, CHARLES P41RR02583-07 0014
SCHOLES, CHARLES P R01GM35103-17
SCHOLES, CHARLES P S07RR07122-23 0091
SCHOLEY, JONATHAN M R01GM46376-01
SCHOLL, THERESA O R01HD18269-07
SCHOLLE, SARAH HUDSON R03HS06962-01
SCHOLZ, JOHN P S07RR07016-18 0360
SCHOLZ, PETER M R29HL40320-04
SCHOMER, DONALD M01RR01032-16 0449
SCHON, ERIC P20HG00424-01 0004
SCHON, ERIC A P01NS11766-17A1 0037
SCHON, ERIC A P50AG08702-03 0002
SCHON, ERIC A R01NS28828-02
SCHONBERG, RUSSELL G R43CA53964-01
SCHONBRUNN, AGNES R01DK32234-09
SCHONFELD, DAVID J R29MH47251-02
SCHONFELD, GUSTAV M01RR00036-31 1044
SCHONFELD, GUSTAV M01RR00036-31 1025
SCHONFELD, GUSTAV M01RR00036-31 1026
SCHONFELD, GUSTAV P01AG05562-07 0005
SCHONFELD, GUSTAV P41RR00954-15 9013
SCHONFELD, GUSTAV R01HL42460-03
SCHONFELD, IRVIN R01OH02571-04
SCHOOK, LAWRENCE B P30CA16059-15 9009
SCHOOK, LAWRENCE B R01ES04348-06
SCHOOLER, C Z01MH00672-26
SCHOOLER, C Z01MH00683-04
SCHOOLER, C Z01MH02495-02
SCHOOLER, C Z01MH02496-02
SCHOOLER, JONATHAN W R29MH45135-02
SCHOOLER, NINA R P50MH45156-02 9001
SCHOOLEY, ROBERT M01RR01066-14 0090
SCHOOLEY, ROBERT P01HL18646-15 9003
SCHOOLEY, ROBERT T M01RR00051-30 0773
SCHOOLEY, ROBERT T M01RR00051-30 0771
SCHOOLEY, ROBERT T M01RR00051-30 0749
SCHOOLEY, ROBERT T R01CA37461-08
SCHOOLEY, ROBERT T U01AI26463-04 0004
SCHOOLNIK, GARY P30DK38707-05 0005
SCHOOLNIK, GARY K P30DK38707-05 0012
SCHOOLNIK, GARY K P30DK38707-05 9003
SCHOOLWERTH, ANTON C R01DK36822-07
SCHOONMAKER, J N M01RR00069-29 0433
SCHOPLER, ERIC R01MH44626-03
SCHOR, CLIFTON M R01EY03532-10
SCHOR, CLIFTON M R01EY08882-01
SCHOR, CLIFTON M S07RR05832-12 0200
SCHOR, NINA F R29CA47161-03
SCHOR, NINA F S07RR05507-29 0484
SCHOR, ROBERT H R01NS24930-05
SCHORK, MICHAEL A P01DE07687-09A1 9002
SCHORLING, JOHN B R01HL43611-01A1
SCHOTT, DOUBET P41RR05351-03 9001
SCHOTT, THOMAS R29MH45050-03
SCHOTTENFELD, DAVID R03CA54119-01
SCHOTTENFELD, RICHARD S R18DA06915-02
SCHOTZ, MICHAEL C P01HL28481-09 0007
SCHOTZ, MICHAEL C P01HL28481-09 0002
SCHOWEN, RICHARD L R01GM20198-17
SCHRAEDER, BARBARA D R01NR01315-07
SCHRAGER S07RR05380-30 0884
SCHRAM, KARL H R01CA43068-05
SCHRAMM, CRAIG M R01HL43285-02
SCHRAMM, LAWRENCE P R37HL16315-18
SCHRAMM, VERN L R01GM21083-16
SCHRAMM, VERN L R01GM41916-03
SCHRAMM, WILLFRIED R44DA06344-02
SCHRAUFSTATTER, INGRID U R29AI27506-03
SCHRECK, RHONA P01DK42792-01A1 9002
SCHREIBER, ALAN D P01HL40387-04 0006
SCHREIBER, ALAN D R01AI22193-07
SCHREIBER, ALAN D R01HL27068-08
SCHREIBER, ALAN D R37HL28207-10
SCHREIBER, GEORGE N01HB97082-03
SCHREIBER, GEORGE B N01HC55026-09
SCHREIBER, HANS P01CA19266-14A1
SCHREIBER, HANS P01CA19266-14A1 0025
SCHREIBER, HANS R01CA37156-07
SCHREIBER, HANS R37CA22677-14
SCHREIBER, JAMES R P50HL15062-20 0029
SCHREIBER, JOHN R R29AI27862-04
SCHREIBER, MICHAEL D R03DA07607-01
SCHREIBER, R{OBERT P01AI24854-05 0002
SCHREIBER, ROBERT D R01CA43059-05
SCHREIBER, SIDNEY S R01HL09562-27
SCHREIBER, STEVEN S K08NS01337-03
SCHREIBER, STUART L P01HG00365-04 0004
SCHREIBER, STUART L R01GM32527-10
SCHREIBER, STUART L R01GM38627-06
SCHREIBER, STUART L R01GM44993-02
SCHREIBER, STUART L. P01GM40660-03 0001
SCHREIBMAN, LAURA E R01MH39434-06A1
SCHREIER, HANS R01AI26339-03
SCHREIER, HANS S07RR05573-13 0085
SCHREIER, HAROLD J R29GM39541-05
SCHREILER, HANS P30CA14599-18 9008
SCHRELNER, GEORGE P01DK09976-27 0017
SCHRIER, RACHEL D S07RR05665-24 0894
SCHRIER, ROBERT P01DK35098-06A1 0006
SCHRIER, ROBERT W P01DK19928-13
SCHRIER, ROBERT W P01DK19928-13 0015
SCHRIER, ROBERT W P01DK19928-13 0016
SCHRIER, ROBERT W P01DK19928-13 0017
SCHRIER, ROBERT W P01DK34039-06A1 0002
SCHRIER, ROBERT W P01DK35098-06A1
SCHRIER, STANLEY L R01DK13682-32
SCHRIGER, DAVID L R18HS06284-01A1
SCHRIOCK, ELDON D M01RR00211-27 0272
SCHRODER, ED S07RR05830-12 0968
SCHROEDER, ALICE S07RR07097-26 0387
SCHROEDER, DOLORES M S07RR07031-26 0107
SCHROEDER, FRIEDHELM R01DK41402-03
SCHROEDER, FRIEDHELM R01GM31651-08A3
SCHROEDER, HAROLD E R03MH46629-02
SCHROEDER, HARRY P50AI23694-06 0011
SCHROEDER, HARRY W P01AR03555-32A1 0006
SCHROEDER, JOHN L R44GM41539-03
SCHROEDER, JOHN L R44HG00057-02
SCHROEDER, KATHLEEN LEE R13DE09884-02
SCHROEDER, KATHRYN L M01RR00034-31 0400
SCHROEDER, STEPHEN R P30HD02528-25A1
SCHROEDER, WANDA T S07RR05745-19 0248
SCHROER, TRINA S07RR07041-26 0394
SCHROER, TRINA A R01GM44589-02
SCHROHENLOHER, RALPH E P01AI18745-10 0003
SCHROIT, ALAN J R01CA47845-03
SCHROIT, ALAN J R01DK41714-03
SCHRON, CHARLES M R01DK31205-10
SCHROTER, GERHARD M01RR00069-29 0414
SCHROTT, HELMUT G M01RR00059-30 0683
SCHROTT, HELMUT G U01HL40195-05
SCHROY, PAUL C S07RR05487-29 0708
SCHTEINGART, DAVID E M01RR00042-31 0611
SCHTEINGART, DAVID E M01RR00042-31 0408
SCHTEINGART, DAVID E R01CA37794-06
SCHUBACH, WILLIAM H R01AI29466-01A1
SCHUBACH, WILLIAM H U01AI25893-05 0008
SCHUBART, ULRICH K R01NS26333-04
SCHUBERT, DAVID R R01NS09658-21
SCHUBERT, M P01CA38552-05A1 0009
SCHUBERT, M Z01NS02791-03
SCHUBERT, M Z01NS02818-02
SCHUBERT, MARK P01CA18029-16 9009
SCHUBERT, WILLIAM K P30HD28827-01
SCHUBERT, WILLIAM K S03RR03125-11
SCHUBERT, WILLIAM K S07RR05535-29
SCHUBERT, WILLIAM K S15HL47701-01
SCHUBIGER, GEROLD A R01GM33656-08
SCHUCKIT, MARC A R01AA05526-09
SCHUELER, RONALD L N01AI05070-03
SCHUELER, RONALD L N01AI05076-02
SCHUETTE, SALLY A P30DK26678-12 9004
SCHUETTE, SALLY A R29DK41353-02
SCHUETZ, ERIN R01ES04628-04
SCHUFFLER, HELEN S07RR06025-02 0025
SCHUG, KENNETH R S03RR03038-09
SCHUKNECHT, HAROLD F R01DC00079-26
SCHULBERG, HERBERT C R01MH45815-02
SCHULDBERG, DAVID R03MH46628-02
SCHULE, B P50DC00422-05 0005
SCHULENBERG, JOHN E R03AA09143-01
SCHULER, MARY A R01GM39025-04
SCHULKIN, JAY J K01MH00678-05
SCHULLER, DAVID P30CA16058-17 9016
SCHULLER, DAVID P30CA16058-17 9017
SCHULLER, DAVID E P30CA16058-17
SCHULLER, HILDEGARD M R01CA42829-05
SCHULLER, HILDEGARD M R55CA51211-01A1
SCHULMAN, EDWARD S R01AI20634-08
SCHULMAN, GERALD P30DK26657-12 0026
SCHULMAN, GERRI S07RR05417-30 0814
SCHULMAN, HOWARD P50MH48108-01 0006
SCHULMAN, HOWARD R01GM30179-10
SCHULMAN, HOWARD R01GM40600-04
SCHULMAN, IRVING M01RR00081-29
SCHULMAN, JOSEPH H N01NS92327-03
SCHULMAN, LA DONNE H R01GM16995-22
SCHULMAN, MARK N01CN85125-02
SCHULOF, RICHARD S U01AI25867-05
SCHULOF, RICHARD S U01AI25867-05 0001
SCHULOF, RICHARD S U01AI25867-05 0002
SCHULOF, RICHARD S U01AI25867-05 0003
SCHULTE, BRADLEY A R01DC00713-02
SCHULTE, JOHN K S07RR05322-30 0279
SCHULTEN, K P41RR05969-02
SCHULTHEIS, LESTER W M01RR00035-31 0418
SCHULTHEISS, TIMOTHY EDWARD R01CA54295-02
SCHULTZ, ALBERT B P30AG08808-03 9001
SCHULTZ, ALBERT B R01AR33948-09
SCHULTZ, ALBERT B R01NS20536-08
SCHULTZ, ARTHUR G R01GM26568-13
SCHULTZ, ARTHUR G R01GM33061-13
SCHULTZ, ARTHUR G R01GM41053-03
SCHULTZ, ARTHUR G S10RR06245-01
SCHULTZ, ELIZABETH P01HL25816-11 9003
SCHULTZ, HAROLD R01HL33797-06
SCHULTZ, KEVIN T. P51RR00167-31 0046
SCHULTZ, PETER G R01AI24695-05
SCHULTZ, PETER G R01GM41679-03
SCHULTZ, PHYLLIS S07RR05758-18 0259
SCHULTZ, RICHARD P01HD21355-04 0004
SCHULTZ, RICHARD M R01HD22681-05
SCHULTZ, RICHARD M U01HD28514-01
SCHULTZ, ROGER A R01CA52121-02
SCHULTZ, TERRY W S03RR03326-10
SCHULZ, HORST H R01HL18089-16
SCHULZ, HORST H R01HL30847-09
SCHULZ, HORST H S06GM08168-13 0008
SCHULZ, PAUL E K11AG00432-03
SCHULZ, RICHARD R01CA48635-03
SCHULZ, ROCKWELL I R01MH48405-01
SCHULZE, DAN S07RR05379-30 0768
SCHULZE, DAN H R29AI24681-06
SCHULZE, IRENE T R01AI23520-06
SCHULZE, KARL P50HD13063-12 0012
SCHUMACHER, BARBARA S07RR05477-29 0420
SCHUMACHER, H RALPH M01RR00040-31 0082
SCHUMACHER, MICHAEL S07RR05675-23 0919
SCHUMACHER, MICHAEL J R01GM41068-02
SCHUMACHER, RALPH H. P01AG03934-10 0007
SCHUMACHER, SUSAN S07RR07236-04 0173
SCHUMACHER, SUSAN J K14HL01983-05
SCHUMACHER, SUSAN J S06GM08019-21 0009
SCHUMACKER, PAUL T R55HL32646-07A1
SCHUMAKER, SALLY A P60AG10484-01 9003
SCHUMAKER, VERNE N P01HL28481-09
SCHUMAKER, VERNE N P01HL28481-09 0001
SCHUMAKER, VERNE N R01GM13914-27
SCHUMAN, HOWARD R01AG08951-01A1
SCHUMANN, DEBRA P01AI26482-03S1 0004
SCHUPBACH, GERTRUD M R01GM40558-04
SCHUPBACH, TRUDI M R13HD27952-01
SCHUR, PETER P60AR36308-07 9004
SCHUR, PETER H P30AR35907-07 0001
SCHUR, PETER H P30AR35907-07 9001
SCHUR, PETER H P30AR35907-07 9005
SCHUR, PETER H P30AR35907-07
SCHURMAN, DAVID R18AR21393-17 0008
SCHURMAN, DAVID J R01AR26833-10
SCHURR, AVITAL S07RR05375-30 0758
SCHURR, J MICHAEL P01GM32681-08 0001
SCHUSTER, DANIEL P R01HL32815-07
SCHUSTER, DANIEL P. P01HL13851-29 0008
SCHUSTER, GARY B R01GM28190-12
SCHUSTER, SHELDON M R01CA28725-11
SCHUSTER, STEPHEN J K08HL02167-02
SCHUSTER, TODD M R01AI11573-18
SCHUTT, CLARENCE E R01AI30743-01
SCHUTT, CLARENCE E R01GM44038-06
SCHUTZBACH, JOHN S R01GM38643-05
SCHUTZER, STEVEN E R01AR41518-01
SCHUYLER, MARK S07RR05583-27 0639
SCHUYLER, MARK R R01HL44253-02
SCHWAB-STONE, MARY U01MH46717-03
SCHWAB, CATHERINE S07RR05704-20 0005
SCHWAB, JOHN H R01AR39480-03
SCHWAB, JOHN M R01GM36286-05A1
SCHWAB, RISE R01AG08092-02
SCHWAB, RISE R29AG06854-04
SCHWAB, THERESE S07RR05654-24 0141
SCHWABER, JERROLD R01AI21165-08
SCHWAIGER, MARKUS M01RR00042-31 0606
SCHWAIGER, MARKUS M01RR00042-31 0589
SCHWAIGER, MARKUS R01HL41047-03
SCHWAN, T G Z01AI00480-06
SCHWAN, T G Z01AI00492-05
SCHWANZEL-FUKUDA, MARLENE R01DC00880-08
SCHWARCZ, ROBERT P50MH44211-03 0004
SCHWARCZ, ROBERT R01NS16102-11
SCHWARCZ, ROBERT R01NS28236-02
SCHWARK, HARRIS D R29NS25729-04

SCHWARK, WAYNE S07RR05462-29 0897
SCHWARTING, GERALD P30HD04147-22A1 9016
SCHWARTING, GERALD A P01HD05515-21 0052
SCHWARTING, ROLAND S07RR05414-30 0998
SCHWARTZ-GIBLIN, SUSAN T R01DA06811-01
SCHWARTZ, ABRAHAM R44CA48570-03
SCHWARTZ, ALAN L P50HL17646-17 0033
SCHWARTZ, ALAN L R01GM38284-06
SCHWARTZ, ALAN L R01HD26169-03
SCHWARTZ, ALAN L. N01HB77031-09
SCHWARTZ, ALAN L. N01HB97071-04
SCHWARTZ, ALAN R K08HL02031-04
SCHWARTZ, ANDREW B R01NS26375-03
SCHWARTZ, ANN G R29CA50383-03
SCHWARTZ, ARNOLD P01HL22619-14
SCHWARTZ, ARNOLD P01HL22619-14 0003
SCHWARTZ, ARNOLD P01HL22619-14 0015
SCHWARTZ, ARNOLD P01HL41496-03 0010
SCHWARTZ, ARNOLD R37HL43231-03
SCHWARTZ, ARTHUR G R01CA52500-01A1
SCHWARTZ, ARTHUR L U10EY06826-05
SCHWARTZ, BENJAMIN D P50AI15322-14 0010
SCHWARTZ, BENJAMIN D R01AI32764-01
SCHWARTZ, BRADFORD S K04HL01870-05
SCHWARTZ, BRADFORD S R01HL43506-07A2
SCHWARTZ, BRIAN R29AI31608-01
SCHWARTZ, CARL E K20MH00891-02
SCHWARTZ, CHARLES C. P01DK38030-05 0002
SCHWARTZ, CHARLES F S07RR05431-30 0852
SCHWARTZ, COLIN P01HL26890-09 9001
SCHWARTZ, COLIN J P01HL26890-09
SCHWARTZ, COLIN J R01HL41175-04
SCHWARTZ, DAVID M01RR00059-30 0723
SCHWARTZ, DAVID S07RR05445-30 0877
SCHWARTZ, DAVID A K01OH00093-02
SCHWARTZ, DAVID A K08ES00203-02
SCHWARTZ, DAVID C R01HG00225-01
SCHWARTZ, DAVID H R01AI32388-01
SCHWARTZ, ELIAS M01RR00240-27 0344
SCHWARTZ, ELIAS M01RR00240-27
SCHWARTZ, ELIAS P60HL38632-04 0009
SCHWARTZ, ELIAS P60HL38632-04 0001
SCHWARTZ, ELIAS R01DK16691-19
SCHWARTZ, ERIC A R37EY02440-14
SCHWARTZ, ERIC L R01MH45969-02
SCHWARTZ, FREDERIC N U76PE00231-01
SCHWARTZ, G M01RR00585-20 0417
SCHWARTZ, G L M01RR00585-20 0538
SCHWARTZ, GEORGE J R01HD13232-13
SCHWARTZ, GERALD S07RR05653-24 0804
SCHWARTZ, GREGORY G K11HL02155-04
SCHWARTZ, HERBERT S S07RR05424-30 0085
SCHWARTZ, ILSA R R01DC00132-15
SCHWARTZ, IRA S R01AR41511-01
SCHWARTZ, IRA S R01GM29265-11
SCHWARTZ, J P Z01NS02752-05
SCHWARTZ, J SANFORD P01HS06481-02
SCHWARTZ, JAMES H R55NS29255-01
SCHWARTZ, JANICE B M01RR00079-29 0361
SCHWARTZ, JANICE B R01AG05940-06
SCHWARTZ, JANICE B R01AG09550-01
SCHWARTZ, JANICE B S15GM47084-01
SCHWARTZ, JEFFREY R01GM34005-13
SCHWARTZ, JOHN H R01DK37105-05
SCHWARTZ, JOSEPH E R01AA08631-01A1
SCHWARTZ, JOYCE S07RR07187-13 0692
SCHWARTZ, JS P01HS06481-02 0001
SCHWARTZ, JS P01HS06481-02 0002
SCHWARTZ, KENNETH A K07HL02043-05
SCHWARTZ, LAWRENCE B R01AI27517-03
SCHWARTZ, LAWRENCE B R37AI20487-09
SCHWARTZ, LAWRENCE M K04AG00492-02
SCHWARTZ, LAWRENCE M R01GM40458-04
SCHWARTZ, MARTIN A R01GM47214-01
SCHWARTZ, MELVIN M R01DK21536-11
SCHWARTZ, MICHAEL P01NS22807-07 0003
SCHWARTZ, MYRNA F K04DC00027-04
SCHWARTZ, NANCY B P01HD09402-16
SCHWARTZ, NANCY B P01HD09402-16 0002
SCHWARTZ, NANCY B R01HD17332-08
SCHWARTZ, NANCY B R37AR19622-15
SCHWARTZ, NEENA B P01HD21921-04 0002
SCHWARTZ, NEENA B P01HD21921-04
SCHWARTZ, NEENA B P30HD28048-01 9005
SCHWARTZ, NEENA B R01HD07504-17A2
SCHWARTZ, NEENA B S07RR07028-26 0016
SCHWARTZ, PATRICIA M01RR00350-25 0457
SCHWARTZ, PATRICIA L M01RR00188-27 0319
SCHWARTZ, PATRICIA L M01RR00188-27 0306
SCHWARTZ, R H Z01AI00485-05
SCHWARTZ, R H Z01AI00613-01
SCHWARTZ, RANDY N01CN15376-00
SCHWARTZ, RICHARD C R29CA45360-05
SCHWARTZ, RICHARD G R01DC00583-04
SCHWARTZ, RICHARD G S07RR07032-26 0027
SCHWARTZ, ROBERT P50HL42267-02 0004
SCHWARTZ, ROBERT P60HL38655-04 0004
SCHWARTZ, ROBERT H M01RR00044-31 0382
SCHWARTZ, ROBERT J R01HL38401-13
SCHWARTZ, ROBERT J R01HL45476-02
SCHWARTZ, ROBERT S M01RR00037-31 0483
SCHWARTZ, ROBERT S P01CA24530-12 0001
SCHWARTZ, ROBERT S R01AG08673-01A2
SCHWARTZ, ROBERT S R01AI26450-05
SCHWARTZ, ROBERT S R01AI28899-02
SCHWARTZ, ROCHELLE D R29NS24577-05
SCHWARTZ, RONALD N01AI05068-03
SCHWARTZ, RONALD G M01RR00044-31 0369
SCHWARTZ, STANLEY M01RR00040-31 0325
SCHWARTZ, STANLEY A R01MH39346-08
SCHWARTZ, STANLEY A R01MH47225-02
SCHWARTZ, STANLEY S M01RR00040-31 0387
SCHWARTZ, STEPHEN M P01HL03174-36
SCHWARTZ, STEPHEN M P01HL03174-36 0001
SCHWARTZ, STEPHEN M P01HL18645-17 0011
SCHWARTZ, STEPHEN M R01HL26405-11
SCHWARTZ, SUSAN M P40RR03640-05 0006
SCHWARTZ, WILLIAM P60HL38632-04 0005
SCHWARTZ, WILLIAM J R01NS24542-06
SCHWARTZBACH, STEVEN S07RR07055-26 0174
SCHWARTZER, THOMAS A U01AI25914-04S2 9001
SCHWARTZKROIN, PHILIP A P01NS20482-08
SCHWARTZKROIN, PHILIP A P01NS20482-08 0015
SCHWARTZKROIN, PHILIP A R01NS18895-09
SCHWARTZKROIN, PHILIP A R01NS15317-12
SCHWARTZMAN, MICHAL P01HL34300-07 0005
SCHWARTZMAN, MICHAL L R01EY06513-05
SCHWARTZMAN, ROBERT JAY R01NS27107-03
SCHWARZ, KARL Q S07RR05403-30 0824
SCHWARZ, KATHLEEN B R01HD28070-01
SCHWARZ, PETER D S07RR05458-29 0837
SCHWARZ, RICHARD H M01RR00318-25
SCHWARZ, RICHARD H S15DA07773-01
SCHWARZ, RICHARD H S15HL47739-01
SCHWARZ, THOMAS S07RR05353-30 0365
SCHWARZ, THOMAS L P50MH48108-01 0004
SCHWARZ, THOMAS L R01GM42376-03
SCHWARZBACH, RICHARD J R44EY08316-02
SCHWARZBAUER, JEAN E R01CA44627-05
SCHWARZENBERG, SARAH J R29DK40332-04
SCHWARZKOPF, STEVEN B K20MH00859-02
SCHWEIKERT, EMILE A S07RR07090-26 0478
SCHWEINFEST, C W Z01CP05569-04
SCHWEINFEST, C W Z01CP05585-03
SCHWEINFEST, C W Z01CP05664-01
SCHWEINLE, JO ELLEN R01AI30286-02
SCHWEIS, JEAN E S03RR03380-08
SCHWEITZER, ERIK P41RR00570-21 0012
SCHWEITZER, ERIK S R01NS23084-07
SCHWEITZER, JOHN B K08NS01230-05
SCHWEITZER, LAURA F R01DC00233-09
SCHWEITZER, STUART S07RR06025-02 0026
SCHWEIZER, EDWARD P30MH48539-01 0002
SCHWENKE, DAWN C R29HL45027-01A1
SCHWENN, MOLLY M01RR00054-30 0406
SCHWENN, MOLLY R U10CA53549-01 0043
SCHWENN, MOLLY R U10CA53549-01
SCHWENN, MOLLY R U10CA53549-01 0001
SCHWENN, MOLLY R U10CA53549-01 0002
SCHWENN, MOLLY R U10CA53549-01 0044
SCHWENN, MOLLY R U10CA53549-01 0023
SCHWENN, MOLLY R U10CA53549-01 0024
SCHWENN, MOLLY R U10CA53549-01 0025
SCHWENN, MOLLY R U10CA53549-01 0026
SCHWENN, MOLLY R U10CA53549-01 0027
SCHWENN, MOLLY R U10CA53549-01 0028
SCHWENN, MOLLY R U10CA53549-01 0029
SCHWENN, MOLLY R U10CA53549-01 0030
SCHWENN, MOLLY R U10CA53549-01 0031
SCHWENN, MOLLY R U10CA53549-01 0032
SCHWENN, MOLLY R U10CA53549-01 0033
SCHWENN, MOLLY R U10CA53549-01 0034
SCHWENN, MOLLY R U10CA53549-01 0035
SCHWENN, MOLLY R U10CA53549-01 0036
SCHWENN, MOLLY R U10CA53549-01 0037
SCHWENN, MOLLY R U10CA53549-01 0038
SCHWENN, MOLLY R U10CA53549-01 0039
SCHWENN, MOLLY R U10CA53549-01 0040
SCHWENN, MOLLY R U10CA53549-01 0041
SCHWENN, MOLLY R U10CA53549-01 0042
SCHWENN, MOLLY R U10CA53549-01 0045
SCHWENN, MOLLY R U10CA53549-01 0046
SCHWENN, MOLLY R U10CA53549-01 0047
SCHWENN, MOLLY R U10CA53549-01 0048
SCHWENN, MOLLY R U10CA53549-01 0049
SCHWENN, MOLLY R U10CA53549-01 0050
SCHWENN, MOLLY R U10CA53549-01 0003
SCHWENN, MOLLY R U10CA53549-01 0004
SCHWENN, MOLLY R U10CA53549-01 0051
SCHWENN, MOLLY R U10CA53549-01 0052
SCHWENN, MOLLY R U10CA53549-01 0053
SCHWENN, MOLLY R U10CA53549-01 0054
SCHWENN, MOLLY R U10CA53549-01 0055
SCHWENN, MOLLY R U10CA53549-01 0056
SCHWENN, MOLLY R U10CA53549-01 0057
SCHWENN, MOLLY R U10CA53549-01 0058
SCHWENN, MOLLY R U10CA53549-01 0059
SCHWENN, MOLLY R U10CA53549-01 0060
SCHWENN, MOLLY R U10CA53549-01 0005
SCHWENN, MOLLY R U10CA53549-01 0006
SCHWENN, MOLLY R U10CA53549-01 0007
SCHWENN, MOLLY R U10CA53549-01 0008
SCHWENN, MOLLY R U10CA53549-01 0009
SCHWENN, MOLLY R U10CA53549-01 0010
SCHWENN, MOLLY R U10CA53549-01 0011
SCHWENN, MOLLY R U10CA53549-01 0012
SCHWENN, MOLLY R U10CA53549-01 0013
SCHWENN, MOLLY R U10CA53549-01 0014
SCHWENN, MOLLY R U10CA53549-01 0015
SCHWENN, MOLLY R U10CA53549-01 0016
SCHWENN, MOLLY R U10CA53549-01 0017
SCHWENN, MOLLY R U10CA53549-01 0018
SCHWENN, MOLLY R U10CA53549-01 0019
SCHWENN, MOLLY R U10CA53549-01 0020
SCHWENN, MOLLY R U10CA53549-01 0021
SCHWENN, MOLLY R U10CA53549-01 0022
SCHWERTZ, DORIE W R29NR02203-03
SCHWERTZ, DORIE W S07RR05776-11 0398
SCHWINN, DEBRA A K08HL02490-02
SCHWOB, JAMES E R29DC00467-03
SCHYMURA, MARIA J S07RR05443-30 0991
SCICCHITANO, DAVID A R29CA51860-01A2
SCICLI, A GUILLERMO P01HL28982-10 0005
SCICLI, A GUILLERMO P01HL28982-10 9001
SCICLI, GUILLOZMO A. P01HL28982-10 0008
SCIOTE, JAMES J K15DE00223-05
SCLABASSI, ROBERT J P20NS30318-01 9001
SCLAFANI, ANTHONY R01DK31135-08
SCLAFANI, ROBERT A R01GM35078-06
SCLOSSMAN, STUART P30CA06516-28 0025
SCOFIELD, VIRGINIA L R29HD23093-05
SCOTCH, NORMAN A S07RR05927-07
SCOTCH, NORMAN A S15CA55972-01
SCOTT, A IAN R01CA44395-05
SCOTT, A IAN R01DK32034-10
SCOTT, A IAN R01GM32596-09
SCOTT, ALAN B R01EY08280-03
SCOTT, ALAN B R01EY08303-02
SCOTT, ALAN B S07RR05981-05
SCOTT, ALAN F P01HG00373-04 0002
SCOTT, ALAN F P01HG00373-04 9001
SCOTT, APRIL E P01DC00168-10 0018
SCOTT, C RONALD M01RR00037-31 0520
SCOTT, DAVID G S06GM08060-21 0006
SCOTT, DAVID W R01AI29691-02
SCOTT, GWENDOLYN B R01AI23524-06A1
SCOTT, GWENDOLYN B U01AI27560-04
SCOTT, JOHN D R01GM44427-03
SCOTT, JOHN F S03RR03499-03
SCOTT, JOHN F S06GM08073-20 0011
SCOTT, JOHN F S06GM08073-20
SCOTT, JOHN W R01DC00113-12
SCOTT, JUNE R R01AI20723-08
SCOTT, JUNE R R01AI24870-04
SCOTT, KATHERINE N P41RR02278-06A1 0004
SCOTT, KATHERINE N P41RR02278-06A1 0005
SCOTT, KATHLEEN J G07LM05295-01
SCOTT, KENNETH R S06GM08244-05 0017
SCOTT, MARCIA S R01HD22952-05
SCOTT, MATTHEW P41RR00592-22 0024
SCOTT, MATTHEW P R01HD18163-09
SCOTT, MICHEAL R R35AG08967-02 0004
SCOTT, MICHELLE P S07RR07043-26 0128
SCOTT, PHILLIP A R01AI30073-02
SCOTT, ROBERT A R01GM42025-03
SCOTT, ROBERT E R01CA28240-12
SCOTT, ROBERT E R01CA51715-01A1
SCOTT, ROLAND B. N01HB97061-03
SCOTT, RONALD P30HD02274-24 9008
SCOTT, SHERYL A R01NS16067-10
SCOTT, SUSAN M01RR00997-16 0341
SCOTT, SUSAN M M01RR00997-16 0398
SCOTT, THOMAS R, JR R01DK30964-08
SCOTT, THOMAS W R01AI22119-05
SCOTT, THOMAS W R01AI26787-04
SCOTT, WALTER A R55AI31375-01
SCOTT, WALTER J S07RR05583-27 0640
SCOTTO, ANTHONY W R01GM44947-02
SCOTTO, ANTHONY W R03RR06854-01
SCOTTO, J Z01CP04475-14
SCOTTO, K P01CA18856-16 0021
SCOVELL, WILLIAM M R15CA52286-01A1
SCOW, R O Z01DK15401-19
SCRIBNER, RICHARD R03AA08361-01A1
SCROGGS, MARK W K11EY00304-02
SCUDDER, CHARLES A R29EY09210-01
SCULLY, PETER P01CA51495-02 9001
SCUTCHFIELD, F DOUGLAS S07RR05974-05
SCUTCHFIELD, F DOUGLAS S15CA55959-01
SCWARTZ, NEENA B S07RR07028-26 0021
SEACH, JAMES N01HO99005-06
SEAGRAVE, J D S07RR05900-06 0628
SEAGRAVE, JEANCLARE S03RR03470-03
SEALEY, JEAN P50HL18323-17 0045
SEALEY, JEAN E P50HL18323-17 9001
SEALEY, JEAN E R01HL40152-05
SEALFON, STUART C K11DK01854-04
SEALOCK, ROBERT R01NS15293-11A1
SEALOCK, ROBERT S07RR05406-30 0901
SEALS, DOUGLAS R K04AG00423-04
SEALS, DOUGLAS R R01AG06537-06
SEALS, DOUGLAS R R01HL39966-04
SEALS, JONATHAN P01AI27135-04 0002
SEALY, LINDA J R01GM39826-04
SEAMAN, WILLIAM E R01CA46812-04
SEAQUIST, ELIZABETH R K08DK01920-03

SEARLES, JOHN S R29AA09312-01
SEARS, AMY P01AI24009-05 0003
SEARS, DAVIDA P01HD03144-24 9001
SEARS, DAVIDA P01HD18955-07 9001
SEARS, DUANE W S07RR07099-25 0392
SEARS, MARVIN L R37EY08879-01
SEASHOLTZ, AUDREY F R29DK42730-01A1
SEASHORE, JOHN H M01RR06022-02 0744
SEASHORE, MARGRETTA M01RR06022-02 0770
SEASHORE, MARGRETTA M01RR06022-02 0771
SEATON, BARBARA A R29GM44554-02
SEBASTIAN, ANTHONY M01RR00079-29 0389
SEBASTIAN, ANTHONY M01RR00079-29 0390
SEBASTIAN, ANTHONY M01RR00079-29 0385
SEBASTIAN, ANTHONY M01RR00079-29 0356
SEBASTIAN, ANTHONY M01RR00079-29 0393
SEBASTIAN, ANTHONY M01RR00083-29 0193
SEBRECHTS, MARC M S07RR07123-22 0590
SEBTI, SAID M R01CA48905-02
SECHREST, LEE R13HS06806-01
SECKER-WALKER, ROGER H P01CA46456-02 0003
SECKER-WALKER, ROGER H R01CA38395-06
SECKER-WALKER, ROGER H R01HL40685-03
SECKER-WALKER, ROGER H R01HL29957-09
SECOMB, TIMOTHY W R01HL34555-07
SECRIST, JOHN A P01CA34200-09 0002
SECRIST, JOHN A P01CA34200-09 0004
SECRIST, JOHN A U01AI25784-05 0002
SEDANO, HEDDIE O S03RR03355-09
SEDAT, JOHN W R01GM25101-14
SEDDON, JOHANNA M N01EY02117-02
SEDDON, JOHANNA M R21EY08541-01A1
SEDENSKY, MARGARET M R29GM41385-03
SEDIVY, JOHN M R01GM41690-02
SEDMAK, DANIEL D R01AI32744-01
SEDMAK, DANIEL D R29AI29002-02
SEDMAN, AILEEN M01RR00042-31 0485
SEDOR, JOHN R R01DK38558-05
SEDVALL, GORAN R37MH44814-03
SEDWICK, W DAVID R01CA52683-01A1
SEDWICK, W DAVID R01ES05540-01
SEE, RONALD E R29DE09678-01
SEED, BRIAN R01AI27849-03
SEED, BRIAN R01DK43031-02
SEEDS, NICHOLAS W R01NS09818-19
SEEF, STEVEN P30CA15704-18 9002
SEEFF, LEONARD N01HB87047-04
SEEGAL, RICHARD F P42ES04913-02 0002
SEEGER, CHRISTOPH R01AI30544-01
SEEGER, CHRISTOPH R29AI24972-05
SEEGER, LEANNE U01CA54012-01
SEEGER, ROBERT S07RR05354-30 0412
SEEGER, ROBERT C R01CA22794-15
SEEGER, ROBERT C R03CA53329-02
SEEGMILLER, EDWIN J. P01AG07996-03 0001
SEEGMILLER, J EDWIN P01AG07996-03
SEEGMILLER, J EDWIN P50AG05131-08 0006
SEEGMILLER, JARVIS E K12AG00353-05
SEEGMILLER, R E S07RR07111-12 0515
SEEHAFER, ROGER W S07RR07032-26 0032
SEELIG, LEONARD L, JR R01AA07381-05
SEELY, OLIVER, JR S06GM08156-15 0008
SEELY, OLIVER, JR S06GM08156-15 0008
SEEMAN, NADRIAN C R01GM29554-10
SEEMAN, PHILIP R01DA07223-01
SEETHARAM, BELLUR R01DK26638-13
SEETHARAM, BELLUR S07RR05434-30 0798
SEETHARAM, SHAKUNTLA S07RR05434-30 0801
SEFTON, BARTHOLOMEW M P30CA14195-18 0045
SEFTON, BARTHOLOMEW M R01CA17289-16
SEFTON, BARTHOLOMEW M R01CA42350-06
SEFTON, MICHAEL V R01HL24020-10A2
SEFTOR, RICHARD E B S07RR05675-23 0945
SEGAL, D Z01CB09289-03
SEGAL, D Z01CB09290-01
SEGAL, D M Z01CB09254-03
SEGAL, DAVID S K05MH70183-18
SEGAL, DAVID S R01DA01568-15
SEGAL, KAREN R R01DK37948-05
SEGAL, MARK R R29GM45543-01
SEGAL, MICHAEL M K08NS01407-03
SEGAL, ROBERT K11DK01878-03
SEGAL, ROSALIND A K08NS01488-01
SEGAL, S Z01CM07257-03
SEGAL, STANTON P01DK40555-04
SEGAL, STANTON P01DK40555-04 0001
SEGAL, STANTON R01DK42785-02
SEGAL, STEVEN P P50MH43694-04 0013
SEGAL, STEVEN P R01MH37310-08A1
SEGAL, STEVEN P R01MH47487-01
SEGAL, STEVEN P R24MH46371-02
SEGAL, STEVEN S R29HL41026-04
SEGAL, STEVEN S S07RR07082-26 0306
SEGALL, GEORGE S07RR05353-30 0366
SEGALL, JEFFREY E R29GM44246-01A2
SEGALL, MIRIAM R01DK40516-02
SEGALOFF, DEBORAH L R01HD22196-07
SEGAR, JEFFREY M01RR00059-30 0742
SEGEL, GEORGE B R01CA34691-08
SEGEL, LEIGH D R01HL30065-07
SEGERSON, EDWARD S07RR07236-04 0174
SEGERSON, THOMAS PATRICK K08DK01883-05
SEGHI, ROBERT S07RR05304-30 0221
SEGHI, ROBERT R R03DE10200-01
SEGRAVES, MARK A R29EY08212-03
SEGRE, GINO V S03RR03546-01
SEGREST, JERE P M01RR00032-31 0380
SEGREST, JERE P R01AI28928-02
SEGREST, JERE P R01HL37833-05
SEGUNDO, JOSE S07RR05354-30 0387
SEHAGAL, PRABHAT K P51RR00168-30 9012
SEHGAL, CHANDRA M R01CA41324-07
SEHGAL, PRABHAT K P51RR00168-30 9007
SEHGAL, PRABHAT K P51RR00168-30 9008
SEHGAL, PRAVINKUMAR B R01AI16262-13
SEHGAL, PRAVINKUMAR B R01CA44365-05
SEIBEL, FREDERICK N01RR12103-00
SEIBER, J N P42ES04699-05 0001
SEIDEL, EDWARD R R01DK34110-06
SEIDEL, GEORGE E, JR R01HD27938-01
SEIDEN, ANNE M R18DA06378-03
SEIDEN, LEWIS S K05MH10562-15
SEIDEN, LEWIS S P50DA00250-20
SEIDEN, LEWIS S P50DA00250-20 0023
SEIDEN, LEWIS S R01DA00085-19
SEIDEN, LEWIS S R37MH11191-26
SEIDENBERG, MARK S P01MH47566-01 0003
SEIDLER, FREDERIC J R01DA05031-03
SEIDLIN, MINDELL M01RR00096-30A1 0233
SEIDLIN, MINDELL R01DA05324-05
SEIDMAN, CHRISTINE R01HL42467-02
SEIDMAN, CHRISTINE R29HL41474-04
SEIDMAN, EDWARD R01MH43084-04S1
SEIDMAN, JONATHAN G R01AI19148-10
SEIDMAN, JONATHAN G R01CA46361-04
SEIDMAN, JONATHAN G R01HL46320-01
SEIDNER, STEVEN, DR S07RR05654-24 0135
SEIFER, DAVID B K11AG00566-01
SEIFER, RONALD R01MH43822-04
SEIFERT, H STEVEN R29AI27195-03
SEIFERT, H STEVEN U01AI31494-01 0002
SEIFTER, JULIAN L P50DK39249-05 0004
SEIGEL, CHARLES M01RR00350-25 0370
SEIGLER, DAVID S S07RR07030-26 0413
SEIGLER, H F P30CA14236-18 9032
SEIGLER, HILLIARD F P30CA14236-18 9021
SEIGLER, HILLIARD F P51RR00165-31 0141
SEIGLER, HILLIARD F R01CA57111-01
SEIL, FREDRICK P01NS17493-08 0012
SEIL, FREDRICK J R13NS29614-01
SEILHEIMER, DAN K R01HL38339-05
SEILKOP, STEVEN K N01ES15324-00
SEITZ, FRANZ P S07RR07245-03 0857
SEITZ, VICTORIA P01HD03008-24 0049
SEITZ, VICTORIA P01HD03008-24 9002
SEIZINGER, BERND R R01CA49455-03
SEJNOWSKI, TERRENCE J R01MH46482-01A1
SEKHAR, CHANDRA V S07RR05801-13 0447
SELANDER, ROBERT K R37AI22144-07
SELAWRY, HELENA P R01DK42421-03
SELBY, JOSEPH V R01DK42439-01A1
SELBY, JOSEPH V R01HL41830-03
SELBY, JOSEPH V U01HL47889-01
SELBY, MAIJA L R01HS06507-02
SELBY, MICHAEL P30AG08051-02 9004
SELDIN, DAVID C K08HL02686-01
SELDIN, MICHAEL F R01HG00101-02
SELEGUE, JOHN P S07RR07114-23 0447
SELIGMAN, MARTIN E R37MH19604-18A1
SELIGMAN, MARTIN E P P50MH45178-02 0010
SELIGMAN, MARTIN E P P50MH45178-02 0007
SELIM, MUSTAFA I R01OH02857-01
SELINFREUND, RICHARD H P01HL38156-05 0002
SELINSKY, BARRY S S07RR07260-02 0548
SELITRENNIKOFF, CLAUDE P U01AI30183-02 0005
SELIVONCHICK, DANIEL P P30ES03850-07 0006
SELKER, ERIC U R01GM35690-06
SELKER, HARRY P R01HS06208-03
SELKIRK, J K Z01ES21156-01
SELKOE, DENNIS J R35AG07911-04 0005
SELKOE, DENNIS J R35AG07911-04
SELKOE, DENNIS J R35AG07911-04 0001
SELKOE, DENNIS J R37AG06173-06
SELL, ELSA J S07RR05675-23 0920
SELL, KENNETH W R13CA54787-01
SELL, STEWART R01CA54526-01
SELLER, THOMAS A P41RR01632-09 0029
SELLERS, EDWARD M R01DA06889-01
SELLERS, J R Z01HL01785-12
SELLERS, J R Z01HL01786-12
SELLERS, J R Z01HL04212-03
SELLERS, THOMAS A S07RR05448-30 0298
SELLERS, THOMAS A S07RR05448-30 0284
SELLERS, TOM P01CA50305-02 9003
SELLIN, JOSEPH H M01RR02558-07 0050
SELLIN, JOSEPH H M01RR02558-07 0027
SELLIN, JOSEPH H R01DK35193-06
SELLNER, PEGGY A R29EY06989-05
SELLS, MARY ANN S07RR05526-29 0084
SELMAN, BRUCE R S07RR07098-26 0333
SELMAN, STEVEN H P01CA48733-02 0004
SELMAN, STEVEN H P01CA48733-02 9001
SELMAN, WARREN R R29NS27641-03
SELMANOFF, MICHAEL K R01HD21351-10A2
SELSING, ERIK R01AI24465-05
SELSTED, MICHAEL E R01AI22931-07
SELSTED, MICHAEL E U01AI31696-01 9002
SELSTED, MICHAEL E U01AI31696-01
SELSTED, MICHAEL E U01AI31696-01 0001
SELTZER, JUDITH A R01HD24571-03
SELTZER, MARSHA M R01AG08768-02
SELTZER, STEPHEN P01CA41167-06 0005
SELTZER, WILLIAM K M01RR00069-29 0445
SELTZMAN, H N01CM07330-05
SELTZMAN, HERBERT H N01CM17568-00
SELVAM, M P Z01BG06046-01
SELVAM, M P Z01BG06047-01
SELVAM, M P Z01BG06048-01
SELVAM, M P Z01BG06049-01
SELVAM, M P Z01BG06050-01
SELVARAJ, PERIASAMY S07RR05364-30 0541
SELVERSTON, ALLEN P01NS25916-04 0001
SELVERSTON, ALLEN I P01NS25916-04
SELVERSTON, ALLEN I R01NS09322-17
SELWYN, ANDREW N01HV18124-02
SELWYN, ANDREW P R01HL38780-03
SELZER, MICHAEL E R01NS14837-10A1
SELZER, ROBERT P41RR01861-07 0008
SELZER, ROBERT H R01HL40098-02
SEMA, INC N01MH10001-00
SEMBA, RICHARD D K11EY00286-05
SEMENKOVICH, CLAY F K11DK01762-05
SEMENZA, GREGG L R01DK39869-05
SEMKOW, THOMAS S07RR05649-25 0786
SEMLER, BERT L R01AI22693-07
SEMLER, BERT L R01AI26765-03S1
SEMMELHACK, MARTIN F R01CA54819-01
SEMMELHACK, MARTIN F R01GM31352-12A2
SEMMLOW, JOHN L R01EY07519-02
SEMPLE-ROWLAND, SUSAN L R01EY08340-02
SEMPLE, MALCOLM P01DC00450-04 0001
SEMPLE, MALCOLM N R29DC00364-05
SEMRAD, CAROL P50DK41146-04 0006
SEN, GANES C R01AI22510-07
SEN, RANJAN K04GM00563-02
SEN, RANJAN R01GM43874-02
SEN, RANJAN R29GM38925-05
SEN, SHUKDEB S06GM08119-18 0014
SEN, SUBHA R01HL27838-09
SEN, SUBRATA S07RR05511-29 0504
SENAY, EDWARD C R18DA06984-02
SENCHAK, MARILYN R01AA08263-02
SENDER, LEONARD S K11DK01990-02
SENEAR, DONALD F R29GM41465-03
SENGELAUB, DALE R R01AG09309-02
SENGER, DONALD R R01CA34025-08
SENGER, DONALD R R01CA43967-05
SENGUPTA-GOPALAN, CH S07RR07154-16 0564
SENGUPTA-GOPALAN, CHAMPA S06GM08136-18 002
SENGUPTA-GOPALAN, CO S07RR07154-16 0563
SENIOR, ALAN E R37GM25349-14
SENIOR, ROBERT M P01HL29594-09
SENIOR, ROBERT M P01HL29594-09 0004
SENOGLES, SUSAN E R29NS28811-01A1
SENS, MARY A R01GM43140-02
SENSEMAN, DAVID M S06GM08194-12 0030
SEO, KYUNG M01RR00069-29 0457
SEPSENWOL, SOL P41RR00570-21 0004
SEQUEST, JERE P M01RR00032-31 0359
SERA, MARIA D S07RR07052-26 0169
SERAFIN, WILLIAM E P01HL36110-07 0004
SERBY, VICTOR M R43CE00014-01
SERCARZ, ELI E P01AR40919-01 0006
SERCARZ, ELI E R01AI11183-19
SERCARZ, ELI E R01AI28419-03
SERCARZ, ELI E R37CA24442-23
SERGE, GINO V P01DK11794-24 0004
SERGENT, JUSTINE R01MH45696-02
SERHAN, CHARLES N P01HL36028-07 9003
SERHAN, CHARLES N R29GM38765-05
SERPERSU, ENGIN H R29GM42661-02
SERRANO, ELBA E S06GM08136-18 0029
SERRANO, LOUIS J P30CA13330-20 9002
SERRERO, GINETTE P01CA37589-08 0002
SERRERO, GINETTE P01DK38639-04 0005
SERRERO, GINETTE S07RR05863-11 0572
SERSEN, EUGENE A P01AG09017-02 9001
SERSHEN, HENRY S07RR05651-24 0146
SERVICE, F JOHN M01RR00585-20 0256
SERVICE, F JOHN U01DK30609-09
SERWER, PHILIP R01GM24365-15
SESHI, BEERELLI S07RR05403-30 0825
SESSLE, BARRY J R01DE04786-14
SESSLER, CURTIS M01RR00065-29 0363
SESSLER, DANIEL I R29GM39723-03
SESSLER, FRANCIS S07RR07241-04 0701
SESSLER, JONATHAN L R01AI28845-02
SESSLER, JONATHAN L R01GM41657-03
SETCHELL, KENNETH D R01CA56303-01
SETH, A Z01CP05565-04
SETH, A Z01CP05566-04
SETH, A Z01CP05588-03
SETH, A K Z01CP05668-01
SETHI, V SAGAR P30CA12197-19 9005
SETLOW, PETER R01GM19698-20
SETLOW, RICHARD B R13CA54130-01

SETLOW, RICHARD B S07RR05731-20
SETLOW, RICHARD B S15NS30127-01
SETO, JOSEPH T S06GM08101-20 0018
SETTLE, R. GREGG P01DC00161-11 0011
SETTON, L M01RR00645-20 0478
SEUANEZ, H N Z01CP05584-04
SEVANIAN, ALEX R01ES03466-06
SEVANIAN, ALEX R01HL45206-01A1
SEVERENCE, CRAIG J S06GM08073-20 0009
SEVERIN, MATTHEW J S07RR05390-30 0660
SEVERSON, HERBERT H R01HL43923-02
SEVILLA, MICHAEL S07RR07131-22 0138
SEVILLA, MICHAEL D R01CA45424-04A1
SEWALL, ASE I N01DK12282-00
SEWALL, ASE I N01DK72289-07
SEWELL, GRANVILLE S07RR05449-30 0322
SEWELL, WILLIAM F R01DC00767-01A1
SEWITCH, DEBORAH E M01RR00040-31 0400
SEXTON, GARY P30AG08017-02 9003
SEXTON, MARY N01HD13119-00
SEYBERT, DAVID W R01AG09033-01A1
SEYBOLD, VIRGINIA S07RR05385-30 0801
SEYBOLD, VIRGINIA S N01DE02579-01
SEYBOLD, VIRGINIA S R01NS17702-08
SEYER, J H P50AR39166-05 9002
SEYFARTH, ROBERT P51RR00169-30 0157
SEYFRED, MARK S07RR07201-12 0639
SEYFRIED, THOMAS N R01NS23355-06
SEYFRIED, THOMAS N R01NS24826-04
SGOUROS, GEORGE P01CA29502-11A1 0060
SGRO, JOSEPH P01NS25630-03 0002
SGRO, JOSEPH P01NS25630-03 9002
SGRO, JOSEPH A. P01NS12587-16 0014
SHA'AFI, RAMADAN I R01AI24935-05
SHABANOWITZ, ROBERT B R29HD28841-01
SHABETAI, RALPH M01RR00827-17 0464
SHABETAI, RALPH S07RR05665-24 0890
SHACHTER, NEIL M01RR00102-28 0152
SHACK, ROLAND P01CA38548-07 0002
SHACKELFORD, PENELOPE G M01RR06021-02 0596
SHACKELFORD, PENELOPE G R01AI19350-07A1
SHACKFORD, STEVEN R P20NS30324-01
SHACKFORD, STEVEN R P20NS30324-01 0001
SHACKFORD, STEVEN R P20NS30324-01 0005
SHACKFORD, STEVEN R P20NS30324-01 9001
SHACKLEFORD, GREGORY M R01CA54436-01
SHACKLETON, CEDRIC H P30HD22224-05S1 0002
SHACKLETON, CEDRIC H R01DK34400-08
SHACKLETON, CEDRIC H S10RR06505-01
SHACKLETON, CEDRIC H L P41RR01614-10 0008
SHACKNEY, STANLEY E R01CA55230-01
SHACKS, SAMUEL S07RR05780-16 0977
SHACKS, SAMUEL J S03RR03412-07
SHACKS, SAMUEL J S06GM08140-17
SHACKS, SAMUEL J S07RR05780-16
SHACKS, SAMUEL J S15CA55939-01
SHADDUCK, JOHN A R01EY08778-02
SHADDUCK, JOHN A S03RR03388-08
SHADDUCK, JOHN A S07RR05854-11
SHADDUCK, JOHN A S15ES05840-01
SHADDUCK, RICHARD K R01CA15237-17
SHADE, ROBERT E P01HL36080-06 9001
SHADE, ROBERT E P01HL36080-06 0006
SHADER, RICHARD I R37MH34223-13
SHADER, RICHARD I R37MH34223-13 0001
SHADER, RICHARD I R37MH34223-13 0002
SHADER, RICHARD I R37MH34223-13 0003
SHADER, RICHARD I R37MH34223-13 0004
SHADLEY, JEFFREY D R01CA49181-04
SHAEFFER, JOSEPH R R01HL29379-09
SHAFER, A W N01HB97081-04
SHAFER, MARY ANN B U01AI31499-01 0005
SHAFER, RICHARD H R01CA27343-12
SHAFER, WILLIAM M R01AI21150-07
SHAFFER, DAVID P50MH43878-03 0038
SHAFFER, DAVID P50MH43878-03 0004
SHAFFER, DAVID P50MH43878-03 0015
SHAFFER, DAVID P50MH43878-03
SHAFFER, DAVID P50MH43878-03 0039
SHAFFER, DAVID P50MH43878-03 0027
SHAFFER, DAVID P50MH43878-03 0037
SHAFFER, JACQUELIN B R01HL39631-05
SHAFIR, ELDAR B R29MH46885-02
SHAFIT-ZAGARDO, BRIDGET P01AG06803-05 0002
SHAFIT-ZAGARDO, BRIDGET P50NS11920-17 0020
SHAFIT-ZAGARDO, BRIDGET R01AG07677-03
SHAFRITZ, DAVID A P30DK41296-03
SHAFRITZ, DAVID A R01CA32605-10
SHAFRITZ, DAVID A R01DK17609-18
SHAGASS, CHARLES R01MH12507-26
SHAH, DINESH M S07RR05424-30 0073
SHAH, DINESH M S07RR05654-24 0137
SHAH, SHANTILAL S07RR05755-18 0241
SHAH, SUDHIR V R01DK41480-04
SHAHIN, R D Z01BA07007-12
SHAHIN, R D Z01BA07008-04
SHAHIN, R D Z01BA07009-02
SHAHIN, R D Z01BA07022-02
SHAIE, K. WARNER R37AG08055-03 9001
SHAIKH, MAJID B S07RR05393-30 0903
SHAIKH, ZAHIR S07RR07086-15 0322
SHAIKH, ZAHIR A R01ES03187-07
SHAIN, ROCHELLE N R01HD24149-04
SHAIN, ROCHELLE N U01AI31498-01 0004
SHAIN, SYDNEY A R01CA53203-01A1
SHAIN, W P41RR01219-10 0006
SHAIN, WILLIAM S07RR05649-25 0794
SHAIN, WILLIAM G R01NS21219-06
SHAIR, HARRY N R01HD28942-01
SHAKIR, AMAL KANBOUR S07RR05570-20 0848
SHAKLEE, PATRICK S07RR05879-09 0604
SHAKUN, MORTIMER S S07RR05778-16 0404
SHALAT, STUART N01ES85235-06
SHALLOWAY, DAVID I K04CA01139-06
SHALLOWAY, DAVID I R01CA32317-11
SHALLOWAY, DAVID I R01CA47333-05
SHALLOWAY, DAVID I S07RR07082-26 0307
SHALON, LINDA S07RR05924-07 0004
SHALWITZ, ROBERT ALAN R29DK40732-04
SHAMOON, HARRY U01DK37863-06
SHANAHAN, FERGUS P30DK36200-05S1 0001
SHANAHAN, FERGUS R29DK40057-04
SHANAHAN, MICHAEL F R01DK36855-05
SHANE, BARRY R01CA41991-07
SHANE, BARRY R01DK42033-02
SHANE, ELIZABETH M01RR00645-20 0497
SHANE, ELIZABETH J M01RR00645-20 0285
SHANELARIS, JAMES R19DA06428-03
SHANER, ANDREW R01MH48081-02
SHANGRAW, ROBERT E S07RR05412-30 0982
SHANK, PETER R R55AI31815-01
SHANK, RONALD C R01ES03726-07
SHANKAR, P MOHANA P01CA52823-02 0004
SHANKARAN, SEETHA U10HD21385-06
SHANKEL, DELBERT M R13CA54695-01
SHANKLAND, S MARTIN R01HD21735-06
SHANKWEILER, DONALD P P01HD01994-26A1 0010
SHANLEY, JOHN D P01CA30206-10 0011
SHANLEY, JOHN D R01HL34813-05A1
SHANLEY, PAUL F R29DK38516-04
SHANNON, BARBARA M R01HL43880-02
SHANNON, JOHN M R01HL45011-02
SHANNON, KENNEY P01CA19014-14 0020
SHANNON, RICHARD P P01DA06306-01A1 0002
SHANNON, ROBERT V R29DC00409-06
SHANNON, ROGER S07RR05749-19 0280
SHANNON, WILLIAM N01AI72642-10
SHANNON, WILLIAM M N01CM87237-03
SHANNON, WILLIAM M P01CA34200-09 9008
SHANNON, WILLIAM M U01AI30279-02 0004
SHAPER, JOEL H R01CA45799-05
SHAPIRO, B Z01CB08382-08
SHAPIRO, DAVID R01HL31184-07
SHAPIRO, DAVID R01HL40466-04
SHAPIRO, DAVID R01HL40584-04
SHAPIRO, DAVID J R01HD16720-10
SHAPIRO, DAVID N R29GM38970-06
SHAPIRO, DOUGLAS Y S06GM08103-18 0022
SHAPIRO, EUGENE D M01RR06022-02 0772
SHAPIRO, EUGENE D M01RR06022-02 0745
SHAPIRO, EUGENE D M01RR06022-02 0661
SHAPIRO, EUGENE D R01AI28308-03
SHAPIRO, EUGENE D R01AR40451-02
SHAPIRO, FREDERIC D R01AR39965-03
SHAPIRO, GAIL G N01HR16050-00
SHAPIRO, HERMAN S07RR05393-30 0904
SHAPIRO, HOWARD M R43HG00441-01
SHAPIRO, HOWARD M R44RR07751-02
SHAPIRO, IRVING M R01AR34411-07
SHAPIRO, IRVING M R01DE09684-01
SHAPIRO, JAY P01AG04402-09
SHAPIRO, JAY R M01RR02719-06 0011
SHAPIRO, JAY R R01AR39870-04
SHAPIRO, JOAN R S15CA56003-01
SHAPIRO, JOAN RANKIN R01CA25956-13
SHAPIRO, LARRY J P30HD19445-05S1 9004
SHAPIRO, LARRY J R01HD12178-13
SHAPIRO, LEWIS P R29DC00494-04
SHAPIRO, LUCILLE P30CA13696-19 9005
SHAPIRO, LUCILLE R01GM32506-10
SHAPIRO, LYNDA P S07RR07080-26 0306
SHAPIRO, M Z01AG00405-05
SHAPIRO, M Z01AI00578-02
SHAPIRO, M Z01CT00008-18
SHAPIRO, MARTIN F R01HS06775-01
SHAPIRO, MICHAEL E R29AI25126-05
SHAPIRO, PETER P30DE09743-02 0009
SHAPIRO, ROBERT E K08NS01518-01
SHAPIRO, SANDOR S R37HL09163-26
SHAPIRO, STEVEN D S07RR05491-29 0466
SHAPIRO, STEVEN M R01DC00369-05
SHAPIRO, THERESA A R01AI28855-02
SHAPIRO, WILLIAM R U10CA36047-07
SHAPLEY, PATRICIA A R01AI28851-02
SHAPLEY, ROBERT S07RR07062-26 0220
SHAPLEY, ROBERT M R01EY01472-17
SHAPSHAK, PAUL R01DA04787-05
SHARE, LEONARD R37HL19209-16
SHARFMAN, W H Z01CM09361-01
SHARIFI, BEHROOZ S07RR05468-29 0390
SHARKEY, ROBERT M R01CA37895-06
SHARKIS, SAUL J P30CA06973-29 9006
SHARKIS, SAUL J R01CA47993-04
SHARKIS, SAUL J R01HL46533-01
SHARMA, HARI M01RR00034-31 0347
SHARMA, MINOTI R01CA46896-03
SHARMA, RAGHUBIR P R01HD28259-01
SHARMA, SARLA S07RR07236-04 0175
SHARMA, SHEELA N01CN95172-09
SHARMA, SURENDRA R01CA54763-01
SHARMA, VIJAY S R01HL31159-15
SHARON, JACQUELINE R01AI23909-06
SHARON, PINHAS S07RR05477-29 0430
SHARP, BURT M R01DA03977-07
SHARP, BURT M R01DA04196-06
SHARP, BURT M S03RR03547-01
SHARP, FRANK R P50NS14543-14 0016
SHARP, FRANK RAY R01NS28167-02
SHARP, GEOFFREY W R01DK31667-09
SHARP, GEOFFREY W R01DK42063-01A1
SHARP, HARVEY L N01DK62274-06
SHARP, JOHN G R01AI25820-03
SHARP, M K S07RR07092-26 0544
SHARP, P P30CA14051-20 9005
SHARP, P P30CA14051-20 9006
SHARP, P P30CA14051-20 9007
SHARP, P P30CA14051-20 9010
SHARP, P S07RR07015-26 0610
SHARP, PHILLIP A P01CA42063-06 0006
SHARP, PHILLIP A P01CA42063-06 9001
SHARP, PHILLIP A P01CA42063-06
SHARP, PHILLIP A R01GM34277-07
SHARP, R MARK P01HL28972-10 9005
SHARP, SANDRA B S06GM08101-20 0042
SHARP, Z DAVE R29DK38546-05
SHARPLESS, K BARRY R37GM28384-11
SHARROCK, WILLIAM J S07RR07052-26 0170
SHARROW, S O Z01CB09255-16
SHASBY, D MICHAEL P50HL14230-20 9003
SHASBY, DOUGLAS M R01HL33540-07
SHASBY, MICHAEL P50HL42385-04 0004
SHASTRI, NILABH R01AI26604-03
SHATOS, MARIE P20NS30324-01 0002
SHATTIL, SANFORD J P01HL40387-04 0003
SHATTUCK-EIDENS, DONNA R44GM40794-03
SHATTUCK, DAVID P S07RR07147-19 0651
SHATZ, CARLA J P50MH48108-01 0008
SHATZ, CARLA J R01EY02858-13
SHAVER, PHILLIP R S07RR07066-26 0257
SHAW, ANDREY SHIN-YEE K08AI00997-03
SHAW, BARBARA R R01CA44709-05
SHAW, DANIEL S R29MH46925-01A1
SHAW, DENISE R R01CA51857-02
SHAW, DENISE R R01HL44363-02
SHAW, DOUGLAS N01HB17089-00
SHAW, GEORGE M P30AI27767-04 9001
SHAW, GEORGE M. P01AI27290-04 9002
SHAW, GEORGE M. P01AI27290-04 0007
SHAW, GERARD PJ R01NS22695-06
SHAW, JERRI N01AI15117-00
SHAW, JOCELYN E R01HD22163-01A2
SHAW, LESLIE M M01RR00040-31 0373
SHAW, PHYLLIS A R01DE08174-05
SHAW, REBECCA J S07RR05776-11 0399
SHAW, S Z01CB09257-16
SHAW, SPENCER R01AA07212-05
SHAW, SYLVIA M01RR00043-31 0468
SHAY, JERRY W R01CA40065-05
SHAY, JERRY W R01CA50195-03
SHAYE, ROBERT S03RR03058-11
SHAYMAN, JAMES P50DK39255-05 0006
SHAYMAN, JAMES A R01DK41487-02
SHAYWITZ, B P01HD21888-04 0001
SHAYWITZ, B P01HD21888-04 0002
SHAYWITZ, BENNETT A P01HD21888-04
SHAYWITZ, BENNETT A P50HD25802-02
SHAYWITZ, SALLY P01HD21888-04 0004
SHEA, BRIAN S07RR05311-30 0009
SHEA, BRIAN T K04DE00255-02
SHEA, BRIAN T R01DE08948-02
SHEA, BRIAN T S07RR05370-30 0616
SHEA, JOHN M N01AR92200-03
SHEA, KENNETH J R01GM33484-07
SHEA, KENNETH J S10RR06714-01
SHEA, KENNETH J S10RR06735-01
SHEA, STEVEN J R01HL38260-03
SHEA, THOMAS C M01RR00827-17 0446
SHEAR, HANNAH L R01AI15235-13
SHEAR, M KATHERINE R01MH45964-02
SHEARER, G M Z01CB09259-13
SHEARER, G M Z01CB09264-04
SHEARER, G M Z01CB09267-09
SHEARER, G M Z01CB09282-05
SHEARER, THOMAS R R01EY03600-10
SHEARER, THOMAS R R01EY05786-06
SHEARER, WILLIAM M01RR00188-27 0339
SHEARER, WILLIAM M01RR00188-27 0336
SHEARER, WILLIAM M01RR00188-27 0341
SHEARER, WILLIAM M01RR00188-27 0342
SHEARER, WILLIAM T M01RR00188-27 0321
SHEARER, WILLIAM T M01RR00188-27 0286
SHEARER, WILLIAM T R01AI32466-01
SHEARER, WILLIAM T R01HD26603-02
SHEARER, WILLIAM T U01AI27551-04
SHEARER, WILLIAM T. N01HR96040-06
SHEARN, ALLEN S07RR07041-26 0392

SHEARN, ALLEN D R01AG01822-12
SHEARN, ALLEN D R01GM33959-06A1
SHEARN, ALLEN D R03CA54838-01
SHEARS, S B Z01ES80046-03
SHECHTER, HAROLD R01CA11185-20
SHEDLOFSKY, STEVEN I M01RR02602-07 0050
SHEEHAN, FLORENCE H R03HL46144-01A1
SHEEHAN, JOSEPH P60AR20621-13 9001
SHEETS, MICHAEL F R29HL44630-02
SHEETZ, MICHAEL P R01GM36277-08
SHEETZ, MICHAEL P R01NS23345-06
SHEFER, RUTH E R44CA50031-02
SHEFER, RUTH E R44HL42176-03
SHEFER, SARAH R37DK26756-13
SHEFFERY, MICHAEL B R01DK37513-06
SHEFFERY, MICHAEL B R01DK41079-03
SHEFFIELD, JOE S07RR07115-24 0577
SHEFFIELD, LEWIS G R29HD24094-03
SHEFFIELD, LEWIS G S07RR07098-26 0334
SHEFFIELD, MATTHEW S07RR05365-30 0105
SHEFFIELD, VAL C R01HG00457-01
SHEFNER, SARAH A R01AA05846-09
SHEFRIN, E A Z01AG00625-02
SHEFT, STANLEY S07RR07210-09 0679
SHEIKH, AZAD S07RR05684-23 0174
SHEIL, JAMES M R01AI27917-03
SHEINER, LEWIS B P50GM26691-13 0015
SHEINER, LEWIS B R01GM26676-13
SHEKELLE, PAUL G R03HS06920-01
SHEKHAR, ANANTHA R29MH45362-03
SHELANSKI, MICHAEL P50NS27680-03 0004
SHELANSKI, MICHAEL L P50AG08702-03
SHELANSKI, MICHAEL L R01NS15076-13
SHELHAMER, J Z01CL00092-02
SHELHAMER, J Z01CL00112-01
SHELHAMER, J H Z01CL00018-05
SHELHAMER, J H Z01CL00020-05
SHELHAMER, J H Z01CL00024-05
SHELHAMER, J H Z01CL00030-04
SHELHAMER, J H Z01CL00055-02
SHELLER, JAMES R S07RR05424-30 0107
SHELLITO, JUDD E R01AA08845-01
SHELLITO, JUDD ERNEST R01HL29246-11
SHELLOCK, FRANK G R01CA44014-04
SHELNESS, GREGORY S S07RR05404-30 0858
SHELTON RICHARD, C R29MH45173-02
SHELTON, KEITH R R01ES02377-10A1
SHELTON, KEITH R S07RR05724-20 0187
SHELTON, RICHARD C S07RR05424-30 0101
SHELTON, ROBERT N S07RR07007-26
SHEN, BETTY W R01HL33254-07
SHEN, CHE-KUN J R01DK29800-11
SHEN, DANNY P01GM32165-09 0005
SHEN, DANNY D R01HL33389-06
SHEN, GUO-LIANG S07RR07175-15 0443
SHEN, LINUS U01AI30183-02 0002
SHEN, SHELDON S07RR07034-26 0068
SHEN, SHIDA R43RR07528-01
SHEN, VICTOR P50AR39191-05 0002
SHEN, VICTOR P50AR39191-05 9001
SHEN, WEI-CHIANG S07RR05792-15 0949
SHEN, Y P51RR00168-30 0136
SHENK, THOMAS E P01CA41086-06 9001
SHENK, THOMAS E P01CA41086-06
SHENK, THOMAS E P01CA41086-06 0001
SHENK, THOMAS E R37CA38965-08
SHENKER, BRUCE J R01DE06014-10
SHENKER, BRUCE J R01DE08587-03
SHENKER, YORAM M01RR03186-06 0011
SHENKER, YORAM M01RR03186-06 0066
SHENKER, YORAM M01RR03186-06 0049
SHENKER, YORAM R29DK38444-05
SHENTON, MARTHA E K01MH00746-04
SHEPARD, J W M01RR00585-20 0416
SHEPARD, THERESA S07RR05909-08 0954
SHEPARD, THOMAS P01DK31232-10 9001
SHEPARD, THOMAS H R01HD00836-27
SHEPARTZ, ALANNA R01GM43501-02
SHEPHERD, ALEX M M01RR01346-10 0193
SHEPHERD, ALEX M M01RR01346-10 0169
SHEPHERD, GORDON M P50NS10174-20 0019
SHEPHERD, GORDON M R01DC00086-24
SHEPHERD, PATRICIA A N01HD62931-08
SHEPHERD, RAYMOND E S07RR05376-30 0035
SHEPHERD, VIRGINIA L R01AI22697-07
SHEPLER, THOMAS R S07RR05983-05 0367
SHEPP, BRYAN E P40RR00419-24
SHEPPARD, DEAN R01HL33259-07
SHEPPARD, LOUIS S07RR07205-11 0648
SHEPRO, DAVID R01HL43875-02
SHER, A Z01AI00246-09
SHER, A Z01AI00251-10
SHER, A Z01AI00579-02
SHER, DAVID S07RR07066-26 0258
SHER, KENNETH J R01AA07231-05
SHERIDAN, JOHN F R01MH46801-01A1
SHERIDAN, JOHN F R29HL38485-04
SHERIDAN, JOHN F S15HL47753-01
SHERIDAN, JUDSON D S07RR07053-26
SHERIDAN, JUDSON D S15AA09242-01
SHERIDAN, JUDSON D S15HL47696-01
SHERIDAN, MARY E S15HL47756-01
SHERIDAN, SUSAN M S07RR07092-26 0503
SHERK, HELEN A R01EY04847-08
SHERMAN, A Z01DK13020-02
SHERMAN, ARNOLD P50MH43271-05 0006
SHERMAN, DAVID G R01NS24224-05
SHERMAN, FRED R01AI29433-01A1
SHERMAN, FRED R01GM12702-27
SHERMAN, IRWIN W R01AI21251-04A1
SHERMAN, J A P01HD18955-07 0005
SHERMAN, JACQUELINE B R01HD24727-02
SHERMAN, JAMES S07RR07037-26 0368
SHERMAN, JAMES A P01HD18955-07
SHERMAN, KAREN J R01CA48996-01A2
SHERMAN, LINDA A P01CA25803-13 0004
SHERMAN, LINDA A R01CA52856-02
SHERMAN, LLOYD R S03RR03114-08
SHERMAN, LORI M01RR00188-27 0334
SHERMAN, MATTHEW L R29CA53599-01A1
SHERMAN, MICHAEL U01CA51992-02 9001
SHERMAN, S MURRAY R01EY03038-12
SHERMAN, S MURRAY R01EY03604-11
SHERMAN, STEPHANIE L R01HD27801-01
SHERMAN, STEVEN J R01HD13449-11
SHERMAN, WARREN V S06GM08043-21 0013
SHERMAN, WARREN V S06GM08043-21
SHERMAN, WILLIAM R P41RR00954-15 9006
SHERMAN, WILLIAM R P60DK20579-14 9005
SHERN, DAVID L R18MH48215-02
SHERN, DAVID L R19MH46365-02
SHERR, CHARLES J P01CA20180-14 0011
SHERR, CHARLES J R35CA47064-04
SHERR, DAVID H R01AI23978-05
SHERRILL, KIMBERLY A K07MH00915-01A1
SHERRY, A DEAN R01HL34557-04
SHERRY, A DEAN S07RR07133-22 0513
SHERRY, BARBARA A R01AI29110-02
SHERRY, DAVID S07RR05655-21 0811
SHERWIN, ROBERT M01RR00125-28 0773
SHERWIN, ROBERT P01DK43078-02 0004
SHERWIN, ROBERT P01DK43078-02 9002
SHERWIN, ROBERT S M01RR00125-28 0729
SHERWIN, ROBERT S M01RR00125-28 0749
SHERWIN, ROBERT S R01DK20495-15
SHERWIN, ROGER W R01AR35584-06
SHERWOOD, ALAN CHARLES R19DA06421-03
SHERWOOD, ANDREW R29HL38950-03
SHERWOOD, JUDITH P60HL38655-04 0001
SHERWOOD, MARK M01RR00082-29 0338
SHERWOOD, MARK B U10EY05604-07
SHERWOOD, ORRIN D R01HD08700-17
SHETLAR, MARTIN D R01GM23526-14
SHETTIGAR, UDIPI R R43HL45354-01A1
SHETTY, VIVEK S07RR05304-30 0228
SHEU, KWAN-FU R R01AA08246-02
SHEU, KWAN-FU REX P01AG03853-09 9003
SHEU, SHEY-SHING R01HL33333-06
SHEVACH, E M Z01AI00224-10
SHEVELL, STEVEN K R01EY04802-09
SHEWACH, DONNA S R29CA46452-04
SHI, WEIMIN R43HD27816-01
SHI, WEIGIANG S07RR05468-29 0392
SHIAVI, RAUL M01RR00071-28A1 0183
SHIBAMOTO, T P42ES04699-05 0007
SHIBATA, DARRYL S07RR05356-30 0435
SHIBATA, ERWIN F R29HL41031-04
SHIBATA, HENRY R U10CA20321-15
SHICHI, HITOSHI R01EY04694-10
SHIDELER, SUSAN E P51RR00169-30 0125
SHIELDS, ANTHONY F P01CA42045-06 0003
SHIELDS, ANTHONY F R01CA39566-08
SHIELDS, DENNIS R37DK21860-14
SHIELDS, DONALD M01RR00865-18 0355
SHIELDS, DONALD W M01RR00865-18 0364
SHIELDS,DENNIS P60DK20541-14 0025
SHIEMKE, ANDREW S07RR05433-30 0253
SHIER, WAYNE T S03RR03083-11
SHIFFERIE, ROBERT P50DE08240-05 0006
SHIFFMAN, CARL A S07RR07143-20 0634
SHIFFMAN, MITCHELL L R29DK43264-01A1
SHIFFMAN, SAUL R01DA06084-02
SHIFFRIN, RICHARD M R37MH12717-23
SHIH, CHIAHO R01CA48198-03
SHIH, DANIEL T B R29HL40573-03
SHIH, J Z01CL02061-02
SHIH, J Z01CL02064-01
SHIH, JEAN C K05MH00796-03
SHIH, JEAN C R01MH37020-07A2
SHIH, JEAN C R37MH39085-07
SHIH, MING-CHE R01GM41669-03
SHIH, T Y Z01CP04963-15
SHIH, T Y Z01CP05594-03
SHIH, T Y Z01CP05658-02
SHIH, VIVIAN E R01EY05633-07
SHIH, VIVIAN E R01NS05096-28
SHIIGI, S M P51RR00163-32 9016
SHIKE, MOSHE N01CN05318-01
SHIKOWITZ, MARK J P01DC00203-09 0007
SHILLITOE, EDWARD J R01DE07007-06
SHILO, BEN-ZION R01GM35998-06
SHILOACH, J Z01DK15500-32
SHIMADA, T Z01HL02310-11
SHIMADA, T Z01HL02331-05
SHIMAMURA, ARTHUR S07RR07006-26 0904
SHIMAMURA, ARTHUR P R29AG09055-02
SHIMASAKI, SHUNICHI P01HD09690-18 0004
SHIMASKI, SHUNICHI P01HD09690-18 9006
SHIMIZU, NOBUYOSHI R01GM24375-14A1
SHIMIZU, YOJI R29AI31126-01
SHIMIZU, YUZURU R01CA49992-03
SHIMIZU, YUZURU R37GM28754-16
SHIMIZU, YUZURU S07RR07086-15 0323
SHIMIZU, YUZUVU U01CA50750-03 0006
SHIMP, CHARLES P S07RR07092-26 0532
SHIN, CHEOLSU R29NS25608-04
SHIN, HYUN S R01CA14113-19
SHIN, HYUN S R01CA49644-03
SHIN, MOON L P50NS20022-08 0004
SHIN, MOON L R01AI19622-09
SHIN, MOON L R01NS15662-12
SHIN, MOON L S07RR05379-30 0770
SHINAGAWA, SUSUMU Z01BD01001-03
SHINAGAWA, SUSUMU Z01BD01002-03
SHINAGI, RAYMOND F N01AI05078-03
SHINE, KENNETH I M01RR00865-18
SHINE, NANCY R29GM43299-03
SHING, YUEN P01CA45548-05 9004
SHINKLE, JAMES R S07RR07261-02 0714
SHINN, MARYBETH R01MH46116-02
SHINNAR, MEIR P41RR02305-08 9002
SHINNAR, MEIR P41RR02305-08 9005
SHINNAR, MEIR P41RR02305-08 9006
SHINNAR, SHLOMO R01NS26151-04
SHINNERS, ELIZABETH N R15AI30074-01A1
SHINNICK-GALLAGHER, PATRICIA R01NS29265-01
SHINOHARA, T Z01EY00250-04
SHINOHARA, TOSHIMICHI Z01EY00132-10
SHINOZUKA, HISASHI R01CA26556-12
SHINOZUKA, HISASHI R01CA53453-01
SHIP, J A Z01DE00500-02
SHIPLEY, G GRAHAM P01HL26335-11A1 0001
SHIPLEY, GARY D R01CA42409-07
SHIPLEY, J P50AA07378-04 0006
SHIPLEY, MICHAEL T P01DC00347-06
SHIPLEY, MICHAEL T P01DC00347-06 0003
SHIPLEY, MICHAEL T R01NS29218-01
SHIPLEY, THOMAS E U01AA08802-02
SHIPMAN, CHARLES U01AI25739-04 0002
SHIPMAN, CHARLES, JR R01DE08510-05
SHIPP, MARGARET A R01CA55095-01
SHIPP, MARGARET A S07RR05526-29 0100
SHIRES III, GEORGE T R29GM39906-03
SHIRES, G. TOM P50GM26145-13 9002
SHIRES, GEORGE M S07RR05845-11
SHIRES, GEORGE T R37GM23000-16
SHIROMANI, PRIYATTAM J P50MH30914-14 0049
SHIROMANI, PRIYATTAM J R01NS30140-01
SHIROMANI, PRIYATTAM J R29NS25212-06
SHIVELY, CAROL A R01HL39789-04
SHIVELY, JOHN S07RR05841-12 0223
SHIVELY, JOHN E P01HL28481-09 9002
SHIVERICK, KATHLEEN T R01DA06890-01
SHIVERICK, KATHLEEN T R01ES04435-04A1
SHIVERICK, KATHLEEN T R01HD18506-07
SHLAFER, MARSHAL R01HL29499-10
SHLICHTA, PAUL J R43CA53966-01A1
SHMOOKLER-REIS, ROBERT J R01AG09413-01A1
SHNEIDMAN, PAUL S K08NS01451-01A1
SHOAF, S Z01AA00292-01
SHOAL, S Z01AA00237-09
SHOBACK, DOLORES M R01DK43400-01
SHOBHA, SRIHARAN S06GM08169-13 0005
SHOCKLEY, DOLORES C R24DA06686-02
SHOCKMAN, GERALD D R01AI05044-28
SHOEMAKER, CHARLES R22AI28499-01A1
SHOEMAKER, CHARLES S07RR05446-30 0272
SHOEMAKER, CHARLES S07RR05446-30 0273
SHOEMAKER, R P01CA38548-07 0003
SHOEMAKER, R Z01CM07199-01
SHOEMAKER, RICHARD K S10RR06301-01
SHOEMAKER, WILLIAM P50AA03510-14 0022
SHOEMAKER, WILLIAM J P50AA06420-08 0003
SHOEMAKER, WILLIAM J R01AA06927-06
SHOEN, FREDERICK P01HL38189-04 9002
SHOFFNER, JOHN M K08NS01336-03
SHOHAM-SALOMON, VARDA R01MH47451-01A1
SHOHAM, MENACHAM S07RR05410-30 0956
SHOHET, S B R01DK16095-17
SHOHET, STEPHEN B P01DK32094-08
SHOLL, SAMUEL P51RR00167-31 0037
SHOLL, SAMUEL S07RR07098-26 0368
SHONFELD, GUSTAV P01DK33487-05 0001
SHOOK, MICHAEL R. S06GM08119-18 0013
SHOOTER, ERIC M R01NS04270-29
SHOPE, JEAN T P50AG08671-03 9003
SHOPP, G S07RR05900-06 0629
SHOPP, GEORGE M N01ES95238-04
SHORE, ELSIE R R01AA08268-02
SHORE, JOSEPH D R01HL25670-10
SHORE, JOSEPH D R01HL45930-02
SHORE, JOSEPH D S03RR03078-11
SHORE, JOSEPH D S07RR05490-29
SHORE, JOSEPH D S15HL47709-01
SHORE, MILES F S15MH49306-01
SHORE, ROY P42ES04895-03 9001

SHORE, ROY E R37CA43175-06
SHORE, STEPHANIE A S07RR05446-30 0278
SHORE, VIRGIE S P01HL18574-16 9002
SHORT, JAY M R01ES04728-03
SHORT, JAY M R43GM46585-01
SHORT, JAY M R44GM42291-02
SHORT, MARION P K08NS01251-04
SHORTHILL, RICHARD W S07RR07092-26 0550
SHORTLE, DAVID P41RR04328-04 0008
SHORTLE, DAVID R R01GM34171-08
SHORTLIFFE, EDWARD H P41LM05208-18S1
SHORTLIFFE, EDWARD H R13HS06647-01S1
SHORTLIFFE, EDWARD H R18HS06330-02
SHORTLIFFE, EDWARD H S03RR03509-03
SHORTY, VERNON R18DA05759-03S1
SHORTY, VERNON U01DA07475-01
SHOU-HUA, L Z01DE00462-04
SHOUKAS, ARTIN A R01HL14529-20
SHOUKAS, ARTIN A R37HL19039-15
SHOULSON, IRA R01NS24778-05
SHOUPE, DONNA M01RR00043-31 0458
SHOUPE, DONNA M01RR00043-31 0492
SHOUSE, MARGARET N R01NS25629-04
SHOVEN, JOHN B S07RR05995-04 0051
SHOWE, LOUISE C R01CA51918-01A1
SHOWE, LOUISE C S07RR05540-29 0557
SHOWS, THOMAS B R01HD05196-20
SHOWS, THOMAS B R01HG00333-19
SHOWS, THOMAS B R01HG00359-04
SHRAGER, R I Z01CT00010-17
SHRAKE, A F Z01BH05014-05
SHRAKE, A F Z01BH05015-09
SHRAKE, A F Z01BH05016-02
SHRAKE, A F Z01BH05024-01
SHREEVE, STEPHEN M R29HL38853-05
SHREEVE, STEPHEN M S07RR05429-30 0199
SHREFFLER, DONALD C R37AI12734-16
SHRIBERG, LAWRENCE D R01DC00496-04
SHRIVER, JOHN S07RR07118-22 0384
SHRIVER, JOHN W K04AR01788-04
SHRIVER, JOHN W R01AR40190-02
SHRIVER, MARK P30CA16087-14 9011
SHROFF, BHAVNA R03DE09935-01
SHROFF, SANJEEV G R01HL36185-06
SHROUT, PATRICK P50MH43878-03 0003
SHROUT, PATRICK E R01MH45763-01A1
SHU, SUYU R01CA49231-04
SHUB, DAVID A R01GM37746-05
SHUB, DAVID A S07RR07122-23 0083
SHUCARD, DAVID W R01HD25718-01A3
SHUKLA, SHIVENDRA D K04DK01782-03
SHUKLA, SHIVENDRA D R01DK35170-06
SHULER, CHARLES P50DE09165-03 0005
SHULER, CHARLES F R01DE07682-04
SHULER, CHARLES F S03RR03538-01
SHULER, MICHAEL L R01CA55138-01
SHULKIN, BARRY L R29CA54216-01
SHULL, GARY P01HL41496-03 0006
SHULL, GARY E R01DK39626-04
SHULL, GARY E R01HL41558-03
SHULL, JAMES D R29HD24189-03
SHULL, L R P42ES04699-05 9001
SHULMAN, GERALD P01DK34576-06 0002
SHULMAN, GERALD P30DK34989-08 0016
SHULMAN, GERALD I M01RR00125-28 0731
SHULMAN, GERALD I M01RR00125-28 0755
SHULMAN, GERALD I M01RR00125-28 0732
SHULMAN, GERALD I R01DK40936-03
SHULMAN, N R Z01DK51000-33
SHULMAN, N R Z01DK51001-33
SHULMAN, ROBERT M01RR00188-27 0332
SHULMAN, ROBERT G P01DK34576-06 9001
SHULMAN, ROBERT G P01DK34576-06
SHULMAN, ROBERT G R01DK43146-02
SHULMAN, ROBERT J M01RR00188-27 0325
SHULTS, WILLIAM T U10EY07687-04
SHULTZ, LEONARD S07RR05545-29 0567
SHULTZ, LEONARD S07RR05545-29 0568
SHULTZ, LEONARD D R01AI30389-02
SHULTZ, LEONARD D R01CA20408-15
SHULTZ, LEONARD D R13AI31415-01
SHUMAN, HOWARD A R01AI19276-10
SHUMAN, HOWARD A R01AI23549-06
SHUMAN, MARC A R01HL21403-12
SHUMAN, MARC A R01HL33277-06
SHUMAN, STEWART H R01GM42498-03
SHUMAN, STEWART H R01GM46330-01
SHUMAN, WILLIAM P P01CA42045-06 9005
SHUNG, K KIRK R01HL28452-09
SHUNG, K KIRK R01HL47011-01
SHUPERT, CHARLOTTE L R55DC01104-01
SHUPNIK, MARGARET A R01HD25719-03
SHUPNIK, MARGARET A R55DK44142-01
SHUPNIK, MARGARET A S07RR05431-30 0841
SHUR, BARRY D R01DE07120-08
SHUR, BARRY D R01HD22590-05
SHUR, BARRY D R01HD23479-04
SHURE, MYRNA B R01MH40801-05
SHUSTER, LOUIS S07RR05382-30 0877
SHUSTER, ROBERT C S07RR05364-30 0542
SHUSTER, TERRENCE A R01EY05291-06
SHUSTER, TERRENCE A S06GM08238-05 0017

SHUTTLEWORTH, TREVOR J P30ES03828-06 0011
SHUTTLEWORTH, TREVOR J R01GM40457-04
SHY, CARL M S07RR05450-30 0334
SHY, MICHAEL E K08NS01261-04
SHYAMALA, GOPALAN R01CA54828-01
SHYU, ANN-BIN R01GM46454-01
SHYU, ANN-BIN S07RR05745-19 0243
SIBAI, BAHA M N01HD13126-00
SIBAI, BAHA M U10HD21414-06
SIBER, GEORGE R R01AI18125-10
SIBER, GEORGE R R01AI24996-05
SIBERSTEIN, DAVID S R29AI28525-03
SIBLEY, CAROL P01GM42508-03 0008
SIBLEY, CHARLES G R01GM40304-04
SIBLEY, D R Z01NS02263-15
SIBLEY, JOHN R18AR21393-17 0017
SIBLEY, RICHARD P01DK13083-24 0167
SICA, ANTHONY L R29HL41008-04
SICA, DOMENIC M01RR00065-29 0342
SICA, DOMENIC A. M01RR00065-29 0300
SICILIANO, MICHAEL J P01CA34936-08 0004
SICK, THOMAS J P01NS05820-26 0023
SIDBURY, J B Z01HD00133-14
SIDDIK, ZAHID H R01CA50380-01A3
SIDDIQI, FASEEB S07RR05401-30 0862
SIDDIQI, TARIQ A R01HD21687-04
SIDDIQUE, TEEPU P50NS21442-07 0004
SIDDIQUI, ALEEM P30DK34914-06 0013
SIDDIQUI, ALEEM R01CA33135-07A2
SIDDIQUI, ALEEM R03AI31994-01
SIDDIQUI, M R01HL43159-03
SIDELL, NEIL R01CA30515-09
SIDEN, E S07RR05362-30 0781
SIDLES, JOHN A S07RR05432-30 0241
SIDMAN, CHARLES P30CA34196-09 9006
SIDMAN, CHARLES S07RR05545-29 0573
SIDMAN, CHARLES S07RR05545-29 0577
SIDMAN, CHARLES L R01AI20232-08
SIDMAN, CHARLES L R01AI25765-05
SIDMAN, CHARLES L S10RR06371-01
SIDMAN, RICHARD L R01NS20820-10A1
SIDMAN, RICHARD L R55EY06631-05A1
SIDMAN, RICHARD L U01EY06859-06S1
SIDNEY, STEPHEN R01DA06609-01
SIDNEY, STEPHEN S07RR05521-29 0065
SIDTIS, JOHN J. P01NS25701-05 9001
SIDTIS, JOHN T. P01NS25701-05 0002
SIDWELL, ROBERT W N01AI15097-00
SIEBENLIST, U Z01AI00431-07
SIEBENS, HILARY S07RR05468-29 0389
SIEBER-BLUM, MAYA S07RR05434-30 0819
SIEBER-BLUM, MAYA F R01HD21423-07
SIEBER, FREDERICK E K08NS01380-03
SIEBER, FRITZ P01CA49089-03 0003
SIEBERT, ELEANOR D S06GM08232-06 0010
SIEBERT, ELEANOR D S06GM08232-06 0010
SIEBERT, JOSEPH S07RR05655-21 0818
SIEBES, MARIA S07RR07035-26 0076
SIEBURG, HANS B R29MH45688-03
SIEBURTH, SCOTT S07RR07067-26 0224
SIEBURTH, SCOTT M R01GM45214-01
SIECK, GARY C R01HL34817-07
SIECK, GARY C R01HL37680-06
SIEFF, COLIN A MB BCH R01DK42260-03
SIEFF, COLIN A R01CA45559-04A1
SIEGAL, GENE P R29CA45727-06
SIEGAL, HARVEY A R18DA05757-03S1
SIEGAL, HARVEY A R18DA06944-02
SIEGAL, HARVEY A U01DA07305-01
SIEGAL, JUDITH S07RR06025-02 0027
SIEGEL, ALBERT S06GM08167-13 0048
SIEGEL, ALLAN R01NS07941-21
SIEGEL, BRYNA S07RR05755-18 0235
SIEGEL, DAVID P50MH42459-06 0004
SIEGEL, DAVID R01HD27020-02
SIEGEL, DONALD L K08HL02621-01
SIEGEL, FRANK L P30HD03352-25 9011
SIEGEL, FRANK L R01NS24969-05
SIEGEL, GEORGE J S07RR05383-30 0569
SIEGEL, J P Z01BD02001-05
SIEGEL, JEROME P50NS23724-06 0005
SIEGEL, JEROME M R01HL41370-04
SIEGEL, JEROME M R01NS14610-12
SIEGEL, KAROLYNN R01MH41967-05
SIEGEL, KAROLYNN R01MH42878-05
SIEGEL, KAROLYNN R01MH47656-01A1
SIEGEL, LAWRENCE S07RR05353-30 0367
SIEGEL, NORMAN M01RR06022-02 0773
SIEGEL, NORMAN P01DK34576-06 0003
SIEGEL, NORMAN J M01RR06022-02 0747
SIEGEL, NORMAN J R01DK44336-01
SIEGEL, SHEPARD R01MH45137-03
SIEGEL, STUART E P30CA14089-16 9010
SIEGEL, WILLIAM C M01RR00030-30 0477
SIEGELBAUM, STEVEN A P01HL30557-08 0001
SIEGELBAUM, STEVEN A R01NS19569-09
SIEGER, LANCE M01RR00425-22S3 0415
SIEGER, LANCE M01RR00425-22S3 0440
SIEGFRIED, JILL M R01CA50694-01A2
SIEGFRIED, JOHN B R01NS30354-01
SIEGLER, MELODY V K04NS01481-02
SIEGLER, ROBERT S R01HD19011-07

SIEGMAN, ARON W S07RR07159-16 0581
SIEGMAN, M G Z01HL05001-02
SIEGMAN, MARION J R01DK37598-04
SIEKEVITZ, MIRIAM L R29AI27053-04
SIEMANN, DIETMAR W P30CA11198-23 9016
SIEMANN, DIETMAR W R01CA36858-08
SIEMANN, DIETMAR W R01CA38637-07
SIEMERS, ERIC M01RR00750-19 0253
SIEMERS, ERIC R S07RR05371-30 0643
SIERRA, MARTHA-LUCIA N01LM03506-01
SIERVOGEL, ROGER M R01HD12252-14
SIERVOGEL, ROGER M R01HD26971-02
SIESJO, BO K R01NS07838-22
SIETSEMA, KATHY E K08HL01642-05
SIEVER, LARRY M01RR00071-28A1 0193
SIEVER, LARRY J R37MH42827-03
SIEVER, LARRY T M01RR00071-28A1 0173
SIEVERT, MARYELLEN R01LM04605-05
SIEVING, PAUL A R01EY06094-06
SIEW, CHAKWAN S07RR05689-23 0855
SIEW, CHAKWAN S07RR05425-30 0853
SIFERS, RICHARD S07RR05425-30 0767
SIFERS, RICHARD N R29DK42806-01A1
SIGAL, ELLIOTT MD PHD K08HL02047-03
SIGAL, LEONARD H S07RR05576-27 0602
SIGEL, BERNARD R01HL41874-03
SIGELMAN, CAROL K R01HD27274-02
SIGGINS, GEORGE P50MH47680-02 0013
SIGGINS, GEORGE R P50AA06420-08 0001
SIGGINS, GEORGE R R01DA03665-09
SIGGINS, GEORGE R R37MH44346-04
SIGLER, PAUL B R01NS25867-04
SIGLER, PAUL B R37GM15225-24
SIGMAN, CAROLINE N01CN95159-05
SIGMAN, CAROLINE C N01CP15723-00
SIGMAN, DAVID S P01GM39558-05 0005
SIGMAN, DAVID S R01GM21199-23
SIGMAN, DAVID S R01HG00255-01
SIGMAN, EUGENE M S07RR05678-23
SIGMAN, MARIAN D R01NS25243-10
SIGNER, ETHAN R R01GM40725-03
SIGNEY, GOTTLIEB O. N01HV18118-02
SIGNS, STEVEN A R03AA08641-02
SIGUEL, EDWARD N R01HL39681-05
SIGURDSON, ELIN R P01CA47997-03 0004
SIGURDSSON, A S07RR05333-30 0876
SIGWORTH, FREDERICK J R01NS21501-07
SIH, CHARLES J R01GM33149-11
SIH, CHARLES J R55GM46290-01
SIITERI, PENTTI K R35CA39825-07
SIKELA, JAMES M R29NS27322-03
SIKIC, BRANIMIR I P01CA49605-03 0005
SIKIC, BRANIMIR I R01CA52168-02
SIKKA, HARISH C R01CA53197-01
SILAGE, DENNIS A P50HL42236-04 9001
SILAVIN, S S07RR05411-30 0961
SILBER, HERBERT B. S06GM08192-12 0012
SILBER, JEFFREY H K04CA01480-03
SILBER, ROBERT R01CA54484-01
SILBERBERG, DONALD H P01NS11037-18
SILBERBERG, DONALD H P01NS11037-18 0054
SILBERGLITT, RICHARD S R43AR41093-01
SILBERMAN, SANDRA L K08AI01033-01
SILBERSTEIN, LESLIE S07RR05415-30 0019
SILBERSTEIN, LESLIE E R29DK39065-04
SILBERT, DAVID F P60DK20579-14 0033
SILBERT, DAVID F R01GM38540-05
SILEN, WILLIAM P30DK34854-08
SILEN, WILLIAM R37DK15681-20
SILER-KHOR, THERESA M P30HD10202-15 9002
SILFLOW, CAROLYN D R01GM31159-09
SILHAVY, THOMAS J R01GM34821-07
SILHAVY, THOMAS J R01GM35791-06
SILICIANO, ROBERT F R01AI28108-04
SILICIFANO, ROBERT F U01AI27336-04 0003
SILINSKY, EUGENE M R01NS12782-13
SILK, JOAN B P51RR00169-30 0158
SILK, JOAN B P51RR00169-30 0159
SILKS, LOUIS A S07RR07160-16 0586
SILL, JOHN C R01HL38668-04
SILLAU, ALBERTO H S06GM08224-07 0019
SILLIMAN, CHRISTOPHER M01RR00069-29 0463
SILLIMAN, CHRISTOPHER M01RR00069-29 0491
SILLIMAN, D N01CO15659-00
SILLIMAN, DAVID N01CO15668-00
SILLIMAN, DAVID N01CO15671-00
SILVA, JORGE E R01DK42431-03
SILVA, PATRICIO P30ES03828-06 0006
SILVA, WALTER I R29NS27259-03
SILVER, J Z01AI00304-10
SILVER, JACK R01AI22005-08
SILVER, JERRY R01NS25713-04
SILVER, JUSTIN R01DK38696-03
SILVER, KENNETH H K08DC00055-01
SILVER, LEE M R01HD20275-08
SILVER, LEE M R01HD24383-04
SILVER, PAMELA A R01GM36373-06
SILVER, RAE R01MH29380-15
SILVER, RAE R01NS24292-04A2
SILVER, RAE S07RR07234-05 0853
SILVER, RICHARD M M01RR01070-15 0147
SILVER, RICHARD P R01AI26655-03

SILVER, RICHARD T U10CA07968-27
SILVER, ROBERT M01RR00069-29 0474
SILVERBERG, BARBARA R44DC00489-03
SILVERBERG, S J M01RR00645-20 0414
SILVERBERG, SHONNI J K08DK01836-05
SILVERMAN, ANN J R01DK42323-02
SILVERMAN, ANN J R01HD10665-16
SILVERMAN, ANN-JUDITH R01NS23858-05
SILVERMAN, DAVID J R01AI17416-08
SILVERMAN, DAVID N R01GM25154-14
SILVERMAN, GARY A R29HD28475-01
SILVERMAN, GREGG J K11AI00866-05
SILVERMAN, GREGG J M01RR00833-17 0172
SILVERMAN, GREGG J P60AR40770-01A1 0003
SILVERMAN, H Z01AG00257-03
SILVERMAN, H S Z01AG00263-02
SILVERMAN, HAROLD P01ES03347-08 0005
SILVERMAN, HOWARD S K08HL02539-01
SILVERMAN, JAN F P01DK36296-05 9001
SILVERMAN, JAY N01LM13511-00
SILVERMAN, JEREMY M P01MH45212-02 9003
SILVERMAN, JOHN N01AI02500-08
SILVERMAN, JOHN N01LM13532-00
SILVERMAN, JOHN N01LM93524-04
SILVERMAN, MARTIN S R01EY07547-03S1
SILVERMAN, MICHAEL R S07RR05878-09
SILVERMAN, MYRNA P50AG05133-08 9005
SILVERMAN, MYRNA P50AG05133-08 0013
SILVERMAN, MYRNA R01AG08276-02
SILVERMAN, PETER B R01DA06269-02
SILVERMAN, PHILIP M R01GM38657-05
SILVERMAN, RICHARD B R01GM32634-12
SILVERMAN, RICHARD B R01NS15703-13
SILVERMAN, ROBERT H R01AI28253-03
SILVERMAN, WAYNE P R01AG09439-01
SILVERMAN, WENDY K R29MH44781-03
SILVERS, J B R01HS06156-01A1
SILVERS, WILLYS K R37CA18640-21
SILVERSTEIN, FAYE S R29NS26142-03
SILVERSTEIN, FRED E R01DK34814-06
SILVERSTEIN, JANET H M01RR00082-29 0477
SILVERSTEIN, JANET H M01RR00082-29 0463
SILVERSTEIN, MARC D R01HL46974-01
SILVERSTEIN, MARSHALL L P50MH41684-07 0075
SILVERSTEIN, RICHARD R01AI30500-01
SILVERSTEIN, ROY L P01HL46403-01 0003
SILVERSTEIN, ROY L P50HL18828-16 0010
SILVERSTEIN, ROY L R01HL42540-03
SILVERSTEIN, SAMUEL C P01AI26886-04 0002
SILVERSTEIN, SAMUEL C R01AI20516-08
SILVERSTEIN, SAMUEL C R01HL32210-08
SILVERSTEIN, SAUL J P01CA23767-13 0007
SILVERSTEIN, SAUL J P01GM38125-04
SILVERSTEIN, SAUL J P01GM38125-04 0003
SILVERSTEIN, SAUL J P01GM38125-04 9001
SILVERSTEIN, SUZANNE M01RR00082-29 0277
SILVERTON, J V Z01HL01005-20
SILVERTON, SUSAN S07RR05337-30 0772
SILVERTON, SUSAN F R29AR40428-01A2
SILVIA, WILLIAM J R29HD24979-03
SIM, TOMMY C M01RR00073-29 0319
SIMA, ANDERS A R01DK43884-01
SIMANSKY, KENNY J R01MH41987-04A1
SIMARD, J MARC R29HL42646-02
SIMCHOWITZ, LOUIS R01GM38094-05
SIMERLY, RICHARD S07RR05694-22 0858
SIMERLY, RICHARD B R01NS26723-03
SIMINOFF, LAURA A R01CA49641-02
SIMINOFF, LAURA A R01HS06579-02
SIMISTER, NEIL S07RR07044-26 0119
SIMISTER, NEIL E R01HD27691-01
SIMKIN, PETER A R01AR32811-08S1
SIMMELINK, JAMES W R01DE02525-25
SIMMEN, ROSALIA C R01HD21961-06
SIMMER, ROBERT L U01AI27220-04 0001
SIMMONDS, HERMIONE A R13DK43185-01
SIMMONS, ANDREA M R01NS28565-02
SIMMONS, CHARLES F K08HL02030-05
SIMMONS, CHARLES J S06GM08102-20 0048
SIMMONS, DANIEL T R01CA36118-07
SIMMONS, DANIEL T S15CA55991-01
SIMMONS, F BLAIR R01DC00099-19
SIMMONS, GAIL S07RR07132-20 0408
SIMMONS, JAMES S07RR05546-26 0578
SIMMONS, JAMES A K02MH00521-07
SIMMONS, MARK A R29NS25999-06
SIMMONS, MICHAEL A P30HD27827-02
SIMMONS, MICHAEL J R01GM40263-13
SIMMONS, RICHARD L R01AI14032-13
SIMMONS, RICHARD L R01GM37753-05
SIMMONS, RICHARD L R01GM41734-02
SIMMONS, RICHARD L R37AI16869-12
SIMMONS, ROBERTA P01DK13083-24 0174
SIMMONS, WILLIAM H R01HL45159-01A1
SIMMS, LILLIAN M S07RR05796-14 0441
SIMMS, ROBERT P60AR20613-14 0026
SIMON, A R S07RR05333-30 0877
SIMON, BRUCE S07RR07205-11 0645
SIMON, BRUCE J R29AR39627-04
SIMON, CHRIS S07RR07026-26 0010
SIMON, ERIC J P01NS15638-13 0002
SIMON, ERIC J R01DA00017-27
SIMON, FRANCIS R P30DK34914-06
SIMON, FRANCIS R R01AA08770-02
SIMON, FRANCIS R R01DK15851-20
SIMON, GREGORY E R03MH47765-01
SIMON, HELEN R29DC00468-03
SIMON, HELEN J S07RR05981-05 0796
SIMON, JAY R P01NS27613-01A2 0003
SIMON, JOHN D R01GM41942-02
SIMON, JOHN D S06GM47165-01 0029
SIMON, KENNETH J R01CA49588-04
SIMON, LEE M01RR01066-14 0076
SIMON, LEE P01AR03564-32 0023
SIMON, MELVIN P30CA32911-08 9004
SIMON, MELVIN I P01AG07687-04
SIMON, MELVIN I R01AI19296-10
SIMON, MELVIN I R01GM34236-07
SIMON, ROGER P P01HL25816-11 0005
SIMON, ROGER P P50NS14543-14 0014
SIMON, RONALD A M01RR00833-17 0167
SIMON, SANFORD R R01HL14262-20
SIMON, SIDNEY A R01DC01065-01
SIMON, TOBY L M01RR00997-16 0312
SIMON, TOBY L M01RR00997-16 0386
SIMON, TOBY L M01RR00997-16 0297
SIMON, TOBY L M01RR00997-16 0388
SIMON, TOBY L M01RR00997-16 0355
SIMON, TOBY L M01RR00997-16 0357
SIMON, TOBY L M01RR00997-16 0360
SIMON, TOBY L M01RR00997-16 0395
SIMON, TOBY L M01RR00997-16 0407
SIMON, TOBY L M01RR00997-16 0402
SIMON, TOBY L M01RR00997-16 0403
SIMON, TOBY L R01HL36158-05
SIMONE, ALBERT J G12RR03061-06
SIMONE, JOSEPH V P30CA21765-14
SIMONE, JOSEPH V S03RR03167-11
SIMONE, JOSEPH V S07RR05584-27
SIMONE, JOSEPH V S15CA55997-01
SIMONI, ROBERT D R01HL26502-11
SIMONI, ROBERT D R37GM18539-21
SIMONI, ROBERT D S10RR06513-01
SIMONS S07RR05380-30 0895
SIMONS, ANNE S07RR07080-26 0316
SIMONS, DANIEL J R01NS19950-09
SIMONS, ELIZABETH R P01AI28408-02 9001
SIMONS, ELIZABETH R P01HL19717-15 0051
SIMONS, ELIZABETH R R01AG10684-01
SIMONS, ELIZABETH R R01DK31056-10
SIMONS, JONATHAN W K11CA01495-02
SIMONS, KURT R01EY07577-02
SIMONS, KURT R01EY07990-03
SIMONS, R P50MH48165-02 0004
SIMONS, ROBERT S07RR07009-26 0944
SIMONS, ROBERT F S07RR07016-18 0353
SIMONS, ROBERT W R01GM35322-07
SIMONS, RONALD L R01HD27724-01
SIMONS, S S Z01DK58002-16
SIMONSON, DONALD C M01RR02635-07 0287
SIMONSON, DONALD C M01RR02635-07 0288
SIMONSON, DONALD C R01DK43505-01A1
SIMPKINS, JAMES W P01AG10485-01
SIMPKINS, JAMES W P01AG10485-01 0004
SIMPKINS, JAMES W S07RR05573-13
SIMPKINS, JAMES W S15AG10237-01
SIMPSON-HERREN, LIND S07RR05676-15 0951
SIMPSON-HERREN, LINDA P01CA34200-09 0014
SIMPSON, D DWAYNE R18DA06162-03
SIMPSON, D L Z01NS02086-18
SIMPSON, DAVID M R01NS28630-01A1
SIMPSON, DIANE M R01CA52977-02
SIMPSON, E RAND U10EY06839-06
SIMPSON, EVAN R P50HD11149-14 0009
SIMPSON, EVAN R R01AG08174-04
SIMPSON, EVAN R R01CA51119-02
SIMPSON, EVAN R R01HD13234-13
SIMPSON, GEORGE P50MH40380-07 0002
SIMPSON, GEORGE M R01MH47162-01
SIMPSON, GREGORY V R01NS27900-02
SIMPSON, JOHN I P01NS13742-15 0011
SIMPSON, LANCE L R01NS22153-08
SIMPSON, LARRY R37AI09102-23
SIMPSON, LARRY S10RR06456-01
SIMPSON, MARCUS B K07HL02339-02
SIMPSON, MELVIN V R01AI29905-01A1
SIMPSON, N Z01CL30002-01
SIMPSON, PATRICIA J. P01HL30616-09 0007
SIMPSON, PAUL C, JR R01HL42150-03
SIMPSON, R T Z01DK15100-21
SIMPSON, ROSS J, JR R01HL44157-03
SIMS, COLIN R44CA42615-03
SIMS, FRED N01LM03509-02
SIMS, GRETHA P60HL38737-04 0004
SIMS, KATHERINE B K11HD00824-06
SIMS, LESLIE B S15ES05834-01
SIMS, PETER J R01HL36061-07
SIMS, PETER J R01HL36946-05
SIMS, RONALD C P42ES04922-03 0005
SINAIKO, ALAN R R01HL34659-06S1
SINAKI, M M01RR00585-20 0387
SINCLAIR, N A P42ES04940-02 0008
SINCLAIR, PETER R R01CA25012-13
SINDEL, LAWRENCE P60HL38639-04 0004
SINDELAR, JODY L R01AA08394-02
SINDELAR, W F Z01CM06654-14
SINDEN, RICHARD R P01ES05652-01 0002
SINDEN, RICHARD R R01GM37677-04A1
SINDEN, RICHARD R S07RR05408-30 0939
SINENSKY, MICHAEL S07RR05964-06 0756
SINENSKY, MICHAEL S07RR05964-06 0762
SINENSKY, MICHAEL S R01DK40804-03
SINENSKY, MICHAEL S S15HD28741-01
SINEX, DONAL G R01DC00341-06
SINEX, DONAL G S07RR05834-12 0546
SING, C F M01RR00585-20 0537
SING, CHARLES F P60HL16008-19 9001
SING, CHARLES F R01HL39107-05
SINGER, A Z01CB09268-04
SINGER, A Z01CB09273-04
SINGER, A Z01CB09275-04
SINGER, ALAN G R01HD19764-08
SINGER, ALAN G S07RR05825-12 0515
SINGER, BEA A R01CA42736-07
SINGER, BEA A R01CA47723-04
SINGER, BURTON H S07RR05443-30 0993
SINGER, BURTON H S07RR05443-30
SINGER, BURTON H S15AR41245-01
SINGER, D Z01CB09270-08
SINGER, D Z01CB09279-06
SINGER, D Z01CB09285-05
SINGER, DANIEL E S07RR05381-30 0795
SINGER, FREDERICK R M01RR00043-31 0084
SINGER, FREDERICK R M01RR00043-31 0442
SINGER, HAROLD A R01HL40992-04
SINGER, JACK W P01CA18029-16 0020
SINGER, JACK W P01CA47748-03 0008
SINGER, JACK W R01HL31782-08
SINGER, KAY H P50AR39162-05 9001
SINGER, LYNN T R01HL38193-03
SINGER, M F Z01CB05244-14
SINGER, MICHAEL C S07RR07091-26 0769
SINGER, PAUL A R01DK40751-04
SINGER, PAUL A S07RR05876-09 0587
SINGER, ROBERT H R01HD18066-08
SINGER, S P41RR04050-03 9001
SINGER, S JONATHAN P01AI23287-06 0005
SINGER, S JONATHAN R01GM15971-24
SINGER, THOMAS P P01HL16251-18 0007
SINGER, THOMAS P P01HL16251-18 0013
SINGER, THOMAS P P01HL16251-18
SINGER, THOMAS P P01HL16251-18 0014
SINGER, THOMAS P P01HL16251-18 0016
SINGERMAN, LAWRENCE J U10EY07788-04
SINGERMAN, LAWRENCE J U10EY02554-12
SINGH, ASHOK K R01DK35804-08
SINGH, HARINDER P01CA19266-14A1 0024
SINGH, INDERJIT R01NS22576-06
SINGH, JARNAIL S03RR03493-03
SINGH, JARNAIL S14GM02867-05
SINGH, MANBIR P41RR01861-07 0007
SINGH, MUKUL S07RR05396-30 0768
SINGH, N K Z01BB02004-02
SINGH, POMILA P01DK35608-06A1 9003
SINGH, POMILA R01CA38651-05
SINGH, RAJ K S07RR05676-15 0949
SINGH, RAJ K S07RR05676-15 0961
SINGH, SATPAL S07RR05454-29 0883
SINGH, SHIVA P R15AI31205-01
SINGH, SHIVA P S03RR03403-07
SINGH, SHIVENDRA V R29CA50638-02
SINGH, U. C P01GM38794-05 0004
SINGHAL, PRAVIN C R01DA06753-01
SINGLETARY, KEITH W R29AA08584-01A1
SINGLETON, DANIEL A R01GM45617-01
SINGMASTER-HERNANDEZ, KAREN A S06GM08192-1
SINHA, B K Z01CM06523-06
SINHA, MADHUR P01DK36296-05 0003
SINHA, MADHUR K P01DK36296-05 0004
SINHA, UMA R43HL47268-01
SININGER, YVONNE S R29DC00021-02
SINNING, ALLAN R S07RR05386-30 0595
SINNOTT, JOAN M K04DC00042-02
SINNOTT, MICHAEL L R01GM42469-03
SINOWAY, LAWRENCE C S07RR05680-23 0913
SINOWAY, LAWRENCE I K08HL01744-05
SINOWAY, LAWRENCE I R29HL44667-02
SINSHEIMER, JOSEPH E R01ES03345-11
SINSHEIMER, JOSEPH E R01ES05047-02
SINSHEIMER, ROBERT S07RR07099-25 0391
SINYA, Y N S07RR05876-09 0588
SIOSHANSI, PIRAN N43DK12275-00
SIOSHANSI, PIRAN N43NS12313-00
SIOSHANSI, PIRAN R43HL46097-01
SIOSHANSI, PIRAN R43HL47255-01
SIOUFI, HABIB A R43AI30814-01A1
SIPE, JACK C M01RR00833-17 0170
SIPE, JEAN D R01AG09006-02
SIPERSTEIN, GARY N R37HD14772-09
SIPERSTEIN, MARVIN D R01CA15979-18
SIPES, I GLENN N01ES85230-04
SIPES, I GLENN S07RR05605-13
SIPIN, A J R43HL46637-01
SIPOS, TIBOR R43DK44047-01
SIPOS, TIBOR R43DK44049-01
SIPPEL, C JEFFREY K08HD00954-02

SIPSKI, MARCA L S07RR05393-30 0905
SIRAGANIAN, R Z01DE00034-23
SIRAGANIAN, R Z01DE00290-12
SIRAGY, HELMY M01RR00847-18 0506
SIRBASKU, DAVID A R01CA38024-07
SIREN, ANA-LEENA R01NS28225-03
SIREN, ANNA-LEENA K R01DA07212-01A1
SIRICA, ALPHONSE E R01CA39225-07
SIRIS, E M01RR00645-20 0422
SIRIS, E M01RR00645-20 0430
SIRIS, ELIZABETH M01RR00645-20 0351
SIRIS, ETHEL M01RR00645-20 0395
SIRIS, ETHEL M01RR00645-20 0504
SIRIS, ETHEL M01RR00645-20 0494
SIROIS, DAVID A K15DE00227-05
SIROTNAK, FRANCIS M P01CA18856-16
SIROTNAK, FRANCIS M P01CA18856-16 0008
SIROTNAK, FRANCIS M P01CA18856-16 9001
SIROTNAK, FRANCIS M R01CA22764-14
SIROTNAK, FRANCIS M R01CA46673-04
SIROTNAK, FRANK P01CA34200-09 0012
SIROVER, MICHAEL A R01CA29414-10
SISCOVICK, DAVID S07RR05714-21 0126
SISCOVICK, DAVID S N01HD13107-00
SISCOVICK, DAVID S R01HL41993-02
SISCOVICK, DAVID S R01HL42456-02
SISCOVICK, DAVID S S07RR05432-30 0235
SISK, CHERYL L K04HD00950-01
SISK, CHERYL L R01HD26483-02
SISK, CHERYL L S07RR07049-26 0437
SISKEN, BETTY S07RR05374-30 0744
SISKEN, BETTY F R01NS29621-01
SISKEN, J E P50AG05144-08 0006
SISKIND, GREGORY W S07RR05396-30
SISKIND, GREGORY W S15DA07798-01
SISKIND, GREGORY W S15HL47697-01
SISSON, JAMES C M01RR00042-31 0337
SISSON, JAMES C M01RR00042-31 0610
SISSON, JOSEPH H R29AA08769-01
SISSON, REBECCA S07RR05604-14 0682
SISTLER, AUDREY B S06GM08025-21 0021
SITKOVSKY, M V Z01AI00427-07
SITRIN, M P30DK42086-02 0006
SITRIN, MICHAEL D P30DK26678-12
SITRIN, MICHAEL D P30DK26678-12 9012
SITRIN, ROBERT G R01HL39672-04
SITTIG, DEAN F R29LM05284-01
SITZMANN, JAMES V R29HL39683-04
SIU, A S07RR05710-21 0029
SIU, ALBERT P60AG10415-01 0001
SIU, ALBERT L K08AG00342-05
SIU, CYNTHIA O P50HL17655-17 9011
SIVAM, SUBBIAH P R29NS26063-04
SIVARAMAKRISHNAN, MA S07RR05511-29 0503
SIVITZ, WILLIAM M01RR00059-30 0710
SIX, ERICH W R01AI04043-30
SIXBEY, JOHN W R01CA38877-07A1
SIXBEY, JOHN W R01CA52258-02
SJOKA, NICHOLAS P30CA44579-04A1 9009
SKACH, WILLIAM R K11CA01614-01
SKALAK, RICHARD P01HL43026-02 0005
SKALAK, THOMAS C K04HL02372-02
SKALAK, THOMAS C R29HL39680-04
SKALKA, ANNA M R35CA47486-02
SKALKA, ANNA MARIE S07RR05539-29 0546
SKARE, JAMES C R01CA49629-03
SKARLATOS, S I Z01HL02832-01
SKATRUD, JAMES B M01RR03186-06 0059
SKATRUD, JAMES B P01HL42242-04 0001
SKAVENSKI, ALEXANDER S07RR07143-20 0635
SKEATH, PERRY R R43CA53993-02
SKEEL, ROLAND T U10CA39227-07
SKEHAN, P Z01CM07192-01
SKENE, J H PATE R01EY07397-06
SKENE, J PATE R01NS20178-07A1
SKIAS, DEMETRIOS S07RR05369-30 0586
SKIBBA, JOSEPH L R01CA41316-07
SKIBO, EDWARD B K04CA01349-04
SKIDGEL, RANDAL A R29DK41431-03
SKILLING, STEPHEN R K11CA01342-04
SKINNER, JAMES E R01NS27745-03
SKINNER, MARGARET W R01DC00581-02
SKINNER, MARTHA M01RR00533-23 0142
SKINNER, MARTHA R01AR40414-01A1
SKINNER, MICHAEL K R01HD20583-06
SKINNER, ROBERT D R01NS21981-06
SKINNER, SHERI M S07RR05425-30 0768
SKINNER, WILLIAM F R29DA05831-03
SKITA, VICTOR R29HL45284-01A1
SKLAR, CHARLES M01RR00096-30A1 0229
SKLAR, JEFFREY L P01CA49605-03 0003
SKLAR, JEFFREY LEWIS K04CA01189-06
SKLAR, JEFFREY LEWIS R01CA38621-08
SKLAR, LARRY A M01RR00997-16 0416
SKLAR, LARRY A P01GM37696-05 0004
SKLAR, LARRY A P01HL43026-02 0002
SKLAR, LARRY A R01AI19032-10
SKLAR, MARSHALL D R01CA51826-02
SKLAREW, ROBERT J R55CA51823-01A1
SKOFF, ROBERT P P50AA07606-04 0007
SKOFF, ROBERT P R01NS15338-14
SKOFF, ROBERT P R01NS18883-09
SKOLL, M AMANDA M01RR00211-27 0314
SKOLNICK, JEFFREY R01GM37408-05A1
SKOLNICK, MALCOLM H R03DA06869-01A1
SKOLNICK, MARK R01CA36362-08
SKOLNICK, MARK H P01CA48711-02
SKOLNICK, MARK H P01CA48711-02 0004
SKOLNICK, MICHAEL P01CA26803-11 0002
SKOLNICK, P Z01DK58501-05
SKOLNIK, DEBORAH C G07LM05390-01
SKOLNIK, EDWARD K11DK01927-03
SKOLNIK, PAUL R K08AI01046-01
SKOLNIK, PAUL R M01RR00054-30 0415
SKORTON, DAVID P50HL32295-07
SKORTON, DAVID J P50HL32295-07 9002
SKORTON, DAVID J P50HL32295-07 0011
SKORTON, DAVID J P50HL32295-07 0008
SKOULTCHI, ARTHUR P60HL38655-04 0006
SKOULTCHI, ARTHUR I R25CA47779-04
SKOULTCHI, ARTHUR I R37CA16368-18
SKOWRON, GAIL R01AI32439-01
SKRINSKA, VICTOR A R29HL38990-05
SKUSE, GARY R R29CA55173-01
SKUTA, GREGORY L U10EY06827-05
SKYLER, JAY S P01HL36588-06 0003
SLABAUGH, MARY B S07RR07079-26 0282
SLACK, JAMES L K11AR01846-02
SLADE, ARIETTA R01HD24676-03
SLADEK, CELIA S07RR05403-30 0826
SLADEK, CELIA D R01NS27975-02
SLADEK, CELIA D R35AG09016-02 0006
SLADEK, JOHN R P01NS24032-06 0001
SLADIK, NORMAN P01CA21737-14 0008
SLAGLE, BETTY L R01CA54557-01
SLAKEY, LINDA L R01HL31854-07
SLAMA, JAMES T R01GM32821-07
SLAMON, DENNIS J P01CA36827-08
SLAPAK, CHRISTOPHER A K08CA01613-01
SLATER, JAY E R29AI29428-01A1
SLATER, JONATHAN S R01CA52994-02
SLATER, N TRAVERSE P01NS17489-10 0012
SLATKIN, MONTGOMERY W R01GM40282-04
SLATOPOLSKY, EDUARDO P01DK09976-27 9002
SLATOPOLSKY, EDUARDO P01DK09976-27 0020
SLATTERY, JOHN T R01NS30108-01
SLATTERY, MARTHA L R01CA48998-01A2
SLAUGHTER, CLIVE A S07RR07175-15 0444
SLAUGHTER, MALCOLM M R01EY05725-08
SLAUGHTER, RICHARD L S07RR07051-26 0736
SLAVIN, JOANNE L P01CA50305-02 0004
SLAVIN, RAYMOND G R01HL30652-08
SLAVKIN, HAROLD C P50DE09165-03
SLAVKIN, HAROLD C P50DE09165-03 0004
SLAVKIN, HAROLD C R01DE06425-08
SLAVKIN, HAROLD C R37DE09002-02
SLAYMAN, CAROLYN W R01GM37279-06
SLAYMAN, CAROLYN W R37GM15761-23
SLAYTER, HENREY S P30CA06516-28 9005
SLAYTER, HENRY S P01HL33014-07 9001
SLAYTER, HENRY S P01HL33014-07 0006
SLEDGE, CLEMENT B M01RR02635-07 0237
SLEDGE, CLEMENT B R01AR35906-07
SLEDGE, WILLIAM H R03MH47023-02
SLEDGE, WILLIAM H R18MH47638-02
SLEDGE, WILLIAM H S07RR05358-30 0499
SLEGEL, DUANE E S07RR05426-30 0148
SLEIGHT, RICHARD G R29GM39035-03
SLEIGHT, RICHARD G S07RR05408-30 0940
SLEMMON, J RANDALL R35AG09016-02 0004
SLENKER, SUZANNE N01HD13135-01
SLEPECKY, NORMA P01DC00380-05 0003
SLEVIN, JOHN T M01RR02602-07 0056
SLEVIN, JOHN T. P01AG05119-07 0006
SLICHTER, SHERRILL J M01RR00037-31 0505
SLICHTER, SHERRILL J R18HL45265-02 0003
SLICHTER, SHERRILL J R18HL45265-02
SLICHTER, SHERRILL J U01HL42799-03
SLIGAR, STEPHEN G R01GM31756-10
SLIGAR, STEPHEN G R01GM33775-07
SLINKER, BRYAN K R01HL37005-06
SLIZOFSKI, WALTER S07RR05413-30 0986
SLOAN, DONALD L S06GM08168-13 0009
SLOAN, FRANK A R01AA08354-02
SLOAN, FRANK A R01AG09468-01
SLOAN, FRANK A R01HS06499-02
SLOAN, GARY L S07RR07151-13 0520
SLOAN, LLOYD R24MH47199-02 0001
SLOAN, MICHAEL A R01DA06625-01A2
SLOAN, PATRICIA R24MH47187-02 0004
SLOAN, RICHARD S07RR05650-25 0110
SLOAN, TOD B S07RR05654-24 0142
SLOANE, BONNIE F R01CA36481-08
SLOANE, BONNIE F R01CA48210-04
SLOANE, DOUGLAS M S07RR07123-22 0594
SLOANE, PHILIP D K08AG00341-05
SLOANE, PHILIP D U01AG10313-01
SLOBIN, LAWRENCE I R01GM25434-11
SLOBODA, ROGER D R01GM43982-02
SLOCUM, H P30CA16056-16 9020
SLOCUM, HARRY K P01CA21071-14 9006
SLOMIANY, AMALIA R01AA05858-10
SLOMIANY, BRONISLAW L R01DE05666-12
SLOMIANY, BRONISLAW L R01DK21684-15
SLONE, MICHAEL A P01NS16332-09A2 0002
SLONIM-NEVO, VERED R01MH45306-03
SLOPIS, JOHN M S07RR05745-19 0226
SLOTKIN, THEODORE P50DA05303-03 0004
SLOTKIN, THEODORE A R01HD09713-15
SLOTNICK, BURTON M R01DC01266-01
SLOTS, JORGEN P50DE07118-07 0002
SLOVAK, MARILYN S07RR05471-29 0594
SLOVIK, DAVID M M01RR01066-14 0112
SLOVITER, HENRY A S07RR07083-26 0495
SLOVITER, ROBERT S07RR05649-25 0798
SLOVITER, ROBERT S07RR05649-25 0790
SLOVITER, ROBERT S R01NS18201-07
SLOVITER, ROBERT S R01NS28140-02
SLOWIACZEK, LOUISA M R29NS29286-01
SLUDER, GREENFIELD R01GM30758-10
SLUSS, PATRICK M R01HD19302-07
SLUSS, PATRICK M U54HD29164-01 0005
SLY, LINDA N01CP15674-01
SLY, WILLIAM S R01DK40163-04
SLY, WILLIAM S R37GM34182-08
SMAIL, EDWIN H P01AI28408-02 0002
SMALDONE, GERALD P50AI16337-13 0006
SMALDONE, GERALD C U01AI25893-05 0006
SMALE, STEPHEN T R29DK43726-01
SMALHEISER, NEIL P01HD09402-16 0007
SMALHEISER, NEIL R R29NS26055-03
SMALL BUSINESS ADMIN N01DA12215-00
SMALL, DONALD M P01HL26335-11A1
SMALL, DONALD M P01HL26335-11A1 0002
SMALL, ENOCH W R01GM25663-14
SMALL, GARY P30AG10123-01 9004
SMALL, GARY W R29MH46424-02
SMALL, GERALD J. P01CA49210-03 0003
SMALL, JEANNE RUDZKI R29GM41415-04
SMALL, JOYCE G R37MH40930-06
SMALL, KENT W K11EY00313-03
SMALL, MICHAEL S07RR05393-30 0906
SMALL, MICHAEL B R55CA53136-01A1
SMALL, STEVEN L K08DC00054-01
SMALLEY, RICHARD V M01RR03186-06 0032
SMALLEY, RICHARD V M01RR03186-06 0033
SMALLEY, SUSAN S07RR05756-18 0303
SMARRELLI, J S07RR07210-09 0677
SMART, ROBERT C R29CA46637-02
SMART, ROBERT C. P01ES00044-26 0009
SMEEDING, TIMOTHY P01AG09743-01 0002
SMEEDING, TIMOTHY P01AG09743-01 0003
SMEEDLING, TIMOTHY M. P01AG07669-03 9002
SMELTZER SUZANNE C S07RR07059-26 0838
SMELTZER, SUZANNE C S07RR07059-26 0835
SMERDON, MICHAEL J R01ES02614-12
SMERDON, MICHAEL J R01ES04106-05
SMITH-GILL, S Z01CB08950-09
SMITH-HARRISON, LEON S07RR05430-30 0227
SMITH, ABIGAIL L P40RR00393-24 0004
SMITH, ABIGAIL L R24RR04507-04
SMITH, ALAN E P01CA50661-03 0002
SMITH, ALAN E R01HL47120-01
SMITH, AMOS B P41RR01348-10 0006
SMITH, AMOS B, III R01CA19033-16
SMITH, AMOS B, III R01CA22807-14
SMITH, AMOS B, III R01GM29028-11
SMITH, AMOS B, III R01NS18254-08A1
SMITH, ANDREW T S07RR07112-24 0431
SMITH, ANN R01DK37463-06
SMITH, ANNE R01DC00559-03
SMITH, ANNE S07RR07032-26 0045
SMITH, ARNOLD L M01RR00037-31 0506
SMITH, ARNOLD L M01RR00037-31 0467
SMITH, ARNOLD L M01RR00037-31 0494
SMITH, ARNOLD L M01RR00037-31 0513
SMITH, ARNOLD L M01RR00037-31 0507
SMITH, ARNOLD L P50DK41978-03
SMITH, ARNOLD L S15AI32170-01
SMITH, ARNOLD L. P51RR00166-30 0119
SMITH, BARBARA A S07RR05944-04 0979
SMITH, BARBARA D R01HL41373-04
SMITH, BRENDA C K08DK01840-03
SMITH, BRENDA C S07RR05680-23 0914
SMITH, BRIAN R P01CA39542-07 9002
SMITH, BRIAN R R01HL47193-01
SMITH, BRIAN R S06GM08139-17 0059
SMITH, BRUCE D R01CA51077-01A1
SMITH, C Z01HL00636-10
SMITH, C B Z01MH00889-12
SMITH, C B Z01MH02536-02
SMITH, C D M01RR00585-20 0527
SMITH, C L Z01NS02788-03
SMITH, C WAYNE P01HL42550-02 0003
SMITH, CARL H R01HD07562-18
SMITH, CAROL E K07NR00020-02
SMITH, CASSANDRA P30CA13696-19 9021
SMITH, CASSANDRA P30CA13696-19 9018
SMITH, CHARLES B P50DA00254-20 0011
SMITH, CHARLES B R01DA05272-04
SMITH, CHARLES D K08NS01421-02
SMITH, CHARLES J R01AI28884-01A1
SMITH, CHARLES V R01GM44263-02
SMITH, CLIFFORD L S06GM08023-20 0002
SMITH, CLIFFORD L S06GM08023-20
SMITH, CRAIG H M01RR00037-31 0464

SMITH, CRAIG H U10EY07694-04
SMITH, DANIEL J P50DE07009-08 0004
SMITH, DANIEL J R01DE06153-09
SMITH, DANIEL J R29DK38883-04
SMITH, DAVID P01DC00347-06 0008
SMITH, DAVID F R01GM45914-01
SMITH, DAVID F R44AI28628-02A1
SMITH, DAVID G P51RR00169-30 0160
SMITH, DAVID G P51RR00169-30 0161
SMITH, DAVID G R24RR05090-04
SMITH, DAVID I R01CA48031-04
SMITH, DAVID I S06GM08167-13 0049
SMITH, DAVID L R01EY07609-03
SMITH, DAVID V R01DC00066-02
SMITH, DAVID V R01DC00353-06
SMITH, DAVID W P01NS05820-26 9003
SMITH, DEAN O R01NS13600-14
SMITH, DEAN O S07RR07098-26
SMITH, DIANE B P60HL15996-19 9004
SMITH, EARL L, III R01EY03611-10
SMITH, EDDIE C S07RR07078-18
SMITH, ELIOT R R01MH46840-01A1
SMITH, ELIZABETH M R01AA08311-03
SMITH, ELIZABETH M R01AA08335-02
SMITH, ELIZABETH M R01MH40025-03A2
SMITH, ELIZABETH M U01AA08804-02
SMITH, ELSKE V S03RR03275-10
SMITH, ELSKE V S07RR07204-11
SMITH, ELVIN E S07RR05814-12
SMITH, EMIL R S07RR05712-20 0114
SMITH, ERIC M R01DK41034-03
SMITH, ERIC P R01HD28430-01
SMITH, ERIC P S07RR05408-30 0941
SMITH, EUCLID O P51RR00165-31 0169
SMITH, EVA D S07RR05776-11 0400
SMITH, FRANCES I R29DK38381-06
SMITH, FRANCINE R R01DK41971-03
SMITH, FRED W R19DA06456-03
SMITH, G DAVID R01DK41387-03
SMITH, G N P50AR39250-05 0001
SMITH, G N P50AR39250-05 9003
SMITH, G RICHARD K02MH00843-03
SMITH, G RICHARD P50MH48197-02
SMITH, GARY J P01CA42765-04 0006
SMITH, GEORGE P R01GM41478-03
SMITH, GEORGIA F K04AI00955-03
SMITH, GEORGIA F R29AI24915-04
SMITH, GEORGIA F S07RR07112-24 0414
SMITH, GERALD R R01GM31693-10
SMITH, GERALD R R01GM32194-09
SMITH, GERARD P K05MH00149-10
SMITH, GERARD P R01MH40010-07
SMITH, GERARD P R37MH15455-21
SMITH, GORDON S R29AA07700-04
SMITH, HAMILTON O R01AI27783-03
SMITH, HAMILTON O S07RR05378-30 0015
SMITH, HAROLD C S07RR05403-30 0827
SMITH, HELENE S P01CA44768-05
SMITH, HELENE S P01CA44768-05 9005
SMITH, HELENE S P01CA44768-05 0002
SMITH, HOWARD E P30HD05797-20 9009
SMITH, IAN M M01RR00059-30 0663
SMITH, ISSAR R01GM19693-17
SMITH, ISSAR R01GM32651-09
SMITH, J W Z01CM09291-06
SMITH, J W Z01CM09308-05
SMITH, J W Z01CM09332-03
SMITH, J W Z01CM09350-02
SMITH, J W Z01CM09354-02
SMITH, J W Z01CM09365-01
SMITH, J W Z01CM09366-01
SMITH, JACK W, JR R01HL38776-05
SMITH, JACK W, JR R01LM04298-06
SMITH, JACKSON B R01HD25629-03
SMITH, JAMES B R01DA01987-11
SMITH, JAMES C R01AG04932-07
SMITH, JAMES E K05DA00114-02
SMITH, JAMES E P50DA06634-01A1
SMITH, JAMES E P50DA06634-01A1 0005
SMITH, JAMES E P50DA06634-01A1 9002
SMITH, JAMES E R01DA03628-08
SMITH, JAMES E R37DA01999-14
SMITH, JAMES P P50HD12639-12
SMITH, JAMES P P50HD12639-12 0018
SMITH, JAMES P R01HD27303-01
SMITH, JAMES P S07RR05710-21
SMITH, JAMES P S07RR05710-21 0018
SMITH, JAMES R P01AG07123-04
SMITH, JAMES R P01AG07123-04 0001
SMITH, JAMES R P01AG07123-04 9001
SMITH, JAMES W N01AI72647-11
SMITH, JAMES W U01AI25859-05 0005
SMITH, JANE E R01AA08331-01A1
SMITH, JANET L R01DK42303-02
SMITH, JEANNE A P60HL28381-09 0003
SMITH, JEFFREY B P50DK39258-05 0005
SMITH, JEFFREY B R01ES05234-02
SMITH, JEFFREY B R01HL44408-01A1
SMITH, JEFFREY C K04HL02204-04
SMITH, JEFFREY C R01HL40959-04
SMITH, JERRY C S07RR07171-08 0159
SMITH, JILL P R29CA50303-03
SMITH, JO-ANNE A P01AR38933-05 0004
SMITH, JOHN S07RR05336-29 0298
SMITH, JOHN A S07RR05486-29 0060
SMITH, JOHN M R01AI20068-09
SMITH, JOHN M S07RR05939-07 0728
SMITH, JOHN M S07RR05939-07 0722
SMITH, JOHN R S03RR03345-09
SMITH, JOSEPH A M01RR00064-27 0372
SMITH, JUDITH L R01NS19864-09
SMITH, KELLY L R43AA08961-01
SMITH, KENDALL A R01AI32031-16
SMITH, KENDRIC C R55CA50220-01A2
SMITH, KENNETH M01RR00997-16 0264
SMITH, KENNETH A S07RR07047-26
SMITH, KENNETH J M01RR00997-16 0387
SMITH, KENNETH J M01RR00997-16 0371
SMITH, KENNETH S K S06GM08139-17 0073
SMITH, KEVIN M R01HL22252-14
SMITH, L DENNIS R01HD04229-22
SMITH, LEWIS J M01RR00048-30 0156
SMITH, LEWIS J M01RR00048-30 0145
SMITH, LEWIS J P50AI11403-19 0012
SMITH, LINDA B S07RR07031-26 0108
SMITH, LLOYD S07RR05684-23 0179
SMITH, LLOYD M R01HG00321-03
SMITH, LOUIS C P30HG00210-01 0002
SMITH, LOUIS C P50AG08664-03 0007
SMITH, LOUIS C P60HL27341-10 0007
SMITH, LYNWOOD H R13DK44205-01
SMITH, M SUSAN R01HD14643-11
SMITH, M SUSAN S07RR05416-30 0575
SMITH, MALCOLM M R01GM28920-11
SMITH, MARGARET M S07RR07079-26 0287
SMITH, MARION E R01NS02785-32
SMITH, MARJORIE N01LM93503-11
SMITH, MARK SCOTT S07RR05655-21 0823
SMITH, MARTIN A R01NS27563-03
SMITH, MARTYN P30ES01896-13 9032
SMITH, MARTYN P42ES04705-05 0001
SMITH, MARTYN T P42ES04705-05
SMITH, MICHAEL P51RR00165-31 9014
SMITH, MICHAEL S07RR07090-26 0479
SMITH, MICHAEL B P01NS23393-06 9001
SMITH, MICHAEL G R44HL43447-02
SMITH, MOYRA P50AA07606-04 0004
SMITH, NATHAN L R43HL46635-01
SMITH, ORVILLE A P01HL16910-18 0007
SMITH, ORVILLE A P51RR00166-30 0187
SMITH, ORVILLE A. P51RR00166-30 0073
SMITH, ORVILLE A. P51RR00166-30 0074
SMITH, P D Z01DE00392-08
SMITH, P D Z01RR10214-07
SMITH, P D Z01RR10349-02
SMITH, PETER G R01NS23502-06
SMITH, PETER K R01HL41087-04
SMITH, PHILIP C R01AG09594-01
SMITH, PHILIP C R29GM41828-03
SMITH, PHILIP HAROLD R29NS26285-04
SMITH, PHILIP J S07RR05448-30 0303
SMITH, PHILIP L P01AG04402-09 0003
SMITH, PHILIP L R01HL37379-05
SMITH, Q P50DE08489-04 0002
SMITH, Q R Z01AG00129-11
SMITH, R GRAHAM R03CA53284-02
SMITH, RANDALL P41LM05205-08 9006
SMITH, RANDALL P41LM05205-08 9008
SMITH, RICHARD M01RR00109-28 0372
SMITH, RICHARD H R44AI26438-03
SMITH, RICHARD T S15AI32211-01
SMITH, ROBERT G R01MH48168-01
SMITH, ROBERT J P50GM36428-07 0001
SMITH, ROBERT L P01DC00380-05 0002
SMITH, ROBERT V S07RR07097-26
SMITH, ROBERTA A R01CA48280-02
SMITH, ROGER P R01HL14127-29
SMITH, RONALD E R01EY06482-04
SMITH, RONALD E U10EY06496-07
SMITH, SCOTT D S07RR05788-15 0897
SMITH, SHELLEY D P60DC00982-02 0003
SMITH, SHELLY D P50HD27802-01S1 0004
SMITH, SHERYL S07RR05413-30 0992
SMITH, SHIRLEY H K11HL01596-05
SMITH, STANLEY D R29AG08820-02
SMITH, STEPHEN P50MH48108-01 0007
SMITH, STEPHEN J R01NS28587-01A1
SMITH, STEPHEN W S07RR07070-26 0461
SMITH, STEVEN S07RR07015-26 0604
SMITH, STEVEN M R01MH44730-03
SMITH, STEVEN O R01GM41412-03
SMITH, STEVEN S S07RR05471-29 0579
SMITH, STUART R01DK16073-17
SMITH, STUART R01DK42636-01A2
SMITH, STUART S15DK44709-01
SMITH, STUART W P01HL28982-10 9002
SMITH, SUZANNE MELEG S07RR05583-27 0641
SMITH, SUZANNE T S07RR05486-29 0058
SMITH, T G Z01NS02767-05
SMITH, TEMPLE P41LM05205-08 9002
SMITH, TEMPLE P41LM05205-08 9004
SMITH, TEMPLE F P41LM05205-08
SMITH, TEMPLE F S07RR05526-29 0101
SMITH, THOMAS S07RR05651-24 0143
SMITH, THOMAS E S06GM08016-21 0062
SMITH, THOMAS J R01GM10704-29
SMITH, THOMAS L S07RR05404-30 0859
SMITH, THOMAS W R37HL36141-07
SMITH, TIMOTHY D N01CM73719-05
SMITH, TIMOTHY W S07RR07092-26 0524
SMITH, VIVIANNE C R01EY07390-05
SMITH, W MCFATE N01HC48060-12
SMITH, WENDY A R01DK37435-06
SMITH, WILLIAM L R01DK42509-02
SMITH, WILLIAM L R37DK22042-14
SMITH, WILLIAM M R01HL33637-07
SMITH, WILLIS W S07RR05970-06 0781
SMITHIES, OLIVER R01HL37001-06
SMITHIES, OLIVER R37GM20069-20
SMITS, ALLAN W R15HL46428-01
SMOLEN, ANDREW R01HD21709-05
SMOLEN, ANDREW R01HD28114-01
SMOLEN, JAMES E R01DK32471-08
SMOLENSKY, MICHAEL H M01RR02558-07 0057
SMOLKA, ADAM S07RR05420-30 0044
SMOLKA, ADAM J R01DK43138-02
SMOLLER, BRUCE S07RR05353-30 0368
SMOOT, DUANE T S06GM08244-05 0026
SMOTHERMAN, WILLIAM P R01HD16102-10
SMOTHERMAN, WILLIAM P R01HD28231-01
SMOTKIN, DAVID R29CA47127-04
SMULSON, MARK E R01CA13195-17
SMULSON, MARK E R01CA25344-13
SMYER, MICHAEL S07RR07082-26 0308
SMYTH, KATHLEEN P50AG08012-04 0006
SMYTH, NANCY S07RR05938-07 0324
SMYTH, ROBERT J JR S07RR07048-26 0655
SMYTHE, CHEVES MCC M01RR02558-07 0059
SNAPE, WILLIAM A M01RR00425-22S3 0408
SNAPE, WILLIAM J M01RR00425-22S3 0460
SNAPE, WILLIAM J, JR P30DK36200-05S1
SNAPE, WILLIAM J, JR R01DK31147-09
SNAPKA, ROBERT M R29CA45208-05
SNAPPER, JAMES R R01HL27274-10
SNAPPER, JAMES R R01HL46971-01
SNEAD, MALCOLM L R01DE06988-07
SNEAD, MALCOLM L R01DE08678-03
SNEAD, ORLANDO C, III R01NS17117-10
SNEDEKER, JEFFREY D K11AI00759-05
SNELL, WILLIAM J R01GM25661-14
SNELLER, M Z01AI00590-02
SNELLING, LINDA K M01RR06022-02 0774
SNIDER, BARRY B R01GM46470-01
SNIDER, GORDON L P01HL19717-15 0008
SNIDER, MICHAEL T N01HR16053-00
SNIDER, WILLIAM P01NS17763-10 0013
SNIDER, WILLIAM D K08NS01202-05
SNODDERLY, D MAX R01EY06591-04
SNODDERLY, MAX P30EY03790-11 9004
SNODDERLY, MAX D S07RR05527-29 0518
SNODGRASS-PILLA, LYNN G07LM05338-01
SNODGRASS, HIRAM R R01DK43517-01A1
SNODGRASS, SAMUEL H R29DA06838-01
SNOOK, SANDRA S07RR05367-30 0571
SNOOK, SANDRA S R29DA07263-02
SNOW, ALAN P50AG05136-08 0007
SNOW, CATHERINE E P01HD23388-04
SNOW, CATHERINE E R13HD26455-01A1
SNOW, DEAN R S07RR07122-23 0095
SNOW, ELIZABETH T R01CA51825-02
SNOW, ELIZABETH T R29CA45664-05
SNOW, ELIZABETH T S07RR05399-30 0931
SNOW, JAMES B P01DC00161-11 9001
SNOW, JULIAN W R15HL40568-01A3
SNOW, MIKEL S07RR05356-30 0436
SNOW, PETER M R29NS28699-02
SNOWDEN, C Z01DE00527-01
SNOWDEN, C Z01DE00528-01
SNOWDEN, C B Z01DE00504-02
SNOWDEN, C B Z01DE00505-02
SNOWDEN, LONNIE R P50MH43694-04 0015
SNOWDEN, LONNIE R R01MH46618-02
SNOWDON, CHARLES T K05MH00177-15
SNOWDON, CHARLES T R01MH29775-14
SNOWDON, DAVID A R01AG09862-02
SNOWDOWNE, KEN S07RR05301-21 0735
SNYDER-KELLER, ABIGAIL M R01MH46577-01A1
SNYDER-MACKLER, LYNN S07RR07016-18 0361
SNYDER, ABRAHAM P01NS06833-25 0027
SNYDER, ANN C R15HD24224-01A3
SNYDER, ANN K R01AA08029-03
SNYDER, CARROL A. P42ES04895-03 0002
SNYDER, CARROLL A. P42ES04895-03 9002
SNYDER, DAVID S07RR05471-29 0588
SNYDER, DONALD L P41RR01380-10 9003
SNYDER, EDWARD L K07HL02035-05
SNYDER, EVAN Y K08NS01403-03
SNYDER, FRED L R01DK42804-01A1
SNYDER, FRED L R01HL35495-05
SNYDER, FRED L S07RR05746-19 0889
SNYDER, FRED L S07RR05746-19 0888
SNYDER, GRAYSON H R01GM26715-13
SNYDER, GREG S07RR07013-26 0965
SNYDER, GREGORY K R01HL32894-06
SNYDER, JEANNE M P01HD13912-12 0006
SNYDER, JEANNE M R01HL32650-07

SNYDER, MARK R01MH47673-01A1
SNYDER, MICHAEL P01HG00365-04 0003
SNYDER, MICHAEL S07RR07015-26 0600
SNYDER, MICHAEL P R01GM36494-06
SNYDER, PETER J M01RR00040-31 0129
SNYDER, PETER J M01RR00040-31 0391
SNYDER, PETER J M01RR00040-31 0210
SNYDER, PETER J M01RR00040-31 0309
SNYDER, PETER J M01RR00040-31 0272
SNYDER, PETER J R01AR41425-01
SNYDER, PETER J R01DK42139-02
SNYDER, ROBERT P30ES05022-04 9001
SNYDER, ROBERT S07RR05909-08 0950
SNYDER, ROBERT W R03EY09202-01
SNYDER, SCOTT S07RR05387-30 0612
SNYDER, SCOTT W K11HD00947-01
SNYDER, SOLOMON H K05DA00074-12
SNYDER, SOLOMON H P50DA00266-20
SNYDER, SOLOMON H P50DA00266-20 0006
SNYDER, SOLOMON H R37MH18501-22
SNYDER, WILLIAM M01RR00633-19 0150
SNYDERMAN, RALPH P01CA29589-10 0003
SNYDERMAN, RALPH S07RR05405-30
SNYDERMAN, RALPH S15HL47779-01
SNYDERMAN, RALPH J M01RR00030-30
SNYDERMAN, SELMA M01RR00096-30A1 0316
SNYDERMAN, SELMA M01RR00096-30A1 0268
SNYDERMAN, SELMA M01RR00096-30A1 0270
SNYDERS, DIRK J S07RR05424-30 0110
SNYDERWINE, E G Z01CP05496-07
SNYDMAN, DAVID M01RR00054-30 0397
SNYDMAN, DAVID R M01RR00054-30 0341
SNYDMAN, DAVID R R01DK31389-10
SO, ANTERO G R01DK26206-12
SO, MAGADALENE Y H R01AI22983-06
SO, MAGDALENE H R01AI20845-09
SOARES, MARCELO B R55HD28422-01
SOARES, MICHAEL J R01HD20676-05
SOAVE, R M01RR00047-31 0304
SOAVE, ROSEMARY M01RR00047-31 0437
SOAVE, ROSEMARY U01AI25917-04 0002
SOBAL, JEFFERY R29DK42787-03
SOBEL, BURTON E P50HL17646-17 9001
SOBEL, BURTON E P50HL17646-17 0009
SOBEL, BURTON E P50HL17646-17
SOBEL, BURTON E. P01HL13851-29 0007
SOBEL, EUGENE L. P50AG05142-08 9008
SOBEL, JOAN H R01HL45936-02
SOBEL, M E Z01CB09131-07
SOBEL, MICHAEL R29HL39903-04
SOBEL, RAYMOND A R01NS26773-03
SOBELL, LINDA C R01AA08593-01A1
SOBERMAN, ROY J P01HL36110-07 0006
SOBERMAN, ROY J R01AI22563-07
SOBERS, CARLTON N01CM73720-07
SOBIN, SIDNEY S MD PHD R01HL42084-03
SOBKOWICZ, HANNA M R01DC00517-04
SOBSEY, MARK S07RR05450-30 0347
SOCCI, ROBIN R S07RR05365-30 0100
SOCIAL AND SCIENTIFIC SYSTS, I N01MH80019-0
SOCIOTECHNICAL RES APPLS, INC N01TI10011-0
SOCKLER, JAMES M S07RR07127-23 0487
SOCKRIDER, MARIANNA M K07HL02606-01
SOCRANSKY, SIGMUND S P01DE02847-23
SOCRANSKY, SIGMUND S P50DE04881-14
SOCRANSKY, SIGMUND S P50DE04881-14 0001
SOCRANSKY, SIGMUND S P50DE04881-14 0002
SODERBERG, LEE S R01DA06662-01A1
SODERHOLM, KARL-JOHAN M R01DE09292-01A1
SODERHOLM, SIDNEY C R01OH02772-02
SODERHOLM, SIDNEY C R29ES04433-05
SODERLAND, CARL R43HL46049-01A1
SODERLING, THOMAS R R01DK17808-18
SODERLING, THOMAS R R01GM41292-04
SODERLING, THOMAS R R01NS27037-03
SODERQUIST, JOHN A S06GM08102-20 0051
SODETZ, JAMES M R01GM42898-03
SODETZ, JAMES M S07RR07160-16
SODETZ, JAMES M S15CA55975-01
SODJA, ANN S06GM08167-13 0050
SODROSKI, JOSEPH U01AI24845-06 0008
SODROSKI, JOSEPH G R01AI24755-05
SODROSKI, JOSEPH G R01AI27702-03
SODROSKI, JOSEPH G R01AI29395-03
SODROSKI, JOSEPH G R01AI31783-01
SODROSKI, JOSEPH G. P30AI28691-03 9001
SOECHTING, JOHN F R01NS15018-12
SOEIRO, RUY U01AI27671-06
SOEJARTO, DOEL N01CM17548-00
SOELDNER, J STEWART P30DK36836-05 9010
SOELDNER, JOHN S R01DK33790-09
SOELDNER, JOHN S R01DK39233-05
SOERGEL, KONRAD H M01RR00058-30 0082
SOETANTO, KAWAN P01CA52823-02 0001
SOFER, WILLIAM H R01GM28791-12
SOFFER, EDY M01RR00059-30 0719
SOFFER, EDY M01RR00059-30 0738
SOFFER, RICHARD L R01HL45313-02
SOGIN, MITCHELL L R01GM32964-09
SOHAL, GURKIRPAL S R01HD18280-07
SOHAL, RAJINDAR S R01AG08459-03
SOHAL, RAJINDAR S S07RR07194-09 0625
SOHMER, BARBARA H K11MH00686-05
SOHN, MIRIAM P01CA41167-06 0008
SOHN, OCK SOON U01CA46589-05 0004
SOHN, RICHARD J S15ES05836-01
SOHN, RICHARD J S15MH49315-01
SOHNLE, PETER G R01AI23705-03
SOIFER, SCOTT J R01HL35518-06
SOIFFER, ROBERT S07RR05526-29 0087
SOIKE, KENNETH F N01AI62521-08
SOIKE, KENNETH F P51RR00164-30 0013
SOIKE, KENNETH F P51RR00164-30 0014
SOINE, WILLIAM H R01GM34507-04A2
SOJKA, NICKOLAS J G20RR06764-01
SOKAL, ROBERT R R01GM28262-11
SOKAS, ROSEMARY K K07ES00204-01
SOKATCH, JOHN R R01DK21737-13
SOKATCH, JOHN R R01GM30428-08A1
SOKIL-MELGAR, JOAN S07RR05853-11 0982
SOKOL, PAUL P S07RR05371-30 0644
SOKOL, REBECCA Z R01ES03749-07
SOKOL, ROBERT J P50AA07606-04 9001
SOKOL, ROBERT J P50AA07606-04
SOKOL, RONALD M01RR00069-29 0475
SOKOL, RONALD M01RR00069-29 0467
SOKOL, RONALD M01RR00069-29 0479
SOKOL, RONALD J M01RR00069-29 0348
SOKOL, RONALD J M01RR00069-29 0299
SOKOL, RONALD J R29DK38446-05
SOKOLOFF, L Z01MH00882-24
SOKOLOSKI, E A Z01HL01002-17
SOLARO, R JOHN R01HL22231-14
SOLARO, R. JOHN P01HL22619-14 0018
SOLDO, BETH J S07RR07136-20 0612
SOLDZ, STEPHEN M R43MH47689-01A1
SOLEMANI, MANOOCHER S07RR05371-30 0645
SOLIMAN, KARAM S06GM08111-19 0026
SOLIMAN, KARAM S06GM08111-19 0026
SOLIMAN, KARAM F G12RR03020-07 0001
SOLIMAN, MAGDI S06GM08111-19 0027
SOLIMAN, MAGDI S06GM08111-19 0027
SOLIMAN, MAGDI R G12RR03020-07 9002
SOLL, ANDREW S07RR05354-30 0396
SOLL, ANDREW H R01DK19984-15
SOLL, ANDREW H R01DK30444-09A2
SOLL, DAVID R P01HD18577-08 9001
SOLL, DAVID R P01HD18577-08
SOLL, DAVID R P01HD18577-08 0001
SOLL, DAVID R R01AI31474-01
SOLL, DIETER G R37GM22854-16
SOLLINGER, HANS W R01DK31774-09
SOLLINGER, HANS W R01DK41627-03
SOLLNER-WEBB, BARBARA T R01GM27720-12
SOLLNER-WEBB, BARBARA T R01GM34231-07
SOLLOTT, S Z01AG00261-04
SOLO, ALAN J S07RR05454-29 0888
SOLOFF, MELVYN S R01HD08406-14
SOLOFF, MELVYN S R01HD26168-03
SOLOMKIN, JOSEPH S R01GM31754-09
SOLOMON, ALAN R01CA10056-25
SOLOMON, D Z01CB00852-38
SOLOMON, D Z01CB00897-08
SOLOMON, D Z01CB09153-04
SOLOMON, D Z01CB09176-03
SOLOMON, DAVID H K12AG00489-02
SOLOMON, E P41RR01209-12 0016
SOLOMON, E P41RR01209-12 0019
SOLOMON, EDWARD I R01DK31450-11
SOLOMON, EDWARD I R01GM40392-04
SOLOMON, FRANK P01CA26712-11S1 0004
SOLOMON, FRANK E R01CA53395-01
SOLOMON, FRANK E R01GM41477-03
SOLOMON, JEROME J R01ES05694-01
SOLOMON, LAURA J P01CA46456-02 0002
SOLOMON, LIZA R03HS06441-02
SOLOMON, M A Z01CL00093-02
SOLOMON, PHYLLIS L R18MH46162-03
SOLOMON, ROBERT A R01NS27325-01A2
SOLOMON, WILLIAM B R29DK39566-03
SOLOMON, ZAHAVA R03MH49007-01
SOLONIUK, DONALD S S07RR05400-30 0041
SOLORZANO, CARMEN P R29CA46292-04
SOLOSKI, MARK J R01AI20922-07
SOLOWAY, ALBERT H R01CA53896-01
SOLOWAY, ROGER D M01RR00073-29 0307
SOLSKY, MARILYN A K11AG00325-06
SOLT, DENNIS S07RR05311-30 0008
SOLTANI, PETER K R43DE09906-01
SOLTER, DAVOR P01HD21355-04 0001
SOLTER, DAVOR P01HD21355-04 9001
SOLTER, DAVOR S07RR05540-29 0559
SOLTERO-HARRINGTON, FRED V S06GM08239-06 0
SOLTIS, EDWARD S07RR05857-11 0927
SOLURSH, M P50DE09170-03 0003
SOLURSH, MICHAEL P01HD18577-08 0002
SOLURSH, MICHAEL P50DE09170-03
SOLURSH, MICHAEL P50HL42266-02 0002
SOLURSH, MICHAEL R01HD05505-19
SOLURSH, MICHAEL R01HL43600-03
SOLWAY, JULIAN K04HL02205-04
SOLWAY, JULIAN R01HL41009-04
SOM, TAPAN S07RR05417-30 0815
SOMERMAN, MARTHA S07RR05317-21 0746
SOMERMAN, MARTHA J R01DE09532-03
SOMERS, SCOTT D R29GM46324-01
SOMERVELL, PHILIP R01MH42473-06 0002
SOMERVILLE, RONALD L R01GM22131-15
SOMJEN, GEORGE G P01NS17771-10 0002
SOMJEN, GEORGE G R01NS18670-08
SOMLO, STEFAN K08DK02015-01
SOMLYO, A V P01HL19242-15 0018
SOMLYO, ANDREW P P01HL15835-19 0019
SOMMADOSSI, JEAN-PIERRE P51RR00165-31 0197
SOMMADOSSI, JEAN-PIERRE U01AI25784-05 9001
SOMMADOSSI, JEAN-PIERRE C R01HL42125-04
SOMMER, BARBARA S07RR05736-19 0199
SOMMER, BARBARA S07RR05755-18 0210
SOMMER, FRANK G R01CA37483-06
SOMMER, GRAHAM F P01CA44665-04 0005
SOMMER, JOACHIM R R01HL12486-22
SOMMER, STEVE S R01HL39762-03
SOMMER, STEVE S R01MH44276-03
SOMMERCORN, J Z01DK69029-03
SOMMERCORN, J Z01DK69030-03
SOMMERCORN, J Z01DK69031-03
SOMMERCORN, J Z01DK69032-04
SOMMERCORN, J Z01DK69043-02
SOMMERFELD, EBERHARD S M01RR00055-30 0580
SONCRANT, T Z01AG00125-13
SONCRANT, T Z01AG00128-11
SONCRANT, T Z01AG00133-09
SONDAK, VERNON K R29CA55299-01
SONDEL, PAUL M M01RR03186-06 0004
SONDEL, PAUL M M01RR03186-06 0060
SONDEL, PAUL M M01RR03186-06 0050
SONDEL, PAUL M M01RR03186-06 0040
SONDEL, PAUL M P01CA20432-14 0031
SONDEL, PAUL M P30CA14520-19 9005
SONDEL, PAUL M R01CA32685-10
SONDEL, PAUL M R03CA53441-02
SONDHEIMER, STEVEN J M01RR00040-31 0367
SONEA, IOANA M S07RR05623-25 0725
SONENBERG, MARTIN R01DK41931-04A2
SONENSHEIN, ABRAHAM L R01GM42219-03
SONENSHEIN, GAIL E P01HL13262-19 0034
SONENSHEIN, GAIL E R01CA36355-08
SONENSTEIN, FREYA L R01HD27119-03
SONES, WILLIAM R43NS29316-01
SONG, B J Z01AA00036-05
SONG, B J Z01AA00037-05
SONG, CHANG W R01CA44114-04A2
SONG, CHANG W R37CA13353-18
SONG, CHUNG-SENG S07RR07187-13 0700
SONG, PILL-SOON R01GM36956-06
SONG, PILL-SOON R01NS15426-12
SONG, PILL-SOON S07RR07055-26
SONGU-MIZE, EMEL R01HL32270-06
SONIS, WILLIAM A K07MH00769-03
SONNEBORN, DAVID R R01GM36474-05
SONNENBERG, FRANK A R01HS06396-01A1
SONNENBERG, FRANK A R29LM05266-02
SONNENBERG, FRANK A S07RR05576-27 0606
SONNENBERG, GABRIELE M01RR00058-30 0255
SONNENBERG, GABRIELE M01RR00058-30 0251
SONNENBLICK, EDMUND H P01HL37412-04 0001
SONNENBLICK, EDMUND H P01HL37412-04
SONNENSCHEIN, CARLOS R01CA13410-17A2
SONNENSTUHL, WILLIAM J R18DA06995-02
SONNTAG, EDITH E P30HD06268-18 9002
SONNTAG, WILLIAM E R01AA08536-02
SONNTAG, WILLIAM E R01AG07752-04
SONO, MASANORI S07RR07160-16 0600
SONSALLA, PATRICIA K R01AG08479-03
SONSALLA, PATRICIA K R01DA06236-02
SONSALLA, PATRICIA K S07RR05576-27 0617
SONTHEIMER, RICHARD D K04AR01784-05
SONTHEIMER, RICHARD D P01AR09989-27 0003
SONTHEIMER, RICHARD D R01AR19101-15
SOOD, ASHWANI S07RR05648-25 0927
SOONG, SENG JAW P30CA13148-20 9009
SOPER, NATHANIEL M01RR00036-31 1027
SOPER, NATHANIEL M01RR00036-31 0964
SOPORI, MOHAN L R01AI31386-01A1
SOPRANO, DIANNE R R29DK41089-03
SOPRANO, DIANNE R R55HD27556-01A1
SOPRANO, KENNETH J P01CA56309-01 0004
SORACI, SALVATORE A, JR K04HD00921-02
SORCI-THOMAS, MARY P50HL14164-20 0050
SORCI-THOMAS, MARY G R29HL41916-03
SORDAHL, LOUIS A S07RR07205-11 0651
SORENSEN, GLORIAN C U01CA51686-03
SORENSEN, JAMES L R18DA06097-03
SORENSEN, RICARDO U M01RR00080-29 0359
SORENSON, ANNAMETTE P01AG07669-03 0002
SORENSON, GEORGE D R01CA47248-03
SORENSON, GEORGE D S07RR05392-30 0705
SORENSON, JAMES R R01HG00643-01
SORENSON, ROBERT R01DK33655-06
SORENSON, ROBERT L R01DK32237-09
SORGE, JOSEPH A N01ES75196-04
SORGE, JOSEPH A R01CA36448-09
SORIANO, PHILIPPE M R01HD24875-03
SORKIN, J Z01AG00215-01
SORKIN, J Z01AG00216-01
SORKIN, LINDA S P01NS11255-17 0028

SOROF, SAM R01CA05945-27
SOROKIN, SERGEI P R01HL33070-08
SOSENKO, ILENE R S M01RR05280-03 0016
SOSIN, MICHAEL R U01AA08773-02
SOSKEL, NORMAN T S07RR05423-30 0061
SOSLAU, GERALD S07RR07241-04 0702
SOSTMAN, DIRK P01CA42745-05 0005
SOTO, CALIXTO G12RR03050-07 0004
SOUBA, WILEY W R01HL44986-02
SOUBA, WILEY W R29CA45327-04
SOUHRADA, M S07RR05692-22 0982
SOUHRADA, MAGDALENA R01HL31940-08
SOULE, HOWARD R R44HL41433-03
SOULES, MICHAEL R M01RR00037-31 0496
SOULES, MICHAEL R M01RR00037-31 0448
SOULES, MICHAEL R M01RR00037-31 0522
SOULES, MICHAEL R M01RR00037-31 0519
SOULES, MICHAEL R R01HD18967-07
SOUTH, MARY ANN S06GM08198-10 0014
SOUTHARD, DOUGLAS R S07RR07095-24 0375
SOUTHARD, JAMES H R01DK35143-06
SOUTHARD, JOHN W U01CA50112-03
SOUTHARD, MARYLEE S07RR07037-26 0369
SOUTHARD, MARYLEE S07RR07037-26 0386
SOUTHERN RES INST N01DA19302-00
SOUTHERN, PETER J P01AG04342-09 0002
SOUTHERN, PETER J R01AI25224-05
SOUTHREN, A LOUIS R01EY01313-16S1
SOUTHWICK, FREDERICK S R01AI23262-07
SOUTO, FERNANDO A S06GM08103-18 0013
SOWADSKI, JANUSZ M R01GM37674-01A3
SOWERS, JAMES R R01HD24497-04
SOWERS, LAWRENCE S07RR05471-29 0596
SOWERS, LAWRENCE C R29GM41336-03
SOWERS, MARY F R29AR39651-03
SOWERS, MARYFRAN P01AG07094-05 0002
SOYBEL, DAVID I S07RR05358-30 0493
SOYFER, VALERY N R01GM44700-03
SPACH, MADISON S P01HL11307-25 0006
SPACH, MADISON S P01HL11307-25
SPACH, MADISON S P01HL11307-25 0002
SPACH, MADISON S P01HL11307-25 0004
SPACH, MADISON S. P01HL11307-25 0008
SPACKMAN, KENT A R29HL41581-04
SPADY, DAVID K R01HL38049-04A2
SPAETH, GEORGE L S07RR05510-28 0057
SPAIN, WILLIAM J K08NS01166-05
SPALHOLZ, B Z01CP05663-01
SPALL, RICHARD D R15GM46004-01
SPANGELO, BRYAN LEE R29DK42059-03
SPANGLER, RUDOLPH S07RR05591-27 0656
SPANGRUDE, G J Z01AI00611-01
SPANN, CHARLES H S03RR03203-11
SPANNHAKE, ERNST W P01ES03505-07
SPANNHAKE, ERNST W P01ES03505-07 0003
SPANNHAKE, ERNST W R01HL30195-09
SPAR, JAMES S07RR05756-18 0315
SPARBER, SHELDON B R01DA01880-12
SPARGO, BENJAMIN H K06HL04418-28
SPARK, RICHARD M01RR01032-16 0461
SPARK, RICHARD F M01RR01032-16 0415
SPARKES, ROBERT S M01RR00865-18 0048
SPARKES, ROBERT S N01CP71081-05
SPARKES, ROBERT S P01HL28481-09 0006
SPARKMAN, DENNIS R P50AG08013-04 0002
SPARKS, BARBARA S07RR05772-17 0338
SPARKS, DAVID L P50AG05144-08 0007
SPARKS, DAVID L R37EY01189-19
SPARKS, HARVEY V R37HL24232-13
SPARKS, JANET D S07RR05403-30 0828
SPARKS, JOHN W P01HD00781-27S1 0039
SPARKS, JOHN W P01HD00781-27S1 0042
SPARKS, LARRY D. P01AG05119-07 0005
SPARKS, RODNEY L R29CA46683-05
SPARLING, PHILIP F R37AI26837-04
SPARLING, PHILIP F U01AI31496-01
SPARLING, PHILIP F U01AI31496-01 0001
SPARLING, PHILLIP B S07RR07024-26 0050
SPARROW, DAVID W R01HL45089-02
SPARROW, JAMES T P60HL27341-10 0002
SPARROW, SARA P01HD03008-24 9001
SPATOLA, ARNO F R01GM33376-07
SPATZ, M Z01NS02357-13
SPATZ, M Z01NS02689-07
SPATZ, M Z01NS02751-05
SPATZ, M Z01NS02797-03
SPAULDING, GLEN S07RR05852-11 0257
SPAULDING, WILLIAM D R01MH44756-02
SPAZIANI, EUGENE P30DK25295-12S1 0012
SPEAKS, CHARLES E P50DC00110-17 0018
SPEALMAN, R D P51RR00168-30 0124
SPEALMAN, R D P51RR00168-30 0125
SPEALMAN, R D P51RR00168-30 0126
SPEALMAN, R D P51RR00168-30 0127
SPEALMAN, ROGER D K02DA00088-10
SPEALMAN, ROGER D R01DA00499-17
SPEALMAN, ROGER D R01DA06303-03
SPEAR ROBERT S07RR06025-02 0030
SPEAR, BRETT T R29GM45253-01A1
SPEAR, GREGORY T R29AI31812-01
SPEAR, JOSEPH F R01HL33593-07
SPEAR, LINDA P K02DA00140-03
SPEAR, LINDA P R01DA04478-05
SPEAR, NORMAN E R37MH35219-12
SPEAR, NORMAN E S03RR03301-10
SPEAR, NORMAN E S07RR07149-18
SPEAR, PATRICIA G R37CA21776-15
SPEAR, PATRICIA G U01AI31494-01 0001
SPEAR, PETER D R01EY01916-16
SPEAR, PETER D R01EY02545-13
SPEAR, ROBERT P42ES04705-05 0009
SPEAR, SHERILYNN R01DA05570-03
SPEAROW, JIMMY L R01HD28253-01
SPEARS, COLIN P R01CA39629-06S1
SPECHT, JAMES S07RR07055-26 0191
SPECHT, LINDA M01RR02172-09 0194
SPECHT, LINDA A K08NS01254-04
SPECHT, SUSAN C P01NS07464-24 0042
SPECIAN, ROBERT D P01DK43785-01 9003
SPECK, DEXTER F P01HL40369-03 0004
SPECK, NANCY A R29CA51065-02
SPECK, NANCY A S07RR05392-30 0706
SPECK, SAMUEL H R01CA43143-06
SPECK, SAMUEL H R01CA52004-02
SPECKER, BONNIE S07RR05535-29 0536
SPECKER, BONNY L R01AR40169-01A2
SPECKER, BONNY L R01AR41366-01
SPECTER, STEVEN S07RR05749-19 0275
SPECTER, STEVEN C R01DA04141-05
SPECTOR, ABRAHAM R01EY00423-23
SPECTOR, ABRAHAM R01EY04919-08
SPECTOR, ABRAHAM R37EY00759-20
SPECTOR, ALAN C. P01DC00161-11 0013
SPECTOR, ARTHUR A P50HL14230-20 0092
SPECTOR, ARTHUR A P50HL14230-20
SPECTOR, ARTHUR A R01DK28516-11
SPECTOR, ARTHUR A R01HL39308-05
SPECTOR, DAVID A M01RR02719-06 0136
SPECTOR, DAVID L P30CA45508-05 9008
SPECTOR, DAVID L R01GM42694-02
SPECTOR, DEBORAH H R01AI20954-05
SPECTOR, ILAN R01GM32776-07
SPECTOR, M P41RR01296-08 0001
SPECTOR, MYRON R01AR40427-01A1
SPECTOR, STEPHEN P50MH45294-03 9002
SPECTOR, STEPHEN A M01RR00827-17 0399
SPECTOR, STEPHEN A M01RR00827-17 0448
SPECTOR, STEPHEN A M01RR00827-17 0508
SPECTOR, STEPHEN A M01RR00827-17 0473
SPECTOR, STEPHEN A M01RR00827-17 0492
SPECTOR, STEPHEN A M01RR00827-17 0474
SPECTOR, STEPHEN A R01AI28270-03
SPECTOR, STEPHEN A U01AI27563-04
SPECTOR, STEPHEN A U01AI27670-05S1
SPECTOR, STEPHEN B M01RR00827-17 0350
SPEEDIE, MARILYN K S07RR05770-13 0932
SPEER, DONALD P S07RR05675-23 0921
SPEICHER, DAVID P01CA25874-12 0012
SPEICHER, DAVID W R01AR39158-03
SPEICHER, DAVID W R01HL38794-05
SPEIDEL, H S06GM08215-09 0008
SPEIDEL, HAROLD K S03RR03401-04
SPEIDEL, HAROLD K S06GM08215-09
SPEIGEL, THERESA A M01RR00040-31 0416
SPEIGLMAN, RICHARD C R01AA08189-03
SPEIR, E Z01HL04893-01
SPEIR, E Z01HL04894-01
SPEISER, PHYLLIS M01RR06020-02 0354
SPEISER, PHYLLIS M01RR06020-02 0427
SPEISER, PHYLLIS M01RR06020-02 0447
SPEISER, PHYLLIS M01RR06020-02 0445
SPEISER, PHYLLIS M01RR06020-02 0432
SPEISER, PHYLLIS M01RR06020-02 0391
SPEISER, PHYLLIS M01RR06020-02 0425
SPEISER, PHYLLIS W S07RR05396-30 0777
SPEIZER, FRANK M01RR02635-07 0233
SPEIZER, FRANK E R01CA49449-03
SPEIZER, FRANK E R01DK36798-07
SPEIZER, FRANK E R01ES04595-05
SPEIZER, FRANK E R01HL36002-07
SPEIZER, FRANK E R01HL36474-06A1
SPEIZER, FRANK E R37CA40356-07
SPELKE, ELIZABETH S R01HD23103-06
SPELMAN, FRANCIS A P01DC00274-08 0004
SPELMAN, FRANCIS A P51RR00166-30 9012
SPELMAN, FRANCIS A P51RR00166-30 9013
SPELMAN, FRANCIS A R03RR06969-01
SPELMAN, FRANCIS A. P51RR00166-30 0130
SPELMAN, FRANCIS A. P51RR00166-30 0131
SPELMAN, FRANCIS A. P51RR00166-30 0132
SPELMAN, FRANCIS A. P51RR00166-30 0133
SPELMAN, FRANCIS A. P51RR00166-30 0129
SPELSBERG, THOMAS C P50HD09140-16 0001
SPELSBERG, THOMAS C P50HD09140-16
SPELSBERG, THOMAS C. P01AG04875-08 0005
SPELTZ, MATTHEW L R01HD25987-03
SPELTZ, MATTHEW L R01MH45437-01A2
SPENCE, ALEXANDER M P01CA42045-06 0001
SPENCE, JOSEPH T S15AI32199-01
SPENCE, M ANNE P01MH46981-01A1 9002
SPENCE, M ANNE P01MH46981-01A1 0001
SPENCE, M ANNE R01MH44742-03
SPENCE, RICHARD K K07HL02532-01A1
SPENCER, ANDREW J R01DE09588-01A1
SPENCER, CAROLE A M01RR00043-31 0377
SPENCER, CAROLE A M01RR00043-31 0378
SPENCER, CAROLE A M01RR00043-31 0452
SPENCER, ELIZABETH K K07MH00763-03
SPENCER, ELIZABETH K S07RR05399-30 0947
SPENCER, FITZGERALD S06GM08025-21 0016
SPENCER, H TRENT S07RR05390-30 0657
SPENCER, JOHN W S06GM08066-20 0005
SPENCER, MARTIN P50GM27345-11 0012
SPENCER, PAULETTE K11DE00260-03
SPENCER, PETER S P01NS19611-08 9001
SPENCER, PETER S P01NS19611-08
SPENCER, R G Z01AG00381-01
SPENCER, R G Z01AG00382-01
SPENCER, ROBERT F R37EY02191-14
SPENCER, THOMAS A S07RR07056-18 0208
SPENDALE, STEVEN M01RR00069-29 0466
SPENGLER, ROBERT F U01CA50109-03
SPENGLER, ROBERT N S07RR05400-30 0042
SPERBER, STEVEN S07RR05576-27 0599
SPERELAKIS, NICHOLAS R01HD26170-02
SPERELAKIS, NICHOLAS R01HL31942-09
SPERELAKIS, NICHOLAS R01HL40572-02
SPERLING, HARRY G S07RR07143-20 0542
SPERLING, MARK P01HD11725-13 0012
SPERLING, MARK A P01HD11725-13 0009
SPERLING, MARK A S07RR05507-29
SPERLING, MARK A S15CA55996-01
SPERLING, MICHAEL R R01NS26178-03
SPERRY, DAVID G R01NS21878-06
SPERRY, JAY S S07RR07086-15 0320
SPETH, ROBERT C R01NS21305-04A2
SPETH, ROBERT C S07RR05465-29 0380
SPEYER, JAMES M01RR00096-30A1 0322
SPEYER, JAMES M01RR00096-30A1 0288
SPICER, DARCY P30CA14089-16 9009
SPICER, ELEANOR K S07RR05358-30 0494
SPICER, LEONARD D P30CA14236-18 9027
SPICER, LEONARD D R01GM41829-03
SPIEGEL, A Z01DK59000-04
SPIEGEL, A Z01DK59001-26
SPIEGEL, A Z01DK59002-26
SPIEGEL, A Z01DK59003-01
SPIEGEL, DAVID R01MH47226-02
SPIEGEL, DAVID A S07RR05369-30 0603
SPIEGEL, SARAH R01GM43880-02
SPIEGEL, SARAH R29GM39718-04
SPIEGELBERG, HANS P01DK42717-02 0003
SPIEGELBERG, HANS L R01AI10734-18
SPIEGELBERG, HANS L U01AI31595-01 0002
SPIEGELBERG, HANS L U01AI31595-01
SPIEGELMAN, BRUCE P01HD24926-03 0004
SPIEGELMAN, BRUCE M P01CA22427-14 0010
SPIEGELMAN, BRUCE M R01DK31405-10
SPIEGELMAN, BRUCE M R01DK42539-02
SPIEGELMAN, DONNA K01OH00106-01
SPIELMAN, ANDREW R01AI29724-02
SPIELMAN, ANDREW R37AI19693-09
SPIELMAN, ANDREW I S07RR07062-26 0222
SPIELMAN, RICHARD P30DK19525-15 0018
SPIELMAN, RICHARD S R01DK35047-07
SPIELMAN, WILLIAM S R01DK39654-04
SPIELVOGEL, BERNARD F R43AI30887-01
SPIELVOGEL, BERNARD F R44CA55543-02
SPIER, CATHERINE S07RR05675-23 0948
SPIERING, ANDREA L S07RR05425-30 0769
SPIES, HAROLD G P30HD18185-08
SPIES, HAROLD G P51RR00163-32 0017
SPIES, HAROLD G R01HD16631-09
SPIES, THOMAS R01AI30581-01A1
SPIES, THOMAS S07RR05526-29 0085
SPIES, THOMAS S07RR05526-29 0092
SPIGA, RALPH R29DA06633-02
SPIKES, JOHN D S07RR07092-26 0515
SPILLER, HART S06GM08062-21 0004
SPINALE, FRANCIS G R29HL45024-01A1
SPINDEL, ELIOT R R01CA39237-07
SPINDEL, ELIOT R R01CA53584-01
SPINDLER, KATHERINE R R01AI23762-04A1
SPINOLA, STANLEY M R29AI27863-02
SPIRA, DAN T P01AI26497-03 0003
SPIRO, MARY J R01HL31315-07
SPIRO, ROBERT C R01CA49243-03
SPIRO, ROBERT G P30DK36836-05 9005
SPIRO, ROBERT G R01DK17477-19
SPIRO, THOMAS G P41RR01348-10 0007
SPIRO, THOMAS G R01GM25158-13
SPIRO, THOMAS G R01GM33576-22
SPIRO, THOMAS G R37GM13498-26
SPIROU, GEORGE A R29DC01387-01
SPITALNIK, STEVEN L P30AG10124-01 0001
SPITALNIK, STEVEN L R01HL46206-01
SPITALNIK, STEVEN L R29CA45690-05
SPITALNIK, STEVEN L S07RR05415-30 0020
SPITZ, MARGARET R R01CA55769-01
SPITZBERG, LARRY A R44EY08156-02
SPITZE, GLENNA D R01AG08644-03
SPITZE, GLENNA D S07RR07122-23 0113
SPITZE, GLENNA D S07RR07122-23 0114
SPITZE, GLENNA D S07RR07122-23 0115
SPITZER, ADRIAN R01DK28477-08A2
SPITZER, ALAN R. M01RR00240-27 0274

SPITZER, ERIC D S07RR05736-19 0200
SPITZER, JOHN J P01GM32654-08
SPITZER, JOHN J P01GM32654-08 0001
SPITZER, JOHN J R01AA07287-05
SPITZER, JOHN J S15NS30115-01
SPITZER, JUDY A P01GM32654-08 0004
SPITZER, JUDY A R01GM30312-10
SPITZER, KENNETH W R01HL42873-03
SPITZER, NICHOLAS P01NS25916-04 0005
SPITZER, NICHOLAS P01NS25916-04 9005
SPITZER, NICHOLAS C R01NS15918-12
SPITZER, VICTOR N01LM13543-00
SPITZER, VICTOR M S07RR05357-30 0456
SPITZNAGEL, JOHN K R01AI26589-03
SPIVACK, JORDAN G P01AI23968-06 0002
SPIVAK, JERRY L R37DK16702-19
SPLITTER, GARY S07RR05912-08 0655
SPOEREL, NIKOLAUS A R29GM40024-04
SPORN, LEE A R29HL43711-02
SPORN, PETER H K08HL02407-03
SPOTH, RICHARD L R01DA07029-01A1
SPOTNITZ, WILLIAM D R29HL43787-01A2
SPRADLIN, J E P01HD18955-07 0002
SPRADLIN, JOSEPH E P01HD26927-01A1
SPRADLING, ALLAN C R01GM27875-12
SPRAGG, ROGER G P50HL23584-13 9001
SPRAGG, ROGER G P50HL23584-13 0007
SPRAGUE, EUGENE A P01HL26890-09 9002
SPRAGUE, GEORGE F, JR R01GM30027-10
SPRAGUE, GEORGE F, JR R01GM38157-05
SPRAGUE, KAREN U R01GM25388-14
SPRAGUE, KAREN U R01GM32851-07
SPRAGUE, RANDY S K08HL01867-05
SPRATT, THOMAS E R29CA53625-01A1
SPRAY, DAVID C P01DK41918-02 0002
SPRAY, DAVID C P01NS07512-23 0042
SPRAY, DAVID C R01EY08969-01
SPRAY, DAVID C R01HL38449-04
SPRAY, DAVID C R01NS16524-11
SPREAT, SCOTT R01MH43851-04
SPRECHER, DENNIS L R01HD18281-07
SPRECHER, HOWARD W R01DK20387-14
SPREMULLI, LINDA L R01GM24963-14
SPREMULLI, LINDA L R01GM32734-08
SPRENT, JONATHAN P01CA25803-13 0007
SPRENT, JONATHAN P01CA25803-13
SPRENT, JONATHAN R01AI21487-08
SPRENT, JONATHAN R37CA38355-08
SPRENT, JONATHON P01CA15822-17 0009
SPRIGGS, DAVID R N01CM07306-03
SPRIGGS, DAVID R R01CA47722-04
SPRINCE, NANCY S07RR05372-30 0657
SPRING, JEFFREY H R01AI28399-03
SPRING, K R Z01HL01266-09
SPRINGER, ALAN D R01EY03552-09
SPRINGER, CHARLES S, JR R01GM32125-08
SPRINGER, GEORG F R01CA22540-27
SPRINGER, JOE E R01NS30248-01
SPRINGER, JOE E R29AG08969-03
SPRINGER, TIMOTHY A R01CA31798-11
SPRINGER, TIMOTHY A R37CA31799-11
SPRINGER, TIMOTHY A S07RR05626-25 0672
SPRINGER, TIMOTHY A U01AI31921-01
SPRINGER, WAYNE R S07RR05665-24 0878
SPRITZ, RICHARD A R01AR39892-03
SPRUANCE, SPOTSWOOD M01RR00064-27 0327
SPUDICH, JAMES A P01GM30387-10 9001
SPUDICH, JAMES A P01GM30387-10 0004
SPUDICH, JAMES A R01GM33289-08
SPUDICH, JAMES A R01GM40509-04
SPUDICH, JAMES A R37GM46551-01
SPUDICH, JOHN L R01GM27750-12
SPUDICH, JOHN L S10RR06486-01
SPUNT, BARRY J R01DA07374-01
SPURR, CHARLES L P30CA12197-19 9006
SPURR, CHARLES L U10CA45808-05
SPURR, G B R22DK39734-02
SQUIER, CHRISTOPHER P30DE10126-01 9003
SQUIER, CHRISTOPHER A K16DE00175-07
SQUIER, CHRISTOPHER A P30DE10126-01 0002
SQUIER, CHRISTOPHER A S03RR03456-05
SQUIER, CHRISTOPHER A S07RR05313-30
SQUIER, CHRISTOPHER A S15DE10070-01
SQUILLANTE, MICHAEL R N44DK12262-01
SQUILLANTE, MICHAEL R R43GM45639-01
SQUILLANTE, MICHAEL R R43RR07524-01
SQUILLANTE, MICHAEL R R44GM42247-03
SQUIRE, LARRY R R37MH24600-18
SQUIRES, CATHERINE L R01GM24751-14
SQUIRES, CATHERINE L R01GM35874-06
SQUIRES, KATHLEEN M01RR00047-31 0461
SQUIRES, ROBERT M01RR00633-19 0418
SQUITIERI, LOUISE S06GM08174-13 0007
SREBRO, RICHARD R01EY08515-02
SREBRO, RICHARD R01EY09041-01
SRERE, PAUL A R01DK11313-24
SRI INTERNATIONAL N01DA07407-00
SRI INTERNATIONAL N01DA98159-00
SRIDARAN, RAJAGOPALA S07RR05907-08 0638
SRIDHARA, S S07RR05773-17 0376
SRIKANTA, SATHYANARAYANA P30DK36836-05 000
SRINIVAS, RANGA V R01CA40440-07
SRINIVASAN, ALAGARSAMY R01AI29306-02
SRINIVASAN, ASOKA S03RR03228-09
SRINIVASAN, ASOKA S06GM08110-20
SRINIVASAN, ASOKA S06GM08110-20 0001
SRINIVASAN, MANDAYAM A R29DC00625-04
SRINIVASAN, PADMINI S07RR07035-26 0084
SRINIVASAN, R S07RR07254-03 0495
SRINIVASAN, SATHANUR R R01HL38844-05 9002
SRIRAM, S S07RR05429-30 0212
SRIRAM, SUBRAMANIAM M01RR00109-28 0331
SRIRAM, SUBRAMANIAM R01NS27513-01A2
SRIVASTAVA, ARUN P60AR20582-14 0001
SRIVASTAVA, ARUN R29AI26323-04
SRIVASTAVA, D K S15GM47031-01
SRIVASTAVA, OM P R01EY06400-04A3
SRIVASTAVA, PRAKASH N R01HD14947-09
SRIVASTAVA, PRAMOD K R03CA54990-01
SRIVASTAVA, PRAMOD K R29CA44786-06
SRIVASTAVA, RACHANA S07RR05664-24 0875
SRIVASTAVA, RAKESH R29AI26334-03
SRIVASTAVA, SATISH K R01EY01677-17
SRIVASTAVA, SHIVA KUMAR R29CA46455-05
SRIVASTAVA, VINOD K S07RR05854-11 0918
SRIVATSAN, ERI S R29CA47206-03
SROUR, EDWARD F S07RR05371-30 0646
ST CLAIR, DARET K R29CA49797-02
ST CLAIR, RICHARD P50HL14164-20
ST CLAIR, RICHARD W P01HL45666-01 9001
ST CLAIR, RICHARD W P50HL14164-20 0035
ST CLAIR, RICHARD W P50HL14164-20 9001
ST CLAIR, WILLIAM H S07RR05404-30 0857
ST GEORGE-HYSLOP, PETER H P01AG02126-11 00
ST GEORGE-HYSLOP, PETER H R01NS29821-01
ST GERMAIN, DONALD L R01DK42271-02
ST JEOR, SACHIKO T R25CA48062-03
ST JOHN, PAUL A S07RR05675-23 0922
ST JOHN, RONALD K N01AI72649-04
ST JOHN, THOS P R01CA42571-07
ST JOHN, WALTER M R01HL20574-14A2
ST JOHN, WALTER M R01HL26091-10
ST LAWRENCE, JANET S R01MH48848-01
ST. CLAIR, E. WILLIAM P50AR39162-05 0004
ST. CLAIR, EUGENE W. M01RR00030-30 0452
STABEN, CHARLES A R01GM46193-01
STABEN, CHARLES A S07RR07114-23 0448
STABLER, BRIAN M01RR00046-31 0464
STABLER, BRIAN M01RR00046-31 0383
STABLER, SALLY P P01AG09417-01 0004
STABLER, SALLY P R01AG09834-01
STABLER, SALLY P S07RR05357-30 0448
STACEY, DENNIS W R01CA48662-03
STACH, BRAD P01HD24234-04 0002
STACHOWIAK, MICHAEL S07RR05872-08 0984
STACK, RICHARD S P50HL17670-17 0037
STACKPOLE, CHRISTOPHER W R01CA49835-02
STACOOOLE, PETER W M01RR00082-29 0468
STACPOOLE, PETER W M01RR00082-29 0467
STACPOOLE, PETER W M01RR00082-29 0281
STACPOOLE, PETER W M01RR00082-29 0472
STACPOOLE, PETER W R01DK40439-04
STADALNIK, ROBERT C R01DK34706-07
STADDON, JOHN E R01MH45856-02
STADER, JOAN A R01GM43514-02
STADIUS, MICHAEL S07RR05353-30 0369
STADTMAN, E R Z01HL00211-18
STADTMAN, T C Z01HL00205-36
STAEHELIN, L A R01GM22912-15
STAEHELIN, L ANDREW R01GM18639-18
STAERZ, UWE S07RR05842-12 0284
STAERZ, UWE D R01HD26841-01A1
STAFFORD, DARREL W R01HL38973-05
STAFFORD, DARREL W. P01HL06350-30 0023
STAFFORD, WALTER F U01CA51880-02 0004
STAGNO, SERGIO P01HD10699-15 0001
STAGNO, SERGIO P30HD28831-01
STAGNO, SERGIO B M01RR00032-31 0278
STAHL, FRANKLIN W R01GM33677-08
STAHL, JEANNE M S06GM45913-01 0002
STAHL, PHILIP D R01GM42259-20
STAHL, PHILIP D R37AI20015-09
STAHL, STEPHEN M M01RR00827-17 0486
STAHL, STEPHEN M P50MH30914-14 0050
STAHL, STEPHEN M R01MH45787-01A1
STAHL, WILLIAM L P01NS20482-08 0010
STAHLMAN, MILDRED T P50HL14214-20 0039
STAHLMAN, MILDRED T P50HL14214-20
STAHN, RUGGLES M R21DK44596-01
STAIANO-COICO, LISA P50GM26145-13 0009
STAIANO-COICO, LISA R01GM42461-03
STAIANO-COICO, LISA S07RR05396-30 0785
STAINSBY, WENDELL N R01AR39378-04
STALEY, KEVIN J K08NS01573-01
STALL, ALAN M S10RR06250-01
STALL, RONALD D R01AA08233-02
STALLCUP, MICHAEL R R01DK43093-02
STALLCUP, WILLIAM B R01NS21990-08
STALLCUP, WILLIAM B. P01HD25938-02 0001
STALLINGS, VIRGINIA M01RR00240-27 0310
STALLINGS, VIRGINIA A M01RR00240-27 0343
STALLONES, LORANN S07RR05458-29 0838
STALVEY, JOHN R D S07RR07208-10 0670
STALVEY, JOHN R D S07RR07208-10 0667
STAMATO, THOMAS R01CA45277-06
STAMATO, THOMAS S07RR05540-29 0554
STAMATO, THOMAS D R01CA48636-05
STAMATO, THOMAS D R01ES02470-10
STAMATOYANNAPOULOS, GEORGE P01DK31232-10 0
STAMATOYANNOPOULOS, GEORGE P01DK31232-10
STAMATOYANNOPOULOS, GEORGE R37HL20899-15
STAMBOLIAN, D E P50DE09164-03 0004
STAMBOLIAN, DWIGHT S07RR07083-26 0482
STAMBROOK, PETER J P01ES05652-01
STAMBROOK, PETER J P01ES05652-01 0001
STAMBROOK, PETER J R01ES05204-03
STAMENKOVIC, IVAN R01GM43257-02
STAMEY, THOMAS A N01CM97568-04
STAMLER, JEREMIAH R01HL21010-15
STAMLER, JEREMIAH R01HL33387-06S1
STAMLER, JEREMIAH R01HL40397-04
STAMLER, JONATHAN S K08HL02582-01
STAMM, LOLA V R29AI24976-05
STAMM, LOLA V U01AI31496-01 0004
STAMM, WALTER E P01AI24756-05 9001
STAMM, WALTER E R01DK40045-03
STAMM, WALTER E U01AI31448-01 9004
STAMM, WALTER E U01AI31448-01 9002
STAMMER, CHARLES H R01GM42685-03
STAMPFER, MARTHA R R37CA24844-13
STAMPFER, MEIR P01CA55075-01 0002
STAMPLEY, ANITA R S07RR05788-15 0893
STANBERRY, LAWRENCE R R01AI22667-06
STANBERRY, LAWRENCE R R01AI29687-02
STANBRIDGE, ERIC J R37CA19401-16
STANCEL, GEORGE M R01HD08615-17A1
STANCEL, GEORGE M R13CA55013-01
STANDAERT, FRANK G S07RR05700-22
STANDAERT, FRANK G S15NS30111-01
STANDART, THOMAS A P01HL39157-05 9001
STANFIELD, B B Z01MH00798-05
STANFIELD, B B Z01MH00799-05
STANFIELD, C A Z01MH01098-05
STANFORD, JANET L K07CA01364-04
STANFORD, JOHN W N01DE12584-00
STANFORD, JOHN W R13DE09648-01A1
STANFORD, LAURENCE R P30HD03352-25 9001
STANFORD, LAURENCE R R01EY04977-09
STANG, PETER J R01CA16903-15
STANGER, CATHERINE R03MH47751-01
STANHOPE, S J Z01CL60016-01
STANINEC, MICHAL S07RR05305-30 0719
STANISWALIS, JOAN S07RR05724-20 0188
STANKO, RONALD M01RR00056-30 0370
STANKO, RONALD M01RR00056-30 0371
STANKO, RONALD T M01RR00056-30 0325
STANKO, RONALD T M01RR00056-30 0285
STANKO, RONALD T M01RR00056-30 0312
STANKOVICH, MARIAN T R01GM29344-10
STANLEY-SAMUELSON, D S07RR07055-26 0195
STANLEY, BARBARA H R01MH41734-04
STANLEY, BILLY G R01NS24268-05A1
STANLEY, CHARLES M01RR00240-27 0336
STANLEY, CHARLES A M01RR00240-27 0334
STANLEY, CHARLES A M01RR00240-27 0308
STANLEY, CHARLES A M01RR00240-27 0202
STANLEY, E F Z01NS02606-08
STANLEY, EVAN R R01CA32551-10
STANLEY, EVAN R R37CA26504-13
STANLEY, FREDERICK M S07RR05399-30 0939
STANLEY, J R Z01CB03667-07
STANLEY, MELINDA A S07RR05745-19 0234
STANLEY, PAMELA P30DK41296-03 0004
STANLEY, PAMELA M R01CA36434-08
STANLEY, PAMELA M R37CA30645-11
STANLEY, WILLIAM C S07RR07098-26 0344
STANNARD, JAN G R01DE10140-01
STANSKI, DONALD R P01AG03104-10 0005
STANSKI, DONALD R R01AG04594-08
STANTON, BONITA F R01HD27114-02
STANTON, BONITA F U01MH48068-02
STANTON, BRUCE A R01DK34533-07
STANTON, BRUCE A S07RR05392-30 0707
STANTON, PATRIC K R01MH45752-02
STANTON, TONI L S06GM08238-05 0018
STAPELLS, DAVID P01DC00223-08 0006
STAPLETON, D P41RR01243-10 0028
STAR, ROBERT A K08DK01888-03
STARCHER, BARRY S07RR05958-06 0747
STARFIELD, BARBARA R01HS06170-03
STARK-SEITZ, RACHEL E R01DC00389-06
STARK, ANN R P50HL34616-07 0005
STARK, DAVID D R01CA50353-02
STARK, DENNIS M P40RR01180-14 0005
STARK, JAMES M K08HL02505-01A1
STARK, JAMES M S07RR05435-30 0982
STARK, KENNETH R18DA06361-03
STARK, RAYMOND I P50HD13063-12 0002
STARK, RAYMOND I P50HD13063-12 0008
STARK, RAYMOND I R01AI32314-01
STARK, RUTH E K04DK01793-04
STARK, RUTH E R01DK36888-05
STARK, RUTH E S07RR07244-03 0489
STARK, RUTH E S07RR07244-03
STARK, WALTER J U10EY06155-07
STARK, WALTER J U10EY06172-07

STARK, WILLIAM S07RR07053-26 0165
STARK, WILLIAM S R01EY07192-04
STARKEY, PRENTICE R01HD26579-02
STARKMAN, M N M01RR00042-31 0527
STARKMAN, MONICA N M01RR00042-31 0005
STARKUS, JOHN G S07RR07026-26 0003
STARL, DENNIS M S07RR07065-26 0069
STARLING, MARK R M01RR00042-31 0488
STARLING, MARK R M01RR00042-31 0582
STARLING, MARK R R01HL36450-06A1
STARMER, C FRANK R01HL32994-08
STARNES, H F, JR R29CA47963-03
STARNES, H FLETCHER M01RR00070-29 0228
STARNES, VAUGHN A M01RR00081-29 0141
STAROS, JAMES V P01CA43720-05 0007
STAROS, JAMES V R01DK25489-11
STARR, STUART E M01RR00240-27 0351
STARR, STUART E R01HD18957-13
STARZL, THOMAS E R37DK29961-11
STASHENKO, PHILIP R01DE09018-03
STASTNY, P P50AR39169-05 0001
STASTNY, PETER P01AI23271-06 9002
STASTNY, PETER P01AI23271-06 0002
STASTNY, PETER R01HL47145-01
STATEN, MYRLENE M01RR00047-31 0474
STATEN, MYRLENE A. M01RR00036-31 0713
STATES, BEATRICE P01DK40555-04 0003
STATES, J CHRISTOPHER R29CA47735-05
STATES, J CHRISTOPHER S03RR03332-07
STATHOPOULOS, ELAINE T R29DC00516-03
STAUB, NORMAN C P01HL25816-11 0016
STAUB, NORMAN C P01HL25816-11 0003
STAUB, NORMAN C P01HL25816-11
STAUB, NORMAN C P50HL19155-15 0012
STAUBUS, ALFRED E P30CA16058-17 9010
STAUDT, L M Z01CB04024-04
STAUFFACHER, CYNTHIA V R01GM44001-01A1
STAUFFER, EDWARD K S07RR05896-09 0619
STAUFFER, GEORGE V R01AI20279-09
STAUFFER, GEORGE V R01GM26878-13
STAUFFER, GEORGE V R01GM38912-04
STAUSFELD, NICHOLAS S07RR07002-26 0876
STAVNEZER, EDWARD R01CA43600-06
STAVNEZER, JANET M R01AI23283-07
STAVNEZER, JANET M R55AI28827-01A2
STAVNEZER, JANET M S07RR05712-20 0115
STAY, BARBARA A P01NS15350-13 0007
STAY, BARBARA A R01AI15230-12
STAYTON, MARK M S07RR07157-16 0574
STEADMAN, C J M01RR00585-20 0468
STEADMAN, HENRY J R01MH48523-01
STEAKLEY, CARYN P30CA51008-02 9006
STEARNS, JAY F R44AI28126-03
STEARNS, MARK E R01CA53813-02
STEARNS, MARK E R29CA45425-05
STEBBINS, WILLIAM P01DC00078-27 0040
STECENKO, ARLENE A K04HL01919-05
STECK, PETER A R55CA56041-01
STECK, T P30DK42086-02 0004
STECK, THEODORE L P60DK20595-14 0017
STECKEL, RICHARD J P30CA16042-17
STECKER, MARK M K08NS01502-01
STEDHAM, MICHAEL A N01CM87258-09
STEEG, P S Z01CB00892-07
STEEGE, DEBORAH A R01GM33349-08
STEEGE, JOHN F M01RR00030-30 0506
STEEL, DUNCAN S07RR07050-26 0128
STEEL, R KNIGHT R13AG09961-01
STEELE, A D Z01AI00606-01
STEELE, ANNE C S03RR03532-02
STEELE, CHARLES R R01DC00108-16
STEELE, CLAUDE M R01MH45889-02
STEELE, GLENN D, JR P01CA44704-04A1
STEELE, MARIANNE K P01HL29714-29 0008
STEELE, MARILYN I K11AI00873-04
STEELE, MARK P K08HL02620-01
STEELE, PAUL E R29AI29676-02
STEELE, ROBERT D R01DK35853-06
STEEN, VIRGINIA R18AR21393-17 0019
STEENBERGEN, CHARLES R29HL39752-04
STEENKAMP, DANIEL J P01HL16251-18 0017
STEER, MICHAEL L R01DK31914-09
STEER, MICHAEL L R37DK31396-09
STEERE, ALLEN C R01AR20358-16
STEERE, ALLEN C R01AR40576-02
STEERS, C WILLIAM S15MH49314-01
STEERS, WILLIAM D K11DK01732-06
STEERS, WILLIAM D R29NS28566-02
STEEVES, RICHARD A R01CA49429-02
STEEVES, RICHARD H R15NR02482-01A1
STEFANATOS, GERRY A R01DC00969-01A1
STEFANI, ENRICO P01HL37044-06 0010
STEFANI, ENRICO R01AR38970-05
STEFANI, ENRICO R01HD25616-03
STEFANO, GEORGE R24MH47392-02 0001
STEFANO, GEORGE B R24MH47392-02
STEFANSSON, KARI P01NS24575-04 0003
STEFANSSON, KARI P50NS21442-07 0006
STEFFEN, DAVID L R01CA30674-10
STEFFES, MICHAEL W R01DK43605-01
STEFLIK, DAVID E R29DE08586-03
STEGEMAN, JOHN J R01ES04220-05
STEGNER, JANE M01RR00750-19 0230
STEHMAN, FREDERICK B M01RR00750-19 0263
STEHOUWER, DONALD J R01NS28850-01A1
STEIGBIGEL, ROY U01AI25993-05 9001
STEIGBIGEL, ROY U01AI25993-05 0003
STEIGBIGEL, ROY T U01AI25893-05
STEIGBIGEL, ROY T U01AI25893-05 0001
STEIGBIGEL, ROY T U01AI25993-05
STEIMER, KATHELYN S U01AI26471-04 0003
STEIN-STREILEIN, JOAN E K04HL01683-05
STEIN-STREILEIN, JOAN E R01HL33372-05
STEIN-STREILEIN, JOAN E R01HL33709-06
STEIN-STREILEIN, JOAN E R01HL43388-02
STEIN, BARRY E R01EY06562-06
STEIN, BARRY E R01NS22543-09
STEIN, DANIEL C R29AI24452-04
STEIN, DONALD G S03RR03095-11
STEIN, DONALD G S07RR07059-26
STEIN, DONALD G S15NS30133-01
STEIN, ELLIOT A R01DA06485-03
STEIN, GARY S R01AR39588-02
STEIN, GARY S R01GM32010-10
STEIN, GRETCHEN H R01AG00947-14
STEIN, JANET L P01CA39240-07 0006
STEIN, JANET L P01CA39240-07 9003
STEIN, JOSEPH P R01CA41829-07
STEIN, JOSEPH P S07RR05402-30 0796
STEIN, K E Z01BA02006-09
STEIN, K E Z01BA02008-04
STEIN, K E Z01BA02009-02
STEIN, KAREN P20NR02962-01 0003
STEIN, LARRY R01DA05107-02
STEIN, LEONARD D R01HD26637-02
STEIN, LEONARD D R29AI25523-04
STEIN, MICHAEL A K08HL02519-02
STEIN, RICHARD S M01RR00095-31 0342
STEIN, ROLAND W P01DK42502-02 0003
STEIN, ROLAND W R29GM39257-04
STEIN, RUTH E P50MH38280-08
STEIN, RUTH E P50MH38280-08 0007
STEIN, RUTH E P50MH38280-08 0008
STEIN, RUTH E P50MH38280-08 0009
STEIN, STUART A R29MH43017-05
STEIN, THOMAS P R01DK35612-08
STEIN, THOMAS P R01DK41927-02
STEIN, ZENA A R01HD26492-02
STEINBACH, JOSEPH H R01NS22356-07
STEINBACH, SUZANNE F S07RR05569-27 0125
STEINBERG, A D Z01AR41020-24
STEINBERG, A D Z01AR41023-17
STEINBERG, A D Z01AR41040-19
STEINBERG, BETTIE M P01DC00203-09
STEINBERG, BETTIE M P01DC00203-09 0001
STEINBERG, BETTIE M S15DK44693-01
STEINBERG, DANIEL K12DK01408-07
STEINBERG, DANIEL P50HL14197-20
STEINBERG, DANIEL R13HL46708-01
STEINBERG, EARL P P01HS06280-03
STEINBERG, EARL P P01HS06280-03 0001
STEINBERG, EARL P P01HS06280-03 0002
STEINBERG, GARY S07RR05353-30 0370
STEINBERG, GARY K R01NS27292-01A2
STEINBERG, HOWARD N R01HL42148-04
STEINBERG, JONATHAN S M01RR00645-20 0498
STEINBERG, JUDITH L S07RR05569-27 0110
STEINBERG, MALCOLM S R01CA13605-18
STEINBERG, MARK L R01CA52915-02
STEINBERG, MARLENE R29MH43352-03
STEINBERG, MARTIN H N01HB73005-21
STEINBERG, ROBERT A R01DK37583-06
STEINBERG, ROY H R37EY01429-18
STEINBERG, S M Z01CM07202-08
STEINBERG, STEVEN S07RR05377-30 0769
STEINBERG, SUSAN F R01HL38976-04
STEINBERG, THOMAS H R29GM45815-01
STEINBERGER, ANNA R01HD17802-08
STEINBROOK, RICHARD S07RR05950-07 0993
STEINDLER, DENNIS A R01NS20856-07
STEINER, CAROL B U01CA50117-03
STEINER, DONALD F P60DK20595-14 9001
STEINER, DONALD F R37DK13914-22
STEINER, HANS S07RR05353-30 0371
STEINER, JAMES S07RR05304-30 0226
STEINER, LISA A R37AI08054-25
STEINER, LISA A S07RR07047-26 0144
STEINER, ROBERT P50HD12629-12 9005
STEINER, ROBERT A P50HD12629-12 0008
STEINER, ROBERT A R01HD12625-13
STEINER, ROBERT A. P51RR00166-30 0120
STEINER, ROBERT A. P51RR00166-30 0151
STEINER, ROBERT A. P51RR00166-30 0121
STEINERT, P Z01AR41084-02
STEINERT, P Z01AR41085-02
STEINERT, P Z01AR41086-02
STEINERT, P Z01AR41087-02
STEINETZ, BERNARD G S07RR05399-30 0932
STEINGOLD, KENNETH M01RR00065-29 0356
STEINGOLD, KENNETH A M01RR00065-29 0295
STEINHARDT, RICHARD A R01AR41129-01
STEINHERZ, PETER G U10CA42764-06
STEINHOFF, FREDRICK R43DE10010-01
STEINKAMP, JOHN A P41RR01315-10 9002
STEINKE, JOHN M R43HL47273-01
STEINKE, JOHN M R44HL44802-02
STEINMAN, CHARLES R R01AR33278-09
STEINMAN, CHARLES R R01AR39939-03
STEINMAN, HOWARD M R01GM40468-04
STEINMAN, LAWRENCE P01GM28428-11 0009
STEINMAN, LAWRENCE R01NS18235-10
STEINMAN, LAWRENCE R01NS28759-01S1
STEINMAN, R M R37AI13013-15
STEINMAN, RALPH M P01AI24775-05 9001
STEINMAN, RALPH M P01AI24775-05 0002
STEINMAN, RALPH M R01AI24540-05
STEINMAN, THEODORE I M01RR01032-16 0474
STEINMETZ, JOSEPH E R29MH44052-04
STEINMETZ, JOSEPH E S07RR07031-26 0109
STEINMETZ, MICHAEL A R01EY09129-01
STEINMETZ, PHILIP R P01HL14388-20 0191
STEINMETZ, PHILIP R R37DK30693-11
STEINMULLER, DAVID R01AI23653-06
STEINSAPIR, JAIME S07RR05365-30 0101
STEINSCHNEIDER, MITCHELL R29DC00657-02
STEINWACHS, DONALD M P50MH43703-05
STEIS, R G Z01CM09305-05
STEIS, R G Z01CM09306-05
STEITZ, JOAN A P01CA16038-18 0010
STEITZ, JOAN A R37GM26154-21
STEITZ, THOMAS A P01GM39546-05 0003
STEITZ, THOMAS H P01GM22778-16 0005
STEKETEE, GAIL S R01MH44190-03
STEKIEL, WILLIAM J P01HL29587-09 0006
STELLA, VALENTINO N01CM97576-02
STELLAR, ELIOT R01NS25079-05
STELLER, HERMANN S07RR07047-26 0135
STELLWAGEN, EARLE P01HL14388-20 0247
STELLWAGEN, EARLE C R01GM22109-16
STELLWAGEN, NANCY C R01GM29690-11
STELMACHOWICZ, PATRICIA P60DC00982-02 0001
STELZNER, DENNIS J R01NS14096-14
STELZNER, THOMAS J S07RR05357-30 0441
STEMBER, MARILYN L R01NR01670-04
STEMBER, MARILYN L S03RR03503-03
STEMBER, MARILYN L S07RR05809-06
STEMBER, MARILYN L S15NR02934-01
STEMERMAN, MICHAEL B P01HL43023-01A2 9001
STEMERMAN, MICHAEL B R01HL33742-08
STENMARK, KURT R P01HL14985-20 0027
STENSAAS, LARRY P01NS07938-22 0031
STENSAAS, LARRY J P01NS07938-22 9002
STENSON, WILLIAM P01DK33487-05 0002
STENSON, WILLIAM F R01DK33165-08
STENT, GUNTHER S R01NS12818-38
STENZEL, KURT M01RR00047-31 0465
STENZEL, KURT H M01RR00047-31 0431
STENZEL, KURT H M01RR00047-31 0446
STEPHAN, WOLFGANG H R55GM46233-01
STEPHEN, R P01AI21912-08 0006
STEPHEN, RAPPAPORT P42ES04705-05 0002
STEPHENS, J C Z01CP05680-01
STEPHENS, J C Z01CP05681-01
STEPHENS, MARY ANN P S07RR07208-10 0672
STEPHENS, RALPH E P30CA16058-17 9013
STEPHENS, RAYMOND E R01GM20644-19
STEPHENS, RICHARD C R18DA05754-03S1
STEPHENS, RICHARD S R01AI32432-01A1
STEPHENS, RICHARD S R01EY07757-04
STEPHENS, RICHARD S U01AI31499-01 0002
STEPHENS, ROBERT J R01EY05910-07
STEPHENS, ROBERT L, JR R29DK42880-02
STEPHENS, RONALD L U10CA12644-20
STEPHENS, TRENT D R15HD28223-01
STEPHENSEN, CHARLES S07RR05829-09 0955
STEPHENSEN, CHARLES R P40RR00463-23 0003
STEPHENSON, EDWIN CLARK R01GM41513-03
STEPHENSON, JOHN L R01DK31550-07
STEPHENSON, JOHN L R01RR06589-01
STEPHENSON, LARRY W R01HL34778-08
STEPHENSON, ROBERT S S06GM08167-13 0051
STEPKOWSKI, STANISLA S07RR05745-19 0240
STEPLEWSKI, XENON P01CA21124-14 0012
STEPLEWSKI, ZENON S U01CA51958-02
STEPLEWSKI, ZENON S U01CA51958-02 9001
STEPONKUS, PETER L R01GM37575-04A1
STEPP, MARY A R01EY08512-02
STEPP, MARY ANN S07RR05527-29 0523
STERGACHIS, ANDREAS S P01AI24756-05 0003
STERLING, CHARLES R U01AI30223-02
STERLING, CHARLES R U01AI30223-02 0001
STERLING, PETER R01EY00828-20
STERLING, PETER R01EY08124-03
STERN, ARNOLD R01ES03425-14
STERN, DAVID F R01CA45708-04A1
STERN, DAVID F S07RR05358-30 0480
STERN, DAVID M R01HL34625-08
STERN, DAVID M R01HL42507-03
STERN, DAVID M R01HL42833-03
STERN, HARRIET N01CN85060-06
STERN, JUDITH P30DK35747-06 9005
STERN, JUDITH M R01MH40459-07
STERN, JUDITH S R01DK18899-17
STERN, MARVIN N01LM13533-00
STERN, MICHAEL K15DE00307-01
STERN, MICHAEL R01GM46566-01

STERN, MICHAEL D P50HL17655-17 9010
STERN, MICHAEL D R01HL42050-03
STERN, MICHAEL P P01HL45522-01A1 9001
STERN, MICHAEL P R01DK42273-01A2
STERN, MICHAEL P R01HL24799-13
STERN, MICHAEL P R37HL36820-05
STERN, PAULA S07RR05311-30 0004
STERN, PAULA H R01AR11262-25
STERN, PAULA H S15AR41231-01
STERN, ROBERT P01CA44768-05 0003
STERN, ROBERT C M01RR00080-29 0392
STERN, ROBERT C P30DK27651-09 9001
STERN, SUSAN N01HB17087-02
STERN, SUSAN A N01AI82684-24
STERN, WALTER H R01EY03228-11
STERN, YAAKOV P01AG07232-03 9001
STERN, YAAKOV R01AG07370-03
STERNAU, LINDA L P50NS30291-01 0004
STERNBERG, E M Z01MH02585-01
STERNBERG, EDITH R01CA46668-04
STERNBERG, EDWARD A S07RR05434-30 0809
STERNBERG, NAT L R01HG00339-03
STERNBERG, PAUL R29EY07892-03
STERNBERG, PAUL U10EY06238-06
STERNBERG, PAUL JR U10EY06274-07
STERNBERG, PAUL W R01HD23690-04
STERNBERG, STEVEN S P30CA08748-26 9011
STERNBERGER, LUDWIG A R01NS24423-06
STERNBERGER, NANCY P01HD16596-08 0006
STERNGLANZ, ROLF R01GM28220-12
STERNINI, CATIA P30DK41301-02 9005
STERNINI, CATIA R01DK38752-05
STERNLIEB, IRMIN R01DK34668-05
STERNS, RONNI S R44AG08605-02
STERNWEIS, PAUL C R01GM31954-09
STETLER-STEVENSON, M Z01CB09181-03
STETLER-STEVENSON, W G Z01CB09179-03
STETLER-STEVENSON, W G Z01CB09164-03
STETLER, DEAN A R01AI24855-04
STETLER, DEAN A S07RR07037-26 0371
STETSON, DAVID P50HL42385-04 0003
STETSON, MILTON H S07RR07016-18 0363
STETSON, MILTON H S07RR07016-18
STETSON, MILTON H S07RR07016-18 0364
STETSON, PHILIP L R01CA46256-04
STETSON, PHILLIP L P30CA46592-04 9003
STETTER, JOSEPH R R44ES05156-03
STEUER, ANTON F N01CP05686-06
STEVEN, A C Z01AR27002-13
STEVEN, WILLIAM M R03DA06822-01A1
STEVENS, ANN R S07RR07023-26
STEVENS, ANN R S15DA07805-01
STEVENS, ANN R S15GM47064-01
STEVENS, C E S15EY09475-01
STEVENS, C EDWARD S07RR05911-08
STEVENS, CHARLES F R01NS12961-17
STEVENS, CLADD E R01AI24239-05
STEVENS, CLAUZELL S06GM08091-20 0029
STEVENS, J R Z01MH02275-07
STEVENS, J R Z01MH02457-03
STEVENS, JACK G R01AI06246-27
STEVENS, JACK G R01NS30420-01
STEVENS, JAMES P30CA46934-04 9005
STEVENS, JAMES R01DK38925-04
STEVENS, JAMES L P01CA37589-08 0007
STEVENS, JAMES L R01ES05670-01
STEVENS, JAMES L S07RR05863-11 0573
STEVENS, JAMES O P50NS09199-21 9001
STEVENS, JAMES O S15CA56025-01
STEVENS, JOSEPH C R37AG04287-09
STEVENS, JUNE R01HL42305-03
STEVENS, JUNE S07RR05420-30 0045
STEVENS, KATHLEEN R S07RR05654-24 0147
STEVENS, KENNETH N R01DC00075-28
STEVENS, RANDALL M S07RR05576-27 0604
STEVENS, RICHARD P01HL36110-07 0005
STEVENS, RICHARD L R01AI23483-04A2
STEVENS, RICHARD L U01AI31599-01 0004
STEVENS, SALLY J U01AA08788-02
STEVENS, SALLY J U01DA07470-01
STEVENS, TOM H R01GM32448-09
STEVENS, TOM H R01GM38006-05
STEVENS, VICTOR U01HL37954-05
STEVENS, WALTER M01RR00064-27
STEVENS, WALTER S03RR03173-10
STEVENS, WALTER S07RR05428-30
STEVENS, WALTER S15HL47748-01
STEVENS, WILLIAM S07RR07118-22 0385
STEVENSON, DAVID M01RR00081-29 0147
STEVENSON, DAVID K M01RR00081-29 0145
STEVENSON, DAVID K P51RR00169-30 0162
STEVENSON, DAVID K U10HD27880-01
STEVENSON, DONALD B M01RR00833-17 0080
STEVENSON, DONALD D M01RR00833-17 0151
STEVENSON, MARGUERIT S07RR07098-26 0347
STEVENSON, MARIO R01AI30386-02
STEVENSON, MARIO R29AI25582-03
STEVENSON, ROBERT N01RR92105-09
STEVENSON, SHARON P60AR20618-13 9005
STEWARD, OSWALD R01NS12333-17
STEWARD, OSWALD R01NS29875-01
STEWARD, RUTH R01HD18055-07A1
STEWART, ABIGAIL S07RR07050-26 0129
STEWART, ALEXANDRIA A R44HL41457-03
STEWART, ANITA R01AG09931-01
STEWART, BOB W R03RR06953-01A1
STEWART, CARLETON P01CA57165-01 9002
STEWART, CARLETON P41RR01315-10 9010
STEWART, CARLETON C P41RR01315-10 0046
STEWART, CARLETON C R01AI19490-10
STEWART, CARLTON P30CA16056-16 9022
STEWART, CYNTHIA S07RR05796-14 0442
STEWART, DOUGLAS K N01HC65038-08
STEWART, GEORGE S06GM08256-03 0003
STEWART, GEORGE C R01GM37990-06
STEWART, GEORGE C R13AI31531-01
STEWART, GWENDOLYN J P50HL45486-01 9002
STEWART, H L Z01CP04548-19
STEWART, J ROBERT P30CA42014-06 9009
STEWART, J ROBERT P30CA42014-06
STEWART, JAMES A P30CA22435-11 9002
STEWART, JAMES A U10CA43189-03
STEWART, JENNIFER K S07RR07204-11 0449
STEWART, JOHN M R01HL33534-05
STEWART, JOHN M R37HL26284-12
STEWART, JUARINE G12RR03062-07 0002
STEWART, JUARINE S06GM08247-04 0010
STEWART, KAREN N01CP61012-08
STEWART, KERRY J M01RR02719-06 0133
STEWART, LAURAINE M01RR00065-29 0374
STEWART, MCDONALD N01LM13547-00
STEWART, MICHAEL J R29AI24615-04
STEWART, STANFORD J R29GM38610-05
STEWART, VALLEY J R01GM36877-06
STEWART, WALTER F R01NS26450-04
STEWART, WILLIAM B P01DC00168-10 0017
STEWMAN, SHELBY R01AG04139-04
STIBITZ, E S Z01BA03003-02
STIEFEL, DORIS S07RR05346-30 0328
STIEFEL, DORIS J P30DE09743-02 0003
STIEHM, E RICHARD P50AI15332-14 0012
STIEHM, E RICHARD R01HD09800-15
STIER, CHARLES T, JR R01HL35522-06
STIFFMAN, ARLENE R R01MH45118-03
STIFTER, CYNTHIA A S07RR07082-26 0309
STILES-DAVIS, JOAN P50NS22343-06A1 0003
STILES, ALAN D R29HL38902-05
STILES, CHARLES P01HD24926-03 0001
STILES, CHARLES D P01CA22427-14 0005
STILES, CHARLES D P01HD24926-03
STILES, CHARLES D R01CA22042-14
STILES, CHARLES D R01GM31489-09
STILES, CHARLES D R13CA56580-01
STILES, GARY L P50HL17670-17 0032
STILES, GARY L R01HL35134-06
STILL, WILLIAM C, JR R01GM44525-02
STILL, WILLIAM C, JR R01HL25634-12
STILLE, JOHN R R29GM44163-02
STILLE, JOHN R S07RR07049-26 0449
STILLMAN, BRUCE S P01CA13106-20 0016
STILLMAN, BRUCE S P01CA13106-20 0017
STILLMAN, BRUCE W R01GM45436-01A1
STILLMAN, BRUCE W R37AI20460-09
STILLMAN, DAVID J R01GM39067-04
STILLWELL, WILLIAM H R15AG09881-01
STIMERS, JOSEPH R R01RR06564-02
STIMERS, JOSEPH R R29HL44660-02
STINE, ELIZABETH A L R29AG08382-05
STINE, KIMO S07RR05377-30 0755
STINEMAN, MARGARET G K08AG00487-02
STINI, WILLIAM A S07RR07002-26 0875
STINNETT, HENRY S07RR05407-30 0043
STINSKI, MARK F P01HD19937-06 0001
STINSKI, MARK F R01AI13562-16
STINSON, EDWARD B P01HL13108-22
STINSON, M W P01DE07585-04 0003
STINSON, MICHAEL P01DC00316-06 0001
STINSON, MURRAY W P50DE08240-05 0004
STINSON, S Z01CM07196-01
STINSON, S Z01CM07197-01
STIPEK, DEBORAH J R01MH46427-01A1
STIREWALT, WILLIAM S R01AR40494-02
STISTES, DANIEL P01AI24286-05 0005
STITES, DANIEL P R01AI23788-04
STITH, R D S07RR05411-30 0963
STITT, BARBARA S07RR07062-26 0223
STITT, BARBARA S07RR07062-26 0224
STITT, FRANK W P50NS30291-01 9001
STITT, JOHN T R01NS11487-17
STITT, JOHN T S03RR03277-10
STITZER, MAXINE L R01DA03893-08
STITZER, MAXINE L R01DA04011-06
STITZER, MAXINE L R01DA05880-07
STITZER, MAXINE L R18DA06165-03
STITZER, SUSAN O P40RR03640-05 0007
STOBO, JOHN D K12DK01298-07
STOCCO, DOUGLAS S07RR05773-17 0370
STOCK, JEFFRY B R01AI20980-07
STOCKDALE, FRANK E R01AG02822-11
STOCKDALE, FRANK E R01AR39320-04
STOCKER, BRUCE A R01AI27722-03
STOCKERT, RICHARD J R01DK32972-08
STOCKMEIER, CRAIG P50MH41684-07 0040
STOCKMEIER, CRAIG P50MH41684-07 0041
STOCKMEIER, CRAIG P50MH41684-07 0042
STOCKMEIER, CRAIG P50MH41684-07 0043
STOCKMEIER, CRAIG P50MH41684-07 0044
STOCKMEIER, CRAIG A R01MH45488-03
STOCKWELL, HEATHER G R29CA45513-05
STODDARD, LAWRENCE T P01HD25995-03
STODDARD, LAWRENCE T P01HD25995-03 0005
STOECKERT, CHRISTIAN J, JR R29HL45123-01A1
STOFF, DAVID M K02MH00590-05
STOFFOLANO, JOHN G J S07RR07048-26 0656
STOFFOLANO, JOHN G J S07RR07048-26 0657
STOHLER, CHRISTIAN S R01DE08606-03
STOHLMAN, STEPHEN A P01NS18146-10 0002
STOICA, GEORGE S07RR05854-11 0920
STOKES, BRADFORT T P50NS10165-20
STOKES, DAVID L R01AR40997-01
STOKES, GERALD V S03RR03520-02
STOKES, IAN A R01AR40093-02
STOKES, IAN F S07RR05429-30 0198
STOKES, JOHN B P30ES03828-06 0012
STOKES, JOHN B, III R01DK25231-13
STOLER, MARK H R01CA43629-06
STOLERMAN, IAN P R01DA04376-05
STOLERMAN, IAN PETER R01DA05543-04
STOLFI, ROBERT L P01CA25842-11 9001
STOLL, BARBARA J U10HD27851-01
STOLLAR, BERNARD D R01GM32375-09
STOLLAR, VICTOR R01AI26371-04
STOLLAR, VICTOR R22AI05920-29
STOLLBERG, JES R01NS26943-02
STOLLE, CATHERINE A R29AR40556-02
STOLLER, ELEANOR P R01AG07794-03
STOLLER, HAROLD M R43NS29317-01
STOLLER, MILTON R43CA53952-01
STOLLER, MILTON R44CA48544-03
STOLLEY, PAUL P30HD26979-02 9006
STOLTE, HILMAR P30ES03828-06 0013
STOLTZFUS, CONRAD M R01CA28051-12
STOLZ, ANDREW A R29DK41014-04
STOLZ, RUTH I S07RR05408-30 0942
STOLZENBERG, ALAN M R01GM33882-07
STOMING, TERRANCE P01HL41544-04 0003
STONE, A L Z01MH02593-01
STONE, ARTHUR S07RR07067-26 0225
STONE, CHARLES K R29HL47003-01
STONE, DENNIS K R01DK33627-07
STONE, DIANA S07RR07097-26 0386
STONE, EDWIN M R29EY08426-02
STONE, ERIC A R37MH45265-03
STONE, JAMES S07RR05545-29 0566
STONE, KATHLEEN S R01NR01552-05
STONE, KATHLEEN S S07RR05944-04 0974
STONE, MARCIA J R44ES05220-02
STONE, MARVIN P01CA41081-06A1 0005
STONE, MARVIN J P01CA41081-06A1 0003
STONE, MARY N01CO84339-19
STONE, MICHAEL P P01ES05355-01A1 0003
STONE, MICHAEL P S10RR06381-01
STONE, PETER R01HL42419-03 9003
STONE, PETER H M01RR02635-07 0245
STONE, PETER H M01RR02635-07 0283
STONE, PHILIP J P01HL19717-15 0003
STONE, PHILLIP J R01HL46338-01
STONE, RICHARD A P51RR00165-31 0180
STONE, RICHARD A R01EY05454-08
STONE, RICHARD A R01EY07354-02
STONE, RICHARD M K08CA01352-02
STONE, SUSAN L R01EY06960-05
STONE, SUSAN L S07RR05399-30 0936
STONE, WILLIAM S07RR07261-02 0715
STONE, WILLIAM H R24RR04301-04
STONEKING, BETH R18MH46146-03
STONEMAN, WILLIAM, III S07RR05388-30
STONER, G L Z01NS02550-10
STONER, GARY D R37CA28950-10
STONESTREET, BARBARA S P50HD11343-14A1 001
STONEY, CATHERINE M R01HL48363-01
STOODT, GEORJEAN N01CN15386-00
STOODT, GEORJEAN R01CA46582-04
STOOKEY, GEORGE K P01DE09835-01A1 0003
STOOKEY, GEORGE K P01DE09835-01A1
STOOKEY, GEORGE K S07RR06037-01
STOOLMAN, L M P60AR20557-13 0061
STOOLMAN, LLOYD M R01CA49256-03
STOOPS, JAMES K R01GM46278-01
STOOPS, JAMES K R01HL42886-03
STOPA, EDWARD G R01AG10682-01
STOPPARD, LAWRENCE T P01HD25995-03 0006
STOPPEL, DAVID A R43HD25382-01A3
STORANDT, MARTHA P01AG03991-08 9002
STORANDT, MARTHA P01AG03991-08 9004
STORANDT, MARTHA P50AG05681-08 9003
STORB, RAINER F P01CA18029-16 0019
STORB, RAINER F P01CA18029-16 0002
STORB, RAINER F P01CA18221-16 9001
STORB, RAINER F P01CA18221-16
STORB, RAINER F P01HL36444-11 0003
STORB, RAINER F P01HL36444-11
STORB, RAINER F R01CA31787-11
STORB, RAINER F R01DK42716-02
STORB, URSULA B R01GM38649-05
STORB, URSULA B R01HD23089-06

STORCH, GREGORY A M01RR06021-02 1005
STORCH, GREGORY A M01RR06021-02 1012
STORCH, GREGORY A U01AI25903-05 9001
STORCH, JUDITH R29DK38389-05
STORCH, THOMAS S07RR05377-30 0758
STORELLA, ROBERT J R01NS28165-01A2
STORER, BARRY E P01CA20432-14 0035
STORER, BARRY E R29CA45313-05
STOREY, BAYARD T P01HD06274-20 0001
STOREY, BAYARD T R01HD15842-09
STOREY, BAYARD T R01HD25867-02
STOREY, BAYARD T R13HD28300-01
STOREY, KENNETH B R01GM43796-02
STORK, GILBERT R01GM05147-35
STORK, GILBERT R01HL25635-12
STORK, PHILIP J K08DK02035-01
STORK, PHILIP J R03DA06895-02
STORM, DANIEL P50AG05136-08 0013
STORM, DANIEL R P01HL44948-01A1 0004
STORM, DANIEL R R01GM31708-09
STORM, DANIEL R R01GM33708-07
STORM, DANIEL R R01NS20498-08
STORM, F KRISTIAN P01CA29605-10 0004
STORM, HANS H N01CP85639-01
STORMO, GARY D R01GM28755-11
STORMO, GARY D R01HG00249-03
STORMO, GARY D R01LM05094-03
STORMO, GARY D S07RR07013-26 0951
STORNETTA, RUTH L R29DA07353-01
STORTHZ, KAREN A R29DE08061-05
STORTI, GEORGE M R43GM45674-01
STORTI, GEORGE M R43MH48255-01
STORTI, ROBERT V R01GM27611-13
STORTI, ROBERT V S07RR05369-30 0600
STORZ, G Z01HD01608-01
STOSSEL, THOMAS P P01AI28465-03 0004
STOSSEL, THOMAS P P50DK39249-05 0015
STOSSEL, THOMAS P R37HL19429-16
STOTO, MICHAEL A N01AI15130-00
STOTT, PHILLIP B U10CA35184-08
STOTTLER, RICHARD H R43HD26690-01A1
STOTTS, NANCY A M01RR00079-29 0398
STOTTS, NANCY A S07RR05604-14 0683
STOTZKY, GUENTHER S07RR07062-26 0225
STOUDEMIRE, ALAN G R01MH47597-01
STOUDEMIRE, BEVERLY A K07HL02682-01
STOUFFER, RICHARD L P51RR00163-32 0034
STOUFFER, RICHARD L P51RR00163-32 9017
STOUFFER, RICHARD L R01HD20869-06
STOUGHTON, W VICKERY G08LM04613-05
STOUT, CHARLES D R01GM36325-07
STOUT, FRANK G S07RR05598-26
STOUT, FRANK G S15HL47711-01
STOUT, JOSEPH T S07RR07082-26 0310
STOUT, ROBERT L R01AA08992-01
STOVALL, MARILYN N01CP95614-05
STOW, JENNIFER P30DK43351-01 9002
STOW, JENNIFER L R29DK42881-02
STOWE, STEVEN M R01LM05334-01
STOYSICH, ANNE M S07RR05390-30 0683
STRAATON, KARIN P60AR20614-14 0006
STRAATSMA, BRADLEY R U10EY06268-07
STRACHER, ALFRED R01HL14020-18
STRACKE, M Z01CB00891-08
STRAHILEVITZ, MIER S07RR05745-19 0232
STRAIN, GEORGE M R15DC01128-01
STRAIN, PHILLIP S R01MH37110-08
STRAIR, ROGER K R01CA54547-01
STRAIR, ROGER K R29CA49047-04
STRALEY, SUSAN C R01AI21017-08
STRAND, EDYTHE A K08DC00043-01A1
STRAND, EDYTHE A S07RR07125-22 0400
STRAND, FLEUR S07RR07062-26
STRAND, FLEUR S15GM47047-01
STRAND, METTE R01AI28206-03
STRAND, METTE R37AI19217-10
STRANDBERG, J P40RR00130-28 0115
STRANDBERG, JOHN D G20RR06785-01
STRANDBERG, JOHN D P01AG08321-03 9001
STRANDBERG, JOHN D P40RR00130-28
STRANDNESS, DONALD E, JR P50HL42270-02
STRANDNESS, DONALD E, JR P50HL42270-02 0002
STRANDNESS, DONALD E, JR P50HL42270-02 0003
STRANDNESS, DONALD E, JR R37HL36095-05
STRANEVA, JOHN E R15HL46405-01
STRANEY, DAVID S07RR07042-26 0408
STRANG, CANDACE J S07RR07090-26 0467
STRANGE, KEVIN S10RR06725-01
STRANGE, WINIFRED R01DC00323-07
STRANTZ, IRMA R18DA07311-02
STRASBURG, GALE S07RR07049-26 0444
STRASSBERG, DONALD S S07RR07092-26 0533
STRASSMAN, ANDREW M R29NS24594-04
STRASSMAN, RICK M01RR00997-16 0300
STRASSMAN, RICK M01RR00997-16 0393
STRASSMAN, RICK M01RR00997-16 0235
STRASSMAN, RICK J R03DA06524-02
STRATES, BASIL S R01AR40064-03
STRATHMANN, RICHARD S07RR07096-26 0055
STRATTON, HAROLD H P20NS30303-01 9001
STRAUBINGER, ROBERT M R01CA55251-01
STRAUBINGER, ROBERT M R29AI28732-02

STRAUCH, ARTHUR R R01HL43370-03
STRAUCH, ARTHUR R R29HL38694-02
STRAUMAN, TIMOTHY J R29MH45800-01A1
STRAUS, DANIEL S R01DK39739-03
STRAUS, DAVID S07RR05773-17 0373
STRAUS, DAVID J R01CA55531-01
STRAUS, K L Z01CM06310-12
STRAUS, RICHARD N01CO15632-00
STRAUS, RICHARD R N01CO15696-01
STRAUS, S E Z01AI00058-18
STRAUS, S E Z01AI00430-07
STRAUS, S E Z01AI00470-06
STRAUS, S E Z01AI00496-05
STRAUS, S E Z01AI00548-03
STRAUS, THOM N01CO15759-00
STRAUS, THOMAS F N01CO15728-00
STRAUSFELD, NICHOLAS J R01EY07151-05
STRAUSS, ARNOLD M P50HL17646-17 9006
STRAUSS, ARNOLD W P01DK33487-05 0003
STRAUSS, ARNOLD W P50HL17646-17 0007
STRAUSS, ARNOLD W R37DK20407-14
STRAUSS, BERNARD P01CA40046-05S2 0002
STRAUSS, BERNARD S P01CA40046-05S2
STRAUSS, BERNARD S R01GM07816-32
STRAUSS, BERNARD S R37CA32436-10
STRAUSS, HAROLD C P50HL17670-17 0039
STRAUSS, HAROLD C P50HL17670-17
STRAUSS, HAROLD C R01HL45132-02
STRAUSS, HAROLD C R37HL19216-16
STRAUSS, HARRY W R01HL32636-06
STRAUSS, HERBERT L R01GM27690-12
STRAUSS, JAMES H R22AI20612-08
STRAUSS, JAMES H R37AI10793-18
STRAUSS, JEROME F P01HD06274-20 0010
STRAUSS, JEROME F, III P01HD06274-20
STRAUSS, JOHN P01HD28372-01 0003
STRAUSS, JOHN P01HD28372-01 0005
STRAUSS, JOHN P01HD28372-01 0006
STRAUSS, JOHN P50HD12639-12 0020
STRAUSS, JOHN R01HD27560-01A1
STRAUSS, JOHN S07RR05710-21 0019
STRAUSS, JOHN S K05MH00340-11
STRAUSS, JOSE R01DK40838-03
STRAUSS, PHYLLIS R S07RR07143-20 0636
STRAUSS, WILLIAM L R01NS23430-01A4
STRAW, RODNEY C S07RR05458-29 0839
STRECHER, VICTOR J R01HL46775-01
STRECHER, VICTOR J R29HL41886-03
STRECHER, VICTOR J S07RR05450-30 0330
STRECKER, ROBERT E R03DA07456-01
STRED, SUSAN E S07RR05402-30 0801
STREET, JOSEPH P S07RR07147-19 0652
STREET, NANCY E R29CA55266-01
STREET, NANCY E S07RR07175-15 0445
STREETEN, BARBARA W R01EY01602-17
STREILEIN, J WAYNE R01CA39078-08
STREILEIN, J WAYNE R37EY05678-08
STREILEIN, WAYNE J R01AI22072-05
STREISAND, JAMES M01RR00064-27 0383
STREISSGUTH, ANN P R01AA01455-16
STREISSGUTH, ANN P R01DA05365-04
STREIT, DONALD A S07RR07082-26 0311
STREITWIESER, ANDREW R01GM30369-10
STREKAS, THOMAS C S03RR03460-05
STREKAS, THOMAS C S07RR07064-24 0208
STREKOWSKI, LUCJAN U01AI27196-04 0002
STRETTON, ANTONY O R01AI15429-13
STRETTON, ANTONY O R01AI20355-09
STRETTON, ANTONY O S07RR07098-26 0360
STREUFERT, SIEGFRIED R01DA06170-02S1
STREWLER, GORDON J R01CA34738-06
STRICHARTZ, GARY P50GM15904-24 0023
STRICHARTZ, GARY R R01GM35647-07
STRICK, PETER L R01NS24328-05
STRICKER, EDWARD M P50MH45156-02
STRICKER, EDWARD M R01MH29670-14
STRICKER, EDWARD M R37MH25140-18
STRICKLAND, DUDLEY P50HL44336-01 0001
STRICKLAND, DUDLEY P50HL44336-01 9001
STRICKLAND, DUDLEY K K04HL02113-04
STRICKLAND, DUDLEY K R01GM42581-03
STRICKLAND, DUDLEY K R01HL30200-07
STRICKLAND, J Z01CP05178-10
STRICKLAND, JAMES H, S07RR05992-04 0816
STRICKLAND, ORA L R01NR02705-01
STRICKLAND, PAUL T R29AR38884-04
STRICKLAND, SIDNEY R01HD17875-08
STRICKLAND, SIDNEY R01HD25922-03
STRICKLAND, TONY L K14HL01988-03
STRICKLER, RONALD C R01HD20055-06
STRICKLIN, GEORGE P R01AR39682-03
STRICOFF, SCOTT R N01ES85215-10
STRIEGEL, JANE E M01RR00334-25 0304
STRIETER, ROBERT M K08HL02401-02
STRIKER, G Z01DK43233-02
STRIKER, L Z01DK43211-07
STRIKER, L Z01DK43214-07
STRIKER, L Z01DK43225-04
STRIKER, L Z01DK43228-04
STRIKER, L Z01DK43232-02
STRIKER, L Z01DK43235-02
STRIKER, L Z01DK43236-01

STRIKER, L Z01DK43238-01
STRINGER, JAMES P01ES05652-01 0004
STRINGER, JAMES R P01AI28392-02 0005
STRINGER, JAMES R R01AI28471-03
STRINGER, JAMES R R01GM39622-04
STRINGER, JANET R29NS28871-02
STRINGER, KATHLEEN S07RR05831-12 0976
STRITTMATER, PHILIP S07RR05678-23 0156
STRITTMATTER, PHILIPP R01GM15924-24
STRITTMATTER, STEPHEN M K08NS01467-02
STRITTMATTER, WARREN J P50AG08664-03 0004
STRITTMATTER, WARREN J P50AG08664-03 9001
STROBEL, HENRY W R01CA53191-01A1
STROBER, SAMUEL N01AI85001-06
STROBER, SAMUEL P01AI29796-08
STROBER, SAMUEL P01AI29796-08 0001
STROBER, SAMUEL P01AI29796-08 9001
STROBER, SAMUEL P01AI29796-08 9002
STROBER, SAMUEL R01AR40227-02
STROBL, JEANNINE S R01CA46350-03
STROHL, KINGMAN P01HL25830-11A1 0009
STROHL, KINGMAN P50HL42215-04 9002
STROHL, KINGMAN P50HL42215-04 0001
STROHL, KINGMAN P K04HL02011-05
STROHL, KINGMAN P M01RR00080-29 0374
STROHL, KINGMAN P P50HL37117-05 0003
STROHL, KINGMAN P P50HL42215-04
STROM, STEPHEN P30CA16059-15 9017
STROM, TERRY B M01RR01032-16 0453
STROM, TERRY B P50DK39249-05 0010
STROM, TERRY B R01AI22882-05S1
STROM, TERRY B U01CA48626-04 0003
STROMBERG, K J Z01BD01005-03
STROME, SUSAN R01GM34059-06
STROMER, ROBERT P01HD25995-03 0007
STROMER, ROBERT P01HD25995-03 0003
STROMER, ROBERT L, JR R01HD26200-01A3
STROMINGER, JACK L P01HD17461-08 0004
STROMINGER, JACK L R01AI15669-14
STROMINGER, JACK L R01AI20182-07
STROMINGER, JACK L R35CA47554-04
STROMINGER, JACK L R37DK30241-10
STROMINGER, JACK L U01AI27221-03 0002
STRONG, DONNA D S07RR05352-30 0766
STRONG, JACK P R10HL33746-07
STRONG, JACK P R10HL45720-01
STRONG, LOUISE C P01CA34936-08
STRONG, LOUISE C P01CA34936-08 0001
STRONG, LOUISE C R01CA38929-07
STRONG, RANDY R01AG09557-01
STROTHER, STEPHEN C R29NS25563-05
STROTHKAMP, KENNETH G R15DK41550-01A1
STROTT, C A Z01HD00194-03
STROTTMAN, PAUL M01RR00059-30 0713
STROTTMANN, PAUL M01RR00059-30 0709
STROUD, ROBERT P41RR01614-10 0001
STROUD, ROBERT M P01GM39552-05 0004
STROUD, ROBERT M R01GM24485-15
STROUD, ROBERT M R01GM32079-09
STROUD, ROBERT M S10RR06474-01
STRUCK, ROBERT F P01CA34200-09 0013
STRUCK, ROBERT F P01CA34200-09
STRUCK, ROBERT F P01CA34200-09 0005
STRUENING, ELMER L R01MH44690-02A1
STRUENING, ELMER L R01MH46130-02
STRUHL, KEVIN R01GM30186-10
STRUHL, KEVIN R01GM46555-01
STRUMWASSER, FELIX P41RR01395-10 0016
STRUMWASSER, FELIX R01NS21046-08
STRUMWASSER, FELIX S07RR05547-23 0079
STRUNK, ROBERT N01HR16051-00
STRUNK, ROBERT C R01DK26609-08
STRUNK, ROBERT S M01RR06021-02 1018
STRUPP, BARBARA S07RR07061-26 0191
STRUVE, FREDERICK A R01DA06643-02
STRYER, LUBERT R01EY02005-15
STRYER, LUBERT R01MH45324-03
STRYER, LUBERT R37GM24032-15
STRYKER, JEFFREY M S07RR07031-26 0110
STRYKER, MICHAEL P R01EY02874-12
STRÖBER, W Z01AI00356-09
STUART, ANN E R01EY03347-13
STUART, CHARLES A M01RR00073-29 0303
STUART, CHARLES A M01RR00073-29 0197
STUART, CHARLES A R01DK33749-05
STUART, DOUGLAS G R01NS25077-05
STUART, FRANK P P01AI29531-02 0003
STUART, FRANK P U01AI31445-01
STUART, GARY W R01HD27555-01
STUART, J M P50AR39166-05 0007
STUART, J M P50AR39166-05 0001
STUART, KENNETH D R01AI17375-10
STUART, KENNETH D R01AI24771-05
STUART, KENNETH D R01GM42188-03
STUART, KENNETH D S07RR05939-07 0729
STUART, KENNETH D S07RR05939-07
STUART, KENNETH D S15AI32184-01
STUART, MARIE J R01AR38847-03
STUART, MARIE J R01HL45969-02
STUART, W DORSEY S15GM47035-01
STUBBE, JO ANNE R37GM29595-13
STUBBE, JOANN P41RR02583-07 0015

STUBBE, JOANNE R01GM32191-10
STUBBS, CHRISTOPHER D P01AA07215-06 0003
STUBBS, CHRISTOPHER D R29AA08022-03
STUBBS, G P41RR02250-06 0001
STUBBS, GERALD P41RR01646-09 0011
STUBBS, GERALD J R01GM33265-09
STUBBS, GERALD J R01GM42287-04
STUBER, MARGARET S07RR05756-18 0316
STUBER, MARGARET S07RR05756-18 0304
STUCKEY, WALTER J U10CA52623-02
STUCKI, JOSEPH W S07RR07030-26 0414
STUDDERT-KENNEDY, MICHAEL P01HD01994-26A1
STUDDERT-KENNEDY, MICHAEL P01HD01994-26A1
STUDDERT-KENNEDY, MICHAEL S07RR05596-27
STUDEBAKER, GERALD A R01DC00154-13
STUDEBAKER, GERALD A S07RR07229-06
STUDIER, F WILLIAM R01GM21872-17
STUEHR, DENNIS J R29CA53914-02
STUEN, CYNTHIA R13AG09398-01
STUIFBERGEN, ALEXA M S07RR07091-26 0770
STUKALIN, R S07RR05915-08 0691
STUKEL, THERESE A R01CA52192-01A1
STUKES, JAMES B S06GM08060-21 0005
STULL, DONALD E R29AG07597-04
STULL, DONALD E S07RR07249-03 0724
STULL, JAMES T P01HL06296-31 9006
STULL, JAMES T P01HL06296-31 0009
STULL, JAMES T R01HD26164-03
STULL, JAMES T R13HL47174-01
STULL, JAMES T R37HL26043-11A1
STULL, TERRENCE L R01AI29611-01A1
STULTING, RD P30EY06360-06 9004
STULTING, ROBERT D R01EY05097-08
STULTING, ROBERT D U10EY06121-07
STULTING, ROBERT D U10EY07482-04
STUM, MARLENE S S07RR07052-26 0171
STUMP, DAVID A P01NS27500-01A2 9001
STUMP, J M Z01CP04269-20
STUMP, ROBERT S07RR05583-27 0642
STUMPF, WALTER P30HD18968-08 9001
STUMPH, WILLIAM E R01GM33512-07
STUNKARD, ALBERT J K05MH00245-13
STUNKARD, ALBERT J P01MH31050-15
STUNKARD, ALBERT J P01MH31050-15 0001
STUNKARD, ALBERT J P01MH31050-15 0002
STUNKARD, ALBERT J P01MH31050-15 0003
STUNKARD, ALBERT J P01MH31050-15 0004
STUNKARD, ALBERT J P01MH31050-15 0005
STUREK, MICHAEL S R29HL41033-02
STURGILL, THOMAS W R01DK41077-03
STURMAN, JOHN A R01HD16634-07
STURMAN, JOHN A R01HD18678-07A1
STURMAN, JOHN A S07RR05838-12 0272
STURMAN, LAWRENCE S15AI32162-01
STURROCK, ANN B S07RR05428-30 0170
STURTEVANT, JULIAN M R01GM04725-35
STUTMAN, OSIAS R01AG02152-10
STUTTS, M JACKSON P01HL34322-06 0003
STUTTS, M JACKSON P50HL42384-04 0002
STUYCK, STEPHEN C N01CO03865-05
STYBLO, TONCRED S07RR05364-30 0543
STYC, KATHLEEN R19MH46177-03
STYNE, DENNIS M P51RR00169-30 0126
STYNE, DENNIS M P51RR00169-30 0127
STYNE, DENNIS M R01HD24959-03
STYRT, BARBARA S07RR05656-24 0846
SU, JUDY Y R01HL20754-14
SU, S SUSAN R01DA05617-01A1
SU, SOL I P30HD06268-18 9003
SU, T P Z01DA00206-06
SU, YU R43GM45677-01
SUAREZ-QUIAN, CARLOS A R29HD23484-04
SUAREZ, BRIAN K R01HL41035-02
SUAREZ, EDWARD C R29HL46283-01
SUAREZ, PEDRO S06GM45455-01 0004
SUAREZ, SUSAN S R01HD19584-06
SUBIN, SIDNEY S K06HL07064-31
SUBJECK, JOHN R R01CA40330-07
SUBJECK, JOHN R R01GM39860-04
SUBRAMANI, SURESH R01DK41737-02
SUBRAMANI, SURESH R01GM31253-09A1
SUBRAMANIAN, KIRANUR S07RR05369-30 0605
SUBRAMANIAN, MARAPPA G R29AA07670-03
SUBRAMANIAN, UMA N01HB97053-05
SUBRAMANIAN, V P41RR02305-08 9003
SUCCOP, P P01ES01566-13 0003
SUCHARD, SUZANNE J R29AI26863-04
SUCHMAN, ANTHONY L R03MH47110-02
SUCHY, FREDERICK J M01RR06022-02 0749
SUCHY, FREDERICK J R01DK43509-01A1
SUCHY, FREDERICK J R01HD20632-06
SUCHY, FREDERICK J R13DK44145-01
SUCIU-FOCA, NICOLE R01AI25210-05
SUDAK, HOWARD P50MH41684-07 0084
SUDAK, HOWARD S P50MH41684-07 0037
SUDDATH, FRED L, JR R01GM36610-07
SUDHOF, THOMAS C R01MH47510-01A1
SUDILOVSKY, OSCAR R01CA35362-06
SUDOL, MARIUS K04CA01605-01
SUDOL, MARIUS R29CA45757-05
SUE, STANLEY R01MH44331-04
SUE, STANLEY R01MH44331-04 0001

SUENRAM, C ALAN P01HL26890-09 9003
SUEOKA, NOBORU R01NS21512-05
SUETA, CARLA M01RR00046-31 0491
SUFFREDINI, A F Z01CL00056-03
SUFFREDINI, A F Z01CL00063-03
SUFIAN, MERYL R18DA05283-03S1
SUFRIN, JANICE S07RR05648-25 0928
SUFRIN, JANICE R U01CA37606-08 0003
SUGA, NOBUO R01DC00175-11
SUGAR, ALAN M P01AI28408-02 0004
SUGAR, ALAN M S07RR05487-29 0698
SUGAR, JOEL U10EY07488-04
SUGARBAKER, DAVID S07RR05950-07 0982
SUGARMAN, JONATHAN R R21DK44594-01
SUGDEN, BILL R01AI29988-02
SUGDEN, BILL R01CA41302-06
SUGDEN, BILL M P01CA22443-14 0004
SUGDEN, BILL M P30CA07175-28 9002
SUGGS, PATRICIA P60AG10484-01 9005
SUGINO, A Z01ES61037-07
SUGINO, A Z01ES61039-07
SUGIYAMA, KATSUMI Z01HL04401-02
SUGRUE, STEPHEN P R01EY07883-03
SUGRUE, STEPHEN P S07RR05381-30 0783
SUH, BO S07RR05551-29 0961
SUH, H H Z01ES90060-02
SUINN, RICHARD M P50DA07074-02 9001
SUINN, RICHARD M P50DA07074-02
SUIT, HERMAN P01CA21239-15 0001
SUIT, HERMAN P01CA21239-15 0002
SUIT, HERMAN D P01CA21239-15
SUIT, HERMAN D R37CA13311-20
SUKALSKI, KATHERINE S07RR05407-30 0052
SUKUMAR, SARASWATI P01HG00202-02 0002
SUKUMAR, SARASWATI R01CA48943-03
SUKUMAR, SARASWATI S07RR05595-27 0673
SUL, HEI S R01DK36264-07
SUL, HEI S R01DK40518-03
SULEIMAN, JOANN D N01LM13520-00
SULIK, KATHLEEN K R01AA08204-03
SULING, WILLIAM J S07RR05676-15 0954
SULIS, CAROL ANN S07RR05569-27 0111
SULKES, MARK A R01GM32777-04A2
SULLIVAN JAY M M01RR00211-27 0291
SULLIVAN, CONSTANCE N01LM03510-01
SULLIVAN, CONSTANCE N01LM13519-00
SULLIVAN, DANIEL MARK K08CA01124-05
SULLIVAN, DAVID A R01EY05612-07
SULLIVAN, DONNA C S07RR05386-30 0596
SULLIVAN, J GREER R29MH47907-02
SULLIVAN, JAY M M01RR00211-27 0309
SULLIVAN, JAY M M01RR00211-27 0111
SULLIVAN, JAY M M01RR00211-27 0337
SULLIVAN, JOHN L R01AI25542-04
SULLIVAN, JOHN L R01AI32391-01
SULLIVAN, JOHN L R01HL42257-09
SULLIVAN, JOHN L U01AI26507-03 0002
SULLIVAN, KEITH P01CA18029-16 9011
SULLIVAN, KEITH P01CA47748-03 9003
SULLIVAN, KEITH P01HL36444-11 0011
SULLIVAN, KEVIN M01RR00833-17 0214
SULLIVAN, KEVIN F P01GM46006-01 0005
SULLIVAN, KEVIN F R29GM39068-04
SULLIVAN, MARK D R01AG08240-03
SULLIVAN, MARTIN J M01RR00030-30 0484
SULLIVAN, RICHARD H S06GM08047-20S1 0033
SULLIVAN, TIMOTHY M01RR00633-19 0392
SULLIVAN, TIMOTHY J P01AI23271-06 0003
SULLIVAN, TIMOTHY J R01AI26646-04
SULLIVAN, WALTER W S03RR03413-07
SULLIVAN, WALTER W S06GM08248-05
SULLIVAN, WALTER W S07RR05907-08
SULLIVAN, WILLIAM T R29GM46409-01
SULS, JERRY M R01HL46448-02
SULSER, FRIDOLIN R37MH29228-15
SULTZER, BARNET M R01AI28526-03
SULTZER, DAVID L K07MH00910-01
SULZER, DAVID R29DA07418-01
SUMAYA, CIRO V U01AI31498-01 0005
SUMAYA, CIRO V U76PE00228-02
SUMBURERU, DALE S07RR05407-30 0047
SUMI, SHUZO M P50AG05136-08 9003
SUMIKAWA, KATUMI R01NS25928-03
SUMIKAWA, KATUMI R01NS27341-02
SUMMERHAYES, IAN P01CA44704-04A1 0004
SUMMERHAYES, IAN C R01CA42944-05
SUMMERS, ANNE O R01GM28211-12
SUMMERS, CAROLE G U10EY06396-07
SUMMERS, DENISE O S03RR03435-05
SUMMERS, DONALD F R01AI12316-15S1
SUMMERS, DONALD F R01AI26350-04
SUMMERS, GAIL C P01GM22167-16 0009
SUMMERS, JESSE W R35CA42542-06
SUMMERS, MICHAEL F R01AI30917-01A1
SUMMERS, MICHAEL F R29GM42561-03
SUMMERS, WILLIAM P01GM39546-05 0004
SUMMITT, ROBERT L M01RR00211-27
SUMMITT, ROBERT L S07RR05423-30
SUMMITT, ROBERT L S15HL47698-01
SUMMY-LONG, JOAN Y R01HD25498-02
SUMNER, DALE R R29AR39827-03
SUMNER, SUSAN S07RR07055-26 0197

SUMNERS, COLIN R01NS19441-08
SUMPIO, BAUER E R29HL40305-04
SUN, ALBERT Y R01AA02054-12
SUN, ALBERT Y R01AA07585-03
SUN, DEMING R29NS29695-01
SUN, GRACE Y R01AA06661-07
SUN, HUN H S07RR07129-22 0504
SUN, TUNG-TIEN P30AR39749-04 9002
SUN, TUNG-TIEN R01AR34511-08
SUN, TUNG-TIEN R01DK39753-04
SUN, TUNG-TIEN R01EY04722-10
SUNDAR RAJ, NIRMALA R01EY03263-12
SUNDARALINGAM, MUTTAIYA R01GM17378-23
SUNDARAM, RAMAKRISHN S07RR05385-30 0809
SUNDARESESN, VENEKTE S07RR05717-21 0131
SUNDAY, MARY E R01HL44984-02
SUNDBERG, DAVID K S07RR05404-30 0860
SUNDBERG, JOHN S07RR05545-29 0571
SUNDBERG, JOHN P R01AR40324-02
SUNDBERG, NORMAN D S07RR07080-26 0317
SUNDBERG, RICHARD J R01GM41105-03
SUNDBERG, RICHARD J S07RR07094-26 0368
SUNDE, ROGER A P01CA45164-04A1 0004
SUNDE, ROGER A R01DK43491-02
SUNDELL, HAKAN W P50HL14214-20 0045
SUNDELL, HAKAN W P50HL14214-20 9002
SUNDELL, HAKAN W R01HD22712-05
SUNDELL, HAKAN W S07RR05424-30 0094
SUNDERLAND, T Z01MH00339-10
SUNDERMAN, F WILLIAM, JR R01ES05331-02
SUNDSTROM, PAULA R01DE10144-01
SUNDSTROM, PAULA S07RR05879-09 0605
SUNDT, THORALF M JR R01NS25374-04
SUNG, FUNG-CHANG S07RR05907-08 0639
SUNG, FUNG-CHANG S07RR05907-08 0640
SUNG, JOHN S06GM08248-05 0017
SUNG, KUO-LI PAUL P01HL43026-02 0003
SUNG, LANPING AMY P01HL43026-02 0001
SUNG, SUN-SANG J R01AI26928-04
SUNSHINE, PHILIP M01RR00081-29 0124
SUOMI, S J Z01HD01106-08
SUOMI, S J Z01HD01107-08
SUOMI, S J Z01HD01111-01
SUPALLA, TED S07RR07069-26 0239
SUPALLA, TED S07RR07069-26 0243
SUPER TEAMS OPERATING CO, INC N01SP12001-0
SUPER, DENNIS M M01RR00080-29 0440
SUPIANO, MARK A K08AG00433-03
SUPIANO, MARK A M01RR00042-31 0289
SUPIANO, MARK A P30AG08808-03 0005
SUPINSKI, GERALD P01HL25830-11A1 0015
SUPKO, JEFFREY S07RR05607-25 0701
SUPKO, JEFFREY G N01CM73701-06
SUPPLE, WILLIAM F, JR R29MH47307-01
SUR, MRIGANKA R01EY07023-07
SUR, MRIGANKA R01EY07719-03S1
SURATT, PAUL M M01RR00847-18 0218
SUREAU, CAMILLE R29AI31072-01
SUREAU, CAMILLE S07RR05519-29 0512
SURESH, CHANDRA R N01EY02112-02
SURGENOR, DOUGLAS M P50HL33774-06 0004
SURGENOR, DOUGLAS M P50HL33774-06
SURKS, MARTIN I R01CA16463-17
SURMEIER, DALTON J R29NS28889-02
SURPRENANT, ANN MARI S07RR07238-04 0477
SURPRENANT, ANNMARIE R01HL38940-05
SURPRENANT, ANNMARIE R01NS25996-04A1
SURREY, SAUL P01HL40387-04 9002
SURREY, SAUL P50HG00425-01 9002
SURREY, SAUL P60HL38632-04 0002
SURREY, SAUL S03RR03149-11
SURREY, SAUL S07RR05506-29
SURREY, SAUL S15HL47718-01
SURTI, URVASHI R01CA43882-05
SURWIT, EARL A R01CA40889-06
SURWIT, RICHARD S K02MH00303-10
SURWIT, RICHARD S M01RR00030-30 0476
SURWIT, RICHARD S M01RR00030-30 0412
SURWIT, RICHARD S M01RR00030-30 0504
SURWIT, RICHARD S R01DK42923-01A1
SURWIT, RICHARD S R01DK43106-01A1
SURYA, BABU V S07RR05402-30 0797
SUSA, JOHN P50HD11343-14A1 9002
SUSKIND, MIRIAM R01AI19036-09
SUSKIND, RAYMOND R P30ES00159-24S1 9001
SUSKIND, ROBERT M K07HL02087-04
SUSLA, G M Z01CL00102-01
SUSLICK, KENNETH S R01HL25934-11
SUSMAN, ELIZABETH J R01HD26004-02
SUSMAN, MILLARD S15CA55969-01
SUSSER, EZRA R29MH47154-02
SUSSKIND, MIRIAM M R01GM36811-07
SUSSMAN, DANIEL S07RR05863-11 0574
SUSSMAN, HOWARD H R01CA13533-20
SUSSMAN, ILENE S07RR05487-29 0697
SUSSMAN, ILENE S07RR05487-29 0706
SUSSMAN, KARL M01RR00051-30 0756
SUSSMAN, KARL M01RR00051-30 0757
SUSSMAN, KARL M01RR00051-30 0758
SUSSMAN, KARL M01RR00051-30 0759
SUSSMAN, NORMAN L R29DK39552-03
SUSSMAN, STEVEN Y R01CA44907-05

SUSZKIW, JANUSZ B R01ES04090-04A1
SUSZKIW, JANUSZ B S07RR05408-30 0943
SUTCH, RICHARD C R01AG08131-02
SUTCLIFFE, J G R01HG00332-03
SUTCLIFFE, J GREGOR M01RR00833-17 0215
SUTCLIFFE, J GREGOR P01NS22347-06 0005
SUTCLIFFE, J GREGOR R01GM32355-07
SUTCLIFFE, J GREGOR R01NS22111-06
SUTER, DIANE S07RR07210-09 0685
SUTER, MAJA M S07RR05462-29 0898
SUTER, MAJA M S07RR05462-29 0899
SUTERA, SALVATORE P R01HL12839-22
SUTHANTHIRAN, KRISHNAN R43CA55417-01
SUTHANTHIRAN, MANIKKAM R01AI26932-01A3
SUTHERLAND, CARL M U10CA23306-12
SUTHERLAND, DAVID M01RR00400-23 0239
SUTHERLAND, DAVID E M01RR00400-23 0097
SUTHERLAND, DAVID E P01DK13083-24 0191
SUTHERLAND, DAVID E P01DK13083-24 0184
SUTHERLAND, DAVID E P01DK13083-24 0185
SUTHERLAND, DAVID E R N01DK92244-05
SUTHERLAND, JOHN C R01HG00371-04
SUTHERLAND, ROBERT S07RR05522-29
SUTHERLAND, ROBERT M R01CA37618-08
SUTHERLAND, ROBERT M R37CA20329-17
SUTHERLAND, ROBERT M S15CA56016-01
SUTHERLING, WILLIAM W R01NS20806-08
SUTHERS, RODERICK A R01NS29467-01
SUTKO, JOHN L R01HL27470-09
SUTPHEN, JAMES L M01RR00847-18 0510
SUTTCLIFFE, GREGOR P50MH47680-02 0003
SUTTER, ERICH E P30EY06883-06 9001
SUTTER, ERICH E R01EY06861-05
SUTTIE, JOHN W P01DK14881-21 0013
SUTTIE, JOHN W P01HL29586-09 0004
SUTTIE, JOHN W S07RR07098-26 0330
SUTTLE, DALE P, JR R01DK36747-06
SUTTLES, JILL S07RR05959-06 0018
SUTTON, DWIGHT N01DC02400-01
SUTTON, DWIGHT P01DC00274-08 0003
SUTTON, DWIGHT S07RR05588-25
SUTTON, FLETCHER S07RR05704-20 0002
SUTTON, GREGORY P M01RR00750-19 0299
SUTULA, THOMAS P R29NS25020-05
SUYAMA, YOSHITAKA R01AI26144-02
SUYAMA, YOSHITAKA S07RR07083-26 0488
SUZUKI, JON B R01DE07204-08
SUZUKI, KINUKO R01NS24453-06
SUZUKI, KUNIHIKO P30HD03110-24 9006
SUZUKI, KUNIHIKO P30HD03110-24
SUZUKI, KUNIHIKO R01NS24289-06
SUZUKI, KUNIHIKO R01NS28997-01
SUZUKI, SHINTARO R01EY08106-03
SUZUKI, SHINTARO R01EY09051-01
SUZUKI, SHINTARO S07RR05810-13 0022
SUZUKI, TSUNEO R01CA35977-08
SUZUKI, TSUNEO R55CA55274-01
SUZUKI, YASUNOSUKE P30ES00928-18 9012
SVANBORG, CATHARINA R13AI31511-01
SVARE, BRUCE B R03DA06472-02
SVED, ALAN F P01NS19608-09 9003
SVED, ALAN F R01HL38786-06
SVENNERHOLM, LARS P50NS20023-08 0014
SVETKEY, LAURA P M01RR00030-30 0388
SVETKEY, LAURA P M01RR00030-30 0445
SVETKEY, LAURA P M01RR00030-30 0480
SVETKEY, LAURA P. M01RR00030-30 0436
SVEUM, LARRY K S06GM08066-20
SVOBODA, KATHY K R01EY08886-01A1
SWAIN, JUDITH L P50HL17670-17 0036
SWAIN, JUDITH L R01HL26831-11
SWAIN, ROBERT S07RR05655-21 0816
SWAIN, SUSAN P01AI23287-06 9003
SWAIN, SUSAN L P01AI23287-06 0001
SWAIN, SUSAN L R01AI22125-07
SWAIN, SUSAN L R01AI26887-04
SWAMINATHA, SANTHANAM R01ES03509-08
SWAMINATHAN, SANKAR K11CA01392-04
SWAMINATHAN, SANTHANAM P01CA51987-02 0002
SWAN, GARY S07RR05522-29 0069
SWAN, GARY E R01AG09341-06A1
SWAN, PATRICIA B S07RR07034-26
SWAN, PATRICIA B S15GM47096-01
SWAN, PATRICIA B S15MH49317-01
SWANBORG, ROBERT H R01NS06985-25
SWANGO, P A Z01DE00464-04
SWANK, R P30CA16056-16 9016
SWANK, RICHARD T R01GM33559-06A2
SWANK, RICHARD T R01HL31698-08
SWANN, ALAN C S15AA09303-01
SWANN, J P41RR01219-10 0007
SWANN, JENNIFER M R29HD28467-01
SWANN, JENNIFER M S06GM08223-08 0032
SWANN, JOHN W R01NS18309-10
SWANN, WILLIAM B K02MH00498-08
SWANN, WILLIAM B R01MH37598-09
SWANSON, G MARIE R01OH02067-08
SWANSON, J Z01AI00193-12
SWANSON, JAMES M R01MH44844-03
SWANSON, JANICE M R01NR01637-06
SWANSON, JOEL A S07RR05381-30 0784
SWANSON, KRISTEN M R29NR01899-04
SWANSON, LARRY W P01DK26741-12 0007
SWANSON, LARRY W R01NS16686-13
SWANSON, MARIE G N01CN05225-08
SWANSON, MARIE G P30CA22453-14 0005
SWANSON, MARIE G P30CA22453-14 9006
SWANSON, MARK N01HD02911-02
SWANSON, MAURICE S R01GM46272-01
SWANSON, MELVIN R44AI27614-02
SWANSON, MELVIN J R43DA06388-01A1
SWANSON, WILLIAM H M01RR00425-22S3
SWANSON, WILLIAM H R29EY07716-01A3
SWANSON, WILLIAM H S07RR05551-29
SWANSTON, ROBERT P01CA19014-14 0018
SWANSTORM, RONALD P01CA19014-14 9004
SWANSTROM, RONALD U01AI25868-05 0005
SWANSTROM, RONALD I R01AI25321-05
SWARBRICK, JAMES S07RR05967-04
SWARBRICK, JAMES S07RR05967-04 0290
SWARBRICK, JAMES S15CA55980-01
SWAROOP, ANAND P30HG00209-02 0006
SWAROOP, ANAND R29EY07961-04
SWARTZ, CONRAD S07RR05366-30 0563
SWARTZ, HAROLD M P41RR01811-06A1
SWARTZ, HAROLD M P41RR01811-06A1 9004
SWARTZ, HAROLD M R01GM34250-06
SWARTZ, KARYL B S03RR03421-06
SWARTZ, KARYL B S06GM08225-07
SWARTZ, KARYL B S06GM08225-07 0012
SWARTZ, KENNETH P R29AG08718-02
SWARTZ, SHARON S07RR05664-24 0876
SWARTZ, STEPHEN L M01RR02635-07 0190
SWEADNER, KATHLEEN J P50NS10828-16 0027
SWEADNER, KATHLEEN J R01HL36271-05
SWEADNER, KATHLEEN J R01NS27653-03
SWEARINGEN, BROOKE K11EY00317-01
SWEATMAN, TREVOR W R29CA44890-04
SWEATT, JOHN S07RR05425-30 0770
SWEAZEY, ROBERT D R29DC00735-02
SWEELEY, CHARLES S07RR05656-24 0852
SWEELEY, CHARLES C R01DK12434-24
SWEENEY, H LEE R01AR35661-04A1
SWEENEY, H LEE S07RR05415-30 0021
SWEENEY, JOHN A P50MH46745-02 0003
SWEENEY, JOHN A P50MH46745-02 9003
SWEENEY, THOMAS L S07RR07074-26
SWEENEY, WILLIAM S06GM08176-12 0027
SWEENEY, WILLIAM S07RR07109-23 0510
SWEER, LEON S S07RR05680-23 0915
SWEET, LAUREL J R43DK44046-01
SWEET, RICHARD L P01AI24768-05
SWEET, RICHARD L P01AI24768-05 0001
SWEET, RICHARD L P01AI24768-05 0003
SWEET, RICHARD L P01AI24768-05 9001
SWEET, RICHARD L P01HD24640-03
SWEET, RICHARD L U01AI31499-01 0004
SWEET, RICHARD L. P01HD24640-03 0003
SWEETNAM, PAUL M R43HL46098-01
SWENDSEID, MARIAN E P01CA42710-06A1 9003
SWENSON, BRENT P51RR00165-31 9005
SWENSON, CHARLES S07RR05372-30 0686
SWENSON, ERIK R R29HL45571-01
SWENSON, MICHAEL R S07RR05665-24 0882
SWENSON, RICHARD B U42RR03591-06
SWENSON, RICHARD P R01GM36490-03
SWENTON, JOHN S R01GM36592-04
SWERDLOFF, RONALD S M01RR00425-22S3 0452
SWERDLOFF, RONALD S M01RR00425-22S3 0304
SWERDLOFF, RONALD S M01RR00425-22S3 0389
SWERDLOFF, RONALD S M01RR00425-22S3 0327
SWERDLOFF, RONALD S P30HD19445-05S1 9001
SWERDLOFF, RONALD S P30HD19445-05S1
SWERLICK, ROBERT S07RR05364-30 0544
SWETTE, LARRY R43HD27815-01A1
SWETTE, LARRY R44HL40256-03
SWETTE, LARRY L R44AA07657-03S1
SWHWARTZ, ROBERT S P01CA24530-12 9001
SWIFT, H P30DK42086-02 9003
SWIFT, HEWSON P30CA14599-18 9003
SWIFT, LARRY P30DK26657-12 9006
SWIFT, LARRY L R01DK42118-02
SWIFT, MICHAEL R R01CA14235-18
SWIFT, MICHAEL R R01CA50489-02
SWIFT, MICHAEL R R01MH45128-01A1
SWIGART, RICHARD H U76PE00202-07
SWINDELL, CHARLES S R01CA41349-06
SWINDELL, CHARLES S R01CA55139-01
SWINYARD, EWART, A N01NS92328-05
SWITALSKI, RICHARD N01CM07313-02
SWITALSKI, RICHARD N N01DE92574-05
SWITZER, ROBERT L R01GM47112-19
SWYT, C R Z01RR10322-03
SWYT, C R Z01RR10356-01
SY, BON K S07RR07064-24 0209
SY, MAN-SUN R01AI27740-03
SY, MAN-SUN R01AR38018-05A1
SYAPIN, PETER S07RR05356-30 0437
SYAPIN, PETER J R29AA07351-06
SYBERT, VIRGINIA P M01RR00037-31 0479
SYED, SALAM S07RR05321-30 0266
SYED, SALAM A R01DE08664-03
SYFTESTAD, GLENN T R01DE06886-09
SYIN, C Z01BB02012-03
SYKES, MEGAN R01AI31158-01
SYKES, MEGAN R01CA55290-01
SYLVESTER, J T R01HL41970-04
SYLVESTER, JIMMIE T P01HL10342-26 0023
SYLVESTER, PAUL W S07RR05465-29 0385
SYLVESTER, PAUL W S07RR05686-11 0979
SYLVESTRE, DIANA K08AI01067-01
SYMINGTON, BANU ERHAN K11HL02216-04
SYMINGTON, FRANK W R29AI28523-03
SYMINGTON, LORRAINE S R01GM41784-03
SYMINTON, FRAUK W P01CA18221-16 0009
SYMKO, OREST S07RR07092-26 0548
SYNDER, EVAN Y P30HD18655-10 0183
SYNDER, GRAYSON H U01AI25721-05 9001
SYNDER, JEANNE P50HD11149-14 0013
SYNER, FRANK N P50AA07606-04 0005
SYPEK, JOSEPH P R29AI24500-05
SYPHERD, PAUL S R01GM23999-13
SYRJALA, K L P01CA38552-05A1 0001
SYSTROM, DAVID M S07RR05486-29 0051
SYTKOWSKI, ARTHUR J R01DK38841-06
SZABA, GEORGE P M01RR00035-31 0392
SZABO, A Z01DK29019-11
SZABO, GABOR R37HL37127-07
SZABO, GEORGE S07RR05319-18 0622
SZABO, GYONGYI R29AA08577-02
SZABO, JOANNE S R29DK40035-03
SZABO, PAUL P01AG03853-09 0014
SZAKAL, ANDRAS K R01AG05374-04A2
SZALAY, JEANNE S07RR07064-24 0210
SZANISZLO, PAUL S07RR07091-26 0771
SZAPIEL, SUSAN V K11EY00305-03
SZAPOCZNIK, JOSE R01DA05334-05
SZAREK, JOHN L R29HL41548-01A3
SZEFLER, STANLEY J N01HR16048-00
SZENT-GYORGYI, ANDREW G R37AR15963-26
SZETO, HAZEL H K02DA00100-08
SZETO, HAZEL H R01DA02475-12
SZILAGYI, JULIANNA E R01HL40134-05
SZKLO, MOYSES N01HC55020-11
SZNOL, M Z01CM09351-02
SZNOL, M Z01CM09355-02
SZNOL, M Z01CM09356-02
SZOKA, FRANCIS C, JR R01AI25099-03
SZOKA, FRANCIS C, JR R01GM30163-08
SZOLOVITS, PETER R01LM04493-07
SZOSTAK, JACK W R01GM45315-01A1
SZTUL, ELIZABETH P30DK34989-08 0017
SZU, S C Z01HD01303-08
SZUBA, MARTIN S07RR05756-18 0294
SZUBE, MARTIN S07RR05756-18 0319
SZUCHET, SARA P01NS24575-04 0002
SZURSZEWSKI, J H M01RR00585-20 0566
SZURSZEWSKI, JOSEPH H R01DK17632-17A1
SZURSZEWSKI, JOSEPH H R37DK17238-18
SZUTS, ETE S07RR05547-23 0078
SZUTS, ETE S07RR05547-23 0081
SZWAJKUN, KONSTANTYN S07RR05700-22 0866
SZWEDA, L I Z01HL00277-01
SZWERGOLD, BENJAMIN R01EY08414-02
SZWERGOLD, BENJAMIN S P01CA41078-05 0005
SZYBALAKI, WACLAW R01HG00504-01 0003
SZYBALSKI, WACLAW R01HG00379-01
SZYBALSKI, WACLAW R01HG00504-01 0004
SZYBALSKI, WACLAW R01HG00504-01
SZYMANSKI, IRMA O K07HL02147-04
T HEAD & COMPANY, INC N01DA10002-00
Tasaki, I Z01MH02396-05
TABAK, LAWRENCE A P50DE07003-08 0009
TABAK, LAWRENCE A R01DE08108-05A1
TABAK, LAWRENCE A R01DE08511-05
TABAKOFF, BORIS R01AA09014-01
TABAS, IRA A R01HL39703-04
TABAS, IRA A S07RR05395-30 0826
TABER, DOUGLASS F S07RR07016-18 0349
TABER, HARRY W R01GM44547-01A1
TABER, HARRY W S07RR05394-30 0724
TABER, LARRY A R55HL46367-01
TABIBZADEH, SIAMAK S R29CA46866-04
TABIN, CLIFFORD J R01HD26842-01A1
TABITA, FRED R R01GM24497-14
TABLIN, F S07RR05457-29 0009
TABOR, C W Z01DK24709-10
TABOR, E Z01CP05646-02
TABOR, E Z01CP05647-02
TABOR, E Z01CP05693-01
TABOR, E Z01CP05694-01
TABOR, E Z01CP05695-01
TABOR, E Z01CP05696-01
TABOR, E Z01CP05697-01
TABOR, M WILSON P42ES04908-03 0002
TACCARDI, BRUNO R01HL43276-03
TACEY, RICHARD N01HD72913-14
TACHE, YVETTE P30DK41301-02 9002
TACHE, YVETTE S07RR05354-30 0390
TACHE, YVETTE F K05MH00663-04
TACHE, YVETTE F R01DK30110-09
TACHE, YVETTE F R01DK33061-07A1
TACHE, YVETTE F R13DK43849-01
TACK, BRIAN F M01RR00833-17 0210
TACK, BRIAN F P01AI17354-10S1 0007
TACK, BRIAN F R01AI19222-10

TACK, BRIAN F R01AI22214-07
TAEGTMEYER, HEINRICH R01HL43133-01A2
TAETLE, RAYMOND P01CA37497-07 0002
TAETLE, RAYMOND U01CA37641-07 9002
TAETLE, RAYMOND U01CA37641-07 0002
TAFFET, GEORGE E K08AG00428-03
TAGER-FLUSBERG, HELEN B R01DC01234-01
TAGER, HOWARD S P60DK20595-14 9002
TAGER, HOWARD S R37DK18347-18
TAGGART, R THOMAS R55DK43721-01
TAGHERT, PAUL H R01NS21749-07
TAHARA, STANLEY M P01NS26991-02 0003
TAI, MEI-SHENG R43HL46585-01
TAI, PHANG C R01GM34766-08
TAI, PHANG C R01GM41845-04
TAI, PHANG C R01GM47638-01
TAI, PHANG C S07RR05711-21 0041
TAICHMAN, LORNE B P01DC00203-09 0005
TAICHMAN, LORNE B R37DE04511-16
TAICHMAN, NORTON S P50DE07118-07
TAICHMAN, NORTON S P50DE07118-07 0004
TAICHMAN, NORTON S P50DE08239-04 0007
TAINER, JOHN A R01AI22160-06
TAINER, JOHN A R01GM39345-04
TAINER, JOHN A R01GM46312-01
TAINSKY, MICHAEL A R01CA42810-04A3
TAINSKY, MICHAEL A P01CA52051-01A1 0005
TAIRA, M Z01HL00654-01
TAIT, ALAN R R29GM39505-03
TAIT, JONATHAN F R29HL40801-04
TAIT, ROBERT P30DK35747-06 0010
TAKACS, JAMES S07RR07055-26 0178
TAKACS, L Z01AA00481-02
TAKACS, L Z01AA00482-02
TAKADA, YOSHIKAZU R01GM47157-01
TAKAHASHI, JOSEPH S R01EY08467-02
TAKAHASHI, JOSEPH S R37MH39592-07
TAKAHASHI, M Z01HL04208-05
TAKAHASHI, TERRY T R29DC00535-03
TAKAYAMA, KUNI K R01GM36054-06
TAKEDA, AKIKA P30CA13943-19 0012
TAKEMORI, A E P01DA05695-03 0005
TAKEMORI, AKIRA E R01DA00289-19
TAKEMOTO-CHOCK, NAOMI K S06GM08073-20 0012
TAKEMOTO, LARRY J R01EY02932-13
TAKEMOTO, LARRY J S10RR06240-01
TAKESHITA, KENICHI K11DK01751-04
TAKEUCHI, ESTHER S R44HL40740-03
TAKEYASU, KUNIO R01GM44373-02
TAKIYYUDDIN, MARWAN A R29HL43275-03
TAKUSAGAWA, FUSAO R01GM37233-04
TALAL, NORMAN R01DE09311-02
TALALAY, PAUL P01CA44530-05
TALALAY, PAUL P01CA44530-05 0001
TALALAY, PAUL R01DK07422-28
TALAMANTES, FRANK P01CA05388-31A1 0037
TALAMANTES, FRANK J R01DK42361-01A2
TALAMANTES, FRANK J R37HD14966-11
TALAMANTES, FRANK J S06GM08132-17 0020
TALAMO, BARBARA R R01AG09200-01A1
TALAMO, BARBARA R R01NS28556-02
TALAN, M I Z01AG00073-03
TALASKA, GLENN S07RR05408-30 0944
TALBERT, JAMES L U10CA35157-08
TALBORT, PAUL A S06GM08037-20 0048
TALBOT, T L Z01RR10162-09
TALBOT, T L Z01RR10256-05
TALBOT, T L Z01RR10303-03
TALBOTT, EVELYN O R01HL44664-01A2
TALCOTT, JAMES A K08CA01418-03
TALL, ALAN R P50HL21006-15 0007
TALL, ALAN R R01HL22682-14
TALL, ALAN R R01HL43165-03
TALLAL, PAULA R03DC01038-01
TALLENTS, ROSS H S07RR05548-26 0580
TALLEY, N J M01RR00585-20 0358
TALLEY, N J M01RR00585-20 0446
TALLEY, NICHOLAS J R55AG09440-01A1
TALLEY, PAUL ALEXIS S06GM08198-10 0001
TALLEY, ROBERT C S03RR03512-03
TALLEY, ROBERT C S07RR05421-27
TALLMADGE, JAMES M S07RR05429-30 0204
TALLMAN, IRVING R01MH46828-01
TALLMAN, RICHARD P41RR01861-07 0010
TALMAGE, DAVID A R29HD26854-02
TALMAN, WILLIAM T P01NS24621-05 0003
TALMAN, WILLIAM T R01HL32205-04A3
TALMAN, WILLIAM T S10RR06533-01
TALVENHEIMO, JANE A S07RR05363-30 0836
TAM, CHICK R S06GM08101-20 0036
TAM, JAMES P R01CA36544-08
TAM, JAMES P R01HL41935-03
TAM, JAMES P U01AI28701-03
TAMANOI, FUYUHIKO R01CA41996-07
TAMANOI, FUYUHIKO R01NS30054-01
TAMARI, YEHUDA R44HL37168-02A6
TAMARI, YEHUDA R44HL41426-02
TAMARIN, ROBERT S07RR07043-26 0129
TAMARKIN, LAWRENCE N43DK12276-00
TAMBORLANE, WILLIAM M01RR00125-28 0774
TAMBORLANE, WILLIAM M01RR00125-28 0592
TAMBORLANE, WILLIAM M01RR06022-02 0592
TAMBORLANE, WILLIAM V M01RR06022-02 0591
TAMBORLANE, WILLIAM V M01RR06022-02 0663
TAMBORLANE, WILLIAM V M01RR06022-02 0604
TAMBORLANE, WILLIAM V M01RR06022-02 0750
TAMBORLANE, WILLIAM V M01RR06022-02 0605
TAMBORLANE, WILLIAM V M01RR06022-02 0751
TAMBORLANE, WILLIAM V M01RR00125-28 0663
TAMBORLANE, WILLIAM V M01RR00125-28 0448
TAMBORLANE, WILLIAM V, JR U01DK30618-09
TAMIR, HADASSAH R01MH37575-09
TAMIR, HADASSAH S07RR05650-25 0111
TAMIS-LEMONDA, CATHERINE R01HD20559-05
TAMKUN, MICHAEL M R29GM41325-03
TAMM, LUKAS K R01AI30557-01A1
TAMM, SIDNEY L R01GM45557-01
TAMMINGA, CAROL P50MH40279-05 9003
TAMMINGA, CAROL A P50MH44211-03 0009
TAMMINGA, CAROL A P50MH44211-03 9002
TAMMINGA, CAROL A P50MH44211-03 0012
TAMMINGA, CAROL A R37MH37073-09
TAMURA, SUSAN Y R43HL46094-01
TAMURA, TSUNENOBU R01HD28119-01
TAN-WILSON, ANNA S07RR07149-18 0426
TAN, ENG P01DK42717-02 0002
TAN, ENG M M01RR00833-17 0169
TAN, ENG M M01RR00833-17 0219
TAN, ENG M P01DK42717-02
TAN, ENG M R37AR32063-10
TAN, ENG M U01AI32834-01
TAN, ENG M U01AI32834-01 0001
TAN, ENG M U01AI32834-01 9001
TAN, KUT-NIE R29AI27983-03
TANAGHO, EMIL A R01NS18029-10
TANAKA, AKIKO R01CA50523-03
TANAKA, DAVID T R29HL43853-02
TANAKA, DUKE S07RR05623-25 0724
TANAKA, JACQUELINE C R01EY06640-06
TANAKA, KAY R01DK38154-05
TANAKA, KAY R37DK17453-19
TANAKA, TOYOICHI R01EY05272-06
TANCER, MANUEL M01RR00046-31 0488
TANCER, MANUEL M01RR00046-31 0531
TANCER, MANUEL M01RR00046-31 0524
TANDON, RAJIV M01RR00042-31 0598
TANDON, RAJIV S07RR05383-30 0570
TANELIAN, DARRELL L R01NS28646-01A1
TANELIAN, DARRELL L S07RR05353-30 0372
TANENHAUS, MICHAEL K R01HD27206-01A1
TANFER, KORAY R01HD26288-02
TANFER, KORAY R01HD26631-03
TANG, BING-KOU R01AA07817-03
TANG, CHA-MIN R29NS28158-02
TANG, CHA-MIN S07RR07083-26 0483
TANG, ERIC M R01ES03124-10
TANG, JORDAN J R01AI26762-04
TANG, JORDAN J R01DK01107-35
TANG, WAI-HONG WILSO S07RR05664-24 0877
TANGA, MARY J N01CM07333-02
TANGA, MARY J N01CP15737-00
TANGALOS, ERIC G P30AG08031-02 9003
TANGNEY, JUNE P R01HD27171-02
TANGREA, J A Z01CN00103-09
TANIGAKI, NOBUYUKI S07RR05648-25 0929
TANIUCHI, H Z01DK25011-17
TANIUCHI, H Z01DK25025-15
TANK, A WILLIAM R01DA05014-02
TANKE, ELIZABETH D R43AI31750-01
TANKERSLEY, D L Z01BH05018-02
TANKERSLEY, D L Z01BH05025-01
TANNEN, RICHARD P50DK39255-05 0007
TANNEN, RICHARD L R37DK25248-15
TANNENBAUM, S P42ES04675-05 0003
TANNENBAUM, S H Z01CL10166-04
TANNENBAUM, STEVEN R P01CA26731-12
TANNENBAUM, STEVEN R P01CA26731-12 0005
TANNENBAUM, STEVEN R P01CA28842-09 0008
TANNENBAUM, STEVEN R P01ES01640-14 0016
TANNENBAUM, STEVEN R P01ES05622-02 0032
TANNENBAUM, STEVEN R P30ES02109-13 9003
TANNER, J Z01BD04015-01
TANNER, MARTIN P60AG10463-01 9003
TANNER, MARTIN A R01CA35464-08
TANNER, T BRADLEY R43MH47615-01A1
TANNOCK, IAN F R01CA51033-02
TANNOUS, RAYMOND U10CA29314-11
TANOUYE, MARK P01GM40499-04 0005
TANOUYE, MARK A R01GM42824-04
TANOWITZ, HERBERT B R01AI12770-14
TANSEY, TERESE S07RR07136-20 0608
TANZER, JASON P60AR20621-13 0029
TANZER, MARVIN L P01HD22610-04 0002
TANZER, MARVIN L R01AR17220-19
TANZER, MARVIN L R37AR12683-23
TANZI, RUDOLPH E R01NS30428-01
TAO, MARIANO R01DK23045-12
TAO, TERENCE C R37AR21673-14
TAORMINA, MICHAEL S07RR05365-30 0106
TAPAROWSKY, ELIZABET S07RR07032-26 0050
TAPAROWSKY, ELIZABETH J R01CA42835-06
TAPLEY, DONALD F M01RR00645-20
TAPLIN, STEPHEN P01CA34847-09 0017
TAPP, DAVID C S07RR05654-24 0113
TAPP, JON P30HD15052-11 9010
TAPPEL, ALOYS L R01DK39225-05
TAPPER, DAVID R01CA40423-05
TARAGIN, MARK S07RR05576-27 0603
TARANGER, JOHN N01HD92905-03
TARANTAL, ALICE F P51RR00169-30 0128
TARANTAL, ALICE F R01AI32299-01
TARANTAL, ALICE F S10RR07172-01
TARAPOREWALA, IRACH S07RR05519-29 0516
TARASCHI, THEODORE P50AA07186-06 0011
TARASCHI, THEODORE F K02AA00088-08
TARASCHI, THEODORE F P01AA07215-06 0004
TARASCHI, THEODORE F R22AI27247-03
TARBELL, JOHN M R01HL35549-06
TARBELL, JOHN M S07RR07082-26 0312
TARBELL, SALLY E S07RR05712-20 0110
TARDIF, SUZETTE D R01RR02022-07
TARDIFF, KENNETH J R01DA06534-02
TARGAN, STEPHAN R P30DK36200-05S1 9001
TARGAN, STEPHEN R P50AI15332-14 0011
TARGAN, STEPHEN R R01DK43026-01A1
TARGAN, STEPHEN R R01DK43211-01A1
TARGOFF, IRA N P01AI21568-07 0007
TARGOFF, IRA N P01AI21568-07 9001
TARGOFF, IRA N R29AI27181-03
TARIOT, PIERRE P01AG03644-07 9002
TARIOT, PIERRE P60AG10463-01 0004
TARIOT, PIERRE N K07MH00733-04
TARIOT, PIERRE N M01RR00044-31 0346
TARIOT, PIERRE N P50MH40381-06 0005
TARLETON, RICK L R01AI22070-05
TARLETON, RICK L S07RR07025-26 0993
TARLOFF, JOAN B R15GM44296-01A1
TARNAWSKI, ANDRZEJ S R01AA07751-03
TARR, CHARLES M P30HD02528-25A1 0001
TARR, CHARLES M R01HL43008-02
TARR, MICHAEL S07RR07015-26 0605
TARR, PHILLIP S07RR05655-21 0815
TARR, PHILLIP I S07RR05432-30 0233
TARTAGLIA, ANTHONY P S07RR05394-30
TARTAGLIONE, TERESA M01RR00037-31 0515
TARTAGLIONE, TERESA A M01RR00037-31 0508
TARTAGLIONE, TERESA A M01RR00037-31 0495
TARTAKOFF, ALAN P30DK27651-09 9006
TARTAKOFF, ALAN M P01AI15351-13 0007
TARTAKOFF, ALAN M P01DK38181-05
TARTAKOFF, ALAN M P01DK38181-05 0003
TARTAKOFF, ALAN M R01GM46569-01
TARTAR, RALPH P50AA08746-02 9003
TARTER, MICHAEL E R01ES05379-02
TARTER, RALPH E P50DA05605-03
TARTOF, KENNETH D R01HG00319-03
TARTTER, VIVIEN S07RR07132-20 0409
TARTTER, VIVIEN C R01DC01250-01
TARULLO, L Z01MH02488-02
TAS CONSULTATION ASSN, INC N01DA11301-00
TASH, JOSEPH S R01GM29496-09
TASH, JOSEPH S S07RR05373-30 0731
TASH, WILLIAM R S15DA07801-01
TASHIAN, RICHARD E R01GM24681-14
TASHJIAN, A.H. P30ES00002-29 0039
TASHJIAN, ARMEN H, JR R01DK10206-26
TASHJIAN, ARMEN H, JR R01DK11011-24S1
TASHKIN, DONALD P M01RR00865-18 0224
TASHKIN, DONALD P R01DA03018-10
TASHKIN, DONALD P. N01HR46022-19
TASSAVA, ROY A P50NS10165-20 0029
TATAKIS, DIMITRIS N R03DE09915-01
TATCHELL, KELLY G R01CA37702-08
TATE, CHARLOTTE A P30DK27685-10 0009
TATE, CHARLOTTE A R01AG06221-06
TATE, CHARLOTTE A S07RR07147-19 0653
TATE, R L Z01CT00201-02
TATE, WILLIAM H S07RR05970-06 0782
TATEMICHI, T M01RR00645-20 0431
TATEMICHI, THOMAS K R01NS26179-04
TATEMOTO, KAZUHIKO R01DK39188-05
TATTERSALL, PETER P01CA16038-18 0017
TATTERSALL, PETER J R01AI26109-04
TATTERSALL, PETER J R01CA29303-11
TAUB, DAVID M U42RR05083-04
TAUB, MARY L R01DK40286-10
TAUB, REBECCA P50HG00425-01 0001
TAUB, REBECCA A R01DK44237-01
TAUBE, HENRY R37GM13638-26
TAUBER, ALFRED I P01AI24760-05 0004
TAUBER, ALFRED I R01HL33565-07
TAUBK, ROBERT N. P30CA13696-19 9026
TAUBMAN, MARK B R01HL43302-03
TAUBMAN, MARTIN A R01DE04733-13
TAUBMAN, MARTIN A R37DE03420-18
TAUN, ROCKY S P01HD21355-04 0006
TAUNTON, ROMA L R01NR02092-03
TAUROG, J P50AR39169-05 0003
TAUROG, JOEL P01AR09989-27 0006
TAUROG, JOEL D R01AR38319-05
TAUSSIG, LYNN M P50HL14136-20 0017
TAVARES, JAMES R01RR06161-01
TAVARES, MARY A R01HS06826-01
TAVARES, RAPHAEL P50MH43520-04 9005
TAVASSOLI, MEHDI R01DK30142-11
TAVLARIDES, LAWRENCE P42ES04913-02 0005

TAVOLONI, NICOLA R01DK42346-08
TAYEK, JOHN S07RR05551-29 0945
TAYEK, JOHN A M01RR00425-22S3 0390
TAYLOR, A N S07RR05915-08 0678
TAYLOR, ADDISON A M01RR00350-25 0449
TAYLOR, ADDISON A M01RR00350-25 0450
TAYLOR, ALLEN R01EY08566-01A1
TAYLOR, ANDREW T, JR R01DK38842-05
TAYLOR, AUBREY E R01HL41961-04
TAYLOR, AUBREY E R37HL22549-15
TAYLOR, BARRY L R01GM29481-09
TAYLOR, BENJAMIN A R01CA33093-10
TAYLOR, BENJAMIN A R01GM18684-20
TAYLOR, BENJAMIN A S15AI32200-01
TAYLOR, BILL P30CA14089-16 9011
TAYLOR, BONNIE J K11HL01822-05
TAYLOR, BRIAN H S07RR07090-26 0468
TAYLOR, BRIAN H S07RR07090-26 0480
TAYLOR, C RICHARD R01AR18140-15
TAYLOR, CHARLES W R03CA53372-02
TAYLOR, CRAIG S07RR07131-22 0139
TAYLOR, CRAIG B R01MH45431-02
TAYLOR, D LANSING R37AR32461-10
TAYLOR, DIANE WALLACE R22AI26153-03
TAYLOR, DONALD F S06GM08033-21
TAYLOR, DOUGLAS D R01CA50458-02
TAYLOR, DOUGLAS D S07RR05895-09 0614
TAYLOR, E H Z01MH02542-02
TAYLOR, EDWARD C R01CA42367-06
TAYLOR, EDWARD C R01DK35642-06
TAYLOR, EDWIN W P01HL20592-15 0001
TAYLOR, ELLISON H R43CA55459-01
TAYLOR, ELLISON H R44DK39921-03
TAYLOR, ETHAN W R29AI30392-02
TAYLOR, FLETCHER B, JR R01GM37704-05
TAYLOR, FREDRICK P30CA34196-09 9014
TAYLOR, HERMAN A K07HL02603-01
TAYLOR, IAN L R01DK38216-06
TAYLOR, IAN L R01DK44072-01
TAYLOR, J Z01ES49002-03
TAYLOR, JACK L G20RR07085-01
TAYLOR, JAMES O N01AG02107-26
TAYLOR, JEREMY M R01AI29196-02
TAYLOR, JEREMY M R29CA45216-04
TAYLOR, JERRY L R01EY06990-05
TAYLOR, JOHN M R01AI26522-14
TAYLOR, JOHN M R01HL37063-06
TAYLOR, JOHN M S07RR05539-29 0550
TAYLOR, JOHN M S15HL47699-01
TAYLOR, JOHN M U01AI31927-01
TAYLOR, JOHN M. P01HL41633-03 0003
TAYLOR, JOHN W R01AI28545-03
TAYLOR, JOHN WATSON R01GM38811-04
TAYLOR, JOHN-STEPHEN A P41RR00954-15 0027
TAYLOR, JOHN-STEPHEN A P41RR00954-15 0028
TAYLOR, JOHN-STEPHEN A P41RR00954-15 0029
TAYLOR, JOHN-STEPHEN A R01CA40463-07
TAYLOR, JUNE S R01CA49516-04
TAYLOR, K GRANT R01DE05102-11A2
TAYLOR, KENNETH A R01GM30598-08A1
TAYLOR, KENNETH B P30CA13148-20 9015
TAYLOR, KENNETH J R01HD24669-03
TAYLOR, LATHROP S07RR05814-12 0153
TAYLOR, LATHROP S07RR05814-12 0145
TAYLOR, LLOYD M01RR00334-25 0284
TAYLOR, LLOYD M M01RR00334-25 0269
TAYLOR, LLOYD M, JR R01HL45267-01A1
TAYLOR, MARY N01LM13517-00
TAYLOR, MICHAEL J R01HD22786-03
TAYLOR, MILTON W R01CA53783-01
TAYLOR, MILTON W R01DK25498-12
TAYLOR, P R Z01CN00101-09
TAYLOR, P R Z01CN00104-09
TAYLOR, P R Z01CN00112-08
TAYLOR, P R Z01CN00143-07
TAYLOR, P R Z01CN00149-03
TAYLOR, P R Z01CN00150-03
TAYLOR, PALMER W R01GM18360-20
TAYLOR, PALMER W R01GM24337-14A1
TAYLOR, REGINALD W K15DE00228-05
TAYLOR, RICHARD A S07RR07078-18 0466
TAYLOR, ROBERT N R29HD22873-05
TAYLOR, RONALD K R22AI25096-05
TAYLOR, RONALD P R55AR41072-01
TAYLOR, S E S07RR05915-08 0672
TAYLOR, S I Z01DK47022-12
TAYLOR, S I Z01DK47026-07
TAYLOR, SCOTT E S07RR05918-08 0710
TAYLOR, SCOTT E S07RR05918-08 0707
TAYLOR, SHELLEY E R37MH42152-05
TAYLOR, STEPHEN C S06GM08140-17 0018
TAYLOR, SUSAN S R01GM19301-20
TAYLOR, SUSAN S R01GM34921-07
TAYLOR, TERRIE E R01AI25568-04
TAYLOR, THOMAS R R01HS06545-01
TAYLOR, WILLIAM P30HD05797-20 0001
TAYLOR, WILLIAM L P30HD28819-01 9004
TAYLOR, WILLIAM L R55GM39234-04
TAYLOR, YVONNE P01CA51116-02 0002
TAYLOR, YVONNE C R29CA47855-04
TCHEN, T T S07RR07051-26 0737
TEACHMAN, JAY D R01HD25274-02
TEAGUE, GREGORY B R01MH47567-02
TEAGUE, GREGORY B R19MH46215-03
TEALE, JUDY M R01AI19896-09
TEALE, JUDY M R01AI20313-08
TEALE, JUDY M R01AI27994-03
TECHNICAL RESOURECES, INC. N01MH70017-00
TEDDER, THOMAS F P01CA34183-08 0014
TEDDER, THOMAS F R01AI26872-04
TEDDER, THOMAS F R55CA54464-01
TEDDER, THOMAS F S07RR05526-29 0103
TEEBOR, GEORGE W R01CA49869-03
TEEBOR, GEORGE W R37CA16669-16
TEETER, JOHN H R01DC00566-03
TEETER, JOHN H S07RR05825-12 0516
TEETER, MARTHA M R01GM38114-05
TEGTMEYER, PETER J P01CA28146-11
TEGTMEYER, PETER J P01CA28146-11 0005
TEGTMEYER, PETER J R37CA18808-17
TEICH, ALBERT H R13HG00119-02
TEICHER, BEVERLY A P01CA19589-14A1 0029
TEICHER, BEVERLY A P01CA38493-06S1 0002
TEICHER, BEVERLY A R01CA47379-04
TEICHER, MARTIN H R29MH43743-04
TEICHER, MARTIN H S07RR05484-29 0032
TEICHGRAEBER, JOHN F S07RR05745-19 0239
TEINTZE, MARTIN R01GM38142-04
TEIRSTEIN, PAUL A M01RR00833-17 0204
TEITELBAUM, ISSAC M01RR00051-30 0769
TEITELBAUM, STEVEN L R01AR32788-08
TEITELBAUM, STEVEN L R01DE05413-12
TEITLER, MILT R01MH40716-05
TEJANI-BUTT, SHANAZ M R01MH45472-02
TEL-POGOSSIAN, MICHEL M P01NS06833-25 9001
TELANG, NITIN T P01CA29502-11A1 9007
TELANG, NITIN T R29CA44741-04
TELCH, MICHAEL J R29MH44701-02
TELEN, MARILYN J K04HL02233-03
TELEN, MARILYN J R01HL33572-07
TELEN, MARILYN J R01HL44042-02
TELFER, WILLIAM R01AI28852-02
TELFER, WILLIAM H R01GM32909-08
TELIAN, STEVEN A K08DC00001-02
TELIAN, STEVEN A U01DC01285-01
TELL, GRETHE P60AG10484-01 9001
TELL, GRETHE S R01AR41344-01
TELL, GRETHE S R55DK43494-01A1
TELLER, DAVIDA Y R01EY04470-09
TEMIN, HOWARD M P01CA22443-14
TEMIN, HOWARD M P01CA22443-14 0001
TEMIN, HOWARD M P30CA07175-28 0002
TEMKIN, NANCY R P01NS17111-11 0011
TEMKIN, NANCY R P01NS17111-11 9002
TEMPEL, ANN R01DA05440-04
TEMPEL, ANN S15MH49332-01
TEMPEL, BRUCE P01HL44948-01A1 0002
TEMPEL, BRUCE L R01NS27206-03
TEMPLE, BRUCE P50AG05136-08 0015
TEMPLE, CARROLL G N01CM07329-01
TEMPLE, CARROLL G S07RR05676-15 0966
TEMPLE, MARK R01AA08564-04
TEMPLETON, ALAN R R01AG02246-12
TEMPLETON, ALAN R R01GM31571-08S1
TEMPLETON, ALAN R S10RR06380-01
TEMPST, PAUL S07RR05534-19 0531
TEN EICK, ROBERT E R01HL27026-11
TEN EICK, ROBERT E R01HL38041-05
TENCZA, MICHAEL G K11DE00312-01
TENDLER, CRAIG L R03HD28583-01
TENEN, DANIEL S07RR05479-29 0446
TENEN, DANIEL S07RR05479-29 0440
TENEN, DANIEL S07RR05479-29 0438
TENEN, DANIEL S07RR05479-29 0434
TENEN, DANIEL G P01CA34183-08 0016
TENEN, DANIEL G R01AI29847-02
TENEN, DANIEL G R01CA41456-06
TENG, B P30DK42086-02 0005
TENG, C T Z01ES70067-08
TENNANT, BUD C N01AI82698-07
TENNEKOON, GIHAN I R01NS21700-08
TENNEKOON, GIHAN I R55NS29710-01
TENNEKOON, GIHAN I S07RR05383-30 0571
TENNER, ANDREA J R01AI27168-03
TENNER, THOMAS S07RR05773-17 0374
TENNER, THOMAS S07RR05773-17 0371
TENNEY, JEFF R19MH46182-03
TENNYSON, VIRGINIA M R01HD17736-08
TENOVER, JOYCE A M01RR00037-31 0488
TENOVER, JOYCE S K08AG00411-05
TENOVER, JOYCE S M01RR00037-31 0458
TENPENNY, P S07RR07210-09 0680
TENSER, RICHARD B S07RR05680-23 0916
TENSOR, RICHARD B P01AI24010-05 0001
TEPHLY, THOMAS R R01GM19420-20
TEPLIN, LINDA A R01MH45583-02
TEPLIN, LINDA A R01MH47994-02
TEPPER, JAMES M R29MH45286-04
TEPPER, JAMES M S07RR07059-26 0841
TEPPER, ROBERT I K11DK01662-05
TEPPO, LYLY N01CP85638-02
TER-POGOSSIAN, MICHEL M P01HL13851-29
TER-POGOSSIAN, MICHEL M P01HL13851-29 9001
TER-POGOSSIAN, MICHEL M P41RR01380-10 0001
TERADA, LANCE S K08HL02375-02
TERASAKI, M Z01NS02841-01
TERASAKI, PAUL I R01DK02375-33
TERASAWA, EI P51RR00167-31 0038
TERASAWA, EI R01HD11355-13
TERASAWA, EI R01HD15433-09
TERASAWA, EI S07RR07098-26 0365
TERCYAK, ANNA P01HL26335-11A1 9002
TERENIUS, LARS Y P50DA05186-05 0007
TERESI, JEANNE A R01AG08948-02
TERHORST, CORNELIS P01AI28046-03 0003
TERHORST, CORNELIS P01AI28046-03 0004
TERHORST, CORNELIS P P01AI28046-03
TERHORST, CORNELIS P R01AI15066-14
TERHORST, CORNELIS P R37AI17651-12
TERHORST, CORNELIUS P U01AI31541-01 0003
TERHUNE, PENELOPE L S07RR05425-30 0771
TERI, LINDA P50AG05136-08 9001
TERI, LINDA R29MH43266-04
TERJUNG, RONALD L R01HL37387-04A1
TERJUNG, RONALD L R37AR21617-14
TERKELTAUB, ROBERT R01DK36702-07
TERMAN, MICHAEL P50MH43878-03 0026
TERMAN, MICHAEL R01MH42931-04A1
TERMINI, JOHN S07RR05841-12 0230
TERNER, JAMES R01GM34443-07
TERNER, JAMES S07RR07204-11 0450
TERNER, JAMES S15GM47034-01
TERPENNING, MARGARET P01DE09142-02 0001
TERRACIO, LOUIS R01HL40424-03
TERRACIO, LOUIS R01HL42249-04
TERRANOVA, PAUL P30HD02528-25A1 9017
TERRANOVA, PAUL F R01CA50616-01A2
TERRANOVA, VICTOR P R01DE08188-04A1
TERRANOVA, VICTOR P R01DE09411-01A1
TERRIN, MICHAEL L U01HL45696-01A1
TERRY, L CASS S07RR05434-30 0810
TERRY, NICHOLAS H P01CA06294-30 9006
TERRY, RICHARD B S07RR05818-12 0156
TERRY, ROBERT D P50AG05131-08 9001
TERRY, ROBERT D P50AG05131-08 0014
TERRY, ROBERT D R01AG08201-04
TERWILLIGER, ERNEST F R01AI28193-03
TERWILLIGER, ERNEST F R01AI31354-01A1
TERWILLIGER, THOMAS C R01GM38714-05
TERZAGHI-HOWE, MARGARET R01CA34695-09
TESCHAN, PAUL E U01DK34534-07
TESH, ROBERT B P01AI28778-02 0003
TESH, ROBERT B P01AI28778-02 9001
TESH, ROBERT B R01AI21049-08
TESH, ROBERT B R01AI28528-03
TESH, ROBERT B R37AI10984-20
TESI, RAYMOND J M01RR00034-31 0420
TESSEL, RICHARD P01HD26927-01A1 0004
TESSEL, RICHARD E S07RR05606-25 0690
TESSER, ABRAHAM R01MH41487-05
TESSLER, ALAN P01NS24707-05 9002
TESSLER, ALAN R P01NS24707-05 0007
TESSLER, RICHARD C K05MH00834-03
TESSLER, RICHARD C R01MH44683-03
TESSMAN, IRWIN R01GM35850-07
TEST, MARY ANN S07RR07098-26 0356
TESTA, JACQUELINE S07RR05736-19 0167
TESTA, JACQUELINE E R03CA54873-01
TESTA, JOSEPH R R01CA45745-04
TESTA, JOSEPH R S07RR05895-09 0612
TETI, DOUGLAS M R29MH44713-03
TEUSCHER, CORY R01HD21926-05
TEUSCHER, CORY R01HD27275-01A1
TEVETHIA, MARY J P01CA27503-12 0005
TEVETHIA, MARY J R55CA24694-14
TEVETHIA, SATVIR P01CA27503-12
TEVETHIA, SATVIR S P01CA27503-12 0004
TEVETHIA, SATVIR S R37CA25000-14
TEW, J C P01DE08972-03 0004
TEW, JOHN P50AI28532-03 0003
TEW, JOHN G R01AI17142-12
TEW, KENNETH D R01CA43783-06
TEW, KENNETH D R01CA43830-06
TEW, KENNETH D S07RR05895-09 0613
TEWARI, KRISHNA K R01GM33725-07
TEWARI, RAM P S07RR05843-11 0547
TEWARSON, REGINALD P R01DK17593-14
TEXTOR, S C M01RR00585-20 0493
TEYLER, TIMOTHY J R01NS28698-01A1
THACH, BRADLEY T R37HD10993-15
THACH, ROBERT E R01AI20484-20
THACH, WILLIAM T, JR R01NS12777-16
THACHER, SCOTT M S07RR05814-12 0146
THACKER, WAYNE R19DA06417-03
THAKER, GUNVANT K R29MH43031-04
THAKUR, MADHUKAR L R01CA51960-02
THAKUR, VASHU S07RR05377-30 0754
THAL, DONNA P01DC01289-01 0001
THAL, DONNA J R29DC00482-04
THAL, DONNA J S06GM45765-01 0007
THAL, LEON P50MH45294-03 9003
THAL, LEON J M01RR00827-17 0356
THAL, LEON J P50AG05131-08 0015
THAL, LEON J U01AG10483-01
THAL, LEON J U01AG10483-01 0001
THALER, HOWARD P01AG03853-09 9004

THALER, HOWARD TZYI P01NS25701-05 9003
THALMANN, ISOLDE P01DC00384-05 0004
THALMANN, ROBERT H R01NS21713-07
THALMANN, RUEDIGER R P01DC00384-05 0002
THALMANN, RUEDIGER R P01DC00384-05
THAMES, HOWARD D, JR R01CA29026-11
THAMES, MARC P01HL14388-20 0243
THAMES, MARC DAVID R01HL30506-10
THANANART, PAT N01HD72922-09
THANAVALA, YASMIN R01AI27976-02
THANDROYEN, FRANCIS S07RR05745-19 0251
THASE, MICHAEL E R01MH41884-04A1
THASE, MICHAEL E U01DA07673-01
THAU, ROSEMARIE B P50HD13541-12 9004
THAUT, MICHAEL S07RR07127-23 0490
THAYER, STANLEY A R01DA06781-01
THAYER, STANLEY A S07RR05385-30 0820
THAYER, WILLIAM S K02AA00087-05
THE BIONETICS CORPORATION N01DA92010-00
THE CDM GROUP, INC N01SP12003-00
THE CIRCLE, INC N01DA08105-00
THE CIRCLE, INC N01MH70018-00
THE CIRCLE, INC N01MH70021-00
THE CIRCLE, INC N01MH80024-00
THEDFORD, ROOSEVELT S03RR03516-03
THEDFORD, ROOSEVELT S06GM08247-04 0017
THEIL, ELIZABETH C R37DK20251-15
THEIS, SAUNDRA L S07RR05776-11 0401
THELEN, ESTHER K02MH00718-04
THELEN, ESTHER R01HD22830-06
THEODORE, JAMES P01HL13108-22 0029
THEODORE, T S Z01AI00527-04
THEODORE, W Z01NS02236-14
THEODORE, W Z01NS02318-15
THEOFILOPOULOS, ARGYRIOS N R01AG09430-01
THEOFILOPOULOS, ARGYRIOS N R01AR31203-09
THEOFILOPOULOS, ARGYRIOS N R01CA52539-01A1
THEOFILOPOULOS, ARGYRIOS N R01AR39555-04
THEOHARIDES, THEOHAR S07RR05319-18 0623
THEOHARIDES, THEOHARIS C R01DK42409-03
THEOLOGIS, ATHANASIOS R01GM35447-06
THERRIEN, BARBARA A R01NR02412-02
THESLEFF, IRMA R01DE09399-02
THET, LYN A P01HL31992-08 0004
THET, LYN A R01HL43256-03
THIAGARAJAN, PERUMAL R01HL40860-04
THIBODEAU, LINDA M R29DC00911-01A1
THIBONNIER, MARC P01HL41618-03 0004
THIBONNIER, MARC R01HL39757-05
THIBOS, LARRY N R01EY05109-07
THIELE, C J Z01CM06813-09
THIELE, DENNIS J M01RR00042-31 0660
THIELE, DENNIS J R01GM41840-03
THIELE, DWAIN L R01AI24639-05
THIEME, THOMAS R R44AI28605-02
THIERRY-PALMER, MYRTLE S06GM08248-05 0018
THIERY, JEAN P R01CA49417-02
THIESSEN, DELBERT D R01MH14076-23
THIGPEN, J E Z01ES22110-03
THIGPEN, JAMES T U10CA16385-17
THILAGAR, ARULASANAM K N01ES85223-05
THILLY, WILLIAM P42ES04675-05 0001
THILLY, WILLIAM G P01ES01640-14 0015
THILLY, WILLIAM G P01ES01640-14
THILLY, WILLIAM G P01ES03926-07
THILLY, WILLIAM G P01ES03926-07 0005
THILLY, WILLIAM G P01ES05622-02 0033
THILLY, WILLIAM G P30ES02109-13
THILLY, WILLIAM G P42ES04675-05
THIMMAPPAYA, BAYAR R01AI18029-09
THISTLE, JOHNSON L M01RR00585-20 0215
THISTLETHWAITE, J RICHARD P60DK20595-14 0025
THISTLETHWAITE, JAMES R P01AI29531-02 0004
THISTLETHWAITE, JAMES R P01AI29531-02 9001
THISTLETHWAITE, JAMES R, JR R29DK40092-04
THOENE, JESS G M01RR00042-31 0489
THOENE, JESS G R01DK25548-10A1
THOENE, JESSEE G M01RR00042-31 0169
THOFT, RICHARD A P30EY08098-03
THOFT, RICHARD A R01EY06185-05A1
THOFT, RICHARD A R01EY06186-07
THOFT, RICHARD A S07RR06024-03
THOFT, RICHARD A S15EY09467-01
THOITS, PEGGY A R01MH43802-04
THOM, STEPHEN R R29ES05211-03
THOMAN, EVELYN B R01MH41244-05
THOMAN, MARILYN L K04AG00374-05
THOMAN, MARILYN L R55AG09948-01
THOMANN, ROBERT V. P42ES04895-03 0013
THOMAS-DOBERSEN, DEBORAH M01RR00069-29 0477
THOMAS, ALVIN V, JR K07HL02607-01
THOMAS, ANDREW P P01AA07215-06 0002
THOMAS, ANDREW P P50AA07186-06 0013
THOMAS, ANDREW P R29DK38422-04
THOMAS, D Z01DE00291-12
THOMAS, DAVID N01CN05230-08
THOMAS, DAVID P60DK20572-14 0045
THOMAS, DAVID B N01HD52901-09
THOMAS, DAVID B R01CA46823-04
THOMAS, DAVID B R01CA49044-02
THOMAS, DAVID B R37CA41530-06
THOMAS, DAVID D R01AR32961-08
THOMAS, DAVID D R01AR39754-03
THOMAS, DAVID D R01GM27906-12
THOMAS, DEBORA DENEE R29AI26804-04
THOMAS, DUNCAN P01HD28372-01 0009
THOMAS, DUNCAN C R01CA42949-05
THOMAS, DUNCAN C R01CA52862-01A1
THOMAS, DUNEAN C P30CA14089-16 9008
THOMAS, E DONNALL P01CA18029-16
THOMAS, E DONNALL P01CA18029-16 9006
THOMAS, E DONNALL P01CA18029-16 9007
THOMAS, E DONNALL P01CA18029-16 0001
THOMAS, E DONNALL P01CA18029-16 0026
THOMAS, EDWIN L R01AI16795-11
THOMAS, EDWIN L R01DE04235-14
THOMAS, EWART A S07RR07005-26
THOMAS, EWART A C S15HD28738-01
THOMAS, GARY R01DK37274-06
THOMAS, GARY S07RR07238-04 0470
THOMAS, GEORGE H P01HD10981-14 0001
THOMAS, GEORGE H P01HD10981-14 0010
THOMAS, GEORGE J, JR R01AI11855-17
THOMAS, GEORGE J, JR R01AI18758-11
THOMAS, GROGAN P01CA17094-16 0027
THOMAS, HUW F R01DE07075-07
THOMAS, JAMES S07RR05450-30 0342
THOMAS, JAMES C U01AI31496-01 0006
THOMAS, JAMES H R01GM39868-04
THOMAS, JAMES P R01EY00360-25
THOMAS, JAMES W P01AI21289-08 0003
THOMAS, JAMES W R01DK32329-09
THOMAS, JO ANN S07RR07002-26 0886
THOMAS, JOCELYN S07RR07169-07 0171
THOMAS, JOHN B R01GM40613-02
THOMAS, JOHN R S07RR05655-21 0825
THOMAS, JUDITH M R01AI22293-06
THOMAS, JULIAN E S06GM08091-20
THOMAS, KAREN S07RR05758-18 0260
THOMAS, KAREN A R29NR02420-02
THOMAS, LAUREE S03RR03186-08
THOMAS, LEWIS J P41RR01380-10 0008
THOMAS, LEWIS J P41RR01380-10 0010
THOMAS, LEWIS J P41RR01380-10 9001
THOMAS, LEWIS J R01GM43239-02
THOMAS, LEWIS J, JR P41RR01380-10
THOMAS, LEWIS J, JR R01HG00331-03
THOMAS, MARILYN N01AI15131-00
THOMAS, MARILYN N01HB87046-08
THOMAS, MATTHEW L R01AI26363-04
THOMAS, MICHAEL J P30CA12197-19 9009
THOMAS, MICHAEL J P30CA12197-19 9013
THOMAS, PAUL E R01GM44982-01A1
THOMAS, PAUL R N01DK12270-00
THOMAS, PETER P01CA44704-04A1 0007
THOMAS, PETER R01ES04214-05
THOMAS, RICHARD G S06GM08094-17 0006
THOMAS, STEPHEN J S07RR07264-01
THOMAS, STEPHEN R R01HL45243-02
THOMAS, SUE A R01NR02043-04
THOMAS, T J S07RR05576-27 0605
THOMAS, TED S S07RR05431-30 0855
THOMAS, THRESIA R01CA42439-06
THOMAS, THRESIA S07RR05576-27 0619
THOMAS, WILLIAM C M01RR00082-29 0319
THOMAS, WILLIAM C P01DK20586-15 9001
THOMAS, WILLIAM C JR M01RR00082-29 0469
THOMAS, WILLIAM E S06GM08037-20 0030
THOMASON, DONALD B R29AR40901-01
THOMASSEN, MARY J R01CA54248-01A1
THOMES, HOWARD D R01CA11430-25 0066
THOMPSON, JAMES C. M01RR00073-29 0267
THOMPSON, A M S07RR05411-30 0962
THOMPSON, ALBERT S03RR03113-10
THOMPSON, ALBERT N S06GM08241-07 0006
THOMPSON, ALBERT N JR S06GM08241-07
THOMPSON, ARTHUR R R01HL31193-06
THOMPSON, AUBREY S07RR07205-11 0652
THOMPSON, BETI P01CA34847-09 9004
THOMPSON, BETI P01CA34847-09 0019
THOMPSON, BRIAN J S07RR07069-26
THOMPSON, BRIAN J S15GM47063-01
THOMPSON, BRIAN J S15MH49278-01
THOMPSON, C S07RR07210-09 0686
THOMPSON, CHARLES M R29ES04434-05
THOMPSON, CHARLES P R01MH44090-03
THOMPSON, CLAUDIA Z01ES46007-01
THOMPSON, CRAIG B M01RR00042-31 0672
THOMPSON, CRAIG B P60AR20557-13 0066
THOMPSON, CRAIG B R01CA48023-03
THOMPSON, DAVID C R01HL47101-01
THOMPSON, DAVID C S07RR05814-12 0154
THOMPSON, DEBRA A R01EY09193-01
THOMPSON, DOROTHY P S06GM08025-21 0014
THOMPSON, E AUBREY P01DK42788-01 0003
THOMPSON, E AUBREY, JR R37CA24347-13
THOMPSON, E BRAD P01DK42788-01
THOMPSON, E BRAD P01DK42788-01 0001
THOMPSON, E BRAD R01CA41407-06
THOMPSON, E BRAD R01DK41058-03
THOMPSON, ELIZABETH A R01GM46255-01
THOMPSON, GLENN C R01DC00381-06
THOMPSON, H STANLEY U10EY07683-04
THOMPSON, HENRY P01CA45164-04A1 0005
THOMPSON, HENRY J R01CA52626-02
THOMPSON, HENRY J S03RR03390-08
THOMPSON, HENRY J S07RR05894-09
THOMPSON, HENRY J S15CA56033-01
THOMPSON, HERBERT W. S06GM08119-18 0015
THOMPSON, J Z01DE00341-11
THOMPSON, JAMES C M01RR00073-29 0293
THOMPSON, JAMES C P01DK35608-06A1
THOMPSON, JAMES C P01DK35608-06A1 0001
THOMPSON, JAMES C R37DK15241-21
THOMPSON, JAMES J P01HL25596-12 9002
THOMPSON, JAMES W R01MH47817-02
THOMPSON, JOHN A R01CA41248-06
THOMPSON, JOHN F K08DK01863-04
THOMPSON, JOHN S M01RR02602-07 0049
THOMPSON, JOHN S N01AI82511-07
THOMPSON, LARRY W R01MH46783-02
THOMPSON, LEE ANNE R03MH46512-02
THOMPSON, LINDA F P41RR00954-15 0025
THOMPSON, LINDA F R01AI18220-10
THOMPSON, LINDA F R55GM39699-05
THOMPSON, M B Z01ES21128-02
THOMPSON, MARTHA E S07RR05336-29 0310
THOMPSON, MELANIE N01AI95027-07
THOMPSON, MICHAEL L S07RR05382-30 0878
THOMPSON, NANCY L R01GM37145-06
THOMPSON, PAUL D R01HL28467-10
THOMPSON, R P50AR39255-05 0001
THOMPSON, RICHARD S07RR07012-25 0023
THOMPSON, RICHARD F. P50AG05142-08 0006
THOMPSON, RICHARD L R01NS25879-04
THOMPSON, ROBERT J. P01HD21354-05 0001
THOMPSON, ROBY C, JR P50AR39255-05
THOMPSON, STANLEY M01RR00059-30 0715
THOMPSON, STUART H R01NS14519-12A1
THOMPSON, SUMNER P01AI19554-08S1 0003
THOMPSON, SUMNER P01AI19554-08S1 0005
THOMPSON, THOMAS E R01GM14628-26
THOMPSON, THOMAS E R37GM23573-14
THOMPSON, TIMOTHY C R01CA50588-03
THOMPSON, TIMOTHY C R01DK43523-01A1
THOMPSON, TRAVIS I P30HD24051-03
THOMPSON, TRAVIS I R01HD22415-03A1
THOMPSON, TRAVIS I R01HD25150-01A2
THOMPSON, W DOUGLAS P01CA42101-06 0005
THOMPSON, W DOUGLAS P01CA42101-06 0009
THOMPSON, WILLIAM S07RR07205-11 0653
THOMPSON, WILLIAM F R01GM43108-02
THOMPSON,W DOUGLAS P01CA42101-06 0004
THOMSEN, DONALD L, JR R01DA04722-05
THOMSEN, DONALD L, JR R13DA07460-01
THOMSON, ELIZABETH J R01HD20491-05
THOMSON, ELIZABETH J R01HD23898-04
THOMSON, ELIZABETH J R01HD26122-03
THOMSON, GLENYS J R01GM35326-06
THOMSON, GLENYS J R01HD12731-13
THOMSON, KENNETH S S07RR05390-30 0658
THOMSON, ROBERT J, JR P01HD21354-05
THOMSON, WILLIAM A S03RR03169-10
THONAR, EUGENE P50AR39239-05 0004
THONAR, EUGENE J R01AG04736-08
THOR, ANN P01CA44768-05 9004
THORBECKE, G JEANETTE P01AG04860-08 0001
THORBECKE, GEERTRUIDA J P01AG04860-08 9001
THORBECKE, GEERTRUIDA J P01AG04860-08
THORBECKE, GEERTRUIDA J R01AG04980-28S3
THORBECKE, GEERTRUIDA J R01CA14462-19
THORGAARD, GARY H. P01ES04766-04 0005
THORGAARD, GARY H R01RR06654-02
THORGEIRSSON, S S Z01CP05453-07
THORGEIRSSON, S S Z01CP05558-04
THORGEIRSSON, S S Z01CP05600-03
THORGEIRSSON, U P Z01CP03509-28
THORGEIRSSON, U P Z01CP05576-04
THORGEIRSSON, U P Z01CP05641-02
THORGEIRSSON, U P Z01CP05700-01
THORLEY-LAWSON, DAVID A R01AI18757-11
THORLEY-LAWSON, DAVID A R37CA31893-10
THORN, BEVERLY E S07RR07151-13 0519
THORNBERRY, TERENCE P R01DA05512-04
THORNBURG, KENT L R01HL43015-03
THORNE, PETER S07RR05372-30 0683
THORNE, PETER S P30ES05605-02 9006
THORNER, JEREMY W R37GM21841-17
THORNER, M O M01RR00847-18 0369
THORNER, MICHAEL O M01RR00847-18 0321
THORNER, MICHAEL O M01RR00847-18 0091
THORNER, MICHAEL O M01RR00847-18 0476
THORNER, MICHAEL O M01RR00847-18 0229
THORNER, MICHAEL O M01RR00847-18 0567
THORNER, MICHAEL O M01RR00847-18 0573
THORNER, MICHAEL O M01RR00847-18 0571
THORNER, MICHAEL O M01RR00847-18 0569
THORNER, MICHAEL O M01RR00847-18 0232
THORNER, MICHAEL O M01RR00847-18 0233
THORNER, MICHAEL O M01RR00847-18 0576
THORNER, MICHAEL O M01RR00847-18 0555
THORNER, MICHAEL O M01RR00847-18 0513
THORNER, MICHAEL O M01RR00847-18 0450
THORNER, MICHAEL O M01RR00847-18 0451
THORNER, MICHAEL O M01RR00847-18 0515
THORNER, MICHAEL O M01RR00847-18 0516

THORNER, MICHAEL O M01RR00847-18 0517
THORNER, MICHAEL O M01RR00847-18 0518
THORNER, MICHAEL O M01RR00847-18 0519
THORNER, MICHAEL O M01RR00847-18 0452
THORNHILL, WILLIAM B R01NS29633-01
THORNTON, AARON R P01DC00361-05S1 0003
THORNTON, ARLAND D R01HD19342-07
THORNTON, EDWARD R R01GM38079-04A1
THORNTON, EDWARD R R01GM41113-03
THORNTON, JOHN S07RR05300-30 0213
THORP, JOHN M01RR00046-31 0532
THORPE, COLIN R01GM26643-13
THORPE, PHILIP E R01CA54168-01
THORPE, SUZANNE R R01DK25373-13
THORPE, SUZANNE R S07RR07160-16 0591
THORSNESS, PETER E S07RR07157-16 0578
THORSTENSON, PATRICIA C S06GM08005-20 0007
THOULESS MARGARET U01AI26503-04 9001
THOULESS, MARGARET P51RR00166-30 0160
THRALL, DONALD E P01CA42745-05 9002
THRALL, DONALD W P01CA42745-05 0001
THRALL, MARY A R01AR37095-05
THRALL, MARY A R01RR06886-01
THRALL, MARY ANNA S07RR05458-29 0840
THRALL, ROGER S R01HL39939-04
THRASHER, TERRY N R01HL41313-04
THRAVES, PETER J R01CA52945-02
THULBORN, KEITH R P01CA48729-03 0003
THULBORN, KEITH R R01HL45176-02
THUMASATHIT, SUTHEE S07RR05372-30 0704
THUMMEL, CARL S R29GM40905-03
THUREEN, PATTI J M01RR00069-29 0435
THUREN, TOM Y S07RR05404-30 0861
THURIN, JAN U01AI28679-03
THURLOW, DAVID L R15GM44309-01A1
THURMAN, RONALD G R01AA03624-13
THURMAN, RONALD G R01ES02759-10
THURMAN, WILLIAM G S03RR03249-09
THURMAN, WILLIAM G S07RR05538-29
THURMAN, WILLIAM G S15AR41246-01
THURMOND, AMY S S07RR05412-30 0970
THURMOND, VERA B S03RR03034-11
THURNAU, GARY R U10HD27889-01
THURSTON, GEORGE D R01ES04612-04S1
THYLETORS, BJORN N01EY92103-24
THYS-JACOBS, SUSAN M01RR00071-28A1 0209
TIBBETTS, CLARK P30HD28819-01 9006
TIBBETTS, CLARK J R01CA34126-09
TICE, RAYMOND N01ES15311-00
TICE, RAYMOND N01ES15321-00
TICE, RAYMOND R R43ES05381-01
TICE, RAYMOND R R44ES05383-02
TICH, NANCY N01CN95214-01
TICKEN, PATRICIA S07RR06014-03 0842
TICKNER, E GLENN R44CA53590-02
TICKU, MAHARAJ K R01AA04090-08
TICKU, MAHARAJ K R01NS15339-12A1
TIDBALL, JAMES G R01AR40343-03
TIDBALL, JAMES G R01HL42227-04
TIDWELL, RICHARD R N01AI72648-08
TIDWELL, RICHARD R P50HL19171-15 0014
TIDWELL, RICHARD R R01AI32912-01
TIEDJE, JAMES M P42ES04911-03 0001
TIEN, ALLEN Y K20MH00881-01A1
TIEN, MING P42ES04922-03 0006
TIENDA, MARTA R01HD25588-02
TIETZ, ELIZABETH S07RR05700-22 0867
TIETZ, ELIZABETH S07RR05700-22 0881
TIETZ, ELIZABETH I R01DA04075-04A2
TIETZE, F Z01DK57503-18
TIFFANY-CASTIGLIONI, S07RR05854-11 0915
TIFFANY, STEPHEN T R01DA04050-05
TIGELAAR, ROBERT E R01AI27404-04
TIGGES, JOHANNES V S07RR07023-26 0975
TIGGES, JOHANNES W P51RR00165-31 0176
TIGGES, MARGARETE S07RR05364-30 0551
TIGGES, MARGARETE H P51RR00165-31 0177
TIGHE, HELEN P P60AR40770-01A1 0004
TIGNOR, GREGORY H S03RR03316-10
TIJIAN, ROBERT P41RR01614-10 0012
TIKKANEN, WAYNE R S06GM08101-20 0043
TILDEN, SAMUEL J M01RR00032-31 0345
TILDEN, VIRGINIA P R03NR02818-01
TILDON, J P01HD16596-08 0001
TILDON, J TYSON P01HD16596-08
TILGHMAN, SHIRLEY M R37CA44976-06
TILLACK, THOMAS W R01GM26234-12
TILLEY, BARBARA C N01AR12202-01
TILLEY, BARBARA C N01NS02382-02
TILLEY, BARBARA C R01CA52605-01
TILLEY, BARBARA C. P01HL28982-10 9003
TILLEY, SHERMAINE A R55AI26081-04
TILLINGHAST, EDWARD S07RR07108-19 0410
TILLINGHAST, EDWARD K R15GM44353-01A1
TILLOTSON, DOUGLAS L R01DK40127-04
TILLOTSON, LACEY M S06GM08025-21 0022
TILNEY, LEWIS G R01HD14474-12
TILNEY, NICHOLAS L R01AI19071-18
TILSON, MARTIN D R01HL29325-08
TIMASHEFF, SERGE N R01CA16707-17
TIMASHEFF, SERGE N R01GM14603-25
TIMBERLAKE, WILLIAM D R01MH37892-08
TIMBERLAKE, WILLIAM E R01GM37886-06
TIMBERLAKE, WILLIAM E R01HG00337-03
TIMKOVICH, RUSSELL R01GM43292-01
TIMKOVICH, RUSSELL S07RR07151-13 0517
TIMKOVICH, RUSSELL S07RR07151-13 0521
TIMMERMANN, BARBARA S07RR07002-26 0859
TIMMONS, THERESE S07RR05425-30 0772
TIMMS, BARRY G R15DK42609-01A1
TIMOR, ILAN P50HD13063-12 0011
TINANOFF, NORMAN R01DE09217-02
TINDALL, DONALD J P50HD09140-16 0015
TINDALL, DONALD J R01CA32387-09
TINDALL, K R Z01ES65050-05
TINDALL, K R Z01ES65051-05
TINDALL, RICHARD S M01RR00633-19 0341
TINDALL, RICHARD S M01RR00633-19 0285
TINETTI, MARY E R01AG07449-03
TINETTI, MARY E U01AG09087-02
TING, C C Z01CB08907-08
TING, JENNY P R01AI29564-01A1
TING, JENNY P Y P01CA29589-10 0007
TING, PAULINE S06GM08244-05 0027
TING, WINDSOR S07RR05576-27 0611
TINOCO, IGNACIO, JR R37GM10840-33
TINTNER, RON M01RR00633-19 0404
TINTNER, RON M01RR00633-19 0378
TINTNER, RON P50AG08013-04 0006
TIPPER, DONALD J S07RR05712-20 0098
TIPPETT, MAURICE L R19DA06411-03
TIPPETT, MAURICE L R19MH46202-03
TIPTON, ARTHUR J R43AR41109-01
TIPTON, ARTHUR J R43DA05983-01A2
TIPTON, CHARLES M R01HL33782-05
TIPTON, CHARLES M S07RR06044-01
TIPTON, DAVID A S07RR05994-03 0298
TISCHLER, ARTHUR S R01CA27808-09
TISHER, C CRAIG R01DK28330-12
TISHER, C CRAIG U01DK39480-04
TISSOT, ROBERT G P01CA49488-01A2 0001
TITUS, MARGARET A R01GM46486-01
TITUS, MARK S07RR05635-18 0782
TITUS, RICHARD G R01AI27511-03
TITUS, RICHARD G R29AI24511-05
TITZE, INGO R P60DC00976-02
TITZE, INGO R P60DC00976-02 0001
TITZE, INGO R R01DC00157-11
TITZE, INGO R R01DC00387-05
TIUS, MARCUS A R01DA06731-02
TIUS, MARCUS A S07RR07026-26 0004
TIWARI, RAJ K P01CA29502-11A1 0035
TJIAN, ROBERT T R37CA25417-13
TJIO, J H Z01DK21008-25
TLSTY, THEA D R01CA51912-01A1
TO BE APPOINTED N01LM63529-15
TOBACK, FREDERICK G R01DK18413-15
TOBACK, FREDERICK G R01DK37227-15
TOBACMAN, LARRY S R29HL38834-05
TOBIAN, LOUIS R01HL44657-01A1
TOBIAS, CORNELIUS A P01CA19138-15 0003
TOBIAS, PETER S M01RR00833-17 0209
TOBIAS, PETER S R29AI25563-04
TOBIASEN, JOYCE M R29DE08153-05
TOBIN, ALLAN J R01NS20356-08
TOBIN, ALLAN J R01NS22256-07
TOBIN, ELAINE M R01GM23167-16
TOBIN, J Z01AG00204-08
TOBIN, J D Z01AG00290-06
TOBIN, J D Z01AG00293-03
TOBIN, MICHAEL J S07RR05451-30 0359
TOBIN, SHELDON S R01AG09198-02
TOBIS, JONATHAN M R01HL45077-01A1
TOBLER, JACK N01ES95263-02
TOCE, JOSEPH A R43HL47230-01
TOCKMAN, M S Z01AG00634-02
TOD, MARY L R29HL43304-02
TODD, JAMES K S07RR06022-02
TODD, LORI A K01OH00103-01
TODD, MARY B R01HL42822-03
TODD, MICHAEL M R01NS24517-06
TODD, PETER J R01GM41617-03
TODD, RICHARD P50MH31302-14 0025
TODD, RICHARD D P50AA03539-14 9004
TODD, RICHARD D R01MH45019-03
TODD, ROBERT F P60AR20557-13 9001
TODD, ROBERT F, III R01CA39064-08
TODD, ROBERT F, III R01CA42246-06
TODD, ROBERT F, III S10RR06414-01
TODD, ROBERTA B P30HD06645-20 9006
TODD, SELDON P, JR R43NR02594-01
TODMAN, PATRICIA R S06GM08266-04 0007
TOEWS, GALEN B R01HL29543-10
TOEWS, MYRON L R01GM34500-08
TOFILON, PHILIP J P01CA06294-30 0072
TOFILON, PHILIP J R01CA46798-03
TOFILON, PHILIP J R01CA50207-02
TOFT, DAVID O P50HD09140-16 0012
TOFT, DAVID O R01HD18287-09
TOGA, ARTHUR S07RR05354-30 0408
TOGA, ARTHUR S07RR05756-18 0312
TOGA, ARTHUR N P41RR01380-10 9002
TOGA, ARTHUR W R01RR05956-02
TOGIAS, ALKIS G S07RR05378-30 0016
TOHEN, MAURICIO R03MH48444-01
TOKES, ZOLTAN A P30CA14089-16 9003
TOKES, ZOLTAN A R01AG09681-01
TOKES, ZOLTON A. P50AG05142-08 0008
TOKUYASU, K P41RR04050-03 9002
TOLAN, DEAN R R29DK38821-05
TOLAN, DEAN R S07RR07043-26 0111
TOLAN, PATRICK H R01MH48248-02
TOLBERT, DANIEL L R01NS20227-08
TOLBERT, KATHRYN R01HD28305-02
TOLBERT, LAREN M S07RR07024-26 0047
TOLBERT, LELLAND M01RR00032-31 0272
TOLBERT, LESLIE P P01NS28495-02 0003
TOLBERT, LESLIE P P01NS28495-02 9001
TOLBERT, LESLIE P R01NS20040-08A1
TOLBERT, LESLIE P S07RR07002-26 0887
TOLEDANO, STUART R U10CA41082-06
TOLEDANO, STUART R U10CA41082-06 0021
TOLEDANO, STUART R U10CA41082-06 0001
TOLEDANO, STUART R U10CA41082-06 0002
TOLEDANO, STUART R U10CA41082-06 0003
TOLEDANO, STUART R U10CA41082-06 0004
TOLEDANO, STUART R U10CA41082-06 0005
TOLEDANO, STUART R U10CA41082-06 0006
TOLEDANO, STUART R U10CA41082-06 0007
TOLEDANO, STUART R U10CA41082-06 0008
TOLEDANO, STUART R U10CA41082-06 0009
TOLEDANO, STUART R U10CA41082-06 0010
TOLEDANO, STUART R U10CA41082-06 0011
TOLEDANO, STUART R U10CA41082-06 0012
TOLEDANO, STUART R U10CA41082-06 0013
TOLEDANO, STUART R U10CA41082-06 0014
TOLEDANO, STUART R U10CA41082-06 0015
TOLEDANO, STUART R U10CA41082-06 0016
TOLEDANO, STUART R U10CA41082-06 0017
TOLEDANO, STUART R U10CA41082-06 0018
TOLEDANO, STUART R U10CA41082-06 0019
TOLEDANO, STUART R U10CA41082-06 0020
TOLEDANO, STUART R U10CA41082-06 0022
TOLEDANO, STUART R U10CA41082-06 0023
TOLEDANO, STUART R U10CA41082-06 0024
TOLEDANO, STUART R U10CA41082-06 0025
TOLEDANO, STUART R U10CA41082-06 0026
TOLEDANO, STUART R U10CA41082-06 0027
TOLEDANO, STUART R U10CA41082-06 0041
TOLEDANO, STUART R U10CA41082-06 0042
TOLEDANO, STUART R U10CA41082-06 0043
TOLEDANO, STUART R U10CA41082-06 0044
TOLEDANO, STUART R U10CA41082-06 0045
TOLEDANO, STUART R U10CA41082-06 0046
TOLEDANO, STUART R U10CA41082-06 0047
TOLEDANO, STUART R U10CA41082-06 0048
TOLEDANO, STUART R U10CA41082-06 0049
TOLEDANO, STUART R U10CA41082-06 0050
TOLEDANO, STUART R U10CA41082-06 0051
TOLEDANO, STUART R U10CA41082-06 0052
TOLEDANO, STUART R U10CA41082-06 0053
TOLEDANO, STUART R U10CA41082-06 0054
TOLEDANO, STUART R U10CA41082-06 0055
TOLEDANO, STUART R U10CA41082-06 0028
TOLEDANO, STUART R U10CA41082-06 0029
TOLEDANO, STUART R U10CA41082-06 0030
TOLEDANO, STUART R U10CA41082-06 0031
TOLEDANO, STUART R U10CA41082-06 0032
TOLEDANO, STUART R U10CA41082-06 0033
TOLEDANO, STUART R U10CA41082-06 0034
TOLEDANO, STUART R U10CA41082-06 0035
TOLEDANO, STUART R U10CA41082-06 0036
TOLEDANO, STUART R U10CA41082-06 0037
TOLEDANO, STUART R U10CA41082-06 0038
TOLEDANO, STUART R U10CA41082-06 0039
TOLEDANO, STUART R U10CA41082-06 0040
TOLEDANO, STUART R U10CA41082-06 0056
TOLEDANO, STUART R U10CA41082-06 0057
TOLEDANO, STUART R U10CA41082-06 0058
TOLEDANO, STUART R U10CA41082-06 0059
TOLEDANO, STUART R U10CA41082-06 0060
TOLENTINO, ERNEST P30CA15704-18 9019
TOLL, LAWRENCE R01DA06682-02
TOLLEFSEN, DOUGLAS M P50HL14147-21 0022
TOLLEFSEN, SHERIDA P01HD20805-05A1 0005
TOLLEFSEN, SHERIDA E K04DK01978-01
TOLLEFSEN, SHERIDA E R01DK42658-01A1
TOLLIN, GORDON R01DK15057-21
TOLMACH, L P01CA51116-02 0005
TOLNAY, STEWART E S07RR07122-23 0116
TOLTZIS, PHILLIP H M01RR00080-29 0431
TOMANEK, ROBERT J P50HL32295-07 9003
TOMARKEN, ANDREW J S07RR07201-12 0640
TOMASEK, PAUL H S07RR07058-26 0184
TOMASELLI, GORDON F K08HL02421-02
TOMASELLO, W MICHAEL P51RR00165-31 0084
TOMASI, THOMAS P30CA16056-16 9019
TOMASI, THOMAS P30CA16056-16 9015
TOMASI, THOMAS P30CA16056-16 9021
TOMASI, THOMAS P41RR01315-10 0026
TOMASI, THOMAS B, JR P30CA16056-16
TOMASI, THOMAS B, JR S07RR05648-25
TOMASI, THOMAS E R15AG09840-01
TOMASOVIC, STEPHEN P R01CA32745-09
TOMASOVIC, STEPHEN P R01CA47786-02
TOMASULO, RICHARD A K08NS01438-01A1

TOMASZ, A P41RR00862-18 0005
TOMASZ, ALEXANDER R37AI16794-10
TOMASZ, MARIA R37CA28681-12
TOMASZ, MARIA S06GM08176-12 0014
TOMASZ, MARIA S07RR07109-23 0511
TOMASZEWSKI, JOHN E S07RR07083-26 0497
TOMBLIN, BRUCE N01DC12107-00
TOMBLIN, JAMES B R01DC00612-03
TOMBOULIAN, PAUL S07RR07131-22 0140
TOMER, K Z01ES50108-03
TOMER, K B Z01ES50080-09
TOMER, K B Z01ES50106-03
TOMER, K B Z01ES50107-03
TOMER, K B Z01ES50116-02
TOMETSKO, ANDREW M R43CA52331-01A1
TOMFORD, WILLIAM W R01AR21896-13
TOMICH, JOHN M R29GM43617-02
TOMIE, DAVID L P30CA16058-17 9014
TOMLINSON, GUS S06GM08092-18 0020
TOMLINSON, HAROLD W R43HL44811-01A1
TOMLINSON, JAMES E R43HL46099-01
TOMPKINS, CONNIE A R29DC00453-04
TOMPKINS, LAURIE S07RR07115-24 0578
TOMPKINS, LAURIE S07RR07115-24 0579
TOMPKINS, LUCY S R01AI23796-06
TOMPKINS, LUCY S R01AI30618-01
TOMPKINS, MARY B R01CA43676-05
TOMPKINS, RONALD G K08DK01746-05
TOMPKINS, RONALD G P50GM21700-15 0012
TOMPKINS, RONALD G R01DK41709-03
TOMPKINS, WAYNE A N01AI72665-08
TOMPKINS, WAYNE A R01AI32310-01
TOMPKINS, WAYNE A R01CA54723-01
TONASCIA, JAMES A N01HR16044-00
TONEGAWA, SUSUMU R35CA53874-01
TONEGAWA, SUSUMU R37AI17879-11
TONG, JENNIFER S07RR05801-13 0443
TONG, SANDRA E R29AI28735-02
TONG, WILLIAM P01CA47997-03 9002
TONG, WILLIAM G R01GM41032-03
TONINO, RICHARD P M01RR00109-28 0339
TONINO, RICHARD P M01RR00109-28 0300
TONIOLO, PAOLO G R01CA51921-01A2
TONKISS S07RR05380-30 0885
TONKS, NICHOLAS K R01CA53840-01A1
TONNER, DENISE M01RR00059-30 0728
TONNER, DENISE R M01RR00059-30 0744
TONSGARD, JAMES S07RR05367-30 0573
TOOD, MARY B P01CA08341-26 0076
TOOLE, BRYAN P P01HD23681-04
TOOLE, BRYAN P R01DE05838-12
TOOLE, BRYAN P. P01HD23681-04 0001
TOOLE, JAMES F R01NS22611-07
TOOLEY, WILLIAM H P50HL27356-10 0005
TOOLEY, WILLIAM H P50HL27356-10
TOOMEY, BEVERLY G R01MH46111-02S1
TOONE, ERIC J S07RR07070-26 0456
TOONE, ERIC J S07RR07070-26 0457
TOOTELL, ROGER B R01EY07980-03
TOOTLE, JOHN S R01EY08281-03
TOPAL, MICHAEL D R01CA46527-13
TOPALIAN, S L Z01CM06664-02
TOPHAM, RICHARD W R01DK38313-04
TOPOL, ERIC J U01HL38529-05
TOPOLSKI, JAMES M R19DA06451-03
TOPP, MICHAEL S07RR07083-26 0484
TOPP, MICHAEL R P41RR01348-10 9002
TOPPINO, THOMAS C S15HD28751-01
TOPRAC, MARCIA G R18MH47634-02
TORAN-ALLERAND, C DOMINIQUE K05MH00192-11A
TORAN-ALLERAND, C DOMINIQUE R01AG08099-03
TORBINER, MARK S07RR05304-30 0219
TORCHIA, D A Z01DE00157-16
TORCHIA, D A Z01DE00507-02
TORDAY, JOHN S P50HL34616-07 0001
TORDOFF, MICHAEL S07RR05825-12 0510
TORDOFF, MICHAEL G R01DK36339-06
TORDOFF, MICHAEL G R01DK40099-04
TORIAN, BRUCE E R29AI28188-05
TORIBARA, TAFT Y P30ES01247-17 9002
TORIZILLI, PETER P60AR38520-04 0005
TORMEY, DOUGLAS U10CA37403-07
TORMEY, DOUGLASS C P01CA20432-14 9001
TORMEY, DOUGLASS C P01CA20432-14 0019
TORMEY, DOUGLASS C P30CA14520-19 9013
TORMEY, DOUGLASS C U10CA21076-16
TORMEY, DOUGLASS C U10CA21115-16
TORMEY, DOUGLASS C U10CA39088-07
TORMEY, JOHN M R01HL31249-08
TORNABENE, THOMAS G S07RR07024-26 0054
TORNABENE, THOMAS G S07RR07024-26
TORNHEIM, KEITH R01DK31559-07A3
TORO, PAUL A R01MH46096-01A2
TOROK-STORB, BEVERLY J P01CA18221-16 0004
TOROK-STORB, BEVERLY J P01HL36444-11 0006
TOROK-STORB, BEVERLY J R01DK34431-07
TOROK-STORH, BEVERLY P01CA47748-03 0007
TORRENCE, P F Z01DK59601-04
TORRENCE, P F Z01DK59602-18
TORRES-BAUZA, LUIS S07RR05419-30 0825
TORRES-BAUZA, LUIS J S06GM08224-07 0021
TORRES-RAINES, ROSARIO S06GM08107-18 0009
TORRES-RUIZ, JOSE A S06GM08239-06 0009
TORRES-RUIZ, JOSE A S06GM08239-06 0009
TORRES, V E M01RR00585-20 0533
TORRES, VICENTE E R01DK44863-01
TORREY, E FULLER R01MH41176-04S1
TORRIANI-GORINI, ANNAMARIA R01GM24009-13
TORTI, FRANK M M01RR00070-29 0227
TORTI, FRANK M R01DK42412-03
TORTI, RICHARD P R43HL46061-01
TOSATO, G Z01BD04001-03
TOSATO, G Z01BD04002-03
TOSATO, G Z01BD04014-01
TOSATO, G Z01BD04016-01
TOSATO, G Z01BD04017-01
TOSI, MICHAEL F K08HL02234-03
TOSKES, PHILIP M01RR00082-29 0456
TOSKES, PHILLIP P M01RR00082-29 0481
TOSNEY, KATHRYN W R01NS27634-03
TOSTES TON, DANIEL C P51RR00168-30 9011
TOSTESON, ANNA R01HS06694-02
TOSTESON, DANIEL C P51RR00168-30
TOSTESTON, DANIEL C P51RR00168-30 9014
TOTH, CAROL A S07RR05591-27 0658
TOTH, FRANK N01CO15637-00
TOTH, FRANK N01CO15639-00
TOTH, FRANK N01CO15650-00
TOTH, FRANK N01CO15670-00
TOTH, FRANK N01CO15686-01
TOTH, FRANK N01CO15700-00
TOTH, FRANK N01CO15734-00
TOTH, FRANK N01CO15747-00
TOTH, FRANK N01CO15748-00
TOTH, FRANK N01CO15764-00
TOTH, FRANK N01CO15773-00
TOTH, FRANK N01CO15775-00
TOTH, LINDA A R01NS26429-03
TOTO, ROBERT D M01RR00633-19 0383
TOTO, ROBERT D M01RR00633-19 0262
TOUCHON, ROBERT C K07HL02079-04
TOUMALA, RUTH N01AI82507-17
TOUR, JAMES M S07RR07160-16 0587
TOURTELLOTTE, WALLACE W P01NS21908-06A1 90
TOURTELLOTTE, WALLACE W P01NS21908-06A1 00
TOURTELLOTTE, WALLACE W R01MH47281-01
TOURVILLE, DONALD R R44CA48530-03
TOUTELLOTE, W P30AI28697-01 9007
TOVERUD, SVEIN U R01HD12496-09S1
TOWBIN, JEFFREY A K08HL02485-02
TOWBIN, KENNETH M01RR06022-02 0617
TOWEY, JAMES PATRICK R01MH44815-02
TOWLE, HOWARD C R01DK39997-04
TOWNES-ANDERSON, ELLEN S R01EY06135-08
TOWNES, TIM M R01HL35559-06
TOWNES, TIM M R01HL43508-03
TOWNS, LEX C S15EY09443-01
TOWNSEL, JAMES G S06GM08037-20
TOWNSEL, JAMES G S06GM08037-20 0038
TOWNSEND, ALAN J S07RR05404-30 0862
TOWNSEND, COURTNEY M P01DK35608-06A1 0003
TOWNSEND, COURTNEY M P01DK35608-06A1 9002
TOWNSEND, CRAIG A R01AI14937-13
TOWNSEND, CRAIG A R01CA54421-01
TOWNSEND, CRAIG A R01ES01670-14
TOWNSEND, CRAIG A S10RR06468-01
TOWNSEND, LEROY B U01AI31718-01 0001
TOWNSEND, LEROY B U01AI31718-01
TOWNSEND, LEROY B. U01AI25739-04 0001
TOWNSEND, MICHAEL E R19DA06419-03
TOWNSEND, RAYMOND R M01RR00073-29 0306
TOWNSEND, RAYMOND R M01RR00073-29 0314
TOWNSEND, ROBERT M R01HD27638-01
TOWNSEND, WILMA R18MH49325-01
TOWNSLEY, MARY I R29HL39045-06
TOWNSWL, JAMES G G12RR03032-07 0001
TOY, PEARL T R01HL36715-05
TOYOOKA, ARTHUR P51RR00163-32 9001
TOZER, THOMAS P42ES04705-05 0008
TOZEREN, AYDIN R01GM41460-03
TRABASSO, THOMAS R R01HD25742-03
TRABER, PETER G M01RR00042-31 0659
TRABER, PETER G R29DK41393-03
TRACHTE, GEORGE J R01HL42525-01A3
TRACHTMAN, HOWARD S07RR05496-29 0904
TRACY, JAMES W P01AI28781-02 0003
TRACY, JAMES W R22AI22520-06
TRACY, PAULA B M01RR00109-28 0325
TRACY, PAULA B P01HL46703-01 0004
TRACY, RUSSELL P P01AG08777-01 0005
TRACY, RUSSELL P P01AG08777-01 0002
TRACY, SARAH W R03HS06985-01
TRAGER, WILLIAM R22AI20938-07A1
TRAGER, WILLIAM F P01GM32165-09 9001
TRAGER, WILLIAM F P01GM32165-09
TRAGER, WILLIAM F P01GM32165-09 0001
TRAGER, WILLIAM F R01GM36922-06
TRAHEY, GREGG E R01CA43334-05
TRAHIOTIS, CONSTANTINE R01DC00234-09
TRAIGER, GEORGE S07RR05606-25 0694
TRAKTMAN, PAULA P01CA29502-11A1 0061
TRAKTMAN, PAULA R01AI21758-07
TRAKTMAN, PAULA S07RR05396-30 0741
TRAMO, MARK JUDE P01NS17778-10 0004
TRAMONTANO, ALFONSO R01GM35318-07
TRAN, CHIEU S07RR07196-11 0628
TRAN, CHIEU D R55RR06887-01
TRAN, ZUNG V R01DK42860-02
TRANEL, DANIEL P01NS19632-09 0003
TRANIELLO, JAMES F A S07RR07043-26 0110
TRANKINA, MICHELE S06GM02721-07 0006
TRANQUADA, ROBERT S07RR05356-30 0439
TRANQUADA, ROBERT E S07RR05356-30 0438
TRANQUADA, ROBERT E S07RR05356-30
TRANQUADA, ROBERT E S15CA55968-01
TRANQUILLO, ROBERT T R29GM46052-01
TRANTOLO, DEBRA J R43DK44385-01
TRAPIDO, EDWARD N01CO03875-05
TRAPIDO, EDWARD P30CA14395-18A1 9010
TRAPNELL, GORDON R R44AG09167-02
TRAPP, BRUCE D P01NS22849-06 0003
TRAPP, BRUCE D R01NS30451-01
TRAPP, BRUCE D R55NS29818-01
TRASK, BARBARA J R01HG00256-01
TRAUGH, JOLINDA A R01GM21424-16
TRAUGH, JOLINDA A R01GM26738-12
TRAUGOTT, UTE P50NS11920-17 0018
TRAUNER, DORIS P01DC01289-01 9001
TRAUNER, DORIS A M01RR00827-17 0457
TRAUNER, DORIS A P50NS22343-06A1 9002
TRAUNER, DORIS A R01HD23854-04A1
TRAUT, ROBERT R R01GM17924-21
TRAUTMAN, PAUL P50MH43878-03 0035
TRAUTMAN, PAUL P50MH43878-03 0018
TRAUTMAN, PAUL S07RR05650-25 0112
TRAVERS, JOSEPH B R01DC00417-05
TRAVI, BRUNO L P50AI30603-01 9003
TRAVI, BRUNO L P50AI30603-01 0001
TRAVIS, ELIZABETH L P01CA06294-30 0078
TRAVIS, ELIZABETH L P01CA06294-30 0067
TRAVIS, ELIZABETH L R01CA38106-07
TRAVIS, GABRIEL H R01EY08043-04
TRAVIS, JAMES R01DE09761-01A1
TRAVIS, JAMES R01HL26148-12
TRAVIS, JAMES R37HL37090-06
TRAVIS, JEFFREY L S07RR07122-23 0084
TRAVIS, W D Z01CB09165-04
TRAVIS, W D Z01CB09166-02
TRAWEEK, S THOMAS S07RR05471-29 0595
TRAWICK, JOHN D S07RR05357-30 0467
TRAYLOR, TEDDY G R01HL13581-24
TRAYNELIS, VINCENT S07RR05372-30 0658
TRAYNOR-KAPLAN, ALEX S07RR05665-24 0884
TRAYSTMAN, RICHARD J M01RR00722-19 0237
TRAYSTMAN, RICHARD J P01NS20020-08 0006
TRAYSTMAN, RICHARD J P01NS20020-08
TRAYSTMAN, RICHARD J P01NS20020-08 0001
TRAYSTMAN, RICHARD J R01DA06658-02
TRAYSTMAN, RICHARD J R01HL36765-05
TREACY, J G Z01DE00543-01
TREIBER, FRANK A R29HL41781-03
TREIMAN, DAVID M M01RR00865-18 0333
TREIMAN, DAVID M M01RR00865-18 0363
TREIMAN, DAVID M N01NS72328-03
TREIMAN, REBECCA A K04HD00769-05
TREISTMAN, STEVEN N R01AA05542-09
TREISTMAN, STEVEN N R01AA08003-04
TREMPE, CLEMENT L U10EY06265-07
TREMPE, CLEMENT L U10EY06753-04
TREMPER, RONALD R19MH46183-03
TREMPY, JANINE E S07RR07079-26 0293
TRENT, CAROL R29GM43333-04
TRENT, JEFFREY M P01CA41183-05 0002
TRENT, JEFFREY M P30CA23074-14 9007
TRENT, JEFFREY M R13CA54767-01
TRENT, JEFFREY M R37CA29476-12
TRENTHAM, DAVID M01RR01032-16 0479
TRENTHAM, DAVID N01AR12205-01
TRENTHAM, DAVID S07RR05479-29 0442
TRENTHAM, DAVID R P01HL15835-19 0037
TRENTIN, JOHN J K06CA14219-30
TREPEL, J B Z01CM06719-03
TREPEL, J B Z01CM06721-04
TRES, LAURA L P30HD18968-08 9004
TRESCHER, WILLIAM H K08NS01482-01
TRESCHER, WILLIAM H S07RR05808-13 0914
TRESTMAN, ROBERT M01RR00071-28A1 0237
TRETIAK, OLEH J P41RR01638-07 0025
TRETIAK, OLEH J P41RR01638-07 9005
TRETIAK, OLEH J P41RR01638-07
TRETIAK, OLEH J P41RR01638-07 9001
TREVINO, DANIEL L S03RR03318-07
TREVISAN, MAURIZIO K04HL02189-03
TREVOR, KATRINA T R01GM44582-02
TREWHELLA, JILL R01GM40528-04
TREWYN, RONALD W P30CA16058-17 9009
TRIARHOU, LAZAROS C R29NS29283-01
TRIBBLE, CURTIS G S07RR05431-30 0846
TRICHE, TIMOTHY J P30CA14089-16 9013
TRICK, GARY P50AG05681-08 0015
TRICKETT, PENELOPE K R01MH48330-01
TRICOLI, JAMES V S07RR05408-30 0945
TRIER, JERRY S P30DK34854-08 9004
TRIER, JERRY S R37DK36835-07
TRIEZENBERG, STEVEN J R01AI27323-03
TRIGG, MICHAEL E. M01RR00059-30 0606

TRIGGLE, DAVID J R01HL16003-20
TRIGGLE, DAVID J S03RR03376-08
TRIGGLE, DAVID J S07RR05454-29
TRIGGLE, DAVID J S07RR05454-29 0889
TRIMBLE, ROBERT B P41RR01614-10 0010
TRIMBLE, ROBERT B R01GM23900-14
TRINCHIERI, GIORGIO R01CA32898-10
TRINCHIERI, GIORGIO R01CA40256-06
TRINCHIERI, GIORGIO R37CA20833-15
TRINCHIERI, GIORGIO S10RR06401-01
TRINKAUS-RANDALL, VICKERY E R01EY06000-06
TRINKAUS, JOHN P R37CA22451-18
TRIOZZI, PIERRE L U01AI25924-05 0002
TRIPATHI, A K Z01BH02004-02
TRIPATHI, BRENDA J R01EY03747-09A1
TRIPATHI, RAMESH C R01EY08707-02
TRIPPEL, STEPHEN B R01AR31068-09
TRITTON, THOMAS R R01CA44729-05
TROBE, JONATHAN D U10EY07675-04
TROBE, JONATHAN DANIEL M01RR00042-31 0525
TROCHIM, WILLIAM MK R01MH46712-01A1
TROCKI, KAREN P50AA05595-11 0016
TROEN, BRUCE R R29CA53910-01
TROGLER, WILLIAM C S06GM47165-01 0030
TROJANOWSKA, MARIA S07RR05420-30 0046
TROJANOWSKI, JOHN C P50MH43880-04 9007
TROJANOWSKI, JOHN Q P01AG09215-02
TROJANOWSKI, JOHN Q P01AG09215-02 9002
TROJANOWSKI, JOHN Q P01AG09215-02 0002
TROJANOWSKI, JOHN Q P30AG10124-01
TROJANOWSKI, JOHN Q P30AG10124-01 9002
TROJANOWSKI, JOHN Q R37CA36245-08
TROLL, LILLIAN S07RR05755-18 0213
TROLL, WALTER P42ES04895-03 0001
TROLL, WALTER R01CA53003-02
TROMMER, BARBARA L K08NS01498-01
TROMMER, BARBARA L S07RR05370-30 0615
TRONCOSO, JUAN C P50AG05146-09 0009
TRONCOSO, JUAN C P50AG05146-09 9003
TRONCOSO, JUAN C R01NS25369-04
TRONICK, EDWARD Z R01DA06882-02
TRONICK, EDWARD Z R01MH43398-02
TRONICK, EDWARD Z R01MH45547-02
TRONICK, S R Z01CP04941-19
TROOST, B TODD P01NS27500-01A2 9002
TROPE, YAACOV R01MH45557-01A1
TROSKO, JAMES E P42ES04911-03 0009
TROST, BARRY M R01GM33049-15
TROST, BARRY M R37GM13598-26
TROTTER, GAYLE S07RR05458-29 0841
TROTTER, JOHN A R01AR39922-03
TROTTER, JOHN L M01RR00036-31 1045
TROTTER, JOHN L M01RR00036-31 0469
TROTTER, ROBERT T II U01DA07295-01
TROTTIER, RALPH S06GM08248-05 0019
TROTTMAN, CHARLES S06GM08047-20S1 0018
TROUG, WILLIAM E P01HL39157-05 0003
TROUSDALE, MELVIN D R01EY02957-13
TROUSDALE, MELVIN D S07RR05810-13 0023
TROUTH, C OVID S06GM08016-21 0056
TROWBRIDGE, IAN S P30CA14195-18 0033
TROWBRIDGE, IAN S R01CA34787-09
TROWBRIDGE, IAN S R37CA17733-17
TROWBRIDGE, IAN S S15GM47082-01
TROWBRIDGE, IAN S U01CA37641-07 0001
TROWBRIDGE, IAN S U01CA37641-07 9001
TROXLER, ROBERT F P01HL13262-19 9003
TROXLER, ROBERT F R01HL37592-05
TROY, CAROL M K08AG00430-03
TROY, CAROL M P50AG08702-03 0004
TROY, FREDERIC A R01AI09352-21
TROYER, DEAN A R01DK34234-07
TRUCCO, MASSIMO R01CA44977-06
TRUCCO, MASSIMO M R01AI23963-04
TRUCKMAN S07RR05380-30 0901
TRUDELL, JAMES R R01GM43701-10
TRUELOVE, EDMOND S07RR05346-30 0321
TRUELOVE, EDMOND S07RR05346-30 0320
TRUGMAN, JOEL M K08NS01174-05
TRUJILLO, ANGELINA L S07RR05421-27 0976
TRUJILLO, EDWARD M S07RR07092-26 0543
TRUJILLO, EUGENE D S03RR03276-08
TRULL, TIMOTHY S07RR07053-26 0143
TRULL, TIMOTHY J S07RR07053-26 0159
TRUMAN, JAMES W R01NS13079-16
TRUMAN, JAMES W R01NS29971-01
TRUMBLE, WILLIAM R S07RR07170-15 0605
TRUMBLY, ROBERT J P01HL36573-06 0009
TRUMP, BENJAMIN N01CP95624-02
TRUMP, BENJAMIN F N01CP15623-00
TRUMP, BENJAMIN F R01DK15440-19
TRUMP, DONALD L U10CA47577-04
TRUMPOWER, BERNARD L R01GM20379-18
TRUPIN, JOEL S K14HL02332-03
TRUPIN, JOEL S S06GM08037-20 0013
TRUPIN, S P41RR05964-02 0009
TRUS, B L Z01CT00090-12
TRUS, B L Z01CT00092-10
TRUSH, MICHAEL A R01ES05131-02
TRUSKEY, GEORGE A R29HL41372-04
TRUSSELL, LAURENCE O R01NS28901-01A1
TRYBUS, KATHLEEN M R29HL38113-05
TRYON, VICTOR V U01AI31498-01 9001
TRYON, VICTOR V U01AI31498-01 0002
TRZEPACZ, PAULA M01RR00056-30 0377
TRZEPACZ, PAULA T R29MH44964-05
TS'O, DANIEL Y R01EY08240-02
TS'O, PAUL O P01CA42762-05
TS'O, PAUL O P01CA42762-05 0002
TSAI, C M Z01BA02010-08
TSAI, C M Z01BA02011-03
TSAI, CHE - CHUNG P51RR00166-30 0180
TSAI, CHE-CHUNG P51RR00166-30 9018
TSAI, CHE-CHUNG P51RR00166-30 0161
TSAI, CHE-CHUNG P51RR00166-30 0162
TSAI, CHE-CHUNG P51RR00166-30 0163
TSAI, CHE-CHUNG P51RR00166-30 0164
TSAI, CHE-CHUNG P51RR00166-30 0165
TSAI, CHE-CHUNG R01CA54757-01
TSAI, CHE'CHEUNG N01AI15120-00
TSAI, JIR M01RR00096-30A1 0260
TSAI, L Z01HL00206-32
TSAI, MING-DAW R01GM30327-10
TSAI, MING-DAW R01GM41788-03
TSAI, MING-JER R01HD17379-08
TSAI, PHILIP H S07RR05653-24 0805
TSAI, S-C Z01HL00627-13
TSAI, SHIEN N01CP73724-07
TSAI, WEI TEK P41RR01632-09 9024
TSAI, WEI-YANN R29AI29004-02
TSALIKIAN, EVA M01RR00059-30 0736
TSALIKIAN, EVA M01RR00059-30 0674
TSANG, K Y Z01CB09025-04
TSANG, PAMELA R29AG08589-02
TSANG, REGINALD C P01HD11725-13
TSANG, REGINALD C P50HD20748-06A1
TSANG, REGINALD C U10HD27853-01
TSANG, SO-FAI K11CA01524-02
TSAO, BETTY P60AR36834-05 0007
TSAO, BETTY S07RR05354-30 0401
TSAO, BETTY P P01AR40919-01 0001
TSAO, FRANCIS H R01HL38744-05
TSCHETTER, LOREN K U10CA35103-08
TSE-DINH, YUK-CHING R01GM42774-02
TSE, CHUNG MING R29DK43778-01
TSE, HARLEY Y R01NS26823-03
TSENG, BEN Y P01CA50528-03 0005
TSENG, LIANG-FU R01DA03811-07
TSENG, LINDA R01HD19247-05
TSENG, SCHEFFER C R01EY06819-06
TSEVAT, JOEL R03HS06673-01
TSIATIS, ANASTASIOS A R01AI31789-01
TSIATIS, ANASTASIOS A R01CA51962-02
TSICHLIS, PHILIP N R01CA38047-07
TSICHLIS, PHILIP N R01CA51893-01A1
TSICHLIS, PHILIP N R13CA54434-01
TSICHLIS, PHILIP N S07RR05895-09 0610
TSIEN, RICHARD W P01HL38156-05 0001
TSIEN, RICHARD W P50MH48108-01
TSIEN, RICHARD W P50MH48108-01 9002
TSIEN, RICHARD W P50MH48108-01 0002
TSIEN, RICHARD W P50MH48108-01 0005
TSIEN, RICHARD W R01NS24067-07
TSIEN, ROGER Y R01NS27177-04
TSILIBARY, EFFIE C R01DK43574-01
TSILIBARY, PHOTINI-EFFIE C R29DK39216-04
TSIN, ANDREW S06GM08194-12
TSIN, ANDREW T C S06GM08194-12 0031
TSIPOURAS, PETROS P01HD22610-04 0005
TSO, MARK O R01EY01903-16
TSO, MARK O R01EY06761-05
TSO, PATRICK P01DK43785-01 0001
TSO, PATRICK P R01DK32288-08
TSOKOS, G C Z01DK43200-12
TSOKOS, G C Z01DK43201-07
TSOKOS, G C Z01DK43202-08
TSOKOS, M Z01CB09187-02
TSOKOS, M Z01CB09354-01
TSOKOS, M Z01CB09355-01
TSONIS, PANAGIOTIS A R29HD27684-02
TSOU, KANG P01MH40899-07 9001
TSOUKAS, CONSTANTINE R01AI28364-03
TSOUKAS, CONSTANTINE S06GM45765-01 0008
TSOUKAS, CONSTANTINE S07RR07004-16 0055
TSUANG, MING T R01DA04604-02
TSUANG, MING T R37MH43518-04
TSUANG, MING T U01MH46318-03
TSUBOTA, H P51RR00168-30 0151
TSUBOTA, STUART S07RR07050-26 0130
TSUI, AMY O R01HD25957-03
TSUI, BENJAMIN M R01CA39463-05
TSUI, LAP-CHEE R01DK34944-07
TSUJIMOTO, Y R01CA50551-03
TSUJIMOTO, Y R01CA51864-02
TSUJIMOTO, YOSHIHIDE S07RR05540-29 0556
TSUKAMOTO, HIDEKAZU R01AA06603-09
TU, ALICE N01ES15325-00
TU, ANTHONY T R37GM15591-24
TU, CHEN-PEI D S07RR07082-26 0313
TU, SHIAO-CHUN R01GM25953-13
TU, SHIAO-CHUN S07RR07147-19 0654
TU, SHIAO-CHUN S15DK44680-01
TUAN, TAI-LAN R29AR40409-01A1
TUBBS, RAYMOND P01CA48919-01A2 9001
TUBERGEN, DAVID G U10CA28851-11
TUBLITZ, NATHAN J K04NS01258-04
TUBMAN, JONATHAN S07RR05938-07 0322
TUCK, MICHAEL L R01HL41295-02
TUCKER, DIANE C R29HL39048-05
TUCKER, DIANE C S07RR07178-14 0672
TUCKER, DON M R01MH42129-03
TUCKER, DON M R01MH42669-02
TUCKER, M A Z01CP04410-15
TUCKER, M BELINDA K01MH00681-05
TUCKER, PHILIP P01AI11851-18 0018
TUCKER, PHILIP W R01AI18016-12
TUCKER, PHILIP W R01CA31534-10
TUCKER, PHILIP W R01GM41497-03
TUCKER, PHILLIP W P01AI31229-01 0004
TUCKER, PHILLIP W P01GM31689-08 0002
TUCKER, RICHARD P S07RR05404-30 0863
TUCKER, ROBERT W P30CA06973-29 9010
TUCKER, ROBERT W R01CA34472-06
TUCKER, STANLEY D R43CA53040-01A1
TUCKER, SUSAN L R29CA48672-03
TUCKETT, ROBERT P R01NS26229-03
TUCKETT, ROBERT P R43EY09483-01
TUCKMAN, HOWARD P R01MH46889-02
TUHRIM, STANLEY R01NS29762-01
TUHRIM, STANLEY R29NS27924-01A2
TUKEY, ROBERT H R01CA37139-08
TUKEY, ROBERT H R01GM36590-06
TULENKO, THOMAS N R01HL30496-07
TULINSKY, ALEXANDER R01HL25942-09
TULINSKY, ALEXANDER R01HL43229-03
TULJAPURKAR, SHRIPAD D R01HD29003-01
TULJAPURKAR, SHRIPAD D R01HD16640-08
TULLER, BETTY H R29DC00411-04
TULLIUS, THOMAS D K04CA01208-05
TULLIUS, THOMAS D R01GM40894-07
TULLIUS, THOMAS D R01GM41930-03
TULLY, J G Z01AI00027-24
TULLY, TIM P01GM33205-08 0006
TULLY, TIM R29NS25621-05
TULMAN, LORRAINE R01NR02340-02
TULSIANI, DAULAT R R01HD25869-02
TUMA, DEAN J R01AA04961-11
TUNE, BRUCE M R01DK33814-06
TUNE, LARRY E K01MH00723-05
TUNE, LARRY E M01RR00035-31 0419
TUNE, LARRY E M01RR00035-31 0394
TUNE, LARRY E R01MH40362-05
TUNG, FRANK Y R01AI31918-01
TUNG, KENNETH U54HD29099-01 0004
TUNG, KENNETH S R01HD14504-11
TUNG, LESLIE R29HL40422-04
TUNG, LIM P30DK19525-15 0020
TUNG, LIM P30DK19525-15 9006
TUNG, MING S R01DE08916-03
TUNIN MACANESPIE, CAROL R29DA05856-03
TOOHY, VINCENT K R29NS29095-01
TUOMANEN, ELAINE I R01AI23459-05A1
TUOMANEN, ELAINE I R01AI27913-03
TUOMILEHTO, JAAKKO R01DK37957-04A1
TURANO, KATHLEEN A R29EY07839-03
TURBEK, JOHN P01HL36552-07 9002
TURCO, SALVATORE J R01AI20941-07
TURCOTTE, JOSEPH G S07RR07086-15 0327
TUREEN, JAY H R01NS27310-03
TUREK, FRED W P01HD21921-04 0003
TUREK, FRED W P30HD28048-01
TUREK, FRED W R01AG09297-01A1
TUREK, FRED W R01HD09885-16
TUREK, LUBOMIR P30DK25295-12S1 0013
TUREK, LUBOMIR P R01CA49912-03
TURGEON, JUDITH L R01HD12137-10
TURIEL, ELLIOT R01MH47250-02
TURINSKY, JIRI R01GM22825-12
TURITTO, VINCENT T R01HL38933-06
TURITTO, VINCENT T S15HL47735-01
TURK, JOHN W K04DK01553-05
TURK, JOHN W R01DK34388-07
TURK, STEVEN R R29DE09066-04
TURKA, LAURENCE A K08DK01899-04
TURKELTAUB, P C Z01BA01008-02
TURKELTAUB, P C Z01BA01009-02
TURKELTAUB, P C Z01BA01011-02
TURKELTAUB, P C Z01BA01012-02
TURKELTAUB, P C Z01BA01014-08
TURKELTAUB, P C Z01BA01016-02
TURKER, MITCHELL S R29AG08199-04
TURKKAN, JAYLAN S R01HL34034-05
TURKKAN, JAYLAN S R01HL40138-05
TURLEY, EVA ANN R01CA51540-01A1
TURNBOUGH, CHARLES L, JR R01GM29466-11
TURNBULL, BRUCE W R01GM28364-11
TURNER, BARBARA S07RR05959-06 0024
TURNER, BARBARA J R01HS06465-02
TURNER, BARBARA S R01NR01549-06
TURNER, BRUCE J S07RR07095-24 0372
TURNER, CHARLES HALL R29AR40688-02
TURNER, CHARLES W S07RR07092-26 0500
TURNER, CHRISTOPHER E R29GM47607-01
TURNER, CHRISTOPHER W R01DC00377-03
TURNER, DAVID C R01NS27409-03
TURNER, DENNIS A R01NS29482-01

TURNER, DOUGLAS H R01GM22939-16
TURNER, DOUGLAS H S10RR06731-01
TURNER, ERNEST A P60HL38737-04 9001
TURNER, ERNEST A P60HL38737-04
TURNER, ERNEST A S06GM08198-10 0015
TURNER, ERNEST A S15HL47717-01
TURNER, JAMES P41RR01219-10 9002
TURNER, JAMES P41RR01219-10 9003
TURNER, JAMES E R01EY04377-08S1
TURNER, JAMES E S07RR05404-30 0864
TURNER, JAMES N R55RR06904-01
TURNER, LISA A R15HD27043-01A1
TURNER, NANCY A R43CA54653-01
TURNER, R Z01HL04603-01
TURNER, R J Z01DE00415-05
TURNER, RALPH M P50DA07697-01 9001
TURNER, RALPH M P50DA07697-01 9002
TURNER, RAYMOND P41RR00592-22 0034
TURNER, ROBERT C R01DK33152-05
TURNER, ROBERT C U10EY07049-05
TURNER, RUSSELL T R01AR35651-05
TURNER, RUSSELL T R01AR41418-01
TURNER, SAMUEL M R01MH42884-02
TURNER, STEPHEN T R01HL30428-08
TURNER, TERENCE J S07RR07114-23 0449
TURNER, TERRY T R01HD09490-15
TURNER, TERRY T R01HD18252-08
TUROS, EDWARD S07RR07066-26 0259
TURRO, NICHOLAS J P41RR06892-01 0002
TURTELTAUB, KENNETH S07RR05917-08 0693
TURVEY, MICHAEL T P01HD01994-26A1 0013
TURVEY, MICHAEL T S07RR05596-27 0130
TUSA, RONALD J R55EY09289-01
TUSZYNSKI, GEORGE S07RR05418-30 0034
TUSZYNSKI, GEORGE P R01HL28149-09
TUSZYNSKI, MARK P01AG10435-01 0003
TUTTLE, JEREMY B R01DK44830-01
TUTTLE, KATHERINE M01RR01346-10 0146
TUTTLE, MARK N01LM03515-05
TWENTE, JOHN S07RR07053-26 0149
TWENTYMAN, CRAIG T K14HL02137-04
TWINING, SALLY S R01EY06663-06
TWINING, SALLY S R01EY08388-02
TWOMBLY, DENNIS A R29AA08172-02
TWYMAN, ROY E K08NS01266-04
TYACK, PETER L R29DC00429-05
TYBURSKI, ROBERT F R19DA06402-03
TYCHSEN, LAWRENCE S07RR05389-30 0650
TYCKO, BENJAMIN R29GM43572-02
TYCKO, BENJAMIN S07RR05950-07 0985
TYE-MURRAY, NANCY P50DC00242-07 0006
TYE-MURRAY, NANCY P50DC00242-07 0003
TYE, BIK-KWOON R01GM34190-12
TYINSKY, MICHAEL P01CA34936-08 0006
TYKOCINSKI, MARK L R29CA47566-04
TYLER, BRETT M R01GM42178-03
TYLER, CHRISTOPHER W R01EY07890-01A3
TYLER, CHRISTOPHER W R01MH49044-01
TYLER, CHRISTOPHER W S07RR05981-05 0808
TYLER, CHRISTOPHER W S15EY09454-01
TYLER, RICHARD S P50DC00242-07 0001
TYLER, WALTER S P01ES00628-19 9001
TYLKOWSKI, C S07RR05362-30 0803
TYLOR, JOHN WATSON R01DA04197-06
TYMOCZKO, JOHN L R15AR40894-01
TYNER, ANGELA R01HD25329-03
TYOR, MALCOLM P M01RR00030-30 0446
TYPRING, STEPHAN K S07RR07205-11 0643
TYRING, STEPHEN K M01RR00073-29 0326
TYRING, STEPHEN K M01RR00073-29 0327
TYRING, STEPHEN K M01RR00073-29 0296
TYRING, STEPHEN K M01RR00073-29 0301
TYRING, STEPHEN K R01AI26896-03
TYROLER, HERMAN A S07RR05450-30 0339
TYRRELL, KIM SUTTON R29HL39871-04
TYSON, CHARLES N01CN95168-04
TYSON, CHARLES A N01ES55109-07
TYSON, GEORGE S07RR05736-19 0166
TYSON, JON E M01RR00633-19 0363
TYSON, JON E R01HD22380-04A1
TYSON, JON E U10HD21373-06
TYTELL, MICHAEL R01EY07616-04
TZAGOLOFF, ALEXANDER A R37HL22174-14
TZAGOURNIS, MANUEL M01RR00034-31
TZIPORI, SAUL S07RR05852-11 0261
U S SMALL BUSINESS ADMIN N01SP01003-00
U S SMALL BUSINESS ADMIN N01SP02004-00
UAUY, RICARDO M01RR00633-19 0342
UAUY, RICARDO M01RR00633-19 0349
UAUY, RICARDO M01RR00633-19 0365
UBELS, JOHN L R01EY05640-07
UCHIDA, K Z01HL00276-01
UCKRUN, FATIH P01CA21737-14 0002
UCKUN, FATIH M R01CA42633-06
UCKUN, FATIH M R01CA51425-02
UDEN, PETER S07RR07048-26 0658
UDEY, M Z01CB03669-02
UDIN, SUSAN B R01EY03470-12
UDRY, J R M01RR00046-31 0312
UDRY, J RICHARD P30HD05798-17
UDRY, J RICHARD R01HD23454-03
UDRY, J RICHARD R37HD12806-10
UDRY, RICHARD J S07RR07072-26 0274
UDUPA, JAYARAM K R01CA50851-03
UEDA, ISSAKU R01GM25716-10
UEDA, TETSUFUMI P01MH42652-05 0004
UEDA, TETSUFUMI R01NS26884-03
UEDA, TETSUFUMI R01NS29278-01
UEHLING, DAVID T R01DK30808-09A1
UEMURA, ETSURO R01NS28416-01A1
UFFEN, ROBERT L S07RR07049-26 0434
UGURBIL, KAMIL P01HL32427-06 0001
UGURBIL, KAMIL R01HL33600-07
UHAL, BRUCE D R29HL45136-02
UHDE, T W Z01MH02515-02
UHDE, T W Z01MH02516-02
UHDE, T W Z01MH02517-02
UHDE, T W Z01MH02518-02
UHDE, T W Z01MH02519-02
UHDE, T W Z01MH02520-02
UHDE, T W Z01MH02521-02
UHDE, T W Z01MH02522-02
UHDE, T W Z01MH02540-01
UHING, RONALD J P01CA29589-10 9003
UHL, G Z01DA09601-03
UHL, G R Z01DA00032-02
UHL, G R Z01DA00114-02
UHL, G R Z01DA00115-03
UHL, G R Z01DA00116-03
UHL, G R Z01DA00117-02
UHL, G R Z01DA00314-01
UHLENBECK, OLKE C R01AI30242-02
UHLENBECK, OLKE C R01GM37552-07
UHLENBECK, OLKE C R37GM36944-06
UHLENHUTH, EBERHARD H M01RR00997-16 0382
UHLENHUTH, EBERHARD H M01RR00997-16 0368
UHLER, MICHAEL D R29GM38788-06
UHLMANN, RICHARD F R01HS06343-03
UHLRICH, DANIEL JAMES R01EY06610-06
UHR, JONATHAN W P01AI11851-18 0010
UHR, JONATHAN W P01AI11851-18
UHR, JONATHAN W P01AI11851-18 0006
UHR, JONATHAN W P01AI11851-18 9001
UHR, JONATHAN W P01AI11851-18 0013
UHR, JONATHAN W P01AI11851-18 0014
UHR, JONATHAN W P01AI11851-18 0015
UHR, JONATHAN W P01CA41081-06A1
UITTO, JOUNI P01AR39740-03 9001
UITTO, JOUNI J P01AR38923-05
UITTO, JOUNI J R01AR28450-09
UITTO, JOUNI J R01AR41439-13
UITTO, JOUNI J R13AR40984-01
ULATMANN, MICHELLE C M01RR00084-29 0215
ULEMAN, JAMES S R01MH43959-04
ULEVITCH, RICHARD J P01GM37696-05
ULEVITCH, RICHARD J P01GM37696-05 0001
ULEVITCH, RICHARD J P01GM37696-05 9001
ULEVITCH, RICHARD J R01AI15136-13
ULEVITCH, RICHARD J R37GM28485-11
ULICK, STANLEY P50HL18323-17 0038
ULINSKI, PHILIP S R01EY08352-02
ULLMAN, BUDDY R01AI23682-07
ULLMAN, DANIEL P30DK40566-02 0003
ULLO, CHARLES A S07RR05778-16 0409
ULLRICH, ROBERT L R01CA43322-07
ULLRICH, S Z01CB05599-01
ULLRICH, STEPHAN S07RR05511-29 0494
ULLRICH, STEPHEN E R01AR40824-01
ULLU, ELISABETTA P01AI28778-02 0001
ULLU, ELISABETTA R01AI28798-02
ULTMAN, JAMES S S07RR07082-26 0314
ULTMANN, JOHN E. P30CA14599-18 9009
ULUG, E T S07RR07036-26 0106
UMBARGER, H EDWIN R01GM12522-27
UMBERSON, DEBRA R29AG08554-02
UMBREIT, J N R29CA44507-05
UMBRICHT, CHRISTOPHER B K11CA01469-03
UMEDA, PATRICK K P50HL17667-17 0069
UMEDA, PATRICK K R01HL44094-02
UMETSU, DALE T K07AI01026-01
UMETSU, DALE T R01AI26322-03
UNADKAT, J D N01AI15118-00
UNADKAT, JASHVANT P50DK41978-03 0003
UNADKAT, JASHVANT D R01HD27110-02
UNADKAT, JASHVANT D R01HD27438-01
UNADKAT, JASHVANT D. P51RR00166-30 0122
UNADKAT, JASHVANT D. P51RR00166-30 0123
UNAKAR, NALIN J R01EY01680-16
UNANUE, EMIL R P01AI24854-05 9001
UNANUE, EMIL R P01AI24854-05
UNANUE, EMIL R P01AI24854-05 0001
UNANUE, EMIL R P01AI31238-01
UNANUE, EMIL R P01AI31238-01 0001
UNANUE, EMIL R P50AI15322-14
UNANUE, EMIL R P50AI15322-14 0012
UNANUE, EMIL R R01AI22033-07
UNANUE, EMIL R R37AI24742-05
UNDEM, BRADLEY J R29HL38095-04
UNDERHILL, CHARLES B R01HD26758-01A1
UNDERHILL, CHARLES B R01HL41565-03
UNDERSOOW, LOUIS E N01ES05294-02
UNDERWOOD, HERBERT A, JR R01NS20961-05
UNDERWOOD, JEFFREY T N01CO15703-00
UNDERWOOD, LOUIS M01RR00046-31 0492
UNDERWOOD, LOUIS M01RR00046-31 0515
UNDERWOOD, LOUIS E R01HD26871-01A1
UNDERWOOD, LOUIS E. M01RR00046-31 0313
UNDERWOOD, LOUISE E M01RR00046-31 0339
UNGER, E Z01HL04852-02
UNGER, E Z01HL04853-02
UNGER, ELIZABETH S07RR05364-30 0545
UNGER, EVAN C R01CA49879-03
UNGER, ROGER P01DK42582-02 0001
UNGER, ROGER H P01DK42582-02
UNGER, ROGER H P01DK42582-02 9002
UNGER, ROGER H R37DK02700-32
UNGERLEIDER, L G Z01MH02035-01
UNGERSTEDT, URBAN P50MH44211-03 0003
UNITED INFORMATION SYS, INC N01TI10013-00
UNITED INFORMATION SYS, INC N01TI10005-00
UNIV ARIZONA N01MH80010-00
UNIV CALIF, SAN FRANCISCO N01DA08402-00
UNIV KENTUCKY RES FDN N01DA19200-00
UNIV OF CALIFORNIA N01DA07307-00
UNIV OF MINNESOTA N01DA98155-00
UNIV OF NEW MEXICO N01AA10006-00
UNIV SOUTHERN CALIF N01MH00013-00
UNK S07RR05717-21 0129
UNK S07RR05717-21 0130
UNK S07RR05718-16 0133
UNK S07RR05908-08 0928
UNKEFER, CLIFFORD J R01GM45262-01
UNKELESS, JAY C P01AI24671-04 0002
UNKELESS, JAY C R01AI24322-06
UNKNOWN S07RR05301-21 0732
UNKNOWN S07RR05862-10 0563
UNKNOWN S07RR07167-14 0603
UNKNOWN S07RR07229-06 0723
UNNASCH, THOMAS P01AI28780-01A1 0002
UNNASCH, THOMAS R R29AI29693-03
UNNERSTALL, JAMES R P50AG08012-04 9003
UNNERSTALL, JAMES R R01AG09587-01A1
UNO, HIDEO P51RR00167-31 0039
UNO, HIDEO P51RR00167-31 9008
UNSER, M Z01RR10225-07
UNSER, M Z01RR10270-05
UNSER, M Z01RR10317-03
UNSER, M Z01RR10318-03
UNSER, M Z01RR10343-02
UNSER, M Z01RR10344-02
UNTERMAN, TERRY G R29DK41430-02
UNTHANK, JOSEPH L R29HL42898-01A2
UNWIN, PETER N R01GM41449-03
UPCHURCH, BENNIE R S07RR05372-30 0697
UPCHURCH, DAWN S07RR05445-30 0878
UPDIKE, STUART J M01RR03186-06 0072
UPDIKE, WANDA S K08AI01028-01
UPDYKE, BRUCE V R01EY05724-06
UPHOUSE, LYNDA S06GM08256-03 0007
UPHOUSE, LYNDA L G20RR06921-01
UPHOUSE, LYNDA L R01HD28419-01
UPHOUSE, LYNDA L S07RR07218-05 0457
UPHOUSE, LYNDA L S07RR07218-05
UPTON, ARTHUR C P30CA13343-18 9007
UPTON, ARTHUR C P30CA13343-18 9008
UPTON, ARTHUR C P30CA13343-18 9010
UPTON, ARTHUR C P30CA13343-18 9011
UPTON, ARTHUR C P30CA13343-18 9012
UPTON, ARTHUR C P30CA13343-18 9013
UPTON, ARTHUR C P30CA13343-18
UPTON, ARTHUR C P30CA13343-18 9001
UPTON, ARTHUR C P30CA13343-18 9002
UPTON, ARTHUR C P30CA13343-18 9003
UPTON, ARTHUR C P30ES00260-29 9011
UPTON, ARTHUR C P30ES00260-29
UPTON, STEVE J R01AI31774-01
URANO, MUNEYASU R01CA26350-12
URAY, NANDOR J R01AA07537-04
URBAN, NICOLE P01CA34847-09 9006
URBAN, NICOLE P01CA34847-09 0016
URBAN, RANDALL J M01RR00073-29 0321
URBANIAK, JAMES R R01HL36046-04
URBANSKI, HENRYK P51RR00163-32 0031
URBANSKI, HENRYK F R29HD24312-03
URBANSKI, HERYK S07RR05694-22 0859
URBERG, KATHRYN A R01DA06213-02
URDANETA, MARIA-LUIS S07RR07217-08 0168
URETSKY, BARRY M01RR00056-30 0360
URQUIZA, ANTHONY J R01MH48251-02
URRY, DAN W R01HL29578-10
URSO, PAUL S06GM08248-05 0012
URTHALER, FERDINAND P50HL17667-17 0071
URTHALER, FERDINAND R01HL31536-08
US SMALL BUSINESS ADMIN N01SP12002-00
US SMALL BUSINESS ADMIN N01SP11002-00
USALA, STEPHEN J R29DK42807-02
USAMI, SHUNICHI P60HL28381-09 0006
USAMI, SUNICHI P01HL43026-02 9003
USINGER, WILLIAM R R43AI29772-01A1
UTELL, MARK J K07ES00220-01
UTELL, MARK J M01RR00044-31 0248
UTELL, MARK J M01RR00044-31 0360
UTELL, MARK J M01RR00044-31 0376
UTELL, MARK J P30ES01247-17 0064
UTELL, MARK J R01ES02679-11
UYEDA, KOSAKU R01DK16194-20

UYENOYAMA, MARCY K R01GM37841-09
UZODINMA, JOHN S06GM08047-20S1 0034
UZZELL, THOMAS S07RR07030-26 0415
VA COMMONWEALTH UNIV N01DA98156-00
VAAGE, JAN R01CA29660-10
VACCARO, CHARLES A. P01HL19717-15 9001
VACQUIER, VICTOR D R01HD12986-14
VADAS, MATHEW A R01CA45822-05
VAFGI, ABBAS P01AG07347-04 0002
VAGHY, PAL L R01HL41088-04
VAGNUCCI, ANTHONY M01RR00056-30 0375
VAGNUCCI, ANTHONY H M01RR00056-30 0216
VAIDYA, AKHIL B R22AI28398-03
VAIDYANATHAN, T K S15DE10074-01
VAIDYANATHAN, TRITALA K R01DE08024-06
VAILLANT, GEORGE E K05MH00364-09
VAILLANT, GEORGE E R37MH42248-05
VAINA, LUCIA R01EY07861-03
VAINIO, HARRI U01CA33193-10
VAKIL, MEENAL P50AI23694-06 0012
VALANIS, BARBARA G R01CA48203-04
VALANIS, BARBARA G S07RR05521-29 0064
VALANTINE, HANNAH S07RR05353-30 0373
VALANTINE, HANNAH A K08HL02447-01A1
VALCIUKAS, JOSE P30ES00928-18 9005
VALDIEVIESE, MANUEL P30CA22453-14 9011
VALDIVIESO, MANUEL P01CA46560-03 0004
VALDMANIS, VIVIAN S07RR05444-30 0262
VALE, RONALD D R01GM38499-04
VALE, WYLIE W P01CA54418-01 9003
VALE, WYLIE W P01DK26741-12
VALE, WYLIE W P01DK26741-12 0001
VALE, WYLIE W P01HD13527-12
VALE, WYLIE W P01HD13527-12 0001
VALE, WYLIE W P50AA06420-08 0006
VALENCIA, ELIECER S R18MH48041-03
VALENTE, ANTHONY J P01HL26890-09 0004
VALENTE, ANTHONY J S07RR07187-13 0706
VALENTINE, FRED M01RR00096-30A1 0275
VALENTINE, FRED M01RR00096-30A1 0309
VALENTINE, FRED M01RR00096-30A1 0310
VALENTINE, FRED M01RR00096-30A1 0264
VALENTINE, FRED M01RR00096-30A1 0302
VALENTINE, FRED M01RR00096-30A1 0303
VALENTINE, FRED M01RR00096-30A1 0304
VALENTINE, FRED M01RR00096-30A1 0305
VALENTINE, FRED M01RR00096-30A1 0298
VALENTINE, FRED T M01RR00096-30A1 0297
VALENTINE, FRED T M01RR00096-30A1 0280
VALENTINE, FRED T M01RR00096-30A1 0241
VALENTINE, FRED T M01RR00096-30A1 0231
VALENTINE, FRED T M01RR00096-30A1 0232
VALENTINE, FRED T M01RR00096-30A1 0222
VALENTINE, FRED T M01RR00096-30A1 0242
VALENTINE, FRED T N01AI72659-08
VALENTINE, FRED T R01AI32429-01
VALENTINE, FRED T U01AI27665-05S2
VALENTINE, FRED T. P30AI27742-03 9007
VALENTINE, FREDERICK T M01RR00096-30A1 012
VALENTINE, JOAN S R01GM28222-12
VALENTINE, NANCY S07RR05484-29 0033
VALENTINO, RITA J K02MH00840-02
VALENTOVIC, MONICA A S07RR05870-10 0997
VALENZUELA, JORGE E. M01RR00043-31 0397
VALENZUELA, GUILLERM S07RR05352-30 0754
VALENZUELA, JORGE E M01RR00043-31 0467
VALERIE, KRISTOFFER C R29CA53199-01A1
VALERIOTE, FRED P30CA22453-14 0004
VALERIOTE, FREDERICK P01CA46560-03 0003
VALERIOTE, FREDERICK A U01CA53001-02 0004
VALERIOTE, FREDERICK A U01CA53001-02
VALES, LYNNE S07RR05576-27 0593
VALLANO, MARY L R01NS27603-02
VALLANO, MARY L R29NS24705-04
VALLANO, MARY LOU P01HL39707-02 0005
VALLE, DAVID L M01RR00052-30 0099
VALLE, DAVID L P01HD10981-14 9001
VALLE, DAVID L R01EY02948-13
VALLE, J R R01MH43390-02S1
VALLE, RAMON S07RR07004-16 0056
VALLEE, RICHARD B R01GM26701-13
VALLEE, RICHARD B R01GM32977-08
VALLERA, DANIEL A R01CA31618-10
VALLERA, DANIEL A R01CA36725-08
VAN ADELSBERG, JANET S K08DK01869-03
VAN BELLE, GERALD U01AG06790-06 0005
VAN BREEMEN, CORNELIUS R01HL40184-05
VAN BREEMEN, CORNELIUS R01HL39831-04
VAN BUSKIRK, E MICHAEL R01EY05231-05
VAN BUSKIRK, E MICHAEL R01EY08247-03
VAN CAMPEN, HANA S07RR07082-26 0315
VAN CAUTER, EVE M01RR00055-30 0536
VAN CAUTER, EVE M01RR00055-30 0572
VAN CITTERS, ROBERT L U76PE00212-07
VAN DE GEIGN, J Z01CM06378-06
VAN DE GEIJN, J Z01CM06329-11
VAN DE GEIJN, J Z01CM06330-11
VAN DE GEIJN, J Z01CM06381-05
VAN DE GEIJN, J Z01CM06394-02
VAN DE KAR, LOUIS D R01DA04865-03
VAN DE KAR, LOUIS D R01MH45812-02
VAN DE WATER, THOMAS R R01DC00088-22

VAN DEMARK, D R P01DE05837-10 0001
VAN DEN BERG, BARBARA J N01HD13134-00
VAN DEN POL, ANTHONY P50NS10174-20 0018
VAN DEN TOP, JERALDINE J G08LM05246-01
VAN DER HELM, DICK R01CA17562-16
VAN DER HELM, DICK R01GM21822-17
VAN DER HORST, CHARLES M01RR00046-31 0397
VAN DER HORST, CHARLES M01RR00046-31 0442
VAN DER HORST, CHARLES M01RR00046-31 0477
VAN DER HORST, CHARLES M01RR00046-31 0467
VAN DER HORST, CHARLES M01RR00046-31 0444
VAN DER HORST, CHARLES M01RR00046-31 0471
VAN DER HORST, CHARLES M01RR00046-31 0461
VAN DER HORST, CHARLES M01RR00046-31 0462
VAN DER HORST, CHARLES M01RR00046-31 0458
VAN DER HORST, CHARLES M01RR00046-31 0438
VAN DER HORST, CHARLES M01RR00046-31 0482
VAN DER HORST, CHARLES M01RR00046-31 0494
VAN DER HORST, CHARLES M01RR00046-31 0495
VAN DER HORST, CHARLES M01RR00046-31 0496
VAN DER HORST, CHARLES M M01RR00046-31 041
VAN DER HORST, CHARLES M U01AI25868-05
VAN DER HOST, CHARLES M01RR00046-31 0527
VAN DER KLOOT, WILLIAM G R01NS10320-19
VAN DER PLOEG, L H R01AI21784-07
VAN DER PLOEG, LEX P01AI26497-03 0004
VAN DER PLOEG, LEX P30CA13696-19 9016
VAN DOP, CORNELIUS S07RR05354-30 0378
VAN DOREN, CLAYTON L R29NS27958-02
VAN DOREN, KEVIN S07RR07068-26 0236
VAN DYCK, CHRISTOPHER H R03MH47459-01A1
VAN DYKE, REBECCA W R01DK38333-04
VAN DYKE, TERRY S07RR07084-26 0328
VAN DYKE, TERRY A R01CA46283-04
VAN DYKE, TERRY A R01DK42910-01A1
VAN ECHO, DAVID A N01CM07303-02
VAN ELDIK, LINDA J R55NS29215-01A1
VAN ELDIK, LINDA J S07RR05424-30 0122
VAN EPPS, DENNIS E P41RR01315-10 0048
VAN ESSEN, DAVID C R01EY02091-15
VAN ESSEN, DAVID C S10RR06509-01
VAN ETTEN, JAMES L R01GM32441-09
VAN ETTEN, ROBERT L R01GM27003-22
VAN GERVEN, DENNIS S07RR07013-26 0958
VAN HAAREN, FRANS R01DA06463-02
VAN HALBEEK, HERMAN R01AI29751-01A1
VAN HERLE, ANDRE S07RR05354-30 0403
VAN HEUSDEN, MIRANDA C R29GM44876-01A1
VAN HEUVEN, WICHARD A U10EY06264-07
VAN HLBEEK, HERMAN P01AI27135-04 0004
VAN HOESEN, GARY W P01NS19632-09 0009
VAN HOESEN, GARY W R01NS14944-12
VAN HOFF, JACK M01RR06022-02 0665
VAN HOFF, JACK M01RR06022-02 0602
VAN HOFF, JACK M01RR06022-02 0702
VAN HOFF, JACK M01RR06022-02 0777
VAN HOFF, JACK M01RR06022-02 0752
VAN HOFF, JACK M01RR06022-02 0775
VAN HOFF, JACK M01RR06022-02 0776
VAN HOFF, JACK M01RR06022-02 0778
VAN HOLDE, KENSAL E. P01ES04766-04 0006
VAN HOLDE, KENSAL E R01GM22916-16
VAN HOOSIER, GERALD S07RR05432-30 0232
VAN HOOSIER, GERALD L, JR P40RR01203-13
VAN HORN, LINDA V U01HL37947-05
VAN HOUTE, J P50DE07009-08 0009
VAN HOUTEN, BENNETT R29CA50681-03
VAN HOUTEN, JUDITH L R01DC00721-02
VAN ITALLIE, CHRISTINA M R01DK41720-03
VAN ITALLIE, THEODORE B P30DK26687-11 9007
VAN KAMMEN, DANIEL P R01MH44841-02
VAN LUNTEREN, ERIC P50HL42215-04 0003
VAN LUNTEREN, ERIK R01HL38701-05
VAN LYSEL, MICHAEL S R01HL38409-05
VAN MEURS, KRISA M01RR00081-29 0144
VAN ORDEN, GUY C R29NS26247-02
VAN ORT, SUZANNE R R01NR03034-01
VAN ORT, SUZANNE R S03RR03513-03
VAN ROEY, PATRICK S07RR05716-20 0143
VAN SCOTT, MICHAEL R P01HL34322-06 0008
VAN SCOTT, MICHAEL R R01HL40367-04
VAN SLUYTERS, RICHAR S07RR05832-12 0201
VAN SLUYTERS, RICHARD C R01EY02193-14
VAN TASELL, DIANNE J P50DC00110-17 0022
VAN THIEL, DAVID P50AA08746-02 0004
VAN THIEL, DAVID H P41RR03631-04 0002
VAN THIEL, DAVID H P50AA08746-02 9001
VAN THIEL, DAVID H R01AA04425-11
VAN THIEL, DAVID H R01AA06601-06
VAN THIEL, DAVID H R01DK39789-03
VAN VOOHRIS, BRADLEY S07RR05372-30 0659
VAN VOORHIS, WESLEY C K04AI01023-01
VAN VOORHIS, WESLEY C R01AI31414-01
VAN VUNAKIS, HELEN K06AI02372-29
VAN VUNAKIS, HELEN R01DA06047-02
VAN WART, HAROLD E R01DE09122-03
VAN WART, HAROLD E R01GM27276-10A2
VAN WART, HAROLD E R01GM27939-11
VAN WART, HAROLD E R01GM46051-01
VAN WINKLE, LON J R01HD21801-06
VAN WYK, JUDSON J M01RR00046-31 0456
VAN WYK, JUDSON J M01RR00046-31 0317

VAN WYLEN, DAVID G R01HL46027-01
VAN WYLEN, DAVID G R29HL40878-04
VAN ZANT, GARY E R01CA40575-07
VANAMAN, THOMAS C R01HL27368-11
VANAMAN, THOMAS C R01NS21868-06
VANBIERVLIET, ALAN R43HD27764-01A1
VANCE, JEFFERY M R01NS29416-01
VANCE, JEFFREY M K08NS01289-04
VANCE, MARY L M01RR00847-18 0522
VANCE, MARY L M01RR00847-18 0524
VANCE, MARY L M01RR00847-18 0525
VANCE, MARY L M01RR00847-18 0526
VANCE, MARY L M01RR00847-18 0574
VANCE, MARY L M01RR00847-18 0575
VANCE, MARY LEE M01RR00847-18 0453
VANDE WOUDE, GEORGE N01CO74101-20
VANDEBERG, JOHN L P01HL28972-10 0003
VANDEBERG, JOHN L P01HL45522-01A1 0004
VANDEBERG, JOHN L R01HL39890-04
VANDELL, DEBORAH L U10HD27040-03
VANDENBARK, ARTHUR A R01NS23221-05
VANDENBERG, CAROL R29HL41656-04
VANDENBERG, HERMAN H S07RR05818-12 0159
VANDENBERGH, JOHN G R01MH45401-03
VANDENBERGH, JOHN G R03DA06689-01A1
VANDENBOSCH, JAMES L R15AI29627-01A1
VANDENBURGH, HERMAN H R01AR39998-03
VANDER JAGT, DAVID S07RR05583-27 0643
VANDER JAGT, DAVID L R22AI21214-08
VANDER JAGT, DAVID L S06GM08139-17 0067
VANDERBERG, JEROME P R22AI24528-03
VANDERKOOI, JANE M P41RR01348-10 0008
VANDERKOOI, JANE M R01GM36393-05
VANDERKOOI, JANE N S07RR07083-26 0485
VANDERLAAN, WILLARD P S07RR05876-09
VANDEVANTER, DONALD R R29CA54998-01
VANDEWATER, LIVINGSTON R01GM36812-05
VANDORSTEN, J PETER U10HD27883-01
VANDYKE, MICHAEL W S07RR05511-29 0498
VANDYKE, T T S07RR05308-30 0241
VANDYKE, TERRY S07RR07084-26 0327
VANETTEN, HANS D S07RR07002-26 0877
VANHOUTTE, PAUL M R01HL31183-08
VANHOUTTE, PAUL M R01HL39423-05
VANHOUTTE, PAUL M R13HL47058-01
VANKAN, PETER S07RR05872-08 0985
VANMETRE, THOMAS E M01RR00722-19 0104
VANN, W F Z01BA02007-09
VANN, W F Z01BA02025-01
VANNIER, MICHAEL W R01DE08909-03
VANNUCCI, ROBERT C R01HD19913-05A1
VANNUCCI, ROBERT C R01HD26144-02
VANSELOW, NEAL A P51RR00164-30
VANVALKENBURGH, BLAI S07RR07009-26 0927
VARDENY, ZEEV V S07RR07092-26 0522
VARDIMON, A D S07RR05689-23 0852
VARELA, BENIGNO L R29DA05510-04
VARESIO, L Z01CM09216-11
VARGA, JOHN K08AR01817-03
VARGAS, FERNANDO F S06GM08224-07 0022
VARGHESE, P J P01HL38079-05 0003
VARKI, AJIT P01AI23287-06 0007
VARKI, AJIT R01GM32373-09
VARKI, AJIT P P30CA23100-11 9005
VARKI, AJIT P R01CA38701-06
VARMA, MADHU R43HD27367-01A1
VARMA, SHAMBHU D R01EY01292-15
VARMUS, HAROLD E R35CA39832-07
VARMUS, HAROLD E U01AI27205-04
VARMUS, HAROLD E U01AI27205-04 0001
VARNER, HUGH H R43CA54036-01
VARNES, JILL W U01CA51687-03
VARNES, MARIE E P01CA51183-01A1 0002
VARNES, MARIE E R01CA40516-07
VARON, SILVIO S R01NS16349-12
VARON, SILVIO S R01NS27047-01A2
VARSHAVSKY, ALEXANDER J R01AG08991-02
VARSHAVSKY, ALEXANDER J R01DK39520-04
VARSHAVSKY, ALEXANDER J R01GM31530-09
VARTICOVSKI, LYUBA R29CA53094-02
VARY, THOMAS C K04GM00570-02
VARY, THOMAS C R01GM39277-03
VASAN, NAGASWAMISRI S07RR05393-30 0907
VASANTHAKUMAR, GEETH S07RR05676-15 0959
VASANTHAKUMAR, GEETH S07RR05676-15 0960
VASANTHAKUMAR, GEETH S07RR05676-15 0963
VASANTHAKUMAR, GEETHA U01AI30279-02 0002
VASCONEZ, HENRY S07RR05374-30 0735
VASIL, MICHAEL L R01AI15940-12
VASILATOS-YOUNKEN, R S07RR07082-26 0316
VASKO, MICHAEL R R01DA07176-01
VASSALLE, MARIO R01HL27038-10
VASSALLO, M M01RR00585-20 0460
VASSEUR, P B S07RR05457-29 0010
VASSILEV S07RR05950-07 0010
VASSILEV, PETER M R01HL47079-01
VATHY, ILONA U R29DA05833-02
VATNER, DOROTHY E K04HL01909-05
VATNER, DOROTHY E P01HL38070-05 9003
VATNER, DOROTHY E R01HL37404-05
VATNER, DOROTHY E R01HL45332-02
VATNER, S F P51RR00168-30 0139

VATNER, STEPHEN F P01HL38070-05 9002
VATNER, STEPHEN F P01HL38070-05 0001
VATNER, STEPHEN F P01HL38070-05
VATNER, STEPHEN F P51RR00168-30 0091
VATNER, STEPHEN F R01HL33107-08
VATS, TRIBHAWAN S U10CA28841-11 0044
VATS, TRIBHAWAN S U10CA28841-11 0024
VATS, TRIBHAWAN S U10CA28841-11 0025
VATS, TRIBHAWAN S U10CA28841-11 0026
VATS, TRIBHAWAN S U10CA28841-11 0027
VATS, TRIBHAWAN S U10CA28841-11 0028
VATS, TRIBHAWAN S U10CA28841-11 0045
VATS, TRIBHAWAN S U10CA28841-11 0046
VATS, TRIBHAWAN S U10CA28841-11 0047
VATS, TRIBHAWAN S U10CA28841-11 0048
VATS, TRIBHAWAN S U10CA28841-11 0049
VATS, TRIBHAWAN S U10CA28841-11 0050
VATS, TRIBHAWAN S U10CA28841-11 0051
VATS, TRIBHAWAN S U10CA28841-11 0052
VATS, TRIBHAWAN S U10CA28841-11 0053
VATS, TRIBHAWAN S U10CA28841-11 0054
VATS, TRIBHAWAN S U10CA28841-11 0055
VATS, TRIBHAWAN S U10CA28841-11 0056
VATS, TRIBHAWAN S U10CA28841-11 0057
VATS, TRIBHAWAN S U10CA28841-11 0058
VATS, TRIBHAWAN S U10CA28841-11 0059
VATS, TRIBHAWAN S U10CA28841-11 0060
VATS, TRIBHAWAN S U10CA28841-11 0029
VATS, TRIBHAWAN S U10CA28841-11 0004
VATS, TRIBHAWAN S U10CA28841-11 0005
VATS, TRIBHAWAN S U10CA28841-11 0006
VATS, TRIBHAWAN S U10CA28841-11 0007
VATS, TRIBHAWAN S U10CA28841-11 0008
VATS, TRIBHAWAN S U10CA28841-11 0009
VATS, TRIBHAWAN S U10CA28841-11 0010
VATS, TRIBHAWAN S U10CA28841-11 0011
VATS, TRIBHAWAN S U10CA28841-11 0012
VATS, TRIBHAWAN S U10CA28841-11 0013
VATS, TRIBHAWAN S U10CA28841-11 0014
VATS, TRIBHAWAN S U10CA28841-11 0015
VATS, TRIBHAWAN S U10CA28841-11 0016
VATS, TRIBHAWAN S U10CA28841-11 0017
VATS, TRIBHAWAN S U10CA28841-11 0018
VATS, TRIBHAWAN S U10CA28841-11 0019
VATS, TRIBHAWAN S U10CA28841-11 0020
VATS, TRIBHAWAN S U10CA28841-11 0021
VATS, TRIBHAWAN S U10CA28841-11 0022
VATS, TRIBHAWAN S U10CA28841-11 0023
VATS, TRIBHAWAN S U10CA28841-11 0030
VATS, TRIBHAWAN S U10CA28841-11
VATS, TRIBHAWAN S U10CA28841-11 0001
VATS, TRIBHAWAN S U10CA28841-11 0002
VATS, TRIBHAWAN S U10CA28841-11 0003
VATS, TRIBHAWAN S U10CA28841-11 0031
VATS, TRIBHAWAN S U10CA28841-11 0032
VATS, TRIBHAWAN S U10CA28841-11 0033
VATS, TRIBHAWAN S U10CA28841-11 0034
VATS, TRIBHAWAN S U10CA28841-11 0035
VATS, TRIBHAWAN S U10CA28841-11 0036
VATS, TRIBHAWAN S U10CA28841-11 0037
VATS, TRIBHAWAN S U10CA28841-11 0038
VATS, TRIBHAWAN S U10CA28841-11 0039
VATS, TRIBHAWAN S U10CA28841-11 0040
VATS, TRIBHAWAN S U10CA28841-11 0041
VATS, TRIBHAWAN S U10CA28841-11 0042
VATS, TRIBHAWAN S U10CA28841-11 0043
VAUCLAIR, J P51RR00165-31 0171
VAUGHAN S07RR05380-30 0893
VAUGHAN, CHRISTOPHER S07RR05431-30 0859
VAUGHAN, DANA K R29EY09038-01
VAUGHAN, DEBORAH W R01AG09869-01
VAUGHAN, HERBERT G P30HD01799-27 9013
VAUGHAN, HERBERT G, JR P30HD01799-27
VAUGHAN, JOHN H M01RR00833-17 0103
VAUGHAN, JOHN H R01AR21175-15
VAUGHAN, THOMAS L R29CA46552-04
VAUGHN-COOKE, ANNA F S06GM08005-20 0008
VAUGHN, BRIAN E S07RR07255-02 0502
VAUGHN, CLARENCE B U10CA52650-02
VAUGHN, E DARRACOTT P50HL18323-17 9003
VAUGHN, HERBERT G P01DC00223-08 0007
VAUGHN, JAMES E P01NS18858-09A2 0016
VAUGHN, JAMES E P01NS18858-09A2
VAUGHN, JAMES E R01NS25784-04
VAUGHN, JAMES E S03RR03430-06
VAUGHN, JAMES E. P01NS18858-09A2 9001
VAUGHN, LINDA K R03DE09998-01
VAUPEL, JAMES W P01AG08761-02
VAUPEL, JAMES W P01AG08761-02 0001
VAUPEL, JAMES W P01AG08761-02 0002
VAZQUEZ, GUILLERMO J U01AI31122-02
VAZQUEZ, JORGE M01RR00056-30 0330
VAZQUEZ, JORGE M01RR00056-30 0374
VAZQUEZ, JORGE A R29DK39157-03
VEBER, M P01CA29502-11A1 0049
VEDAL, SVERRE R01ES04757-03
VEDEJS, EDWIN R01CA17918-17
VEDEJS, EDWIN R01GM44724-01A1
VEECH, R L Z01AA00024-13
VEECH, R L Z01AA00049-02
VEECH, R L Z01AA00050-02
VEECH, R L Z01AA00057-01

VEENSTRA, RICHARD D P01HL39707-02 0004
VEENSTRA, RICHARD D R01HL42220-04
VEGA, GLORIA P50GM21681-27 0005
VEGA, WILLIAM A R01DA05912-03
VEHASKARI, V MATTI R29DK39101-04
VEHASKARI, VESA MATTI M01RR06021-02 1013
VEILLE, JEAN-CLAUDE L R29HL38296-05
VEIS, ARTHUR R01DE08525-05
VEIS, ARTHUR R37AR13921-31
VEIS, ARTHUR R37DE01374-31
VEIS, ARTHUR S07RR05311-30 0002
VEIS, ARTHUR S07RR05311-30 0003
VELAZQUEZ-LOZADA, JOSE M S06GM08267-04 0007
VELAZQUEZ, MARISSEL K08HL02244-04
VELDHUIS, JOHANNE D M01RR00847-18 0242
VELDHUIS, JOHANNES M01RR00847-18 0582
VELDHUIS, JOHANNES D M01RR00847-18 0527
VELDHUIS, JOHANNES D M01RR00847-18 0528
VELDHUIS, JOHANNES D M01RR00847-18 0334
VELDHUIS, JOHANNES D M01RR00847-18 0529
VELDHUIS, JOHANNES D M01RR00847-18 0455
VELDHUIS, JOHANNES D M01RR00847-18 0530
VELDHUIS, JOHANNES D M01RR00847-18 0459
VELDHUIS, JOHANNES D M01RR00847-18 0461
VELDHUIS, JOHANNES D M01RR00847-18 0479
VELDHUIS, JOHANNES D M01RR00847-18 0414
VELDHUIS, JOHANNES D M01RR00847-18 0416
VELDHUIS, JOHANNES D M01RR00847-18 0538
VELDHUIS, JOHANNES D R01HD16806-08
VELEZ, ROMAN K07HL02671-01
VELICER, LELAND F S07RR05623-25 0718
VELICER, WAYNE F P01CA50087-03 9001
VELLUTINO, FRANK R S07RR07122-23 0096
VELOSA, J A M01RR00585-20 0463
VELTEN, JEFF P S07RR07154-16 0554
VELTEN, JEFF P S07RR07154-16 0555
VELTON, JEFF S06GM08136-18 0019
VENABLE, R M Z01BB03009-02
VENDER, ROBERT S07RR05418-30 0035
VENG-PEDERSEN, PETER S07RR05877-09 0597
VENKATACHALAM, MANJERI A R01DK37139-05
VENKATARAMAN, K S07RR05471-29 0580
VENKATESAN, S Z01AI00467-06
VENKATESAN, S Z01AI00528-03
VENKATESH, NAGAMMAL R29HL38366-04
VENTER, J C Z01NS02710-07
VENTER, J C Z01NS02806-02
VENTOR, J C Z01NS02754-05
VENTURA, C Z01AG00259-03
VENTURA, JOSEPH P50MH30911-14 9005
VENTURA, MARLENE R R01NR01636-05
VENTURE, C Z01AG00260-03
VEOMETT, GEORGE S07RR07055-26 0168
VERA, CHRISTIAN L P01NS11066-17 0005
VERA, MARSIOL S06GM08103-18 0021
VERANI, MARIO S M01RR00350-25 0369
VERBALIS, JOSEPH G P41RR03631-04 0003
VERBRUGGE, LOIS S07RR07050-26 0131
VERBRUGGE, LOIS M K01AG00394-05
VERCELLI, DONATA R29CA56277-01
VERCELLOTTI, GREGORY M R01HL33793-05
VERCELLOTTI, SHARON V R43AI31740-01
VERDERAME, MICHAEL F R01CA52791-02
VERDERY, ROY B K01AG00414-02
VERDERY, ROY B P01AG04402-09 0006
VERDIN, E Z01NS02830-01
VERDINE, GREGORY L R01GM44853-02
VERDOLINI-MARSTEN, K S07RR07035-26 0086
VEREGGE, SYLVIA ANN S06GM08192-12 0014
VERES, Z Z01HL00274-02
VERFAELLIE, MIEKE H P50NS26985-03 0001
VERGARA, JULIO L R01AR25201-12
VERGARO, JULIO S07RR05354-30 0421
VERHAGE, HAROLD G R01HD20571-05A1
VERHAVE, THOM S07RR07064-24
VERKMAN, ALAN S R01DK35124-06
VERKMAN, ALAN S R01DK39354-04
VERKMAN, ALLAN S P50HL42368-04 0003
VERMA, AJIT K R01CA35368-08
VERMA, AJIT K R01CA42585-05
VERMA, INDER M P01CA54418-01
VERMA, INDER M P30CA14195-18 0044
VERMA, INDER M P30CA14195-18 0026
VERMA, INDER M R35CA44360-04
VERMA, OM P S06GM08091-20 0018
VERMEULEN, MARY W R29HL46966-01
VERMEULEN, MARY W S07RR05486-29 0059
VERNADAKIS, ANTONIA O R01AA08026-03
VERNON, D SUE R43MH47211-01A1
VERNON, GRACE S07RR07150-17 0553
VERNON, ROBERT B R01HD25059-03
VERONESI, UMBERTO R01CA38193-07
VERONESI, UMBERTO U01CA38567-06
VERRAN, JOYCE A U01NR02153-04
VERRIER, RICHARD L R01HL33567-08
VERRILLO, RONALD T P01DC00380-05
VERRILLO, RONALD T R01DC00098-19
VERRILLO, RONALD T R01DC01243-01
VERRILLO, RONALD T S07RR07068-26 0237
VERRUSIO, A CARL S07RR05689-23
VERTEL, BARBARA S07RR05366-30 0564
VERTEL, BARBARA M R01DK28433-11

VERTES, ROBERT P R01MH45075-04
VERTREES, JAMES C R43AG09725-01
VERTREES, JAMES C R44AG03796-02
VESELL, ELLIOT S S07RR05680-23 0923
VESLEY, DONALD S07RR05448-30 0290
VESLEY, DONALD S07RR05448-30 0288
VESSEY, DONALD A R01DK19212-15A1
VESTAL, MARVIN L R43GM46169-01
VESTAL, MARVIN L R44GM43669-02
VESTAL, ROBERT E R01AG09559-01
VEZZA, ANNE C R22AI20597-07
VIA, DAVID P R01HL34111-07
VICARIO, DAVID S R01MH40900-05S1
VICHINSKY, ELLIOT P60HL20985-14 0019
VICHINSKY, ELLIOTT N01HB77030-08
VICHINSKY, ELLIOTT N01HB97054-04
VICINI, STEFANO P01NS28130-02 0003
VICKERY, ANN C R22AI20052-08
VICKERY, LARRY E R01DK30109-09
VICKERY, LARRY E R01GM43548-02
VICKERY, ROBERT K S07RR07092-26 0535
VICKREY, BARBARA R01HS06856-01
VICKREY, BARBARA S07RR05756-18 0317
VICKROY, THOMAS W R29NS28568-02
VICTOR, JONATHAN S07RR05396-30 0766
VICTOR, JONATHAN D R01EY07977-03
VICTOR, JONATHAN D R01EY09314-01
VICTOR, RONALD G P01HL06296-31 0017
VICTOR, RONALD G R01HL44010-02
VICTOR, THOMAS A R01CA49564-02
VIDEKA-SHERMAN, LYNN S07RR07122-23 0110
VIDEKA-SHERMAN, LYNN S07RR07122-23 0111
VIDRICH, ALDA R29DK40939-03
VIEGAS, STEVEN F R29AR38640-05
VIELAND, VERONICA J K21MH00884-02
VIEMEISTER, NEAL F P50DC00110-17 0019
VIEMEISTER, NEAL F R01DC00683-02
VIERA, L S07RR05728-20 0205
VIERCK, CHARLES P01NS14899-13 0008
VIERCK, CHARLES J JR P01NS27511-03 0003
VIERCK, CHARLES J, JR R01NS07261-25
VIERLING, ELIZABETH R01GM42762-03
VIERLING, JOHN M R01DK33883-07
VIETTI, TERESA J U10CA30969-11
VIEWEG, VICTOR R M01RR00847-18 0531
VIG, PETER S R01DE06881-09
VIG, PETER S R01DE09883-02
VIG, PETER S S07RR05338-26
VIGLIANTI, GREGORY A R55AI31355-01
VIGNERY, AGNES M K04AR01694-05
VIGNERY, AGNES M R01AR35004-06
VIJAY, INDER K R01DK19682-14
VIJAY, INDER K R01GM44651-02
VIJAY, INDER K S07RR07042-26
VIJAY, INDER K S15GM47069-01
VIJAYAGOPAL, PARAKAT R01HL42993-03
VIJAYAN, VIJAYA K R01AG06159-04A1
VIK, DENNIS P R29AI29742-02
VIK, STEVEN B R01GM40508-04
VIK, TERRY A K11HD00874-03
VILCEK, JAN T R35CA49731-01A2
VILEISIS, RITA A. P01HD21354-05 0002
VILLA-KOMAROFF, LYDIA P30HD18655-10 9010
VILLA-KOMAROFF, LYDIA R01NS27832-03
VILLABLANCA, JAIME R P01HD05958-20 0008
VILLAFRANCA, JOSEPH J R01GM29139-11
VILLAFRANCA, JOSEPH J R01GM23529-15
VILLALTA, FERNANDO R29AI25637-04
VILLALTA, FERNANDO S06GM08037-20 0040
VILLANUEVA, GERMAN B R01HL43252-02
VILLAR, HUGO O R03DA07100-01
VILLAREJO, MERNA R R01GM33778-07
VILLARREAL, JOHN R S06GM08038-21 0012
VILLARREAL, LUIS P R01GM36605-06
VILLEE, CLAUDE A P30HD06645-20 9007
VILLEE, CLAUDE A P30HD06645-20 9001
VILLEMEZ, CLARENCE L, JR R01AI23996-03
VILLEPONTEAU, BRYANT S07RR07050-26 0132
VILLEREAL, MITCHEL L R01GM41400-03
VILLEREAL, MITCHELL L P60DK20595-14 0022
VILLINGER, FRANCOIS P51RR00165-31 0199
VIMAL, RAM L R01EY09511-01
VIMR, ERIC R R01AI23039-05
VINCE, ROBERT S07RR05634-24
VINCE, ROBERT S07RR05634-24 0510
VINCE, ROBERT S15CA55965-01
VINCENT, JENNIFER S07RR05655-21 0817
VINCENT, ROBERT S07RR05372-30 0660
VINCI, ROBERT S07RR05569-27 0115
VINCIGUERRA, VINCENT P U10CA35279-08
VINE, ANDREW K U10EY06282-07
VINE, ANDREW K U10EY08591-02
VINEGAR, ALLEN P30ES00159-24S1 0037
VINEIS, PAOLO R01CA51086-01A2
VINGI, ROBERT N01CO15638-00
VINGI, ROBERT N01CO15692-00
VINGI, ROBERT E N01CO15669-00
VINICOR, FRANK P60DK20542-14 9007
VINICOR, FRANK P60DK20542-14 9010
VINIK, AARON P60DK20572-14 0044
VINIK, AARON I P30DK34933-06A1 9004
VINIK, AARON I R01CA54641-02

VINOGRADOV, SERGE N R01DK38674-05
VINOKUR, AMIRAM S07RR07050-26 0133
VINTER, D P30CA13148-20 9022
VINTERS, HARRY P30AG10123-01 9003
VINTERS, HARRY V R29NS26312-04
VINTON, NANCY E M01RR00054-30 0404
VIOLA, MICHAEL V R01AG10683-01
VIOLA, RONALD E S07RR07249-03 0726
VIOLANTE, MICHAEL R R43AI31763-01
VIOLANTI, JOHN M R03MH47091-01
VIRELLA, GABRIEL T S07RR05767-17 0326
VIRGENE KAYSER, JONE S07RR05604-14 0678
VIRMANI, RENU R01AG06942-05
VIRMANI, RENU R10HL45718-01
VIRSHUP, DAVID M R01AI31657-01
VISCARDI, ROSE M R29HL44853-01A1
VISCIDI, RAPHAEL P R01AI30916-01
VISCIDI, RAPHAEL P R01HL43586-03
VISHWANATHA, JAMBOOR K R01GM46459-01
VISKOCHIL, DAVID H K08NS01492-01
VISNER, MARC S R29HL46280-01
VISNER, MARC S S07RR05712-20 0071
VISTICA, D Z01CM07194-01
VISTICA, D Z01CM07195-01
VISWANATH, NAGALAPUR S07RR05425-30 0773
VIT, ROBERT N01CM73709-10
VITALIANO, PETER P M01RR00037-31 0462
VITALIANO, PETER P R01AG10760-01
VITALIANO, PETER P R01MH43267-04
VITEK, JERROLD L K08NS01328-04
VITETTA, ELLEN P01AI11851-18 0017
VITETTA, ELLEN S P01AI11851-18 0016
VITETTA, ELLEN S P01AI11851-18 0008
VITETTA, ELLEN S P01CA41081-06A1 9001
VITETTA, ELLEN S R01AI21229-07
VITETTA, ELLEN S R37CA28149-11
VITETTA, ELLEN S U01AI27336-04 0002
VITIELLO, MICHAEL V M01RR00037-31 0524
VITIELLO, MICHAEL V R01MH45186-02
VITKOVIC, L Z01AI00562-03
VITULLI, WILLIAM F P40RR01254-11 0002
VIVIAN, DINA R29MH44665-02
VIVINO, M A Z01CT00137-08
VIVINO, M A Z01CT00222-01
VLAHCEVIC, Z. RENO P01DK38030-05 0001
VLAHCEVIC, ZDRAVKO R P01DK38030-05
VLAHOV, DAVID R01DA04334-05
VLASSARA, HELEN M01RR00102-28 0100
VLASSARA, HELEN R01AG06943-05
VLASSARA, HELEN R01AG08245-03
VLASSARA, HELEN R01AG09453-01A1
VLOCK, DANIEL R R01CA42922-04A1
VLOCK, DANIEL R R01CA49708-03
VLODAVSKY, ISRAEL R01CA30289-09
VNENCAK-JONES, CINDY P30DK26657-12 0027
VOCI, JAMES M K11AG00533-01
VODA, ANN M01RR00064-27 0329
VOEIKEL, NORBERT F. P01HL14985-20 0026
VOELKEL, NOBERT F. P01HL14985-20 9005
VOELKEL, STEVEN A R43RR06803-01
VOELKER, DENNIS R R01GM32453-09
VOELKER, DENNIS R R01HL45286-02
VOELKER, JAMES R M01RR00750-19 0246
VOELKER, JAMES R R01AG09560-01
VOELKER, R A Z01ES61024-09
VOELKER, R A Z01ES61048-01
VOELLER, KYTJA R01MH44689-02
VOELLMY, RICHARD W R01GM31125-10
VOET, DONALD H R01GM42571-02
VOGEL, CARL WILHEIM P50AI26821-04 0002
VOGEL, GERALD L R01DE04385-15
VOGEL, GERALD W R01MH40880-06
VOGEL, JONATHAN R01CA52408-01A1
VOGEL, KATHRYN G R01AR36110-07
VOGEL, KATHRYN G S06GM08139-17 0062
VOGEL, MICHAEL W R55NS29277-01A1
VOGEL, STEFANIE N R01AI18797-09
VOGELSANG, GEORGIA R01CA44783-05
VOGELSTEIN, BERT P01CA41183-05 0003
VOGELSTEIN, BERT R01CA43460-09
VOGELSTEIN, BERT R37CA35494-08
VOGELZANG, NICHOLAS J U10CA41287-06
VOGL, THOMAS N01NS02389-02
VOGLER, GEORGE P R01GM43475-02
VOGLER, WILLIAM R R01CA29850-07A2
VOGLER, WILLIAM R U10CA49762-01A2
VOGT, MARGUERITE M P30CA14195-18 0046
VOGT, MARGUERITE M R01CA13608-19
VOGT, PETER K R35CA42564-06
VOGT, RICHARD GUPTON R01DC00588-04
VOGT, THOMAS M R01AR35583-06
VOGT, THOMAS M. N01HC48057-12
VOGT, VOLKER M R37CA20081-15
VOGTSBERGER, KENNETH N R18DA05741-03S1
VOHR, BETTY P50HD11343-14A1 0019
VOICE, THOMAS P42ES04911-03 9001
VOICE, THOMAS P42ES04911-03 0002
VOIGHT, ROBERT A P30CA43703-04A1 9008
VOIGT, HERBERT F R01DC01099-01
VOJCIC, L K Z01BF04014-01
VOLANAKIS, JOHN P50AI23694-06 0007
VOLANAKIS, JOHN E P01AR03555-32A1
VOLANAKIS, JOHN E P01AR03555-32A1 0009
VOLANAKIS, JOHN E R01AI21067-08
VOLANAKIS, JOHN E R37AI15607-13
VOLAND, JOSEPH R R29AI31870-01
VOLAVKA, JAN R01MH41772-05
VOLBERDING, PAUL A P01AI24286-05 9001
VOLBERDING, PAUL A P01AI24286-05
VOLBERDING, PAUL A P30AI27763-04
VOLBRECHT, VICKI S07RR07127-23 0500
VOLD, BARBARA S07RR05522-29 0067
VOLD, BARBARA S R01GM29231-10A1
VOLD, TERJE G R15GM46107-01
VOLICER, LADISLAV P01AG00001-17A2 0021
VOLICER, LADISLAV P01HD22539-04 0005
VOLINI, MARGUERITE R01GM44546-02
VOLKERT, FREDRIC C R01GM40614-03
VOLKERT, MICHAEL R R01GM37052-04A3
VOLKERT, MICHAEL R S07RR05712-20 0072
VOLKMAN, ALVIN R01AI17162-10
VOLKMAN, DAVID J R01AI29008-02
VOLKMAR, F P01MH47200-02 0002
VOLKMAR, FRED R P01HD03008-24 0050
VOLKMAR, FRED R R01MH46961-01
VOLKOW, NORA S07RR05736-19 0163
VOLKOW, NORA D P01NS15638-13 0011
VOLKOW, NORA D R01DA06278-02
VOLKOW, NORA D R01DA06891-02
VOLLHARDT, K PETER C R01GM22479-16
VOLLMER, DENNIS G S07RR05389-30 0651
VOLLMER, WILLIAM M R01HL41964-03
VOLLMER, WILLIAM M R29HL41039-04
VOLLMER, WILLIAM M S07RR05521-29 0063
VOLLOCH, VLADIMIR S07RR05711-21 0033
VOLLOCH, VLADIMIR Z R01GM41243-03
VOLLOCH, VLADIMIR Z R55GM45237-01
VOLMAN, SUSAN F R29MH47330-01A1
VOLPE, BRUCE T R01MH40090-05
VOLPE, JOSEPH J M01RR06021-02 0715
VOLPE, JOSEPH J P30HD18655-10
VOLPE, JOSEPH J R01HD07464-18
VOLPICELLI, JOSEPH R R29AA07517-03
VOLSKY, DAVID J U01AI25902-05 0002
VOLSKY, DAVID J P30CA36727-08 9006
VOLSKY, DAVID J R01CA37465-07
VOLSKY, DAVID J R01HL43628-03
VOLSKY, DAVID J U01AI27397-04 0004
VOLTMER, RITA K R25AD00056-01
VOLTZOW, JANICE S06GM08102-20 0055
VOMSAAL, FREDERICK S07RR07053-26 0144
VON HIPPEL, PETER H R01GM29158-10S1
VON HIPPEL, PETER H R37GM15792-25
VON HOFF, DANIEL D M01RR01346-10 0176
VON HOFF, DANIEL D M01RR01346-10 0194
VON HOFF, DANIEL D M01RR01346-10 0195
VON HOFF, DANIEL D M01RR01346-10 0196
VON HOFF, DANIEL D M01RR01346-10 0197
VON HOFF, DANIEL D M01RR01346-10 0198
VON HOFF, DANIEL D N01CM07305-02
VON HOFF, DANIEL D U01CA50771-03 0004
VON KORFF, M P01DE08773-03 0002
VON KORFF, MICHAEL R R01HS06168-03
VON RAMM, OLAF T R01CA37586-11
VON REYN, C FORDHAM S07RR05392-30 0708
VON REYN, CHARLES F R01AI30373-01A1
VON STRANDTMANN, MAXIMILLIAN R44HD25796-02
VONDERHAAR, B K Z01CB08226-15
VONDRA, JOAN T R03MH46455-01A2
VONHOFE, ERIC S07RR05712-20 0111
VONHOFE, ERIC H R55CA51103-01A1
VONLANTHEN, MARYELLE S07RR05654-24 0134
VOOGT, JAMES L R01HD24190-04
VOOGT, JAMES L R03DA06790-01A1
VORE, MARY E R01HD13250-13
VORHEES, CHARLES V R01DA06733-01A1
VORHEES, CHARLES V R01HD21806-05
VORNOV, JAMES J K08NS01310-04
VOS, JEAN-MICHEL H R01CA51096-01A2
VOSBURGH, EVAN S07RR05487-29 0711
VOUROS, PAUL S07RR07143-20 0637
VOYKSNER, ROBERT D R01DA06315-03
VOYTA, JOHN C R44HD26205-02
VRANA, KENT S07RR05433-30 0255
VRANA, KENT E R01GM38931-01A3
VRIESENDORP, FRANCINE J K08NS01530-01
VRTUNSKI, P BART P50MH41684-07 0073
VRTUNSKI, P BART R01MH46630-02
VUCHINICH, RUDY E P50AA07606-04 9004
VUCHINICH, SAMUEL R29MH45073-03
VUCHINICH, SAMUEL S07RR07079-26 0290
VUJCIC, L K Z01BF04015-01
VUJCIC, L K Z01BF04016-01
VUK-PAVLOVIC, STANIMIR R29CA45312-05
VUKAJLOVICH, STANLEY W R29AI24565-05
VULLIET, P R S07RR05457-29 0011
VULLIET, PHILIP R R01NS28765-02
VYAS, GIRISH N N01HB67020-11
VYAS, GIRISH N P30AI27763-04 9006
W LIU, CHUNG-CHIUN P41RR02024-08 9001
Williams, Donna M Z01DK25073-03
WAALKES, M P Z01CP05488-06
WABER, DEBORAH P R01NS22108-06
WABL, MATTHIAS R R01AI30177-02
WABL, MATTHIAS R R01GM37699-05
WABNER, CINDY M01RR00633-19 0409
WACHAL, MARILYN R19MH47699-02
WACHSMAN, WILLIAM P01CA50528-03 0004
WACKETT, LAWRENCE P R29GM41235-03
WACKYM, PHILLIP A K08DC00062-01
WADA, Y Z01DK25060-06
WADDEN, RICHARD A R01OH02804-01
WADDEN, THOMAS A K01MH00702-05
WADDLE, FLOYD R S06GM08206-10 0004
WADE, BRUCE R24MH47188-02 0005
WADE, GEORGE N K05MH00321-11A1
WADE, GEORGE N R01DK32976-08
WADE, GEORGE N R01NS10873-19
WADE, JAMES B R01DK32839-08
WADE, JAMES B. P01HL27867-10 9001
WADE, JAMES L U10CA45807-06
WADE, MICHAEL J R01GM22523-16
WADE, NANCY A K11AI00944-02
WADE, ROBERT S07RR05379-30 0760
WADE, WILLIAM S07RR07055-26 0175
WADE, WILLIAM F R29AI31160-01
WADHWANI, K C Z01AG00121-14
WADSWORTH, B JO U01CA50135-03
WADSWORTH, JO N01CN15388-00
WADSWORTH, PATRICIA S07RR07048-26 0659
WAECHTER, CHARLES J R01GM36065-06
WAGENAAR, ALEX C P50AA06282-09 0002
WAGENAAR, ALEXANDER C R01AA09142-01
WAGENKNECHT, TERENCE C R01AR40615-01A1
WAGENKNECHT, TERENCE C R29GM38161-05
WAGER, ELIZABETH S07RR05354-30 0411
WAGERLE, L CRAIG R01DA06484-02
WAGGONER, ALAN S R01NS19353-10
WAGMAN, LAWRENCE D U10CA43595-05
WAGNER, ELIZABETH M. P01HL10342-26 0032
WAGNER, ANN E S07RR05458-29 0842
WAGNER, BARRY M S07RR07123-22 0592
WAGNER, BETTY J R01EY02299-14
WAGNER, CONRAD R01DK15289-16
WAGNER, DAVID A R43DK44399-01
WAGNER, DAVID K S07RR05434-30 0815
WAGNER, DENISA D P01HL30616-09 9001
WAGNER, DENISA D P01HL42443-03 0004
WAGNER, DENISA D P01HL42443-03 9002
WAGNER, DENISA D R01HL41002-04
WAGNER, EDWARD H P01CA34847-09 9002
WAGNER, EDWARD K R37CA11861-22
WAGNER, FRED S07RR07055-26 0193
WAGNER, GERHARD R01CA54513-01A1
WAGNER, GERHARD R01GM38608-05
WAGNER, H G Z01NS02718-06
WAGNER, HANS E S07RR05591-27 0659
WAGNER, HENRY N P01CA32845-29 9001
WAGNER, HENRY N, JR P01CA32845-29
WAGNER, HENRY N, JR P01NS15080-12
WAGNER, JANICE D K01RR00072-01
WAGNER, JANICE D P01HL45666-01 9005
WAGNER, JOHN A P01CA22427-14 0011
WAGNER, JOHN A R01CA40929-07
WAGNER, JOHN A R01EY06454-07
WAGNER, JOHN A S07RR05526-29 0077
WAGNER, JOSEPH E N01CM17534-00
WAGNER, JOSEPH E P40RR00471-22
WAGNER, JOSEPH L G20RR06768-01
WAGNER, JOSEPH L N01RR62123-09
WAGNER, JOSEPH L U42RR05088-04
WAGNER, P Z01CB05265-09
WAGNER, PETER D P01HL17731-17
WAGNER, PETER D P01HL17731-17 0015
WAGNER, PETER D P01HL17731-17 0006
WAGNER, PETER J R01GM39821-03
WAGNER, RICHARD K R01HD23340-04
WAGNER, ROBERT R P30CA44579-04A1 9008
WAGNER, ROBERT R P30CA44579-04A1
WAGNER, ROBERT R R37AI11112-25
WAGNER, ROGER C R01HL33936-07
WAGNER, WILLIAM D P50HL14164-20 9006
WAGNER, WILLIAM D P50HL14164-20 0029
WAGNER, WILLIAM D R01HL45848-01A1
WAGNER, WILTZ W, JR R01HL36033-07
WAGNER, WILTZ W, JR R13HL47343-01
WAGNILD, GAIL S07RR05758-18 0261
WAGSTAFF, JOSEPH K08HD00966-01
WAHBA, ALBERT J R01GM25451-12
WAHL, GEOFFREY M P01HG00202-02 0004
WAHL, GEOFFREY M R01GM27754-12
WAHL, GEOFFREY M U01CA48405-04
WAHL, L M Z01DE00456-04
WAHL, RICHARD M01RR00042-31 0602
WAHL, RICHARD L M01RR00042-31 0657
WAHL, RICHARD L R01CA53172-01
WAHL, RICHARD L R55CA52880-01A1
WAHL, S M Z01DE00046-19
WAHL, S M Z01DE00513-02
WAHLESTEDT, CLAES R01DA06805-01
WAHLESTEDT, CLAES S07RR05396-30 0767
WAIGHT, DAVID S07RR05372-30 0705
WAINER, BRUCE H R01NS17661-10
WAINER, BRUCE H R01NS25787-04A1
WAISMAN, Y Z01CL00110-01
WAIT, RICHARD B R01DK39966-03

WAITE, B MOSELEY P30CA12197-19 9003
WAITE, B MOSELEY R01HL31338-08
WAITE, LINDA S07RR05710-21 0017
WAITE, LINDA J P01AG08291-03 0002
WAITE, LINDA J P01AG08291-03 0003
WAITE, LINDA J P50HD12639-12 0014
WAITE, LINDA J P50HD12639-12 0016
WAKADE, ARUN R R01HL18601-12A3
WAKADE, ARUN R R01HL22170-12
WAKATSUKI, S P41RR01209-12 0022
WAKATSUKI, S P41RR01209-12 0023
WAKATSUKI, S P41RR01209-12 0024
WAKATSUKI, S P41RR01209-12 0025
WAKE, DAVID B S07RR07006-26 0919
WAKEFIELD, GREGORY H P01DC00274-08 0007
WAKEFIELD, GREGORY H R01DC00706-02
WAKEFIELD, L M Z01CP05398-08
WAKELAND, EDWARD K R01AI17966-11
WAKELAND, EDWARD K R01GM39578-03
WAKELAND, EDWARD K R01HL47138-01
WAKELANDS, EDWARD P01DK39079-05 0003
WAKIL, SALIH J R01GM19091-21
WAKIMOTO, BARBARA T S07RR07096-26 0060
WAKSMAN, BYRON H R13MH46982-02
WAKSMONSKI, CAROL A P01DA06306-01A1 9001
WALASZEK, ZBIGNIEW R01CA47342-03
WALBOT, VIRGINIA E R01GM32422-09
WALBURN, FRED N01HC48061-12
WALCZAK, C A Z01DE00250-14
WALDEN, TEDRA S07RR07201-12 0641
WALDER, JOSEPH A P01HL40453-04
WALDER, JOSEPH A P30DK25295-12S1 9014
WALDMAN, BARBARA C S07RR05371-30 0647
WALDMAN, FRED P01CA44768-05 0004
WALDMAN, FREDERIC M R01CA49056-03
WALDMAN, LEWIS K R01HL45897-01
WALDMAN, ROBERT H S07RR05391-30
WALDMAN, ROBERT H S07RR05391-30 0930
WALDMAN, ROBERT H S15CA55927-01
WALDMAN, STEPHANIE M01RR02635-07 0275
WALDMANN, T A Z01CB04002-22
WALDO, ALBERT L M01RR00080-29 0366
WALDO, ALBERT L N01HC65047-08
WALDO, ALBERT L R01HL38408-02A1
WALDORF, DANIEL R01DA06487-02
WALDORF, DANIEL O R01HD26282-02
WALDORF, RONALD A R43AA08958-01
WALDREN, CHARLES P41RR01315-10 0020
WALDREN, CHARLES A R01CA36447-06
WALDREP, J CLIFFORD R01EY07154-05
WALDRON, JAMES P50HL27353-10 9001
WALDRON, MANJULA B R03DC01031-01A1
WALDROP, TONY G P01HL06296-31 0016
WALDSCHMIDT, THOMAS J R29AI31265-01
WALENGA, RONALD P30DK27651-09 9011
WALFIELD, ALAN M R43AI32227-01
WALFORD, ROY R01AG00424-29
WALFORD, ROY S07RR05354-30 0409
WALFORD, ROY L R01AG08936-02
WALIA, SATISH S07RR07131-22 0141
WALIA, SATISH S07RR07131-22 0142
WALICKE, PATRICIA A P01NS28121-01A1S1 0005
WALKENBACH, RONALD J R01EY02597-14
WALKER-JONES, DOROTHY G S06GM08016-21 0082
WALKER, ALEXIS J S07RR07079-26 0291
WALKER, BRUCE D R01AI28568-03
WALKER, BRUCE D R01AI30914-01
WALKER, BRUCE D R01AI31563-01
WALKER, BRUCE D R01AI32469-01
WALKER, BRUCE E R01CA39456-03
WALKER, CLAY B P50DE07117-07 0002
WALKER, CLAY B R01DE06070-08
WALKER, DAVID S07RR05427-30 0156
WALKER, DAVID H R01AI21242-08
WALKER, DAVID H R01AI31431-01
WALKER, DERALD R R01MH48073-01
WALKER, DERALD R R18MH49072-01
WALKER, DON W R01AA00200-19
WALKER, E C Z01RR10335-02
WALKER, EDWARD A M01RR00037-31 0523
WALKER, EDWIN B U01AI25859-05 0002
WALKER, ELAINE F K02MH00876-02
WALKER, ELAINE F R01MH46496-02
WALKER, FRANCES A R01DK31038-10
WALKER, FREDERICK J R01HL40328-04
WALKER, GEORGE E S15HD28745-01
WALKER, GEORGE E S15MH49333-01
WALKER, GLENDA C R15NR02757-01
WALKER, GRAHAM C P01ES03926-07 0006
WALKER, GRAHAM C R01CA21615-14A1
WALKER, GRAHAM C R01GM31030-10
WALKER, J MICHAEL R01DA04988-04
WALKER, JEFFERY W R01HL44114-02
WALKER, JOHN C R29GM39993-04
WALKER, KAY B M01RR00064-27 0374
WALKER, LYNN S R01HD23264-05
WALKER, M Z01HL00657-01
WALKER, MARY EDITH P30CA21765-14 9007
WALKER, PATRICK S07RR05377-30 0760
WALKER, PATRICK D R29GM40037-05
WALKER, R DALE R01AA07103-05
WALKER, R DALE U10AA08436-03
WALKER, ROBERT S07RR05623-25 0720
WALKER, W ALLAN P01DK33506-08
WALKER, W ALLAN P01DK33506-08 0001
WALKER, W ALLAN R22HD12437-12
WALKER, W GORDON R01DK39885-05
WALKER, W GORDON R21DK44562-01
WALKER, W. ALLAN P30DK34854-08 9006
WALKER, WILLIAM S R01AI17979-09
WALKLEY, STEVEN P30HD01799-27 9002
WALKLEY, STEVEN U R01NS18804-08
WALL, CONRAD III R01DC00290-05
WALL, JACK R R01EY05062-07
WALL, JAMES C R15NS28502-01A1
WALL, JOHN T, JR R01NS21105-07
WALL, JOSEPH P41RR01777-08 9001
WALL, JOSEPH P41RR01777-08 9002
WALL, JOSEPH P41RR01777-08 9003
WALL, JOSEPH P41RR01777-08 9004
WALL, JOSEPH P41RR01777-08 9005
WALL, JOSEPH S P41RR01777-08
WALL, JOSEPH S P41RR01777-08 0001
WALL, MICHAEL A K07HL02104-05
WALL, MONROE P01CA50529-01A2 0001
WALL, MONROE E P01CA48112-01A3 0004
WALL, MONROE E S07RR05791-15 0514
WALL, MONROE E U01CA52956-02 0004
WALL, RANDOLF P01CA12800-18A1 0048
WALL, RANDOLPH P01CA12800-18A1
WALL, RANDOLPH R01GM40185-04
WALL, TERESA N01DK72292-06
WALLACE, ANDREW G S07RR05392-30
WALLACE, ANDREW G S15CA55938-01
WALLACE, B A S07RR07104-25 0563
WALLACE, BRUCE G R01NS29673-01
WALLACE, BRUCE R P01CA30206-10 0009
WALLACE, CHARLES P50MH30911-14 9001
WALLACE, CHARLES J R01MH43364-02
WALLACE, CHARLES R S07RR07161-14 0850
WALLACE, DAVID B R43GM44461-01A1
WALLACE, DOUGLAS C P30AG10130-01 0001
WALLACE, DOUGLAS C P30AG10130-01 9004
WALLACE, DOUGLAS C R01HL45572-01
WALLACE, DOUGLAS C R01NS21328-08
WALLACE, HAROLD J, JR U10CA35091-08
WALLACE, JAMES A S06GM08139-17 0063
WALLACE, JEANNE M. N01HR76030-05
WALLACE, LANE J S15CA55956-01
WALLACE, MARTHA C S07RR05300-30 0205
WALLACE, R BRUCE P30CA33572-11 9011
WALLACE, R BRUCE R01HG00099-02
WALLACE, ROBERT N01AG02106-18
WALLACE, ROBERT B N02HI09501-06
WALLACE, ROBERT B P01AG07094-05
WALLACE, ROBERT B P01AG07094-05 9001
WALLACE, ROBERT B P01AG07094-05 0001
WALLACE, ROBERT B P20AG09682-01 0002
WALLACE, ROBERT B P20AG09682-01 9001
WALLACE, ROBERT B P20AG09682-01
WALLACE, ROBERT B U01NR02638-02
WALLACE, ROBERT W P01DK38518-05 0002
WALLACE, ROGER B P42ES04911-03 0004
WALLACE, STEPHEN S07RR05767-17 0327
WALLACE, SUSAN S R01CA52040-01A1
WALLACE, SUSAN S R37CA33657-11
WALLACE, WILLIAM C. P50AG05138-08 0014
WALLACE, WILLIAM D S03RR03040-10
WALLACE, WILLIAM R S07RR05928-06
WALLACH, EDWARD E R01HD19430-07
WALLACK, LAWRENCE N01CN64097-11
WALLACK, MARC KENNETH R01CA45358-03
WALLANDER, JAN L K04HD00867-01A2
WALLANDER, JAN L R01HD25310-01A2
WALLE, THOMAS M01RR01070-15 0132
WALLE, THOMAS R01GM41141-03
WALLE, THOMAS R01GM46000-01
WALLEN, C ANNE S07RR05404-30 0865
WALLEN, KIM P51RR00165-31 0087
WALLER, PATRICIA F R01AA09026-01
WALLERSTEIN, ROBERT S07RR05755-18 0234
WALLHAGEN, MARGARET S07RR05604-14 0684
WALLICK, EARL T P01HL22619-14 9002
WALLICK, EARL T P01HL22619-14 0004
WALLIG, MATTHEW A R01DK41215-03
WALLIG, MATTHEW A S07RR05460-29 0365
WALLIN, REIDAR R01HL32070-07
WALLIS, JOHN W, JR R29GM41409-03
WALLIS, ROBERT S R29AI25076-04
WALLIS, ROIANN S07RR05756-18 0308
WALLMAN, JOSHUA R01EY02727-13
WALLMAN, JOSHUA S06GM08168-13 0012
WALLOW, INGOLF H L R01EY01634-16
WALLSTON, KENNETH A R01NR01007-06A2
WALMSLEY, JUDITH A S06GM08194-12 0032
WALRAVENS, PHILIP A M01RR00069-29 0198
WALROND, JOHN P R29NS25572-03
WALROND, JOHN P S07RR05458-29 0843
WALSER, MACKENZIE M01RR00722-19 0048
WALSER, MACKENZIE R01DK32008-09
WALSER, MACKENZIE R01DK32009-08
WALSETH, TIMOTHY F S07RR05385-30 0810
WALSETH, TIMOTHY F S07RR05385-30 0811
WALSH, B TIMOTHY M01RR00645-20 0496
WALSH, B TIMOTHY R01MH42206-04
WALSH, BERNARD T R01MH38355-09
WALSH, BRIAN S07RR05950-07 0001
WALSH, BRIAN W M01RR02635-07 0195
WALSH, CHARLES J S07RR07084-26 0329
WALSH, CHRISTINA M01RR00096-30A1 0284
WALSH, CHRISTINA M01RR00096-30A1 0312
WALSH, CHRISTOPHER T P01HL42443-03 0001
WALSH, CHRISTOPHER T R01GM21643-18
WALSH, CHRISTOPHER T R01GM31574-09
WALSH, CHRISTOPHER T R37GM20011-20
WALSH, DAVID A R01AG08106-03
WALSH, DIANA S07RR05927-07 0957
WALSH, DONAL A R01DK13613-23
WALSH, DONAL A R55DK21019-14
WALSH, EDWARD P60DC00982-02 0004
WALSH, EDWARD E R01AI20608-06
WALSH, EDWARD J R01DC01007-02
WALSH, JOHN P01AG09793-01 0003
WALSH, JOHN H P30DK41301-02
WALSH, JOHN H R01DK35740-07
WALSH, JOHN H R37DK17294-18
WALSH, JOHN V R01DK31620-09
WALSH, KENNETH R01AR40197-01A1
WALSH, KENNETH R01HL45345-02
WALSH, KENNETH A R01HL40990-04
WALSH, KENNETH A S07RR05432-30 0248
WALSH, KENNETH B R55HL45789-01A1
WALSH, MARGARET S07RR05305-30 0744
WALSH, MARY F S06GM08167-13 0052
WALSH, PETER P30ES02109-13 0010
WALSH, PETER N P50HL45486-01 0003
WALSH, PETER N R01HL25661-10
WALSH, PETER N R01HL46213-01
WALSH, RAYMOND S07RR05359-30 0521
WALSH, RAYMOND F S07RR05394-30 0726
WALSH, RICHARD A R01HL33579-07
WALSH, THOMAS J R29ES04262-06
WALTENBAUGH, CARL R R01AA08275-01A1
WALTER, GERNOT F R01CA36111-07
WALTER, HEATHER J P50MH43520-04 0002
WALTER, PETER R01GM32384-09
WALTER, PETER R01GM37485-05
WALTER, RONALD B R01CA56728-02
WALTERS, EDGAR T R01MH38726-07A1
WALTERS, GLENN A R43GM41504-01A1
WALTERS, J R Z01NS02139-17
WALTERS, JOHN D R01DE09851-01
WALTERS, LAUREL L R29AI28003-04
WALTERS, LEROY N01LM13531-00
WALTERS, LEROY B P50LM04492-07
WALTERS, MARIAN R R01DK31847-07
WALTERS, MARIAN R R01DK43846-01
WALTERS, MARY J P30CA08748-26 9019
WALTERS, MARY J P30CA08748-26 9030
WALTHALL, W WILLIAM S07RR07171-08 0160
WALTON, JONATHAN S07RR07049-26 0435
WALTON, PETER L N01CO94386-11
WALTON, PETER L N44CO05180-01
WALTON, ROSE A U01AI25893-05 0009
WALTRIP, ROYCE W P50MH44211-03 0014
WALTRIP, ROYCE W, II K20MH00814-02
WALZ, DANIEL A R01HL27073-09
WALZ, FREDERICK G, JR R01GM40289-03
WALZER, PETER N01AI72646-07
WALZER, PETER D U01AI25897-05 0001
WALZER, PETER D U01AI31702-01
WAMSLEY, JAMES KEVIN R01DA05167-04
WAN, KEE KWONG S07RR05370-30 0610
WAN, YU-JUI Y R29CA53596-01A1
WAN, YU-JUI YVONNE S07RR05551-29 0958
WAND, A JOSHUA S07RR07030-26 0416
WAND, ANDREW J R01GM35940-06
WAND, GARY S R01AA09000-01
WAND, GARY S R29AA07384-04
WANDELL, BRIAN A R01EY03164-13
WANDELL, BRIAN A S07RR07005-26 0344
WANDS, JACK R K05AA00048-12
WANDS, JACK R R01AA08169-03
WANDS, JACK R R01CA35711-08
WANDS, JACK R R01HD20469-07
WANDS, JACK R R37AA02666-15
WANECK, GERALD L R29GM46467-01
WANG, AN-CHUAN S07RR05767-17 0328
WANG, ANDREW H R01CA52506-02
WANG, ANDREW H R01GM41612-02
WANG, ANDREW H J S07RR07030-26 0417
WANG, BI-CHENG R01GM41936-03
WANG, BI-CHENG S07RR07084-26 0330
WANG, C Y S07RR07049-26 0436
WANG, CHANG U01AI30238-02 0002
WANG, CHI-SUN R01HD23472-03
WANG, CHIH-LUEH A R01HL41411-07
WANG, CHING C R01AI21786-07
WANG, CHING C R01AI30475-01
WANG, CHING C R22AI24011-06
WANG, CHING Y R01CA23800-13
WANG, CHING Y R01CA49783-03
WANG, CHRISTINA S07RR05468-29 0403
WANG, F Z01HL04213-02
WANG, FREDERICK C S R01CA52244-02
WANG, FREDERICK C S U01AI32246-01 0002

WANG, GING K R01GM35401-07
WANG, HOWARD H R01GM41796-03
WANG, JAMES C R01CA47958-04
WANG, JAMES C R37GM24544-15
WANG, JEAN Y R01CA43054-05
WANG, JOHN L R01GM27203-10
WANG, JOHN L R01GM38740-04
WANG, JOSEPH S07RR07154-16 0557
WANG, JUI H R01GM41610-03
WANG, KENNING S07RR05959-06 0027
WANG, KUAN R01DK20270-13
WANG, LEE-HO S07RR05745-19 0254
WANG, LU-HAI R01CA29339-12
WANG, MEI-CHENG R01AI29197-03
WANG, NANCY R55CA52761-01A1
WANG, REBECCA S07RR05611-22 0707
WANG, REX Y R01MH41440-06
WANG, REX Y S07RR05736-19 0180
WANG, RICHARD S07RR07053-26 0136
WANG, RONG R44DE08905-03
WANG, SAN YOU R29DK39755-04
WANG, SHOOU-LIH S07RR06004-04 0039
WANG, SHOOU-LIH S07RR06004-04 0040
WANG, STEWART C K11AI01030-01
WANG, SUE M R29HL43034-03
WANG, T Z01CN00159-01
WANG, TAITZER P01HL22619-14 0009
WANG, TERESA S R01AI28873-02
WANG, TERESA S R01CA14835-18
WANG, TERESA S R01CA54415-01
WANG, TIMOTHY C K08DK01937-02
WANG, TINGCHUNG R01HL45129-01A1
WANG, WILLIAM S-Y S07RR07006-26 0893
WANG, WINFRED N01HB77037-09
WANG, WINFRED N01HB97066-04
WANG, YI-TIN S07RR07114-23 0450
WANG, YU-HWA E R01AG07444-04
WANG, YU-HWA E R01AG09278-02
WANG, YU-LI R01GM32476-07
WANG, YU-LI R01GM41681-01
WANG, ZHIYUE P41RR02305-08 9007
WANI, ALTAF A R01ES02388-09
WANNER, ADAM R01HL20989-14
WANSBROUGH, SCOTT R S07RR05426-30 0149
WANSLEY, RICHARD A U76PE00032-08
WANSLEY, RICHARD A U76PE00449-02
WAPNIR, J S07RR05576-27 0608
WARA, D. P01HD24640-03 9003
WARA, DIANE W M01RR00079-29 0399
WARA, DIANE W M01RR01271-10 0114
WARA, DIANE W M01RR01271-10 0103
WARA, DIANE W M01RR01271-10 0118
WARA, DIANE W M01RR01271-10 0104
WARA, DIANE W M01RR01271-10 0079
WARA, DIANE W M01RR01271-10 0086
WARA, DIANE W P60HL20985-14 0002
WARA, DIANE W U01AI27541-04
WARBURTON, DAVID R01HL44060-01A1
WARBURTON, DAVID R01HL44977-01A1
WARBURTON, DOROTHY P30CA13696-19 9024
WARBURTON, DOROTHY P R55HG00366-04
WARBURTON, DORTHY P20HG00424-01 0002
WARBURTON, WILLIAM K R44GM43675-02
WARD, ARTHUR A P01NS20482-08 9001
WARD, DAVID C R01AI19973-09
WARD, DAVID C R01GM40115-03
WARD, DAVID C R01HG00246-03
WARD, DAVID C R01HG00272-02
WARD, DAVID C R01HG00307-04
WARD, DEBBIE S07RR05758-18 0262
WARD, ELIZABETH S R29AI31592-01
WARD, ELIZABETH SALL S07RR07175-15 0446
WARD, FRANCES E N01AI15116-00
WARD, HONORINE D R29AI27218-02
WARD, J M Z01CP05301-10
WARD, J M Z01CP05303-10
WARD, JOEL I N01AI15124-00
WARD, JOEL I R01AI31580-01
WARD, JOHN D P01NS12587-16 9004
WARD, JOHN D. P01NS12587-16 0001
WARD, JOHN F R01CA46295-03
WARD, JOHN F R13CA53089-01S1
WARD, JOHN F R37CA26279-12
WARD, JOHN H M01RR00064-27 0352
WARD, JOHN H P01CA48711-02 0003
WARD, JOHN R N01AR12204-20
WARD, KATHY R01CA46574-05
WARD, MARCIA M R01HL41635-03
WARD, PATRICK E R01HL45791-01
WARD, PETER A P01HL31963-08
WARD, PETER A P01HL31963-08 0001
WARD, PETER A P01HL31963-08 0005
WARD, PETER A R37GM29507-10
WARD, R H R01AR40057-03
WARD, R H R01GM41746-03
WARD, RICHARD H R01HD23492-04
WARD, RICHARD L S07RR05951-07 0736
WARD, ROBERT S R43GM44437-01A1
WARD, SAMUEL R01GM25243-14
WARD, STEVEN C S07RR07208-10 0668
WARD, STEVEN W S07RR05576-27 0612
WARD, W DIXON P50DC00110-17 0001
WARD, WALTER F. P01AG01188-13 0012
WARD, WALTER R S07RR07187-13 0701
WARD, WARREN W R43EY09015-01A1
WARD, WILLIAM F R01HL25106-10
WARD, WILLIAM L R19DA06437-03
WARD, WILLIAM L R19MH46227-03
WARD, WILLIAM S R29HD28501-01
WARDEN, J T S07RR07104-25 0564
WARDLAW, SHARON M01RR00645-20 0483
WARDLAW, SHARON P50HD05077-21 0033
WARE, ANTHONY S07RR05479-29 0447
WARE, ANTHONY J P01DA06306-01A1 0003
WARE, BENJAMIN R S07RR07068-26
WARE, BENJAMIN R S15HD28776-01
WARE, J ANTHONY K04HL02271-02
WARE, J ANTHONY S07RR05479-29 0433
WARE, JAMES P50HL34616-07 9001
WARE, JAMES H S07RR05446-30
WARE, JAMES H S15CA55943-01
WARE, JOE A R29HL38820-05
WARE, JOHN E P01AG08291-03 0005
WARE, JOHN E JR R01HS06073-03S1
WARE, JOY P30CA16059-15 9016
WARE, JOY L R01CA50609-02
WARE, RUSSELL E K11HL02015-05
WARE, WENDY A S07RR07034-26 0069
WAREING, THOMAS H S07RR05491-29 0467
WARGOVICH, MICHAEL J R01CA52006-01A1
WARGOVICH, MICHAEL J S07RR05511-29 0501
WARING, GEORGE O P51RR00165-31 0143
WARING, GEORGE O P51RR00165-31 0191
WARING, GEORGE O, III U10EY03761-11
WARING, RICHARD B R29GM41009-03
WARKENTIN, PHYLLIS I K07HL02341-03
WARLTIER, DAVID C R01HL32911-06
WARNECKE, RICHARD B P01CA42760-06
WARNECKE, RICHARD B P01CA42760-06 0001
WARNECKE, RICHARD B P01CA42760-06 9002
WARNER, ANGELEINE E S07RR05446-30 0279
WARNER, CAROL M R01HD13748-13
WARNER, DAVID O R01HL45532-02
WARNER, DAVID O R29GM40909-03
WARNER, DAVID S R29GM39771-04
WARNER, HOMER R R01LM05202-01A1
WARNER, ISIAH M R01GM39844-03
WARNER, JONATHAN R P30CA13330-20 9012
WARNER, JONATHAN R R01GM25532-14
WARNER, MARGARET ROSE R29HL41599-03
WARNICK, G RUSSELL P01HL30086-09 9002
WARNKE, ROGER P01CA34233-09 9002
WARNKE, ROGER A R01CA33119-07A1
WARNOCK, DAVID G P50DK39258-05
WARNOCK, DAVID G R01DK19407-15A3
WARR, GREGORY W S07RR05767-17 0329
WARR, WILLIAM B R01DC00372-06
WARRELL, R P01CA29502-11A1 0054
WARREN, CHRISTOPHER S07RR05486-29 0052
WARREN, CHRISTOPHER S07RR05486-29 0046
WARREN, CHRISTOPHER D R01DK40930-02
WARREN, DONALD W R01DE06957-08
WARREN, DONALD W R01DE07105-07
WARREN, GUYLYN R S06GM08218-08 0009
WARREN, H SHAW R29AI28943-02
WARREN, JAMES C R01DK15708-20
WARREN, JEFFERY SCOTT R29HL40526-03
WARREN, JOHN W P01AG04393-07
WARREN, JOHN W P01AG04393-07 0005
WARREN, JOHN W P01AG04393-07 9004
WARREN, L P41RR00317-25 0006
WARREN, MICHELLE P R01HD22171-06
WARREN, MICHELLE P S03RR03462-05
WARREN, REED S07RR07093-24 0777
WARREN, RICHARD M R01DC00208-07
WARREN, RICHARD M S07RR07181-13 0538
WARREN, RONALD Q S07RR05519-29 0514
WARREN, SANFORD E M01RR01032-16 0405
WARREN, STEPHEN L K08CA01339-01A2
WARREN, STEPHEN L S07RR05358-30 0488
WARREN, STEPHEN T R01HD20521-06
WARREN, STEPHEN T R01HG00038-02
WARREN, STEVEN F P30HD15052-11
WARREN, SUSAN R29NS27996-02
WARREN, SUSAN S07RR05386-30 0597
WARREN, WARREN S R01GM35253-07
WARREN, WILLIAM H, JR R01AG05223-06
WARSHAW, DAVID M P01HL28001-10 0008
WARSHAW, DAVID M R01AR34872-07
WARSHAW, DAVID M R01HL45161-02
WARSHAW, GREGG A K07AG00466-01
WARSHAW, JOSEPH B P30HD27757-02
WARSHAWSKY, D P30ES00159-24S1 0036
WARSHAWSKY, DAVID P01ES05652-01 9002
WARSHAWSKY, DAVID P42ES04908-03 0003
WARSHAWSKY, DAVID R01ES04203-05
WARSHAWSKY, DAVID R01OH02277-02
WARSHEL, ARIEH R01GM24492-14
WARSHEL, ARIEH R01GM40283-04
WARTELL, ROGER S07RR07024-26 0032
WARTELL, ROGER M R01GM38045-01A2
WARTELL, ROGER M S07RR07024-26 0051
WARTELL, ROGER M S15HL47726-01
WARTERS, RAYMOND L R01CA25957-12
WARTERS, RAYMOND L R01CA45154-05
WARWICK, WARREN J R01HL37504-05
WASFI, SADIQ H S06GM08182-12 0006
WASHABAUGH, MICHAEL S07RR05445-30 0879
WASHABAUGH, MICHAEL W R29GM42878-03
WASHBURN, RONALD G K04AI01036-01
WASHBURN, RONALD G R29AI25037-05
WASHECKA, ROBERT M S07RR05736-19 0182
WASHINGTON, ARTHUR S06GM08094-17 0008
WASHINGTON, ARTHUR C S06GM08094-17
WASHINGTON, NANCY D S03RR03154-10
WASHINGTON, O S07RR05333-30 0878
WASHINGTON, ROBERT O S03RR03543-01
WASI, PRAWASE R01HL34408-21
WASILENKO, WILLIAM J R29CA53085-02
WASKELL, LUCY A R01GM35533-06
WASKIN, HETTY A M01RR00030-30 0513
WASMUND, LOIDE M S06GM08003-21 0009
WASMUTH, JOHN J R01HD18642-08
WASMUTH, JOHN J R01HG00320-03
WASMUTH, JOHN J R01NS25631-04
WASSEF, ADEL A. M01RR00073-29 0275
WASSER, S K Z01RR00089-02
WASSER, SAMUEL K R01MH45863-02
WASSERMAN, DAVID P60DK20593-13 0001
WASSERMAN, DAVID H R01DK42488-02
WASSERMAN, EDWARD A R01MH47313-01
WASSERMAN, FREDERICK S07RR07043-26 0116
WASSERMAN, HARRY H R01GM07874-27
WASSERMAN, HARRY H R37GM13854-22
WASSERMAN, KARLMAN R01HL11907-19
WASSERMAN, MARVIN S07RR07064-24 0211
WASSERMAN, ROBERT H R37DK04652-31
WASSERMAN, STEPHEN U01AI31595-01 0001
WASSERMAN, TODD M01RR00036-31 0981
WASSERMAN, TODD H R13CA54258-01
WASSERSTEIN, ALAN G M01RR00040-31 0409
WASSERSTROM, JOHN A R01HL30724-10
WASSERTHEIL-SMOLLER, SYLVIA R01HL41445-04
WASSERTHEIL-SMOLLER, SYLVIA R03HL46559-01
WASSOM, DONALD L R01AI24355-06
WASSOM, DONALD L R22AI26904-03
WASSON, JOHN H R01HS06420-02
WASSUM, DONALD L P01AI28781-02 0002
WASTERLAIN, CLAUDE G R01NS13515-13
WASZCZAK, B S07RR05830-12 0960
WASZCZAK, BARBARA LEE R01NS23541-05
WATANABE, AUGUST M P01HL06308-31 0039
WATANABE, KEIKO S07RR05864-10 0937
WATANABE, KYOICHI A P30CA08748-26 9013
WATANABE, KYOICHI A R01CA18601-16
WATANABE, KYOICHI A R01CA33907-08A1
WATANABE, KYOICHI A S15CA55937-01
WATANABE, KYOTCHI A P01CA18856-16 0009
WATANABE, M P51RR00168-30 0150
WATANABE, MICHIKO R29HL38172-04
WATCHKO, JON F K08HL02491-02
WATERBORG, JAKOB H S07RR05997-04 0817
WATERHOUSE, BARRY D K04NS01233-05
WATERHOUSE, BARRY D R01DA05117-01A2
WATERMAN, MICHAEL R R01DK28350-11
WATERMAN, MICHAEL R R01GM37942-05
WATERMAN, MICHAEL S R01GM36230-06
WATERS, EVERETT R01MH44935-02
WATERS, ROBERT M R19MH46194-03
WATERS, ROBERT S R01NS25824-02
WATERS, WILLIAM J R01AA08277-02
WATERSTON, ROBERT H R01HG00136-02
WATERSTON, ROBERT H R01HG00375-04
WATERSTON, ROBERT H R37GM23883-15
WATFORD, MALCOLM R01DK37301-03
WATKINS, D I P51RR00168-30 0152
WATKINS, DAVID P30DK43351-01 0001
WATKINS, HALCYON O K14HL01978-04
WATKINS, HALCYON O S06GM08061-17 0019
WATKINS, JEFFREY C R01NS26540-04
WATKINS, MICHAEL J S07RR07103-25 0499
WATKINS, NELLOUISE D S14GM44780-02
WATKINS, PAUL B R01GM38149-06
WATKINS, PAUL B R55ES05770-01
WATKINS, ROBERT A P51RR00164-30 9001
WATKINS, ROBERT A P51RR00164-30 9002
WATKINS, ROBERT A P51RR00164-30 9004
WATKINS, RUTH W S07RR07133-22 0515
WATKINS, SANDRA L M01RR00037-31 0517
WATKINS, SIMON P30CA47904-04 9016
WATLINGTON, CHARLES O M01RR00065-29 0281
WATLINGTON, CHARLES O R01DK35341-07
WATLINGTON, ROY A S06GM08266-04 0001
WATRAS, JAMES M P01HL33026-07 0002
WATSON, BRANT D R01NS23244-06
WATSON, CHARLES S R01DC00250-09
WATSON, CHERYL S R29HD22746-05
WATSON, D Z01CP05238-10
WATSON, D K Z01CP05574-04
WATSON, D K Z01CP05665-01
WATSON, DAVID S07RR05535-29 0537
WATSON, DEENA D R18DA05176-03S1
WATSON, EDNA S S14GM02866-07 0001
WATSON, EILEEN L R01DE05249-12
WATSON, EILEEN L R01DE08295-04
WATSON, ELAINE S07RR05464-29 0378

WATSON, GORDON S07RR05545-29 0572
WATSON, JACK T P41RR00480-23
WATSON, JACK T P41RR00480-23 9001
WATSON, JACK T P41RR00480-23 9003
WATSON, JOHN A R01HL40445-04
WATSON, JOSEPH B P01HD25831-01A1 0001
WATSON, MAXINE S07RR07031-26 0111
WATSON, PETER A R01HL42365-02
WATSON, PHILIP D R01HL24314-12
WATSON, ROBERT E S07RR05374-30 0743
WATSON, RONALD P50AA08037-04 0002
WATSON, RONALD R P50AA08037-04
WATSON, RONALD R R01DA04827-03
WATSON, STANLEY J M01RR00042-31 0287
WATSON, STANLEY J P01MH42251-05 0003
WATSON, STANLEY J P01MH42251-05 0004
WATSON, STANLEY J P30DK34933-06A1 9003
WATSON, STANLEY J, JR P01MH42251-05
WATSON, WINSOR H S07RR07108-19 0411
WATSON, WINSOR H, III R15NS29555-01
WATSON,JACK T P41RR00480-23 9002
WATT, CARL B R01EY05622-07
WATT, DAVID S P50AG05144-08 0008
WATT, DEAN D S07RR05390-30 0666
WATT, GERALD D S15DK44694-01
WATT, WARD B R01GM26758-07S1
WATT, WARD B S07RR07005-26 0345
WATTENBERG, LEE W R01CA50980-02
WATTENMAKER, WILLIAM D R29MH45585-03
WATTERS, JOHN K U01DA06908-02
WATTERSON, D. MARTIN P01CA48799-03 9001
WATTERSON, DANIEL M R01GM30861-10
WATTERSON, MARTIN P30HD28819-01 9002
WATTS, ALAN G R01NS29728-01A1
WATTS, FRANK P30CA21765-14 9014
WATTS, NELSON B M01RR00039-31 0382
WATTS, PARRIS S07RR07053-26 0146
WATTS, RAYMOND G K11HL02601-01
WAUD, WILLIAM S07RR05676-15 0958
WAUGH, RICHARD E P01HL18208-17 9005
WAUGH, RICHARD E P01HL18208-17 0012
WAUGH, RICHARD E R01HL31524-08
WAWER, MARIA J R01AI29314-02
WAWER, MARIA J R01HD28306-02
WAX, JUDY N01CB71085-10
WAX, MARTIN B R01EY06810-07
WAXDAL, MYRON N01AI95010-04
WAXHAM, MELVIN N K04NS01509-01
WAXHAM, MELVIN NEAL R01NS26086-04
WAXMAN, DAVID J P01CA19589-14A1 0030
WAXMAN, DAVID J R01CA49248-01A2
WAXMAN, DAVID J R01DK33765-08
WAY, JAMES L R01ES05139-03
WAY, JEFFREY C R29HD25557-03
WAYBILL, MARY M K08DK02017-01
WAYLAND, BRADFORD B S07RR07083-26 0498
WAYMIRE, JACK C R01NS11061-13
WAYNE STATE UNIV N01MH80012-00
WAYNE, NANCY L R29HD28336-01
WAYNER, MATTHEW J S07RR07217-08
WAYNER, MATTHEW J S15GM47053-01
WAYS, DOUGLAS K R29CA43823-05
WAZER, DAVID M01RR00054-30 0425
WEATHERLY, NORMAN S07RR05449-30 0326
WEATHERSTONE, KATHLE S07RR05373-30 0732
WEAVER, CONNIE M R01AR39560-01A1
WEAVER, CONNIE M R01AR40553-02
WEAVER, DAVID S R01AG09827-01
WEAVER, DAVID T R01CA52694-02
WEAVER, DAVID T R29GM39312-04
WEAVER, DAVID T S07RR05526-29 0088
WEAVER, JAMES C R01GM34077-07A1
WEAVER, ROBERT S07RR07037-26 0377
WEAVER, ROBERT E S07RR07037-26 0367
WEAVER, SHIRLEY A U76PE00474-01
WEAVER, STEVEN G R01GM30140-10
WEAVER, TIMOTHY P50HD20748-06A1 0006
WEAVER, TIMOTHY E R01HL36055-06
WEAVER, W DOUGLAS R01HL38454-04
WEBB, CAROL F S07RR05538-29 0545
WEBB, CAROL FRANCES R55GM46462-01
WEBB, D S Z01BD03013-02
WEBB, D S Z01BD03015-02
WEBB, D S Z01BD03033-01
WEBB, D S Z01BD03034-01
WEBB, JERRY G R01HL42077-03
WEBB, R CLINTON P01HL18575-16A1
WEBB, R CLINTON P01HL18575-16A1 0018
WEBB, SUSAN R R01CA41993-05
WEBB, THOMAS E N01CN05261-01
WEBB, THOMAS E R01CA51756-01A1
WEBB, WATT W P41RR04224-04
WEBB, WATT W P41RR04224-04 9001
WEBB, WATT W P41RR04224-04 9002
WEBB, WATT W P41RR04224-04 9003
WEBB, WATT W P41RR04224-04 9004
WEBB, WATT W P41RR04224-04 9005
WEBB, WATT W P41RR04224-04 9006
WEBB, WATT W P41RR04224-04 9007
WEBB, WATT W P41RR04224-04 9008
WEBB, WATT W P41RR04224-04 9009
WEBBER, BONNIE L R01LM05217-01
WEBBER, LARRY S R01HL38844-05 9001
WEBBER, LARRY S U01HL39906-05
WEBBER, MUTKA S07RR05656-24 0853
WEBBER, RICHARD J K04AR01799-04
WEBER, ANNEMARIE A P01HL15835-19 0001
WEBER, BARBARA L K08CA01511-02
WEBER, BRUCE H S06GM08258-02
WEBER, CHRISTINE A R01CA52679-01A1
WEBER, COLLIN J R01DK39088-01A3
WEBER, DENNIS S07RR05864-10 0936
WEBER, ECKARD R01DA06726-02
WEBER, ECKARD R01MH40303-07A1
WEBER, ECKARD S07RR07238-04 0473
WEBER, FREDERICK L M01RR00080-29 0417
WEBER, GEORGE R35CA42510-06
WEBER, GEORGE S07RR05371-30 0648
WEBER, GEORGE H R43CI00020-01
WEBER, GREGORIO R01GM11223-29
WEBER, JAMES L R01HG00248-04
WEBER, JAMES L S15HL47755-01
WEBER, KARL T R01HL31701-09
WEBER, LEE A R01GM43167-03
WEBER, MICHAEL J P01CA40042-07 9001
WEBER, MICHAEL J P01CA40042-07 0001
WEBER, MICHAEL J R01CA47815-03
WEBER, MICHAEL J R37CA39076-08
WEBER, PAUL A U10EY06831-05
WEBER, PETER C P50DK39249-05 0016
WEBER, PETER C R01AI29961-02
WEBER, STEPHEN G R01GM44842-01A1
WEBER, STEPHEN J. N01HV98108-05
WEBER, WENDELL W R01CA39018-06A2
WEBER, WENDELL W R01GM44965-02
WEBER, WENDELL W S07RR05383-30 0572
WEBSTER-STRATTON, CAROLYN H R01NR01075-07
WEBSTER, CHARLES W P50AG05133-08 0014
WEBSTER, DALE A S07RR07027-26
WEBSTER, DALE A S07RR07027-26 0014
WEBSTER, DENISE S07RR05809-06 0478
WEBSTER, DENISE S07RR05809-06 0476
WEBSTER, DOUGLAS B P01DC00379-05 0002
WEBSTER, DOUGLAS B R01DC00206-08S1
WEBSTER, H F Z01NS01995-19
WEBSTER, JAMES E S06GM08091-20 0031
WEBSTER, KEITH A R29HL44578-02
WEBSTER, ROBERT E R01GM18305-20
WEBSTER, ROBERT G R01AI20591-08
WEBSTER, ROBERT G R01AI29680-02
WEBSTER, ROBERT G R37AI08831-23
WEBSTER, ROBERT O P50HL30572-08 0004
WEBSTER, TERESA P41LM05205-08 9005
WEBSTER, TERESA P41LM05205-08 0002
WEBSTER, WAYNE N01CL92100-04
WECHSLER, STEVEN L R01EY07566-04
WECHSLER, STEVEN L R01EY08697-02
WECKER, DONALD N01CO15722-01
WECKER, LYNN R01MH33443-13
WEDEEN, VAN J P01CA48729-03 0004
WEDEEN, VAN J S07RR07047-26 0141
WEDELL, DOUGLAS H S07RR07160-16 0592
WEDER, ALAN B P01HL18575-16A1 0019
WEDLER, FREDERICK C S07RR07082-26 0317
WEDNER, H JAMES P50AI15322-14 0008
WEDNER, H JAMES U01AI30752-01
WEEKS, BRAD R S07RR05854-11 0922
WEEKS, DANIEL L R29GM40308-04
WEEKS, JANIS S07RR07080-26 0311
WEEKS, JANIS C K04NS01473-01
WEEKS, JANIS C R01NS23208-06
WEEKS, RICHARD N01CO05709-01
WEEKS, RICK N01CO15651-00
WEEKS, RICK N01CO15695-00
WEEMS, L S06GM08215-09 0009
WEESE-MAYER, DEBRA S07RR05477-29 0417
WEESE-MAYER, DEBRA E U01HD28971-01
WEFEL, J S P30DE10126-01
WEFEL, JAMES S R01DE04486-11
WEGIEL, JERZY S07RR05838-12 0274
WEGLICKI, WILLIAM B P01HL38079-05
WEGLICKI, WILLIAM B P01HL38079-05 0001
WEGLICKI, WILLIAM B P01HL38079-05 0002
WEHNER, JEANNE M K02AA00141-01
WEHNER, JEANNE M P50AA03527-14 0017
WEHNER, JEANNE M R01AA07567-02
WEHR, T A Z01MH02424-04
WEHR, T A Z01MH02494-02
WEHRENBERG, WILLIAM B K04DK01874-03
WEHRLI, FELIX W R01AR40671-01A1
WEI, EDWARD P42ES04705-05 0011
WEI, EDWARD T R37DA00091-21
WEI, JEANNE Y K04AG00436-04
WEI, JEANNE Y K12AG00294-07
WEI, JEANNE Y P30AG08812-02 9005
WEI, JEANNE Y P30AG08812-02
WEI, JEANNE Y R01AG07225-03
WEI, JEN Y R01NS28433-02
WEI, LEE-JEN R01AI29131-03
WEI, LEE-JEN R01CA56844-01
WEI, WEI-ZEN R01CA42522-04A1
WEI, WEI-ZEN S07RR05529-29 0526
WEI, WEI-ZEN S15CA55973-01
WEI, YEN R01DE09848-01
WEICHSEL, MORTON A M01RR00425-22S3 0433
WEICHSELBAUM, RALPH P01CA40046-05S2 0001
WEICHSELBAUM, RALPH R R01CA41068-05
WEICHSELBAUM, RALPH R R01CA42596-05
WEICK, JAMES K U10CA04919-32
WEICKMANN, JOACHIM L R44DE09063-02
WEIDANZ, WILLIAM P R01AI12710-16
WEIDEN, PETER J R29MH43635-06
WEIDMAN, MARGARET J S07RR05388-30 0615
WEIDNER, GERDI S07RR07067-26 0226
WEIDNER, NOEL P01HL36110-07 0009
WEIDNER, NOEL U01AI31599-01 0005
WEIDNER, NOEL U01AI31599-01 0006
WEIDNER, NOEL U01AI31599-01 0007
WEIFFENBACH, J M Z01DE00212-14
WEIGEL, NANCY P30HD07495-19 9018
WEIGEL, NANCY L R01HD22061-04A3
WEIGEL, PAUL H R01GM35978-06A1
WEIGENT, DOUGLAS A R01NS24636-04A1
WEIGERT, MARTIN G R37GM20964-18
WEIGHT, F F Z01AA00479-08
WEIGHT, F F Z01AA00480-08
WEIGLE, D. SCOTT P51RR00166-30 0124
WEIGLE, D. SCOTT P51RR00166-30 0125
WEIGLE, DAVID S R01DK38847-05
WEIGLE, KRISTEN A P50AI30603-01 9001
WEIGLE, KRISTIN A P50AI30603-01 0002
WEIGLE, WILLIAM O P01AG01743-12 0005
WEIGLE, WILLIAM O R01AG00783-12
WEIGLE, WILLIAM O R37AI15761-12
WEIHS, KAREN L K20MH00906-01A1
WEIKEL, CYNTHIA S M01RR00035-31 0420
WEIKEL, CYNTHIA S M01RR00722-19 0256
WEIKEL, CYNTHIA S P01AI26512-03 0002
WEIKEL, CYNTHIA S R01DK37075-05A2
WEIL, ANTHONY P60DK20593-13 9004
WEIL, ANTHONY P60DK20593-13 9005
WEIL, DAVID N S07RR05995-04 0052
WEIL, GARY J R22AI22488-07
WEIL, GARY J R22AI25587-03
WEIL, JOHN V P01HL14985-20
WEIL, JOHN V P01HL14985-20 0028
WEIL, JOHN V P01HL14985-20 0016
WEIL, P A P01DK42502-02 0004
WEIL, PETER A R01GM40517-04
WEILER, JOHN M R01AI22350-05
WEILER, KAY B S07RR07035-26 0085
WEILER, MOLLY S S07RR05456-29 0362
WEILER, PHILIP P30AG10129-01 9001
WEILL, HANS P50HL15092-20
WEIN, ALAN J U01DK44998-01
WEINBACH, E C Z01AI00098-35
WEINBAUM, SHELDON R01HL26090-09
WEINBERG, C Z01ES40004-14
WEINBERG, DAVID P01AI23360-07 9001
WEINBERG, GENE B U01CA50118-02
WEINBERG, J. BRICE P50AR39162-05 0002
WEINBERG, JOANNE R01AA07789-04
WEINBERG, JOEL P50DK39255-05 0005
WEINBERG, JOEL M R01DK34275-07
WEINBERG, KENNETH I R29AI25071-02
WEINBERG, RICHARD B R01HL30897-09
WEINBERG, RICHARD J R01NS29879-01
WEINBERG, ROBERT A R13CA55385-01
WEINBERG, ROBERT A R35CA39826-07
WEINBERG, RONA S R01DK41938-03
WEINBERGER, DANIEL A S07RR07113-24 0565
WEINBERGER, JUDAH P01AI26886-04 0005
WEINBERGER, JUDAH Z R01HL42392-03
WEINBERGER, MILES M M01RR00059-30 0707
WEINBERGER, MORRIS S07RR05405-30 0876
WEINBERGER, MYRON R01HL30561-08
WEINBERGER, MYRON H M01RR00750-19 0106
WEINBERGER, MYRON H M01RR00750-19 0273
WEINBERGER, OFRA R01HL43528-03
WEINBERGER, STEVEN P50HL19170-15 0012
WEINER, ALAN M R01GM31073-10
WEINER, ALAN M R01GM41624-03
WEINER, BONNIE U01HL38556-05
WEINER, CARL P R01HD24494-04
WEINER, DAVID B R01AI32788-01
WEINER, DAVID B R29AI28767-03
WEINER, DEBRA S07RR05405-30 0877
WEINER, DORA B R01LM04901-03
WEINER, GEORGE S07RR05372-30 0684
WEINER, GEORGE J R55CA55178-01
WEINER, HENRY K05AA00028-13
WEINER, HENRY P50AA07611-04 0001
WEINER, HENRY R03AA08532-02
WEINER, HENRY R37AA05812-08
WEINER, HOWARD L M01RR02635-07 0171
WEINER, HOWARD L M01RR02635-07 0253
WEINER, HOWARD L N01NS02397-02
WEINER, HOWARD L R01NS23132-07
WEINER, HOWARD L R01NS29352-01A1
WEINER, LESLIE B P01NS18146-10 0005
WEINER, LESLIE P K12AG00521-01
WEINER, LESLIE P P01NS18146-10
WEINER, LESLIE P P01NS18146-10 9001
WEINER, LESLIE P P01NS26991-02
WEINER, LOUIS M R01CA50633-03
WEINER, LOUIS M U01CA51880-02 0003

WEINER, MARC M01RR01346-10 0199
WEINER, MICHAEL W R01DK33293-08
WEINER, MYRON F M01RR00633-19 0371
WEINER, MYRON F P50AG08013-04 9001
WEINER, MYRON R M01RR00633-19 0336
WEINER, NORMAN P50AA03527-14 0020
WEINER, NORMAN P50NS09199-21 0006
WEINER, RICHARD D P50MH40159-08 0003
WEINER, RICHARD D R37MH30723-14
WEINER, RICHARD I R01DK40945-03
WEINER, RICHARD I R01HD08924-16
WEINER, SAUL S07RR06004-04 0041
WEINER, STEPHEN R01DE06954-07
WEINERMAN, S P01CA29502-11A1 0053
WEINERT , TED A R01GM45276-01
WEINERT, CLARANN R01CA46330-03
WEINERT, CLARANN R01NR01852-02
WEINERT, TED A S07RR07002-26 0878
WEINGARTNER, H Z01AG00188-01
WEINGEIST, THOMAS A U10EY06269-07
WEINGEIST, THOMAS A U10EY06843-04
WEINHOLD, KENT J P01CA43447-06 0009
WEINHOLD, KENT J P30AI28662-03 9003
WEINHOLD, KENT J R01AI29852-02
WEINHOLD, PAUL A R01HD02871-21
WEINMAN, STEVEN A R29DK42917-01A1
WEINMANN, GAIL G P01ES03505-07 0006
WEINMANN, ROBERTO S07RR05540-29 0555
WEINRAUB, MARSHA S07RR07115-24 0588
WEINRAUB, MARSHA U10HD25455-03
WEINREB, ROBERT N R01EY05990-07
WEINREB, ROBERT N R01EY06006-04
WEINREB, STEVEN M R01CA34303-09
WEINREB, STEVEN M R01GM32299-13A1
WEINREICH, DANIEL R01NS22069-07
WEINREICH, DANIEL R01NS25598-04
WEINRICH, MICHAEL R01DC00856-02
WEINRICH, SALLY P R01NR02259-02
WEINROTT, MARK R R44MH44952-02
WEINSHANK, RICHARD L R44MH48240-02
WEINSHILBOUM, RICHARD M R01GM28157-11
WEINSHILBOUM, RICHARD M R01GM35720-06
WEINSIER, M01RR00032-31 0280
WEINSIER, ROLAND L M01RR00032-31 0377
WEINSIER, ROLAND L P01CA28103-13 9012
WEINSTEIN, ALAN M R01DK29857-10
WEINSTEIN, BERNARD I P01CA49062-02 0004
WEINSTEIN, GERALD D R01AR27110-11
WEINSTEIN, HAREL K05DA00060-12
WEINSTEIN, HAREL R01DA06620-02
WEINSTEIN, HAREL R01GM41373-03
WEINSTEIN, I BERNARD P01CA21111-15
WEINSTEIN, I BERNARD P01CA21111-15 0004
WEINSTEIN, I BERNARD P01ES05294-02 0003
WEINSTEIN, I BERNARD P30CA13696-19
WEINSTEIN, I BERNARD P50MH43520-04 9006
WEINSTEIN, I BERNARD R37CA26056-12
WEINSTEIN, J N Z01CB08341-13
WEINSTEIN, J N Z01CB08366-08
WEINSTEIN, J N Z01CB08392-03
WEINSTEIN, MAXINE S07RR07136-20 0611
WEINSTEIN, MELVIN P U01AI25914-04S2 0002
WEINSTEIN, MILTON C R01HL46315-01
WEINSTEIN, MILTON C R01HS06258-03
WEINSTEIN, PHILIP R R01NS22022-06A1
WEINSTEIN, ROBERT P60HL15157-20 0024
WEINSTEIN, SIDNEY R44EY05368-02A4
WEINSTEIN, STEVEN P K08DK02057-01
WEINSTOCK, GEORGE M R01GM35247-07
WEINSTOCK, JOEL V R01DK38327-05
WEINSTOCK, MARTIN A R29CA49531-02
WEINTRAUB, B D Z01DK55000-19
WEINTRAUB, B D Z01DK55002-11
WEINTRAUB, B D Z01DK55015-02
WEINTRAUB, HAROLD P01DK31232-10 0004
WEINTRAUB, HAROLD P30CA15704-18 9020
WEINTRAUB, HAROLD M R01GM26176-13
WEINTRAUB, HAROLD M R35CA42506-06
WEINTRAUB, SANDRA M01RR01032-16 0410
WEINTRAUB, SANDRA S07RR05479-29 0445
WEIR, BRUCE S P01GM45344-01
WEIR, BRUCE S P01GM45344-01 0002
WEIR, BRUCE S R01GM32518-08
WEIR, BRYCE K R01NS25946-04
WEIR, ELEANOR C P40RR00393-24 0009
WEIR, GORDON C R01DK35449-08
WEIR, LAWRENCE R29AR40580-01A1
WEIR, LAWRENCE S07RR05587-20 0650
WEIR, MICHAEL S15GM47088-01
WEIR, MICHAEL P R29GM42752-03
WEIS, ALEXANDER N01NS02386-01
WEIS, ARTHUR E S07RR07008-26 0065
WEIS, JOHN H P30AR35907-07 9003
WEIS, JOHN H R01AI24158-04A1
WEIS, JOHN H S07RR05428-30 0185
WEIS, JOHN H S07RR05428-30 0164
WEIS, ROBERT M S07RR07048-26 0660
WEIS, ROBERT M S07RR07048-26 0661
WEISBART, RICHARD H R01CA30280-10
WEISBERG, R Z01HD00066-21
WEISBLAT, DAVID A R29HD23328-05
WEISBLUM, BERNARD R01AI18283-11
WEISBURGER, JOHN H R01CA42381-05
WEISE, FRIEDA O N01LM13503-00
WEISE, WOLFGANG J S07RR05487-29 0694
WEISEL, CLIFFORD S07RR05576-27 0618
WEISEL, JOHN W R01HL30954-07
WEISEL, JOHN W S10RR06522-01
WEISENBERGER, JANET M R01DC00306-08
WEISER, BARBARA U01AI25893-05 0003
WEISER, BARBARA U01AI25993-05 0004
WEISER, MILTON M R01DK25754-10
WEISER, WEISHUI Y R01AI22801-06
WEISFELDT, MYRON N01AG92116-01
WEISFELDT, MYRON L P50HL17655-17
WEISGRABER, KARL H. P01HL41633-03 0002
WEISIGER, RICHARD P30DK26743-11 9011
WEISIGER, RICHARD A R01DK32898-09
WEISMAN, GARY A R01GM36887-04
WEISMAN, MICHAEL H M01RR00827-17 0316
WEISMAN, MICHAEL H M01RR00827-17 0495
WEISMAN, MICHAEL H M01RR00827-17 0496
WEISMAN, MICHAEL H M01RR00827-17 0318
WEISMAN, MICHAEL H M01RR00827-17 0440
WEISMAN, MICHAEL H M01RR00827-17 0425
WEISMAN, MICHAEL H M01RR00827-17 0459
WEISMAN, MICHAEL H M01RR00827-17 0394
WEISMAN, MICHAEL H M01RR00827-17 0384
WEISMAN, MICHAEL H M01RR00827-17 0361
WEISMAN, MICHAEL H M01RR00827-17 0468
WEISMAN, MICHAEL H M01RR00827-17 0478
WEISMANN, DOUGLAS N M01RR00059-30 0697
WEISNER, CONSTANCE P50AA05595-11 0024
WEISNER, CONSTANCE P50AA05595-11 0021
WEISNER, CONSTANCE P50AA05595-11 0022
WEISS, SUSAN P01NS11037-18 0059
WEISS, ALISON A R01AI23695-05
WEISS, ARTHUR R01GM39553-04
WEISS, BAHR S07RR07201-12 0642
WEISS, BENJAMIN R37MH42148-05
WEISS, BERNARD M01RR00042-31 0661
WEISS, BERNARD P30ES01247-17 0082
WEISS, BERNARD R01ES05433-02
WEISS, CAROL D K11AI00979-02
WEISS, DANIEL S07RR05755-18 0228
WEISS, ELLEN R R29GM43582-03
WEISS, ELLEN R S07RR05406-30 0902
WEISS, ELLEN R S07RR05406-30 0891
WEISS, FRIEDBERT R01DA07348-01
WEISS, FRIEDBERT R29AA08164-03
WEISS, G Z01CT00014-25
WEISS, G Z01CT00024-15
WEISS, GEOFFREY R M01RR01346-10 0200
WEISS, GEOFFREY R M01RR01346-10 0201
WEISS, GEOFFREY R U10CA22433-14
WEISS, GERALD K R55NS23262-04A1
WEISS, GERALD K S06GM08139-17 0064
WEISS, GERSON R01HD22338-07
WEISS, HARVEY J R01HL27346-13
WEISS, HARVEY R R01NS25100-03
WEISS, JAMES L R01HL43722-02
WEISS, JAMES N K04HL01890-05
WEISS, JAMES N R01HL36729-06
WEISS, JAMES N R01HL44880-02
WEISS, JAMES W R01HL46951-01
WEISS, JERROLD P R01AI18571-10
WEISS, JOHN H K08AG00495-02
WEISS, KEVIN B R13HS06782-01S1
WEISS, KLAUDIUSZ R R37MH36730-10
WEISS, LAWRENCE S07RR05471-29 0590
WEISS, LAWRENCE M R29CA50341-01A2
WEISS, LEON P R01DK19920-16
WEISS, MARISA C S07RR05415-30 0022
WEISS, MARK P01DC00178-10 0011
WEISS, MARTIN M R25RR07690-01
WEISS, MICHAEL A R01DK40949-03
WEISS, MICHAEL A R01GM45290-01
WEISS, MICHAEL A R01HD26465-02
WEISS, MITCHELL G K01MH00616-05
WEISS, MITCHELL G R03MH47104-01
WEISS, NOEL S R35CA39779-07
WEISS, RAYMOND B U10CA26806-12
WEISS, RICHARD S07RR07009-26 0933
WEISS, RICHARD L R01GM36552-06
WEISS, ROBERT M01RR00059-30 0711
WEISS, ROBERT B P30HG00199-01 0001
WEISS, ROBERT B R01HG00517-01
WEISS, ROBERT M R37DK38311-14
WEISS, ROBERT S R01AG07363-04
WEISS, ROBIN N01OD92119-06
WEISS, ROGER S07RR05484-29 0034
WEISS, ROGER D R29DA05944-03
WEISS, ROGER D U01DA07693-01
WEISS, S R Z01MH02527-02
WEISS, S R Z01MH02528-02
WEISS, S R Z01MH02529-02
WEISS, S R Z01MH02530-02
WEISS, SCOTT N01HR16049-00
WEISS, SCOTT T P50HL19170-15 0014
WEISS, SCOTT T R01HL34645-07
WEISS, STANLEY J R01MH45545-03
WEISS, STEPHEN J R01AI21301-08
WEISS, STEPHEN J R01AI23876-04A1
WEISS, STEPHEN J R01HL28024-10
WEISS, SUSAN R R01AI17418-11
WEISS, THOMAS F P01DC00119-16 0002
WEISS, THOMAS F R01DC00238-08
WEISS, THOMAS F R01DC00473-04
WEISSFELD, JOEL L R01HL47862-01
WEISSLER, JONATHAN M01RR00633-19 0333
WEISSMAN, A Z01CB09291-01
WEISSMAN, A Z01CB09292-01
WEISSMAN, A Z01CB09295-02
WEISSMAN, BERNARD E R01CA44470-03S1
WEISSMAN, BERNARD E S07RR05406-30 0892
WEISSMAN, DAVID N M01RR00997-16 0392
WEISSMAN, DAVID N M01RR00997-16 0351
WEISSMAN, DAVID N R01HL43529-03
WEISSMAN, DAVID N R01HL44071-02
WEISSMAN, IRVING L P01CA49605-03 0004
WEISSMAN, IRVING L R35CA42551-06
WEISSMAN, MICHAEL P50MH43878-03 0024
WEISSMAN, MICHAEL P50MH43878-03 0021
WEISSMAN, MYMA P50MH43878-03 0002
WEISSMAN, MYRNA M R01DA07201-01
WEISSMAN, MYRNA M R37MH28274-16
WEISSMAN, SAMUEL M P30CA16359-17 9019
WEISSMAN, SHERMAN M P01CA16038-18
WEISSMAN, SHERMAN M P30CA16359-17 9004
WEISSMAN, SHERMAN M P30DK34989-08 0010
WEISSMAN, SHERMAN M R35CA42556-06
WEISSMANN, CHARLES P01NS22786-07 0002
WEISSMANN, GERALD R01HL19721-16
WEISSMANN, GERALD R37AR11949-24
WEISZ, DONALD J R01MH42800-03
WEISZ, JOHN R R01MH38240-08
WEISZ, JOHN R R01MH49522-01
WEITH, H LEE P30AI27713-04 9002
WEITH, H LEE R01LM05118-03
WEITLAUF, HARRY S07RR05773-17 0372
WEITLAUF, HARRY M R01HD17437-10
WEITZ, CHARLES J K11EY00289-04
WEITZMAN, SIGMUND A R01CA47549-03
WEKSLER, BABETTE B P50HL18828-16 0005
WEKSLER, BABETTE B R01HL35724-07
WEKSLER, MARC E M01RR00047-31 0396
WEKSLER, MARC E R37AG08707-02
WEKSLER, MARC E S07RR05396-30 0761
WEKSTEIN, DAVID R P50AG05144-08 9003
WELCH, FINIS R R01HD21713-03A2
WELCH, KENNETH P01NS23393-06 0003
WELCH, KENNETH M P01NS23393-06
WELCH, KENNETH M R13NS29978-01
WELCH, MICHAEL J P01HL13851-29 0001
WELCH, MICHAEL J P01NS06833-25 9003
WELCH, MICHAEL J R01CA48286-03
WELCH, NOREEN P30HD04024-23 9006
WELCH, RODNEY A R01AI20323-09
WELCH, SANDRA P P50DA05274-04 0011
WELCH, SANDRA P R29DA06031-02
WELCH, STEVEN C S07RR07147-19 0655
WELCH, WILLIAM J R01GM33551-09
WELDER, ALLISON A R29DA05699-03
WELGUS, HOWARD G P01HL29594-09 0006
WELGUS, HOWARD G R01AR35805-08
WELKOWITZ, JOAN P50MH35976-10 9007
WELLE, STEPHEN P60AG10463-01 0003
WELLE, STEPHEN L R01AG09833-01
WELLEMS, T E Z01AI00483-06
WELLER, ELIZABETH B R01MH44315-03
WELLER, ELIZABETH B R01MH45534-01A1
WELLER, PETER F R01AI20241-08
WELLER, PETER F R01AI22571-06A1
WELLER, ROSALYN E R29EY07147-05
WELLER, SANDRA K R01AI21747-07
WELLMAN, HENRY M R01HD22149-05
WELLMAN, SUSAN E S07RR05386-30 0598
WELLNER, DANIEL S07RR05396-30 0734
WELLS-PARKER, ELISABETH N R01AA07796-03
WELLS-PARKER, ELIZAB S07RR07215-05 0452
WELLS, ALVIN F S07RR07121-13 0473
WELLS, CAROL L R01AI23484-06
WELLS, DAN E R55HG00172-01A1
WELLS, DAN E S07RR07147-19 0656
WELLS, ELIZABETH A R01DA07047-02
WELLS, EUGENE N01LM93526-03
WELLS, H BRADLEY U01HL40232-05
WELLS, INA G N01LM13518-00
WELLS, INA G N01LM83525-04
WELLS, JACK N R01GM21220-15
WELLS, JACK N R01HL19325-15
WELLS, JAMES W P01HL37412-04 0006
WELLS, JOHN R P30CA16042-17 9004
WELLS, JOSEPH R01NS23266-05
WELLS, K E S07RR05710-21 0031
WELLS, KAREN C R01DA07203-01
WELLS, KENNETH R01HS06802-01
WELLS, KENNETH R01MH46370-02
WELLS, KENNETH R01MH48144-01A1
WELLS, KENNETH B K12MH00990-01
WELLS, KENNETH B R01MH42229-03S2A1
WELLS, M Z01BF04001-06
WELLS, MICHAEL A R01AI29434-02
WELLS, MICHAEL A R01HL39116-05
WELLS, NORMA P30DE09743-02 0016
WELLS, NORMA S07RR05346-30 0327

WELLS, ROBERT D R01GM30822-10
WELLS, ROBERT J U10CA26126-13
WELLS, SAMUEL A M01RR00036-31 1029
WELLS, THELMA P60AG10463-01 0001
WELLS, THELMA J R01NR01917-04A1
WELLS, THELMA J S07RR05952-06 0742
WELLS, WILLIAM W R01CA51972-02
WELLSTEIN, ANTON U01CA51908-02 0004
WELLY, DEVIN M01RR00065-29 0331
WELSCH, CLIFFORD W R01CA37613-07
WELSCH, CLIFFORD W R01CA42876-04A2
WELSH, C J Z01CN00158-01
WELSH, C JANE R01NS29133-01A1
WELSH, FRANK A R01NS29331-01
WELSH, JANE C S07RR05854-11 0916
WELSH, MARCIA G R01HD24717-03
WELSH, MICHAEL P50HL42385-04 9001
WELSH, MICHAEL P50HL42385-04 0002
WELSH, MICHAEL P50HL42385-04 0001
WELSH, MICHAEL J P30CA46592-04 9009
WELSH, MICHAEL J P30HD18258-08 9008
WELSH, MICHAEL J P50HL42385-04
WELSH, MICHAEL J R01HD17121-07
WELSH, MICHAEL J R01HL29851-09
WELSH, RAYMOND M R01CA34461-09
WELSH, RAYMOND M, JR R01AI17672-12
WELSH, RAYMOND M, JR R01AR35506-06
WELSHONS, WADE V R29CA50354-02
WELSHONS, WADE V S07RR05949-07 0735
WELT, CAROL S07RR05393-30
WELT, CAROL S15AA09253-01
WELT, CAROL S15GM47097-01
WELTE, JOHN W R01AA08157-01A2
WELTE, JOHN W S07RR05938-07 0314
WELTI, R S07RR07036-26 0105
WELTMAN, ARTHUR L R01DK38930-05
WELTY, FRANCINE K K08HL02626-01
WELTY, THOMAS K R01CA49522-03
WELTY, THOMAS K U01HL41652-04
WEMMER, DAVID E P41RR01237-09
WEMMER, DAVID E R01GM43129-02
WEN, PATRICK Y K11CA01492-02
WENDER, PAUL A R01CA31841-11
WENDER, PAUL A R01CA31845-11
WENDER, PAUL H R01MH41935-03
WENDT, STANLEY S07RR05677-23 0972
WENGER, DAVID A R01DK38795-06
WENGER, GALEN R R01DA05815-03
WENK, GARY L P01HD24448-04 0004
WENK, MARTIN L N01ES05303-02
WENK, MARTIN L N01ES15319-00
WENNBERG, JOHN E P01HS06336-03
WENNBERG, JOHN E R18HS05745-04
WENNBERG, RICHARD P R01HD25241-02
WENNER, DENNIS R18MH49382-01
WENSEL, THEODORE G R01EY07981-03
WENSINK, PIETER C R01GM21626-17
WENSINK, PIETER C R01GM46237-01
WENSTRUP, JEFFREY J R29DC00937-01
WENSTRUP, JEFFREY J S07RR05806-13 0909
WENSTRUP, RICHARD J R01AR40586-01A1
WENTHOLD, R J Z01DC00003-03
WENTOWSKI, GLORIA J R24AA08671-02
WENZEL, SALLY S07RR05842-12 0286
WENZEL, SALLY E K08HL02254-02
WERB, ZENA P01HD26732-01A1 0003
WERB, ZENA R01HD23539-04
WERBER, ANDREW H R03AA08554-02
WERBER, ANDREW H S07RR05394-30 0722
WERBER, ANDREW H S07RR05394-30 0711
WERBLIN, FRANK S R01EY00561-22
WERDEGAR, DAVID R18DA06979-02
WERKMEISTER, JAMES R K11DE00321-01
WERLIN, STEVE M01RR00058-30 0257
WERLING, LINDA S07RR05359-30 0522
WERLING, LINDA L R29DA06667-01A1
WERNER, CAROL M S07RR07092-26 0542
WERNER, JOHN S R01AG04058-07
WERNER, LYNNE A R01DC00396-06
WERNER, LYNNE A R13DC01069-01
WERNER, RUDOLF P30CA14395-18A1 9018
WERNER, RUDOLF K R01GM40583-02
WERNZ, JAMES M01RR00096-30A1 0318
WERREN, JOHN H R01HD24310-02
WERSHIL, BARRY P01DK33506-08 0009
WERTZ, DOROTHY C N01HD13136-00
WERTZ, GAIL W R01AI20181-10
WERTZ, GAIL W R37AI12464-16
WESDEMIOTIS, CHRYS R15GM44341-01A1
WESS, J Z01NS02800-03
WESSEL, GARY M R29HD28152-01
WESSELS, MICHAEL R R01AI28040-02
WESSELS, MICHAEL R R01AI29952-01A1
WESSENDORF, MARTIN W R01DA05466-04
WESSINGER, WILLIAM D R01DA04278-04A2
WESSLER, SUSAN R R01GM32528-09
WESSLING-RESNICK, M S07RR05446-30 0267
WESSON, DONALD R R01DA06038-02
WEST, A BRIAN S07RR05358-30 0481
WEST, DAVID B R29DK44446-01
WEST, DEE N01CN05224-07
WEST, DEE W S15CA56031-01
WEST, FREDERICK R29GM44720-01A1
WEST, FREDERICK B S07RR07092-26 0534
WEST, HELEN L P50AG08013-04 9004
WEST, JAMES B R44HL44822-02
WEST, JAMES R R01AA07313-05
WEST, JAMES R R01DA07364-01
WEST, JAMES R R37AA05523-10
WEST, JOHN B P01HL17731-17 0001
WEST, MARK O R01DA06886-01
WEST, MARK O R29DA04551-05
WEST, MARK O S07RR07058-26 0185
WEST, MICHAEL P30CA13330-20 9003
WEST, MICHAEL A R29GM44764-02
WEST, ROBERT W, JR R55GM39052-04
WEST, S Z01AG00627-02
WEST, SHEILA K R01EY08776-02
WEST, SUZANNE L R03HS06906-01
WESTAWAY, DAVID A R35AG08967-02 0003
WESTBROOK, CAROL A R03CA53267-01
WESTBROOK, CAROL A R29CA44700-05
WESTBROOK, EDWIN M P41RR06017-02
WESTBROOK, EDWIN M R01AI28535-03
WESTBROOK, EDWIN M R01GM44292-01
WESTBROOK, GARY L R01MH46613-02
WESTBROOK, GARY L R29NS26494-04
WESTBURY, JOHN R R01DC00820-02
WESTCOTT, JAY Y R29HL44122-02
WESTENSKOW, DWAYNE S03RR03559-01
WESTENSKOW, DWAYNE R R43NS29311-02
WESTENSKOW, DWAYNE R R44GM41558-02A1
WESTERFIELD, MONTE P01HD22486-05 9004
WESTERFIELD, MONTE P01HD22486-05 0002
WESTERFIELD, MONTE R01NS21132-07
WESTERFIELD, MONTE S03RR03138-06
WESTERINK, MARIA ANNA JULIA R29AI26279-03
WESTERMAN, GARY H S07RR05390-30 0652
WESTERMARK, BENGT P01CA25874-12 0014
WESTFALL, DAVID P R01DK44817-01
WESTFALL, DAVID P R01HL38126-05
WESTFALL, THOMAS C R01DA02668-12
WESTFALL, THOMAS C R01HL35202-05
WESTFALL, THOMAS C S15DA07793-01
WESTHEAD, E W S07RR07048-26 0662
WESTHEAD, EDWARD W R01NS26606-03
WESTHEAD, EDWARD W S15NS30128-01
WESTHEIMER, GERALD R37EY00220-30
WESTHOFF, CAROLYN L R01CA50658-01A2
WESTIN, ELIZABETH S07RR05998-04 0032
WESTIN, ERIC P30CA16059-15 9013
WESTLER, WILLIAM P41RR02301-07 0006
WESTLEY, JOHN L R01GM30971-07
WESTLUND, KARIN N K04NS01445-02
WESTLUND, KARIN N P01NS11255-17 9004
WESTLUND, KARIN N R01NS28064-01A2
WESTLUND, KARIN N. P01NS11255-17 0020
WESTNEAT, DAVID F S07RR07114-23 0451
WESTOFF, CHARLES F N01HD72901-07
WESTOFF, CHARLES F P30HD08008-15S3
WESTON, A Z01CP05435-07
WESTON, A Z01CP05480-06
WESTON, JAMES A P01HD22486-05
WESTON, JAMES A R01DE04316-14A2
WESTON, JAMES A R01NS29438-01
WESTON, SUE S07RR05346-30 0312
WESTON, WILLIAM L R01AI16637-11
WESTOVER CONSULTANTS, INC N01DA02208-00
WESTPHAL, H Z01HD00071-19
WESTRUM, LESNICK P30HD02274-24 9006
WESTRUM, LESNICK E P50AG05136-08 0014
WESTRUM, LESNICK E R01DE04942-11
WESTRUM, LESNICK E R01NS09678-19
WETHERS, DORIS N01HB97067-03
WETHERS, DORIS L N01HB77042-06
WETMUR, JAMES R01ES05046-03
WETMUR, JAMES G R01HG00446-01
WETSEL, RICK A K04AI00919-03
WETSEL, RICK A R55AI25011-04A1
WETSEL, W C Z01ES90054-04
WETTERHAHN, KAREN E R01CA34869-09
WETTERHAHN, KAREN E R01CA45735-04A1
WETTERHAHN, KAREN E S07RR07056-18
WETTSTEIN, FELIX O R01CA50339-03
WETTSTEIN, FELIX O R37CA18151-16
WETTSTEIN, JOSEPH G P51RR00168-30 0128
WETTSTEIN, JOSEPH G P51RR00168-30 0129
WETTSTEIN, JOSEPH G P51RR00168-30 0130
WETTSTEIN, JOSEPH G P51RR00168-30 0131
WETTSTEIN, JOSEPH G P51RR00168-30 0132
WETTSTEIN, PETER J R01AI16052-16
WETTSTEIN, PETER J R01GM41260-05
WETTSTEIN, PETER J S07RR06017-04 0044
WEWERS, MARK D R29HL40871-03
WEWERS, MARY E M01RR00034-31 0427
WEWERS, MARY ELLEN M01RR00034-31 0392
WEWERS, MARY ELLEN S07RR05944-04 0975
WEXLER, HARRY S07RR05859-09 0930
WEXLER, HARRY K P50DA07700-01 0003
WEXLER, ISAIAH D K11HD00878-03
WEXLER, NANCY S R01NS22031-07
WEYAND, ERIC S07RR05909-08 0955
WEYAND, ERIC H R29CA49826-03
WEYAND, ERIC H S15ES05844-01
WEYAND, THEODORE G R01EY06818-05
WEYANT, R S Z01RR00086-02
WHALEN, DOUGLAS H R01DC00825-01A1
WHALEN, L RAY R01NS28510-03
WHALEN, LAWRENCE R S07RR05458-29 0844
WHALEN, ROBERT L R44HL37879-03
WHANG-PENG, J Z01CM06119-22
WHANGER, PHILIP D R01DK38306-19A1
WHANGER, PHILIP D S07RR07079-26 0279
WHATLEY, RALPH E R29HL43689-01A2
WHATLEY, RALPH E S07RR05428-30 0188
WHEAT, JOSEPH M01RR00750-19 0298
WHEAT, JOSEPH M01RR00750-19 0301
WHEAT, JOSEPH M01RR00750-19 0289
WHEAT, L JOSEPH M01RR00750-19 0278
WHEAT, LAWRENCE J U01AI25859-05 0003
WHEATLEY, MARGARET A P01CA52823-02 0006
WHEELER, ARTHUR P S07RR05424-30 0118
WHEELER, BRUCE C R03RR06870-01
WHEELER, BRUCE C S07RR07030-26 0418
WHEELER, COSETTE M R01AI32917-01
WHEELER, COZETTE M S07RR05583-27 0644
WHEELER, DARRELL D R01DA05919-02
WHEELER, DAVID M R29GM39568-04
WHEELER, DESMOND M S S07RR07055-26 0179
WHEELER, DESMOND MS S07RR07055-26 0182
WHEELER, DESMOND MS S07RR07055-26 0185
WHEELER, DIANA ESTHER R29AI27403-03
WHEELER, FRANCES C N01CN15382-00
WHEELER, KENNETH T, JR R01CA45156-05
WHEELER, MATTHEW B S07RR07030-26 0419
WHEELER, NICHOLAS C R01CA55150-01
WHEELER, RICHARD H P30CA13148-20 9021
WHEELER, T S07RR05728-20 0201
WHEELESS, LEON L R01CA33148-10
WHEELESS, LEON L R01HL45998-01
WHEELOCK, MARGARET J R29CA44464-06
WHELAN, WILLIAM J R01DK37500-04A1
WHELAN, WILLIAM J S07RR05363-30 0837
WHELCHEL, JOHN D M01RR00039-31 0422
WHELESS, JAMES M01RR02558-07 0067
WHELTON, PAUL K M01RR00722-19 0259
WHELTON, PAUL K M01RR00722-19 0257
WHELTON, PAUL K M01RR00722-19 0258
WHELTON, PAUL K M01RR00722-19 0239
WHELTON, PAUL K M01RR00722-19 0240
WHELTON, PAUL K M01RR00722-19 0241
WHELTON, PAUL K U01HL37924-06
WHELTON, PAUL K. M01RR00722-19 0175
WHIKEHART, DAVID R R01EY02949-13
WHIKEHART, DAVID R S07RR05807-13 0466
WHIKEHART, DAVID R S07RR05807-13 0467
WHIPP, BRIAN S07RR05354-30 0419
WHIPPLE, BEVERLY S07RR07059-26 0836
WHISENNAND, HARTWELL P01DK44080-01 9002
WHISNANT, CAROL C N01ES15317-00
WHISNANT, JACK P P50NS06663-25
WHISNANT, JACK P P50NS06663-25 0055
WHISNANT, JACK P P50NS06663-25 0056
WHISNANT, JACK P P50NS06663-25 0057
WHISNANT, JACK P P50NS06663-25 0058
WHISNANT, JACK P P50NS06663-25 9001
WHITACRE, CAROLINE C P01MH44660-04 0004
WHITACRE, CAROLINE C R01NS23561-04A1
WHITACRE, CAROLINE C U01AI25924-05 9001
WHITAKER, AGNES H R01MH45834-01A1
WHITAKER, JOHN N M01RR00032-31 0229
WHITAKER, JOHN N P01NS29719-01
WHITAKER, JOHN N P01NS29719-01 0003
WHITAKER, JOHN N R01NS23240-07
WHITALL, JILL S07RR07098-26 0343
WHITCOMB, RANDALL M01RR01066-14 0015
WHITCOMB, RANDALL W U54HD29164-01 0003
WHITCUP, S M Z01EY00268-01
WHITCUP, S M Z01EY00269-01
WHITCUP, S M Z01EY00270-01
WHITE S07RR05380-30 0886
WHITE , BRUCE A R01DK43064-02
WHITE , ALICE D S07RR05450-30 0329
WHITE, B J Z01DK25064-05
WHITE, CARL S07RR05842-12 0290
WHITE, CARL W R55HL39185-04A2
WHITE, CATHERINE A R15AI31214-01
WHITE, CATHERINE A S07RR07147-19 0657
WHITE, CATHERINE M S07RR05425-30 0774
WHITE, CATHY M01RR00188-27 0329
WHITE, CHARLES L P50AG08013-04 9002
WHITE, CHRISTOPHER B S07RR05983-05 0364
WHITE, DAVID C S07RR07088-24 0354
WHITE, EDWARD L R01NS20149-08
WHITE, EILEEN R01CA53370-01
WHITE, EILEEN S07RR07058-26 0186
WHITE, EMILY P01CA34847-09 0012
WHITE, EMILY P01CA34847-09 9003
WHITE, EMILY R29CA44790-05
WHITE, FRANCIS J R01DA04093-07
WHITE, FRANCIS J R01MH40832-06
WHITE, GARY L G20RR07089-01
WHITE, GILBERT C P50HL26309-11 0004
WHITE, H STEVE R01NS22200-06
WHITE, H STEVE S15HL47746-01
WHITE, HAROLD B S07RR07016-18 0347

WHITE, HAROLD B S07RR07016-18 0348
WHITE, HILLARY D R29CA45049-05
WHITE, HOWARD D R01HL41776-03
WHITE, J EMILY S07RR05714-21 0127
WHITE, JACQUELYN W R01MH45083-02
WHITE, JAMES D R01AI10964-18
WHITE, JAMES D R01ES03334-05
WHITE, JAMES G P01GM22167-16 0005
WHITE, JAMES G R37HL11880-23
WHITE, JANE H S07RR07123-22 0600
WHITE, JEFFREY D K02MH00801-03
WHITE, JEFFREY D R01MH42074-04A1
WHITE, JOEL M P01DE09859-01 0005
WHITE, JOHN N01LM13510-00
WHITE, JOHN S07RR05377-30 0770
WHITE, JOHN R S07RR05686-11 0976
WHITE, JON S07RR05359-30 0523
WHITE, JUDITH M R01AI22470-05
WHITE, KALPANA P P01GM33205-08 0003
WHITE, KALPANA P R01NS23510-06
WHITE, KALPANA P R01NS29826-01
WHITE, KEVIN S07RR05300-30 0206
WHITE, L R Z01AG07040-02
WHITE, MAURICE A R01HL42304-03
WHITE, MICHAEL J P30HD28251-01 9002
WHITE, MICHAEL M R01NS23885-06
WHITE, MICHAEL W R01GM42791-03
WHITE, MORRIS F P30DK36836-05 0007
WHITE, MORRIS F R01DK43808-01
WHITE, MORRIS F R55DK38712-04A1
WHITE, NEIL H M01RR00042-31 0583
WHITE, NEIL H M01RR00042-31 0495
WHITE, PERRIN R01DK37867-06
WHITE, PERRIN C R01DK42169-02
WHITE, PERRIN C S07RR05396-30 0778
WHITE, R ALLEN R01CA11430-25 0068
WHITE, RAYMOND P30HG00199-01 0003
WHITE, RAYMOND L P30CA42014-06 9002
WHITE, RAYMOND L P30CA42014-06 9003
WHITE, RAYMOND L R01HG00367-04
WHITE, RICHARD P S07RR05423-30 0062
WHITE, ROBERT M01RR00125-28 0775
WHITE, ROBERT I M01RR00125-28 0754
WHITE, ROBERT L R29GM40196-04
WHITE, ROBERTA F R01OH02767-01A1
WHITE, ROY L R01HL42074-01A3
WHITE, ROY L S07RR05417-30 0816
WHITE, SCOTT C S07RR07066-26 0260
WHITE, STEPHEN W R01GM44973-02
WHITE, STEVEN R K08HL02484-02
WHITE, SUSAN R S07RR05465-29 0382
WHITE, TIMOTHY P01DE07687-09A1 0003
WHITEHEAD, MARK C R29DC00452-05
WHITEHEAD, VICTOR M U10CA33587-09
WHITEHEAD, VICTOR M U10CA33587-09 0036
WHITEHEAD, VICTOR M U10CA33587-09 0001
WHITEHEAD, VICTOR M U10CA33587-09 0002
WHITEHEAD, VICTOR M U10CA33587-09 0003
WHITEHEAD, VICTOR M U10CA33587-09 0004
WHITEHEAD, VICTOR M U10CA33587-09 0005
WHITEHEAD, VICTOR M U10CA33587-09 0006
WHITEHEAD, VICTOR M U10CA33587-09 0007
WHITEHEAD, VICTOR M U10CA33587-09 0008
WHITEHEAD, VICTOR M U10CA33587-09 0009
WHITEHEAD, VICTOR M U10CA33587-09 0010
WHITEHEAD, VICTOR M U10CA33587-09 0011
WHITEHEAD, VICTOR M U10CA33587-09 0012
WHITEHEAD, VICTOR M U10CA33587-09 0013
WHITEHEAD, VICTOR M U10CA33587-09 0014
WHITEHEAD, VICTOR M U10CA33587-09 0015
WHITEHEAD, VICTOR M U10CA33587-09 0037
WHITEHEAD, VICTOR M U10CA33587-09 0016
WHITEHEAD, VICTOR M U10CA33587-09 0017
WHITEHEAD, VICTOR M U10CA33587-09 0018
WHITEHEAD, VICTOR M U10CA33587-09 0019
WHITEHEAD, VICTOR M U10CA33587-09 0020
WHITEHEAD, VICTOR M U10CA33587-09 0021
WHITEHEAD, VICTOR M U10CA33587-09 0022
WHITEHEAD, VICTOR M U10CA33587-09 0023
WHITEHEAD, VICTOR M U10CA33587-09 0024
WHITEHEAD, VICTOR M U10CA33587-09 0025
WHITEHEAD, VICTOR M U10CA33587-09 0026
WHITEHEAD, VICTOR M U10CA33587-09 0027
WHITEHEAD, VICTOR M U10CA33587-09 0028
WHITEHEAD, VICTOR M U10CA33587-09 0029
WHITEHEAD, VICTOR M U10CA33587-09 0030
WHITEHEAD, VICTOR M U10CA33587-09 0031
WHITEHEAD, VICTOR M U10CA33587-09 0032
WHITEHEAD, VICTOR M U10CA33587-09 0033
WHITEHEAD, VICTOR M U10CA33587-09 0038
WHITEHEAD, VICTOR M U10CA33587-09 0039
WHITEHEAD, VICTOR M U10CA33587-09 0040
WHITEHEAD, VICTOR M U10CA33587-09 0041
WHITEHEAD, VICTOR M U10CA33587-09 0042
WHITEHEAD, VICTOR M U10CA33587-09 0043
WHITEHEAD, VICTOR M U10CA33587-09 0044
WHITEHEAD, VICTOR M U10CA33587-09 0045
WHITEHEAD, VICTOR M U10CA33587-09 0046
WHITEHEAD, VICTOR M U10CA33587-09 0047
WHITEHEAD, VICTOR M U10CA33587-09 0048
WHITEHEAD, VICTOR M U10CA33587-09 0049
WHITEHEAD, VICTOR M U10CA33587-09 0050
WHITEHEAD, VICTOR M U10CA33587-09 0051
WHITEHEAD, VICTOR M U10CA33587-09 0052
WHITEHEAD, VICTOR M U10CA33587-09 0053
WHITEHEAD, VICTOR M U10CA33587-09 0054
WHITEHEAD, VICTOR M U10CA33587-09 0055
WHITEHEAD, VICTOR M U10CA33587-09 0034
WHITEHEAD, VICTOR M U10CA33587-09 0056
WHITEHEAD, VICTOR M U10CA33587-09 0057
WHITEHEAD, VICTOR M U10CA33587-09 0058
WHITEHEAD, VICTOR M U10CA33587-09 0035
WHITEHEAD, VICTOR M U10CA33587-09 0059
WHITEHEAD, VICTOR M U10CA33587-09 0060
WHITEHEAD, WILLIAM E K05MH00133-14
WHITEHEAD, WILLIAM E M01RR02719-06 0135
WHITEHEAD, WILLIAM E M01RR02719-06 0139
WHITEHEAD, WILLIAM E M01RR02719-06 0140
WHITEHEAD, WILLIAM E M01RR02719-06 0021
WHITEHEAD, WILLIAM E P01AG04402-09 0008
WHITEHOUSE, CRAIG M R44GM41565-03
WHITEHOUSE, FRED W U01DK30636-09
WHITEHOUSE, PETER J P50AG08012-04 9001
WHITEHOUSE, PETER J P50AG08012-04
WHITEHOUSE, WAYNE G. P01MH44193-03 9004
WHITELEY, JOHN M R01CA11778-22
WHITELEY, JOHN M R01GM45727-01
WHITELY, RICHARD J M01RR00032-31 0303
WHITELY, RICHARD J M01RR00032-31 0292
WHITELY, RICHARD J P01AI24009-05 0001
WHITESIDE, THERESA L. P30CA47904-04 9006
WHITESIDE, THERESA N01CN15393-01
WHITESIDE, THERESA L P01CA47445-03 0002
WHITESIDE, THERESA L P01CA47445-03 0003
WHITESIDES, GEORGE M P01GM39589-05 0001
WHITESIDES, GEORGE M R37GM30367-10
WHITFIELD, CAROL S07RR05680-23 0919
WHITFIELD, G KERR R29DK40372-03
WHITFIELD, G KERR S07RR05675-23 0938
WHITFORD, GARY M R01DE06429-08
WHITIEY, RICHARD D N01AI15113-00
WHITING, JAMES S R01HL42997-02
WHITLEY, CHESTER B R01DK39891-04
WHITLEY, R J M01RR00032-31 0230
WHITLEY, RICHARD J M01RR00032-31 0277
WHITLEY, RICHARD J M01RR00032-31 0363
WHITLEY, RICHARD J M01RR00032-31 0314
WHITLEY, RICHARD J M01RR00032-31 0318
WHITLEY, RICHARD J M01RR00032-31 0319
WHITLEY, RICHARD J M01RR00032-31 0310
WHITLEY, RICHARD J M01RR00032-31 0353
WHITLEY, RICHARD J M01RR00032-31 0354
WHITLEY, RICHARD J M01RR00032-31 0351
WHITLEY, RICHARD J M01RR00032-31 0337
WHITLEY, RICHARD J M01RR00032-31 0338
WHITLEY, RICHARD J M01RR00032-31 0339
WHITLEY, RICHARD J P30AI27767-04 9002
WHITLEY, RICHARD J R13AI31040-01
WHITLEY, RICHARD J U01AI25784-05
WHITLOCK, JAMES P, JR R01ES03719-07
WHITLOCK, JAMES P, JR R35CA53887-01
WHITLON, DONNA S R29DC00653-02
WHITLOW, JESSE W, JR R25AD00033-01
WHITLOW, PATRICK U01HL38518-05
WHITMAN, CHRISTIAN P R29GM41239-03
WHITMAN, R DOUGLAS S07RR07051-26 0738
WHITMIRE, DAVID R R29AA08258-03
WHITNEY, GLAYDE D R01DC00150-11
WHITNEY, J BARRY P01HL41544-04 0005
WHITNEY, PAUL M R03MH46400-01A1
WHITSEL, BARRY L R01MH48654-01
WHITSELL, JEFFREY A P30HD28827-01 9001
WHITSELL, RICHARD R S07RR05424-30 0092
WHITSETT, JEFFREY P01HL41496-03 0004
WHITSETT, JEFFREY A P01HD11725-13 0006
WHITSETT, JEFFREY A P50HD20748-06A1 9003
WHITSETT, JEFFREY A R01HL28623-10
WHITSETT, JEFFREY A R01HL38859-05
WHITSON, S WILLIAM R15DE09872-01
WHITT, J KENNETH M01RR00046-31 0416
WHITT, J KENNETH M01RR00046-31 0401
WHITT, J KENNETH P01NS26680-04A1 0002
WHITTAKER, J RICHARD R01HD21823-06
WHITTAKER, J RICHARD S07RR05547-23 0076
WHITTAKER, J RICHARD S07RR05547-23 0072
WHITTAKER, JAMES W R01GM42680-03
WHITTAKER, JONATHAN R01DK42171-02
WHITTAM, THOMAS S K04AI00964-02
WHITTAM, THOMAS S R22AI24566-05
WHITTEMORE, ALICE S R35CA47448-03
WHITTEMORE, ANTHONY S07RR05950-07 0980
WHITTEMORE, RUTH M01RR06022-02 0779
WHITTEMORE, RUTH M01RR06022-02 0755
WHITTEMORE, SCOTT R R01NS26887-03
WHITTEN, CHARLES F P60HL16008-19
WHITTEN, CHARLES F P60HL16008-19 0011
WHITTEN, CHARLES F S03RR03331-09
WHITTEN, CHARLES W S07RR05426-30 0150
WHITTEN, DAVID G R01CA48961-03
WHITTEN, KIM N01AI05081-05
WHITTINGHAM, TIM S P01HL25830-11A1 0013
WHITTINGTON, WILLIAM L P01AI19554-08S1 0006
WHITTLE, BARRY P50MH43878-03 0040
WHITTON, J LINDSAY P01AG04342-09 0007
WHITTON, J LINDSAY R01AI27028-03
WHITTON, LINDSAY P50NS12428-17 0009
WHITTUM-HUDSON, JUDITH R01EY03324-11
WHITTY, ALBERT J S07RR05641-17
WHITWORTH, DONALD P, JR R44AG10347-02
WHITWORTH, RANDOLPH R24MH47167-02 0009
WHORTON, A RICHARD P01HL42444-02 0003
WHORTON, A RICHARD R01HL44740-02
WHYBROW, PETER C P01MH44210-03
WHYBROW, PETER C P01MH44210-03 0001
WHYTE, JOHN R29NS27715-01A2
WHYTE, MICHAEL M M01RR00036-31 1000
WIANT, JOSEPH R19MH46211-03
WIBERG, KENNETH B R01GM37650-05
WICHA, MAX S P30CA46592-04
WICHA, MAX S P30CA46592-04 9011
WICHMAN, HOLLY A R29GM38727-06
WICK, BRUCE C K11EY00282-05
WICK, TIMOTHY M R29HL44960-01A1
WICKENS, MARVIN P K04GM00521-04
WICKLINE, SAMUEL A R01HL42950-03
WICKNER, R B Z01DK24940-18
WICKNER, S Z01CB08710-14
WICKNER, WILLIAM T R01GM38895-05
WICKNER, WILLIAM T R37GM23377-16
WICKS, WESLEY D S07RR07088-24 0353
WICKS, WESLEY D S07RR07088-24 0346
WICKSTROM, ERIC S07RR07121-13 0472
WIDAMAN, KEITH F R55HD22953-05
WIDDICOMBE, JONATHAN P50HL42368-04 0001
WIDDICOMBE, JONATHAN H P50HL42368-04
WIDDOWS, RICHARD S07RR07032-26 0037
WIDERA, GEORG M01RR00833-17 0202
WIDERA, GEORG R01AI23927-06
WIDGER, WILLIAM R R01GM46297-01
WIDGER, WILLIAM R S07RR07147-19 0658
WIDIGER, T P01MH47200-02 0001
WIDLANSKI, THEODORE S07RR07031-26 0112
WIDLANSKI, THEODORE S R01GM45572-01A1
WIDMAIER, ERIC P R01DK41263-03
WIDMER, CHARLES G K04DE00333-01
WIDMER, CHARLES G R01DE10130-01
WIDMER, CHARLES G S07RR05308-30 0235
WIDMER, GIOVANNI R01AI29390-01A1
WIDNESS, JOHN A R01HL47453-01
WIDOM, JONATHAN R01GM41915-04
WIEBEL, W WAYNE R01DA06589-02
WIEBEL, W WAYNE R18DA05285-03S2
WIEBEN, ERIC D P50HD09140-16 0013
WIEBERS, DAVID O R01NS28492-01A1
WIEBEU, ERIC D P30CA15083-18 9013
WIECHMANN, ALLAN F R29EY08006-04
WIECZOREK, DAVID P01HL46826-01 0004
WIECZOREK, DAVID F R29AR39423-04
WIECZOREK, WILLIAM F R29AA08920-01
WIED, GEORGE L R35CA42517-06
WIEDERANDERS, MARK R19MH46296-03
WIEDMEIER, SUSAN E K08AI00958-02
WIEDMER, THERESE R29HL40796-04
WIEGAND, LAUREL K08HL02289-03
WIELAND, DONALD M R01HL27555-10
WIELAND, DONALD M R01NS25656-04
WIEMAN, THOMAS J R01CA47377-03
WIEMER, DAVID F R01GM44986-02
WIEMER, DAVID F R01GM46631-01
WIENCEK, JOHN S07RR07058-26 0187
WIENCKE, JOHN P42ES04705-05 0004
WIENER, JOSEPH R01HL23603-14
WIENS, DELBERT S07RR07092-26 0536
WIENTJES, M GUILL R01AI28757-03
WIER, WITHROW G R01HL29473-11
WIERASZKO, ANDRZEJ R01NS27866-02
WIERENGA, WENDEL U01AI25696-05 0005
WIERMAN, MARGARET E R29HD25275-03
WIERNIK, PETER H P30CA13330-20 9005
WIERNIK, PETER H U10CA14958-17
WIESCHAUS, ERIC F R01HD22780-05
WIESCHAUS, ERIC F R37HD15587-11
WIESEL, TORSTEN R37EY05253-10
WIESEL, TORSTEN N P30EY08570-02
WIESEL, TORSTEN N R01EY05251-09
WIESENFELD, MARTIN U10CA52352-02
WIESNER, RUSSELL H N01DK02253-05
WIESSMAN, IRVING P01AI19512-09 0014
WIEST, PETER M K11AI00780-04
WIGDAHL, BRIAN P01NS27405-03 0002
WIGDAHL, BRIAN R01AI24484-05
WIGDAHL, BRIAN R01CA54559-01
WIGGERT, BARBARA Z01EY00070-14
WIGGINS, HARVEY W R44NS27394-02
WIGGINS, JAMES M01RR00069-29 0464
WIGGINS, RICHARD CALVIN R01NS13799-11
WIGGINS, ROGER P50DK39255-05 9001
WIGGINS, ROGER P50DK39255-05
WIGGINS, ROGER C P01DK38149-04
WIGGINS, ROGER C P01DK38149-04 0003
WIGGINS, ROGER C P01DK38149-04 9001
WIGHT, CHARLES A S07RR07092-26 0537
WIGHT, THOMAS N P01AR21557-13 0005
WIGHT, THOMAS N P01HL18645-17 9002
WIGHT, THOMAS N P01HL18645-17 0008
WIGHT, THOMAS N P50DE08229-05 0007

WIGHTMAN, FREDERIC P01DC00116-16 0022
WIGHTMAN, FREDERIC L P30HD03352-25 9002
WIGHTMAN, FREDERIC L R01HD23333-03
WIGHTMAN, MARK R S07RR07072-26 0275
WIGHTMAN, R MARK R01NS15841-13
WIGINTON, DAN A R01GM42969-02
WIGLER, MICHAEL P01CA46370-04 0001
WIGLER, MICHAEL P01CA46370-04 9001
WIGLER, MICHAEL H P01CA46370-04
WIGLER, MICHAEL H P30CA45508-05 9006
WIGLER, MICHAEL H R01DK43070-02
WIGLER, MICHAEL H R35CA39829-07
WIGLEY, DAVID E S07RR07002-26 0888
WIKLER, DANIEL I R13HG00431-01S1
WIKSTRAND, CAROL J P50NS20023-08 0002
WIKSWO, JOHN P, JR R01NS19794-09
WIKSWO, JOHN P, JR R01NS24751-05
WILBUR, JOELLEN S07RR05776-11 0402
WILCOX, A Z01ES44003-14
WILCOX, BRUCE S07RR05352-30 0752
WILCOX, CHRISTINE P01AG10446-01 0003
WILCOX, CHRISTINE L R29NS29046-01
WILCOX, CHRISTOPHER M01RR00082-29 0448
WILCOX, CHRISTOPHER S M01RR00082-29 0465
WILCOX, CHRISTOPHER S R01DK36079-06
WILCOX, CRAIG S R01GM34846-07
WILCOX, DEAN E S07RR07056-18 0209
WILCOX, GEORGE L K02DA00145-02
WILCOX, GEORGE L R01DA01933-09
WILCOX, GEORGE L R01DA04274-05
WILCOX, JOSIAH N R01HL47838-01
WILCOX, KENT W R01AI17246-11
WILCOX, KIM S07RR07037-26 0375
WILCOX, RICH S07RR05849-11 0256
WILCOX, RICHARD E S07RR07091-26 0772
WILCZYNSKI, SHARON P R29CA53005-02
WILCZYNSKI, WALTER R01MH45350-03
WILCZYNSKI, WALTER R13MH47289-01
WILCZYNSKI, WALTER S15AI32174-01
WILD, JAMES R R01GM33191-07
WILD, JAMES R S07RR07090-26
WILD, JAMES R S15DK44692-01
WILD, ROBERT A K07HL02669-01
WILD, ROBERT A R55HD26893-01A1
WILDE, CHARLES E U01AI31494-01 0006
WILDER, DAVID G K01OH00090-02
WILDER, LORA B M01RR00722-19 0260
WILDER, R L Z01AR41048-12
WILDER, R L Z01AR41066-09
WILDER, R L Z01AR41088-01
WILDING, GEORGE R29CA50590-03
WILDT, DAVID E R01HD23853-03
WILENSKY, ALAN P01NS17111-11 0013
WILENSKY, ALAN J M01RR00037-31 0498
WILENSKY, JACOB T U10EY05446-07
WILENSKY, JACOB T U10EY06832-05
WILEY, CLAYTON P50MH45294-03 9008
WILEY, CLAYTON A P50MH45294-03 0007
WILEY, CLAYTON A R01MH46790-02
WILEY, CLAYTON A R01NS25178-05
WILEY, CLAYTON A R01NS27417-03
WILEY, DON C P01GM39589-05
WILEY, DON C P01GM39589-05 0002
WILEY, DON C R01AI13654-15
WILEY, DON C R01AI21324-08
WILEY, DON C R01AI25287-05
WILEY, EDWARD S07RR05596-27 0127
WILEY, ELIZABETH L S07RR05426-30 0151
WILEY, H STEVEN S07RR05428-30 0163
WILEY, HENRY S K04DK01827-04
WILEY, JAMES N01CP15732-00
WILEY, JOHN D S15DK44657-01
WILEY, JOHN W P51RR00167-31
WILEY, JOSEPH M K08CA01371-04
WILEY, K S07RR07210-09 0682
WILEY, LYNN M P51RR00169-30 0129
WILEY, LYNN M P51RR00169-30 0130
WILEY, LYNN M P51RR00169-30 0131
WILEY, LYNN M R01ES05409-01A1
WILEY, ROBERT A S03RR03454-05
WILEY, ROBERT A S07RR05877-09
WILEY, RONALD G S07RR05424-30 0112
WILFERT, CATHERINE M M01RR00030-30 0494
WILFERT, CATHERINE M U01AI27535-03
WILFERT, CATHERINE M U01AI27535-03 0001
WILIMAS, JUDITH A M01RR00211-27 0331
WILIMAS, JUDITH A R25CA23944-11
WILK, SHERWIN K05MH00350-11
WILK, SHERWIN R01NS17392-11
WILKENING, RANDALL B P50HD20761-06A1 0005
WILKERSON, ROBERT D R01DA04038-06
WILKERSON, WILLIAM R S15DK44679-01
WILKES, BARRY M R01HL40914-02
WILKES, BARRY M R01HL44373-01A1
WILKIE, DIANA S07RR05758-18 0263
WILKINS, CHARLES L R01GM44606-01A1
WILKINS, JEFFERY N R01DA06551-02
WILKINS, JEFFREY N R01DA05685-03
WILKINS, TRACY D R01AI15749-13
WILKINS, TRACY D R01CA23857-14
WILKINSON, BRIAN J R15GM42080-01A2
WILKINSON, DONALD R S06GM08182-12 0007
WILKINSON, GRANT R P01GM31304-09
WILKINSON, GRANT R P01GM31304-09 0006
WILKINSON, GRANT R R37GM46622-13
WILKINSON, J ERBY S07RR05845-11 0554
WILKINSON, KEITH S07RR05364-30 0546
WILKINSON, KEITH D K04HL01929-05
WILKINSON, KEITH D P30AG10130-01 0004
WILKINSON, KEITH D R01GM30308-10
WILKINSON, MILES S07RR07238-04 0474
WILKINSON, MILES F R01HD27233-01A1
WILKINSON, MILES F R29GM39586-04
WILKINSON, ROBERT S R29NS24752-05
WILKINSON, WILLIAM H P60HL38655-04 0013
WILKISON, DOUGLAS M S07RR05434-30 0796
WILKOFF, LEE J S07RR05676-15 0964
WILKUS, ROBERT P01NS17111-11 0015
WILLARD, ALAN P01NS14899-13 0013
WILLARD, ALAN L R01NS24362-05
WILLARD, DEREK H S15MH49281-01
WILLARD, HUNTINGTON F R01GM45441-01
WILLARD, HUNTINGTON F R01HG00107-05
WILLARD, HUNTINGTON F R01HG00013-02
WILLARD, MARK B R37EY02682-17
WILLEKE, KLAUS R01OH01301-08
WILLENBUCHER, ROBERT F K11DK02053-01
WILLERFORD, DENNIS M K08AI01012-01
WILLERSON, JAMES T P50HL17669-17 0035
WILLETT, GERALD D S07RR05360-30 0777
WILLETT, JAMES D S07RR07228-02
WILLETT, NORMAN P R25RR07654-01
WILLETT, WALTER C P01CA55075-01 0005
WILLETT, WALTER C P01CA55075-01
WILLETT, WALTER C P01CA55075-01 0001
WILLETT, WALTER C R01CA50385-03
WILLETT, WALTER C R01HL35464-06
WILLIAM, CHERYL L P41RR01315-10 0047
WILLIAMS, DAVID E. P01ES04766-04 0007
WILLIAMS, ALAN E N01HB97079-04
WILLIAMS, ANITA P60HL28391-09 0011
WILLIAMS, ARTHUR S06GM08247-04 0012
WILLIAMS, ARTHUR L G12RR03062-07 0001
WILLIAMS, BEN T R43AI30865-01
WILLIAMS, BOBBY G. P30CA21765-14 9008
WILLIAMS, C H JR R01GM21444-26
WILLIAMS, CAROL L R29CA52471-01A1
WILLIAMS, CAROLYN S03RR03469-04
WILLIAMS, CHRISTINA L P01AG09525-01 0004
WILLIAMS, CHRISTINE L K07HL01934-05
WILLIAMS, CHRISTOPHER J R03HL46674-01
WILLIAMS, CLAYTON C S07RR07092-26 0510
WILLIAMS, DALE O N01HC55015-14
WILLIAMS, DARRELL D P51RR00166-30 9017
WILLIAMS, DARRELL D. P51RR00166-30 0181
WILLIAMS, DARRELL D. P51RR00166-30 0182
WILLIAMS, DAVID P60DK20572-14 0043
WILLIAMS, DAVID R01HL42419-03 9004
WILLIAMS, DAVID A R01HL46528-01
WILLIAMS, DAVID E R29HL38650-05
WILLIAMS, DAVID L R37DK18171-17
WILLIAMS, DAVID O U01HL38532-05
WILLIAMS, DAVID R R01EY04367-09
WILLIAMS, DAVID R R01GM41560-09
WILLIAMS, DAVID R R01GM42897-10A2
WILLIAMS, DAVID R R29AG07904-02
WILLIAMS, DAVID S S07RR05962-05 0017
WILLIAMS, DIANE L S03RR03528-02
WILLIAMS, DOUGLAS P01HD11944-12 0009
WILLIAMS, DWIGHT M P01AI22380-07 0004
WILLIAMS, EDNA N01AI95025-05
WILLIAMS, EDWARD H R29EY07107-04
WILLIAMS, ELAINE S07RR05780-16 0978
WILLIAMS, EVAN S06GM08248-05 0013
WILLIAMS, EVAN F S15HL47732-01
WILLIAMS, FRANK G R01NS28016-02
WILLIAMS, GARY M R01CA39545-06
WILLIAMS, GARY M R01ES05642-01
WILLIAMS, GARY M R13CA53160-01
WILLIAMS, GEORGE W N01DK62285-10
WILLIAMS, GEORGE W U01DK35073-07
WILLIAMS, GEORGE W. N01HR86036-06
WILLIAMS, GORDON S07RR05950-07 0011
WILLIAMS, GORDON H M01RR02635-07 0284
WILLIAMS, GORDON H M01RR02635-07 0238
WILLIAMS, GORDON H M01RR02635-07 0244
WILLIAMS, GORDON H R01HL45438-02
WILLIAMS, GORDON H R01HL46373-01
WILLIAMS, GREGORY M S06GM08258-02 0005
WILLIAMS, HEATHER R29DC00553-03
WILLIAMS, HENRY S G12RR03026-05S1
WILLIAMS, HIBBARD E S03RR03244-09
WILLIAMS, HIBBARD E S07RR05684-23
WILLIAMS, HIBBARD E S15EY09468-01
WILLIAMS, HIBBARD E U76PE00491-01
WILLIAMS, HIBBARD E U76PE00434-02
WILLIAMS, HIBBARD E U76PE00437-02
WILLIAMS, HIBBARD E U76PE00438-02
WILLIAMS, JAMES C JR R29DK39023-05
WILLIAMS, JAMES F R01CA21375-14
WILLIAMS, JAMES F R01CA32940-10
WILLIAMS, JANET B W P50MH43520-04 9001
WILLIAMS, JEFFREY F P01AI16312-13 0003
WILLIAMS, JEFFREY F P01AI16312-13 9001
WILLIAMS, JERRY P01CA43791-04A1 0004
WILLIAMS, JERRY P01CA43791-04A1 9002
WILLIAMS, JERRY P30CA06973-29 9017
WILLIAMS, JERRY R P01CA43791-04A1
WILLIAMS, JOANN C R29GM45902-01
WILLIAMS, JOHN P30DK34933-06A1 9006
WILLIAMS, JOHN S07RR07238-04 0475
WILLIAMS, JOHN A R01DK41122-03
WILLIAMS, JOHN A R01DK41225-03
WILLIAMS, JOHN L P50AR39226-05 9003
WILLIAMS, JOHN L P50AR39226-05 0004
WILLIAMS, JOHN L P50AR39226-05 9001
WILLIAMS, JOHN T K02DA00141-02
WILLIAMS, JOHN T R01DA04523-05
WILLIAMS, JOHN T R01MH45003-02
WILLIAMS, JOHN W S06GM08091-20 0030
WILLIAMS, JOY P S03RR03026-11
WILLIAMS, KEITH R29NS30000-01
WILLIAMS, KENNETH R R01GM31539-09
WILLIAMS, KENNETH R R01GM37573-04
WILLIAMS, KEVIN J R29HL38956-06
WILLIAMS, LESTER F S07RR05424-30 0067
WILLIAMS, LESTER F, JR R01DK15304-18
WILLIAMS, LEWIS T P01HL43821-02
WILLIAMS, LEWIS T P01HL43821-02 0001
WILLIAMS, LEWIS T R01HL32898-08
WILLIAMS, M S Z01BF02001-15
WILLIAMS, MARILYN A R01EY06409-06
WILLIAMS, MARK L R18DA05156-03S1
WILLIAMS, MARK L U01DA06906-02
WILLIAMS, MARSHALL V K04ES00163-04
WILLIAMS, MARVIN T S03RR03031-11
WILLIAMS, MARY P01AR39448-04 9001
WILLIAMS, MARY ANN S07RR07006-26 0901
WILLIAMS, MARY C P01HL24075-13 0003
WILLIAMS, MARY C S07RR07169-07 0170
WILLIAMS, MARY L R01AR29908-09
WILLIAMS, MELVIN S03RR03052-09
WILLIAMS, MICHAEL E R29CA46723-04
WILLIAMS, MOSES L S03RR03150-08
WILLIAMS, O DALE N01HV08112-03
WILLIAMS, P I S06GM08206-10 0006
WILLIAMS, P I S06GM08206-10 0006
WILLIAMS, PAMELA R01AG08562-03
WILLIAMS, PAUL T K04HL02183-04
WILLIAMS, PAUL T R01HL38763-04
WILLIAMS, PHILLIP E P60DK20593-13 9001
WILLIAMS, R SANDERS P50HL17670-17 0034
WILLIAMS, RALPH C, JR R01AR40438-01A1
WILLIAMS, RALPH C, JR R55AR13824-21A2
WILLIAMS, RAY C K16DE00275-02
WILLIAMS, REDFORD B P30AG09463-01 9002
WILLIAMS, REDFORD B, JR K05MH70482-18
WILLIAMS, REDFORD B, JR R01HL44998-01A1
WILLIAMS, RICHARD D R55DK43538-01A1
WILLIAMS, ROBERT B R01CA54345-01
WILLIAMS, ROBERT C S07RR07112-24 0412
WILLIAMS, ROBERT M R01CA43969-05
WILLIAMS, ROBERT M R01GM40988-03
WILLIAMS, ROBERT M S07RR07127-23 0498
WILLIAMS, ROBERT S R01AR40849-01
WILLIAMS, ROBERT S R01HL35639-08
WILLIAMS, ROBERT W R01EY08868-01
WILLIAMS, ROGER M01RR00064-27 0300
WILLIAMS, ROGER R R01HL24855-11S1
WILLIAMS, RUTH E S03RR03407-07
WILLIAMS, S LLOYD R29MH43285-04
WILLIAMS, SCOTT M S07RR07043-26 0130
WILLIAMS, STUART K R01DK43620-02
WILLIAMS, THEODORE P R01EY07753-03
WILLIAMS, THOMAS M R29CA54428-02
WILLIAMS, TODD D S10RR06294-01
WILLIAMS, WICK R P01CA34936-08 0005
WILLIAMS, WILLIAM V R01AR41547-01
WILLIAMS, WILLIAM V R01GM46400-01
WILLIAMS, WILLIAM V R29AI28503-03
WILLIAMS, WINFRED W JR M01RR02635-07 0289
WILLIAMSON, ALEX N S03RR03213-06
WILLIAMSON, ALEX N S06GM08019-21
WILLIAMSON, ALEX N S06GM08019-21 0003
WILLIAMSON, ALEX N S07RR07236-04
WILLIAMSON, ANNE R29NS30012-01
WILLIAMSON, DANIEL M01RR00188-27 0264
WILLIAMSON, DANIEL P30HD24064-04 9002
WILLIAMSON, DAVID S07RR05736-19 0149
WILLIAMSON, JEFFREY F R01CA46640-04
WILLIAMSON, JO SIEW-PING P01NS18146-10 000
WILLIAMSON, JOHN R P01MH43787-03 0001
WILLIAMSON, JOHN R R01DK15120-21
WILLIAMSON, JOSEPH R P60DK20579-14 9003
WILLIAMSON, JOSEPH R R01EY06600-06
WILLIAMSON, JOSEPH R R01HL39934-04
WILLIAMSON, PATRICK S07RR07110-24 0369
WILLIARD, PAUL G K04CA01330-04
WILLIARD, PAUL G R01GM35982-06
WILLIARD, PAUL G S10RR06462-01
WILLING, MARCIA C S07RR05432-30 0231
WILLINGHAM, M C Z01CB08010-18
WILLINGHAM, WILLIAM M S03RR03372-08
WILLINGHAM, WILLIAM M S06GM08211-09 0006
WILLINGHAM, WILLIAM M S06GM08211-09
WILLIS, IAN M R01GM42728-03

WILLIS, JOHN P41RR05964-02 0008
WILLIS, JUDITH H R01GM44511-02
WILLIS, PARK W N01HC55008-10
WILLIS, ROBERT J R01HD22211-05
WILLIS, SHERRY L. R37AG08055-03 0003
WILLIS, WILLIAM D, JR P01NS11255-17
WILLIS, WILLIAM D, JR R01NS09743-22
WILLMAN, CHERYL L R01DK43042-02
WILLMAN, CHERYL L S07RR05583-27 0645
WILLOTT, JAMES F R37AG07554-04
WILLOWS, A O DENNIS R01NS22974-06
WILLS, JOHN W R01CA47482-05
WILLS, NANCY K R01DK29962-11
WILLS, NANCY K S07RR07205-11 0654
WILLS, THOMAS A R01DA05950-03
WILLSON, JAMES K P01CA51183-01A1 9001
WILLSON, JAMES K P01CA51183-01A1 0001
WILLSON, RICHARD C R29GM44344-02
WILLY, JAMES C P30ES01247-17 0099
WILMER, LEONARD S03RR03370-08
WILMER, LEONARD S14GM05364-03
WILMORE, DOUGLAS W M01RR02635-07 0216
WILMORE, DOUGLAS W M01RR02635-07 0271
WILMORE, DOUGLAS W M01RR02635-07 0272
WILMORE, DOUGLAS W M01RR02635-07 0177
WILMORE, DOUGLAS W P50GM36428-07 0003
WILMORE, DOUGLAS W P50GM36428-07 9001
WILMORE, DOUGLAS W P50GM36428-07
WILNER, MARY A R44NR02210-02
WILSMAN, NORMAN J R01AR35155-07
WILSNACK, SHARON C R37AA04610-10
WILSON-DUCLOS, CHRISTINE R01MH42473-06 000
WILSON, ALLAN C P30ES01896-13 9033
WILSON, ALLAN C R37GM21509-17
WILSON, BARBARA D R01HL40944-03
WILSON, BARRY S P30DK34933-06A1 9005
WILSON, BRUCE S07RR05656-24 0829
WILSON, CHARLES P01NS02808-30 0003
WILSON, CHARLES P41RR00592-22 0006
WILSON, CHARLES P41RR00592-22 0007
WILSON, CHARLES B P01CA13525-19
WILSON, CHARLES B R13CA54736-01
WILSON, CHARLES J P01NS26473-04 0004
WILSON, CHRISTOPHER P50DK41978-03 0001
WILSON, CHRISTOPHER B P01HL39157-05 0002
WILSON, CHRISTOPHER B R37HD18184-12
WILSON, CRAIG M K11AI00892-04
WILSON, CURTIS P01DK42717-02 0001
WILSON, CURTIS B P01AG04342-09 0005
WILSON, CURTIS B R01DK20043-14
WILSON, CURTIS B R01DK40251-04
WILSON, D P50NS10939-18A1S1 9004
WILSON, D P50NS10939-18A1S1 0029
WILSON, DANA E M01RR00064-27 0059
WILSON, DANNY N01CP85604-06
WILSON, DARCY B P01CA15822-17 0001
WILSON, DARCY B P01CA15822-17 9001
WILSON, DARCY B R37AI22519-08
WILSON, DARRELL S07RR05353-30 0374
WILSON, DAVID A P01NS20020-08 0004
WILSON, DAVID F R01NS27027-03
WILSON, DAVID J U10EY06259-07
WILSON, DAVID W U01AI27196-04 0004
WILSON, DEBORAH R S07RR05425-30 0775
WILSON, DENNIS E P51RR00169-30 9006
WILSON, DIANE S07RR07016-18 0362
WILSON, DONALD A R01DC00866-01A1
WILSON, DONELLA P60HL38737-04 0002
WILSON, DONELLA J S06GM08037-20 0051
WILSON, DORIS B R01HD12308-07A2
WILSON, DORIS B R01NS20055-08A1
WILSON, E LYNETTE R01CA49419-03
WILSON, ELAINE R19DA06442-03
WILSON, ELIZABETH M R01HD16910-10
WILSON, EMERY A M01RR02602-07
WILSON, EMERY A S07RR05374-30
WILSON, EMERY A S15CA55933-01
WILSON, F E S07RR07036-26 0103
WILSON, FRANKLIN D R01HD25592-02
WILSON, G TERENCE P50AA08747-02 0001
WILSON, G TERENCE R01AA00259-20
WILSON, GEORGE S R01DK30718-06
WILSON, GLENN L R01ES03456-08
WILSON, GOLDER N R01HD26324-01A1
WILSON, GRAEME S S07RR05807-13 0469
WILSON, GRAEME S S07RR05807-13 0470
WILSON, GRAEME S S07RR05807-13 0471
WILSON, GRAEME S S07RR05807-13 0468
WILSON, GRAEME S S07RR05807-13
WILSON, HUGH R R01EY02158-11
WILSON, I DODD S07RR05350-30
WILSON, IAN A P01GM38794-05 0005
WILSON, IAN A R01AI23498-06
WILSON, IAN A R01GM38419-04A1
WILSON, IAN A R01GM46192-01
WILSON, IRWIN B R01HL22242-14
WILSON, JAMES M P01DK42718-02 0001
WILSON, JAMES M P01DK42718-02 9002
WILSON, JAMES M P01DK42718-02 9004
WILSON, JAMES M R01DK42193-02
WILSON, JAMES N P60AR20557-13 0067
WILSON, JAMES R P50AA03527-14 0001
WILSON, JAMES R R01AA08118-03
WILSON, JAMES R R01EY04976-07
WILSON, JEAN D R01DK03892-32S1
WILSON, JEAN D S07RR07175-15 0447
WILSON, JEAN M R29DK43329-01A1
WILSON, JEAN M S07RR05675-23 0923
WILSON, JOAN W P30CA15704-18 9006
WILSON, JOHN P41RR02305-08 0019
WILSON, JOHN E R01NS09910-20
WILSON, JOHN H R01DK42678-02
WILSON, JOHN H R01GM38219-05
WILSON, KARL A S07RR07149-18 0427
WILSON, KATHRINE S07RR05378-30 0017
WILSON, L Z01BG04009-01
WILSON, LABRESIA S07RR05471-29 0581
WILSON, LAIRD JR S07RR05369-30 0599
WILSON, LEANNE P30DE09743-02 0015
WILSON, LESLIE R01NS13560-15
WILSON, MARIE P50DE04898-14 0002
WILSON, MARK P50DE08240-05 0011
WILSON, MARK S07RR07023-26 0981
WILSON, MARK E P01HL45666-01 9003
WILSON, MARK E R01HD16305-09
WILSON, MARK E R01HD18120-07
WILSON, MARK E S07RR05330-30 0027
WILSON, MARK E. P51RR00165-31 9003
WILSON, MARLENE A R29DA05932-03
WILSON, MARTIN C R01EY04112-10
WILSON, MARY E R29AI30126-01A1
WILSON, MICHAEL P50MH47680-02 0005
WILSON, NANCY Z R01MH43029-05
WILSON, NANCY Z R18MH47814-02
WILSON, NANCY Z R19MH46188-03
WILSON, OWEN B R43DA07017-01
WILSON, PATRICIA D R01AG06533-06
WILSON, PATRICIA D R01DK40698-03
WILSON, PATRICIA D R01DK44833-01
WILSON, PHILLIP D R01HL39614-01A3
WILSON, RAYMOND W K11AR01813-03
WILSON, RICHARD A S07RR07082-26 0318
WILSON, S H Z01CB05214-20
WILSON, S H Z01CB05269-04
WILSON, S H Z01CB05270-04
WILSON, SANDRA R R01HL41819-03
WILSON, SCOTT B R43MH46153-01A2
WILSON, STEPHEN S07RR07062-26 0226
WILSON, STUART D M01RR00058-30 0132
WILSON, STUART D M01RR00058-30 0047
WILSON, SUSAN W N01CO23913-33
WILSON, THEODORE A R01HL45545-01
WILSON, THOMAS A S07RR05736-19 0178
WILSON, THOMAS G R01GM33422-06
WILSON, THOMAS H R37DK05736-30
WILSON, TIMOTHY D R01MH41841-06
WILSON, VICTOR J R01NS02619-32
WILSON, W DAVID S07RR07171-08 0164
WILSON, W E Z01ES90033-09
WILSON, W E Z01ES90034-08
WILSON, W E Z01ES90068-01
WILSON, WILKIE A P01NS17771-10 0004
WILSON, WILKIE A P50NS06233-25 0043
WILSON, WILLIAM G M01RR00847-18 0532
WILSON, WILLIAM G M01RR00847-18 0583
WILSON, WILLIAM H R29MH46700-03
WILSON, WILLIAM R N01CM07321-03
WILT, FRED H R37HD15043-11
WILTROUT, R H Z01CM09262-10
WILTROUT, R H Z01CM09348-02
WILUSZ, JEFFREY S07RR05393-30 0908
WIMALASENA, JAYANTHA R01AA08328-02
WIMALASENA, JAYANTHA R55CA53506-01A1
WIMER, RICHARD S07RR05841-12 0221
WIMMER, ECKARD P01CA28146-11 0006
WIMMER, ECKARD U01AI25993-05 0001
WIMMER, ECKARD A R37AI15122-18
WIMSATT, JEFFREY H K01RR00061-02
WINAND, NENA K11AR01812-03
WINANS, STEPHEN C R29GM42893-03
WINAWER, SIDNEY J R01CA26852-10S1
WINBORN, WILLIAM B S07RR07187-13 0695
WINCHESTER, ROBERT J R01AR39626-04
WINCHESTER, ROBERT J R01AR40495-02
WINCHESTER, ROBERT J R37AI19411-10
WINCHESTER, ROBERT J S07RR05589-24
WINCHESTER, ROBERT J S15AR41252-01
WINCHURCH, RICHARD A R01AG09304-01A1
WINDEBANK, A. S. M01RR00585-20 0348
WINDEBANK, ANTHONY P01NS14304-13 0039
WINDELER, ALFRED S R44GM40825-03
WINDER, WILLIAM W R01DK40448-04
WINDER, WILLIAM W S07RR07111-12
WINDER, WILLIAM W S07RR07111-12 0516
WINDHAGER, ERICH E R01DK11489-23A2
WINDLE, BRADFORD E R29CA54785-01
WINDLE, BRADFORD E S07RR05956-06 0743
WINDLE, JOLENE J R01EY09213-01
WINDLE, JOLENE J S07RR05956-06 0744
WINDLE, MICHAEL S07RR05938-07 0315
WINDLE, MICHAEL T R01AA07861-04
WINDLE, MICHAEL T R01AA08051-01A4
WINDRIDGE, GRAHAM C S07RR05697-22
WINDRIDGE, GRAHAM C S15HL47760-01
WINE, JEFFREY P50HL42368-04 0002
WINE, JEFFREY J R03DK43384-01
WINEFORDNER, JAMES D R01GM38434-05
WINEGAR, RICHARD A R29GM46563-01
WINEGRAD, SAUL R01HL16010-28
WINEMAN, NANCY M R01NR02662-02
WINER, JEFFERY A R01NS16832-11
WINESKI, LAWRENCE S06GM08248-05 0020
WINESKI, LAWRENCE E S07RR05907-08 0641
WINEY, MARK E S07RR07013-26 0950
WINFIELD, HOWARD S07RR05372-30 0685
WINFIELD, JOHN B P60AR30701-10
WINFIELD, JOHN B R01AR30863-10
WING, EDWARD J R01AI24141-04A1
WING, EDWARD J S07RR05592-21
WING, RENA R M01RR00056-30 0290
WING, RENA R R01DK29757-11
WING, RENA R R01HL41330-03
WING, RENA R R01MH44828-01A3
WING, STEVEN B R01HL42320-03
WINGARD, JOHN M01RR00052-30 0208
WINGARD, JOHN R P01CA15396-18 9005
WINGE, DENNIS R R01ES03817-10
WINGER, GAIL D P50DA00254-20 0013
WINGER, GAIL D R01DA04403-05
WINGET, RODNER R R43AR40645-01A1
WINGET, RODNER R R44HL40772-03
WINGFIELD, ARTHUR R37AG04517-08
WINGFIELD, WAYNE E S07RR05458-29 0845
WINKELMANN, DONALD S07RR05576-27 0615
WINKELMANN, DONALD A R29AR38454-05
WINKELMANN, JOHN M01RR00400-23 0296
WINKELMANN, JOHN C R29HL39834-04
WINKELMANN, JOHN C R55DK44134-01
WINKELSTEIN, ALAN R01CA24429-16
WINKELSTEIN, ALAN S15DK44698-01
WINKELSTEIN, JERRY A R01AI19278-08S1
WINKELSTEIN, WARREN P30AI27763-04 9004
WINKLER, BARRY S R01EY05100-08
WINKLER, BARRY S S15EY09447-01
WINKLER, HERBERT H R01AI15035-14
WINKLER, HERBERT H R37AI19659-09
WINKLER, JEFFREY DAVID K04CA01337-05
WINKLER, MALCOLM E R01GM37561-06
WINKLER, MALCOLM E R01GM46570-01
WINKLER, MATTHEW M S07RR07091-26 0773
WINKLES, JEFFREY A R29HL39727-04
WINN, H RICHARD R01NS19643-08
WINN, H RICHARD R01NS21076-08
WINN, ROBERT K R01HL43141-02
WINN, RODGER J P01CA52051-01A1 9002
WINN, RODGER J U10CA45809-04
WINNIFORD, MICHAEL D P50HL32295-07 0010
WINNIK, WILMA S07RR07064-24 0212
WINOGRAD, CAROL H P50MH40041-08 0004
WINOKUR, ANDREW M01RR00040-31 0405
WINOKUR, ANDREW P50MH43880-04 9006
WINOKUR, ANDREW R01MH46594-01A1
WINOKUR, ANDREW R01NS29573-01A1
WINOTO, ASTAR R01AI31558-01
WINOTO, ASTAR S07RR07006-26 0900
WINSBOROUGH, HALLIMAN P30HD05876-21 9001
WINSHIP, CHRISTOPHER R01HD25748-03
WINSTON, FRED M R01GM32967-08
WINSTON, FRED M R01GM45720-01
WINSTON, GARY W R29AA06758-05
WINTER, CHARLES H S07RR07051-26 0739
WINTER, EDWARD P R01GM45772-01
WINTER, HARLAND U01AI25934-05 0002
WINTER, JERROLD C R01DA03385-06
WINTER, WALTER P S06GM08244-05 0028
WINTERS, KEN C R01DA05104-02
WINTERS, KEN C R21AA08764-01
WINTERS, STEPHEN J M01RR00056-30 0343
WINTERS, STEPHEN J R01HD19546-05
WINTON, ELLIOTT F P51RR00165-31 0144
WINTON, ELLIOT F M01RR00039-31 0429
WINTROUB, BRUCE U M01RR00079-29 0377
WINTROUB, BRUCE U R01AR31901-09
WIRA, CHARLES R R55AI13541-14A1
WIRA, CHARLES R S07RR05392-30 0709
WIRANOWSKA, MARZENNA R01NS28989-02
WIRGIN, ISAAC I R01ES05541-01
WIRGIN, ISAAC I R29ES05003-03
WIRGIN, ISAAC I S07RR05399-30 0943
WIRSIG-WIECHMANN, CELESTE R R29NS27586-03
WIRTH, DYANN F R01AI21365-05
WIRTH, DYANN F R22AI27872-02
WIRTH, P J Z01CP05659-02
WISE, BRADLEY C R01MH45181-03
WISE, DAVID A P01AG05842-06
WISE, DAVID A P01AG05842-06 0001
WISE, DAVID A R37AG08146-03
WISE, DAVID A S07RR05995-04
WISE, DAVID A S15AG10245-01
WISE, DONALD L R01AI27272-03
WISE, DONALD L S07RR07143-20 0638
WISE, GARY E R01DE08911-01A3
WISE, JO ANN R01GM38070-04
WISE, KENSAL D N01NS02396-01
WISE, KENSALL D N01NS92359-03
WISE, KIM S R01AI31656-01

WISE, KIM S R01AR35587-06
WISE, LEIGH S P60DK20541-14 0023
WISE, MARK E R29HD22747-04
WISE, PHYLLIS M R01HD15955-09
WISE, PHYLLIS M R37AG02224-12
WISE, ROBERT N01HR46021-18
WISE, ROY A R37DA01720-15
WISE, S P Z01MH01092-13
WISE, STEPHEN S07RR05366-30 0565
WISEMAN, R W Z01ES23000-05
WISER, MARK F S07RR05444-30 0263
WISH, ERIC D U18DA07082-02
WISHNOK, JOHN S P01CA26731-12 9001
WISHNOK, JOHN S P01ES05622-02 9001
WISNER, KATHERINE L R29MH44287-04
WISNIESKI, BERNADINE J R01GM22240-16
WISNIEWSKI, HENRY K P01AG04220-07A1 0009
WISNIEWSKI, HENRY M S07RR05838-12
WISNIEWSKI, HENRYK M P01AG04220-07A1
WISNIEWSKI, HENRYK M R01HD22634-05
WISSLER, ROBERT W R10HL33740-07
WISSLER, ROBERT W R10HL45715-01
WISSOW, LAWRENCE S R01MH46134-03
WISTOW, G J Z01EY00255-04
WIT, ANDREW L P01HL30557-08 0007
WIT, ANDREW L R37HL31393-08
WIT, ANDREW L. P01HL30557-08 0010
WITEBSKY, F G Z01CL10172-03
WITEBSKY, F G Z01CL10187-02
WITEBSKY, F G Z01CL10201-01
WITELSON, SANDRA F R01NS18954-08
WITHERS, H RODNEY R01CA44881-05
WITHERS, H RODNEY R37CA31612-10
WITHERSPOON, ROBERT P P01CA18221-16 0002
WITHROW, STEPHEN J P01CA29582-10A1 0005
WITKIN, J M Z01DA00104-01
WITKIN, JOAN W R01AG05366-05
WITKOP, CARL J P01GM22167-16 0006
WITKOP, CARL J P01GM22167-16 9001
WITKOP, CARL J P01GM22167-16 0001
WITKOP, CARL J P01GM22167-16 0003
WITKOVSKY, PAUL P30EY01842-15
WITKOVSKY, PAUL R01EY03570-12
WITKOWSKI, JAN A R13HG00436-01
WITMAN, GEORGE P30CA12708-21 9003
WITMAN, GEORGE B, III R01GM30626-10A1
WITMAN, GEORGE B, III R01HD23858-04
WITRAK, MARTHA S07RR07068-26 0238
WITSCH, HANSPETER R P51RR00169-30 0167
WITSCHI, HANSPETER P01ES00628-19 0011
WITSCHI, HANSPETER R P51RR00169-30 0168
WITTE, LARRY D P50HL21006-15 9004
WITTE, LARRY D P50HL21006-15 0014
WITTE, MARLYS P50AA08037-04 0004
WITTE, MARLYS H S03RR03004-10
WITTE, OWEN N R35CA53867-01
WITTE, PAMELA L S07RR05368-30 0576
WITTE, SCOTT T S07RR07034-26 0070
WITTEN, MARK L S07RR05675-23 0924
WITTENBERG, BEATRICE A R01HL19299-15
WITTENBERG, BEATRICE A R01HL40998-04
WITTENBERG, CURT P01GM46006-01 0006
WITTENBERG, CURT R01GM43487-02
WITTENBERG, JONATHAN B K06HL00733-28
WITTER, FRANK R U01HD21386-05S1
WITTERS, LEE A R01DK35712-07
WITTERS, LEE A S07RR05392-30 0710
WITTES, JANET N01AI15105-00
WITTINGHOFER, ALFRED U01CA51992-02 0002
WITTMERS, LORENTZ E S07RR05896-09 0623
WITTNER, MURRAY R01AI29747-01A1
WITTNER, MURRAY R01MH45654-02
WITTRIG, ERIN S07RR05704-20 0007
WITZ, GISELA R01ES02558-08A1
WITZBURG, ROBERT A S07RR05569-27 0116
WITZTUM, JOSEPH L M01RR00827-17 0485
WITZTUM, JOSEPH L M01RR00827-17 0444
WITZTUM, JOSEPH L M01RR00827-17 0489
WITZTUM, JOSEPH L M01RR00827-17 0319
WITZTUM, JOSEPH L M01RR00827-17 0321
WITZTUM, JOSEPH L M01RR00827-17 0498
WITZTUM, JOSEPH L P50HL14197-20 0006
WITZTUM, JOSEPH L P50HL14197-20 9002
WITZTUM, JOSEPH L P50HL14197-20 0018
WODA, BRUCE A R01DK40707-03
WODA, BRUCE A S07RR05712-20 0112
WODARSKI, JOHN S S07RR07249-03
WODARSKI, JOHN S S15AG10231-01
WOELFEL, ALAN K M01RR00046-31 0423
WOELFL, NANCY N01LM13504-00
WOESSNER, J FREDERICK, JR R01HD06773-20
WOESSNER, J FREDERICK, JR R37AR16940-19
WOGAN, G N P42ES04675-05 0002
WOGAN, GERALD N P01CA26731-12 0009
WOGAN, GERALD N P01CA28842-09 0012
WOGAN, GERALD N P01ES01640-14 0019
WOGAN, GERALD N P01ES05622-02
WOGAN, GERALD N P01ES05622-02 0029
WOHL, MARY ELLEN B P50HL34616-07 0007
WOHL, ROBERT P01HL18577-16 9002
WOHLRAB, HARTMUT R01GM33357-08
WOHLRAB, HARTMUT S07RR05711-21 0037
WOJCHOWSKI, DON M R01HL44491-01A1
WOJCHOWSKI, DON M R29DK40242-04
WOJCHOWSKI, DON M S07RR07082-26 0319
WOJCHOWSKI, DON M S15GM47085-01
WOJCIK, WALTER J R01MH45223-03
WOJDANI, ARISTO S06GM08140-17 0019
WOJTA, DANIEL M01RR00036-31 1030
WOLANCZYK, JAN P R29EY08676-02
WOLCHIK, SHARLENE A P50MH39246-07 0002
WOLCOTT, R MICHAEL S07RR05822-12 0502
WOLCOTT, ROBERT M R03AA09067-01
WOLD, BARBARA J R01AR40780-01
WOLD, FINN R01GM31305-10
WOLD, MARC S R01GM44721-02
WOLD, WILLIAM S R01AI29492-02
WOLD, WILLIAM S R01CA24710-13
WOLDOW, ASHER S07RR05611-22 0703
WOLF, ALFRED P P01NS15638-13 9001
WOLF, ALFRED P P01NS15638-13
WOLF, ALFRED P R01NS15380-16
WOLF, ALFRED P S07RR05731-20 0146
WOLF, BARRY M01RR00065-29 0322
WOLF, BARRY R01DK33022-08
WOLF, BARRY R01HD23223-04
WOLF, BRYAN A R01DK43354-01A1
WOLF, DAVID E R01HD23294-05
WOLF, DON P P30HD18185-08 9004
WOLF, DON P U01HD28484-01
WOLF, DONALD P P51RR00163-32 0035
WOLF, DOUGLAS A R01AG08651-03
WOLF, DOUGLAS A R13HD28258-01
WOLF, DOUGLAS A S15AG10247-01
WOLF, FREDRIC M P50AG08671-03 0007
WOLF, GERALD L R01CA49785-03
WOLF, GREGORY T M01RR00042-31 0562
WOLF, JAMES L R43HL46075-01
WOLF, MARY P30ES00928-18 9013
WOLF, MARYANN S07RR07179-14 0687
WOLF, MATTHEW B R01HL39691-04
WOLF, MERRILL K R01NS11425-17A1
WOLF, MERRILL K S07RR05712-20 0116
WOLF, NORMAN P01AG01751-13 9002
WOLF, NORMAN S P01AG01751-13 0005
WOLF, NORMAN S R01AG07724-04
WOLF, PHILIP A N01EY92109-04
WOLF, PHILIP A R01AG08122-03
WOLF, PHILIP A R01NS17950-10
WOLF, PHILIP A. N01HC38038-19
WOLF, RICHARD E, JR R01GM27113-11
WOLF, ROBERT P30CA54174-01 9002
WOLF, ROBERT H G20RR07052-01
WOLF, ROBERT H P51RR00164-30 9005
WOLF, ROBERT H P51RR00164-30 9006
WOLF, STEVEN L R01NS28784-01A1
WOLF, STEVEN L S07RR05364-30 0547
WOLF, STEVEN L U01AG09124-02
WOLF, WALTER R55CA48255-01A3
WOLF, WENDY J K07HL02440-02
WOLFE, ALAN J R29GM46221-01
WOLFE, BARRY P01AG09973-01 0003
WOLFE, BARRY B R01AG09884-01
WOLFE, BARRY B R01NS26934-04
WOLFE, FREDERICK R18AR21393-17 0012
WOLFE, FREDERICK R18AR21393-17 0026
WOLFE, JEREMY M R01EY05087-08
WOLFE, JOHN H K01RR00035-05
WOLFE, JOHN H R01DK42707-02
WOLFE, RALPH S R01AI12277-18
WOLFE, ROBERT M01RR00073-29 0242
WOLFE, ROBERT R M01RR00073-29 0216
WOLFE, ROBERT R M01RR00073-29 0221
WOLFE, ROBERT R M01RR00073-29 0313
WOLFE, ROBERT R R01DK33952-08
WOLFE, ROBERT R R01DK34817-07
WOLFE, ROBERT R R01DK37484-03
WOLFE, ROBERT R R01DK38010-04
WOLFE, ROBERT R R01GM41089-03
WOLFE, WALTER G P01HL31992-08 9002
WOLFECK, BEVERLY P01DC01289-01 9002
WOLFENDEN, RICHARD V R37GM18325-21
WOLFENDEN, RICHARD V S10RR06317-01
WOLFERSBERGER, MICHAEL G R01GM41766-02
WOLFF, DONALD J R01NS11252-18
WOLFF, J Z01DK45014-21
WOLFF, J Z01DK45016-21
WOLFF, JON A M01RR03186-06 0034
WOLFF, JON A R01DK42709-02
WOLFF, L P50DE08489-04 0001
WOLFF, L Z01CB08952-05
WOLFF, MARK S S07RR05778-16 0406
WOLFF, MARK S S07RR05778-16 0407
WOLFF, MARY S R01ES05638-01
WOLFF, PETER H R01HD26630-02
WOLFFE, A Z01DK36106-04
WOLFFE, A Z01HD01900-01
WOLFLE, THOMAS L P40RR01375-10
WOLFMAN, ALAN S R29GM41220-04
WOLFNER, MARIANA F R01GM44659-01A1
WOLFSON, ROBERT N. P50HD11089-14 0023
WOLFSON, LESLIE U01AG09675-02
WOLFSON, MARLA R R29HD26341-02
WOLFSON, SIDNEY K, JR S03RR03157-09
WOLGEMUTH, DEBRA P50HD05077-21 0034
WOLGEMUTH, DEBRA P50HD05077-21 9003
WOLGEMUTH, DEBRA J R01HD18122-08
WOLGEMUTH, DEBRA J R55HD28374-01
WOLGIN, DAVID L R01DA04592-02
WOLIN, MICHAEL S P01HL43023-01A2 0002
WOLIN, MICHAEL S R01HL31069-08
WOLINSKY, EVE J R01NS28704-02
WOLINSKY, EVE J S07RR05399-30 0926
WOLINSKY, FREDRIC D R37AG09692-02
WOLINSKY, JERRY S R01AI26943-03
WOLINSKY, LAWRENCE E R03DE09831-01
WOLKIN, ADAM R01MH46465-01A1
WOLKOFF, ALLAN W P01DK41918-02
WOLKOFF, ALLAN W P01DK41918-02 0001
WOLKOFF, ALLAN W R01DK23026-13
WOLKOWITZ, OWEN S07RR05755-18 0223
WOLKOWITZ, OWEN S07RR05755-18 0225
WOLKOWITZ, OWEN M R29MH43612-05
WOLLACK, JAN B K08NS01514-02
WOLLENZIEN, PAUL L R01GM43237-02
WOLLMAN, HARRY S07RR05413-30
WOLLMAN, HARRY S15AI32205-01
WOLLMAN, HARRY S15MH49280-01
WOLOSCHAK, MICHAEL K11DK02009-01
WOLOSIN, JOSE M R01EY07773-04
WOLOSIN, JOSE M R01EY09074-01
WOLPAW, JONATHAN R R01NS22189-07
WOLPOFF, MILFORD S07RR07050-26 0134
WOLSDORF, JOSEPH M01RR02172-09 0080
WOLSTENHOLME, DAVID R R01GM18375-20
WOLTER, JANET M U10CA20371-15
WOLTERING, EUGENE M01RR00334-25 0242
WOLTERING, EUGENE A. M01RR00334-25 0231
WOLTZ, DAN J S07RR07092-26 0502
WOLYNES, PETER G R01GM44557-02
WOMACK, JAMES E N01CM37536-12
WOMER, R P01CA47983-04 9001
WOMERSLEY, CHRISTOPH S07RR07026-26 0005
WONDERGEM, ROBERT R01AA08867-01
WONDERLICH, STEVEN S07RR05407-30 0046
WONDISFORD, FREDRIC E R29DK43653-01
WONG-RILEY, MARGARET T R01EY05439-05
WONG-RILEY, MARGARET T R01NS18122-09A2
WONG-STAAL, F U01AI30238-02 0001
WONG-STAAL, FLOSSIE R01AI29889-02
WONG-STAAL, FLOSSIE R01AI31378-01A1
WONG-STAAL, FLOSSIE R01CA52412-01A1
WONG-STAAL, FLOSSIE U01AI30238-02
WONG, A P41RR01243-10 0020
WONG, ALBERT J R01CA51093-02
WONG, ALBERT J R01CA53149-01A1
WONG, BRIAN P01AI28392-02 0004
WONG, BRIAN U01AI31702-01 0004
WONG, C J Z01DA00505-01
WONG, CHI-HUEY M01RR00833-17 0206
WONG, CHI-HUEY R01GM44154-03
WONG, DAVID T K04DE00318-01
WONG, DAVID T R29DE08680-04
WONG, DAVID T W S07RR05318-30 0253
WONG, DAVID T W S15EY09450-01
WONG, DEAN F P01HD24448-04 0005
WONG, DEAN F P01NS15080-12 0012
WONG, DEAN F P50MH44211-03 0011
WONG, DONA L P01MH39437-07 0001
WONG, DONALD R01DC00600-03
WONG, EDWARD S M01RR00065-29 0289
WONG, ERIC A S07RR07095-24 0373
WONG, FULTON P30EY05722-06A1 9003
WONG, FULTON R01EY06862-06
WONG, GEORGE Y P01CA52477-01A1 9002
WONG, GLENDA L R01AR33098-09
WONG, JEFFERY Y C R01CA42329-05
WONG, JOHN W P41RR01380-10 0002
WONG, JOHNSON T R29AI27050-04
WONG, LAURENCE P01HL25596-12 0002
WONG, PATRICK Y R13AR41034-01
WONG, PATRICK Y-K P01HL34300-07 9002
WONG, PATRICK Y-K P01HL43023-01A2 0001
WONG, PATRICK Y-K R37HL25316-12A1
WONG, PAUL K R01CA45124-06
WONG, PAUL K Y R01AI28283-03
WONG, PETER C S07RR05401-30 0863
WONG, PETER M R29DK41298-03
WONG, ROBERT K R01NS24519-06
WONG, ROBERT K R01NS24682-06
WONG, TIMOTHY P50AG05136-08 0009
WONG, WAI-HOI S07RR07143-20 0535
WOO, DAVID D R01DK40700-02
WOO, SAVIO P01DK44080-01 0001
WOO, SAVIO R01HL40162-05
WOO, SAVIO L P01DK44080-01
WOO, SAVIO L P30HD07495-19 9012
WOO, SAVIO L R37HD17711-09
WOO, SAVIO L-Y R01AR39683-03
WOOD KLINGER, KATHERINE N01CP71127-06
WOOD, ALASTAIR M01RR00095-31 0356
WOOD, ALASTAIR M01RR00095-31 0375
WOOD, ALASTAIR J M01RR00095-31 0337
WOOD, ALASTAIR J J P01GM31304-09 0014
WOOD, ALASTAIR J.J. M01RR00095-31 0311
WOOD, ALASTAIR JJ M01RR00095-31 0235

WOOD, ALEX U01CA51992-02 0003
WOOD, CHARLES R01AI30356-01A1
WOOD, DAVID O K04AI00815-05
WOOD, DAVID O R01AI20384-09
WOOD, FRANK P50DA06634-01A1 0006
WOOD, GARY S R29AR40844-01
WOOD, GARY W R01HD17678-08
WOOD, HARLAND G R01GM29569-11
WOOD, HARLAND G R01GM40786-04
WOOD, HARLAND G R37GM24913-14
WOOD, JACKIE D R01DK41825-02
WOOD, JO ANNE S07RR07067-26 0227
WOOD, JOHN G P30AG10130-01 0002
WOOD, JOHN G R01NS17731-11
WOOD, JOHN G R01NS27847-02
WOOD, LAWRENCE MD PHD R01HL35440-06
WOOD, MICHAEL B R01AR38671-05
WOOD, MICHELLE S07RR07080-26 0305
WOOD, MORTON R01DE09393-01A1
WOOD, PAMELA R R01HL45297-02
WOOD, PATRICIA A S07RR05394-30 0713
WOOD, PATRICK P01NS28059-01A1 0004
WOOD, PETER D R01HL45733-01A1
WOOD, PETER D U01HL40205-05
WOOD, PHILIP A P40RR00463-23 0005
WOOD, R PATRICK N01DK02254-03
WOOD, ROBERT W P50HL19171-15 0017
WOOD, ROBERT W R18DA05752-03S1
WOOD, RONALD W K02DA00117-05
WOOD, RONALD W R01DA04438-06
WOOD, RONALD W R01DA05080-04
WOOD, STEPHEN C R01HL40537-01A3
WOOD, W B P41RR00592-22 0025
WOOD, W GIBSON R01AA07292-05A1
WOOD, WILLIAM B R01HD11762-14
WOOD, WILLIAM B R37HD14958-11
WOODBURY, DIXON M K06NS13838-30
WOODBURY, MAX A R37AG03188-10
WOODBURY, RICHARD G S07RR05995-04 0053
WOODCOCK, C P41RR01219-10 0004
WOODCOCK, C L S07RR07048-26 0663
WOODCOCK, CHRISTOPHER L R01GM43786-02
WOODE, MOSES K S03RR03174-07
WOODFIN, BEULAH M S07RR05583-27 0646
WOODHEAD, JEROLD C M01RR00059-30 0691
WOODIN, TERRY S S03RR03093-10
WOODLAND, ROBERT T R01AI30890-08
WOODLAND, ROBERT T S07RR05712-20 0100
WOODLEY, CHARLES L S07RR05386-30 0599
WOODLEY, DAVID T R01AR33625-09
WOODLEY, DAVID T R01AR41551-01 0002
WOODRUFF-PAK, DIANA S07RR05611-22 0706
WOODRUFF-PAK, DIANA S07RR07115-24 0589
WOODRUFF-PAK, DIANA S R01AG09752-01
WOODRUFF, MICHAEL L R01ES04070-06
WOODRUFF, WILLIAM H R01DK36263-07
WOODRUFF, WILLIAM H R01GM45807-01
WOODRUM, DAVID E P01HL39157-05 0004
WOODS, BRYAN T S07RR05484-29 0024
WOODS, DAVID L R01DC01049-02
WOODS, GERALD M N01HB77044-07
WOODS, J S P42ES04696-05 0002
WOODS, JAMES H P50DA00254-20
WOODS, JAMES H P50DA00254-20 0010
WOODS, JAMES H R01DA05325-04
WOODS, JAMES R, JR R01DA04415-06
WOODS, JAMES S R01ES03628-06
WOODS, LORI L R01HD24915-04
WOODS, NANCY S07RR05758-18 0264
WOODS, NANCY S07RR05758-18 0265
WOODS, NANCY F P50NR02323-03
WOODS, NANCY F R55NR01054-07
WOODS, SCOTT W R01MH45966-02
WOODS, STEPHEN C R01DK17844-16
WOODS, STEPHEN C. P51RR00166-30 0126
WOODS, VIRGIL L, JR R01HL30480-08
WOODS, W THOMAS R01HL42258-04
WOODS, WILLIAM G R01CA46907-03
WOODS, WILLIAM G U10CA07306-28
WOODS, WILLIAM H S14GM02716-05 0002
WOODSIDE, WILLIAM F R01DK41562-02
WOODSON, GAYLE E K08DC00009-04
WOODSON, ROBERT D K07HL02143-04
WOODSON, SARAH S07RR07042-26 0409
WOODTLI, ANNE S07RR05913-08 0662
WOODWARD, ARTHUR E S06GM08168-13 0013
WOODWARD, CLARE K R01GM26242-13
WOODWARD, DONALD J P01MH44337-03
WOODWARD, DONALD J P01MH44337-03 9001
WOODWARD, DONALD J P01NS19608-09 0009
WOODWARD, DONALD J R01DA02338-12
WOODWARD, JEAN B S07RR05877-09 0593
WOODWARD, JEROLD G R01CA39070-06
WOODWARD, JOHN J R29AA08089-04
WOODWARD, JOHN J S15AA09258-01
WOODWORTH, C D Z01CP05625-02
WOODWORTH, ROBERT C R01DK21739-10
WOODWORTH, ROBERT C S07RR05429-30 0202
WOODY, CHARLES D P01HD05958-20 0002
WOODY, GEORGE E P50DA05186-05 0001
WOODY, GEORGE E R01DA05593-03
WOODY, ROBERT W R01GM22994-16
WOODY, ROBERT W R01GM23697-14
WOOGEN, SCOTT S07RR05430-30 0228
WOOL, IRA G R01GM21769-17
WOOL, IRA G R01GM33702-06
WOOLF, NIGEL K R01DC00386-05
WOOLF, PAUL D S07RR05403-30 0829
WOOLFORD, JOHN L, JR R01GM28301-12
WOOLFORD, JOHN L, JR R01GM38782-05
WOOLLACOTT, MARJORIE H R01AG05317-04A3
WOOLLETT, LAURA A S07RR05426-30 0152
WOOLSEY, THOMAS A P01NS17763-10 0004
WOOLSEY, THOMAS A P01NS17763-10 0008
WOOLSEY, THOMAS A P01NS17763-10
WOOLSEY, THOMAS A P01NS17763-10 9002
WOOLSEY, THOMAS A R01NS28781-02
WOOLSON, ROBERT F. P01NS24621-05 9001
WOOLSON, ROBERT P50MH43271-05 9001
WOOLSON, ROBERT F R01MH46011-02
WOOLSON, ROBERT F R01NS27960-02
WOOLVERTON, WILLIAM P50DA00250-20 0026
WOOLVERTON, WILLIAM L K02DA00161-01
WOOLVERTON, WILLIAM L P01GM22220-15 0007
WOOLVERTON, WILLIAM L P50DA00250-20 0022
WOOSLEY, RAYMOND L P01GM31304-09 0008
WOOTEN, BILLY R S07RR07085-26 0344
WOOTEN, MARIE W R01AA08753-01A1
WORCESTER, ELAINE M R29DK41725-03
WORD, RUTH A S07RR05426-30 0153
WORDEN, JOHN K P01CA46456-02
WORDEN, JOHN K P01CA46456-02 0001
WORGUL, BASIL V R01EY02648-13
WORK, JACK P50DK39258-05 0007
WORK, JACK P50DK39258-05 9001
WORLAND, STEPHEN T R01GM42651-02
WORLAND, STEPHEN T S15AI32210-01
WORLEY, DAVID E S06GM08218-08 0011
WORLEY, NANCY K R29MH44648-04
WORLEY, PAUL F R01EY08900-01
WORMAN, HOWARD J K11DK01790-05
WORMINGTON, W MICHAEL R01HD17691-10
WORRINGHAM, CHARLES J R29NS27761-03
WORSTER, DALE E M01RR00059-30 0553
WORTHEN, G SCOTT P01HL34303-07 0008
WORTHEN, G SCOTT P50HL40784-03 0002
WORTHEN, G SCOTT S07RR05842-12 0288
WORTHINGTON, BONNIE S M01RR00037-31 0453
WORTIS, HENRY H R01CA52658-02
WORTIS, HENRY H R37AI15803-13
WORTIS, HENRY H S15CA56020-01
WORTMAN, CAMILLE B P01AG05561-06A1 0004
WORTMAN, CAMILLE B R01AG10757-01
WOSTER, PATRICK J S07RR07051-26 0740
WOTRING, LINDA P30CA46592-04 9012
WOWER, JACEK S07RR07048-26 0664
WOYCHIK, RICHARD P R01HD25323-03
WOZNIAK, DAVID F P50AG05681-08 0012
WOZNIAK, K Z01AA00289-01
WRAIGHT, COLIN A S07RR07030-26 0420
WRATHALL, JEAN P01NS28130-02 9002
WRATHALL, JEAN P01NS28130-02 0002
WRAY, S Z01NS02824-01
WRAY, SUSAN S07RR07021-26 0529
WRAY, SUSAN D S07RR07021-26
WRAY, SUSAN D S15CA55951-01
WREDE, ARNOLD F R18DA06104-03
WRENN, ROBERT W S07RR05365-30 0102
WRENSCH, MARGARET R R01CA52689-01A1
WRIGHT, ANDREW R01GM38035-05
WRIGHT, ANDREW R55AI20337-07
WRIGHT, ANTHONY S07RR07143-20 0536
WRIGHT, ANTHONY A R01MH35202-08A5
WRIGHT, BARBARA A G07LM05201-01A1
WRIGHT, BARBARA E R01AG03884-10
WRIGHT, CHARLES S07RR07060-26 0452
WRIGHT, CHRISTINE S R01AI17992-11
WRIGHT, CHRISTOPHER V R01HD28062-01
WRIGHT, CRAIG D N01AI05071-04
WRIGHT, CYNTHIA F R01AI31220-01
WRIGHT, DAVID A P30CA16672-17 9017
WRIGHT, ERNEST S07RR05354-30 0418
WRIGHT, ERNEST M R01DK19567-15
WRIGHT, ERNEST M R01NS09666-18
WRIGHT, FRANCIS S N01NS72326-02
WRIGHT, FRED D P50MH45178-02 0008
WRIGHT, GEORGE N01AI72644-09
WRIGHT, GEORGE E R01GM21747-16
WRIGHT, GEORGE L, JR R01CA26659-11S1
WRIGHT, HARVEL A R43ES05904-01
WRIGHT, HERBERT N P01DC00220-08 0001
WRIGHT, J GORDON M01RR00034-31 0424
WRIGHT, J GORDON M01RR00034-31 0425
WRIGHT, JAMES S07RR05377-30 0752
WRIGHT, JAMES C R15AI31180-01
WRIGHT, JAMES D U01AA08775-02
WRIGHT, JEFFREY S07RR05655-21 0822
WRIGHT, JO R R01HL30923-09
WRIGHT, JOHN C R01MH44311-03
WRIGHT, JOHN R R25CA48924-03
WRIGHT, JOHN R S06GM08003-21 0007
WRIGHT, JOHN TIMOTHY R29DE08994-03
WRIGHT, KRISTINA S07RR07171-08 0161
WRIGHT, MAGGIE S S03RR03284-10
WRIGHT, MICHAEL P R43AI31757-01
WRIGHT, MICHAEL P R43CA56263-01
WRIGHT, PETER E P01GM38794-05 0006
WRIGHT, PETER E P01HL16411-18 0016
WRIGHT, PETER E R01DK34909-07
WRIGHT, PETER E R01GM36643-06
WRIGHT, PETER F N01AI05050-04
WRIGHT, PETER F N01AI05062-04
WRIGHT, RICHARD M U54HD29099-01 9002
WRIGHT, ROBIN L R01GM45726-01
WRIGHT, RONALD A S07RR05463-29
WRIGHT, SAMUEL D P01AI24775-05 0004
WRIGHT, SAMUEL D R01AI22003-08
WRIGHT, SAMUEL D R01AI30556-01A1
WRIGHT, SETH W S07RR05424-30 0105
WRIGHT, STEPHEN P01DK41006-03 0002
WRIGHT, SUSAN C R01CA47669-05
WRIGHT, THEODORE R R01GM19242-20
WRIGHT, TIMOTHY M K04AR01737-05
WRIGHT, TIMOTHY M R01AR38905-05
WRIGHT, TIMOTHY M R01CA55333-01
WRIGHT, TIMOTHY M S15AR41229-01
WRIGHT, WILLIAM W P01AG08321-03 0003
WRIGHT, WILLIAM W R01HD17989-07
WRIGHT, WOODRING E R01AG07992-03
WRIGHT, WOODRING E R37AG01228-13
WRIGLEY, J MICHAEL R29AG10756-01
WRIGLEY, J MICHAEL S07RR07178-14 0670
WRIGLEY, J MICHAEL S07RR07178-14 0671
WROBLEWSKA, ZOFIA P01AI23968-06 0004
WROBLEWSKI, JARDA P01NS28130-02 9001
WRONSKI, THOMAS J R01AG09241-01
WU-HSIEH, BETTY R29AI25134-05
WU-WANG, CHI-YING S07RR06004-04 0042
WU-YUAN, CHRISTINE D R01DE08558-03
WU, ANNA S07RR05841-12 0228
WU, ANNA M P30CA33572-11 9010
WU, BARBARA R29GM42465-03
WU, C Z01CB05263-10
WU, CHOU BING R01AR41074-01
WU, CHUN-FANG P01NS15350-13 0006
WU, CHUN-FANG R01NS18500-09
WU, CHUNG-I K04HG00005-03
WU, CHUNG-I R01GM39902-05
WU, GEORGE Y K04CA01110-05
WU, GEORGE Y R01DK42182-02
WU, GLORIA R03EY09635-01
WU, GUANG-JER S07RR05364-30 0548
WU, HENRY C R01GM28810-11
WU, HENRY C R01GM28811-12
WU, HO-I N01CO33858-24
WU, HO-I N01OD12109-00
WU, J H DAVID S07RR07069-26 0245
WU, JOSEPH P50MH30914-14 0055
WU, JOSEPH CHONG-SANG R01MH42955-03A1
WU, KENNETH K N01HC55022-13
WU, KENNETH K P50NS23327-07
WU, KENNETH K P50NS23327-07 0007
WU, KENNETH K P50NS23327-07 0009
WU, KENNETH K P50NS23327-07 9001
WU, LICIA S07RR07160-16 0601
WU, MING-CHI S07RR07195-12 0712
WU, PYNG-PYNG N01CO15727-01
WU, REEN P01ES00628-19 0009
WU, REEN P51RR00169-30 0169
WU, REEN P51RR00169-30 0170
WU, REEN R01HL35635-04
WU, SAMUEL M R01EY04446-10
WU, YN-LOW H S07RR05305-30 0731
WU,CHUN-FANG P01HD18577-08 0003
WUCHINICH, DAVID G R43HL44771-01A1
WUEPPER, KIRK D R13AR09431-26
WUJEK, JEROME R R43NS29914-01
WULFECK, BEVERLY P50NS22343-06A1 0005
WULFECK, BEVERLY B R29DC00787-02
WULFERT, EDELGARD R01HD26245-01A2
WULFF, DANIEL L R01GM28370-12
WULFF, WILLIAM D R01CA32974-09
WULFF, WILLIAM D R01GM33589-07A2
WUNDERLICH, J Z01CB09250-25
WURSTER, DALE E S15GM47055-01
WURSTER, DALE ERICE S07RR05877-09 0594
WURTELE, SANDY K R29MH42795-05
WURTMAN, JUDITH M01RR00088-28 0273
WURTMAN, JUDITH M01RR00088-28 0264
WURTMAN, JUDITH M01RR00088-28 0266
WURTMAN, JUDITH M01RR00088-28 0267
WURTMAN, RICHARD M01RR00088-28 0268
WURTMAN, RICHARD M01RR00088-28 0269
WURTMAN, RICHARD M01RR00088-28 0259
WURTMAN, RICHARD M01RR00088-28 0281
WURTMAN, RICHARD J R37MH28783-15
WURTMAN, RICHARD J. M01RR00088-28 0240
WURTMAN, RICHARD J. M01RR00088-28 0224
WURTMAN, RICHARD L M01RR00088-28 0262
WURTZ, R H Z01EY00109-11
WURTZEL, ELEANORE T S06GM08225-07 0015
WUTHIER, ROY E R01AR18983-15
WYAND, MICHAEL S N01AI15114-00
WYAND, MIKE U01AI28167-02 9001
WYATT, GAIL E K02MH00269-10
WYATT, R J Z01MH02280-07

WYATT, ROBERT J M01RR00211-27 0229
WYCKOFF, HAROLD W P01GM22778-16 0003
WYDE, PHILIP R N01AI15099-00
WYDE, PHILIP R N01AI82519-03
WYER, ROBERT S JR R01MH38585-07
WYKLE, MAY R01AG08288-02
WYKLE, ROBERT L R01AI17287-10
WYKLE, ROBERT L R01HL26818-11
WYLER, ALLEN R R01NS28712-01A1
WYLER, DAVID J R22AI17615-11
WYLIE-ROSETT, JUDITH R01HL39032-05
WYMAN, JEAN F R01NR02561-02
WYMAN, JEAN F U01AG05170-07 0001
WYMAN, ROBERT P01GM39813-04 0007
WYNDER, ERNEST L. P30CA17613-17 9010
WYNDER, ERNST L P01CA32617-09A1
WYNDER, ERNST L P01CA50956-02
WYNDER, ERNST L P30CA17613-17
WYNDER, ERNST L P30CA17613-17 9002
WYNDER, ERNST L P30CA17613-17 9003
WYNDER, ERNST L P30CA17613-17 9004
WYNDER, ERNST L P30CA17613-17 9005
WYNDER, ERNST L P30CA17613-17 9006
WYNDER, ERNST L P30CA17613-17 9007
WYNDER, ERNST L P30CA17613-17 9008
WYNDER, ERNST L P30CA17613-17 9009
WYNDER, ERNST L R01CA45504-04
WYNDER, ERNST L S03RR03290-10
WYNDER, ERNST L S07RR05775-16
WYNDER, ERNST L S15CA56015-01
WYNN, KAREN S07RR07002-26 0889
WYNNE, LYMAN P50MH30911-14 0028
WYNNE, LYMAN C R01MH39663-06
WYRICK, PRISCILLA B R01AI13446-12A1
WYRICK, PRISCILLA B S07RR05406-30 0903
WYRICK, PRISCILLA B U01AI31496-01 0005
WYSE, D GEORGE N01HC65046-10
WYSE, GORDON A S07RR07048-26 0665
WYSOCKI, CHARLES J P50DC00214-06 0003
WYSOCKI, CHARLES J R01DC00298-07
WYSOCKI, LARRY S07RR05842-12 0287
WYSOLMERSKI, ROBERT S07RR05388-30 0620
WYSOLMERSKI, ROBERT B R29HL45788-01
WYSS, J MICHAEL R01HL37722-04A1
WYSS, MICHAEL P30AG10163-01 0003
WOOLLEY, DOUGLAS C S07RR05680-23 0910
XI-QUING, C Z01BB02001-02
XI-QUING, C Z01BB02003-02
XIAO, FEI S07RR05477-29 0421
XIAO, R P Z01AG00279-01
XIAO, R P Z01AG00280-01
XIE, DONG-LIN S07RR05477-29 0428
XIONG, CHENG R43AI30834-01
XU, GUANG-WEI N01CP15620-00
XUONG, NGUYEN-HUU P41RR01644-09
XUONG, NGUYEN-HUU R55DK44125-01
Y P01AR32087-09 0014
Y-T TUNG, F P51RR00168-30 0166
YAAR, MINA R01AG08909-03
YABLONKA-REUVENI, ZIPORA R29AR39677-03
YABLONSKI, MICHAEL E R01EY07836-04
YACK, H JOHN S07RR07066-26 0261
YACOWITZ, HAROLD N44ES92004-07
YAEGER, MICHAEL J S07RR05623-25 0717
YAGER, JAMES P30ES03819-06A1 9015
YAGER, JAMES D R01CA36701-08
YAGI, MAYUMI R29CA45236-06
YAGI, MAYUMI S07RR05939-07 0730
YAGI, TAKAO M01RR00833-17 0220
YAGI, TAKAO R01GM33712-05
YAGIL, YORAM S07RR05403-30 0830
YAGODA, ALAN P01CA05826-29 0154
YAHR, MELVIN P M01RR00071-28A1 0194
YAHR, PAULINE I K02MH00478-07
YAHR, PAULINE I R37MH26481-16
YAIRI, EHUD R01DC00459-03
YAKSH, TONY L R01AI26249-05
YAKSH, TONY L R01DA02110-13
YAKSH, TONY L R01NS16541-12
YALOWICH, JACK C R01CA51657-03
YALOWICH, JACK C S07RR05416-30 0576
YAMA, MARK F S07RR07170-15 0608
YAMADA, K Z01DE00524-01
YAMADA, K Z01DE00525-01
YAMADA, KELVIN A K08NS01443-02
YAMADA, TADATAKA P30DK34933-06A1
YAMADA, TADATAKA R01DK33500-09
YAMADA, TADATAKA R01DK34306-08
YAMADA, Y Z01DE00483-03
YAMADA, Y Z01DE00484-03
YAMADA, Y Z01DE00485-03
YAMAGUCHI, GARY T S07RR07112-24 0419
YAMAGUCHI, HIROSHI R01HL35807-05
YAMAGUCHI, HIROSHI S07RR05712-20 0073
YAMAKAWA, K Z01HL04207-06
YAMAMOTO, BRYAN KEN R29NS24814-05
YAMAMOTO, JANET K R01AI30904-01A2
YAMAMOTO, JANET K R01CA39016-06
YAMAMOTO, JOE S03RR03012-10
YAMAMOTO, KEITH R P01HL43821-02 0006
YAMAMOTO, KEITH R R37CA20535-15
YAMAMURA, HENRY I P01DK36289-06A1 0007
YAMAMURA, HENRY I P01DK36289-06A1
YAMAMURA, HENRY I R01MH45051-02
YAMAMURA, YASUHIRO G12RR03050-07 0002
YAMAMURA, YASUHIRO G12RR03050-07 0007
YAMAMURA, YASUHIRO R01DA06037-02
YAMASAKI, HIROSHI R01CA40534-07
YAMASAKI, RYOHEI R01AI22998-06
YAMASHIRO, S P41RR01243-10 0026
YAMASHIRO, S P41RR01861-07 0012
YAMASHIRO, STANLEY M R01HL16390-18
YAMAUCHI, MITSO R01AR30587-08
YAMAUCHI, MITSUO K04DE00233-04
YAMAUCHI, MITSUO R01AR19969-12
YAMAUCHI, MITSUO R01DE08522-05
YAMAZAKI, AKIO R01EY07546-05
YAMAZAKI, AKIO R01EY09631-01
YAMAZAKI, KUNIO R01GM32096-12
YAN, PEARLLY S S07RR07053-26 0158
YANAGAWA, NORIMOTO R01DK40973-02
YANAGIMACHI, RYUZO R01HD03402-24
YANAGISAWA, YUKIO S07RR05446-30 0280
YANAGISHITA, M Z01DE00431-04
YANAI, JOSEPH R01DA06670-01
YANCEY, ANTRONETTE K K08CA01646-01
YANCEY, KIM B S07RR05983-05 0365
YANCH, JACQUELYN C S07RR07047-26 0142
YANCHICK, VICTOR A S07RR06009-03
YANCHICK, VICTOR A S15HL47712-01
YANDELL, DAVID W R01EY08690-02
YANDELL, DAVID W R29EY07573-04
YANDRASITZ, JOHN P01DK40555-04 9002
YANEZ, LUIS R43CA55433-01
YANG, CHAO-YUH P60HL27341-10 9004
YANG, CHUNG S P30ES05022-04 9003
YANG, CHUNG S R01ES03938-06
YANG, CHUNG S R37CA37037-08
YANG, DAVID C R01GM25848-10
YANG, FUNMEI P01AG06872-05 0002
YANG, GILBERT K R29GM42704-03
YANG, H-Y T Z01MH01559-10
YANG, HENRY S07RR05551-29 0957
YANG, J C Z01CM06660-08
YANG, JEN T R01GM10880-32
YANG, KE S R43HL47278-01
YANG, NIEN-CHU C R01GM44158-01A1
YANG, SOO Y R01HL47141-01
YANG, THOMAS P R01GM44286-01A1
YANG, VICTOR C R29HL38353-05
YANG, XIAOWEI R43NS29598-01
YANG, XIONG-LI R01EY08338-02
YANG, YIH-MING P60HL38639-04 0008
YANG, YU-CHUNG R01DK43105-01A1
YANKASKAS, JAMES P50HL42384-04 9001
YANKASKAS, JAMES R P01HL34322-06 9002
YANKASKAS, JAMES R R01HL41983-04
YANKELL, SAMUEL L S07RR05337-30 0773
YANKNER, BRUCE A K08NS01240-05
YANKNER, BRUCE A R29AG09229-02
YANOFF, JAY M S03RR03440-06
YANOFSKY, CHARLES R01GM41296-03
YANOFSKY, CHARLES R37GM09738-29
YANTIS, STEVEN S07RR07041-26 0397
YANY, H-Y T Z01MH02301-06
YANZ, JERRY L P01GM22167-16 0007
YAO, JEFFREY K R01MH43742-04
YAO, MENG-CHAO R01GM26210-12
YARASHESKI, K E P41RR00954-15 9011
YARASHESKI, KEVIN E K01AG00444-03
YARBROUGH, LYNWOOD R R01GM38872-04
YARCHOAN, R Z01CM07209-03
YARCHOAN, R Z01CM07210-02
YARCHOAN, R Z01CM07211-02
YARCHOAN, R Z01CM07216-01
YARCHOAN, R Z01CM07217-01
YARDEN, YOSEF R01CA51712-02
YARED, AIDA R29DK39343-04
YARLETT, NIGEL R R29AI25361-02
YARMOLINSKY, M Z01CB05267-07
YARMUSH, MARTIN L K04CA01401-03
YARMUSH, MARTIN L R29CA45272-05
YAROSH, DANIEL B R44CA52401-02
YARUS, MICHAEL J R37GM30881-10
YASBIN, RONALD E R01DE08506-05
YASBIN, RONALD E S07RR07159-16
YASBIN, RONALD E S15GM47056-01
YASKO, J P30CA47904-04 9017
YASSIN, RIHAB S07RR05413-30 0987
YASUI, LINDA S R29CA45011-06
YASWEN, PAUL R55CA54247-01
YATES, ALLAN J P50NS10165-20 0023
YATES, ALLAN J R01CA50486-03
YATES, ALLAN J U01CA50910-03
YATES, BILLY J R01DC00693-02
YATES, JOHN P01GM44119-02 0004
YATES, JOHN L R01CA43122-05
YATES, LAWRENCE S07RR07077-24 0267
YATES, LAWRENCE D R01AR39728-03
YATES, SUZANNE M S06GM08225-07 0017
YATVIN, MILTON B R01CA49416-02
YATVIN, MILTON B R13CA54684-01
YAU, KING-WAI R01EY06837-05
YAZULLA, STEPHEN R01EY01682-16
YE, RICHARD D M01RR00833-17 0211
YE, RICHARD D R29GM46572-01
YEAGER, ANDREW M R01CA40282-04A1
YEAGER, ANDREW M S07RR05378-30 0018
YEAGER, HENRY N01CP85606-03
YEAGER, MARK J K08HL02129-05
YEATES, DONOVAN B R01ES04317-05
YEATES, TERRY L S06GM08139-17 0041
YEATES, TODDS P01GM31299-09 0003
YEAWORTH, ROSALEE S07RR05942-06 0008
YEDIDIA, MICHAEL J R01HS06539-01
YEE, AMY S R01GM44634-01A1
YEE, DOUGLAS R29CA52592-02
YEE, DOUGLAS S15CA55960-01
YEE, GARY C M01RR00082-29 0289
YEE, GARY C S07RR05573-13 0089
YEE, JIING-KUAN R29AI29485-02
YEE, THOMAS W S07RR07133-22 0511
YEH, EDWARD P01AR03564-32 0021
YEH, EDWARD T R01HL45851-01
YEH, EDWARD T H S07RR05486-29 0053
YEH, FRANK Y S03RR03424-06
YEH, G C Z01CN00155-01
YEH, HERMES H K04NS01340-03
YEH, HERMES H R01NS24830-05
YEH, I-TIEN S07RR07083-26 0486
YEH, J P42ES04940-02 9001
YEH, JAMES K P01CA29502-11A1 0038
YEH, JOHN M01RR02635-07 0285
YEH, JOHN R03HD28584-01
YEH, S Y Z01DA00307-03
YEH, YU-YAN S07RR07082-26 0320
YEHUDA, RACHEL R03MH49536-01
YEI, SS Z01BH05021-03
YELIN, E. P60AR20684-14 0031
YELIN, EDWARD P60AR20684-14 9002
YELLEN, GARY I R01NS29693-01
YELLIN, ALBERT E M01RR00043-31 0381
YELLIN, EDWARD P01HL37412-04 0009
YEN, ANDREW R01CA33505-10
YEN, ANDREW S07RR05462-29 0900
YEN, DUEN H R43EY09325-01
YEN, L P51RR00168-30 0158
YEN, L P51RR00168-30 0159
YEN, L P51RR00168-30 0163
YEN, SAMEUL S M01RR00827-17 0323
YEN, SAMUEL M01RR00827-17 0385
YEN, SAMUEL M01RR00827-17 0403
YEN, SAMUEL S M01RR00827-17 0426
YEN, SAMUEL S M01RR00827-17 0324
YEN, SAMUEL S M01RR00827-17 0327
YEN, SAMUEL S M01RR00827-17 0359
YEN, SAMUEL S M01RR00827-17 0472
YEN, SAMUEL S M01RR00827-17 0476
YEN, SAMUEL S M01RR00827-17 0494
YEN, SAMUEL S M01RR00827-17 0477
YEN, SAMUEL S M01RR00827-17 0501
YEN, SAMUEL S M01RR00827-17 0436
YEN, SAMUEL S M01RR00827-17 0180
YEN, SAMUEL S M01RR00827-17 0437
YEN, SAMUEL S M01RR00827-17 0502
YEN, SAMUEL S P30CA23100-11 9002
YEN, SAMUEL S P50HD12303-13 9001
YEN, SAMUEL S P50HD12303-13
YEN, SAMUEL S P50HD12303-13 0001
YEN, SHU-HUI C R01AG04145-09
YEN, SHU-HUI C R37AG01136-14
YEO, CHARLES J R01CA56130-01
YEO, CHARLES J R29DK41178-03
YEOMAN, LYNN C R01CA50391-02
YER, PHILIP E M01RR00036-31 1034
YERBY, MARK S N01NS72330-01
YERGEY, A L Z01HD01400-09
YERGEY, A L Z01HD01401-09
YESAVAGE, JEROME A P50MH40041-08
YESAVAGE, JEROME A P50MH40041-08 0001
YESAVAGE, JEROME A P50MH40041-08 9001
YESAVAGE, JEROME A R01AA07035-06
YESAVAGE, JEROME A R01MH45143-02
YESAVAGE, JEROME A R37MH35182-08
YEUNG, CHO-YAU S07RR05369-30 0608
YEUNG, MARIA K R29DE08932-03
YEWDELL, J Z01AI00541-04
YEWDELL, J W Z01AI00542-04
YEWDELL, J W Z01AI00619-01
YEZIERSKI, ROBERT P P01NS28059-01A1 0006
YEZIERSKI, ROBERT P R01NS19509-08A2
YIELDING, K LEMONE S03RR03350-09
YIELDING, K LEMONE S07RR07205-11
YIELDING, K LEMONE S15CA56007-01
YIELDING, K LEMONE S15MH49517-01
YILMA, TILAHUN U01AI29207-03
YIM, GEORGE K S07RR05586-24 0112
YIM, GEORGE K S07RR05586-24 0113
YIM, M B Z01HL00272-03
YIN, FRANK C N01AG12118-00
YIN, FRANK C S07RR05378-30 0019
YIN, FRANK CHI-PONG R01HL33621-07
YIN, HELEN L R01HL29113-11
YIN, HELEN LU S07RR07175-15 0448
YIN, T C P01DC00116-16 0013
YING, SHAO-YAO R01HD26635-03

YINGLING, CHARLES S07RR05755-18 0211
YIP, JOSEPH W R01HD25539-02
YIP, JOSEPH W R01NS23916-06
YIP, VERA S S07RR05428-30 0184
YOBURN, BYRON C P50DA05186-05 0003
YOBURN, BYRON C R01DA04185-06
YOCH, DUANE S07RR07160-16 0598
YODA, ATSUNOBU R01HL16549-16
YODER, CRAIG R N01CP95651-02
YODER, PAUL J R29HD22812-04
YOFFE, BORIS S07RR05425-30 0776
YOGANATHAN, AJIT S07RR07024-26 0034
YOGANATHAN, AJIT P R01HL45485-01
YOGEV, RAM U01AI27559-04
YOHEM, KARIN H S07RR05675-23 0925
YOHN, DAVID S R13CA54764-01
YOHN, JOSEPH J K08AR01868-01
YOKEL, ROBERT S07RR05857-11 0928
YOKEL, ROBERT A K04ES00174-05
YOKEL, ROBERT A R01ES04640-01A2
YOKOYAMA, M T S07RR07049-26 0423
YOKOYAMA, SHOZO R01AA08241-03
YOKOYAMA, SHOZO R01GM42379-02
YOKOYAMA, WAYNE M R29AI29981-02
YOLKEN, ROBERT H R01DK33089-08
YOLKEN, ROBERT H U01AI27565-04
YOLKEN, ROBERT H U01AI30420-02
YONAS, HOWARD R01HL27208-09
YONATH, ADA R01GM34360-07
YONEDA, TOSHIYUKI P01DE08569-03 0005
YONETANI, TAKASHI R37HL14508-23
YONGJIA, YU N44ES92001-03
YONGMIN, KIM P01HL03174-36 9003
YONGUE, BRANDON G K01MH00803-03
YONGUE, BRANDON G R01MH45951-02
YOO, TAI JUNE R01DC00652-03
YOPP, JOHN H S07RR07118-22
YOPP, JOHN H S15GM47041-01
YORDE, DONALD E P01HD20743-05 9002
YOREK, MARK A P30DK25295-12S1 0011
YORK, ALISON S07RR07254-03 0500
YORK, DONALD H R01NS24960-05
YORK, JAMES L R01AA06867-04A1
YORK, JAMES L R01AA08636-02
YORK, RUTH R01NR02443-02
YOSHIDA, AKIRA Y R01AA05763-09
YOSHIDA, AKIRA Y R37HL29515-12
YOSHIMURA, FAYTH K R01CA44166-06
YOSHINO, TIMOTHY P P01AI28781-02 0004
YOSHINO, TIMOTHY P R01AI15503-14
YOSHIO, SAKURAI N01CM17535-00
YOSHIO, SAKURAI N01CM36011-15
YOSHIOKA, TOSHIMASA R29DK40527-04
YOSHIZAWA, CARL P01CA33619-09 0010
YOST, GAROLD S K04HL02119-05
YOST, GAROLD S R01AA06555-04A2
YOST, GAROLD S R01HL13645-21
YOST, WILLIAM A P50DC00293-07 0005
YOST, WILLIAM A P50DC00293-07
YOST, WILLIAM A R13DC00275-08
YOTHER, JANET L R01AI28457-03
YOU, MING S07RR05700-22 0868
YOUDERIAN, PHILIP A R01GM34150-08S1
YOUDERIAN, PHILIP A R01HG00250-04
YOULE, R Z01NS02674-07
YOULE, R J Z01NS02823-02
YOUNATHAN, EZZAT S R01DK40401-02
YOUNG, A BRYON M01RR02602-07 0035
YOUNG, A BYRON M01RR02602-07 0044
YOUNG, ALFRED B R01CA44522-04
YOUNG, ALICE M K02DA00132-03
YOUNG, ALICE M R01DA03796-07
YOUNG, ALICE M S06GM08167-13 0053
YOUNG, ANNE B P01NS19613-07 0002
YOUNG, ANNE B P50AG08671-03 0003
YOUNG, ANNE B P50NS15655-12 0005
YOUNG, ANTHONY P30CA06927-29 9019
YOUNG, ANTHONY P S07RR05607-25 0702
YOUNG, ANTHONY PETER R01EY05063-09
YOUNG, CHARLES N01CN15337-01
YOUNG, CHARLES SH P01GM38125-04 0004
YOUNG, CHARLES W P01CA05826-29 0143
YOUNG, CHARLES Y R01DK41995-01A2
YOUNG, DAVID B R01HL21435-13
YOUNG, DAVID M S03RR03091-11
YOUNG, DAVID M S06GM08218-08
YOUNG, DAVID M S07RR07100-13
YOUNG, DONALD A R01DK16177-20
YOUNG, DONN P30CA16058-17 9012
YOUNG, ELEANOR A P20NR03039-01 0001
YOUNG, ELEANOR A R01DK35039-03
YOUNG, ELEANOR A S06GM08170-11A2 0002
YOUNG, ELIZABETH A K02MH00427-07
YOUNG, ELIZABETH A R29MH45232-02
YOUNG, ELTON T, II R01GM26079-13
YOUNG, ELTON T, II R01GM33779-08
YOUNG, ERIC M01RR00334-25 0288
YOUNG, ERIC P30DK40566-02 9002
YOUNG, ERIC D P60DC00979-02 0001
YOUNG, ERIC D R01DC00115-16
YOUNG, FRANKLIN A S15DK44673-01
YOUNG, FRANKLIN A, JR S03RR03164-11
YOUNG, FRANKLIN A, JR S07RR05767-17
YOUNG, GERALD A R01DA01050-17
YOUNG, H A Z01CM09283-07
YOUNG, H A Z01CM09303-05
YOUNG, H A Z01CM09326-03
YOUNG, H A Z01CM09345-02
YOUNG, HAROLD F P01NS12587-16
YOUNG, HAROLD F R01NS29267-01
YOUNG, J GERALD P50MH30929-15 9004
YOUNG, JAMES B M01RR00350-25 0357
YOUNG, JAMES B N01HC55004-13
YOUNG, JAMES F U01AI28171-03
YOUNG, JAMES H R01LM05140-02
YOUNG, JAMES J M01RR01346-10
YOUNG, JAMES J S07RR05654-24
YOUNG, JAMES W K08CA00961-05
YOUNG, JAMES W R29AI26875-02
YOUNG, JANIS S07RR07009-26 0949
YOUNG, JOHN D R01CA47307-04
YOUNG, KAREN M R29AI24432-04
YOUNG, KEVIN D R01GM40947-03
YOUNG, LAURENCE R S07RR07047-26 0147
YOUNG, LEONA G P51RR00165-31 0187
YOUNG, LILY Y. P42ES04895-03 0010
YOUNG, LOWELL S N01AI72637-07
YOUNG, LOWELL S R01AI25769-05
YOUNG, LOWELL S S07RR05566-28 0585
YOUNG, M S07RR05362-30 0792
YOUNG, M A P51RR00168-30 0134
YOUNG, M F Z01DE00379-09
YOUNG, M RITA R01CA48080-02
YOUNG, MARK A S07RR07035-26 0093
YOUNG, MARTIN H S07RR05712-20 0074
YOUNG, MICHAEL W R01GM25103-14
YOUNG, N Z01HL02315-09
YOUNG, N Z01HL02319-07
YOUNG, PAUL E S06GM08153-16 0006
YOUNG, PEGGY N01CO15636-03
YOUNG, PEGGY L N01CO54052-16
YOUNG, R P30CA06927-29 9017
YOUNG, R P30CA06927-29 9018
YOUNG, R P30CA06927-29 9020
YOUNG, R P30CA06927-29 9021
YOUNG, R P30CA06927-29 9022
YOUNG, R P30CA06927-29 9023
YOUNG, R P30CA06927-29 9024
YOUNG, RICHARD A R01GM34365-07
YOUNG, RICHARD A U01AI26463-04
YOUNG, RICHARD A U01AI26463-04 0001
YOUNG, RICHARD S R01NS24605-06
YOUNG, ROBERT P30CA06927-29 9016
YOUNG, ROBERT C P30CA06927-29
YOUNG, ROBERT C R01MH42522-04
YOUNG, ROBERT C S07RR05539-29
YOUNG, ROBERT C S07RR05895-09
YOUNG, ROBERT C S15AI32175-01
YOUNG, ROBERT C S15CA56024-01
YOUNG, ROCKEFELLER S R01EY08384-01A2
YOUNG, ROGER C K08HD00827-05
YOUNG, ROSALIE R24MH47181-02 0001
YOUNG, RY S07RR07090-26 0469
YOUNG, RYLAND F R01GM27099-12
YOUNG, STEPHEN J P50AG05131-08 0020
YOUNG, STEPHEN L P01HL31992-08 0007
YOUNG, STEPHEN L R01HL32188-08
YOUNG, STEVE P41RR00592-22 0023
YOUNG, STEVE J P41RR00592-22 0033
YOUNG, STEVEN G. P01HL41633-03 0005
YOUNG, STUART W R01AA07862-02
YOUNG, THERESA B M01RR03186-06 0037
YOUNG, THERESA B P01HL42242-04 0003
YOUNG, VERNON M01RR00088-28 0270
YOUNG, VERNON M01RR00088-28 0282
YOUNG, VERNON M01RR00088-28 0283
YOUNG, VERNON M01RR00088-28 0278
YOUNG, VERNON M01RR00088-28 0279
YOUNG, VERNON M01RR00088-28 0280
YOUNG, VERNON R M01RR00088-28 0263
YOUNG, VERNON R M01RR00088-28 0257
YOUNG, VERNON R M01RR00088-28 0258
YOUNG, VERNON R M01RR00088-28 0237
YOUNG, VERNON R R01DK42101-02
YOUNG, VERNON R R22DK15856-18
YOUNG, VERNON R R37AG07388-04
YOUNG, W S Z01MH02498-02
YOUNG, WALTER F N01CN15380-00
YOUNG, WILLIAM L R01NS27713-01A1S1
YOUNG, WILLIAM W, JR R01GM42698-03
YOUNG, WISE P50NS10164-19
YOUNG, WISE P50NS10164-19 0025
YOUNG, WISE R01NS15590-13
YOUNG, WISE R01NS27226-02
YOUNGENTOB, STEVEN L P01DC00220-08 0002
YOUNGMAN, PHILIP J R01GM35495-07
YOUNGNER, JULIUS S R01AI06264-27
YOUNGS, CURTIS R S07RR07034-26 0071
YOUNKIN, DONALD P41RR02305-08 0021
YOUNKIN, STEVEN R35AG08992-01 0007
YOUNKIN, STEVEN G P50AG08012-04 0002
YOUNKIN, STEVEN G R01AG06656-05
YOUNT, RALPH G R37DK05195-31
YOURTREE, DAVID M P01DE09696-01 0003
YOUSSOUFIAN, HAGOP K11HL02277-03
YOUVAN, DOUGLAS C R01GM42645-03
YU, ALICE L M01RR00827-17 0395
YU, ALICE L M01RR00827-17 0449
YU, AMY WAN-HUA S07RR07132-20 0410
YU, BYUNG P P01AG01188-13 0013
YU, C P R01HL38503-10
YU, CHANG-AN R01GM30721-10
YU, CHANG-AN S07RR07077-24 0269
YU, DAVID T Y P01AR40919-01 0005
YU, DIHUA R03CA54989-01
YU, ELENA S H R01AG10327-01
YU, ELENA S H R01CA49569-03
YU, HING-SING S07RR05654-24 0143
YU, JIA-HUEY R01DE08050-04A1
YU, JOHN M01RR00833-17 0189
YU, JOHN C R01DK40218-03
YU, K F Z01HD00841-10
YU, L C Z01AR27012-07
YU, LEI P30AG10133-01 0004
YU, LEI R29NS28190-02
YU, M W Z01BH05022-02
YU, M W Z01BH05026-01
YU, MIMI C P01CA17054-16 0004
YU, MIMI C R01CA40468-06
YU, NAI-TENG R01EY01746-16
YU, NAI-TENG R01GM18894-21
YU, ROBERT K R01NS11853-17
YU, ROBERT K R01NS23102-05A1
YU, ROBERT K R01NS26994-04
YUAN, DOROTHY C R01CA51426-01A3
YUAN, DOROTHY C R01GM37743-08
YUAN, FOU-XIAO S07RR05551-29 0967
YUAN, J Z01DK25066-05
YUAN, J H Z01ES21150-01
YUDKOFF, MARC M01RR00240-27 0279
YUDKOFF, MARC R01HD25277-03
YUDKOFF, MARC R01NS27889-01A3
YUE, BEATRICE Y R01EY03890-10
YUE, BEATRICE Y R01EY05628-06
YUE, DAVID Y MD PHD R29HL43307-03
YUE, KWOK T R29GM38555-05
YUE, KWOK T S07RR07023-26 0976
YUEN, PICK-HOONG R01CA52421-02
YUEN, PICK-HOONG S07RR05511-29 0490
YUHKI, N Z01CP05529-05
YUHKI, N Z01CP05653-02
YUHKI, N Z01CP05682-01
YUILL, THOMAS M S03RR03466-05
YUILL, THOMAS M S07RR05912-08
YUILL, THOMAS M S15HD28744-01
YUN, JOHN C H S06GM08016-21 0048
YUNG, WAI-KWAN A R01CA51148-02
YUNGINGER, JOHN W M01RR00585-20 0258
YUNGINGER, JOHN W N01AI72621-10
YUNGINGER, JOHN W R01AI25187-05
YUNIS, ADEL A M01RR05280-03 0015
YUNIS, EDMOND J P01HL29583-09 0004
YUNIS, EDMOND J R01AG02329-15
YUNIS, EDMOND J R01CA20531-15
YUNIS, JORGE J R01CA33314-10
YUNIS, JORGE J R01CA51664-02
YUNIS, KHALID A M01RR00633-19 0422
YURCHENCO, PETER D R01DK36425-06
YURCHENCO, PETER D R01DK41500-02
YURKOW, EDWARD J S07RR05909-08 0951
YUSPA, S H Z01CP04504-19
YUSPA, S H Z01CP05445-07
YUTRZENKA, GERALD J R03DA06476-02
ZABIK, JOSEPH E S07RR05586-24 0114
ZABRISKIE, JOHN B M01RR00102-28 0042
ZABRISKIE, JOHN B R01AI18149-09
ZABRISKIE, JOHN B. M01RR00102-28 0155
ZABRISKIE, JOHN B. M01RR00102-28 0143
ZABROCKY, KAREN M R29AG09208-01A1
ZACHARIAH, P K M01RR00585-20 0436
ZACHARIAH, P K M01RR00585-20 0482
ZACHARY, WAYNE W R44GM42331-03
ZACHMAN, RICHARD D M01RR03186-06 0047
ZACHMAN, RICHARD D M01RR03186-06 0048
ZACK, DONALD J K11EY00297-04
ZACKARY, JIM B M01RR02719-06 0018
ZACNY, JAMES P R03DA07103-01
ZACUR, HOWARD P30HD06268-18 9006
ZADUNAISKY, JOSE P30ES03828-06 0014
ZADUNAISKY, JOSE A R01EY01340-17
ZAGER, PHILIP M01RR00997-16 0367
ZAGER, PHILIP G M01RR00997-16 0350
ZAGER, PHILIP G M01RR00997-16 0383
ZAGER, RICHARD A R01DK38432-04
ZAGON, IAN S R01NS20500-07
ZAGON, IAN S R01NS21246-08
ZAGZEBSKI, JAMES A R01CA39224-10
ZAHLER, RAPHAEL S07RR05358-30 0500
ZAHLER, STANLEY A R01GM43979-02
ZAHM, DANIEL S R01NS23805-06
ZAHN-WAXLER, C Z01MH02447-03
ZAHN-WAXLER, C Z01MH02499-02
ZAHN-WAXLER, C Z01MH02559-01
ZAHN, T P Z01MH00484-31
ZAHN, T P Z01MH00486-19
ZAHN, T P Z01MH00491-15

ZAHNER, GWENDOLYN S07RR05358-30 0482
ZAHNISER, NANCY R P01AG04418-08 0002
ZAHNISER, NANCY R R01DA04216-04
ZAHNISER, NANCY R R01NS26851-03
ZAIA, JOHN S07RR05471-29 0578
ZAIA, JOHN S07RR05471-29 0585
ZAIA, JOHN A P01CA30206-10 0005
ZAIA, JOHN A U01AI25959-05
ZAIA, JOHN A U01AI25959-05 0004
ZAIDEL, ERAN K05MH00179-13
ZAIDEL, ERAN R01NS20187-08
ZAIDEN, JAMES R S07RR05364-30 0549
ZAIDER, MARCO P01CA12536-20 0017
ZAIDI, QASIM R29EY07556-04
ZAIN, SAYEDA B P01AG02126-11 0008
ZAIN, SAYEEDA P30CA11198-23 9021
ZAJAC-KAYE, M Z01CM06727-02
ZAJAC-KAYE, M Z01CM06734-02
ZAJAC, FELIX E, III R01NS17662-10
ZAJAC, WALTER W S07RR07260-02 0549
ZAK, RADOVAN P01HL20592-15 0015
ZAK, RADOVAN R01HL45646-01A1
ZAKIAN, VIRGINIA A R01GM26938-12A1
ZAKIAN, VIRGINIA A R01GM43265-02
ZAKIM, DAVID S07RR05396-30 0762
ZAKON, HAROLD H K04NS01278-04
ZAKON, HAROLD H R01NS25513-03
ZALESKE, DAVID J R29AR39380-03
ZALESKI, JAN S07RR05909-08 0952
ZALEWSKI, A A Z01NS02254-15
ZALEWSKI, ANDREW P S07RR05414-30 0995
ZALKIN, HOWARD R01GM24658-21
ZALKOW, L H N01CM17570-00
ZALKOW, LEON H N01CM17550-00
ZALKOW, LEON H R01DA06305-02
ZALKOW, LEON H U01CA52995-02 0001
ZALMAN, LEORA S R01CA47869-03
ZALUDEK, SUSAN K G07LM05312-01
ZALUPS, RUDOLFS K R29ES05157-04
ZALUTSKY, MICHAEL R P30CA14236-18 9022
ZALUTSKY, MICHAEL R P50NS20023-08 0016
ZALUTSKY, MICHAEL R R01CA42324-06
ZAMANSKY, HAROLD S S07RR07143-20 0639
ZAMBON, JOSEPH P50DE04898-14 0001
ZAMBON, JOSEPH J P01DE09545-01A1 0003
ZAMBON, JOSEPH J P50DE08240-05 0005
ZAMBONI, LUCIANO P30HD19445-05S1 9005
ZAMBRYSKI, PATRICIA C R01GM45244-01
ZAMECNIK, PAUL C U01AI24846-06
ZAMPIGHI, GUIDO A R01EY04110-09
ZANAKIS, MICHAEL F R43NS27396-01A3
ZANE, NOLAN R01MH44331-04 0003
ZANER, KEN S R01GM37590-04
ZANER, KENNETH S P01DK38452-05 0003
ZANETTI, MAURIZIO R01HD25787-02
ZANEVELD, LOURENS J R01HD19555-08
ZANG, EDITH A P01CA32617-09A1 9001
ZANG, EDITH A P01CA50956-02 9002
ZANJANI, ESMAIL D R01HL40722-13
ZANJANI, ESMAIL D R01HL46556-01
ZANNIS, VASSILIS P50HL47124-01 9002
ZANNIS, VASSILIS I R01HL33952-08
ZANOLI, MICHAEL D S07RR05404-30 0866
ZAPATA, JESSE T R24DA07234-01
ZAPKA, JANE M R01HS06874-01
ZAPOL, WARREN M R01HL42397-02
ZARBL, HELMUT P01ES03926-07 0007
ZARBL, HELMUT R01CA47571-04
ZARBL, HELMUT R01CA50378-02
ZARCONE, VINCENT P P50MH30854-14 0010
ZARE, RICHARD N R01MH45423-03
ZARET, BARRY L R01HL42419-03 9005
ZARET, KENNETH S R01GM36477-06
ZARINS, CHRISTOPHER K P50HL15062-20 0032
ZARINS, CHRISTOPHER K R01HL41267-04
ZARKIN, GARY A R01AG08319-02
ZARKOWER, ARIAN S07RR07082-26 0321
ZARLING, DAVID A R01GM38424-05
ZARLING, JOYCE M R01AI28065-03
ZAROUKIAN, MICHAEL S07RR05656-24 0830
ZASLOFF, MICHAEL P30HD26979-02 9001
ZASSENHAUS, H PETER S07RR05388-30 0624
ZATZ, M Z01MH00422-20
ZAUDERER, MAURICE R01AG08179-04
ZAUDERER, MAURICE R01AI22009-07
ZAVA, DAVID T R43HD27738-01
ZAVALA, FIDEL R29AI27458-03
ZAWALICH, WALTER S R01DK41230-03
ZBAR, B Z01CB08577-06
ZBAR, B Z01CB08578-02
ZEALEAR, DAVID L R01DC01149-02
ZEANAH, CHARLES H K01MH00691-03
ZEBROWITZ, LESLIE A R01MH42684-05
ZEBROWSKI, PATRICIA S07RR07035-26 0100
ZECH, L A Z01CB08300-19
ZECHMEISTER, EUGENE S07RR07210-09 0689
ZEE, DAVID S P01NS16375-11 0003
ZEE, DAVID S P60DC00979-02 0007
ZEE, DAVID S R37EY01849-16
ZEECE, MICHAEL S07RR07055-26 0196
ZEGANS, LEONARD S07RR05755-18 0208
ZEGER, SCOTT L R29AI25529-04
ZEHNBAUER, BARBARA P01CA15396-18 9001
ZEHNER, ZENDRA E R01HL45422-02
ZEHRER, JACINTA L M01RR00400-23 0280
ZEICHNER, AMOS S07RR07025-26 0994
ZEIDEL, MARK L P50DK39249-05 0003
ZEIDEL, MARK L R01DK43955-01
ZEIGER, E Z01ES21094-05
ZEIGER, E Z01ES21103-05
ZEIGER, E Z01ES60102-13
ZEIGER, ROBERT S N01HR16045-00
ZEIGLER, HARRIS P R37MH08366-29
ZEIMER, RAN C R01EY03841-10
ZEIMER, RAN C R01EY06976-04
ZEIMER, RAN C R01EY07768-04
ZEISEL, STEVEN H M01RR00533-23 0180
ZEISEL, STEVEN H M01RR00533-23 0207
ZEISEL, STEVEN H P01CA09525-01 0005
ZEISEL, STEVEN H R01HD26553-03
ZEISS, C RAYMOND P50AI11403-19 0010
ZEITLER, ROD U01DK30659-09
ZEITLER, RODNEY R M01RR00059-30 0636
ZEITLIN, PAMELA L K08HL02188-04
ZEKOWSKI, STEVEN S07RR05507-29 0485
ZELDIN, SHEPHERD N01HD13114-00
ZELDIS, JEROME B K08HL01917-05
ZELEN, MARVIN P30CA06516-28 9004
ZELENKA, P Z01EY00238-06
ZELEZNIK, ANTHONY J R01HD12014-13
ZELEZNIK, ANTHONY J R01HD16842-07A2
ZELIKOVIC, ISRAEL S07RR05655-21 0820
ZELINSKY, ELIZABETH S07RR07012-25 0024
ZELLER, KATHLEEN M01RR00633-19 0270
ZELLERS, EDWARD T K01OH00077-03
ZELLERS, EDWARD T R01OH02663-03
ZEMAN, ELAINE M R29CA53516-01
ZEMKE, RUTH S07RR07012-25 0025
ZEMLICKA, JIRI R01CA32779-07
ZENG, YI-TAO R01HL29623-09
ZENO, SUSAN M R44HD24023-03
ZENSER, TERRY V S07RR05388-30 0614
ZENTALL, THOMAS R R01MH45979-01A1
ZEPELIN, HAROLD R01MH42547-02
ZEPELIN, HAROLD S07RR07131-22 0143
ZERBE, GARY P50HD20761-06A1 9003
ZERBE, GARY O P01AG04418-08 9002
ZERBE, GARY O P50NS09199-21 9002
ZERHOUNI, ELIAS A U01CA45202-04S1
ZERHOUNI, ELIAS A U01CA49076-03
ZERN, MARK A R01AA06386-08
ZERN, MARK A R01DK41875-03
ZERNIK, JOSEPH P60AR20621-13 0030
ZERNIK, JOSEPH R01DE10131-01
ZERO, DOMENICK T S07RR05548-26 0579
ZERVAS, NICHOLAS T R01HL22573-14
ZERWEKH, JOSEPH P01DK20543-15 0008
ZERWEKH, JOSEPH P01DK20543-15 0009
ZERWEKH, JOSEPH E K04DK01787-05
ZETTER, BRUCE R P01CA45548-05 0004
ZETTER, BRUCE R R37CA37393-10
ZHANG, C Z01AI00459-06
ZHANG, JILUN R43CA54035-01A1
ZHANG, KANYIN S07RR05635-18 0783
ZHANG, MOE-ZHU R44GM42322-02
ZHANG, YOU-XUN S07RR05569-27 0126
ZHAO, JUNGUO R43ES05742-01
ZHENG, YUNKAI N01CP15618-00
ZHOU, FENG P01AA08553-02 0004
ZHOU, G Z01RR10307-03
ZHOU, G Z01RR10368-01
ZHU, J Z01MH02505-02
ZHU, J Z01MH02506-02
ZHU, QINGLIN P41LM05205-08 9009
ZHU, S Z01ES21160-01
ZIEGELSTEIN, R Z01AG00272-01
ZIEGLER, EKHARD E M01RR00059-30 0644
ZIEGLER, EKHARD E M01RR00059-30 0647
ZIEGLER, EKHARD E M01RR00059-30 0626
ZIEGLER, EKHARD E R01HD26872-01A1
ZIEGLER, FREDERICK E R01GM33180-11
ZIEGLER, HARRIS PHIL S07RR07109-23 0512
ZIEGLER, HARRY K R01AI25132-04A1
ZIEGLER, MICHAEL G M01RR00827-17 0460
ZIEGLER, MICHAEL G M01RR00827-17 0505
ZIEGLER, MICHAEL G R01HL35924-04A2
ZIEGLER, R G Z01CP05128-12
ZIEGLER, RICHARD J R01NS29320-01
ZIEGLER, ROLF R01AI26905-03
ZIEL, HARRY K DR N01CP95680-04
ZIELKE, H P01HD16596-08 0002
ZIELKE, H RONALD N01HD13138-00
ZIER, KAREN S R01AI30546-02
ZIERDT, C H Z01CL10009-17
ZIERDT, C H Z01CL10133-03
ZIERDT, C H Z01CL10175-03
ZIERDT, C H Z01CL10176-03
ZIERDT, C H Z01CL10181-02
ZIESKE, JAMES P30EY03790-11 9003
ZIESKE, JAMES D R01EY05665-07
ZIESKE, JAMES D S15EY09446-01
ZIFF, EDWARD B R01CA44042-05
ZIFFER, H Z01DK29005-17
ZIGLER, EDWARD F P01HD03008-24
ZIGLER, EDWARD F P01HD03008-24 0041
ZIGLER, J S Z01EY00105-12
ZIGMAN, SEYMOUR R01EY00459-22
ZIGMAN, WARREN B R29HD24170-04
ZIGMOND, MICHAEL J K05MH00058-16
ZIGMOND, MICHAEL J P01NS19608-09
ZIGMOND, MICHAEL J P01NS19608-09 9004
ZIGMOND, MICHAEL J P01NS19608-16 0002
ZIGMOND, MICHAEL J R01MH43947-04
ZIGMOND, RICHARD E K05MH00162-16
ZIGMOND, RICHARD E R01NS12651-16
ZIGMOND, RICHARD E R13NS29616-01
ZIGMOND, RICHARD E S07RR05410-30 0954
ZIGMOND, SALLY H R01AI19883-09
ZILL, NICHOLAS R01MH45491-01A1
ZIMBA, LYNN D S07RR07035-26 0098
ZIMM, BRUNO H R01GM11916-28
ZIMMER, JAMES P60AG10463-01 9002
ZIMMER, STEPHEN G P50AG05144-08 0009
ZIMMER, STEVAN K11HL02014-05
ZIMMER, STEVEN S07RR05374-30 0742
ZIMMERBERG, BETTY R01AA08605-01A1
ZIMMERBERG, J Z01HD01409-06
ZIMMERBERG, J Z01HD01415-01
ZIMMERER, EDMUND J R15GM46014-01
ZIMMERMAN, ANITA L R01EY07774-04
ZIMMERMAN, BEN G R01HL39698-04
ZIMMERMAN, BEN G R01HL44370-01A1
ZIMMERMAN, DONALD M01RR00585-20 0339
ZIMMERMAN, EARL A P30AG08017-02
ZIMMERMAN, EARL G S07RR07195-12 0718
ZIMMERMAN, ERNEST S07RR05535-29 0538
ZIMMERMAN, GUY A R01HL44525-02
ZIMMERMAN, JERRY J M01RR03186-06 0029
ZIMMERMAN, ROBERT P30HD26979-02 9002
ZIMMERMAN, S B Z01DK36105-09
ZIMMERMAN, STEVEN C R29GM38010-05
ZIMMERMAN, STUART O R01CA11430-25
ZIMMERMAN, STUART O R01CA11430-25 0067
ZIMMERMAN, THEODORE S P01HL31950-08 0005
ZIMMERMAN, THEODORE S P01HL31950-08 9002
ZIMMERMAN, VEVA S03RR03110-04
ZIMMERMAN, WILLIAM S07RR07050-26 0135
ZIMMERMAN, WILLIAM F R01EY00675-19
ZIMMERMAN, WILLIAM F S07RR07110-24
ZIMMERMAN, WILLIAM F S07RR07110-24 0370
ZIMMERMAN, WILLIAM F S15EY09477-01
ZIMMERMANN, ROBERT A R01GM22807-16
ZIMMERMANN, ROBERT A S07RR07048-26 0666
ZIMMET, PAUL Z R01DK25446-12A1
ZIMRIN, ANN B K11HL02646-01
ZIND, BARBARA M01RR00069-29 0408
ZINK, BRIAN J S07RR05394-30 0718
ZINK, CHRISTINE P40RR00130-28 0113
ZINK, M CHRISTINE R29NS28357-02
ZINMAN, BERNARD R21DK44597-01
ZINMAN, BERNARD U01DK30632-09
ZINN, CHARLES J N01CO03876-05
ZINN, KAI G R01NS28182-02
ZIOMEK, CAROL A R01HD23668-05
ZIOMEK, CAROL A U01HD21942-06
ZIPES, DOUGLAS P M01RR00750-19 0249
ZIPES, DOUGLAS P R01HL42370-03
ZIPF, WILLIAM B M01RR00034-31 0417
ZIPF, WILLIAM B M01RR00034-31 0418
ZIPPEN, CALVIN N01CN05247-04
ZIPSER, BIRTIT S07RR07049-26 0450
ZIPSER, DAVID R01MH45271-03
ZIPSER, ROBERT D P30DK36200-05S1 9002
ZIPURSKY, ROBERT S07RR05353-30 0375
ZIPURSKY, STEPHEN L R01EY08772-02
ZIPURSKY, STEPHEN L R01EY09045-05
ZIRKEN, BARRY R. P01DK19300-16 0008
ZIRKIN, BARRY R P01AG08321-03
ZIRKIN, BARRY R P01AG08321-03 0002
ZIRKIN, BARRY R P30HD06268-18 9005
ZIRKIN, BARRY R R01HD07204-19
ZIRKIN, BARRY R R01HD09921-14
ZIRVI, KARIMULLAH S07RR06004-04 0043
ZISCOVICI, S Z01CL10184-02
ZISCOVICI, S Z01CL10185-02
ZISCOVICI, S Z01CL10186-02
ZISCOVICI, S Z01CL10202-01
ZISCOVICI, S Z01CL10203-01
ZISKIND-CONHAIM, LEA K04NS01314-04
ZISKIND-CONHAIM, LEA R01NS23808-05
ZISKIND, ANDREW S07RR05379-30 0766
ZISOOK, SIDNEY P50MH30914-14 0056
ZISOOK, SIDNEY P50MH45294-03 0005
ZISSLER, JAMES F R01GM44507-02
ZITO, JOSEPH P50MH41960-05S1 0003
ZITO, JULIE M R01MH44688-02
ZITOMER, RICHARD S R01GM26061-12
ZIVIN, JUSTIN A P01NS28121-01A1S1
ZIVIN, JUSTIN A P01NS28121-01A1S1 0001
ZIVIN, JUSTIN A R01NS23814-05
ZIYADEH, FUAD N R29DK39565-04
ZLOTNIK, HINDA S06GM08224-07 0023
ZOELLER, RAPHAEL ANDREW R29DK40192-04
ZOELLER, ROBERT T R01AA08887-01
ZOELLER, THOMAS S07RR05387-30 0606
ZOGHBI, HUDA Y P01HD24234-04 0005

ZOGHBI, HUDA Y R01NS27699-03
ZOGHBI, WILLIAM A M01RR00350-25 0358
ZOLA-MORGAN, STUART M R01NS19063-08
ZOLAN, MIRIAM S07RR07031-26 0113
ZOLAN, MIRIAM E R29GM43930-02
ZOLLA-PAZNER, SUSAN R01AI32424-01
ZOLLER, MARK J P30CA45508-05 9009
ZOLNAI, ZSOLT P41RR02301-07 0004
ZON, LEONARD I K11HL02347-03
ZON, LEONARD I P01HL32262-10 0008
ZONANA, JONATHAN R01AR40741-01A1
ZONDERMAN, A B Z01AG00185-03
ZONE, JOHN M01RR00064-27 0391
ZONE, JOHN J M01RR00064-27 0357
ZOOK, JOHN M K04DC00038-03
ZOOK, JOHN M R01DC01303-01
ZORN, MARK B R03EY09198-01
ZORN, NANCY E S07RR05749-19 0276
ZORNOW, MARK H R01NS29403-01
ZORUMSKI, CHARLES F K11MH00630-05
ZORUMSKI, CHARLES F P50AG05681-08 0013
ZORUMSKI, CHARLES F R29MH45493-03
ZUAZAGA, CONCHITA P01NS07464-24 0031
ZUAZAGA, CONCHITA P01NS07464-24 9003
ZUAZAGA, CONCHITA S06GM08102-20 0057
ZUBENKO, GEORGE S K02MH00540-06
ZUBENKO, GEORGE S R01MH43261-04
ZUBENKO, GEORGE S R01MH45968-02
ZUBER, PETER S07RR05822-12 0497
ZUBER, PETER A R29GM39479-05
ZUBIETA, JON S07RR07122-23 0092
ZUCALI, JAMES R R01AI24709-05
ZUCCARELLI, ANTHONY S07RR05352-30 0751
ZUCKER-FRANKLIN, DOR S07RR05399-30 0940
ZUCKER-FRANKLIN, DOROTHEA R01HL42103-02
ZUCKER-FRANKLIN, DOROTHEA R01DK12274-24
ZUCKER, CHARLES P01NS25916-04 9003
ZUCKER, CHARLES L R01EY07552-04
ZUCKER, IRVING R01HD02982-25
ZUCKER, IRVING R01HD14595-12
ZUCKER, IRVING S07RR07006-26
ZUCKER, IRVING S15HD28749-01
ZUCKER, IRVING S15MH49298-01
ZUCKER, IRVING H R01HL38690-05
ZUCKER, MARJORIE B R37HL27752-09
ZUCKER, ROBERT A R01AA07065-05
ZUCKER, ROBERT S R01NS15114-13
ZUCKER, STEPHEN D K11DK02047-01
ZUCKER, STEVEN B U76PE00211-07
ZUCKER, STEVEN B U76PE00467-01
ZUCKERMAN, ALAN P50AI26821-04 0005
ZUCKERMAN, BERT M S07RR07048-26 0667
ZUCKERMAN, KENNETH S R01DK41935-03
ZUCKERMAN, RALPH S07RR07129-22 0503
ZUCKERMANN, FEDERICO S07RR05460-29 0366
ZUCKIER, LIONEL S K11CA01503-02
ZUKER, CHARLES S P01NS25916-04 0006
ZUKER, CHARLES S R01EY06979-05
ZUKIN, RUTH S R01DA05618-03
ZUKIN, RUTH S R01NS20752-06
ZUKIN, STEPHEN R R01DA03383-09
ZUKOWSKA - GROJEC, ZOFIA R29HL40718-01A3
ZULL, JAMES E R01GM45687-01A1
ZULL, JAMES E S07RR07113-24 0572
ZUNIGA, MARTHA C S06GM08132-17 0021
ZUR, MARGALIT P01HL29019-10 0002
ZURAW, BRUCE P01DK42717-02 0005
ZURAW, BRUCE L M01RR00833-17 0082
ZURAW, BRUCE L R29HL39773-04
ZURAW, BRUCE L U01AI32834-01 0002
ZUREK, PATRICK M R01DC00270-07
ZURIER, ROBERT R R01AR38501-06
ZURIF, EDGAR P01DC00081-26 0014
ZUSMAN, DAVID R R01GM20509-19
ZWANZIG, R Z01DK29027-03
ZWEBEN, ALLEN S07RR07181-13 0539
ZWEBEN, ALLEN U10AA08442-03
ZWEIER, JAY L P50HL17655-17 0036
ZWEIER, JAY L R29HL38324-05
ZWEIER, JAY L S10RR06448-01
ZWEIG, M Z01CL10152-05
ZWEIG, M H Z01CL10149-05
ZWEIG, M H Z01CL10153-05
ZWEIMAN, BURTON R01AI14332-15
ZWELLING, LEONARD A R01CA40090-05A2
ZWELLING, LEONARD A S07RR05511-29 0505
ZWERLING, CRAIG S07RR05372-30 0661
ZWICK, JANET R19DA06432-03
ZWIEB, CHRISTIAN S07RR05958-06 0746
ZWIEBEL, JAMES A S07RR05360-30 0778
ZWILLICH, CLIFFORD W R01HL42911-03
ZWILLICH, SAMUEL H P01AI29522-02 0002
ZWILLING, BRUCE P30CA16058-17 9011
ZWILLING, BRUCE S R01MH45679-03
ZWILLING, BRUCE S U01AI25924-05 0004
ZWISLOCKI, JOZEF J R01DC00074-29
ZWISLOCKI, JOZET J P01DC00380-05 0001
ZWIZINSKI, CRAIG W R01GM40463-03
ZYDNEY, ANDREW L R01HL39455-03
ZYMAN, PAMELA S07RR05654-24 0120
ZYSKIND, JUDITH W S06GM45765-01 0010
0QUENDO, CARMEN A S06GM08159-13 0003